# Income
# Tax Regulations

Including Proposed Regulations

*As of June 10, 2021*

## Volume 3

## § 1.1401-1–END

**Wolters Kluwer Editorial Staff Publication**

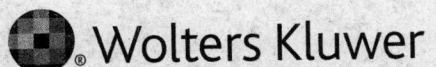 Wolters Kluwer

This publication is designed to provide accurate and authoritative information in regard to the subject matter covered. It is sold with the understanding that the publisher is not engaged in rendering legal, accounting, or other professional service. If legal advice or other expert assistance is required, the services of a competent professional person should be sought.

ISBN 978-0-8080-5615-7 (4-Volume Set)

Do not send returns to the above address. If for any reason you are not satisfied with your book purchase, it can easily be returned within 30 days of shipment. Please go to *support.cch.com/returns* to initiate your return. If you require further assistance with your return, please call: (800) 344-3734 M-F, 8 a.m. – 6 p.m. CT.

Printed in the United States of America

SUSTAINABLE FORESTRY INITIATIVE
Certified Sourcing
www.sfiprogram.org
SFI-01681

# Tax on Self-Employment Income

### See p. 20,601 for regulations not amended to reflect law changes

## [Reg. §1.1401-1]

**§1.1401-1. Tax on self-employment income.**—(a) There is imposed, in addition to other taxes, a tax upon the self-employment income of every individual at the rates prescribed in section 1401(a) (old-age, survivors, and disability insurance) and (b) (hospital insurance). (See subparagraphs (1) and (2) of paragraph (b) of this section.) This tax shall be levied, assessed, and collected as part of the income tax imposed by subtitle A of the Code and, except as otherwise expressly provided, will be included with the tax imposed by section 1 or 3 in computing any deficiency or overpayment and in comput-

(1) For Old-age, Survivors, and Disability Insurance:

| Taxable year | Percent |
|---|---|
| Beginning after December 31, 1983 and before January 1, 1988 | 11.40 |
| Beginning after December 31, 1987 and before January 1, 1990 | 12.12 |
| Beginning after December 31, 1989 | 12.40 |

(2)(i) For Hospital Insurance:

| Taxable year | Percent |
|---|---|
| Beginning after December 31, 1983 and before January 1, 1985 | 2.60 |
| Beginning after December 31, 1984 and before January 1, 1986 | 2.70 |
| Beginning after December 31, 1985 | 2.90 |

(ii) For Additional Medicare Tax:

| Taxable year | Percent |
|---|---|
| Beginning after December 31, 2012 | 0.9 |

(c) In general, self-employment income consists of the net earnings derived by an individual (other than a nonresident alien) from a trade or business carried on by him as sole proprietor or by a partnership of which he is a member, including the net earnings of certain employees as set forth in §1.1402(c)-3, and of crew leaders, as defined in section 3121(o) (see such section and the regulations thereunder in Part 31 of this chapter (Employment Tax Regulations)).

| Filing Status | Threshold |
|---|---|
| Married individual filing a joint return | $250,000 |
| Married individual filing a separate return | $125,000 |
| Any other case | $200,000 |

Note: These threshold amounts are specified under section 1401(b)(2)(A).

(2) *Coordination with Federal Insurance Contributions Act.*—(i) *General rule.*—Under section 1401(b)(2)(B), the applicable threshold specified under section 1401(b)(2)(A) is reduced (but not below zero) by the amount of wages (as defined in section 3121(a)) taken into account in determining Additional Medicare Tax under section 3101(b)(2) with respect to the taxpayer. This rule does not apply to Railroad Retirement Tax Act (RRTA) compensation (as defined in section 3231(e)).

(ii) *Examples.*—The rules provided in paragraph (d)(2)(i) of this section are illustrated by the following examples:

*Example 1.* A, a single filer, has $130,000 in self-employment income and $0 in wages. A is not liable to pay Additional Medicare Tax.

*Example 2.* B, a single filer, has $220,000 in self-employment income and $0 in wages. B is liable to pay Additional Medicare Tax on $20,000 ($220,000 in self-employment income minus the threshold of $200,000).

*Example 3.* C, a single filer, has $145,000 in self-employment income and $130,000 in wages. C's wages are not in excess of $200,000 so C's employer did not withhold Additional Medicare Tax. However, the $130,000 of wages reduces the self-employment income threshold to $70,000 ($200,000 threshold minus the $130,000 of wages). C is liable to pay Additional Medicare Tax on $75,000 of self-employment income ($145,000 in self-employment income minus the reduced threshold of $70,000).

*Example 4.* E, who is married and files a joint return, has $140,000 in self-employment income. F, E's spouse, has $130,000 in wages. F's wages are not in excess of $200,000 so F's employer did not withhold Additional Medicare Tax. However, the $130,000 of F's wages reduces E's self-employment income threshold to $120,000 ($250,000 threshold minus the $130,000 of wages). E and F are liable to pay Additional Medicare Tax on $20,000 of E's self-employment income ($140,000 in self-employment income minus the reduced threshold of $120,000).

*Example 5.* D, who is married and files married filing separately, has $150,000 in self-employment income and $200,000 in

ing the interest and additions to any deficiency, overpayment, or tax. Since the tax on self-employment income is part of the income tax, it is subject to the jurisdiction of the Tax Court of the United States to the same extent and in the same manner as the other taxes under subtitle A of the Code. Furthermore, with respect to taxable years beginning after December 31, 1966, this tax must be taken into account in computing any estimate of the taxes required to be declared under section 6015.

(b) The rates of tax on self-employment income are as follows (these regulations do not reflect off-Code revisions to the following rates):

See, however, the exclusions, exceptions, and limitations set forth in §§1.1402(a)-1 through 1.1402(h)-1.

(d) *Special rules regarding Additional Medicare Tax.*—(1) *General rule.*—An individual is liable for Additional Medicare Tax to the extent that his or her self-employment income exceeds the following threshold amounts.

wages. D's wages are not in excess of $200,000 so D's employer did not withhold Additional Medicare Tax. However, the $200,000 of wages reduces the self-employment income threshold to $0 ($125,000 threshold minus the $200,000 of wages). D is liable to pay Additional Medicare Tax on $75,000 of wages ($200,000 in wages minus the $125,000 threshold for a married filing separately return) and on $150,000 of self-employment income ($150,000 in self-employment income minus the reduced threshold of $0).

(e) *Effective/applicability date.*—Paragraphs (b) and (d) of this section apply to quarters beginning on or after November 29, 2013. [Reg. §1.1401-1.]

☐ [T.D. 6196, 8-13-56. *Amended by T.D. 6691, 12-2-63, T.D. 6993, 1-17-69; T.D. 7333, 12-19-74 and T.D. 9645, 11-26-2013.*]

## [Reg. §1.1402(a)-1]

**§1.1402(a)-1. Definition of net earnings from self-employment.**—(a) Subject to the special rules set forth in §§1.1402(a)-3 to 1.1402(a)-17, inclusive, and to the exclusions set forth in §§1.1402(c)-2 to 1.1402(c)-7, inclusive, the term "net earnings from self-employment" means—

(1) The gross income derived by an individual from any trade or business carried on by such individual, less the deductions allowed by chapter 1 of the Code which are attributable to such trade or business, plus

(2) His distributive share (whether or not distributed), as determined under section 704, of the income (or minus the loss), described in section 702(a)(9) and as computed under section 703, from any trade or business carried on by any partnership of which he is a member.

(b) Gross income derived by an individual from a trade or business includes payments received by him from a partnership of which he is a member for services rendered to the partnership or for the use of capital by the partnership, to the extent the payments are determined without regard to the income of the partnership. However, such payments received from a partnership not engaged in a trade or business within the meaning of section 1402(c) and §1.1402(c)-1 do not constitute gross income derived by an individual from a trade or business. See section 707(c) and the regulations thereunder, relating to guaranteed payments to a member of a partnership for services or the use of capital. See also section 706(a) and the regulations thereunder, relating to the taxable year of the partner in which such guaranteed payments are to be included in computing taxable income.

(c) Gross income derived by an individual from a trade or business includes gross income received (in the case of an individual reporting income on the cash receipts and disbursements method) or accrued (in the case of an individual reporting income on the accrual method) in the taxable year from a trade or business even though such income may be attributable in whole or in part to services rendered or other acts performed in a prior taxable year as to which the individual was not subject to the tax on self-employment income. [Reg. § 1.1402(a)-1.]

☐ [*T.D.* 6196, 8-13-56. *Amended by T.D.* 6691, 12-2-63, *and T.D.* 7333, 12-19-74.]

### [Reg. § 1.1402(a)-2]

**§ 1.1402(a)-2. Computation of net earnings from self-employment.**—(a) *General rule.*—In general, the gross income and deductions of an individual attributable to a trade or business (including a trade or business conducted by an employee referred to in paragraphs (b), (c), (d), or (e) of § 1.1402(c)-3), for the purpose of ascertaining his net earnings from self-employment, are to be determined by reference to the provisions of law and regulations applicable with respect to the taxes imposed by sections 1 and 3. Thus, if an individual uses the accrual method of accounting in computing taxable income from a trade or business for the purpose of the tax imposed by section 1 or 3, he must use the same method in determining net earnings from self-employment. Likewise, if a taxpayer engaged in a trade or business of selling property on the installment plan elects, under the provisions of section 453, to use the installment method in computing income for purposes of the tax under section 1 or 3, he must use the same method in determining net earnings from self-employment. Income which is excludable from gross income under any provision of subtitle A of the Internal Revenue Code is not taken into account in determining net earnings from self-employment except as otherwise provided in § 1.1402(a)-9, relating to certain residents of Puerto Rico, in § 1.1402(a)-11, relating to ministers or members of religious orders, and in § 1.1402(a)-12, relating to the term "possession of the United States" as used for purposes of the tax on self-employment income. Thus, in the case of a citizen of the United States conducting, in a foreign country, a trade or business in which both personal services and capital are material income-producing factors, any part of the income therefrom which is excluded from gross income as earned income under the provisions of section 911 and the regulations thereunder is not taken into account in determining net earnings from self-employment.

(b) *Trade or business carried on.*—The trade or business must be carried on by the individual, either personally or through agents or employees. Accordingly, income derived from a trade or business carried on by an estate or trust is not included in determining the net earnings from self-employment of the individual beneficiaries of such estate or trust.

(c) *Aggregate net earnings.*—Where an individual is engaged in more than one trade or business within the meaning of section 1402(c) and § 1.1402(c)-1, his net earnings from self-employment consist of the aggregate of the net income and losses (computed subject to the special rules provided in § § 1.1402(a)-1 to 1.1402(a)-17, inclusive) of all such trades or businesses carried on by him. Thus, a loss sustained in one trade or business carried on by an individual will operate to offset the income derived by him from another trade or business.

(d) *Partnerships.*—The net earnings from self-employment of an individual include, in addition to the earnings from a trade or business carried on by him, his distributive share of the income or loss, described in section 702(a)(9), from any trade or business carried on by each partnership of which he is a member. An individual's distributive share of such income or loss of a partnership shall be determined as provided in section 704, subject to the special rules set forth in section 1402(a) and in § § 1.1402(a)-1 to 1.1402(a)-17, inclusive, and to the exclusions provided in section 1402(c) and § § 1.1402(c)-2 to 1.1402(c)-7, inclusive. For provisions relating to the computation of the taxable income of a partnership, see section 703.

(e) *Different taxable years.*—If the taxable year of a partner differs from that of the partnership, the partner shall include, in computing net earnings from self-employment, his distributive share of the income or loss, described in section 702(a)(9), of the partnership for its taxable year ending with or within the taxable year of the partner. For the special rule in case of the termination of a partner's taxable year as result of death, see § § 1.1402(f) and 1.1402(f)-1.

(f) *Meaning of partnerships.*—For the purpose of determining net earnings from self-employment, a partnership is one which is recognized as such for income tax purposes. For income tax purposes, the term "partnership" includes not only a partnership as known at common law, but, also, a syndicate, group, pool, joint venture, or other unincorporated organization which carries on any trade or business, financial operation, or venture, and which is not, within the meaning of the Code, a trust, estate, or a corporation. An organization described in the preceding sentence shall be treated as a partnership for purposes of the tax on self-employment income even though such organization has elected, pursuant to section 1361 and the regulations thereunder, to be taxed as a domestic corporation.

(g) *Nature of partnership interest.*—The net earnings from self-employment of a partner include his distributive share of the income or loss, described in section 702(a)(9), of the partnership of which he is a member, irrespective of the nature of his membership. Thus, in determining his net earnings from self-employment, a limited or inactive partner includes his distributive share of such partnership income or loss. In the case of a partner who is a member of a partnership with respect to which an election has been made pursuant to section 1361 and the regulations thereunder to be taxed as a domestic corporation, net earnings from self-employment include his distributive share of the income or loss, described in section 702(a)(9), from the trade or business carried on by the partnership computed without regard to the fact that the partnership has elected to be taxed as a domestic corporation.

(h) *Proprietorship taxed as domestic corporation.*—A proprietor of an unincorporated business enterprise with respect to which an election has been made pursuant to section 1361 and the regulations thereunder to be taxed as a domestic corporation shall compute his net earnings from self-employment without regard to the fact that such election has been made. [Reg. § 1.1402(a)-2.]

☐ [*T.D.* 6691, 12-2-63. *Amended by T.D.* 7333, 12-19-74.]

### [Reg. § 1.1402(a)-3]

**§ 1.1402(a)-3. Special rules for computing net earnings from self-employment.**—For the purpose of computing net earnings from self-employment, the gross income derived by an individual from a trade or business carried on by him, the allowable deductions attributable to such trade or business, and the individual's distributive share of the income or loss, described in section 702(a)(9), from any trade or business carried on by a partnership of which he is a member shall be computed in accordance with the special rules set forth in § § 1.1402(a)-4 to 1.1402(a)-17, inclusive. [Reg. § 1.1402(a)-3.]

☐ [*T.D.* 6691, 12-2-63. *Amended by T.D.* 7710, 7-28-80.]

### [Reg. § 1.1402(a)-4]

**§ 1.1402(a)-4. Rentals from real estate.**—(a) *In general.*—Rentals from real estate and from personal property leased with the real estate (including such rentals paid in crop shares) and the deductions attributable thereto, unless such rentals are received by an individual in the course of a trade or business as a real-estate dealer, are excluded. Whether or not an individual is engaged in the trade or business of a real-estate dealer is determined by the application of the principles followed in respect of the taxes imposed by sections 1 and 3. In general, an individual who is engaged in the business of selling real estate to customers with a view to the gains and profits that may be derived from such sales is a real-estate dealer. On the other hand, an individual who merely holds real estate for investment or speculation and receives rentals therefrom is not considered a real-estate dealer. Where a real-estate dealer holds real estate for investment or speculation in addition to real estate held for sale to customers in the ordinary course of his trade or business as a real-estate dealer, only the rentals from the real estate held for sale to customers in the ordinary course of his trade or business as a real-estate dealer, and the deductions attributable thereto, are included in determining net earnings from self-employment; the rentals from the real estate held for investment or speculation, and the deductions attributable thereto, are excluded. Rentals paid in crop shares include income derived by an owner or lessee of land under an agreement entered into with another person pursuant to which such other person undertakes to produce a crop or livestock on such land and pursuant to which (1) the crop or livestock, or the proceeds thereof, are to be divided between such owner or lessee and such other person, and (2) the share of the owner or lessee depends on the amount of the crop or livestock produced. See, however, paragraph (b) of this section.

(b) *Special rule for "includible farm rental income".*—(1) *In general.*—Notwithstanding the rules set forth in paragraph (a) of this section, there shall be included in determining net earnings from self-employment for taxable years ending after 1955 any income derived by an owner or tenant of land, if the following requirements are met with respect to such income:

(i) The income is derived under an arrangement between the owner or tenant of land and another person which provides that such other person shall produce agricultural or horticultural commodities on such land, and that there shall be material participation by the owner or tenant in the production or the management of the production of such agricultural or horticultural commodities; and

(ii) There is material participation by the owner or tenant with respect to any such agricultural or horticultural commodity.

Income so derived shall be referred to in this section as "includible farm rental income".

(2) *Requirement that income be derived under an arrangement.*—In order for rental income received by an owner or tenant of land to be treated as includible farm rental income, such income must be derived pursuant to a sharefarming or other rental arrangement which contemplates material participation by the owner or tenant in the production or management of production of agricultural or horticultural commodities.

(3) *Nature of arrangement.*—(i) The arrangement between the owner or tenant and the person referred to in subparagraph (1) of this paragraph may be either oral or written. The arrangement must impose upon such other person the obligation to produce one or more agricultural or horticultural commodities (including livestock, bees, poultry, and fur-bearing animals and wildlife) on the land of the owner or tenant. In addition, it must be within the contemplation of the parties that the owner or tenant will participate in the production or the management of the production of the agricultural or horticultural commodities required to be produced by the other person under such arrangement to an extent which is material with respect either to the production or to the management of production of such commodities or is material with respect to the production and management of production when the total required participation in connection with both is considered.

(ii) The term "production", wherever used in this paragraph, refers to the physical work performed and the expenses incurred in producing a commodity. It includes such activities as the actual work of planting, cultivating, and harvesting crops, and the furnishing of machinery, implements, seed, and livestock. An arrangement will be treated as contemplating that the owner or tenant will materially participate in the "production" of the commodities required to be produced by the other person under the arrangement if under the arrangement it is understood that the owner or tenant is to engage to a material degree in the physical work related to the production of such commodities. The mere undertaking to furnish machinery, implements, and livestock and to incur expenses is not, in and of itself, sufficient. Such factors may be significant, however, in cases where the degree of physical work intended of the owner or tenant is not material. For example, if under the arrangement it is understood that the owner or tenant is to engage periodically in physical work to a degree which is not material in and of itself and, in addition, to furnish a substantial portion of the machinery, implements, and livestock to be used in the production of the commodities or to furnish or advance funds or assume financial responsibility for a substantial part of the expense involved in the production of the commodities, the arrangement will be treated as contemplating material participation of the owner or tenant in the production of such commodities.

(iii) The term "management of the production", wherever used in this paragraph, refers to services performed in making managerial decisions relating to the production, such as when to plant, cultivate, dust, spray, or harvest the crop, and includes advising and consulting, making inspections, and making decisions as to matters such as rotation of crops, the type of crops to be grown, the type of livestock to be raised, and the type of machinery and implements to be furnished. An arrangement will be treated as contemplating that the owner or tenant is to participate materially in the "management of the production" of the commodities required to be produced by the other person under the arrangement if the owner or tenant is to engage to a material degree in the management decisions related to the production of such commodities. The services which are considered of particular importance in making such management decisions are those services performed in making inspections of the production activities and in advising and consulting with such person as to the production of the commodities. Thus, if under the arrangement it is understood that the owner or tenant is to advise or consult periodically with the other person as to the production of the commodities required to be produced by such person under the arrangement and to inspect periodically the production activities on the land, a strong inference will be drawn that the arrangement contemplates participation by the owner or tenant in the management of the production of such commodities. The mere undertaking to select the crops or livestock to be produced or the type of machinery and implements to

be furnished or to make decisions as to the rotation of crops generally is not, in and of itself, sufficient. Such factors may be significant, however, in making the over-all determination of whether the arrangement contemplates that the owner or tenant is to materially participate in the management of the production of the commodities. Thus, if in addition to the understanding that the owner or tenant is to advise or consult periodically with the other person as to the production of the commodities and inspect periodically the production activities on the land, it is also understood that the owner is to select the type of crops and livestock to be produced and the type of machinery and implements to be furnished and to make decisions as to the rotation of crops, the arrangement will be treated as contemplating material participation of the owner or tenant in the management of production of such commodities.

(4) *Actual participation.*—In order for the rental income received by the owner or tenant of land to be treated as includible farm rental income, not only must it be derived pursuant to the arrangement described in subparagraph (1) of this paragraph, but also the owner or tenant must actually participate to a material degree in the production or in the management of the production of any of the commodities required to be produced under the arrangement, or he must actually participate in both the production and the management of the production to an extent that his participation in the one when combined with his participation in the other will be considered participation to a material degree. If the owner or tenant shows that he periodically advises or consults with the other person, who under the arrangement produces the agricultural or horticultural commodities, as to the production of any of these commodities and also shows that he periodically inspects the production activities on the land, he will have presented strong evidence of the existence of the degree of participation contemplated by section 1402(a)(1). If, in addition to the foregoing, the owner or tenant shows that he furnishes a substantial portion of the machinery, implements, and livestock used in the production of the commodities or that he furnishes or advances funds, or assumes financial responsibility, for a substantial part of the expense involved in the production of the commodities, he will have established the existence of the degree of participation contemplated by section 1402(a)(1) and this paragraph.

(5) *Employees or agents.*—An agreement entered into by an employee or agent of an owner or tenant and another person is considered to be an arrangement entered into by the owner or tenant for purposes of satisfying the requirement set forth in paragraph (b)(2) that the income must be derived under an arrangement between the owner or tenant and another person. For purposes of determining whether the arrangement satisfies the requirement set forth in paragraph (b)(3) that the parties contemplate that the owner or tenant will materially participate in the production or management of production of a commodity, services which will be performed by an employee or agent of the owner or tenant are not considered to be services which the arrangement contemplates will be performed by the owner or tenant. Services actually performed by such employee or agent are not considered services performed by the owner or tenant in determining the extent to which the owner or tenant has participated in the production or management of production of a commodity. For taxable years beginning before January 1, 1974, contemplated or actual services of an agent or an employee of the owner or tenant are deemed to be contemplated or actual services of the owner or tenant under paragraphs (b)(3) and (b)(4) of this section.

(6) *Examples.*—Application of the rules prescribed in this paragraph may be illustrated by the following examples:

*Example (1).* After the death of her husband, Mrs. A rents her farm, together with its machinery and equipment, to B for one-half of the proceeds from the commodities produced on such farm by B. It is agreed that B will live in the tenant house on the farm and be responsible for the over-all operation of the farm, such as planting, cultivating, and harvesting the field crops, caring for the orchard and harvesting the fruit and caring for the livestock and poultry. It also is agreed that Mrs. A will continue to live in the farm residence and help B operate the farm. Under the agreement it is contemplated that Mrs. A will regularly operate and clean the cream separator and feed the poultry flock and collect the eggs. When possible she will assist B in such work as spraying the fruit trees, penning livestock, culling the poultry, and controlling weeds. She will also assist in preparing the meals when B engages seasonal workers. The agreement between Mrs. A and B clearly provides that she will materially participate in the over-all production operations to be conducted on her farm by B. In actual practice, Mrs. A performs such regular and intermittent services. The regularly performed services are material to the production of an agricultural commodity, and the intermittent services performed are material to the production operations to which they relate. The furnishing of a substantial portion of the farm machinery and equipment also adds support to a conclusion that Mrs. A has materially participated. Accordingly, the rental income Mrs. A re-

**Reg. §1.1402(a)-4(b)(6)**

ceives from her farm should be included in net earnings from self-employment.

*Example (2).* D agrees to produce a crop on C's cotton farm under an arrangement providing that C and D will each receive one-half of the proceeds from such production. C agrees to furnish all the necessary equipment, and it is understood that he is to advise D when to plant the cotton and when it needs to be chopped, plowed, sprayed, and picked. It is also understood that during the growing season C is to inspect the crop every few days to determine whether D is properly taking care of the crop. Under the arrangement, D is required to furnish all labor needed to grow and harvest the crop. C, in fact, renders such advice, makes such inspections, and furnishes such equipment. C's contemplated participation in management decisions is considered material with respect to the management of the cotton production operation. C's actual participation pursuant to the arrangement is also considered to be material with respect to the management of the production of cotton. Accordingly, the income C receives from his cotton farm is to be included in computing his net earnings from self-employment.

*Example (3).* E owns a grain farm and turns its operation over to his son, F. By the oral rental arrangement between E and F, the latter agrees to produce crops of grain on the farm, and E agrees that he will be available for consultation and advice and will inspect and help to harvest the crops. E furnishes most of the equipment, including a tractor, a combine, plows, wagons, drills, and harrows: he continues to live on the farm and does some of the work such as repairing barns and farm machinery, going to town for supplies, cutting weeds, etc.; he regularly inspects the crops during the growing season; and he helps F to harvest the crops. Although the final decisions are made by F, he frequently consults with his father regarding the production of the crops. An evaluation of all of E's actual activities indicates that they are sufficiently substantial and regular to support a conclusion that he is materially participating in the crop production operations and the management thereof. If it can be shown that the degree of E's actual participation was contemplated by the arrangement, E's income from the grain farm will be included in computing net earnings from self-employment.

*Example (4).* G owns a fully-equipped farm which he rents to H under an arrangement which contemplates that G shall materially participate in the management of the production of crops raised on the farm pursuant to the arrangement. G lives in town about 5 miles from the farm. About twice a month he visits the farm and looks over the buildings and equipment. G may occasionally, in an emergency, discuss with H some phase of a crop production activity. In effect, H has complete charge of the management of farming operations regardless of the understanding between him and G. Although G pays one-half of the cost of the seed and fertilizer and is charged for the cost of materials purchased by H to make all necessary repairs, G's activities do not constitute material participation in the crop production activities. Accordingly, G's income from the crops is not included in computing net earnings from self-employment.

*Example (5).* I owned a farm several miles from the town in which he lived. He rented the farm to J under an arrangement which contemplated I's material participation in the management of production of wheat. I furnished one-half of the seed and fertilizer and all the farm equipment and livestock. He employed K to perform all the services in advising, consulting, and inspecting contemplated by the arrangement. I is not materially participating in the management of production of wheat by J. The work done by I's employee, K, is not attributable to I in determining the extent of I's participation. I's rental income from the arrangement is, therefore, not to be included in computing his net earnings from self-employment. For taxable years beginning before January 1, 1974, however, I's rental income would be includible in those earnings.

*Example (6).* L, a calendar-year taxpayer, appointed M as his agent to rent his fully equipped farm for 1974. M entered into a rental arrangement with N under which M was to direct the planting of crops, inspect them weekly during the growing season, and consult with N on any problems that might arise in connection with irrigation, etc., while N furnished all the labor needed to grow and harvest the crops. M did in fact fulfill its responsibilities under the arrangement. Although the arrangement entered into by M and N is considered to have been made by L, M's services are not attributable to L, and L's furnishing of a fully equipped farm is insufficient by itself to constitute material participation in the production of the crops. Accordingly, L's rental income from the arrangement is not included in his net earnings from self-employment for that year. For taxable years beginning before January 1, 1974, however, L's rental income would be includible in those earnings.

(c) *Rentals from living quarters.*—(1) *No services rendered for occupants.*—Payments for the use or occupancy of entire private residences or living quarters in duplex or multiple-housing units are generally rentals from real estate. Except in the case of real-estate

dealers, such payments are excluded in determining net earnings from self-employment even though such payments are in part attributable to personal property furnished under the lease.

(2) *Services rendered for occupants.*—Payments for the use or occupancy of rooms or other space where services are also rendered to the occupant, such as for the use or occupancy of rooms or other quarters in hotels, boarding houses, or apartment houses furnishing hotel services, or in tourist camps or tourist homes, or payments for the use or occupancy of space in parking lots, warehouses, or storage garages, do not constitute rentals from real estate; consequently, such payments are included in determining net earnings from self-employment. Generally, services are considered rendered to the occupant if they are primarily for his convenience and are other than those usually or customarily rendered in connection with the rental of rooms or other space for occupancy only. The supplying of maid service, for example, constitutes such service; whereas the furnishing of heat and light, the cleaning of public entrances, exits, stairways and lobbies, the collection of trash, and so forth, are not considered as services rendered to the occupant.

(3) *Example.*—The application of this paragraph may be illustrated by the following example:

*Example.* A, an individual, owns a building containing four apartments. During the taxable year, he receives $1,400 from apartments numbered 1 and 2, which are rented without services rendered to the occupants, and $3,600 from apartments numbered 3 and 4, which are rented with services rendered to the occupants. His fixed expenses for the four apartments aggregate $1,200 during the taxable year. In addition, he has $500 of expenses attributable to the services rendered to the occupants of apartments 3 and 4. In determining his net earnings from self-employment, A includes the $3,600 received from apartments 3 and 4, and the expenses of $1,100 ($500 plus one-half of $1,200) attributable thereto. The rentals and expenses attributable to apartments 1 and 2 are excluded. Therefore, A has $2,500 of net earnings from self-employment for the taxable year from the building.

(d) *Treatment of business income which includes rentals from real estate.*—Except in the case of a real-estate dealer, where an individual or a partnership is engaged in a trade or business the income of which is classifiable in part as rentals from real estate, only that portion of such income which is not classifiable as rentals from real estate, and the expenses attributable to such portion, are included in determining net earnings from self-employment. [Reg. § 1.1402(a)-4.]

☐ [T.D. 6691, 12-2-63. Amended by T.D. 7710, 7-28-80.]

**[Reg. § 1.1402(a)-5]**

§ 1.1402(a)-5. Dividends and interest.—(a) All dividends on shares of stock are excluded unless they are received by an individual in the course of his trade or business as a dealer in stocks or securities.

(b) Interest on any bond, debenture, note, or certificate, or other evidence of indebtedness, issued with interest coupons or in registered form by any corporation (including one issued by a government or political subdivision thereof) is excluded unless such interest is received in the course of a trade or business as a dealer in stocks or securities. However, interest with respect to which a credit against tax is allowable as provided in section 35, that is, interest on certain obligations of the United States and its instrumentalities, is not included in net earnings from self-employment even though received in the course of a trade or business as a dealer in stocks or securities. Only interest on bonds, debentures, notes, or certificates, or other evidence of indebtedness, issued with interest coupons or in registered form by a corporation, is excluded in the case of all persons other than dealers in stocks or securities; other interest received in the course of any trade or business (such as interest received by a pawnbroker on his loans or interest received by a merchant on his accounts or notes receivable) is not excluded.

(c) Dividends and interest of the character excludable under paragraphs (a) and (b) of this section received by an individual on stocks or securities held for speculation or investment are excluded whether or not the individual is a dealer in stocks or securities.

(d) A dealer in stocks or securities is a merchant of stocks or securities with an established place of business, regularly engaged in the business of purchasing stocks or securities and reselling them to customers; that is, he is one who as a merchant buys stocks or securities and sells them to customers with a view to the gains and profits that may be derived therefrom. Persons who buy and sell or hold stocks or securities for investment or speculation, irrespective of whether such buying or selling constitutes the carrying on of a trade or business, are not dealers in stocks or securities. [Reg. § 1.1402(a)-5.]

☐ [T.D. 6691, 12-2-63.]

**[Reg. § 1.1402(a)-6]**

**§ 1.1402(a)-6. Gain or loss from disposition of property.—**
(a) There is excluded any gain or loss: (1) Which is considered as gain or loss from the sale or exchange of a capital asset; (2) from the cutting of timber or the disposal of timber, coal, or iron ore, even though held primarily for sale to customers, if section 631 is applicable to such gain or loss; and (3) from the sale, exchange, involuntary conversion, or other disposition of property if such property is neither (i) stock in trade or other property of a kind which would properly be includible in inventory if on hand at the close of the taxable year, nor (ii) property held primarily for sale to customers in the ordinary course of a trade or business. For the purpose of the special rule in subparagraph (3) of this paragraph, it is immaterial whether a gain or loss is treated as a capital gain or loss or as an ordinary gain or loss for purposes other than determining net earnings from self-employment. For instance, where the character of a loss is governed by the provisions of section 1231, such loss is excluded in determining net earnings from self-employment even though such loss is treated under section 1231 as an ordinary loss. For the purposes of this special rule, the term "involuntary conversion" means a compulsory or involuntary conversion of property into other property or money as a result of its destruction in whole or in part, theft or seizure, or an exercise of the power of requisition or condemnation or the threat or imminence thereof; and the term "other disposition" includes the destruction or loss, in whole or in part, of property by fire, storm, shipwreck, or other casualty, or by theft, even though there is no conversion of such property into other property or money.

(b) The application of this section may be illustrated by the following example:

*Example.* During the taxable year 1954, A, who owns a grocery store, realized a net profit of $1,500 from the sale of groceries and a gain of $350 from the sale of a refrigerator case. During the same year, he sustained a loss of $2,000 as a result of damage by fire to the store building. In computing taxable income, all of these items are taken into account. In determining net earnings from self-employment, however, only the $1,500 of profit derived from the sale of groceries is included. The $350 gain and the $2,000 loss are excluded. [Reg. § 1.1402(a)-6.]

☐ [*T.D. 6691, 12-2-63. Amended by T.D. 6841, 7-26-65.*]

**[Reg. § 1.1402(a)-7]**

**§ 1.1402(a)-7. Net operating loss deduction.—**The deduction provided by section 172, relating to net operating losses sustained in years other than the taxable year, is excluded. [Reg. § 1.1402(a)-7.]

☐ [*T.D. 6691, 12-2-63.*]

**[Reg. § 1.1402(a)-8]**

**§ 1.1402(a)-8. Community income.—**(a) *In case of an individual.—*If any of the income derived by an individual from a trade or business (other than a trade or business carried on by a partnership) is community income under community property laws applicable to such income, all of the gross income, and the deductions attributable to such income, shall be treated as the gross income and deductions of the husband unless the wife exercises substantially all of the management and control of such trade or business, in which case all of such gross income and deductions shall be treated as the gross income and deductions of the wife. For the purpose of this special rule, the term "management and control" means management and control in fact, not the management and control imputed to the husband under the community property laws. For example, a wife who operates a beauty parlor without any appreciable collaboration on the part of her husband will be considered as having substantially all of the management and control of such business despite the provision of any community property law vesting in the husband the right of management and control of community property; and the income and deductions attributable to the operation of such beauty parlor will be considered the income and deductions of the wife.

(b) *In case of a partnership.—*Even though a portion of a partner's distributive share of the income or loss, described in section 702(a)(9), from a trade or business carried on by a partnership is community income or loss under the community property laws applicable to such share, all of such distributive share shall be included in computing the net earnings from self-employment of such partner; no part of such share shall be taken into account in computing the net earnings from self-employment of the spouse of such partner. In any case in which both spouses are members of the same partnership, the distributive share of the income or loss of each spouse is included in computing the net earnings from self-employment of that spouse. [Reg. § 1.1402(a)-8.]

☐ [*T.D. 6691, 12-2-63.*]

**[Reg. § 1.1402(a)-9]**

**§ 1.1402(a)-9. Puerto Rico.—**(a) *Residents.—*A resident of Puerto Rico, whether or not a bona fide resident thereof during the entire taxable year, and whether or not an alien, a citizen of the United States, or a citizen of Puerto Rico, shall compute his net earnings from self-employment in the same manner as would a citizen of the United States residing in the United States. See paragraph (d) of § 1.1402(b)-1 for regulations relating to nonresident aliens. For the purposes of the tax on self-employment income, the gross income of such a resident of Puerto Rico also includes income from Puerto Rican sources. Thus, under this special rule, income from Puerto Rican sources will be included in determining net earnings from self-employment of a resident of Puerto Rico engaged in the active conduct of a trade or business in Puerto Rico despite the fact that, under section 933, such income may not be taken into account for purposes of the tax under section 1 or 3.

(b) *Nonresidents.—*A citizen of Puerto Rico who is also a citizen of the United States and who is not a resident of Puerto Rico will compute his net earnings from self-employment in the same manner and subject to the same provisions of law and regulations as other citizens of the United States. [Reg. § 1.1402(a)-9.]

☐ [*T.D. 6691, 12-2-63.*]

**[Reg. § 1.1402(a)-10]**

**§ 1.1402(a)-10. Personal exemption deduction.—**The deduction provided by section 151, relating to personal exemptions, is excluded. [Reg. § 1.1402(a)-10.]

☐ [*T.D. 6691, 12-2-63.*]

**[Reg. § 1.1402(a)-11]**

**§ 1.1402(a)-11. Ministers and members of religious orders.—**
(a) *In general.—*For each taxable year ending after 1954 in which a minister or member of a religious order is engaged in a trade or business, within the meaning of section 1402(c) and § 1.1402(c)-5, with respect to service performed in the exercise of his ministry or in the exercise of duties required by such order, net earnings from self-employment from such trade or business include the gross income derived during the taxable year from any such service, less the deductions attributable to such gross income. For each taxable year ending on or after December 31, 1957, such minister or member of a religious order shall compute his net earnings from self-employment derived from the performance of such service without regard to the exclusions from gross income provided by section 107 (relating to rental value of parsonages) and section 119 (relating to meals and lodging furnished for the convenience of the employer). Thus, a minister who is subject to self-employment tax with respect to his services as a minister will include in the computation of his net earnings from self-employment for a taxable year ending on or after December 31, 1957, the rental value of a home furnished to him as remuneration for services performed in the exercise of his ministry or the rental allowance paid to him as remuneration for such services irrespective of whether such rental value or rental allowance is excluded from gross income by section 107. Similarly, the value of any meals or lodging furnished to a minister or to a member of a religious order in connection with service performed in the exercise of his ministry or as a member of such order will be included in the computation of his net earnings from self-employment for a taxable year ending on or after December 31, 1957, notwithstanding the exclusion of such value from gross income by section 119.

(b) *In employ of American employer.—*If a minister or member of a religious order engaged in a trade or business described in section 1402(c) and § 1.1402(c)-5 is a citizen of the United States and performs service, in his capacity as a minister or member of a religious order, as an employee of an American employer, as defined in section 3121(h) and the regulations thereunder in Part 31 of this chapter (Employment Tax Regulations), his net earnings from self-employment derived from such service shall be computed as provided in paragraph (a) of this section but without regard to the exclusions from gross income provided in section 911, relating to earned income from sources without the United States, and section 931, relating to income from sources within certain possessions of the United States. Thus, even though all the income of the minister or member for service of the character to which this paragraph is applicable was derived from sources without the United States, or from sources within certain possessions of the United States, and therefore may be excluded from gross income, such income is included in computing net earnings from self-employment.

(c) *Minister in a foreign country whose congregation is composed predominantly of citizens of the United States.—*(1) *Taxable years ending after 1956.—*For any taxable year ending after 1956, a minister of a church, who is engaged in a trade or business within the meaning of section 1402(c) and §1.1402(c)-5, is a citizen of the United States, is performing service in the exercise of his ministry in a foreign country, and has a congregation composed predominantly of United States citizens, shall compute his net earnings from self-employment derived from his services as a minister for such taxable year without regard to the exclusion from gross income provided in section 911, relating to earned income from sources without the United States. For taxable years ending on or after December 31, 1957, such minister shall also disregard sections 107 and 119 in the computation of his net earnings from self-employment. (See paragraph (a) of this section.) For purposes of section 1402(a)(8) and this paragraph a "congregation composed predominantly of citizens of the United States" means a congregation the majority of which throughout the greater portion of its minister's taxable year were United States citizens.

(2) *Election for taxable years ending after 1954 and before 1957.*— (i) A minister described in subparagraph (1) of this paragraph who, for a taxable year ending after 1954 and before 1957, had income from service described in such subparagraph which would have been included in computing net earnings from self-employment if such income had been derived in a taxable year ending after 1956 by an individual who had filed a waiver certificate under section 1402(e), may elect to have section 1402(a)(8) and subparagraph (1) of this paragraph apply to his income from such service for his taxable years ending after 1954 and before 1957. If such minister filed a waiver certificate prior to August 1, 1956, in accordance with §1.1402(e)(1)-1, or he files such a waiver certificate on or before the due date of his return (including any extensions thereof) for his last taxable year ending before 1957, he must make such election on or before the due date of his return (including any extensions thereof) for such taxable year or before April 16, 1957, whichever is the later. If the waiver certificate is not so filed, the minister must make his election on or before the due date of the return (including any extensions thereof) for his first taxable year ending after 1956. Notwithstanding the expiration of the period prescribed by section 1402(e)(2) for filing such waiver, the minister may file a waiver certificate at the time he makes the election. In no event shall an election be valid unless the minister files prior to or at the time of the election a waiver certificate in accordance with §1.1402(e)(1)-1.

(ii) The election shall be made by filing with the district director of internal revenue with whom the waiver certificate, Form 2031, is filed a written statement indicating that, by reason of the Social Security Amendments of 1956, the minister desires to have the Federal old-age, survivors, and disability insurance system established by title II of the Social Security Act extended to his services performed in a foreign country as a minister of a congregation composed predominantly of United States citizens beginning with the first taxable year ending after 1954 and prior to 1957 for which he had income from such services. The statement shall be dated and signed by the minister and shall clearly state that it is an election for retroactive self-employment tax coverage under the Self-Employment Contributions Act of 1954. In addition, the statement shall include the following information:

(a) The name and address of the minister.

(b) His social security account number, if he has one.

(c) That he is a duly ordained, commissioned, or licensed minister of a church.

(d) That he is a citizen of the United States.

(e) That he is performing services in the exercise of his ministry in a foreign country.

(f) That his congregation is composed predominantly of citizens of the United States.

(g) (1) That he has filed a waiver certificate and, if so, where and under what circumstances the certificate was filed and the taxable year for which it is effective; or (2) That he is filing a waiver certificate with his election for retroactive coverage and, if so, the taxable year for which it is effective.

(h) That he has or has not filed income tax returns for his taxable years ending after 1954 and before 1957. If he has filed such returns, he shall state the years for which they were filed and indicate the district director of internal revenue with whom they were filed.

(iii) Notwithstanding section 1402(e)(3), a waiver certificate filed pursuant to §1.1402(e)(1)-1 by a minister making an election under this paragraph shall be effective (regardless of when such certificate is filed) for such minister's first taxable year ending after 1954 in which he had income from service described in subparagraph (1) of this paragraph or for the taxable year of the minister prescribed by section 1402(e)(3), if such taxable year is earlier, and for all succeeding taxable years.

(iv) No interest or penalty shall be assessed or collected for failure to file a return within the time prescribed by law if such failure arises solely by reason of an election made by a minister pursuant to this paragraph or for any underpayment of self-employment income tax arising solely by reason of such election, for the period ending with the date such minister makes an election pursuant to this paragraph.

(d) *Treatment of certain remuneration paid in 1955 and 1956 as wages.*—For treatment of remuneration paid to an individual for service described in section 3121(b)(8)(A) which was erroneously treated by the organization employing him as employment within the meaning of chapter 21 of the Internal Revenue Code, see §1.1402(e)(4)-1. [Reg. §1.1402(a)-11.]

☐ [*T.D.* 6691, 12-2-63. *Amended by T.D.* 9194, 4-6-2005.]

### [Reg. §1.1402(a)-12]

**§1.1402(a)-12. Continental shelf and certain possessions of the United States.**—(a) *Certain possessions.*—For purposes of the tax on self-employment income, the exclusion from gross income provided by section 931 (relating to bona fide residents of certain possessions of the United States) will not apply. Net earnings from self-employment are subject to the tax on self-employment income even if such amounts are excluded from gross income under section 931.

(b) *Continental shelf.*—For the definition of the term "United States" and for other geographical definitions relating to the continental shelf, see section 638 and §1.638-1.

(c) *Effective/applicability date.*—This section applies to taxable years ending after April 9, 2008. [Reg. §1.1402(a)-12.]

☐ [*T.D.* 6691, 12-2-63. *Amended by T.D.* 7277, 5-14-73; *T.D.* 9194, 4-6-2005 *and T.D.* 9391, 4-4-2008.]

### [Reg. §1.1402(a)-13]

**§1.1402(a)-13. Income from agricultural activity.**—(a) *Agricultural trade or business.*—(1) An agricultural trade or business is one in which, if the trade or business were carried on exclusively by employees, the major portion of the services would constitute agricultural labor as defined in section 3121(g) and the regulations thereunder in Part 31 of this chapter (Employment Tax Regulations). In case the services are in part agricultural and in part nonagricultural, the time devoted to the performance of each type of service is the test to be used to determine whether the major portion of the services would constitute agricultural labor. If more than half of the time spent in performing all the services is spent in performing services which would constitute agricultural labor under section 3121(g), the trade or business is agricultural. If only half, or less, of the time spent in performing all the services is spent in performing services which would constitute agricultural labor under section 3121(g), the trade or business is not agricultural. In every case the time spent in performing the services will be computed by adding the time spent in the trade or business during the taxable year by every individual (including the individual carrying on such trade or business and the members of his family) in performing such services. The operation of this special rule is not affected by section 3121(c), relating to the included-excluded rule for determining employment.

(2) The rules prescribed in subparagraph (1) of this paragraph have no application where the nonagricultural services are performed in connection with an enterprise which constitutes a trade or business separate and distinct from the trade or business conducted as an agricultural enterprise. Thus, the operation of a roadside automobile service station on farm premises constitutes a trade or business separate and distinct from the agricultural enterprise, and the gross income derived from such service station, less the deductions attributable thereto, is to be taken into account in determining net earnings from self-employment.

(b) *Farm operator's income for taxable years ending before 1955.*— Income derived in a taxable year ending before 1955 from any agricultural trade or business (see paragraph (a) of this section), and all deductions attributable to such income, are excluded in computing net earnings from self-employment.

(c) *Farm operator's income for taxable years ending after 1954.*—Income derived in a taxable year ending after 1954 from an agricultural trade or business (see paragraph (a) of this section) is includible in computing net earnings from self-employment. Income derived from an agricultural trade or business includes income derived by an individual under an agreement entered into by such individual with another person pursuant to which such individual undertakes to produce agricultural or horticultural commodities (including livestock, bees, poultry, and fur-bearing animals and wildlife) on land owned or leased by such other person and pursuant to which the agricultural or horticultural commodities produced by such individual, or the proceeds therefrom, are to be divided between such individual and such other person, and the amount of such individual's share depends on the amount of the agricultural or horticultural commodities produced. However, except as provided in paragraph (d) of this section, relating to arrangements involving material participation, the income derived under such an agreement by the owner or lessee of the land is not includible in computing net earnings from self-employment. See § 1.1402(a)-4. For options relating to the computation of net earnings from self-employment, see § § 1.1402(a)-14 and 1.1402(a)-15.

(d) *Includible farm rental income for taxable years ending after 1955.—* For taxable years ending after 1955, income derived from an agricultural trade or business (see paragraph (a) of this section) includes also income derived by the owner or tenant of land under an arrangement between such owner or tenant and another person, if such arrangement provides that such other person shall produce agricultural or horticultural commodities (including livestock, bees, poultry, and fur-bearing animals and wildlife) on such land, and that there shall be material participation by the owner or tenant in the production or the management of the production of such agricultural or horticultural commodities, and if there is material participation by the owner or tenant with respect to any such agricultural or horticultural commodity. See paragraph (b) of § 1.1402(a)-4. For options relating to the computation of net earnings from self-employment, see § § 1.1402(a)-14 and 1.1402(a)-15.

(e) *Income from service performed after 1956 as a crew leader.—*Income derived by a crew leader (see section 3121(o) and the regulations thereunder in Part 31 of this chapter (Employment Tax Regulations)) from service performed after 1956 in furnishing individuals to perform agricultural labor for another person and from service performed after 1956 in agricultural labor as a member of the crew is considered to be income derived from a trade or business for purposes of § 1.1402(c)-1. Whether such trade or business is an agricultural trade or business shall be determined by applying the rules set forth in this section. [Reg. § 1.1402(a)-13.]

☐ [*T.D.* 6691, 12-2-63.]

### [Reg. § 1.1402(a)-14]

**§ 1.1402(a)-14. Options available to farmers in computing net earnings from self-employment for taxable years ending after 1954 and before December 31, 1956.—**[This regulation is now obsolete.—CCH.]

### [Reg. § 1.1402(a)-15]

**§ 1.1402(a)-15. Options available to farmers in computing net earnings from self-employment for taxable years ending on or after December 31, 1956.—**(a) *Computation of net earnings.—*In the case of any trade or business which is carried on by an individual or by a partnership and in which, if such trade or business were carried on exclusively by employees, the major portion of the services would constitute agricultural labor as defined in section 3121(g) (see paragraph (a) of § 1.1402(a)-13), net earnings from self-employment may, for a taxable year ending on or after December 31, 1956, at the option of the taxpayer, be computed as follows:

(1) *In case of an individual.—*(i) *Gross income of less than specified amount.—*If the gross income, computed as provided in paragraph (b) of this section, from such trade or business is $2,400 or less ($1,800 or less for a taxable year ending on or after December 31, 1956, and beginning before January 1, 1966), the taxpayer may, at his option, treat as net earnings from self-employment from such trade or business an amount equal to $66^2/_3$ percent of such gross income. If the taxpayer so elects, the amount equal to $66^2/_3$ percent of such gross income shall be used in computing his self-employment income in lieu of his actual net earnings from such trade or business, if any.

(ii) *Gross income in excess of specified amount.—*If the gross income, computed as provided in paragraph (b) of this section, from such trade or business is more than $2,400 ($1,800 for a taxable year ending on or after December 31, 1956, and beginning before January 1, 1966), and the net earnings from self-employment from such trade or business (computed without regard to this section) are less than $1,600 ($1,200 for a taxable year ending on or after December 31, 1956, and beginning before January 1, 1966), the taxpayer may, at his option, treat $1,600 ($1,200 for a taxable year ending on or after December 31, 1956, and beginning before January 1, 1966) as net earnings from self-employment. If the taxpayer so elects, $1,600 ($1,200 for a taxable year ending on or after December 31, 1956, and beginning before January 1, 1966) shall be used in computing his self-employment income in lieu of his actual net earnings from such trade or business, if any. However, if the taxpayer's actual net earnings from such trade or business, as computed in accordance with the applicable provisions of § § 1.1402(a)-1 to 1.1402(a)-13, inclusive, are $1,600 or more ($1,200 or more for a taxable year ending on or after December 31, 1956, and beginning before January 1, 1966) such actual net earnings shall be used in computing his self-employment income.

(2) *In case of a member of a partnership.—*(i) *Distributive share of gross income of less than specified amount.—*If a taxpayer's distributive

share of the gross income of a partnership (as such gross income is computed under the provisions of paragraph (b) of this section) derived from such trade or business (after such gross income has been reduced by the sum of all payments to which section 707(c) applies) is $2,400 or less ($1,800 or less for a taxable year ending on or after December 31, 1956, and beginning before January 1, 1966), the taxpayer may, at his option, treat as his distributive share of income described in section 702(a)(9) derived from such trade or business an amount equal to $66^2/_3$ percent of his distributive share of such gross income (after such gross income has been reduced by the sum of all payments to which section 707(c) applies). If the taxpayer so elects, the amount equal to $66^2/_3$ percent of his distributive share of such gross income shall be used by him in the computation of his net earnings from self-employment in lieu of the actual amount of his distributive share of income described in section 702(a)(9) from such trade or business, if any.

(ii) *Distributive share of gross income in excess of specified amount.—*If a taxpayer's distributive share of the gross income of a partnership (as such gross income is computed under the provisions of paragraph (b) of this section) derived from such trade or business (after such gross income has been reduced by the sum of all payments to which section 707(c) applies) is more than $2,400 ($1,800 for a taxable year ending on or after December 31, 1956, and beginning before January 1, 1966) and the actual amount of his distributive share (whether or not distributed) of income described in section 702(a)(9) derived from such trade or business (computed without regard to this section) is less than $1,600 ($1,200 for a taxable year ending on or after December 31, 1956, and beginning before January 1, 1966), the taxpayer may, at his option, treat $1,600 ($1,200 for a taxable year ending on or after December 31, 1956, and beginning before January 1, 1966) as his distributive share of income described in section 702(a)(9) derived from such trade or business. If the taxpayer so elects, $1,600 ($1,200 for a taxable year ending on or after December 31, 1956, and beginning before January 1, 1966) shall be used by him in the computation of his net earnings from self-employment in lieu of the actual amount of his distributive share of income described in section 702(a)(9) from such trade or business, if any. However, if the actual amount of the taxpayer's distributive share of income described in section 702(a)(9) from such trade or business, as computed in accordance with the applicable provisions of § § 1.1402(a)-1 to 1.1402(a)-13, inclusive, is $1,600 or more ($1,200 or more for a taxable year ending on or after December 31, 1956, and beginning before January 1, 1966), such actual amount of the taxpayer's distributive share shall be used in computing his net earnings from self-employment.

(iii) *Cross reference.—*For a special rule in the case of certain deceased partners, see paragraph (c) of § 1.1402(f)-1.

(b) *Computation of gross income.—*For purposes of this section gross income has the following meanings:

(1) In the case of any such trade or business in which the income is computed under a cash receipts and disbursements method, the gross receipts from such trade or business reduced by the cost or other basis of property which was purchased and sold in carrying on such trade or business (see paragraphs (a) and (c), other than paragraph (a)(5), of § 1.61-4), adjusted (after such reduction) in accordance with the applicable provisions of § § 1.1402(a)-3 to 1.1402(a)-13, inclusive.

(2) In the case of any such trade or business in which the income is computed under an accrual method (see paragraphs (b) and (c), other than paragraph (b)(5), of § 1.61-4), the gross income from such trade or business, adjusted in accordance with the applicable provisions of § § 1.1402(a)-3 to 1.1402(a)-13, inclusive.

(c) *Two or more agricultural activities.—*If an individual (including a member of a partnership) derives gross income (as defined in paragraph (b) of this section) from more than one agricultural trade or business, such gross income (including his distributive share of the gross income of any partnership derived from any such trade or business) shall be deemed to have been derived from one trade or business. Thus, such an individual shall aggregate his gross income derived from each agricultural trade or business carried on by him (which includes, under paragraph (b) of § 1.1402(a)-1, any guaranteed payment, within the meaning of section 707(c), received by him from a farm partnership of which he is a member) and his distributive share of partnership gross income (after such gross income has been reduced by any guaranteed payment within the meaning of section 707(c)) derived from each farm partnership of which he is a member. Such gross income is the amount to be considered for purposes of the optional method provided in this section for computing net earnings from self-employment. If the aggregate gross income of an individual includes income derived from an agricultural trade or business carried on by him and a distributive share of partnership income derived from an agricultural trade or business carried on by a partnership of which he is a member, such aggregate gross income shall be treated as income derived from a single trade or business carried on by him, and such individual shall apply the optional method applicable to individuals set forth in paragraph (a)(1) of this section for purposes of computing his net earnings from self-employment.

(d) *Examples.*—The application of this section may be illustrated by the following examples:

*Example (1).* F is engaged in the business of farming and computes his income under the cash receipts and disbursements method. He files his income tax returns on the basis of the calendar year. During the year 1966, F's gross income from the business of farming (computed in accordance with paragraph (b)(1) of this section) is $2,325. His actual net earnings from self-employment derived from such business are $1,250. As his net earnings from self-employment, F may report $1,250 or, by the optional computation method, he may report $1,550 (66 2/3 percent of $2,325).

*Example (2).* G is engaged in the business of farming and computes his income under the accrual method. His income tax returns are filed on the calendar year basis. For the year 1966, G's gross income from the operation of his farm (computed in accordance with paragraph (b)(2) of this section) is $2,800. He has actual net earnings from self-employment derived from such farm in the amount of $1,250. As his net earnings from self-employment derived from his farm, G may report his actual net earnings of $1,250, or by the optional method he may report $1,600. If G's actual net earnings from self-employment from his farming activities for 1966 were in an amount of $1,600 or more, he would be required to report such amount in computing his self-employment income.

*Example (3).* M, who files his income tax returns on a calendar year basis, is one of the three partners of the XYZ Company, a partnership, engaged in the business of farming. The taxable year of the partnership is the calendar year, and its income is computed under the cash receipts and disbursements method. For M's services in connection with the planting, cultivating, and harvesting of the crops during the year 1966 the partnership agrees to pay him $500, the full amount of which is determined without regard to the income of the partnership and constitutes a guaranteed payment within the meaning of section 707(c). This guaranteed payment to M is the only such payment made during such year. The gross income derived from the business for the year 1966 computed in accordance with paragraph (b)(1) of this section and after being reduced by the guaranteed payment of $500 made to M, is $3,000. One-third of the $3,000 ($1,000), is M's distributive share of such gross income. Under paragraph (c) of this section, the guaranteed payment ($500) received by M and his distributive share of the partnership gross income ($1,000) are deemed to have been derived from one trade or business, and such amounts must be aggregated for purposes of the optional method of computing net earnings from self-employment. Since M's combined gross income from his two agricultural businesses ($1,000 and $500) is not more than $2,400 and since such income is deemed to be derived from one trade or business, M's net earnings from self-employment derived from such farming business may, at his option, be deemed to be $1,000 (66 2/3 percent of $1,500).

*Example (4).* A is one of the two partners of the AB partnership which is engaged in the business of farming. The taxable year of the partnership is the calendar year and its income is computed under the accrual method. A files his income tax returns on the calendar year basis. The partnership agreement provides for an equal sharing in the profits and losses of the partnership by the two partners. A is an experienced farmer and for his services as manager of the partnership's farm activities during the year 1966 he receives $6,000 which amount constitutes a guaranteed payment within the meaning of section 707(c). The gross income of the partnership derived from such business for the year 1966, computed in accordance with paragraph (b)(2) of this section and after being reduced by the guaranteed payment made to A, is $9,600. A's distributive share of such gross income is $4,800 and his distributive share of income described in section 702(a)(9) derived from the partnership's business is $1,900. Under paragraph (c) of this section, the guaranteed payment received by A and his distributive share of the partnership gross income are deemed to have been derived from one trade or business, and such amounts must be aggregated for purposes of the optional method of computing his net earnings from self-employment. Since the aggregate of A's guaranteed payment ($6,000) and his distributive share of partnership gross income ($4,800) is more than $2,400 and since the aggregate of A's guaranteed payment ($6,000) and his distributive share ($1,900) of partnership income described in section 702(a)(9) is not less than $1,600, the optional method of computing net earnings from self-employment is not available to A.

*Example (5).* F is a member of the EFG partnership which is engaged in the business of farming. F files his income tax returns on the calendar year basis. The taxable year of the partnership is the calendar year, and its income is computed under a cash receipts and

disbursements method. Under the partnership agreement the partners are to share equally the profits or losses of the business. The gross income derived from the partnership business for the year 1966, computed in accordance with paragraph (b)(1) of this section is $7,500. F's share of such gross income is $2,500. Due to drought and an epidemic among the livestock, the partnership sustains a net loss of $7,800 for the year 1966 of which loss F's share is $2,600. Since F's distributive share of gross income derived from such business is in excess of $2,400 and since F does not receive income described in section 702(a)(9) of $1,600 or more from such business, he may, at his option, be deemed to have received $1,600 as his distributive share of income described in section 702(a)(9) from such business. [Reg. § 1.1402(a)-15.]

☐ [*T.D. 6691, 12-2-63. Amended by T.D. 6993, 1-17-69.*]

### [Reg. § 1.1402(a)-16]

**§ 1.1402(a)-16. Exercise of option.**—A taxpayer shall, for each taxable year with respect to which he is eligible to use the optional method described in § 1.1402(a)-14 or § 1.1402(a)-15, make a determination as to whether his net earnings from self-employment are to be computed in accordance with such method. If the taxpayer elects the optional method for a taxable year, he shall signify such election by computing net earnings from self-employment under the optional method as set forth in Schedule F (Form 1040) of the income tax return filed by the taxpayer for such taxable year. If the optional method is not elected at the time of the filing of the return for a taxable year with respect to which the taxpayer is eligible to elect such optional method, such method may be elected on an amended return (or on such other form as may be prescribed for such use) filed within the period prescribed by section 6501 and the regulations thereunder for the assessment of the tax for such taxable year. If the optional method is elected on a return for a taxable year, the taxpayer may revoke such election by filing an amended return (or such other form as may be prescribed for such use) for the taxable year within the period prescribed by section 6501 and the regulations thereunder for the assessment of the tax for such taxable year. If the taxpayer is deceased or unable to make an election, the person designated in section 6012(b) and the regulations thereunder may, within the period prescribed in this section elect the optional method for any taxable year with respect to which the taxpayer is eligible to use the optional method and revoke an election previously made by or for the taxpayer. [Reg. § 1.1402(a)-16.]

☐ [*T.D. 6691, 12-2-63.*]

### [Reg. § 1.1402(a)-17]

**§ 1.1402(a)-17. Retirement payments to retired partners.**—(a) *In general.*—There shall be excluded, in computing net earnings from self-employment for taxable years ending on or after December 31, 1967, certain payments made on a periodic basis by a partnership, pursuant to a written plan of the partnership, to a retired partner on account of his retirement. The exclusion applies only if the payments are made pursuant to a plan which meets the requirements prescribed in paragraph (b) of this section, and, in addition, the conditions set forth in paragraph (c) of this section are met.

(b) *Retirement plan of partnership.*—(1) To meet the requirements of section 1402(a)(10), the written plan of the partnership must set forth the terms and conditions of the program or system established by the partnership for the purpose of making payments to retired partners on account of their retirement. To qualify as payments on account of retirement, the payments must constitute bona fide retirement income. Thus, payments of benefits not customarily included in a pension or retirement plan such as layoff benefits are not payments on account of retirement. Eligibility for retirement generally is established on the basis of age, physical condition, or a combination of age or physical condition and years of service. Generally, retirement benefits are measured by, and based on, such factors as years of service and compensation received. In determining whether the plan of the partnership provides for payments on account of retirement, factors, formulas, etc., reflected in public, and in broad based private, pension or retirement plans in prescribing eligibility requirements and in computing benefits may be taken into account.

(2) The plan of the partnership must provide for payments on account of retirement—

(i) To partners generally or to a class or classes of partners,

(ii) On a periodic basis, and

(iii) Which continue at least until the partner's death.

For purposes of subdivision (i) of this subparagraph, a class of partners may, in an appropriate case, contain only one member. Payments are made on a periodic basis if made at regularly recurring intervals (usually monthly) not exceeding one year.

(c) *Conditions relating to exclusion.*—(1) *In general.*—A payment made pursuant to a written plan of a partnership which meets the requirements of paragraph (b) of this section shall be excluded, in computing net earnings from self-employment, only if—

(i) The retired partner to whom the payment is made rendered no service with respect to any trade or business carried on by the partnership (or its successors) during the taxable year of the partnership (or its successors), which ends within or with the taxable year of the retired partner and in which the payment was received by him;

(ii) No obligation (whether certain in amount or contingent on a subsequent event) exists (as of the close of the partnership's taxable year referred to in subdivision (i) of this subparagraph) from the other partners to the retired partner except with respect to retirement payments under the plan or rights such as benefits payable on account of sickness, accident, hospitalization, medical expenses, or death; and

(iii) The retired partner's share (if any) of the capital of the partnership has been paid to him in full before the close of the partnership's taxable year referred to in subdivision (i) of this subparagraph.

By application of the conditions set forth in this subparagraph, either all payments on account of retirement received by a retired partner during the taxable year of the partnership ending within or with his taxable year are excluded or none of the payments are excluded. Subdivision (ii) of this subparagraph has application only to obligations from other partners in their capacity as partners as distinguished from an obligation which arose and exists from a transaction unrelated to the partnership or to a trade or business carried on by the partnership. The effect of the conditions set forth in subdivisions (ii) and (iii) of this subparagraph is that the exclusion may apply with respect to payments received by a retired partner during the taxable year of the partnership ending within or with his taxable year only if at the close of the partnership's taxable year the retired partner had no financial interest in the partnership except for the right to retirement payments.

(2) *Examples.*—The application of subparagraph (1) of this paragraph may be illustrated by the following examples. Each example assumes that the partnership plan pursuant to which the payments are made meets the requirements of paragraph (b) of this section.

*Example (1).* A, who files his income tax returns on a calendar year basis, is a partner in the ABC partnership. The taxable year of the partnership is the period July 1 to June 30, inclusive. A retired from the partnership on January 1, 1973, and receives monthly payments on account of his retirement. As of June 30, 1973, no obligation existed from the other partners to A (except with respect to retirement payments under the plan) and A's share of the capital of the partnership had been paid to him in full. The monthly retirement payments received by A from the partnership in his taxable year ending on December 31, 1973, are not excluded from net earnings from self-employment since A rendered service to the partnership during a portion of the partnership's taxable year (July 1, 1972, through June 30, 1973) which ends within A's taxable year ending on December 31, 1973.

*Example (2).* D, a partner in the DEF partnership, retired from the partnership as of the close of December 31, 1972. The taxable year of both D and the partnership is the calendar year. During the partnership's taxable year ending December 31, 1973, D rendered no service with respect to any trade or business carried on by the partnership. On or before December 31, 1973, all obligations (other than with respect to retirement payments under the plan) from the other partners to D have been liquidated, and D's share of the capital of the partnership has been paid to him. Retirement payments received by D pursuant to the partnership's plan in his taxable year ending December 31, 1973, are excluded in determining his net earnings from self-employment (if any) for that taxable year.

*Example (3).* Assume the same facts as in example (2) except that as of the close of December 31, 1973, D has a right to a fixed percentage of any amounts collected by the partnership after that date which are attributable to services rendered by him prior to his retirement for clients of the partnership. The monthly payments received by D in his taxable year ending December 31, 1973, are not excluded from net earnings from self-employment since as of the close of the partnership's taxable year which ends with D's taxable year, an obligation (other than an obligation with respect to retirement payments) exists from the other partners to D. [Reg. §1.1402(a)-17.]

□ [*T.D. 7333, 12-19-74.*]

### [Reg. §1.1402(a)-18]

**§1.1402(a)-18. Split-dollar life insurance arrangements.**—See §§1.61-22 and 1.7872-15 for rules relating to the treatment of split-dollar life insurance arrangements.

□ [*T.D. 9092, 9-11-2003.*]

### [Reg. §1.1402(b)-1]

**§1.1402(b)-1. Self-employment income.**—(a) *In general.*—Except for the exclusions in paragraphs (b) and (c) of this section and the exception in paragraph (d) of this section, the term "self-employment income" means the net earnings from self-employment derived by an individual during a taxable year.

(b) *Maximum self-employment income.*—(1) *General rule.*—Subject to the special rules described in subparagraph (2) of this paragraph, the maximum self-employment income of an individual for a taxable year (whether a period of 12 months or less) is—

(i) For any taxable year beginning in a calendar year after 1974, an amount equal to the contribution and benefit base (as determined under section 230 of the Social Security Act) which is effective for such calendar year; and

(ii) For any taxable year—

| | |
|---|---:|
| Ending before 1955 | $3,600 |
| Ending after 1954 and before 1959 | 4,200 |
| Ending after 1958 and before 1966 | 4,800 |
| Ending after 1965 and before 1968 | 6,600 |
| Ending after 1967 and beginning before 1972 | 7,800 |
| Beginning after 1971 and before 1973 | 9,000 |
| Beginning after 1972 and before 1974 | 10,800 |
| Beginning after 1973 and before 1975 | 13,200 |

(2) *Special rules.*—(i) If an individual is paid wages as defined in subparagraph (3) of this paragraph in a taxable year, the maximum self-employment income for such taxable year is computed as provided in subdivision (ii) or (iii) of this subparagraph.

(ii) If an individual is paid wages as defined in subparagraph (3)(i) or (ii) of this paragraph in a taxable year, the maximum self-employment income of such individual for such taxable year is the excess of the amounts indicated in subparagraph (1) of this paragraph over the amount of the wages, as defined in subparagraph (3)(i) and (ii) of this paragraph, paid to him during the taxable year. For example, if for his taxable year beginning in 1974, an individual has $15,000 of net earnings from self-employment and during such taxable year is paid $1,000 of wages as defined in section 3121(a) (see subparagraph (3)(i) of this paragraph), he has $12,200 ($13,200 – $1,000) of self-employment income for the taxable year.

(iii) For taxable years ending on or after December 31, 1968, wages, as defined in subparagraph (3)(iii) of this paragraph, are taken into account in determining the maximum self-employment income of an individual for purposes of the tax imposed under section 1401(b) (hospital insurance), but not for purposes of the tax imposed under section 1401(a) (old-age, survivors, and disability insurance). If an individual is paid wages as defined in subparagraph (3)(iii) of this paragraph in a taxable year, his maximum self-employment income for such taxable year for purposes of the tax imposed under section 1401(a) is computed under subparagraph (1) of this paragraph or subdivision (ii) of this subparagraph (whichever is applicable), and his maximum self-employment income for such taxable year for purposes of the tax imposed under section 1401(b) is the excess of his section 1401(a) maximum self-employment income over the amount of wages, as defined in subparagraph (3)(iii) of this paragraph, paid to him during the taxable year. For purposes of this subdivision, wages as defined in subparagraph (3)(iii) of this paragraph are deemed paid to an individual in the period with respect to which the payment is made, that is, the period in which the compensation was earned or deemed earned within the meaning of section 3231(e). For an explanation of the term "compensation" and for provisions relating to when compensation is earned, see the regulations under section 3231(e) in Part 31 of this chapter (Employment Tax Regulations). The application of the rules set forth in this subdivision may be illustrated by the following example:

*Example.* M, a calendar-year taxpayer, has $15,000 of net earnings from self-employment for 1974 and during the taxable year is paid $1,000 of wages as defined in section 3121(a) (see subparagraph (3)(i) of this paragraph) and $1,600 of compensation subject to tax under section 3201 (see subparagraph (3)(iii) of this paragraph). Of the $1,600 of taxable compensation, $1,200 represents compensation for services rendered in 1974 and the balance ($400) represents compensation which pursuant to the provisions of section 3231(e) is earned or deemed earned in 1973. M's maximum self-employment income for 1974 for purposes of the tax imposed under section 1401(a), computed as provided in subdivision (ii) of this subparagraph, is $12,200 ($13,200 – $1,000), and for purposes of the tax imposed under section 1401(b) is $11,000 ($12,200 – $1,200). However, M may recompute his maximum self-employment income for 1973 for purposes of the tax imposed under section 1401(b) by taking into account the $400 of compensation which is deemed paid in 1973.

(3) *Meaning of term "wages".*—For the purpose of the computation described in subparagraph (2) of this paragraph, the term "wages" includes:

(i) Wages as defined in section 3121(a);

(ii) Such remuneration paid to an employee for services covered by—

(a) An agreement entered into pursuant to section 218 of the Social Security Act (42 U.S.C. 418), which section provides for extension of the Federal old-age, survivors and disability insurance system to State and local government employees under voluntary agreements between the States and the Secretary of Health, Education, and Welfare (Federal Security Administrator before April 11, 1953), or

(b) An agreement entered into pursuant to the provisions of section 3121(1), relating to coverage of citizens of the United States who are employees of foreign subsidiaries of domestic corporations, as would be wages under section 3121(a) if such services constituted employment under section 3121(b). For an explanation of the term "wages", see the regulations under section 3121(a) in Part 31 of this chapter (Employment Tax Regulations); and

(iii) Compensation, as defined in section 3231(e), which is subject to the employee tax imposed by section 3201 or the employee representative tax imposed by section 3211.

(c) *Minimum net earnings from self-employment.*—Self-employment income does not include the net earnings from self-employment of an individual when the amount of such earnings for the taxable year is less than $400. Thus, an individual having only $300 of net earnings from self-employment for the taxable year would not have any self-employment income. However, an individual having net earnings from self-employment of $400 or more for the taxable year may, by application of paragraph (b)(2) of this section, have less than $400 of self-employment income for purposes of the tax imposed under section 1401(a) and the tax imposed under section 1401(b) or may have self-employment income of $400 or more for purposes of the tax imposed under section 1401(a) and of less than $400 for purposes of the tax imposed under section 1401(b). This could occur in a case in which the amount of the individual's net earnings from self-employment is $400 or more for a taxable year and the amount of such net earnings from self-employment plus the amount of wages, as defined in paragraph (b)(3) of this section, paid to him during the taxable year exceed the maximum self-employment income, as set forth in paragraph (b)(1) of this section, for the taxable year. However, the result occurs only if such maximum self-employment income exceeds the amount of such wages. The application of this paragraph may be illustrated by the following example:

*Example.* For 1974 M, a calendar-year taxpayer, has net earnings from self-employment of $2,000 and wages (as defined in paragraph (b)(3)(i) and (ii) of this section) of $12,500. Since M's net earnings from self-employment plus his wages exceed the maximum self-employment income for 1974 ($13,200), his self-employment income for 1974 is $700 ($13,200 − $12,500). If M also had wages, as defined in paragraph (b)(3)(iii) of this section, of $200, his self-employment income would be $700 for purposes of the tax imposed under section 1401(a) and $500 ($13,200 − $12,700 ($12,500 + $200)) for purposes of the tax imposed under section 1401(b).

For provisions relating to when wages as defined in paragraph (b)(3)(iii) of this section are treated as paid, see paragraph (b)(2)(iii) of this section.

(d) *Nonresident aliens.*—A nonresident alien individual never has self-employment income. While a nonresident alien individual who derives income from a trade or business carried on within the United States, Puerto Rico, the Virgin Islands, Guam, or American Samoa (whether by agents or employees, or by a partnership of which he is a member) may be subject to the applicable income tax provisions on such income, such nonresident alien individual will not be subject to the tax on self-employment income, since any net earnings which he may have from self-employment do not constitute self-employment income. For the purpose of the tax on self-employment income, an individual who is not a citizen of the United States but who is a resident of the Commonwealth of Puerto Rico, the Virgin Islands, or, for taxable years beginning after 1960, of Guam or American Samoa is not considered to be a nonresident alien individual. [Reg. § 1.1402(b)-1.]

☐ [*T.D.* 6196, 8-13-56. *Amended by T.D.* 6691, 12-2-63, *T.D.* 6993, 1-17-69 *and T.D.* 7333, 12-19-74.]

### [Reg. § 1.1402(c)-1]

§ 1.1402(c)-1. **Trade or business.**—In order for an individual to have net earnings from self-employment, he must carry on a trade or business, either as an individual or as a member of a partnership. Except for the exclusions discussed in § § 1.1402(c)-2 to 1.1402(c)-7, inclusive, the term "trade or business", for the purpose of the tax on self-employment income, shall have the same meaning as when used

in section 162. An individual engaged in one of the excluded activities specified in such sections of the regulations may also be engaged in carrying on activities which constitute a trade or business for purposes of the tax on self-employment income. Whether or not he is also engaged in carrying on a trade or business will be dependent upon all of the facts and circumstances in the particular case. An individual who is a crew leader, as defined in section 3121(o) (see such section and the regulations thereunder in Part 31 of this chapter (Employment Tax Regulations)), is considered to be engaged in carrying on a trade or business with respect to services performed by him after 1956 in furnishing individuals to perform agricultural labor for another person or services performed by him after 1956 as a member of the crew. [Reg. § 1.1402(c)-1.]

☐ [*T.D.* 6196, 8-13-56. *Amended by T.D.* 6691, 12-2-63 *and T.D.* 6978, 10-29-68.]

### [Reg. § 1.1402(c)-2]

§ 1.1402(c)-2. **Public office.**—(a) *In general.*—(1) *General rule.*—Except as otherwise provided in subparagraph (2) of this paragraph, the performance of the functions of a public office does not constitute a trade or business.

(2) *Fee basis public officials.*—(i) *In general.*—If an individual receives fees after 1967 for the performance of the functions of a public office of a State or a political subdivision thereof for which he is compensated solely on a fee basis, and if the service performed in such office is eligible for (but is not made the subject of) an agreement between the State and the Secretary of Health, Education, and Welfare pursuant to section 218 of the Social Security Act to extend social security coverage thereto, the service for which such fees are received constitutes a trade or business within the meaning of section 1402(c) and § 1.1402(c)-1. If an individual performs service for a State or a political subdivision thereof in any period in more than one position, each position is treated separately for purposes of the preceding sentence. See also paragraph (f) of § 1.1402(c)-3 relating to the performance of service by an individual as an employee of a State or a political subdivision thereof in a position compensated solely on a fee basis.

(ii) *Election with respect to fees received in 1968.*—(A) Any individual who in 1968 receives fees for service performed by him with respect to the functions of a public office of a State or a political subdivision thereof in any period in which the functions are performed in a position compensated solely on a fee basis may elect, if the performance of the service for which such fees are received constitutes a trade or business pursuant to the provisions of subdivision (i) of this subparagraph, to have such performance of service treated as excluded from the term "trade or business" for the purpose of the tax on self-employment income, pursuant to the provisions of section 122(c)(2) of the Social Security Amendments of 1967 (as quoted in § 1.1402(c)). Such election shall not be limited to service to which the fees received in 1968 are attributable but must also be applicable to service (if any) in subsequent years which, except for the election, would constitute a trade or business pursuant to the provisions of subdivision (i) of this subparagraph. An election made pursuant to the provisions of this subparagraph is irrevocable.

(B) The election referred to in subdivision (ii)(A) of this subparagraph shall be made by filing a certificate of election of exemption (Form 4415) on or before the due date of the income tax return (see section 6072), including any extension thereof (see section 6081), for the taxable year of the individual making the election which begins in 1968. The certificate of election of exemption shall be filed with an internal revenue office in accordance with the instructions on the certificate.

(b) *Meaning of public office.*—The term "public office" includes any elective or appointive office of the United States or any possession thereof, of the District of Columbia, of a State or its political subdivisions, or of a wholly-owned instrumentality of any one or more of the foregoing. For example, the President, the Vice President, a governor, a mayor, the Secretary of State, a member of Congress, a State representative, a county commissioner, a judge, a justice of the peace, a county or city attorney, a marshal, a sheriff, a constable, a registrar of deeds, or a notary public performs the functions of a public office. (However, the service of a notary public could not be made the subject of a section 218 agreement under the Social Security Act because notaries are not "employees" within the meaning of that section. Accordingly, such service does not constitute a trade or business.) [Reg. § 1.1402(c)-2.]

☐ [*T.D.* 6691, 12-2-63. *Amended by T.D.* 7333, 12-19-74 *and T.D.* 7372, 7-23-75.]

### [Reg. § 1.1402(c)-3]

§ 1.1402(c)-3. **Employees.**—(a) *General rule.*—Generally, the performance of service by an individual as an employee, as defined in the Federal Insurance Contributions Act (chapter 21 of the Internal Revenue Code) does not constitute a trade or business within the meaning of section 1402(c) and §1.1402(c)-1. However, in six cases set forth in paragraphs (b) to (g), inclusive, of this section, the performance of service by an individual is considered to constitute a trade or business within the meaning of section 1402(c) and §1.1402(c)-1. (As to when an individual is an employee, see section 3121(d) and (o) and section 3506 and the regulations under those sections in part 31 of this chapter (Employment Tax Regulations).)

(b) *Newspaper vendors.*—Service performed by an individual who has attained the age of 18 constitutes a trade or business for purposes of the tax on self-employment income within the meaning of section 1402(c) and §1.1402(c)-1 if performed in, and at the time of, the sale of newspapers or magazines to ultimate consumers, under an arrangement under which the newspapers or magazines are to be sold by him at a fixed price, his compensation being based on the retention of the excess of such price over the amount at which the newspapers or magazines are charged to him, whether or not he is guaranteed a minimum amount of compensation for such service, or is entitled to be credited with the unsold newspapers or magazines turned back.

(c) *Sharecroppers.*—Service performed by an individual under an arrangement with the owner or tenant of land pursuant to which—

(1) Such individual undertakes to produce agricultural or horticultural commodities (including livestock, bees, poultry, and furbearing animals and wildlife) on such land,

(2) The agricultural or horticultural commodities produced by such individual, or the proceeds therefrom, are to be divided between such individual and such owner or tenant, and

(3) The amount of such individual's share depends on the amount of the agricultural or horticultural commodities produced, constitutes a trade or business within the meaning of section 1402(c) and §1.1402(c)-1.

(d) *Employees of foreign government, instrumentality wholly owned by foreign government, or international organization.*—Service performed in the United States, as defined in section 3121(e)(2) (see such section and the regulations thereunder in Part 31 of this chapter (Employment Tax Regulations)), by an individual who is a citizen of the United States constitutes a trade or business within the meaning of section 1402(c) and §1.1402(c)-1 if such service is excepted from employment, for purposes of the Federal Insurance Contributions Act (chapter 21 of the Code), by—

(1) Section 3121(b)(11), relating to service in the employ of a foreign government (for regulations under section 3121(b)(11), see §31.3121(b)(11)-1 of this chapter);

(2) Section 3121(b)(12), relating to service in the employ of an instrumentality wholly owned by a foreign government (for regulations under section 3121(b)(12), see §31.3121(b)(12)-1 of this chapter); or

(3) Section 3121(b)(15), relating to service in the employ of an international organization (for regulations under section 3121(b)(15), see §31.3121(b)(15)-1 of this chapter).

This paragraph is applicable to service performed in any taxable year ending on or after December 31, 1960, except that it does not apply to service performed before 1961 in Guam or American Samoa.

(e) *Ministers and members of religious orders.*—(1) *Taxable years ending before 1968.*—Service described in section 1402(c)(4) performed by an individual during taxable years ending before 1968 for which a certificate filed pursuant to section 1402(e) is in effect constitutes a trade or business within the meaning of section 1402(c) and §1.1402(c)-1. See also §1.1402(c)-5.

(2) *Taxable years ending after 1967.*—Service described in section 1402(c)(4) performed by an individual during taxable years ending after 1967 constitutes a trade or business within the meaning of section 1402(c) and §1.1402(c)-1 unless an exemption under section 1402(e) (see §§1.1402(e)-1A through 1.1402(e)-4A) is efffective with respect to such individual for the taxable year during which the service is performed. See also §1.1402(c)-5.

(f) *State and local government employees compensated on fee basis.*—(1) *In general.*—(i) Section 1402(c)(2)(E) and this paragraph are applicable only with respect to fees received by an individual after 1967 for services performed by him as an employee of a State or a political subdivision thereof in a position compensated solely on a fee basis. If an individual performs service for a State or a political subdivision thereof in more than one position, each position is treated separately for purposes of determining whether the service performed in such position is performed by an employee and whether compensation for service performed in the position is solely on a fee basis.

(ii) If an individual receives fees after 1967 for service performed by him as an employee of a State or a political subdivision

thereof in a position compensated solely on a fee basis, the service for which such fees are received constitutes a trade or business within the meaning of section 1402(c) and §1.1402(c)-1 except that if service performed in such position is covered under an agreement entered into by the State and the Secretary of Health, Education, and Welfare pursuant to section 218 of the Social Security Act at the time a fee is received, the service to which such fee relates does not constitute a trade or business. See also paragraph (a) of §1.1402(c)-2, relating, in part, to the performance of the functions of a public office of a State or a political subdivision thereof by an individual.

(2) *Election with respect to fees received in 1968.*—(i) Any individual who in 1968 receives fees for service as an employee of a State or a political subdivision thereof in a position compensated solely on a fee basis may elect, if the performance of the service for which such fees are received constitutes a trade or business pursuant to the provisions of subparagraph (1) of this paragraph, to have such performance of service treated as excluded from the term "trade or business" for the purpose of the tax on self-employment income, pursuant to the provisions of section 122(c)(2) of the Social Security Amendments of 1967 (as quoted in §1.1402(c)). Such election shall not be limited to service to which the fees received in 1968 are attributable but must also be applicable to service (if any) in subsequent years which, except for the election, would constitute a trade or business pursuant to the provisions of subparagraph (1) of this paragraph. An election made pursuant to the provisions of this subparagraph is irrevocable.

(ii) The election referred to in subdivision (i) of this subparagraph shall be made by filing a certificate of election of exemption (Form 4415) on or before the due date of the income tax return (see section 6072), including any extension thereof (see section 6081), for the taxable year of the individual making the election which begins in 1968. The certificate of election of exemption shall be filed with an internal revenue office in accordance with the instructions on the certificate.

(g) *Individuals engaged in fishing.*—For taxable years ending after December 31, 1954, service performed by an individual on a boat engaged in catching fish or other forms of aquatic animal life (hereinafter "fish") constitutes a trade or business within the meaning of section 1402(c) and §1.1402(c)-1 if the service is excepted from the definition of employment by section 3121(b)(20) and §31.3121(b)(20)-1(a). However, the preceding sentence does not apply to services performed after December 31, 1954, and before October 4, 1976, on a boat engaged in catching fish if the owner or operator of the boat treated the individual as an employee in the manner described in §31.3121(b)(20)-1(b). [Reg. §1.1402(c)-3.]

☐ [*T.D.* 6691, 12-2-63. *Amended by T.D.* 6978, 10-29-68, *T.D.* 7333, 12-19-74, *T.D.* 7691, 4-8-80 *and T.D.* 7716, 8-26-80.]

### [Reg. §1.1402(c)-4]

**§1.1402(c)-4. Individuals under Railroad Retirement System.**—The performance of service by an individual as an employee or employee representative as defined in section 3231(b) and (c), respectively (see §§31.3231(b)-1 and 31.3231(c)-1 of Part 31 of this chapter (Employment Tax Regulations)), that is, an individual covered under the railroad retirement system, does not constitute a trade or business. [Reg. §1.1402(c)-4.]

☐ [*T.D.* 6691, 12-2-63.]

### [Reg. §1.1402(c)-5]

**§1.1402(c)-5. Ministers and members of religious orders.**—(a) *In general.*—(1) *Taxable years ending before 1968.*—For taxable years ending before 1955, a duly ordained, commissioned, or licensed minister of a church or a member of a religious order is not engaged in carrying on a trade or business with respect to service performed by him in the exercise of his ministry or in the exercise of duties required by such order. However, for taxable years ending after 1954 and before 1968, any individual who is a duly ordained, commissioned, or licensed minister of a church or a member of a religious order (other than a member of a religious order who has taken a vow of poverty as a member of such order) may elect, as provided in §1.1402(e)(1)-1, to have the Federal old-age, survivors, and disability insurance system established by title II of the Social Security Act extended to service performed by him in his capacity as such a minister or member. If such a minister or a member of a religious order makes an election pursuant to §1.1402(e)(1)-1 he is, with respect to service performed by him in such capacity, engaged in carrying on a trade or business for each taxable year to which the election is effective. An election by a minister or member of a religious order has no application to service performed by such minister or member which is not in the exercise of his ministry or in the exercise of duties required by such order.

(2) *Taxable years ending after 1967.*—For any taxable year ending after 1967, a duly ordained, commissioned, or licensed minister of a church or a member of a religious order (other than a member of a religious order who has taken a vow of poverty as a member of such order) is engaged in carrying on a trade or business with respect to service performed by him in the exercise of his ministry or in the exercise of duties required by such order unless an exemption under section 1402(e) (see §§ 1.1402(e)-1A through 1.1402(e)-4A) is effective with respect to such individual for the taxable year during which the service is performed. An exemption which is effective with respect to a minister or a member of a religious order has no application to service performed by such minister or member which is not in the exercise of his ministry or in the exercise of duties required by such order.

(b) *Service by a minister in the exercise of his ministry.*—(1)(i) A certificate of election filed by a duly ordained, commissioned, or licensed minister of a church under the provisions of § 1.1402(e)(1)-1 has application only to service performed by him in the exercise of his ministry.

(ii) An exemption under section 1402(e) (see §§ 1.1402(e)-1A through 1.1402(e)-4A) which is effective with respect to a duly ordained, commissioned, or licensed minister of a church has application only to service performed by him in the exercise of his ministry.

(2) Except as provided in paragraph (c)(3) of this section, service performed by a minister in the exercise of his ministry includes the ministration of sacerdotal functions and the conduct of religious worship, and the control, conduct, and maintenance of religious organizations (including the religious boards, societies, and other integral agencies of such organizations), under the authority of a religious body constituting a church or church denomination. The following rules are applicable in determining whether services performed by a minister are performed in the exercise of his ministry:

(i) Whether service performed by a minister constitutes the conduct of religious worship or the ministration of sacerdotal functions depends on the tenets and practices of the particular religious body constituting his church or church denomination.

(ii) Service performed by a minister in the control, conduct, and maintenance of a religious organization relates to directing, managing, or promoting the activities of such organization. Any religious organization is deemed to be under the authority of a religious body constituting a church or church denomination if it is organized and dedicated to carrying out the tenets and principles of a faith in accordance with either the requirements or sanctions governing the creation of institutions of the faith. The term "religious organization" has the same meaning and application as is given to the term for income tax purposes.

(iii) If a minister is performing service in the conduct of religious worship or the ministration of sacerdotal functions, such service is in the exercise of his ministry whether or not it is performed for a religious organization. The application of this rule may be illustrated by the following example:

*Example.* M, a duly ordained minister, is engaged to perform service as chaplain at N University. M devotes his entire time to performing his duties as chaplain which include the conduct of religious worship, offering spiritual counsel to the university students, and teaching a class in religion. M is performing service in the exercise of his ministry.

(iv) If a minister is performing service for an organization which is operated as an integral agency of a religious organization under the authority of a religious body constituting a church or church denomination, all service performed by the minister in the conduct of religious worship, in the ministration of sacerdotal functions, or in the control, conduct, and maintenance of such organization (see subparagraph (2)(ii) of this paragraph) is in the exercise of his ministry. The application of this rule may be illustrated by the following example:

*Example.* M, a duly ordained minister, is engaged by the N Religious Board to serve as director of one of its departments. He performs no other service. The N Religious Board is an integral agency of O, a religious organization operating under the authority of a religious body constituting a church denomination. M is performing service in the exercise of his ministry.

(v) If a minister, pursuant to an assignment or designation by a religious body constituting his church, performs service for an organization which is neither a religious organization nor operated as an integral agency of a religious organization, all service performed by him, even though such service may not involve the conduct of religious worship or the ministration of sacerdotal functions, is in the exercise of his ministry. The application of this rule may be illustrated by the following example:

*Example.* M, a duly ordained minister, is assigned by X, the religious body constituting his church, to perform advisory service to Y Company in connection with the publication of a book dealing

with the history of M's church denomination. Y is neither a religious organization nor operated as an integral agency of a religious organization. M performs no other service for X or Y. M is performing service in the exercise of his ministry.

(c) *Service by a minister not in the exercise of his ministry.*—(1)(i) A certificate filed by a duly ordained, commissioned, or licensed minister of a church under the provisions of § 1.1402(e)(1)-1 has no application to service performed by him which is not in the exercise of his ministry.

(ii) An exemption under section 1402(e) (see §§ 1.1402(e)-1A through 1.1402(e)-4A) which is effective with respect to a duly ordained, commissioned, or licensed minister of a church has no application to service performed by him which is not in the exercise of his ministry.

(2) If a minister is performing service for an organization which is neither a religious organization nor operated as an integral agency of a religious organization and the service is not performed pursuant to an assignment or designation by his ecclesiastical superiors, then only the service performed by him in the conduct of religious worship or the ministration of sacerdotal functions is in the exercise of his ministry. See, however, subparagraph (3) of this paragraph. The application of the rule in this subparagraph may be illustrated by the following example:

*Example.* M, a duly ordained minister, is engaged by N University to teach history and mathematics. He performs no other service for N although from time to time he performs marriages and conducts funerals for relatives and friends. N University is neither a religious organization nor operated as an integral agency of a religious organization. M is not performing the service for N pursuant to an assignment or designation by his ecclesiastical superiors. The service performed by M for N University is not in the exercise of his ministry. However, service performed by M in performing marriages and conducting funerals is in the exercise of his ministry.

(3) Service performed by a duly ordained, commissioned, or licensed minister of a church as an employee of the United States, or a State, Territory, or possession of the United States, or the District of Columbia, or a foreign government, or a political subdivision of any of the foregoing, is not considered to be in the exercise of his ministry for purposes of the tax on self-employment income, even though such service may involve the ministration of sacerdotal functions or the conduct of religious worship. Thus, for example, service performed by an individual as a chaplain in the Armed Forces of the United States is considered to be performed by a commissioned officer in his capacity as such, and not by a minister in the exercise of his ministry. Similarly, service performed by an employee of a State as a chaplain in a State prison is considered to be performed by a civil servant of the State and not by a minister in the exercise of his ministry.

(d) *Service in the exercise of duties required by a religious order.*—(1) *Certificate of election.*—A certificate of election filed by a member of a religious order (other than a member of a religious order who has taken a vow of poverty as a member of such order) under the provisions of § 1.1402(e)(1)-1 has application to all duties required of him by such order.

(2) *Exemption.*—An exemption under section 1402(e) (see §§ 1.1402(e)-1A through 1.1402(e)-4A) which is effective with respect to a member of a religious order (other than a member of a religious order who has taken a vow of poverty as a member of such order) has application only to the duties required of him by such order.

(3) *Service.*—For purposes of subparagraphs (1) and (2) of this paragraph, the nature or extent of the duties required of the member by the order is immaterial so long as it is a service which he is directed or required to perform by his ecclesiastical superiors. [Reg. § 1.1402(c)-5.]

☐ [T.D. 6691, 12-2-63. *Amended by* T.D. 6978, 10-29-68.]

**[Reg. § 1.1402(c)-6]**

**§ 1.1402(c)-6. Members of certain professions.**—(a) *Periods of exclusion.*—(1) *Taxable years ending before 1955.*—For taxable years ending before 1955, an individual is not engaged in carrying on a trade or business with respect to the performance of service in the exercise of his profession as a physician, lawyer, dentist, osteopath, veterinarian, chiropractor, naturopath, optometrist, Christian Science practitioner, architect, certified public accountant, accountant registered or licensed as an accountant under State or municipal law, full-time practicing public accountant, funeral director, or professional engineer.

(2) *Taxable years ending in 1955.*—Except as provided in paragraph (b) of this section, for a taxable year ending in 1955 an individual is not engaged in carrying on a trade or business with respect to the performance of service in the exercise of his profession

as a physician, lawyer, dentist, osteopath, veterinarian, chiropractor, naturopath, optometrist, or Christian Science practitioner.

(3) *Taxable years ending after 1955.*—(i) *Doctors of medicine.*—For taxable years ending after 1955 and before December 31, 1965, an individual is not engaged in carrying on a trade or business with respect to the performance of service in the exercise of his profession as a doctor of medicine. For taxable years ending after December 30, 1965, an individual is engaged in carrying on a trade or business with respect to the performance of service in the exercise of his profession as a doctor of medicine.

(ii) *Christian Science practitioners.*—Except as provided in paragraph (b)(1), of this section, for taxable years ending after 1955 and before 1968, an individual is not engaged in carrying on a trade or business with respect to the performance of service in the exercise of his profession as a Christian Science practitioner. For provisions relating to the performance of service in taxable years ending after 1967 by an individual in the exercise of his profession as a Christian Science practitioner, see paragraph (b)(2) of this section.

(b) *Christian Science practitioner.*—(1) *Certain taxable years ending before 1968; election.*—For taxable years ending after 1954 and before 1968, a Christian Science practitioner may elect, as provided in § 1.1402(e)(1)-1, to have the Federal old-age, survivors, and disability insurance system established by title II of the Social Security Act extended to service performed by him in the exercise of his profession as a Christian Science practitioner. If an election is made pursuant to § 1.1402(e)(1)-1, the Christian Science practitioner is, with respect to the performance of service in the exercise of such profession, engaged in carrying on a trade or business for each taxable year for which the election is effective. An election by a Christian Science practitioner has no application to service performed by him which is not in the exercise of his profession as a Christian Science practitioner.

(2) *Taxable years ending after 1967; exemption.*—For a taxable year ending after 1967, a Christian Science practitioner is, with respect to the performance of service in the exercise of his profession as a Christian Science practitioner, engaged in carrying on a trade or business unless an exemption under section 1402(e) (see §§ 1.1402(e)-1A through 1.1402(e)-4A) if effective with respect to him for the taxable year during which the service is performed. An exemption which is effective with respect to a Christian Science practitioner has no application to service performed by him which is not in the exercise of his profession as a Christian Science practitioner.

(c) *Meaning of terms.*—The designations in this section are to be given their commonly accepted meanings. For taxable years ending after 1955, an individual who is a doctor of osteopathy, and who is not a doctor of medicine within the commonly accepted meaning of that term, is deemed, for purposes of this section, not to be engaged in carrying on a trade or business in the exercise of the profession of doctor of medicine.

(d) *Legal requirements.*—The exclusions specified in paragraph (a) of this section apply only if the individuals meet the legal requirements, if any, for practicing their professions in the place where they perform the service.

(e) *Partnerships.*—In the case of a partnership engaged in the practice of any of the designated excluded professions, the partnership shall not be considered as carrying on a trade or business for the purpose of the tax on self-employment income, and none of the distributive shares of the income or loss, described in section 702(a)(9), of such partnership shall be included in computing net earnings from self-employment of any member of the partnership. On the other hand, where a partnership is engaged in a trade or business not within any of the designated excluded professions, each partner must include his distributive share of the income or loss, described in section 702(a)(9), of such partnership in computing his net earnings from self-employment, irrespective of whether such partner is engaged in the practice of one or more of such professions and contributes his professional services to the partnership. [Reg. § 1.1402(c)-6.]

☐ *[T.D. 6691, 12-2-63. Amended by T.D. 6978, 10-29-68.]*

### [Reg. § 1.1402(c)-7]

§ 1.1402(c)-7. **Members of religious groups opposed to insurance.**—The performance of service by an individual—

(a) Who is a member of a recognized religious sect or division thereof, and

(b) Who is an adherent of established tenets or teachings of such sect or division by reason of which he is conscientiously opposed to acceptance of the benefits of any private or public insurance which makes payments in the event of death, disability, old age, or retire-

ment or makes payments toward the cost of, or provides services for, medical care (including the benefits of any insurance system established by the Social Security Act),

during any taxable year for which he is granted a tax exemption, pursuant to section 1402(h), does not constitute a trade or business within the meaning of section 1402(c) and § 1.1402(c)-1. See also §§ 1.1402(h) and 1.1402(h)-1. [Reg. § 1.1402(c)-7.]

☐ *[T.D. 6993, 1-17-69.]*

### [Reg. § 1.1402(d)-1]

§ 1.1402(d)-1. **Employee and wages.**—For the purpose of the tax on self-employment income, the term "employee" and the term "wages" shall have the same meaning as when used in the Federal Insurance Contributions Act. For an explanation of these terms, see Subpart B of Part 31 of this chapter (Employment Tax Regulations). [Reg. § 1.1402(d)-1.]

☐ *[T.D. 6196, 8-13-56. Amended by T.D. 6691, 12-2-63.]*

### [Reg. § 1.1402(e)-1A]

§ 1.1402(e)-1A. **Application of regulations under section 1402(e).**—The regulations in §§ 1.1402(e)-2A through 1.1402(e)-4A relate to section 1402(e) as amended by section 115(b)(2) of the Social Security Amendments of 1967 (81 Stat. 839) and apply to taxable years ending after 1967. Section 1.1402(e)-5A reflects changes made by section 1704(a) of the Tax Reform Act of 1986 (100 Stat. 2085, 2779) and applies to applications for exemption under section 1402(e) filed after December 31, 1986. For regulations under section 1402(e) (as in effect prior to amendment by the Social Security Amendments of 1967) applicable to taxable years ending before 1968, see §§ 1.1402(e)(1)-1 through 1.1402(e)(6)-1. [Reg. § 1.1402(e)-1A.]

☐ *[T.D. 6978, 10-29-68. Amended by T.D. 8221, 8-30-88.]*

### [Reg. § 1.1402(e)-2A]

§ 1.1402(e)-2A. **Ministers, members of religious orders and Christian Science practitioners; application for exemption from self-employment tax.**—(a) *In general.*—(1) Subject to the limitations set forth in subparagraphs (2) and (3) of this paragraph, any individual who is (i) a duly ordained, commissioned, or licensed minister of a church or a member of a religious order (other than a member of a religious order who has taken a vow of poverty as a member of such order) or (ii) a Christian Science practitioner may request an exemption from the tax on self-employment income (see §§ 1.1401 and 1.1401-1) with respect to services performed by him in his capacity as a minister or member, or as a Christian Science practitioner, as the case may be. Such a request shall be made by filing an application for exemption on Form 4361 in the manner provided in paragraph (b) of this section and within the time specified in § 1.1402(e)-3A. For provisions relating to the taxable year or years for which an exemption from the tax on self-employment income with respect to service performed by a minister or member or a Christian Science practitioner in his capacity as such is effective, see § 1.1402(e)-4A. For additional provisions applicable to services performed by individuals referred to in this subparagraph, see paragraph (e) of § 1.1402(c)-3 and § 1.1402(c)-5 relating to ministers and members of religious orders, and paragraphs (a)(3)(ii) and (b) of § 1.1402(c)-6 relating to Christian Science practitioners.

(2) The application for exemption shall contain, or there shall be filed with such application, a statement to the effect that the individual making application for exemption is conscientiously opposed to, or because of religious principles is opposed to, the acceptance (with respect to services performed by him in his capacity as a minister, member, or Christian Science practitioner) of any public insurance which makes payments in the event of death, disability, old age, or retirement or makes payments toward the cost of, or provides services for, medical care (including the benefits of any insurance system established by the Social Security Act). Thus, ministers, members of religious orders, and Christian Science practitioners requesting exemption from social security coverage must meet either of two alternative tests: (1) A religious principles test which refers to the institutional principles and discipline of the particular religious denomination to which he belongs, or (2) a conscientious opposition test which refers to the opposition because of religious considerations of individual ministers, members of religious orders, and Christian Science practitioners (rather than opposition based upon the general conscience of any such individual or individuals). The term "public insurance," as used in section 1402(e) and this paragraph, refers to governmental, as distinguished from private, insurance and does not include insurance carried with a commercial insurance carrier. To be eligible to file an application for exemption on Form 4361, a minister, member, or Christian Science practitioners need not be opposed to the acceptance of all public insurance making payments of this specified type; he must, however, be opposed on religious grounds to the acceptance of any such payment which, in whole or in part, is

based on, or measured by earnings from, services performed by him in his capacity as a minister or member (see §1.1402(c)-5) or in his capacity as a Christian Science practitioner (see paragraph (b)(2) of §1.1402(c)-6). For example, a minister performing service in the exercise of his ministry may be eligible to file an application for exemption on Form 4361 even though he is not opposed to the acceptance of benefits under the Social Security Act with respect to service performed by him which is not in the exercise of his ministry.

(3) An exemption from the tax imposed on self-employment income with respect to service performed by a minister, member, or Christian Science practitioner in his capacity as such may not be granted to a minister, member, or practitioner who (in accordance with the provisions of section 1402(e) as in effect prior to amendment by section 115(b)(2) of the Social Security Amendments of 1967 (81 Stat. 839)) filed a valid waiver certificate on Form 2031 electing to have the Federal old-age, survivors, and disability insurance system established by title II of the Social Security Act extended to service performed by him in the exercise of his ministry or in the exercise of duties required by the order of which he is a member, or in the exercise of his profession as a Christian Science practitioner. For provisions relating to waiver certificates on Form 2031, see §§1.1402(e)(1)-1 through 1.1402(e)(6)-1.

(b) *Application for exemption.*—An application for exemption on Form 4361 shall be filed in triplicate with the internal revenue officer or the internal revenue office, as the case may be, designated in the instructions relating to the application for exemption. The application for exemption must be filed within the time prescribed in §1.1402(e)-3A. If the last original Federal income tax return of an individual to whom paragraph (a) of this section applies which was filed before the expiration of such time limitation for filing an application for exemption shows no liability for tax on self-employment income, such return will be treated as an application for exemption, provided that before February 28, 1975 such individual also files a properly executed Form 4361.

(c) *Approval of application for exemption.*—The filing of an application for exemption on Form 4361 by a minister, a member of a religious order, or a Christian Science practitioner does not constitute an exemption from the tax on self-employment income with respect to services performed by him in his capacity as a minister, member, or practitioner. The exemption is granted only if the application is approved by an appropriate internal revenue officer. See §1.1402(e)-4A relating to the period for which an exemption is effective. [Reg. §1.1402(e)-2A.]

☐ [*T.D.* 7333, 12-19-74.]

### [Reg. §1.1402(e)-3A]

**§1.1402(e)-3A. Time limitation for filing application for exemption.**—(a) *General rule.*—(1) Any individual referred to in paragraph (a) of §1.1402(e)-2A who desires an exemption from the tax on self-employment income with respect to service performed by him in his capacity as a minister or member of a religious order or as a Christian Science practitioner must file the application for exemption (Form 4361) prescribed by §1.1402(e)-2A on or before whichever of the following dates is later:

(i) The due date of the income tax return (see section 6072), including any extension thereof (see section 6081), for his second taxable year ending after 1967, or

(ii) The due date of the income tax return, including any extension thereof, for his second taxable year beginning after 1953 for which he has net earnings from self-employment of $400 or more, any part of which—

(*a*) In the case of a duly ordained, commissioned, or licensed minister of a church, consists of remuneration for service performed in the exercise of his ministry,

(*b*) In the case of a member of a religious order who has not taken a vow of poverty as a member of such order, consists of remuneration for service performed in the exercise of duties required by such order, or

(*c*) In the case of a Christian Science practitioner, consists of remuneration for service performed in the exercise of his profession as a Christian Science practitioner.

See paragraph (c) of this section for provisions relating to the computation of net earnings from self-employment.

(2) If a minister, a member of a religious order, or a Christian Science practitioner derives gross income in a taxable year both from service performed in such capacity and from the conduct of another trade or business, and the deductions allowed by chapter 1 of the Internal Revenue Code which are attributable to the gross income derived from service performed in such capacity equal or exceed the gross income derived from service performed in such capacity, no part of the net earnings from self-employment (computed as pre-

scribed in paragraph (c) of this section) for the taxable year shall be considered as derived from service performed in such capacity.

(3) The application of the rules set forth in subparagraphs (1) and (2) of this paragraph may be illustrated by the following examples:

*Example (1).* M, who makes his income tax returns on a calendar year basis, was ordained as a minister in January 1960. During each of two or more taxable years ending before 1968 M has net earnings from self-employment in excess of $400, some part of which is from service performed in the exercise of his ministry. M has not filed an effective waiver certificate on Form 2031 (see paragraph (a)(3) of §1.1402(e)-2A). If M desires an exemption from the tax on self-employment income with respect to service performed in the exercise of his ministry, he must file an application for exemption on or before the due date of his income tax return for 1969 (his second taxable year ending after 1967), or any extension thereof.

*Example (2).* M, who makes his income tax returns on a calendar year basis, was ordained as a minister in January 1966. M has net earnings of $350 for the taxable year 1966 and has net earnings in excess of $400 for each of his taxable years 1967 and 1968 (some part or all of which is derived from service performed in the exercise of his ministry). M has not filed an effective waiver certificate on Form 2031 (see paragraph (a)(3) of §1.1402(e)-2A). If M desires an exemption from the tax on self-employment income with respect to service performed in the exercise of his ministry, he must file an application for exemption on or before the due date of his income tax return for 1969 (his second taxable year ending after 1967), or any extension thereof.

*Example (3).* Assume the same facts as in example (2) except that M has net earnings in excess of $400 for each of his taxable years 1967 and 1969 (but less than $400 in 1968). The application for exemption must be filed on or before the due date of his income tax return for 1969, or any extension thereof.

*Example (4).* M was ordained as a minister in May 1973. During each of the taxable years 1973 and 1975, M, who makes his income tax returns on a calendar year basis, derives net earnings in excess of $400 from his activities as a minister. M has net earnings of $350 for the taxable year 1974, $200 of which is derived from service performed by him in the exercise of his ministry. If M desires an exemption from the tax on self-employment income with respect to service performed in the exercise of his ministry, he must file an application for exemption on or before the due date of his income tax return for 1975, or any extension thereof.

*Example (5).* M, who was ordained a minister in January 1973, is employed as a toolmaker by the XYZ Corporation for the taxable years 1973 and 1974 and also engages in activities as a minister on weekends. M makes his income tax returns on the basis of a calendar year. During each of the taxable years 1973 and 1974 M receives wages of $14,000 from the XYZ Corporation and derives net earnings of $400 from his activities as a minister. If M desires an exemption from the tax on self-employment income with respect to service performed in the exercise of his ministry, he must file an application for exemption on or before the due date of his income tax return for 1974, or any extension thereof. It should be noted that although by reason of section 1402(b)(1)(G) and (H) no part of the $400 represents "self-employment income," nevertheless the entire $400 constitutes "net earnings from self-employment" for purposes of fulfilling the requirements of section 1402(e)(2).

*Example (6).* M, who files his income tax returns on a calendar year basis, was ordained as a minister in March 1973. During 1973 he receives $410 for service performed in the exercise of his ministry. In addition to his ministerial services, M is engaged during the year 1973 in a mercantile venture from which he derives net earnings from self-employment in the amount of $4,000. The expenses incurred by him in connection with his ministerial services during 1973 and which are allowable deductions under chapter 1 of the Internal Revenue Code amount to $410. During 1974 and 1975, M has net earnings from self-employment in amounts of $4,600 and $4,800, respectively, and some part of each of these amounts is from the exercise of his ministry. The deductions allowed in each of the years 1974 and 1975 by chapter 1 which are attributable to the gross income derived by M from the exercise of his ministry in each of such years, respectively, do not equal or exceed such gross income in such year. If M desires an exemption from the tax on self-employment income with respect to service performed in the exercise of his ministry, he must file an application for exemption on or before the due date of his income tax return for 1975, or an extension thereof.

(b) *Effect of death.*—The right of an individual to file an application for exemption shall cease upon his death. Thus, the surviving spouse, administrator, or executor of a decedent shall not be permitted to file an application for exemption for such decedent.

(c) *Computation of net earnings.*—(1) *Taxable years ending before 1968.*—For purposes of this section net earnings from self-employment for taxable years ending before 1968 shall be determined without regard to the fact that, without an election under section 1402(e) (as in effect prior to amendment by section 115(b)(2) of the Social Security Amendments of 1967, see §1.1402(e)-1A), the performance of services by a duly ordained, commissioned, or licensed minister of a church in the exercise of his ministry, or by a member of a religious order in the exercise of duties required by such order, or the performance of service by an individual in the exercise of his profession as a Christian Science practitioner, does not constitute a trade or business for purposes of the tax on self-employment income.

(2) *Taxable years ending after 1967.*—For purposes of this section and §1.1402(e)-4A net earnings from self-employment for taxable years ending after 1967 shall be determined without regard to section 1402(c)(4) and (5). See §1.1402(c)-3(e)(2) and §1.1402(c)-5 relating to ministers and members of religious orders, and paragraphs (a)(3)(ii) and (b) of §1.1402(c)-6 relating to Christian Science practitioners. [Reg. §1.1402(e)-3A.]

☐ [*T.D. 7333, 12-19-74.*]

### [Reg. §1.1402(e)-4A]

**§1.1402(e)-4A. Period for which exemption is effective.**—(a) *In general.*—If an application for exemption on Form 4361—

(1) Is filed by a minister, a member of a religious order, or a Christian Science practitioner eligible to file such an application (see particularly paragraph (a)(2) and (3) of §1.1402(e)-2A), and

(2) Is approved (see paragraph (c) of §1.1402(e)-2A),

the exemption from the tax on self-employment income shall be effective for the first taxable year ending after 1967 for which such minister, member, or practitioner has net earnings from self-employment of $400 or more any part of which was derived from the performance of service in his capacity as a minister, member, or practitioner, and for all succeeding taxable years. See, however, paragraphs (b)(1)(ii) and (d)(2) of §1.1402(c)-5 relating to ministers and members of religious orders and paragraph (b)(2) of §1.1402(c)-6 relating to Christian Science practitioners.

(b) *Exemption irrevocable.*—An exemption granted to a minister, a member of a religious order, or a Christian Science practitioner pursuant to the provisions of section 1402(e) is irrevocable. [Reg. §1.1402(e)-4A.]

☐ [*T.D. 7333, 12-19-74.*]

### [Reg. §1.1402(e)-5A]

**§1.1402(e)-5A. Applications for exemption from self-employment taxes filed after December 31, 1986, by ministers, certain members of religious orders, and Christian Science practitioners.**—(a) *In general.*—(1) Except as provided in paragraph (a)(2) of this section, this section applies to any individual who is a duly ordained, commissioned, or licensed minister of a church, member of a religious order (other than a member of a religious order who has taken a vow of poverty as a member of such order), or a Christian Science practitioner who files an application after December 31, 1986, for exemption from the tax on self-employment income (see section 1401 and §1.1401-1) with respect to services performed by him or her in his or her capacity as a minister, member, or practitioner pursuant to §§1.1402(e)-2A through 1.1402(e)-4A. This section does not apply to applications for exemption under section 1402(e) that are filed before January 1, 1987.

(2) *Application of this section to Christian Science practitioners.*—Paragraph (b) of this section does not apply to Christian Science practitioners. Thus, Christian Science practitioners filing applications for exemption from self-employment taxes under section 1402(e) should follow the procedures set forth in §§1.1402(e)-2A through 1.1402(e)-4A, and are not required to include the statement described in paragraph (b)(1)(ii) of this section. However, see paragraph (c) of this section for verification procedures with respect to applications for exemption from self-employment taxes filed after December 31, 1986, by Christian Science practitioners.

(b) *Church or order must be informed.*—(1) *In general.*—Any individual, other than a Christian Science practitioner, who files an application for exemption from the tax on self-employment income under section 1402(e) after December 31, 1986:

(i) Shall file such application in accordance with the procedures set forth in §§1.1402(e)-2A through 1.1402(e)-4A, and

(ii) Shall include with such application a statement to the effect that the individual making application for exemption has informed the ordaining, commissioning, or licensing body of the church or order that he or she is opposed to the acceptance (for services performed as a minister or member of a religious order not under a vow of poverty) of any public insurance that makes payments in the event of death, disability, old age, or retirement, or that makes payments toward the cost of, or provides services for, medical care (including the benefits of any insurance system established by the Social Security Act).

(2) *Statement to be filed with Form.*—If the form provided by the Service for applying for exemption under 1402(e) does not contain the statement set forth in paragraph (b)(1)(ii) of this section, any individual required to include this statement with his or her application under this paragraph (b) shall file such statement with the individual's application at the time and place prescribed for filing such application under §§1.1402(e)-2A and 1.1402(e)-3A. The statement shall contain the information set forth in paragraph (b)(1)(ii) of this section and shall be signed by such individual under penalties of perjury.

(c) *Verification of Application.*—(1) *In general.*—The Service will approve an application for an exemption filed by an individual to whom this section applies only after verifying that the individual applying for the exemption is aware of the grounds on which the individual may receive an exemption under section 1402(e) (see §1.1402(e)-2A) and that the individual seeks exemption on such grounds in accordance with the procedures set forth in paragraph (c)(2) of this section.

(2) *Verification procedure.*—Upon receipt of an application for exemption from self-employment taxes under section 1402(e) and this section, the Service will mail to the applicant a statement that describes the grounds on which an individual may receive an exemption under section 1402(e). The individual filing the application shall certify that he or she has read the statement and that he or she seeks exemption from self-employment taxes on the grounds listed in the statement. The certification shall be made by signing a copy of the statement under penalties of perjury and mailing the signed copy to the Service Center from which the statement was issued not later than 90 days after the date on which the statement was mailed to the individual. If the signed copy of the statement is not mailed to the Service Center within 90 days of the date on which the statement was mailed to the individual, that individual's exemption will not be effective until the date that the signed copy of the statement is received at the Service Center. [Reg. §1.1402(e)-5A.]

☐ [*T.D. 8821, 8-30-88.*]

### [Reg. §1.1402(f)-1]

**§1.1402(f)-1. Computation of partner's net earnings from self-employment for taxable years ending as result of his death.**—(a) *Taxable years ending after August 28, 1958.*—(1) *In general.*—The rules for the computation of a partner's net earnings from self-employment are set forth in paragraphs (d) to (g), inclusive, of §1.1402(a)-2. In addition to the net earnings from self-employment computed under such rules for the last taxable year of a deceased partner, if a partner's taxable year ends after August 28, 1958, solely because of death, and on a day other than the last day of the partnership's taxable year, the deceased partner's net earnings from self-employment for such year shall also include so much of the deceased partner's distributive share of partnership ordinary income or loss (see subparagraph (3) of this paragraph) for the taxable year of the partnership in which his death occurs as is attributable to an interest in the partnership prior to the month following the month of his death.

(2) *Computation.*—(i) The deceased partner's distributive share of partnership ordinary income or loss for the partnership taxable year in which he died shall be determined by applying the rules contained in paragraphs (d) to (g), inclusive, of §1.1402(a)-2, except that paragraph (e) shall not apply.

(ii) The portion of such distributive share to be included under this section in the deceased partner's net earnings from self-employment for his last taxable year shall be determined by treating the ordinary income or loss constituting such distributive share as having been realized or sustained ratably over the period of the partnership taxable year during which the deceased partner had an interest in the partnership and during which his estate, or any other person succeeding by reason of his death to rights with respect to his partnership interest, held such interest in the partnership or held a right with respect to such interest. The amount to be included under this section in the deceased partner's net earnings from self-employment for his last taxable year will, therefore, be determined by multiplying the deceased partner's distributive share of partnership ordinary income or loss for the partnership taxable year in which he died, as determined under subdivision (i) of this subparagraph, by a fraction, the denominator of which is the number of calendar months in the partnership taxable year over which the ordinary income or loss constituting the deceased partner's distributive share of partnership income or loss for such year is treated as having been realized or sustained under the preceding sentence and the numerator of which is the number of calendar months in such partnership taxable year that precede the month following the month of his death.

(3) *Definition of "deceased partner's distributive share."*—For the purpose of this section, the term "deceased partner's distributive share" includes the distributive share of his estate or of any other person succeeding, by reason of his death, to rights with respect to his partnership interest. It does not include any share attributable to a partnership interest which was not held by the deceased partner at the time of his death. Thus, if a deceased partner's estate should acquire an interest in a partnership additional to the interest to which it succeeded upon the death of the deceased partner, the amount of the distributive share attributable to such additional interest acquired by the estate would not be included in computing the "deceased partner's distributive share" of the partnership's ordinary income or loss for the partnership taxable year.

(4) *Examples.*—The application of this paragraph may be illustrated by the following examples:

*Example (1).* B, an individual who files his income tax returns on the calendar year basis, is a member of the ABC partnership, the taxable year of which ends on June 30. B dies on October 17, 1958, and his estate succeeds to his partnership interest and continues as a partner in its own right under local law until June 30, 1959. B's distributive share of the partnership's ordinary income, as determined under paragraphs (d) to (g), inclusive, of § 1.1402(a)-2, for the taxable year of the partnership ended June 30, 1958 is $2,400. His distributive share, including the share of his estate, of such partnership's ordinary income, as determined under paragraphs (d) to (g), inclusive, of § 1.1402(a)-2 (with the exception of paragraph (e)), for the taxable year of the partnership ended June 30, 1959 is $4,500. The portion of such $4,500 attributable to an interest in the partnership prior to the month following the month in which he died is $4,500 × $^4/_{12}$ (4 being the number of months in the partnership taxable year in which B died which precede the month following the month of his death and 12 being the number of months in such partnership taxable year in which B and his estate had an interest in the partnership) or $1,500. The amount to be included in the deceased partner's net earnings from self-employment for his last taxable year in $3,900 ($2,400 plus $1,500).

*Example (2).* If in the preceding example B's estate is entitled to only $1,000, the amount of B's distributive share of partnership ordinary income for the period July 1, 1958 through October 17, 1958, such $1,000 is considered to have been realized ratably over the period preceding B's death and will be included in B's net earnings from self-employment for his last taxable year.

*Example (3).* X, who reports his income on a calendar year basis, is a member of a partnership which also reports its income on a calendar year basis. X dies on June 30, 1959, and his estate succeeds to his partnership interest and continues as a partner in its own right under local law. On September 15, 1959, X's estate sells the partnership interest to which it succeeded on the death of X. X's distributive share of partnership income for 1959 is $5,500. $600 of such amount is X's share of the gain from the sale of a capital asset which occurs on May 1, 1959, and $400 of such amount is the estate's share of the gain from the sale of a capital asset which occurs on July 15, 1959. The remainder of such amount is income from services rendered. X's distributive share of partnership ordinary income for 1959, as determined under paragraphs (d) to (g), inclusive, of § 1.1402(a)-2 (with the exception of paragraph (e)), is $4,500 ($5,500 minus $1,000). The portion of such share attributable to an interest in the partnership prior to the month following the month of his death is $4,500 × 6/8.5 (6 being the number of months in the partnership taxable year in which X died as precede the month following the month of his death and 8.5 being the number of months in such partnership taxable year in which X and his estate had an interest in the partnership) or $3,176.47.

(b) *Options available to farmers.*—(1) *Special rule.*—In determining whether the optional method available to a member of a farm partnership in computing his net earnings from self-employment may be applied, and in applying such method, it is necessary to determine the partner's distributive share of partnership gross income and the partner's distributive share of income described in section 702(a)(9). See section 1402(a) and § 1.1402(a)-15. If section 1402(f) and this section apply, or may be made applicable under section 403(b)(2) of the Social Security Amendments of 1958 and paragraph (c) of this section, for the last taxable year of a deceased partner, such partner's distributive share of income described in section 702(a)(9) for his last taxable year shall be determined by including therein any amount which is included under section 1402(f) and this section in his net earnings from self-employment for such taxable year. Such a partner's distributive share of partnership gross income for his last taxable year shall be determined by including therein so much of the deceased partner's distributive share (see paragraph (a)(3) of this section) of partnership gross income, as defined in section 1402(a) and paragraph (b) of § 1.1402(a)-15, for the partnership taxable year in which he died as is attributable to an interest in the partnership

prior to the month following the month of his death. Such allocation shall be made in the same manner as is prescribed in paragraph (a)(2) of this section for determining the portion of a deceased partner's distributive share of partnership ordinary income or loss to be included under section 1402(f) and this section in his net earnings from self-employment for his last taxable year.

(2) *Examples.*—The principles set forth in this paragraph may be illustrated by the following examples:

*Example (1).* X, an individual who files his income tax returns on a calendar year basis, is a member of the XYZ farm partnership, the taxable year of which ends on March 31. X dies on May 31, 1967, and his estate succeeds to his partnership interest and continues as a partner in its own right under local law until March 31, 1968. X's distributive share of the partnership's ordinary income, determined under paragraphs (d) to (g), inclusive, of § 1.1402(a)-2, for the taxable year of the partnership ended March 31, 1967, is $1,600. His distributive share, including the share of his estate, of such partnership's ordinary loss as determined under paragraphs (d) to (g), inclusive, of § 1.1402(a)-2 (with the exception of paragraph (e)), for the taxable year of the partnership ended March 31, 1968, is $1,200. The portion of such $1,200 attributable to an interest in the partnership prior to the month following the month in which he died is $1,200 × $^2/_{12}$ (2 being the number of months in the partnership taxable year in which X died which precede the month following the month of his death and 12 being the number of months in such partnership taxable year in which X and his estate had an interest in the partnership) or $200. X is also a member of the ABX farm partnership, the taxable year of which ends on May 31. His distributive share of the partnership loss described in section 702(a)(9) for the partnership taxable year ending May 31, 1967, is $300. Section 1402(f) and this section do not apply with respect to such $300 since X's last taxable year ends, as a result of his death, with the taxable year of the ABX partnership. Under this paragraph the $200 loss must be included in determining X's distributive share of XYZ partnership income described in section 702(a)(9) for the purpose of applying the optional method available to farmers for computing net earnings from self-employment. Further, the resulting $1,400 of income must be aggregated, pursuant to paragraph (c) of § 1.1402(a)-15, with the $300 loss, X's distributive share of ABX partnership loss described in section 702(a)(9), for purposes of applying such option. The representative of X's estate may exercise the option described in paragraph (a)(2)(ii) of § 1.1402(a)-15, provided the portion of X's distributive share of XYZ partnership gross income for the taxable year ended March 31, 1968, attributable to an interest in the partnership prior to the month following the month in which he died (the allocation being made in the manner prescribed for allocating his $1,200 distributive share of XYZ partnership loss for such year), when aggregated with his distributive share of XYZ partnership gross income for the partnership taxable year ended March 31, 1967, and with his distributive share of ABX partnership gross income for the partnership taxable year ended May 31, 1967, results in X having more than $2,400 of gross income from the trade or business of farming. If such aggregate amount of gross income is not more than $2,400, the option described in paragraph (a)(2)(i) of § 1.1402(a)-15, is available.

*Example (2).* A, a sole proprietor engaged in the business of farming, files his income tax returns on a calendar year basis. A is also a member of a partnership engaged in an agricultural activity. The partnership files its returns on the basis of a fiscal year ending March 31. A dies June 29, 1967. A's gross income from farming as a sole proprietor for the 6-month period comprising his taxable year which ends because of death is $1,600 and his actual net earnings from self-employment based thereon are $400. As of March 31, 1967, A's distributive share of the gross income of the farm partnership is $2,200 and his distributive share of income described in section 702(a)(9) based thereon is $1,000. The amount of A's distributive share of the partnership's ordinary income for its taxable year ended March 31, 1968, which may be included in his net earnings from self-employment under section 1402(f) and paragraph (a) of this section is $300. The amount of the deceased partner's distributive share of partnership gross income attributable to an interest in the partnership prior to the month following the month of his death as is determined, pursuant to subparagraph (1) of this paragraph, under paragraph (a) of this section is $2,000. An aggregation of the above figures produces a gross income from farming of $5,800 and actual net earnings from self-employment of $1,700. Under these circumstances none of the options provided by section 1402(a) may be used. If the actual net earnings from self-employment had been less than $1,600, the option described in paragraph (a)(2)(ii) of § 1.1402(a)-15 would have been available.

(c) *Taxable years ending after 1955 and on or before August 28, 1958.*—(1) *Requirement of election.*—If a partner's taxable year ended, as a result of his death, after 1955 and on or before August 28, 1958, the rules set forth in paragraph (a) of this section may be made applicable in computing the deceased partner's net earnings from self-employment for his last taxable year provided that—

(i) Before January 1, 1960, there is filed, by the person designated in section 6012(b)(1) and paragraph (b)(1) of §1.6012-3, a return (or amended return) of the tax imposed by chapter 2 for the taxable year ending as a result of death, and

(ii) Such return, if filed solely for the purpose of reporting net earnings from self-employment resulting from the enactment of section 1402(f), is accompanied by the amount of tax attributable to such net earnings.

(2) *Administrative rule of special application.*—Notwithstanding the provisions of sections 6601, 6651, and 6653 (see such sections and the regulations thereunder) no interest or penalty shall be assessed or collected on the amount of any self-employment tax due solely by reason of the operation of section 1402(f) in the case of an individual who died after 1955 and before August 29, 1958. [Reg. §1.1402(f)-1.]

☐ [*T.D. 6691, 12-2-63. Amended by T.D. 6993, 1-17-69.*]

## [Reg. §1.1402(g)-1]

**§1.1402(g)-1. Treatment of certain remuneration erroneously reported as net earnings from self-employment.**—(a) *General rule.*—If an amount is erroneously paid as self-employment tax, for any taxable year ending after 1954 and before 1962, with respect to remuneration for service (other than service described in section 3121(b)(8)(A)) performed in the employ of an organization described in section 501(c)(3) and exempt from income tax under section 501(a), and if such remuneration is reported as self-employment income on a return filed on or before the due date prescribed for filing such return (including any extension thereof), the individual who paid such amount (or a fiduciary acting for such individual or his estate, or his survivor (within the meaning of section 205(c)(1)(C) of the Social Security Act)), may request that such remuneration be deemed to constitute net earnings from self-employment. If such request is filed during the period September 14, 1960, to April 16, 1962, inclusive, and on or after the date on which the organization which paid such remuneration to such individual for services performed in its employ has filed, pursuant to section 3121(k), a certificate waiving exemption from taxes under the Federal Insurance Contributions Act, and if no credit or refund of any portion of the amount erroneously paid for such taxable year as self-employment tax (other than a credit or refund which would be allowable if such tax were applicable with respect to such remuneration) has been obtained before the date on which such request is filed or, if obtained, the amount credited or refunded (including any interest under section 6611) is repaid on or before such date, then, for purposes of the Self-Employment Contributions Act of 1954 and the Federal Insurance Contributions Act, any amount of such remuneration which is paid to such individual before the calendar quarter in which such request is filed (or before the succeeding quarter if such certificate first becomes effective with respect to services performed by such individual in such succeeding quarter) and with respect to which no tax (other than an amount erroneously paid as tax) has been paid under the Federal Insurance Contributions Act, shall be deemed to constitute net earnings from self-employment and not remuneration for employment. If the certificate filed by such organization pursuant to section 3121(k) is not effective with respect to services performed by such individual on or before the first day of the calendar quarter in which the request is filed, then, for purposes of section 3121(b)(8)(B)(ii) and (iii), such individual shall be deemed to have become an employee of such organization (or to have become a member of a group, described in section 3121(k)(1)(E), of employees of such organization) on the first day of the succeeding quarter.

(b) *Request for validation.*—(1) No particular form is prescribed for making a request under paragraph (a) of this section. The request should be in writing, should be signed and dated by the person making the request, and should indicate clearly that it is a request that, pursuant to section 1402(g) of the Code, remuneration for service described in section 3121(b)(8) (other than service described in section 3121(b)(8)(A)) erroneously reported as self-employment income for one or more specified years be deemed to constitute net earnings from self-employment and not remuneration for employment. In addition, the following information shall be shown in connection with the request:

(i) The name, address, and social security account number of the individual with respect to whose remuneration the request is made.

(ii) The taxable year or years (ending after 1954 and before 1962) to which the request relates.

(iii) A statement that the remuneration was erroneously reported as self-employment income on the individual's return for each year specified and that the return was filed on or before its due date (including any extension thereof).

(iv) Location of the office of the district director with whom each return was filed.

(v) A statement that no portion of the amount erroneously paid by the individual as self-employment tax with respect to the remuneration has been credited or refunded (other than a credit or refund which would have been allowable if the tax had been applicable with respect to the remuneration); or, if a credit or refund of any portion of such amount has been obtained, a statement identifying the credit or refund and showing how and when the amount credited or refunded, together with any interest received in connection therewith, was repaid.

(vi) The name and address of the organization which paid the remuneration to the individual.

(vii) The date on which the organization filed a waiver certificate on Form SS-15, and the location of the office of the district director with whom it was filed.

(viii) The date on which the certificate became effective with respect to services performed by the individual.

(ix) If the request is made by a person other than the individual to whom the remuneration was paid, the name and address of that person and evidence which shows the authority of such person to make the request.

(2) The request should be filed with the district director of internal revenue with whom the latest of the returns specified in the request pursuant to subparagraph (1)(iii) of this paragraph was filed.

(c) *Cross references.*—For regulations relating to exemption from income tax of an organization described in section 501(c)(3), see §1.501(c)(3)-1. [Reg. §1.1402(g)-1.]

☐ [*T.D. 6691, 12-2-63 and T.D. 9849, 3-11-2019.*]

## [Reg. §1.1402(h)-1]

**§1.1402(h)-1. Members of certain religious groups opposed to insurance.**—(a) *In general.*—An individual—

(1) Who is a member of a recognized religious sect or division thereof and

(2) Who is an adherent of established tenets or teachings of such sect or division and by reason thereof is conscientiously opposed to acceptance of the benefits of any private or public insurance which makes payments in the event of death, disability, old age, or retirement or makes payments toward the cost of, or provides services for, medical care (including the benefits of any insurance system established by the Social Security Act), may file an application for exemption from the tax under section 1401. The form of insurance to which section 1402(h) and this section refer does not include liability insurance of a kind that provides only for the protection of other persons, or property of other persons, who may be injured or damaged by or on property belonging to, or by an action of, an individual who otherwise meets the requirements of this section. An application for exemption under section 1402(h) and this section shall be made in the manner provided in paragraph (b) of this section and within the time specified in paragraph (c) of this section. For provisions relating to the filing of an application for exemption by a fiduciary or survivor, see paragraph (d) of this section.

(b) *Application for exemption.*—The application for exemption shall be filed on Form 4029 in duplicate with the internal revenue official or office designated on the form. The filing of a return by a member of a religious group opposed to insurance showing no self-employment income or self-employment tax shall not be construed as an application for exemption referred to in paragraph (a) of this section.

(c) *Time limitation for filing application for exemption.*—(1) *Taxable years ending before December 31, 1967.*—A member of a religious group opposed to insurance within the meaning of paragraph (a) of this section—

(i) Who has self-employment income (determined without regard to subsections (c)(6) and (h) of section 1402 and this section) for one or more taxable years ending before December 31, 1967, and

(ii) Who desires to be exempt from the payment of the self-employment tax under section 1401,
must file the application for exemption on or before December 31, 1968.

(2) *Taxable year ending on or after December 31, 1967.*—(i) *General rule.*—Except as provided in subdivision (ii) of this subparagraph, a member of a religious group opposed to insurance within the meaning of paragraph (a) of this section—

(*a*) Who has no self-employment income (determined without regard to subsections (c)(6) and (h) of section 1402 and this section) for any taxable year ending before December 31, 1967, and

(*b*) Who desires to be exempt from the payment of the self-employment tax under section 1401 for any taxable year ending on or after December 31, 1967, must file the application for exemption on or before the due date of the income tax return (see section 6072), including any extension thereof (see section 6081), for the first taxable year ending on or after December 31, 1967, for which he has self-employment income (determined without regard to subsections (c)(6) and (h) of section 1402 and this section).

(ii) *Exception to general rule.*—If an individual to whom subdivision (i) of this subparagraph applies—

(a) Is notified in writing by a district director of internal revenue or the Director of International Operations that he has not filed the application for exemption on or before the date specified in such subdivision (i), and

(b) Files the application for exemption on or before the last day of the third calendar month following the calendar month in which he is so notified,

such application shall be considered a timely filed application for exemption.

(d) *Application by fiduciary or survivor.*—If an individual who was a member of a religious group opposed to insurance dies before the expiration of the time prescribed in section 1402(h)(2) and paragraph (c) of this section during which an application could have been filed by him, an application for exemption with respect to such deceased individual may be filed by a fiduciary acting for such individual's estate or by such individual's survivor within the meaning of section 205(c)(1)(C) of the Social Security Act. An application for exemption with respect to a deceased individual executed by a fiduciary or survivor may be approved only if it could have been approved if the individual were not deceased and had filed the application on the date the application was filed by the fiduciary or executor.

(e) *Approval of application for exemption.*—(1) *In general.*—The filing of an application for exemption on Form 4029 by a member of a religious group opposed to insurance does not constitute an exemption from the payment of the tax on self-employment income. An individual who files such an application is exempt from the payment of the tax only if the application is approved by the official with whom the application is required to be filed (see paragraph (b) of this section).

(2) *Conditions relating to approval or disapproval of application.*—An application for exemption on Form 4029 will not be approved unless the Secretary of Health, Education, and Welfare finds with respect to the religious sect or division thereof of which the individual filing the application is a member—

(i) That the sect or division thereof has the established tenets or teachings by reason of which the individual applicant is conscientiously opposed to the benefits of insurance of the type referred to in section 1402(h) (see paragraph (a) of this section),

(ii) That it is the practice, and has been for a period of time which the Secretary of Health, Education, and Welfare deems to be substantial, for members of such sect or division thereof to make provisions for their dependent members which, in the judgment of such Secretary, is reasonable in view of the general level of living of the members of the sect or division thereof; and

(iii) That the sect or division thereof has been in existence continuously since December 31, 1950.

In addition, an application for exemption on Form 4029 will not be approved if any benefit or other payment under title II or title XVIII of the Social Security Act became payable (or, but for section 203,

relating to reduction of insurance benefits, or 222(b), relating to reduction of insurance benefits on account of refusal to accept rehabilitation services, of the Social Security Act would have been payable) at or before the time of the filing of the application for exemption. Any determination required to be made pursuant to the preceding sentence will be made by the Secretary of Health, Education, and Welfare.

(f) *Period for which exemption is effective.*—(1) *General rule.*—An application for exemption shall be in effect (if approved as provided in paragraph (e) of this section) for all taxable years beginning after December 31, 1950 except as otherwise provided in subparagraph (2) of this paragraph.

(2) *Exceptions.*—An application for exemption referred to in subparagraph (1) of this paragraph shall not be effective for any taxable year which—

(i) Begins (a) before the taxable year in which the individual filing the application first met the requirements of subparagraphs (1) and (2) of paragraph (a) of this section, or (b) before the time as of which the Secretary of Health, Education, and Welfare finds that the sect or division thereof of which the individual is a member met the requirements of subparagraphs (C) and (D) of section 1402(h)(1) (see subdivisions (i) and (ii) of paragraph (e)(2) of this section), or

(ii) Ends (a) after the time at which the individual filing the application ceases to meet the requirements of subparagraphs (1) and (2) of paragraph (a) of this section, or (b) after the time as of which the Secretary of Health, Education, and Welfare finds that the sect or division thereof of which the individual is a member ceases to meet the requirements of subparagraphs (C) and (D) of section 1402(h)(1) (see subdivisions (i) and (ii) of paragraph (e)(2) of this section).

(g) *Refund or credit.*—An application for exemption on Form 4029 filed on or before December 31, 1968 (if approved as provided in paragraph (e) of this section), shall constitute a claim for refund or credit of any tax on self-employment income under section 1401 (or under section 480 of the Internal Revenue Code of 1939) paid or incurred in respect of any taxable year beginning after December 31, 1950, and ending before December 31, 1967, for which an exemption is granted. Refund or credit of any tax referred to in the preceding sentence may be made, pursuant to the provisions of section 501(c) of the Social Security Amendments of 1967 (81 Stat. 933), notwithstanding that the refund or credit would otherwise be prevented by operation of any law or rule of law. No interest shall be allowed or paid in respect of any refund or credit made or allowed in connection with a claim for refund or credit made on Form 4029. [Reg. § 1.1402(h)-1.]

☐ [T.D. 6993, 1-17-69.]

**[Reg. § 1.1403-1]**

**§ 1.1403-1. Cross references.**—For provisions relating to the requirement for filing returns with respect to net earnings from self-employment, see § 1.6017-1. For provisions relating to declarations of estimated tax on self-employment income, see § § 1.6015(a)-1 to 1.6015(j)-1, inclusive. For other administrative provisions relating to the tax on self-employment income, see the applicable sections of the regulations in this part (§ 1.6001-1 et seq.) and the applicable sections of the regulations in Part 301 of this chapter (Regulations on Procedure and Administration). [Reg. § 1.1403-1.]

☐ [T.D. 6196, 8-13-56. Amended by T.D. 7427, 8-9-76.]

# Net Investment Income Tax

See p. 20,601 for regulations not amended to reflect law changes

## [Reg. § 1.1411-0]

(4) Total section 1411 NOL amount of a net operating loss deduction.

(5) Examples.

(i) Effective/applicability date.

*§1.1411-5 Trades and businesses to which tax applies.*

(a) In general.

(b) Passive activity.

(1) In general.

(2) Application of income recharacterization rules.

(i) Income and gain recharacterization.

(ii) Gain recharacterization.

(iii) Exception for certain portfolio recharacterizations.

(3) Examples.

(c) Trading in financial instruments or commodities.

(1) Definition of financial instruments.

(2) Definition of commodities.

(d) Effective/applicability date.

*§1.1411-6 Income on investment of working capital subject to tax.*

(a) General rule.

(b) Example.

(c) Effective/applicability date.

*§1.1411-7 Exception for dispositions of certain active interests in partnerships and S corporations.* [Reserved]

*§1.1411-8 Exception for distributions from qualified plans.*

(a) General rule.

(b) Rules relating to distributions.

(1) Actual distributions.

(2) Amounts treated as distributed.

(3) Amounts includible in gross income.

(4) Amounts related to employer securities.

(i) Dividends related to employer securities.

(ii) Amounts related to the net unrealized appreciation in employer securities.

(c) Effective/applicability date.

*§1.1411-9 Exception for self-employment income.*

(a) General rule.

(b) Special rule for traders.

(c) Examples.

(d) Effective/applicability date.

*§1.1411-10 Controlled foreign corporations and passive foreign investment companies.*

(a) In general.

(b) Amounts derived from a trade or business described in §1.1411-5.

(1) In general.

(2) Coordination rule for changes in trade or business status.

(c) Calculation of net investment income.

(1) Dividends.

(i) Distributions of previously taxed earnings and profits.

(A) Rules when an election under paragraph (g) of this section is not in effect with respect to the shareholder.

*(1)* General rule.

*(2)* Exception for distributions attributable to earnings and profits previously taken into account for purposes of section 1411.

(B) Rule when an election under paragraph (g) of this section is in effect with respect to the shareholder.

(C) Special rule for certain distributions related to 2013 taxable years.

*(1)* Scope.

*(2)* Rule.

*(3)* Ordering rule.

(ii) Excess distributions that constitute dividends.

(2) Net gain.

(i) Gains treated as excess distributions.

(ii) Inclusions and deductions with respect to section 1296 mark to market elections.

(iii) Gain or loss attributable to the disposition of stock of CFCs and QEFs.

(iv) Gain or loss attributable to the disposition of interests in domestic partnerships or S corporations that own directly or indirectly stock of CFCs or QEFs.

(3) Application of section 1248.

(4) Amounts distributed by an estate or trust.

(5) Properly allocable deductions.

(i) General rule.

(ii) Additional rules.

(d) Conforming basis adjustments.

(1) Basis adjustments under sections 961 and 1293.

(i) Stock held by individuals, estates, or trusts.

(ii) Stock held by domestic partnerships or S corporations.

(A) Rule when an election under paragraph (g) of this section is not in effect.

(B) Rules when an election under paragraph (g) of this section is in effect.

(2) Special rules for partners that own interests in domestic partnerships that own directly or indirectly stock of CFCs or QEFs.

(3) Special rules for S corporation shareholders that own interests in S corporations that own directly or indirectly stock of CFCs or QEFs.

(4) Special rules for participants in common trust funds.

(e) Conforming adjustments to modified adjusted gross income and adjusted gross income.

(1) Individuals.

(2) Estates and trusts.

(f) Application to estates and trusts.

(g) Election with respect to CFCs and QEFs.

(1) Effect of election.

(2) Years to which election applies.

(i) In general.

(ii) Termination of interest in CFC or QEF.

(iii) Termination of partnership.

(3) Who may make the election.

(4) Time and manner for making the election.

(i) Individuals, estates, and trusts.

(A) General rule.

(B) Special rule for charitable remainder trusts (CRTs).

(ii) Certain domestic passthrough entities.

(iii) Taxable years that begin before January 1, 2014.

(A) Individuals, estates, or trusts.

(B) Certain domestic passthrough entities.

(iv) Time for making election.

(h) Examples.

(i) Effective/applicability date.

[Reg. §1.1411-0.]

☐ [*T.D.* 9644, 11-26-2013 (*corrected* 3-31-2014).]

**[Reg. §1.1411-1]**

**§1.1411-1. General rules.**—(a) *General rule.*—Except as otherwise provided, all Internal Revenue Code (Code) provisions that apply for chapter 1 purposes in determining taxable income (as defined in section 63(a)) of a taxpayer also apply in determining the tax imposed by section 1411.

(b) *Adjusted gross income.*—All references to an individual's adjusted gross income are treated as references to adjusted gross income as defined in section 62, and all references to an estate's or trust's adjusted gross income are treated as references to adjusted gross income as defined in section 67(e). However, there may be additional adjustments to adjusted gross income because of investments in controlled foreign corporations (CFCs) or passive foreign investment companies (PFICs). See §1.1411-10(e).

(c) *Effect of section 1411 and the regulations thereunder for other purposes.*—The inclusion or exclusion of items of income, gain, loss, or deduction in determining net investment income for purposes of section 1411, and the assignment of items of income, gain, loss, or deduction to a particular category of net investment income under section 1411(c)(1)(A), does not affect the treatment of any item of income, gain, loss, or deduction under any provision of the Code other than section 1411.

(d) *Definitions.*—The following definitions apply for purposes of calculating net investment income under section 1411 and the regulations thereunder—

(1) The term *gross income from annuities* under section 1411(c)(1)(A) includes the amount received as an annuity under an annuity, endowment, or life insurance contract that is includible in gross income as a result of the application of section 72(a) and section 72(b), and an amount not received as an annuity under an annuity contract that is includible in gross income under section 72(e). In the case of a sale of an annuity, to the extent the sales price of the annuity does not exceed its surrender value, the gain recognized would be treated as gross income from an annuity within the meaning of section 1411(c)(1)(A)(i) and §1.1411-4(a)(1)(i). However, if the sales price of the annuity exceeds its surrender value, the seller would treat the gain equal to the difference between the basis in the annuity and the surrender value as gross income from an annuity described in section 1411(c)(1)(A)(i) and §1.1411-4(a)(1)(i) and the excess of the sales price over the surrender value as gain from the disposition of property included in section 1411(c)(1)(A)(iii) and §1.1411-4(a)(1)(iii). The term *gross income from annuities* does not include amounts paid in consideration for services rendered. For example, distributions from

a foreign retirement plan that are paid in the form of an annuity and include investment income that was earned by the retirement plan does not constitute income from an annuity within the meaning of section 1411(c)(1)(A)(i).

(2) The term *controlled foreign corporation (CFC)* is as defined in section 953(c)(1)(B) or 957(a).

(3) The term *gross income from dividends* includes any item treated as a dividend for purposes of chapter 1. See also §1.1411-10 for additional amounts that constitute gross income from dividends. The term *gross income from dividends* includes, but is not limited to, amounts treated as dividends—

(i) Pursuant to subchapter C that are included in gross income (including constructive dividends);

(ii) Pursuant to section 1248(a), other than as provided in §1.1411-10;

(iii) Pursuant to §1.367(b)-2(e)(2);

(iv) Pursuant to section 1368(c)(2); and

(v) Substitute dividends that represent payments made to the transferor of a security in a securities lending transaction or a sale-repurchase transaction.

(4) The term *excluded income* means:

(i) Items of income excluded from gross income in chapter 1. For example, interest on state and local bonds excluded from gross income under section 103 and gain from the sale of a principal residence excluded from gross income under section 121.

(ii) Items of income not included in net investment income, as determined under §§1.1411-4 and 1.1411-10. For example, wages, unemployment compensation, Alaska Permanent Fund Dividends, alimony, and Social Security Benefits.

(iii) Items of gross income and net gain specifically excluded by section 1411, the regulations thereunder, or other guidance published in the Internal Revenue Bulletin. For example, gains from the disposition of property used in a trade of business not described in section 1411(c)(2) under §1.1411-4(d)(4)(i), distributions from certain Qualified Plans described in section 1411(c)(5) and §1.1411-8, income taken into account in determining self-employment income that is subject to tax under section 1401(b) described in section 1411(c)(6) and §1.1411-9, and section 951(a) inclusions from a CFC for which a §1.1411-10(g) election is not in effect.

(5) The term *individual* means any natural person.

(6) The term *gross income from interest* includes any item treated as interest income for purposes of chapter 1 and substitute interest that represents payments made to the transferor of a security in a securities lending transaction or a sale-repurchase transaction.

(7) The term *married* and *married taxpayer* has the same meaning as in section 7703.

(8) The term *net investment income (NII)* means net investment income as defined in section 1411(c) and §1.1411-4, as adjusted pursuant to the rules described in §1.1411-10(c).

(9) The term *passive foreign investment company (PFIC)* is as defined in section 1297(a).

(10) The term *gross income from rents* includes amounts paid or to be paid principally for the use of (or the right to use) tangible property.

(11) The term *gross income from royalties* includes amounts received from mineral, oil, and gas royalties, and amounts received for the privilege of using patents, copyrights, secret processes and formulas, goodwill, trademarks, tradebrands, franchises, and other like property.

(12) The term *trade or business* refers to a trade or business within the meaning of section 162.

(13) The term *United States person* is as defined in section 7701(a)(30).

(14) The term *United States shareholder* is as defined in section 951(b).

(e) *Disallowance of certain credits against the section 1411 tax.*— Amounts that may be credited against only the tax imposed by chapter 1 of the Code may not be credited against the section 1411 tax imposed by chapter 2A of the Code unless specifically provided in the Code. For example, the foreign income, war profits, and excess profits taxes that are allowed as a foreign tax credit by section 27(a), section 642(a), and section 901, respectively, are not allowed as a credit against the section 1411 tax.

(f) *Application to taxable years beginning before January 1, 2014.*— (1) *Retroactive application of regulations.*—Taxpayers that are subject to section 1411, and any other taxpayer to which these regulations may apply (such as partnerships and S corporations), may apply §§1.1411-1 through 1.1411-10 (including the ability to make any election(s) contained therein) in any taxable year that begins after December 31, 2012, but before January 1, 2014, for which the period of limitation under section 6501 has not expired.

(2) *Reliance and transitional rules.*—For taxable years beginning before January 1, 2014, the Internal Revenue Service will not challenge a taxpayer's computation of tax under section 1411 if the taxpayer has made a reasonable, good faith effort to comply with the requirements of section 1411. For example, a taxpayer's compliance with the provisions of the proposed and final regulations under section 1411 (REG-130507-11 or REG-130843-13), generally, will be considered a reasonable, good faith effort to comply with the requirements of section 1411 if reliance on such regulation projects under section 1411 are applied in their entirety, and the taxpayer makes reasonable adjustments to ensure that their section 1411 tax liability in the taxable years beginning after December 31, 2013, is not inappropriately distorted by the positions taken in taxable years beginning after December 31, 2012, but before January 1, 2014. A similar rule applies to any other taxpayer to which these regulations may apply (such as partnerships and S corporations).

(g) *Effective/applicability date.*—This section applies to taxable years beginning after December 31, 2013. However, taxpayers may apply this section to taxable years beginning after December 31, 2012, in accordance with paragraph (f) of this section. [Reg. §1.1411-1.]

☐ [T.D. 9644, 11-26-2013.]

## [Reg. §1.1411-2]

**§1.1411-2. Application to individuals.**—(a) *Individual to whom tax applies.*—(1) *In general.*—Section 1411 applies to an individual who is a citizen or resident of the United States (within the meaning of section 7701(a)(30)(A)). Section 1411 does not apply to nonresident alien individuals (within the meaning of section 7701(b)(1)(B)). See paragraph (a)(2)(vi) of this section for special rules regarding bona fide residents of United States territories.

(2) *Special rules.*—(i) *Dual resident individuals treated as residents of a foreign country under an income tax treaty.*—A dual resident taxpayer (as defined in §301.7701(b)-7(a)(1)) who determines that he or she is a resident of a foreign country for treaty purposes pursuant to an income tax treaty between the United States and the foreign country and who claims benefits of the treaty as a nonresident of the United States will be treated as a nonresident alien of the United States for purposes of paragraph (a)(1) of this section.

(ii) *Dual-status resident aliens.*—A dual-status individual who is a resident of the United States for a portion of a taxable year and a nonresident alien for the other portion of the taxable year will not be subject to section 1411 with respect to the portion of the year for which that individual is treated as a nonresident alien. The only income the individual must take into account for purposes of section 1411 is the income he or she receives during the portion of the year for which he or she is treated as a resident of the United States. The threshold amount under paragraph (d)(1) of this section applies.

(iii) *Joint returns in the case of a nonresident alien individual married to a United States citizen or resident.*—(A) *Default treatment.*—In the case of a United States citizen or resident who is married to a nonresident alien individual, the spouses will be treated as married filing separately for purposes of section 1411. For purposes of calculating the tax imposed under section 1411(a)(1), the United States citizen or resident spouse will be subject to the threshold amount for a married taxpayer filing a separate return in paragraph (d)(1)(ii) of this section, and the nonresident alien spouse will not be subject to tax under section 1411. In accordance with the rules for married individuals filing separate returns, the spouse that is a United States citizen or resident must determine his or her own net investment income and modified adjusted gross income.

(B) *Taxpayer election.*—Married taxpayers who file a joint Federal income tax return pursuant to a section 6013(g) election for purposes of chapter 1 and chapter 24 also may elect to be treated as making a section 6013(g) election for purposes of chapter 2A (relating to the tax imposed by section 1411).

(1) *Effect of election.*—For purposes of calculating the tax imposed under section 1411(a)(1), the effect of an election under section 6013(g) is to include the combined income of the United States citizen or resident spouse and the nonresident spouse in the section 1411(a)(1) calculation and to apply the threshold amount for a taxpayer making a joint return as set out in paragraph (d)(1)(i) of this section.

(2) *Procedural requirements for making election.*—Taxpayers with a section 6013(g) election in effect for chapter 1 and chapter 24 purposes for any taxable year beginning after December 31, 2012, or taxpayers making a section 6013(g) election for chapter 1 and chapter 24 purposes in any taxable year beginning after December 31, 2012, who want to apply their section 6013(g) election for purposes of chapter 2A must make the election for the first taxable year beginning after December 31, 2013, in which the United States taxpayer is

subject to tax under section 1411. The determination of whether the United States taxpayer is subject to tax under section 1411 is made without regard to the effect of the section 6013(g) election described in paragraph (a)(2)(iii)(B) of this section. The election, if made, must be made in the manner prescribed by forms, instructions, or in other guidance on an original or amended return for the taxable year for which the election is made. An election can be made on an amended return only if the taxable year for which the election is made, and all taxable years that are affected by the election, are not closed by the period of limitations on assessments under section 6501. Further, once made, the duration and termination of the section 6013(g) election for chapter 2A is governed by the rules of section 6013(g)(2) through (g)(6) and the regulations thereunder.

(3) *Ineffective elections.*—In the event a taxpayer makes an election described in paragraph (a)(2)(iii)(B) of this section and subsequently determines that such taxpayer does not meet the criteria for making such election in such tax year described in paragraph (a)(2)(iii)(B)(2) of this section, then such original election will have no effect for that year and all future years. In such a case, the taxpayer should make appropriate adjustments to properly reflect the ineffective election. However, notwithstanding the previous sentence, if a taxpayer meets the criteria for the same election in a subsequent year, such taxpayer is deemed to treat such original election as being made in that subsequent year unless the taxpayer files (or amends) the return for such subsequent year to report the taxpayer's net investment income tax without the original election. Furthermore, this paragraph (a)(2)(iii)(B)(3) shall not apply if a taxpayer does not meet the criteria described in paragraph (a)(2)(iii)(B)(2) of this section for making such election in such tax year solely as a result of the carryback of a net operating loss pursuant to section 172.

(iv) *Joint returns for a year in which nonresident alien married to a United States citizen or resident becomes a United States resident.*—(A) *Default treatment.*—In the case of a United States citizen or resident who is married to an individual who is a nonresident alien individual at the beginning of any taxable year, but is a United States resident at the close of such taxable year, each spouse will be treated as married filing separately for the entire year for purposes of section 1411. For purposes of calculating the tax imposed under section 1411(a)(1), each spouse will be subject to the threshold amount for a married taxpayer filing a separate return in paragraph (d)(1)(ii) of this section. The spouse who becomes a United States resident during the tax year will be subject to section 1411 only with respect to income received for the portion of the year for which he or she is treated as a United States resident. Each spouse must determine his or her own net investment income and modified adjusted gross income.

(B) *Taxpayer election.*—Married taxpayers who file a joint Federal income tax return pursuant to a section 6013(h) election for purposes of chapter 1 and chapter 24 also may elect to be treated as making a section 6013(h) election for purposes of chapter 2A for such tax year.

(1) *Effect of election.*—For purposes of calculating the tax imposed under section 1411(a)(1), the effect of an election under section 6013(h) is to include the combined income of the United States citizen or resident spouse and the dual-status resident spouse in the section 1411(a)(1) calculation and to apply the threshold amount for a taxpayer making a joint return as set out in paragraph (d)(1)(i) of this section.

(2) *Procedural requirements for making election.*—Taxpayers who make a section 6013(h) election for purposes of chapter 1 and chapter 24 for any taxable year beginning after December 31, 2012, may elect to have their section 6013(h) election apply for purposes of chapter 2A. The election, if made, must be made in the manner prescribed by forms, instructions, or in other guidance on an original or amended return for the taxable year for which the election is made. An election can be made on an amended return only if the taxable year for which the election is made, and all taxable years that are affected by the election, are not closed by the period of limitations on assessments under section 6501. Further, in all cases, once made, the section 6013(h) election is governed by the rules of section 6013(h)(2) and the regulations thereunder.

(iv) *Grantor trusts.*—For rules regarding the treatment of owners of grantor trusts, see § 1.1411-3(b)(1)(v).

(v) *Bankruptcy estates.*—A bankruptcy estate administered under chapter 7 (relating to liquidations) or chapter 11 (relating to reorganizations) of the Bankruptcy Code (Title 11 of the United States Code) of a debtor who is an individual is treated as a married taxpayer filing a separate return for purposes of section 1411. See § 1.1411-2(d)(1)(ii).

(vi) *Bona fide residents of United States territories.*—(A) *Applicability.*—An individual who is a bona fide resident of a United States territory is subject to the tax imposed by section 1411(a)(1) only if the individual is required to file an income tax return with the United States upon application of section 931, 932, 933, or 935 and the regulations thereunder. With respect to an individual described in this paragraph (a)(2)(vi)(A), the amount excluded from gross income under section 931 or 933 and any deduction properly allocable or chargeable against amounts excluded from gross income under section 931 or 933, respectively, is not taken into account in computing modified adjusted gross income under paragraph (c) of this section or net investment income (within the meaning of § 1.1411-1(d)).

(B) *Coordination with exception for nonresident aliens.*—An individual who is both a bona fide resident of a United States territory and a nonresident alien individual with respect to the United States is not subject to taxation under section 1411(a)(1).

(C) *Definitions.*—For purposes of this section—

(1) *Bona fide resident.*—The term *bona fide resident* has the meaning provided under section 937(a).

(2) *United States territory.*—The term *United States territory* means American Samoa, Guam, the Northern Mariana Islands, Puerto Rico, or the United States Virgin Islands.

(b) *Calculation of tax.*—(1) *In general.*—In the case of an individual described in paragraph (a)(1) of this section, the tax imposed by section 1411(a)(1) for each taxable year is equal to 3.8 percent of the lesser of—

(i) Net investment income for such taxable year; or

(ii) The excess (if any) of—

(A) The modified adjusted gross income (as defined in paragraph (c) of this section) for such taxable year; over

(B) The threshold amount (as defined in paragraph (d) of this section).

(2) *Example.*—During Year 1 (a year in which section 1411 is in effect), A, an unmarried United States citizen, has modified adjusted gross income (as defined in paragraph (c) of this section) of $190,000, which includes $50,000 of net investment income. A has a zero tax imposed under section 1411 because the threshold amount for a single individual is $200,000 (as provided in paragraph (d)(1)(iii) of this section). If during Year 2, A has modified adjusted gross income of $220,000, which includes $50,000 of net investment income, then the individual has a section 1411 tax of $760 (3.8% multiplied by $20,000, the lesser of $50,000 net investment income or $20,000 excess of modified adjusted gross income over the threshold amount).

(c) *Modified adjusted gross income.*—(1) *General rule.*—For purposes of section 1411, the term *modified adjusted gross income* means adjusted gross income increased by the excess of—

(i) The amount excluded from gross income under section 911(a)(1); over

(ii) The amount of any deductions (taken into account in computing adjusted gross income) or exclusions disallowed under section 911(d)(6) with respect to the amounts described in paragraph (c)(1)(i) of this section.

(2) *Rules with respect to CFCs and PFICs.*—Additional rules in § 1.1411-10(e)(1) apply to an individual that is a United States shareholder of a controlled foreign corporation (CFC) or that is a United States person that directly or indirectly owns an interest in a passive foreign investment company (PFIC).

(d) *Threshold amount.*—(1) *In general.*—The term *threshold amount* means—

(i) In the case of a taxpayer making a joint return under section 6013 or a surviving spouse (as defined in section 2(a)), $250,000;

(ii) In the case of a married taxpayer filing a separate return, $125,000; and

(iii) In the case of any other individual, $200,000.

(2) *Taxable year of less than twelve months.*—(i) *General rule.*—In the case of an individual who has a taxable year consisting of less than twelve months (short taxable year), the threshold amount under paragraph (d)(1) of this section is not reduced or prorated. For example, in the case of an unmarried decedent who dies on June 1, the threshold amount is $200,000 for the decedent's short taxable year that begins on January 1 and ends on June 1.

(ii) *Change of annual accounting period.*—Notwithstanding paragraph (d)(2)(i) of this section, an individual who has a short taxable year resulting from a change of annual accounting period reduces the threshold amount to an amount that bears the same ratio to the full threshold amount provided under paragraph (d)(1) of this section as the number of months in the short taxable year bears to twelve.

(e) *Effective/applicability date.*—This section applies to taxable years beginning after December 31, 2013. However, taxpayers may apply this section to taxable years beginning after December 31, 2012, in accordance with §1.1411-1(f). [Reg. §1.1411-2.]

☐ [*T.D. 9644, 11-26-2013 (corrected 3-31-2014).*]

### [Reg. §1.1411-3]

**§1.1411-3. Application to estates and trusts.**—(a) *Estates and trusts to which tax applies.*—(1) *In general.*—(i) *General application.*—Section 1411 and the regulations thereunder apply to all estates and trusts that are subject to the provisions of part I of subchapter J of chapter 1 of subtitle A of the Internal Revenue Code, unless specifically exempted under paragraph (b) of this section.

(ii) *Calculation of tax.*—The tax imposed by section 1411(a)(2) for each taxable year is equal to 3.8 percent of the lesser of—

(A) The estate's or trust's undistributed net investment income for such taxable year; or

(B) The excess (if any) of—

(1) The estate's or trust's adjusted gross income (as defined in section 67(e) and as adjusted under §1.1411-10(e)(2), if applicable) for such taxable year; over

(2) The dollar amount at which the highest tax bracket in section 1(e) begins for such taxable year.

(2) *Taxable year of less than twelve months.*—(i) *General rule.*—In the case of an estate or trust that has a taxable year consisting of less than twelve months (short taxable year), the dollar amount described in paragraph (a)(1)(ii)(B)(2) of this section is not reduced or prorated.

(ii) *Change of annual accounting period.*—Notwithstanding paragraph (a)(2)(i) of this section, an estate or trust that has a short taxable year resulting from a change of annual accounting period (but not from an individual's death) reduces the dollar amount described in paragraph (a)(1)(ii)(B)(2) of this section to an amount that bears the same ratio to that dollar amount as the number of months in the short taxable year bears to twelve.

(3) *Rules with respect to CFCs and PFICs.*—Additional rules in §1.1411-10 apply to an estate or trust that holds an interest in a controlled foreign corporation (CFC) or a passive foreign investment company (PFIC).

(b) *Application to certain trusts and estates.*—(1) *Exception for certain trusts and estates.*—The following trusts are not subject to the tax imposed by section 1411:

(i) A trust or decedent's estate all of the unexpired interests in which are devoted to one or more of the purposes described in section 170(c)(2)(B).

(ii) A trust exempt from tax under section 501.

(iii) A charitable remainder trust described in section 664. However, see paragraph (d) of this section for special rules regarding the treatment of annuity or unitrust distributions from such a trust to persons subject to tax under section 1411.

(iv) Any other trust, fund, or account that is statutorily exempt from taxes imposed in subtitle A. For example, see sections 220(e)(1), 223(e)(1), 529(a), and 530(a).

(v) A trust, or a portion thereof, that is treated as a grantor trust under subpart E of part I of subchapter J of chapter 1. However, in the case of any such trust or portion thereof, each item of income or deduction that is included in computing taxable income of a grantor or another person under section 671 is treated as if it had been received by, or paid directly to, the grantor or other person for purposes of calculating such person's net investment income.

(vi) Electing Alaska Native Settlement Trusts subject to taxation under section 646.

(vii) Cemetery Perpetual Care Funds to which section 642(i) applies.

(viii) Foreign trusts (as defined in section 7701(a)(31)(B) and §301.7701-7(a)(2)) (but see §§1.1411-3(e)(3)(ii) and 1.1411-4(e)(1)(ii) for rules related to distributions from foreign trusts to United States beneficiaries).

(ix) Foreign estates (as defined in section 7701(a)(31)(A)) (but see §1.1411-3(e)(3)(ii) for rules related to distributions from foreign estates to United States beneficiaries).

(2) *Special rules for certain taxable trusts and estates.*—(i) *Qualified funeral trusts.*—For purposes of the calculation of any tax imposed by section 1411, section 1411 and the regulations thereunder are applied to each qualified funeral trust (within the meaning of section 685) by treating each beneficiary's interest in each such trust as a separate trust.

(ii) *Bankruptcy estates.*—A bankruptcy estate in which the debtor is an individual is treated as a married taxpayer filing a separate return for purposes of section 1411. See §1.1411-2(a)(2)(v) and (d)(1)(ii).

(c) *Application to electing small business trusts (ESBTs).*—(1) *General application.*—The S portion and non-S portion (as defined in §1.641-1(b)(2) and (3), respectively) of a trust that has made an ESBT election under section 1361(e)(3) and §1.1361-1(m)(2) are treated as separate trusts for purposes of the computation of undistributed net investment income in the manner described in paragraph (e) of this section, but are treated as a single trust for purposes of determining the amount subject to tax under section 1411. If a grantor or another person is treated as the owner of a portion of the ESBT, the items of income and deduction attributable to the grantor portion (as defined in §1.641(c)-1(b)(1)) are included in the grantor's calculation of net investment income and are not included in the ESBT's computation of tax described in paragraph (c)(1)(ii) of this section.

(2) *Computation of tax.*—This paragraph (c)(2) provides the method for an ESBT to compute the tax under section 1411.

(i) *Step one.*—The S portion and non-S portion computes each portion's undistributed net investment income as separate trusts in the manner described in paragraph (e) of this section and then combine these amounts to calculate the ESBT's undistributed net investment income.

(ii) *Step two.*—The ESBT calculates its adjusted gross income (as defined in paragraph (a)(1)(ii)(B)(1) of this section). The ESBT's adjusted gross income is the adjusted gross income of the non-S portion, increased or decreased by the net income or net loss of the S portion, after taking into account all deductions, carryovers, and loss limitations applicable to the S portion, as a single item of ordinary income (or ordinary loss).

(iii) *Step three.*—The ESBT pays tax on the lesser of—

(A) The ESBT's total undistributed net investment income; or

(B) The excess of the ESBT's adjusted gross income (as calculated in paragraph (c)(2)(ii) of this section) over the dollar amount at which the highest tax bracket in section 1(e) begins for the taxable year.

(3) *Example.*—(i) In Year 1 (a year that section 1411 is in effect), the non-S portion of Trust, an ESBT, has dividend income of $15,000, interest income of $10,000, and capital loss of $5,000. Trust's S portion has net rental income of $21,000 and a capital gain of $7,000. The Trustee's annual fee of $1,000 is allocated 60% to the non-S portion and 40% to the S portion. Trust makes a distribution from income to a single beneficiary of $9,000.

(ii) *Step one.*—(A) Trust must compute the undistributed net investment income for the S portion and non-S portion in the manner described in paragraph (c) of this section.

The undistributed net investment income for the S portion is $27,600 and is determined as follows:

| | |
|---|---:|
| Net Rental Income | $21,000 |
| Capital Gain | $7,000 |
| Trustee Annual Fee | ($400) |
| Total S portion undistributed net investment income | $27,600 |

(B) The undistributed net investment income for the non-S portion is $12,400 and is determined as follows:

| | |
|---|---:|
| Dividend Income | $15,000 |
| Interest Income | $10,000 |
| Deductible Capital Loss | ($3,000) |
| Trustee Annual Fee | ($600) |
| Distributable net income distribution | ($9,000) |
| Total non-S portion undistributed net investment income | $12,400 |

(C) Trust combines the undistributed net investment income of the S portion and non-S portion from (ii)(A) and (B) to arrive at Trust's combined undistributed net investment income.

| | |
|---|---:|
| S portion's undistributed net investment income | $27,600 |
| Non-S portion's undistributed net investment income | $12,400 |
| Combined undistributed net investment income | $40,000 |

(iii) *Step two.*—(A) The ESBT calculates its adjusted gross income. Pursuant to paragraph (c)(2)(ii) of this section, the ESBT's adjusted gross income is the non-S portion's adjusted gross income increased or decreased by the net income or net loss of the S portion.

| | |
|---|---:|
| Dividend Income | $15,000 |
| Interest Income | $10,000 |
| Deductible Capital Loss | ($3,000) |
| Trustee Annual Fee | ($600) |
| Distributable net income distribution | ($9,000) |
| S Portion Income | $27,600 |
| Adjusted gross income | $40,000 |

(C) The S portion's single item of ordinary income used in the ESBT's adjusted gross income calculation is $27,600. This item of income is determined by starting with net rental income of $21,000 and capital gain of $7,000 and reducing it by the S portion's $400 share of the annual trustee fee.

(iv) *Step three.*—Trust pays tax on the lesser of—

(A) The combined undistributed net investment income ($40,000); or

(B) The excess of adjusted gross income ($40,000) over the dollar amount at which the highest tax bracket in section 1(e) applicable to a trust begins for the taxable year.

(d) *Application to charitable remainder trusts (CRTs).*—(1) *Operational rules.*—(i) *Treatment of annuity or unitrust distributions.*—If one or more items of net investment income comprise all or part of an annuity or unitrust distribution from a CRT, such items retain their character as net investment income in the hands of the recipient of that annuity or unitrust distribution.

(ii) *Apportionment among multiple beneficiaries.*—In the case of a CRT with more than one annuity or unitrust beneficiary, the net investment income is apportioned among such beneficiaries based on their respective shares of the total annuity or unitrust amount paid by the CRT for that taxable year.

(iii) *Accumulated net investment income.*—The accumulated net investment income of a CRT is the total amount of net investment income received by a CRT for all taxable years that begin after December 31, 2012, less the total amount of net investment income distributed for all prior taxable years of the trust that begin after December 31, 2012.

(2) *Application of Section 664.*—(i) *General rule.*—The Federal income tax rate of the item of net investment income, to be used to determine the proper classification of that item within the appropriate income category as described in § 1.664-1(d)(1)(i)(b), is the sum of the income tax rate applicable to that item under chapter 1 and the tax rate under section 1411. Thus, the accumulated net investment income and excluded income (as defined in § 1.1411-1(d)(4)) of a CRT in the same income category constitute separate classes of income within that category as described in § 1.664-1(d)(1)(i)(b).

(ii) *Special rules for CRTs with income from CFCs or PFICs.*—[Reserved]

(iii) *Examples.*—The following examples illustrate the provisions of this paragraph (d)(2).

*Example 1.* (i) In 2009, A formed CRT as a charitable remainder annuity trust. The trust document requires an annual annuity payment of $50,000 to A for 15 years. For purposes of this example, assume that CRT is a valid charitable remainder trust under section 664 and has not received any unrelated business taxable income during any taxable year.

(ii) As of January 1, 2013, CRT has the following items of undistributed income within its § 1.664-1(d)(1) categories and classes:

| Category | Class | Tax Rate | Amount |
|---|---|---|---:|
| Ordinary Income | Interest | 39.6% | $4,000 |
| | Net Rental Income | 39.6% | $8,000 |
| | Non-Qualified Dividend Income | 39.6% | $2,000 |
| | Qualified Dividend Income | 20.0% | $10,000 |
| Capital Gain | Short-Term | 39.6% | $39,000 |
| | Unrecaptured Section 1250 Gain | 25.0% | $1,000 |
| | Long-Term | 20.0% | $560,000 |
| Other Income | | | None |
| Total undistributed income as of January 1, 2013 | | | $624,000 |

Pursuant to § 1.1411-3(d)(1)(iii), none of the $624,000 of undistributed income is accumulated net investment income (ANII) because none of it was received by CRT after December 31, 2012. Thus, the entire $624,000 of undistributed income is excluded income (as defined in § 1.1411-1(d)(4)).

(iii) During 2013, CRT receives $7,000 of interest income, $9,000 of qualified dividend income, $4,000 of short-term capital gain, and $11,000 of long-term capital gain. Prior to the 2013 distribution of $50,000 to A, CRT has the following items of undistributed income within its § 1.664-1(d)(1) categories and classes after the application of paragraph (d)(2) of this section:

| Category | Class | Excluded / ANII | Tax Rate | Amount |
|---|---|---|---|---:|
| Ordinary Income | | | | |
| | Interest | NII | 43.4% | $7,000 |
| | Interest | Excluded | 39.6% | $4,000 |
| | Net Rental Income | Excluded | 39.6% | $8,000 |
| | Non-Qualified Dividend Income | Excluded | 39.6% | $2,000 |
| | Qualified Dividend Income | NII | 23.8% | $9,000 |
| | Qualified Dividend Income | Excluded | 20.0% | $10,000 |
| Capital Gain | | | | |
| | Short-Term | NII | 43.4% | $4,000 |
| | Short-Term | Excluded | 39.6% | $39,000 |
| | Unrecaptured Section 1250 Gain | Excluded | 25.0% | $1,000 |
| | Long-Term | NII | 23.8% | $11,000 |
| | Long-Term | Excluded | 20.0% | $560,000 |
| Other Income | | | | None |

(iv) The $50,000 distribution to A for 2013 will include the following amounts:

| Category | Class | Excluded / ANII | Tax Rate | Amount |
|---|---|---|---|---|
| Ordinary Income | | | | |
| | Interest | NII | 43.4% | $7,000 |
| | Interest | Excluded | 39.6% | $4,000 |
| | Net Rental Income | Excluded | 39.6% | $8,000 |
| | Non-Qualified Dividend Income | Excluded | 39.6% | $2,000 |
| | Qualified Dividend Income | NII | 23.8% | $9,000 |
| | Qualified Dividend Income | Excluded | 20.0% | $10,000 |
| Capital Gain | | | | |
| | Short-Term | NII | 43.4% | $4,000 |
| | Short-Term | Excluded | 39.6% | $6,000 |
| | Unrecaptured Section 1250 Gain | Excluded | 25.0% | None |
| | Long-Term | NII | 23.8% | None |
| | Long-Term | Excluded | 20.0% | None |

The amount included in A's 2013 net investment income is $20,000. This amount is comprised of $7,000 of interest income, $9,000 of qualified dividend income, and $4,000 of short-term capital gain.

| Category | Class | Excluded / ANII | Tax Rate | Amount |
|---|---|---|---|---|
| Ordinary Income | | | | |
| | Interest | | | None |
| | Net Rental Income | | | None |
| | Non-Qualified Dividend Income | | | None |
| | Qualified Dividend Income | | | None |
| Capital Gain | | | | |
| | Short-Term | Excluded | 39.6% | $33,000 |
| | Unrecaptured Section 1250 Gain | Excluded | 25.0% | $1,000 |
| | Long-Term | ANII | 23.8% | $11,000 |
| | Long-Term | Excluded | 20.0% | $560,000 |
| Other Income | | | | None |

*Example 2* [Reserved].

(3) *Elective simplified method.*—[Reserved]

(e) *Calculation of undistributed net investment income.*—(1) *In general.*—This paragraph (e) provides special rules for the computation of certain deductions and for the allocation of net investment income between an estate or trust and its beneficiaries. Generally, an estate's or trust's net investment income is calculated in the same manner as that of an individual. See §1.1411-10(c) for special rules regarding CFCs, PFICs, and estates and trusts holding interests in such entities.

(2) *Undistributed net investment income.*—An estate's or trust's undistributed net investment income is the estate's or trust's net investment income reduced by distributions of net investment income to beneficiaries and by deductions under section 642(c) in the manner described in paragraphs (e)(3) and (e)(4) of this section.

(3) *Distributions of net investment income to beneficiaries.*—(i) In computing the estate's or trust's undistributed net investment income, net investment income is reduced by distributions of net investment income made to beneficiaries. The deduction allowed under this paragraph (e)(3) is limited to the lesser of the amount deductible to the estate or trust under section 651 or section 661, as applicable, or the net investment income of the estate or trust. In the case of a deduction under section 651 or section 661 that consists of both net investment income and excluded income (as defined in §1.1411-1(d)(4)), the distribution must be allocated between net investment income and excluded income in a manner similar to §1.661(b)-1 as if net investment income constituted gross income and excluded income constituted amounts not includible in gross income. See §1.661(c)-1 and *Example 1* in paragraph (e)(5) of this section.

(ii) If one or more items of net investment income comprise all or part of a distribution for which a deduction is allowed under paragraph (e)(3)(i) of this section, such items retain their character as net investment income under section 652(b) or section 662(b), as applicable, for purposes of computing net investment income of the recipient of the distribution who is subject to tax under section 1411. The provisions of this paragraph (e)(3)(ii) also apply to distributions to United States beneficiaries of current year income described in section 652 or section 662, as applicable, from foreign estates and foreign nongrantor trusts.

(4) *Deduction for amounts paid or permanently set aside for a charitable purpose.*—In computing the estate's or trust's undistributed net investment income, the estate or trust is allowed a deduction for amounts of net investment income that are allocated to amounts allowable under section 642(c). In the case of an estate or trust that has items of income consisting of both net investment income and excluded income, the allowable deduction under this paragraph (e)(4) must be allocated between net investment income and excluded income in accordance with §1.642(c)-2(b) as if net investment

income constituted gross income and excluded income constituted amounts not includible in gross income. For an estate or trust with deductions under both sections 642(c) and 661, see §1.662(b)-2 and *Example 2* in paragraph (e)(5) of this section.

(5) *Examples.*—The following examples illustrate the provisions of this paragraph (e). In each example, Year 1 is a year in which section 1411 is in effect and the taxpayer is not a foreign estate or trust:

*Example 1. Calculation of undistributed net investment income (with no deduction under section 642(c)).* (i) In Year 1, Trust has dividend income of $15,000, interest income of $10,000, capital gain of $5,000, and $75,000 of taxable income relating to a distribution from an individual retirement account (as defined under section 408). Trust has no expenses. Trust distributes $10,000 of its current year trust accounting income to A, a beneficiary of Trust.

(ii) Trust's distributable net income is $100,000 ($15,000 in dividends plus $10,000 in interest plus $75,000 of taxable income from an individual retirement account), from which the $10,000 distribution to A is paid. Trust's deduction under section 661 is $10,000. Under §1.662(b)-1, the deduction reduces each class of income comprising distributable net income on a proportional basis. The $10,000 distribution equals 10% of distributable net income ($10,000 divided by $100,000). Therefore, the distribution consists of dividend income of $1,500, interest income of $1,000, and ordinary income attributable to the individual retirement account of $7,500. Because the $5,000 of capital gain allocated to principal for trust accounting purposes did not enter into distributable net income, no portion of that amount is included in the $10,000 distribution, nor does it qualify for the deduction under section 661.

(iii) Trust's net investment income is $30,000 ($15,000 in dividends plus $10,000 in interest plus $5,000 in capital gain). Trust's $75,000 of taxable income attributable to the individual retirement account is excluded income under §1.1411-1(d)(4). Trust's undistributed net investment income under paragraph (e)(2) of this section is $27,500, which is Trust's net investment income ($30,000) less the amount of dividend income ($1,500) and interest income ($1,000) distributed to A. The $27,500 of undistributed net investment income is comprised of the capital gain allocated to principal ($5,000), the remaining undistributed dividend income ($13,500), and the remaining undistributed interest income ($9,000).

(iv) Under paragraph (e)(3) of this section and pursuant to §1.1411-4(a)(1), A's net investment income includes dividend income of $1,500 and interest income of $1,000, but does not include the $7,500 of ordinary income attributable to the individual retirement account because it is excluded from net investment income under §1.1411-8.

*Example 2. Calculation of undistributed net investment income (with deduction under section 642(c)).* (i) Same facts as *Example 1*, except Trust is required to distribute $30,000 to A. In addition, Trust has a $10,000 deduction under section 642(c) (deduction for amounts paid for a charitable purpose). Trust also makes an additional discretionary distribution of $20,000 to B, a beneficiary of Trust. As in *Example 1*, Trust's net investment income is $30,000 ($15,000 in dividends plus $10,000 in interest plus $5,000 in capital gain). In accordance with §§ 1.661(b)-2 and 1.662(b)-2, the items of income must be allocated between the mandatory distribution to A, the discretionary distribution to B, and the $10,000 distribution to a charity.

(ii) For purposes of the mandatory distribution to A, Trust's distributable net income is $100,000. See § 1.662(b)-2, *Example* 1(b). Trust's deduction under section 661 for the distribution to A is $30,000. Under § 1.662(b)-1, the deduction reduces each class of income comprising distributable net income on a proportional basis. The $30,000 distribution equals 30% of distributable net income ($30,000 divided by $100,000). Therefore, the distribution consists of dividend income of $4,500, interest income of $3,000, and ordinary income attributable to the individual retirement account of $22,500. A's mandatory distribution thus consists of $7,500 of net investment income and $22,500 of excluded income.

(iii) Trust's remaining distributable net income is $70,000. Trust's remaining undistributed net investment income is $22,500. The $10,000 deduction under section 642(c) is allocated in the same manner as the distribution to A, where the $10,000 distribution equals 10% of distributable net income ($10,000 divided by $100,000). For purposes of determining undistributed net investment income, Trust's net investment income is reduced by $2,500 under paragraph (e)(4) of this section (dividend income of $1,500, interest income of $1,000, but with no reduction for amounts attributable to the individual retirement account of $7,500).

(iv) With respect to the discretionary distribution to B, Trust's remaining distributable net income is $60,000. Trust's remaining undistributed net investment income is $20,000. Trust's deduction under section 661 for the distribution to B is $20,000. The $20,000 distribution equals 20% of distributable net income ($20,000 divided by $100,000). Therefore, the distribution consists of dividend income of $3,000, interest income of $2,000, and ordinary income attributable to the individual retirement account of $15,000. B's distribution consists of $5,000 of net investment income and $15,000 of excluded income.

(v) Trust's undistributed net investment income is $15,000 after taking into account distribution deductions and section 642(c) in accordance with paragraphs (e)(3) and (e)(4) of this section, respectively. To arrive at Trust's undistributed net investment income of $15,000, Trust's net investment income of $30,000 is reduced by $7,500 of the mandatory distribution to A, $2,500 of the section 642(c) deduction, and $5,000 of the discretionary distribution to B. The undistributed net investment income consists of the remaining dividend income of $6,000 ($15,000 less $4,500 less $1,500 less $3,000), interest income of $4,000 ($10,000 less $1,000 less $3,000 less $2,000), and the $5,000 of undistributed capital gain.

*Example 3. Fiscal Year Estate.* (i) D died in 2011. D's estate (Estate) filed its first return that established its fiscal year ending October 31, 2011. During Estate's fiscal year ending October 31, 2013, it earned $10,000 of interest, $1,000 of dividends, and $15,000 of short-term gains. The Estate distributed its interest and dividends to S, D's spouse and sole beneficiary, on a quarterly basis; the last quarter's payment for that taxable year was made to S on December 5, 2013. Pursuant to § 1.662(c)-1, S is deemed to have received the first three payments for that taxable year, regardless of the actual payment dates, on October 31, 2013, the last day of Estate's taxable year. Estate makes a timely section 663(b) election to treat the fourth quarter distribution to S as having been made on October 31, 2013, the last day of Estate's preceding taxable year. Accordingly, S is deemed to have received $10,000 of interest and $1,000 of dividends on October 31, 2013.

(ii) Because Estate's fiscal year ending October 31, 2013, began on November 1, 2012, the Estate is not subject to section 1411 on income received during that taxable year. Therefore, none of the income received by Estate during its fiscal year ending October 31, 2013, is net investment income. Pursuant to paragraph (e)(3)(ii) of this section, because none of the distributed interest or dividend income constituted net investment income to Estate, the $10,000 of interest and $1,000 of dividends that Estate distributed to S does not constitute net investment income to S.

(f) *Effective/applicability date.*—This section applies to taxable years beginning after December 31, 2013, except that paragraph (d) of this section applies to taxable years of CRTs that begin after December 31, 2012. However, taxpayers other than CRTs may apply this section to taxable years beginning after December 31, 2012, in accordance with § 1.1411-1(f). [Reg. § 1.1411-3.]

☐ [*T.D. 9644, 11-26-2013 (corrected 3-31-2014).*]

**[Reg. § 1.1411-4]**

**§ 1.1411-4. Definition of net investment income.**—(a) *In general.*—For purposes of section 1411 and the regulations thereunder, net investment income means the excess (if any) of—

(1) The sum of—

(i) Gross income from interest, dividends, annuities, royalties, and rents, except to the extent excluded by the ordinary course of a trade or business exception described in paragraph (b) of this section;

(ii) Other gross income derived from a trade or business described in § 1.1411-5; and

(iii) Net gain (to the extent taken into account in computing taxable income) attributable to the disposition of property, except to the extent excluded by the exception described in paragraph (d)(4)(i)(A) of this section for gain or loss attributable to property held in a trade or business not described in § 1.1411-5; over

(2) The deductions allowed by subtitle A that are properly allocable to such gross income or net gain (as determined in paragraph (f) of this section).

(b) *Ordinary course of a trade or business exception.*—Gross income described in paragraph (a)(1)(i) of this section is excluded from net investment income if it is derived in the ordinary course of a trade or business not described in § 1.1411-5. See § 1.1411-6 for rules regarding working capital. To determine whether gross income described in paragraph (a)(1)(i) of this section is derived in a trade or business, the following rules apply.

(1) In the case of an individual, estate, or trust that owns or engages in a trade or business directly (or indirectly through ownership of an interest in an entity that is disregarded as an entity separate from its owner under § 301.7701-3), the determination of whether gross income described in paragraph (a)(1)(i) of this section is derived in a trade or business is made at the individual, estate, or trust level.

(2) In the case of an individual, estate, or trust that owns an interest in a passthrough entity (for example, a partnership or S corporation), and that entity is engaged in a trade or business, the determination of whether gross income described in paragraph (a)(1)(i) of this section is—

(i) Derived in a trade or business described in § 1.1411-5(a)(1) is made at the owner level; and

(ii) Derived in a trade or business described in § 1.1411-5(a)(2) is made at the entity level.

(3) The following examples illustrate the provisions of this paragraph (b). For purposes of these examples, assume that the taxpayer is a United States citizen, uses a calendar taxable year, and Year 1 and all subsequent years are taxable years in which section 1411 is in effect:

*Example 1. Multiple passthrough entities.* A, an individual, owns an interest in UTP, a partnership, which is engaged in a trade or business. UTP owns an interest in LTP, also a partnership, which is not engaged in a trade or business. LTP receives $10,000 in dividends, $5,000 of which is allocated to A through UTP. The $5,000 of dividends is not derived in a trade or business because LTP is not engaged in a trade or business. This is true even though UTP is engaged in a trade or business. Accordingly, the ordinary course of a trade or business exception described in paragraph (b) of this section does not apply, and A's $5,000 of dividends is net investment income under paragraph (a)(1)(i) of this section.

*Example 2. Multiple passthrough entities.* B, an individual, owns an interest in UTP2, a partnership, which is not engaged in a trade or business. UTP2 owns an interest in LTP2, also a partnership, which is engaged in a commercial lending trade or business. LTP2 is not engaged in a trade or business described in § 1.1411-5(a)(2). LTP2's trade or business is not a passive activity (within the meaning of section 469) with respect to B. LTP2 earns $10,000 of interest income from its trade or business which is allocated to B through UTP2. Although UTP2 is not engaged in a trade or business, the $10,000 of interest income is derived in the ordinary course of LTP2's lending trade or business. Because LTP2 is not engaged in a trade or business described in § 1.1411-5(a)(2) and because LTP2's trade or business is not a passive activity with respect to B (as described in § 1.1411-5(a)(1)), the ordinary course of a trade or business exception described in paragraph (b) of this section applies, and B's $10,000 of interest is not included as net investment income under paragraph (a)(1)(i) of this section.

*Example 3. Entity engaged in trading in financial instruments.* C, an individual, owns an interest in PRS, a partnership, which is engaged in a trade or business of trading in financial instruments (as defined in § 1.1411-5(a)(2)). PRS' trade or business is not a passive activity (within the meaning of section 469) with respect to C. In addition, C is not directly engaged in a trade or business of trading in financial instruments or commodities. PRS earns interest of $50,000, and C's distributive share of the interest is $25,000. Because PRS is engaged in a trade or business described in § 1.1411-5(a)(2), the ordinary course of a trade or business exception described in paragraph (b) of this section does not apply, and C's $25,000 distributive share of the interest is net investment income under paragraph (a)(1)(i) of this section.

*Example 4. Application of ordinary course of a trade or business exception.* D, an individual, owns stock in S corporation, S. S is engaged in a banking trade or business (that is not a trade or business of trading in financial instruments or commodities), and S's trade or business is not a passive activity (within the meaning of section 469) with respect to D because D materially participates in the activity. S earns $100,000 of interest in the ordinary course of its trade or business, of which $5,000 is D's pro rata share. For purposes of paragraph (b) of this section, the interest income is derived in the ordinary course of S's banking business because it is not derived from working capital under section 1411(c)(3) and § 1.1411-6(a) (because it is considered to be derived in the ordinary course of a trade or business under the principles of § 1.469-2T(c)(3)(ii)(A)). Because S is not engaged in a trade or business described in § 1.1411-5(a)(2) and because S's trade or business is not a passive activity with respect to D (as described in § 1.1411-5(a)(1)), the ordinary course of a trade or business exception described in paragraph (b) of this section applies, and D's $5,000 of interest is not included under paragraph (a)(1)(i) of this section.

(c) *Other gross income from a trade or business described in § 1.1411-5.*—For a trade or business described in § 1.1411-5, paragraph (a)(1)(ii) of this section includes all other gross income (within the meaning of section 61) that is not gross income described in paragraph (a)(1)(i) of this section or net gain described in paragraph (a)(1)(iii) of this section.

(d) *Net gain.*—This paragraph (d) describes special rules for purposes of paragraph (a)(1)(iii) of this section.

(1) *Definition of disposition.*—For purposes of section 1411 and the regulations thereunder, the term *disposition* means a sale, exchange, transfer, conversion, cash settlement, cancellation, termination, lapse, expiration, or other disposition (including a deemed disposition, for example, under section 877A).

(2) *Limitation.*—The calculation of net gain may not be less than zero. Losses allowable under section 1211(b) are permitted to offset gain from the disposition of assets other than capital assets that are subject to section 1411.

(3) *Net gain attributable to the disposition of property.*—(i) *General rule.*—Net gain attributable to the disposition of property is the gain described in section 61(a)(3) recognized from the disposition of property reduced, but not below zero, by losses deductible under section 165, including losses attributable to casualty, theft, and abandonment or other worthlessness. The rules in subchapter O of chapter 1 and the regulations thereunder apply. See, for example, § 1.61-6(b). For purposes of this paragraph, net gain includes, but is not limited to, gain or loss attributable to the disposition of property from the investment of working capital (as defined in § 1.1411-6); gain or loss attributable to the disposition of a life insurance contract; and gain attributable to the disposition of an annuity contract to the extent the sales price of the annuity exceeds the annuity's surrender value.

(ii) *Examples.*—The following examples illustrate the provisions of this paragraph (d)(3). For purposes of these examples, assume that the taxpayer is a United States citizen, uses a calendar taxable year, and Year 1 and all subsequent years are taxable years in which section 1411 is in effect:

*Example 1. Calculation of net gain.* (i) In Year 1, A, an unmarried individual, realizes a capital loss of $40,000 on the sale of P stock and realizes a capital gain of $10,000 on the sale of Q stock, resulting in a net capital loss of $30,000. Both P and Q are C corporations. A has no other capital gain or capital loss in Year 1. In addition, A receives wages of $300,000 and earns $5,000 of gross income from interest. For income tax purposes, under section 1211(b), A may use $3,000 of the net capital loss against other income. Under section 1212(b)(1), the remaining $27,000 is a capital loss carryover. For purposes of determining A's Year 1 net gain under paragraph (a)(1)(iii) of this section, A's gain of $10,000 on the sale of the Q stock is reduced by A's loss of $40,000 on the sale of the P stock. In addition, A may reduce net investment income by the $3,000 of the excess of capital losses over capital gains allowed for income tax purposes under section 1211(b).

(ii) In Year 2, A has a capital gain of $30,000 on the sale of Y stock. Y is a C corporation. A has no other capital gain or capital loss in Year 2. For income tax purposes, A may reduce the $30,000 gain by the Year 1 section 1212(b) $27,000 capital loss carryover. For purposes of determining A's Year 2 net gain under paragraph (a)(1)(iii) of this section, A's $30,000 gain may also be reduced by the $27,000 capital loss carryover from Year 1. Therefore, in Year 2, A has $3,000 of net gain for purposes of paragraph (a)(1)(iii) of this section.

*Example 2. Calculation of net gain.* The facts are the same as in *Example 1*, except that in Year 1, A also realizes a gain of $20,000 on the sale of Rental Property D, all of which is treated as ordinary income under section 1250. For income tax purposes, under section 1211(b), A may use $3,000 of the net capital loss against other income. Under section 1212(b)(1) the remaining $27,000 is a capital loss carryover. For purposes of determining A's net gain under paragraph (a)(1)(iii) of this section, A's gain of $10,000 on the sale of the Q stock is reduced by A's loss of $40,000 on the sale of the P stock. A's $20,000 gain on the sale of Rental Property D is reduced to the extent of the $3,000 loss allowed under section 1211(b). Therefore, A's net gain for Year 1 is $17,000 ($20,000 gain treated as ordinary income on the sale of Rental Property D reduced by $3,000 loss allowed under section 1211).

*Example 3. Section 121(a) exclusion.* (i) In Year 1, A, an unmarried individual, sells a house that A has owned and used as A's principal residence for the five years preceding the sale and realizes $200,000 in gain. In addition to the gain realized from the sale of A's principal residence, A also realizes $7,000 in long-term capital gain. A has a $5,000 short-term capital loss carryover from a year preceding the effective date of section 1411.

(ii) For income tax purposes, under section 121(a), A excludes the $200,000 gain realized from the sale of A's principal residence from A's Year 1 gross income. In determining A's Year 1 adjusted gross income, A also reduces the $7,000 capital gain by the $5,000 capital loss carryover allowed under section 1211(b).

(iii) For section 1411 purposes, under section 121(a), A excludes the $200,000 gain realized from the sale of A's principal residence from A's Year 1 gross income and, consequently, from A's net investment income. In determining A's Year 1 net gain under paragraph (a)(1)(iii) of this section, A reduces the $7,000 capital gain by the $5,000 capital loss carryover allowed under section 1211(b).

*Example 4. Section 1031 like-kind exchange.* (i) In Year 1, A, an unmarried individual who is not a dealer in real estate, purchases Greenacre, a piece of undeveloped land, for $10,000. A intends to hold Greenacre for investment.

(ii) In Year 3, A enters into an exchange in which A transfers Greenacre, now valued at $20,000, and $5,000 cash for Blackacre, another piece of undeveloped land, which has a fair market value of $25,000. The exchange is a transaction for which no gain or loss is recognized under section 1031.

(iii) In Year 3, for income tax purposes, A does not recognize any gain from the exchange of Greenacre for Blackacre. A's basis in Blackacre is $15,000 ($10,000 substituted basis in Greenacre plus $5,000 additional cost of acquisition). For purposes of section 1411, A's net investment income for Year 3 does not include any realized gain from the exchange of Greenacre for Blackacre.

(iv) In Year 5, A sells Blackacre to an unrelated party for $35,000 in cash.

(v) In Year 5, for income tax purposes, A recognizes capital gain of $20,000 ($35,000 sale price minus $15,000 basis). For purposes of section 1411, A's net investment income includes the $20,000 gain recognized from the sale of Blackacre.

(4) *Gains and losses excluded from net investment income.*—(i) *Exception for gain or loss attributable to property held in a trade or business not described in § 1.1411-5.*—(A) *General rule.*—Net gain does not include gain or loss attributable to property (other than property from the investment of working capital (as described in § 1.1411-6)) held in a trade or business not described in § 1.1411-5.

(B) *Special rules for determining whether property is held in a trade or business.*—To determine whether net gain described in paragraph (a)(1)(iii) of this section is from property held in a trade or business—

(1) A partnership interest or S corporation stock generally is not property held in a trade or business. Therefore, gain from the sale of a partnership interest or S corporation stock is generally gain described in paragraph (a)(1)(iii) of this section. However, net gain does not include certain gain or loss attributable to the disposition of certain interests in partnerships and S corporations as provided in § 1.1411-7.

(2) In the case of an individual, estate, or trust that owns or engages in a trade or business directly (or indirectly through ownership of an interest in an entity that is disregarded as an entity separate from its owner under § 301.7701-3), the determination of whether net gain described in paragraph (a)(1)(iii) of this section is attributable to property held in a trade or business is made at the individual, estate, or trust level.

(3) In the case of an individual, estate, or trust that owns an interest in a passthrough entity (for example, a partnership or S corporation), and that entity is engaged in a trade or business, the determination of whether net gain described in paragraph (a)(1)(iii) of this section from such entity is attributable to—

(i) Property held in a trade or business described in § 1.1411-5(a)(1) is made at the owner level; and

(ii) Property held in a trade or business described in §1.1411-5(a)(2) is made at the entity level.

(C) *Examples.*—The following examples illustrate the provisions of this paragraph (d)(4)(i). For purposes of these examples, assume the taxpayer is a United States citizen, uses a calendar taxable year, and Year 1 and all subsequent years are taxable years in which section 1411 is in effect:

*Example 1. Gain from rental activity.* A, an unmarried individual, rents a boat to B for $100,000 in Year 1. A's rental activity does not involve the conduct of a section 162 trade or business, and under section 469(c)(2), A's rental activity is a passive activity. In Year 2, A sells the boat to B, and A realizes and recognizes taxable gain attributable to the disposition of the boat of $500,000. Because the exception provided in paragraph (d)(4)(i)(A) of this section requires a trade or business, this exception is inapplicable, and therefore, A's $500,000 gain will be taken into account under §1.1411-4(a)(1)(iii).

*Example 2. Installment sale.* (i) PRS, a partnership for Federal income tax purposes, operates an automobile dealership. B and C, unmarried individuals, each own a 40% interest in PRS and both materially participate in the activities of PRS for all relevant years. Therefore, with respect to B and C, PRS is not a trade or business described in section 1411(c)(2) and §1.1411-5. D owns the remaining 20% of PRS. Assume, for purposes of this example, that PRS is a passive activity with respect to D, and therefore is a trade or business described in section 1411(c)(2)(A) and §1.1411-5(a)(1).

(ii)(A) In Year 0, a year preceding the effective date of section 1411, PRS relocates its dealership to a larger location. As a result of the relocation, PRS sells its old dealership facility to a real estate developer in exchange for $1,000,000 cash and a $4,500,000 promissory note, fully amortizing over the subsequent 15 years, and bearing adequate stated interest. PRS reports the sale transaction under section 453. PRS's adjusted tax basis in the old dealership facility is $1,075,000. Assume for purposes of this example that PRS has $300,000 of recapture income (within the meaning of section 453(i)); the buyer is not related to PRS, B, C, or D; and the buyer is not assuming any liabilities of PRS in the transaction.

(B) For chapter 1 purposes, PRS has realized gain on the transaction of $4,425,000 ($5,500,000 less $1,075,000). Pursuant to section 453(i), PRS will take into account $300,000 of the recapture income in Year 0, and the gain in excess of the recapture income ($4,125,000) will be taken into account under the installment method. For purposes of section 453, PRS's profit percentage is 75% ($4,125,000 gain divided by $5,500,000 gross selling price). In Year 0, PRS will take into account $750,000 of capital gain attributable to the $1,000,000 cash payment. In the subsequent 15 years, PRS will receive annual payments of $300,000 (plus interest). Each payment will result in PRS recognizing $225,000 of capital gain (75% of $300,000).

(iii)(A) In Year 1, PRS receives a payment of $300,000 plus the applicable amount of interest. For purposes of chapter 1, PRS recognizes $225,000 of capital gain. B and C's distributive share of the gain is $90,000 each and D's distributive share of the gain is $45,000.

(B) The old dealership facility constituted property held in PRS's trade or business. In the case of section 453 installment sales, section 453 governs the timing of the gain recognition, but does not alter the character of the gain. See §1.1411-1(a). The determination of whether the gain is attributable to the disposition of property used in a trade or business described in paragraph (d)(4)(i) of this section constitutes an element of the gain's character for Federal tax purposes. As a result, the applicability of paragraph (d)(4)(i) of this section is determined in Year 0 and applies to all gain received on the promissory note during the 15 year payment period. This result is consistent with the section 469 determination of the passive or nonpassive classification of the gain under §1.469-2T(c)(2)(i)(A).

(C) In the case of D, PRS's trade or business is described in section 1411(c)(2)(A) and §1.1411-5(a)(1). Therefore, the exclusion in paragraph (d)(4)(i) of this section does not apply, and D must include the $45,000 of gain in D's net investment income.

(D) In the case of B and C, PRS's trade or business is not described in section 1411(c)(2) or §1.1411-5. Therefore, B and C exclude the $90,000 gain from net investment income pursuant to paragraph (d)(4)(i) of this section.

(iv) In Year 2, C dies and C's 40% interest in PRS passes to Estate.

(v)(A) In Year 3, PRS receives a payment of $300,000 plus the applicable amount of interest. For purposes of chapter 1, PRS recognizes $225,000 of capital gain. B and Estate each have a distributive share of the gain equal to $90,000 and D's distributive share of the gain is $45,000.

(B) The calculation of net investment income for B and D in Year 3 is the same as in (iii) for Year 1.

(C) In the case of Estate, the distributive share of the $90,000 gain constitutes income in respect of a decedent (IRD) under section 691(a)(4) and subchapter K. See §1.1411-1(a). Assume that Estate paid estate taxes of $5,000 that were attributable to the $90,000 of IRD. Pursuant to section 691(c)(4), the amount of gain taken into account in computing Estate's taxable income in Year 3 is $85,000 ($90,000 reduced by the $5,000 of allocable estate taxes). Pursuant to section 691(a)(3) and §1.691(a)-3(a), the character of the gain to the Estate is the same character as the gain would have been if C had survived to receive it. Although the amount of taxable gain for chapter 1 has been reduced, the remaining $85,000 retains its character attributable to the disposition of property used in a trade or business described in paragraph (d)(4)(i) of this section. Therefore, Estate may exclude the $85,000 gain from net investment income pursuant to paragraph (d)(4)(i) of this section.

(ii) *Other gains and losses excluded from net investment income.*—Net gain, as determined under paragraph (d) of this section, does not include gains and losses excluded from net investment income by any other provision in §§1.1411-1 through 1.1411-10. For example, see §1.1411-7 (certain gain or loss attributable to the disposition of certain interests in partnerships and S corporations) and §1.1411-8(b)(4)(ii) (net unrealized appreciation attributable to employer securities realized on a disposition of those employer securities).

(iii) *Adjustment for capital loss carryforwards for previously excluded income.*—[Reserved]

(e) *Net investment income attributable to certain entities.*—(1) *Distributions from estates and trusts.*—(i) *In general.*—Net investment income includes a beneficiary's share of distributable net income, as described in sections 652(a) and 662(a), to the extent that, under sections 652(b) and 662(b), the character of such income constitutes gross income from items described in paragraphs (a)(1)(i) and (ii) of this section or net gain attributable to items described in paragraph (a)(1)(iii) of this section, with further computations consistent with the principles of this section, as provided in §1.1411-3(e).

(ii) *Distributions of accumulated net investment income from foreign nongrantor trusts to United States beneficiaries.*—[Reserved]

(2) *CFCs and PFICs.*—For purposes of calculating net investment income, additional rules in §1.1411-10(c) apply to an individual, an estate, or a trust that is a United States shareholder that owns an interest in a controlled foreign corporation (CFC) or that is a United States person that directly or indirectly owns an interest in a passive foreign investment company (PFIC).

(3) *Treatment of income from common trust funds.*—[Reserved]

(f) *Properly allocable deductions.*—(1) *General rule.*—(i) *In general.*—Unless provided elsewhere in §§1.1411-1 through 1.1411-10, only properly allocable deductions described in this paragraph (f) may be taken into account in determining net investment income.

(ii) *Limitations.*—Any deductions described in this paragraph (f) in excess of gross income and net gain described in section 1411(c)(1)(A) are not taken into account in determining net investment income in any other taxable year, except as allowed under chapter 1.

(2) *Properly allocable deductions described in section 62.*—(i) *Deductions allocable to gross income from rents and royalties.*—Deductions described in section 62(a)(4) allocable to rents and royalties described in paragraph (a)(1)(i) of this section are taken into account in determining net investment income.

(ii) *Deductions allocable to gross income from trades or businesses described in §1.1411-5.*—Deductions described in section 62(a)(1) allocable to income from a trade or business described in §1.1411-5 are taken into account in determining net investment income to the extent the deductions have not been taken into account in determining self-employment income within the meaning of §1.1411-9.

(iii) *Penalty on early withdrawal of savings.*—Deductions described in section 62(a)(9) are taken into account in determining net investment income.

(iv) *Net operating loss.*—The total section 1411 NOL amount of a net operating loss deduction allowed under section 172 is allowed as a properly allocable deduction in determining net investment income for any taxable year. See paragraph (h) of this section for the calculation of the total section 1411 NOL amount of a net operating loss deduction.

(v) *Examples.*—The following examples illustrate the provisions of this paragraph (f)(2). For purposes of these examples, assume the taxpayer is a United States citizen, uses a calendar taxable year, and Year 1 and all subsequent years are taxable years in which section 1411 is in effect:

*Example 1.* (i) A, an individual, is a 40% shareholder in SCo, an S corporation. SCo is engaged in a trade or business described in section 1411(c)(2)(A). SCo is the only passive activity owned by A. In Year 1, SCo reported a loss of $11,000 to A which was comprised of gross operating income of $29,000 and operating deductions of $40,000. A's at risk amount at the beginning of Year 1 is $7,000. There were no other events that affected A's at risk amount in Year 1.

(ii) For purposes of calculating A's net investment income, A's $29,000 distributive share of SCo's gross operating income is income within the meaning of section 1411(c)(1)(A)(ii).

(iii) As a result of A's at risk limitation, for chapter 1 purposes, A may only deduct $7,000 of the operating deductions in excess of the gross operating income. The remaining $4,000 deductions are suspended because A's amount at risk at the end of Year 1 is zero.

(iv) For purposes of section 469, A has passive activity gross income of $29,000 and passive activity deductions of $36,000 ($40,000 of operating deductions allocable to A less $4,000 suspended under section 465). Because A has no other passive activity income from any other source, section 469 limits A's passive activity deductions to A's passive activity gross income. As a result, section 469 allows A to deduct $29,000 of SCo's operating deductions and suspends the remaining $7,000.

(v) For purposes of calculating A's net investment income, A has $29,000 of properly allocable deductions allowed by section 1411(c)(1)(B) and paragraph (f)(2)(ii) of this section.

*Example 2.* (i) Same facts as *Example 1.* In Year 2, SCo reported net income of $13,000 to A, which was comprised of gross operating income of $43,000 and operating deductions of $30,000. There were no other events that affected A's at risk amount in Year 2.

(ii) For purposes of calculating A's net investment income, A's $43,000 distributive share of gross operating income is income within the meaning of section 1411(c)(1)(A)(ii).

(iii) Pursuant to section 465(a)(2), A's deductions attributable to the gross income of SCo include the $30,000 deduction allocable to A in Year 2 plus the $4,000 loss that was suspended and carried over to Year 2 from Year 1 pursuant to section 465(a)(2). Under section 465(a)(2), the $4,000 of losses from Year 1 are treated as deductions from the activity in Year 2. As a result, A's net operating income from SCo in Year 2 is $9,000 ($43,000 -$30,000 -$4,000) in Year 2. A's amount at risk at the end of Year 2 is $9,000.

(iv) For purposes of section 469, A has passive activity gross income of $43,000. A's passive activity deductions attributable to SCo are the sum of the Year 2 operating deductions allocable to A from S ($30,000), deductions formerly suspended by section 465 ($4,000), and passive activity losses suspended by section 469 ($7,000). Therefore, in Year 2, A has passive activity deductions of $41,000. Because A's passive activity gross income exceeds A's passive activity deductions, section 469 does not limit any of the deductions in Year 2. At the end of Year 2, A has no suspended passive activity losses.

(v) Although A's distributive share of Year 2 deductions allocable to SCo's operating income was $30,000; the operative provisions of sections 465 and 469 do not change the character of the deductions when such amounts are suspended under either section. Furthermore, section 465(a)(2) and §§ 1.469-1(f)(4) and 1.469-2T(d)(1) treat amounts suspended from prior years as deductions in the current year. See § 1.1411-1(a). Therefore, for purposes of calculating A's net investment income, A has $41,000 of properly allocable deductions allowed by section 1411(c)(1)(B) and paragraph (f)(2)(ii) of this section.

(3) *Properly allocable deductions described in section 63(d).*—In determining net investment income, the following itemized deductions are taken into account:

(i) *Investment interest expense.*—Investment interest (as defined in section 163(d)(3)) to the extent allowed under section 163(d)(1). Any investment interest not allowed under section 163(d)(1) is treated as investment interest paid or accrued by the taxpayer in the succeeding taxable year. The following example illustrates the provisions of this paragraph. For purposes of this example, assume that the taxpayer uses a calendar taxable year, and Year 1 and all subsequent years are taxable years in which section 1411 is in effect:

(A) In Year 1, A, an unmarried individual, pays interest of $4,000 on debt incurred to purchase stock. Under § 1.163-8T, this interest is allocable to the stock and is investment interest within the meaning of section 163(d)(3). A has no investment income as defined by section 163(d)(4). A has $10,000 of income from a trade or business that is a passive activity (as defined in § 1.1411-5(a)(1)) with respect to A. For income tax purposes, under section 163(d)(1), A may not deduct the $4,000 investment interest in Year 1 because A does not have any section 163(d)(4) net investment income. Under section 163(d)(2), the $4,000 investment interest is a carryforward of disallowed interest that is treated as investment interest paid by A in the succeeding taxable year. Similarly, for purposes of determining A's

Year 1 net investment income, A may not deduct the $4,000 investment interest.

(B) In Year 2, A has $5,000 of section 163(d)(4) net investment income. For both income tax purposes and for determining section 1411 net investment income, A's $4,000 carryforward of interest expense disallowed in Year 1 may be deducted in Year 2.

(ii) *Investment expenses.*—Investment expenses (as defined in section 163(d)(4)(C)).

(iii) *Taxes described in section 164(a)(3).*—State, local, and foreign income, war profits, and excess profit taxes described in section 164(a)(3) that are allocable to net investment income pursuant to paragraph (g)(1) of this section. Except to the extent specifically expected from section 275(a)(4), foreign income, war profits, and excess profit taxes are not allowed as deductions under section 164(a)(3) in determining net investment income if the taxpayer claims the benefit of the foreign tax credit under section 901 with respect to the same taxable year. For rules applicable to refunds of taxes described in this paragraph, see paragraph (g)(2) of this section.

(iv) *Items described in section 72(b)(3).*—In the case of an amount allowed as a deduction to the annuitant for the annuitant's last taxable year under section 72(b)(3), such amount is allowed as a properly allocable deduction in the same taxable year if the income from the annuity (had the annuitant lived to receive such income) would have been included in net investment income under paragraph (a)(1)(i) of this section (and not excluded from net investment income by reason of § 1.1411-8).

(v) *Items described in section 691(c).*—Deductions for estate and generation-skipping taxes allowed by section 691(c) that are allocable to net investment income; provided, however, that any portion of the section 691(c) deduction described in section 691(c)(4) is taken into account instead in computing net gain under paragraph (d) and not under this paragraph (f)(3)(v).

(vi) *Items described in section 212(3).*—Amounts described in section 212(3) and § 1.212-1(l) to the extent they are allocable to net investment income pursuant to paragraph (g)(1) of this section.

(vii) *Amortizable bond premium.*—A deduction allowed under section 171(a)(1) for the amortizable bond premium on a taxable bond (for example, see § 1.171-2(a)(4)(i)(C) for the treatment of a bond premium carryforward as a deduction under section 171(a)(1)).

(viii) *Fiduciary expenses.*—In the case of an estate or trust, amounts described in § 1.212-1(i) to the extent they are allocable to net investment income pursuant to paragraph (g)(1) of this section.

(4) *Loss deductions.*—(i) *General rule.*—Losses described in section 165, whether described in section 62 or section 63(d), are allowed as properly allocable deductions to the extent such losses exceed the amount of gain described in section 61(a)(3) and are not taken into account in computing net gain by reason of paragraph (d) of this section.

(ii) *Examples.*—The following examples illustrate the provisions of this paragraph (f)(4). For purposes of these examples, assume the taxpayer is a United States citizen, uses a calendar taxable year, and Year 1 and all subsequent years are taxable years in which section 1411 is in effect:

*Example 1.* (i) A, an unmarried individual, owns an interest in PRS, a partnership for Federal income tax purposes. PRS is engaged in a trading business described in section 1411(c)(2)(B) and § 1.1411-5(a)(2) and has made a valid and timely election under section 475(f)(2). A's distributive share from PRS in Year 1 consists of $125,000 of interest and dividends and $60,000 of ordinary losses from the trading business. In addition to A's investment in PRS, A sold undeveloped land in Year 1 for a long-term capital gain of $50,000. A has no capital losses carried over from a preceding year.

(ii) For purposes of chapter 1, A includes the $125,000 of interest and dividends, $60,000 of ordinary loss, and $50,000 of long-term capital gain in the computation of A's adjusted gross income.

(iii) For purposes of calculating net investment income, A includes the $125,000 of interest and dividends. Pursuant to paragraph (d) of this section, A takes into account the $60,000 of ordinary loss from PRS and the $50,000 of long term capital gain in the computation of A's net gain. A's losses ($60,000) exceed A's gains ($50,000). Therefore, A's net gain under paragraph (d) of this section is zero. Additionally, A is allowed a deduction under paragraph (f)(4)(i) of this section for $10,000 (the amount of ordinary losses that were allowable under chapter 1 in excess of the amounts taken into account in computing net gain). A's net investment income in Year 1 is $115,000.

*Example 2.* (i) In Year 1, T, a nongrantor trust, incurs a capital loss of $5,000 on the sale of publicly traded stocks. In addition, T receives $17,000 of interest and dividend income. T has no capital losses carried over from a preceding year.

(ii) For purposes of chapter 1, T includes the $17,000 of interest and dividends and only $3,000 of the capital loss in the computation of adjusted gross income. The remaining $2,000 capital loss is carried over to Year 2.

(iii) For purposes of calculating net investment income, T includes the $17,000 of interest and dividends in net investment income. Pursuant to paragraph (d) of this section, T takes into account the $3,000 capital loss allowed by chapter 1. T's losses ($3,000) exceed T's gains ($0). Therefore, T's net gain under paragraph (d) of this section is zero. However, T is allowed a deduction under paragraph (f)(4)(i) of this section for $3,000 (the amount of losses that were allowable under chapter 1 in excess of the amounts taken into account in computing net gain). T's net investment income in Year 1 is $14,000.

*Example 3.* (i) In Year 1, B, an unmarried individual, incurs a short-term capital loss of $15,000 on the sale of publicly traded stocks. B also receives annuity income of $50,000. In addition, B disposes of property used in his sole proprietorship (which is not a trade or business described in section 1411(c)(2) or §1.1411-5(a) for a gain of $21,000. Pursuant to section 1231, the gain of $21,000 is treated as a long-term capital gain for purposes of chapter 1. B has no capital losses carried over from a preceding year.

(ii) For purposes of chapter 1, B includes the $50,000 of annuity income in the computation of adjusted gross income. The $21,000 long-term capital gain is offset by the $15,000 short-term capital loss, so B includes $6,000 of net long-term capital gain in the computation of adjusted gross income.

(iii) For purposes of calculating net investment income, B includes the $50,000 of annuity income in net investment income. Pursuant to paragraph (d)(4)(i) of this section, B's net gain does not include the $21,000 long-term capital gain because it is attributable to property held in B's sole proprietorship (a nonpassive activity). Pursuant to paragraph (d) of this section, T takes into account the $15,000 capital loss allowed by chapter 1. B's losses ($15,000) exceed B's gains ($0). Therefore, A's net gain under paragraph (d) of this section is zero. However, B is allowed a deduction under paragraph (f)(4)(i) of this section for $15,000 (the amount of losses that were allowable under chapter 1 in excess of the amounts taken into account in computing net gain). B's net investment income in Year 1 is $35,000.

(5) *Ordinary loss deductions for certain debt instruments.*—An amount treated as an ordinary loss by a holder of a contingent payment debt instrument under §1.1275-4(b) or an inflation-indexed debt instrument under §1.1275-7(f)(1).

(6) *Other deductions.*—Any other deduction allowed by subtitle A that is identified in published guidance in the **Federal Register** or in the Internal Revenue Bulletin (see §601.601(d)(2)(ii)(b) of this chapter) as properly allocable to gross income or net gain under this section.

(7) *Application of limitations under sections 67 and 68.*—Any deductions described in this paragraph (f) that are subject to section 67 (the 2-percent floor on miscellaneous itemized deductions) or section 68 (the overall limitation on itemized deductions) are allowed in determining net investment income only to the extent the items are deductible for chapter 1 purposes after the application of sections 67 and 68. For this purpose, section 67 applies before section 68. The amount of deductions subject to sections 67 and 68 that may be deducted in determining net investment income after the application of sections 67 and 68 is determined as described in paragraph (f)(7)(i) and (f)(7)(ii) of this section.

(i) *Deductions subject to section 67.*—The amount of miscellaneous itemized deductions (as defined in section 67(b)) tentatively deductible in determining net investment income after applying section 67 (but before applying section 68) is the lesser of:

(A) The portion of the taxpayer's miscellaneous itemized deductions (before the application of section 67) that is properly allocable to items of income or net gain included in determining net investment income, or

(B) The taxpayer's total miscellaneous itemized deductions allowed after the application of section 67, but before the application of section 68.

(ii) *Deductions subject to section 68.*—The amount of itemized deductions allowed in determining net investment income after applying sections 67 and 68 is the lesser of:

(A) The sum of the amount determined under paragraph (f)(7)(i) of this section and the amount of itemized deductions not subject to section 67 that are properly allocable to items of income or net gain included in determining net investment income, or

(B) The total amount of itemized deductions allowed after the application of sections 67 and 68.

(iii) *Itemized deductions.*—For purposes of paragraph (f)(7)(ii), itemized deductions do not include any deduction described in section 68(c).

(iv) *Example.*—The following example illustrates the provisions of this paragraph (f)(7). For purposes of these examples, assume the taxpayer is a United States citizen, uses a calendar taxable year, and Year 1 and all subsequent years are taxable years in which section 1411 is in effect:

(A) A, an unmarried individual, has adjusted gross income in Year 1 as follows:

| | |
|---|---|
| Wages | $1,600,000 |
| Interest income | 400,000 |
| Adjusted gross income | $2,000,000 |

In addition, A has the following items of expense qualifying as itemized deductions:

| | |
|---|---|
| Investment expenses | $70,000 |
| Job-related expenses | 30,000 |
| Investment interest expense | 75,000 |
| State income taxes | 120,000 |

A's investment expenses and job-related expenses are miscellaneous itemized deductions. In addition, A's investment interest expense and investment expenses are properly allocable to net investment income (within the meaning of this section). A's job-related expenses are not properly allocable to net investment income. Of the state income tax expense, A applied a reasonable method pursuant to paragraph (g)(1) of this section to properly allocate $20,000 to net investment income.

(B) A's 2-percent floor under section 67 is $40,000 (2% of $2,000,000). For Year 1, assume the section 68 limitation starts at adjusted gross income of $200,000. The section 68 overall limitation disallows $54,000 of A's itemized deductions that are subject to section 68 (3% of the excess of the $2,000,000 adjusted gross income over the $200,000 limitation threshold).

(C)(1) A's total miscellaneous itemized deductions allowable before the application of section 67 is $100,000 ($70,000 in investment expenses plus $30,000 in job-related expenses), and the total miscellaneous deductions allowed after the application of section 67 is $60,000 ($100,000 minus $40,000).

(2) The amount of the miscellaneous itemized deductions properly allocable to net investment income after the application of section 67 is $60,000 (the lesser of $70,000 in investment expenses that are deductible as a miscellaneous itemized deduction and properly allocable to net investment income or $60,000 of miscellaneous itemized deductions allocable to net investment income allowed after the application of section 67).

(D)(1) The amount of itemized deductions allocable to net investment income after applying section 67 to deductions that are also miscellaneous itemized deductions but before applying section 68 is $155,000. This amount is the sum of $60,000 of miscellaneous itemized deductions determined in (C)(2), plus $20,000 in state income tax properly allocable to net investment income, plus $75,000 of investment interest expense. However, under section 68(c)(2), the $75,000 deduction for investment interest expenses is not subject to the section 68 limitation on itemized deductions and is excluded from the computation under §1.1411-4(f)(7). Thus, the amount of itemized deductions allocable to net investment income and subject to section 68, after applying section 67 but before applying section 68, is $80,000.

(2) A's total itemized deductions allowed subject to the limitation under section 68 and after application of section 67, but before the application of section 68, are the following:

| | |
|---|---|
| Miscellaneous itemized deductions | $60,000 |
| State income tax | $120,000 |
| Deductions subject to section 68 | $180,000 |

(3) Of A's itemized deductions that are subject to the limitation under section 68, the amount allowed after the application of section 68 is $126,000 ($180,000 minus the $54,000 disallowed in (B)).

(E) Under paragraph (f)(7)(ii) of this section, the amount of itemized deductions allowed in determining net investment income after applying sections 67 and 68 is the lesser of $80,000 (the sum of $60,000 determined under paragraph (C)(2) and $20,000 state income tax allocable to net investment income) or $126,000 (determined under (D)(3)). Therefore, A's itemized deductions that are properly allocable to net investment income are $155,000 ($80,000 of properly allocable itemized deductions subject to section 67 or 68 plus $75,000 of investment interest expense (which is not subject to either section 67 or section 68 limitations)).

(g) *Special rules.*—(1) *Deductions allocable to both net investment income and excluded income.*—In the case of a properly allocable deduction described in section 1411(c)(1)(B) and paragraph (f) of this section that is allocable to both net investment income and excluded income, the portion of the deduction that is properly allocable to net investment income may be determined by taxpayers using any reasonable method. Examples of reasonable methods of allocation include, but are not limited to, an allocation of the deduction based on the ratio of the amount of a taxpayer's gross income (including net gain) described in §1.1411-4(a)(1) to the amount of the taxpayer's adjusted gross income (as defined under section 62 (or section 67(e) in the case of an estate or trust)). In the case of an estate or trust, an allocation of a deduction pursuant to rules described in §1.652(b)-3(b) (and §1.641(c)-1(h) in the case of an ESBT) is also a reasonable method.

(2) *Recoveries of properly allocable deductions.*—(i) *General rule.*—If a taxpayer is refunded, reimbursed, or otherwise recovers any portion of an amount deducted as a section 1411(c)(1)(B) properly allocable deduction in a prior year, and such amount is not otherwise included in net investment income in the year of recovery under section 1411(c)(1)(A), the amount of the recovery will reduce the taxpayer's total section 1411(c)(1)(B) properly allocable deductions in the year of recovery (but not below zero). The preceding sentence applies regardless of whether the amount of the recovery is excluded from gross income by reason of section 111.

(ii) *Recoveries of items allocated between net investment income and excluded income.*—In the case of a refund of any item that was deducted under section 1411(c)(1)(B) in a prior year and the gross amount of the deduction was allocated between items of net investment income and excluded income pursuant to paragraph (g)(1) of this section, the amount of the reduction in section 1411(c)(1)(B) properly allocable deductions in the year of receipt under this paragraph (g)(2) is the total amount of the refund multiplied by a fraction. The numerator of the fraction is the amount of the total deduction allocable to net investment income in the prior year to which the refund relates. The denominator of the fraction is the total amount of the deduction in the prior year to which the refund relates.

(iii) *Recoveries with no prior year benefit.*—For purposes of this paragraph (g)(2), section 111 applies to reduce the amount of any reduction required by paragraph (g)(2)(i) of this section to the extent that such previously deducted amount did not reduce the tax imposed by section 1411. To the extent a deduction is taken into account in computing a taxpayer's net operating loss deduction under paragraph (h) of this section, section 111(c) applies. Except as provided in the preceding sentence, for purposes of this paragraph (g)(2), no reduction of section 1411(c)(1)(B) properly allocable deductions is required in a year when such recovered item is attributable to an amount deducted in a taxable year—

(A) Preceding the effective date of section 1411, or

(B) In which the taxpayer was not subject to section 1411 solely because that individual's (as defined in §1.1411-2(a)) modified adjusted gross income (as defined in §1.1411-2(c)) does not exceed the applicable threshold in §1.1411-2(d) or such estate's or trust's (as defined in §1.1411-3(a)(1)(i)) adjusted gross income does not exceed the amount described in section 1411(a)(2)(B)(ii) and §1.1411-3(a)(1)(ii)(B)(2).

(iv) *Examples.*—The following examples illustrate the provisions of this paragraph (g)(2). For purposes of these examples, assume the taxpayer is a United States citizen, uses a calendar taxable year, and Year 1 and all subsequent years are taxable years in which section 1411 is in effect:

*Example 1. Recovery of amount included in income.* A, an individual, is a 40% limited partner in LP. LP is a passive activity to A. In Year 1, A's distributive share of section 1411(c)(1)(A)(ii) income and properly allocable deductions described in §1.1411-4(f)(2)(ii) were $50,000 and $37,000, respectively. In Year 2, LP received a refund of a properly allocable deduction described in §1.1411-4(f)(2)(ii). A's distributive share of the recovered deduction is $2,000. Since the $2,000 recovery constitutes gross income described in section 1411(c)(1)(A)(ii) in Year 2, A does not reduce any properly allocable deductions attributable to Year 2.

*Example 2. State income tax refund.* In Year 1, D, an individual, allocated $15,000 of taxes out of a total of $75,000 to net investment income under paragraph (f)(3)(iii) of this section. D received no tax benefit from the deduction in Year 1 for chapter 1 purposes due to the alternative minimum tax, but it did reduce D's section 1411 tax. In Year 3, D received a refund of $5,000. For chapter 1 purposes, D excludes the $5,000 refund from gross income in Year 3 by reason of section 111. In Year 3, D allocated $30,000 of state income taxes out of

a total of $90,000 to net investment income under paragraph (f)(3)(iii) of this section. Although the refund is excluded from D's gross income, D must nonetheless reduce Year 3's section 1411(c)(1)(B) properly allocable deductions by $1,000 ($5,000 x ($15,000/$75,000)). D's allocation of 33 1/3% of section 164(a)(3) taxes in Year 3 to net investment income is irrelevant to the calculation of the amount of the reduction required by this paragraph (g)(2).

*Example 3. State income tax refund with no prior year benefit.* Same facts as *Example 2*, except in Year 1, D's section 1411(c)(1)(B) properly allocable deductions exceeded D's section 1411(c)(1)(A) income by $300. As a result, D was not subject to section 1411 in Year 1. Pursuant to paragraph (g)(2)(iii) of this section, D does not reduce Year 3's section 1411(c)(1)(B) properly allocable deductions for recoveries of amounts to the extent that such deductions did not reduce the tax imposed by section 1411. Therefore, D must reduce Year 3's section 1411(c)(1)(B) properly allocable deductions by $700 ($1,000 less $300).

(3) *Deductions described in section 691(b).*—For purposes of paragraph (f) of this section, properly allocable deductions include items of deduction described in section 691(b), provided that the item otherwise would have been deductible to the decedent under §1.1411-4(f). For example, an estate may deduct the decedent's unpaid investment interest expense in computing its net investment income because section 691(b) specifically allows the deduction under section 163, and §1.1411-4(f)(3)(i) allows those deductions as well. However, an estate or trust may not deduct a payment of real estate taxes on the decedent's principal residence that were unpaid at death in computing its net investment income because, although real estate taxes are deductible under section 164 and specifically are allowed by section 691(b), the real estate taxes would not have been a properly allocable deduction of the decedent under §1.1411-4(f).

(4) *Amounts described in section 642(h).*—For purposes of the calculation of net investment income under this section, one or more beneficiaries succeeding to the property of the estate or trust, within the meaning of section 642(h), shall—

(i) Treat excess capital losses of the estate or trust described in section 642(h)(1) as capital losses of the beneficiary in the calculation of net gain in paragraph (d) and paragraph (f)(4) of this section, as applicable, in a manner consistent with section 642(h)(1);

(ii) Treat excess net operating losses of the estate or trust described in section 642(h)(1) as net operating losses of the beneficiary in the calculation of net investment income in paragraphs (f)(2)(iv) and (h) of this section in a manner consistent with section 642(h)(1); and

(iii) Treat the deductions described in paragraph (f) of this section (other than those taken into account under paragraph (g)(4)(i) or (ii) of this section) that exceed the gross investment income described in paragraph (a)(1) of this section (after taking into account any modifications, adjustments, and special rules for calculating net investment income in section 1411 and the regulations thereunder) of a terminating estate or trust as a section 1411(c)(1)(B) deduction of the beneficiary in a manner consistent with section 642(h)(2).

(5) *Treatment of self-charged interest income.*—Gross income from interest (within the meaning of section 1411(c)(1)(A)(i) and paragraph (a)(1)(i) of this section) that is received by the taxpayer from a nonpassive activity of such taxpayer, solely for purposes of section 1411, is treated as derived in the ordinary course of a trade or business not described in §1.1411-5. The amount of interest income that is treated as derived in the ordinary course of a trade or business not described in §1.1411-5, and thus excluded from the calculation of net investment income, under this paragraph (g)(5) is limited to the amount that would have been considered passive activity gross income under the rules of §1.469-7 if the payor was a passive activity of the taxpayer. For purposes of this rule, the term nonpassive activity does not include a trade or business described in §1.1411-5(a)(2). However, this rule does not apply to the extent the corresponding deduction is taken into account in determining self-employment income that is subject to tax under section 1401(b).

(6) *Treatment of certain nonpassive rental activities.*—(i) *Gross income from rents.*—To the extent that gross rental income described in paragraph (a)(1)(i) of this section is treated as not derived from a passive activity by reason of §1.469-2(f)(6) or as a consequence of a taxpayer grouping a rental activity with a trade or business activity under §1.469-4(d)(1), such gross rental income is deemed to be derived in the ordinary course of a trade or business within the meaning of paragraph (b) of this section.

(ii) *Gain or loss from the disposition of property.*—To the extent that gain or loss resulting from the disposition of property is treated as nonpassive gain or loss by reason of §1.469-2(f)(6) or as a consequence of a taxpayer grouping a rental activity with a trade or business activity under §1.469-4(d)(1), then such gain or loss is deemed to be derived from property used in the ordinary course of a trade or business within the meaning of paragraph (d)(4)(i) of this section.

(7) *Treatment of certain real estate professionals.*—(i) *Safe Harbor.*— In the case of a real estate professional (as defined in section 469(c)(7)(B)) that participates in a rental real estate activity for more than 500 hours during such year, or has participated in such real estate activity for more than 500 hours in any five taxable years (whether or not consecutive) during the ten taxable years that immediately precede the taxable year, then—

(A) Such gross rental income from that rental activity is deemed to be derived in the ordinary course of a trade or business within the meaning of paragraph (b) of this section; and

(B) Gain or loss resulting from the disposition of property used in such rental real estate activity is deemed to be derived from property used in the ordinary course of a trade or business within the meaning of paragraph (d)(4)(i) of this section.

(ii) *Definitions.*—(A) *Participation.*—For purposes of establishing participation under this paragraph (g)(7), any participation in the activity that would count towards establishing material participation under section 469 shall be considered.

(B) *Rental real estate activity.*—The term *rental real estate activity* used in this paragraph (g)(7) is a rental activity within the meaning of §1.469-1T(e)(3). An election to treat all rental real estate as a single rental activity under §1.469-9(g) also applies for purposes of this paragraph (g)(7). However, any rental real estate that the taxpayer grouped with a trade or business activity under §1.469-4(d)(1)(i)(A) or (d)(1)(i)(C) is not a rental real estate activity.

(iii) *Effect of safe harbor.*—The inability of a real estate professional to satisfy the safe harbor in this paragraph (g)(7) does not preclude such taxpayer from establishing that such gross rental income and gain or loss from the disposition of property, as applicable, is not included in net investment income under any other provision of section 1411.

(8) *Treatment of former passive activities.*—(i) *Section 469(f)(1)(A) losses.*—Losses allowed in computing taxable income by reason of the rules governing former passive activities in section 469(f)(1)(A) are taken into account in computing net gain under paragraph (d) of this section or as properly allocable deductions under paragraph (f) of this section, as applicable, in the same manner as such losses are taken into account in computing taxable income (as defined in section 63). The preceding sentence applies only to the extent the net income or net gain from the former passive activity (as defined in section 469(f)(3)) is included in net investment income.

(ii) *Section 469(f)(1)(C) losses.*—Losses allowed in computing taxable income by reason of section 469(f)(1)(C) are taken into account in computing net gain under paragraph (d) of this section or as properly allocable deductions under paragraph (f) of this section, as applicable, in the same manner as such losses are taken into account in computing taxable income (as defined in section 63).

(iii) *Examples.*—The following examples illustrate the provisions of this paragraph (g)(8). For purposes of these examples, assume the taxpayer is a United States citizen, uses a calendar taxable year, and Year 1 and all subsequent years are taxable years in which section 1411 is in effect:

*Example 1.* (i) B, an individual taxpayer, owns a 50% interest in SCorp, an S corporation engaged in the trade or business of retail clothing sales. B also owns a single family rental property, a passive activity. B materially participates in the retail sales activity of SCorp, but B has $10,000 of suspended losses from prior years when the retail sales activity of SCorp was a passive activity of B. Therefore, the retail sales activity of SCorp is a former passive activity within the meaning of section 469(f)(3).

(ii) In Year 1, B reports $205,000 of wages, $7,000 of nonpassive net income, $500 of interest income (attributable to working capital) from SCorp's retail sales activity, and $1,000 of net rental income from the single family rental property. B's Year 1 modified adjusted gross income (as defined in §1.1411-2(c)) is $205,500; which includes $205,000 of wages, $500 of interest income, $7,000 of nonpassive income from SCorp, $7,000 of section 469(f)(1)(A) losses, $1,000 of passive income from the single family rental property and $1,000 of section 469(f)(1)(C) losses.

(iii) For purposes of the calculation of B's Year 1 net investment income, B includes the $500 of interest income and $1,000 of net passive income from the single family rental property. The $7,000 of nonpassive income from SCorp's retail sales activity is excluded from net investment income because the income is not attributable to a trade or business described in §1.1411-5. Therefore, pursuant to the rules of paragraph (g)(8)(i) of this section, the $7,000 of section

469(f)(1)(A) losses are not taken into account in computing B's net investment income. However, pursuant to the rules of paragraph (g)(8)(ii) of this section, the $1,000 of passive losses allowed by reason of section 469(f)(1)(C), which are allowed as a deduction in Year 1 by reason of B's $1,000 of passive income from the single family rental property are allowed in computing B's net investment income. As a result, B's net investment income is $500 ($500 of interest income plus $1,000 of passive rental income less $1,000 of section 469(f)(1)(C) losses). Although the $500 of interest income is attributable to SCorp and includable in B's net investment income, such income is not taken into account when calculating the amount of section 469(f)(1)(A) losses allowed in the current year. Therefore, such income is not taken into account in computing the amount of section 469(f)(1)(A) losses allowed by reason of paragraph (g)(8)(i) of this section. Pursuant to section 469(b), B carries forward $2,000 of suspended passive losses attributable to SCorp's retail sales activity to Year 2.

*Example 2.* Same facts as *Example 1.* In Year 2, B materially participates in the retail sales activity of SCorp, and disposes of his entire interest in SCorp for a $9,000 long-term capital gain. Pursuant to §1.469-2T(e)(3), the $9,000 gain is characterized as nonpassive income. Pursuant to section 469(f)(1)(A), the remaining $2,000 of suspended passive loss is allowed because the $9,000 gain is treated as nonpassive income. Assume that under section 1411(c)(4) and §1.1411-7, B takes into account only $700 of the $9,000 gain in computing net investment income for Year 2. Pursuant to paragraph (g)(8)(i) of this section, B may take into account $700 of the $2,000 loss allowed by section 469(f)(1)(A) in computing net investment income for Year 2. Pursuant to paragraph (g)(8)(i) of this section, B may not deduct the remaining $1,300 passive loss allowed for chapter 1 in calculating net investment income for Year 2.

(9) *Treatment of section 469(g)(1) losses.*—Losses allowed in computing taxable income by reason of section 469(g) are taken into account in computing net gain under paragraph (d) of this section or as properly allocable deductions under paragraph (f) of this section, as applicable, in the same manner as such losses are taken into account in computing taxable income (as defined in section 63).

(10) *Treatment of section 707(c) guaranteed payments.*—[Reserved]

(11) *Treatment of section 736 payments.*—[Reserved]

(12) *Income and deductions from certain notional principal contracts.*—[Reserved]

(13) *Treatment of income or loss from REMIC residual interests.*—[Reserved]

(h) *Net operating loss.*—(1) *General rule.*—For purposes of paragraph (f)(2)(iv) of this section, the total section 1411 NOL amount of a net operating loss deduction for a taxable year is calculated by first determining the applicable portion of the taxpayer's net operating loss for each loss year under paragraph (h)(2) of this section. Next, the applicable portion for each loss year is used to determine the section 1411 NOL amount for each net operating loss carried from a loss year and deducted in the taxable year as provided in paragraph (h)(3) of this section. The section 1411 NOL amounts of each net operating loss carried from a loss year and deducted in the taxable year are then added together as provided in paragraph (h)(4) of this section. This sum is the total section 1411 NOL amount of the net operating loss deduction for the taxable year that is allowed as a properly allocable deduction in determining net investment income for the taxable year. For purposes of this paragraph (h), both the amount of a net operating loss for a loss year and the amount of a net operating loss deduction refer to such amounts as determined for purposes of chapter 1.

(2) *Applicable portion of a net operating loss.*—In any taxable year beginning after December 31, 2012, in which a taxpayer incurs a net operating loss, the applicable portion of such loss is the lesser of:

(i) The amount of the net operating loss for the loss year that the taxpayer would incur if only items of gross income that are used to determine net investment income and only properly allocable deductions are taken into account in determining the net operating loss in accordance with section 172(c) and (d); or

(ii) The amount of the taxpayer's net operating loss for the loss year.

(3) *Section 1411 NOL amount of a net operating loss carried to and deducted in a taxable year.*—The section 1411 NOL amount of each net operating loss that is carried from a loss year that is allowed as a deduction is the total amount of such net operating loss carried from the loss year allowed as a deduction under section 172(a) in the taxable year multiplied by a fraction. The numerator of the fraction is the applicable portion of the net operating loss for that loss year, as determined under paragraph (h)(2) of this section. The denominator

of the fraction is the total amount of the net operating loss for the same loss year.

(4) *Total section 1411 NOL amount of a net operating loss deduction.*—The section 1411 NOL amounts of each net operating loss carried to and deducted in the taxable year as determined under paragraph (h)(3) of this section are added together to determine the *total* section 1411 NOL amount of the net operating loss deduction for the taxable year that is properly allocable to net investment income.

(5) *Examples.*—The following examples illustrate the provisions of this paragraph (h). For purposes of these examples, assume the taxpayer is a United States citizen, uses a calendar taxable year, and Year 1 and all subsequent years are taxable years in which section 1411 is in effect:

*Example 1.* (i)(A) In Year 1, A, an unmarried individual, has the following items of income and deduction: $200,000 in wages, $50,000 in gross income from a trade or business of trading in financial instruments or commodities (as defined in §1.1411-5(a)(2)) (trading activity), $10,000 of dividends, $1,000,000 in loss from his sole proprietorship (which is not a trade or business described in §1.1411-5), $12,000 of non-business investment expenses, and $250,000 in trading loss deductions. As a result, for income tax purposes A sustains a section 172(c) net operating loss of $1,000,000. A makes an election under section 172(b)(3) to waive the carryback period for this net operating loss.

(B) For purposes of section 1411, A's net investment income for Year 1 is the excess (if any) of $60,000 ($50,000 trading activity gross income plus $10,000 dividend income) over $262,000 ($250,000 trading loss deductions plus $12,000 nonbusiness expenses).

(C) The amount of the net operating loss for Year 1 determined under section 172 that A would incur if only items of gross income that are used to determine net investment income and only properly allocable deductions are taken into account is $200,000. This amount is the excess of $250,000 trading loss deductions, over $50,000 trading activity gross income. Under section 172(d)(4), in determining the net operating loss, the $12,000 nonbusiness expenses are allowed only to the extent of the $10,000 dividend income. The $200,000 net operating loss determined using only properly allocable deductions and gross income items used in determining net investment income is less than A's actual net operating loss for Year 1 of $1,000,000, and accordingly the applicable portion for Year 1 is $200,000. The ratio used to calculate section 1411 NOL amounts of A's Year 1 net operating loss is $200,000 (net operating loss determined using only properly allocable deductions and gross income items used in determining net investment income)/$1,000,000 (net operating loss), or 0.2.

(ii) For Year 2, A has $250,000 of wages, no gross income from the trading activity, $300,000 of income from his sole proprietorship, and $10,000 in trading loss deductions. For income tax purposes, A deducts $540,000 of the net operating loss carried over from Year 1. In addition, under §1.1411-2(c), the $540,000 net operating loss will be allowed as a deduction in computing A's Year 2 modified adjusted gross income. Because A's modified adjusted gross income is $0, A is not subject to net investment income tax. For purposes of A's net investment income calculation, the section 1411 NOL amount of the $540,000 net operating loss from Year 1 that A deducts in Year 2 is $108,000 ($540,000 multiplied by 0.2 (the fraction determined based on the applicable portion of the net operating loss in the loss year)). The amount of the Year 1 net operating loss carried over to Year 3 is $460,000. For purposes of A's net investment income calculation, this net operating loss carryover amount includes a section 1411 NOL amount of $92,000 ($460,000 multiplied by 0.2). The section 1411 NOL amount may be applied in determining A's net investment income in Year 3.

(iii)(A) For Year 3, A has $400,000 of wages, $200,000 in trading gains which are gross income from the trading activity, $250,000 of income from his sole proprietorship, and $10,000 in trading loss deductions. For income tax purposes, A deducts the remaining $460,000 of the net operating loss from Year 1. In addition, under §1.1411-2(c), the $460,000 net operating loss deduction reduces A's Year 3 modified adjusted gross income to $380,000.

(B) A's section 1411 NOL amount of the net operating loss deduction for Year 3 is $92,000, which is the $460,000 net operating loss deduction for Year 3 multiplied by 0.2.

(C) A's net investment income for Year 3 before the application of paragraph (f)(2)(iv) of this section is $190,000 ($200,000 in gross income from the trading activity, minus $10,000 in trading loss deductions). After the application of paragraph (f)(2)(iv) of this section, A's net investment income for Year 3 is $98,000 ($190,000 minus $92,000, the total section 1411 NOL amount of the net operating loss deduction).

*Example 2.* (i) The facts for Year 1 are the same as in *Example 1.*

(ii)(A) For Year 2, A has $100,000 in wages, $200,000 in gross income from the trading activity, $15,000 of dividends, $250,000 in losses from the sole proprietorship, $10,000 of non-business invest-

ment expenses, and $355,000 in trading loss deductions. As a result, for income tax purposes A sustains a section 172(c) net operating loss of $300,000. A makes an election under section 172(b)(3) to waive the carryback period for the Year 2 net operating loss.

(B) For purposes of section 1411, A's net investment income for Year 2 is the excess (if any) of $215,000 ($200,000 trading activity gross income plus $15,000 dividend income) over $365,000 ($355,000 trading loss deductions plus $10,000 nonbusiness expenses).

(C) The amount of the net operating loss for Year 2 determined under section 172 that A would incur if only items of gross income that are used to determine net investment income and only properly allocable deductions are taken into account is $150,000. This amount is the excess of $365,000 ($355,000 trading loss deductions plus $10,000 nonbusiness expenses) over $215,000 ($200,000 trading activity gross income plus $15,000 dividend income). Under section 172(d)(4), in determining the net operating loss, the $10,000 nonbusiness expenses are allowed in full against the $15,000 dividend income. The $150,000 net operating loss determined using only properly allocable deductions and gross income items used in determining net investment income is less than A's actual net operating loss for Year 2 of $300,000, and accordingly the applicable portion is $150,000. The ratio used to calculate the section 1411 NOL amount of A's Year 2 net operating loss is $150,000 (the applicable portion)/$300,000 (net operating loss), or 0.5.

(iii) For Year 3, A has $250,000 of wages, no gross income from the trading activity, $300,000 of income from his sole proprietorship, and $10,000 in trading loss deductions. For income tax purposes, A deducts $540,000 of the net operating loss from Year 1. In addition, under §1.1411-2(c), the $540,000 net operating loss will be allowed as a deduction in computing A's Year 3 modified adjusted gross income. Because A's modified adjusted gross income is $0, A is not subject to net investment income tax. The section 1411 NOL amount of the $540,000 net operating loss from Year 1 that A deducts in Year 3 is $108,000 ($540,000 multiplied by 0.2 (the fraction used to calculate the section 1411 NOL amount of the net operating loss)), and this is also the total section 1411 NOL amount for Year 3. The amount of the Year 1 net operating loss carried over to Year 4 is $460,000. This net operating loss carryover amount includes a section 1411 NOL amount of $92,000 ($460,000 multiplied by 0.2) that may be applied in determining net investment income in Year 4. None of the Year 2 net operating loss is deducted in Year 3 so that the $300,000 Year 2 net operating loss (including the section 1411 NOL amount of $150,000) is carried to Year 4.

(iv)(A) For Year 4, A has $150,000 of wages, $450,000 in trading gains which are gross income from the trading activity, $250,000 of income from his sole proprietorship, and $10,000 in trading loss deductions. For income tax purposes, A deducts the remaining $460,000 of the net operating loss carryover from Year 1 and the $300,000 net operating loss carryover from Year 2, for a total net operating loss deduction in Year 4 of $760,000. In addition, under §1.1411-2(c), the $760,000 net operating loss deduction reduces A's Year 4 modified adjusted gross income to $80,000.

(B) A's total section 1411 NOL amount of the net operating loss deduction for Year 4 is $242,000, which is the sum of the $92,000 ($460,000 net operating loss carryover from Year 1 and deducted in Year 4 multiplied by 0.2 (the ratio used to calculate the section 1411 NOL amount of the Year 1 net operating loss)) plus $150,000 ($300,000 net operating loss carryover from Year 2 and deducted in Year 4 multiplied by 0.5 (the ratio used to calculate the section 1411 NOL amount of the Year 2 net operating loss)).

(C) A's net investment income for Year 4 before the application of paragraph (f)(2)(iv) of this section is $440,000 ($450,000 in gross income from the trading activity, minus $10,000 in trading loss deductions). After the application of paragraph (f)(2)(iv) of this section, A's net investment income for Year 4 is $198,000 ($440,000 minus $242,000, the total section 1411 NOL amount of the Year 4 net operating loss deduction).

(i) *Effective/applicability date.*—This section applies to taxable years beginning after December 31, 2013. However, taxpayers may apply this section to taxable years beginning after December 31, 2012, in accordance with §1.1411-1(f). [Reg. §1.1411-4.]

☐ [T.D. 9644, 11-26-2013 (*corrected* 3-31-2014).]

## [Reg. §1.1411-5]

**§1.1411-5. Trades or businesses to which tax applies.**—(a) *In general.*—A trade or business is described in this section if such trade or business involves the conduct of a trade or business, and such trade or business is either—

(1) A passive activity (within the meaning of paragraph (b) of this section) with respect to the taxpayer; or

(2) The trade or business of a trader trading in financial instruments (as defined in paragraph (c)(1) of this section) or commodities (as defined in paragraph (c)(2) of this section).

(b) *Passive activity.*—(1) *In general.*—A passive activity is described in this section if—

(i) Such activity is a trade or business; and

(ii) Such trade or business is a passive activity with respect to the taxpayer within the meaning of section 469 and the regulations thereunder.

(2) *Application of income recharacterization rules.*—(i) *Income and gain recharacterization.*—To the extent that any income or gain from a trade or business is recharaterized as "not from a passive activity" by reason of § 1.469-2T(f)(2), § 1.469-2(f)(5), or § 1.469-2(f)(6), such trade or business does not constitute a passive activity within the meaning of paragraph (b)(1)(ii) of this section solely with respect to such recharacterized income or gain.

(ii) *Gain recharacterization.*—To the extent that any gain from a trade or business is recharacterized as "not from a passive activity" by reason of § 1.469-2(c)(2)(iii) and does not constitute portfolio income under § 1.469-2(c)(2)(iii)(F), such trade or business does not constitute a passive activity within the meaning of paragraph (b)(1)(ii) of this section solely with respect to such recharacterized gain.

(iii) *Exception for certain portfolio recharacterizations.*—To the extent that any income or gain from a trade or business is recharacterized as "not from a passive activity" and is further characterized as portfolio income under § 1.469-2 (f)(10) or § 1.469-2(c)(2)(iii)(F), then such trade or business constitutes a passive activity within the meaning of paragraph (b)(1)(ii) of this section solely with respect to such recharacterized income or gain.

(3) *Examples.*—The following examples illustrate the principles of paragraph (b)(1) of this section and the ordinary course of a trade or business exception in § 1.1411-4(b). In each example, unless otherwise indicated, the taxpayer uses a calendar taxable year, the taxpayer is a United States citizen, and Year 1 and all subsequent years are taxable years in which section 1411 is in effect:

*Example 1. Rental activity.* A, an unmarried individual, rents a commercial building to B for $50,000 in Year 1. A is not involved in the activity of the commercial building on a regular and continuous basis, therefore, A's rental activity does not involve the conduct of a trade or business, and under section 469(c)(2), A's rental activity is a passive activity. Because paragraph (b)(1)(i) of this section is not satisfied, A's rental income of $50,000 is not derived from a trade or business described in paragraph (b)(1) of this section. However, A's rental income of $50,000 still constitutes gross income from rents within the meaning of § 1.1411-4(a)(1)(i) because rents are included in the determination of net investment income under § 1.1411-4(a)(1)(i) whether or not derived from a trade or business described in paragraph (b)(1) of this section.

*Example 2. Application of grouping rules under section 469.* In Year 1, A, an unmarried individual, owns an interest in PRS, a partnership for Federal income tax purposes. PRS is engaged in two activities, X and Y, which constitute trades or businesses, and neither of which constitute trading in financial instruments or commodities (within the meaning of paragraph (a)(2) of this section). Pursuant to § 1.469-4, A has properly grouped X and Y together as one activity (the grouped activity). A participates in X for more than 500 hours during Year 1 and would be treated as materially participating in activity X within the meaning of § 1.469-5T(a)(1) if A's material participation were determined only with respect to activity X. A only participates in Y for 50 hours during Year 1. If not for the grouping of the X and Y activities together, A would not be treated as materially participating in Y within the meaning of § 1.469-5T(a). However, pursuant to § § 1.469-4 and 1.469-5T(a)(1), A materially participates in the grouped activity. Therefore, for purposes of paragraph (b)(1)(ii) of this section, neither X nor Y is a passive activity with respect to A. Accordingly, with respect to A, neither X nor Y is a trade or business described in paragraph (b)(1) of this section.

*Example 3. Application of the rental activity exceptions.* B, an unmarried individual, is a partner in PRS, which is engaged in an equipment leasing activity. The average period of customer use of the equipment is seven days or less (and therefore meets the exception in § 1.469-1T(e)(3)(ii)(A)). B materially participates in the equipment leasing activity (within the meaning of § 1.469-5T(a)). The equipment leasing activity constitutes a trade or business. In Year 1, B has modified adjusted gross income (as defined in § 1.1411-2(c)) of $300,000, all of which is derived from PRS. All of the income from PRS is derived in the ordinary course of the equipment leasing activity, and all of PRS's property is held in the equipment leasing activity. Of B's allocable share of income from PRS, $275,000 constitutes gross income from rents (within the meaning of § 1.1411-4(a)(1)(i)). While $275,000 of the gross income from the equipment leasing activity meets the definition of rents in § 1.1411-4(a)(1)(i), the activity meets one of the exceptions to rental

activity in § 1.469-1T(e)(3)(ii) and B materially participates in the activity. Therefore, the trade or business is not a passive activity with respect to B for purposes of paragraph (b)(1)(ii) of this section. Because the rents are derived in the ordinary course of a trade or business not described in paragraph (a) of this section, the ordinary course of a trade or business exception in § 1.1411-4(b) applies, and the rents are not described in § 1.1411-4(a)(1)(i). Furthermore, because the equipment leasing trade or business is not a trade or business described in paragraph (a)(1) or (a)(2) of this section, the $25,000 of other gross income is not net investment income under § 1.1411-4(a)(1)(ii). However, the $25,000 of other gross income may be net investment income by reason of section 1411(c)(3) and § 1.1411-6 if it is attributable to PRS's working capital. Finally, gain or loss from the sale of the property held in the equipment leasing activity will not be subject to § 1.1411-4(a)(1)(iii) because, although it is attributable to a trade or business, it is not a trade or business to which the section 1411 tax applies.

*Example 4. Application of section 469 and other gross income under § 1.1411-4(a)(1)(ii).* Same facts as *Example 3*, except B does not materially participate in the equipment leasing trade or business and therefore the trade or business is a passive activity with respect to B for purposes of paragraph (b)(1)(ii) of this section. Accordingly, the $275,000 of gross income from rents is described in § 1.1411-4(a)(1)(i) because the rents are derived from a trade or business that is a passive activity with respect to B. Furthermore, the $25,000 of other gross income from the equipment leasing trade or business is described in § 1.1411-4(a)(1)(ii) because the gross income is derived from a trade or business described in paragraph (a)(1) of this section. Finally, gain or loss from the sale of the property used in the equipment leasing trade or business is subject to § 1.1411-4(a)(1)(iii) because the trade or business is a passive activity with respect to B, as described in paragraph (b)(1)(ii) of this section.

*Example 5. Application of the portfolio income rule and section 469.* C, an unmarried individual, is a partner in PRS, a partnership engaged in a trade or business that does not involve a rental activity. C does not materially participate in PRS within the meaning of § 1.469-5T(a). Therefore, the trade or business of PRS is a passive activity with respect to C for purposes of paragraph (a)(1) of this section. C's $500,000 allocable share of PRS's income consists of $450,000 of gross income from a trade or business and $50,000 of gross income from dividends and interest (within the meaning of § 1.1411-4(a)(1)(i)) that is not derived in the ordinary course of the trade or business of PRS. Therefore, C's $500,000 allocable share of PRS's income is subject to section 1411. C's $50,000 allocable share of PRS's income from dividends and interest is subject to § 1.1411-4(a)(1)(i) because the share is gross income from dividends and interest that is not derived in the ordinary course of a trade or business (that is, the ordinary course of a trade or business exception in § 1.1411-4(b) is inapplicable). C's $450,000 allocable share of PRS's income is subject to § 1.1411-4(a)(1)(ii) because it is gross income from a trade or business that is a passive activity.

(c) *Trading in financial instruments or commodities.*—(1) *Definition of financial instruments.*—For purposes of section 1411 and the regulations thereunder, the term *financial instruments* includes stocks and other equity interests, evidences of indebtedness, options, forward or futures contracts, notional principal contracts, any other derivatives, or any evidence of an interest in any of the items described in this paragraph (c)(1). An evidence of an interest in any of the items described in this paragraph (c)(1) includes, but is not limited to, short positions or partial units in any of the items described in this paragraph (c)(1).

(2) *Definition of commodities.*—For purposes of section 1411 and the regulations thereunder, the term *commodities* refers to items described in section 475(e)(2).

(d) *Effective/applicability date.*—This section applies to taxable years beginning after December 31, 2013. However, taxpayers may apply this section to taxable years beginning after December 31, 2012, in accordance with § 1.1411-1(f). [Reg. § 1.1411-5.]

☐ [*T.D.* 9644, 11-26-2013 (*corrected* 3-31-2014).]

### [Reg. § 1.1411-6]

**§ 1.1411-6. Income on investment of working capital subject to tax.**—(a) *General rule.*—For purposes of section 1411, any item of gross income from the investment of working capital will be treated as not derived in the ordinary course of a trade or business, and any net gain that is attributable to the investment of working capital will be treated as not derived in the ordinary course of a trade or business. In determining whether any item is gross income from or net gain attributable to an investment of working capital, principles similar to those described in § 1.469-2T(c)(3)(ii) apply. See § 1.1411-4(f) for rules regarding properly allocable deductions with respect to an investment of working capital and § 1.1411-7 for rules relating to the adjustment to net gain on the disposition of interests in a partnership or S corporation.

(b) *Example.*—The following example illustrates the principles of this section. Assume for purposes of the example that the taxpayer uses a calendar taxable year, the taxpayer is a United States citizen, and Year 1 and all subsequent years are taxable years in which section 1411 is in effect:

*Example.* (i) A, an unmarried individual, operates a restaurant, which is a section 162 trade or business but is not a trade or business described in § 1.1411-5(a)(1) with respect to A. A owns and conducts the restaurant business through S, an S corporation wholly-owned by A. S is able to pay all of the restaurant's current obligations with cash flow generated by the restaurant. S utilizes an interest-bearing checking account at a local bank to make daily deposits of cash receipts generated by the restaurant, and also to pay the recurring ordinary and necessary business expenses of the restaurant. The average daily balance of the checking account is approximately $2,500, but at any given time the balance may be significantly more or less than this amount depending on the short-term cash flow needs of the business. In addition, S has set aside $20,000 for the potential future needs of the business in case the daily cash flow into and from the checking account becomes insufficient to pay the restaurant's recurring business expenses. S does not currently need to spend or use the $20,000 capital to conduct the restaurant business, and S deposits and maintains the $20,000 in an interest-bearing savings account at a local bank.

(ii) Both the $2,500 average daily balance of the checking account and the $20,000 savings account balance constitute working capital under § 1.469-2T(c)(3)(ii) and, pursuant to paragraph (a) of this section, the interest generated by this working capital will not be treated as derived in the ordinary course of S's restaurant business. Accordingly, the interest income derived by S from its checking and savings accounts and allocated to A under section 1366 constitutes gross income from interest under § 1.1411-4(a)(1)(i).

(c) *Effective/applicability date.*—This section applies to taxable years beginning after December 31, 2013. However, taxpayers may apply this section to taxable years beginning after December 31, 2012, in accordance with § 1.1411-1(f). [Reg. § 1.1411-6.]

☐ [*T.D.* 9644, 11-26-2013.]

### [Reg. § 1.1411-7]

**§ 1.1411-7. Exception for dispositions of interests in partnerships and S corporations.**—[Reserved]

☐ [*T.D.* 9644, 11-26-2013.]

### [Reg. § 1.1411-8]

**§ 1.1411-8. Exception for distributions from qualified plans.**—(a) *General rule.*—Net investment income does not include any distribution from a qualified plan or arrangement. For this purpose, the term qualified plan or arrangement means any plan or arrangement described in section 401(a), 403(a), 403(b), 408, 408A, or 457(b).

(b) *Rules relating to distributions.*—This paragraph (b) provides rules for purposes of paragraph (a) of this section. For purposes of section 1411(c)(5) and this section, a distribution means the following:

(1) *Actual distributions.*—Any amount actually distributed from a qualified plan or arrangement, as defined in paragraph (a) of this section, is a distribution within the meaning of section 1411(c)(5), and thus is not included in net investment income. Examples include a rollover to an eligible retirement plan within the meaning of section 402(c)(8)(B), a distribution of a plan loan offset amount within the meaning of Q&A-13(b) of § 1.72(p)-1, and certain corrective distributions under the Internal Revenue Code (Code).

(2) *Amounts treated as distributed.*—Any amount that is treated as distributed from a qualified plan or arrangement under the Code for purposes of income tax is a distribution within the meaning of section 1411(c)(5), and thus is not included in net investment income. Examples include a conversion to a Roth IRA described in section 408A and a deemed distribution under section 72(p).

(3) *Amounts includible in gross income.*—Any amount that is not treated as a distribution but is otherwise includible in gross income pursuant to a rule relating to amounts held in a qualified plan or arrangement described in paragraph (a) of this section is a distribution within the meaning of section 1411(c)(5), and thus is not included in net investment income. For example, any income of the trust of a qualified plan or arrangement that is applied to purchase a participant's life insurance coverage (the P.S. 58 costs) is a distribution within the meaning of section 1411(c)(5), and thus is not included in net investment income.

(4) *Amounts related to employer securities.*—(i) *Dividends related to employer securities.*—Any dividend that is deductible under section 404(k) and is paid in cash directly to plan participants or beneficiaries is a distribution within the meaning of section 1411(c)(5), and thus is not included in net investment income. However, any amount paid as a dividend after the employer securities have been distributed from a qualified plan is not a distribution within the meaning of section 1411(c)(5), and thus is included in net investment income.

(ii) *Amounts related to the net unrealized appreciation in employer securities.*—The amount of any net unrealized appreciation attributable to employer securities (within the meaning of section 402(e)(4)) realized on a disposition of those employer securities is a distribution within the meaning of section 1411(c)(5), and thus is not included in net investment income. However, any appreciation in value of the employer securities after the distribution from the qualified plan is not a distribution within the meaning of section 1411(c)(5), and is included in net investment income.

(c) *Effective/applicability date.*—This section applies to taxable years beginning after December 31, 2013. However, taxpayers may apply this section to taxable years beginning after December 31, 2012, in accordance with § 1.1411-1(f). [Reg. § 1.1411-8.]

☐ [*T.D.* 9644, 11-26-2013.]

### [Reg. § 1.1411-9]

**§ 1.1411-9. Exception for self-employment income.**—(a) *General rule.*—Except as provided in paragraph (b) of this section, net investment income does not include any item taken into account in determining self-employment income that is subject to tax under section 1401(b) for such taxable year. For purposes of section 1411(c)(6) and this section, *taken into account* means income included and deductions allowed in determining net earnings from self-employment. However, amounts excepted in determining net earnings from self-employment under section 1402(a)(1)-(17), and thus excluded from self-employment income under section 1402(b), are not taken into account in determining self-employment income and thus may be included in net investment income if such amounts are described in § 1.1411-4. Except as provided in paragraph (b) of this section, if net earnings from self-employment consist of income or loss from more than one trade or business, all items taken into account in determining the net earnings from self-employment with respect to these trades or businesses (see § 1.1402(a)-2(c)) are considered taken into account in determining the amount of self-employment income that is subject to tax under section 1401(b) and therefore not included in net investment income.

(b) *Special rule for traders.*—In the case of gross income described in §§ 1.1411-4(a)(1)(ii) and (a)(1)(iii) derived from a trade or business of trading in financial instruments or commodities (as described in § 1.1411-5(a)(2)), the deductions described in § 1.1411-4(f)(2)(ii) properly allocable to the taxpayer's trade or business of trading in financial instruments or commodities are taken into account in determining the taxpayer's self-employment income only to the extent that such deductions reduce the taxpayer's net earnings from self-employment (after aggregating under § 1.1402(a)-2(c) the net earnings from self-employment from any trade or business carried on by the taxpayer as an individual or as a member of a partnership). Any deductions described in § 1.1411-4(f)(2)(ii) that exceed the amount of net earnings from self-employment, in the aggregate (if applicable), are allowed in determining the taxpayer's net investment income under section 1411 and the regulations thereunder.

(c) *Examples.*—The following examples illustrate the provisions of this section. For purposes of these examples, assume the taxpayer is a United States citizen, uses a calendar taxable year, and Year 1 and all subsequent years are taxable years in which section 1411 is in effect:

*Example 1. Exclusion from self-employment income.* A is a general partner in PRS, a partnership carrying on a trade or business that is not a trade or business of trading in financial instruments or commodities (within the meaning of § 1.1411-5(a)(2)). During Year 1, A's distributive share from PRS is $1 million, $300,000 of which is attributable to the gain on the sale of PRS's capital assets. Section 1402(a)(3)(A) provides an exclusion from net earnings from self-employment for any gain or loss from the sale or exchange of a capital asset. For Year 1, A has $700,000 self-employment income subject to self-employment tax. This $700,000 subject to self-employment tax is not included as part of net investment income under paragraph (a) of this section. However, the $300,000 attributable to the gain on PRS's sale of a capital asset is excluded from net earnings from self-employment, and from self-employment income, and thus is not covered by the exception in section 1411(c)(6). Therefore, the $300,000 attributable to the gain on PRS's sale of a capital asset is included as net investment income if the other requirements of section 1411 are satisfied.

*Example 2. Two trades or businesses.* B is an individual engaged in two trades or businesses, Business X and Business Y, neither of which is the trade or business of trading in financial instruments or commodities (as described in § 1.1411-5(a)(2)). B carries on Business X as a sole proprietor and B is also a general partner in a partnership that carries on Business Y. Business Y is a nonpassive activity of B. During Year 1, B had net earnings from self-employment consisting of the aggregate of a $50,000 loss (that is, after application of the exclusions under section 1402(a)(1)-(17)) from Business X, and $70,000 in income (after application of the exclusions under section 1402(a)(1)-(17)) from B's distributive share from the partnership from carrying on Business Y. Thus, B's net earnings from self-employment in Year 1 are $20,000. For Year 1, all of B's income, deductions, gains, and losses from Business X and distributive share from the partnership carrying on Business Y, other than those amounts excluded due to application of section 1402(a)(1)-(17), are taken into account in determining B's net earnings from self-employment and self-employment income for such taxable year. Accordingly, in calculating B's net investment income (as defined in § 1.1411-4) for Year 1, B will not take into account the items of income, loss, gain, and deduction that comprise B's $50,000 loss attributable to Business X (after application of the exclusions under section 1402(a)(1)-(17)), and the items of income, loss, gain, and deduction that comprise B's $70,000 distributable share attributable to B's general partnership interest (after application of the exclusions under section 1402(a)(1)-(17)). Rather, only items of income, loss, gain, and deduction from the two separate businesses that were excluded from the calculation of B's net earnings from self-employment income due to the application of the exclusions under section 1402(a)(1)-(17), such as any capital gains and losses excluded under section 1402(a)(3), are considered for purposes of calculating B's net investment income for Year 1 in connection with these two trades or businesses.

*Example 3. Special rule for trader with single trade or business.* D is an individual engaged in the trade or business of trading in commodities (as described in § 1.1411-5(a)(2)). D made a valid and timely election under section 475(f)(2). D derives $400,000 of trading gains, which are gross income described in § 1.1411-4(a)(1) and $15,000 of expenses described in § 1.1411-4(f)(2)(ii) from carrying on the trade or business. Pursuant to sections 475(f)(1)(D) and 1402(a)(3)(A), none of the gross income is taken into account in determining D's net earnings from self-employment and self-employment income. Therefore, under paragraph (a) of this section, the $400,000 of gross income is not covered by the exception in section 1411(c)(6). Because D had $0 net earnings from self-employment, the $15,000 of deductions did not reduce D's net earnings from self-employment under paragraph (b) of this section and § 1.1411-(4)(f)(2)(ii). Therefore, the $15,000 of deductions may reduce D's gross income of $400,000 for purposes of section 1411.

*Example 4. Special rule for trader with multiple trades or businesses.* E is an individual engaged in two trades or businesses, Business X (which is not a trade or business of trading in financial instruments or commodities) and Business Y (which is a trade or business of trading in financial instruments or commodities (as described in § 1.1411-5(a)(2)). E made a valid and timely election under section 475(f) with respect to Business Y. During Year 1, E had net earnings from self-employment from Business X of $35,000. During Year 1, E also had $300,000 of trading gains, which are gross income described in § 1.1411-4(a)(1) and $40,000 of expenses described in § 1.1411-4(f)(2)(ii) from Business Y. E's $300,000 of gross income from Business Y is excluded from net earnings from self-employment and self-employment income pursuant to sections 475(f)(1)(D) and 1402(a)(3)(A). E's $40,000 of deductions from Business Y reduce E's $35,000 of net earnings from self-employment from Business X to $0. Pursuant to paragraph (b) of this section and § 1.1411-4(f)(2)(ii), the remaining $5,000 of deductions from Business Y are taken into account in determining E's net investment income (by reducing E's gross income of $300,000 from Business Y to $295,000) for purposes of section 1411.

(d) *Effective/applicability date.*—This section applies to taxable years beginning after December 31, 2013. However, taxpayers may apply this section to taxable years beginning after December 31, 2012, in accordance with § 1.1411-1(f). [Reg. § 1.1411-9.]

☐ [*T.D.* 9644, 11-26-2013.]

**[Reg. § 1.1411-10]**

**§ 1.1411-10. Controlled foreign corporations and passive foreign investment companies.**—(a) *In general.*—This section provides rules that apply to an individual, estate, or trust that is a United States shareholder of a controlled foreign corporation (CFC), or that is a United States person that directly or indirectly owns an interest in a passive foreign investment company (PFIC). In addition, this section provides rules that apply to an individual, estate, or trust that owns an interest in a domestic partnership or an S corporation that is either

a United States shareholder of a CFC or that has made an election under section 1295 to treat a PFIC as a qualified electing fund (QEF). References in this section to an election under paragraph (g) of this section being in effect relate to an election that is applicable to the person that is determining the section 1411 consequences with respect to holding a particular CFC or QEF.

(b) *Amounts derived from a trade or business described in § 1.1411-5.*—(1) *In general.*—Except as provided in paragraph (b)(2) of this section, an amount included in gross income under section 951(a) or section 1293(a) that is also income derived from a trade or business described in section 1411(c)(2) and § 1.1411-5 (applying the relevant rules in § 1.1411-4(b)) is taken into account as net investment income under section 1411(c)(1)(A)(ii) and § 1.1411-4(a)(1)(ii) for purposes of section 1411 and the regulations thereunder when it is taken into account for purposes of chapter 1, and the rules in paragraphs (c) through (g) of this section do not apply to that amount. For purposes of section 1411 and the regulations thereunder, an amount included in gross income under section 1296(a) that is also income derived from a trade or business described in section 1411(c)(2) and § 1.1411-5 (applying the relevant rules in § 1.1411-4(b)), is net investment income within the meaning of section 1411(c)(1)(A)(ii) and § 1.1411-4(a)(1)(ii), and the rules in paragraph (c)(2)(ii) of this section do not apply to that amount.

(2) *Coordination rule for changes in trade or business status.*—With respect to stock of a CFC or QEF for which an election under paragraph (g) of this section is not in effect, the rules in paragraphs (c) through (f) of this section apply to a distribution of earnings and profits described in paragraph (c)(1)(i)(A) of this section that was not taken into account as net investment income under paragraph (b) of this section.

(c) *Calculation of net investment income.*—(1) *Dividends.*—For purposes of section 1411(c)(1)(A)(i) and § 1.1411-4(a)(1)(i), net investment income is calculated by taking into account the amount of dividends described in this paragraph (c)(1).

(i) *Distributions of previously taxed earnings and profits.*—(A) *Rules when an election under paragraph (g) of this section is not in effect with respect to the shareholder.*—(1) *General rule.*—Except as otherwise provided in this paragraph (c)(1)(i), with respect to stock of a CFC or QEF for which an election under paragraph (g) of this section is not in effect, a distribution of earnings and profits that is not treated as a dividend for chapter 1 purposes under section 959(d) or section 1293(c) is a dividend for purposes of section 1411(c)(1)(A)(i) and § 1.1411-4(a)(1)(i) if the distribution is attributable to amounts that are or have been included in gross income for chapter 1 purposes under section 951(a) or section 1293(a) in a taxable year beginning after December 31, 2012. Solely, for this purpose, distributions of earnings and profits attributable to amounts that are or have been included in gross income for chapter 1 purposes under section 951(a) or section 1293(a) are considered first attributable to those earnings and profits, if any, derived from the current taxable year, and then from prior taxable years beginning with the most recent prior taxable year, and with respect to amounts included under section 951(a), without regard to whether the earnings and profits are described in section 959(c)(1) or section 959(c)(2).

(2) *Exception for distributions attributable to earnings and profits previously taken into account for purposes of section 1411.*—A distribution of earnings and profits that is not treated as a dividend for chapter 1 purposes under section 959(d) or section 1293(c) is not treated as a dividend for purposes of section 1411(c)(1)(A)(i) and § 1.1411-4(a)(1)(i), to the extent that an individual, estate, or trust establishes, by providing information that is similar to, and in the same manner as, the information described in § 1.959-1(d) (relating to previously taxed earnings and profits), that the distribution is attributable to—

(i) Amounts included in gross income by any person for chapter 1 purposes under section 951(a) or section 1293(a) that have been taken into account by any person as net investment income by reason of paragraph (b) of this section or an election under paragraph (g) of this section; or

(ii) Amounts included in gross income by any person as a dividend pursuant to section 1248(a) that, by reason of paragraph (c)(3)(ii) of this section, have been taken into account by any person as net investment income under section 1411(c)(1)(A)(i) and § 1.1411-4(a)(1)(i).

(B) *Rule when an election under paragraph (g) of this section is in effect with respect to the shareholder.*—Except as otherwise provided in this paragraph (c)(1)(i), if an election under paragraph (g) of this section is in effect, a distribution of earnings and profits that is not treated as a dividend for chapter 1 purposes under section 959(d) or section 1293(c) is not treated as a dividend for purposes of section 1411(c)(1)(A)(i) and § 1.1411-4(a)(1)(i).

(C) *Special rule for certain distributions related to 2013 taxable years.*—*(1) Scope.*—The rule in this paragraph (c)(1)(i)(C) applies to individuals, estates, and trusts that were subject to section 1411 during a taxable year that began after December 31, 2012, and before January 1, 2014, and that satisfy all of the conditions set forth in paragraph (c)(1)(i)(C)(2) of this section. This rule also applies to all domestic partnerships and S corporations that satisfy all of the conditions set forth in paragraph (c)(1)(i)(C)(2) of this section.

(2) *Rule.*—A distribution of earnings and profits from a CFC or QEF, with respect to which an election under paragraph (g) is in effect, that is not treated as a dividend for chapter 1 purposes under section 959(d) or section 1293(c) is a dividend for purposes of section 1411(c)(1)(A)(i) and § 1.1411-4(a)(1)(i) to the extent that—

(i) The distribution of earnings and profits is attributable to an amount included by an individual, estate, trust, domestic partnership, S corporation or common trust fund in gross income for chapter 1 purposes under section 951(a) or section 1293(a) with respect to the CFC or QEF for a taxable year that began after December 31, 2012, and before January 1, 2014;

(ii) The individual, estate, trust, domestic partnership, S corporation, or common trust fund made the election under paragraph (g) of this section with respect to the CFC or QEF in a taxable year that began after December 31, 2013; and

(iii) The individual, estate, trust, domestic partnership, S corporation, or common trust fund did not make the election described in paragraph (g)(4)(iii) of this section (concerning making an election under paragraph (g) of this section for a taxable year that begins before January 1, 2014).

(3) *Ordering rule.*—Solely, for purposes of this paragraph (c)(1)(i)(C)(3), distributions of earnings and profits attributable to amounts that have been included in gross income for chapter 1 purposes under section 951(a) or section 1293(a) are considered first attributable to the earnings and profits derived from a taxable year that began after December 31, 2012, and before January 1, 2014.

(ii) *Excess distributions that constitute dividends.*—To the extent an excess distribution within the meaning of section 1291(b) constitutes a dividend within the meaning of section 316(a), the amount is included in net investment income for purposes of section 1411(c)(1)(A)(i) and § 1.1411-4(a)(1)(i).

(2) *Net gain.*—For purposes of section 1411(c)(1)(A)(iii) and § 1.1411-4(a)(1)(iii), the rules in this paragraph (c)(2) apply in determining net gain attributable to the disposition of property.

(i) *Gains treated as excess distributions.*—Gains treated as excess distributions under section 1291(a)(2) are included in determining net gain attributable to the disposition of property for purposes of section 1411(c)(1)(A)(iii) and § 1.1411-4(a)(1)(iii).

(ii) *Inclusions and deductions with respect to section 1296 mark to market elections.*—Amounts included in gross income under section 1296(a)(1) and amounts allowed as a deduction under section 1296(a)(2) are taken into account in determining net gain attributable to the disposition of property for purposes of section 1411(c)(1)(A)(iii) and § 1.1411-4(a)(1)(iii).

(iii) *Gain or loss attributable to the disposition of stock of CFCs and QEFs.*—With respect to stock of a CFC or QEF for which an election under paragraph (g) of this section is not in effect, for purposes of calculating the net gain under §§ 1.1411-4(a)(1)(iii) and 1.1411-4(d) that is attributable to the direct or indirect disposition of that stock (including for purposes of determining gain or loss on the direct or indirect disposition of that stock by a domestic partnership, S corporation, or common trust fund), basis is determined in accordance with the provisions of paragraph (d) of this section.

(iv) *Gain or loss attributable to the disposition of interests in domestic partnerships or S corporations that own directly or indirectly stock of CFCs or QEFs.*—With respect to stock of a CFC or QEF for which an election under paragraph (g) of this section is not in effect, for purposes of calculating the net gain under §§ 1.1411-4(a)(1)(iii) and 1.1411-4(d) that is attributable to the disposition of an interest in a domestic partnership or S corporation that directly or indirectly owns that stock, basis is determined in accordance with the provisions of paragraph (d) of this section.

(3) *Application of section 1248.*—With respect to stock of a CFC or QEF for which an election under paragraph (g) of this section is not in effect, for purposes of section 1411 and § 1.1411-4—

(i) In determining the gain recognized on the sale or exchange of stock of a foreign corporation for section 1248(a) purposes, basis is determined in accordance with the provisions of paragraph (d) of this section; and

(ii) Section 1248(a) applies without regard to the exclusion for certain earnings and profits under sections 1248(d)(1) and (d)(6),

except that those exclusions will apply with respect to the earnings and profits of a foreign corporation that are attributable to:

(A) Amounts taken into account as net investment income under paragraph (b) of this section; and

(B) Amounts previously included in gross income for chapter 1 purposes under section 951(a) or section 1293(a) in a taxable year beginning before December 31, 2012, and that have not yet been distributed. For this purpose, the determination of whether earnings and profits that are attributable to amounts previously taxed in a taxable year beginning before December 31, 2012, have been distributed is determined based on the rules described in paragraph (c)(1)(i) of this section.

(4) *Amounts distributed by an estate or trust.*—Net investment income of a beneficiary of an estate or trust includes the beneficiary's share of distributable net income, as described in sections 652 and 662 and as modified by paragraph (f) of this section, to the extent that the beneficiary's share of distributable net income includes items that, if they had been received directly by the beneficiary, would have been described in this paragraph (c).

(5) *Properly allocable deductions.*—(i) *General rule.*—For purposes of section 1411(c)(1)(B) and § 1.1411-4(f), the section 163(d)(1) investment expense deduction may be calculated by—

(A) Increasing the amount of investment income determined for chapter 1 purposes under section 163(d)(4)(B) by the amount of dividends described in § 1.1411-10(c) that are derived from a CFC or QEF with respect to which an election under paragraph (g) of this section is not in effect;

(B) Decreasing the amount of investment income determined for chapter 1 purposes under section 163(d)(4)(B) by the amount included in gross income for chapter 1 purposes under section 951(a) or section 1293(a) that is attributable to a CFC or QEF with respect to which an election under paragraph (g) of this section is not in effect; and

(C) Increasing or decreasing, as applicable, the amount of investment income for chapter 1 purposes under section 163(d)(4)(B) by the difference between the amount calculated with respect to a disposition under paragraphs (c)(2)(iii) and (c)(2)(iv) of this section and the amount of the gain or loss attributable to the relevant disposition as calculated for chapter 1 purposes.

(ii) *Additional rules.*—For purposes of section 1411(c)(1)(B) and § 1.1411-4(f), if the method of calculation described in paragraph (c)(5)(i) of this section is applied:

(A) The amount of investment interest not allowed as a deduction under section 163(d)(2) must be calculated consistent with the method of calculation described in paragraph (c)(5)(i).

(B) The method of calculation must be adopted by an individual, estate, or trust no later than the first year in which the individual, estate, or trust is subject to section 1411.

(C) The method of calculation must be applied with respect to all CFCs and QEFs for all taxable years with respect to which an election under paragraph (g) of this section is not in effect.

(D) A method of calculation under this paragraph is a method of accounting, which must be applied consistently, and may only be changed by the taxpayer by securing the consent of the Commissioner in accordance with § 1.446-1(e) and following the administrative procedures issued under § 1.446-1(e)(3)(ii).

(d) *Conforming basis adjustments.*—(1) *Basis adjustments under sections 961 and 1293.*—(i) *Stock held by individuals, estates, or trusts.*—With respect to stock of a CFC or QEF which is held by an individual, estate, or trust, either directly or indirectly through one or more entities each of which is foreign, for which an election under paragraph (g) of this section is not in effect—

(A) The basis increases made pursuant to sections 961(a) and 1293(d) for amounts included in gross income for chapter 1 purposes under sections 951(a) and 1293(a) in taxable years beginning after December 31, 2012, are not taken into account for purposes of section 1411 and the regulations thereunder; and

(B) The basis decreases made pursuant to sections 961(b) and 1293(d) attributable to amounts treated as dividends for purposes of section 1411 under paragraph (c)(1)(i) of this section are not taken into account for purposes of section 1411 and the regulations thereunder.

(ii) *Stock held by domestic partnerships or S corporations.*—(A) *Rule when an election under paragraph (g) of this section is not in effect.*—The rules of this paragraph (d)(1)(ii)(A) apply with respect to stock of a CFC or QEF held directly by a domestic partnership or S corporation, or indirectly through one or more entities each of which is foreign, for which an election under paragraph (g) of this section is not in effect. If an individual, estate, or trust is a shareholder of an S corporation, or if an individual, estate, or trust directly, or through one or more tiers of passthrough entities (including an S corporation), owns an interest in a domestic partnership, the S corporation or domestic partnership, as the case may be, will not take into account for purposes of section 1411 and the regulations thereunder the basis increases made by the domestic partnership or S corporation pursuant to sections 961(a) and 1293(d) for amounts included in gross income for chapter 1 purposes under sections 951(a) and 1293(a) for taxable years beginning after December 31, 2012, and the basis decreases made by the domestic partnership or S corporation pursuant to sections 961(b) and 1293(d) attributable to amounts treated as dividends for purposes of section 1411 under paragraph (c)(1)(i) of this section (the *section 1411 recalculated basis*). If the domestic partnership or S corporation disposes of the stock of a CFC or QEF, the section 1411 recalculated basis will be used to determine the distributive share or pro rata share of the gain or loss for purposes of section 1411 for partners or shareholders.

(B) *Rules when an election under paragraph (g) of this section is in effect.*—If an election under paragraph (g) of this section is in effect with respect to stock of a CFC or QEF held directly or indirectly by a domestic partnership or S corporation, the partner's distributive share or the shareholder's pro rata share of the gain or loss for purposes of section 1411 is the same as the distributive share or pro rata share of the gain or loss for purposes of chapter 1. See *Example 6* of paragraph (h) of this section.

(2) *Special rules for partners that own interests in domestic partnerships that own directly or indirectly stock of CFCs or QEFs.*—The rules of this paragraph (d)(2) apply with respect to stock of a CFC or QEF for which an election under paragraph (g) of this section is not in effect, and that is held by a domestic partnership, either directly or indirectly through one or more entities each of which is foreign. In such a case, the basis increases provided under section 705(a)(1)(A) to the partners for purposes of chapter 1 that are attributable to amounts that the domestic partnership includes or included in gross income under section 951(a) or section 1293(a) for a taxable year beginning after December 31, 2012, are not taken into account for purposes of section 1411. Instead, each partner's adjusted basis in the partnership interest is increased by its share of any distributions to the partnership from the CFC or QEF that are treated as dividends for purposes of section 1411 under paragraph (c)(1)(i) of this section. Similar rules apply when the stock of the CFC or QEF is held in a tiered partnership structure. For purposes of determining net investment income under section 1411 and the regulations thereunder, the partner's adjusted basis in the partnership interest as calculated under this paragraph (d)(2) is used to determine all tax consequences related to tax basis (for example, loss limitation rules and the characterization of partnership distributions).

(3) *Special rules for S corporation shareholders that own interests in S corporations that own directly or indirectly stock of CFCs or QEFs.*—The rules of this paragraph (d)(3) apply with respect to stock of a CFC or QEF for which an election under paragraph (g) of this section is not in effect, and that is held by an S corporation, directly or indirectly through one or more entities each of which is foreign. In such case, the basis increases provided in section 1367(a)(1)(A) to its shareholders for chapter 1 purposes that are attributable to amounts that the S corporation includes or included in gross income for chapter 1 purposes under section 951(a) or section 1293(a) for taxable years beginning after December 31, 2012, are not taken into account for purposes of section 1411. Instead, each shareholder's adjusted basis of stock in the S corporation is increased by its share of the distributions to the S corporation from the CFC or QEF that are treated as dividends for purposes of section 1411 under paragraph (c)(1)(i) of this section. Similar rules apply when the S corporation holds an interest in a CFC or QEF through a partnership. For purposes of determining net investment income under section 1411 and the regulations thereunder, the shareholder's adjusted basis in the stock of the S corporation as calculated under this paragraph (d)(3) is used to determine all tax consequences related to tax basis (for example, loss limitation rules and the characterization of S corporation distributions).

(4) *Special rules for participants in common trust funds.*—Rules similar to the rules in paragraphs (d)(2) and (3) of this section apply to ownership interests in common trust funds (as defined in section 584).

(e) *Conforming adjustments to modified adjusted gross income and adjusted gross income.*—(1) *Individuals.*—Solely for purposes of section 1411(a)(1)(B)(i) and the regulations thereunder, the term *modified adjusted gross income* means modified adjusted gross income as defined in § 1.1411-2(c)(1)—

(i) Increased by amounts included in net investment income under paragraphs (c)(1)(i), (c)(1)(ii), (c)(2)(i), and (c)(4) of this section that are not otherwise included in gross income for chapter 1 purposes;

(ii) Increased or decreased, as applicable, by the difference between the amount calculated with respect to a disposition under paragraphs (c)(2)(iii) and (iv) of this section and the amount of the gain or loss attributable to the relevant disposition as calculated for chapter 1 purposes;

(iii) Decreased by any amount included in gross income for chapter 1 purposes under section 951(a) or section 1293(a) attributable to a CFC or QEF with respect to which no election under paragraph (g) of this section is in effect; and

(iv) To the extent the section 163(d)(1) investment interest expense deduction is calculated using the method of calculation set forth in paragraph (c)(5) of this section and the deduction is taken into account under § 1.1411-4(f)(2), increased or decreased, as appropriate, by the difference between the amount of the section 163(d)(1) investment interest expense deduction calculated under paragraph (c)(5) of this section and the amount calculated for chapter 1 purposes.

(2) *Estates and trusts.*—Solely for purposes of section 1411(a)(2)(B)(i) and the regulations thereunder, the term *adjusted gross income* means adjusted gross income as defined in § 1.1411-3(a)(1)(ii)(B)(*1*) adjusted by the following amounts to the extent those amounts are not distributed by the estate or trust—

(i) Increased by amounts included in net investment income under paragraphs (c)(1)(i), (c)(1)(ii), (c)(2)(i), and (c)(4) of this section that are not otherwise included in gross income for chapter 1 purposes;

(ii) Increased or decreased, as applicable, by the difference between the amount calculated with respect to a disposition under paragraphs (c)(2)(iii) and (iv) of this section and the amount of the gain or loss attributable to the relevant disposition as calculated for chapter 1 purposes;

(iii) Decreased by any amount included in gross income for chapter 1 purposes under section 951(a) or section 1293(a) attributable to a CFC or QEF with respect to which no election under paragraph (g) of this section is in effect; and

(iv) To the extent the section 163(d)(1) investment interest expense deduction is calculated using the method of calculation set forth in paragraph (c)(5) of this section and taken into account under § 1.1411-4(f)(2), increased or decreased, as appropriate, by the difference between the amount of the section 163(d)(1) investment interest expense deduction calculated under paragraph (c)(5) of this section and the amount calculated for chapter 1 purposes.

(f) *Application to estates and trusts.*—All of the items described in paragraph (c) of this section are included in the net investment income of an estate or trust or its beneficiaries. The amounts described in paragraphs (e)(2)(i) through (iv) of this section, regardless of whether the estate or trust receives those amounts directly or indirectly through another estate or trust, increase or decrease, as applicable, the estate's or trust's distributable net income for purposes of section 1411. The estate or trust, or the beneficiaries thereof, must take those amounts into account in a manner reasonably consistent with the general operating rules for estates and trusts in § 1.1411-3 and subchapter J in computing the undistributed net investment income of the estate or trust and the net investment income of the beneficiaries.

(g) *Election with respect to CFCs and QEFs.*—(1) *Effect of election.*—If an election under paragraph (g) of this section is made with respect to a CFC or QEF, amounts included in gross income for chapter 1 purposes under section 951(a) or section 1293(a)(1)(A) with respect to the CFC or QEF in taxable years beginning with the taxable year for which the election is made are treated as net investment income for purposes of § 1.1411-4(a)(1)(i), and amounts included in gross income under section 1293(a)(1)(B) with respect to the QEF in taxable years beginning with the taxable year for which the election is made are taken into account in calculating net gain attributable to the disposition of property under § 1.1411-4(a)(1)(iii). See paragraphs (c)(1)(i)(B) and (c)(1)(i)(C) of this section for the effect of this election on certain distributions of previously taxed earnings and profits.

(2) *Years to which election applies.*—(i) *In general.*—An election under paragraph (g) of this section applies to the taxable year for which it is made and all subsequent taxable years, and applies to all subsequently acquired interests in the CFC or QEF. An election under paragraph (g) of this section is irrevocable.

(ii) *Termination of interest in CFC or QEF.*—Complete termination of a person's interest in the CFC or QEF does not terminate the person's election under paragraph (g) of this section with respect to the CFC or QEF. Thus, if the person reacquires stock of the CFC or QEF, that stock is considered to be stock for which an election under paragraph (g) of this section has been made and is in effect.

(iii) *Termination of partnership.*—If a domestic partnership that makes the election under paragraph (g) of this section is terminated pursuant to section 708(b)(1)(B), the election is binding on the new partnership.

(3) *Who may make the election.*—An individual, estate, trust, domestic partnership, S corporation, or common trust fund may make an election under paragraph (g) of this section with respect to each CFC or QEF that it holds directly or indirectly through one or more entities, each of which is foreign. In addition, an individual, estate, trust, domestic partnership, S corporation, or common trust fund may make an election under paragraph (g) of this section with respect to a CFC or QEF that it holds indirectly through a domestic partnership, S corporation, estate, trust, or common trust fund if the domestic partnership, S corporation, estate, trust, or common trust fund does not make the election. The election, if made, for an estate or trust must be made by the fiduciary of that estate or trust.

(4) *Time and manner for making the election.*—(i) *Individuals, estates, and trusts.*—(A) *General rule.*—Except as otherwise provided in this paragraph, in order for an election under paragraph (g) of this section by an individual, estate, or trust (other than a CRT) with respect to a CFC or QEF to be effective, the election must be made no later than the first taxable year beginning after December 31, 2013, during which the individual, estate, or trust—

    (1) Includes an amount in gross income for chapter 1 purposes under section 951(a) or section 1293(a) with respect to the CFC or QEF; and

    (2) Is subject to tax under section 1411 or would be subject to tax under section 1411 if the election were made with respect to the stock of the CFC or QEF.

(B) *Special rule for charitable remainder trusts (CRTs).*—Except as otherwise provided in this paragraph, in order for an election under paragraph (g) of this section by a CRT with respect to a CFC or QEF to be effective, the election must be made no later than the first taxable year beginning after December 31, 2013, during which the CRT includes an amount in gross income for chapter 1 purposes under section 951(a) or section 1293(a) with respect to the CFC or QEF.

(ii) *Certain domestic passthrough entities.*—Except as otherwise provided in this paragraph, in order for an election under paragraph (g) of this section by a domestic partnership, S corporation, or common trust fund with respect to a CFC or a QEF to be effective, the election must be made no later than the first taxable year beginning after December 31, 2013, during which the domestic partnership S corporation, or common trust fund—

(A) Includes an amount in gross income for chapter 1 purposes under section 951(a) or section 1293(a) with respect to the CFC or QEF; and

(B) Has a direct or indirect owner that is subject to tax under section 1411 or would be subject to tax under section 1411 if the election were made.

(iii) *Taxable years that begin before January 1, 2014.*—(A) *Individuals, estates, or trusts.*—An individual, estate, or trust may make an election under paragraph (g) of this section for a taxable year that begins before January 1, 2014.

(B) *Certain domestic passthrough entities.*—A domestic partnership, S corporation, or common trust fund may make an election under paragraph (g) of this section for a taxable year that begins before January 1, 2014, provided that all of its partners, shareholders, or participants, as the case may be, consent to the election. In the case of a partner, shareholder, or participant that is a partnership, S corporation, or common trust fund, all of the partners, shareholders, and participants also must consent to the election.

(iv) *Time for making election.*—In all cases, the election under paragraph (g) of this section must be made in the manner prescribed by forms, instructions, or in other guidance on the individual's, estate's, trust's, domestic partnership's, S corporation's, or common trust fund's original or amended return for the taxable year for which the election is made. An election can be made on an amended return only if the taxable year for which the election is made, and all taxable years that are affected by the election, are not closed by the period of limitations on assessments under section 6501. An individual, estate, trust, domestic partnership, S corporation, or common trust fund may not seek an extension of time to make the election under any other provision of the law, including § 301.9100 of this chapter.

(h) *Examples.*—The following examples illustrate the rules of this section. In each example, unless otherwise indicated, the individuals, the foreign corporation (FC), the QEF (QEF), and the partnership (PRS) use a calendar taxable year. Further, the gross income or gain with respect to an interest in FC is not derived in a trade or business described in § 1.1411-5.

*Example 1.* (i) *Facts.* A, a United States citizen, is the sole shareholder of FC, a controlled foreign corporation (within the meaning of section 957). A is a United States shareholder (within the meaning of

section 951(b)) with respect to FC. In 2012, A includes $40,000 in gross income for chapter 1 purposes under section 951(a)(1)(A) with respect to FC. On December 31, 2012, A's basis in the stock of FC for chapter 1 purposes is $500,000, which includes an increase to basis under section 961(a) of $40,000. The amount of FC's earnings and profits that are described in section 959(c)(2) is $40,000, the amount of FC's earnings and profits that are described in section 959(c)(3) is $20,000, and FC does not have any earnings and profits that are described in section 959(c)(1). No election is made under paragraph (g) of this section. During 2013, A does not include any amounts in income under section 951(a) with respect to FC, A does not receive any distributions from FC, and there is no change in the amount of FC's earnings and profits. In 2014, A includes $10,000 in gross income for chapter 1 purposes under section 951(a)(1)(A) with respect to FC. As a result, A's basis in the stock of FC for chapter 1 purposes increases by $10,000 to $510,000 pursuant to section 961(a). During 2015, FC distributes $30,000 to A, which is not treated as a dividend for purposes of chapter 1 under section 959(d). As a result, A's basis in the stock of FC for chapter 1 purposes is decreased by $30,000 to $480,000 pursuant to section 961(b).

(ii) *Results for section 1411 purposes.* In 2014, A does not include the $10,000 section 951(a) income inclusion in A's net investment income under section 1411(c)(1)(A)(i) and § 1.1411-4(a)(1)(i). Pursuant to paragraph (e)(1)(iii) of this section, A decreases A's modified adjusted gross income for section 1411 purposes by $10,000 in 2014, and pursuant to paragraph (d)(1)(i) of this section, A's adjusted basis is not increased by $10,000 and remains at $500,000. In 2015, pursuant to paragraph (c)(2)(i) of this section, A includes $10,000 of the distribution of previously taxed earnings and profits as a dividend for purposes of determining A's net investment income because $10,000 of the $30,000 distribution is attributable to amounts that A included in gross income for chapter 1 purposes under section 951(a) in a tax year that began after December 31, 2012. Pursuant to paragraph (e)(1)(i) of this section, A increases A's modified adjusted gross income for section 1411 purposes by $10,000 in 2015. Under paragraph (d)(1)(i) of this section, A's adjusted basis is not decreased by the $10,000 that is treated as a dividend for section 1411 purposes, and thus, A's adjusted basis in FC for section 1411 purposes is decreased under section 961 only by $20,000 to $480,000.

*Example 2.* (i) *Facts.* Same facts as *Example 1.* In addition, during 2016, A includes $15,000 in gross income for chapter 1 purposes under section 951(a)(1)(A) with respect to FC. As a result, A's basis in the stock of FC for chapter 1 purposes increases by $15,000 to $495,000 pursuant to section 961(a). During 2017, A sells all of A's shares of FC for $550,000 and, prior to the application of section 1248, recognizes $55,000 ($550,000 minus $495,000) of long-term capital gain for chapter 1 purposes. For purposes of calculating the amount included in income as a dividend pursuant to section 1248(a) for chapter 1 purposes, the earnings and profits of FC attributable to A's shares in FC which were accumulated after December 31,1962 and during the period which A held the stock while FC was a controlled foreign corporation is $55,000, $35,000 of which is excluded pursuant to section 1248(d)(1). Therefore, after the application of section 1248, for chapter 1 purposes, upon the sale of the FC stock, A recognizes $35,000 of long-term capital gain and a $20,000 dividend.

(ii) *Results for section 1411 purposes.* (A) In 2016, A does not include the $15,000 section 951(a)(1)(A) income inclusion in A's net investment income under section 1411(c)(1)(A)(i) and § 1.1411-1(a)(1)(i). Pursuant to paragraph (e)(1)(ii) of this section, A decreases A's modified adjusted gross income for section 1411 purposes by $15,000, and, pursuant to paragraph (d)(1)(i) of this section, A's adjusted basis remains at $480,000.

(B) During 2017, prior to the application of section 1248, A recognizes $70,000 ($550,000 minus $480,000) of gain for section 1411 purposes. Pursuant to paragraph (c)(3) of this section, for section 1411 purposes, section 1248(a) applies to the gain on the sale of FC calculated for section 1411 purposes ($70,000) and section 1248(d)(1) does not apply, except with respect to the $20,000 of earnings and profits of FC that are attributable to amounts previously included in income for chapter 1 purposes under section 951 for a taxable year beginning before December 31, 2012. Accordingly, for purposes of calculating the amount of income includible as a dividend under section 1248(a), A has $55,000 of earnings and profits, $20,000 of which is excluded pursuant to section 1248(d)(1). Therefore, after the application of section 1248, for section 1411 purposes A has $35,000 of long-term capital gain and a $35,000 dividend. For purposes of calculating net investment income in 2017, A includes $35,000 as a dividend under section 1411(c)(1)(A)(i) and § 1.1411-4(a)(1)(i) and $35,000 as a gain under section 1411(c)(1)(A)(iii) and § 1.1411-4(a)(1)(iii).

*Example 3.* (i) *Facts.* Same facts as *Example 2,* except that A timely makes an election under paragraph (g)(4)(i) of this section for 2014 (and thus for all subsequent years).

(ii) *Results for section 1411 purposes.* A does not have any adjustments to A's modified adjusted gross income for section 1411 purposes for 2014, 2015, 2016 or 2017 because the election under paragraph (g)(4)(i) of this section was timely made. Pursuant to paragraph (g)(2) of this section, for purposes of calculating A's net investment income in 2014, the $10,000 that A included in income for chapter 1 purposes under section 951(a) is net investment income for purposes of section 1411(c)(1)(A)(i) and §1.1411-4(a)(1)(i). A has no amount of net investment income with respect to FC in 2015. Pursuant to paragraph (g)(2) of this section, for purposes of calculating A's net investment income in 2016, the $15,000 that A included in income for chapter 1 purposes under section 951(a) is net investment income for purposes of section 1411(c)(1)(A)(i) and §1.1411-4(a)(1)(i). For purposes of calculating A's net investment income in 2017, the amount of gain on the disposition of the FC shares is the same as the amount calculated for chapter 1 purposes. Applying section 1248, A includes $35,000 as a gain under section 1411(c)(1)(A)(iii) and §1.1411-4(a)(1)(iii), and $20,000 as a dividend under section 1411(c)(1)(A)(i) and §1.1411-4(a)(1)(i).

*Example 4. Domestic partnership holding QEF stock.* (i) *Facts.* (A) C, a United States citizen, owns a 50% interest in PRS, a domestic partnership. D, a United States citizen, and E, a United States citizen, each own a 25% interest in PRS. All allocations of partnership income and losses are pro rata based on ownership interests. PRS owns an interest in QEF, a foreign corporation that is a passive foreign investment company (within the meaning of section 1297(a)). PRS, a United States person, made an election under section 1295 with respect to QEF applicable to the first year of its holding period in QEF. As of December 31, 2012, for chapter 1 purposes, C's basis in his partnership interest is $100,000, D's basis in his partnership interest is $50,000, E's basis in his partnership interest is $50,000, and PRS's adjusted basis in its QEF stock is $80,000, which includes an increase in basis under section 1293(d) of $40,000. As of December 31, 2012, the amount of QEF's earnings that have been included in income by PRS under section 1293(a), but have not been distributed by QEF, is $40,000. PRS also has cash of $60,000 and domestic C corporation stock with an adjusted basis of $60,000. During 2013, PRS does not include any amounts in income under section 1293(a) with respect to QEF, PRS does not receive any distributions from QEF, and there are no adjustments to the basis of C, D, or E in their interests in PRS.

(B) During 2014, PRS has income of $40,000 under section 1293(a) with respect to QEF and has no other partnership income. PRS does not make an election under paragraph (g) of this section.

(C) During 2015, QEF distributes $60,000 to PRS. PRS has no income for the year.

(ii) *Results for 2014.* (A) For chapter 1 purposes, as a result of the $40,000 income inclusion under section 1293(a), PRS's basis in its QEF stock is increased by $40,000 under section 1293(d)(1) to $120,000. Under §1.1293-1(c)(1) and section 702, C's, D's, and E's distributive shares of the section 1293(a) income inclusion are $20,000, $10,000, and $10,000, respectively. Under section 705(a)(1)(A), C increases his adjusted basis in his partnership interest by $20,000 to $120,000, and D and E each increase his adjusted basis in his partnership interest by $10,000 to $60,000.

(B) For section 1411 purposes, pursuant to paragraph (d)(1)(ii) of this section, PRS's basis in QEF is not increased by the $40,000 income inclusion (it remains at $80,000). Because PRS did not make an election under paragraph (g) of this section, C, D and E do not have net investment income with respect to the income inclusion, and pursuant to paragraph (d)(2) of this section, they do not increase their adjusted bases in their interests in PRS (each remains at $50,000). Pursuant to paragraph (e)(1)(ii) of this section, C reduces his modified adjusted gross income by $20,000, and D and E each reduce their modified adjusted gross income by $10,000.

(iii) *Results for 2015.* (A) For chapter 1 purposes, the distribution of $60,000 from QEF to PRS is not a dividend under section 1293(c), and PRS decreases its basis in QEF by $60,000 under section 1293(d)(2) to $60,000.

(B) Pursuant to paragraph (c)(1)(i) of this section, $40,000 of the distribution is a dividend for section 1411 purposes because PRS included $40,000 in gross income for chapter 1 purposes under

section 1293(a) in a tax year that began after December 31, 2012. For section 1411 purposes, pursuant to paragraph (d)(1)(ii) of this section, section 1293(d) will not apply to reduce PRS's basis in QEF to the extent of the $40,000 of the distribution that is treated as a dividend under paragraph (c)(2)(i) of this section. Thus, PRS's basis in QEF is decreased only by $20,000 for purposes of section 1411 and is $60,000. The $40,000 distribution of previously taxed earnings and profits that is treated as a dividend for section 1411 purposes is allocated $20,000 to C, $10,000 to D, and $10,000 to E. Because PRS did not make an election under paragraph (g) of this section, pursuant to paragraph (c)(2)(i) of this section, C has $20,000 of net investment income, and D and E each has $10,000 of net investment income as a result of the distribution by QEF, and pursuant to paragraph (d)(2) of this section, C increases his adjusted basis in PRS by $20,000 to $120,000, and D and E each increases his adjusted basis in PRS by $10,000 to $60,000. Pursuant to paragraph (e)(1)(i) of this section, C increases his modified adjusted gross income by $20,000, and D and E each increases his modified adjusted gross income by $10,000.

*Example 5. Sale of partnership interest.* (i) *Facts.* Same facts as *Example 4.* In addition, in 2016, D sells his entire interest in PRS to F for $100,000.

(ii) *Results for 2016.* For chapter 1 purposes, D has a gain of $40,000 ($100,000 minus $60,000). For section 1411 purposes, D has a gain of $40,000 ($100,000 minus $60,000), and thus, has net investment income of $40,000. No adjustments to modified adjusted gross income are necessary under paragraph (e) of this section.

*Example 6. Domestic partnership's sale of QEF stock.* (i) *Facts.* Same facts as *Example 4.* In addition, in 2016 PRS has income of $60,000 under section 1293(a) with respect to QEF, and in 2017, PRS sells its entire interest in QEF for $170,000.

(ii) *Results for 2016.* (A) For chapter 1 purposes, as a result of the $60,000 income inclusion under section 1293(a), PRS's basis in its QEF stock is increased by $60,000 under section 1293(d)(1) to $120,000. Under §1.1293-1(c)(1) and section 702, C's, D's, and E's distributive shares of the section 1293(a) income inclusion are $30,000, $15,000, and $15,000 respectively. Under section 705(a)(1)(A), C increases his adjusted basis in his partnership interest by $30,000 to $150,000, and D and E each increases his adjusted basis in his partnership interest by $15,000 to $75,000.

(B) For section 1411 purposes, pursuant to paragraph (d)(1)(ii) of this section, PRS's basis in QEF is not increased by the $60,000 income inclusion (it remains at $60,000). Because PRS did not make an election under paragraph (g) of this section, C, D and E do not have net investment income with respect to the income inclusion, and pursuant to paragraph (d)(2) of this section, they do not increase their adjusted bases in their interests in PRS (C remains at $120,000, and D and E each remain at $60,000). Pursuant to paragraph (e)(1)(ii) of this section, C reduces his modified adjusted gross income by $30,000, and D and E each reduce their modified adjusted gross income by $15,000.

(iii) *Results for 2017.* (A) For chapter 1 purposes, PRS has a gain of $50,000 ($170,000 minus $120,000), which is allocated 50% ($25,000) to C, 25% ($12,500) to D, and 25% ($12,500) to E.

(B) Based on PRS's basis in the stock of QEF for section 1411 purposes, PRS has a gain for section 1411 purposes of $110,000 ($170,000 minus $60,000), which in the absence of an election by PRS under paragraph (g) of this section, results in gain of $55,000 to C, $27,500 to D, and $27,500 to E. Therefore, C has net investment income of $55,000, and D and E each have net investment income of $27,500. Pursuant to paragraph (e)(1)(ii) of this section, C increases his modified adjusted gross income by $30,000, and D and E each increase their modified adjusted gross income by $15,000.

(i) *Effective/applicability date.*—This section applies to taxable years beginning after December 31, 2013. However, taxpayers may apply this section to taxable years beginning after December 31, 2012, in accordance with §1.1411-1(f). [Reg. §1.1411-10.]

□ [T.D. 9644, 11-26-2013 (*corrected* 3-31-2014).]

# Withholding of Tax on Nonresident Aliens and Foreign Corporations

## NONRESIDENT ALIENS AND FOREIGN CORPORATIONS

See p. 20,601 for regulations not amended to reflect law changes

### [Reg. §1.1441-0]

**§1.1441-0. Outline of regulation provisions for section 1441.—**
This section lists captions contained in §§1.1441-1 through 1.1441-9.

*§1.1441-1. Requirement for the deduction and withholding of tax on payments to foreign persons.*
  (a) Purpose and scope.
  (b) General rules of withholding.
    (1) Requirement to withhold on payments to foreign persons.

  (2) Determination of payee and payee's status.
    (i) In general.
    (ii) Payments to a U.S. agent of a foreign person.
    (iii) Payments to wholly-owned entities.
      (A) Foreign-owned domestic entity.
      (B) Foreign entity.
    (iv) Payments to a U.S. branch of certain foreign banks or foreign insurance companies
      (A) U.S. branch treated as a U.S. person in certain cases.

(B) Consequences to the withholding agent.

(C) Consequences to the U.S. branch.

(D) Definition of payment to a U.S. branch.

(E) Payments to other U.S. branches.

(v) Payments to a foreign intermediary.

(A) Payments treated as made to persons for whom the intermediary collects the payment.

(B) Payments treated as made to foreign intermediary.

(vi) Other payees.

(vii) Rules for reliably associating a payment with a withholding certificate or other appropriate documentation.

(A) Generally.

(B) Special rules applicable to a withholding certificate from a nonqualified intermediary or flow-through entity.

(C) Special rules applicable to a withholding certificate provided by a qualified intermediary that does not assume primary withholding responsibility.

(D) Special rules applicable to a withholding certificate provided by a qualified intermediary that assumes primary withholding responsibility under chapter 3 and chapter 4 of the Internal Revenue Code.

(E) Special rules applicable to a withholding certificate provided by a qualified intermediary that assumes primary Form 1099 reporting and backup withholding responsibility but not primary withholding under chapter 3 and chapter 4.

(F) Special rules applicable to a withholding certificate provided by a qualified intermediary that assumes primary withholding responsibility under chapter 3 and chapter 4 and primary Form 1099 reporting and backup withholding responsibility and a withholding certificate provided by a withholding foreign partnership or a withholding foreign trust.

(3) Presumptions regarding payee's status in the absence of documentation.

(i) General rules.

(ii) Presumptions of classification as individual, corporation, partnership, etc.

(A) In general.

(B) No documentation provided.

(C) Documentary evidence furnished for offshore obligation.

(iii) Presumption of U.S. or foreign status.

(A) Payments to exempt recipients.

(1) In general.

(2) Special rule for withholdable payments made to exempt recipients.

(B) Scholarships and grants.

(C) Pensions, annuities, etc.

(D) Payments with respect to offshore obligations.

(E) Certain payments for services.

(iv) Grace period.

(v) Special rules applicable to payments to foreign intermediaries.

(A) Reliance on claim of status as foreign intermediary.

(B) Beneficial owner documentation or allocation information is lacking or unreliable.

(vi) U.S. branches and territory financial institutions not treated as U.S. persons.

(vii) Joint payees.

(A) In general.

(B) Special rule for offshore obligations.

(viii) Rebuttal of presumptions.

(ix) Effect of reliance on presumptions and of actual knowledge or reason to know otherwise.

(A) General rule.

(B) Actual knowledge or reason to know that amount of withholding is greater than is required under the presumptions or that reporting of the payment is required.

(x) Examples.

(4) List of exemptions from, or reduced rates of, withholding under chapter 3 of the Code.

(5) Establishing foreign status under applicable provisions of chapter 61 of the Code.

(6) Rules of withholding for payments by a foreign intermediary or certain U.S. branches.

(i) In general.

(ii) Examples.

(7) Liability for failure to obtain documentation timely or to act in accordance with applicable presumptions.

(i) General rule.

(ii) Proof that tax liability has been satisfied.

(A) In general.

(B) Special rule for establishing that income is effectively connected with the conduct of a U.S. trade or business.

(iii) Liability for interest and penalties.

(iv) Special rule for determining validity of withholding certificate containing inconsequential errors.

(v) Special effective date.

(8) Adjustments, refunds, or credits of overwithheld amounts.

(9) Payments to joint owners.

(c) Definitions.

(1) Withholding.

(2) Foreign and U.S. person.

(i) In general.

(ii) Dual residents.

(3) Individual.

(i) Alien individual.

(ii) Nonresident alien individual.

(4) Certain foreign corporations.

(5) Financial institution and foreign financial institution (or FFI).

(6) Beneficial owner.

(i) General rule.

(ii) Special rules.

(A) General rule.

(B) Foreign partnerships.

(C) Foreign simple trusts and foreign grantor trusts.

(D) Other foreign trusts and foreign estates.

(7) Withholding agent.

(8) Person.

(9) Source of income.

(10) Chapter 3 of the Code (or chapter 3).

(11) Reduced rate.

(12) Payee.

(13) Intermediary.

(14) Nonqualified intermediary.

(15) Qualified intermediary.

(16) Withholding certificate.

(17) Documentary evidence; other appropriate documentation.

(18) Documentation.

(19) Payor.

(20) Exempt recipient.

(21) Non-exempt recipient.

(22) Reportable amounts.

(23) Flow-through entity.

(24) Foreign simple trust.

(25) Foreign complex trust.

(26) Foreign grantor trust.

(27) Partnership.

(28) Nonwithholding foreign partnership (or NWP).

(29) Withholding foreign partnership (or WP).

(30) Possession of the United States or U.S. territory.

(31) Amount subject to chapter 3 withholding.

(32) EIN.

(33) Flow-through withholding certificate.

(34) Foreign payee.

(35) Intermediary withholding certificate.

(36) Nonwithholding foreign trust (or NWT).

(37) Payment with respect to an offshore obligation.

(38) Permanent residence address.

(i) In general.

(ii) Hold mail instruction.

(39) Standing instructions to pay amounts.

(40) Territory financial institution.

(41) TIN.

(42) Withholding foreign trust (or WT).

(43) Certified deemed-compliant FFI.

(44) Chapter 3 withholding rate pool.

(45) Chapter 3 status.

(46) Chapter 4 of the Code (or chapter 4).

(47) Chapter 4 status.

(48) Chapter 4 withholding rate pool.

(49) Deemed-compliant FFI.

(50) GIIN (or Global Intermediary Identification Number).

(51) NFFE.

(52) Nonparticipating FFI.

(53) Participating FFI.

(54) Preexisting obligation.

(55) Registered deemed-compliant FFI.

(56) Withholdable payment.

(d) Beneficial owner's or payee's claim of U.S. status.

(1) In general.

(2) Payments for which a Form W-9 is otherwise required.

(3) Payments for which a Form W-9 is not otherwise required.

(4) When a payment to an intermediary or flow-through entity may be treated as made to a U.S. payee.

(e) Beneficial owner's claim of foreign status.

(1) Withholding agent's reliance.

(i) In general.

(ii) Payments that a withholding agent may treat as made to a foreign person that is a beneficial owner.

(A) General rule.

(B) Additional requirements.

(2) Beneficial owner withholding certificate.

(i) In general.

(ii) Requirements for validity of certificate.

(A) In general.

(B) Requirement to collect foreign TIN and date of birth.

(1) In general.

(2) Definitions.

(3) Requirements for reasonable explanation of the absence of a foreign TIN.

(4) Exceptions to the requirement to obtain a foreign TIN (or reasonable explanation for its absence).

(i) Jurisdictions with which the United States does not have an agreement relating to the exchange of tax information.

(ii) Jurisdictions that do not issue foreign TINs.

(iii) Account holder that is a government, international organization, foreign central bank of issue, or resident of a U.S. territory.

(5) Transition rules for the foreign TIN requirement for a beneficial owner withholding certificate signed before January 1, 2018.

(i) Payments made before January 1, 2020.

(ii) Payments made after December 31, 2019.

(iii) Limitation on standard of knowledge.

(6) Transition rule for the date of birth requirement for a beneficial owner withholding certificate signed before January 1, 2018.

(3) Intermediary, flow-through, or U.S. branch withholding certificate.

(i) In general.

(ii) Intermediary withholding certificate from a qualified intermediary.

(iii) Intermediary withholding certificate from a nonqualified intermediary.

(iv) Withholding statement provided by nonqualified intermediary.

(A) In general.

(B) General requirements.

(C) Content of withholding statement.

(1) In general.

(2) Nonqualified intermediary withholding statement for withholdable payments.

(3) Alternative withholding statement.

(4) Example.

(D) Alternative procedures.

(1) In general.

(2) Withholding rate pools.

(i) In general.

(ii) Withholding rate pools for chapter 4 purposes.

(3) Allocation information.

(4) Failure to provide allocation information.

(5) Cure provision.

(6) Form 1042-S reporting in case of allocation failure.

(7) Liability for tax, interest, and penalties.

(8) Applicability to flow-through entities and certain U.S. branches.

(E) Notice procedures.

(v) Withholding certificate from certain U.S. branches (including territory financial institutions).

(vi) Reportable amounts.

(4) Applicable rules.

(i) Who may sign the certificate.

(A) In general.

(B) Electronic signatures.

(ii) Period of validity.

(A) General rule.

(1) Withholding certificates and documentary evidence.

(2) Documentary evidence for treaty claims and treaty statements.

(B) Indefinite validity period.

(C) Withholding certificate for effectively connected income.

(D) Change in circumstances.

(1) Defined.

(2) Obligation to notify a withholding agent of a change in circumstances.

(3) Withholding agent's obligation with respect to a change in circumstances.

(iii) Retention of documentation.

(iv) Electronic transmission of information

(A) In general.

(B) Requirements.

(1) In general.

(2) Same information as paper Form W-8.

(3) Perjury statement and signature requirements.

(i) Perjury statement.

(ii) Electronic signature.

(4) Requests for electronic Form W-8 data.

(C) Form 8233.

(D) Forms and documentary evidence received by facsimile or email.

(E) Third party repositories.

(F) Examples.

(1) Example 1.

(2) Example 2.

(3) Example 3.

(v) Additional procedures for certificates provided electronically.

(vi) Acceptable substitute form.

(vii) Requirement of taxpayer identifying number.

(viii) Reliance rules.

(A) Classification.

(B) Status of payee as an intermediary or as a person acting for its own account.

(C) Reliance on a prior version of a withholding certificate.

(ix) Certificates to be furnished to withholding agent for each obligation unless exception applies.

(A) Exception for certain branch or account systems or system maintained by agent.

(B) Reliance on certification provided by introducing brokers.

(1) In general.

(2) Example.

(C) Reliance on documentation and certifications provided between principals and agents.

(1) Withholding agent as agent.

(2) Withholding agent as principal.

(D) Reliance upon documentation for accounts acquired in merger or bulk acquisition for value.

(5) Qualified intermediaries.

(i) In general.

(ii) Definition of qualified intermediary.

(iii) Withholding agreement.

(A) In general.

(B) Terms of the withholding agreement.

(iv) Assignment of primary withholding responsibility.

(v) Withholding statement.

(A) In general.

(B) Content of withholding statement.

(C) Withholding rate pools
(1) In general.
(2) Withholding rate pool requirements for a withholdable payment.
(3) Alternative procedure for U.S. non-exempt recipients.
(D) Example.
(6) Qualified derivatives dealers.
(f) Effective/applicability date.
(1) In general.
(2) Lack of documentation for past years.
(3) Special rules related to section 871(m).

§ 1.1441-2. *Amounts subject to withholding.*
(a) In general.
(b) Fixed or determinable annual or periodical income.
(1) In general.
(i) Definition.
(ii) Manner of payment.
(iii) Determinability of amount.
(2) Exceptions.
(3) Original issue discount.
(i) Amount subject to tax.
(ii) Amounts subject to withholding.
(iii) Exceptions to withholding.
(4) Securities lending transactions and equivalent transactions.
(5) REMIC residual interests.
(6) Dividend equivalents.
(c) Other income subject to withholding.
(d) Exceptions to withholding where no money or property is paid or lack of knowledge.
(1) General rule.
(2) Cancellation of debt.
(3) Satisfaction of liability following underwithholding by withholding agent.
(4) Withholding exemption inapplicable.
(e) Payment.
(1) General rule.
(2) Income allocated under section 482.
(3) Blocked income.
(4) Special rules for dividends.
(5) Certain interest accrued by a foreign corporation.
(6) Payments other than in U.S. dollars.
(7) Payments of dividend equivalents.
(i) In general.
(ii) Payment.
(iii) Premiums and other upfront payments.
(f) Effective/applicability date.

§ 1.1441-3. *Determination of amounts to be withheld.*
(a) General rule.
(1) Withholding on gross amount.
(2) Coordination with chapter 4.
(b) Withholding on payments on certain obligations.
(1) Withholding at time of payment of interest.
(2) No withholding between interest payment dates.
(i) In general.
(ii) Anti-abuse rule.
(c) Corporate distributions.
(1) General rule.
(2) Exception to withholding on distributions.
(i) In general.
(ii) Reasonable estimate of accumulated and current earnings and profits on the date of payment.
(A) General rule.
(B) Procedures in case of underwithholding.
(C) Reliance by intermediary on reasonable estimate.
(D) Example.
(3) Special rules in the case of distributions from a regulated investment company.
(i) General rule
(ii) Reliance by intermediary on reasonable estimate.
(4) Coordination with withholding under section 1445.
(i) In general.
(A) Withholding under section 1441.
(B) Withholding under both sections 1441 and 1445.
(C) Coordination with REIT/QIE withholding.
(ii) Intermediary reliance rule.
(d) Withholding on payments that include an undetermined amount of income.

(1) In general.
(2) Withholding on certain gains.
(e) Payments other than in U.S. dollars.
(1) In general.
(2) Payments in foreign currency.
(f) Tax liability of beneficial owner satisfied by withholding agent.
(1) General rule.
(2) Example.
(g) Conduit financing arrangements
(1) Duty to withhold.
(2) Effective date.
(h) Dividend equivalents.
(1) Withholding on gross amount.
(2) Reliance by withholding agent on reasonable determinations.
(3) Effective/applicability date.
(i) Effective/applicability date.

§ 1.1441-4. *Exemptions from withholding for certain effectively connected income and other amounts.*
(a) Certain income connected with a U.S. trade or business.
(1) In general.
(2) Withholding agent's reliance on a claim of effectively connected income.
(i) In general.
(ii) Special rules for U.S. branches of foreign persons.
(A) U.S. branches of certain foreign banks or foreign insurance companies.
(B) Other U.S. branches.
(3) Income on notional principal contracts.
(i) General rule.
(ii) Exception for certain payments.
(iii) Exception for specified notional principal contracts.
(b) Compensation for personal services of an individual.
(1) Exemption from withholding.
(2) Manner of obtaining withholding exemption under tax treaty.
(i) In general.
(ii) Withholding certificate claiming withholding exemption.
(iii) Review by withholding agent.
(iv) Acceptance by withholding agent.
(v) Copies of Form 8233.
(3) Withholding agreements.
(4) Final payment exemption.
(5) Requirement of return.
(6) Personal exemption.
(i) In general.
(ii) Multiple exemptions.
(iii) Special rule where both certain scholarship and compensation income are received.
(c) Special rules for scholarship and fellowship income.
(1) In general.
(2) Alternate withholding election.
(d) Annuities received under qualified plans.
(e) Per diem of certain alien trainees.
(f) Failure to receive withholding certificates timely or to act in accordance with applicable presumptions.
(g) Effective/applicability date.

§ 1.1441-5. *Withholding on payments to partnerships, trusts, and estates.*
(a) In general.
(b) Rules applicable to U.S. partnerships, trusts, and estates.
(1) Payments to U.S. partnerships, trusts, and estates.
(2) Withholding by U.S. payees.
(i) U.S. partnerships.
(A) In general.
(B) Effectively connected income of partners.
(ii) U.S. simple trusts.
(iii) U.S. complex trusts and U.S. estates.
(iv) U.S. grantor trusts.
(v) Subsequent distribution
(vi) Coordination with chapter 4 requirements for U.S. partnerships, trusts, and estates.
(c) Foreign partnerships.
(1) Determination of payee.
(i) Payments treated as made to partners.
(ii) Payments treated as made to the partnership.
(iii) Rules for reliably associating a payment with documentation.

**Reg. § 1.1441-0**

(iv) Coordination with chapter 4 for payments made to foreign partnerships.

    (v) Examples.

  (2) Withholding foreign partnerships.

    (i) Reliance on claim of withholding foreign partnership status.

    (ii) Withholding agreement.

    (iii) Withholding responsibility.

    (iv) Withholding certificate from a withholding foreign partnership.

  (3) Nonwithholding foreign partnerships.

    (i) Reliance on claim of foreign partnership status.

    (ii) Reliance on claim of reduced withholding by a partnership for its partners.

    (iii) Withholding certificate from a nonwithholding foreign partnership.

    (iv) Withholding statement provided by nonwithholding foreign partnership and coordination with chapter 4.

    (v) Withholding and reporting by a foreign partnership.

  (d) Presumption rules.

    (1) In general.

    (2) Determination of partnership status as U.S. or foreign in the absence of documentation.

    (3) Determination of partners' status in the absence of certain documentation.

    (4) Determination by a withholding foreign partnership of the status of its partners.

  (e) Foreign trusts and estates.

    (1) In general.

    (2) Payments to foreign complex trusts and foreign estates.

    (3) Payees of payments to foreign simple trusts and foreign grantor trusts.

    (i) Payments for which beneficiaries and owners are payees.

    (ii) Payments for which trust is payee.

    (iii) Coordination with chapter 4 for payments made to foreign simple trusts and foreign grantor trusts.

    (4) Reliance on claim of foreign complex trust or foreign estate status.

    (5) Foreign simple trust and foreign grantor trust.

    (i) Reliance on claim of foreign simple trust or foreign grantor trust status.

    (ii) Reliance on claim of reduced withholding by a foreign simple trust or foreign grantor trust for its beneficiaries or owners.

    (iii) Withholding certificate from foreign simple trust or foreign grantor trust.

    (iv) Withholding statement provided by foreign simple trust or foreign grantor trust and coordination with chapter 4.

    (v) Withholding foreign trusts.

    (6) Presumption rules

    (i) In general

    (ii) Determination of status as U.S. or foreign trust or estate in the absence of documentation.

    (iii) Determination of beneficiary or owner's status in the absence of certain documentation.

  (f) Failure to receive withholding certificate timely or to act in accordance with applicable presumptions.

  (g) Effective/applicability date.

**§1.1441-6. Claim of reduced withholding under an income tax treaty.**

  (a) In general.

  (b) Reliance on claim of reduced withholding under an income tax treaty.

    (1) In general.

    (i) Identification of limitation on benefits provisions.

    (ii) Reason to know based on existence of treaty.

    (2) Payment to fiscally transparent entity.

    (i) In general.

    (ii) Certification by qualified intermediary.

    (iii) Dual treatment.

    (iv) Examples.

    (3) Certified TIN.

    (4) Claim of benefits under an income tax treaty by a U.S. person.

  (c) Exemption from requirement to furnish a taxpayer identifying number and special documentary evidence rules for certain income.

    (1) General rule.

    (2) Income to which special rules apply.

    (3) Certificate of residence.

    (4) Documentary evidence establishing residence in the treaty country.

    (i) Individuals.

    (ii) Persons other than individuals.

    (5) Statements regarding entitlement to treaty benefits.

    (i) Statement regarding conditions under a limitation on benefits provision.

    (ii) Statement regarding whether the taxpayer derives the income.

  (d) Joint owners.

  (e) Competent authority.

  (f) Failure to receive withholding certificate timely.

  (g) Special taxpayer identifying number rule for certain foreign individuals claiming treaty benefits.

    (1) General rule.

    (2) Special rule.

    (3) Requirement that an ITIN be requested during the first business day following payment.

    (4) Definition of unexpected payment.

    (5) Examples.

  (h) Dividend equivalents.

  (i) Effective/applicability dates.

    (1) General rule.

    (2) Dividend equivalents.

**§1.1441-7. General provisions relating to withholding agents.**

  (a) Withholding agent defined.

    (1) In general.

    (2) Withholding agent with respect to dividend equivalents.

    (3) Examples.

    (4) Effective/applicability date.

  (b) Standards of knowledge.

    (1) In general.

    (2) Reason to know.

    (3) Financial institutions—limits on reason to know.

    (i) In general.

    (ii) Limits on reason to know for preexisting obligations.

    (4) Rules applicable to withholding certificates.

    (i) In general.

    (ii) Examples.

    (5) Withholding certificate—establishment of foreign status.

    (i) Classification of U.S. status, U.S. address, or U.S. telephone number.

    (ii) U.S. place of birth.

    (iii) Standing instructions with respect to offshore obligations.

    (6) Withholding certificate—claim of reduced rate of withholding under.

    (i) Permanent residence address.

    (ii) Mailing address.

    (iii) Standing instructions.

    (7) Documentary evidence.

    (8) Documentary evidence—establishment of foreign status.

    (i) Documentary evidence received prior to January 1, 2001.

    (ii) Documentary evidence received after December 31, 2000.

      (A) Treatment of individual's foreign status.

      (B) Presumption of entity's foreign status.

    (iii) U.S. place of birth.

    (iv) Standing instructions with respect of offshore obligations.

    (9) Documentary evidence—claim of reduced rate of withholding under treaty.

    (i) Permanent residence address and mailing address.

    (ii) Standing instructions.

    (10) Indirect account holders.

    (11) Limits on reason to know for multiple obligations belonging to a single person.

    (12) Reasonable explanation supporting claim of foreign status.

    (13) Additional guidance.

  (c) Agent.

    (1) In general.

    (2) Authorized agent.

    (3) Liability of withholding agent acting through an agent.

  (d) United States obligations.

  (e) Assumed obligations.

  (f) Conduit financing arrangements.

    (1) Liability of withholding agent.

    (2) Exception for withholding agents that do not know of conduit financing arrangement.

    (i) In general.

☐ [*T.D.* 8734, 10-6-97 (T.D. 8804 delayed the effective date of T.D. 8734 from January 1, 1999, to January 1, 2000; T.D. 8856 further delayed the effective date of T.D. 8734 until January 1, 2001). *Amended by T.D.* 8881, 5-15-2000; *T.D.* 9023, 11-21-2002; *T.D.* 9272, 7-31-2006, *T.D.* 9415, 7-11-2008, *T.D.* 9808, 12-30-2016 (corrected 6-29-2017) *and T.D.* 9890, 12-27-2019.]

[Reg. § 1.1441-1]

**§ 1.1441-1. Requirement for the deduction and withholding of tax on payments to foreign persons.**—(a) *Purpose and scope.*—This section, § § 1.1441-2 through 1.1441-9, and 1.1443-1 provide rules for withholding under sections 1441, 1442, and 1443 when a payment is made to a foreign person. This section provides definitions of terms used in chapter 3 of the Internal Revenue Code (Code) and regulations thereunder. It prescribes procedures to determine whether an amount must be withheld under chapter 3 of the Code and documentation that a withholding agent may rely upon to determine the status of a payee or a beneficial owner as a U.S. person or as a foreign person and other relevant characteristics of the payee that may affect a withholding agent's obligation to withhold under chapter 3 of the Code and the regulations thereunder. Special procedures regarding payments to foreign persons that act as intermediaries are also provided. Section 1.1441-2 defines the income subject to withholding under sections 1441, 1442, and 1443 and the regulations under these sections. Section 1.1441-3 provides rules regarding the amount subject to withholding and rules for coordinating withholding under this section with withholding under section 1445 and under chapter 4 of the Code. Section 1.1441-4 provides exemptions from withholding for, among other things, certain income effectively connected with the conduct of a trade or business in the United States, including certain compensation for the personal services of an individual. Section 1.1441-5 provides rules for withholding on payments made to flow-through entities and other similar arrangements. Section 1.1441-6 provides rules for claiming a reduced rate of withholding under an income tax treaty. Section 1.1441-7 defines the term withholding agent and provides due diligence rules governing a withholding agent's obligation to withhold. Section 1.1441-8 provides rules for relying on claims of exemption from withholding for payments to a foreign government, an international organization, a foreign central bank of issue, or the Bank for International Settlements. Sections 1.1441-9 and 1.1443-1 provide rules for relying on claims of exemption from withholding for payments to foreign tax exempt organizations and foreign private foundations.

(b) *General rules of withholding.*—(1) *Requirement to withhold on payments to foreign persons.*—A withholding agent must withhold 30 percent of any payment of an amount subject to withholding made to a payee that is a foreign person unless it can reliably associate the payment with documentation upon which it can rely to treat the payment as made to a payee that is a U.S. person or as made to a beneficial owner that is a foreign person entitled to a reduced rate of withholding. However, a withholding agent making a payment to a foreign person need not withhold where the foreign person assumes responsibility for withholding on the payment under chapter 3 of the Code and the regulations thereunder as a qualified intermediary (see paragraphs (e)(5) and (e)(6) of this section), as a U.S. branch of a foreign person (see paragraph (b)(2)(iv) of this section), as a withholding foreign partnership (see § 1.1441-5(c)(2)(i)), or as a withholding foreign trust (see § 1.1441-5(e)(5)(v)). When withholding under chapter 4 was applied to a payment, the withholding obligation under this section is satisfied. See § 1.1441-3(a)(2). This section (dealing with general rules of withholding and claims of foreign or U.S. status by a payee or a beneficial owner) and § § 1.1441-4, 1.1441-5, 1.1441-6, 1.1441-8, 1.1441-9, and 1.1443-1 provide rules for determining whether documentation is required as a condition for reducing the rate of withholding on a payment to a foreign beneficial owner or to a U.S. payee and if so, the nature of the documentation upon which a withholding agent may rely in order to reduce such rate. Paragraph (b)(2) of this section prescribes the rules for the determination of who the payee is, the extent to which a payment is treated as made to a foreign payee, and reliable association of a payment with documentation. Paragraph (b)(3) of this section describes the applicable presumptions for determining the payee's status as U.S. or foreign and the payee's other characteristics (*e.g.,* as an owner or intermediary, as an individual, partnership, corporation, etc.). Paragraph (b)(4) of this section lists the types of payments for which the 30-percent withholding rate may be reduced. Because the treatment of a payee as a U.S. or a foreign person also has consequences for purposes of making an information return under the provisions of chapter 61 of the Code and for withholding under other provisions of the Code, such as sections 3402, 3405, or 3406, paragraph (b)(5) of this section lists applicable provisions outside chapter 3 of the Code that require certain payees to establish their foreign status (*e.g.,* in order to be exempt from information reporting). Paragraph (b)(6) of this section describes the withholding obligations of a foreign person making a payment that it has received in its capacity as an intermediary. Paragraph (b)(7) of this section describes the liability of a withholding agent that fails to withhold at the required 30-percent rate in the absence of documentation. Paragraph (b)(8) of this section deals with adjustments and refunds in the case of overwithholding. Paragraph (b)(9) of this section deals with determining the status of the payee when the payment is jointly owned. See paragraph (c)(6) of this section for a definition of beneficial owner. See § 1.1441-7(a) for a definition of withholding agent. See § 1.1441-2(a) for the determination of an amount subject to withholding. See § 1.1441-2(e) for the definition of a payment and when it is considered made. Except as otherwise provided, the provisions of this section apply only for purposes of determining a withholding agent's obligation to withhold under chapter 3 of the Code and the regulations thereunder.

(2) *Determination of payee and payee's status.*—(i) *In general.*—Except as otherwise provided in this paragraph (b)(2) and § 1.1441-5(c)(1) and (e)(3), a payee is the person to whom a payment is made, regardless of whether such person is the beneficial owner of the amount (as defined in paragraph (c)(6) of this section). A foreign payee is a payee who is a foreign person. A U.S. payee is a payee who is a U.S. person. Generally, the determination by a withholding agent of the U.S. or foreign status of a payee and of its other relevant characteristics (*e.g.,* as a beneficial owner or intermediary, or as an individual, corporation, or flow-through entity) is made on the basis of a withholding certificate that is a Form W-8 or a Form 8233 (indicating foreign status of the payee or beneficial owner) or a Form W-9 (indicating U.S. status of the payee). The provisions of this paragraph (b)(2), paragraph (b)(3) of this section, and § 1.1441-5(c), (d), and (e) dealing with determinations of payee and applicable presumptions in the absence of documentation apply only to payments of amounts subject to withholding under chapter 3 of the Code (within the meaning of § 1.1441-2(a)). However, for a payment that is both an amount subject to withholding under chapter 3 and a withholdable payment under chapter 4, first apply the rules of § 1.1471-3 for determining the payee of a withholdable payment under chapter 4 and the applicable presumptions in the absence of documentation applicable to such payments. See also § 1.6049-5(d) for payments of amounts that are not subject to withholding under chapter 3 of the Code (or the regulations thereunder) but that may be reportable under provisions of chapter 61 of the Code (and the regulations thereunder). See paragraph (d) of this section for docu-

mentation upon which the withholding agent may rely in order to treat the payee or beneficial owner as a U.S. person. See paragraph (e) of this section for documentation upon which the withholding agent may rely in order to treat the payee or beneficial owner as a foreign person. For applicable presumptions of status in the absence of documentation, see paragraph (b)(3) of this section and §1.1441-5(d). For definitions of a foreign person and U.S. person, see paragraph (c)(2) of this section.

(ii) *Payments to a U.S. agent of a foreign person.*—A withholding agent making a payment to a U.S. person (other than to a U.S. branch that is treated as a U.S. person pursuant to paragraph (b)(2)(iv) of this section) and who has actual knowledge that the U.S. person receives the payment as an agent of a foreign person must treat the payment as made to the foreign person. However, the withholding agent may treat the payment as made to the U.S. person if the U.S. person is a financial institution and the withholding agent has no reason to believe that the financial institution will not comply with its obligation to withhold. See paragraph (c)(5) of this section for the definition of a financial institution.

(iii) *Payments to wholly-owned entities.*—(A) *Foreign-owned domestic entity.*—A payment to a wholly-owned domestic entity that is disregarded for federal tax purposes under §301.7701-2(c)(2) of this chapter as an entity separate from its owner and whose single owner is a foreign person shall be treated as a payment to the owner of the entity, subject to the provisions of paragraph (b)(2)(iv) of this section. For purposes of this paragraph (b)(2)(iii)(A), a domestic entity means a person that would be treated as a U.S. person if it had an election in effect under §301.7701-3(c)(1)(i) of this chapter to be treated as a corporation. For example, a limited liability company, A, organized under the laws of the State of Delaware, opens an account at a U.S. bank. Upon opening of the account, the bank requests A to furnish a Form W-9 as required under section 6049(a) and the regulations under that section. A does not have an election in effect under §301.7701-3(c)(1)(i) of this chapter and, therefore, is not treated as an organization taxable as a corporation, including for purposes of the exempt recipient provisions in §1.6049-4(c)(1). If A has a single owner and the owner is a foreign person (as defined in paragraph (c)(2) of this section), then A may not furnish a Form W-9 because it may not represent that it is a U.S. person for purposes of the provisions of chapters 3, 4, and 61 of the Code, and section 3406. Therefore, A must furnish a Form W-8 with the name, address, and taxpayer identifying number (TIN) (if required) of the foreign person who is the single owner in the same manner as if the account were opened directly by the foreign single owner. See §§1.894-1(d) and 1.1441-6(b)(2) for special rules where the entity's owner is claiming a reduced rate of withholding under an income tax treaty.

(B) *Foreign entity.*—A payment to a wholly-owned foreign entity that is disregarded under §301.7701-2(c)(2) of this chapter as an entity separate from its owner shall be treated as a payment to the single owner of the entity, subject to the provisions of paragraph (b)(2)(iv) of this section if the foreign owner has a U.S. branch in the United States. For purposes of this paragraph (b)(2)(iii)(B), a foreign entity means a person that would be treated as a foreign person if it had an election in effect under §301.7701-3(c)(1)(i) of this chapter to be treated as a corporation. See §§1.894-1T(d) and 1.1441-6(b)(2) for special rules where the foreign entity or its owner is claiming a reduced rate of withholding under an income tax treaty. Thus, for example, if the foreign entity's single owner is a U.S. person, the payment shall be treated as a payment to a U.S. person. Therefore, based on the saving clause in U.S. income tax treaties, such an entity may not claim benefits under an income tax treaty even if the entity is organized in a country with which the United States has an income tax treaty in effect and treats the entity as a non-fiscally transparent entity. See §1.894-1T(d)(6), *Example 10.* Unless it has actual knowledge or reason to know that the foreign entity to whom the payment is made is disregarded under §301.7701-2(c)(2) of this chapter, a withholding agent may treat a foreign entity as an entity separate from its owner unless it can reliably associate the payment with a withholding certificate from the entity's owner.

(iv) *Payments to a U.S. branch of certain foreign banks or foreign insurance companies.*—(A) *U.S. branch treated as a U.S. person in certain cases.*—A payment to a U.S. branch of a foreign person is a payment to a foreign person. However, a U.S. branch of a foreign person that is described in this paragraph (b)(2)(iv)(A) may agree to be treated as a U.S. person for purposes of withholding on specified payments to the U.S. branch. If a U.S. branch agrees to be treated as a U.S. person with a withholding agent, it is required to act as a U.S. person with respect to all other withholding agents, including when acting as an intermediary with respect to withholdable payments for purposes of chapter 4. See §1.1471-3(a)(3)(vi). In such cases, the U.S. branch is treated as a payee that is a U.S. person. See paragraph (C) of this section for additional requirements for the U.S. branch when treated

as a payor that is a U.S. person. Notwithstanding the preceding sentence, a withholding agent making a payment to a U.S. branch treated as a U.S. person under this paragraph (b)(2)(iv)(A) shall not treat the branch as a U.S. person for purposes of reporting the payment made to the branch. Therefore, a payment to such U.S. branch shall be reported on Form 1042-S under §1.1461-1(c) and §1.1474-1(d)(1)(i) for a payment of U.S. source FDAP income that is a chapter 4 reportable amount as defined in §1.1471-1(b)(18). Further, a U.S. branch that is treated as a U.S. person under this paragraph (b)(2)(iv)(A) shall not be treated as a U.S. person for purposes of the withholding certificate it provides to a withholding agent. Therefore, the U.S. branch must furnish a U.S. branch withholding certificate on a Form W-8IMY as provided in paragraph (e)(3)(v) of this section and not a Form W-9. An agreement to treat a U.S. branch as a U.S. person must be evidenced by a U.S. branch withholding certificate described in paragraph (e)(3)(v) of this section furnished by the U.S. branch to the withholding agent. A U.S. branch described in this paragraph (b)(2)(iv)(A) and eligible to be treated as a U.S. person is any U.S. branch of a foreign bank subject to regulatory supervision by the Federal Reserve Board or a U.S. branch of a foreign insurance company required to file an annual statement on a form approved by the National Association of Insurance Commissioners with the Insurance Department of a State, a Territory, or the District of Columbia. In addition, a territory financial institution (including a territory financial institution that is a flow-through entity) will be treated as a U.S. branch for purposes of this paragraph (b)(2)(iv)(A) and therefore is eligible to be treated as a U.S. person. The Internal Revenue Service (IRS) may approve a list of U.S. branches that may be eligible for treatment as U.S. persons under this paragraph (b)(2)(iv)(A) (see §601.601(d)(2) of this chapter). See §1.6049-5(c)(5)(vi) for the treatment of U.S. branches as U.S. payors if they make a payment that is subject to reporting under chapter 61 of the Code. Also see §1.6049-5(d)(1)(ii) for the treatment of U.S. branches as foreign payees under chapter 61 of the Code.

(B) *Consequences to the withholding agent.*—Any person that is otherwise a withholding agent regarding a payment to a U.S. branch described in paragraph (b)(2)(iv)(A) of this section shall treat the payment in one of the following ways—

(1) As a payment to a U.S. person, in which case the withholding agent is not responsible for withholding on such payment to the extent it can reliably associate the payment with a withholding certificate described in paragraph (e)(3)(v) of this section that has been furnished by the U.S. branch under its agreement with the withholding agent to be treated as U.S. person;

(2) As a payment directly to the persons whose names are on withholding certificates or other appropriate documentation forwarded by the U.S. branch to the withholding agent when no agreement is in effect to treat the U.S. branch as a U.S. person for such payment, to the extent the withholding agent can reliably associate the payment with such certificates or documentation;

(3) As a payment to a foreign person of income that is effectively connected with the conduct of a trade or business in the United States if the withholding agent has obtained an EIN for the branch and cannot reliably associate the payment with a withholding certificate from a U.S. branch (or any other certificate or other appropriate documentation from another person). See §1.1441-4(a)(2)(ii); or

(4) As a payment to a foreign person of income that is not effectively connected with the conduct of a trade or business in the United States if the withholding agent has not obtained an EIN for the branch and cannot reliably associate the payment with a withholding certificate from the U.S. branch.

(C) *Consequences to the U.S. branch.*—A U.S. branch that is treated as a U.S. person under paragraph (b)(2)(iv)(A) of this section shall be treated as a separate person for purposes of section 1441(a) and all other provisions of chapters 3 and 4 of the Code and the regulations thereunder (other than for purposes of reporting the payment to the U.S. branch under §1.1461-1(c) and §1.1474-1(d)(1)(i) for a chapter 4 reportable amount by a withholding agent) or for purposes of the documentation such a branch must furnish under paragraph (e)(3)(v) of this section) for any payment that it receives as such. Thus, the U.S. branch shall be responsible for withholding on a payment as a U.S. person in accordance with the provisions under chapters 3 and 4 of the Code and the regulations thereunder and other applicable withholding provisions of the Code. For this purpose, it shall obtain and retain documentation from payees or beneficial owners of the payments that it receives as an intermediary as a U.S. person in the same manner as if it were a separate entity. For example, if a U.S. branch receives a payment as an intermediary on behalf of customers of its home office and the home office is a qualified intermediary, the U.S. branch must obtain a qualified intermediary withholding certificate described in paragraph (e)(3)(ii) of this section from its home office. Similarly, if a U.S. branch of an FFI treated as a U.S. person receives a payment on behalf of another branch of the FFI that is treated as a nonparticipating FFI, the U.S. branch must withhold on the payment made to the other branch as if it were a separate person to the extent required under chapter 4. In addition, a U.S. branch that has not provided documentation to the withholding agent for a payment that is, in fact, not effectively connected income is a withholding agent with respect to that payment. See paragraph (b)(6) of this section and §1.1441-4(a)(2)(ii).

(D) *Definition of payment to a U.S. branch.*—A payment is treated as a payment to a U.S. branch of a foreign bank or foreign insurance company if the payment is credited to an account maintained in the United States in the name of a U.S. branch of the foreign person, or the payment is made to an address in the United States where the U.S. branch is located and the name of the U.S. branch appears on documents (in written or electronic form) associated with the payment (e.g., the check mailed or a letter addressed to the branch).

(E) *Payments to other U.S. branches.*—Similar withholding procedures may apply to payments to U.S. branches that are not described in paragraph (b)(2)(iv)(A) of this section to the extent permitted by the IRS. Any such branch must establish that its situation is analogous to that of a U.S. branch described in paragraph (b)(2)(iv)(A) of this section. In the alternative, the branch must establish that the withholding and reporting requirements under chapter 3 of the Code and the regulations thereunder impose an undue administrative burden and that the collection of the tax imposed by section 871(a) or 881(a) on the foreign person (or its members in the case of a foreign partnership) will not be jeopardized by the exemption from withholding. Generally, an undue administrative burden will be found to exist in a case where the person entitled to the income, such as a foreign insurance company, receives from the withholding agent income on securities issued by a single corporation, some of which is, and some of which is not, effectively connected with conduct of a trade or business within the United States and the criteria for determining the effective connection are unduly difficult to apply because of the circumstances under which such securities are held. No exemption from withholding shall be granted under this paragraph (b)(2)(iv)(E) unless the person entitled to the income complies with such other requirements as may be imposed by the IRS and unless the IRS is satisfied that the collection of the tax on the income involved will not be jeopardized by the exemption from withholding. The IRS may prescribe such procedures as are necessary to make these determinations (see §601.601(d)(2) of this chapter).

(v) *Payments to a foreign intermediary.*—(A) *Payments treated as made to persons for whom the intermediary collects the payment.*—Except as otherwise provided in paragraph (b)(2)(v)(B) of this section, the payee of a payment to a person that the withholding agent may treat as a foreign intermediary in accordance with the provisions of paragraph (b)(3)(ii)(C) or (b)(3)(v)(A) of this section is the person or persons for whom the intermediary collects the payment. Thus, for example, the payee of a payment that the withholding agent can reliably associate with a withholding certificate from a qualified intermediary (defined in paragraph (e)(5)(ii) of this section) that does not assume primary withholding responsibility or a payment to a nonqualified intermediary are the persons for whom the qualified intermediary or nonqualified intermediary acts and not to the intermediary itself. See paragraph (b)(3)(v) of this section for presumptions that apply if the payment cannot be reliably associated with valid documentation. For similar rules for payments to flow-through entities, see §1.1441-5(c)(1) and (e)(3).

(B) *Payments treated as made to foreign intermediary.*—The payee of a payment to a person that the withholding agent may treat as a qualified intermediary is the qualified intermediary to the extent that the qualified intermediary assumes primary withholding responsibility under paragraph (e)(5)(iv) of this section for the payment. For example if a qualified intermediary assumes primary withholding responsibility under chapter 3 of the Internal Revenue Code but does not assume primary reporting or withholding responsibility under chapter 61 or section 3406 of the Internal Revenue Code and therefore provides Forms W-9 for U.S. non-exempt recipients, the qualified intermediary is the payee except to the extent the payment is reliably associated with a Form W-9 from a U.S. non-exempt recipient.

(vi) *Other payees.*—A payment to a person described in §1.6049-4(c)(1)(ii) that the withholding agent would treat as a payment to a foreign person without obtaining documentation for purposes of information reporting under section 6049 (if the payment were interest) is treated as a payment to a foreign payee for purposes of chapter 3 of the Code and the regulations thereunder (or to a foreign beneficial owner to the extent provided in paragraph (e)(1)(ii)(A)(6) or (7) of this section). Further, a payment that the withholding agent can reliably associate with documentary evidence described in §1.6049-5(c)(1) relating to the payee is treated as a

payment to a foreign payee. See §1.1441-5(b)(1) and (c)(1) for payee determinations for payments to partnerships. See §1.1441-5(e) for payee determinations for payments to foreign trusts or foreign estates.

(vii) *Rules for reliably associating a payment with a withholding certificate or other appropriate documentation.*—(A) *Generally.*—The presumption rules of paragraph (b)(3) of this section and §§1.1441-5(d) and (e)(6) and 1.6049-5(d) apply to any payment, or portion of a payment, that a withholding agent cannot reliably associate with valid documentation. Generally, a withholding agent can reliably associate a payment with valid documentation if, prior to the payment, it holds valid documentation (either directly or through an agent), it can reliably determine how much of the payment relates to the valid documentation, and it has no actual knowledge or reason to know that any of the information, certifications, or statements in, or associated with, the documentation, are incorrect. Special rules apply for payments made to intermediaries, flow-through entities, and certain U.S. branches. See paragraph (b)(2)(vii)(B) through (F) of this section. The documentation referred to in this paragraph (b)(2)(vii) is documentation described in paragraphs (c)(16) and (17) of this section upon which a withholding agent may rely to treat the payment as a payment made to a payee or beneficial owner, and to ascertain the characteristics of the payee or beneficial owner that are relevant to withholding or reporting under chapter 3 of the Internal Revenue Code and the regulations thereunder. A withholding agent that is not required to obtain documentation with respect to a payment is considered to lack documentation for purposes of this paragraph (b)(2)(vii). For example, a withholding agent paying U.S. source interest to a person that is an exempt recipient, as defined in §1.6049-4(c)(1)(ii), is not required to obtain documentation from that person in order to determine whether an amount paid to that person is reportable under an applicable information reporting provision under chapter 61 of the Internal Revenue Code. The withholding agent must, however, treat the payment as made to an undocumented person for purposes of chapter 3 of the Internal Revenue Code. Therefore, the presumption rules of paragraph (b)(3)(iii) of this section apply to determine whether the person is presumed to be a U.S. person (in which case, no withholding is required under this section), or whether the person is presumed to be a foreign person (in which case 30-percent withholding is required under this section). See paragraph (b)(3)(v) of this section for special reliance rules in the case of a payment to a foreign intermediary and §1.1441-5(d) and (e)(6) for special reliance rules in the case of a payment to a flow-through entity.

(B) *Special rules applicable to a withholding certificate from a nonqualified intermediary or flow-through entity.*—(1) In the case of a payment made to a nonqualified intermediary, a flow-through entity (as defined in paragraph (c)(23) of this section), or a U.S. branch described in paragraph (b)(2)(iv) of this section (other than a U.S. branch that is treated as a U.S. person), a withholding agent can reliably associate the payment with valid documentation only to the extent that, prior to the payment, the withholding agent can allocate the payment to a valid nonqualified intermediary, flow-through entity, or U.S. branch withholding certificate (and a withholding certificate provided by a nonparticipating FFI with respect to a portion of a payment that is a withholdable payment allocated to an exempt beneficial owner as described in §1.1471-3(c)(3)(iii)(B)(4)); the withholding agent can reliably determine how much of the payment relates to valid documentation provided by a payee as determined under paragraph (c)(12) of this section (i.e., a person that is not itself an intermediary, flow-through entity, or U.S. branch); and the withholding agent has sufficient information to report the payment on Form 1042-S or Form 1099, if reporting is required. See, however, paragraph (e)(3)(iv) of this section for when a nonqualified intermediary may report payees to the withholding agent in a chapter 4 withholding rate pool, in which case a withholding agent need not associate the portion of the payment attributable to such payees with documentation from each such payee. See also paragraph (e)(3)(iii) of this section for the requirements of a nonqualified intermediary withholding certificate, paragraph (e)(3)(v) of this section for the requirements of a U.S. branch withholding certificate, and §§1.1441-5(c)(3)(iii) and (e)(5)(iii) for the requirements of a flow-through withholding certificate (including the requirements for a withholding certificate associated with a withholdable payment). Thus, a payment cannot be reliably associated with valid documentation provided by a payee to the extent such documentation is lacking or unreliable, or to the extent that information required to allocate and report all or a portion of the payment to each payee is lacking or unreliable. If a withholding certificate attached to an intermediary, U.S. branch, or flow-through withholding certificate is another intermediary, U.S. branch, or flow-through withholding certificate, the rules of this paragraph (b)(2)(vii)(B) apply by treating the share of the payment allocable to the other intermediary, U.S. branch, or flow-through entity as if the payment were made directly to such other entity. See paragraph (e)(3)(iv)(D) of this section for rules permitting information allocating a payment to documentation to be received after the payment is made.

(2) The rules of paragraph (b)(2)(vii)(B)(*1*) of this section are illustrated by the following examples. Each example illustrates a payment that is not a withholdable payment and, as a result of which, neither the chapter 4 status of the NQI nor payee specific documentation with respect to the chapter 4 status is required to be provided to the withholding agent (and no withholding applies under chapter 4 on each payment). See paragraph (e)(3)(iv)(C) of this section for the requirements of a withholding statement provided by a nonqualified intermediary that receives a withholdable payment and for an example illustrating the requirements of an NQI providing a withholding statement to a withholding agent for a withholdable payment.

*Example 1.* WA, a withholding agent, makes a payment of U.S. source interest with respect to a grandfathered obligation as described in §1.1471-2(b) (and thus the payment is not a withholdable payment) to NQI, an intermediary that is a nonqualified intermediary. NQI provides a valid intermediary withholding certificate under paragraph (e)(3)(iii) of this section. NQI does not, however, provide valid documentation from the persons on whose behalf it receives the interest payment, and, therefore, the interest payment cannot be reliably associated with valid documentation provided by a payee. WA must apply the presumption rules of paragraph (b)(3)(v) of this section to the payment.

*Example 2.* The facts are the same as in *Example 1*, except that NQI does attach valid beneficial owner withholding certificates (as defined in paragraph (e)(2)(i) of this section) from A, B, C, and D establishing their statuses as foreign persons. NQI does not, however, provide WA with any information allocating the payment among A, B, C, and D and, therefore, WA cannot determine the portion of the payment that relates to each beneficial owner withholding certificate. The interest payment cannot be reliably associated with valid documentation from a payee, and WA must apply the presumption rules of paragraph (b)(3)(v) of this section to the payment. See, however, paragraph (e)(3)(iv)(D) of this section providing for alternative procedures that allow a nonqualified intermediary to provide allocation information after a payment is made.

*Example 3.* The facts are the same as in *Example 2*, except that NQI provides allocation information associated with its intermediary withholding certificate indicating that 25% of the interest payment is allocable to A and 25% to B. NQI does not provide any allocation information regarding the remaining 50% of the payment. WA may treat 25% of the payment as made to A and 25% as made to B. The remaining 50% of the payment cannot be reliably associated with valid documentation from a payee, however, since NQI did not provide information allocating the payment. Thus, the remaining 50% of the payment is subject to the presumption rules of paragraph (b)(3)(v) of this section.

*Example 4.* WA makes a payment of U.S. source interest to NQI1, an intermediary that is not a qualified intermediary. NQI1 provides WA with a valid nonqualified intermediary withholding certificate as well valid beneficial owner withholding certificates from A and B and a valid nonqualified intermediary withholding certificate from NQI2. NQI2 has provided valid beneficial owner documentation from C sufficient to establish C's status as a foreign person. Based on information provided by NQI1, WA can allocate 20% of the interest payment to A, and 20% to B. Based on information that NQI2 provided NQI1 and that NQI1 provides to WA, WA can allocate 60% of the payment to NQI2, but can only allocate one half of that payment (30%) to C. Therefore, WA cannot reliably associate the remainder of the payment made to NQI2 (30% of the total payment) with valid documentation and must apply the presumption rules of paragraph (b)(3)(v) of this section to that portion of the payment.

(C) *Special rules applicable to a withholding certificate provided by a qualified intermediary that does not assume primary withholding responsibility.*—(*1*) If a payment is made to a qualified intermediary that does not assume primary withholding responsibility under chapters 3 and 4 of the Code or primary Form 1099 reporting and backup withholding responsibility under chapter 61 and section 3406 of the Code for the payment, a withholding agent can reliably associate the payment with valid documentation only to the extent that, prior to the payment, the withholding agent has received a valid qualified intermediary withholding certificate described in paragraph (e)(3)(ii) of this section and the withholding agent can reliably determine the portion of the payment that relates to a chapter 3 withholding rate pool, as defined in paragraph (c)(44) of this section; a chapter 4 withholding rate pool (including for a withholdable payment as described in paragraph (e)(5)(v)(C)(*2*) of this section), as defined in paragraph (c)(48) of this section; or a pool attributable to U.S. exempt recipients. In the case of a withholding rate pool attribu-

table to a U.S. non-exempt recipient, a payment cannot be reliably associated with valid documentation unless, prior to the payment, the qualified intermediary has provided the U.S. person's Form W-9 (or, in the absence of the form, the name, address, and TIN, if available, of the U.S. person) and sufficient information for the withholding agent to report the payment on Form 1099. See, however, paragraph (e)(5)(v)(C)(*3*) of this section for alternative procedures for allocating payments among U.S. non-exempt recipients and paragraphs (e)(5)(v)(C)(*1*) and (2) of this section for when a chapter 4 withholding rate pool of U.S. payees may be provided by a qualified intermediary instead of documentation with respect to each U.S. non-exempt recipient.

(2) The rules of this paragraph (b)(2)(vii)(C) are illustrated by the following examples:

*Example 1.* WA, a withholding agent, makes a payment of U.S. source dividends that is a withholdable payment to QI. QI provides WA with a valid qualified intermediary withholding certificate on which it indicates that it does not assume primary withholding responsibility under chapters 3 and 4 or primary Form 1099 reporting and backup withholding responsibility under chapter 61 and section 3406. QI does not provide any information allocating the dividend to withholding rate pools. WA cannot reliably associate the payment with valid payee documentation and therefore must apply the presumption rules applicable to a withholdable payment under §1.1471-3(f)(5) to determine the status of the payee for purposes of chapter 4. See *Example 2* for an application of the presumption rules under §1.1471-3(f).

*Example 2.* WA makes a payment of U.S. source dividends that is a withholdable payment to QI, which is an NFFE. QI has 5 customers: A, B, C, D, and E, all of whom are individuals except for C. QI has obtained valid documentation from A and B establishing their entitlement to a 15% rate of tax on U.S. source dividends under an income tax treaty. C is a U.S. person that is an exempt recipient as defined in paragraph (c)(20) of this section. D and E are U.S. non-exempt recipients who have provided Forms W-9 to QI. A, B, C, D, and E are each entitled to 20% of the dividend payment. QI provides WA with a valid qualified intermediary withholding certificate as described in paragraph (e)(3)(ii) of this section with which it associates the Forms W-9 from D and E. QI associates the following allocation information with its qualified intermediary withholding certificate: 40% of the payment is allocable to the 15% chapter 3 withholding rate pool, and 20% is allocable to each of D and E. QI does not provide any allocation information regarding the remaining 20% of the payment. WA cannot reliably associate 20% of the payment with valid documentation and, therefore, must apply the presumption rules applicable to a withholdable payment. Because QI is receiving a withholdable payment as an intermediary, under paragraph (b)(3)(iii) of this section WA must apply the presumption rule of §1.1471-3(f)(5) to treat the portion of the payment that cannot reliably be associated with valid documentation as made to a nonparticipating FFI account holder of QI. As a result, WA is required to withhold at a 30% rate of tax under chapter 4. See §1.1441-3(a)(2) permitting WA to credit the amount withheld under chapter 4 against the liability for tax due on the payment under section 1441 or 1442. The 40% of the payment allocable to the 15% withholding rate pool and the portion of the payments allocable to D and E are payments that can be reliably associated with documentation.

(D) *Special rules applicable to a withholding certificate provided by a qualified intermediary that assumes primary withholding responsibility under chapter 3 and chapter 4 of the Internal Revenue Code.*—(*1*) In the case of a payment made to a qualified intermediary that assumes primary withholding responsibility under chapters 3 and 4 of the Code with respect to that payment (but does not assume primary Form 1099 reporting and backup withholding responsibility under chapter 61 of the Code and section 3406), a withholding agent can reliably associate the payment with valid documentation only to the extent that, prior to the payment, the withholding agent has received a valid qualified intermediary withholding certificate and the withholding agent can reliably determine the portion of the payment that relates to the withholding rate pool for which the qualified intermediary assumes primary withholding responsibility and the portion of the payment attributable to withholding rate pools for each U.S. non-exempt recipient for whom the qualified intermediary has provided a Form W-9 (or, in absence of the form, the name, address, and TIN, if available, of the U.S. non-exempt recipient). See paragraph (e)(5)(iv) of this section (requiring a qualified intermediary assuming primary withholding responsibility under chapter 3 to assume primary withholding responsibility under chapter 4). See also paragraph (e)(5)(v)(C)(*3*) of this section for alternative allocation procedures for payments made to U.S. persons that are not exempt recipients and paragraphs (e)(5)(v)(C)(*1*) and (2) of this section for when a qualified intermediary may provide a chapter 4 withholding rate pool of U.S. payees to a withholding agent instead of documentation with respect to each U.S. non-exempt recipient.

*(2) Examples.*—The following examples illustrate the rules of paragraph (b)(2)(vii)(D)(*1*) of this section. See also the example in paragraph (e)(5)(v)(D) for rules for reporting of U.S. non-exempt recipients when a qualified intermediary that is an FFI reports a U.S. account under chapter 4.

*Example 1.* WA makes a payment of U.S. source interest that is a withholdable payment to QI, a qualified intermediary that is an NFFE. QI provides WA with a withholding certificate that indicates that QI will assume primary withholding responsibility under chapters 3 and 4 of the Code with respect to the payment. In addition, QI attaches a Form W-9 from A, a U.S. non-exempt recipient, as defined in paragraph (c)(21) of this section, and provides the name, address, and TIN of B, a U.S. person that is also a non-exempt recipient but who has not provided a Form W-9. QI associates a withholding statement with its qualified intermediary withholding certificate indicating that 10% of the payment is attributable to A and 10% to B, and that QI will assume primary withholding responsibility under chapters 3 and 4 with respect to the remaining 80% of the payment. WA can reliably associate the entire payment with valid documentation. Although under the presumption rule of paragraph (b)(3)(v) of this section, an undocumented person receiving U.S. source interest is generally presumed to be a foreign person, WA has actual knowledge that B is a U.S. non-exempt recipient and therefore must report the payment on Form 1099 and backup withhold on the interest payment under section 3406.

*Example 2.* The facts are the same as in *Example 1*, except that no information has been provided for the 20% of the payment that is allocable to A and B. Thus, QI has accepted withholding responsibility for 80% of the payment but has provided no information for the remaining 20%. In this case, 20% of the payment cannot be reliably associated with valid documentation, and, under paragraph (b)(3)(iii) of this section, WA must apply the presumption rule of § 1.1471-3(f)(5) to treat the payment as made to a nonparticipating FFI and withhold 30% of the gross amount of the payment (because the payment is a withholdable payment and is treated as made to a foreign payee under paragraph (b)(3)(v) of this section). See *Example* 2 in paragraph (b)(2)(vii)(C)(*2*) and § 1.1471-3(f)(1).

(E) *Special rules applicable to a withholding certificate provided by a qualified intermediary that assumes primary Form 1099 reporting and backup withholding responsibility but not primary withholding under chapter 3 and chapter 4.*—(*1*) If a payment is made to a qualified intermediary that assumes primary Form 1099 reporting and backup withholding responsibility for the payment (but does not assume primary withholding responsibility under chapters 3 and 4 of the Code), a withholding agent can reliably associate the payment with valid documentation only to the extent that, prior to the payment, the withholding agent has received a valid qualified intermediary withholding certificate and the withholding agent can reliably determine the portion of the payment that relates to a withholding rate pool or pools provided as part of the qualified intermediary's withholding statement and the portion of the payment for which the qualified intermediary assumes primary Form 1099 reporting and backup withholding responsibility. See paragraph (e)(5)(v)(C)(*2*) of this section for when a qualified intermediary may include a chapter 4 withholding rate pool on a withholding statement provided to a withholding agent with respect to a withholdable payment.

(*2*) The following example illustrates the rules of paragraph (b)(2)(vii)(D)(*1*) of this section:

*Example.* WA, a withholding agent, makes a payment of U.S. source dividends that is a withholdable payment to QI, a qualified intermediary that is a participating FFI. QI has provided WA with a valid qualified intermediary withholding certificate. QI states on its withholding statement accompanying the certificate that it assumes primary Form 1099 reporting and backup withholding responsibility but does not assume primary withholding responsibility under chapters 3 and 4 of the Code. QI represents that 15% of the dividend is subject to a 30% rate of withholding, 75% of the dividend is subject to a 15% rate of withholding. QI represents that it assumes primary Form 1099 reporting and backup withholding for the remaining 10% of the payment and will not need to provide a chapter 4 withholding rate pool with respect to this portion of the payment or documentation with respect to U.S. non-exempt recipients. WA can reliably associate the entire payment with valid documentation.

(F) *Special rules applicable to a withholding certificate provided by a qualified intermediary that assumes primary withholding responsibility under chapter 3 and chapter 4 and primary Form 1099 reporting and backup withholding responsibility and a withholding certificate provided by a withholding foreign partnership or a withholding foreign trust.*—If a payment is made to a qualified intermediary that assumes both primary withholding responsibility under chapters 3 and 4 of the Code and primary Form 1099 reporting and backup withholding responsibility under chapter 61 and section 3406 of the Code for the

payment, a withholding agent can reliably associate a payment with valid documentation provided that it receives a valid qualified intermediary withholding certificate as described in paragraph (e)(3)(ii) of this section. In the case of a payment made to a withholding foreign partnership or a withholding foreign trust, the withholding agent can reliably associate the payment with valid documentation to the extent it can associate the payment with a valid withholding certificate described in § 1.1441-5(c)(2)(iv) or in § 1.1441-5(e)(5)(v) (respectively). See paragraph (e)(5)(iv) of this section, providing that a qualified intermediary assuming primary withholding responsibility under chapter 3 must also assume primary withholding responsibility under chapter 4 with respect to a withholdable payment.

(3) *Presumptions regarding payee's status in the absence of documentation.*—(i) *General rules.*—A withholding agent that cannot, prior to the payment, reliably associate (within the meaning of paragraph (b)(2)(vii) of this section) a payment of an amount subject to withholding (as described in § 1.1441-2(a)) with valid documentation may rely on the presumptions of this paragraph (b)(3) to determine the status of the person receiving the payment as a U.S. or a foreign person and the person's other relevant characteristics (*e.g.*, as an owner or intermediary, as an individual, trust, partnership, or corporation). The determination of withholding and reporting requirements applicable to payments to a person presumed to be a foreign person is governed only by the provisions of chapters 3 and 4 of the Code and the regulations thereunder. For the determination of withholding and reporting requirements applicable to payments to a person presumed to be a U.S. person, see chapter 61 of the Code, section 3402, 3405, or 3406, and, with respect to the reporting requirements of a participating FFI or registered deemed-compliant FFI, see chapter 4 of the Code and the related regulations. A presumption that a payee is a foreign payee is not a presumption that the payee is a foreign beneficial owner. Therefore, the provisions of this paragraph (b)(3) have no effect for purposes of reducing the withholding rate if associating the payment with documentation of foreign beneficial ownership is required as a condition for such rate reduction. See paragraph (b)(3)(ix) of this section for consequences to a withholding agent that fails to withhold in accordance with the presumptions set forth in this paragraph (b)(3) or if the withholding agent has actual knowledge or reason to know of facts that are contrary to the presumptions set forth in this paragraph (b)(3). See paragraph (b)(2)(vii) of this section for rules regarding the extent to which a withholding agent can reliably associate a payment with documentation.

(ii) *Presumptions of classification as individual, corporation, partnership, etc.*—(A) *In general.*—A withholding agent that cannot reliably associate a payment with a valid withholding certificate or that has received valid documentary evidence under §§ 1.1441-1(e)(1)(ii)(A)(2) and 1.6049-5(c)(1) or (4) but cannot determine a payee's classification from the documentary evidence must apply the rules of this paragraph (b)(3)(ii) to determine the payee's classification as an individual, trust, estate, corporation, or partnership. The fact that a payee is presumed to have a certain status under the provisions of this paragraph (b)(3)(ii) does not mean that it is excused from furnishing documentation if documentation is otherwise required to obtain a reduced rate of withholding under this section. For example, if, for purposes of this paragraph (b)(3)(ii), a payee is presumed to be a tax-exempt organization based on § 1.6049-4(c)(1)(ii)(B), the withholding agent cannot rely on this presumption to reduce the rate of withholding on payments to such person (if such person is also presumed to be a foreign person under paragraph (b)(3)(iii)(A) of this section) because a reduction in the rate of withholding for payments to a foreign tax-exempt organization generally requires that a valid Form W-8 described in § 1.1441-9(b)(2) be furnished to the withholding agent.

(B) *No documentation provided.*—If the withholding agent cannot reliably associate a payment with a valid withholding certificate or valid documentary evidence, it must presume that the payee is an individual, a trust, or an estate, if the payee appears to be such person (*e.g.*, based on the payee's name or information in the customer file). In the absence of reliable indications that the payee is an individual, a trust, or an estate, the withholding agent must presume that the payee is a corporation or one of the persons enumerated under § 1.6049-4(c)(1)(ii)(B) through (Q) if it can be so treated under § 1.6049-4(c)(1)(ii)(A)(*1*) or any one of the paragraphs under § 1.6049-4(c)(1)(ii)(B) through (Q) without the need to furnish documentation. If the withholding agent cannot treat a payee as a person described in § 1.6049-4(c)(1)(ii)(A)(*1*) through (Q), then the payee shall be presumed to be a partnership. If such a partnership is presumed to be foreign, it is not the beneficial owner of the income paid to it. See paragraph (c)(6) of this section. If such a partnership is presumed to be domestic, it is a U.S. non-exempt recipient for purposes of chapter 61 of the Code.

(C) *Documentary evidence furnished for offshore obligation.*—If the withholding agent receives valid documentary evidence, as described in §1.6049-5(c)(1) or (c)(4), with respect to an offshore obligation from an entity but the documentary evidence does not establish the entity's classification as a corporation, trust, estate, or partnership, the withholding agent may presume (in the absence of actual knowledge otherwise) that the entity is the type of person enumerated under §1.6049-4(c)(1)(ii)(B) through (Q) if it can be so treated under any one of those paragraphs without the need to furnish documentation. If the withholding agent cannot treat a payee as a person described in §1.6049-4(c)(1)(ii)(B) through (Q), then the payee shall be presumed to be a corporation unless the withholding agent knows, or has reason to know, that the entity is not classified as a corporation for U.S. tax purposes. If a payee is, or is presumed to be, a corporation under this paragraph (b)(3)(ii)(C) and a foreign person under paragraph (b)(3)(iii) of this section, a withholding agent shall not treat the payee as the beneficial owner of income if the withholding agent knows, or has reason to know, that the payee is not the beneficial owner of the income. For this purpose, a withholding agent will have reason to know that the payee is not a beneficial owner if the documentary evidence indicates that the payee is a bank, broker, intermediary, custodian, or other agent, or is treated under §1.6049-4(c)(1)(ii)(B) through (Q) as such a person. A withholding agent may, however, treat such a person as a beneficial owner if the foreign person provides a statement, in writing and signed by a person with authority to sign the statement, that is attached to the documentary evidence and that states that the foreign person is the beneficial owner of the income.

(iii) *Presumption of U.S. or foreign status.*—A payment that the withholding agent cannot reliably associate with documentation is presumed to be made to a U.S. person, except as otherwise provided in this paragraph (b)(3)(iii), in paragraphs (b)(3)(iv) and (v) of this section, or in §1.1441-5(d) or (e). A withholding agent must treat a payee that is presumed or known to be a trust but for which the withholding agent cannot determine the type of trust in accordance with the presumptions specified in §1.1441-5(e)(6)(ii). In the case of a payment that is a withholdable payment, a withholding agent must apply the presumption rule under §1.1471-3(f) for purposes of chapter 4.

(A) *Payments to exempt recipients.*—(1) *In general.*—If a withholding agent cannot reliably associate a payment with documentation from the payee and the payee is an exempt recipient (as determined under the provisions of §1.6049-4(c)(1)(ii) in the case of interest, or under similar provisions under chapter 61 of the Code applicable to the type of payment involved, but not including a payee that the withholding agent may treat as a foreign intermediary in accordance with paragraph (b)(3)(v) of this section), the payee is presumed to be a foreign person and not a U.S. person—

(i) If the withholding agent has actual knowledge of the payee's employer identification number and that number begins with the two digits "98";

(ii) If the withholding agent's communications with the payee are mailed to an address in a foreign country;

(iii) If the name of the payee indicates that the entity is the type of entity that is on the per se list of foreign corporations contained in §301.7701-2(b)(8)(i) of this chapter (and, in the case of a name which contains the designation "corporation" or "company," the withholding agent has a document that reasonably demonstrates the payee was incorporated in the relevant jurisdiction);

(iv) If the payment is made with respect to an offshore obligation (as defined in paragraph (c)(37) of this section); or

(v) With respect to an account opened after July 1, 2014, if the withholding agent has a telephone number for the person outside of the United States.

(2) *Special rule for withholdable payments made to exempt recipients.*—Notwithstanding the provisions of paragraph (b)(3)(iii)(A)(1) of this section, a payment that is also a withholdable payment made to an entity determined to be an exempt recipient under §1.6049-4(c)(1)(ii)(A)(1), (F), (G), (H), (M), (O), (P), or (Q) in the case of interest (or under similar provisions in chapter 61 applicable to the type of income) shall be presumed made to a foreign payee in the absence of documentation (including documentary evidence) establishing the entity as a U.S. person. Additionally, a withholding agent may apply the rule provided in this paragraph (b)(3)(iii)(A)(2) instead of the rule in provided in paragraph (b)(3)(iii)(A)(1) of this section for all payments with respect to an obligation. The provisions of this paragraph (b)(3)(iii)(A)(2) will not apply, however, to a withholdable payment made with respect to a preexisting obligation to a payee that the withholding agent determined prior to July 1, 2014, to be a U.S. exempt recipient.

(B) *Scholarships and grants.*—A payment representing taxable scholarship or fellowship grant income that does not represent compensation for services (but is not excluded from tax under section 117) and that a withholding agent cannot reliably associate with documentation is presumed to be made to a foreign person if the withholding agent has a record that the payee has a U.S. visa that is not an immigrant visa. See section 871(c) and §1.1441-4(c) for applicable tax rate and withholding rules.

(C) *Pensions, annuities, etc.*—A payment from a trust described in section 401(a), an annuity plan described in section 403(a), a payment with respect to any annuity, custodial account, or retirement income account described in section 403(b), or a payment from an individual retirement account or individual retirement annuity described in section 408 that a withholding agent cannot reliably associate with documentation is presumed to be made to a U.S. person only if the withholding agent has a record of a Social Security number for the payee and relies on a mailing address described in the following sentence. A mailing address is an address used for purposes of information reporting or otherwise communicating with the payee that is an address in the United States or in a foreign country with which the United States has an income tax treaty in effect and the treaty provides that the payee, if an individual resident in that country, would be entitled to an exemption from U.S. tax on amounts described in this paragraph (b)(3)(iii)(C). Any payment described in this paragraph (b)(3)(iii)(C) that is not presumed to be made to a U.S. person is presumed to be made to a foreign person. A withholding agent making a payment to a person presumed to be a foreign person may not reduce the 30-percent amount of withholding required on such payment unless it receives a withholding certificate described in paragraph (e)(2)(i) of this section furnished by the beneficial owner. For reduction in the 30-percent rate, see §§1.1441-4(e) or 1.1441-6(b).

(D) *Payments with respect to offshore obligations.*—A payment is presumed made to a foreign payee if the payment is made outside the United States (as defined in §1.6049-5(e)) with respect to an offshore obligation (as defined in paragraph (c)(37) of this section) and the withholding agent does not have actual knowledge that the payee is a U.S. person. See §1.6049-5(d)(2) and (3) for exceptions to this rule.

(E) *Certain payments for services.*—A payment for services is presumed to be made to a foreign person if—

(1) The payee is an individual;

(2) The withholding agent does not know, or have reason to know, that the payee is a U.S. citizen or resident;

(3) The withholding agent does not know, or have reason to know, that the income is (or may be) effectively connected with the conduct of a trade or business within the United States; and

(4) All of the services for which the payment is made were performed by the payee outside of the United States.

(iv) *Grace period.*—A withholding agent may choose to apply the provisions of §1.6049-5(d)(2)(ii) regarding a 90-day grace period for purposes of this paragraph (b)(3) (by applying the term withholding agent instead of the term payor) to amounts described in §1.1441-6(c)(2) and to amounts covered by a Form 8233 described in §1.1441-4(b)(2)(ii). Thus, for these amounts, a withholding agent may choose to treat the payee as a foreign person and withhold under chapter 3 of the Code (and the regulations thereunder) while awaiting documentation. For purposes of determining the rate of withholding under this section, the withholding agent must withhold at the unreduced 30-percent rate at the time that the amounts are credited to an account. For reporting of amounts credited both before and after the grace period, see §1.1461-1(c)(4)(i)(A). The following adjustments shall be made at the expiration of the grace period:

(A) If, at the end of the grace period, the documentation is not furnished in the manner required under this section and the account holder is presumed to be a U.S. non-exempt recipient, then backup withholding only applies to amounts credited to the account after the expiration of the grace period. Amounts credited to the account during the grace period shall be treated as owned by a foreign payee and adjustments must be made to correct any underwithholding on such amounts in the manner described in §1.1461-2.

(B) If, at the end of the grace period, the documentation is not furnished in the manner required under this section, or if documentation is furnished that does not support the claimed rate reduction, and the account holder is presumed to be a foreign person then adjustments must be made to correct any underwithholding on amounts credited to the account during the grace period, based on the adjustment procedures described in §1.1461-2.

(v) *Special rules applicable to payments to foreign intermediaries.*—(A) *Reliance on claim of status as foreign intermediary.*—The presumption rules of paragraph (b)(3)(v)(B) of this section apply to a payment made to an intermediary (whether the intermediary is a qualified or nonqualified intermediary) that has provided a valid withholding certificate under paragraph (e)(3)(ii) or (iii) of this section (or has provided documentary evidence described in paragraph (b)(3)(ii)(C) of this section that indicates it is a bank, broker, custodian, intermediary, or other agent) to the extent the withholding agent cannot treat the payment as being reliably associated with valid documentation under the rules of paragraph (b)(2)(vii) of this section. For this purpose, a U.S. person's foreign branch that is a qualified intermediary defined in paragraph (e)(5)(ii) of this section shall be treated as a foreign intermediary. A payee that the withholding agent may not reliably treat as a foreign intermediary under this paragraph (b)(3)(v)(A) is presumed to be a payee other than an intermediary whose classification as an individual, corporation, partnership, etc., must be determined in accordance with paragraph (b)(3)(ii) of this section to the extent relevant. In addition, such payee is presumed to be a U.S. or a foreign payee based upon the presumptions described in paragraph (b)(3)(iii) of this section. The provisions of paragraph (b)(3)(v)(B) of this section are not relevant to a withholding agent that can reliably associate a payment with a qualified intermediary to the extent person representing to be a qualified intermediary has assumed primary withholding responsibility in accordance with paragraph (e)(5)(iv) of this section.

(B) *Beneficial owner documentation or allocation information is lacking or unreliable.*—Except as otherwise provided in this paragraph (b)(3)(v)(B), any portion of a payment that the withholding agent may treat as made to a foreign intermediary (whether a nonqualified or a qualified intermediary) but that the withholding agent cannot treat as reliably associated with valid documentation under the rules of paragraph (b)(2)(vii) of this section is presumed made to an unknown, undocumented foreign payee. As a result, a withholding agent must deduct and withhold 30 percent from any payment of an amount subject to withholding. If a withholding certificate attached to an intermediary certificate is another intermediary withholding certificate or a flow-through withholding certificate, the rules of this paragraph (b)(3)(v)(B) (or §1.1441-5(d)(3) or (e)(6)(iii)) apply by treating the portion of the payment allocable to the other intermediary or flow-through entity as if it were made directly to the other intermediary or flow-through entity. Any payment of an amount subject to withholding that is presumed made to an undocumented foreign person must be reported on Form 1042-S. See §1.1461-1(c). See §1.6049-5(d) for payments that are not subject to withholding under chapter 3. However, in the case of a payment that is a withholdable payment made to a foreign intermediary, the presumption rules under §1.1471-3(f)(5) shall apply.

(vi) *U.S. branches and territory financial institutions not treated as U.S. persons.*—The rules of paragraph (b)(3)(v)(B) of this section shall apply to payments to a U.S. branch or a territory financial institution described in paragraph (b)(2)(iv)(A) of this section that has provided a withholding certificate as described in paragraph (e)(3)(v) of this section on which it has not agreed to be treated as a U.S. person.

(vii) *Joint payees.*—(A) *In general.*—Except as provided in paragraph (b)(3)(vii)(B) of this section and this paragraph (b)(3)(vii)(A), if a withholding agent makes a payment to joint payees and cannot reliably associate the payment with valid documentation from all payees, the payment is presumed made to an unidentified U.S. person. If, however, a withholding agent makes a payment that is a withholdable payment and any joint payee does not appear, by its name and other information contained in the account file, to be an individual, then the entire amount of the payment will be treated as made to an undocumented foreign person. See paragraph (b)(3)(iii) of this section for presumption rules that apply in the case of a payment that is a withholdable payment. However, if one of the joint payees provides a Form W-9 furnished in accordance with the procedures described in §§31.3406(d)-1 through 31.3406(d)-5 of this chapter, the payment shall be treated as made to that payee. See §31.3406(h)-2 of this chapter for rules to determine the relevant payee if more than one Form W-9 is provided. For purposes of applying this paragraph (b)(3), the grace period rules in paragraph (b)(3)(iv) of this section shall apply only if each payee meets the conditions described in paragraph (b)(3)(iv) of this section.

(B) *Special rule for offshore obligations.*—If a withholding agent makes a payment to joint payees and cannot reliably associate a payment with valid documentation from all payees, the payment is presumed made to an unknown foreign payee (as defined in §1.6049-5(c)(1)) with respect to an offshore obligation (as defined in §1.6049-5(e)) with respect to an offshore obligation (as defined in §1.6049-5(c)(1)).

(viii) *Rebuttal of presumptions.*—A payee or beneficial owner may rebut the presumptions described in this paragraph (b)(3) by providing reliable documentation to the withholding agent or, if applicable, to the IRS.

(ix) *Effect of reliance on presumptions and of actual knowledge or reason to know otherwise.*—(A) *General rule.*—Except as otherwise provided in paragraph (b)(3)(ix)(B) of this section, a withholding agent that withholds on a payment under section 3402, 3405, or 3406 in accordance with the presumptions set forth in this paragraph (b)(3) shall not be liable for withholding under this section even if it is later established that the beneficial owner of the payment is, in fact, a foreign person. Similarly, a withholding agent that withholds on a payment under this section in accordance with the presumptions set forth in this paragraph (b)(3) shall not be liable for withholding under section 3402 or 3405 or for backup withholding under section 3406 even if it is later established that the payee or beneficial owner is, in fact, a U.S. person. A withholding agent that, instead of relying on the presumptions described in this paragraph (b)(3), relies on its own actual knowledge to withhold a lesser amount, not withhold, or not report a payment, even though reporting of the payment or withholding a greater amount would be required if the withholding agent relied on the presumptions described in this paragraph (b)(3), shall be liable for tax, interest, and penalties to the extent provided under section 1461 and the regulations under that section. See paragraph (b)(7) of this section for provisions regarding such liability if the withholding agent fails to withhold in accordance with the presumptions described in this paragraph (b)(3).

(B) *Actual knowledge or reason to know that amount of withholding is greater than is required under the presumptions or that reporting of the payment is required.*—Notwithstanding the provisions of paragraph (b)(3)(ix)(A) of this section, a withholding agent may not rely on the presumptions described in this paragraph (b)(3) to the extent it has actual knowledge or reason to know that the status or characteristics of the payee or of the beneficial owner are other than what is presumed under this paragraph (b)(3) and, if based on such knowledge or reason to know, it should withhold (under this section or another withholding provision of the Code) an amount greater than would be the case if it relied on the presumptions described in this paragraph (b)(3) or it should report (under this section or under another provision of the Code) an amount that would not otherwise be reportable if it relied on the presumptions described in this paragraph (b)(3). In such a case, the withholding agent must rely on its actual knowledge or reason to know rather than on the presumptions set forth in this paragraph (b)(3). Failure to do so and, as a result, failure to withhold the higher amount or to report the payment, shall result in liability for tax, interest, and penalties to the extent provided under sections 1461 and 1463 and the regulations under those sections.

(x) *Examples.*—The provisions of this paragraph (b)(3) are illustrated by the following examples:

*Example 1.* A withholding agent, W, makes a payment of U.S. source interest with respect to a grandfathered obligation as described in §1.1471-2(b) (and thus the payment is not a withholdable payment) to X, Inc. with respect to an account W maintains for X, Inc. outside the United States. W cannot reliably associate the payment to X, Inc. with documentation. Under §1.6049-4(c)(1)(ii)(A)(1), W may treat X, Inc. as a corporation that is an exempt recipient under chapter 61. Thus, under the presumptions described in paragraph (b)(3)(iii) of this section as applicable to a payment to an exempt recipient that is not a withholdable payment, W must presume that X, Inc. is a foreign person (because the payment is made with respect to an offshore obligation). However, W knows that X, Inc. is a U.S. person who is an exempt recipient. W may not rely on its actual knowledge to not withhold under this section. If W's knowledge is, in fact, incorrect, W would be liable for tax, interest, and, if applicable, penalties under section 1461. W would be permitted to reduce or eliminate its liability for the tax by establishing, in accordance with paragraph (b)(7) of this section, that the tax is not due or has been satisfied. If W's actual knowledge is, in fact, correct, W may nevertheless be liable for tax, interest, or penalties under section 1461 for the amount that W should have withheld or eliminate its liability for the tax by establishing, in accordance with paragraph (b)(7) of this section, that its actual knowledge was, in fact, correct and that no tax or a lesser amount of tax was due.

*Example 2.* A withholding agent, W, makes a payment of U.S. source interest with respect to a grandfathered obligation as described in §1.1471-2(b) (and thus the payment is not a withholdable payment) to Y who does not qualify as an exempt recipient under §1.6049-4(c)(1)(ii). W cannot reliably associate the payment to Y with documentation. Under the presumptions described in paragraph (b)(3)(iii) of this section, W must presume that Y is a U.S. person who is not an exempt recipient for purposes of section 6049. However, W knows that Y is a foreign person. W may not rely on its actual knowledge to withhold under this section rather than backup withhold under section 3406. If W's knowledge is, in fact, incorrect, W would be liable for tax, interest, and, if applicable, penalties, under

(ii) Payments to a foreign person that are governed by section 6041A (dealing with remuneration for services and certain sales) are exempt from information reporting under § 1.6041A-1(d)(3).

(iii) Payments to a foreign person that are governed by section 6042 (dealing with dividends) are exempt from information reporting under § 1.6042-3(b)(1)(iii) through (vi).

(iv) Payments to a foreign person that are governed by section 6044 (dealing with patronage dividends) are exempt from information reporting under § 1.6044-3(c)(1).

(v) Payments to a foreign person that are governed by section 6045 (dealing with broker proceeds) are exempt from information reporting under § 1.6045-1(g).

(vi) Payments to a foreign person that are governed by section 6049 (dealing with interest) to a foreign person are exempt from information reporting under § 1.6049-5(b)(6) through (15).

(vii) Payments to a foreign person that are governed by section 6050N (dealing with royalties) are exempt from information reporting under § 1.6050N-1(c).

(viii) Payments to a foreign person that are governed by section 6050P (dealing with income from cancellation of debt) are exempt from information reporting under section 6050P or the regulations under that section except to the extent provided in Notice 96-61 (1996-2 CB 227); see also § 601.601(b)(2) of this chapter.

(ix) Payments to a foreign person that are governed by section 6050W (dealing with payment card and third party network transactions) are exempt from information reporting under § 1.6050W-1(a)(5)(ii).

(6) *Rules of withholding for payments by a foreign intermediary or certain U.S. branches.*—(i) *In general.*—A foreign intermediary described in paragraph (e)(3)(i) of this section or a U.S. branch or territory financial institution described in paragraph (b)(2)(iv) of this section that receives an amount subject to withholding (as defined in § 1.1441-2(a)) shall be required to withhold (if another withholding agent has not withheld the full amount required) and report such payment under chapter 3 of the Code and the regulations thereunder except as otherwise provided in this paragraph (b)(6). A nonqualified intermediary, U.S. branch, or territory financial institution described in paragraph (b)(2)(iv) of this section (other than a U.S. branch or territory financial institution that is treated as a U.S. person) shall not be required to withhold or report if it has provided a valid nonqualified intermediary withholding certificate or a U.S. branch withholding certificate, it has provided all of the information required by paragraph (e)(3)(iv) of this section (withholding statement), and it does not know, and has no reason to know, that another withholding agent failed to withhold the correct amount or failed to report the payment correctly under § 1.1461-1(c). The withholding requirement of a nonqualified intermediary under the previous sentence also excludes a case in which withholding under chapter 4 was imposed by a withholding agent on the payment. See § 1.1441-3(a)(2) (coordinating withholding under chapter 3 with withholding applied under chapter 4 of the Code). A qualified intermediary's obligations to withhold and report shall be determined in accordance with its qualified intermediary withholding agreement.

(ii) *Examples.*—The following examples illustrate the rules of paragraph (b)(6)(i) of this section and coordinate rules for withholding that apply under chapter 4 with those that apply under chapter 3. See also paragraph (e)(3)(iv)(C) of this section for the requirements of withholding statements provided by nonqualified intermediaries.

*Example 1.* FB, a foreign bank, acts as intermediary for five different individuals, A, B, C, D, and E, each of whom owns U.S. securities that generate U.S. source dividends (that are withholdable payments). The dividends are paid by USWA, a U.S. withholding agent. FB furnished USWA with a nonqualified intermediary withholding certificate, described in paragraph (e)(3)(iii) of this section, on which FB certifies its status as a participating FFI (such that withholding under chapter 4 does not apply), to which it attached valid withholding certificates for A, B, C, D, and E. The withholding certificates from A and B claim a 15% reduced rate of withholding under an income tax treaty. C, D, and E claim no reduced rate of withholding. FB provides a withholding statement that meets all of the requirements of paragraph (e)(3)(iv) of this section, including information allocating 20% of each dividend payment to each of A, B, C, D, and E. FB does not have actual knowledge or reason to know that USWA did not withhold the correct amounts or report the dividends on Forms 1042-S to each of A, B, C, D, and E. FB is not required to withhold or to report the dividends to A, B, C, D, and E.

*Example 2.* The facts are the same as in *Example 1*, except that FB did not provide any information for USWA to determine how much of the dividend payments were made to A, B, C, D, and E. Because USWA could not reliably associate the dividend payments with documentation under paragraph (b)(2)(vii) of this section with respect to a payment that is a withholdable payment, USWA applied the presumption rule of § 1.1471-3(f)(5) and withheld 30% from all

dividend payments under chapter 4 and filed a Form 1042-S reporting the payment to an account holder of FB that is a non-participating FFI. FB is deemed to know that USWA did not report the payment to A, B, C, D, and E because it did not provide all of the information required on a withholding statement under paragraph (e)(3)(iv) of this section (*i.e.,* allocation information). Although FB is not required to withhold on the payment under this section because the full 30% withholding was imposed by USWA, it is required to report the payments on Forms 1042-S to A, B, C, D, and E. FB's intentional failure to do so will subject it to intentional disregard penalties under sections 6721 and 6722.

(7) *Liability for failure to obtain documentation timely or to act in accordance with applicable presumptions.*—(i) *General rule.*—A withholding agent that cannot reliably associate a payment with valid documentation on the date of payment and that does not withhold under this section, or withholds at less than the 30-percent rate prescribed under section 1441(a) and paragraph (b)(1) of this section, is liable under section 1461 for the tax required to be withheld under chapter 3 of the Code and the regulations thereunder, without the benefit of a reduced rate unless—

(A) The withholding agent has appropriately relied on the presumptions described in paragraph (b)(3) of this section (including the grace period described in paragraph (b)(3)(iv) of this section) in order to treat the payee as a U.S. person or, if applicable, on the presumptions described in § 1.1441-4(a)(2)(ii) or (a)(3)(i) to treat the payment as effectively connected income;

(B) The withholding agent can demonstrate to the satisfaction of the district director or the Assistant Commissioner (International) that the proper amount of tax, if any, was in fact paid to the IRS;

(C) No documentation is required under section 1441 or this section in order for a reduced rate of withholding to apply; or

(D) The withholding agent has complied with the provisions of § 1.1441-6(c) or (g).

(ii) *Proof that tax liability has been satisfied.*—(A) *In general.*—Proof of payment of tax may be established for purposes of paragraph (b)(7)(i)(B) of this section on the basis of a Form 4669 (or such other form as the IRS may prescribe in published guidance (see § 601.601(d)(2) of this chapter)) establishing the amount of tax, if any, actually paid by or for the beneficial owner on the income. Proof that a reduced rate of withholding was, in fact, appropriate under the provisions of chapter 3 of the Code and the regulations thereunder may also be established after the date of payment by the withholding agent on the basis of a valid withholding certificate or other appropriate documentation received after that date that was effective as of the date of payment. A withholding certificate furnished after the date of payment will be considered effective as of the date of the payment if the certificate contains a signed affidavit (either at the bottom of the form or on an attached page) that states that the information and representations contained on the certificate were accurate as of the time of the payment. A withholding certificate received within 30 days after the date of the payment will not be considered to be unreliable solely because it does not contain the affidavit described in the preceding sentence. However, in the case of a withholding certificate of an individual received more than a year after the date of payment, the withholding agent will be required to obtain, in addition to the withholding certificate and affidavit, documentary evidence, as described in § 1.1471-3(c)(5)(i), that supports the individual's claim of foreign status or documentary evidence described in § 1.1441-6(c)(4)(i) to support any treaty claim made on the certificate. In the case of a withholding certificate of an entity received more than a year after the date of payment, the withholding agent will be required to obtain, in addition to the withholding certificate and affidavit, documentary evidence described in § 1.1471-3(c)(5)(i) that supports the entity's claim of foreign status or documentary evidence described in § 1.1441-6(c)(4)(ii) to support any treaty claim made on the certificate. If documentation other than a withholding certificate is submitted from a payee more than a year after the date of payment, the withholding agent will be required to obtain from the payee a withholding certificate and affidavit supporting the claim of chapter 3 status as of the time of the payment. See, however, paragraph (b)(7)(ii)(B) of this section for special rules that apply when a withholding certificate is received after the date of the payment to claim that income is effectively connected with the conduct of a U.S. trade or business. See § 1.1471-3(c)(7)(ii) for additional requirements that may apply under chapter 4 for documentation obtained after the date of payment of a withholdable payment.

(B) *Special rules for establishing that income is effectively connected with the conduct of a U.S. trade or business.*—A withholding certificate received after the date of payment to claim under § 1.1441-4(a)(1) that income is effectively connected with the conduct of a U.S. trade or business will be considered effective as of the date of the payment if the certificate contains a signed affidavit (either at the bottom of the form or on an attached page) that states that the information and representations contained on the certificate were accurate as of the time of the payment. The signed affidavit must also state that the beneficial owner has included the income on its U.S. income tax return for the taxable year in which it is required to report the income or, alternatively, that the beneficial owner intends to include the income on a U.S. income tax return for the taxable year in which it is required to report the income and the due date for filing such return (including any applicable extensions) is after the date on which the affidavit is signed. A certificate received within 30 days after the date of the payment will not be considered to be unreliable solely because it does not contain the affidavit described in the preceding sentences.

(iii) *Liability for interest and penalties.*—For payments made after December 31, 2000, if a withholding agent fails to deduct and withhold any tax imposed under sections 1441 or 1442, and the tax against which such tax may be credited under section 1462 is paid, then the amount of tax required to be deducted and withheld shall not be collected from the withholding agent. However, the withholding agent is not relieved from liability for interest or any penalties or additions to the tax otherwise applicable in respect of the failure to deduct and withhold. See section 1463. Further, in the event that a tax liability is assessed against the beneficial owner under section 871, 881, or 882 and interest under section 6601(a) is assessed against, and collected from, the beneficial owner, the interest charge imposed on the withholding agent shall be abated to that extent so as to avoid the imposition of a double interest charge.

(iv) *Special rule for determining validity of withholding certificate containing inconsequential errors.*—A withholding agent may treat a withholding certificate as valid when the certificate includes an error described as an inconsequential error in §1.1471-3(c)(7)(i) for which the withholding agent obtains documentation sufficient for supporting a payee's claim of status as a foreign person or, for a payee that is an entity, its classification to the extent permitted under §1.1471-3(c)(7)(i). For example, if the country of residence is abbreviated in an ambiguous way on a beneficial owner withholding certificate provided to establish the beneficial owner's foreign status, a withholding agent may treat the withholding certificate as valid if it has obtained documentary evidence supporting that the beneficial owner's residence is in a country other than the United States.

(v) *Special effective date.*—See paragraph (f)(2)(ii) of this section for the special effective date applicable to this paragraph (b)(7).

(8) *Adjustments, refunds, or credits of overwithheld amounts.*—If the amount withheld under section 1441, 1442, or 1443 is greater than the tax due by the withholding agent or the taxpayer, adjustments may be made in accordance with the procedures described in §1.1461-2(a). Alternatively, refunds or credits may be claimed in accordance with the procedures described in §1.1464-1, relating to refunds or credits claimed by the beneficial owner, or §1.6414-1, relating to refunds or credits claimed by the withholding agent. If an amount was withheld under section 3406 or is subsequently determined to have been paid to a foreign person, see paragraph (b)(3)(vii) of this section and §31.6413(a)-3(a)(1) of this chapter.

(9) *Payments to joint owners.*—A payment to joint owners that requires documentation in order to reduce the rate of withholding under chapter 3 of the Code and the regulations thereunder does not qualify for such reduced rate unless the withholding agent can reliably associate the payment with documentation from each owner. Notwithstanding the preceding sentence, a payment to joint owners qualifies as a payment exempt from withholding under this section if any one of the owners provides a certificate of U.S. status on a Form W-9 in accordance with paragraph (d)(2) or (3) of this section or the withholding agent can associate the payment with an intermediary or flow-through withholding certificate upon which it can rely to treat the payment as made to a U.S. payee under paragraph (d)(4) of this section. See §31.3406(h)-2(a)(3)(i)(B) of this chapter.

(c) *Definitions.*—The following definitions apply for purposes of sections 1441 through 1443, 1461, and regulations under those sections. For definitions of terms used in these regulations that are defined under sections 1471 through 1474, see subparagraphs (43) through (56) of this paragraph.

(1) *Withholding.*—The term *withholding* means the deduction and withholding of tax at the applicable rate from the payment.

(2) *Foreign and U.S. person.*—(i) *In general.*—The term foreign person means any person that is not a U.S. person, including a QI branch of a U.S. financial institution (as defined in §1.1471-1(b)(109). Such a branch continues to be a U.S. payor for purposes of chapter 61 of the Code. See §1.6049-5(c)(4). A U.S. person is a person described in section 7701(a)(30), the U.S. government (including an agency or instrumentality thereof), a State (including an agency or instrumen-

tality thereof), or the District of Columbia (including an agency or instrumentality thereof).

(ii) *Dual residents.*—Individuals will not be treated as U.S. persons for purposes of this section for a taxable year or any portion of a taxable year for which they are a dual resident taxpayer (within the meaning of §301.7701(b)-7(a)(1) of this chapter) who is treated as a nonresident alien pursuant to §301.7701(b)-7(a)(1) of this chapter for purposes of computing their U.S. tax liability.

(3) *Individual.*—(i) *Alien individual.*—The term *alien individual* means an individual who is not a citizen or a national of the United States. See §1.1-1(c).

(ii) *Nonresident alien individual.*—The term *nonresident alien individual* means persons described in section 7701(b)(1)(B), alien individuals who are treated as nonresident aliens pursuant to §301.7701(b)-7 of this chapter for purposes of computing their U.S. tax liability, or an alien individual who is a resident of Puerto Rico, Guam, the Commonwealth of Northern Mariana Islands, the U.S. Virgin Islands, or American Samoa as determined under §301.7701(b)-1(d) of this chapter. An alien individual who has made an election under section 6013(g) or (h) to be treated as a resident of the United States is nevertheless treated as a nonresident alien individual for purposes of withholding under chapter 3 of the Code and the regulations thereunder.

(4) *Certain foreign corporations.*—For purposes of this section, a corporation created or organized in Guam, the Commonwealth of Northern Mariana Islands, the U.S. Virgin Islands, and American Samoa, is not treated as a foreign corporation if the requirements of sections 881(b)(1)(A), (B), and (C) are met for such corporation. Further, a payment made to a foreign government or an international organization shall be treated as a payment made to a foreign corporation for purposes of withholding under chapter 3 of the Code and the regulations thereunder.

(5) *Financial institution and foreign financial institution (or FFI).*—The term financial institution means a person described in §1.1471-1(b)(50). The term foreign financial institution or FFI has the meaning set forth in §1.1471-1(b)(47).

(6) *Beneficial owner.*—(i) *General rule.*—This paragraph (c)(6) defines the term *beneficial owner* for payments of income other than a payment for which a reduced rate of withholding is claimed under an income tax treaty. The term *beneficial owner* means the person who is the owner of the income for tax purposes and who beneficially owns that income. A person shall be treated as the owner of the income to the extent that it is required under U.S. tax principles to include the amount paid in gross income under section 61 (determined without regard to an exclusion or exemption from gross income under the Internal Revenue Code). Beneficial ownership of income is determined under the provisions of section 7701(l) and the regulations under that section and any other applicable general U.S. tax principles, including principles governing the determination of whether a transaction is a conduit transaction. Thus, a person receiving income in a capacity as a nominee, agent, or custodian for another person is not the beneficial owner of the income. In the case of a scholarship, the student receiving the scholarship is the beneficial owner of that scholarship. In the case of a payment of an amount that is not income, the beneficial owner determination shall be made under this paragraph (c)(6) as if the amount were income.

(ii) *Special rules.*—(A) *General rule.*—The beneficial owners of income paid to an entity described in this paragraph (c)(6)(ii) are those persons described in paragraphs (c)(6)(ii)(B) through (D) of this section.

(B) *Foreign partnerships.*—The beneficial owners of income paid to a foreign partnership (whether a nonwithholding or a withholding foreign partnership) are the partners in the partnership, unless they themselves are not the beneficial owners of the income under this paragraph (c)(6). For example, a partnership (first tier) that is a partner in another partnership (second tier) is not the beneficial owner of income paid to the second tier partnership since the first tier partnership is not the owner of the income under U.S. tax principles. Rather, the partners of the first tier partnership are the beneficial owners (to the extent they are not themselves persons that are not beneficial owners under this paragraph (c)(6)). See §1.1441-5(b) for applicable withholding procedures for payments to a domestic partnership. See also §1.1441-5(c)(3)(ii) for applicable withholding procedures for payments to a foreign partnership where one of the partners (at any level in the chain of tiers) is a domestic partnership.

(C) *Foreign simple trusts and foreign grantor trusts.*—The beneficial owners of income paid to a foreign simple trust, as described in paragraph (c)(23) of this section, are the beneficiaries of the trust, unless they themselves are not the beneficial owners of the income under this paragraph (c)(6). The beneficial owners of income paid to a foreign grantor trust, as described in paragraph (c)(26) of this section, are the persons treated as the owners of the trust, unless they themselves are not the beneficial owners of the income under this paragraph (c)(6).

(D) *Other foreign trusts and foreign estates.*—The beneficial owner of income paid to a foreign complex trust as defined in paragraph (c)(25) of this section or to a foreign estate is the foreign complex trust or estate itself.

(7) *Withholding agent.*—For a definition of the term *withholding agent* and applicable rules, see §1.1441-7.

(8) *Person.*—For purposes of the regulations under chapter 3 of the Code, the term *person* shall mean a person described in section 7701(a)(1) and the regulations under that section and a U.S. branch to the extent treated as a U.S. person under paragraph (b)(2)(iv) of this section. For purposes of the regulations under chapter 3 of the Code, the term *person* does not include a wholly-owned entity that is disregarded for federal tax purposes under §301.7701-2(c)(2) of this chapter as an entity separate from its owner. See paragraph (b)(2)(iii) of this section for procedures applicable to payments to such entities.

(9) *Source of income.*—The source of income is determined under the provisions of part I (section 861 and following), subchapter N, chapter 1 of the Code and the regulations under those provisions.

(10) *Chapter 3 of the Code (or chapter 3).*—For purposes of the regulations under sections 1441, 1442, and 1443, any reference to chapter 3 of the Code (or chapter 3) shall not include references to sections 1445 and 1446, unless the context indicates otherwise.

(11) *Reduced rate.*—For purposes of regulations under chapter 3 of the Code, and other withholding provisions of the Code, the term *reduced rate*, when used in regulations under chapter 3 of the Code, shall include an exemption from tax.

(12) *Payee.*—For purposes of chapter 3 of the Code, the term payee of a payment is determined under paragraph (b)(2) of this section, §1.1441-5(c)(1) (relating to partnerships), and §1.1441-5(e)(2) and (3) (relating to trusts and estates) and includes foreign persons, U.S. exempt recipients, and U.S. non-exempt recipients. A nonqualified intermediary and a qualified intermediary (to the extent it does not assume primary withholding responsibility) are not payees if they are acting as intermediaries and not the beneficial owner of income. In addition, a flow-through entity (other than a withholding foreign partnership, withholding foreign trust, or qualified intermediary that assumes primary withholding responsibility) is not a payee unless the income is (or is deemed to be) effectively connected with the conduct of a trade or business in the United States. See §1.6049-5(d)(1) for rules to determine the payee for purposes of chapter 61 of the Code. See §§1.1441-1(b)(3), 1.1441-5(d), and (e)(6) and §1.6049-5(d)(3) for presumption rules that apply if a payee's identity cannot be determined on the basis of valid documentation. For purposes of chapter 4, the term payee has the meaning set forth in §1.1471-3(a) with respect to a withholdable payment.

(13) *Intermediary.*—An *intermediary* means, with respect to a payment that it receives, a person that, for that payment, acts as a custodian, broker, nominee, or otherwise as an agent for another person, regardless of whether such other person is the beneficial owner of the amount paid, a flow-through entity, or another intermediary.

(14) *Nonqualified intermediary.*—A *nonqualified intermediary* means any intermediary that is not a U.S. person and not a qualified intermediary, as defined in paragraph (e)(5)(ii) of this section, or a qualified intermediary that is not acting in its capacity as a qualified intermediary with respect to a payment. For example, to the extent an entity that is a qualified intermediary provides another withholding agent with a foreign beneficial owner withholding certificate as defined in paragraph (e)(2)(i) of this section, the entity is not acting in its capacity as a qualified intermediary. Notwithstanding the preceding sentence, a qualified intermediary is acting as a qualified intermediary to the extent it provides another withholding agent with Forms W-9, or other information regarding U.S. non-exempt recipients pursuant to its qualified intermediary agreement with the IRS.

(15) *Qualified intermediary.*—The term *qualified intermediary* is defined in paragraph (e)(5)(ii) of this section.

(16) *Withholding certificate.*—The term withholding certificate means a Form W-8 described in paragraph (e)(2)(i) of this section (relating to foreign beneficial owners), paragraphs (e)(3)(i) or (e)(5)(i) of this section (relating to foreign intermediaries or qualified intermediaries), §1.1441-5(c)(2)(iv), (c)(3)(iii), and (e)(5)(iii) (relating to flow through entities), a Form 8233 described in §1.1441-4(b)(2), a

Form W-9 as described in paragraph (d) of this section, a statement described in §1.871-14(c)(2)(v) (relating to portfolio interest), or any other certificates that under the Code or regulations certifies or establishes the status of a payee or beneficial owner as a U.S. or a foreign person.

(17) *Documentary evidence; other appropriate documentation.*—The terms documentary evidence or other appropriate documentation refer to documentary evidence that may be provided for payments made outside the United States with respect to offshore obligations in accordance with §1.6049-5(c)(1) or any other evidence that under the Code or regulations certifies or establishes the status of a payee or beneficial owner as a U.S. or foreign person. See §§1.1441-6(b)(2), (c)(3) and (4) (relating to treaty benefits), and 1.6049-5(c)(1) and (4) (relating to chapter 61 reporting). Also see §1.1441-4(a)(3)(ii) regarding documentary evidence for notional principal contracts.

(18) *Documentation.*—The term *documentation* refers to both withholding certificates, as defined in paragraph (c)(16) of this section, and documentary evidence or other appropriate documentation, as defined in paragraph (c)(17) of this section.

(19) *Payor.*—The term *payor* is defined in §31.3406(a)-2 of this chapter and §1.6049-4(a)(2) and generally includes a withholding agent, as defined in §1.1441-7(a). The term also includes any person that makes a payment to an intermediary, flow-through entity, or U.S. branch that is not treated as a U.S. person to the extent the intermediary, flow-through, or U.S. branch provides a Form W-9 or other appropriate information relating to a payee so that the payment can be reported under chapter 61 of the Internal Revenue Code and, if required, subject to backup withholding under section 3406. This latter rule does not preclude the intermediary, flow-through entity, or U.S. branch from also being a payor.

(20) *Exempt recipient.*—The term *exempt recipient* means a person that is exempt from reporting under chapter 61 of the Internal Revenue Code and backup withholding under section 3406 and that is described in §§1.6041-3(q), 1.6045-2(b)(2)(i), and 1.6049-4(c)(1)(ii), and §5f.6045-1(c)(3)(i)(B) of this chapter. Exempt recipients are not exempt from withholding under chapter 3 of the Internal Revenue Code unless they are U.S. persons or foreign persons entitled to an exemption from withholding under chapter 3.

(21) *Non-exempt recipient.*—A *non-exempt recipient* is any person that is not an exempt recipient under paragraph (c)(20) of this section.

(22) *Reportable amounts.*—*Reportable amounts* are defined in paragraph (e)(3)(vi) of this section.

(23) *Flow-through entity.*—A flow-through entity means any entity that is described in this paragraph (c)(23) and that may provide documentation on behalf of its partners, beneficiaries, or owners to a withholding agent. The entities described in this paragraph are a foreign partnership (other than a withholding foreign partnership), a foreign simple trust (other than a withholding foreign trust) that is described in paragraph (c)(24) of this section, a foreign grantor trust (other than a withholding foreign trust) that is described in paragraph (c)(26) of this section, or, for any payments for which a reduced rate of withholding under an income tax treaty is claimed, any entity to the extent the entity is considered to be fiscally transparent under section 894 with respect to the payment by an interest holder's jurisdiction.

(24) *Foreign simple trust.*—A *foreign simple trust* is a foreign trust that is described in section 651(a).

(25) *Foreign complex trust.*—A foreign complex trust is a foreign trust other than a foreign simple trust or foreign grantor trust.

(26) *Foreign grantor trust.*—A *foreign grantor trust* is a foreign trust but only to the extent all or a portion of the income of the trust is treated as owned by the grantor or another person under sections 671 through 679.

(27) *Partnership.*—The term *partnership* means any entity treated as a partnership under §301.7701-2 or -3 of this chapter.

(28) *Nonwithholding foreign partnership (or NWP).*—A nonwithholding foreign partnership is a foreign partnership that is not a withholding foreign partnership, as defined in §1.1441-5(c)(2)(i).

(29) *Withholding foreign partnership (or WP).*—A withholding foreign partnership is defined in §1.1441-5(c)(2)(i).

(30) *Possessions of the United States or U.S. territory.*—For purposes of the regulations under chapters 3 and 61 of the Code, the term possessions of the United States or U.S. territory means Guam,

American Samoa, the Northern Mariana Islands, Puerto Rico, or the Virgin Islands.

(31) *Amount subject to chapter 3 withholding.*—An amount subject to withholding under chapter 3 is an amount described in §1.1441-2(a).

(32) *EIN.*—The term EIN means an employer identification number (also known as a federal tax identification number) described in §301.6109-1(a)(1)(i).

(33) *Flow-through withholding certificate.*—The term flow-through withholding certificate means a Form W-8IMY submitted by a foreign partnership, foreign simple trust, or foreign grantor trust.

(34) *Foreign payee.*—The term foreign payee means any payee other than a U.S. payee.

(35) *Intermediary withholding certificate.*—The term intermediary withholding certificate means a Form W-8IMY submitted by an intermediary or qualified intermediary.

(36) *Nonwithholding foreign trust (or NWT).*—The term nonwithholding foreign trust or NWT means a foreign trust as defined in section 7701(a)(31)(B) that is a simple trust or grantor trust and is not a withholding foreign trust.

(37) *Payment with respect to an offshore obligation.*—The term payment with respect to an offshore obligation means a payment made outside of the United States, within the meaning of §1.6049-5(e), with respect to an offshore obligation (as defined in §1.6049-5(c)(1), §1.6041-1(d), or §1.6042-3(b) (depending on the type of payment)).

(38) *Permanent residence address.*—(i) *In general.*—The term *permanent residence address* is the address in the country of which the person claims to be a resident for purposes of that country's income tax. In the case of a withholding certificate furnished in order to claim a reduced rate of withholding under an income tax treaty, whether a person is a resident of a treaty country must be determined in the manner prescribed under the applicable treaty. See §1.1441-6(b). The address of a financial institution with which the person maintains an account, a post office box, or an address used solely for mailing purposes is not a permanent residence address unless such address is the only address used by the person and appears as the person's registered address in the person's organizational documents. Further, an address that is provided subject to a hold mail instruction (as defined in paragraph (c)(38)(ii) of this section) is not a permanent residence address unless the person provides the documentary evidence described in paragraph (c)(38)(ii) of this section. If the person is an individual who does not have a tax residence in any country, the permanent residence address is the place at which the person normally resides. If the person is an entity and does not have a tax residence in any country, then the permanent residence address of the entity is the place at which the person maintains its principal office.

(ii) *Hold mail instruction.*—The term *hold mail instruction* means a current instruction by a person to keep the person's mail until such instruction is amended. An instruction to send all correspondence electronically is not a hold mail instruction. An address that is subject to a hold mail instruction may be used as a permanent residence address if the person has also provided the withholding agent with documentary evidence described in §1.1471-3(c)(5)(i) (without regard to the requirement in §1.1471-3(c)(5)(i) that the documentary evidence contain a permanent residence address). The documentary evidence described in §1.1471-3(c)(5)(i) must support the person's claim of foreign status or, in the case of a person that is claiming treaty benefits, must support residence in the country where the person is claiming a reduced rate of withholding under an income tax treaty. If, after a withholding certificate is provided, a person's permanent residence address is subsequently subject to a hold mail instruction, the addition of the hold mail instruction is a change in circumstances requiring the person to provide the documentary evidence described in this paragraph (c)(38)(ii) in order for a withholding agent to use the address as a permanent residence address.

(39) *Standing instructions to pay amounts.*—The term standing instructions to pay amounts has the meaning set forth in §1.1471-1(b)(126).

(40) *Territory financial institution.*—The term territory financial institution has the meaning set forth in §1.1471-1(b)(130).

(41) *TIN.*—The term TIN means the tax identifying number assigned to a person under section 6109.

(42) *Withholding foreign trust (or WT).*—The term withholding foreign trust (or WT) means a foreign grantor trust or foreign simple trust that has executed the agreement described in §1.1441-5(e)(5)(v).

(43) *Certified deemed-compliant FFI.*—The term certified deemed-compliant FFI means an FFI described in §1.1471-5(f)(2).

(44) *Chapter 3 withholding rate pool.*—The term chapter 3 withholding rate pool has the meaning described in paragraph (e)(5)(v)(C)(1) of this section.

(45) *Chapter 3 status.*—The term chapter 3 status refers to the attributes of a payee relevant for determining the rate of withholding with respect to a payment made to the payee for purposes of chapter 3.

(46) *Chapter 4 of the Code (or chapter 4).*—The term chapter 4 of the Code (or chapter 4) means sections 1471 through 1474 and the regulations thereunder.

(47) *Chapter 4 status.*—The term chapter 4 status means a person's status as a U.S. person, a specified U.S. person, an individual that is a foreign person, a participating FFI, a deemed-compliant FFI, a restricted distributor, an exempt beneficial owner, a nonparticipating FFI, a territory financial institution, an excepted NFFE, or a passive NFFE.

(48) *Chapter 4 withholding rate pool.*—The term chapter 4 withholding rate pool has the meaning set forth §1.1471-1(b)(20). For when a withholding statement may include a chapter 4 withholding rate pool of U.S. payees for purposes of this section and §1.1441-5, however, see paragraph (e)(3)(iv)(A) of this section (for a withholding statement provided by a nonqualified intermediary) or paragraph (e)(5)(v)(C)(2) of this section (for a withholding statement provided by a qualified intermediary).

(49) *Deemed-compliant FFI.*—The term deemed-compliant FFI means an FFI that is treated, pursuant to section 1471(b)(2) and §1.1471-5(f), as meeting the requirements of section 1471(b). The term deemed-compliant FFI also includes a QI branch of a U.S. financial institution that is a reporting Model 1 FFI.

(50) *GIIN (or Global Intermediary Identification Number).*—The term GIIN or Global Intermediary Identification Number means the identification number that is assigned to a participating FFI or registered deemed-compliant FFI. The term GIIN or Global Intermediary Identification Number also includes the identification number assigned to a reporting Model 1 FFI (as defined in §1.1471-1(b)(114)) for purposes of identifying such entity to withholding agents. All GIINs will appear on the IRS FFI list.

(51) *NFFE.*—The term NFFE or non-financial foreign entity has the meaning set forth in §1.1471-1(b)(80).

(52) *Nonparticipating FFI.*—The term nonparticipating FFI means an FFI other than a participating FFI, a deemed-compliant FFI, or an exempt beneficial owner.

(53) *Participating FFI.*—The term participating FFI has the meaning set forth in §1.1471-1(b)(91).

(54) *Preexisting obligation.*—The term preexisting obligation has the meaning set forth in §1.1471-1(b)(104).

(55) *Registered deemed-compliant FFI.*—The term registered deemed-compliant FFI has the meaning set forth in §1.1471-5(f)(1).

(56) *Withholdable payment.*—The term withholdable payment has the meaning set forth in §1.1473-1(a).

(d) *Beneficial owner's or payee's claim of U.S. status.*—(1) *In general.*—Under paragraph (b)(1) of this section, a withholding agent is not required to withhold under chapter 3 of the Code on payments to a U.S. payee, to a person presumed to be a U.S. payee in accordance with the provisions of paragraph (b)(3) of this section, or to a person that the withholding agent may treat as a U.S. beneficial owner of the payment. Absent actual knowledge or reason to know otherwise, a withholding agent may rely on the provisions of this paragraph (d) in order to determine whether to treat a payee or beneficial owner as a U.S. person.

(2) *Payments for which a Form W-9 is otherwise required.*—A withholding agent may treat as a U.S. payee any person who is required to furnish a Form W-9 and who furnishes it in accordance with the procedures described in §§31.3406(d)-1 through 31.3406(d)-5 of this chapter (including the requirement that the payee furnish its taxpayer identifying number (TIN)) if the withholding agent meets all the requirements described in §31.3406(h)-3(e) of this chapter regarding reliance by a payor on a Form W-9. Providing a Form W-9 or valid substitute form shall serve as a statement that the person whose name is on the form is a U.S. person. Therefore, a foreign person, including a U.S. branch treated as a U.S. person under paragraph (b)(2)(iv) of this section, shall not provide a Form W-9. A U.S. branch of a foreign person may establish its status as a foreign person

required to be allocated to the extent it is required to be reported on Form 1099 or Form 1042-S. See §1.6049-8 (regarding reporting of bank deposit interest to certain foreign persons). If a payee receives income through another nonqualified intermediary, flow-through entity, or U.S. branch or territory financial institution described in paragraph (e)(2)(iv) of this section (other than a U.S. branch or territory financial institution treated as a U.S. person), the withholding statement must also state, with respect to the payee, the name, address, and TIN, if known, of the other nonqualified intermediary or U.S. branch from which the payee directly receives the payment or the flow-through entity in which the payee has a direct ownership interest. If another nonqualified intermediary, flow-through entity, or U.S. branch fails to allocate a payment, the name of the nonqualified intermediary, flow-through entity, or U.S. branch that failed to allocate the payment shall be provided with respect to such payment.

(iii) If a payee is identified as a foreign person, the nonqualified intermediary must specify the rate of withholding to which the payee is subject, the payee's country of residence and, if a reduced rate of withholding is claimed, the basis for that reduced rate (e.g., treaty benefit, portfolio interest, exempt under section 501(c)(3), 892, or 895). The allocation statement must also include the TINs of those foreign persons for whom such a number is required under paragraph (e)(4)(vii) of this section or §1.1441-6(b)(1) (regarding claims for treaty benefits for which a TIN is provided unless a foreign tax identifying number described in §1.1441-6(b)(1) is provided). In the case of a claim of treaty benefits, the nonqualified intermediary's withholding statement must also state whether the limitation on benefits and section 894 statements required by §1.1441-6(c)(5) have been provided, if required, in the beneficial owner's Form W-8 or associated with such owner's documentary evidence.

(iv) The withholding statement must also contain any other information the withholding agent reasonably requests in order to fulfill its obligations under chapter 3 and chapter 61 of the Code, and section 3406.

(2) *Nonqualified intermediary withholding statement for withholdable payments.*—This paragraph (e)(3)(iv)(C)(2) modifies the requirements of a withholding statement described in paragraph (e)(3)(iv)(C)(1) of this section that is provided by a nonqualified intermediary with respect to a reportable amount that is a withholdable payment. For such a payment, the requirements applicable to a withholding statement described in paragraph (e)(3)(iv)(A) through (e)(3)(iv)(C)(1) of this section shall apply, except that—

(i) The withholding statement must include the chapter 4 status (using the applicable status code used for filing Form 1042-S) and GIIN (when required for chapter 4 purposes under §1.1471-3(d)) of each other intermediary or flow-through entity that is a foreign person and that receives the payment, excluding an intermediary or flow-through entity that is an account holder of or interest holder in a withholding foreign partnership, withholding foreign trust, or intermediary acting as a qualified intermediary for the payment;

(ii) If the nonqualified intermediary that is a participating FFI or registered deemed-compliant FFI provides a withholding statement described in §1.1471-3(c)(3)(iii)(B)(2) (describing an FFI withholding statement), the withholding statement may include chapter 4 withholding rate pools with respect to the portions of the payment allocated to nonparticipating FFIs and recalcitrant account holders (to the extent permitted on an FFI withholding statement described in that paragraph) in lieu of providing specific payee information with respect to such persons on the statement (including persons subject to chapter 4 withholding) as described in paragraph (e)(3)(iv)(C)(1) of this section;

(iii) If the nonqualified intermediary provides a withholding statement described in §1.1471-3(c)(3)(iii)(B)(3) (describing a chapter 4 withholding statement), the withholding statement may include chapter 4 withholding rate pools with respect to the portions of the payment allocated to nonparticipating FFIs; and

(iv) For a payment allocated to a payee that is a foreign person (other than a person included in a chapter 4 withholding rate pool described in paragraphs (e)(3)(iv)(C)(2)(ii) and (iii) of this section) that is reported on a withholding statement described in §1.1471-3(c)(3)(iii)(B)(2) or (3), the withholding statement must include the chapter 4 status of the payee (unless an exception applies for purposes of providing such status under chapter 4) and, for a payee other than an individual, the recipient code for chapter 4 purposes used for filing Form 1042-S; and

(v) To the extent that a withholdable payment is not reportable on a Form 1042-S, Form 1099 under the rules of chapter 61, or Form 8966 "FATCA Report," no allocation of the payment is required on the withholding statement.

(3) *Alternative withholding statement.*—(i) In lieu of a withholding statement containing all of the information described in paragraph (e)(3)(iv)(C)(1) and (2) of this section, a withholding agent may accept from a nonqualified intermediary a withholding statement that meets all of the requirements of this paragraph (e)(3)(iv)(C)(3)(i) with respect to a payment. The withholding statement described in this paragraph (e)(3)(iv)(C)(3)(i) may be provided only by a nonqualified intermediary that provides the withholding agent with the withholding certificates from the beneficial owners (that is, not documentary evidence) before the payment is made.

(A) The withholding statement is not required to contain all of the information specified in paragraphs (e)(3)(iv)(C)(1) and (2) of this section that is also included on a withholding certificate (for example, name, address, TIN (if any), chapter 4 status, GIIN (if any)). The withholding statement is also not required to specify the rate of withholding to which each foreign payee is subject, provided that all of the information necessary to make such determination is provided on the withholding certificate. A withholding agent that uses the withholding statement may not apply a different rate from that which the withholding agent may reasonably conclude from the information on the withholding certificate.

(B) The withholding statement must allocate the payment to every payee required to be reported as described in paragraph (e)(3)(iv)(C)(1)(ii) of this section.

(C) The withholding statement must also contain any other information the withholding agent reasonably requests in order to fulfill its obligations under chapters 3, 4, and 61, and section 3406.

(D) The withholding statement must contain a representation from the nonqualified intermediary that the information on the withholding certificates is not inconsistent with any other account information the nonqualified intermediary has for the beneficial owners for determining the rate of withholding with respect to each payee (applying the standards of knowledge applicable to a withholding agent's reliance on a withholding certificate in the regulations under section 1441 and, for a withholdable payment, the regulations under section 1471).

(ii) In lieu of a withholding statement that includes a recipient code for chapter 4 purposes used for filing Form 1042-S, a withholding agent may accept a nonqualified intermediary withholding statement that contains all of the information described in paragraph (e)(3)(iv)(C)(1) and (2) of this section (or an alternative withholding statement permitted under paragraph (e)(3)(iv)(C)(3)(i) of this section) but that does not provide a recipient code for chapter 4 purposes used for filing Form 1042-S for a payee as required in paragraph (e)(3)(iv)(C)(2)(iv) of this section if the withholding agent is able to determine such payee's recipient code based on other information included on or with the withholding statement or in the withholding agent's records with respect to the payee.

(4) *Example.*—This example illustrates the principles of paragraph (e)(3)(iv)(C) of this section. WA makes a withholdable payment of U.S. source dividends to NQI, a nonqualified intermediary. NQI provides WA with a valid intermediary withholding certificate under paragraph (e)(3)(iii) of this section that includes NQI's certification of its status for chapter 4 purposes as a participating FFI. NQI provides a withholding statement on which NQI allocates 20% of the payment to a chapter 4 withholding rate pool of recalcitrant account holders of NQI for purposes of chapter 4 and allocates 80% of the payment equally to A and B, individuals that are account holders of NQI. NQI also provides WA with valid beneficial owner withholding certificates from A and B establishing their status as foreign persons entitled to a 15% rate of withholding under an applicable income tax treaty. Because NQI has certified its status as a participating FFI, withholding under chapter 4 is not required with respect to NQI. See §1.1471-2(a)(4). Based on the documentation NQI provided to WA with respect to A and B, WA can reliably associate the payment with valid documentation on the portion of the payment allocated to them and, because the payment is a withholdable payment, may rely on the allocation of the payment for NQI's recalcitrant account holders in a chapter 4 withholding rate pool in lieu of payee information with respect to such account holders. See paragraph (e)(3)(iv)(C)(2) of this section for the special rules for a withholding statement provided by a nonqualified intermediary for a withholdable payment. Also see §1.1471-2(a) for WA's withholding requirements under chapter 4 with respect to the portion of the payment allocated to NQI's recalcitrant account holders and §1.1441-3(a)(2) for coordinating withholding under chapter 3 for payments to which withholding is applied under chapter 4.

(D) *Alternative procedures.*—(1) *In general.*—Under the alternative procedures of this paragraph (e)(3)(iv)(D), a nonqualified intermediary may provide information allocating a payment of a reportable amount to each payee (including U.S. exempt recipients) otherwise required under paragraph (e)(3)(iv)(B)(2) of this section after a payment is made. To use the alternative procedure of this paragraph (e)(3)(iv)(D), the nonqualified intermediary must inform the withholding agent on a statement associated with its nonqualified intermediary withholding certificate that it is using the procedure under this paragraph (e)(3)(iv)(D) and the withholding agent must agree to the procedure. If the requirements of the alternative procedure are met, a withholding agent, including the nonqualified intermediary using the procedures, can treat the payment as reliably associated with documentation and, therefore, the presumption rules of paragraph (b)(3) of this section and §§ 1.1441-5(d) and (e)(6) and 1.6049-5(d) do not apply even though information allocating the payment to each payee has not been received prior to the payment. See paragraph (e)(3)(iv)(D)(7) of this section, however, for a nonqualified intermediary's liability for tax and penalties if the requirements of this paragraph (e)(3)(iv)(D) are not met. These alternative procedures shall not be used for payments that are allocable to U.S. non-exempt recipients except as provided in paragraph (e)(3)(iv)(D)(2)(*ii*) of this section. Therefore, a nonqualified intermediary is required to provide a withholding agent with information allocating payments of reportable amounts to U.S. non-exempt recipients prior to the payment being made by the withholding agent.

(2) *Withholding rate pools.*—(i) *In general.*—In place of the information required in paragraph (e)(3)(iv)(C)(2) of this section allocating payments to each payee, the nonqualified intermediary must provide a withholding agent with withholding rate pool information prior to the payment of a reportable amount. The withholding statement must contain all other information required by paragraph (e)(3)(iv)(C) of this section. Further, each payee listed in the withholding statement must be assigned to an identified withholding rate pool. To the extent a nonqualified intermediary is required to provide, or does provide, documentation, the alternative procedures do not relieve the nonqualified intermediary from the requirement to provide documentation prior to the payment being made. Therefore, withholding certificates or other appropriate documentation and all information required by paragraph (e)(3)(iv)(C) of this section (other than allocation information) must be provided to a withholding agent before any new payee receives a reportable amount. In addition, the withholding statement must be updated by assigning a new payee to a withholding rate pool prior to the payment of a reportable amount. A withholding rate pool is a payment of a single type of income, determined in accordance with the categories of income used to file Form 1042-S, that is subject to a single rate of withholding. A withholding rate pool may be established by any reasonable method to which the nonqualified intermediary and a withholding agent agree (*e.g.*, by establishing a separate account for a single withholding rate pool, or by dividing a payment made to a single account into portions allocable to each withholding rate pool). The nonqualified intermediary shall determine withholding rate pools based on valid documentation or, to the extent a payment cannot be reliably associated with valid documentation, the presumption rules of paragraph (b)(3) of this section and §§ 1.1441-5(d) and (e)(6) and 1.6049-5(d).

(ii) *Withholding rate pools for chapter 4 purposes.*—This paragraph (e)(3)(iv)(D)(2)(*ii*) modifies the provisions of paragraph (e)(3)(iv)(D)(2)(*i*) of this section with respect to the withholding rate pools permitted for the alternative procedures described in paragraph (e)(3)(iv)(D)(1) of this section in the case of a payment that is allocable on a withholding statement to a chapter 4 withholding rate pool as described in this paragraph. In the case of a withholdable payment, a nonqualified intermediary may include reportable amounts allocable to a chapter 4 withholding rate pool (other than a chapter 4 withholding rate pool of U.S. payees) in a 30-percent rate pool together with a withholding rate pool for amounts subject to chapter 3 withholding at the 30-percent rate. For a payment of a reportable amount that is allocable to a chapter 4 withholding rate pool of U.S. payees on a withholding statement, a nonqualified intermediary may include such amount in a single withholding rate pool with the amount of the payment that is exempt from withholding under chapter 3 instead of providing documentation regarding U.S. non-exempt recipients included in the pool or separately allocating the amount to the chapter 4 withholding rate pool. To the extent that a nonqualified intermediary allocates an amount to any chapter 4 withholding rate pool, the nonqualified intermediary is required to notify the withholding agent of the allocation before receiving the payment and is not required to provide documentation with respect to the payees included in such pool. The nonqualified intermediary shall determine the chapter 4 withholding rate pools permitted to be used under this paragraph (e)(3)(iv)(D)(2)(*ii*) in accordance with the nonqualified intermediary's applicable chapter 4 status and under § 1.1471-3(c)(3)(iii)(B)(2) (for an FFI withholding statement) or (c)(3)(iii)(B)(3) (for a chapter 4 withholding statement) or under § 1.6049-4(c)(4) for a chapter 4 withholding rate pool of U.S. payees (or similar applicable coordination rule in chapter 61 for payments other than interest). Additionally, the nonqualified intermediary shall identify those payees to which withholding under chapter 4 applies that are not included in a chapter 4 reporting pool (including payees that could be included in a chapter 4 withholding rate pool for whom the nonqualified intermediary chooses to provide payee specific information).

(3) *Allocation information.*—The nonqualified intermediary must provide the withholding agent with sufficient information to allocate the income in each withholding rate pool to each payee (including U.S. exempt recipients or any chapter 4 withholding rate pool identified by the withholding agent under paragraph (e)(3)(iv)(D)(2)(*ii*) of this section) within the pool no later than January 31 of the year following the year of payment. Any payments that are not allocated to payees for whom documentation has been provided or a chapter 4 withholding rate pool referred to in the previous sentence shall be allocated to an undocumented payee in accordance with the presumption rules of paragraph (b)(3) of this section and §§ 1.1441-5(d) and (e)(6) and 1.6049-5(d), and 1.1471-3(f)(5) (for a withholdable payment for chapter 4 purposes). Notwithstanding the preceding sentence, deposit interest (including original issue discount) described in section 871(i)(2)(A) or 881(d) and interest or original issue discount on short-term obligations as described in section 871(g)(1)(B) or 881(e) is not required to be allocated to a U.S. exempt recipient or a foreign payee, except as required under § 1.6049-8 (regarding reporting of deposit interest paid to certain foreign persons).

(4) *Failure to provide allocation information.*—Except as provided in paragraph (e)(3)(iv)(D)(5) of this section, if a nonqualified intermediary fails to provide allocation information, if required, by January 31 for any withholding rate pool to the extent required in paragraph (e)(3)(iv)(D)(3) of this section, a withholding agent shall not apply the alternative procedures of this paragraph (e)(3)(iv)(D) to any payments of reportable amounts paid after January 31 in the taxable year following the calendar year for which allocation information was not given and any subsequent taxable year. Further, the alternative procedures shall be unavailable for any other withholding rate pool (other than a chapter 4 withholding rate pool as otherwise permitted) even though allocation information was given for that other pool. Therefore, the withholding agent must withhold on a payment of a reportable amount in accordance with the presumption rules of paragraph (b)(3) of this section, and §§ 1.1441-5(d) and (e)(6) and 1.6049-5(d), and 1.1471-3(f)(5) (for a withholdable payment for chapter 4 purposes), unless the nonqualified intermediary provides all of the information, including information sufficient to allocate the payment to each specific payee or chapter 4 withholding rate pool (as permitted), required by paragraph (e)(3)(iv)(A) through (C) of this section prior to the payment. A nonqualified intermediary must allocate at least 90 percent of the income required to be allocated for each withholding rate pool as required under this paragraph (e)(3)(iv)(D)(4) or the nonqualified intermediary will be treated as having failed to provide allocation information for purposes of this paragraph (e)(3)(iv)(D). For purposes of the allocation, a nonqualified intermediary is required to identify by January 31 the portion of the payment that is allocated to each chapter 4 withholding rate pool (rather than the payees included in each such pool). See paragraph (e)(3)(iv)(D)(7) of this section for liability for tax and penalties if a nonqualified intermediary fails to provide allocation information in whole or in part.

(5) *Cure provision.*—A nonqualified intermediary may cure any failure to provide allocation information by providing the required allocation information to the withholding agent no later than February 14 following the calendar year of payment. If the withholding agent receives the allocation information by that date, it may apply the adjustment procedures of § 1.1461-2 (or of § 1.1474-2 for an amount withheld under chapter 4) to any excess withholding for payments made on or after February 1 and on or before February 14. Any nonqualified intermediary that fails to cure by February 14 may request the ability to use the alternative procedures of this paragraph (e)(3)(iv)(D) by submitting a request, in writing, to the IRS. The request must state the reason that the nonqualified intermediary did not comply with the alternative procedures of this paragraph (e)(3)(iv)(D) and steps that the nonqualified intermediary has taken, or will take, to ensure that no failures occur in the future. If the IRS determines that the alternative procedures of this paragraph (e)(3)(iv)(D) may apply, a determination to that effect will be issued by the IRS to the nonqualified intermediary.

(6) *Form 1042-S reporting in case of allocation failure.*—If a nonqualified intermediary fails to provide allocation information by February 14 following the year of payment for a withholding rate pool, the withholding agent must file Forms 1042-S for payments made to each payee in that pool (other than U.S. exempt recipients) in the prior calendar year by pro rating the payment to each payee (including U.S. exempt recipients) listed in the withholding statement for that withholding rate pool, treating as a payee for this purpose each chapter 4 withholding rate pool identified by the nonqualified intermediary under paragraph (e)(3)(iv)(D)(2)(*ii*) of this section. If the nonqualified intermediary fails to allocate 10 percent or less of an amount required to be allocated for a withholding rate pool, a withholding agent shall report the unallocated amount as

paid to a single unknown payee in accordance with the presumption rules of paragraph (b) of this section and §§1.1441-5(d) and (e)(6) and 1.6049-5(d), and §1.1471-3(f)(5) (for a withholdable payment for chapter 4 purposes). The portion of the payment that can be allocated to specific recipients, as defined in §1.1461-1(c)(1)(ii), shall be reported to each recipient in accordance with the rules of §1.1461-1(c) and §1.1474-1(d)(2) (for a withholdable payment).

(7) *Liability for tax, interest, and penalties.*—If a nonqualified intermediary fails to provide allocation information by February 14 following the year of payment for all or a portion of the payments made to any withholding rate pool, the withholding agent from whom the nonqualified intermediary received payments of reportable amounts shall not be liable for any tax, interest, or penalties, due solely to the errors or omissions of the nonqualified intermediary. See §1.1441-7(b)(2) through (10) for the due diligence requirements of a withholding agent. Because failure by the nonqualified intermediary to provide allocation information results in a payment not being reliably associated with valid documentation, the beneficial owners for whom the nonqualified intermediary acts are not entitled to a reduced rate of withholding. Therefore, the nonqualified intermediary, as a withholding agent, shall be liable for any tax not withheld by the withholding agent in accordance with the presumption rules, interest on the under withheld tax if the nonqualified intermediary fails to pay the tax timely, and any applicable penalties, including the penalties under sections 6656 (failure to deposit), 6721 (failure to file information returns) and 6722 (failure to file payee statements). Failure to provide allocation information for more than 10 percent of the payments made to a particular withholding rate pool will be presumed to be an intentional failure within the meaning of sections 6721(e) and 6722(c). The nonqualified intermediary may rebut the presumption.

(8) *Applicability to flow-through entities and certain U.S. branches.*—See paragraph (e)(3)(v) of this section and §1.1441-5(c)(3)(iv) and (e)(5)(iv) for the applicability of this paragraph (e)(3)(iv) to U.S. branches described in paragraph (b)(2)(iv) of this section (other than U.S. branches treated as U.S. persons) and flow-through entities.

(E) *Notice procedures.*—The IRS may notify a withholding agent that the alternative procedures of paragraph (e)(3)(iv)(D) of this section are not applicable to a specified nonqualified intermediary, a U.S. branch described in paragraph (b)(2)(iv) of this section, or a flow-through entity. If a withholding agent receives such a notice, it must commence withholding under this section or chapter 4 (if applicable) in accordance with the presumption rules of paragraph (b)(3) and §§1.1441-5(d) and (e)(6), 1.6049-5(d), and 1.1471-3(f)(5) (for a withholdable payment for chapter 4 purposes) unless the nonqualified intermediary, U.S. branch, or flow-through entity complies with the procedures in paragraphs (e)(3)(iv)(A) through (C) of this section. In addition, the IRS may notify a withholding agent, in appropriate circumstances, that it must apply the presumption rules of paragraph (b)(3) of this section and §§1.1441-5(d) and (e)(6), 1.6049-5(d), and §1.1471-3(f)(5) (for a withholdable payment for chapter 4 purposes) to payments made to a nonqualified intermediary, a U.S. branch, or a flow-through entity even if the nonqualified intermediary, U.S. branch, or flow-through entity provides allocation information prior to the payment. A withholding agent that receives a notice under this paragraph (e)(3)(iv)(E) must commence withholding in accordance with the presumption rules within 30 days of the date of the notice. The IRS may withdraw its prohibition against using the alternative procedures of paragraph (e)(3)(iv)(D) of this section, or its requirement to follow the presumption rules, if the nonqualified intermediary, U.S. branch, or flow-through entity can demonstrate to the satisfaction of the IRS that it is capable of complying with the rules under chapter 3 of the Code and any other conditions required by the IRS.

(v) *Withholding certificate from certain U.S. branches (including territory financial institutions).*—A U.S. branch certificate is a withholding certificate provided by a U.S. branch (including a territory financial institution) described in paragraph (b)(2)(iv) of this section that is not the beneficial owner of the income. The withholding certificate is provided with respect to reportable amounts and must state that such amounts are not effectively connected with the conduct of a trade or business in the United States. The withholding certificate must either transmit the appropriate documentation for the persons for whom the branch receives the payment (*i.e.*, as an intermediary) or be provided as evidence of its agreement with the withholding agent to be treated as a U.S. person with respect to any payment associated with the certificate. A U.S. branch withholding certificate is valid only if it is furnished on a Form W-8, an acceptable substitute form, or such other form as the IRS may prescribe, it is signed under penalties of perjury by a person authorized to sign for the branch, its validity has not expired, and it contains the informa-

tion, statements, and certifications described in this paragraph (e)(3)(v). If the certificate is furnished to transmit withholding certificates and other documentation, it must contain the information, certifications, and statements described in paragraphs (e)(3)(v)(A) through (C) of this section and in paragraphs (e)(3)(iii) and (iv) (alternative procedures) of this section, applying the term U.S. branch instead of the term nonqualified intermediary. If the certificate is furnished pursuant to an agreement to treat the U.S. branch or territory financial institution as a U.S. person (which agreement must be for purposes of chapter 4 in addition to this section in the case of a payment that is a withholdable payment), the information and certifications required on the withholding certificate are limited to the following—

(A) The name of the territory financial institution or person of which the U.S. branch is a part, the address of the territory financial institution or U.S. branch;

(B) A certification that the payments associated with the certificate are not effectively connected with the conduct of its trade or business in the United States;

(C) The EIN of the U.S. branch or territory financial institution;

(D) When required for chapter 4 purposes, the chapter 4 status and GIIN (if applicable) of the entity of which the U.S. branch is a part; and

(E) Any other information, certifications, or statements as may be required by the form or accompanying instructions in addition to, or in lieu of, the information and certification described in this paragraph (e)(3)(v).

(vi) *Reportable amounts.*—For purposes of chapter 3 of the Internal Revenue Code, a nonqualified intermediary, qualified intermediary, flow-through entity, and U.S. branch described in paragraph (b)(2)(iv) of this section (other than a U.S. branch that agrees to be treated as a U.S. person) must provide a withholding certificate and associated documentation and other information with respect to reportable amounts. For purposes of the regulations under chapter 3 of the Internal Revenue Code, the term reportable amount means an amount subject to withholding within the meaning of §1.1441-2(a), bank deposit interest (including original issue discount) and similar types of deposit interest described in section 871(i)(2)(A) or 881(d) that are from sources within the United States, and any amount of interest or original issue discount from sources within the United States on the redemption of certain short-term obligations described in section 871(g)(1)(B) or 881(e). Reportable amounts shall not include amounts received on the sale or exchange (other than a redemption) of an obligation described in section 871(g)(1)(B) or 881(e) that is effected at an office outside the United States. See §1.6045-1(g)(3) to determine whether a sale is effected at an office outside the United States. Reportable amounts also do not include payments with respect to deposits with banks and other financial institutions that remain on deposit for a period of two weeks or less, to amounts of original issue discount arising from a sale and repurchase transaction that is completed within a period of two weeks or less, or to amounts described in §1.6049-5(b)(7), (10) or (11) (relating to certain obligations issued in bearer form). While short-term OID and bank deposit interest are not subject to withholding under chapter 3 of the Internal Revenue Code, such amounts may be subject to information reporting under section 6049 if paid to a U.S. person who is not an exempt recipient described in §1.6049-4(c)(1)(ii) and to backup withholding under section 3406 in the absence of documentation. See §1.6049-5(d)(3)(iii) for applicable procedures when such amounts are paid to a foreign intermediary.

(4) *Applicable rules.*—The provisions in this paragraph (e)(4) describe procedures applicable to withholding certificates on Form W-8 or Form 8233 (or a substitute form) or documentary evidence furnished to establish foreign status. These provisions do not apply to Forms W-9 (or their substitutes). For corresponding provisions regarding Form W-9 (or a substitute form), see section 3406 and the regulations under that section.

(i) *Who may sign the certificate.*—(A) *In general.*—A withholding certificate (including an acceptable substitute) may be signed by any person authorized to sign a declaration under penalties of perjury on behalf of the person whose name is on the certificate as provided in section 6061 and the regulations under that section (relating to who may sign generally for an individual, estate, or trust, which includes certain agents who may sign returns and other documents), section 6062 and the regulations under that section (relating to who may sign corporate returns), and section 6063 and the regulations under that section (relating to who may sign partnership returns). A person authorized to sign a withholding certificate includes an officer or director of a corporation, a partner of a partnership, a trustee of a trust, an executor of an estate, any foreign equivalent of the former titles, and any other person that has been provided written authorization by the individual or entity named on the certificate to sign documentation on such person's behalf.

(B) *Electronic signatures.*—A withholding agent, regardless of whether the withholding agent has established an electronic system pursuant to paragraph (e)(4)(iv)(A) or (e)(4)(iv)(C) of this section, may accept a withholding certificate with an electronic signature, provided the electronic signature meets the requirements of paragraph (e)(4)(iv)(B)(3)(ii) of this section. In addition, the withholding certificate must reasonably demonstrate to the withholding agent that the form has been electronically signed by the recipient identified on the form (or a person authorized to sign for the recipient). For example, a withholding agent may treat as signed for purposes of the requirements for a valid withholding certificate, a withholding certificate that has in the signature block the name of the person authorized to sign, a time and date stamp, and a statement that the certificate has been electronically signed. However, a withholding agent may not treat a withholding certificate with a typed name in the signature line and no other information as signed for purposes of the requirements for a valid withholding certificate. A withholding agent may also rely upon, in addition to the contents of a withholding certificate, other documentation or information it has collected to support that a withholding certificate was electronically signed by the recipient identified on the form (or other person authorized to sign for the recipient), provided that the withholding agent does not have actual knowledge that the documentation or information is incorrect.

(ii) *Period of validity.*—(A) *General rule.*—(1) *Withholding certificates and documentary evidence.*—Except as provided otherwise in paragraphs (e)(4)(ii)(B) and (C) of this section and this paragraph (e)(4)(ii)(A), a withholding certificate described in paragraph (e)(2)(i) of this section, or a certificate described in § 1.871-14(c)(2)(v) (furnished to qualify interest as portfolio interest for purposes of sections 871(h) and 881(c)), will remain valid until the earlier of the last day of the third calendar year following the year in which the withholding certificate is signed or the day that a change in circumstances occurs that makes any information on the certificate incorrect. For example, a withholding certificate signed on September 30, 2015, remains valid through December 31, 2018, unless circumstances change that make the information on the form no longer correct. Documentary evidence described in § 1.6049-5(c)(1) provided to establish a payee's foreign status shall remain valid until the last day of the third calendar year following the year in which the documentary evidence is provided to the withholding agent except as provided in paragraph (e)(4)(ii)(B) of this section; however, if such documentary evidence contains an expiration date, it may be treated as valid until that expiration date if doing so would provide a longer period of validity than the three-year period. Additionally, a withholding certificate or documentary evidence with a period of validity that is valid on December 31, 2013, will not be treated as invalid based solely on the period described in this paragraph (e)(4)(ii) before January 1, 2015. Notwithstanding the validity periods prescribed by this paragraph (e)(4)(ii)(A) and paragraphs (e)(4)(ii)(B) and (C) of this section, a withholding certificate and documentary evidence will cease to be valid if a change in circumstances makes the information on the documentation incorrect.

(2) *Documentary evidence for treaty claims and treaty statements.*—Documentary evidence described in § 1.1441-6(c)(3) or (4) shall remain valid until the last day of the third calendar year following the year in which the documentary evidence is provided to the withholding agent, except as provided in paragraph (e)(4)(ii)(B) of this section. A statement regarding entitlement to treaty benefits described in § 1.1441-6(c)(5) (treaty statement) shall remain valid until the last day of the third calendar year following the year in which the treaty statement is provided to the withholding agent except as provided in this paragraph (e)(4)(ii)(A)(2). A treaty statement provided by an entity that identifies a limitation on benefits provision for a publicly traded corporation shall not expire at the time provided in the preceding sentence if a withholding agent determines, based on publicly available information at each time for which the treaty statement would otherwise be renewed, that the entity is publicly traded. Notwithstanding the second sentence of this paragraph (e)(4)(ii)(A)(2), a treaty statement provided by an entity that identifies a limitation on benefits provision for a government or tax-exempt organization (other than a tax-exempt pension trust or pension fund) shall remain valid indefinitely. Notwithstanding the validity periods (or exceptions thereto) prescribed in this paragraph (e)(4)(ii)(A)(2), a treaty statement will cease to be valid if a change in circumstances makes the information on the statement unreliable or incorrect. For accounts opened and treaty statements obtained prior to January 6, 2017 (including those from publicly traded corporations, governments, and tax-exempt organizations), the treaty statement will expire January 1, 2020.

(B) *Indefinite validity period.*—Notwithstanding paragraph (e)(4)(ii)(A) of this section, the certificates (or parts of certificates) and documentary evidence described in paragraphs (e)(4)(ii)(B)(1) through (11) of this section shall remain valid until a change in circumstances makes the information on the documentation incorrect under paragraph (e)(4)(ii)(D)(3). See, however, § 1.1471-3(c)(6)(ii) for when a withholding certificate or documentary evidence remains valid (or is subject to renewal) when also provided with respect to a withholdable payment made to an entity (including an intermediary) for purposes of whether a withholding agent may continue to rely on the entity's claim of chapter 4 status. Additionally, the provisions of paragraphs (e)(4)(ii)(B)(1), (2), and (11) of this section do not apply to documentary evidence or a withholding certificate furnished prior to July 1, 2014. (For documentary evidence or a withholding certificate furnished after December 31, 2000, and before July 1, 2014, see this section as in effect and contained in 26 CFR part 1, as revised April 1, 2013.)

(1) A beneficial owner withholding certificate (other than the portion of the certificate making a claim for treaty benefits) and documentary evidence supporting a claim of foreign status when both are provided together by an individual claiming foreign status, if the withholding agent does not have a current U.S. residence address or U.S. mailing address for the payee, does not have one or more current U.S. telephone numbers that are the only telephone numbers the withholding agent has for the payee, and, for a payment described in § 1.6049-5(c)(1), the withholding agent has not been provided standing instructions to make a payment to an account in the United States for the obligation. For purposes of the preceding sentence, a beneficial owner withholding certificate and documentary evidence supporting the individual's claim of foreign status will be treated as provided together if they are provided within 30 days of each other, regardless of which the withholding agent receives first.

(2) A beneficial owner withholding certificate (other than the portion of the certificate making a claim for treaty benefits) and documentary evidence provided by an entity supporting the entity's claim of foreign status, if both are received by the withholding agent before the validity period of either the withholding certificate or the documentary evidence would otherwise expire under paragraph (e)(4)(ii)(A) of this section. See, however, § 1.1471-3(c)(6)(ii) for rules regarding indefinite validity for chapter 4 purposes.

(3) A beneficial owner withholding certificate provided by an entity claiming status as a tax-exempt entity under section 501(c) that is not a foreign private foundation under section 509, provided that the withholding agent reports at least one payment annually to the entity under § 1.1461-1(c).

(4) A certificate described in paragraph (e)(3)(ii) of this section (a qualified intermediary withholding certificate) but not including the withholding certificates, documentary evidence, statements, or other information associated with the certificate.

(5) A certificate described in paragraph (e)(3)(iii) of this section (a nonqualified intermediary certificate), but not including the withholding certificates, documentary evidence, statements, or other information associated with the certificate.

(6) A certificate described in paragraph (e)(3)(v) of this section (a U.S. branch (including a territory financial institution) withholding certificate that is not provided by the beneficial owner), but not including the withholding certificates, documentary evidence, statements, or other information associated with the certificate.

(7) A certificate furnished by a person representing to be an integral part of a foreign government (within the meaning of § 1.892-2T(a)(2)) in accordance with § 1.1441-8(b), or by a person representing to be a foreign central bank of issue (within the meaning of § 1.861-2(b)(4)) or the Bank for International Settlements in accordance with § 1.1441-8(c)(1).

(8) A withholding certificate provided by a withholding foreign trust described in § 1.1441-5(e)(5)(v).

(9) A certificate described in § 1.1441-5(c)(2)(iv) (dealing with a certificate from a person representing to be a withholding foreign partnership).

(10) A certificate described in § 1.1441-5(c)(3)(iii) (a withholding certificate from a nonwithholding foreign partnership) or in § 1.1441-5(e)(5)(iii) (a withholding certificate of a foreign simple or foreign grantor trust) but not including the withholding certificates, documentary evidence, statements, or other information required to be associated with the certificate; and

(11) Documentary evidence that is not generally renewed or amended (such as a certificate of incorporation).

(C) *Withholding certificate for effectively connected income.*—Notwithstanding paragraph (e)(4)(ii)(B) of this section, the period of validity of a withholding certificate furnished to a withholding agent to claim a reduced rate of withholding for income that is effectively connected with the conduct of a trade or business within the United

States shall be limited to the three-year period described in paragraph (e)(4)(ii)(A) of this section.

(D) *Change in circumstances.*—*(1) Defined.*—A certificate or documentation becomes invalid from the date of a change in circumstances affecting the correctness of the certificate or documentation to the extent provided in this paragraph (e)(4)(ii)(D). For purposes of this section, a person is considered to have a change in circumstances only if such change affects the person's claim of chapter 3 status. Thus, for example, a change of address is not a change in circumstances with respect to a claim of only foreign status under this paragraph (e)(4)(ii)(D) if the change is to another address outside the United States, but is a change in circumstances if the change is to an address in the United States. However, see paragraph (e)(2)(ii)(B)(*1*) of this section for a special rule for a change of address for purposes of reliance on a foreign TIN (or a reasonable explanation for the absence of a foreign TIN) included on a beneficial owner withholding certificate.

(2) *Obligation to notify a withholding agent of a change in circumstances.*—If a change in circumstances makes any information on a certificate or other documentary evidence incorrect, then the person whose name is on the certificate or other documentation must inform the withholding agent within 30 days of the change and furnish a new certificate or new documentary evidence. If an intermediary (including a U.S. branch or territory financial institution described in paragraph (b)(2)(iv)(A) of this section) or a flow-through entity becomes aware that a certificate or other appropriate documentation it has furnished to the person from whom it collects a payment is no longer valid because of a change in the circumstances of the person who issued the certificate or furnished the other appropriate documentation, then the intermediary or flow-through entity must notify the person from whom it collects the payment of the change of circumstances within 30 days of the date that it knows or has reason to know of the change in circumstances. It must also obtain a new withholding certificate or new appropriate documentation to replace the existing certificate or documentation the validity of which has expired due to the change in circumstances to continue to treat the person who provided the certificate or documentary evidence under its claimed chapter 3 status.

(3) *Withholding agent's obligation with respect to a change in circumstances.*—A withholding agent may rely on a certificate without having to inquire into possible changes of circumstances that may affect the validity of the statement, unless it knows or has reason to know that circumstances have changed, as permitted under paragraph (e)(4)(viii) of this section. A withholding agent is required to notify any person providing documentary evidence (in lieu of a withholding certificate) of the person's obligation to notify the withholding agent of a change in circumstances. However, a withholding agent may choose to apply the provisions of paragraph (b)(3)(iv) of this section regarding the 90-day grace period as of that date while awaiting a new certificate or documentation or while seeking information regarding changes, or suspected changes, in the person's circumstances. A withholding agent may also require a new certificate at any time prior to a payment, even though the withholding agent has no actual knowledge or reason to know that any information stated on the certificate has changed.

(iii) *Retention of documentation.*—A withholding agent must retain each withholding certificate and other documentation for purposes of this section for as long as it may be relevant to the determination of the withholding agent's tax liability under section 1461 and § 1.1461-1. A withholding agent may retain a withholding certificate or documentary evidence that is an original, certified copy, or a scanned document (as described in paragraph (e)(4)(iv)(D) of this section). A withholding agent may also retain a withholding certificate by other means (such as microfiche) that allows a reproduction of the document provided that the withholding agent has recorded its receipt of a form described in the preceding sentence and is able to produce a hard copy of the form. See § 1.6049-5(c)(1) for the requirements for maintaining documentary evidence that also apply for purposes of determining a payee's U.S. or foreign status for purposes of chapter 3.

(iv) *Electronic transmission of information.*—(A) *In general.*—A withholding agent may establish a system for a beneficial owner or payee to electronically furnish a Form W-8, an acceptable substitute Form W-8, or such other form as the IRS may prescribe. The system must meet the requirements described in paragraph (e)(4)(iv)(B) of this section. See paragraph (e)(4)(iv)(D) of this section for other cases in which a Form W-8 (or other documentation) may be furnished electronically.

(B) *Requirements.*—(1) *In general.*—The electronic system must ensure that the information received is the information sent, and must document all occasions of user access that result in the submission renewal, or modification of a Form W-8. In addition, the design and operation of the electronic system, including access procedures, must make it reasonably certain that the person accessing the system and furnishing Form W-8 is the person named in the Form.

(2) *Same information as paper Form W-8.*—The electronic transmission must provide the withholding agent or payor with exactly the same information as the paper Form W-8.

(3) *Perjury statement and signature requirements.*—The electronic transmission must contain an electronic signature by the person whose name is on the Form W-8 and the signature must be under penalties of perjury in the manner described in this paragraph (e)(4)(iv)(B)(3).

(i) *Perjury statement.*—The perjury statement must contain the language that appears on the paper Form W-8. The electronic system must inform the person whose name is on the Form W-8 that the person must make the declaration contained in the perjury statement and that the declaration is made by signing the Form W-8. The instructions and the language of the perjury statement must immediately follow the person's certifying statements and immediately precede the person's electronic signature.

(ii) *Electronic signature.*—The act of the electronic signature must be effected by the person whose name is on the electronic Form W-8. The signature must also authenticate and verify the submission. For this purpose, the terms *authenticate* and *verify* have the same meanings as they do when applied to a written signature on a paper Form W-8. An electronic signature can be in any form that satisfies the foregoing requirements. The electronic signature must be the final entry in the person's Form W-8 submission.

(4) *Requests for electronic Form W-8 data.*—Upon request by the Internal Revenue Service during an examination, the withholding agent must supply a hard copy of the electronic Form W-8 and a statement that, to the best of the withholding agent's knowledge, the electronic Form W-8 was filed by the person whose name is on the form. The hard copy of the electronic Form W-8 must provide exactly the same information as, but need not be identical to, the paper Form W-8.

(C) *Form 8233.*—A withholding agent may establish a system for a beneficial owner or payee to provide Form 8233 electronically, provided the system meets the requirements of paragraph (e)(4)(iv)(B)(1) through (4) of this section (replacing "Form W-8" with "Form 8233" each place it appears).

(D) *Forms and documentary evidence received by facsimile or email.*—A withholding agent may rely upon an otherwise valid Form W-8 (or documentary evidence) received by facsimile or a form or document scanned and received electronically, such as, for example, an image embedded in an email or as a Portable Document Format (.pdf) attached to an email. A withholding agent may not rely on a form or document received by such means, however, if the withholding agent knows that the form or document was transmitted to the withholding agent by a person not authorized to do so by the person required to execute the form. A withholding agent may establish other procedures to authenticate and verify a form or document sent by such means and may reject any form or document that fails to satisfy the requirements of such procedures. A taxpayer may apply this paragraph (e)(4)(iv)(D) to all of its open tax years, including tax years that are currently under examination by the IRS.

(E) *Third party repositories.*—A withholding certificate will be considered furnished for purposes of this section (including paragraph (e)(1)(ii)(A)(1) of this section) by the person providing the certificate, and a withholding agent may rely on an otherwise valid withholding certificate received electronically from a third party repository, if the withholding certificate was uploaded or provided to a third party repository and there are processes in place to ensure that the withholding certificate can be reliably associated with a specific request from the withholding agent and a specific authorization from the person providing the certificate (or an agent of the person providing the certificate) for the withholding agent making the request to receive the withholding certificate. For purposes of the preceding sentence, a withholding agent must be able to reliably associate each payment with a specific request and authorization except when the withholding agent is permitted to rely on the withholding certificate on an obligation-by-obligation basis or as otherwise permitted under paragraph (e)(4)(ix) of this section (treating the withholding certificate as obtained by the withholding agent and furnished by a customer for purposes of this paragraph (e)(4)(iv)(E)). A third party repository may also be used for withholding statements, and a withholding agent may also rely on an otherwise valid withholding statement, if the intermediary providing the withholding certificates and withholding statement through the repository provides an updated withholding statement in the event of any change in the information previously provided (for example, a change in the composition of a partnership or a change in the allocation of payments to the partners) and ensures there are processes in place to update withholding agents when there is a new withholding statement (and withholding certificates, as necessary) in the event of any change that would affect the validity of the prior withholding certificates or withholding statement. A third party repository, for purposes of this paragraph, is an entity that maintains withholding certificates (including certificates accompanied by withholding statements) but is not an agent of the applicable withholding agent or the person providing the certificate.

(F) *Examples.*—This paragraph contains examples to illustrate the rules of paragraph (e)(4)(iv)(E) of this section.

(1) *Example 1.* A, a foreign corporation, completes a Form W-8BEN-E and a Form W-8ECI and uploads the forms to X, a third party repository (X is an entity that maintains withholding certificates on an electronic data aggregation site). WA, a withholding agent, enters into a contract with A under which it will make payments to A of U.S. source FDAP that are not effectively connected with A's conduct of a trade or business in the United States. X is not an agent of WA or A. Before receiving a payment, A sends WA an email with a link that authorizes WA to access A's Form W-8BEN-E on X's system. The link does not authorize WA to access A's Form W-8ECI. X's system meets the requirements of a third party repository, and WA can treat the Form W-8BEN-E as furnished by A.

(2) *Example 2.* The facts are the same as Example 1 of this paragraph (e)(4)(iv)(F), and WA and A enter into a second contract under which WA will make payments to A that are effectively connected with A's conduct of a trade or business in the United States. A sends WA an email with a link that gives WA access to A's Form W-8ECI on X's system. The link in this second email does not give WA access to A's Form W-8BEN-E. A's email also clearly indicates that the link is associated with payments received under the second contract. X's system meets the requirements of a third party repository, and WA can treat the Form W-8ECI as furnished by A.

(3) *Example 3.* FP is a foreign partnership that is acting on behalf of its partners, A and B, who are both foreign individuals. FP completes a Form W-8IMY and uploads it to X, a third party repository. FP also uploads Forms W-8BEN from both A and B and a valid withholding statement allocating 50% of the payment to A and 50% to B. WA is a withholding agent that makes payments to FP as an intermediary for A and B. FP sends WA an email with a link to its Form W-8IMY on X's system. The link also provides WA access to FP's withholding statement and A's and B's Forms W-8BEN. FP also has processes in place that ensure it will provide a new withholding statement or withholding certificate to X's repository in the event of a change in the information previously provided that affects the validity of the withholding statement and that ensure it will update WA if there is a new withholding statement. X's system meets the requirements of a third party repository, and WA can treat the Form W-8IMY (and withholding statement) as furnished by FP. In addition, because FP is acting as an agent of A and B, the beneficial owners, WA can treat the Forms W-8BEN for A and B as furnished by A and B.

(v) *Additional procedures for certificates provided electronically.*—The IRS may prescribe procedures in a revenue procedure (see §601.601(d)(2) of this chapter) or may issue other appropriate guidance (including a written directive for revenue agents) to further prescribe the conditions by which the IRS will determine that a system developed by a withholding agent to permit beneficial owners and payees to provide Forms W-8 electronically satisfies the requirements of paragraph (e)(4)(iv)(B) of this section.

(vi) *Acceptable substitute form.*—A withholding agent may substitute its own form instead of an official Form W-8 or 8233 (or such other official form as the IRS may prescribe). Such a substitute for an official form will be acceptable if it contains provisions that are substantially similar to those of the official form, it contains the same certifications relevant to the transactions as are contained on the official form and these certifications are clearly set forth, and the substitute form includes a signature-under penalties-of-perjury statement identical to the one stated on the official form. The substitute form is acceptable even if it does not contain all of the provisions contained on the official form, so long as it contains those provisions that are relevant to the transaction for which it is furnished (including those required for purposes of chapter 4). For example, a withholding agent that pays no income for which treaty benefits are claimed may develop a substitute form that is identical to the official form, except that it does not include information regarding claims of benefits under an income tax treaty. Similarly, a withholding agent that is not required to determine the chapter 4 status of a payee providing a form may develop a substitute form that does not

contain chapter 4 statuses. A withholding agent who uses a substitute form must furnish instructions relevant to the substitute form only to the extent and in the manner specified in the instructions to the official form. A withholding agent may use a substitute form that is written in a language other than English and may accept a form that is filled out in a language other than English, but the withholding agent must make available an English translation of the form and its contents to the IRS upon request. A withholding agent may refuse to accept a certificate from a payee or beneficial owner (including the official Form W-8 or 8233) if the certificate provided is not an acceptable substitute form provided by the withholding agent, but only if the withholding agent furnishes the payee or beneficial owner with an acceptable substitute form within 5 business days of receipt of an unacceptable form from the payee or beneficial owner. In that case, the substitute form is acceptable only if it contains a notice that the withholding agent has refused to accept the form submitted by the payee or beneficial owner and that the payee or beneficial owner must submit the acceptable form provided by the withholding agent in order for the payee or beneficial owner to be treated as having furnished the required withholding certificate.

(vii) *Requirement of taxpayer identifying number.*—A TIN must be stated on a withholding certificate when required by this paragraph (e)(4)(vii) for the withholding certificate to be valid for purposes of this section. A TIN is required to be stated on—

(A) A withholding certificate on which a beneficial owner is claiming the benefit of a reduced rate under an income tax treaty (other than for amounts described in §1.1441-6(c)(2) or amounts for which a foreign tax identifying number has been provided, as described in §1.1441-6(c)(2));

(B) A withholding certificate on which a beneficial owner is claiming exemption from withholding because income is effectively connected with a U.S. trade or business;

(C) A withholding certificate on which a beneficial owner is claiming exemption from withholding under section 871(f) for certain annuities received under qualified plans;

(D) A withholding certificate on which a beneficial owner is claiming an exemption based solely on a foreign organization's claim of tax exempt status under section 501(c) or private foundation status (however, a TIN is not required from a foreign private foundation that is subject to the 4-percent tax under section 4948(a) on income if that income would be exempt from withholding but for section 4948(a) (e.g., portfolio interest));

(E) A withholding certificate from a person representing to be a qualified intermediary described in paragraph (e)(5)(ii) of this section;

(F) A withholding certificate from a person representing to be a withholding foreign partnership or a withholding foreign trust;

(G) A withholding certificate provided by a foreign organization that is described in section 501(c);

(H) A withholding certificate from a person representing to be a U.S. branch or territory financial institution described in paragraph (b)(2)(iv) of this section; and

(I) A withholding certificate provided by an entity acting as a qualified securities lender, as defined for purposes of chapter 3, with respect to a substitute dividend paid in a securities lending or similar transaction.

(viii) *Reliance rules.*—A withholding agent may rely on the information and certifications stated on withholding certificates or other documentation without having to inquire into the veracity of this information or certification, unless it has actual knowledge or reason to know that the information or certification is incorrect. In the case of amounts described in §1.1441-6(c)(2), a withholding agent described in §1.1441-7(b)(3) has reason to know that the information or certifications on a certificate are incorrect only to the extent provided in §1.1441-7(b)(4) through (6). See §1.1441-6(b)(1) for reliance on representations regarding eligibility for a reduced rate under an income tax treaty. Paragraphs (e)(4)(viii)(A) and (B) of this section provide examples of such reliance.

(A) *Classification.*—A withholding agent may rely on the claim of entity classification indicated on the withholding certificate that it receives from or for the beneficial owner, unless it has actual knowledge or reason to know that the classification claimed is incorrect. A withholding agent may not rely on a person's claim of classification other than as a corporation if the name of the corporation indicates that the person is a per se corporation described in §301.7701-2(b)(8)(i) of this chapter unless the certificate contains a statement that the person is a grandfathered per se corporation described in §301.7701-2(b)(8) of this chapter and that its grandfathered status has not been terminated. In the absence of reliable representation or information regarding the classification of the payee or beneficial owner, see §1.1441-1(b)(3)(ii) for applicable presumptions.

(B) *Status of payee as an intermediary or as a person acting for its own account.*—A withholding agent may rely on the type of certificate furnished as indicative of the payee's status as an intermediary or as an owner, unless the withholding agent has actual knowledge or reason to know otherwise. For example, a withholding agent that receives a beneficial owner withholding certificate from a foreign financial institution may treat the institution as the beneficial owner, unless it has information in its records that would indicate otherwise or the certificate contains information that is not consistent with beneficial owner status (*e.g.*, sub-account numbers that do not correspond to accounts maintained by the withholding agent for such person or names of one or more persons other than the person submitting the withholding certificate). If the financial institution also acts as an intermediary, the withholding agent may request that the institution furnish two certificates, *i.e.*, a beneficial owner certificate described in paragraph (e)(2)(i) of this section for the amounts that it receives as a beneficial owner, and an intermediary withholding certificate described in paragraph (e)(3)(i) of this section for the amounts that it receives as an intermediary. In the absence of reliable representation or information regarding the status of the payee as an owner or as an intermediary, see paragraph (b)(3)(v)(A) for applicable presumptions.

(C) *Reliance on a prior version of a withholding certificate.*—Upon the issuance by the IRS of an updated version of a withholding certificate, a withholding agent may continue to accept the prior version of the withholding certificate until the later of six full months after the revision date shown on the updated withholding certificate or the end of the calendar year the updated withholding certificate is issued, unless the IRS has issued guidance that indicates that the period for accepting a prior version is shortened or extended (including in the instructions to the form), such as when there is a new payee status required to be established using the form. A withholding agent may continue to rely upon a previously signed prior version of the withholding certificate until its period of validity expires.

(ix) *Certificates to be furnished to withholding agent for each obligation unless exception applies.*—Unless otherwise provided in paragraphs (e)(4)(ix)(A) through (D) of this section, a withholding agent that is a financial institution with which a customer may open an account shall obtain a withholding certificate or documentary evidence on an obligation-by-obligation basis and may not rely upon such documentation collected by another person or another branch of the withholding agent.

(A) *Exception for certain branch or account systems or system maintained by agent.*—A withholding agent may rely on a withholding certificate or documentary evidence furnished by a customer as part of a single branch system, universal account system, or shared account system described in § 1.1471-3(c)(8) (substituting the term chapter 3 status for chapter 4 status each place it appears in that paragraph. Furthermore, a withholding agent may rely on a shared documentation system maintained by an agent as described in § 1.1471-3(c)(9)(i) (also substituting the term chapter 3 status for chapter 4 status each place it appears in that paragraph).

(B) *Reliance on certification provided by introducing brokers.*—(1) *In general.*—A withholding agent may rely on the certification of a broker indicating the broker's determination of a payee's chapter 3 status and that the broker holds a valid beneficial owner withholding certificate described in paragraph (e)(2)(i) of this section or other appropriate documentation for that beneficial owner with respect to any readily tradable instrument, as defined in § 31.3406(h)-1(d) of this chapter, if the broker is a United States person (including a U.S. branch treated as a U.S. person under paragraph (b)(2)(iv) of this section) that is acting as the agent of a beneficial owner. A withholding agent may also rely on a certification described in the preceding sentence that is provided by a qualified intermediary that makes payments to beneficial owners that it receives from the withholding agent. The certification must be in writing or in electronic form and contain all of the information required of a nonqualified intermediary under paragraphs (e)(3)(iv)(B) and (C) of this section. If a broker chooses to use this paragraph (e)(4)(ix)(B), that broker will be solely responsible for applying the rules of § 1.1441-7(b) to the withholding certificates or other appropriate documentation and shall be liable for any underwithholding as a result of the broker's failure to apply such rules. See § 1.1471-3(c)(9)(iii) for a similar allowance that applies to a broker's determination of a payee's chapter 4 status for purposes of chapter 4. For purposes of this paragraph (e)(4)(ix)(B), the term *broker* means a person treated as a broker under § 1.6045-1(a).

(2) *Example.*—The following example illustrates the rules of this paragraph (e)(4)(x)(B) with respect to a U.S. broker:

*Example.* SCO is a U.S. securities clearing organization that provides clearing services for correspondent broker, CB, a U.S. corporation. Pursuant to a fully disclosed clearing agreement, CB fully discloses the identity of each of its customers to SCO. Part of SCO's clearing duties include the crediting of income and gross proceeds of readily tradable instruments (as defined in § 31.3406(h)-1(d)) to each customer's account. For each disclosed customer that is a foreign beneficial owner, CB provides SCO with information required under paragraphs (e)(3)(iv)(B) and (C) of this section that is necessary to apply the correct rate of withholding and to file Forms 1042-S. SCO may use the representations and beneficial owner information provided by CB to determine the proper amount of withholding and to file Forms 1042-S. CB is responsible for determining the validity of the withholding certificates or other appropriate documentation under § 1.1441-1(b).

(C) *Reliance on documentation and certifications provided between principals and agents.*—(1) *Withholding agent as agent.*—A withholding agent that acts on behalf of a principal may rely upon documentation (or copies of documentation) obtained from the principal, and, with respect to a principal that is a U.S. withholding agent, a qualified intermediary (when acting as such for determining a payee's status), or a withholding foreign partnership or withholding foreign trust with respect to a partner, owner, or beneficiary in the partnership or trust, the withholding agent may rely upon certification provided by the principal for purposes of determining a payee's chapter 3 status. Thus an agent (such as a paying agent or transfer agent) may not rely upon a certification provided by a principal that is a participating FFI but is not also a qualified intermediary, withholding foreign partnership, or withholding foreign trust for purposes of this section, even though it may rely on the certification when provided solely for purposes of chapter 4 under § 1.1471-3(c)(9)(iv).

(2) *Withholding agent as principal.*—A withholding agent may also rely on documentation collected by an agent of the withholding agent in order to fulfill its chapter 3 obligations because such agent's actions are imputed to the principal (the withholding agent). For example, a withholding agent may contract an agent to collect Forms W-8 from account holders on its behalf, but the withholding agent remains liable for any tax liability resulting from a failure of the agent to comply with the requirements of chapter 3.

(D) *Reliance upon documentation for accounts acquired in merger or bulk acquisition for value.*—A withholding agent that acquires an account from a predecessor or transferor in a merger or bulk acquisition of accounts for value is permitted to rely upon valid documentation (or copies of valid documentation) collected by the predecessor or transferor for determining the chapter 3 status of an account holder of such an account. In addition, a withholding agent that acquires an account in a merger or bulk acquisition of accounts for value, other than a related party transaction, from a U.S. withholding agent (or a qualified intermediary when the withholding agent is also a qualified intermediary) may also rely upon the predecessor's or transferor's determination of the account holder's chapter 3 status for a transition period of the lesser of six months from the date of the merger or until the acquirer knows that the claim of entity classification and status is inaccurate or a change in circumstances occurs with respect to the account. At the end of the transition period, the acquirer will be permitted to rely upon the predecessor's determination as to the chapter 3 status of the account holder only if the documentation that the acquirer has for the account holder, including documentation obtained from the predecessor or transferor, supports the status claimed. An acquirer that discovers at the end of the transition period that the chapter 3 status assigned by the predecessor or transferor to the account holder was incorrect and has not withheld as it would have been required to but for its reliance upon the predecessor's determination, will be required to withhold on future payments, if any, made to the account holder the amount of tax that should have been withheld during the transition period but for the erroneous classification as to the account holder's status. For purposes of this paragraph (e)(4)(ix)(D), a related party transaction is a merger or sale of accounts in which the acquirer is in the same expanded affiliated group, within the meaning of § 1.1471-5(i)(2), as the predecessor or transferor either prior to or after the merger or acquisition or the predecessor or transferor (or shareholders of the predecessor or transferor) obtain a controlling interest in the acquirer or in a newly formed entity created for purposes of the merger or acquisition. See § 1.1471-3(c)(9)(v) for a similar reliance rule that applies for purposes of chapter 4.

(5) *Qualified intermediaries.*—(i) *In general.*—A qualified intermediary, as defined in paragraph (e)(5)(ii) of this section, may furnish a qualified intermediary withholding certificate to a withholding agent. The withholding certificate provides certifications on behalf of other persons for the purpose of claiming and verifying reduced rates of withholding under section 1441 or 1442 and for the purpose of reporting and withholding under other provisions of the Code, such as the provisions under chapter 61 and section 3406 (and the

regulations under those provisions), or for the qualified derivative dealer (if applicable). Furnishing such a certificate is in lieu of transmitting to a withholding agent withholding certificates or other appropriate documentation for the persons for whom the qualified intermediary receives the payment, including interest holders in a qualified intermediary that is fiscally transparent under the regulations under section 894. Although the qualified intermediary is required to obtain withholding certificates or other appropriate documentation from beneficial owners, payees, or interest holders pursuant to its agreement with the IRS, it is generally not required to attach such documentation to the intermediary withholding certificate. Notwithstanding the preceding sentence, a qualified intermediary must provide a withholding agent with the Forms W-9, or disclose the names, addresses, and taxpayer identifying numbers, if known, of those U.S. non-exempt recipients for whom the qualified intermediary receives reportable amounts (within the meaning of paragraph (e)(3)(vi) of this section) to the extent required in the qualified intermediary's agreement with the IRS. When a qualified intermediary is acting as a qualified derivatives dealer, the withholding certificate entitles a withholding agent to make payments with respect to potential section 871(m) transactions that are not underlying securities and dividend equivalent payments on underlying securities to the qualified derivatives dealer free of withholding. A withholding agent is required to withhold on all other U.S. source FDAP payments made to a qualified derivatives dealer as required by applicable law. Paragraph (e)(6) of this section contains detailed rules prescribing the circumstances in which a qualified intermediary can act as a qualified derivatives dealer. A person may claim qualified intermediary status before an agreement is executed with the IRS if it has applied for such status and the IRS authorizes such status on an interim basis under such procedures as the IRS may prescribe.

(ii) *Definition of qualified intermediary.*—With respect to a payment to a foreign person, the term qualified intermediary means a person that is a party to a withholding agreement with the IRS where such person is—

(A) A foreign financial institution that is a participating FFI (including a reporting Model 2 FFI), a registered deemed-compliant FFI (including a reporting Model 1 FFI), an FFI treated as a deemed-compliant FFI under an applicable IGA that is subject to due diligence and reporting requirements with respect to its U.S. accounts similar to those applicable to a registered deemed-compliant FFI under § 1.1471-5(f)(1), excluding a U.S. branch of any of the foregoing entities, or any other category of FFI identified in a qualified intermediary withholding agreement as eligible to act as a qualified intermediary;

(B) A foreign branch or office of a U.S. financial institution or a foreign branch or office of a U.S. clearing organization that is either a reporting Model 1 FFI or agrees to the reporting requirements applicable to a participating FFI with respect to its U.S. accounts;

(C) A foreign person that is a home office or has a branch that is an eligible entity as described in paragraph (e)(6)(ii) of this section, without regard to the requirement that the person be a qualified intermediary; or

(D) Any other person acceptable to the IRS.

(iii) *Withholding agreement.*—(A) *In general.*—The IRS may, upon request, enter into a withholding agreement with a foreign person described in paragraph (e)(5)(ii) of this section pursuant to such procedures as the IRS may prescribe in published guidance (see § 601.601(d)(2) of this chapter). Under the withholding agreement, a qualified intermediary shall generally be subject to the applicable withholding and reporting provisions applicable to withholding agents and payors under chapters 3, 4, and 61 of the Code, section 3406, the regulations under those provisions, and other withholding provisions of the Code, except to the extent provided under the agreement.

(B) *Terms of the withholding agreement.*—The withholding agreement shall specify the obligations of the qualified intermediary under chapters 3 and 4 including, for a qualified intermediary that is an FFI, the documentation, withholding, and reporting obligations required of a participating FFI or registered deemed-compliant FFI (including a reporting Model 1 FFI as defined in § 1.1471-1(b)(114)) with respect to each branch of the qualified intermediary other than a U.S. branch that is treated as a U.S. person under paragraph (b)(2)(iv)(A) of this section. The withholding agreement will specify the type of certifications and documentation upon which the qualified intermediary may rely to ascertain the classification (*e.g.*, corporation or partnership) status (*i.e.*, U.S. or foreign and chapter 4 status) of beneficial owners and payees who receive reportable amounts, reportable payments, and withholdable payments collected by the qualified intermediary for purposes of chapters 3, 4, and 61, section 3406, and, if necessary, entitlement to the benefits of a reduced rate under an income tax treaty. The withholding agreement

shall specify if, and to what extent, the qualified intermediary may assume primary withholding responsibility in accordance with paragraph (e)(5)(iv) of this section. It shall also specify the extent to which applicable return filing and information reporting requirements are modified so that, in appropriate cases, the qualified intermediary may report payments to the IRS on an aggregated basis, without having to disclose the identity of beneficial owners and payees. However, the qualified intermediary may be required to provide to the IRS the name and address of those foreign customers who benefit from a reduced rate under an income tax treaty pursuant to the withholding agreement for purposes of verifying entitlement to such benefits, particularly under an applicable limitation on benefits provision. Under the withholding agreement, a qualified intermediary may agree to act as an acceptance agent to perform the duties described in § 301.6109-1(d)(3)(iv)(A) of this chapter. The withholding agreement may specify the manner in which applicable procedures for adjustments for underwithholding and overwithholding, including refund procedures, apply to qualified intermediaries and the extent to which applicable procedures may be modified. In particular, a withholding agreement may allow a qualified intermediary to claim refunds of overwithheld amounts. In addition, the withholding agreement shall specify the manner in which the IRS will verify compliance with the agreement, including the time and manner for which a qualified intermediary will be required to certify to the IRS regarding its compliance with the withholding agreement (including its performance of a periodic review) and the types of information required to be disclosed as part of the certification. In appropriate cases, the IRS may require review procedures be performed by an approved reviewer (in addition to those performed as part of the periodic review) and may conduct a review of the reviewer's findings. The withholding agreement may include provisions for the assessment and collection of tax in the event that failure to comply with the terms of the withholding agreement results in the failure by the withholding agent or the qualified intermediary to withhold and deposit the required amount of tax. Further, the withholding agreement may specify the procedures by which amounts withheld are to be deposited, if different from the deposit procedures under the Code and applicable regulations. To determine whether to enter a withholding agreement and the terms of any particular withholding agreement, the IRS will consider the type of local know-your-customer laws and practices to which the entity is subject (if the entity is an FFI), as well as the extent and nature of supervisory and regulatory control exercised under the laws of the foreign country over the foreign entity.

(iv) *Assignment of primary withholding responsibility.*—Any person (whether a U.S. person or a foreign person) who meets the definition of a withholding agent under § 1.1441-7(a) (for payments subject to chapter 3 withholding) and § 1.1473-1(d) (for withholdable payments) is required to withhold and deposit any amount withheld under § § 1.1461-1(a) and 1.1474-1(b) and to make the returns prescribed by § § 1.1461-1(b) and (c), and by 1.1474-1(c), and (d). Under its qualified intermediary withholding agreement, a qualified intermediary may, however, inform a withholding agent from which it receives a payment that it will assume the primary obligation to withhold, deposit, and report amounts under chapters 3 and 4 of the Code and/or under chapter 61 and section 3406 of the Code. For assuming withholding obligations as described in the previous sentence, a qualified intermediary that assumes primary withholding responsibility for payments made to an account under chapter 3 is also required to assume primary withholding responsibility under chapter 4 for payments made to the account that are withholdable payments. Additionally, a qualified intermediary may represent that it assumes chapter 61 reporting and section 3406 obligations for a payment when the qualified intermediary meets the requirements of § 1.6049-4(c)(4)(i) or (ii) for the payment. If a withholding agent makes a payment of an amount subject to withholding under chapter 3, a reportable payment (as defined in section 3406(b)), or a withholdable payment to a qualified intermediary that represents to the withholding agent that it has assumed primary withholding responsibility for the payment, the withholding agent is not required to withhold on the payment. The withholding agent is not required to determine that the qualified intermediary actually performs its primary withholding responsibilities. A qualified intermediary that assumes primary withholding responsibility under chapters 3 and 4 or primary reporting and backup withholding responsibility under chapter 61 and section 3406 is not required to assume primary withholding responsibility for all accounts it has with a withholding agent but must assume primary withholding responsibility for all payments made to any one account that it has with the withholding agent.

(v) *Withholding statement.*—(A) *In general.*—A qualified intermediary must provide each withholding agent from which it receives reportable amounts as a qualified intermediary with a written statement (the withholding statement) containing the information specified in paragraph (e)(5)(v)(B) of this section. A withholding statement is not required, however, if all of the information a withholding agent needs to fulfill its withholding and reporting requirements is contained in the withholding certificate. The qualified intermediary withholding agreement will require the qualified intermediary to include information in its withholding statement relating to withholdable payments for purposes of withholding under chapter 4 as described in paragraph (e)(5)(v)(C)(2) of this section. The withholding statement forms an integral part of the qualified intermediary's qualified intermediary withholding certificate, and the penalties of perjury statement provided on the withholding certificate shall apply to the withholding statement as well. The withholding statement may be provided in any manner, and in any form, to which qualified intermediary and the withholding agent mutually agree, including electronically. If the withholding statement is provided electronically, the statement must satisfy the requirements described in paragraph (e)(3)(iv) of this section (applicable to a withholding statement provided by a nonqualified intermediary). The withholding statement shall be updated as often as necessary for the withholding agent to meet its reporting and withholding obligations under chapters 3, 4, and 61 and section 3406. For purposes of this section, a withholding agent will be liable for tax, interest, and penalties in accordance with paragraph (b)(7) of this section to the extent it does not follow the presumption rules of paragraph (b)(3) of this section, §§ 1.1441-5(d) and (e)(6), and 1.6049-5(d) for a payment, or portion thereof, for which it does not have a valid withholding statement prior to making a payment.

(B) *Content of withholding statement.*—The withholding statement must contain sufficient information for a withholding agent to apply the correct rate of withholding on payments from the accounts identified on the statement and to properly report such payments on Forms 1042-S and Forms 1099, as applicable. The withholding statement must—

    (1) Designate those accounts for which the qualified intermediary acts as a qualified intermediary;

    (2) Designate those accounts for which qualified intermediary assumes primary withholding responsibility under chapter 3 and chapter 4 of the Code and/or primary reporting and backup withholding responsibility under chapter 61 and section 3406;

    (3) If applicable, designate those accounts for which the qualified intermediary is acting as a qualified securities lender with respect to a substitute dividend paid in a securities lending or similar transaction;

    (4) If a qualified intermediary is acting as a qualified derivatives dealer, designate the accounts:

        (i) For which the qualified derivatives dealer is receiving payments with respect to potential section 871(m) transactions or underlying securities as a qualified derivatives dealer;

        (ii) For which the qualified derivatives dealer is receiving payments with respect to potential section 871(m) transactions (and that are not underlying securities) for which withholding is not required;

        (iii) For which qualified derivatives dealer is receiving payments with respect to underlying securities for which withholding is required; and

        (iv) If applicable, identifying the home office or branch that is treated as the owner for U.S. federal income tax purposes; and

    (5) Provide information regarding withholding rate pools, as described in paragraph (e)(5)(v)(C) of this section.

(C) *Withholding rate pools.*—(1) *In general.*—Except to the extent it has assumed both primary withholding responsibility under chapters 3 and 4 of the Code and primary Form 1099 reporting and backup withholding responsibility under chapter 61 and section 3406 with respect to a payment, a qualified intermediary shall provide as part of its withholding statement the chapter 3 withholding rate pool information that is required for the withholding agent to meet its withholding and reporting obligations under chapters 3 and 61 of the Code and section 3406. See, however, paragraph (e)(5)(v)(C)(2) of this section for when a qualified intermediary may provide a chapter 4 withholding rate pool (as described in paragraph (c)(48) of this section) with respect to a payment that is a withholdable payment. A chapter 3 withholding rate pool is a payment of a single type of income, determined in accordance with the categories of income reported on Form 1042-S, that is subject to a single rate of withholding paid to a payee that is a foreign person and for which withholding under chapter 4 does not apply. A chapter 3 withholding rate pool may be established by any reasonable method on which the qualified intermediary and a withholding agent agree (*e.g.*, by establishing a separate account for a single chapter 3 withholding rate pool, or by dividing a payment made to a single account into portions allocable to each chapter 3 withholding rate pool). A qualified intermediary may include a separate pool for account holders that are U.S. exempt recipients or may include such accounts in a chapter 3 withholding rate pool to which withholding does not apply. The withholding statement must identify the chapter 4 exemption code (as provided in the instructions to Form 1042-S) applicable to the chapter 3 withholding rate pools contained on the withholding statement. To the extent a qualified intermediary does not assume primary Form 1099 reporting and backup withholding responsibility under chapter 61 and section 3406, a qualified intermediary's withholding statement must establish a separate withholding rate pool for each U.S. non-exempt recipient account holder that the qualified intermediary has disclosed to the withholding agent unless the qualified intermediary uses the alternative procedures in paragraph (e)(5)(v)(C)(3) of this section or the account holder is a payee that the qualified intermediary is permitted to include in a chapter 4 withholding rate pool of U.S. payees. A qualified intermediary that is a participating FFI or registered deemed-compliant FFI may include a chapter 4 withholding rate pool of U.S. payees on a withholding statement by applying the rules under paragraph (e)(3)(iv)(A) of this section (by substituting "qualified intermediary" for "nonqualified intermediary") with respect to an account that it maintains (as described in § 1.1471-5(b)(5)) for the payee of the payment. A qualified intermediary shall determine withholding rate pools based on valid documentation that it obtains under its withholding agreement with the IRS, or if a payment cannot be reliably associated with valid documentation, under the applicable presumption rules. If a qualified intermediary has an account holder that is another intermediary (whether a qualified intermediary or a nonqualified intermediary) or a flow-through entity, the qualified intermediary may combine the account holder information provided by the other intermediary or flow-through entity with the qualified intermediary's direct account holder information to determine the qualified intermediary's chapter 3 withholding rate pools and each of the qualified intermediary's chapter 4 withholding rate pools to the extent provided in its withholding agreement with the IRS.

    (2) *Withholding rate pool requirements for a withholdable payment.*—This paragraph (e)(5)(v)(C)(2) modifies the requirements of a withholding statement described in paragraph (e)(5)(v)(C)(1) of this section provided by a qualified intermediary with respect to a withholdable payment (including a reportable amount that is a withholdable payment). For such a payment, the regulations applicable to a withholding statement described in paragraph (e)(5)(v)(C)(1) of this section shall apply, except that—

        (i) If the qualified intermediary provides a withholding statement described in § 1.1471-3(c)(3)(iii)(B)(2) (describing an FFI withholding statement), the withholding statement may include a chapter 4 withholding rate pool with respect to the portion of the payment allocated to a single pool of recalcitrant account holders (without the need to subdivide into the pools described in § 1.1471-4(d)(6)), including both account holders of the qualified intermediary and of any participating FFI, registered deemed-compliant FFI, or other qualified intermediary for whom the first-mentioned qualified intermediary receives the payment, and nonparticipating FFIs (to the extent permitted) in lieu of reporting chapter 3 withholding rate pools with respect to such persons as described in paragraph (e)(5)(v)(C)(1) of this section); or

        (ii) If the qualified intermediary provides a withholding statement described in § 1.1471-3(c)(3)(iii)(B)(3) (describing a chapter 4 withholding statement), the withholding statement may include a chapter 4 withholding rate pool with respect to the portion of the payment allocated to nonparticipating FFIs.

    (3) *Alternative procedure for U.S. non-exempt recipients.*—If permitted under its withholding agreement with the IRS, a qualified intermediary may, by mutual agreement with a withholding agent, establish a single zero withholding rate pool that includes U.S. non-exempt recipient account holders for whom the qualified intermediary has provided Forms W-9 prior to the withholding agent paying any reportable payments, as defined in the qualified intermediary withholding agreement, and foreign persons for which no withholding is required under chapters 3 and 4, and may include payments allocated to a chapter 4 withholding rate pool of U.S. payees. In such a case, the qualified intermediary may also establish a separate withholding rate pool (subject to 28-percent withholding, or other applicable statutory back-up withholding tax rate) that includes only U.S. non-exempt recipient account holders for whom a qualified intermediary has not provided Forms W-9 prior to the withholding agent paying any reportable payments. If a qualified intermediary chooses the alternative procedure of this paragraph (e)(5)(v)(C)(3), the qualified intermediary must provide the information required by its withholding agreement to the withholding agent no later than January 15 of the year following the year in which the payments are paid. Failure to provide such information will result in the application of penalties to the qualified intermediary under sections 6721 and 6722, as well as any other applicable penalties, and may result in the termination of the qualified intermediary's withholding agree-

ment with the IRS. A withholding agent shall not be liable for tax, interest, or penalties for failure to backup withhold or report information under chapter 61 of the Code due solely to the errors or omissions of the qualified intermediary. If a qualified intermediary fails to provide the allocation information required by this paragraph (e)(5)(v)(C)(3), with respect to U.S. non-exempt recipients, the withholding agent shall report the unallocated amount paid from the withholding rate pool to an unknown recipient, or otherwise in accordance with the appropriate Form 1099 and the instructions accompanying the form.

(D) *Example.*—The following example illustrates the application of paragraph (e)(5)(v)(C) of this section for a qualified intermediary providing chapter 4 withholding rate pools on an FFI withholding statement provided to a withholding agent. WA makes a payment of U.S. source interest that is a withholdable payment to QI, a qualified intermediary that is an FFI and a non-U.S. payor (as defined in §1.6049-5(c)(5)), and A and B are account holders of QI (as defined under §1.1471-5(a)) and are both U.S. nonexempt recipients (as defined paragraph (c)(21) of this section). Ten percent of the payment is attributable to both A and B. A has provided WA with a Form W-9, but B has not provided WA with a Form W-9. QI assumes primary withholding responsibility under chapters 3 and 4 with respect to the payment, 80 percent of which is allocable to foreign payees who are account holders other than A and B. As a participating FFI, QI is required to report with respect to its U.S. accounts under §1.1471-4(d) (as incorporated into its qualified intermediary agreement). Provided that QI reports A's account as a U.S. account under the requirements referenced in the preceding sentence, QI is not required to provide WA with a Form W-9 from A and may instead include A in a chapter 4 withholding rate pool of U.S. payees, allocating 10% of the payment to this pool. See §1.6049-4(c)(4)(iii) concerning when reporting under section 6049 for a payment of interest is not required when an FFI that is a non-U.S. payor reports an account holder receiving the payment under its chapter 4 requirements. With respect to B, the interest payment is subject to backup withholding under section 3406. Because B is a recalcitrant account holder of QI for withholdable payments and because QI assumes primary chapter 4 withholding responsibility, however, QI may include the portion of the payment allocated to B with the remaining 80% of the payment for which QI assumes primary withholding responsibility. WA can reliably associate the full amount of the payment based on the withholding statement and does so regardless of whether WA knows B is a U.S. non-exempt recipient that is receiving a portion of the payment. See §31.3406(g)-1(e) (providing exemption to backup withholding when withholding was applied under chapter 4).

(6) *Qualified derivatives dealers.*—(i) *In general.*—To act as a qualified derivatives dealer under a qualified intermediary withholding agreement, the home office or branch that is a qualified intermediary must be an eligible entity as described in paragraph (e)(6)(ii) of this section and, in accordance with the qualified intermediary agreement, must—

(A) Furnish to a withholding agent a qualified intermediary withholding certificate (described in paragraph (e)(3)(ii) of this section) that indicates that the home office or branch receiving the payment is a qualified derivatives dealer with respect to the payments associated with the withholding certificate;

(B) Agree to assume the primary withholding and reporting responsibilities, including the documentation provisions under chapters 3, 4, and 61, and section 3406, the regulations under those provisions, and other provisions of the Internal Revenue Code, for payments made as a qualified derivatives dealer with respect to potential section 871(m) transactions. For this purpose, a qualified derivatives dealer is required to obtain a withholding certificate or other appropriate documentation from each counterparty to whom the qualified derivatives dealer makes a reportable payment (including a dividend equivalent payment within the meaning of §1.871-15(i)). The qualified derivatives dealer is also required to determine whether any payment it makes with respect to a potential section 871(m) transaction is, in whole or in part, a dividend equivalent;

(C) Agree to remain liable for tax under section 881, if any, on any payment with respect to a potential section 871(m) transaction (including a dividend equivalent payment within the meaning of §1.871-15(i)) and underlying securities as defined in §1.871-15(a)(15) (including dividends) it receives as a qualified derivatives dealer, or in the case of dividend equivalents received in its equity derivatives dealer capacity, the taxes required pursuant to §1.871-15(q);

(D) Comply with the compliance review procedures applicable to a qualified intermediary that acts as a qualified derivatives dealer under the qualified intermediary withholding agreement, which will specify the time and manner in which a qualified derivatives dealer must:

(1) Certify to the IRS that it has complied with the obligations to act as a qualified derivatives dealer (including its performance of a periodic review applicable to a qualified derivatives dealer);

(2) Report to the IRS any amounts subject to reporting on Forms 1042-S (including dividend equivalent payments that it made);

(3) Report to the IRS on the appropriate U.S. federal tax return, its tax liabilities, including its tax liability pursuant to §1.871-15(q)(1) and any other taxes on payments with respect to potential section 871(m) transactions or underlying securities as defined in §1.871-15(a)(15) it receives; and

(4) Respond to inquiries from the IRS about obligations it has assumed as a qualified derivatives dealer in a timely manner;

(E) Agree to act as a qualified derivatives dealer for all payments made as a principal with respect to potential section 871(m) transactions and all payments received as a principal with respect to potential section 871(m) transactions and underlying securities as defined in §1.871-15(a)(15) (including dividend equivalent payments within the meaning of §1.871-15(i)), excluding any payments made or received by the qualified derivatives dealer to the extent the payment is treated as effectively connected with the conduct of a trade or business within the United States within the meaning of section 864, and not act as a qualified derivatives dealer for any other payments. For purposes of this paragraph (E), any securities lending or sale-repurchase transaction that the qualified intermediary enters into that is a section 871(m) transaction is treated as entered into as a principal unless the qualified intermediary determines that it is acting as an intermediary with respect to that transaction; and

(F) Each home office or branch must qualify and be approved for qualified derivatives dealer status and must represent itself as a qualified derivatives dealer on its Form W-8IMY and separately identify the home office or branch as the recipient on a withholding statement (if necessary). The home office means a foreign person, excluding any branches of the foreign person, that applies for qualified derivatives dealer status. Each home office or branch that obtains qualified derivatives dealer status must be treated as a separate qualified derivatives dealer.

(ii) *Definition of eligible entity.*—An eligible entity is a home office or branch that is a qualified intermediary and that, treating the home office or branch as a separate entity, is—

(A) An equity derivatives dealer subject to regulatory supervision as a dealer by a governmental authority in the jurisdiction in which it was organized or operates;

(B) A bank or bank holding company subject to regulatory supervision as a bank or bank holding company (as applicable) by a governmental authority in the jurisdiction in which it was organized or operates or an entity that is wholly-owned (directly or indirectly) by a bank or bank holding company subject to regulatory supervision as a bank or bank holding company (as applicable) by a governmental authority in the jurisdiction in which the bank or bank holding company (as applicable) was organized or operates and that in its equity derivatives dealer capacity—

(1) Issues potential section 871(m) transactions to customers; and

(2) Receives dividends with respect to stock or dividend equivalent payments with respect to potential section 871(m) transactions that hedge potential section 871(m) transactions that it issued;

(C) A foreign branch of a U.S. financial institution, if the foreign branch would meet the requirements of paragraph (A) or (B) of this section if it were a separate entity; or

(D) Any person otherwise acceptable to the IRS.

(f) *Effective/applicability date.*—(1) *In general.*—Except as otherwise provided in paragraphs (e)(2)(ii)(B), (e)(4)(iv)(D), (f)(2), and (f)(3) of this section, this section applies to payments made on or after January 6, 2017. (For payments made after June 30, 2014 (except for payments to which paragraph (e)(4)(iv)(D) applies, in which case, substitute March 5, 2014, for June 30, 2014), and before January 6, 2017, see this section as in effect and contained in 26 CFR part 1, as revised April 1, 2016. For payments made after December 31, 2000, and before July 1, 2014, see this section as in effect and contained in 26 CFR part 1, as revised April 1, 2013.)

(2) *Lack of documentation for past years.*—A taxpayer may elect to apply the provisions of paragraphs (b)(7)(i)(B), (ii), and (iii) of this section, dealing with liability for failure to obtain documentation timely, to all of its open tax years, including tax years that are currently under examination by the IRS. The election is made by simply taking action under those provisions in the same manner as the taxpayer would take action for payments made after December 31, 2000.

(3) *Special rules related to section 871(m).*—Paragraphs (b)(4)(xxi), (b)(4)(xxiii), (e)(3)(ii)(E), and (e)(6) of this section apply to payments

made on or after September 18, 2015. Paragraphs (e)(5)(ii)(C) and (e)(5)(v)(B)(4) of this section apply to payments made on or after on January 19, 2017. [Reg. § 1.1441-1.]

☐ [*T.D.* 6187, 7-5-56. *Amended by T.D.* 6592, 2-27-62; *T.D.* 6908, 12-30-66; *T.D.* 7157, 12-29-71; *T.D.* 7385, 10-28-75; *T.D.* 7670, 1-30-80; *T.D.* 8734, 10-6-97; *T.D.* 8804, 12-30-98; *T.D.* 8856, 12-29-99 (*corrected* 3-27-2000); *T.D.* 8881, 5-15-2000 (*corrected* 4-5-2001); *T.D.* 9023, 11-21-2002; *T.D.* 9253, 3-13-2006; *T.D.* 9323, 4-11-2007 *T.D.* 9658, 2-28-2014 (*corrected* 6-30-2014), *T.D.* 9734, 9-17-2015 (*corrected* 12-4-2015), *T.D.* 9808, 12-30-2016 (*corrected* 6-29-2017), *T.D.* 9815, 1-19-2017 (*corrected* 10-25-2017) *and T.D.* 9890, 12-27-2019.]

### [Reg. § 1.1441-2]

**§ 1.1441-2. Amounts subject to withholding.**—(a) *In general.*—For purposes of the regulations under chapter 3 of the Internal Revenue Code, the term *amounts subject to withholding* means amounts from sources within the United States that constitute either fixed or determinable annual or periodical income described in paragraph (b) of this section or other amounts subject to withholding described in paragraph (c) of this section. For purposes of this paragraph (a), an amount shall be treated as being from sources within the United States if the source of the amount cannot be determined at the time of payment. See § 1.1441-3(d)(1) for determining the amount to be withheld from a payment in the absence of information at the time of payment regarding the source of the amount. Amounts subject to withholding include amounts that are not fixed or determinable annual or periodical income and upon which withholding is specifically required under a provision of this section or another section of the regulations under chapter 3 of the Internal Revenue Code (such as corporate distributions upon which withholding is required under § 1.1441-3(c)(1) that do not constitute dividend income). Amounts subject to withholding do not include—

(1) Amounts described in § 1.1441-1(b)(4)(i) to the extent they involve interest on obligations in bearer form or on foreign-targeted registered obligations (but, in the case of a foreign-targeted registered obligation, only to the extent of those amounts paid to a registered owner that is a financial institution within the meaning of section 871(h)(5)(B) or a member of a clearing organization which member is the beneficial owner of the obligation);

(2) Amounts described in § 1.1441-1(b)(4)(ii) (dealing with bank deposit interest and similar types of interest (including original issue discount) described in section 871(i)(2)(A) or 881(d));

(3) Amounts described in § 1.1441-1(b)(4)(iv) (dealing with interest or original issue discount on certain short-term obligations described in section 871(g)(1)(B) or 881(e));

(4) Amounts described in § 1.1441-1(b)(4)(xx) (dealing with income from certain gambling winnings exempt from tax under section 871(j));

(5) Amounts paid as part of the purchase price of an obligation sold or exchanged between interest payment dates, unless the sale or exchange is part of a plan the principal purpose of which is to avoid tax and the withholding agent has actual knowledge or reason to know of such plan;

(6) Original issue discount paid as part of the purchase price of an obligation sold or exchanged in a transaction other than a redemption of such obligation, unless the purchase is part of a plan the principal purpose of which is to avoid tax and the withholding agent has actual knowledge or reason to know of such plan; and

(7) Insurance premiums paid with respect to a contract that is subject to the section 4371 excise tax.

(8) Amounts of United States source gross transportation income, as defined in section 887(b)(1), that is taxable under section 887(a).

(b) *Fixed or determinable annual or periodical income.*—(1) *In general.*—(i) *Definition.*—For purposes of chapter 3 of the Internal Revenue Code and the regulations thereunder, fixed or determinable annual or periodical income includes all income included in gross income under section 61 (including original issue discount) except for the items specified in paragraph (b)(2) of this section. Items of income that are excluded from gross income under a provision of law without regard to the U.S. or foreign status of the owner of the income, such as interest excluded from gross income under section 103(a) or qualified scholarship income under section 117, shall not be treated as fixed or determinable annual or periodical income under chapter 3 of the Internal Revenue Code. Income excluded from gross income under section 892 (income of foreign governments) or section 115 (income of a U.S. possession) is fixed or determinable annual or periodical income since the exclusion from gross income under those sections is dependent on the foreign status of the owner of the income. See § 1.306-3(h) for treating income from the disposition of section 306 stock as fixed or determinable annual or periodical income.

(ii) *Manner of payment.*—The term *fixed or determinable annual or periodical* is merely descriptive of the character of a class of income. If an item of income falls within the class of income contemplated in the statute and described in paragraph (a) of this section, it is immaterial whether payment of that item is made in a series of payments or in a single lump sum. Further, the income need not be paid annually if it is paid periodically; that is to say, from time to time, whether or not at regular intervals. The fact that a payment is not made annually or periodically does not, however, prevent it from being fixed or determinable annual or periodical income (e.g., a lump sum payment). In addition, the fact that the length of time during which the payments are to be made may be increased or diminished in accordance with someone's will or with the happening of an event does not disqualify the payment as determinable or periodical. For this purpose, the share of the fixed or determinable annual or periodical income of an estate or trust from sources within the United States which is required to be distributed currently, or which has been paid or credited during the taxable year, to a nonresident alien beneficiary of such estate or trust constitutes fixed or determinable annual or periodical income.

(iii) *Determinability of amount.*—An item of income is fixed when it is to be paid in amounts definitely pre-determined. An item of income is determinable if the amount to be paid is not known but there is a basis of calculation by which the amount may be ascertained at a later time. For example, interest is determinable even if it is contingent in that its amount cannot be determined at the time of payment of an amount with respect to a loan because the calculation of the interest portion of the payment is contingent upon factors that are not fixed at the time of the payment. For purposes of this section, an amount of income does not have to be determined at the time that the payment is made in order to be determinable. An amount of income described in paragraph (a) of this section which the withholding agent knows is part of a payment it makes but which it cannot calculate exactly at the time of payment, is nevertheless determinable if the determination of the exact amount depends upon events expected to occur at a future date. In contrast, a payment which may be income in the future based upon events that are not anticipated at the time the payment is made is not determinable. For example, loan proceeds may become income to the borrower when and to the extent the loan is canceled without repayment. While the cancellation of the debt is income to the borrower when it occurs, it is not determinable at the time the loan proceeds are disbursed to the borrower if the lack of repayment leading to the cancellation of part or all of the debt was not anticipated at the time of disbursement. The fact that the source of an item of income cannot be determined at the time that the payment is made does not render a payment not determinable. See § 1.1441-3(d)(1) for determining the amount to be withheld from a payment in the absence of information at the time of payment regarding the source of the amount.

(2) *Exceptions.*—For purposes of chapter 3 of the Code and the regulations thereunder, the items of income described in this paragraph (b)(2) are not fixed or determinable annual or periodical income—

(i) Gains derived from the sale of property (including market discount and option premiums), except for gains described in paragraph (b)(3) or (c) of this section; and

(ii) Any other income that the Internal Revenue Service (IRS) may determine, in published guidance (see § 601.601(d)(2) of this chapter), is not fixed or determinable annual or periodical income.

(3) *Original issue discount.*—(i) *Amount subject to tax.*—An amount representing original issue discount is fixed or determinable annual or periodical income that is subject to tax under sections 871(a)(1)(C) and 881(a)(3) to the extent provided in those sections and this paragraph (b)(3) if not otherwise excluded under paragraph (a) of this section. An amount of original issue discount is subject to tax with respect to a foreign beneficial owner of an obligation carrying original issue discount upon a sale or exchange of the obligation or when a payment is made on such obligation. The amount taxable is the amount of original issue discount that accrued while the foreign person held the obligation up to the time that the obligation is sold or exchanged or that a payment is made on the obligation, reduced by any amount of original issue discount that was taken into account prior to that time (due to a payment made on the obligation). In the case of a payment made on the obligation, the tax due on the amount of original issue discount may not exceed the amount of the payment reduced by the tax imposed on any portion of the payment that is qualified stated interest.

(ii) *Amounts subject to withholding.*—A withholding agent must withhold on the taxable amount of original issue discount paid on the redemption of an original issue discount obligation unless an exception to withholding applies (e.g., portfolio interest or treaty exception). In addition, withholding is required on the taxable amount of original issue discount upon the sale or exchange of an original issue discount obligation, other than in a redemption, to the extent the withholding agent has actual knowledge or reason to know that the sale or exchange is part of a plan the principal purpose of which is to avoid tax. If a withholding agent cannot determine the taxable amount of original issue discount on the redemption of an original issue discount obligation (or on the sale or exchange of such an obligation if the principal purpose of the sale is to avoid tax), then it must withhold on the entire amount of original issue discount accrued from the date of issue until the date of redemption (or the date the obligation is sold or exchanged) determined on the basis of the most recently published "List of Original Issue Discount Instruments" (IRS Publication 1212, available from the IRS Forms Distribution Center) or similar list published by the IRS as if the beneficial owner of the obligation had held the obligation since its original issue.

(iii) *Exceptions to withholding.*—To the extent that this paragraph (b)(3) applies to require withholding by a person other than an issuer of an original issue discount obligation, or the issuer's agent, it shall apply only to obligations issued after December 31, 2000.

(4) *Securities lending transactions and equivalent transactions.*—See §§ 1.871-7(b)(2) and 1.881-2(b)(2) regarding the character of substitute payments as fixed and determinable annual or periodical income. Such amounts constitute income subject to withholding to the extent they are from sources within the United States, as determined under section §§ 1.861-2(a)(7) and 1.861-3(a)(6). See §§ 1.6042-3(a)(2) and 1.6049-5(a)(5) for reporting requirements applicable to substitute dividend and interest payments, respectively.

(5) *REMIC residual interests.*—Amounts subject to withholding include an excess inclusion described in § 1.860G-3(b)(2) and the portion of an amount described in § 1.860G-3(b)(1) that is an excess inclusion.

(6) *Dividend equivalents.*—Amounts subject to withholding include a dividend equivalent described in section 871(m) and the regulations thereunder. For this purpose, the amount of a dividend equivalent includes any gross amount that is used in computing any net amount that is transferred to or from the taxpayer under the terms of the transaction or any other payment described in section 871(m) and the regulations thereunder.

(c) *Other income subject to withholding.*—Withholding is also required on the following items of income—

(1) Gains described in sections 631(b) or (c), relating to treatment of gain on disposal of timber, coal, or domestic iron ore with a retained economic interest; and

(2) Gains subject to the 30-percent tax under section 871(a)(1)(D) or 881(a)(4), relating to contingent payments received from the sale or exchange of patents, copyrights, and similar intangible property.

(d) *Exceptions to withholding where no money or property is paid or lack of knowledge.*—(1) *General rule.*—A withholding agent who is not related to the recipient or beneficial owner has an obligation to withhold under section 1441 only to the extent that, at any time between the date that the obligation to withhold would arise (but for the provisions of this paragraph (d)) and the due date for the filing of return on Form 1042 (including extensions) for the year in which the payment occurs, it has control over, or custody of money or property owned by the recipient or beneficial owner from which to withhold an amount and has knowledge of the facts that give rise to the payment. The exemption from the obligation to withhold under this paragraph (d) shall not apply, however, to distributions with respect to stock or if the lack of control or custody of money or property from which to withhold is part of a pre-arranged plan known to the withholding agent to avoid withholding under section 1441, 1442, or 1443. For purposes of this paragraph (d), a withholding agent is related to the recipient or beneficial owner if it is related within the meaning of section 482. Any exemption from withholding pursuant to this paragraph (d) applies without a requirement that documentation be furnished to the withholding agent. However, documentation may have to be furnished for purposes of the information reporting provisions under chapter 61 of the Code and backup withholding under section 3406. The exemption from withholding under this paragraph (d) is not a determination that the amounts are not fixed or determinable annual or periodical income, nor does it constitute an exemption from reporting the amount under § 1.1461-1(b) and (c).

(2) *Cancellation of debt.*—A lender of funds who forgives any portion of the loan is deemed to have made a payment of income to the borrower under § 1.61-12 at the time the event of forgiveness occurs. However, based on the rules of paragraph (d)(1) of this section, the lender shall have no obligation to withhold on such amount to the extent that it does not have custody or control over money or property of the borrower at any time between the time that the loan is forgiven and the due date (including extensions) of the Form 1042 for the year in which the payment is deemed to occur. A payment received by the lender from the borrower in partial settlement of the debt obligation does not, for this purpose, constitute an amount of money or property belonging to the borrower from which the withholding tax liability can be satisfied.

(3) *Satisfaction of liability following underwithholding by withholding agent.*—A withholding agent who, after failing to withhold the proper amount from a payment, satisfies the underwithheld amount out of its own funds may cause the beneficial owner to realize income to the extent of such satisfaction or may be considered to have advanced funds to the beneficial owner. Such determination depends upon the contractual arrangements governing the satisfaction of such tax liability (e.g., arrangements in which the withholding agent agrees to pay the amount due under section 1441 for the beneficial owner) or applicable laws governing the transaction. If the satisfaction of the tax liability is considered to constitute an advance of funds by the withholding agent to the beneficial owner and the withholding agent fails to collect the amount from the beneficial owner, a cancellation of indebtedness may result, giving rise to income to the beneficial owner under § 1.61-12. While such income is annual or periodical fixed or determinable, the withholding agent shall have no liability to withhold on such income to the extent the conditions set forth in paragraphs (d)(1) and (2) of this section are satisfied with respect to this income. Contrast the rules of this paragraph (d)(3) with the rules in § 1.1441-3(f)(1) dealing with a situation in which the satisfaction of the beneficial owner's tax liability itself constitutes additional income to the beneficial owner. See, also, § 1.1441-3(c)(2)(ii)(B) for a special rule regarding underwithholding on corporate distributions due to underestimating an amount of earnings and profits.

(4) *Withholding exemption inapplicable.*—The exemption in § 1.1441-2(d) from the obligation to withhold shall not apply to amounts described in § 1.860G-3(b)(1) (regarding certain partnership allocations of REMIC net income with respect to a REMIC residual interest).

(e) *Payment.*—(1) *General rule.*—A payment is considered made to a person if that person realizes income whether or not such income results from an actual transfer of cash or other property. For example, realization of income from cancellation of debt results in a deemed payment. A payment is considered made when the amount would be includible in the income of the beneficial owner under the U.S. tax principles governing the cash basis method of accounting. A payment is considered made whether it is made directly to the beneficial owner or to another person for the benefit of the beneficial owner (e.g., to the agent of the beneficial owner). Thus, a payment of income is considered made to a beneficial owner if it is paid in complete or partial satisfaction of the beneficial owner's debt to a creditor. In the event of a conflict between the rules of this paragraph (e)(1) governing whether a payment has occurred and its timing and the rules of § 31.3406(a)-4 of this chapter, the rules in § 31.3406(a)-4 of this chapter shall apply to the extent that the application of section 3406 is relevant to the transaction at issue.

(2) *Income allocated under section 482.*—A payment is considered made to the extent income subject to withholding is allocated under section 482. Further, income arising as a result of a secondary adjustment made in conjunction with a reallocation of income under section 482 from a foreign person to a related U.S. person is considered paid to a foreign person unless the taxpayer to whom the income is reallocated has entered into a repatriation agreement with the IRS and the agreement eliminates the liability for withholding under this section. For purposes of determining the liability for withholding, the payment of income is deemed to have occurred on the last day of the taxable year in which the transactions that give rise to the allocation of income and the secondary adjustments, if any, took place.

(3) *Blocked income.*—Income is not considered paid if it is blocked under executive authority, such as the President's exercise of emergency power under the Trading with the Enemy Act (50 U.S.C. App. 5), or the International Emergency Economic Powers Act (50 U.S.C. 1701 et seq).. However, on the date that the blocking restrictions are removed, the income that was blocked is considered constructively received by the beneficial owner (and therefore paid for purposes of this section) and subject to withholding under § 1.1441-1. Any exemption from withholding pursuant to this paragraph (e)(3) applies without a requirement that documentation be furnished to the withholding agent. However, documentation may have to be furnished for purposes of the information reporting provisions under chapter 61 of the Code and backup withholding under section 3406. The exemption from withholding granted by this paragraph (e)(3) is not a determination that the amounts are not fixed or determinable annual or periodical income.

(4) *Special rules for dividends.*—For purposes of sections 1441 and 6042, in the case of stock for which the record date is earlier than the payment date, dividends are considered paid on the payment date. In the case of a corporate reorganization, if a beneficial owner is required to exchange stock held in a former corporation for stock in a new corporation before dividends that are to be paid with respect to the stock in the new corporation will be paid on such stock, the dividend is considered paid on the date that the payee or beneficial owner actually exchanges the stock and receives the dividend. See § 31.3406(a)-4(a)(2) of this chapter.

(5) *Certain interest accrued by a foreign corporation.*—For purposes of sections 1441 and 6049, a foreign corporation shall be treated as having made a payment of interest as of the last day of the taxable year if it has made an election under § 1.884-4(c)(1) to treat accrued interest as if it were paid in that taxable year.

(6) *Payments other than in U.S. dollars.*—For purposes of section 1441, a payment includes amounts paid in a medium other than U.S. dollars. See § 1.1441-3(e) for rules regarding the amount subject to withholding in the case of such payments.

(7) *Payments of dividend equivalents.*—(i) *In general.*—Subject to paragraphs (e)(7)(iv), (vi), and (vii) of this section, a payment of a dividend equivalent is not considered to be made until the later of when—

(A) The amount of a dividend equivalent is determined as provided in § 1.871-15(j)(2), and

(B) A payment occurs with respect to the section 871(m) transaction after the amount of a dividend equivalent is determined as provided in § 1.871-15(j)(2).

(ii) *Payment.*—For purposes of paragraph (e)(7) of this section, a payment occurs with respect to a section 871(m) transaction when—

(A) Money or other property is paid to or by the long party, unless the section 871(m) transaction is described in § 1.871-15(i)(3)(i), in which case a payment is treated as being made at the end of the applicable calendar quarter;

(B) The long party sells, exchanges, transfers, or otherwise disposes of the section 871(m) transaction (including by settlement, offset, termination, expiration, lapse, or maturity); or

(C) The section 871(m) transaction is transferred to an account that is not maintained by the withholding agent or the long party terminates the account relationship with the withholding agent.

(iii) *Premiums and other upfront payments.*—When a long party pays a premium or other upfront payment to the short party at the time a section 871(m) transaction is issued, the premium or other upfront payment is not treated as a payment for purposes of paragraph (e)(7)(ii)(A) of this section.

(iv) *Option to withhold on dividend payment date.*—A withholding agent may withhold on the payment date described in paragraph (e)(4) of this section for the applicable dividend on the underlying security (the dividend payment date) if it withholds on that date for all section 871(m) transactions of the same type (for example, securities lending or sale-repurchase transaction, NPC, or ELI) and satisfies the requirements to paragraph (e)(7)(v) of this section.

(v) *Changes to time of withholding.*—This paragraph describes how a withholding agent changes the time that it withholds on a dividend equivalent payment to a time described in paragraph (e)(7)(i) or (iv) of this section and these requirements must be satisfied for a withholding agent to change the time it withholds. A withholding agent must apply the change consistently to all transactions of the same type entered into on or after the change. For transactions of the same type entered into before the change, a withholding agent must withhold under the original approach throughout the term of the transaction. When a withholding agent changes the time that it will withhold, the withholding agent must notify each payee in writing that it will withhold using the approach described in paragraph (e)(7)(i) or (iv) of this section, as applicable, before the time for determining the payee's first dividend equivalent payment (as determined under § 1.871-15(j)(2)). With respect to transactions held by an intermediary or foreign flow-through entity, a withholding agent is treated as providing notice to each payee holding that transaction through the entity when it notifies the intermediary or foreign flow-through entity of the time it will withhold, as described in the preceding sentence, provided that the intermediary or foreign flow-through entity agrees to provide the same notice to each payee. The withholding agent must attach a statement to its relevant income tax return (filed by the due date, including extensions) for the year of the change notifying the IRS of the change and when it applies, identifying the type of section 871(m) transaction to which the change applies, and certifying that it has notified its

payees. For purposes of this paragraph, a withholding agent will be considered to have entered into a transaction on the first date the withholding agent becomes responsible for withholding on the transaction (based on the rule in paragraph (e)(7)(ix) of this section).

(vi) *Withholding by qualified derivatives dealers.*—A withholding agent that is acting as a qualified derivatives dealer must withhold with respect to a dividend equivalent payment on the payment date described in paragraph (e)(4) of this section for the applicable dividend on the underlying security and must notify each payee in writing that it will withhold on the dividend payment date before the time for determining the payee's first dividend equivalent payment (as determined under § 1.871-15(j)(2)).

(vii) *Withholding with respect to derivatives that reference partnerships.*—To the extent that a withholding agent is required to withhold with respect to a partnership interest described in § 1.871-15(m), the liability for withholding arises on March 15 of the year following the year in which the payment of a dividend equivalent (determined under § 1.871-15(i)) occurs.

(viii) *Notification to holders of withholding timing.*—If a withholding agent is required to notify a payee of when it will withhold under paragraph (e)(7)(v) of this section, it may use the reporting methods prescribed in § 1.871-15(p)(3)(i).

(ix) *Withholding agent responsibility.*—A withholding agent is only responsible for dividend equivalent amounts determined (as provided in § 1.871-15(j)(2)) during the period the withholding agent is a withholding agent for the section 871(m) transaction.

(f) *Effective/applicability date.*—This section applies to payments made after December 31, 2000. Paragraph (a)(8) of this section applies to payments made on or after January 6, 2017; however, taxpayers may apply paragraph (a)(8) to any open tax year. Paragraphs (b)(5) and (d)(4) of this section apply to payments made after August 1, 2006. Paragraph (b)(6) of this section applies to payments made on or after January 23, 2012. Paragraph (e)(7) of this section applies to payments made on or after January 19, 2017. [Reg. § 1.1441-2.]

☐ [T.D. 6187, 7-5-56. *Amended by* T.D. 6464, 5-11-60, T.D. 6592, 2-27-62, T.D. 6841, 7-26-65, T.D. 6873, 1-24-66, T.D. 6908, 12-30-66; T.D. 7977, 9-19-84; T.D. 8734, 10-6-97; T.D. 8804, 12-30-98; T.D. 8856, 12-29-99; T.D. 8881, 5-15-2000; T.D. 9272, 7-31-2006; T.D. 9415, 7-11-2008 *(corrected* 8-5-2008*);* T.D. 9572, 1-19-2012, T.D. 9648, 12-4-2013, T.D. 9734, 9-17-2015, T.D. 9808, 12-30-2016, T.D. 9815, 1-19-2017 *(corrected* 10-25-2017) *and* T.D. 9890, 12-27-2019.]

**[Reg. § 1.1441-3]**

**§ 1.1441-3. Determination of amounts to be withheld.**—(a) *General rule.*—(1) *Withholding on gross amount.*—Except as otherwise provided in regulations under section 1441, the amount subject to withholding under § 1.1441-1 is the gross amount of income subject to withholding that is paid to a foreign person. The gross amount of income subject to withholding may not be reduced by any deductions, except to the extent that one or more personal exemptions are allowed as provided under § 1.1441-4(b)(6).

(2) *Coordination with chapter 4.*—A withholding agent making a payment that is both a withholdable payment and an amount subject to withholding under § 1.1441-2(a) and that has withheld tax as required under chapter 4 from such payment is not required to withhold under this section notwithstanding paragraph (a)(1) of this section. See § 1.1474-6(b)(1) for the allowance for a withholding agent to credit withholding applied under chapter 4 against its liability for tax due under sections 1441, 1442, or 1443, and see § 1.1474-6(b)(1) for the rule allowing a withholding agent to credit withholding applied under chapter 4 against its liability for tax due under sections 1441, 1442, or 1443, and § 1.1474-6(b)(2) for when such withholding is considered applied by a withholding agent. If the withholdable payment is not required to be withheld upon under chapter 4, then the withholding agent must apply the provisions of § 1.1441-1 to determine whether withholding is required under sections 1441, 1442, or 1443.

(b) *Withholding on payments on certain obligations.*—(1) *Withholding at time of payment of interest.*—When making a payment on an interest-bearing obligation, a withholding agent must withhold under § 1.1441-1 upon the gross amount of stated interest payable on the interest payment date, regardless of whether the payment constitutes a return of capital or the payment of income within the meaning of section 61. To the extent an amount was withheld on an amount of capital rather than interest, see the rules for adjustments, refunds, or credits under § 1.1441-1(b)(8).

(2) *No withholding between interest payment dates.*—(i) *In general.*—A withholding agent is not required to withhold under § 1.1441-1 upon interest accrued on the date of a sale or exchange of a

debt obligation when that sale occurs between two interest payment dates (even though the amount is treated as interest under §1.61-7(c) or (d) and is subject to tax under section 871 or 881). See §1.6045-1(c) for reporting requirements by brokers with respect to sale proceeds. See §1.61-7(c) regarding the character of payments received by the acquirer of an obligation subsequent to such acquisition (that is, as a return of capital or interest accrued after the acquisition). Any exemption from withholding pursuant to this paragraph (b)(2)(i) applies without a requirement that documentation be furnished to the withholding agent. However, documentation may have to be furnished for purposes of the information reporting provisions under section 6045 or 6049 and backup withholding under section 3406. The exemption from withholding granted by this paragraph (b)(2) is not a determination that the accrued interest is not fixed or determinable annual or periodical income under section 871(a) or 881(a).

(ii) *Anti-abuse rule.*—The exemption in paragraph (b)(2)(i) of this section does not apply if the sale of securities is part of a plan the principal purpose of which is to avoid tax by selling and repurchasing securities and the withholding agent has actual knowledge or reason to know of such plan.

(c) *Corporate distributions.*—(1) *General rule.*—A corporation making a distribution with respect to its stock or any intermediary (described in §1.1441-1(c)(13)) making a payment of such a distribution is required to withhold under section 1441, 1442, or 1443 on the entire amount of the distribution, unless it elects to reduce the amount of withholding under the provisions of this paragraph (c). Any exceptions from withholding provided by this paragraph (c) apply without any requirement to furnish documentation to the withholding agent. However, documentation may have to be furnished for purposes of the information reporting provisions under section 6042 or 6045 and backup withholding under section 3406. See §1.1461-1(c) to determine whether amounts excepted from withholding under this section are considered amounts that are subject to reporting.

(2) *Exception to withholding on distributions.*—(i) *In general.*—An election described in paragraph (c)(1) of this section is made by actually reducing the amount of withholding at the time that the payment is made. An intermediary that makes a payment of a distribution is not required to reduce the withholding based on the distributing corporation's estimates under this paragraph (c)(2), even if the distributing corporation itself elects to reduce the withholding on payments of distributions that it itself makes to foreign persons. Conversely, an intermediary may elect to reduce the amount of withholding with respect to the payment of a distribution even if the distributing corporation does not so elect for the payments of distributions that it itself makes of distributions to foreign persons. The amounts with respect to which a distributing corporation or intermediary may elect to reduce the withholding are as follows:

(A) A distributing corporation or intermediary may elect to not withhold on a distribution to the extent it represents a nontaxable distribution payable in stock or stock rights.

(B) A distributing corporation or intermediary may elect to not withhold on a distribution to the extent it represents a distribution in part or full payment in exchange for stock.

(C) A distributing corporation or intermediary may elect to not withhold on a distribution (actual or deemed) to the extent it is not paid out of accumulated earnings and profits or current earnings and profits, based on a reasonable estimate determined under paragraph (c)(2)(ii) of this section.

(D) A regulated investment company or intermediary may elect to not withhold on a distribution representing a capital gain dividend (as defined in section 852(b)(3)(C)) or an exempt interest dividend (as defined in section 852(b)(5)(A)) based on the applicable procedures described under paragraph (c)(3) of this section.

(E) A U.S. Real Property Holding Corporation (defined in section 897(c)(2)) or a real estate investment trust (defined in section 856) or intermediary may elect to not withhold on a distribution to the extent it is subject to withholding under section 1445 and the regulations under that section. See paragraph (c)(4) of this section for applicable procedures.

(ii) *Reasonable estimate of accumulated and current earnings and profits on the date of payment.*—(A) *General rule.*—A reasonable estimate for purposes of paragraph (c)(2)(i)(C) of this section is a determination made by the distributing corporation at a time reasonably close to the date of payment of the extent to which the distribution will constitute a dividend, as defined in section 316. The determination is based upon the anticipated amount of accumulated earnings and profits and current earnings and profits for the taxable year in which the distribution is made, the distributions made prior to the distribution for which the estimate is made and all other relevant facts and circumstances. A reasonable estimate may be made based on the procedures described in §31.3406(b)(2)-4(c)(2) of this chapter.

(B) *Procedures in case of underwithholding.*—A distributing corporation or intermediary that is a withholding agent with respect to a distribution and that determines at the end of the taxable year in which the distribution is made that it underwithheld under section 1441 on the distribution shall be liable for the amount underwithheld as a withholding agent under section 1461. However, for purposes of this section and §1.1461-1, any amount underwithheld paid by a distributing corporation, its paying agent, or an intermediary shall not be treated as income subject to additional withholding even if that amount is treated as additional income to the shareholders unless the additional amount is income to the shareholder as a result of a contractual arrangement between the parties regarding the satisfaction of the shareholder's tax liabilities. In addition, no penalties shall be imposed for failure to withhold and deposit the tax if—

(1) The distributing corporation made a reasonable estimate as provided in paragraph (c)(2)(ii)(A) of this section; and

(2) Either—

(i) The corporation or intermediary pays over the underwithheld amount on or before the due date for filing a Form 1042 for the calendar year in which the distribution is made, pursuant to §1.1461-2(b); or

(ii) The corporation or intermediary is not a calendar year taxpayer and it files an amended return on Form 1042X (or such other form as the Commissioner may prescribe) for the calendar year in which the distribution is made and pays the underwithheld amount and interest within 60 days after the close of the taxable year in which the distribution is made.

(C) *Reliance by intermediary on reasonable estimate.*—For purposes of determining whether the payment of a corporate distribution is a dividend, a withholding agent that is not the distributing corporation may, absent actual knowledge or reason to know otherwise, rely on representations made by the distributing corporation regarding the reasonable estimate of the anticipated accumulated and current earnings and profits made in accordance with paragraph (c)(2)(ii)(A) of this section. Failure by the withholding agent to withhold the required amount due to a failure by the distributing corporation to reasonably estimate the portion of the distribution treated as a dividend or to properly communicate the information to the withholding agent shall be imputed to the distributing corporation. In such a case, the Internal Revenue Service (IRS) may collect from the distributing corporation any underwithheld amount and subject the distributing corporation to applicable interest and penalties as a withholding agent.

(D) *Example.*—The rules of this paragraph (c)(2) are illustrated by the following example:

*Example.* (i) *Facts.* Corporation X, a publicly traded corporation with both U.S. and foreign shareholders and a calendar year taxpayer, has an accumulated deficit in earnings and profits at the close of 2000. In 2001, Corporation X generates $1 million of current earnings and profits each month and makes an $18 million distribution, resulting in a $12 million dividend. Corporation X plans to make an additional $18 million distribution on October 1, 2002. Approximately one month before that date, Corporation X's management receives an internal report from its legal and accounting department concerning Corporation X's estimated current earnings and profits. The report states that Corporation X should generate only $5.1 million of current earnings and profits by the close of the third quarter due to costs relating to substantial organizational and product changes, but these changes will enable Corporation X to generate $1.3 million of earnings and profits monthly for the last quarter of the 2002 fiscal year. Thus, the total amount of current and earnings and profits for 2002 is estimated to be $9 million.

(ii) *Analysis.* Based on the facts in paragraph (i) of this *Example,* including the fact that earnings and profits estimate was made within a reasonable time before the distribution, Corporation X can rely on the estimate under paragraph (c)(2)(ii)(A) of this section. Therefore, Corporation X may treat $9 million of the $18 million of the October 1, 2002, distribution to foreign shareholders as a nondividend distribution.

(3) *Special rules in the case of distributions from a regulated investment company.*—(i) *General rule.*—If the amount of any distributions designated as being subject to section 852(b)(3)(C) or (5)(A), or 871(k)(1)(C) or (2)(C), exceeds the amount that may be designated under those sections for the taxable year, then no penalties will be asserted for any resulting underwithholding if the designations were based on a reasonable estimate (made pursuant to the same procedures as are described in paragraph (c)(2)(ii)(A) of this section) and the adjustments to the amount withheld are made within the time period described in paragraph (c)(2)(ii)(B) of this section. Any adjustment to the amount of tax due and paid to the IRS by the withholding agent as a result of underwithholding shall not be treated as a distribution for purposes of section 562(c) and the regulations thereunder. Any amount of U.S. tax that a foreign shareholder is treated as

having paid on the undistributed capital gain of a regulated investment company under section 852(b)(3)(D) may be claimed by the foreign shareholder as a credit or refund under §1.1464-1.

(ii) *Reliance by intermediary on reasonable estimate.*—For purposes of determining whether a payment is a distribution designated as subject to section 852(b)(3)(C) or (5)(A), or 871(k)(1)(C) or (2)(C), a withholding agent that is not the distributing regulated investment company may, absent actual knowledge or reason to know otherwise, rely on the designations that the distributing company represents have been made in accordance with paragraph (c)(3)(i) of this section. Failure by the withholding agent to withhold the required amount due to a failure by the regulated investment company to reasonably estimate the required amounts or to properly communicate the relevant information to the withholding agent shall be imputed to the distributing company. In such a case, the IRS may collect from the distributing company any underwithheld amount and subject the company to applicable interest and penalties as a withholding agent.

(4) *Coordination with withholding under section 1445.*—(i) *In general.*—A distribution from a U.S. Real Property Holding Corporation (USRPHC) (or from a corporation that was a USRPHC at any time during the five-year period ending on the date of distribution) with respect to stock that is a U.S. real property interest under section 897(c) or from a Real Estate Investment Trust (REIT) or other entity that is a qualified investment entity (QIE) under section 897(h)(4) with respect to its stock is subject to the withholding provisions under section 1441 (or section 1442 or 1443) and section 1445. A USRPHC making a distribution shall be treated as satisfying its withholding obligations under both sections if it withholds in accordance with one of the procedures described in either paragraph (c)(4)(i)(A) or (B) of this section. A USRPHC must apply the same withholding procedure to all the distributions made during the taxable year. However, the USRPHC may change the applicable withholding procedure from year to year. For rules regarding distributions by REITs and other entities that are QIEs, see paragraph (c)(4)(i)(C) of this section. To the extent withholding under sections 1441, 1442, or 1443 applies under this paragraph (c)(4)(i) to any portion of a distribution that is a withholdable payment, see paragraph (a)(2) for rules coordinating withholding under chapter 4.

(A) *Withholding under section 1441.*—The USRPHC may choose to withhold on a distribution only under section 1441 (or 1442 or 1443) and not under section 1445. In such a case, the USRPHC must withhold under section 1441 (or 1442 or 1443) on the full amount of the distribution, whether or not any portion of the distribution represents a return of basis or capital gain. If a reduced tax rate under an income tax treaty applies to the distribution by the USRPHC, then the applicable rate of withholding on the distribution shall be no less than 15 percent for distributions after February 16, 2016, and no less than 10 percent for distributions on or before February 16, 2016, unless the applicable treaty specifies an applicable lower rate for distributions from a USRPHC, in which case the lower rate may apply.

(B) *Withholding under both sections 1441 and 1445.*—As an alternative to the procedure described in paragraph (c)(4)(i)(A) of this section, a USRPHC may choose to withhold under both sections 1441 (or 1442 or 1443) and 1445 under the procedures set forth in this paragraph (c)(4)(i)(B). The USRPHC must make a reasonable estimate of the portion of the distribution that is a dividend under paragraph (c)(2)(ii)(A) of this section, and must—

(1) Withhold under section 1441 (or 1442 or 1443) on the portion of the distribution that is estimated to be a dividend under paragraph (c)(2)(ii)(A) of this section; and

(2) Withhold under section 1445(e)(3) and §1.1445-5(e) on the remainder of the distribution or on such smaller portion based on a withholding certificate obtained in accordance with §1.1445-5(e)(3)(iv).

(C) *Coordination with REIT/QIE withholding.*—Withholding is required under section 1441 (or 1442 or 1443) on the portion of a distribution from a REIT or other entity that is a QIE that is not designated (for REITs) or reported (for regulated investment companies that are QIEs) as a capital gain dividend, a return of basis, or a distribution in excess of a shareholder's adjusted basis in the stock of the REIT or QIE that is treated as a capital gain under section 301(c)(3). A distribution in excess of a shareholder's adjusted basis in the stock of the REIT or QIE is, however, subject to withholding under section 1445, unless the interest in the REIT or QIE is not a U.S. real property interest (*e.g.*, an interest in a domestically controlled REIT or QIE under section 897(h)(2)). In addition, withholding is required under section 1445 on the portion of the distribution designated (for REITs) or reported (for regulated investment companies that are QIEs) as a capital gain dividend to the extent that it is

attributable to the sale or exchange of a U.S. real property interest. See §1.1445-8.

(ii) *Intermediary reliance rule.*—A withholding agent that is not the distributing USRPHC must withhold under paragraph (c)(4)(i) of this section, but may, absent actual knowledge or reason to know otherwise, rely on representations made by the USRPHC regarding the determinations required under paragraph (c)(4)(i) of this section. Failure by the withholding agent to withhold the required amount due to a failure by the distributing USRPHC to make these determinations in a reasonable manner or to properly communicate the determinations to the withholding agent shall be imputed to the distributing USRPHC. In such a case, the IRS may collect from the distributing USRPHC any underwithheld amount and subject the distributing USRPHC to applicable interest and penalties as a withholding agent.

(d) *Withholding on payments that include an undetermined amount of income.*—(1) *In general.*—Where the withholding agent makes a payment and does not know at the time of payment the amount that is subject to withholding because the determination of the source of the income or the calculation of the amount of income subject to tax depends upon facts that are not known at the time of payment, then the withholding agent must withhold an amount under §1.1441-1 based on the entire amount paid that is necessary to ensure that the tax withheld is not less than 30 percent (or other applicable percentage) of the amount that could be from sources within the United States or income subject to tax. See §1.1471-2(a)(5) for similar rules under chapter 4 that apply to payments made to payees that are entities. The amount so withheld shall not exceed 30 percent of the amount paid. With respect to a payment described in paragraph (d)(1) or (2) of this section, the withholding agent may elect to retain 30 percent of the payment to hold in escrow until the earlier of the date that the amount of income from sources within the United States or the taxable amount can be determined or one year from the date the amount is placed in escrow, at which time the withholding becomes due under §1.1441-1, or, to the extent that withholding is not required, the escrowed amount must be paid to the payee.

(2) *Withholding on certain gains.*—Absent actual knowledge or reason to know otherwise, a withholding agent may rely on a claim regarding the amount of gain described in §1.1441-2(c) if the beneficial owner withholding certificate, or other appropriate withholding certificate, states the beneficial owner's basis in the property giving rise to the gain. In the absence of a reliable representation on a withholding certificate, the withholding agent must withhold an amount under §1.1441-1 that is necessary to assure that the tax withheld is not less than 30 percent (or other applicable percentage) of the recognized gain. For this purpose, the recognized gain is determined without regard to any deduction allowed by the Code from the gains. The amount so withheld shall not exceed 30 percent of the amount payable by reason of the transaction giving rise to the recognized gain. See §1.1441-1(b)(8) regarding adjustments in the case of overwithholding.

(e) *Payments other than in U.S. dollars.*—(1) *In general.*—The amount of a payment made in a medium other than U.S. dollars is measured by the fair market value of the property or services provided in lieu of U.S. dollars. The withholding agent may liquidate the property prior to payment in order to withhold the required amount of tax under section 1441 or obtain payment of the tax from an alternative source. However, the obligation to withhold under section 1441 is not deferred even if no alternative source can be located. Thus, for purposes of withholding under chapter 3 of the Code, the provisions of §31.3406(h)-2(b)(2)(ii) of this chapter (relating to backup withholding from another source) shall not apply. If the withholding agent satisfies the tax liability related to such payments, the rules of paragraph (f) of this section apply.

(2) *Payments in foreign currency.*—If the amount subject to withholding tax is paid in a currency other than the U.S. dollar, the amount of withholding under section 1441 shall be determined by applying the applicable rate of withholding to the foreign currency amount and converting the amount withheld into U.S. dollars on the date of payment at the spot rate (as defined in §1.988-1(d)(1)) in effect on that date. A withholding agent making regular or frequent payments in foreign currency may use a month-end spot rate or a monthly average spot rate. In addition, such as withholding agent may use the spot rate on the date the amount of tax is deposited (within the meaning of §1.6302-2(a)), provided that such deposit is made within seven days of the date of the payment giving rise to the obligation to withhold. A spot rate convention must be used consistently for all non-dollar amounts withheld and from year to year. Such convention cannot be changed without the consent of the Commissioner. The U.S. dollar amount so determined shall be treated by the beneficial owner as the amount of tax paid on the

income for purposes of determining the final U.S. tax liability and, if applicable, claiming a refund or credit of tax.

(f) *Tax liability of beneficial owner satisfied by withholding agent.*—(1) *General rule.*—In the event that the satisfaction of a tax liability of a beneficial owner by a withholding agent constitutes income to the beneficial owner and such income is of a type that is subject to withholding, the amount of the payment deemed made by the withholding agent for purposes of this paragraph (f) shall be determined under the gross-up formula provided in this paragraph (f)(1). Whether the payment of the tax by the withholding agent constitutes a satisfaction of the beneficial owner's tax liability and whether, as such, it constitutes additional income to the beneficial owner, must be determined under all the facts and circumstances surrounding the transaction, including any agreements between the parties and applicable law. The formula described in this paragraph (f)(1) is as follows:

$$\text{Payment} = \frac{\text{Gross payment without withholding}}{1 - (\text{tax rate})}$$

(2) *Example.*—The following example illustrates the provisions of this paragraph (f):

*Example.* College X awards a qualified scholarship within the meaning of section 117(b) to foreign student, FS, who is in the United States on an F visa. FS is a resident of a country that does not have an income tax treaty with the United States. The scholarship is $20,000 to be applied to tuition, mandatory fees and books, plus benefits in kind consisting of room and board and roundtrip air transportation. College X agrees to pay any U.S. income tax owed by FS with respect to the scholarship. The fair market value of the room and board measured by the amount College X charges non-scholarship students is $6,000. The cost of the roundtrip air transportation is $2,600. Therefore, the total fair market value of the scholarship received by FS is $28,600. However, the amount taxable is limited to the fair market value of the benefits in kind ($8,600) because the portion of the scholarship amount for tuition, fees, and books is not included in gross income under section 117. The applicable rate of withholding is 14 percent under section 1441(b). Therefore, under the gross-up formula, College X is deemed to make a payment of $10,000 ($8,600 divided by (1 − .14). The U.S. tax that must be deducted and withheld from the payment under section 1441(b) is $1,400 (.14 × $10,000). College X reports scholarship income of $30,000 and $1,400 of U.S. tax withheld on Forms 1042 and 1042-S.

(g) *Conduit financing arrangements.*—(1) *Duty to withhold.*—A financed entity or other person required to withhold tax under section 1441 with respect to a financing arrangement that is a conduit financing arrangement within the meaning of §1.881-3(a)(2)(iv) shall be required to withhold under section 1441 as if the district director had determined, pursuant to §1.881-3(a)(3), that all conduit entities that are parties to the conduit financing arrangement should be disregarded. The amount of tax required to be withheld shall be determined under §1.881-3(d). The withholding agent may withhold tax at a reduced rate if the financing entity establishes that it is entitled to the benefit of a treaty that provides a reduced rate of tax on a payment of the type deemed to have been paid to the financing entity. Section 1.881-3(a)(3)(ii)(E) shall not apply for purposes of determining whether any person is required to deduct and withhold tax pursuant to this paragraph (g), or whether any party to a financing arrangement is liable for failure to withhold or entitled to a refund of tax under sections 1441 or 1461 to 1464 (except to the extent the amount withheld exceeds the tax liability determined under §1.881-3(d)). See §1.1441-7(f) relating to withholding tax liability of the withholding agent in conduit financing arrangements subject to §1.881-3.

(2) *Effective date.*—This paragraph (g) is effective for payments made by financed entities on or after September 11, 1995. This paragraph shall not apply to interest payments covered by section 127(g)(3) of the Tax Reform Act of 1984, and to interest payments with respect to other debt obligations issued prior to October 15, 1984 (whether or not such debt was issued by a Netherlands Antilles corporation).

(h) *Dividend equivalents.*—(1) *Withholding on gross amount.*—The gross amount of a dividend equivalent described in section 871(m) and the regulations thereunder is subject to withholding in an amount equal to the gross amount of the dividend equivalent used in computing any net amount that is transferred to or from the taxpayer. Withholding is required on the amount of the dividend equivalent calculated under §1.871-15(j).

(2) *Reliance by withholding agent on reasonable determinations.*—For purposes of determining whether a payment is a dividend equivalent and the timing and amount of a dividend equivalent under section

871(m), a withholding agent may rely on the information received from the party to the transaction that is required (as provided in §1.871-15(p)) to make those determinations, unless the withholding agent knows or has reason to know that the information is incorrect. When a withholding agent fails to withhold the required amount because the party described in §1.871-15(p) fails to reasonably determine or timely provide information regarding whether a transaction is a section 871(m) transaction, the timing and amount of any dividend equivalent, or any other information required to be provided pursuant to §1.871-15(p), and the withholding agent relied, absent actual knowledge to the contrary, on that party's determination or did not timely receive required information, then the failure to withhold is imputed to the party required to make the determinations described in §1.871-15(p). In that case, the IRS may collect any underwithheld amount from the party to the transaction that was required to make the determinations described in §1.871-15(p) or timely provide the information and subject that party to applicable interest and penalties as if the party were a withholding agent with respect to the payment of the dividend equivalent made pursuant to the section 871(m) transaction.

(3) *Effective/applicability date.*—Except for the first sentence of paragraph (h)(1), this paragraph (h) applies to payments made on or after September 18, 2015. The first sentence of paragraph (h)(1) of this section, applies to payments made on or after January 23, 2012.

(i) *Effective/applicability date.*—Except as otherwise provided in paragraphs (g)(2) and (h)(3) of this section, this section applies to payments made on or after January 6, 2017. (For payments made after June 30, 2014, and before January 6, 2017, see this section as in effect and contained in 26 CFR part 1, revised April 1, 2016. For payments made after December 31, 2000, see this section as in effect and contained in 26 CFR part 1 as revised April 1, 2013.) [Reg. §1.1441-3.]

☐ [T.D. 6187, 7-5-56. *Amended by* T.D. 6592, 2-27-62; T.D. 6636, 2-25-63; T.D. 6669, 8-26-63; T.D. 6777, 12-15-64; T.D. 6908, 12-30-66; T.D. 7378, 9-29-75; T.D. 7977, 9-19-84; T.D. 8611, 8-10-95; T.D. 8734, 10-6-97; T.D. 8804, 12-30-98; T.D. 8856, 12-29-99; T.D. 8881, 5-15-2000; T.D. 9253, 3-13-2006; T.D. 9572, 1-19-2012; T.D. 9648, 12-4-2013, T.D. 9658, 2-28-2014, T.D. 9734, 9-17-2015 *and* T.D. 9808, 12-30-2016 (*corrected* 6-29-2017).]

### [Reg. §1.1441-4]

**§1.1441-4. Exemptions from withholding for certain effectively connected income and other amounts.**—(a) *Certain income connected with a U.S. trade or business.*—(1) *In general.*—No withholding is required under section 1441 on income otherwise subject to withholding if the income is (or is deemed to be) effectively connected with the conduct of a trade or business within the United States and is includible in the beneficial owner's gross income for the taxable year. For purposes of this paragraph (a), an amount is not deemed to be includible in gross income if the amount is (or is deemed to be) effectively connected with the conduct of a trade or business within the United States and the beneficial owner claims an exemption from tax under an income tax treaty because the income is not attributable to a permanent establishment in the United States. To claim a reduced rate of withholding because the income is not attributable to a permanent establishment, see §1.1441-6(b)(1). This paragraph (a) does not apply to income of a foreign corporation to which section 543(a)(7) applies for the taxable year or to compensation for personal services performed by an individual. See paragraph (b) of this section for compensation for personal services performed by an individual.

(2) *Withholding agent's reliance on a claim of effectively connected income.*—(i) *In general.*—Absent actual knowledge or reason to know otherwise, a withholding agent may rely on a claim of exemption based upon paragraph (a)(1) of this section if, prior to the payment to the foreign person, the withholding agent can reliably associate the payment with a Form W-8 upon which it can rely to treat the payment as made to a foreign beneficial owner in accordance with §1.1441-1(e)(1)(ii). For purposes of this paragraph (a), a withholding certificate is valid only if, in addition to other applicable requirements, it includes the taxpayer identifying number of the person whose name is on the Form W-8 and represents, under penalties of perjury, that the amounts for which the certificate is furnished are effectively connected with the conduct of a trade or business in the United States and is includable in the beneficial owner's gross income for the taxable year. In the absence of a reliable claim that the income is effectively connected with the conduct of a trade or business in the United States, the income is presumed not to be effectively connected, except as otherwise provided in paragraph (a)(2)(ii) or (3) of this section. See §1.1441-1(e)(4)(ii)(C) for the period of validity applicable to a certificate provided under this section and §1.1441-1(e)(4)(ii)(D) for changes in circumstances arising during the taxable year indicating that the income to which the certificate relates

is not, or is no longer expected to be, effectively connected with the conduct of a trade or business within the United States. A withholding certificate shall be effective only for the item or items of income specified therein. The provisions of §1.1441-1(b)(3)(iv) dealing with a 90-day grace period shall apply for purposes of this section.

(ii) *Special rules for U.S. branches of foreign persons.*—(A) *U.S. branches of certain foreign banks or foreign insurance companies.*—A payment to a U.S. branch described in §1.1441-1(b)(2)(iv)(B)(3) is presumed to be effectively connected with the conduct of a trade or business in the United States without the need to furnish a certificate if the withholding agent obtains an EIN for the entity, unless the U.S. branch provides a U.S. branch withholding certificate described in §1.1441-1(e)(3)(v) that represents otherwise. If no certificate is furnished but the income is not, in fact, effectively connected income, then the branch must withhold whether the payment is collected on behalf of other persons or on behalf of another branch of the same entity. See §1.1441-1(b)(2)(iv) and (b)(6) for general rules applicable to payments to U.S. branches of foreign persons.

(B) *Other U.S. branches.*—See §1.1441-1(b)(2)(iv)(E) for similar procedures for other U.S. branches to the extent provided in a determination letter from the IRS.

(3) *Income on notional principal contracts.*—(i) *General rule.*—Except as otherwise provided in paragraph (a)(3)(iii) of this section, a withholding agent that pays amounts attributable to a notional principal contract described in §1.863-7(a) or §1.988-2(e) shall have no obligation to withhold on the amounts paid under the terms of the notional principal contract regardless of whether a withholding certificate is provided. However, a withholding agent must file returns under §1.1461-1(b) and (c) reporting the income that it must treat as effectively connected with the conduct of a trade or business in the United States under the provisions of this paragraph (a)(3). Except as otherwise provided in paragraph (a)(3)(ii) of this section, a withholding agent must treat the income as effectively connected with the conduct of a U.S. trade or business if the income is paid to, or to the account of, a qualified business unit of a foreign person located in the United States or, if the payment is paid to, or to the account of, a qualified business unit of a foreign person located outside the United States, the withholding agent knows, or has reason to know, the payment is effectively connected with the conduct of a trade or business within the United States. Income on a notional principal contract does not include the amount characterized as interest under the provisions of §1.446-3(g)(4).

(ii) *Exception for certain payments.*—A payment shall not be treated as effectively connected with the conduct of a trade or business within the United States for purposes of paragraph (a)(3)(i) of this section even if no withholding certificate is furnished if the payee provides a representation in a master agreement that governs the transactions in notional principal contracts between the parties (for example an International Swaps and Derivatives Association (ISDA) Agreement, including the Schedule thereto) or in the confirmation on the particular notional principal contract transaction that the payee is a U.S. person or a non-U.S. branch of a foreign person.

(iii) *Exception for specified notional principal contracts.*—A withholding agent that makes a payment attributable to a specified notional principal contract described in section 871(m) and the regulations thereunder that is not treated as effectively connected with the conduct of a trade or business within the United States is obligated to withhold on the amount of the payment that is a dividend equivalent.

(b) *Compensation for personal services of an individual.*—(1) *Exemption from withholding.*—Withholding is not required under §1.1441-1 from salaries, wages, remuneration, or any other compensation for personal services of a nonresident alien individual if such compensation is effectively connected with the conduct of a trade or business within the United States and—

(i) Such compensation is subject to withholding under section 3402 (relating to withholding on wages) and the regulations under that section;

(ii) Such compensation would be subject to withholding under section 3402 but for the provisions of section 3401(a) (not including section 3401(a)(6)) and the regulations under that section. This paragraph (b)(1)(ii) does not apply to payments to a nonresident alien individual from any trust described in section 401(a), any annuity plan described in section 403(a), any annuity, custodial account, or retirement income account described in section 403(b), or an individual retirement account or individual retirement annuity described in section 408. Instead, these payments are subject to withholding under this section to the extent they are exempted from the definition of wages under section 3401(a)(12) or to the extent they are from an annuity, custodial account, or retirement income account

described in section 403(b), or an individual retirement account or individual retirement annuity described in section 408. Thus, for example, payments to a nonresident alien individual from a trust described in section 401(a) are subject to withholding under section 1441 and not under section 3405 or section 3406;

(iii) Such compensation is for services performed by a nonresident alien individual who is a resident of Canada or Mexico and who enters and leaves the United States at frequent intervals;

(iv) Such compensation is, or will be, exempt from the income tax imposed by chapter 1 of the Code by reason of a provision of the Internal Revenue Code or a tax treaty to which the United States is a party;

(v) Such compensation is paid after January 3, 1979 as a commission or rebate paid by a ship supplier to a nonresident alien individual, who is employed by a nonresident alien individual, foreign partnership, or foreign corporation in the operation of a ship or ships of foreign registry, for placing orders for supplies to be used in the operation of such ship or ships with the supplier. See section 162(c) and the regulations thereunder for denial of deductions for illegal bribes, kickbacks, and other payments; or

(vi) Compensation that is exempt from withholding under section 3402 by reason of section 3402(e), provided that the employee and his employer enter into an agreement under section 3402(p) to provide for the withholding of income tax upon payments of amounts described in §31.3401(a)-3(b)(1) of this chapter. An employee who desires to enter into such an agreement should furnish his employer with Form W-4 (withholding exemption certificate) (or such other form as the Internal Revenue Service (IRS) may prescribe). See section 3402(f) and the regulations thereunder and §31.3402(p)-1 of this chapter.

(2) *Manner of obtaining withholding exemption under tax treaty.*—(i) *In general.*—In order to obtain the exemption from withholding by reason of a tax treaty provided by paragraph (b)(1)(iv) of this section, a nonresident alien individual must submit a withholding certificate (described in paragraph (b)(2)(ii) of this section) to each withholding agent from whom amounts are to be received. A separate withholding certificate must be filed for each taxable year of the alien individual. If the withholding agent is satisfied that an exemption from withholding is warranted (see paragraph (b)(2)(iii) of this section), the withholding certificate shall be accepted in the manner set forth in paragraph (b)(2)(iv) of this section. The exemption from withholding becomes effective for payments made at least ten days after a copy of the accepted withholding certificate is forwarded to the IRS. The withholding agent may rely on an accepted withholding certificate only if the IRS has not objected to the certificate. For purposes of this paragraph (b)(2)(i), the IRS will be considered to have not objected to the certificate if it has not notified the withholding agent within a 10-day period beginning from the date that the withholding certificate is forwarded to the IRS pursuant to paragraph (b)(2)(v) of this section. After expiration of the 10-day period, the withholding agent may rely on the withholding certificate retroactive to the date of the first payment covered by the certificate. The fact that the IRS does not object to the withholding certificate within the 10-day period provided in this paragraph (b)(2)(i) shall not preclude the IRS from examining the withholding agent at a later date with respect to facts that the withholding agent knew or had reason to know regarding the payment and eligibility for a reduced rate and that were not disclosed to the IRS as part of the 10-day review process.

(ii) *Withholding certificate claiming withholding exemption.*—The statement claiming an exemption from withholding shall be made on Form 8233 (or an acceptable substitute or such other form as the IRS may prescribe). Form 8233 shall be dated, signed by the beneficial owner under penalties of perjury, and contain the following information—

(A) The individual's name, permanent residence address, taxpayer identifying number (or a copy of a completed Form W-7 or SS-5 showing that a number has been applied for), and the U.S. visa number, if any;

(B) The individual's current immigration status and visa type;

(C) The individual's original date of entry into the United States;

(D) The country that issued the individual's passport and the number of such passport, or the individual's permanent address if a citizen of Canada or Mexico;

(E) The taxable year, for which the statement is to apply the compensation to which it relates, and the amount (or estimated amount if exact amount not known) of such compensation;

(F) A statement that the individual is not a citizen or resident of the United States;

(G) The number of personal exemptions claimed by the individual;

(H) A statement as to whether the compensation to be paid to him or her during the taxable year is or will be exempt from income tax and the reason why the compensation is exempt;

(I) If the compensation is exempt from withholding by reason of an income tax treaty to which the United States is a party, the tax treaty and provision under which the exemption from withholding is claimed and the country of which the individual is a resident;

(J) Sufficient facts to justify the claim in exemption from withholding; and

(K) Any other information as may be required by the form or accompanying instructions in addition to, or in lieu of, the information described in this paragraph (b)(2)(ii).

(iii) *Review by withholding agent.*—The exemption from withholding provided by paragraph (b)(1)(iv) of this section shall not apply unless the withholding agent accepts (in the manner provided in paragraph (b)(2)(iv) of this section) the statement on Form 8233, "Exemption From Withholding on Compensation for Independent (and Certain Dependent) Personal Services of a Nonresident Alien Individual," (or successor form) supplied by the nonresident alien individual. Before accepting the statement, the withholding agent must examine the statement. If the withholding agent knows or has reason to know that any of the facts or assertions on Form 8233 may be false or that the eligibility of the individual's compensation for the exemption cannot be readily determined, the withholding agent may not accept the statement on Form 8233 and is required to withhold under this section. If the withholding agent accepts the statement and subsequently finds that any of the facts or assertions contained on Form 8233 may be false or that the eligibility of the individual's compensation for the exemption can no longer be readily determined, then the withholding agent shall promptly so notify the IRS by letter, and the withholding agent is not relieved of liability to withhold on any amounts still to be paid. If the withholding agent is notified by the IRS that the eligibility of the individual's compensation for the exemption is in doubt or that such compensation is not eligible for the exemption, the withholding agent is required to withhold under this section. The rules of this paragraph (b)(2) are illustrated by the following examples.

*Example 1.* C, a nonresident alien individual, submits Form 8233 to W, a withholding agent. The statement on Form 8233 does not include all the information required by paragraph (b)(2)(ii) of this section. Therefore, W has reason to know that he or she cannot readily determine whether C's compensation for personal services is eligible for an exemption from withholding and, therefore, W must withhold.

*Example 2.* D, a nonresident alien individual, is performing services for W, a withholding agent. W has accepted a statement on Form 8233 submitted by D, according to the provisions of this section. W receives notice from the IRS that the eligibility of D's compensation for a withholding exemption is in doubt. Therefore, W has reason to know that the eligibility of the compensation for a withholding exemption cannot be readily determined, as of the date W receives the notification, and W must withhold tax under section 1441 on amounts paid after receipt of the notification.

*Example 3.* E, a nonresident alien individual, submits Form 8233 to W, a withholding agent for whom E is to perform personal services. The statement contains all the information requested on Form 8233. E claims an exemption from withholding based on a personal exemption amount computed on the number of days E will perform personal services for W in the United States. If W does not know or have reason to know that any statement on the Form 8233 is false or that the eligibility of E's compensation for the withholding exemption cannot be readily determined, W can accept the statement on Form 8233 and exempt from withholding the appropriate amount of E's income.

(iv) *Acceptance by withholding agent.*—If after the review described in paragraph (b)(2)(iii) of this section the withholding agent is satisfied that an exemption from withholding is warranted, the withholding agent may accept the statement by making a certification, verified by a declaration that it is made under the penalties of perjury, on Form 8233. The certification shall be—

(A) That the withholding agent has examined the statement,

(B) That the withholding agent is satisfied that an exemption from withholding is warranted, and

(C) That the withholding agent does not know or have reason to know that the individual's compensation is not entitled to the exemption or that the eligibility of the individual's compensation for the exemption cannot be readily determined.

(v) *Copies of Form 8233.*—The withholding agent shall forward one copy of each Form 8233 that is accepted under paragraph (b)(2)(iv) of this section to the IRS within five days of such acceptance. The withholding agent shall retain a copy of Form 8233.

(3) *Withholding agreements.*—Compensation for personal services of a nonresident alien individual who is engaged during the taxable year in the conduct of a trade or business within the United States may be wholly or partially exempted from the withholding required by §1.1441-1 if an agreement is reached between the IRS and the alien individual with respect to the amount of withholding required. Such agreement shall be available in the circumstances and in the manner set forth by the Internal Revenue Service, and shall be effective for payments covered by the agreement that are made after the agreement is executed by all parties. The alien individual must agree to timely file an income tax return for the current taxable year.

(4) *Final payment exemption.*—(i) *General rule.*—Compensation for independent personal services of a nonresident alien individual who is engaged during the taxable year in the conduct of a trade or business within the United States may be wholly or partially exempted from the withholding required by §1.1441-1 from the final payment of compensation for independent personal services. This exemption does not apply to wages. This exemption from withholding is available only once during an alien individual's taxable year and is obtained by the alien individual presenting to the withholding agent a letter in duplicate from a district director stating the amount of compensation subject to the exemption and the amount that would otherwise be withheld from such final payment under section 1441 that shall be paid to the alien individual due to the exemption. The alien individual shall attach a copy of the letter to his or her income tax return for the taxable year for which the exemption is effective.

(ii) *Final payment of compensation for personal services.*—For purposes of this paragraph, final payment of compensation for personal services means the last payment of compensation, other than wages, for personal services rendered within the United States that the individual expects to receive from any withholding agent during the taxable year.

(iii) *Manner of applying for final payment exemption.*—In order to obtain the final payment exemption provided by paragraph (b)(4)(i) of this section, the nonresident alien individual (or his or her agent) must file the forms and provide the information required by the district director. Ordinary and necessary business expenses may be taken into account if substantiated to the satisfaction of the district director. The alien individual must submit a statement, signed by him or her and verified by a declaration that it is made under the penalties of perjury, that all the information provided is true and that to his or her knowledge no relevant information has been omitted. The information required to be submitted includes, but is not limited to—

(A) A statement by each withholding agent from whom amounts of gross income effectively connected with the conduct of a trade or business within the United States have been received by the alien individual during the taxable year, of the amount of such income paid and the amount of tax withheld, signed and verified by a declaration that it is made under penalties of perjury;

(B) A statement by the withholding agent from whom the final payment of compensation for personal services will be received, of the amount of such final payment and the amount which would be withheld under §1.1441-1 if a final payment exemption under paragraph (b)(4)(i) of this section is not granted, signed and verified by a declaration that it is made under penalties of perjury;

(C) A statement by the individual that he or she does not intend to receive any other amounts of gross income effectively connected with the conduct of a trade or business within the United States during the current taxable year;

(D) The amount of tax which has been withheld (or paid) under any other provision of the Code or regulations with respect to any income effectively connected with the conduct of a trade or business within the United States during the current taxable year;

(E) The amount of any outstanding tax liabilities (and interest and penalties relating thereto) from the current taxable year or prior taxable periods; and

(F) The provision of any income tax treaty under which a partial or complete exemption from withholding may be claimed, the country of the individual's residence, and a statement of sufficient facts to justify an exemption pursuant to such treaty.

(iv) *Letter to withholding agent.*—If the district director is satisfied that the information provided under paragraph (b)(4)(iii) of this section is sufficient, the district director will, after coordination with the Director of the Foreign Operations District, ascertain the amount of the alien individual's tentative income tax for the taxable year with respect to gross income that is effectively connected with the conduct of a trade or business within the United States. After the tentative tax has been ascertained, the district director will provide the alien individual with a letter to the withholding agent stating the amount of the final payment of compensation for personal services that is exempt from withholding, and the amount that would otherwise be withheld under section 1441 that shall be paid to the alien individual due to the exemption. The amount of compensation for personal services exempt from withholding under this paragraph (b)(4) shall not exceed $5,000.

*Example 1.* On July 15, 1983, B, a nonresident alien individual, appears before a district director with the information required by paragraph (b)(4)(iii) of this section. B has received personal service income in 1983 from which $3,000 has been withheld under section 1441. On August 1, 1983, B will receive $5,000 in personal service income from W. B does not intend to receive any other income subject to U.S. tax during 1983. Taking into account B's substantiated deductible business expenses, the district director computes the tentative tax liability on B's income effectively connected with the conduct of a trade or business in the United States during 1983 (including the $5,000 payment to be made on August 1, 1983) to be $3,300. B does not owe U.S. tax for any other taxable periods. The amount of B's final payment exemption is determined as follows:

*(1)* The amount of total withholding is $4,500 ($3,000 previously withheld plus $1,500, 30% of the $5,000 final payment);

*(2)* The amount of tentative excess withholding is $1,200 (total withholding of $4,500 minus B's tentative tax liability of $3,300); and

*(3)* To allow B to receive $1,200 of the amount which would otherwise have been withheld from the final payment, the district director allows a withholding exemption for $4,000 of B's final payment. W must withhold $300 from the final payment.

*Example 2.* The facts are the same as in Example 1 except B will receive a final payment of compensation on August 1, 1983, in the amount of $10,000 and B's tentative tax liability is $3,900. The amount of B's final payment exemption is determined as follows:

*(1)* The amount of total withholding is $6,000 ($3,000 previously withheld plus $3,000, 30% of the $10,000 final payment);

*(2)* The amount of tentative excess withholding is $2,100 (total withholding of $6,000 minus B's tentative tax liability of $3,900); and

*(3)* To allow B to receive $2,100 of the amount which would otherwise be withheld from the final payment, $7,000 of the final payment would have to be exempt from withholding; however, as no more than $5,000 of the final payment can be exempt from withholding under this paragraph (b)(4), the district director allows a withholding exemption for $5,000 of B's final payment. B must file a claim for refund at the end of the taxable year to obtain a refund of $600. W must withhold $1,500 from the final payment.

*(5) Requirement of return.*—The tentative tax determined by the district director under paragraph (b)(4)(iv) of this section or by the Director of the Foreign Operations District under the withholding agreement procedure of paragraph (b)(3) of this section shall not constitute a final determination of the income tax liability of the nonresident alien individual, nor shall such determination constitute a tax return of the nonresident alien individual for any taxable period. An alien individual who applies for or obtains an exemption from withholding under the procedures of paragraphs (b)(2), (3), or (4) of this section is not relieved of the obligation to file a return of income under section 6012.

*(6) Personal exemption.*—*(i) In general.*—To determine the tax to be withheld at source under §1.1441-1 from remuneration paid for personal services performed within the United States by a nonresident alien individual and from scholarship and fellowship income described in paragraph (c) of this section, a withholding agent may take into account one personal exemption pursuant to sections 873(b)(3) and 151 regardless of whether the income is effectively connected. For purposes of withholding under section 1441 on remuneration for personal services, the exemption must be prorated upon a daily basis for the period during which the personal services are performed within the United States by the nonresident alien individual by dividing by 365 the number of days in the period during which the individual is present in the United States for the purpose of performing the services and multiplying the result by the amount of the personal exemption in effect for the taxable year. See §31.3402(f)(6)-1 of this chapter.

*(ii) Multiple exemptions.*—More than one personal exemption may be claimed in the case of a resident of a contiguous country or a national of the United States under section 873(b)(3). In addition, residents of a country with which the United States has an income tax treaty in effect may be eligible to claim more than one personal exemption if the treaty so provides. Claims for more than one personal exemption shall be made on the withholding certificate furnished to the withholding agent. The exemption must be prorated on a daily basis in the same manner as described in paragraph (b)(6)(i) of this section.

*(iii) Special rule where both certain scholarship and compensation income are received.*—The fact that both non-compensatory scholarship income and compensation income (including compensatory scholarship income) are received during the taxable year does not entitle the

taxpayer to claim more than one personal exemption amount (or more than the additional amounts permitted under paragraph (b)(6)(ii) of this section). Thus, if a nonresident alien student receives non-compensatory taxable scholarship income from one withholding agent and compensation income from another withholding agent, no more than the total personal exemption amount permitted under the Internal Revenue Code or under an income tax treaty may be taken into account by both withholding agents. For this purpose, the withholding agent may rely on a representation from the beneficial owner that the exemption amount claimed does not exceed the amount permissible under this section.

*(c) Special rules for scholarship and fellowship income.*—*(1) In general.*—Under section 871(c), certain amounts paid as a scholarship or fellowship for study, training, or research in the United States to a nonresident alien individual temporarily present in the United States as a nonimmigrant under section 101(a)(15)(F), (J), (M), or (Q) of the Immigration and Nationality Act are treated as income effectively connected with the conduct of a trade or business within the United States. The amounts described in the preceding sentence are those amounts that do not represent compensation for services. Such amounts (as described in the second sentence of section 1441(b)) are subject to withholding under section 1441, but at the lower rate of 14 percent. That rate may be reduced under the provisions of an income tax treaty. Claims of a reduced rate under an income tax treaty shall be made under the procedures described in §1.1441-6(b)(1). Therefore, claims for reduction in withholding under an income tax treaty on amounts described in this paragraph (c)(1) may not be made on a Form 8233. However, if the payee is receiving both compensation for personal services (including compensatory scholarship income) and non-compensatory scholarship income described in this paragraph (c)(1) from the same withholding agent, claims for reduction of withholding on both types of income may be made on Form 8233.

*(2) Alternate withholding election.*—A withholding agent may elect to withhold on the amounts described in paragraph (c)(1) of this section at the rates applicable under section 3402, as if the income were wages. Such election shall be made by obtaining a Form W-4 (or an acceptable substitute or such other form as the IRS may prescribe) from the beneficial owner. The fact that the withholding agent asks the beneficial owner to furnish a Form W-4 for such fellowship or scholarship income or to take such income into account in preparing such Form W-4 shall serve as notice to the beneficial owner that the income is being treated as wages for purposes of withholding tax under section 1441.

*(d) Annuities received under qualified plans.*—Withholding is not required under section §1.1441-1 in the case of any amount received as an annuity if the amount is exempt from tax under section 871(f) and the regulations under that section. The withholding agent may exempt the payment from withholding if, prior to payment, it can reliably associate the payment with documentation upon which it can rely to treat the payment as made to a beneficial owner in accordance with §1.1441-1(e)(1)(ii). A beneficial owner withholding certificate furnished for purposes of claiming the benefits of the exemption under this paragraph (d) is valid only if, in addition to other applicable requirements, it contains a taxpayer identifying number.

*(e) Per diem of certain alien trainees.*—Withholding is not required under section 1441(a) and §1.1441-1 on per diem amounts paid for subsistence by the United States Government (directly or by contract) to any nonresident alien individual who is engaged in any program of training in the United States under the Mutual Security Act of 1954, as amended (22 U.S.C. chapter 24). This rule shall apply even though such amounts are subject to tax under section 871. Any exemption from withholding pursuant to this paragraph (e) applies without a requirement that documentation be furnished to the withholding agent. However, documentation may have to be furnished for purposes of the information reporting provisions under section 6041 and backup withholding under section 3406. The exemption from withholding granted by this paragraph (e) is not a determination that the amounts are not fixed or determinable annual or periodical income.

*(f) Failure to receive withholding certificates timely or to act in accordance with applicable presumptions.*—See applicable procedures described in §1.1441-1(b)(7) in the event the withholding agent does not hold an appropriate withholding certificate or other appropriate documentation at the time of payment or does not act in accordance with applicable presumptions described in paragraph (a)(2)(i), (2)(ii), or (3) of this section.

*(g) Effective/applicability date.*—This section applies to payments made on or after January 6, 2017. (For payments made after June 30, 2014, and before January 6, 2017, see this section as in effect and contained in 26 CFR part 1, revised April 1, 2016. For payments made

after December 31, 2000, see this section as in effect and contained in 26 CFR part 1 revised April 1, 2013.) [Reg. §1.1441-4.]

☐ [T.D. 6187, 7-5-56. *Amended by* T.D. 6229, 4-22-57; T.D. 6592, 2-27-62; T.D. 6908, 12-30-66; T.D. 6922, 6-16-67; T.D. 7378, 9-29-75; T.D. 7582, 1-2-79; T.D. 7777, 5-18-81; T.D. 7842, 11-2-82; T.D. 7977, 9-19-84; T.D. 8015, 3-25-85; T.D. 8288, 2-2-90; T.D. 8734, 10-6-97; T.D. 8804, 12-30-98; T.D. 8856, 12-29-99; T.D. 8881, 5-15-2000; T.D. 9572, 1-19-2012 (*corrected* 3-7-2012); T.D. 9648, 12-4-2013; T.D. 9658, 2-28-2014, T.D. 9808, 12-30-2016 (*corrected* 6-29-2017) *and* T.D. 9890, 12-27-2019.]

### [Reg. §1.1441-5]

**§1.1441-5. Withholding on payments to partnerships, trusts, and estates.**—(a) *In general.*—This section describes the rules that apply to payments made to partnerships, trusts, and estates. Paragraph (b) of this section prescribes the rules that apply to a withholding agent making a payment to a U.S. partnership, trust, or estate. It also prescribes the obligations of a U.S. partnership, trust, or estate that makes a payment to a foreign partner, beneficiary, or owner. Paragraph (c) of this section prescribes rules that apply to a withholding agent that makes a payment to a foreign partnership. Paragraph (d) of this section provides presumption rules that apply to payments made to foreign partnerships. Paragraph (e) of this section prescribes rules, including presumption rules, that apply to a withholding agent that makes a payment to a foreign trust or foreign estate.

(b) *Rules applicable to U.S. partnerships, trusts, and estates.*—(1) *Payments to U.S. partnerships, trusts, and estates.*—No withholding is required under section 1.1441-1(b)(1) on a payment of an amount subject to withholding (as defined in §1.1441-2(a)) that a withholding agent may treat as made to a U.S. payee. Therefore, if a withholding agent can reliably associate (within the meaning of §1.1441-1(b)(vii)) a Form W-9 provided in accordance with §1.1441-1(d)(2) or (4) by a U.S. partnership, U.S. trust, or a U.S. estate the withholding agent may treat the payment as made to a U.S. payee and the payment is not subject to withholding under section 1441 even though the partnership, trust, or estate may have foreign partners, beneficiaries, or owners. A withholding agent is also not required to withhold under section 1441 on a payment it makes to an entity presumed to be a U.S. payee under paragraphs (d)(2) and (e)(6)(ii) of this section.

(2) *Withholding by U.S. payees.*—(i) *U.S. partnerships.*—(A) *In general.*—A U.S. partnership is required to withhold under §1.1441-1 as a withholding agent on an amount subject to withholding (as defined in §1.1441-2(a)) that is includible in the gross income of a partner that is a foreign person. Subject to paragraph (b)(2)(v) of this section, a U.S. partnership shall withhold when any distributions that include amounts subject to withholding (including guaranteed payments made by a U.S. partnership) are made. To the extent a foreign partner's distributive share of income subject to withholding has not actually been distributed to the foreign partner, the U.S. partnership must withhold on the foreign partner's distributive share of the income on the earlier of the date that the statement required under section 6031(b) is mailed or otherwise provided to the partner or the due date for furnishing the statement.

(B) *Effectively connected income of partners.*—Withholding on items of income that are effectively connected income in the hands of the partners who are foreign persons is governed by section 1446 and not by this section. In such a case, partners in a domestic partnership are not required to furnish a withholding certificate in order to claim an exemption from withholding under section 1441(c)(1) and §1.1441-4.

(ii) *U.S. simple trusts.*—A U.S. trust that is described in section 651(a) (a U.S. simple trust) is required to withhold under chapter 3 of the Internal Revenue Code as a withholding agent on the distributable net income includible in the gross income of a foreign beneficiary to the extent the distributable net income is an amount subject to withholding (as defined in §1.1441-2(a)). A U.S. simple trust shall withhold when a distribution is made to a foreign beneficiary. The U.S. trust may make a reasonable estimate of the portion of the distribution that constitutes distributable net income consisting of an amount subject to withholding and apply the appropriate rate of withholding to the estimated amount. If, at the end of the taxable year in which the distribution is made, the U.S. simple trust determines that it underwithheld under section 1441 or 1442, the trust shall be liable as a withholding agent for the amount under withheld under section 1461. No penalties shall be imposed for failure to withhold and deposit the tax if the U.S. simple trust's estimate was reasonable and the trust pays the underwithheld amount on or before the due date of Form 1042 under section 1461. Any payment of underwithheld amounts by the U.S. simple trust shall not be treated as income subject to additional withholding even if that amount is treated as additional income to the foreign beneficiary, unless the additional amount is income to the foreign beneficiary as a result of a contractual arrangement between the parties regarding the satisfaction of the foreign beneficiary's tax liability. To the extent a U.S. simple trust is required to, but does not, distribute such income to a foreign beneficiary, the U.S. trust must withhold on the foreign beneficiary's allocable share at the time the income is required (without extension) to be reported on Form 1042-S under §1.1461-1(c).

(iii) *U.S. complex trusts and U.S. estates.*—A U.S. trust that is not a trust described in section 651(a) (see paragraph (b)(2)(ii) of this section) or sections 671 through 679 (see paragraph (b)(2)(iv) of this section) (a U.S. complex trust) is required to withhold under chapter 3 of the Internal Revenue Code (Code) as a withholding agent on the distributable net income includible in the gross income of a foreign beneficiary to the extent the distributable net income consists of an amount subject to withholding (as defined in §1.1441-2(a)) that is, or is required to be, distributed currently. The U.S. complex trust shall withhold when a distribution is made to a foreign beneficiary. The trust may use the same procedures regarding an estimate of the amount subject to withholding as a U.S. simple trust under paragraph (b)(2)(ii) of this section. To the extent an amount subject to withholding is required to be, but is not actually, distributed, the U.S. complex trust must withhold on the foreign beneficiary's allocable share at the time the income is required to be reported on Form 1042-S under §1.1461-1(c), without extension. A U.S. estate is required to withhold under chapter 3 of the Code on the distributable net income includible in the gross income of a foreign beneficiary to the extent the distributable net income consists of an amount subject to withholding (as defined in §1.1441-2(a)) that is actually distributed. A U.S. estate may also use the reasonable estimate procedures of paragraph (b)(2)(ii) of this section. However, those procedures apply to an estate that has a taxable year other than a calendar year only if the estate files an amended return on Form 1042 for the calendar year in which the distribution was made and pays the underwithheld tax and interest within 60 days after the close of the taxable year in which the distribution was made.

(iv) *U.S. grantor trusts.*—A U.S. trust that is described in section 671 through 679 (a U.S. grantor trust) must withhold on any income includible in the gross income of a foreign person that is treated as an owner of the grantor trust to the extent the amount includible consists of an amount that is subject to withholding (as described in §1.1441-2(a)). The withholding must occur at the time the income is received by, or credited to, the trust.

(v) *Subsequent distribution.*—If a U.S. partnership or U.S. trust withholds on a foreign partner, beneficiary, or owner's share of an amount subject to withholding before the amount is actually distributed to the partner, beneficiary, or owner, withholding is not required when the amount is subsequently distributed.

(vi) *Coordination with chapter 4 requirements for U.S. partnerships, trusts, and estates.*—To the extent that a U.S. partnership is required to withhold on an amount under chapter 4 with respect to a partner, beneficiary, or owner, the partnership, trust, or estate must apply the rules described in §1.1473-1(a)(5) to determine when it must withhold on the amount under chapter 4. In a case in which withholding applies under chapter 4 to such an amount, see §1.1441-3(a)(2) to coordinate with withholding that otherwise applies to such an amount under this paragraph (b).

(c) *Foreign partnerships.*—(1) *Determination of payee.*—(i) *Payments treated as made to partners.*—Except as otherwise provided in paragraph (c)(1)(ii) or (iv) of this section, the payees of a payment to a person that the withholding agent may treat as a nonwithholding foreign partnership under paragraph (c)(3)(i) or (d)(2) of this section are the partners (looking through partners that are foreign intermediaries or flow-through entities) as follows—

(A) If the withholding agent can reliably associate a partner's distributive share of the payment with a valid Form W-9 provided under §1.1441-1 (d), the partner is a U.S. payee;

(B) If the withholding agent can reliably associate a partner's distributive share of the payment with a valid Form W-8, or other appropriate documentation, provided under §1.1441-1 (e)(1)(ii), the partner is a payee that is a foreign beneficial owner;

(C) If the withholding agent can reliably associate a partner's distributive share of the payment with a qualified intermediary withholding certificate under §1.1441-1(e)(3)(ii), a nonqualified intermediary withholding certificate under §1.1441-1(e)(3)(iii), or a U.S. branch certificate under §1.1441-1(e)(3)(v) (including one provided by a territory financial institution), then the rules of §1.1441-1(b)(2)(v) shall apply to determine who the payee is in the same manner as if the partner's distributive share of the payment had been paid directly to such intermediary or U.S. branch or territory financial institution;

(D) If the withholding agent can reliably associate the partner's distributive share with a withholding foreign partnership certificate under paragraph (c)(2)(iv) of this section or a nonwithholding foreign partnership certificate under paragraph (c)(3)(iii) of this section, then the rules of this paragraph (c)(1)(i) or paragraph (c)(1)(ii) of this section shall apply to determine whether the payment is treated as made to the partners of the higher-tier partnership under this paragraph (c)(1)(i) or to the higher-tier partnership itself (under the rules of paragraph (c)(1)(ii) of this section) in the same manner as if the partner's distributive share of the payment had been paid directly to the higher-tier foreign partnership;

(E) If the withholding agent can reliably associate the partner's distributive share with a withholding certificate described in paragraph (e) of this section regarding a foreign trust or estate, then the rules of paragraph (e) of this section shall apply to determine who the payees are; and

(F) If the withholding agent cannot reliably associate the partner's distributive share with a withholding certificate or other appropriate documentation, the partners are considered to be the payees and the presumptions described in paragraph (d)(3) of this section shall apply to determine their classification and status.

(ii) *Payments treated as made to the partnership.*—A payment to a person that the withholding agent may treat as a foreign partnership is treated as a payment to the foreign partnership and not to its partners only if—

(A) The withholding agent can reliably associate the payment with a withholding certificate described in paragraph (c)(2)(iv) of this section (withholding certificate of a withholding foreign partnership);

(B) The withholding agent can reliably associate the payment with a withholding certificate described in paragraph (c)(3)(iii) of this section (nonwithholding foreign partnership) certifying that the payment is income that is effectively connected with the conduct of a trade or business in the United States; or

(C) The withholding agent can treat the income as effectively connected income under the presumption rules of § 1.1441-4(a)(2)(ii) or (3)(i).

(iii) *Rules for reliably associating a payment with documentation.*— For rules regarding the reliable association of a payment with documentation, see § 1.1441-1(b)(2)(vii). In the absence of documentation, see § § 1.1441-1(b)(3) and 1.6049-5(d) and paragraphs (d) and (e)(6) of this section for applicable presumptions.

(iv) *Coordination with chapter 4 for payments made to foreign partnerships.*—A withholding agent that makes a payment of U.S. source FDAP income to a foreign partnership that is a withholdable payment to which withholding under chapter 4 applies must apply the rules described in § 1.1473-1(a)(5)(vi) to determine when the payment is treated as made to a partner in the partnership for purposes of chapter 4. In a case in which withholding applies under chapter 4 to a withholdable payment made to a foreign partnership, see § 1.1441-3(a)(2) to coordinate with withholding otherwise required under this paragraph (c) with respect to the amount of the payment included in the gross income of a partner. For when a withholding agent may reliably associate a withholdable payment with a chapter 4 withholding rate pool in lieu of obtaining documentation for each payee include in the pool, see § 1.1441-1(e)(3)(iv)(C)(2) (substituting the term *nonwithholding foreign partnership* for the term *nonqualified intermediary*).

(v) *Examples.*—The rules of paragraphs (c)(1)(i) and (ii) of this section are illustrated by the following examples. Each example assumes that all payments are not withholdable payments and thus no withholding applies under chapter 4.

*Example 1.* FP is a nonwithholding foreign partnership organized in Country X. FP has two partners, FC, a foreign corporation, and USP, a U.S. partnership. USWH, a U.S. withholding agent, makes a payment of U.S. source interest to FP that is not a withholdable payment. FP has provided USWH with a valid nonwithholding foreign partnership certificate, as described in paragraph (c)(3)(iii) of this section, with which it associates a beneficial owner withholding certificate from FC and a Form W-9, "Request for Taxpayer Identification Number and Certification," from USP together with the withholding statement required by paragraph (c)(3)(iv) of this section. USWH can reliably associate the payment of interest with the withholding certificates from FC and USP. Under paragraph (c)(1)(i) of this section, the payees of the interest payment are FC and USP.

*Example 2.* The facts are the same as in *Example 1*, except that FP1, a nonwithholding foreign partnership, is a partner in FP rather than USP. FP1 has two partners, A and B, both foreign persons. FP provides USWH with a valid nonwithholding foreign partnership certificate, as described in paragraph (c)(3)(iii) of this section, with which it associates a beneficial owner withholding certificate from FC and a nonwithholding foreign partnership certificate from FP1. In addition, foreign beneficial owner withholding certificates from A

and B are associated with the nonwithholding foreign partnership withholding certificate from FP1. FP also provides the withholding statement required by paragraph (c)(3)(iv) of this section. USWH can reliably associate the interest payment with the withholding certificates provided by FC, A, and B. Therefore, under paragraph (c)(1)(i) of this section, the payees of the interest payment are FC, A, and B.

*Example 3.* USWH makes a payment of U.S. source dividends to WFP, a withholding foreign partnership, that is not a withholdable payment. WFP has two partners, FC1 and FC2, both foreign corporations. USWH can reliably associate the payment with a valid withholding foreign partnership withholding certificate from WFP. Therefore, under paragraph (c)(1)(ii)(A) of this section, WFP is the payee of the interest.

*Example 4.* USWH makes a payment of U.S. source royalties that is not a withholdable payment to FP, a foreign partnership. USWH can reliably associate the royalties with a valid withholding certificate from FP on which FP certifies that the income is effectively connected with the conduct of a trade or business in the United States. Therefore, under paragraph (c)(1)(ii)(B) of this section, FP is the payee of the royalties.

(2) *Withholding foreign partnerships.*—(i) *Reliance on claim of withholding foreign partnership status.*—A withholding foreign partnership is a foreign partnership that has entered into an agreement with the IRS, as described in paragraph (c)(2)(ii) of this section, with respect to distributions and guaranteed payments it makes to its partners. A withholding agent that can reliably associate a payment with a certificate described in paragraph (c)(2)(iv) of this section may treat the person to whom it makes the payment as a withholding foreign partnership for purposes of withholding under chapters 3 and 4 of the Code, information reporting under chapter 61 of the Code, backup withholding under section 3406, and withholding under other provisions of the Code. Furnishing such a certificate is in lieu of transmitting to a withholding agent withholding certificates or other appropriate documentation for its partners. Although the withholding foreign partnership generally will be required to obtain withholding certificates or other appropriate documentation from its partners pursuant to its agreement with the IRS, it generally will not be required to attach such documentation to its withholding foreign partnership withholding certificate to the extent it is permitted to act as a withholding foreign partnership with respect to the payment under its agreement. In addition, the IRS may permit a foreign partnership to act as a qualified intermediary under § 1.1441-1(e)(5)(ii)(D) with respect to its partners in appropriate circumstances.

(ii) *Withholding agreement.*—The IRS may, upon request, enter into a withholding agreement with a foreign partnership pursuant to such procedures as the IRS may prescribe in published guidance (see § 601.601(d)(2) of this chapter). Under the withholding agreement, a foreign partnership shall generally be subject to the applicable withholding and reporting provisions applicable to withholding agents and payors as defined in § 1.6049-4(a) under chapters 3, 4, and 61 of the Code, section 3406, the regulations under those provisions, and other withholding provisions of the Code, except to the extent provided under the withholding agreement. Under the withholding agreement, a foreign partnership may agree to act as an acceptance agent to perform the duties described in § 301.6109-1(d)(3)(iv)(A) of this chapter. For a foreign partnership that is an FFI, the withholding agreement will require the partnership to assume the requirements of a participating FFI, a registered deemed-compliant FFI, or an FFI treated as a deemed-compliant FFI under an applicable IGA that is subject to due diligence and reporting requirements with respect to its U.S. accounts similar to those applicable to a registered deemed-compliant FFI under § 1.1471-5(f)(1). The withholding agreement may specify the manner in which applicable procedures for adjustments for underwithholding and overwithholding, including refund procedures, apply to the withholding foreign partnership and its partners and the extent to which applicable procedures may be modified. In particular, the withholding agreement may allow a withholding foreign partnership to claim refunds of overwithheld amounts on behalf of its customers. In addition, the withholding agreement must specify the manner in which the IRS will verify the partnership's compliance with its agreement, including the requirements for a periodic review of the partnership's compliance with the withholding agreement and the procedures for the partnership to certify to its compliance with the withholding agreement. A withholding foreign partnership must file a return on Form 1042, "Annual Withholding Tax Return for U.S. Source Income of Foreign Persons," and information returns on Form 1042-S, "Foreign Person's U.S. Source Income Subject to Withholding." The withholding agreement may also require a withholding foreign partnership to file a partnership return under section 6031(a) and partner statements under 6031(b), including for each U.S. partner to the extent required in the agreement. Additionally, a partnership that is an FFI will be required to file Form 8966, "FATCA Report" to the extent provided in the withholding agreement.

(iii) *Withholding responsibility.*—A withholding foreign partnership must assume primary withholding responsibility under both chapters 3 and 4 of the Code to the extent required in the withholding agreement. It is not required to provide information to the withholding agent regarding each partner's distributive share of the payment (including a withholdable payment). The withholding foreign partnership will be responsible for reporting the payments under §§ 1.1461-1(c), 1.1474-1(d), and chapter 61 of the Code and filing Form 1042 (to the extent required in the withholding agreement). A withholding agent making a payment to a withholding foreign partnership is not required to withhold any amount under chapters 3 and 4 of the Code on the payment unless it has actual knowledge or reason to know that the foreign partnership is not acting as a withholding foreign partnership with respect to the payment or has not withheld to the extent required. The withholding foreign partnership shall withhold the payments under the same procedures and at the same time as prescribed for withholding by a U.S. partnership under paragraph (b)(2) of this section, except that, for purposes of determining the partner's status, the provisions of paragraph (d)(4) of this section shall apply.

(iv) *Withholding certificate from a withholding foreign partnership.*—The rules of § 1.1441-1(e)(4) shall apply to withholding certificates described in this paragraph (c)(2)(iv). A withholding certificate furnished by a withholding foreign partnership is valid with regard to any partner on whose behalf the certificate is furnished only if it is furnished on a Form W-8, an acceptable substitute form, or such other form as the IRS may prescribe, it is signed under penalties of perjury by a partner with authority to sign for the partnership, its validity has not expired, and it contains the information, statement, and certifications described in this paragraph (c)(2)(iv) as follows—

(A) The name, permanent residence address (as described in § 1.1441-1(e)(2)(ii)), the employer identification number of the partnership, the country under the laws of which the partnership is created or governed, the chapter 4 status of the partnership if required for purposes of chapter 4 or if the partnership provides (or will provide) a withholding statement associated with the Form W-8 allocating a payment to a chapter 4 withholding rate pool of U.S. payees under § 1.6049-4(c)(4) with respect to its partners, and the GIIN of the partnership (if applicable). If the partnership provides (or will provide) a chapter 4 withholding rate pool of U.S. payees as described in the preceding sentence, the partnership must certify to its chapter 4 status as a participating FFI (including a reporting Model 2 FFI) or registered deemed-compliant FFI (including a reporting Model 1 FFI);

(B) A certification that the partnership is a withholding foreign partnership within the meaning of paragraph (c)(2)(i) of this section, and, for a partnership that is an FFI receiving a withholdable payment, a certification that the partnership is acting as a participating FFI, a registered deemed-compliant FFI, or a nonreporting IGA FFI (as defined in § 1.1471-1(b)(83)); and

(C) Any other information, certifications or statements as may be required by the withholding foreign partnership agreement with the IRS or the form or accompanying instructions in addition to, or in lieu of, the information, statements, and certifications described in this paragraph (c)(2)(iv).

(3) *Nonwithholding foreign partnerships.*—(i) *Reliance on claim of foreign partnership status.*—A withholding agent may treat a person as a nonwithholding foreign partnership if it receives from that person a nonwithholding foreign partnership withholding certificate as described in paragraph (c)(3)(iii) of this section. A withholding agent that does not receive a nonwithholding foreign partnership withholding certificate or does not receive a valid withholding certificate from an entity it knows, or has reason to know, is a foreign partnership must apply the presumption rules of §§ 1.1441-1(b)(3) and 1.6049-5(d) and paragraphs (d) and (e)(6) of this section. In addition, to the extent a withholding agent cannot, prior to a payment, reliably associate the payment with valid documentation from a payee that is associated with the nonwithholding foreign partnership withholding certificate or has insufficient information to report the payment on Form 1042-S or Form 1099, to the extent reporting is required, the withholding agent must apply the presumption rules. See § 1.1441-1(b)(2)(vii)(A) and (B) for rules regarding reliable association. See, however, § 1.1441-1(e)(3)(iv)(C)(2) for when a withholding agent may reliably associate a withholdable payment with a chapter 4 withholding rate pool in lieu of obtaining documentation for each payee included in the pool (substituting the term nonwithholding foreign partnership for the term nonqualified intermediary). See also § 1.1441-1(e)(3)(iv)(A) for when a withholding agent may reliably associate a payment with a chapter 4 withholding rate pool of U.S. payees. See paragraph (c)(3)(iv) of this section and § 1.1441-1(e)(3)(iv)

for alternative procedures permitting allocation information to be received after a payment is made.

(ii) *Reliance on claim of reduced withholding by a partnership for its partners.*—This paragraph (c)(3)(ii) describes the manner in which a withholding agent may rely on a claim of reduced withholding when making a payment to a nonwithholding foreign partnership. To the extent that a withholding agent treats a payment to a nonwithholding foreign partnership as a payment to the nonwithholding foreign partnership's partners (whether direct or indirect) in accordance with paragraph (c)(1)(i) of this section, it may rely on a claim for reduced withholding by the partner if, prior to the payment, the withholding agent can reliably associate the payment (within the meaning of § 1.1441-1(b)(2)(vii)) with a valid withholding certificate or other appropriate documentation from the partner that establishes entitlement to a reduced rate of withholding. A withholding certificate or other appropriate documentation that establishes entitlement to a reduced rate of withholding is a beneficial owner withholding certificate described in § 1.1441-1(e)(2)(i), documentary evidence described in § 1.1441-6(c)(3) or (4) or § 1.6049-5(c)(1) (for a partner claiming to be a foreign person and a beneficial owner, determined under the provisions of § 1.1441-1(c)(6)), a Form W-9 described in § 1.1441-1(d) (for a partner claiming to be a U.S. payee), a withholding foreign partnership withholding certificate described in paragraph (c)(2)(iv) of this section, or a withholding statement allocating the payment to a chapter 4 withholding rate pool of U.S. payees. For when the withholding agent can reliably associate the payment with a chapter 4 withholding rate pool, see paragraph (c)(3)(i) of this section. See also § 1.1441-3(a)(2) (coordinating withholding under chapter 3 when withholding under chapter 4 is applied to a payment). Unless a nonwithholding foreign partnership withholding certificate is provided for income claimed to be effectively connected with the conduct of a trade or business in the United States, a claim must be presented for each portion of the payment that represents an item of income includible in the distributive share of a partner as required under paragraph (c)(3)(iii)(C) of this section. When making a claim for several partners, the partnership may present a single nonwithholding foreign partnership withholding certificate to which the partners' certificates or other appropriate documentation are associated. Where the nonwithholding foreign partnership withholding certificate is provided for income claimed to be effectively connected with the conduct of a trade or business in the United States under paragraph (c)(3)(iii)(D) of this section, the claim may be presented without having to identify any partner's distributive share of the payment.

(iii) *Withholding certificate from a nonwithholding foreign partnership.*—A nonwithholding foreign partnership shall provide a nonwithholding foreign partnership withholding certificate with respect to reportable amounts received by the nonwithholding foreign partnership. A nonwithholding foreign partnership withholding certificate is valid only to the extent it is furnished on a Form W-8 (or an acceptable substitute form or such other form as the IRS may prescribe), it is signed under penalties of perjury by a partner with authority to sign for the partnership, its validity has not expired, and it contains the information, statements, and certifications described in this paragraph (c)(3)(iii) and paragraph (c)(3)(iv) of this section, and the withholding certificates and other appropriate documentation for all the persons to whom the certificate relates are associated with the certificate. The rules of § 1.1441-1(e)(4) shall apply to withholding certificates described in this paragraph (c)(3)(iii). No withholding certificates or other appropriate documentation from persons who derive income through a partnership (whether or not U.S. exempt recipients) are required to be associated with the nonwithholding foreign partnership withholding certificate if the certificate is furnished solely for income claimed to be effectively connected with the conduct of a trade or business in the United States. Withholding certificates and other appropriate documentation that may be associated with the nonwithholding foreign partnership withholding certificate consist of beneficial owner withholding certificates under § 1.1441-1(e)(2)(i), intermediary withholding certificates under § 1.1441-1(e)(3)(i), withholding foreign partnership withholding certificates under paragraph (c)(2)(iv) of this section, nonwithholding foreign partnership withholding certificates under this paragraph (c)(3)(iii), withholding certificates from foreign trusts or estates under paragraph (e) of this section, documentary evidence described in § 1.1441-6(c)(3) or (4) or documentary evidence described in § 1.6049-5(c)(1), and any other documentation or certificates applicable under other provisions of the Internal Revenue Code or regulations that certify or establish the status of the payee or beneficial owner as a U.S. or a foreign person. Nothing in this paragraph (c)(3)(iii) shall require a nonwithholding foreign partnership to furnish original documentation. Copies of certificates or documentary evidence may be transmitted to the U.S. withholding agent, in which case the nonwithholding foreign partnership must retain the original documentation for the same time period that the copy is required to be retained by the withholding agent under §1.1441-1(e)(4)(iii) and must provide it to the withholding agent upon request. The information, statement, and certifications required on the withholding certificate are as follows—

(A) The name, permanent residence address (as described in §1.1441-1(e)(2)(ii)), the employer identification number of the partnership, if any, the country under the laws of which the partnership is created or governed, and the chapter 4 status of the partnership (for a nonwithholding foreign partnership receiving a withholdable payment or providing a withholding statement associated with the Form W-8 allocating a payment to a chapter 4 withholding rate pool of U.S. payees), and the GIIN of the partnership (if applicable);

(B) A certification that the person whose name is on the certificate is a foreign partnership;

(C) A withholding statement associated with the nonwithholding foreign partnership withholding certificate that provides all of the information required by paragraph (c)(3)(iv) of this section and §1.1441-1(e)(3)(iv). No withholding statement is required, however, for a nonwithholding foreign partnership withholding certificate furnished for income claimed to be effectively connected with the conduct of a trade or business in the United States;

(D) A certification that the income is effectively connected with the conduct of a trade or business in the United States, if applicable; and

(E) Any other information, certifications, or statements required by the form or accompanying instructions in addition to, or in lieu of, the information and certifications described in this paragraph (c)(3)(iii).

(iv) *Withholding statement provided by nonwithholding foreign partnership and coordination with chapter 4.*—The provisions of §1.1441-1(e)(3)(iv) (regarding a withholding statement) shall apply to a nonwithholding foreign partnership by substituting the term nonwithholding foreign partnership for the term nonqualified intermediary, including when a nonwithholding foreign partnership may provide to a withholding agent a withholding statement that includes a chapter 4 withholding rate pool in lieu of information with respect to each partner that is a payee of a payment.

(v) *Withholding and reporting by a foreign partnership.*—A nonwithholding foreign partnership described in this paragraph (c)(3) that receives an amount subject to withholding (as defined in §1.1441-2(a)) shall be required to withhold and report such payment under chapter 3 of the Code and the regulations thereunder except as otherwise provided in this paragraph (c)(3)(v). A nonwithholding foreign partnership shall not be required to withhold and report if it has provided a valid nonwithholding foreign partnership withholding certificate, it has provided all of the information required by paragraph (c)(3)(iv) of this section (withholding statement), and it does not know, and has no reason to know, that another withholding agent failed to withhold the correct amount or failed to report the payment correctly under §1.1461-1(c). A nonwithholding foreign partnership is also not required to withhold and report under this paragraph (c)(3) to the extent that withholding under chapter 4 was applied to a payment that is includible in the gross income of a partner in the partnership. See also §1.1441-3(a)(2) for coordination rules when withholding under chapter 4 has been applied to a withholdable payment. A withholding foreign partnership's obligations to withhold and report shall be determined in accordance with its withholding foreign partnership agreement.

(d) *Presumption rules.*—(1) *In general.*—This paragraph (d) contains the applicable presumptions for a withholding agent (including a partnership) to determine the classification and status of a partnership and its partners in the absence of documentation. The provisions of §1.1441-1(b)(3)(iv) (regarding the 90-day grace period) and §1.1441-1(b)(3)(vii) through (ix) shall apply for purposes of this paragraph (d).

(2) *Determination of partnership status as U.S. or foreign in the absence of documentation.*—In the absence of a valid representation of U.S. partnership status in accordance with paragraph (b)(1) of this section or of foreign partnership status in accordance with paragraph (c)(2)(i) or (c)(3)(i) of this section, the withholding agent shall determine the classification of the payee under the presumptions set forth in §1.1441-1(b)(3)(ii). If the withholding agent treats the payee as a partnership under §1.1441-1(b)(3)(ii), the withholding agent shall apply the presumptions set forth in §1.1441-1(b)(3)(iii)(A)(*1*) (applied by substituting the term *partnership* for the term *exempt recipient*) to determine whether to treat the partnership as a U.S. person or foreign person. For rules regarding reliable association with a withholding certificate from a domestic or a foreign partnership, see §1.1441-1(b)(2)(vii).

(3) *Determination of partners' status in the absence of certain documentation.*—If a nonwithholding foreign partnership has provided a nonwithholding foreign partnership withholding certificate under paragraph (c)(3)(iii) of this section that would be valid except that the withholding agent cannot reliably associate all or a portion of the payment with valid documentation from a partner of the partnership, then the withholding agent may apply the presumption rule of this paragraph (d)(3) with respect to all or a portion of the payment for which documentation has not been received. See §1.1441-1(b)(2)(vii)(A) and (B) for rules regarding reliable association. The presumption rule of this paragraph (d)(3) also applies to a person that is presumed to be a foreign partnership under the rule of paragraph (d)(2) of this section. Any portion of a payment that the withholding agent cannot treat as reliably associated with valid documentation from a partner may be presumed made to a foreign payee. As a result, any payment of an amount subject to withholding is subject to withholding at a rate of 30 percent. Any payment that is presumed to be made to an undocumented foreign payee must be reported on Form 1042-S. See §1.1461-1(c). For a payment described in this paragraph (d)(3) that is a withholdable payment, see §1.1471-3(f)(5) for the presumption rule for determining the payee's chapter 4 status to determine whether withholding under chapter 4 applies to the payment.

(4) *Determination by a withholding foreign partnership of the status of its partners.*—Except as otherwise provided in the agreement described in paragraph (c)(2) of this section, a withholding foreign partnership shall determine whether the partners or some other persons are the payees of the partners' distributive shares of any payment made by a withholding foreign partnership by applying the rules of §1.1441-1(b)(2), paragraph (c)(1) of this section (in the case of a partner that is a foreign partnership), and paragraph (e)(3) of this section (in the case of a partner that is a foreign estate or a foreign trust). Further, the provisions of paragraph (d)(3) of this section shall apply to determine the status of partners and the applicable withholding rates to the extent that, at the time the foreign partnership is required to withhold on a payment, it cannot reliably associate the amount with documentation for any one or more of its partners.

(e) *Foreign trusts and estates.*—(1) *In general.*—This paragraph (e) provides rules applicable to payments of amounts subject to withholding (as defined in §1.1441-2(a)) that a withholding agent may treat as made to any foreign trust or a foreign estate. For rules relating to payments to a U.S. trust or a U.S. estate, see paragraph (b) of this section. For the definitions of foreign simple trust, foreign complex trust, and foreign grantor trust, see §1.1441-1(c)(24), (25), and (26).

(2) *Payments to foreign complex trusts and foreign estates.*—Under §1.1441-1(c)(6)(ii)(D), a foreign complex trust or foreign estate is generally considered to be the beneficial owner of income paid to the foreign complex trust or foreign estate. See paragraph (e)(4) of this section for rules describing when a withholding agent may treat a payment as made to a foreign complex trust or a foreign estate.

(3) *Payees of payments to foreign simple trusts and foreign grantor trusts.*—(i) *Payments for which beneficiaries and owners are payees.*—For purposes of the regulations under chapters 3 and 61 of the Internal Revenue Code and section 3406, a foreign simple trust is not a beneficial owner or a payee of a payment. Also, a foreign grantor trust (or a portion of a trust that is a foreign grantor trust) is not considered a beneficial owner or a payee of a payment. Except as otherwise provided in paragraph (e)(3)(ii) of this section, the payees of a payment made to a person that the withholding agent may treat as a foreign simple trust or a foreign grantor trust (or a portion of a trust that is a foreign grantor trust) are determined under the rules of this paragraph (e)(3)(i). The payees shall be treated as the beneficial owners if they may be so treated under §1.1441-1(c)(6)(ii)(C) and they provide documentation supporting their status as the beneficial owners. The payees of a payment to a foreign simple trust or foreign grantor trust are determined as follows—

(A) If the withholding agent can reliably associate a payment with a valid Form W-9 provided under §1.1441-1(d) from a beneficiary or owner of the foreign trust, then the beneficiary or owner is a U.S. payee;

(B) If the withholding agent can reliably associate a payment with a valid Form W-8, or other appropriate documentation, provided under §1.1441-1(e)(1)(ii) from a beneficiary or owner of the foreign trust, then the beneficiary or owner is a payee that is a foreign beneficial owner;

(C) If the withholding agent can reliably associate a payment with a qualified intermediary withholding certificate under §1.1441-1(e)(3)(ii), a nonqualified intermediary withholding certificate under §1.1441-1(e)(3)(ii), or a U.S. branch withholding certificate under §1.1441-1(e)(3)(v), then the rules of §1.1441-1(b)(2)(v) shall apply to determine the payee in the same manner as if the payment had been paid directly to such intermediary or U.S. branch;

(D) If the withholding agent can reliably associate a payment with a withholding foreign partnership withholding certificate under paragraph (c)(2)(iv) of this section or a nonwithholding foreign partnership withholding certificate under paragraph (c)(3)(iii) of this section, then the rules of paragraph (c)(1)(i) or (ii) of this section shall apply to determine the payee;

(E) If the withholding agent can reliably associate the payment with a foreign simple trust withholding certificate or a foreign grantor trust withholding certificate (both described in paragraph (e)(5)(iii) of this section) from a second or higher-tier foreign simple trust or foreign grantor trust, then the rules of this paragraph (e)(3)(i) or paragraph (e)(3)(ii) of this section shall apply to determine whether the payment is treated as made to a beneficiary or owner of the higher-tier trust or to the trust itself in the same manner as if the payment had been made directly to the higher-tier trust; and

(F) If the withholding agent cannot reliably associate a payment with a withholding certificate or other appropriate documentation, the payees shall be determined by applying the presumptions described in paragraph (e)(6) of this section.

(ii) *Payments for which trust is payee.*—A payment to a person that the withholding agent may treat as made to a foreign trust under paragraph (e)(5)(iii) of this section is treated as a payment to the trust, and not to a beneficiary of the trust, only if—

(A) The withholding agent can reliably associate the payment with a foreign complex trust withholding certificate under paragraph (e)(4) of this section;

(B) The withholding agent can reliably associate the payment with a foreign simple trust withholding certificate under paragraph (e)(5)(iii) of this section certifying that the payment is income that is treated as effectively connected with the conduct of a trade or business in the United States; or

(C) The withholding agent can treat the income as effectively connected income under the presumption rules of §1.1441-4(a)(3)(i).

(iii) *Coordination with chapter 4 for payments made to foreign simple trusts and foreign grantor trusts.*—A withholding agent that makes a payment of U.S. source FDAP income to a foreign simple trust or foreign grantor trust that is a withholdable payment to which withholding under chapter 4 applies must apply the rules described in §1.1473-1(a)(5)(vi) to determine when the payment is treated as made to a beneficiary or owner of the trust for purposes of chapter 4. In a case in which withholding applies under chapter 4 to a withholdable payment made to a foreign simple trust or foreign grantor trust, see §1.1441-3(a)(2) to coordinate withholding otherwise required under this paragraph (e) with respect to the amount of the payment included in the gross income of the payee of the payment. For when a withholding agent may reliably associate a withholdable payment with a chapter 4 withholding rate pool in lieu of obtaining documentation for each payee included in the pool, see §1.1441-1(e)(3)(iv)(C)(2) (substituting the term *nonwithholding foreign trust* for the term *nonqualified intermediary*).

(4) *Reliance on claim of foreign complex trust or foreign estate status.*—A withholding agent may treat a payment as made to a foreign complex trust or a foreign estate if the withholding agent can reliably associate the payment with a beneficial owner withholding certificate described in §1.1441-1(e)(2)(i) or other documentary evidence under §1.1441-6(c)(3) or (4) (regarding a claim for treaty benefits) or §1.6049-5(c)(1) (regarding documentary evidence to establish foreign status for purposes of chapter 61 of the Internal Revenue Code) that establishes the foreign complex trust or foreign estate's status as a beneficial owner. See paragraph (e)(6) of this section for presumption rules if documentation is lacking.

(5) *Foreign simple trust and foreign grantor trust.*—(i) *Reliance on claim of foreign simple trust or foreign grantor trust status.*—A withholding agent may treat a person as a foreign simple trust or foreign grantor trust if it receives from that person a foreign simple trust or foreign grantor trust withholding certificate as described in paragraph (e)(5)(iii) of this section. A withholding agent must apply the presumption rules of §§1.1441-1(b)(3) and 1.6049-5(d) and paragraphs (d) and (e)(6) of this section to the extent it cannot, prior to the payment, reliably associate a payment (within the meaning of §1.1441-1(b)(2)(vii)) with a valid foreign simple trust or foreign grantor trust withholding certificate, it cannot reliably determine how much of the payment relates to valid documentation provided by a payee (*e.g.,* a person that is not itself a nonqualified intermediary, flow-through entity, or U.S. branch) associated with the foreign simple trust or foreign grantor trust withholding certificate, or it does not have sufficient information to report the payment on Form 1042-S or Form 1099, if reporting is required. See §1.1441-1(b)(2)(vii)(A) and (B). See, however, §1.1441-1(e)(3)(iv)(C)(2) for when a withholding

agent may reliably associate a withholdable payment with a chapter 4 withholding rate pool in lieu of obtaining documentation for each payee included in a pool (substituting the term *nonwithholding foreign trust* for the term *nonqualified intermediary*). See also §1.1441-1(e)(3)(iv)(A) for when a withholding agent may reliably associate a payment with a chapter 4 withholding rate pool of U.S. payees.

(ii) *Reliance on claim of reduced withholding by a foreign simple trust or foreign grantor trust for its beneficiaries or owners.*—This paragraph (e)(5)(ii) describes the manner in which a withholding agent may rely on a claim of reduced withholding when making a payment to a foreign simple trust or foreign grantor trust. To the extent that a withholding agent treats a payment to a foreign simple trust or foreign grantor trust as a payment to payees other than the trust in accordance with paragraph (e)(3)(i) of this section, it may rely on a claim for reduced withholding by a beneficiary or owner if, prior to the payment, the withholding agent can reliably associate the payment (within the meaning of §1.1441-1(b)(2)(vii)) with a valid withholding certificate or other appropriate documentation from a payee or beneficial owner that establishes entitlement to a reduced rate of withholding. A withholding certificate or other appropriate documentation that establishes entitlement to a reduced rate of withholding is a beneficial owner withholding certificate described in §1.1441-1(e)(2)(i) or documentary evidence described in §1.1441-6(c)(3) or (4) or in §1.6049-5(c)(1) (for a beneficiary or owner claiming to be a foreign person and a beneficial owner, determined under the provisions of §1.1441-1(c)(6)), a Form W-9 described in §1.1441-1(d) (for a beneficiary or owner claiming to be a U.S. payee), a withholding foreign partnership withholding certificate described in paragraph (c)(2)(iv) of this section, or a withholding statement allocating the payment to a chapter 4 withholding rate pool of U.S. payees. For when the withholding agent can reliably associate the payment with a chapter 4 withholding rate pool, see paragraph (c)(3)(i) of this section. See also §1.1441-3(a)(2) (coordinating withholding under chapter 3 when withholding under chapter 4 is applied to a withholdable payment). Unless a foreign simple trust or foreign grantor trust withholding certificate is provided for income treated as income effectively connected with the conduct of a trade or business in the United States, a claim must be presented for each payee's portion of the payment. When making a claim for several payees, the trust may present a single foreign simple trust or foreign grantor trust withholding certificate with which the payees' certificates or other appropriate documentation are associated. Where the foreign simple trust or foreign grantor trust withholding certificate is provided for income that is treated as effectively connected with the conduct of a trade or business in the United States under paragraph (e)(5)(iii)(D) of this section, the claim may be presented without having to identify any beneficiary's or grantor's distributive share of the payment.

(iii) *Withholding certificate from foreign simple trust or foreign grantor trust.*—A withholding certificate furnished by a foreign simple trust or a foreign grantor trust that is not a withholding foreign trust (within the meaning of paragraph (e)(5)(v) of this section) is valid only if it is furnished on a Form W-8, an acceptable substitute form, or such other form as the IRS may prescribe, it is signed under penalties of perjury by a trustee, its validity has not expired, it contains the information, statements, and certifications required by this paragraph (e)(5)(iii) and §1.1441-1(e)(3)(iv), and the withholding certificates or other appropriate documentation for all of the payees (as determined under paragraph (e)(3)(i) of this section) to whom the certificate relates are associated with the foreign simple trust or foreign grantor trust withholding certificate. The rules of §1.1441-1(e)(4) shall apply to withholding certificates described in this paragraph (e)(5)(iii). No withholding certificates or other appropriate documentation from persons who derive income through a foreign simple trust or a foreign grantor trust (whether or not U.S. exempt recipients) are required to be associated with the foreign simple trust or foreign grantor trust withholding certificate if the certificate is furnished solely for income that is treated as effectively connected with the conduct of a trade or business in the United States. Withholding certificates and other appropriate documentation (as determined under paragraph (e)(3)(i) of this section) that may be associated with a foreign simple trust or foreign grantor trust withholding certificate consist of beneficial owner withholding certificates under §1.1441-1(e)(2)(i), intermediary withholding certificates under §1.1441-1(e)(3)(i), withholding foreign partnership withholding certificates under paragraph (c)(2)(iv) of this section, nonwithholding foreign partnership withholding certificates under paragraph (c)(3)(iii) of this section, withholding certificates from foreign trusts or estates under paragraph (e)(4) or (5)(iii) of this section, documentary evidence described in §§1.1441-6(c)(3) or (4), or 1.6049-5(c)(1), and any other documentation or certificates applicable under other provisions of the Internal Revenue Code or regulations that certify or establish the status of the payee or beneficial owner as a U.S. or a foreign person. Nothing in this paragraph (e)(5)(iii) shall require a foreign simple trust or foreign grantor trust to provide original documentation. Copies of certificates or documentary evidence may be passed up to the U.S. withholding agent, in which case the foreign simple trust or foreign grantor trust must retain the original documentation for the same time period that the copy is required to be retained by the withholding agent under §1.1441-1(e)(4)(iii) and must provide it to the withholding agent upon request. The information, statement, and certifications required on a foreign simple trust or foreign grantor trust withholding certificate are as follows:

(A) The name, permanent residence address (as described in §1.1441-1(e)(2)(ii)), the employer identification number, if required, of the trust, the country under the laws of which the trust is created, the chapter 4 status of the trust if required for purposes of chapter 4 or if the trust provides (or will provide) a withholding statement associated with the Form W-8 allocating a payment to a chapter 4 withholding rate pool of U.S. payees under §1.6049-4(c)(4) with respect to the nonwithholding foreign trust's owners and beneficiaries, and the GIIN of the trust (if applicable). If a nonwithholding foreign trust provides (or will provide) a chapter 4 withholding rate pool of U.S. payees as described in the preceding sentence, the trust must certify to its chapter 4 status as a participating FFI (including a reporting Model 2 FFI) or registered deemed-compliant FFI (including a reporting Model 1 FFI);

(B) A certification that the person whose name is on the certificate is a foreign simple trust or a foreign grantor trust;

(C) A withholding statement associated with the foreign simple trust or foreign grantor trust withholding certificate that provides all of the information required by paragraph (e)(5)(iv) of this section. No withholding statement is required, however, for a foreign simple trust withholding certificate furnished for income that is treated as effectively connected with the conduct of a trade or business in the United States;

(D) A certification on a foreign simple trust withholding certificate that the income is treated as effectively connected with the conduct of a trade or business in the United States, if applicable; and

(E) Any other information, certifications, or statements required by the form or accompanying instructions in addition to, or in lieu of, the information, certifications, and statements described in this paragraph (e)(5)(iii);

(iv) *Withholding statement provided by a foreign simple trust or foreign grantor trust and coordination with chapter 4.*—The provisions of §1.1441-1(e)(3)(iv) (regarding a withholding statement) shall apply to a foreign simple trust or foreign grantor trust by substituting the term *foreign simple trust* or *foreign grantor trust* for the term *nonqualified intermediary*, including when a withholding statement provided by a foreign simple trust or foreign grantor trust may include a chapter 4 withholding rate pool in lieu of information with respect to each owner or beneficiary that is a payee of a payment.

(v) *Withholding foreign trusts.*—The IRS may enter into a withholding agreement with a foreign trust to treat the trust or estate as a withholding foreign trust. Such a withholding agreement shall generally follow the same principles as a withholding agreement with a withholding foreign partnership under paragraph (c)(2)(ii) of this section. A withholding agent may treat a payment to a withholding foreign trust in the same manner the withholding agent would treat a payment (including a withholdable payment) to a withholding foreign partnership. See §1.1441-1(e)(5)(ii)(D). For a withholding foreign trust that is an FFI, the withholding agreement will require the withholding foreign trust to assume the requirements of either a participating FFI, registered deemed-compliant FFI, or an FFI treated as a deemed-compliant FFI under an applicable IGA that is subject to due diligence and reporting requirements with respect to its U.S. accounts similar to those applicable to a registered deemed-compliant FFI under §1.1471-5(f)(1).

(6) *Presumption rules.*—(i) *In general.*—This paragraph (e)(6) contains the applicable presumptions for a withholding agent (including a trust or estate) to determine the classification and status of a trust or estate and its beneficiaries or owners in the absence of valid documentation. The provisions of §1.1441-1(b)(3)(iv) (regarding the 90-day grace period) and §1.1441-1(b)(3)(vii) through (ix) shall apply for purposes of this paragraph (e)(6).

(ii) *Determination of status as U.S. or foreign trust or estate in the absence of documentation.*—In the absence of valid documentation that establishes the U.S. status of a trust or estate under paragraph (b)(1) of this section and of documentation that establishes the foreign status of a trust or estate under paragraph (e)(4) or (e)(5)(iii) of this section, the withholding agent shall determine the classification of the payee based upon the presumptions set forth in §1.1441-1(b)(3)(ii). If, based upon those presumptions, the withholding agent classifies the payee as a trust or estate, the withholding agent shall apply the presumptions set forth in

§1.1441-1(b)(3)(iii)(A)(*1*) (applied by substituting the term *trust* for the term *exempt recipient*) to determine whether the trust or estate is a U.S. person or foreign person. An undocumented payee presumed to be a foreign trust shall be presumed to be a foreign complex trust. If a withholding agent has documentary evidence that establishes that an entity is a foreign trust, but the withholding agent cannot determine whether the foreign trust is a complex trust, a simple trust, or foreign grantor trust, the withholding agent shall presume that the trust is a foreign complex trust. Notwithstanding the preceding sentence, in the case of a foreign trust with a settlor that is a U.S. person for which a withholding agent has both a U.S. address and TIN, the withholding agent shall presume that the trust is a grantor trust when it cannot determine the status of the trust as a simple trust, complex trust, or grantor trust. See §1.1471-3(f)(4) and (5) to determine the status of the payee for purposes of chapter 4.

(iii) *Determination of beneficiary or owner's status in the absence of certain documentation.*—If a foreign simple trust or foreign grantor trust has provided a foreign simple trust or foreign grantor trust withholding certificate under paragraph (e)(5)(iii) of this section but the payment to such trust cannot be reliably associated with valid documentation from a specific beneficiary or owner of the trust, then any portion of a payment that a withholding agent cannot treat as reliably associated with valid documentation from a beneficiary or owner may be presumed made to a foreign payee. As a result, any payment of an amount subject to withholding is subject to withholding at a rate of 30 percent. Any such payment that is presumed to be made to an undocumented foreign person must be reported on Form 1042-S. See §1.1461-1(c).

(f) *Failure to receive withholding certificate timely or to act in accordance with applicable presumptions.*—See applicable procedures described in §1.1441-1(b)(7) in the event the withholding agent does not hold an appropriate withholding certificate or other appropriate documentation at the time of payment or fails to rely on the presumptions set forth in §1.1441-1(b)(3) or in paragraph (d) or (e) of this section. For a payment that is a withholdable payment, see §1.1471-3(f) for the presumption rule for determining the payee's chapter 4 status.

(g) *Effective/applicability date.*—This section applies to payments made on or after January 6, 2017. (For payments made after June 30, 2014, and before January 6, 2017, see this section as in effect and contained in 26 CFR Part 1, as revised April 1, 2016. For payments made after December 31, 2000, and before July 1, 2014, see this section as in effect and contained in 26 CFR Part 1, as revised April 1, 2013.) [Reg. §1.1441-5.]

☐ [*T.D.* 6187, 7-5-56. *Amended by T.D.* 6238, 6-10-57; *T.D.* 6908, 12-30-66; *T.D.* 7277, 5-14-73; *T.D.* 7842, 11-2-82; *T.D.* 7977, 9-19-84; *T.D.* 8160, 9-8-87; *T.D.* 8411, 4-24-92; *T.D.* 8734, 10-6-97; *T.D.* 8804, 12-30-98; *T.D.* 8856, 12-29-99; *T.D.* 8881, 5-15-2000 (*corrected* 4-5-2001), *T.D.* 9658. 2-28-2014 *and T.D.* 9808, 12-30-2016.]

## [Reg. §1.1441-6]

**§1.1441-6. Claim of reduced withholding under an income tax treaty.**—(a) *In general.*—The rate of withholding on a payment of income subject to withholding may be reduced to the extent provided under an income tax treaty in effect between the United States and a foreign country. Most benefits under income tax treaties are to foreign persons who reside in the treaty country. In some cases, benefits are available under an income tax treaty to U.S. citizens or U.S. residents or to residents of a third country. See paragraph (b)(5) of this section for claims of benefits by U.S. persons. If the requirements of this section are met, the amount withheld from the payment may be reduced at source to account for the treaty benefit. See, however, §1.1471-2(a) and §1.1472-1(b) for when withholding at source on a withholdable payment may not be reduced to account for a treaty benefit such that the beneficial owner of the payment may need to file a claim for refund to obtain a refund for the overwithheld amount of tax. See also §1.1441-4(b)(2) for rules regarding claims of a reduced rate of withholding under an income tax treaty in the case of compensation from personal services and §1.1441-4(c)(1) for rules regarding claims of a reduced rate of withholding under an income tax treaty in the case of scholarship and fellowship income.

(b) *Reliance on claim of reduced withholding under an income tax treaty.*—(1) *In general.*—The withholding imposed under section 1441, 1442, or 1443 on any payment to a foreign person is eligible for reduction under the terms of an income tax treaty only to the extent that such payment is treated as derived by a resident of an applicable treaty jurisdiction, such resident is a beneficial owner, and all other requirements for benefits under the treaty are satisfied. See section 894 and the regulations under section 894 to determine whether a resident of a treaty country derives the income. Absent actual knowledge or reason to know otherwise, a withholding agent may rely on a claim that a beneficial owner is entitled to a reduced rate of withholding based upon an income tax treaty if, prior to the payment, the withholding agent can reliably associate the payment with a beneficial owner withholding certificate, as described in §1.1441-1(e)(2), that contains the information necessary to support the claim, or, in the case of a payment of income described in paragraph (c)(2) of this section made outside the United States with respect to an offshore obligation, documentary evidence described in paragraphs (c)(3), (c)(4), and (c)(5) of this section. See §1.6049-5(e) for the definition of payments made outside the United States and §1.6049-5(c)(1) for the definition of an offshore obligation. For purposes of this paragraph (b)(1), a beneficial owner withholding certificate described in §1.1441-1(e)(2)(i) contains information necessary to support the claim for a treaty benefit only if it includes the beneficial owner's taxpayer identifying number (except as otherwise provided in paragraph (c)(1) and (g) of this section, or the beneficial owner provides its foreign tax identifying number issued by its country of residence and such country has with the United States an income tax treaty or information exchange agreement in effect), includes the representations that the beneficial owner derives the income under section 894 and the regulations under section 894, if required, and with regard to a beneficial owner that is an entity, includes a statement that the entity meets the limitation on benefits provisions of the treaty, if any. For claims for treaty benefits for scholarship and fellowship income, the beneficial owner withholding certificate must contain the beneficial owner's U.S. taxpayer identifying number (not a foreign taxpayer identifying number). The withholding certificate must also contain any other representations required by this section and any other information, certifications, or statements as may be required by the form or accompanying instructions in addition to, or in place of, the information and certifications described in this section. Absent actual knowledge or reason to know that the claims are unreliable or incorrect (applying the standards of knowledge in §1.1441-7(b)), a withholding agent may rely on the claims made on a withholding certificate or on documentary evidence. A withholding agent may also rely on the information contained in a withholding statement provided under §§1.1441-1(e)(3)(iv) and 1.1441-5(c)(3)(iv) and (e)(5)(iv) to determine whether the appropriate statements regarding section 894 and limitation on benefits have been provided in connection with documentary evidence. The Internal Revenue Service (IRS) may apply the provisions of §1.1441-1(e)(1)(ii)(B) to notify the withholding agent that the certificate cannot be relied upon to grant benefits under an income tax treaty. See §1.1441-1(e)(4)(viii) regarding reliance on a withholding certificate by a withholding agent. The provisions of §1.1441-1(b)(3)(iv) dealing with a 90-day grace period shall apply for purposes of this section.

(i) *Identification of limitation on benefits provisions.*—In conjunction with the representation that the beneficial owner meets the limitation on benefits provision of the applicable treaty, if any, required by paragraph (b)(1) of this section, a beneficial owner withholding certificate must also identify the specific limitation on benefits provision of the article (if any, or a similar provision) of the treaty upon which the beneficial owner relies to claim the treaty benefit. A withholding agent may rely on the beneficial owner's claim regarding its reliance on a specific limitation on benefits provision absent actual knowledge that such claim is unreliable or incorrect.

(ii) *Reason to know based on existence of treaty.*—For purposes of this paragraph (b)(1), a withholding agent's reason to know that a beneficial owner's claim to a reduced rate of withholding under an income tax treaty is unreliable or incorrect includes a circumstance where the beneficial owner is claiming benefits under an income tax treaty that does not exist or is not in force. A withholding agent may determine whether a tax treaty is in existence and is in force by checking the list maintained on the IRS Web site at https://www.irs.gov/businesses/international-businesses/united-states-income-tax-treaties-a-to-z (or any replacement page on the IRS Web site) or in the State Department's annual Treaties in Force publication.

(2) *Payment to fiscally transparent entity.*—(i) *In general.*—If the person claiming a reduced rate of withholding under an income tax treaty is an interest holder of an entity that is considered to be fiscally transparent (as defined in the regulations under section 894) by the interest holder's jurisdiction with respect to an item of income, then, with respect to such income derived by that person through the entity, the entity shall be treated as a flow-through entity and may provide a flow-through withholding certificate with which the withholding certificate or other documentary evidence of the interest holder that supports the claim for treaty benefits is associated. In the case of a payment that is a withholdable payment, see, however, §1.1471-3(c) for determining the payee of the payment and §§1.1471-2(a) and 1472-1(b) for when withholding at source may apply to the payment based on the status of the payee notwithstanding a claim for treaty benefits made under this paragraph (b)(2) by an interest holder in the payee. In such a case, the interest holder may file a claim for refund of the overwithheld amount of tax. For purposes of this paragraph (b)(2)(i), interest holders do not include any direct or indirect interest holders that are themselves treated as fiscally transparent entities with respect to that income by the interest holder's jurisdiction. See §1.1441-1(c)(23) and (e)(3)(i) for the definition of flow-through entity and flow-through withholding certificate. The entity may provide a beneficial owner withholding certificate, or beneficial owner documentation, with respect to any remaining portion of the income to the extent the entity is receiving income and is not treated as fiscally transparent by its own jurisdiction. Further, the entity may claim a reduced rate of withholding with respect to the portion of a payment for which it is not treated as fiscally transparent if it meets all the requirements to make such a claim and, in the case of treaty benefits, it provides the documentation required by paragraph (b)(1) of this section. If dual claims, as described in paragraph (b)(2)(iii) of this section, are made, multiple withholding certificates may have to be furnished. Multiple withholding certificates may also have to be furnished if the entity receives income for which a reduction of withholding is claimed under a provision of the Internal Revenue Code (*e.g.*, portfolio interest) and income for which a reduction of withholding is claimed under an income tax treaty.

(ii) *Certification by qualified intermediary.*—Notwithstanding paragraph (b)(2)(i) of this section, a foreign entity that is fiscally transparent, as defined in the regulations under section 894, that is also a qualified intermediary for purposes of claiming a reduced rate of withholding under an income tax treaty for its interest holders (who are deriving the income paid to the entity as residents of an applicable treaty jurisdiction) may furnish a single qualified intermediary withholding certificate, as described in §1.1441-1(e)(3)(ii), for amounts for which it claims a reduced rate of withholding under an income tax treaty on behalf of its interest holders.

(iii) *Dual treatment.*—Under paragraph (b)(2)(i) of this section, a withholding agent may make a payment to a foreign entity that is simultaneously claiming to be the beneficial owner of a portion of the income (whether or not it is also claiming a reduced rate of tax on its own behalf) and a reduced rate on behalf of persons in their capacity as interest holders in the entity with respect to the same, or a different, portion of the income. If the same portion of a payment may be reliably associated with both the entity's claim and an interest holder's claim, the withholding agent may choose to reject both claims and request new documentation and information allocating the payment among the beneficial owners of the payment or the withholding agent may choose which claim to apply. If the entity and the interest holder's claims are reliably associated with separate portions of the payment, the withholding agent may, at its option, accept such dual claims based on withholding certificates or other appropriate documentation furnished by the entity and its interest holders with respect to their respective shares of the payment even though this will result in the withholding agent treating the entity differently with respect to different portions of the same payment. Alternatively, the withholding agent may choose to apply only the claim made by the entity, provided the entity may be treated as a beneficial owner of the income. If the withholding agent does not accept claims for a reduced rate of withholding presented by any one or more of the interest holders, or by the entity, any interest holder or the entity may subsequently claim a refund or credit of any amount so withheld to the extent the interest holder's or entity's share of such withholding exceeds the amount of tax due.

(iv) *Examples.*—The following examples illustrate the rules of paragraph (b)(2) of this section. Each of the following examples describes a payment of U.S. source royalties, which are not withholdable payments under chapter 4. See §1.1473-1(a)(4)(iii) (describing nonfinancial payments that are not treated as withholdable payments). Thus, withholding under chapter 4 shall not apply with respect to the U.S. source royalties in any of the following examples:

(A) *Example 1.*—(i) *Facts.* Entity E is a business organization formed under the laws of country Y. Country Y has an income tax treaty with the United States. The treaty contains a limitation on benefits provision. E receives U.S. source royalties from withholding agent W and claims a reduced rate of withholding under the U.S.-Y tax treaty on its own behalf (rather than on behalf of its interest holders). E furnishes a beneficial owner withholding certificate described in paragraph (b)(1) of this section that represents that E is a resident of country Y (within the meaning of the U.S.-Y tax treaty), is the beneficial owner of the income, derives the income under section 894 and the regulations under section 894, and is not precluded from claiming benefits by the treaty's limitation on benefits provision.

(ii) *Analysis.* Absent actual knowledge or reason to know otherwise, as described in paragraph (b)(1) of this section, W may rely on the representations made by E to apply a reduced rate of withholding.

Reg. §1.1441-6(b)(2)(iv)(A)(ii)

(B) *Example 2.*—(i) *Facts.* The facts are the same as under *Example 1,* except that one of E's interest holders, H, is an entity organized in country Z. The U.S.-Z tax treaty reduces the rate on royalties to zero whereas the rate on royalties under the U.S.-Y tax treaty applicable to E is 5%. H is not fiscally transparent under country Z's tax law with respect to such income. H furnishes a beneficial owner withholding certificate to E that represents that H derives, within the meaning of section 894 and the regulations under section 894, its share of the royalty income paid to E as a resident of country Z, is the beneficial owner of the royalty income, and is not precluded from claiming treaty benefits by virtue of the limitation on benefits provision in the U.S.-Z treaty. E furnishes to W a flow-through withholding certificate described in § 1.1441-1(e)(3)(i) to which it attaches H's beneficial owner withholding certificate and a withholding statement for the portion of the payment that H claims as its distributive share of the royalty income. E also furnishes to W a beneficial owner withholding certificate for itself for the portion of the payment that H does not claim as its distributive share.

(ii) *Analysis.* Absent actual knowledge or reason to know otherwise, as described in paragraph (b)(1) of this section, W may rely on the documentation furnished by E to treat the royalty payment to a single foreign entity (E) as derived by different residents of tax treaty countries as a result of the claims presented under different treaties. W may, at its option, grant dual treatment, that is, a reduced rate of zero percent under the U.S.-Z treaty on the portion of the royalty payment that H claims to derive as a resident of country Z and a reduced rate of 5% under the U.S.-Y treaty for the balance. However, under paragraph (b)(2)(iii) of this section, W may, at its option, treat E as the only relevant person deriving the royalty and grant benefits under the U.S.-Y treaty only.

(C) *Example 3.*—(i) *Facts.* E is a business organization formed under the laws of country X. Country X has an income tax treaty with the United States. E has two interest holders, H1, organized in country Y, and H2, organized in country Z. E receives from W, a U.S. withholding agent, a payment of U.S. source royalties and interest, with respect to an obligation issued before July 1, 2014, that is eligible for the portfolio interest exception under sections 871(h) and 881(c), provided W receives the appropriate beneficial owner statement required under section 871(h)(5). E is classified as a corporation under U.S. tax law principles. Country X, E's country of organization, treats E as an entity that is not fiscally transparent with respect to items of income under the regulations under section 894. Under the U.S.-X income tax treaty, royalties are subject to a 5% rate of withholding. Country Y, H1's country of organization, treats E as fiscally transparent with respect to items of income under section 894 and H1 as not fiscally transparent with respect to items of income. Under the country Y-U.S. income tax treaty, royalties are exempt from U.S. tax. Country Z, H2's country of organization, treats E as not fiscally transparent under section 894 with respect to items of income. E provides W with a flow-through beneficial owner withholding certificate with which it associates a beneficial owner withholding certificate from H1. H1's withholding certificate states that H1 is a resident of country Y, derives the royalty income under section 894, meets the applicable limitation on benefits provisions of the U.S.-Y treaty, and is the beneficial owner of the income. The withholding statement attached to E's flow-through withholding certificate allocates one-half of the royalty payment to H1. E also provides W with a beneficial owner withholding certificate for the interest income and the remaining one-half of the royalty income. The withholding certificate states that E is a resident of country X, derives the royalty income under section 894, meets the limitation on benefits provisions of the U.S.-X treaty, and is the beneficial owner of the income.

(ii) *Analysis.* Absent actual knowledge or reason to know that the claims are incorrect, as described in paragraph (b)(1), W may treat one-half of the royalty derived by E as subject to a 5% withholding rate and one-half of the royalty as derived by H1 and subject to no withholding. Further, it may treat all of the interest as being paid to E and as qualifying for the portfolio interest exception. W can, at its option, treat the entire royalty as paid to E and subject it to withholding at a 5% rate of withholding. In that case, H1 would be entitled to claim a refund with respect to its one-half of the royalty.

(D) *Example 4.*—(1) *Facts.* Entity E is a business organization formed under the laws of Country Y. Country Y has an income tax treaty with the United States that contains a limitation on benefits provision. E receives U.S. source royalties from withholding agent W. E furnishes a beneficial owner withholding certificate to W claiming a reduced rate of withholding under the U.S.-Country Y tax treaty. However, E's beneficial owner withholding certificate does not specifically identify the limitation on benefits provision that E satisfies.

(2) *Analysis.* Because E's withholding certificate does not specifically identify the limitation on benefits provision under the U.S.-Country Y tax treaty that E satisfies as required by paragraph (b)(1)(i) of this section, W cannot rely on E's withholding certificate to apply the reduced rate of withholding claimed by E.

(3) *Certified TIN.*—The IRS may issue guidance requiring a foreign person claiming treaty benefits and for whom a TIN is required to establish with the IRS, at the time the TIN is requested or after the TIN is issued, that the person is a resident in a treaty country and meets other conditions (such as limitation on benefits provisions) of the treaty. See § 601.601(d)(2) of this chapter.

(4) *Claim of benefits under an income tax treaty by a U.S. person.*—In certain cases, a U.S. person may claim the benefit of an income tax treaty. For example, under certain treaties, a U.S. citizen residing in the treaty country may claim a reduced rate of U.S. tax on certain amounts representing a pension or an annuity from U.S. sources. Claims of treaty benefits by a U.S. person may be made by furnishing a Form W-9 to the withholding agent or such other form as the IRS may prescribe in published guidance (see § 601.601(d)(2) of this chapter).

(c) *Exemption from requirement to furnish a taxpayer identifying number and special documentary evidence rules for certain income.*—(1) *General rule.*—In the case of income described in paragraph (c)(2) of this section, a withholding agent may rely on a beneficial owner withholding certificate described in paragraph (b)(1) of this section without regard to the requirement that the withholding certificate include the beneficial owner's taxpayer identifying number. In the case of a payment of income not described in paragraph (c)(2) of this section, a withholding agent may rely on a withholding certificate that includes the beneficial owner's foreign taxpayer identifying number described in paragraph (b)(1) of this section instead of the beneficial owner's taxpayer identifying number. In the case of payments of income described in paragraph (c)(2) of this section made outside the United States (as defined in § 1.6049-5(e)) with respect to an offshore obligation (as defined in § 1.6049-5(c)(1)), a withholding agent may, as an alternative to a withholding certificate described in paragraph (b)(1) of this section, rely on a certificate of residence described in paragraph (c)(3) of this section or documentary evidence described in paragraph (c)(4) of this section, relating to the beneficial owner, that the withholding agent has reviewed and maintains in its records in accordance with § 1.1441-1(e)(4)(iii). In the case of a payment to a person other than an individual, the certificate of residence or documentary evidence must be accompanied by the statements described in paragraphs (c)(5)(i) and (ii) of this section regarding limitation on benefits and whether the amount paid is derived by such person or by one of its interest holders. The withholding agent maintains the reviewed documents by retaining the original, certified copy, or photocopy (microfiche, electronic scan, or similar means of electronic storage) of such documents. With respect to documentary evidence, the withholding agent must also note in its records the date on which the documents were received and reviewed. This paragraph (c)(1) shall not apply to amounts that are exempt from withholding based on a claim that the income is effectively connected with the conduct of a trade or business in the United States.

(2) *Income to which special rules apply.*—The income to which paragraph (c)(1) of this section applies is dividends and interest from stocks and debt obligations that are actively traded, dividends from any redeemable security issued by an investment company registered under the Investment Company Act of 1940 (15 U.S.C. 80a-1), dividends, interest, or royalties from units of beneficial interest in a unit investment trust that are (or were upon issuance) publicly offered and are registered with the Securities and Exchange Commission under the Securities Act of 1933 (15 U.S.C. 77a), and amounts paid with respect to loans of securities described in this paragraph (c)(2). With respect to a dividend equivalent described in section 871(m) and the regulations thereunder, this paragraph (c)(2) applies to the extent that the underlying security described in section 871(m) and the regulations thereunder satisfies the requirements of this paragraph (c)(2). For purposes of this paragraph (c)(2), a stock or debt obligation is actively traded if it is actively traded within the meaning of section 1092(d) and § 1.1092(d)-1 when documentation is provided.

(3) *Certificate of residence.*—A certificate of residence referred to in paragraph (c)(1) of this section is a certification issued by an appropriate tax official of the treaty country of which the taxpayer claims to be a resident that the taxpayer has filed its most recent income tax return as a resident of that country (within the meaning of the applicable tax treaty). The certificate of residence must have been issued by such official within three years prior to its being presented to the withholding agent, or such other period as the IRS may prescribe in published guidance (see § 601.601(d)(2) of this chapter). See § 1.1441-1(e)(4)(ii)(A) for the period during which a withholding agent may rely on a certificate of residence. The competent authorities may agree to a different procedure for certifying residence, in which case such procedure shall govern for payments made

to a person claiming to be a resident of the country with which such an agreement is in effect.

(4) *Documentary evidence establishing residence in the treaty country.*—(i) *Individuals.*—For an individual, the documentary evidence referred to in paragraph (c)(1) of this section is any documentation that includes the individuals name, address, and photograph, is an official document issued by an authorized governmental body (i.e., a government or agency thereof, or a municipality), and has been issued no more than three years prior to presentation to the withholding agent. A document older than three years may be relied upon as proof of residence only if it is accompanied by additional evidence of the person's residence in the treaty country (e.g., a bank statement, utility bills, or medical bills). Documentary evidence must be in the form of original documents or certified copies thereof.

(ii) *Persons other than individuals.*—For a person other than an individual, the documentary evidence referred to in paragraph (c)(1) of this section is any documentation that includes the name of the entity and the address of its principal office in the treaty country, and is an official document issued by an authorized governmental body (e.g., a government or agency thereof, or a municipality).

(5) *Statements regarding entitlement to treaty benefits.*—(i) *Statement regarding conditions under a limitation on benefits provision.*—In addition to the documentary evidence described in paragraph (c)(4)(ii) of this section, a taxpayer that is not an individual must provide a statement that it meets one or more of the conditions set forth in the limitation on benefits article (if any, or in a similar provision) contained in the applicable tax treaty and must identify the specific limitation on benefits provision of the article (if any, or a similar provision) of the treaty upon which the taxpayer relies to claim the treaty benefit. A withholding agent may rely on the taxpayer's claim on a treaty statement regarding its reliance on a specific limitation on benefits provision absent actual knowledge that such claim is unreliable or incorrect.

(ii) *Statement regarding whether the taxpayer derives the income.*— A taxpayer that is not an individual must also provide, in addition to the documentary evidence and the statement described in paragraph (c)(5)(i) of this section, a statement that any income for which it intends to claim benefits under an applicable income tax treaty is income that will properly be treated as derived by itself as a resident of the applicable treaty jurisdiction within the meaning of section 894 and the regulations thereunder. This requirement does not apply if the taxpayer furnishes a certificate of residence that certifies that fact.

(d) *Joint owners.*—In the case of a payment to joint owners, each owner must furnish a withholding certificate or, if applicable, documentary evidence or a certificate of residence. The applicable rate of withholding on a payment of income to joint owners shall be the highest applicable rate.

(e) *Competent authority.*—The procedures described in this section may be modified to the extent the U.S. competent authority may agree with the competent authority of a country with which the United States has an income tax treaty in effect.

(f) *Failure to receive withholding certificate timely.*—See applicable procedures described in §1.1441-1(b)(7) in the event the withholding agent does not hold an appropriate withholding certificate or other appropriate documentation at the time of payment.

(g) *Special taxpayer identifying number rule for certain foreign individuals claiming treaty benefits.*—(1) *General rule.*—Except as provided in paragraph (c) or (g)(2) of this section, for purposes of paragraph (b)(1) of this section, a withholding agent may not rely on a beneficial owner withholding certificate, described in paragraph (b)(1) of this section, that does not include the beneficial owner's taxpayer identifying number (TIN).

(2) *Special rule.*—For purposes of satisfying the TIN requirement of paragraph (b)(1) of this section, a withholding agent may rely on a beneficial owner withholding certificate, described in such paragraph, without regard to the requirement that the withholding certificate include the beneficial owner's TIN, if—

(i) A withholding agent, who is also an acceptance agent, as defined in §301.6109-1(d)(3)(iv) of this chapter (the payor), has entered into an acceptance agreement that permits the acceptance agent to request an individual taxpayer identification number (ITIN) on an expedited basis because of the circumstances of payment or unexpected nature of payments required to be made by the payor;

(ii) The payor was required to make an unexpected payment to the beneficial owner who is a foreign individual;

(iii) An ITIN for the beneficial owner cannot be received by the payor from the Internal Revenue Service (IRS) because the IRS is not issuing ITINs at the time of payment or any time prior to the time

of payment when the payor has knowledge of the unexpected payment;

(iv) The unexpected payment to the beneficial owner could not be reasonably delayed to permit the payor to obtain an ITIN for the beneficial owner on an expedited basis; and

(v) The payor satisfies the provisions of paragraph (g)(3) of this section.

(3) *Requirement that an ITIN be requested during the first business day following payment.*—The payor must submit a beneficial owner payee application for an ITIN (Form W-7 "Application for IRS Individual Taxpayer Identification Number") that complies with the requirements of §301.6109-1(d)(3)(ii) of this chapter, and also the certification described in §301.6109-1(d)(3)(iv)(A)(4) of this chapter, to the IRS during the first business day after payment is made.

(4) *Definition of unexpected payment.*—For purposes of this section, an *unexpected payment* is a payment that, because of the nature of the payment or the circumstances in which it is made, could not reasonably have been anticipated by the payor or beneficial owner during a time when the payor or beneficial owner could obtain an ITIN from the IRS. For purposes of this paragraph (g)(4), a payor or beneficial owner will not lack the requisite knowledge of the forthcoming payment solely because the amount of the payment is not fixed.

(5) *Examples.*—The rules of this paragraph (g) are illustrated by the following examples:

*Example 1.* G, a citizen and resident of Country Y, a country with which the United States has an income tax treaty that exempts U.S. source gambling winnings from U.S. tax, is visiting the United States for the first time. During his visit, G visits Casino B, a casino that has entered into a special acceptance agent agreement with the IRS that permits Casino B to request an ITIN on an expedited basis. During that visit, on a Sunday, G wins $5000 in slot machine play at Casino B and requests immediate payment from Casino B. ITINs are not available from the IRS on Sunday and would not again be available until Monday. G, who does not have an individual taxpayer identification number, furnishes a beneficial owner withholding certificate, described in §1.1441-1(e)(2), to the Casino upon winning at the slot machine. The beneficial owner withholding certificate represents that G is a resident of Country Y (within the meaning of the U.S.—Y tax treaty) and meets all applicable requirements for claiming benefits under the U.S.—Y tax treaty. The beneficial owner withholding certificate does not, however, contain an ITIN for G. On the following Monday, Casino B faxes a completed Form W-7, including the required certification, for G, to the IRS for an expedited ITIN. Pursuant to paragraph (b) and (g)(2) of this section, absent actual knowledge or reason to know otherwise, Casino B, may rely on the documentation furnished by G at the time of payment and pay the $5000 to G without withholding U.S. tax based on the treaty exemption.

*Example 2.* The facts are the same as *Example 1*, except G visits Casino B on Monday. G requests payment Monday afternoon. In order to pay the winnings to G without withholding the 30 percent tax, Casino B must apply for and obtain an ITIN for G because an expedited ITIN is available from the IRS at the time of the $5000 payment to G.

*Example 3.* The facts are the same as *Example 1*, except G requests payment fifteen minutes before the time when the IRS begins issuing ITINs. Under these facts, it would be reasonable for Casino B to delay payment to G. Therefore, Casino B must apply for and obtain an ITIN for G if G wishes to claim an exemption from U.S. withholding tax under the U.S.—Y tax treaty at the time of payment.

*Example 4.* P, a citizen and resident of Country Z, is a lawyer and a well-known expert on real estate transactions. P is scheduled to attend a three-day seminar on complex real estate transactions, as a participant, at University U, a U.S. university, beginning on a Saturday and ending on the following Monday, which is a holiday. University U has entered into a special acceptance agent agreement with the IRS that permits University U to request an ITIN on an expedited basis. Country Z is a country with which the United States has an income tax treaty that exempts certain income earned from the performance of independent personal services from U.S. tax. It is P's first visit to the United States. On Saturday, prior to the start of the seminar, Professor Q, one of the lecturers at the seminar, cancels his lecture. That same day the Dean of University U offers P $5000, to replace Professor Q at the seminar, payable at the conclusion of the seminar on Monday. P agrees. P gives her lecture Sunday afternoon. ITINs are not available from the IRS on that Saturday, Sunday, or Monday. After the seminar ends on Monday, P, who does not have an ITIN, requests payment for her teaching. P furnishes a beneficial owner withholding certificate, described in §1.1441-1(e)(2), to University U that represents that P is a resident of Country Z (within the meaning of the U.S.—Z tax treaty) and meets all applicable requirements for claiming benefits under the U.S.—Z tax treaty. The beneficial owner withholding certificate does not, however, contain an

Reg. §1.1441-6(g)(5)

ITIN for P. On Tuesday, University U faxes a completed Form W-7, including the required certification, for P, to the IRS for an expedited ITIN. Pursuant to paragraph (b) and (g)(2) of this section, absent actual knowledge or reason to know otherwise, University U may rely on the documentation furnished by P and pay $5000 to P without withholding U.S. tax based on the treaty exemption.

(h) *Dividend equivalents.*—The rate of withholding on a dividend equivalent may be reduced to the extent provided under an income tax treaty in effect between the United States and a foreign country. For this purpose, a dividend equivalent as described in section 871(m) and the regulations thereunder is treated as a dividend from sources within the United States. To receive a reduced rate of withholding with respect to a dividend equivalent, a foreign person must satisfy the other requirements described in this section.

(i) *Effective/applicability dates.*—(1) *General rule.*—Except as otherwise provided in paragraphs (i)(2) and (3) of this section, this section applies to payments made on or after January 6, 2017. (For payments made after June 30, 2014 (except for payments to which paragraph (c)(1) applies, in which case substitute March 5, 2014, for June 30, 2014), and before January 6, 2017, see this section as in effect and contained in 26 CFR part 1, revised April 1, 2016. For payments made after December 31, 2001, and before July 1, 2014, see this section as in effect and contained in 26 CFR part 1 revised April 1, 2013.)

(2) *Dividend equivalents.*—Paragraph (h) of this section applies to payments made on or after December 5, 2013.

(3) *Effective/applicability date.*—Paragraphs (b)(1)(i) and (ii), (b)(2)(iv)(D), and (c)(5)(i) of this section apply to withholding certificates and treaty statements provided on or after January 6, 2017. [Reg. § 1.1441-6.]

□ [T.D. 7157, 12-29-71. *Amended by T.D.* 7842, 11-2-82; *T.D.* 7977, 9-19-84; *T.D.* 8734, 10-6-97; *T.D.* 8804, 12-30-98; *T.D.* 8856, 12-29-99 *(corrected 3-27-2000); T.D.* 8881, 5-15-2000; *T.D.* 8977, 1-16-2002; *T.D.* 9023, 11-21-2002; *T.D.* 9253, 3-13-2006 *(corrected 5-1-2006); T.D.* 9648, 12-4-2013, *T.D.* 9658, 2-28-2014, *T.D.* 9808, 12-30-2016 *and T.D.* 9890, 12-27-2019 *(corrected 3-5-2020).*]

## [Reg. § 1.1441-7]

**§ 1.1441-7.  General provisions relating to withholding agents.**—(a) *Withholding agent defined.*—(1) *In general.*—For purposes of chapter 3 of the Internal Revenue Code and the regulations under such chapter, the term *withholding agent* means any person, U.S. or foreign, that has the control, receipt, custody, disposal, or payment of an item of income of a foreign person subject to withholding, including (but not limited to) a foreign intermediary described in § 1.1441-1(e)(3)(i), a foreign partnership, or a U.S. branch described in § 1.1441-1(b)(2)(iv)(A) or (E). See §§ 1.1441-1(b)(2) and (3) and 1.1441-5(c), (d), and (e), for rules to determine whether a payment is considered made to a foreign person. Any person who meets the definition of a withholding agent is required to deposit any tax withheld under § 1.1461-1(a) and to make the returns prescribed by § 1.1461-1(b) and (c), except as otherwise may be required by a qualified intermediary withholding agreement, a withholding foreign partnership agreement, or a withholding foreign trust agreement. When several persons qualify as withholding agents with respect to a single payment, only one tax is required to be withheld and deposited. See § 1.1461-1. A person who, as a nominee described in § 1.6031(c)-1T, has furnished to a partnership all of the information required to be furnished under § 1.6031(c)-1T(a) shall not be treated as a withholding agent if it has notified the partnership that it is treating the provision of information to the partnership as a discharge of its obligations as a withholding agent.

(2) *Withholding agent with respect to dividend equivalents.*—Each person that is a party to any contract or arrangement that provides for the payment of a dividend equivalent, as described in section 871(m) and the regulations thereunder, is treated as having control and custody of the payment.

(3) *Examples.*—The following examples illustrate the rules of paragraphs (a)(1) and (a)(2) of this section:

*Example 1.* USB is a broker organized in the United States. USB pays U.S. source dividends and interest, which are amounts subject to withholding under § 1.1441-2(a), to FC, a foreign corporation that has an investment account with USB. USB is a withholding agent as defined in paragraph (a)(1) of this section.

*Example 2.* USB is a bank organized in the United States. FB is a bank organized in country X. FB has an omnibus account with USB through which FB invests in debt and equity instruments that pay amounts subject to withholding as defined in § 1.1441-2(a). FB is a nonqualified intermediary, as defined in § 1.1441-1(c)(14). Both USB and FB are withholding agents as defined in paragraph (a)(1) of this section.

*Example 3.* The facts are the same as in *Example 2,* except that FB is a qualified intermediary. Both USB and FB are withholding agents as defined in paragraph (a)(1) of this section.

*Example 4.* FB is a bank organized in country X. FB has a branch in the United States. FB's branch has customers that are foreign persons who receive amounts subject to withholding, as defined in § 1.1441-2(a). FB is a withholding agent under paragraph (a)(1) of this section and is required to withhold and report payments of amounts subject to withholding in accordance with chapter 3 of the Internal Revenue Code.

*Example 5.* X is a foreign corporation. X pays dividends to shareholders who are foreign persons. Under section 861(a)(2)(B), a portion of the dividends are from sources within the United States and constitute amounts subject to withholding within the meaning of § 1.1441-2(a). The dividends are not subject to tax under section 884(a). See section 884(e)(3). X is a withholding agent under paragraph (a)(1) of this section.

*Example 6.* FC, a foreign corporation, enters into a notional principal contract (NPC) with Bank X, a bank organized in the United States. The NPC is a specified NPC for purposes of section 871(m) and the regulations thereunder. FC is the long party to the contract and Bank X is the short party. The NPC references a specified number of shares of dividend-paying common stock issued by a domestic corporation. As the long party, FC receives payments from Bank X based on any appreciation in the value of the common stock and dividends paid with respect to the common stock. As the short party, Bank X receives payment from FC based on any depreciation in the value of the common stock and a payment based on LIBOR. Bank X is a withholding agent because Bank X is deemed to have control and custody of a dividend equivalent as a party to the NPC. If FC's tax liability under section 881 has not been satisfied in full by Bank X as withholding agent, FC is required to file a return on Form 1120-F (U.S. Income Tax Return of a Foreign Corporation).

*Example 7.* CO is a domestic clearing organization. CO serves as a central counterparty clearing and settlement service provider for derivatives exchanges in the United States. CB is a broker organized in Country X, a foreign country, and a clearing member of CO. CB is a nonqualified intermediary, as defined in § 1.1441-1(c)(14). FC is a foreign corporation that has an account with CB. FC instructs CB to purchase a call option that is a specified ELI (as described in § 1.871-15(e)). CB effects the trade for FC on the exchange. The exchange matches FC's order with an order for a written call option with the same terms. The exchange then sends the matched trade to CO, which clears the trade. CB and the clearing member representing the person who sold the call option settle the trade with CO. Upon receiving the matched trade, the option contracts are novated and CO becomes the counterparty to CB and the counterparty to the clearing member representing the person who sold the call option. To the extent that there is a dividend equivalent with respect to the call option, both CO and CB are withholding agents as described in paragraph (a)(1) of this section. As a withholding agent, CO and CB must each determine whether it is obligated to withhold under chapter 3 of the Internal Revenue Code and the regulations thereunder.

*Example 8.* FCO is a foreign clearing organization. FCO serves as a central counterparty clearing and settlement service provider for derivatives exchanges in Country A, a foreign country. CB is a broker organized in Country A, and a clearing member of FCO. CB is a nonqualified intermediary, as defined in § 1.1441-1(c)(14). FC is a foreign corporation that has an account with CB. FC instructs CB to purchase a call option that is a section 871(m) transaction. CB effects the trade for FC on the exchange. The exchange matches FC's order with an order for a written call option with the same terms. The exchange then sends the matched trade to FCO, which clears the trade. CB and the clearing member representing the call option seller settle the trade with FCO. Upon receiving the matched trade, the option contracts are novated and FCO becomes the counterparty to CB and the counterparty to the clearing member representing the call option seller. To the extent that there is a dividend equivalent with respect to the call option, both FCO and CB are withholding agents as described in paragraph (a)(1) of this section.

*Example 9.* The facts are the same as Example 8, except that CB is a qualified intermediary, as defined in § 1.1441-1(c)(15), that has assumed the primary obligation to withhold, deposit, and report amounts under chapters 3 and 4 of Internal Revenue Code. CB provides a written statement to FCO representing that it has assumed primary withholding responsibility for any dividend equivalent payment with respect to the call option. FCO, therefore, is not required to withhold on a dividend equivalent payment to CB.

(4) *Effective/applicability date.*—Paragraph (a)(2) of this section and *Example 6* apply on or after January 23, 2012. *Example 7, Example 8,* and *Example 9* of paragraph (a)(3) of this section apply beginning January 19, 2017.

(b) *Standards of knowledge.*—(1) *In general.*—A withholding agent must withhold at the full 30-percent rate under section 1441, 1442, or 1443(a) or at the full 4-percent rate under section 1443(b) if it has actual knowledge or reason to know that a claim of U.S. status or of a reduced rate of withholding under section 1441, 1442, or 1443 is unreliable or incorrect. A withholding agent shall be liable for tax, interest, and penalties to the extent provided under sections 1461 and 1463 and the regulations under those sections if it fails to withhold the correct amount despite its actual knowledge or reason to know the amount required to be withheld. For purposes of the regulations under sections 1441, 1442, and 1443, a withholding agent may rely on information or certifications contained in, or associated with, a withholding certificate or other documentation furnished by or for a beneficial owner or payee unless the withholding agent has actual knowledge or reason to know that the information or certifications are incorrect or unreliable and, if based on such knowledge or reason to know, it should withhold (under chapter 3 of the Code or another withholding provision of the Code) an amount greater than would be the case if it relied on the information or certifications, or it should report (under chapter 3 of the Code or under another provision of the Code) an amount that would not otherwise be reportable if it relied on the information or certifications. See § 1.1441-1(e)(4)(viii) for applicable reliance rules. A withholding agent that has received notification by the Internal Revenue Service (IRS) that a claim of U.S. status or of a reduced rate is incorrect has actual knowledge beginning on the date that is 30 calendar days after the date the notice is received. A withholding agent that fails to act in accordance with the presumptions set forth in § § 1.1441-1(b)(3), 1.1441-4(a), 1.1441-5(d) and (e), or 1.1441-9(b)(3) may also be liable for tax, interest, and penalties. See § 1.1441-1(b)(3)(ix) and (7). In the case of a withholding agent making a withholdable payment to a payee that the withholding agent is required to treat as a foreign entity, see § 1.1471-3(e) for standards of knowledge and § § 1.1471-2 and 1.1472-1(b) for withholding that may apply under chapter 4. A withholding agent is allowed to apply the rules under paragraphs (b)(5) and (b)(8) of this section as in effect and contained in 26 CFR part 1 revised April 1, 2013, to accounts opened, and obligations entered into, by an entity on or after July 1, 2014, and before January 1, 2015.

(2) *Reason to know.*—A withholding agent shall be considered to have reason to know if its knowledge of relevant facts or of statements contained in the withholding certificates or other documentation is such that a reasonably prudent person in the position of the withholding agent would question the chapter 3 claims made. For an obligation other than a preexisting obligation, a withholding agent will have reason to know that a chapter 3 claim made by the holder of the obligation (account holder) is unreliable or incorrect if any information contained in its account opening files or other files pertaining to the obligation (account information), including documentation collected for purposes of AML due diligence (as defined under § 1.1471-1(b)(4)), conflicts with the account holder's claim. A withholding agent will not, however, be considered to have reason to know that a person's chapter 3 claim is unreliable or incorrect based on documentation collected for AML due diligence until the date that is 30 days after the obligation is executed (or the account is opened for an obligation that is an account with a financial institution).

(3) *Financial institutions—limits on reason to know.*—(i) *In general.*—For purposes of this paragraph (b)(3) and paragraphs (b)(4) through (10) of this section, the terms withholding certificate, documentary evidence, and documentation are defined in § 1.1441-1(c)(16), (17), and (18). Except as otherwise provided in paragraphs (b)(4) through (9) of this section, a withholding agent that is a financial institution under § 1.1471-5(e), an insurance company (without regard to whether such company is a specified insurance company), or a broker or dealer in securities that maintains or opens an account for a beneficial owner (a direct account holder) has reason to know that documentation provided by the direct account holder is unreliable or incorrect only if one or more of the circumstances described in paragraphs (b)(4) through (9) of this section exist. If a direct account holder has provided documentation that is unreliable or incorrect under the rules of paragraph (b)(4) through (9) of this section, the withholding agent may require new documentation. Alternatively, the withholding agent may rely on the documentation originally provided if the rules of paragraphs (b)(4) through (9) of this section permit such reliance based on additional statements and documentation obtained by the withholding agent from the beneficial owner. Paragraph (b)(10) of this section provides rules regarding reason to know for withholding agents that receive beneficial owner documentation from persons (indirect account holders) that have an account relationship with, or an ownership interest in, a direct account holder of the withholding agent. Paragraph (b)(11) of this section provides limitations on a withholding agent's reason to know for multiple obligations held by the same person. Paragraph (b)(12) of this section defines a reasonable explanation provided by an individual with respect to the individual's claim of foreign status. For

rules regarding reliance on Form W-9, see § 31.3406(h)-3(e)(2) of this chapter. For payments that are withholdable payments, see § 1.1471-3(e)(3) and (4) for additional rules regarding a withholding agent's reason to know with respect to a payee's claim of chapter 4 status and § 1.1471-3(f) for presumption rules that apply when the claim of chapter 4 status is unreliable or incorrect.

(ii) *Limits on reason to know for preexisting obligations.*—With respect to a preexisting obligation, a withholding agent that has documented the foreign status of the direct account holder for purposes of chapter 3 or chapter 61 before July 1, 2014, may continue to rely on such documentation without regard to a U.S. phone number or U.S. place of birth. If, however, the withholding agent reviews documentation for an individual account holder claiming foreign status that contains a U.S. place of birth (as described in paragraph (b)(5)(ii) of this section) or if the withholding agent is notified of a change in circumstances under the criteria of paragraphs (b)(5) and (8) of this section (as effective on July 1, 2014), the obligation will be treated as having experienced a change in circumstances under § 1.1441-1(e)(4)(ii)(D) as of the date that the withholding agent reviews the documentation or receives the notification, and the withholding agent will then have reason to know that the documentation is unreliable or incorrect. With respect to an obligation held by an entity, a withholding agent is not required to treat the additional U.S. indicia described in this paragraph (b) as a change in circumstances under § 1.1441-1(e)(4)(ii)(D) before January 1, 2015. See § 1.1441-1(b)(3)(iv) for the grace period following a change in circumstances. For purposes of this rule, a direct account holder will be considered documented prior to July 1, 2014, without regard to whether the withholding agent obtains renewal documentation for the account holder on or after July 1, 2014, pursuant to the requirements of § 1.1441-1(e)(4)(ii)(A).

(4) *Rules applicable to withholding certificates.*—(i) *In general.*—A withholding agent has reason to know that a beneficial owner withholding certificate provided by a direct account holder is unreliable or incorrect if the withholding certificate is incomplete with respect to any item on the certificate that is relevant to the claims made by the direct account holder, the withholding certificate contains any information that is inconsistent with the direct account holder's claim, the withholding agent has account information that is inconsistent with the direct account holder's claim, or the withholding certificate lacks information necessary to establish entitlement to a reduced rate of withholding. For purposes of establishing a direct account holder's status as a foreign person or resident of a treaty country a withholding certificate shall be considered unreliable or inconsistent with an account holder's claims only if it is not reliable under the rules of paragraphs (b)(5) and (6) of this section. See, however, § 1.1441-1(e)(2)(ii)(B) for additional reliance standards that apply to a withholding certificate that is required to include an account holder's foreign TIN. A withholding agent that relies on an agent to review and maintain a withholding certificate is considered to know or have reason to know the facts within the knowledge of the agent.

(ii) *Examples.*—The rules of paragraph (b)(4) of this section are illustrated by the following examples:

*Example 1.* F, a foreign person that has a direct account relationship with USB, a bank that is a U.S. person, provides USB with a beneficial owner withholding certificate for the purpose of claiming a reduced rate of withholding on U.S. source dividends (which is a withholdable payment). F resides in a treaty country that has a limitation on benefits provision in its income tax treaty with the United States. The withholding certificate includes a certification of F's status for chapter 4 purposes to except the payment from withholding under chapter 4, but does not contain a statement regarding limitation on benefits or deriving the income under section 894 as required by § 1.1441-6(b)(1). USB cannot rely on the withholding certificate to grant a reduced rate of withholding for chapter 3 purposes because it is incomplete with respect to the claim made by F.

*Example 2.* F, a foreign person and entity that has a direct account relationship with USB, a broker that is a U.S. person, provides USB with a withholding certificate for the purpose of claiming the portfolio interest exception under section 881(c) with respect to interest paid on an obligation issued before July 1, 2014. The payment of interest is not a withholdable payment under § 1.1471-2(b) (referring to payments made with respect to grandfathered obligations), and, therefore, withholding does not apply to the payment under chapter 4. See § 1.1441-3(c)(4)(i) for rules coordinating withholding under chapters 3 and 4. F indicates on its withholding certificate, however, that it is a partnership. USB may not treat F as a beneficial owner of the interest for purposes of the portfolio interest exception because F has indicated on its withholding certificate that it is a foreign partnership, and such entity classification is inconsistent with its claim as a beneficial owner.

(5) *Withholding certificate—establishment of foreign status.*—A withholding agent has reason to know that a beneficial owner withholding certificate (as defined in §1.1441-1(e)(2), but excluding a Form W-8ECI) provided by a direct account holder is unreliable or incorrect for purposes of establishing the account holder's status as a foreign person as set forth in paragraphs (b)(5)(i) through (iii) of this section.

(i) *Classification of U.S. status, U.S. address, or U.S. telephone number.*—A withholding certificate is unreliable or incorrect if the withholding agent has classified the person as a U.S. person in its account information, the withholding certificate has a current permanent residence address (as defined in §1.1441-1(e)(2)(ii)) in the United States, the withholding certificate has a current mailing address in the United States, the withholding agent has a current residence or mailing address as part of its account information that is an address in the United States, or the direct account holder notifies the withholding agent of a new residence or mailing address in the United States (whether or not provided on a withholding certificate). A withholding agent also has reason to know that a withholding certificate provided by a person is unreliable or incorrect if the withholding agent has a current telephone number for the account holder in the United States and has no telephone number for the account holder outside of the United States. When any of the foregoing U.S. indicia are present, a withholding agent may nevertheless rely on the beneficial owner withholding certificate to establish the account holder's foreign status if it may do so under the provisions of paragraph (b)(5)(i)(A) or (B) of this section.

(A) A withholding agent may treat a direct account holder as a foreign person if the beneficial owner withholding certificate has been provided by an individual and—

(1) The withholding agent has in its possession or obtains documentary evidence establishing foreign status (as described in §1.1471-3(c)(5)(i)) that does not contain a U.S. address and the individual provides the withholding agent with a reasonable explanation, in writing, supporting the claim of foreign status (as defined in paragraph (b)(12) of this section);

(2) For a payment made outside the U.S. with respect to an offshore obligation (as described in §1.6049-5(c)(1)), the withholding agent has in its possession or obtains documentary evidence establishing foreign status (as described in §1.1471-3(c)(5)(i)), that does not contain a U.S. address;

(3) For a payment made with respect to an offshore obligation (with offshore obligation defined as in §1.6049-5(c)(1)), the withholding agent classifies the individual as a resident of the country in which the obligation is maintained, the withholding agent is required to report a payment made to the individual annually on a tax information statement that is filed with the tax authority of the country in which the office is located as part of that country's resident reporting requirements, and that country has a tax information exchange agreement or income tax treaty in effect with the United States; or

(4) For a case in which the withholding agent classified the account holder as a U.S. person in its account information, the withholding agent has in its possession or obtains documentary evidence described in §1.1471-3(c)(5)(i)(B) evidencing citizenship in a country other than the United States.

(B) A withholding agent may treat a direct account holder as a foreign person if the beneficial owner withholding certificate has been provided by an entity that the withholding agent does not know, or does not have reason to know, is a flow-through entity and—

(1) The withholding agent has in its possession or obtains documentation establishing foreign status that substantiates that the entity is actually organized or created under the laws of a foreign country; or

(2) For a payment made with respect to an offshore obligation (with offshore obligation defined as in §1.6049-5(c)(1)), the withholding agent classifies the entity as a resident of the country in which the account is maintained, the withholding agent is required to report a payment made to the entity annually on a tax information statement that is filed with the tax authority of the country in which the office is located as part of that country's resident reporting requirements, and that country has a tax information exchange agreement or income tax treaty in effect with the United States.

(ii) *U.S. place of birth.*—A withholding agent has reason to know that a withholding certificate claiming foreign status provided by a direct account holder that is an individual is unreliable or incorrect if the withholding agent has, either on accompanying documentation or as part of its account information, an unambiguous indication of a place of birth for the individual in the United States. A withholding agent may treat the individual as a foreign person, notwithstanding the U.S. place of birth, if the withholding agent has in its possession or obtains documentary evidence described in

§1.1471-3(c)(5)(i)(B) evidencing citizenship in a country other than the United States and either a copy of the individual's Certificate of Loss of Nationality of the United States or a reasonable written explanation of the account holder's renunciation of U.S. citizenship or the reason the account holder did not obtain U.S. citizenship at birth.

(iii) *Standing instructions with respect to offshore obligations.*—A beneficial owner withholding certificate is unreliable or incorrect if it is provided with respect to an offshore obligation (as defined in §1.6049-5(c)(1)) of a direct account holder that has provided standing instructions to pay amounts to an address or an account maintained in the United States. The withholding agent may treat the account holder as a foreign person, however, if the account holder provides either a reasonable explanation in writing that supports its foreign status or documentary evidence establishing foreign status described in §1.1471-3(c)(5)(i).

(6) *Withholding certificate—claim of reduced rate of withholding under treaty.*—A withholding agent has reason to know that a withholding certificate (other than Form W-9) provided by a direct account holder is unreliable or incorrect for purposes of establishing that the account holder is a resident of a country with which the United States has an income tax treaty if it is described in paragraphs (b)(6)(i) through (iii) of this section.

(i) *Permanent residence address.*—A beneficial owner withholding certificate is unreliable or incorrect if the permanent residence address on the beneficial owner withholding certificate is not in the country whose treaty is invoked, or the direct account holder notifies the withholding agent of a new permanent residence address that is not in the treaty country. A withholding agent may, however, treat a direct account holder as entitled to a reduced rate of withholding under an income tax treaty if the account holder provides a reasonable explanation for the permanent residence address outside the treaty country (e.g., the address is the address of a branch of the beneficial owner located outside the treaty country in which the entity is a resident) or the withholding agent has in its possession or obtains documentary evidence described in §1.1471-3(c)(5)(i) that establishes residency in a treaty country.

(ii) *Mailing address.*—A beneficial owner withholding certificate is unreliable or incorrect if the permanent residence address on the withholding certificate is in the applicable treaty country but the withholding certificate contains a mailing address outside the treaty country or the withholding agent has a current mailing address as part of its account information for the direct account holder that is outside the treaty country. A mailing address that is a P.O. Box, in-care-of address, or address at a financial institution (if the financial institution is not a beneficial owner) shall not preclude a withholding agent from treating the account holder as a resident of a treaty country if such address is in the treaty country. If a withholding agent has a mailing address (whether or not contained on the withholding certificate) outside the applicable treaty country, the withholding agent may nevertheless treat a direct account holder as a resident of an applicable treaty country if—

(A) The withholding agent has in its possession or obtains documentary evidence described in §1.1471-3(c)(5)(i) supporting the account holder's claim of residence in the applicable treaty country (and the additional documentation does not contain an address outside the treaty country);

(B) The withholding agent has in its possession, or obtains, documentation that establishes that the direct account holder is an entity organized in a treaty country (or an entity managed and controlled in a treaty country, if the applicable treaty so requires);

(C) The withholding agent knows that the address outside the applicable treaty country (other than a P.O. box, or in-care-of address) is a branch of the account holder that is an entity that is a resident of the applicable treaty country; or

(D) The withholding agent obtains a written statement from the direct account holder that reasonably establishes entitlement to treaty benefits.

(iii) *Standing instructions.*—A beneficial owner withholding certificate is unreliable or incorrect to establish entitlement to a reduced rate of withholding under an income tax treaty if the direct account holder has standing instructions to pay amounts directing the withholding agent to pay amounts from its account to an address or an account outside the treaty country unless the account holder provides a reasonable explanation, in writing, or the withholding agent has in its possession or obtains documentary evidence described in §1.1471-3(c)(5)(i) establishing the account holder's residence in the applicable treaty country.

(7) *Documentary evidence.*—A withholding agent shall not treat documentary evidence provided by a direct account holder as valid if the documentary evidence does not reasonably establish the identity

of the person presenting the documentary evidence. For example, documentary evidence is not valid if it is provided in person by a direct account holder that is a natural person and the photograph or signature on the documentary evidence, if any, does not match the appearance or signature of the person presenting the document. A withholding agent shall not rely on documentary evidence to reduce the rate of withholding that would otherwise apply under the presumption rules of §§ 1.1441-1(b)(3), 1.1441-5(d) and (e)(6), and 1.6049-5(d) if the documentary evidence contains information that is inconsistent with the direct account holder's claim of a reduced rate of withholding, the withholding agent has other account information that is inconsistent with the direct account holder's claim, or the documentary evidence lacks information necessary to establish entitlement to a reduced rate of withholding. For example, if a direct account holder provides documentary evidence to claim treaty benefits and the documentary evidence establishes the direct account holder's status as a foreign person and a resident of a treaty country, but the account holder fails to provide the treaty statements required by § 1.1441-6(c)(5), the documentary evidence does not establish the direct account holder's entitlement to a reduced rate of withholding. For purposes of establishing a direct account holder's status as a foreign person or resident of a country with which the United States has an income tax treaty, documentary evidence shall be considered unreliable or incorrect only if it is not reliable under the rules of paragraph (b)(8) or (9) of this section.

(8) *Documentary evidence—establishment of foreign status.*—A withholding agent has reason to know that documentary evidence is unreliable or incorrect for purposes of establishing the direct account holder's status as a foreign person if the documentary evidence is described in paragraphs (b)(8)(i), (ii), (iii), or (iv) of this section.

(i) *Documentary evidence received prior to January 1, 2001.*—A withholding agent shall not treat documentary evidence provided by a direct account holder before January 1, 2001, as valid for purposes of establishing the account holder's status as a foreign person if it has actual knowledge that the account holder is a U.S. person or if it has a mailing or residence address for the account holder in the United States. If a withholding agent has an address for the direct account holder in the United States, the withholding agent may nevertheless treat the account holder as a foreign person if it can so treat the account holder under the rules of paragraph (b)(8)(ii) of this section. See, however, paragraph (b)(3)(ii) of this section regarding changes in circumstances with respect to preexisting obligations.

(ii) *Documentary evidence received after December 31, 2000.*—A withholding agent shall not treat documentary evidence provided by an account holder after December 31, 2000, as valid for purposes of establishing the direct account holder's foreign status if the withholding agent does not have a permanent residence address for the account holder. Documentary evidence is also unreliable or incorrect to establish a direct account holder's status as a foreign person if the withholding agent has classified the account holder as a U.S. person in its account information, if the withholding agent has a current mailing or permanent residence address (whether or not on the documentation) for the direct account holder in the United States, the direct account holder notifies the withholding agent of a new residence or mailing address in the United States, or if the withholding agent has a current telephone number for the account holder in the United States and has no telephone number for the account holder outside of the United States. Notwithstanding the foregoing, a withholding agent may rely on documentary evidence as establishing the direct account holder's foreign status if it may do so under the provisions of paragraph (b)(8)(ii)(A) or (B) of this section.

(A) *Treatment of individual's foreign status.*—A withholding agent may treat a direct account holder that is an individual as a foreign person even if it has any of the U.S. indicia described in this paragraph for the account holder if—

(1) The withholding agent has in its possession or obtains additional documentary evidence supporting the claim of foreign status (described in § 1.1471-3(c)(5)(i)) that does not contain a U.S. address and a reasonable explanation in writing supporting the account holder's foreign status;

(2) The withholding agent obtains a valid beneficial owner withholding certificate on Form W-8 and the Form W-8 contains a permanent residence address outside the United States and a mailing address outside the United States (or if a mailing address is inside the United States the account holder provides a reasonable explanation in writing supporting the account holder's foreign status); or

(3) For a payment made with respect to an offshore obligation (with offshore obligation defined as in § 1.6049-5(c)(1)), the withholding agent classifies the individual as a resident of the country in which the obligation is maintained, the withholding agent is required to report a payment made to the individual annually on a tax information statement that is filed with the tax authority of the country in which the office is located as part of that country's resident reporting requirements, and that country has a tax information exchange agreement or income tax treaty in effect with the United States.

(B) *Presumption of entity's foreign status.*—A withholding agent may treat a direct account holder that is an entity (other than a flow-through entity) as a foreign person even if it has any of the U.S. indicia described in this paragraph for the account holder in the United States if—

(1) The withholding agent has in its possession or obtains documentary evidence establishing foreign status that substantiates that the entity is actually organized or created under the laws of a foreign country;

(2) The withholding agent obtains a valid beneficial owner withholding certificate on Form W-8 and the Form W-8 contains a permanent residence address outside the United States and a mailing address outside the United States (or if a mailing address is inside the United States the account holder provides additional documentary evidence sufficient to establish the account holder's foreign status); or

(3) For a payment made with respect to an offshore obligation (with offshore obligation defined as in § 1.6049-5(c)(1)), the withholding agent classifies the entity as a resident of the country in which the account is maintained, the withholding agent is required to report a payment made to the entity annually on a tax information statement that is filed with the tax authority of the country in which the office is located as part of that country's resident reporting requirements, and that country has a tax information exchange agreement or income tax treaty in effect with the United States.

(iii) *U.S. place of birth.*—A withholding agent has reason to know that documentary evidence provided by a direct account holder to support an individual's foreign status is unreliable or incorrect if the withholding agent has, either on the documentary evidence or as part of its account information, an unambiguous indication of a place of birth for the individual in the United States. A withholding agent may treat the individual as a foreign person, notwithstanding the U.S. birth place, if the withholding agent has in its possession or obtains documentary evidence described in § 1.1471-3(c)(5)(i)(B) evidencing citizenship in a country other than the United States and a copy of the individual's Certificate of Loss of Nationality of the United States. Alternatively, a withholding agent may treat the individual as a foreign person if the withholding agent obtains a valid beneficial owner withholding certificate on Form W-8 from the individual that establishes the account holder's foreign status, documentary evidence described in § 1.1471-3(c)(5)(i)(B) evidencing citizenship in a country other than the United States, and a reasonable written explanation of the individual's renunciation of U.S. citizenship or the reason the individual did not obtain U.S. citizenship at birth.

(iv) *Standing instructions with respect to offshore obligations.*—Documentary evidence is unreliable or incorrect if it is provided with respect to an offshore obligation (as defined in § 1.6049-5(c)(1)) of a direct account holder that has provided the withholding agent with standing instructions to pay amounts to an address or an account maintained in the United States. The withholding agent may treat the direct account holder as a foreign person, however, if the account holder provides either a reasonable explanation in writing that supports its foreign status or a valid beneficial owner withholding certificate claiming foreign status.

(9) *Documentary evidence—claim of reduced rate of withholding under treaty.*—A withholding agent has reason to know that documentary evidence is unreliable or incorrect for purposes of establishing that a direct account holder is a resident of a country with which the United States has an income tax treaty if it is described in paragraph (b)(9)(i) or (ii) of this section.

(i) *Permanent residence address and mailing address.*—Documentary evidence is unreliable or incorrect if the withholding agent has a current mailing or current permanent residence address for the direct account holder (whether or not on the documentary evidence) that is outside the applicable treaty country, or the withholding agent has no permanent residence address for the account holder. If a withholding agent has a current mailing or current permanent residence address for the direct account holder outside the applicable treaty country, the withholding agent may nevertheless treat a direct account holder as a resident of an applicable treaty country if the withholding agent—

(A) Has in its possession or obtains additional documentary evidence described in § 1.1471-3(c)(5)(i) supporting the direct account holder's claim of residence in the applicable treaty country (and the documentary evidence does not contain an address outside the applicable treaty country, a P.O. box, an in-care-of address, or the address of a financial institution);

(B) Has in its possession or obtains documentary evidence described in §1.1471-3(c)(5)(i) that establishes the direct account holder is an entity organized in a treaty country (or an entity managed and controlled in a treaty country, if the applicable treaty so requires); or

(C) Obtains a valid beneficial owner withholding certificate on Form W-8 that contains a permanent residence address and a mailing address in the applicable treaty country.

(ii) *Standing instructions.*—Documentary evidence is unreliable or incorrect if the direct account holder has provided the withholding agent with standing instructions to pay amounts to an address or an account maintained outside the treaty country unless the direct account holder provides a reasonable explanation, in writing, establishing the direct account holder's residence in the applicable treaty country, or a valid beneficial owner withholding certificate that contains a permanent residence address and a mailing address in the applicable treaty country.

(10) *Indirect account holders.*—A withholding agent that receives documentation from a payee through a nonqualified intermediary, a flow-through entity, or a U.S. branch (including a territory financial institution) described in §1.1441-1(b)(2)(iv) (other than a U.S. branch or territory financial institution that is treated as a U.S. person) has reason to know that the documentation is unreliable or incorrect if a reasonably prudent person in the position of a withholding agent would question the claims made. This standard requires, but is not limited to, a withholding agent's compliance with the rules of paragraphs (b)(10)(i) through (iv).

(i) The withholding agent must review the withholding statement described in §1.1441-1(e)(3)(iv) and may not rely on information in the statement to the extent the information does not support the claims made for any payee. For this purpose, a withholding agent may not treat a payee as a foreign person if an address in the United States is provided for such payee and may not treat a person as a resident of a country with which the United States has an income tax treaty if the address for that person is outside the applicable treaty country. Notwithstanding a U.S. address or an address outside a treaty country, the withholding agent may treat a payee as a foreign person or a foreign person as a resident of a treaty country if the withholding statement is accompanied by a valid withholding certificate and documentary evidence (as described in §1.1471-3(c)(5)(i)) or a reasonable explanation is provided, in writing, by the nonqualified intermediary, flow-through entity, or U.S. branch supporting the payee's foreign status or the foreign person's residency in a treaty country.

(ii) The withholding agent must review each withholding certificate in accordance with the requirements of paragraphs (b)(5) and (6) of this section and verify that the information on the withholding certificate is consistent with the information on the withholding statement required under §1.1441-1(e)(3)(iv). If there is a discrepancy between the withholding certificate and the withholding statement, the withholding agent may choose to rely on the withholding certificate, if valid, and instruct the nonqualified intermediary, flow-through entity, or U.S. branch to correct the withholding statement or apply the presumption rules of §§1.1441-1(b), 1.1441-5(d) and (e)(6), 1.6049-5(d), and 1.1471-3(f) (for a withholdable payment for chapter 4 purposes) to the payment allocable to the payee who provided the withholding certificate. If the withholding agent chooses to rely upon the withholding certificate, the withholding agent is required to instruct the intermediary or flow-through entity to correct the withholding statement and confirm that the intermediary or flow-through entity does not know or have reason to know that the withholding certificate is unreliable or inaccurate.

(iii) The withholding agent must review the documentary evidence provided by the nonqualified intermediary, flow-through entity, or U.S. branch to determine that there is no obvious indication that the payee is a U.S. non-exempt recipient or that the documentary evidence does not establish the identity of the person who provided the documentation (*e.g.*, the documentary evidence does not appear to be an identification document).

(iv) If the beneficial owner is claiming a reduced rate of withholding under an income tax treaty, the rules of §1.1441-6(b)(1)(ii) also apply to determine whether the withholding agent has reason to know that a claim for treaty benefits is unreliable or incorrect.

(11) *Limits on reason to know for multiple obligations belonging to a single person.*—A withholding agent that maintains multiple obligations for a single person will have reason to know that a claim of foreign status for the person is inaccurate based on account information for another obligation held by the person only to the extent that—

(i) The withholding agent's computerized systems link the obligations by reference to a data element such as client number, EIN, or foreign tax identifying number and consolidates the account information and payment information for the obligations; or

(ii) The withholding agent has treated the obligations as consolidated obligations for purposes of sharing documentation pursuant to §1.1441-1(e)(4)(ix).

(12) *Reasonable explanation supporting claim of foreign status.*—A reasonable explanation supporting an individual's claim of foreign status for purposes of paragraphs (b)(5) and (8) of this section means a written statement prepared by the individual or the individual's completion of a checklist provided by the withholding agent, stating that the individual meets the requirements of one of paragraphs (b)(12)(i) through (iv) of this section.

(i) The individual certifies that he or she—

(A) Is a student at a U.S. educational institution and holds the appropriate visa;

(B) Is a teacher, trainee, or intern at a U.S. educational institution or a participant in an educational or cultural exchange visitor program, and holds the appropriate visa;

(C) Is a foreign individual assigned to a diplomatic post or a position in a consulate, embassy, or international organization in the United States; or

(D) Is a spouse or unmarried child under the age of 21 years of one of the persons described in paragraphs (b)(12)(i)(A) through (C) of this section;

(ii) The individual provides information demonstrating that he or she has not met the substantial presence test set forth in §301.7701(b)-1(c) of this chapter (*e.g.*, a written statement indicating the number of days present in the United States during the three-year period that includes the current year);

(iii) The individual certifies that he or she meets the closer connection exception described in §301.7701(b)-2, states the country to which the individual has a closer connection, and demonstrates how that closer connection has been established; or

(iv) With respect a payment entitled to a reduced rate of tax under a U.S. income tax treaty, the individual certifies that he or she is treated as a resident of a country other than the United States and is not treated as a U.S. resident or U.S. citizen for purposes of that income tax treaty.

(13) *Additional guidance.*—The IRS may prescribe other circumstances for which a withholding certificate or documentary evidence is unreliable or incorrect in addition to the circumstances described in paragraph (b) of this section to establish an account holder's status as a foreign person or a beneficial owner entitled to a reduced rate of withholding in published guidance (see §601.601(d)(2) of this chapter).

(c) *Agent.*—(1) *In general.*—A withholding agent may authorize an agent to fulfill its obligations under chapter 3 if the requirements of paragraph (c)(2) of this section are satisfied. The acts of an agent of a withholding agent (including the receipt of withholding certificates, the payment of amounts of income subject to withholding, and the deposit of tax withheld) are imputed to the withholding agent on whose behalf it is acting.

(2) *Authorized agent.*—An agent is an authorized agent only if—

(i) There is a written agreement between the withholding agent and the person acting as agent that clearly provides which obligations under chapter 3 that the agent is authorized to fulfill;

(ii) A Form 8655, "Reporting Agent Authorization," is filed with the IRS by a withholding agent if its agent (including any sub-agent) acts as a reporting agent for filing Form 1042 on behalf of the withholding agent and the agent (or sub-agent) identifies itself (instead of the withholding agent) as the filer on the Form 1042;

(iii) Books and records and relevant personnel of the agent (including any sub-agent) are available to the withholding agent (on a continuous basis, including after termination of the relationship) in order to evaluate the withholding agent's compliance with the provisions of chapters 3, 4, and 61 of the Code, section 3406, and the regulations under those provisions; and

(iv) The U.S. withholding agent remains fully liable for the acts of its agent (or for any sub-agent) and does not assert any of the defenses that may otherwise be available, including under common law principles of agency in order to avoid tax liability under the Code.

(3) *Liability of withholding agent acting through an agent.*—An authorized agent is subject to the same withholding and reporting obligations that apply to any withholding agent under the provisions of chapter 3 of the Code and the regulations thereunder. See the instructions to Form 1042-S for the manner for filing the form when an authorized agent acts on behalf of a withholding agent. Except as otherwise provided in the QI, WP, and WT agreements, an author-

ized agent does not benefit from the special procedures or exceptions that may apply to a QI, WP, or WT. A withholding agent acting through an authorized agent is liable for any failure of the agent, such as failure to withhold an amount or make payment of tax, in the same manner and to the same extent as if the agent's failure had been the failure of the withholding agent. For this purpose, the agent's actual knowledge or reason to know shall be imputed to the withholding agent. The withholding agent's liability shall exist irrespective of the fact that the authorized agent is also a withholding agent and is itself separately liable for failure to comply with the provisions of the regulations under section 1441, 1442, or 1443. However, the same tax, interest, or penalties shall not be collected more than once.

(d) *United States obligations.*—If the United States is a withholding agent for an item of interest, including original issue discount, on obligations of the United States or of any agency or instrumentality thereof, the withholding obligation of the United States is assumed and discharged by—

(1) The Commissioner of the Public Debt, for interest paid by checks issued through the Bureau of the Public Debt;

(2) The Treasurer of the United States, for interest paid by him or her, whether by check or otherwise;

(3) Each Federal Reserve Bank, for interest paid by it, whether by check or otherwise; or

(4) Such other person as may be designated by the IRS.

(e) *Assumed obligations.*—If, in connection with the sale of a corporation's property, payment on the bonds or other obligations of the corporation is assumed by a person, then that person shall be a withholding agent to the extent amounts subject to withholding are paid to a foreign person. Thus, the person shall withhold such amounts under §1.1441-1 as would be required to be withheld by the seller or corporation had no such sale or assumption been made.

(f) *Conduit financing arrangements.*—(1) *Liability of withholding agent.*—Subject to paragraph (f)(2) of this section, any person that is required to deduct and withhold tax under §1.1441-3(g) is made liable for that tax by section 1461. A person that is required to deduct and withhold tax but fails to do so is liable for the payment of the tax and any applicable penalties and interest.

(2) *Exception for withholding agents that do not know of conduit financing arrangement.*—(i) *In general.*—A withholding agent will not be liable under paragraph (f)(1) of this section for failing to deduct and withhold with respect to a conduit financing arrangement unless the person knows or has reason to know that the financing arrangement is a conduit financing arrangement. This standard shall be satisfied if the withholding agent knows or has reason to know of facts sufficient to establish that the financing arrangement is a conduit financing arrangement, including facts sufficient to establish that the participation of the intermediate entity in the financing arrangement is pursuant to a tax avoidance plan. A withholding agent that knows only of the financing transactions that comprise the financing arrangement will not be considered to know or have reason to know of facts sufficient to establish that the financing arrangement is a conduit financing arrangement.

(ii) *Examples.*—The following examples illustrate the operation of paragraph (d)(2) of this section. Each example assumes that withholding under chapter 4 does not apply.

*Example 1.* (i) DS is a U.S. subsidiary of FP, a corporation organized in Country N, a country that does not have an income tax treaty with the United States. FS is a special purpose subsidiary of FP that is incorporated in Country T, a country that has an income tax treaty with the United States that prohibits the imposition of withholding tax on payments of interest. FS is capitalized with $10,000,000 in debt from BK, a Country N bank, and $1,000,000 in capital from FS.

(ii) On May 1, 1995, C, a U.S. person, purchases an automobile from DS in return for an installment note. On July 1, 1995, DS sells a number of installment notes, including C's, to FS in exchange for $10,000,000. DS continues to service the installment notes for FS, and C is not notified of the sale of its obligation and continues to make payments to DS. But for the withholding tax on payments of interest by DS to BK, DS would have borrowed directly from BK, pledging the installment notes as collateral.

(iii) The C installment note is a financing transaction, whether held by DS or by FS, and the FS note held by BK also is a financing transaction. After FS purchases the installment note, and during the time the installment note is held by FS, the transactions constitute a financing arrangement, within the meaning of §1.881-3(a)(2)(i). BK is the financing entity, FS is the intermediate entity, and C is the financed entity. Because the participation of FS in the financing arrangement reduces the tax imposed by section 881 and because there was a tax avoidance plan, FS is a conduit entity.

(iv) Because C does not know or have reason to know of the tax avoidance plan (and by extension that the financing arrangement is a conduit financing arrangement), C is not required to withhold tax

under section 1441. However, DS, who knows that FS's participation in the financing arrangement is pursuant to a tax avoidance plan and is a withholding agent for purposes of section 1441, is not relieved of its withholding responsibilities.

*Example 2.* Assume the same facts as in *Example 1* except that C receives a new payment booklet on which DS is described as "agent." Although C may deduce that its installment note has been sold, without more C has no reason to know of the existence of a financing arrangement. Accordingly, C is not liable for failure to withhold, although DS still is not relieved of its withholding responsibilities.

*Example 3.* (i) DC is a U.S. corporation that is in the process of negotiating a loan of $10,000,000 from BK1, a bank located in Country N, a country that does not have an income tax treaty with the United States. Before the loan agreement is signed, DC's tax lawyers point out that interest on the loan would not be subject to withholding tax if the loan were made by BK2, a subsidiary of BK1 that is incorporated in Country T, a country that has an income tax treaty with the United States that prohibits the imposition of withholding tax on payments of interest. BK1 makes a loan to BK2 to enable BK2 to make the loan to DC. Without the loan from BK1 to BK2, BK2 would not have been able to make the loan to DC.

(ii) The loan from BK1 to BK2 and the loan from BK2 to DC are both financing transactions and together constitute a financing arrangement within the meaning of §1.881-3(a)(2)(i). BK1 is the financing entity, BK2 is the intermediate entity, and DC is the financed entity. Because the participation of BK2 in the financing arrangement reduces the tax imposed by section 881 and because there is a tax avoidance plan, BK2 is a conduit entity.

(iii) Because DC is a party to the tax avoidance plan (and accordingly knows of its existence), DC must withhold tax under section 1441. If DC does not withhold tax on its payment of interest, BK2, a party to the plan and a withholding agent for purposes of section 1441, must withhold tax as required by section 1441.

*Example 4.* (i) DC is a U.S. corporation that has a long-standing banking relationship with BK2, a U.S. subsidiary of BK1, a bank incorporated in Country N, a country that does not have an income tax treaty with the United States. DC has borrowed amounts of as much as $75,000,000 from BK2 in the past. On January 1, 1995, DC asks to borrow $50,000,000 from BK2. BK2 does not have the funds available to make a loan of that size. BK2 considers asking BK1 to enter into a loan with DC but rejects this possibility because of the additional withholding tax that would be incurred. Accordingly, BK2 borrows the necessary amount from BK1 with the intention of on-lending to DC. BK1 does not make the loan directly to DC because of the withholding tax that would apply to payments of interest from DC to BK1. DC does not negotiate with BK1 and has no reason to know that BK1 was the source of the loan.

(ii) The loan from BK2 to DC and the loan from BK1 to BK2 are both financing transactions and together constitute a financing arrangement within the meaning of §1.881-3(a)(2)(i). BK1 is the financing entity, BK2 is the intermediate entity, and DC is the financed entity. The participation of BK2 in the financing arrangement reduces the tax imposed by section 881. Because the participation of BK2 in the financing arrangement reduces the tax imposed by section 881 and because there was a tax avoidance plan, BK2 is a conduit entity.

(iii) Because DC does not know or have reason to know of the tax avoidance plan (and by extension that the financing arrangement is a conduit financing arrangement), DC is not required to withhold tax under section 1441. However, BK2, who is also a withholding agent under section 1441 and who knows that the financing arrangement is a conduit financing arrangement, is not relieved of its withholding responsibilities.

(g) *Effective/applicability date.*—Except as otherwise provided in paragraph (a)(4) of this section, this section applies to payments made on or after January 6, 2017. (For payments made after June 30, 2014, and before January 6, 2017, see this section as in effect and contained in 26 CFR part 1, as revised April 1, 2016. For payments made after December 31, 2000, and before July 1, 2014, see this section as in effect and contained in 26 CFR part 1, as revised April 1, 2013.) [Reg. §1.1441-7.]

☐ [T.D. 7977, 9-19-84. *Amended by* T.D. 8611, 8-10-95; T.D. 8734, 10-6-97; T.D. 8804, 12-30-98; T.D. 8856, 12-29-99; T.D. 8881, 5-15-2000 (*corrected* 4-5-2001); T.D. 9572, 1-19-2012 (*corrected* 3-7-2012); T.D. 9648, 12-4-2013, T.D. 9658, 2-28-2014, T.D. 9734, 9-17-2015, T.D. 9808, 12-30-2016, T.D. 9815, 1-19-2017 (*corrected* 10-25-2017) *and* T.D. 9890, 12-27-2019.]

**[Reg. §1.1441-8]**

**§1.1441-8. Exemption from withholding for payments to foreign governments, international organizations, foreign central banks of issue, and the Bank for International Settlements.**—(a) *Foreign governments.*—Under section 892, certain specific types of income received by foreign governments are excluded from gross income and are exempt from taxation, unless derived from the conduct of a commercial activity or received from or by a controlled commercial entity. Accordingly, withholding is not required under §1.1441-1 with regard to any item of income which is exempt from taxation under section 892.

(b) *Reliance on claim of exemption by foreign government.*—Absent actual knowledge or reason to know otherwise, the withholding agent may rely upon a claim of exemption made by the foreign government if, prior to the payment, the withholding agent can reliably associate the payment with documentation upon which it can rely to treat the payment as made to a beneficial owner in accordance with §1.1441-1(e)(1)(ii). A Form W-8 furnished by a foreign government for purposes of claiming an exemption under this paragraph (b) is valid only if, in addition to other applicable requirements, it certifies that the income is, or will be, exempt from taxation under section 892 and the regulations under that section and whether the person whose name is on the certificate is an integral part of a foreign government (as defined in §1.892-2T(a)(2)) or a controlled entity (as defined in §1.892-2T(a)(3)).

(c) *Income of a foreign central bank of issue or the Bank for International Settlements.*—(1) *Certain interest income.*—Section 895 provides for the exclusion from gross income of certain income derived by a foreign central bank of issue, or by the Bank for International Settlements, from obligations of the United States or of any agency or instrumentality thereof or from interest on deposits with persons carrying on the banking business if the bank is the owner of the obligations or deposits and does not hold the obligations or deposits for, or use them in connection with, the conduct of a commercial banking function or other commercial activity by such bank. See §1.895-1. Absent actual knowledge or reason to know that a foreign central bank of issue, or the Bank for International Settlements, is operating outside the scope of the exclusion granted by section 895 and the regulations under that section, the withholding agent may rely on a claim of exemption if, prior to the payment, the withholding agent can reliably associate the payment with documentation upon which it can rely to treat the foreign central bank of issue or the Bank for International Settlements as the beneficial owner of the payment in accordance with §1.1441-1(e)(1)(ii). A Form W-8 furnished by a foreign central bank of issue or the Bank for International Settlements for purposes of claiming an exemption under this paragraph (c)(1) is valid only if, in addition to other applicable requirements, it certifies that the person whose name is on the certificate is a foreign central bank of issue, or the Bank for International Settlements, and that the bank does not, and will not, hold the obligations or the bank deposits covered by the Form W-8 for, or use them in connection with, the conduct of a commercial banking function or other commercial activity.

(2) *Bankers' acceptances.*—Interest derived by a foreign central bank of issue from bankers' acceptances is exempt from tax under sections 871(i)(2)(C) and 881(d) and §1.861-2(b)(4). With respect to bankers' acceptances, a withholding agent may treat a payee as a foreign central bank of issue without requiring a withholding certificate if the name of the payee and other facts surrounding the payment reasonably indicate that the payee or beneficial owner is a foreign central bank of issue, as defined in §1.861-2(b)(4).

(d) *Exemption for payments to international organizations.*—A payment to an international organization (within the meaning of section 7701(a)(18)) is exempt from withholding on any payment. A withholding agent may treat a payee as an international organization without requiring a withholding certificate if the name of the payee is one that is designated as an international organization by executive order (pursuant to 22 U.S.C. 288 through 288(f)) and other facts surrounding the transaction reasonably indicate that the international organization is the beneficial owner of the payment.

(e) *Failure to receive withholding certificate timely and other applicable procedures.*—See applicable procedures described in §1.1441-1(b)(7) in the event the withholding agent does not hold a valid withholding certificate described in paragraph (b) or (c)(1) of this section or other appropriate documentation at the time of payment. Further, the provisions of §1.1441-1(e)(4) shall apply to withholding certificates and other documents related thereto furnished under the provisions of this section.

(f) *Effective date.*—(1) *In general.*—This section applies to payments made after December 31, 2000.

(2) *Transition rules.*—For purposes of this section, the validity of a Form 8709 that was valid on January 1, 1998, under the regulations in effect prior to January 1, 2001 (see 26 CFR part 1, revised April 1, 1999) and expired, or will expire, at any time during 1998, is extended until December 31, 1998. The validity of a Form 8709 that is valid on or after January 1, 1999, remains valid until its validity expires under the regulations in effect prior to January 1, 2001 (see 26 CFR part 1, revised April 1, 1999) but in no event shall such a form remain valid after December 31, 2000. The rule in this paragraph (f)(2), however, does not apply to extend the validity period of a Form 8709 that expires solely by reason of changes in the circumstances of the person whose name is on the certificate. Notwithstanding the first three sentences of this paragraph (f)(2), a withholding agent may choose to not take advantage of the transition rule in this paragraph (f)(2) with respect to one or more withholding certificates valid under the regulations in effect prior to January 1, 2001 (see 26 CFR part 1, revised April 1, 1999) and, therefore, to require withholding certificates conforming to the requirements described in this section (new withholding certificates). For purposes of this section, a new withholding certificate is deemed to satisfy the documentation requirement under the regulations in effect prior to January 1, 2001 (see 26 CFR part 1, revised April 1, 1999). Further, a new withholding certificate remains valid for the period specified in §1.1441-1(e)(4)(ii), regardless of when the certificate is obtained. [Reg. §1.1441-8.]

☐ *[T.D. 8211, 6-24-88. Redesignated and amended by T.D. 8734, 10-6-97 and amended by T.D. 8804, 12-30-98 and T.D. 8856, 12-29-99.]*

## [Reg. §1.1441-9]

**§1.1441-9. Exemption from withholding on exempt income of a foreign tax-exempt organization, including foreign private foundations.**—(a) *Exemption from withholding for exempt income.*—No withholding is required under section 1441(a) or 1442, and the regulations under those sections, on amounts paid to a foreign organization that is described in section 501(c) to the extent that the amounts are not income includible under section 512 in computing the organization's unrelated business taxable income. See, however, §1.1443-1 for withholding on payments of unrelated business income to foreign tax-exempt organizations and on payments subject to tax under section 4948. For a foreign organization to claim an exemption from withholding under section 1441(a) or 1442 based on its status as an organization described in section 501(c), it must furnish the withholding agent with a withholding certificate described in paragraph (b)(2) of this section. A foreign organization described in section 501(c) may choose to claim a reduced rate of withholding under the procedures described in other sections of the regulations under section 1441 and not under this section. In particular, if an organization chooses to claim benefits under an income tax treaty, the withholding procedures applicable to claims of such a reduced rate are governed solely by the provisions of §1.1441-6 and not of this section.

(b) *Reliance on foreign organization's claim of exemption from withholding.*—(1) *General rule.*—A withholding agent may rely on a claim of exemption under this section only if, prior to the payment, the withholding agent can reliably associate the payment with a valid withholding certificate described in paragraph (b)(2) of this section.

(2) *Withholding certificate.*—A withholding certificate under this paragraph (b)(2) is valid only if it is a Form W-8 and if, in addition to other applicable requirements, the Form W-8 includes the taxpayer identifying number of the organization whose name is on the certificate, and it certifies that the Internal Revenue Service (IRS) has issued a favorable determination letter (and the date thereof) that is currently in effect, what portion, if any, of the amounts paid constitute income includible under section 512 in computing the organization's unrelated business taxable income, and, if the organization is described in section 501(c)(3), whether it is a private foundation described in section 509. Notwithstanding the preceding sentence, if the organization cannot certify that it has been issued a favorable determination letter that is still in effect, its withholding certificate is nevertheless valid under this paragraph (b)(2) if the organization attaches to the withholding certificate an opinion that is acceptable to the withholding agent from a U.S. counsel (or any other person as the IRS may prescribe in published guidance (see §601.601(d)(2) of this chapter)) concluding that the organization is described in section 501(c). If the determination letter or opinion of counsel to which the withholding certificate refers concludes that the organization is described in section 501(c)(3), and the certificate further certifies that the organization is not a private foundation described in section 509, an affidavit of the organization setting forth sufficient facts concerning the operations and support of the organization for the Internal Revenue Service (IRS) to determine that such organization would be likely to qualify as an organization described in section 509(a)(1), (2), (3), or (4) must be attached to the withholding certificate. An organization that provides an opinion of U.S. counsel or an affidavit may provide the same opinion or affidavit to more than one withholding agent provided that the opinion is acceptable to each withholding agent who receives it in conjunction with a withholding certificate. Any such opinion of counsel or affidavit must be renewed whenever

there is a change in facts or circumstances that are relevant to determine the organization's status under section 501(c) or, if relevant, that the organization is or is not a private foundation described in section 509.

(3) *Presumptions in the absence of documentation.*—Notwithstanding paragraph (b)(1) of this section, if the organization's certification with respect to whether amounts paid constitute income includible under section 512 in computing the organization's unrelated business taxable income is not reliable or is lacking but all other certifications are reliable, the withholding agent may rely on the certificate but the amounts paid are presumed to be income includible under section 512 in computing the organization's unrelated business taxable income. If the certification regarding private foundation status is not reliable, the withholding agent may rely on the certificate but the amounts paid are presumed to be paid to a foreign beneficial owner that is a private foundation.

(4) *Reason to know.*—Reliance by a withholding agent on the information and certifications stated on a withholding certificate is subject to the agent's actual knowledge or reason to know that such information or certification is incorrect as provided in §1.1441-7(b). For example, a withholding agent must cease to treat a foreign organization's claim for exemption from withholding based on the organization's tax-exempt status as valid beginning on the earlier of the date on which such agent knows that the IRS has given notice to such foreign organization that it is not an organization described in section 501(c) or the date on which the IRS gives notice to the public that such foreign organization is not an organization described in section 501(c). Similarly, a withholding agent may no longer rely on a certification that an amount is not subject to tax under section 4948 beginning on the earlier of the date on which such agent knows that the IRS has given notice to such foreign organization that it is subject to tax under section 4948 or the date on which the IRS gives notice that such foreign organization is a private foundation within the meaning of section 509(a).

(c) *Failure to receive withholding certificate timely and other applicable procedures.*—See applicable procedures described in §1.1441-1(b)(7) in the event the withholding agent does not hold a valid withholding certificate or other appropriate documentation at the time of payment. Further, the provisions of §1.1441-1(e)(4) shall apply to withholding certificates and other documents related thereto furnished under the provisions of this section.

(d) *Effective date.*—(1) *In general.*—This section applies to payments made after December 31, 2000.

(2) *Transition rules.*—For purposes of this section, the validity of a Form W-8, 1001, or 4224 or a statement that was valid on January 1, 1998, under the regulations in effect prior to January 1, 2001 (see 26 CFR parts 1 and 35a, revised April 1, 1999) and expired, or will expire, at any time during 1998, is extended until December 31, 1998. The validity of a Form W-8, 1001, or 4224 or a statement that is valid on or after January 1, 1999 remains valid until its validity expires under the regulations in effect prior to January 1, 2001 (see 26 CFR parts 1 and 35a, revised April 1, 1999) but in no event shall such form or statement remain valid after December 31, 2000. The rule in this paragraph (d)(2), however, does not apply to extend the validity period of a Form W-8, 1001, or 4224 or a statement that expires solely by reason of changes in the circumstances of the person whose name is on the certificate. Notwithstanding the first three sentences of this paragraph (d)(2), a withholding agent may choose to not take advantage of the transition rule in this paragraph (d)(2) with respect to one or more withholding certificates valid under the regulations in effect prior to January 1, 2001 (see 26 CFR parts 1 and 35a, revised April 1, 1999) and, therefore, to require withholding certificates conforming to the requirements described in this section (new withholding certificates). For purposes of this section, a new withholding certificate is deemed to satisfy the documentation requirement under the regulations in effect prior to January 1, 2001 (see 26 CFR parts 1 and 35a, revised April 1, 1999). Further, a new withholding certificate remains valid for the period specified in §1.1441-1(e)(4)(ii), regardless of when the certificate is obtained. [Reg. §1.1441-9.]

□ [*T.D.* 8734, 10-6-97. *Amended by T.D.* 8804, 12-30-98; *T.D.* 8856, 12-29-99 *and T.D.* 8881, 5-15-2000.]

### [Reg. §1.1441-10]

**§1.1441-10. Withholding agents with respect to fast-pay arrangements.**—(a) *In general.*—A corporation that issues fast-pay stock in a fast-pay arrangement described in §1.7701(l)-3(b)(1) is a withholding agent with respect to payments made on the fast-pay stock and payments deemed made under the recharacterization rules of §1.7701(l)-3. Except as provided in this paragraph (a) or in paragraph

(b) of this section, the withholding tax rules under section 1441 and section 1442 apply with respect to a fast-pay arrangement described in §1.7701(l)-3(c)(1)(i) in accordance with the recharacterization rules provided in §1.7701(l)-3(c). In all cases, notwithstanding paragraph (b) of this section, if at any time the withholding agent knows or has reason to know that the Commissioner has exercised the discretion under either §1.7701(l)-3(c)(1)(ii) to apply the recharacterization rules of §1.7701(l)-3(c), or §1.7701(l)-3(d) to depart from the recharacterization rules of §1.7701(l)-3(c) for a taxpayer, the withholding agent must withhold on payments made (or deemed made) to that taxpayer in accordance with the characterization of the fast-pay arrangement imposed by the Commissioner under §1.7701(l)-3.

(b) *Exception.*—If at any time the withholding agent knows or has reason to know that any taxpayer entered into a fast-pay arrangement with a principal purpose of applying the recharacterization rules of §1.7701(l)-3(c) to avoid tax under section 871(a) or section 881, then for each payment made or deemed made to such taxpayer under the arrangement, the withholding agent must withhold, under section 1441 or section 1442, the higher of—

(1) The amount of withholding that would apply to such payment determined under the form of the arrangement; or

(2) The amount of withholding that would apply to deemed payments determined under the recharacterization rules of §1.7701(l)-3(c).

(c) *Liability.*—Any person required to deduct and withhold tax under this section is made liable for that tax by section 1461, and is also liable for applicable penalties and interest for failing to comply with section 1461.

(d) *Examples.*—The following examples illustrate the rules of this section:

*Example 1.* REIT W issues shares of fast-pay stock to foreign individual A, a resident of Country C. United States source dividends paid to residents of C are subject to a 30 percent withholding tax. W issues all shares of benefited stock to foreign individuals who are residents of Country D. D's income tax convention with the United States reduces the United States withholding tax on dividends to 15 percent. Under §1.7701(l)-3(c), the dividends paid by W to A are deemed to be paid by W to the benefited shareholders. W has reason to know that A entered into the fast-pay arrangement with a principal purpose of using the recharacterization rules of §1.7701(l)-3(c) to reduce United States withholding tax. W must withhold at the 30 percent rate because the amount of withholding that applies to the payments determined under the form of the arrangement is higher than the amount of withholding that applies to the payments determined under §1.7701(l)-3(c).

*Example 2.* The facts are the same as in *Example 1* of this paragraph (d) except that W does not know, or have reason to know, that A entered into the arrangement with a principal purpose of using the recharacterization rules of §1.7701(l)-3(c) to reduce United States withholding tax. Further, the Commissioner has not exercised the discretion under §1.7701(l)-3(d) to depart from the recharacterization rules of §1.7701(l)-3(c). Accordingly, W must withhold tax at a 15 percent rate on the dividends deemed paid to the benefited shareholders.

(e) *Effective date.*—This section applies to payments made (or deemed made) on or after January 6, 1999. [Reg. §1.1441-10.]

□ [*T.D.* 8853, 1-7-2000.]

### [Reg. §1.1442-1]

**§1.1442-1. Withholding of tax on foreign corporations.**—For regulations concerning the withholding of tax at source under section 1442 in the case of foreign corporations, foreign governments, international organizations, foreign tax-exempt corporations, or foreign private foundations, see §§1.1441-1 through 1.1441-9. [Reg. §1.1442-1.]

□ [*T.D.* 6187, 7-5-56. *Amended by T.D.* 6908, 12-30-66 *and T.D.* 8734, 10-6-97 (T.D. 8804 delayed the effective date of T.D. 8734 from January 1, 1999, to January 1, 2000; T.D. 8856 further delayed the effective date of T.D. 8734 until January 1, 2001).]

### [Reg. §1.1442-2]

**§1.1442-2. Exemption under a tax treaty.**—For regulations providing for a claim of reduced withholding tax under section 1442 by certain foreign corporations pursuant to the provisions of an income tax treaty, see §1.1441-6. [Reg. §1.1442-2.]

□ [*T.D.* 6908, 12-30-66. *Amended by T.D.* 8734, 10-6-97 (T.D. 8804 delayed the effective date of T.D. 8734 from January 1, 1999, to January 1, 2000; T.D. 8856 further delayed the effective date of T.D. 8734 until January 1, 2001).]

## [Reg. § 1.1442-3]

**§ 1.1442-3. Tax exempt income of a foreign tax-exempt corporation.**—For regulations providing for a claim of exemption for income exempt from tax under section 501(a) of a foreign tax-exempt corporation, see § 1.1441-9. See § 1.1443-1 for withholding rules applicable to foreign private foundations and to the unrelated business income of foreign tax-exempt organizations. [Reg. § 1.1442-3.]

☐ [*T.D. 8734,* 10-6-97 (T.D. 8804 delayed the effective date of T.D. 8734 from January 1, 1999, to January 1, 2000; T.D. 8856 further delayed the effective date of T.D. 8734 until January 1, 2001).]

## [Reg. § 1.1443-1]

**§ 1.1443-1. Foreign tax-exempt organizations.**—(a) *Income includible in computing unrelated business taxable income.*—In the case of a foreign organization that is described in section 501(c), amounts paid or effectively connected taxable income allocable to the organization that are includible under section 512 and section 513 in computing the organization's unrelated business taxable income are subject to withholding under § § 1.1441-1, 1.1441-4, 1.1441-6, and 1.1446-1 through 1.1446-6, in the same manner as payments or allocations of effectively connected taxable income of the same amounts made to any foreign person that is not a tax-exempt organization. Therefore, a foreign organization receiving amounts includible under section 512 and section 513 in computing the organization's unrelated business taxable income may claim an exemption from withholding or a reduced rate of withholding with respect to that income in the same manner as a foreign person that is not a tax-exempt organization. See § 1.1441-9(b)(3) for a presumption that amounts are includible under section 512 and section 513 in computing the organization's unrelated business taxable income in the absence of reliable certification. See also § 1.1446-3(c)(3), applying this presumption in the context of section 1446.

(b) *Income subject to tax under section 4948.*—(1) *In general.*—The gross investment income (as defined in section 4940(c)(2)) of a foreign private foundation is subject to withholding under section 1443(b) at the rate of 4 percent to the extent that the income is from sources within the United States and is subject to the tax imposed by section 4948(a) and the regulations under that section. Withholding under this paragraph (b) is required irrespective of the fact that the income may be effectively connected with the conduct of a trade or business in the United States by the foreign organization. See § 1.1441-9(b)(3) for applicable presumptions that amounts are subject to tax under section 4948. The withholding imposed under this paragraph (b)(1) does not obviate a private foundation's obligation to file any return required by law with respect to such organization, such as the form that the foundation is required to file under section 6033 for the taxable year.

(2) *Reliance on a foreign organization's claim of foreign private foundation status.*—For reliance by a withholding agent on a foreign organization's claim of foreign private foundation status, see § 1.1441-9(b) and (c).

(3) *Applicable procedures.*—A withholding agent withholding the 4-percent amount pursuant to paragraph (b)(1) of this section shall treat such withholding as withholding under section 1441(a) or 1442(a) for all purposes, including reporting of the payment on a Form 1042 and a Form 1042-S pursuant to § 1.1461-1(b) and (c). Similarly, the foreign private foundation shall treat the 4-percent withholding as withholding under section 1441(a) or 1442(a), including for purposes of claims for refunds and credits.

(4) *Claim of benefits under an income tax treaty.*—The withholding procedures applicable to claims of a reduced rate under an income tax treaty are governed solely by the provisions of § 1.1441-6 and not by this section.

(c) *Effective date.*—(1) *In general.*—This section applies to payments made after December 31, 2000, except that the references in paragraph (a) of this section to effectively connected taxable income and withholding under section 1446 shall apply to partnership taxable years beginning after May 18, 2005, or such earlier time as the regulations under § § 1.1446-1 through 1.1446-5 apply by reason of an election under § 1.1446-7.

(2) *Transition rules.*—For purposes of this section, the validity of an affidavit or opinion of counsel described in § 1.1443-1(b)(4)(i) in effect prior to January 1, 2001 (see § 1.1443-1(b)(4)(i) as contained in 26 CFR part 1, revised April 1, 1999) is extended until December 31, 2000. However, a withholding agent may chose to not take advantage of the transition rule in this paragraph (c)(2) with respect to one or more withholding certificates valid under the regulations in effect prior to January 1, 2001 (see CFR part 1, revised April 1, 1999) and, therefore, to require withholding certificates conforming to the requirements described in this section (new withholding certificates).

For purposes of this section, a new withholding certificate is deemed to satisfy the documentation requirement under the regulations in effect prior to January 1, 2001 (see 26 CFR part 1, revised April 1, 1999). Further, a new withholding certificate remains valid for the period specified in § 1.1441-1(e)(4)(ii), regardless of when the certificate is obtained. [Reg. § 1.1443-1.]

☐ [*T.D. 6187,* 7-5-56. *Amended by T.D. 6908,* 12-30-66; *T.D. 7229,* 12-20-72; *T.D. 7247,* 12-29-72; *T.D. 8734,* 10-6-97; *T.D. 8804,* 12-30-98; *T.D. 8856,* 12-29-99; *T.D. 9200,* 5-13-2005 *and T.D. 9394,* 4-28-2008.]

## [Reg. § 1.1445-1]

**§ 1.1445-1. Withholding on dispositions of U.S. real property interests by foreign persons: In general.**—(a) *Purpose and scope of regulations.*—These regulations set forth rules relating to the withholding requirements of section 1445. In general, section 1445(a) provides that any person who acquires a U.S. real property interest from a foreign person must withhold a tax of 15 percent (10 percent in the case of dispositions described in paragraph (b)(2) of this section) from the amount realized by the transferor foreign person (or a lesser amount established by agreement with the Internal Revenue Service). Section 1445(e) provides special rules requiring withholding on distributions and certain other transactions by corporations, partnerships, trusts, and estates. This § 1.1445-1 provides general rules concerning the withholding requirement of section 1445(a), as well as definitions applicable under both sections 1445(a) and 1445(e). Section 1.1445-2 provides for various situations in which withholding is not required under section 1445(a). Section 1.1445-3 provides for adjustments to the amount required to be withheld by transferees under section 1445(a). Section 1.1445-4 prescribes the duties of agents in transactions subject to withholding under either section 1445(a) or 1445(e). Section 1.1445-5 provides rules concerning the withholding required under section 1445(e), while § 1.1445-6 provides for adjustments to the amount required to be withheld under section 1445(e). Finally, § 1.1445-7 provides rules concerning the treatment of a foreign corporation that has made an election under section 897(i) to be treated as a domestic corporation.

(b) *Duty to withhold.*—(1) *In general.*—Except as provided in paragraph (b)(2) and § § 1.1445-2 and 1.1445-3, transferees of U.S. real property interests are required to deduct and withhold a tax equal to 15 percent of the amount realized by the transferor if the transferor is a foreign person. Neither the transferee's duty to withhold nor the amount required to be withheld is affected by the amount of cash to be paid by the transferee. Amounts withheld must be reported and paid over in accordance with the requirements of paragraph (c) of this section. Failures to withhold and pay over are subject to the liabilities set forth in paragraph (e) of this section. If two or more persons are joint transferees of a U.S. real property interest, each such person is subject to the obligation to withhold. That obligation is fulfilled with respect to each such person if any one of them withholds and pays over the required amount in accordance with the rules of this section. If the amount realized (as defined in paragraph (g)(5) of this section) by the transferor is zero, then no withholding is required. For example, if a real property interest is transferred as a gift (i.e., the recipient does not assume any liabilities or furnish any other consideration to the transferor) then no withholding is required.

(2) *Reduced rate for certain residences.*—Transferees of U.S. real property interests are required to deduct and withhold a tax equal to 10 percent of the amount realized by the transferor if the transferor is a foreign person and the following requirements are satisfied:

(i) the property is acquired by the transferee for use by the transferee as a residence;

(ii) the amount realized for the property does not exceed $1,000,000; and

(iii) section 1445(b)(5) does not apply to the disposition. See § 1.1445-2(d)(1).

(3) *U.S. real property interest owned jointly by foreign and non-foreign transferors.*—The amount subject to withholding under paragraph (b)(1) of this section with respect to the transfer of a U.S. real property interest owned by one or more foreign persons (as defined in § 1.897-1(k)) and one or more non-foreign persons shall be determined by allocating the amount realized from the transfer between (or among) such transferors based upon the capital contribution of each transferor with respect to the property and by aggregating the amounts allocated to any foreign person (or persons). For this purpose, a husband and wife will each be deemed to have contributed 50 percent of the aggregate capital contributed by such husband and wife. See § 1.1445-1(f)(3)(iv) with respect to the crediting of the amount withheld between or among joint foreign transferors.

(4) *Options to acquire a U.S. real property interest.*—(i) *No withholding on grant of option.*—No withholding is required under section 1445

with respect to any amount realized by the grantor on the grant of an option to acquire a U.S. real property interest.

(ii) *No withholding upon lapse of option.*—No withholding is required under section 1445 with respect to any amount realized by the grantor upon the lapse of an option to acquire a U.S. real property interest.

(iii) *Withholding required upon the sale or exchange of option.*—A transferee of an option to acquire a U.S. real property interest must deduct and withhold a tax equal to 15 percent of the amount realized by the transferor upon the disposition. This paragraph (b)(4)(iii) does not apply to require withholding upon the initial grant of an option.

(iv) *Withholding required on exercise of option.*—If the holder exercises an option to purchase a U.S. real property interest, the amount paid for the option shall be considered an amount realized by the grantor/transferor upon the transfer of the property with respect to which the option was granted, and shall thus be subject to withholding on the day that such underlying property is transferred. The preceding sentence applies regardless of whether or not the terms of the option specifically provide that the option price is applied to the purchase price.

(5) *Exceptions and modifications.*—The duty to withhold under section 1445(a) is subject to the exceptions and modifications contained in §§ 1.1445-2 and 1.1445-3. Generally, § 1.1445-2 provides rules for determining that withholding is not required because either the transferor is not a foreign person or the interest transferred is not a U.S. real property interest. In addition, § 1.1445-2 provides exceptions to the withholding requirement, including a rule that exempts from withholding any person who acquires a U.S. real property interest for use as a residence for a contract price of $300,000 or less. If withholding is required under section 1445(a), § 1.1445-3 allows the amount withheld to be modified pursuant to a withholding certificate issued by the Internal Revenue Service. If a transferee cannot withhold the full amount required because the first payment of consideration for the transfer does not involve sufficient cash (or other liquid assets convertible into cash, such as foreign currency), then a withholding certificate must be obtained pursuant to § 1.1445-3.

(c) *Reporting and paying over of withheld amounts.*—(1) *In general.*—A transferee must report and pay over any tax withheld by the 20th day after the date of the transfer. Forms 8288 and 8288-A are used for this purpose, and must be filed at the location as provided in the instructions to Forms 8288 and 8288-A. Pursuant to section 7502 and regulations thereunder, the timely mailing of Forms 8288 and 8288-A will be treated as their timely filing. Form 8288-A will be stamped by the IRS to show receipt, and a stamped copy will be mailed by the IRS to the transferor (at the address reported on the form) for the transferor's use. See §§ 1.1445-1(f) and 1.1445-3(f). Forms 8288 and 8288-A are required to include the identifying numbers of both the transferor and the transferee, as provided in paragraph (d) of this section. If any identifying number as required by such forms is not provided, the transferee must still report and pay over any tax withheld on Form 8288, although the transferor cannot obtain a credit or refund of tax on the basis of a Form 8288-A that does not include the transferor's identifying number (see paragraph (f)(2) of this section).

(2) *Pending application for withholding certificate.*—(i) *In general.*—(A) *Delayed reporting and payment with respect to application submitted by transferee.*—If an application for a withholding certificate with respect to a transfer of a U.S. real property interest is submitted to the Internal Revenue Service by the transferee on the day of or at any time prior to the transfer, the transferee must withhold 15 percent (10 percent in the case of dispositions described in paragraph (b)(2) of this section) of the amount realized as required by paragraph (b) of this section. However, the amount withheld, or a lesser amount as determined by the Service, need not be reported and paid over to the Service until the 20th day following the Service's final determination with respect to the application for a withholding certificate. For this purpose, the Service's final determination occurs on the day when the withholding certificate is mailed to the transferee by the Service or when a notification denying the request for a withholding certificate is mailed to the transferee by the Service. An application is submitted to the Service on the day it is actually received by the Service at the address provided in § 1.1445-1(g)(10) or, under the rules of section 7502, on the day it is mailed to the Service at the address provided in § 1.1445-1(g)(10).

(B) *Delayed reporting and payment with respect to application submitted by transferor.*—If an application for a withholding certificate with respect to a transfer of a U.S. real property interest is submitted to the Internal Revenue Service by the transferor on the day of or any time prior to the transfer, such transferor must provide notice to the

transferee prior to the transfer. No particular form is required but the notice must set forth the name, address, and taxpayer identification number of the transferor, a brief description of the property which is the subject of the application, and the date the application was submitted to the Service. The transferee must withhold 15 percent (10 percent in the case of dispositions described in paragraph (b)(2) of this section) of the amount realized as required in paragraph (b) of this section but need not report or pay over to the Service such amount (or a lesser amount as determined by the Service) until the 20th day following the Service's final determination with respect to the application. The Service will send a copy of the withholding certificate or copy of the notification denying the request for a withholding certificate to the transferee. For this purpose, the Service's final determination will be deemed to occur on the day when the copy of the withholding certificate or the copy of the notification denying the request for a withholding certificate is mailed by the Service to the transferee (or transferees). An application is submitted to the Service on the day it is actually received by the Service at the address provided in § 1.1445-1(g)(10) or, under the rules of § 7502, on the day it is mailed to the Service at the address provided in § 1.1445-1(g)(10).

(ii) *Anti-abuse rule.*—(A) *In general.*—A transferee that in reliance upon the rules of this paragraph (c)(2) fails to report and pay over amounts withheld by the 20th day following the date of the transfer, shall be subject to the payment of interest and penalties if the relevant application for a withholding certificate (or an amendment to the application for a withholding certificate) was submitted for a principal purpose of delaying the transferee's payment to the IRS of the amount withheld. Interest and penalties shall be assessed on the amount that is ultimately paid over (or collected pursuant to the agreement) with respect to the period between the 20th day after the date of the transfer and the date on which payment is made (or collected).

(B) *Presumption.*—A principal purpose of delaying payment of the amount withheld shall be presumed if—

(1) The transferee applies for a withholding certificate pursuant to § 1.1445-3(c) based on a determination of the transferor's maximum tax liability, and

(2) Such liability is ultimately determined to be equal to 90 percent or more of the amount that was otherwise required to be withheld and paid over.

However, the presumption created by the previous sentence may be rebutted by evidence establishing that delaying payment of the amount withheld was not a principal purpose of the transaction.

(d) *Contents of Forms 8288 and 8288-A.*—(1) *Transactions subject to section 1445(a).*—Any person that is required to file Forms 8288 and 8288-A pursuant to section 1445(a) and the rules of this section must set forth thereon the following information:

(i) The name, identifying number, and home address (in the case of an individual) or office address (in the case of any entity) of the transferee(s) filing the return;

(ii) The name, identifying number, and home address (in the case of an individual) or office address (in the case of any entity) of the transferor(s);

(iii) A brief description of the U.S. real property interest transferred, including its location and the nature of any substantial improvements in the case of real property, and the class or type and amount of interests transferred in the case of interests in a corporation that constitute U.S. real property interests;

(iv) The date of the transfer;

(v) The amount realized by the transferor, as defined in paragraph (g)(5) of this section;

(vi) The amount withheld by the transferee and whether withholding is at the statutory or reduced rate; and

(vii) Such other information as the Commissioner may require.

For purposes of paragraph (d)(1)(i) and (ii), mailing addresses may be provided in addition to, but not in lieu of, home addresses or office addresses.

(2) *Transactions subject to section 1445(e).*—Any person that is required to file Forms 8288 and 8288-A pursuant to the rules of § 1.1445-5 must set forth thereon the following information:

(i) The name, identifying number, and office address of the entity or fiduciary filing the return;

(ii) The amount withheld by the entity or fiduciary;

(iii) The date of the transfer;

(iv) In the case of a transaction subject to withholding pursuant to section 1445(e)(1) and § 1.1445-5(c):

(A) A brief description of the U.S. real property interest transferred, as described in paragraph (d)(1)(iii) of this section;

(B) The name, identifying number, and home address (in the case of an individual) or office address (in the case of an entity) of each holder of an interest in the entity that is a foreign person; and

(C) Each such interest-holder's pro rata share of the amount withheld;

(v) In the case of a distribution subject to withholding pursuant to section 1445(e)(2) and § 1.1445-5(d):

(A) A brief description of the U.S. real property interest transferred, as described in paragraph (d)(1)(iii) of this section; and

(B) The amount of gain recognized upon the distribution by the corporation.

(vi) In the case of a distribution subject to withholding pursuant to section 1445(e)(3) and § 1.1445-5(e):

(A) A brief description of the property distributed by the corporation;

(B) The name, identifying number, and home address (in the case of an individual) or office address (in the case of an entity) of each holder of an interest in the entity that is a foreign person;

(C) The amount realized upon the distribution by each such foreign interest holder; and

(D) Each foreign interest-holder's pro rata share of the amount withheld; and

(vii) Such other information as the Commissioner may require.

(e) *Liability of transferee upon failure to withhold.*—(1) *In general.*—Every person required to deduct and withhold tax under section 1445 is made liable for that tax by section 1461. Therefore, a person that is required to deduct and withhold tax but fails to do so may be held liable for the payment of the tax and any applicable penalties and interest.

(2) *Transferor's liability not otherwise satisfied.*—(i) *Tax and penalties.*—Except as provided in paragraph (e)(3) of this section, if a transferee is required to deduct and withhold tax under section 1445 but fails to do so, then the tax shall be assessed against and collected from that transferee. Such person may also be subject to any of the civil and criminal penalties that apply. Corporate officers or other responsible persons may be subject to a civil penalty under section 6672 equal to the amount that should have been withheld and paid over.

(ii) *Interest.*—If a transferee is required to deduct and withhold tax under section 1445 but fails to do so, then such transferee shall be liable for the payment of interest pursuant to section 6601 and the regulations thereunder. Interest shall be payable with respect to the period between—

(A) The last date on which the tax imposed under section 1445 was required to be paid over by the transferee, and

(B) The date on which such tax is actually paid. Interest shall be payable with respect to the entire amount that is required to be deducted and withheld. However, if the Service issues a withholding certificate providing for withholding of a reduced amount, then, for the period after the issuance of the certificate, interest shall be payable with respect to that reduced amount.

(3) *Transferor's liability otherwise satisfied.*—(i) *Tax and penalties.*—If a transferee is required to deduct and withhold tax under section 1445 but fails to do so, and the transferor's tax liability with respect to the transfer was satisfied (or was established to be zero) by—

(A) The transferor's filing of an income tax return (and payment of any tax due) with respect to the transfer, or

(B) The issuance of a withholding certificate by the Internal Revenue Service establishing that the transferor's maximum tax liability is zero,

then the tax required to be withheld under section 1445 shall not be collected from the transferee. Such transferee's liability for tax, and the requirement that such person file Forms 8288 and 8288-A, shall be deemed to have been satisfied as of the date on which the transferor's income tax return was filed or the withholding certificate was issued. No penalty shall be imposed on or collected from such person for failure to return or pay the tax, unless such failure was fraudulent and for the purpose of evading payment. A transferee that seeks to avoid liability for tax and penalties pursuant to the rule of paragraph (e)(3)(i) must provide sufficient information for the Service to determine whether the transferor's tax liability was satisfied (or was established to be zero).

(ii) *Interest.*—If a transferee is required to deduct and withhold tax under section 1445 but fails to do so, then such person shall be liable for the payment of interest under section 6601 and regulations thereunder. Such transferee's liability for the payment of interest shall not be excused by reason of the deemed satisfaction, pursuant to subdivision (i) of this paragraph (e)(3), of the transferee's liability under section 1445, because the deemed satisfaction of that liability is the equivalent of the late payment of a liability, on which

interest must be paid. Interest shall be payable with respect to the period between—

(A) The last date on which the tax imposed under section 1445 was required to be paid over, and

(B) The date (established from information supplied to the Service by the transferee) on which any tax due is paid with respect to the transferor's relevant income tax return, or the date the withholding certificate is issued establishing that the transferor's maximum tax liability is zero.

Interest shall be payable with respect to the entire amount that is required to be deducted and withheld. However, if the Service issues a withholding certificate providing for withholding of a reduced amount, then for the period after the issuance of the certificate interest shall be payable with respect to that reduced amount.

(4) *Coordination with entity withholding rules.*—For purposes of section 1445(e) and §§ 1.1445-5, 1.1445-6, 1.1445-7, and 1.1445-8T, the rules of this paragraph (e) shall be applied by—

(i) Substituting the words "person required to withhold" for the word "transferee" each place it appears in this paragraph (e), and

(ii) Substituting the words "person subject to withholding" for the word "transferor" each place it appears in this paragraph (e).

(f) *Effect of withholding on transferor.*—(1) *In general.*—The withholding of tax under section 1445(a) does not excuse a foreign person that disposes of a U.S. real property interest from filing a U.S. tax return with respect to the income arising from the disposition. Form 1040NR, 1041, or 1120F, as appropriate, must be filed, and any tax due must be paid, by the filing deadline generally applicable to such person. (The return may be filed by such later date as is provided in an extension granted by the Internal Revenue Service.) Any tax withheld under section 1445(a) shall be credited against the amount of income tax as computed in such return.

(2) *Manner of obtaining credit or refund.*—A stamped copy of Form 8288-A will be provided to the transferor by the Service (under paragraph (c) of this section) if the Form 8288-A is complete, including the transferor's identifying number. Except as provided in paragraph (f)(3) of this section, a stamped copy of Form 8288-A must be attached to the transferor's return to establish the amount withheld that is available as a credit. If the amount withheld under section 1445(a) constitutes less than the full amount of the transferor's U.S. tax liability for that taxable year, then a payment of estimated tax may be required to be made pursuant to section 6154 or 6654 prior to the filing of the income tax return for that year. Alternatively, if the amount withheld under section 1445(a) exceeds the transferor's maximum tax liability with respect to the disposition (as determined by the IRS), then the transferor may seek an early refund of the excess pursuant to § 1.1445-3T(g), or a normal refund upon filing of a tax return.

(3) *Special rules.*—(i) *Failure to receive Form 8288-A.*—If a stamped copy of Form 8288-A has not been provided to the transferor by the Service, the transferor may establish the amount of tax withheld by the transferee by attaching to its return substantial evidence (*e.g.,* closing documents) of such amount. Such a transferor must attach to its return a statement which supplies all of the information required by § 1.1445-1(d), including the transferor's identifying number.

(ii) *U.S. persons subjected to withholding.*—If a transferee withholds tax under section 1445(a) with respect to a person who is not a foreign person, such person may credit the amount of any tax withheld against his income tax liability in accordance with the provisions of this § 1.1445-1(f) or apply for an early refund under § 1.1445-3(g).

(iii) *Refund in case of installment sale.*—A transferor that takes gain into account in accordance with the provisions of section 453 shall not be entitled to a refund of the amount withheld, unless a withholding certificate providing for such a refund is obtained from the Internal Revenue Service pursuant to the provisions of § 1.1445-3.

(iv) *Joint foreign transferors.*—If two or more foreign persons jointly transfer a U.S. real property interest, each transferor shall be credited with such portion of the amount withheld as such transferors mutually agree. Such transferors must request that the transferee reflect the agreed-upon crediting of the amount withheld on the Forms 8288-A filed by the transferee. If the foreign transferors fail to request that the transferee reflect the agreed-upon crediting of the amount withheld by the 10th day after the date of transfer, the transferee must credit the amount withheld equally between (or among) the foreign transferors. In such case, the transferee is indemnified pursuant to section 1461 against any claim by a transferor objecting to the resulting division of credits. For rules regarding the amount realized allocated to joint foreign and non-foreign transferors, see § 1.1445-1(b)(2).

(g) *Definitions.*—(1) *In general.*—Unless otherwise specified, the definitions of terms provided in §1.897-1 shall apply for purposes of this section and §§1.1445-2 through 1.1445-7. For purposes of section 1445 and the regulations thereunder, definitions of other relevant terms are provided in this paragraph (g). In addition, the term "residence" is defined in §1.1445-2(d)(1), the terms "transferor's agent" and "transferee's agent" are defined in §1.1445-4(f), and the term "relevant taxpayer" is defined in §1.1445-6(a)(2).

(2) *Transfer.*—The term "transfer" means any transaction that would constitute a disposition for any purpose of the Internal Revenue Code and regulations thereunder. For purposes of §§1.1445-5 and 1.1445-6, the term includes distributions to shareholders of a corporation, partners of a partnership, and beneficiaries of a trust or estate.

(3) *Transferor.*—The term "transferor" means any person, foreign or domestic, that disposes of a U.S. real property interest by sale, exchange, gift or any other transfer. The term "U.S. real property interest" is defined in §1.897-1(c).

(4) *Transferee.*—The term "transferee" means any person, foreign or domestic, that acquires a U.S. real property interest by purchase, exchange, gift, or any other transfer.

(5) *Amount realized.*—The amount realized by the transferor for the transfer of a U.S. real property interest is the sum of:

(i) The cash paid, or to be paid,

(ii) The fair market value of other property transferred, or to be transferred, and

(iii) The outstanding amount of any liability assumed by the transferee or to which the U.S. real property interest is subject immediately before and after the transfer. The term "cash paid or to be paid" does not include stated or unstated interest or original issue discount (as determined under the rules of sections 1271 through 1275).

(6) *Contract price.*—The contract price of a U.S. real property interest is the sum that is agreed to by the transferee and transferor as the total amount of consideration to be paid for the property. That amount will generally be equal to the amount realized by the transferor, as defined in paragraph (b)(5) of this section.

(7) *Fair market value.*—The fair market value of property means the price at which the property would change hands between an unrelated willing buyer and willing seller, neither being under any compulsion to buy or to sell and both having reasonable knowledge of all relevant facts.

(8) *Date of transfer.*—The date of transfer of a U.S. real property interest is the first date on which consideration is paid (or a liability assumed) by the transferee. However, for purposes of section 1445(e)(2), (3), and (4) and §1.1445-5(c)(1)(iii) and 1.1445-5(c)(3) only, the date of transfer is the date of the distribution that gives rise to the obligation to withhold. For purposes of this paragraph (g)(8), the payment of consideration does not include the payment, prior to the passage of legal or equitable title (other than pursuant to an initial contract for purchase), of earnest money, a good-faith deposit, or any similar sum that is primarily intended to bind the transferee or transferor to the entering or performance of a contract. Such a payment will not constitute a payment of consideration solely because it may ultimately be applied against the amount owed to the transferor by the transferee. Such a payment is presumed to be earnest money, a good faith deposit, or a similar sum if it is subject to forfeiture in the event of a failure to enter into a contract or a breach of contract. However, a payment that is not forfeitable may nevertheless be found to constitute earnest money, a good faith deposit, or a similar sum.

(9) *Identifying number.*—Pursuant to §1.897-1(p), an individual's identifying number is the social security number or the identification number assigned by the Internal Revenue Service (see §301.6109-1 of this chapter). The identifying number of any other person is its United States employer identification number.

(10) *Address for correspondence.*—Any written communication to the Internal Revenue Service described in this section is to be mailed to the address specified in the Instructions for Form 8288 under the heading "Where To File."

(h) *Applicability dates.*—The requirement in paragraphs (c)(2)(i)(B), (d)(1)(i) and (ii), (d)(2)(i), (d)(2)(iv)(B), and (d)(2)(vi)(B) of this section that taxpayer identification numbers be provided (in all cases) is applicable for dispositions of U.S. real property interests occurring after November 3, 2003. The withholding rates set forth in paragraphs (a), (b)(1), (b)(2), (b)(4)(iii), (c)(2)(i)(A), and (c)(2)(i)(B) of this section apply to dispositions after February 16, 2016. For dispositions on or before February 16, 2016, see paragraphs (a), (b)(1),

(b)(3)(iii), (c)(2)(i)(A), and (c)(2)(i)(B) of this section as contained in 26 CFR part 1 revised as of April 1, 2015. [Reg. §1.1445-1.]

☐ [*T.D. 8113*, 12-18-86. *Amended by T.D. 8647*, 12-20-95 *T.D. 9082*, 8-4-2003 *and T.D. 9751*, 2-17-2016.]

## [Reg. §1.1445-2]

**§1.1445-2. Situations in which withholding is not required under section 1445(a).**—(a) *Purpose and scope of section.*—This section provides rules concerning various situations in which withholding is not required under section 1445(a). In general, a transferee has a duty to withhold under section 1445(a) only if both of the following are true:

(1) The transferor is a foreign person; and

(2) The transferee is acquiring a U.S. real property interest.

Thus, paragraphs (b) and (c) of this section provide rules under which a transferee of property can ascertain that he has no duty to withhold because one or the other of the two key elements is missing. Under paragraph (b), a transferee may determine that no withholding is required because the transferor is not a foreign person. Under paragraph (c), a transferee may determine that no withholding is required because the property acquired is not a U.S. real property interest. Finally, paragraph (d) of this section provides rules concerning exceptions to the withholding requirement.

(b) *Transferor not a foreign person.*—(1) *In general.*—No withholding is required under section 1445 if the transferor of a U.S. real property interest is not a foreign person. Therefore, paragraph (b)(2) of this section provides rules pursuant to which the transferor can provide a certification of non-foreign status to inform the transferee that withholding is not required. A transferee that obtains such a certification must retain that document for five years, as provided in paragraph (b)(3) of this section. Except to the extent provided in paragraph (b)(4) of this section, the obtaining of this certification excuses the transferee from any liability otherwise imposed by section 1445 and §1.1445-1(e). However, section 1445 and the rules of this section do not impose any obligation upon a transferee to obtain a certification from the transferor; thus, a transferee may instead rely upon other means to ascertain the non-foreign status of the transferor. If, however, the transferee relies upon other means and the transferor was, in fact, a foreign person, then the transferee is subject to the liability imposed by section 1445 and §1.1445-1(e).

A transferee is in no event required to rely upon other means to ascertain the non-foreign status of the transferor and may demand a certification of non-foreign status. If the certification is not provided, the transferee may withhold tax under section 1445 and will be considered, for purposes of sections 1461 through 1463, to have been required to withhold such tax.

(2) *Transferor's certification of non-foreign status.*—(i) *In general.*—A transferee of a U.S. real property interest is not required to withhold under section 1445(a) if, prior to or at the time of the transfer, the transferor furnishes to the transferee a certification that—

(A) States that the transferor is not a foreign person,

(B) Sets forth the transferor's name, identifying number and home address (in the case of an individual) or office address (in the case of an entity), and

(C) Is signed under penalties of perjury.

In general, a foreign person is a nonresident alien individual, foreign corporation, foreign partnership, foreign trust, or foreign estate, but not a qualified foreign pension fund (as defined in section 897(l)) or an entity all of the interests of which are held by a qualified foreign pension fund. In this regard, see §1.897-1(k). However, a foreign corporation that has made a valid election under section 897(i) is generally not treated as a foreign person for purposes of section 1445. In this regard, see §1.1445-7. Pursuant to §1.897-1(p), an individual's identifying number is the individual's Social Security number and any other person's identifying number is its U.S. employer identification number. A certification pursuant to this paragraph (b) must be verified as true and signed under penalties of perjury by a responsible officer in the case of a corporation, by a general partner in the case of a partnership, and by a trustee, executor, or equivalent fiduciary in the case of a trust or estate. No particular form is needed for a certification pursuant to this paragraph (b), nor is any particular language required, so long as the document meets the requirements of this paragraph (b)(2)(i). Samples of acceptable certifications are provided in paragraph (b)(2)(iii) of this section.

(ii) *Foreign corporation that has made election under section 897(i).*—A foreign corporation that has made a valid election under section 897(i) to be treated as a domestic corporation for purposes of section 897 may provide a certification of non-foreign status pursuant to this paragraph (b)(2). However, an electing foreign corporation must attach to such certification a copy of the acknowledgement of the election provided to the corporation by the Internal Revenue Service pursuant to §1.897-3(d)(4). An acknowledgement is valid for this purpose only if it states that the information required by § 1.897-3 has been determined to be complete.

(iii) *Disregarded entities.*—A disregarded entity may not certify that it is the transferor of a U.S. real property interest, as the disregarded entity is not the transferor for U.S. tax purposes, including sections 897 and 1445. Rather, the owner of the disregarded entity is treated as the transferor of property and must provide a certificate of non-foreign status to avoid withholding under section 1445. A disregarded entity for these purposes means an entity that is disregarded as an entity separate from its owner under § 301.7701-3 of this chapter, a qualified REIT subsidiary as defined in section 856(i), or a qualified subchapter S subsidiary under section 1361(b)(3)(B). Any domestic entity must include in its certification of non-foreign status with respect to the transfer a certification that it is not a disregarded entity. This paragraph (b)(2)(iii) and the sample certification provided in paragraph (b)(2)(iv)(B) of this section (to the extent it addresses disregarded entities) is applicable for dispositions occurring [after]September 4, 2003.

(iv) *Sample certifications.*—(A) *Individual transferor.*—"Section 1445 of the Internal Revenue Code provides that a transferee (buyer) of a U.S. real property interest must withhold tax if the transferor (seller) is a foreign person. To inform the transferee (buyer) that withholding of tax is not required upon my disposition of a U.S. real property interest, I, [*name of transferor*], hereby certify the following:

1. I am not a nonresident alien for purposes of U.S. income taxation;

2. My U.S. taxpayer identifying number (Social Security number) is _____; and

3. My home address is

_____

I understand that this certification may be disclosed to the Internal Revenue Service by the transferee and that any false statement I have made here could be punished by fine, imprisonment, or both.

Under penalties of perjury I declare that I have examined this certification and to the best of my knowledge and belief it is true, correct, and complete.
[Signature and Date]"

(B) *Entity transferor.*—"Section 1445 of the Internal Revenue Code provides that a transferee of a U.S. real property interest must withhold tax if the transferor is a foreign person. For U.S. tax purposes (including section 1445), the owner of a disregarded entity (which has legal title to a U.S. real property interest under local law) will be the transferor of the property and not the disregarded entity. To inform the transferee that withholding of tax is not required upon the disposition of a U.S. real property interest by [name of transferor], the undersigned hereby certifies the following on behalf of [name of the transferor]:

1. [Name of transferor] is not a foreign corporation, foreign partnership, foreign trust, or foreign estate (as those terms are defined in the Internal Revenue Code and Income Tax Regulations);

2. [Name of transferor] is not a disregarded entity as defined in § 1.1445-2(b)(2)(iii);

3. [Name of transferor]'s U.S. employer identification number is _____; and

4. [Name of transferor]'s office address is _____

[Name of transferor] understands that this certification may be disclosed to the Internal Revenue Service by transferee and that any false statement contained herein could be punished by fine, imprisonment, or both.

Under penalties of perjury I declare that I have examined this certification and to the best of my knowledge and belief it is true, correct, and complete, and I further declare that I have authority to sign this document on behalf of [name of transferor].
[Signature(s) and date]
[Title(s)]"

(v) *Form W-9.*—For purposes of paragraph (b)(2)(i) of this section, a certification of non-foreign status includes a valid Form W-9, *Request for Taxpayer Identification Number and Certification*, or its successor, submitted to the transferee by the transferor.

(3) *Transferee must retain certification.*—If a transferee obtains a transferor's certification pursuant to the rules of this paragraph (b), then the transferee must retain that certification until the end of the fifth taxable year following the taxable year in which the transfer takes place. The transferee must retain the certification, and make it available to the Internal Revenue Service when requested in accordance with the requirements of section 6001 and regulations thereunder.

(4) *Reliance upon certification not permitted.*—(i) *In general.*—A transferee may not rely upon a transferor's certification pursuant to this paragraph (b) under the circumstances set forth in either subdivision (ii) or (iii) of this paragraph (b)(4). In either of those circumstances, a transferee's withholding obligation shall apply as if a certification had never been obtained, and the transferee is fully liable pursuant to section 1445 and § 1445-1(e) for any failure to withhold.

(ii) *Failure to attach IRS acknowledgment of election.*—A transferee that knows that the transferor is a foreign corporation may not rely upon a certification of non-foreign status provided by the corporation on the basis of election under section 897(i), unless there is attached to the certification a copy of the acknowledgment by the Internal Revenue Service of the corporation's election, as required by paragraph (b)(2)(ii) of this section.

(iii) *Knowledge of falsity.*—A transferee is not entitled to rely upon a transferor's certification if prior to or at the time of the transfer the transferee either—

(A) Has actual knowledge that the transferor's certification is false; or

(B) Receives a notice that the certification is false from a transferor's or transferee's agent, pursuant to § 1.1445-4.

(iv) *Belated notice of false certification.*—If after the date of the transfer a transferee receives a notice that a certification is false, then that transferee is entitled to rely upon the certification only with respect to consideration that was paid prior to receipt of the notice. Such a transferee is required to withhold a full 15 percent of the amount realized from the consideration that remains to be paid to the transferor if possible. Thus, if 15 percent or more of the amount realized remains to be paid to the transferor then the transferee is required to withhold and pay over the full 15 percent. The transferee must do so by withholding and paying over the entire amount of each successive payment of consideration to the transferor until the full 15 percent of the amount realized has been withheld and paid over. Amounts so withheld must be reported and paid over by the 20th day following the date on which each such payment of consideration is made. A transferee that is subject to the rules of this paragraph (b)(4)(iv) may not obtain a withholding certificate pursuant to § 1.1445-3, but must instead withhold and pay over the amounts required by this paragraph. For dispositions described in § 1.1445-1(b)(2), this paragraph shall be applied by replacing "15 percent" with "10 percent" each time it appears.

(c) *Transferred property not a U.S. real property interest.*—(1) *In general.*—No withholding is required under section 1445 if the transferee acquires only property that is not a U.S. real property interest. As defined in section 897(c) and § 1.897-1(c), a U.S. real property interest includes certain interests in U.S. corporations, as well as direct interests in real property and certain associated personal property. This paragraph (c) provides rules pursuant to which a person acquiring an interest in a U.S. corporation may determine that withholding is not required because that interest is not a U.S. real property interest. To determine whether an interest in tangible property constitutes a U.S. real property interest the acquisition of which would be subject to withholding, see § 1.897-1(b) and (c).

(2) *Interests in publicly traded entities.*—No withholding is required under section 1445(a) upon the acquisition of an interest in a domestic corporation if any class of stock of the corporation is regularly traded on an established securities market. This exemption shall apply if the disposition is incident to an initial public offering of stock pursuant to a registration statement filed with the Securities and Exchange Commission. Similarly, no withholding is required under section 1445(a) upon the acquisition of an interest in a publicly traded partnership or trust. However, the rule of this paragraph (c)(2) shall not apply to the acquisition, from a single transferor (or related transferors as defined in § 1.897-1(i)) in a single transaction (or related transactions), of an interest described in § 1.897-1(c)(2)(iii)(B) (relating to substantial amounts of non-publicly traded interests in publicly traded corporations) or to similar interests in publicly traded partnerships or trusts. The person making an acquisition described in the preceding sentence must otherwise determine whether withholding is required, pursuant to section 1445 and the regulations thereunder. Transactions shall be deemed to be related if they are undertaken within 90 days of one another or if it can otherwise be shown that they were undertaken in pursuance of a prearranged plan.

(3) *Transferee receives statement that interest in corporation is not a U.S. real property interest.*—(i) *In general.*—No withholding is required under section 1445(a) upon the acquisition of an interest in a domestic corporation, if the transferor provides the transferee with a copy of a statement, issued by the corporation pursuant to § 1.897-2(h), certifying that the interest is not a U.S. real property interest. In

general, a corporation may issue such a statement only if the corporation was not a U.S. real property holding corporation at any time during the previous five years (or the period in which the interest was held by its present holder, if shorter) or if interests in the corporation ceased to be United States real property interests under section 897(c)(1)(B). (A corporation may not provide such a statement based on its determination that the interest in question is an interest solely as a creditor.) See §1.897-2(f) and (h). The corporation may provide such a statement directly to the transferee at the transferor's request. The transferor must request such a statement prior to the transfer, and shall, to the extent possible, specify the anticipated date of the transfer. A corporation's statement may be relied upon for purposes of this paragraph (c)(3) only if the statement is dated not more than 30 days prior to the date of the transfer. A transferee may also rely upon a corporation's statement that is voluntarily provided by the corporation in response to a request from the transferee, if that statement otherwise complies with the requirements of this paragraph (c)(3) and §1.897-2(h).

(ii) *Reliance on statement not permitted.*—A transferee is not entitled to rely upon a statement that a corporation is not a U.S. real property holding corporation if, prior to or at the time of the transfer, the transferee either—

(A) Has actual knowledge that the statement is false, or

(B) Receives a notice that the statement is false from a transferor's or transferee's agent, pursuant to §1.1445-4.

Such a transferee's withholding obligations shall apply as if a statement had never been given, and such a transferee may be held fully liable pursuant to §1.1445-1(e) for any failure to withhold.

(iii) *Belated notice of false statement.*—If after the date of the transfer, a transferee receives notice that a statement provided under §1.1445-2(c)(3)(i) (that an interest in a corporation is not a U.S. real property interest) is false, then such transferee may rely on the statement only with respect to consideration that was paid prior to the receipt of the notice. Such a transferee is required to withhold a full 15 percent of the amount realized from the consideration that remains to be paid to the transferor, if possible. Thus, if 15 percent or more of the amount realized remains to be paid to the transferor, then the transferee is required to withhold any pay over the full 15 percent. The transferee must do so by withholding and paying over the entire amount of each successive payment of consideration to the transferor, until the full 15 percent of the amount realized has been withheld and paid over. Amounts so withheld must be reported and paid over by the 20th day following the date on which each such payment of consideration is made. A transferee that is subject to the rules of this paragraph 1.1445-2(c)(3)(iii) may not obtain a withholding certificate pursuant to §1.1445-3, but must instead withhold and pay over the amounts required by this paragraph.

(d) *Exceptions to requirement of withholding.*—(1) *Purchase of residence for $300,000 or less.*—No withholding is required under section 1445(a) if one or more individual transferees acquire a U.S. real property interest for use as a residence and the amount realized on the transaction is $300,000 or less. For purposes of this section, a U.S. real property interest is acquired for use as a residence if on the date of the transfer the transferee (or transferees) has definite plans to reside at the property for at least 50 percent of the number of days that the property is used by any person during each of the first two 12-month periods following the date of the transfer. The number of days that the property will be vacant is not taken into account in determining the number of days such property is used by any person. A transferee shall be considered to reside at a property on any day on which a member of the transferee's family, as defined in section 267(c)(4), resides at the property. No form or other document need be filed with the Internal Revenue Service to establish a transferee's entitlement to rely upon the exception provided by this paragraph (d)(1). A transferee who fails to withhold in reliance upon this exception, but who does not in fact reside at the property for the minimum number of days set forth above, shall be liable for the failure to withhold (if the transferor was a foreign person and did not pay the full U.S. tax due on any gain recognized upon the transfer). However, if the transferee establishes that the failure to reside the minimum number of days was caused by a change in circumstances that could not reasonably have been anticipated at the time of the transfer, then the transferee shall not be liable for the failure to withhold. The exception provided by paragraph (d)(1) does not apply in any case where the transferee is other than an individual even if the property is acquired for or on behalf of an individual who will use the property as a residence. However, this exception applies regardless of the organizational structure of the transferor (i.e., regardless of whether the transferor is an individual, partnership, trust, corporation, etc.).

(2) *Coordination with nonrecognition provisions.*—(i) *In general.*—A transferee shall not be required to withhold under section 1445(a) with respect to the transfer of a U.S. real property interest if—

(A) The transferor notifies the transferee, in the manner described in paragraph (d)(2)(iii) of this section, that by reason of the operation of a nonrecognition provision of the Internal Revenue Code or the provisions of any United States treaty the transferor is not required to recognize any gain or loss with respect to the transfer; and

(B) By the 20th day after the date of the transfer the transferee mails a copy of the transferor's notice to the Internal Revenue Service, at the address provided in §1.1445-1(g)(10), together with a cover letter setting forth the name, identifying number, and home address (in the case of an individual) or office address (in the case of an entity) of the transferee providing the notice to the Service.

The rule of this paragraph (d)(2)(i) is subject to the exceptions set forth in paragraph (d)(2)(ii). For purposes of this paragraph (d)(2) a nonrecognition provision is any provision of the Internal Revenue Code for not recognizing gain or loss.

(ii) *Exceptions.*—A transferee may not rely upon the rule of paragraph (d)(2)(i) of this section, and must therefore withhold under section 1445(a) with respect to the transfer of a U.S. real property interest, if either:

(A) The transferor qualifies for nonrecognition treatment with respect to part, but not all, of the gain realized by the transferor upon the transfer; or

(B) The transferee knows or has reason to know that the transferor is not entitled to the nonrecognition treatment claimed by the transferor.

In either of the above circumstances the transferee or transferor may request a withholding certificate from the Internal Revenue Service pursuant to the rules of §1.1445-3.

(iii) *Contents of the notice.*—No particular form is required for a transferor's notice to a transferee that the transferor is not required to recognize gain or loss with respect to a transfer. The notice must be verified as true and signed under penalties of perjury by the transferor, by a responsible officer in the case of a corporation, by a general partner in the case of a partnership, and by a trustee or equivalent fiduciary in the case of a trust or estate. The following information must be set forth in paragraphs labeled to correspond with the designation set forth as follows—

(A) A statement that the document submitted constitutes a notice of a nonrecognition transaction or a treaty provision pursuant to the requirements of §1.1445-2(d)(2);

(B) The name, identifying number, and home address (in the case of an individual) or office address (in the case of an entity) of the transferor submitting the notice;

(C) A statement that the transferor is not required to recognize any gain or loss with respect to the transfer;

(D) A brief description of the transfer; and

(E) A brief summary of the law and facts supporting the claim that recognition of gain or loss is not required with respect to the transfer.

(iv) *No notice allowed.*—The provisions of this paragraph (d)(2) do not apply to exclusions from income under section 121, to simultaneous like-kind exchanges under section 1031 that do not qualify for nonrecognition treatment in their entirety (see paragraph (d)(2)(ii)(A) of this section), and to nonsimultaneous like-kind exchanges under section 1031 where the transferee cannot determine that the exchange has been completed and all the conditions for nonrecognition have been satisfied at the time it is otherwise required to pay the section 1445 withholding tax and file the withholding tax return (Form 8288, "U.S. Withholding Tax Return for Dispositions by Foreign Persons of U.S. Real Property Interests"). In these cases, the transferee is excused from withholding only upon the timely application for and receipt of a withholding certificate under §1.1445-3 (see §1.1445-3(b)(5) and (6) for specific rules applicable to transactions under sections 121 and 1031). This paragraph (d)(2)(iv) is applicable for dispositions and exchanges occurring [after] September 4, 2003.

(3) *Special procedural rules applicable to foreclosures.*—(i) *Amount to be withheld.*—(A) *Foreclosures.*—A transferee that acquires a U.S. real property interest pursuant to a repossession or foreclosure on such property under a mortgage, security agreement, deed of trust or other instrument securing a debt must withhold tax under section 1445(a) equal to 15 percent (10 percent in the case of dispositions described in §1.1445-1(b)(2)) of the amount realized on such sale. Such amount must be reported and paid over to the Service under the general rules of §1.1445-1. However, if the transferee complies with the notice requirements of §1.1445-2(d)(3)(ii) and (iii), such transferee may report and pay over to the Service on or before the

20th day following the final determination by a court or trustee with jurisdiction over the foreclosure action, the lesser of:

(1) the amount otherwise required to be withheld under section 1445(a), or

(2) the "alternative amount" as defined in the succeeding sentence.

The alternative amount is the entire amount, if any, determined by a court or trustee with jurisdiction over the matter, that accrues to the debtor/transferor out of the amount realized from the foreclosure sale. The amount of any mortgage, lien, or other security agreement secured by the property, that is terminated, assumed by another person, or otherwise extinguished (as to the debtor/transferor) shall not be treated as an amount that accrues to the debtor/transferor for purposes of this §1.1445-2(d)(3)(i)(A). If the alternative amount is zero, no withholding is required. Any difference between the amount withheld at the time of the foreclosure sale and the amount to be reported and paid over to the Service must be transferred to the court or trustee with jurisdiction over the foreclosure action. Amounts withheld, if any, are to be reported and paid over to the Service by using Forms 8288 and 8288-A in conformity with §1.1445-1(d).

(B) *Deeds in lieu of foreclosures.*—A transferee of a U.S. real property interest pursuant to a deed in lieu of foreclosure must withhold tax equal to 15 percent (10 percent in the case of dispositions described in §1.1445-1(b)(2)) of the amount realized by the debtor/transferor on the transfer. However, no withholding is required if:

(1) The transferee is the only person with a security interest in the property,

(2) No cash or other property (other than incidental fees incurred with respect to the transfer) is paid, directly or indirectly, to any person with respect to the transfer, and

(3) The notice requirements of §1.1445-2(d)(3) are satisfied.

The amount withheld, if any, must be reported and paid over to the Service not later than the 20th day following the date of transfer. In a case where withholding would otherwise be required, a withholding certificate may be requested in accordance with §1.1445-3.

(ii) *Notice to the court or trustee in a foreclosure action.*—(A) *Notice on day of purchase.*—A transferee in a foreclosure sale that chooses to use the special rules applicable to foreclosures must provide notice to the court or trustee with jurisdiction over the foreclosure action on the day the property is transferred with respect to such transferee's withholding obligation. No particular form is necessary but the notice must set forth the transferee's name, home address in the case of an individual, office address in the case of an entity, a brief description of the property, the date of the transfer, the amount realized on the sale of the foreclosed property and the amount withheld under section 1445(a).

(B) *Notice whether amount withheld or alternative amount is reported and paid over the Service.*—A purchaser/transferee in a foreclosure that chooses to use the special rules applicable to foreclosures must provide notice to the court or trustee with jurisdiction over the foreclosure action regarding whether the amount withheld or the alternative amount will be (or has been) reported and paid over to the Service. The notice should set forth all the information required by the preceding paragraph (d)(3)(ii)(A), the amount withheld or alternative amount that will be (or has been) reported and paid over to the Service, and the amount that will be (or has been) paid over to the court or trustee.

(iii) *Notice to the Service.*—(A) *General rule.*—A transferee that in reliance upon the rules of this paragraph (d)(3) withholds an alternative amount (or does not withhold because the alternative amount is zero) must, on or before the 20th day following the final determination by a court or trustee in a foreclosure action or on or before the 20th day following the date of the transfer with respect to a transfer pursuant to a deed in lieu of foreclosure, provide notice thereof to the Assistant Commissioner (International) at the address provided in §1.1445-1(g)(10). (The filing of such a notice shall not relieve a creditor of any obligation it may have to file a notice pursuant to section 6050J and the regulations thereunder.) No particular form is required but the following information must be set forth in paragraphs labelled to correspond with the numbers set forth below.

(1) A statement that the notice constitutes a notice of foreclosure action or transfer pursuant to a deed in lieu of foreclosure under §1.1445-2(d)(3).

(2) The name, identifying number, and home address (in the case of an individual) or office address (in the case of an entity) of the purchaser/transferee.

(3) The name, identifying number, and home address (in the case of an individual) or office address (in the case of an entity) of the debtor/transferor.

(4) In a foreclosure action, the date of the final determination by a court or trustee regarding the distribution of the amount realized from the foreclosure sale. In a transfer pursuant to a deed in lieu of foreclosure, the date the property is transferred to the purchaser/transferee.

(5) A brief description of the property.

(6) The amount realized from the foreclosure sale or with respect to the transfer pursuant to a deed in lieu of foreclosure.

(7) The alternative amount.

(B) *Special rule for lenders required to file Form 1099-A where the alternative amount is zero.*—A person required under section 6050J to file Form 1099-A does not have to comply with the notice requirement of §1.1445-2(d)(3)(iii)(A) if the alternative amount is zero. In such case, the filing of the Form 1099-A will be deemed to satisfy the notice requirement of §1.1445-2(d)(3)(iii)(A).

(iv) *Requirements not applicable.*—A transferee is not required to withhold tax or provide notice pursuant to the rules of this paragraph (d)(3) if no substantive withholding liability applies to the transfer of the property by the debtor/transferor. For example, if the debtor/transferor provides the transferee with a certification of non-foreign status pursuant to paragraph (b) of this section, then no substantive withholding liability would exist with respect to the acquisition of the property from the debtor transferor. In such a case, no withholding of tax or notice to the Internal Revenue Service is required of the transferee with respect to the repossession or foreclosure.

(v) *Anti-abuse rule.*—If a U.S. real property interest is transferred in foreclosure or pursuant to a deed in lieu of foreclosure for a principal purpose of avoiding the requirements of section 1445(a), then the provisions of this paragraph (d)(3) shall not apply to the transfer and the transferee shall be fully liable for any failure to withhold with respect to the transfer. A principal purpose to avoid section 1445(a) will be presumed (subject to rebuttal on the basis of all relevant facts and circumstances) if:

(A) The transferee acquires property in which it, or a related party, has a security interest;

(B) The security interest did not arise in connection with the debtor/transferor's or a related party's or predecessor in interest's acquisition, improvement, or maintenance of the property; and

(C) The total amount of all debts secured by the property exceeds 90 percent of the fair market value of the property.

(4) *Installment payments.*—A transferee of a U.S. real property interest is not required to withhold under section 1445 when making installment payments on an obligation arising out of a disposition that took place before January 1, 1985. With respect to dispositions that take place after December 31, 1984, the transferee shall be required to satisfy its entire withholding obligation within the time specified in §1.1445-1(c) regardless of the amount actually paid by the transferee. Thereafter, no withholding is required upon further installment payments on an obligation arising out of the transfer. A transferee that is unable to satisfy its entire withholding obligation within the time specified in §1.1445-1(c) may request a withholding certificate pursuant to §1.1445-3.

(5) *Acquisitions by governmental bodies.*—No withholding of tax is required under section 1445 with respect to any acquisition of property by the United States, a state or possession of the United States, a political subdivision thereof, or the District of Columbia.

(6) [Reserved.]

(7) *Withholding certificate obtained by transferee or transferor.*—No withholding is required under section 1445(a) if the transferee is provided with a withholding certificate that so specifies. Either the transferor or the transferee may seek a withholding certificate from the Internal Revenue Service, pursuant to the provisions of §1.1445-3.

(8) *Amount realized by transferor is zero.*—If the amount realized by the transferor on a transfer of a U.S. real property interest is zero, no withholding is required.

(e) *Applicability dates.*—The requirement in paragraphs (d)(2)(i)(B), (d)(2)(iii)(B), and (d)(3)(iii)(A)(2) and (3) of this section that taxpayer identification numbers be provided (in all cases) is applicable for dispositions of U.S. real property interests occurring after November 3, 2003. The exclusion of entities described in section 897(l) from the definition of foreign person in paragraph (b)(2)(i) of this section applies to dispositions and distributions after December 18, 2015, and the withholding rates set forth in paragraphs (b)(4)(iv), (c)(3)(iii), and (d)(3)(i) of this section apply to dispositions after February 16, 2016. For dispositions on or before February 16, 2016, see paragraphs (b)(4)(iv), (c)(3)(iii), and (d)(3)(i) of this section as contained in 26 CFR part 1 revised as of April 1, 2015. Paragraph (b)(2)(v) of this section applies to certifications provided on or after May 7, 2019, except that a taxpayer may choose to apply paragraph (b)(2)(v) of this section with respect to certifications provided before May 7, 2019. [Reg. §1.1445-2.]

□ [*T.D.* 8113, 12-18-86. *Amended by T.D.* 8198, 5-4-88, *T.D.* 9082, 8-4-2003, *T.D.* 9751, 2-17-2016 *and T.D.* 9926, 11-27-2020.]

### [Reg. §1.1445-3]

**§1.1445-3. Adjustments to amount required to be withheld pursuant to withholding certificate.**—(a) *In general.*—Withholding under section 1445(a) may be reduced or eliminated pursuant to a withholding certificate issued by the Internal Revenue Service in accordance with the rules of this section. A withholding certificate may be issued by the Service in cases where reduced withholding is appropriate (see paragraph (c) of this section), where the transferor is exempt from U.S. tax (see paragraph (d) of this section), or where an agreement for the payment of tax is entered into with the Service (see paragraph (e) of this section). A withholding certificate that is obtained prior to a transfer notifies the transferee that no withholding is required. A withholding certificate that is obtained after a transfer has been made may authorize a normal refund or an early refund pursuant to paragraph (g) of this section. Either a transferee or transferor may apply for a withholding certificate. The Internal Revenue Service will act upon an application for a withholding certificate not later than the 90th day after it is received. Solely for this purpose (i.e., determining the day upon which the 90-day period commences), an application is received by the Service on the date that all information necessary for the Service to make a determination is provided by the applicant. In no event, however, will a withholding certificate be issued without the transferor's identifying number. (For rules regarding whether an application for a withholding certificate has been timely submitted, see §1.1445-1(c)(2).) The Service may deny a request for a withholding certificate where, after due notice, an applicant fails to provide information necessary for the Service to make a determination. The Service will act upon an application for an early refund not later than the 90th day after it is received. An application for an early refund must either (1) include a copy of a withholding certificate issued by the Service with respect to the transaction, or (2) be combined with an application for a withholding certificate. Where an application for an early refund is combined with an application for a withholding certificate, the Service will act upon both applications not later than the 90th day after receipt. In the case of an application for a certificate based on nonconforming security under paragraph (e)(3)(v) of this section, and in unusually complicated cases, the Service may be unable to provide a final withholding certificate by the 90th day. In such a case the Service will notify the applicant, by the 45th day after receipt of the application, that additional processing time will be necessary. The Service's notice may request additional information or explanation concerning particular aspects of the application, and will provide a target date for final action (contingent upon the applicant's timely submission of any requested information). A withholding certificate issued pursuant to the provisions of this section serves to fulfill the requirements of section 1445(b)(4) concerning qualifying statements, section 1445(c)(1) concerning the transferor's maximum tax liability, or section 1445(c)(2) concerning the Secretary's authority to prescribe reduced withholding.

(b) *Applications for withholding certificates.*—(1) *In general.*—An application for a withholding certificate must be submitted to the address provided in §1.1445-1(g)(10). An application for a withholding certificate must be signed by a responsible officer in the case of a corporation, by a general partner in the case of a partnership, by a trustee, executor, or equivalent fiduciary in the case of a trust or estate, and in the case of an individual by the individual himself. A duly authorized agent may sign the application but the application must contain a valid power of attorney authorizing the agent to sign the application on behalf of the applicant. The person signing the application must verify under penalties of perjury that all representations made in connection with the application are true, correct, and complete to his knowledge and belief. No particular form is required for an application, but the application must set forth the information described in paragraphs (b)(2), (3), and (4), and to the extent applicable, paragraph (b)(5) or (6) of this section.

(2) *Parties to the transaction.*—The application must set forth the name, address, and identifying number of the person submitting the application (specifying whether that person is the transferee or transferor), and the name, address, and identifying number of other parties to the transaction (specifying whether each such party is a transferee or transferor). The Service will deny the application if complete information, including the identifying numbers of all the parties, is not provided. Thus, for example, the applicant should determine if an identifying number exists for each party, and, if that exists for a particular party, the applicant should notify the particular party of the obligation to get an identifying number before the

application can be submitted to the Service. The address provided in the case of an individual must be that individual's home address, and the address provided in the case of an entity must be that entity's office address. A mailing address may be provided in addition to, but not in lieu of, a home address or office address.

(3) *Real property interest to be transferred.*—The application must set forth information concerning the U.S. real property interest with respect to which the withholding certificate is sought, including the type of interest, the contract price, and, in the case of an interest in real property, its location and general description, or in the case of an interest in a U.S. real property holding corporation, the class or type and amount of the interest.

(4) *Basis for certificate.*—(i) *Reduced withholding.*—If a withholding certificate is sought on the basis of a claim that reduced withholding is appropriate, the application must include:

(A) A calculation of the maximum tax that may be imposed on the disposition in accordance with paragraph (c)(2) of this section. Such calculation must be accompanied by a copy of the relevant contract and depreciation schedules or other evidence that confirms the contract price and adjusted basis of the property. If no depreciation schedules are provided, the application must state the nature of the use of the property and why depreciation was not allowable. Evidence that supports any claimed adjustment to the maximum tax on the disposition must also be provided;

(B) A calculation of the transferor's unsatisfied withholding liability, or evidence supporting the claim that no such liability exists, in accordance with paragraph (c)(3) of this section; and

(C) In the case of a request for a special reduction of withholding pursuant to paragraph (c)(4) of this section, a statement of law and facts in support of the request.

(ii) *Exemption.*—If a withholding certificate is sought on the basis of the transferor's exemption from U.S. tax, the application must set forth a brief statement of the law and facts that support the claimed exemption. In this regard, see paragraph (d) of this section.

(iii) *Agreement.*—If a withholding certificate is sought on the basis of an agreement for the payment of tax, the application must include a signed copy of the agreement proposed by the applicant and a copy of the security instrument (if any) proposed by the applicant. In this regard, see paragraph (e) of this section.

(5) *Special rule for exclusions from income under section 121.*—A withholding certificate may be sought on the basis of a section 121 exclusion as a reduction in the amount of tax due under paragraph (c)(2)(v) of this section. The application must include information establishing that the transferor, who is a nonresident alien individual at the time of the sale (and is therefore subject to sections 897 and 1445) is entitled to claim the benefits of section 121. For example, a claim for reduced withholding as a result of section 121 must include information that the transferor occupied the U.S. real property interest as his or her personal residence for the required period of time.

(6) *Special rule for like-kind exchanges under Section 1031.*—A withholding certificate may be requested with respect to a like-kind exchange under section 1031 as a transaction subject to a nonrecognition provision under paragraph (c)(2)(ii) of this section. The application must include information substantiating the requirements of section 1031. The IRS may require additional information during the course of the application process to determine that the requirements of section 1031 are satisfied. In the case of a deferred like-kind exchange, the withholding agent is excused from reporting and paying the withholding tax to the IRS within 20 days after the transfer only if an application for a withholding certificate is submitted prior to or on the date of transfer. See §1.1445-1(c)(2) for rules concerning delayed reporting and payment where an application for a withholding certificate has been submitted to the IRS prior to or on the date of transfer.

(c) *Adjustment of amount required to be withheld.*—(1) *In general.*—The Internal Revenue Service may issue a withholding certificate that excuses withholding or that permits the transferee to withhold an adjusted amount reflecting the transferor's maximum tax liability. The transferor's maximum tax liability is the sum of—

(i) The maximum amount which could be imposed as tax under section 871 or 882 upon the transferor's disposition of the subject real property interest, as determined under paragraph (c)(2) of this section, and

(ii) The transferor's unsatisfied withholding liability with respect to the subject real property interest, as determined under paragraph (c)(3) of this section.

In addition, the Internal Revenue Service may issue a withholding certificate that permits the transferee to withhold a reduced amount if the Service determines pursuant to paragraph (c)(4) of this section that reduced withholding will not jeopardize the collection of tax.

(2) *Maximum tax imposed on disposition.*—The first element of the transferor's maximum tax liability is the maximum amount which the transferor could be required to pay as tax upon the disposition of the subject real property interest. In the case of an individual transferor that amount will generally be the contract price of the property minus its adjusted basis, multiplied by the maximum individual income tax rate applicable to long-term capital gain. In the case of a corporate transferor, that amount will generally be the contract price of the property minus its adjusted basis, multiplied by the maximum corporate income tax rate applicable to long-term capital gain. However, that amount must be adjusted to take into account the following:

(i) Any reduction of tax to which the transferor is entitled under the provisions of a U.S. income tax treaty;

(ii) The effect of any nonrecognition provision that is applicable to the transaction;

(iii) Any losses realized and recognized upon the previous disposition of U.S. real property interests during the taxable year;

(iv) Any amount that is required to be treated as ordinary income; and

(v) Any other factor that may increase or reduce the tax upon the disposition.

(3) *Transferor's unsatisfied withholding liability.*—(i) *In general.*—The second element of the transferor's maximum tax liability is the transferor's unsatisfied withholding liability. That liability is the amount of any tax that the transferor was required to but did not withhold and pay over under section 1445 upon the acquisition of the subject U.S. real property interest or a predecessor interest. The transferor's unsatisfied withholding liability is included in the calculation of maximum tax liability so that such prior withholding liability can be satisfied by the transferee's withholding upon the current transfer. Alternatively, the transferor's unsatisfied withholding liability may be disregarded for purposes of calculating the maximum tax liability, if either—

(A) Such prior withholding liability is fully satisfied by a payment that is made with the application submitted pursuant to this section; or

(B) An agreement is entered into for the payment of that liability pursuant to the rules of paragraph (e) of this section. Because section 1445 only requires withholding after December 31, 1984, no transferor's unsatisfied withholding liability can exist unless the transferor acquired the subject or predecessor real property interest after that date. For purposes of this paragraph (c), a predecessor interest is one that was exchanged for the subject U.S. real property interest in a transaction in which the transferor was not required to recognize the full amount of the gain or loss realized upon the transfer.

(ii) *Evidence that no unsatisfied withholding liability exists.*—For purposes of paragraph (b)(4)(i)(B) of this section (concerning information that must be submitted with an application for a withholding certificate), evidence that the transferor has no unsatisfied withholding liability includes any one of the following documents:

(A) Evidence that the transferor acquired the subject or predecessor real property interest prior to January 1, 1985;

(B) A copy of the Form 8288 that was filed by the transferor, and proof of payment of the amount shown due thereon, with respect to the transferor's acquisition of the subject or predecessor real property interest;

(C) A copy of a withholding certificate with respect to the transferor's acquisition of the subject or predecessor real property interest, plus a copy of Form 8288 and proof of payment with respect to any withholding required under that certificate;

(D) A copy of the non-foreign certification furnished by the person from whom the subject or predecessor U.S. real property interest was acquired, executed at the time of that acquisition;

(E) Evidence that the transferor purchased the subject or predecessor real property for $300,000 or less, and a statement, signed by the transferor under penalties of perjury, that the transferor purchased the property for use as a residence within the meaning of § 1.1445-2(d)(1);

(F) Evidence that the person from whom the transferor acquired the subject or predecessor U.S. real property interest fully paid any tax imposed on that transaction pursuant to section 897;

(G) A copy of a notice of nonrecognition treatment provided to the transferor pursuant to § 1.1445-2(d)(2) by the person from whom the transferor acquired the subject or predecessor U.S. real property interest; and

(H) A statement, signed by the transferor under penalties of perjury, setting forth the facts and circumstances that supported the transferor's conclusion that no withholding was required under sec-

tion 1445(a) with respect to the transferor's acquisition of the subject or predecessor real property interest.

(4) *Special reduction of amount required to be withheld.*—The Internal Revenue Service may, in its discretion, issue a withholding certificate that permits the transferee to withhold a reduced amount based upon a determination that reduced withholding will not jeopardize the collection of tax. A transferor that requests a withholding certificate pursuant to this paragraph (c)(4) is required pursuant to paragraph (b)(4)(i)(C) of this section to submit a statement of law and facts in support of the request. That statement must explain why the transferor is unable to enter into an agreement for the payment of tax pursuant to paragraph (e) of this section.

(d) *Transferor's exemption from U.S. tax.*—(1) *In general.*—The Internal Revenue Service will issue a withholding certificate that excuses all withholding by a transferee if it is established that:

(i) The transferor's gain from the disposition of the subject U.S. real property interest will be exempt from U.S. tax, and

(ii) The transferor has no unsatisfied withholding liability.
For the available exemptions, see paragraph (d)(2) of this section. The transferor's unsatisfied withholding liability shall be determined in accordance with the provisions of paragraph (c)(3) of this section. A transferor that is entitled to a reduction of (rather than an exemption from) U.S. tax may obtain a withholding certificate to that effect pursuant to the provisions of paragraph (c) of this section.

(2) *Available exemptions.*—A transferor's gain from the disposition of a U.S. real property interest may be exempt from U.S. tax because either:

(i) The transferor is an integral part or controlled entity of a foreign government and the disposition of the subject property is not a commercial activity, as determined pursuant to section 892 and the regulations thereunder; or

(ii) The transferor is entitled to the benefits of an income tax treaty that provides for such an exemption (subject to the limitations imposed by section 1125(c) of Pub. L. 96-499, which, in general, overrides such benefits as of January 1, 1985).

(e) *Agreement for the payment of tax.*—(1) *In general.*—The Internal Revenue Service will issue a withholding certificate that excuses withholding or that permits a transferee to withhold a reduced amount, if either the transferee or the transferor enters into an agreement for the payment of tax pursuant to the provisions of this paragraph (e). An agreement for the payment of tax is a contract between the Service and any other person that consists of two necessary elements. Those elements are—

(i) A contract between the Service and the other person, setting forth in detail the rights and obligations of each; and

(ii) A security instrument or other form of security acceptable to the Director, Foreign Operations District.

(2) *Contents of agreement.*—(i) *In general.*—An agreement for the payment of tax must cover an amount described in subdivision (ii) or (iii) of this paragraph (e)(2). The agreement may either provide adequate security for the payment of the chosen amount in accordance with paragraph (e)(3) of this section, or provide for the payment of that amount through a combination of security and withholding of tax by the transferee.

(ii) *Tax that would otherwise be withheld.*—An agreement for the payment of tax may cover the amount of tax that would otherwise be required to be withheld pursuant to section 1445(a). In addition to the amount computed pursuant to section 1445(a), the applicant must agree to pay interest upon that amount, at the rate established under section 6621, with respect to the period between the date on which the tax imposed by section 1445(a) would otherwise be due (*i.e.*, the 20th day after the date of transfer) and the date on which the transferor's payment of tax with respect to the disposition will be due under the agreement. The amount of interest agreed upon must be paid by the applicant regardless of whether or not the Service is required to draw upon any security provided pursuant to the agreement. The interest may be paid either with the return or by the Service drawing upon the security.

(iii) *Maximum tax liability.*—An agreement for the payment of tax may cover the transferor's maximum tax liability, determined in accordance with paragraph (c) of this section. The agreement must also provide for the payment of an additional amount equal to 25 percent of the amount determined under paragraph (c) of this section. This additional amount secures the interest and penalties that would accrue between the date of a failure to file a return and pay tax with respect to the disposition, and the date on which the Service collects upon that liability pursuant to the agreement. Such additional amount will only be collected if the Service finds it necessary to draw upon any security provided due to the transferor's failure to file a return and pay tax with respect to the relevant disposition.

(3) *Major types of security.*—(i) *In general.*—The following are the major types of security acceptable to the Service. Further details with respect to the terms and conditions of each type may be specified by Revenue Procedure.

(ii) *Bond with surety or guarantor.*—The Service may accept as security with respect to a transferor's tax liability a bond that is executed with a satisfactory surety or guarantor. Only the following persons may act as surety or guarantor for this purpose:

(A) A surety company holding a certificate of authority from the Secretary as an acceptable surety on Federal bonds, as listed in Treasury Department Circular No. 570, published annually in the Federal Register on the first working day of July;

(B) A person that is engaged within or without the United States in the conduct of a banking, financing, or similar business under the principles of § 1.864-4(c)(5) and that is subject to U.S. or foreign local or national regulation of such business, if that person is otherwise acceptable to the Service; and

(C) A person that is engaged within or without the United States in the conduct of an insurance business that is subject to U.S. or foreign local or national regulation, if that person is otherwise acceptable to the Service.

(iii) *Bond with collateral.*—The Service may accept as security with respect to a transferor's tax liability a bond that is secured by acceptable collateral. All collateral must be deposited with a responsible financial institution acting as escrow agent or, in the Service's discretion, with the Service. Only the following types of collateral are acceptable:

(A) Bonds, notes, or other public debt obligations of the United States, in accordance with the rules of 31 CFR Part 225; and

(B) A certified cashier's, or treasurer's check, drawn on an entity acceptable to the Service that is engaged within or without the United States in the conduct of a banking, financing, or similar business under the principles of § 1.864-4(c)(5) and that is subject to U.S. or foreign local or national regulation of such business.

(iv) *Letter of credit.*—The Service may accept as security with respect to a transferor's tax liability an irrevocable letter of credit. The Service may accept a letter of credit issued by an entity acceptable to the Service that is engaged within or without the United States in the conduct of a banking, financing or similar business under the principles of § 1.884-4(c)(5) and that is subject to U.S. or foreign local or national regulation of such business. However, the Director will accept a letter of credit from an entity that is not engaged in trade or business in the United States only if such letter may be drawn on an advising bank within the United States.

(v) *Guarantees and other nonconforming security.*—(A) *Guarantee.*—The Service may in its discretion accept as security with respect to a transferor's tax liability the applicant's guarantee that it will pay such liability. The Service will in general accept such a guarantee only from a corporation, foreign or domestic, any class of stock of which is regularly traded on an established securities market on the date of the transfer.

(B) *Other forms of security.*—The Service may in unusual circumstances and at its discretion accept any form of security that it finds to be adequate. An application for a withholding certificate that proposes a form of security that does not conform with any of the preferred types set forth in paragraph (e)(3)(ii) through (iv) of this section or any relevant Revenue Procedure must include:

(1) A detailed statement of the facts and circumstances supporting the use of the proposed form of security, and

(2) A memorandum of law concerning the validity and enforceability of the proposed form of security.

(4) *Terms of security instrument.*—Any security instrument that is furnished pursuant to this section must provide that—

(i) The amount of each deposit of estimated tax that will be required with respect to the gain realized on the subject disposition may be collected by levy upon the security as of the date following the date on which each such deposit is due (unless such deposit is timely made);

(ii) The entire amount of the liability may be collected by levy upon the security at any time during the nine months following the date on which the payment of tax with respect to the subject disposition is due, subject to release of the security upon the full payment of the tax and any interest and penalties due. If the transferor requests an extension of time to file a return with respect to the disposition, then the Director may require that the term of the security instrument be extended until the date that is nine months after the filing deadline as extended.

(f) *Amendments to application for withholding certificate.*—(1) *In general.*—An applicant for a withholding certificate may amend an otherwise complete application by submitting an amending statement to the address provided in § 1.1445-1(g)(10). The amending statement shall provide the information required by § 1.1445-3(f)(3) and must be signed and accompanied by a penalties of perjury statement in accordance with § 1.1445-3(b)(1).

(2) *Extension of time for the Service to process requests for withholding certificates.*—(i) *In general.*—If an amending statement is submitted, the time in which the Internal Revenue Service must act upon the amended application shall be extended by 30 days.

(ii) *Substantial amendments.*—If an amending statement is submitted and the Service finds that the statement substantially amends the facts of the underlying application or substantially alters the terms of the withholding certificate as requested in the initial application, the time within which the Service must act upon the amended application shall be extended by 60 days. The applicant shall be so notified.

(iii) *Amending statement received after the requested withholding certificate has been signed on behalf of the Service.*—If an amending statement is received after the withholding certificate, drafted in response to the underlying application, has been signed on behalf of the Service and prior to the day such certificate is mailed to the applicant, the time in which the Service must act upon the amended application shall be extended by 90 days. The applicant will be so notified.

(3) *Information required to be submitted.*—No particular form is required for an amending statement but the statement must provide the following information:

(i) *Identification of applicant.*—The amending statement must set forth the name, address and identifying number of the person submitting the amending statement (specifying whether that person is the transferee or transferor).

(ii) *Date of underlying application.*—The amending statement must set forth the date of the underlying application for a withholding certificate.

(iii) *Real property interest to be (or that has been) transferred.*—The amending statement must set forth a brief description of the real property interest with respect to which the underlying application for a withholding certificate was submitted.

(iv) *Amending information.*—The amending statement must fully set forth the basis for the amendment including any modification of the facts supporting the application for a withholding certificate and any change sought in the terms of the withholding certificate.

(g) *Early refund of overwithheld amounts.*—If a transferor receives a withholding certificate pursuant to this section, and an amount greater than that specified in the certificate was withheld by the transferee, then pursuant to the rules of this paragraph (g) the transferor may apply for a refund (without interest) of the excess amount prior to the date on which the transferor's tax return is due (without extensions). (Any interest payable on refunds issued after the filing of a tax return shall be determined in accordance with the provisions of section 6611 and regulations thereunder.) An application for an early refund must be delivered to the address provided in § 1.1445-1(g)(10). No particular form is required for the application, but the following information must be set forth in separate paragraphs numbered to correspond with the number given below:

(1) Name, address, and identifying number of the transferor seeking the refund;

(2) Amount required to be withheld pursuant to the withholding certificate issued by Internal Revenue Service;

(3) Amount withheld by the transferee (attach a copy of Form 8288-A stamped by IRS pursuant to § 1.1445-1(c));

(4) Amount to be refunded to the transferor. An application for an early refund cannot be processed unless the required copy of Form 8288-A (or substantial evidence of the amount withheld in the case of a failure to receive Form 8288-A as provided in § 1.1445-1(f)(3)) is attached to the application. If an application for a withholding certificate based upon the transferor's maximum tax liability is submitted after the transfer takes place, then that application may be combined with an application for an early refund. The Service will act upon a claim for refund within the time limits set forth in paragraph (a) of this section.

(h) *Effective date for taxpayer identification numbers.*—The requirement in paragraphs (b)(2), (f)(3)(i), and (g)(1) of this section that taxpayer identification numbers be provided (in all cases) is applicable for dispositions of U.S. real property interests occurring after November 3, 2003. [Reg. § 1.1445-3.]

☐ [*T.D.* 8113, 12-18-86. *Amended by T.D.* 9082, 8-4-2003 *and T.D.* 9751, 2-17-2016.]

## [Reg. §1.1445-4]

**§1.1445-4. Liability of agents.**—(a) *Duty to provide notice of false certification or statement to transferee.*—A transferee's or transferor's agent must provide notice to the transferee if either—

(1) The transferee is furnished with a non-U.S. real property interest statement pursuant to §1.1445-2(c)(3) and the agent knows that the statement is false; or

(2) The transferee is furnished with a non-foreign certification pursuant to §1.1445-2(b)(2) and either (i) the agent knows that the certification is false, or (ii) the agent represents a transferor that is a foreign corporation.

An agent that represents a transferor that is a foreign corporation is not required to provide notice to the transferee if the foreign corporation provided a nonforeign certification to the transferee prior to such agent's employment and the agent does not know that the corporation did so.

(b) *Duty to provide notice of false certification or statement to entity or fiduciary.*—A transferee's or transferor's agent must provide notice to an entity or fiduciary that plans to carry out a transaction described in section 1445(e)(1), (2), (3), or (4) if either—

(1) The entity or fiduciary is furnished with a non-U.S. real property interest statement pursuant to §1.1445-5(b)(4)(iii) and the agent knows that such statement is false; or

(2) The entity or fiduciary is furnished with a non-foreign certification pursuant to §1.1445-5(b)(3)(ii) and either (i) the agent knows that such certification is false, or (ii) the agent represents a foreign corporation that made such a certification.

(c) *Procedural requirements.*—(1) *Notice to transferee, entity, or fiduciary.*—An agent who is required by this section to provide notice must do so in writing as soon as possible after learning of the false certification or statement, but not later than the date of the transfer (prior to the transferee's payment of consideration). If an agent first learns of a false certification or statement after the date of the transfer, notice must be given by the third day following that discovery. The notice must state that the certification or statement is false and may not be relied upon. The notice must also explain the possible consequences to the recipient of a failure to withhold. The notice need not disclose the information on which the agent's statement is based. The following is an example of an acceptable notice: "This is to notify you that you may be required to withhold tax in connection with *(describe transaction)*. You have been provided with a certification of nonforeign status (or a non-U.S. real property interest statement) in connection with that transaction. I have learned that that document is false. Therefore, you may not rely upon it as a basis for failing to withhold under section 1445 of the Internal Revenue Code. Section 1445 provides that any person who acquires a U.S. real property interest from a foreign person after February 16, 2016, must withhold a tax equal to 15 percent (10 percent in the case of dispositions described in §1.1445-1(b)(2)) of the total purchase price. (The term 'U.S. real property interest' includes real property, stock in U.S. corporations whose assets are primarily real property, and some personal property associated with realty.) Any person who is required to withhold but fails to do so can be held liable for the tax. Thus, if you do not withhold the 15 percent tax (10 percent tax in the case of dispositions described in §1.1445-1(b)(2)) from the total that you pay on this transaction, you could be required to pay the tax yourself, if what you are acquiring is a U.S. real property interest and the transferor is a foreign person. Tax that is withheld must be promptly paid over to the IRS using Form 8288. For further information see sections 897 and 1445 of the Internal Revenue Code and the related regulations."

(2) *Notice to be filed with IRS.*—An agent who is required by paragraph (a) or (b) of this section to provide notice to a transferee, entity, or fiduciary must furnish a copy of that notice to the Internal Revenue Service by the date on which the notice is required to be given to the transferee, entity, or fiduciary. The copy of the notice must be delivered to the address provided in §1.1445-1(g)(10), and must be accompanied by a cover letter stating that the copy is being filed pursuant to the requirements of this §1.1445-4(c)(2).

(d) *Effect on recipient.*—A transferee, entity, or fiduciary that receives a notice pursuant to this section prior to the date of the transfer from any agent of the transferor or transferee may not rely upon the subject certification or statement for purposes of excusing withholding pursuant to §1.1445-2 or §1.1445-5. Therefore, the recipient of a notice may be held liable for any failure to deduct and withhold tax under section 1445 as if such certification or statement had never been given. For special rules concerning the effect of the receipt of a notice after the date of the transfer, see §§1.1445-2(b)(4)(iv) and 1.1445-5(c), (d) and (e).

(e) *Failure to provide notice.*—Any agent who is required to provide notice but who fails to do so in the manner required by paragraph (a)

or (b) of this section shall be held liable for the tax that the recipient of the notice would have been required to withhold under section 1445 if such notice had been given. However, an agent's liability under this paragraph (e) is limited to the amount of compensation that that agent derives from the transaction. In addition, an agent who assists in the preparation of, or fails to disclose knowledge of, a false certification or statement may be liable for civil or criminal penalties.

(f) *Definition of transferor's or transferee's agent.*—(1) *In general.*—For purposes of this section, the terms "transferor's agent" and "transferee's agent" mean any person who represents the transferor or transferee (respectively)—

(i) In any negotiation with another person (or another person's agent) relating to the transaction; or

(ii) In settling the transaction.

(2) *Transactions subject to section 1445(e).*—In the case of transactions subject to section 1445(e), the following definitions apply.

(i) The term "transferor's agent" means any person that represents or advises an entity or fiduciary with respect to the planning, arrangement, or consummation by the entity of a transaction described in section 1445(e)(1), (2), (3), or (4).

(ii) The term "transferee's agent" means any person that represents or advises the holder of an interest in an entity with respect to the planning, arrangement or consummation by the entity of a transaction described in section 1445(e)(1), (2), (3), or (4).

(3) *Exclusion of settlement officers and clerical personnel.*—For purposes of this section, a person shall not be treated as a transferor's agent or transferee's agent with respect to any transaction solely because such person performs one or more of the following activities:

(i) The receipt and disbursement of any portion of the consideration for the transaction;

(ii) The recording of any document in connection with the transaction; or

(iii) Typing, copying, and other clerical tasks;

(iv) The obtaining of title insurance reports and reports concerning the condition of the real property that is the subject of the transaction; or

(v) The transmission or delivery of documents between the parties.

(4) *Exclusion for governing body of a condominium association and the board of directors of a cooperative housing corporation.*—The members of a board, committee or other governing body of a condominium association and the board of directors and officers of a cooperative housing corporation will not be deemed agents of the transferor or transferee if such individuals function exclusively in their capacity as representatives of such association or corporation with respect to the transaction. In addition, the managing agent of a cooperative housing corporation or condominium association will not be deemed to be an agent of the transferee or transferor if such person functions exclusively in its capacity as a managing agent. If a person's activities include advising the transferee or transferor with respect to the transfer, this exclusion shall not apply. [Reg. §1.1445-4.]

☐ [*T.D.* 8113, 12-18-86. *Amended by T.D.* 9082, 8-4-2003 *and T.D.* 9751, 2-17-2016.]

### [Reg. §1.1445-5]

**§1.1445-5. Special rules concerning distributions and other transactions by corporations, partnerships, trusts, and estates.**—(a) *Purpose and scope.*—This section provides special rules concerning the withholding that is required under section 1445(e) upon distributions and other transactions involving domestic or foreign corporations, partnerships, trusts, and estates. Paragraph (b) of this section provides rules that apply generally to the various withholding requirements set forth in this section. Under section 1445(e)(1) and paragraph (c) of this section, a domestic partnership or the fiduciary of a domestic trust or estate is required to withhold tax upon the entity's disposition of a U.S. real property interest if any foreign persons are partners or beneficiaries of the entity. Paragraph (d) provides rules concerning the requirement of section 1445(e)(2) that a foreign corporation withhold tax upon its distribution of a U.S. real property interest to its interest-holders. Finally, under section 1445(e)(3) and paragraph (e) of this section a domestic U.S. real property holding corporation is required to withhold tax upon certain distributions to interest-holders that are foreign persons. Paragraphs (f) and (g) of this section are reserved to provide rules concerning transactions involving interests in partnerships, trusts, and estates that will be subject to withholding pursuant to section 1445(e)(4) and (5).

(b) *Rules of general application.*—(1) *Double withholding not required.*—If tax is required to be withheld with respect to a transfer of property in accordance with the rules of this section, then no additional tax is required to be withheld by the transferee of the property with respect to that transfer pursuant to the general rules of section 1445(a) and §1.1445-1. For rules coordinating the withholding under section 1441 (or section 1442 or 1443) and under section 1445 on distributions from a corporation, see §1.1441-3(b)(4). If a transfer of a U.S. real property interest described in section 1445(e) is exempt from withholding under the rules of this section, then no withholding is required under the general rules of section 1445(a) and §1.1445-1.

(2) *Coordination with nonrecognition provisions.*—(i) *In general.*—Withholding shall not be required under the rules of this section with respect to a transfer described in section 1445(e) of a U.S. real property interest if—

(A) By reason of the operation of a nonrecognition provision of the Internal Revenue Code or the provisions of any treaty of the United States no gain or loss is required to be recognized by the foreign person with respect to which withholding would otherwise be required; and

(B) The entity or fiduciary that is otherwise required to withhold complies with the notice requirements of paragraph (b)(2)(ii) of this section. The entity or fiduciary must determine whether gain or loss is required to be recognized pursuant to the rules of section 897 and the applicable nonrecognition provisions of the Internal Revenue Code. An entity or fiduciary may obtain a withholding certificate from the Internal Revenue Service that confirms the applicability of a nonrecognition provision, but is not required to do so. For purposes of this paragraph (b)(2), a nonrecognition provision is any provision of the Internal Revenue Code for not recognizing gain or loss. If nonrecognition treatment is available only with respect to part of the gain realized on a transfer, the exemption from withholding provided by this paragraph (b)(2) shall not apply. In such cases a withholding certificate may be sought pursuant to the provisions of §1.1445-6.

(ii) *Notice of nonrecognition transfer.*—An entity or fiduciary that fails to withhold tax with respect to a transfer in reliance upon the rules of this paragraph (b)(2) must by the 20th day after the date of the transfer deliver a notice thereof to the address provided in §1.1445-1(g)(10). No particular form is required for a notice of transfer, but the following information must be set forth in paragraphs labelled to correspond with the letter set forth below:

(A) A statement that the document submitted constitutes a notice of a nonrecognition transfer pursuant to the requirements of §1.1445-5(b)(2)(ii);

(B) The name, office address, and identifying number of the entity of fiduciary submitting the notice;

(C) The name, identifying number, and home address (in the case of an individual) or office address (in the case of an entity) of each foreign person with respect to which withholding would otherwise be required;

(D) A brief description of the transfer; and

(E) A brief statement of the law and facts supporting the claim that recognition of gain or loss is not required with respect to the transfer.

(3) *Interest-holder not a foreign person.*—(i) *In general.*—Pursuant to the provisions of paragraphs (c) and (e) of this section, an entity or fiduciary is required to withhold with respect to certain transfers of property if a holder of an interest in the entity is a foreign person. For purposes of determining whether a holder of an interest is a foreign person, an entity or fiduciary may rely upon a certification of non-foreign status provided by that person in accordance with paragraph (b)(3)(ii) of this section. Except to the extent provided in paragraph (b)(3)(iii) of this section, such a certification excuses the entity or fiduciary from any liability otherwise imposed pursuant to section 1445(e) and regulations thereunder. However, no obligation is imposed upon an entity or fiduciary to obtain certifications from interest-holders; an entity or fiduciary may instead rely upon other means to ascertain the non-foreign status of an interest-holder. If the entity or fiduciary does rely upon other means but the interest-holder proves, in fact, to be a foreign person, then the entity or fiduciary is subject to any liability imposed pursuant to section 1445 and regulations thereunder. An entity or fiduciary is not required to rely upon other means to ascertain the non-foreign status of an interest-holder and may demand a certification of non-foreign status. If the certification is not provided, the entity or fiduciary may withhold tax under section 1445 and will be considered, for purposes of sections 1461 through 1463, to have been required to withhold such tax.

(ii) *Interest-holder's certification of non-foreign status.*—(A) *In general.*—For purposes of this section, an entity or fiduciary may treat any holder of an interest in the entity as a U.S. person if that interest-holder furnishes to the entity or fiduciary a certification stating that the interest-holder is not a foreign person, in accordance with the

provisions of paragraph (b)(3)(ii)(B) of this section. In general, a foreign person is a nonresident alien individual, foreign corporation, foreign partnership, foreign trust, or foreign estate, but not a resident alien individual. In general, a foreign person is a nonresident alien individual, foreign corporation, foreign partnership, foreign trust, or foreign estate, but not a qualified foreign pension fund (as defined in section 897(l)) or an entity all of the interests of which are held by a qualified foreign pension fund.

(B) *Procedural rules.*—An interest-holder's certification of non-foreign status must—

(1) State that the interest-holder is not a foreign person;

(2) Set forth the interest-holder's name, identifying number, home address (in the case of an individual) or office address (in the case of an entity), and place of incorporation (in the case of a corporation); and

(3) Be signed under penalties of perjury.

Pursuant to §1.897-1(p), an individual's identifying number is the individual's Social Security number and any other person's identifying number is its U.S. employer identification number. The certification must be signed by a responsible officer in the case of a corporation, by a general partner in the case of a partnership, and by a trustee, executor, or equivalent fiduciary in the case of a trust or estate. No particular form is needed for a certification pursuant to this paragraph (b)(3)(ii)(B), nor is any particular language required, so long as the document meets the requirements of this paragraph. Samples of acceptable certifications are provided in paragraph (b)(3)(ii)(D) of this section. An entity may rely upon a certification pursuant to this paragraph (b)(3)(ii)(B) for a period of two calendar years following the close of the calendar year in which the certification was given. If an interest holder becomes a foreign person within the period described in the preceding sentence, the interest holder must notify the entity prior to any further dispositions or distributions and upon receipt of such notice (or any other notification of the foreign status of the interest holder) the entity may no longer rely upon the prior certification. An entity that obtains and relies upon a certification must retain that certification with its books and records for a period of three calendar years following the close of the last calendar year in which the entity relied upon the certification.

(C) *Foreign corporation that has made an election under section 897(i).*—A foreign corporation that has made a valid election under section 897(i) to be treated as a domestic corporation for purposes of section 897 may provide a certifi-cation of non-foreign status pursuant to this paragraph (b)(3)(ii). However, an electing foreign corporation must attach to such certification a copy of the acknowledgment of the election provided to the corporation by the Internal Revenue Service pursuant to §1.897-3(d)(4).

An acknowledgment is valid for this purpose only if it states that the information required by §1.897-3 has been determined to be complete.

(D) *Sample certifications.*—(1) *Individual interest-holder.*—"Under section 1445(e) of the Internal Revenue Code, a corporation, partnership, trust or estate must withhold tax with respect to certain transfers of property if a holder of an interest in the entity is a foreign person. To inform [*name of entity*]that no withholding is required with respect to my interest in it, I, [*name of interest-holder*], hereby certify the following:

1. I am not a nonresident alien for purposes of U.S. income taxation;

2. My U.S. taxpayer identifying number (Social Security number) is ——; and

3. My home address is

_____

_____

I agree to inform [name of entity] promptly if I become a nonresident alien at any time during the three years immediately following the date of this notice.

I understand that this certification may be disclosed to the Internal Revenue Service by [*name of entity*] and that any false statement I have made here could be punished by fine, imprisonment, or both.

Under penalties of perjury I declare that I have examined this certification and to the best of my knowledge and belief it is true, correct, and complete.
[*Signature and date*]"

(2) *Entity interest-holder.*—"Under section 1445(e) of the Internal Revenue Code, a corporation, partnership, trust, or estate must withhold tax with respect to certain transfers of property if a holder of an interest in the entity is a foreign person. To inform [*name of entity*]that no withholding is required with respect to [*name of interest-holder*]'s interest in it, the undersigned hereby certifies the following on behalf of [*name of interest-holder*]:

1. [*Name of interest-holder*] is not a foreign corporation, foreign partnership, foreign trust, or foreign estate (as those terms are defined in the Internal Revenue Code and Income Tax Regulations);

2. [*Name of interest-holder*]'s U.S. employer identification number is _____; and

3. [*Name of interest-holder*]'s office address is

_____

and place of incorporation (if applicable) is

_____

[Name of interest holder] agrees to inform [name of entity]if it becomes a foreign person at any time during the three year period immediately following the date of this notice.

[*Name of interest-holder*] understands that this certification may be disclosed to the Internal Revenue Service by [*name of entity*] and that any false statement contained herein could be punished by fine, imprisonment, or both.

Under penalties of perjury I declare that I have examined this certification and to the best of my knowledge and belief it is true, correct, and complete, and I further declare that I have authority to sign this document on behalf of [*name of interest-holder*].

[*Signature and date*]

[*Title*]"

(iii) *Reliance upon certification not permitted.*—An entity or fiduciary may not rely upon an interest-holder's certification of non-foreign status if, prior to or at the time of the transfer with respect to which withholding would be required, the entity or fiduciary either—

(A) Has actual knowledge that the certification is false;

(B) Has received a notice that the certification is false from a transferor's or transferee's agent, pursuant to § 1.1445-4; or

(C) Has received from a corporation that it knows to be a foreign corporation a certification that does not have attached to it a copy of the IRS acknowledgment of the corporation's election under section 897(i), as required by paragraph (b)(3)(ii)(C) of this section.

Such an entity's or fiduciary's withholding obligations shall apply as if a statement had never been given, and such an entity or fiduciary may be held fully liable pursuant to § 1.1445-1(e) for any failure to withhold. For special rules concerning an entity's belated receipt of a notice concerning a false certification, see paragraphs (c)(2)(ii) and (e)(2)(iii) of this section.

(iv) *Form W-9.*—For purposes of paragraph (b)(3)(i) of this section, a certification of non-foreign status includes a valid Form W-9, *Request for Taxpayer Identification Number and Certification*, or its successor, submitted to the transferee by the transferor.

(4) *Property transferred not a U.S. real property interest.*—(i) *In general.*—Pursuant to the provisions of paragraphs (c) and (d) of this section, an entity or fiduciary is required to withhold with respect to certain transfers of property, if the property transferred is a U.S. real property interest. (In addition, taxable distributions of U.S. real property interests by domestic or foreign partnerships, trusts, and estates will be subject to withholding pursuant to section 1445(e)(4) and paragraph (f) of this section after publication of a Treasury decision under sections 897(e)(2) and (g).) As defined in section 897(c) and § 1.897-1(c), a U.S. real property interest includes certain interests in U.S. corporations, as well as direct interests in real property and certain associated personal property. This paragraph (b)(4) provides rules pursuant to which an entity (or fiduciary thereof) that transfers an interest in a U.S. corporation may determine that withholding is not required because the interest transferred is not a U.S. real property interest. To determine whether an interest in tangible property constitutes a U.S. real property interest the transfer of which would be subject to withholding, see § 1.897-1(b) and (c).

(ii) *Interests in publicly traded entities.*—Withholding is not required under paragraph (c) or (d) of this section upon an entity's transfer of an interest in a domestic corporation if any class of stock of the corporation is regularly traded on an established securities market. This exemption shall apply to a disposition incident to an initial public offering of stock pursuant to a registration statement filed with the Securities and Exchange Commission. Similarly, no withholding is required under paragraph (c) or (d) of this section upon an entity's transfer of an interest in a publicly traded partnership or trust. However, the rule of this paragraph (b)(4)(ii) shall not apply to the transfer, to a single transferee (or related transferees as defined in § 1.897-1(i)) in a single transaction (or related transactions), of an interest described in § 1.897-1(c)(2)(iii)(B) (relating to substantial amounts of non-publicly traded interests in publicly traded corporations) or of similar interests in publicly traded partnerships or trusts. The entity making a transfer described in the preceding sentence must otherwise determine whether withholding is required, pursuant to section 1445(e) and the regulations thereunder. Transactions shall be deemed to be related if they are undertaken within 90 days

of one another or if if can otherwise be shown that they were undertaken in pursuance of a prearranged plan.

(iii) *Corporation's statement that interest is not a U.S. real property interest.*—(A) *In general.*—No withholding is required under paragraph (c) or (d) of this section upon an entity's transfer of an interest in a domestic corporation if, prior to the transfer, the entity or fiduciary obtains a statement, issued by the corporation pursuant to § 1.897-2(h), certifying that the interest is not a U.S. real property interest. In general, a corporation may issue such a statement only if the corporation was not a U.S. real property holding corporation at any time during the previous five years (or the period in which the interest was held by its present holder, if shorter) or if interests in the corporation ceased to be United States real property interests under section 897(c)(1)(B). (A corporation may not provide such a statement based on its determination that the interest in question is an interest solely as a creditor.) See § 1.897-2(f) and (h). A corporation's statement may be relied upon for purposes of this paragraph (b)(4)(iii) only if the statement is dated not more than 30 days prior to the date of the transfer.

(B) *Reliance on statement not permitted.*—An entity or fiduciary is not entitled to rely upon a statement that an interest in a corporation is not a U.S. real property interest if, prior to or at the time of the transfer, the entity or fiduciary either—

(1) Has actual knowledge that the statement is false, or

(2) Receives a notice that the statement is false from a transferor's or transferee's agent, pursuant to § 1.1445-4.

Such an entity's or fiduciary's withholding obligations shall apply as if a statement had never been given, and such an entity or fiduciary may be held fully liable pursuant to § 1.1445-1(e) for any failure to withhold. For special rules concerning an entity's belated receipt of a notice concerning a false statement, see paragraphs (c)(2)(iii) and (d)(2)(i) of this section.

(5) *Reporting and paying over of withheld amounts.*—(i) *In general.*—An entity or fiduciary must report and pay over to the Internal Revenue Service any tax withheld pursuant to section 1445(e) and this section by the 20th day after the date of the transfer (as defined in § 1.1445-1(g)(8)). Forms 8288 and 8288-A are used for this purpose and must be filed at the location as provided in the instructions to Forms 8288 and 8288-A. The contents of Forms 8288 and 8288-A are described in § 1.1445-1(d). Pursuant to section 7502 and regulations thereunder, the timely mailing of Forms 8288 and 8288-A by U.S. mail will be treated as their timely filing. Form 8288-A will be stamped by the Internal Revenue Service to show receipt, and a stamped copy will be mailed by the Service to the interest holder if the Form 8288 is complete, including the transferor's identifying number, at the address shown on the form, for the interest-holder's use. See paragraph (b)(7) of this section.

If an application for a withholding certificate with respect to a transfer of a U.S. real property interest was submitted to the Internal Revenue Service on the day of or at any time prior to the transfer, the entity or fiduciary must withhold the amount required under section 1445(e) and the rules of this section. However, the amount withheld, or a lesser amount as determined by the Service, need not be reported and paid over to the Service until the 20th day following the Service's final determination. For this purpose, the Service's final determination occurs on the day when the withholding certificate is mailed to the applicant by the Service or when notification denying the request for a withholding certificate is mailed to the applicant by the Service. An application is submitted to the Service on the day it is actualy received by the Service at the address provided in § 1.1445-1(g)(10) or, under the rules of section 7502, on the day it is mailed to the Service at the address provided in § 1.1445-1(g)(10), concerning the issuance of withholding certificates see § 1.1445-6.

(ii) *Anti-abuse rule.*—An entity or fiduciary that in reliance upon the rules of this paragraph (b)(5)(ii) fails to report and pay over amounts withheld by the 20th day following the date of the transfer, shall be subject to the payment of interest and penalties if the relevant application for a withholding certificate (or an amendment of the application for a withholding certificate) was submitted for a principle purpose of delaying the payment to the IRS of the amount withheld. Interest and penalties shall be assessed on the amount that is ultimately paid over with respect to the period between the 20th day after the date of the transfer and the date on which payment is made.

(6) *Liability upon failure to withhold.*—For rules regarding liability upon failure to withhold under section 1445(e) and this § 1.1445-5, see § 1.1445-1(e).

(7) *Effect of withholding by entity or fiduciary upon interest holder.*—The withholding of tax under section 1445(e) does not excuse a foreign person that is subject to U.S. tax by reason of the operation of section 897 from filing a U.S. tax return. Thus, Form 1040NR, 1041, or

1120F as appropriate must be filed and any tax due must be paid by the filing date otherwise applicable to such person (or any extension therof). The tax withheld with respect to the foreign person under section 1445(e) (as shown on Form 8288-A) shall be credited against the amount of income tax as computed in such return, but only if the stamped copy of Form 8288-A provided to the entity or fiduciary (under paragraph (b)(5) of this section) is attached to the return or substantial evidence of the amount of tax withheld is attached to the return in accordance with the succeeding sentence. If a stamped copy of Form 8288-A has not been provided to the interest-holder by the Service, the interest-holder may establish the amount of tax withheld by the entity or fiduciary by attaching to its return substantial evidence of such amount. Such an interest-holder must attach to its return a statement which supplies all of the information required by § 1.1445-1(d)(2). If the amount withheld under section 1445(e) constitutes less than the full amount of the foreign person's U.S. tax liability for that taxable year, then a payment of estimated tax may be required to be made pursuant to section 6154 or 6654 prior to the filing of the income tax return for that year. Alternatively, if the amount withheld under section 1445(e) exceeds the foreign person's maximum tax liability with respect to the transaction (as *reflected* in a withholding certificate issued by the Internal Revenue Service pursuant to § 1.1445-6), then the foreign person may seek an early refund of the excess pursuant to § 1.1445-6(g). A foreign person that takes gain into account in accordance with the provisions of section 453 shall not be entitled to a refund of the amount withheld unless a withholding certificate providing for such a refund is obtained pursuant to § 1.1445-6.

If an entity or fiduciary withholds tax under section 1445(e) with respect to a beneficial owner of an interest who is not a foreign person, such beneficial owner may credit the amount of any tax withheld against his income tax liability in accordance with the provisions of this § 1.1445-5(b)(7) or apply for an early refund under § 1.1445-6(g).

(8) *Effective dates.*—(i) *Partnership, trust, and estate dispositions of U.S. real property interests.*—The provisions of section 1445(e)(1) and paragraph (c) of this section, requiring withholding upon certain dispositions of U.S. real property interests by domestic partnerships, trusts and estates, shall apply to any disposition on or after January 1, 1985.

(ii) *Certain distributions by foreign corporations.*—The provisions of section 1445(e)(2) and paragraph (d) of this section requiring withholding upon distributions of U.S. real property interest by foreign corporations, shall apply to distributions made on or after January 1, 1985.

(iii) *Distributions by certain domestic corporations to foreign shareholders.*—The provisions of section 1445(e)(3) and paragraph (e)(1) of this section, requiring withholding upon distributions in redemption of stock under section 302(a) or liquidating distributions under Part II of subchapter C of the Internal Revenue Code by U.S. real property holding corporations to foreign shareholders, shall apply to distributions made on or after January 1, 1985. The provisions of section 1445(e)(3) and paragraph (e)(1) of this section requiring withholding on distributions under section 301 by U.S. real property holding corporations to foreign shareholders shall apply to distributions made after August 20, 1996. The provisions of paragraph (e) of this section providing for the coordination of withholding between sections 1445 and 1441 (or 1442 or 1443) for distributions under section 301 by U.S. real property holding corporations to foreign shareholders apply to distributions after December 31, 2000 (see § 1.1441-3(c)(4) and (h)).

(iv) *Taxable distributions by domestic or foreign partnerships, trusts, and estates.*—The provisions of section 1445(e)(4), requiring withholding upon certain taxable distributions by domestic or foreign partnerships, trusts, and estates, shall apply to distributions made on or after the effective date of a Treasury decision under section 897(e)(2)(B)(ii) and (g).

(v) [Removed]

(vi) *Tiered partnerships.*—No withholding is required upon the disposition of a U.S. real property interest by a partnership which is directly owned, in whole or in part, by another domestic partnership

(but only to the extent that the amount realized is attributable to the partnership interest of that other partnership) until the effective date of a Treasury Decision published under section 1445(e) providing rules governing this matter.

(c) *Dispositions of U.S. real property interests by domestic partnerships, trusts, and estates.*—(1) *Withholding required.*—(i) *In general.*—If a domestic partnership, trust, or estate disposes of a U.S. real property interest and any partner, beneficiary, or owner of the entity is a foreign person, then the partnership or the trustee, executor, or equivalent fiduciary of the trust or estate must withhold tax with respect to each such foreign person in accordance with the provisions of subdivision (ii), (iii), or (iv) of this paragraph (c)(1) (as applicable). The withholding obligation imposed by this paragraph (c) applies to the fiduciary of a trust even if the grantor of the trust or another person is treated as the owner of the trust or any portion thereof for purposes of the Internal Revenue Code. Thus, the withholding obligation imposed by this paragraph (c) applies to the trustee of a land trust or similar arrangement, even if such a trustee is not ordinarily treated under the applicable provisions of local law as a true fiduciary.

(ii) *Disposition by partnership.*—A partnership must withhold a tax equal to the rate specified in section 1445(e)(1) multiplied by the amount of each foreign partner's distributive share of the gain realized by the partnership upon the disposition of each U.S. real property interest. Such distributive share of the gain must be determined pursuant to the principles of section 704 and the regulations thereunder. For the rules applicable to partnerships, interests in which are regularly traded on an established securities market, see § 1.1445-8.

(iii) *Disposition by trust or estate.*—(A) *In general.*—A trustee, fiduciary, executor or equivalent fiduciary (hereafter collectively referred to as the fiduciary) of a trust or estate having one or more foreign beneficiaries must withhold tax in accordance with the rules of this § 1.1445-5(c)(1)(iii). Such a fiduciary must establish a U.S. real property interest account and must enter in such account all gains and losses realized during the taxable year of the trust or estate from dispositions of U.S. real property interests. The fiduciary must withhold a tax equal to the rate specified in section 1445(e)(1) multiplied by the amount of any distribution to a foreign beneficiary that is attributable to the balance in the U.S. real property interest account on the day of the distribution. A distribution from a trust or estate to a beneficiary (domestic or foreign) shall, solely for purposes of section 1445(e)(1), be deemed to be attributable first to any balance in the U.S. real property interest account and then to other amounts. However, a distribution that occurs prior to the transfer of a U.S. real property interest in a taxable year or at any other time when the amount contained in the U.S. real property interest account is zero, is not subject to withholding under this § 1.1445-5(c)(1)(iii). The U.S. real property interest account is reduced by the amount distributed to all beneficiaries (domestic and foreign) attributable to such account during the taxable year of the trust or estate. Any ending balance of the U.S. real property interest account not distributed by the close of the taxable year of the trust or estate is cancelled and is not carried over (or carried back) to any other year. Thus, the beginning balance of such account in any taxable year of the trust or estate is always zero. For rules applicable to grantor trusts see § 1.1445-5(c)(1)(iv). For rules applicable to trusts, interests in which are regularly traded on an established securities market and real estate investment trusts, see § 1.1445-8.

(B) *Example.*—The following example illustrates the rules of paragraph (c)(1)(iii)(A) of this section.

On January 1, 1994, A establishes a domestic trust (which has as its taxable year, the calendar year) for the benefit of B, a nonresident alien, and C, a U.S. citizen. The trust is not a trust subject to sections 671 through 679. Under the terms of the trust, the trustee, T, is given discretion to distribute income and corpus of the trust to provide for the reasonable needs of B and C. During the trust's 1994 tax year, T disposes of three parcels of vacant land located in the United States. The following chart illustrates the computation of the amount subject to withholding under section 1445 with respect to distributions made by T to B and C during 1994. In 1994, the relevant rate of withholding (that is, the rate specified in section 1445(e)(1)) was 35%.

| Date | Parcel sold | Gains or (loss) realized | Distributions to C | Distributions to B (before withholding) | Section 1445 withholding (35% rate) | U.S. real property interest account |
|------|------|------|------|------|------|------|
| 1/01/94 | | | | | | -0- |
| 3/01/94 | Parcel 1 | 140,000 | | | | 140,000 |
| 3/05/94 | | | 5,000 | 10,000 | 3,500 | 125,000 |
| 3/15/94 | | | 10,000 | 5,000 | 1,750 | 110,000 |
| 5/01/94 | Parcel 2 | 300,000 | | | | 410,000 |
| 5/15/94 | Parcel 3 | (50,000) | | | | 360,000 |
| 12/01/94 | | | 170,000 | 170,000 | 59,500 | 20,000 |
| 1/01/95 | | | | | | -0- |

Reg. § 1.1445-5(c)(1)(iii)(B)

(iv) *Disposition by grantor trust.*—The trustee or equivalent fiduciary of a trust that is subject to the provisions of subpart E of part 1 of subchapter J ( sections 671 through 679) must withhold a tax equal to the rate specified in section 1445(e)(1) multiplied by the amount of the gain realized from each disposition of a U.S. real property interest to the extent such gain is allocable to a portion of the trust treated as owned by a foreign person under subpart E of part I of subchapter J.

(2) *Withholding not required under paragraph (c).*—(i) [Removed]

(ii) *Interest-holder not a foreign person.*—(A) *In general.*—A domestic partnership, trust, or estate that disposes of a U.S. real property interest shall not be required to withhold with respect to any partner or beneficiary that it determines, pursuant to the rules of paragraph (b)(3) of this section, not to be a foreign person.

(B) *Belated notice of false certification.*—If after the date of the transfer a partnership or fiduciary learns that a partner's or beneficiary's certification of non-foreign status is false, then that partnership or fiduciary shall be required to withhold, with respect to the foreign partner or beneficiary that gave the false certification, the lesser of—

(1) The amount otherwise required to be withheld under the rules of this paragraph (c), or

(2) An amount equal to that partner's or beneficiary's remaining interests in the income or assets of the partnership, trust, or estate.

Amounts so withheld must be reported and paid over by the 60th day following the date on which the partnership or fiduciary learns that the certification is false. For rules concerning the notifications of false certifications that may be required to be given to partnerships and fiduciaries, see § 1.1445-4(b).

(iii) *Property disposed of not a U.S. real property interest.*—(A) *In general.*—No withholding is required under this paragraph (c) if a domestic partnership, trust, or estate that disposes of property determines pursuant to the rules of paragraph (b)(4) of this section that the property disposed of is not a U.S. real property interest.

(B) *Belated notice of false statement.*—If after the date of the transfer a partnership or fiduciary learns that a corporation's statement (that an interest in the corporation is not a U.S. real property interest) is false, then that partnership or fiduciary shall be required to withhold, with respect to each foreign partner or beneficiary, the lesser of—

(1) The amount otherwise required to be withheld under the rules of this paragraph (c), or

(2) An amount equal to that partner's or beneficiary's remaining interests in the income or assets of the partnership, trust, or estate.

Amounts so withheld must be reported and paid over by the 60th day following the date on which the partnership or fiduciary learns that the statement is false. For rules concerning the notifications of false statements that may be required to be given to partnerships or fiduciaries, see § 1.1445-4(b).

(iv) *Withholding certificate.*—No withholding is required under this paragraph (c) with respect to the transfer of a U.S. real property interest if the Internal Revenue Service issues a withholding certificate that so provides. For rules concerning the issuance of withholding certificates, see § 1.1445-6.

(v) *Nonrecognition transactions.*—For special rules concerning transactions entitled to nonrecognition of gain or loss, see paragraph (b)(2) of this section.

(3) *Large partnerships or trusts.*—(i) *In general.*—If a partnership or trust has more than 100 partners or beneficiaries, then the partnership or fiduciary of the trust may elect to withhold in accordance with the provisions of this § 1.1445-5(c)(3) in lieu of withholding in the manner required by § 1.1445-5(c)(1). However, the rules of this § 1.1445-5(c)(3) shall not apply to any partnership or trust interests in which are regularly traded on an established securities market except as described in § 1.1445-8(c)(1). The rules of this § 1.1445-5(c)(3) shall not apply to any real estate investment trust. *See* § 1.1445-8.

(ii) *Amount to be withheld.*—A partnership or trust electing to withhold under this paragraph (c)(3) shall withhold from each distri-

bution to a foreign person an amount equal to the rate specified in section 1445(e)(1) multiplied by of the amount attributable to section 1445(e)(1) transfers.

(iii) *Amounts attributable to section 1445(e)(1) transfers.*—A distribution is attributable to section 1445(e)(1) transfers to the extent of the partner's or beneficiary's proportionate share of the current balance of the entity's section 1445(e)(1) account. A distribution from a partnership or trust that has made an election under this § 1.1445-5(c)(3) shall be deemed first to be attributable to a section 1445(e)(1) transfer to the extent of the balance in the section 1445(e)(1) account. An entity's section 1445(e)(1) account shall be equal to—

(A) The total amount of net gain realized by the entity upon all transfers of U.S. real property interests carried out by the entity after the date of its election under this § 1.1445-5(c)(3); minus

(B) The total amount of all distributions by the entity to domestic and foreign distributees from such account.

(iv) *Special rules for entities that make recurring sales of growing crops and timber.*—An entity that makes an election under § 1.1445-5(c)(3) and that makes recurring sales of growing crops and timber may further elect to determine the amount subject to withholding under the rules of this § 1.1445-5(c)(3)(iv). Such an entity must withhold from each distribution to a foreign partner or beneficiary an amount equal to 15 percent of such partner's or beneficiary's proportionate share of the current balance of the entity's gross section 1445(e)(1) account. An entity's gross section 1445(e)(1) account equals—

(A) The total amount realized by the entity upon all transfers of U.S. real property interests carried out by the entity after the date of its election under this § 1.1445-5(c)(3)(iv); minus

(B) The total amount of all distributions to domestic and foreign distributees from such account.

An entity that elects to compute the amount subject to withholding under this § 1.1445-5(c)(3)(iv), shall make such election in accordance with § 1.1445-5(c)(3)(vi) and shall be subject to the provisions otherwise applicable under § 1.1445-5(c)(3).

(v) *Procedural rules.*—An election under paragraph (c)(3) may be made by filing a notice thereof at the address provided in § 1.1445-1(g)(10). The notice must be submitted by a general partner (in the case of a partnership) or the trustee or equivalent fiduciary (in the case of a trust). The notice must set forth the name, office address, and identifying number of the partnership or fiduciary making the election, and, in the case of a partnership, must include the name, office address, and identifying number of the general partner submitting the election. An election under this paragraph (c)(3) may be revoked only with the consent of the Internal Revenue Service. Consent of the Service may be requested by filing an application to revoke the election at the address stated above. This application must include all information provided to the Service with the election notice and must provide an explanation of the reasons for revoking the election. The application to revoke an election must also specify the amount remaining to be distributed in the section 1445(e)(1) account or the gross section 1445(e)(1) account. An entity that ceases to qualify under section 1.1445-5(c)(3) because such entity does not have more than 100 partners or beneficiaries may revoke its election only with the consent of the Internal Revenue Service.

(d) *Distributions of U.S. real property interests by foreign corporations.*—(1) *In general.*—A foreign corporation that distributes a U.S. real property interest must deduct and withhold a tax equal to the rate specified in section 1445(e)(2) multiplied by of the amount of gain recognized by the corporation on the distribution. The amount of gain required to be recognized by the corporation must be detemined pursuant to the rules of section 897 and any other applicable section. For special rules concerning the applicability of a nonrecognition provision to a distribution, see paragraph (b)(2) of this section. The withholding liability imposed by this paragraph (d) applies to the same taxpayer that owes the related substantive income tax liability pursuant to the operation of section 897. Only one such liability will be assessed and collected from a foreign corporation, but separate penalties for failures to comply with the two requirements will be asserted.

(2) *Withholding not required.*—(i) *Property distributed not a U.S. real property interest.*—(A) *In general.*—No withholding is required

under this paragraph (d) if a foreign corporation that distributes property determines pursuant to the rules of paragraph (b)(3) of this section that the property distributed is not a U.S. real property interest.

(B) *Belated notice of false statement.*—If after the date of a distribution described in paragraph (d)(1) of this section a foreign corporation learns that another corporation's statement (that an interest in that other corporation is not a U.S. real property interest) is false, then the foreign corporation may not rely upon that statement for any purpose. Such a foreign corporation's withholding obligations under this paragaph (d) shall apply as if a statement had never been given, and such a corporation may be held fully liable pursuant to § 1.1445-5(b)(5) for any failure to withhold. Amounts withheld pursuant to the rule of this paragraph (d)(2)(i)(B) must be reported and paid over by the 60th day following the date on which the foreign corporation learns that the statement is false. No penalties or interest will be assessed for failures to withhold prior to that date. For rules concerning the notifications of false statements that may be required to be given to foreign corporations, see § 1.1445-4(b).

(ii) *Withholding certificate.*—No withholding is required under this paragraph (d) with respect to a foreign corporation's distribution of a U.S. real property interest if the distributing corporation obtains a withholding certificate from the Internal Revenue Service that so provides. For rules concerning the issuance of withholding certificates, see § 1.1445-6.

(e) *Distributions to foreign persons by U.S. real property holding corporations.*—(1) *In general.*—A domestic corporation that distributes any property to a foreign person that holds an interest in the corporation must deduct and withhold a tax equal to 15 percent of the fair market value of the property distributed to the foreign person, if—

(i) The foreign person's interest in the corporation constitutes a U.S. real property interest under the provisions of section 897 and regulations thereunder; and

(ii) There is a distribution of property in redemption of stock treated as an exchange under section 302(a), in liquidation of the corporation pursuant to the provisions of Part II of subchapter C of the Internal Revenue Code (sections 331 through section 346), or with respect to stock under section 301 that is not made out of earnings and profits of the corporation.

(2) *Coordination rules for Section 301 distributions.*—If a domestic corporation makes a distribution of property under section 301 to a foreign person whose interest in such corporation constitutes a U.S. real property interest under the provisions of section 897 and the regulations thereunder, then see § 1.1441-3(c)(4) for rules coordinating withholding obligations under sections 1445 and 1441 (or 1442 or 1443)).

(3) *Withholding not required.*—(i) *Foreign person's interest not a U.S. real property interest.*—Withholding is required under this paragraph (e) only with respect to distributions to foreign persons holding interests in the corporation that constitute U.S. real property interests. In general, a foreign person's interest in a domestic corporation constitutes a U.S. real property interest if the corporation was a U.S. real property holding corporation at any time during the shorter of (A) the period in which the foreign person held the interest or (B) the previous five years (but not earlier than June 19, 1980). See section 897(c) and §§ 1.897-1(c) and 1.897-2(b) and (h). However, an interest in such a corporation ceases to be a U.S. real property interest after all of the U.S. real property interests held by the corporation itself are disposed of in transactions on which gain or loss is recognized. See section 897(c)(1)(B) and § 1.897-2(f)(2). Thus, if a U.S. real property holding corporation in the process of liquidation does not elect section 337 nonrecognition treatment upon its sale of all U.S. real property interests held by the corporation, and recognizes gain or loss upon such sales, interests in that corporation cease to be U.S. real property interests. Therefore, no withholding would be required with respect to that corporation's subsequent liquidating distribution to a foreign shareholder of property other than a U.S. real property interest.

(ii) *Nonrecognition transactions.*—For special rules concerning the applicability of a nonrecognition provision to a distribution described in paragraph (e)(1) of this section, see paragraph (b)(2) of this section.

(iii) *Interest-holder not a foreign person.*—(A) *In general.*—A domestic corporation shall not be required to withhold under this paragraph (e) with respect to a distribution of property to any distributee that it determines, pursuant to the rules of paragraph (b)(3) of this section, not to be a foreign person.

(B) *Belated notice of false certification.*—If after the date of a distribution described in paragraph (e)(1) of this section a domestic

corporation learns that an interest-holder's certification of non-foreign status is false, then the corporation may rely upon that certification only if the person providing the false certification holds (or held) less than 10 percent of the value of the outstanding stock of the corporation. With respect to less than 10 percent interest-holders, no withholding is required under this paragraph (e) upon receipt of a belated notice of false certification. With respect to 10 percent or greater interest-holders, the corporation's withholding obligations under this paragraph (e) shall apply as if a certification had never been given, and such a corporation may be held fully liable pursuant to § 1.1445-5(b)(6) for any failure to withhold as of the date specified in this § 1.1445-5(e)(3)(iii)(B). Amounts withheld pursuant to the rule of this paragraph (e)(3)(iii)(B) must be reported and paid over by the 60th day following the date on which the corporation learns that the certification is false. No penalties or interest for failures to withhold will be assessed prior to that date. For rules concerning the notifications of false certifications that may be required to be given to U.S. real property holding corporations, see § 1.1445-4(b).

(iv) *Withholding certificate.*—No withholding, or reduced withholding, is required under this paragraph (e) with respect to a domestic corporation's distribution of property if the distributing corporation obtains a withholding certificate from the Internal Revenue Service that so provides. For rules concerning the issuance of withholding certificates, see § 1.1445-6.

(f) *Taxable distributions by domestic or foreign partnerships, trusts, or estates.*—[Reserved]

(g) *Dispositions of interests in partnerships, trusts, and estates.*—[Reserved]

(h) *Applicability dates.*—The requirement in paragraphs (b)(2)(ii)(B) and (C) of this section that taxpayer identification numbers be provided (in all cases) is is applicable for dispositions of U.S. real property interests occurring after November 3, 2003. The withholding rates set forth in paragraphs (c)(3)(iv) and (e)(1) of this section apply to distributions after February 16, 2016. For distributions on or before February 16, 2016, see paragraphs (c)(3)(iv) and (e)(1) of this section as contained in 26 CFR part 1 revised as of April 1, 2015. Paragraph (b)(3)(iv) of this section applies to certifications provided on or after May 7, 2019, except that a taxpayer may choose to apply paragraph (b)(3)(iv) of this section with respect to certifications provided before May 7, 2019. Paragraphs (c) and (d) of this section apply to distributions on or after November 30, 2020. [Reg. § 1.1445-5.]

☐ [*T.D.* 8113, 12-18-86. *Amended by T.D.* 8198, 5-4-88; *T.D.* 8321, 12-6-90; *T.D.* 8647, 12-20-95; *T.D.* 8734, 10-6-97 (T.D. 8804 delayed the effective date of T.D. 8734 from January 1, 1999, to January 1, 2000; T.D. 8856 further delayed the effective date of T.D. 8734 until January 1, 2001), *T.D.* 9082, 8-4-2003, *T.D.* 9751, 2-17-2016 (*corrected* 4-25-2016) *and T.D.* 9926, 11-27-2020.]

## [Reg. § 1.1445-6]

**§ 1.1445-6. Adjustments pursuant to withholding certificate of amount required to be withheld under section 1445(e).—**
(a) *Withholding certificate for purposes of section 1445(e).*—(1) *In general.*—Pursuant to the provisions of § 1.1445-5(c)(2)(iv), (d)(2)(ii), and (e)(2)(iv), withholding under section 1445(e) may be reduced or eliminated pursuant to a withholding certificate issued by the Internal Revenue Service in accordance with the rules of this § 1.1445-6. A withholding certificate may be issued in cases where adjusted withholding is appropriate (e.g., because of the applicability of a nonrecognition provision—see paragraph (c) of this section), where the relevant taxpayers are exempt from U.S. tax (see paragraph (d) of this section), or where an agreement for the payment of tax is entered into with the Service (see paragraph (e) of this section). A withholding certificate that is obtained prior to a transfer allows the entity or fiduciary to withhold a reduced amount or excuses withholding entirely. A withholding certificate that is obtained after a transfer has been made may authorize a normal refund or an early refund pursuant to paragraph (g) of this section. The Internal Revenue Service will act upon an application for a withholding certificate not later than the 90th day after it is received. (The Service may deny a request for a withholding certificate where, after due notice, an applicant fails to provide the information necessary to make a determination.) Solely for this purpose (i.e., determining the day upon which the 90 day period commences), an application is received by the Service on the date when all information necessary for the Service to make a determination is provided by the applicant. In no event, however, will a withholding certificate be issued without the transferor's identifying number. (For rules regarding whether an application has been timely submitted, see § 1.1445-5(b)(5).) The Internal Revenue Service will act upon an application for an early refund not later than the 90th day after it is received. An application for an early refund must either (i) include a copy of a withholding certificate issued by the Service with respect to the transaction, or (ii) be combined with an application for

a withholding certificate. Where an application for an early refund is combined with an application for a withholding certificate, the Service will act upon both applications not later than the 90th day after receipt. Either an entity, a fiduciary, or a relevant taxpayer (as defined in paragraph (a)(2) of this section) may apply for a withholding certificate. An entity or fiduciary may apply for a withholding certificate with respect to all or less than all relevant taxpayers. For special rules concerning the issuance of a withholding certificate to a foreign corporation that has made an election under section 897(i), see § 1.1445-7(d).

(2) *Relevant taxpayer.*—For purposes of this section, the term "relevant taxpayer" means any foreign person that will bear substantive income tax liability by reason of the operation of section 897 with respect to a transaction upon which withholding is required under section 1445(e).

(b) *Applications for withholding certificates.*—(1) *In general.*—An application for a withholding certificate pursuant to this § 1.1445-6 must be submitted in the manner provided in § 1.1445-3(b). However, in lieu of the information required to be submitted pursuant to § 1.1445-3(b)(4), the applicant must provide the information required by paragraph (b)(2) of this section. In addition, the information required by paragraph (b)(3) of this section must be submitted with the application.

(2) *Basis for certificate.*—(i) *Adjusted withholding.*—If a withholding certificate is sought on the basis of a claim that adjusted withholding is appropriate, the application must include a calculation, in accordance with paragraph (c) of this section, of the maximum tax that may be imposed on each relevant taxpayer with respect to which adjusted withholding is sought. The application must also include all evidence necessary to substantiate the claimed calculation, such as records of adjustments to basis or appraisals of fair market value.

(ii) *Exemption.*—If a withholding certificate is sought on the basis of a relevant taxpayer's exemption from U.S. tax, the application must set forth a brief statement of the law and facts that support the claimed exemption. See paragraph (d) of this section.

(iii) *Agreement.*—If a withholding certificate is sought on the basis of an agreement for the payment of tax, the application must include a copy of the agreement proposed by the applicant and a copy of the security instrument (if any) proposed by the applicant. In this regard, see paragraph (e) of this section.

(3) *Relevant taxpayers.*—An application for withholding certificate pursuant to this section must include all of the following information: the name, identifying number, and home address (in the case of an individual) or office address (in the case of an entity) of each relevant taxpayer with respect to which adjusted withholding is sought.

(c) *Adjustment of amount required to be withheld.*—The Internal Revenue Service may issue a withholding certificate that excuses withholding, or that permits an entity or fiduciary to withhold an adjusted amount reflecting the relevant taxpayers' maximum tax liability. A relevant taxpayer's maximum tax liability is the maximum amount which that taxpayer could be required to pay as tax by reason of the transaction upon which withholding is required. In the case of an individual taxpayer that amount will generally be the gain realized by the individual, multiplied by the maximum individual income tax rate applicable to long term capital gain. In the case of a corporate taxpayer, that amount will generally be the gain realized by the corporation, multiplied by the maximum corporate income tax rate applicable to long term capital gain. However, that amount must be adjusted to take into account the following:

(1) Any reduction of tax to which the relevant taxpayer is entitled under the provisions of a U.S. income tax treaty;

(2) The effect of any nonrecognition provision that is applicable to the transaction;

(3) Any losses previously realized and recognized by the relevant taxpayer during the taxable year by reason of the operation of section 897;

(4) Any amount realized upon the subject transfer by the relevant taxpayer that is required to be treated as ordinary income under any provision of the Code; and

(5) Any other factor that may increase or reduce the tax upon the transaction.

(d) *Relevant taxpayer's exemption from U.S. tax.*—(1) *In general.*—The Internal Revenue Service will issue a withholding certificate that excuses withholding by an entity or fiduciary if it is established that a relevant taxpayer's income from the transaction will be exempt from U.S. tax. For the available exemptions, see paragraph (d)(2) of this section. If a relevant taxpayer is entitled to a reduction of (rather than an exemption from) U.S. tax, then the entity or fiduciary may obtain

a withholding certificate to that effect pursuant to the provisions of paragraph (c) of this section.

(2) *Available exemptions.*—A relevant taxpayer's income from a transaction with respect to which withholding is required under section 1445(e) may be exempt from U.S. tax because either:

(i) The relevant taxpayer is an integral part or controlled entity of a foreign government and the subject income is exempt from U.S. tax pursuant to section 892 and the regulations thereunder; or

(ii) The relevant taxpayer is entitled to the benefits of an income tax treaty that provides for such an exemption (subject to the limitations imposed by section 1125(c) of Pub. L. 96-499, which, in general, overrides such benefits as of January 1, 1985).

(e) *Agreement for the payment of tax.*—(1) *In general.*—The Internal Revenue Service will issue a withholding certificate that excuses withholding or that permits an entity or fiduciary to withhold a reduced amount, if the entity, fiduciary, or a relevant taxpayer enters into an agreement for the payment of tax pursuant to the provisions of this paragraph (e). An agreement for the payment of tax is a contract between the Service and the entity, fiduciary, or relevant taxpayer that consists of two necessary elements. Those elements are—

(i) A contract between the Service and the other person, setting forth in detail the rights and obligations of each; and

(ii) A security instrument or other form of security acceptable to the Assistant Commissioner (International).

(2) *Contents of agreement.*—(i) *In general.*—An agreement for the payment of tax must cover an amount described in subdivision (ii) or (iii) of this paragraph (e)(2). The agreement may either provide adequate security for the payment of the chosen amount with respect to the relevant taxpayer in accordance with paragraph (e)(3) of this section, or provide for the payment of that amount through a combination of security and withholding of tax by the entity or fiduciary.

(ii) *Tax that would otherwise be withheld.*—An agreement for the payment of tax may cover the amount of tax that would otherwise be required to be withheld with respect to the relevant taxpayer pursuant to section 1445(e). In addition to the amount computed pursuant to section 1445(e), the applicant must agree to pay interest upon that amount, at the rate established under section 6621, with respect to the period between the date on which withholding tax under section 1445(e) would otherwise be due and the date on which the relevant taxpayer's payment of tax with respect to the disposition will be due. The amount of interest agreed upon must be paid by the applicant regardless of whether or not the Service is required to draw upon any security provided pursuant to the agreement. The interest may be paid either with the return or by the Service drawing upon the security.

(iii) *Maximum tax liability.*—An agreement for the payment of tax may cover the relevant taxpayer's maximum tax liability, determined in accordance with paragraph (c) of this section. The agreement must also provide for the payment of an additional amount equal to 25 percent of the amount determined under paragraph (c) of this section. This additional amount secures the interest and penalties that would accrue between the date of the relevant taxpayer's failure to file a return and pay tax with respect to the disposition, and the date on which the Service collects upon that liability pursuant to the agreement.

(iv) *Allocation of payment.*—An agreement for the payment of tax pursuant to this section must set forth an allocation of the payment provided for by the agreement among the relevant taxpayers with respect to which the withholding certificate is sought. In the case of an agreement that covers an amount described in subdivision (ii) of this paragraph (e)(2), such allocation must be based upon the amount that would otherwise be required to be withheld with respect to each relevant taxpayer. In the case of an agreement that covers an amount described in subdivision (iii) of this paragraph (e)(2), such allocation must be based upon each relevant taxpayer's maximum tax liability.

(3) *Major types of security.*—The major types of security that are acceptable to the Internal Revenue Service for purposes of this section are described in § 1.1445-3(e)(3).

(4) *Terms of security instrument.*—Any security instrument that is furnished pursuant to this section must contain the terms described in § 1.1445-3(e)(4).

(f) *Amendments to application for withholding certificates.*—(1) *In general.*—An applicant for a withholding certificate may amend an otherwise complete application by submitting an amending statement to the address provided in § 1.1445-1(g)(10). The amending statement shall provide the information required by § 1.1445-6(f)(3) and must be signed and accompanied by a penalties of perjury statement in accordance with §1.1445-6(b).

(2) *Extension of time for the Service to process requests for withholding certificates.*—(i) *In general.*—If an amending statement is submitted, the time in which the Internal Revenue Service must act upon the amended application shall be extended by 30 days.

(ii) *Substantial amendments.*—If an amending statement is submitted and the Service finds that the statement substantially amends to the facts of the underlying application or substantially alters the terms of the withholding certificate as requested in the initial application, the time within which the Service must act upon the amended application shall be extended by 60 days. The applicant shall be so notified.

(iii) *Amending statement received after the requested withholding certificate has been signed on behalf of the Service.*—If an amending statement is received after the withholding certificate, drafted in response to the underlying application, has been signed on behalf of the Service and prior to the day such certificate is mailed to the applicant, the time in which the Service must act upon the amended application shall be extended by 90 days.

(3) *Information required to be submitted.*—No particular form is required for an amending statement but the statement must provide the following information:

(i) *Identification of applicant.*—The amending statement must set forth the name, address, and identifying number of the person submitting the amending statement.

(ii) *Date of application.*—The amending statement must set forth the date of the underlying application for a withholding certificate.

(iii) *Real property interest to be (or that has been) transferred.*—The amending statement must set forth a brief description of the real property interest with respect to which the underlying application for a withholding certificate was submitted.

(iv) *Amending information.*—The amending statement must fully set forth the basis for the amendment including any modification of the facts supporting the application for a withholding certificate and any change sought in the terms of the withholding certificate.

(g) *Early refund of overwithheld amounts.*—If the Internal Revenue Service issues a withholding certificate pursuant to this section, and an amount greater than that specified in the certificate was withheld by the entity or fiduciary, then pursuant to the rules of this paragraph (g) a relevant taxpayer may apply for an early refund of a proportionate share of the excess amount (without interest) prior to the date on which the relevant taxpayer's return is due (without extensions). An application for an early refund must be delivered to the address provided in §1.1445-1(g)(10). No particular form is required for the application, but the following information must be set forth in separate paragraphs numbered to correspond with the numbers given below:

(1) Name, address, and identifying number of the relevant taxpayer seeking the refund;

(2) Amount required to be withheld pursuant to withholding certificate;

(3) Amount withheld by entity or fiduciary (attach a copy of Form 8388-A stamped by IRS pursuant to §1.1445-5(b)(4) or provide substantial evidence of the amount withheld in the case of a failure to receive Form 8288-A, as provided in §1.1445-5(b)(7));

(4) Amount to be refunded to the relevant taxpayer.

An application for an early refund cannot be processed unless the required copy of Form 8288-A or substantial evidence of the amount withheld in the case of a failure to receive Form 8288-A (as provided in §1.1445-5(b)(7)) is attached to the application. If an application for a withholding certificate is submitted after the transfer takes place, then that application may be combined with an application for an early refund. The Service will act upon a claim for refund within the time limits set forth in §1.1445-6(a)(1).

(h) *Effective date for taxpayer identification numbers.*—The requirement in paragraphs (b)(3), (f)(3)(i), and (g)(1) of this section that taxpayer identification numbers be provided (in all cases) is applicable for dispositions of U.S. real property interests occurring after November 3, 2003. [Reg. §1.1445-6.]

☐ [*T.D.* 8113, 12-18-86. *Amended by T.D.* 9082, 8-4-2003 *and T.D.* 9751, 2-17-2016.]

## [Reg. §1.1445-7]

**§1.1445-7. Treatment of foreign corporation that has made an election under section 897(i) to be treated as a domestic corporation.**—(a) *In general.*—Pursuant to section 897(i) a foreign corporation may elect to be treated as a domestic corporation for purposes of sections 897 and 6039C. A foreign corporation that has made such an election shall also be treated as a domestic corporation for purposes of the withholding required under section 1445, in accordance with the provisions of this section.

(b) *Withholding under section 1445(a).*—(1) *Dispositions by corporation.*—A foreign corporation that has made an election under section 897(i) may provide a transferee with a certification of non-foreign status in connection with the corporation's disposition of a U.S. real property interest. However, in accordance with the provisions of §§1.1445-2(b)(2)(ii) and 1.1445-5(b)(3)(ii)(C), such an electing foreign corporation must attach to such certification a copy of the acknowledgment of the election provided to the corporation by the Internal Revenue Service pursuant to §1.897-3(d)(4) which states that the information required by §1.897-3 has been determined to be complete.

(2) *Dispositions of interests in corporation.*—Dispositions of interests in electing foreign corporations shall be subject to the withholding requirements of section 1445(a) and the rules of §§1.1445-1 through 1.1445-4. Therefore, if a foreign person disposes of an interest in such a corporation, and that interest is a U.S. real property interest under the provisions of section 897 and regulations thereunder, then the transferee is required to withhold under section 1445(a).

(c) *Withholding under section 1445(e).*—Because a foreign corporation that has made an election under section 897(i) is treated as a domestic corporation for purposes of determining withholding obligations under section 1445, such a corporation is not subject to the requirement of section 1445(e)(2) that a foreign corporation withhold at the corporate capital gain rate from the gain recognized upon the distribution of a U.S. real property interest. Such a corporation is subject to the provisions of section 1445(e)(3). Thus, if interests in an electing corporation constitute U.S. real property interests, then the corporation is required to withhold with respect to the non-dividend distribution of any property to an interest-holder that is a foreign person. See §1.1445-5(e). Dividend distributions (distributions that are described in section 301) shall be treated as provided in sections 897(f), 1441 and 1442. In addition, if interests in an electing foreign corporation do not constitute U.S. real property interests, then distributions by such corporation shall be treated as provided in sections 897(f) (if applicable), 1441 and 1442. Approved by the Office of Management and Budget under control number 545-0902. [Reg. §1.1445-7.]

☐ [*T.D.* 8113, 12-18-86.]

## [Reg. §1.1445-8]

**§1.1445-8. Special rules regarding publicly traded partnerships, publicly traded trusts and real estate investment trusts (REITS).**—(a) *Entities to which this section applies.*—The rules of this section apply to—

(1) Any partnership or trust, interests in which are regularly traded on an established securities market (regardless of the number of its partners or beneficiaries), and

(2) Any REIT (regardless of the form of its organization).

For purposes of paragraph (a)(1) of this section, the rules of section 1445(e)(1) and this section shall not apply to a publicly traded partnership (as defined in section 7704) which is treated as a corporation under section 7704(a), or to those entities that are classified as "associations" and taxed as corporations. See §301.7701-2.

(b) *Obligation to withhold.*—(1) *In general.*—An entity described in paragraph (a) of this section is not required to withhold under the provisions of §1.1445-5(c), which states the withholding requirements of domestic partnerships, trusts and estates upon the disposition of U.S. real property interests. Except as otherwise provided in this paragraph (b), an entity described in paragraph (a) of this section shall be liable to withhold tax upon the distribution of any amount attributable to the disposition of a U.S. real property interest, with respect to each holder of an interest in the entity that is a foreign person. The amount to be withheld is described in paragraph (c) of this section.

(2) *Publicly traded partnerships.*—Publicly traded partnerships which comply with the withholding procedures under section 1446 will be deemed to have satisfied their withholding obligations under this paragraph (b).

(3) *Special rule for certain distributions to nominees.*—In the case of a person that—

(i) Is a nominee (as defined in paragraph (d) of this section),

(ii) Receives a distribution attributable to the disposition of a U.S. real property interest directly from an entity described in paragraph (a) of this section or indirectly from such entity through a nominee,

(iii) Receives the distribution for payment to any foreign person, or the account of any foreign person, and

(iv) Receives a qualified notice pursuant to paragraph (f) of this section,

then the obligation to withhold in accordance with the general rules of section 1445(e)(1) and this paragraph (b) shall be imposed solely on that person to the extent of the amount specified by the qualified notice. A person obligated to withhold by reason of this paragraph (b)(3) is referred to as a withholding agent.

(4) *Person designated to act for withholding agent.*—The rules stated in § 1.1441-7(b)(1) and (2) regarding a person designated to act for a withholding agent shall apply for purposes of this section.

(5) *Effect of withholding exemption granted under § 1.1441-4(f).*—A letter issued by a district director under the provisions of § 1.1441-4(f), which exempts a person from withholding under section 1441 or section 1442, shall also exempt that person from withholding under this paragraph (b), if—

(i) The letter identifies another person as the withholding agent for purposes of section 1441 or 1442, and

(ii) Such other person enters into a written agreement, with the district director who issued the letter, to be the withholding agent for purposes of this paragraph (b).

The exemption granted, and the corresponding withholding obligation imposed, by this paragraph (b)(5) shall apply with respect to the first distribution made after execution of the agreement described in the preceding sentence and shall continue to apply to all distributions made during the period in which the exemption granted under § 1.1441-4(f) is in effect.

(6) *Payment other than in money.*—The rule stated in § 1.1441-7(c) regarding payment other than in money shall apply for purposes of this section.

(c) *Amount to be withheld.*—(1) *Distribution from a publicly traded partnership or publicly traded trust.*—The amount to be withheld under this section with respect to a distribution by a publicly traded partnership or publicly traded trust shall be computed in the manner described in § 1.1445-5(c)(3)(ii) and (iii), subject to the rules of this section.

(2) *REITs.*—(i) *In general.*—The amount to be withheld with respect to a distribution by a REIT, under this section shall be equal to the highest rate specified in section 1445(e)(1) multiplied by the amount described in paragraph (c)(2)(ii) of this section.

(ii) *Amount subject to withholding.*—(A) *In general.*—Except as otherwise provided in paragraph (c)(2)(ii)(C) of this section, the amount subject to withholding is the amount of any distribution, determined with respect to each share or certificate of beneficial interest, designated by a REIT as a capital gain dividend, multiplied by the number of shares or certificates of beneficial interest owned by the foreign person. Solely for purposes of this paragraph, the largest amount of any distribution occurring after March 7, 1991 that could be designated as a capital gain dividend under section 857(b)(3)(C) shall be deemed to have been designated by a REIT as a capital gain dividend regardless of the amount actually designated.

(B) *Distribution attributable to net short-term capital gain from the disposition of a U.S. real property interest.*—[Reserved]

(C) *Designation of prior distribution as capital gain dividend.*—If a REIT makes an actual designation of a prior distribution, in whole or in part, as a capital gain dividend, such prior distribution shall not be subject to withholding under this section. Rather, a REIT must characterize and treat as a capital gain dividend distribution (solely for purposes of section 1445(e)(1)) each distribution, determined with respect to each share or certificate of beneficial interest, made on the day of, or any time subsequent to, such designation as a capital gain dividend until such characterized amounts equal the amount of the prior distribution designated as a capital gain dividend. The provisions of this paragraph shall not be applicable in any taxable year in which the REIT adopts a formal or informal resolution or plan of complete liquidation.

(iii) *Example.*—The following example illustrates the rules of paragraph (c)(2)(ii)(C) of this section.

In the first quarter of 1988, XYZ REIT makes a dividend distribution of $2X. In the second quarter of 1988, XYZ sells real property, recognizing a long term capital gain of $15X, and makes a dividend distribution of $5X. In the third quarter of 1988, XYZ makes

a distribution of $3X. In the fourth quarter of 1988, XYZ sells real property recognizing a long term capital loss of $2X. Within 30 days after the close of the taxable year, XYZ designates a capital gain dividend for the year of $13X. It subsequently makes a fourth quarter distribution of $7X. Since XYZ has made an actual designation of prior distributions during the taxable year as capital gain dividends, withholding on those prior distributions will not be required. However, the REIT must characterize, solely for purposes of § 1445(e)(1), a total amount of $13X of dividend distributions as capital gain dividends. Therefore, the fourth quarter dividend distribution of $7X must be characterized as a capital gain dividend subject to withholding under this section. In addition, XYZ will be required to characterize an additional $6X of subsequent dividend distributions as capital gain dividends.

(d) *Definition of nominee.*—For purposes of this section, the term "nominee" means a domestic person that holds an interest in an entity described in paragraph (a) of this section on behalf of another domestic or foreign person.

(e) *Determination of non-foreign status by withholding agent.*—A withholding agent may rely on a certificate of non-foreign status pursuant to § 1.1445-2(b) or on the statements and address provided to it on Form W-9 or a form that is substantially similar to such form, to determine whether an interest holder is a domestic person. Reliance on these documents will excuse the withholding agent from liability imposed under section 1445(e)(1) in the absence of actual knowledge that the interest holder is a foreign person. A withholding agent may also employ other means to determine the status of an interest holder, but, if the agent relies on such other means and the interest holder proves, in fact, to be a foreign person, then the withholding agent is subject to any liability imposed pursuant to section 1445 and the regulations thereunder for failure to withhold.

(f) *Qualified notice.*—A qualified notice for purposes of paragraph (b)(3)(iv) of this section is a notice provided in the manner described in § 1.1446-4(b)(4) by a partnership, trust, or REIT regarding a distribution that is attributable to the disposition of a United States real property interest. In the case of a REIT, a qualified notice is only a notice of a distribution, all or any portion of which the REIT actually designates, or characterizes in accordance with paragraph (c)(2)(ii)(C) of this section, as a capital gain dividend in the manner described in § 1.1446-4(b)(4), with respect to each share or certificate of beneficial interest. A deemed designation under paragraph (c)(2)(ii)(A) of this section may not be the subject of a qualified notice under this paragraph (f). A person described in paragraph (b)(3) of this section is treated as receiving a qualified notice when the notice is provided in accordance with § 1.1446-4(b)(4).

(g) *Reporting and paying over withheld amounts.*—With respect to an amount withheld under this section, a withholding agent is not required to conform to the requirements of § 1.1445-5(b)(5) but is required to report and pay over to the Internal Revenue Service any amount required to be withheld pursuant to the rules and procedures of section 1461, the regulations thereunder and § 1.6302-2. Forms 1042 and 1042S are to be used for this purpose.

(h) *Early refund procedure not available.*—The early refund procedure set forth in § 1.1445-6(g) shall not apply to amounts withheld under the rules of this section. For adjustment of over-withheld amounts, see § 1.1461-4.

(i) *Liability upon failure to withhold.*—For rules regarding liability upon failure to withhold under § 1445(e) and this section, see § 1.1445-1(e).

(j) *Applicability dates.*—Paragraph (c)(2)(i) of this section applies to distributions on or after November 30, 2020. Paragraph (f) of this section applies to distributions made on or after January 1, 2022. For distributions made before January 1, 2022, see § 1.1445-8(f) as contained in 26 CFR part 1, revised as of April 1, 2020. [Reg. § 1.1445-8.]

☐ [*T.D. 8321, 12-6-90. Amended by T.D. 8647, 12-20-95 and T.D. 9926,* 11-27-2020.]

### [Reg. § 1.1445-10T]

**§ 1.1445-10T. Special rule for foreign governments (Temporary).**—(a) This section provides a temporary regulation that, if and when adopted as a final regulation, will add a new paragraph (d)(6) to § 1.1445-2. Paragraph (b) of this section would then appear as paragraph (d) (6) of § 1.1445-2.

(b) *Foreign government.*—(1) *As transferor.*—A foreign government is subject to U.S. taxation under section 897 on the disposition of a U.S. real property interest except to the extent specifically otherwise provided in the regulations issued under section 892. A foreign government that disposes of a U.S. real property interest that is not subject to taxation as specifically provided by the regulations under section 892 may present a notice of nonrecognition treatment pursuant to paragraph (d)(2) of this section that specifically cites the provision of such regulation, and thereby avoids withholding by the transferee of the property. A foreign government that disposes of a U.S. real property interest or the transferee of the property may obtain a withholding certificate from the Internal Revenue Service that confirms the applicability of section 892, but neither is required to do so. Rules concerning the issuance of withholding certificates are provided in § 1.1445-3.

(2) *As transferee.*—A foreign government or international organization that acquires a U.S. real property interest is fully subject to section 1445 and the regulations thereunder. Therefore, such an entity is required to withhold tax upon the acquisition of a U.S. real property interest from a foreign person.

(c) *Effective date.*—The rules of this section shall be effective for transfers, exchanges, distributions and other dispositions occurring on or after June 6, 1988. [Temporary Reg. § 1.1445-10T.]

☐ [T.D. 8198, 5-4-88.]

#### [Reg. § 1.1445-11T]

**§ 1.1445-11T. Special rules requiring withholding under § 1.1445-5 (Temporary).**—(a) *Purpose and scope.*—This section provides temporary regulations that, if and when adopted as a final regulation, will add certain new paragraphs within § 1.1445-5(b) and (c). The paragraphs of this section would then appear as set forth below. Paragraph (b) of this section would then appear as paragraph (b)(8)(v) of § 1.1445-5. Paragraph (c) of this section would then appear as paragraph (c)(2)(i) of § 1.1445-5. Paragraph (d) of this section would then appear as paragraph (g) of § 1.1445-5.

(b) *Disposition of interests in partnerships, trusts, and estates.*—The provisions of section 1445(e)(5), requiring withholding upon certain dispositions of interests in partnerships, trusts, and estates, that own directly or indirectly a U.S. real property interest shall apply to dispositions on or after the effective date of a later Treasury decision under section 897(g) of the Code except in the case of dispositions of interests in partnerships in which fifty percent of the value of the gross assets consist of U.S. real property interests and ninety percent or more of the value of the gross assets consist of U.S. real property interests plus any cash or cash equivalents. The provisions of section 1445(e)(5), shall apply, however, to dispositions after June 6, 1988, of interests in partnerships in which fifty percent or more of the value of the gross assets consist of U.S. real property interests, and ninety percent or more of the value of the gross assets consist of U.S. real property interests plus any cash or cash equivalents. See paragraph (d) of this section.

(c) *Transactions covered elsewhere.*—No withholding is required under this paragraph (c) with respect to the distribution of a U.S. real property interest by a partnership, trust, or estate. Such distributions shall be subject to withholding under section 1445(e)(4) and paragraph (f) of this § 1.1445-5 on the effective date of a later Treasury decision published under section 897(g) of the Code. No withholding is required at this time for distributions described in the preceding sentence. See paragraph (b)(8)(iv) of this § 1.1445-5. No withholding is required under this paragraph with respect to the disposition of an interest in a trust, estate, or partnership except in the case of a partnership in which fifty percent or more of the value of the gross assets consist of U.S. real property interests, and ninety percent or more of the value of the gross assets consist of U.S. real property interests plus any cash or cash equivalents. See paragraph (b)(8)(v) of § 1.1445-5. Withholding shall be required as provided in section 1445(e)(5) and paragraph (g) of this section with respect to the disposition after June 6, 1988, of an interest in a partnership in which fifty percent or more of the value of the gross assets consist of U.S. real property interests, and ninety percent or more of the value of the gross assets consist of U.S. real property interests plus any cash or cash equivalents.

(d) *Dispositions of interests in partnerships, trusts, and estates.*—(1) *Withholding required on disposition of certain partnership interests.*—Withholding is required under section 1445(e)(5) and this paragraph with respect to the disposition by a foreign partner of an interest in a domestic or foreign partnership in which fifty percent or more of the value of the gross assets consist of U.S. real property interests, and ninety percent or more of the value of the gross assets consist of U.S. real property interests plus any cash or cash equivalents. For purposes of this paragraph cash equivalents means any asset readily convertible into cash (whether or not denominated in U.S. dollars),

including, but not limited to, bank accounts, certificates of deposit, money market accounts, commercial paper, U.S. and foreign treasury obligations and bonds, corporate obligations and bonds, precious metals or commodities, and publicly traded instruments. The taxpayer on filing an income tax return for the year of the disposition may demonstrate the extent to which the gain on the disposition of the interest is not attributable to U.S. real property interests. A taxpayer is also permitted by § 1.1445-3 to apply for a withholding certificate in instances where reduced withholding is appropriate.

(2) *Withholding not required.*—(i) *Transferee receives statement that interest in partnership is not described in paragraph (d)(1).*—No withholding is required under paragraph (d)(1) of this section upon the disposition of a partnership interest otherwise described in that paragraph if the transferee is provided a statement, issued by the partnership and signed by a general partner under penalties of perjury no earlier than 30 days before the transfer, certifying that fifty percent or more of the value of the gross assets does not consist of U.S. real property interests, or that ninety percent or more of the value of the gross assets of the partnership does not consist of U.S. real property interests plus cash or cash equivalents.

(ii) *Reliance on statement not permitted.*—A transferee is not entitled to rely upon a statement described in paragraph (d)(2)(i) of this section if, prior to or at the time of the transfer, the transferee either—

(A) Has actual knowledge that the statement is false, or

(B) Receives a notice, pursuant to § 1.1445-4.

Such a transferee's withholding obligations shall apply as if the statement had never been given, and such a transferee may be held fully liable pursuant to § 1.1445-1(e) for any failure to withhold.

(iii) *Belated notice of false statement.*—If, after the date of the transfer, a transferee receives notice that a statement provided under paragraph (d)(2)(i) of this section is false, then such transferee may rely on the statement only with respect to consideration that was paid prior to the receipt of the notice. Such a transferee is required to withhold a full 10 percent of the amount realized from the consideration that remains to be paid to the transferor. Thus, if 10 percent or more of the amount realized remains to be paid to the transferor, then the transferee is required to withhold and pay over the full 10 percent. The transferee must do so by withholding and paying over the entire amount of each successive payment of consideration to the transferor, until the full 10 percent of the amount realized has been withheld and paid over. Amounts so withheld must be reported and paid over by the 20th day following the date on which each such payment of consideration is made. A transferee that is subject to the rules of this § 1.1445-10T(d)(2)(iii) may not obtain a withholding certificate pursuant to § 1.1445-3, but must instead withhold and pay over the amounts required by this paragraph.[1]

(e) *Effective date.*—The rules of this section are effective for transactions after June 6, 1988. [Temporary Reg. § 1.1445-11T.]

☐ [T.D. 8198, 5-4-88. *Amended by T.D. 9751, 2-17-2016.*]

#### [Reg. § 1.1446-0]

**§ 1.1446-0. Table of contents.**—This section lists the captions contained in §§ 1.1446-1 through 1.1446-7.

---

[1] Section 324(a) of the Protecting Americans from Tax Hikes Act of 2015 (Public Law 114-113) increased the withholding rate under section 1445(e)(5) to 15 percent, applicable to dispositions after February 16, 2016.

(iii) Effect of Forms W-8BEN, W-8IMY, W-8ECI, W-8EXP, W-9, and statement.

(A) Partnership reliance on withholding certificate.

(B) Reason to know.

(C) Subsequent knowledge and impact on penalties.

(iv) Requirements for certificates to be valid.

(A) When period of validity expires.

(B) Required information for Forms W-8BEN, W-8IMY, W-8ECI, and W-8EXP.

(v) Partner must provide new withholding certificate when there is a change in circumstances.

(vi) Partnership must retain withholding certificates.

(3) Presumptions in the absence of valid Form W-8BEN, Form W-8IMY, Form W-8ECI, Form W-8EXP, Form W-9, or statement.

(4) Consequences when partnership knows or has reason to know that Form W-8BEN, Form W-8IMY, Form W-8ECI, Form W-8EXP, or Form W-9 is incorrect or unreliable and does not withhold.

(5) Acceptable substitute form.

*§1.1446-2 Determining a partnership's effectively connected taxable income allocable to foreign partners under section 704.*

(a) In general.

(b) Computation.

(1) In general.

(2) Income and gain rules.

(i) Application of the principles of section 864.

(ii) Income treated as effectively connected.

(iii) Exempt income.

(3) Deductions and losses.

(i) Oil and gas interests.

(ii) Charitable contributions.

(iii) Net operating losses and other suspended or carried losses.

(iv) Interest deductions.

(v) Limitation on capital losses.

(vi) Other deductions.

(vii) Limitations on deductions.

(4) Other rules.

(i) Exclusion of items allocated to U.S. partners.

(ii) Partnership credits.

(5) Examples.

*§1.1446-3 Time and manner of calculating and paying over the 1446 tax.*

(a) In general.

(1) Calculating 1446 tax.

(2) Applicable percentage.

(i) In general.

(ii) Special types of income or gain.

(b) Installment payments.

(1) In general.

(2) Calculation.

(i) General application of the principles of section 6655.

(ii) Annualization methods.

(iii) Partner's estimated tax payments.

(iv) Partner whose interest terminates during the partnership's taxable year.

(v) Exceptions and modifications to the application of the principles under section 6655.

(A) Inapplicability of special rules for large corporations.

(B) Inapplicability of special rules regarding early refunds.

(C) Period of underpayment.

(D) Other taxes.

(E) 1446 tax treated as tax under section 11.

(F) Application of section 6655(f).

(G) Application of section 6655(i).

(H) Current year tax safe harbor.

(I) Prior year tax safe harbor.

(3) 1446 tax safe harbor.

(i) In general.

(ii) Permission to change to standard annualization method.

(c) Coordination with other withholding rules.

(1) Fixed or determinable, annual or periodical income.

(2) Real property gains.

(i) Domestic partnerships.

(ii) Foreign partnerships.

(3) Coordination with section 1443.

(4) Coordination with section 1446(f).

(d) Reporting and crediting the 1446 tax.

(1) Reporting 1446 tax.

(i) Reporting of installment tax payments and notification to partners of installment tax payments.

(ii) Payment due dates.

(iii) Annual return and notification to partners.

(iv) Information provided to beneficiaries of foreign trusts and estates.

(v) Attachments required of foreign trusts and estates.

(vi) Attachments required of beneficiaries of foreign trusts and estates.

(vii) Information provided to beneficiaries of foreign trusts and estates that are partners in certain publicly traded partnerships.

(2) Crediting 1446 tax against a partner's U.S. tax liability.

(i) In general.

(ii) Substantiation for purposes of claiming the credit under section 33.

(iii) Special rules for apportioning the tax credit under section 33.

(A) Foreign trusts and estates.

(B) Use of domestic trusts to circumvent section 1446.

(iv) Refunds to withholding agent.

(v) 1446 tax treated as cash distribution to partners.

(vi) Examples.

(e) Liability of partnership for failure to withhold.

(1) In general.

(2) Proof that tax liability has been satisfied and deemed payment of 1446 tax.

(3) Liability for interest, penalties, and additions to the tax.

(i) Partnership.

(ii) Foreign partner.

(4) Examples.

(f) Effect of withholding on partner.

*§1.1446-4 Publicly traded partnerships.*

(a) In general.

(b) Definitions.

(1) Publicly traded partnership.

(2) Applicable percentage.

(3) Nominee.

(4) Qualified notice.

(c) Paying and reporting 1446 tax.

(d) Rules for nominees required to withhold tax under section 1446.

(1) In general.

(2) Exception to nominee's withholding.

(e) Determining foreign status of partners.

(f) Distributions subject to withholding.

(1) In general.

(2) In-kind distributions.

(3) Ordering rule relating to distributions.

(4) Coordination with section 1445(e) (1).

*§1.1446-5 Tiered partnership structures.*

(a) In general.

(b) Reporting requirements.

(1) In general.

(2) Publicly traded partnerships.

(c) Look through rules for foreign upper-tier partnerships.

(d) Publicly traded partnerships.

(1) Upper-tier publicly traded partnership.

(2) Lower-tier publicly traded partnership.

(e) Election by a domestic upper-tier partnership to apply look through rules.

(1) In general.

(2) Information required for valid election statement.

(3) Consent of lower-tier partnership.

(f) Examples.

*§1.1446-6 Special rules to reduce a partnership's 1446 tax with respect to a foreign partner's allocable share of effectively connected taxable income.*

(a) In general.

(1) Purpose and scope.

(2) Reasonable reliance on a certificate.

(b) Foreign partners to whom this section applies.

(1) In general.

(2) Definitions.

(i) U.S. income tax return.

(ii) Timely-filed.

(iii) Qualifying U.S. income tax return.

(3) Special rules.

(c) Reduction of 1446 tax with respect to a foreign partner.

(1) General rules.
  (i) Certified deductions and losses.
    (A) Deductions and losses from the partnership.
    (B) Deductions and loss from other sources.
    (C) Limit on the consideration of a partner's net operating loss deduction.
    (D) Limitation on losses subject to certain partner level limitations.
    (E) Certification of deductions and losses to other partnerships.
    (F) Partner level use of deductions and losses certified to a partnership.
  (ii) De minimis certificate for nonresident alien individual partners.
    (A) In general.
    (B) Requirements for exception.
  (iii) Consideration of certain current year state and local taxes.
(2) Form and time of certification.
  (i) Form of certification.
  (ii) Time of certification provided to partnership.
    (A) First certificate submitted for a partnership's taxable year.
    (B) Updated certificates and status updates.
      (1) Preceding year tax returns not yet filed.
      (2) Other circumstances requiring an updated certificate.
      (3) Form and content of updated certificate.
      (4) Partnership consideration of an updated certificate.
(3) Notification to partnership when a partner's certificate cannot be relied upon.
(4) Partner to receive copy of notice.
(5) Notification to partnership when no foreign partner's certificate can be relied upon.
(6) Partnership notification to partner regarding use of deductions and losses.
(7) Partner's certificate valid only for partnership taxable year for which submitted.
(d) Effect of certificate of deductions and losses on partner and partnership.
  (1) Effect on partner.
    (i) No effect on liability for income tax of foreign partner.
    (ii) No effect on partner's estimated tax obligations.
    (iii) No effect on partner's obligation to file U.S. income tax return.
  (2) Effect on partnership.
    (i) Reasonable reliance to relieve partnership from addition to tax under section 6665.
    (ii) Continuing liability for withholding tax under section 1461 and for applicable interest and penalties.
      (A) In general.
      (B) Certificate defective because of amount or character of deductions and losses.
  (3) Partnership level rules and requirements.
    (i) Filing requirement.
    (ii) Reasonable cause for failure to timely file a valid certificate and computation.
      (A) Determining reasonable cause.
      (B) Notification.
(e) Examples.
(f) Effective/Applicability date.
(g) Transition rule.

**§ 1.1446-7** *Applicability dates.*
[Reg. § 1.1446-0.]

☐ [*T.D. 9200, 5-13-2005. Amended by T.D. 9394, 4-28-2008 and T.D. 9926, 11-27-2020.*]

### [Reg. § 1.1446-1]

**§ 1.1446-1. Withholding tax on foreign partners' share of effectively connected taxable income.**—(a) *In general.*—If a domestic or foreign partnership has effectively connected taxable income (ECTI) as computed under § 1.1446-2 for any partnership tax year, and any portion of such taxable income is allocable under section 704 to a foreign partner, then the partnership must pay a withholding tax under section 1446 (1446 tax) at the time and in the manner prescribed in this section, and §§ 1.1446-2 through 1.1446-6.

(b) *Steps in determining 1446 tax obligation.*—In general, a partnership determines its 1446 tax as follows. The partnership determines whether it has any foreign partners in accordance with paragraph (c) of this section. If the partnership does not have any foreign partners (including any person presumed to be foreign under paragraph (c) of this section and any domestic trust treated as foreign under § 1.1446-3(d)) during its taxable year, it generally will not have a 1446 tax obligation. If the partnership has one or more foreign partners, it then determines under § 1.1446-2 whether it has ECTI any portion of which is allocable under section 704 to one or more of the foreign partners. If the partnership has ECTI allocable under section 704 to one or more of its foreign partners, the partnership computes its 1446 tax, pays over 1446 tax, and reports the amount paid in accordance with the rules in § 1.1446-3. For special rules applicable to publicly traded partnerships, see § 1.1446-4. For special rules applicable to tiered partnership structures, see § 1.1446-5. For special rules that may apply in determining the amount of 1446 tax due with respect to a partner, see § 1.1446-6.

(c) *Determining whether a partnership has a foreign partner.*—(1) *In general.*—Except as otherwise provided in this section, § 1.1446-3, and § 1.1446-5, only a partnership that has at least one foreign partner during the partnership's taxable year can have a 1446 tax liability. Generally, the term foreign partner means any partner of the partnership that is not a U.S. person within the meaning of section 7701(a)(30). Thus, a partner of the partnership is generally a foreign partner if the partner is a nonresident alien, foreign partnership (see § 1.1446-5 for rules that allow a lower-tier partnership to look through an upper-tier foreign partnership to the partners of such partnership for purposes of computing its 1446 tax), foreign corporation (which includes a foreign government pursuant to section 892(a)(3)), foreign estate or trust (see paragraph (c) (2) of this section for rules that instruct a partnership to consider the grantor or other owner of a trust under subpart E of subchapter J as the partner for purposes of computing the partnership's 1446 tax), as those terms are defined under section 7701 and the regulations thereunder, or a foreign organization described in section 501(c), or other foreign person. A person also is a foreign partner if the person is presumed to be a foreign person under paragraph (c)(3) of this section. For purposes of this section, a partner that is treated as a U.S. person for all income tax purposes (by election or otherwise, see e.g., sections 953(d) and 1504(d)) will not be a foreign partner, provided the partner has provided the partnership a valid Form W-9, "Request for Taxpayer Identification Number and Certification," or the partnership uses other means to determine that the partner is not a foreign partner (see paragraph (c)(3) of this section). A partner that is treated as a U.S. person only for certain specified purposes is considered a foreign partner for purposes of section 1446, and a partnership must pay 1446 tax on the portion of ECTI allocable to that partner. For example, a partnership must generally pay 1446 tax on ECTI allocable to a foreign corporate partner that has made an election under section 897(i).

(2) *Submission of Forms W-8BEN, W-8IMY, W-8ECI, W-8EXP, and W-9.*—(i) *In general.*—Except as otherwise provided in this paragraph (c)(2) or paragraph (c)(3) of this section, a partnership must generally determine whether a partner is a foreign partner, and the partner's tax classification (e.g., corporate or non-corporate), by obtaining a withholding certificate from the partner that is a Form W-8BEN, "Certificate of Foreign Status of Beneficial Owner for United States Tax Withholding," Form W-8IMY, "Certificate of Foreign Intermediary, Flow-Through Entity, or Certain U.S. Branches for United States Tax Withholding," Form W-8ECI, "Certificate of Foreign Person's Claim for Exemption from Withholding on Income Effectively Connected With the Conduct of a Trade or Business in the United States," Form W-8EXP, "Certificate of Foreign Government or other Foreign Organization for United States Tax Withholding," or a Form W-9, as applicable, or an acceptable substitute form permitted under paragraph (c)(5) of this section. Generally, a foreign partner that is a nonresident alien, a foreign estate or trust (other than a grantor trust described in this paragraph (c) (2)), a foreign corporation, or a foreign government should provide a valid Form W-8BEN.

(ii) *Withholding certificate applicable to each type of partner.*—A partner that submits a valid Form W-8 (e.g., Form W-8BEN) for purposes of section 1441 or 1442 will generally satisfy the documentation requirements of this section provided that the submission of such form is not inconsistent with the rules of this paragraph (c)(2) or paragraph (c)(3) of this section. The following rules shall apply for purposes of this section.

(A) *U.S. person.*—A partner that is a U.S. person (other than a grantor trust described in this paragraph (c)(2)), including a domestic partnership and domestic simple or complex trust (including an estate), shall provide a valid Form W-9.

(B) *Nonresident alien.*—A Form W-8 (e.g., Form W-8BEN) submitted by a nonresident alien for purposes of withholding under section 1441 will generally be accepted for purposes of section 1446. If no such form is submitted for purposes of section 1441, such nonresident alien shall submit Form W-8BEN for purposes of section 1446.

(C) *Foreign partnership.*—A partner that is a foreign partnership generally shall provide a valid Form W-8IMY for purposes of section 1446. See § 1.1446-5 (permitting a lower-tier partnership to look through an upper-tier foreign partnership in certain circumstances when computing 1446 tax).

(D) *Disregarded entities.*—An entity that is disregarded as an entity separate from its owner under § 301.7701-3 of this chapter (whether domestic or foreign) shall not submit a Form W-8 (e.g., Form W-8BEN) or Form W-9. Instead, the owner of such entity for Federal tax purposes shall submit appropriate documentation to comply with this section. See § § 301.7701-1 through 301.7701-3 of this chapter for determining the U.S. Federal tax classification of a partner.

(E) *Domestic and foreign grantor trusts.*—To the extent that a grantor or other person is treated as the owner of any portion of a trust under subpart E of subchapter J of the Internal Revenue Code, such trust shall provide documentation under this paragraph (c)(2) to identify the trust as a grantor trust and provide documentation on behalf of the grantor or other person treated as the owner of all or a portion of such trust as required by this paragraph (c)(2). If such trust is a foreign trust, the trust shall submit Form W-8IMY to the partnership identifying itself as a foreign grantor trust and shall provide such documentation (e.g., Forms W-8BEN, W-8IMY, W-8ECI, W-8EXP, or W-9) and information pertaining to its grantor or other owner to the partnership that permits the partnership to reliably associate (within the meaning of § 1.1441-1(b)(2)(vii)) such portion of the trust's allocable share of partnership ECTI with the grantor or other person that is the owner of such portion of the trust. If such trust is a domestic trust, the trust shall furnish the partnership a statement under penalty of perjury that the trust is, in whole or in part, a domestic grantor trust and such statement shall identify that portion of the trust that is treated as owned by a grantor or another person under subpart E of subchapter J of the Internal Revenue Code. The trust shall also provide such documentation and information (e.g., Forms W-8BEN, W-8IMY, W-8ECI, W-8EXP, or W-9) pertaining to its grantor or other owner(s) to the partnership that permits the partnership to reliably associate (within the meaning of § 1.1441-1(b)(2)(vii)) such portion of the trust's allocable share of partnership ECTI with the grantor or other person that is the owner of such portion of the trust.

(F) *Nominees.*—Where a nominee holds an interest in a partnership on behalf of another person, the beneficial owner of the partnership interest, not the nominee, shall submit a Form W-8 (e.g., Form W-8BEN) or Form W-9 to the partnership or nominee that is the withholding agent.

(G) *Foreign governments, foreign tax-exempt organizations and other foreign persons.*—A Form W-8 (e.g., Form W-8EXP) submitted by a partner that is a foreign government, foreign tax-exempt organization, or other foreign person for purposes of withholding under § § 1441 through 1443 will also operate to establish the foreign status of such partner under this section. However, except as set forth in § 1.1446-3(c)(3) (regarding certain tax-exempt organizations described in section 501(c)), the submission of Form W-8EXP will have no effect on whether there is a 1446 tax due with respect to such partner's allocable share of partnership ECTI. For example, a partnership must still pay 1446 tax with respect to a foreign government partner's allocable share of ECTI because such partner is treated as a foreign corporation under section 892(a)(3). If no Form W-8 is submitted for purposes of withholding under sections 1441 through 1443, then such government, tax-exempt organization, or person must generally submit Form W-8BEN.

(H) *Foreign corporations, certain foreign trusts, and foreign estates.*—Consistent with the rules of this paragraph (c)(2) and paragraph (c)(3) of this section, a foreign corporation, a foreign trust (other than a foreign grantor trust described in paragraph (c)(2)(ii)(E) of this section), or a foreign estate may generally submit any appropriate Form W-8 (e.g., Form W-8BEN) to the partnership to establish its foreign status for purposes of section 1446.

(iii) *Effect of Forms W-8BEN, W-8IMY, W-8ECI, W-8EXP, W-9, and statement.*—(A) *Partnership reliance on withholding certificate.*—In general, for purposes of this section, a partnership may rely on a valid Form W-8 (e.g., Form W-8BEN) or Form W-9, or statement described in this paragraph (c)(2) from a partner, beneficial owner, or grantor trust to determine whether that person, beneficial owner, or the owner of a grantor trust, is a non-foreign or foreign partner for purposes of computing 1446 tax, and if such person is a foreign partner, to determine whether or not such person is a corporation for U.S. tax purposes. The rules of paragraph (c)(3) of this section shall

apply to a partnership that receives a Form W-8IMY from a foreign grantor trust or a statement described in this paragraph (c)(2) from a domestic grantor trust, but does not receive a Form W-8 (e.g., Form W-8BEN) or Form W-9 identifying such grantor or other person. Further, a partnership may not rely on a Form W-8 or Form W-9, or statement described in this paragraph (c)(2), and such form or statement is therefore not valid for any installment period or Form 8804 filing date during which the partnership has actual knowledge or has reason to know that any information on the withholding certificate or statement is incorrect or unreliable and, if based on such knowledge or reason to know, the partnership should pay 1446 tax in an amount greater than would be the case if it relied on the certificate or statement.

(B) *Reason to know.*—A partnership has reason to know that information on a withholding certificate or statement is incorrect or unreliable if its knowledge of relevant facts or statements contained on the form or other documentation is such that a reasonably prudent person in the position of the withholding agent would question the claims made. See § § 1.1441-1(e)(4)(viii) and 1.1441-7(b)(1) and (2).

(C) *Subsequent knowledge and impact on penalties.*—If the partnership does not have actual knowledge or reason to know that a Form W-8BEN, Form W-8IMY, Form W-8ECI, Form W-8EXP, Form W-9, or statement received from a partner, beneficial owner, or grantor trust contains incorrect or unreliable information, but it subsequently determines that the certificate or statement contains incorrect or unreliable information, and, based on such knowledge the partnership should pay 1446 tax in an amount greater than would be the case if it relied on the certificate or statement, then the partnership will not be subject to penalties for its failure to pay the 1446 tax in reliance on such certificate or statement for any installment payment date prior to the date that the determination is made. See § § 1.1446-1(c)(4) and 1.1446-3 concerning penalties for failure to pay the withholding tax when a partnership knows or has reason to know that a withholding certificate or statement is incorrect or unreliable.

(iv) *Requirements for certificates to be valid.*—Except as otherwise provided in this paragraph (c), for purposes of this section, the validity of a Form W-9 shall be determined under section 3406 and § 31.3406(h)-3(e) of this chapter which establish when such form may be reasonably relied upon. A Form W-8BEN, Form W-8IMY, Form W-8ECI, or Form W-8EXP is only valid for purposes of this section if its validity period has not expired, the partner submitting the form has signed it under penalties of perjury, and it contains all the required information.

(A) *When period of validity expires.*—For purposes of this section, a Form W-8BEN, Form W-8IMY, Form W-8ECI, or Form W-8EXP submitted by a partner shall be valid until the end of the period of validity determined for such form under § 1.1441-1(e). With respect to a foreign partnership submitting Form W-8IMY, the period of validity of such form shall be determined under § 1.1441-1(e) as if such foreign partnership submitted the form required of a nonwithholding foreign partnership. See § 1.1441-1(e)(4)(ii).

(B) *Required information for Forms W-8BEN, W-8IMY, W-8ECI, and W-8EXP.*—Forms W-8BEN, W-8IMY, W-8ECI, and W-8EXP submitted under this section must contain the partner's name, permanent address and Taxpayer Identification Number (TIN), the country under the laws of which the partner is formed, incorporated or governed (if the person is not an individual), the classification of the partner for U.S. Federal tax purposes (e.g., partnership, corporation), and any other information required to be submitted by the forms or instructions for such form, as applicable.

(v) *Partner must provide new withholding certificate when there is a change in circumstances.*—The principles of § 1.1441-1(e)(4)(ii)(D) shall apply when a change in circumstances has occurred (including situations where the status of a U.S. person changes) that requires a partner to provide a new withholding certificate.

(vi) *Partnership must retain withholding certificates.*—A partnership or nominee who has responsibility for paying 1446 tax under this section or § 1.1446-4 must retain each withholding certificate, statement, and other information received from its direct and indirect partners for as long as it may be relevant to the determination of the withholding agent's 1446 tax liability under section 1461 and the regulations thereunder.

(3) *Presumptions in the absence of valid Form W-8BEN, Form W-8IMY, Form W-8ECI, Form W-8EXP, Form W-9, or statement.*—Except as otherwise provided in this paragraph (c)(3), a partnership that does not receive a valid Form W-8BEN, Form W-8IMY, Form W-8ECI, Form W-8EXP, Form W-9, or statement required by paragraph (c)(2) of this section from a partner, beneficial owner, or grantor trust, or a partnership that receives a withholding certificate

or statement but has actual knowledge or reason to know that the information on the certificate or statement is incorrect or unreliable, must presume that the partner is a foreign person. Except as provided in §1.1446-3(a)(2) and §1.1446-5(c)(2), a partnership that knows that a partner is an individual shall treat the partner as a nonresident alien. Except as provided in §1.1446-3(a)(2) and §1.1446-5(c)(2), a partnership that knows that a partner is an entity shall treat the partner as a corporation if the entity is a corporation as defined in §301.7701-2(b)(8) of this chapter. See §1.1446-3(a)(2) which prohibits a partnership in certain circumstances from considering preferential tax rates in computing its 1446 tax when the presumption and rules of this paragraph (c)(3) apply. In all other cases, the partnership shall treat the partner as either a nonresident alien or a foreign corporation, whichever classification results in a higher 1446 tax being due, and shall pay the 1446 tax in accordance with this presumption. Except as provided in §1.1446-5(c)(2), the presumption set forth in this paragraph (c)(3) that a partner is a foreign person shall not apply to the extent that the partnership relies on other means to ascertain the non-foreign status of a partner and the partnership is correct in its determination that such partner is a U.S. person. A partnership is in no event required to rely upon other means to determine the non-foreign status of a partner and may demand that a partner furnish an acceptable certificate under this section. If a certificate is not provided in such circumstances, the partnership may presume that the partner is a foreign partner, and for purposes of sections 1461 through 1463, will be considered to have been required to pay 1446 tax on such partner's allocable share of partnership ECTI.

(4) *Consequences when partnership knows or has reason to know that Form W-8BEN, Form W-8IMY, Form W-8ECI, Form W-8EXP, or Form W-9 is incorrect or unreliable and does not withhold.*—If a partnership has actual knowledge or has reason to know that a Form W-8BEN, Form W-8IMY, Form W-8ECI, Form W-8EXP, Form W-9, or statement required by paragraph (c)(2) of this section submitted by a partner, beneficial owner, or grantor trust contains incorrect or unreliable information (either because the certificate or statement when given to the partnership contained incorrect information or because there has been a change in facts that makes information on the certificate or statement incorrect), and the partnership pays less than the full amount of 1446 tax due on ECTI allocable to that partner, the partnership shall be fully liable under section 1461 and §1.1461-3 (§1.1461-1 for publicly traded partnerships subject to §1.1446-4) and §1.1446-3, and for all applicable penalties and interest, for any failure to pay the 1446 tax for the period during which the partnership has such knowledge or reason to know that the certificate contained incorrect or unreliable information and for all subsequent installment periods. If a partner, beneficial owner, or grantor trust submits a new valid Form W-8BEN, Form W-8IMY, Form W-8ECI, Form W-8EXP, Form W-9, or statement, as applicable, the partnership may rely on that documentation when paying 1446 tax (or any installment of such tax) for any payment date that has not passed at the time such form is received.

(5) *Acceptable substitute form.*—A partnership or withholding agent responsible for paying 1446 tax (or any installment of such tax) may substitute its own form for the official version of Form W-8 (e.g., Form W-8BEN) that is recognized under this section to ascertain the identity of its partners, provided such form is consistent with §1.1441-1(e)(4)(vi). All references under this section or §§1.1446-2 through 1.1446-6 to a Form W-8 (e.g., Form W-8BEN, Form W-8IMY, Form W-8ECI, Form W-8EXP) shall include the acceptable substitute form recognized under this paragraph (c)(5). [Reg. §1.1446-1.]

☐ [*T.D. 9200, 5-13-2005. Amended by T.D. 9394, 4-28-2008.*]

**[Reg. §1.1446-2]**

**§1.1446-2. Determining a partnership's effectively connected taxable income allocable to foreign partners under section 704.**—(a) *In general.*—A partnership's effectively connected taxable income (ECTI) is generally the partnership's taxable income as computed under section 703, with adjustments as provided in section 1446(c) and this section, and computed with consideration of only those partnership items which are effectively connected (or treated as effectively connected) with the conduct of a trade or business in the United States. For purposes of determining the section 1446 withholding tax (1446 tax) or any installment of such tax under §1.1446-3, partnership ECTI allocable under section 704 to foreign partners is the sum of the allocable shares of ECTI of each of the partnership's foreign partners as determined under paragraph (b) of this section. See §1.1446-6 (special rules permitting the partnership to consider partner-level deductions and losses to reduce the partnership's 1446 tax). The calculation of partnership ECTI allocable to foreign partners as set forth in paragraph (b) of this section and the partnership's withholding tax obligation are partnership-level computations solely

for purposes of determining the 1446 tax. Therefore, any deduction that is not taken into account in calculating a partner's allocable share of partnership ECTI (e.g., percentage depletion), but which is a deduction that under U.S. tax law the foreign partner is otherwise entitled to claim, can still be claimed by the foreign partner when computing its U.S. tax liability and filing its U.S. income tax return, subject to any restriction or limitation that otherwise may apply.

(b) *Computation.*—(1) *In general.*—A foreign partner's allocable share of partnership ECTI for the partnership's taxable year that is allocable under section 704 to a particular foreign partner is equal to that foreign partner's distributive share of partnership gross income and gain for the partnership's taxable year that is effectively connected and properly allocable to the partner under section 704 and the regulations thereunder, reduced by the foreign partner's distributive share of partnership deductions for the partnership taxable year that are connected with such income under section 873(a) or 882(c) and properly allocable to the partner under section 704 and the regulations thereunder, in each case, after application of the rules of this section. See §1.1446-6 (special rules permitting the partnership to consider partner-level deductions and losses to reduce the partnership's 1446 tax). For these purposes, a foreign partner's distributive share of effectively connected gross income and gain and the deductions connected with such income shall be computed by considering allocations that are respected under the rules of section 704 and §1.704-1(b)(1), including special allocations in the partnership agreement (as defined in §1.704-1(b)(2)(ii) (*h*)), and adjustments to the basis of partnership property described in section 743 pursuant to an election by the partnership under section 754 (see §1.743-1(j)). The character of effectively connected partnership items (capital versus ordinary) shall be separately considered only to the extent set forth in paragraph (b)(3)(v) of this section and, when applicable, sections 1.1446-3(a)(2) (consideration of preferential rates when computing 1446 tax) and section 1.1446-6 (special rules permitting the partnership to consider partner-level deductions and losses to reduce the partnership's 1446 tax).

(2) *Income and gain rules.*—For purposes of computing a foreign partner's allocable share of partnership ECTI under this paragraph (b), the following rules shall apply with respect to partnership income and gain.

(i) *Application of the principles of section 864.*—The determination of whether a partnership's items of gross income are effectively connected shall be made by applying the principles of section 864 and the regulations thereunder.

(ii) *Income treated as effectively connected.*—A partnership's items of gross income that are effectively connected include any income that is treated as effectively connected income, including partnership income subject to a partner's election under section 871(d) or section 882(d), any partnership income treated as effectively connected with the conduct of a U.S. trade or business pursuant to section 897, and any other items of partnership income treated as effectively connected under another provision of the Internal Revenue Code, without regard to whether those amounts are taxable to the partner. A partner that makes the election under section 871(d) or section 882(d) shall furnish to the partnership a statement that indicates that such election has been made. See §1.871-10(d)(3). If a partnership receives a valid Form W-8ECI from a partner, the partner is deemed, for purposes of section 1446, to have effectively connected income subject to withholding under section 1446 to the extent of the items identified on the form.

(iii) *Exempt income.*—A foreign partner's allocable share of partnership ECTI does not include income or gain exempt from U.S. tax by reason of a provision of the Internal Revenue Code. A foreign partner's allocable share of partnership ECTI also does not include income or gain exempt from U.S. tax by operation of any U.S. income tax treaty or reciprocal agreement. In the case of income excluded by reason of a treaty provision, such income must be derived by a resident of an applicable treaty jurisdiction, the resident must be the beneficial owner of the item, and all other requirements for benefits under the treaty must be satisfied. The partnership must have received from the partner a valid withholding certificate, that is, Form W-8BEN (see §1.1446-1(c)(2)(iii) regarding when a Form W-8BEN is valid for purposes of this section), containing the information necessary to support the claim for treaty benefits required in the forms and instructions. In addition, for purposes of this section, the withholding certificate must contain the beneficial owner's taxpayer identification number.

(3) *Deductions and losses.*—For purposes of computing a foreign partner's allocable share of partnership ECTI under this paragraph (b), the following rules shall apply with respect to deductions and losses.

(i) *Oil and gas interests.*—The deduction for depletion with respect to oil and gas wells shall be allowed, but the amount of such deduction shall be determined without regard to sections 613 and 613A.

(ii) *Charitable contributions.*—The deduction for charitable contributions provided in section 170 shall not be allowed.

(iii) *Net operating losses and other suspended or carried losses.*—Except as provided in §1.1446-6, the net operating loss deduction of any foreign partner provided in section 172 shall not be taken into account. Further, except as provided in §1.1446-6, the partnership shall not take into account any suspended losses (e.g., losses in excess of a partner's basis in the partnership, see section 704(d)) or any capital loss carrybacks or carryovers available to a foreign partner.

(iv) *Interest deductions.*—The rules of this paragraph (b)(3)(iv) shall apply for purposes of determining the amount of interest expense that is allocable to income which is (or is treated as) effectively connected with the conduct of a trade or business for purposes of calculating a foreign partner's allocable share of partnership ECTI. In the case of a non-corporate foreign partner, the rules of §1.861-9T(e)(7) shall apply. In the case of a corporate foreign partner, the rules of §1.882-5 shall apply by treating the partnership as a foreign corporation and using the partner's pro-rata share of the partnership's assets and liabilities for these purposes. For these purposes, the rules governing elections under §1.882-5(a)(7) shall be made at the partnership level.

(v) *Limitation on capital losses.*—Losses from the sale or exchange of capital assets allocable under section 704 to a partner shall be allowed only to the extent of gains from the sale or exchange of capital assets allocable under section 704 to such partner.

(vi) *Other deductions.*—No deduction shall be allowed for personal exemptions provided in section 151 or the additional itemized deductions for individuals provided in part VII of subchapter B of the Internal Revenue Code (section 211 and following).

(vii) *Limitations on deductions.*—Except as provided in §1.1446-6 and this paragraph (b)(3), any limitations on losses or deductions that apply at the partner level when determining ECTI allocable to a foreign partner shall not be taken into account.

(4) *Other rules.*—(i) *Exclusion of items allocated to U.S. partners.*—Except as provided in §1.1446-5(e), in computing partnership ECTI, the partnership shall not take into account any item of income, gain, loss, or deduction to the extent allocable to any partner that is not a foreign partner, as that term is defined in §1.1446-1(c).

(ii) *Partnership credits.*—See §1.1446-3(a) providing that the 1446 tax is computed without regard to a partner's distributive share of the partnership's tax credits.

(5) *Examples.*—The following examples illustrate the application of this section. In considering the examples, disregard the potential application of §1.1446-3(b)(2)(v)(F) (relating to the de minimis exception to paying 1446 tax). The examples are as follows:

*Example 1. Limitation on capital losses.* PRS partnership has two equal partners, A and B. A is a nonresident alien and B is a U.S. citizen. A provides PRS with a valid Form W-8BEN, and B provides PRS with a valid Form W-9. PRS has the following annualized tax items for the relevant installment period, all of which are effectively connected with its U.S. trade or business and are allocated equally between A and B: $100 of long-term capital gain, $400 of long-term capital loss, $300 of ordinary income, and $100 of ordinary deductions. Assume that these allocations are respected under section 704(b) and the regulations thereunder. Accordingly, A's allocable share of PRS's effectively connected items includes $50 of long-term capital gain, $200 of long-term capital loss, $150 of ordinary income, and $50 of ordinary deductions. In determining A's allocable share of partnership ECTI, the amount of the long-term capital loss that may be taken into account pursuant to paragraph (b)(3)(v) of this section is limited to A's allocable share of gain from the sale or exchange of capital assets. Accordingly, A's share of partnership ECTI allocable under section 704 pursuant to §1.1446-2 is $100 ($150 of ordinary income less $50 of ordinary deductions, plus $50 of capital gain less $50 of capital loss).

*Example 2. Limitation on capital losses—special allocations.* PRS partnership has two equal partners, A and B. A and B are both nonresident aliens. A and B each provide PRS with a valid Form W-8BEN. PRS has the following annualized tax items for the relevant installment period, all of which are effectively connected with its U.S. trade or business: $200 of long-term capital gain, $200 of long-term capital loss, and $400 of ordinary income. A and B have equal shares in the ordinary income, however, pursuant to the partnership agreement, capital gains and losses are subject to special allocations. The long-term capital gain is allocable to A, and the long-term capital loss is

allocable to B. Assume that these allocations are respected under section 704(b) and the regulations thereunder. Pursuant to paragraph (b)(3)(v) of this section, A's allocable share of partnership ECTI under §1.1446-2 is $400 (consisting of $200 of ordinary income and $200 of long-term capital gain), and B's allocable share of partnership ECTI is $200 (consisting of $200 of ordinary income).

*Example 3. Withholding tax obligation where partner has net operating losses.* PRS partnership has two equal partners, FC, a foreign corporation, and DC, a domestic corporation. FC and DC provide a valid Form W-8BEN and Form W-9, respectively, to PRS. Both FC and PRS are on a calendar taxable year. PRS is engaged in the conduct of a trade or business in the United States and for its first installment period during its taxable year has $100 of annualized ECTI that is allocable to FC. As of the beginning of the taxable year, FC had an unused effectively connected net operating loss carryover in the amount of $300. FC's net operating loss carryover is not taken into account in determining FC's allocable share of partnership ECTI under §1.1446-2 and, absent the application of §1.1446-6 (permitting a foreign partner to certify deductions and losses reasonably expected to be available to reduce the partner's U.S. income tax liability on the effectively connected income or gain allocable from the partnership), is not considered in computing the 1446 tax installment payment due on behalf of FC. Accordingly, PRS must pay 1446 tax with respect to the $100 of ECTI allocable to FC.

[Reg. §1.1446-2.]

☐ [*T.D. 9200, 5-13-2005. Amended by T.D. 9394, 4-28-2008.*]

## [Reg. §1.1446-3]

**§1.1446-3. Time and manner of calculating and paying over the 1446 tax.**—(a) *In general.*—(1) *Calculating 1446 tax.*—This section provides rules for calculating, reporting, and paying over the section 1446 withholding tax (1446 tax). A partnership's 1446 tax equals the amount determined under this section and shall be paid in installments during the partnership's taxable year (see paragraph (d)(1) of this section for installment payment due dates), with any remaining tax due paid with the partnership's annual return required to be filed pursuant to paragraph (d) of this section. For these purposes, a partnership shall not take into account either a partner's liability for any other tax imposed under any other provision of the Internal Revenue Code (e.g., section 55 or 884) or a partner's distributive share of the partnership's tax credits when determining the amount of the partnership's 1446 tax.

(2) *Applicable percentage.*—(i) *In general.*—Except as provided in this paragraph (a)(2), in the case of a foreign partner that is a corporation for U.S. tax purposes, the applicable percentage is the highest rate of tax specified in section 11(b) for such taxable year. Except as provided in this paragraph (a)(2) and §1.1446-5, in the case of a foreign partner that is not a corporation for U.S. tax purposes (e.g., a partnership, individual, trust or estate), the applicable percentage is the highest rate of tax specified in section 1.

(ii) *Special types of income or gain.*—Except as otherwise provided, a partnership is permitted to consider as the applicable percentage under this paragraph (a)(2) the highest rate of tax applicable to a particular type of income or gain allocable to a partner (e.g., long-term capital gain allocable to a non-corporate partner, unrecaptured section 1250 gain, collectibles gain under section 1(h)), to the extent of a partner's allocable share of such income or gain. Consideration of the highest rate of tax applicable to a particular type of income or gain under the previous sentence shall be made without regard to the amount of such partner's income. A partnership is not permitted to consider the highest rate of tax applicable to a particular type of income or gain under this paragraph (a)(2)(ii) if the application of the preferential rate depends upon the corporate or non-corporate status of the person reporting the income or gain and, either no documentation has been provided to the partnership under §1.1446-1 to establish the corporate or non-corporate status of the partner required to pay tax on the income or gain, or the partnership is otherwise required to compute and pay 1446 tax on such portion of the income or gain using the highest applicable percentage under section 1446(b). See e.g., §§1.1446-1(c)(3) (presumption of foreign status in the absence of documentation) and 1.1446-5(c)(2) (requirement to pay 1446 tax at higher of rates in section 1446(b) where a lower-tier partnership cannot reliably associate income with a partner of the upper-tier partnership).

(b) *Installment payments.*—(1) *In general.*—Except as provided in §1.1446-4 for certain publicly traded partnerships, a partnership must pay its 1446 tax by making installment payments of the 1446 tax based on the amount of partnership effectively connected taxable income (ECTI) allocable under section 704 to its foreign partners, without regard to whether the partnership makes any distributions to its partners during the partnership's taxable year. The amount of the installment payments is determined in accordance with this paragraph (b), and the tax must be paid at the times set forth in paragraph (d) of this section. Subject to paragraphs (b)(2)(v) and (b)(3)(ii) of this section, in computing its first installment of 1446 tax for a taxable year, a partnership must decide whether it will pay its 1446 tax for the entire taxable year by using the safe harbor set forth in paragraph (b)(3)(i) of this section, or by using one of several annualization methods available under paragraph (b)(2)(ii) of this section for computing partnership ECTI allocable to foreign partners. In the case of a partnership's underpayment of an installment of 1446 tax, the partnership shall be subject to an addition to the tax equal to the amount determined under section 6655, as modified by this section, as if such partnership were a corporation, as well as any other applicable interest and penalties. See § 1.1446-3(f). Section 6425 (permitting an adjustment for an overpayment of estimated tax by a corporation) shall not apply to a partnership's payment of its 1446 tax.

(2) *Calculation.*—(i) *Application of the principles of section 6655.*—(A) *In general.*—Installment payments of 1446 tax required during the partnership's taxable year are based upon partnership ECTI for the portion of the partnership taxable year to which the payments relate, and, except as set forth in this paragraph (b)(2) or paragraph (b)(3) of this section, shall be calculated using the principles of section 6655. The principles of section 6655, except as otherwise provided in §1.6655-2, are applied to annualize the partnership's items of effectively connected income, gain, loss, and deduction to determine each foreign partner's allocable share of partnership ECTI. Each foreign partner's allocable share of partnership ECTI is then multiplied by the relevant applicable percentage for the type of income allocable to the foreign partner under paragraph (a)(2) of this section. The respective 1446 tax amounts are then added for each foreign partner to yield an annualized 1446 tax with respect to such partner. The installment of 1446 tax due with respect to a foreign partner equals the excess of the section 6655(e)(2)(B)(ii) percentage of the annualized 1446 tax for that partner (or, if applicable, the adjusted seasonal amount) for the relevant installment period, over the aggregate amount of 1446 tax installment payments previously paid with respect to that partner during the partnership's taxable year. The partnership's total 1446 tax installment payment equals the sum of the installment payments due for such period on behalf of all the partnership's foreign partners.

(B) *Calculation rules when certificates are submitted under §1.1446-6.*—(1) To the extent applicable, in computing the 1446 tax due with respect to a foreign partner, a partnership may consider a certificate received from such partner under § 1.1446-6(c)(1)(i) or (ii) and the amount of state and local taxes permitted to be considered under § 1.1446-6(c)(1)(iii). For the purposes of applying this paragraph (b)(2)(i)(B), a partnership shall first annualize the partner's allocable share of the partnership's items of effectively connected income, gain, deduction, and loss before—

(i) Considering under § 1.1446-6(c)(1)(i) the partner's certified deductions and losses;

(ii) Determining under § 1.1446-6(c)(1)(ii) whether the 1446 tax otherwise due with respect to that partner is less than $1,000 (determined with regard to any certified deductions or losses); or

(iii) Considering under § 1.1446-6(c)(1)(iii) the amount of state and local taxes withheld and remitted on behalf of the partner.

(2) The amount of the limitation provided in § 1.1446-6(c)(1)(i)(C) shall be based on the partner's allocable share of these annualized amounts. For any installment period in which the partnership considers a partner's certificate, the partnership must also consider the following events to the extent they occur prior to the due date for paying the 1446 tax for such installment period—

(i) The receipt of an updated certificate or status update from the partner under § 1.1446-6(c)(2)(ii)(B) certifying an amount of deductions or losses that is less than the amount reflected on the superseded certificate (see § 1.1446-6(e)(2) *Example 4*);

(ii) The failure to receive an updated certificate or status update from the partner that should have been provided under § 1.1446-6(c)(2)(ii)(B); and

(iii) The receipt of a notification from the IRS under § 1.1446-6(c)(3) or (5) (see § 1.1446-6(e)(2) *Example 5*).

(ii) *Annualization methods.*—A partnership that decides to annualize its income for the taxable year shall use one of the annualization methods set forth in section 6655(e) and the regulations thereunder, and as described in the forms and instructions for Form 8804, "Annual Return for Partnership Withholding Tax (Section 1446)," Form 8805, "Foreign Partner's Information Statement of Section 1446 Withholding Tax," and Form 8813, "Partnership Withholding Tax Payment Voucher."

(iii) *Partner's estimated tax payments.*—In computing its installment payments of 1446 tax, a partnership may not take into account a partner's estimated tax payments.

(iv) *Partner whose interest terminates during the partnership's taxable year.*—If a partner's interest in the partnership terminates prior to the end of the partnership's taxable year, the partnership shall take into account the income that is allocable to the partner for the portion of the partnership taxable year that the person was a partner.

(v) *Exceptions and modifications to the application of the principles under section 6655.*—To the extent not otherwise modified in § § 1.1446-1 through 1.1446-7 or inconsistent with those rules, the principles of section 6655 apply to the calculation of the installment payments of 1446 tax made by a partnership as set forth in this paragraph (b)(2)(v).

(A) *Inapplicability of special rules for large corporations.*—The principles of section 6655(d)(2), concerning large corporations (as defined in section 6655(g)(2)), shall not apply.

(B) *Inapplicability of special rules regarding early refunds.*—The principles of section 6655(h), applicable to amounts excessively credited or refunded under section 6425, shall not apply. See paragraph (b)(1) of this section providing that section 6425 shall not apply for purposes of the 1446 tax. This paragraph (b)(2)(v)(B) shall apply to 1446 tax paid by a partnership or nominee, as well as to amounts that a partner is deemed to have paid for estimated tax purposes by reason of the partnership's or nominee's 1446 tax payments under § 1.1446-3(d)(1)(i).

(C) *Period of underpayment.*—The period of the underpayment set forth in section 6655(b)(2) shall end on the earlier of the date the partnership is required to file Form 8804 (as provided in paragraph (d)(1)(iii) of this section and without regard to extensions), or with respect to any portion of the underpayment, the date on which such portion is paid.

(D) *Other taxes.*—Section 6655 shall be applied without regard to any references to alternative minimum taxable income and modified alternative minimum taxable income.

(E) *1446 tax treated as tax under section 11.*—The principles of section 6655(g)(1) shall be applied to treat the 1446 tax as a tax imposed by section 11, and any partnership required to pay such tax shall be treated as a corporation.

(F) *Application of section 6655(f).*—A partnership subject to section 1446 shall apply section 6655(f) after aggregating the 1446 tax due (or any installment of such tax) for all its foreign partners. See § 1.1446-6(c)(1)(ii) for an exception to this rule when a nonresident alien partner certifies to the partnership that the partnership investment is the nonresident alien partner's only activity giving rise to effectively connected items.

(G) *Application of section 6655(i).*—If a partnership has a taxable year of less than 12 months, the partnership is required to pay 1446 tax (including installments of such tax) in accordance with this section § 1.1446-3, if the partnership has ECTI allocable under section 704 to foreign partners. In such a case, the partnership shall adjust its installment payments of 1446 tax in a reasonable manner (e.g., the annualized amounts of ECTI estimated to be allocable to a foreign partner, and the section 6655(e)(2)(B)(ii) percentage to be applied to each installment) to account for the short-taxable year. However, if the partnership's taxable year is a period of less than 4 months, the partnership shall not be required to make installment payments of 1446 tax, but will only be required to file Forms 8804 and 8805 in accordance with this section § 1.1446-3, and report and pay the appropriate 1446 tax for the short-taxable year.

(H) *Current year tax safe harbor.*—The safe harbor set forth in section 6655(d)(1)(B)(i) shall apply to a partnership subject to section 1446.

(I) *Prior year tax safe harbor.*—The safe harbor set forth in section 6655(d)(1)(B)(ii) shall not apply and instead the safe harbor set forth in paragraph (b)(3) of this section applies.

(3) *1446 tax safe harbor.*—(i) *In general.*—The addition to tax under section 6655 shall not apply to a partnership with respect to a current installment of 1446 tax if—

(A) The average of the amount of the current installment and prior installments during the taxable year is at least 25 percent of the total 1446 tax (without regard to § 1.1446-6) for the prior taxable year;

(B) The prior taxable year consisted of twelve months;

(C) The partnership timely files (including extensions) an information return under section 6031 for the prior year; and

(D) The amount of ECTI for the prior taxable year is not less than 50 percent of the ECTI shown on the annual return of section 1446 withholding tax that is (or will be) timely filed for the current year.

(ii) *Permission to change to standard annualization method.*—Except as otherwise provided in this paragraph (b)(3)(ii), if a partnership decides to pay its 1446 tax for the first installment period based upon the safe harbor method set forth in paragraph (b)(3)(i), the partnership must use the safe harbor method for each installment payment made during the partnership's taxable year. Notwithstanding the previous sentence, if a partnership paying over 1446 tax during the taxable year pursuant to this paragraph (b)(3) determines during an installment period (based upon the standard option annualization method set forth in section 6655(e) and the regulations thereunder, as modified by the forms and instructions to Forms 8804, 8805, and 8813) that it will not qualify for the safe harbor in this paragraph (b)(3) because the prior year's ECTI will not meet the 50-percent threshold in paragraph (b)(3)(i)(D) of this section, then the partnership is permitted, without being subject to the addition to the tax under section 6655 (as applied through this section), to pay over its 1446 tax for the period in which such determination is made, and all subsequent installment periods during the taxable year, using the standard option annualization method. A change pursuant to this paragraph shall be disclosed in a statement attached to the Form 8804 the partnership files for the taxable year and shall include information to allow the IRS to determine whether the change was appropriate.

(c) *Coordination with other withholding rules.*—(1) *Fixed or determinable, annual or periodical income.*—Fixed or determinable, annual or periodical income subject to tax under section 871(a) or section 881 is not subject to withholding under section 1446, and such income is subject to the withholding requirements of sections 1441 and 1442 and the regulations thereunder.

(2) *Real property gains.*—(i) *Domestic partnerships.*—Except as otherwise provided in this paragraph (c)(2), a domestic partnership that is otherwise subject to the withholding requirements of sections 1445 and 1446 will be subject to the payment and reporting requirements of section 1446 only and not section 1445(e)(1) and the regulations thereunder, with respect to partnership gain from the disposition of a U.S. real property interest (as defined in section 897(c)). A partnership that has complied with the requirements of section 1446 will be deemed to satisfy the withholding requirements of section 1445 and the regulations thereunder. However, a domestic partnership that would otherwise be exempt from section 1445 withholding by operation of a nonrecognition provision must continue to comply with the requirements of § 1.1445-5(b)(2). In the event that amounts are withheld under section 1445(e) at the time of the disposition of a U.S. real property interest, such amounts may be credited against the partnership's 1446 tax. A partnership that fails to comply fully with the requirements of section 1446 pursuant to this paragraph (c)(2) shall be liable for any unpaid 1446 tax and subject to any applicable addition to the tax, interest, and penalties under section 1446. See § 1.1446-4(f)(4) for rules coordinating the withholding liability of publicly traded partnerships under sections 1445 and 1446.

(ii) *Foreign partnerships.*—A foreign partnership that is subject to withholding under section 1445(a) during its taxable year may credit the amount withheld under section 1445(a) against its section 1446 tax liability for that taxable year only to the extent such amount is allocable to foreign partners.

(3) *Coordination with section 1443.*—A partnership that has ECTI allocable under section 704 to a foreign organization described in section 501(c) shall be required to pay 1446 tax on such ECTI only to the extent such ECTI is includible under section 512 and section 513 in computing the organization's unrelated business taxable income. The certificate procedure available under § 1.1441-9(b)(1) by which a partner may set forth the amounts it believes will and will not be includible in its computation of unrelated business taxable income under section 512 and section 513 shall also apply to a partner in a partnership subject to section 1446. Such certificate shall be made by a partner in the same manner as under § 1.1441-9(b)(2). A partnership that determines that the partner's certificate as to certain partnership items is unreliable or lacking must presume, consistent with § 1.1441-9(b)(3) (regarding amounts includible under section 512 in computing the organization's unrelated business taxable income), that such partnership items would be includible in computing the partner's UBTI.

(4) *Coordination with section 1446(f).*—A partnership that is directly or indirectly subject to withholding under section 1446(f)(1) during its taxable year may credit the amount withheld under section 1446(f)(1) against its section 1446 tax liability for that taxable year only to the extent the amount is allocable to foreign partners.

(d) *Reporting and crediting the 1446 tax.*—(1) *Reporting 1446 tax.*—This paragraph (d) sets forth the rules for reporting and crediting the 1446 tax paid by a partnership. To the extent that 1446 tax is paid on ECTI allocable to a domestic trust (including a grantor or other person treated as an owner of a portion of such trust) or a grantor or other person treated as the owner of a portion of a foreign trust, the rules of this paragraph (d) applicable to a foreign trust or its beneficiaries shall be applied to such domestic or foreign trust and its beneficiaries or owners, as applicable, so that appropriate credit for the 1446 tax may be claimed by the trust, beneficiary, grantor, or other person.

(i) *Reporting of installment tax payments and notification to partners of installment tax payments.*—Each partnership required to make an installment payment of 1446 tax must file Form 8813, "Partnership Withholding Tax Payment Voucher (Section 1446)," in accordance with the instructions to that form. Form 8813 is generally used to transmit an installment payment of 1446 tax to the IRS with respect to partnership ECTI estimated to be allocated to foreign partners. However, see § 1.1446-6(d)(3) (relating to circumstances where a partnership must file Form 8813 when no payment is required under section 1446). Except as provided in this section, a partnership must notify each foreign partner of the 1446 tax paid on the partner's behalf when the partnership makes an installment payment of 1446 tax. The notice required to be given to a foreign partner under the previous sentence must be provided within 10 days of the installment payment due date, or, if paid later, the date such installment payment is made. A foreign partner generally may credit an installment of 1446 tax paid by the partnership on the partner's behalf against the partner's estimated tax that the partner must pay during the partner's own taxable year. See § 1.1446-5(b) (relating to tiered partnership structures). However, a foreign partner may not obtain an early refund of such amounts under the estimated tax rules. See § 1.1446-3(b)(2)(v)(B). See paragraph (d)(2) of this section for the amount of 1446 tax a partner may credit against its U.S. income tax liability. No particular form is required for a partnership's notification to a foreign partner, but each notification must include the partnership's name, the partnership's Taxpayer Identification Number (TIN), the partnership's address, the partner's name, the partner's TIN, the partner's address, the annualized ECTI estimated to be allocated to the foreign partner (or prior year's safe harbor amount, if applicable), and the amount of tax paid on behalf of the partner for both the current and any prior installment periods during the partnership's taxable year. Notwithstanding any other provision of this paragraph (d), a withholding agent is not required to notify a partner of an installment of 1446 tax paid on the partner's behalf, unless requested by the partner, if—

(A) The partnership's agent responsible for providing notice pursuant to this paragraph is the same person that acts as an agent of the foreign partner for purposes of filing the partner's U.S. Federal income tax return for the partner's taxable year that includes the installment payment date; or

(B) The partnership has at least 500 foreign partners and the total 1446 tax that the partnership determines will be required to be paid for the partnership taxable year on behalf of such partner (based on paragraph (b)(2)(ii) or (3) of this section) with respect to the partner's allocable share of ECTI is less than $1,000.

(ii) *Payment due dates.*—The 1446 tax is calculated based on partnership ECTI allocable under section 704 to foreign partners during the partnership's taxable year, as determined under section 706. Installment payments of the 1446 tax generally must be made during the partnership's taxable year in which such income is derived. A partnership must pay to the Internal Revenue Service a portion of its estimated annual 1446 tax in installments on or before the 15th day of the fourth, sixth, ninth, and twelfth months of the partnership's taxable year as provided in section 6655. Any additional amount determined to be due is to be paid with the filing of the annual return of tax required under paragraph (d)(1)(iii) of this section and clearly designated as for the prior taxable year. Form 8813 should not be submitted for a payment made under the preceding sentence.

(iii) *Annual return and notification to partners.*—Every partnership (except a publicly traded partnership subject to § 1.1446-4) that has effectively connected gross income for the partnership's taxable year allocable under section 704 to one or more of its foreign partners (or is treated as having paid 1446 tax under § 1.1446-5(b)), must file Form 8804, "Annual Return for Partnership Withholding Tax (Section 1446)." Additionally, every partnership that is required to file Form 8804 also must file Form 8805, "Foreign Partner's Information Statement of Section 1446 Withholding Tax," for each of its foreign partners on whose behalf it paid 1446 tax, and furnish Form 8804 and the Forms 8805 to the Internal Revenue Service and the respective Form 8805 to each of its partners. Notwithstanding the previous sentence, a partnership that considers a foreign partner's certificate under

§ 1.1446-6 when computing its 1446 tax on Form 8804 is required to furnish such partner and the Internal Revenue Service a Form 8805, even if the form submitted to the partner shows no payment of 1446 tax on behalf of the partner. Forms 8804 and 8805 are separate from Form 1065, "U.S. Return of Partnership Income," and the attachments thereto, and are not to be filed as part of the partnership's Form 1065. A partnership must generally file Forms 8804 and 8805 on or before the due date for filing the partnership's Form 1065. See § 1.6031(a)-1(c) for rules concerning the due date of a partnership's Form 1065. However, with respect to partnerships described in § 1.6081-5(a)(1), Forms 8804 and 8805 are not due until the 15th day of the sixth month following the close of the partnership's taxable year.

(iv) *Information provided to beneficiaries of foreign trusts and estates.*—A foreign trust or estate that is a partner in a partnership subject to withholding under section 1446 shall be provided Form 8805 by the partnership. The foreign trust or estate must provide to each of its beneficiaries a copy of the Form 8805 furnished by the partnership. In addition, the foreign trust or estate must provide a statement for each of its beneficiaries to inform each beneficiary of the amount of the credit that may be claimed under section 33 (as determined under this section) for the 1446 tax paid by the partnership. Until an official Internal Revenue Service form is available, the statement from a foreign trust or estate that is described in this paragraph (d)(1)(iv) shall contain the following information—

(A) Name, address, and TIN of the foreign trust or estate;

(B) Name, address, and TIN of the partnership;

(C) The amount of the partnership's ECTI allocated to the foreign trust or estate for the partnership taxable year (as shown on the Form 8805 provided to the trust or estate);

(D) The amount of 1446 tax paid by the partnership on behalf of the foreign trust or estate (as shown on Form 8805 to the trust or estate);

(E) Name, address, and TIN of the beneficiary of the foreign trust or estate;

(F) The amount of the partnership's ECTI allocated to the trust or estate for purposes of section 1446 that is to be included in the beneficiary's gross income; and

(G) The amount of 1446 tax paid by the partnership on behalf of the foreign trust or estate that the beneficiary is entitled to claim on its return as a credit under section 33.

(v) *Attachments required of foreign trusts and estates.*—The statement furnished to each foreign beneficiary under this paragraph (d)(1) must also be attached to the foreign trust or estate's U.S. Federal income tax return filed for the taxable year that includes the installment periods to which the statement relates.

(vi) *Attachments required of beneficiaries of foreign trusts and estates.*—The beneficiary of the foreign trust or estate must attach the statement provided by the trust or estate pursuant to paragraph (d)(1)(iv) of this section, along with a copy of the Form 8805 furnished by the partnership to such trust or estate, to its U.S. income tax return for the year in which it claims a credit for the 1446 tax. See § 1.1446-3(d)(2)(ii) for additional rules regarding a partner or beneficial owner claiming a credit for the 1446 tax.

(vii) *Information provided to beneficiaries of foreign trusts and estates that are partners in certain publicly traded partnerships.*—A statement similar to the statement required by paragraph (d)(1)(iv) of this section shall be provided by trusts or estates that hold interests in publicly traded partnerships subject to § 1.1446-4.

(2) *Crediting 1446 tax against a partner's U.S. tax liability.*—(i) *In general.*—A partnership's payment of 1446 tax on the portion of ECTI allocable to a foreign partner generally relates to the partner's U.S. income tax liability for the partner's taxable year in which the partner is subject to U.S. tax on that income. Subject to paragraphs (d)(2)(ii) and (iii) of this section, a partner may claim as a credit under section 33 the 1446 tax paid by the partnership with respect to ECTI allocable to that partner. The partner may not claim an early refund of these amounts under the estimated tax rules. See paragraph (d)(1)(i) of this section regarding a partner's ability to credit an installment of 1446 tax paid on the partner's behalf against the partner's estimated tax payments due for the taxable year. See also § 1.1446-5(b) (relating to tiered partnership structures).

(ii) *Substantiation for purposes of claiming the credit under section 33.*—A partner may credit the amount paid under section 1446 with respect to such partner against its U.S. income tax liability only if it attaches proof of payment to its U.S. income tax return for the partner's taxable year in which the items comprising such partner's allocable share of partnership ECTI are included in the partner's income. Except as provided in the next sentence, proof of payment consists of a copy of the Form 8805 the partnership provides to the

partner (or in the case of a beneficiary of a foreign trust or estate, the statement required under paragraph (d)(1)(iv) or (vii) of this section to be provided by such trust or estate and a copy of the related Form 8805 furnished to such trust or estate), but only if the name and TIN on the Form 8805 (or the statement provided by a foreign trust or estate) match the name and TIN on the partner's U.S. tax return, and such form (or statement) identifies the partner (or beneficiary) as the person entitled to the credit under section 33. In the case of a partner of a publicly traded partnership that is subject to withholding on distributions under § 1.1446-4, proof of payment consists of a copy of the Form 1042-S, "Foreign Person's U.S. Source Income Subject to Withholding," provided to the partner by the partnership.

(iii) *Special rules for apportioning the tax credit under section 33.*—(A) *Foreign trusts and estates.*—Section 1446 tax paid on the portion of ECTI allocable under section 704 to a foreign trust or estate that the foreign trust or estate may claim as a credit under section 33 shall bear the same ratio to the total 1446 tax paid on behalf of the trust or estate as the total ECTI allocable to such trust or estate and not distributed (or treated as distributed) to the beneficiaries of such trust or estate, and, accordingly not deducted under section 651 or section 661 in calculating the trust or estate's taxable income, bears to the total ECTI allocable to such trust or estate. The 1446 tax that a foreign trust or estate is not entitled to claim as a credit under this paragraph (d)(2) may be claimed as a credit by the beneficiary of such trust or estate that includes the partnership ECTI allocated to the trust or estate in gross income under section 652 or section 662 (whether distributed or deemed to be distributed and with the same character as effectively connected income as in the hands of the trust or estate). In the case of a foreign trust or estate with multiple beneficiaries, each beneficiary may claim a portion of the 1446 tax that may be claimed by all beneficiaries under the previous sentence as a credit in the same proportion as the amount of ECTI included in such beneficiary's gross income bears to the total amount of ECTI included by all beneficiaries. The trust or estate must provide each beneficiary with a copy of the Form 8805 provided to it by the partnership and prepare the statement required by paragraph (d)(1)(iv) of this section.

(B) *Use of domestic trusts to circumvent section 1446.*—This paragraph (d)(2)(iii)(B) shall apply if a partnership knows or has reason to know that a foreign person holds its interest in the partnership through a domestic trust, and such domestic trust was formed or availed of with a principal purpose of avoiding the 1446 tax. The use of a domestic trust may have a principal purpose of avoiding the 1446 tax even though the tax avoidance purpose is outweighed by other purposes when taken together. In such case, a partnership is required to pay 1446 tax under this paragraph as if the domestic trust was a foreign trust for purposes of section 1446 and the regulations thereunder. Accordingly, all applicable additions to the tax, interest, and penalties shall apply to the partnership for its failure to pay 1446 tax under this paragraph (d)(2)(iii)(B), commencing with the installment period during which the partnership knows or has reason to know that this paragraph (d)(2)(iii)(B) applies. A publicly traded partnership within the meaning of § 1.1446-4 (or a nominee required to pay 1446 tax under § 1.1446-4) will not be considered to know or have reason to know a domestic trust is being used to avoid the 1446 tax under this paragraph (d)(2)(iii)(B), provided the interest held in such entity by the domestic trust is publicly traded.

(iv) *Refunds to withholding agent.*—A withholding agent (i.e., the partnership) may obtain a refund of the 1446 tax paid (or deemed paid under § 1.1446-5(b)) to the extent of the excess of the amount paid to the Internal Revenue Service by the partnership, over the partnership's section 1446 tax liability as determined by the sum of the total tax creditable to each partner indicated on all Forms 8805 for the taxable year. If a partnership issues Form 8805 to a partner, then the partnership may not claim a refund for any amount of tax shown on that form as paid on behalf of the partner. If a partnership incorrectly withholds upon a United States person under section 1446 of the Internal Revenue Code and issues a Form 8805 to that person, the partnership may not file for a refund of the amount incorrectly withheld. Instead, the United States person may file for a refund of that amount on its annual return. For rules concerning refunds to withholding agents who pay 1446 tax on distributions of effectively connected income or gain under § 1.1446-4 (i.e., publicly traded partnerships or nominees), see § 1.1464-1.

(v) *1446 tax treated as cash distribution to partners.*—Except as otherwise provided in this paragraph (d)(2)(v), a partnership's payment of 1446 tax on behalf of a foreign partner is treated under section 1446(d) and this section as a deemed distribution of money to the partner on the earliest of the day on which the partnership paid the tax, the last day of the partnership's taxable year for which the amount was paid, or the last day on which the partner owned an interest in the partnership during the taxable year for which the tax was paid. However, a deemed distribution of money under section

1446(d) resulting from a partnership's installment payment of 1446 tax on behalf of a partner is treated as an advance or drawing of money under § 1.731-1(a)(1)(ii) to the extent of the partner's distributive share of income for the partnership taxable year. The rule treating a deemed distribution as an advance or drawing of money under this paragraph (d)(2)(v) applies only for purposes of determining the tax results of the deemed distribution to the partner under sections 705, 731, and 733, and does not affect the date that the partnership is considered to have paid any installment of 1446 tax for purposes of section 6655 (as applied through this section) or the date a foreign partner is deemed to have paid estimated tax by reason of such installment payment. See paragraph (d)(1)(i) of this section (permitting a partner to credit 1446 tax paid on the partner's behalf against the partner's estimated tax obligation). An amount treated as an advance or drawing of money is taken into account at the end of the partnership taxable year or the last day during the partnership's taxable year on which the partner owned an interest in the partnership. Any 1446 tax paid after the close of the partnership's taxable year, including amounts paid with the filing of Form 8804, that are on account of partnership ECTI allocated to partners for the prior taxable year shall be treated under section 1446(d) and this section as a distribution from the partnership on the earlier of the last day of the partnership's prior taxable year for which the tax is paid, or the last day in such prior taxable year on which such foreign partner held an interest in the partnership.

(vi) *Examples.*—The following examples illustrate the application of this section. In considering the examples, disregard the potential application of paragraph (b)(2)(v)(F) of this section (relating to the de minimis exception to paying 1446 tax). The examples are as follows:

(A) *Example 1. Simple trust that reports entire amount of ECTI.*—PRS is a partnership that has two partners, FT, a foreign trust, and A, a U.S. person. FT is a simple trust under section 651. FT and A each provide PRS with a valid Form W-8BEN and Form W-9, respectively. FT has one beneficiary, NRA, a nonresident alien. PRS and FT each maintain a calendar taxable year. PRS estimated for each installment period during the partnership's taxable year that FT would be allocated $100 of ECTI for the taxable year, and that all such ECTI would be ordinary in character. Assume that the allocation of the $100 would be respected under section 704(b) and the regulations thereunder. PRS pays installments of 1446 tax based upon its estimates and timely pays a total of $37 of 1446 tax over the course of the partnership's taxable year ($100 ECTI × .37). Assume that PRS' estimates of ECTI allocable to FT during the taxable year equal the actual amount of ECTI allocable to FT for the taxable year. Assume also that FT's only income for the taxable year is the $100 of income from PRS, and that, pursuant to the terms of the trust's governing instrument and local law, the $100 of ECTI is not included in FT's fiduciary accounting income and the deemed distribution of the $37 withholding tax paid under paragraph (d)(2)(v) of this section is not included in FT's fiduciary accounting income. Accordingly, the $100 of ECTI is not income required to be distributed by FT, and FT may not claim a deduction under section 651 for this amount. FT must report the $100 of ECTI in its gross income and may claim a credit under section 33 as determined under paragraph (d)(2)(iii) of this section of $37 for the 1446 tax paid by PRS. NRA is not required to include any of the ECTI in gross income and accordingly may not claim a credit for any amount of the $37 of 1446 tax PRS paid.

(B) *Example 2. Simple trust that distributes a portion of ECTI to the beneficiary.*.—Assume the same facts as in paragraph (d)(2)(vi)(A) of this section (*Example 1*), except that PRS distributes $60 to FT, which FT includes in its fiduciary accounting income under local law. FT will report the $100 of ECTI in its gross income and may claim a deduction for the $60 required to be distributed under section 651(a) to NRA. Pursuant to paragraph (d)(2)(iii) of this section, FT may claim a $14.8 credit under section 33 for the 1446 tax PRS paid ($40/$100 multiplied by $37). NRA is required to include the $60 of the ECTI in gross income under section 652 (as ECTI) and may claim a $22.2 credit under section 33 for the 1446 tax PRS paid ($37 less $14.8 or $60/$100 multiplied by $37).

(C) *Example 3. Complex trust that distributes entire ECTI to the beneficiary.*—Assume the same facts as in paragraph (d)(2)(vi)(A) of this section (*Example 1*), except that FT is a complex trust under section 661. PRS distributes $60 to FT, which FT includes in its fiduciary accounting income. FT distributes the $60 of fiduciary accounting income to NRA and also properly distributes an additional $40 to NRA from FT's principal. FT will report the $100 of ECTI in its gross income and may deduct the $60 required to be distributed to NRA under section 661(a)(1) and may deduct the $40 distributed to NRA under section 661(a)(2). Pursuant to paragraph (d)(2)(iii) of this section, FT may not claim a credit under section 33 for any of the $37 of 1446 tax paid by PRS. NRA is required to include

$100 of the ECTI in gross income under section 662 (as ECTI) and may claim a $37 credit under section 33 for the 1446 tax paid by PRS ($37 less $0).

(e) *Liability of partnership for failure to withhold.*—(1) *In general.*—Every partnership required to pay 1446 tax is made liable for that tax by section 1461. Therefore, a partnership that is required to pay 1446 tax but fails to do so, or pays less than the amount required under this section, is liable under section 1461 for the payment of the tax required to be withheld under chapter 3 of the Internal Revenue Code and the regulations thereunder unless, and to the extent, the partnership can demonstrate pursuant to paragraph (e)(2) of this section, to the satisfaction of the Commissioner or his delegate, that a foreign partner has paid the full amount of tax required to be paid by such partner to the Internal Revenue Service. See paragraph (e)(3) of this section and section 1463 regarding a partnership's liability for penalties and interest even though a foreign partner has satisfied the underlying tax liability. See also § 1.1461-3 for applicable penalties when a partnership fails to pay 1446 tax. See paragraph (b) of this section for an addition to the tax under section 6655 when there is an underpayment of 1446 tax.

(2) *Proof that tax liability has been satisfied and deemed payment of 1446 tax.*—Proof of payment of tax may be established for purposes of paragraph (e)(1) of this section consistent with § 1.1445-1(e)(3). Under that standard, a partnership must provide sufficient information to the IRS to determine that the partner's tax liability was satisfied or established to be zero in accordance with the rules of this section. Under this section, a partnership's liability for 1446 tax shall be deemed to have been satisfied (deemed payment), to the extent of the 1446 tax due with respect to the ECTI allocable to a foreign partner, on the later of the date that such partner is considered to have paid all tax that is required to be shown on such partner's U.S. income tax return under section 6513(a) and (b)(2) (prescribing the date tax is considered paid for purposes of sections 6511(b)(2), (c), and 6512), or the last date for payment of the 1446 tax without extensions (the unextended due date for Form 8804). The deemed payment rule of this paragraph (e)(2) shall apply for purposes sections of 1446, 1461, and 1463, and any additions to the tax, interest, or penalties potentially applicable to such partnership under section 1446, including sections 6601, 6651, and 6655. Any deemed payment of 1446 tax under this paragraph (e)(2) shall not be treated as a deemed distribution under section 1446(d) and this section.

(3) *Liability for interest, penalties, and additions to the tax.*—(i) *Partnership.*—Notwithstanding paragraph (e)(2) of this section, a partnership that fails to pay 1446 tax is not relieved from liability under section 6655 (as applied through this section) or for interest under section 6601, when applicable. See § 1.1463-1. Such liability may exist even if there is no underlying tax liability due from a foreign partner on its allocable share of partnership ECTI. The addition to the tax under section 6655 or the interest charge under section 6601 that is required by those sections shall be imposed as set forth in those sections, as modified by this section. The section 6601 interest charge shall accrue beginning on the last date prescribed for payment of the 1446 tax due under section 1461 (which is the due date, without extensions, for filing Form 8804). The section 6601 interest charge shall stop accruing on the 1446 tax liability on the date, and to the extent, that the unpaid tax liability under section 1446 is satisfied (or is deemed satisfied under this paragraph (e)). Further, a partnership's liability under section 6655 (as applied through this section) for any underpaid installment payment shall accrue beginning on the relevant installment payment date, and shall stop accruing on the earlier of the date (and to the extent) that the 1446 tax liability is actually satisfied or the date prescribed in paragraph (b)(2)(v)(C) of this section. See paragraph (e)(4) of this section for examples illustrating that a partner's payment of estimated tax has no effect on the partnership's calculation of its addition to the tax under section 6655 and this section. See § 1.1461-3 for a list of the additions to tax, interest, and penalties that may apply to a partnership that fails to comply with section 1446. See § 1.1446-6(d)(2)(i) for exceptions to the application of the addition to the tax under section 6655 (as applied through this section) when a partnership reasonably relies on a foreign partner's certificate to reduce 1446 tax.

(ii) *Foreign partner.*—A foreign partner is permitted to reduce any addition to the tax under section 6654 or section 6655 by the amount of any section 6655 addition to the tax paid by the partnership with respect to the partnership's failure to pay adequate installment payments of the 1446 tax on ECTI allocable to the foreign partner.

(4) *Examples.*—The following examples illustrate the application of this section. In considering the examples, disregard the potential application of paragraph (b)(2)(v)(F) of this section (relating to the de minimis exception to paying 1446 tax). Further, in each of the examples where a partnership is deemed to have paid 1446 tax with

respect to ECTI allocable to a partner, it is assumed that the partnership has presented to the IRS the appropriate information under paragraph (e)(2) of this section for the IRS to conclude that the deemed payment is appropriate. The examples are as follows:

(i) *Example 1. Foreign partnership fails to pay 1446 tax and sole foreign partner fails to pay all tax required to be shown on partner's U.S. income tax return.*—(A) PRS is a foreign partnership engaged in a trade or business in the United States and has two equal partners, A, a U.S. person, and B, a nonresident alien. PRS is described in §1.6081-5(a) (PRS keeps its books and records outside the United States and Puerto Rico) and, therefore, is required to file Form 8804 by the 15th day of the 6th month following the close of its taxable year. Both partners and PRS are calendar year taxpayers. PRS has received a valid Form W-9 and W-8BEN from A and B, respectively, but has not received any other documents or certificates. B is engaged in multiple trades or businesses (including the PRS partnership) that give rise to effectively connected income. PRS will use an acceptable annualization method under this section for computing its 1446 tax.

(B) In PRS's first year of operations (Year 1), PRS estimates for each installment period described in §1.1446-3 that B will be allocated $100 of ordinary ECTI for the taxable year. Therefore, for each installment period PRS is required to pay one fourth of the tax on the annualized ECTI allocable to B, or $9.25 (.25 X ($100 X .37)). PRS fails to make any installment payments. PRS's operations actually result in $100 of ECTI allocated to B. Therefore, PRS was required to have paid 1446 tax of $37 on or before the due date, without extensions, for filing its Form 8804 which is June 15, Year 2 (the last date prescribed for payment of the 1446 tax). PRS does not file Forms 8804 or 8805.

(C) B pays estimated taxes and makes the following payments on the following dates: June 15, Year 1 - $20, September 15, Year 1 - $15, and January 15, Year 2 - $10. B's total estimated tax payments equal $45. B files its U.S. Federal income tax return timely on June 15, Year 2, and reports all effectively connected income required to be shown on its return. Assume that B's total correct tax liability as shown on the return is $50. B does not make a payment with its return and so B still owes $5 to the Internal Revenue Service (excluding any interest, penalties, and additions to the tax that may apply). Assume that B is not subject to an addition to the tax under section 6654.

(D) Under the rules of paragraph (e)(2) of this section, for purposes of sections 1446, 1461, and 1463, PRS is not considered to have paid any 1446 tax because B has not paid all of B's U.S. income tax liability.

(E) Further, under the principles of section 6655 and the rules of §1.1446-3(e), a partner's estimated tax payments will not affect the calculation of a partnership's addition to the tax. Accordingly, PRS will be liable under the principles of section 6655 and §1.1446-3 for failing to withhold for each installment payment. The addition to the tax will accrue beginning with the due date of each installment payment on the $9.25 underpayment for each respective installment period and will continue to accrue until June 15, Year 2 (the date prescribed in paragraph (b)(2)(v)(C) of this section).

(F) Further, beginning on June 15, Year 2 (the last date prescribed for payment of 1446 tax without extensions), PRS will be liable for interest under section 6601 with respect to the unpaid 1446 tax, $37. This interest will stop accruing on the earlier of the date that the 1446 tax is paid by PRS or is deemed paid under paragraph (e)(2) of this section by reason of B's payment of its full tax liability.

(G) Further, beginning on June 15, Year 2 (the due date for filing Form 8804), PRS will be liable for the addition to the tax under section 6651(a)(1) for failing to file Form 8804. This addition to the tax accrues on the amount required to be shown as the 1446 tax liability on Form 8804, $37. This addition to the tax will accrue at the rate of 5 percent per month until the date that PRS files Form 8804 for Year 1, or the maximum accrual of the penalty (25 percent of the tax required to be shown on the return) under that section has been reached.

(H) PRS may be liable for other penalties and additions to the tax for its failure to withhold or to furnish statements to its foreign partner B. See §1.1461-3 for a list of the penalties that may apply.

(ii) *Example 2. Foreign partnership fails to pay 1446 tax but sole foreign partner pays all tax required to be shown on the partner's U.S. income tax return.*—The facts are the same as paragraph (e)(4)(i)(A) of this section (*Example 1*), except that B pays $5 with the filing of B's return and has therefore paid all tax required to be shown on B's return within the meaning of paragraph (e)(2) of this section.

(A) For purposes of sections 1446, 1461, and 1463, PRS is deemed to have paid its 1446 tax liability under paragraph (e) (2) of this section as of the later of the date that B is considered to have paid its tax under section 6513(a) and (b)(2) (June 15, Year 2) and the last date for PRS to pay its 1446 tax without extensions (also June 15, Year 2). Therefore, PRS is deemed to have paid all of its 1446 tax liability as of June 15, Year 2. PRS has no continuing liability for 1446 tax

under section 1461, however, additions to the tax, interest, and penalties may apply.

(B) For purposes of section 6655 and §1.1446-3, under paragraph (e)(2) PRS is deemed to have paid its 1446 tax on June 15, Year 2. Even if B had fully paid its tax liability as of March 15, Year 2, the rule in paragraph (e) (2) of this section would not deem PRS to have paid its 1446 tax until June 15, Year 2. As a result, B's estimated tax payments will have no effect on PRS's calculation of its addition to the tax. The addition to the tax under 6655 and §1.1446-3 shall begin to accrue on each installment date with respect to the underpaid installment ($8.75), and will stop accruing on June 15, Year 2, the date prescribed in paragraph (b)(2)(v)(C) of this section.

(C) Because PRS is deemed to have paid its full 1446 tax liability as of June 15, Year 2 (the last date prescribed for payment of 1446 tax without extensions), PRS is not subject to an interest charge under section 6601, or a failure to file penalty under section 6651 (see section 6651(b)(1)).

(D) PRS may be liable for other penalties and additions to the tax for its failure to withhold or to furnish statements to its foreign partner B. See §1.1461-3 for a list of the penalties that may apply.

(E) If PRS had several foreign partners, PRS would conduct the same analysis as set forth above with respect to each partner. That is, under paragraph (e) of this section, PRS may be deemed to have paid 1446 tax with respect to the ECTI allocable to some but not all of its foreign partners.

(iii) *Example 3. Domestic partnership fails to pay 1446 tax but sole foreign partner fully pays all tax required to be shown on partner's U.S. income tax return.*—The facts are the same as paragraph (e)(4)(ii) introductory text of this section (*Example 2*), except that PRS is a domestic partnership whose last date prescribed for paying 1446 tax without extensions (i.e., generally the unextended due date for Form 8804) is March 15, Year 2.

(A) For purposes of sections 1446, 1461, and 1463, PRS is deemed to have paid its 1446 tax liability on the later of the date that B is considered to have paid tax under section 6513(a) and (b)(2) (June 15, Year 2) and the last date for paying 1446 tax without extensions (i.e., the unextended due date for Form 8804, March 15, Year 2). Accordingly, PRS is not considered to have fully paid its 1446 tax liability until June 15, Year 2. PRS has no continuing liability for 1446 tax under section 1461, however, additions to the tax, interest, and penalties may apply.

(B) For purposes of section 6655 and §1.1446-3, PRS is subject to an underpayment addition to the tax that accrues on the same amount as in paragraphs (e)(4)(i) and (ii) of this section (*Examples 1* and *2*), respectively, in paragraphs (e)(4)(i) and (e)(4)(ii) of this section, respectively because PRS is not deemed to have paid 1446 tax under paragraph (e)(2) of this section until June 15, Year 2. The addition to the tax will stop accruing on the date prescribed in paragraph (b)(2)(v)(C) of this section (i.e., March 15, Year 2, the due date, without extensions, for filing Form 8804).

(C) For purposes of section 6601, as of the last date prescribed for paying 1446 tax without extensions (March 15, Year 2), PRS has not paid or been deemed to have paid any 1446 tax. Accordingly, the interest charge under section 6601 shall begin to accrue on March 15, Year 2, and shall accrue until the 1446 liability is paid or deemed to have been paid. In this case, the interest charge will accrue until June 15, Year 2, the date that PRS is deemed to have paid its 1446 tax under paragraph (e)(2) of this section.

(D) For purposes of section 6651(a)(1), as of March 15, Year 2, PRS's amount required to be shown as tax on its Form 8804 is $37. This amount cannot be reduced under section 6651(b)(1) because PRS is not deemed to have paid 1446 tax under paragraph (e)(2) of this section until June 15, Year 2, a date falling after the last date for PRS to pay its 1446 tax, March 15, Year 2. Accordingly, the failure to file penalty will begin to accrue on March 15, Year 2 (filing due date for Form 8804), and shall stop accruing on the earlier of the date that PRS files Form 8804 or the maximum accrual of the penalty (25 percent of the amount required to be shown as tax on the return) is reached.

(E) PRS may be liable for other penalties and additions to the tax for its failure to withhold or to furnish statements to its foreign partner B. See §1.1461-3 for a list of the penalties that may apply.

(f) *Effect of withholding on partner.*—The payment of the 1446 tax by a partnership does not excuse a foreign partner to which a portion of ECTI is allocable from filing a U.S. tax or informational return, as appropriate, with respect to that income. Information concerning installment payments of 1446 tax paid during the partnership's taxable year on behalf of a foreign partner shall be provided to such foreign partner in accordance with paragraph (d) of this section and such information may be taken into account by the foreign partner when computing the partner's estimated tax liability during the taxable year. Form 1040NR, "U.S. Nonresident Alien Income Tax Return," Form 1065, "U.S. Return of Partnership Income," Form

1120F, "U.S. Income Tax Return of a Foreign Corporation," or such other return as appropriate, must be filed by the partner, and any tax due must be paid, by the filing deadline (including extensions) generally applicable to such person. Pursuant to paragraph (d) of this section, a partner may generally claim a credit under section 33 for its share of any 1446 tax paid by the partnership against the amount of income tax (or 1446 tax in the case of tiers of partnerships) as computed in such partner's return. See § 1.1446-3(e)(3)(ii) for rules permitting a partner to reduce its addition to tax under section 6654 or section 6655. [Reg. § 1.1446-3.]

☐ [*T.D. 9200, 5-13-2005. Amended by T.D. 9394, 4-28-2008 (corrected 6-10-2020), T.D. 9821, 7-18-2017, T.D. 9892, 1-29-2020 and T.D. 9926, 11-27-2020.*]

### [Reg. § 1.1446-4]

**§ 1.1446-4. Publicly traded partnerships.**—(a) *In general.*—This section sets forth rules for applying the section 1446 withholding tax (1446 tax) to publicly traded partnerships. A publicly traded partnership (as defined in paragraph (b) of this section) that has effectively connected gross income, gain or loss must pay 1446 tax by withholding from distributions to a foreign partner. Publicly traded partnerships that withhold on distributions must pay over and report any 1446 tax as provided in paragraph (c) of this section, and generally are not to pay over and report the 1446 tax under the rules in § 1.1446-3. The amount of the withholding tax on distributions, other than distributions excluded under paragraph (f) of this section, that are made during any partnership taxable years, equals the applicable percentage (defined in paragraph (b)(2) of this section) of such distributions. For penalties and additions to the tax for failure to comply with this section, see § § 1.1461-1 and 1.1461-3.

(b) *Definitions.*—(1) *Publicly traded partnership.*—For purposes of this section, the term publicly traded partnership has the same meaning as in section 7704 (including the regulations thereunder), but does not include a publicly traded partnership treated as a corporation under that section.

(2) *Applicable percentage.*—For purposes of this section, applicable percentage shall have the meaning as set forth in § 1.1446-3(a)(2), except that the partnership or nominee required to pay 1446 tax may not consider a preferential rate in computing the 1446 tax due with respect to a partner.

(3) *Nominee.*—For purposes of this section, the term nominee means a person that holds an interest in a publicly traded partnership on behalf of a foreign person and that is either a U.S. person, a qualified intermediary (as defined in § 1.1441-1(e)(5)(ii)) that assumes primary withholding responsibility for the distribution, or a U.S. branch of a foreign person that agrees to be treated as a U.S. person (as described in § 1.1441-1(b)(2)(iv)) with respect to the distribution. For purposes of this paragraph (b)(3), a U.S. branch or a qualified intermediary is a nominee only if it assumes primary withholding responsibility for the distribution for all purposes of chapters 3 and 4 of subtitle A of the Code.

(4) *Qualified notice.*—For purposes of this section, a qualified notice is a notice from a publicly traded partnership that states the amount of a distribution that is attributable to each type of income described in paragraphs (f)(3)(i) through (v) of this section. A qualified notice may also include the information described in § 1.1446(f)-4(b)(3) (relating to the 10-percent exception to withholding under section 1446(f)(1)) and the information described in § 1.1446(f)-4(c)(2)(iii) (relating to an adjustment to the amount realized for withholding under section 1446(f)(1)). The notice must be posted in a readily accessible format in an area of the primary public website of the publicly traded partnership that is dedicated to this purpose, and a copy of the notice must be delivered to any registered holder that is a nominee. A qualified notice must be posted and delivered to the registered holder by the date required for providing notice with respect to distributions described in 17 CFR 240.10b-17(b)(1) or (3) issued pursuant to the Securities Exchange Act of 1934 (15 U.S.C. 78a) and contain the information described therein as it would relate to the distribution. The publicly traded partnership must keep the notice accessible to the public for ten years on its primary public website or the primary public website of any successor organization. No specific format is required unless otherwise prescribed by the Commissioner in forms or instructions or in publications or guidance published in the Internal Revenue Bulletin (see § § 601.601(d)(2) and 601.602 of this chapter). See paragraph (d) of this section regarding when a nominee is considered to have received a qualified notice.

(c) *Paying and reporting 1446 tax.*—The withholding tax required under this section is to be paid pursuant to the rules and procedures of section 1461, § § 1.1461-1, 1.1461-2, and 1.6302-2, as supplemented by the rules of this section. A withholding agent under this section

must use Form 1042, "Annual Withholding Tax Return for U.S. Source Income of Foreign Persons," and Form 1042-S, "Foreign Person's U.S. Source Income Subject to Withholding," to report withholding from distributions under this section. See § 1.1461-1(b). Further, a withholding agent under this section may obtain a refund for 1446 tax paid in accordance with section 1464 and the regulations thereunder. See § 1.1446-3(d)(1)(iv) and (vii) (relating to a foreign trust or estate that holds an interest in a publicly traded partnership) and § 1.1446-5(d) (relating to a publicly traded partnership that is part of a tiered partnership structure) for additional guidance.

(d) *Rules for nominees required to withhold tax under section 1446.*—(1) *In general.*—A nominee that receives a distribution from a publicly traded partnership (or another nominee) that is to be paid to (or for the account of) any foreign person is treated as a withholding agent under this section. A nominee that fails to withhold pursuant to this section is subject to liability under section 1461, as well as applicable penalties and interest, as if the nominee were the partnership responsible for withholding. A nominee that receives a qualified notice that meets the requirements in paragraph (b)(4) of this section must withhold based on the amounts specified on the qualified notice. A nominee is treated as receiving a qualified notice on the date that the notice is posted to the publicly traded partnership's website or is received by the nominee in accordance with paragraph (b)(4) of this section. If a nominee properly withholds based on the amounts specified on a qualified notice, the nominee is not liable for any underwithholding on amounts that are effectively connected income, gain, or loss. Rather, the publicly traded partnership that issued the qualified notice is liable under section 1461 for underwithholding on such amounts. If a nominee does not receive a qualified notice that meets the requirements in paragraph (b)(4) of this section, or to the extent the qualified notice does not specify an amount, the nominee must withhold on the full amount of the distribution with respect to—

(i) A foreign partner that is a corporation, at the greater of the highest rate of tax specified in section 11(b) or 881 (without regard to any reduction in the rate of tax permitted under an applicable income tax treaty);

(ii) A foreign partner that is not a corporation, at the greater of the highest rate of tax specified in section 1 or 871 (without regard to any reduction in the rate of tax permitted under an applicable income tax treaty); or

(iii) A foreign partner whose classification cannot be determined, at the higher of the rate determined under paragraph (d)(1)(i) or (ii) of this section.

(2) *Exception to nominee's withholding.*—A nominee is not required to withhold under paragraph (d)(1) of this section to the extent that it makes a payment of a distribution to a qualified intermediary or U.S. branch that is also a nominee for the distribution under paragraph (b)(3) of this section. For purposes of the preceding sentence, a nominee may treat a qualified intermediary or U.S. branch as a nominee for a distribution based on, respectively, a valid qualified intermediary withholding certificate described in § 1.1441-1(e)(3)(ii) or a valid U.S. branch withholding certificate described in § 1.1446(f)-4(a)(2)(ii)(B) on which the qualified intermediary or U.S. branch represents that it assumes primary withholding responsibility with respect to the distribution.

(e) *Determining foreign status of partners.*—Except as provided in this paragraph (e), the rules of § 1.1446-1 shall apply in determining whether a partner of a publicly traded partnership is a foreign partner for purposes of the 1446 tax. A partnership or nominee obligated to withhold under this section shall be entitled to rely on any of the forms acceptable under § 1.1446-1 that it receives from persons on whose behalf it holds interests in the partnership to the same extent a partnership is entitled to rely on such forms under those rules. If a partnership or nominee pays a distribution to an entity that provides a valid qualified intermediary withholding certificate described in § 1.1441-1(e)(3)(ii) indicating that the entity does not assume primary withholding responsibility for the distribution, for withholding under this section the partnership or nominee may instead rely on a withholding statement that allocates the distribution to—

(1) A chapter 3 withholding rate pool (as described in § 1.1441-1(e)(5)(v)(C)) consisting of account holders that are foreign persons subject to withholding at the highest rate of tax specified in section 1;

(2) A chapter 3 withholding rate pool (as described in § 1.1441-1(e)(5)(v)(C)) consisting of account holders that are foreign persons subject to withholding at the highest rate of tax specified in section 11(b);

(3) A chapter 3 withholding rate pool (as described in § 1.1441-1(e)(5)(v)(C)) consisting of account holders that are foreign persons not subject to withholding; or

(4) Each account holder for which a form acceptable under §1.1446-1 is provided.

(f) *Distributions subject to withholding.*—(1) *In general.*—Except as provided in this paragraph (f)(1), a publicly traded partnership must withhold at the applicable percentage with respect to any actual distribution made to a foreign partner. The amount of a distribution subject to 1446 tax includes the amount of any 1446 tax required to be withheld on the distribution. In the case of a partnership (upper-tier partnership) that receives a partnership distribution from another partnership in which it is a partner (lower-tier partnership) (i.e., a tiered structure described in §1.1446-5), any 1446 tax that was paid by the lower-tier partnership may be credited by the upper-tier partnership and shall be treated as a distribution under section 1446. For example, a foreign publicly traded partnership, UTP, owns an interest in domestic publicly traded partnership, LTP. LTP makes a distribution subject to section 1446 of $100 to UTP during its taxable year beginning January 1, 2020, and withholds 37 percent (the highest rate in section 1) ($37) of that distribution under section 1446. UTP receives a net distribution of $63 which it immediately redistributes to its partners. UTP has a liability to pay 37 percent of the total actual and deemed distribution it makes to its foreign partners as a section 1446 withholding tax. UTP may credit the $37 withheld by LTP against this liability as if it were paid by UTP. See §§1.1462-1(b) and 1.1446-5(b)(1). When UTP distributes the $63 it actually receives from LTP to its partners, UTP is treated for purposes of section 1446 as if it made a distribution of $100 to its partners ($63 actual distribution and $37 deemed distribution). UTP's partners (U.S. and foreign) may claim a credit against their U.S. income tax liability for their allocable share of the $37 of 1446 tax paid on their behalf.

(2) *In-kind distributions.*—If a publicly traded partnership distributes property other than money, the partnership shall not release the property until it has funds sufficient to enable the partnership to pay over in money the required 1446 tax.

(3) *Ordering rule relating to distributions.*—Distributions from publicly traded partnerships are deemed to be paid out of the following types of income in the order indicated—

(i) Amounts attributable to income described in section 1441 or 1442 that are not effectively connected with the conduct of a trade or business in the United States and are subject to withholding under §1.1441-2(a);

(ii) Amounts attributable to income described in section 1441 or 1442 that are not effectively connected with the conduct of a trade or business in the United States and are not subject to withholding under §1.1441-2(a);

(iii) Amounts attributable to income effectively connected with the conduct of a trade or business in the United States that are not subject to withholding under §§1.1446-1 through 1.1446-6;

(iv) Amounts subject to withholding under §§1.1446-1 through 1.1446-6; and

(v) Amounts not listed in paragraphs (f)(3)(i) through (iv) of this section.

(4) *Coordination with section 1445(e)(1).*—Except as otherwise provided in this section, a publicly traded partnership that complies with the requirements of withholding under section 1446 and this section will be deemed to have satisfied the requirements of section 1445(e)(1) and the regulations thereunder. Notwithstanding the excluded amounts set forth in paragraph (f)(3) of this section, distributions subject to withholding at the applicable percentage shall include the following—

(i) Amounts subject to withholding under section 1445(e)(1) upon distribution pursuant to an election under §1.1445-5(c)(3) of the regulations; and

(ii) Amounts not subject to withholding under section 1445 because the distributee is a partnership or is a foreign corporation that has made an election under section 897(i). [Reg. §1.1446-4.]

☐ [*T.D.* 9200, 5-13-2005 *Amended by T.D.* 9926, 11-27-2020 (*corrected* 3-5-2021).]

### [Reg. §1.1446-5]

**§1.1446-5. Tiered partnership structures.**—(a) *In general.*—The rules of this section shall apply in cases where a partnership (lower-tier partnership) that has effectively connected taxable income (ECTI), has a partner that is a partnership (upper-tier partnership). Except as provided in paragraph (e) of this section, if an upper-tier domestic partnership directly owns an interest in a lower-tier partnership, the lower-tier partnership is not required to pay the section 1446 withholding tax (1446 tax) with respect to the upper-tier partnership's allocable share of net income, regardless of whether the upper-tier domestic partnership's partners are foreign. Paragraph (b) of this section prescribes the reporting requirements for upper-tier and lower-tier partnerships subject to section 1446. Paragraph (c) of

this section prescribes rules requiring a lower-tier partnership to look through an upper-tier foreign partnership to a partner of such upper-tier partnership to the extent it has sufficient documentation to determine the status of such partner and determine such partner's indirect share of the lower-tier partnership's effectively connected taxable income (ECTI). Paragraph (d) of this section prescribes rules applicable to a publicly traded partnership in a tiered partnership structure. Paragraph (e) of this section prescribes rules permitting a domestic upper-tier partnership to elect to apply the look through rules of paragraph (c) of this section. Paragraph (f) of this section sets forth examples illustrating the rules of this section.

(b) *Reporting requirements.*—(1) *In general.*—Notwithstanding paragraph (c) of this section, to the extent that an upper-tier partnership that is a foreign partnership is a partner in a lower-tier partnership, and the lower-tier partnership has paid 1446 tax (including installment payments of such tax) with respect to ECTI allocable to the upper-tier partnership, the lower-tier partnership shall comply with §§1.1446-1 through 1.1446-3 and provide the upper-tier partnership notice of such payments and a copy of the statements and forms filed with respect to the upper-tier partnership's interest in the lower-tier partnership (e.g., Form 8805, "Foreign Partner's Information Statement of Section 1446 Withholding Tax"). The upper-tier partnership may treat the 1446 tax (or any installment of such tax) paid by the lower-tier partnership on its behalf as a credit against its liability to pay 1446 tax (or any installment of such tax), as if the upper-tier partnership actually paid over the amounts at the time that the amounts were paid by the lower-tier partnership. See §1.1462-1(b) and §1.1446-3(d). To the extent required in §1.1446-3(d)(1)(iii), the upper-tier partnership will file Form 8804, "Annual Return for Partnership Withholding Tax (Section 1446)," and Form 8805, "Foreign Partner's Information Statement of Section 1446 Withholding Tax," for each of its foreign partners with respect to its 1446 tax obligation. To the extent the upper-tier partnership does not claim a refund of the 1446 tax it paid (or is considered to have paid), the upper-tier partnership will pass the credit for the 1446 tax paid to its partners on the Forms 8805 it issues. See §1.1446-3(d). The rules of this paragraph (b) shall apply to an upper-tier and lower-tier partnership to the extent that an election has been made and consented to under paragraph (e) of this section.

(2) *Publicly traded partnerships.*—In the case of an upper-tier foreign partnership that is a publicly traded partnership, the rules of §1.1446-4(c) shall apply. See also paragraph (d) of this section.

(c) *Look through rules for foreign upper-tier partnerships.*—For purposes of computing the 1446 tax obligation of a lower-tier partnership, if an upper-tier foreign partnership owns an interest in the lower-tier partnership, the upper-tier partnership's allocable share of ECTI from the lower-tier partnership shall be treated as allocable to a partner of the upper-tier partnership, to the extent of such partner's indirect share of such ECTI (as if such partner were a direct partner in the lower-tier partnership), if—

(1) The upper-tier foreign partnership furnishes the lower-tier partnership a valid Form W-8IMY, "Certificate of Foreign Intermediary, Flow Through Entity, or Certain U.S. Branches for United States Tax Withholding," indicating that it is a look-through foreign partnership for purposes of section 1446; and

(2) The lower-tier partnership can reliably associate (within the meaning of §1.1441-1(b)(2)(vii)) effectively connected partnership items allocable to the upper-tier partnership (and indirectly to such partner) with a Form W-8 (e.g., Form W-8BEN), Form W-9, "Request for Taxpayer Identification Number and Certification," or other form acceptable under §1.1446-1, establishing the status of such partner provided by the upper-tier partnership. The lower-tier partnership required to pay 1446 tax must be able to provide the information necessary for the IRS to determine the chain of ownership, allocation of effectively connected items at each partnership level, as well as to the ultimate beneficial owner of the effectively connected items, and whether the amount of 1446 tax paid was appropriate. This information should permit each partnership in the tiered structure and the IRS to reliably associate any effectively connected items allocable to such upper-tier partnership, as well as to the ultimate beneficial owner of the effectively connected items. The principles of §1.1441-1(b)(2)(vii) shall apply to determine whether a lower-tier partnership can reliably associate effectively connected partnership items allocable to the upper-tier partnership with a partner of the upper-tier partnership. To the extent the lower-tier partnership receives a valid Form W-8IMY from the upper-tier partnership but cannot reliably associate a portion of the upper-tier partnership's allocable share of effectively connected partnership items with a partner of such upper-tier partnership, then the lower-tier partnership shall pay 1446 tax on such portion at the higher of the applicable percentages in section 1446(b). See §1.1446-3(a)(2) for the treatment of any income or gain potentially subject to a preferential rate. If a lower-tier partnership has not received a valid Form W-8IMY from

the upper-tier partnership, the lower-tier partnership shall withhold on the upper-tier partnership's entire allocable share of ECTI at the higher of the applicable percentages in section 1446(b). The look through regime set forth in this paragraph (c) is for purposes of computing the lower-tier partnership's 1446 tax obligation only and does not alter the persons considered to be partners in the lower-tier partnership for partnership reporting purposes (e.g., issuing Form 8805, Schedule K-1).

(d) *Publicly traded partnerships.*—(1) *Upper-tier publicly traded partnership.*—The rules set forth in paragraph (c) shall not apply to look through an upper-tier partnership whose interests are publicly traded (as defined in §1.1446-4(b)(1)).

(2) *Lower-tier publicly traded partnership.*—The look through rules of paragraph (c) of this section shall apply, if the requirements of that paragraph are met, to a lower-tier partnership that is a publicly traded partnership within the meaning of §1.1446-4(b)(1) only if the upper-tier partnership is not described in paragraph (d)(1) of this section. For example, a lower-tier publicly traded partnership (or nominee) shall look through an upper-tier foreign partnership (or domestic partnership to the extent an election is made and consented to under paragraph (e) of this section) when computing its 1446 tax liability, provided the upper-tier partnership is not a publicly traded partnership and the appropriate documentation needed to satisfy the standards set forth in §1.1441-1(b)(2)(vii) and paragraph (c) of this section have been furnished.

(e) *Election by a domestic upper-tier partnership to apply look through rules.*—(1) *In general.*—Subject to the rules of this paragraph (e), a domestic partnership that is a partner in a lower-tier partnership may elect to apply the rules of this section 1.1446-5 and have the lower-tier partnership look through such upper-tier partnership to the partners of such domestic partnership for purposes of computing the lower-tier partnership's 1446 tax liability. A domestic partnership shall make this election by attaching to the Form W-9 submitted to the lower-tier partnership, a written statement and information (described in paragraph (e)(2) of this section) that identifies the upper-tier partnership as a domestic partnership and that states that such partnership is making the election under this paragraph (e). This paragraph (e)(1) shall not apply to a publicly traded partnership described in §1.1446-4(b)(1). See paragraph (d)(1) of this section.

(2) *Information required for valid election statement.*—In addition to the requirements of paragraphs (e)(1) and (3) of this section, the election statement submitted under this paragraph (e)(2) is not valid and cannot be accepted by the lower-tier partnership pursuant to paragraph (e)(3) of this section unless the upper-tier partnership attaches valid documentation pursuant to §1.1446-1 (e.g., Form W-8BEN) with respect to one or more of its foreign partners. The information and documentation submitted with the election must comply with the rules of this section to permit the lower-tier partnership to reliably associate (within the meaning of §1.1441-1(b)(2)(vii)) at least a portion of the upper-tier partnership's allocable share of ECTI with one or more foreign partners of the upper-tier partnership. The election statement must identify the upper-tier partnership by name, address, and TIN, and specify the percentage interest the domestic partnership holds in the lower-tier partnership. The statement may also include such information the upper-tier partnership deems necessary to enable the lower-tier partnership to apply the provisions of this section. If at any time the upper-tier partnership determines that the information or documentation previously provided to the lower- tier partnership is no longer correct, the upper-tier partnership shall update such information and documentation. Except as provided in paragraph (e)(3) of this section, an election that is effective under this paragraph (e) shall apply for subsequent taxable years until such upper-tier partnership revokes the election in writing. A revocation under this section shall be effective for any installment due date arising more than 15 days subsequent to the date that the lower-tier partnership receives such revocation.

(3) *Consent of lower-tier partnership.*—An election made under this paragraph (e) is not effective until the lower-tier partnership consents in writing to the upper-tier partnership that it agrees to apply the provisions of this section. A lower-tier partnership may not consent to an election submitted under this paragraph (e) for any installment date or Form 8804 filing date arising within 15 days of the lower-tier partnership's receipt of such election. The lower-tier partnership's written consent must specify the extent to which it will look through the upper-tier partnership in computing its 1446 tax (or any installment of such tax). To the extent that the lower-tier partnership does not consent to an election to apply the look through provisions of paragraph (c) of this section, the lower-tier partnership shall consider such portion of the upper-tier partnership's allocable share of ECTI as allocable to a domestic person for purposes of computing its 1446 tax obligation. A lower-tier partnership that has

consented to an election under this paragraph (e) may revoke or modify its consent, in writing, at any time.

(f) *Examples.*—The following examples illustrate the provisions of this section. In considering the examples, disregard the potential application of §1.1446-3(b)(2)(v)(F) (relating to the de minimis exception to paying 1446 tax). The examples are as follows:

*Example 1. Sufficient documentation—tiered partnership structure.* (i) Nonresident alien (NRA) and foreign corporation (FC) are partners in PRS, a foreign partnership, and share profits and losses in PRS 70 and 30 percent, respectively. All of PRS's partnership items are allocated based upon each partner's respective ownership interest and it is assumed that these allocations are respected under section 704(b) and the regulations thereunder. NRA and FC each furnish PRS with a valid Form W-8BEN establishing themselves as a foreign individual and foreign corporation, respectively. PRS holds a 40 percent interest in the profits, losses and capital of LTP, a lower-tier partnership. NRA holds the remaining 60 percent interest in profits, losses and capital of LTP. All of LTP's partnership items are allocated based upon each partner's respective ownership interest and it is assumed that these allocations are respected under section 704(b) and the regulations thereunder. LTP has $100 of annualized ECTI for the relevant installment period. All of this income is ordinary income and there is no potential application of a preferential rate applicable percentage under §1.1446-3(a)(2). Further, §1.1446-6 does not apply. PRS has no income other than the income allocated from LTP. PRS provides LTP with a valid Form W-8IMY indicating that it is a foreign partnership and attaches the valid Form W-8BENs executed by NRA and FC, as well as a statement describing the allocation of PRS's effectively connected items among its partners. The information that PRS submits to LTP is sufficient to permit LTP to reliably associate (within the meaning of §1.1441-1(b)(2)(vii)) PRS's allocable share of effectively connected items with NRA and FC pursuant to this section. Further, NRA provides a valid Form W-8BEN to LTP.

(ii) LTP must pay 1446 tax on the $60 allocable to its direct partner NRA using the applicable percentage for non-corporate partners (the highest rate in section 1).

(iii) With respect to the effectively connected partnership items that LTP can reliably associate with NRA through PRS (70 percent of PRS's 40 percent allocable share ($40), or $28), LTP will pay 1446 tax on NRA's allocable share of LTP's ECTI (as determined by looking through PRS) using the applicable percentage for non-corporate partners (the highest rate in section 1).

(iv) With respect to the effectively connected partnership items that LTP can reliably associate with FC through PRS (30 percent of PRS's 40 percent allocable share ($40), or $12), LTP will pay 1446 tax on FC's allocable share of LTP's ECTI (as determined by looking through PRS) using the applicable percentage for corporate partners (the highest rate in section 11).

(v) LTP's payment of the 1446 tax is treated as a distribution to NRA and PRS, its direct partners, that those partners may credit against their respective tax obligations. PRS will report its 1446 tax obligation with respect to its direct foreign partners, NRA and FC, on the Form 8804 and Forms 8805 that it files with the Internal Revenue Service pursuant to paragraph (b) of this section and will credit the amount withheld by LTP on its Form 8804. This credit will satisfy PRS's 1446 tax liability as reported on the Form 8804 it files because PRS's only income is from LTP, and LTP paid 1446 tax with respect to all of PRS's allocable share in LTP by looking through to PRS's partners NRA and FC. Further, PRS will pass along the credit for the 1446 tax withheld by LTP to its partners, NRA and FC on the Form 8805 issued to each partner. The credit passed to each partner on Form 8805 will be treated as a distribution to the respective partners under section 1446(d).

*Example 2. Insufficient documentation—tiered partnership structure.* (i) LTP is a domestic partnership that has two equal partners A and PRS. A is a nonresident alien and PRS is a foreign partnership that has two equal foreign partners, C and D. Neither A nor PRS provides LTP with a valid Form W-8 or Form W-9. Neither C nor D provides PRS with a valid Form W-8 or Form W-9. Pursuant to §1.1446-1(c)(3), LTP must presume that PRS is a foreign person subject to withholding under section 1446 at the higher of the highest rate under section 1 or section 11(b)(1). LTP has also not received any documentation with respect to A. LTP must presume that A is a foreign person, and, if LTP knows that A is an individual, compute and pay 1446 tax, subject to §1.1446-3(a)(2), based on that knowledge.

(ii) Assume a change of facts where C provides a form W-8 (e.g., Form W-8BEN) to PRS, and PRS in turn, furnishes that form to LTP along with its Form W-8IMY, and information regarding how effectively connected items are allocated to C and D. Based upon the additional facts, LTP can reliably associate one-half of PRS's allocable share of ECTI with documentation related with C. Therefore, under paragraph (c)(2) of this section, LTP will look through PRS to C when computing its 1446 tax to the extent of C's indirect share and will not look through with respect to the remainder of PRS's allocable share (D's indirect share).

[Reg. §1.1446-5.]

☐ [*T.D. 9200, 5-13-2005. Amended by T.D. 9394, 4-28-2008.*]

### [Reg. §1.1446-6]

**§1.1446-6. Special rules to reduce a partnership's 1446 tax with respect to a foreign partner's allocable share of effectively connected taxable income.**—(a) *In general.*—(1) *Purpose and scope.*—This section provides rules regarding when a partnership required to pay withholding tax under section 1446 (1446 tax), or an installment of 1446 tax, may consider certain partner-level deductions and losses in computing its 1446 tax obligation under §1.1446-3, or otherwise not pay a de minimis amount of 1446 tax due with respect to a nonresident alien individual partner. A partnership determines the applicability of the rules of this section on a partner-bypartner basis for each installment period and when completing its Form 8804, "Annual Return for Partnership Withholding Tax (Section 1446)," and paying 1446 tax for the partnership taxable year. Except with respect to certain state and local taxes paid by the partnership on behalf of the partner, to apply the rules of this section with respect to a foreign partner, the partnership must receive a certificate from such partner for each partnership taxable year. Paragraph (b) of this section identifies the foreign partners to which this section applies. Paragraph (c) of this section identifies the deductions and losses that a foreign partner may certify to the partnership as well as the state and local taxes paid by the partnership on behalf of the foreign partner that can be taken into account without a certification, and establishes an exception that permits a partnership to not pay a de minimis amount of 1446 tax with respect to a nonresident alien partner. Paragraph (c) of this section also sets forth the requirements for a valid certificate. Paragraphs (a)(2) and (d) of this section establish when a partnership may rely on and consider a foreign partner's certificate in computing its 1446 tax, and the effects of relying on such certificate. Paragraph (d) of this section also describes the effects of a partnership relying on a certificate (including an updated certificate) and the reporting requirements of a partnership with respect to a certificate. Paragraph (e) of this section sets forth examples that illustrate the rules of this section. Paragraph (f) of this section provides the Effective/Applicability date. Paragraph (g) of this section provides a transition rule.

(2) *Reasonable reliance on a certificate.*—Subject to §1.1446-2 and the rules of this section, a partnership receiving a certificate (including an updated certificate or status update under paragraph (c)(2)(ii)(B) of this section) of deductions and losses from a partner provided in accordance with the provisions of this section may reasonably rely on such certificate (to the extent of the certified deductions and losses or other representations set forth in the certificate) until such time that it has actual knowledge or reason to know that the certificate is defective or that the time for receiving an updated certificate or status update from the partner under paragraph (c)(2)(ii)(B) of this section has expired. For this purpose, a partnership shall be considered to have actual knowledge or reason to know that a certificate is defective upon receipt of written notification from the IRS under paragraph (c)(3) or (c)(5) of this section.

(b) *Foreign partner to whom this section applies.*—(1) *In general.*—Except as otherwise provided in paragraph (b)(3) of this section, a foreign partner to whom this section applies is a foreign partner that meets the requirements of this paragraph (b)(1).

(i) The partner has provided valid documentation to the partnership to which a certificate is submitted under this section in accordance with §1.1446-1.

(ii) If the partner's current taxable year is the first taxable year in which the partner submits a certificate to any partnership, the partner has filed (or will file) a qualifying U.S. income tax return for each of its three taxable years ending before the end of the partnership's taxable year for which the partner is submitting a certificate (regardless of whether it was a partner in that partnership during each of these years). A qualifying U.S. income tax return for a taxable year that is prior to the first taxable year the partner submits a certificate to any partnership is a U.S. income tax return filed within the time specified in paragraph (b)(2)(iii) of this section.

(iii) If the current taxable year of the partner is not the first taxable year in which the partner submits a certificate to any partnership, the partner met the requirements in paragraph (b)(1)(ii) of this section for the first taxable year in which it submitted a certificate to any partnership and has filed (or will file) a qualifying U.S. income tax return for its first taxable year in which it submitted a certificate to any partnership and each subsequent taxable year ending before the beginning of the current taxable year (regardless of whether it was a partner in any partnership during each of those years). A qualifying U.S. income tax return for a taxable year that is prior to the taxable year the partner submits a certificate to any partnership is a

U.S. income tax return filed within the time specified in paragraph (b)(2)(iii) of this section.

(iv) The partner files a qualifying U.S. income tax return (within the meaning of paragraph (b)(2)(iii) of this section) for its taxable year in which a certificate is provided to any partnership.

(2) *Definitions.*—(i) *U.S. income tax return.*—A U.S. income tax return means a Form 1040NR, "U.S. Nonresident Alien Income Tax Return," in the case of a nonresident alien individual and a Form 1120F, "U.S. Income Tax Return of a Foreign Corporation," in the case of a foreign corporation.

(ii) *Timely-filed.*—Only for purposes of this section, a U.S. income tax return shall be considered timely-filed if the return is filed on or before the due date set forth in section 6072(c), plus any extension of time to file such return granted under section 6081.

(iii) *Qualifying U.S. income tax return.*—A U.S. income tax return shall constitute a qualifying U.S. income tax return if the return reports income or gain that is effectively connected with a U.S. trade or business or deductions or losses properly allocated and apportioned to such activities and if the return is described in paragraph (b)(2)(iii)(A), (B), or (C) of this section. A protective return described in §1.874-1(b)(6) or §1.882-4(a)(3)(vi) is not a qualifying U.S. income tax return for purposes of this section.

(A) A U.S. income tax return for a partner's preceding taxable year in which it did not submit a certificate to any partnership (but not including a taxable year following the first taxable year in which the partner submitted a certificate to any partnership), with a due date as set forth in section 6072(c), not including any extensions of time to file, which falls before the beginning of the current partnership taxable year for which the certificate is provided is described in this paragraph (b)(2)(iii)(A) if the return is filed and all amounts due with respect to such return (including interest, penalties, and additions to tax, if any) are paid on or before the earlier of—

*(1)* The date that is one year after the due date set forth in section 6072(c) for such return, not including any extensions of time to file; or

*(2)* The date on which the certificate for the current partnership taxable year is submitted to the partnership.

(B) A U.S. income tax return for a partner's preceding taxable year in which it did not submit a certificate to any partnership (but not including a taxable year following the first taxable year in which the partner submitted a certificate to any partnership), with a due date as set forth in section 6072(c), not including any extensions of time to file, which falls within the current partnership taxable year for which the certificate is provided is described in this paragraph (b)(2)(iii)(B) if the return is timely-filed and all amounts due with respect to such return are timely paid.

(C) A U.S. income tax return for a taxable year in which the partner submits a certificate to any partnership and for a taxable year following the first taxable year in which the partner submits a certificate to any partnership is described in this paragraph (b)(2)(iii)(C) if the return is timely-filed and all amounts due with such return are timely paid with respect to such return.

(3) *Special rules.*—(i) In the case of a partnership (upper-tier partnership) that is a partner in another partnership (lower-tier partnership)—

(A) The rules of this section may apply to reduce or eliminate the 1446 tax (or any installment of such tax) of the lower-tier partnership with respect to a foreign partner of the upper-tier partnership only to the extent the provisions of §1.1446-5 apply to look through the upper-tier partnership to the foreign partner of such upper-tier partnership and the certificate described in paragraph (c) of this section is provided by such foreign partner to the upper-tier partnership and, in turn, provided to the lower-tier partnership with other appropriate documentation (see §1.1446-5(c) and (e));

(B) An upper-tier partnership that submits a certificate of deductions and losses or a de minimis certificate to a lower-tier partnership may not submit that certificate to another lower-tier partnership;

(C) An upper-tier partnership that relies on a certificate submitted to it by a foreign partner under this section for computing its 1446 tax due on effectively connected taxable income (ECTI) allocable to that partner (other than ECTI allocable to it from a lower-tier partnership) may not submit that certificate to any lower-tier partnership; and

(D) In addition to any other information required by this section, a lower-tier partnership must submit with a Form 8813, "Partnership Withholding Tax Payment Voucher (Section 1446)," and Form 8805, "Foreign Partner's Information Statement of Section 1446 Withholding Tax," for which it relies on a certificate from an upper-tier partnership to reduce the 1446 tax due with respect to a foreign partner of the upper-tier partnership, sufficient information so that the IRS may reliably associate the ECTI and the certificate of deductions and losses with the partner in the upper-tier partnership submitting the certificate, including the name, taxpayer identification number (TIN) and allocation of effectively connected items at each partnership tier, as well as to the ultimate upper-tier partner submitting the certificate.

(ii) This section shall not apply to a partner that is a foreign estate or its beneficiaries.

(iii) This section shall not apply to a partner that is a trust or to its beneficiaries, except to the extent that such trust is owned by a grantor or other person under subpart E of subchapter J of the Internal Revenue Code, the documentation requirements of §1.1446-1 have been met by the grantor or other owner of such trust, and the certificate described in paragraph (c) of this section is provided by the grantor or other owner of such trust to the partnership.

(iv) This section shall not apply to a partner in a publicly-traded partnership subject to §1.1446-4.

(c) *Reduction of 1446 tax with respect to a foreign partner.*—(1) *General rules.*—Under paragraph (c)(1)(i) of this section a foreign partner to whom this section applies may certify to a partnership for a partnership taxable year that it has certain deductions (other than charitable deductions) and losses properly allocated and apportioned to gross income that is effectively connected (or treated as effectively connected) with the conduct of the partner's trade or business in the United States, and that the partner reasonably expects those deductions and losses to be available and claimed on the partner's U.S. income tax return to be filed for that taxable year. Under paragraph (c)(1)(ii) of this section, a nonresident alien individual partner to whom this section applies may also certify to a partnership for a partnership taxable year that its only investment or activity giving rise to effectively connected items for the partnership's taxable year that ends with or within the partner's taxable year is (and will be) the partner's investment in the partnership. A certificate submitted by a foreign partner to a partnership under this section must be in accordance with the form and requirements set forth in paragraph (c)(2)(ii) of this section. Under paragraph (c)(1)(iii) of this section, a partnership may take into account certain state and local taxes withheld by the partnership on behalf of the partner.

(i) *Certified deductions and losses.*—(A) *Deductions and losses from the partnership.*—Under this paragraph (c)(1)(i)(A), a partner may certify to a partnership for a partnership taxable year deductions (other than charitable deductions) and losses properly allocated and apportioned to gross income which is effectively connected (or treated as effectively connected) with the conduct of the partner's trade or business in the United States, that are reported on a Form 1065 (Schedule K-1), "Partner's Share of Income, Credits, Deductions, etc.," issued (or to be issued) to the partner by the partnership for a prior partnership taxable year, that are (or will be) reported on a qualifying U.S. income tax return for a partner's taxable year that ends before the installment due date or the close of the partnership taxable year for which the partner is certifying such deductions and losses, and that the partner reasonably expects to be available and claimed on a qualifying U.S. income tax return for the partner's taxable year ending with or after the close of the partnership taxable year. A partner that has a loss reported on a Form 1065 (Schedule K-1) issued (or to be issued) to the partner by the partnership for a prior partnership taxable year, but that is not (and will not be) reported on a qualifying U.S. income tax return for a prior taxable year of the partner because the loss is suspended under section 704(d) may also certify such suspended loss to the partnership under this paragraph (c)(1)(i)(A).

(B) *Deductions and losses from other sources.*—Under this paragraph (c)(1)(i)(B), a foreign partner may certify to a partnership for a partnership taxable year deductions (other than charitable deductions) and losses properly allocated and apportioned to gross income that is effectively connected (or treated as effectively connected) with the conduct of the partner's trade or business in the United States and that are from sources other than the partnership to whom the certificate is submitted if the deductions and losses are (or will be) reported on a qualifying U.S. income tax return of the partner for a taxable year that ends before the installment due date or the close of the partnership taxable year for which the partner is certifying the deductions and losses and the partner reasonably expects the deductions and losses to be available and claimed on the qualifying U.S. income tax return filed for its taxable year ending with or after the close of the partnership taxable year. Any deductions and losses certified under this paragraph (c)(1)(i)(B) that are allocated to the partner from another partnership must be reported on a Form 1065 (Schedule K-1) issued (or to be issued) to the partner by such other partnership. However, the partner may not certify any deduction or loss allocated to it from another partnership that is suspended under section 704(d).

(C) *Limit on the consideration of a partner's net operating loss deduction.*—A partnership may not consider a net operating loss deduction (as determined under section 172) certified by the partner under this paragraph (c)(1)(i) in an amount greater than the percentage limitation, if any, provided in section 56(a)(4) and (d) multiplied by the partner's allocable share of ECTI from the partnership reduced by all other certified deductions and losses whether or not taken into account by the partnership, as well as deductions considered under paragraph (c)(1)(iii) of this section.

(D) *Limitation on losses subject to certain partner level limitations.*—Pursuant to paragraph (c)(2)(i) of this section, a partner must identify any certified losses or deductions that are subject to special limitations at the partner level (for example, sections 465 and 469) and provide information to the partnership that will allow the partnership to take the special limitations into account. For example, where a partner certifies a loss to the partnership that is a passive activity loss under section 469, the partner shall identify the activities the partnership conducts that the partner expects will be passive activities. The partnership shall then ensure that these limitations are taken into account when determining the 1446 tax due with respect to the partner.

(E) *Certification of deductions and losses to other partnerships.*—Deductions and losses certified to a partnership for a taxable year of the partnership may not be certified for the taxable year of another partnership that begins or ends with or within the taxable year of the partnership to which the deductions and losses were certified.

(F) *Partner level use of deductions and losses certified to a partnership.*—Any deductions and losses certified to a partnership for a taxable year of the partner and considered by the partnership in computing its section 1446 tax due may not be considered by that partner for the same taxable year in computing the amount of its required installments under section 6654(d) or 6655(d) on income unrelated to the partnership to which the partner has submitted the certificate.

(ii) *De minimis certificate for nonresident alien individual partners.*—(A) *In general.*—Under this paragraph (c)(1)(ii), a nonresident alien individual partner to whom this section applies and that satisfies the requirements of paragraph (c)(1)(ii)(B) of this section may certify to a partnership that its only activity giving rise to effectively connected income, gain, deduction, or loss for the partnership's taxable year that ends with or within the partner's taxable year is (and will be) the partner's investment in the partnership. A partnership that receives a certificate from a nonresident alien partner under this paragraph (c)(1)(ii) and that may reasonably rely on such certificate is not required to pay 1446 tax (or any installment of such tax) with respect to such partner if the partnership estimates that the annualized (or, in the case of a partnership completing its Form 8804, the actual) 1446 tax otherwise due with respect to such partner is less than $1,000, without taking into account any deductions or losses certified by the partner to the partnership under paragraph (c)(1)(i) of this section or any amounts under paragraph (c)(1)(iii) of this section.

(B) *Requirements for exception.*—The requirements of this paragraph (c)(1)(ii)(B) are met if the nonresident individual alien partner's only activity giving rise to effectively connected income, gain, deduction, or loss for the partnership taxable year that ends with or within the partner's taxable year is (and will be) the partner's investment in the partnership. For this purpose, if the partner has (or has reason to expect to have) income or gain described in section 864(c)(6), such income or gain shall be considered derived from a separate investment activity. A certificate submitted by a nonresident alien individual partner under this paragraph (c)(1)(ii) is valid even if such certificate does not certify deductions and losses to partnership under this section. A nonresident alien individual partner that submits a certificate to a partnership under this paragraph (c)(1)(ii) must notify the partnership in writing and revoke such certificate within 10 days of the date that the partner invests or otherwise engages in another activity that may give rise to effectively connected income, gain, deduction, or loss for the partner's taxable year. For example, while an investment in a U.S. real property interest (as defined in section 897(c)) would not give rise to an activity requiring a notification (unless an election is in effect under section 871(d)), the disposition of the U.S. real property interest would give rise to an activity requiring a notification.

(iii) *Consideration of certain current year state and local taxes.*—In addition to any deductions and losses certified by a foreign partner to a partnership under paragraph (c)(1)(i) of this section, the partnership may consider as a deduction of such partner 90-percent of any state and local income taxes withheld and remitted by the partnership on behalf of such partner with respect to the partner's allocable share of partnership ECTI. The partnership may consider the amount of state and local taxes of the foreign partner determined under this paragraph (c)(1)(iii) regardless of whether the foreign partner submits a certificate to the partnership under paragraph (c)(1)(i) or (ii) of this section.

(2) *Form and time of certification.*—(i) *Form of certification.*—A partner's certification to a partnership under paragraph (c)(1)(i) or (iii) of this section shall be made using Form 8804-C, "Certificate Of Partner-Level Items to Reduce Section 1446 Withholding" in accordance with the instructions of the form and the rules of this section.

(ii) *Time for certification provided to partnership.*—(A) *First certificate submitted for a partnership's taxable year.*—Provided the other requirements of this section are met, a partnership may only rely on the first certificate received from a foreign partner for any 1446 tax installment due or Form 8804 filing due (without regard to extensions) on or after the date on which the certificate is received. See §1.1446-3 for 1446 tax installment due dates. See also paragraph (e) of this section for examples illustrating the rules of this paragraph (c)(2).

(B) *Updated certificates and status updates.*—(1) *Preceding year tax returns not yet filed.*—If a foreign partner's U.S. income tax return for a preceding taxable year has not been filed as of the time the partner submits to the partnership its first certificate under this paragraph (c), the certificate shall specify this fact and set forth the filing due date for such return set forth in section 6072(c), plus any extension of time to file such return granted under section 6081 and the regulations under section 6081. The partner shall also submit an updated certificate to the partnership in accordance with this paragraph (c) within 10 days of the date the partner files its U.S. income tax return for any such taxable year. In addition, prior to the partnership's final 1446 tax installment due date the partner shall provide to the partnership, under penalties of perjury, a status update regarding any U.S. income tax return for the prior taxable year that has not (or will not) be filed as of the final installment due date. The status update must identify the due date, set forth in section 6072(c), plus any extension of time to file such return granted under section 6081 and the regulations under section 6081, for any un-filed return identified in the first certificate and state whether the first certificate submitted may continue to be considered by the partnership. If the partnership does not receive an updated certificate or a status update from the partner prior to the partnership's final installment due date, the partnership shall disregard the partner's certificate when computing the 1446 tax due with respect to that partner for the final installment period and when completing its Form 8804 for the taxable year. In addition, the foreign partner shall not be permitted to submit an additional or substitute certificate for the disregarded certificate. See §1.1446-3(b)(2)(i) for computation requirements for installment payments of 1446 tax when a partnership receives, or fails to receive, an updated certificate or status update. See also paragraph (e)(2) *Examples 4 and 8* of this section. Notwithstanding this paragraph (c)(2)(ii)(B)(1), a partner that can meet the requirements of this section for a subsequent partnership taxable year may submit a certificate to the partnership under this section for such taxable year.

(2) *Other circumstances requiring an updated certificate.*—If at any time during the partnership taxable year the partner determines that its most recent certificate furnished to the partnership for such taxable year is incorrect, then the partner shall submit to the partnership an updated certificate in accordance with this paragraph (c) within 10 days of such determination. For example, if the partner determines that the amount or character of the certified deductions or losses is incorrect, the partner shall submit an updated certificate to the partnership. See §1.1446-3(b)(2)(i) for computation requirements for installment payments of 1446 tax when a partnership receives an updated certificate.

(3) *Form and content of updated certificate.*—The updated certificate required by this paragraph (c)(2)(ii) must be provided using the form and instructions identified in paragraph (c)(2)(i) of this section. The updated certificate must indicate that it is an updated certificate filed in accordance with this paragraph (c)(2)(ii). The partner is not required to attach to the updated certificate a copy of the certificate that is being updated (superseded certificate).

(4) *Partnership consideration of an updated certificate.*—A partnership may consider an updated certificate, that meets the requirements of this paragraph (c), that is received prior to an installment due date in the same partnership taxable year for which the superseded certificate was provided, or prior to the due date of its Form 8804 (without regard to extensions) to be filed for the year the superseded certificate was provided. A partnership must consider an updated certificate that meets all the requirements of this paragraph (c) if it would increase the amount of 1446 tax the partnership would pay by the next installment due date, if any, or the due date of its

Form 8804. An updated certificate considered by the partnership under this paragraph (c)(2)(ii)(B)(4) supersedes all prior certificates submitted by the foreign partner for the same partnership taxable year, beginning with the installment period or Form 8804 filing date for which the partnership considers the updated certificate. See paragraph (e)(2) *Example 4* of this section.

(3) *Notification to partnership when a partner's certificate cannot be relied upon.*—If the IRS determines, in its discretion based on all the facts and circumstances, that a foreign partner's certificate is defective (or that it lacks information sufficient to make this determination after providing written request for such information to the partnership), the IRS shall notify the partnership of such determination in writing. Upon receipt of such written notification, the partnership shall not rely on any certificate submitted by that foreign partner for the partnership taxable year to which the defective certificate relates (or any subsequent partnership taxable year), until the IRS provides written notification to the partnership revoking or modifying the original written notification. For purposes of this section, a foreign partner's certificate of deductions and losses shall be defective if—

(i) The partner is not described in paragraph (b) of this section;

(ii) Any deductions or losses set forth in such certificate are not described in paragraph (c)(1)(i) of this section;

(iii) The timing requirements under paragraph (c)(2) of this section for submitting an original certificate, an updated certificate or a status update to the partnership are not met;

(iv) The certificate does not include all of the information required by paragraph (c)(2)(i) of this section;

(v) Any representation made on the certificate is incorrect;

(vi) The actual amount of deductions and losses available to the partner is less than the amount of deductions and losses certified to the partnership for the partnership taxable year and considered by the partnership in determining its 1446 tax due; or

(vii) There is a failure to comply with any other provision of this section.

(4) *Partner to receive copy of notice.*—If the IRS notifies a partnership under paragraph (c)(3) of this section that a certificate of a foreign partner is defective, the IRS shall send a copy of such notice to the partner's address as shown on the certificate. The partnership shall also promptly furnish a copy of the IRS notice to such partner.

(5) *Notification to partnership when no foreign partner's certificate can be relied upon.*—If the IRS determines, in its discretion based on all the facts and circumstances, that there would be a substantial reduction in section 1446 tax as a result of the submission of one or more defective certificates or that a substantial portion of all certificates being submitted by partners to the partnership and by the partnership to the IRS are defective (or lack information sufficient to make this determination), then the IRS shall notify the partnership of such determination in writing. Upon receipt of such written notification, the partnership shall not rely on any certificate submitted by any partner for the partnership taxable year to which the notice relates or any subsequent partnership taxable year, until the IRS provides written notification to the partnership revoking or modifying the original notice.

(6) *Partnership notification to partner regarding use of deductions and losses.*—Unless §1.1446-3(d)(1)(i)(A) or (B) applies (relating to waiver of notice of tax paid during the partnership taxable year), a partnership must notify each foreign partner of the amount of such partner's certified deductions and losses and state and local taxes, if any, taken into account under this paragraph (c) in determining the 1446 tax due with respect to such partner for each installment period or Form 8804 filing date, as applicable.

(7) *Partner's certificate valid only for partnership taxable year for which submitted.*—A partnership that receives a certificate from a partnership under this paragraph (c) shall consider such certificate only for the partnership taxable year for which the certificate is submitted, as set forth on the certificate.

(d) *Effect of certificate of deductions and losses on partners and partnership.*—(1) *Effect on partner.*—(i) *No effect on liability for income tax of foreign partner.*—A foreign partner that certifies deductions and losses to a partnership under this section is not relieved of liability for income tax on its allocable share of ECTI from the partnership. Further, the submission of a certificate under this section does not constitute an acceptance by the IRS of the amount or character of the deductions or losses certified therein.

(ii) *No effect on partner's estimated tax obligations.*—A foreign partner that certifies deductions and losses to a partnership under this section is not relieved of any estimated tax obligation otherwise applicable to such partner with respect to income or gain allocated to such partner from the partnership.

Reg. §1.1446-6(d)(1)(ii)

(iii) *No effect on partner's obligation to file U.S. income tax return.*—The submission of a certificate under paragraph (c) of this section does not relieve the foreign partner from its obligation to file a U.S. income tax return even if as a result of the partnership considering the certificate the partner would have no additional tax due with such return. See also § 1.1446-3(f).

(2) *Effect on partnership.*—(i) *Reasonable reliance to relieve partnership from addition to tax under section 6655.*—A partnership that has reasonably relied on a certificate received from a foreign partner and complied with the filing requirements of paragraph (d)(3)(i) of this section, shall not be liable for any addition to tax under section 6655 (as applied through § 1.1446-3) for any period during which the partnership reasonably relied on such certificate, even if such certificate is later determined to be defective or the partner submits an updated certificate under paragraph (c)(2) of this section that increases the 1446 tax due with respect to such partner.

(ii) *Continuing liability for withholding tax under section 1461 and for applicable interest and penalties.*—(A) *In general.*—Except as otherwise provided in this section, a partnership that has reasonably relied on a certificate received from a foreign partner and complied with the filing requirements of paragraph (d)(3)(i) of this section, is not relieved from liability for the 1446 tax (or any installment of such tax) under section 1461, any additions to the tax, interest or penalties. However, the partnership may be relieved of additions to the tax or penalties in certain circumstances. See §§ 301.6651-1(c) and 301.6724-1 of this chapter. Further, see § 1.1446-3(e) which deems a partnership to have paid 1446 tax with respect to ECTI allocable to a partner in certain circumstances. See also paragraph (e)(2) *Example 5* of this section.

(B) *Certificate defective because of amount or character of deductions and losses.*—If a certificate is determined to be defective because the actual amount of deductions and losses available to the partner is less than the amount reflected on the certificate (other than when it is determined that the partner certified the same deduction or loss to more than one partnership), or because the character of the certified deductions and losses is erroneous, the partnership shall be liable for 1446 tax under section 1461 (or any installment of such tax) with respect to such partner to the extent the partnership considered an amount of certified deductions and losses greater than the amount actually available to the partner and permitted to be used under §§ 1.1446-1 through 1.1446-5 and this section, or to the extent the proper character of the certified deductions and losses results in a greater amount of 1446 tax due with respect to such partner. See paragraph (e)(2) *Example 6* of this section.

(3) *Partnership level rules and requirements.*—(i) *Filing requirement.*—A partnership that relies in whole or in part on a certificate received from a partner under this section in computing its 1446 tax due with respect to such partner must still file Form 8813 or Form 8804 and 8805, whichever is applicable, for the period for which the certificate is considered, even if as a result of relying on the certificate no 1446 tax (or an installment of such tax) is due with respect to such foreign partner. See generally § 1.1446-3(d)(1). Except as otherwise provided in this paragraph (d)(3)(i), the partnership must attach a copy of the foreign partner's certificate, and the computation of the 1446 tax due with respect to such partner, to both the Form 8813 and Form 8805 filed with the IRS for any installment period or year for which such certificate is considered in computing the partnership's 1446 tax. See § 1.1446-3(d)(1)(iii) requiring the partnership to furnish Form 8805 to the IRS and such foreign partner even if no 1446 tax is paid on behalf of the partner. The partnership must include in that computation the amount of state and local taxes described in paragraph (c)(1)(iii) of this section taken into account in computing the 1446 tax due with respect to that partner. The partnership must also attach a computation of the 1446 tax due with respect to a partner for whom only state and local taxes described in paragraph (c)(1)(iii) are taken into account. For an installment period other than the first installment period for which the partnership considers a foreign partner's certificate or updated certificate, the partnership may, instead of attaching any partner's certificate, attach to Form 8813 a list containing the name, TIN, the amount of certified deductions and losses, and the amount of state and local taxes the partnership may consider under paragraph (c)(1)(iii) of this section for each foreign partner whose certificate was relied upon. For purposes of the preceding sentence, if the partnership is relying on a certificate received under paragraph (c)(1)(ii) of this section, instead of providing the amounts described in the prior sentence, it should attach a statement to Form 8813 which provides that, relying on that certificate, no 1446 tax is due with respect to that partner.

(ii) *Reasonable cause for failure to timely file a valid certificate and computation.*—This paragraph (d)(3)(ii) provides the sole source of relief for a partnership that fails to timely file a valid certificate or attach a computation of 1446 tax as required under paragraph

(d)(3)(i) of this section. To permit the partnership to reasonably rely on such certificate, the partnership shall be considered to have satisfied the requirements of paragraph (d)(3)(i) of this section if the partnership demonstrates that such failure was due to reasonable cause and not willful neglect and if once the partnership becomes aware of the failure, the partnership attaches the certificate and computation, as well as a written statement setting forth the reasons for the failure to comply with the requirements of paragraph (d)(3)(i) of this section, to an amended Form 8813 or amended Forms 8804 and 8805 for the relevant period. All such submissions should be sent to the address provided in the instructions to Form 8804-C.

(A) *Determining reasonable cause.*—In determining whether the partnership has reasonable cause, the Director shall consider whether the partnership acted reasonably and in good faith considering all the facts and circumstances.

(B) *Notification.*—If the IRS has notified, as provided in paragraph (c)(3) of this section, the partnership that the certificate is defective or that no foreign partner's certificate may be relied upon, as provided in paragraph (c)(5) of this section, the partnership will be deemed not to have acted reasonably and in good faith. Otherwise, the Director shall notify the partnership in writing within 120 days of the amended filing if it is determined that the failure to comply was not due to reasonable cause, or if additional time will be needed to make such determination. If the Director fails to notify the partnership within 120 days of the amended filing, the partnership shall be considered to have demonstrated to the Director that such failure was due to reasonable cause and not willful neglect.

(e) *Examples.*—(1) The rules of this section are illustrated by the examples in paragraph (e)(2) of this section. In 2008, the relevant rate of withholding for foreign partners that were not corporations (that is, the highest rate in section 1 as specified in § 1.1446-3(a)(2)(i)) was 35%, and the due date for filing Form 8804 for domestic calendar year partnerships (that is, the date specified in § 1.1446-3(d)(1)(iii)) was April 15. Except as otherwise provided, in each example assume:

(i) Section 1.1446-3(b)(2)(v)(F) (relating to the de minimis exception to paying 1446 tax) does not apply;

(ii) Paragraph (c)(1)(ii) of this section (relating to a nonresident alien individual partner whose sole investment generating effectively connected income or gain is the partnership) does not apply;

(iii) All income and losses are ordinary;

(iv) For purposes of applying paragraph (c)(1)(i)(C) of this section, the percentage limitation under section 56(a)(4) and (d) is 90 percent;

(v) Any loss is not a passive activity loss within the meaning of section 469;

(vi) The partnership uses an acceptable annualization method under § 1.1446-3;

(vii) NRA is a nonresident alien individual who maintains a calendar taxable year for U.S. tax purpose;

(viii) B and C are U.S. individuals who maintain a calendar taxable year; and

(ix) Any partnership maintains a calendar taxable year.

(2) The examples are as follows:

*Example 1. Qualifying U.S. income tax return.* (i) NRA and B form a partnership (PRS) in year 4 to conduct a trade or business in the United States. NRA and B provide PRS appropriate documentation under § 1.1446-1 to establish their status for purposes of section 1446. NRA submits a certificate to PRS (using Form 8804-C) on March 20, year 4, to be considered by PRS in determining its 1446 tax due with respect to NRA for the first installment period in the year 4. The Form 8804-C states that NRA reasonably expects to have an effectively connected net operating loss of $5,000 available to offset its allocable share of ECTI from PRS in year 4. Prior to year 4, NRA had not submitted a certificate to a partnership under this section. NRA filed (or will file) its year 1 U.S. income tax return on March 11, year 3; its year 2 U.S. income tax return on February 12, year 4; its year 3 U.S. income tax return on April 13, year 4; and its year 4 U.S. income tax return on May 14, year 5. NRA paid (or will pay) all amounts due with respect to the returns (including interest, penalties, and additions to tax, if any) by the date they are filed. NRA's years 1 though 3 U.S. income tax returns report income or gain effectively connected with a U.S. trade or business or deductions or losses properly allocated and apportioned to such activities.

(ii) To be eligible to submit a certificate of deductions and losses to PRS under this section, NRA must satisfy the requirements of paragraph (b)(1) of this section. In accordance with § 1.1446-1, NRA provided valid documentation to PRS to establish its status for purposes of section 1446. NRA's year 1 U.S. income tax return is a qualifying U.S. income tax return because it reported income or gain effectively connected with a U.S. trade or business or deductions or losses properly allocated and apportioned to such activities and is described under paragraph (b)(2)(iii)(A) of this section. Although

NRA filed its year 1 return after the due date of the return (determined under section 6072(c) without regard to any extension of time to file) the return was filed on March 11, year 3, which was on or before the earlier of June 15, year 3, the date one year after its section 6072(c) due date without regard to any extension of time to file, and March 20, year 4, the date on which NRA submitted the certificate to PRS. NRA's year 2 U.S. income tax return is a qualifying U.S. income tax return because it reported income or gain effectively connected with a U.S. trade or business or deductions or losses properly allocated and apportioned to such activities and is described under paragraph (b)(2)(iii)(A) of this section. Although NRA filed its year 2 return after the due date of the return (determined under section 6072(c) without regard to any extension of time to file) the return was filed on February 12, year 4, which was on or before the earlier of June 15, year 4, the date one year after its section 6072(c) due date without regard to any extension of time to file, and March 20, year 4, the date on which NRA submitted the certificate to PRS. NRA's year 3 U.S. income tax return is a qualifying U.S. income tax return because it reported income or gain effectively connected with a U.S. trade or business or deductions or losses properly allocated and apportioned to such activities and is described under paragraph (b)(2)(iii)(B) of this section. Because NRA filed its year 3 U.S. income tax return on April 13, year 4, the return will be considered timelyfiled under paragraph (b)(2)(ii) of this section, as the due date under section 6072(c) was June 15, year 4. NRA's year 4 U.S. income tax return is a qualifying U.S. income tax return because it reported income or gain effectively connected with a U.S. trade or business or deductions or losses properly allocated and apportioned to such activities and is described under paragraph (b)(2)(iii)(C) of this section. Because NRA filed its year 4 U.S. income tax return on May 14, year 5, the return will be considered timelyfiled under paragraph (b)(2)(ii) of this section. Accordingly, NRA meets the conditions of paragraph (b)(1) of this section and is eligible to provide a certificate of deductions and losses to PRS for year 4.

*Example 2. Subsequent year qualifying U.S. income tax return.* (i) Assume the same facts as in Example 1. Further, NRA and C form a second partnership (XYZ) in year 7 to conduct a trade or business in the United States. NRA and C provide XYZ appropriate documentation under §1.1446-1 to establish their status for purposes of section 1446. NRA did not submit a certificate under this section to any partnership for years 5 and 6. NRA submits a certificate to XYZ (using Form 8804-C) on April 10, year 7, to be considered by XYZ in determining its 1446 tax due with respect to NRA for its first installment period in year 7. The certificate states that NRA reasonably expects to have an effectively connected net operating loss of $8,000 available to offset its allocable share of ECTI from XYZ in year 7. Further, the certificate contains all of the necessary representations required under this section. NRA will file its U.S. income tax return for year 5 on March 25, year 7, (after its section 6072(c) due date and any extension of time to file that could have been granted under section 6081), its U.S. income tax return for year 6 on April 26, year 7; and its U.S. income tax return for year 7 on May 27, year 8. NRA will pay all amounts due with the returns (including interest, penalties, and additions to tax, if any) by the dates they are filed. NRA's years 5, 6, and 7 U.S. income tax returns will report income or gain that is effectively connected with a U.S. trade or business or deductions or losses properly allocated and apportioned to such activities.

(ii) To be eligible to submit a certificate of deductions and losses to XYZ under this section, NRA must satisfy the requirements of paragraph (b)(1) of this section. NRA provided valid documentation to XYZ in accordance with §1.1446-1. As described in Example 1, NRA's year 4 U.S. income tax return is a qualifying U.S. income tax return because it will report income or gain effectively connected with a U.S. trade or business and is described under paragraph (b)(2)(iii)(C) of this section. Although NRA's year 5 U.S. income tax return reports income or gain effectively connected with a U.S. trade or business or deductions or losses properly allocated and apportioned to such activities it is not qualifying U.S. tax return under paragraph (b)(2)(iii) of this section. Because NRA submitted a certificate to PRS in year 4, to constitute a qualifying U.S. tax income return the year 5 U.S. income tax return must be timely-filed and all amounts due with such return must be timely paid. See paragraph (b)(2)(iii)(C) of this section. However, NRA will not file its U.S. income tax return for year 5 until March 25, year 7, (after its section 6072(c) due date and any extension of time to file that could have been granted under section 6081). Because the year 5 tax return is not a qualifying U.S. income tax return under paragraph (b)(2)(iii) of this section, NRA does not satisfy the requirements of paragraph (b)(1)(ii) of this section and, therefore, may not submit a certificate of deductions and losses to XYZ under this section in year 7.

*Example 3. General application of the rules of this section.* NRA and B form a partnership (PRS) to conduct a trade or business in the United States. NRA and B are equal partners under the partnership agreement. NRA and B provide PRS appropriate documentation under §1.1446-1 to establish their status for purposes of section 1446. Prior

to the formation of PRS, NRA had not invested in or engaged in the conduct of a U.S. trade or business. PRS incurs a $1,500 effectively connected net operating loss in years 1 and 2. The loss incurred in each is allocated equally between NRA and B. NRA has filed a qualifying U.S. income tax return (within the meaning of paragraph (b)(2)(iii) of this section) for years 1 and 2 that report its allocable share of effective connected net operating loss allocated to it from PRS, as reported on the Form 1065 (Schedule K-1) issued to NRA for each year.

(i) In year 3, NRA may not submit a certificate to PRS under paragraph (c) because it will not have filed qualifying U.S. income tax returns for the preceding three years. In year 3, PRS has ECTI of $1,000 that is allocated equally between NRA and B. PRS satisfies its 1446 tax obligation with respect to NRA for year 3.

(ii) In year 4, PRS estimates that it will have ECTI of $4,000, which will be allocated equally between NRA and B. On or before April 15th of year 4 (the first installment due date), NRA submits a certificate to PRS under this section (using Form 8804-C) certifying that it reasonably expects to have an effectively connected net operating loss of $1,000 ($750 loss in both years 1 and 2, less $500 of income in year 3) available to offset its allocable share of ECTI from PRS in year 4. As of the date the certificate is submitted, NRA has received the Form 1065 (Schedule K-1) from PRS for year 3 but has not yet filed its U.S. income tax return for year 3.

(iii) With respect to year 4, and based upon paragraph (b)(1) of this section, NRA can include year 3 (NRA's preceding taxable year) as one of the preceding three years that it has filed or will file qualifying U.S. income tax returns (within the meaning of paragraph (b)(2)(iii) of this section). Therefore, provided PRS has, in accordance with paragraph (a)(2) of this section, no actual knowledge or reason to know the certificate is defective, PRS may reasonably rely on NRA's certificate. Accordingly, PRS may consider NRA's certificate to reduce the 1446 tax that would otherwise be required to be paid on NRA's behalf. Specifically, subject to paragraph (c)(1)(i)(C) of this section, the $1,000 of net losses that have been reported on Forms 1065 (Schedule K-1) issued to NRA that are available to reduce NRA's U.S. income tax on NRA's allocable share of effectively connected income or gain allocable from PRS may be used to reduce the $2,000 of ECTI estimated to be allocable to NRA. As a result, PRS must pay 1446 tax on only $1,100 of NRA's allocable share of partnership ECTI for the first installment period in year 5 ($2,000 – ($1,000 × .90)). PRS must pay 1446 tax of $96.25 for its first installment period with respect to the ECTI allocable to NRA ($1,100 (net ECTI after considering certified losses) x .35 (withholding tax rate) x .25 (section 6655(e)(2)(B) percentage for the first installment period)). See §1.1446-3(b)(2). Pursuant to paragraph (d)(3) of this section, PRS must attach NRA's certificate and PRS's computation of its 1446 tax obligation with respect to NRA to its Form 8813, "Partnership Withholding Tax Payment Voucher (Section 1446)," filed for the first installment period. Under paragraph (c)(2)(ii)(B) of this section, NRA is required to provide an updated certificate on or before the 10th day after NRA files its U.S. income tax return for year 3, even if the updated certificate results in no change to the amount of deductions and losses reported on the superseded certificate.

(iv) The results are the same if NRA had not yet received a Form 1065 (Schedule K-1) from PRS for year 3. See paragraph (c)(1)(i)(A) of this section.

*Example 4. Updated certificate submitted for losses.* On January 1, year 8, NRA and B form a partnership (PRS) to conduct a trade or business in the United States. NRA and B are equal partners in PRS. NRA and B provide PRS appropriate documentation under §1.1446-1 to establish their status for purposes of section 1446. During years 1 through 7 NRA held an interest in another partnership (XYZ) that conducted a trade or business in the United States. NRA timely-filed (within the meaning of paragraph (b)(2) of this section) U.S. income tax returns for years 1 through 6 reporting its allocable year of ECTI (or loss) from XYZ (and timely paid all tax shown on such returns). NRA files its U.S. income tax return for year 7 on June 9, year 8 (and timely pays all tax due with such return). Therefore, NRA has filed qualifying U.S. income tax returns (within the meaning of paragraph (b)(2)(iii) of this section) for years 1 through 7. During years 1 through 7, NRA's only investment generating effectively connected items was its interest in XYZ. The XYZ partnership liquidated and ceased doing business on December 31, year 7.

(i) On or before April 15, year 8, PRS receives from NRA a valid certificate under this section using Form 8804-C in which NRA certifies that it reasonably expects to have available effectively connected net operating losses in the amount of $5,000. Among other statements made in accordance with paragraph (c) of this section, NRA represents that it has not yet filed its year 7 U.S. income tax return, but will timely file such return (and timely pay all tax due with such return). For its first installment period in year 8, PRS estimates that it will earn taxable income of $10,000 for the year which will be allocated equally to NRA and B (NRA's allocable share of PRS's ECTI is $5,000).

(ii) Provided PRS has, in accordance with paragraph (a)(2) of this section, no actual knowledge or reason to know the certificate is defective, PRS may reasonably rely on NRA's certificate when computing its 1446 tax obligation for the first installment period. PRS is limited under paragraph (c)(1)(i)(C) of this section and PRS may only consider $4,500 ($5,000 × .90) of the certified net operating loss. After consideration of the certified loss, PRS owes 1446 tax in the amount of $43.75 for the first installment period ($5,000 estimated allocable ECTI less $4,500 (certified loss as limited under paragraph (c)(1)(i)(C)) × .35 (1446 tax applicable percentage) x .25 (section 6655(e)(2)(B) percentage for the first installment period)). See § 1.1446-3(b)(2). Pursuant to paragraph (d)(3) of this section, PRS must attach a copy of NRA's certificate and the computation of 1446 tax due with respect to NRA to the Form 8813 filed with respect to NRA.

(iii) PRS's estimate of ECTI allocable to NRA for the second installment period remains unchanged from the first installment period. On June 10, year 8, NRA provides PRS an updated certificate reporting that NRA now reasonably expects to have an effectively connected net operating loss of $4,000 available to offset its allocable share of ECTI from PRS in year 4. NRA provided the updated certificate within 10 days of filing its U.S. income tax return for the year 7 taxable year, as required by paragraph (c)(2)(ii)(B) of this section. Provided the updated certificate is otherwise valid, PRS may rely on the updated certificate for the second installment period (due date June 15, year 8). Even if the updated certificate were not valid, PRS could no longer rely on the original certificate.

(iv) Under paragraph (d) of this section, PRS is not relieved from liability for the 1446 tax due with respect to NRA under section 1461 if it relies on a certificate determined to be defective, or if it receives an updated certificate reporting an amount of deductions and losses less than the amount reported on the superseded certificate. Under the principles of section 6655 (as applied through § 1.1446-3), PRS is required to have paid 50-percent of the annualized 1446 tax due with respect to NRA on or before the due date of the second installment period (section 6655(e)(2)(B) percentage for the second installment period). Under paragraph (c)(2)(ii)(B) of this section, because NRA's updated certificate is valid for the second installment period, if PRS considers a certificate for that period it must consider the updated certificate. Under paragraph (c)(1)(i)(C) of this section, PRS can only consider $3,600 ($4,000 × .90) of NRA's updated effectively connected net operating loss. Assuming PRS considers NRA's updated certificate for the second installment period, PRS must have paid a total of $245 of 1446 tax with respect to the ECTI estimated to be allocable to NRA as of the second installment due date ($1,400 ($5,000 ECTI less $3,600 net operating loss deduction) × .35 (withholding tax rate) x .50 (section 6655(e)(2)(B) percentage for the second installment period)). After considering PRS's payment of 1446 tax for the first installment period, PRS is required to pay $201.25 for the second installment period ($245 less previous payment of $43.75). See § 1.1446-3(b)(2). Further, if PRS considers NRA's updated certificate for the second installment period, when PRS files Form 8813 it must attach the updated certificate along with PRS's computation of 1446 tax due with respect to NRA.

(v) Under paragraph (d) of this section, PRS is not liable for the addition to the tax under section 6655 (as applied through § 1.1446-3) for the first installment period because PRS reasonably relied on NRA's certificate of losses for that period.

(vi) Assume that PRS's estimate of its ECTI allocable to NRA for the third and fourth installment periods is the same as for the first and second installment periods. Assume PRS may reasonably rely on NRA's updated certificate in calculating its payment of 1446 tax for the third and fourth installment periods. The third installment of 1446 tax would be $122.50 (($5,000 − $3,600) × .35 × .75 = $367.50 − $245 (total previous payments)). The fourth installment of 1446 tax would be $122.50 (($5,000- $3,600) × .35 × 1.00 = $490 − $367.50 (total previous payments)). See § 1.1446- 3(b)(2). PRS must attach to each Form 8813 a computation of the 1446 tax due with respect to NRA that takes into account the amount of effectively connected net operating loss reported on NRA's updated certificate.

(vii) Because NRA's certified net operating loss has not changed for the third and fourth installments, in lieu of attaching NRA's certificate, PRS may attach a statement containing NRA's name, TIN, and the certified net operating loss amount. However, PRS must attach NRA's certificate and a computation of the 1446 tax due with respect to NRA that takes into account NRA's certified net operating loss to the Form 8805 filed with respect to NRA. See paragraph (d)(3) of this section.

*Example 5. IRS determines in subsequent taxable year that partner's certificate is defective because partner failed to timely file a U.S. income tax return.* NRA and B form a partnership (PRS) in year 1 to conduct a trade or business in the United States. NRA and B provide PRS appropriate documentation under § 1.1446-1 to establish their status for purposes of section 1446. In year 4, NRA timely submits a

certificate under this section (using Form 8804-C) to be considered by PRS for its first installment period. The certificate reports that NRA reasonably expects to have an effectively connected net operating loss of $5,000 available to offset its allocable share of ECTI from PRS in year 4. Further, the certificate contains all of the necessary representations required under this section. PRS estimates for each installment period that NRA's allocable share of ECTI will be $5,000 for the taxable year. PRS's actual operating results for the year result in $5,000 of ECTI allocable to NRA.

(i) PRS reasonably relies on (within the meaning of paragraph (a)(2) of this section) NRA's certificate when computing each installment payment during year 4 and the 1446 tax due on Form 8804 and appropriately considers the limitation in paragraph (c)(1)(i)(C) of this section. As a result, PRS paid $175 of 1446 tax on behalf of NRA for the taxable year ($5,000 of ECTI less $4,500 net operating loss deduction x .35 applicable percentage). As required under paragraph (d) of this section, PRS attached the certificate to the Form 8813 for the first installment period and the Form 8805 for year 4. Because NRA did not submit an updated certificate to PRS in year 4, PRS attached to the Forms 8813 for the second, third and fourth installment periods a statement containing NRA's name, TIN, and the certified net operating loss as well as the computation of 1446 tax due with respect to NRA reflecting the amount of net operating loss considered.

(ii) In year 5, NRA timely submits to PRS a certificate under this section to be considered for the first installment period. The certificate represents that NRA reasonably expects to have an effectively connected net operating loss of $5,000 available to offset its allocable share of ECTI from PRS in year 5. For the first installment period, PRS estimates that NRA's allocable share of partnership ECTI is $5,000. PRS reasonably relies on the certificate for the first installment period and determines that it is required to make a 1446 tax installment payment of $43.75 ($5,000 allocable ECTI less $4,500 (certified net operating loss as limited under paragraph (c)(1)(i)(C) of this section) x .35 (1446 tax applicable percentage) x .25 (section 6655(e)(2)(B) percentage for the first installment period)). See § 1.1446-3(b)(2). PRS makes the installment payment with the Form 8813 filed for the first installment period, and complies with paragraph (d)(3) of this section by attaching NRA's certificate and the computation of 1446 tax due with respect to NRA to the Form 8813.

(iii) The IRS provides written notification to PRS on June 1, year 5, (pursuant to paragraph (c)(3) of this section) that the certificate received from NRA in year 4 is defective because NRA failed to file a qualifying U.S. income tax return (within the meaning of paragraph (b)(2)(iii) of this section) for one of the preceding taxable years as required under paragraph (b)(1) of this section. The notice further states that PRS is not to rely on any certificate received from NRA in year 5.

(iv) Under paragraph (d)(2)(ii) of this section, because the certificate submitted by NRA in year was determined to be defective for a reason other than the amount or character of the certified deductions and losses, under section 1461 PRS is fully liable for the 1446 tax due with respect to NRA's allocable share of ECTI year 4 without regard to the certificate. The total 1446 tax due for year 4 without regard to the certificate is $1,750 ($5,000 ECTI x .35) and PRS paid $175 of 1446 tax in year 4. Therefore, PRS owes $1,575 of 1446 tax. However, PRS may be deemed to have paid the outstanding 1446 tax due if NRA paid all of its U.S. tax due in year 4. See § 1.1446-3(e).

(v) However, because PRS did not have actual knowledge or reason to know that the certificate NRA submitted in year 4 was defective, PRS reasonably relied on the certificate for purposes of paragraph (d)(2) of this section. Therefore, PRS is not liable for an addition to the tax with respect to its underpayment of 1446 tax under the principles of section 6655 (as applied through § 1.1446-3) for any installment period in year 4.

(vi) However, PRS is generally liable for interest under section 6601 and for the failure to pay addition to tax under section 6651(a)(2) on the $1,575 of 1446 tax due for year 4 for the period from April 15, year 5 (last date prescribed for payment of 1446 tax) to the date PRS pays the 1446 tax or is deemed to have paid the 1446 tax under § 1.1446-3(e).

(vii) With respect to the year 5, PRS reasonably relied on NRA's certificate when computing its first installment payment (due on April 15, year 5). Therefore, in accordance with paragraph (d)(2)(i) of this section, PRS will not be liable for an addition to the tax under the principles of section 6655 (as applied through § 1.1446-3) for the first installment period. However, because the IRS provided written notification to PRS on June 1, year 5, to disregard any certificate received from NRA for year 5, PRS may not rely on any certificate received from NRA certificate (or any new certificate provided by NRA) when it computes its second installment payment in year 5. PRS is not permitted to consider any certificate submitted by NRA until the IRS provides written notification to PRS revoking or modifying the original notice. PRS's second installment payment in year 5 must include the additional amount of 1446 tax it would have paid for the first installment period without regard to the certificate received from NRA.

*Example 6. IRS determines in subsequent taxable year that partner's certificate is defective because partner's actual losses are less than amount certified and considered by the partnership.* Assume the same facts as in *Example 5*, except that the IRS determines that NRA's certificate submitted in year 4 is defective because the actual effectively connected net operating loss available to NRA for year 4 was $1,000 rather than the $5,000 certified.

(i) Under paragraph (d)(2)(ii) of this section, PRS is not relieved from its liability for 1446 tax under section 1461 when it relies on a certificate of losses from a foreign partner that is later determined to be defective. However, when the IRS determines that a partner's certificate is defective because of the amount of the certified deductions and losses, the partnership is liable for the 1446 tax, interest, additions to tax, and penalties to the extent the amount of certified deductions and losses taken into account when computing 1446 tax (or, unless there was reasonable reliance on the certificate, any installment of such tax) is greater than the actual amount of available deductions and losses. Here, PRS considered the certified deductions and losses in the amount of $4,500. The IRS subsequently determined that NRA only had $1,000 of actual losses, only $900 of which were permitted to be considered under paragraph (c)(1)(i)(C) of this section. Accordingly, PRS is liable for the 1446 tax due with respect to the portion of the overstated losses that it considered when computing its 1446 tax. The remaining 1446 tax due for year 4 is $1,260 ($3,600 ($4,500 less $900) of excess losses considered x .35). However, PRS may be deemed to have paid the $1,260 of 1446 tax under § 1.1446-3(e) if NRA has paid all of NRA's U.S. income tax.

(ii) If PRS had considered only $900 (or a lesser amount) of NRA's certified net operating loss when computing and paying its 1446 tax during year 4 then, under paragraph (d)(2)(iii) of this section, PRS would not be liable for 1446 tax because it did not consider a net operating loss greater than the amount actually available to NRA.

*Example 7. Partner with different taxable year than partnership.* PRS partnership has two equal partners, FC, a foreign corporation, and DC, a domestic corporation. PRS conducts a trade or business in the United States and generates effectively connected income. FC maintains a June 30 fiscal taxable year end, while DC and PRS maintain a calendar taxable year end. FC and DC provide a valid Form W-8BEN and Form W-9, respectively, to PRS. FC and DC are the only persons that have ever been partners in PRS. For its year 1 through year 3 taxable years, PRS issued Forms 1065 (Schedule K-1) reporting in the aggregate $100 of net loss to each partner. For its year 4 taxable year, PRS issued Forms 1065 (Schedule K-1) to its partners reporting $150 of loss to each partner. All of the losses reported on the Forms 1065 (Schedule K-1) are effectively connected to PRS's and FC's trade or business in the United States.

(i) Assume that FC submits a valid certificate under this section certifying losses to the partnership for the partnership's year 5 taxable year. Further, assume that FC's only source of effectively connected income, gain, deduction, or loss is the activity of PRS.

(ii) For PRS's first installment period in year 5, FC may only certify deductions and losses under this section in the amount of $100 (the losses as reported on the Forms 1065 (Schedule K-1) issued for PRS's year 1 through year 3 taxable years). Under section 706, the taxable income of a partner shall include the income, gain, loss, deduction, or credit of the partnership for the partnership taxable year ending within or with the taxable year of the partner. PRS's year 4 calendar taxable year ends during FC's fiscal taxable year ending June 30, year 5. Therefore, under paragraph (c)(1) of this section, as of April 15, year 5 (the last date FC may submit its first certificate under paragraph (c) of this section to have it considered for PRS's first installment due date of April 15, year 5), FC's allocable share of the PRS losses for years 1 through 3 are the only losses that FC can represent have been or will be reported on an FC U.S. income tax return filed for a taxable year ending prior to such installment due date.

(iii) The result in paragraph (ii) of this *Example 7* is the same for the year 5 second installment period, the due date of which is June 15, year 5.

(iv) FC may submit an updated certificate under this section after June 30, year 5, which includes the $150 loss for year 4. PRS may consider such an updated certificate for its third installment period (due date September 15, year 5), provided the updated certificate is received by the due date for such installment in accordance with paragraph (c) of this section.

*Example 8. Failure to provide status update with respect to prior year unfiled returns.* FC, a foreign corporation, and DC, a domestic corporation, form a partnership (PRS) to conduct a trade or business in the United States. FC and DC provide PRS appropriate documentation under § 1.1446-1 to establish their status for purposes of section 1446. FC and DC are equal partners in PRS, and all partnership items are allocated equally between FC and DC.

(i) In the current taxable year FC submits a certificate under this section using Form 8804-C prior to PRS's first installment due date. FC represents that it has filed or will file a qualifying U.S. income tax return (within the meaning of paragraph (b)(2)(iii) of this section) in each of the preceding three taxable years. FC specifies that it has not filed its U.S. income tax return for the immediately preceding taxable year. FC also represents that it will timely file its U.S. income tax return for the partnership taxable year during which the certificate is considered (and will timely pay all tax due with such return). Assume all other requirements under paragraph (c) of this section are met for FC's certificate to be valid.

(ii) Provided that PRS does not possess actual knowledge or reason to know that FC's certificate is defective under paragraph (a)(2) of this section, PRS may reasonably rely on FC's certificate for its first, second, and third installment payments.

(iii) If FC does not submit to PRS either an updated certificate or a status update as required by paragraph (c)(2)(ii)(B)(1) of this section by December 15th (PRS's final installment due date), PRS must disregard FC's certificate when computing its fourth installment payment of 1446 tax and when completing its Form 8804 for the taxable year. PRS's payment of 1446 tax for its fourth installment period must include the additional amount of 1446 tax it would have paid in the first, second and third installment periods had it not considered FC's certificate. Further, even if the status update is provided by December 15th, PRS may only rely on the certificate if the status update does not contradict the original certificate and such update indicates that the immediately preceding year's return will be timely filed. Finally, even if the status update is provided by December 15th, FC must also submit an updated certificate to the partnership in accordance with paragraph (c) of this section within 10 days of the date FC timely files its U.S. income tax return for the preceding taxable year.

*Example 9. Partnership consideration of certified deductions and losses or de minimis certificate.* For purposes of this example assume paragraph (c)(1)(ii) of this section may apply. On January 1, year 4, NRA and B form a partnership (PRS) to conduct a trade or business in the United States. NRA and B are equal partners in PRS and all partnership items are shared equally. NRA and B provide PRS appropriate documentation under § 1.1446-1 to establish their status for purposes of section 1446. During years 1 through 3, NRA's only activity generating effectively connected items was an interest in partnership XYZ. XYZ allocated NRA a loss for all three years. NRA filed qualifying U.S. income tax returns (within the meaning of paragraph (b)(2)(iii) of this section) reporting its allocable share of losses from XYZ in years 1 through 3. The XYZ partnership dissolved on December 31, year 3.

(i) In year 4, NRA's only activity giving rise to effectively connected income, gain, deduction, or loss is its interest in PRS. NRA submits to PRS a valid certificate (using Form 8804-C) certifying under paragraph (c)(1)(i) its effectively connected net operating losses from years 1 through 3 and under (c)(1)(ii) of this section that its only activity giving rise to effectively connected income, gain, deduction, or loss for the PRS taxable year that ends with or within its taxable year is (and will be) its investment in PRS.

(ii) During year 4, PRS allocates ECTI to NRA. If the 1446 tax otherwise due on the annualized amount allocated to NRA is less than $1,000, determined without regard to any deductions and losses certified by NRA under paragraph (c)(1)(i) of this section, PRS may consider the certificate received from NRA under paragraph (c)(1)(ii) of this section and not pay 1446 tax (or any installment of such tax) with respect to NRA. Alternatively, PRS may consider the deductions and losses certified by NRA under paragraph (c)(1)(i) of this section.

(iii) Regardless of whether PRS considers NRA's certification under paragraph (c)(1)(i) or (c)(1)(ii) of this section in computing its 1446 tax due with respect to NRA, PRS must file Form 8813 for all installment periods as well as a Form 8805 for NRA with its Form 8804. If PRS considers NRA's certification under paragraph (c)(1)(i) or (c)(1)(ii) of this section, PRS must attach to each Form 8813, as well as to the Form 8805, a computation of the 1446 tax with respect to NRA that takes into account its consideration of NRA's certificate. In addition, PRS must attach NRA's certificate to the Form 8813 for the first installment period it considers the certificate, as well as to the Form 8805. For all subsequent installment periods, PRS may attach a statement containing NRA's name, and TIN. If PRS is relying on NRA's certified losses under paragraph (c)(1)(i) of this section, the statement must indicate the amount of losses and deductions NRA certified. If PRS is relying on NRA's certification under paragraph (c)(ii) of this section, the statement must indicate that it is relying on NRA meeting the requirements under paragraph (c)(1)(ii) of this section and the 1446 tax on the annualized amount allocated to NRA is less than $1,000. See paragraph (d)(3)(i) of this section.

*Example 10. Application of transition rule.* NRA and B form a partnership (PRS) on January 1, 2004, to conduct a trade or business in the United States. NRA and B are equal partners in PRS and all partnership items are shared equally. NRA and B provide PRS appropriate documentation under §1.1446-1 to establish their status for purposes of section 1446. For its 2004 through 2007 tax years, PRS issued Forms 1065 (Schedule K-1) to NRA and B reporting a $1,000 net loss from its U.S. trade or business to each partner for each year (for an aggregate loss of $4,000 per partner). During the 2004 through 2007 tax years, NRA's only activity generating effectively connected items was its investment in PRS.

(i) On February 10, 2008, NRA submitted a certificate to PRS, reporting its aggregate $4,000 effectively connected loss to PRS, that met the requirements of §1.1446-6T(c) (See 26 CFR Part 1, revised as of April 1, 2007), as in effect before January 1, 2008. The certificate stated that NRA had timely filed its U.S. income tax returns for the 2004, 2005 and 2006 tax years, and that it would timely file a U.S. income tax return for its 2007 tax year. For the first and second installments period in 2008, PRS estimates that it will earn ECTI of $10,000.

(ii) Because the certificate submitted by NRA to PRS on February 10, 2008, met the requirements of §1.1446-6T (See 26 CFR Part 1, revised as of April 1, 2007), as in effect before January 1, 2008, PRS may consider such certificate when computing its 1446 tax due for the first and second installment period even if the certificate does not meet all the requirements of paragraph (c) of this section.

(iii) NRA timely files its U.S. income tax return for the 2007 tax year on July 24, 2008. In accordance with paragraph (c)(2)(ii)(B)(1) of this section, within 10 days of filing such return NRA prepares an updated certificate to be submitted to PRS certifying that it reasonably expects to have only $3,500 of losses available to reduce its allocable share of ECTI from PRS. Because the updated certificate will be submitted after July 28, 2008, to be valid the updated certificate must meet the requirements of paragraph (c) this section.

(f) *Effective/Applicability date.*—Except as otherwise provided in this paragraph (f), the rules of this section are applicable to partnership taxable years beginning after December 31, 2007. The rules of paragraphs (b)(3)(i)(B) through (D) shall apply to partnership taxable years beginning after July 28, 2008.

(g) *Transition rule.*—A certificate that met the requirements of §1.1446-6T(c) (See 26 CFR Part 1, revised as of April 1, 2007), as in effect before January 1, 2008, submitted on or before July 28, 2008 by a partner that met the requirements of §1.1446-6T(b) (See 26 CFR Part 1, revised as of April 1, 2007), as in effect before January 1, 2008, shall not be considered defective because it does not meet the requirements of this section. However, any certificate (including any updated certificates and status updates) submitted, or required to be submitted, under paragraph (c) of this section after July 28, 2008, must meet the requirements of this section. See paragraph (e)(2) *Example 10* of this section. [Reg. §1.1446-6.]

☐ [*T.D. 9394*, 4-28-2008 (*corrected* 4-1-2009). *Amended by T.D. 9926*, 11-27-2020.]

### [Reg. §1.1446-7]

**§1.1446-7. Applicability dates.**—Sections 1.1446-1 through 1.1446-5 shall apply to partnership taxable years beginning after May 18, 2005. However, a partnership may elect to apply all of the provisions of §§1.1446-1 through 1.1446-5 to partnership taxable years beginning after December 31, 2004. A partnership shall make the election under this section by complying with the provisions of §§1.1446-1 through §1.1446-5 and attaching a statement to the Form 8804 or Form 1042 annual return, filed for the taxable year in which the regulation provisions first apply, that indicates that the partnership is making the election under this section. The revisions to §§1.1446-3(b)(2), 1.1446-3(b)(3)(i)(A) and 1.1446-5(c)(2) contained in the final regulations published in 2008 apply to partnership taxable years beginning after December 31, 2007. See §1.1446-6(f) and (g) for the Effective/Applicability date and Transition rule to §1.1446-6. Section 1.1446-3 generally applies to returns filed on or after January 30, 2020 and §1.1446-3T (as contained in 26 CFR part 1, revised as of April 1, 2019) generally applies to returns filed before January 30, 2020. The addition of §1.1446-3(c)(4) applies to transfers of partnership interests that occur on or after January 29, 2021, except that a taxpayer may choose to apply §1.1446-3(c)(4) to transfers of partnership interests that occur on or after January 1, 2018. Sections 1.1446-3(a)(2)(i), (d)(2)(vi), and (e)(4) and 1.1446-4(f)(1) apply to partnership taxable years beginning on or after November 30, 2020. For partnership taxable years beginning before November 30, 2020, see those sections as in effect and contained in 26 CFR part 1, revised as of April 1, 2020. Section 1.1446-4(b)(3) and (4), (c), (d), (e), and (f)(3) apply to distributions made on or after January 1, 2022. For distributions made before January 1, 2022, see §§1.1446-4(b)(3) and (4), (c), (d), (e) and (f)(3), as contained in 26 CFR part 1, revised as of April 1, 2020. [Reg. §1.1446-7.]

☐ [*T.D. 9200*, 5-13-2005. *Amended by T.D. 9394*, 4-28-2008 *and T.D. 9926*, 11-27-2020.]

### [Reg. §1.1446(f)-1]

**§1.1446(f)-1. General rules.**—(a) *Overview.*—This section and §§ 1.1446(f)-2 through 1.1446(f)-5 provide rules for withholding, reporting, and paying tax under section 1446(f) upon the sale, exchange, or other disposition of certain interests in partnerships. This section provides definitions and general rules that apply for purposes of section 1446(f). Section 1.1446(f)-2 provides withholding rules for the transfer of a non-publicly traded partnership interest under section 1446(f)(1). Section 1.1446(f)-3 provides rules that apply when a partnership is required to withhold under section 1446(f)(4) on distributions made to the transferee in an amount equal to the amount that the transferee failed to withhold plus interest. Section 1.1446(f)-4 provides special rules for the sale, exchange, or disposition of publicly traded partnership interests, for which the withholding obligation under section 1446(f)(1) is generally imposed on certain brokers that act on behalf of the transferor. Section 1.1446(f)-5 provides rules that address the liability for failure to withhold under section 1446(f) and rules regarding the liability of a transferor's or transferee's agent.

(b) *Definitions.*—This paragraph (b) provides definitions that apply for purposes of this section and §§1.1446(f)-2 through 1.1446(f)-5.

(1) The term *broker* means any person, foreign or domestic, that, in the ordinary course of a trade or business during the calendar year, stands ready to effect sales made by others, and that, in connection with a transfer of a PTP interest, receives all or a portion of the amount realized on behalf of the transferor. The term broker includes a clearing organization (as defined in §1.1471-1(b)(21)). In the case of a U.S. clearing organization clearing or settling sales of PTP interests, however, see §1.1446(f)-4(a)(3) for an exception from the requirement to withhold on a sale of a PTP interest. The term broker does not include an escrow agent that does not effect sales other than transactions that are incidental to the purpose of escrow (such as sales to collect on collateral).

(2) The term *controlling partner* means a partner that, together with any person that bears a relationship described in section 267(b) or 707(b)(1) to the partner, owns directly or indirectly a 50 percent or greater interest in the capital, profits, deductions, or losses of the partnership at any time within the 12 months before the determination date (see paragraph (c)(4) of this section).

(3) The term *effect* has the meaning provided in §1.6045-1(a)(10).

(4) The term *foreign person* means a person that is not a United States person, including a QI branch of a U.S. financial institution (as defined in §1.1471-1(b)(109)).

(5) The term *PTP interest* means an interest in a publicly traded partnership if the interest is publicly traded on an established securities market or is readily tradable on a secondary market (or the substantial equivalent thereof).

(6) The term *publicly traded partnership* has the same meaning as in section 7704 and §§1.7704-1 through 1.7704-4 but does not include a publicly traded partnership treated as a corporation under that section.

(7) The term *TIN* means the tax identifying number assigned to a person under section 6109.

(8) The term *transfer* means a sale, exchange, or other disposition, and includes a distribution from a partnership to a partner, as well as a transfer treated as a sale or exchange under section 707(a)(2)(B).

(9) The term *transferee* means any person, foreign or domestic, that acquires a partnership interest through a transfer, and includes a partnership that makes a distribution.

(10) Except as otherwise provided in this paragraph, the term *transferor* means any person, foreign or domestic, that transfers a partnership interest. In the case of a trust, to the extent all or a portion of the income of the trust is treated as owned by the grantor or another person under sections 671 through 679 (such trust, a grantor trust), the term transferor means the grantor or such other person.

(11) The term *transferor's agent* or *transferee's agent* means any person who represents the transferor or transferee (respectively) in any negotiation with another person relating to the transaction or in settling the transaction. A person will not be treated as a transferor's agent or a transferee's agent solely because it performs one or more of the activities described in §1.1445-4(f)(3) (relating to activities of settlement officers and clerical personnel).

(12) The term *United States person* or *U.S. person* means a person described in section 7701(a)(30).

(c) *General rules of applicability.*—(1) *In general.*—This paragraph (c) provides general rules that apply for purposes of this section and §§1.1446(f)-2 through 1.1446(f)-5.

(2) *Certifications.*—(i) *In general.*—This paragraph (c)(2) provides rules that are applicable to certifications described in this section and §§1.1446(f)-2 through 1.1446(f)-5, except as otherwise provided

therein, or as may be prescribed by the Commissioner in forms or instructions or in publications or guidance published in the Internal Revenue Bulletin (see §§ 601.601(d)(2) and 601.602 of this chapter). A certification must provide the name and address of the person providing it. A certification must also be signed under penalties of perjury and, if the certification is provided by the transferor, must include a TIN if the transferor has, or is required to have, a TIN. A transferee (or other person required to withhold) may not rely on a certification if it knows that a transferor has, or is required to have, a TIN, and that TIN has not been provided with the certification. A certification includes any documents associated with the certification, such as statements from the partnership, IRS forms, withholding certificates, withholding statements, certifications, or other documentation. Documents associated with the certification form an integral part of the certification, and the penalties of perjury statement provided on the certification also applies to the associated documents. A certification (other than the certification described in § 1.1446(f)-2(d)(2)) may not be relied upon if it is obtained earlier than 30 days before the transfer or any time after the transfer.

(ii) *Penalties of perjury.*—A certification signed under penalties of perjury must provide the following: "Under penalties of perjury, I declare that I have examined the information on this document, and to the best of my knowledge and belief, it is true, correct, and complete."

(iii) *Authority to sign certifications on behalf of a business entity.*— A certification provided by a business entity must be signed by an individual who is an officer, director, general partner, or managing member of the entity, or other individual that has authority to sign for the entity under local law.

(iv) *Electronic submission.*—A certification may be sent electronically, including as text in an email, an image embedded in an email, or a Portable Document Format (.pdf) attached to an email. An electronic certification, however, may not be relied upon if the person receiving the submission knows that the certification was transmitted by a person not authorized to do so by the person required to execute the certification.

(v) *Retention period.*—Any person that relies on a certification pursuant to this section and §§ 1.1446(f)-2 through 1.1446(f)-5 must retain the certification (including any documentation) for as long as it may be relevant to the determination of its withholding obligation under section 1446(f) or its withholding tax liability under section 1461.

(vi) *Submission to IRS.*—The recipient of a certification is not required to mail a copy to the IRS, except as provided in § 1.1446(f)-2(b)(7) and (c)(4)(vi) (involving certifications relating to an income tax treaty), or as may be prescribed by the Commissioner in forms or instructions or in publications or guidance published in the Internal Revenue Bulletin (see §§ 601.601(d)(2) and 601.602 of this chapter).

(vii) *Grantor trusts.*—A certification provided by a transferor that is a grantor or other owner of a grantor trust must identify the portion of the amount realized that is attributable to the grantor or other owner. A certification provided by a foreign grantor trust on behalf of a transferor that is a grantor or owner must also include a Form W-8IMY, *Certificate of Foreign Intermediary, Foreign Flow-Through Entity, or Certain U.S. Branches for United States Tax Withholding and Reporting)*, (or similar statement for a domestic grantor trust with a foreign grantor or owner), that includes a withholding statement that provides the percentage of the amount realized allocable to each grantor or owner of the trust, and any applicable certification for each grantor or owner. In the case of a certification so provided, a grantor or owner of the trust is treated as having provided the certification to the transferee (or broker).

(3) *Books and records.*—A partnership that relies on its books and records pursuant to this section and §§ 1.1446(f)-2 through 1.1446(f)-5 (including for purposes of providing a certification or other statement) must identify in its books and records the date on which the transfer occurred, the information on which the partnership relied, and the provisions of this section and §§ 1.1446(f)-2 through 1.1446(f)-5 supporting an exception from, or adjustment to, the partnership's obligation to withhold. The identification required by this paragraph (c)(3) must be made no later than 30 days after the date of the transfer. The partnership must retain the identified information in its books and records for the longer of five calendar years following the close of the last calendar year in which it relied on the information or for as long as it may be relevant to the determination of its withholding obligation under section 1446(f) or its withholding tax liability under section 1461.

(4) *Determination date.*—(i) *In general.*—This paragraph (c)(4) provides rules for the determination date. The same determination date must be used for all purposes with respect to a transfer. Any statement, certification, or books and records with regard to a transfer must state the determination date. The determination date of a transfer must be one of the following—

(A) The date of the transfer;

(B) Any date that is no more than 60 days before the date of the transfer; or

(C) The date that is the later of—

(1) The first day of the partnership's taxable year in which the transfer occurs, as determined under section 706; or

(2) The date, before the date of the transfer, of the most recent event described in § 1.704-1(b)(2)(iv)(*f*)(5) or § 1.704-1(b)(2)(iv)(*s*)(1) (revaluation event), irrespective of whether the capital accounts of the partners are adjusted in accordance with § 1.704-1(b)(2)(iv)(f).

(ii) *Controlling partner.*—The determination date for a transferor that is a controlling partner is determined without regard to paragraph (c)(4)(i)(C) of this section.

(5) *IRS forms and instructions.*—Any reference to an IRS form includes its successor form. Any form must be filed in the manner prescribed by the Commissioner in forms or instructions or in publications or guidance published in the Internal Revenue Bulletin (see §§ 601.601(d)(2) and 601.602 of this chapter).

(d) *Coordination with section 1445.*—A transferee that is otherwise required to withhold under section 1445(e)(5) or § 1.1445-11T(d)(1) with respect to the amount realized, as well as under section 1446(f)(1), will be subject to the payment and reporting requirements of section 1445 only, and not section 1446(f)(1), with respect to that amount. However, if the transferor has applied for a withholding certificate under the last sentence of § 1.1445-11T(d)(1), the transferee must withhold the greater of the amounts required under section 1445(e)(5) or 1446(f)(1). A transferee that has complied with the withholding requirements under either section 1445(e)(5) or 1446(f)(1), as applicable under this paragraph (d), will be deemed to satisfy the withholding requirement.

(e) *Applicability date.*—This section applies to transfers that occur on or after January 29, 2021. [Reg. § 1.1446(f)-1.]

☐ [*T.D. 9926, 11-27-2020.*]

### [Reg. § 1.1446(f)-2]

**§ 1.1446(f)-2. Withholding on the transfer of a non-publicly traded partnership interest.**—(a) *Transferee's obligation to withhold.*— Except as otherwise provided in this section, a transferee is required to withhold under section 1446(f)(1) a tax equal to 10 percent of the amount realized on any transfer of a partnership interest. This section does not apply to a transfer of a PTP interest that is effected through one or more brokers, including a distribution made with respect to a PTP interest held in an account with a broker. For rules regarding those transfers, see § 1.1446(f)-4.

(b) *Exceptions to withholding.*—(1) *In general.*—A transferee is not required to withhold under this section if it properly relies on a certification or its books and records as described in this paragraph (b). A transferee may not rely on a certification if it has actual knowledge that the certification is incorrect or unreliable. A partnership that is a transferee because it makes a distribution may not rely on its books and records if it knows, or has reason to know, that the information is incorrect or unreliable.

(2) *Certification of non-foreign status by transferor.*—A transferee may rely on a certification of non-foreign status from the transferor that states that the transferor is not a foreign person, states the transferor's name, TIN, and address, and is signed under penalties of perjury. For purposes of this paragraph (b)(2), a certification of non-foreign status includes a valid Form W-9, *Request for Taxpayer Identification Number and Certification*. For purposes of this paragraph (b)(2), a transferee may rely on a valid Form W-9 from the transferor that it already possesses if the form meets these requirements of this paragraph (b)(2).

(3) *No realized gain by transferor.*—(i) *In general.*—A transferee (other than a partnership that is a transferee because it makes a distribution) may rely on a certification from the transferor that states that the transfer of the partnership interest would not result in any realized gain (including ordinary income arising from the application of section 751 and § 1.751-1) to the transferor as of the determination date (see § 1.1446(f)-1(c)(4)). See paragraph (b)(6) of this section for rules that apply when the transferor realizes gain but is not required to recognize the gain under a provision of the Internal Revenue Code.

(ii) *No section 751 income.*—For purposes of paragraph (b)(3)(i) of this section, a transferor may rely on a certification from the partnership stating that the transfer of the partnership interest would not result in any ordinary income arising from the application of section 751 and §1.751-1 to the transferor as of the determination date. The certification from the partnership must be attached to, and forms part of, the certification of no realized gain that the transferor provides to the transferee.

(iii) *Partnership distributions.*—A partnership that is a transferee because it makes a distribution may rely on its books and records, or on a certification from the transferor, to determine that the distribution would not result in any realized gain to the transferor as of the determination date.

(4) *Less than 10 percent effectively connected gain.*—(i) *In general.*—A transferee (other than a partnership that is a transferee because it makes a distribution) may rely on a certification from the partnership that states that—

(A) If the partnership sold all of its assets at fair market value as of the determination date in the manner described in §1.864(c)(8)-1(c), either—

(1) The partnership would have no gain that would have been effectively connected with the conduct of a trade or business within the United States, or, if the partnership would have a net amount of such gain, the amount of the partnership's net gain that would have been effectively connected with the conduct of a trade or business within the United States would be less than 10 percent of the total net gain; or

(2) The transferor would not have a distributive share of net gain from the partnership that would have been effectively connected with the conduct of a trade or business in the United States, or, if the transferor would have a distributive share of such gain from the partnership, the transferor's distributive share of net gain from the partnership that would have been effectively connected with the conduct of a trade or business within the United States would be less than 10 percent of the transferor's distributive share of the total net gain from the partnership; or

(B) The partnership was not engaged in a trade or business within the United States at any time during the taxable year of the partnership through the date of transfer.

(ii) *Partnership distributions.*—A partnership that is a transferee because it makes a distribution may rely on its books and records to determine that paragraph (b)(4)(i)(A) of this section is satisfied as of the determination date or paragraph (b)(4)(i)(B) of this section is satisfied for the taxable year of the partnership through the date of transfer.

(5) *Less than 10 percent effectively connected income.*—(i) *In general.*—A transferee (other than a partnership that is a transferee because it makes a distribution) may rely on a certification from the transferor that states that—

(A) The transferor was a partner in the partnership throughout the look-back period described in paragraph (b)(5)(ii) of this section;

(B) The transferor's distributive share of gross effectively connected income from the partnership, as reported on a Schedule K-1 (Form 1065), *Partner's Share of Income, Deductions, Credits, etc.*, or other statement required to be furnished under §1.6031(b)-1T, including any gross effectively connected income included in the distributive share of a partner that bears a relationship to the transferor described in section 267(b) or 707(b)(1), was less than $1 million for each of the taxable years within the look-back period described in paragraph (b)(5)(ii) of this section;

(C) The transferor's distributive share of gross effectively connected income from the partnership, as reported on a Schedule K-1 (Form 1065), or other statement required to be furnished under §1.6031(b)-1T, for each of the taxable years within the look-back period described in paragraph (b)(5)(ii) of this section, was less than 10 percent of the transferor's total distributive share of gross income from the partnership for that year as determined under subchapter K of the Internal Revenue Code (as provided on a Schedule K-1 (Form 1065) or other statement required to be furnished under §1.6031(b)-1T); and

(D) The transferor's distributive share of income or gain from the partnership that is effectively connected with the conduct of a trade or business within the United States or deductions or losses properly allocated and apportioned to that income in each of the taxable years within the look-back period described in paragraph (b)(5)(ii) of this section has been reported on a Federal income tax return (either filed by the transferor or, in the case of transferor that is a partnership, filed by its direct or indirect nonresident alien individual or foreign corporate partners) on or before the due date (including extensions), and all amounts due with respect to the reported amounts have been timely paid to the IRS, provided that the return was required to be filed when the transferor furnishes the certification (taking into account any extensions of time to file).

(ii) *Look-back period.*—(A) *In general.*—The transferor's look-back period is the transferor's immediately prior taxable year and the two preceding taxable years.

(B) *Immediately prior taxable year.*—The transferor's immediately prior taxable year is the transferor's most recent taxable year–

(1) With or within which a taxable year of the partnership ended; and

(2) For which a Schedule K-1 (Form 1065) was due (including extensions) or furnished (if earlier) before the transfer.

(C) *Limitation.*—A transferee may not rely on a certification that is provided before the transferor's receipt of the Schedule K-1 (Form 1065) described in paragraph (b)(5)(ii)(B) of this section.

(iii) *No distributive share of gross income.*—A transferor that did not have a distributive share of gross income in any year described in paragraph (b)(5)(ii)(A) of this section cannot provide the certification described in this paragraph (b)(5).

(iv) *Partnership distributions.*—A partnership that is a transferee by reason of making a distribution may rely on its books and records to determine that the requirements in paragraphs (b)(5)(i)(A) through (C) of this section have been satisfied (subject to the rules in paragraphs (b)(5)(ii) and (iii) of this section). The partnership must also obtain a representation from the transferor stating that the requirement in paragraph (b)(5)(i)(D) of this section has been satisfied.

(6) *Certification of nonrecognition by transferor.*—(i) *In general.*—A transferee may rely on a certification from the transferor that states that by reason of the operation of a nonrecognition provision of the Internal Revenue Code the transferor is not required to recognize any gain or loss with respect to the transfer. The certification must briefly describe the transfer and provide the relevant law and facts relating to the certification.

(ii) *Partial nonrecognition.*—Paragraph (b)(6)(i) of this section does not apply if only a portion of the gain realized on the transfer is subject to a nonrecognition provision. However, see paragraph (c)(4)(v) of this section for rules applicable to a transferor's claim for partial nonrecognition.

(7) *Income tax treaties.*—(i) *In general.*—A transferee may rely on a certification from the transferor that states that the transferor is not subject to tax on any gain from the transfer pursuant to an income tax treaty in effect between the United States and a foreign country if the requirements of this paragraph (b)(7) are met. The transferor makes the certification on a withholding certificate (on a Form W-8BEN, *Certificate of Foreign Status of Beneficial Owner for United States Tax Withholding and Reporting (Individuals)*, or Form W-8BEN-E, *Certificate of Status of Beneficial Owner for United States Tax Withholding and Reporting (Entities)*) that meets the requirements for validity under §1.1446-1(c)(2)(iv) (or an applicable substitute form that meets the requirements under §1.1446-1(c)(5)) and that contains the information necessary to support the claim for treaty benefits. A transferee may rely on a certification of treaty benefits only if, within 30 days after the date of the transfer, the transferee mails a copy of the certification to the Internal Revenue Service, at the address provided in §1.1445-1(g)(10), together with a cover letter providing the name, TIN, and address of the transferee and the partnership in which an interest was transferred.

(ii) *Treaty claim for less than all of the gain.*—Paragraph (b)(7)(i) of this section does not apply if treaty benefits apply to only a portion of the gain from the transfer. However, see paragraph (c)(4)(vi) of this section for rules applicable to situations in which treaty benefits apply to only a portion of the gain.

(iii) *Exclusive means to claim an exception from withholding based on treaty benefits.*—A transferor claiming treaty benefits with respect to all of the gain from the transfer must use the exception in this paragraph (b)(7) and not any other exception or determination procedure in paragraphs (b) and (c) of this section to claim an exception to withholding by reason of a claim of treaty benefits.

(c) *Determining the amount to withhold.*—(1) *In general.*—A transferee that is required to withhold under this section must withhold 10 percent of the amount realized on the transfer of the partnership interest, except as otherwise provided in this paragraph (c). Any procedures in this paragraph (c) apply solely for purposes of determining the amount to withhold under section 1446(f)(1) and this section. A transferee may not rely on a certification if it has actual knowledge that the certification is incorrect or unreliable. A partnership that is a transferee because it makes a distribution may not rely on its books and records if it knows, or has reason to know, that the information is incorrect or unreliable.

(2) *Amount realized.*—(i) *In general.*—The amount realized on the transfer of the partnership interest is determined under section 1001 (including §§ 1.1001-1 through 1.1001-5) and section 752 (including §§ 1.752-1 through 1.752-7). Thus, the amount realized includes the amount of cash paid (or to be paid), the fair market value of other property transferred (or to be transferred), the amount of any liabilities assumed by the transferee or to which the partnership interest is subject, and the reduction in the transferor's share of partnership liabilities. In the case of a distribution, the amount realized is the sum of the amount of cash distributed (or to be distributed), the fair market value of property distributed (or to be distributed), and the reduction in the transferor's share of partnership liabilities.

(ii) *Alternative procedures for transferee to determine share of partnership liabilities.*—(A) *In general.*—A transferee (other than a partnership that is a transferee because it makes a distribution), as an alternative to determining the share of partnership liabilities under paragraph (c)(2)(i) of this section, may use the procedures of this paragraph (c)(2)(ii) to determine the extent to which a reduction in partnership liabilities is included in the amount realized.

(B) *Certification of liabilities by transferor.*—Except as otherwise provided in this section, a transferee may rely on a certification from a transferor, other than a controlling partner, that provides the amount of the transferor's share of partnership liabilities reported on the most recent Schedule K-1 (Form 1065) issued by the partnership. If the transferor's actual share of liabilities at the time of the transfer differs from the amount reported on that Schedule K-1 (Form 1065), the certification will not be treated as incorrect or unreliable if the transferor also certifies that it does not have actual knowledge of any events occurring after receiving the Schedule K-1 (Form 1065) and before the date of the transfer that would cause the amount of the transferor's share of partnership liabilities at the time of the transfer to differ by more than 25 percent from the amount shown on the Schedule K-1 (Form 1065). A transferee may not rely on a certification if the last day of the partnership taxable year for which the Schedule K-1 (Form 1065) was provided was more than 22 months before the date of the transfer.

(C) *Certification of liabilities by partnership.*—A transferee may rely on a certification from a partnership that provides the amount of the transferor's share of partnership liabilities on the determination date. If the transferor's actual share of liabilities at the time of the transfer differs from the amount on the certification, the certification will not be treated as incorrect or unreliable if the partnership also certifies that it does not have actual knowledge of any events occurring after the determination date and before the date on which the partnership provides the certification to the transferee that would cause the amount of the transferor's share of partnership liabilities at the time of the transfer to differ by more than 25 percent from the amount shown on the certification by the partnership for the determination date.

(iii) *Partnership's determination of partnership liabilities for distributions.*—A partnership that is a transferee because it makes a distribution may rely on its books and records to determine the extent to which the transferor's share of partnership liabilities on the determination date are included in the amount realized. The information in the books and records will not be treated as incorrect or unreliable unless the partnership has actual knowledge, on or before the date of the distribution, of any events occurring after the determination date that would cause the amount of the transferor's share of partnership liabilities at the time of the transfer to differ by more than 25 percent from the amount determined by the partnership as of the determination date.

(iv) *Certification by a foreign partnership of modified amount realized.*—(A) *In general.*—When a transferor is a foreign partnership, a transferee may use the procedures of this paragraph (c)(2)(iv) to determine the amount realized. For purposes of this paragraph (c)(2)(iv)(A), the transferee may treat the modified amount realized as the amount realized to the extent that it may rely on a certification from the transferor providing the modified amount realized.

(B) *Determining modified amount realized.*—The modified amount realized is determined by multiplying the amount realized (as determined under this paragraph (c)(2), without regard to this paragraph (c)(2)(iv)) by the aggregate percentage computed as of the determination date. The aggregate percentage is the percentage of the gain (if any) arising from the transfer that would be allocated to presumed foreign taxable persons. For purposes of this paragraph (c)(2)(iv)(B), a presumed foreign taxable person is any direct or indirect partner of the transferor that has not provided either a certification of non-foreign status that meets the requirements of paragraph (b)(2) of this section or a certification of treaty benefits that states that the partner is not subject to tax on any gain from the transfer pursuant to an income tax treaty in effect between the United

States and a foreign country. A valid certification of treaty benefits must meet the requirements of paragraph (b)(7) of this section (as applied to the partner claiming treaty benefits), including the requirement that the transferee mail a copy of the certification to the IRS within the time prescribed. For purposes of this paragraph (c)(2)(iv), an indirect partner is a person that owns an interest in the transferor indirectly through one or more foreign partnerships.

(C) *Certification.*—The certification is made by providing a withholding certificate (on Form W-8IMY, *Certificate of Foreign Intermediary, Foreign Flow-Through Entity, or Certain U.S. Branches for United States Tax Withholding and Reporting*) that includes a withholding statement that provides the percentage of gain allocable to each direct or indirect partner and that provides whether each such person is a United States person, a foreign partner eligible for treaty benefits, or a presumed foreign taxable person. The certification must also include the certification of non-foreign status or the certification of treaty benefits from each direct or indirect partner that is not a presumed foreign taxable person.

(3) *Lack of money or property or lack of knowledge regarding liabilities.*—The amount to withhold equals the amount realized determined without regard to any decrease in the transferor's share of partnership liabilities if—

(i) The amount otherwise required to be withheld under this paragraph (c) would exceed the amount realized determined without regard to the decrease in the transferor's share of partnership liabilities; or

(ii) The transferee is unable to determine the amount realized because it does not have actual knowledge of the transferor's share of partnership liabilities (and has not received or cannot rely on a certification described in paragraph (c)(2)(ii)(B) or (C) of this section).

(4) *Certification of maximum tax liability.*—(i) *In general.*—A transferee may use the procedures of this paragraph (c)(4) for determining the amount to withhold for purposes of section 1446(f)(1) and paragraph (a) of this section. A transferee (other than a partnership that is a transferee because it makes a distribution) may rely on a certification from a transferor that is a foreign corporation, a nonresident alien individual, a foreign partnership, or a foreign trust regarding the transferor's maximum tax liability as described in paragraph (c)(4)(ii) of this section. A partnership that is a transferee because it makes a distribution may instead rely on its books and records to determine the transferor's maximum tax liability if the books and records includes the information required by paragraphs (c)(4)(iii) and (iv) of this section. A transferor that is a foreign partnership or a foreign trust is treated as a nonresident alien individual for purposes of determining the transferor's maximum tax liability.

(ii) *Maximum tax liability.*—For purposes of this paragraph (c)(4), the term *maximum tax liability* means the amount of the transferor's effectively connected gain (as determined under paragraph (c)(4)(iii)(E) of this section) multiplied by the applicable percentage, as defined in § 1.1446-3(a)(2).

(iii) *Required information.*—The certification must include—

(A) A statement that the transferor is either a nonresident alien individual, a foreign corporation, a foreign partnership, or a foreign trust;

(B) The transferor's adjusted basis in the transferred interest on the determination date;

(C) The transferor's amount realized (determined in accordance with paragraph (c)(2) of this section) on the determination date;

(D) Whether the transferor remains a partner immediately after the transfer;

(E) The amount of outside ordinary gain and outside capital gain that would be recognized and treated as effectively connected gain under § 1.864(c)(8)-1(b) on the determination date (effectively connected gain);

(F) The transferor's maximum tax liability on the determination date;

(G) A representation from the transferor that the transferor determined the amounts described in paragraph (c)(4)(iii)(E) of this section based on the statement described in paragraph (c)(4)(iv) of this section, if applicable; and

(H) A representation from the transferor that it has provided the transferee with a copy of the statement described in paragraph (c)(4)(iv) of this section.

(iv) *Partnership statement.*—A transferor may make the representation in paragraph (c)(4)(iii)(G) of this section only if the partnership provides to the transferor a statement (that meets the requirements for a certification under the general rules for applicability in § 1.1446(f)-1(c)) that includes—

(A) The partnership's name, address, and TIN; and

**Reg. §1.1446(f)-2(c)(4)(iv)(A)**

(B) The transferor's aggregate deemed sale EC ordinary gain, within the meaning of §1.864(c)(8)-1(c)(3)(ii)(A) (if any) and the transferor's aggregate deemed sale EC capital gain, within the meaning of §1.864(c)(8)-1(c)(3)(ii)(B) (if any), in each case, on the determination date.

(v) *Partial nonrecognition.*—If a nonrecognition provision applies to only a portion of the gain realized on the transfer, a certification described in paragraph (c)(4)(i) may be relied upon only if the certification also includes the information required in paragraph (b)(6) of this section (substituting "a portion of the gain or loss" for "any gain or loss" in paragraph (b)(6)(i) of this section).

(vi) *Income tax treaties.*—If only a portion of the gain on the transfer is not subject to tax pursuant to an income tax treaty in effect between the United States and a foreign country, a certification described in paragraph (c)(4)(i) of this section may be relied upon only if the requirements of paragraph (b)(7)(i) of this section have been met, including the requirement to obtain the applicable withholding certificate indicating that the gain from the transfer is not subject to tax pursuant to an income tax treaty (substituting "a portion of the gain" for "any gain" in paragraph (b)(7)(i) of this section), and the requirement to mail a copy of the withholding certificate to the IRS.

(d) *Reporting and paying withheld amounts.*—(1) *In general.*—A transferee required to withhold under this section must report and pay any tax withheld by the 20th day after the date of the transfer using Forms 8288, *U.S. Withholding Tax Return for Dispositions by Foreign Persons of U.S. Real Property Interests*, and 8288-A, *Statement of Withholding on Dispositions by Foreign Persons of U.S. Real Property Interests*, in accordance with the instructions to those forms. The IRS will stamp Form 8288-A to show receipt and mail a stamped copy to the transferor (at the address reported on the form). See paragraph (e)(2) of this section for the procedures for the transferor to claim a credit for amounts withheld. Forms 8288 and 8288-A must include the TINs of both the transferor and the transferee. If any required TIN is not provided, the transferee must still report and pay any tax withheld on Form 8288.

(2) *Certification of withholding to partnership for purposes of section 1446(f)(4).*—A transferee (other than a partnership that is a transferee because it makes a distribution) must certify to the partnership the extent to which it has satisfied its obligation to withhold under this section no later than 10 days after the transfer. The certification must either include a copy of Form 8288-A that the transferee files with respect to the transfer, or state the amount realized and the amount withheld on the transfer. The certification must also include any certifications that the transferee relied on to apply an exception to withholding under paragraph (b) of this section or to determine the amount to withhold under paragraph (c) of this section. A transferee that relied on a certification to apply an exception or adjustment to withholding remains liable under this section when the partnership knows, or has reason to know, that the certification is incorrect or unreliable. See §1.1446(f)-3 for rules regarding a partnership's obligation to withhold on distributions to a transferee when this certification establishes only partial satisfaction of the required amount, is not provided, or cannot be relied upon.

(e) *Effect of withholding on transferor.*—(1) *In general.*—The withholding of tax by a transferee under this section does not relieve a foreign person from filing a U.S. tax return with respect to the transfer. See §§1.6012-1(b)(1), 1.6012-2(g)(1), and 1.6031(a)-1. Further, the withholding of tax by a transferee does not relieve a nonresident alien individual or foreign corporation subject to tax on gain by reason of section 864(c)(8) from paying any tax due with the return that has not been fully satisfied through withholding.

(2) *Manner of obtaining credit.*—(i) *Individuals or corporations.*—Except as provided in paragraph (e)(3) of this section, an individual or corporation may claim a credit under section 33 for the amount withheld under this section by attaching to its applicable return the stamped copy of Form 8288-A provided to it under paragraph (d)(1) of this section.

(ii) *Partnerships, trusts, or estates.*—For a rule allowing a foreign partnership that is a transferor to claim a credit for the amount withheld under this section against its tax liability under section 1446(a), see §1.1446-3(c)(4). For the rule providing the extent to which a foreign trust or estate may claim a credit for an amount withheld under this section, see §1.1462-1. Except as provided in paragraph (e)(3) of this section, a foreign partnership, trust, or estate claiming a credit for an amount withheld must attach to its applicable return the stamped copy of Form 8288-A provided to it under paragraph (d)(1) of this section. A foreign trust or estate must also provide any other information required in forms or instructions to

any beneficiary or owner that is liable for tax on any of the gain under section 864(c)(8).

(3) *Failure to receive Form 8288-A.*—If a stamped copy of Form 8288-A has not been provided to the transferor by the IRS, the transferor may establish the amount of tax withheld by the transferee by attaching to its return substantial evidence of the amount. The transferor must attach to its return a statement that includes all of the information otherwise required to be provided on Form 8288-A.

(f) *Applicability date.*—This section applies to transfers that occur on or after January 29, 2021. [Reg. §1.1446(f)-2.]

☐ [*T.D.* 9926, 11-27-2020.]

**[Reg. §1.1446(f)-3]**

**§1.1446(f)-3. Partnership's requirement to withhold under section 1446(f)(4) on distributions to transferee.**—(a) *Partnership's obligation to withhold amounts not withheld by the transferee.*—(1) *In general.*—If a transferee fails to withhold any amount required to be withheld under §1.1446(f)-2, the partnership in which the interest was transferred must withhold from any distributions with respect to the transferred interest pursuant to this section. To determine its withholding obligation under this paragraph (a)(1), a partnership may rely on a certification received from the transferee described in §1.1446(f)-2(d)(2) unless it knows, or has reason to know, that the certification is incorrect or unreliable. A partnership that already possesses a certification of non-foreign status (including a Form W-9) for the transferor that meets the requirements provided in §1.1446(f)-2(b)(2) may instead rely on this certification to determine that it has no withholding obligation under this paragraph (a)(1) unless it knows, or has reason to know, that the certification is incorrect or unreliable. A partnership that receives a certification described in §1.1446(f)-2(d)(2) that is inconsistent with the information on the certification of non-foreign status in its possession is treated as having actual knowledge, or reason to know, that the certification of non-foreign status is incorrect or unreliable.

(2) *Notification by IRS.*—A partnership that receives notification from the IRS that a transferee has provided incorrect information regarding the amount realized or amount withheld on the certification described in §1.1446(f)-2(d)(2), or has failed to pay the IRS the amount reported as withheld on the certification, must withhold the amount prescribed in the notification on distributions with respect to the transferred interest made on or after the date that is 15 days after it receives the notification. The IRS will not issue a notification on the basis that the amount realized on the certification described in §1.446(f)-2(d)(2) is incorrect if it determines that the transferee properly relied on a certification that included the incorrect information to compute the amount realized pursuant to §1.1446(f)-2(c)(2).

(3) *Subsequent transferees.*—A partnership is not required to withhold under paragraph (a)(1) or (2) of this section on distributions that are made after the date on which the transferee disposes of the transferred interest, unless the partnership has actual knowledge that any person that acquires the transferee's interest in the partnership is a related person, i.e., a person that bears a relationship described in section 267(b) or 707(b)(1) with respect to the transferee or the transferor from which the transferee acquired the interest. A related person that acquires the transferee's interest is treated as liable for tax under section 1461 to the same extent that the transferee is liable for its failure to withhold under §1.1446(f)-2.

(b) *Exceptions to withholding.*—(1) *Withholding has been satisfied by transferee.*—A partnership is not required to withhold under paragraph (a)(1) of this section if it relies on a certification described in §1.1446(f)-2(d)(2) received from the transferee (within the time prescribed in §1.1446(f)-2(d)(2)) that states that an exception to withholding described in §1.1446(f)-2(b) applies or that the transferee withheld the full amount required to be withheld (taking into account any adjustments under §1.1446(f)-2(c)) under §1.1446(f)-2.

(2) *PTP interests.*—A partnership is not required to withhold under this section on distributions made with respect to a PTP interest.

(3) *Distributing partnerships.*—A partnership that is a transferee because it makes a distribution is not required to withhold under this section.

(c) *Withholding rules.*—(1) *Timing of withholding.*—(i) *In general.*—A partnership required to withhold under paragraph (a)(1) of this section must withhold on distributions made with respect to a transferred interest beginning on the later of—

(A) The date that is 30 days after the date of transfer; or

(B) The date that is 15 days after the date on which the partnership acquires actual knowledge that the transfer has occurred.

(ii) *Satisfaction of withholding obligation.*—A partnership is treated as satisfying its withholding obligation under paragraph (a)(1) of this section and may stop withholding on distributions with respect to a transferred interest on the earlier of—

(A) The date on which the partnership completes withholding and paying the amount required to be withheld under paragraph (c)(2) of this section; or

(B) The date on which the partnership receives and may rely on a certification from the transferee described in §1.1446(f)-2(d)(2) (without regard to whether the certification is received by the time prescribed in §1.1446(f)-2(d)(2)) that claims an exception to withholding under §1.1446(f)-2(b).

(2) *Amount to withhold.*—(i) *In general.*—A partnership required to withhold under paragraph (a)(1) of this section must withhold the full amount of each distribution made with respect to the transferred interest until it has withheld—

(A) A tax of 10 percent of the amount realized (determined solely under §1.1446(f)-2(c)(2)(i)) on the transfer, reduced by any amount withheld by the transferee; plus

(B) Any interest computed under paragraph (c)(2)(ii) of this section.

(ii) *Computation of interest.*—The amount of interest required to be withheld under paragraph (a)(1) of this section is the amount of interest that would be required to be paid under section 6601 and §301.6601-1 of this chapter if the amount that should have been withheld by the transferee was considered an underpayment of tax. For purposes of this paragraph (c)(2)(ii), interest is payable between the date that is 20 days after the date of the transfer and the date on which the tax due under paragraph (a)(1) of this section is paid to the IRS.

(iii) *Certifications required.*—For purposes of paragraph (c)(2)(i)(A) of this section, a partnership must determine the amount realized on the transfer and any amount withheld by the transferee based on a certification from the transferee described in §1.1446(f)-2(d)(2), without regard to whether the certification is received by the time prescribed in §1.1446(f)-2(d)(2). A partnership that does not receive or cannot rely on a certification from the transferee described in §1.1446(f)-2(d)(2) must withhold tax equal to the full amount of each distribution made with respect to a transferred interest until it receives a certification that it can rely on.

(3) *Coordination with other withholding provisions.*—Any amount required to be withheld on a distribution under any other provision of the Internal Revenue Code is not also required to be withheld under section 1446(f)(4) or this section.

(d) *Reporting and paying withheld amounts.*—The partnership must report and pay the tax withheld using Forms 8288, *U.S. Withholding Tax Return for Dispositions by Foreign Persons of U.S. Real Property Interests*, and 8288-C, *Statement of Withholding Under Section 1446(f)(4) for Withholding on Dispositions by Foreign Persons of Partnership Interests*, as provided in forms, instructions, or other guidance.

(e) *Effect of withholding on transferor and transferee.*—(1) *Transferor.*—The withholding of tax by a partnership under this section does not relieve a foreign person from filing a U.S. income tax return with respect to the transfer. See §§1.6012-1(b)(1), 1.6012-2(g)(1), and 1.6031(a)-1. Further, the withholding of tax by a partnership does not relieve a nonresident alien individual or foreign corporation subject to tax on gain by reason of section 864(c)(8) from paying any tax due with the return that has not been fully satisfied through withholding. An individual or corporation is not allowed a credit under section 33 for amounts withheld on distributions to the transferee under this section. See, however, §§1.1446(f)-5(a) and 1.1463-1(a), which generally provide that tax will not be recollected if paid by another person.

(2) *Transferee.*—A transferee is treated as satisfying its withholding tax liability under §1.1446(f)-2 to the extent that a partnership withholds tax (which does not include interest) under this section. Interest computed under paragraph (c)(2)(ii) of this section that is withheld by the partnership from the transferee is treated as interest paid by the transferee with respect to its withholding tax liability under §1.1446(f)-2. An excess amount under this section is the amount of tax and interest withheld under this section that exceeds the transferee's withholding tax liability under §1.1446(f)-2 plus any interest owed by the transferee with respect to such liability. A transferee may claim a refund for the excess amount if payments have been made in excess of the tax which is properly due by the transferee for the tax period.

(f) *Applicability date.*—This section applies to transfers that occur on or after January 1, 2022. [Reg. §1.1446(f)-3.]

☐ [*T.D. 9926, 11-27-2020.*]

[Reg. §1.1446(f)-4]

**§1.1446(f)-4. Withholding on the transfer of a publicly traded partnership interest.**—(a) *Obligation to withhold on a transfer of a PTP interest.*—(1) *In general.*—If a transfer of a PTP interest is effected through one or more brokers (as defined in §1.1446(f)-1(b)(1)), the transferee is not required to withhold under section 1446(f)(1) and §1.1446(f)-2. Rather, any broker required to withhold under paragraph (a)(2) of this section must withhold a tax equal to 10 percent of the amount realized (as defined in paragraph (c)(2) of this section) on the transfer of a PTP interest, except as otherwise provided in this section. For cases in which a publicly traded partnership is liable for withholding under this section, see paragraphs (b)(3)(i) and (c)(2)(iii) of this section.

(2) *Broker's requirement to withhold.*—(i) *In general.*—Except as otherwise provided in this section, a broker is required to withhold under this section if it pays an amount realized to another broker that it is required to treat as a foreign person, or if a broker pays an amount realized to a foreign transferor that is its customer.

(ii) *Payments to foreign brokers.*—A broker that pays an amount realized from the transfer of a PTP interest to another broker that it is required to treat as a foreign person must withhold under this section unless the first-mentioned broker obtains documentation on which it may rely establishing that the second-mentioned broker is described in paragraph (a)(2)(ii)(A) or (B) of this section. A broker must treat any broker to which it pays an amount realized from the transfer of a PTP interest as a foreign person unless it obtains, or already possesses, documentation (including a certification of non-foreign status) on which it may rely that establishes that the other broker is a U.S. person. A broker may rely on documentation described in this paragraph (a)(2)(ii), or in paragraph (a)(2)(ii)(A) or (B) of this section, unless it has actual knowledge that the documentation is unreliable or incorrect.

(A) A broker is described in this paragraph (a)(2)(ii)(A) if it is a qualified intermediary (as defined in §1.1441-1(e)(5)(ii)) that provides a valid qualified intermediary withholding certificate (as described in §1.1441-1(e)(3)(ii)) that states that it assumes primary withholding responsibility for the payment.

(B) A broker is described in this paragraph (a)(2)(ii)(B) if it is a U.S. branch of a foreign person (as described in §1.1441-1(b)(2)(iv)) that provides a valid U.S. branch withholding certificate (as described in §1.1441-1(e)(3)(v), but without regard to the requirement in §1.1441-1(e)(3)(v) that the certificate state that the amount is not effectively connected with a trade or business within the United States) that states that the U.S. branch agrees to be treated as a U.S. person with respect to the payment.

(iii) *Payments to foreign transferors that are customers of the broker.*—A broker that pays an amount realized to a foreign transferor that is its customer (as defined in §1.6045-1(a)(2)) from the transfer of a PTP interest is required to withhold under this section unless an exception under paragraph (b) of this section applies.

(3) *Exception from certain withholding by U.S. clearing organizations.*—A broker that is a U.S. clearing organization clearing or settling a sale of a PTP interest is not required to withhold on the amount realized from the sale. However, see §1.1461-1(c)(2)(i)(R)(2) for the requirement that a U.S. clearing organization acting as a central counterparty report on Form 1042-S sales of PTP interests that it clears and settles on a net basis.

(4) *Exception when withholding already satisfied.*—A broker that receives from another broker an amount realized from the transfer of a PTP interest is required to withhold under this section unless the other broker has withheld the full amount required. A broker that receives from another broker an amount realized from the transfer of a PTP interest may treat the withholding as having been satisfied on the full amount required unless it knows or has reason to know that the withholding obligation has not already been satisfied. A broker that is a qualified intermediary determines its withholding requirement for purposes of this paragraph (a)(4) in accordance with its qualified intermediary agreement.

(5) *Documentation obtained from another person to determine a broker's status.*—A U.S. clearing organization may act as an agent for a broker receiving an amount realized from another broker that is a member of the clearing organization for purposes of furnishing valid documentation described in paragraph (a)(2) of this section of the first-mentioned broker's status to such other broker, provided the clearing organization notifies the first-mentioned broker and such broker has the ability to opt out. A broker that obtains documentation from a clearing organization under this paragraph (a)(5) for a broker to which the first-mentioned broker is paying an amount realized may rely on such documentation unless it has actual knowledge that the documentation is incorrect or unreliable.

(6) *Date of withholding with respect to a transfer other than a distribution.*—For a transfer of a PTP interest that is not a distribution, a broker is required to apply the principles of § 31.3406(a)-4(b)(1) of this chapter to determine the date on which to withhold under this section.

(7) *Payments to qualified intermediaries not assuming primary withholding responsibility.*—With respect to the transfer of a PTP interest, if a broker pays the amount realized to a foreign person that the broker may treat as a qualified intermediary (as defined in § 1.1441-1(e)(5)(ii)) that does not assume primary withholding responsibility for the payment based on a valid qualified intermediary withholding certificate described in § 1.1441-1(e)(3)(ii) upon which the broker may rely under paragraph (a)(2) of this section, the broker may withhold as provided in this paragraph (a)(7). Under this paragraph (a)(7), a broker may withhold under this section by reference to the amount of the payment that the broker can reliably determine, based on the withholding statement provided with the withholding certificate, is allocable to—

(i) Foreign transferors included in a chapter 3 withholding rate pool (as described in § 1.1441-1(e)(5)(v)(C)) that are subject to a 10 percent rate of withholding on the payment of the amount realized;

(ii) Foreign transferors included in a chapter 3 withholding rate pool (as described in § 1.1441-1(e)(5)(v)(C)) that qualify for an exception from withholding on the payment of the amount realized under paragraph (b) of this section;

(iii) Each foreign transferor for which a form acceptable under § 1.1446-1 is provided; or

(iv) U.S. transferors, based on a valid Form W-9 provided for each such transferor to the extent that the transferor is not included in a chapter 4 withholding rate pool of U.S. payees (as described in § 1.1441-1(e)(5)(v)(C), to the extent permitted for purposes of chapter 4 of the Internal Revenue Code).

(8) *Qualified intermediary or U.S. branch withholding requirement.*—A broker that is a qualified intermediary (as defined in § 1.1441-1(e)(5)(ii)) or U.S. branch must assume primary withholding responsibility under this section for a distribution from a publicly traded partnership for which the qualified intermediary or U.S. branch acts as a nominee for purposes of section 1446(a). See § 1.1446-4(b)(3).

(b) *Exceptions to withholding.*—(1) *In general.*—A broker is not required to withhold under this section if it properly relies on a certification described in paragraph (b)(2), (5), or (6) of this section, a qualified notice described in paragraph (b)(3) of this section, or if the exception described in paragraph (b)(4) of this section applies. A broker may not rely on a certification described in this paragraph (b) if it has actual knowledge that the certification is incorrect or unreliable.

(2) *Certification of non-foreign status.*—A broker may rely on a certification of non-foreign status that it obtains from the transferor. A certification of non-foreign status under this section means a Form W-9, *Request for Taxpayer Identification Number and Certification*, or valid substitute form, that meets the requirements of § 1.1441-1(d)(2). For purposes of this paragraph (b)(2), a broker may rely on a valid form that it already possesses from the transferor. A broker may instead rely on certification from a second broker (as defined in § 1.6045-1(a)(1)) that acts as an agent for the transferor when the second broker does not receive the amount realized from the transfer of the PTP interest. This certification must state that the second broker has collected a valid certification of non-foreign status (within the meaning of this paragraph (b)(2)) from the transferor, and it must include the transferor's TIN and status as a foreign or U.S. person.

(3) *Less than 10 percent effectively connected gain by partnership.*—(i) *In general.* A broker may rely on a qualified notice described in paragraph (b)(3)(iii) of this section that states that the 10-percent exception applies, as determined under paragraph (b)(3)(ii) of this section. In a case in which a broker properly relies on a qualified notice under paragraph (b)(1) of this section that results in underwithholding on a transfer of a PTP interest, the publicly traded partnership that issued the notice is solely liable for the underwithheld tax under section 1461. A publicly traded partnership's liability referenced in the preceding sentence, however, applies only when the publicly traded partnership fails to make a reasonable estimate of the amounts required for determining the applicability of the 10-percent exception.

(ii) *10-percent exception.*—(A) *In general.*—The 10-percent exception applies to a transfer if, on the PTP designated date described in paragraph (b)(3)(ii)(B) of this section—

*(1)* If the publicly traded partnership sold all of its assets at fair market value in the manner described in § 1.864(c)(8)-1(c), either—

*(i)* The amount of net gain that would have been effectively connected with the conduct of a trade or business within the United States would be less than 10 percent of the total net gain; or

*(ii)* No gain would have been effectively connected with the conduct of a trade or business in the United States; or

*(2)* The partnership was not engaged in a trade or business within the United States at any time during the taxable year of the partnership through the PTP designated date.

(B) *PTP designated date.*—The PTP designated date for a transfer is any date for a deemed sale determination that is designated by the publicly traded partnership in a qualified notice described in paragraph (b)(3)(iii) of this section, provided that the PTP designated date occurs on or after the date that is 92 days before the date on which the publicly traded partnership posted the qualified notice naming the PTP designated date.

(iii) *Qualified notice.*—(A) *In general.*—Except as provided in paragraphs (b)(3)(iii)(B) and (C) of this section, a qualified notice described in this paragraph (b)(3)(iii) is the most recent qualified notice (within the meaning of § 1.1446-4(b)(4)) posted by the publicly traded partnership.

(B) *Qualified notice posting date requirement.*—A qualified notice is described in this paragraph (b)(3)(iii) only if the publicly traded partnership has posted it within the 92-day period ending on the date of the transfer. For a transfer that is a distribution by the publicly traded partnership, the qualified notice is described in paragraph (b)(3)(iii) of this section only if the qualified notice is posted with respect to the distribution.

(C) *Recent posting of qualified notice.*—If the most recent qualified notice posted by the publicly traded partnership was posted during the 10-day period ending on the date of the transfer, a broker may instead rely on the immediately preceding qualified notice (within the meaning of § 1.1446-4(b)(4)) posted by the publicly traded partnership, provided that it satisfies the condition described in paragraph (b)(3)(iii)(B) of this section.

(4) *Amount subject to withholding under section 3406.*—A broker is not required to withhold under this section if the amount realized from the transfer of the PTP interest is subject to withholding under § 31.3406(b)(3)-2 of this chapter.

(5) *Income tax treaties.*—A broker may rely on a certification from the transferor that states that the transferor is not subject to tax on any gain from the transfer pursuant to an income tax treaty in effect between the United States and a foreign country if the requirements of this paragraph (b)(5) are met. The transferor makes the certification on a withholding certificate (on a Form W-8BEN, *Certificate of Foreign Status of Beneficial Owner for United States Tax Withholding and Reporting (Individuals)*, or Form W-8BEN-E, *Certificate of Status of Beneficial Owner for United States Tax Withholding and Reporting (Entities))* that meets the requirements for validity under § 1.1446-1(c)(2)(iv) (or an applicable substitute form that meets the requirements under § 1.1446-1(c)(5)) and that contains the information necessary to support the claim for treaty benefits. For purposes of this paragraph (b)(5), a broker may rely on a withholding certificate that it already possesses from the transferor that meets the requirements of this paragraph (b)(5) unless it has actual knowledge that the information is incorrect or unreliable. The exception in this paragraph (b)(5) does not apply if treaty benefits apply to only a portion of the gain from the transfer.

(6) *Foreign dealers that provide Form W-8ECI.*—A broker may rely on a certification provided by a transferor that certifies that it is a dealer in securities (as defined in section 475(c)(1)) and that any gain from the transfer of the PTP interest is effectively connected with the conduct of a trade or business within the United States without regard to the provisions of section 864(c)(8). The certification described in the preceding sentence is made on a Form W-8ECI, *Certificate of Foreign Person's Claim That Income Is Effectively Connected With the Conduct of a Trade or Business in the United States*, that meets the requirements for validity under § 1.1446-1(c)(2)(iv) (or an applicable substitute form that meets the requirements under § 1.1446-1(c)(5)) and that contains any other information required in the instructions to the form. A broker may rely on a withholding certificate that it already possesses from the transferor that meets the requirements of this paragraph (b)(6) unless it has actual knowledge that the information is incorrect or unreliable.

(c) *Determining the amount to withhold.*—(1) *In general.*—A broker that is required to withhold under this section must withhold 10 percent of the amount realized on the transfer of the PTP interest, except as provided in this paragraph (c). Any procedures in this paragraph (c) apply solely for purposes of determining the amount to withhold under section 1446(f)(1) and this section. A broker may not rely on a certification described in this paragraph (c) if it has actual knowledge that the certification is incorrect or unreliable.

(2) *Amount realized.*—(i) *In general.*—Solely for purposes of this section, the amount realized is the amount of gross proceeds (as defined in §1.6045-1(d)(5)) paid or credited upon the transfer to the customer or other broker (as applicable), or, in the case of a distribution, the amount determined under paragraph (c)(2)(iii) of this section.

(ii) *Certification by a foreign partnership of modified amount realized.*—(A) *In general.*—When a transferor is a foreign partnership, a broker may use the procedures of this paragraph (c)(2)(ii) to determine the amount realized. For purposes of this paragraph (c)(2)(ii)(A), the broker may treat the modified amount realized as the amount realized to the extent it may rely on a certification from the transferor providing the modified amount realized.

(B) *Determining modified amount realized.*—The modified amount realized is determined by multiplying the amount realized (as determined under this paragraph (c)(2), without regard to this paragraph (c)(2)(ii)) by the aggregate percentage computed as of the determination date (see §1.1446(f)-1(c)(4)). The aggregate percentage is the percentage of the gain (if any) arising from the transfer that would be allocated to presumed foreign taxable persons. For purposes of this paragraph (c)(2)(ii)(B), a presumed foreign taxable person is any direct or indirect partner of the transferor that has not provided either a certification of non-foreign status that meets the requirements of paragraph (b)(2) of this section or a certification of treaty benefits that states that the partner is not subject to tax on any gain from the transfer pursuant to an income tax treaty in effect between the United States and a foreign country. A valid certification of treaty benefits must meet the requirements of paragraph (b)(5) of this section (as applied to the partner claiming treaty benefits). For purposes of this paragraph (c)(2)(ii), an indirect partner is a person that owns an interest in the transferor indirectly through one or more foreign partnerships.

(C) *Certification.*—The certification is made by providing a withholding certificate (on Form W-8IMY, *Certificate of Foreign Intermediary, Foreign Flow-Through Entity, or Certain U.S. Branches for United States Tax Withholding and Reporting*) that includes a withholding statement that provides the percentage of gain allocable to each direct or indirect partner and that provides whether each such person is a United States person, a foreign partner eligible for treaty benefits, or a presumed foreign taxable person. The certification must also include the certification of non-foreign status or the certification of treaty benefits from each direct or indirect partner that is not a presumed foreign taxable person. For purposes of this paragraph (c)(2)(ii), a broker may rely on a withholding certificate and withholding statement that it already possesses from the partnership unless it has actual knowledge that the information is incorrect or unreliable.

(iii) *Determination of amount realized on a distribution.*—The amount realized on a distribution from a publicly traded partnership is the amount of the distribution reduced by the portion of the distribution that is attributable to the cumulative net income of the partnership. The cumulative net income is the net income earned by the publicly traded partnership since its formation that has not been previously distributed by the partnership. A publicly traded partnership identifies such excess portion of the distribution as an amount in excess of cumulative net income on a qualified notice (within the meaning of §1.1446-4(b)(4)) posted with respect to the distribution. If a broker properly withholds based on the qualified notice (applying the rules of §1.1446-4(d)(1) to the distribution), the broker is not liable for any underwithholding on any amount attributable to an amount in excess of cumulative net income. Rather, the publicly traded partnership that issued the qualified notice is solely liable for the underwithheld tax under section 1461 on such amount that results from a broker's reliance on the notice.

(d) *Reporting and paying withheld amounts.*—A broker that is required to withhold under this section must pay the withheld tax pursuant to the deposit rules in §1.6302-2. For rules regarding reporting on Forms 1042, *Annual Withholding Tax Return for U.S. Source Income of Foreign Persons*, and 1042-S, *Foreign Person's U.S. Source Income Subject to Withholding*, that apply to a broker that withholds under this section, see §1.1461-1(b) and (c). For rules regarding when an amount realized on the transfer of a PTP interest is reportable on a Form 1042-S (including in certain cases in which withholding is not required), see §1.1461-1(c)(2)(i)(Q) and (R). A broker that pays the amount realized to a foreign partnership must issue a Form 1042-S directly to the partnership rather than issuing a form to each of the partners of the partnership. *See* §1.1461-1(c)(1)(ii)(A)(8) (treating the foreign partnership as a recipient for reporting purposes). A broker making a payment to a U.S. branch treated as a U.S. person must

treat the branch as a U.S. person for purposes of reporting the payment made to the branch. Therefore, a payment to that U.S. branch must be reported on Form 1042-S. *See* §1.1461-1(c). A Form 1042-S issued directly to the transferor must include the TIN of the transferor unless the broker does not know the TIN at the time of issuance.

(e) *Effect of withholding on transferor.*—(1) *In general.*—The withholding of tax under this section does not relieve a foreign person from filing a U.S. tax return with respect to the transfer. *See* §§1.6012-1(b)(1), 1.6012-2(g)(1), and 1.6031(a)-1. Further, the withholding of tax by a broker does not relieve a nonresident alien individual or foreign corporation subject to tax on gain by reason of section 864(c)(8) from paying any tax due with the return that has not been fully satisfied through withholding.

(2) *Manner of obtaining credit.*—(i) *Individuals and corporations.*—An individual or corporation may claim a credit under section 33 for the amount withheld under this section by attaching to its applicable return a copy of a Form 1042-S that includes its TIN (or as otherwise provided in IRS forms or instructions).

(ii) *Partnerships, trusts, or estates.*—For a rule allowing a foreign partnership that is a transferor to claim a credit for the amount withheld under this section against its obligation to withhold under section 1446(a), see §1.1446-3(c)(4). For the rule providing the extent to which a foreign trust or estate may claim a credit for an amount withheld under this section, see §1.1462-1. A foreign partnership, trust, or estate claiming a credit for an amount withheld must attach to its applicable return the Form 1042-S provided to it under paragraph (d) of this section (or as otherwise provided in IRS forms or instructions). A foreign trust or estate must also provide any information required in forms or instructions to any beneficiary or owner that is liable for tax on any of the gain under section 864(c)(8).

(f) *Applicability date.*—This section applies to transfers that occur on or after January 1, 2022. [Reg. §1.1446(f)-4.]

☐ [T.D. 9926, 11-27-2020.]

**[Reg. §1.1446(f)-5]**

**§1.1446(f)-5. Liability for failure to withhold.**—(a) *Liability for failure to withhold.*—Every person required to withhold and pay tax under section 1446(f), but that fails to do so, is liable for the tax under section 1461, plus any applicable interest, penalties, or additions to tax. A partnership that failed to withhold and pay tax under §1.1446(f)-3 is liable only for the amount of tax that it failed to collect (but not any interest computed on that amount under §1.1446(f)-3(c)(2)(ii)), plus any interest, penalties, or additions to tax with regard to the partnership's failure to withhold.

(b) *Tax liability otherwise satisfied.*—Under section 1463, if the tax required to be withheld under section 1446(f) is paid by another person required to withhold under section 1446(f), or by the nonresident alien individual or foreign corporation subject to tax on gain resulting from section 864(c)(8), the tax will not be recollected. The person required to withhold must establish proof of payment by another person required to withhold or by the nonresident alien individual or foreign corporation subject to the tax on gain resulting from section 864(c)(8). The person required to withhold may show that a reduced rate of withholding was appropriate by establishing the amount of tax due by the foreign transferor (as defined in §1.864(c)(8)-1(g)(3)) on gain resulting from section 864(c)(8). The person required to withhold under section 1446(f) is not relieved from liability for any interest, penalties, or additions to tax that would otherwise apply. However, if the person required to withhold establishes to the satisfaction of the Commissioner that no gain on the transfer is treated as effectively connected with the conduct of a trade or business within the United States trade or business under section 864(c)(8), no interest, penalties, or additions to tax will apply.

(c) *Liability of agents.*—(1) *Duty to provide notice of false certification.*—A transferee's or transferor's agent (other than a broker required to withhold under §1.1446(f)-4) must provide notice to a transferee (or other person required to withhold) if that person is furnished with a certification described in §§1.1446(f)-1 through 1.1446(f)-4 that the agent knows is false. A person required to withhold may not rely on a certification if it receives the notice described in this paragraph (c)(1).

(2) *Procedural requirements.*—Any agent who is required to provide notice under paragraph (c)(1) of this section must do so in writing (including by electronic submission) as soon as possible after learning of the false certification. If the agent first learns of the false certification before the date of transfer, notice must be given by the third day following that discovery but no later than the date of transfer (before the transferee's payment of consideration). If an agent first learns of a false certification after the date of transfer,

notice must be given by the third day following that discovery. The notice must also explain the possible consequences to the recipient of a failure to withhold. The notice need not disclose the information on which the agent's statement is based. The agent must also furnish a copy of the notice to the IRS by the date on which the notice is required to be given to the recipient. The copy of the notice must be delivered to the address provided in §1.1445-1(g)(10) and must be accompanied by a cover letter stating that the copy is being filed pursuant to the requirements of this paragraph (c)(2).

(3) *Failure to provide notice.*—Any agent who is required to provide notice under paragraph (c)(1) of this section, but fails to do so in the manner required in paragraph (c)(2) of this section, is liable for the tax that the person who should have been provided notice in accordance with paragraph (c)(2) of this section was required to withhold under section 1446(f) if the notice had been given.

(4) *Limitation on liability.*—An agent's liability under paragraph (c)(3) of this section is limited to the amount of compensation that the agent derives from the transaction. In addition, an agent that assists in the preparation of, or fails to disclose knowledge of, a false certification may be liable for civil and criminal penalties.

(d) *Applicability date.*—This section applies to transfers that occur on or after January 29, 2021. [Reg. §1.1446(f)-5.]

☐ [*T.D.* 9926, 11-27-2020.]

# Application of Withholding Provisions

See p. 20,601 for regulations not amended to reflect law changes

### [Reg. §1.1461-1]

**§1.1461-1. Payment and returns of tax withheld.**—(a) *Payment of withheld tax.*—(1) *Deposits of tax.*—Every withholding agent who withholds tax pursuant to chapter 3 of the Internal Revenue Code (Code) and the regulations under such chapter shall deposit such amount of tax as provided in §1.6302-2(a). If for any reason the total amount of tax required to be returned for any calendar year pursuant to paragraph (b) of this section has not been deposited pursuant to §1.6302-2, the withholding agent shall pay the balance of tax due for such year at such place as the Internal Revenue Service (IRS) shall specify. The tax shall be paid when filing the return required under paragraph (b)(1) of this section for such year, unless the IRS specifies otherwise. With respect to withholding under section 1446, this section shall apply only to publicly traded partnerships and nominees that withhold under §1.1446-4 and brokers and publicly traded partnerships that withhold (or are otherwise liable for underwithholding) under §1.1446(f)-4 on transfers of publicly traded partnership interests. See §1.1461-3 regarding withholding tax liabilities under sections 1446(a) and 1446(f) and penalties that apply for failure to withhold under either of those sections.

(2) *Penalties for failure to pay tax.*—For penalties and additions to the tax for failure to timely pay the tax required to be withheld under chapter 3 of the Code, see sections 6656, 6672, and 7202 and the regulations under those sections.

(b) *Income tax return.*—(1) *General rule.*—A withholding agent shall make an income tax return on Form 1042 (or such other form as the IRS may prescribe) for income paid during the preceding calendar year that the withholding agent is required to report on an information return on Form 1042-S (or such other form as the IRS may prescribe) under paragraph (c)(1) of this section. See sections 6011 and §1.6011-1(c). The withholding agent must file the return on or before March 15 of the calendar year following the year in which the income was paid. The return must show the aggregate amount of income paid and tax withheld required to be reported on all the Forms 1042-S for the preceding calendar year by the withholding agent, in addition to such information as is required by the form and accompanying instructions. See §1.1474-1(c) for the requirement to show the aggregate chapter 4 reportable amounts and tax withheld on Form 1042. A single Form 1042 may be filed by a withholding agent to report amounts under chapters 3 and 4, including tax withheld. Withholding certificates or other statements or information provided to a withholding agent are not required to be attached to the return. A return must be filed under this paragraph (b)(1) even though no tax was required to be withheld during the preceding calendar year. The withholding agent must retain a copy of Form 1042 for the applicable statute of limitations on assessments and collection with respect to the amounts required to be reported on the Form 1042. See section 6501 and the regulations thereunder for the applicable statute of limitations. Adjustments to the total amount of tax withheld, as described in §1.1461-2, shall be stated on the return as prescribed by the form and accompanying instructions.

(2) *Amended returns.*—An amended return may be filed on a Form 1042 or such other form as the IRS may prescribe. An amended return must include such information as the form or accompanying instructions shall require, including, with respect to any information that has changed from the time of the filing of the return, the information that was shown on the original return and the corrected information.

(c) *Information returns.*—(1) *Filing requirement.*—(i) *In general.*—A withholding agent (other than an individual who is not acting in the course of a trade or business with respect to a payment) must make an information return on Form 1042-S, "Foreign Person's U.S. Source Income Subject to Withholding," (or such other form as the IRS may prescribe) to report the amounts subject to reporting, as defined in paragraph (c)(2) of this section, that were paid during the preceding calendar year. Notwithstanding the preceding sentence, any person that withholds or is required to withhold an amount under section 1441, 1442, or 1443, or §1.1446-4(a) (applicable to publicly traded partnerships required to pay tax under section 1446(a) on distributions) or §1.1446(f)-4(a) (applicable to brokers required to withhold on transfers of publicly traded partnership interests) must file a Form 1042-S for the payment withheld upon whether or not that person is engaged in a trade or business and whether or not the payment is an amount subject to reporting. A Form 1042-S shall be prepared for each recipient of an amount subject to reporting and for each single type of income payment. The Form 1042-S shall be prepared in such manner as the form and accompanying instructions prescribe. One copy of the Form 1042-S shall be filed with the IRS on or before March 15th of the calendar year following the year in which the amount subject to reporting was paid. It shall be filed with a transmittal form as provided in the instructions to the Form 1042-S and to the transmittal form. Withholding certificates, documentary evidence, or other statements or documentation provided to a withholding agent are not required to be attached to the form. Another copy of the Form 1042-S must be furnished to the recipient for whom the form is prepared (or any other person, as required under this paragraph (c) or the instructions to the form) on or before March 15 of the calendar year following the year in which the amount subject to reporting was paid. The withholding agent must retain a copy of each Form 1042-S for the statute of limitations on assessment and collection applicable to the Form 1042 to which the Form 1042-S relates. A withholding agent required by this section to furnish a recipient copy of Form 1042-S may furnish such copy electronically by complying with the requirements provided in §1.6050W-2(a)(2) through (5) applicable to statements required under section 6050W (substituting the phrase "Form 1042-S" for the phrases "statement required under section 6050W" or "statements required by section 6050W(f)" each place they appear). A withholding agent that meets the requirements of that section for providing electronic copies to recipients may apply these rules to payments made in calendar year 2016.

(ii) *Recipient.*—(A) *Defined.*—For purposes of this section, the term *recipient* means—

(1) A beneficial owner as defined in §1.1441-1(c)(6), including a foreign estate or a foreign complex trust, as defined in §1.1441-1(c)(25);

(2) A qualified intermediary as defined in §1.1441-1(e)(5)(ii);

(3) A withholding foreign partnership as defined in §1.1441-5(c)(2) or a withholding foreign trust under §1.1441-5(e)(5)(v);

(4) A territory financial institution treated as a U.S. person under §1.1441-1(b)(2)(iv)(A);

(5) A U.S. branch that is treated as a U.S. person under §1.1441-1(b)(2)(iv)(A);

(6) A nonwithholding foreign partnership or a foreign simple trust as defined in §1.1441-1(c)(24), but only to the extent the income is (or is treated as) effectively connected with the conduct of a trade or business in the United States by such entity, or if the nonwithholding foreign partnership or foreign simple trust is also described in paragraph (c)(1)(ii)(A)(9) or (c)(1)(ii)(A)(10) of this section;

(7) A payee, as defined in §1.1441-1(b)(2) that is presumed to be a foreign person under the presumption rules of §1.1441-1(b)(3); 1.1441-5(d) or (e)(6), or 1.6049-5(d);

(8) A partner (including a foreign partnership or a partner for which a qualified intermediary provides partner-specific documentation under §1.1446-4(e)) receiving a distribution from a

publicly traded partnership subject to withholding under section 1446(a) and §1.1446-4 on distributions of effectively connected income, and a partner (including a foreign partnership or a partner for which a qualified intermediary provides partner-specific documentation under §1.1446(f)-4(a)(7)) receiving an amount realized from a transfer of a publicly traded partnership interest under section 1446(f)(1) and §1.1446(f)-4.

(9) A foreign intermediary, nonwithholding foreign partnership, or nonwithholding foreign trust that is a participating FFI or registered deemed-compliant FFI with respect to a chapter 4 reporting pool of U.S. payees;

(10) A participating FFI or a registered deemed-compliant FFI that is a recipient of a withholdable payment described in §1.1474-1(d)(1)(ii)(A)(*1*)(*iii*); and

(11) Any other person as required on Form 1042-S or the instructions to the form.

(B) *Persons that are not recipients.*—A recipient does not include—

(1) A nonqualified intermediary, except with respect to a payment (or portion of a payment) for which a nonqualified intermediary that is an FFI is a recipient reporting as described in §1.1474-1(d)(1)(ii)(A)(*1*)(*iii*), or if the nonqualified intermediary is also described in paragraph (c)(1)(ii)(A)(*9*) or (c)(1)(ii)(A)(*10*) of this section;

(2) A payee included in a chapter 3 or chapter 4 withholding rate pool;

(3) A flow-through entity, as defined in §1.1441-1(c)(23) (to the extent it is receiving amounts subject to reporting other than income effectively connected with the conduct of a trade or business in the United States), that is not a recipient described in paragraphs (c)(1)(ii)(A)(*9*) or (c)(1)(ii)(A)(*10*) of this section;

(4) A U.S. branch (including a territory financial institution) described in §1.1441-1(b)(2)(iv)(A) that is not treated as a U.S. person under that section and is not a recipient described in paragraphs (c)(1)(ii)(A)(*9*) or (*10*) of this section;

(5) A foreign broker withheld upon under §1.1446(f)-4(a)(2)(ii) by another broker paying an amount realized from the transfer of a PTP interest.

(C) *Coordination with chapter 4 reporting.*—See §1.1474-1(d)(1)(ii)(A) for persons that are defined as recipients of a withholdable payment of U.S. source FDAP income for purposes of chapter 4 in addition to the persons that are recipients under this paragraph (c)(1)(ii).

(2) *Amounts subject to reporting.*—(i) *In general.*—Subject to the exceptions described in paragraph (c)(2)(ii) of this section, amounts subject to reporting on Form 1042-S are amounts paid to a foreign payee or partner (including persons presumed to be foreign) that are amounts subject to withholding as defined in §1.1441-2(a), distributions of effectively connected income under §1.1446-4, or amounts realized from transfers of PTP interests under §1.1446(f)-4. Amounts subject to reporting include amounts subject to withholding even if no amount is deducted and withheld from the payment because of a treaty or Internal Revenue Code exception to taxation or because an amount withheld was reimbursed to the payee under the adjustment procedures of §1.1461-2. In addition, amounts subject to reporting include any amounts paid to a foreign payee on which a withholding agent withheld (including under §1.1441-2(e)(7)) an amount (either under chapter 3 of the Internal Revenue Code or section 3406) whether or not the amount is subject to withholding. Amounts subject to reporting include, but are not limited to, the following items—

(A) The entire amount of a corporate distribution (whether actual or deemed) irrespective of any estimate of the portion of the distribution that represents a taxable dividend;

(B) Interest, including the portion of a notional principal contract payment that is characterized as interest. Interest shall also be reported on Form 1042-S if it is bank deposit interest paid to nonresident alien individuals as required under §1.6049-8;

(C) Rents;

(D) Royalties;

(E) Compensation for dependent and independent personal services performed in the United States;

(F) Annuities;

(G) Pension distributions and other deferred income;

(H) Gambling winnings that are not exempt from tax under section 871(j);

(I) Income from the cancellation of indebtedness unless the withholding agent is unrelated to the debtor and does not have knowledge of the facts that give rise to the payment (see §1.1441-2(d));

(J) Amounts that are (or are presumed to be) effectively connected with the conduct of a trade or business in the United States (including deposit interest as defined in sections 871(i)(2)(A) and 881(d)) even if no withholding certificate is required to be furnished by the payee or beneficial owner. In the case of amounts paid on a notional principal contract described in §1.1441-4(a)(3) that are presumed to be effectively connected with the conduct of a trade or business in the United States, the amount required to be reported is limited to the amount of cash paid from the notional principal contract;

(K) Scholarship, fellowship, or grant income and compensation for personal services that is not excludible from gross income under section 117 (whether or not the taxable scholarship, fellowship, grant income, or compensation for personal services is exempt from tax under an income tax treaty) paid to foreign students, trainees, teachers, or researchers;

(L) Dividend equivalents as described in section 871(m) and the regulations thereunder;

(M) Any dividend or any payment that references a dividend from an underlying security pursuant to a securities lending or sale-repurchase transaction paid to a qualified derivatives dealer even when the withholding agent is not required to withhold on the payment pursuant to §1.1441-1(b)(4)(xxi), (xxii), or (xxiii);

(N) Amounts paid to foreign governments, international organizations, or the Bank for International Settlements, whether or not documentation must be provided;

(O) Original issue discount paid on the redemption of an OID obligation. The amount to be reported is the amount of OID includible in the gross income of the holder of the obligation, if known, or, if not known, the total amount of original issue discount determined as if the holder held the obligation from its original issuance. A withholding agent may determine the total amount of OID by using the most recently published "List of Original Issue Discount Instruments," (Publication 1212, available from the IRS Forms Distribution Centers);

(P) The amount of any distribution made by a publicly traded partnership that is an amount subject to withholding under §1.1446-4, or that is paid to a qualified intermediary or a U.S. branch of a foreign person that agrees to be treated as a U.S. person;

(Q) Except with respect to a broker that is a U.S. clearing organization, an amount realized on the transfer of a PTP interest under §1.1446(f)-4 (unless an exception to withholding applies under §1.1446(f)-4(b)(2) through (4)); and

(R) In the case of a broker that is a U.S. clearing organization—

(1) An amount realized (as determined under §1.1446(f)-4(c)(2)(iii)) on a distribution made by a publicly traded partnership for which withholding is required under §1.1446(f)-4(a); and

(2) An amount realized on the sale of a PTP interest cleared and settled through a net settlement system maintained by the clearing organization acting as a central counterparty in the sale (with the reporting on the non-netted amount), unless an exception to withholding would apply under §1.1446(f)-4(b)(2) or (3).

(ii) *Exceptions to reporting.*—The amounts listed in this paragraph (c)(2)(ii) are not required to be reported on Form 1042-S—

(A) Interest (including original issue discount) that is deposit interest under sections 871(i)(2)(A) and 881(d) and that is not effectively connected with the conduct of a trade or business in the United States, unless reporting is required under §1.6049-8 (regarding payments to certain foreign residents) or is interest that is effectively connected with the conduct of a trade or business in the United States;

(B) Interest or original issue discount on certain short-term obligations, described in section 871(g)(1)(B) or 881(a)(3);

(C) Interest paid on obligations sold between interest payment dates and the portion of the purchase price of an OID obligation that is sold or exchanged in a transaction other than a redemption, unless the sale or exchange is part of a plan, the principal purpose of which is to avoid tax and the withholding agent has actual knowledge or reason to know of such plan (see §1.1441-2(a)(5) and (6));

(D) Any item required to be reported on a Form W-2, including an item required to be shown on Form W-2 solely by reason of §1.6041-2 (relating to return of information for payments to employees) or §1.6052-1 (relating to information regarding payment of wages in the form of group-term life insurance);

(E) Any item required to be reported on Form 1099, and such other forms as are prescribed pursuant to the information reporting provisions of sections 6041 through 6050W and the regulations under those sections;

(F) Amounts paid on a notional principal contract described in §1.1441-4(a)(3)(i) that are not effectively connected with the conduct of a trade or business in the United States (or not treated as effectively connected pursuant to §1.1441-4(a)(3)(ii));

**Reg. §1.1461-1(c)(2)(ii)(F)**

(G) Amounts required to be reported on Form 8288 (U.S. Withholding Tax Return for Dispositions by Foreign Persons of U.S. Real Property Interests) or Form 8804 (Annual Return for Partnership Withholding Tax (section 1446)). A withholding agent that must report a distribution partly on a Form 8288 or 8804 and partly on a Form 1042-S may elect to report the entire amount on a Form 8288 or 8804;

(H) Interest (including original issue discount) paid with respect to foreign-targeted registered obligations issued before January 1, 2016, that are described in §1.871-14(e)(2) to the extent the documentation requirements described in §1.871-14(e)(3) and (e)(4) are required to be satisfied (taking into account the provisions of §1.871-14(e)(4)(ii), if applicable);

(I) Interest on a foreign-targeted bearer obligation (see §§1.1441-1(b)(4)(i) and 1.1441-2(a)) issued before March 19, 2012;

(J) Except as provided in §1.1461-1(c)(2)(i)(M), any payment to a qualified derivatives dealer when the withholding agent is not required to withhold on the payment pursuant to §1.1441-1(b)(4)(xxi), (xxii), or (xxiii). This exception does not apply to withholding agents that are qualified derivatives dealers;

(K) Gain described in section 301(c)(3); and

(L) Amounts described in §1.1441-1(b)(4)(xviii) (dealing with certain amounts paid by the U.S. government).

(iii) *Applicability date.*—Paragraph (c)(2) of this section applies beginning January 19, 2017.

(3) *Required information.*—The information required to be furnished under this paragraph (c)(3) shall be based upon the information provided by or on behalf of the recipient of an amount subject to reporting (as corrected and supplemented based on the withholding agent's actual knowledge) or the presumption rules of §§1.1441-1(b)(3), 1.1441-4(a), 1.1441-5(d) and (e); 1.1441-9(b)(3), 1.1446-1(c)(3) (as applied to publicly traded partnerships required to pay tax under section 1446 on distributions of effectively connected income) or 1.6049-5(d). The reference in the previous sentence to presumption rules applicable to withholding under section 1446 shall apply to partnership taxable years beginning after May 18, 2005, or such earlier time as the regulations under §§1.1446-1 through 1.1446-5 apply by reason of an election under §1.1446-7. The Form 1042-S must include the following information, if applicable—

(i) The name, address, taxpayer identifying number of the withholding agent, and the withholding agent's status for chapter 3 purposes (based on the status codes applicable for chapter 3 purposes provided on the form);

(ii) A description of each category of income paid based on the income codes provided on the form (e.g., interest, dividends, royalties, etc.) and the aggregate amount in each category expressed in U.S. dollars;

(iii) For a payment not subject to withholding under chapter 4, the rate of withholding applied or the basis for exempting the payment from withholding under chapter 3, and the exemption applicable to the payment for chapter 4 purposes (based on the exemption codes provided on the form);

(iv) The name and address of the recipient;

(v) The name and address of any nonqualified intermediary, flow-through entity, or U.S. branch as described in §1.1441-1(b)(2)(iv) (other than a branch that is treated as a U.S. person) to which the payment was made;

(vi) The taxpayer identifying number of the recipient if required under §1.1441-1(e)(4)(vii) or if actually known to the withholding agent making the return;

(vii) The taxpayer identifying number of a nonqualified intermediary or flow-through entity (to the extent it is not a recipient) or other flow-through entity to the extent it is known to the withholding agent;

(viii) The country (based on the country codes provided on the form) of the recipient and of any nonqualified intermediary or flow-through entity the name of which appears on the form; and

(ix) Such information as the form or the instructions may require in addition to, or in lieu of, information required under this paragraph (c)(3).

(4) *Method of reporting.*—(i) *Payments by U.S. withholding agents to recipients.*—A withholding agent that is a U.S. person (other than a foreign branch of a U.S. person that is a qualified intermediary as defined in §1.1441-1(e)(5)(ii) that makes payments of amounts subject to reporting on Form 1042-S must file a separate Form 1042-S for each recipient who receives such amount. For purposes of this paragraph (c)(4), a U.S. person includes a U.S. branch (including a territory financial institution) described in §1.1441-1(b)(2)(iv)(A) that is treated as a U.S. person. Except as may otherwise be required on Form 1042-S or the instructions to the form, only payments for which the income code, exemption code, withholding rate, and recipient code are the same may be reported on a single Form 1042-S. See

paragraph (c)(4)(ii) of this section for reporting of payments made to a person that is not a recipient. See §1.1474-1(d)(4) for additional requirements that may apply for reporting on Form 1042-S with respect to a withholdable payment that is a chapter 4 reportable amount.

(A) *Payments to beneficial owners.*—If a U.S. withholding agent makes a payment directly to a beneficial owner it must complete Form 1042-S treating the beneficial owner as the recipient. Under the grace period rule of §1.1441-1(b)(3)(iv), a U.S. withholding agent may, under certain circumstances, treat a payee as a foreign person while the withholding agent awaits a valid withholding certificate. A U.S. withholding agent who relies on the grace period rule to treat a payee as a foreign person must file a Form 1042-S to report all payments on Form 1042-S during the period that person was presumed to be foreign even if that person is later determined to be a U.S. person based on appropriate documentation or is presumed to be a U.S. person after the grace period ends. In the case of joint owners, a withholding agent may provide a single Form 1042-S made out to the owner whose status the U.S. withholding agent relied upon to determine the applicable rate of withholding. If, however, any one of the owners requests its own Form 1042-S, the withholding agent must furnish a Form 1042-S to the person who requests it. If more than one Form 1042-S is issued for a single payment, the aggregate amount paid and tax withheld that is reported on all Forms 1042-S cannot exceed the total amounts paid to joint owners and the tax withheld thereon.

(B) *Payments to a qualified intermediary, a withholding foreign partnership, or a withholding foreign trust.*—A U.S. withholding agent that makes payments to a qualified intermediary (whether or not the qualified intermediary assumes primary withholding responsibility for purposes of chapter 3 and chapter 4 of the Code), a withholding foreign partnership, or a withholding foreign trust shall complete Forms 1042-S treating the qualified intermediary, withholding foreign partnership, or withholding foreign trust as the recipient. The U.S. withholding agent must complete a separate Form 1042-S for each chapter 3 and chapter 4 withholding rate pool with respect to each qualified intermediary. A qualified intermediary that does not assume primary withholding responsibility on all payments it receives provides information regarding the proportions of income subject to a particular withholding rate (*i.e.*, a chapter 3 withholding rate pool) to the withholding agent on a withholding statement associated with a qualified intermediary withholding certificate. In such a case, the U.S. withholding agent must complete a separate Form 1042-S for each chapter 3 and chapter 4 withholding rate pool with respect to the qualified intermediary. To the extent a qualified intermediary is required to report a payment under chapter 61, it may provide a U.S. withholding agent with information regarding withholding rate pools for U.S. non-exempt recipients (as defined under §1.1441-1(c)(21)). Amounts paid with respect to such withholding rate pools must be reported on a Form 1099 completed for each U.S. non-exempt recipient to the extent such U.S. non-exempt recipient is subject to Form 1099 reporting and is not reported on Form 1042-S. See, however, §1.1441-1(e)(5)(v)(C) for when a qualified intermediary may provide a chapter 4 withholding rate pool of U.S payees (in lieu of reporting such payees on a withholding statement) and for the withholding rate pools (including chapter 4 withholding rate pools) otherwise reportable on a withholding statement provided by a qualified intermediary.

(C) *Amounts paid to U.S. branches treated as U.S. persons.*—A U.S. withholding agent making a payment to a U.S. branch of a foreign person (including a territory financial institution) described in §1.1441-1(b)(2)(iv)(A) shall complete Form 1042-S as follows—

(1) If the branch has provided the U.S. withholding agent with a withholding certificate that evidences its agreement with the withholding agent to be treated as a U.S. person, the U.S. withholding agent files Forms 1042-S treating the U.S. branch or territory financial institution as the recipient;

(2) If the branch has provided the U.S. withholding agent with a withholding certificate that transmits information regarding beneficial owners, qualified intermediaries, withholding foreign partnerships, or other recipients, the U.S. withholding agent must complete a separate Form 1042-S for each recipient whose documentation is associated with the U.S. branch's or territory financial institution's withholding certificate; or

(3) If the U.S. withholding agent cannot reliably associate a payment with a valid withholding certificate from the U.S. branch, it shall treat the U.S. branch as the recipient and report the income as effectively connected with the conduct of a trade or business in the United States except as otherwise provided in §1.1441-1(b)(2)(iv)(B)(4).

(D) *Dual Claims.*—A U.S. withholding agent may make a payment to a foreign entity that is simultaneously claiming a reduced rate of tax on its own behalf for a portion of the payment and a reduced rate on behalf of persons in their capacity as interest holders in that entity on the remaining portion. See § 1.1441-6(b)(2)(iii). If the claims are consistent and the withholding agent accepts the multiple claims, the withholding agent must file a separate Form 1042-S for those payments for which the entity is treated as the beneficial owner and Forms 1042-S for each of the interest holders in the entity for which the interest holder is treated as the recipient. For those payments for which the interest holder in an entity is treated as the recipient, the U.S. withholding agent shall prepare the Form 1042-S in the same manner as a payment made to a nonqualified intermediary or flow-through entity as set forth in paragraph (c)(4)(ii) of this section. If the claims are consistent but the withholding agent has not chosen to accept the multiple claims, or if the claims are inconsistent, the withholding agent must file a separate Form 1042-S for the person or persons it has chosen to treat as the recipients.

(ii) *Payments made by U.S. withholding agents to persons that are not recipients.*—(A) *Amounts paid to a nonqualified intermediary, a flow-through entity, and certain U.S. branches.*—If a U.S. withholding agent makes a payment to a nonqualified intermediary, a flow-through entity, or a U.S. branch (including a territory financial institution) described in § 1.1441-1(b)(2)(iv) (other than a U.S. branch or territory financial institution that is treated as a U.S. person), it must complete a separate Form 1042-S for each recipient to the extent the withholding agent can reliably associate a payment with valid documentation (within the meaning of § 1.1441-1(b)(2)(vii)) from the recipient which is associated with the withholding certificate provided by the nonqualified intermediary, flow-through entity, or U.S. branch or territory financial institution. See § 1.1474-1(d)(4)(i) for when a withholding agent may report a chapter 4 reportable amount made to such an entity in a chapter 4 withholding rate pool. See also § 1.1441-1(e)(3)(iv)(A) for when a withholding statement provided by a nonqualified intermediary may include a chapter 4 withholding rate pool of U.S. payees. If a payment is reported by the withholding agent in a chapter 4 withholding rate pool, the withholding agent must report on Form 1042-S the nonqualified intermediary or flow-through entity as a recipient associated with the applicable chapter 4 withholding rate pool. If a payment is made through tiers of nonqualified intermediaries or flow-through entities, the withholding agent must nevertheless complete Form 1042-S for the recipient to the extent it can reliably associate the payment with documentation from the recipient. A withholding agent that is completing a Form 1042-S for a recipient that receives a payment through a nonqualified intermediary, a flow-through entity, or a U.S. branch or territory financial institution must include on the Form 1042-S the name of the nonqualified intermediary, flow-through entity, U.S. branch or territory financial institution from which the recipient directly receives the payment. If a U.S. withholding agent cannot reliably associate the payment, or any portion of the payment, with valid documentation from a recipient either because no such documentation has been provided or because the nonqualified intermediary, flow-through entity, or U.S. branch or territory financial institution has failed to provide sufficient allocation information so that the withholding agent can associate the payment, or any portion thereof, with valid documentation, then the withholding agent must report the payments as made to an unknown recipient in accordance with the appropriate presumption rules for that payment. Thus, if the payment is not a withholdable payment and under the presumption rules the payment is presumed to be made to a foreign person, the withholding agent must generally withhold 30 percent of the payment and report the payment on Form 1042-S made out to an unknown recipient and shall also include the name of the nonqualified intermediary, flow-through entity, U.S. branch or territory financial institution that received the payment on behalf of the unknown recipient. If, however, the recipient is presumed to be a U.S. nonexempt recipient (as defined in § 1.1441-1(c)(21)), the withholding agent must withhold on the payment as required under section 3406 and report the payment as required under chapter 61 of the Code. See § 1.1474-1(d)(4) for reporting requirements that apply to payments of chapter 4 reportable amounts paid to nonqualified intermediaries and flow-through entities. If, however, the payment is a withholdable payment, the withholding agent must report the payment as made to a chapter 4 withholding rate pool of nonparticipating FFIs in accordance with the presumption rule under § 1.1471-3(f)(5). For a payment to a foreign partnership on the transfer of a publicly traded partnership interest subject to § 1.1446(f)-4(a), see paragraph (c)(1)(ii)(A)(8) of this section (treating the foreign partnership as a recipient).

(B) *Disregarded entities.*—If a U.S. withholding agent makes a payment to a disregarded entity but receives a valid withholding certificate or other documentary evidence from a foreign person that is the single owner of a disregarded entity, the withholding agent must file a Form 1042-S treating the foreign single owner as the recipient. The taxpayer identifying number on the Form 1042-S, if required, must be the foreign single owner's TIN.

(iii) *Reporting by qualified intermediaries, withholding foreign partnerships, and withholding foreign trusts.*—A qualified intermediary, a withholding foreign partnership, and a withholding foreign trust shall report payments on Form 1042-S as provided in their agreements with the IRS and the instructions to the form.

(iv) *Reporting by a nonqualified intermediary, flow-through entity, and certain U.S. branches.*—A nonqualified intermediary, flow-through entity, or U.S. branch (including a territory financial institution) described in § 1.1441-1(e)(2)(iv) (other than a U.S. branch or territory financial institution that is treated as a U.S. person) is a withholding agent and must file Forms 1042-S for amounts paid to recipients in the same manner as a U.S. withholding agent. A Form 1042-S will not be required, however, if another withholding agent has reported the same amount for which the nonqualified intermediary, flow-through entity, or U.S. branch would be required to file a return and the entire amount that should be withheld from such payment has been withheld (including withholding and reporting in accordance with the applicable presumption rule for the payment). A nonqualified intermediary, flow-through entity, or U.S. branch must report payments made to recipients to the extent it has failed to provide the appropriate documentation to another withholding agent together with the information required for that withholding agent to reliably associate the payment with the recipient documentation or to the extent it knows, or has reason to know, that less than the required amount has been withheld. A nonqualified intermediary or flow-through entity that is required to report a payment on Form 1042-S must follow the same rules as apply to a U.S. withholding agent under paragraphs (c)(4)(i) and (ii) of this section.

(v) *Pro rata reporting for allocation failures.*—If a nonqualified intermediary, flow-through entity, or U.S. branch (including a territory financial institution) described in § 1.1441-1(b)(2)(iv) (other than a U.S. branch or territory financial institution treated as a U.S. person) uses the alternative procedures of § 1.1441-1(e)(3)(iv)(D) and fails to provide information sufficient to allocate the amount subject to reporting paid to a withholding rate pool to the payees identified for that pool, then the withholding agent shall report the payment in accordance with the rule provided in § 1.1441-1(e)(3)(iv)(D)(6).

(vi) *Other withholding agents.*—Any person that is a withholding agent not described in paragraph (c)(4)(i), (iii), or (iv) of this section (e.g., a foreign person that is not a qualified intermediary, flow-through entity, or U.S. branch) shall file Form 1042-S in the same manner as a U.S. withholding agent and in accordance with the instructions to the form.

(5) *Magnetic media reporting.*—A withholding agent that makes 250 or more Form 1042-S information returns for a taxable year must file Form 1042-S returns on magnetic media. See, however, § 301.1474-1(a) of this chapter for the requirements for a withholding agent that is a financial institution to file Forms 1042-S on magnetic media. See, also, § 301.6011-2 of this chapter for requirements applicable to a withholding agent that files Forms 1042-S with the IRS on magnetic media and publications of the IRS relating to magnetic media filing.

(d) *Report of taxpayer identifying numbers.*—When so required under procedures that the IRS may prescribe in published guidance (see § 601.601(d)(2) of this chapter), a withholding agent must attach to the Form 1042 a list of all the taxpayer identifying numbers (and corresponding names) that have been furnished to the withholding agent and upon which the withholding agent has relied to grant a reduced rate of withholding and that are not otherwise required to be reported on a Form 1042-S under the provisions of this section.

(e) *Indemnification of withholding agent.*—A withholding agent is indemnified against the claims and demands of any person for the amount of any tax it deducts and withholds in accordance with the provisions of chapter 3 of the Code and the regulations under that chapter. A withholding agent that withholds based on a reasonable belief that such withholding is required under chapter 3 of the Code and the regulations under that chapter is treated for purposes of section 1461 and this paragraph (e) as having withheld tax in accordance with the provisions of chapter 3 of the Code and the regulations under that chapter. In addition, a withholding agent is indemnified against the claims and demands of any person for the amount of any payments made in accordance with the grace period provisions set forth in § 1.1441-1(b)(3)(iv). This paragraph (e) does not apply to relieve a withholding agent from tax liability under chapter 3 of the Code or the regulations under that chapter.

(f) *Amounts paid not constituting gross income.*—Any amount withheld in accordance with § 1.1441-3 shall be reported and paid in accordance with this section, even though the amount paid to the beneficial owner may not constitute gross income in whole or in part. For this purpose, a reference in this section and §1.1461-2 to an amount shall, where appropriate, be deemed to refer to the amount subject to withholding under §1.1441-3.

(g) *Extensions of time to file Forms 1042 and 1042-S.*—The IRS may grant an extension of time in which to file a Form 1042 or a Form 1042-S. Form 2758, Application for Extension of Time to File Certain Excise, Income, Information, and Other Returns (or such other form as the IRS may prescribe), must be used to request an extension of time for a Form 1042. Form 8809, Request for Extension of Time to File Information Returns (or such other form as the IRS may prescribe) must be used to request an extension of time for a Form 1042-S. The request must contain a statement of the reasons for requesting the extension and such other information as the forms or instructions may require. It must be mailed or delivered not later than March 15 of the year following the end of the calendar year for which the return will be filed.

(h) *Penalties.*—For penalties and additions to the tax for failure to file returns or furnish statements in accordance with this section, see sections 6651, 6662, 6663, 6721, 6722, 6723, 6724(c), 7201, 7203, and the regulations under those sections.

(i) *Applicability date.*—This section applies to payments made on or after January 1, 2022. For payments made before January 1, 2022, see this section as in effect and contained in 26 CFR part 1, as revised April 1, 2020. [Reg. §1.1461-1.]

☐ [*T.D.* 6187, 7-5-56. *Amended by T.D.* 6213, 11-20-56; *T.D.* 6908, 12-30-66; *T.D.* 7157, 12-29-71; *T.D.* 7977, 9-19-84; *T.D.* 8734, 10-6-97; *T.D.* 8804, 12-30-98; *T.D.* 8856, 12-29-99; *T.D.* 8881, 5-15-2000 (*corrected* 4-5-2001); *T.D.* 8952, 6-25-2001; *T.D.* 9200, 5-13-2005; *T.D.* 9507, 12-2-2010; *T.D.* 9572, 1-19-2012; *T.D.* 9648, 12-4-2013, *T.D.* 9658, 2-28-2014 (*corrected* 6-3-2014), *T.D.* 9734, 9-17-2015 (*corrected* 12-4-2015), *T.D.* 9808, 12-30-2016, *T.D.* 9815, 1-19-2017 (*corrected* 10-25-2017) *and T.D.* 9926, 11-27-2020.]

### [Reg. §1.1461-2]

**§1.1461-2. Adjustments for overwithholding or underwithholding of tax.**—(a) *Adjustments of overwithheld tax.*—(1) *In general.*—Except as otherwise provided in this paragraph (a)(1), a withholding agent that has overwithheld under chapter 3 of the Internal Revenue Code, and made a deposit of the tax as provided in §1.6302-2(a), may adjust the overwithheld amount either pursuant to the reimbursement procedure described in paragraph (a)(2) of this section or pursuant to the set-off procedure described in paragraph (a)(3) of this section. The rules in the preceding sentence do not apply to partnerships or nominees required to withhold under section 1446(a), other than on a distribution by a publicly traded partnership subject to withholding under §1.1446-4(a) and a payment of an amount realized on the transfer of an interest in a publicly traded partnership subject to §1.1446(f)-4.

(2) *Reimbursement of tax.*—(i) *General rule.*—Under the reimbursement procedure, the withholding agent repays the beneficial owner or payee for the amount of tax overwithheld. In such a case, the withholding agent may reimburse itself by reducing, by the amount of tax actually repaid to the beneficial owner or payee, the amount of any deposit of tax made by the withholding agent under §1.6302-2(a)(1)(iii) for any subsequent payment period occurring before the end of the calendar year following the calendar year of overwithholding. Any such reduction that occurs for a payment period in the calendar year following the calendar year of overwithholding shall be allowed only if—

(A) The repayment to the beneficial owner or payee occurs before the earlier of the due date (not including extensions) for filing Form 1042-S for the calendar year of overwithholding or the date the Form 1042-S is actually filed with the IRS; and

(B) The withholding agent states on a timely filed (not including extensions) Form 1042 for the calendar year of overwithholding, that the filing of the Form 1042 constitutes a claim for credit in accordance with §1.6414-1.

(ii) *Record maintenance.*—If the beneficial owner is repaid an amount of withholding tax under the provisions of this paragraph (a)(2), the withholding agent shall keep as part of its records a receipt showing the date and amount of repayment and the withholding agent must provide a copy of such receipt to the beneficial owner. For this purpose, a canceled check or an entry in a statement is sufficient provided that the check or statement contains a specific notation that it is a refund of tax overwithheld.

(3) *Set-offs.*—Under the set-off procedure, the withholding agent may repay the beneficial owner or payee by applying the amount overwithheld against any amount which otherwise would be required under chapter 3 of the Code or the regulations thereunder to be withheld from income paid by the withholding agent to such person before the earlier of the due date (without regard to extensions) for filing the Form 1042-S for the calendar year of overwithholding or the date that the Form 1042-S is actually filed with the IRS. For purposes of making a return on Form 1042 or 1042-S (or an amended form) for the calendar year of overwithholding and for purposes of making a deposit of the amount withheld, the reduced amount shall be considered the amount required to be withheld from such income under chapter 3 of the Code and the regulations thereunder.

(4) *Examples.*—The principles of this paragraph (a) are illustrated by the following examples:

*Example 1.* (i) N is a nonresident alien individual who is a resident of the United Kingdom. In December 2001, a domestic corporation C pays a dividend of $100 to N, at which time C withholds $30 and remits the balance of $70 to N. On February 10, 2002, prior to the time that C files its Form 1042 and Form 1042-S with respect to the payment, N furnishes a valid Form W-8 described in §1.1441-1(e)(2)(i) upon which C may rely to reduce the rate of withholding to 15% under the provisions of the U.S.-U.K. tax treaty. Consequently, N advises C that its tax liability is only $15 and not $30 and requests reimbursement of $15. Although C has already deposited the $30 that was withheld, as required by §1.6302-2(a)(1)(iv), C repays N in the amount of $15.

(ii) During 2001, C makes no other payments upon which tax is required to be withheld under chapter 3 of the Code; accordingly, its return on Form 1042 for such year, which is filed on March 15, 2002, shows total tax withheld of $30, an adjusted total tax withheld of $15, and $30 previously paid for such year. Pursuant to §1.6414-1(b), C claims a credit for the overpayment of $15 shown on the Form 1042 for 2001. Accordingly, it is permitted to reduce by $15 any deposit required by §1.6302-2 to be made of tax withheld during the calendar year 2002. The Form 1042-S required to be filed by C with respect to the dividend of $100 paid to N in 2001 is required to show tax withheld under chapter 3 of $30 and tax repaid to N of $15.

*Example 2.* The facts are the same as in *Example 1.* In addition, during 2002, C makes payments to N upon which it is required to withhold $200 under chapter 3 of the Code, all of which is withheld in June 2002. Pursuant to §1.6302-2(a)(1)(iii), C deposits the amount of $185 on July 15, 2002 ($200 less the $15 for which credit is claimed on the Form 1042 for 2001). On March 15, 2003, C Corporation files its return on Form 1042 for calendar year 2002, which shows total tax withheld of $200, $185 previously deposited by C, and $15 allowable credit.

*Example 3.* The facts are the same as in *Example 1.* Under §1.6302-2(a)(1)(ii), C is required to deposit on a quarter-monthly basis the tax withheld under chapter 3 of the Code. C withholds tax of $100 between February 8 and February 15, 2002, and deposits $75 [($100 × 90%) less $15] of the withheld tax within 3 banking days after February 15, 2002, and by depositing $10 [($100-$15) less $75] within 3 banking days after March 15, 2002.

(b) *Withholding of additional tax when underwithholding occurs.*—A withholding agent may withhold from future payments (including distributions of effectively connected income subject to withholding under §1.1446-4 and the amount realized from the transfer of an interest in a publicly traded partnership subject to §1.1446(f)-4) made to a beneficial owner the tax that should have been withheld from previous payments to that beneficial owner under chapter 3 of the Code. In the alternative, the withholding agent may satisfy the tax from property that it holds in custody for the beneficial owner or property over which it has control. Such additional withholding or satisfaction of the tax owed may only be made before the date that the Form 1042 is required to be filed (not including extensions) for the calendar year in which the underwithholding occurred. See §1.6302-2 for making deposits of tax or §1.1461-1(a) for making payment of the balance due for a calendar year. See also §§1.1461-1, 1.1461-3, and 1.1446-1 through 1.1446-7 for rules relating to withholding under section 1446.

(c) *Definition.*—For purposes of this section, the term *payment period* means the period for which the withholding agent is required by §1.6302-2(a)(1) to make a deposit of tax withheld under chapter 3 of the Code.

(d) *Applicability date.*—This section applies to payments made on or after January 1, 2022. For payments made before January 1, 2022, see this section as in effect and contained in 26 CFR part 1, as revised April 1, 2020. [Reg. §1.1461-2.]

☐ [*T.D.* 6187, 7-5-56. *Amended by T.D.* 6213, 11-20-56, *T.D.* 6922, 6-16-67, *T.D.* 7157, 12-29-71, *T.D.* 7284, 8-2-73; *T.D.* 7977, 9-19-84; *T.D.* 8734, 10-6-97; *T.D.* 8804, 12-30-98; *T.D.* 8856, 12-29-99; *T.D.* 9200, 5-13-2005, *T.D.* 9658, 2-28-2014, *T.D.* 9808, 12-30-2016 *and T.D.* 9926, 11-27-2020.]

### [Reg. §1.1461-3]

**§1.1461-3. Withholding under section 1446.**—For rules relating to the withholding tax liability of a partnership, nominee, or transferee under section 1446, see §§1.1446-1 through 1.1446-7 and 1.1446(f)-1 through 1.1446(f)-5. For interest, penalties, and additions to the tax for failure to timely pay the tax required to be paid under section 1446, see sections 6601, 6651, 6655 (in the case of publicly traded partnerships, see section 6656), 6672, and 7202 and the regulations under those sections. For additional penalties and additions to such tax for failure to comply with the regulations under section 1446, see sections 6651, 6662, 6663, 6721, 6722, 6723, 6724(c), 7201, 7203, and the regulations under those sections. The references in this section to §§1.1446-1 through 1.1446-7 apply to partnership taxable years beginning after May 18, 2005, or such earlier time as the regulations under §§1.1446-1 through 1.1446-5 apply by reason of an election under §1.1446-7, and the references in this section to §§1.1446(f)-1 through 1.1446(f)-5 shall apply with respect to returns for transfers that occur on or after January 29, 2021. [Reg. §1.1461-3.]

☐ [*T.D. 9200, 5-13-2005. Amended by T.D. 9926, 11-27-2020.*]

### [Reg. §1.1462-1]

**§1.1462-1. Withheld tax as credit to recipient of income.**— (a) *Creditable tax.*—The entire amount of the income from which the tax is required to be withheld (including amounts calculated under the gross-up formula in §1.1441-3(f)(1)) shall be included in gross income in the return required to be made by the beneficial owner of the income, without deduction for the amount required to be or actually withheld, but the amount of tax actually withheld shall be allowed as a credit against the total income tax computed in the beneficial owner's return.

(b) *Amounts paid to persons who are not the beneficial owner.*— Amounts withheld at source under chapter 3 of the Internal Revenue Code on payments to (or effectively connected taxable income allocable to) a fiduciary, partnership, or intermediary are deemed to have been paid by the taxpayer ultimately liable for the tax upon such income. Thus, for example, if a beneficiary of a trust is subject to the taxes imposed by section 1, 2, 3, or 11 upon any portion of the income received from a foreign trust, the part of any amount withheld at source which is properly allocable to the income so taxed to such beneficiary shall be credited against the amount of the income tax computed upon the beneficiary's return, and any excess shall be refunded. See §1.1446-3 for examples applying this rule in the context of a partnership interest held by a foreign trust or estate. Further, if a partnership withholds an amount under chapter 3 of the Internal Revenue Code with respect to the allocable share of a partner that is a partnership (upper-tier partnership) or with respect to the allocable share of partners in an upper-tier partnership, such amount is deemed to have been withheld by the upper-tier partnership. See §1.1446-5 for rules applicable to tiered partnership structures. References in this paragraph (b) to withholding under section 1446 shall apply to partnership taxable years beginning after May 18, 2005, or such earlier time as the regulations under §§1.1446-1 through 1.1446-5 apply by reason of an election under §1.1446-7.

(c) *Effective date.*—Unless otherwise provided in this section, this section applies to payments made after December 31, 2000. [Reg. §1.1462-1.]

☐ [*T.D. 6187, 7-5-56. Amended by T.D. 7977, 9-19-84; T.D. 8734, 10-6-97; T.D. 8804, 12-30-98; T.D. 8856, 12-29-99 and T.D. 9200, 5-13-2005.*]

### [Reg. §1.1463-1]

**§1.1463-1. Tax paid by recipient of income.**—(a) *Tax paid.*—If the tax required to be withheld under chapter 3 of the Internal Revenue Code is paid by the beneficial owner of the income or by the withholding agent, it shall not be re-collected from the other, regardless of the original liability therefor. However, this section does not relieve the person that did not withhold tax from liability for interest or any penalties or additions to tax otherwise applicable. See §1.1441-7(b) for additional applicable rules. See §§1.1446-3(e) and (f) and 1.1446(f)-5(a) for application of the rule of this paragraph (a), and for additional rules, in which the withholding tax was required to be paid under section 1446. The references in the previous sentence to §1.1446-3(e) and (f) apply to partnership taxable years beginning after May 18, 2005, or such earlier time as the regulations under §§1.1446-1 through 1.1446-5 apply by reason of an election under §1.1446-7, and the reference in the previous sentence to §1.1446(f)-5(a) shall apply to the tax required to be withheld under section 1446(f) for transfers that occur on or after January 29, 2021.

(b) *Effective date.*—Unless otherwise provided in this section, this section applies to failures to withhold occurring after December 31, 2000. [Reg. §1.1463-1.]

☐ [*T.D. 6187, 7-5-56. Amended by T.D. 8734, 10-6-97; T.D. 8804, 12-30-98; T.D. 8856, 12-29-99, T.D. 9200, 5-13-2005 and T.D. 9926, 11-27-2020.*]

### [Reg. §1.1464-1]

**§1.1464-1. Refunds or credits.**—(a) *In general.*—The refund or credit under chapter 65 of the Code of an overpayment of tax which has actually been withheld at the source under chapter 3 of the Code shall be made to the taxpayer from whose income the amount of such tax was in fact withheld. To the extent that the overpayment under chapter 3 was not in fact withheld at the source, but was paid, by the withholding agent the refund or credit under chapter 65 of the overpayment shall be made to the withholding agent. Thus, where a debtor corporation assumes liability pursuant to its tax-free covenant for the tax required to be withheld under chapter 3 upon interest and pays the tax in behalf of its bondholder, and it can be shown that the bondholder is not in fact liable for any tax, the overpayment of tax shall be credited or refunded to the withholding agent in accordance with chapter 65 since the tax was not actually deducted and withheld from the interest paid to the bondholder. In further illustration, where a withholding agent who is required by chapter 3 to withhold $300 tax from rents paid to a nonresident alien individual mistakenly withholds $320 and mistakenly pays $350 as internal revenue tax, the amount of $30 shall be credited or refunded to the withholding agent in accordance with chapter 65 and the amount of $20 shall be credited or refunded in accordance with such chapter to the person from whose income such amount has been withheld. With respect to section 1446(a), this section applies only to a publicly traded partnership or nominee described in §1.1446-4 and, with respect to section 1446(f), only to a publicly traded partnership or broker described in §1.1446(f)-4.

(b) *Tax repaid to payee.*—For purposes of this section and §1.6414-1, any amount of tax withheld under chapter 3 of the Code, which, pursuant to paragraph (a)(1) of §1.1461-2, is repaid by the withholding agent to the person from whose income such amount was erroneously withheld shall be considered as tax which, within the meaning of sections 1464 and 6414, was not actually withheld by the withholding agent.

(c) *Applicability date.*—The last sentence of paragraph (a) of this section applies to nominees and publicly traded partnerships described in §1.1446-4 for partnership taxable years beginning after April 29, 2008, and to brokers required to withhold and publicly traded partnerships liable for underwithholding under §1.1446(f)-4 on transfers that occur on or after January 1, 2022. [Reg. §1.1464-1.]

☐ [*T.D. 6187, 7-5-56. Amended by T.D. 6922, 6-16-67; T.D. 8804, 12-30-98, T.D. 9394, 4-28-2008 (corrected 4-1-2009) and T.D. 9926, 11-27-2020.*]

### [Reg. §1.1471-0]

**§1.1471-0. Outline of regulation provisions for sections 1471 through 1474.**—This section lists the table of contents for §§1.1471-1 through 1.1474-7 and §301.1474-1 of this chapter.

*§1.1471-1 Scope of chapter 4 and definitions.*

(a) Scope of chapter 4 of the Internal Revenue Code.

(b) Definitions.

  (1) Account.
  (2) Account holder.
  (3) Active NFFE.
  (4) AML due diligence.
  (5) Annuity contract.
  (6) Assumes primary withholding responsibility.
  (7) Backup withholding.
  (8) Beneficial owner.
  (9) Blocked account.
  (10) Branch.
  (11) Broker.
  (12) Cash value.
  (13) Cash value insurance contract.
  (14) Certified deemed-compliant FFI.
  (15) Change in circumstances.
  (16) Chapter 3.
  (17) Chapter 4.
  (18) Chapter 4 reportable amount.
  (19) Chapter 4 status.
  (20) Chapter 4 withholding rate pool.
  (21) Clearing organization.
  (22) Complex trust.
  (23) Consolidated obligations.
  (24) Custodial account.
  (25) Custodial institution.
  (26) Customer master file.

(27) Deemed-compliant FFI.
(28) Deferred annuity contract.
(29) Depository account.
(30) Depository institution.
(31) Direct reporting NFFE.
(32) Documentary evidence.
(33) Documentation.
(34) Dormant account.
(35) Effective date of the FFI agreement.
(36) EIN.
(37) Election to be withheld upon.
(38) Electronically searchable information.
(39) Entity.
(40) Entity account.
(41) Excepted NFFE.
(42) Exempt beneficial owner.
(43) Exempt recipient.
(44) Expanded affiliated group.
(45) FATF.
(46) FATF-compliant jurisdiction.
(47) FFI.
(48) FFI agreement.
(49) Financial account.
(50) Financial institution.
(51) Flow-through entity.
(52) Flow-through withholding certificate.
(53) Foreign entity.
(54) Foreign passthru payment.
(55) Foreign payee.
(56) Foreign person.
(57) GIIN.
(58) Grandfathered obligation.
(59) Grantor trust.
(60) Gross proceeds.
(61) Group annuity contract.
(62) Group insurance contract.
(63) Immediate annuity.
(64) Individual account.
(65) Insurance company.
(66) Insurance contract.
(67) Intergovernmental agreement (IGA).
(68) Intermediary.
(69) Intermediary withholding certificate.
(70) Investment entity.
(71) Investment-linked annuity contract.
(72) Investment-linked insurance contract.
(73) IRS FFI list.
(74) Life annuity contract.
(75) Life insurance contract.
(76) Limited branch.
(77) Limited FFI.
(78) Model 1 IGA.
(79) Model 2 IGA.
(80) NFFE.
(81) Non-exempt recipient.
(82) Nonparticipating FFI.
(83) Nonreporting IGA FFI.
(84) Non-U.S. account.
(85) NQI.
(86) NWP.
(87) NWT.
(88) Offshore obligation.
(89) Owner.
(90) Owner-documented FFI.
(91) Participating FFI.
(92) Participating FFI group.
(93) Partnership.
(94) Passive NFFE.
(95) Passthru payment.
(96) Payee.
(97) Payment with respect to an offshore obligation.
(98) Payor.
(99) Permanent residence address.
(100) Person.
(101) Preexisting account.
(102) Preexisting entity account.
(103) Preexisting individual account.
(104) Preexisting obligation.
(105) Pre-FATCA Form W-8.

(106) Prima facie FFI.
(107) QI.
(108) QI agreement.
(109) QI branch of a U.S. financial institution.
(110) Recalcitrant account holder.
(111) Registered deemed-compliant FFI.
(112) Relationship manager.
(113) Reportable payment.
(114) Reporting Model 1 FFI.
(115) Reporting Model 2 FFI.
(116) Responsible officer.
(117) Restricted distributor.
(118) Simple trust.
(119) Specified insurance company.
(120) Specified U.S. person.
(121) Sponsored FFI.
(122) Sponsored FFI group.
(123) Sponsored direct reporting NFFE.
(124) Sponsoring entity.
(125) Standardized industry coding system.
(126) Standing instructions to pay amounts.
(127) Subject to withholding.
(128) Substantial U.S. owner.
(129) Territory entity.
(130) Territory financial institution.
(131) Territory financial institution treated as a U.S. person.
(132) Territory NFFE.
(133) TIN.
(134) U.S. account.
(135) U.S. branch treated as a U.S. person.
(136) U.S. financial institution.
(137) U.S. indicia.
(138) U.S. owned foreign entity.
(139) U.S. payee.
(140) U.S. payor.
(141) U.S. person.
(142) U.S. source FDAP income.
(143) U.S. territory.
(144) U.S. withholding agent.
(145) Withholdable payment.
(146) Withholding.
(147) Withholding agent.
(148) Withholding certificate.
(149) WP.
(150) Written statement.
(151) WT.
(c) Effective/applicability date.

§1.1471-2 *Requirement to deduct and withhold tax on withholdable payments to certain FFIs.*
(a) Requirement to withhold on payments to FFIs.
(1) General rule of withholding.
(2) Special withholding rules.
(i) Requirement to withhold on payments of U.S. source FDAP income to participating FFIs and deemed-compliant FFIs that are NQIs, NWPs, or NWTs, and U.S. branches acting as intermediaries.
(ii) Residual withholding responsibility of intermediaries and flow-through entities.
(iii) Requirement to withhold if a participating FFI or registered deemed-compliant FFI makes an election to be withheld upon.
(A) Election to be withheld upon for U.S. source FDAP income.
(B) Election to be withheld upon for gross proceeds.
(iv) Withholding obligation of a territory financial institution.
(v) Withholding obligation of a foreign branch of a U.S. financial institution.
(vi) Payments of gross proceeds.
(3) Coordination of withholding under sections 1471(a) and (b).
(4) Payments for which no withholding is required.
(i) Exception to withholding if the withholding agent lacks control, custody, or knowledge.
(A) In general.
(B) Example.
(ii) Exception to withholding for certain payments made prior to July 1, 2016 (transitional).
(iii) Payments to a participating FFI.
(iv) Payments to a deemed-compliant FFI.
(v) Payments to an exempt beneficial owner.
(vi) Payments to a territory financial institution.

(vii) Payments to an account held with a clearing organization with FATCA-compliant membership.

(viii) Payments to certain excepted accounts.

(5) Withholding requirements if source or character of payment is unknown.

(b) Grandfathered obligations.

(1) Grandfathered treatment of outstanding obligations.

(2) Definitions.

(i) Grandfathered obligation.

(ii) Obligation.

(iii) Date outstanding.

(iv) Material modification.

(3) Application to flow-through entities.

(i) Partnerships.

(ii) Simple trusts.

(iii) Grantor trusts.

(4) Determination by withholding agent of grandfathered treatment.

(i) In general.

(ii) Determination of material modification.

(iii) Record retention.

(c) Effective/applicability date.

§1.1471-3 *Identification of payee.*

(a) Payee defined.

(1) In general.

(2) Payee with respect to a financial account.

(3) Exceptions.

(i) Certain foreign agents or intermediaries.

(ii) Foreign flow-through entity.

(iii) U.S. intermediary or agent of a foreign person.

(iv) Territory financial institution.

(v) Disregarded entity or limited branch.

(vi) U.S. branch of treated as a U.S. person.

(vii) Foreign branch of a U.S. person.

(b) Determination of payee's status.

(1) Determining whether a payment is received by an intermediary.

(2) Determination of entity type.

(3) Determination of whether the payment is made to a QI, WP, or WT.

(4) Determination of whether the payee is receiving effectively connected income.

(c) Rules for reliably associating a payment with a withholding certificate or other appropriate documentation.

(1) In general.

(2) Reliably associating a payment with documentation if a payment is made through an intermediary or flow-through entity that is not the payee.

(i) In general.

(ii) Exception to entity account documentation rules for an offshore account of an intermediary or flow-through entity.

(3) Requirements for validity of certificates.

(i) Form W-9.

(ii) Beneficial owner withholding certificate (Form W-8BEN).

(iii) Withholding certificate of an intermediary, flow-through entity, or U.S. branch (Form W-8IMY).

(A) In general.

(B) Withholding statement.

(1) In general.

(2) Special requirements for an FFI withholding statement.

(3) Special requirements for a chapter 4 withholding statement.

(4) Special requirements for an exempt beneficial owner withholding statement.

(5) Nonqualified intermediary withholding statement.

(C) Failure to provide allocation information.

(D) Special rules applicable to a withholding certificate of a QI that assumes primary withholding responsibility under chapter 3.

(E) Special rules applicable to a withholding certificate of a QI that does not assume primary withholding responsibility under chapter 3.

(F) Special rules applicable to a withholding certificate of a territory financial institution that agrees to be treated as a U.S. person.

(G) Special rules applicable to a withholding certificate of a territory financial institution that does not agree to be treated as a U.S. person.

(H) Rules applicable to a withholding certificate of a U.S. branch.

(iv) Certificate for exempt status (Form W-8EXP).

(v) Certificate for effectively connected income (Form W-8ECI).

(4) Requirements for written statements.

(5) Requirements for documentary evidence.

(i) Foreign status.

(A) Certificate of residence.

(B) Individual government identification.

(C) QI documentation.

(D) Entity government documentation.

(E) Third-party credit report.

(ii) Chapter 4 status.

(A) General documentary evidence.

(B) Preexisting obligation documentary evidence.

(C) Payee-specific documentary evidence.

(6) Applicable rules for withholding certificates, written statements, and documentary evidence.

(i) Who may sign the withholding certificate or written statement.

(ii) Period of validity.

(A) General rule.

(B) Indefinite validity.

(C) Indefinite validity in the case of certain offshore obligations.

(D) Exception for certificate for effectively connected income.

(E) Change in circumstances.

(1) Defined.

(2) Obligation to notify withholding agent of a change in circumstances.

(3) Withholding agent's obligation with respect to a change in circumstances.

(iii) Record retention.

(A) In general.

(B) Exception for documentary evidence received with respect to offshore obligations.

(iv) Electronic transmission of withholding certificate, written statement, and documentary evidence.

(v) Acceptable substitute withholding certificate.

(A) In general.

(B) Non-IRS form for individuals.

(vi) Electronic confirmation of TIN on withholding certificate.

(vii) Reliance on a prior version of a withholding certificate.

(7) Curing documentation errors.

(i) Curing inconsequential errors on a withholding certificate.

(ii) Documentation received after the time of payment.

(8) Documentation furnished on account-by-account basis unless exception provided for sharing documentation within expanded affiliated group.

(i) Single branch systems.

(ii) Universal account systems.

(iii) Shared account systems.

(iv) Document sharing for gross proceeds.

(v) Preexisting account.

(9) Reliance on documentation collected by or certifications provided by other persons.

(i) Shared documentation system maintained by an agent.

(ii) Third-party data providers.

(iii) Reliance on certification provided by introducing brokers.

(iv) Reliance on documentation and certifications provided between principals and agents.

(A) In general.

(B) Reliance upon certification of the principal.

(C) Document sharing.

(D) Examples.

(v) Reliance upon documentation for accounts acquired in merger or bulk acquisition for value.

(d) Documentation requirements to establish payee's chapter 4 status.

(1) Reliance on pre-FATCA Form W-8.

(2) Identification of U.S. persons.

(i) In general.

(ii) Reliance on documentary evidence.

(iii) Preexisting obligations.

(3) Identification of individuals that are foreign persons.

(i) In general.

(ii) Exception for offshore obligations.

(4) Identification of participating FFIs and registered deemed-compliant FFIs.

(i) In general.

(ii) Exception for payments made prior to January 1, 2017, with respect to preexisting obligations (transitional).

(iii) Exception for offshore obligations.

(iv) Exceptions for payments to reporting Model 1 FFIs.

(v) Reason to know.

(vi) Sponsored investment entities and sponsored controlled foreign corporations.

(A) In general.

(B) Payments made prior to January 1, 2017 (transitional).

(C) Payments made after December 31, 2016, to payees documented prior to January 1, 2017.

(5) Identification of certified deemed-compliant FFIs.

(i) In general.

(ii) Sponsored, closely-held investment vehicles.

(A) In general.

(B) Offshore obligations.

(iii) Certain investment entities that do not maintain financial accounts.

(A) In general.

(B) Offshore obligations.

(6) Identification of owner-documented FFIs.

(i) In general.

(ii) Auditor's letter substitute.

(iii) Documentation for owners and debt holders of payee.

(iv) Content of FFI owner reporting statement.

(v) Exception for preexisting obligations (transitional).

(vi) Exception for offshore obligations.

(vii) Exception for certain offshore obligations of $1,000,000 or less.

(7) Nonreporting IGA FFIs.

(i) In general.

(ii) Exception for offshore obligations.

(8) Identification of nonparticipating FFIs.

(i) In general.

(ii) Special documentation rules for payments made to an exempt beneficial owner through a nonparticipating FFI.

(9) Identification of exempt beneficial owners.

(i) Identification of foreign governments, governments of U.S. territories, international organizations, and foreign central banks of issue.

(A) In general.

(B) Exception for offshore obligations.

(C) Exception for preexisting offshore obligations.

(ii) Identification of retirement funds.

(A) In general.

(B) Exception for offshore obligations.

(C) Exception for preexisting offshore obligations.

(iii) Identification of entities wholly owned by exempt beneficial owners.

(10) Identification of territory financial institutions.

(i) Identification of territory financial institutions that are beneficial owners.

(A) In general.

(B) Exception for preexisting offshore obligations.

(ii) Identification of territory financial institutions acting as intermediaries or that are flow-through entities.

(iii) Reason to know.

(11) Identification of excepted NFFEs.

(i) Identification of excepted nonfinancial group entities.

(A) In general.

(B) Exception for offshore obligations.

(ii) Identification of excepted nonfinancial start-up companies.

(A) In general.

(B) Exception for offshore obligations.

(C) Exception for preexisting offshore obligations.

(iii) Identification of excepted nonfinancial entities in liquidation or bankruptcy.

(A) In general.

(B) Exception for offshore obligations.

(C) Exception for preexisting offshore obligations.

(iv) Identification of section 501(c) organizations.

(A) In general.

(B) Reason to know.

(v) Identification of non-profit organizations.

(A) In general.

(B) Exception for offshore obligations.

(C) Exception for preexisting offshore obligations.

(D) Reason to know.

(vi) Identification of NFFEs that are publicly traded corporations.

(A) Exception for offshore obligations.

(B) Exception for preexisting offshore obligations.

(vii) Identification of NFFE affiliates.

(A) Exception for offshore obligations.

(B) Exception for preexisting offshore obligations.

(viii) Identification of excepted territory NFFEs.

(A) Exception for payments made prior to January 1, 2017, with respect to preexisting obligations of $1,000,000 or less (transitional).

(B) Exception for offshore obligations.

(C) Exception for preexisting offshore obligations of $1,000,000 or less.

(ix) Identification of active NFFEs.

(A) Exception for offshore obligations.

(B) Exception for preexisting offshore obligations.

(C) Limit on reason to know.

(x) Identifying a direct reporting NFFE (other than a sponsored direct reporting NFFE).

(A) In general.

(B) Exception for offshore obligations.

(C) Special rule for preexisting offshore obligations.

(xi) Identifying a sponsored direct reporting NFFE.

(A) In general.

(1) Payments made prior to January 1, 2017 (transitional).

(2) Payments made after December 31, 2016, to payees documented prior to January 1, 2017.

(B) Exception for offshore obligations.

(xii) Identification of excepted inter-affiliate FFI.

(A) In general.

(B) Offshore obligations.

(C) Reason to know.

(12) Identification of passive NFFEs.

(i) Exception for offshore obligations.

(ii) Special rule for preexisting offshore obligations.

(iii) Required owner certification for passive NFFEs.

(A) In general.

(B) Exception for preexisting obligations of $1,000,000 or less (transitional).

(e) Standards of knowledge.

(1) In general.

(2) Notification by the IRS.

(3) GIIN verification.

(i) In general.

(ii) Special rules for reporting Model 1 FFIs.

(iii) Special rules for direct reporting NFFEs.

(iv) Special rules for sponsored direct reporting NFFEs and sponsoring entities.

(A) Sponsored direct reporting NFFEs.

(B) Sponsoring entities (transitional).

(4) Reason to know.

(i) Reason to know regarding an entity's chapter 4 status.

(ii) Reason to know applicable to withholding certificates.

(A) In general.

(B) Withholding certificate provided by an FFI.

(iii) Reason to know applicable to written statements.

(iv) Reason to know applicable to documentary evidence.

(A) In general.

(B) Standards of knowledge applicable to certain types of documentary evidence.

(v) Specific standards of knowledge applicable when only documentary evidence is a code or classification described in paragraph (c)(5)(ii)(B) of this section.

(A) U.S. indicia for entities.

(B) Documentation required to cure U.S. indicia.

(vi) Specific standards of knowledge applicable to documentation received from intermediaries and flow-through entities.

(A) In general.

(B) Limits on reason to know with respect to documentation received from participating FFIs and registered deemed-compliant FFIs that are intermediaries or flow-through entities.

(vii) Limits on reason to know.

(A) Scope of review for preexisting obligations of entities.

(B) Reason to know there are U.S. indicia associated with preexisting obligations.

(C) Reason to know there are U.S. indicia associated with preexisting offshore obligations.

(D) Limits on reason to know for multiple obligations belonging to a single person.

(viii) Reasonable explanation supporting claim of foreign status.

(5) Conduit financing arrangements.

(6) Additional guidance.

(f) Presumptions regarding chapter 4 status of the person receiving the payment in the absence of documentation.

(1) In general.

(2) Presumptions of classification as an individual or entity and entity as the beneficial owner.

(3) Presumptions of U.S. or foreign status.

(4) Presumption of chapter 4 status for a foreign entity.

(5) Presumption of chapter 4 status of payee with respect to a payment to an intermediary or flow-through entity.

(6) Presumption of effectively connected income for payments to certain U.S. branches.

(7) Joint payees.

(i) In general.

(ii) Exception for offshore obligations.

(8) Rebuttal of presumptions.

(9) Effect of reliance on presumptions and of actual knowledge or reason to know otherwise.

(i) In general.

(ii) Actual knowledge or reason to know that amount of withholding is greater than is required under the presumptions or that reporting of the payment is required.

(g) Effective/applicability date.

**§ 1.1471-4 FFI agreement.**

(a) In general.

(1) Withholding.

(2) Identification and documentation of account holders.

(3) Reporting.

(4) Expanded affiliated group.

(5) Verification.

(6) Event of default.

(7) Refunds.

(b) Withholding requirements.

(1) In general.

(2) Withholding determination.

(3) Satisfaction of withholding requirements.

(i) In general.

(ii) Withholding not required.

(iii) Election to withhold under section 3406.

(4) Foreign passthru payments.

(5) Withholding on limited FFIs and limited branches.

(i) Limited FFIs.

(ii) Limited branches.

(6) Special rule for dormant accounts.

(7) Withholding requirements for U.S. branches of FFIs treated as U.S. persons.

(c) Due diligence for the identification and documentation of account holders and payees.

(1) Scope of paragraph.

(2) General rules for the identification and documentation of account holders and payees.

(i) Overview.

(ii) Standards of knowledge.

(A) In general.

(B) Limits on reason to know with respect to certain accounts acquired in merger of bulk acquisition.

(1) In general.

(2) Participating FFIs and certain deemed-compliant FFIs that apply the due diligence rules, and U.S. financial institutions.

(iii) Change in circumstances.

(A) Obligation to identify a change in circumstances.

(B) Definition of change in circumstances.

(C) Requirements following a change in circumstances.

(iv) Record retention.

(v) Documentation rules for U.S. branches of FFIs that are treated as U.S. persons.

(3) Identification and documentation procedure for entity accounts and payees.

(i) In general.

(ii) Timeframe for applying identification and documentation procedure for entity accounts and payees.

(iii) Documentation exception for certain preexisting entity accounts.

(A) Accounts to which this exception applies.

(B) Aggregation of entity accounts.

(C) Election to forgo exception.

(4) Identification and documentation procedure for individual accounts other than preexisting accounts.

(i) In general.

(ii) Reliance on third-party for identification of individual accounts other than preexisting accounts.

(iii) Alternative identification and documentation procedure for certain cash value insurance or annuity contracts.

(A) Group cash value insurance contracts or group annuity contracts.

(B) Accounts held by beneficiaries of a cash value insurance contract that is a life insurance contract.

(5) Identification and documentation procedure for preexisting individual accounts.

(i) In general.

(ii) Special rule for preexisting individual accounts previously documented as U.S. accounts for purposes of chapter 3 or 61.

(iii) Exceptions for certain low value preexisting individual accounts.

(A) Accounts to which an exception applies.

(B) Aggregation of accounts.

(C) Election to forgo exception.

(iv) Specific identification and documentation procedures for preexisting individual accounts.

(A) In general.

(B) U.S. indicia and relevant documentation rules.

(1) U.S. indicia.

(2) Documentation to be retained upon identifying U.S. indicia.

(i) Designation of account holder as a U.S. citizen or resident.

(ii) Unambiguous indication of a U.S. place of birth.

(iii) U.S. address or U.S. mailing address.

(iv) Only U.S. telephone numbers.

(v) U.S. telephone numbers and non-U.S. telephone numbers.

(vi) Standing instructions to pay amounts.

(vii) Power of attorney or signatory authority granted to a person with a U.S. address or "in-care-of" address or "hold mail" address.

(C) Electronic search for identifying U.S. indicia.

(D) Enhanced review for identifying U.S. indicia in the case of certain high-value accounts.

(1) In general.

(2) Relationship manager inquiry.

(3) Additional review of non-electronic records.

(4) Limitations on the enhanced review in the case of comprehensive electronically searchable information.

(E) Exception for preexisting individual accounts previously documented as held by foreign individuals.

(6) Examples.

(7) Certifications of responsible officer.

(d) Account reporting.

(1) Scope of paragraph.

(2) Reporting requirements in general.

(i) Accounts subject to reporting.

(ii) Financial institution required to report an account.

(A) In general.

(B) Special reporting of account holders of territory financial institutions.

(C) Special reporting of account holders of a sponsored FFI.

(D) Special reporting of accounts held by owner-documented FFIs.

(E) Requirement to identify the GIIN of a branch that maintains an account.

(F) Reporting by participating FFIs and registered deemed-compliant FFIs (including QIs, WPs, WTs, and certain U.S. branches not treated as U.S. persons) for accounts of nonparticipating FFIs (transitional).

(G) Combined reporting on Form 8966 following merger or bulk acquisition.

(iii) Special U.S. account reporting rules for U.S. payors.

(A) Special reporting rule for U.S. payors other than U.S. branches.

(B) Special reporting rules for U.S. branches treated as U.S. persons.

(C) Rules for U.S. branches of FFIs not treated as U.S. persons.

(3) Reporting of accounts under section 1471(c)(1).

(i) In general.

(ii) Accounts held by specified U.S. persons.

(iii) Accounts held by U.S. owned foreign entities.

(iv) Special reporting of accounts held by owner-documented FFIs.
(v) Form for reporting accounts under section 1471(c)(1).
(vi) Time and manner of filing.
(vii) Extensions in filing.
(4) Descriptions applicable to reporting requirements of § 1.1471-4(d)(3).
(i) Address.
(ii) Account number.
(iii) Account balance or value.
(A) In general.
(B) Currency translation of account balance or value.
(iv) Payments made with respect to an account.
(A) Depository accounts.
(B) Custodial accounts.
(C) Other accounts.
(D) Transfers and closings of deposit, custodial, insurance, and annuity financial accounts.
(E) Amount and character of payments subject to reporting.
(F) Currency translation.
(v) Record retention requirements.
(5) Election to perform chapter 61 reporting.
(i) In general.
(A) Election under section 1471(c)(2).
(B) Election to report in a manner similar to section 6047(d).
(ii) Additional information to be reported.
(iii) Special reporting of accounts held by owner-documented FFIs.
(iv) Branch reporting.
(v) Time and manner of making the election.
(vi) Revocation of election.
(vii) Filing of information under election.
(6) Reporting on recalcitrant account holders.
(i) In general.
(ii) Definition of dormant account.
(iii) End of dormancy.
(iv) Forms.
(v) Time and manner of filing.
(vi) Extensions in filing.
(vii) Record retention requirements.
(7) Special reporting rules with respect to the 2014 and 2015 calendar years.
(i) In general.
(ii) Participating FFIs that report under § 1.1471-4(d)(3).
(A) Reporting with respect to the 2014 calendar year.
(B) Reporting with respect to the 2015 calendar year.
(iii) Participating FFIs that report under § 1.1471-4(d)(5).
(iv) Forms for reporting.
(A) In general.
(B) Special determination date and timing for reporting with respect to the 2014 calendar year.
(8) Reporting requirements of QIs, WPs and WTs.
(9) Examples.
(e) Expanded affiliated group requirements.
(1) In general.
(2) Limited branches.
(i) In general.
(ii) Branch defined.
(iii) Limited branch defined.
(iv) Conditions for limited branch status.
(v) Term of limited branch status (transitional).
(vi) Exception from restriction on opening U.S. accounts and nonparticipating FFI accounts.
(3) Limited FFI.
(i) In general.
(ii) Limited FFI defined.
(iii) Conditions for limited FFI status.
(iv) Period for limited FFI status (transitional).
(v) Exception from registration requirement.
(A) Conditions for exception.
(B) Confirmation requirements of lead FI.
(vi) Exception from restriction on opening U.S. accounts and nonparticipating FFI accounts.
(4) Special rule for QIs.
(f) Verification.
(1) In general.
(2) Compliance program.
(i) In general.
(ii) Consolidated compliance program.
(A) In general.

(B) Requirements of compliance FI.
(1) Periodic certification.
(i) In general.
(ii) Late-joining electing FFIs.
(2) Preexisting account certification.
(3) Certification of compliance.
(i) In general.
(ii) Certification of effective internal controls.
(iii) Qualified certification.
(iv) Material failures defined.
(4) IRS review of compliance.
(i) General inquiries.
(ii) Inquiries regarding substantial non-compliance.
(g) Event of default.
(1) Defined.
(2) Notice of event of default.
(3) Remediation of event of default.
(h) Collective credit or refund procedures for overpayments.
(1) In general.
(2) Persons for which a collective refund is not permitted.
(3) Payments for which a collective refund is permitted.
(4) Procedural and other requirements for collective refund.
(i) Legal prohibitions on reporting U.S. accounts and withholding.
(1) In general.
(2) Requesting waiver or closure of a U.S. account.
(i) In general.
(ii) Valid and effective waiver for a U.S. account.
(iii) Closure or transfer of U.S. account.
(3) Legal prohibitions preventing withholding.
(i) In general.
(ii) Block or transfer accounts or obligations.
(j) Effective/applicability date.
(1) In general.
(2) Special applicability date.
**§ 1.1471-5 Definitions applicable to section 1471.**
(a) U.S. accounts.
(1) In general.
(2) Definition of U.S. account.
(3) Account holder.
(i) In general.
(ii) Financial accounts held by agents that are not financial institutions.
(iii) Jointly held accounts.
(iv) Account holder for insurance and annuity contracts.
(v) Examples.
(4) Exceptions to U.S. account status.
(i) Exception for certain individual accounts of participating FFIs.
(ii) Election to forgo exception.
(iii) Example.
(b) Financial accounts.
(1) In general.
(i) Depository account.
(ii) Custodial account.
(iii) Equity or debt interest.
(A) Equity or debt interests in an investment entity.
(B) Certain equity or debt interests in a holding company or treasury center.
(C) Equity or debt interests in other financial institutions.
(iv) Insurance and annuity contracts.
(2) Exceptions.
(i) Certain savings accounts.
(A) Retirement and pension accounts.
(B) Non-retirement savings accounts.
(C) Rollovers.
(D) Coordination with section 6038D.
(E) Account that is tax-favored.
(ii) Certain term life insurance contracts.
(iii) Account held by an estate.
(iv) Certain escrow accounts.
(v) Certain annuity contracts.
(vi) Account or product excluded under an intergovernmental agreement.
(3) Definitions.
(i) Depository account.
(A) In general.
(B) Exceptions.
(ii) Custodial account.
(iii) Equity interest in certain entities.

(A) Partnership.

(B) Trust.

(iv) Regularly traded on an established securities market.

(v) Value of interest determined, directly or indirectly, primarily by reference to assets that give rise (or could give rise) to withholdable payments.

(A) Equity interest.

(B) Debt interest.

(vi) Return earned on the interest (including upon a sale, exchange, or redemption) determined, directly or indirectly, primarily by reference to one or more investment entities or passive NFFEs.

(A) Equity interest.

(B) Debt interest.

(vii) Cash value insurance contract.

(A) In general.

(B) Cash value.

(C) Amounts excluded from cash value.

(D) Policyholder dividend.

(4) Account balance or value.

(i) In general.

(ii) Special rule for immediate annuity.

(A) Immediate annuities without minimum benefit guarantees.

(B) Immediate annuities with a minimum benefit guarantee.

(C) Net present value of amounts payable in future periods.

(iii) Account aggregation requirements.

(A) In general.

(B) Aggregation rule for relationship managers.

(C) Examples.

(iv) Currency translation of balance or value.

(5) Account maintained by financial institution.

(c) U.S. owned foreign entity.

(d) Definition of FFI.

(e) Definition of financial institution.

(1) In general.

(2) Banking or similar business.

(i) In general.

(ii) Exception for certain lessors and lenders.

(iii) Application of section 581.

(iv) Effect of local regulation.

(3) Holding financial assets for others as a substantial portion of its business.

(i) Substantial portion.

(A) In general.

(B) Special rule for start-up entities.

(ii) Income attributable to holding financial assets and related financial services.

(iii) Effect of local regulation.

(4) Investment entity.

(i) In general.

(ii) Financial assets.

(iii) Primarily conducts as a business.

(A) In general.

(B) Special rule for start-up entities.

(iv) Primarily attributable to investing, reinvesting, or trading in financial assets.

(A) In general.

(B) Special rule for start-up entities.

(v) Examples.

(5) Exclusions.

(i) Excepted nonfinancial group entities.

(A) In general.

(B) Nonfinancial group.

(C) Holding company.

(D) Treasury center.

(E) Captive finance company.

(ii) Excepted nonfinancial start-up companies or companies entering a new line of business.

(A) In general.

(B) Exception for investment funds.

(iii) Excepted nonfinancial entities in liquidation or bankruptcy.

(iv) Excepted inter-affiliate FFI.

(v) Section 501(c) entities.

(vi) Non-profit organizations.

(6) Reserving activities of an insurance company.

(f) Deemed-compliant FFIs.

(1) Registered deemed-compliant FFIs.

(i) Registered deemed-compliant FFI categories.

(A) Local FFIs.

(B) Nonreporting members of participating FFI groups.

(C) Qualified collective investment vehicles.

(D) Restricted funds.

(E) Qualified credit card issuers and servicers.

(F) Sponsored investment entities and controlled foreign corporations.

(ii) Procedural requirements for registered deemed-compliant FFIs.

(iii) Deemed-compliant FFI that is merged or acquired.

(iv) IRS review of compliance by registered deemed-compliant FFIs.

(A) General inquiries.

(B) Inquiries regarding substantial non-compliance.

(2) Certified deemed-compliant FFIs.

(i) Nonregistering local bank.

(ii) FFIs with only low-value accounts.

(iii) Sponsored, closely-held investment vehicles.

(iv) Limited life debt investment entities (transitional).

(v) Certain investment entities that do not maintain financial accounts.

(3) Owner-documented FFIs.

(i) In general.

(ii) Requirements of owner-documented FFI status.

(4) Definition of a restricted distributor.

(g) Recalcitrant account holders.

(1) Scope.

(2) Recalcitrant account holder.

(3) Start of recalcitrant account holder status.

(i) Preexisting accounts identified under the procedures described in § 1.1471-4(c) for identifying U.S. accounts.

(A) In general.

(B) Accounts other than high-value accounts.

(C) High-value accounts.

(D) Preexisting accounts that become high-value accounts.

(ii) Accounts that are not preexisting accounts and accounts requiring name/TIN correction.

(iii) Accounts with changes in circumstances.

(4) End of recalcitrant account holder status.

(h) Passthru payment.

(1) Defined.

(2) Foreign passthru payment.

(i) Expanded affiliated group.

(1) Scope of paragraph.

(2) Expanded affiliated group defined.

(3) Member of expanded affiliated group.

(4) Ownership test.

(i) Corporations.

(A) Stock not to include certain preferred stock.

(B) Valuation.

(ii) Partnerships.

(iii) Trusts.

(5) Treatment of warrants, options, and obligations convertible into equity for determining ownership.

(6) Exception for FFIs holding certain capital investments.

(7) Seed capital.

(8) Anti-abuse rule.

(9) Exception for limited life debt investment entities.

(10) Partnerships, trusts, and other non-corporate entities.

(j) Sponsoring entity verification.

(1) In general.

(2) Compliance program.

(3) Certification of compliance.

(i) Certification requirement.

(A) In general.

(B) Extension of time for the certification period ending on December 31, 2017.

(ii) Late-joining sponsored FFIs.

(iii) Certification period.

(iv) Additional certifications or information.

(v) Certifications regarding sponsoring entity and sponsored FFI requirements.

(vi) Certifications regarding internal controls.

(A) Certification of effective internal controls.

(B) Qualified certification.

(vii) Material failures defined.

(4) IRS review of compliance.

(i) General inquiries.

(ii) Inquiries regarding substantial non-compliance.

(3) Gross proceeds defined.
   (i) Sale or other disposition.
      (A) In general.
      (B) Special rule for sales effected by brokers.
      (C) Special rule for gross proceeds from sales settled by a clearing organization.
   (ii) Property of a type that can produce interest or dividend payments that would be U.S. source FDAP income.
      (A) In general.
      (B) Contracts producing dividend equivalent payments.
      (C) Regulated investment company distributions.
   (iii) Payment of gross proceeds.
      (A) When gross proceeds are paid.
      (B) Amount of gross proceeds.
  (4) Payments not treated as withholdable payments.
   (i) Certain short-term obligations.
   (ii) Effectively connected income.
   (iii) Excluded nonfinancial payments.
   (iv) Gross proceeds from sales of excluded property.
   (v) Fractional shares.
   (vi) Offshore payments of U.S. source FDAP income prior to 2017 (transitional).
   (vii) Collateral arrangements prior to 2017 (transitional).
   (viii) Certain dividend equivalents.
  (5) Special payment rules for flow-through entities, complex trusts, and estates.
   (i) In general.
   (ii) Partnerships.
   (iii) Simple trusts.
   (iv) Complex trusts and estates.
   (v) Grantor trusts.
   (vi) Special rule for an NWP or NWT.
   (vii) Special rules for determining when gross proceeds are treated as paid to a partner, owner, or beneficiary of a flow-through entity.
  (6) Reporting of withholdable payments.
  (7) Example.
(b) Substantial U.S. owner.
  (1) Definition.
  (2) Indirect ownership of foreign entities.
   (i) Indirect ownership of stock.
   (ii) Indirect ownership in a foreign partnership or ownership of a beneficial interest in a foreign trust.
   (iii) Ownership and holdings through options.
   (iv) Determination of proportionate interest.
   (v) Interests owned or held by a related person.
  (3) Beneficial interest in a foreign trust.
   (i) In general.
   (ii) Determining the 10 percent threshold in the case of a beneficial interest in a foreign trust.
  (4) Exceptions.
   (i) De minimis amount or value exception.
   (ii) Trusts wholly owned by certain U.S. persons.
  (5) Special rule for certain financial institutions.
  (6) Determination dates for substantial U.S. owners.
  (7) Examples.
(c) Specified U.S. person.
(d) Withholding agent.
  (1) In general.
  (2) Participating FFIs and registered deemed-compliant FFIs as withholding agents.
  (3) Grantor trusts as withholding agents.
  (4) Deposit and return requirements.
  (5) Multiple withholding agents.
  (6) Exception for certain individuals.
(e) Foreign entity.
(f) Effective/applicability date.
**§ 1.1474-1** *Liability for withheld tax and withholding agent reporting.*
(a) Payment and returns of tax withheld.
  (1) In general.
  (2) Withholding agent liability.
  (3) Use of agents.
   (i) In general.
   (ii) Authorized agent.
   (iii) Liability of withholding agent acting through an agent.
  (4) Liability for failure to obtain documentation timely or to act in accordance with applicable presumptions.
   (i) In general.
   (ii) Withholding satisfied by another withholding agent.
(b) Payment of withheld tax.

  (1) In general.
  (2) Special rule for foreign passthru payments and payments of gross proceeds that include an undetermined amount of income subject to tax.
(c) Income tax return.
  (1) In general.
  (2) Participating FFIs, registered deemed-compliant FFIs, and U.S. branches treated as U.S. persons.
  (3) Amended returns.
(d) Information returns for payment reporting.
  (1) Filing requirement.
   (i) In general.
   (ii) Recipient.
      (A) Defined.
      (B) Persons that are not recipients.
  (2) Amounts subject to reporting.
   (i) In general.
   (ii) Exception to reporting.
   (iii) Coordination with chapter 3.
  (3) Required information.
  (4) Method of reporting.
   (i) Payments by U.S. withholding agent to recipients.
      (A) Payments to certain entities that are beneficial owners.
      (B) Payments to participating FFIs, deemed-compliant FFIs, and certain QIs.
      (C) Amounts paid to a U.S. branch.
      (D) Amounts paid to territory financial institutions that are flow-through entities or acting as intermediaries.
      (E) Amounts paid to NFFEs.
   (ii) Payments made by withholding agents to certain entities that are not recipients.
      (A) Entities that provide information for a withholding agent to perform specific payee reporting.
      (B) Nonparticipating FFI that is a flow-through entity or intermediary.
      (C) Disregarded entities.
   (iii) Reporting by participating FFIs and deemed-compliant FFIs (including QIs, WPs, and WTs) and U.S. branches not treated as U.S. persons.
      (A) In general.
      (B) Special reporting requirements of participating FFIs, deemed-compliant FFIs, FFIs that make an election under section 1471(b)(3), and U.S. branches not treated as U.S. persons.
      (C) Reporting by a U.S. branch treated as a U.S. person.
   (iv) Reporting by territory financial institutions.
   (v) Nonparticipating FFIs.
   (vi) Other withholding agents.
   (vii) Combined Form 1042-S reporting.
(e) Magnetic media reporting.
(f) Indemnification of withholding agent.
(g) Extensions of time to file Forms 1042 and 1042-S.
(h) Penalties.
(i) Additional reporting requirements with respect to U.S. owned foreign entities and owner-documented FFIs.
  (1) Reporting by certain withholding agents with respect to owner-documented FFIs.
  (2) Reporting by certain withholding agents with respect to U.S. owned foreign entities that are NFFEs.
  (3) Cross reference to reporting by participating FFIs.
  (4) Extensions of time to file.
(j) Effective/applicability date.
**§ 1.1474-2** *Adjustments for overwithholding or underwithholding of tax.*
(a) Adjustments of overwithheld tax.
  (1) In general.
  (2) Overwithholding.
  (3) Reimbursement of tax.
   (i) General rule.
   (ii) Record maintenance.
  (4) Set-offs.
  (5) Examples.
(b) Withholding of additional tax when underwithholding occurs.
(c) Effective/applicability date.
**§ 1.1474-3** *Withheld tax as credit to beneficial owner of income.*
(a) Creditable tax
(b) Amounts paid to persons that are not the beneficial owners
(c) Effective/applicability date
**§ 1.1474-4** *Tax paid only once.*
(a) Tax paid.
(b) Effective/applicability date.
**§ 1.1474-5** *Refunds or credits.*

(a) Refund and credit.

   (1) In general.

   (2) Limitation to refund and credit for a nonparticipating FFI.

   (3) Requirement to provide additional documentation for certain beneficial owners.

      (i) In general.

      (ii) Claim of reduced withholding under an income tax treaty.

      (iii) Additional documentation to be furnished to the IRS for certain NFFEs.

(b) Tax repaid to payee.

(c) Effective/applicability date.

*§ 1.1474-6 Coordination of chapter 4 with other withholding provisions.*

(a) In general.

(b) Coordination of withholding for amounts subject to withholding under sections 1441, 1442, and 1443.

   (1) In general.

   (2) When withholding is applied.

   (3) Special rule for certain substitute dividend payments.

(c) Coordination with amounts subject to withholding under section 1445.

   (1) In general.

   (2) Determining the amount of the distribution from certain domestic corporations subject to section 1445 or chapter 4 withholding.

      (i) Distribution from qualified investment entity.

      (ii) Distribution from a United States real property holding corporation.

(d) Coordination with section 1446.

   (1) In general.

   (2) Determining the amount of distribution subject to section 1446.

(e) Example.

(f) Coordination with section 3406.

(g) Effective/applicability date.

*§ 1.1474-7 Confidentiality of information.*

(a) Confidentiality of information.

(b) Exception for disclosure of participating FFIs.

(c) Effective/applicability date.

*§ 301.1474-1 Required use of magnetic media for financial institutions filing Form 1042-S or Form 8966.*

(a) Financial institutions filing certain information returns.

(b) Waiver.

(c) Failure to file.

(d) Meaning of terms.

   (1) Magnetic media.

   (2) Financial institution.

(e) Effective/applicability date.

[Reg. § 1.1471-0.]

   ☐ [*T.D. 9610*, 1-17-2013 (*corrected* 9-9-2013). *Amended by T.D. 9809*, 12-30-2016, *T.D. 9852*, 3-21-2019 *and T.D. 9890*, 12-27-2019.]

**[Reg. § 1.1471-1]**

**§ 1.1471-1. Scope of chapter 4 and definitions.**—(a) *Scope of chapter 4 of the Internal Revenue Code.*—Sections 1.1471-1 through 1.1474-7 provide rules for withholding when a withholding agent makes a payment to an FFI or NFFE and prescribe the requirements for and definitions relevant to FFIs and NFFEs to which withholding will not apply. Section 1.1471-1 provides definitions for terms used in chapter 4 of the Internal Revenue Code (Code) and the regulations thereunder. Section 1.1471-2 provides rules for withholding under section 1471(a) on payments to FFIs, including the exception from withholding for payments made with respect to certain grandfathered obligations. Section 1.1471-3 provides rules for determining the payee of a payment and the documentation requirements to establish a payee's chapter 4 status. Section 1.1471-4 describes the requirements of an FFI agreement under section 1471(b) and the application of sections 1471(b) and (c) to an expanded affiliated group of FFIs. Section 1.1471-5 defines terms relevant to section 1471 and the FFI agreement and defines categories of FFIs that will be deemed to have met the requirements of section 1471(b) pursuant to section 1471(b)(2). Section 1.1471-6 defines classes of beneficial owners of payments that are exempt from withholding under chapter 4. Section 1.1472-1 provides rules for withholding when a withholding agent makes a payment to an NFFE, and defines categories of NFFEs that are not subject to withholding. Section 1.1473-1 provides definitions of the statutory terms in section 1473. Section 1.1474-1 provides rules relating to a withholding agent's liability for withheld tax, filing of income tax and information returns, and depositing of tax withheld. Section 1.1474-2 provides rules relating to adjustments for overwithholding and underwithholding of tax. Section 1.1474-3 provides the circumstances in which a credit is allowed to a beneficial owner for a

withheld tax. Section 1.1474-4 provides that a chapter 4 withholding obligation need only be collected once. Section 1.1474-5 contains rules relating to credits and refunds of tax withheld. Section 1.1474-6 provides rules coordinating withholding under sections 1471 and 1472 with withholding provisions under other sections of the Code. Section 1.1474-7 provides the confidentiality requirement for information obtained to comply with the requirements of chapter 4. Any reference in the provisions of sections 1471 through 1474 to an amount that is stated in U.S. dollars includes the foreign currency equivalent of that amount. Except as otherwise provided, the provisions of sections 1471 through 1474 and the regulations thereunder apply only for purposes of chapter 4. See § 301.1474-1 of this chapter for the requirements for reporting on magnetic media that apply to financial institutions making payments or otherwise reporting accounts pursuant to chapter 4.

   (b) *Definitions.*—Except as otherwise provided in this paragraph (b) or under the terms of an applicable Model 2 IGA, the following definitions apply for purposes of sections 1471 through 1474 and the regulations under those sections.

   (1) *Account.*—The term *account* means a financial account as defined in § 1.1471-5(b).

   (2) *Account holder.*—The term *account holder* means the person who holds an account, as determined under § 1.1471-5(a)(3).

   (3) *Active NFFE.*—The term *active NFFE* has the meaning set forth in § 1.1472-1(c)(1)(iv).

   (4) *AML due diligence.*—The term *AML due diligence* means the customer due diligence procedures of a financial institution pursuant to the anti-money laundering or similar requirements to which the financial institution, or branch thereof, is subject. This includes identifying the customer (including the owners of the customer), understanding the nature and purpose of the account, and ongoing monitoring.

   (5) *Annuity contract.*—The term *annuity contract* means a contract under which the issuer agrees to make payments for a period of time determined in whole or in part by reference to the life expectancy of one or more individuals. The term also includes a contract that is considered to be an annuity contract in accordance with the law, regulation, or practice of the jurisdiction in which the contract was issued, and under which the issuer agrees to make payments for a term of years. For purposes of the preceding sentence, it is immaterial whether a contract satisfies any of the substantive U.S. tax rules (for example, sections 72(s), 72(u), 817(h), and the investor control prohibition) applicable to the taxation of a contract holder or issuer.

   (6) *Assumes primary withholding responsibility.*—The term *assumes primary withholding responsibility* refers to when a QI, territory financial institution, or U.S. branch assumes responsibility for withholding on a payment for purposes of chapters 3 and 4 as if it were a U.S. person. A QI may only assume primary withholding responsibility if it does not make an election to be withheld upon with respect to the payment.

   (7) *Backup withholding.*—The term *backup withholding* means the withholding required under section 3406.

   (8) *Beneficial owner.*—Except as provided in § 1.1472-1(d), § 1.1471-6(d)(4), and § 1.1471-6(f), the term *beneficial owner* has the meaning set forth in § 1.1441-1(c)(6).

   (9) *Blocked account.*—The term *blocked account* has the meaning set forth in § 1.1471-4(e)(2)(iii)(B).

   (10) *Branch.*—With respect to a financial institution, the term *branch* means a unit, business, or office of a financial institution that is treated as a branch under the regulatory regime of a country or that is otherwise regulated under the laws of a country as separate from other offices, units, or branches of the financial institution and also includes an entity that is disregarded as an entity separate from the financial institution (including branches maintained by such disregarded entity). A branch includes a unit, business, or office of a financial institution located in a country in which it is resident, and a unit, business, or office of a financial institution located in the country in which the financial institution is created or organized. All units, businesses, and offices of a participating FFI located in a single country, and all entities disregarded as entities separate from a participating FFI and located in a single country, shall be treated as a single branch and may use the same GIIN. An account will be treated as maintained by a branch or disregarded entity if the rights and obligations of the account holder and the participating FFI with regard to such account (including any assets held in the account) are governed by the laws of the country of the branch or disregarded entity.

(11) *Broker.*—The term *broker* means any person, U.S. or foreign, that, in the ordinary course of a trade or business during the calendar year, stands ready to effect sales to be made by others. Examples of a broker include an obligor that regularly issues and retires its own debt obligations, a corporation that regularly redeems its own stock, and a clearing organization that effects sales of securities for its members. A broker does not include an international organization described in §1.1471-6(c) that redeems or retires an obligation of which it is the issuer, a stock transfer agent that records transfers of stock for a corporation if the nature of the activities of the agent is such that the agent ordinarily would not know the gross proceeds from sales, an escrow agent that effects no sales other than transactions incidental to the purpose of the escrow (such as sales to collect on collateral), or a corporation that issues and retires long-term debt on an irregular basis.

(12) *Cash value.*—The term *cash value* has the meaning set forth in §1.1471-5(b)(3)(vii)(B).

(13) *Cash value insurance contract.*—The term *cash value insurance contract* has the meaning set forth in §1.1471-5(b)(3)(vii).

(14) *Certified deemed-compliant FFI.*—The term *certified deemed-compliant FFI* means an FFI described in §1.1471-5(f)(2).

(15) *Change in circumstances.*—The term *change in circumstances* has the meaning set forth in §1.1471-3(c)(6)(ii)(E) for withholding agents and, in the case of a participating FFI, has the meaning set forth in §1.1471-4(c)(2)(iii).

(16) *Chapter 3.*—For purposes of chapter 4, the term *chapter 3* means sections 1441 through 1464 and the regulations thereunder, but does not include sections 1445 and 1446 and the regulations thereunder, unless the context indicates otherwise.

(17) *Chapter 4.*—The term *chapter 4* means sections 1471 through 1474 and the regulations thereunder.

(18) *Chapter 4 reportable amount.*—The term *chapter 4 reportable amount* has the meaning set forth in §1.1474-1(d)(2)(i).

(19) *Chapter 4 status.*—The term *chapter 4 status* means a person's status as a U.S. person, a specified U.S. person, an individual that is a foreign person, a participating FFI, a deemed-compliant FFI, a restricted distributor, an exempt beneficial owner, a nonparticipating FFI, a territory financial institution, an excepted NFFE, or a passive NFFE.

(20) *Chapter 4 withholding rate pool.*—The term *chapter 4 withholding rate pool* means a pool of payees that are nonparticipating FFIs provided on a chapter 4 withholding statement (as described in §1.1471-3(c)(3)(iii)(B)(3)) to which a withholdable payment is allocated. The term *chapter 4 withholding rate pool* also means a pool provided on an FFI withholding statement (as described in §1.1471-3(c)(3)(iii)(B)(2)) to which a withholdable payment is allocated to—

(i) A pool of payees consisting of each class of recalcitrant account holders described in §1.1471-4(d)(6) (or with respect to an FFI that is a QI, a single pool of recalcitrant account holders without the need to subdivide into each class of recalcitrant account holders described in §1.1471-4(d)(6)), including a separate pool of account holders to which the escrow procedures for dormant accounts apply; or

(ii) A pool of payees that are U.S. persons as described in §1.1471-3(c)(3)(iii)(B)(2).

(21) *Clearing organization.*—The term *clearing organization* means an entity that is in the business of holding securities for its member organizations or clearing trades of securities and transferring, or instructing the transfer of, securities by credit or debit to the account of a member without the necessity of physical delivery of the securities.

(22) *Complex trust.*—A *complex trust* is a trust that is not a simple trust or a grantor trust.

(23) *Consolidated obligations.*—The term *consolidated obligations* means multiple obligations that a withholding agent (including a withholding agent that is an FFI) has chosen to treat as a single obligation in order to treat the obligations as preexisting obligations pursuant to paragraph (b)(104)(ii) of this section or in order to share documentation between the obligations pursuant to §1.1471-3(c)(8). A withholding agent that has opted to treat multiple obligations as consolidated obligations pursuant to the previous sentence must also treat the obligations as a single obligation for purposes of satisfying the standards of knowledge requirements set forth in §§1.1471-3(e) and 1.1471-4(c)(2)(ii), and for purposes of determining the balance or value of any of the obligations when applying any of the account thresholds applicable to due diligence or reporting as set forth in §§1.1471-3(c)(6)(ii), 1.1471-3(d), 1.1471-4(c), 1.1471-5(a)(4), and 1.1471-5(b)(3)(vii). For example, with respect to consolidated obligations, if a withholding agent has reason to know that the chapter 4 status assigned to the account holder or payee of one of the consolidated obligations is inaccurate, then it has reason to know that the chapter 4 status assigned for all other consolidated obligations of the account holder or payee is inaccurate. Similarly, to the extent that an account balance or value is relevant for purposes of applying any account threshold to one or more of the consolidated obligations, the withholding agent must aggregate the balance or value of all such consolidated obligations.

(24) *Custodial account.*—The term *custodial account* has the meaning set forth in §1.1471-5(b)(3)(ii).

(25) *Custodial institution.*—The term *custodial institution* has the meaning set forth in §1.1471-5(e)(1)(ii).

(26) *Customer master file.*—A *customer master file* includes the primary files of a withholding agent, participating FFI, or deemed-compliant FFI for maintaining account holder information, such as information used for contacting account holders and for satisfying AML due diligence.

(27) *Deemed-compliant FFI.*—The term *deemed-compliant FFI* means an FFI that is treated, pursuant to section 1471(b)(2) and §1.1471-5(f), as meeting the requirements of section 1471(b). The term *deemed-compliant FFI* also includes a QI branch of a U.S. financial institution that is a reporting Model 1 FFI.

(28) *Deferred annuity contract.*—The term *deferred annuity contract* means an annuity contract other than an immediate annuity contract.

(29) *Depository account.*—The term *depository account* has the meaning set forth in §1.1471-5(b)(3)(i).

(30) *Depository institution.*—The term *depository institution* has the meaning set forth in §1.1471-5(e)(1)(i).

(31) *Direct reporting NFFE.*—The term *direct reporting NFFE* has the meaning set forth in §1.1472-1(c)(3).

(32) *Documentary evidence.*—The term *documentary evidence* means documents, other than a withholding certificate or written statement, that a withholding agent is permitted to rely upon to determine the chapter 4 status of a person in accordance with §1.1471-3(c)(5).

(33) *Documentation.*—The term *documentation* means withholding certificates, written statements, documentary evidence, and other documents that may be relevant in determining a person's chapter 4 status, including any document containing a determination of the account holder's citizenship or residency for tax or AML due diligence purposes or an account holder's claim of citizenship or residency for tax or AML due diligence purposes.

(34) *Dormant account.*—The term *dormant account* has the meaning set forth in §1.1471-4(d)(6)(ii).

(35) *Effective date of the FFI agreement.*—The term *effective date of the FFI agreement* with respect to an FFI or a branch of an FFI that is a participating FFI means the date on which the IRS issues a GIIN to the FFI or branch. For participating FFIs that receive a GIIN prior to June 30, 2014, the effective date of the FFI agreement is June 30, 2014.

(36) *EIN.*—The term *EIN* means an employer identification number (also known as a federal tax identification number) described in §301.6109-1(a)(1)(i) of this chapter.

(37) *Election to be withheld upon.*—The term *election to be withheld upon* has the meaning set forth in §1.1471-2(a)(2)(iii).

(38) *Electronically searchable information.*—The term *electronically searchable information* means information that a withholding agent or FFI maintains in its tax reporting files, customer master files, or similar files, and that is stored in the form of an electronic database against which standard queries in programming languages, such as Structured Query Language, may be used. Information, data, or files are not electronically searchable merely because they are stored in an image retrieval system (such as portable document format (.pdf) or scanned documents).

(39) *Entity.*—The term *entity* means any person other than an individual.

(40) *Entity account.*—The term *entity account* means an account held by one or more entities.

(41) *Excepted NFFE.*—The term *excepted NFFE* means a NFFE that is described in §1.1472-1(c)(1).

(42) *Exempt beneficial owner.*—The term *exempt beneficial owner* means any person described in §1.1471-6(b) through (g) or that is otherwise treated as an exempt beneficial owner pursuant to a Model 1 IGA or Model 2 IGA.

(43) *Exempt recipient.*—The term *exempt recipient* means a person described in §1.6049-4(c)(1)(ii) (for interest, dividends, and royalties), a person described in §1.6045-2(b)(2)(i) (for broker proceeds), and a person described in §1.6041-3(q) (for rents, amounts paid on notional principal contracts, and other fixed or determinable income).

(44) *Expanded affiliated group.*—The term *expanded affiliated group* has the meaning set forth in §1.1471-5(i)(2).

(45) *FATF.*—The term *FATF* means the Financial Action Task Force, an inter-governmental body that develops and promotes international policies to combat money laundering and terrorist financing.

(46) *FATF-compliant jurisdiction.*—The term *FATF-compliant jurisdiction* means a jurisdiction that —

(i) Is not subject to a FATF call on its members and other jurisdictions to apply counter-measures to protect the international financial system from the on-going and substantial money laundering and terrorist financing risks emanating from the jurisdiction;

(ii) Is not a jurisdiction with strategic AML/CFT (anti-money laundering and combating the financing of terrorism) deficiencies that has not made sufficient progress in addressing the deficiencies or has not committed to an action plan developed with the FATF to address the deficiencies; and

(iii) Is not a jurisdiction with strategic AML/CFT deficiencies that the FATF has identified as not making sufficient progress on its action plan agreed upon with the FATF.

(47) *FFI.*—The term *FFI* or *foreign financial institution* has the meaning set forth in §1.1471-5(d).

(48) *FFI agreement.*—The term *FFI agreement* means an agreement that is described in §1.1471-4(a). An FFI agreement includes a QI agreement, a WP agreement, and a WT agreement that is entered into by an FFI (other than an FFI that is a registered deemed-compliant FFI, including a reporting Model 1 FFI) and that has an effective date or renewal date on or after June 30, 2014. The term *FFI agreement* also includes a QI agreement that is entered into by a foreign branch of a U.S. financial institution (other than a branch that is a reporting Model 1 FFI) and that has an effective date or renewal date on or after June 30, 2014.

(49) *Financial account.*—The term *financial account* has the meaning set forth in §1.1471-5(b).

(50) *Financial institution.*—The term *financial institution* has the meaning set forth in §1.1471-5(e) and includes a financial institution as defined in an applicable Model 1 or Model 2 IGA.

(51) *Flow-through entity.*—The term *flow-through entity* means a partnership, simple trust, or grantor trust, as determined under U.S. tax principles.

(52) *Flow-through withholding certificate.*—The term *flow-through withholding certificate* means a Form W-8IMY submitted by a foreign partnership, foreign simple trust, or foreign grantor trust.

(53) *Foreign entity.*—The term *foreign entity* has the meaning set forth in §1.1473-1(e).

(54) *Foreign passthru payment.*—The term *foreign passthru payment* has the meaning set forth in §1.1471-5(h)(2).

(55) *Foreign payee.*—The term *foreign payee* means any payee other than a U.S. payee.

(56) *Foreign person.*—The term *foreign person* means any person other than a U.S. person and includes a QI branch of a U.S. financial institution.

(57) *GIIN.*—The term *GIIN* or *Global Intermediary Identification Number* means the identification number that is assigned to a participating FFI or registered deemed-compliant FFI. The term *GIIN* or *Global Intermediary Identification Number* also includes the identification number assigned to a reporting Model 1 FFI for purposes of identifying such entity to withholding agents. All GIINs will appear on the IRS FFI list.

(58) *Grandfathered obligation.*—The term *grandfathered obligation* has the meaning set forth in §1.1471-2(b).

(59) *Grantor trust.*—A *grantor trust* is a trust with respect to which one or more persons are treated as owners of all or a portion of the trust under sections 671 through 679. If only a portion of the trust

is treated as owned by a person, that portion is a grantor trust with respect to that person.

(60) *Gross proceeds.*—The term *gross proceeds* has the meaning set forth in §1.1473-1(a)(3).

(61) *Group annuity contract.*—The term *group annuity contract* means an annuity contract under which the obligees are individuals who are affiliated through an employer, trade association, labor union, or other association or group.

(62) *Group insurance contract.*—The term *group insurance contract* means an insurance contract that—

(i) Provides coverage on individuals who are affiliated through an employer, trade association, labor union, or other association or group; and

(ii) Charges a premium for each member of the group (or member of a class within the group) that is determined without regard to the individual health characteristics other than age, gender, and smoking habits of the member (or class of members) of the group.

(63) *Immediate annuity.*—The term *immediate annuity* means an annuity contract that—

(i) Is purchased with a single premium or annuity consideration; and

(ii) No later than one year from the purchase date of the contract commences to pay annually or more frequently substantially equal periodic payments.

(64) *Individual account.*—The term *individual account* means an account held by one or more individuals.

(65) *Insurance company.*—The term *insurance company* means an entity or arrangement —

(i) That is regulated as an insurance business under the laws, regulations, or practices of any jurisdiction in which the company does business;

(ii) The gross income of which (for example, gross premiums and gross investment income) arising from insurance, reinsurance, and annuity contracts for the immediately preceding calendar year exceeds 50 percent of total gross income for such year; or

(iii) The aggregate value of the assets of which associated with insurance, reinsurance, and annuity contracts at any time during the immediately preceding calendar year exceeds 50 percent of total assets at any time during such year.

(66) *Insurance contract.*—The term *insurance contract* means a contract (other than an annuity contract) under which the issuer in exchange for consideration agrees to pay an amount upon the occurrence of a specified contingency involving mortality, morbidity, accident, liability, or property risk.

(67) *Intergovernmental agreement (IGA).*—The term *intergovernmental agreement* or *IGA* means any applicable Model 1 or Model 2 IGA.

(68) *Intermediary.*—The term *intermediary* has the meaning set forth in §1.1441-1(c)(13).

(69) *Intermediary withholding certificate.*—The term *intermediary withholding certificate* means a Form W-8IMY submitted by an intermediary.

(70) *Investment entity.*—The term *investment entity* has the meaning set forth in §1.1471-5(e)(1)(iii).

(71) *Investment-linked annuity contract.*—The term *investment-linked annuity contract* means an annuity contract under which benefits or premiums are adjusted to reflect the investment return or market value of assets associated with the contract.

(72) *Investment-linked insurance contract.*—The term *investment-linked insurance contract* means an insurance contract under which benefits, premiums, or the period of coverage are adjusted to reflect the investment return or market value of assets associated with the contract.

(73) *IRS FFI list.*—The term *IRS FFI list* means the list published by the IRS that contains the names and GIINs for all participating FFIs, registered deemed-compliant FFIs, and reporting Model 1 FFIs.

(74) *Life annuity contract.*—The term *life annuity contract* means an annuity contract that provides for payments over the life or lives of one or more individuals.

(75) *Life insurance contract.*—The term *life insurance contract* means an insurance contract under which the issuer, in exchange for consideration, agrees to pay an amount upon the death of one or more individuals. That a contract provides one or more payments

(for example, for endowment benefits or disability benefits) in addition to a death benefit will not cause the contract to be other than a life insurance contract. For purposes of the preceding sentence, it is immaterial whether a contract satisfies any of the substantive U.S. tax rules (for example, sections 101(f), 817(h), 7702, or investor control prohibition) applicable to the taxation of the contract holder or issuer.

(76) *Limited branch.*—The term *limited branch* has the meaning set forth in § 1.1471-4(e)(2)(iii). With respect to a reporting Model 2 FFI, a limited branch is a branch of the reporting Model 2 FFI that operates in a jurisdiction that prevents such branch from fulfilling the requirements of a participating FFI or deemed-compliant FFI, or that cannot fulfill the requirements of a participating FFI or deemed-compliant FFI due to the expiration of the transitional rule for limited branches under § 1.1471-4(e)(2)(v), and for which the reporting Model 2 FFI meets the terms of the applicable Model 2 IGA with respect to the branch.

(77) *Limited FFI.*—The term *limited FFI* has the meaning set forth in § 1.1471-4(e)(3)(ii). With respect to a reporting Model 2 FFI, a limited FFI is a related entity that operates in a jurisdiction that prevents the entity from fulfilling the requirements of a participating FFI or deemed-compliant FFI or that cannot fulfill the requirements of a participating FFI or deemed-compliant FFI due to the expiration of the transitional rule for limited FFIs under § 1.1471-4(e)(3)(iv), and for which the reporting Model 2 FFI meets the requirements of the applicable Model 2 IGA with respect to the entity.

(78) *Model 1 IGA.*—The term *Model 1 IGA* means an agreement or arrangement between the United States or the Treasury Department and a foreign government or one or more agencies thereof to implement FATCA through reporting by financial institutions to such foreign government or agency thereof, followed by automatic exchange of the reported information with the IRS. The IRS will publish a list identifying all countries that are treated as having in effect a Model 1 IGA.

(79) *Model 2 IGA.*—The term *Model 2 IGA* means an agreement or arrangement between the United States or the Treasury Department and a foreign government or one or more agencies thereof to facilitate the implementation of FATCA through reporting by financial institutions directly to the IRS in accordance with the requirements of an FFI agreement, supplemented by the exchange of information between such foreign government or agency thereof and the IRS. The IRS will publish a list identifying all countries that are treated as having in effect a Model 2 IGA.

(80) *NFFE.*—The term *NFFE* or *non-financial foreign entity* means a foreign entity that is not a financial institution (including a territory NFFE). The term also means a foreign entity treated as an NFFE pursuant to a Model 1 IGA or Model 2 IGA.

(81) *Non-exempt recipient.*—The term *non-exempt recipient* means a person that is not an exempt recipient.

(82) *Nonparticipating FFI.*—The term *nonparticipating FFI* means an FFI other than a participating FFI, a deemed-compliant FFI, or an exempt beneficial owner.

(83) *Nonreporting IGA FFI.*—The term *nonreporting IGA FFI* means an FFI that is a resident of, or located or established in, a Model 1 or Model 2 IGA jurisdiction, as the context requires, and that meets the requirements of one of the following—

(i) A nonreporting financial institution described in Annex II of the Model 1 IGA;

(ii) A nonreporting financial institution described in Annex II of the Model 2 IGA;

(iii) A registered deemed-compliant FFI described in § 1.1471-5(f)(1)(i)(A) through (F);

(iv) A certified deemed-compliant FFI described in § 1.1471-5(f)(2)(i) through (v); or

(v) An exempt beneficial owner described in § 1.1471-6.

(84) *Non-U.S. account.*—The term *non-U.S. account* means an account that is not a U.S. account and that does not have an account holder that is a nonparticipating FFI or recalcitrant account holder.

(85) *NQI.*—The term *NQI* or *nonqualified intermediary* has the meaning set forth in § 1.1441-1(c)(14).

(86) *NWP.*—The term *NWP* or *nonwithholding foreign partnership* means a foreign partnership that is not a withholding foreign partnership.

(87) *NWT.*—The term *NWT* or *nonwithholding foreign trust* means a foreign trust as defined in section 7701(a)(31)(B) that is a simple trust or grantor trust and is not a withholding foreign trust.

(88) *Offshore obligation.*—The term *offshore obligation* means an offshore obligation defined in § 1.6049-5(c)(1) (by substituting the terms *withholding agent* or *financial institution* for the term *payor*).

(89) *Owner.*—The term *owner* means a person described in § 1.1473-1(b)(1), without regard to whether such person is a U.S. person and without regard to whether such person owns a ten percent interest in the entity. The term also includes a person that owns a discretionary interest in a trust and receives a distribution during the calendar year.

(90) *Owner-documented FFI.*—The term *owner-documented FFI* means an FFI described in § 1.1471-5(f)(3).

(91) *Participating FFI.*—The term *participating FFI* means an FFI that has agreed to comply with the requirements of an FFI agreement with respect to all branches of the FFI, other than a branch that is a reporting Model 1 FFI or a U.S. branch. The term *participating FFI* also includes an FFI described in a Model 2 IGA that has agreed to comply with the requirements of an FFI agreement with respect to a branch (a *reporting Model 2 FFI*), and a QI branch of a U.S. financial institution, unless such branch is a reporting Model 1 FFI.

(92) *Participating FFI group.*—The term *participating FFI group* means an expanded affiliated group that includes one or more participating FFIs and meets the requirements of § 1.1471-4(e)(1). The term *participating FFI group* also means an expanded affiliated group in which one or more members of the group is a reporting Model 1 FFI and each member of the group that is an FFI is a registered deemed-compliant FFI, nonreporting IGA FFI, limited FFI, or retirement fund described in § 1.1471-6(f).

(93) *Partnership.*—The term *partnership* has the meaning set forth in § 301.7701-2(c)(1) of this chapter.

(94) *Passive NFFE.*—The term *passive NFFE* means an NFFE other than an excepted NFFE.

(95) *Passthru payment.*—The term *passthru payment* has the meaning set forth in § 1.1471-5(h).

(96) *Payee.*—The term *payee* has the meaning set forth in § 1.1471-3(a).

(97) *Payment with respect to an offshore obligation.*—The term *payment with respect to an offshore obligation* means a payment made outside of the United States, within the meaning of § 1.6049-5(e), with respect to an offshore obligation.

(98) *Payor.*—The term *payor* has the meaning set forth in §§ 31.3406(a)-2 and 1.6049-4(a)(2) and generally includes a withholding agent.

(99) *Permanent residence address.*—The term *permanent residence address* has the meaning set forth in § 1.1441-1(c)(38).

(100) *Person.*—The term *person* has the meaning set forth in section 7701(a)(1) and the regulations thereunder and includes an entity or arrangement that is an insurance company. The term *person* also includes, with respect to a withholdable payment, a QI branch of a U.S. financial institution.

(101) *Preexisting account.*—The term *preexisting account* means a financial account that is a preexisting obligation.

(102) *Preexisting entity account.*—The term *preexisting entity account* means a preexisting account held by one or more entities.

(103) *Preexisting individual account.*—The term *preexisting individual account* means a preexisting account held by one or more individuals.

(104) *Preexisting obligation.*—(i) The term *preexisting obligation* means any account, instrument, contract, debt, or equity interest maintained, executed, or issued by the withholding agent that is outstanding on June 30, 2014. With respect to a participating FFI, the term *preexisting obligation* means any account, instrument, or contract (including any debt or equity interest) maintained, executed, or issued by the FFI that is outstanding on the effective date of the FFI agreement. With respect to a registered deemed-compliant FFI, a preexisting obligation means any account, instrument, or contract (including any debt or equity interest) that is maintained, executed, or issued by the FFI prior to the later of the date that the FFI registers as a deemed-compliant FFI pursuant to § 1.1471-5(f)(1) and receives a GIIN or the date the FFI is required to implement its account opening procedures under § 1.1471-5(f). Notwithstanding the previous provisions of this paragraph (b)(104)(i), a preexisting obligation includes an obligation held by an entity that is issued, opened, or executed on or after July 1, 2014, and before January 1, 2015, by or with a withholding agent or FFI that treats the obligation as a preexisting

obligation. See §§ 1.1471-2(a)(4)(ii), 1.1472-1(b)(2), and 1.1471-4(c)(3) for the due diligence requirements applicable to preexisting obligations for withholding agents and participating FFIs.

(ii) The term *preexisting obligation* also includes any obligation (referring to an account, instrument, contract, debt, or equity interest) of an account holder or payee, regardless of the date such obligation was entered into, if—

(A) The account holder or payee also holds with the withholding agent (or a member of the withholding agent's expanded affiliated group or sponsored FFI group) an account, instrument, contract, or equity interest that is a preexisting obligation under paragraph (b)(104)(i) of this section;

(B) The withholding agent (and, as applicable, the member of the withholding agent's expanded affiliated group or sponsored FFI group) treats both of the aforementioned obligations, and any other obligations of the payee or account holder that are treated as preexisting obligations under this paragraph (b)(104)(ii), as consolidated obligations; and

(C) With respect to an obligation that is subject to AML due diligence, the withholding agent is permitted to satisfy such AML due diligence for the obligation by relying upon the AML due diligence performed for the preexisting obligation described in paragraph (b)(104)(i) of this section.

(105) *Pre-FATCA Form W-8.*—The term *pre-FATCA Form W-8* means a version of a Form W-8 that was issued by the IRS prior to 2013 (including an acceptable substitute form based on such version) and that does not contain chapter 4 statuses but otherwise meets the requirements of § 1.1441-1(e)(1)(ii) applicable to such certificate (or substitute form) and has not expired, or a Form W-8 that was issued prior to 2013 and furnished by an individual to establish such individual's foreign status but otherwise meets the requirements of § 1.1441-1(e)(1)(ii) applicable to such certificate and has not expired.

(106) *Prima facie FFI.*—The term *prima facie FFI* means an entity described in § 1.1471-2(a)(4)(ii)(B).

(107) *QI.*—The term *QI* or *qualified intermediary* has the meaning set forth in § 1.1441-1(e)(5)(ii).

(108) *QI agreement.*—The term *QI agreement* means the agreement described in § 1.1441-1(e)(5)(iii).

(109) *QI branch of a U.S. financial institution.*—The term *QI branch of a U.S. financial institution* means a foreign branch of a U.S. financial institution for which a QI agreement is in effect.

(110) *Recalcitrant account holder.*—The term *recalcitrant account holder* has the meaning set forth in § 1.1471-5(g).

(111) *Registered deemed-compliant FFI.*—The term *registered deemed-compliant FFI* means an FFI described in § 1.1471-5(f)(1). The term *registered deemed-compliant FFI* also includes a QI branch of a U.S. financial institution that is a reporting Model 1 FFI.

(112) *Relationship manager.*—A *relationship manager* is an officer or other employee of an FFI who is assigned responsibility for specific account holders on an on-going basis (including as an officer or employee that is a member of an FFI's private banking department), advises account holders regarding their banking, investment, trust, fiduciary, estate planning, or philanthropic needs, and recommends, makes referrals to, or arranges for the provision of financial products, services, or other assistance by internal or external providers to meet those needs. Notwithstanding the previous sentence, a person is only a relationship manager with respect to an account that has a balance or value of more than $1,000,000, taking into account the aggregation rules described in § 1.1471-5(b)(4)(iii)(A) and (B).

(113) *Reportable payment.*—The term *reportable payment* means a payment of interest or dividends (as defined in section 3406(b)(2)) and other reportable payments (as defined in section 3406(b)(3)).

(114) *Reporting Model 1 FFI.*—The term *reporting Model 1 FFI* means an FFI with respect to which a foreign government or agency thereof agrees to obtain and exchange information pursuant to a Model 1 IGA, other than an FFI that is treated as a nonparticipating FFI under the Model 1 IGA.

(115) *Reporting Model 2 FFI.*—The term *reporting Model 2 FFI* means a participating FFI that is described in § 1.1471-1(b)(91).

(116) *Responsible officer.*—The term *responsible officer* means, with respect to a participating FFI, an officer of any participating FFI or reporting Model 1 FFI in the participating FFI's expanded affiliated group with sufficient authority to fulfill the duties of a responsible officer described in § 1.1471-4, which include the requirement to periodically certify to the IRS regarding the FFI's compliance with its FFI agreement. The term *responsible officer* means, in the case of a registered deemed-compliant FFI, an officer of any deemed-compliant FFI or participating FFI in the deemed-compliant FFI's expanded affiliated group with sufficient authority to ensure that the FFI meets the applicable requirements of § 1.1471-5(f). The term *responsible officer* means, with respect to a sponsoring entity, an officer of the sponsoring entity or an officer of an entity that establishes and maintains policies and procedures for, and has general oversight over, the sponsoring entity, provided such officer has sufficient authority to fulfill the duties of a responsible officer described in § 1.1471-5(j) or § 1.1472-1(f) (as applicable). If a participating FFI elects to be part of a consolidated compliance program, the term *responsible officer* means an officer of the compliance FI (as described in § 1.1471-4(f)) with sufficient authority to fulfill the duties of a responsible officer described in § 1.1471-4(f)(2) and (3) on behalf of each FFI in the compliance group. In the case of an FI or sponsoring entity that is an investment entity, for purposes of this paragraph (b)(116), the responsible officer may be, in lieu of an officer of the investment entity, an individual who is a director, managing member, or general partner of the investment entity or, if the general partner or managing member of the investment entity is itself an entity, an individual who is an officer, director, managing member, or general partner of such other entity.

(117) *Restricted distributor.*—The term *restricted distributor* means an entity described in § 1.1471-5(f)(4).

(118) *Simple trust.*—The term *simple trust* means a trust that meets the requirements of section 651(a)(1) and (2).

(119) *Specified insurance company.*—The term *specified insurance company* has the meaning set forth in § 1.1471-5(e)(1)(iv).

(120) *Specified U.S. person.*—The term *specified U.S. person* or *specified United States person* has the meaning set forth in § 1.1473-1(c).

(121) *Sponsored FFI.*—The term *sponsored FFI* means any entity described in § 1.1471-5(f)(1)(i)(F) (describing sponsored investment entities and sponsored controlled foreign corporations) or § 1.1471-5(f)(2)(iii) (describing sponsored, closely held investment vehicles). The term *sponsored FFI* also means a sponsored investment entity, a sponsored controlled foreign corporation, or a sponsored, closely held investment vehicle treated as deemed-compliant under an applicable Model 2 IGA.

(122) *Sponsored FFI group.*—The term *sponsored FFI group* means a group of sponsored FFIs that share the same sponsoring entity.

(123) *Sponsored direct reporting NFFE.*—The term *sponsored direct reporting NFFE* has the meaning set forth in § 1.1472-1(c)(5).

(124) *Sponsoring entity.*—The term *sponsoring entity* means (i) an entity that registers with the IRS and agrees to perform the due diligence, withholding, and reporting obligations of one or more FFIs pursuant to § 1.1471-5(f)(1)(i)(F) or (f)(2)(iii); or (ii) an entity that registers with the IRS and agrees to perform the due diligence and reporting obligations of one or more direct reporting NFFEs pursuant to § 1.1472-1(c)(5).

(125) *Standardized industry coding system.*—The term *standardized industry coding system* means a coding system used by the withholding agent or FFI to classify account holders by business type for purposes other than U.S. tax purposes and that was implemented by the withholding agent by the later of January 1, 2012, or six months after the date the withholding agent was formed or organized.

(126) *Standing instructions to pay amounts.*—The term *standing instructions to pay amounts* means current payment instructions provided by the account holder, or an agent of the account holder, that will repeat without further instructions being provided by the account holder. Therefore, for example, a payment instruction to make an isolated payment is not a standing instruction to pay amounts, even if the instructions are given one year in advance. However, an instruction to make payments indefinitely is a standing instruction to pay amounts for the period during which such instructions are in effect, even if such instructions are amended after a single payment.

(127) *Subject to withholding.*—The term *subject to withholding*, with respect to an amount, means an amount for which withholding is required under chapter 4 or an amount for which chapter 4 withholding was otherwise applied.

(128) *Substantial U.S. owner.*—The term *substantial U.S. owner* or *substantial United States owner* has the meaning set forth in § 1.1473-1(b). In the case of a reporting Model 2 FFI, in applying this section with respect to a passive NFFE the term *substantial U.S. owner* means a controlling person as defined in the applicable Model 2 IGA.

(129) *Territory entity.*—The term *territory entity* means any entity that is incorporated or organized under the laws of any U.S. territory.

(130) *Territory financial institution.*—The term *territory financial institution* means a financial institution that is incorporated or organized under the laws of any U.S. territory, not including a territory entity that is an investment entity but that is not a depository institution, custodial institution, or specified insurance company.

(131) *Territory financial institution treated as a U.S. person.*—The term *territory financial institution treated as a U.S. person* means a territory financial institution that is treated as a U.S. person under § 1.1471-3(a)(3)(iv).

(132) *Territory NFFE.*—The term *territory NFFE* means a territory entity that is not a financial institution, including a territory entity that is an investment entity but is not a depository institution, custodial institution, or specified insurance company.

(133) *TIN.*—The term *TIN* means the tax identifying number assigned to a person under section 6109.

(134) *U.S. account.*—The term *U.S. account* or *United States account* has the meaning set forth in § 1.1471-5(a).

(135) *U.S. branch treated as a U.S. person.*—The term *U.S. branch treated as a U.S. person* means a U.S. branch that agrees to be treated as a U.S. person as described in § 1.1441-1(b)(2)(iv)(A). For the due diligence, withholding, and reporting requirements of a U.S. branch of an FFI treated as a U.S. person for purposes of chapter 4, see § 1.1471-4(b)(7), (c)(2)(v), (d)(2)(iii)(B), § 1.1472-1(a), and § 1.1474-1(i)(1) and (2).

(136) *U.S. financial institution.*—The term *U.S. financial institution* means a financial institution that is a U.S. person, including a U.S. branch treated as a U.S. person.

(137) *U.S. indicia.*—The term *U.S. indicia* has the meaning set forth in § 1.1471-4(c)(5)(iv)(B) when applied to an individual and as set forth in § 1.1471-3(e)(4)(v)(A) when applied to an entity.

(138) *U.S. owned foreign entity.*—The term *U.S. owned foreign entity* or *United States owned foreign entity* has the meaning set forth in § 1.1471-5(c).

(139) *U.S. payee.*—The term *U.S. payee* means any payee that is a U.S. person.

(140) *U.S. payor.*—The term *U.S. payor* means a U.S. payor or U.S. middleman as defined in § 1.6049-5(c)(5).

(141) *U.S. person.*—(i) Except as otherwise provided in paragraph (b)(141)(ii) of this section, the term *U.S. person* or *United States person* means a person described in section 7701(a)(30), the United States government (including an agency or instrumentality thereof), a State (including an agency or instrumentality thereof), or the District of Columbia (including an agency or instrumentality thereof). The term *U.S. person* or *United States person* also means a foreign insurance company that has made an election under section 953(d), provided that either the foreign insurance company is not a specified insurance company (as described in § 1.1471-5(e)(1)(iv)), or the foreign insurance company is a specified insurance company and is licensed to do business in any State.

(ii) The term *U.S. person* or *United States person* does not include a foreign insurance company that has made an election under section 953(d) if it is a specified insurance company and is not licensed to do business in any State. An individual will not be treated as a U.S. person for a taxable year or any portion of a taxable year that the individual is a dual resident taxpayer (within the meaning of § 301.7701(b)-7(a)(1) of this chapter) who is treated as a nonresident alien pursuant to § 301.7701(b)-7 of this chapter for purposes of computing the individual's U.S. tax liability. A U.S. person does not include an alien individual who has made an election under section 6013(g) or (h) to be treated as a resident of the United States.

(142) *U.S. source FDAP income.*—The term *U.S. source FDAP income* has the meaning set forth in § 1.1473-1(a)(2).

(143) *U.S. territory.*—The term *U.S. territory* or *possession of the United States* means American Samoa, Guam, the Northern Mariana Islands, Puerto Rico, or the U.S. Virgin Islands.

(144) *U.S. withholding agent.*—The term *U.S. withholding agent* means a withholding agent that is either a U.S. person or a U.S. branch of a foreign person.

(145) *Withholdable payment.*—The term *withholdable payment* has the meaning set forth in § 1.1473-1(a).

(146) *Withholding.*—The term *withholding* means the deduction and withholding of tax at the applicable rate from a payment.

(147) *Withholding agent.*—The term *withholding agent* has the meaning set forth in § 1.1473-1(d).

(148) *Withholding certificate.*—The term *withholding certificate* means a Form W-8, Form W-9, or any other certificate that under the Code or regulations certifies or establishes the chapter 4 status of a payee or beneficial owner.

(149) *WP.*—The term *WP* or *withholding foreign partnership* means a foreign partnership that has executed the agreement described in § 1.1441-5(c)(2)(ii).

(150) *Written statement.*—The term *written statement* has the meaning set forth in § 1.1471-3(c)(4).

(151) *WT.*—The term *WT* or *withholding foreign trust* means a foreign grantor trust or foreign simple trust that has executed the agreement described in § 1.1441-5(e)(5)(v).

(c) *Applicability date.*—This section generally applies beginning on January 6, 2017, except for paragraphs (b)(116) and (121) of this section, which apply beginning on March 25, 2019. However, taxpayers may apply these provisions as of January 28, 2013. (For the rules that otherwise apply beginning on January 6, 2017, and before March 25, 2019, see this section as in effect and contained in 26 CFR part 1 revised April 1, 2018. For rules that otherwise apply beginning on January 28, 2013, and before January 6, 2017, see this section as in effect and contained in 26 CFR part 1 revised April 1, 2016.) [Reg. § 1.1471-1.]

☐ [T.D. 9610, 1-17-2013 (corrected 9-9-2013). Amended by T.D. 9657, 2-28-2014 T.D. 9809, 12-30-2016, T.D. 9852, 3-21-2019 and T.D. 9890, 12-27-2019.]

**[Reg. § 1.1471-2]**

**§ 1.1471-2. Requirement to deduct and withhold tax on withholdable payments to certain FFIs.**—(a) *Requirement to withhold on payments to FFIs.*—(1) *General rule of withholding.*—Under section 1471(a), notwithstanding any exemption from withholding under any other provision of the Code or regulations, a withholding agent must withhold 30 percent of any withholdable payment made after June 30, 2014, to a payee that is an FFI unless either the withholding agent can reliably associate the payment with documentation upon which it is permitted to rely to treat the payment as exempt from withholding under paragraph (a)(4) of this section or the payment is made under a grandfathered obligation that is described in paragraph (b) of this section or constitutes gross proceeds from the disposition of such an obligation. A withholding agent that is making a payment must determine who the payee is under § 1.1471-3(a) with respect to that payment and the chapter 4 status of such payee. See § 1.1471-3 for requirements for determining the chapter 4 status of a payee, including additional documentation requirements that apply when a payment is made to an intermediary or flow-through entity that is not the payee. Withholding under this section applies without regard to whether the payee receives a withholdable payment as a beneficial owner or as an intermediary. See paragraph (a)(2)(iv) of this section for a description of the withholding requirements imposed on territory financial institutions as withholding agents under chapter 4. In the case of a withholdable payment to a NFFE, a withholding agent is required to determine whether withholding applies under section 1472 and § 1.1472-1. Except as otherwise provided in the regulations under chapter 4, a withholding obligation arises on the date a payment is made, as determined under § 1.1473-1(a).

(2) *Special withholding rules.*—(i) *Requirement to withhold on payments of U.S. source FDAP income to participating FFIs and deemed-compliant FFIs that are NQIs, NWPs, or NWTs, and U.S. branches acting as intermediaries.*—A withholding agent that, after June 30, 2014, makes a payment of U.S. source FDAP income to a participating FFI or deemed-compliant FFI that is an NQI receiving the payment as an intermediary, or a NWP or NWT, must withhold 30 percent of the payment unless the withholding is reduced under this paragraph (a)(2)(i). A withholding agent is not required to withhold on a payment, or portion of a payment, that it can reliably associate, in the manner described in § 1.1471-3(c)(2), with a valid intermediary or flow-through withholding certificate that meets the requirements of § 1.1471-3(d)(4) and a withholding statement that meets the requirements of § 1.1471-3(c)(3)(iii)(B) and that allocates the payment or portion of the payment to payees for which no withholding is required under chapter 4. Further, a withholding agent is not required to withhold on a payment that it can reliably associate with documentation indicating that the payee is a U.S. branch treated as a U.S. person (as defined in § 1.1471-1(b)(135)) or is a U.S. branch of an FFI that is not treated as a U.S. person but that applies the rules described in § 1.1471-4(d)(2)(iii)(C). See also § 1.1471-3(c)(3)(iii)(H) for the rules for valid documentation of a U.S. branch.

(ii) *Residual withholding responsibility of intermediaries and flow-through entities.*—An intermediary or flow-through entity that receives a withholdable payment after June 30, 2014, is required to withhold on such payment to the extent required under chapter 4. Notwithstanding the previous sentence, an intermediary or flow-through entity is not required to withhold if another withholding agent has withheld the full amount required. Further, an NQI, NWP, or NWT is not required to withhold with respect to a withholdable payment under chapter 4 if it has provided a valid intermediary withholding certificate or flow-through withholding certificate and all of the information required by §1.1471-3(c)(3)(iii), and it does not know, and has no reason to know, that another withholding agent failed to withhold the correct amount. A QI's, WP's, or WT's obligation to withhold and report is determined in accordance with its QI agreement, WP agreement, or WT agreement.

(iii) *Requirement to withhold if a participating FFI or registered deemed-compliant FFI makes an election to be withheld upon.*—A person that otherwise would be a payee with respect to a payment but that makes an election to be withheld upon does not agree to accept primary withholding responsibility for the payment under chapter 3 or 4. Accordingly, such person cannot be treated as the payee and the withholding agent must determine whether it must withhold based on the chapter 4 status of the payee on whose behalf the person is receiving the payment. The election to be withheld upon is only available to the extent provided in paragraph (a)(2)(iii)(A) and (B) of this section. The election is not available to an entity that is required to accept primary withholding responsibility for the payment, such as a WP or WT receiving a payment of U.S. source FDAP income, or an entity that already must be withheld upon because it may not accept primary withholding responsibility for the payment and, as such, already must pass up documentation with respect to the payee to the withholding agent, such as a participating FFI that is an NQI receiving a payment of U.S. source FDAP income.

(A) *Election to be withheld upon for U.S. source FDAP income.*—A withholding agent is required to withhold with respect to a payment, or portion of a payment, that is U.S. source FDAP income subject to withholding that is made after June 30, 2014, to a QI that has elected in accordance with this paragraph to be withheld upon, unless such withholding agent also makes an election to be withheld upon under this paragraph (a)(2)(iii)(A) or is an FFI that may not accept primary withholding responsibility for the payment. In such case, the withholding agent must withhold 30 percent of the portion of the payment that is allocable, pursuant to a withholding statement described in §1.1471-3(c)(3)(iii)(B) provided by the QI, to recalcitrant account holders and nonparticipating FFIs. If no such allocation information is provided, the withholding agent must apply the presumption rules of §1.1471-3(f) to determine the chapter 4 status of the payee. A QI that is an FFI and that makes the election to be withheld upon with respect to a payment of U.S. source FDAP income may not assume primary withholding responsibility under chapter 3 for that payment. Conversely, a QI that is an FFI and that does not make the election to be withheld upon with respect to a payment of U.S. source FDAP income is required to assume primary withholding responsibility under chapter 3 for that payment. The election to be withheld upon is only available with respect to a payment of U.S. source FDAP income if—

(1) The withholding agent is a participating FFI, reporting Model 1 FFI, QI, or a U.S. withholding agent;

(2) The person who receives the payment is a participating FFI or registered deemed-compliant FFI that acts as a QI with respect to the payment;

(3) The person who receives the payment provides the withholding agent, at or before the time of the payment, with a valid intermediary withholding certificate with respect to the payment that notifies the withholding agent that it has elected to be withheld upon, certifies that it is not assuming primary withholding responsibility under chapter 3, and designates whether such election is made for all accounts held with the withholding agent or for the specific accounts identified on the withholding certificate; and

(4) The intermediary withholding certificate is accompanied by a withholding statement described in §1.1471-3(c)(3)(iii)(B).

(B) *Election to be withheld upon for gross proceeds.*—[Reserved].

(iv) *Withholding obligation of a territory financial institution.*—A territory financial institution that is a flow-through entity or that acts as an intermediary with respect to a withholdable payment has an obligation to withhold (to the extent required under this section and §1.1472-1(b)) if it agrees to be treated as a U.S. person with respect to the payment for purposes of both chapter 4 and §1.1441-1(b)(2)(iv)(A). A territory financial institution that is a flow-through entity or that acts as an intermediary with respect to a withholdable payment is not required to withhold under paragraph (a)(1) of this section or §1.1472-1(b), however, if it has provided the withholding agent that is a U.S. withholding agent, participating FFI,

reporting Model 1 FFI, or QI with all of the documentation described in §1.1471-3(c)(3)(iii) (in which it has not agreed to be treated as a U.S. person with respect to the payment), and it does not know, or have reason to know, that another withholding agent failed to withhold the correct amount or failed to report the payment correctly under §1.1474-1(d).

(v) *Withholding obligation of a foreign branch of a U.S. financial institution.*—A foreign branch of a U.S. financial institution is a U.S. withholding agent and a payee that is a U.S. person, and is generally not an FFI. However, a foreign branch of a U.S. financial institution that is also a reporting Model 1 FFI is both a withholding agent and a registered deemed-compliant FFI. Additionally, a QI branch of a U.S. financial institution is both a withholding agent and either a participating FFI or a registered deemed-compliant FFI. Therefore, a foreign branch of a U.S. financial institution is not subject to withholding under chapter 4 but has an obligation to withhold under this section and §1.1472-1 and may be liable for the tax if it fails to do so. See §1.1471-2(a) (requirement to withhold on payments to FFIs) and §1.1471-3(a)(3)(iii) (U.S. intermediary or agent of a foreign person). A foreign branch that is a reporting Model 1 FFI or a reporting Model 2 FFI may apply the procedures under Annex I of an applicable IGA to document the chapter 4 status of a payee of a withholdable payment that is a holder of an account maintained by the branch in the Model 1 or Model 2 IGA jurisdiction. A QI branch of a U.S. financial institution must withhold in accordance with this chapter as provided in the QI agreement in addition to meeting its obligations under either §1.1471-4(b) and its FFI agreement or §1.1471-5(f).

(vi) *Payments of gross proceeds.*—[Reserved].

(3) *Coordination of withholding under sections 1471(a) and (b).*—The following entities are deemed to satisfy their withholding obligations under section 1471(a) and this section: participating FFIs that comply with the withholding requirements of §1.1471-4(b); exempt beneficial owners; section 501(c) entities described in §1.1471-5(e)(5)(v); and nonprofit organizations described in §1.1471-5(e)(5)(vi). See §1.1471-5(f) for when a deemed-compliant FFI is deemed to satisfy its withholding obligations under section 1471(a) and this section.

(4) *Payments for which no withholding is required.*—A withholding agent that has determined, in accordance with the documentation requirements and other rules provided in §1.1471-3, that the payee of a withholdable payment is a foreign entity must determine whether the payment is exempt from withholding. Paragraphs (a)(4)(i) through (viii) of this section describe the circumstances in which a withholdable payment is not subject to withholding under section 1471(a) and this section.

(i) *Exception to withholding if the withholding agent lacks control, custody, or knowledge.*—(A) *In general.*—A withholding agent that is not related to the payee or beneficial owner has an obligation to withhold under chapter 4 only to the extent that, at any time between the date that the obligation to withhold would arise (but for the provisions of this paragraph (a)(4)(i)) and the due date for filing the return on Form 1042 (including extensions) for the year in which the payment occurs, it has control over or custody of money or property owned by the payee or beneficial owner from which to withhold an amount and has knowledge of the facts that give rise to the payment. The exemption from the obligation to withhold under this paragraph (a)(4)(i) does not apply, however, to payments with respect to stock or other securities or if the lack of control or custody of money or property from which to withhold is part of a pre-arranged plan known to the withholding agent to avoid withholding under section 1471 or 1472. A withholding agent does not lack control over money or property for purposes of this paragraph (a)(4)(i) if the withholding agent directs another party to make the payment. Thus, for example, a principal does not cease to have control over a payment when it contracts with a paying agent to make the payments to its account holders in lieu of paying the account holders directly. Further, a withholding agent does not lack knowledge of the facts that give rise to a payment merely because the withholding agent does not know the character or source of the payment for U.S. tax purposes. See paragraph (a)(5) of this section for rules addressing a withholding agent's obligations when the withholding agent has knowledge of the facts that give rise to the payment, but the character or source of the payment is not known. For purposes of this paragraph (a)(4)(i), a withholding agent is related to the payee or beneficial owner if it is related within the meaning of section 482. Any exemption from withholding pursuant to this paragraph (a)(4)(i) applies without a requirement that documentation be furnished to the withholding agent. The special rules set forth in §1.1441-2(d)(2) through (4), regarding the obligation of a withholding agent with respect to cancellation of debt, the satisfaction of a tax liability following underwithholding by a withholding agent, and amounts described in §1.860G-3(b)(1) (regarding certain partnership allocations of REMIC net income with respect to a REMIC residual interest) also apply for purposes of chapter 4.

(B) *Example.*—A, an individual, owns stock in DC, a domestic corporation, through a custodian, Bank 1, that is a participating FFI. A also has a money market account at Bank 2, which is also a participating FFI. DC pays a dividend of $1,000 that is deposited in A's custodial account at Bank 1. A then directs Bank 1 to transfer $1,000 to A's money market account at Bank 2. With respect to the payment of the dividend into A's custodial account with Bank 1, both DC and Bank 1 are withholding agents making a withholdable payment for which they have custody, control, and knowledge. See § 1.1473-1(a)(2)(vii)(B) and (d). Therefore, both DC and Bank 1 have an obligation to withhold on the payment unless they can reliably associate the payment with documentation sufficient to treat the respective payees as not subject to withholding under chapter 4. With respect to the wire transfer of $1,000 from A's account at Bank 1 to A's account at Bank 2, neither Bank 1 nor Bank 2 is required to withhold with respect to the transfer because neither bank has knowledge of the facts that gave rise to the payment. Even though Bank 1 is a custodian with respect to A's interest in DC and has knowledge regarding the $1,000 dividend paid to A, once Bank 1 credits the $1,000 dividend to A's account, the $1,000 becomes A's property. When A transfers the $1,000 to its account at Bank 2, this constitutes a separate payment about which Bank 1 has no knowledge regarding the type of payment made. Further, Bank 2 only has knowledge that it receives $1,000 to be credited to A's account but has no knowledge regarding the type of payment made. Accordingly, Bank 1 and Bank 2 have no withholding obligation with respect to the transfer from A's custodial account at Bank 1 to A's money market account at Bank 2.

(ii) *Exception to withholding for certain payments made prior to July 1, 2016 (transitional).*—(A) *In general.*—For any withholdable payment made prior to July 1, 2016, with respect to a preexisting obligation for which a withholding agent does not have documentation indicating the payee's status as a nonparticipating FFI, the withholding agent is not required to withhold under this section and section 1471(a) unless the payee is a prima facie FFI.

(B) *Prima facie FFIs.*—If the payee is a prima facie FFI, the withholding agent must treat the payee as a nonparticipating FFI beginning on January 1, 2015, until the date the withholding agent obtains documentation sufficient to establish a different chapter 4 status of the payee. A prima facie FFI means any payee if—

(1) The withholding agent has available as part of its electronically searchable information a designation for the payee as a QI or NQI; or

(2) For an account maintained in the United States, the payee is presumed to be a foreign entity under § 1.1471-3(f) or is documented as a foreign entity for purposes of chapter 3 or 61, and the withholding agent has recorded as part of its electronically searchable information one of the following North American Industry Classification System or Standard Industrial Classification codes indicating that the payee is a financial institution:

(i) Commercial Banking (NAICS 522110).

(ii) Savings Institutions (NAICS 522120).

(iii) Credit Unions (NAICS 522130).

(iv) Other Depository Credit Intermediation (NAICS 522190).

(v) Investment Banking and Securities Dealing (NAICS 523110).

(vi) Securities Brokerage (NAICS 523120).

(vii) Commodity Contracts Dealing (NAICS 523130).

(viii) Commodity Contracts Brokerage (NAICS 523140).

(ix) Miscellaneous Financial Investment Activities (NAICS 523999).

(x) Open-End Investment Funds (NAICS 525910).

(xi) Commercial Banks, NEC (SIC 6029).

(xii) Branches and Agencies of Foreign Banks (branches) (SIC 6081).

(xiii) Foreign Trade and International Banking Institutions (SIC 6082).

(xiv) Asset-Backed Securities (SIC 6189).

(xv) Security & Commodity Brokers, Dealers, Exchanges & Services (SIC 6200).

(xvi) Security Brokers, Dealers & Flotation Companies (SIC 6211).

(xvii) Commodity Contracts Brokers & Dealers (SIC 6221).

(xviii) Unit Investment Trusts, Face-Amount Certificate Offices, and Closed-End Management Investment Offices (SIC 6726).

(iii) *Payments to a participating FFI.*—Except to the extent provided in paragraph (a)(2)(i) of this section, a withholding agent is not required to withhold under section 1471(a) and this section on a withholdable payment made to a payee that the withholding agent can treat as a participating FFI in accordance with § 1.1471-3(d)(4). For this purpose, a limited branch of a participating FFI is treated as a nonparticipating FFI.

(iv) *Payments to a deemed-compliant FFI.*—Except to the extent provided in paragraph (a)(2)(i) or (iii) of this section, a withholding agent is not required to withhold under section 1471(a) and this section on a withholdable payment made to a payee that the withholding agent can treat as a deemed-compliant FFI in accordance with § 1.1471-3(d)(4) through (7). For this purpose, a limited branch of a deemed-compliant FFI is treated as a nonparticipating FFI.

(v) *Payments to an exempt beneficial owner.*—A withholding agent is not required to withhold under section 1471(a) and this section on a withholdable payment to the extent that the withholding agent can reliably associate the payment with documentation to determine the portion of the payment that is allocable to an exempt beneficial owner in accordance with § 1.1471-3(d)(8). For example, a withholding agent is not required to withhold under this section on a withholdable payment made to a payee that is an exempt beneficial owner with respect to the payment, to a nonparticipating FFI to the extent that the nonparticipating FFI receives the payment as an intermediary on behalf of one or more of its account holders that are exempt beneficial owners, or to a flow-through entity to the extent that the flow-through entity receives the payment with respect to one or more of its partners, beneficiaries, or owners (as applicable) that are exempt beneficial owners. See § 1.1471-3(d)(8)(ii) for special rules for a withholding agent to determine the portion of a withholdable payment that is beneficially owned by an exempt beneficial owner in the case of a payment made to a nonparticipating FFI.

(vi) *Payments to a territory financial institution.*—A withholding agent is not required to withhold under section 1471(a) and this section on a withholdable payment made to a payee that the withholding agent can treat as a territory financial institution that beneficially owns the payment in accordance with § 1.1471-3(d)(10)(i). A withholding agent also is not required to withhold under this section on a withholdable payment that the withholding agent can treat, in accordance with § 1.1471-3(d)(10)(ii), as made to a territory financial institution that is a flow-through entity or that acts as an intermediary with respect to the payment and that has agreed to be treated as a U.S. person for purposes of chapters 3 and 4 with respect to the payment. A territory financial institution's agreement to be treated as a U.S. person for purposes of this section must be evidenced by a withholding certificate described in § 1.1471-3(c)(3)(iii)(F) furnished by the territory financial institution to the withholding agent.

(vii) *Payments to an account held with a clearing organization with FATCA-compliant membership.*—[Reserved].

(viii) *Payments to certain excepted accounts.*—A withholding agent is not required to withhold under chapter 4 on a withholdable payment made to an account described in § 1.1471-5(b)(2).

(5) *Withholding requirements if source or character of payment is unknown.*—(i) *General rule.*—If a withholding agent has knowledge of the facts that give rise to a payment but is unable to determine at the time of payment the character of the payment sufficiently to determine whether it is a withholdable payment, such payment must be treated as a withholdable payment. If a withholding agent has knowledge of the facts that give rise to a payment but is unable to determine at the time of payment the source of the payment, such payment must be treated as U.S. source income. For example, if a withholding agent does not know at the time of payment the amount of the payment that is a withholdable payment, because that calculation depends on facts that are not known at the time of payment (for example, because the withholding agent does not know whether services were performed in the United States or whether the payment constitutes income to the recipient) the withholding agent must withhold an amount necessary to ensure that the amount withheld is not less than 30 percent of the amount that could be a withholdable payment, subject to the limitation that the withheld amount must not exceed 30 percent of the amount paid. Notwithstanding this paragraph (a)(5), a withholding agent may presume a payment to be effectively connected with the conduct of a trade or business in the United States, and thus, not a withholdable payment, if it can do so under § 1.1471-3(f)(6) (regarding payments to certain U.S. branches).

(ii) *Optional escrow procedure.*—With respect to a payment described in paragraph (a)(5) of this section, the withholding agent may elect to retain 30 percent of the payment to hold in escrow until the earlier of the date that the amount of the withholdable payment can be determined or one year from the date the amount is placed in escrow, at which time either the withholding becomes due under this section or, to the extent that it is determined that the payment is of a type for which no withholding is required, the escrowed amount must be paid to the payee.

(b) *Grandfathered obligations.*—(1) *Grandfathered treatment of outstanding obligations.*—Notwithstanding § 1.1473-1(a), a withholdable payment does not include any payment made under a grandfathered obligation described in paragraph (b)(2)(i)(A) of this section, or any gross proceeds from the disposition of such an obligation. Notwithstanding § 1.1471-5(h), a foreign passthru payment does not include any payment made under a grandfathered obligation described in paragraph (b)(2)(i)(A) or (B) of this section, or any gross proceeds from the disposition of such an obligation. A premium paid with regard to an insurance contract or annuity contract that is a grandfathered obligation is treated as a payment made under a grandfathered obligation.

(2) *Definitions.*—The following definitions apply solely for purposes of this paragraph (b).

(i) *Grandfathered obligation.*—(A) The term *grandfathered obligation* means—

(1) Any obligation outstanding on July 1, 2014;

(2) Any obligation that gives rise to a withholdable payment solely because the obligation is treated as giving rise to a dividend equivalent pursuant to section 871(m) and the regulations thereunder, provided that the obligation is executed on or before the date that is six months after the date on which obligations of its type are first treated as giving rise to dividend equivalents;

(3) Any agreement requiring a secured party to make a payment with respect to, or to repay, collateral posted to secure a grandfathered obligation. If collateral (or a pool of collateral) secures both grandfathered obligations and obligations that are not grandfathered, the collateral posted to secure the grandfathered obligations may be determined by allocating (pro rata by value) the collateral (or each item comprising the pool of collateral) to all outstanding obligations secured by the collateral (or pool of collateral) or, if the collateral cannot be allocated pro rata to all obligations, by allocating all collateral to obligations that are not grandfathered and withholding to the extent required under chapter 4; and

(4) Any obligation that gives rise to substitute interest (as defined in § 1.861-2(a)(7)) that arises from the payee posting a grandfathered obligation described in paragraph (b)(2)(i)(A)(1) of this section as collateral.

(B) Solely for purposes of a foreign passthru payment, the term *grandfathered obligation* also includes any obligation that is executed on or before the date that is six months after the date on which final regulations defining the term foreign passthru payment are filed with the Federal Register.

(ii) *Obligation.*—(A) Except as otherwise provided in paragraph (b)(2)(ii)(B) of this section, the term *obligation* means any legally binding agreement or instrument. An obligation for purposes of this paragraph (b)(2)(i) includes, for example—

(1) A debt instrument (for example, a bond, guaranteed investment certificate, or term deposit);

(2) An agreement to extend credit for a fixed term (for example, a line of credit or a revolving credit facility), provided that the agreement as of its issue date fixes the material terms (including a stated maturity date) under which the credit will be provided;

(3) A derivatives transaction entered into between counterparties under an ISDA Master Agreement that is evidenced by a confirmation;

(4) A life insurance contract under which the entire contract value is payable no later than upon the death of the individual(s) insured under the contract but, in the case of a life insurance contract that contains a provision that permits the substitution of a new individual as the insured under the contract, only until a substitution occurs; and

(5) An immediate annuity contract payable for a period certain or for the life of the annuitant.

(B) An *obligation* for purposes of this paragraph (b)(2)(ii) does not include any legal agreement or instrument that—

(1) Is treated as equity for U.S. tax purposes;

(2) Lacks a stated expiration or term (for example, a savings deposit or demand deposit, a deferred annuity contract, or an annuity contract that permits a substitution of a new individual as the annuitant under the contract);

(3) Is a brokerage agreement, custodial agreement, investment linked insurance contract, investment linked annuity contract, or similar agreement to hold financial assets for the account of others and to make and receive payments of income and other amounts with respect to such assets; or

(4) Is a master agreement that merely sets forth standard terms and conditions that are intended to apply to a series of transactions between parties but that does not set forth all of the specific terms necessary to conclude a particular transaction.

(iii) *Date outstanding.*—Except as provided in the following sentence, an obligation that constitutes indebtedness for U.S. tax purposes is outstanding on the date provided in paragraph (b)(2)(i) if it has an issue date before such date. In all other cases, including an agreement described in paragraph (b)(2)(ii)(A)(2) of this section, an obligation is outstanding on the date provided in paragraph (b)(2)(i) if a legally binding agreement establishing the obligation was executed between the parties to the agreement before such date. Any material modification of an outstanding obligation will result in the obligation being treated as newly issued or executed as of the effective date of such modification.

(iv) *Material modification.*—In the case of an obligation that constitutes indebtedness for U.S. tax purposes, a material modification is any significant modification of the debt instrument as defined in § 1.1001-3(e). For life insurance contracts, a material modification includes any substitution of the insured under the contract. In all other cases, whether a modification of an obligation is material is determined based on the facts and circumstances.

(3) *Application to flow-through entities.*—(i) *Partnerships.*—A payment made under a grandfathered obligation includes a payment made to a partnership with respect to such obligation and a payment made with respect to a partnership's disposition of such obligation. A payment made under a grandfathered obligation also includes the income from such obligation that is includible in the gross income of a partner with respect to a capital or profits interest in the partnership and the gross proceeds allocated to a partner from the disposition of such obligation as determined under § 1.1473-1(a)(5)(vii).

(ii) *Simple trusts.*—A payment made under a grandfathered obligation includes a payment made to a simple trust with respect to such obligation, including a payment made with respect to a simple trust's disposition of such obligation. A payment made under a grandfathered obligation also includes income from such obligation that is includible in the income of a beneficiary and further includes a beneficiary's share of the gross proceeds from a disposition of such obligation as determined under § 1.1473-1(a)(5)(vii).

(iii) *Grantor trusts.*—A payment made under a grandfathered obligation includes a payment made to a grantor trust with respect to such obligation, including a payment made with respect to the trust's disposition of such obligation. A payment made under a grandfathered obligation also includes income from such obligation that is includible in the gross income of a person that is treated as an owner of the trust and the gross proceeds from the disposition of such obligation to the extent such owner is treated as owning the portion of the trust that consists of the obligation.

(4) *Determination by withholding agent of grandfathered treatment.*—(i) *In general.*—A withholding agent other than the issuer of the obligation (or agent of the issuer) may, absent actual knowledge, rely on a written statement by the issuer of the obligation to determine if such obligation meets the requirements for grandfathered treatment provided under this paragraph (b).

(ii) *Determination of material modification.*—For purposes of paragraph (b)(2)(iv) of this section (defining material modification), a withholding agent, other than the issuer of the obligation (or an agent of the issuer), is required to treat a modification of the obligation as material only if the withholding agent has actual knowledge thereof, such as in the event the withholding agent receives a disclosure indicating that there has been or will be a material modification to such obligation. The issuer of the obligation (or an agent of the issuer) that is a withholding agent is required to treat a modification of the obligation as material if the withholding agent knows or has reason to know that a material modification has occurred with respect to the obligation.

(iii) *Record retention.*—A withholding agent that relies on a document provided by the issuer of an obligation as described in paragraph (b)(4)(i) or (ii) of this section must retain such document in its records for the applicable period of limitations on assessment and collection with respect to amounts paid under the obligation or from disposition of the obligation.

(c) *Effective/applicability date.*—This section applies on January 6, 2017. However, taxpayers may apply these provisions as of January 28, 2013. (For the rules that apply beginning on January 28, 2013, and before January 6, 2017, see this section as in effect and contained in 26 CFR part 1 revised April 1, 2016.) [Reg. § 1.1471-2.]

☐ [T.D. 9610, 1-17-2013 (*corrected* 9-9-2013). *Amended by* T.D. 9657, 2-28-2014 (*corrected* 6-30-2014) *and* T.D. 9809, 12-30-2016 (*corrected* 6-29-2017).]

[Reg. §1.1471-3]

§1.1471-3. **Identification of payee.**—(a) *Payee defined.*—(1) *In general.*—Except as otherwise provided in this paragraph (a), for purposes of chapter 4 a payee is the person to whom a payment is made, regardless of whether such person is the beneficial owner of the amount.

(2) *Payee with respect to a financial account.*—For purposes of payments made to a financial account and except as otherwise provided in paragraph (a)(3) of this section, the payee is the holder of the financial account.

(3) *Exceptions.*—(i) *Certain foreign agents or intermediaries.*—(A) Except as otherwise provided in paragraphs (a)(3)(iv) and (vi) of this section (applicable to territory financial institutions and certain U.S. branches), a foreign person that is acting as an agent or intermediary with respect to a payment in accordance with paragraph (b)(1) of this section is not the payee if such foreign person is—

(1) An NFFE, unless the NFFE is a QI that has assumed primary withholding responsibility; or

(2) In the case of a payment of U.S. source FDAP income, a participating FFI, deemed-compliant FFI, or restricted distributor, unless the participating FFI, deemed-compliant FFI, or restricted distributor is a QI that has assumed primary withholding responsibility.

(B) In the case of an agent or intermediary described in paragraph (a)(3)(i)(A) of this section, the payee is the person or persons for whom the agent or intermediary collects the payment. Thus, for example, the payee of a payment of U.S. source FDAP income that the withholding agent can reliably associate with a withholding certificate from a QI that does not assume primary withholding responsibility with respect to the payment under chapter 3, or a payment to a participating FFI that is an NQI, is the person or persons for whom the QI or NQI acts.

(ii) *Foreign flow-through entity.*—(A) A foreign entity that is a flow-through entity is a payee with respect to a payment only if the flow-through entity is—

(1) An FFI that is not a participating FFI or deemed-compliant FFI, or restricted distributor receiving a payment of U.S. source FDAP income;

(2) An excepted NFFE that is not acting as an agent or intermediary with respect to the payment;

(3) A WP or WT that is not acting as an agent or intermediary with respect to the payment; or

(4) Receiving income that is (or is deemed to be) effectively connected with the conduct of a trade or business in the United States, or receiving a payment of gross proceeds from the sale of property that can produce income that is effectively connected with the conduct of a trade or business in the United States and that is excluded from the definition of a withholdable payment under §1.1473-1(a)(4).

(B) A withholding agent that makes a withholdable payment to a flow-through entity that is not described in paragraphs (a)(3)(ii)(A)(1) through (3) of this section will be required to treat the partner, beneficiary, or owner (as applicable) as the payee (looking through partners, beneficiaries, and owners that are themselves flow-through entities that are not described in paragraphs (a)(3)(ii)(A)(1) through (3)).

(iii) *U.S. intermediary or agent of a foreign person.*—A withholding agent that makes a withholdable payment to a U.S. person and has actual knowledge that the person receiving the payment is acting as an intermediary or agent of a foreign person with respect to the payment must treat such foreign person, and not the intermediary or agent, as the payee of such payment. Notwithstanding the previous sentence, a withholding agent that makes a withholdable payment to a U.S. financial institution or a U.S. insurance broker (to the extent such withholdable payment is a payment of premiums) that is acting as an intermediary or agent with respect to the payment on behalf of one or more foreign persons may treat the U.S. financial institution or U.S. insurance broker as the payee if the withholding agent does not have reason to know that the U.S. financial institution or U.S. insurance broker will not comply with its obligations to withhold under sections 1471 and 1472.

(iv) *Territory financial institution.*—A withholding agent that makes a withholdable payment to a territory financial institution that is a flow-through entity or is acting as an intermediary or agent with respect to the payment may treat the territory financial institution as the payee only if the territory financial institution has agreed (as evidenced by a withholding certificate described in paragraphs (c)(3)(iii)(A) and (F) of this section) to be treated as a U.S. person with respect to the payment for purposes of both chapters 3 and 4. In all other cases, the withholding agent must treat as the payee the part-

ner, beneficiary, or owner (as applicable) of the territory financial institution that is a flow-through entity (looking through partners, beneficiaries, and owners that are themselves flow-through entities that are not described in paragraphs (a)(3)(ii)(A)(1) through (3)) or the person on whose behalf the territory financial institution is acting.

(v) *Disregarded entity or limited branch.*—Except as otherwise provided in paragraph (a)(3)(v) through (vii) of this section, a withholding agent that makes a withholdable payment to an entity that is disregarded for U.S. federal tax purposes under §301.7701-2(c)(2)(i) of this chapter as an entity separate from its single owner must treat the single owner as the payee. The rules under §1.1471-3(d)(4) and (e)(3) apply to determine the circumstances under which a withholding agent may treat a payment made to a disregarded entity owned by an FFI as made to a payee that is a participating FFI or registered deemed-compliant FFI, and not as a payment made to a payee that is a nonparticipating FFI. A withholding agent that makes a payment to a limited branch (including an entity disregarded as a separate entity from its owner if such owner is an FFI and the disregarded entity is unable to comply with the terms of an FFI agreement with respect to accounts that it maintains) will be required to treat the payment as being made to a nonparticipating FFI.

(vi) *U.S. branch treated as a U.S. person.*—A withholdable payment to a U.S. branch is a payment to a U.S. person if the U.S. branch is treated as a U.S. person (as defined in §1.1471-1(b)(135)). In such case, the U.S. branch is treated as the payee. A U.S. branch treated as a U.S. person, however, is not treated as a U.S. person for purposes of the withholding certificate it may provide to a withholding agent for purposes of chapter 4. Accordingly, a U.S. branch treated as a U.S. person must furnish a withholding certificate on a Form W-8 to certify its chapter 4 status (and not a Form W-9, "Request for Taxpayer Identification Number and Certification"). See also paragraph (f)(6) of this section for the rules under which a withholding agent can presume a payment to a U.S. branch constitutes income that is effectively connected with a U.S. trade or business. A U.S. branch treated as a U.S. person may not make an election to be withheld upon, as described in section 1471(b)(3) and §1.1471-2(a)(2)(iii), for purposes of chapter 4. See §1.1471-4(c)(2)(v) for the rule requiring a U.S. branch treated as a U.S. person to apply the due diligence rules applicable to a U.S. withholding agent. See also §1.1474-1(i)(1) and (2) for the requirement of a U.S. branch to report information regarding certain U.S. owners of owner documented FFIs and passive NFFEs. See §1.1471-4(d) for rules for when a U.S. branch reports as a U.S. person.

(vii) *Foreign branch of a U.S. person.*—A payment to a foreign branch of a U.S. person is generally a payment to a U.S. payee. However, a payment to a foreign branch of a U.S. financial institution will be treated as a payment to an FFI if the foreign branch is a QI that is acting as an intermediary with respect to the payment. Therefore, a foreign branch that is a QI will provide the withholding agent with an intermediary withholding certificate and the withholding agent will report the payment as having been made to the foreign branch on a Form 1042-S.

(b) *Determination of payee's status.*—Except as otherwise provided in this section, a withholding agent must base its determination of the chapter 4 status of a payee on documentation that the withholding agent can reliably associate with such payment. If a withholding agent makes a payment to a person that is not the payee, the withholding agent will be required to determine the chapter 4 status of each intermediary or flow-through entity in the payment chain until the withholding agent is able to identify the payee. Paragraph (c) of this section provides rules for when a withholding agent can reliably associate a payment with appropriate documentation. Paragraph (d) of this section provides documentation requirements applicable to each class of payees, including exceptions for payments made with respect to offshore obligations or preexisting obligations. Paragraph (e) provides standards for determining when a withholding agent will be considered to have reason to know that a claim of exemption from withholding is unreliable or incorrect. Paragraph (f) of this section provides presumptions that apply for purposes of determining a payee's chapter 4 status in the absence of documentation or if the documentation provided is unreliable or incorrect.

(1) *Determining whether a payment is received by an intermediary.*—A withholding agent must treat the person who receives a payment as an intermediary if it can reliably associate the payment with a valid intermediary withholding certificate on which the person who receives the payment claims to be a QI or NQI. A U.S. person's foreign branch that is acting in its capacity as a QI is treated as a foreign intermediary. A withholding agent that makes a payment with respect to an offshore obligation must also treat the person who receives the payment as an intermediary if the person has provided written notification, whether or not such notification is signed, that it

accepts the payment on behalf of another person or persons. A withholding agent may rely on the type of certificate furnished as determinative of whether the person who receives the payment is an intermediary, unless the withholding agent knows or has reason to know that the certificate is incorrect. For example, a withholding agent that receives a beneficial owner withholding certificate from an FFI may treat the FFI as the beneficial owner unless it has information in its records that would indicate otherwise or the certificate contains information that is not consistent with beneficial owner status (for example, sub-account numbers that do not correspond to accounts maintained by the withholding agent for such person or names of one or more persons other than the person submitting the withholding certificate). If the FFI receives a payment in part as a beneficial owner and in part as an intermediary, the withholding agent may request that the FFI furnish two certificates, that is, a beneficial owner certificate for the amounts it receives as a beneficial owner, and an intermediary withholding certificate for the amounts it receives as an intermediary. A withholding agent that cannot reliably associate a payment with documentation sufficient to treat the person who receives the payment as an intermediary or as other than an intermediary pursuant to this paragraph (b)(1) must follow the presumption rules set forth in paragraph (f)(5) of this section to determine whether it must treat the person who receives the payment as an intermediary. A determination that a payment is made to an intermediary under this paragraph (b)(1) is not a determination that the payment can be reliably associated with documentation. See paragraph (c)(2) of this section for rules on reliably associating a payment with documentation if such payment is made through an intermediary.

(2) *Determination of entity type.*—A person's entity classification for purposes of chapter 4 is the person's entity classification for U.S. federal income tax purposes. Thus, for example, an entity that is disregarded as a legal entity in its country of organization or an arrangement that does not have a legal personality and is not a juridical person in the country in which it was organized will be treated as an entity for purposes of chapter 4 if it is an entity for U.S. federal income tax purposes. A withholding agent may rely upon a person's entity classification contained in a valid Form W-8 or W-9 if the withholding agent has no reason to know that the entity classification is incorrect. A withholding agent that makes a payment with respect to an offshore obligation may also rely upon a written notification provided by the person who receives the payment, regardless of whether such notification is signed, that indicates the person's entity classification (other than as a QI, WP, or WT) unless the withholding agent knows or has reason to know that the entity classification indicated by the person who receives the payment is incorrect. A withholding agent may not rely on a person's claim of classification other than as a corporation if the person's name indicates that the person is a per se corporation described in § 301.7701-2(b)(8) of this chapter unless the certificate or written statement contains a statement that the person is a grandfathered per se corporation described in § 301.7701-2(b)(8) and that its grandfathered status has not been terminated.

(3) *Determination of whether the payment is made to a QI, WP, or WT.*—A withholding agent may treat the person who receives a payment as a QI, WP, or WT if the withholding agent can reliably associate the payment with a valid Form W-8IMY, as described in paragraph (c)(3)(iii) of this section, that indicates that the person who receives the payment is a QI, WP, or WT, provides the person's QI-EIN, WP-EIN, or WT-EIN, and the person's GIIN, if applicable.

(4) *Determination of whether the payee is receiving effectively connected income.*—A withholding agent may treat a payment as being made to a payee that is receiving income that is effectively connected with a trade or business in the United States, or gross proceeds from the sale of property that can produce income that is effectively connected with the conduct of a trade or business in the United States, if it can reliably associate the payment with a valid Form W-8ECI described in paragraph (c)(3)(v) of this section or if it can do so under the presumption rule in paragraph (f)(6) of this section.

(c) *Rules for reliably associating a payment with a withholding certificate or other appropriate documentation.*—(1) *In general.*—A withholding agent can reliably associate a withholdable payment with valid documentation if, before the payment, it has obtained (either directly from the payee or through its agent) valid documentation appropriate to the payee's chapter 4 status as described in paragraph (d) of this section, it can reliably determine how much of the payment relates to the valid documentation, and it does not know or have reason to know that any of the information, certifications, or statements in, or associated with, the documentation are unreliable or incorrect. Thus, a withholding agent cannot reliably associate a withholdable payment with valid documentation provided by a payee to the extent such documentation appears unreliable or incorrect with respect to

the claims made, or to the extent that information required to allocate all or a portion of the payment to each payee is unreliable or incorrect. A withholding agent may rely on information and certifications contained in withholding certificates or other documentation without having to inquire into the truthfulness of the information or certifications, unless it knows or has reason to know that the information or certifications are untrue. A withholding agent may rely upon the same documentation for purposes of both chapters 3 and 4 provided the documentation is sufficient to meet the requirements of each chapter. Alternatively, a withholding agent may elect to rely upon the presumption rules of paragraph (f) of this section in lieu of obtaining documentation from the payee. A withholding certificate will be considered provided by a payee if a withholding agent obtains the certificate from a third party repository (rather than directly from the payee or through its agent) and the requirements in § 1.1441-1(e)(4)(iv)(E) are satisfied. A withholding certificate obtained from a third party repository must still be reviewed by the withholding agent in the same manner as any other documentation to determine whether it may be relied upon for chapter 4 purposes. A withholding agent may rely on an electronic signature on a withholding certificate if the requirements in § 1.1441-1(e)(4)(i)(B) are satisfied.

(2) *Reliably associating a payment with documentation if a payment is made through an intermediary or flow-through entity that is not the payee.*—(i) *In general.*—A withholding agent that makes a payment to a foreign intermediary or foreign flow-through entity that is not the payee under paragraph (a) of this section can reliably associate the payment with valid documentation if, in addition to the documentation described in paragraph (d) of this section that is relevant to each payee, the withholding agent also has obtained a valid Form W-8IMY, described in paragraph (c)(3)(iii) of this section, from the intermediary or flow-through entity (and, with respect to a payment made through a chain of intermediaries or flow-through entities, has received a valid Form W-8IMY from each intermediary or flow-through entity in that chain). An intermediary or flow-through entity that is a participating FFI or registered deemed-compliant FFI receiving a payment of U.S. source FDAP income may, in lieu of providing the withholding agent with documentation for each payee, provide pooled allocation information to the extent and in the manner permitted by paragraph (c)(3)(iii)(B)(2) of this section. With respect to the documentation provided for the owners of a foreign flow-through entity, the foreign flow-through entity is permitted to provide the documentary evidence described in paragraph (d) of this section applicable to each payee in lieu of a withholding certificate, regardless of whether the payment is made with respect to an offshore obligation.

(ii) *Exception to entity account documentation rules for an offshore account of an intermediary or flow-through entity.*—In the case of an offshore account held by an intermediary or flow-through entity not receiving a payment of U.S. source FDAP income, an FFI may, in lieu of obtaining a withholding certificate, reliably associate such account with valid documentation if the FFI has obtained a written statement certifying as to the account holder's chapter 4 status and stating that the account holder is a flow-through entity or is acting as an intermediary with respect to the payment. In such case, the intermediary or flow-through entity will also be required to provide the withholding statement that generally accompanies the Form W-8IMY, designating the payees and the appropriate amount that should be allocated to each payee, and valid documentation for each payee. If no such withholding statement or underlying documentation is provided, the payment will be treated as made to a nonparticipating FFI.

(3) *Requirements for validity of certificates.*—(i) *Form W-9.*—A valid Form W-9, or a substitute form, must meet the requirements prescribed in § 31.3406(h)-3 of this chapter, including the requirement that the form contain the payee's name and TIN, and be signed and dated under penalties of perjury by the payee or a person authorized to sign for the payee pursuant to sections 6061 through 6063 and the regulations thereunder. A foreign person, including a U.S. branch of a foreign person that is treated as a U.S. person under § 1.1441-1(b)(2)(iv), or a foreign branch of a U.S. financial institution that is a QI, may not provide a Form W-9.

(ii) *Beneficial owner withholding certificate (Form W-8BEN).*—A beneficial owner withholding certificate includes a Form W-8BEN (or a substitute form) and such other form as the IRS may prescribe. A beneficial owner withholding certificate is valid only if its validity period has not expired, it is signed under penalties of perjury by a person with authority to sign for the person whose name is on the form, and it contains—

(A) The person's name, permanent residence address, and TIN (if required);

(B) A certification that the person is not a U.S. citizen (if the person is an individual) or a certification of the country under the laws of which the person is created, incorporated, or governed (for a person other than an individual);

    (C) The person's entity classification for U.S. tax purposes;

    (D) The person's chapter 4 status; and

    (E) Such other information required under paragraph (d) of this section applicable to the chapter 4 status selected or otherwise required by the regulations under section 1471 or 1472, or by the form or its accompanying instructions in addition to, or in lieu of, the information described in this paragraph (c)(3)(ii).

    (iii) *Withholding certificate of an intermediary, qualified intermediary, flow-through entity, or U.S. branch (Form W-8IMY).*—(A) *In general.*—A withholding certificate of an intermediary, qualified intermediary, flow-through entity, or U.S. branch of such entity (whether or not such branch is treated as a U.S. person) is valid for purposes of chapter 4 only if it is furnished on a Form W-8IMY, an acceptable substitute form, or such other form as the IRS may prescribe, it is signed under penalties of perjury by a person with authority to sign for the person named on the form, its validity period has not expired, and it contains the following information, statements, and certifications—

    (1) The name and permanent residence address of the person.

    (2) The country under the laws of which the person is created, incorporated, or governed.

    (3) The person's entity classification for U.S. tax purposes.

    (4) The person's chapter 4 status.

    (5) A GIIN, in the case of a participating FFI or a registered deemed-compliant FFI (including a QI, WP, or WT that is a participating FFI or registered deemed-compliant FFI), and an EIN in the case of a QI, WP, or WT. Additionally, if a branch (other than a U.S. branch) of a participating FFI or registered deemed-compliant FFI outside of its country of residence acts as an intermediary, a GIIN of such branch must be provided on the withholding certificate. In the case of a U.S. branch, see the rules in paragraph (c)(3)(iii)(H) of this section.

    (6) In the case of an intermediary certificate, a certification that, with respect to accounts listed on the withholding statement, the intermediary is not acting for its own account.

    (7) With respect to a withholding certificate of a QI, a certification that it is acting as a QI with respect to the accounts listed on the withholding statement.

    (8) In the case of a participating FFI or registered deemed-compliant FFI (including a U.S. branch of either such entities that is not treated as a U.S. person) that is an NQI, NWP, NWT, or a QI that makes an election to be withheld upon, an FFI withholding statement that meets the requirements of paragraphs (c)(3)(iii)(B)(1) and (2) of this section.

    (9) In the case of a territory financial institution that does not agree to be treated as a U.S. person or a U.S. branch that is not a U.S. branch of a participating FFI, registered deemed-compliant FFI, or nonparticipating FFI, a chapter 4 withholding statement that meets the requirements of paragraphs (c)(3)(iii)(B)(1) and (3) of this section.

    (10) In the case of an NFFE or certified deemed-compliant FFI that is an NQI, NWP, or NWT and is not the payee, a chapter 4 withholding statement that meets the requirements of paragraphs (c)(3)(iii)(B)(1) and (3) of this section.

    (11) In the case of a nonparticipating FFI receiving a payment on behalf of one or more exempt beneficial owners, an exempt beneficial owner withholding statement that meets the requirements of paragraphs (c)(3)(iii)(B)(1) and (4) of this section.

    (12) Any other information, certifications, or statements as may be required by the form or its accompanying instructions in addition to, or in lieu of, the information and certifications described in this paragraph.

    (B) *Withholding statement.*—(1) *In general.*—A withholding statement forms an integral part of the withholding certificate and the penalties of perjury statement provided on the withholding certificate applies to the withholding statement as well. The withholding statement may be provided in any manner, and in any form, to which the person submitting the form and the withholding agent mutually agree, including electronically. A withholding statement may be provided electronically only if it meets the requirements of §1.1441-1(e)(3)(iv)(B). The withholding statement must be updated as often as necessary for the withholding agent to meet its reporting and withholding obligations under chapter 4. A withholding agent will be liable for tax, interest, and penalties under §1.1474-1(a) to the extent it does not follow the presumption rules of paragraph (f) of this section for any payment, or portion thereof, for which a withholding statement is required and the withholding agent does not have a valid withholding statement prior to making a payment. A withholding agent that is making a withholdable payment for which

a withholding statement is also required for purposes of chapter 3 may only rely upon the withholding statement if, in addition to providing the information required by paragraph (c)(3)(iii)(B) of this section, the withholding statement also includes all of the information required for purposes of chapter 3 and specifies the chapter 4 status of each payee or pool of payees identified on the withholding statement for purposes of chapter 3.

    (2) *Special requirements for an FFI withholding statement.*—(i) An FFI withholding statement may include either payee-specific information or pooled information that indicates the portion of the payment allocable to a chapter 4 withholding rate pool of U.S. payees, each class of recalcitrant account holders described in §1.1471-1(b)(20)(i), or a class of nonparticipating FFIs. In addition, an FFI withholding statement may include an allocation of a portion of the payment to a pool of account holders (other than nonqualified intermediaries and flow-through entities) for whom no reporting is required on any of Forms 1042-S, 1099, and 8966, provided that the FFI provides to the withholding agent for each account holder payee-specific information (including the payee's chapter 4 status (using the applicable status code used for filing Form 1042-S)) and any other information required for purposes of chapter 3 or 61 on the withholding statement, and the FFI provides documentation for each account holder in the pool (an *exempt payee pool*). For example, a participating FFI may provide on its withholding statement an exempt payee pool for a payment of U.S. source interest on a bank deposit not subject to withholding or reporting under chapter 4 that is allocable to a pool of foreign account holders (that is, a withholdable payment that is not reported on any of Forms 1042-S, 1099, and 8966) and provide to the withholding agent documentation for each account holder included in the pool. If payee-specific information is provided for purposes of chapter 4 it must indicate both the portion of the payment allocated to each payee and each payee's chapter 4 status (using the applicable status code used for filing Form 1042-S). A participating FFI that applies the escrow procedures described in §1.1471-4(b)(6) for dormant accounts must also indicate the portion of the payment allocated to a chapter 4 withholding rate pool of recalcitrant account holders that hold dormant accounts for which the participating FFI (and not the withholding agent) will withhold in escrow. The withholding statement provided by a participating FFI that applies the election to backup withhold under §1.1471-4(b)(3)(iii) must also indicate the portion of the reportable payment that is a withholdable payment allocated to each recalcitrant account holder subject to backup withholding under section 3406. See section 3406 for when backup withholding is required, including the exception to backup withholding under §31.3406(g)-1(e). Regardless of whether the FFI withholding statement provides information on a pooled or payee-specific basis, a withholding statement provided by an FFI other than an FFI acting as a WP, WT, or QI with respect to the account must also identify each intermediary or flow-through entity that receives the payment and such entity's chapter 4 status (using the applicable status code used for filing Form 1042-S) and GIIN (when required under paragraph (d) of this section), when applicable. An FFI withholding statement must also include any other information that the withholding agent or payor reasonably requests in order to fulfill its obligations under chapter 4, and chapters 3 and 61, if applicable.

    (ii) An FFI withholding statement provided by a reporting Model 2 FFI or a reporting Model 1 FFI may indicate, with respect to a withholdable payment, that the payment is allocable to a chapter 4 withholding rate pool of U.S. payees, which is comprised of account holders receiving a payment that is not subject to withholding under chapter 3 or 4 or to backup withholding under section 3406 and that are, with respect to a reporting Model 2 FFI, the holders of non-consenting U.S. accounts as described in an applicable IGA when the FFI reports the accounts in one of the pools described in §1.1471-4(d)(6) for the year in which the payment is made; or with respect to a reporting Model 1 FFI, the holders of accounts that have U.S. indicia for which appropriate documentation sufficient to treat the accounts as held by other than specified U.S. persons has not been provided pursuant to an applicable Model 1 IGA and the reporting Model 1 FFI reports the accounts as U.S. reportable accounts pursuant to the applicable Model 1 IGA for the year in which the payment is made.

    (iii) An FFI withholding statement provided by a participating FFI or registered deemed-compliant FFI that is a non-U.S. payor (a payor other than a U.S. payor as defined in §1.6049-5(c)(5)) may indicate, with respect to a withholdable payment, that the payment is allocable to a chapter 4 withholding rate pool of U.S. payees (in addition to the U.S. payees described in paragraph (c)(3)(iii)(B)(2)(ii) of this section), which is comprised of account holders that are not subject to withholding under chapter 3 or 4 or to backup withholding under section 3406 and that are, with respect to a participating FFI (including a reporting Model 2 FFI), account holders that hold U.S. accounts (as defined in §1.1471-1(b)(134) and an applicable Model 2 IGA) that the FFI reports as U.S. accounts pursuant to §1.1471-4(d)(3) or (5) for the year in which the payment is made; with respect to a registered deemed-compliant FFI (other than a reporting Model 1 FFI), account holders of U.S. accounts that the FFI reports pursuant to the conditions of its applicable deemed-compliant status under §1.1471-5(f)(1) for the year in which the payment is made; or with respect to a reporting Model 1 FFI, account holders of U.S. accounts that the reporting Model 1 FFI reports as reportable U.S. accounts pursuant to an applicable Model 1 IGA, and which includes the U.S. TINs of such account holders, for the year in which the payment is made.

*(iv)* An FFI withholding statement provided by a participating FFI or a registered deemed-compliant FFI may include a certification that the FFI is reporting, for the year in which the payment is made, an account held by a passive NFFE with one or more substantial U.S. owners (or, with respect to a reporting Model 1 FFI or reporting Model 2 FFI, one or more controlling persons that are specified U.S. persons, as defined in an applicable IGA) as a U.S. account (excluding a non-consenting U.S. account or an account held by a recalcitrant account holder) or, with respect to a reporting Model 1 FFI, a U.S. reportable account, in accordance with the terms of the FFI agreement or an applicable IGA.

*(v)* An FFI withholding statement provided by a participating FFI or a reporting Model 1 FFI may include a certification that the FFI is reporting to the IRS for the year of the payment all of the information described in §1.1471-4(d) or §1.1474-1(i)(1) (as applicable) with respect to all specified U.S. persons described in §1.1471-3(d)(6)(iv)(A)(1) and (2) with respect to an account holder or payee that the FFI has agreed to treat as an owner-documented FFI.

*(3) Special requirements for a chapter 4 withholding statement.*—A chapter 4 withholding statement must contain the name, address, TIN (if any), entity type, and chapter 4 status (using the applicable status code used for filing Form 1042-S) of each payee, the amount allocated to each payee, a valid withholding certificate or other appropriate documentation sufficient to establish the chapter 4 status of each payee, and each intermediary or flow-through entity that receives the payment on behalf of the payee, in accordance with paragraph (d) of this section, and any other information the withholding agent reasonably requests in order to fulfill its obligations under chapter 4. Notwithstanding the prior sentence, a chapter 4 withholding statement is permitted to provide pooled allocation information with respect to payees that are treated as nonparticipating FFIs (in lieu of providing the withholding agent with documentation for each payee). A chapter 4 withholding statement may include an allocation of a portion of the payment to a pool of payees (rather than to each payee) for whom no reporting is required on any of Forms 1042-S, 1099, and 8966, provided each payee is identified on the withholding statement and documentation is provided to the withholding agent for each payee included in the pool. If the withholdable payment is a reportable amount under chapter 3, see the provisions of §1.1441-1(e)(3)(iv)(C) for any additional information that may be required on the withholding statement (including pooled information under the alternative procedures described in §1.1441-1(e)(3)(iv)(D), if applicable).

*(4) Special requirements for an exempt beneficial owner withholding statement.*—An exempt beneficial owner withholding statement must include the name, address, TIN (if any), entity type, and chapter 4 status (using the applicable status code used for filing Form 1042-S) of each exempt beneficial owner on behalf of which the nonparticipating FFI is receiving the payment, the amount of the payment allocable to each exempt beneficial owner, a valid withholding certificate or other documentation sufficient to establish the chapter 4 status of each exempt beneficial owner in accordance with paragraph (d) of this section, and any other information the withholding agent reasonably requests in order to fulfill its obligations under chapter 4. The withholding statement must allocate the remainder of the payment that is not allocated to an exempt beneficial owner to the nonparticipating FFI receiving the payment. With respect to the amount of the payment allocable to each exempt beneficial owner and subject to withholding under chapter 3, see §1.1441-1(e)(3)(iv).

*(5) Nonqualified intermediary withholding statement.*—A withholding agent that is making a withholdable payment to a nonqualified intermediary for which a withholding statement is required under chapters 3 or 4 may accept a withholding statement that meets the requirements described in §1.1441-1(e)(3)(iv)(C)(3)(*i*) or (*ii*).

(C) *Failure to provide allocation information.*—A withholding certificate that fails to provide allocation information or any of the required documentation for one or more of the payees will not be treated as invalid with respect to the persons for whom valid documentation and allocation information is properly provided. The portion of the payment that is not reliably associated with underlying

documentation or that is not properly allocated will be treated in accordance with the presumption rules set forth in paragraph (f) of this section. For example, assume a withholding certificate that is provided by a participating FFI that is an NQI includes an FFI withholding statement that indicates that 50 percent of the payment is allocable to payees that are exempt for purposes of chapter 4 but does not allocate the remaining 50 percent of the payment for purposes of chapter 4. In such case, the withholding agent may treat 50 percent of the payment as exempt from chapter 4 and the remaining 50 percent that was not allocated will be treated, under the presumption rules set forth in paragraph (f) of this section, as made to a pool of payees that are nonparticipating FFIs.

(D) *Special rules applicable to a withholding certificate of a QI that assumes primary withholding responsibility under chapter 3.*—A QI that assumes primary withholding responsibility under chapter 3 for a payment may not make an election to be withheld upon, as described in §1.1471-2(a)(2)(iii), with respect to that payment. Thus, if a QI assumes primary withholding responsibility under chapter 3 with respect to a payment of U.S. source FDAP income, in addition to the other requirements described in paragraph (c)(3)(iii)(A) of this section, a withholding agent can reliably associate the payment with a valid withholding certificate only when the QI has also indicated on the intermediary withholding certificate that it will assume primary withholding responsibility for that payment for purposes of chapter 4.

(E) *Special rules applicable to a withholding certificate of a QI that does not assume primary withholding responsibility under chapter 3.*—A QI that does not assume primary withholding responsibility under chapter 3 with respect to a payment of U.S. source FDAP income will be required to make the election to be withheld upon with respect to that payment. Thus, if a QI does not assume primary withholding responsibility under chapter 3, a withholding agent can reliably associate a payment of U.S. source FDAP income with a valid withholding certificate only when, in addition to the other information required by paragraph (c)(3)(iii)(A) of this section, the withholding certificate indicates that the QI does not assume primary withholding responsibility for that payment for purposes of chapter 4.

(F) *Special rules applicable to a withholding certificate of a territory financial institution that agrees to be treated as a U.S. person.*—A withholding agent may reliably associate a payment with an intermediary withholding certificate or flow-through withholding certificate of a territory financial institution that agrees to be treated as a U.S. person if, in addition to the other information required by paragraph (c)(3)(iii)(A) of this section, the certificate contains an EIN of the territory financial institution and a certification that the territory financial institution agrees to be treated as a U.S. person and accepts primary withholding responsibility with respect to the payment for purposes of both chapters 3 and 4.

(G) *Special rules applicable to a withholding certificate of a territory financial institution that does not agree to be treated as a U.S. person.*—A withholding agent may reliably associate a payment with an intermediary withholding certificate or a flow-through withholding certificate of a territory financial institution that does not agree to be treated as a U.S. person if, in addition to the information required by paragraph (c)(3)(iii)(A) of this section, the certificate indicates that the institution has not agreed to be treated as a U.S. person for purposes of chapter 4 and the institution provides a withholding statement described in paragraphs (c)(3)(iii)(B)(*1*) and (*3*) of this section.

(H) *Rules applicable to a withholding certificate of a U.S. branch.*—A withholding agent may reliably associate a payment with a withholding certificate of a U.S. branch of an FFI that is treated as a U.S. person for purposes of §1.1441-1(b)(2)(iv) if, in addition to the other information required by paragraph (c)(2)(iii)(A) of this section, the certificate contains the EIN of the U.S. branch and a certification that the U.S. branch is described in paragraph §1.1441-1(b)(2)(iv) and, accordingly, is required to accept primary withholding responsibility with respect to the payment for purposes of both chapters 3 and 4. A withholding agent may reliably associate a payment with a withholding certificate of a U.S. branch of an FFI that is not treated as a U.S. person and that applies the rules described in §1.1471-4(d)(2)(iii)(C) if, in addition to the other information required by paragraph (c)(2)(iii)(A) of this section, the certificate contains the EIN of the U.S. branch and a certification that the U.S. branch applies the rules described in §1.1471-4(d)(2)(iii)(C). However, the requirement to obtain the certification that a U.S. branch applies the rules described in §1.1471-4(d)(2)(iii)(C) shall not apply to payments made on or before June 30, 2017.

*(iv) Certificate for exempt status (Form W-8EXP).*—A Form W-8EXP is valid only if it contains the name, address, and chapter 4 status of the payee, the relevant certifications or documentation, and

any other requirements indicated in the instructions to the form, and is signed under penalties of perjury by a person with authority to sign for the payee.

(v) *Certificate for effectively connected income (Form W-8ECI).*—A Form W-8ECI is valid only if, in addition to meeting the requirements in the instructions to the form, it contains the name, address, and TIN of the payee (other than a GIIN), represents that the amounts for which the certificate is furnished are effectively connected with the conduct of a trade or business in the United States and are includable in the payee's gross income for the taxable year (or are gross proceeds from the sale of property that can produce income that is effectively connected with the conduct of a trade or business in the United States), and is signed under penalties of perjury by a person with authority to sign for the payee.

(4) *Requirements for written statements.*—A written statement is a statement by the payee, or other person receiving the payment, that provides the person's chapter 4 status and any other information reasonably requested by the withholding agent to fulfill its obligations under chapter 4 with respect to the payment, such as whether the person is receiving the payment as a beneficial owner, intermediary, or flow-through entity. A written statement is valid only if it is provided by a person with respect to an offshore obligation, contains the name of the person, the person's address, the certifications relevant to the person's chapter 4 status (as contained on a withholding certificate), any additional information required with respect to the chapter 4 status claimed as provided under paragraph (d) of this section (for example, a GIIN), and a signed and dated certification that the information provided on the form is accurate and will be updated by the individual within 30 days of a change in circumstances that causes the form to become incorrect. A written statement may be submitted in any form that is acceptable to the withholding agent, including a statement made as part of the account opening documentation. A written statement may be used in lieu of a withholding certificate only to the extent provided under §1.1471-3(d), as applicable to the chapter 4 status claimed.

(5) *Requirements for documentary evidence.*—Documentary evidence with respect to a payee is only reliable if it contains sufficient information to support the payee's claim of chapter 4 status.

(i) *Foreign status.*—Acceptable documentary evidence supporting a claim of foreign status includes the following types of documentation if the documentation contains a permanent residence address for the person named on the documentation (or indicates the country in which a person that is an individual is a resident or citizen or the country in which a person that is an entity has a permanent residence or is incorporated or organized, if the withholding agent has otherwise obtained a current permanent residence address for the person)—

(A) *Certificate of residence.*—A certificate of residence issued by an appropriate tax official of the country in which the payee claims to be a resident that indicates that the payee has filed its most recent income tax return as a resident of that country;

(B) *Individual government identification.*—With respect to an individual, any valid identification issued by an authorized government body (for example, a government or agency thereof, or a municipality), that is typically used for identification purposes;

(C) *QI documentation.*—With respect to an account maintained in a jurisdiction with anti-money laundering rules that have been approved by the IRS in connection with a QI agreement (as referenced in §1.1441-1(e)(5)(iii)), any of the documents other than a Form W-8 or W-9 referenced in the jurisdiction's attachment to the QI agreement for identifying individuals or entities;

(D) *Entity government documentation.*—With respect to an entity, any documentation that substantiates that the entity is actually organized or created under the laws of a foreign country; and

(E) *Third-party credit report.*—For a payment made with respect to an offshore obligation to an individual, a third-party credit report that is obtained pursuant to the conditions described in §1.1471-4(c)(4)(ii).

(ii) *Chapter 4 status.*—Acceptable documentary evidence supporting an entity's claim of chapter 4 status includes—

(A) *General documentary evidence.*—With respect to an entity other than a participating FFI or registered deemed-compliant FFI, any organizational document (such as articles of incorporation or a trust agreement), financial statement, third-party credit report, letter from a government agency, or statement from a government website, agency, or registrar (such as an SEC report) to the extent permitted in paragraphs (d) and (e) of this section;

(B) *Preexisting obligation documentary evidence.*—With respect to a preexisting obligation of an entity, any classification in the withholding agent's records with respect to the payee that was determined based on documentation supplied by the payee (or other person receiving the payment) or a standardized industry coding system and that was recorded by the withholding agent consistent with its normal business practices for AML or another regulatory purpose (other than for tax purposes), to the extent permitted by paragraph (d) of this section and provided there is no U.S. indicia associated with the payee for which appropriate curing documentation has not been obtained as set forth in paragraph (e) of this section; and

(C) *Payee-specific documentary evidence.*—A letter from an auditor or attorney with a location in the United States that is not related to the withholding agent or payee and is subject to the authority of a regulatory body that governs the auditor's or attorney's review of the chapter 4 status of the payee, any bankruptcy filing, corporate resolution, copy of a stock market index or other document to the extent permitted in the specific payee documentation requirements in paragraph (d) and (e) of this section.

(6) *Applicable rules for withholding certificates, written statements, and documentary evidence.*—The provisions in this paragraph (c)(6) describe standards generally applicable to withholding certificates on Forms W-8 (or substitute forms), written statements, and documentary evidence furnished to establish the payee's chapter 4 status. These provisions do not apply to Forms W-9 (or their substitutes). For corresponding provisions regarding the Form W-9 (or a substitute Form W-9), see section 3406 and the regulations thereunder.

(i) *Who may sign the withholding certificate or written statement.*—A withholding certificate (including an acceptable substitute) or written statement may be signed by any person authorized to sign a declaration under penalties of perjury on behalf of the person whose name is on the certificate or written statement, as provided in sections 6061 through 6063 and the regulations thereunder. A person authorized to sign a withholding certificate or written statement includes an officer or director of a corporation, a partner of a partnership, a trustee of a trust, an executor of an estate, any foreign equivalent of the former titles, and any other person that has been provided written authorization by the individual or entity named on the certificate or written statement to sign documentation on such person's behalf.

(ii) *Period of validity.*—(A) *General rule.*—Except as provided otherwise in paragraphs (c)(6)(ii)(B) and (C) of this section, a withholding certificate or written statement will remain valid until the last day of the third calendar year following the year in which the withholding certificate or written statement is signed. Documentary evidence is generally valid until the last day of the third calendar year following the year in which the documentary evidence is provided to the withholding agent. Nevertheless, documentary evidence that contains an expiration date may be treated as valid until that expiration date if doing so would provide a longer period of validity than the three-year period. Notwithstanding the validity periods permitted by paragraphs (c)(6)(ii)(A) through (D) of this section, a withholding certificate, written statement, and documentary evidence will cease to be valid if the withholding agent has knowledge of a change in circumstances that makes the information on the documentation incorrect. Therefore, a withholding agent is required to institute procedures to ensure that any change to the customer master files that constitutes a change in circumstances described in paragraph (c)(6)(ii)(E) of this section is identified by the withholding agent. In addition, a withholding agent is required to notify any person providing documentation of the person's obligation to notify the withholding agent of a change in circumstances.

(B) *Indefinite validity.*—Notwithstanding paragraph (c)(6)(ii)(A) of this section, the following certificates (or parts of certificates), written statements, or documentary evidence shall remain valid until the withholding agent has knowledge of a change in circumstances that makes the information on the documentation incorrect—

(1) A withholding certificate or written statement provided by a participating FFI or registered deemed-compliant FFI that has furnished a valid GIIN that has been verified by the withholding agent in the manner set forth in paragraph (e)(3) of this section;

(2) A beneficial owner withholding certificate and documentary evidence supporting the individual's claim of foreign status when both are provided together (as defined in §1.1441-1(e)(4)(ii)(B)(1)) by an individual claiming foreign status, if the withholding agent does not have a current U.S. residence or U.S. mailing address for the payee and does not have one or more current U.S. telephone numbers that are the only telephone numbers the withholding agent has for the payee;

(3) A beneficial owner withholding certificate that is provided by an entity described in paragraph (c)(6)(ii)(C)(2) of this section (other than an entity described in paragraph (c)(6)(ii)(C)(2)(iii) of this section) and documentary evidence establishing the entity's foreign status when both are received by the withholding agent before the validity period of either would otherwise expire under paragraph (c)(6)(ii)(A) of this section;

(4) A withholding certificate of an intermediary, flow-through entity, or U.S. branch (not including the withholding certificates, written statements, or documentary evidence of the payees, or withholding statements associated with the withholding certificate);

(5) A withholding certificate, written statement, or documentary evidence furnished by a foreign government, government of a U.S. territory, foreign central bank (including the Bank for International Settlements), international organization, or entity that is wholly owned by any such entities;

(6) Documentary evidence that is not generally renewed or amended (such as a certificate of incorporation); and

(7) For the validity period of a beneficial owner withholding certificate provided by an entity described in paragraph (c)(6)(ii)(C)(2)(iii) of this section, see § 1.1441-1(e)(4)(ii).

(C) *Indefinite validity in the case of certain offshore obligations.*—Notwithstanding paragraph (c)(6)(ii)(A) of this section, the following certificates, written statements, and documentary evidence that are provided with respect to offshore obligations shall remain valid until a change in circumstances occurs that makes the information on the documentation incorrect—

(1) A withholding certificate or documentary evidence provided by an individual claiming foreign status if the withholding agent does not have a current U.S. residence or U.S. mailing address for the payee, does not have one or more current U.S. telephone numbers that are the only telephone numbers the withholding agent has for the payee, and has not been provided standing instructions to make a payment in the United States for the obligation;

(2) A withholding certificate, written statement, or documentary evidence provided by one of the following entities if such entity is the payee—

(i) A retirement fund described in § 1.1471-6(f) or an entity that is wholly owned by such a retirement fund;

(ii) An excepted nonfinancial group entity described in § 1.1471-5(e)(5)(i);

(iii) A section 501(c) entity described in § 1.1471-5(e)(5)(v);

(iv) A non-profit organization described in § 1.1471-5(e)(5)(vi);

(v) A nonreporting IGA FFI;

(vi) A territory financial institution;

(vii) An NFFE whose stock is regularly traded as described in § 1.1472-1(c)(1)(i);

(viii) An NFFE affiliate described in § 1.1472-1(c)(1)(ii);

(ix) An active NFFE that the withholding agent has determined, through its AML due diligence, is engaged in a business other than that of a financial institution, and ongoing monitoring of the account for purposes of AML due diligence does not indicate that the determination is incorrect; and

(x) A sponsored FFI described in § 1.1471-5(f)(1)(i)(F);

(3) A withholding certificate or written statement of an owner-documented FFI, but not including the withholding statements, documentary evidence, and withholding certificates of its owners (unless such documentation is permitted indefinite validity under another provision);

(4) An owner reporting statement associated with a withholding certificate of an owner-documented FFI, provided the account balance of all accounts held by such owner-documented FFI with the withholding agent does not exceed $1,000,000 on the later of June 30, 2014, or the last day of the calendar year in which the account was opened, and the last day of each subsequent calendar year preceding the payment, applying the aggregation principles of § 1.1471-5(b)(4)(iii), and the owner-documented FFI does not have any contingent beneficiaries or designated classes with unidentified beneficiaries; and

(5) A withholding certificate of a passive NFFE or excepted territory NFFE, provided the account balance of all accounts held by such entity with the withholding agent does not exceed $1,000,000 on the later of June 30, 2014, or the last day of the calendar year in which the account was opened, and the last day of each subsequent calendar year preceding the payment, applying the aggregation principles of § 1.1471-5(b)(4)(iii), and the withholding agent does not know or have reason to know that the entity has any contingent beneficiaries or designated classes with unidentified beneficiaries.

(D) *Exception for certificate for effectively connected income.*—Notwithstanding paragraphs (c)(6)(ii)(B) to (C) of this section, the period of validity of a withholding certificate furnished to a withholding agent to claim a reduced rate of withholding for income that is effectively connected with the conduct of a trade or business within the United States shall be limited to the three-year period described in paragraph (c)(6)(ii)(A) of this section.

(E) *Change in circumstances.*—*(1) Defined.*—For purposes of this chapter, a person is considered to have a change in circumstances only if such change would affect the chapter 4 status of the person. A change in circumstances includes any change that results in the addition of information described in paragraph (e)(4) relevant to a person's claim of foreign status (that is, U.S. indicia that is not otherwise cured by documentation on file and that is relevant to the chapter 4 status claimed) or otherwise conflicts with such person's claim of chapter 4 status. Unless stated otherwise, a change of address or telephone number is a change in circumstances for purposes of this paragraph (c)(6)(ii)(E) only if it changes to an address or telephone number in the United States. A change in circumstances affecting the withholding information provided to the withholding agent, including allocation information or withholding pools contained in a withholding statement or owner reporting statement, will terminate the validity of the withholding certificate with respect to the information that is no longer reliable, until the information is updated.

(2) *Obligation to notify withholding agent of a change in circumstances.*—If a change in circumstances makes any information on a certificate or other documentation incorrect, then the person whose name is on the certificate or other documentation must inform the withholding agent within 30 days of the change and furnish a new certificate, a new written statement, or new documentary evidence. Notwithstanding the previous sentence, if an FFI's chapter 4 status changes solely because the jurisdiction in which the FFI is resident, organized, or located is later treated as having an IGA in effect (including a jurisdiction that had a Model 2 IGA in effect and is later treated as having a Model 1 IGA in effect) or ceases to be treated as having an IGA in effect, in lieu of providing a new withholding certificate, the FFI may, within 30 days of such change in circumstances, provide to the withholding agent oral or written confirmation (including by e-mail) of the change in the FFI's chapter 4 status. If an intermediary or a flow-through entity becomes aware that a certificate or other appropriate documentation it has furnished to the person from whom it collects a payment is no longer valid because of a change in the circumstances of the person who issued the certificate or furnished the other appropriate documentation, then the intermediary or flow-through entity must notify the person from whom it collects the payment of the change in circumstances within 30 days of the date that it knows or has reason to know of the change in circumstances. It must also obtain a new withholding certificate or new appropriate documentation to replace the existing certificate or documentation the validity of which has expired due to the change in circumstances.

(3) *Withholding agent's obligation with respect to a change in circumstances.*—A certificate or other documentation becomes invalid on the date that the withholding agent holding the certificate or documentation knows or has reason to know that circumstances affecting the correctness of the certificate or documentation have changed. A withholding agent will not have reason to know of a change in circumstances with respect to an FFI's chapter 4 status that results solely because a jurisdiction is later treated as having an IGA in effect (including a jurisdiction that had a Model 2 IGA in effect and is later treated as having a Model 1 IGA in effect) until the withholding agent obtains the confirmation of a change in the FFI's chapter 4 status described in paragraph (c)(6)(ii)(E)(2) of this section (which will become part of the FFI's withholding certificate or other documentation retained by the withholding agent). A withholding agent will have reason to know of a change in circumstances with respect to an FFI's chapter 4 status that results solely because the jurisdiction in which the FFI is resident, organized, or located ceases to be treated as having an IGA in effect on the date that the jurisdiction ceases to be treated as having an IGA in effect. A withholding agent may choose to treat a person as having the same chapter 4 status that it had prior to the change in circumstances until the earlier of 90 days from the date that the certificate or documentation became invalid due to the change in circumstances or the date that a new certificate or new documentation is obtained. See, however, § 1.1441-1(e)(4)(ii)(D) for requirements, including the requirement to withhold under chapter 3 or section 3406, applicable when a change in circumstances occurs for purposes of chapter 3 and the related grace period allowed under § 1.1441-1(b)(3)(iv). A withholding agent may rely on a certificate without having to inquire into possible changes of circumstances that may affect the validity of the statement, unless it knows or has reason to know that circumstances have

changed. A withholding agent may require a new certificate or additional documentation at any time prior to a payment, regardless of whether the withholding agent knows or has reason to know that any information stated on the certificate or documentation has changed.

(4) [Reserved]. For further guidance, see § 1.1471-3T(c)(6)(ii)(E)(4).

(iii) *Record Retention.*—(A) *In general.*—A withholding agent must retain each withholding certificate, written statement, or copy of documentary evidence for as long as it may be relevant to the determination of the withholding agent's tax liability under section 1474(a) and § 1.1474-1. A withholding agent may retain an original, certified copy, or photocopy (including a microfiche, electronic scan, or similar means of electronic storage) of the withholding certificate, written statement, or documentary evidence. With respect to documentary evidence, the withholding agent must also note in its records the date on which the document was received and reviewed. Any documentation that is stored electronically must be made available in hard copy form to the IRS upon request during an examination.

(B) *Exception for documentary evidence received with respect to offshore obligations.*—A withholding agent that is making a payment with respect to an offshore obligation and is not required to retain copies of documentation reviewed pursuant to its AML due diligence, may, in lieu of retaining the documents as set forth in paragraph (c)(6)(iii)(A), retain a notation of the type of documentation reviewed, the date the documentation was reviewed, the document's identification number (if any) (for example, a passport number), and whether such documentation contained any U.S. indicia. The previous sentence applies with respect to an offshore obligation that is also a preexisting obligation, except, in such case, the requirement to record whether the documentation contained U.S. indicia does not apply. See also § 1.1471-4(c)(2)(iv) for the record retention requirements of a participating FFI.

(iv) *Electronic transmission of withholding certificate, written statement, and documentary evidence.*—A withholding agent may accept a withholding certificate (including an acceptable substitute form), a written statement, or other such form as the IRS may prescribe, electronically in accordance with the requirements set forth in § 1.1441-1(e)(4)(iv).

(v) *Acceptable substitute withholding certificate.*—(A) *In general.*—A withholding agent may substitute its own form for an official Form W-8 (or such other official form as the IRS may prescribe). A substitute form will be acceptable if it contains provisions that are substantially similar to those of the official form, it contains the same certifications relevant to the transactions as are contained on the official form and these certifications are clearly set forth, and the substitute form includes a signature-under-penalties-of-perjury statement identical to the one on the official form. The substitute form is acceptable even if it does not contain all of the provisions contained on the official form, so long as it contains those provisions that are relevant to the transaction for which it is furnished. A withholding agent may choose to provide a substitute form that does not include all of the chapter 4 statuses provided on the official version but the substitute form must include any chapter 4 status for which withholding may apply, such as the categories for a nonparticipating FFI or passive NFFE. A withholding agent that uses a substitute form must furnish instructions relevant to the substitute form only to the extent and in the manner specified in the instructions to the official form. A withholding agent may use a substitute form that is written in a language other than English and may accept a form that is filled out in a language other than English, but the withholding agent must make available an English translation of the form and its contents to the IRS upon request. A withholding agent may refuse to accept a certificate (including the official Form W-8) from a person if the certificate provided is not an acceptable substitute form provided by the withholding agent, but only if the withholding agent furnishes the person with an acceptable substitute form within five business days of receipt of an unacceptable form from the person. In that case, the substitute form is acceptable only if it contains a notice that the withholding agent has refused to accept the form submitted by the person and that the person must submit the acceptable form provided by the withholding agent in order for the person to be treated as having furnished the required withholding certificate.

(B) *Non-IRS form for individuals.*—A withholding agent may also substitute its own form for an official Form W-8BEN (for individuals), regardless of whether the substitute form is titled a Form W-8. However, in addition to the name and address of the individual that is the payee or beneficial owner, the substitute form must provide all countries in which the individual is resident for tax purposes, country of birth, a tax identification number (if any) for each country of residence, the individual's date of birth, and must

contain a signed and dated certification made under penalties of perjury that the information provided on the form is accurate and will be updated by the individual within 30 days of a change in circumstances that causes the form to become incorrect. Notwithstanding the previous sentence, the signed certification provided on a form need not be signed under penalties of perjury if the form is accompanied by documentary evidence that supports the individual's claim of foreign status. Such documentary evidence may be the same documentary evidence that is used to support foreign status in the case of a payee whose account has U.S. indicia as described in paragraph (e) of this section or § 1.1471-4(c)(4)(i)(A). The form may also request other information required for purposes of tax or AML due diligence in the United States or in other countries.

(vi) *Electronic confirmation of TIN on withholding certificate.*— The Commissioner may prescribe procedures in a revenue procedure or other appropriate guidance to require a withholding agent to confirm electronically with the IRS information concerning any TIN stated on a withholding certificate.

(vii) *Reliance on a prior version of a withholding certificate.*— Upon the issuance by the IRS of an updated version of a withholding certificate, a withholding agent may continue to accept the prior version of the withholding certificate in accordance with the requirements of § 1.1441-1(e)(4)(viii)(C) and without regard to whether a withholdable payment associated with the certificate is subject to withholding under § 1.1441-2(a).

(7) *Curing documentation errors.*—The provisions in this paragraph (c)(7) describe standards generally applicable to withholding certificates (Forms W-8 or substitute forms), written statements, and documentary evidence furnished to establish the payee's chapter 4 status. These provisions do not apply to Forms W-9 (or their substitutes). For corresponding provisions regarding the Form W-9 (or a substitute Form W-9), see section 3406 and the regulations thereunder.

(i) *Curing inconsequential errors on a withholding certificate.*—A withholding agent may treat a withholding certificate as valid, notwithstanding that the withholding certificate contains an inconsequential error, if the withholding agent has sufficient documentation on file to supplement the information missing from the withholding certificate due to the error. In such case, the documentation relied upon to cure the inconsequential error must be conclusive. For example, a withholding certificate in which the individual submitting the form abbreviated the country of residence in an ambiguous way may be treated as valid, notwithstanding the abbreviation, if the withholding agent has government issued identification for the person from a country that reasonably matches the abbreviation. On the other hand, an ambiguous abbreviation for the country of residence that does not reasonably match the country of residence shown on the person's passport is not an inconsequential error. A failure to select an entity type on a withholding certificate is not an inconsequential error, even if the withholding agent has an organization document for the entity that provides sufficient information to determine the person's entity type, if the person was eligible to make an election under § 301.7701-3(c)(1)(i) of this chapter (that is, a check-the-box election). A failure to check a box to make a required certification on the withholding certificate or to provide a country of residence or a country under which treaty benefits are sought is not an inconsequential error. In addition, information on a withholding certificate that contradicts other information contained on the withholding certificate or in the customer master file is not an inconsequential error.

(ii) *Documentation received after the time of payment.*—Proof that withholding was not required under the provisions of chapter 4 and the regulations thereunder also may be established after the date of payment by the withholding agent on the basis of a valid withholding certificate and/or other appropriate documentation that was furnished after the date of payment but that was effective as of the date of payment. A withholding certificate furnished after the date of payment will be considered effective as of the date of the payment if the certificate contains a signed affidavit (either at the bottom of the form or on an attached page) that states that the information and representations contained on the certificate were accurate as of the time of the payment. A certificate obtained within 30 days after the date of the payment will not be considered to be unreliable solely because it does not contain an affidavit. However, in the case of a withholding certificate of an individual received more than a year after the date of payment, the withholding agent will be required to obtain, in addition to the withholding certificate and affidavit, documentary evidence described in paragraph (c)(5)(i) of this section that supports the individual's claim of foreign status. In the case of a withholding certificate of an entity received more than a year after the date of payment, the withholding agent will be required to obtain, in addition to the withholding certificate and affidavit, documentary evidence specified in paragraph (c)(5)(ii) of this section that supports the chapter 4 status claimed. If documentation other than a withholding certificate is submitted from a payee more than a year after the date of payment, the withholding agent will be required to also obtain from the payee a withholding certificate and affidavit supporting the chapter 4 status claimed as of the date of the payment. See, however, § 1.1441-1(b)(7)(ii) for special rules that apply when a withholding certificate is received after the date of payment to claim that income is effectively connected with the conduct of a U.S. trade or business (as applied for purposes of this paragraph (c)(7)(ii) to a claim to establish that the payment is not a withholdable payment under § 1.1473-1(a)(4)(ii) rather than to claim an exemption described in § 1.1441-4(a)(1)).

(8) *Documentation furnished on account-by-account basis unless exception provided for sharing documentation within expanded affiliated group.*—Except as otherwise provided in this paragraph (c)(8), a withholding agent that is a financial institution with which a customer may open an account must obtain withholding certificates, written statements, Forms W-9, or documentary evidence on an account-by-account basis. Notwithstanding the previous sentence, a withholding agent may rely upon the withholding certificate, written statement, or documentary evidence furnished by a customer under any one or more of the circumstances described in this paragraph (c)(8).

(i) *Single branch systems.*—A withholding agent may rely on documentation furnished by a customer for another account if both accounts are held at the same branch location and both accounts are treated as consolidated obligations.

(ii) *Universal account systems.*—A withholding agent may rely on documentation furnished by a customer for an account held at another branch location of the same withholding agent or at a branch location of a member of the expanded affiliated group of the withholding agent if the withholding agent treats all accounts that share documentation as consolidated obligations and the withholding agent and the other branch location or expanded affiliated group member are part of a universal account system that uses a customer identifier that can be used to retrieve systematically all other accounts of the customer. A withholding agent that opts to rely upon the chapter 4 status designated for the payee in the universal account system without obtaining and reviewing copies of the documentation supporting the status must be able to produce all documentation (or a notation of the documentary evidence reviewed if the withholding agent is not required to retain copies of the documentary evidence) relevant to the chapter 4 status claimed upon request by the IRS and will be liable for any underwithholding that results from any failure to assign the correct status based upon the available information.

(iii) *Shared account systems.*—A withholding agent may rely on documentation furnished by a customer for an account held at another branch location of the same withholding agent or at a branch location of a member of the expanded affiliated group of the withholding agent if the withholding agent treats all accounts that share documentation as a consolidated obligation and the withholding agent and the other branch location or expanded affiliated group member share an information system, electronic or otherwise, that is described in this paragraph (c)(8)(iii). The system must allow the withholding agent to easily access data regarding the nature of the documentation, the information contained in the documentation (including a copy of the documentation itself), and the validity status of the documentation. The information system must also allow the withholding agent to easily transmit data into the system regarding any facts of which it becomes aware that may affect the reliability of the documentation. The withholding agent must be able to establish, to the extent applicable, how and when it has transmitted data regarding any facts of which it became aware that may affect the reliability of the documentation and must be able to establish that any data it has transmitted to the information system has been processed and appropriate due diligence has been exercised regarding the validity of the documentation. A withholding agent that opts to rely upon the chapter 4 status designated for the payee in the shared account system without obtaining and reviewing copies of documentation supporting the status must be able to produce all documentation (or a notation of the documentary evidence reviewed if the withholding agent is not required to retain copies of the documentary evidence) relevant to the chapter 4 status claimed upon request by the IRS and will be liable for any underwithholding that results from any failure to assign the correct status based upon the available information.

(iv) *Document sharing for gross proceeds.*—[Reserved].

(v) *Preexisting account.*—A withholding agent may rely on documentation furnished by a payee for a preexisting account held at another branch location of the same withholding agent or at a branch location of a member of the expanded affiliated group of the withholding agent if the withholding agent obtains and reviews copies of such documentation supporting the chapter 4 status designated for the payee and the withholding agent has no reason to know that, at the time the documentation is obtained by the withholding agent, the documentation is unreliable or incorrect. For example, the withholding agent may not rely on documentation furnished by a payee for a preexisting account held at another branch location of the same withholding agent or at a branch location of a member of the expanded affiliated group of the withholding agent if, based on information in the withholding agent's account records, the withholding agent has reason to know that such documentation is unreliable or incorrect.

(9) *Reliance on documentation collected by or certifications provided by other persons.*—(i) *Shared documentation system maintained by an agent.*—A withholding agent may rely on documentation collected by an agent (including a fund advisor for mutual funds, hedge funds, or a private equity group) of the withholding agent. The agent may retain the documentation as part of an information system maintained for a single withholding agent or multiple withholding agents provided that under the system, any withholding agent on behalf of which the agent retains documentation may easily access data regarding the nature of the documentation, the information contained in the documentation (including a copy of the documentation itself) and its validity, and must allow such withholding agent to easily transmit data, either directly into an electronic system or by providing such information to the agent, regarding any facts of which it becomes aware that may affect the reliability of the documentation. The withholding agent must be able to establish, to the extent applicable, how and when it has transmitted data regarding any facts of which it became aware that may affect the reliability of the documentation and must be able to establish that any data it has transmitted has been processed and appropriate due diligence has been exercised regarding the validity of the documentation. The agent must have a system in effect to ensure that any information it receives regarding facts that affect the reliability of the documentation or the chapter 4 status assigned to the customer are provided to all withholding agents for which the agent retains the documentation and any chapter 4 status assigned by the agent is amended to incorporate such information. A withholding agent that opts to rely upon the chapter 4 status assigned by the agent without obtaining and reviewing copies of the documentation supporting the status must be able to produce all documentation relevant to the chapter 4 status claimed upon request by the IRS and will be liable for any underwithholding that results from a failure of the agent to assign the correct status based upon the available information. See § 1.1474-1(a) for a withholding agent's liability when it relies upon an agent for chapter 4 purposes. This paragraph (c)(9)(i) does not apply to a withholding certificate provided by a QI, a withholding certificate provided by a territory financial institution that elects to be treated as a U.S. person, or any withholding statement, unless the person submitting the form specifically identifies the withholding agents for which the certificates and/or statements are provided.

(ii) *Third-party data providers.*—A withholding agent may rely upon documentation collected by a third-party data provider with respect to an entity, subject to the conditions described in this paragraph (c)(9)(ii).

(A) The third-party data provider must have collected documentation that is sufficient to determine the chapter 4 status of the entity under paragraph (d) of this section.

(B) The third-party data provider must be in the business of providing credit reports or business reports to customers unrelated to it and must have reviewed all information it has for the entity and verified that such additional information does not conflict with the chapter 4 status claimed by the entity. For purposes of this paragraph (c)(9)(ii)(B), a customer is related to a third-party data provider if they have a relationship with each other that is described in section 267(b).

(C) The third-party data provider must notify the entity submitting the documentation that such entity must notify the third-party data provider in the event of a change in circumstances within 30 days of the change in circumstances, and the third-party data provider must be obligated under its contract with the withholding agent to notify the withholding agent if a change in circumstances occurs.

(D) The withholding agent may not rely upon a chapter 4 status provided by a third-party data provider if the withholding agent knows or has reason to know that the chapter 4 status is unreliable or incorrect based on information in the withholding agent's account records, or if the documentation or information provided by the third-party data provider does not support the chapter 4 status claimed.

(E) The withholding agent must be able to submit copies of the documentation received from the third-party data provider upon request to the IRS and will remain liable for any underwithholding that occurs as a result of its reliance on information provided by the third-party data provider if the documentation is invalid or unreliable.

(F) This paragraph (c)(9)(ii) does not apply to a withholding statement or a withholding certificate that contains an election to accept withholding or reporting responsibility (such as one made by a QI, territory financial institution, or U.S. branch) provided by a third-party data provider.

(iii) *Reliance on certification provided by introducing brokers.*— (A) A withholding agent may rely on a certification of a payee's chapter 4 status and indicating that the broker holds valid documentation sufficient to determine the payee's chapter 4 status under paragraph (d) of this section with respect to any readily tradable instrument as defined in § 31.3406(h)-1(d) of this chapter if the conditions in paragraph (c)(9)(iii)(B) of this section are satisfied and the broker is either—

(1) A U.S. person (including a U.S. branch that is treated as a U.S. person) that is acting as the agent of the payee; or

(2) A participating FFI or a reporting Model 1 FFI that is acting as the agent of the payee with respect to an obligation and receiving all payments from the withholding agent with respect to such obligation as an intermediary on behalf of the payee.

(B) The certification from the broker must be in writing or in electronic form and contain all of the information required of a chapter 4 withholding statement described in paragraph (c)(3)(iii)(B)(3). Notwithstanding this paragraph (c)(9)(iii), a withholding agent may not rely upon a certification provided by a broker if it knows or has reason to know that the broker has not obtained valid documentation as represented or the information contained in the certification is otherwise inaccurate. A broker that chooses to provide a certification under this paragraph (c)(9)(iii) will be responsible for applying the rules set forth in the regulations under section 1471 and 1472 to the withholding certificates, written statements, or documentary evidence obtained from the payee and shall be liable for any underwithholding that occurs as a result of the broker's failure to reasonably apply such rules.

(iv) *Reliance on documentation and certifications provided between principals and agents.*—(A) *In general.*—Subject to the conditions under § 1.1474-1(a)(3), a withholding agent is permitted to use an agent to fulfill its chapter 4 obligations and such agent's actions are imputed to the principal. However, an agent that makes a payment pursuant to an agency arrangement (paying agent) is also a withholding agent with respect to the payment unless an exception under § 1.1473-1(d) applies. Therefore, the paying agent will have its own obligation to determine the chapter 4 status of the payee and withhold upon the payment if required. Although a paying agent is generally a withholding agent for purposes of chapter 4, the financial accounts to which it makes payments are not necessarily financial accounts of the paying agent. See the rules under § 1.1471-5(b)(5) to determine when a financial institution maintains a financial account. In addition, the status of a payment as made with respect to an offshore obligation or as a preexisting obligation will be determined based on such obligation's status in relation to the principal. Further, the due diligence required with respect to the payment will be determined by the status of the principal and not the paying agent. Consequently, a payment that is made, for example, by a paying agent that is a foreign entity on behalf of a principal that is a U.S. withholding agent will be subject to the due diligence applicable to the principal. See § 1.1474-1(a)(3) for rules regarding the reporting obligations of a principal and agent in the case of a payment made by an agent of behalf of a principal.

(B) *Reliance upon certification of the principal.*—An agent that makes a payment on behalf of a principal that it may treat, pursuant to paragraph (d) of this section, as a U.S. withholding agent, participating FFI, or reporting Model 1 FFI may rely upon a certification provided by the principal indicating that the principal has obtained valid documentation sufficient to determine the chapter 4 status of the payee and may rely upon the principal's determination as to the payee's chapter 4 status. In such a case, the agent will be permitted to rely upon the certification provided by the principal when determining whether it is required to withhold on the payment and will not be liable for any underwithholding that occurs as a result of the principal's failure to properly determine the chapter 4 status of the payee unless the agent knows or has reason to know the certification provided by the principal is inaccurate.

(C) *Document sharing.*—In lieu of obtaining a certification from the principal as described in paragraph (c)(9)(iv)(B) of this section, or when reliance upon such certification is not permitted, an agent that makes a payment on behalf of a principal may rely upon

copies of documentation provided to the principal with respect to the payment. However, in such case, both the principal and the agent are obligated to determine the chapter 4 status of the payee based upon the documentation and ensure that adequate withholding occurs with respect to the payment. While a principal is imputed the knowledge of the agent with respect to the payment, the agent is not imputed the knowledge of the principal.

(D) *Examples.*—(1) *Example 1.*—*Paying agent that does not collect documentation.* A fund, P, that is a participating FFI contracts with a U.S. person, A, to make payments to its account holders with respect to their equity interests in P. P contracts with another agent, B, to obtain documentation sufficient to determine the chapter 4 status of such account holders. Based on the documentation it collects, B determines that none of P's account holders are subject to withholding. P provides a certification to A indicating that it has obtained documentation sufficient to determine the chapter 4 status of P's account holders and that each payee is not subject to withholding under chapter 4. As the actions of B, as P's agent, are attributed to P, P may provide a certification to A indicating that it has determined the chapter 4 status of its payees, even if it is B, and not P, who made the determinations. However, P will be liable for any underwithholding that results from a failure by B to reasonably apply the rules under chapter 4. A is permitted to rely upon the certification provided by P and, accordingly, is not required to withhold on the payments made to P's account holders and would not be liable for any underwithholding that results if the determinations made by B are incorrect unless A had reason to know that chapter 4 status claimed was inaccurate.

(ii) *Example 2.*—*Paying agent that collects documentation.* A fund, P, that is a participating FFI contracts with a U.S. person, A, to make a payment to its account holders on its behalf. P also contracts with A to obtain documentation sufficient to determine the chapter 4 status of P's account holders. Based on the documentation it collects, A determines that none of P's account holders are subject to withholding. As the actions of A, as P's agent, are imputed to P, P will be liable for any underwithholding that results from a failure by A to reasonably apply the rules under chapter 4. P is also required to retain the documentation upon which A relied in determining the chapter 4 status of its account holders. Because A performed the due diligence on behalf of P, A will have reason to know if any of the chapter 4 determinations made based on the documentation received were made incorrectly, and, as a withholding agent with respect to the payment, is liable, in addition to P, for any underwithholding that results from an incorrect determination that withholding was not required. This result applies regardless of whether A retains copies of the documentation obtained with respect to P's account holders or receives a certification from P indicating that P has obtained documentation sufficient to determine the chapter 4 status of its account holders and that each payee is not subject to withholding under chapter 4.

(v) *Reliance upon documentation for accounts acquired in merger or bulk acquisition for value.*—A withholding agent that acquires an account from a predecessor or transferor in a merger or bulk acquisition of accounts for value is permitted to rely upon valid documentation (or copies of valid documentation) collected by the predecessor or transferor. In addition, a withholding agent that acquires an account in a merger or bulk acquisition of accounts for value, other than a related party transaction, from a U.S. withholding agent, a participating FFI that has completed all due diligence required under its agreement with respect to the accounts transferred, or a reporting Model 1 FFI that has completed all due diligence required pursuant to the applicable Model 1 IGA, may also rely upon the predecessor's or transferor's determination of the chapter 4 status of an account holder for a transition period of the lesser of six months from the date of the merger or until the acquirer knows that the claim of status is inaccurate or a change in circumstances occurs. At the end of the transition period, the acquirer will be permitted to rely upon the predecessor's determination as to the chapter 4 status of the account holder only if the documentation that the acquirer has for the account holder, including documentation obtained from the predecessor or transferor, supports the chapter 4 status claimed. An acquirer that discovers at the end of the transition period that the chapter 4 status assigned by the predecessor or transferor to the account holder was incorrect and, as a result, has not withheld as it would have been required to but for its reliance upon the predecessor's determination, will be required to withhold on payments made after the transition period, if any, to the account holder equal to the amount of tax that should have been withheld during the transition period but for the erroneous classification as to the account holder's status. For purposes of this paragraph (c)(9)(v), a related party transaction is a merger or sale of accounts in which either the acquirer is in the same expanded affiliated group as the predecessor or transferor prior to or after the merger or acquisition or the predecessor or transferor (or shareholders of the predecessor or transferor) obtains a controlling interest in the acquirer or in a newly formed entity created for purposes of the merger or acquisition. See § 1.1471-4(c)(2)(ii)(B) for an additional allowance for a participating FFI to rely upon the determination made by another participating FFI as to the chapter 4 status of an account obtained as part of a merger or bulk acquisition for value.

(d) *Documentation requirements to establish payee's chapter 4 status.*— Unless the withholding agent knows or has reason to know otherwise, a withholding agent may rely on the provisions of this paragraph (d) to determine the chapter 4 status of a payee (or other person that receives a payment). Except as otherwise provided in this paragraph (d), a withholding agent is required to obtain a valid withholding certificate or a Form W-9 from a payee in order to treat the payee as having a particular chapter 4 status. Paragraphs (d)(1) through (12) of this section indicate when it is appropriate for a withholding agent to rely upon a written statement, documentary evidence, or other information in lieu of a Form W-8 or W-9. Paragraphs (d)(1) through (12) of this section also prescribe additional documentation requirements that must be met in certain cases in order to treat a payee as having a specific chapter 4 status and specific standards of knowledge that apply to a particular payee, in addition to the general standards of knowledge set forth in paragraph (e) of this section. This paragraph (d) also provides the circumstances in which special documentation rules are permitted with respect to preexisting obligations. A withholding agent may not rely on documentation described in this paragraph (d) if the documentation is not valid or cannot reliably be associated with the payment pursuant to the requirements of paragraph (c) of this section, or the withholding agent knows or has reason to know that such documentation is incorrect or unreliable as described in paragraphs (d) and (e) of this section. If the chapter 4 status of a payee cannot be determined under this paragraph (d) based on documentation received, a withholding agent must apply the presumption rules in paragraph (f) to determine the chapter 4 status of the payee.

(1) *Reliance on pre-FATCA Form W-8.*—To establish a payee's status as a foreign individual, foreign government, government of a U.S. territory, or international organization, a withholding agent may rely upon a pre-FATCA Form W-8 in lieu of obtaining an updated version of the withholding certificate. This reliance is only available in the case of a payee that is an international organization if such payee is described under section 7701(a)(18). To establish the chapter 4 status of a payee that is not a foreign individual, a foreign government, or an international organization, a withholding agent may, for payments made prior to January 1, 2017, rely upon a pre-FATCA Form W-8 in lieu of obtaining an updated version of the withholding certificate if the withholding agent has one or more forms of documentary evidence described in paragraphs (c)(5)(ii), as necessary, to establish the chapter 4 status of the payee and the withholding agent has obtained any additional documentation or information required for the particular chapter 4 status (such as withholding statements, certifications as to owners, or required documentation for underlying owners), as set forth under the specific payee rules in paragraphs (d)(2) through (12) of this section. See paragraph (d)(4)(ii) and (iv) of this section for specific requirements applicable when relying upon a pre-FATCA Form W-8 for a participating FFI or registered deemed-compliant FFI. This paragraph (d)(1) does not apply to nonregistering local banks, FFIs with only low-value accounts, sponsored FFIs, owner-documented FFIs, territory financial institutions that are not the beneficial owners of the payment, foreign central banks (other than a foreign central bank specifically identified as an exempt beneficial owner under a Model 1 IGA or Model 2 IGA), or international organizations not described under section 7701(a)(18).

(2) *Identification of U.S. persons.*—(i) *In general.*—A withholding agent must treat a payee as a U.S. person, including a payee that is a foreign branch of a U.S. person (other than a branch that is treated as a QI) or is an FFI that has elected to be treated as a U.S. person for tax purposes under section 953(d), if it has a valid Form W-9 associated with the payee or if it must presume the payee is a U.S. person under the presumption rules set forth in paragraph (f) of this section. Consistent with the presumption rules in paragraph (f)(3) of this section, a withholding agent must treat a payee that has provided a valid Form W-9 as a specified U.S. person unless the Form W-9 contains a certification that the payee is other than a specified U.S. person. Notwithstanding the foregoing, a withholding agent receiving a Form W-9 indicating that the payee is other than a specified U.S. person must treat the payee as a specified U.S. person if the withholding agent knows or has reason to know that the payee's claim that it is other than a specified U.S. person is incorrect. For example, a withholding agent that receives a Form W-9 from a payee that is an individual would be required to treat the payee as a specified U.S. person regardless of whether the Form W-9 indicates that the payee is not a specified U.S. person, because an individual

that is a U.S. person is not excepted from the definition of a specified U.S. person.

(ii) *Reliance on documentary evidence.*—A withholding agent may also treat the payee as a U.S. person that is other than a specified U.S. person if the withholding agent has documentary evidence described in paragraphs (c)(5)(i)(C) and (D) of this section or general documentary evidence (as described in paragraph (c)(5)(ii)(A) of this section) that both establishes that the payee is a U.S. person and establishes (either through the documentation or the application of the rules in § 1.6049-4(c)(1)(ii) or paragraph (f)(3) of this section) that the payee is an exempt recipient. For purposes of the previous sentence, an exempt recipient means with respect to a withholding agent other than a participating FFI or registered deemed-compliant FFI, an exempt recipient under § 1.6049-4(c)(1)(ii) or, with respect to a withholding agent that is a participating FFI or registered deemed-compliant FFI, a U.S. person other than a specified U.S. person as described under § 1.1473-1(c).

(iii) *Preexisting obligations.*—As an alternative to applying the rules in paragraphs (d)(2)(i) and (ii) of this section, a withholding agent that makes a payment with respect to a preexisting obligation may treat a payee as a U.S. person if it has a notation in its files that it has previously reviewed a Form W-9 that established that the payee is a U.S. person and has retained the payee's TIN. A withholding agent, other than a participating FFI or registered deemed-compliant FFI, may also treat a payee of a payment with respect to a preexisting obligation as a U.S. person if it has previously classified the payee as a U.S. person for purposes of chapter 3 or 61 and established (through the documentation or the application of the rules in § 1.6049-4(c)(1)(ii)) that the payee is an exempt recipient for purposes of chapter 61.

(3) *Identification of individuals that are foreign persons.*—(i) *In general.*—A withholding agent may treat a payee as an individual that is a foreign person if the withholding agent has a withholding certificate identifying the payee as such a person.

(ii) *Exception for offshore obligations.*—A withholding agent that makes a payment with respect to an offshore obligation may treat the payee as an individual that is a foreign person if it obtains documentary evidence supporting the payee's claim of status as a foreign individual (as described in paragraph (c)(5)(i)) or if the payee is presumed to be an individual that is a foreign person under the presumption rules set forth in paragraph (f) of this section.

(4) *Identification of participating FFIs and registered deemed-compliant FFIs.*—(i) *In general.*—Except as otherwise provided in paragraphs (d)(4)(ii) through (iv) or paragraphs (e)(3)(i) and (ii) of this section, a withholding agent may treat a payee as a participating FFI or registered deemed-compliant FFI only if the withholding agent has a withholding certificate identifying the payee as a participating FFI, registered deemed-compliant FFI, or branch thereof (including an entity that is disregarded as an entity separate from the FFI), and the withholding certificate contains a GIIN described in paragraph (e)(3) of this section that is verified against the published IRS FFI list in the manner described in paragraph (e)(3) of this section (indicating when a withholding agent may rely upon a GIIN). For when a withholding agent may treat a payee as a registered deemed-compliant FFI that is a sponsored investment entity or sponsored controlled foreign corporation, see paragraph (d)(4)(vi) of this section. See paragraph (c)(3)(iii) of this section for additional requirements that apply to a valid withholding certificate provided by a participating FFI or registered deemed-compliant FFI that is a flow-through entity or is acting as an intermediary with respect to the payment.

(ii) *Exception for payments made prior to January 1, 2017, with respect to preexisting obligations (transitional).*—For payments made prior to January 1, 2017, with respect to a preexisting obligation, a withholding agent may treat a payee as a participating FFI or registered deemed-compliant FFI, or branch thereof (including an entity that is disregarded as an entity separate from the FFI), if the payee has provided the withholding agent with a pre-FATCA Form W-8 and (either orally or in writing) its GIIN and has indicated whether it is a participating FFI or a registered deemed-compliant FFI (or whether such branch or disregarded entity is treated as a participating FFI or a registered deemed-compliant FFI), and the withholding agent has verified the GIIN of the FFI, branch, or disregarded entity, as the context requires, in the manner described in paragraph (e)(3) of this section.

(iii) *Exception for offshore obligations.*—A withholding agent that makes a payment, other than a payment of U.S. source FDAP income, with respect to an offshore obligation may treat a payee as a participating FFI or registered deemed-compliant FFI, or branch thereof (including an entity that is disregarded as an entity separate from the FFI), if the payee provides the withholding agent with its

GIIN and states whether the payee is a participating FFI or a registered deemed-compliant FFI, and the withholding agent verifies the GIIN in the manner described in paragraph (e)(3) of this section. A withholding agent that makes a payment of U.S. source FDAP income with respect to an offshore obligation may treat the payee as a participating FFI or registered deemed-compliant FFI, or branch thereof (including an entity that is disregarded as an entity separate from the FFI) if—

(A) The payee provides the withholding agent with—

*(1)* A written statement that contains the payee's GIIN, states that the payee is the beneficial owner of the payment, and indicates whether the payee is treated as a participating FFI or a registered deemed-compliant FFI, as appropriate; and

*(2)* Documentary evidence supporting the payee's claim of foreign status; and

(B) The withholding agent verifies the GIIN in the manner described in paragraph (e)(3) of this section.

(iv) *Exceptions for payments to reporting Model 1 FFIs.*—(A) For payments made prior to January 1, 2015, a withholding agent may treat a payee that is an FFI or branch of an FFI (including an entity that is disregarded as an entity separate from the FFI) as a reporting Model 1 FFI if it receives a withholding certificate from the payee indicating that the payee is a reporting Model 1 FFI and the country in which the payee is a reporting Model 1 FFI, regardless of whether the certificate contains a GIIN for the payee.

(B) For payments made prior to January 1, 2015, with respect to a preexisting obligation, a withholding agent may treat a payee as a reporting Model 1 FFI if it obtains a pre-FATCA Form W-8 from the payee, and the payee indicates (either orally or in writing) that it is a reporting Model 1 FFI and the country in which it is a reporting Model 1 FFI, regardless of whether the certificate contains a GIIN for the payee.

(C) For payments made prior to January 1, 2015, with respect to an offshore obligation, a withholding agent may treat a payee as a reporting Model 1 FFI if the payee informs the withholding agent that the payee is a reporting Model 1 FFI and provides the country in which the payee is a reporting Model 1 FFI. In the case of a payment of U.S. source FDAP income, such payee must also provide a written statement that it is the beneficial owner and documentary evidence supporting the payee's claim of foreign status (as described in paragraph (c)(5)(i) of this section).

(D) For payments made on or after January 1, 2015, that do not constitute U.S. source FDAP income, the withholding agent may continue to treat a payee as a reporting Model 1 FFI if the payee provides the withholding agent with its GIIN, either orally or in writing, and the withholding agent verifies the GIIN in the manner described in paragraph (e)(3) of this section.

(v) *Reason to know.*—See paragraph (e) of this section for when a withholding agent will have reason to know that a withholding certificate or written statement provided by a payee claiming status as a participating FFI or registered deemed-compliant FFI is incorrect or invalid.

(vi) *Sponsored investment entities and sponsored controlled foreign corporations.*—(A) *In general.*—A withholding agent may treat a payee as a sponsored investment entity or sponsored controlled foreign corporation if the withholding agent has a withholding certificate identifying the payee as a sponsored investment entity or sponsored controlled foreign corporation (as applicable) and the withholding certificate includes the GIIN of the sponsored investment entity or sponsored controlled foreign corporation entity (as applicable), which the withholding agent has verified against the published IRS FFI list in the manner described in paragraph (e)(3)(i) of this section.

(B) *Payments made prior to January 1, 2017 (transitional).*—For payments made prior to January 1, 2017, a sponsored investment entity or sponsored controlled foreign corporation may provide the GIIN of its sponsoring entity on the withholding certificate, which the withholding agent must verify against the published IRS FFI list in the manner described in paragraph (e)(3)(i) of this section.

(C) *Payments made after December 31, 2016, to payees documented prior to January 1, 2017.*—For a payment made after December 31, 2016, to a payee that the withholding agent has documented prior to January 1, 2017, as a sponsored investment entity or sponsored controlled foreign corporation with a valid withholding certificate that includes the GIIN of the sponsoring entity, the withholding agent must obtain and verify the GIIN of the sponsored investment entity or sponsored controlled foreign corporation against the published IRS FFI list in the manner described in paragraph (e)(3)(i) of this section by March 31, 2017. Notwithstanding the preceding sentence, a GIIN is not required for a payee that provides a valid withholding certificate prior to January 1, 2017, that identifies the

payee as a sponsored FFI and includes the GIIN of the sponsoring entity if the withholding agent determines, based on information provided on the withholding certificate, that the sponsored entity is resident, organized, or located in a jurisdiction that is treated as having a Model 1 IGA in effect. A withholding agent required to obtain a GIIN of the sponsored investment entity or sponsored controlled foreign corporation under this paragraph (d)(4)(vi)(C) may obtain such GIIN by oral or written confirmation (including by e-mail) rather than obtaining a new withholding certificate, provided that the withholding agent retains a record of the confirmation, which will become part of the withholding certificate.

(5) *Identification of certified deemed-compliant FFIs.*—(i) *In general.*—Except as otherwise provided in this paragraph (d)(5), a withholding agent may treat a payee as a certified deemed-compliant FFI, other than a sponsored, closely held investment vehicle, if the withholding agent has a withholding certificate that identifies the payee as a certified deemed-compliant FFI, and the withholding certificate contains a certification by the payee that it meets the requirements to qualify as the type of certified deemed-compliant FFI identified on the withholding certificate. See paragraph (c)(3)(iii) of this section for additional requirements that apply to a valid withholding certificate provided by a certified deemed-compliant FFI that is a flow-through entity or is acting as an intermediary with respect to the payment, or by a U.S. branch of a certified deemed-compliant FFI.

(ii) *Sponsored, closely held investment vehicles.*—(A) *In general.*—A withholding agent may treat a payee as a sponsored, closely held investment vehicle described in § 1.1471-5(f)(2)(iii) if the withholding agent can reliably associate the payment with a withholding certificate that identifies the payee as a sponsored, closely held investment vehicle and includes the sponsoring entity's GIIN, which the withholding agent has verified against the published IRS FFI list in the manner described in paragraph (e)(3) of this section. In addition to the standards of knowledge rules indicated in paragraph (e) of this section, a withholding agent will have reason to know that the payee is not a sponsored, closely held investment vehicle described in § 1.1471-5(f)(2)(iii) if its AML due diligence indicates that the payee has in excess of 20 individual investors that own direct and/or indirect interests in the payee. See paragraph (c)(3)(iii) of this section for additional requirements that apply to a valid withholding certificate provided by a sponsored, closely held investment vehicle that is a flow-through entity or is acting as an intermediary with respect to the payment, or by a U.S. branch of such vehicle.

(B) *Offshore obligations.*—A withholding agent that makes a payment with respect to an offshore obligation may treat a payee as a sponsored, closely held investment vehicle if it obtains a written statement that indicates that the payee is a sponsored, closely held investment vehicle, and provides the sponsoring entity's GIIN, which the withholding agent has verified in the manner described in paragraph (e)(3) of this section. In the case of a payment of U.S. source FDAP income, the written statement must also indicate that the payee is the beneficial owner and must be supplemented with documentary evidence supporting the payee's claim of foreign status (as described in paragraph (c)(5)(i) of this section).

(iii) *Certain investment entities that do not maintain financial accounts.*—(A) *In general.*—A withholding agent may treat a payee as an investment entity that does not maintain financial accounts described in § 1.1471-5(f)(2)(v) if the withholding agent can reliably associate the payment with a withholding certificate that identifies the payee as an investment entity that does not maintain financial accounts. In addition to the standards of knowledge rules indicated in paragraph (e) of this section, a withholding agent will have reason to know that the payee is not an investment entity that does not maintain financial accounts described in § 1.1471-5(f)(2)(v) if its AML due diligence documentation indicates that the payee has financial accounts.

(B) *Offshore obligations.*—A withholding agent that makes a payment with respect to an offshore obligation may treat a payee as an investment advisor and investment manager described in § 1.1471-5(f)(2)(v) if it obtains a written statement that indicates that the payee is an investment advisor and investment manager. In the case of a payment of U.S. source FDAP income, the written statement must also indicate that the payee is the beneficial owner and must be supplemented with documentary evidence supporting the payee's claim of foreign status (as described in paragraph (c)(5)(i) of this section).

(6) *Identification of owner-documented FFIs.*—(i) *In general.*—A withholding agent may treat a payee as an owner-documented FFI if all the following requirements of paragraphs (d)(6)(i)(A) through (F) of this section are met. A withholding agent may not rely upon a withholding certificate to treat a payee as an owner-documented FFI, either in whole or in part, if the withholding certificate does not

contain all of the information and associated documentation required by paragraphs (d)(6)(i)(A), (C), and (D) of this section.

(A) The withholding agent has a withholding certificate that identifies the payee as an owner-documented FFI that is not acting as an intermediary;

(B) The withholding agent is a U.S. financial institution, participating FFI, or reporting Model 1 FFI that agrees pursuant to §1.1471-5(f)(3) to act as a designated withholding agent with respect to the payee;

(C) The payee submits to the withholding agent an FFI owner reporting statement that meets the requirements of paragraph (d)(6)(iv) of this section;

(D) The payee submits to the withholding agent valid documentation meeting the requirements of paragraph (d)(6)(iii) of this section with respect to each person identified on the FFI owner reporting statement;

(E) The withholding agent does not know or have reason to know that the payee (or any other FFI that is an owner of the payee and that the designated withholding agent is treating as an owner-documented FFI) maintains any financial account for a nonparticipating FFI; and

(F) The withholding agent does not know or have reason to know that the payee is a member of an expanded affiliated group with any FFI that is a depository institution, custodial institution, or specified insurance company, or that the FFI has any specified U.S. persons that own an equity interest in the FFI or a debt interest (other than a debt interest that is not a financial account or that has a balance or value not exceeding $50,000) in the FFI other than those identified on the FFI owner reporting statement described in paragraph (d)(6)(iv) of this section.

(ii) *Auditor's letter substitute.*—A payee may, in lieu of providing an FFI owner reporting statement and documentation for each owner of the FFI as described in paragraphs (d)(6)(i)(C) and (D) of this section, provide a letter from an auditor or an attorney that is licensed in the United States or whose firm has a location in the United States, signed no more than four years prior to the date of the payment, that certifies that the firm or representative has reviewed the payee's documentation with respect to all of its owners and debt holders described in paragraph (d)(6)(iv) of this section in accordance with §1.1471-4(c) and that the payee meets the requirements of §1.1471-5(f)(3). The payee must also provide an FFI owner reporting statement and a Form W-9, with any applicable waiver, for each specified U.S. person that owns a direct or indirect interest in the payee or that holds debt interests described in paragraph (d)(6)(iv) of this section. A withholding agent may rely upon the letter described in this paragraph (d)(6)(ii) if it does not know or have reason to know that any of the information contained in the letter is unreliable or incorrect.

(iii) *Documentation for owners and debt holders of payee.*—Acceptable documentation for an individual owning an equity interest in the payee or a debt holder described in paragraph (d)(6)(iv) of this section means a valid withholding certificate, valid Form W-9 (including any necessary waiver), or documentary evidence establishing the foreign status of the individual as set forth in paragraph (d)(3)(ii) of this section (regardless of whether the payment is made with respect to an offshore obligation). Acceptable documentation for a specified U.S. person means a valid Form W-9 (including any necessary waiver). Acceptable documentation for all other persons owning an equity or debt interest in the payee means documentation described in this paragraph (d), applicable to the chapter 4 status claimed by the person. The rules for reliably associating a payment with a withholding certificate or documentary evidence set forth in paragraph (c) of this section, the rules for payee documentation provided in this paragraph (d), and the standards of knowledge set forth in paragraph (e) of this section will apply to documentation submitted by the owners and debt holders by substituting the phrase "owner of the payee" or "debt holder" for "payee."

(iv) *Content of FFI owner reporting statement.*—The FFI owner reporting statement provided by an owner-documented FFI must contain the information required by this paragraph (d)(6)(iv) and is subject to the general rules applicable to all withholding statements described in paragraph (c)(3)(iii)(B)(1) of this section. An FFI that is a partnership, simple trust, or grantor trust may substitute an NWP withholding statement described in §1.1441-5(c)(3)(iv) or a foreign simple trust or foreign grantor trust withholding statement described in §1.1441-5(e)(5)(iv) for the FFI owner reporting statement, provided that the NWP withholding certificate or foreign simple trust or foreign grantor trust withholding certificate contains all of the information required in this paragraph (d)(6)(iv). The owner reporting statement will expire on the last day of the third calendar year following the year in which the statement was provided to the withholding agent unless an exception in paragraph (c)(6)(ii) of this section (for example, accounts with a balance or value of $1,000,000

or less) or this paragraph (d)(6) applies. The owner-documented FFI will also be required to provide the withholding agent with an updated owner reporting statement if there is a change in circumstances as required under paragraph (c)(6)(ii)(E) of this section.

(A) The FFI owner reporting statement must provide the following information:

(1) The name, address, TIN (if any), and chapter 4 status of every individual and specified U.S. person that owns a direct or indirect equity interest in the payee (looking through all entities other than specified U.S. persons).

(2) The name, address, TIN (if any), and chapter 4 status of every individual and specified U.S. person that owns a debt interest in the payee (including any indirect debt interest, which includes debt interests in any entity that directly or indirectly owns the payee or any direct or indirect equity interest in a debt holder of the payee), in either such case if the debt interest constitutes a financial account in excess of $50,000 (disregarding all such debt interests owned by participating FFIs, registered deemed-compliant FFIs, certified deemed-compliant FFIs, excepted NFFEs, exempt beneficial owners, or U.S. persons other than specified U.S. persons).

(3) Any other information the withholding agent reasonably requests in order to fulfill its obligations under chapter 4.

(B) The information on the FFI owner reporting statement may contain names of equity and debt holders that are prepopulated by the withholding agent based on prior information provided to the withholding agent by the payee if the prepopulated form instructs the payee to amend the statement if the contents are inaccurate, incomplete, or have changed, and the payee confirms in writing that the FFI owner reporting statement submitted to the withholding agent is accurate and complete.

(C) The FFI owner reporting statement may be submitted in any form that meets the requirements of this paragraph, including a form used for purposes of AML due diligence.

(v) *Exception for preexisting obligations (transitional).*—A withholding agent may treat a payment made prior to January 1, 2017, with respect to a preexisting obligation as made to an owner-documented FFI if the withholding agent has collected, for purposes of satisfying its AML due diligence, documentation with respect to each individual and specified U.S. person that owns a direct or indirect interest in the payee, other than an interest as a creditor, within four years of the date of payment, that documentation is sufficient to satisfy the AML due diligence requirements of the jurisdiction in which the withholding agent maintains the account, the withholding agent has sufficient information to report all specified U.S. persons that own an interest in the payee, and the withholding agent does not know, or have reason to know, that any nonparticipating FFI owns an equity interest in the FFI or that any nonparticipating FFI or specified U.S. person owns a debt interest in the FFI constituting a financial account in excess of $50,000.

(vi) *Exception for offshore obligations.*—A withholding agent that is making a payment, other than a payment of U.S. source FDAP income, with respect to an offshore obligation may, in lieu of obtaining a withholding certificate as otherwise required under paragraph (d)(6)(i)(A) of this section, rely upon a written statement that indicates the payee meets the requirements to qualify as an owner-documented FFI under §1.1471-5(f)(3) and is not acting as an intermediary, if the withholding agent provides a written notice to the payee indicating that the payee is required to update the written statement and all associated documentation (such as the FFI owner reporting statement and underlying documentation) within 30 days of a change in circumstances.

(vii) *Exception for certain offshore obligations of $1,000,000 or less.*—(A) A withholding agent may treat the payment as being made to an owner-documented FFI if—

(1) The payment is made with respect to an offshore obligation that has a balance or value not exceeding $1,000,000 on the later of June 30, 2014, or the last day of the calendar year in which the account was opened, and the last day of each subsequent year preceding the payment, applying the aggregation principles of §1.1471-5(b)(4);

(2) The withholding agent has collected documentation or a certification as to the payee's owners (either for purposes of complying with its AML due diligence or for purposes of satisfying the requirements of this paragraph (d)(6)(vii)) sufficient to identify every individual and specified U.S. person that owns any direct or indirect interest in the payee (other than an interest as a creditor) and determine the chapter 4 status of such person;

(3) The documentation described in paragraph (d)(6)(vii)(A)(2) of this section is sufficient to satisfy the AML due diligence requirements of the jurisdiction in which the withholding agent maintains the account (and such jurisdiction is a FATF-compliant jurisdiction);

(4) The withholding agent has sufficient information to report all specified U.S. persons that own an interest in the payee in accordance with § 1.1474-1(d); and

(5) The withholding agent does not know, or have reason to know, that the payee has any contingent beneficiaries or designated classes with unidentified beneficiaries or owners, that any nonparticipating FFI owns a direct or indirect equity interest in the payee, or that any specified U.S. persons or nonparticipating FFIs own a debt interest constituting a financial account in excess of $50,000 in the payee (other than specified U.S. persons that the withholding agent has sufficient information to report).

(B) For example, a withholding agent that is required to obtain a certification from the payee identifying all persons owning an interest in the payee as part of its AML due diligence will not be required to obtain an FFI owner reporting statement, provided the other conditions of this paragraph (d)(6)(vii) are met. On the other hand, a withholding agent that has only obtained documentation for persons owning a certain threshold percentage of the payee will be required to obtain additional documentation to satisfy the requirements of this paragraph (d)(6)(vii). A withholding agent that treats a payee as an owner-documented FFI pursuant to this paragraph (d)(6)(vii) will not be required to obtain new documentation, including the FFI owner reporting statement, until there is a change in circumstances or until the account balance or value exceeds $1,000,000 on the last day of the calendar year.

(7) *Nonreporting IGA FFIs.*—(i) *In general.*—A withholding agent may treat a payee as a nonreporting IGA FFI described in § 1.1471-1(b)(83)(ii) (unless such FFI is treated as a registered deemed-compliant FFI under Annex II of the Model 2 IGA) or as a nonreporting IGA FFI described in § 1.1471-1(b)(83)(i), (iv), or (v) if the withholding agent has a withholding certificate identifying the payee, or the relevant branch of the payee, as a nonreporting IGA FFI. A withholding agent may treat a payee as a nonreporting IGA FFI described in § 1.1471-1(b)(83)(ii) that is treated as a registered deemed-compliant FFI under Annex II of the Model 2 IGA or as a nonreporting IGA FFI described in § 1.1471-1(b)(83)(iii) if the withholding agent has a withholding certificate identifying the payee, or the relevant branch of the payee, as a nonreporting IGA FFI, and the withholding certificate contains a GIIN for the payee that is verified against the published IRS FFI list in the manner described in paragraph (e)(3) of this section.

(ii) *Exception for offshore obligations.*—A withholding agent that makes a payment with respect to an offshore obligation may treat a payee as a nonreporting IGA FFI if it can reliably associate the payment with a written statement identifying the payee (or the relevant branch of the payee) as a nonreporting IGA FFI and, with respect to a payment of U.S. source FDAP income, the written statement indicates that the payee is the beneficial owner of the income and is accompanied by documentary evidence supporting a claim of foreign status (as described in paragraph (c)(5)(i) of this section). A withholding agent that makes a payment with respect to an offshore obligation may also treat a payee as a nonreporting IGA FFI if the withholding agent has a permanent residence address for the payee, or an address of the relevant branch of the payee, and has obtained a notification, either orally or in writing, indicating that the payee is not acting as an intermediary and general documentary evidence (as described in paragraph (c)(5)(ii)(A) of this section) that provides the withholding agent with sufficient information to reasonably determine that the payee is an entity listed as a nonreporting IGA FFI pursuant to a Model 1 or Model 2 IGA.

(8) *Identification of nonparticipating FFIs.*—(i) *In general.*—A withholding agent is required to treat a payee as a nonparticipating FFI if the withholding agent can reliably associate the payment with a withholding certificate identifying the payee as a nonparticipating FFI, the withholding agent knows or has reason to know that the payee is a nonparticipating FFI, or the withholding agent is required to treat the payee as a nonparticipating FFI under the presumption rules described in paragraph (f) of this section.

(ii) *Special documentation rules for payments made to an exempt beneficial owner through a nonparticipating FFI.*—A withholding agent may treat a payment made to a nonparticipating FFI as beneficially owned by an exempt beneficial owner if the withholding agent can reliably associate the payment with—

(A) A withholding certificate that identifies the payee as a nonparticipating FFI that is either acting as an intermediary or is a flow-through entity; and

(B) An exempt beneficial owner withholding statement that meets the requirements of paragraphs (c)(3)(iii)(B)(1) and (4) of this section and contains the associated documentation necessary to establish the chapter 4 status of the exempt beneficial owner in accordance with paragraph (d)(9) of this section as if the exempt beneficial owner were the payee.

(9) *Identification of exempt beneficial owners.*—(i) *Identification of foreign governments, governments of U.S. territories, international organizations, and foreign central banks of issue.*—(A) *In general.*—A withholding agent may treat a payee as a foreign government, government of a U.S. territory, international organization, or foreign central bank of issue if it has a withholding certificate that identifies the payee as such an entity, indicates that the payee is the beneficial owner of the payment, and indicates that the payee is not engaged in commercial financial activities with respect to the payments or accounts identified on the form. A withholding agent may treat a payee as an international organization without requiring a withholding certificate if the name of the payee is one that is designated as an international organization by executive order (pursuant to 22 U.S.C. 288 through 288f) and other facts surrounding the transaction reasonably indicate that the international organization is not receiving the payment as an intermediary on behalf of another person. A withholding agent may treat a payee as an exempt beneficial owner pursuant to a Model 1 IGA or Model 2 IGA if it has a withholding certificate that identifies the payee as such an entity and indicates that the payee is the beneficial owner of the payment.

(B) *Exception for offshore obligations.*—A withholding agent that makes a payment, other than a payment of U.S. source FDAP income, with respect to an offshore obligation may treat a payee as a foreign government, government of a U.S. territory, international organization, or foreign central bank of issue if the payee provides a written statement that it is such an entity and the written statement indicates that the payee receives the payment as a beneficial owner (within the meaning provided in § 1.1471-6). A written statement provided by a foreign central bank of issue must also state that the foreign central bank of issue does not receive the payment in connection with a commercial activity as provided in § 1.1471-6(h).

(C) *Exception for preexisting offshore obligations.*—A withholding agent that makes a payment, other than a payment of U.S. source FDAP income, with respect to an offshore obligation that is also a preexisting obligation may treat the payee as a foreign government, government of a U.S. territory, international organization, or foreign central bank of issue if—

(1) The payee is generally known to the withholding agent to be, the payee's name and the facts surrounding the payment reasonably indicate, or the withholding agent has preexisting account documentary evidence (as described in paragraph (c)(5)(ii)(B) of this section) that reasonably indicates that the payee is a foreign government or government of a U.S territory, a political subdivision of a foreign government or government of a U.S. territory, any wholly owned agency or instrumentality of any one or more of the foregoing, an international organization, a foreign central bank of issue, or the Bank for International Settlements; and

(2) The withholding agent does not know that the payee is not the beneficial owner, within the meaning of § 1.1471-6(b) through (e) (disregarding any presumption that a financial institution is assumed to be an intermediary absent documentation indicating otherwise) or a foreign central bank of issue receiving the payment in connection) with a commercial activity.

(ii) *Identification of retirement funds.*—(A) *In general.*—A withholding agent may treat a payee as a retirement fund described in § 1.1471-6(f) if it has a withholding certificate in which the payee certifies that it is a retirement fund meeting the requirements of § 1.1471-6(f).

(B) *Exception for offshore obligations.*—A withholding agent that makes a payment with respect to an offshore obligation may treat the payment as being made to a retirement fund described in § 1.1471-6(f) if it obtains a written statement in which the payee certifies that it is a retirement fund under the laws of its local jurisdiction meeting the requirements of § 1.1471-6(f) and, with respect to a payment of U.S. source FDAP income, documentary evidence supporting a claim of foreign status (as described in paragraph (c)(5)(i) of this section). A withholding agent that makes a payment with respect to an offshore obligation may also treat the payment as made to a retirement fund if it obtains general documentary evidence (as described in paragraph (c)(5)(ii)(A) of this section) that provides the withholding agent with sufficient information to establish that the payee is a retirement fund meeting the requirements of § 1.1471-6(f).

(C) *Exception for preexisting offshore obligations.*—A withholding agent that makes a payment with respect to an offshore obligation that is also a preexisting obligation, may treat the payee as a retirement fund described in § 1.1471-6(f) if the withholding agent has general documentary evidence or preexisting account documentary evidence (as described in paragraphs (c)(5)(ii)(A) or (B)) that establishes that the payee is a foreign entity that qualifies as a retirement fund in the country in which the payee is organized.

(iii) *Identification of entities wholly owned by exempt beneficial owners.*—A withholding agent may treat a payee as an entity described in § 1.1471-6(g) (referring to certain entities wholly owned by exempt beneficial owners) if the withholding agent has—

(A) A withholding certificate or, for a payment made with respect to an offshore obligation, a written statement that identifies the payee as an investment entity that is the beneficial owner of the payment;

(B) An owner reporting statement that contains the name, address, TIN (if any), chapter 4 status (identifying the type of exempt beneficial owner), and a description of the type of documentation (Form W-8 or other documentary evidence) provided to the withholding agent for every person that owns a direct equity interest, or a debt interest constituting a financial account, in the payee, and that is subject to the general rules applicable to all withholding statements described in paragraph (c)(3)(iii)(B)(1) of this section; and

(C) Documentation for every person identified on the owner reporting statement establishing, pursuant to the documentation requirements described in this paragraph (d)(9), that such person is an exempt beneficial owner (without regard to whether the person is a beneficial owner of the payment).

(10) *Identification of territory financial institutions.*— (i) *Identification of territory financial institutions that are beneficial owners.*—(A) *In general.*—A withholding agent may treat a payee as a territory financial institution if the withholding agent has a withholding certificate identifying the payee as a territory financial institution that beneficially owns the payment. See paragraph (d)(11)(viii) of this section for rules for documenting territory NFFEs.

(B) *Exception for preexisting offshore obligations.*—A withholding agent that makes a payment with respect to an offshore obligation that is also a preexisting obligation may treat the payee as a territory financial institution if the withholding agent receives written notification, whether signed or not, that the payee is the beneficial owner of the payment and the withholding agent has general documentary evidence (as described in paragraph (c)(5)(ii)(A) of this section) or preexisting account documentary evidence (as described in paragraph (c)(5)(ii)(B) of this section) establishing that the payee was organized or incorporated under the laws of any U.S. territory and is a depository institution, custodial institution, or specified insurance company.

(ii) *Identification of territory financial institutions acting as intermediaries or that are flow-through entities.*—A withholding agent may treat a payment as being made to a territory financial institution that is acting as an intermediary or that is a flow-through entity if the withholding agent has an intermediary withholding certificate or flow-through withholding certificate as described in paragraph (c)(3)(iii) of this section that identifies the person who receives the payment as a territory financial institution. A withholding agent that obtains the documentation described in the preceding sentence may treat the territory financial institution as the payee if the withholding certificate contains a certification that the territory financial institution agrees to be treated as a U.S. person with respect to the payment. If the withholding certificate does not contain such a certification, then the withholding agent must treat the person on whose behalf the territory financial institution receives the payment as the payee. See paragraph (c)(3)(iii) of this section for additional documentation that must accompany the withholding certificate of the territory financial institution in this case.

(iii) *Reason to know.*—In addition to the general standards of knowledge described in paragraph (e) of this section, a withholding agent will have reason to know that an entity is not a territory financial institution if the withholding agent has: a current residence or mailing address, either in the entity's account files or on documentation provided by the payee, for the entity that is outside the U.S. territory in which the entity claims to be organized; a current telephone number for the payee that has a country code other than the country code for the U.S. territory or has an area code other than the area code(s) of the applicable U.S. territory and no telephone number for the payee in the applicable U.S. territory; or standing instructions for the withholding agent to pay amounts from its account to an address or account outside the applicable U.S. territory. A withholding agent that has knowledge of a current address, current telephone number, or standing payment instructions for the entity outside of the applicable U.S. territory, may nevertheless treat the entity as a territory financial institution if it obtains documentary evidence that establishes that the entity was organized in the applicable U.S. territory.

(11) *Identification of excepted NFFEs.*—(i) *Identification of excepted nonfinancial group entities.*—(A) *In general.*—A withholding agent may treat a payee as an excepted nonfinancial group entity described

in § 1.1471-5(e)(5)(i) if the withholding agent has a withholding certificate identifying the payee as such an entity.

(B) *Exception for offshore obligations.*—A withholding agent that makes a payment with respect to an offshore obligation may treat a payee as an excepted nonfinancial group entity described in § 1.1471-5(e)(5)(i) if the withholding agent obtains:

(1) A written statement in which the payee certifies that it is a foreign entity operating primarily as an excepted nonfinancial group entity for a group that primarily engages in a business other than a financial business described in § 1.1471-5(e)(4) and, with respect to a payment of U.S. source FDAP income, documentary evidence supporting a claim of foreign status (as described in paragraph (c)(5)(i) of this section); or

(2) General documentary evidence (as described in paragraph (c)(5)(ii)(A) of this section) that provides the withholding agent with sufficient information to establish that the payee is an excepted nonfinancial group entity described in § 1.1471-5(e)(5)(i).

(ii) *Identification of excepted nonfinancial start-up companies.*— (A) *In general.*—A withholding agent may treat a payee as an excepted nonfinancial start-up company described in § 1.1471-5(e)(5)(ii) if the withholding agent has a withholding certificate that identifies the payee as a start-up company that intends to operate as other than a financial institution and the withholding certificate provides a formation date for the payee that is less than 24 months prior to the date of the payment.

(B) *Exception for offshore obligations.*—A withholding agent that makes a payment with respect to an offshore obligation may treat a payee as an excepted nonfinancial start-up company described in § 1.1471-5(e)(5)(ii) if it obtains—

(1) A written statement from the payee in which the payee certifies that it is a foreign entity formed for the purpose of operating a business other than that of a financial institution and provides the entity's formation date which was less than 24 months prior to the date of the payment and, with respect to a payment of U.S. source FDAP income, documentary evidence supporting a claim of foreign status (as described in paragraph (c)(5)(i) of this section); or

(2) General documentary evidence (as described in paragraph (c)(5)(ii)(A) of this section) that provides the withholding agent with sufficient information to establish that the payee is a foreign entity other than a financial institution and has a formation date which is less than 24 months prior to the date of the payment.

(C) *Exception for preexisting offshore obligations.*—A withholding agent may treat a payment made with respect to an offshore obligation that is also a preexisting obligation as made to a start-up company described in § 1.1471-5(e)(5)(ii) if the withholding agent has general documentary evidence (as described in paragraph (c)(5)(ii)(A) of this section) or preexisting account documentary evidence (as described in paragraph (c)(5)(ii)(B) of this section) that provides the withholding agent sufficient information to establish that the payee is, or intends to be, engaged in a business other than as a financial institution and establishes that the payee is a foreign entity that was organized less than 24 months prior to the date of the payment.

(iii) *Identification of excepted nonfinancial entities in liquidation or bankruptcy.*—(A) *In general.*—A withholding agent may treat a payee as an excepted nonfinancial entity in liquidation or bankruptcy, as described in § 1.1471-5(e)(5)(iii), if the withholding agent has a withholding certificate that identifies the payee as such an entity and the withholding agent has no knowledge that the payee has claimed to be such an entity for more than three years. A withholding agent may continue to treat a payee as an entity described in this paragraph for longer than three years if it obtains, in addition to a withholding certificate, documentary evidence such as a bankruptcy filing or other public document that supports the payee's claim that it remains in liquidation or bankruptcy.

(B) *Exception for offshore obligations.*—A withholding agent that makes a payment with respect to an offshore obligation may treat the payee as an excepted nonfinancial entity in liquidation or bankruptcy, as described in § 1.1471-5(e)(5)(iii) if the withholding agent has general documentary evidence (as described in paragraph (c)(5)(ii)(A) of this section) or a copy of a bankruptcy filing, or similar documentation, establishing that the payee is a foreign entity in liquidation or bankruptcy and establishing that prior to the liquidation or bankruptcy filing, the payee was engaged in a business other than that of a financial institution. A withholding agent may also treat the payee with respect to an offshore obligation as an excepted nonfinancial entity in liquidation or bankruptcy, as described in § 1.1471-5(e)(5)(iii), if the withholding agent obtains a written statement stating that the payee is a foreign entity in the process of liquidating or reorganizing with the intent to continue or recommence its former business as a nonfinancial institution, the withholding agent has no knowledge that the payee has claimed to be such an entity for more than three years (unless the withholding agent has obtained additional documentary evidence to support the claim that the entity remains in bankruptcy or liquidation), and, with respect to a payment of U.S. source FDAP income, documentary evidence supporting a claim of foreign status (as described in paragraph (c)(5)(i) of this section).

(C) *Exception for preexisting offshore obligations.*—A withholding agent that makes a payment with respect to an offshore obligation that is also a preexisting obligation may treat a payee as an excepted nonfinancial entity in liquidation or bankruptcy, as described in § 1.1471-5(e)(5)(iii), if the withholding agent has preexisting account documentary evidence (as described in paragraph (c)(5)(ii)(B) of this section) that unambiguously indicates that the payee is not a financial institution and is a foreign entity that entered liquidation or bankruptcy within the three years preceding the date of the payment.

(iv) *Identification of section 501(c) organizations.*—(A) *In general.*—A withholding agent may treat a payee as a 501(c) organization described in § 1.1471-5(e)(5)(v) if the withholding agent can reliably associate the payment with a withholding certificate that identifies the payee as a section 501(c) organization and the payee provides either a certification that the payee has been issued a determination letter by the IRS that is currently in effect concluding that the payee is a section 501(c) organization and providing the date of the letter, or a copy of an opinion from U.S. counsel certifying that the payee is a section 501(c) organization (without regard to whether the payee is a foreign private foundation).

(B) *Reason to know.*—A withholding agent must cease to treat a foreign organization's claim that it is a section 501(c) organization as valid beginning on the earlier of the date on which such agent knows that the IRS has given notice to such foreign organization that it is not a section 501(c) organization or 90 days after the date on which the IRS gives notice to the public that such foreign organization is not a section 501(c) organization. Further, a withholding agent will have reason to know that a payee is not a section 501(c) organization if it has determined, pursuant to its AML due diligence, that the payee has beneficial owners (as defined for purposes of the AML due diligence).

(v) *Identification of non-profit organizations.*—(A) *In general.*—A withholding agent may treat a payee as a non-profit organization described in § 1.1471-5(e)(5)(vi) if the withholding agent has a withholding certificate that identifies the payee as a non-profit organization.

(B) *Exception for offshore obligations.*—A withholding agent may treat a payment with respect to an offshore obligation as made to a nonprofit organization without obtaining a withholding certificate for the payee if the payee—

(1) Has provided a written statement indicating that the payee is a non-profit organization described in § 1.1471-5(e)(5)(vi) and, with respect to a payment of U.S. source FDAP income, has provided documentary evidence supporting a claim of foreign status (as described in paragraph (c)(5)(i) of this section); or

(2) Is required to be reported by the withholding agent as a tax-exempt charitable organization under the information reporting laws of the country in which the account is maintained or is permitted an exemption from withholding due to its status as a tax exempt charitable organization under the laws of the country in which the account is maintained, and the withholding agent obtains general documentary evidence (as described in paragraph (c)(5)(ii)(A) of this section) establishing that the payee was organized for charitable purposes in the same country in which the account is maintained by the withholding agent for the purposes described in § 1.1471-5(e)(5)(vi) and that the payee has no beneficial owners (as that term is used for purposes of that country's AML due diligence).

(C) *Exception for preexisting offshore obligations.*—A withholding agent that makes a payment with respect to an offshore obligation that is also a preexisting obligation may treat the payee as a nonprofit organization described in § 1.1471-5(e)(5)(vi) if the payee—

(1) Provides a letter of local counsel that certifies that the payee qualifies as a tax-exempt entity in its local jurisdiction; or

(2) Provides a letter issued by the tax authority of the country in which the payee is organized or a statement provided on the website of such tax authority indicating that the payee is a tax-exempt entity or charitable organization in the payee's country of organization.

(D) *Reason to know.*—A withholding agent will have reason to know that a payee is not a nonprofit organization if it has deter-

mined, pursuant to its AML due diligence, that the payee has beneficial owners (as defined for purposes of the AML due diligence).

(vi) *Identification of NFFEs that are publicly traded corporations.*—A withholding agent may treat a payee as an NFFE described in § 1.1472-1(c)(1)(i) (applying to an entity the stock of which is regularly traded on an established securities market) if it has a withholding certificate that certifies that the payee is such an entity and provides the name of a securities exchange upon which the payee's stock is regularly traded.

(A) *Exception for offshore obligations.*—A withholding agent that makes a payment with respect to an offshore obligation may treat a payee as an NFFE described in § 1.1472-1(c)(1)(i) if the withholding agent obtains—

(1) A written statement that the payee is a foreign corporation that is not a financial institution, that its stock is regularly traded on an established securities market, the name of one of the exchanges upon which the payee's stock is traded, and, with respect to a payment of U.S. source FDAP income, documentary evidence supporting a claim of foreign status (as described in paragraph (c)(5)(i) of this section); or

(2) Any documentation establishing that the payee is listed on a public securities exchange or on a stock market index and general documentary evidence (as described in paragraph (c)(5)(ii)(A) of this section) establishing that the payee is a foreign corporation other than a financial institution.

(B) *Exception for preexisting offshore obligations.*—A withholding agent that makes a payment with respect to an offshore obligation that is also a preexisting obligation may treat the payee as an entity described in § 1.1472-1(c)(1)(i) if the withholding agent has any documentation confirming that the payee is listed on a public securities exchange or on a stock market index and preexisting account documentary evidence (as described in paragraph (c)(5)(ii)(B) of this section) establishing that the payee is a foreign corporation other than a financial institution.

(vii) *Identification of NFFE affiliates.*—A withholding agent may treat a payee as an NFFE described in § 1.1472-1(c)(1)(ii) (applying to an affiliate of an entity the stock of which is regularly traded on an established exchange) if it has a beneficial owner withholding certificate that identifies the payee as a foreign corporation that is an affiliate of an entity, described § 1.1472-1(c)(1)(i), whose stock is regularly traded on an established exchange and provides the name of the entity that is regularly traded and one of the exchanges upon which the entity's stock is listed.

(A) *Exception for offshore obligations.*—A withholding agent that makes a payment with respect to an offshore obligation may treat a payment as being made to an NFFE described in § 1.1472-1(c)(1)(ii) if the withholding agent obtains—

(1) Documentary evidence or other information confirming that the payee is affiliated with an entity listed on a public securities exchange or on a stock market index and general documentary evidence (as described in paragraph (c)(5)(ii)(A) of this section) that indicates that the payee is a foreign corporation other than a financial institution; or

(2) A written statement that the payee is a foreign corporation that is not a financial institution, that the payee is an affiliate of another nonfinancial entity whose stock is regularly traded on an established securities exchange, providing the name of the payee's affiliate and one of the exchanges upon which the affiliate's stock is traded and, in the case of a payment of U.S. source FDAP income, documentary evidence supporting the payee's claim of foreign status (as described in paragraph (c)(5)(i) of this section).

(B) *Exception for preexisting offshore obligations.*—A withholding agent that makes a payment with respect to an offshore obligation that is also a preexisting obligation may treat the payee as an NFFE described in § 1.1472-1(c)(1)(ii) if the withholding agent has—

(1) Documentation or other information confirming that the payee is affiliated with a corporation that is listed on a public securities exchange or on a stock market index;

(2) Preexisting account documentary evidence (as described in paragraph (c)(5)(ii)(B) of this section) that unambiguously indicates that the payee is a corporation that is not a financial institution; and

(3) In the case of a payment of U.S. source FDAP income, documentary evidence supporting the payee's claim of foreign status (as described in paragraph (c)(5)(i) of this section).

(viii) *Identification of excepted territory NFFEs.*—A withholding agent may treat a payee as an excepted territory NFFE described in § 1.1472-1(c)(1)(iii) if it has a withholding certificate that identifies the payee as an NFFE that was organized in a U.S. territory and includes a certification for chapter 4 purposes that all of its owners are bona fide residents of that U.S. territory.

(A) *Exception for payments made prior to January 1, 2017, with respect to preexisting obligations of $1,000,000 or less (transitional).*—A withholding agent that makes a payment prior to January 1, 2017, with respect to a preexisting obligation with a balance or value not exceeding $1,000,000 on June 30, 2014, and December 31, 2015, applying the aggregation principles of § 1.1471-5(b)(4)(iii), may treat a payee as an excepted territory NFFE described in § 1.1472-1(c)(1)(iii) if the withholding agent—

(1) Has a pre-FATCA Form W-8 identifying the payee as a foreign entity with a permanent residence address in a U.S. territory; and

(2) Has general documentary evidence (as described in paragraph (c)(5)(ii)(A) of this section), preexisting account documentary evidence (as described in paragraph (c)(5)(ii)(B) of this section), or a prospectus establishing that the payee is an entity other than a depository institution, custodial institution, or specified insurance company; and

(3) Is subject, with respect to such obligation, to the laws of a FATF-compliant jurisdiction and as part of its AML due diligence has not identified any owners of the payee that are not bona fide residents of the U.S. territory in which the payee is organized.

(B) *Exception for offshore obligations.*—A withholding agent that makes a payment with respect to an offshore obligation may treat a payment as being made to an excepted territory NFFE described in § 1.1472-1(c)(1)(iii) if it has—

(1) A written statement providing that the payee is an entity other than a depository institution, custodial institution, or specified insurance company, was organized in a U.S. territory, and is wholly owned by one or more bona fide residents of that U.S. territory, and, with respect to a payment of U.S. source FDAP income, the written statement must indicate that the payee is the beneficial owner of the income and be accompanied by documentary evidence supporting a claim of foreign status (as described in paragraph (c)(5)(i) of this section); or

(2) General documentary evidence (as described in paragraph (c)(5)(ii)(A) of this section) or a prospectus establishing that the payee is an entity other than a depository institution, custodial institution, or specified insurance company, establishing that the payee was organized in a U.S. territory, and establishing that the payee is wholly owned by one or more bona fide residents of that U.S. territory.

(C) *Exception for preexisting offshore obligations of $1,000,000 or less.*—A withholding agent that makes a payment with respect to an offshore obligation that is also a preexisting obligation with a balance or value not exceeding $1,000,000 on June 30, 2014 (or the effective date of the FFI agreement for a withholding agent that is a participating FFI) and the last day of each subsequent calendar year preceding the payment, applying the aggregation principles of § 1.1471-5(b)(4)(iii), may rely upon its review conducted for AML due diligence purposes to determine whether the owners of the payee are bona fide residents of the U.S. territory in which the payee is organized, in lieu of obtaining a written statement or documentary evidence described in paragraph (d)(11)(viii)(B) of this section. The preceding sentence applies only if the withholding agent is subject, with respect to such account, to the laws of a FATF-compliant jurisdiction and has identified the residence of the owners. The withholding agent relying upon this paragraph (d)(11)(viii)(C) must still obtain a written statement, documentary evidence (as provided in paragraph (d)(11)(viii)(B) of this section), or preexisting account documentary evidence (as described in paragraph (c)(5)(ii)(B) of this section) establishing that the payee is an entity other than a depository institution, custodial institution, or specified insurance company organized in a U.S. territory.

(ix) *Identification of active NFFEs.*—A withholding agent may treat a payee as an active NFFE described in § 1.1472-1(c)(1)(iv) if it has a withholding certificate identifying the payee as an active NFFE.

(A) *Exception for offshore obligations.*—A withholding agent that makes a payment with respect to an offshore obligation may treat the payee as an active NFFE if the withholding agent has—

(1) General documentary evidence (as described in paragraph (c)(5)(ii)(A) of this section) providing sufficient information to determine that the payee is a foreign entity engaged in an active trade or business other than that of a financial institution; or

(2) A written statement stating that the payee is a foreign entity engaged in an active business other than that of a financial institution and, in the case of a payment of U.S. source FDAP income, documentary evidence supporting the payee's claim of foreign status (as described in paragraph (c)(5)(i) of this section).

(B) *Exception for preexisting offshore obligations.*—A withholding agent that makes a payment with respect to an offshore obligation that is also a preexisting obligation may treat the payee as an active NFFE if the withholding agent has preexisting account documentary evidence (as described in paragraph (c)(5)(ii)(B) of this section) that unambiguously indicates that the payee is a foreign entity engaged in a trade or business other than that of a financial institution and, in the case of a payment of U.S. source FDAP income, documentary evidence supporting the payee's claim of foreign status (as described in paragraph (c)(5)(i) of this section).

(C) *Limit on reason to know.*—A withholding agent relying on documentary evidence to determine that a payee is an active NFFE will not be required to determine that the payee meets the income and asset thresholds but rather must determine only that the payee is primarily engaged in a business other than that of a financial institution.

(x) *Identifying a direct reporting NFFE (other than a sponsored direct reporting NFFE).*—(A) *In general.*—A withholding agent may treat a payment as having been made to a direct reporting NFFE (other than a sponsored direct reporting NFFE) if it has a withholding certificate that identifies the payee as a direct reporting NFFE and the withholding certificate contains a GIIN for the payee that is verified against the published IRS FFI list in the manner described in paragraph (e)(3)(iii) of this section (indicating when a withholding agent may rely upon a GIIN).

(B) *Exception for offshore obligations.*—A withholding agent that makes a payment with respect to an offshore obligation may treat the payment as made to a direct reporting NFFE if the withholding agent has—

(1)(i) General documentary evidence (as described in paragraph (c)(5)(ii)(A) of this section) for the payee providing sufficient information to determine that the payee is a foreign entity that is not a financial institution; or

(ii) A written statement that the payee is a foreign entity that is not a financial institution and, for a payment of U.S. source FDAP income, documentary evidence supporting the payee's claim of foreign status (as described in paragraph (c)(5)(i) of this section), and

(2) Received (either orally or in writing) a GIIN from the direct reporting NFFE and has verified the GIIN in the manner described in paragraph (e)(3)(iii) of this section.

(C) *Special rule for preexisting offshore obligations.*—A withholding agent that makes a payment with respect to an offshore obligation that is also a preexisting obligation may treat the payee as a direct reporting NFFE if the withholding agent has preexisting account documentary evidence (as described in paragraph (c)(5)(ii)(B) of this section) providing sufficient information to determine that the payee is a foreign entity that is not a financial institution and it has received (either orally or in writing) a GIIN from the direct reporting NFFE and has verified the GIIN in the manner described in paragraph (e)(3)(iii) of this section.

(xi) *Identifying a sponsored direct reporting NFFE.*—(A) *In general.*—A withholding agent may treat a payment as having been made to a sponsored direct reporting NFFE if it has a withholding certificate that identifies the payee as a sponsored direct reporting NFFE and the withholding certificate includes the sponsored direct reporting NFFE's GIIN, which the withholding agent has verified against the published IRS FFI list in the manner described in paragraph (e)(3)(iv) of this section (indicating when a withholding agent may rely upon a GIIN).

(1) *Payments made prior to January 1, 2017 (transitional).*—For payments prior to January 1, 2017, a sponsored direct reporting NFFE may provide the GIIN of its sponsoring entity on the withholding certificate, which the withholding agent must verify against the published IRS FFI list in the manner described in paragraph (e)(3)(iv) of this section.

(2) *Payments made after December 31, 2016, to payees documented prior to January 1, 2017.*—For a payment made after December 31, 2016, to a payee that the withholding agent has documented prior to January 1, 2017, as a sponsored direct reporting NFFE with a valid withholding certificate that includes the GIIN of the sponsoring entity, the withholding agent must obtain and verify the GIIN of the sponsored direct reporting NFFE against the published IRS FFI list in the manner described in paragraph (e)(3)(i) of this section by March 31, 2017. A withholding agent required to obtain a GIIN of the sponsored direct reporting NFFE in the preceding sentence may obtain such GIIN by oral or written confirmation (including by e-mail) rather than obtaining a new withholding certificate, provided that the withholding agent retains a record of the confirmation, which will become part of the withholding certificate.

(B) *Exception for offshore obligations.*—A withholding agent that makes a payment with respect to an offshore obligation may treat the payment as made to a sponsored direct reporting NFFE if the withholding agent has—

(1) A written statement that the payee is a foreign entity that is a sponsored direct reporting NFFE and, for a payment of U.S. source FDAP income, documentary evidence supporting the payee's claim of foreign status (as described in paragraph (c)(5)(i) of this section), and

(2) Received (either orally or in writing) the GIIN of the sponsored direct reporting NFFE and has verified the GIIN in the manner described in paragraph (e)(3)(iv) of this section. For payments prior to January 1, 2017, such requirement may be fulfilled by receiving (either orally or in writing) the GIIN of the sponsoring entity to the extent that the sponsored direct reporting NFFE has not obtained a GIIN.

(xii) *Identification of excepted inter-affiliate FFI.*—(A) *In general.*—A withholding agent may treat a payee as an excepted inter-affiliate FFI described in § 1.1471-5(e)(5)(iv) if it has obtained a withholding certificate identifying the payee as such an entity.

(B) *Offshore obligations.*—A withholding agent that makes a payment with respect to an offshore obligation may treat the payment as made to an excepted inter-affiliate FFI described in § 1.1471-5(e)(5)(iv) if the withholding agent obtains a written statement in which the payee certifies that it is a foreign entity operating as an excepted inter-affiliate FFI and that it is a member of an expanded affiliated group of participating FFIs or registered deemed-compliant FFIs. In the case of a payment of U.S. source FDAP income, the written statement must also indicate that the payee is the beneficial owner and must be supplemented with documentary evidence supporting the payee's claim of foreign status (as described in paragraph (c)(5)(i) of this section).

(C) *Reason to know.*—A withholding agent that is not a member of the payee's expanded affiliated group has reason to know that an entity is not an excepted inter-affiliate FFI if it makes any payments (other than a payment of bank deposit interest) to such entity.

(12) *Identification of passive NFFEs.*—A withholding agent may treat a payment as having been made to a passive NFFE if it has a withholding certificate that identifies the payee as a passive NFFE.

(i) *Exception for offshore obligations.*—A withholding agent that makes a payment with respect to an offshore obligation may treat the payment as made to a passive NFFE if the withholding agent has—

(A) General documentary evidence (as described in paragraph (c)(5)(ii)(A) of this section) for the payee providing sufficient information to determine that the payee is a foreign entity that is not a financial institution; or

(B) A written statement that the payee is a foreign entity that is not a financial institution and, for a payment of U.S. source FDAP income, documentary evidence supporting the payee's claim of foreign status (as described in paragraph (c)(5)(i) of this section).

(ii) *Special rule for preexisting offshore obligations.*—A withholding agent that makes a payment with respect to an offshore obligation that is also a preexisting obligation may treat the payee as a passive NFFE if the withholding agent has preexisting account documentary evidence (as described in paragraph (c)(5)(ii)(B) of this section) providing sufficient information to determine that the payee is a foreign entity that is not a financial institution and, with respect to a payment of U.S. source FDAP income, documentary evidence supporting the payee's claim of foreign status (as described in paragraph (c)(5)(i) of this section).

(iii) *Required owner certification for passive NFFEs.*—(A) *In general.*—A passive NFFE will be required to provide to the withholding agent either a written certification (contained on a withholding certificate or in a written statement) that it does not have any substantial U.S. owners or the name, address, and TIN of each substantial U.S. owner of the NFFE, to avoid being withheld upon under § 1.1472-1(b).

(B) *Exception for preexisting obligations of $1,000,000 or less (transitional).*—A withholding agent that makes a payment prior to January 1, 2017, with respect to a preexisting obligation with a balance or value not exceeding $1,000,000 on June 30, 2014, and December 31, 2015, applying the aggregation principles of § 1.1471-5(b)(4)(iii), may rely upon its review conducted for AML due diligence purposes to identify any substantial U.S. owners of the payee in lieu of obtaining the certification or information required in paragraph (d)(12)(iii)(A) of this section if the withholding agent is subject, with respect to such obligation, to the laws of a FATF-compliant jurisdiction and has identified the residence of any con-

trolling persons (within the meaning of the withholding agent's AML due diligence rules). A withholding agent that makes a payment with respect to an offshore obligation that is also a preexisting obligation with a balance or value not exceeding $1,000,000 on June 30, 2014, (or the effective date of the FFI agreement for a withholding agent that is a participating FFI) and the last day of each subsequent calendar year preceding the payment, applying the aggregation principles of § 1.1471-5(b)(4)(iii), may rely upon its review conducted for AML due diligence purposes to identify any substantial U.S. owners of the payee in lieu of obtaining the certification or information required in paragraph (d)(12)(iii)(A) of this section if the withholding agent is subject, with respect to such obligation, to the laws of a FATF-compliant jurisdiction and has identified the residence of any controlling persons (within the meaning of the withholding agent's AML due diligence rules).

(e) *Standards of knowledge.*—(1) *In general.*—The standards of knowledge discussed in this section apply for purposes of determining the chapter 4 status of payees, beneficial owners, intermediaries, flow-through entities, and persons that own an interest in an owner-documented FFI. A withholding agent shall be liable for tax, interest, and penalties to the extent provided under section 1474 and the regulations under that section if it fails to withhold the correct amount despite knowing or having reason to know the amount required to be withheld. A withholding agent that cannot reliably associate the payment with documentation and fails to act in accordance with the presumption rules set forth in paragraph (f) of this section may also be liable for tax, interest, and penalties. See paragraph (e)(4) in this section for the specific standards of knowledge applicable to a person's specific claims of chapter 4 status.

(2) *Notification by the IRS.*—A withholding agent that has received notification by the IRS that a claim of status as a U.S. person, a participating FFI, a deemed-compliant FFI, or other entity entitled to a reduced rate of withholding under section 1471 or 1472 is incorrect knows that such a claim is incorrect beginning on the date that is 30 days after the date the notice is received.

(3) *GIIN verification.*—(i) *In general.*—A withholding agent that has received a payee's claim of status as a participating FFI or registered deemed-compliant FFI, and that is required under paragraph (d)(4) of this section to confirm that the FFI or branch thereof (including an entity that is disregarded as an entity separate from the FFI) claiming status as a participating FFI or registered deemed-compliant FFI has a GIIN that appears on the published IRS FFI list, has reason to know that such payee is not such a financial institution if the payee's name (including a name reasonably similar to the name the withholding agent has on file for the payee) and GIIN do not appear on the most recently published IRS FFI list within 90 days of the date that the claim is made. For purposes of this paragraph (e)(3)(i), the GIIN that the withholding agent must confirm is, with respect to a payee that is a participating FFI or registered deemed-compliant FFI, the GIIN assigned to the FFI identifying its country of residence for tax purposes (or place of organization if the FFI has no country of residence) or, with respect to a payment that is made to a branch (including a disregarded entity) of a participating FFI or registered deemed-compliant FFI located outside of the FFI's country of residence or organization, the GIIN of the branch (or disregarded entity) receiving the payment. The withholding agent will have reason to know that a withholdable payment is made to a branch (including a disregarded entity) of a participating or registered deemed-compliant FFI that is not itself a participating FFI or registered deemed-compliant FFI when the withholding agent is directed to make the payment to an address in a jurisdiction other than that of the participating FFI or registered deemed-compliant FFI (or branch (including a disregarded entity) of such FFI) that is identified as the FFI (or branch (including a disregarded entity) of such FFI) that is supposed to receive the payment and for which the FFI's GIIN is not confirmed as described in the preceding sentence. The preceding sentence does not apply to an FFI that is an investment entity. If an FFI (other than an investment entity) directs the withholding agent to make the payment to an account held by the FFI and maintained by another financial institution, the FFI must provide to the withholding agent a statement in writing that the FFI is not directing the payment to any branch of such FFI that is not a participating FFI or a registered deemed-compliant FFI. An FFI whose registration with the IRS as a participating FFI or a registered deemed-compliant FFI is in process but has not yet received a GIIN may provide a withholding agent with a Form W-8 claiming the chapter 4 status it applied for and writing "applied for" in the box for the GIIN. In such case, the withholding agent will have 90 days from the date it receives the Form W-8 to obtain a GIIN and to verify the accuracy of the GIIN against the published IRS FFI list before it has reason to know that the payee is not a participating FFI or registered deemed-compliant FFI. If an FFI is removed from the published IRS FFI list, the withholding agent knows that such FFI is not a participating FFI or

registered deemed-compliant FFI on the earlier of the date that the withholding agent discovers that the FFI has been removed from the list or the date that is one year from the date the FFI's GIIN was actually removed from the list.

(ii) *Special rules for reporting Model 1 FFIs.*—Prior to January 1, 2015, a withholding agent that receives an FFI's claim of status as a reporting Model 1 FFI will not be required to confirm that the FFI has a GIIN that appears on the published IRS FFI list. A withholding agent has reason to know that the FFI is not a reporting Model 1 FFI if the withholding agent does not have a permanent residence address for the FFI, or an address of the relevant branch of the FFI, located in the country in which the FFI claims to be a reporting Model 1 FFI, or the withholding agent is making a payment to a branch of the FFI at an address in a country that does not have in effect a Model 1 IGA.

(iii) *Special rules for direct reporting NFFEs.*—A withholding agent that has received a payee's claim of status as a direct reporting NFFE and that is required under paragraph (d)(11)(x) of this section to confirm that the entity claiming status as a direct reporting NFFE has a GIIN that appears on the published IRS FFI list, has reason to know that such payee is not such a NFFE if the payee's name (including a name reasonably similar to the name the withholding agent has on file for the payee) and GIIN do not appear on the most recently published IRS FFI list within 90 days of the date that the claim is made. A payee whose registration with the IRS as a direct reporting NFFE is in process but has not yet received a GIIN may provide a withholding agent with a Form W-8 claiming the chapter 4 status it applied for and writing "applied for" in the box for the GIIN. In such case, the withholding agent will have 90 days from the date it receives the Form W-8 to verify the accuracy of the GIIN against the published IRS FFI list before it has reason to know that the payee is not a direct reporting NFFE. If a direct reporting NFFE is removed from the published IRS FFI list, the withholding agent knows that such NFFE is not a direct reporting NFFE on the earlier of the date that the withholding agent discovers that the NFFE has been removed from the list or the date that is one year from the date the NFFE's GIIN was actually removed from the list.

(iv) *Special rules for sponsored direct reporting NFFEs and sponsoring entities.*—(A) *Sponsored direct reporting NFFEs.*—A withholding agent that has received a payee's claim of status as a sponsored direct reporting NFFE and that is required under paragraph (d)(11)(xi) of this section to confirm that the entity claiming status as a sponsored direct reporting NFFE has a GIIN that appears on the published IRS FFI list, has reason to know that such payee is not such a NFFE if the payee's name (including a name reasonably similar to the name the withholding agent has on file for the payee) and GIIN do not appear on the most recently published IRS FFI list within 90 days of the date that the claim is made. A sponsored direct reporting NFFE whose registration with the IRS as a sponsored direct reporting NFFE is in process but has not yet received a GIIN may provide a withholding agent with a Form W-8 claiming the chapter 4 status it applied for and writing "applied for" in the box for the GIIN. In such case, the withholding agent will have 90 days from the date it receives the Form W-8 to verify the accuracy of the GIIN against the published IRS FFI list before it has reason to know that the payee is not a sponsored direct reporting NFFE. If a sponsored direct reporting NFFE is removed from the published IRS FFI list, the withholding agent knows that such NFFE is not a sponsored direct reporting NFFE on the earlier of the date that the withholding agent discovers that the sponsored entity has been removed from the list or the date that is one year from the date the sponsored entity's GIIN was actually removed from the list.

(B) *Sponsoring entities (transitional).*—For payments made prior to January 1, 2017, a withholding agent that has received a payee's claim of status as a sponsored direct reporting NFFE has reason to know that such payee is not such a NFFE if the name of its sponsoring entity (including a name reasonably similar to the name the withholding agent has on file for the sponsoring entity) and the GIIN of its sponsoring entity do not appear on the most recently published IRS FFI list within 90 days of the date that the claim is made. A sponsoring entity whose registration with the IRS is in process but has not yet received a GIIN may provide a withholding agent with a Form W-8 claiming the chapter 4 status it applied for and writing "applied for" in the box for the GIIN. In such case, the withholding agent will have 90 days from the date it receives the Form W-8 to verify the accuracy of the GIIN against the published IRS FFI list before it has reason to know that the payee is not a sponsored direct reporting NFFE. If the sponsoring entity of the NFFE is removed from the published IRS FFI list, the withholding agent knows that such NFFE is not a sponsored direct reporting NFFE on the earlier of the date that the withholding agent discovers

that the sponsoring entity has been removed from the list or the date that is one year from the date the sponsoring entity's GIIN was actually removed from the list.

(4) *Reason to know.*—A withholding agent has reason to know that a claim of chapter 4 status is unreliable or incorrect if its knowledge of relevant facts or statements contained in the withholding certificate or other documentation is such that a reasonably prudent person in the position of the withholding agent would question the claim being made. For an obligation other than a preexisting obligation, a withholding agent has reason to know that a person's claim of chapter 4 status is unreliable or incorrect if any information contained in its account opening files or other customer account files, including documentation collected for AML due diligence purposes, conflicts with the chapter 4 status being claimed. A withholding agent will not, however, have reason to know that a person's claim of chapter 4 status is unreliable or incorrect based on documentation collected for AML due diligence purposes until the date that is 30 days after the obligation is created. In addition to the specific standards of knowledge set forth in this paragraph (e) regarding a person's claim of chapter 4 status, a withholding agent is also required to apply any specific standards of knowledge applicable to the chapter 4 status claimed as set forth in paragraph (d) of this section. A withholding agent that has obtained documentation to reliably associate a payment to a foreign person under paragraph (c) of this section has reason to know that the person's claim of foreign status is unreliable or incorrect only to the extent provided in this paragraph (e)(4). See also § 1.1441-1(e)(4)(ii)(D) for requirements that apply when a change in circumstances occurs for purposes of chapter 3 and the related grace period allowed under § 1.1441-1(b)(3)(iv). The limits on reason to know for multiple obligations held by the same person set forth in § 1.1441-7(b)(11) shall apply by substituting the term *chapter 4 status* for the term *foreign status*. See § 1.1471-3(e)(4)(vii) for the limits on reason to know with respect to a preexisting obligation.

(i) *Reason to know regarding an entity's chapter 4 status.*—A withholding agent has reason to know that a withholding certificate, written statement, or documentary evidence provided by or on behalf of an entity is unreliable or incorrect if there is information on the face of the documentation or in the withholding agent's account files that conflicts with the entity's claim regarding its chapter 4 status. For example, a withholding agent has reason to know that an entity's claim that it is an excepted NFFE is unreliable or incorrect if the withholding agent has obtained a financial statement or credit report for AML purposes that indicates that the entity is engaged in business as a financial institution. See also paragraph (e)(4) of this section for the 30-day period before a withholding agent has reason to know a claim is unreliable or incorrect based on AML information. Further, a withholding agent that has classified an entity as engaged in a particular type of business based on its records, such as through the use of a standardized industry coding system, AML or other regulatory purpose that requires the withholding agent to periodically monitor and periodically update the business classification based on the withholding agent's records, the withholding agent has reason to know that the chapter 4 status claimed by the entity is unreliable or incorrect only if the entity's claim conflicts with the withholding agent's classification of the entity's business type.

(ii) *Reason to know applicable to withholding certificates.*—(A) *In general.*—A withholding agent has reason to know that a withholding certificate provided by a person is unreliable or incorrect if the withholding certificate is incomplete with respect to any item on the certificate that is relevant to the claims made by the person, the withholding certificate contains any information that is inconsistent with the person's claim, the withholding agent has other account information that is inconsistent with the person's claim, or the withholding certificate lacks information necessary to establish entitlement to an exemption from withholding for chapter 4 purposes. Except as otherwise provided in this paragraph (e)(4)(ii)(A), a withholding agent that is a financial institution or other entity described in § 1.1441-7(b)(3) and that has obtained a withholding certificate to reliably associate a payment to a foreign person under paragraph (c) of this section has reason to know that the person's claim of foreign status is unreliable or incorrect only if there are U.S. indicia, as described in § 1.1441-7(b)(5), associated with the person and for which appropriate documentation sufficient to cure the U.S. indicia has not been obtained in accordance with § 1.1441-7(b) within 90 days of when the U.S. indicia was first identified by the withholding agent. See also § 1.1441-1(e)(4)(ii)(D) for requirements that apply when a change in circumstances occurs for purposes of chapter 3 and the related grace period allowed under § 1.1441-1(b)(3)(iv). A withholding agent that relies on an agent to review and maintain a withholding certificate is considered to know or have reason to know the facts within the knowledge of the agent.

(B) *Withholding certificate provided by an FFI.*—A withholding agent that obtains a withholding certificate to reliably associate a payment to a participating FFI, a registered deemed-compliant FFI, a sponsoring entity, or a sponsored FFI does not need to apply the standards of knowledge described in §1.1441-7(b)(5) if it has confirmed the FFI's GIIN on the current published IRS FFI list, in the manner described under paragraph (e)(3) of this section, within 90 days of receipt of the withholding certificate.

(iii) *Reason to know applicable to written statements.*—A withholding agent must apply the standards of knowledge applicable to withholding certificates, as set forth in paragraph (e)(4)(ii) of this section, to determine whether it has reason to know that a written statement is unreliable or incorrect in terms of establishing a person's claim of foreign status. The rules under paragraph (e)(4)(ii) shall be applied by substituting the term *written statement* for the term *withholding certificate.*

(iv) *Reason to know applicable to documentary evidence.*—(A) *In general.*—A withholding agent may not treat documentary evidence provided by a person as valid if the documentary evidence does not reasonably establish the identity of the person presenting the documentary evidence. For example, documentary evidence is not valid if it is provided in person by an individual and the photograph or signature on the documentary evidence does not match the appearance or signature of the person presenting the document. A withholding agent may not treat documentary evidence as valid if the documentary evidence contains information that is inconsistent with the person's claim as to its chapter 4 status, the withholding agent has other account information that is inconsistent with the person's chapter 4 status, or the documentary evidence lacks information necessary to establish the person's chapter 4 status. Additionally, a withholding agent that is a financial institution under §1.1471-5(e), or other entity as described in §1.1441-7(b)(3) that has obtained documentary evidence to reliably associate a payment to a foreign person under paragraph (c) of this section has reason to know that the person's claim of foreign status is unreliable or incorrect only if there are U.S. indicia, as described in §1.1441-7(b)(8), associated with the person and appropriate documentation sufficient to cure the U.S. indicia has not been obtained in accordance with §1.1441-7(b) within 90 days of when the U.S. indicia was first identified by the withholding agent. See also §1.1441-1(e)(4)(ii)(D) for requirements when a change in circumstances occurs for purposes of chapter 3 and the related grace period allowed under §1.1441-1(b)(3)(iv).

(B) *Standards of knowledge applicable to certain types of documentary evidence.*—(1) *Financial statement.*—A withholding agent that obtains a financial statement for purposes of establishing that a foreign payee meets a certain asset threshold has reason to know that the chapter 4 status claimed is unreliable or incorrect only if the total assets shown on the financial statement for the payee, and if relevant the payee's expanded affiliated group, are not within the permissible thresholds, or the footnotes to the financial statement indicate that the payee is not a foreign entity or is not a type of FFI eligible for the chapter 4 status claimed. A withholding agent that obtains a financial statement for purposes of establishing that the payee is an active NFFE will be required to review the balance sheet and income statement to determine whether the payee meets the income and asset thresholds set forth in §1.1472-1(c)(1)(iv) and the footnotes of the financial statement for an indication that the payee is not a foreign entity or is a financial institution. A withholding agent that obtains a financial statement for purposes of establishing a chapter 4 status for a payee that does not require the payee to meet an asset or income threshold will be required to review only the footnotes to the financial statement to determine whether the financial statement supports the claim of chapter 4 status. A withholding agent that is not relying upon a financial statement to establish the chapter 4 status of the payee (for example because it has other documentation that establishes the payee's chapter 4 status) is not required to independently evaluate the financial statement solely because the withholding agent also has collected the financial statement in the course of its account opening or other procedures.

(2) *Organizational documents.*—A withholding agent that obtains organizational documents for a payee solely for the purpose of supporting the chapter 4 status claimed by the entity will only be required to review the document sufficiently to establish that the entity is a foreign person and that the purposes for which the entity was formed and its basic activities appear to be of a type consistent with the chapter 4 status claimed, unless otherwise specified in paragraph (d) of this section. A withholding agent that obtains organizational documents for the purpose of establishing that an entity has a particular chapter 4 status will only be required to review the document to the extent needed to establish that the entity is a foreign person, that the requirements applicable to the particular

chapter 4 status are met, and that the document was executed, but will not be required to review the remainder of the document.

(v) *Specific standards of knowledge applicable when only documentary evidence is a code or classification described in paragraph (c)(5)(ii)(B) of this section.*—A withholding agent may not rely upon a classification described in paragraph (c)(5)(ii)(B) of this section or a standardized industry coding system to treat an entity as having a foreign status if there are U.S. indicia described in paragraph (e)(4)(v)(A) of this section associated with the entity, unless such U.S. indicia are cured in the manner set forth in paragraph (e)(4)(v)(B) of this section.

(A) *U.S. indicia for entities.*—The term *U.S. indicia* when used with respect to an entity includes, for purposes of this paragraph (e)(4)(v) any of the following—

(1) Classification of an account holder as a U.S. resident in the withholding agent's customer files;

(2) A current U.S. residence address or U.S. mailing address;

(3) With respect to an offshore obligation, standing instructions to pay amounts to a U.S. address or an account maintained in the United States;

(4) A current telephone number for the entity in the United States but no telephone number for the entity outside of the United States;

(5) A current telephone number for the entity in the United States in addition to a telephone number for the entity outside of the United States;

(6) A power of attorney or signatory authority granted to a person with a U.S. address; and

(7) An "in-care-of" address or "hold mail" address that is the sole address provided for the entity.

(B) *Documentation required to cure U.S. indicia.*—A withholding agent may rely upon a code or classification described in paragraph (c)(5)(ii)(B) of this section to treat an entity as having a foreign chapter 4 status if there are U.S. indicia associated with the entity and the withholding agent obtains the relevant documentation described in this paragraph (e)(4)(v)(B).

(1) If there are U.S. indicia described in paragraphs (e)(4)(v)(A)(1) through (4) of this section associated with the entity, the withholding agent may treat the entity as a foreign person only if the withholding agent obtains a withholding certificate for the entity and one form of documentary evidence, described in paragraph (c)(5) of this section, that establishes the entity's status as a foreign person (such as a certificate of incorporation).

(2) If there are U.S. indicia described in paragraphs (e)(4)(v)(A)(1) through (4) of this section associated with the entity and the withholding agent is making a payment with respect to an offshore obligation, the withholding agent may also treat the entity as a foreign person if the withholding agent obtains a withholding certificate for the entity and the withholding agent treats the entity as foreign for purposes of foreign tax reporting. A withholding agent will treat an entity as foreign for purposes of foreign tax reporting only if the withholding agent classifies the entity as a resident of the country in which the obligation is maintained, the withholding agent is required to report a payment made to the entity annually on a tax information statement that is filed with the tax authority of the country in which the account is maintained as part of that country's resident reporting requirements, and that country has a tax information exchange agreement or income tax treaty in effect with the United States.

(3) If there are indicia described in paragraphs (e)(4)(v)(A)(5) through (7) of this section associated with the entity, the withholding agent may treat the entity as a foreign person if the withholding agent obtains a withholding certificate or one form of documentary evidence, described in paragraph (c)(5) of this section, that establishes the entity's status as a foreign person (such as a certificate of incorporation).

(vi) *Specific standards of knowledge applicable to documentation received from intermediaries and flow-through entities.*—(A) *In general.*—A withholding agent that receives documentation from a payee through an intermediary or flow-through entity is required to review all documentation obtained with respect to the payee and all intermediaries and/or flow-through entities in the chain of payment, applying the standards of knowledge set forth in paragraph (e) of this section. This standard requires, but is not limited to, a withholding agent's compliance with the rules of paragraphs (e)(4)(vi)(A)(1) and (2) of this section.

(1) The withholding agent is required to review the withholding statement or owner reporting statement provided and may not rely on information in the statement to the extent the information does not support the claims made regarding the chapter 4 status of the person. For this purpose, a withholding agent may not treat a

**Reg. § 1.1471-3(e)(4)(vi)(A)(1)**

person as a foreign person if an address in the United States is provided for such person unless the withholding statement is accompanied by a valid withholding certificate and documentary evidence establishing foreign status (as described in paragraph (c)(5)(i) of this section).

(2) The withholding agent must review each withholding certificate and written statement in accordance with paragraph (e)(4)(i) through (iii) of this section and all documentary evidence in accordance with paragraph (e)(4)(i) and (iv) of this section, and must verify that the information contained on the withholding certificate, written statement, and documentary evidence is consistent with the information on the withholding statement or owner reporting statement. If there is a discrepancy between the withholding certificate, written statement, or documentary evidence and the withholding statement or owner reporting statement, the withholding agent may choose to rely on the withholding certificate, written statement, or documentary evidence provided such documentation is valid and the intermediary or flow-through entity does not indicate that the documentation is unreliable or inaccurate, or may apply the presumption rules set forth in paragraph (f) of this section. If the withholding agent chooses to rely upon the withholding certificate, written statement, or documentary evidence, the withholding agent is required to instruct the intermediary or flow-through entity to correct the withholding statement and confirm that the intermediary or flow-through entity does not know or have reason to know that the documentation is unreliable or inaccurate.

(B) *Limits on reason to know with respect to documentation received from participating FFIs and registered deemed-compliant FFIs that are intermediaries or flow-through entities.*—A withholding agent that receives documentation from a participating FFI or registered deemed-compliant FFI that is not the payee must apply the requirements of paragraph (e)(4)(vi)(A) of this section, except that the withholding agent may rely upon the chapter 4 status provided by the participating FFI or registered deemed-compliant FFI in the withholding statement, including a chapter 4 status determined under the requirements of (and documentation or information that is publicly available that determines the chapter 4 status of the payee permitted under) an applicable IGA for an account holder, provided that the withholding agent has the information necessary to report on Form 1042-S, unless the withholding agent has information that conflicts with the chapter 4 status provided. See § 1.1441-1(e)(3)(iv)(C)(2)(*iv*) (requiring that a nonqualified intermediary withholding statement for a reportable amount that is a withholdable payment include the recipient code for chapter 4 purposes used for filing Form 1042-S for an entity payee). If underlying documentation is provided for the payee and information in the documentation or in the withholding agent's records conflicts with the chapter 4 status claimed by the payee, the withholding agent has reason to know that the chapter 4 status claimed is unreliable or incorrect. A withholding agent is not, however, required to verify information contained in documentation provided by an intermediary or flow-through entity that is a participating FFI or registered deemed-compliant FFI that is not facially incorrect and is not required to obtain supporting documentation for the payee in addition to a withholding certificate unless the withholding agent obtains such documentation for purposes of chapter 3 or 61 or unless the withholding agent knows that the review conducted by the participating FFI or registered deemed-compliant FFI for purposes of chapter 4 was not adequate. For example, a withholding agent that receives a withholding statement from a participating FFI that is an intermediary stating that the payee is a registered deemed-compliant FFI is only required to determine that any withholding certificate provided for the payee contains a GIIN and that the GIIN does not appear to be facially invalid (for example, because it does not contain the correct amount of digits), but is not subject to the requirements set forth in paragraph (e)(3) of this section. Similarly, a withholding agent that receives from a participating FFI that is a partnership a withholding statement claiming that the payee is an active NFFE has reason to know that the claim is unreliable or incorrect if it receives a withholding statement that contains a U.S. address for the payee unless the partnership also provides a copy of documentation sufficient to cure the U.S. indicia in the manner set forth in this paragraph (e) or the withholding statement indicates that appropriate documentation sufficient to cure the U.S. indicia in the manner set forth in this paragraph (e) has been obtained and provides details of such documentation, such as the type of documentation and an identification number of the person contained in the document.

(vii) *Limits on reason to know.*—(A) *Scope of review for preexisting obligations of entities.*—For purposes of determining whether a withholding agent that makes a payment with respect to a preexisting obligation to an entity has reason to know that the chapter 4 status applied to the entity is unreliable or incorrect, the withholding agent is only required to review information contradicting the chapter 4 status claimed if such information is contained in the current

customer master file, the most recent withholding certificate, written statement, and documentary evidence for the person, the most recent account opening contract, the most recent documentation obtained by the withholding agent for purposes of AML due diligence or for other regulatory purposes, any power of attorney or signature authority forms currently in effect, and any standing instructions to pay amounts that is currently in effect.

(B) *Reason to know there are U.S. indicia associated with preexisting obligations.*—With respect to a preexisting obligation, a withholding agent may apply the limits on reason to know described in § 1.1441-7(b)(3)(ii) for a person that the withholding agent has previously documented for purposes of chapter 3 or 61. A withholding agent that applies the limits on reason to know described in § 1.1441-7(b)(3)(ii) must, however, review for U.S. indicia any additional documentation upon which the withholding agent is relying to determine the chapter 4 status of the person, if any.

(C) *Reason to know there are U.S. indicia associated with preexisting offshore obligations.*—For payments made outside of the United States with respect to an offshore obligation that is also a preexisting obligation and with respect to a withholding agent that had not already documented the payee for purposes of chapter 3 or 61, the withholding agent, in lieu of searching the account files addressed in paragraph (e)(4)(vii)(A) of this section to determine whether there are U.S. indicia associated with the payee (or other person who receives the payment), may instead rely upon a search of its electronically searchable information associated with such person. A withholding agent that relies upon an electronic search pursuant to this paragraph (e)(4)(vii)(C) must also review for U.S. indicia any documentation upon which the withholding agent relies to determine the chapter 4 status of the person and any documentation that the withholding agent had been relying upon to determine the residency or citizenship of the person.

(D) *Limits on reason to know for multiple obligations belonging to a single person.*—A withholding agent that maintains multiple obligations for a single person will have reason to know that a chapter 4 status assigned to the person is inaccurate based on information contained in the customer files for another obligation held by the person only to the extent that—

(1) The withholding agent's computerized systems link the obligations by reference to a data element such as client number, EIN, or foreign tax identifying number and consolidates the customer information and payment information for the obligations; or

(2) The withholding agent has treated the obligations as consolidated obligations for purposes of sharing documentation pursuant to paragraph (c)(8) of this section or for purposes of treating one or more accounts as preexisting obligations.

(viii) *Reasonable explanation supporting claim of foreign status.*—A reasonable explanation supporting a claim of foreign status for an individual has the meaning described in § 1.1441-7(b)(12).

(5) *Conduit financing arrangements.*—The rules set forth in § 1.1441-7(f), regarding a withholding agent's liability for failing to withhold in the case in which the financing arrangement is a conduit financing arrangement, apply for purposes determining a withholding agent's liability for any withholding required under chapter 4.

(6) *Additional guidance.*—The IRS may prescribe other circumstances for which a withholding certificate or documentary evidence to establish a payee's chapter 4 status is unreliable or incorrect in addition to the circumstances described in this paragraph (e).

(f) *Presumptions regarding chapter 4 status of the person receiving the payment in the absence of documentation.*—(1) *In general.*—A withholding agent that cannot, prior to the payment, reliably associate (within the meaning of paragraph (c) of this section) the payment with valid documentation may rely on the presumptions of this paragraph (f) to determine the status of the payee (or other person receiving the payment) as a U.S. or foreign person and such person's other relevant characteristics (for example, as a nonparticipating FFI). Paragraph (f)(2) of this section provides the presumption rules with respect to classification as an individual or entity. Paragraph (f)(3) of this section provides the presumption rules to determine a payee's U.S. or foreign status. Paragraph (f)(4) of this section provides the presumption rules with respect to an entity's chapter 4 status. Paragraph (f)(5) of this section provides the presumption rules with respect to an intermediary or flow-through entity. Paragraph (f)(6) of this section provides the presumption rules with respect to effectively connected income paid to a U.S. branch of a payee. Paragraph (f)(7) of this section provides the presumption rules that apply to a payment made to joint payees. Paragraph (f)(8) of this section provides rules for how a payee may rebut the presumptions described in this paragraph (f). Paragraph (f)(9) of this section provides the consequences to a withholding agent that fails to withhold in accordance with the presumptions set forth in this paragraph (f) or that has actual knowledge or reason to know facts that are contrary to the presumptions set forth in this paragraph (f).

(2) *Presumptions of classification as an individual or entity and entity as the beneficial owner.*—A withholding agent that cannot reliably associate a payment with a valid withholding certificate, or that has received valid documentary evidence (as described in paragraph (c)(5) of this section), but cannot determine a payee's status as an individual or an entity from the documentary evidence, must apply the presumption rules of §1.1441-1(b)(3)(ii) to determine the payee's classification as an individual, trust, partnership, corporation, intermediary, or flow-through entity. Additionally, a withholding agent that receives valid documentary evidence with respect to an entity must apply the rules under §1.1441-1(b)(3)(ii) to determine when it may treat such entity as a beneficial owner.

(3) *Presumptions of U.S. or foreign status.*—If a withholding agent cannot reliably associate a payment with a valid withholding certificate or valid documentary evidence from which it is possible to determine the payee's U.S. or foreign status, it must apply the presumption rules of §1.1441-1(b)(3)(iii) to determine the U.S. or foreign status of the payee (substituting the term *withholdable payment* for the term *payment*). In the case of a payment that a withholding agent can reliably associate with valid documentation that indicates the payment is made to a U.S. person but does not indicate whether the person is a specified U.S. person, the payment will be presumed made to a specified U.S. person unless the withholding agent can apply the presumption rules of §1.6049-4(c)(1)(ii)(B), (C), (D), (E), (I), (J), (K), (L), or (N), to presume that the person is other than a specified U.S. person, or the person's name reasonably indicates that the person is a bank (for example because it contains the word Bank or a foreign equivalent).

(4) *Presumption of chapter 4 status for a foreign entity.*—If a withholding agent cannot reliably associate a valid withholding certificate or valid documentary evidence sufficient to determine the chapter 4 status of the entity receiving payment under paragraph (d) of this section (for example, as a participating FFI, nonparticipating FFI, or NFFE), it must presume that the entity is a nonparticipating FFI.

(5) *Presumption of chapter 4 status of payee with respect to a payment to an intermediary or flow-through entity.*—If a withholding agent makes a payment to a foreign flow-through entity or intermediary, including a payment that it is required to treat as made to such an entity under paragraphs (f)(2) and (3) of this section, and cannot reliably associate such payment with valid documentation under paragraph (c) of this section, the withholding agent must presume that the payment is made to a nonparticipating FFI.

(6) *Presumption of effectively connected income for payments to certain U.S. branches.*—A withholding agent that makes a payment to a U.S. branch described in this paragraph (f)(6) may presume, in the absence of documentation indicating otherwise, that the U.S. branch is the payee of a payment that is effectively connected with the conduct of a trade or business in the United States if the withholding agent has obtained an EIN from the U.S. branch (either orally or in writing). A U.S. branch is described in this paragraph (f)(6) if it is a U.S. branch of a foreign bank subject to regulatory supervision by the Federal Reserve Board or a U.S. branch of a foreign insurance company required to file an annual statement on a form approved by the National Association of Insurance Commissioners with the Insurance Department of a State, a Territory, or the District of Columbia. A payment is treated as made to a U.S. branch of a foreign bank or foreign insurance company if the payment is credited to an account maintained in the United States in the name of a U.S. branch of the foreign person, or the payment is made to an address in the United States where the U.S. branch is located and the name of the U.S. branch appears on documents (in written or electronic form) associated with the payment (for example, the check mailed or letter addressed to the branch).

(7) *Joint payees.*—(i) *In general.*—If a withholding agent makes a payment to joint payees and cannot reliably associate the payment with valid documentation from each payee but all of the joint payees appear to be individuals, then the payment is presumed made to an unidentified U.S. person. If any joint payee does not appear, by its name and other information contained in the account file, to be an individual, then the entire payment will be treated as made to a nonparticipating FFI. However, if one of the joint payees provides a Form W-9 in accordance with the procedures described in §§31.3406(d)-1 through 31.3406(d)-5 of this chapter, the payment shall be treated as made to that payee.

(ii) *Exception for offshore obligations.*—If a withholding agent makes a payment outside the United States with respect to an offshore obligation held by joint payees and cannot reliably associate a

payment with valid documentation from each payee but all of the joint payees appear to be individuals, then the payment is presumed made to an unknown foreign individual if the payment with respect to the offshore obligation is made outside the United States (as described in §1.6049-5(e)).

(8) *Rebuttal of presumptions.*—A payee may rebut the presumptions described in paragraphs (f)(2) through (7) of this section by providing reliable documentation to the withholding agent or, if applicable, to the IRS.

(9) *Effect of reliance on presumptions and of actual knowledge or reason to know otherwise.*—(i) *In general.*—Except as otherwise provided in this paragraph (f)(9), a withholding agent that withholds on a payment under section 1471 or 1472 in accordance with the presumptions set forth in this paragraph (f) shall not be liable for withholding under this section even if it is later established that the payee has a chapter 4 status other than the status presumed. A withholding agent that fails to report and withhold in accordance with the presumptions described in paragraphs (f)(2) through (7) of this section with respect to a payment that it cannot reliably associate with valid documentation shall be liable for tax, interest, and penalties. See §1.1474-1(a) for the extent of a withholding agent's liability for failing to withhold in accordance with the presumptions described in this paragraph (f).

(ii) *Actual knowledge or reason to know that amount of withholding is greater than is required under the presumptions or that reporting of the payment is required.*—Notwithstanding the provisions of paragraph (f)(9)(i) of this section, a withholding agent that knows or has reason to know that the status or characteristics of the person are other than what is presumed under this paragraph (f) may not rely on the presumptions described in this paragraph (f) to the extent that, if it determined the status of the person based on such knowledge or reason to know, it would be required to withhold (under this section or another withholding provision of the Code) an amount greater than would be the case if it relied on the presumptions described in this paragraph (f). In such a case, the withholding agent must rely on its knowledge or reason to know rather than on the presumptions set forth in this paragraph (f). Failure to do so shall result in liability for tax, interest, and penalties to the extent described in §1.1474-1(a).

(g) *Effective/applicability date.*—This section applies on January 6, 2017. However, taxpayers may apply these provisions as of January 28, 2013. A taxpayer may apply paragraph (c)(6)(iv) of this section to all of its open tax years. (For the rules that apply beginning on January 28, 2013, and before January 6, 2017, see this section as in effect and contained in 26 CFR part 1 revised April 1, 2016.) [Reg. §1.1471-3.]

☐ [*T.D.* 9610, 1-17-2013 (*corrected* 9-9-2013). *Amended by T.D.* 9657, 2-28-2014, *T.D.* 9809, 12-30-2016 (*corrected* 6-29-2017) *and T.D.* 9890, 12-27-2019.]

### [Reg. §1.1471-4]

§1.1471-4. **FFI agreement.**—(a) *In general.*—An FFI agreement will be in effect in accordance with section 1471(b) if an FFI registers with the IRS pursuant to procedures prescribed by the IRS and agrees to comply with the terms of an FFI agreement. The FFI agreement will incorporate the requirements set forth in this section, any modifications set forth in an applicable Model 2 IGA, and any provisions applicable to a reporting Model 1 FFI.

(1) *Withholding.*—A participating FFI is required to deduct and withhold tax with respect to payments made to recalcitrant account holders and nonparticipating FFIs to the extent required under paragraph (b) of this section. A participating FFI that is prohibited by foreign law from withholding as required under paragraph (b) of this section with respect to an account must close such account within a reasonable period of time or must otherwise block or transfer such account as described in paragraph (i) of this section.

(2) *Identification and documentation of account holders.*—A participating FFI is required to obtain such information regarding each holder of each account maintained by the participating FFI to determine whether each account is a U.S. account or an account held by a recalcitrant account holder or nonparticipating FFI in accordance with the due diligence procedures for identifying and documenting account holders described in paragraph (c) of this section.

(3) *Reporting.*—A participating FFI is required to report the information described in paragraph (d) of this section annually with respect to U.S. accounts under section 1471(c) and accounts held by recalcitrant account holders. A participating FFI must also comply with the filing requirements described in §1.1474-1(c) and (d) to report payments that are chapter 4 reportable amounts paid to recalcitrant account holders and nonparticipating FFIs (including the transitional reporting of foreign reportable amounts paid to nonpar-

ticipating FFIs for calendar years 2015 and 2016 described in §1.1471-4(d)(2)(ii)(F)). A participating FFI that is unable to obtain a waiver, if required by foreign law, to report an account as required under paragraph (d) of this section must close or transfer such account within a reasonable period of time as described in paragraph (i) of this section.

(4) *Expanded affiliated group.*—Except as otherwise provided in Model 1 IGA or Model 2 IGA, in order for any FFI that is a member of an expanded affiliated group to be a participating FFI, each FFI that is a member of the expanded affiliated group must be a participating FFI, deemed-compliant FFI, or exempt beneficial owner as described in paragraph (e) of this section. For a limited period described in paragraph (e)(2) or (3) of this section, however, a branch of an FFI or an FFI that is a member of an expanded affiliated group and is unable under foreign law to satisfy the requirements of this section may instead obtain status as a limited branch of a participating FFI or limited FFI if the branch or FFI meets the requirements set forth in paragraph (e)(2) or (3) of this section (as applicable).

(5) *Verification.*—A participating FFI is required to adopt a compliance program as described in paragraph (f) of this section under the authority of the responsible officer, who will be required to certify periodically to the IRS on behalf of the FFI regarding the participating FFI's compliance with the requirements of the FFI agreement. If the IRS identifies concerns about the participating FFI's compliance, the IRS may request additional information to verify compliance with the requirements of the FFI agreement as described in paragraph (f)(4) of this section.

(6) *Event of default.*—A participating FFI is required to cure an event of default with respect to the FFI agreement as defined in paragraph (g) of this section. Upon the occurrence of an event of default, the IRS will deliver to a participating FFI a notice of default and will allow the FFI an opportunity to cure the event of default as described in paragraph (g) of this section.

(7) *Refunds.*—A participating FFI may file a collective refund on behalf of certain account holders and payees for amounts withheld by the participating FFI or its withholding agent under chapter 4 in excess of the account holder or payee's U.S. tax liability to the extent permitted in paragraph (h) of this section. A participating FFI may also make an adjustment for overwithholding using either the reimbursement procedure described in §1.1474-2(a)(3) or the set-off procedure described in §1.1474-2(a)(4).

(b) *Withholding requirements.*—(1) *In general.*—Except as otherwise provided in a Model 2 IGA, a participating FFI is required to deduct and withhold a tax equal to 30 percent of any withholdable payment made by such participating FFI to an account held by a recalcitrant account holder or to a nonparticipating FFI after June 30, 2014, to the extent required under paragraph (b)(3) of this section. See paragraph (b)(2) of this section for rules for a participating FFI to identify the payee of a payment in order to determine whether withholding is required under this paragraph (b). See paragraph (b)(4) of this section for the extent of a participating FFI's requirement to deduct and withhold tax on a foreign passthru payment made by such participating FFI to an account held by a recalcitrant account holder or to a nonparticipating FFI. See paragraph (b)(5) of this section for the rules for withholding on payments to limited branches and limited FFIs. See paragraph (b)(6) for the special allowance to set aside in escrow amounts withheld with respect to dormant accounts. See paragraph (b)(7) of this section for the withholding requirements of certain U.S. branches of FFIs. See §1.1471-2 for the exceptions to and special rules for withholding and the exclusion from the definitions of the terms *withholdable payment* and *foreign passthru payment* that applies to any payment made under a grandfathered obligation or the gross proceeds from the disposition of such an obligation. See §1.1474-1(d)(4)(iii) for the requirement of participating FFIs to report payments that are chapter 4 reportable amounts. See §1.1474-6 for the coordination of withholding on payments under this paragraph (b) with the other withholding provisions under the Code.

(2) *Withholding determination.*—Except as otherwise provided under §1.1471-2 and, with respect to certain preexisting accounts, under paragraph (c) of this section, a participating FFI is required to determine whether withholding applies at the time a payment is made by reliably associating the payment with valid documentation described in paragraph (c) of this section for the payee of the payment. For a payment made to an account, if the account is held by one or more individuals, the payee is each individual account holder. For a payment made to an account held by an entity, except as otherwise provided in §1.1471-3(a)(3), the payee is the account holder. If the participating FFI makes a withholdable payment to a payee that is an entity and the payment is made with respect to an obligation that is not an account, except as otherwise provided in §1.1471-3(a)(3), the payee is the person to whom the payment is

made. See §1.1473-1(a) to determine when a payment is made in the case of a withholdable payment. If a participating FFI cannot reliably associate a payment (or any portion of a payment) with valid documentation, the rules described in paragraph (c) of this section shall apply to determine the chapter 4 status of the account holder (and payee if other than the account holder). Notwithstanding the foregoing, a participating FFI may establish after the date of payment that withholding was not required to the extent permitted under §1.1471-3(c)(7) or may apply the procedures provided in §1.1474-2 when overwithholding occurs.

(3) *Satisfaction of withholding requirements.*—(i) *In general.*—A participating FFI that complies with the withholding obligations of this paragraph (b) with respect to accounts held by recalcitrant account holders and payees that are nonparticipating FFIs shall be deemed to satisfy its withholding obligations under sections 1471(a) and 1472 with respect to such account holders and payees.

(ii) *Withholding not required.*—A participating FFI that is an NQI, NWP, NWT, or that is a QI that elects under section 1471(b)(3) not to assume withholding responsibility for a payment and that provides its withholding agent with the information necessary to allocate all or a portion of the payment to each payee as part of a withholding certificate described in §1.1471-3(c)(3)(iii) will generally not be required to withhold under paragraph (b)(1) of this section. See §1.1471-2(a)(2)(ii), however, for the circumstances under which a participating FFI that is an NQI, NWP, or NWT has a residual withholding responsibility. See also §1.1471-3(c)(9)(iii)(B) for the circumstances under which a participating FFI that is a broker has a residual withholding responsibility as an intermediary of the payment and may also be liable for any underwithholding that occurs. See §§1.1471-2(a) and 1.1472-1(a)(2)(i) and the QI, WP, or WT agreement for the withholding requirements of a participating FFI that is a QI, WP, or WT for purposes of chapter 4.

(iii) *Election to withhold under section 3406.*—A participating FFI may elect to satisfy its withholding obligation under paragraph (b)(1) of this section with respect to recalcitrant account holders that are also U.S. non-exempt recipients subject to backup withholding under section 3406 receiving withholdable payments, to the extent that the payments also constitute reportable payments, by applying withholding under section 3406 at the backup withholding rate to such withholdable payments. A participating FFI may make the election described in this paragraph only if it complies with the information reporting rules under chapter 61 with respect to payments to which backup withholding applies. Nothing in this paragraph relieves a participating FFI of its requirement to backup withhold under section 3406 with respect to reportable payments that are not also withholdable payments. See §1.1474-6(f) for the general rule that satisfying withholding requirements under chapter 4 will satisfy backup withholding requirements under section 3406 for a payment that is both a withholdable payment and a reportable payment.

(4) *Foreign passthru payments.*—A participating FFI is not required to deduct and withhold tax on a foreign passthru payment made by such participating FFI to an account held by a recalcitrant account holder or to a nonparticipating FFI before the later of January 1, 2019, or the date of publication in the **Federal Register** of final regulations defining the term *foreign passthru payment.*

(5) *Withholding on limited FFIs and limited branches.*—(i) *Limited FFIs.*—A participating FFI is required to withhold on a withholdable payment made to a limited FFI identifying itself as a nonparticipating FFI. A participating FFI that is a member of an expanded affiliated group that includes one or more limited FFIs will also be required to treat any such limited FFI as a nonparticipating FFI with respect to withholdable payments made to such limited FFI. A participating FFI will be considered to have made a withholdable payment to a limited FFI if such participating FFI receives a withholdable payment with respect to a security or instrument held on behalf of a limited FFI (or an account maintained by the limited FFI). A participating FFI will also be considered to have made a withholdable payment to a limited FFI when the limited FFI receives a payment with respect to a transaction between the limited FFI and such participating FFI that is in the same expanded affiliated group and such transaction hedges or otherwise provides total return exposure to another transaction between such participating FFI and a third party that gives rise to a withholdable payment.

(ii) *Limited branches.*—A participating FFI is required to withhold on a withholdable payment made to a limited branch identifying itself as a nonparticipating FFI. A branch of the participating FFI other than the limited branch is also required to withhold on a withholdable payment when it receives the payment on behalf of a limited branch of the participating FFI. A branch of the participating FFI other than a limited branch will be considered to have received a withholdable payment on behalf of a limited branch when such other branch receives a withholdable payment with respect to a security or instrument it holds on behalf of a limited branch (or an account maintained by the limited branch). A branch of a participating FFI other than a limited branch will be considered to hold a security or instrument on behalf of a limited branch when it executes a transaction with a limited branch that hedges or otherwise provides total return exposure to another transaction between such other branch and a third party that gives rise to a withholdable payment.

(6) *Special rule for dormant accounts.*—A participating FFI that makes a withholdable payment not otherwise subject to withholding under chapter 3 or backup withholding under section 3406 to a recalcitrant account holder of a dormant account that it maintains must withhold on the account for purposes of chapter 4. However, the participating FFI may, in lieu of depositing the tax withheld, set aside the amount withheld in escrow until the date that the account ceases to be a dormant account. In such case, the tax withheld becomes due 90 days following the date that the account ceases to be a dormant account if the account holder does not provide the documentation required under paragraph (c) of this section or becomes refundable to the account holder if the account holder provides the documentation required under paragraph (c) of this section establishing that withholding does not apply. A participating FFI that maintains a dormant account of a recalcitrant account holder and that elects to escrow withheld tax pursuant to this paragraph (b)(6) may not delegate the responsibility to escrow withheld tax to the withholding agent from which it is receiving payment. Once a dormant account escheats irrevocably to a foreign government under the relevant laws in the jurisdiction in which the participating FFI (or branch thereof) operates, the participating FFI is no longer required to deposit with the IRS the amount held in escrow with respect to the account. See paragraph (d)(6)(ii) of this section for the definition of dormant account.

(7) *Withholding requirements for U.S. branches of FFIs treated as U.S. persons.*—A U.S. branch of an FFI treated as a U.S. person must satisfy its backup withholding obligations under section 3406(a) with respect to accounts held at the U.S. branch by account holders that are payees treated as other than exempt recipients under chapter 61. See §§ 1.1441-1(b)(2)(iv)(C), 1.1471-2(a), and 1.1472-1(a) for additional withholding obligations for a U.S. branch of an FFI treated as a U.S. person. See paragraph (d)(2)(iii)(B) of this section for the reporting requirements applicable to U.S. branches of FFIs that are treated as U.S. persons.

(c) *Due diligence for the identification and documentation of account holders and payees.*—(1) *Scope of paragraph.*—Except to the extent that a participating FFI relies on the due diligence procedures set forth in an applicable Model 2 IGA, a participating FFI must follow this paragraph (c) to identify and document the chapter 4 status of each holder of an account maintained by the participating FFI to determine if the account is a U.S. account, non-U.S. account, or an account held by a recalcitrant account holder or nonparticipating FFI. Paragraph (c)(2) of this section provides the general rules for identification and documentation of account holders and payees, and paragraph (c)(2)(v) provides documentation requirements for certain U.S. branches of FFIs. Paragraph (c)(3) of this section provides the rules for documenting entity accounts and payees. Paragraph (c)(4) of this section provides the general rules for documenting individual accounts other than preexisting accounts. Paragraph (c)(5) of this section provides the identification and documentation procedure for preexisting individual accounts. Paragraph (c)(6) of this section provides examples illustrating the application of the documentation exceptions for entity accounts and individual accounts. Paragraph (c)(7) of this section outlines the certification requirement relating to the due diligence procedures of this paragraph (c) with respect to preexisting accounts within the specified periods of time.

(2) *General rules for the identification and documentation of account holders and payees.*—(i) *Overview.*—Except as otherwise provided in paragraphs (c)(3)(iii) and (c)(5)(iii) of this section (documentation exceptions for certain preexisting accounts), a participating FFI is required to identify among accounts maintained by the participating FFI each account that is a U.S. account or an account held by a recalcitrant account holder or nonparticipating FFI, and to report information about such accounts in the manner provided in paragraph (d) of this section and § 1.1474-1(d)(4)(iii). See § 1.1471-5(a)(3) for rules to determine the holder of an account. The participating FFI is also required to retain a record of the documentation collected or otherwise maintained that meets the requirements described in this paragraph (c) when making certain payments to an account holder or payee (if other than an account holder) to determine whether withholding applies under paragraph (b) of this section or whether reporting applies under § 1.1474-1(d)(4)(iii)(C) and any payee for

which it provides the certification described in § 1.1471-3(c)(9)(iii)(A) to another withholding agent.

(ii) *Standards of knowledge.*—(A) *In general.*—A participating FFI may rely on valid documentation that is collected pursuant to the due diligence procedures set forth in this paragraph (c) or that is otherwise maintained in the participating FFI's files, unless the participating FFI knows or has reason to know that such documentation is unreliable or incorrect. For purposes of a participating FFI documenting an account holder under this paragraph (c), the requirements for the validity of withholding certificates, written statements, and documentary evidence provided in § 1.1471-3(c) shall apply regardless of whether the participating FFI makes a payment to the account. Except as otherwise provided paragraph (c)(2)(ii)(B) of this section (certain mergers or bulk acquisitions) and in paragraph (c)(5)(iv) of this section (preexisting individual accounts), to determine whether a participating FFI knows or has reason to know that the documentation collected or otherwise maintained with respect to the account holder is unreliable or incorrect, the standards of knowledge provided in § 1.1471-3(e) shall apply regardless of whether the participating FFI makes a payment to the account. See § 1.1471-3(c)(8) and (9) for the requirement to obtain documentation on an account-by-account basis and the exceptions to this requirement.

(B) *Limits on reason to know with respect to certain accounts acquired in merger or bulk acquisition.*—A participating FFI that acquires accounts of another financial institution either in a merger or bulk acquisition of accounts for value (other than a related party transaction described in § 1.1471-3(c)(9)(v)) may apply the limitations on reason to know provided in paragraphs (c)(2)(ii)(B)(*1*) or (*2*) of this section (as applicable and subject to the conditions therein), or the rules of § 1.1471-3(c)(9)(v) to rely upon documentation collected by another financial institution for an account acquired either in a merger or bulk acquisition of accounts for value.

(*1*) *In general.*—The participating FFI may treat accounts acquired in a transaction described in this paragraph (c)(2)(ii)(B) as preexisting accounts for purposes of applying the identification and documentation procedures of this paragraph (c) by substituting the date of acquisition of such accounts for the effective date of the FFI agreement.

(*2*) *Participating FFIs and certain deemed-compliant FFIs that apply the due diligence rules, and U.S. financial institutions.*—If a participating FFI (transferee FFI) acquires accounts of another participating FFI or deemed-compliant FFI (including a U.S. branch of either such FFI) that applies the due diligence requirements of this paragraph (c) as a condition of its status (as described in § 1.1471-5(f)), or of a U.S. financial institution (transferor FI), the transferee FFI may rely on the chapter 4 status determination made by the transferor FI for an account holder and will not be subject to the standards of knowledge set forth in paragraph (c)(2)(ii)(A) of this section until there is a change in circumstances with respect to the account if the following conditions are met—

(*i*) The transferee FFI does not have actual knowledge that the chapter 4 status determination provided by the transferor FI is unreliable or incorrect;

(*ii*) For the certification period following the acquisition of such accounts (described in paragraph (f)(3)(i) of this section), the transferee FFI acquiring the accounts tests a sample of the acquired accounts to determine if the chapter 4 status determinations made by the transferor FI are reliable;

(*iii*) In the case of a transferor FI that is a participating FFI or a registered deemed-compliant FFI (or a U.S. branch of either such entity that is not treated as a U.S. person) or that is a deemed-compliant FFI that applies the requisite due diligence rules of this paragraph (c) as a condition of its status, the transferor FI provides a written representation to the transferee FFI acquiring the accounts that the transferor FI has applied the due diligence procedures of this paragraph (c) with respect to the transferred accounts and, in the case of a transferor FI that is a participating FFI, has complied with the requirements of paragraph (f)(2) of this section; and

(*iv*) In the case of a transferor FI that is a U.S. financial institution or that is a U.S. branch of a participating FFI or of a registered deemed-compliant FFI that is treated as a U.S. person, the transferee FFI may rely on the chapter 4 status determinations for a payee that is an entity only if prior to the date of transfer the U.S. financial institution or U.S. branch made a withholdable payment to the payee or, for a payee that is an individual, only if the U.S. financial institution or U.S. branch made a reportable payment (as defined under section 3406(b)) to the payee.

(iii) *Change in circumstances.*—(A) *Obligation to identify a change in circumstances.*—A participating FFI is required to institute procedures to ensure that any change in circumstances, as described in paragraph (c)(2)(iii)(B) of this section, is identified by the participating FFI, including procedures to ensure that a relationship manager identifies any change in circumstances with respect to an account. For example, if a relationship manager is notified that the account holder has a mailing address in the United States when there was no U.S. address previously associated with the account, the participating FFI will be required to treat the new address as a change in circumstances and will be required to retain a record of the appropriate documentation from the account holder as described in paragraph (c)(5)(iv)(B)(2)(iii) of this section.

(B) *Definition of change in circumstances.*—For purposes of this section, a change in circumstances (as defined in § 1.1471-3(c)(6)(ii)(E)) includes any change or addition of information to the account holder's account (including the addition, substitution, or other change of an account holder) or any change or addition of information to any account associated with such account (applying the account aggregation rules described in § 1.1471-5(b)(4)(iii) or by treating the accounts as consolidated obligations) if such change or addition of information affects the chapter 4 status of the account holder. For example, if a holder of an account (including a preexisting account) opens another account that is linked to such account in the participating FFI's computerized system as described under § 1.1471-5(b)(4)(iii) and as part of the participating FFI's account opening procedures the account holder provides a U.S. telephone number for such other account, this is a change in circumstances with respect to the first mentioned account. With respect to a preexisting account that meets a documentation exception described in paragraphs (c)(3)(iii) and (c)(5)(iii) of this section, a change in circumstances also includes a change in account balance or value as of the end of the first subsequent year that causes the account no longer to meet the documentation exception.

(C) *Requirements following a change in circumstances.*—With respect to an individual account or an account held by a passive NFFE for which there is a change in circumstances with respect to the information regarding its owners, following a change in circumstances the participating FFI must retain a record of the appropriate documentation described in paragraph (c)(3) or (c)(5)(iv)(B)(2) of this section within the time period provided by § 1.1471-5(g)(3)(iii) or, if unable to do so, must treat such account as held by a recalcitrant account holder. With respect to an account held by an entity other than a passive NFFE described in the preceding sentence, following a change in circumstances, the participating FFI must retain a record of the appropriate documentation described in paragraph (c)(3) of this section by the date that is 90 days after the change in circumstances or, if unable to do so, must treat such account as held by a nonparticipating FFI.

(iv) *Record retention.*—A participating FFI must retain a record of the documentation collected (or otherwise maintained) to establish the chapter 4 status of an account holder or payee pursuant to the requirements of this paragraph (c)(2)(iv). A participating FFI will be treated as having retained a record of a withholding certificate, written statement, or documentary evidence if the participating FFI retains either an original, certified copy, or photocopy (including a microfiche, scan, or similar means of record retention) of the withholding certificate, written statement, or documentary evidence collected to determine the chapter 4 status of the account holder for six calendar years following the year in which the due diligence procedures of this paragraph (c) were performed for the account. With respect to documentary evidence for an offshore obligation, however, a participating FFI that is not required to retain copies of documentation reviewed pursuant to its AML due diligence will be treated as having retained a record of such documentation if the participating FFI retains a record in its files noting the date the documentation was reviewed, each type of document, the document's identification number (if any) (for example, passport number), and whether any U.S. indicia were identified. The previous sentence applies with respect to an offshore obligation that is also a preexisting obligation, except, in such case, the requirement to record whether the documentation contained U.S. indicia does not apply. A participating FFI must also retain a record of any searches, including search results provided by third-party credit agencies as described in paragraph (c)(4)(ii) of this section, results from electronic searches, and requests made and responses to relationship manager inquiries for six calendar years following the year in which the due diligence procedures of this paragraph (c) were performed for the account. A participating FFI may be required to extend the six year retention period if the IRS requests such extension prior to the end of the six year retention period. Notwithstanding the preceding sentences, a participating FFI must retain a record of the chapter 4 status of an account holder or payee for as long as the FFI maintains the account or obligation. See § 1.1471-3(c)(6)(iii)(A) for the record retention period applicable to a participating FFI that is a withholding agent with respect to documentation collected (or otherwise maintained) for a payee.

(v) *Documentation rules for U.S. branches of FFIs that are treated as U.S. persons.*—A U.S. branch of an FFI that is treated as a U.S. person shall apply the due diligence requirements of § 1.1471-3 to determine the chapter 4 status of account holders and payees that are entities and shall apply the documentation requirements of chapter 3 or 61 (as applicable) with respect to individual account holders. See paragraph (b)(7) of this section for withholding rules and paragraph (d)(2)(iii)(B) of this section for reporting rules applicable to such U.S. branches.

(3) *Identification and documentation procedure for entity accounts and payees.*—(i) *In general.*—With respect to accounts held by entities, unless the documentation exception described in paragraph (c)(3)(iii) of this section applies, a participating FFI must determine if the account is a U.S. account or an account held by a recalcitrant account holder or nonparticipating FFI by applying the principles of § 1.1471-3(b), (c), and (d) to establish the chapter 4 status of each account holder and each payee regardless of whether the participating FFI makes a payment to the account. If an account holder receiving a payment is not the payee of the payment under §§ 1.1471-3(a) and 1.1472-1(d)(3), the participating FFI is also required to establish the chapter 4 status of the payee or payees in order to determine whether withholding applies under paragraph (b) of this section.

(ii) *Timeframe for applying identification and documentation procedure for entity accounts and payees.*—For preexisting entity accounts (including entity accounts that are opened on or after July 1, 2014, and before January 1, 2015, that the FFI treats as preexisting obligations under § 1.1471-1(b)(104)(i)), a participating FFI must perform the requisite identification and documentation procedures within six months of the effective date of the FFI agreement for any account holder that is a prima facie FFI, as defined in § 1.1471-2(a)(4)(ii)(B), and within two years of the effective date of the FFI agreement for all other entity accounts, except as otherwise provided in paragraph (c)(3)(iii) of this section. For accounts that are not preexisting accounts, the participating FFI must perform the requisite identification and documentation procedures by the earlier of the date a withholdable payment or a foreign passthru payment is made with respect to the account or within 90 days of the date the participating FFI opens the account. Notwithstanding the foregoing sentences of this paragraph (c)(3)(ii), with respect to a preexisting obligation issued in nonregistered (bearer) form by an investment entity, the investment entity is required to perform the requisite identification and documentation procedures at the time a payment is collected by the beneficial owner of the payment (including a beneficial owner that collects the payment through an intermediary or agent). If the participating FFI cannot obtain all the documentation described in § 1.1471-3(d) or if the participating FFI knows or has reason to know that the documentation provided for an entity account is unreliable or incorrect (by applying the standards of knowledge applicable to entities in § 1.1471-3(e) as modified by paragraph (c)(2)(ii)), the participating FFI shall apply the presumption rules of § 1.1471-3(f) (as applicable to entities) to determine the chapter 4 status of the account holder. In the case of an account held by a passive NFFE that provides the documentation described in § 1.1471-3(d)(12) to establish its status as a passive NFFE but fails to provide the information regarding its owners, see § 1.1471-5(g)(2)(iv) for the requirement to treat the account as held by a recalcitrant account holder.

(iii) *Documentation exception for certain preexisting entity accounts.*—(A) *Accounts to which this exception applies.*—Unless the participating FFI elects otherwise pursuant to paragraph (c)(3)(iii)(C) of this section, a participating FFI is not required to perform the identification and documentation procedure contained in this paragraph (c)(3) with respect to a preexisting entity account the aggregate balance or value of which is $250,000 or less if no holder of such account that has previously been documented by the FFI as a U.S. person for purposes of chapter 3 or 61 is a specified U.S. person. For purposes of applying this exception, the account balance must be determined as of the effective date of the FFI agreement and the aggregation rules of paragraph (c)(3)(iii)(B) of this section shall apply. An account that meets this exception will cease to meet this exception as of the end of any subsequent calendar year in which the account balance or value exceeds $1,000,000, applying the aggregation rules of paragraph (c)(3)(iii)(B) of this section, or as of the date on which there is another change in circumstances with respect to the account or any account aggregated with the account. The exception to the identification and documentation procedure described in this paragraph (c)(3)(iii)(A) does not apply to an entity account opened on or after July 1, 2014, and before January 1, 2015, that the FFI treats as a preexisting account under § 1.1471-1(b)(104)(i).

(B) *Aggregation of entity accounts.*—For purposes of determining the aggregate balance or value of accounts held by an entity in applying the exception in this paragraph (c)(3)(iii), an FFI is required to aggregate the balance or value of all accounts held (in whole or in part) by the same account holder to the extent required under §1.1471-5(b)(4)(iii)(A) and (B).

(C) *Election to forgo exception.*—A participating FFI may elect to forgo the exception described in this paragraph (c)(3)(iii) by applying the identification and documentation procedures provided in this paragraph (c)(3) within the time period provided by paragraph (c)(3)(ii) of this section or otherwise applying the presumption rules of §1.1471-3(f) to determine the chapter 4 status of the account holder.

(4) *Identification and documentation procedure for individual accounts other than preexisting accounts.*—(i) *In general.*—With respect to an individual account that is not a preexisting account or an account described under paragraph (c)(4)(iii)(B) of this section or §1.1471-5(a)(4)(i) (providing an exception to U.S. account status for certain depository accounts with an aggregate balance or value of $50,000 or less), a participating FFI must determine if the account is a U.S. account or non-U.S. account by retaining a record of certain documentation to establish the chapter 4 status of each account holder. Specifically, a participating FFI must retain a record of documentary evidence that meets the requirements of §1.1471-3(c)(5) (as applicable to individuals), the information described in paragraph (c)(4)(ii) or (c)(4)(iii)(A) of this section, or a withholding certificate to establish an account holder's status as a foreign person. Except as otherwise provided in paragraph (c)(4)(iii)(A) of this section, the participating FFI must also review all information collected in connection with the opening or maintenance of each account, including documentation collected as part of the participating FFI's account opening procedures and documentation collected for other regulatory purposes, and apply the standards of knowledge in paragraph (c)(2)(ii) of this section to determine if an account holder's claim of foreign status is unreliable or incorrect. If the participating FFI is not able to establish an account holder's status as a foreign person, the participating FFI must retain a record of either a Form W-9 or U.S. TIN (in any manner) and a valid and effective waiver described in section 1471(b)(1)(F)(i), if necessary, to establish an account holder's status as a U.S. person and to confirm that the account is a U.S. account. A participating FFI must complete the requisite identification and documentation procedures with respect to each account within the time period provided by §1.1471-5(g)(3)(ii), or, if unable to do so, it must treat such account as held by a recalcitrant account holder. The presumption rules of §1.1471-3(f) do not apply to individual account holders of a participating FFI.

(ii) *Reliance on third party for identification of individual accounts other than preexisting accounts.*—A participating FFI may establish an account holder's status as a foreign person based on information provided by a third-party credit agency only if the following conditions are met—

(A) As part of the participating FFI's account opening procedures, the account holder provides a residence address outside the United States and attests in writing that the account holder is not a U.S. citizen or resident;

(B) The third-party credit agency verifies the account holder's claimed residence with at least one government data source from the jurisdiction in which the participating FFI (or branch thereof) operates or the account holder claims residence; and

(C) The participating FFI (or branch thereof) relies on the information provided by the third-party credit agency for purposes of satisfying AML due diligence with respect to the account in a FATF-compliant jurisdiction.

(iii) *Alternative identification and documentation procedure for certain cash value insurance or annuity contracts.*—(A) *Group cash value insurance contracts or group annuity contracts.*—A participating FFI may treat an account that is a group cash value insurance contract or group annuity contract and that meets the requirements of this paragraph (c)(4)(iii)(A) as a non-U.S. account until the date on which an amount is payable to an employee/certificate holder or beneficiary, if the participating FFI obtains a certification from an employer that no employee/certificate holder (account holder) is a U.S. person. A participating FFI is also not required to review all the account information collected by the FFI to determine if an account holder's claim of foreign status is unreliable or incorrect. An account that is a group cash value insurance contract or group annuity contract meets the requirements of this paragraph (c)(4)(iii)(A) if—

(1) The group life insurance contract or a group annuity contract issued to an employer and covers twenty-five or more employee/certificate holders;

(2) The employee/certificate holders are entitled to receive any contract value and to name beneficiaries for the benefit payable upon the employee's death; and

(3) The aggregate amount payable to any employee/certificate holder or beneficiary does not exceed $1,000,000.

(B) *Accounts held by beneficiaries of a cash value insurance contract that is a life insurance contract.*—A participating FFI may presume that an individual beneficiary (other than the owner) of a cash value insurance contract that is a life insurance contract (account holder) receiving a death benefit is a foreign person and treat such account as a non-U.S. account unless the participating FFI has actual knowledge or reason to know that the beneficiary is a U.S. person. A participating FFI has reason to know that a beneficiary of a cash value insurance contract is a U.S. person if the information collected by the participating FFI and associated with the beneficiary contains U.S. indicia as described paragraph (c)(5)(iv)(B)(1) of this section. If a participating FFI has actual knowledge or reason to know that the beneficiary is a U.S. person, the participating FFI must retain a record of the appropriate documentation described in paragraph (c)(5)(iv)(B)(2) of this section.

(5) *Identification and documentation procedure for preexisting individual accounts.*—(i) *In general.*—With respect to a preexisting individual account, unless the account is an account described in §1.1471-5(a)(4)(i) (providing exception to U.S. account status for certain depository accounts with an aggregate balance or value of $50,000 or less), a participating FFI may follow the identification and documentation procedures described below in paragraph (c)(5)(ii) through (iv) of this section (as applicable), in lieu of the identification and documentation procedures described in paragraph (c)(4) of this section, to determine if an account that is a preexisting account is a U.S. account, non-U.S. account, or account held by a recalcitrant account holder. A participating FFI must first determine whether there are any U.S. indicia associated with the account (as defined in paragraph (c)(5)(iv)(B)(1) of this section), and second, if there are U.S. indicia associated with the account, retain a record of the documentation described in paragraph (c)(5)(iv)(B)(2) of this section to establish the account holder's chapter 4 status. For this purpose, the presumption rules of §1.1471-3(f) do not apply. A participating FFI must complete the requisite identification and documentation procedures with respect to each account within the time period provided by §1.1471-5(g)(3)(i) or (ii) (as applicable) or, if unable to do so, must treat such account as held by a recalcitrant account holder. A participating FFI may continue to treat an account with no U.S. indicia or an account that meets a documentation exception described in paragraph (c)(5)(iii) of this section or §1.1471-5(a)(4)(i) (providing exception to U.S. account status for certain depository accounts with an aggregate balance or value of $50,000 or less) as a non-U.S. account, until there is a change in circumstances with respect to the account as described in paragraph (c)(2)(iii) of this section.

(ii) *Special rule for preexisting individual accounts previously documented as U.S. accounts for purposes of chapter 3 or 61.*—If a participating FFI has documented an individual account holder as a U.S. person for purposes of chapter 3 or 61 and such account holder is a specified U.S. person, the account holder's account will be treated as a U.S. account for chapter 4 purposes and the identification and documentation procedures in paragraph (c)(5)(i) and (iv) of this section will not apply.

(iii) *Exceptions for certain low value preexisting individual accounts.*—(A) *Accounts to which an exception applies.*—Unless the participating FFI elects otherwise pursuant to paragraph (c)(5)(iii)(C) of this section, a participating FFI is not required to perform requisite identification and documentation procedures described in paragraph (c)(5)(i) and (iv) of this section with respect to either a preexisting individual account, other than a cash value insurance or annuity contract, the aggregate balance or value of which is $50,000 or less, or a preexisting individual account that is a cash value insurance or annuity contract described in §1.1471-5(b)(1)(iv) the aggregate balance or value of which is $250,000 or less. For purposes of applying these exceptions, the account balance must be determined as of the effective date of the FFI agreement and the aggregation rules of paragraph (c)(5)(iii)(B) of this section shall apply. An account that meets either of these exceptions will cease to meet these exceptions as of the end of any subsequent calendar year in which the account balance or value exceeds $1,000,000, applying the aggregation rules of paragraph (c)(3)(iii)(B) of this section, or until there is another change in circumstances with respect to the account or any account aggregated with the account.

(B) *Aggregation of accounts.*—For purposes of determining the aggregate balance or value of a preexisting individual account, other than an account that is cash value insurance or annuity contract, an FFI is required to aggregate the balance or value of all accounts that are not cash value insurance or annuity contracts to the extent required under §1.1471-5(b)(4)(iii)(A) or (B). For purposes of determining the aggregate balance or value of preexisting individual account that is a cash value insurance or annuity contract, an FFI will be required to aggregate the balance or value of all accounts that are cash value insurance or annuity contracts to the extent required under § 1.1471-5(b)(4)(iii)(A) or (B).

(C) *Election to forgo exception.*—A participating FFI may elect to forgo the exceptions described in paragraph (c)(5)(iii) of this section by applying the identification and documentation procedures provided in this paragraph (c) within the time provided by paragraph (c)(5)(i) of this section or otherwise treating the account as held by a recalcitrant account holder pursuant to § 1.1471-5(g).

(iv) *Specific identification and documentation procedures for preexisting individual accounts.*—(A) *In general.*—A participating FFI applying the identification and documentation procedures of this paragraph (c)(5)(iv) must review its preexisting individual accounts (applying the electronic search described in paragraph (c)(5)(iv)(C) of this section and, if appropriate, the enhanced review for high-value accounts described in paragraph (c)(5)(iv)(D) of this section) to determine if there are any U.S. indicia (as described in paragraph (c)(5)(iv)(B)(*1*) of this section) associated with the account. If no U.S. indicia are identified with respect to an account, the participating FFI may treat the account as a non-U.S. account. If U.S. indicia are identified with respect to an account, the participating FFI must retain a record of the appropriate documentation described in paragraph (c)(5)(iv)(B)(2) of this section to establish the account holder's status as a foreign person. A participating FFI that follows the procedures described in this paragraph (c)(5)(iv) (as applicable) with respect to its preexisting individual accounts will not be treated as having reason to know that the determination made with respect to the account was unreliable or incorrect because of information contained in any account files that the participating FFI did not review and was not required to review under the applicable identification procedure. Thus, for example, if a participating FFI was only required to perform an electronic search with respect to a preexisting individual account and no U.S. indicia were identified in the results of the electronic search, the participating FFI would not have reason to know that the individual account holder was a U.S. person, even if the participating FFI had on file (but was not required to and did not review) a copy of the individual's passport that indicates that the individual was born in the United States.

(B) *U.S. indicia and relevant documentation rules.*—(*1*) *U.S. indicia.*—A participating FFI must review an account holder's account information to the extent required under paragraphs (c)(5)(iv)(C) and (D) of this section for any of the following U.S. indicia:

(i) Designation of the account holder as a U.S. citizen or resident;

(ii) A U.S. place of birth;

(iii) A current U.S. residence address or U.S. mailing address (including a U.S. post office box);

(iv) A current U.S. telephone number (regardless of whether such number is the only telephone number associated with the account holder);

(v) Standing instructions to pay amounts from the account to an account maintained in the United States;

(vi) A current power of attorney or signatory authority granted to a person with a U.S. address; or

(vii) An "in-care-of" address or a "hold mail" address that is the sole address the FFI has identified for the account holder.

(2) *Documentation to be retained upon identifying U.S. indicia.*—If U.S. indicia are identified with respect to an account holder's account information, a participating FFI must retain a record of the documentation described in paragraphs (c)(5)(iv)(B)(2)(*i*) through (*vii*) of this section, applicable to the U.S. indicia identified, to establish the account holder's status as a foreign person. If the participating FFI cannot establish an account holder's status as a foreign person based on such documentation, the participating FFI must retain a record of a Form W-9 and a valid and effective waiver as described in section 1471(b)(1)(F)(ii), if necessary, to confirm that the account is a U.S. account or, if unable to do so, must treat the account as held by a recalcitrant account holder.

(i) *Designation of account holder as a U.S. citizen or resident.*—If the information required to be reviewed with respect to the account contains a designation of an account holder as a U.S. citizen or resident, the participating FFI must retain a record of a withholding certificate and documentary evidence described in § 1.1471-3(c)(5)(i)(B) evidencing citizenship in a country other than the United States in order to establish the account holder's status as a foreign person.

(ii) *Unambiguous indication of a U.S. place of birth.*—If information required to be reviewed with respect to the account unambiguously indicates a U.S. place of birth for an account holder, the participating FFI must retain a record of a form of documentary

evidence described in § 1.1471-3(c)(5)(i)(B) evidencing citizenship in a country other than the United States and a copy of the individual's Certificate of Loss of Nationality of the United States, or, alternatively, a withholding certificate, a form of documentary evidence described in § 1.1471-3(c)(5)(i)(B) evidencing citizenship in a country other than the United States, and a reasonable written explanation of the account holder's renunciation of U.S. citizenship or the reason the account holder did not obtain U.S. citizenship at birth in order to establish the account holder's status as a foreign person.

(iii) *U.S. address or U.S. mailing address.*—If information required to be reviewed with respect to the account contains a U.S. address or a U.S. mailing address for an account holder, the participating FFI must retain a record of a withholding certificate and a form of documentary evidence described in § 1.1471-3(c)(5)(i)(A) through (C) in order to establish the account holder's status as a foreign person.

(iv) *Only U.S. telephone numbers.*—If information required to be reviewed with respect to the account contains one or more telephone numbers in the United States and no other telephone numbers for an account holder, the participating FFI must retain a record of a withholding certificate and a form of documentary evidence described in § 1.1471-3(c)(5)(i)(A) through (C) in order to establish the account holder's status as a foreign person.

(v) *U.S. telephone numbers and non-U.S. telephone numbers.*—If information required to be reviewed with respect to the account contains one or more telephone numbers in the United States and at least one telephone number outside the United States for an account holder, the participating FFI must retain a record of a withholding certificate or a form of documentary evidence described in § 1.1471-3(c)(5)(i)(A) through (C) in order to establish the account holder's status as a foreign person.

(vi) *Standing instructions to pay amounts.*—If information required to be reviewed with respect to the account contains standing instructions to pay amounts from the account to an account maintained in the United States for an account holder, the participating FFI must retain a record of a withholding certificate and either a form of documentary evidence described in § 1.1471-3(c)(5)(i)(A) through (C) or a written reasonable explanation (as defined in § 1.1441-7(b)(12)) establishing the account holder's status as a foreign person.

(vii) *Power of attorney or signatory authority granted to a person with a U.S. address or "in-care-of" address or "hold mail" address.*—If information required to be reviewed with respect to the account includes a power of attorney or signatory authority granted to a person with a U.S. address or contains an "in-care-of" address or "hold mail" address that is the sole address identified for the account holder, the participating FFI must retain a record of either a withholding certificate or a form of documentary evidence described in § 1.1471-3(c)(5)(i)(A) through (C) in order to establish the account holder's status as a foreign person.

(C) *Electronic search for identifying U.S. indicia.*—Except as provided in paragraph (c)(5)(iv)(D) of this section relating to the enhanced review for high-value accounts, a participating FFI may rely solely on a review of the electronically searchable information associated with an account and maintained by the participating FFI to determine if there are any of the U.S. indicia described in paragraph (c)(5)(iv)(B)(1) of this section associated with the account. For purposes of this paragraph (c)(5)(iv)(C), however, an FFI will not be required to treat as U.S. indicia an in-care-of address or a hold mail address that is the sole address identified for the account holder.

(D) *Enhanced review for identifying U.S. indicia in the case of certain high-value accounts.*—(*1*) *In general.*—With respect to preexisting individual accounts that have a balance or value that exceeds $1,000,000 as of the effective date of the FFI agreement, or at the end of any subsequent calendar year ("high-value accounts"), a participating FFI must apply the enhanced review described in this paragraph (c)(5)(iv)(D) in addition to the electronic search described in paragraph (c)(5)(iv)(C) of this section to identify any U.S. indicia described in paragraph (c)(5)(iv)(B)(1) of this section associated with the account. For purposes of determining the balance or value of an account, a participating FFI must apply the aggregation rules § 1.1471-5(b)(4)(iii)(A) and (B). If a participating FFI applied the enhanced review described in this paragraph (c)(5)(iv)(D) to an account in a previous year, the participating FFI will not be required to reapply such procedures to such account in a subsequent year.

(2) *Relationship manager inquiry.*—With respect to all high-value accounts, a participating FFI must identify accounts to which a relationship manager is assigned (including any accounts aggregated with such account) and for which the relationship manager has actual knowledge that the account holder is a U.S. citizen or resident.

*(3) Additional review of non-electronic records.*—Except as provided in paragraph (c)(5)(iv)(E) of this section, and except with respect to any account for which the participating FFI has retained a record of a withholding certificate and documentary evidence described in §1.1471-3(c)(5) establishing the account holder's foreign status, a participating FFI must review to identify any U.S. indicia in the current customer master file of a high-value account and, if not contained in the current customer master file, the following documents described in paragraphs (c)(5)(iv)(D)(3)(i) through (v) of this section that are associated with such an account and were obtained by the participating FFI within the five calendar years preceding the later of the effective date of the FFI agreement, or the end of the calendar year in which the account exceeded the $1,000,000 threshold described in paragraph (c)(5)(iv)(D)(1) of this section. The documents to be reviewed by the participating FFI if not contained in the current customer master file are—

    *(i)* The most recent withholding certificate, written statement, and documentary evidence;

    *(ii)* The most recent account opening contract or documentation;

    *(iii)* The most recent documentation obtained by the participating FFI for purposes of AML due diligence or for other regulatory purposes;

    *(iv)* Any power of attorney or signature authority forms currently in effect; and

    *(v)* Any standing instructions to pay amounts to another account.

    *(4) Limitations on the enhanced review in the case of comprehensive electronically searchable information.*—A participating FFI is not required to apply the enhanced review of paragraph (c)(5)(iv)(D)(3) of this section and may instead rely on the electronic search described in paragraph (c)(5)(iv)(C) of this section to identify U.S. indicia to the extent the following information is available in the FFI's electronically searchable information—

    *(i)* The account holder's nationality and/or residence status;

    *(ii)* The account holder's current residence address and mailing address;

    *(iii)* The account holder's current telephone number(s);

    *(iv)* Whether there are standing instructions to pay amounts to another account;

    *(v)* Whether there is a current "in-care-of" address or "hold mail" address for the account holder if no other residence or mailing address is found for the account; and

    *(vi)* Whether there is any power of attorney or signatory authority for the account.

    *(E) Exception for preexisting individual accounts previously documented as held by foreign individuals.*—A participating FFI that has previously obtained documentation from an account holder to establish the account holder's status as a foreign individual in order to meet its obligations under its QI, WP, or WT agreement with the IRS, or to fulfill its reporting obligations as a U.S. payor under chapter 61, is not required to perform the electronic search described in paragraph (c)(5)(iv)(C) of this section or the enhanced review described in paragraph (c)(5)(iv)(D)(3) of this section for such account. Additionally, a participating FFI with a U.S. payor as its paying agent is not required to perform the electronic search described in paragraph (c)(5)(iv)(C) of this section or the enhanced review described in paragraph (c)(5)(iv)(D)(3) of this section for an account for which its paying agent that is a U.S. payor has previously obtained documentation to establish the account holder's status as a foreign individual under chapter 61. The participating FFI is required, however, to perform the relationship manager inquiry described in paragraph (c)(5)(iv)(D)(2) of this section if the account is a high-value account described in paragraph (c)(5)(iv)(D)(1) of this section. For purposes of this paragraph (c)(5)(iv)(E), a participating FFI has documented an account holder's foreign status under chapter 61 if the participating FFI (or its paying agent that is a U.S. payor) has retained a record of the documentation required under chapter 61 to establish the foreign status of an individual and the account received a reportable payment as defined under section 3406(b) in any prior year that was properly reported in that year. In the case of a participating FFI that is a QI, WP, or WT, the participating FFI has documented an account holder's foreign status under its QI, WP, or WT agreement (as applicable) if the participating FFI has met the relevant documentation and reporting requirements of its agreement with respect to an account holder that received a reportable amount in any year in which its agreement was in effect.

    *(6) Examples.*—The following examples illustrate the documentation exceptions provided in paragraphs (c)(3)(iii) and (c)(5)(iii) of this section:

*Example 1. Aggregation rules applicable to preexisting individual accounts.* U, a U.S. resident individual, holds 100 shares of common stock of FFI1, an investment entity. On the effective date of FFI1's FFI agreement, the common stock held by U is worth $45,000. U also holds shares of preferred stock of FFI1. On the effective date of FFI1's FFI agreement, U's preferred stock in FFI1 is worth $35,000. Neither FFI1's common stock nor FFI1's preferred stock is regularly traded on an established securities market. U also holds debt instruments issued by FFI1 that are not regularly traded on an established securities market. On the effective date of FFI1's FFI agreement, U's FFI1 debt instruments are worth $15,000. U's common and preferred equity interests are associated with U and with one another by reference to U's foreign tax identification number in FFI1's computerized information management system. However, U's debt instruments are not associated with U's equity interests in FFI1's computerized information management system. None of these accounts are managed by a relationship manager. Previously, FFI1 was not required to and did not obtain a Form W-9 from U for purposes of chapter 3 or 61. U's FFI1 debt interests are eligible for the paragraph (c)(5)(iii)(A) documentation exception because that account does not exceed the $50,000 threshold described in paragraph (c)(5)(iii)(A)(1) of this section, taking into account the aggregation rule described in paragraph (c)(5)(iii)(A)(2) of this section. However, U's common and preferred equity interests are not eligible for the paragraph (c)(5)(iii)(A) documentation exception because the accounts exceed the $50,000 threshold described in paragraph (c)(5)(iii)(A)(1) of this section, taking into account the aggregation rules described in §1.1471-5(b)(4)(iii) pursuant to the requirements of paragraph (c)(5)(iii)(A)(2) of this section.

*Example 2. Aggregation rules for owners of entity accounts.* In Year 1, U, a U.S. resident individual, maintains a depository account that is a preexisting account in CB, a commercial bank. The balance in U's depository account on the effective date of CB's FFI agreement is $20,000. U also owns 100% of Entity X, which maintains a depository account that is a preexisting account in CB, and 50% of Entity Y, which maintains a depository account that is a preexisting account in CB. The balance in Entity X's account on the effective date of CB's FFI agreement is $130,000, and the balance in Entity Y's account on the effective date of CB's FFI agreement is $110,000. All three accounts are associated with one another in CB's computerized information management system by reference to U's foreign tax identification number. None of the accounts are managed by a relationship manager. Previously, CB was not required to and did not obtain a Form W-9 from U for purposes of chapter 3 or 61. U's depository account qualifies for the §1.1471-5(a)(4)(i) exception to U.S. account status because it does not exceed the $50,000 threshold, taking into account the aggregation rule described in §1.1471-5(a)(4)(iii)(A). Entity X's account and Entity Y's account both qualify for the paragraph (c)(3)(iii) documentation exception because the accounts do not exceed the $250,000 threshold described in paragraph (c)(3)(iii)(B)(1) of this section taking into account the aggregation rules described in §1.1471-5(b)(4)(iii) pursuant to the requirements of paragraph (c)(3)(iii)(B)(2) of this section.

    *(7) Certifications of responsible officer.*—In order for a participating FFI to comply with the requirements of an FFI agreement with respect to its identification procedures for preexisting accounts, a responsible officer of the participating FFI must certify to the IRS regarding the participating FFI's compliance with the diligence requirements of this paragraph (c). The responsible officer must certify that the participating FFI has completed the review of all high-value accounts as required under paragraphs (c)(5)(iv)(D) and (E) of this section and treats any account holder of an account for which the participating FFI has not retained a record of any required documentation as a recalcitrant account holder as required under this section and §1.1471-5(g). The responsible officer must also certify that the participating FFI has completed the account identification procedures and documentation requirements of this paragraph (c) for all other preexisting accounts or, if it has not retained a record of the documentation required under this paragraph (c) with respect to an account, treats such account in accordance with the requirements of this section and §1.1471-5(g) or §1.1471-3(f) (as applicable). The responsible officer must also certify to the best of the responsible officer's knowledge after conducting a reasonable inquiry, that the participating FFI did not have any formal or informal practices or procedures in place from August 6, 2011, through the date that is two years after the effective date of the FFI's FFI agreement to assist account holders in the avoidance of chapter 4. A reasonable inquiry for purposes of this paragraph (c)(7) is a review of the participating FFI's procedures and a written inquiry, such as email requests to relevant lines of business, that requires responses from relevant customer on-boarding and management personnel as to whether they engaged in any such practices during that period. Practices or procedures that assist account holders in the avoidance of chapter 4 include, for example, suggesting that account holders split up ac-

counts to avoid classification as a high-value account; suggesting that account holders of U.S. accounts close, transfer, or withdraw from their account to avoid reporting; intentional failures to disclose a known U.S. account; suggesting that an account holder remove U.S. indicia from its account information; or facilitating the manipulation of account balances or values to avoid thresholds. If the responsible officer is unable to make any of the certifications described in this paragraph (c)(7), the responsible officer must make a qualified certification to the IRS stating that such certification cannot be made and that corrective actions will be taken by the responsible officer. The certifications described in this paragraph (c)(7) must be submitted to the IRS by the due date of the FFI's first certification of compliance required under paragraph (f)(3) of this section.

(d) *Account reporting.*—(1) *Scope of paragraph.*—This paragraph (d) provides rules addressing the information reporting requirements applicable to participating FFIs with respect to U.S. accounts, accounts held by owner-documented FFIs, and recalcitrant account holders. Paragraph (d)(2) of this section describes the accounts subject to reporting under this paragraph (d), and specifies the participating FFI that is responsible for reporting an account or account holder. Paragraph (d)(3) of this section describes the information required to be reported and the manner of reporting by a participating FFI under section 1471(c)(1) with respect to a U.S. account or an account held by an owner-documented FFI. Paragraph (d)(4) of this section provides definitions of terms applicable to paragraph (d)(3). Paragraph (d)(5) of this section describes the conditions for a participating FFI to elect to report its U.S. accounts and accounts held by owner-documented FFIs under section 1471(c)(2) and the information required to be reported under such election. Paragraph (d)(6) of this section provides rules for a participating FFI to report its recalcitrant account holders. Paragraph (d)(7) of this section provides special transitional reporting rules applicable to reports due in 2015 and 2016. Paragraph (d)(8) of this section provides the reporting requirements of a participating FFI that is a QI, WP, or WT with respect to U.S. accounts. See chapter 61 for reporting requirements that may apply to a payor that is a participating FFI or registered deemed compliant FFI with respect to payees. See § 301.1474-1(a) of this chapter for the requirement for a financial institution to file the information required under this paragraph (d) on magnetic media.

(2) *Reporting requirements in general.*—(i) *Accounts subject to reporting.*—Subject to the rules of paragraph (d)(7) of this section, a participating FFI shall report by the time and in the manner prescribed in paragraph (d)(3)(vi) of this section, the information described in paragraph (d)(3) of this section with respect to accounts maintained at any time during each calendar year for which the participating FFI is responsible for reporting under paragraph (d)(2)(ii) of this section and that it is required to treat as U.S. accounts or accounts held by owner-documented FFIs, including accounts that are identified as U.S. accounts by the end of such calendar year pursuant to a change in circumstances during such year as described in paragraph (c)(2)(iii) of this section. Alternatively, a participating FFI may elect to report under paragraph (d)(5) of this section with respect to such accounts for each calendar year. With respect to accounts held by recalcitrant account holders, a participating FFI is required to report with respect to each calendar year under paragraph (d)(6) of this section and not under paragraph (d)(3) or (5) of this section. For separate reporting requirements of participating FFIs with respect to foreign reportable amounts and for transitional rules for participating FFIs to report certain foreign reportable amounts paid to accounts held by nonparticipating FFIs, see § 1.1471-4(d)(2)(ii)(F).

(ii) *Financial institution required to report an account.*—(A) *In general.*—Except as otherwise provided in paragraphs (d)(2)(ii)(B) through (G) of this section, the participating FFI that maintains the account is responsible for reporting the account in accordance with the requirements of paragraph (d)(2)(iii), (d)(3), or (d)(5) of this section (as applicable) for each calendar year. Except as otherwise provided in paragraph (d)(2)(ii)(C) of this section, a participating FFI is responsible for reporting accounts held by recalcitrant account holders that it maintains in accordance with the requirements of paragraph (d)(6) of this section. A participating FFI is not required to report the information required under paragraph (d)(6) of this section with respect to an account held by a recalcitrant account holder of another participating FFI even if that other participating FFI holds the account as an intermediary on behalf of such account holder and regardless of whether the participating FFI is required to report payments made to the recalcitrant account holder of such other FFI under § 1.1474-1(d)(4)(iii).

(B) *Special reporting of account holders of territory financial institutions.*—In the case of an account held by a territory financial institution that is a flow-through entity or acting as an intermediary with respect to a withholdable payment—

(1) If the territory financial institution agrees to be treated as a U.S. person with respect to the payment under § 1.1471-3(c)(3)(iii)(F), a participating FFI is not required to report under paragraph (d)(2)(i) of this section with respect to the account holders of the territory financial institution; or

(2) If the territory financial institution does not agree to be treated as a U.S. person with respect to a withholdable payment, the participating FFI must report with respect to each specified U.S. person or substantial U.S. owner of an entity that is treated as a passive NFFE with respect to which the territory financial institution acts as an intermediary or is a flow-through entity and provides the participating FFI with the information and documentation required under § 1.1471-3(c)(3)(iii)(G). The participating FFI shall be treated as having satisfied these reporting requirements if it reports with respect to each such specified U.S. person or substantial U.S. owner of a passive NFFE either—

(i) The information required by chapter 61 and described in paragraph (d)(5)(ii) or (d)(5)(iii) of this section (except account number); or

(ii) The information described in paragraph (d)(3)(ii), (d)(3)(iii), or (d)(3)(iv) of this section (except account number and account balance or value).

(C) *Special reporting of account holders of a sponsored FFI.*—A sponsoring entity that has agreed to fulfill the reporting responsibilities of this paragraph (d) on behalf of a sponsored FFI shall report in accordance with the requirements of paragraph (d)(2)(iii), (3), or (5) of this section (as applicable) with respect to each U.S. account and paragraph (d)(6) of this section with respect to each account held by a recalcitrant account holder of the sponsored FFI to the extent and in the manner required if such sponsored FFI were a participating FFI. The sponsoring entity shall identify each sponsored FFI for which it is reporting to the extent required on the forms for reporting U.S. accounts and recalcitrant account holders and the accompanying instructions to the forms.

(D) *Special reporting of accounts held by owner-documented FFIs.*—A participating FFI that maintains an account held by an FFI that it has agreed to treat as an owner-documented FFI under § 1.1471-3(d)(6) shall report the information described in paragraph (d)(3)(iv) or (d)(5)(iii) of this section with respect to each specified U.S. person identified in § 1.1471-3(d)(6)(iv)(A)(1) and (2). See § 1.1474-1(i) for the reporting obligations of a participating FFI with respect to a payee of an obligation other than an account that it has agreed to treat as an owner-documented FFI.

(E) *Requirement to identify the GIIN of a branch that maintains an account.*—A participating FFI may report under paragraph (d)(3) or (d)(5) of this section either with respect to all of its U.S. accounts and recalcitrant accounts, or separately with respect to any clearly identified group of accounts (such as by line of business or the location of where the account is maintained). A participating FFI shall include the GIIN assigned to the participating FFI or its branches to identify the jurisdiction of the FFI or branch that maintains the accounts subject to reporting under paragraph (d)(3) or (d)(5) of this section. Additionally, a participating FFI shall file with the IRS the information required to be reported on accounts that it maintains in accordance with the forms and their accompanying instructions provided by the IRS. For the definition of a branch that applies for purposes of this paragraph (d), see paragraph (e)(2)(ii) of this section.

(F) *Reporting by participating FFIs (including QIs, WPs, WTs, and certain U.S. branches not treated as U.S. persons) for accounts of nonparticipating FFIs (transitional).*—Except as otherwise provided in the instructions to Form 8966, "FATCA Report" or in this paragraph (d)(2)(ii)(F), if a participating FFI (including a QI, WP, WT, or U.S. branch of a participating FFI that is not treated as a U.S. person) maintains an account for a nonparticipating FFI (including a limited branch and limited FFI treated as a nonparticipating FFI), the participating FFI must report on Form 8966 the name and address of the nonparticipating FFI, and the aggregate amount of foreign source payments, as described in paragraph (d)(4)(iv) of this section, paid to or with respect to each such account (foreign reportable amount) for each of the calendar years 2015 and 2016. If, however, the participating FFI is prohibited under domestic law from reporting on a specific payee basis without consent from the nonparticipating FFI account holder and the participating FFI has not been able to obtain such consent, the participating FFI may instead report the aggregate number of accounts held by such non-consenting nonparticipating FFIs and the aggregate amount of foreign reportable amounts paid with respect to such accounts, as described in paragraph (d)(4)(iv) of this section, during the calendar year. A participating FFI may, in lieu of reporting only foreign reportable amounts, report all income, gross proceeds, and redemptions (irrespective of the source) paid to the nonparticipating FFI's account by the participating FFI during the calendar year. With respect to calendar year 2015, however, a participating FFI is not required to report gross proceeds described in paragraph (d)(4)(iv)(B)(3) of this section paid to an account held by a nonparticipating FFI. In addition, the participating FFI must retain the account statements related to such nonparticipating FFI accounts. See paragraphs (d)(6)(iv), through (vii) of this section for rules relating to reporting on recalcitrant account holders. Form 8966 shall be filed electronically with the IRS on or before March 31 of the year following the end of the calendar year to which the form relates.

(G) *Combined reporting on Form 8966 following merger or bulk acquisition.*—If a participating FFI (successor) acquires accounts of another participating FFI (predecessor) in a merger or bulk acquisition of accounts, the successor may assume the predecessor's obligations to report the acquired accounts under paragraph (d) of this section with respect to the calendar year in which the merger or acquisition occurs (acquisition year), provided that the requirements in paragraphs (d)(2)(ii)(G)(1) through (4) of this section are satisfied. If the requirements of paragraphs (d)(2)(ii)(G)(1) through (4) of this section are not satisfied, both the predecessor and the successor are required to report the acquired accounts for the portion of the acquisition year that it maintains the account.

(1) The successor must acquire substantially all of the accounts maintained by the predecessor, or substantially all of the accounts maintained at a branch of the predecessor, in a merger or bulk acquisition of accounts for value.

(2) The successor must agree to report the acquired accounts for the acquisition year on Form 8966 to the extent required in § 1.1471-4(d)(3) or (d)(5).

(3) The successor may not elect to report under section 1471(c)(2) and § 1.1471-4(d)(5) with respect to any acquired account that is a U.S. account for the acquisition year.

(4) The successor must notify the IRS on the form and in the manner prescribed by the IRS that Form 8966 is being filed on a combined basis.

(iii) *Special U.S. account reporting rules for U.S. payors.*—(A) *Special reporting rule for U.S. payors other than U.S. branches.*—Participating FFIs that are U.S. payors (other than U.S. branches) shall be treated as having satisfied the chapter 4 reporting requirements described in paragraph (d)(2)(i) of this section with respect to accounts that the participating FFI is required to treat as U.S. accounts, or accounts held by owner-documented FFIs, if the participating FFI reports with respect to each such account either—

(1) The information required by chapter 61 and described in paragraph (d)(5)(ii) or (d)(5)(iii) of this section; or

(2) The information described in paragraph (d)(3)(ii), (d)(3)(iii), or (d)(3)(iv) of this section. However, such participating FFI that is required to report on such accounts under chapter 61 is not relieved of that obligation.

(B) *Special reporting rules for U.S. branches treated as U.S. persons.*—A U.S. branch treated as a U.S. person (as defined in § 1.1471-1(b)(135)) shall be treated as having satisfied the reporting requirements described in paragraph (d)(2)(i) of this section if it reports under—

(1) Chapter 61 with respect to account holders that are U.S. non-exempt recipients;

(2) Chapter 61 with respect to persons subject to withholding under section 3406;

(3) Section 1.1474-1(i) with respect to substantial U.S. owners of NFFEs that are not excepted NFFEs as defined in § 1.1472-1(c) and;

(4) Section 1.1474-1(i) with respect to specified U.S. persons identified in § 1.1471-3(d)(6)(iv)(A)(1) and (2) of owner-documented FFIs.

(C) *Rules for U.S. branches of FFIs not treated as U.S. persons.*—A U.S. branch of an FFI that is not treated as a U.S. person shall apply the due diligence rules in paragraph (c)(2) of this section to document its accounts and payees, and shall report its U.S. accounts and accounts held by owner-documented FFIs under paragraph (d)(3), (d)(5), or (d)(6) of this section, as if the U.S. branch were a participating FFI. In addition, the U.S. branch shall apply the withholding requirements in paragraph (b) of this section as if the U.S. branch were a participating FFI.

(3) *Reporting of accounts under section 1471(c)(1).*—(i) *In general.*—The participating FFI (or branch thereof) is responsible for reporting an account that it is required to treat as a U.S. account or accounts held by owner-documented FFIs under paragraph (d)(2)(ii) of this section and required to report such account under this paragraph (d)(3) for each calendar year unless it elects to report its U.S. accounts or accounts held by owner-documented FFIs under paragraph (d)(5) of this section.

(ii) *Accounts held by specified U.S. persons.*—In the case of an account described in paragraph (d)(3)(i) of this section that is held by one or more specified U.S. persons, a participating FFI is required to report the following information under this paragraph (d)(3)—

(A) The name, address, and TIN of each account holder that is a specified U.S. person;

(B) The account number;

(C) The account balance or value of the account;

(D) The payments made with respect to the account, as described in paragraph (d)(4)(iv) of this section, during the calendar year; and

(E) Such other information as is otherwise required to be reported under this paragraph (d)(3) or in the form described in paragraph (d)(3)(v) of this section and its accompanying instructions.

(iii) *Accounts held by U.S. owned foreign entities.*—With respect to each U.S. account described in paragraph (d)(3)(i) of this section that is held by a passive NFFE that is a U.S. owned foreign entity, a participating FFI is required to report under this paragraph (d)(3)(iii)—

(A) The name of the U.S. owned foreign entity that is the account holder;

(B) The name, address, and TIN of each substantial U.S. owner of such entity;

(C) The account number;

(D) The account balance or value of the account held by the NFFE;

(E) The payments made with respect to the account, as described in paragraph (d)(4)(iv) of this section, during the calendar year; and

(F) Such other information as is otherwise required to be reported under this paragraph (d)(3) or in the form described in paragraph (d)(3)(v) of this section and its accompanying instructions.

(iv) *Special reporting of accounts held by owner-documented FFIs.*—With respect to each account held by an owner-documented FFI, a participating FFI is required to report under this paragraph (d)(3)(iv)—

(A) The name of the owner-documented FFI;

(B) The name, address, and TIN of each specified U.S. person identified in § 1.1471-3(d)(6)(iv)(A)(1) and (2);

(C) The account number of the account held by the owner-documented FFI;

(D) The account balance or value of the account held by the owner-documented FFI;

(E) The payments made with respect to the account held by the owner-documented FFI, as described in paragraph (d)(4)(iv) of this section, during the calendar year; and

(F) Such other information as is otherwise required to be reported under this paragraph (d)(3) or in the form described in paragraph (d)(3)(vi) of this section and its accompanying instructions.

(v) *Form for reporting accounts under section 1471(c)(1).*—The information described in paragraphs (d)(3)(ii) through (iv) of this section shall be reported on Form 8966, "FATCA Report," (or such other form as the IRS may prescribe) with respect to each account subject to reporting under paragraph (d)(3)(i) of this section maintained at any time during the calendar year. This form shall be filed in accordance with its requirements and its accompanying instructions.

(vi) *Time and manner of filing.*—Except as provided in paragraph (d)(7)(iv)(B) of this section, Form 8966 shall be filed electronically with the IRS on or before March 31 of the year following the end of the calendar year to which the form relates. See the accompanying instructions to this form for electronic filing instructions.

(vii) *Extensions in filing.*—The IRS shall grant an automatic 90-day extension of time in which to file Form 8966. Form 8809-I, "Application for Extension of Time to File FATCA Form 8966," (or such other form as the IRS may prescribe) must be used to request such extension of time and must be filed no later than the due date of Form 8966. Under certain hardship conditions, the IRS may grant an additional 90-day extension. A request for extension due to hardship must contain a statement of the reasons for requesting the extension and such other information as the forms or instructions may require.

(4) *Descriptions applicable to reporting requirements of § 1.1471-4(d)(3).*—(i) *Address.*—The address to be reported with respect to an account held by a specified U.S. person is the residence address recorded by the participating FFI for the account holder or, if no residence address is associated with the account holder, the address for the account used for mailing or for other purposes by the participating FFI. In the case of an account held by a passive NFFE that is a U.S. owned foreign entity, the address to be reported is the

address of each substantial U.S. owner of such entity. In the case of an account held by an owner-documented FFI, the address to be reported is the address of each specified U.S. person identified in § 1.1471-3(d)(6)(iv)(A)(1) and (2).

(ii) *Account number.*—The account number to be reported with respect to an account is the identifying number assigned by the participating FFI for purposes other than to satisfy the reporting requirements of this paragraph (d), or, if no such number is assigned to the account, a unique serial number or other number such participating FFI assigns to the financial account for purposes of reporting under paragraph (d)(3) of this section that distinguishes the account from other accounts maintained by such institution.

(iii) *Account balance or value.*—(A) *In general.*—The participating FFI shall report the average balance or value of the account if the FFI reports average balance or value to the account holder for a calendar year. If the participating FFI does not report the average balance or value of the account to the account holder, the participating FFI shall report the balance or value of the account as of the end of the calendar year as determined in accordance with § 1.1471-5(b)(4). In the case of an account that is a cash value insurance or annuity contract, a participating FFI shall report the balance or value of the account as determined in accordance with § 1.1471-5(b)(4).

(B) *Currency translation of account balance or value.*—The account balance or value of an account may be reported in U.S. dollars or in the currency in which the account is denominated. In the case of an account denominated in one or more foreign currencies, the participating FFI may elect to report the account balance or value in a currency in which the account is denominated and is required to identify the currency in which the account is reported. If the participating FFI elects to report such an account in U.S. dollars, the participating FFI must calculate the account balance or value of the account in the manner described in § 1.1471-5(b)(4).

(iv) *Payments made with respect to an account.*—(A) *Depository accounts.*—The payments made during a calendar year with respect to a depository account consist of the aggregate gross amount of interest paid or credited to the account during the year.

(B) *Custodial accounts.*—The payments made during a calendar year with respect to a custodial account consist of—

(1) The aggregate gross amount of dividends paid or credited to the account during the calendar year;

(2) The aggregate gross amount of interest paid or credited to the account during the calendar year;

(3) The gross proceeds from the sale or redemption of property paid or credited to the account during the calendar year with respect to which the FFI acted as a custodian, broker, nominee, or otherwise as an agent for the account holder; and

(4) The aggregate gross amount of all other income paid or credited to the account during the calendar year.

(C) *Other accounts.*—In the case of an account described in § 1.1471-5(b)(1)(iii) (relating to a debt or equity interest other than an interest as a partner in a partnership) or § 1.1471-5(b)(1)(iv) (relating to cash value insurance contracts and annuity contracts), the payments made during the calendar year with respect to such account are the gross amounts paid or credited to the account holder during the calendar year including payments in redemption (in whole or part) of the account. In the case of an account that is a partner's interest in a partnership, the payments made during the calendar year with respect to such account are the amount of the partner's distributive share of the partnership's income or loss for the calendar year, without regard to whether any such amount is distributed to the partner during the year, and any guaranteed payments for the use of capital. The payments required to be reported under this paragraph (d)(4)(iv)(C) with respect to a partner may be determined based on the partnership's tax returns or, if the tax returns are unavailable by the due date for filing Form 8966, the partnership's financial statements or any other reasonable method used by the partnership for calculating the partner's share of partnership income by such date.

(D) *Transfers and closings of deposit, custodial, insurance, and annuity financial accounts.*—In the case of an account closed or transferred in its entirety during a calendar year that is a depository account, custodial account, or a cash value insurance contract or annuity contract, the payments made with respect to the account shall be—

(1) The payments and income paid or credited to the account that are described in paragraph (d)(4)(iv)(A) or (B) of this section for the calendar year until the date of transfer or closure; and

(2) The amount or value withdrawn or transferred from the account in connection with the closure or transfer of the account.

(E) *Amount and character of payments subject to reporting.*—For purposes of reporting under paragraph (d)(3) of this section, the amount and character of payments made with respect to an account may be determined under the same principles that the participating FFI uses to report information on its resident account holders to the tax administration of the jurisdiction in which the FFI (or branch thereof) is located. Thus, the amount and character of items of income described in paragraphs (d)(4)(iv)(A), (B), and (C) need not be determined in accordance with U.S. federal income tax principles. If any of the types of payments described in paragraph (d)(4)(iv) of this section are not reported to the tax administration of the jurisdiction in which the participating FFI (or branch thereof) is located, such amounts may be determined in the same manner as is used by the participating FFI for purposes of reporting to the account holder. If any of the types of payments described in this paragraph (d)(4)(iv) is neither reported to the tax administration of the jurisdiction in which the FFI (or branch thereof) is located nor reported to the account holder for the year for which reporting is required under paragraph (d) of this section, such item must be determined and reported either in accordance with U.S. federal tax principles or in accordance with any reasonable method of reporting that is consistent with the accounting principles generally applied by the participating FFI. Once a participating FFI (or branch thereof) has applied a method to determine such amounts, it must apply such method consistently for all account holders and for all subsequent years unless the Commissioner consents to a change in such method. Consent will be automatically granted for a change to rely on U.S. federal income tax principles to determine such amounts.

(F) *Currency translation.*—A payment described in this paragraph (d)(4)(iv) may be reported in the currency in which the payment is denominated or in U.S. dollars. In the case of payments denominated in one or more foreign currencies, a participating FFI may elect to report the payments in a currency in which payments are denominated and is required to identify the currency in which the account is reported. If such a payment is reported in U.S. dollars, the participating FFI must calculate the amount in the manner described in § 1.1471-5(b)(4).

(v) *Record retention requirements.*—A participating FFI that produces, in the ordinary course of its business, account statements that summarize the activity (including withdrawals, transfers, and closures) of an account for any calendar year in which the account was required to be reported under paragraph (d)(3) of this section must retain a record of such account statements. The record must be retained for the longer of six years or the retention period under the FFI's normal business procedures. A participating FFI may be required to extend the six year retention period if the IRS requests such an extension prior to the expiration of the six year period.

(5) *Election to perform chapter 61 reporting.*—(i) *In general.*—(A) *Election under section 1471(c)(2).*—Except as otherwise provided in this paragraph (d)(5), a participating FFI may elect under section 1471(c)(2) and this paragraph (d)(5) to report under sections 6041, 6042, 6045, and 6049, as appropriate, with respect to any account required to be reported under this paragraph (d). Such reporting must be done as if such participating FFI were a U.S. payor and each holder of an account that is a specified U.S. person, passive NFFE that is a U.S. owned foreign entity, or owner-documented FFI were a payee who is an individual and citizen of the United States. If a participating FFI makes such an election, the FFI is required to report the information required under this paragraph (d)(5) with respect to each such U.S. account or account held by an owner-documented FFI, regardless of whether the account holder of such account qualifies as a recipient exempt from reporting by a payor or middleman under sections 6041, 6042, 6045, or 6049, including the reporting of payments made to such account of amounts that are subject to reporting under any of these sections. A participating FFI that elects to report an account under the election described in this paragraph (d)(5) is required to report the information described in paragraph (d)(5)(ii) or (iii) of this section for a calendar year regardless of whether a reportable payment was made to the U.S. account during the calendar year. A participating FFI that reports an account under the election described in this paragraph (d)(5) is not required to report the information described in paragraph (d)(3) of this section with respect to the account. The election under section 1471(c)(2) described in this paragraph (d)(5)(i)(A) does not apply to cash value insurance contracts or annuity contracts that are financial accounts described in § 1.1471-5(b)(1)(iv). See paragraph (d)(5)(i)(B) of this section for an election to report cash value insurance contracts or annuity contracts that are U.S. accounts held by specified U.S. persons in a manner similar to section 6047(d).

(B) *Election to report in a manner similar to section 6047(d).*—Except as otherwise provided in this paragraph (d)(5), a participating FFI may elect to report with respect to any of its cash value insurance contracts or annuity contracts that are U.S. accounts held by specified U.S. persons under section 6047(d), modified as follows. The amount to be reported is any amount paid under the contract during such reporting period as if such participating FFI were a U.S. payor. Each holder of a U.S. account that is a specified U.S. person is treated for purposes of reporting under this paragraph (d)(5)(i)(B) as a contract holder or payee who is an individual and citizen of the United States.

(ii) *Additional information to be reported.*—In addition to the information otherwise required to be reported under sections 6041, 6042, 6045, 6047(d) (in the manner described in paragraph (d)(5)(i)(B) of this section with respect to U.S. accounts held by specified U.S. persons), and 6049, including the reporting of payments made to such accounts subject to reporting under the applicable section, a participating FFI that elects to report under this paragraph (d)(5)(ii) must report with respect to each account that it is required to treat as a U.S. account—

(A) In the case of an account holder that is a specified U.S. person—

(1) The name, address, and TIN of the account holder; and

(2) The account number; and

(B) In the case of an account holder that is a U.S. owned foreign entity that is a passive NFFE—

(1) The name of such entity;

(2) The name, address, and TIN of each substantial U.S. owner of such entity; and

(3) The account number.

(iii) *Special reporting of accounts held by owner-documented FFIs.*—With respect to each account held by an owner-documented FFI, a participating FFI that elects to report under this paragraph (d)(5) must report payments made to the owner-documented FFI under the requirements of sections 6041, 6042, 6045, 6047(d), and 6049, the other information required under each applicable section, and the following information—

(A) The name of such FFI;

(B) The name, address, and TIN of each specified U.S. person identified in §1.1471-3(d)(6)(iv)(A)(1) and (2); and

(C) The account number for the account held by the owner-documented FFI.

(iv) *Branch reporting.*—A participating FFI that reports the information described in paragraphs (d)(5)(ii) and (iii) of this section shall also report the jurisdiction of the branch that maintains the account being reported.

(v) *Time and manner of making the election.*—A participating FFI (or one or more branches of the participating FFI) may make the election described in this paragraph (d)(5) by reporting the information described in this paragraph (d)(5) on the form described in paragraph (d)(5)(vii) of this section on the next reporting date following the end of the calendar year for which the election is made. A participating FFI may make an election under this paragraph (d)(5) either with respect to all of its U.S. accounts and recalcitrant accounts or, separately, with respect to any clearly identified group of accounts (such as by line of business or the location where the account is maintained).

(vi) *Revocation of election.*—A participating FFI may revoke the election described in paragraph (d)(5)(i) of this section (as a whole or with regard to any clearly identified group of accounts) by reporting the information described in paragraph (d)(3) this section beginning on the first reporting date with respect to the calendar year that follows the calendar year for which it last reports an account under this paragraph (d)(5).

(vii) *Filing of information under election.*—In the case of an account holder that is a specified U.S. person, the information required to be reported under the election described in this paragraph (d)(5) shall be filed with the IRS and issued to the account holder in the time and manner prescribed in sections 6041, 6042, 6045, 6047(d), and 6049 and in accordance with the forms referenced therein and their accompanying instructions provided by the IRS for reporting under each of these sections. If the account holder is a passive NFFE that is a U.S. owned foreign entity or owner-documented FFI, however, the information required to be reported under the election described in this paragraph (d)(5) shall be filed on Form 8966 in accordance with its requirements and its accompanying instructions.

(6) *Reporting on recalcitrant account holders.*—(i) *In general.*—Except as otherwise provided in a Model 2 IGA, a participating FFI, as part of its reporting responsibilities under this paragraph (d), shall report to the IRS for each calendar year the information described for each of the classes of account holders described in paragraphs (d)(6)(i)(A) through (E) of this section. See §1.1474-1(d)(4)(ii) for a participating FFI or registered deemed-compliant FFI's requirement

to report chapter 4 reportable amounts paid to such account holders and tax withheld.

(A) The aggregate number and aggregate balance or value of accounts held by recalcitrant account holders at the end of the calendar year that are described in §1.1471-5(g)(2)(iv) (referencing passive NFFEs that are recalcitrant account holders).

(B) The aggregate number and aggregate balance or value of accounts held by recalcitrant account holders at the end of the calendar year that are described in §1.1471-5(g)(2)(ii) and (iii) (referencing U.S. persons that are recalcitrant account holders).

(C) The aggregate number and aggregate balance or value of accounts held by recalcitrant account holders at the end of the calendar year, other than accounts described in paragraph (d)(6)(i)(A), (B), or (E) of this section, that have U.S. indicia.

(D) The aggregate number and aggregate balance or value of accounts held by recalcitrant account holders at the end of the calendar year, other than accounts described in paragraph (d)(6)(i)(A) or (E) of this section, that do not have U.S. indicia.

(E) The aggregate number and aggregate balance or value of accounts held by recalcitrant account holders at the end of the calendar year that are dormant accounts.

(ii) *Definition of dormant account.*—A dormant account is an account (other than a cash value insurance contract or annuity contract) that is a dormant or inactive account under applicable laws or regulations or the normal operating procedures of the participating FFI that are consistently applied for all accounts maintained by such institution in a particular jurisdiction. If neither applicable laws or regulations nor the normal operating procedures of the participating FFI maintaining the account address dormant or inactive accounts, an account will be a dormant account if—

(A) The account holder has not initiated a transaction with regard to the account or any other account held by the account holder with the FFI in the past three years; and

(B) The account holder has not communicated with the FFI that maintains such account regarding the account or any other account held by the account holder with the FFI in the past six years.

(iii) *End of dormancy.*—An account that is a dormant account under paragraph (d)(6)(ii) of this section ceases to be a dormant account when—

(A) The account holder initiates a transaction with regard to the account or any other account held by the account holder with the FFI;

(B) The account holder communicates with the FFI that maintains such account regarding the account or any other account held by the account holder with the FFI; or

(C) The account ceases to be a dormant account under applicable laws or regulations or the participating FFI's normal operating procedures.

(iv) *Forms.*—Reporting under paragraph (d)(6)(i) of this section shall be filed on Form 8966 in accordance with its requirements and accompanying instructions.

(v) *Time and manner of filing.*—Except as provided in paragraph (d)(7)(iv)(B) of this section, Form 8966 shall be filed electronically with the IRS on or before March 31 of the year following the end of the calendar year to which the form relates. See the accompanying instructions to this form for electronic filing instructions.

(vi) *Extensions in filing.*—The IRS shall grant an automatic 90-day extension of time in which to file Form 8966. Form 8809-I, "Application for Extension of Time to File FATCA Form 8966," (or such other form as the IRS may prescribe) must be used to request such extension of time and must be filed no later than the due date of Form 8966. Under certain hardship conditions, the IRS may grant an additional 90-day extension. A request for extension due to hardship must contain a statement of the reasons for requesting the extension and such other information as the forms or instructions may require.

(vii) *Record retention requirements.*—A participating FFI that produces, in the ordinary course of its business, account statements that summarize the activity (including withdrawals, transfers, and closures) of an account held by a recalcitrant account holder described in paragraph (d)(6)(i)(B) of this section for any calendar year in which the account was required to be reported under paragraph (d)(6) of this section must retain a record of such account statements. Such record must be retained for the longer of six years or the retention period under the FFI's normal business procedures. A participating FFI may be required to extend the six year retention period if the IRS requests such an extension prior to the expiration of the six year period.

(7) *Special reporting rules with respect to the 2014 and 2015 calendar years.*—(i) *In general.*—If the effective date of the FFI agreement of a participating FFI is on or before December 31, 2015, the participating

FFI is required to report U.S. accounts and accounts held by owner-documented FFIs that it maintained (or that it is otherwise required to report under paragraph (d)(2)(ii) of this section) during the 2014 and 2015 calendar years in accordance with paragraph (d)(7)(ii) or (iii) of this section.

(ii) *Participating FFIs that report under §1.1471-4(d)(3).*—With respect to accounts that a participating FFI is required to report in accordance with paragraph (d)(2) of this section, the participating FFI may, instead of the information described in paragraphs (d)(3)(ii) and (iii) of this section, report only the following information—

(A) *Reporting with respect to the 2014 calendar year.*—With respect to accounts maintained during the 2014 calendar year—

(1) The name, address, and TIN of each specified U.S. person who is an account holder and, in the case of any account holder that is a passive NFFE that is a U.S. owned foreign entity or that is an owner-documented FFI, the name of such entity and the name, address, and TIN of each substantial U.S. owner of such NFFE or, in the case of an owner-documented FFI, of each specified U.S. person identified in §1.1471-3(d)(6)(iv)(A)(1) and (2);

(2) The account balance or value as of the end of the relevant calendar year, or if the account was closed after the effective date of the FFI agreement, the amount or value withdrawn or transferred from the account in connection with closure; and

(3) The account number of the account.

(B) *Reporting with respect to the 2015 calendar year.*—With respect to the 2015 calendar year, the participating FFI may report only—

(1) The information described in paragraph (d)(7)(ii)(A) of this section; and

(2) The payments made with respect to the account except for those payments described in paragraph (d)(4)(iv)(B)(3) of this section (certain gross proceeds).

(iii) *Participating FFIs that report under §1.1471-4(d)(5).*—A participating FFI that elects to report under paragraph (d)(5) of this section may report only the information described in paragraphs (d)(7)(ii)(A)(1) and (3) of this section for its 2014 calendar year. With respect to its 2015 calendar year, a participating FFI is required to report all of the information required to be reported under paragraphs (d)(5)(i) through (iii) of this section but may exclude from such reporting amounts reportable under section 6045.

(iv) *Forms for reporting.*—(A) *In general.*—Except as provided in paragraph (d)(7)(iv)(B) of this section, reporting under paragraph (d)(7)(ii) of this section shall be made on Form 8966 (or such other form as the IRS may prescribe), in the manner described in paragraph (d)(3)(vi) of this section. Reporting under paragraph (d)(7)(iii) of this section shall be made in accordance with paragraph (d)(5)(vii) of this section.

(B) *Special determination date and timing for reporting with respect to the 2014 calendar year.*—With respect to the 2014 calendar year, a participating FFI must report under paragraph (d)(3) or (5) of this section on all accounts that are identified and documented under paragraph (c) of this section as U.S. accounts or accounts held by owner-documented FFIs as of December 31, 2014, (or as of the date an account is closed if the account is closed prior to December 31, 2014) if such account was outstanding on or after the effective date of the participating FFI's FFI agreement. Reporting for the 2014 calendar year shall be filed with the IRS on or before March 31, 2015. However, a U.S. payor (including a U.S. branch treated as a U.S. person (as defined in §1.1471-1(b)(135))) that reports in accordance with paragraph (d)(2)(iii) of this section may report all or a portion of its U.S. accounts and accounts held by owner-documented FFIs in accordance with the dates otherwise applicable to reporting under chapter 61 with respect to the 2014 calendar year.

(8) *Reporting requirements of QIs, WPs, and WTs.*—In general, the reporting requirements with respect to the U.S. accounts maintained by a participating FFI that is a QI, WP, or WT will be consistent with the reporting requirements with respect to such accounts of a participating FFI that is not a QI, WP, or WT. See the QI, WP, or WT agreement for the coordination of the chapter 4 reporting obligations of a participating FFI that also is a QI, WP, or WT.

(9) *Examples.*—The following examples illustrate the provisions of this paragraph:

*Example 1. Financial institution required to report U.S. account.* PFFI1, a participating FFI, issues shares of stock that are financial accounts under §1.1471-5(b). Such shares are held in custody by PFFI2, another participating FFI, on behalf of U, a specified U.S. person that holds an account with PFFI2. The shares of PFFI1 held by PFFI2 will not be subject to reporting by PFFI1 if PFFI1 may treat

PFFI2 as a participating FFI under §1.1471-3(d)(4). See paragraph (d)(2)(ii)(A) of this section.

*Example 2. Financial institution required to report U.S. account.* U, a specified U.S. person, holds shares in PFFI1, a participating FFI that invests in other financial institutions (a fund of funds). The shares of PFFI1 are financial accounts under §1.1471-5(b)(3)(iii). PFFI1 holds shares that are also financial accounts under §1.1471-5(b)(3)(iii) in PFFI2, another participating FFI. The shares of PFFI2 held by PFFI1 are not subject to reporting by PFFI2, if PFFI2 may treat PFFI1 as a participating FFI under §1.1471-3(d)(4). See paragraph (d)(2)(ii)(A) of this section.

*Example 3. U.S. owned foreign entity.* FC, a passive NFFE, holds a custodial account with PFFI1, a participating FFI. U, a specified U.S. person, owns 3% of the only class of stock of FC. Q, another specified U.S. person, owns 12% of the only class of stock of FC. U is not a substantial U.S. owner of FC. See §1.1473-1(b). Q is a substantial U.S. owner of FC and FC identifies her as such to PFFI1. PFFI1 does not elect to report under paragraph (d)(5) of this section. PFFI1 must complete and file the reporting form described in paragraph (d)(3)(v) of this section and report the information described in paragraph (d)(3)(iii) with respect to both FC and Q. See paragraph (d)(3)(ii) of this section.

*Example 4. Election to perform Form 1099 reporting with regard to an NFFE.* Same facts as in *Example 3*, except that PFFI1 has made the election in accordance with paragraph (d)(5) of this section. PFFI1 must complete and file the forms described in paragraph (d)(5)(vii) for FC, treating FC as if it were an individual and citizen of the United States and must identify Q as a substantial U.S. owner of FC on such form. See paragraph (d)(5)(ii) of this section. PFFI1 shall not complete the forms described in paragraph (d)(5)(vii) with regard to U.

*Example 5. Owner-documented FFI.* DC, an owner-documented FFI under §1.1471-3(d)(6), holds a custodial account with PFFI1, a participating FFI. U, a specified U.S. person, owns 3% of the only class of stock of DC. Q, another specified U.S. person, owns 12% of the only class of stock of DC. Both U and Q are persons identified in §1.1471-3(d)(6)(iv)(A)(1) and DC identifies U and Q to PFFI1 and otherwise provides to PFFI1 all of the information required to be reported with respect to DC. PFFI1 must complete and file a form described in paragraph (d)(3)(v) of this section with regard to U and Q. See paragraph (d)(3)(iii) of this section.

*Example 6. Election to perform Form 1099 reporting with regard to an owner-documented FFI.* Same facts as in *Example 5*, except that PFFI1 has made the election in accordance with paragraph (d)(5) of this section. PFFI1 must complete and file the forms described in paragraph (d)(5)(vii) for U and Q.

*Example 7. Sponsored FFI.* DC2 is an FFI that has agreed to have a sponsoring entity, PFFI1, fulfill DC2's chapter 4 responsibilities under §1.1471-5(f)(2)(iii). U, a specified U.S. person, holds an equity interest in DC2 that is a financial account under §1.1471-5(b)(3)(iii). PFFI1 must complete and file a form described in paragraph (d)(3)(v) of this section with regard to U's account on behalf of DC2. See paragraph (d)(2)(ii)(C) of this section.

(e) *Expanded affiliated group requirements.*—(1) *In general.*—Except as otherwise provided in this paragraph (e)(1) or paragraphs (e)(2) and (e)(3) of this section, each FFI that is a member of an expanded affiliated group must have the chapter 4 status of a participating FFI, deemed-compliant FFI, or exempt beneficial owner as a condition for any member of such group to obtain the status of a participating FFI or registered deemed-compliant FFI. Accordingly, except as otherwise provided in paragraph (e)(3)(v) of this section, each FFI other than a certified deemed-compliant FFI or exempt beneficial owner in an expanded affiliated group must submit a registration form to the IRS in such manner as the IRS may prescribe requesting an FFI agreement, registered deemed-compliant status, or limited FFI status as a condition for any member to become a participating FFI or registered deemed-compliant FFI. Except as provided in paragraph (e)(2) of this section, each FFI other than a certified deemed-compliant FFI or exempt beneficial owner that is a member of such group must also agree to all of the requirements for the status for which it applies with respect to all accounts maintained at all of its branches, offices, and divisions. For the withholding requirements of a participating FFI with respect to its limited branches and its affiliates that are limited FFIs, see paragraph (b)(5) of this section. Notwithstanding the foregoing, an FFI (or branch thereof) that is treated as a participating FFI or a deemed-compliant FFI pursuant to a Model 1 IGA or Model 2 IGA will maintain such status provided that it meets the terms for such status pursuant to such agreement.

(2) *Limited branches.*—(i) *In general.*—An FFI that otherwise satisfies the requirements for participating FFI status as described in this section will be allowed to become a participating FFI notwithstanding that one or more of its branches cannot satisfy all of the requirements of a participating FFI as described in this section if—

(A) All branches (as defined in paragraph (e)(2)(ii) of this section) that cannot satisfy all of the requirements of a participating FFI as described in this section are limited branches as described in paragraph (e)(2)(iii) of this section;

(B) The FFI maintains at least one branch that complies with all of the requirements of a participating FFI, even if the only branch that can comply is a U.S. branch; and

(C) The FFI agrees to and complies with the conditions in paragraph (e)(2)(iv) of this section.

(ii) *Branch defined.*—The term *branch* has the meaning set forth in § 1.1471-1(b)(10).

(iii) *Limited branch defined.*—A limited branch is a branch of an FFI that, under the laws of the jurisdiction that apply with respect to the accounts maintained by the branch, cannot satisfy the conditions of both paragraphs (e)(2)(iii)(A) and (B) of this section, but with respect to which the FFI will agree to the conditions of paragraph (e)(2)(iv) of this section.

(A) With respect to accounts that pursuant to this section the participating FFI is required to treat as U.S. accounts, either report such accounts to the IRS as described in paragraph (d) of this section, close such accounts within a reasonable period of time, or transfer such accounts to a U.S. financial institution, a branch of the FFI that will so report, a participating FFI, or a reporting Model 1 FFI.

(B) With respect to recalcitrant account holders and accounts held by nonparticipating FFIs, withhold with respect to each such account as required under paragraph (b) of this section, block each such account (as defined in this paragraph), close each such account within a reasonable period of time, or transfer each such account to a U.S. financial institution, a branch of the FFI that will so report, a participating FFI, or a reporting Model 1 FFI. For purposes of this paragraph (e)(2)(iii)(B), an account is a blocked account if the FFI prohibits the account holder from effecting any transactions with respect to an account until such time as the account is closed, transferred, or the account holder provides the documentation described in paragraph (c) of this section for the FFI to determine the U.S. or non-U.S. status of the account and report the account if required under paragraph (d) of this section.

(iv) *Conditions for limited branch status.*—An FFI with one or more limited branches must satisfy the following requirements when applying for participating FFI status with the IRS—

(A) Identify the relevant jurisdiction of each branch for which it seeks limited branch status;

(B) Agree that each such branch will identify its account holders under the due diligence requirements applicable to participating FFIs under paragraph (c) of this section, retain a record of account holder and payee documentation pertaining to those identification requirements for the longer of six years from the effective date of the FFI agreement or for as long as the branch maintains the account or obligation, and report to the IRS with respect to accounts that it is required to treat as U.S. accounts to the extent permitted under the relevant laws pertaining to the branch;

(C) Agree to treat each such branch as an entity separate from its other branches for purposes of the withholding requirements described in paragraph (b)(5) of this section;

(D) Except as otherwise provided in paragraph (e)(2)(vi) of this section, agree that each such branch will not open accounts that it is required to treat as U.S. accounts or accounts held by nonparticipating FFIs, including accounts transferred from any branch of the FFI or from any member of its expanded affiliated group; and

(E) Agree that each limited branch will identify itself to withholding agents as a nonparticipating FFI (including to affiliates of the FFI in the same expanded affiliated group that are withholding agents).

(v) *Term of limited branch status (transitional).*—An FFI that becomes a participating FFI with one or more limited branches will cease to be a participating FFI after December 31, 2016, unless otherwise provided pursuant to Model 1 IGA or Model 2 IGA. A branch will cease to be a limited branch as of the beginning of the third calendar quarter following the date on which the branch is no longer prohibited from complying with the requirements of a participating FFI as described in this section. In such case, a participating FFI will retain its status as a participating FFI if it notifies the IRS by the date such branch ceases to be a limited branch that it will comply with the requirements of an FFI agreement with respect to such branch, or if otherwise provided pursuant to a Model 1 IGA or Model 2 IGA.

(vi) *Exception from restriction on opening U.S. accounts and accounts held by nonparticipating FFIs.*—Notwithstanding the requirements of paragraph (e)(2)(iv)(D) of this section, a branch may open U.S. accounts for persons resident in the same jurisdiction in which such branch is located or operating and accounts for nonparticipating FFIs that are resident in the same jurisdiction provided that—

(A) The branch does not solicit U.S. accounts or accounts for nonparticipating FFIs from persons not resident in the same jurisdiction in which such branch is located or operating; and

(B) The branch is not used by the FFI or any FFI in its expanded affiliated group to circumvent the obligations of such FFI under section 1471.

(3) *Limited FFI.*—(i) *In general.*—An FFI will be allowed to become either a participating FFI or a registered deemed-compliant FFI notwithstanding that one or more of the FFIs in the expanded affiliated group of which the FFI is a member cannot comply with all of the requirements of a participating FFI as described in this section if each such FFI is a limited FFI under paragraph (e)(3)(ii) of this section.

(ii) *Limited FFI defined.*—A limited FFI is a member of an expanded affiliated group that includes one or more participating FFIs that agrees to the conditions described in paragraph (e)(3)(iii) of this section to become a limited FFI and if under the laws of each jurisdiction that apply with respect to the accounts maintained by the affiliate, the affiliate cannot satisfy the conditions of both paragraphs (e)(3)(ii)(A) and (B) of this section.

(A) With respect to accounts that are U.S. accounts, report such accounts to the IRS as described in paragraph (d) of this section, close such accounts within a reasonable period of time, or transfer such accounts to a U.S. financial institution, a participating FFI, or a reporting Model 1 FFI.

(B) With respect to recalcitrant account holders and accounts held by nonparticipating FFIs, withhold with respect to each such account as required under paragraph (b) of this section, block each such account, close each such account within a reasonable period of time, or transfer each such account to a U.S. financial institution, a participating FFI, or a reporting Model 1 FFI. See paragraph (e)(2)(iii)(B) of this section for when an account is considered blocked.

(iii) *Conditions for limited FFI status.*—An FFI that seeks to become a limited FFI must—

(A) Except as otherwise provided in paragraph (e)(3)(v) of this section, register as part of its expanded affiliated group's FFI agreement process for limited FFI status;

(B) Agree as part of such registration to identify its account holders under the due diligence requirements applicable to participating FFIs under paragraph (c) of this section, retain a record of account holder and payee documentation pertaining to those identification requirements for the longer of six years from the effective date of its registration as a limited FFI or for as long as the FFI maintains the account or obligation, and report with respect to accounts that it is required to treat as U.S. accounts to the extent permitted under the relevant laws pertaining to the FFI;

(C) Except as otherwise provided in paragraph (e)(3)(vi) of this section, agree as part of such registration that it will not open accounts that it is required to treat as U.S. accounts or accounts held by nonparticipating FFIs, including accounts transferred from any member of its expanded affiliated group; and

(D) Agree as part of such registration that it will identify itself to withholding agents as a nonparticipating FFI.

(iv) *Period for limited FFI status (transitional).*—A limited FFI will cease to be a limited FFI after December 31, 2016. An FFI will also cease to be a limited FFI when it becomes a participating FFI or deemed-compliant FFI, or as of the beginning of the third calendar quarter following the date on which the FFI is no longer prohibited from complying with the requirements of a participating FFI as described in this section. In such case, participating FFIs and deemed-compliant FFIs that are members of the same expanded affiliated group will retain their status if, by the date that an FFI ceases to be a limited FFI, such FFI enters into an FFI agreement or becomes a registered deemed-compliant FFI, unless otherwise provided pursuant to an applicable Model 1 IGA or Model 2 IGA.

(v) *Exception from registration requirement.*—(A) *Conditions for exception.*—An FFI that seeks to become a limited FFI is excepted from the registration requirement of paragraph (e)(3)(iii)(A) of this section provided that—

(1) The FFI is prohibited under local law from registering as a limited FFI;

(2) A member of the FFI's expanded affiliated group that is a U.S. financial institution or an FFI seeking status as (or that is) a participating FFI or reporting Model 1 FFI registers as a lead FI (defined in the Instructions for Form 8957, "Foreign Account Tax Compliance Act (FATCA) Registration") with respect to the limited FFI; and

(3) The lead FI identifies the limited FFI on the lead FI's FATCA registration. However, if the limited FFI is prohibited under applicable law from being identified by its legal name on the FATCA

registration website, the lead FI may use the term *Limited FFI* in place of the limited FFI's name and indicate the limited FFI's jurisdiction of residence or organization.

(B) *Confirmation requirements of lead FI.*—By identifying a limited FFI on the FATCA registration website pursuant to paragraph (e)(3)(v)(A)(2) of this section, the lead FI is confirming that—

(1) The limited FFI has represented to the lead FI that it will meet the conditions for limited FFI status described in paragraph (e)(3)(iii) of this section;

(2) The limited FFI has agreed to notify the lead FI within 30 days of the date that such FFI ceases to meet the requirements of a limited FFI or the date that such FFI can comply with the requirements of a participating FFI or deemed-compliant FFI (and will separately register for that status); and

(3) The lead FI, if it receives a notification described in paragraph (e)(3)(v)(B)(2) of this section or otherwise knows that the limited FFI has not complied with the conditions for limited FFI status or can comply with the requirements of a participating FFI or deemed-compliant FFI, will, within 90 days of such notification or acquiring such knowledge, remove the FFI from the lead FI's registration on the FATCA registration website and maintain a record of the date on which the FFI ceased to be a limited FFI and (if applicable) the circumstances of the limited FFI's non-compliance, which will be available to the IRS upon request.

(vi) *Exception from restriction on opening U.S. accounts and accounts held by nonparticipating FFIs.*—Notwithstanding paragraph (e)(3)(iii)(C) of this section, a limited FFI may open U.S. accounts for persons resident in the same jurisdiction in which such FFI is resident or organized and accounts for nonparticipating FFIs that are resident in the same jurisdiction provided that—

(A) Such FFI does not solicit U.S. accounts or accounts for nonparticipating FFIs from persons not resident in the same jurisdiction in which the FFI is resident or organized; and

(B) The FFI is not used by another FFI in the FFI's expanded affiliated group to circumvent the obligations of such other FFI under section 1471.

(4) *Special rule for QIs.*—An FFI that has in effect a QI agreement with the IRS will be allowed to become a limited FFI notwithstanding that none of the FFIs in the expanded affiliated group of which the FFI is a member can comply with the requirements of a participating FFI as described in this section if the FFI that is a QI meets the conditions of a limited FFI under paragraph (e)(3)(iii) of this section.

(f) *Verification.*—(1) *In general.*—This paragraph (f) describes the requirement for a participating FFI to establish and implement a compliance program for satisfying its requirements under this section. Paragraph (f)(2) of this section provides the requirement for a participating FFI to establish a compliance program and the option for a group of FFIs to adopt a consolidated compliance program. Paragraph (f)(3) of this section describes the periodic certification that the participating FFI must make to the IRS regarding the participating FFI's compliance with the requirements of an FFI agreement. Paragraph (f)(4) describes IRS information requests related to compliance with an FFI agreement.

(2) *Compliance program.*—(i) *In general.*—The participating FFI must appoint a responsible officer to oversee the participating FFI's compliance with the requirements of the FFI agreement. The responsible officer must (either personally or through designated persons) establish a compliance program that includes policies, procedures, and processes sufficient for the participating FFI to satisfy the requirements of the FFI agreement. The responsible officer (or designee) must periodically review the sufficiency of the FFI's compliance program and the FFI's compliance with the requirements of an FFI agreement during the certification period described in paragraph (f)(3) of this section. The results of the periodic review must be considered by the responsible officer in making the periodic certifications required under paragraph (f)(3) of this section.

(ii) *Consolidated compliance program.*—(A) *In general.*—A participating FFI that is a member of an expanded affiliated group that includes one or more FFIs may elect to be part of a consolidated compliance program (and perform a consolidated periodic review) under the authority of a participating FFI, reporting Model 1 FFI, or U.S. financial institution (compliance FI) that is a member of the electing FFI's expanded affiliated group, regardless of whether all such members so elect. In addition, when an FFI elects to be part of a consolidated compliance program, each branch that it maintains (including a limited branch or a branch described in § 1.1471-5(f)(1)), other than a branch located in a Model 1 IGA jurisdiction, must be subject to periodic review as part of such program and included on the periodic certification (described in paragraph (f)(2)(ii)(B)(1) of this section). To the extent that a compliance FI satisfies the certification requirements of paragraph (f)(2)(ii)(B) of this section on behalf of

an electing FFI, such electing FFI does not have a certification requirement under paragraph (f)(3) of this section. See § 1.1471-5(j) for the requirement of a sponsoring entity to establish and implement a compliance program for its sponsored FFIs.

(B) *Requirements of compliance FI.*—A participating FFI, reporting Model 1 FFI, or U.S. financial institution that agrees to establish and maintain a consolidated compliance program and perform a consolidated periodic review on behalf of one or more FFIs (the compliance group), must agree to identify itself as the compliance FI and identify each FFI for which it acts (an electing FFI) to the extent required by the IRS as part of the FFI registration process or certification procedures. The agreement between the compliance FI and each electing FFI must permit either the compliance FI or the electing FFI to terminate the agreement upon a finding by the IRS or by either party that the other party to the agreement is not fulfilling its obligations under the agreement or is no longer able to fulfill such obligations.

(1) *Periodic certification.*—(i) *In general.*—On or before July 1 of the calendar year following the end of the certification period, the responsible officer of the compliance FI must make the certification described in either paragraph (f)(3)(ii) or (iii) of this section with respect to all electing FFIs for which it acts during the certification period on the form and in the manner prescribed by the IRS. The certification must be made on behalf of all electing FFIs in the compliance group during the certification period, except as otherwise provided in paragraph (f)(2)(ii)(B)(1)(ii) of this section. The first certification period for a compliance group begins on the later of the date the compliance FI is issued a GIIN or June 30, 2014, and ends at the close of the third full calendar year following such date. Each subsequent certification period is the three-calendar-year period following the previous certification period.

(ii) *Late-joining electing FFIs.*—In general, with respect to a certification period, a compliance FI is not required to make a certification for an electing FFI that first elects to be part of the consolidated compliance program of the compliance FI during the six-month period before the end of the certification period, provided that the compliance FI makes certifications for such electing FFI for subsequent certification periods, and the first such certification covers both the subsequent certification period and the portion of the prior certification period of the compliance group during which such FFI was an electing FFI in the consolidated compliance program of the compliance FI. However, the preceding sentence does not apply to an electing FFI that, immediately before the electing FFI elects to be part of the consolidated compliance program, was a participating FFI or registered deemed-compliant FFI. The compliance FI may certify for an electing FFI described in the preceding sentence for the portion of the certification period of the compliance group before the date that the electing FFI elects to be part of the consolidated compliance program if the compliance FI obtains from the FFI (or the FFI's former compliance FI, if applicable) a written certification that the FFI has complied with its applicable chapter 4 requirements during such portion of the certification period, provided that: the compliance FI does not know that such certification is unreliable or incorrect; and the certification for the electing FFI for the subsequent certification period covers both the subsequent certification period and the portion of the prior certification period during which such FFI was an electing FFI in the consolidated compliance program of the compliance FI.

(2) *Preexisting account certification.*—The responsible officer of a compliance FI must make the certification described in paragraph (c)(7) of this section (preexisting account certification of a participating FFI) with respect to each electing FFI that elects to be part of the consolidated compliance program under the compliance FI during the certification period. However, a preexisting account certification is not required for an electing FFI if immediately before electing to be part of the consolidated compliance program under the compliance FI the FFI was a participating FFI or a registered deemed-compliant FFI that is a local FFI or restricted fund, and the FFI (or the FFI's former compliance FI, if applicable) provides a written certification to the compliance FI that the FFI has made the preexisting account certification required under paragraph (c)(7) of this section or § 1.1471-5(f)(1)(i)(A)(7) or (f)(1)(i)(D)(6) (as applicable), unless the compliance FI knows that such written certification is unreliable or incorrect. In addition, a preexisting account certification is not required for an electing FFI that elects to be part of the consolidated compliance program under the compliance FI during the two year period before the end of the certification period, provided that the compliance FI makes the preexisting account certification for such FFI for the subsequent certification period. The certification required under this paragraph (f)(2)(ii)(B)(2) for the certification period must be submitted by the due date of the FFI's certification of compliance required under paragraph (f)(2)(ii)(B)(1)(i) of this section for the

certification period, on the form and in the manner prescribed by the IRS.

(3) *Certification of compliance.*—(i) *In general.*—In addition to the certifications required under paragraph (c)(7) of this section, on or before July 1 of the calendar year following the end of each certification period, the responsible officer must make the certification described in either paragraph (f)(3)(ii) or (iii) of this section on the form and in the manner prescribed by the IRS. The first certification period begins on the effective date of the FFI agreement and ends at the close of the third full calendar year following the effective date of the FFI agreement. Each subsequent certification period is the three-calendar-year period following the previous certification period, unless the FFI agreement provides for a different period. The responsible officer must either certify that the participating FFI maintains effective internal controls or, if the participating FFI has identified an event of default (defined in paragraph (g) of this section) or a material failure (defined in paragraph (f)(3)(iv) of this section) that it has not corrected as of the date of the certification, must make the qualified certification described in paragraph (f)(3)(iii) of this section. The certification of compliance described in paragraph (f)(3)(ii) or (iii) of this section may be modified through an amendment to the FFI agreement to include any additional certifications or information (such as quantitative or factual information related to the FFI's compliance with the FFI agreement), provided that any additional information or certifications are published at least 90 days before being incorporated into the FFI agreement to allow for public comment.

(ii) *Certification of effective internal controls.*—The responsible officer must certify to the following statements—

(A) The responsible officer (or designee) has established a compliance program that is in effect as of the date of the certification and that has been subjected to the review as described in paragraph (f)(2)(i) of this section;

(B) With respect to material failures—

*(1)* There are no material failures for the certification period; or

*(2)* If there are any material failures, appropriate actions were taken to remediate such failures and to prevent such failures from reoccurring; and

(C) With respect to any failure to withhold, deposit, or report to the extent required under the FFI agreement, the FFI has corrected such failure by paying any taxes due (including interest and penalties) and filing the appropriate return (or amended return).

(iii) *Qualified certification.*—If the responsible officer has identified an event of default or a material failure that the participating FFI has not corrected as of the date of the certification, the responsible officer must certify to the following statements—

(A) With respect to the event of default or material failure—

*(1)* The responsible officer (or designee) has identified an event of default as defined in paragraph (g)(1) of this section; or

*(2)* The responsible officer has determined that as of the date of the certification, there are one or more material failures with respect to the participating FFI's compliance with the FFI agreement and that appropriate actions will be taken to prevent such failures from reoccurring;

(B) With respect to any failure to withhold, deposit, or report to the extent required under the FFI agreement, the FFI will correct such failure by paying any taxes due (including interest and penalties) and filing the appropriate return (or amended return); and

(C) The responsible officer (or designee) will respond to any notice of default (if applicable) or will provide to the IRS, to the extent requested, a description of each material failure and a written plan to correct each such failure.

(iv) *Material failures defined.*—A material failure is a failure of the participating FFI to fulfill the requirements of the FFI agreement if the failure was the result of a deliberate action on the part of one or more employees of the participating FFI (its agent, sponsor, or compliance FI) to avoid the requirements of the FFI agreement or was an error attributable to a failure of the participating FFI to implement internal controls sufficient for the participating FFI to meet the requirements of this section. A material failure will not constitute an event of default unless such material failure occurs in more than limited circumstances when a participating FFI has not substantially complied with the requirements of an FFI agreement. Material failures include the following—

(A) The deliberate or systemic failure of the participating FFI to report accounts that it was required to treat as U.S. accounts, withhold on passthru payments to the extent required, deposit taxes withheld, or accurately report recalcitrant account holders or payees that are nonparticipating FFIs as required;

(B) A criminal or civil penalty or sanction imposed on the participating FFI (or any branch or office thereof) by a regulator or other governmental authority or agency with oversight over the participating FFI's compliance with the AML due diligence procedures to which it (or any branch or office thereof) is subject and that is imposed based on a failure to properly identify account holders under the requirements of those procedures; and

(C) A potential future tax liability related to the participating FFI's compliance (or lack thereof) with the FFI agreement for which the FFI establishes, for financial statement purposes, a tax reserve or provision.

(4) *IRS review of compliance.*—(i) *General inquiries.*—The IRS, based upon the information reporting forms described in paragraphs (d)(3)(v), (d)(5)(vii), or (d)(6)(iv) of this section filed with the IRS (or the absence of such reporting) for each calendar year, may request additional information with respect to the information reported (or required to be reported) on the forms or may request the account statements described in paragraph (d)(4)(v) of this section, or confirmation that the FFI has no accounts that it was required to report. The IRS may also request any additional information to determine an FFI's compliance with its FFI agreement and to assist the IRS with its review of account holder compliance with tax reporting requirements.

(ii) *Inquiries regarding substantial non-compliance.*—If, based on the information reporting forms described in paragraphs (d)(3)(v), (d)(5)(vii), or (d)(6)(iv) of this section filed with the IRS for each calendar year, the certifications made by the responsible officer described in paragraph (f)(3) of this section, or any other information related to the participating FFI's compliance with its FFI agreement, the IRS determines in its discretion that the participating FFI may not have substantially complied with the requirements of its FFI agreement, the IRS may request from the responsible officer (or designee) information necessary to verify the participating FFI's compliance with the FFI agreement. The IRS may request, for example, a description or copy of the participating FFI's policies and procedures for fulfilling the requirements of the FFI agreement, a description of the participating FFI's procedures for conducting its periodic review, or a copy of any written reports documenting the findings of such review in order to evaluate the sufficiency of the participating FFI's compliance program and review of such program. The IRS may also request the performance of specified review procedures by a person (including an external auditor or third-party consultant) that the IRS identifies as competent to perform such procedures given the facts and circumstances surrounding the FFI's potential failure to comply with the FFI agreement. The IRS may make these requests to a sponsoring entity with respect to any sponsored FFI.

(g) *Event of default.*—(1) *Defined.*—An event of default occurs if a participating FFI fails to perform material obligations required with respect to the due diligence, verification, withholding, or reporting requirements of the FFI agreement or if the IRS determines that the participating FFI has failed to substantially comply with the requirements of the FFI agreement. An event of default also includes the occurrence of the following—

(i) Failure to obtain, in any case in which foreign law would (but for a waiver) prevent the reporting of U.S. accounts required under paragraph (d) of this section, valid and effective waivers from holders of U.S. accounts or failure to otherwise close or transfer such U.S. accounts as required under paragraph (i) of this section;

(ii) Failure to significantly reduce, over a period of time, the number of account holders or payees that the participating FFI is required to treat as recalcitrant account holders or nonparticipating FFIs, as a result of the participating FFI failing to comply with the due diligence procedures for the identification and documentation of account holders and payees, as set forth in paragraph (c) of this section;

(iii) Failure, in any case in which foreign law prevents or otherwise limits withholding to the extent required under paragraph (b) of this section, to fulfill the requirements of paragraph (i) of this section;

(iv) Failure to establish or maintain a compliance program for fulfilling the requirements of the FFI agreement or to perform a periodic review of the participating FFI's compliance;

(v) Failure to take timely corrective actions to remedy a material failure described in paragraph (f)(3)(iv) of this section after making the qualified certification described in paragraph (f)(3)(iii) of this section;

(vi) Failure to make the initial certification required under paragraph (c)(7) of this section or to make the periodic certification required under paragraph (f)(3) of this section within the specified time period;

(vii) Making incorrect claims for refund under the collective refund procedures described in paragraph (h) of this section;

**Reg. §1.1471-4(g)(1)(vii)**

(viii) Failure to cooperate with an IRS request for additional information or making any fraudulent statement or misrepresentation of material fact to the IRS; or

(ix) Any transaction relating to sponsorship, promotion, or noncustodial distribution for or on behalf of any Local FFI, as described in § 1.1471-5(f)(1)(i)(A), that is an investment entity.

(2) *Notice of event of default.*—Following an event of default known by or disclosed to the IRS, the IRS will deliver to the participating FFI a notice of default specifying the event of default. The IRS will request that the participating FFI remediate the event of default within 45 days (unless additional time is requested and agreed to by the IRS). The participating FFI must respond to the notice of default and provide information responsive to an IRS request for information or state the reasons why the participating FFI does not agree that an event of default has occurred. Taking into account the terms of any applicable Model 2 IGA, if the participating FFI does not provide a response within the specified time period, the IRS may, at its sole discretion, deliver a notice of termination that terminates the FFI's participating FFI status. If the FFI's participating FFI status is terminated, in addition to the requirements in § 1.1471-3(c)(6)(ii)(E)(2), the FFI must, within 30 days of the termination, send notice of the termination to each withholding agent from which it receives payments and each financial institution with which it holds an account for which a withholding certificate or other documentation was provided. An FFI that has had its participating FFI status terminated may not reregister on the FATCA registration website as a participating FFI or registered deemed-compliant FFI unless it receives written approval from the IRS to register. A participating FFI may request, within 90 days of a notice of default or notice of termination, reconsideration of a notice of default or notice of termination by written request to the IRS.

(3) *Remediation of event of default.*—A participating FFI will be permitted to remediate an event of default to the extent that it agrees with the IRS on a remediation plan. Such a plan may, for example, allow a participating FFI to remediate an event of default described in paragraph (g)(1)(iii) of this section by providing specific information regarding its U.S. accounts when the FFI has been unable to report all of the information with respect to such accounts as required under paragraph (d) of this section and has been unable to close or transfer such accounts. The IRS may, as part of a remediation plan, require additional information from the FFI or the performance of the specified review procedures described in paragraph (f)(4)(ii) of this section.

(h) *Collective credit or refund procedures for overpayments.*—(1) *In general.*—Except as otherwise provided in the FFI agreement, if there has been an overpayment of tax with respect to an account holder or payee of a participating FFI or reporting Model 1 FFI resulting from tax withheld under chapter 4 by either the participating FFI or reporting Model 1 FFI or by its withholding agent during a calendar year and the amount withheld has not been recovered under the reimbursement or set-off procedures described in § 1.1474-2(a) (applied by either the withholding agent or the participating FFI or reporting Model 1 FFI), the participating FFI or reporting Model 1 FFI may request a credit or refund from the IRS of the overpayment to the extent permitted under this paragraph (h) on behalf of such account holder or payee. For purposes of this paragraph (h), an overpayment means an amount withheld in excess of the account holder or payee's U.S. tax liability with respect to the payment (including overwithholding as defined § 1.1474-2(a)(2)). If a participating FFI or reporting Model 1 FFI does not elect the procedure provided in this paragraph (h) to request a credit or refund, the participating FFI or reporting Model 1 FFI is required to (or must request that its withholding agent) file and furnish within a reasonable period a Form 1042-S (or such other form as the IRS may prescribe) and Form 1042 (or amended forms) to report to any account holder or payee that has requested such form with regard to the tax withheld by the participating FFI or reporting Model 1 FFI or its withholding agent.

(2) *Persons for which a collective refund is not permitted.*—A participating FFI or reporting Model 1 FFI cannot include in its collective refund claim any payments made to an account holder or payee that is a nonparticipating FFI, a participating FFI or reporting Model 1 FFI that is a flow-through entity (including a WP or WT) or that is acting as an intermediary (including a QI), a U.S. person, or a passive NFFE that is a flow-through entity with respect to taxes allocated to its substantial U.S. owners. A participating FFI or reporting Model 1 FFI must follow the procedures set forth under sections 6402 and 6414 and the regulations thereunder, as modified by this paragraph (h), to claim the credit or refund. No credit or refund will be allowed after the expiration of the statutory period of limitation for refunds under section 6511.

(3) *Payments for which a collective refund is permitted.*—A collective refund is permitted only for payments withheld upon under chapter 4.

(4) *Procedural and other requirements for collective refund.*—A participating FFI or reporting Model 1 FFI may use the collective refund procedures of this paragraph (h) under the following conditions—

(i) All account holders and payees for which the participating FFI or reporting Model 1 FFI seeks a refund must have been included on a Form 1042-S in a reporting pool of nonparticipating FFIs or recalcitrant account holders described in § 1.1474-1(d)(4)(iii) with respect to the payments for which refund is sought and the participating FFI or reporting Model 1 FFI (or the withholding agent) has not filed or furnished a Form 1042-S to any such account holder or payee with respect to which the refund is sought;

(ii) If a refund is sought on the grounds that the account holder or payee of a payment that is U.S. source FDAP income subject to withholding under chapter 3 is entitled to a reduced rate of tax by reason of any treaty obligation of the United States, the participating FFI or reporting Model 1 FFI has also obtained valid documentation that meets the requirements of chapter 3 for a reduced rate of tax and such documentation is available to the IRS upon request with respect to each such account holder or payee; and

(iii) In filing a claim for refund with the IRS under this paragraph (h), the participating FFI or reporting Model 1 FFI submits the following, together with its Form 1042 (or amended Form 1042) on which it provides a reconciliation of amounts withheld and claims a credit or refund, a schedule identifying the taxes withheld with respect to each account holder or payee to which the claim relates, and, if applicable, a copy of the Form 1042-S (or such other form as the IRS may prescribe) furnished to the participating FFI or reporting Model 1 FFI by its withholding agent reporting the taxes withheld to which the claim relates, and a statement that includes the following representations and explanation—

(A) The reason(s) for the overpayment;

(B) A representation that the participating FFI or reporting Model 1 FFI or its withholding agent deposited the tax for which a refund is being sought under section 6302 and has not applied the reimbursement or set-off procedure of § 1.1474-2 to adjust the tax withheld to which the claim relates;

(C) A representation that the participating FFI or reporting Model 1 FFI has repaid or will repay the amount for which refund is sought to the appropriate account holders or payees;

(D) A representation that the participating FFI or reporting Model 1 FFI retains a record showing the total amount of tax withheld, credits from other withholding agents, tax assumed by the participating FFI or reporting Model 1 FFI, adjustments for underwithholding, and reimbursements for overwithholding as its relates to each account holder and payee and also showing the repayment to such account holders or payees for the amount of tax for which a refund is being sought;

(E) A representation that the participating FFI or reporting Model 1 FFI retains valid documentation that meets the requirements of chapters 3 (if applicable) and 4 to substantiate the amount of overwithholding with respect to each account holder and payee for which a refund is being sought and that such documentation is available to the IRS upon request; and

(F) A representation that the participating FFI or reporting Model 1 FFI will not issue a Form 1042-S (or such other form as the IRS may prescribe) to any account holder or payee for which a refund is being sought.

(i) *Legal prohibitions on reporting U.S. accounts and withholding.*—(1) *In general.*—Except to the extent otherwise provided in a Model 2 IGA, a participating FFI (or branch thereof) that is prohibited by foreign law from reporting the information required under paragraph (d) of this section with respect to a U.S. account must follow the procedures of paragraph (i)(2) of this section to obtain a valid and effective waiver of such law and, if such waiver is not obtained within a reasonable period of time, to close or transfer such account. A participating FFI (or branch thereof) that is prohibited by law from withholding with respect to a recalcitrant account holder or nonparticipating FFI as required under paragraph (b) of this section is required to perform the procedures of paragraph (i)(3) of this section to obtain an authorization to withhold on payments made to the account holder or payee to the extent required under paragraph (b) of this section, close the account or terminate the obligation (as applicable), or to sell the assets in the account that produce (or could produce) withholdable payments and, if such authorization is not obtained within a reasonable period of time, to transfer or block such account or obligation. An FFI that cannot comply with any of the requirements of this paragraph (i) is not eligible to enter into an FFI agreement with the IRS, but may obtain status as a limited FFI if the FFI meets the requirements and agrees to the conditions of paragraph (e)(3) of this section. If a branch of an FFI cannot comply with the requirements of this paragraph (i), then the FFI must agree to the conditions of a limited branch as described in paragraph (e)(2) of this section to obtain status as a participating FFI.

(2) *Requesting waiver or closure of a U.S. account.*—(i) *In general.*—If a participating FFI (or branch thereof) is prohibited by law from reporting the information required under paragraph (d) of this section with respect to a U.S. account that it maintains unless a valid and effective waiver of such law is obtained, the participating FFI must request a valid and effective waiver (including by obtaining waivers from all relevant account holders if necessary). For accounts other than preexisting accounts, the participating FFI must obtain a valid and effective waiver upon opening the account or, if prohibitions on disclosure cannot by law be waived, the participating FFI must refrain from opening accounts that are U.S. accounts or must transfer such accounts as described in paragraph (i)(2)(iii) of this section. Beginning on the date provided in § 1.1471-5(g)(3) and until such time as the holder of a U.S. account either consents to disclosure or closure of the account or until the account is transferred, the participating FFI is required to treat the account as held by a recalcitrant account holder.

(ii) *Valid and effective waiver for a U.S. account.*—For purposes of this paragraph (i)(2), a valid and effective waiver is a waiver that, under the applicable law governing the participating FFI's agreement with the account holder, permits the participating FFI (or branch thereof) to report to the IRS all of the information specified in paragraph (d) of this section with respect to the U.S. account and permits the FFI to provide the IRS with additional information concerning such account as specified in paragraph (f) or (g) of this section.

(iii) *Closure or transfer of U.S. account.*—If the participating FFI (or branch thereof) is prohibited by law from reporting a U.S. account to the IRS under paragraph (d) of this section and the participating FFI either does not obtain a valid and effective waiver (and Form W-9) or prohibitions on disclosure cannot by law be waived, the participating FFI (or branch thereof) must close or transfer the account within a reasonable time. If the participating FFI cannot close or transfer the account absent the account holder consenting to closure, the participating FFI must request such a consent from such account holder and, if obtained, close or transfer the account within a reasonable period of time.

(3) *Legal prohibitions preventing withholding.*—(i) *In general.*—If the participating FFI (or branch thereof) is prohibited by law from withholding with respect to payments subject to withholding under paragraph (b) of this section, the participating FFI (or a branch thereof) must obtain the authorization described in this paragraph (i)(3)(i) from each account holder or payee receiving such payments to either withhold, close the account or terminate the obligation, or sell all of the assets in the account that produce (or could produce) withholdable payments. If the participating FFI does not receive such authorization from the account holder or payee within a reasonable period of time, the participating FFI must block or transfer such accounts or obligations as described in paragraph (i)(3)(ii) of this section.

(ii) *Block or transfer accounts or obligations.*—If the participating FFI does not receive the authorization described in paragraph (i)(3)(i) of this section from the account holder or payee within a reasonable period of time and is prohibited by law from closing accounts or terminating obligations with account holders or payees as described in paragraph (i)(3)(i) of this section, the participating FFI must either block or transfer such accounts or obligations prior to the date on which the participating FFI would otherwise be required to withhold under paragraph (b) of this section. See paragraph (e)(2)(iii)(B) of this section for when an account is considered blocked. A transfer of an account or obligation must be made to a branch of the FFI that may so withhold or to a participating FFI or reporting Model 1 FFI.

(j) *Effective/applicability date.*—(1) *In general.*—This section generally applies beginning on January 6, 2017, except for paragraphs (f)(2)(ii)(A), (f)(2)(ii)(B)(1) and (2), (f)(3)(i), and (g)(2) of this section, which apply March 25, 2019. However, taxpayers may apply these provisions as of January 28, 2013. (For the rules that otherwise apply beginning on January 6, 2017, and before March 25, 2019, see this section as in effect and contained in 26 CFR part 1 revised April 1, 2018. For rules that apply beginning on January 23, 2013 and before January 6, 2017, see this section as in effect and contained in 26 CFR part 1 revised April 1, 2016.)

(2) *Special applicability date.*—Paragraph (d)(4)(iv)(C) of this section applies beginning with reporting with respect to calendar year 2017. (For rules that apply to reporting under paragraph (d)(4)(iv)(C) with respect to calendar years before 2017, see this section as in effect

and contained in 26 CFR part 1 revised April 1, 2016.) [Reg. § 1.1471-4.]

☐ [*T.D.* 9610, 1-17-2013 (*corrected* 9-9-2013). *Amended by T.D.* 9657, 2-28-2014 (*corrected* 6-30-2014), *T.D.* 9809, 12-30-2016 (*corrected* 6-29-2017), *T.D.* 9852, 3-21-2019 (*corrected* 4-3-2019) *and T.D.* 9890, 12-27-2019.]

**[Reg. § 1.1471-5]**

**§ 1.1471-5. Definitions applicable to section 1471.**—(a) *U.S. accounts.*—(1) *In general.*—This paragraph (a) defines the term *U.S. account* and describes when a person is treated as the holder of a financial account (account holder). This paragraph also provides rules for determining when an exception to U.S. account status applies for certain depository accounts, including account aggregation requirements relevant to applying the exception.

(2) *Definition of U.S. account.*—Subject to the exception described in paragraph (a)(4)(i) of this section, a U.S. account is any financial account maintained by an FFI that is held by one or more specified U.S. persons or U.S. owned foreign entities. For the definition of the term financial account, see paragraph (b) of this section. For the definition of the term specified U.S. person, see § 1.1473-1(c). For the definition of the term U.S. owned foreign entity, see paragraph (c) of this section. For reporting requirements of participating FFIs with respect to U.S. accounts, see § 1.1471-4(d).

(3) *Account holder.*—(i) *In general.*—Except as otherwise provided in this paragraph (a)(3), the account holder is the person listed or identified as the holder or owner of the account with the FFI that maintains the account, regardless of whether such person is a flow-through entity. Thus, for example, except as otherwise provided in paragraph (a)(3)(ii) of this section, if a trust (including a simple or grantor trust) or an estate is listed as the holder or owner of a financial account, the trust or estate is the account holder, rather than its owners or beneficiaries. Similarly, except as otherwise provided in this paragraph (a)(3), if a partnership is listed as the holder or owner of a financial account, the partnership is the account holder, rather than the partners in the partnership. In the case of an account held by an entity that is disregarded for U.S. federal tax purposes under § 301.7701-2(c)(2)(i) of this chapter, the account shall be treated as held by the person owning such entity. With respect to an account held by an exempt beneficial owner, such account is treated as held by an exempt beneficial owner only when all payments made to such account would be treated as made to an exempt beneficial owner. See § 1.1471-6(h) for when a payment derived from certain commercial activities is not treated as made to an exempt beneficial owner.

(ii) *Financial accounts held by agents that are not financial institutions.*—A person, other than a financial institution, that holds a financial account for the benefit or account of another person as an agent, custodian, nominee, signatory, investment advisor, or intermediary, is not treated as an account holder with respect to such account for purposes of this section. Instead, such other person is treated as the account holder.

(iii) *Jointly held accounts.*—With respect to a jointly held account, each joint holder is treated as an account holder for purposes of determining whether the account is a U.S. account. Thus, an account is a U.S. account if any of the account holders is a specified U.S. person or a U.S. owned foreign entity and the account is not otherwise excepted from U.S. account status under paragraph (a)(4) of this section. When more than one U.S. person is a joint holder, each U.S. person will be treated as an account holder and will be attributed the entire balance of the jointly held account, including for purposes of applying the aggregation rules set forth in paragraph (b)(4)(iii) of this section.

(iv) *Account holder for insurance and annuity contracts.*—An insurance or annuity contract is held by each person that is entitled to access the contract's value (for example, through a loan, withdrawal, surrender, or otherwise) or change a beneficiary under the contract. If no person can access the contract's value or change a beneficiary, the account holders are any person named in the contract as an owner and any person who is entitled to receive a future payment under the terms of the contract. When an obligation to pay an amount under the contract becomes fixed, each person entitled to receive a payment is an account holder.

(v) *Examples.*—The following examples illustrate the provisions of paragraph (a)(3) of this section:

*Example 1. Account held by agent.* F, a nonresident alien, holds a power of attorney from U, a specified U.S. person, that authorizes F to open, hold, and make deposits and withdrawals with respect to a depository account on behalf of U. The balance of the account for the calendar year is $100,000. F is listed as the holder of the depository account at a participating FFI, but because F holds the account as an agent for the benefit of U, F is not ultimately entitled to the funds in the account. Because the depository account is treated as held by U, a specified U.S. person, the account is a U.S. account.

*Example 2. Jointly held accounts.* U, a specified U.S. person, holds a depository account in a participating FFI. The balance of the account for the calendar year is $100,000. The account is jointly held with A, an individual who is a nonresident alien. Because one of the joint holders is a specified U.S person, the account is a U.S. account.

*Example 3. Jointly held accounts.* U and Q, both specified U.S. persons, hold a depository account in a participating FFI. The balance of the account for the calendar year is $100,000. The account is a U.S. account and both U and Q are treated as holders of the account.

(4) *Exceptions to U.S. account status.*—(i) *Exception for certain individual accounts of participating FFIs.*—Unless a participating FFI elects under paragraph (a)(4)(ii) of this section not to apply this paragraph (a)(4)(i), the term *U.S. account* shall not include any depository account maintained by such financial institution during a calendar year if the account is held solely by one or more individuals and, with respect to each holder of such account, the aggregate balance or value of all depository accounts held by each such individual does not exceed $50,000 as of the end of the calendar year or on the date the account is closed. For rules for determining the account balance or value, see paragraphs (a)(3)(iii) and (b)(4) of this section.

(ii) *Election to forgo exception.*—A participating FFI may elect to disregard the exception described in paragraph (a)(4)(i) of this section by reporting all U.S. accounts, including those accounts that would otherwise meet the conditions of the exception.

(iii) *Example.*—*Aggregation rules for exception to U.S. account status for certain depository accounts.* In Year 1, a U.S. resident individual, U, holds a depository account with CB, a commercial bank that is a participating FFI. The balance in U's CB account at the end of Year 1 is $35,000. In Year 1, U also holds a custodial account with CB's brokerage business. The custodial account has a $45,000 balance as of the end of Year 1. CB's retail banking and brokerage businesses share computerized information management systems that associate U's depository account and U's custodial account with U and with one another within the meaning of paragraph (b)(4)(iii)(A) of this section. For purposes of applying the $50,000 threshold described in paragraph (a)(4)(i) of this section, however, a depository account is aggregated only with other depository accounts. Therefore, U's depository account is eligible for the paragraph (a)(4)(i) exception to U.S. account status because the balance of the depository account does not exceed $50,000.

(b) *Financial accounts.*—(1) *In general.*—Except as otherwise provided in this paragraph (b), the term *financial account* means—

(i) *Depository account.*—Any depository account (as defined in paragraph (b)(3)(i) of this section) maintained by a financial institution;

(ii) *Custodial account.*—Any custodial account (as defined in paragraph (b)(3)(ii) of this section) maintained by a financial institution;

(iii) *Equity or debt interest.*—(A) *Equity or debt interests in an investment entity.*—Any equity or debt interest (other than interests regularly traded on an established securities market under paragraph (b)(3)(iv) of this section) in an investment entity described in paragraph (e)(4)(i)(B) or (C) of this section (including an entity that is also a depository institution, custodial institution, insurance company, or investment entity described in paragraph (e)(4)(i)(A) of this section);

(B) *Certain equity or debt interests in a holding company or treasury center.*—Any equity or debt interest (other than interests regularly traded on an established securities market under paragraph (b)(3)(iv) of this section) in a holding company or treasury center described in paragraph (e)(1)(v) of this section if—

(1) The expanded affiliated group of which the entity is a member includes one or more investment entities described in paragraph (e)(4)(i)(B) or (C) of this section or passive NFFEs and the income derived by such investment entities or passive NFFEs is 50 percent or more of the aggregate income earned by the expanded affiliated group;

(2) The return earned on the interest is determined, directly or indirectly, primarily by reference to one or more investment entities described in paragraph (e)(4)(i)(B) or (C) of this section or one or more passive NFFEs that are members of the entity's expanded affiliated group (as determined under paragraph (b)(3)(vi) of this section);

(3) The value of the interest is determined, directly or indirectly, primarily by reference to assets that give rise (or could give rise) to withholdable payments (as determined under paragraph (b)(3)(v)) of this section); or

(4) The interest is issued with a principal purpose of avoiding the reporting or withholding requirements of chapter 4;

(C) *Equity or debt interests in other financial institutions.*—Any equity or debt interest (other than interests regularly traded on an established securities market under paragraph (b)(3)(iv) of this section) in an entity that is a depository institution, custodial institution, investment entity described in paragraph (e)(4)(i)(A) of this section, or insurance company if—

(1) The value of the interest is determined, directly or indirectly, primarily by reference to assets that give rise (or could give rise) to withholdable payments (as determined under paragraph (b)(3)(v) of this section); or

(2) The interest is issued with a principal purpose of avoiding the reporting or withholding requirements of chapter 4.

(iv) *Insurance and annuity contracts.*—A contract issued or maintained by an insurance company, a holding company (as described in paragraph (e)(5)(i)(C) of this section) of an insurance company, or a financial institution described in paragraphs (e)(1)(i), (ii), (iii), or (v) of this section, if the contract is a cash value insurance contract (as defined in paragraph (b)(3)(vii) of this section) or an annuity contract.

(2) *Exceptions.*—A financial account does not include an account described in this paragraph (b)(2).

(i) *Certain savings accounts.*—(A) *Retirement and pension accounts.*—A retirement or pension account that satisfies the following conditions under the laws of the jurisdiction where the account is maintained:

(1) The account is subject to regulation as a personal retirement account or is part of a registered or regulated retirement or pension plan for the provision of retirement or pension benefits (including disability or death benefits);

(2) The account is tax-favored (as described in paragraph (b)(2)(i)(E) of this section);

(3) Annual information reporting is required to the relevant tax authorities with respect to the account;

(4) Withdrawals are conditioned on reaching a specified retirement age, disability, or death, or penalties apply to withdrawals made before such specified events; and

(5) Either—

(i) Annual contributions are limited to $50,000 or less, or

(ii) There is a maximum lifetime contribution limit to the account of $1,000,000 or less.

(B) *Non-retirement savings accounts.*—An account (other than an insurance or annuity contract) that satisfies the following conditions under the laws of the jurisdiction where the account is maintained:

(1) The account is subject to regulation as a savings vehicle for purposes other than for retirement;

(2) The account is tax-favored (as described in paragraph (b)(2)(i)(E) of this section);

(3) Withdrawals are conditioned on meeting specific criteria related to the purpose of the savings account (for example, the provision of educational or medical benefits), or penalties apply to withdrawals made before such criteria are met; and

(4) Annual contributions are limited to $50,000 or less;

(C) *Rollovers.*—An account that otherwise satisfies the requirements of paragraph (b)(2)(i)(A) or (B) of this section will not fail to satisfy such requirements solely because such account may receive assets or funds transferred from one or more accounts that meet the requirements of paragraph (b)(2)(i)(A) or (B) of this section, one or more retirement or pension funds that meet the requirements of § 1.1471-6(f), one or more accounts described in paragraph (b)(2)(vi) of this section, or one or more entities identified as nonreporting financial institutions under the terms of an applicable Model 1 or Model 2 IGA because they are retirement or pension funds.

(D) *Coordination with section 6038D.*—The exclusions provided under paragraph (b)(2)(i) of this section shall not apply for purposes of determining whether an account or other arrangement is a financial account for purposes of section 6038D.

(E) *Account that is tax-favored.*—For purposes of this paragraph (b)(2)(i), an account is tax-favored under the laws of a jurisdiction where the account is maintained if—

(1) Contributions to the account that would otherwise be subject to tax under such laws are deductible or excluded from the gross income of the account holder or taxed at a reduced rate; or

(2) Taxation of investment income from the account is deferred or taxed at a reduced rate.

(ii) *Certain term life insurance contracts.*—A life insurance contract with a coverage period that will end before the insured individual attains age 90, provided that the contract satisfies the following conditions—

(A) Periodic premiums, which do not decrease over time, are payable at least annually during the period the contract is in existence or until the insured attains age 90, whichever is shorter;

(B) The contract has no contract value that any person can access (by withdrawal, loan, or otherwise) without terminating the contract;

(C) The amount (other than a death benefit) payable upon cancellation or termination of the contract cannot exceed the aggregate premiums paid for the contract, less the sum of mortality, morbidity, and expense charges (whether or not actually imposed) for the period or periods of the contract's existence and any amounts paid prior to the cancellation or termination of the contract; and

(D) The contract is not held by a transferee for value.

(iii) *Account held by an estate.*—An account that is held solely by an estate if the documentation for such account includes a copy of the deceased's will or death certificate.

(iv) *Certain escrow accounts.*—An escrow account that is established in connection with—

(A) A court order or judgment; or

(B) A sale, exchange, or lease of real or personal property, provided that the account meets the following conditions—

(1) The account is funded solely with a down payment, earnest money, deposit in an amount appropriate to secure an obligation of one of the parties directly related to the transaction, or a similar payment, or with a financial asset that is deposited in the account in connection with the sale, exchange, or lease of the property;

(2) The account is established and used solely to secure the obligation of the purchaser to pay the purchase price for the property, the seller to pay any contingent liability, or the lessor or lessee to pay for any damages relating to the leased property as agreed under the lease;

(3) The assets of the account, including the income earned thereon, will be paid or otherwise distributed for the benefit of the purchaser, seller, lessor, or lessee (including to satisfy such person's obligation) when the property is sold, exchanged, or surrendered, or the lease terminates;

(4) The account is not a margin or similar account established in connection with a sale or exchange of a financial asset; and

(5) The account is not associated with a credit card account.

(v) *Certain annuity contracts.*—A non-investment linked, non-transferable, immediate life annuity contract (including a disability annuity) that monetizes a retirement or pension account described in paragraph (b)(2)(i)(A) or (b)(2)(vi) of this section.

(vi) *Account or product excluded under an intergovernmental agreement.*—An account or product that is excluded from the definition of financial account under the terms of an applicable Model 1 IGA or Model 2 IGA.

(3) *Definitions.*—The following definitions apply for purposes of chapter 4—

(i) *Depository account.*—(A) *In general.*—Except as otherwise provided in this paragraph (b)(3)(i), the term *depository account* means any account that is—

(1) A commercial, checking, savings, time, or thrift account, or an account that is evidenced by a certificate of deposit, thrift certificate, investment certificate, passbook, certificate of indebtedness, or any other instrument for placing money in the custody of an entity engaged in a banking or similar business for which such institution is obligated to give credit (regardless of whether such instrument is interest bearing or non-interest bearing), including, for example, a credit balance with respect to a credit card account issued by a credit card company that is engaged in a banking or similar business; or

(2) Any amount held by an insurance company under a guaranteed investment contract or under a similar agreement to pay or credit interest thereon or to return the amount held.

(B) *Exceptions.*—A depository account does not include—

(1) A negotiable debt instrument that is traded on a regulated market or over-the-counter market and distributed and held through financial institutions; or

(2) An advance premium or premium deposit described in paragraph (b)(3)(vii)(C)(5) of this section.

(ii) *Custodial account.*—The term *custodial account* means an arrangement for holding a financial instrument, contract, or invest-

ment (including, but not limited to, a share of stock in a corporation, a note, bond, debenture, or other evidence of indebtedness, a currency or commodity transaction, a credit default swap, a swap based upon a nonfinancial index, a notional principal contract as defined in §1.446-3(c), an insurance or annuity contract, and any option or other derivative instrument) for the benefit of another person.

(iii) *Equity interest in certain entities.*—(A) *Partnership.*—In the case of a partnership that is a financial institution, the term *equity interest* means either a capital or profits interest in the partnership.

(B) *Trust.*—In the case of a trust that is a financial institution, an *equity interest* means an interest held by—

(1) A person who is an owner of all or a portion of the trust under sections 671 through 679;

(2) A beneficiary who is entitled to a mandatory distribution from the trust as defined in §1.1473-1(b)(3); or

(3) A beneficiary who may receive a discretionary distribution as defined in §1.1473-1(b)(3) from the trust but only if such person receives a distribution in the calendar year.

(iv) *Regularly traded on an established securities market.*—To determine if debt or equity interests described in paragraph (b)(1)(iii) of this section are regularly traded, the principles of §1.1472-1(c)(1)(i)(A)(2)(*i*) and (*ii*) shall apply with respect to the interests, and the principles of §1.1472-1(c)(1)(i)(B)(1) shall apply for this purpose in the case of an initial public offering of such interests. See §1.1472-1(c)(1)(i)(C) for the definition of an established securities market. For purposes of paragraph (b)(1)(iii) of this section, an interest is not regularly traded on an established securities market if the holder of the interest (excluding a financial institution acting as an intermediary) is registered on the books of the investment entity. The preceding sentence shall not apply to the extent a holder's interest is registered prior to July 1, 2014, on the books of the investment entity.

(v) *Value of interest determined, directly or indirectly, primarily by reference to assets that give rise (or could give rise) to withholdable payments.*—(A) *Equity interest.*—The value of an equity interest is determined, directly or indirectly, primarily by reference to assets that give rise (or could give rise) to withholdable payments if the return earned on such interest (including upon a sale, exchange, or redemption) is determined primarily by reference to profits or assets of a U.S. person or equity interests in a U.S. person.

(B) *Debt interest.*—The value of a debt interest is determined, directly or indirectly, primarily by reference to assets that give rise (or could give rise) to withholdable payments if—

(1) Debt is convertible into equity interests in a U.S. person; or

(2) The return earned on such interest (including upon a sale, exchange, or redemption) is determined primarily by reference to profits or assets of a U.S. person or equity interests in a U.S. person.

(vi) *Return earned on the interest (including upon a sale, exchange, or redemption) determined, directly or indirectly, primarily by reference to one or more investment entities or passive NFFEs.*—(A) *Equity interest.*—The return earned on an equity interest is determined, directly or indirectly, primarily by reference to one or more investment entities described in paragraph (e)(4)(i)(B) or (C) of this section or passive NFFEs that are members of the entity's expanded affiliated group if the return on such interest (including upon a sale, exchange, or redemption) is determined primarily by reference to profits or assets of, or equity interests in, one or more investment entities described in paragraph (e)(4)(i)(B) or (C) of this section or passive NFFEs that are members of the entity's expanded affiliated group.

(B) *Debt interest.*—The return earned on a debt interest is determined, directly or indirectly, primarily by reference to one or more investment entities described in paragraph (e)(4)(i)(B) or (C) of this section or passive NFFEs that are members of the entity's expanded affiliated group if—

(1) Debt is convertible into equity interests in one or more investment entities described in paragraph (e)(4)(i)(B) or (C) of this section or passive NFFEs that are members of the entity's expanded affiliated group; or

(2) The return on such interest (including upon a sale, exchange, or redemption) is determined primarily by reference to profits or assets of, or equity interests in, one or more investment entities described in paragraph (e)(4)(i)(B) or (C) of this section or passive NFFEs that are members of the entity's expanded affiliated group.

(vii) *Cash value insurance contract.*—(A) *In general.*—The term *cash value insurance contract* means an insurance contract (other than an indemnity reinsurance contract between two insurance companies and a term life insurance contract described in paragraph (b)(2)(ii) of this section) that has an aggregate cash value greater than $50,000 at any time during the calendar year, applying the rules set forth in paragraph (b)(4)(iii) of this section. A participating FFI may elect to disregard the $50,000 threshold in the preceding sentence by reporting all contracts with a cash value greater than zero.

(B) *Cash value.*—Except as otherwise provided in paragraph (b)(3)(vii)(C) of this section, the term *cash value* means any amount (determined without reduction for any charge or policy loan) that—

(1) Is payable under the contract to any person upon surrender, termination, cancellation, or withdrawal; or

(2) Any person can borrow under or with regard to (for example, by pledging as collateral) the contract.

(C) *Amounts excluded from cash value.*—Cash value does not include an amount payable—

(1) Solely by reason of the death of an individual insured under a life insurance contract;

(2) As a personal injury or sickness benefit or a benefit providing indemnification of an economic loss incurred upon the occurrence of the event insured against;

(3) As a refund of a previously paid premium (less cost of insurance charges whether or not actually imposed) under an insurance contract (other than a life insurance or annuity contract) due to cancellation or termination of the contract, decrease in risk exposure during the effective period of the contract, or arising from the correction of a posting or similar error with regard to the premium for the contract; or

(4) As a policyholder dividend (other than a termination dividend) provided that the dividend relates to an insurance contract under which the only benefits payable are described in paragraph (b)(3)(vii)(C)(2) of this section.

(5) As a return of an advance premium or premium deposit for an insurance contract for which the premium is payable at least annually if the amount of the advance premium or premium deposit does not exceed the next annual premium that will be payable under the contract.

(D) *Policyholder dividend.*—(1) For purposes of paragraph (b)(3)(vii)(C)(4) of this section and except as otherwise provided in this paragraph, a policyholder dividend means any dividend or similar distribution to policyholders in their capacity as such, including—

(i) An amount paid or credited (including as an increase in benefits) if the amount is not fixed in the contract but rather depends on the experience of the insurance company or the discretion of management;

(ii) A reduction in the premium that, but for the reduction, would have been required to be paid; and

(iii) An experience rated refund or credit based solely upon the claims experience of the contract or group involved.

(2) A policyholder dividend cannot exceed the premiums previously paid for the contract, less the sum of the cost of insurance and expense charges (whether or not actually imposed) during the contract's existence and the aggregate amount of any prior dividends paid or credited with regard to the contract.

(3) A policyholder dividend does not include any amount that is in the nature of interest that is paid or credited to a contract holder to the extent that such amount exceeds the minimum rate of interest required to be credited with respect to contract values under local law.

(4) *Account balance or value.*—This paragraph (b)(4) provides rules for determining the balance or value of a financial account for purposes of chapter 4. For example, the rules of this paragraph apply for purposes of determining whether an FFI meets the requirements of paragraph (f)(2)(i), (f)(2)(ii) or (f)(3) of this section to certify to a deemed-compliant FFI status. The rules of this paragraph also apply to a participating FFI's due diligence and reporting obligations to the extent required under §1.1471-4(c) or (d) and to a U.S. withholding agent's due diligence obligations to the extent required under §1.1471-3.

(i) *In general.*—Except as otherwise provided in paragraph (b)(4)(ii) of this section with respect to immediate annuities, the balance or value of a financial account is the balance or value calculated by the financial institution for purposes of reporting to the account holder. In the case of an account described in paragraph (b)(1)(iii) of this section, the balance or value of an equity interest is the value calculated by the financial institution for the purpose that requires the most frequent determination of value, and the balance or value of a debt interest is its principal amount. Except as provided in paragraph (b)(3)(vii) of this section, the balance or value of an insurance or annuity contract is the balance or value as of either the calendar year end or the most recent contract anniversary date. The balance or value of the account is not to be reduced by any liabilities

or obligations incurred by an account holder with respect to the account or any of the assets held in the account and is not to be reduced by any fees, penalties, or other charges for which the account holder may be liable upon terminating, transferring, surrendering, liquidating, or withdrawing cash from the account. Each holder of a jointly held account is attributed the entire balance or value of the joint account. See §1.1473-1(b)(3) for rules regarding the valuation of trust interests that also apply under this paragraph (b)(4)(i) to determine the value of trust interests that are financial accounts.

(ii) *Special rule for immediate annuity.*—(A) *Immediate annuities without minimum benefit guarantees.*—If the value of an immediate annuity contract with no minimum benefit guarantee is not reported to the account holder, the account balance or value of the contract is the sum of the net present values on the valuation date of the amounts reasonably expected to be payable in future periods under the contract.

(B) *Immediate annuities with a minimum benefit guarantee.*—The account balance or value of an annuity contract with a minimum guarantee is the sum of the net present values on the valuation date of—

(1) The non-guaranteed amounts reasonably expected to be payable in future periods; and

(2) The guaranteed amounts payable in future periods.

(C) *Net present value of amounts payable in future periods.*—The net present value of an amount payable in a future period shall be determined using—

(1) A reasonable actuarial valuation method, and

(2) The mortality tables and interest rate(s)—

(i) Prescribed pursuant to section 7520 and the regulations thereunder; or

(ii) Used by the issuer of the contract to determine the amounts payable under the contract.

(iii) *Account aggregation requirements.*—(A) *In general.*—To the extent a financial institution is required under chapter 4 to determine the aggregate balance or value of an account, the financial institution is required to aggregate the account balance or value of all accounts that are held (in whole or in part) by the same person and that are maintained by the financial institution or members of its expanded affiliated group, but only to the extent that the financial institution's computerized systems link the accounts by reference to a data element, such as client number, EIN, or foreign tax identifying number, and allow the account balances of such accounts to be aggregated. Notwithstanding the rules set forth in this paragraph (b)(4)(iii), a financial institution is required to aggregate the balance or value of accounts that it treats as consolidated obligations.

(B) *Aggregation rule for relationship managers.*—To the extent a financial institution is required under chapter 4 to apply the aggregation rules of this paragraph (b)(4)(iii), the financial institution also is required to aggregate all accounts that a relationship manager knows are directly or indirectly owned, controlled, or established (other than in a fiduciary capacity) by the same person, as well as all accounts that the relationship manager has associated with one another through a relationship code, customer identification number, TIN, or similar indicator, or that the relationship manager would typically associate with each other under the procedures of the financial institution (or the department, division, or unit with which the relationship manager is associated).

(C) *Examples.*—The following examples illustrate the account aggregation requirements of this paragraph (b)(4)(iii):

*Example 1. FFI not required to aggregate accounts for U.S. account exception.* A U.S. resident individual, U, holds a depository account with Branch 1 of CB, a commercial bank that is a participating FFI. The balance in U's Branch 1 account at the end of Year 1 is $35,000. U also holds a depository account with Branch 2 of CB, with a $45,000 balance at the end of Year 1. CB's retail banking businesses share computerized information management systems across its branches, but U's accounts are not associated with one another in the shared computerized information system. In addition, CB has not assigned a relationship manager to U or U's accounts. Because the accounts are not associated in CB's system or by a relationship manager, CB is not required to aggregate the accounts under paragraph (b)(4)(iii) and both accounts are eligible for the exception to U.S. account status described in paragraph (a)(4)(i) of this section as neither account exceeds the $50,000 threshold.

*Example 2. FFI required to aggregate accounts for U.S. account exception.* Same facts as *Example 1*, except that both of U's depository accounts are associated with U and with one another by reference to CB's internal identification number. The system shows the account balances for both accounts, and such balances may be electronically aggregated, though the system does not show a combined balance for the accounts. In determining whether such accounts meet the exception to U.S. account status described in paragraph (a)(4)(i) of this section for certain depository accounts with an aggregate balance or value of $50,000 or less, CB is required to aggregate the account balances of all depository accounts under the rules of paragraph (b)(4)(iii) of this section. Under those rules, U is treated as holding depository accounts with CB with an aggregate balance of $80,000. Accordingly, neither account is eligible for the exception to U.S. account status, because the accounts, when aggregated, exceed the $50,000 threshold.

*Example 3. Aggregation rules for joint accounts maintained by a participating FFI.* In Year 1, a U.S. resident individual, U, holds a custodial account that is a preexisting account at custodial institution CI, a participating FFI. The balance in U's CI custodial account at the end of Year 1 is $35,000. U also holds a joint custodial account that is a preexisting account with her sister, A, a nonresident alien for U.S. federal income tax purposes, with another custodial institution, CI2. The balance in the joint account at the end of Year 1 is also $35,000. CI and CI2 are part of the same expanded affiliated group and share computerized information management systems. Both U's custodial account at CI and U and A's custodial account at CI2 are associated with U and with one another by reference to CI's internal identification number and the system allows the balances to be aggregated. In determining whether such accounts meet the documentation exception described in §1.1471-4(c)(4)(iv) for certain preexisting individual accounts with an aggregate balance or value of $50,000 or less, CI is required to aggregate the account balances of accounts held in whole or in part by the same account holder under the rules of paragraph (b)(4)(iii) of this section. Under those rules, U is treated as having financial accounts with C1 and CI2, each with an aggregate balance of $70,000. Accordingly, neither account is eligible for the documentation exception.

Example 4. *Aggregation for applying indefinite validity periods.* In Year 1, an owner-documented FFI, O, holds an offshore account with Branch 1 of CB, a commercial bank that is a U.S. withholding agent. The balance in O's CB account at the end of Year 1 is $600,000. In Year 1, O also holds an account in the United States with Branch 2 of CB. The Branch 2 account has a $450,000 balance at the end of Year 1. CB's banking businesses share computerized information management systems across its branches. O's accounts are associated with one another in the shared computerized information system and the system allows the balances to be aggregated. In determining whether CB is permitted to apply an indefinite validity period for the documentation submitted for O's account at Branch 1 pursuant to §1.1471-3(c)(6)(ii)(C)(4) (permitting indefinite validity for a withholding statement of an owner-documented FFI if the balance or value of all accounts held by the owner-documented FFI does not exceed $1,000,000), CB is required to aggregate the account balance of O's accounts at Branch 1 and Branch 2 to the extent required under the rules of paragraph (b)(4)(iii) of this section. Accordingly, O is treated as holding financial accounts with CB with an aggregate balance of $1,050,000 and the documentation submitted for O's account at Branch 1 is not eligible for the indefinite validity period described under §1.1471-3(c)(6)(ii)(C)(4).

(iv) *Currency translation of balance or value.*—If the balance or value of a financial account, other obligation, or the aggregate amount payable under a group life or group annuity contract described in §1.1471-4(c)(4) is denominated in a currency other than U.S. dollars, a withholding agent must calculate the balance or value by applying a spot rate determined under §1.988-1(d) to translate such balance or value into the U.S. dollar equivalent. For the purpose of a participating or registered deemed-compliant FFI reporting an account under §1.1471-4(d), the spot rate must be determined as of the last day of the calendar year (or, in the case of an insurance contract or annuity contract, the most recent contract anniversary date, when applicable) for which the account is being reported or, if the account was closed during such calendar year, the date the account was closed. In the case of an FFI determining whether an account meets (or continues to meet) a preexisting account documentation exception described in §1.1471-4(c)(3)(iii) or (c)(5)(iii), or whether the account is an account described in paragraph (a)(4)(i) of this section, the spot rate must be determined on the date for which the FFI is determining the threshold amount as prescribed in those provisions.

(5) *Account maintained by financial institution.*—A custodial account is maintained by the financial institution that holds custody over the assets in the account (including a financial institution that holds assets in street name for an account holder in such institution). A depository account is maintained by the financial institution that is obligated to make payments with respect to the account (excluding an agent of a financial institution regardless of whether such agent is a financial institution under paragraph (e)(1) of this section). Any

equity or debt interest in a financial institution that constitutes a financial account under paragraph (b)(1)(iii) of this section is maintained by such financial institution. A cash value insurance contract or an annuity contract described in paragraph (b)(1)(iv) of this section is maintained by the financial institution that is obligated to make payments with respect to the contract.

(c) *U.S. owned foreign entity.*—The term *U.S. owned foreign entity* means any foreign entity that has one or more substantial U.S. owners (as defined in §1.1473-1(b)). See §1.1473-1(e) for the definition of foreign entity for purposes of chapter 4. For the requirements applicable to determining direct and indirect ownership in an entity, see §1.1473-1(b)(2).

(d) *Definition of FFI.*—The term *FFI* means, with respect to any entity that is not resident in, or organized under the laws of, as applicable, a country that has in effect a Model 1 IGA or Model 2 IGA, any financial institution (as defined in paragraph (e) of this section) that is a foreign entity. The term *FFI* also means, with respect to any entity that is resident in, or organized under the laws of, as applicable, a country that has in effect a Model 1 IGA or Model 2 IGA, any entity that is treated as a FATCA Partner Financial Institution pursuant to such Model 1 IGA or Model 2 IGA. See, however, §1.1471-2(a)(2)(v) for when certain branches of U.S. financial institutions may be treated as FFIs. A territory financial institution is not an FFI under this paragraph (d).

(e) *Definition of financial institution.*—(1) *In general.*—Except as otherwise provided in paragraph (e)(5) of this section, the term *financial institution* means any entity that—

(i) Accepts deposits in the ordinary course of a banking or similar business (as defined in paragraph (e)(2) of this section) (depository institution);

(ii) Holds, as a substantial portion of its business (as defined in paragraph (e)(3) of this section), financial assets for the benefit of one or more other persons (custodial institution);

(iii) Is an investment entity (as defined in paragraph (e)(4) of this section);

(iv) Is an insurance company or a holding company (as described in paragraph (e)(5)(i)(C) of this section) that is a member of an expanded affiliated group that includes an insurance company, and the insurance company or holding company issues, or is obligated to make payments with respect to, a cash value insurance or annuity contract described in paragraph (b)(1)(iv) of this section (specified insurance company); or

(v) Is an entity that is a holding company or treasury center (as described in paragraphs (e)(5)(i)(C) and (e)(5)(i)(D)(1) of this section) that—

(A) Is part of an expanded affiliated group that includes a depository institution, custodial institution, specified insurance company, or investment entity described in paragraphs (e)(4)(i)(B) or (C) of this section; or

(B) Is formed in connection with or availed of by a collective investment vehicle, mutual fund, exchange traded fund, private equity fund, hedge fund, venture capital fund, leveraged buyout fund, or any similar investment vehicle established with an investment strategy of investing, reinvesting, or trading in financial assets.

(2) *Banking or similar business.*—(i) *In general.*—Except as otherwise provided in paragraph (e)(2)(ii) of this section, an entity is considered to be engaged in a banking or similar business if, in the ordinary course of its business with customers, the entity accepts deposits or other similar investments of funds and regularly engages in one or more of the following activities—

(A) Makes personal, mortgage, industrial, or other loans or provides other extensions of credit;

(B) Purchases, sells, discounts, or negotiates accounts receivable, installment obligations, notes, drafts, checks, bills of exchange, acceptances, or other evidences of indebtedness;

(C) Issues letters of credit and negotiates drafts drawn thereunder;

(D) Provides trust or fiduciary services;

(E) Finances foreign exchange transactions; or

(F) Enters into, purchases, or disposes of finance leases or leased assets.

(ii) *Exception for certain lessors and lenders.*—An entity is not considered to be engaged in a banking or similar business for purposes of this paragraph (e)(2) if the entity solely accepts deposits from persons as collateral or security pursuant to a sale or lease of property or pursuant to a similar financing arrangement between such entity and the person holding the deposit with the entity.

(iii) *Application of section 581.*—Entities engaged in a banking or similar business include, but are not limited to, entities that would qualify as banks under section 585(a)(2) (including banks as defined in section 581 and any corporation to which section 581 would apply but for the fact that it is a foreign corporation).

(iv) *Effect of local regulation.*—Whether an entity is subject to the banking and credit laws of a foreign country, the United States, a State, a U.S. territory, or a subdivision thereof, or is subject to supervision and examination by agencies having regulatory oversight of banking or similar institutions, is relevant to, but not necessarily determinative of, whether that entity qualifies as a financial institution under section 1471(d)(5)(A). Whether an entity conducts a banking or similar business is determined based upon the character of the actual activities of such entity.

(3) *Holding financial assets for others as a substantial portion of its business.*—(i) *Substantial portion.*—(A) *In general.*—An entity holds financial assets for the account of others as a substantial portion of its business if the entity's gross income attributable to holding financial assets and related financial services equals or exceeds 20 percent of the entity's gross income during the shorter of—

(1) The three-year period ending on December 31 of the year preceding the year in which the determination is made; or

(2) The period during which the entity has been in existence before the determination is made.

(B) *Special rule for start-up entities.*—An entity with no operating history as of the date of the determination is considered to hold financial assets for the account of others as a substantial portion of its business if the entity expects to meet the gross income threshold described in paragraph (e)(3)(i)(B) of this section based on its anticipated functions, assets, and employees, with due consideration given to any purpose or functions for which the entity is licensed or regulated (including those of any predecessor).

(ii) *Income attributable to holding financial assets and related financial services.*—For purposes of this paragraph (e)(3), the term *income attributable to holding financial assets and related financial services* means custody, account maintenance, and transfer fees; commissions and fees earned from executing and pricing securities transactions; income earned from extending credit to customers with respect to financial assets held in custody by the entity (or acquired through such extension of credit); income earned on the bid-ask spread of financial assets; fees for providing financial advice with respect to financial assets held in (or potentially to be held in) custody by the entity; and fees for clearance and settlement services.

(iii) *Effect of local regulation.*—Whether an entity is subject to the banking and credit, broker-dealer, fiduciary, or other similar laws and regulations of the United States, a State, a U.S. territory, a political subdivision thereof, or a foreign country, or to supervision and examination by agencies having regulatory oversight of banks, credit issuers, or other financial institutions, is relevant to, but not necessarily determinative of, whether that entity holds financial assets for the account of others as a substantial portion of its business.

(4) *Investment entity.*—(i) *In general.*—The term *investment entity* means any entity that is described in paragraph (e)(4)(i)(A), (B), or (C) of this section.

(A) The entity primarily conducts as a business one or more of the following activities or operations for or on behalf of a customer—

(1) Trading in money market instruments (checks, bills, certificates of deposit, derivatives, etc.); foreign currency; foreign exchange, interest rate, and index instruments; transferable securities; or commodity futures;

(2) Individual or collective portfolio management; or

(3) Otherwise investing, administering, or managing funds, money, or financial assets on behalf of other persons.

(B) The entity's gross income is primarily attributable to investing, reinvesting, or trading in financial assets (as defined in paragraph (e)(4)(ii) of this section) and the entity is managed by another entity that is described in paragraph (e)(1)(i), (ii), (iv), or (e)(4)(i)(A) of this section. For purposes of this paragraph (e)(4)(i)(B), an entity is managed by another entity if the managing entity performs, either directly or through another third-party service provider, any of the activities described in paragraph (e)(4)(i)(A) of this section on behalf of the managed entity.

(C) The entity functions or holds itself out as a collective investment vehicle, mutual fund, exchange traded fund, private equity fund, hedge fund, venture capital fund, leveraged buyout fund, or any similar investment vehicle established with an investment strategy of investing, reinvesting, or trading in financial assets.

(ii) *Financial assets.*—For purposes of this paragraph, the term *financial asset* means a security (as defined in section 475(c)(2) without regard to the last sentence thereof), partnership interest, commodity (as defined in section 475(e)(2)), notional principal contract (as de-

fined in §1.446-3(c)), insurance contract or annuity contract, or any interest (including a futures or forward contract or option) in a security, partnership interest, commodity, notional principal contract, insurance contract, or annuity contract.

(iii) *Primarily conducts as a business.*—(A) *In general.*—An entity is treated as primarily conducting as a business one or more of the activities described in paragraph (e)(4)(i)(A) of this section if the entity's gross income attributable to such activities equals or exceeds 50 percent of the entity's gross income during the shorter of—

(1) The three-year period ending on December 31 of the year preceding the year in which the determination is made; or

(2) The period during which the entity has been in existence.

(B) *Special rule for start-up entities.*—An entity with no operating history as of the date of the determination is treated as primarily conducting as a business one or more of the activities described in paragraph (e)(4)(i)(A) of this section if such entity expects to meet the gross income threshold described in paragraph (e)(4)(iii)(A) of this section based on its anticipated functions, assets, and employees, with due consideration given to any purpose or functions for which the entity is licensed or regulated (including those of any predecessor).

(iv) *Primarily attributable to investing, reinvesting, or trading in financial assets.*—(A) *In general.*—An entity's gross income is primarily attributable to investing, reinvesting, or trading in financial assets for purposes of paragraph (e)(4)(i)(B) of this section if the entity's gross income attributable to investing, reinvesting, or trading in financial assets equals or exceeds 50 percent of the entity's gross income during the shorter of—

(1) The three-year period ending on December 31 of the year preceding the year in which the determination is made; or

(2) The period during which the entity has been in existence.

(B) *Special rule for start-up entities.*—An entity with no operating history as of the date of the determination will be considered to have income that is primarily attributable to investing, reinvesting, or trading in financial assets for purposes of paragraph (e)(4)(i)(B) of this section if such entity expects to meet the income threshold described in paragraph (e)(4)(iv)(A) of this section based on its anticipated functions, assets, and employees, with due consideration given to any purpose or functions for which the entity is licensed or regulated (including those of any predecessor).

(v) *Examples.*—The following examples illustrate the provisions of paragraph (e)(4) of this section:

*Example 1. Investment advisor.* Fund Manager is an investment entity within the meaning of paragraph (e)(4)(i)(A) of this section. Fund Manager, among its various business operations, organizes and manages a variety of funds, including Fund A, a fund that invests primarily in equities. Fund Manager hires Investment Advisor, a foreign entity, to provide advice and discretionary management of a portion of the financial assets held by Fund A. Investment Advisor earned more than 50% of its gross income for the last three years from providing similar services. Because Investment Advisor primarily conducts a business of managing financial assets on behalf of clients, Investment Advisor is an investment entity under paragraph (e)(4)(i)(A) of this section and an FFI under paragraph (e)(1)(iii) of this section.

*Example 2. Entity that is managed by an FFI.* The facts are the same as in *Example 1.* In addition, in every year since it was organized, Fund A has earned more than 50% of its gross income from investing in financial assets. Accordingly, Fund A is an investment entity under paragraph (e)(4)(i)(B) of this section because it is managed by Fund Manager and Investment Advisor and its gross income is primarily attributable to investing, reinvesting, or trading in financial assets.

*Example 3. Investment manager.* Investment Manager, a U.S. entity, is an investment entity within the meaning of paragraph (e)(4)(i)(A) of this section. Investment Manager organizes and registers Fund A in Country A. Investment Manager is authorized to facilitate purchases and sales of financial assets held by Fund A in accordance with Fund A's investment strategy. In every year since it was organized, Fund A has earned more than 50% of its gross income from investing, reinvesting, or trading in financial assets. Accordingly, Fund A is an investment entity under paragraph (e)(4)(i)(B) of this section and an FFI under paragraph (e)(1)(iii) of this section.

*Example 4. Foreign real estate investment fund that is managed by an FFI.* The facts are the same as in *Example 3*, except that Fund A's assets consist solely of non-debt, direct interests in real property located within and without the United States. Fund A is not an investment entity under paragraph (e)(4)(i)(B) of this section, even though it is managed by Investment Manager, because less than 50%

of its gross income is attributable to investing, reinvesting, or trading in financial assets.

*Example 5. Trust managed by an individual.* On January 1, 2013, X, an individual, establishes Trust A, a nongrantor foreign trust for the benefit of X's children, Y and Z. X appoints Trustee A, an individual, to act as the trustee of Trust A. Trust A's assets consists solely of financial assets, and its income consists solely of income from those financial assets. Pursuant to the terms of the trust instrument, Trustee A manages and administers the assets of the trust. Trustee A does not hire any entity as a third-party service provider to perform any of the activities described in paragraph (e)(4)(i)(A) of this section. Trust A is not an investment entity under paragraph (e)(4)(i)(B) of this section because it is managed solely by Trustee A, an individual.

*Example 6. Trust managed by a trust company.* The facts are the same as in *Example 5*, except that X hires Trust Company, an FFI, to act as trustee on behalf of Trust A. As trustee, Trust Company manages and administers the assets of Trust A in accordance with the terms of the trust instrument for the benefit of Y and Z. Because Trust A is managed by an FFI, Trust A is an investment entity under paragraph (e)(4)(i)(B) of this section and an FFI under paragraph (e)(1)(iii) of this section.

*Example 7. Individual introducing broker.* IB, an individual introducing broker, primarily conducts a business of providing advice to clients, has discretionary authority to manage clients' assets, and uses the services of a foreign entity to conduct and execute trades on behalf of clients. IB provides services as an investment advisor and manager to Entity, a foreign corporation. Entity has earned 50% or more of its gross income for the past three years from investing, reinvesting, or trading in financial assets. Because IB is an individual, notwithstanding that IB primarily conducts certain investment-related activities, IB is not an investment entity under paragraph (e)(4)(i)(A) of this section. Further, Entity is not an investment entity under paragraph (e)(4)(i)(B) of this section because Entity is managed by IB, an individual.

*Example 8. Entity introducing broker.* IB, a foreign entity introducing broker, primarily conducts a business of providing advice to clients, has discretionary authority to manage clients' assets, and uses the services of a foreign entity to conduct and execute trades on behalf of clients. IB provides its services as an investment advisor and manager to Entity, a foreign corporation. Entity has earned 50% or more of its gross income for the past three years from investing, reinvesting, or trading in financial assets. Because IB is an entity that primarily conducts certain investment-related activities, IB is an investment entity under paragraph (e)(4)(i)(A) of this section. Further, Entity is an investment entity under paragraph (e)(4)(i)(B) of this section because it is managed by IB, an investment entity that performs certain of the activities described in paragraph (e)(4)(i)(A) of this section on behalf of Entity.

(5) *Exclusions.*—A financial institution does not include an entity described in this paragraph, provided that the entity is not also described in paragraph (e)(1)(iv) of this section. For the treatment of foreign entities described in this paragraph under section 1472, see § 1.1472-1(c)(1)(v).

(i) *Excepted nonfinancial group entities.*—(A) *In general.*—A foreign entity that is a member of a nonfinancial group (as defined in paragraph (e)(5)(i)(B) of this section) if—

(1) The entity is not a depository institution or custodial institution (other than for members of its expanded affiliated group);

(2) The entity is a holding company, treasury center, or captive finance company and substantially all the activities of such entity are to perform one or more of the functions described in paragraphs (e)(5)(i)(C), (D), or (E) of this section; and

(3) The entity does not hold itself out as, and was not formed in connection with or availed of by, an arrangement or investment vehicle that is a private equity fund, venture capital fund, leveraged buyout fund, or any similar investment vehicle established with an investment strategy to acquire or fund companies and to treat the interests in those companies as capital assets held for investment purposes. For purposes of determining whether an entity was formed in connection with or availed of by such an arrangement or investment vehicle, any entity that existed at least six months prior to its acquisition by such arrangement or investment vehicle and that, prior to the acquisition, regularly conducted activities described in paragraph (e)(5)(i)(C), (D), or (E) of this section will not be considered to have been formed in connection with or availed of by the arrangement or investment vehicle, in the absence of other facts suggesting the existence of an investment strategy described in the prior sentence.

(B) *Nonfinancial group.*—An expanded affiliated group defined in paragraph (i)(2) of this section is a nonfinancial group if, taking into account the application of this section—

(1) For the three-year period (or the period during which the expanded affiliated group has been in existence, if shorter) ending on December 31 (or the end of the fiscal year of one or more members of the group) of the year preceding the year in which the determination is made, no more than 25 percent of the gross income of the expanded affiliated group (excluding income derived by any member that is an entity described in paragraph (e)(5)(ii) or (iii) of this section, income derived from transactions between members of the expanded affiliated group, and interest income on notes issued by customers to a member of the expanded affiliated group that is a captive finance company to finance the customer's purchase of inventory or goods that are manufactured by a member of the expanded affiliated group) consists of passive income (as defined in § 1.1472-1(c)(1)(iv)); no more than five percent of the gross income of the expanded affiliated group is derived by members of the expanded affiliated group that are FFIs (excluding income derived from transactions between members of the expanded affiliated group or by any member of the expanded affiliated group that is a certified deemed-compliant FFI); and no more than 25 percent of the value of assets held by the expanded affiliated group (excluding assets held by a member that is an entity described in paragraph (e)(5)(ii) or (iii) of this section, assets resulting from transactions between related members of the expanded affiliated group, and receivables that are notes issued by customers to a member of the expanded affiliated group that is a captive finance company to finance the customer's purchase of inventory or goods that are manufactured by a member of the expanded affiliated group) are assets that produce or are held for the production of passive income; and

(2) Any member of the expanded affiliated group that is an FFI is a participating FFI, deemed-compliant FFI, or an exempt beneficial owner. However, an acquisition by a member of the expanded affiliated group of an FFI that is not a participating FFI, deemed-compliant FFI, or an exempt beneficial owner, or a change in the chapter 4 status of a member of the expanded affiliated group, will not cause a nonfinancial group to cease to be a nonfinancial group until 90 days after the acquisition or change in chapter 4 status.

(C) *Holding company.*—For purposes of this paragraph (e)(5)(i), an entity is a holding company if its primary activity consists of holding (directly or indirectly) all or part of the outstanding stock of one or more members of its expanded affiliated group. A partnership or any other non-corporate entity shall be treated as a holding company if substantially all the activities of such partnership (or other entity) consist of holding more than 50 percent of the voting power and value of the stock of one or more common parent corporation(s) of one or more expanded affiliated group(s). If a partnership or other non-corporate entity owns more than 50 percent of the voting power and value of the stock of more than one common parent corporation of an expanded affiliated group, each common parent corporation's expanded affiliated group will be treated as a separate expanded affiliated group for purposes of applying the rules of this section unless a non-corporate entity is treated as the common parent entity of the expanded affiliated group in accordance with § 1.1471-5(i)(10).

(D) *Treasury center.*—(1) Except as otherwise provided in this paragraph, an entity is a treasury center for purposes of this paragraph (e)(5)(i) if the primary activity of such entity is to enter into investment, hedging, and financing transactions with or for members of its expanded affiliated group for purposes of—

(i) Managing the risk of price changes or currency fluctuations with respect to property that is held or to be held by the expanded affiliated group (or any member thereof);

(ii) Managing the risk of interest rate changes, price changes, or currency fluctuations with respect to borrowings made or to be made by the expanded affiliated group (or any member thereof);

(iii) Managing the risk of interest rate changes, price changes, or currency fluctuations with respect to assets or liabilities to be reflected in financial statements of the expanded affiliated group (or any member thereof);

(iv) Managing the working capital of the expanded affiliated group (or any member thereof) such as by pooling the cash balances of affiliates (including both positive and deficit cash balances) or by investing or trading in financial assets solely for the account and risk of such entity or any member of its expanded affiliated group; or

(v) Acting as a financing vehicle for the expanded affiliated group (or any member thereof).

(2) An entity is not a treasury center if any equity or debt interest in the entity is held by a person that is not a member of the entity's expanded affiliated group and the redemption or retirement amount or return earned on such interest is determined primarily by reference to—

**Reg. § 1.1471-5(e)(5)(i)(D)(2)**

*(i)* The investment, hedging, and financing activities of the treasury center with members outside of its expanded affiliated group; or

*(ii)* Any member of the group that is an investment entity described in (e)(4)(i)(B) or passive NFFE (as described in paragraph (b)(3)(vi) of this section with respect to either such entity).

(E) *Captive finance company.*—For purposes of this paragraph (e)(5)(i), an entity is a captive finance company if the primary activity of such entity is to enter into financing (including the extension of credit) or leasing transactions with or for suppliers, distributors, dealers, franchisees, or customers of such entity or of any member of such entity's expanded affiliated group that is an active NFFE.

(ii) *Excepted nonfinancial start-up companies or companies entering a new line of business.*—(A) *In general.*—A foreign entity that is investing capital in assets with the intent to operate a new business or line of business other than that of a financial institution or passive NFFE for a period of—

*(1)* In the case of an entity intending to operate a new business, 24 months from the initial organization of such entity; and

*(2)* In the case of an entity with the intent to operate a new line of business, 24 months from the date of the board resolution (or its equivalent) approving the new line of business, provided that such entity qualified as an active NFFE for the 24 months preceding the date of such approval.

(B) *Exception for investment funds.*—An entity is not described in this paragraph (e)(5)(ii) if the entity functions (or holds itself out) as an investment fund, such as a private equity fund, venture capital fund, leveraged buyout fund, or any investment vehicle whose purpose is to acquire or fund companies and hold interests in those companies as capital assets for investment purposes.

(iii) *Excepted nonfinancial entities in liquidation or bankruptcy.*—A foreign entity that was not a financial institution or passive NFFE at any time during the past five years and that is in the process of liquidating its assets or reorganizing with the intent to continue or recommence operations as a nonfinancial entity.

(iv) *Excepted inter-affiliate FFI.*—A foreign entity that is a member of a participating FFI group if—

(A) The entity does not maintain financial accounts (other than accounts maintained for members of its expanded affiliated group);

(B) The entity does not hold an account (other than depository accounts in the country in which the entity is operating to pay for expenses in that country) with or receive payments from any withholding agent other than a member of its expanded affiliated group;

(C) The entity does not make withholdable payments to any person other than to members of its expanded affiliated group that are not limited FFIs or limited branches; and

(D) The entity has not agreed to report under § 1.1471-4(d)(2)(ii)(C) or otherwise act as an agent for chapter 4 purposes on behalf of any financial institution, including a member of its expanded affiliated group.

(v) *Section 501(c) entities.*—A foreign entity that is described in section 501(c) other than an insurance company described in section 501(c)(15).

(vi) *Non-profit organizations.*—A foreign entity that is established and maintained in its country of residence exclusively for religious, charitable, scientific, artistic, cultural or educational purposes if—

(A) The entity is exempt from income tax in its country of residence;

(B) The entity has no shareholders or members who have a proprietary or beneficial interest in its income or assets;

(C) Neither the laws of the entity's country of residence nor the entity's formation documents permit any income or assets of the entity to be distributed to, or applied for the benefit of, an individual or noncharitable entity other than pursuant to the conduct of the entity's charitable activities, or as payment of reasonable compensation for services rendered or the use of property, or as payment representing the fair market value of property that the entity has purchased; and

(D) The laws of the entity's country of residence or the entity's formation documents require that, upon the entity's liquidation or dissolution, all of its assets be distributed to an entity that meets the requirements of § 1.1471-6(b) or another organization that meets the requirements of this paragraph (e)(5)(vi) or escheat to the government of the entity's country of residence or any political subdivision thereof.

(6) *Reserving activities of an insurance company.*—The reserving activities of an insurance company will not cause the company to be a financial institution described in (e)(1)(i), (ii), or (iii) of this section.

(f) *Deemed-compliant FFIs.*—The term *deemed-compliant FFI* includes a registered deemed-compliant FFI (as defined in paragraph (f)(1) of this section), a certified deemed-compliant FFI (as defined in paragraph (f)(2) of this section), a nonreporting IGA FFI (as defined in § 1.1471-1(b)(83)), and, to the extent provided in paragraph (f)(3) of this section, an owner-documented FFI. A deemed-compliant FFI will be treated pursuant to section 1471(b)(2) as having met the requirements of section 1471(b). A deemed-compliant FFI that complies with the due diligence and withholding requirements applicable to such entity as provided in this paragraph (f) will also be deemed to have met its withholding obligations under sections 1471(a) and 1472(a). For this purpose, an intermediary or flow-through entity that has a residual withholding obligation under § 1.1471-2(a)(2)(ii) must fulfill such obligation to be considered a deemed-compliant FFI.

(1) *Registered deemed-compliant FFIs.*—A registered deemed-compliant FFI means an FFI that meets the procedural requirements described in paragraph (f)(1)(ii) of this section and that either is described in any of paragraphs (f)(1)(i)(A) through (F) of this section or is treated as a registered deemed-compliant FFI under a Model 2 IGA. A registered deemed-compliant FFI also includes any FFI, or branch of an FFI, that is a reporting Model 1 FFI that complies with the registration requirements of a Model 1 IGA.

(i) *Registered deemed-compliant FFI categories.*—(A) *Local FFIs.*—An FFI is described in this paragraph (f)(1)(i)(A) if the FFI meets the following requirements.

*(1)* The FFI is licensed and regulated as a financial institution under the laws of its country of incorporation or organization (which must be a FATF-compliant jurisdiction at the time the FFI registers for deemed-compliant status).

*(2)* The FFI does not have a fixed place of business outside its country of incorporation or organization. For this purpose, a fixed place of business does not include a location that is not advertised to the public and from which the FFI performs solely administrative support functions.

*(3)* The FFI does not solicit customers or account holders outside its country of incorporation or organization. For this purpose, an FFI will not be considered to have solicited customers or account holders outside its country of incorporation or organization merely because it operates a website, provided that the website does not specifically indicate that the FFI maintains accounts for or provides services to nonresidents, and does not otherwise target or solicit U.S. customers or account holders. An FFI will also not be considered to have solicited customers or account holders outside its country of incorporation or organization merely because it advertises in print media or on a radio or television station that is distributed or aired primarily within its country of incorporation or organization but is also incidentally distributed or aired in other countries, provided that the advertisement does not specifically indicate that the FFI maintains accounts for or provides services to nonresidents and does not otherwise target or solicit U.S. customers or account holders.

*(4)* The FFI is required under the laws of its country of incorporation or organization to identify resident account holders for purposes of either information reporting or withholding of tax with respect to accounts held by residents or is required to identify resident accounts for purposes of satisfying such country's AML due diligence requirements.

*(5)* At least 98 percent of the accounts by value maintained by the FFI as of the last day of the preceding calendar year are held by residents (including residents that are entities) of the country in which the FFI is incorporated or organized. An FFI that is incorporated or organized in a member state of the European Union may treat account holders that are residents (including residents that are entities) of other member states of the European Union as residents of the country in which the FFI is incorporated or organized for purposes of this calculation.

*(6)* By the later of June 30, 2014, or the date it registers as a deemed-compliant FFI, the FFI implements policies and procedures, consistent with those set forth for a participating FFI under § 1.1471-4(c), to monitor whether the FFI opens or maintains an account for a specified U.S. person who is not a resident of the country in which the FFI is incorporated or organized (including a U.S. person that was a resident when the account was opened but subsequently ceases to be a resident), an entity controlled or beneficially owned (as determined under the FFI's AML due diligence) by one or more specified U.S. persons that are not residents of the country in which the FFI is incorporated or organized, or a nonparticipating FFI. Such policies and procedures must provide that if any

such account is discovered, the FFI will close such account, transfer such account to a participating FFI, reporting Model 1 FFI, or U.S. financial institution, or withhold and report on such account as would be required under §1.1471-4(b) and (d) if the FFI were a participating FFI.

(7) With respect to each preexisting account held by a nonresident of the country in which the FFI is organized or held by an entity, the FFI reviews those accounts in accordance with the procedures described in §1.1471-4(c) applicable to preexisting accounts to identify any U.S. account or account held by a nonparticipating FFI, and certifies to the IRS that it did not identify any such account as a result of its review, that it has closed any such accounts that were identified or transferred them to a participating FFI, reporting Model 1 FFI, or U.S. financial institution, or that it agrees to withhold and report on such accounts as would be required under §1.1471-4(b) and (d) if it were a participating FFI. Such certification must be submitted by the due date of the FFI's first certification of compliance required under paragraph (f)(1)(ii)(B) of this section.

(8) In the case of an FFI that is a member of an expanded affiliated group, each FFI in the group is incorporated or organized in the same country and, with the exception of any member that is a retirement plan described in §1.1471-6(f), meets the requirements set forth in this paragraph (f)(1)(i)(A) and the procedural requirements of paragraph (f)(1)(ii) of this section.

(9) The FFI does not have policies or practices that discriminate against opening or maintaining accounts for individuals who are specified U.S. persons and who are residents of the FFI's country of incorporation or organization.

(B) *Nonreporting members of participating FFI groups.*—An FFI that is a member of a participating FFI group is described in this paragraph (f)(1)(i)(B) if it meets the following requirements.

(1) By the later of June 30, 2014, or the date it registers with the IRS pursuant to paragraph (f)(1)(ii) of this section, the FFI implements policies and procedures to ensure that within six months of opening a U.S. account or an account held by a recalcitrant account holder or a nonparticipating FFI, the FFI either transfers such account to an affiliate that is a participating FFI, reporting Model 1 FFI, or U.S. financial institution, closes the account, or becomes a participating FFI.

(2) The FFI reviews its accounts that were opened prior to the time it implements the policies and procedures (including time frames) described in paragraph (f)(1)(i)(B)(1) of this section, using the procedures described in §1.1471-4(c) applicable to preexisting accounts of participating FFIs, to identify any U.S. account or account held by a nonparticipating FFI. Within six months of the identification of any account described in this paragraph, the FFI transfers the account to an affiliate that is a participating FFI, reporting Model 1 FFI, or U.S. financial institution, closes the account, or becomes a participating FFI.

(3) By the later of June 30, 2014, or the date it registers with the IRS pursuant to paragraph (f)(1)(ii) of this section, the FFI implements policies and procedures to ensure that it identifies any account that becomes a U.S. account or an account held by a recalcitrant account holder or a nonparticipating FFI due to a change in circumstances. Within six months of the date on which the FFI first has knowledge or reason to know of the change in the account holder's chapter 4 status, the FFI transfers any such account to an affiliate that is a participating FFI, reporting Model 1 FFI, or U.S. financial institution, closes the account, or becomes a participating FFI.

(C) *Qualified collective investment vehicles.*—An FFI is described in this paragraph (f)(1)(i)(C) if it meets the following requirements.

(1) The FFI is an FFI solely because it is an investment entity, and it is regulated as an investment fund either in its country of incorporation or organization or in all of the countries in which it is registered and all of the countries in which it operates. A fund will be considered to be regulated as an investment fund under this paragraph if its manager is regulated with respect to the investment fund in all of the countries in which the investment fund is registered and in all of the countries in which the investment fund operates.

(2) Each holder of record of direct debt interests in the FFI in excess of $50,000, of any direct equity interests in the FFI (for example the holders of its units or global certificates), and of any other account holder of the FFI is a participating FFI, a registered deemed-compliant FFI, a retirement plan described in §1.1471-6(f), a non-profit organization described in paragraph (e)(5)(vi) of this section, a U.S. person that is not a specified U.S. person, a nonreporting IGA FFI, or an exempt beneficial owner. Notwithstanding the prior sentence, an FFI will not be prohibited from qualifying as a qualified collective investment vehicle solely because it has issued interests in such bearer form provided that the FFI ceased issuing interests in such form after December 31, 2012, retires all such interests upon surren-

der, and establishes policies and procedures to redeem or immobilize all such interests prior to January 1, 2017, and that prior to payment the FFI documents the account holder in accordance with the procedures set forth in §1.1471-4(c) applicable to accounts other than preexisting accounts and agrees to withhold and report on such accounts as would be required under §1.1471-4(b) and (d) if it were a participating FFI. For purposes of this paragraph (f)(1)(i)(C), an FFI may disregard equity interests owned by specified U.S. persons acquired with seed capital within the meaning of paragraph (i)(4) of this section if the specified U.S. person is described in paragraph (i)(3)(i) and (ii) of this section (substituting the term *U.S. person* for the terms *FFI* and *member*), and the specified U.S. person neither has held, nor intends to hold, such interest for more than three years.

(3) In the case of an FFI that is part of an expanded affiliated group, all other FFIs in the expanded affiliated group are participating FFIs, registered deemed-compliant FFIs, sponsored FFIs described in paragraph (f)(1)(i)(F)(1) or(2) of this section, nonreporting IGA FFIs, or exempt beneficial owners.

(D) *Restricted funds.*—An FFI is described in this paragraph (f)(1)(i)(D) if it meets the following requirements.

(1) The FFI is an FFI solely because it is an investment entity, and it is regulated as an investment fund under the laws of its country of incorporation or organization (which must be a FATF-compliant jurisdiction at the time the FFI registers for deemed-compliant status) or in all of the countries in which it is registered and in all of the countries in which it operates. A fund will be considered to be regulated as an investment fund for purposes of this paragraph if its manager is regulated with respect to the fund in all of the countries in which the investment fund is registered and in all of the countries in which the investment fund operates.

(2) Interests issued directly by the fund are redeemed by or transferred by the fund rather than sold by investors on any secondary market. Notwithstanding the prior sentence, an FFI will not be prohibited from qualifying as a restricted fund solely because it issued interests in bearer form provided that the FFI ceased issuing interests in bearer form after December 31, 2012, retires all such interests upon surrender, and establishes policies and procedures to redeem or immobilize all such interests prior to January 1, 2017, and that prior to payment the FFI documents the account holder in accordance with the procedures set forth in §1.1471-4(c) applicable to accounts other than preexisting accounts and agrees to withhold and report on such accounts as would be required under §1.1471-4(b) and (d) if it were a participating FFI. For purposes of this paragraph (f)(1)(i)(D), interests in the FFI that are issued by the fund through a transfer agent or distributor that does not hold the interests as a nominee of the account holder will be considered to have been issued directly by the fund.

(3) Interests that are not issued directly by the fund are sold only through distributors that are participating FFIs, registered deemed-compliant FFIs, nonregistering local banks described in paragraph (f)(2)(i) of this section, or restricted distributors described in paragraph (f)(4) of this section. For purposes of this paragraph (f)(1)(i)(D) and paragraph (f)(4) of this section, a distributor means an underwriter, broker, dealer, or other person who participates, pursuant to a contractual arrangement with the FFI, in the distribution of securities and holds interests in the FFI as a nominee.

(4) The FFI ensures that by the later of December 31, 2014, or six months after the date the FFI registers as a deemed-compliant FFI, each agreement that governs the distribution of its debt or equity interests prohibits sales and other transfers of debt or equity interests in the FFI (other than interests that are both distributed by and held through a participating FFI) to specified U.S. persons, nonparticipating FFIs, or passive NFFEs with one or more substantial U.S. owners. In addition, by that date, the FFI's prospectus and all marketing materials must indicate that sales and other transfers of interests in the FFI to specified U.S. persons, nonparticipating FFIs, or passive NFFEs with one or more substantial U.S. owners are prohibited unless such interests are both distributed by and held through a participating FFI.

(5) The FFI ensures that by the later of December 31, 2014, or six months after the date the FFI registers as a deemed-compliant FFI, each agreement entered into by the FFI that governs the distribution of its debt or equity interests requires the distributor to notify the FFI of a change in the distributor's chapter 4 status within 90 days of the change. The FFI must, with respect to any distributor that ceases to qualify as a distributor identified in paragraph (f)(1)(i)(D)(3) of this section, terminate its distribution agreement with the distributor, or cause the distribution agreement to be terminated, within 90 days of the notification of the distributor's change in status and, with respect to all debt and equity interests of the FFI issued through that distributor, redeem those interests, convert those interests to direct holdings in the fund, or cause those interests to be transferred to another distributor identified in paragraph (f)(1)(i)(D)(3) of this section within six months of the distributor's change in status.

*(6)* With respect to any of the FFI's preexisting direct accounts that are held by the beneficial owner of the interest in the FFI, the FFI reviews those accounts in accordance with the procedures (and time frames) described in §1.1471-4(c) applicable to preexisting accounts to identify any U.S. account or account held by a nonparticipating FFI. Notwithstanding the previous sentence, the FFI will not be required to review the account of any individual investor that purchased its interest at a time when all of the FFI's distribution agreements and its prospectus contained an explicit prohibition of the issuance and/or sale of shares to U.S. entities and U.S. resident individuals. An FFI will not be required to review the account of any investor that purchased its interest in bearer form until the time of payment, but at such time will be required to document the account in accordance with procedures set forth in §1.1471-4(c) applicable to accounts other than preexisting accounts. The FFI is required to certify to the IRS either that it did not identify any U.S. account or account held by a nonparticipating FFI as a result of its review or, if any such accounts were identified, that the FFI will either redeem such accounts, transfer such accounts to an affiliate or other FFI that is a participating FFI, reporting Model 1 FFI, or U.S. financial institution, or withhold and report on such accounts as would be required under §1.1471-4(b) and (d) if it were a participating FFI. Such certification must be submitted to the IRS by the due date of the FFI's first certification of compliance required under paragraph (f)(1)(ii)(B) of this section.

*(7)* By the later of June 30, 2014, or the date that it registers as a deemed-compliant FFI, the FFI implements the policies and procedures described in §1.1471-4(c) to ensure that it either—

*(i)* Does not open or maintain an account for, or make a withholdable payment to, any specified U.S. person, nonparticipating FFI, or passive NFFE with one or more substantial U.S. owners and, if it discovers any such accounts, closes all accounts for any such person within six months of the date that the FFI had reason to know the account holder became such a person; or

*(ii)* Withholds and reports on any account held by, or any withholdable payment made to, any specified U.S. person, nonparticipating FFI, or passive NFFE with one or more substantial U.S. owners to the extent and in the manner that would be required under §1.1471-4(b) and (d) if the FFI were a participating FFI.

*(8)* For an FFI that is part of an expanded affiliated group, all other FFIs in the expanded affiliated group are participating FFIs, registered deemed-compliant FFIs, sponsored FFIs described in paragraph (f)(1)(i)(F)(1) or (2) of this section, nonreporting IGA FFIs, or exempt beneficial owners.

(E) *Qualified credit card issuers and servicers.*—An FFI is described in this paragraph (f)(1)(i)(E) if the FFI meets the following requirements.

*(1)* The FFI is an FFI solely because it is an issuer or servicer of credit cards that accepts deposits, on its own behalf or, in the case of a servicer, on behalf of a credit card issuer, only when a customer makes a payment in excess of a balance due with respect to the credit card account and the overpayment is not immediately returned to the customer.

*(2)* By the later of June 30, 2014, or the date it registers as a deemed-compliant FFI, the FFI implements policies and procedures to either prevent a customer deposit in excess of $50,000 or to ensure that any customer deposit in excess of $50,000 is refunded to the customer within 60 days. For this purpose, a customer deposit does not refer to credit balances to the extent of disputed charges but does include credit balances resulting from merchandise returns.

(F) *Sponsored investment entities and controlled foreign corporations.*—An FFI is described in this paragraph (f)(1)(i)(F) if the FFI is described in paragraph (f)(1)(i)(F)(1) or (2) of this section and the sponsoring entity meets the requirements of paragraph (f)(1)(i)(F)(3) of this section.

*(1)* An FFI is a sponsored investment entity described in this paragraph (f)(1)(i)(F)(1) if—

*(i)* It is an investment entity that is not a QI, WP (except to the extent permitted in the WP agreement), or WT; and

*(ii)* An entity, other than a nonparticipating FFI, has agreed with the FFI to act as a sponsoring entity for the FFI.

*(2)* An FFI is a sponsored controlled foreign corporation described in this paragraph (f)(1)(i)(F)(2) if the FFI meets the following requirements—

*(i)* The FFI is a controlled foreign corporation as defined in section 957(a) that is not a QI, WP, or WT;

*(ii)* The FFI is wholly owned, directly or indirectly, by a U.S. financial institution that agrees with the FFI to act as a sponsoring entity for the FFI; and

*(iii)* The FFI shares a common electronic account system with the sponsoring entity that enables the sponsoring entity to identify all account holders and payees of the FFI and to access all account and customer information maintained by the FFI including,

but not limited to, customer identification information, customer documentation, account balance, and all payments made to the account holder or payee.

*(3)* A sponsoring entity described in paragraph (f)(1)(i)(F)(1)(ii) or(f)(1)(i)(F)(2)(ii) of this section meets the requirements of this paragraph (f)(1)(i)(F)(3) if the sponsoring entity-

*(i)* Is authorized to act on behalf of the FFI (such as a fund manager, trustee, corporate director, or managing partner) to fulfill all due diligence, withholding, and reporting responsibilities that the FFI would have assumed if it were a participating FFI;

*(ii)* Has registered with the IRS as a sponsoring entity;

*(iii)* Has registered the FFI with the IRS by the later of January 1, 2017, or the date that the FFI identifies itself as qualifying under this paragraph (f)(1)(i)(F);

*(iv)* Agrees to perform, on behalf of the FFI, all due diligence, withholding, reporting, and other requirements that the FFI would have been required to perform if it were a participating FFI;

*(v)* Identifies the FFI in all reporting completed on the FFI's behalf to the extent required under §§1.1471-4(d)(2)(ii)(C) and 1.1474-1;

*(vi)* Complies with the verification procedures described in paragraph (j) of this section; and

*(vii)* Has not had its status as a sponsoring entity revoked.

*(4)* The IRS may revoke a sponsoring entity's status with respect to one or more sponsored FFIs based on the provisions of paragraphs (k)(2), (3), and (4) of this section (describing notice of event of default, remediation, and termination procedures) if there is an event of default as defined in paragraph (k)(1) of this section.

*(5)* A sponsoring entity is not liable for any failure to comply with the obligations contained in paragraph (f)(1)(i)(F)(3) of this section unless the sponsoring entity is a withholding agent that is separately liable for the failure to withhold on or report with respect to a payment made by the sponsoring entity on behalf of the sponsored FFI. A sponsored FFI will remain liable for any failure of its sponsoring entity to comply with the obligations contained in paragraph (f)(1)(i)(F)(3) of this section that the sponsoring entity has agreed to undertake on behalf of the FFI, even if the sponsoring entity is also a withholding agent and is itself separately liable for the failure to withhold on or report with respect to a payment made by the sponsoring entity on behalf of the sponsored FFI. The same tax, interest, or penalties, however, shall not be collected more than once.

(ii) *Procedural requirements for registered deemed-compliant FFIs.*—A registered deemed-compliant FFI described in paragraph (f)(1)(i)(A) through (E) of this section may use one or more agents to perform the necessary due diligence to identify its account holders and to take any required action associated with obtaining and maintaining its deemed-compliant status. The FFI, however, remains responsible for ensuring that the requirements for its deemed-compliant status are met. Unless otherwise provided in this section, a registered deemed-compliant FFI described in paragraph (f)(1)(i)(A) through (E) of this section is required to—

(A) Register with the IRS pursuant to procedures prescribed by the IRS and agree to comply with the terms of its registered deemed-compliant status.

(B) Have its responsible officer certify, on or before July 1 of the calendar year following the end of each certification period, that all of the requirements for the deemed-compliant status claimed by the FFI have been satisfied during the certification period. The responsible officer may certify collectively for the FFI's expanded affiliated group that all of the requirements for the deemed-compliant status claimed by each member of the expanded affiliated group that is a registered deemed-compliant FFI (other than a member that is a reporting Model 1 FFI or deemed-compliant FFI under an applicable Model 1 IGA) have been satisfied. The certification must be made on the form and in the manner prescribed by the IRS. The first certification period begins on the later of the date the FFI registers as a deemed-compliant FFI and is issued a GIIN, or June 30, 2014, and ends at the close of the third full calendar year following that date. Each subsequent certification period is the three calendar year period following the previous certification period.

(C) Maintain in its records the confirmation from the IRS of the FFI's registration as a deemed-compliant FFI and GIIN or such other information as the IRS specifies in forms or other guidance; and

(D) Agree to notify the IRS if there is a change in circumstances that would make the FFI ineligible for the deemed-compliant status for which it has registered, and to do so within six months of the change in circumstances unless the FFI is able to resume its eligibility for its registered-deemed compliant status within the six month notification period.

(iii) *Deemed-compliant FFI that is merged or acquired.*—A deemed-compliant FFI that becomes a participating FFI or a member of a participating FFI group as a result of a merger or acquisition will not be required to redetermine the chapter 4 status of any account maintained by the FFI prior to the date of the merger or acquisition unless that account has a subsequent change in circumstances.

(iv) *IRS review of compliance by registered deemed-compliant FFIs.*—(A) *General inquiries.*—With respect to a registered deemed-compliant FFI described in paragraph (f)(1)(i)(A), (C), or (D) of this section, the IRS, based upon the information reporting forms described in §1.1471-4(d)(3)(v), (d)(5)(vii), or (d)(6)(iv) filed with the IRS for each calendar year (if applicable), may request additional information with respect to the information reported (or required to be reported) on the forms, the account statements described in §1.1471-4(d)(4)(v), or confirmation that the FFI has no reporting requirements for the calendar year. The IRS may request additional information from the FFI to determine the FFI's compliance with §1.1471-4 (if applicable) and to assist the IRS with its review of account holder compliance with tax reporting requirements. For IRS review of compliance with respect to a registered deemed-compliant FFI described in paragraph (f)(1)(i)(F) of this section (describing sponsored investment entities and controlled foreign corporations), see paragraph (j)(4) of this section.

(B) *Inquiries regarding substantial non-compliance.*—With respect to a registered deemed-compliant FFI described in paragraph (f)(1)(i)(A) through (E) of this section, the IRS may determine in its discretion that the FFI may not have substantially complied with the requirements of the deemed-compliant status claimed by the FFI. This determination is based on the information reporting forms described in §1.1471-4(d)(3)(v), (d)(5)(vii), or (d)(6)(iv) filed with the IRS for each calendar year (if applicable), the certifications made by the responsible officer described in paragraph (f)(1)(ii)(B) of this section (or the absence of such certifications), or any other information related to the FFI's compliance with the requirements of the deemed-compliant status claimed by the FFI. In such a case, the IRS may request from the responsible officer (or designee) information necessary to verify the FFI's compliance with the requirements for the deemed-compliant status claimed by the FFI. For example, in the case of a local FFI under paragraph (f)(1)(i)(A) of this section, the IRS may request a description or copy of the FFI's policies and procedures for identifying accounts held by specified U.S. persons not resident in the jurisdiction in which the FFI is incorporated or organized, identifying entities controlled or beneficially owned by such persons, and identifying nonparticipating FFIs. The IRS may also request the performance of specified review procedures by a person (including an external auditor or third-party consultant) that the IRS identifies as competent to perform such procedures given the facts and circumstances surrounding the FFI's potential failure to comply with the requirements of the deemed-compliant category claimed by the FFI. If the IRS determines that the FFI has not complied with the requirements of the deemed-compliant status claimed by the FFI, the IRS may terminate the FFI's deemed-compliant status. If the FFI's deemed-compliant status is terminated, the FFI must send notice of the termination to each withholding agent from which it receives payments and each financial institution with which it holds an account for which a withholding certificate or other documentation was provided within 30 days after the termination. An FFI that has had its deemed-compliant status terminated may not reregister on the FATCA registration website as a registered deemed-compliant FFI or register on the FATCA registration website as a participating FFI unless it receives written approval from the IRS. A registered deemed-compliant FFI may request, within 90 days of a notice of termination, reconsideration of the notice of termination by written request to the IRS.

(2) *Certified deemed-compliant FFIs.*—A certified deemed-compliant FFI means an FFI described in any of paragraphs (f)(2)(i) through (v) of this section that has certified as to its status as a deemed-compliant FFI by providing a withholding agent with the documentation described in §1.1471-3(d)(5) applicable to the relevant deemed-compliant category. A certified deemed-compliant FFI is not required to register with the IRS.

(i) *Nonregistering local bank.*—An FFI is described in this paragraph (f)(2)(i) if the FFI meets the following requirements.

(A) The FFI operates solely as (and is licensed and regulated under the laws of its country of incorporation or organization as)—

(1) A bank; or

(2) A credit union or similar cooperative credit organization that is operated without profit.

(B) The FFI's business consists primarily of receiving deposits from and making loans to, with respect to a bank, retail customers that are unrelated to such bank and, with respect to a credit union or similar cooperative credit organization, members, provided that no such member has a greater than 5 percent interest in such credit union or cooperative credit organization. For purposes of this paragraph (f)(2)(i)(B), a customer is related to a bank if the customer and the bank have a relationship described in section 267(b). For purposes of determining whether a member has a greater than 5 percent interest in a credit union or cooperative credit organization, the member must aggregate the ownership or beneficial interests in the credit union or cooperative credit organization that are owned or held by a related member. A member of a credit union or cooperative credit organization is related to another member if the relationship of such members is described in section 267(b).

(C) The FFI does not have a fixed place of business outside its country of incorporation or organization. For this purpose, a fixed place of business does not include a location that is not advertised to the public and from which the FFI performs solely administrative support functions.

(D) The FFI does not solicit customers or account holders outside its country of incorporation or organization. For this purpose, an FFI will not be considered to have solicited customers or account holders outside its country of incorporation or organization merely because it operates a website, provided that the website does not permit account opening, does not indicate that the FFI maintains accounts for or provides services to nonresidents, and does not otherwise target or solicit U.S. customers or account holders. An FFI will also not be considered to have solicited customers or account holders outside its country of incorporation or organization merely because it advertises in print media or on a radio or television station that is distributed or aired primarily within its country of incorporation or organization but is also incidentally distributed or aired in other countries, provided that the advertisement does not indicate that the FFI maintains accounts for or provides services to nonresidents and does not otherwise target or solicit U.S. customers or account holders.

(E) The FFI does not have more than $175 million in assets on its balance sheet and, if the FFI is a member of an expanded affiliated group, the group does not have more than $500 million in total assets on its consolidated or combined balance sheets.

(F) With respect to an FFI that is part of an expanded affiliated group, each member of the expanded affiliated group is incorporated or organized in the same country and does not have a fixed place of business outside of that country. For this purpose, a fixed place of business does not include a location that is not advertised to the public and from which the FFI performs solely administrative support functions. Further, each FFI in the group, other than an FFI described in paragraph (f)(2)(ii) of this section or §1.1471-6(f), meets the requirements set forth in this paragraph (f)(2)(i). For this purpose, a fixed place of business does not include a location that is not advertised to the public and from which the FFI performs solely administrative support functions.

(ii) *FFIs with only low-value accounts.*—An FFI is described in this paragraph (f)(2)(ii) if the FFI meets the following requirements:

(A) The FFI is not an investment entity.

(B) No financial account maintained by the FFI (or, in the case of an FFI that is a member of an expanded affiliated group, by any member of the expanded affiliated group) has a balance or value in excess of $50,000. The balance or value of a financial account shall be determined by applying the rules described in paragraph (b)(4) of this section, substituting the term *financial account* for the term *depository account* and the term *person* for the term *individual*.

(C) The FFI does not have more than $50 million in assets on its balance sheet as of the end of its most recent accounting year. In the case of an FFI that is a member of an expanded affiliated group, the entire expanded affiliated group does not have more than $50 million in assets on its consolidated or combined balance sheet as of the end of its most recent accounting year.

(iii) *Sponsored, closely held investment vehicles.*—Subject to the provisions of paragraph (f)(2)(iii)(E) of this section, an FFI is described in this paragraph (f)(2)(iii) if it meets the requirements described in paragraphs (f)(2)(iii)(A) through (D) of this section.

(A) The FFI is an FFI solely because it is an investment entity and is not a QI, WP, or WT.

(B) A participating FFI, reporting Model 1 FFI, or U.S. financial institution agrees to fulfill all due diligence, withholding, and reporting responsibilities that the FFI would have assumed if it were a participating FFI.

(C) Twenty or fewer individuals own all of the debt and equity interests in the FFI (disregarding debt interests owned by U.S. financial institutions, participating FFIs, registered deemed-compliant FFIs, and certified deemed-compliant FFIs and equity interests owned by an entity if that entity owns 100 percent of the equity interests in the FFI and is itself a sponsored FFI under this paragraph (f)(2)(iii)).

(D) The sponsoring entity complies with the following requirements—

*(1)* The sponsoring entity has registered with the IRS as a sponsoring entity;

*(2)* The sponsoring entity agrees to perform, on behalf of the FFI, all due diligence, withholding, reporting, and other requirements that the FFI would have been required to perform if it were a participating FFI and retains documentation collected with respect to the FFI for a period of six years;

*(3)* The sponsoring entity identifies the FFI in all reporting completed on the FFI's behalf to the extent required under §§ 1.1471-4(d)(2)(ii)(C) and 1.1474-1;

*(4)* Complies with the verification procedures described in paragraph (j) of this section; and

*(5)* The sponsoring entity has not had its status as a sponsor revoked.

(E) The IRS may revoke a sponsoring entity's status as a sponsoring entity with respect to one or more sponsored FFIs based on the provisions of paragraphs (k)(2), (3), and (4) of this section (describing notice of event of default, remediation, and termination procedures) if there is an event of default as defined in paragraph (k)(1) of this section. A sponsoring entity is not liable for any failure to comply with the obligations contained in paragraph (f)(2)(iii)(D) of this section unless the sponsoring entity is a withholding agent that is separately liable for the failure to withhold on or report with respect to a payment made by the sponsoring entity on behalf of the sponsored FFI. A sponsored FFI will remain liable for any failure of its sponsoring entity to comply with the obligations contained in paragraph (f)(2)(iii)(D) of this section that the sponsoring entity has agreed to undertake on behalf of the FFI, even if the sponsoring entity is also a withholding agent and is itself separately liable for the failure to withhold on or report with respect to a payment made by the sponsoring entity on behalf of the sponsored FFI. The same tax, interest, or penalties, however, shall not be collected more than once.

*(iv) Limited life debt investment entities (transitional).*—An FFI is described in this paragraph (f)(2)(iv) if the FFI is the beneficial owner of the payment (or of payments made with respect to the account) and the FFI meets the following requirements.

(A) The FFI is an investment entity that issued one or more classes of debt or equity interests to investors pursuant to a trust indenture or similar agreement and all of such interests were issued on or before January 17, 2013.

(B) The FFI was in existence as of January 17, 2013, and has entered into a trust indenture or similar agreement that requires the FFI to pay to investors holding substantially all of the interests in the FFI, no later than a set date or period following the maturity of the last asset held by the FFI, all amounts that such investors are entitled to receive from the FFI.

(C) The FFI was formed and operated for the purpose of purchasing or acquiring specific types of debt instruments or interests therein and holding those assets subject to reinvestment only under prescribed circumstances to maturity.

(D) Substantially all of the assets of the FFI consist of debt instruments or interests therein (including assets acquired pursuant to a foreclosure, restructuring, workout, or similar event with respect to a debt instrument).

(E) All payments made to the investors of the FFI (other than holders of a de minimis interest) are either cleared through a clearing organization or custodial institution that is a participating FFI, reporting Model 1 FFI, or U.S. financial institution or made through a transfer agent that is a participating FFI, reporting Model 1 FFI, or U.S. financial institution.

(F) The FFI's trustee or fiduciary is not authorized through a fiduciary duty or otherwise to fulfill the obligations of a participating FFI under § 1.1471-4 and no other person has the authority to fulfill the obligations of a participating FFI under § 1.1471-4 on behalf of the FFI.

*(v) Certain investment entities that do not maintain financial accounts.*—An FFI is described in this paragraph (f)(2)(v) if the FFI meets the following requirements.

(A) The FFI is a financial institution solely because it is described in paragraph (e)(4)(i)(A) of this section.

(B) The FFI does not maintain financial accounts.

*(3) Owner-documented FFIs.—(i) In general.*—An owner-documented FFI means an FFI that meets the requirements of paragraph (f)(3)(ii) of this section. An FFI may only be treated as an owner-documented FFI with respect to payments received from and accounts held with a designated withholding agent (or with respect to payments received from and accounts held with another FFI that is also treated as an owner-documented FFI by such designated withholding agent). A designated withholding agent is a U.S. financial institution, participating FFI, or reporting Model 1 FFI that agrees to undertake the additional due diligence and reporting required under paragraphs (f)(3)(ii)(D) and (E) of this section in order to treat the FFI

as an owner-documented FFI. An FFI meeting the requirements of this paragraph (f)(3) will only be treated as a deemed-compliant FFI with respect to a payment or account for which it does not act as an intermediary.

*(ii) Requirements of owner-documented FFI status.*—An FFI meets the requirements of this paragraph (f)(3)(ii) only if—

(A) The FFI is an FFI solely because it is an investment entity;

(B) The FFI is not owned by or in an expanded affiliated group with any FFI that is a depository institution, custodial institution, or specified insurance company;

(C) The FFI does not maintain a financial account for any nonparticipating FFI;

(D) The FFI provides the designated withholding agent with all of the documentation described in § 1.1471-3(d)(6) and agrees to notify the withholding agent if there is a change in circumstances; and

(E) The designated withholding agent agrees to report to the IRS (or, in the case of a reporting Model 1 FFI, to the relevant foreign government or agency thereof) all of the information described in § 1.1471-4(d) or § 1.1474-1(i) (as appropriate) with respect to any specified U.S. persons that are identified in § 1.1471-3(d)(6)(iv)(A)(1) and (2). Notwithstanding the previous sentence, the designated withholding agent is not required to report information with respect to an indirect owner of the FFI that holds its interest through a participating FFI, a deemed-compliant FFI (other than an owner-documented FFI), an entity that is a U.S. person, an exempt beneficial owner, or an excepted NFFE.

*(4) Definition of a restricted distributor.*—An entity is a restricted distributor for purposes of paragraph (f)(1)(i)(D) of this section (relating to registered deemed-compliant restricted funds) if it operates as a distributor that holds debt or equity interests in a restricted fund as a nominee and meets the following requirements.

(i) The distributor provides investment services to at least 30 customers unrelated to each other and fewer than half of the distributor's customers are related to each other. For purposes of this paragraph (f)(4)(i), customers are related to each other if they have a relationship with each other described in section 267(b).

(ii) The distributor is required to perform AML due diligence procedures under the anti-money laundering laws of its country of incorporation or organization (which must be a FATF-compliant jurisdiction).

(iii) The distributor operates solely in its country of incorporation or organization, does not have a fixed place of business outside that country, and, if such distributor belongs to an expanded affiliated group, has the same country of incorporation or organization as all other members of its expanded affiliated group. For this purpose, a fixed place of business does not include a location that is not advertised to the public and from which the FFI performs solely administrative support functions.

(iv) The distributor does not solicit customers or account holders outside its country of incorporation or organization. For this purpose, a distributor will not be considered to have solicited customers or account holders outside its country of organization merely because it operates a website, provided that the website does not permit account opening by persons identified as nonresidents, does not specifically state that nonresidents may acquire securities from the distributor, and does not otherwise target U.S. customers or account holders. A distributor will also not be considered to have solicited customers or account holders outside its country of incorporation or organization merely because it advertises in print media or on a radio or television station that is distributed or aired primarily within its country of incorporation or organization but is also incidentally distributed or aired in other countries, provided that the advertisement does not indicate that the distributor maintains accounts for or provides services to nonresidents and does not otherwise target or solicit U.S. customers or account holders.

(v) The distributor does not have more than $175 million in total assets under management and has no more than $7 million in gross revenue on its income statement for the most recent financial accounting year and, if the distributor belongs to an expanded affiliated group, the entire group does not have more than $500 million in total assets under management or more than $20 million in gross revenue for its most recent financial accounting year on a combined or consolidated income statement.

(vi) The distributor provides the restricted fund (or another distributor of the restricted fund that is a participating FFI or registered deemed-compliant FFI, and with which the distributor has entered into its distribution agreement) with a valid Form W-8 indicating that the distributor satisfies the requirements to be a restricted distributor.

(vii) The agreement governing the distributor's distribution of debt or equity interests of the restricted fund—

(A) Prohibits the distributor from distributing any securities to specified U.S. persons, passive NFFEs that have one or more substantial U.S. owners, and nonparticipating FFIs;

(B) Requires that if the distributor does distribute securities to any of the persons described in this paragraph (f)(4)(vii), it will cause the restricted fund to redeem or retire those interests, or it will transfer those interests to a distributor that is a participating FFI or reporting Model 1 FFI, within six months and the commission paid to the distributor will be forfeited to the restricted fund or to the participating FFI to which those interests are transferred; and

(C) Requires the distributor to notify the restricted fund (or another distributor of the restricted fund that is a participating FFI, reporting Model 1 FFI, or registered deemed-compliant FFI and with which the distributor has entered into its distribution agreement) of a change in the distributor's chapter 4 status within 90 days of the change in status.

(viii) With respect to sales after December 31, 2011, and prior to the time the restrictions described in paragraph (f)(4)(vii) of this section were incorporated into the distribution agreement, either the agreement governing the distributor's distribution of debt or equity interests of the relevant FFI contained a prohibition of the sale of such securities to U.S. entities or U.S. resident individuals, or the distributor reviews all accounts relating to such sales in accordance with the procedures (and time frames) described in § 1.1471-4(c) applicable to preexisting accounts and certifies that it has caused the restricted fund to redeem or retire, or it has transferred all securities sold to any of the persons described in paragraph (f)(4)(vii) of this section. If the distribution agreement addressed in the prior sentence contained only a prohibition on the sale of securities to U.S. resident individuals, the distributor will not be required to review the individual accounts relating to such sales but must review and make certifications with respect to all entity accounts in the manner described in the previous sentence.

(g) *Recalcitrant account holders.*—(1) *Scope.*—This paragraph (g) provides rules for determining when an account holder of a participating FFI or registered deemed-compliant FFI is a recalcitrant account holder. Paragraph (g)(2) of this section defines the term recalcitrant account holder. Paragraphs (g)(3) and (4) of this section provide timing rules for when an account holder will begin to be treated as a recalcitrant account holder by a participating FFI and when an account holder will cease to be treated as a recalcitrant account holder by such institution. For rules for determining the holder of an account, see paragraph (a)(3) of this section. For the withholding requirements of an FFI with respect to its recalcitrant account holders, see paragraph (f) of this section and § 1.1471-4(b). For the reporting requirements of an FFI with respect to its recalcitrant account holders, see § 1.1471-4(d)(6), and, for the reporting required with respect to payments made to such account holders, see § 1.1474-1(d)(4)(iii). A U.S. branch treated as a U.S. person shall apply the presumption rules of § 1.1471-3(f) (for foreign entity account holders) and chapter 3 or 61 (for individual payees) to determine the status of a payee if it cannot reliably associate a payment made to the payee with valid documentation and does not apply this paragraph (g).

(2) *Recalcitrant account holder.*—The term *recalcitrant account holder* means any holder of an account maintained by an FFI if such account holder is not an FFI (or presumed to be an FFI under § 1.1471-3(f)), the account does not meet the requirements of the exception to U.S. account status described in paragraph (a)(4) of this section (for depository accounts with a balance of $50,000 or less) and does not qualify for any of the exceptions from the documentation requirements described in § 1.1471-4(c)(3)(iii), (c)(4)(iii), (c)(5)(iii), (c)(5)(iv)(E) (or the participating FFI elects to forego such exceptions) and—

(i) The account holder fails to comply with requests by the FFI for the documentation or information that is required under § 1.1471-4(c) for determining the status of such account as a U.S. account or other than a U.S. account;

(ii) The account holder fails to provide a valid Form W-9 upon request from the FFI or fails to provide a correct name and TIN combination upon request from the FFI when the FFI has received notice from the IRS indicating that the name and TIN combination reported by the FFI for the account holder is incorrect;

(iii) If foreign law would (but for a waiver) prevent reporting by the FFI (or branch or division thereof) of the information described in § 1.1471-4(d)(3) or (5) with respect to such account, the account holder (or substantial U.S. owner of an account holder that is a U.S. owned foreign entity) fails to provide a valid and effective waiver to permit such reporting; or

(iv) The account holder provides the documentation described in § 1.1471-3(d)(12) to establish its status as a passive NFFE (other than a WP or WT) but fails to provide the information regarding its owners required under § 1.1471-3(d)(12)(iii).

(3) *Start of recalcitrant account holder status.*—(i) *Preexisting accounts identified under the procedures described in § 1.1471-4(c) for identifying U. S. accounts.*—(A) *In general.*—An account holder of a preexisting account described in paragraph (g)(2) of this section maintained by a participating FFI will be treated as a recalcitrant account holder beginning on the dates provided in paragraphs (g)(3)(B) through (D) of this section. An account holder of a preexisting account described in paragraph (g)(2) of this section that is maintained by a registered deemed-compliant FFI will be treated as a recalcitrant account holder beginning on the dates provided in paragraph (f) of this section (setting forth the time by which the FFI must identify its accounts in accordance with the requirements of § 1.1471-4(c) in order to meet the requirements of its applicable registered deemed-compliant status).

(B) *Accounts other than high-value accounts.*—Account holders of preexisting accounts maintained by a participating FFI that are not high-value accounts (as described in § 1.1471-4(c)(5)(iv)(D)) and that are described in paragraph (g)(2) of this section will be treated as recalcitrant account holders beginning on the date that is two years after the effective date of the FFI agreement.

(C) *High-value accounts.*—Account holders of preexisting accounts maintained by a participating FFI that are high-value accounts (as described in § 1.1471-4(c)(5)(iv)(D)) and that are described in paragraph (g)(2) of this section will be treated as recalcitrant account holders beginning on the date that is one year after the effective date of the FFI agreement.

(D) *Preexisting accounts that become high-value accounts.*—With respect to a calendar year beginning after December 31, 2015, an account holder that is described in paragraph (g)(2) of this section and that holds a preexisting account that a participating FFI identifies as a high-value account pursuant to § 1.1471-4(c)(5)(iv)(D) will be treated as a recalcitrant account holder beginning on the earlier of the date a withholdable payment is made to the account following end of the calendar year in which the account is identified as a high-value account or the date that is six months after the calendar year end.

(ii) *Accounts that are not preexisting accounts and accounts requiring name/TIN correction.*—An account holder of an account other than a preexisting account and that is described in paragraph (g)(2) of this section will be treated as a recalcitrant account holder beginning on the date that is the earlier of 90 days after the account is opened by the participating FFI or the date that a withholdable payment that is subject to withholding under § 1.1441-2(a) is made to the account. An account holder for which the participating FFI received a notice from the IRS indicating that the name and TIN combination provided for the account holder is incorrect will be treated as a recalcitrant account holder following the date of such notice within the time prescribed in § 31.3406(d)-5(a) of this chapter.

(iii) *Accounts with changes in circumstances.*—An account holder holding an account that is described in paragraph (g)(2) of this section following a change in circumstances (other than a change in account balance or value in a subsequent year that causes an individual account to be identified as a high-value account) will be treated as a recalcitrant account holder beginning on the date that is 90 days after the change in circumstances. For the definition of a change in circumstances with respect to an account, see § 1.1471-4(c)(2)(iii).

(4) *End of recalcitrant account holder status.*—An account holder that is treated as a recalcitrant account holder under paragraphs (g)(2) and (3) of this section will cease to be so treated as of the date on which the account holder is no longer described in paragraph (g)(2) of this section.

(h) *Passthru payment.*—(1) *Defined.*—The term *passthru payment* means any withholdable payment and any foreign passthru payment.

(2) *Foreign passthru payment.*—[Reserved].

(i) *Expanded affiliated group.*—(1) *Scope of paragraph.*—This paragraph (i) defines the term *expanded affiliated group* for purposes of chapter 4. For the requirements of a participating FFI with respect to members of its expanded affiliated group that are FFIs, see § 1.1471-4(e).

(2) *Expanded affiliated group defined.*—Except as otherwise provided in this paragraph (i), an expanded affiliated group is defined in accordance with the principles of section 1504(a) to mean one or more chains of members connected through ownership by a common parent entity if the common parent entity directly owns stock or other equity interests meeting the requirements of paragraph (i)(4) of this section in at least one of the other members (for purposes of this paragraph (i), the constructive ownership rules of section 318 do not

apply). Generally, only a corporation shall be treated as the common parent entity of an expanded affiliated group, unless the taxpayer elects to follow the approach described in paragraph (i)(10) of this section.

(3) *Member of an expanded affiliated group.*—The term *member of an expanded affiliated group* means a corporation or any entity other than a corporation (such as a partnership or trust) with respect to which the ownership requirements of paragraph (i)(4) of this section are met, regardless of whether such entity is a U.S. person or a foreign person, but excluding corporations described in paragraphs (1), (4), (6), (7), or (8) of section 1504(b).

(4) *Ownership test.*—The ownership requirements of this paragraph (i)(4) are met if—

(i) *Corporations.*—For purposes of paragraph (i)(2) of this section, a corporation (except the common parent entity) will be considered owned by another member entity or by the common parent entity if more than 50 percent of the total voting power of the stock of such corporation and more than 50 percent of the total value of the stock of such corporation is owned directly by one or more other members of the group (including the common parent entity).

(A) *Stock not to include certain preferred stock.*—For purposes of this paragraph (i)(4), the term *stock* does not include any stock which is described in section 1504(a)(4).

(B) *Valuation.*—For purposes of section 1471(e) and this section, all shares of stock within a single class are considered to have the same value in determining the ownership percentage. Thus, control premiums and minority blockage discounts within a single class are not taken into account.

(ii) *Partnerships.*—For purposes of paragraph (i)(2) of this section, a partnership will be considered owned by another member entity (including the common parent entity) if more than 50 percent (by value) of the capital or profits interest in the partnership is owned directly by one or more other members of the group (including the common parent entity).

(iii) *Trusts.*—For purposes of paragraph (i)(2) of this section, a trust will be considered owned by another member entity or by the common parent entity if more than 50 percent (by value) of the beneficial interest in such trust is owned directly by one or more other members of the group (including the common parent entity). A beneficial interest in a trust includes an interest held by an entity treated as a grantor or other owner of the trust under sections 671 through 679 and a beneficial trust interest.

(5) *Treatment of warrants, options, and obligations convertible into equity for determining ownership.*—For purposes of paragraph (i)(4) of this section, ownership of warrants, options, obligations convertible into the equity of a corporation or entity other than a corporation, and other similar interests is not considered for purposes of determining whether an entity is a member of an expanded affiliated group, except as follows:

(i) Ownership of a warrant, option, obligation convertible into stock, or other similar instrument creating an interest in a corporation will be considered for purposes of paragraph (i)(4) of this section to the extent that the common parent or member of the expanded affiliated group that holds such instrument also maintains voting rights with respect to such corporation. However, interests described in § 1.1504-4(d)(2) will not be treated as options.

(ii) Ownership of a warrant, option, obligation convertible into an equity interest, or other similar instrument creating an interest in a corporation or entity other than a corporation will be considered for purposes of paragraph (i)(4) of this section to the extent that such instrument is reasonably certain to be exercised, based on all of the facts and circumstances and in accordance with the principles set forth in § 1.1504-4(g).

(6) *Exception for FFIs holding certain capital investments.*—Notwithstanding paragraphs (i)(2) and (i)(4) of this section, an investment entity will not be considered a member of an expanded affiliated group as a result of a contribution of seed capital by a member of such expanded affiliated group if—

(i) The member that owns the investment entity is an FFI that is in the business of providing seed capital to form investment entities, the interests in which it intends to sell to investors that do not have a relationship with each other described in section 267(b);

(ii) The investment entity is created in the ordinary course of such other FFI's business described in paragraph (i)(6)(i) of this section;

(iii) As of the date the FFI acquired the equity interest, any equity interest in the investment entity in excess of 50 percent of the total value of the stock of the investment entity is intended to be held by such other FFI (including ownership by other members of such

other FFI's expanded affiliated group) for no more than three years from the date on which such other FFI first acquired an equity interest in the investment entity; and

(iv) In the case of an equity interest that has been held by such other FFI for over three years from the date referenced in paragraph (i)(6)(iii) of this section, the aggregate value of the equity interest held by such other FFI and the equity interests held by other members of its expanded affiliated group is 50 percent or less of the total value of the stock of the investment entity.

(7) *Seed capital.*—For purposes of this paragraph (i), the term *seed capital* means an initial capital contribution made to an investment entity that is intended as a temporary investment and is deemed by the manager of the entity to be necessary or appropriate for the establishment of the entity, such as for the purpose of establishing a track record of investment performance for such entity, achieving economies of scale for diversified investment, avoiding an artificially high expense to return ratio, or similar purposes.

(8) *Anti-abuse rule.*—A change in ownership, voting rights, or the form of an entity that results in an entity meeting or not meeting the ownership requirements described in paragraph (i)(4) of this section will be disregarded for purposes of determining whether an entity is a member of an expanded affiliated group if the change is pursuant to a plan a principal purpose of which is to avoid reporting or withholding that would otherwise be required under any chapter 4 provision. For purposes of this paragraph (i)(8), a change in voting rights includes a separation of voting rights and value.

(9) *Exception for limited life debt investment entities.*—Notwithstanding paragraphs (i)(2) and (4) of this section, an entity that meets the requirements of paragraph (f)(2)(iv) of this section, including the requirements to have been in existence as of January 17, 2013, and to have issued interests in the entity on or before January 17, 2013, will not be considered a member of an expanded affiliated group as a result of any member of such expanded affiliated group owning interests in such entity.

(10) *Partnerships, trusts, and other non-corporate entities.*—For purposes of determining the composition of an expanded affiliated group, an entity other than a corporation may elect to be treated as the common parent entity. Taxpayers following this approach may not, in a later year, follow the rule described in paragraph (i)(2) of this section without the approval of the Commissioner. See also paragraph (e)(5)(i)(C) of this section.

(j) *Sponsoring entity verification.*—(1) *In general.*—This paragraph (j) describes the requirements for a sponsoring entity of a sponsored FFI to establish and implement a compliance program for satisfying its requirements as a sponsoring entity and to provide a certification of compliance with its requirements. This paragraph (j) also describes the procedures for the IRS to review the sponsoring entity's compliance with respect to each sponsored FFI for purposes of satisfying the requirements of paragraph (f)(1)(i)(F) or (f)(2)(iii) of this section or an applicable Model 2 IGA. For purposes of a sponsoring entity's certification of compliance under this paragraph (j), a sponsoring entity must have in place a written sponsorship agreement described in paragraph (j)(6) of this section with each sponsored FFI. See paragraph (j)(3)(v)(B) of this section for the certification regarding a sponsoring entity's sponsorship agreement with each sponsored FFI.

(2) *Compliance program.*—The sponsoring entity must appoint a responsible officer to oversee the compliance of the sponsoring entity with respect to each sponsored FFI for purposes of satisfying the requirements of paragraph (f)(1)(i)(F) or (f)(2)(iii) of this section or an applicable Model 2 IGA. The responsible officer must (either personally or through designated persons) establish a compliance program that includes policies, procedures, and processes sufficient for the sponsoring entity to satisfy the requirements described in the preceding sentence. The responsible officer (or designee) must periodically review the sufficiency of the sponsoring entity's compliance program, the sponsoring entity's compliance with respect to each sponsored FFI for purposes of satisfying the requirements of paragraph (f)(1)(i)(F) or (f)(2)(iii) of this section or an applicable Model 2 IGA, and the compliance of each sponsored FFI with the due diligence, withholding, and reporting requirements of § 1.1471-4 or an applicable Model 2 IGA during the certification period described in paragraph (j)(3)(iii) of this section. The results of the periodic review must be considered by the responsible officer in making the periodic certifications described in paragraph (j)(3) of this section.

(3) *Certification of compliance.*—(i) *Certification requirement.*—(A) *In general.*—In addition to the certification required under paragraph (j)(5) of this section (preexisting account certification), and except as otherwise provided in paragraph (j)(3)(i)(B) or (j)(3)(ii) of this section, on or before July 1 of the calendar year following the certification period, the responsible officer of the sponsoring entity

must make the certification described in paragraph (j)(3)(v) of this section and either the certification described in paragraph (j)(3)(vi)(A) of this section or the certification described in paragraph (j)(3)(vi)(B) of this section with respect to all sponsored FFIs for which the sponsoring entity acts during the certification period on the form and in the manner prescribed by the IRS. To the extent that a sponsoring entity satisfies the certification requirements of paragraph (j)(3) of this section on behalf of a sponsored FFI, the sponsored FFI does not have a certification requirement under paragraph (f)(1)(ii)(B) of this section.

(B) *Extension of time for the certification period ending on December 31, 2017.*—The certifications required for a certification period ending on December 31, 2017, must be submitted on or before March 31, 2019.

(ii) *Late-joining sponsored FFIs.*—In general, with respect to a certification period, a sponsoring entity is not required to make a certification for a sponsored FFI that first agrees to be sponsored by the sponsoring entity during the six-month period before the end of the sponsoring entity's certification period, provided that the sponsoring entity makes certifications for such sponsored FFI for subsequent certification periods and the first such certification covers both the subsequent certification period and the portion of the prior certification period of the sponsoring entity during which such FFI was sponsored by the sponsoring entity. However, the preceding sentence does not apply to a sponsored FFI that, immediately before the FFI agrees to be sponsored by the sponsoring entity, was a participating FFI, registered deemed-compliant FFI, or sponsored, closely held investment vehicle of another sponsoring entity. The sponsoring entity may certify for a sponsored FFI described in the preceding sentence for the portion of the certification period of the sponsoring entity before the date that the FFI first agrees to be sponsored by the sponsoring entity if the sponsoring entity obtains from the FFI (or the FFI's sponsoring entity, if applicable) a written certification that the FFI has complied with its applicable chapter 4 requirements during such portion of the certification period, provided that: the sponsoring entity does not know that such certification is unreliable or incorrect; and the certification for the sponsored FFI for the subsequent certification period covers both the subsequent certification period and the portion of the prior certification period during which such FFI was sponsored by the sponsoring entity.

(iii) *Certification period.*—The first certification period of a sponsoring entity begins on the later of the date the sponsoring entity is issued a GIIN to act as a sponsoring entity or June 30, 2014, and ends at the close of the third full calendar year following such date. Each subsequent certification period is the three-calendar-year period following the previous certification period.

(iv) *Additional certifications or information.*—The certification of compliance described in paragraph (j)(3) of this section may be modified to include additional certifications or information (such as quantitative or factual information related to the sponsoring entity's compliance with respect to each sponsored FFI for purposes of satisfying the requirements of paragraph (f)(1)(i)(F) or (f)(2)(iii) of this section or an applicable Model 2 IGA), provided that such additional information or certifications are published at least 90 days before being made effective in order to allow for public comment.

(v) *Certifications regarding sponsoring entity and sponsored FFI requirements.*—The responsible officer of the sponsoring entity must certify to the following statements—

(A) The sponsoring entity meets all of the requirements of a sponsoring entity as described in paragraph (f)(1)(i)(F)(3) or (f)(2)(iii)(D) of this section or an applicable Model 2 IGA, including the chapter 4 status required of such entity;

(B) The sponsoring entity has a written sponsorship agreement with each sponsored FFI authorizing the sponsoring entity to fulfill the requirements of paragraph (f)(1)(i)(F) or (f)(2)(iii) of this section or an applicable Model 2 IGA with respect to each sponsored FFI; and

(C) Each sponsored FFI treated as a sponsored investment entity, a sponsored controlled foreign corporation, or a sponsored, closely held investment vehicle by the sponsoring entity meets the requirements of its respective status.

(vi) *Certifications regarding internal controls.*—(A) *Certification of effective internal controls.*—The responsible officer of the sponsoring entity must certify to the following statements—

(1) The responsible officer of the sponsoring entity has established a compliance program that is in effect as of the date of the certification and that has been subject to the review as described in paragraph (j)(2) of this section;

(2) With respect to material failures (defined in paragraph (j)(3)(vii) of this section)—

(i) There are no material failures for the certification period; or

(ii) If there were any material failures, appropriate actions were taken to remediate such failures and to prevent such failures from reoccurring; and

(3) With respect to any failure to withhold, deposit, or report to the extent required under § 1.1471-4 or an applicable Model 2 IGA with respect to any sponsored FFI for any year during the certification period, the sponsored FFI has corrected such failure by paying (or directing the sponsoring entity to pay) any taxes due (including interest and penalties) and filing (or directing the sponsoring entity to file) the appropriate return (or amended return).

(B) *Qualified certification.*—If the responsible officer of the sponsoring entity has identified an event of default (defined in paragraph (k)(1) of this section) or a material failure (defined in paragraph (j)(3)(vii) of this section) that the sponsoring entity has not corrected as of the date of the certification, the responsible officer must certify to the following statements—

(1) The responsible officer of the sponsoring entity has established a compliance program that is in effect as of the date of the certification and that has been subjected to the review as described in paragraph (j)(2) of this section;

(2) With respect to the event of default or material failure—

(i) The responsible officer (or designee) has identified an event of default; or

(ii) The responsible officer has determined that there are one or more material failures as defined in paragraph (j)(3)(vii) of this section and that appropriate actions will be taken to prevent such failures from reoccurring;

(3) With respect to any failure to withhold, deposit, or report to the extent required under § 1.1471-4 or an applicable Model 2 IGA with respect to any sponsored FFI for any year during the certification period, the sponsored FFI will correct such failure by paying (or directing the sponsoring entity to pay) any taxes due (including interest and penalties) and filing (or directing the sponsoring entity to file) the appropriate return (or amended return); and

(4) The responsible officer (or designee) will respond to any notice of default under paragraph (k)(2) of this section or will provide to the IRS a description of each material failure and a written plan to correct each such failure when requested under paragraph (j)(4) of this section.

(vii) *Material failures defined.*—A material failure is a failure of the sponsoring entity with respect to each sponsored FFI to satisfy the requirements of paragraph (f)(1)(i)(F) or (f)(2)(iii) of this section or an applicable Model 2 IGA if the failure was the result of a deliberate action on the part of one or more employees of the sponsoring entity or was an error attributable to a failure of the sponsoring entity to implement internal controls sufficient for the sponsoring entity to meet its requirements. A material failure will not constitute an event of default unless such material failure occurs in more than limited circumstances when a sponsoring entity has not substantially complied with the requirements described in the preceding sentence. Material failures include the following—

(A) With respect to any sponsored FFI, the deliberate or systematic failure of the sponsoring entity to report accounts that such sponsored FFI was required to treat as U.S. accounts, withhold on passthru payments to the extent required, deposit taxes withheld to the extent required, accurately report recalcitrant account holders (or non-consenting U.S. accounts under an applicable Model 2 IGA), or accurately report with respect to nonparticipating FFIs as required under § 1.1471-4(d)(2)(ii)(F) or an applicable Model 2 IGA;

(B) A criminal or civil penalty or sanction imposed on the sponsoring entity or any sponsored FFI (or any branch or office of the sponsoring entity or any sponsored FFI) by a regulator or other governmental authority or agency with oversight over the sponsoring entity's or sponsored FFI's compliance with the AML due diligence procedures to which it (or any branch or office thereof) is subject and that is imposed based on a failure to properly identify account holders under the requirements of those procedures;

(C) A potential future tax liability of any sponsored FFI related to its compliance (or lack thereof) with the due diligence, withholding, and reporting requirements of § 1.1471-4 or an applicable Model 2 IGA for which such sponsored FFI has established, for financial statement purposes, a tax reserve or provision;

(D) A potential contractual liability under the agreement described in paragraph (j)(3)(v)(B) of this section of the sponsoring entity to any sponsored FFI related to such sponsoring entity's compliance (or lack thereof) with paragraph (f)(1)(i)(F) or (f)(2)(iii) of this section or an applicable Model 2 IGA for which the sponsoring entity has established, for financial statement purposes, a reserve or provision; and

(E) Failure to register with the IRS as a sponsoring entity or to register each sponsored FFI required to be registered under paragraph (f)(1)(i)(F)(3)(iii) of this section or an applicable Model 2 IGA.

(4) *IRS review of compliance.*—(i) *General inquiries.*—The IRS, based upon the information reporting forms described in § 1.1471-4(d)(3)(v), (d)(5)(vii), or (d)(6)(iv) filed with the IRS (or the absence of such reporting) by the sponsoring entity for each calendar year with respect to any sponsoring FFI, may request additional information with respect to the information reported (or required to be reported) on the forms, the account statements described in § 1.1471-4(d)(4)(v) with respect to one or more sponsored FFIs, or confirmation that the FFI has no reporting requirements. The IRS may also request any additional information from the sponsoring entity (including a copy of each sponsorship agreement the sponsoring entity has entered into with each sponsored FFI) necessary to determine the compliance with the due diligence, withholding, and reporting requirements of § 1.1471-4 or an applicable Model 2 IGA with respect to each sponsored FFI and to assist the IRS with its review of account holder compliance with tax reporting requirements.

(ii) *Inquiries regarding substantial non-compliance.*—The IRS may determine in its discretion that a sponsoring entity may not have substantially complied with the requirements of paragraph (f)(1)(i)(F) or (f)(2)(iii) of this section or an applicable Model 2 IGA with respect to any sponsored FFI. This determination is based on the information reporting forms described in § 1.1471-4(d)(3)(v), (d)(5)(vii), or (d)(6)(iv) filed with the IRS by the sponsoring entity for each calendar year with respect to any sponsored FFI (or the absence of reporting), the certifications made by the responsible officer described in paragraphs (j)(3) and (5) of this section (or the absence of such certifications), or any other information related to the sponsoring entity's compliance with respect to any sponsored FFI for purposes of satisfying the requirements of paragraph (f)(1)(i)(F) or (f)(2)(iii) of this section or an applicable Model 2 IGA. In such a case, the IRS may request from the responsible officer (or designee) information necessary to verify the sponsoring entity's compliance with such requirements. The IRS may request, for example, a description or copy of the sponsoring entity's policies and procedures for fulfilling the requirements of paragraph (f)(1)(i)(F) or (f)(2)(iii) of this section or an applicable Model 2 IGA, a description or copy of the sponsoring entity's procedures for conducting its periodic review, or a copy of any written reports documenting the findings of such review. The IRS may also request the performance of specified review procedures by a person (including an external auditor or third-party consultant) that the IRS identifies as competent to perform such procedures given the facts and circumstances surrounding the sponsoring entity's potential failure to comply with respect to each sponsored FFI with the requirements of paragraph (f)(1)(i)(F) or (f)(2)(iii) of this section or an applicable Model 2 IGA.

(iii) *Compliance procedures for a sponsored FFI subject to a Model 2 IGA.*—In the case of a sponsored FFI subject to the requirements of an applicable Model 2 IGA, the procedures described in paragraph (j)(4) of this section apply, except as otherwise provided in the applicable Model 2 IGA.

(5) *Preexisting account certification.*—The responsible officer of a sponsoring entity must make the certification described in § 1.1471-4(c)(7) (preexisting account certification of a participating FFI) with respect to each sponsored FFI that enters into the sponsorship agreement with the sponsoring entity during the certification period (as defined in paragraph (j)(3)(iii) of this section). However, the preexisting account certification is not required for a sponsored FFI that, immediately before the FFI first agrees to be sponsored by the sponsoring entity, was a participating FFI, a sponsored FFI of another sponsoring entity, or a registered deemed-compliant FFI that is a local FFI or a restricted fund, if the FFI (or the FFI's former sponsoring entity, if applicable) provides a written certification to the sponsoring entity that the FFI has made the preexisting account certification required under § 1.1471-4(c)(7) or paragraph (f)(1)(i)(A)(7) or (f)(1)(i)(D)(6) of this section (as applicable), unless the sponsoring entity knows that such written certification is unreliable or incorrect. In addition, the preexisting account certification is not required for a sponsored FFI that enters into the sponsorship agreement with the sponsoring entity during the two year period before the end of the sponsoring entity's certification period, provided that the sponsoring entity makes the preexisting account certification for such FFI for the subsequent certification period. The certification described in this paragraph (j)(5) for the certification period must be submitted by the due date of the sponsoring entity's certification of compliance required under paragraph (j)(3)(i) of this section for the certification period (or the extended due date described in paragraph (j)(3)(i)(B) of this section for the certification period ending on December 31, 2017), on the form and in the manner

prescribed by the IRS. With respect to a sponsored FFI for which the sponsoring entity makes a preexisting account certification, a preexisting obligation means any account, instrument, or contract (including any debt or equity interest) maintained, executed, or issued by the sponsored FFI that is outstanding on the earlier of the date the FFI is issued a GIIN as a sponsored FFI or the date the FFI first agrees to be sponsored by the sponsoring entity.

(6) *Sponsorship agreement.*—A sponsoring entity must have a written sponsorship agreement (which may be part of another agreement between the sponsoring entity and the sponsored FFI) that refers to the requirements of a sponsored FFI under FATCA and that must be in place with each sponsored FFI for which the sponsoring entity acts by the later of March 31, 2019, or the date that the sponsoring entity begins acting as a sponsoring entity for the applicable sponsored FFI.

(k) *Sponsoring entity event of default.*—(1) *Defined.*—An event of default with regard to a sponsoring entity occurs if the sponsoring entity fails to perform material obligations required with respect to the due diligence, withholding, and reporting requirements of § 1.1471-4 or an applicable Model 2 IGA with respect to any sponsored FFI, to establish or maintain a compliance program as described in paragraph (j)(2) of this section, or to perform a periodic review described in paragraph (j)(2) of this section. An event of default also includes the occurrence of any of the following—

(i) With respect to any sponsored FFI, failure to obtain, in any case in which foreign law would (but for a waiver) prevent the reporting of U.S. accounts required under § 1.1471-4(d), valid and effective waivers from holders of U.S. accounts or failure to otherwise close or transfer such U.S. accounts as required under § 1.1471-4(i);

(ii) With respect to any sponsored FFI, failure to significantly reduce, over a period of time, the number of account holders or payees that such sponsored FFI is required to treat as recalcitrant account holders or nonparticipating FFIs, as a result of the sponsoring entity failing to comply with the due diligence procedures set forth in § 1.1471-4(c);

(iii) With respect to any sponsored FFI, failure to fulfill the requirements of § 1.1471-4(i) in any case in which foreign law prevents or otherwise limits withholding under § 1.1471-4(b);

(iv) Failure to take timely corrective actions to remedy a material failure described in paragraph (j)(3)(vii) of this section after making a qualified certification described in paragraph (j)(3)(vi)(B) of this section;

(v) Failure to make the preexisting account certification required under paragraph (j)(5) of this section or the periodic certification required under paragraph (j)(3) of this section with respect to any sponsored FFI within the specified time period;

(vi) Making incorrect claims for refund on behalf of any sponsored FFI;

(vii) Failure to cooperate with an IRS request for additional information under paragraph (j)(4) of this section;

(viii) Making any fraudulent statement or misrepresentation of material fact to the IRS or representing to a withholding agent or the IRS its status as a sponsoring entity for an entity other than an entity for which it acts as a sponsoring entity;

(ix) The sponsoring entity is no longer authorized to perform the requirements of a sponsoring entity with respect to one or more sponsored FFIs; or

(x) Failure to have the written sponsorship agreement described in paragraph (j)(3)(v)(B) of this section in effect with each sponsored FFI.

(2) *Notice of event of default.*—Following an event of default known by or disclosed by the sponsoring entity to the IRS, the IRS will deliver to the sponsoring entity a notice of default specifying the event of default and, if applicable, identifying each sponsored FFI to which the notice relates. The IRS will request that the sponsoring entity remediate the event of default within 45 days (unless additional time is requested and agreed to by the IRS). The sponsoring entity must respond to the notice of default and provide information responsive to an IRS request for information or state the reasons why the sponsoring entity does not agree that an event of default has occurred.

(3) *Remediation of event of default.*—A sponsoring entity will be permitted to remediate an event of default to the extent that it agrees with the IRS on a remediation plan. Such a plan may, for example, allow a sponsoring entity to remediate an event of default described in paragraph (k)(1) of this section with respect to a sponsored FFI by providing specific information regarding the U.S. accounts maintained by such sponsored FFI when the sponsoring entity has been unable to report all of the information with respect to such accounts as required under § 1.1471-4(d) and has been unable to close or transfer such accounts. The IRS may, as part of a remediation plan,

require additional information from the sponsoring entity or the performance of the specified review procedures described in paragraph (j)(4)(ii) of this section.

(4) *Termination.*—(i) *In general.*—If the sponsoring entity does not provide a response to a notice of default within the period specified in paragraph (k)(2) of this section or does not remediate the event of default as described in paragraph (k)(3) of this section, the IRS may deliver a notice of termination that terminates the sponsoring entity's status, the status of one or more sponsored FFIs as deemed-compliant FFIs, or the status of both the sponsoring entity and one or more sponsored FFIs.

(ii) *Termination of sponsoring entity.*—If the IRS terminates the status of the sponsoring entity, the sponsoring entity must send notice of the termination within 30 days after the date of termination to each sponsored FFI for which it acts, as well as to each withholding agent from which each sponsored FFI receives payments and each financial institution with which each sponsored FFI holds an account for which a withholding certificate or other documentation was provided. A sponsoring entity that has had its status terminated cannot register on the FATCA registration website to act as a sponsoring entity for any sponsored FFI or for any entity that is a sponsored entity under a Model 1 IGA unless it receives written approval from the IRS to register. Unless the status of a sponsored FFI has been terminated, the sponsored FFI may register on the FATCA registration website as a participating FFI or registered deemed-compliant FFI (as applicable). However, a sponsored FFI whose sponsoring entity has been terminated may not register or represent its status as a sponsored FFI of a sponsoring entity that has a relationship described in section 267(b) or 707(b) with the sponsoring entity that was terminated without receiving written approval from the IRS.

(iii) *Termination of sponsored FFI.*—If the IRS notifies the sponsoring entity that the status of a sponsored FFI is terminated (but not the sponsoring entity's status), the sponsoring entity must remove the sponsored FFI from the sponsoring entity's registration account on the FATCA registration website and send notice of the termination within 30 days after the date of termination to each withholding agent from which the sponsored FFI receives payments and each financial institution with which it holds an account for which a withholding certificate or other documentation was provided with respect to such sponsored FFI. A sponsored FFI that has had its status as a sponsored FFI terminated (independent from a termination of status of its sponsoring entity) may not register on the FATCA registration website as a participating FFI or registered deemed-compliant FFI unless it receives written approval from the IRS.

(iv) *Reconsideration of notice of default or notice of termination.*—A sponsoring entity or sponsored FFI may request, within 90 days of a notice of default or notice of termination, reconsideration of the notice of default or notice of termination by written request to the IRS.

(v) *Sponsoring entity of sponsored FFIs subject to a Model 2 IGA.*—Subject to the provisions of an applicable Model 2 IGA, the IRS may revoke the status of a sponsoring entity with respect to one or more sponsored FFIs subject to a Model 2 IGA based on the provisions of paragraphs (k)(2), (3), and (4) of this section (describing notice of event of default and termination procedures) if there is an event of default as defined in paragraph (k)(1) of this section.

(l) *Trustee-documented trust verification.*—(1) *Compliance program.*—A trustee of a trust treated as a trustee-documented trust under an applicable Model 2 IGA must establish and implement a compliance program for purposes of satisfying the requirements of an applicable Model 2 IGA with respect to each such trust. The trustee must appoint a responsible officer who must (either personally or through designated persons) establish policies, procedures, and processes sufficient for the trustee to implement the compliance program. The responsible officer (or designee) must periodically review the sufficiency of the trustee's compliance program and the trustee's compliance with respect to each trust for purposes of satisfying the requirements of an applicable Model 2 IGA for each certification period described in paragraph (l)(2) of this section. The results of the periodic review must be considered by the responsible officer in making the certification described in paragraph (l)(2) of this section.

(2) *Certification of compliance.*—(i) *Certification requirement.*—(A) *In general.*—Except as otherwise provided in paragraph (l)(2)(i)(B) or (l)(2)(ii) of this section, on or before July 1 of the calendar year following the end of the certification period, the responsible officer of the trustee must make a certification for the certification period with respect to all trustee-documented trusts described in paragraph (l)(1) of this section on the form and in the manner prescribed by the IRS.

(B) *Extension of time for the certification period ending on December 31, 2017.*—The certifications required for a certification period ending on December 31, 2017, must be submitted on or before March 31, 2019.

(ii) *Late-joining trustee-documented trusts.*—In general, with respect to a certification period, the responsible officer of a trustee is not required to make a certification for a trustee-documented trust for which the trustee first agreed to act as the trustee under Annex II of an applicable IGA during the six-month period before the end of the trustee's certification period, provided that the responsible officer of the trustee makes certifications for such trustee-documented trust for subsequent certification periods and the first such certification covers both the subsequent certification period and the portion of the prior certification period of the trustee during which the trustee acted as the trustee of the trustee-documented trust. However, the preceding sentence does not apply to a trustee-documented trust that, immediately before the trustee first agrees to act as the trustee under Annex II of an applicable IGA, was a trustee-documented trust of another trustee. The trustee of a trustee-documented trust may certify for a trustee-documented trust described in the preceding sentence for the portion of the certification period of the trustee before the date that the trustee first agrees to act as the trustee under Annex II of an applicable IGA if the trustee obtains from the trustee-documented trust (or the trust's former trustee, if applicable) a written certification that the trust has complied with its applicable chapter 4 requirements during such portion of the certification period, provided that: the trustee does not know that such certification is unreliable or incorrect; and the certification for the trustee-documented trust for the subsequent certification period covers both the subsequent certification period and the portion of the prior certification period during which the trustee acts as the trustee under Annex II of an applicable IGA.

(iii) *Certification period.*—The first certification period of the trustee begins on the later of the date the trustee is issued a GIIN to act as a trustee of a trustee-documented trust or June 30, 2014, and ends at the close of the third full calendar year following such date. Each subsequent certification period is the three-calendar-year period following the previous certification period.

(iv) *Certifications.*—The responsible officer of the trustee must certify to the following statements—

(A) The responsible officer of the trustee has established a compliance program that is in effect as of the date of the certification and has performed a periodic review described in paragraph (l)(1) of this section for the certification period; and

(B) The trustee has reported to the IRS on Form 8966, "FATCA Report" (or such other form as the IRS may prescribe), all of the information required to be reported pursuant to the applicable Model 2 IGA with respect to all U.S. accounts of each trustee-documented trust for which the trustee acts during the certification period by the due date of Form 8966 (including extensions) for each year.

(3) *IRS review of compliance by trustees of trustee-documented trusts.*—(i) *General inquiries.*—Based upon the information reporting forms filed with the IRS (or the absence of such reporting) by a trustee with respect to any trustee-documented trust subject to a Model 2 IGA for each calendar year, and subject to the requirements of an applicable Model 2 IGA, the IRS may request from the trustee additional information with respect to the information reported on the forms with respect to any trustee-documented trust or a confirmation that the trustee has no reporting requirements with respect to any trustee-documented trust. The IRS may also request any additional information to determine the trustee's compliance for purposes of satisfying the trust's requirements as a trustee-documented trust under an applicable Model 2 IGA or to assist the IRS with its review of account holder compliance with tax reporting requirements.

(ii) *Inquiries regarding substantial non-compliance.*—The IRS may determine in its discretion that the trustee may not have substantially complied with the requirements applicable to a trustee of a trustee-documented trust. This determination is based on the information reporting forms filed with the IRS by a trustee with respect to any trustee-documented trust subject to a Model 2 IGA for each calendar year (or the absence of such reporting), the certification described in paragraph (l)(2) of this section (or the absence of such certification), or any other information related to the trustee's compliance with respect to any trustee-documented trust for purposes of satisfying the trust's applicable Model 2 IGA requirements. In such a case, the IRS may request from the responsible officer information necessary to verify the trustee's compliance with such requirements. The IRS may also request the performance of specified review procedures by a person (including an external auditor or third-party consultant) that the IRS identifies as competent to perform such procedures given the circumstances surrounding the trustee's potential failure to comply with the requirements of an applicable Model 2 IGA with respect to one or more trustee-documented trusts. The IRS may notify the applicable Model 2 IGA jurisdiction that the trustee has not complied with its requirements as a trustee of one or more trustee-documented trusts.

(m) *Applicability date.*—This section generally applies beginning on January 6, 2017, except for paragraphs (f)(1)(i)(F)(3)(vi), (f)(1)(i)(F)(4), (f)(1)(iv), (f)(2)(iii)(D)(4), (f)(2)(iii)(E), (j), (k), and (l) of this section, which apply March 25, 2019. However, taxpayers may apply these provisions as of January 28, 2013. (For the rules that otherwise apply beginning on January 6, 2017, and before March 25, 2019, see this section as in effect and contained in 26 CFR part 1 revised April 1, 2018. For the rules that otherwise apply beginning on January 28, 2013, and before January 6, 2017, see this section as in effect and contained in 26 CFR part 1 revised April 1, 2016.) [Reg. § 1.1471-5.]

☐ [*T.D.* 9610, 1-17-2013 (*corrected* 9-9-2013). *Amended by T.D.* 9657, 2-28-2014, *T.D.* 9809, 12-30-2016 (*corrected* 6-29-2017) *and T.D.* 9852, 3-21-2019 (*corrected* 4-3-2019).]

**[Reg. § 1.1471-6]**

**§ 1.1471-6. Payments beneficially owned by exempt beneficial owners.**—(a) *In general.*—This section describes classes of beneficial owners that are identified in section 1471(f) (exempt beneficial owners). Except as otherwise provided in paragraphs (d) (regarding securities held by foreign central banks of issue) and (f) (regarding retirement funds) of this section, a person must be a beneficial owner of a payment to be treated as an exempt beneficial owner with respect to the payment. The following classes of persons are exempt beneficial owners: any foreign government, any political subdivision of a foreign government, or any wholly owned agency or instrumentality of any one or more of the foregoing described in paragraph (b) of this section; any international organization or any wholly owned agency or instrumentality thereof described in paragraph (c) of this section; any foreign central bank of issue described in paragraph (d) of this section; any government of a U.S. territory described in paragraph (e) of this section; certain foreign retirement funds described in paragraph (f) of this section; and certain entities described in paragraph (g) of this section that are wholly owned by one or more other exempt beneficial owners. In addition, an exempt beneficial owner includes any person treated as an exempt beneficial owner pursuant to a Model 1 IGA or Model 2 IGA. See § § 1.1471-2(a)(4)(v) and 1.1472-1(c)(2) for the exemptions from withholding for payments beneficially owned by an exempt beneficial owner; § 1.1471-3(d)(9) for the documentation requirements applicable to a withholding agent for purposes of determining when a withholdable payment is beneficially owned by an exempt beneficial owner; and § 1.1471-3(d)(8)(ii) for when a withholding agent may treat a payment made to a nonparticipating FFI as beneficially owned by an exempt beneficial owner.

(b) *Any foreign government, any political subdivision of a foreign government, or any wholly owned agency or instrumentality of any one or more of the foregoing.*—Solely for purposes of this section and except as provided in paragraph (h) of this section, the term *any foreign government, any political subdivision of a foreign government, or any wholly owned agency or instrumentality of any one or more of the foregoing* means only the integral parts, controlled entities, and political subdivisions of a foreign sovereign.

(1) *Integral part.*—Solely for purposes of this paragraph (b), an *integral part* of a foreign sovereign is any person, body of persons, organization, agency, bureau, fund, instrumentality, or other body, however designated, that constitutes a governing authority of a foreign country. The net earnings of the governing authority must be credited to its own account or to other accounts of the foreign sovereign, with no portion inuring to the benefit of any private person as defined in paragraph (b)(3) of this section. An integral part does not include any individual who is a sovereign, official, or administrator acting in a private or personal capacity. All the facts and circumstances will be taken into account in determining whether an individual is acting in a private or personal capacity.

(2) *Controlled entity.*—Solely for purposes of this paragraph (b), a *controlled entity* means an entity that is separate in form from a foreign sovereign or that otherwise constitutes a separate juridical entity, provided that—

(i) The entity is wholly owned and controlled by one or more foreign sovereigns directly or indirectly through one or more controlled entities;

(ii) The entity's net earnings are credited to its own account or to other accounts of one or more foreign sovereigns, with no portion of its income inuring to the benefit of any private person as defined in paragraph (b)(3) of this section; and

(iii) The entity's assets vest in one or more foreign sovereigns upon dissolution.

(3) *Inurement to the benefit of private persons.*—Solely for purposes of this paragraph (b)—

(i) Income does not inure to the benefit of private persons if such persons (within the meaning of section 7701(a)(1)) are the intended beneficiaries of a governmental program carried on by a foreign sovereign, and the program activities constitute governmental functions under the regulations under section 892.

(ii) Income is considered to inure to the benefit of private persons if such income benefits—

(A) Private persons through the use of a governmental entity as a conduit for personal investment;

(B) Private persons through the use of a governmental entity to conduct a commercial business, such as a commercial banking business, that provides financial services to private persons; or

(C) Private persons who divert such income from its intended use by exerting influence or control through means explicitly or implicitly approved of by the foreign sovereign.

(c) *Any international organization or any wholly owned agency or instrumentality thereof.*—Except as provided in paragraph (h) of this section, the term *any international organization or any wholly owned agency or instrumentality thereof* means any entity described in section 7701(a)(18). The term also includes any intergovernmental or supranational organization—

(1) That is comprised primarily of foreign governments;

(2) That is recognized as an intergovernmental or supranational organization under a foreign law similar to 22 U.S.C. 288-288f or that has in effect a headquarters agreement with a foreign government; and

(3) Whose income does not inure to the benefit of private persons under the principles of paragraph (b)(3)(ii) of this section, as applied to the intergovernmental or supranational organization in place of the government or governmental entity.

(d) *Foreign central bank of issue.*—(1) *In general.*—Solely for purposes of this section and except as provided in paragraph (h) of this section, the term *foreign central bank of issue* means an institution that is by law or government sanction the principal authority, other than the government itself, issuing instruments intended to circulate as currency. Such an institution is generally the custodian of the banking reserves of the country under whose law it is organized.

(2) *Separate instrumentality.*—A foreign central bank of issue may include an instrumentality that is separate from a foreign government, whether or not owned in whole or in part by a foreign government. For example, foreign banks organized along the lines of, and performing functions similar to, the Federal Reserve System qualify as foreign central banks of issue for purposes of this section.

(3) *Bank for International Settlements.*—The Bank for International Settlements is a foreign central bank of issue for purposes of this section.

(4) *Income on certain transactions.*—Solely for purposes of determining whether an entity is an exempt beneficial owner of a payment under this paragraph (d), a foreign central bank of issue is a beneficial owner with respect to income earned on cash and securities, including cash and securities held as collateral or securities held in connection with a securities lending transaction, held by the foreign central bank of issue in the ordinary course of its operations as a central bank of issue.

(e) *Governments of U.S. territories.*—Except as provided in paragraph (h) of this section, whether a person or entity constitutes a government of a U.S. territory for purposes of this section is determined by applying principles analogous to those set forth in paragraph (b) of this section.

(f) *Certain retirement funds.*—A fund is described in this paragraph (f) if it is described in paragraphs (f)(1) through (6) of this section. In addition, if a withholding agent may treat a withholdable payment as made to a payee that is a retirement fund in accordance with § 1.1471-3, then the withholding agent may also treat such retirement fund as the beneficial owner of the payment. See § 1.1471-3(d)(9)(ii).

(1) *Treaty-qualified retirement fund.*—A fund established in a country with which the United States has an income tax treaty in force, provided that the fund is entitled to benefits under such treaty on income that it derives from sources within the United States (or would be entitled to such benefits if it derived any such income) as a resident of the other country that satisfies any applicable limitation on benefits requirement, and is operated principally to administer or provide pension or retirement benefits;

(2) *Broad participation retirement fund.*—A fund established to provide retirement, disability, or death benefits, or any combination thereof, to beneficiaries that are current or former employees (or persons designated by such employees) of one or more employers in consideration for services rendered, provided that the fund—

(i) Does not have a single beneficiary with a right to more than five percent of the fund's assets;

(ii) Is subject to government regulation and provides annual information reporting about its beneficiaries to the relevant tax authorities in the country in which the fund is established or operates; and

(iii) Satisfies one or more of the following requirements—

(A) The fund is generally exempt from tax on investment income under the laws of the country in which it is established or operates due to its status as a retirement or pension plan;

(B) The fund receives at least 50 percent of its total contributions (other than transfers of assets from accounts described in § 1.1471-5(b)(2)(i)(A) (referring to retirement and pension accounts), from retirement and pension accounts described in an applicable Model 1 or Model 2 IGA, or from other retirement funds described in this paragraph (f) or in an applicable Model 1 or Model 2 IGA) from the sponsoring employers;

(C) Distributions or withdrawals from the fund are allowed only upon the occurrence of specified events related to retirement, disability, or death (except rollover distributions to accounts described in § 1.1471-5(b)(2)(i)(A) (referring to retirement and pension accounts), to retirement and pension accounts described in an applicable Model 1 or Model 2 IGA, or to other retirement funds described in this paragraph (f) or in an applicable Model 1 or Model 2 IGA), or penalties apply to distributions or withdrawals made before such specified events; or

(D) Contributions (other than certain permitted make-up contributions) by employees to the fund are limited by reference to earned income of the employee or may not exceed $50,000 annually.

(3) *Narrow participation retirement funds.*—A fund established to provide retirement, disability, or death benefits to beneficiaries that are current or former employees (or persons designated by such employees) of one or more employers in consideration for prior services rendered, provided that—

(i) The fund has fewer than 50 participants;

(ii) The fund is sponsored by one or more employers and each of these employers are not investment entities or passive NFFEs;

(iii) Employee and employer contributions to the fund (other than transfers of assets from other retirement plans described in paragraph (f)(1) of this section, from accounts described in § 1.1471-5(b)(2)(i)(A) (referring to retirement and pension accounts), or retirement and pension accounts described in an applicable Model 1 or Model 2 IGA) are limited by reference to earned income and compensation of the employee, respectively;

(iv) Participants that are not residents of the country in which the fund is established or operated are not entitled to more than 20 percent of the fund's assets; and

(v) The fund is subject to government regulation and provides annual information reporting about its beneficiaries to the relevant tax authorities in the country in which the fund is established or operates.

(4) *Fund formed pursuant to a plan similar to a section 401(a) plan.*—A fund formed pursuant to a pension plan that would meet the requirements of section 401(a), other than the requirement that the plan be funded by a trust created or organized in the United States.

(5) *Investment vehicles exclusively for retirement funds.*—A fund established exclusively to earn income for the benefit of one or more retirement funds described in paragraphs (f)(1) through (5) of this section or in an applicable Model 1 or Model 2 IGA, accounts described in § 1.1471-5(b)(2)(i)(A) (referring to retirement and pension accounts), or retirement and pension accounts described in an applicable Model 1 or Model 2 IGA.

(6) *Pension fund of an exempt beneficial owner.*—A fund established and sponsored by an exempt beneficial owner described in paragraph (b), (c), (d), or (e) of this section or an exempt beneficial owner (other than a fund that qualifies as an exempt beneficial owner) described in an applicable Model 1 or Model 2 IGA to provide retirement, disability, or death benefits to beneficiaries or participants that are current or former employees of the exempt beneficial owner (or persons designated by such employees), or that are not current or former employees, but the benefits provided to such beneficiaries or participants are in consideration of personal services performed for the exempt beneficial owner.

(7) *Example.*—FP, a foreign pension fund established in Country X, is generally exempt from income taxation in Country X, and is operated principally to provide retirement benefits in such country. The U.S.-Country X income tax treaty is identical in all material respects to the 2006 U.S. model income tax convention. FP is a resident of Country X under Article 4(2)(a) and a qualified person under Article 22(2)(d) of the U.S.-Country X income tax treaty. Therefore, FP is a pension fund described in paragraph (f)(1) of this section.

(g) *Entities wholly owned by exempt beneficial owners.*—A person is described in this paragraph (g) if it is an FFI solely because it is an investment entity, each direct holder of an equity interest in the investment entity is an exempt beneficial owner described in paragraph (b), (c), (d), (e), (f), or (g) of this section or an exempt beneficial owner described in an applicable Model 1 or Model 2 IGA, and each direct holder of a debt interest in the investment entity is either a depository institution (with respect to a loan made to such entity), an exempt beneficial owner described in paragraph (b), (c), (d), (e), (f), or (g) of this section, or an exempt beneficial owner described in an applicable Model 1 or Model 2 IGA.

(h) *Exception for commercial activities.*—(1) *General rule.*—An exempt beneficial owner described in paragraph (b), (c), (d), or (e) of this section will not be treated as an exempt beneficial owner with respect to a payment that is derived from an obligation held in connection with a commercial financial activity of a type engaged in by an insurance company, custodial institution, or depository institution (including the accepting of deposits). Thus, for example, a central bank of issue that conducts a commercial financial activity, such as acting as an intermediary on behalf of persons other than in the bank's capacity as a central bank of issue, is not an exempt beneficial owner under paragraph (d)(1) of this section with respect to payments received in connection with an account held in connection with such activity.

(2) *Limitation.*—Paragraph (h)(1) of this section will not apply to treat an exempt beneficial owner as engaged in a commercial financial activity if—

(i) The entity undertakes commercial financial activity described in paragraph (h)(1) of this section solely for or at the direction of other exempt beneficial owners and such commercial financial activity is consistent with the purposes of the entity;

(ii) The entity has no outstanding debt that would be a financial account under § 1.1471-5(b)(1)(iii); and

(iii) The entity otherwise maintains financial accounts only for exempt beneficial owners, or, in the case of a foreign central bank of issue as described in paragraph (d), the entity only maintains financial accounts that are depository accounts for current or former employees of the entity (and the spouses and children of such employees) or financial accounts for exempt beneficial owners.

(i) *Effective/applicability date.*—This section applies on January 6, 2017. However, taxpayers may apply these provisions as of January 28, 2013. (For the rules that apply beginning on January 28, 2013, and before January 6, 2017, see this section as in effect and contained in 26 CFR part 1 revised April 1, 2016.) [Reg. § 1.1471-6.]

☐ [*T.D.* 9610, 1-17-2013 (*corrected* 9-9-2013). *Amended by T.D.* 9657, 2-28-2014 *and T.D.* 9809, 12-30-2016.]

### [Reg. § 1.1472-1]

**§ 1.1472-1. Withholding on NFFEs.**—(a) *In general.*—This section provides rules that a withholding agent must apply to determine its obligations to withhold under section 1472 on withholdable payments made to a payee that is a NFFE. A participating FFI that complies with its withholding obligations under § 1.1471-4(b) will be deemed to satisfy its obligations under section 1472 with respect to withholdable payments made to NFFEs that are account holders. The rules of this section will apply, however, in the case of a participating FFI acting as a withholding agent with respect to a payment made to a NFFE that is not an account holder (for example, a payment with respect to a contract that does not constitute a financial account). See § 1.1473-1(a)(4)(vi), however, for rules excepting from the definition of withholdable payment certain payments of U.S. source FDAP income made prior to January 1, 2017, with respect to an offshore obligation and § 1.1471-2(b) for rules excepting from the definition of withholdable payment a grandfathered obligation. See also § 1.1471-2(a)(2)(ii), (iv), (v), and (vi) for special rules of withholding that apply for purposes of this section and § 1.1471-2(a)(5) for withholding requirements if the source or character of a payment is unknown. The following entities are deemed to satisfy their withholding obligations under section 1472: exempt beneficial owners; section 501(c) entities described in § 1.1471-5(e)(5)(v); and nonprofit organizations described in § 1.1471-5(e)(5)(vi). See § 1.1471-5(f) for when a deemed-compliant FFI is deemed to satisfy its withholding obligations with respect to payments made to NFFEs that are account holders under section 1472.

(b) *Withholdable payments made to an NFFE.*—(1) *In general.*—Except as otherwise provided in paragraph (b)(2) of this section (providing transitional relief) or paragraph (c)(1) or (2) of this section (providing exceptions for payments to an excepted NFFE or an exempt beneficial owner), §1.1471-2(a)(4)(i) (providing an exception to withholding if the withholding agent lacks control, custody, or knowledge), §1.1471-2(a)(4)(vii) (providing an exception to withholding for payments made to an account held with or equity interests traded through a clearing organization with FATCA-compliant membership), or §1.1471-2(a)(4)(viii) (providing an exception to withholding for payments to certain excepted accounts), a withholding agent must withhold 30 percent of any withholdable payment made after June 30, 2014, to a payee that is a NFFE unless—

(i) The beneficial owner of such payment is the NFFE or any other NFFE;

(ii) The withholding agent can, pursuant to paragraph (d) of this section, treat the beneficial owner of the payment as an NFFE that does not have any substantial U.S. owners, or as an NFFE that has identified its substantial U.S. owners; and

(iii) The withholding agent reports the information described in §1.1474-1(i)(2) relating to any substantial U.S. owners of the beneficial owner of such payment.

(2) *Transitional relief.*—For any withholdable payment made prior to July 1, 2016, with respect to a preexisting obligation to a payee that is not a prima facie FFI and for which a withholding agent does not have documentation indicating the payee's status as a passive NFFE when the NFFE has failed to provide the owner certification as required under §1.1471-3(d)(12)(iii), the withholding agent is not required to withhold under this section or report under §1.1474-1(i)(2) (describing the reporting obligations of withholding agents with respect to NFFEs).

(c) *Exceptions.*—(1) *Payments to an excepted NFFE.*—A withholding agent is not required to withhold under section 1472(a) and paragraph (b) of this section on a withholdable payment (or portion thereof) if the withholding agent can treat the payment as made to a payee that is an excepted NFFE. For purposes of this paragraph, the term *excepted NFFE* means a payee that the withholding agent may treat as a NFFE that is a QI, WP, or WT. Additionally, the term *excepted NFFE* means, with respect to the payment, a NFFE described in paragraphs (c)(1)(i) through (vii) of this section to the extent the withholding agent may treat the NFFE as the beneficial owner of the payment.

(i) *Publicly traded corporation.*—A NFFE is described in this paragraph (c)(1)(i) if it is a corporation the stock of which is regularly traded on one or more established securities markets for the calendar year.

(A) *Regularly traded.*—For purposes of this section, stock of a corporation is *regularly traded* on one or more established securities markets for a calendar year if—

(1) One or more classes of stock of the corporation that, in the aggregate, represent more than 50 percent of the total combined voting power of all classes of stock of such corporation entitled to vote and of the total value of the stock of such corporation are listed on such market or markets during the prior calendar year; and

(2) With respect to each class relied on to meet the more-than-50-percent listing requirement of paragraph (c)(1)(i)(A)(1) of this section—

(i) Trades in each such class are effected, other than in de minimis quantities, on such market or markets on at least 60 days during the prior calendar year; and

(ii) The aggregate number of shares in each such class that are traded on such market or markets during the prior year are at least 10 percent of the average number of shares outstanding in that class during the prior calendar year.

(B) *Special rules regarding the regularly traded requirement.*—(1) *Year of initial public offering.*—For the calendar year in which a corporation initiates a public offering of a class of stock for trading on one or more established securities markets, as defined in paragraph (c)(1)(i)(C) of this section, such class of stock meets the requirements of this paragraph (c)(1)(i) for such year if the stock is regularly traded in more than de minimis quantities on 1/6 of the days remaining after the date of the offering in the quarter during which the offering occurs, and on at least 15 days during each remaining quarter of the calendar year. If a corporation initiates a public offering of a class of stock in the fourth quarter of the calendar year, such class of stock meets the requirements of this paragraph (c)(1)(i) in the calendar year of the offering if the stock is regularly traded on such established securities market, other than in de minimis quantities, on the greater of 1/6 of the days remaining after the date of the offering in the quarter during which the offering occurs, or 5 days.

(2) *Classes of stock treated as meeting the regularly traded requirement.*—A class of stock meets the trading requirements of this paragraph (c)(1)(i) for a calendar year if the stock is traded during such year on an established securities market located in the United States and is regularly quoted by dealers making a market in the stock. A dealer makes a market in a stock only if the dealer regularly and actively offers to, and in fact does, purchase the stock from, and sell the stock to, customers who are not related persons (as defined in section 954(d)(3)) with respect to the dealer in the ordinary course of a trade or business.

(3) *Anti-abuse rule.*—Any trade conducted with a principal purpose of meeting the regularly traded requirements of this paragraph (c)(1)(i) shall be disregarded. Further, a class of stock shall not be treated as regularly traded if there is a pattern of trades conducted to meet the requirements of this paragraph (c)(1)(i). Similarly, paragraph (c)(1)(i)(B)(1) of this section shall not apply to a public offering of stock that has as one of its principal purposes qualification of the class of stock as regularly traded under the reduced regularly traded requirements for the calendar year of an initial public offering. For purposes of applying the immediately preceding sentence, consideration will be given to whether the regularly traded requirements of this paragraph (c)(1)(i) are satisfied in the calendar year immediately following the initial public offering.

(C) *Established securities market.*—(1) *In general.*—For purposes of this paragraph (c)(1)(i), the term *established securities market* means, for any calendar year—

(i) A foreign securities exchange that is officially recognized, sanctioned, or supervised by a governmental authority of the foreign country in which the market is located, and has an annual value of shares traded on the exchange (or a predecessor exchange) exceeding $1 billion during each of the three calendar years immediately preceding the calendar year in which the determination is being made;

(ii) A national securities exchange that is registered under section 6 of the Securities Exchange Act of 1934 (15 USC 78f) with the Securities and Exchange Commission;

(iii) Any exchange designated under a Limitation on Benefits article of an income tax treaty with the United States that is in force; or

(iv) Any other exchange that the Secretary may designate in published guidance.

(2) *Foreign exchange with multiple tiers.*—If an exchange in a foreign country has more than one tier or market level on which stock may be separately listed or traded, each such tier shall be treated as a separate exchange.

(3) *Computation of dollar value of stock traded.*—For purposes of paragraph (c)(1)(i)(C)(1)(i) of this section, the value in U.S. dollars of shares traded during a calendar year shall be determined on the basis of the dollar value of such shares traded as reported by the World Federation of Exchanges located in Paris (or a successor institution), or, if not so reported, by converting into U.S. dollars the aggregate value in local currency of the shares traded using an exchange rate equal to the average of the spot rates on the last day of each month of the calendar year.

(ii) *Certain affiliated entities related to a publicly traded corporation.*—A NFFE is described in this paragraph (c)(1)(ii) if it is a corporation that is a member of the same expanded affiliated group (as defined in §1.1471-5(i)) as a corporation described in paragraph (c)(1)(i) of this section (without regard to whether such corporation is a NFFE).

(iii) *Certain territory entities.*—A NFFE is described in this paragraph (c)(1)(iii) if it is a territory entity that is directly or indirectly wholly owned by one or more bona fide residents of the U.S. territory under the laws of which the entity is organized. The term *bona fide resident of a U.S. territory* means an individual who qualifies as a bona fide resident under section 937(a) and §1.937-1.

(iv) *Active NFFEs.*—A NFFE is described in this paragraph (c)(1)(iv) (and thus constitutes an active NFFE) if it is an entity and for the preceding calendar or fiscal year less than 50 percent of its gross income is passive income and the weighted average of the percentage of assets held by it that produce or are held for the production of passive income (weighted by total assets and measured quarterly) is less than 50 percent, as determined after the application of paragraph (c)(1)(iv)(B) of this section (passive assets). For purposes of the calculations described in the preceding sentence, a NFFE may use any accounting method permitted under paragraph (c)(1)(iv)(C) of this section but must apply a uniform method for measuring assets for the calendar or fiscal year.

(A) *Passive income.*—Except as provided in paragraph (c)(1)(iv)(B) of this section, the term *passive income* means the portion of gross income that consists of—

(1) Dividends, including substitute dividend amounts;

(2) Interest;

(3) Income equivalent to interest, including substitute interest and amounts received from or with respect to a pool of insurance contracts if the amounts received depend in whole or part upon the performance of the pool;

(4) Rents and royalties, other than rents and royalties derived in the active conduct of a trade or business conducted, at least in part, by employees of the NFFE;

(5) Annuities;

(6) The excess of gains over losses from the sale or exchange of property that gives rise to passive income described in paragraphs (c)(1)(iv)(A)(1) through (5) of this section;

(7) The excess of gains over losses from transactions (including futures, forwards, and similar transactions) in any commodities, but not including—

(i) Any commodity hedging transaction described in section 954(c)(5)(A), determined by treating the entity as a controlled foreign corporation; or

(ii) Active business gains or losses from the sale of commodities, but only if substantially all the foreign entity's commodities are property described in paragraph (1), (2), or (8) of section 1221(a);

(8) The excess of foreign currency gains over foreign currency losses (as defined in section 988(b)) attributable to any section 988 transaction;

(9) Net income from notional principal contracts as defined in § 1.446-3(c)(1);

(10) Amounts received under cash value insurance contracts; or

(11) Amounts earned by an insurance company in connection with its reserves for insurance and annuity contracts.

(B) *Exceptions from passive income treatment.*—Notwithstanding paragraph (c)(1)(iv)(A) of this section, the term *passive income* does not include—

(1) Any income from interest, dividends, rents, or royalties that is received or accrued from a related person to the extent such amount is properly allocable to income of such related person that is not passive income. For purposes of this paragraph (c)(1)(iv)(B)(1), the term "related person" has the meaning given such term by section 954(d)(3) determined by substituting "foreign entity" for "controlled foreign corporation" each place it appears in section 954(d)(3); or

(2) In the case of a foreign entity that regularly acts as a dealer in property described in paragraph (c)(1)(iv)(A)(6) of this section (referring to the sale or exchange of property that gives rise to passive income), forward contracts, option contracts, or similar financial instruments (including notional principal contracts and all instruments referenced to commodities)—

(i) Any item of income or gain (other than any dividends or interest) from any transaction (including hedging transactions and transactions involving physical settlement) entered into in the ordinary course of such dealer's trade or business as such a dealer; and

(ii) If such dealer is a dealer in securities (within the meaning of section 475(c)(2)), any income from any transaction entered into in the ordinary course of such trade or business as a dealer in securities.

(C) *Methods of measuring assets.*—For purposes of this paragraph (c)(1)(iv), the value of a NFFE's assets is determined based on the fair market value or book value of the assets that is reflected on the NFFE's balance sheet (as determined under either a U.S. or an international financial accounting standard).

(v) *Excepted nonfinancial entities.*—A NFFE is described in this paragraph (c)(1)(v) if it is an entity described in § 1.1471-5(e)(5) (referring to holding companies, treasury centers, and captive finance companies that are members of a nonfinancial group; start-up companies; entities that are liquidating or emerging from bankruptcy; and non-profit organizations).

(vi) *Direct reporting NFFEs.*—A NFFE is described in this paragraph (c)(1)(vi) if it meets the requirements described in § 1.1472-1(c)(3) to be treated as a direct reporting NFFE.

(vii) *Sponsored direct reporting NFFEs.*—A NFFE is described in this paragraph (c)(1)(vii) if it meets the requirements described in § 1.1472-1(c)(5) to be treated as a sponsored direct reporting NFFE.

(2) *Payments made to an exempt beneficial owner.*—A withholding agent is not required to withhold on a withholdable payment (or

portion thereof) under section 1472(a) and paragraph (b) of this section if the withholding agent may treat the payment as made to an exempt beneficial owner.

(3) *Definition of direct reporting NFFE.*—A direct reporting NFFE means a NFFE that elects to report information about its direct or indirect substantial U.S. owners to the IRS and meets the following requirements—

(i) The NFFE must register on Form 8957, "FATCA Registration," (or such other form as the IRS may prescribe) with the IRS to obtain a GIIN pursuant to the procedures prescribed by the IRS;

(ii) The NFFE must report directly to the IRS on Form 8966, "FATCA Report," (or such other form as the IRS may prescribe) the following information for each calendar year (or, may be required by the IRS to certify on Form 8966, or in such other manner as the IRS may prescribe, that the NFFE has no substantial U.S. owners):

(A) The name, address, and TIN of each substantial U.S. owner (as defined in § 1.1473-1(b)) of such NFFE;

(B) The total of all payments made to each substantial U.S. owner (including the gross amounts paid or credited to the substantial U.S. owner with respect to such owner's equity interest in the NFFE during the calendar year, which include payments in redemption or liquidation (in whole or part) of the substantial U.S. owner's equity interest in the NFFE);

(C) The value of each substantial U.S. owner's equity interest in the NFFE determined by applying the rules described in § 1.1471-5(b)(4) (substituting the term *equity* for the terms *account* and *financial account*);

(D) The name, address, and GIIN of the NFFE; and

(E) Any other information as required by Form 8966 (or such other form as the IRS may prescribe) and its accompanying instructions;

(iii) The NFFE must obtain a written certification (contained on a withholding certificate or in a written statement) from each person that would be treated as a substantial U.S. owner of the NFFE if such person were a specified U.S. person. Such written certification must indicate whether the person is a substantial U.S. owner of the NFFE, and if so, the name, address and TIN of the person. If the NFFE has reason to know that such written certification is unreliable or incorrect, it must contact the person and request a revised written certification. If no revised written certification is received, the NFFE must treat the person as a substantial U.S. owner and report on Form 8966 the information required under paragraph (c)(3)(ii) of this section. The NFFE has reason to know that such a written certification is unreliable or incorrect if the certification is inconsistent with information in the NFFE's possession, including information that the NFFE provides to a financial institution in order for the financial institution to meet its AML or other account identification due diligence procedures with respect to the NFFE's account, information that is publicly available, or U.S. indicia as described in § 1.1441-7(b) for which appropriate documentation sufficient to cure the U.S. indicia in the manner set forth in § 1.1441-7(b)(8) has not been obtained;

(iv) The NFFE must keep records that it produces in the ordinary course of its business that summarize the activity (including the gross amounts described in paragraph (c)(3)(ii)(B) of this section that are paid or credited to each of its substantial U.S. owners) relating to its transactions with respect to the equity of the NFFE held by each of its substantial U.S. owners for any calendar year in which the owner was required to be reported under paragraph (c)(3)(ii) of this section. The records must be retained for the longer of six years or the retention period under the NFFE's normal business procedures. A NFFE may be required to extend the six year retention period if the IRS requests such an extension prior to the expiration of the six year period;

(v) The NFFE must respond to requests made by the IRS for additional information with respect to any substantial U.S. owner that is subject to reporting by the NFFE or with respect to the records described in paragraph (c)(3)(iii) or (iv) of this section;

(vi) The NFFE must make a periodic certification to the IRS on or before July 1 of the calendar year following the end of each certification period relating to its compliance with respect to the election described in paragraphs (c)(3) and (4) of this section on the form and in the manner prescribed by the IRS. The first certification period begins on the later of the date a GIIN is issued or June 30, 2014, and ends at the close of the third full calendar year following that date. Each subsequent certification period is the three calendar year period following the close of the previous certification period. The certification will require an officer of the NFFE to certify to the following statements—

(A)(1) The NFFE has not had any events of default described in paragraph (c)(4)(v) of this section; or

(2) If there are any events of default, appropriate measures were taken to remediate such failures and to prevent such failures from recurring; and

(B) With respect to any failure to report to the extent required under paragraph (c)(3)(ii), the NFFE has corrected such failure by filing the appropriate information returns; and

(vii) The NFFE has not had its status as a direct reporting NFFE revoked by the IRS.

(4) *Election to be treated as a direct reporting NFFE.*—(i) *Manner of making election.*—A NFFE may elect to be treated as a direct reporting NFFE by registering on Form 8957 (or such other form as the IRS may prescribe) with the IRS to obtain a GIIN pursuant to the procedures prescribed by the IRS.

(ii) *Effective date of election.*—The election is effective upon the issuance of a GIIN to the NFFE.

(iii) *Revocation of election by NFFE.*—The election may be revoked by the NFFE by canceling its registration account on the FATCA registration website and notifying the IRS of its revocation in such manner as the IRS may prescribe in the Instructions for Form 8966, "FATCA Report." The NFFE must also notify within 30 days its sponsoring entity (if applicable) and each withholding agent and financial institution from which it receives payments or with which it holds an account for which a withholding certificate or written statement prescribed in §1.1471-3(d)(11)(x)(B) (as applicable) was provided on which the NFFE certified its status as a direct reporting NFFE if it revokes its election.

(iv) *Revocation of election by Commissioner.*—The election may be revoked by the Commissioner upon an event of default described in paragraph (c)(4)(v) of this section and following the notice and remediation procedures described in paragraphs (vi) and (vii) of this section. If the Commissioner revokes the NFFE's status as a direct reporting NFFE, the NFFE must provide notification within 30 days of the revocation to each withholding agent and financial institution from which the NFFE receives payments or with which it holds an account for which a withholding certificate or written statement (as permitted for chapter 4 purposes) was provided by the NFFE to represent its status as a direct reporting NFFE.

(v) *Event of default.*—An event of default occurs if a direct reporting NFFE fails to perform any of the obligations described in (c)(3)(i) through (vi) of this section. An event of default also includes any misrepresentation of a material fact to the IRS.

(vi) *Notice of event of default.*—Following an event of default known by or disclosed to the IRS, the IRS will deliver to the NFFE a notice of default specifying the event of default. The IRS will request that the NFFE remediate the event of default within a specified time period. The NFFE must respond to the notice of default and provide information responsive to an IRS request for information or state the reasons why the NFFE does not agree that an event of default has occurred. If the NFFE does not provide a response within the specified time period, the IRS may, at its sole discretion, deliver a notice to the NFFE that its election to be treated as a direct reporting NFFE has been revoked. A NFFE may request, within 90 days of receipt, reconsideration of a notice of default or notice of revocation by written request to the IRS.

(vii) *Remediation of event of default.*—A NFFE will be permitted to remediate an event of default to the extent it agrees with the IRS on a remediation plan. The IRS may, as part of a remediation plan, require additional information from the NFFE.

(5) *Election by a direct reporting NFFE to be treated as a sponsored direct reporting NFFE.*—(i) *Definition of sponsored direct reporting NFFE.*—A NFFE is a sponsored direct reporting NFFE if the NFFE is a direct reporting NFFE and if another entity, other than a nonparticipating FFI, has agreed with the NFFE to act as its sponsoring entity, as described in paragraph (c)(5)(ii) of this section.

(ii) *Requirements for sponsoring entity of a sponsored direct reporting NFFE.*—A sponsoring entity meets the requirements of this paragraph (c)(5)(ii) if the sponsoring entity—

(A) Is authorized to act on behalf of the NFFE;

(B) Has registered with the IRS as a sponsoring entity;

(C) Has registered the NFFE with the IRS as a sponsored direct reporting NFFE by the later of January 1, 2017, or the date that the NFFE identifies itself to a withholding agent or financial institution as qualifying as a sponsored direct reporting NFFE under paragraph (c)(5) of this section;

(D) Agrees to perform, on behalf of the NFFE, all due diligence, reporting, and other requirements that the NFFE would have been required to perform as a direct reporting NFFE;

(E) Identifies the NFFE in all reporting completed on the NFFE's behalf;

(F) Complies with the certification and other requirements in paragraphs (f) and (g) of this section;

(G) Has not had its status as a sponsoring entity revoked; and

(H) Agrees to notify all relevant withholding agents and the IRS if its status as a sponsoring entity is revoked, if it otherwise ceases to be the sponsoring entity of any of its sponsored direct reporting NFFEs (for example, if the sponsored direct reporting NFFE changes sponsors), or if the status of any of its sponsored direct reporting NFFEs has been revoked.

(iii) *Revocation of status as sponsoring entity.*—The IRS may revoke a sponsoring entity's status as a sponsoring entity with respect to all sponsored direct reporting NFFEs if there is an event of default as defined in paragraph (g) of this section with respect to any sponsored direct reporting NFFE.

(iv) *Liability of sponsoring entity.*—A sponsoring entity is not liable for any failure to comply with the obligations contained in paragraph (c)(5)(ii) of this section. A sponsored direct reporting NFFE will remain liable for all of its chapter 4 obligations without regard to any failure of its sponsoring entity to comply with the obligations contained in paragraph (c)(5)(ii) of this section that the sponsoring entity has agreed to undertake on behalf of the NFFE.

(d) *Rules for determining payee and beneficial owner.*—(1) *In general.*—For purposes of this section, except in the case of a payee that is a QI, WP, or WT, a withholding agent may treat a withholdable payment as beneficially owned by the payee as determined under §1.1471-3. Thus, a withholding agent may treat a withholdable payment as beneficially owned by an excepted NFFE (other than a QI, WP, or WT) if the withholding agent can reliably associate the payment with valid documentation to determine the payee's status as an excepted NFFE under the rules of §1.1471-3(d).

(2) *Payments made to a NFFE that is a QI, WP, or WT.*—A withholding agent may treat the payee of a withholdable payment as a NFFE that is a QI, WP, or WT if the withholding agent can reliably associate the payment with valid documentation to determine the payee's status as such under the rules of §1.1471-3(b)(3) and (d).

(3) *Payments made to a partner or beneficiary of an NFFE that is an NWP or NWT.*—A withholding agent may treat a partner or beneficiary of an NFFE that is an NWP or NWT, respectively, as the payee of a withholdable payment under this section if the withholding agent can reliably associate the payment with a valid Form W-8 or written notification that the NFFE is a flow-through entity as described in §1.1471-3(c)(2), including valid documentation sufficient to establish the chapter 4 status of each payee of the payment that is a partner or beneficiary, respectively, by applying the rules described in §1.1471-3(d).

(4) *Payments made to a beneficial owner that is an NFFE.*—A withholding agent may treat the beneficial owner of a withholdable payment as an NFFE that does not have any substantial U.S. owners or that has identified all of its substantial U.S. owners if it can reliably associate the payment with valid documentation identifying the beneficial owner as an NFFE that does not have any substantial U.S. owners or that has identified all of its substantial U.S. owners by applying the rules described in §1.1471-3(d).

(5) *Absence of valid documentation.*—A withholding agent that cannot reliably associate the payment with documentation as described in any of paragraphs (d)(2) through (4) of this section must treat the payment as made to a payee in accordance with the presumption rules under §1.1471-3(f).

(e) *Information reporting requirements.*—(1) *Reporting on withholdable payments.*—A withholding agent that treats a withholdable payment as made to any payee described in paragraph (d) of this section must provide information about such payee on Form 1042-S and file a withholding income tax return on Form 1042 to the extent required under §1.1474-1(d) and (c), respectively.

(2) *Reporting on substantial U.S. owners.*—A withholding agent that receives information about any substantial U.S. owners of an NFFE that is not an excepted NFFE must report information about the NFFE's substantial U.S. owners in accordance with §1.1474-1(i)(2). See §1.1471-4(d) for the reporting requirements of a participating FFI with respect to the substantial U.S. owners of account holders that are NFFEs.

(f) *Sponsoring entity verification.*—(1) *In general.*—This paragraph (f) describes the requirements for a sponsoring entity to provide a certification of compliance with respect to each sponsored direct reporting NFFE for purposes of satisfying the requirements of paragraph (c)(5) of this section and defines the certification period for such certifications. This paragraph (f) also describes the procedures for the IRS to review the sponsoring entity's compliance with such requirements during the certification period. Finally, this paragraph

(f) describes the requirement that a sponsoring entity have in place a written sponsorship agreement with each sponsored direct reporting NFFE for which it acts and specifies the terms of such agreement. See paragraph (g)(1)(i) of this section, describing an event of default for a sponsoring entity that does not have a sponsorship agreement with each sponsored direct reporting NFFE for which it acts as a sponsoring entity. References in this paragraph (f) or paragraph (g) of this section to a sponsored direct reporting NFFE mean a sponsored direct reporting NFFE for which the sponsoring entity acts as a sponsoring entity under paragraph (c)(5)(ii) of this section.

(2) *Certification of compliance.*—(i) *Certification requirement.*— (A) *In general.*—The sponsoring entity must appoint a responsible officer to oversee the sponsoring entity's compliance with respect to each sponsored direct reporting NFFE for purposes of satisfying the requirements of paragraph (c)(5) of this section. Except as otherwise provided in paragraph (f)(2)(i)(B) or (f)(2)(ii) of this section, on or before July 1 of the calendar year following the certification period, the responsible officer of the sponsoring entity must make a certification for the certification period with respect to all sponsored direct reporting NFFEs for which the sponsoring entity acts during the certification period on the form and in the manner prescribed by the IRS. To the extent that a sponsoring entity satisfies the certification requirements of paragraph (f)(2) of this section on behalf of a sponsored direct reporting NFFE, the NFFE does not have a certification requirement under paragraph (c)(3)(vi) of this section.

(B) *Extension of time for the certification period ending on December 31, 2017.*—The certifications required for a certification period ending on December 31, 2017, must be submitted on or before March 31, 2019.

(ii) *Late-joining sponsored direct reporting NFFEs.*—In general, with respect to a certification period, a sponsoring entity is not required to make a certification for a sponsored direct reporting NFFE that first agrees to be sponsored by the sponsoring entity during the six-month period before the end of the sponsoring entity's certification period, provided that the sponsoring entity makes certifications for such sponsored direct reporting NFFE for subsequent certification periods, and the first such certification covers both the subsequent certification period and the portion of the prior certification period of the sponsoring entity during which the sponsored direct reporting NFFE was sponsored by the sponsoring entity. However, the preceding sentence does not apply to a sponsored direct reporting NFFE that, immediately before the NFFE agrees to be sponsored by the sponsoring entity, was a direct reporting NFFE or sponsored direct reporting NFFE of another sponsoring entity. The sponsoring entity may certify for a sponsored direct reporting NFFE described in the preceding sentence for the portion of the certification period of the sponsoring entity before the date that the NFFE first agrees to be sponsored by the sponsoring entity if the sponsoring entity obtains from the NFFE (or the NFFE's sponsoring entity, if applicable) a written certification that the NFFE has complied with its applicable chapter 4 requirements during such portion of the certification period, provided that: the sponsoring entity does not know that such certification is unreliable or incorrect; and the certification for the sponsored direct reporting NFFE for the subsequent certification period covers both the subsequent certification period and the portion of the prior certification period during which such NFFE was sponsored by the sponsoring entity.

(iii) *Certification period.*—The first certification period of a sponsoring entity begins on the later of the date the sponsoring entity is issued a GIIN to act as a sponsoring entity or June 30, 2014, and ends at the close of the third full calendar year after such date. Each subsequent certification period is the three-calendar-year period following the close of the previous certification period.

(iv) *Certifications.*—The certification will require the responsible officer of the sponsoring entity to certify to the following statements—

(A) The sponsoring entity meets all of the requirements of a sponsoring entity described in paragraph (c)(5)(ii) of this section;

(B) The sponsoring entity has the written sponsorship agreement described in paragraph (f)(4) of this section in effect with each sponsored direct reporting NFFE;

(C) There were no events of default (as defined in paragraph (g) of this section) with respect to the sponsoring entity, or, to the extent there were any such events of default, appropriate measures were taken by the sponsoring entity to remediate and prevent such events from reoccurring; and

(D) With respect to any failure to report to the extent required under paragraph (c)(3)(ii) of this section with respect to one or more sponsored direct reporting NFFEs, the sponsoring entity has corrected such failure by filing the appropriate information returns.

(3) *IRS review of compliance.*—(i) *General inquiries.*—The IRS, based upon the information reporting forms described in paragraph (c)(3)(ii) of this section filed with the IRS (or the absence of such reporting) by the sponsoring entity for each calendar year with respect to any sponsored direct reporting NFFE, may request additional information with respect to the information reported (or required to be reported) on the forms about any substantial U.S. owner reported on the form or the records for each direct reporting NFFE described in paragraph (c)(3)(iv) of this section. The IRS may also request any additional information from the sponsoring entity (including a copy of each sponsorship agreement the sponsoring entity has entered into with each sponsored FFI) to determine its compliance with paragraph (f) of this section with respect to each sponsored direct reporting NFFE and to assist the IRS with its review of any substantial U.S. owners' compliance with tax reporting requirements.

(ii) *Inquiries regarding substantial non-compliance.*—The IRS may determine in its discretion that a sponsoring entity may not have substantially complied with the requirements of a sponsoring entity with respect to each sponsored direct reporting NFFE for purposes of satisfying the requirements of paragraph (c)(5) of this section. This determination is based on the information reporting forms referenced in paragraph (c)(3)(ii) of this section filed with the IRS by the sponsoring entity for each calendar year with respect to any sponsored direct reporting NFFE (or the absence of such reporting), the certification made by the responsible officer described in paragraph (f)(2) of this section (or the absence of such certification), or any other information related to the sponsoring entity's compliance with the requirements of a sponsoring entity with respect to each sponsored direct reporting NFFE for purposes of satisfying the requirements of paragraph (c)(5) of this section. In such a case, the IRS may request from the responsible officer information necessary to verify the sponsoring entity's compliance with such requirements. The IRS may also request the performance of specified review procedures by a person (including an external auditor or third-party consultant) that the IRS identifies as competent to perform such procedures given the circumstances surrounding the sponsoring entity's potential failure to comply with the requirements of a sponsoring entity.

(4) *Sponsorship agreement.*—The sponsoring entity must have a written sponsorship agreement (which may be part of another agreement between the sponsoring entity and the sponsored direct reporting NFFE) in place with each sponsored direct reporting NFFE for which it acts by the later of March 31, 2019, or the date that the sponsoring entity begins acting as a sponsoring entity for the applicable sponsored direct reporting NFFE, under which—

(i) The sponsored direct reporting NFFE agrees to provide the sponsoring entity access to the sponsored direct reporting NFFE's books and records regarding each of its owners (including AML/KYC documentation regarding the sponsored direct reporting NFFE's owners provided by the sponsored direct reporting NFFE with respect to each financial account it holds) and such other information sufficient for the sponsoring entity to determine the direct and indirect substantial U.S. owners of the sponsored direct reporting NFFE, including the information about such owners required under paragraph (c)(3)(ii) of this section to be reported on Form 8966, "FATCA Report" (or such other form as the IRS may prescribe);

(ii) The sponsored direct reporting NFFE obtains a valid and effective waiver of any legal prohibitions on reporting the information about its direct and indirect substantial U.S. owners required under paragraph (c)(3)(ii) of this section to be reported on Form 8966 (or such other form as the IRS may prescribe);

(iii) The sponsored direct reporting NFFE authorizes the sponsoring entity to act on the sponsored direct reporting NFFE's behalf with respect to the sponsored direct reporting NFFE's obligations as a sponsored direct reporting NFFE (for example, authorizing the sponsoring entity to file Form 8966 on the sponsored direct reporting NFFE's behalf, responding to the IRS inquiries described in paragraph (f)(3) of this section, and providing the certification described in paragraph (f)(2) of this section);

(iv) The sponsored direct reporting NFFE agrees to identify to the sponsoring entity on request each withholding agent and financial institution to which the sponsored direct reporting NFFE reports its status as a sponsored direct reporting NFFE and agrees to provide to the sponsoring entity a copy of the withholding certificate or written statement prescribed in § 1.1471-3(d)(11)(x)(B) (as applicable) that the sponsored direct reporting NFFE provides to each such withholding agent or financial institution;

(v) The sponsored direct reporting NFFE represents that it does not have any formal or informal practices or procedures to assist its substantial U.S. owners with the avoidance of the requirements of chapter 4;

Reg. § 1.1472-1(f)(4)(v)

(vi) The sponsored direct reporting NFFE agrees to cooperate with the sponsoring entity in responding to any IRS inquiries under paragraph (f)(3) of this section with respect to the sponsored direct reporting NFFE; and

(vii) The sponsoring entity retains the records described in paragraphs (c)(3)(iii) and (iv) of this section for the longer of six years or the retention period under the sponsoring entity's normal business procedures. A sponsoring entity may be required to extend the retention period if the IRS requests such an extension before the expiration of the period.

(g) *Sponsoring entity event of default.*—(1) *Defined.*—An event of default by the sponsoring entity means the occurrence of any of the following—

(i) Failure to have the written sponsorship agreement described in paragraph (f)(4) of this section in effect with each sponsored direct reporting NFFE;

(ii) Failure to satisfy the requirements of paragraph (c)(3)(iii) of this section with respect to each sponsored direct reporting NFFE that the NFFE would have been required to satisfy as a direct reporting NFFE;

(iii) Failure to report to the IRS on Form 8966, "FATCA Report," (or such other form as the IRS may prescribe) all of the information required under paragraph (c)(3)(ii) of this section with respect to each sponsored direct reporting NFFE and each of its substantial U.S. owners (or report to the IRS on Form 8966 that the sponsored direct reporting NFFE had no substantial U.S. owners) by the due date of the form (including any extensions);

(iv) Failure to make the certification required under paragraph (f)(2) of this section;

(v) Failure to cooperate with an IRS request for additional information described in paragraph (f)(3) of this section, including requests for the records described in paragraph (c)(3)(iv) of this section and requests to extend the retention period for these records as described in (f)(4)(vii) of this section;

(vi) Making any fraudulent statement or misrepresentation of material fact to the IRS or representing to a withholding agent or the IRS its status as a sponsoring entity under paragraph (c)(5) of this section for an entity other than an entity for which it acts as a sponsoring entity; or

(vii) Failure to obtain from each sponsored direct reporting NFFE the information required to report on Form 8966.

(2) *Notice of event of default.*—Following an event of default known by or disclosed to the IRS, the IRS will deliver to the sponsoring entity a notice of default specifying the event of default and, if applicable, identifying each sponsored direct reporting NFFE to which the notice relates. The IRS will request that the sponsoring entity remediate the event of default within 45 days (unless additional time is requested and agreed to by the IRS). The sponsoring entity must respond to the notice of default and provide information responsive to an IRS request for information or state the reasons why the sponsoring entity does not agree that an event of default has occurred.

(3) *Remediation of event of default.*—A sponsoring entity will be permitted to remediate an event of default to the extent that it agrees with the IRS on a remediation plan. The IRS may, as part of a remediation plan, require additional information from the sponsoring entity, remedial actions, or the performance of the specified review procedures described in paragraph (f)(3)(ii) of this section.

(4) *Termination.*—(i) *In general.*—If the sponsoring entity does not provide a response to a notice of default within the period specified in paragraph (g)(2) of this section, or if the sponsoring entity does not satisfy the conditions of the remediation plan within the time period specified by the IRS, the IRS may deliver a notice of termination that terminates the sponsoring entity's status, the status of one or more sponsored direct reporting NFFEs as a direct reporting NFFE, or the status of both the sponsoring entity and one or more sponsored direct reporting NFFEs.

(ii) *Termination of sponsoring entity.*—If the IRS notifies the sponsoring entity that its status is terminated, the sponsoring entity must send notice of the termination within 30 days after the date of termination to each withholding agent from which each sponsored direct reporting NFFE receives payments and each financial institution with which each sponsored direct reporting NFFE holds an account for which a withholding certificate or written statement prescribed in § 1.1471-3(d)(11)(x)(B) (as applicable) was provided. A sponsoring entity that has had its status terminated cannot reregister on the FATCA registration website to act as a sponsoring entity for any sponsored direct reporting NFFE unless it receives written approval from the IRS. Unless the status of the sponsored direct reporting NFFEs has been terminated, the sponsored direct reporting

NFFEs may register on the FATCA registration website as direct reporting NFFEs or as sponsored direct reporting NFFEs of another sponsoring entity, other than a sponsoring entity that is related to the sponsoring entity that was terminated (absent written approval from the IRS allowing the registration). An entity is related to the terminated sponsoring entity if they have a relationship with each other that is described in section 267(b) or 707(b).

(iii) *Termination of sponsored direct reporting NFFE.*—If the IRS notifies the sponsoring entity that the status of a sponsored direct reporting NFFE is terminated (but not the sponsoring entity's status), the sponsoring entity must remove the sponsored direct reporting NFFE from the sponsoring entity's registration account on the FATCA registration website and send notice of the termination within 30 days after the date of termination to each withholding agent from which the sponsored direct reporting NFFE receives payments and each financial institution with which it holds an account for which a withholding certificate or written statement prescribed in § 1.1471-3(d)(11)(x)(B) (as applicable) was provided with respect to such sponsored direct reporting NFFE. A sponsored direct reporting NFFE that has had its status as a sponsored direct reporting NFFE terminated (independent from a termination of status of its sponsoring entity) may not register on the FATCA registration website as a direct reporting NFFE or as a sponsored direct reporting NFFE of another sponsoring entity unless it receives written approval from the IRS.

(iv) *Reconsideration of notice of default or notice of termination.*—A sponsoring entity or sponsored direct reporting NFFE may request, within 90 days of a notice of default or notice of termination, reconsideration of the notice of default or notice of termination by written request to the IRS.

(h) *Applicability date.*—This section generally applies beginning on January 6, 2017, except for paragraphs (c)(5)(iii), (f), and (g) of this section, which apply March 25, 2019. However, taxpayers may apply these provisions as of January 28, 2013. (For the rules that otherwise apply beginning on January 6, 2017, and before March 25, 2019, see this section as in effect and contained in 26 CFR part 1 revised April 1, 2018. For rules that otherwise apply beginning on January 28, 2013, and before January 6, 2017, see this section as in effect and contained in 26 CFR part 1 revised April 1, 2016.) [Reg. § 1.1472-1.]

☐ [T.D. 9610, 1-17-2013 (*corrected* 9-9-2013). *Amended by T.D. 9657,* 2-28-2014, *T.D. 9809,* 12-30-2016 *and T.D. 9852,* 3-21-2019 (*corrected* 4-3-2019).]

## [Reg. § 1.1473-1]

**§1.1473-1. Section 1473 definitions.**—(a) *Definition of withholdable payment.*—(1) *In general.*—Except as otherwise provided in this paragraph (a) and § 1.1473-2(b) (regarding grandfathered obligations), the term *withholdable payment* means—

(i) Any payment of U.S. source FDAP income (as defined in paragraph (a)(2) of this section); and

(ii) For any sales or other dispositions occurring after December 31, 2018, any gross proceeds from the sale or other disposition (as defined in paragraph (a)(3)(i) of this section) of any property of a type that can produce interest or dividends that are U.S. source FDAP income.

(2) *U.S. source FDAP income defined.*—(i) *In general.*—(A) *FDAP income defined.*—For purposes of chapter 4, the term *FDAP income* means fixed or determinable annual or periodic income that is described in § 1.1441-2(b)(1) or § 1.1441-2(c) (excluding income described in paragraph (a)(2)(vi) of this section or § 1.1441-2(b)(2) (such as gains derived from the sale of certain property)) and including the types of income enumerated in paragraphs (a)(2)(iii) through (v) of this section.

(B) *U.S. source.*—The term *U.S. source* means derived from sources within the United States. A payment is derived from sources within the United States if it is income treated as derived from sources within the United States under sections 861 through 865 and other relevant provisions of the Code. In the case of a payment of FDAP income for which the source cannot be determined at the time of payment, see § 1.1471-2(a)(5).

(C) *Exceptions to withholding on U.S. source FDAP income not applicable under chapter 4.*—Except as otherwise provided in paragraph (a)(4) of this section, no exception to withholding on U.S. source FDAP income for purposes other than chapter 4 applies for purposes of determining whether a payment of such income is a withholdable payment under chapter 4. Thus, for example, an exclusion from an amount subject to withholding under § 1.1441-2(a) or an exclusion from taxation under section 881 does not apply for purposes of determining whether such income constitutes a withholdable payment.

(ii) *Special rule for certain interest.*—Interest that is described in section 861(a)(1)(A) (relating to interest paid by foreign branches of domestic corporations and partnerships) is treated as U.S. source FDAP income.

(iii) *Original issue discount.*—The rules described in §1.1441-2(b)(3)(ii) for determining when an amount representing original issue discount is subject to withholding for chapter 3 purposes apply for purposes of determining when original issue discount from sources within the United States is U.S. source FDAP income.

(iv) *REMIC residual interests.*—U.S. source FDAP income includes an amount described in §1.1441-2(b)(5).

(v) *Withholding liability of payee that is satisfied by withholding agent.*—If a withholding agent satisfies a withholding liability arising under chapter 4 with respect to a withholdable payment from the withholding agent's own funds, the satisfaction of such liability is treated as an additional payment of U.S. source FDAP income to the payee to the extent that the withholding agent's satisfaction of such withholding liability also satisfies a tax liability of the payee under section 881 or 871 with respect to the same payment, and the satisfaction of the tax liability constitutes additional income to the payee under §1.1441-3(f) that is U.S. source FDAP income. In such case, the amount of any additional payment treated as made by the withholding agent for purposes of this paragraph (a)(2)(v) and any tax liability resulting from such payment shall be determined under §1.1441-3(f). See §1.1474-6 regarding the coordination of the withholding requirements under chapters 3 and 4 in the case of a withholdable payment that is also subject to withholding under chapter 3.

(vi) *Special rule for sales of interest bearing debt obligations.*—Income that is otherwise described as U.S. source FDAP income in paragraphs (a)(2)(i) through (v) of this section does not include an amount of interest accrued on the date of a sale or exchange of an interest bearing debt obligation if the sale occurs between two interest payment dates and is not part of a plan described in §1.1441-3(b)(2)(ii).

(vii) *Payment of U.S. source FDAP income.*—(A) *Amount of payment of U.S. source FDAP income.*—The amount of U.S. source FDAP income is the gross amount of the payment of such income, unreduced by any deductions or offsets. The rules of §1.1441-3(b)(1) shall apply to determine the amount of an interest payment on an interest-bearing obligation. In the case of a corporate distribution, the distributing corporation or intermediary shall determine the portion of the distribution that is treated as U.S. source FDAP income under this paragraph (a)(2) in the same manner as the distributing corporation or intermediary determines the portion of the distribution subject to withholding under §1.1441-3(c). Any portion of a payment on a debt instrument or a corporate distribution that does not constitute U.S. source FDAP income under this paragraph (a)(2) solely because of a provision other than the source rules of sections 861 through 865 shall be taken into account as gross proceeds under paragraph (a)(3) of this section. For rules regarding the determination of the amount of a payment of U.S. source FDAP income under paragraph (a)(2) of this section made in a medium other than U.S. dollars, see §1.1441-3(e). For determining the amount of a payment of a dividend equivalent, see section 871(m) and the regulations thereunder.

(B) *When payment of U.S. source FDAP income is made.*—A payment is considered made when the amount would be includible in the income of the beneficial owner under the U.S. tax principles governing the cash method of accounting. If an FFI acts as an intermediary with respect to a payment of U.S. source FDAP income, the FFI will be treated as making a payment of such U.S. source FDAP income to the person with respect to which the FFI acts as an intermediary when it pays or credits such amount to such person. The following rules also apply for purposes of this paragraph (a)(2)(vii)(B): §§1.1441-2(e)(2) (regarding when a payment is considered made in the case of income allocated under section 482); 1.1441-2(e)(3) (regarding blocked income); 1.1441-2(e)(4) (regarding when a dividend is considered paid); and 1.1441-2(e)(5) (regarding when interest is considered paid if a foreign person has made an election under §1.884-4(c)(1)).

(3) *Gross proceeds defined.*—(i) *Sale or other disposition.*—(A) *In general.*—Except as otherwise provided in this paragraph (a)(3)(i), the term *sale or other disposition* means any sale, exchange, or disposition of property described in paragraph (a)(3)(ii) of this section that requires recognition of gain or loss under section 1001(c), determined without regard to whether the owner of such property is subject to U.S. federal income tax with respect to such sale, exchange, or disposition. The term sale or other disposition includes (but is not limited to) sales of securities; redemptions of stock; retirements and redemptions of indebtedness; entering into short sales; and a closing

transaction under a forward contract, option, or other instrument that is otherwise a sale. Such term further includes a distribution from a corporation to the extent the distribution is a return of capital or a capital gain to the beneficial owner of the payment. Such term does not include grants or purchases of options, exercises of call options for physical delivery, transfers of securities for which gain or loss is excluded from recognition under section 1058, or mere executions of contracts that require delivery of personal property or an interest therein. For purposes of this section only, a constructive sale under section 1259 or a mark to fair market value under section 475 or 1296 is not a sale or disposition.

(B) *Special rule for sales effected by brokers.*—In the case of a sale effected by a broker (with the term *effect* defined in §1.6045-1(a)(10)), a sale means a sale as defined in §1.6045-1(a)(9) with respect to property described in paragraph (a)(3)(ii) of this section.

(C) *Special rule for gross proceeds from sales settled by a clearing organization.*—In the case of a clearing organization that settles sales and purchases of securities between members of such organization on a net basis, the gross proceeds from sales or dispositions are limited to the net amount paid or credited to a member's account that is associated with sales or other dispositions of property described in paragraph (a)(3)(ii) of this section by such member as of the time that such transactions are settled under the settlement procedures of such organization.

(ii) *Property of a type that can produce interest or dividend payments that would be U.S. source FDAP income.*—(A) *In general.*—Property is of a type that can produce interest or dividends payments that would be U.S. source FDAP income if the property is of a type that ordinarily gives rise to the payment of interest or dividends that would constitute U.S. source FDAP income, regardless of whether any such payment is made during the period such property is held by the person selling or disposing of such property. Thus, for example, stock issued by a domestic corporation is property of a type that can produce dividends from sources within the United States if a dividend from such corporation would be from sources within the United States, regardless of whether the stock pays dividends at regular intervals and regardless of whether the issuer has any plans to pay dividends or has ever paid a dividend with respect to the stock.

(B) *Contracts producing dividend equivalent payments.*—In the case of any contract that results in the payment of a dividend equivalent as defined in section 871(m) and the regulations thereunder (including as part of a termination payment), such contract shall be treated as property that is described in paragraph (a)(3)(ii)(A) of this section, without regard to whether the taxpayer is a foreign person subject to U.S. federal income tax with respect to such transaction. To the extent that the proceeds from a termination payment include the payment of a dividend equivalent, the gross amount of such proceeds will not include the amount of such dividend equivalent.

(C) *Regulated investment company distributions.*—The amount of a distribution that is designated as a capital gain dividend under section 852(b)(3)(C) or 871(k)(2) is a payment of gross proceeds to the extent attributable to property described in paragraph (a)(3)(ii)(A) of this section.

(iii) *Payment of gross proceeds.*—(A) *When gross proceeds are paid.*—With respect to a sale that is effected by a broker that results in a payment of gross proceeds as defined in this paragraph (a)(3), the date the gross proceeds are considered paid is the date that the proceeds of such sale are credited to the account of or otherwise made available to the person entitled to the payment.

(B) *Amount of gross proceeds.*—Except as otherwise provided in this paragraph (a)(3)—

(1) The amount of gross proceeds from a sale or other disposition means the total amount realized as a result of a sale or other disposition of property described in paragraph (a)(3)(ii) under section 1001(b);

(2) In the case of a sale effected by a broker, the amount of gross proceeds from a sale or other disposition means the total amount paid or credited to the account of the person entitled to the payment increased by any amount not so paid by reason of the repayment of margin loans. The broker may (but is not required to) take commissions with respect to the sale into account in determining the amount of gross proceeds;

(3) In the case of a corporate distribution, the amount treated as gross proceeds excludes the amount described in paragraph (a)(2)(vii)(A) of this section that is treated as U.S source FDAP income;

*(4)* In the case of a sale of an obligation described in paragraph (a)(2)(vi), gross proceeds includes any interest accrued between interest payment dates other than an amount described in paragraph (a)(2)(vi) of this section that is treated as U.S. source FDAP income; and

*(5)* In the case of a sale, retirement, or redemption of a debt obligation, gross proceeds excludes the amount of original issue discount treated as U.S. source FDAP income under paragraph (a)(2)(iii) of this section.

(4) *Payments not treated as withholdable payments.*—The following payments are not withholdable payments under paragraph (a)(1) of this section—

(i) *Certain short-term obligations.*—A payment of interest or original issue discount on short-term obligations described in section 871(g)(1)(B)(i).

(ii) *Effectively connected income.*—Any payment to the extent it gives rise to an item of income that is taken into account under section 871(b)(1) or 882(a)(1) for the taxable year. An item of income is taken into account under section 871(b)(1) or 882(a)(1) when the income is (or is deemed to be) effectively connected with the conduct of a trade or business in the United States and is includible in the beneficial owner's gross income for the taxable year. An amount of income shall not be treated as taken into account under section 871(b)(1) or 882(a)(1) if the income is (or is deemed to be) effectively connected with the conduct of a trade or business in the United States and the beneficial owner claims an exception from tax under an income tax treaty because the income is not attributable to a permanent establishment in the United States.

(iii) *Excluded nonfinancial payments.*—Payments for the following: services (including wages and other forms of employee compensation (such as stock options)), the use of property, office and equipment leases, software licenses, transportation, freight, gambling winnings, awards, prizes, scholarships, and interest on outstanding accounts payable arising from the acquisition of goods or services. Notwithstanding the preceding sentence, excluded nonfinancial payments do not include: payments in connection with a lending transaction (including loans of securities), a forward, futures, option, or notional principal contract, or a similar financial instrument; premiums for insurance contracts or annuity contracts; amounts paid under cash value insurance or annuity contracts; dividends; interest (including substitute interest described in § 1.861-2(a)(7)) other than interest described in the preceding sentence; gross proceeds other than gross proceeds described in paragraph (a)(4)(iv) of this section; investment advisory fees; custodial fees; and bank or brokerage fees.

(iv) *Gross proceeds from sales of excluded property.*—Gross proceeds from the sale or other disposition of any property that can produce U.S. source FDAP income if all such U.S. source FDAP income would be excluded from the definition of withholdable payment under paragraphs (a)(4)(i) through (iii) of this section.

(v) *Fractional shares.*—Payments arising in sales described in § 1.6045-1(c)(3)(ix).

(vi) *Offshore payments of U.S. source FDAP income prior to 2017 (transitional).*—A payment with respect to an offshore obligation (as defined in § 1.1471-1(b)(88)) made prior to January 1, 2017, if such payment is U.S. source FDAP income and made by a person that is not acting as an intermediary or as a WP or WT with respect to the payment. Additionally, a payment with respect to an account, obligation, contract, or other instrument that is issued or maintained by an entity other than a financial institution and that would be treated as an offshore obligation under § 1.6049-5(c)(1) (applied by substituting the term *entity* for the term *financial institution* (as defined in § 1.1471-5(e)) in each place that it appears), made prior to January 1, 2017, if such payment is U.S. source FDAP and made by a person that is not acting as an intermediary or as a WP or WT with respect to the payment is not a withholdable payment under paragraph (a)(1) of this section. The exception for offshore payments of U.S. source FDAP income provided in the preceding sentences shall not apply, however, in the case of a flow-through entity that has a residual withholding requirement with respect to its partners, owners, or beneficiaries under § 1.1471-2(a)(2)(ii), or in the case of payments made with respect to debt or equity issued by a U.S. person (excluding interest payments made by a foreign branch of a U.S. financial institution with respect to depository accounts it maintains). For purposes of this paragraph (a)(4)(vi), an intermediary includes a person that acts as a qualified securities lender as defined for purposes of chapter 3 and does not include a person acting as an insurance broker with respect to premiums.

(vii) *Collateral arrangements prior to 2017 (transitional).*—A payment made prior to January 1, 2017, by a secured party, or to a secured party other than a nonparticipating FFI, with respect to

collateral securing one or more transactions under a collateral arrangement, provided that only a commercially reasonable amount of collateral is held by the secured party (or by a third party for the benefit of the secured party) as part of the collateral arrangement. For purposes of this paragraph (a)(4)(vii), the term *transaction* generally includes a debt instrument, a derivative financial instrument (including a notional principal contract, future, forward, and option), and any securities lending transaction, sale-repurchase transaction, margin loan, or substantially similar transaction that is subject to a collateral arrangement. Solely for purposes of this paragraph (a)(4)(vii), a secured party may provide documentation to the withholding agent indicating that it is the beneficial owner of a payment described in this paragraph (a)(4)(vii), and a withholding agent may rely on such certification for purposes of its requirements under § 1.1471-3(d) for determining whether withholding under chapter 4 applies.

(viii) *Certain dividend equivalents.*—Amounts paid with respect to a notional principal contract described in § 1.871-15(a)(7), an equity-linked instrument described in § 1.871-15(a)(4), or a securities lending or sale-repurchase transaction described in § 1.871-15(a)(13) that are exempt from withholding under section 1441(a) as dividend equivalents under section 871(m) if the transaction is not a section 871(m) transaction within the meaning of § 1.871-15(a)(12), if the transaction is subject to the exception described in § 1.871-15(k), or to the extent the payment is not a dividend equivalent pursuant to § 1.871-15(c)(2).

(5) *Special payment rules for flow-through entities, complex trusts, and estates.*—(i) *In general.*—This paragraph (a)(5) provides special rules for a flow-through entity, complex trust, or estate to determine when such entity must treat a payment of U.S. source FDAP income that is also a withholdable payment as having been paid by such entity to its partners, owners, or beneficiaries (as applicable depending on the type of entity).

(ii) *Partnerships.*—An amount of U.S. source FDAP income that is also a withholdable payment is treated as being paid to a partner under rules similar to the rules prescribing when withholding is required for chapter 3 purposes as described in § 1.1441-5(b)(2)(i)(A).

(iii) *Simple trusts.*—An amount of U.S. source FDAP income that is also a withholdable payment is treated as being paid to a beneficiary of a simple trust under rules similar to the rules prescribing when withholding is required for chapter 3 purposes as described in § 1.1441-5(b)(2)(ii).

(iv) *Complex trusts and estates.*—An amount of U.S. source FDAP income that is also a withholdable payment is treated as being paid to a beneficiary of a complex trust or estate under rules similar to the rules prescribing when withholding is required for chapter 3 purposes as described in § 1.1441-5(b)(2)(iii).

(v) *Grantor trusts.*—If an amount of U.S. source FDAP income that is also a withholdable payment is paid to a grantor trust, a person treated as an owner of all or a portion of such trust is treated as having been paid such income by the trust at the time it is received by or credited to the trust or portion thereof.

(vi) *Special rule for an NWP or NWT.*—In the case of a partnership, simple trust, or complex trust that is an NWP or NWT, the rules described in paragraphs (a)(5)(ii) and (iii) of this section shall not apply, and U.S. source FDAP income that is also a withholdable payment is treated as being paid to the partner or beneficiary at the time the income is paid to the partnership or trust, respectively.

(vii) *Special rules for determining when gross proceeds are treated as paid to a partner, owner, or beneficiary of a flow-through entity.*—[Reserved].

(6) *Reporting of withholdable payments.*—See § 1.1474-1(c) and (d) for a description of the income tax return and information reporting requirements applicable to a withholding agent that has made a withholdable payment.

(7) *Example.*—*Satisfaction of payee's chapter 4 liability by withholding agent.* Recalcitrant account holder (RA) is entitled to receive a payment of $100 of U.S. source interest from withholding agent, WA. The payment is subject to withholding under chapter 4, but is not subject to withholding under section 1442, and RA has no substantive tax liability under section 881 with respect to this payment. WA pays the full $100 to RA and, after the date of payment, pays the $30 of tax due under chapter 4 to the IRS from its own funds. Because no underlying tax liability of RA is satisfied, and further because WA and RA did not execute any agreement for WA to pay this tax and WA did not have an obligation to pay this tax apart from the requirements of chapter 4, WA's payment of the tax does not give rise

to a deemed payment of U.S. source FDAP income to RA under paragraph (a)(2)(v) of this section. Thus, WA is not required to pay any additional tax with respect to this payment for purposes of chapter 4.

(b) *Substantial U.S. owner.*—(1) *Definition.*—Except as otherwise provided in paragraph (b)(4) or (5) of this section, the term *substantial United States owner* (or *substantial U.S. owner*) means:

(i) With respect to any foreign corporation, any specified U.S. person that owns, directly or indirectly, more than 10 percent of the stock of such corporation (by vote or value);

(ii) With respect to any foreign partnership, any specified U.S. person that owns, directly or indirectly, more than 10 percent of the profits interests or capital interests in such partnership; and

(iii) In the case of a trust-

(A) Any specified U.S. person treated as an owner of any portion of the trust under sections 671 through 679; and

(B) Any specified U.S. person that holds, directly or indirectly, more than 10 percent of the beneficial interests of the trust.

(2) *Indirect ownership of foreign entities.*—For purposes of determining a person's interest in a foreign entity, the following rules shall apply.

(i) *Indirect ownership of stock.*—Stock of a foreign corporation that is owned directly or indirectly by an entity (other than a participating FFI, a deemed-compliant FFI (excluding an owner-documented FFI), a U.S. financial institution, a U.S. person that is not a specified U.S. person, an exempt beneficial owner, or an excepted NFFE) that is a corporation, partnership, or trust shall be considered as being owned proportionately by such entity's shareholders, partners, or, in the case of a trust, persons treated as owners under sections 671 through 679 of any portion of the trust that includes the stock, and the beneficiaries of the trust. Stock considered to be owned by a person by reason of the application of the preceding sentence shall, for purposes of applying such sentence, be treated as actually owned by such person.

(ii) *Indirect ownership in a foreign partnership or ownership of a beneficial interest in a foreign trust.*—A capital or profits interest in a foreign partnership or an ownership or beneficial interest (as described in paragraph (b)(3) of this section) in a foreign trust that is owned or held directly or indirectly by an entity (other than a participating FFI, a deemed-compliant FFI (excluding an owner-documented FFI), a U.S. financial institution, a U.S. person that is not a specified U.S. person, an exempt beneficial owner, or an excepted NFFE) that is a corporation, partnership, or trust shall be considered as being owned or held proportionately by such entity's shareholders, partners, or, in the case of a trust, persons treated as owners under sections 671 through 679 of any portion of the trust that includes the partnership or beneficial trust interest, and the beneficiaries of the trust. Partnership or beneficial trust interests considered to be owned or held by a person by reason of the application of the preceding sentence shall, for purposes of applying such sentence, be treated as actually owned or held by such person.

(iii) *Ownership and holdings through options.*—If a specified U.S. person holds, directly or indirectly (applying the principles of paragraphs (b)(2)(i) and (ii) of this section) an option to acquire stock in a foreign corporation, a capital or profits interest in a foreign partnership, or an ownership or beneficial interest in a foreign trust, such person is considered to own the underlying equity or other ownership interest in such foreign entity for purposes of this paragraph (b). For purposes of the preceding sentence, an option to acquire such an option, and each one of a series of such options, shall be considered an option to acquire such stock or other ownership interest described in this paragraph (b)(2)(iii).

(iv) *Determination of proportionate interest.*—For purposes of this paragraph (b), and except as otherwise provided in paragraph (b)(3) of this section, the determination of a person's proportionate interest in a foreign corporation, partnership, or trust is based on all of the relevant facts and circumstances. In making this determination, any arrangement that artificially decreases a specified U.S. person's proportionate interest in any such entity will be disregarded in determining whether such person is a substantial U.S. owner. In lieu of applying the rules of this paragraph (b)(2) to determine whether an owner's proportionate interest in a foreign entity meets the 10 percent threshold described in paragraph (b)(1) of this section, the entity or its withholding agent may opt to treat the owner as a substantial U.S. owner.

(v) *Interests owned or held by a related person.*—For purposes of determining whether a specified U.S. person is a substantial U.S. owner in a foreign entity described in paragraphs (b)(2)(i) through (iv) of this section, if a specified U.S. person owns or holds, directly or indirectly, any interest in the foreign entity, that interest must be aggregated with any such interest in the foreign entity owned or held, directly or indirectly, by a related person. For purposes of the preceding sentence, a related person is a person or spouse of a person described in § 1.267(c)-1(a)(4), determined by reference to such specified U.S. person.

(3) *Beneficial interest in a foreign trust.*—(i) *In general.*—For purposes of paragraph (b)(1)(iii)(B) of this section, a person holds a beneficial interest in a foreign trust if such person has the right to receive directly or indirectly (for example, through a nominee) a mandatory distribution or may receive, directly or indirectly, a discretionary distribution from the trust. For purposes of this section, a *mandatory distribution* means a distribution that is required to be made pursuant to the terms of the trust document. A *discretionary distribution* means a distribution that is made to a person at the discretion of the trustee or a person with a limited power of appointment of such trust.

(ii) *Determining the 10 percent threshold in the case of a beneficial interest in a foreign trust.*—A person will be treated as holding directly or indirectly more than 10 percent of the beneficial interest in a foreign trust if—

(A) The person receives, directly or indirectly, only discretionary distributions from the trust and the fair market value of the currency or other property distributed, directly or indirectly, from the trust to such person during the prior calendar year exceeds 10 percent of the value of either all of the distributions made by the trust during that year or all of the assets held by the trust at the end of that year;

(B) The person is entitled to receive, directly or indirectly, mandatory distributions from the trust and the value of the person's interest in the trust, as determined under section 7520, exceeds 10 percent of the value of all the assets held by the trust as of the end of the prior calendar year; or

(C) The person is entitled to receive, directly or indirectly, mandatory distributions and may receive, directly or indirectly, discretionary distributions from the trust, and the value of the person's interest in the trust, determined as the sum of the fair market value of all of the currency or other property distributed from the trust at the discretion of the trustee during the prior calendar year to the person and the value of the person's interest in the trust as determined under section 7520 at the end of that year, exceeds either 10 percent of the value of all distributions made by such trust during the prior calendar year or 10 percent of the value of all the assets held by the trust at the end of that year.

(4) *Exceptions.*—(i) *De minimis amount or value exception.*—A specified U.S. person is not treated as a substantial U.S. owner if—

(A) The fair market value of the currency or other property distributed, directly or indirectly, from the trust to such specified U.S. person during the prior calendar year is $5,000 or less and,

(B) In the case of a specified U.S. person that is entitled to receive mandatory distributions, the value of such person's interest in the trust is $50,000 or less.

(ii) *Trusts wholly owned by certain U.S. persons.*—A trust that is treated as owned only by U.S. persons under sections 671 through 679 is not required to treat any of its beneficiaries as substantial U.S. owners.

(5) *Special rule for certain financial institutions.*—In the case of any financial institution described in § 1.1471-5(e)(1)(iii) or (iv) (referring to investment entities and specified insurance companies), this section shall be applied by substituting "0 percent" for "10 percent" in each place that it appears. Additionally, in the case of a financial institution described in § 1471-5(e)(1)(iii) that is a trust, the rules of paragraph (b)(3) and (4) of this section (referring to beneficial interests in a trust) shall be applied by substituting "calendar year" for "prior calendar year" in each place that it appears.

(6) *Determination dates for substantial U.S. owners.*—A foreign entity may make the determination of whether it has one or more direct or indirect substantial U.S. owners as of the last day of such entity's accounting year or as of the date on which such foreign entity provides the documentation described in § 1.1471-3(d) to the withholding agent for which such determination is required to be made. See § 1.1471-4(c) for when a participating FFI is required to obtain documentation with respect to its account holders.

(7) *Examples.*—The following examples illustrate the provisions of paragraph (b) of this section:

*Example 1. Indirect ownership.* U, a specified U.S. person, owns directly 100% of the sole class of stock of F1, a foreign corporation. F1 owns directly 90% of the sole class of stock of F2, a foreign corporation, and U owns directly the remaining 10% of the sole class of stock of F2. F2 owns directly 10% of the sole class of stock of F3, a foreign corporation, and U owns directly 3% of the sole class of stock of F3. U is treated as owning 13% (3% directly and 10% indirectly) of the sole class of stock of F3 and 100% (10% directly and 90% indirectly) of the sole class of stock of F2 for purposes of this paragraph (b). U is a substantial U.S. owner of F1, F2, and F3.

*Example 2. Indirect ownership through entities that are specified U.S. persons.* U, a specified U.S. person, owns directly 100% of the sole class of stock of US1, a U.S. corporation that is a specified U.S. person. US1 owns directly 100% of the sole class of stock of US2, a U.S. corporation that is a specified U.S. person. US2 owns directly 15% of the sole class of stock of FC, a foreign corporation. For purposes of this paragraph (b), U, US1, and US2 are all substantial U.S. owners of FC.

*Example 3. Determining the 10% threshold in the case of a beneficial interest in a foreign trust.* U, a U.S. citizen, holds an interest in FT1, a foreign trust, under which U may receive discretionary distributions from FT1. U also holds an interest in FT2, a foreign trust, and FT2, in turn, holds an interest in FT1 under which FT2 may receive discretionary distributions from FT1. U receives $25,000 from FT1 in Year 1. FT2 receives $120,000 from FT1 in Year 1 and distributes the entire amount to its beneficiaries in Year 1. The distribution from FT1 is FT2's only source of income and FT2's distributions in Year 1 total $120,000. U receives $40,000 from FT2 in Year 1. FT1's distributions in Year 1 total $750,000. U's discretionary interest in FT1 is valued at $65,000 at the end of Year 1 and therefore does not meet the 10% threshold as determined under paragraph (b)(3)(ii)(A). U's discretionary interest in FT2, however, is valued at $40,000 at the end of Year 1 and therefore meets the 10% threshold as determined under paragraph (b)(3)(ii)(A).

*Example 4. Determining ownership (determination date).* F, a foreign corporation that is an NFFE, has a calendar year accounting year. On December 31 of Year 1, U, a specified U.S. person, owns 12% of the sole class of outstanding stock of F. In March of Year 2, F redeems a portion of U's stock and reduces U's ownership of F to 9%. In May of Year 2, F opens an account with P, a participating FFI, and delivers to P the documentation required under §1.1471-3(d). At the time F opens its account with P, U is the only specified U.S. person that directly or indirectly owns stock in F. Because of the redemption, U's interest in F is 9% on the date F opens its account with P. Pursuant to paragraph (b)(6) of this section, F may determine whether it has a substantial U.S. owner as of the date it provides the documentation required under §1.1471-3(d) to P, which would be the day it opens the account. As a result, F may indicate in its §1.1471-3(d) documentation that it has no substantial U.S. owners.

(c) *Specified U.S. person.*—The term *specified United States person* (or *specified U.S. person*) means any U.S. person other than—

(1) A corporation the stock of which is regularly traded on one or more established securities markets, as described in §1.1472-1(c)(1)(i);

(2) Any corporation that is a member of the same expanded affiliated group as a corporation described in §1.1472-1(c)(1)(i);

(3) Any organization exempt from taxation under section 501(a) or an individual retirement plan as defined in section 7701(a)(37);

(4) The United States or any wholly owned agency or instrumentality thereof;

(5) Any State, the District of Columbia, any U.S. territory, any political subdivision of any of the foregoing, or any wholly owned agency or instrumentality of any one or more of the foregoing;

(6) Any bank as defined in section 581;

(7) Any real estate investment trust as defined in section 856;

(8) Any regulated investment company as defined in section 851 or any entity registered with the Securities Exchange Commission under the Investment Company Act of 1940 (15 U.S.C. 80a-64);

(9) Any common trust fund as defined in section 584(a);

(10) Any trust that is exempt from tax under section 664(c) or is described in section 4947(a)(1);

(11) A dealer in securities, commodities, or derivative financial instruments (including notional principal contracts, futures, forwards, and options) that is registered as such under the laws of the United States or any State;

(12) A broker; and

(13) Any tax exempt trust under a section 403(b) plan or section 457(g) plan.

(d) *Withholding agent.*—(1) *In general.*—Except as provided in this paragraph (d), the term *withholding agent* means any person, U.S. or foreign, in whatever capacity acting, that has the control, receipt, custody, disposal, or payment of a withholdable payment or foreign passthru payment.

(2) *Participating FFIs and registered deemed-compliant FFIs as withholding agents.*—The term withholding agent includes a participating FFI that has the control, receipt, custody, disposal, or payment of a passthru payment (as defined in §1.1471-5(h)). The term withholding

agent also includes a registered deemed-compliant FFI to the extent that such FFI is required to withhold on a passthru payment as part of the conditions for maintaining its status as a deemed-compliant FFI under §1.1471-5(f)(1)(ii). For the withholding requirements of a participating FFI, including the requirement to withhold with respect to limited branches and limited FFIs that are in the same expanded affiliated group as the participating FFI, see §§1.1471-4(b) and 1.1472-1(a).

(3) *Grantor trusts as withholding agents.*—The term withholding agent includes a grantor trust with respect to a withholdable payment or a foreign passthru payment (in the case of a grantor trust that is a participating FFI) made to a person treated as an owner of the trust under sections 671 through 679. For purposes of determining when a payment is treated as made to such a person, see §1.1473-1(a)(5)(v).

(4) *Deposit and return requirements.*—See §1.1474-1(b) for a withholding agent's requirement to deposit any tax withheld, and §1.1474-1(c) and (d) for the requirement to file income tax and information returns (including the special allowance in §1.1474-1(b)(2) for participating FFIs with respect to dormant accounts).

(5) *Multiple withholding agents.*—When several persons qualify as a withholding agent with respect to a single payment, only one tax is required to be withheld and deposited. See §1.1474-1(a). A person who, as a nominee described in §1.6031(c)-1T, has furnished to a partnership all of the information required to be furnished under §1.6031(c)-1T(a) shall not be treated as a withholding agent if the person has notified the partnership that it is treating the provision of information to the partnership as a discharge of its obligations as a withholding agent.

(6) *Exception for certain individuals.*—An individual is not a withholding agent with respect to a withholdable payment made by the individual outside the course of such individual's trade or business (including as an agent with respect to making or receiving such payment).

(e) *Foreign entity.*—The term *foreign entity* means any entity that is not a U.S. person and includes a territory entity.

(f) *Effective/applicability date.*—This section generally applies on January 6, 2017. However, taxpayers may apply these provisions as of January 28, 2013. Paragraph (a)(4)(viii) of this section applies to payments made on or after September 18, 2015. (For the rules that apply beginning on January 28, 2013, and before January 6, 2017, see this section as in effect and contained in 26 CFR part 1 revised April 1, 2016.) [Reg. §1.1473-1.]

☐ [T.D. 9610, 1-17-2013 (corrected 9-9-2013). Amended by T.D. 9657, 2-28-2014, T.D. 9734, 9-17-2015 and T.D. 9809, 12-30-2016.]

**[Reg. §1.1474-1]**

**§1.1474-1. Liability for withheld tax and withholding agent reporting.**—(a) *Payment and returns of tax withheld.*—(1) *In general.*—A withholding agent is required to deposit any tax withheld pursuant to chapter 4 as provided under paragraph (b) of this section and to make the returns prescribed by paragraphs (c) and (d) of this section. When several persons qualify as withholding agents with respect to a single payment, only one tax is required to be withheld and deposited.

(2) *Withholding agent liability.*—A withholding agent that is required to withhold with respect to a payment under §1.1471-2(a), 1.1471-4(b) (in the case of a participating FFI), or 1.1472-1(b) but fails either to withhold or to deposit any tax withheld as required under paragraph (b) of this section is liable for the amount of tax not withheld and deposited.

(3) *Use of agents.*—(i) *In general.*—Except as otherwise provided in this paragraph (a)(3), a withholding agent may authorize an agent to fulfill its obligations under chapter 4. The acts of an agent of a withholding agent (including the receipt of withholding certificates, the payment of amounts subject to withholding, the withholding and deposit of tax withheld, and the reporting required on the relevant form) are imputed to the withholding agent on whose behalf it is acting.

(ii) *Authorized agent.*—An agent is authorized only if—

(A) There is a written agreement between the withholding agent and the person acting as agent;

(B) A Form 8655, "Reporting Agent Authorization," is filed with the IRS by a withholding agent if its agent (including any sub-agent) acts as a reporting agent for filing Form 1042 on behalf of the withholding agent and the agent (or sub-agent) identifies itself as the filer on the Form 1042;

(C) Books and records and relevant personnel of the agent (including any sub-agent) are available to the withholding agent (on a continuous basis, including after termination of the relationship) in order to evaluate the withholding agent's compliance with the provisions of chapter 4; and

(D) The withholding agent remains fully liable for the acts of its agent (or any sub-agent) and does not assert any of the defenses that may otherwise be available, including under common law principles of agency, in order to avoid tax liability under the Code.

(iii) *Liability of withholding agent acting through an agent.*—A withholding agent acting through an agent is liable for any failure of the agent, such as a failure to withhold an amount or make a payment of tax, in the same manner and to the same extent as if the agent's failure had been the failure of the withholding agent. For this purpose, the agent's actual knowledge or reason to know shall be imputed to the withholding agent. Except as otherwise provided in the QI, WP, or WT agreement, an agent of a withholding agent is subject to the same withholding and reporting obligations that apply to any withholding agent under the provisions of chapter 4 and does not benefit from the special procedures or exceptions that apply to a QI, WP, or WT. If the agent is a foreign person, however, a U.S. withholding agent may treat the acts of the foreign agent as its own for purposes of determining whether it has complied with the provisions of chapter 4. The withholding agent's liability under paragraph (a)(2) of this section will exist even if the agent is also a withholding agent and is itself separately liable for failure to comply with the provisions of chapter 4. The same tax, interest, or penalties, however, shall not be collected more than once.

(4) *Liability for failure to obtain documentation timely or to act in accordance with applicable presumptions.*—(i) *In general.*—A withholding agent that cannot reliably associate a payment with documentation on the date of payment and that does not withhold under §1.1471-2(a), 1.1471-4(b), or 1.1472-1(b), or withholds at less than the 30 percent rate prescribed, is liable under this section for the tax required to be withheld under §1.1471-2(a), 1.1471-4(b), or 1.1472-1(b) (including interest, penalties, or additions to tax otherwise applicable in respect of the failure to deduct and withhold) unless—

(A) The withholding agent has appropriately relied on the presumptions described in §1.1471-3(f) in order to treat the payment as exempt from withholding; or

(B) The withholding agent obtained after the date of payment valid documentation that meets the requirements of §1.1471-3(c)(7) to establish that the payment was, in fact, exempt from withholding.

(ii) *Withholding satisfied by another withholding agent.*—If a withholding agent fails to deduct and withhold any amount required to be deducted and withheld under §1.1471-2(a), 1.1471-4(b), or 1.1472-1(b), and the tax is satisfied by another withholding agent or is otherwise paid, then the amount of tax required to be deducted and withheld shall not be collected from the first-mentioned withholding agent. However, the withholding agent is not relieved from liability in any such case for any interest or penalties or additions to tax otherwise applicable in respect of the failure to deduct and withhold.

(b) *Payment of withheld tax.*—(1) *In general.*—Except as otherwise provided in this paragraph (b), every withholding agent who withholds tax pursuant to chapter 4 shall deposit such tax within the time provided in §1.6302-2(a) by electronic funds transfer as provided under §31.6302-1(h) of this chapter. If for any reason the total amount of tax required to be deposited for any calendar year pursuant to the income tax return described in paragraph (c) of this section has not been deposited pursuant to §1.6302-2, the withholding agent shall pay the balance of such tax due for such year at such place as the IRS shall specify. The tax shall be paid when filing the return described in paragraph (c)(1) of this section for such year, unless the IRS specifies otherwise. See §1.1471-4(b)(6) for the special rule allowing participating FFIs to set aside in escrow amounts withheld with respect to dormant accounts.

(2) *Special rule for foreign passthru payments and payments of gross proceeds that include an undetermined amount of income subject to tax.*— [Reserved].

(c) *Income tax return.*—(1) *In general.*—Every withholding agent shall file an income tax return on Form 1042, "Annual Withholding Tax Return for U.S. Source Income of Foreign Persons," (or such other form as the IRS may prescribe) to report chapter 4 reportable amounts (as defined in paragraph (d)(2)(i) of this section). This income tax return shall be filed on the same income tax return used to report amounts subject to reporting for chapter 3 purposes as described in §1.1461-1(b). The return must show the aggregate amount of payments that are chapter 4 reportable amounts and must

report the tax withheld for the preceding calendar year by the withholding agent, in addition to any information required by the form and its accompanying instructions. Withholding certificates and other statements or information provided to a withholding agent are not required to be attached to the return. A Form 1042 must be filed under this paragraph (c)(1) even if no tax was required to be withheld for chapter 4 purposes during the preceding calendar year. The withholding agent must retain a copy of Form 1042 for the applicable period of limitations on assessment and collection with respect to the amounts required to be reported on the Form 1042. See section 6501 and the regulations thereunder for the applicable period of limitations. Adjustments to the total amount of tax withheld described in §1.1474-2 shall be stated on the return as prescribed by the form and its accompanying instructions.

(2) *Participating FFIs, registered deemed-compliant FFIs, and U.S. branches treated as U.S. persons.*—A participating FFI or registered deemed-compliant FFI shall file Form 1042 in accordance with paragraph (c)(1) of this section to report chapter 4 reportable amounts for which the participating FFI or registered deemed-compliant FFI is required to file Form 1042-S, as described in paragraph (d)(4)(iii) of this section. XOXO A participating FFI or registered deemed-compliant FFI with a U.S. branch that is treated as a U.S. person must exclude from Form 1042 payments made and taxes withheld by such U.S. branch. A U.S. branch that is treated as a U.S. person shall file a separate Form 1042 in accordance with paragraph (c)(1) of this section and the instructions on the form to report chapter 4 reportable amounts.

(3) *Amended returns.*—An amended return under this paragraph (c)(3) must be filed on Form 1042. An amended return must include such information as the form or its accompanying instructions shall require, including, with respect to any information that has changed from the time of the filing of the return, the information that was shown on the original return and the corrected information.

(d) *Information returns for payment reporting.*—(1) *Filing requirement.*—(i) *In general.*—Except as otherwise provided in paragraph (d)(4) of this section or in the instructions to Form 1042-S, every withholding agent must file an information return on Form 1042-S, "Foreign Person's U.S. Source Income Subject to Withholding," (or such other form as the IRS may prescribe) to report to the IRS chapter 4 reportable amounts as described in paragraph (d)(2)(i) of this section that were paid to a recipient during the preceding calendar year. Except as otherwise provided in paragraphs (d)(4)(ii)(B) (certain unknown recipients) and (d)(4)(i)(B) and (d)(4)(iii)(A) of this section (describing payees includable in reporting pools of a participating FFI or registered deemed-compliant FFI), a separate Form 1042-S must be filed with the IRS for each recipient of an amount subject to reporting under paragraph (d)(2)(i) of this section and for each separate type of payment made to a single recipient in accordance with paragraph (d)(4)(i) of this section. The Form 1042-S shall be prepared in such manner as the form and its accompanying instructions prescribe. One copy of the Form 1042-S shall be filed with the IRS on or before March 15 of the calendar year following the year in which the amount subject to reporting was paid, with a transmittal form as provided in the instructions to the form. Withholding certificates, certifications, documentary evidence, or other statements or documentation provided to a withholding agent are not required to be attached to the form. A copy of the Form 1042-S must be furnished to the recipient for whom the form is prepared (or any other person, as required under this paragraph or the instructions to the form) and to any intermediary or flow-through entity described in paragraph (d)(3)(vii) of this section on or before March 15 of the calendar year following the year in which the amount subject to reporting was paid. A person required by this paragraph (d)(1)(i) to furnish a copy of Form 1042-S to the recipient for whom it is prepared may furnish the copy of Form 1042-S in an electronic format in lieu of a paper format provided it meets the requirements of §1.1461-1(c)(1)(i)(A). The withholding agent must retain a copy of each Form 1042-S for the period of limitations on assessment and collection applicable to the tax reportable on the Form 1042 to which the Form 1042-S relates (determined as set forth in paragraph (c)(1) of this section). See paragraph (d)(4)(iii) of this section for the additional reporting requirements of participating FFIs and deemed-compliant FFIs.

(ii) *Recipient.*—(A) *Defined.*—Except as otherwise provided in paragraph (d)(1)(ii)(B) of this section, the term *recipient* under this paragraph (d) means a person that is a recipient of a chapter 4 reportable amount, and includes—

(1) With respect to a payment of U.S. source FDAP income—

(i) A QI (including a QI that is a foreign branch of a U.S. person);

(ii) A WP or WT;

*(iii)* A participating FFI or a registered deemed-compliant FFI that is an NQI, NWP, NWT, and a U.S. branch of an FFI that is not treated as a U.S. person that applies the rules described in § 1.1471-4(d)(2)(iii)(C) and that provides its withholding agent with sufficient information to determine the portion of the payment allocable to its reporting pools of recalcitrant account holders, payees that are nonparticipating FFIs, and payees that are U.S. persons described in paragraph (d)(4)(i)(B) of this section;

*(iv)* An account holder or payee to the extent that the withholding agent issues a Form 1042-S to such account holder or payee;

*(v)* An FFI that is a beneficial owner of the payment (including a limited branch of the FFI);

*(vi)* A U.S. branch of an FFI treated as a U.S. person;

*(vii)* A territory financial institution treated as a U.S. person;

*(viii)* An excepted NFFE and passive NFFE that also is not a flow-through entity and that is not acting as an agent or intermediary with respect to the payment;

*(ix)* A foreign person that is a partner or beneficiary in a flow-through entity that is a NFFE (looking through a partner or beneficiary that is a foreign intermediary or flow-through entity);

*(x)* An exempt beneficial owner of a payment, including when the payment is made to such owner through an FFI (including a nonparticipating FFI) that provides documentation and information sufficient for a withholding agent to determine the portion of the payment allocable to such owner; and

*(xi)* Any person (including a flow-through entity or U.S. branch) receiving such income that is (or is deemed to be) effectively connected with the conduct of its trade or business in the United States;

*(2)* With respect to a payment other than U.S. source FDAP income. [Reserved]; and

*(3)* Any other person required to be reported as a recipient by Form 1042-S, its accompanying instructions, under an FFI agreement, or paragraph (d)(4)(iii) of this section with respect to the Form 1042-S reporting requirements of a participating FFI.

*(B) Persons that are not recipients.*—Persons that are not recipients include—

*(1)* With respect to a payment of U.S. source FDAP income—

*(i)* A certified deemed-compliant FFI that is an NQI, NWP, or NWT and that fails to provide its withholding agent with sufficient information to allocate the payment to its account holders and payees;

*(ii)* A financial institution (other than a nonparticipating FFI) to the extent that the withholding agent issues a Form 1042-S to the FFI's account holder or payee;

*(iii)* A participating FFI or a registered deemed-compliant FFI that is an NQI, NWP, or NWT, and a U.S. branch of an FFI that is not treated as a U.S. person that applies the rules described in § 1.1471-4(d)(2)(iii)(C) to the extent it provides its withholding agent with sufficient information to allocate the payment to its account holders and payees that are exempt from withholding under chapter 4;

*(iv)* An account holder or payee of a participating FFI or registered deemed-compliant FFI, and an account holder or payee of a U.S. branch of an FFI that is not treated as a U.S. person that applies the rules described in § 1.1471-4(d)(2)(iii)(C)that is included in the FFI's reporting pools described in paragraph (d)(4)(i)(B) of this section;

*(v)* A nonparticipating FFI that acts as an intermediary with respect to a payment or that is a flow-through entity (including a limited branch);

*(vi)* An account holder or payee of a nonparticipating FFI except to the extent described in paragraph (d)(1)(ii)(A)(*1*)(*x*) of this section for an exempt beneficial owner;

*(vii)* Except as provided in paragraph (d)(1)(ii)(A)(*1*) of this section, an entity that is disregarded under § 301.7701-2(c)(2) of this chapter as an entity separate from its owner;

*(viii)* A territory financial institution to the extent provided in paragraph (d)(4)(i)(D)(2) and (3) of this section; and

*(ix)* A passive NFFE or an excepted NFFE that is a flow-through entity or acts as an intermediary;

*(2)* With respect to a payment other than U.S. source FDAP income. [Reserved]; and

*(3)* Any other person not treated as a recipient on Form 1042-S, its accompanying instructions, or under an FFI agreement.

*(2) Amounts subject to reporting.*—(i) *In general.*—Subject to paragraph (d)(2)(iii) of this section, the term *chapter 4 reportable amount* means each of the following amounts reportable on a Form 1042-S for purposes of chapter 4—

*(A)* An amount of a withholdable payment that is subject to withholding under chapter 4 paid after June 30, 2014;

*(B)* An amount of a withholdable payment of U.S. source FDAP income (including an amount that would be a withholdable payment but for the fact that it is an amount effectively connected with a U.S. trade or business, as described in § 1.1471-3(a)(4)(ii)) that is also reportable on Form 1042-S under § 1.1461-1(c)(2)(i); or

*(C)* A foreign passthru payment subject to withholding under chapter 4.

*(ii) Exception to reporting.*—Except as otherwise provided in this paragraph (d)(2)(ii), a chapter 4 reportable amount does not include an amount paid to a U.S. person if the withholding agent treats such U.S. person as a payee for purposes of determining whether withholding is required under §§ 1.1471-2 and 1.1472-1. A chapter 4 reportable amount does, however, include an amount paid to a participating FFI or registered deemed-compliant FFI to the extent allocable to its reporting pool of payees that are U.S. persons as described in paragraph (d)(4)(i)(B) of this section.

*(iii) Coordination with chapter 3.*—A payment that is not subject to reporting under this paragraph (d)(2) may be subject to chapter 3 reporting on Form 1042-S to the extent provided on such form and its accompanying instructions or under § 1.1461-1(c)(2). The recipient information and other information required to be reported on Form 1042-S for purposes of chapter 4 shall be in addition to the information required to be provided on Form 1042-S for purposes of chapter 3.

*(3) Required information.*—The information required to be furnished under this paragraph (d)(3) shall be based upon the information provided by or on behalf of the recipient of an amount subject to reporting (as corrected and supplemented based on the withholding agent's actual knowledge) or the presumption rules provided under § 1.1471-3(f) for a U.S. withholding agent and under § 1.1471-4(c)(3)(ii) and (c)(4)(i) for a participating FFI. The Form 1042-S must include the following information, if applicable—

*(i)* The name, address, and EIN or GIIN (as applicable) of the withholding agent (as required on the instructions to the form) and the withholding agent's status for chapter 3 and chapter 4 purposes (as defined in the instructions to the form);

*(ii)* A description of each category of income or payment made based on the income and payment codes provided on the form (for example, interest, dividends, and gross proceeds) and the aggregate amount in each category expressed in U.S. dollars;

*(iii)* The rate and amount of withholding applied or, in the case of a payment of U.S. source FDAP income not subject to withholding and reportable under paragraph (d)(2)(i)(A) of this section, the basis for exempting the payment from withholding under chapter 4 based on exemption codes provided on the form;

*(iv)* The name and address of the recipient and its TIN or GIIN (as applicable) and foreign taxpayer identification number and date of birth (as required on the instructions to the form);

*(v)* In the case of a payment to a person (including a flow-through entity or U.S. branch) for which the payment is reported as effectively connected with its conduct of a trade or business in the United States or, in the case of a U.S. branch that is treated as a U.S. person, the EIN used by the person or U.S. branch to file its U.S. income tax returns;

*(vi)* The name, address of any FFI, flow-through entity that is an NFFE, or U.S. branch or territory financial institution that is not treated as a U.S. person when an account holder or owner of such entity (including an unknown recipient or owner) is treated as the recipient of the payment;

*(vii)* The EIN or GIIN (as applicable), status for chapter 3 and chapter 4 purposes (as required on the instructions to the form) of an entity reported under paragraph (d)(3)(vi) of this section;

*(viii)* The country of incorporation or organization (based on the country codes provided on the form) of any entity the name of which appears on the form; and

*(ix)* Such information as the form or instructions may require in addition to, or in lieu of, information required under this paragraph (d)(3).

*(4) Method of reporting.*—(i) *Payments by U.S. withholding agent to recipients.*—Except as otherwise provided in this paragraph (d)(4) or on the Form 1042-S and its accompanying instructions, a withholding agent that is a U.S. person (including a U.S. branch that is treated as a U.S. person and excluding a foreign branch of a U.S. person that is a QI) and that makes a payment of a chapter 4 reportable amount must file a separate form for each recipient that receives such amount. Except as otherwise provided on Form 1042-S or its instructions, only payments for which the income or payment code, exemption code, withholding rate, and recipient code are the same may be reported on a single form filed with the IRS. See paragraph (d)(4)(ii) of this

section for reporting of payments made to a person that is not a recipient and that is otherwise required to be reported on Form 1042-S.

(A) *Payments to certain entities that are beneficial owners.*—If the beneficial owner of a payment made by a U.S. withholding agent is an exempt beneficial owner, an FFI, an NFFE, or a territory entity, it must complete Form 1042-S treating such entity as the recipient of the payment.

(B) *Payments to participating FFIs, deemed-compliant FFIs, and certain QIs.*—Except as otherwise provided in this paragraph (d)(4)(i)(B), a U.S. withholding agent that makes a payment of a chapter 4 reportable amount to a participating FFI or deemed-compliant FFI that is an NQI, NWP, or NWT must complete a Form 1042-S treating such FFI as the recipient. With respect to a payment of U.S. source FDAP income made to a participating FFI or registered deemed-compliant FFI that is an NQI, NWP, or NWT or QI that elects to be withheld upon under section 1471(b)(3) and from whom the withholding agent receives an FFI withholding statement allocating the payment (or portion of the payment) to a chapter 4 withholding rate pool, a U.S. withholding agent must complete a separate Form 1042-S issued to the participating FFI, registered deemed-compliant FFI, or QI (as applicable) as the recipient with respect to each such pool identified on an FFI withholding statement, described in §1.1471-3(c)(3)(iii)(B)(2). If, however, a participating FFI, deemed-compliant FFI, or QI (as applicable) has made an election under §1.1471-4(b)(3)(iii), for the portion of the payment that the FFI allocates to each recalcitrant account holder that is subject to backup withholding under section 3406, the withholding agent must report on Form 1099 the amount of the payment and tax withheld in accordance with the form's requirements and accompanying instructions. See §1.1471-2(a)(2)(i) for the requirement of a withholding agent to withhold on payments of U.S. source FDAP income made to a participating FFI or registered deemed-compliant FFI that is an NQI, NWP, or NWT. See also §1.1471-2(a)(2)(iii) in the case of payments made to a QI. See §1.1461-1(c)(4)(A) for the extent to which reporting is required under that section for U.S. source FDAP income that is reportable on Form 1042-S under chapter 3 and not subject to withholding under chapter 4, in which case the U.S. withholding agent must report in the manner described under §1.1461-1(c)(4)(ii) and paragraph (d)(4)(ii)(A) of this section. See paragraph (d)(4)(ii)(A) of this section for reporting rules applicable if participating FFIs or deemed-compliant FFIs provide specific payee information for reporting to the recipient of the payment for Form 1042-S reporting purposes. See paragraph (d)(4)(iii) of this section for the residual reporting responsibilities of an NQI, NWP, or NWT that is an FFI.

(C) *Amounts paid to a U.S. branch.*—A U.S. withholding agent making a payment of U.S. source FDAP income to a U.S. branch shall complete Form 1042-S as follows—

(1) If the U.S. branch is treated as a U.S. person, if the withholding agent treats amounts paid as effectively connected with the conduct of the branch's trade or business in the United States, or if the U.S. branch is the beneficial owner of the payment, the withholding agent must file Form 1042-S reporting the U.S. branch as the recipient;

(2) If the U.S. branch of an FFI is not treated as a U.S. person and applies the rules described in §1.1471-4(d)(2)(iii)(C) and provides the withholding agent with a withholding certificate that transmits information regarding its reporting pools referenced in paragraph (d)(4)(i)(B) of this section or information regarding each recipient that is an account holder or payee of the U.S. branch, the withholding agent must complete a separate Form 1042-S issued to the U.S. branch for each such pool to the extent required on the form and its accompanying instructions or must complete a separate Form 1042-S issued to each recipient whose documentation is associated with the U.S. branch's withholding certificate as described in paragraph (d)(4)(ii)(A) of this section and report the U.S. branch as an entity not treated as a recipient; or

(3) If the U.S. branch of an FFI is not treated as a U.S. person and applies the rules described in §1.1471-4(d)(2)(iii)(C) to the extent it fails to provide sufficient information regarding its account holders or payees, the withholding agent shall report the recipient of the payment as an unknown recipient to the extent recipient information is not provided and report the U.S. branch as provided in paragraph (d)(4)(ii)(A) of this section for an entity not treated as a recipient.

(D) *Amounts paid to territory financial institutions that are flow-through entities or acting as intermediaries.*—A U.S. withholding agent making a withholdable payment to a territory financial institution that is a flow-through entity or that acts as an intermediary must complete Form 1042-S as follows—

(1) If the territory financial institution is treated as a U.S. person or is the beneficial owner of the payment, the withholding agent must file Form 1042-S treating the territory financial institution as the recipient;

(2) If the territory financial institution is not treated as a U.S. person and provides the withholding agent with a withholding certificate that transmits information regarding each recipient that is an partner, beneficiary, owner, account holder, or payee, the withholding agent must complete a separate Form 1042-S for each recipient whose documentation is associated with the territory financial institution's withholding certificate as described in paragraph (d)(4)(ii)(A) of this section and must report the territory financial institution under that paragraph; or

(3) If the territory financial institution is not treated as a U.S. person, to the extent its fails to provide sufficient information regarding its partners, beneficiaries, owners, account holders or payees, the withholding agent shall report the recipient of the payment as an unknown recipient and report the territory financial institution as provided in paragraph (d)(4)(ii)(A) of this section for an entity not treated as a recipient.

(E) *Amounts paid to NFFEs.*—A U.S. withholding agent that makes payments of chapter 4 reportable amounts to an excepted or passive NFFE shall complete Forms 1042-S treating the NFFE as the recipient, except when the NFFE is a flow-through entity or acting as an intermediary and the partner or beneficiary is treated as the payee. In cases in which the chapter 4 reportable amount is also an amount of U.S. source FDAP income reportable on Form 1042-S (described in §1.1441-2(a)), see also §1.1461-1(c)(4)(ii)(A) for the extent to which reporting is required with respect to the partners, beneficiaries, or owners of such entities.

(ii) *Payments made by withholding agents to certain entities that are not recipients.*—(A) *Entities that provide information for a withholding agent to perform specific payee reporting.*—If a U.S. withholding agent makes a payment of a chapter 4 reportable amount to a flow-through entity that is a passive NFFE, a nonparticipating FFI receiving a payment on behalf of an exempt beneficial owner, or a participating FFI or deemed-compliant FFI that is an NQI, NWP, or NWT, except as otherwise provided in paragraph (d)(4)(i)(B) of this section, the withholding agent must complete a separate Form 1042-S for each recipient that is a partner, beneficiary, owner, or account holder of such entity to the extent the withholding agent can reliably associate the payment with valid documentation (under the rules of §1.1471-3(c) and (d)) provided by such entity, as applicable, with respect to each such recipient. If a payment is made through tiers of such entities, the withholding agent must nevertheless complete Form 1042-S for the recipient to the extent it can reliably associate the payment with documentation provided with respect to that recipient. A withholding agent that is completing a Form 1042-S for a recipient described in this paragraph (d)(4)(ii)(A) must include on the form the information described in paragraph (d)(3)(vii) of this section for the entity through which the recipient directly receives the payment.

(B) *Nonparticipating FFI that is a flow-through entity or intermediary.*—If a withholding agent makes a payment of a chapter 4 reportable amount to a nonparticipating FFI that it is required to treat as an intermediary with regard to a payment or as a flow-through entity under rules described in §1.1471-3(c)(3)(iii), and except as otherwise provided in paragraph (d)(1)(ii)(A)(1)(x) of this section (relating to an exempt beneficial owner), the withholding agent must report the recipient of the payment as an unknown recipient and report the nonparticipating FFI as provided in paragraph (d)(4)(ii)(A) of this section for an entity not treated as a recipient.

(C) *Disregarded entities.*—If a U.S. withholding agent makes a payment to a disregarded entity and receives a valid withholding certificate or other documentary evidence from the person that is the single owner of such disregarded entity, the withholding agent must file a Form 1042-S treating the single owner as the recipient in accordance with the instructions to the Form 1042-S.

(iii) *Reporting by participating FFIs and deemed-compliant FFIs (including QIs, WPs, and WTs) and U.S. branches of FFIs not treated as U.S. persons.*—(A) *In general.*—Except as otherwise provided in paragraph (d)(4)(iii)(B) (relating to NQIs, NWPs, NWTs, and FFIs electing under section 1471(b)(3)) and §1.1471-4(d)(2)(ii)(F) (relating to transitional payee-specific reporting for payments to nonparticipating FFIs), a participating FFI or deemed-compliant FFI (including a QI, WP, or WT), and a U.S. branch of an FFI that is not treated as a U.S. person that applies the rules described in §1.1471-4(d)(2)(iii)(C) that makes a payment that is a chapter 4 reportable amount to a recalcitrant account holder or nonparticipating FFI must complete a Form 1042-S to report such payments. A participating FFI or registered deemedcompliant FFI (including a QI, WP, or WT), and a U.S. branch of an FFI that is not treated as a U.S. person that applies the rules described in § 1.1471-4(d)(2)(iii)(C) may report in pools consisting of its recalcitrant account holders and payees that are nonparticipating FFIs. With respect to recalcitrant account holders, the FFI may report in pools consisting of recalcitrant account holders within a particular status described in § 1.1471-4(d)(6) and within a particular income code. Except as otherwise provided in § 1.1471-4(d)(2)(ii)(F), with respect to payees that are nonparticipating FFIs, the FFI may report in pools consisting of one or more nonparticipating FFIs that fall within a particular income code and within a particular status code described in the instructions to Form 1042-S. Alternatively, a participating FFI or registered deemed-compliant FFI (including a QI, WP, or WT) and a U.S. branch of an FFI that is not treated as a U.S. person that applies the rules described in § 1.1471-4(d)(2)(iii)(C) may (and a certified deemed-compliant FFI is required to) perform payee-specific reporting to report a chapter 4 reportable amount paid to a recalcitrant account holder or a nonparticipating FFI when withholding was applied (or should have applied) to the payment.

(B) *Special reporting requirements of participating FFIs, deemed-compliant FFIs, FFIs that make an election under section 1471(b)(3), and U.S. branches of FFIs not treated as U.S. persons.*—Except as otherwise provided in § 1.1471-4(d)(2)(ii)(F), a participating FFI or deemedcompliant FFI that is an NQI, NWP, or NWT, and a U.S. branch of an FFI that is not treated as a U.S. person that applies the rules described in § 1.1471-4(d)(2)(iii)(C) or an FFI that has made an election under section 1471(b)(3) and has provided sufficient information to its withholding agent to withhold and report the payment is not required to report the payment on Form 1042-S as described in paragraph (d)(4)(iii)(A) of this section if the payment is made to a nonparticipating FFI or recalcitrant account holder and its withholding agent has withheld the correct amount of tax on such payment and correctly reported the payment on a Form 1042-S. Such FFI or branch is required to report a payment, however, when the FFI knows, or has reason to know, that less than the required amount has been withheld by the withholding agent on the payment or the withholding agent has not correctly reported the payment on Form 1042-S. In such case, the FFI or branch must report on Form 1042-S to the extent required under paragraph (d)(4)(iii)(A) of this section. See, however, § 1.1471-4(d)(6) for the requirement to report certain aggregate information regarding accounts held by recalcitrant account holders on Form 8966, "FATCA Report," regardless of whether withholdable payments are made to such accounts.

(C) *Reporting by a U.S. branch treated as a U.S. person.*—A U.S. branch treated as a U.S. person (as defined in § 1.1471-1(b)(135)) must report amounts paid to recipients on Forms 1042-S in the same manner as a U.S. withholding agent under paragraph (d)(4)(i) of this section.

(iv) *Reporting by territory financial institutions.*—A territory financial institution that is not treated as a U.S. person will not be required to report on Form 1042-S if another withholding agent has reported the same amount with regard to the same recipient for which such entity would otherwise be required to file a return under this paragraph (d)(4)(iv) and such withholding agent has withheld the entire amount required to be withheld from such payment. A territory financial institution must, however, report payments made to recipients for whom it has failed to provide the appropriate documentation to another withholding agent or to the extent it knows, or has reason to know, that less than the required amount has been withheld. A territory financial institution that is treated as a U.S. person or is otherwise required under this paragraph (d)(4)(iv) to report amounts paid to recipients on Forms 1042-S must report in the same manner as a U.S. withholding agent.

(v) *Nonparticipating FFIs.*—A nonparticipating FFI that is a flow-through entity or that acts as an intermediary with respect to a payment may file Forms 1042 and 1042-S only to report and allocate tax withheld to the account holders, partners, owners, or beneficiaries of the nonparticipating FFI.

(vi) *Other withholding agents.*—Any person that is a withholding agent that is not described in any of paragraphs (d)(4)(i) through (v) of this section shall file Forms 1042-S in the same manner as a U.S. withholding agent and in accordance with the instructions to the form.

(vii) *Combined Form 1042-S reporting.*—A withholding agent required to report on Form 1042-S under paragraph (d)(4) of this section (other than a nonparticipating FFI reporting under paragraph (d)(4)(v) of this section) may rely on the procedures used for chapter 3 purposes (provided in published guidance) for reporting on Form 1042-S (even if the withholding agent is not required to report under chapter 3) for combined reporting following a merger or acquisition, provided that all of the requirements for such reporting provided in the Instructions for Form 1042-S are satisfied.

(e) *Magnetic media reporting.*—A withholding agent that is not a financial institution and that is required to file 250 or more Form 1042-S information returns for a taxable year must file Form 1042-S returns on magnetic media. See § 301.6011-2(b) of this chapter for the requirements of a withholding agent that is not a financial institution with respect to the filing of Forms 1042-S on magnetic media. See § 301.1474-1(a) of this chapter for the requirements applicable to a withholding agent that is a financial institution with respect to the filing of Forms 1042-S on magnetic media.

(f) *Indemnification of withholding agent.*—A withholding agent is indemnified against the claims and demands of any person for the amount of any tax it deducts and withholds in accordance with the provisions of chapter 4 and the regulations thereunder. A withholding agent that withholds based on a reasonable belief that such withholding is required under chapter 4 and the regulations thereunder is treated for purposes of section 1474 and this paragraph (f) as having withheld tax in accordance with the provisions of chapter 4 and the regulations thereunder. This paragraph (f) does not relieve a withholding agent from tax liability under chapter 3 or chapter 4 or the regulations under those chapters.

(g) *Extensions of time to file Forms 1042 and 1042-S.*—The IRS may grant an extension of time to file Form 1042 or 1042-S as described in § 1.1461-1(g).

(h) *Penalties.*—For penalties and additions to tax for failure to file returns or file and furnish statements in accordance with this section, see sections 6651, 6662, 6663, 6721, 6722, 6723, 6724(c), 7201, 7203, and the regulations under those sections. For penalties and additions to tax for failure to timely pay the tax required to be withheld under chapter 4, see sections 6656, 6672, 7202, and the regulations under those sections.

(i) *Additional reporting requirements with respect to U.S. owned foreign entities and owner-documented FFIs.*—(1) *Reporting by certain withholding agents with respect to owner-documented FFIs.*—(i) Beginning on July 1, 2014, if a withholding agent (other than an FFI reporting accounts held by owner-documented FFIs under § 1.1471-4(d)) makes a withholdable payment to an entity account holder or payee of an obligation and the withholding agent treats the entity as an owner-documented FFI under § 1.1471-3(d)(6), the withholding agent is required to report for July 1 through December 31, 2014, with respect to each specified U.S. person identified in § 1.1471-3(d)(6)(iv)(A)(1) and (2) the information described in paragraph (i)(1)(iii) of this section.

(ii) Beginning in calendar year 2015, if a withholding agent (other than an FFI reporting accounts held by owner-documented FFIs under § 1.1471-4(d)) makes during a calendar year a withholdable payment to an entity account holder or payee of an obligation and the withholding agent treats the entity as an owner-documented FFI under § 1.1471-3(d)(6), the withholding agent is required to report for such calendar year with respect to each specified U.S. person identified in § 1.1471-3(d)(6)(iv)(A)(1) and (2) the information described in paragraph (i)(1)(iii) of this section.

(iii) The information that a withholding agent (other than an FFI reporting accounts held by owner-documented FFIs under § 1.1471-4(d)) is required to report under paragraphs (i)(1)(i) and (ii) of this section must be made on Form 8966 (or such other form as the IRS may prescribe) and filed on or before March 31 of the calendar year following the year in which the withholdable payment was made. A withholding agent is not required to report under paragraph (i)(1)(i) or (ii) of this section on a withholdable payment made to a participating FFI or reporting Model 1 FFI that is allocated to a payee that is an owner-documented FFI on an FFI withholding statement when the participating FFI or reporting Model 1 FFI includes on the statement the certification described in § 1.1471-3(c)(3)(iii)(B)(2)(v), provided that the withholding agent does not know or have reason to know that the certification is incorrect or unreliable. The report must contain the following information—

(A) The name of the owner-documented FFI;

(B) The name, address, and TIN of each specified U.S. person identified in § 1.1471-3(d)(6)(iv)(A)(1) and (2);

(C) For the period from July 1 through December 31, 2014, the total of all withholdable payments made to the owner-documented FFI, and with respect to payments made after the 2014 calendar year, the total of all withholdable payments made to the owner-documented FFI during the calendar year;

(D) The account balance or value of the account held by the owner-documented FFI; and

(E) Any other information required on Form 8966 and its accompanying instructions provided for purposes of such reporting.

(2) *Reporting by certain withholding agents with respect to U.S. owned foreign entities that are passive NFFEs.*—Beginning on July 1, 2014, in addition to the reporting on Form 1042-S required under

paragraph (d)(4)(i)(E) of this section, a withholding agent (other than an FFI reporting accounts held by NFFEs under §1.1471-4(d)) that makes a withholdable payment to, and receives information about any substantial U.S. owners of, a passive NFFE that is not an excepted NFFE as defined in §1.1472-1(c) shall file a report with the IRS for the period from July 1 through December 31, 2014, and in each subsequent calendar year in which a withholdable payment is made with respect to any substantial U.S. owners of such NFFE. Such report must be made on Form 8966 (or such other form as the IRS may prescribe) and filed on or before March 31 of the calendar year following the year in which the withholdable payment was made. A withholding agent is not required to report under this paragraph (i)(2) on a withholdable payment made to a participating FFI or a registered deemed-compliant FFI that is allocated to a payee that is a passive NFFE with one or more substantial U.S. owners on an FFI withholding statement when the participating FFI or registered deemed-compliant FFI includes on the statement the certification described in §1.1471-3(c)(3)(iii)(B)(2)(iv), provided that the withholding agent does not know or have reason to know that the certification is incorrect or unreliable. In the case of an entity to which the preceding sentence does not apply that is a flow-through entity or is acting as an intermediary receiving a withholdable payment allocable to a passive NFFE with one or more substantial U.S. owners, the entity is not required to report with respect to the passive NFFE under this paragraph (i)(2) if it provides to the withholding agent from which it receives the payment documentation sufficient for the withholding agent to report information with respect to the passive NFFE under this paragraph (i)(2), provided that the intermediary or flow-through entity does not know or have reason to know that the withholding agent does not report with respect to the passive NFFE under this paragraph (i)(2). The report must contain the following information—

(i) Name of the NFFE that is owned by a substantial U.S. owner;

(ii) The name, address, and TIN of each substantial U.S. owner of such NFFE;

(iii) For the period from July 1, 2014 through December 31, 2014, the total of all withholdable payments made to the NFFE and, with respect to payments made after the 2014 calendar year, the total of all withholdable payments made to the NFFE during the calendar year; and

(iv) Any other information as required by the form and its accompanying instructions.

(3) *Cross reference to reporting by participating FFIs.*—For the reporting requirements of a participating FFI with respect to an account holder that is a U.S. owned foreign entity or that it treats as an owner-documented FFI, see §1.1471-4(d).

(4) *Extensions of time to file.*—The IRS shall grant an automatic 90-day extension of time in which to file Form 8966 as required under paragraph (i)(1) or (i)(2) of this section. Form 8809-I, "Application of Extension of Time to File FATCA Form 8966," (or such other form as the IRS may prescribe) must be used to request such extension of time and must be filed no later than the due date of Form 8966. Under certain hardship conditions, the IRS may grant an additional 90-day extension. A request for extension due to hardship must contain a statement of the reasons for requesting the extension and such other information as the form or instructions may require.

(j) *Effective/applicability date.*—This section applies on January 6, 2017. However, taxpayers may apply these provisions as of January 28, 2013. (For the rules that apply beginning on January 28, 2013, and before January 6, 2017, see this section as in effect and contained in 26 CFR part 1 revised April 1, 2016.) [Reg. §1.1474-1.]

☐ [*T.D. 9610, 1-17-2013 (corrected 9-9-2013). Amended by T.D. 9657, 2-28-2014, T.D. 9809, 12-30-2016 (corrected 6-29-2017) and T.D. 9890, 12-27-2019.*]

### [Reg. §301.1474-1]

**§301.1474-1. Required use of magnetic media for financial institutions filing Form 1042-S or Form 8966.**—(a) *Financial institutions filing certain information returns.*—If a financial institution is required to file a Form 1042-S, "Foreign Person's U.S. Source Income Subject to Withholding," (or such other form as the IRS may prescribe) under §1.1474-1(d) of this chapter, the financial institution must file the information required by the applicable forms and schedules on magnetic media. Additionally, if a financial institution is required to file Form 8966, "FATCA Report," (or such other form as the IRS may prescribe) to report certain information about U.S. accounts, substantial U.S. owners of foreign entities, or owner-documented FFIs as required under this chapter, the financial institution must file the required information on magnetic media or other machine-readable form. Returns filed on magnetic media must be made in accordance with applicable regulations, revenue procedures, publications, forms,

instructions, and the IRS.gov Internet site. In prescribing regulations, revenue procedures, publications, forms, and instructions, including those on the IRS.gov Internet site, the Commissioner may direct the type of magnetic media or other machine-readable form used for filing.

(b) *Waiver.*—The Commissioner may grant waivers from the requirements of this section in cases of undue hardship. A request for waiver must be made in accordance with applicable revenue procedures or publications. The waiver also will be subject to such terms and conditions regarding the method of filing as may be prescribed by the Commissioner.

(c) *Failure to file.*—If a financial institution fails to file a Form 1042-S or a Form 8966 on magnetic media when required to do so by this section, the financial institution is deemed to have failed to comply with the information reporting requirements under section 6721 of the Code. See section 6724(c) for failure to meet magnetic media requirements. In determining whether there is reasonable cause for failure to file the return, §301.6651-1(c) and rules similar to the rules in §301.6724-1(c)(3) (undue economic hardship related to filing information returns on magnetic media) will apply.

(d) *Meaning of terms.* The following definitions apply for purposes of this section.—(1) *Magnetic media.*—The term *magnetic media* means any magnetic media permitted under applicable regulations, revenue procedures, publications, forms, or instructions. These generally include magnetic tape, tape cartridge, and diskette, as well as other media, such as electronic filing, specifically permitted under the applicable regulations, revenue procedures, publications, forms, or instructions.

(2) *Financial institution.*—The term *financial institution* has the meaning set forth in section 1471(d)(5) of the Code and the regulations thereunder.

(e) *Effective/applicability date.*—This section applies to any Form 1042-S or Form 8966 (or any other form that the IRS may prescribe) filed with respect to calendar years ending after December 31, 2013. [Reg. §301.1474-1.]

☐ [*T.D. 9610, 1-17-2013. Amended by T.D. 9809, 12-30-2016.*]

### [Reg. §1.1474-2]

**§1.1474-2. Adjustments for overwithholding or underwithholding of tax.**—(a) *Adjustments of overwithheld tax.*—(1) *In general.*—Except as otherwise provided by this section, a withholding agent that has overwithheld tax under chapter 4 and made a deposit of the tax as provided in §1.6302-2(a) may adjust the amount of overwithheld tax either pursuant to the reimbursement procedure described in paragraph (a)(3) of this section or pursuant to the set-off procedure described in paragraph (a)(4) of this section. Adjustments under this paragraph (a) may only be made within the time prescribed under paragraph (a)(3) or (a)(4) of this section. After such time, a refund of the amount of overwithheld tax can only be claimed pursuant to the procedures described in §1.1474-5 and chapter 65 of the Code and the regulations thereunder.

(2) *Overwithholding.*—For purposes of this section, the term *overwithholding* means an amount actually withheld (determined before application of the adjustment procedures under this section and regardless of whether such overwithholding was in error or appeared correct at the time it occurred) from an item of income or other payment pursuant to chapter 4 that is in excess of the greater of—

(i) The amount required to be withheld with respect to such item of income or other payment under chapter 4; and

(ii) The actual tax liability of the beneficial owner that is attributable to the income or payment from which the amount was withheld.

(3) *Reimbursement of tax.*—(i) *General rule.*—Under the reimbursement procedure, the withholding agent may repay the beneficial owner or payee for an amount of overwithheld tax. In such case, the withholding agent may reimburse itself by reducing, by the amount actually repaid to the beneficial owner or payee, the amount of any deposit of tax made by the withholding agent under §1.6302-2(a)(1)(iii) for any subsequent payment period occurring before the end of the calendar year following the calendar year of overwithholding. A withholding agent must obtain valid documentation as described under §1.1471-3(c)(6) with respect to the beneficial owner or payee supporting a reduced rate of withholding before reducing the amount of any deposit of tax under this paragraph (a)(3)(i). Any such reduction that occurs for a payment period in the calendar year following the calendar year of overwithholding shall be allowed only if—

(A) The repayment of the beneficial owner or payee occurs before the earlier of the due date (without regard to extensions) for filing the Form 1042-S for the calendar year of overwithholding or the date that the Form 1042-S is actually filed with the IRS;

(B) The withholding agent states on a timely filed (not including extensions) Form 1042-S the amount of tax withheld and the amount of any actual repayment; and

(C) The withholding agent states on a timely filed (not including extensions) Form 1042 for the calendar year of overwithholding that the filing of the Form 1042 constitutes a claim for credit in accordance with § 1.6414-1.

(ii) *Record maintenance.*—If the beneficial owner or payee is repaid an amount of overwithheld tax under the provisions of this paragraph (a)(3), the withholding agent shall keep as part of its records a receipt showing the date and amount of repayment, and the withholding agent must provide a copy of such receipt to the beneficial owner or payee. For this purpose, a canceled check or an entry in a statement is sufficient, provided that the check or statement contains a specific notation that it is a refund of tax overwithheld.

(4) *Set-offs.*—Under the set-off procedure, the withholding agent may repay the beneficial owner or payee for an amount of overwithheld tax by applying the amount overwithheld against any amount which otherwise would be required under chapter 3 or 4 to be withheld from the amount paid by the withholding agent to such person before the earlier of the due date (without regard to extensions) for filing the Form 1042-S for the calendar year of overwithholding or the date that the Form 1042-S is actually filed with the IRS. For purposes of making a return on Form 1042 or 1042-S (or an amended form) for the calendar year of overwithholding and for purposes of making a deposit of the amount withheld, the reduced amount shall be considered the amount required to be withheld from such payment under chapter 3 or 4, respectively.

(5) *Examples.*—The principles of this paragraph (a) are illustrated by the following examples:

*Example 1.* (i) Fund A is a unit investment trust that is an FFI and a resident of Country X. Fund A also qualifies for the benefits of the income tax treaty between the United States and Country X. On December 1, 2016, domestic corporation C pays a dividend of $100 to Fund A, at which time C withholds $30 of tax pursuant to § 1.1471-2(a) and remits the balance of $70 to Fund A, because it does not hold valid documentation that Fund A is a participating FFI or deemed-compliant FFI. On February 10, 2017, prior to the time that C is obligated to file its Form 1042, Fund A furnishes a valid Form W-8BEN described in § § 1.1441-1(e)(2)(i) and 1.1471-3(c)(3)(ii) upon which C may rely to treat Fund A as the beneficial owner of the income and as a participating FFI so that C may reduce the rate of withholding to 15% under the provisions of the United States-Country X income tax treaty with respect to the payment. C repays the excess tax withheld of $15 to Fund A.

(ii) During the 2016 calendar year, C makes no other payments upon which tax is required to be withheld under chapter 3 or 4; accordingly, its Form 1042 for such year, filed on March 15, 2017, shows total tax withheld of $30, an adjusted total tax withheld of $15, and tax deposited of $30 for such year. Pursuant to § 1.6414-1, C claims a credit for the overpayment of $15 shown on the Form 1042 for 2016. Accordingly, C is permitted to reduce by $15 any deposit required by § 1.6302-2 to be made of tax withheld during the 2017 calendar year with respect to taxes due under chapter 3 or 4. The Form 1042-S required to be filed by C with respect to the dividend of $100 paid to Fund A in 2016 is required to show tax withheld of $30 and tax repaid of $15 to Fund A.

*Example 2.* (i) In November 2016, Bank A, a foreign bank organized in Country X that is an NQI, receives on behalf of one of its account holders, Z, an individual, a $100 dividend payment from C, a domestic corporation. At the time of payment, C withholds $30 pursuant to § 1.1471-2(a) and remits the balance of $70 to Bank A, because it does not hold valid documentation that it may rely on to treat Bank A as a participating FFI or deemed-compliant FFI. In December 2016, prior to the time that C files its Forms 1042 and 1042-S, Bank A furnishes a valid Form W-8IMY and FFI withholding statement described in § 1.1471-3(c)(3)(iii) that establishes Bank A's status as a participating FFI that is an NQI, as well as a valid Form W-8BEN that has been completed by Z as described in § 1.1471-3(c)(3)(ii) and § 1.1441-1(e)(2)(i) upon which C may rely to treat the payment as made to Z, a nonresident alien individual who is a resident of Country X eligible for a reduced rate of withholding of 15% under the income tax treaty between the United States and Country X. Although C has already deposited the $30 that was withheld, as required by § 1.6302-2(a)(1)(iv), C remits the amount of $15 to Bank A for the benefit of Z.

(ii) During the 2016 calendar year, C makes no other payments upon which tax is required to be withheld under chapter 3 or 4; accordingly, its return on Form 1042 for such year, which is filed on March 15, 2017, shows total tax withheld of $30, an adjusted total tax withheld of $15, and tax deposited of $30. Pursuant to § 1.6414-1(b), C

claims a credit for the overpayment of $15 shown on the Form 1042 for 2014. Accordingly, it is permitted to reduce by $15 any deposit required by § 1.6302-2 to be made of tax withheld during the 2017 calendar year. The Form 1042-S required to be filed by C for 2016 with respect to the dividend of $100 beneficially owned by Z is required to show tax withheld of $30 and tax repaid of $15 to Z.

(b) *Withholding of additional tax when underwithholding occurs.*—A withholding agent that has underwithheld under chapter 4 may apply the procedures described in § 1.1461-2(b) (by substituting the term "chapter 4" for "chapter 3") to satisfy its withholding obligations under chapter 4 with respect to a payee or beneficial owner.

(c) *Effective/applicability date.*—This section applies January 28, 2013. [Reg. § 1.1474-2.]

☐ [*T.D.* 9610, 1-17-2013.]

## [Reg. § 1.1474-3]

**§ 1.1474-3. Withheld tax as credit to beneficial owner of income.**—(a) *Creditable tax.*—The entire amount of the income, if any, attributable to a payment from which tax is required to be withheld under chapter 4 (including income deemed paid by a withholding agent under § 1.1473-1(a)(2)(v)) shall be included in gross income in a return required to be made by the beneficial owner of the income, without deduction for the amount required to be or actually withheld, but the amount of tax actually withheld shall be allowed as a credit against the total income tax computed in the beneficial owner's return.

(b) *Amounts paid to persons that are not the beneficial owners.*—Amounts actually deducted and withheld under chapter 4 on payments made to a fiduciary, agent, partnership, trust, or intermediary are deemed to have been paid by the beneficial owner of the item of income or other payment subject to withholding under chapter 4, except when the fiduciary, agent, partnership, trust, or intermediary pays the tax from its own funds and does not in turn withhold with respect to the payment made to such person. Thus, for example, if a beneficiary of a trust is subject to the taxes imposed by section 1, 2, 3, or 11 upon any amount of distributable net income or other taxable distribution received from a foreign trust, the part of any amount withheld at source under chapter 4 that is properly allocable to the income so taxed to such beneficiary shall be credited against the amount of the income tax computed upon the beneficiary's return, and any excess shall be refunded to the beneficiary in accordance with § 1.1474-5 and chapter 65 of the Code.

(c) *Effective/applicability date.*—This section applies January 28, 2013. [Reg. § 1.1474-3.]

☐ [*T.D.* 9610, 1-17-2013.]

## [Reg. § 1.1474-4]

**§ 1.1474-4. Tax paid only once.**—(a) *Tax paid.*—If the tax required to be withheld under chapter 4 on a payment is paid by the payee, beneficial owner, or the withholding agent, it shall not be re-collected from any other, regardless of the original liability therefor. However, this section does not relieve a person that was required to, but did not, withhold tax from liability for interest or any penalties or additions to tax otherwise applicable.

(b) *Effective/applicability date.*—This section applies January 28, 2013. [Reg. § 1.1474-4.]

☐ [*T.D.* 9610, 1-17-2013.]

## [Reg. § 1.1474-5]

**§ 1.1474-5. Refunds or credits.**—(a) *Refund and credit.*—(1) *In general.*—Except to the extent otherwise provided in this section, a refund or credit of tax which has actually been withheld at the source at the time of payment under chapter 4 shall be made to the beneficial owner of the payment to which the amount of withheld tax is attributable if the beneficial owner or payee meets the requirements of this paragraph (a) and any other requirements that may be required under chapter 65. To the extent that the amount withheld under chapter 4 is not actually withheld at source, but is later paid by the withholding agent to the IRS, the refund or credit under chapter 65 of the Code shall be made to the withholding agent to the extent the withholding agent provides documentation with respect to the beneficial owner or payee described in paragraphs (a)(2) and (3) of this section sufficient for the beneficial owner or payee to have obtained a refund of the tax and sufficient for the withholding agent to have applied a reduced rate or exemption from withholding under chapter 4. The preceding sentence shall not, however, apply to a nonparticipating FFI that is acting as a withholding agent with respect to one or more of its account holders. In such a case, only the account holders of the nonparticipating FFI will be entitled to a credit or refund of an amount withheld under chapter 4, to the extent otherwise allowable under this section. Additionally, there are collective refund procedures for a participating FFI or reporting Model 1 FFI to claim a refund or credit on behalf of certain direct account holders that are beneficial owners of the payment under §1.1471-4(h) (in lieu of such account holders claiming refund or credit under this paragraph (a)(1)).

(2) *Limitation to refund and credit for a nonparticipating FFI.*—Notwithstanding paragraph (a)(1) of this section, a nonparticipating FFI (determined as of the time of payment) that is the beneficial owner of an item of income or other payment that is subject to withholding under chapter 4 shall not be entitled to any credit or refund pursuant to section 1474(b)(2) and this section unless it is entitled to a reduced rate of tax with respect to the income or other payment by reason of any treaty obligation of the United States. If the nonparticipating FFI is entitled to a reduced rate of tax with respect to an item of income or other payment by reason of any treaty obligation of the United States, the amount of any credit or refund with respect to such tax shall not exceed the amount of credit or refund attributable to such reduction in rate on the item of income or other payment, and no interest otherwise allowable under section 6611 shall be allowed or paid with respect to such credit or refund.

(3) *Requirement to provide additional documentation for certain beneficial owners.*—(i) *In general.*—Except as provided in paragraph (a)(3)(ii) of this section, no refund or credit shall be allowed under paragraph (a)(1) of this section to the beneficial owner of the income or other payment to which the amount of such withheld tax was attributable if such beneficial owner is an NFFE, unless the NFFE attaches to its income tax return the information described in paragraph (a)(3)(iii) of this section.

(ii) *Claim of reduced withholding under an income tax treaty.*—Paragraph (a)(3)(i) of this section does not apply to the extent that the beneficial owner is entitled to a reduced rate of tax with respect to the income or other payment by reason of any treaty obligation of the United States.

(iii) *Additional documentation to be furnished to the IRS for certain NFFEs.*—The information described in this paragraph (a)(3)(iii) is—

(A) A certification that the beneficial owner does not have any substantial U.S. owners;

(B) The form described in §1.1474-1(i)(2) relating to each substantial U.S. owner of such entity; or

(C) Other appropriate documentation to establish withholding was not required under chapter 4.

(b) *Tax repaid to payee.*—For purposes of this section and §1.6414-1, any amount of tax withheld under chapter 4, which, pursuant to §1.1474-2(a)(1), is repaid by the withholding agent to the beneficial owner of the income or payment to which the withheld amount is attributable shall be considered as tax which, within the meaning of sections 1474 and 6414, was not actually withheld by the withholding agent.

(c) *Effective/applicability date.*—This section applies January 28, 2013. [Reg. §1.1474-5.]

☐ [T.D. 9610, 1-17-2013.]

**[Reg. §1.1474-6]**

**§1.1474-6. Coordination of chapter 4 with other withholding provisions.**—(a) *In general.*—This section coordinates the withholding requirements of a withholding agent when a withholdable payment or foreign passthru payment is subject to withholding under both chapter 4 and another Code provision. See §1.1473-1(a) for the definition of withholdable payment and see §1.1471-5(h)(2) for the definition of foreign passthru payment.

(b) *Coordination of withholding for amounts subject to withholding under sections 1441, 1442, and 1443.*—(1) *In general.*—In the case of a withholdable payment that is both subject to withholding under chapter 4 and is an amount subject to withholding under §1.1441-2(a), a withholding agent may credit the withholding applied under chapter 4 against its liability for any tax due under sections 1441, 1442, or 1443. See §1.1474-1(c) and (d) for the income tax return and information return reporting requirements that apply in the case of a payment that is a withholdable payment subject to withholding under chapter 4 that is also an amount subject to withholding under §1.1441-2(a).

(2) *When withholding is applied.*—For purposes of paragraph (b)(1) of this section, withholding is applied by a withholding agent under section 1441 (or section 1442 or 1443) or chapter 4 (as applicable) when the withholding agent has withheld on the payment and has designated the withholding as having been made under section 1441 (or section 1442 or 1443) or chapter 4 to the extent required in the reporting described in §1.1474-1(c) and (d). For purposes of

allowing an offset of withholding and allowing a credit to a withholding agent against its liability for such tax as described in paragraph (b)(1) of this section, withholding is treated as applied for purposes of paragraph (a) of this section only when the withholding agent has actually withheld on a payment and has not made any adjustment for overwithheld tax applicable to the amount withheld that would otherwise be permitted with respect to the payment.

(3) *Special rule for certain substitute dividend payments.*—In the case of a dividend equivalent under section 871(m) paid pursuant to a securities lending transaction described in section 1058 (or a substantially similar transaction), or pursuant to a sale-repurchase transaction, a withholding agent may offset its obligation to withhold under chapter 4 for amounts withheld by another withholding agent under chapters 3 and 4 with respect to the same underlying security in such a transaction, but only to the extent that there is sufficient evidence as required under chapter 3 that tax was actually withheld on a prior dividend equivalent paid to the withholding agent or a prior withholding agent with respect to the same underlying security in such transaction.

(c) *Coordination with amounts subject to withholding under section 1445.*—(1) *In general.*—An amount subject to withholding under section 1445 is not subject to withholding under chapter 4 as described in paragraphs (c)(2)(i) and (ii) of this section.

(2) *Determining the amount of the distribution from certain domestic corporations subject to section 1445 or chapter 4 withholding.*—(i) *Distribution from qualified investment entity.*—In the case of a passthru payment (including a withholdable payment) subject to withholding under chapter 4 that is a distribution with respect to the stock of a qualified investment entity as described in section 897(h)(4)(A), withholding under chapter 4 does not apply when withholding under section 1445 applies to such amounts. With respect to the portion of such distribution that is not subject to withholding under section 1445 but is subject to withholding under section 1441 (or section 1442 or 1443) and chapter 4, the coordination rule described in paragraph (b)(1) of this section shall apply.

(ii) *Distribution from a United States real property holding corporation.*—A distribution (or portion of a distribution) from a United States real property holding corporation (or from a corporation that was a United States real property holding corporation at any time during the five-year period ending on the date of the distribution) with respect to its stock that is a United States real property interest under section 897(c) is subject to withholding under chapter 4 and is also subject to the withholding provisions of section 1441 (or section 1442 or 1443) and section 1445. In such case, to the extent that the United States real property holding corporation chooses to withhold on a distribution only under section 1441 (or section 1442 or 1443) pursuant to §1.1441-3(c)(4)(i)(A), the coordination rule described in paragraph (b)(1) of this section shall apply to such distribution. Alternatively, to the extent that the United States real property holding corporation chooses to withhold under both section 1441 (or section 1442 or 1443) and section 1445 pursuant to §1.1441-3(c)(4)(i)(B), the coordination rule described in paragraph (b)(1) of this section shall apply to the portion of such distribution described in §1.1441-3(c)(4)(i)(B)(1), and withholding under section 1445 shall apply to the amount of such distribution described in §1.1441-3(c)(4)(i)(B)(2). A withholding agent other than a United States real property holding corporation may rely, absent actual knowledge or reason to know otherwise, on the representations of the United States real property holding corporation making the distribution regarding the portion of the distribution that is estimated to be a dividend under §1.1441-3(c)(2)(ii)(A), and in the case of a failure by the withholding agent to withhold under chapter 4 due to this reliance, the required amount shall be imputed to the United States real property holding corporation.

(d) *Coordination with section 1446.*—(1) *In general.*—Except as otherwise provided in paragraph (d)(2) of this section, a withholdable payment or a foreign passthru payment subject to withholding under section 1446 shall not be subject to withholding under chapter 4. See §1.1473-1(a)(4)(ii) for the exclusion from withholdable payment and the requirements for such exclusion for any item of income that is taken into account under section 871(b)(1) or 882(a)(1) for the taxable year.

(2) *Determining the amount of distribution subject to section 1446.*—[Reserved].

(e) *Example.*—*Chapter 4 withholding satisfies chapter 3 withholding obligation.* WA, a U.S. withholding agent, makes a payment consisting of a dividend from sources within the United States to NPFFI. NPFFI is a nonparticipating FFI that is a resident of Country X, a country that has an income tax treaty in force with the United States that would allow WA to reduce the rate of withholding for section 1442 purposes on a payment of U.S. source dividends paid to NPFFI to 15%. Because the payment is a withholdable payment and NPFFI is a nonparticipating FFI, WA withholds on the payment at the rate of 30% under chapter 4. WA does not make any adjustment for overwithholding that is otherwise permitted with respect to this payment. Although the payment is also an amount subject to withholding under section 1442, WA is not required to withhold any tax on this payment under section 1442. WA may credit its withholding applied under chapter 4 against the amount of tax otherwise required to be withheld on this payment under section 1442. See § 1.1474-5(a)(2) for the credit and refund procedures for nonparticipating FFIs that are entitled to a reduced rate of tax with respect to an amount subject to withholding under chapter 4 by reason of any treaty obligation of the United States.

(f) *Coordination with section 3406.*—A participating FFI that makes a withholdable payment that is also a reportable payment (as defined in the relevant sections of chapter 61) to a recalcitrant account holder that is a U.S. non-exempt recipient is not required to withhold under section 3406 if it withholds on the payment at a 30-percent rate in accordance with its withholding obligations under chapter 4. See, however, § 1.1471-4(b)(3)(iii) for the election to withhold on recalcitrant account holders that are non-exempt U.S. recipients under section 3406 instead of withholding under chapter 4.

(g) *Effective/applicability date.*—This section applies on January 6, 2017. However, taxpayers may apply these provisions as of January 28, 2013. (For the rules that apply beginning on January 28, 2013, and before January 6, 2017, see this section as in effect and contained in 26 CFR part 1 revised April 1, 2016.) [Reg. § 1.1474-6.]

☐ [*T.D. 9610*, 1-17-2013. *Amended by T.D. 9657*, 2-28-2014 *and T.D. 9809*, 12-30-2016.]

### [Reg. § 1.1474-7]

**§ 1.1474-7. Confidentiality of information.**—(a) *Confidentiality of information.*—Pursuant to section 1474(c)(1), the provisions of § 31.3406(f)-1(a) of this chapter shall apply (substituting "sections 1471 through 1474" for "section 3406") to information obtained or used in connection with the requirements of chapter 4.

(b) *Exception for disclosure of participating FFIs.*—Pursuant to section 1474(c)(2), the identity of a participating FFI or deemed-compliant FFI shall not be treated as return information for purposes of section 6103.

(c) *Effective/applicability date.*—This section applies January 28, 2013. [Reg. § 1.1474-7.]

☐ [*T.D. 9610*, 1-17-2013.]

## Consolidated Returns

# RETURNS AND PAYMENT OF TAX

See p. 20,601 for regulations not amended to reflect law changes

### [Reg. § 1.1502-0]

**§ 1.1502-0. Effective dates.**—(a) The regulations under section 1502 are applicable to taxable years beginning after December 31, 1965, except as otherwise provided therein.

(b) The provisions of §§ 1.1502-0A through 1.1502-3A, 1.1502-10A through 1.1502-19A, and 1.1502-30A through 1.1502-51A (as contained in the 26 CFR part 1 edition revised April 1, 1996) are applicable to taxable years beginning before January 1, 1966. [Reg. § 1.1502-0.]

☐ [*T.D. 6894*, 9-7-66. *Amended by T.D. 8677*, 6-26-96.]

### [Reg. § 1.1502-1]

**§ 1.1502-1. Definitions.**—(a) *Group.*—The term "group" means an affiliated group of corporations as defined in section 1504. See § 1.1502-75 (d) as to when a group remains in existence. Except as the context otherwise requires, references to a group are references to a consolidated group (as defined in paragraph (h) of this section).

(b) *Member.*—The term *member* means a corporation (including the common parent) that is included in the group, or as the context may require, a corporation that is included in a subgroup.

(c) *Subsidiary.*—The term "subsidiary" means a corporation other than the common parent which is a member of such group.

(d) *Consolidated return year.*—The term "consolidated return year" means a taxable year for which a consolidated return is filed or required to be filed by such group.

(e) *Separate return year.*—The term "separate return year" means a taxable year of a corporation for which it files a separate return or for which it joins in the filing of a consolidated return by another group.

(f) *Separate return limitation year.*—(1) *In general.*—Except as provided in paragraphs (f)(2) and (3) of this section, the term *separate return limitation year* (or *SRLY*) means any separate return year of a member or of a predecessor of a member.

(2) *Exceptions.*—The term *separate return limitation year* (or *SRLY*) does not include:

(i) A separate return year of the corporation which is the common parent for the consolidated return year to which the tax attribute is to be carried (except as provided in § 1.1502-75(d)(2)(ii) and subparagraph (3) of this paragraph),

(ii) A separate return year of any corporation which was a member of the group for each day of such year, or

(iii) A separate return year of a predecessor of any member if such predecessor was a member of the group for each day of such year,

provided that an election under section 1562(a) (relating to the privilege to elect multiple surtax exemptions) was never effective (or is no longer effective as a result of a termination of such election) for such

year. An election under section 1562(a) which is effective for a taxable year beginning in 1963 and ending in 1964 shall be disregarded.

(3) *Reverse acquisitions.*—In the event of an acquisition to which § 1.1502-75(d)(3) applies, all taxable years of the first corporation and of each of its subsidiaries ending on or before the date of the acquisition shall be treated as separate return limitation years, and the separate return years (if any) of the second corporation and each of its subsidiaries shall not be treated as separate return limitation years (unless they were so treated immediately before the acquisition). For example, if corporation P merges into corporation T, and the persons who were stockholders of P immediately before the merger, as a result of owning the stock of P, own more than 50 percent of the fair market value of the outstanding stock of T, then a loss incurred before the merger by T (even though it is the common parent), or by a subsidiary of T, is treated as having been incurred in a separate return limitation year. Conversely, a loss incurred before the merger by P, or by a subsidiary of P in a separate return year during all of which such subsidiary was a member of the group of which P was the common parent and for which section 1562 was not effective, is treated as having been incurred in a year which is not a separate return limitation year.

(4) *Predecessor and successors.*—The term *predecessor* means a transferor or distributor of assets to a member (the successor) in a transaction—

(i) To which section 381(a) applies; or

(ii) That occurs on or after January 1, 1997, in which the successor's basis for the assets is determined, directly or indirectly, in whole or in part, by reference to the basis of the assets of the transferor or distributor, but in the case of a transaction that occurs before June 25, 1999, only if the amount by which basis differs from value, in the aggregate, is material. For a transaction that occurs before June 25, 1999, only one member may be considered a predecessor to or a successor of one other member.

(g) *Consolidated return change of ownership.*—(1) *In general.*—A consolidated return change of ownership occurs during any taxable year (referred to in this subparagraph as the "year of change") of the corporation which is the common parent for the taxable year to which the tax attribute is to be carried, if, at the end of the year of change—

(i) Any one or more of the persons described in section 382(a)(2) own a percentage of the fair market value of the outstanding stock of such corporation which is more than 50 percentage points greater than such person or persons owned at—

(*a*) The beginning of such taxable year, or

(*b*) The beginning of the preceding taxable year, and

(ii) The increase in percentage points at the end of such year is attributable to—

(*a*) A purchase (within the meaning of section 382(a)(4)) by such person or persons of such stock, the stock of another corporation owning stock in such corporation, or an interest in a partnership or trust owning stock in such corporation, or *(b)* A decrease in the amount of such stock outstanding or the amount of stock outstanding of another corporation owning stock in such corporation, except a decrease resulting from a redemption to pay death taxes to which section 303 applies.

For purposes of subdivision (i)*(a)* and *(b)* of this subparagraph, the beginning of the taxable years specified therein shall be the beginning of such taxable years or October 1, 1965, whichever occurs later.

(2) *Operating rules.*—For purposes of this paragraph—

(i) The term "stock" means all shares except nonvoting stock which is limited and preferred as to dividends, and

(ii) Section 318 (relating to constructive ownership of stock) shall apply in determining the ownership of stock, except that section 318(a)(2)(C) and (3)(C) shall be applied without regard to the 50-percent limitation contained therein.

(3) *Old members.*—The term "old members" of a group means—

(i) Those corporations which were members of such group immediately preceding the first day of the taxable year in which the consolidated return change of ownership occurs, or

(ii) If the group was not in existence prior to the taxable year in which the consolidated return change of ownership occurs, the corporation which is the common parent for the taxable year to which the tax attribute is to be carried.

(4) *Reverse acquisitions.*—If there has been a consolidated return change of ownership of a corporation under subparagraph (1) of this paragraph and the stock or assets of such corporation are subsequently acquired by another corporation in an acquisition to which § 1.1502-7(d)(3) applies so that the group of which the former corporation is the common parent is treated as continuing in existence, then the "old members", as defined in subparagraph (3) of this paragraph, of such group immediately before the acquisition shall continue to be treated as "old members" immediately after the acquisition. For example, assume that corporations P and S comprise group PS, and PS undergoes a consolidated return change of ownership. Subsequently, the stock of P, the common parent, is acquired by corporation T, the common parent of group TU, in an acquisition to which section 368(a)(1)(B) and § 1.1502-75(d)(3) apply. The PS group is treated as continuing in existence with T as the common parent. P and S continue to be treated as old members, as defined in subparagraph (3) of this paragraph.

(h) *Consolidated group.*—The term "consolidated group" means a group filing (or required to file) consolidated returns for the tax year.

(i) [Reserved]

(j) *Affiliated.*—Corporations are affiliated if they are members of a group with each other.

(k) *Nonlife insurance company.*—The term *nonlife insurance company* means a member that is an insurance company other than a *life insurance company*, each as defined in section 816(a).

(l) *Applicability date.*—Paragraph (k) of this section applies to taxable years beginning after December 31, 2020. However, a taxpayer may choose to apply paragraph (k) of this section to taxable years beginning on or before December 31, 2020. [Reg. § 1.1502-1.]

☐ [*T.D. 6894, 9-7-66. Amended by T.D. 7246, 12-29-72; T.D. 8319, 11-19-90; T.D. 8560, 8-12-94; T.D. 8677, 6-26-96, T.D. 8823, 6-25-99 and T.D. 9927, 10-23-2020.*]

### [Reg. § 1.1502-2]

**§ 1.1502-2. Computation of tax liability.**—(a) *Taxes imposed.*—The tax liability of a group for a consolidated return year is determined by adding together—

(1) The tax imposed by section 11(a) in the amount described in section 11(b) on the consolidated taxable income for the year (reduced by the taxable income of a member described in paragraphs (a)(5) through (8) of this section);

(2) The tax imposed by section 541 on the consolidated undistributed personal holding company income;

(3) If paragraph (a)(2) of this section does not apply, the aggregate of the taxes imposed by section 541 on the separate undistributed personal holding company income of the members which are personal holding companies;

(4) If neither paragraph (a)(2) nor (3) of this section apply, the tax imposed by section 531 on the consolidated accumulated taxable income (see § 1.1502-43);

(5) The tax imposed by section 594(a) in lieu of the taxes imposed by section 11 on the taxable income of a life insurance department of the common parent of a group which is a mutual savings bank;

(6) The tax imposed by section 801 on consolidated life insurance company taxable income;

(7) The tax imposed by section 831(a) on consolidated insurance company taxable income of the members which are subject to such tax;

(8) Any increase in tax described in section 1351(d)(1) (relating to recoveries of foreign expropriation losses); and

(9) The tax imposed by section 59A on base erosion payments of taxpayers with substantial gross receipts.

(b) *Credits.*—A group is allowed as a credit against the taxes described in paragraph (a) of this section (except for paragraph (a)(9) of this section) of this section: the general business credit under section 38 (see § 1.1502-3), the foreign tax credit under section 27 (see § 1.1502-4), and any other applicable credits provided under the Internal Revenue Code. Any increase in tax due to the recapture of a tax credit will be taken into account. See section 59A and the regulations thereunder for credits allowed against the tax described in paragraph (a)(9) of this section.

(c) *Allocation of dollar amounts.*—For purposes of this section, if a member or members of the consolidated group are also members of a controlled group that includes corporations that are not members of the consolidated group, any dollar amount described in any section of the Internal Revenue Code is apportioned among all members of the controlled group in accordance with the provisions of the applicable section and the regulations thereunder.

(d) *Applicability date.*—This section applies to taxable years for which the original consolidated Federal income tax return is due (without extension) after December 6, 2019. [Reg. § 1.1502-2.]

☐ [*T.D. 6894, 9-7-66. Amended by T.D. 7093, 3-12-71, T.D. 7937, 1-26-84, T.D. 8677, 6-26-96, T.D. 8823, 6-25-99 and T.D. 9885, 12-2-2019.*]

### [Reg. § 1.1502-3]

**§ 1.1502-3. Consolidated tax credits.**—(a) *Determination of amount of consolidated credit.*—(1) *In general.*—The credit allowed by section 38 for a consolidated return year of a group shall be equal to the consolidated credit earned. The consolidated credit earned is equal to the aggregate of the credit earned (as determined under subparagraph (2) of this paragraph) by all members of the group for the consolidated return year.

(2) *Determination of credit earned.*—The credit earned of a member of the group is an amount equal to 7 percent of such member's qualified investment (determined under section 46(c)). For purposes of computing a member's qualified investment, the basis of property shall not include any gain or loss realized with respect to such property by another member in an inter company transaction (as defined in § 1.1502-13(b)), whether or not such gain or loss is deferred. Thus, if section 38 property acquired in an intercompany transaction has a basis of $100 to the purchasing member, and if the selling member has a $20 gain with respect to such property, the basis of such property for purposes of computing the purchaser's qualified investment is only $80. Such $80 basis shall also be used for purposes of applying section 47 to such property. See paragraph (f) of this section.

(3) *Consolidated limitation based on amount of tax.*—(i) Notwithstanding the amount of the consolidated credit earned for the taxable year, the consolidated credit allowed by section 38 to the group for the consolidated return year is limited to—

*(a)* So much of the consolidated liability for tax as does not exceed $25,000, plus

*(b)* For taxable years ending on or before March 9, 1967, 25 percent of the consolidated liability for tax in excess of $25,000, or

*(c)* For taxable years ending after March 9, 1967, 50 percent of the consolidated liability for tax in excess of $25,000.

The $25,000 amount referred to in the preceding sentence shall be reduced by any part of such $25,000 amount apportioned under § 1.46-1 to component members of the controlled group (as defined in section 46(a)(5)) which do not join in the filing of the consolidated return. For further rules for computing the limitation based on amount of tax with respect to the suspension period (as defined in section 48(j)), see section 46(a)(2). The amount determined under this subparagraph is referred to in this section as the "consolidated limitation based on amount of tax."

(ii) If an organization to which section 593 applies or a cooperative organization described in section 1381(a) joins in the filing of the consolidated return, the $25,000 amount referred to in subdivision (i) of this subparagraph (reduced as provided in such subdivision) shall be apportioned equally among the members of the group filing the consolidated return. The amount so apportioned equally to any such organization shall then be decreased in accordance with the provisions of section 46(d). Finally, the sum of all such equal portions (as decreased under section 46(d)) of each member of the group shall be substituted for the $25,000 amount referred to in subdivision (i) of this subparagraph.

(4) *Consolidated liability for tax.*—For purposes of subparagraph (3) of this paragraph, the consolidated liability for tax shall be the income tax imposed for the taxable year upon the group by chapter 1 of the Code, reduced by the consolidated foreign tax credit allowable under §1.1502-4. The tax imposed by section 56 (relating to minimum tax for tax preferences), section 531 (relating to accumulated earnings tax), section 541 (relating to personal holding company tax), and any additional tax imposed by section 1351(d)(1) (relating to recoveries of foreign expropriation losses), shall not be considered tax imposed by chapter 1 of the Code. In addition, any increase in tax resulting from the application of section 47 (relating to certain dispositions, etc., of section 38 property) shall not be treated as tax imposed by chapter 1 for purposes of computing the consolidated liability for tax.

(b) *Carryback and carryover of unused credits.*—(1) *Allowance of unused credit as consolidated carryback or carryover.*—A group shall be allowed to add to the amount allowable as a credit under paragraph (a)(1) of this section for any consolidated return year an amount equal to the aggregate of the consolidated investment credit carryovers and carrybacks to such year. The consolidated investment credit carryovers and carrybacks to the taxable year shall consist of any consolidated unused credits of the group, plus any unused credits of members of the group arising in separate return years of such members, which may be carried over or back to the taxable year under the principles of section 46(b). However, such consolidated carryovers and carrybacks shall not include any consolidated unused

| | Credit earned | Consolidated credit earned | Consolidated limitation based on amount of tax |
|---|---|---|---|
| 1966: | | | |
| P . . . . . . . . . . . . . . . . . . . . . . . . . . . . . . . . . . . . . . . . | $60,000 | | |
| S . . . . . . . . . . . . . . . . . . . . . . . . . . . . . . . . . . . . . . . . | $30,000 | $90,000 | $100,000 |
| 1967: | | | |
| P . . . . . . . . . . . . . . . . . . . . . . . . . . . . . . . . . . . . . . . . | $40,000 | | |
| S . . . . . . . . . . . . . . . . . . . . . . . . . . . . . . . . . . . . . . . . | $25,000 | $65,000 | $50,000 |

(ii) P's and S's credit earned for 1966 are aggregated, and the group's consolidated credit earned, $90,000, is allowable in full to the group as a credit under section 38 for 1966 since such amount is less than the consolidated limitation based on amount of tax for 1966, $100,000.

(iii) Since the consolidated limitation based on amount of tax for 1967 is $50,000, only $50,000 of the $65,000 consolidated credit earned for such year is allowable to the group under section 38 as a credit for 1967. The consolidated unused credit for 1967 of $15,000 ($65,000 less

credits apportioned to a corporation for a separate return year pursuant to paragraph (c) of §1.1502-79 and shall be subject to the limitations contained in paragraphs (c) and (e) of this section. A consolidated unused credit for any consolidated return year is the excess of the consolidated credit earned over the consolidated limitation based on amount of tax for such year.

(2) *Absorption rules.*—For purposes of determining the amount, if any, of an unused credit (whether consolidated or separate) which can be carried to a taxable year (consolidated or separate), the amount of such unused credit which is absorbed in a prior consolidated return year under section 46(b) shall be determined by—

(i) Applying all unused credits which can be carried to such prior year in the order of the taxable years in which such unused credits arose, beginning with the taxable year which ends earliest, and

(ii) Applying all such unused credits which can be carried to such prior year from taxable years ending on the same date on a pro rata basis.

(3) *Example.*—The provisions of paragraphs (a) and (b) of this section may be illustrated by the following example:

*Example.* (i) Corporation P is incorporated on January 1, 1966. On that same day P incorporates corporation S, a wholly owned subsidiary. P and S file consolidated returns for calendar years 1966 and 1967. P's and S's credit earned, the consolidated credit earned, and the consolidated limitation based on amount of tax for 1966 and 1967 are as follows:

$50,000) is a consolidated investment credit carryback and carryover to the years prescribed in section 46(b). In this case the consolidated unused credit is a consolidated investment credit carryback to 1966 (since P and S were not in existence in 1964 and 1965) and a consolidated investment credit carryover to 1968 and subsequent years. The portion of the consolidated unused credit for 1967 which is allowable as a credit for 1966 is $10,000. This amount shall be added to the amount allowable as a credit to the group for 1966. The balance of the consolidated unused credit for 1967 to be carried to 1968 is $5,000. These amounts are computed as follows:

| | | | |
|---|---|---|---|
| Consolidated carryback to 1966 . . . . . . . . . . . . . . . . . . . . . . . . . . . . . . . . . . . . . . . . . . | | | $15,000 |
| 1966 consolidated limitation based on tax . . . . . . . . . . . . . . . . . . . . . . . . . | | $100,000 | |
| Less: Consolidated credit earned for 1966 . . . . . . . . . . . . . . . . . | $90,000 | | |
| Consolidated unused credits attributable to years preceding 1967 . . . . . . . . . . . . . . . | 0 | $90,000 | |
| Limit on amount of 1967 consolidated unused credit which may be added as a credit for 1966 . . . . . . . . . . . . . . . . . . . . . . . . . . . . . | | | $10,000 |
| Balance of 1967 consolidated unused credit to be carried to 1968 . . . . . . . . . . . . . . . . . . . . . | | | $5,000 |

(c) *Limitation on investment credit carryovers and carrybacks from separate return limitation years applicable for consolidated return years for which the due date of the return is on or before March 13, 1998.*—(1) *General rule.*—In the case of an unused credit of a member of the group arising in a separate return limitation year (as defined in §1.1502-1(f)) of such member (and in a separate return limitation year of any predecessor of such member), the amount which may be included under paragraph (b) of this section (computed without regard to the limitation contained in paragraph (e) of this section) shall not exceed the amount determined under paragraph (c)(2) of this section.

(2) *Computation of limitation.*—The amount referred to in paragraph (c)(1) of this section with respect to a member of the group is the excess, if any, of—

(i) The limitation based on amount of tax of the group, minus such limitation recomputed by excluding the items of income, deduction, and foreign tax credit of such member; over

(ii) The sum of the investment credit earned by such member for such consolidated return year, and the unused credits attributable to such member which may be carried to such consolidated return year arising in unused credit years ending prior to the particular separate return limitation year.

(3) *Special effective date.*—This paragraph (c) applies to consolidated return years for which the due date of the income tax return (without extensions) is on or before March 13, 1998. See paragraph

(d) of this section for the rule that limits the group's use of a section 38 credit carryover or carryback from a SRLY for a consolidated return year for which the due date of the income tax return (without extensions) is after March 13, 1998. See also paragraph (d)(4) of this section for an optional effective date rule (generally making the rules of this paragraph (c) inapplicable to a consolidated return year beginning after December 31, 1996, if the due date of the income tax return (without extensions) for such year is on or before March 13, 1998).

(4) *Examples.*—The provisions of this paragraph (c) may be illustrated by the following examples:

*Example 1.* (i) Assume the same facts as in the example contained in paragraph (b)(3) of this section, except that all the stock of corporation T, also a calendar year taxpayer, is acquired by P on January 1, 1968, and that P, S, and T file a consolidated return for 1968. In 1966, T had an unused credit of $10,000 which has not been absorbed and is available as an investment credit carryover to 1968. Such carryover is from a separate return limitation year. P's and S's credit earned for 1968 is $10,000 each, and T's credit earned is $8,000; the consolidated credit earned is therefore $28,000. The group's consolidated limitation based on amount of tax for 1968 is $50,000. Such limitation recomputed by excluding the items of income, deduction, and foreign tax credit of T is $30,000. Thus, the amount determined under paragraph (c)(2)(i) of this section is $20,000 ($50,000 minus $30,000). Accordingly, the limitation on the carryover of T's unused credit is $12,000, the excess of $20,000 over $8,000 (the sum of T's credit earned for the taxable year and any carryovers from prior unused credit years (none in this case)). Therefore T's $10,000 unused credit from 1966 may be carried over to the consolidated return year without limitation.

(ii) The group's consolidated credit earned for 1968, $28,000, is allowable in full as a credit under section 38 since such amount is less than the consolidated limitation based on amount of tax, $50,000.

(iii) The group's consolidated investment credit carryover to 1968 is $15,000, consisting of the consolidated unused credits of the group ($5,000) plus T's separate return year unused credit ($10,000). The entire $15,000 consolidated carryover shall be added to the amount allowable to the group as a credit under section 38 for 1968,

| | | | |
|---|---|---|---|
| T's carryover to 1968 . . . . . . . . . . . . . | | | $10,000 |
| Consolidated limitation based on amount of tax minus recomputed limitation . . . . . . . . . . . . . | | $12,000 | |
| Less: T's credit earned for 1968 . . . . . . . . . . . . . | $8,000 | | |
| Unused credits attributable to T arising in unused credit years preceding 1966 . . . . . . | 0 | $8,000 | |
| Limit on amount of 1966 unused credit of T which may be added to consolidated investment credit carryover . . . . . . . . . . . . . | | | $4,000 |
| Balance of 1966 unused credit of T to be carried to 1969 (subject to the limitation contained in paragraph (c) of this section) . . . . . . . . . . . . . | | | $6,000 |

(d) *Limitation on tax credit carryovers and carrybacks from separate return limitation years applicable for consolidated return years for which the due date of the return is after March 13, 1998.*—(1) *General rule.*—The aggregate of a member's unused section 38 credits arising in SRLYs that are included in the consolidated section 38 credits for all consolidated return years of the group may not exceed—

(i) The aggregate for all consolidated return years of the member's contributions to the consolidated section 38(c) limitation for each consolidated return year; reduced by

(ii) The aggregate of the member's section 38 credits arising and absorbed in all consolidated return years (whether or not absorbed by the member).

(2) *Computational rules.*—(i) *Member's contribution to the consolidated section 38(c) limitation.*—If the consolidated section 38(c) limitation for a consolidated return year is determined by reference to the consolidated tentative minimum tax (see section 38(c)(1)(A)), then a member's contribution to the consolidated section 38(c) limitation for such year equals the member's share of the consolidated net income tax minus the member's share of the consolidated tentative minimum tax. If the consolidated section 38(c) limitation for a consolidated return year is determined by reference to the consolidated net regular tax liability (see section 38(c)(1)(B)), then a member's contribution to the consolidated section 38(c) limitation for such year equals the member's share of the consolidated net income tax minus 25 percent of the quantity which is equal to so much of the member's share of the consolidated net regular tax liability less its portion of the $25,000 amount specified in section 38(c)(1)(B). The group computes the member's shares by applying to the respective consolidated amounts the principles of section 1552 and the percentage method under § 1.1502-33(d)(3), assuming a 100% allocation of any decreased tax liability. The group must make proper adjustments so that taxes and credits not taken into account in computing the limitation under section 38(c) are not taken into account in computing the member's share of the consolidated net income tax, etc. (See, for example, the taxes described in section 26(b) that are disregarded in computing regular tax liability.) Also, the group may apportion all or a part of the $25,000 amount (or lesser amount if reduced by section 38(c)(3)) for any year to one or more members.

(ii) *Years included in computation.*—For purposes of computing the limitation under this paragraph (d), the consolidated return years of the group include only those years, including the year to which a credit is carried, that the member has been continuously included in the group's consolidated return, but exclude—

(A) For carryovers, any years ending after the year to which the credit is carried; and

(B) For carrybacks, any years ending after the year in which the credit arose.

(iii) *Subgroups and successors.*—The SRLY subgroup principles under § 1.1502-21(c)(2) apply for purposes of this paragraph (d). The predecessor and successor principles under § 1.1502-21(f) also apply for purposes of this paragraph (d).

(iv) *Overlap with section 383.*—The principles under § 1.1502-21(g) apply for purposes of this paragraph (d). For example, an overlap of paragraph (d) of this section and the application of section 383 with respect to a credit carryover occurs if a corporation becomes a member of a consolidated group (the SRLY event) within six months of the change date of an ownership change giving rise to a section 383 credit limitation with respect to that carryover (the section 383 event), with the result that the limitation of this para-

graph (d) does not apply. See § § 1.1502-21(g)(2)(ii)(A) and 1.383-1; see also § 1.1502-21(g)(4) (subgroup rules).

(3) *Effective date.*—(i) *In general.*—This paragraph (d) generally applies to consolidated return years for which the due date of the income tax return (without extensions) is after March 13, 1998.

(A) *Contribution years.*—Except as provided in paragraph (d)(4)(ii) of this section, a group does not take into account a consolidated taxable year for which the due date of the income tax return (without extensions) is on or before March 13, 1998, in determining a member's (or subgroup's) contributions to the consolidated section 38(c) limitation under this paragraph (d).

(B) *Special subgroup rule.*—In the event that the principles of § 1.1502-21(g)(1) do not apply to a particular credit carryover in the current group, then solely for purposes of applying paragraph (d) of this section to determine the limitation with respect to that carryover and with respect to which the SRLY register (the aggregate of the member's or subgroup's contribution to consolidated section 38(c) limitation reduced by the aggregate of the member's or subgroup's section 38 credits arising and absorbed in all consolidated return years) began in a taxable year for which the due date of the return is on or before May 25, 2000, the principles of § 1.1502-21(c)(2) shall be applied without regard to the phrase "or for a carryover that was subject to the overlap rule described in paragraph (g) of this section or § 1.1502-15(g) with respect to another group (the former group)."

(ii) *Overlap rule.*—Paragraph (d)(2)(iv) of this section (relating to overlap with section 383) applies to taxable years for which the due date (without extensions) of the consolidated return is after May 25, 2000. For purposes of this section, only an ownership change to which section 383, as amended by the Tax Reform Act of 1986 (100 Stat. 2085), applies and which results in a section 383 credit limitation shall constitute a section 383 event.

(4) *Optional effective date of January 1, 1997.*—(i) For consolidated taxable years beginning on or after January 1, 1997, for which the due date of the income tax return (without extensions) is on or before March 13, 1998, in lieu of paragraphs (c) and (e)(3) of this section (relating to the general business credit), § 1.1502-4(f)(3) and (g)(3) (relating to the foreign tax credit), the next to last sentence of § 1.1502-9A(a)(2), § 1.1502-9A(b)(1)(v) (relating to overall foreign losses), and § 1.1502-55(h)(4)(iii) (relating to the alternative minimum tax credit), a consolidated group may apply the corresponding provisions as they appear in 1998-1 C.B. 655 through 661 (see § 601.601(d)(2) of this chapter) (treating references in such corresponding provisions to § § 1.1502-9(b)(1)(ii), (iii), and (iv) as references to § § 1.1502-9A(b)(1)(ii), (iii), and (iv)). Also, in the case of a consolidated return change of ownership that occurs on or after January 1, 1997, in a taxable year for which the due date of the income tax return (without extensions) is on or before March 13, 1998, a consolidated group may choose not to apply paragraph (e) of this section and § 1.1502-4(g) to taxable years ending after December 31, 1996. A consolidated group making the choices described in the two preceding sentences generally must apply all such corresponding provisions (including not applying paragraph (e) of this section and § 1.1502-4(g)) for all relevant years. However, a consolidated group making the election provided in § 1.1502-9A(b)(1)(vi) (electing not to apply § 1.1502-9A(b)(1)(v) to years beginning before January 1, 1998) may nevertheless choose to apply all such corresponding provisions referred to in this paragraph (d)(4)(i) other than the provision corresponding to § 1.1502-9A(b)(1)(v) for all relevant years.

Reg. § 1.1502-3(d)(4)(i)

(ii) If a consolidated group chooses to apply the corresponding provisions referred to in paragraph (d)(4)(i) of this section, the consolidated group shall not take into account a consolidated taxable year beginning before January 1, 1997, in determining a member's (or subgroup's) contributions to the consolidated section 38(c) limitation under this paragraph (d).

(5) *Example.*—The following example illustrates the provisions of this paragraph (d):

*Example.* (i) Individual A owns all of the stock of P and T. P is the common parent of the P group. P acquires all the stock of T at the beginning of Year 2. T carries over an unused section 38 general business credit from Year 1 of $100,000. The table in paragraph (i) of this *Example* shows the group's net consolidated income tax, consolidated tentative minimum tax, and consolidated net regular tax liabilities, and T's share of such taxes computed under the principles of section 1552 and the percentage method under § 1.1502-33(d)(3), assuming a 100% allocation of any decreased tax liability, for Year 2. (The effects of the lower section 11 brackets are ignored, there are no other tax credits affecting a group amount or member's share, and $1,000s are omitted.)

**Year 2**

| | Group | P's share of col. 1 | T's share of col. 1 |
|---|---|---|---|
| 1. consolidated taxable income | $2,000 | $1,200 | $800 |
| 2. consolidated net regular tax | $700 | $420 | $280 |
| 3. consolidated alternative minimum taxable income | $4,000 | $3,200 | $800 |
| 4. consolidated tentative minimum tax | $800 | $640 | $160 |
| 5. consolidated net income tax | $800 | $520 | $280 |
| 6. greater of line 4 or 25% of (line 2 minus $25,000) *for the group* | $800 | | |
| 7. consolidated § 38(c) limitation (line 5 minus line 6) | $0 | | |

(ii) T's Year 1 is a SRLY with respect to the P group. See § 1.1502-1(f)(2)(ii). T did not undergo an ownership change giving rise to a section 383 credit limitation within 6 months of joining the P group. Thus, T's $100,000 general business credit arising in Year 1 is subject to a SRLY limitation in the P group. The amount of T's unused section 38 credits from Year 1 that are included in the consolidated section 38 credits for Year 2 may not exceed T's contribution to the consolidated section 38(c) limitation. For Year 2, the group determines the consolidated section 38(c) limitation by reference to consolidated tentative minimum tax for Year 2. Therefore, T's contribution to the consolidated section 38(c) limitation for Year 2 equals its share of consolidated net income tax minus its share of consolidated tentative minimum tax. T's contribution is $280,000 minus $160,000, or $120,000. However, because the group has a consolidated section 38 limitation of zero, it may not include any of T's unused section 38 credits in the consolidated section 38 credits for Year 2.

(iii) The following table shows similar information for the group for Year 3:

**Year 3**

| | Group | P's share of col. 1 | T's share of col. 1 |
|---|---|---|---|
| 1. consolidated taxable income | $1,200 | $1,500 | $(300) |
| 2. consolidated net regular tax | $420 | $525 | $(105) |
| 3. consolidated alternative minimum taxable income | $1,500 | $1,700 | $(200) |
| 4. consolidated tentative minimum tax | $300 | $340 | $(40) |
| 5. consolidated net income tax | $420 | $525 | $(105) |
| 6. greater of line 4 or 25% of (line 2 minus $25,000) *for the group* | $300 | | |
| 7. consolidated § 38(c) limitation (line 5 minus line 6) | $120 | | |

(iv) The amount of T's unused section 38 credits from Year 1 that are included in the consolidated section 38 credits for Year 3 may not exceed T's aggregate contribution to the consolidated section 38(c) limitation for Years 2 and 3. For Year 3, the group determines the consolidated section 38(c) limitation by reference to the consolidated tentative minimum tax for Year 3. Therefore, T's contribution to the consolidated section 38(c) limitation for Year 3 equals its share of consolidated net income tax minus its share of consolidated tentative minimum tax. Applying the principles of section 1552 and § 1.1502-33(d) (taking into account, for example, that T's positive earnings and profits adjustment under § 1.1502-33(d) reflects its losses actually absorbed by the group), T's contribution is $(105,000) minus $(40,000), or $(65,000). T's aggregate contribution to the consolidated section 38(c) limitation for Years 2 and 3 is $120,000 + $(65,000), or $55,000. The group may include $55,000 of T's Year 1 unused section 38 credits in its consolidated section 38 tax credit in Year 3.

(e) *Limitation on investment credit carryovers where there has been a consolidated return change of ownership.*—(1) *General rule.*—If a consolidated return change of ownership (as defined in paragraph (g) of § 1.1502-1) occurs during the taxable year or an earlier taxable year, the amount which may be included under paragraph (b) of this section in the consolidated investment credit carryovers to the taxable year with respect to the aggregate unused credits attributable to old members of the group (as defined in paragraph (g)(3) of § 1.1502-1) arising in taxable years (consolidated or separate) ending on the same day and before the taxable year in which the consolidated return change of ownership occurred shall not exceed the amount determined under subparagraph (2) of this paragraph.

(2) *Computation of limitation.*—The amount referred to in subparagraph (1) of this paragraph shall be the excess of the consolidated limitation based on the amount of tax for the taxable year, recomputed by including only the items of income, deduction, and foreign tax credit of the old members, over the sum of—

(i) The aggregate investment credits earned by the old members for the taxable year, and

(ii) The aggregate unused investment credits attributable to the old members which may be carried to the taxable year arising in unused credit years ending prior to the particular unused credit year or years.

(3) *Special effective date.*—This paragraph (e) applies only to a consolidated return change of ownership that occurred during a consolidated return year for which the due date of the income tax return (without extensions) is on or before March 13, 1998. See paragraph (d)(4) of this section for an optional effective date rule (generally making the rules of this paragraph (e) also inapplicable if the consolidated return change of ownership occurred on or after January 1, 1997, and during a consolidated return year for which the due date of the income tax return (without extensions) is on or before March 13, 1998).

(f) *Early dispositions, etc., of section 38 property.*—(1) *Dispositions of section 38 property during and after consolidated return year.*—If property is subject to section 47(a)(1) or (2) with respect to a member during a consolidated return year, any increase in tax shall be added to the tax liability of the group under § 1.1502-2 (regardless of whether the property was placed in service in a consolidated or separate return year). Also, if property is subject to section 47(a)(1) or (2) with respect to a corporation during a taxable year for which such corporation files on a separate return basis, any increase in tax shall be added to the tax liability of such corporation (regardless of whether such property was placed in service in a consolidated or separate return year).

(2) *Exception for transfer to another member.*—(i) Except as provided in subdivisions (ii) and (iii) of this subparagraph, a transfer of section 38 property from one member of the group to another member of such group during a consolidated return year shall not be treated as a disposition or cessation within the meaning of section 47(a)(1). If such section 38 property is disposed of, or otherwise ceases to be section 38 property or becomes public utility property with respect to the transferee, before the close of the estimated useful life which was taken into account in computing qualified investment, then section 47(a)(1) or (2) shall apply to the transferee with respect to such property (determined by taking into account the period of

use, qualified investment, other dispositions, etc., of the transferor). Any increase in tax due to the application of section 47(a)(1) or (2) shall be added to the tax liability of such transferee (or the tax liability of a group, if the transferee joins in the filing of a consolidated return).

(ii) Except as provided in subdivision (iii) of this subparagraph, if section 38 property is disposed of during a consolidated return year by one member of the group to another member of such group which is an organization to which section 593 applies or a cooperative organization described in section 1381(a), the tax under chapter 1 of the Code for such consolidated return year shall be increased by an amount equal to the aggregate decrease in the credits allowed under section 38 for all prior taxable years which would result solely from treating such property, for purposes of determining qualified investment, as placed in service by such organization to which section 593 applies or such cooperative organization described in section 1381(a), as the case may be, but with due regard to the use of the property before such transfer.

(iii) Section 47(a)(1) shall apply to a transfer of section 38 property by a corporation during a consolidated return year if such corporation is liquidated in a transaction to which section 334(b)(2) applies.

(3) *Examples.*—The provisions of this paragraph may be illustrated by the following examples:

*Example (1).* P, S, and T file a consolidated return for calendar year 1967. In such year S places in service section 38 property having an estimated useful life of more than 8 years. In 1968, P, S, and T file a consolidated return, and in such year S sells such property to T. Such sale will not cause section 47(a)(1) to apply.

*Example (2).* Assume the same facts as in example (1), except that P, S, and T filed separate returns for 1967. The sale from S to T will not cause section 47(a)(1) to apply.

*Example (3).* Assume the same facts as in example (1), except that P, S, and T continue to file consolidated returns through 1971 and in such year T disposes of the property to individual A. Section 47(a)(1) will apply to the group and any increase in tax shall be added to the tax liability of the group. For the purposes of determining the actual period of use by T, such period shall include S's period of use.

*Example (4).* Assume the same facts as in example (3), except that T files a separate return in 1971. Again, the actual periods of use by S and T will be combined in applying section 47. If the disposition results in an increase in tax under section 47(a)(1), such additional tax shall be added to the separate tax liability of T.

*Example (5).* Assume the same facts as in example (1), except that in 1969, P sells all the stock of T to a third party. Such sale will not cause section 47(a)(1) to apply.

[Reg. § 1.1502-3.]

☐ [T.D. 6894, 9-7-66. *Amended by* T.D. 7246, 12-29-72; T.D. 8597, 7-12-95; T.D. 8751, 1-9-98; T.D. 8766, 3-13-98 *and* T.D. 8884, 5-24-2000 (*corrected* 8-7-2000).]

### [Reg. § 1.1502-4]

**§ 1.1502-4. Consolidated foreign tax credit.**—(a) *In general.*—The foreign tax credit under section 901 is allowed to the group only if the agent for the group (as defined in § 1.1502-77(a)) chooses to use the credit in the computation of the consolidated tax liability of the group for the consolidated return year. If that choice is made, section 275(a)(4) provides that no deduction against taxable income may be taken on the consolidated return for foreign taxes paid or accrued by any member. However, if section 275(a)(4) does not apply, a deduction against consolidated taxable income may be allowed for certain taxes for which a credit is not allowed, even though the choice is made to claim a credit for other taxes. See, for example, sections 901(j)(3), 901(k)(7), 901(l)(4), 901(m)(6), and 908(b).

(b) *Computation of foreign tax credit.*—The foreign tax credit for the consolidated return year is determined on a consolidated basis under the principles of sections 901 through 909 and 960. All foreign income taxes paid or accrued by members of the group for the year (including those deemed paid under section 960 and paragraph (d) of this section) must be aggregated.

(c) *Computation of limitation on credit.*—For purposes of computing the group's limiting fraction under section 904, the following rules apply:

(1) *Computation of taxable income from foreign sources.*—(i) *Separate categories.*—The group must compute a separate foreign tax credit limitation for income in each separate category (as defined in § 1.904-5(a)(4)(v)) for purposes of this section. The numerator of the limiting fraction in any separate category is the consolidated taxable income of the group determined in accordance with § 1.1502-11, taking into account adjustments required under section 904(b), if any, from sources without the United States in that category, determined

in accordance with the rules of § § 1.904-4 and 1.904-5 and the section 861 regulations (as defined in § 1.861-8(a)(1)).

(ii) *Adjustments under sections 904(f) and (g).*—The rules for allocation and recapture of separate limitation losses and overall foreign losses under section 904(f) and § 1.1502-9 apply to determine the foreign source and U.S. source taxable income in each separate category of the consolidated group. Similarly, the rules for allocation and recapture of overall domestic losses under section 904(g) and § 1.1502-9 apply to determine the foreign source and U.S. source taxable income in each separate category of the consolidated group. See § 1.904(g)-3 for allocation rules under sections 904(f) and 904(g). The rules of sections 904(f) and 904(g) do not operate to recharacterize foreign income tax attributable to any separate category.

(iii) *Computation of consolidated net operating loss.*—The source and separate category of the group's consolidated net operating loss ("CNOL"), as that term is defined in § 1.1502-21(e), for the taxable year, if any, is determined based on the amounts of any separate limitation losses and U.S. source loss that are not allocated to reduce U.S. source income or income in other separate categories under the rules of sections 904(f) and 904(g) in computing the group's consolidated foreign tax credit limitations for the taxable year under paragraphs (c)(1)(i) and (ii) of this section.

(iv) *Characterization of CNOL carried to a separate return year.*—(A) *In general.*—The total amount of CNOL attributable to a member that is carried to a separate return year is determined under the rules of § 1.1502-21(b)(2). The source and separate category of the portion of the CNOL that is attributable to a member is determined under this paragraph (c)(1)(iv).

(B) *Tentative apportionment.*—For the portion of the CNOL that is attributable to the member described in paragraph (c)(1)(iv) of this section, the consolidated group determines a tentative allocation and apportionment to each statutory and residual grouping (as described in § 1.861-8(a)(4) with respect to section 904 as the operative section) under the principles of § 1.1502-9(c)(2)(i), (ii), (iv), and (v) by treating the portion of the group's CNOL in each statutory and residual grouping as if it were a CSLL account, as that term is described in § 1.1502-9(b)(4). This determination is made as of the end of the taxable year of the consolidated group in which the CNOL arose or, if earlier and applicable, when the member leaves the consolidated group.

(C) *Adjustments.*—(1) If the total tentative apportionment for all statutory and residual groupings exceeds the portion of the CNOL attributable to the member described in paragraph (c)(1)(iv)(A) of this section (the "excess amount"), then the tentative apportionment in each grouping is reduced by an amount equal to the excess amount multiplied by a fraction, the numerator of which is the tentative apportionment in that grouping, and the denominator of which is the total tentative apportionments in all groupings.

(2) If the total tentative apportionment for all statutory and residual groupings is less than the total CNOL attributable to the member described in paragraph (c)(1)(iv)(A) (the "deficiency"), then the tentative apportionment in each grouping is increased by an amount equal to the deficiency multiplied by a fraction, the numerator of which is the CNOL in that grouping that was not tentatively apportioned, and the denominator of which is the total CNOL in all groupings that was not tentatively apportioned.

(v) *Consolidated net capital losses.*—The principles of the rules in paragraphs (c)(1)(i) through (iv) of this section apply for purposes of determining the source and separate category of consolidated net capital losses described in § 1.1502-22(e).

(2) *Computation of consolidated taxable income.*—The denominator of the limiting fraction in any separate category is the consolidated taxable income of the group determined in accordance with § 1.1502-11, taking into account adjustments required under section 904(b), if any.

(3) *Computation of tax against which credit is taken.*—The tax against which the limiting fraction under section 904(a) is applied will be the consolidated tax liability of the group determined under § 1.1502-2, but without regard to § 1.1502-2(a)(2) through (4) and (8) and (9), and without regard to any credit against such liability. See sections 26(b) and 901(a).

(d) *Carryover and carryback of unused foreign tax.*—(1) *Allowance of unused foreign tax as consolidated carryover or carryback.*—The consolidated group's carryovers and carrybacks of unused foreign tax (as defined in § 1.904-2(c)(1)) to the taxable year is determined on a consolidated basis under the principles of section 904(c) and § 1.904-2 and is deemed to be paid or accrued to a foreign country or possession for that year. The consolidated group's unused foreign tax carryovers and carrybacks to the taxable year consist of any unused foreign tax of the consolidated group, plus any unused foreign tax of members for separate return years, which may be carried over or back to the taxable year under the principles of section 904(c) and §1.904-2. The consolidated group's unused foreign tax carryovers and carrybacks do not include any unused foreign taxes apportioned to a corporation for a separate return year pursuant to §1.1502-79(d). A consolidated group's unused foreign tax in each separate category is the excess of the foreign taxes paid, accrued or deemed paid under section 960 by the consolidated group over the limitation in the applicable separate category for the consolidated return year. See paragraph (c) of this section.

(2) *Absorption rules.*—For purposes of determining the amount, if any, of an unused foreign tax which can be carried to a taxable year (whether a consolidated or separate return year), the amount of the unused foreign tax that is absorbed in a prior consolidated return year under section 904(c) shall be determined by—

(i) Applying all unused foreign taxes which can be carried to a prior year in the order of the taxable years in which those unused foreign taxes arose, beginning with the taxable year that ends earliest; and

(ii) Applying all unused foreign taxes which can be carried to such prior year from taxable years ending on the same date on a pro rata basis.

(e) *Example.*—The following example illustrates the application of this section:

(1) *Facts.* (i) Domestic corporation P is incorporated on January 1, Year 1. On that same day, P incorporates domestic corporations S and T as wholly owned subsidiaries. P, S, and T file consolidated returns for Years 1 and 2 on the basis of a calendar year. T engages in business solely through a qualified business unit in Country A. S engages in business solely through qualified business units in Countries A and B. P does business solely in the United States. During Year 1, T sold an item of inventory to P at a gain of $2,000. Under §1.1502-13 the intercompany gain has not been taken into account as of the close of Year 1. The taxable income of each member for Year 1 from foreign and U.S. sources, and the foreign taxes paid on such foreign income, are as follows:

Table 1 to paragraph (e)(1)(i)

| Corporation | U.S. Source taxable income | Foreign branch category foreign source taxable income | Foreign branch category foreign tax paid | Total taxable income |
|---|---|---|---|---|
| P | $40,000 | | | $40,000 |
| T | | $20,000 | $12,000 | 20,000 |
| S | | 20,000 | 9,000 | 20,000 |
| Group | $40,000 | $40,000 | $21,000 | $80,000 |

(ii) The separate taxable income of each member was computed by taking into account the rules under §1.1502-12. Accordingly, T's intercompany gain of $2,000 is not included in T's taxable income for Year 1. The group's consolidated taxable income (computed in accordance with §1.1502-11) is $80,000. The consolidated tax liability against which the credit may be taken (computed in accordance with paragraph (c)(3) of this section) is $16,800.

(2) *Analysis.* Under section 904(d) and paragraph (c)(1)(i) of this section, the aggregate amount of foreign income taxes paid to all foreign countries with respect to the foreign branch category income of $21,000 ($12,000 + $9,000) that may be claimed as a credit in Year 1 is limited to $8,400 ($16,800 x $40,000/$80,000). Assuming P, as the agent for the group, chooses to use the foreign taxes paid as a credit, the group may claim a $8,400 foreign tax credit.

(f) *Applicability date.*—This section applies to taxable years for which the original consolidated Federal income tax return is due (without extensions) after January 11, 2021. [Reg. §1.1502-4.]

☐ [*T.D.* 6894, 9-7-66. *Amended by T.D.* 7637, 8-6-79; *T.D.* 7728, 10-31-80; *T.D.* 8597, 7-12-95; *T.D.* 8751, 1-9-98; *T.D.* 8766, 3-13-98, *T.D.* 8884, 5-24-2000 *T.D.* 9885, 12-2-2019 *and T.D.* 9922, 11-2-2020.]

**[Reg. §1.1502-5]**

**§1.1502-5. Estimated tax.**—(a) *General rule.*—(1) *Consolidated estimated tax.*—If a group files a consolidated return for two consecutive taxable years, it must make payments of estimated tax on a consolidated basis for each subsequent taxable year, until such time as separate returns are properly filed. Until such time, the group is treated as a single corporation for purposes of section 6154 (relating to payment of estimated tax by corporations). If separate returns are filed by the members for a taxable year, the amount of any estimated tax payments made with respect to a consolidated payment of estimated tax for such year shall be credited against the separate tax liabilities of the members in any manner designated by the common parent which is satisfactory to the Commissioner. The consolidated payments of estimated tax shall be deposited with the authorized financial institution with which the common parent deposits its estimated tax payments. A statement should be attached to the payment setting forth the name, address, employer identification number, and internal revenue service center of each member.

(2) *First two consolidated return years.*—For the first 2 years for which a group files a consolidated return, it may make payments of estimated tax on either a consolidated or separate basis. If a consolidated return is filed for such year, the amount of any estimated tax payments made for such year by any member shall be credited against the tax liability of the group.

(3) *Effective date.*—This section applies to taxable years for which the due date (without extensions) for filing returns is after August 6, 1979. For prior taxable years see 26 CFR §1.1502-5. (Revised as of April 1, 1978.)

(b) *Addition to tax for failure to pay estimated tax under section 6655.*—(1) *Consolidated return filed.*—For the first two taxable years for which

a group files a consolidated return, the group may compute the amount of the penalty (if any) under section 6655 on a consolidated basis or separate member basis, regardless of the method of payment. Thereafter, for a taxable year for which the group files a consolidated return, the group must compute the penalty on a consolidated basis.

(2) *Computation of penalty on consolidated basis.*—(i) This paragraph (b)(2) gives the rules for computing the penalty under section 6655 on a consolidated basis.

(ii) The tax and facts shown on the return for the preceding taxable year referred to in section 6655(d)(1) and (2) are, if a consolidated return was filed for that preceding year, such items shown on the consolidated return for that preceding year or, if one was not filed for that preceding year, the aggregate taxes and the facts shown on the separate returns of the common parent and any other corporation that was a member of the same affiliated group as the common parent for that preceding year.

(iii) If estimated tax was not paid on a consolidated basis, then the amount of the group's payments of estimated tax for the taxable year is the aggregate of the payments made by all members for the year.

(iv) Section 6655(d)(1) applies only if the common parent's consolidated return, or each member's separate return, for the preceding taxable year (as the case may be) was a taxable year of 12 months.

(3) *Computation of penalty on separate member basis.*—To compute any penalty under section 6655 on a separate member basis, for purposes of section 6655(b)(1), the "tax shown on the return for the taxable year" is the portion of the tax shown on the consolidated return allocable to the member under paragraph (b)(5) of this section. If the member was included in the consolidated return filed by the group for the preceding taxable year then—

(i) For purposes of section 6655(d)(1), the "tax shown on the return" for any member shall be the portion of the tax shown on the consolidated return for the preceding year allocable to the member under paragraph (b)(5) of this section.

(ii) For purposes of section 6655(d)(2), the "facts shown on the return" shall be the facts shown on the consolidated return for the preceding year and the tax computed under that section shall be allocated under the rules of paragraph (b)(5) of this section.

(4) *Consolidated payments if separate returns filed.*—If the group does not file a consolidated return for the taxable year, but makes payments of estimated tax on a consolidated basis, for purposes of section 6655(b)(2), the "amount, if any of the installment paid" by any member is an amount apportioned to the member in a manner designated by the common parent that is satisfactory to the Commissioner. If the member was included in the consolidated return filed by the group for the preceding taxable year, the amount of a member's penalty under section 6655 is computed on the separate member basis described in paragraph (b)(3)(i) and (ii) of this section.

(5) *Rules for allocation of consolidated tax liability.*—For purposes of subparagraphs (1) and (2) of this paragraph, the tax shown on a

consolidated return shall be allocated to the members of the group under the method which the group has elected pursuant to section 1552 and § 1.1502-33(d)(2).

(c) *Examples.*—The provisions of this section may be illustrated by the following examples:

*Example (1).* Corporations P and S-1 file a consolidated return for the first time for calendar year 1978. P and S-1 also file consolidated returns for 1979 and 1980. For 1978 and 1979, P and S-1 may make payments of estimated tax on either a separate or consolidated basis. For 1980, however, the group must pay its estimated tax on a consolidated basis. In determining whether P and S-1 come within the exception provided in section 6655(d)(1) for 1980, the "tax shown on the return" is the tax shown on the consolidated return for 1979.

*Example (2).* Assume the same facts as in example (1). Assume further that corporation S-2 is a member of the group during 1979, and joins in the filing of the consolidated return for such year, but ceases to be a member of the group on September 15, 1980. In determining whether the group (which no longer includes S-2) comes within the exception provided in section 6655(d)(1) for 1980, the "tax shown on the return" is the tax shown on the consolidated return for 1979.

*Example (3).* Assume the same facts as in example (1). Assume further that corporation S-2 becomes a member of the group on July 1, 1980, and joins in the filing of the consolidated return for 1980. In determining whether the group (which now includes S-2) comes within the exception provided in section 6655(d)(1) for 1980, the "tax shown on the return" is the tax shown on the consolidated return for 1979. Any tax of S-2 for any separate return year is not included as a part of the "tax shown on the return" for purposes of applying section 6655(d)(1).

*Example (4).* Corporations X and Y filed consolidated returns for the calendar years 1977 and 1978 and separate returns for 1979. In determining whether X or Y comes within the exception provided in section 6655(d)(1) for 1979, the "tax shown on the return" is the amount of tax shown on the consolidated return for 1978 allocable to X and to Y in accordance with paragraph (b)(5) of this section.

(d) *Cross reference.*—For provisions relating to quick refunds of corporate estimated tax payments, see § 1.1502-78, and § 1.6425-1 through § 1.6425-3, of this chapter. [Reg. § 1.1502-5.]

☐ [*T.D. 6894, 9-7-66. Amended by T.D. 7059, 9-16-70; T.D. 7637, 8-6-79 and T.D. 8952, 6-25-2001.*]

### [Reg. § 1.1502-6]

**§ 1.1502-6. Liability for tax.**—(a) *Several liability of members of group.*—Except as provided in paragraph (b) of this section, the common parent corporation and each subsidiary which was a member of the group during any part of the consolidated return year shall be severally liable for the tax for such year computed in accordance with the regulations under section 1502 prescribed on or before the due date (not including extensions of time) for the filing of the consolidated return for such year.

(b) *Liability of subsidiary after withdrawal.*—If a subsidiary has ceased to be a member of the group and if such cessation resulted from a bona fide sale or exchange of its stock for fair value and occurred prior to the date upon which any deficiency is assessed, the Commissioner may, if he believes that the assessment or collection of the balance of the deficiency will not be jeopardized, make assessment and collection of such deficiency from such former subsidiary in an amount not exceeding the portion of such deficiency which the Commissioner may determine to be allocable to it. If the Commissioner makes assessment and collection of any part of a deficiency from such former subsidiary, then for purposes of any credit or refund of the amount collected from such former subsidiary the agency of the common parent under the provisions of § 1.1502-77 shall not apply.

(c) *Effect of intercompany agreements.*—No agreement entered into by one or more members of such group with any other member of such group or with any other person shall in any case have the effect of reducing the liability prescribed under this section. [Reg. § 1.1502-6.]

☐ [*T.D. 6894, 9-7-66. Amended by T.D. 9002, 6-27-2002.*]

### [Reg. § 1.1502-9]

**§ 1.1502-9. Consolidated overall foreign losses, separate limitation losses, and overall domestic losses.**—(a) *In general.*—This section provides rules for applying section 904(f) and (g) (including its definitions and nomenclature) to a group and its members. Generally, section 904(f) concerns rules relating to overall foreign losses (OFLs) and separate limitation losses (SLLs) and the consequences of such losses. Under section 904(f)(5), losses are computed separately in each category of income described in section 904(d)(1) or

§ 1.904-4(m) (separate category). Section 904(g) concerns rules relating to overall domestic losses (ODLs) and the consequences of such losses. Paragraph (b) of this section defines terms and provides computational and accounting rules, including rules regarding recapture. Paragraph (c) of this section provides rules that apply to OFLs, SLLs, and ODLs when a member becomes or ceases to be a member of a group. Paragraph (d) of this section provides a predecessor and successor rule. Paragraph (e) of this section provides effective dates.

(b) *Consolidated application of section 904(f) and (g).*—A group applies section 904(f) and (g) for a consolidated return year in accordance with that section, subject to the following rules:

(1) *Computation of CSLI or CSLL and consolidated U.S.-source taxable income or CDL.*—The group computes its consolidated separate limitation income (CSLI) or consolidated separate limitation loss (CSLL) for each separate category under the principles of § 1.1502-11 by aggregating each member's foreign-source taxable income or loss in such separate category computed under the principles of § 1.1502-12, and taking into account the foreign portion of the consolidated items described in § 1.1502-11(a)(2) through (a)(8) for such separate category. The group computes its consolidated U.S.-source taxable income or consolidated domestic loss (CDL) under similar principles.

(2) *Netting CSLLs, CSLIs, and consolidated U.S.-source taxable income.*—The group applies section 904(f)(5) to determine the extent to which a CSLL for a separate category reduces CSLI for another separate category or consolidated U.S.-source taxable income.

(3) *Netting CDL and CSLI.*—The group applies section 904(g)(2) to determine the extent to which a CDL reduces CSLI.

(4) *CSLL, COFL, and CODL accounts.*—To the extent provided in section 904(f), the amount by which a CSLL for a separate category (the loss category) reduces CSLI for another separate category (the income category) will result in the creation of (or addition to) a CSLL account for the loss category with respect to the income category. Likewise, the amount by which a CSLL for a loss category reduces consolidated U.S.-source taxable income will create (or add to) a consolidated overall foreign loss account (a COFL account). To the extent provided in section 904(g), the amount by which a CDL reduces CSLI will result in the creation of (or addition to) a consolidated overall domestic loss (CODL) account for the income category reduced by the CDL.

(5) *Recapture of COFL, CSLL, and CODL accounts.*—In the case of a COFL account for a loss category, section 904(f)(1) and section 904(f)(3) recharacterize some or all of the foreign-source income in the loss category as U.S.-source income. In the case of a CSLL account for a loss category with respect to an income category, section 904(f)(5)(C) and section 904(f)(5)(F) recharacterize some or all of the foreign-source income in the loss category as foreign-source income in the income category. In the case of a CODL account, section 904(g)(3) recharacterizes some of the U.S.-source income as foreign-source income in the separate category that was offset by the CDL. The COFL account, CSLL account, or CODL account is reduced to the extent income is recharacterized with respect to such account.

(6) *Intercompany transactions.*—(i) *Nonapplication of section 904(f) disposition rules.*—Neither section 904(f)(3) (in the case of a COFL account) nor section 904(f)(5)(F) (in the case of a CSLL account) applies at the time of a disposition that is an intercompany transaction to which § 1.1502-13 applies. Instead, section 904(f)(3) and section 904(f)(5)(F) apply only at such time and only to the extent that the group is required under § 1.1502-13 (without regard to section 904(f)(3) and section 904(f)(5)(F)) to take into account any intercompany items resulting from the disposition, based on the COFL or CSLL account existing at the end of the consolidated return year during which the group takes the intercompany items into account.

(ii) *Examples.*—Paragraph (b)(6)(i) of this section is illustrated by the following examples. The identity of the parties and the basic assumptions set forth in § 1.1502-13(c)(7)(i) apply to the examples. Except as otherwise stated, assume further that the consolidated group recognizes no foreign source income other than as a result of the transactions described. The examples are as follows:

*Example 1.* (i) On June 10, year 1, S transfers nondepreciable property with a basis of $100 and a fair market value of $250 to B in a transaction to which section 351 applies. The property was predominantly used without the United States in a trade or business within the meaning of section 904(f)(3). B continues to use the property without the United States. The group has a COFL account in the relevant loss category of $120 as of December 31, year 1.

(ii) Because the contribution from S to B is an intercompany transaction, section 904(f)(3) does not apply to result in any gain recognition in year 1. See paragraph (b)(5)(i) of this section.

(iii) On January 10, year 4, B ceases to be a member of the group. Because S did not recognize gain in year 1 under section 351, no gain is taken into account in year 4 under §1.1502-13. Thus, no portion of the group's COFL account is recaptured in year 4. For rules requiring apportionment of a portion of the COFL account to B, see paragraph (c)(2) of this section.

*Example 2.* (i) The facts are the same as in paragraph (i) of *Example 1.* On January 10, year 4, B sells the property to X for $250. As of December 31, year 4, the group's COFL account is $40. (The COFL account was reduced between year 1 and year 4 due to unrelated foreign-source income taken into account by the group.)

(ii) B takes into account gain of $200 in year 4. The $40 COFL account in year 4 recharacterizes $40 of the gain as U.S. source. See section 904(f)(3).

*Example 3.* (i) On June 10, year 1, S sells nondepreciable property with a basis of $100 and a fair market value of $250 to B for $250 cash. The property was predominantly used without the United States in a trade or business within the meaning of section 904(f)(3). The group has a COFL account in the relevant loss category of $120 as of December 31, year 1. B predominantly uses the property in a trade or business without the United States.

(ii) Because the sale is an intercompany transaction, section 904(f)(3) does not require the group to take into account any gain in year 1. Thus, under paragraph (b)(5)(i) of this section, the COFL account is not reduced in year 1.

(iii) On January 10, year 4, B sells the property to X for $300. As of December 31, year 4, the group's COFL account is $60. (The COFL account was reduced between year 1 and year 4 due to unrelated foreign-source income taken into account by the group.)

(iv) In year 4, S's $150 intercompany gain and B's $50 corresponding gain are taken into account to produce the same effect on consolidated taxable income as if S and B were divisions of a single corporation. See §1.1502-13(c). All of B's $50 corresponding gain is recharacterized under section 904(f)(3). If S and B were divisions of a single corporation and the intercompany sale were a transfer between the divisions, B would succeed to S's $100 basis in the property and would have $200 of gain ($60 of which would be recharacterized under section 904(f)(3)), instead of a $50 gain. Consequently, S's $150 intercompany gain and B's $50 corresponding gain are taken into account, and $10 of S's gain is recharacterized under section 904(f)(3) as U.S. source income to reflect the $10 difference between B's $50 recharacterized gain and the $60 recomputed gain that would have been recharacterized.

(c) *Becoming or ceasing to be a member of a group.*—(1) *Adding separate accounts on becoming a member.*—At the time that a corporation becomes a member of a group (a new member), the group adds to the balance of its COFL, CSLL or CODL account the balance of the new member's corresponding OFL account, SLL account or ODL account. A new member's OFL account corresponds to a COFL account if the account is for the same loss category. A new member's SLL account corresponds to a CSLL account if the account is for the same loss category and with respect to the same income category. A new member's ODL account corresponds to a CODL account if the account is with respect to the same income category. If the group does not have a COFL, CSLL or CODL account corresponding to the new member's account, it creates a COFL, CSLL or CODL account with a balance equal to the balance of the member's account.

(2) *Apportionment of consolidated account to departing member.*—(i) *In general.*—A group apportions to a member that ceases to be a member (a departing member) a portion of each COFL, CSLL and CODL account as of the end of the year during which the member ceases to be a member and after the group makes the additions or reductions to such account required under paragraphs (b)(4), (b)(5), and (c)(1) of this section (other than an addition under paragraph (c)(1) of this section attributable to a member becoming a member after the departing member ceases to be a member). The group computes such portion under paragraph (c)(2)(ii) of this section, as limited by paragraph (c)(2)(iii) of this section. The departing member carries such portion to its first separate return year after it ceases to be a member. Also, the group reduces each account by such portion and carries such reduced amount to its first consolidated return year beginning after the year in which the member ceases to be a member. If two or more members cease to be members in the same year, the group computes the portion allocable to each such member (and reduces its accounts by such portion) in the order that the members cease to be members.

(ii) *Departing member's portion of group's account.*—A departing member's portion of a group's COFL, CSLL or CODL account for a loss category is computed based upon the member's share of the group's assets that generate income subject to recapture at the time that the member ceases to be a member. Under the characterization principles of §§1.861-9T(g)(3) and 1.861-12T, the group identifies the assets of the departing member and the remaining members that

generate U.S.-source income (domestic assets) and foreign-source income (foreign assets) in each separate category. The assets are characterized based upon the income that the assets are reasonably expected to generate after the member ceases to be a member. The member's portion of a group's COFL or CSLL account for a loss category is the group's COFL or CSLL account, respectively, multiplied by a fraction, the numerator of which is the value of the member's foreign assets for the loss category and the denominator of which is the value of the foreign assets of the group (including the departing member) for the loss category. The member's portion of a group's CODL account for each income category is the group's CODL account multiplied by a fraction, the numerator of which is the value of the member's domestic assets and the denominator of which is the value of the domestic assets of the group (including the departing member). The value of the domestic and foreign assets is determined under the asset valuation rules of §1.861-9T(g)(1) and (2) using either tax book value, fair market value, or alternative tax book value under the method chosen by the group for purposes of interest apportionment as provided in §1.861-9T(g)(1)(ii). For purposes of this paragraph (c)(2)(ii), §1.861-9T(g)(2)(iv) (assets in intercompany transactions) shall apply, but §1.861-9T(g)(2)(iii) (adjustments for directly allocated interest) shall not apply. If the group uses the tax book value method, the member's portions of COFL, CSLL, and CODL accounts are limited by paragraph (c)(2)(iii) of this section. In addition, for purposes of this paragraph (c)(2)(ii), the tax book value of assets transferred in intercompany transactions shall be determined without regard to previously deferred gain or loss that is taken into account by the group as a result of the transaction in which the member ceases to be a member. The assets should be valued at the time the member ceases to be a member, but values on other days may be used unless this creates substantial distortions. For example, if a member ceases to be a member in the middle of the group's consolidated return year, an average of the values of assets at the beginning and end of the year (as provided in §1.861-9T(g)(2)) may be used or, if a member ceases to be a member in the early part of the group's consolidated return year, values at the beginning of the year may be used, unless this creates substantial distortions.

(iii) *Limitation on member's portion for groups using tax book value method.*—If a group uses the tax book value method of valuing assets for purposes of paragraph (c)(2)(ii) of this section and the aggregate of a member's portions of COFL and CSLL accounts for a loss category (with respect to one or more income categories) determined under paragraph (c)(2)(ii) of this section exceeds 150 percent of the actual fair market value of the member's foreign assets in the loss category, the member's portion of the COFL or CSLL accounts for the loss category shall be reduced (proportionately, in the case of multiple accounts) by such excess. In addition, if the aggregate of a member's portions of CODL accounts (with respect to one or more income categories) determined under paragraph (c)(2)(ii) of this section exceeds 150 percent of the actual fair market value of the member's domestic assets, the member's portion of the CODL accounts shall be reduced (proportionately, in the case of multiple accounts) by such excess. This rule does not apply in the case of COFL or CSLL accounts if the departing member and all other members that cease to be members as part of the same transaction own all (or substantially all) the foreign assets in the loss category. In the case of CODL accounts, this rule does not apply if the departing member and all other members that cease to be members as part of the same transaction own all (or substantially all) the domestic assets.

(iv) *Determination of values of domestic and foreign assets binding on departing member.*—The group's determination of the value of the member's and the group's domestic and foreign assets for a loss category is binding on the member, unless the Commissioner concludes that the determination is not appropriate. The common parent of the group must attach a statement to the return for the taxable year that the departing member ceases to be a member of the group that sets forth the name and taxpayer identification number of the departing member, the amount of each COFL and CSLL for each loss category and each CODL that is apportioned to the departing member under this paragraph (c)(2), the method used to determine the value of the member's and the group's domestic and foreign assets in each such loss category, and the value of the member's and the group's domestic and foreign assets in each such loss category. The common parent must also furnish a copy of the statement to the departing member.

(v) *Anti-abuse rule.*—If a corporation becomes a member and ceases to be a member, and a principal purpose of the corporation becoming and ceasing to be a member is to transfer the corporation's OFL account, SLL account or ODL account to the group or to transfer the group's COFL, CSLL or CODL account to the corporation, appropriate adjustments will be made to eliminate the benefit of such a transfer of accounts. Similarly, if any member acquires assets or disposes of assets (including a transfer of assets between members of the group and the departing member) with a principal purpose of affecting the apportionment of accounts under paragraph (c)(2)(i) of this section, appropriate adjustments will be made to eliminate the benefit of such acquisition or disposition.

(vi) *Examples.*—The following examples illustrate the rules of this paragraph (c):

*Example 1.* (i) On November 6, year 1, S, a member of the P group, a consolidated group with a calendar consolidated return year, ceases to be a member of the group. On December 31, year 1, the P group has a $40 COFL account for the general category, a $20 CSLL account for the general category (that is, the loss category) with respect to the passive category (that is, the income category), and a $10 CODL account with respect to the passive category (that is, the income category). No member of the group has foreign-source income or loss in year 1. The group apportions its interest expense according to the tax book value method.

(ii) On November 6, year 1, the group identifies S's assets and the group's assets (including S's assets) expected to produce foreign-source general category income. Use of end-of-the-year values will not create substantial distortions in determining the relative values of S's and the group's relevant assets on November 6, year 1. The group determines that S's relevant assets have a tax book value of $2,000 and a fair market value of $2,200. Also, the group's relevant assets (including S's assets) have a tax book value of $8,000. On November 6, year 1, S has no assets expected to produce U.S. source income.

(iii) Under paragraph (c)(2)(ii) of this section, S takes a $10 COFL account for the general category ($40 × $2000/$8000) and a $5 CSLL account for the general category with respect to the passive category ($20 × $2000/$8000). S does not take any portion of the CODL account. The limitation described in paragraph (c)(2)(iii) of this section does not apply because the aggregate of the COFL and CSLL accounts for the general category that are apportioned to S ($15) is less than 150% of the actual fair market value of S's general category foreign assets ($2,200 x 150%).

*Example 2.* (i) Assume the same facts as in *Example 1,* except that the fair market value of S's general category foreign assets is $4 as of November 6, year 1.

(ii) Under paragraph (c)(2)(iii) of this section, S's COFL and CSLL accounts for the general category must be reduced by $9, which is the excess of $15 (the aggregate amount of the accounts apportioned under paragraph (c)(2)(ii) of this section) over $6 (150% of the $4 actual fair market value of S's general category foreign assets). S thus takes a $4 COFL account for the general category ($10 - ($9 × $10/$15)) and a $2 CSLL account for the general category with respect to the passive category ($5 - ($9 x $5/$15)).

*Example 3.* (i) Assume the same facts as in *Example 1,* except that S also has assets that are expected to produce U.S. source income.

(ii) On November 6, year 1, the group identifies S's assets and the group's assets (including S's assets) expected to produce U.S. source income. Use of end-of-the-year values will not create substantial distortions in determining the relative values of S's and the group's relevant assets on November 6, year 1. The group determines that S's relevant assets have a tax book value of $3,000 and a fair market value of $2,500. Also, the group's relevant assets (including S's assets) have a tax book value of $6,000.

(iii) Under paragraph (c)(2)(ii) of this section, S takes a $5 CODL account ($10 x $3,000/$6,000), in addition to the COFL and CSLL accounts determined in Example 1. The limitation described in paragraph (c)(2)(iii) of this section does not apply because the CODL account that is apportioned to S ($5) is less than 150% of the actual fair market value of S's U.S. assets ($2,500 × 150%).

(d) *Predecessor and successor.*—A reference to a member includes, as the context may require, a reference to a predecessor or successor of the member. See § 1.1502-1(f).

(e) *Effective/applicability date.*—This section applies to consolidated return years beginning on or after January 1, 2012, for which the return is due (without extensions) after June 22, 2012. Taxpayers may choose to apply the provisions of this section to other consolidated return years beginning after December 31, 2006, including periods covered by 26 CFR 1.1502-9T (revised as of April 1, 2010). For rules relating to overall foreign losses and separate limitation losses in consolidated return years beginning on or before December 21, 2007, see 26 CFR 1.1502-9 (revised as of April 1, 2007). [Reg. § 1.1502-9.]

☐ [*T.D.* 8833, 8-10-99. *Amended by T.D.* 9371, 12-20-2007 *and T.D.* 9595, 6-21-2012.]

### [Reg. § 1.1502-9A]

**§ 1.1502-9A. Application of overall foreign loss recapture rules to corporations filing consolidated returns due on or before August 11, 1999.**—(a) *Scope.*—(1) *Effective date.*—This section applies only to consolidated return years for which the due date of the income tax return (without extensions) is on or before August 11, 1999.

(2) *In general.*—An affiliated group of corporations filing a consolidated return sustains an overall foreign loss (a consolidated overall foreign loss) in any taxable year in which its gross income from sources without the United States subject to a separate limitation (as defined in § 1.904(f)-1(c)(2)) is exceeded by the sum of the deductions properly allocated and apportioned thereto. However, for taxable years prior to 1983, affiliated groups may have determined their overall foreign losses for income subject to the passive interest limitation, DISC dividend limitation, and general limitation on a combined basis in accordance with the rules in § 1.904(f)-1(c)(1). The rules contained in § § 1.904(f)-1 through 1.904(f)-6 are applicable to affiliated groups filing consolidated returns. This section provides special rules for applying those sections to such groups. Paragraph (b) provides rules for additions and subtractions of a portion of overall foreign losses to and from consolidated overall foreign loss accounts. Paragraph (c) requires that separate notional overall foreign loss accounts be kept for each member of the group that contributes to a consolidated overall foreign loss account and provides for allocation of a portion of the group's overall foreign loss account to a member when the member leaves the group prior to recapture of the entire amount of the loss account. These rules are similar to the rules provided in § 1.1502-21(b)(2) (or § 1.1502-79A, as appropriate) concerning the apportionment of consolidated net operating losses to a member who leaves the group. However, the rules differ somewhat because the absorption rule of § 1.1502-21(b)(1) (or § 1.1502-79A, as appropriate) is applied year-by-year, consistently with the sequence rules of section 172(b), and recapture of overall foreign losses is based on overall foreign loss accounts that may consist of losses in more than one year. Paragraph (d) provides rules for recapture of amounts in consolidated overall foreign loss accounts. Paragraph (e) provides special rules pertaining to section 904(f)(3) dispositions between members of a group. Paragraphs (b), (c), and (e) also contain special rules that apply to overall foreign losses that arise in separate return limitation years; the principles therein also apply to overall foreign losses when there has been a consolidated return change of ownership (as defined in § 1.1502-1(g)). See § 1.1502-9T(b)(1)(v) for the rule that ends the separate return limitation year limitation for consolidated return years for which the due date of the income tax return (without extensions) is after March 13, 1998, and § 1.1502-9T(b)(1)(vi) for an election to continue the separate return limitation year limitation for consolidated return years beginning before January 1, 1998. See also § 1.1502-3(d)(4) for an optional effective date rule (generally making the rules of paragraphs (b)(1)(iii) and (iv) of this section inapplicable for a consolidated return year beginning after December 31, 1996, if the due date of the income tax return (without extensions) for such year is on or before March 13, 1998).

(b) *Consolidated overall foreign loss accounts.*—Any group that sustains an overall foreign loss (or acquires a member with a balance in an overall foreign loss account) must establish a consolidated overall foreign loss account for such loss, and amounts shall be added to and subtracted from such account as provided in § § 1.904(f)-1 through 1.904(f)-6 and this section.

(1) *Additions to the consolidated overall foreign loss accounts.*—(i) *Consolidated overall foreign losses.*—Any consolidated overall foreign loss shall be added to the applicable consolidated overall foreign loss account for such separate limitation, to the extent that the overall foreign loss has reduced United States source income, in accordance with the rules of § § 1.904(f)-1 and 1.904(f)-3.

(ii) *Overall foreign losses from separate return years.*—If a corporation joins in the filing of a consolidated return in a taxable year in which such corporation has a balance in an overall foreign loss account from a prior separate return year that is not a separate return limitation year, such balance shall be added to the applicable consolidated overall foreign loss account in such year and treated as a consolidated overall foreign loss incurred in the previous year (and shall therefore be subject to recapture, in accordance with paragraph (d) of this section, beginning in the same year in which it is added to the consolidated overall foreign loss account).

(iii) *Overall foreign losses from separate return limitation years.*—If a corporation joins in the filing of a consolidated return in a taxable year in which such corporation has a balance in an overall foreign loss account from a prior separate return limitation year, such balance shall be added to the applicable consolidated overall foreign loss account in such consolidated return year to the extent of the lesser of the balance in the overall foreign loss account from the separate return limitation year or 50 percent (or such larger percentage as the taxpayer may elect) of the difference between the consolidated foreign source taxable income subject to the same separate limitation (computed in accordance with § § 1.904(f)-2(b) and 1.1502-4(d)(1) minus such consolidated foreign source taxable income recomputed by excluding the items of income and deduction of such corporation (but not less than zero). The amount added to a consolidated overall foreign loss account in any taxable year under this paragraph (b)(1)(iii) shall be treated as a consolidated overall foreign loss in the previous year (and shall therefore be subject to recapture, in accordance with paragraph (d) of this section, beginning in the same year in which it is added to the consolidated overall foreign loss account).

(iv) *Overall foreign losses that are part of a net operating loss or net capital loss carried over from a separate return limitation year.*—Overall foreign losses that are part of a net operating loss or net capital loss carryover from a separate return limitation year of a member that is absorbed in a consolidated return year shall be treated as though they were added to an overall foreign loss account in a separate return limitation year of such member and will be subject to the limitation on recapture of SRLY losses contained in paragraph (b)(1)(iii) of this section. See paragraph (c)(2) of this section for rules regarding the addition of such losses to the applicable overall foreign loss account of such member.

(v) *Special effective date for SRLY limitation.*—Except as provided in paragraph (b)(1)(vi) of this section, paragraphs (b)(1)(iii) and (iv) of this section apply only to consolidated return years for which the due date of the income tax return (without extensions) is on or before March 13, 1998. For consolidated return years for which the due date of the income tax return (without extensions) is after March 13, 1998, the rules of paragraph (b)(1)(ii) of this section shall apply to overall foreign losses from separate return years that are separate return limitation years. For purposes of applying paragraph (b)(1)(ii) of this section in such years, the group treats a member with a balance in an overall foreign loss account from a separate return limitation year on the first day of the first consolidated return year for which the due date of the income tax return (without extensions) is after March 13, 1998, as a corporation joining the group on such first day. An overall foreign loss that is part of a net operating loss or net capital loss carryover from a separate return limitation year of a member that is absorbed in a consolidated return year for which the due date of the income tax return (without extensions) is after March 13, 1998, shall be added to the appropriate consolidated overall foreign loss account in the year that it is absorbed. For consolidated return years for which the due date of the income tax return (without extensions) is after March 13, 1998, similar principles apply to overall foreign losses when there has been a consolidated return change of ownership (regardless of when the change of ownership occurred). See also § 1.1502-3(d)(4) for an optional effective date rule (generally making this paragraph (b)(1)(v) applicable to a consolidated return year beginning after December 31, 1996, if the due date of the income tax return (without extensions) for such year is on or before March 13, 1998).

(vi) *Election to defer application of special effective date.*—A consolidated group may elect not to apply paragraph (b)(1)(v) of this section to consolidated return years beginning before January 1, 1998. To make this election, a consolidated group must write "Election Pursuant to Notice 98-40" across the top of page 1 of an original or amended tax return for each consolidated return year subject to the election. For the first consolidated return year to which the overall foreign loss provisions of paragraph (b)(1)(v) of this section apply (i.e., the first year beginning on or after January 1, 1998), such consolidated group must write "Notice 98-40 Election in Effect in Prior Years" across the top of page 1 of the consolidated tax return for that year. For purposes of applying paragraph (b)(1)(ii) of this section with respect to such year, any member with a balance in an overall foreign loss account from a separate return limitation year on the first day of such year shall be treated as joining the group on such first day.

(2) *Reductions of the consolidated overall foreign loss accounts.*— (i) *Amounts allocated to members leaving the group.*—When a member leaves the group, each applicable consolidated overall foreign loss account shall be reduced by the amount allocated from such account to such member in accordance with paragraph (c)(3)(i) of this section.

(ii) *Amounts recaptured.*—A consolidated overall foreign loss account shall be reduced by the amount of any overall foreign loss under the same separate limitation that is recaptured from consolidated income in accordance with § 1.904(f)-2.

(c) *Allocation of overall foreign losses among members of an affiliated group.*—(1) *Notional overall foreign loss accounts.*—Separate notional overall foreign loss accounts shall be established for each member of a group that contributes to a consolidated overall foreign loss account. Additions to and reductions of such notional accounts shall be made when additions or reductions are made to consolidated overall foreign loss accounts in accordance with paragraph (b) of this section and § 1.904(f)-1.

(i) *Additions to notional accounts.*—(A) *Consolidated overall foreign losses.*—When a consolidated overall foreign loss is added to a consolidated overall foreign loss account, each member shall add its pro rata share of the amount of such loss to the member's notional overall foreign loss account. A member's pro rata share of a consolidated overall foreign loss for any taxable year is determined by multiplying the consolidated loss by a fraction. The numerator of this fraction is the amount by which the member's separate gross income for the taxable year from sources without the United States subject to the applicable separate limitation is exceeded by the sum of the deductions properly allocated and apportioned thereto (including such member's share of any consolidated net operating loss deduction and consolidated net capital loss carryovers and carrybacks to the taxable year), for each member with such deductions in excess of such income. The denominator of this fraction is the sum of the numerators of this fraction for all such members of the group.

(B) *Overall foreign losses from separate return years and separate return limitation years.*—When an amount from a member's overall foreign loss account from a separate return year or separate return limitation year is added to a consolidated overall foreign loss account in accordance with paragraph (b)(1)(ii) or (iii) of this section, such amount shall also be added to that member's notional overall foreign loss account for such separate limitation.

(ii) *Reductions of notional accounts.*—When a consolidated overall foreign loss account is reduced by recapture, in accordance with paragraph (b)(2)(ii) of this section, each member of the group shall reduce its notional overall foreign loss account for that separate limitation by its pro rata share of the amount by which the consolidated overall foreign loss account is reduced. A member's pro rata share of the amount by which a consolidated overall foreign loss account is reduced is determined by multiplying the amount recaptured by a fraction, the numerator of which is the amount in such member's notional account under such separate limitation, and the denominator of which is the amount in the consolidated overall foreign loss account under such separate limitation before reduction for the amount recaptured for that taxable year.

(2) *Overall foreign losses that are part of a net operating loss or net capital loss from a separate return limitation year.*—An overall foreign loss that is part of a net operating loss or net capital loss carryover from a separate return limitation year of a member that is absorbed in a consolidated return year shall be treated as an overall foreign loss of such member (rather than the group) and shall be added to such member's separate overall foreign loss account to the extent it reduces United States source income, in accordance with § 1.904(f)-1(d)(5). Such overall foreign losses shall be added to the appropriate consolidated overall foreign loss account in later years in accordance with paragraph (b)(1)(iii) of this section.

(3) *Allocation of a portion of overall foreign loss accounts to a member leaving the group.*—(i) *Consolidated overall foreign losses.*—When a corporation ceases to be a member of an affiliated group filing consolidated returns, a portion of the balance in each applicable consolidated overall foreign loss account shall be allocated to such corporation. The amount allocated to such corporation shall be equal to the amount, if any, in such member's notional overall foreign loss account under the same separate limitation.

(ii) *Overall foreign losses from separate return limitation years.*— When a corporation ceases to be a member of an affiliated group filing consolidated returns, it shall take with it the remaining portion of each separate overall foreign loss account for overall foreign losses from separate return limitation years (including amounts added to such accounts under paragraph (c)(2) of this section).

(d) *Recapture of consolidated overall foreign losses.*—The amount in any consolidated overall foreign loss account shall be recaptured under §§ 1.904(f)-1 through 1.904(f)-6 by recharacterizing consolidated foreign source taxable income subject to the separate limitation under which the loss arose as United States source taxable income. For purposes of recapture, consolidated foreign source taxable income subject to the separate limitation under which the loss arose shall be determined in accordance with §§ 1.904(f)-2 and 1.1502-4. Amounts in a member's excess loss account that are included in income under § 1.1502-19 shall be subject to recapture to the extent that they are included in consolidated foreign source taxable income subject to the separate limitation under which the loss arose.

(e) *Dispositions of property between members of the same affiliated group during a consolidated return year.*—(1) *In general.*—Except as provided in paragraph (2) with respect to overall foreign losses of a selling member from a separate return limitation year, the rules of § 1.1502-13 with respect to intercompany transactions will apply to dispositions of property to which section 904(f)(3)(A) applies.

(2) *Recapture of overall foreign loss from a separate return limitation year.*—Paragraph (1) will not apply and gain will be recognized to the extent that the selling member has a balance in its overall foreign loss account from a separate return limitation year unless the selling member adds the entire amount of its overall foreign loss account from separate return limitation years to the applicable consolidated overall foreign loss account and treats such amount as an overall foreign loss incurred in the previous year. Such loss shall be subject to recapture, in accordance with paragraph (d) of §1.1502-9, beginning in the same year in which it is added to the consolidated overall foreign loss account.

(f) *Illustrations.*—The provisions of this section are illustrated by the following examples. All foreign source income or loss in these examples is subject to the general limitation.

*Example (1).* A, B, and C are the members of an affiliated group of corporations (as defined in section 1504), and all use the calendar year as their taxable year. For 1983, A, B, and C file a consolidated return. ABC has United States source income of $1,000 and foreign source losses (overall foreign loss) of $400. In accordance with paragraph (b)(1)(i) of this section, ABC adds $400 to its consolidated overall foreign loss account at the end of 1983. For 1983, the separate foreign source taxable income (or loss) of A is $400, of B is ($200), and of C is ($600). Under paragraph (c)(1) of this section, B and C must establish separate notional overall foreign loss accounts. Under paragraph (c)(1)(i)(A) of this section, the amount added to each notional account is the pro rata share of the consolidated overall foreign loss of each member contributing to such loss. The pro rata share is determined by multiplying the consolidated loss by the member's proportionate share of the total foreign source losses of all members having such losses. B's foreign source loss is $200 and C's foreign source loss is $600, totaling $800. B must add $400 × 200/800, or $100, to its notional overall foreign loss account. C must add $400 × 600/800, or $300, to its notional overall foreign loss account.

*Example (2).* The facts are the same as in example (1). In 1984, ABC has consolidated foreign source taxable income of $200. Under paragraph (d) of this section and §1.904(f)-2, ABC is required to recapture $100 of the amount in its consolidated overall foreign loss account, which reduces that account by $100 under paragraph (b)(2)(ii) of this section. In accordance with paragraph (c)(1)(ii) of this section, B reduces its notional account by $100 × 100/400, or $25, and C reduces its notional account by $100 × 300/400, or $75. At the end of 1984 ABC has $300 in its consolidated overall foreign loss account, B has $75 in its notional account, and C has $225 in its notional account.

*Example (3).* D and E are members of an affiliated group and file separate returns using the calendar year as their taxable year for 1980. In 1980, D has an overall foreign loss of $200, which it adds to its overall foreign loss account, and E has no overall foreign losses. For 1981, D and E file a consolidated return, and DE must establish a consolidated overall foreign loss account, to which D's overall foreign loss from 1980 is added under paragraph (b)(1)(ii) of this section. D also adds the same amount $200 to its notional overall foreign loss account under paragraph (c)(1)(i)(B) of this section. In 1981, DE has consolidated foreign source taxable income of $300. Since the amount added to the consolidated overall foreign loss account in 1981 is treated as a consolidated overall foreign loss from 1980, DE must recapture $150 in 1981 under paragraph (d) of this section and §1.904(f)-2. DE's consolidated overall foreign loss account is reduced by $150 under paragraph (b)(2)(ii) of this section, and D's notional account is reduced by $150 under paragraph (c)(1)(ii) of this section, leaving balances of $50 in each of those accounts at the end of 1981.

| Consolidated foreign source taxable income | $400 |
| Consolidated foreign source taxable income recomputed by excluding H's foreign source income and deductions | −200 |
| | $200 |
| × 50% | $100 |
| Amount from H's separate return limitation year overall foreign loss account added to the consolidated overall foreign loss account | $100 |

This amount is subject to recapture beginning in the same taxable year, as it is treated as a consolidated overall foreign loss incurred in a previous year. Therefore, under paragraph (d) of this section and §1.904(f)-2, JH also recaptures this $100, reducing the consolidated overall foreign loss account to $0. H has $300 remaining in its separate overall foreign loss account at the end of 1984.

(iv) In 1985, H has separate taxable income of $400, comprised of $100 of United States source taxable income and $300 of foreign

*Example (4).* F and G are not members of an affiliated group in 1980, and G has an overall foreign loss of $200, which it adds to its overall foreign loss account. F has no overall foreign loss. On January 1, 1981, F acquires G, and FG files a consolidated return for the calendar year 1981. In 1981, F has no foreign source taxable income or loss, and G has $100 of foreign source taxable income. FG's consolidated foreign source taxable income, $100, minus such income without G's items of income and deduction, $0, is $100. Therefore 50% of that amount, $50, of G's overall foreign loss from its 1980 separate return limitation year is added to FG's consolidated overall foreign loss account under paragraph (b)(1)(iii) of this section, and the same amount is added to G's notional account under paragraph (c)(1)(i)(B) of this section. In accordance with paragraph (d) of this section and §1.904(f)-2, FG must recapture the $50 balance in its consolidated overall foreign loss account in 1981 because the amount added from G's separate return limitation year is treated as a 1980 consolidated overall foreign loss. At the end of 1981, FG has a balance of $0 in its consolidated overall foreign loss account, G has $0 in its notional account, and G also has $150 remaining from its 1980 overall foreign loss that has not yet been added to the consolidated overall foreign loss account.

On January 1, 1982, F sells G and G leaves the affiliated group. Under paragraph (c)(3)(i) of this section, G takes with it the balance in its overall foreign loss account from 1980 (its prior separate return limitation year) that has not been added to the consolidated account. G has $150 of overall foreign loss in its overall foreign loss account. Because the amount in the consolidated overall foreign loss account is zero, no amount from that account is allocated to G.

*Example (5).* (i) In 1982 corporation H has United States source income of $300 and foreign source losses of $500, resulting in a net operating loss of $200 and a balance in H's overall foreign loss account at the end of 1982 of $300.

(ii) On January 1, 1983, H is acquired by J, and for the calendar year 1983 JH files a consolidated return. JH has consolidated taxable income of $700 in 1983, including a consolidated net operating loss deduction of $100. This net operating loss deduction is $100 of H's $200 net operating loss from 1982 (a separate return limitation year), which is limited by §1.1502-21A(c). For 1983, H has separate taxable income of $100, comprised of $100 of United States source taxable income and zero foreign source taxable income, and J has separate taxable income of $700, comprised of $700 of United States source taxable income and zero foreign source taxable income. Under paragraph (c)(2) of this section, H adds $100 to its separate overall foreign loss account, since that amount of its net operating loss has reduced United States source income. H has $400 in its separate overall foreign loss account at the end of 1983, none of which has been added to a consolidated overall foreign loss account.

(iii) In 1984, H has separate taxable income of $400, comprised of $100 of United States source taxable income and $300 of foreign source taxable income. J has separate taxable income of $900, comprised of $700 of United States source taxable income and $200 of foreign source taxable income. JH has consolidated taxable income of $1200, which includes $100 of consolidated net operating loss deduction from H's 1982 net operating loss. Since this net operating loss deduction is allocated to foreign source income, it does not reduce United States source income and will not be added to an overall foreign loss account. Under paragraph (b)(1)(iii) of this section, $100 from H's overall foreign loss is added to the consolidated overall foreign loss account computed as follows:

source taxable income. J has separate taxable income of $300 comprised of $600 of United States source taxable income and $300 of foreign source losses. JH has consolidated taxable income of $700, all of which is United States source. Under paragraph (b)(1)(iii) of this section, an additional $150 from H's separate overall foreign loss is added to the consolidated overall foreign loss account, computed as follows:

| | |
|---|---|
| Consolidated foreign source taxable income | |
| Consolidated foreign source taxable income recomputed by excluding H's foreign source income and deductions | $0 |
| | −(300) |
| | $300 |
| × 50% | $150 |
| Amount from H's separate return limitation year overall foreign loss account added to the consolidated overall foreign loss account | $150 |

Thus, an additional $150 of H's separate overall foreign loss is added to the consolidated overall foreign loss account, and, under paragraph (c)(1)(i)(B) of this section, the same amount is added to J's notional account. While this amount is subject to recapture beginning in the same taxable year, JH has no consolidated foreign source taxable income in 1985, so no overall foreign loss is recaptured. H has a remaining balance of $150 in its separate return limitation year overall foreign loss account and HJ has $150 in its consolidated overall foreign loss account.

*Example (6).* A, B, and C are members of an affiliated group of corporations (as defined in section 1504), and all use the calendar year as their taxable year. For 1986, A, B, and C file a consolidated return. A has an overall foreign loss account which arose in a separate return limitation year. The amount in the overall foreign loss account is $2,000. A makes a disposition of all its assets to B on January 1, 1986. The gain on the transfer is $1,500, all of which would be recognized under section 904(f)(3). However, if A adds the total amount of its overall foreign loss from separate return limitation years to ABC's consolidated overall foreign loss account, no gain will be recognized on the transfer until the intercompany gain is taken into account under §1.1502-13. In the interim, any foreign source gain of the purchasing member (or any other member of the consolidated group) may be used to recapture on a consolidated basis the amount in ABC's consolidated overall foreign loss account. [Reg. §1.1502-9A.]

☐ [*T.D. 8153, 8-21-87. Amended by T.D. 8597, 7-12-95; T.D. 8677, 6-26-96; T.D. 8751, 1-9-98; T.D. 8766, 3-13-98; T.D. 8800, 12-28-98 and T.D. 8823, 6-25-99. Redesignated and amended by T.D. 8833, 8-10-99. Amended by T.D. 8884, 5-24-2000.*]

**[Reg. §1.1502-11]**

**§1.1502-11. Consolidated taxable income.**—(a) *In general.*—The consolidated taxable income for a consolidated return year shall be determined by taking into account—

(1) The separate taxable income of each member of the group (see §1.1502-12 for the computation of separate taxable income);

(2) Any consolidated net operating loss deduction (see §1.1502-21 (or 1.1502-21A, as appropriate) for the computation of the consolidated net operating loss deduction);

(3) Any consolidated capital gain net income (net capital gain for taxable years beginning before January 1, 1977) (see §1.1502-22 (or 1.1502-22A, as appropriate) for the computation of the consolidated capital gain net income (net capital gain for taxable years beginning before January 1, 1977));

(4) Any consolidated section 1231 net loss (see §1.1502-23 (or 1.1502-23A, as appropriate) for the computation of the consolidated section 1231 net loss);

(5) Any consolidated charitable contributions deduction (see §1.1502-24 for the computation of the consolidated charitable contributions deduction);

(6) Any consolidated section 922 deduction (see §1.1502-25 for the computation of the consolidated section 922 deduction);

(7) Any consolidated dividends received deduction (see §1.1502-26 for the computation of the consolidated dividends received deduction); and

(8) Any consolidated section 247 deduction (see §1.1502-27 for the computation of the consolidated section 247 deduction).

(b) *Elimination of circular stock basis adjustments when there is no excluded COD income.*—(1) *In general.*—If one member (P) disposes of the stock of another member (S), this paragraph (b) limits the use of S's deductions and losses in the year of disposition and the carryback of items to prior years. The purpose of the limitation is to prevent P's income or gain from the disposition of S's stock from increasing the absorption of S's deductions and losses, because the increased absorption would reduce P's basis (or increase its excess loss account) in S's stock under §1.1502-32 and, in turn, increase P's income or gain. See paragraph (b)(3) of this section for the application of these principles to P's deduction or loss from the disposition of S's stock, and paragraph (b)(4) of this section for the application of these principles to multiple stock dispositions. This paragraph (b) applies only when no member realizes discharge of indebtedness income that is excluded from gross income under section 108(a) (excluded COD income) during the taxable year of the disposition. See paragraph (c) of this section for rules that apply when a member realizes excluded COD income during the taxable year of the disposition. See §1.1502-19(c) for the definition of disposition.

(2) *Limitation on deductions and losses.*—(i) *Determination of amount of limitation.*—If P disposes of one or more shares of S's stock, the extent to which S's deductions and losses for the tax year of the disposition (and its deductions and losses carried over from prior years) may offset income and gain is subject to limitation. The amount of S's deductions and losses that may offset income and gain is determined by tentatively computing taxable income (or loss) for the year of disposition (and any prior years to which the deductions or losses may be carried) without taking into account P's income and gain from the disposition.

(ii) *Application of limitation.*—S's deductions and losses offset income and gain only to the extent of the amount determined under paragraph (b)(2)(i) of this section. To the extent S's deductions and losses in the year of disposition cannot offset income or gain because of the limitation under this paragraph (b), the items are carried to other years under the applicable provisions of the Internal Revenue Code and regulations as if they were the only items incurred by S in the year of disposition. For example, to the extent S incurs an operating loss in the year of disposition that is limited, the loss is treated as a separate net operating loss attributable to S arising in that year. The tentative computation does not affect the manner in which S's unlimited deductions and losses are absorbed or the manner in which deductions and losses of other members are absorbed. (If the amount of S's unlimited deductions and losses actually absorbed is less than the amount absorbed in the tentative computation, P's stock basis adjustments under §1.1502-32 reflect only the amounts actually absorbed.)

(iii) *Examples.*—For purposes of the examples in this paragraph (b), unless otherwise stated, P owns all of the only class of S's stock for the entire year, S owns no stock of lower-tier members, the tax year of all persons is the calendar year, all persons use the accrual method of accounting, the facts set forth the only corporate activity, all transactions are between unrelated persons, and tax liabilities are disregarded. The principles of this paragraph (b)(2) are illustrated by the following examples.

*Example 1. Limitation on losses with respect to stock gain.* (a) P has a $500 basis in S's stock. For Year 1, P has ordinary income of $30 (determined without taking P's gain or loss from the disposition of S's stock into account) and S has an $80 ordinary loss. P sells S's stock for $520 at the close of Year 1.

(b) To determine the amount of the limitation on S's loss under paragraph (b)(2)(i) of this section, and the effect under §1.1502-32(b) of the absorption of S's loss on P's basis in S's stock, P's gain or loss from the disposition of S's stock is not taken into account. The group is tentatively treated as having a consolidated net operating loss of $50 (P's $30 of income minus S's $80 loss). Thus, $50 of S's loss is limited under this paragraph (b).

(c) Because $30 of S's loss is absorbed in the determination of consolidated taxable income under paragraph (b)(2)(ii) of this section, P's basis in S's stock is reduced under §1.1502-32(b) from $500 to $470 immediately before the disposition. Consequently, P recognizes a $50 gain from the sale of S's stock and the group has consolidated taxable income of $50 for Year 1 (P's $30 of ordinary income and $50 gain from the sale of S's stock, less the $30 of S's loss). In addition, S's limited loss of $50 is treated as a separate net operating loss attributable to S and, because S ceases to be a member, the loss is apportioned to S under §1.1502-21 (or §1.1502-79A, as appropriate) and carried to its first separate return year.

*Example 2. Carrybacks and carryovers.* (a) For Year 1, the P group has consolidated taxable income of $30, and a consolidated net capital loss of $100 ($50 attributable to P and $50 to S). At the beginning of Year 2, P has a $300 basis in S's stock. For Year 2, P has ordinary income of $30, and a $20 capital gain (determined without taking the $100 consolidated net capital loss carryover or P's gain or loss from the disposition of S's stock into account), and S has a $100 ordinary loss. P sells S's stock for $280 at the close of Year 2.

(b) To determine the amount of the limitation under paragraph (b)(2)(i) of this section on S's losses, and the effect of the absorption of S's losses on P's basis in S's stock under §1.1502-32(b), P's gain or loss from the disposition of S's stock is not taken into account. For Year 2, the P group is tentatively treated as having a $70 consolidated net operating loss (S's $100 ordinary loss, less P's $30 of ordinary income). The P group is also treated as having no consolidated net capital gain in Year 2, because P's $20 capital gain is reduced by $20 of the consolidated net capital loss carryover from Year 1 under section 1212(a) (the absorption of which is attributed equally to P and S). In addition, of the $70 consolidated net operating loss, $30 is carried back to Year 1 and offsets P's ordinary income in that year, and $40 is carried forward. Consequently, $40 of S's operating loss from Year 2, and $40 of the consolidated net capital loss carryover from Year 1 attributable to S, are limited under this paragraph (b).

(c) Under paragraph (b)(2)(ii) of this section, the limitation under this paragraph (b) does not affect the absorption of any deductions and losses attributable to P, $60 of S's operating loss from Year 2, and $10 of the consolidated net capital loss from Year 1 attributable to S. Consequently, P's basis in S's stock is reduced under §1.1502-32(b) by $70, from $300 to $230, and P recognizes a $50 gain from the sale of S's stock in Year 2. Thus, the P group is treated as having a $20 unlimited net operating loss that is carried back to Year 1:

| | |
|---|---:|
| Ordinary income: | |
|   P | $30 |
|   S (excluding the $40 limited loss) | (60) |
|     Sub Total | $(30) |
| Consolidated net capital gain: | |
|   P ($20 + $50 from S stock – $50 from Year 1) | $20 |
|   S (–$10 from Year 1) | (10) |
|     Sub Total | $10 |
| Consolidated taxable income | $(20) |

(d) Under paragraph (b)(2)(ii) of this section, S's $40 ordinary loss from Year 2 that is limited under this paragraph (b) is treated as a separate net operating loss arising in Year 2. Similarly, $40 of the consolidated net capital loss from Year 1 attributable to S is treated as a separate net capital loss carried over from Year 1. Because S ceases to be a member, the $40 net operating loss from Year 2 and the $40 consolidated net capital loss from Year 1 are allocated to S under §§1.1502-21 and 1.1502-22, respectively (or §1.1502-79A, as appropriate) and are carried to S's first separate return year.

*Example 3. Allocation of basis adjustments.* (a) For Year 1, the P group has consolidated taxable income of $100. At the beginning of Year 2, P has a $40 basis in each of the 10 shares of S's stock. For Year 2, P has an $80 ordinary loss (determined without taking into account P's gain or loss from the disposition of S's stock) and S has an $80 ordinary loss. P sells 2 shares of S's stock for $85 each at the close of Year 2.

(b) Under paragraph (b)(2)(i) of this section, the amount of the limitation on S's loss is determined by tentatively treating the P group as having a $160 consolidated net operating loss for Year 2. Of this amount, $100 is carried back under section 172 and absorbed in Year 1 ($50 attributable to S and $50 attributable to P). Consequently, $30 of S's loss is limited under this paragraph (b).

(c) Under paragraph (b)(2)(ii) of this section, the limitation under this paragraph (b) does not affect the absorption of P's $80 ordinary loss or $50 of S's ordinary loss. Consequently, P's basis in each share of S's stock is reduced from $40 to $35 under §1.1502-32(b), and P recognizes a $100 gain from the sale of the 2 shares. Thus, the P group is treated as having a $30 unlimited net operating loss:

| | |
|---|---:|
| Ordinary loss: | |
|   P | $(80) |
|   S (excluding the $30 limited loss) | (50) |
|     Sub Total | $(130) |
| Consolidated net capital gain: | |
|   P | $100 |
|   S | 0 |
|     Sub Total | $100 |
| Unlimited consolidated net operating loss | $(30) |

(d) A portion of the $130 of unlimited operating losses for Year 2 is fully absorbed in that year, and a portion is carried back to Year 1. Thus, $61.50 of P's $80 loss ($100 multiplied by $80/$130) and $38.50 of S's $50 unlimited loss ($100 multiplied by $50/$130) are absorbed in Year 2. P's remaining $18.50 of loss and S's remaining $11.50 of loss are not subject to limitation and are carried back and absorbed in Year 1.

(e) Under paragraph (b)(2)(ii) of this section, S's $30 of loss limited under this paragraph (b) is treated as a separate net operating loss.

(3) *Loss dispositions.*—(i) *General rule.*—The principles of paragraph (b)(2) of this section apply to the extent necessary to carry out the purposes of paragraph (b)(1) of this section if P recognizes a deduction or loss from the disposition of S's stock.

(ii) *Example.*—The principles of this paragraph (b)(3) are illustrated by the following example.

*Example.* (a) P has a $400 basis in S's stock. For Year 1, P has a capital gain of $100 (determined without taking P's gain or loss from the disposition of S's stock into account) and S has both a $60 capital loss and a $200 ordinary loss. P sells S's stock for $140 at the close of Year 1.

(b) Under paragraph (b)(3) of this section, the amount of S's ordinary and capital losses that may offset income and gain is determined by tentatively computing the group's consolidated net operating loss and consolidated net capital loss without taking into account P's loss from the disposition of S's stock. The limitation is necessary to prevent P's loss from the disposition of S's stock from affecting the absorption of S's losses and thereby the adjustments to P's basis in S's stock under §1.1502-32(b) (which would, in turn, affect P's loss).

(c) Under the principles of paragraph (b)(2)(i) of this section, the amount of the limitation on S's loss is determined by tentatively treating the P group as having a $40 consolidated net capital gain and a $200 ordinary loss, which results in a $160 consolidated net operating loss for Year 1, all of which is attributable to S. Thus, $160 of S's ordinary loss is limited under this paragraph (b). See also §§1.337(d)-2, 1.1502-35, and 1.1502-36 for rules relating to basis adjustments and allowance of stock loss on dispositions of stock of a subsidiary member.

(4) *Multiple dispositions.*—(i) *Stock of a member.*—To the extent income, gain, deduction, or loss from a prior disposition of S's stock is deferred under any rule of law, the limitation under paragraph (b)(2) of this section is determined by treating the year the deferred amount is taken into account as the year of the disposition.

(ii) *Stock of different members.*—If S is a higher-tier corporation with respect to another member (T), and all of T's items of income, gain, deduction, and loss (including the absorption of T's deduction or loss) would be fully reflected in P's basis in S's stock under §1.1502-32, the limitation under paragraph (b)(2)(i) of this section with respect to T's deductions and losses is determined without taking into account any income, gain, deduction, or loss from the disposition of the stock of S or T (or of the stock of members owned in the chain connecting S and T). However, this paragraph (b) does not otherwise limit the absorption of one member's deduction or loss with respect to the disposition of another member's stock.

(iii) *Examples.*—The principles of this paragraph (b)(4) are illustrated by the following examples.

*Example 1. Chain of subsidiaries.* (a) P owns all of S's stock with a $500 basis, and S owns all of T's stock with a $500 basis. For Year 1, P has ordinary income of $30, S has no income or loss, and T has an $80 ordinary loss. P sells S's stock for $520 at the close of Year 1.

(b) Under paragraph (b)(4) of this section, to determine the amount of the limitation under paragraph (b) of this section on T's loss, and the effect of the absorption of T's loss on P's basis in S's stock under §1.1502-32(b), P's gain or loss from the disposition of S's stock is not taken into account. The group is tentatively treated as having a consolidated net operating loss of $50 (P's $30 of income minus T's $80 loss). Because only $30 of T's loss offsets income or gain, P's basis in S's stock is reduced under §1.1502-32(b) from $500 to $470 immediately before the disposition of S's stock. Thus, P takes into account a $50 gain from the sale of S's stock.

(c) The facts are the same as in paragraph (a) of this *Example 1*, except that S has a $10 excess loss account in T's stock (rather than a $500 basis). Under paragraph (b)(4) of this section, neither P's gain or loss from the disposition of S's stock nor S's gain or loss from the disposition of T's stock (under §1.1502-19) are taken into account for purposes of the tentative computations and the effect of any absorption under §1.1502-32(b) on P's basis in S's stock and S's excess loss account in T's stock. The group is tentatively treated as having a consolidated net operating loss of $50 (P's $30 of income minus T's $80 loss), and only $30 of T's loss may offset the group's income or gain. Under §1.1502-32(b), the absorption of $30 of T's loss increases S's excess loss account in T's stock to $40 and, under §1.1502-19, the excess loss account is taken into account. Moreover, under §1.1502-32(b), P's basis in S's stock is increased immediately before the sale by $10 (S's $40 gain under §1.1502-19(b) minus T's $30 loss absorbed and tiered up under §1.1502-32(b)), from $500 to $510. Thus, P takes into account a $10 gain from the sale of S's stock, and S takes into account a $40 gain from its excess loss account in T's stock.

*Example 2. Brother-sister subsidiaries.* (a) P owns all of the stock of S1 and S2, each with a $50 basis. For Year 1, the group has a $100 consolidated net operating loss ($50 of which is attributable to S1, and $50 to S2) determined without taking gain or loss from the disposition of member stock into account. At the close of Year 1, P sells the stock of S1 and S2 for $100 each.

(b) Paragraph (b)(4) of this section does not limit the loss of S1 or S2 with respect to the disposition of stock of the other. Consequently, each subsidiary's loss may offset P's gain from the disposition of the stock of the other subsidiary. Because this absorption results in a $50 reduction in P's basis in the stock of each subsidiary under §1.1502-32(b), P's aggregate gain from the stock dispositions is increased from $100 to $200, $100 of which is offset by the losses of the subsidiaries.

(5) *Effective date.*—This paragraph (b) applies to stock dispositions occurring in consolidated return years beginning on or after January 1, 1995. For prior years, see §1.1502-11(b) as contained in the 26 CFR part 1 edition revised as of April 1, 1994.

(c) *Elimination of circular stock basis adjustments when there is excluded COD income.*—(1) *In general.*—If one member (P) disposes of the stock of another member (S) in a year during which any member realizes excluded COD income, this paragraph (c) limits the use of S's deductions and losses in the year of disposition and the carryback of items to prior years, the amount of the attributes of certain members that can be reduced in respect of excluded COD income of certain other members, and the attributes that can be used to offset an excess loss account taken into account by reason of the application of §1.1502-19(c)(1)(iii)(B). In addition to the purpose set forth in paragraph (b)(1) of this section, the purpose of these limitations is to prevent the reduction of tax attributes in respect of excluded COD income from affecting P's income, gain, or loss on the disposition of S stock (including a disposition of S stock that results from the application of §1.1502-19(c)(1)(iii)(B)) and, in turn, affecting the attributes available for reduction pursuant to sections 108 and 1017 and §1.1502-28. See §1.1502-19(c) for the definition of disposition.

(2) *Computation of tax liability, reduction of attributes, and computation of limits on absorption and reduction of attributes.*—If a member realizes excluded COD income in the taxable year during which P disposes of S stock, the steps used to compute tax liability, to effect the reduction of attributes, and to compute the limitations on the absorption and reduction of attributes are as follows. These steps also apply to determine whether and to what extent an excess loss account must be taken into account as a result of the application of §1.1502-19(b)(1) and (c)(1)(iii)(B).

(i) *Limitation on deductions and losses to offset income or gain.*—First, the determination of the extent to which S's deductions and losses for the tax year of the disposition (and its deductions and losses carried over from prior years) may offset income and gain is made pursuant to paragraphs (b)(2) and (3) of this section.

(ii) *Tentative adjustment of stock basis.*—Second, §1.1502-32 is tentatively applied to adjust the basis of the S stock to reflect the amount of S's income and gain included, and unlimited deductions and losses that are absorbed, in the tentative computation of taxable

income or loss for the year of the disposition (and any prior years) that is made pursuant to paragraph (b)(2) of this section, but not to reflect the realization of excluded COD income and the reduction of attributes in respect thereof.

(iii) *Tentative computation of stock gain or loss.*—Third, in the case of a disposition of S stock that does not result from the application of §1.1502-19(c)(1)(iii)(B), P's income, gain, or loss from the disposition of S stock is computed. For this purpose, the result of the computation pursuant to paragraph (c)(2)(ii) of this section is treated as the basis of such stock.

(iv) *Tentative computation of tax imposed.*—Fourth, the tax imposed by chapter 1 of the Internal Revenue Code for the year of disposition (and any prior years) is tentatively computed. For this purpose, in the case of a disposition of S stock that does not result from the application of §1.1502-19(c)(1)(iii)(B), the tentative computation of tax imposed takes into account P's income, gain, or loss from the disposition of S stock computed pursuant to paragraph (c)(2)(iii) of this section. The tentative computation of tax imposed is made without regard to whether all or a portion of an excess loss account in a share of S stock is required to be taken into account pursuant to §1.1502-19(b)(1) and (c)(1)(iii)(B).

(v) *Tentative reduction of attributes.*—Fifth, the rules of sections 108 and 1017 and §1.1502-28 are tentatively applied to reduce the attributes remaining after the tentative computation of tax imposed pursuant to paragraph (c)(2)(iv) of this section.

(vi) *Actual adjustment of stock basis.*—Sixth, §1.1502-32 is applied to reflect the amount of S's income and gain included, and unlimited deductions and losses that are absorbed, in the tentative computation of tax imposed for the year of the disposition (and any prior years) made pursuant to paragraph (c)(2)(iv) of this section, and the excluded COD income applied to reduce attributes and the attributes tentatively reduced in respect of the excluded COD income pursuant to paragraph (c)(2)(v) of this section.

(vii) *Actual computation of stock gain or loss.*—Seventh, the group's actual gain or loss on the disposition of S stock (including a disposition that results from the application of §1.1502-19(c)(1)(iii)(B)) is computed. The result of the computation pursuant to paragraph (c)(2)(vi) of this section is treated as the basis of such stock.

(viii) *Actual computation of tax imposed.*—Eighth, the tax imposed by chapter 1 of the Internal Revenue Code for the year of the disposition (and any prior years) is computed. The actual tax imposed on the group for the year of the disposition is computed by applying the limitation computed pursuant to paragraph (c)(2)(i) of this section, and by including the gain or loss recognized on the disposition of S stock computed pursuant to paragraph (c)(2)(vii) of this section. However, attributes that were tentatively used in the computation of tax imposed pursuant to paragraph (c)(2)(iv) of this section and attributes that were tentatively reduced pursuant to paragraph (c)(2)(v) of this section cannot offset any excess loss account taken into account as a result of the application of §1.1502-19(b)(1) and (c)(1)(iii)(B).

(ix) *Actual reduction of attributes.*—Ninth, the rules of sections 108 and 1017 and §1.1502-28 are actually applied to reduce the attributes remaining after the actual computation of tax imposed pursuant to paragraph (c)(2)(viii) of this section.

(A) *S or a lower-tier corporation realizes excluded COD income.*—If S or a lower-tier corporation of S realizes excluded COD income, the aggregate amount of excluded COD income that is applied to reduce attributes to members other than S and any lower-tier corporation of S pursuant to this paragraph (c)(2)(ix) shall not exceed the aggregate amount of excluded COD income that was tentatively applied to reduce attributes attributable to members other than S and any lower-tier corporation of S pursuant to paragraph (c)(2)(v) of this section. The amount of the actual reduction of attributes attributable to S and any lower-tier corporation of S that may be reduced in respect of the excluded COD income of S or a lower-tier corporation of S shall not be so limited.

(B) *A member other than S or a lower-tier corporation realizes excluded COD income.*—If a member other than S or a lower-tier corporation of S realizes excluded COD income, the aggregate amount of excluded COD income that is applied to reduce attributes (other than credits) attributable to S and any lower-tier corporation of S pursuant to this paragraph (c)(2)(ix) shall not exceed the aggregate amount of excluded COD income that was tentatively applied to reduce attributes (other than credits) attributable to S and any lower-tier corporation of S pursuant to paragraph (c)(2)(v) of this section. The amount of the actual reduction of attributes attributable to any member other than S and any lower-tier corporation of S that may be reduced in respect of the excluded COD income of S or a lower-tier corporation of S shall not be so limited.

(3) *Special rules.*—(i) If the reduction of attributes attributable to a member is prevented as a result of a limitation described in paragraph (c)(2)(ix)(B) of this section, the excluded COD income that would have otherwise been applied to reduce such attributes is applied to reduce the remaining attributes of the same type that are available for reduction under § 1.1502-28(a)(4), on a pro rata basis, prior to reducing attributes of a different type. The reduction of such remaining attributes, however, is subject to any applicable limitation described in paragraph (c)(2)(ix)(B) of this section.

(ii) To the extent S's deductions and losses in the year of disposition (or those of a lower-tier corporation of S) cannot offset income or gain because of the limitation under paragraph (b) of this section or this paragraph (c) and are not reduced pursuant to sections 108 and 1017 and § 1.1502-28, such items are carried to other years under the applicable provisions of the Internal Revenue Code and regulations as if they were the only items incurred by S (or a lower-tier corporation of S) in the year of disposition. For example, to the extent S incurs an operating loss in the year of disposition that is limited and is not reduced pursuant to section 108 and § 1.1502-28, the loss is treated as a separate net operating loss attributable to S arising in that year.

(4) *Definition of lower-tier corporation.*—A corporation is a lower-tier corporation of S if all of its items of income, gain, deduction, and loss (including the absorption of deduction or loss and the reduction of attributes other than credits) would be fully reflected in P's basis in S's stock under § 1.1502-32.

(5) *Examples.*—For purposes of the examples in this paragraph (c), unless otherwise stated, the tax year of all persons is the calendar year, all persons use the accrual method of accounting, the facts set forth the only corporate activity, all transactions are between unrelated persons, tax liabilities are disregarded, and no election under section 108(b)(5) is made. The principles of this paragraph (c) are illustrated by the following examples:

*Example 1. Departing member realizes excluded COD income.* (i) *Facts.* P owns all of S's stock with a $90 basis. For Year 1, P has ordinary income of $30, and S has an $80 ordinary loss and $100 of excluded COD income from the discharge of non-intercompany indebtedness. P sells the S stock for $20 at the close of Year 1. As of the beginning of Year 2, S has Asset A with a basis of $0 and a fair market value of $20.

(ii) *Analysis.* The steps used to compute the tax imposed on the group, to effect the reduction of attributes, and to compute the limitations on the use and reduction of attributes are as follows:

(A) *Computation of limitation on deductions and losses to offset income or gain.* To determine the amount of the limitation under paragraph (c)(2)(i) of this section on S's loss and the effect of the absorption of S's loss on P's basis in S's stock under § 1.1502-32(b), P's gain or loss from the disposition of S's stock is not taken into account. The group is tentatively treated as having a consolidated net operating loss of $50 (P's $30 of income minus S's $80 loss). Thus, $30 of S's loss is unlimited and $50 of S's loss is limited under paragraph (c)(2)(i) of this section. Under the principles of § 1.1502-21(b)(2)(iv), all of the consolidated net operating loss is attributable to S.

(B) *Tentative adjustment of stock basis.* Then, pursuant to paragraph (c)(2)(ii) of this section, § 1.1502-32 is tentatively applied to adjust the basis of S stock. For this purpose, however, adjustments attributable to the excluded COD income and the reduction of attributes in respect thereof are not taken into account. Under § 1.1502-32(b), the absorption of $30 of S's loss decreases P's basis in S's stock by $30 to $60.

(C) *Tentative computation of stock gain or loss.* Then, P's income, gain, or loss from the sale of S stock is computed pursuant to paragraph (c)(2)(iii) of this section using the basis computed in the previous step. Thus, P is treated as recognizing a $40 loss from the sale of S stock.

(D) *Tentative computation of tax imposed.* Pursuant to paragraph (c)(2)(iv) of this section, the tax imposed for the year of disposition is then tentatively computed, taking into account P's $40 loss on the sale of the S stock computed pursuant to paragraph (c)(2)(iii) of this section. The group has a $50 consolidated net operating loss for Year 1 that, under the principles of § 1.1502-21(b)(2)(iv), is wholly attributable to S and a consolidated capital loss of $40 that, under the principles of § 1.1502-21(b)(2)(iv), is wholly attributable to P.

(E) *Tentative reduction of attributes.* Next, pursuant to paragraph (c)(2)(v) of this section, the rules of sections 108 and 1017 and § 1.1502-28 are tentatively applied to reduce attributes remaining after the tentative computation of the tax imposed. Pursuant to § 1.1502-28(a)(2), the tax attributes attributable to S would first be reduced to take into account its $100 of excluded COD income. Accordingly, the consolidated net operating loss for Year 1 would be

reduced by $50, the portion of that consolidated net operating loss attributable to S under the principles of § 1.1502-21(b)(2)(iv), to $0. Then, pursuant to § 1.1502-28(a)(4), S's remaining $50 of excluded COD income would reduce the consolidated capital loss attributable to P of $40 by $40 to $0. The remaining $10 of excluded COD income would have no effect.

(F) *Actual adjustment of stock basis.* Pursuant to paragraph (c)(2)(vi) of this section, § 1.1502-32 is applied to reflect the amount of S's income and gain included, and unlimited deductions and losses that are absorbed, in the tentative computation of the tax imposed for the year of the disposition and the excluded COD income tentatively applied to reduce attributes and the attributes reduced in respect of the excluded COD income pursuant to the previous step. Under § 1.1502-32(b), the absorption of $30 of S's loss, the application of $90 of S's excluded COD income to reduce attributes of P and S, and the reduction of the $50 loss attributable to S in respect of the excluded COD income results in a positive adjustment of $10 to P's basis in the S stock. P's basis in the S stock, therefore, is $100.

(G) *Actual computation of stock gain or loss.* Pursuant to paragraph (c)(2)(vii) of this section, P's actual gain or loss on the sale of the S stock is computed using the basis computed in the previous step. Accordingly, P recognizes an $80 loss on the disposition of the S stock.

(H) *Actual computation of tax imposed.* Pursuant to paragraph (c)(2)(viii) of this section, the tax imposed is computed by taking into account P's $80 loss from the sale of S stock. Before the application of § 1.1502-28, therefore, the group has a consolidated net operating loss of $50 that is wholly attributable to S under the principles of § 1.1502-21(b)(2)(iv), and a consolidated capital loss of $80 that is wholly attributable to P under the principles of § 1.1502-21(b)(2)(iv).

(I) *Actual reduction of attributes.* Pursuant to paragraph (c)(2)(ix) of this section, sections 108 and 1017 and § 1.1502-28 are then actually applied to reduce attributes remaining after the actual computation of the tax imposed. Pursuant to § 1.1502-28(a)(2), the tax attributes attributable to S must first be reduced to take into account its $100 of excluded COD income. Accordingly, the consolidated net operating loss for Year 1 is reduced by $50, the portion of that consolidated net operating loss attributable to S under the principles of § 1.1502-21(b)(2)(iv), to $0. Then, pursuant to § 1.1502-28(a)(4), S's remaining $50 of excluded COD income reduces consolidated tax attributes. In particular, without regard to the limitation imposed by paragraph (c)(2)(ix)(A) of this section, the $80 consolidated capital loss, which under the principles of § 1.1502-21(b)(2)(iv) is attributable to P, would be reduced by $50 from $80 to $30. However, the limitation imposed by paragraph (c)(2)(ix)(A) of this section prevents the reduction of the consolidated capital loss attributable to P by more than $40. Therefore, the consolidated capital loss attributable to P is reduced by only $40 in respect of S's excluded COD income. The remaining $10 of excluded COD income has no effect.

*Example 2. Member other than departing member realizes excluded COD income.* (i) *Facts.* P owns all of S1's and S2's stock. P's basis in S2's stock is $600. For Year 1, P has ordinary income of $30, S1 has a $100 ordinary loss and $100 of excluded COD income from the discharge of non-intercompany indebtedness, and S2 has $200 of ordinary loss. P sells the S2 stock for $600 at the close of Year 1. As of the beginning of Year 2, S1 has Asset A with a basis of $0 and a fair market value of $10.

(ii) *Analysis.* The steps used to compute the tax imposed on the group, to effect the reduction of attributes, and to compute the limitations on the use and reduction of attributes are as follows:

(A) *Computation of limitation on deductions and losses to offset income or gain.* To determine the amount of the limitation under paragraph (c)(2)(i) of this section on S2's loss and the effect of the absorption of S2's loss on P's basis in S2's stock under § 1.1502-32(b), P's gain or loss from the sale of S2's stock is not taken into account. The group is tentatively treated as having a consolidated net operating loss of $270 (P's $30 of income minus S1's $100 loss and S2's $200 loss). Consequently, $20 of S2's loss from Year 1 is unlimited and $180 of S2's loss from Year 1 is limited under paragraph (c)(2)(i) of this section. Under the principles of § 1.1502-21(b)(2)(iv), $90 of the consolidated net operating loss is attributable to S1 and $180 of the consolidated net operating loss is attributable to S2.

(B) *Tentative adjustment of stock basis.* Then, pursuant to paragraph (c)(2)(ii) of this section, § 1.1502-32 is tentatively applied to adjust the basis of S2's stock. For this purpose, however, adjustments to the basis of S2's stock attributable to the reduction of attributes in respect of S1's excluded COD income are not taken into account. Under § 1.1502-32(b), the absorption of $20 of S2's loss decreases P's basis in S2's stock by $20 to $580.

(C) *Tentative computation of stock gain or loss.* Then, P's income, gain, or loss from the disposition of S2 stock is computed pursuant to paragraph (c)(2)(iii) of this section using the basis computed in the previous step. Thus, P is treated as recognizing a $20 gain from the sale of the S2 stock.

(D) *Tentative computation of tax imposed.* Pursuant to paragraph (c)(2)(iv) of this section, the tax imposed for the year of disposition is then tentatively computed, taking into account P's $20 gain from the sale of S2 stock computed pursuant to paragraph (c)(2)(iii) of this section. Although S2's limited loss cannot be used to offset P's $20 gain from the sale of S2's stock under the rules of this section, S1's loss will offset that gain. Therefore, the group is tentatively treated as having a consolidated net operating loss of $250, $70 of which is attributable to S1 and $180 of which is attributable to S2 under the principles of § 1.1502-21(b)(2)(iv).

(E) *Tentative reduction of attributes.* Next, pursuant to paragraph (c)(2)(v) of this section, the rules of sections 108 and 1017 and § 1.1502-28 are tentatively applied to reduce attributes remaining after the tentative computation of the tax imposed. Pursuant to § 1.1502-28(a)(2), the tax attributes attributable to S1 would first be reduced to take into account its $100 of excluded COD income. Accordingly, the consolidated net operating loss for Year 1 would be reduced by $70, the portion of that consolidated net operating loss attributable to S1 under the principles of § 1.1502-21(b)(2)(iv), to $0. Then, pursuant to § 1.1502-28(a)(4), S1's remaining $30 of excluded COD income would reduce the consolidated net operating loss for Year 1 attributable to S2 of $180 by $30 to $150.

(F) *Actual adjustment of stock basis.* Pursuant to paragraph (c)(2)(vi) of this section, § 1.1502-32 is applied to reflect the amount of S2's income and gain included, and unlimited deductions and losses that are absorbed, in the tentative computation of the tax imposed for the year of the disposition and the excluded COD income tentatively applied to reduce attributes and the attributes reduced in respect of the excluded COD income pursuant to the previous step. Under § 1.1502-32(b), the absorption of $20 of S2's loss to offset a portion of P's income and the application of $30 of S1's excluded COD income to reduce attributes attributable to S2 results in a negative adjustment of $50 to P's basis in the S2 stock. P's basis in the S2 stock, therefore, is $550.

(G) *Actual computation of stock gain or loss.* Pursuant to paragraph (c)(2)(vii) of this section, P's actual gain or loss on the sale of the S2 stock is computed using the basis computed in the previous step. Therefore, P recognizes a $50 gain on the disposition of the S2 stock.

(H) *Actual computation of tax imposed.* Pursuant to paragraph (c)(2)(viii) of this section, the tax imposed is computed by taking into account P's $50 gain from the disposition of the S2 stock. Before the application of § 1.1502-28, therefore, the group has a consolidated net operating loss of $220, $40 of which is attributable to S1 and $180 of which is attributable to S2 under the principles of § 1.1502-21(b)(2)(iv).

(I) *Actual reduction of attributes.* Pursuant to paragraph (c)(2)(ix) of this section, sections 108 and 1017 and § 1.1502-28 are then actually applied to reduce attributes remaining after the actual computation of the tax imposed. Pursuant to § 1.1502-28(a)(2), the tax attributes attributable to S1 must first be reduced to take into account its $100 of excluded COD income. Accordingly, the consolidated net operating loss for Year 1 is reduced by $40, the portion of that consolidated net operating loss attributable to S1 under the principles of § 1.1502-21(b)(2)(iv), to $0. Then, pursuant to § 1.1502-28(a)(4), without regard to the limitation imposed by paragraph (c)(2)(ix)(B) of this section, S1's remaining $60 of excluded COD income would reduce S2's net operating loss of $180 to $120. However, the limitation imposed by paragraph (c)(2)(ix)(B) of this section prevents the reduction of S2's loss by more than $30. Therefore, S2's loss of $180 is reduced by $30 to $150 in respect of S1's excluded COD income. The remaining $30 of excluded COD income has no effect.

*Example 3. Lower-tier corporation of departing member realizes excluded COD income.* (i) *Facts.* P owns all of S1's stock, S2's stock, and S3's stock. S1 owns all of S4's stock. P's basis in S1's stock is $50 and S1's basis in S4's stock is $50. For Year 1, P has $50 of ordinary loss, S1 has $100 of ordinary loss, S2 has $150 of ordinary loss, S3 has $50 of ordinary loss, and S4 has $50 of ordinary loss and $80 of excluded COD income from the discharge of non-intercompany indebtedness. P sells the S1 stock for $100 at the close of Year 1. As of the beginning of Year 2, S4 has Asset A with a fair market value of $10. After the computation of tax imposed for Year 1 and before the application of sections 108 and 1017 and § 1.1502-28, Asset A has a basis of $0.

(ii) *Analysis.* The steps used to compute the tax imposed on the group, to effect the reduction of attributes, and to compute the limitations on the use and reduction of attributes are as follows:

(A) *Computation of limitation on deductions and losses to offset income or gain.* To determine the amount of the limitation under paragraph (c)(2)(i) of this section on S1's and S4's losses and the effect of the absorption of S1's and S4's losses on P's basis in S1's stock under § 1.1502-32(b), P's gain or loss from the sale of S1's stock is not taken into account. The group is tentatively treated as having a consolidated net operating loss of $400. Consequently, $100 of S1's loss and $50 of S4's loss is limited under paragraph (c)(2)(i) of this section.

(B) *Tentative adjustment of stock basis.* Then, pursuant to paragraph (c)(2)(ii) of this section, § 1.1502-32 is tentatively applied to adjust the basis of S1's stock. For this purpose, adjustments to the basis of S1's stock attributable to S4's realization of excluded COD income and the reduction of attributes in respect of such excluded COD income are not taken into account. There is no adjustment under § 1.1502-32 to the basis of the S1 stock. Therefore, P's basis in the S1 stock for this purpose is $50.

(C) *Tentative computation of stock gain or loss.* Then, P's income, gain, or loss from the sale of S1 stock is computed pursuant to paragraph (c)(2)(iii) of this section using the basis computed in the previous step. Thus, P is treated as recognizing a $50 gain from the sale of the S1 stock.

(D) *Tentative computation of tax imposed.* Pursuant to paragraph (c)(2)(iv) of this section, the tax imposed for the year of disposition is then tentatively computed, taking into account P's $50 gain from the sale of the S1 stock computed pursuant to paragraph (c)(2)(iii) of this section. Although S1's and S4's limited losses cannot be used to offset P's $50 gain from the sale of S1's stock under the rules of this section, $10 of P's loss, $30 of S2's loss, and $10 of S3's loss will offset that gain. Therefore, the group is tentatively treated as having a consolidated net operating loss of $350, $40 of which is attributable to P, $100 of which is attributable to S1, $120 of which is attributable to S2, $40 of which is attributable to S3, and $50 of which is attributable to S4 under the principles of § 1.1502-21(b)(2)(iv).

(E) *Tentative reduction of attributes.* Next, pursuant to paragraph (c)(2)(v) of this section, the rules of sections 108 and 1017 and § 1.1502-28 are tentatively applied to reduce attributes remaining after the tentative computation of the tax imposed. Pursuant to § 1.1502-28(a)(2), the tax attributes attributable to S4 would first be reduced to take into account its $80 of excluded COD income. Accordingly, the consolidated net operating loss for Year 1 would be reduced by $50, the portion of the consolidated net operating loss attributable to S4 under the principles of § 1.1502-21(b)(2)(iv), to $300. Then, pursuant to § 1.1502-28(a)(4), S4's remaining $30 of excluded COD income would reduce the consolidated net operating loss for Year 1 that is attributable to other members. Therefore, the consolidated net operating loss for Year 1 would be reduced by $30. Of that amount, $4 is attributable to P, $10 is attributable to S1, $12 is attributable to S2, and $4 is attributable to S3.

(F) *Actual adjustment of stock basis.* Pursuant to paragraph (c)(2)(vi) of this section, § 1.1502-32 is applied to reflect the amount of S1's and S4's income and gain included, and unlimited deductions and losses that are absorbed, in the tentative computation of tax imposed for the year of the disposition and the excluded COD income tentatively applied to reduce attributes and the attributes reduced in respect of the excluded COD income pursuant to the previous step. Under § 1.1502-32(b), the application of $80 of S4's excluded COD income to reduce attributes, and the reduction of S4's loss in the amount of $50 and S1's loss in the amount of $10 in respect of the excluded COD income results in a positive adjustment of $20 to P's basis in the S1 stock. Accordingly, P's basis in S1 stock is $70.

(G) *Actual computation of stock gain or loss.* Pursuant to paragraph (c)(2)(vii) of this section, P's actual gain or loss on the sale of the S1 stock is computed using the basis computed in the previous step. Accordingly, P recognizes a $30 gain on the disposition of the S1 stock.

(H) *Actual computation of tax imposed.* Pursuant to paragraph (c)(2)(viii) of this section, the tax imposed is computed by taking into account P's $30 gain from the sale of S1 stock. Before the application of § 1.1502-28, therefore, the group has a consolidated net operating loss of $370, $44 of which is attributable to P, $100 of which is attributable to S1, $132 of which is attributable to S2, $44 of which is attributable to S3, and $50 of which is attributable to S4.

(I) *Actual reduction of attributes.* Pursuant to paragraph (c)(2)(ix) of this section, sections 108 and 1017 and § 1.1502-28 are then actually applied to reduce attributes remaining after the actual computation of the tax imposed. Pursuant to § 1.1502-28(a)(2), the tax attributes attributable to S4 must first be reduced to take into account its $80 of excluded COD income. Accordingly, the consolidated net operating loss for Year 1 is reduced by $50, the portion of that consolidated net operating loss attributable to S4 under the principles of § 1.1502-21(b)(2)(iv), to $320. Then, pursuant to § 1.1502-28(a)(4), without regard to the limitation imposed by paragraph (c)(2)(ix)(A) of this section, S4's remaining $30 of excluded COD income would reduce the consolidated net operating loss for Year 1 by $30 ($4.12 of the consolidated net operating loss attributable to P, $9.38 of the consolidated net operating loss attributable to S1, $12.38 of the consolidated net operating loss attributable to S2, and $4.12 of the consolidated net operating loss attributable to S3) to $290. However, the limitation imposed by paragraph (c)(2)(ix)(A) of this section prevents the reduction of the consolidated net operating loss attributable to P, S2, and S3 by more than $4, $12, and $4 respectively. The $.62 of excluded COD income that would have otherwise reduced the consolidated net operating loss attributable to P, S2, and S3 is applied to reduce the consolidated net operating loss attributable to S1. Therefore, S1 carries forward $90 of loss.

*Example 4. Excess loss account taken into account.* (i) *Facts.* P is the common parent of a consolidated group. On Day 1 of Year 2, P acquired all of the stock of S1. As of the beginning of Year 2, S1 had a $30 net operating loss carryover from Year 1, a separate return limitation year. A limitation under §1.1502-21(c) applies to the use of that loss by the P group. For Years 1 and 2, the P group had no consolidated taxable income or loss. On Day 1 of Year 3, S1 acquired all of the stock of S2 for $10. In Year 3, P had ordinary income of $10, S1 had ordinary income of $25, and S2 had an ordinary loss of $50. In addition, in Year 3, S2 realized $20 of excluded COD income from the discharge of non-intercompany indebtedness. After the discharge of this indebtedness, S2 had no liabilities. As of the beginning of Year 4, S2 had Asset A with a fair market value of $10. After the computation of tax imposed for Year 3 and before the application of sections 108 and 1017 and §1.1502-28, Asset A has a basis of $0. S2 had no taxable income (or loss) for Year 1 and Year 2.

(ii) *Analysis.* The steps used to compute the tax imposed on the group, to effect the reduction of attributes, and to compute the limitations on the use and reduction of attributes are as follows:

(A) *Computation of limitation on deductions and losses to offset income or gain, tentative basis adjustments, tentative computation of stock gain or loss.* Because it is not initially apparent that there has been a disposition of stock, paragraph (c)(2)(i) of this section does not limit the use of deductions to offset income or gain, no adjustments to the basis are required pursuant to paragraph (c)(2)(ii) of this section, and no stock gain or loss is computed pursuant to paragraph (c)(2)(iii) of this section or taken into account in the tentative computation of tax imposed pursuant to paragraph (c)(2)(iv) of this section.

(B) *Tentative computation of tax imposed.* Pursuant to paragraph (c)(2)(iv) of this section, the tax imposed for Year 3 is tentatively computed. For Year 3, the P group has a consolidated taxable loss of $15, all of which is attributable to S2 under the principles of §1.1502-21(b)(2)(iv).

(C) *Tentative reduction of attributes.* Next, pursuant to paragraph (c)(2)(v) of this section, the rules of sections 108 and 1017 and §1.1502-28 are tentatively applied to reduce attributes remaining after the tentative computation of tax imposed. Pursuant to §1.1502-28(a)(2), the tax attributes attributable to S2 would first be reduced to take into account its $20 of excluded COD income. Accordingly, the consolidated net operating loss for Year 3 is reduced by $15, the portion of that consolidated net operating loss attributable to S2 under the principles of §1.1502-21(b)(2)(iv), to $0. The remaining $5 of excluded COD income is not applied to reduce attributes as there are no remaining attributes that are subject to reduction.

(D) *Actual adjustment of stock basis.* Pursuant to paragraph (c)(2)(vi) of this section, §1.1502-32 is applied to reflect the amount of S2's income and gain included, and unlimited deductions and losses that are absorbed, in the tentative computation of tax imposed for the year of the disposition and the excluded COD income tentatively applied to reduce attributes and the attributes reduced in respect of the excluded COD income pursuant to the previous step. Under §1.1502-32, the absorption of $35 of S2's loss, the application of $15 in respect of S2's excluded COD income to reduce attributes, and the reduction of $15 in respect of the loss attributable to S2 reduced in respect of the excluded COD income results in a negative adjustment of $35 to the basis of the S2 stock. Therefore, S1 has an excess loss account of $25 in the S2 stock.

(E) *Actual computation of stock gain or loss.* Pursuant to paragraph (c)(2)(vii) of this section, S1's actual gain or loss, if any, on the S2 stock is computed. Because S2 realized $5 of excluded COD income that was not applied to reduce attributes, pursuant to §1.1502-19(b)(1) and (c)(1)(iii)(B), S1 is required to take into account $5 of its excess loss account in the S2 stock.

(F) *Actual computation of tax imposed.* Pursuant to paragraph (c)(2)(viii) of this section, the tax imposed is computed by taking into account the $5 of the excess loss account in the S2 stock required to be taken into account. See §1.1502-28(b)(6) (requiring an excess loss account that is required to be taken into account as a result of the application of §1.1502-19(c)(1)(iii)(B) to be included in the group's tax return for the year that includes the date of the debt discharge). However, pursuant to paragraph (c)(2)(viii) of this section, such amount may not be offset by any of the consolidated net operating loss attributable to S2. It may, however, subject to applicable limitations, be offset by the separate net operating loss of S1 from Year 1.

(G) *Actual reduction of attributes.* Pursuant to paragraph (c)(2)(ix) of this section, sections 108 and 1017 and §1.1502-28 are then actually applied to reduce attributes remaining after the actual computation of the tax imposed. Attributes will be actually reduced in the same way that they were tentatively reduced.

(6) *Additional rules for multiple dispositions.*—[Reserved]

(7) *Effective date.*—This paragraph (c) applies to dispositions of subsidiary stock that occur after March 22, 2005. Taxpayers may apply §1.1502-11(c) of REG-167265-03 (2004-15 IRB 730) (see §601.601(d)(2) of this chapter) in whole, but not in part, to any disposition of subsidiary stock that occurs on or before March 22, 2005, if a member of the group realized excluded COD income after August 29, 2003, in the taxable year that includes the date of the disposition of such subsidiary stock.

(d) *Disallowance of loss attributable to pre-1966 distributions.*—No loss shall be allowed upon the sale or other disposition of stock, bonds, or other obligations of a member or former member to the extent that such loss is attributable to a distribution made in an affiliated year beginning before January 1, 1966, out of earnings and profits accumulated before the distributing corporation became a member. [Reg. §1.1502-11.]

☐ [T.D. 6894, 9-7-66. *Amended by* T.D. 7246, 12-29-72; T.D. 7728, 10-31-80; T.D. 8560, 8-12-94; T.D. 8677, 6-26-96; T.D. 8823, 6-25-99; T.D. 9048, 3-11-2003; T.D. 9187, 3-2-2005 T.D. 9192, 3-21-2005 (*corrected* 4-15-2005); T.D. 9254, 3-9-2006 *and* T.D. 9424, 9-9-2008.]

**[Reg. §1.1502-12]**

**§1.1502-12. Separate taxable income.**—The separate taxable income of a member (including a case in which deductions exceed gross income) is computed in accordance with the provisions of the Code covering the determination of taxable income of separate corporations, subject to the following modifications:

(a) Transactions between members and transactions with respect to stock, bonds, or other obligations of members shall be reflected according to the provisions of §1.1502-13;

(b) Any deduction which is disallowed under §§1.1502-15A or 1.1502-15 shall be taken into account as provided in those sections;

(c) The limitation on deductions provided in section 615(c) or section 617(h) shall be taken into account as provided in §1.1502-16;

(d) The method of accounting under which such computation is made and the adjustments to be made because of any change in method of accounting shall be determined under §1.1502-17;

(e) Inventory adjustments shall be made as provided in §1.1502-18;

(f) Any amount included in income under §1.1502-19 shall be taken into account;

(g) In the computation of the deduction under section 167, property shall not lose its character as new property as a result of a transfer from one member to another member during a consolidated return year if—

(1) The transfer occurs on or before January 4, 1973, or

(2) The transfer occurs after January 4, 1973, and the transfer is an intercompany transaction as defined in §1.1502-13 or the basis of the property in the hands of the transferee is determined (in whole or in part) by reference to its basis in the hands of the transferor;

(h) No net operating loss deduction shall be taken into account;

(i) [Reserved]

(j) No capital gains or losses shall be taken into account;

(k) No gains and losses subject to section 1231 shall be taken into account;

(l) No deduction under section 170 with respect to charitable contributions shall be taken into account;

(m) No deduction under section 922 (relating to the deduction for Western Hemisphere trade corporations) shall be taken into account;

(n) No deductions under section 243(a)(1), 244(a), 245, or 247 (relating to deductions with respect to dividends received and dividends paid) shall be taken into account;

(o) Basis shall be determined under §§1.1502-31 and 1.1502-32, and earnings and profits shall be determined under §1.1502-33; and

(p) The limitation on deductions provided in section 613A shall be taken into account for each member's oil and gas properties as provided in §1.1502-44.

(q) A thrift institution's deduction under section 593(b)(2) (relating to the addition to the reserve for bad debts of a thrift institution under the percentage of taxable income method) shall be determined under §1.1502-42.

(r) See §§1.337(d)-2, 1.1502-35, and 1.1502-36 for rules relating to basis adjustments and allowance of stock loss on dispositions or transfers of subsidiary stock.

(s) See §1.1502-51 for rules relating to the computation of a member's GILTI inclusion amount under section 951A and related basis adjustments.

(t) See §1.1502-50 for rules relating to the computation of a member's deduction under section 250. [Reg. §1.1502-12.]

☐ [T.D. 6894, 9-7-66. *Amended by* T.D. 7192, 6-29-72; T.D. 7246, 12-29-72; T.D. 7725, 9-30-80; T.D. 7876, 3-14-83; T.D. 8294, 3-9-90; T.D. 8319, 11-19-90; T.D. 8364, 9-13-91; T.D. 8597, 7-12-95; T.D. 8677, 6-26-96; T.D. 8823, 6-25-99; T.D. 9048, 3-11-2003 T.D. 9187, 3-2-2005;

*T.D. 9254, 3-9-2006, T.D. 9424, 9-9-2008; T.D. 9866, 6-14-2019 and T.D. 9901, 7-9-2020.]*

[Reg. § 1.1502-13]

**§1.1502-13. Intercompany transactions.**—(a) *In general.*—(1) *Purpose.*—This section provides rules for taking into account items of income, gain, deduction, and loss of members from intercompany transactions. The purpose of this section is to provide rules to clearly reflect the taxable income (and tax liability) of the group as a whole by preventing intercompany transactions from creating, accelerating, avoiding, or deferring consolidated taxable income (or consolidated tax liability).

(2) *Separate entity and single entity treatment.*—Under this section, the selling member (S) and the buying member (B) are treated as separate entities for some purposes but as divisions of a single corporation for other purposes. The *amount* and *location* of S's intercompany items and B's corresponding items are determined on a separate entity basis (separate entity treatment). For example, S determines its gain or loss from a sale of property to B on a separate entity basis, and B has a cost basis in the property. The *timing*, and the *character, source,* and other *attributes* of the intercompany items and corresponding items, although initially determined on a separate entity basis, are redetermined under this section to produce the effect of transactions between divisions of a single corporation (single entity treatment). For example, if S sells land to B at a gain and B sells the land to a nonmember, S does not take its gain into account until B's sale to the nonmember.

(3) *Timing rules as a method of accounting.*—(i) *In general.*—The timing rules of this section are a method of accounting for intercompany transactions, to be applied by each member in addition to the member's other methods of accounting. See § 1.1502-17 and, with regard to consolidated return years beginning on or after November 7, 2001, § 1.446-1(c)(2)(iii). To the extent the timing rules of this section are inconsistent with a member's otherwise applicable methods of accounting, the timing rules of this section control. For example, if S sells property to B in exchange for B's note, the timing rules of this section apply instead of the installment sale rules of section 453. S's or B's application of the timing rules of this section to an intercompany transaction clearly reflects income only if the effect of that transaction as a whole (including, for example, related costs and expenses) on consolidated taxable income is clearly reflected.

(ii) *Automatic consent for joining and departing members.*—(A) *Consent granted.*—Section 446(e) consent is granted under this section to the extent a change in method of accounting is necessary solely by reason of the timing rules of this section—

(1) For each member, with respect to its intercompany transactions, in the first consolidated return year which follows a separate return year and in which the member engages in an intercompany transaction; and

(2) For each former member, with respect to its transactions with members that would otherwise be intercompany transactions if the former member were still a member, in the first separate return year in which the former member engages in such a transaction.

(B) *Cut-off basis.*—Any change in method of accounting described in paragraph (a)(3)(ii)(A) of this section is to be effected on a cut-off basis for transactions entered into on or after the first day of the year for which consent is granted under paragraph (a)(3)(ii)(A) of this section.

(4) *Application of other rules of law.*—See § 1.1502-80(a) regarding the general applicability of other rules of law and a limitation on duplicative adjustments. The rules of this section apply in addition to other applicable law (including nonstatutory authorities). For example, this section applies in addition to sections 267(f) (additional rules for certain losses), 269 (acquisitions to evade or avoid income tax), and 482 (allocations among commonly controlled taxpayers). Thus, an item taken into account under this section can be deferred, disallowed, or eliminated under other applicable law, for example, section 1091 (losses from wash sales).

(5) *References.*—References in other sections to this section include, as appropriate, references to prior law. For effective dates and prior law see paragraph (1) of this section.

(6) *Overview.*—(i) *In general.*—The principal rules of this section that implement single entity treatment are the matching rule and the acceleration rule of paragraphs (c) and (d) of this section. Under the matching rule, S and B are generally treated as divisions of a single corporation for purposes of taking into account their items from intercompany transactions. The acceleration rule provides additional rules for taking the items into account if the effect of treating S and B as divisions cannot be achieved (for example, if S or B becomes a nonmember). Paragraph (b) of this section provides definitions. Paragraph (e) of this section provides simplifying rules for certain transactions. Paragraphs (f) and (g) of this section provide additional rules for stock and obligations of members. Paragraphs (h) and (j) of this section provide anti-avoidance rules and miscellaneous operating rules.

(ii) *Table of examples.*—Set forth below is a table of the examples contained in this section.

(b) *Definitions.*—For purposes of this section—

(1) *Intercompany transactions.*—(i) *In general.*—An intercompany transaction is a transaction between corporations that are members of the same consolidated group immediately after the transaction. S is the member transferring property or providing services, and B is the member receiving the property or services. Intercompany transactions include—

(A) S's sale of property (or other transfer, such as an exchange or contribution) to B, whether or not gain or loss is recognized;

(B) S's performance of services for B, and B's payment or accrual of its expenditure for S's performance;

(C) S's licensing of technology, rental of property, or loan of money to B, and B's payment or accrual of its expenditure; and

(D) S's distribution to B with respect to S stock.

(ii) *Time of transaction.*—If a transaction occurs in part while S and B are members and in part while they are not members, the transaction is treated as occurring when performance by either S or B takes place, or when payment for performance would be taken into account under the rules of this section if it were an intercompany transaction, whichever is earliest. Appropriate adjustments must be made in such cases by, for example, dividing the transaction into two separate transactions reflecting the extent to which S or B has performed.

(iii) *Separate transactions.*—Except as otherwise provided in this section, each transaction is analyzed separately. For example, if S simultaneously sells two properties to B, one at a gain and the other at a loss, each property is treated as sold in a separate transaction. Thus, the gain and loss cannot be offset or netted against each other for purposes of this section. Similarly, each payment or accrual of interest on a loan is a separate transaction. In addition, an accrual of premium is treated as a separate transaction, or as an offset to interest that is not a separate transaction, to the extent required under separate entity treatment. If two members exchange property, each member is S with respect to the property it transfers and B with respect to the property it receives. If two members enter into a notional principal contract, each payment under the contract is a separate transaction and the member making the payment is B with respect to that payment and the member receiving the payment is S. See paragraph (j)(4) of this section for rules aggregating certain transactions.

(2) *Intercompany items.*—(i) *In general.*—S's income, gain, deduction, and loss from an intercompany transaction are its intercompany items. For example, S's gain from the sale of property to B is intercompany gain. An item is an intercompany item whether it is directly or indirectly from an intercompany transaction.

(ii) *Related costs or expenses.*—S's costs or expenses related to an intercompany transaction are included in determining its intercompany items. For example, if S sells inventory to B, S's direct and indirect costs properly includible under section 263A are included in determining its intercompany income. Similarly, related costs or expenses that are not capitalized under S's separate entity method of accounting are included in determining its intercompany items. For example, deductions for employee wages, in addition to other related costs, are included in determining S's intercompany items from performing services for B, and depreciation deductions

are included in determining S's intercompany items from renting property to B.

(iii) *Amounts not yet recognized or incurred.*—S's intercompany items include amounts from an intercompany transaction that are not yet taken into account under its separate entity method of accounting. For example, if S is a cash method taxpayer, S's intercompany income might be taken into account under this section even if the cash is not yet received. Similarly, an amount reflected in basis (or an amount equivalent to basis) under S's separate entity method of accounting that is a substitute for income, gain, deduction or loss from an intercompany transaction is an intercompany item.

(3) *Corresponding items.*—(i) *In general.*—B's income, gain, deduction, and loss from an intercompany transaction, or from property acquired in an intercompany transaction, are its corresponding items. For example, if B pays rent to S, B's deduction for the rent is a corresponding deduction. If B buys property from S and sells it to a nonmember, B's gain or loss from the sale to the nonmember is a corresponding gain or loss; alternatively, if B recovers the cost of the property through depreciation, B's depreciation deductions are corresponding deductions. An item is a corresponding item whether it is directly or indirectly from an intercompany transaction (or from property acquired in an intercompany transaction).

(ii) *Disallowed or eliminated amounts.*—B's corresponding items include amounts that are permanently disallowed or permanently eliminated, whether directly or indirectly. Thus, corresponding items include amounts disallowed under section 265 (expenses relating to tax-exempt income), and amounts not recognized under section 311(a) (nonrecognition of loss on distributions), section 332 (nonrecognition on liquidating distributions), or section 355(c) (certain distributions of stock of a subsidiary). On the other hand, an amount is not permanently disallowed or permanently eliminated (and therefore is not a corresponding item) to the extent it is not recognized in a transaction in which B receives a successor asset within the meaning of paragraph (j)(1) of this section. For example, B's corresponding items do not include amounts not recognized from a transaction with a nonmember to which section 1031 applies or from another transaction in which B receives exchanged basis property.

(4) *Recomputed corresponding items.*—The recomputed corresponding item is the corresponding item that B would take into account if S and B were divisions of a single corporation and the intercompany transaction were between those divisions. For example, if S sells property with a $70 basis to B for $100, and B later sells the property to a nonmember for $90, B's corresponding item is its $10 loss, and the recomputed corresponding item is $20 of gain (determined by comparing the $90 sales price with the $70 basis the property would have if S and B were divisions of a single corporation). Although neither S nor B actually takes the recomputed corresponding item into account, it is computed as if B did take it into account (based on reasonable and consistently applied assumptions, including any provision of the Internal Revenue Code or regulations that would affect its timing or attributes).

(5) *Treatment as a separate entity.*—Treatment as a separate entity means treatment without application of the rules of this section, but with the application of the other consolidated return regulations. For example, if S sells the stock of another member to B, S's gain or loss

on a separate entity basis is determined with the application of § 1.1502-80(b) (non-applicability of section 304), but without redetermination under paragraph (c) or (d) of this section.

(6) *Attributes.*—The attributes of an intercompany item or corresponding item are all of the item's characteristics, except *amount, location,* and *timing,* necessary to determine the item's effect on taxable income (and tax liability). For example, attributes include character, source, treatment as excluded from gross income or as a noncapital, nondeductible amount, and treatment as built-in gain or loss under section 382(h) or 384. In contrast, the characteristics of property, such as a member's holding period, or the fact that property is included in inventory, are not attributes of an item, but these characteristics might affect the determination of the attributes of items from the property.

(c) *Matching rule.*—For each consolidated return year, B's corresponding items and S's intercompany items are taken into account under the following rules:

(1) *Attributes and holding periods.*—(i) *Attributes.*—The separate entity attributes of S's intercompany items and B's corresponding items are redetermined to the extent necessary to produce the same effect on consolidated taxable income (and consolidated tax liability) as if S and B were divisions of a single corporation, and the intercompany transaction were a transaction between divisions. Thus, the activities of both S and B might affect the attributes of both intercompany items and corresponding items. For example, if S holds property for sale to unrelated customers in the ordinary course of its trade or business, S sells the property to B at a gain and B sells the property to an unrelated person at a further gain, S's intercompany gain and B's corresponding gain might be ordinary because of S's activities with respect to the property. Similar principles apply if S performs services, rents property, or engages in any other intercompany transaction.

(ii) *Holding periods.*—The holding period of property transferred in an intercompany transaction is the aggregate of the holding periods of S and B. However, if the basis of the property is determined by reference to the basis of other property, the property's holding period is determined by reference to the holding period of the other property. For example, if S distributes stock to B in a transaction to which section 355 applies, B's holding period in the distributed stock is determined by reference to B's holding period in the stock of S.

(2) *Timing.*—(i) *B's items.*—B takes its corresponding items into account under its accounting method, but the redetermination of the attributes of a corresponding item might affect its timing. For example, if B's sale of property acquired from S is treated as a dealer disposition because of S's activities, section 453(b) prevents any corresponding income of B from being taken into account under the installment method.

(ii) *S's items.*—S takes its intercompany item into account to reflect the difference for the year between B's corresponding item taken into account and the recomputed corresponding item.

(3) *Divisions of a single corporation.*—As divisions of a single corporation, S and B are treated as engaging in their actual transaction and owning any actual property involved in the transaction (rather than treating the transaction as not occurring). For example, S's sale of land held for investment to B for cash is not disregarded, but is treated as an exchange of land for cash between divisions (and B therefore succeeds to S's basis in the property). Similarly, S's issuance of its own stock to B in exchange for property is not disregarded, B is treated as owning the stock it receives in the exchange, and section 1032 does not apply to B on its subsequent sale of the S stock. Although treated as divisions, S and B nevertheless are treated as:

(i) Operating separate trades or businesses. See, e.g., § 1.446-1(d) (accounting methods for a taxpayer engaged in more than one business).

(ii) Having any special status that they have under the Internal Revenue Code or regulations. For example, a bank defined in section 581, a domestic building and loan association defined in section 7701(a)(19), and an insurance company to which section 801 or 831 applies are treated as divisions having separate special status. On the other hand, the fact that a member holds property for sale to customers in the ordinary course of its trade or business is not a special status.

(4) *Conflict or allocation of attributes.*—This paragraph (c)(4) provides special rules for redetermining and allocating attributes under paragraph (c)(1)(i) of this section.

(i) *Offsetting amounts.*—(A) *In general.*—To the extent B's corresponding item offsets S's intercompany item in amount, the attrib-

utes of B's corresponding item, determined based on both S's and B's activities, control the attributes of S's offsetting intercompany item. For example, if S sells depreciable property to B at a gain and B depreciates the property, the attributes of B's depreciation deduction (ordinary deduction) control the attributes of S's offsetting intercompany gain. Accordingly, S's gain is ordinary.

(B) *B controls unreasonable.*—To the extent the results under paragraph (c)(4)(i)(A) are inconsistent with treating S and B as divisions of a single corporation, the attributes of the offsetting items must be redetermined in a manner consistent with treating S and B as divisions of a single corporation. To the extent, however, that B's corresponding item on a separate entity basis is excluded from gross income, is a noncapital, nondeductible amount, or is otherwise permanently disallowed or eliminated, the attributes of B's corresponding item always control the attributes of S's offsetting intercompany item.

(ii) *Allocation.*—To the extent S's intercompany item and B's corresponding item do not offset in amount, the attributes redetermined under paragraph (c)(1)(i) of this section must be allocated to S's intercompany item and B's corresponding item by using a method that is reasonable in light of all the facts and circumstances, including the purposes of this section and any other rule affected by the attributes of S's intercompany item and B's corresponding item. A method of allocation or redetermination is unreasonable if it is not used consistently by all members of the group from year to year.

(5) *Special status.*—Notwithstanding the general rule of paragraph (c)(1)(i) of this section, to the extent an item's attributes determined under this section are permitted or not permitted to a member under the Internal Revenue Code or regulations by reason of the member's special status, the attributes required under the Internal Revenue Code or regulations apply to that member's items (but not the other member). For example, if S is a bank to which section 582(c) applies, and sells debt securities at a gain to B, a nonbank, the character of S's intercompany gain is ordinary as required under section 582(c), but the character of B's corresponding item as capital or ordinary is determined under paragraph (c)(1)(i) of this section without the application of section 582(c). For other special status issues, see, for example, sections 595(b) (foreclosure on property securing loans), 818(b) (life insurance company treatment of capital gains and losses), and 1503(c) (limitation on absorption of certain losses).

(6) *Treatment of intercompany items if corresponding items are excluded or nondeductible.*—(i) *In general.*—Under paragraph (c)(1)(i) of this section, S's intercompany item might be redetermined to be excluded from gross income or treated as a noncapital, nondeductible amount. For example, S's intercompany loss from the sale of property to B is treated as a noncapital, nondeductible amount if B distributes the property to a nonmember shareholder at no further gain or loss (because, if S and B were divisions of a single corporation, the loss would not have been recognized under section 311(a)). Paragraph (c)(6)(ii) of this section, however, provides limitations on the application of this rule to intercompany income or gain. See also § § 1.1502-32 and 1.1502-33 (adjustments to S's stock basis and earnings and profits to reflect amounts so treated).

(ii) *Limitation on treatment of intercompany items as excluded from gross income.*—Notwithstanding the general rule of paragraph (c)(1)(i) of this section, S's intercompany income or gain is redetermined to be excluded from gross income only to the extent one of the following applies:

(A) *Disallowed amounts.*—B's corresponding item is a deduction or loss and, in the taxable year the item is taken into account under this section, it is permanently and explicitly disallowed under another provision of the Internal Revenue Code or regulations. For example, deductions that are disallowed under section 265 are permanently and explicitly disallowed. An amount is not permanently and explicitly disallowed, for example, to the extent that—

(1) The Internal Revenue Code or regulations provide that the amount is not recognized (for example, a loss that is realized but not recognized under section 332 or section 355(c) is not permanently and explicitly disallowed, notwithstanding that it is a corresponding item within the meaning of paragraph (b)(3)(ii) of this section (certain disallowed or eliminated amounts));

(2) A related amount might be taken into account by B with respect to successor property, such as under section 280B (demolition costs recoverable as capitalized amounts);

(3) A related amount might be taken into account by another taxpayer, such as under section 267(d) (disallowed loss under section 267(a) might result in nonrecognition of gain for a related person);

(4) A related amount might be taken into account as a deduction or loss, including as a carryforward to a later year, under

any provision of the Internal Revenue Code or regulations (whether or not the carryforward expires in a later year); or

(5) The amount is reflected in the computation of any credit against (or other reduction of) Federal income tax (whether allowed for the taxable year or carried forward to a later year).

(B) *Section 311.*—The corresponding item is a loss that is realized, but not recognized under section 311(a) on a distribution to a nonmember (even though the loss is not a permanently and explicitly disallowed amount within the meaning of paragraph (c)(6)(ii)(A) of this section).

(C) *Certain intercompany gains on stock.*—(1) *In general.*—Notwithstanding paragraph (c)(6)(ii)(A)(1) of this section, intercompany gain with respect to a member's stock that was created by reason of an intercompany transfer of the stock, and that would not otherwise be taken into account upon a subsequent elimination of the stock's basis but for the transfer, is redetermined to be excluded from gross income if—

(i) B or S becomes a successor (as defined in paragraph (j)(2) of this section) to the other party (either B or S), or a third member becomes a successor to both B and S;

(ii) Immediately before the intercompany gain would be taken into account, the successor member holds the member's stock with respect to which the intercompany gain was realized;

(iii) The successor member's basis in the member's stock that reflects the intercompany gain that is taken into account is eliminated without the recognition of gain or loss (and such eliminated basis is not further reflected in the basis of any successor asset);

(iv) The effects of the intercompany transaction have not previously been reflected, directly or indirectly, on the group's consolidated return; and

(v) The group has not derived, and no taxpayer will derive, any Federal income tax benefit from the intercompany transaction that gave rise to the intercompany gain or the redetermination of the intercompany gain (including any adjustment to basis in member stock under §1.1502-32). For this purpose, the redetermination of the intercompany gain is not itself considered a Federal income tax benefit.

(2) *Effect on earnings and profits and investment adjustments.*—Any amount excluded from gross income under paragraph (c)(6)(ii)(C)(1) of this section shall not be taken into account as earnings and profits of any member and shall not be treated as tax-exempt income under §1.1502-32(b)(2)(ii).

(D) *Other amounts.*—(1) The Commissioner may determine that treating S's intercompany item as excluded from gross income is consistent with the purposes of this section and other applicable provisions of the Internal Revenue Code, regulations, and published guidance, if the following conditions are met, depending on whether the intercompany item is an item of income or an item of gain:

(i) In the case of an intercompany item of income, the corresponding item is permanently disallowed; or

(ii) If the intercompany item constitutes gain, the conditions described in paragraphs (c)(6)(ii)(C)(1)(iv) and (c)(6)(ii)(C)(1)(v) of this section are satisfied.

(2) A determination by the Commissioner may be obtained only through a letter ruling request.

(7) *Examples.*—(i) *In general.*—For purposes of the examples in this section, unless otherwise stated, P is the common parent of the P consolidated group, P owns all of the only class of stock of subsidiaries S and B, X is a person unrelated to any member of the P group, the taxable year of all persons is the calendar year, all persons use the accrual method of accounting, tax liabilities are disregarded, the facts set forth the only corporate activity, no member has any special status, and the transaction is not otherwise subject to recharacterization. If a member acts as both a selling member and a buying member (e.g., with respect to different aspects of a single transaction, or with respect to related transactions), the member is referred to as M, M1, or M2 (rather than as S or B).

(ii) *Matching rule.*—The matching rule of this paragraph (c) is illustrated by the following examples.

(A) *Example 1. Intercompany sale of land followed by sale to a nonmember.* (1) *Facts.* S holds land for investment with a basis of $70. S has held the land for more than one year. On January 1 of Year 1, S sells the land to B for $100. B also holds the land for investment. On July 1 of Year 3, B sells the land to X for $110.

(2) *Definitions.* Under paragraph (b)(1) of this section, S's sale of the land to B is an intercompany transaction, S is the selling member, and B is the buying member. Under paragraphs (b)(2) and (3) of this section, S's $30 gain from the sale to B is its intercompany item, and B's $10 gain from the sale to X is its corresponding item.

(3) *Attributes.* Under the matching rule of paragraph (c) of this section, S's $30 intercompany gain and B's $10 corresponding gain are taken into account to produce the same effect on consolidated taxable income (and consolidated tax liability) as if S and B were divisions of a single corporation. In addition, the holding periods of S and B for the land are aggregated. Thus, the group's entire $40 of gain is long-term capital gain. Because both S's intercompany item and B's corresponding item on a separate entity basis are long-term capital gain, the attributes are not redetermined under paragraph (c)(1)(i) of this section.

(4) *Timing.* For each consolidated return year, S takes its intercompany item into account under the matching rule to reflect the difference for the year between B's corresponding item taken into account and the recomputed corresponding item. If S and B were divisions of a single corporation and the intercompany sale were a transfer between the divisions, B would succeed to S's $70 basis in the land and would have a $40 gain from the sale to X in Year 3, instead of a $10 gain. Consequently, S takes no gain into account in Years 1 and 2, and takes the entire $30 gain into account in Year 3, to reflect the $30 difference in that year between the $10 gain B takes into account and the $40 recomputed gain (the recomputed corresponding item). Under §§1.1502-32 and 1.1502-33, P's basis in its S stock and the earnings and profits of S and P do not reflect S's $30 gain until the gain is taken into account in Year 3. (Under paragraph (a)(3) of this section, the results would be the same if S sold the land to B in an installment sale to which section 453 would otherwise apply, because S must take its intercompany gain into account under this section.)

(5) *Intercompany loss followed by sale to a nonmember at a gain.* The facts are the same as in *Example 1* in paragraph (c)(7)(ii)(A)(1) of this section, except that S's basis in the land is $130 (rather than $70). The attributes and timing of S's intercompany loss and B's corresponding gain are determined under the matching rule in the manner provided in *Example 1* in paragraphs (c)(7)(ii)(A)(3) and (4) of this section. If S and B were divisions of a single corporation and the intercompany sale were a transfer between the divisions, B would succeed to S's $130 basis in the land and would have a $20 loss from the sale to X instead of a $10 gain. Thus, S takes its entire $30 loss into account in Year 3 to reflect the $30 difference between B's $10 gain taken into account and the $20 recomputed loss. (The results are the same under section 267(f).) S's $30 loss is long-term capital loss, and B's $10 gain is long-term capital gain.

(6) *Intercompany gain followed by sale to a nonmember at a loss.* The facts are the same as in *Example 1* in paragraph (c)(7)(ii)(A)(1) of this section except that B sells the land to X for $90 (rather than $110). The attributes and timing of S's intercompany gain and B's corresponding loss are determined under the matching rule. If S and B were divisions of a single corporation and the intercompany sale were a transfer between the divisions, B would succeed to S's $70 basis in the land and would have a $20 gain from the sale to X instead of a $10 loss. Thus, S takes its entire $30 gain into account in Year 3 to reflect the $30 difference between B's $10 loss taken into account and the $20 recomputed gain. S's $30 gain is long-term capital gain, and B's $10 loss is long-term capital loss.

(7) *Intercompany gain followed by distribution to a nonmember at a loss.* The facts are the same as in *Example 1* in paragraph (c)(7)(ii)(A)(1) of this section except that B distributes the land to X, a minority shareholder of B, and at the time of the distribution the land has a fair market value of $90. The attributes and timing of S's intercompany gain and B's corresponding loss are determined under the matching rule. Under section 311(a), B does not recognize its $10 loss on the distribution to X. If S and B were divisions of a single corporation and the intercompany sale were a transfer between divisions, B would succeed to S's $70 basis in the land and would have a $20 gain from the distribution to X instead of an unrecognized $10 loss. Under paragraph (b)(3)(ii) of this section, B's loss that is not recognized under section 311(a) is a corresponding item. Thus, S takes its $30 gain into account under the matching rule in Year 3 to reflect the difference between B's $10 corresponding unrecognized loss and the $20 recomputed gain. B's $10 corresponding loss offsets $10 of S's intercompany gain and, under paragraph (c)(4)(i) of this section, the attributes of B's corresponding item control the attributes of S's intercompany item. Paragraph (c)(6) of this section does not prevent the redetermination of S's intercompany item as excluded from gross income. (See paragraph (c)(6)(ii)(B) of this section.) Thus, $10 of S's $30 gain is redetermined to be excluded from gross income.

(8) *Intercompany sale followed by section 1031 exchange with nonmember.* The facts are the same as in *Example 1* in paragraph (c)(7)(ii)(A)(1) of this section, except, that instead of selling the land to X, B exchanges the land for land owned by X in a transaction to which section 1031 applies. There is no difference in Year 3 between B's $0 corresponding item taken into account and the $0 recomputed corresponding item. Thus, none of S's intercompany gain is taken into account under the matching rule as a result of the section 1031 exchange. Instead, B's gain is preserved in the land received from X

and, under the successor asset rule of paragraph (j)(1) of this section, S's intercompany gain is taken into account by reference to the replacement property. (If B takes gain into account as a result of boot received in the exchange, S's intercompany gain is taken into account under the matching rule to the extent the boot causes a difference between B's gain taken into account and the recomputed gain.)

(9) *Intercompany sale followed by section 351 transfer to nonmember.* The facts are the same as in *Example 1* in paragraph (c)(7)(ii)(A)(1) of this section, except that, instead of selling the land to X, B transfers the land to X in a transaction to which section 351(a) applies and X remains a nonmember. There is no difference in Year 3 between B's $0 corresponding item taken into account and the $0 recomputed corresponding item. Thus, none of S's intercompany gain is taken into account under the matching rule as a result of the section 351(a) transfer. However, S's entire gain is taken into account in Year 3 under the acceleration rule of paragraph (d) of this section (because X, a nonmember, reflects B's $100 cost basis in the land under section 362).

(B) *Example 2. Dealer activities.* (1) *Facts.* S holds land for investment with a basis of $70. On January 1 of Year 1, S sells the land to B for $100. B develops the land as residential real estate, and sells developed lots to customers during Year 3 for an aggregate amount of $110.

(2) *Attributes.* S and B are treated under the matching rule as divisions of a single corporation for purposes of determining the attributes of S's intercompany item and B's corresponding item. Thus, although S held the land for investment, whether the gain is treated as from the sale of property described in section 1221(1) is based on the activities of both S and B. If, based on both's S's and B's activities, the land is described in section 1221(1), both S's gain and B's gain are ordinary income.

(C) *Example 3. Intercompany section 351 transfer.* (1) *Facts.* S holds land with a $70 basis and a $100 fair market value for sale to customers in the ordinary course of business. On January 1 of Year 1, S transfers the land to B in exchange for all of the stock of B in a transaction to which section 351(a) applies. S has no gain or loss under section 351(a), and its basis in the B stock is $70 under section 358. Under section 362, B's basis in the land is $70. B holds the land for investment. On July 1 of Year 3, B sells the land to X for $100. Assume that if S and B were divisions of a single corporation, B's gain from the sale would be ordinary income because of S's activities.

(2) *Timing and attributes.* Under paragraph (b)(1) of this section, S's transfer to B is an intercompany transaction. Under paragraph (c)(3) of this section, S is treated as transferring the land in exchange for B's stock even though, as divisions, S could not own stock of B. S has no intercompany item, but B's $30 gain from its sale of the land to X is a corresponding item because the land was acquired in an intercompany transaction. B's $30 gain is ordinary income that is taken into account under B's method of accounting.

(3) *Intercompany section 351 transfer with boot* The facts are the same as in *Example 3* in paragraph (c)(7)(ii)(C)(1) of this section, except, that S receives $10 cash in addition to the B stock in the transfer. S recognizes $10 of gain under section 351(b), and its basis in the B stock is $70 under section 358. Under section 362, B's basis in the land is $80. S takes its $10 intercompany gain into account in Year 3 to reflect the $10 difference between B's $20 corresponding gain taken into account and the $30 recomputed gain. Both S's $10 gain and B's $20 gain are ordinary income.

(4) *Partial disposition.* The facts are the same as in *Example 3* in paragraph (c)(7)(ii)(C)(3) of this section, except B sells a only a one-half, undivided interest in the land to X for $50. The timing and attributes are determined in the manner provided in *Example 3* in paragraph (c)(7)(ii)(C)(2) of this section, except that S takes only $5 of its gain into account in Year 3 to reflect the $5 difference between B's $10 gain taken into account and the $15 recomputed gain.

(D) *Example 4. Depreciable property.* (1) *Facts.* On January 1 of Year 1, S buys 10-year recovery property for $100 and depreciates it under the straight-line method. On January 1 of Year 3, S sells the property to B for $130. Under section 168(i)(7), B is treated as S for purposes of section 168 to the extent B's $130 basis does not exceed S's adjusted basis at the time of the sale. B's additional basis is treated as new 10-year recovery property for which B elects the straight-line method of recovery. (To simplify the example, the half-year convention is disregarded.)

(2) *Depreciation through Year 3; intercompany gain.* S claims $10 of depreciation for each of Years 1 and 2 and has an $80 basis at the time of the sale to B. Thus, S has a $50 intercompany gain from its sale to B. For Year 3, B has $10 of depreciation with respect to $80 of its basis (the portion of its $130 basis not exceeding S's adjusted basis). In addition, B has $5 of depreciation with respect to the $50 of its additional basis that exceeds S's adjusted basis.

(3) *Timing.* S's $50 gain is taken into account to reflect the difference for each consolidated return year between B's depreciation taken into account with respect to the property and the recomputed

depreciation. For Year 3, B takes $15 of depreciation into account. If the intercompany transaction were a transfer between divisions of a single corporation, B would succeed to S's adjusted basis in the property and take into account only $10 of depreciation for Year 3. Thus, S takes $5 of gain into account in Year 3. In each subsequent year that B takes into account $15 of depreciation with respect to the property, S takes into account $5 of gain.

(4) *Attributes.* Under paragraph (c)(1)(i) of this section, the attributes of S's gain and B's depreciation must be redetermined to the extent necessary to produce the same effect on consolidated taxable income as if the intercompany transaction were between divisions of a single corporation (the group must have a net depreciation deduction of $10). In each year, $5 of B's corresponding depreciation deduction offsets S's $5 intercompany gain taken into account and, under paragraph (c)(4)(i) of this section, the attributes of B's corresponding item control the attributes of S's intercompany item. Accordingly, S's intercompany gain that is taken into account as a result of B's depreciation deduction is ordinary income.

(5) *Sale of property to a nonmember.* The facts are the same as in *Example 4* in paragraph (c)(7)(ii)(D)(1) of this section, except that B sells the property to X on January 1 of Year 5 for $110. As set forth in *Example 4* in paragraphs (c)(7)(ii)(D)(3) and (4) of this section, B has $15 of depreciation with respect to the property in each of Years 3 and 4, causing S to take $5 of intercompany gain into account in each year as ordinary income. The $40 balance of S's intercompany gain is taken into account in Year 5 as a result of B's sale to X, to reflect the $40 difference between B's $50 gain taken into account and the $50 of recomputed gain ($110 of sale proceeds minus the $60 basis B would have if the intercompany sale were a transfer between divisions of a single corporation). Treating S and B as divisions of a single corporation, $40 of the gain is section 1245 gain and $10 is section 1231 gain. On a separate entity basis, S would have more than $10 treated as section 1231 gain, and B would have no amount treated as section 1231 gain. Under paragraph (c)(4)(ii) of this section, all $10 of the section 1231 gain is allocated to S. S's remaining $30 of gain, and all of B's $10 gain, is treated as section 1245 gain.

(E) *Example 5. Intercompany sale followed by installment sale.* (1) *Facts.* S holds land for investment with a basis of $70x. On January 1 of Year 1, S sells the land to B for $100x. B also holds the land for investment. On July 1 of Year 3, B sells the land to X in exchange for X's $110x note. The note bears a market rate of interest in excess of the applicable Federal rate, and provides for principal payments of $55x in Year 4 and $55x in Year 5. The interest charge under section 453A(c) applies to X's note.

(2) *Timing and attributes.* S takes its $30x gain into account to reflect the difference in each consolidated return year between B's gain taken into account for the year and the recomputed gain. Under section 453, B takes into account $5x of gain in Year 4 and $5x of gain in Year 5. Thus, S takes into account $15x of gain in Year 4 and $15x of gain in Year 5 to reflect the $15x difference in each of those years between B's $5x gain taken into account and the $20x recomputed gain. Both S's $30x gain and B's $10x gain are subject to the section 453A(c) interest charge beginning in Year 3.

(3) *Election out under section 453(d).* If, under the facts in *Example 5* in paragraph (c)(7)(ii)(E)(1) of this section, the P group wishes to elect not to apply section 453 with respect to S's gain, an election under section 453(d) must be made for Year 3 with respect to B's gain. This election will cause B's $10x gain to be taken into account in Year 3. Under the matching rule, this will result in S's $30x gain being taken into account in Year 3. (An election by the P group solely with respect to S's gain has no effect because the gain from S's sale to B is taken into account under the matching rule, and therefore must reflect the difference between B's gain taken into account and the recomputed gain.)

(4) *Sale to a nonmember at a loss, but overall gain.* The facts are the same as in *Example 5* in paragraph (c)(7)(ii)(E)(1) of this section, except that B sells the land to X in exchange for X's $90x note (rather than $110x note). If S and B were divisions of a single corporation, B would succeed to S's basis in the land, and the sale to X would be eligible for installment reporting under section 453, because it resulted in an overall gain. However, because only gains may be reported on the installment method, B's $10x corresponding loss is taken into account in, Year 3. Under paragraph (b)(4) of this section the recomputed corresponding item is $20x gain that would be taken into account under the installment method, $0 in Year 3 and $10x in each of Years 4 and 5. Thus, in Year 3 S takes $10x of gain into account to reflect the difference between B's $10x loss taken into account and the $0 recomputed gain for Year 3. Under paragraph (c)(4)(i) of this section, B's $10x corresponding loss offsets $10x of S's intercompany gain, and B's attributes control. S takes $10x of gain into into account in each of Years 4 and 5 to reflect the difference in those years between B's $0 gain taken into account and the $10x recomputed gain that would be taken into account under the installment method. only the $20x of S's gain taken into account in Years 4 and 5 is subject to the interest charge under section 453A(c) begin-

ning in Year 3. (If P elects under section 453(d) for Year 3 not to apply section 453 with respect to the gain, all of S's $30x gain will be taken into account in Year 3 to reflect the difference between B's $10x loss taken into account and the $20x recomputed gain.)

(5) *Intercompany loss, installment gain.* The facts are the same as in *Example 5* in paragraph (c)(7)(ii)(E)(*1*) of this section, except that S has a $130x (rather than $70x) basis in the land. Under paragraph (c)(1)(i) of this section, the separate entity attributes of S's and B's items from the intercompany transaction must be redetermined to produce the same effect on consolidated taxable income (and tax liability) as if the transaction had been a transfer between divisions. If S and B were divisions of a single corporation, B would succeed to S's basis in the land and the group would have $20x loss from the sale to X, installment reporting would be unavailable, and the interest charge under section 453A(c) would not apply. Accordingly, B's gain from the transaction is not eligible for installment treatment under section 453. B takes its $10x gain into account in Year 3, and S takes its $30x of loss into account in Year 3 to reflect the difference between B's $10x gain and the $20x recomputed loss.

(6) *Recapture income.* The facts are the same as in *Example 5* in paragraph (c)(7)(ii)(E)(*1*) of this section, except that S bought depreciable property (rather than land) for $100x, claimed depreciation deductions, and reduced the property's basis to $70x before Year 1. (To simplify the example, B's depreciation is disregarded.) If the intercompany sale of property had been a transfer between divisions of a single corporation, $30x of the $40x gain from the sale to X would be section 1245 gain (which is ineligible for installment reporting) and $10x would be section 1231 gain (which is eligible for installment reporting). On a separate entity basis, S would have $30x of section 1245 gain and B would have $10x of section 1231 gain. Accordingly, the attributes are not redetermined under paragraph (c)(1)(i) of this section. All of B's $10x gain is eligible for installment reporting and is taken into account $5x each in Years 4 and 5 (and is subject to the interest charge under section 453A(c)). S's $30x gain is taken into account in Year 3 to reflect the difference between B's $0 gain taken into account and the $30x of recomputed gain. (If S had bought the depreciable property for $110x and its recomputed basis under section 1245 had been $110x (rather than $100x), B's $10x gain and S's $30x gain would both be recapture income ineligible for installment reporting.)

(F) *Example 6. Intercompany sale of installment obligation.* (1) *Facts.* S holds land for investment with a basis of $70x. On January 1 of Year 1, S sells the land to X in exchange for X's $100x note, and S reports its gain on the installment method under section 453. X's note bears interest at a market rate of interest in excess of the applicable Federal rate, and provides for principal payments of $50x in Year 5 and $50x in Year 6. Section 453A applies to X's note. On July 1 of Year 3, S sells X's note to B for $100x, resulting in $30x gain from S's prior sale of the land to X under section 453B(a).

(2) *Timing and attributes.* S's sale of X's note to B is an intercompany transaction, and S's $30x gain is intercompany gain. S takes $15x of the gain into account in each of Years 5 and 6 to reflect the $15x difference in each year between B's $0 gain taken into account and the $15x recomputed gain. S's gain continues to be treated as its gain from the sale to X, and the deferred tax liability remains subject to the interest charge under section 453A(c).

(3) *Worthlessness.* The facts are the same as in *Example 6* in paragraph (c)(7)(ii)(F)(*1*) of this section, except that X's note becomes worthless on December 1 of Year 3 and B has a $100x short-term capital loss under section 165(g) on a separate entity basis. Under paragraph (c)(1)(i) of this section, B's holding period for X's note is aggregated with S's holding period. Thus, B's loss is a long-term capital loss. S takes its $30x gain into account in Year 3 to reflect the $30x difference between B's $100x loss taken into account and the $70x recomputed loss. Under paragraph (c)(1)(i) of this section, S's gain is long-term capital gain.

(4) *Pledge.* The facts are the same as in *Example 6* in paragraph (c)(7)(ii)(F)(*1*) of this section, except, that, on December 1 of Year 3, B borrows $100x from an unrelated bank and secures the indebtedness with X's note. X's note remains subject to section 453A(d) following the sale to B. Under section 453A(d), B's $100x of proceeds from the secured indebtedness is treated as an amount received on December 1 of Year 3 by B on X's note. Thus, S takes its entire $30x gain into account in Year 3.

(G) *Example 7. Performance of services.* (1) *Facts.* S is a driller of water wells. B operates a ranch in a remote location, and B's taxable income from the ranch is not subject to section 447. B's ranch requires water to maintain its cattle. During Year 1, S drills an artesian well on B's ranch in exchange for $100 from B, and S incurs $80 of expenses (e.g., for employees and equipment). B capitalizes its $100 cost for the well under section 263, and takes into account $10 of cost recovery deductions in each of Years 2 through 11. Under its separate entity method of accounting, S would take its income and expenses into

account in Year 1. If S and B were divisions of a single corporation, the costs incurred in drilling the well would be capitalized.

(2) *Definitions.* Under paragraph (b)(1) of this section, the service transaction is an intercompany transaction, S is the selling member, and B is the buying member. Under paragraph (b)(2)(ii) of this section, S's $100 of income and $80 of related expenses are both included in determining its intercompany income of $20.

(3) *Timing and attributes.* S's $20 of intercompany income is taken into account under the matching rule to reflect the $20 difference between B's corresponding items taken into account (based on its $100 cost basis in the well) and the recomputed corresponding items (based on the $80 basis that B would have if S and B were divisions of a single corporation and B's basis were determined by reference to S's $80 of expenses). In Year 1, S takes into account $80 of its income and the $80 of expenses. In each of Years 2 through 11, S takes $2 of its $20 intercompany income into account to reflect the annual $2 difference between B's $10 of cost recovery deductions taken into account and the $8 of recomputed cost recovery deductions. S's $100 income and $80 expenses, and B's cost recovery deductions, are ordinary items (because S's and B's items would be ordinary on a separate entity basis, the attributes are not redetermined under paragraph (c)(1)(i) of this section). If S's offsetting $80 of income and expense would not be taken into account in the same year under its separate entity method of accounting, they nevertheless must be taken into account under this section in a manner that clearly reflects consolidated taxable income. See paragraph (a)(3)(i) of this section.

(4) *Sale of capitalized services.* The facts are the same as in *Example 7* in paragraph (c)(7)(ii)(G)(*1*) of this section, except that B sells the ranch before Year 11 and recognizes gain attributable to the well. To the extent of S's income taken into account as a result of B's cost recovery deductions, as well as S's offsetting $80 of income and expense, the timing and attributes are determined in the manner provided in *Example 7* in paragraph (c)(7)(ii)(G)(3) of this section. The attributes of the remainder of S's $20 of income and B's gain from the sale are redetermined to produce the same effect on consolidated taxable income as if S and B were divisions of a single corporation. Accordingly, S's remaining intercompany income is treated as recapture income or section 1231 gain, even though it is from S's performance of services.

(H) *Example 8. Rental of property.* B operates a ranch that requires grazing land for its cattle. S owns undeveloped land adjoining B's ranch. On January 1 of Year 1, S leases grazing rights to B for Year 1. B's $100 rent expense is deductible for Year 1 under its separate entity accounting method. Under paragraph (b)(1) of this section, the rental transaction is an intercompany transaction, S is the selling member, and B is the buying member. S takes its $100 of income into account in Year 1 to reflect the $100 difference between B's rental deduction taken into account and the $0 recomputed rental deduction. S's income and B's deduction are ordinary items (because S's intercompany item and B's corresponding item would both be ordinary on a separate entity basis, the attributes are not redetermined under paragraph (c)(1)(i) of this section).

(I) *Example 9. Intercompany sale of a partnership interest.* (1) *Facts.* S owns a 20% interest in the capital and profits of a general partnership. The partnership holds land for investment with a basis equal to its value, and operates depreciable assets which have value in excess of basis. S's basis in its partnership interest equals its share of the adjusted basis of the partnership's land and depreciable assets. The partnership has an election under section 754 in effect. On January 1 of Year 1, S sells its partnership interest to B at a gain. During Years 1 through 10, the partnership depreciates the operating assets, and B's depreciation deductions from the partnership reflect the increase in the basis of the depreciable assets under section 743(b).

(2) *Timing and attributes.* S's gain is taken into account during Years 1 though 10 to reflect the difference in each year between B's depreciation deductions from the partnership taken into account and the recomputed depreciation deductions from the partnership. Under paragraphs (c)(1)(i) and (c)(4)(i) of this section, S's gain taken into account is ordinary income. (The acceleration rule does not apply to S's gain as a result of the section 743(b) adjustment, because the adjustment is solely with respect to B and therefore no nonmember reflects any part of the intercompany transaction.)

(3) *Partnership sale of assets.* The facts are the same as in *Example 9* in paragraph (c)(7)(ii)(I)(*1*) of this section, and the partnership sells some of its depreciable assets to X at a gain on December 31 of Year 4. In addition to the intercompany gain taken into account as a result of the partnership's depreciation, S takes intercompany gain into account in Year 4 to reflect the difference between B's partnership items taken into account from the sale (which reflect the basis increase under section 743(b)) and the recomputed partnership items. The attributes of S's additional gain are redetermined to produce the same effect on consolidated taxable income as if S and B were

divisions of a single corporation (recapture income or section 1231 gain).

(4) *B's sale of partnership interest.* The facts are the same as in *Example 9* in paragraph (c)(7)(ii)(I)(1) of this section, and on December 31 of Year 4, B sells its partnership interest to X at no gain or loss. In addition to the intercompany gain taken into account as a result of the partnership's depreciation, the remaining balance of S's intercompany gain is taken into account in Year 4 to reflect the difference between B's $0 gain taken into account from the sale of the partnership interest and the recomputed gain The character of S's remaining intercompany item and B's corresponding item are determined on a separate entity basis under section 751, and then redetermined to the extent necessary to produce the same effect as treating the intercompany transaction as occurring between divisions of a single corporation.

(5) *No section 754 election.* The facts are the same as in *Example 9* in paragraph (c)(7)(ii)(I)(4) of this section, except that the partnership does not have a section 754 election in effect, and B recognizes a capital loss from its sale of the partnership interest to X on December 31 of Year 4. Because there is no difference between B's depreciation deductions from the partnership taken into account and the recomputed depreciation deductions, S does not take any of its gain into account during Years 1 through 4 as a result of B's partnership's items. Instead, S's entire intercompany gain is taken into account in Year 4 to reflect the difference between B's loss taken into account from the sale to X and the recomputed gain or loss.

(J) *Example 10. Net operating losses subject to section 382 or the SRLY rules.* (1) *Facts.* On January 1 of Year 1, P buys all of S's stock. S has net operating loss carryovers from prior years. P's acquisition results in an ownership change under section 382 with respect to S's loss carryovers, and S has a net unrealized built-in gain (within the meaning of section 382(h)(3)). S owns nondepreciable property with a $70 basis and $100 value. On July 1 of Year 3, S sells the property to B for $100, and its $30 gain is recognized built-in gain (within the meaning of section 382(h)(2)) on a separate entity basis. On December 1 of Year 5, B sells the property to X for $90.

(2) *Timing and attributes.* S's $30 gain is taken into account in Year 5 to reflect the $30 difference between B's $10 loss taken into account and the recomputed $20 gain. S and B are treated as divisions of a single corporation for purposes of applying section 382 in connection with the intercompany transaction. Under a single entity analysis, the single corporation has losses subject to limitation under section 382, and this limitation may be increased under section 382(h) if the single corporation has recognized built-in gain with respect to those losses. B's $10 corresponding loss offsets $10 of S's intercompany gain, and thus, under paragraph (c)(4)(i) of this section, $10 of S's intercompany gain is redetermined not to be recognized built-in gain. S's remaining $20 intercompany gain continues to be treated as recognized built-in gain.

(3) *B's recognized built-in gain.* The facts are the same as in *Example 10* in paragraph (c)(7)(ii)(J)(1) of this section, except that the property declines in value after S becomes a member of the P group, S sells the property to B for its $70 basis, and B sells the property to X for $90 during Year 5. Treating S and B as divisions of a single corporation, S's sale to B does not cause the property to cease to be built-in gain property. Thus, B's $20 gain from its sale to X is recognized built-in gain that increases the section 382 limitation applicable to S's losses.

(4) *SRLY limitation.* The facts are the same as in *Example 10* in paragraph (c)(7)(ii)(J)(1) of this section, except that P's acquisition of S is not subject to the overlap rule of §1.1502-21(g), and S's net operating loss carryovers are subject to the separate return limitation year (SRLY) rules. See §1.1502-21(c). The application of the SRLY rules depends on S's status as a separate corporation having losses from separate return limitation years. Under paragraph (c)(5), the attribute of S's intercompany item as it relates to S's SRLY limitation is not redetermined, because the SRLY limitation depends on S's special status. Accordingly, S's $30 intercompany gain is included in determining its SRLY limitation for Year 5.

(K) *Example 11. Section 475.* (1) *Facts.* S, a dealer in securities within the meaning of section 475(c), owns a security with a basis of $70. The security is held for sale to customers and is not identified under section 475(b) as within an exception to marking to market. On July 1 of Year 1, S sells the security to B for $100. B is not a dealer and holds the security for investment. On December 31 of Year 1, the fair market value of the security is $100. On July 1 of Year 2, B sells the security to X for $110.

(2) *Attributes.* Under section 475, a dealer in securities can treat a security as within an exception to marking to market under section 475(b) only if it timely identifies the security as so described. Under the matching rule, attributes must be redetermined by treating S and B as divisions of a single corporation. As a result of S's activities, the single corporation is treated as a dealer with respect to securities, and B must continue to mark to market the security acquired from S.

Thus, B's corresponding items and the recomputed corresponding items are determined by continuing to treat the security as not within an exception to marking to market. Under section 475(d)(3), it is possible for the character of S's intercompany items to differ from the character of B's corresponding items.

(3) *Timing and character.* S has a $30 gain when it disposes of the security by selling it to B. This gain is intercompany gain that is taken into account in Year 1 to reflect the $30 difference between B's $0 gain taken into account from marking the security to market under section 475 and the recomputed $30 gain that would be taken into account. The character of S's gain and B's gain are redetermined as if the security were transferred between divisions. Accordingly, S's gain is ordinary income under section 475(d)(3)(A)(i), but under section 475(d)(3)(B)(ii) B's $10 gain from its sale to X is capital gain that is taken into account in Year 2.

(4) *Nondealer to dealer.* The facts are the same as in *Example 11* in paragraph (c)(7)(ii)(K)(1) of this section, except that S is not a dealer and holds the security for investment with a $70 basis, B is a dealer to which section 475 applies and, immediately after acquiring the security from S for $100, B holds the security for sale to customers in the ordinary course of its trade or business. Because S is not a dealer and held the security for investment, the security is treated as properly identified as held for investment under section 475(b)(1) until it is sold to B. Under section 475(b)(3), the security thereafter ceases to be described in section 475(b)(1) because B holds the security for sale to customers. The mark-to-market requirement applies only to changes in the value of the security after B's acquisition. B's mark-to-market gain taken into account and the recomputed mark-to-market gain are both determined based on changes from the $100 value of the security at the time of B's acquisition. There is no difference between B's $0 mark-to-market gain taken into account in Year 1 and the $0 recomputed mark-to-market gain. Therefore, none of S's gain is taken into account in Year 1 as a result of B's marking the security to market in Year 1. In Year 2, B has a $10 gain when it disposes of the security by selling it to X, but would have had a $40 gain if S and B were divisions of a single corporation. Thus, S takes its $30 gain into account in Year 2 under the matching rule. Under section 475(d)(3), S's gain is capital gain even though B's subsequent gain or loss from marking to market or disposing of the security is ordinary gain or loss. If B disposes of the security at a $10 loss in Year 2, S's gain taken into account in Year 2 is still capital because on a single entity basis section 475(d)(3) would provide for $30 of capital gain and $10 of ordinary loss. Because the attributes are not redetermined under paragraph (c)(1)(i) of this section, paragraph (c)(4)(i) of this section does not apply. Furthermore, if B held the security for investment, and so identified the security under section 475(b)(1), the security would continue to be excepted from marking to market.

(L) *Example 12. Section 1092.* (1) *Facts.* On July 1 of Year 1, S enters into offsetting long and short positions with respect to actively traded personal property. The positions are not section 1256 contracts, and they are the only positions taken into account for purposes of applying section 1092. On August 1 of Year 1, S sells the long position to B at an $11 loss, and there is $11 of unrealized gain in the offsetting short position. On December 1 of Year 1, B sells the long position to X at no gain or loss. On December 31 of Year 1, there is still $11 of unrealized gain in the short position. On February 1 of Year 2, S closes the short position at an $11 gain.

(2) *Timing and attributes.* If the sale from S to B were a transfer between divisions of a single corporation, the $11 loss on the sale to X would have been deferred under section 1092(a)(1)(A). Accordingly, there is no difference in Year 1 between B's corresponding item of $0 and the recomputed corresponding item of $0. S takes its $11 loss into account in Year 2 to reflect the difference between B's corresponding item of $0 taken into account in Year 2 and the recomputed loss of $11 that would have been taken into account in Year 2 under section 1092(a)(1)(B) if S and B had been divisions of a single corporation. (The results are the same under section 267(f).)

(M) *Example 13.* [Reserved.]

(N) *Example 14. Source of income under section 863.* (1) *Intercompany sale—(i) Facts.* S manufactures inventory property solely in the United States and recognizes $75x of income on sales to B in Year 1. B conducts further production activity on the inventory property solely in Country Y and then sells the inventory property to X in Country Y and recognizes $25x of income on the sale to X, also in Year 1. Title passes from S to B, and from B to X, in Country Y. Assume that applying §1.863-3 on a single entity basis, including the formula for apportionment of multi-country production activities by reference to the basis of production assets, $10x would be treated as foreign source income and $90x would be treated as U.S. source income (that is, 10 percent of the production occurred outside the United States and 90 percent occurred within the United States, as measured by the basis of assets used in production activities with respect to the property). Assume further that, on a separate entity basis, S would have $0x of foreign source income and $75x of U.S. source income and all of B's $25x of income would be foreign source income.

(ii) *Analysis.* Under the matching rule, both S's $75x intercompany item and B's $25x corresponding item are taken into account in Year 1. In determining the source of S and B's income from the inventory property sales, the attributes of S's intercompany item and B's corresponding item are redetermined to the extent necessary to produce the same effect on consolidated taxable income (and consolidated tax liability) as if S and B were divisions of a single corporation. See paragraph (c)(1)(i) of this section. On a single entity basis, S and B would have $10x that would be treated as foreign source income and $90x that would be treated as U.S. source income, but without application of this section (that is, on a separate entity basis), S would have $75x of U.S. source income and B would have $25x of foreign source income. Under paragraph (c)(4)(ii) of this section, a redetermined attribute must be allocated between S and B using a reasonable method. On a separate entity basis B would have only foreign source income and S would have only U.S. source income. Accordingly, under paragraph (c)(1)(i) of this section, $15x of B's $25x sales income that would be treated as foreign source income on a separate entity basis is redetermined to be U.S. source income.

(2) *Sale of property reflecting intercompany services or intangibles*—(i) *Facts.* S earns $10x of income performing services in the United States for B. B capitalizes S's fees into the basis of inventory property that it manufactures in the United States and sells to an unrelated person in Year 1 at a $90x profit, with title passing in Country Y. Assume that on a single entity basis, $100x is treated as U.S. source income and $0x is treated as foreign source income. Further assume that on a separate entity basis, S would have $10x of U.S. source income, and B would have $90x of U.S. source income, with neither having any foreign source income.

(ii) *Analysis.* Under the matching rule, S's $10x income and B's $90x income are taken into account in Year 1. In determining the source of S and B's income, the attributes of S's intercompany item and B's corresponding item are redetermined to the extent necessary to produce the same effect on consolidated taxable income (and consolidated tax liability) as if S and B were divisions of a single corporation. Because the results are the same on a single entity basis and a separate entity basis ($100x of U.S. source income and $0x of foreign source income), the attributes are not redetermined under paragraph (c)(1)(i) of this section.

(O) *Example 15. Section 1248.* (1) *Facts.* On January 1 of Year 1, S forms FT, a wholly owned foreign subsidiary, with a $10 contribution. During Years 1 through 3, FT has earnings and profits of $40. None of the earnings and profits is taxed as subpart F income under section 951, and FT distributes no dividends to S during this period. On January 1 of Year 4, S sells its FT stock to B for $50. While B owns FT, FT has a deficit in earnings and profits of $10. On July 1 of Year 6, B sells its FT stock for $70 to X, an unrelated foreign corporation.

(2) *Timing.* S's $40 of intercompany gain is taken into account in Year 6 to reflect the difference between B's $20 of gain taken into account and the $60 recomputed gain.

(3) *Attributes.* Under the matching rule, the attributes of S's intercompany gain and B's corresponding gain are redetermined to have the same effect on consolidated taxable income (and consolidated tax liability) as if S and B were divisions of a single corporation. On a single entity basis, there is $60 of gain and the portion which is characterized as a dividend under section 1248 is determined on the basis of FT's $30 of earnings and profits at the time of the sale of FT to X (the sum of FT's $40 of earnings and profits while held by S and FT's $10 deficit in earnings and profits while held by B). Therefore, $30 of the $60 gain is treated as a dividend under section 1248. The remaining $30 is treated as capital gain. On a separate entity basis, all of S's $40 gain would be treated as a dividend under section 1248 and all of B's $20 gain would be treated as capital gain. Thus, as a result of the single entity determination, $10 that would be treated as a dividend under section 1248 on a separate entity basis is redetermined to be capital gain. Under paragraph (c)(4)(ii) of this section, this redetermined attribute must be allocated between S's intercompany item and B's corresponding item by using a reasonable method. On a separate entity basis, only S would have any amount treated as a dividend under section 1248 available for redetermination. Accordingly, $10 of S's income is redetermined to be not subject to section 1248, with the result that $30 of S's intercompany gain is treated as a dividend and the remaining $10 is treated as capital gain. All of B's corresponding gain is treated as capital gain, as it would be on a separate entity basis.

(4) *B has loss.* The facts are the same as in *Example 15* in paragraph (c)(7)(ii)(O)(1) of this section, except that FT has no earnings and profits or deficit in earnings and profits while B owns FT, and B sells the FT stock to X for $40. On a single entity basis, there is $30 of gain, and section 1248 is applied on the basis of FT's $40 earnings and profits at the time of the sale of FT to X. Under section 1248, the amount treated as a dividend is limited to $30 (the amount of the gain). On a separate entity basis, S's entire $40 gain would be treated as a dividend under section 1248, and B's $10 loss would be a capital loss. B's $10 corresponding loss offsets $10 of S's intercom-

pany gain and, under paragraph (c)(4)(i) of this section, the attributes of B's corresponding item control. Accordingly, $10 of S's gain must be redetermined to be capital gain. B's $10 loss remains a capital loss. (If, however, S sold FT to B at a loss and B sold FT to X at a gain, it may be unreasonable for the attributes of B's corresponding gain to control S's offsetting intercompany loss. If B's attributes were to control, for example, the group could possibly claim a larger foreign tax credit than would be available if S and B were divisions of a single corporation.)

(P) *Example 16. Intercompany stock distribution followed by section 332 liquidation.* (1) *Facts.* P owns all of the stock of S, S owns all the stock of T, a member of the P group, and T owns all of the stock of T1, also a member of the P group. On January 1 of Year 1, S distributes all of the T stock to P in a distribution to which section 301 applies. At the time of this distribution, the value of the T stock is $100 and S has a $40 basis in the T stock. Under section 311(b), the distribution creates $60 of intercompany gain to S. Under section 301(d), P's basis in the T stock is $100. S will take its $60 intercompany gain into account under the matching rule. On January 1 of Year 4, in an independent transaction, S distributes all of its assets to P in a complete liquidation to which section 332 applies, and, under paragraph (j)(2) of this section, P succeeds to S's $60 gain. On January 1 of Year 7, T distributes all of its T1 stock to P in a transaction to which section 355 applies. At the time of this distribution, P has a basis in the T stock of $100, the value of the T stock (without regard to T1) is $75, and the value of the T1 stock is $25. Under section 358, P allocates $25 of its $100 basis in the T stock to the T1 stock, and, under paragraph (j)(1) of this section, the T1 stock becomes a successor asset to the T stock. On January 1 of Year 9, in an independent transaction, T distributes all of its assets to P in a complete liquidation to which section 332 applies.

(2) *Analysis.* Under paragraphs (b)(1) and (f)(2) of this section, S's distribution in Year 1 of the T stock to P is an intercompany transaction, S is the selling member, and P is the buying member. In Year 9 when T liquidates, P has no gain or loss under section 332. Under paragraph (b)(3)(ii) of this section, P's $0 gain or loss with respect to the T stock under section 332 is a corresponding item. P takes $45 (75/100 × $60) of its intercompany gain into account under the matching rule in Year 9 to reflect the difference between P's $0 of unrecognized gain and P's $45 of recomputed unrecognized gain. (If P and S were divisions of a single corporation, P would have had a $40 basis in the T stock, and, after the Year 7 distribution of the T1 stock, would have held the T stock with a $30 basis.) However, paragraph (c)(6) of this section does not prevent the redetermination of P's intercompany gain as excluded from gross income provided P succeeds to S's intercompany item; P and S are a single entity; P's basis in the T stock that reflects the $45 intercompany gain taken into account is eliminated without the recognition of gain or loss (and this eliminated basis is not further reflected in the basis of any successor asset); the group has not derived and no taxpayer will derive any Federal income tax benefit from the basis in the T stock and will not derive any Federal income tax benefit from a redetermination of this portion of the gain; and the effects of the intercompany transaction have not previously been reflected, directly or indirectly, on the P group's consolidated return. (See paragraph (c)(6)(ii)(C) of this section.) Accordingly, under paragraph (c)(6)(ii)(C) of this section, the $45 intercompany gain that P takes into account is redetermined to be excluded from gross income. P's basis in its T1 stock continues to reflect $15 of intercompany gain.

(Q) *Example 17. Intercompany stock sale followed by section 355 distribution.* (1) *Facts.* The facts are the same as *Example 16* in paragraph (c)(7)(ii)(P) of this section, except that T does not distribute the stock of T1, instead, in Year 7, T makes a distribution of $50 to P in a transaction to which section 301 applies. Under § 1.1502-32, P's basis in its T stock is reduced by $50 and, under paragraph (f)(2)(ii) of this section, the intercompany distribution is excluded from P's gross income. Further, in Year 9, instead of liquidating T, P distributes the T stock to its shareholders in a transaction to which section 355 applies.

(2) *Analysis.* On the distribution of the T stock in Year 9, P has $0 of unrecognized gain under section 355(c). Under paragraph (b)(3)(ii) of this section, P's $0 of unrecognized gain or loss with respect to the T stock under section 355(c) is a corresponding item. P takes its $60 intercompany gain into account under the matching rule in Year 9 to reflect the difference between P's $0 of unrecognized gain and P's $60 of recomputed gain ($50 unrecognized gain and $10 recognized gain). (If P and S were divisions of a single corporation, P would have had a $40 basis in the T stock, and, after the Year 7 distribution, would have held the T stock with a $10 excess loss account.) See *Example 2* in paragraph (f)(7) of this section. Paragraph (c)(6) of this section does not prevent the redetermination of P's intercompany gain as excluded from gross income provided P succeeds to S's intercompany item; P and S are a single entity; P's basis in the T stock that reflects the $60 intercompany gain taken into account is eliminated without the recognition of gain or loss (and this

eliminated basis is not further reflected in any successor asset); the group has not derived any Federal income tax benefit from the basis in the T stock and will not derive any Federal income tax benefit from a redetermination of this portion of the gain; and the effects of the intercompany transaction have not previously been reflected, directly or indirectly, on the P group's consolidated return. (See paragraph (c)(6)(ii)(C) of this section.) The intercompany transaction with respect to the T stock resulted in an increase in the basis of the T stock, and this increase in the basis of the T stock prevented P from holding the T stock with a $10 excess loss account (as a result of the Year 7 distribution) at the time of the section 355 distribution. Accordingly, the group derived a Federal income tax benefit from the intercompany transaction to the extent of $10 and, under paragraph (c)(6)(ii)(C) of this section, only $50 of the $60 intercompany gain that P takes into account is redetermined to be excluded from gross income.

(3) *Application of section 355(e)*. If it were determined that section 355(e) applied to P's distribution of the T stock, P would recognize $0 of gain and derive a Federal income tax benefit to the extent of the full $60 increase in the basis of the T stock. Therefore, no portion of P's intercompany gain would be redetermined to be excluded from gross income under paragraph (c)(6)(ii)(C) of this section.

(R) *Example 18. Redetermination of attributes for section 250 purposes*. (1) *Facts*. S manufactures equipment in the United States and recognizes $75 of gross income included in gross DEI (as defined in § 1.250(b)-1(c)(15)) on the sale of Asset, which is not depreciable property, to B in Year 1 for $100. In Year 2, B sells Asset to X for $125 and recognizes $25 of gross income. The sale is a FDDEI sale (as defined in § 1.250(b)-1(c)(8)), and thus the $25 of income is included in B's gross FDDEI (as defined in § 1.250(b)-1(c)(16)) for Year 2.

(2) *Timing and attributes*. S's $75 of intercompany income is taken into account in Year 2 under the matching rule to reflect the $75 difference between B's $25 corresponding item taken into account (based on B's $100 cost basis in Asset) and the recomputed corresponding item (based on the $25 basis that B would have if S and B were divisions of a single corporation and B's basis were determined by reference to S's basis). In determining whether S's gross income included in gross DEI from the sale of Asset is included in gross FDDEI, S and B are treated as divisions of a single corporation. See paragraph (a)(6) of this section. In determining the amount of income included in gross DEI that is included in gross FDDEI, the attributes of S's intercompany item and B's corresponding item may be redetermined to the extent necessary to produce the same effect on consolidated taxable income (and consolidated tax liability) as if S and B were divisions of a single corporation. See paragraph (c)(1)(i) of this section. Applying section 250 and § 1.1502-50 on a single entity basis, all $100 of income included in gross DEI would be gross FDDEI. On a separate entity basis, S would have $75 of gross income included in gross DEI that is included in gross RDEI (as defined in § 1.250(b)-1(c)(14)) and B would have $25 of gross income included in gross DEI that is included in gross FDDEI. Thus, on a separate entity basis, S and B would have, in the aggregate, $100 of gross income included in gross DEI, of which only $25 is included gross FDDEI. Accordingly, under single entity treatment, $75 that would be treated as gross income included in gross DEI that is included in gross RDEI on a separate entity basis is redetermined to be included in gross FDDEI.

(3) *Intercompany sale for loss*. The facts are the same as in paragraph (c)(7)(ii)(R)(1) of this section (the facts in *Example 18*), except that S recognizes $25 of loss on the sale of Asset. S's $25 of intercompany loss is taken into account under the matching rule to reflect the $25 difference between B's $25 corresponding item taken into account (based on B's $100 cost basis in Asset) and the recomputed corresponding item (based on the $125 basis that B would have if S and B were divisions of a single corporation and B's basis were determined by reference to S's $125 of costs). Applying section 250 and § 1.1502-50 on a single entity basis, $0 of income would be included in gross DEI. In order to reflect this result, under the matching rule, S's $25 loss is allocated and apportioned solely to B's $25 of gross income from the sale of Asset for purposes of determining B's DEI and FDDEI. Furthermore, B's $25 of gross income is not taken into account for purposes of apportioning any other deductions under section 861 and the regulations under that section for purposes of determining any member's DEI or FDDEI.

(iii) *Effective/applicability date*.—(A) *In general*.—Paragraphs (c)(6)(ii)(C) and (D) of this section, *Example 16* in paragraph (c)(7)(ii)(P) of this section, and *Example 17* in paragraph (c)(7)(ii)(Q) of this section apply with respect to items taken into account on or after March 4, 2011.

(B) *Prior periods*.—For items taken into account on or after March 7, 2008, and before March 4, 2011, see § 1.1502-13T(c)(6)(ii)(C) and (f)(7), *Examples 7* and *8* as contained in 26 CFR part 1 in effect on

April 1, 2009. For items taken into account before March 7, 2008, see § 1.1502-13 as contained in 26 CFR part 1 in effect on April 1, 2007.

(d) *Acceleration rule*.—S's intercompany items and B's corresponding items are taken into account under this paragraph (d) to the extent they cannot be taken into account to produce the effect of treating S and B as divisions of a single corporation. For this purpose, the following rules apply:

(1) *S's items*.—(i) *Timing*.—S takes its intercompany items into account to the extent they cannot be taken into account to produce the effect of treating S and B as divisions of a single corporation. The items are taken into account immediately before it first becomes impossible to achieve this effect. For this purpose, the effect cannot be achieved—

(A) To the extent an intercompany item or corresponding item will not be taken into account in determining the group's consolidated taxable income (or consolidated tax liability) under the matching rule (for example, if S or B becomes a nonmember, or if S's intercompany item is no longer reflected in the difference between B's basis (or an amount equivalent to basis) in property and the basis (or equivalent amount) the property would have if S and B were divisions of a single corporation); or

(B) To the extent a nonmember reflects, directly or indirectly, any aspect of the intercompany transaction (e.g., if B's cost basis in property purchased from S is reflected by a nonmember under section 362 following a section 351 transaction).

(ii) *Attributes*.—The attributes of S's intercompany items taken into account under this paragraph (d)(1) are determined as follows:

(A) *Sale, exchange, or distribution*.—If the item is from an intercompany sale, exchange, or distribution of property, its attributes are determined under the principles of the matching rule as if B sold the property, at the time the item is taken into account under paragraph (d)(1)(i) of this section, for a cash payment equal to B's adjusted basis in the property (i.e., at no net gain or loss), to the following person:

(1) *Property leaves the group*.—If the property is owned by a nonmember immediately after S's item is taken into account, B is treated as selling the property to that nonmember. If the nonmember is related for purposes of any provision of the Internal Revenue Code or regulations to any party to the intercompany transaction (or any related transaction) or to the common parent, the nonmember is treated as related to B for purposes of that provision. For example, if the nonmember is related to P within the meaning of section 1239(b), the deemed sale is treated as being described in section 1239(a). See paragraph (j)(6) of this section, under which property is not treated as being owned by a nonmember if it is owned by the common parent after the common parent becomes the only remaining member.

(2) *Property does not leave the group*.—If the property is not owned by a nonmember immediately after S's item is taken into account, B is treated as selling the property to an affiliated corporation that is not a member of the group.

(B) *Other transactions*.—If the item is from an intercompany transaction other than a sale, exchange, or distribution of property (e.g., income from S's services capitalized by B), its attributes are determined on a separate entity basis.

(2) *B's items*.—(i) *Attributes*.—The attributes of B's corresponding items continue to be redetermined under the principles of the matching rule, with the following adjustments:

(A) If S and B continue to join with each other in the filing of consolidated returns, the attributes of B's corresponding items (and any applicable holding periods) are determined by continuing to treat S and B as divisions of a single corporation.

(B) Once S and B no longer join with each other in the filing of consolidated returns, the attributes of B's corresponding items are determined as if the S division (but not the B division) were transferred by the single corporation to an unrelated person. Thus, S's activities (and any applicable holding period) before the intercompany transaction continue to affect the attributes of the corresponding items (and any applicable holding period).

(ii) *Timing*.—If paragraph (d)(1) of this section applies to S, B nevertheless continues to take its corresponding items into account under its accounting method. However, the redetermination of the attributes of a corresponding item under this paragraph (d)(2) might affect its timing.

(3) *Examples*.—The acceleration rule of this paragraph (d) is illustrated by the following examples.

*Example 1. Becoming a nonmember—timing.* (a) *Facts.* S owns land with a basis of $70. On January 1 of Year 1, S sells the land to B for

$100. On July 1 of Year 3, P sells 60% of S's stock to X for $60 and, as a result, S becomes a nonmember.

(b) *Matching rule.* Under the matching rule, none of S's $30 gain is taken into account in Years 1 through 3 because there is no difference between B's $0 gain or loss taken into account and the recomputed gain or loss.

(c) *Acceleration of S's intercompany items.* Under the acceleration rule of paragraph (d) of this section, S's $30 gain is taken into account in computing consolidated taxable income (and consolidated tax liability) immediately before the effect of treating S and B as divisions of a single corporation cannot be produced. Because the effect cannot be produced once S becomes a nonmember, S takes its $30 gain into account in Year 3 immediately before becoming a nonmember. S's gain is reflected under § 1.1502-32 in P's basis in the S stock immediately before P's sale of the stock. Under § 1.1502-32, P's basis in the S stock is increased by $30, and therefore P's gain is reduced (or loss is increased) by $18 (60% of $30). See also §§ 1.1502-33 and 1.1502-76(b). (The results would be the same if S sold the land to B in an installment sale to which section 453 would otherwise apply, because S must take its intercompany gain into account under this section.)

(d) *B's corresponding items.* Notwithstanding the acceleration of S's gain, B continues to take its corresponding items into account under its accounting method. Thus, B's items from the land are taken into account based on subsequent events (e.g., its sale of the land).

(e) *Sale of B's stock.* The facts are the same as in paragraph (a) of this *Example 1,* except that P sells 60% of B's stock (rather than S stock) to X for $60 and, as a result, B becomes a nonmember. Because the effect of treating S and B as divisions of a single corporation cannot be produced once B becomes a nonmember, S takes its $30 gain into account under the acceleration rule immediately before B becomes a nonmember. (The results would be the same if S sold the land to B in an installment sale to which section 453 would otherwise apply, because S must take its intercompany gain into account under this section.)

(f) *Discontinue filing consolidated returns.* The facts are the same as in paragraph (a) of this *Example 1,* except that the P group receives permission under § 1.1502-75(c) to discontinue filing consolidated returns beginning in Year 3. Under the acceleration rule, S takes its $30 gain into account on December 31 of Year 2.

(g) *No subgroups.* The facts are the same as in paragraph (a) of this *Example 1,* except that P simultaneously sells all of the stock of both S and B to X (rather than 60% of S's stock), and S and B become members of the X consolidated group. Because the effect of treating S and B as divisions of a single corporation in the P group cannot be produced once S and B become nonmembers, S takes its $30 gain into account under the acceleration rule immediately before S and B become nonmembers. (Paragraph (j)(5) of this section does not apply to treat the X consolidated group as succeeding to the P group because the X group acquired only the stock of S and B.) However, so long as S and B continue to join with each other in the filing of consolidated returns, B continues to treat S and B as divisions of a single corporation for purposes of determining the attributes of B's corresponding items from the land.

*Example 2. Becoming a nonmember—attributes.* (a) *Facts.* S holds land for investment with a basis of $70. On January 1 of Year 1, S sells the land to B for $100. B holds the land for sale to customers in the ordinary course of business, and expends substantial resources over a two-year period subdividing, developing, and marketing the land. On July 1 of Year 3, before B has sold any of the land, P sells 60% of S's stock to X for $60 and, as a result, S becomes a nonmember.

(b) *Attributes.* Under the acceleration rule, the attributes of S's gain are redetermined under the principles of the matching rule as if B sold the land to an affiliated corporation that is not a member of the group for a cash payment equal to B's adjusted basis in the land (because the land continues to be held within the group). Thus, whether S's gain is capital gain or ordinary income depends on the activities of both S and B. Because S and B no longer join with each other in the filing of consolidated returns, the attributes of B's corresponding items (e.g., from its subsequent sale of the land) are redetermined under the principles of the matching rule as if the S division (but not the B division) were transferred by the single corporation to an unrelated person at the time of P's sale of the S stock. Thus, B continues to take into account the activities of S with respect to the land before the intercompany transaction.

(c) *Depreciable property.* The facts are the same as in paragraph (a) of this *Example 2,* except that the property sold by S to B is depreciable property. Section 1239 applies to treat all of S's gain as ordinary income because it is taken into account as a result of B's deemed sale of the property to a affiliated corporation that is not a member of the group (a related person within the meaning of section 1239(b)).

*Example 3. Selling member's disposition of installment note.* (a) *Facts.* S owns land with a basis of $70. On January 1 of Year 1, S sells the land to B in exchange for B's $110 note. The note bears a market rate of interest in excess of the applicable Federal rate, and provides for

principal payments of $55 in Year 4 and $55 in Year 5. On July 1 of Year 3, S sells B's note to X for $110.

(b) *Timing.* S's intercompany gain is taken into account under this section, and not under the rules of section 453. Consequently, S's sale of B's note does not result in its intercompany gain from the land being taken into account (e.g., under section 453B). The sale does not prevent S's intercompany items and B's corresponding items from being taken into account in determining the group's consolidated taxable income under the matching rule, and X does not reflect any aspect of the intercompany transaction (X has its own cost basis in the note). S will take the intercompany gain into account under the matching rule or acceleration rule based on subsequent events (e.g., B's sale of the land). See also paragraph (g) of this section for additional rules applicable to B's note as an intercompany obligation.

*Example 4. Cancellation of debt and attribute reduction under section 108(b).* (a) *Facts.* S holds land for investment with a basis of $0. On January 1 of Year 1, S sells the land to B for $100. B also holds the land for investment. During Year 3, B is insolvent and B's nonmember creditors discharge $60 of B's indebtedness. Because of insolvency, B's $60 discharge is excluded from B's gross income under section 108(a), and B reduces the basis of the land by $60 under sections 108(b) and 1017.

(b) *Acceleration rule.* As a result of B's basis reduction under section 1017, $60 of S's intercompany gain will not be taken into account under the matching rule (because there is only a $40 difference between B's $40 basis in the land and the $0 basis the land would have if S and B were divisions of a single corporation). Accordingly, S takes $60 of its gain into account under the acceleration rule in Year 3. S's gain is long-term capital gain, determined under paragraph (d)(1)(ii) of this section as if B sold the land to an affiliated corporation that is not a member of the group for $100 immediately before the basis reduction.

(c) *Purchase price adjustment.* Assume instead that S sells the land to B in exchange for B's $100 purchase money note, B remains solvent, and S subsequently agrees to discharge $60 of the note as a purchase price adjustment to which section 108(e)(5) applies. Under applicable principles of tax law, $60 of S's gain and $60 of B's basis in the land are eliminated and never taken into account. Similarly, the note is not treated as satisfied and reissued under paragraph (g) of this section.

*Example 5. Section 481.* (a) *Facts.* S operates several trades or businesses, including a manufacturing business. S receives permission to change its method of accounting for valuing inventory for its manufacturing business. S increases the basis of its ending inventory by $100, and the related $100 positive section 481(a) adjustment is to be taken into account ratably over six taxable years, beginning in Year 1. During Year 3, S sells all of the assets used in its manufacturing business to B at a gain. Immediately after the transfer, B does not use the same inventory valuation method as S. On a separate entity basis, S's sale results in an acceleration of the balance of the section 481(a) adjustment to Year 3.

(b) *Timing and attributes.* Under paragraph (b)(2) of this section, the balance of S's section 481(a) adjustment accelerated to Year 3 is intercompany income. However, S's $100 basis increase before the intercompany transaction eliminates the related difference for this amount between B's corresponding items taken into account and the recomputed corresponding items in subsequent periods. Because the accelerated section 481(a) adjustment will not be taken into account in determining the group's consolidated taxable income (and consolidated tax liability) under the matching rule, the balance of S's section 481 adjustment is taken into account under the acceleration rule as ordinary income at the time of the intercompany transaction. (If S's sale had not resulted in accelerating S's section 481(a) adjustment on a separate entity basis, S would have no intercompany income to be taken into account under this section.)

(e) *Simplifying rules.*—(1) *Dollar-value LIFO inventory* methods.— (i) *In general.*—This paragraph (e)(1) applies if either S or B uses a dollar-value LIFO inventory method to account for intercompany transactions. Rather than applying the matching rule separately to each intercompany inventory transaction, this paragraph (e)(1) provides methods to apply an aggregate approach that is based on dollar-value LIFO inventory accounting. Any method selected under this paragraph (e)(1) must be applied consistently.

(ii) *B uses dollar-value LIFO.*—(A) *In general.*—If B uses a dollar-value LIFO inventory method to account for its intercompany inventory purchases, and includes all of its inventory costs incurred for a year in its cost of goods sold for the year (that is, B has no inventory increment for the year), S takes into account all of its intercompany inventory items for the year. If B does not include all of its inventory costs incurred for the year in its cost of goods sold for the year (that is, B has an inventory increment for the year), S does not take all of its intercompany inventory income or loss into account. The amount not taken into account is determined under either the increment averaging method of paragraph (e)(1)(ii)(B) of this section or the increment valuation method of paragraph (e)(1)(ii)(C) of this section. Separate computations are made for each pool of B that receives intercompany purchases from S, and S's amount not taken into account is layered based on B's LIFO inventory layers.

(B) *Increment averaging method.*—Under this paragraph (e)(1)(ii)(B), the amount not taken into account is the amount of S's intercompany inventory income or loss multiplied by the ratio of the LIFO value of B's current-year costs of its layer of increment to B's total inventory costs incurred for the year under its LIFO inventory method. If B includes more than its inventory costs incurred during any subsequent year in its cost of goods sold (a decrement), S takes into account the intercompany inventory income or loss layers in the same manner and proportion as B takes into account its inventory decrements.

(C) *Increment valuation method.*—Under this paragraph (e)(1)(ii)(C), the amount not taken into account is the amount of S's intercompany inventory income or loss for the appropriate period multiplied by the ratio of the LIFO value of B's current-year costs of its layer of increment to B's total inventory costs incurred in the appropriate period under its LIFO inventory method. The principles of paragraph (e)(1)(ii)(B) of this section otherwise apply. The appropriate period is the period of B's year used to determine its current-year costs.

(iii) *S uses dollar-value LIFO.*—If S uses a dollar-Value LIFO inventory method to account for its intercompany inventory sales, S may use any reasonable method of allocating its LIFO inventory costs to intercompany transactions. LIFO inventory costs include costs of prior layers if a decrement occurs. For example, a reasonable allocation of the most recent costs incurred during the consolidated return year can be used to compute S's intercompany inventory income or loss for the year if S has an inventory increment and uses the earliest acquisitions costs method, but S must apportion costs from the most recent appropriate layers of increment if an inventory decrement occurs for the year.

(iv) *Other reasonable methods.*—S or B may use a method not specifically provided in this paragraph (e)(1) that is expected to reasonably take into account intercompany items and corresponding items from intercompany inventory transactions. However, if the method used results, for any year, in a cumulative amount of intercompany inventory items not taken into account by S that significantly exceeds the cumulative amount that would not be taken into account under paragraph (e)(1)(ii) or (iii) of this section, S must take into account for that year the amount necessary to eliminate the excess. The method is thereafter applied with appropriate adjustments to reflect the amount taken into account.

(v) *Examples.*—The inventory rules of this paragraph (e)(1) are illustrated by the following examples.

*Example 1. Increment averaging method.* (a) *Facts.* Both S and B use a double-extension, dollar-value LIFO inventory method, and both value inventory increments using the earliest acquisitions cost valuation method. During Year 2, S sells 25 units of product Q to B on January 15 at $10/unit. S sells another 25 units on April 15, on July 15, and on September 15, at $12/unit. S's earliest cost of product Q is $7.50/unit and S's most recent cost of product Q is $8.00/unit. Both S and B have an inventory increment for the year. B's total inventory costs incurred during Year 2 are $6,000 and the LIFO value of B's Year 2 layer of increment is $600.

(b) *Intercompany inventory income.* Under paragraph (e)(1)(iii) of this section, S must use a reasonable method of allocating its LIFO inventory costs to intercompany transactions. Because S has an inventory increment for Year 2 and uses the earliest acquisitions cost method, a reasonable method of determining its intercompany cost of goods sold for product Q is to use its most recent costs. Thus, its intercompany cost of goods sold is $800 ($8.00 most recent cost, multiplied by 100 units sold to B), and its intercompany inventory income is $350 ($1,150 sales proceeds from B minus $800 cost).

(c) *Timing.* (i) Under the increment averaging method of paragraph (e)(1)(ii)(B) of this section, $35 of S's $350 of intercompany inventory income is not taken into account in Year 2, computed as follows:

$$\frac{\text{LIFO value of B's Year 2 layer of increment}}{\text{B's total inventory costs for Year 2}} = \frac{\$600}{\$6,000} = 10\%$$

$$10\% \times \text{S's \$350 intercompany inventory income} = \$35$$

(ii) Thus, $315 of S's intercompany inventory income is taken into account in Year 2 ($350 of total intercompany inventory income minus $35 not taken into account).

(d) *S incurs a decrement.* The facts are the same as in paragraph (a) of this *Example 1,* except that in Year 2, S incurs a decrement equal to 50% of its Year 1 layer. Under paragraph (e)(1)(iii) of this section, S must reasonably allocate the LIFO cost of the decrement to the cost of goods sold to B to determine S's intercompany inventory income.

(e) *B incurs a decrement.* The facts are the same as in paragraph (a) of this *Example 1,* except that B incurs a decrement in Year 2. S must take into account the entire $350 of Year 2 intercompany inventory income because all 100 units of product Q are deemed sold by B in Year 2.

*Example 2. Increment valuation method.* (a) The facts are the same as in Example 1. In addition, B's use of the earliest acquisition's cost method of valuing its increments-results in B valuing its year-end inventory using costs incurred from January through March. B's costs incurred during the year are: $1,428 in the period January through March; $1,498 in the period April through June; $1,524 in the period July through September; and $1,550 in the period October through December. S's intercompany inventory income for these periods is: $50 in the period January through March ((25 × $10) – (25 × $8)); $100 in the period April through June ((25 × $12) – (25 × $8)); $100 in the period July through September ((25 × $12) – (25 × $8)); and $100 in the period October through December ((25 × $12) – (25 × $8)).

(b) *Timing.* (i) Under the increment valuation method of paragraph (e)(1)(ii)(C) of this section, $21 of S's $350 of intercompany inventory income is not taken into account in Year 2, computed as follows:

$$\frac{\text{LIFO value of B's Year 2 layer of increment}}{\text{B's total inventory costs from January through March of Year 2}} = \frac{\$600}{\$1,428} = 42\%$$

$$42\% \times \text{S's \$50 intercompany inventory income for the period from January through March} = \$21$$

(ii) Thus, $329 of S's intercompany inventory income is taken into account in Year 2 ($350 of total intercompany inventory income minus $21 not taken into account).

(c) *B incurs a subsequent decrement.* The facts are the same as in paragraph (a) of this *Example 2.* In addition, assume that in Year 3, B experiences a decrement in its pool that receives intercompany purchases from S. B's decrement equals 20% of the base-year costs for its Year 2 layer. The fact that B has incurred a decrement means that all of its inventory costs incurred for Year 3 are included in cost of goods sold. As a result, S takes into account its entire amount of intercompany inventory income from its Year 3 sales. In addition, S takes into account $4.20 of its Year 2 layer of intercompany inventory income not already taken into account (20% of $21).

*Example 3. Other reasonable inventory methods.* (a) *Facts.* Both S and B use a dollar-value LIFO inventory method for their inventory transactions. During Year 1, S sells inventory to B and to X. Under paragraph (e)(1)(iv) of this section, to compute its intercompany inventory income and the amount of this income not taken into account, S computes its intercompany inventory income using the transfer price of the inventory items less a FIFO cost for the goods, takes into account these items based on a FIFO cost flow assumption for B's corresponding items, and the LIFO methods used by S and B are ignored for these computations. These computations are comparable to the methods used by S and B for financial reporting purposes, and the book methods and results are used for tax purposes. S adjusts the amount of intercompany inventory items not taken into account as required by section 263A.

(b) *Reasonable method.* The method used by S is a reasonable method under paragraph (e)(1)(iv) of this section if the cumulative amount of intercompany inventory items not taken into account by S is not significantly greater than the cumulative amount that would not be taken into account under the methods specifically described in paragraph (e)(1) of this section. If, for any year, the method results in a cumulative amount of intercompany inventory items not taken into account by S that significantly exceeds the cumulative amount that would not be taken into account under the methods specifically provided, S must take into account for that year the amount necessary to eliminate the excess. The method is thereafter applied with appropriate adjustments to reflect the amount taken into account (e.g., to prevent the amount from being taken into account more than once).

(2) *Reserve accounting.*—(i) *Banks and thrifts.*—Except as provided in paragraph (g)(4)(v) of this section (deferral of items from an intercompany obligation), a member's addition to, or reduction of, a reserve for bad debts that is maintained under section 585 is taken into account on a separate entity basis. For example, if S makes a loan to a nonmember and subsequently sells the loan to B, any deduction for an addition to a bad debt reserve under section 585 and any recapture income (or reduced bad debt deductions) are taken into account on a separate entity basis rather than as intercompany items or corresponding items taken into account under this section. Any gain or loss of S from its sale of the loan to B is taken into account under this section, however, to the extent it is not attributable to recapture of the reserve.

(ii) *Insurance companies.*—(A) *Direct insurance.*—If a member provides insurance to another member in an intercompany transaction, the transaction is taken into account by both members on a separate entity basis. For example, if one member provides life insurance coverage for another member with respect to its employees, the premiums, reserve increases and decreases, and death benefit payments are determined and taken into account by both members on a separate entity basis rather than taken into account under this section as intercompany items and corresponding items.

(B) *Reinsurance.*—(1) *In general.*—Paragraph (e)(2)(ii)(A) of this section does not apply to a reinsurance transaction that is an intercompany transaction. For example, if a member assumes all or a portion of the risk on an insurance contract written by another member, the amounts transferred as reinsurance premiums, expense allowances, benefit reimbursements, reimbursed policyholder dividends, experience rating adjustments, and other similar items are taken into account under the matching rule and the acceleration rule. For purposes of this section, the assuming company is treated as B and the ceding company is treated as S.

(2) *Reserves determined on a separate entity basis.*—For purposes of determining the amount of a member's increase or decrease in reserves, the amount of any reserve item listed in section 807(c) or 832(b)(5) resulting from a reinsurance transaction that is an intercompany transaction is determined on a separate entity basis. But see section 845, under which the Commissioner may allocate between or among the members any items, recharacterize any such items, or make any other adjustments necessary to reflect the proper source and character of the separate taxable income of a member.

(3) *Consent to treat intercompany transactions on a separate entity basis.*—(i) *General rule.*—The common parent may request consent to take into account on a separate entity basis items from intercompany transactions other than intercompany transactions with respect to stock or obligations of members. Consent may be granted for all items, or for items from a class or classes of transactions. The consent is effective only if granted in writing by the Internal Revenue Service. Unless revoked with the written consent of the Internal Revenue Service, the separate entity treatment applies to all affected intercompany transactions in the consolidated return year for which consent is granted and in all subsequent consolidated return years. Consent under this paragraph (e)(3) does not apply for purposes of taking into account losses and deductions deferred under section 267(f).

(ii) *Time and manner for requesting consent.*—The request for consent described in paragraph (e)(3)(i) of this section must be made in the form of a ruling request. The request must be signed by the common parent, include any information required by the Internal Revenue Service, and be filed on or before the due date of the consolidated return (not including extensions of time) for the first consolidated return year to which the consent is to apply. The Internal Revenue Service may impose terms and conditions for granting consent. A copy of the consent must be attached to the group's consolidated returns (or amended returns) as required by the terms of the consent.

(iii) *Effect of consent on methods of accounting.*—A consent for separate entity accounting under this paragraph (e)(3), and a revocation of that consent, may require changes in members' methods of accounting for intercompany transactions. Because the consent, or a revocation of the consent, is effective for all intercompany transactions occurring in the consolidated return year for which the consent or revocation is first effective, any change in method is effected on a cut-off basis. Section 446(e) consent is granted for any changes in methods of accounting for intercompany transactions that are necessary solely to conform a member's methods to a binding consent with respect to the group under this paragraph (e)(3) or the revocation of that consent, provided the changes are made in the first consolidated return year for which the consent or revocation under

this paragraph (e)(3) is effective. Therefore, section 446(e) consent must be separately requested under applicable administrative procedures if a member has failed to conform its practices to the separate entity accounting provided under this paragraph (e)(3) or the revocation of that treatment in the first consolidated return year for which the consent to use separate entity accounting or revocation of that consent is effective.

(iv) *Consent to treat intercompany transactions on a separate entity basis under prior law.*—A group that has received consent that is in effect as of the first day of the first consolidated return year beginning on or after July 12, 1995 to treat certain intercompany transactions as provided in §1.1502-13(c)(3) of the regulations (as contained in the 26 CFR part 1 edition revised as of April 1, 1995) will be considered to have obtained the consent of the Commissioner to take items from intercompany transactions into account on a separate entity basis as provided in paragraph (e)(3)(i) of this section. This treatment is applicable only to the items, class or classes of transactions for which consent was granted under prior law.

(f) *Stock of members.*—(1) *In general.*—In addition to the general rules of this section, the rules of this paragraph (f) apply to stock of members.

(2) *Intercompany distributions to which section 301 applies.*—(i) *In general.*—This paragraph (f)(2) provides rules for intercompany transactions to which section 301 applies (intercompany distributions). For purposes of determining whether a distribution is an intercompany distribution, it is treated as occurring under the principles of the entitlement rule of paragraph (f)(2)(iv) of this section. A distribution is not an intercompany distribution to the extent it is deducted by the distributing member. See, for example, section 1382(c)(1).

(ii) *Distributee member.*—An intercompany distribution is not included in the gross income of the distributee member (B). However, this exclusion applies to a distribution only to the extent there is a corresponding negative adjustment reflected under §1.1502-32 in B's basis in the stock of the distributing member (S). For example, no amount is included in B's gross income under section 301(c)(3) from a distribution in excess of the basis of the stock of a subsidiary that results in an excess loss account under §1.1502-32(a) which is treated as negative basis under §1.1502-19. B's dividend received deduction under section 243(a)(3) is determined without regard to any intercompany distributions under this paragraph (f)(2) to the extent they are not included in gross income. See §1.1502-26(b) (applicability of the dividends received deduction to distributions not excluded from gross income, such as a distribution from the common parent to a subsidiary owning stock of the common parent).

(iii) *Distributing member.*—The principles of section 311(b) apply to S's loss, as well as gain, from an intercompany distribution of property. Thus, S's loss is taken into account under the matching rule if the property is subsequently sold to a nonmember. However, section 311(a) continues to apply to distributions to nonmembers (for example, loss is not recognized).

(iv) *Entitlement rule.*—(A) *In general.*—For all Federal income tax purposes, an intercompany distribution is treated as taken into account when the shareholding member becomes entitled to it (generally on the record date). For example, if B becomes entitled to a cash distribution before it is made, the distribution is treated as made when B becomes entitled to it. For this purpose, B is treated as entitled to a distribution no later than the time the distribution is taken into account under the Internal Revenue Code (e.g., under section 305(c)). To the extent a distribution is not made, appropriate adjustments must be made as of the date it was taken into account.

(B) *Nonmember shareholders.*—If nonmembers own stock of the distributing corporation at the time the distribution is treated as occurring under this paragraph (f)(2)(iv), appropriate adjustments must be made to prevent the acceleration of the distribution to members from affecting distributions to nonmembers.

(3) *Boot in an intercompany reorganization.*—(i) *Scope.*—This paragraph (f)(3) provides additional rules for an intercompany transaction in which the receipt of money or other property (nonqualifying property) results in the application of section 356. For example, the distribution of stock of a lower-tier member to a higher tier member in an intercompany transaction to which section 355 would apply but for the receipt of nonqualifying property is a transaction to which this paragraph (f)(3) applies. This paragraph (f)(3) does not apply if a party to the transaction becomes a member or nonmember as part of the same plan or arrangement. For example, if S merges into a nonmember in a transaction described in section 368(a)(1)(A), this paragraph (f)(3) does not apply.

(ii) *Treatment.*—Nonqualifying property received as part of a transaction described in this paragraph (f)(3) is treated as received by the member shareholder in a separate transaction. See, for example, sections 302 and 311 (rather than sections 356 and 361). The nonqualifying property is treated as taken into account immediately after the transaction if section 354 would apply but for the fact that nonqualifying property is received. It is treated as taken into account immediately before the transaction if section 355 would apply but for the fact that nonqualifying property is received. The treatment under this paragraph (f)(3)(ii) applies for all Federal income tax purposes.

(4) *Acquisition by issuer of its own stock.*—If a member acquires its own stock, or an option to buy or sell its own stock, in an intercompany transaction, the member's basis in that stock or option is treated as eliminated for all purposes. Accordingly, S's intercompany items from the stock or options of B are taken into account under this section if B acquires the stock or options in an intercompany transaction (unless, for example, B acquires the stock in exchange for successor property within the meaning of paragraph (j)(1)(1) of this section in a nonrecognition transaction). For example, if B redeems its stock from S in a transaction to which section 302(a) applies, S's gain from the transaction is taken into account immediately under the acceleration rule.

(5) *Certain liquidations and distributions.*—(i) *Netting allowed.*—S's intercompany item from a transfer to B of the stock of another corporation (T) is taken into account under this section in certain circumstances even though the T stock is never held by a nonmember after the intercompany transaction. For example, if S sells all of T's stock to B at a gain, and T subsequently liquidates into B in a separate transaction to which section 332 applies, S's gain is taken into account under the matching rule. Under paragraph (c)(6)(ii) of this section, S's intercompany gain taken into account as a result of a liquidation under section 332 or a comparable nonrecognition transaction is not redetermined to be excluded from gross income. Under this paragraph (f)(5)(i), if S has both intercompany income or gain and intercompany deduction or loss attributable to stock of the same corporation having the same material terms, only the income or gain in excess of the deduction or loss is subject to paragraph (c)(6)(ii) of this section. This paragraph (f)(5)(i) applies only to a transaction in which B's basis in its T stock is permanently eliminated in a liquidation under section 332 or any comparable nonrecognition transaction, including—

(A) A merger of B into T under section 368(a);

(B) A distribution by B of its T stock in a transaction described in section 355; or

(C) A deemed liquidation of T resulting from an election under section 338(h)(10).

(ii) *Elective relief.*—(A) *In general.*—If an election is made pursuant to this paragraph (f)(5)(ii), certain transactions are recharacterized to prevent S's items from being taken into account or to provide offsets to those items. This paragraph (f)(5)(ii) applies only if T is a member throughout the period beginning with S's transfer and ending with the completion of the nonrecognition transaction.

(B) *Section 332.*—(1) *In general.*—If section 332 would otherwise apply to T's (old T's) liquidation into B, and B transfers substantially all of old T's assets to a new member (new T), and if a direct transfer of substantially all of old T's assets to new T would qualify as a reorganization described in section 368(a), then, for all Federal income tax purposes, T's liquidation into B and B's transfer of substantially all of old T's assets to new T will be disregarded and instead, the transaction will be treated as if old T transferred substantially all of its assets to new T in exchange for new T stock and the assumption of T's liabilities in a reorganization described in section 368(a). (Under paragraph (j)(1) of this section, B's stock in new T would be a successor asset to B's stock in old T, and S's gain would be taken into account based on the new T stock.)

(2) *Time limitation and adjustments.*—The transfer of old T's assets to new T qualifies under paragraph (f)(5)(ii)(B)(1) of this section only if B has entered into a written plan, on or before the due date of the group's consolidated income tax return (including extensions) for the tax year that includes the date of old T's liquidation, to transfer the old T assets to new T, and the statement described in paragraph (f)(5)(ii)(E) of this section is included on or with a timely filed consolidated income tax return (including extensions) for the tax year that includes the date of the liquidation. However, in the case of a liquidation of old T on or after October 25, 2007, by a taxpayer whose original tax return for the year of liquidation was filed on or before November 3, 2009, see §1.1502-13T(f)(5)(ii)(F)(3)as contained in 26 CFR part 1, revised April 1, 2012. In either case, the transfer of substantially all of T's assets to new T must be completed within 12 months of the filing of the return. Appropriate adjustments are made to reflect any events occurring before the formation of new T and to reflect any assets not transferred to new T, or liabilities not assumed by new T. For example, if B retains an asset of old T, the

asset is treated under paragraph (f)(3) of this section as acquired by new T but distributed to B immediately after the reorganization.

(3) *Downstream merger, etc.*—The principles of this paragraph (f)(5)(ii)(B) apply, with appropriate adjustments, if B's basis in the T stock is eliminated in a transaction similar to a section 332 liquidation, such as a transaction described in section 368 in which B merges into T. For example, if S and B are subsidiaries, and S sells all of T's stock to B at a gain followed by B's merger into T in a separate transaction described in section 368(a), S's gain is not taken into account solely as a result of the merger if T (as successor to B) forms new T with substantially all of T's former assets.

(C) *Sections 338(h)(10) and 336(e).*—(1) *In general.*—This paragraph (f)(5)(ii)(C) applies to a deemed liquidation of T under section 332 as the result of an election under section 338(h)(10) or section 336(e). This paragraph (f)(5)(ii)(C) does not apply if paragraph (f)(5)(ii)(B) of this section is applied to the deemed liquidation. Under this paragraph, B is treated with respect to each share of its T stock as recognizing as a corresponding item any loss or deduction it would recognize (determined after adjusting stock basis under §1.1502-32) if section 331 applied to the deemed liquidation. For all other Federal income tax purposes, the deemed liquidation remains subject to section 332.

(2) *Limitation on amount of loss.*—The amount of B's loss or deduction under this paragraph (f)(5)(ii)(C) is limited as follows—

(i) The aggregate amount of loss recognized with respect to T stock cannot exceed the amount of S's intercompany income or gain that is in excess of S's intercompany deduction or loss with respect to shares of T stock having the same material terms as the shares giving rise to S's intercompany income or gain; and

(ii) The aggregate amount of loss recognized under this paragraph (f)(5)(ii)(C) from T's deemed liquidation cannot exceed the net amount of deduction or loss (if any) that would be taken into account from the deemed liquidation if section 331 applied with respect to all T shares.

(3) *Asset sale, etc.*—The principles of this paragraph (f)(5)(ii)(C) apply, with appropriate adjustments, if T transfers all of its assets to a nonmember and completely liquidates in a transaction comparable to the section 338(h)(10) transaction described in paragraph (f)(5)(ii)(C)(1) of this section. For example, if S sells all of T's stock to B at a gain followed by T's merger into a nonmember in exchange for a cash payment to B in a transaction treated for Federal income tax purposes as T's sale of its assets to the nonmember and complete liquidation, the merger is ordinarily treated as a comparable transaction.

(D) *Section 355.*—If B distributes the T stock in an intercompany transaction to which section 355 applies (including an intercompany transaction to which 355 applies because of the application of paragraph (f)(3) of this section), the redetermination of the basis of the T stock under section 358 could cause S's gain or loss to be taken into account under this section. This paragraph (f)(5)(ii)(D) applies to treat B's distribution as subject to section 301 and 311 (as modified by this paragraph (f)), rather than section 355. The election will prevent S's gain or loss from being taken into account immediately to the extent matching remains possible, but B's gain or loss from the distribution will also be taken into account under this section.

(E) *Election.*—An election to apply paragraph (f)(5)(ii) of this section is made in a separate statement entitled, "[INSERT NAME AND EMPLOYER IDENTIFICATION NUMBER OF COMMON PARENT] HEREBY ELECTS THE APPLICATION OF §1.1502-13(f)(5)(ii) FOR AN INTERCOMPANY TRANSACTION INVOLVING [INSERT NAME AND EMPLOYER IDENTIFICATION NUMBER OF S] AND [INSERT NAME AND EMPLOYER IDENTIFICATION NUMBER OF T]." A separate election must be made for each such application. The election must be filed by including the statement on or with the consolidated group's income tax return for the year of T's liquidation (or other transaction). The Commissioner may impose reasonable terms and conditions to the application of paragraph (f)(5)(ii) of this section that are consistent with the purposes of such section. The statement must—

(1) Identify S's intercompany transaction and T's liquidation (or other transaction); and

(2) Specify which provision of paragraph (f)(5)(ii) of this section applies and how it alters the otherwise applicable results under this section (including, for example, the amount of S's intercompany items and the amount deferred or offset as a result of paragraph (f)(5)(ii) of this section).

(F) *Effective/applicability date.*—(1) *General rule.*—Paragraphs (f)(5)(ii)(B)(1) and (2) of this section apply to transactions in which old T's liquidation into B occurs on or after October 25, 2007.

*(2) Prior periods.*—For transactions in which old T's liquidation into B occurs before October 25, 2007, see paragraphs (f)(5)(ii)(B)(1) and (2) of this section in effect prior to October 25, 2007, as contained in 26 CFR part 1, revised April 1, 2009.

*(6) Stock of common parent.*—In addition to the general rules of this section, this paragraph (f)(6) applies to parent stock (P stock) and positions in P stock held or entered into by another member. For this purpose, P stock is any stock of the common parent held (directly or indirectly) by another member or any stock of a member (the issuer) that was the common parent if the stock was held (directly or indirectly) by another member while the issuer was the common parent.

*(i) Loss stock.*—(A) *Recognized loss.*—Any loss recognized, directly or indirectly, by a member with respect to P stock is permanently disallowed and does not reduce earnings and profits. See § 1.1502-32(b)(3)(iii)(A) for a corresponding reduction in the basis of the member's stock.

(B) *Other cases.*—If a member, M, owns P stock, the stock is subsequently owned by a nonmember, and, immediately before the stock is owned by the nonmember, M's basis in the share exceeds its fair market value, then, to the extent paragraph (f)(6)(i)(A) of this section does not apply, M's basis in the share is reduced to the share's fair market value immediately before the share is held by the nonmember. For example, if M owns shares of P stock with a $100x basis and M becomes a nonmember at a time when the P shares have a value of $60x, M's basis in the P shares is reduced to $60x immediately before M becomes a nonmember. Similarly, if M contributes the P stock to a nonmember in a transaction subject to section 351, M's basis in the shares is reduced to $60x immediately before the contribution. See § 1.1502-32(b)(3)(iii)(B) for a corresponding reduction in the basis of M's stock.

(C) *Waiver of built-in loss on P stock.*—(1) *In general.*—If a nonmember that owns P stock with a basis in excess of its fair market value becomes a member of the P consolidated group in a qualifying cost basis transaction, the group may make an irrevocable election to reduce the basis of the P stock to its fair market value immediately before the nonmember becomes a member of the P group. If the nonmember was a member of another consolidated group immediately before becoming a member of the P group, the reduction in basis is treated as occurring immediately after it ceases to be a member of the prior group. A qualifying cost basis transaction is the purchase (i.e., a transaction in which basis is determined under section 1012) by members of the P consolidated group (while they are members) in a 12-month period of an amount of the nonmember's stock satisfying the requirements of section 1504(a)(2).

*(2) Election.*—The election described in paragraph (f)(6)(i)(C)(1) of this section must be made in a separate statement entitled, "ELECTION TO REDUCE BASIS OF P STOCK UNDER § 1.1502-13(f)(6) HELD BY [INSERT NAME AND EMPLOYER IDENTIFICATION NUMBER OF MEMBER WHOSE BASIS IN P STOCK IS REDUCED]." The election must be filed by including the statement on or with the consolidated group's income tax return for the year in which the nonmember becomes a member. The statement must identify the member's basis in the P stock (taking into account the effect of this election) and the number of shares of P stock held by the member.

*(ii) Gain stock.*—For dispositions of P stock occurring before May 16, 2000, see § 1.1502-13(f)(6)(ii) as contained in 26 CFR part 1 in effect on April 1, 2000. For dispositions of P stock occurring on or after May 16, 2000, see § 1.1032-3.

*(iii) Mark-to-market of P stock.*—Paragraphs (f)(6)(i) and (ii) of this section shall not apply to any gain or loss from a share of P stock held by a member, M, if—

(A) M regularly trades in P stock (of the same class) with customers in the ordinary course of its business as a dealer;

(B) The gain or loss on the share is taken into account by M pursuant to section 475(a);

(C) M's basis in the share is not adjusted by reference to the basis of any other property or by reference to income, gain, deduction, or loss from other property; and

(D) Neither M nor any other member of the group has structured or engaged in any transaction while a member (or in anticipation of becoming a member), during the taxable year or in any year within the preceding five taxable years that is open for assessment under section 6501, with a principal purpose of avoiding gain or creating loss on P stock subject to section 475(a).

*(iv) Options, warrants, and other positions.*—(A) *In general.*—This paragraph (f)(6) applies with appropriate adjustments to positions in P stock to the extent that P's gain or loss from an equivalent

position would not be recognized under section 1032. Thus, if M purchases an option to buy or sell P stock and sells the option at a loss, the loss is permanently disallowed under paragraph (f)(6)(i)(A) of this section. Similarly, if M is the grantor of such an option and becomes a nonmember, then the principles of paragraph (f)(6)(i)(B) of this section apply to the extent that M would recognize loss from cash settlement of the option at its fair market value immediately before M becomes a nonmember, and proper adjustments must be made in the amount of any gain or loss subsequently realized from the position by M. If P grants M an option to acquire P stock in a transaction meeting the requirements of § 1.1032-3, M is treated as having purchased the option from P for fair market value with cash contributed to M by P.

(B) *Mark-to-market of positions in P stock.*—For purposes of paragraph (f)(6)(iii) of this section, gain or loss with respect to a position taken into account under section 1256(a) is treated as taken into account under section 475(a) to the extent that the gain or loss would be taken into account under the principles of section 475.

*(v) Effective date.*—This paragraph (f)(6) applies to gain or loss taken into account on or after July 12, 1995, and to transactions occurring on or after July 12, 1995. For example, if S sells P stock to B at a loss prior to July 12, 1995, and B sells the P stock to a nonmember after July 12, 1995, S's loss is disallowed because it is taken into account after July 12, 1995. If a taxpayer takes a gain or loss into account or engages in a transaction on or after July 12, 1995, during a tax year ending prior to December 31, 1995, the taxpayer may treat the gain or loss or the transaction under the rules of § 1.1502-13T(f)(6) (published in 1995-32 I.R.B. 47), instead of under the rules of this paragraph (f)(6).

*(7) Examples—In general.*—The application of this section to intercompany transactions with respect to stock of members is illustrated by the following examples.

*Example 1. Dividend exclusion and property distribution.* (a) *Facts.* S owns land with a $70 basis and $100 value. On January 1 of Year 1, P's basis in S's stock is $100. During Year 1, S declares and makes a dividend distribution of the land to P. Under section 311(b), S has a $30 gain. Under section 301(d), P's basis in the land is $100. On July 1 of Year 3, P sells the land to X for $110.

(b) *Dividend elimination and stock basis adjustments.* Under paragraph (b)(1) of this section, S's distribution to P is an intercompany distribution. Under paragraph (f)(2)(ii) of this section, P's $100 of dividend income is not included in gross income. Under § 1.1502-32, P's basis in S's stock is reduced from $100 to $0 in Year 1.

(c) *Matching rule and stock basis adjustments.* Under the matching rule (treating S as the buying member and S as the selling member), S takes its $30 gain into account in-Year 3 to reflect the $30 difference between P's $10 gain taken into account and the $40 recomputed gain. Under § 1.1502-32, P's basis in S's stock is increased from $0 to $30 in Year 3.

(d) *Loss property.* The facts are the same as in paragraph (a) of this *Example except,* that S has a $130 (rather than $70) basis in the land. Under paragraph (f)(2)(iii) of this section, the principles of section 311(b) apply to S's loss from the intercompany distribution. Thus, S has a $30 loss that is taken into account under the matching rule in Year 3 to reflect the $30 difference between P's $10 gain taken into account and the $20 recomputed loss. (The results are the same under section 267(f).) Under § 1.1502-32, P's basis in S's stock is reduced from $100 to $0 in Year 1, and from $0 to a $30 excess loss account in Year 3. (If P had distributed the land to its shareholders, rather than selling the land to X, P would take its $10 gain under section 311(b) into account, and S would take its $30 loss into account under the matching rule with $10 offset by P's gain and $20 recharacterized as a noncapital, nondeductible amount.)

(e) *Entitlement rule.* The facts are the same as in paragraph (a) of this *Example 1,* except that, after P becomes entitled to the distribution but before the distribution is made, S issues additional stock to the public and becomes a nonmember. Under paragraph (f)(2)(i) of this section, the determination of whether a distribution is an intercompany distribution is made under the entitlement rule of paragraph (f)(2)(iv) of this section. Treating S's distribution as made when P becomes entitled to it results in the distribution being an intercompany distribution. Under paragraph (f)(2)(ii) of this section, the distribution is not included in P's gross income. S's $30 gain from the distribution is intercompany gain that is taken into account under the acceleration rule immediately before S becomes a nonmember. Thus, there is a net $70 decrease in P's basis in its S stock under § 1.1502-32 ($100 decrease for the distribution and a $30 increase for S's $30 gain). Under paragraph (f)(2)(iv) of this section, P does not take the distribution into account again under separate return rules when received, and P is not entitled to a dividends received deduction.

*Example 2. Excess loss accounts.* (a) *Facts.* S owns all of T's only class of stock with a $10 basis and $100 value. S has substantial earnings and profits, and T has $10 of earnings and profits. On

January 1 of Year 1, S declares and distributes a dividend of all of the T stock to P. Under section 311(b), S has a $90 gain. Under section 301(d), P's basis in the T stock is $100. During Year 3, T borrows $90 and declares and makes a $90 distribution to P to which section 301 applies, and P's basis in the T stock is reduced under §1.1502-32 from $100 to $10. During Year 6, T has $5 of earnings that increase P's basis in the T stock under §1.1502-32 from $10 to $15. On December 1 of Year 9, T issues additional stock to X and, as a result, T becomes a nonmember.

(b) *Dividend exclusion.* Under paragraph (f)(2)(ii) of this section, P's $100 of dividend income from S's distribution of the T stock, and its $10 of dividend income from T's $90 distribution, are not included in gross income.

(c) *Matching and acceleration rules.* Under §1.1502-19(b)(1), when T becomes a nonmember P must include in income the amount of its excess loss account (if any) in T stock. P has no excess loss account in the T stock. Therefore P's corresponding item from the deconsolidation of T is $0. Treating S and P as divisions of a single corporation, the T stock would continue to have a $10 basis after the distribution, and the adjustments under §1.1502-32 for T's $90 distribution and $5 of earnings would result in a $75 excess loss account. Thus, the recomputed corresponding item from the deconsolidation is $75. Under the matching rule, S takes $75 of its $90 gain into account in Year 9 as a result of T becoming a nonmember, to reflect the difference between P's $0 gain taken into account and the $75 recomputed gain. S's remaining $15 of gain is taken into account under the matching and acceleration rules based on subsequent events (for example, under the matching rule if P subsequently sells its T stock, or under the acceleration rule if S becomes a nonmember).

(d) *Reverse sequence.* The facts are the same as in paragraph (a) of this *Example 2,* except that T borrows $90 and makes its $90 distribution to S before S distributes T's stock to P. Under paragraph (f)(2)(ii) of this section, T's $90 distribution to S ($10 of which is a dividend) is not included in S's gross income. The corresponding negative adjustment under §1.1502-32 reduces S's basis in the T stock from $10 to an $80 excess loss account. Under section 311(b), S has a $90 gain from the distribution of T stock to P. Under section 301(d) P's initial basis in the T stock is $10 (the stock's fair market value), and the basis increases to $15 under §1.1502-32 as a result of T's earnings in Year 6. The timing and attributes of S's gain are determined in the manner provided in paragraph (c) of this *Example 2.* Thus, $75 of S's gain is taken into account under the matching rule in Year 9 as a result of T becoming a nonmember, and the remaining $15 is taken into account under the matching and acceleration rules based on subsequent events.

(e) *Partial stock sale.* The facts are the same as in paragraph (a) of this *Example 2,* except that P sells 10% of T's stock to X on December 1 of Year 9 for $1.50 (rather than T's issuing additional stock and becoming a nonmember). Under the matching rule, S takes $9 of its gain into account to reflect the difference between P's $0 gain taken into account ($1,50 sale proceeds minus $1.50 basis) and the $9 recomputed gain ($1.50 sale proceeds plus $7.50 excess loss account).

(f) *Loss, rather than cash distribution.* The facts are the same as in paragraph (a) of this *Example 2,* except that T retains the loan proceeds and incurs a $90 loss in Year 3 that is absorbed by the group. The timing and attributes of S's gain are determined in the same manner provided in paragraph (c) of this *Example 2.* Under §1.1502-32, the loss in Year 3 reduces P's basis in the T stock from $100 to $10, and T's $5 of earnings in Year 6 increase the basis to $15. Thus, $75 of S's gain is taken into account under the matching rule in Year 9 as a result of T becoming a nonmember, and the remaining $15 is taken into account under the matching and acceleration rules based on subsequent events. (The timing and attributes of S's gain would be determined in the same manner provided in paragraph (d) of this *Example 2* if T incurred the $90 loss before S's distribution of the T stock to P.)

(g) *Stock sale, rather than stock distribution.* The facts are the same as in paragraph (a) of this *Example except,* that S sells the T stock to P for $100 (rather than distributing the stock). The timing and attributes of S's gain are determined in the same manner provided in paragraph (c) of this *Example 2.* Thus, $75 of S's gain is taken into account under the matching rule in Year 9 as a result of T becoming a nonmember, and the remaining $15 is taken into account under the matching and acceleration rules based on subsequent events.

*Example 3. Intercompany reorganization.* (a) *Facts.* P forms S and B by contributing $200 to the capital of each. During Years 1 through 4, S and B each earn $50, and under §1.1502-32 P adjusts its basis in the stock of each to $250. (See §1.1502-33 for adjustments to earnings and profits.) On January 1 of Year 5, the fair market value of S's assets and its stock is $500, and S merges into B in a tax-free reorganization. Pursuant to the plan of reorganization, P receives B stock with a fair market value of $350 and $150 of cash.

(b) *Treatment as a section 301 distribution.* The merger of S into B is a transaction to which paragraph (f)(3) of this section applies. P is

treated as receiving additional B stock with a fair market value of $500 and, under section 358, a basis of $250. Immediately after the merger, $150 of the stock received is treated as redeemed, and the redemption is treated under section 302(d) as a distribution to which section 301 applies. Because the $150 distribution is treated as not received as part of the merger, section 356 does not apply and no basis adjustments are required under section 358(a)(1)(A) and (B). Because B is treated under section 381(c)(2) as receiving S's earnings and profits and the redemption is treated as occurring after the merger, $100 of the distribution is treated as a dividend under section 301 and P's basis in the B stock is reduced correspondingly under §1.1502-32. The remaining $50 of the distribution reduces P's basis in the B stock. Section 301(c)(2) and §1.1502-32. Under paragraph (f)(2)(ii) of this section, P's $100 of dividend income is not included in gross income. Under §1.302-2(c), proper adjustments are made to P's basis in its B stock to reflect its basis in the B stock redeemed, with the result that P's basis in the B stock is reduced by the entire $150 distribution.

(c) *Depreciated property.* The facts are the same as in paragraph (a) of this *Example 3,* except that property of S with a $200 basis and $150 fair market value is distributed to p (rather than cash of B). As in paragraph (b) of this *Example 3,* P is treated as receiving additional B stock in the merger and a $150 distribution to which section 301 applies. Under paragraph (f)(2)(iii) of this section, the principles of section 311(b) apply to B's $50 loss and the loss is taken into account under the matching and acceleration rules based on subsequent events (e.g., under the matching rule if P subsequently sells the property, or under the acceleration rule if B becomes a nonmember). The results are the same under section 267(f).

(d) *Divisive transaction.* Assume instead that, pursuant to a plan, S distributes the stock of a lower-tier subsidiary in a spin-off transaction to which section 355 applies together with $150 of cash. The distribution of stock is a transaction to which paragraph (f)(3) of this section applies. P is treated as receiving the $150 of cash immediately before the section 355 distribution, as a distribution to which section 301 applies. Section 356(b) does not apply and no basis adjustments are required under section 358(a)(1)(A) and (B). Because the $150 distribution is treated as made before the section 355 distribution, the distribution reduces P's basis in the S stock under §1.1502-32, and the basis allocated under section 358(c) between the S stock and the lower-tier subsidiary stock received reflects this basis reduction.

*Example 4. All cash intercompany reorganization under section 368(a)(1)(D).* (a) *Facts.* P owns all of the stock of M and B. M owns all of the stock of S with a basis of $25. On January 1 of Year 2, the fair market value of S's assets and its stock is $100, and S sells all of its assets to B for $100 cash and liquidates. The transaction qualifies as a reorganization described in section 368(a)(1)(D). Pursuant to §1.368-2(l), B will be deemed to issue a nominal share of B stock to S in addition to the $100 of cash actually exchanged for the S assets, and S will be deemed to distribute all of the consideration to M. M will be deemed to distribute the nominal share of B stock to P.

(b) *Treatment as a section 301 distribution.* The sale of S's assets to B is a transaction to which paragraph (f)(3) of this section applies. In addition to the nominal share issued by B to S under §1.368-2(l), S is treated as receiving additional B stock with a fair market value of $100 (in lieu of the $100) and, under section 358, a basis of $25 which S distributes to M in liquidation. Immediately after the sale, the B stock (with the exception of the nominal share which is still held by M) received by M is treated as redeemed for $100, and the redemption is treated under section 302(d) as a distribution to which section 301 applies. M's basis of $25 in the B stock is reduced under §1.1502-32(b)(3)(v), resulting in an excess loss account of $75 in the nominal share. (See §1.302-2(c)). M's deemed distribution of the nominal share of B stock to P under §1.368-2(l) will result in M generating an intercompany gain under section 311(b) of $75, to be subsequently taken into account under the matching and acceleration rules.

*Example 5. Stock redemptions and distributions.* (a) *Facts.* Before becoming a member of the P group, S owns P stock with a $30 basis. on January 1 of Year 1, P buys all of S's stock. On July 1 of Year 3, P redeems the P stock held by S for $100 in a transaction to which section 302(a) applies.

(b) *Gain under section 302.* Under paragraph (f)(4) of this section, P's basis in the P stock acquired from S is treated as eliminated. As a result of this elimination, S's intercompany item will never be taken into account under the matching rule because P's basis in the stock does not reflect S's intercompany item. Therefore, S's $70 gain is taken into account under the acceleration rule in Year 3. The attributes of S's item are determined under paragraph (d)(1)(ii) of this section by applying the matching rule as if p had sold the stock to an affiliated corporation that is not a member of the group at no gain or loss. Although P's corresponding item from a sale of its stock would have been excluded from gross income under section 1032, paragraph (c)(6)(ii) of this section prevents S's gain from being treated as excluded from gross income; instead S's gain is capital gain.

(c) *Gain under section 311.* The facts are the same as in paragraph (a) of this *Example* except, except that S distributes the P stock to P in a transaction to which section 301 applies (rather than the stock being redeemed), and S has a $70 gain under section 311(b). The timing and attributes of S's gain are determined in the manner provided in paragraph (b) of this *Example 4.*

(d) *Loss stock.* The facts are the same as in paragraph (a) of this *Example 4,* except that S has a $130 (rather than $30) basis in the P stock and has a $30 loss under section 302(a). The limitation under paragraph (c)(6)(ii) of this section does not apply to intercompany losses. Thus, S's loss is taken into account in Year 3 as a noncapital, nondeductible amount.

*Example 6. Intercompany stock sale followed by section 332 liquidation.* (a) *Facts.* S owns all of the stock of T, with a $70 basis and $100 value, and T's assets have a $10 basis and $100 value. On January 1 of Year 1, S sells all of T's stock to B for $100. On July 1 of Year 3, when T's assets are still worth $100, T distributes all of its assets to B in an unrelated complete liquidation to which section 332 applies.

(b) *Timing and attributes.* Under paragraph (b)(3)(ii) of this section, B's unrecognized gain or loss under section 332 is a corresponding item for purposes of applying the matching rule. In Year 3 when T liquidates, B has $0 of unrecognized gain or loss under section 332 because B has a $100 basis in the T stock and receives a $100 distribution with respect to its T stock. Treating S and B as divisions of a single corporation, the recomputed corresponding item would have been $30 of unrecognized gain under section because B would have succeeded to S's $70 basis in the T stock. Thus, under the matching rule, S's $30 intercompany gain is taken into account in Year 3 as a result of T's liquidation. Under paragraph (c)(1)(i) of this section, the attributes of S's gain and B's corresponding item are redetermined as if S and B were divisions of a single corporation. Although S's gain ordinarily would be redetermined to be treated as excluded from gross income to reflect the nonrecognition of B's gain under section 332, S's gain remains capital gain because B's unrecognized gain under section 332 is not permanently and explicitly disallowed under the Code. See paragraph (c)(6)(ii) of this section. However, relief may be elected under paragraph (f)(5)(ii) of this section.

(c) *Intercompany sale at a loss.* The facts are the same as in paragraph (a) of this *Example 5,* except that S has a $130 (rather than $70) basis in the T stock. The limitation under paragraph (c)(6)(ii) of this section does not apply to intercompany losses. Thus, S's intercompany loss is taken into account in Year 3 as a noncapital, nondeductible amount. However, relief may be elected under paragraph (f)(5)(ii) of this section.

*Example 7. Intercompany stock sale followed by section 355 distribution.* (a) *Facts.* S owns all of the stock of T with a $70 basis and a $100 value. On January 1 of Year 1, S sells all of T's stock to M for $100. on June 1l of Year 6, M distributes all of its T stock to its nonmember shareholders in a transaction to which section 355 applies. At the time of the distribution, M has a basis in T stock of $100 and T has a value of $150.

(b) *Timing and attributes.* Under paragraph (b)(3)(ii) of this section, M's $50 gain not recognized on the distribution under section 355 is a corresponding item. Treating S and M as divisions of a single corporation, the recomputed corresponding item would be $80 of unrecognized gain under section 355 because M would have succeeded to S's $70 basis in the T stock. Thus, under the matching rule, S's $30 intercompany gain is taken into account in Year 6 as a result of the distribution. Under paragraph (c)(1)(i) of this section, the attributes of S's intercompany item and M's corresponding item are redetermined to produce the same effect on consolidated taxable income as if S and M were divisions of a single corporation. Although S's gain ordinarily would be redetermined to be treated as excluded from gross income to reflect the nonrecognition of M's gain under section 355(c), S's gain remains capital gain because M's unrecognized gain under section 355(c) is not permanently and explicitly disallowed under the Code. See paragraph (c)(6)(ii) of this section. Because M's distribution of the T stock is not an intercompany transaction, relief is not available under paragraph (f)(5)(ii) of this section.

(c) *Section 355 distribution within the group.* The facts are the same as under paragraph (a) of this *Example 6,* except that M distributes the T stock to B (another member of the group), and B takes a $75 basis in the T stock under section 358. Under paragraph (j)(2) of this section, B is a successor to M for purposes of taking S's intercompany gain into account, and therefore both M and B might have corresponding items with respect to S's intercompany gain. To the extent it is possible, matching with respect to B's corresponding items produces the result most consistent with treating S, M, and B as divisions of a single corporation. See paragraphs (j)(3) and (j)(4) of this section.

However, because there is only $5 difference between B's $75 basis in the T stock and the $70 basis the stock would have if S, M, and B were divisions of a single corporation, only $5 can be taken into account under the matching rule with respect to B's corresponding items. (This $5 is taken into account with respect to B's corresponding items based on subsequent events.) The remaining $25 of S's $30 intercompany gain is taken into account in Year 6 under the matching rule with respect to M's corresponding item from its distribution of the T stock. The attributes of S's remaining $25 of gain are determined in the same manner as in paragraph (b) of this *Example 6.*

(d) *Relief elected.* The facts are the same as in paragraph (c) of this *Example 6* except that P elects relief pursuant to paragraph (f)(5)(ii)(D) of this section. As a result of the election, M's distribution of the T stock is treated as subject to sections 301 and 311 instead of section 355. Accordingly, M recognizes $50 of intercompany gain from the distribution, B takes a basis in the stock equal to its fair market value of $150, and S and M take their intercompany gains into account with respect to B's corresponding items based on subsequent events. (None of S's gain is taken into account in Year 6 as a result of M's distribution of the T stock.)

(g) *Obligations of members.*—(1) *In general.*—In addition to the general rules of this section, the rules of this paragraph (g) apply to intercompany obligations.

(2) *Definitions.*—For purposes of this section, the following definitions apply—

(i) *Obligation of a member* is a debt or security of a member.

(A) *Debt of a member* is any obligation of the member constituting indebtedness under general principles of Federal income tax law (for example, under nonstatutory authorities, or under section 108, section 163, or § 1.1275-1(d)), but not an executory obligation to purchase or provide goods or services.

(B) *Security of a member* is any security of the member described in section 475(c)(2)(D) or (E), and any commodity of the member described in section 475(e)(2)(A), (B), or (C), but not if the security or commodity is a position with respect to the member's stock. See paragraphs (f)(4) and (f)(6) of this section for special rules applicable to positions with respect to a member's stock.

(ii) *Intercompany obligation* is an obligation between members, but only for the period during which both parties are members.

(iii) *Intercompany obligation subgroup* is comprised of two or more members that include the creditor and debtor on an intercompany obligation if the creditor and debtor bear the relationship described in section 1504(a)(1) to each other through an intercompany obligation subgroup parent.

(iv) *Intercompany obligation subgroup parent* is the corporation (including either the creditor or debtor) that bears the same relationship to the other members of the intercompany obligation subgroup as a common parent bears to the members of a consolidated group. Any reference to an intercompany obligation subgroup parent includes, as the context may require, a reference to a predecessor or successor. For this purpose, a predecessor is a transferor of assets to a transferee (the successor) in a transaction to which section 381(a) applies.

(v) *Tax benefit* is the benefit of, for Federal tax purposes, a net reduction in income or gain, or a net increase in loss, deduction, credit, or allowance. A tax benefit includes, but is not limited to, the use of a built-in item or items from an intercompany obligation to reduce gain or increase loss on the sale of member stock, or to create or absorb a tax attribute of a member or subgroup.

(vi) *Eighty-percent chain* is a chain of two or more corporations in which stock meeting the requirements of section 1504(a)(2) of each lower-tier member is held directly by a higher-tier member of such chain.

(3) *Deemed satisfaction and reissuance of intercompany obligations in triggering transactions.*—(i) *Scope.*—(A) *Triggering transactions.*—For purposes of this paragraph (g)(3), a triggering transaction includes the following:

(1) *Assignment and extinguishment transactions.*—Any intercompany transaction in which a member realizes an amount, directly or indirectly, from the assignment or extinguishment of all or part of its remaining rights or obligations under an intercompany obligation or any comparable transaction in which a member realizes any such amount, directly or indirectly, from an intercompany obligation (for example, a mark to fair market value of an obligation or a bad debt deduction). However, a reduction of the basis of an intercompany obligation pursuant to § 1.1502-36(d) (attribute reduction to prevent duplication of loss), or pursuant to sections 108 and 1017 and § 1.1502-28 (basis reductions upon the exclusion from gross income of discharge of indebtedness) or any other provision that adjusts the basis of an intercompany obligation as a substitute for income, gain, deduction, or loss, is not a comparable transaction.

Reg. § 1.1502-13(g)(3)(i)(A)(1)

*(2) Outbound transactions.*—Any transaction in which an intercompany obligation becomes an obligation that is not an intercompany obligation.

(B) *Exceptions.*—Except as provided in paragraph (g)(3)(i)(C) of this section, a transaction is not a triggering transaction as described in paragraph (g)(3)(i)(A) of this section if any of the exceptions in this paragraph (g)(3)(i)(B) apply. In making this determination, if a creditor or debtor realizes an amount in a transaction in which a creditor assigns all or part of its rights under an intercompany obligation to the debtor, or a debtor assigns all or part of its obligations under an intercompany obligation to the creditor, the transaction will be treated as an extinguishment and will be excepted from the definition of "triggering transaction" only if either of the exceptions in paragraphs (g)(3)(i)(B)(5) or (6) of this section apply. The exceptions are as follows.

*(1) Intercompany section 361, 332, or 351 exchange.*—The transaction is an intercompany exchange to which section 361(a), sections 332 and 337(a), or (except as provided in the following sentence) section 351 applies in which no amount of income, gain, deduction or loss is recognized by the creditor or debtor. The assignment of an intercompany obligation by a creditor member in an intercompany exchange to which section 351 applies is a triggering transaction, notwithstanding the preceding sentence, if a member of the group is described in, or engages in a transaction that is described in, any of the following paragraphs.

*(i)* The transferor or transferee member has a loss subject to a limitation (for example, a loss from a separate return limitation year that is subject to limitation under § 1.1502-21(c), or a dual consolidated loss that is subject to limitation under § 1.1503(d)-4), but only if the other member is not subject to a comparable limitation;

*(ii)* The transferor or transferee member has a special status within the meaning of § 1.1502-13(c)(5) (for example, a bank defined in section 581, or a life insurance company subject to tax under section 801) that the other member does not also possess;

*(iii)* A member of the group realizes discharge of indebtedness income that is excluded from gross income under section 108(a) within the same taxable year as that of the exchange, and the tax attributes attributable to either the transferor or the transferee member are reduced under sections 108, 1017, and § 1.1502-28 (except if the attribute reduction results solely from the application of § 1.1502-28(a)(4) (reduction of certain tax attributes attributable to other members));

*(iv)* The transferee member has a nonmember shareholder;

*(v)* The transferee member issues preferred stock to the transferor member in exchange for the assignment of the intercompany obligation; or

*(vi)* The stock of the transferee member (or a higher-tier member other than a higher-tier member of an 80-percent chain that includes the transferor and transferee) is disposed of within 12 months from the assignment of the intercompany obligation, unless at the time of the assignment, the transferor member, transferee member (or in the case of successive section 351 exchanges, each transferor and transferee member) and the debtor member are all in the same 80-percent chain; and all of the stock of the transferee (or in the case of successive section 351 exchanges, the lowest-tier transferee) held by members of the group is disposed of as part of the same plan or arrangement, either directly or indirectly, to persons that are not members of the group.

*(2) Intercompany assumption transaction.*—All of the debtor's obligations under an intercompany obligation are assumed in connection with the debtor's sale or other disposition of property (other than solely money) in an intercompany transaction in which gain or loss is recognized under section 1001.

*(3) Exception to the application of section 108(e)(4).*—The obligation became an intercompany obligation by reason of an event described in § 1.108-2(e)(2) (exception to the application of section 108(e)(4) in the case of acquisitions by securities dealers).

*(4) Reserve accounting.*—The amount realized is from reserve accounting under section 585 (see paragraph (g)(4)(v) of this section for special rules).

*(5) Intercompany extinguishment transaction.*—All or part of the rights and obligations under the intercompany obligation are extinguished in an intercompany transaction (other than an exchange or deemed exchange of an intercompany obligation for a newly issued intercompany obligation), the adjusted issue price of the obligation is equal to the creditor's basis in the obligation, and the debtor's corresponding item and the creditor's intercompany item (after taking into account the special rules of paragraph (g)(4)(i)(C) of this section) with respect to the obligation offset in amount.

*(6) Routine modification of intercompany obligation.*—All of the rights and obligations under the intercompany obligation are extinguished in an intercompany transaction that is an exchange (or deemed exchange) for a newly issued intercompany obligation, and the issue price of the newly issued obligation equals both the adjusted issue price of the extinguished obligation and the creditor's basis in the extinguished obligation. Solely for purposes of the preceding sentence, a newly issued intercompany obligation includes an obligation that is issued (or deemed issued) by a member other than the original debtor if such other member assumes the original debtor's obligations under the original obligation in a transaction that is described in either paragraph (g)(3)(i)(B)(1) or (g)(3)(i)(B)(2) of this section and the assumption results in a significant modification of the original obligation under § 1.1001-3(e)(4) and a deemed exchange under § 1.1001-3(b).

*(7) Outbound distribution of newly issued intercompany obligation.*—The intercompany obligation becomes an obligation that is not an intercompany obligation in a transaction in which a member that is a party to the reorganization exchanges property in pursuance of the plan of reorganization for a newly issued intercompany obligation of another member that is a party to the reorganization and distributes such intercompany obligation to a nonmember shareholder or nonmember creditor in a transaction to which section 361(c) applies.

*(8) Outbound subgroup exception.*—The intercompany obligation becomes an obligation that is not an intercompany obligation in a transaction in which the members of an intercompany obligation subgroup cease to be members of a consolidated group, neither the creditor nor the debtor recognize any income, gain, deduction, or loss with respect to the intercompany obligation, and such members constitute an intercompany obligation subgroup of another consolidated group immediately after the transaction.

(C) *Tax benefit rule.*—If an assignment or extinguishment of an intercompany obligation in an intercompany transaction is otherwise excepted from the definition of triggering transaction under paragraph (g)(3)(i)(B)(1), (2), (5), or (6) of this section (and not also under paragraph (g)(3)(i)(B)(3) or (4) of this section), and the assignment or extinguishment is engaged in with a view to shift items of built-in gain, loss, income, or deduction from the obligation from one member to another member in order to secure a tax benefit (as defined in paragraph (g)(2)(v) of this section) that the group or its members would not otherwise enjoy in a consolidated or separate return year, then the assignment or extinguishment will be a triggering transaction to which paragraph (g)(3)(ii) of this section applies.

(ii) *Application of deemed satisfaction and reissuance.*—This paragraph (g)(3)(ii) applies if a triggering transaction occurs.

(A) *General rule.*—If the intercompany obligation is debt of a member, then (except as provided in the following sentence) the debt is treated for all Federal income tax purposes as having been satisfied by the debtor for cash in an amount equal to its fair market value, and then as having been reissued as a new obligation (with a new holding period but otherwise identical terms) for the same amount of cash, immediately before the triggering transaction. However, if the creditor realizes an amount with respect to the debt in the triggering transaction that differs from the debt's fair market value, and the triggering transaction is not an exchange (or deemed exchange) of debt of a member for newly issued debt of a member, then the debt is treated for all Federal income tax purposes as having been satisfied by the debtor for cash in an amount equal to such amount realized, and reissued as a new obligation (with a new holding period but otherwise identical terms) for the same amount of cash, immediately before the triggering transaction. If the triggering transaction is a mark to fair market value under section 475, then the intercompany obligation will be deemed satisfied and reissued for its fair market value (as determined under section 475 and applicable regulations) and section 475 will not otherwise apply with respect to that triggering transaction. If the intercompany obligation is a security of a member, similar principles apply (with appropriate adjustments) to treat the security as having been satisfied and reissued immediately before the triggering transaction.

(B) *Treatment as separate transaction.*—The deemed satisfaction and deemed reissuance are treated as transactions separate and apart from the triggering transaction. The deemed satisfaction and reissuance of a member's debt will not cause the debt to be recharacterized as other than debt for Federal income tax purposes.

(4) *Special rules.*—(i) *Timing and attributes.*—For purposes of applying the matching rule and the acceleration rule to a transaction involving an intercompany obligation (other than a transaction to which paragraph (g)(5) of this section applies)—

(A) Paragraph (c)(6)(i) of this section (treatment of intercompany items if corresponding items are excluded or nondeductible) will not apply to exclude any amount of income or gain attributable to a reduction of the basis of the intercompany obligation pursuant to §1.1502-36(d), or pursuant to sections 108 and 1017 and §1.1502-28 or any other provision that adjusts the basis of an intercompany obligation as a substitute for income or gain;

(B) Paragraph (c)(6)(ii) of this section (limitation on treatment of intercompany income or gain as excluded from gross income) does not apply to prevent any intercompany income or gain from the intercompany obligation from being excluded from gross income;

(C) Any income, gain, deduction, or loss from the intercompany obligation is not subject to section 108(a), section 354, section 355(a)(1), section 1091, or, in the case of an extinguishment of an intercompany obligation in a transaction in which the creditor transfers the obligation to the debtor in exchange for stock in such debtor, section 351(a); and

(D) Section 108(e)(7) does not apply upon the extinguishment of an intercompany obligation.

(ii) *Newly issued obligation in intercompany exchange.*—If an intercompany obligation is exchanged (or is deemed exchanged) for a newly issued intercompany obligation and the exchange (or deemed exchange) is not a routine modification of an intercompany obligation (as described in paragraph (g)(3)(i)(B)(*6*) of this section), then the newly issued obligation will be treated for all Federal income tax purposes as having an issue price equal to its fair market value.

(iii) *Off-market issuance.*—If an intercompany obligation is issued at a rate of interest that is materially off-market (off-market obligation) with a view to shift items of built-in gain, loss, income, or deduction from the obligation from one member to another member in order to secure a tax benefit (as defined in paragraph (g)(2)(v) of this section), then the intercompany obligation will be treated, for all Federal income tax purposes, as originally issued for its fair market value, and any difference between the amount loaned and the fair market value of the obligation will be treated as transferred between the creditor and the debtor at the time the obligation is issued. For example, if S lends $100 to B in return for an off-market B note valued at $130, and the note is issued with a view to shift items from the note to secure a tax benefit, then the B note will be treated as issued for $130. The $30 difference will be treated as a distribution or capital contribution between S and B (as appropriate) at the time of issuance, and this amount will be reflected in future payments on the note as bond issuance premium. An adjustment to an off-market obligation under this paragraph (g)(4)(iii) will be made without regard to the application of, and in lieu of any adjustment under, section 467 (certain payments for the use of property or services), 482 (allocations among commonly controlled taxpayers), 483 (interest on certain deferred payments), 1274 (determination of issue price for certain debt instruments issued for property), or 7872 (treatment of loans with below-market interest rates).

(iv) *Deferral of loss or deduction with respect to nonmember indebtedness acquired in certain debt exchanges.*—If a creditor transfers an intercompany obligation to a nonmember (former intercompany obligation) in exchange for newly issued debt of a nonmember (nonmember debt), and the issue price of the nonmember debt is not determined by reference to its fair market value (for example, the issue price is determined under section 1273(b)(4) or 1274(a) or any other provision of applicable law), then any loss of the creditor otherwise allowable on the subsequent disposition of the nonmember debt, or any comparable tax benefit that would otherwise be available in any other transaction that directly or indirectly results from the disposition of the nonmember debt, is deferred until the date the debtor retires the former intercompany obligation.

(v) *Bad debt reserve.*—A member's deduction under section 585 for an addition to its reserve for bad debts with respect to an intercompany obligation is not taken into account, and is not treated as realized for purposes of paragraph (g)(3)(i)(A)(*1*) of this section, until the intercompany obligation is extinguished or becomes an obligation that is not an intercompany obligation.

(5) *Deemed satisfaction and reissuance of obligations becoming intercompany obligations.*—(i) *Application of deemed satisfaction and reissuance.*—This paragraph (g)(5) applies if an obligation that is not an intercompany obligation becomes an intercompany obligation.

(B) *Exceptions.*—This paragraph (g)(5) does not apply to an intercompany obligation if either of the following exceptions apply.

(*1*) *Exception to the application of section 108(e)(4).*—The obligation becomes an intercompany obligation by reason of an event

described in §1.108-2(e)(2) (exception to the application of section 108(e)(4) in the case of acquisitions by securities dealers); or

(*2*) *Inbound subgroup exception.*—The obligation becomes an intercompany obligation in a transaction in which the members of an intercompany obligation subgroup cease to be members of a consolidated group, neither the creditor nor the debtor recognize any income, gain, deduction, or loss with respect to the intercompany obligation, and such members constitute an intercompany obligation subgroup of another consolidated group immediately after the transaction.

(ii) *Deemed satisfaction and reissuance.*—(A) *General rule.*—If the intercompany obligation is debt of a member, then the debt is treated for all Federal income tax purposes, immediately after it becomes an intercompany obligation, as having been satisfied by the debtor for cash in an amount determined under the principles of §1.108-2(f), and then as having been reissued as a new obligation (with a new holding period but otherwise identical terms) for the same amount of cash. If the intercompany obligation is a security of a member, similar principles apply (with appropriate adjustments) to treat the security, immediately after it becomes an intercompany obligation, as satisfied and reissued by the debtor for cash in an amount equal to its fair market value.

(B) *Treatment as separate transaction.*—The deemed satisfaction and deemed reissuance are treated as transactions separate and apart from the transaction in which the debt becomes an intercompany obligation, and the tax consequences of the transaction in which the debt becomes an intercompany obligation must be determined before the deemed satisfaction and reissuance occurs. (For example, if the debt becomes an intercompany obligation in a transaction to which section 351 applies, any limitation imposed by section 362(e) on the basis of the intercompany obligation in the hands of the transferee member is determined before the deemed satisfaction and reissuance.) The deemed satisfaction and reissuance of a member's debt will not cause the debt to be recharacterized as other than debt for Federal income tax purposes.

(6) *Special rules.*—(i) *Timing and attributes.*—If paragraph (g)(5) of this section applies to an intercompany obligation—

(A) Section 108(e)(4) does not apply;

(B) The attributes of all items taken into account from the satisfaction of the intercompany obligation are determined on a separate entity basis, rather than by treating S and B as divisions of a single corporation; and

(C) Any intercompany gain or loss realized by the creditor is not subject to section 354 or section 1091.

(ii) *Waiver of loss carryovers from separate return limitation years.*—Solely for purposes of §1.1502-32(b)(4) and the effect of any election under that provision, any loss taken into account under paragraph (g)(5) of this section by a corporation that becomes a member as a result of the transaction in which the obligation becomes an intercompany obligation is treated as a loss carryover from a separate return limitation year.

(iii) *Deduction of repurchase premium in certain debt exchanges.*—If an obligation to which paragraph (g)(5) of this section applies is acquired in exchange for the issuance of an obligation to a nonmember and the issue price of this newly issued obligation is not determined by reference to its fair market value (for example, the issue price is determined under section 1273(b)(4) or 1274(a) or any other provision of applicable law), then, under the principles of §1.163-7(c), any repurchase premium from the deemed satisfaction of the intercompany obligation under paragraph (g)(5)(ii) of this section will be amortized by the debtor over the term of the obligation issued to the nonmember in the same manner as if it were original issue discount and the obligation to the nonmember had been issued directly by the debtor.

(7) *Examples.*—(i) *In general.*—For purposes of the examples in this paragraph (g), unless otherwise stated, interest is qualified stated interest under §1.1273-1(c), and the intercompany obligations are capital assets and are not subject to section 475.

(ii) The application of this section to obligations of members is illustrated by the following examples:

*Example 1. Interest on intercompany obligation.* (i) *Facts.* On January 1 of year 1, B borrows $100 from S in return for B's note providing for $10 of interest annually at the end of each year, and repayment of $100 at the end of year 5. B fully performs its obligations. Under their separate entity methods of accounting, B accrues a $10 interest deduction annually under section 163, and S accrues $10 of interest income annually under section 61(a)(4) and §1.446-2.

(ii) *Matching rule.* Under paragraph (b)(1) of this section, the accrual of interest on B's note is an intercompany transaction. Under the matching rule, S takes its $10 of income into account in each of years 1 through 5 to reflect the $10 difference between B's $10 of interest expense taken into account and the $0 recomputed expense. S's income and B's deduction are ordinary items. (Because S's intercompany item and B's corresponding item would both be ordinary on a separate entity basis, the attributes are not redetermined under paragraph (c)(1)(i) of this section.)

(iii) *Original issue discount*. The facts are the same as in paragraph (i) of this *Example 1*, except that B borrows $90 (rather than $100) from S in return for B's note providing for $10 of interest annually and repayment of $100 at the end of year 5. The principles described in paragraph (ii) of this *Example 1* for stated interest also apply to the $10 of original issue discount. Thus, as B takes into account its corresponding expense under section 163(e), S takes into account its intercompany income under section 1272. S's income and B's deduction are ordinary items.

(iv) *Tax-exempt income*. The facts are the same as in paragraph (i) of this *Example 1*, except that B's borrowing from S is allocable under section 265 to B's purchase of state and local bonds to which section 103 applies. The timing of S's income is the same as in paragraph (ii) of this *Example 1*. Under paragraph (c)(4)(i) of this section, the attributes of B's corresponding item of disallowed interest expense control the attributes of S's offsetting intercompany interest income. Paragraph (c)(6) of this section does not prevent the redetermination of S's intercompany item as excluded from gross income because section 265(a)(2) permanently and explicitly disallows B's corresponding deduction and because, under paragraph (g)(4)(i)(B) of this section, paragraph (c)(6)(ii) of this section does not apply to prevent any intercompany income from the B note from being excluded from gross income. Accordingly, S's intercompany income is treated as excluded from gross income.

*Example 2. Intercompany obligation becomes nonintercompany obligation.* (i) *Facts.* On January 1 of year 1, B borrows $100 from S in return for B's note providing for $10 of interest annually at the end of each year, and repayment of $100 at the end of year 5. As of January 1 of year 3, B has paid the interest accruing under the note and S sells B's note to X for $70, reflecting an increase in prevailing market interest rates. B is never insolvent within the meaning of section 108(d)(3).

(ii) *Deemed satisfaction and reissuance*. Because the B note becomes an obligation that is not an intercompany obligation, the transaction is a triggering transaction under paragraph (g)(3)(i)(A)(2) of this section. Under paragraph (g)(3)(ii) of this section, B's note is treated as satisfied and reissued for its fair market value of $70 immediately before S's sale to X. As a result of the deemed satisfaction of the note for less than its adjusted issue price, B takes into account $30 of discharge of indebtedness income under §1.61-12. On a separate entity basis, S's $30 loss would be a capital loss under section 1271(a)(1). Under the matching rule, however, the attributes of S's intercompany item and B's corresponding item must be redetermined to produce the same effect as if the transaction had occurred between divisions of a single corporation. Under paragraph (c)(4)(i) of this section, the attributes of B's $30 of discharge of indebtedness income control the attributes of S's loss. Thus, S's loss is treated as ordinary loss. B is also treated as reissuing, immediately after the satisfaction, a new note to S with a $70 issue price, a $100 stated redemption price at maturity, and a $70 basis in the hands of S. S is then treated as selling the new note to X for the $70 received by S in the actual transaction. Because S has a basis of $70 in the new note, S recognizes no gain or loss from the sale to X. After the sale, the new note held by X is not an intercompany obligation, it has a $70 issue price, a $100 stated redemption price at maturity, and a $70 basis. The $30 of original issue discount will be taken into account by B and X under sections 163(e) and 1272.

(iii) *Creditor deconsolidation*. The facts are the same as in paragraph (i) of this *Example 2*, except that P sells S's stock to X (rather than S selling B's note to X). Because the B note becomes an obligation that is not an intercompany obligation, the transaction is a triggering transaction under paragraph (g)(3)(i)(A)(2) of this section. Under paragraph (g)(3)(ii) of this section, B's note is treated as satisfied and reissued for its $70 fair market value immediately before S becomes a nonmember. The treatment of S's $30 of loss and B's $30 of discharge of indebtedness income is the same as in paragraph (ii) of this *Example 2*. The new note held by S upon deconsolidation is not an intercompany obligation, it has a $70 issue price, a $100 stated redemption price at maturity, and a $70 basis. The $30 of original issue discount will be taken into account by B and S under sections 163(e) and 1272.

(iv) *Debtor deconsolidation*. The facts are the same as in paragraph (i) of this *Example 2*, except that P sells B's stock to X (rather than S selling B's note to X). The results to S and B are the same as in paragraph (iii) of this *Example 2*.

(v) *Subgroup exception*. The facts are the same as in paragraph (i) of this *Example 2*, except that P owns all of the stock of S, S owns all of the stock of B, and P sells all of the S stock to X, the parent of another consolidated group. Because B and S, members of an intercompany obligation subgroup, cease to be members of the P group in a transaction that does not cause either member to recognize an item with respect to the B note, and such members constitute an intercompany obligation subgroup in the X group, P's sale of S stock is not a triggering transaction under paragraph (g)(3)(i)(B)(8) of this section, and the note is not treated as satisfied and reissued under paragraph (g)(3)(ii) of this section. After the sale, the note held by S has a $100 issue price, a $100 stated redemption price at maturity, and a $100 basis. The results are the same if the S stock is sold to an individual and the S-B affiliated group elects to file a consolidated return for the period beginning on the day after S and B cease to be members of the P group.

(vi) *Section 338 election*. The facts are the same as paragraph (i) of this *Example 2*, except that P sells S's stock to X and a section 338 election is made with respect to the stock sale. Under section 338, S is treated as selling all of its assets to new S, including the B note, at the close of the acquisition date. The aggregate deemed sales price (within the meaning of §1.338-4) allocated to the B note is $70. Because the B note becomes an obligation that is not an intercompany obligation, the transaction is a triggering transaction under paragraph (g)(3)(i)(A)(2) of this section. Under paragraph (g)(3)(ii) of this section, B's note is treated as satisfied and reissued immediately before S's deemed sale to new S for $70, the amount realized with respect to the note (the aggregate deemed sales price allocated to the note under §1.338-6). The results to S and B are the same as in paragraph (ii) of this *Example 2*.

(vii) *Appreciated note*. The facts are the same as in paragraph (i) of this *Example 2*, except that S sells B's note to X for $130 (rather than $70), reflecting a decline in prevailing market interest rates. Because the B note becomes an obligation that is not an intercompany obligation, the transaction is a triggering transaction under paragraph (g)(3)(i)(A)(2) of this section. Under paragraph (g)(3)(ii) of this section, B's note is treated as satisfied and reissued for its fair market value of $130 immediately before S's sale to X. As a result of the deemed satisfaction of the note for more than its adjusted issue price, B takes into account $30 of repurchase premium under §1.163-7(c). On a separate entity basis, S's $30 gain would be a capital gain under section 1271(a)(1). Under the matching rule, however, the attributes of S's intercompany item and B's corresponding item must be redetermined to produce the same effect as if the transaction had occurred between divisions of a single corporation. Under paragraph (c)(4)(i) of this section, the attributes of B's premium deduction control the attributes of S's gain. Accordingly, S's gain is treated as ordinary income. B is also treated as reissuing, immediately after the satisfaction, a new note to S with a $130 issue price, $100 stated redemption price at maturity, and $130 basis in the hands of S. S is then treated as selling the new note to X for the $130 received by S in the actual transaction. Because S has a basis of $130 in the new note, S recognizes no gain or loss from the sale to X. After the sale, the new note held by X is not an intercompany obligation, it has a $130 issue price, a $100 stated redemption price at maturity, and a $130 basis. The treatment of B's $30 of bond issuance premium under the new note is determined under §1.163-13.

(viii) *Deferral of loss or deduction with respect to nonmember indebtedness acquired in debt exchange*. The facts are the same as in paragraph (i) of this *Example 2*, except that S sells B's note to X for a non-publicly traded X note with an issue price and face amount of $100 and a fair market value of $70, and that, subsequently, S sells the X note for $70. Because the B note becomes an obligation that is not an intercompany obligation, the transaction is a triggering transaction under paragraph (g)(3)(i)(A)(2) of this section. Under paragraph (g)(3)(ii) of this section, B's note is treated as satisfied and reissued immediately before S's sale to X for $100, the amount realized with respect to the note (determined under section 1274). As a result of the deemed satisfaction, neither S nor B take into account any items of income, gain, deduction, or loss. S is then treated as selling the new B note to X for the X note received by S in the actual transaction. Because S has a basis of $100 in the new note, S recognizes no gain or loss from the sale to X. After the sale, the new B note held by X is not an intercompany obligation, it has a $100 issue price, a $100 stated redemption price at maturity, and a $100 basis. S also holds an X note with a basis of $100 but a fair market value of $70. When S disposes of the X note, S's loss on the disposition is deferred under paragraph (g)(4)(iv) of this section, until B retires its note (the former intercompany obligation in the hands of X).

*Example 3. Loss or bad debt deduction with respect to intercompany obligation*. (i) *Facts*. On January 1 of year 1, B borrows $100 from S in return for B's note providing for $10 of interest annually at the end of each year, and repayment of $100 at the end of year 5. On January 1 of year 3, the fair market value of the B note has declined to $60 and S sells the B note to P for property with a fair market value of $60. B is never insolvent within the meaning of section 108(d)(3). The B note is not a security within the meaning of section 165(g)(2).

(ii) *Deemed satisfaction and reissuance.* Because S realizes an amount of loss from the assignment of the B note, the transaction is a triggering transaction under paragraph (g)(3)(i)(A)(1) of this section. Under paragraph (g)(3)(ii) of this section, B's note is treated as satisfied and reissued for its fair market value of $60 immediately before S's sale to P. As a result of the deemed satisfaction of the note for less than its adjusted issue price ($100), B takes into account $40 of discharge of indebtedness income under §1.61-12. On a separate entity basis, S's $40 loss would be a capital loss under section 1271(a)(1). Under the matching rule, however, the attributes of S's intercompany item and B's corresponding item must be redetermined to produce the same effect as if the transaction had occurred between divisions of a single corporation. Under paragraph (c)(4)(i) of this section, the attributes of B's $40 of discharge of indebtedness income control the attributes of S's loss. Thus, S's loss is treated as ordinary loss. B is also treated as reissuing, immediately after the satisfaction, a new note to S with a $60 issue price, $100 stated redemption price at maturity, and $60 basis in the hands of S. S is then treated as selling the new note to P for the $60 of property received by S in the actual transaction. Because S has a basis of $60 in the new note, S recognizes no gain or loss from the sale to P. After the sale, the note is an intercompany obligation, it has a $60 issue price and a $100 stated redemption price at maturity, and the $40 of original issue discount will be taken into account by B and P under sections 163(e) and 1272.

(iii) *Partial bad debt deduction.* The facts are the same as in paragraph (i) of this *Example 3,* except that S claims a $40 partial bad debt deduction under section 166(a)(2) (rather than selling the note to P). Because S realizes a deduction from a transaction comparable to an assignment of the B note, the transaction is a triggering transaction under paragraph (g)(3)(i)(A)(1) of this section. Under paragraph (g)(3)(ii) of this section, B's note is treated as satisfied and reissued for its fair market value of $60 immediately before section 166(a)(2) applies. The treatment of S's $40 loss and B's $40 of discharge of indebtedness income are the same as in paragraph (ii) of this *Example 3.* After the reissuance, S has a basis of $60 in the new note. Accordingly, the application of section 166(a)(2) does not result in any additional deduction for S. The $40 of original issue discount on the new note will be taken into account by B and S under sections 163(e) and 1272.

(iv) *Insolvent debtor.* The facts are the same as in paragraph (i) of this *Example 3,* except that B is insolvent within the meaning of section 108(d)(3) at the time that S sells the note to P. As explained in paragraph (ii) of this *Example 3,* the transaction is a triggering transaction and the B note is treated as satisfied and reissued for its fair market value of $60 immediately before S's sale to P. On a separate entity basis, S's $40 loss would be capital, B's $40 income would be excluded from gross income under section 108(a), and B would reduce attributes under section 108(b) or section 1017 (see also §1.1502-28). However, under paragraph (g)(4)(i)(C) of this section, section 108(a) does not apply to characterize B's income as excluded from gross income. Accordingly, the attributes of S's loss and B's income are redetermined in the same manner as in paragraph (ii) of this *Example 3.*

*Example 4. Intercompany nonrecognition transactions.* (i) *Facts.* On January 1 of year 1, B borrows $100 from S in return for B's note providing for $10 of interest annually at the end of each year, and repayment of $100 at the end of year 5. As of January 1 of year 3, B has fully performed its obligations, but the note's fair market value is $130, reflecting a decline in prevailing market interest rates. On January 1 of year 3, S transfers the note and other assets to a newly formed corporation, Newco, for all of Newco's common stock in an exchange to which section 351 applies.

(ii) *No deemed satisfaction and reissuance.* Because the assignment of the B note is an exchange to which section 351 applies and neither S nor B recognize gain or loss, the transaction is not a triggering transaction under paragraph (g)(3)(i)(B)(1) of this section, and the note is not treated as satisfied and reissued under paragraph (g)(3)(ii) of this section.

(iii) *Receipt of other property.* The facts are the same as in paragraph (i) of this *Example 4,* except that the other assets transferred to Newco have a basis of $100 and a fair market value of $260, and S receives, in addition to Newco common stock, $15 of cash. Because S would recognize $15 of gain under section 351(b), the assignment of the B note is a triggering transaction under paragraph (g)(3)(i)(A)(1) of this section. Under paragraph (g)(3)(ii) of this section, B's note is treated as satisfied and reissued for its fair market value of $130 immediately before the transfer to Newco. As a result of the deemed satisfaction of the note for more than its adjusted issue price, B takes into account $30 of repurchase premium under §1.163-7(c). On a separate entity basis, S's $30 gain would be a capital gain under section 1271(a)(1). Under the matching rule, however, the attributes of S's intercompany item and B's corresponding item must be redetermined to produce the same effect as if the transaction had occurred between divisions of a single corporation. Under paragraph

(c)(4)(i) of this section, the attributes of B's premium deduction control the attributes of S's gain. Accordingly, S's gain is treated as ordinary income. B is also treated as reissuing, immediately after the satisfaction, a new note to S with a $130 issue price, $100 stated redemption price at maturity, and $130 basis in the hands of S. S is then treated as transferring the new note to Newco for the Newco stock and cash received by S in the actual transaction. Because S has a basis of $130 in the new B note, S recognizes no gain or loss with respect to the transfer of the note in the section 351 exchange, and S recognizes $10 of gain with respect to the transfer of the other assets under section 351(b). After the transfer, the note has a $130 issue price and a $100 stated redemption price at maturity. The treatment of B's $30 of bond issuance premium under the new note is determined under §1.163-13.

(iv) *Transferee loss subject to limitation.* The facts are the same as in paragraph (i) of this *Example 4,* except that T is a member with a loss from a separate return limitation year that is subject to limitation under §1.1502-21(c) (a SRLY loss), and on January 1 of year 3, S transfers the assets and the B note to T in an exchange to which section 351 applies. Because the transferee, T, has a loss that is subject to a limitation, the assignment of the B note is a triggering transaction under paragraph (g)(3)(i)(A)(1) of this section (the exception in paragraph (g)(3)(i)(B)(1) of this section does not apply). Under paragraph (g)(3)(ii) of this section, B's note is treated as satisfied and reissued for its fair market value, immediately before S's transfer to T. As a result of the deemed satisfaction of the note for more than its adjusted issue price, B takes into account $30 of repurchase premium under §1.163-7(c). On a separate entity basis, S's $30 gain would be a capital gain under section 1271(a)(1). Under the matching rule, however, the attributes of S's intercompany item and B's corresponding item must be redetermined to produce the same effect as if the transaction had occurred between divisions of a single corporation. Under paragraph (c)(4)(i) of this section, the attributes of B's premium deduction control the attributes of S's gain. Accordingly, S's gain is treated as ordinary income. B is also treated as reissuing, immediately after the satisfaction, a new note to S with a $130 issue price, $100 stated redemption price at maturity, and $130 basis in the hands of S. The treatment of B's $30 of bond issuance premium under the new note is determined under §1.163-13. S is then treated as transferring the new note to T as part of the section 351 exchange. Because T will have a fair market value basis in the reissued B note immediately after the exchange, T's intercompany item from the subsequent retirement of the B note will not reflect any of S's built-in gain (and the amount of T's SRLY loss that may be absorbed by such item will be limited to any appreciation in the B note accruing after the exchange).

(v) *Intercompany obligation transferred in section 332 transaction.* The facts are the same as in paragraph (i) of this *Example 4,* except that S transfers the B note to P in complete liquidation under section 332. Because the transaction is an exchange to which section 332 and section 337(a) applies, and neither S nor B recognize gain or loss, the transaction is not a triggering transaction under paragraph (g)(3)(i)(B)(1) of this section, and the note is not treated as satisfied and reissued under paragraph (g)(3)(ii) of this section.

*Example 5. Assumption of intercompany obligation.* (i) *Facts.* On January 1 of year 1, B borrows $100 from S in return for B's note providing for $10 of interest annually at the end of each year, and repayment of $100 at the end of year 5. The note is fully recourse and is incurred for use in Business Z. As of January 1 of year 3, B has fully performed its obligations, but the note's fair market value is $110 reflecting a decline in prevailing market interest rates. Business Z has a fair market value of $95. On January 1 of year 3, B transfers all of the assets of Business Z and $15 of cash (substantially all of B's assets) to member T in exchange for the assumption by T of all of B's obligations under the note in a transaction in which gain or loss is recognized under section 1001. The terms and conditions of the note are not modified in connection with the sales transaction, the transaction does not result in a change in payment expectations, and no amount of income, gain, deduction, or loss is recognized by S, B, or T with respect to the note.

(ii) *No deemed satisfaction and reissuance.* Because all of B's obligations under the B note are assumed by T in connection with the sale of the Business Z assets, the assignment of B's obligations under the note is not a triggering transaction under paragraph (g)(3)(i)(B)(2) of this section, and the note is not treated as satisfied and reissued under paragraph (g)(3)(ii) of this section.

*Example 6. Extinguishment of intercompany obligation.* (i) *Facts.* On January 1 of year 1, B borrows $100 from S in return for B's note providing for $10 of interest annually at the end of each year, and repayment of $100 at the end of year 20. The note is a security within the meaning of section 351(d)(2). As of January 1 of year 3, B has fully performed its obligations, but the fair market value of the B note is $130, reflecting a decline in prevailing market interest rates, and S transfers the note to B in exchange for $130 of B stock in a transaction to which both section 351 and section 354 applies.

(ii) *No deemed satisfaction and reissuance.* As a result of the satisfaction of the note for more than its adjusted issue price, B takes into account $30 of repurchase premium under § 1.163-7(c). Although the transfer of the B note is a transaction to which both section 351 and section 354 applies, under paragraph (g)(4)(i)(C) of this section, any gain or loss from the intercompany obligation is not subject to either section 351(a) or section 354, and therefore, S has a $30 gain under section 1001. Because the note is extinguished in a transaction in which the adjusted issue price of the note is equal to the creditor's basis in the note, and the debtor's and creditor's items offset in amount, the transaction is not a triggering transaction under paragraph (g)(3)(i)(B)(5) of this section, and the note is not treated as satisfied and reissued under paragraph (g)(3)(ii) of this section. On a separate entity basis, S's $30 gain would be a capital gain under section 1271(a)(1). Under the matching rule, however, the attributes of S's intercompany item and B's corresponding item must be redetermined to produce the same effect as if the transaction had occurred between divisions of a single corporation. Under paragraph (c)(4)(i) of this section, the attributes of B's premium deduction control the attributes of S's gain. Accordingly, S's gain is treated as ordinary income. Under paragraph (g)(4)(i)(D) of this section, section 108(e)(7) does not apply upon the extinguishment of the B note, and therefore, the B stock received by S in the exchange will not be treated as section 1245 property.

*Example 7. Exchange of intercompany obligations.* (i) *Facts.* On January 1 of year 1, B borrows $100 from S in return for B's note providing for $10 of interest annually at the end of each year, and repayment of $100 at the end of year 20. As of January 1 of year 3, B has fully performed its obligations and, pursuant to a recapitalization to which section 368(a)(1)(E) applies, B issues a new note to S in exchange for the original B note. The new B note has an issue price, stated redemption price at maturity, and stated principal amount of $100, but contains terms that differ sufficiently from the terms of the original B note to cause a realization event under § 1.1001-3. The original B note and the new B note are both securities (within the meaning of section 354(a)(1)).

(ii) *No deemed satisfaction and reissuance.* Because the original B note is extinguished in exchange for a newly issued B note and the issue price of the new B note is equal to both the adjusted issue price of the original B note and S's basis in the original B note, the transaction is not a triggering transaction under paragraph (g)(3)(i)(B)(6) of this section, and the note is not treated as satisfied and reissued under paragraph (g)(3)(ii) of this section. B has neither income from discharge of indebtedness under section 108(e)(10) nor a deduction for repurchase premium under § 1.163-7(c). Although the exchange of the original B note for the new B note is a transaction to which section 354 applies, under paragraph (g)(4)(i)(C) of this section, any gain or loss from the intercompany obligation is not subject to section 354. Under section 1001, S has no gain or loss from the exchange of notes.

*Example 8. Tax benefit rule.* (i) *Facts.* On January 1 of year 1, B borrows $100 from S in return for B's note providing for $10 of interest annually at the end of each year, and repayment of $100 at the end of year 5. As of January 1 of year 3, B has fully performed its obligations, but the note's fair market value has depreciated, reflecting an increase in prevailing market interest rates. On that date, S transfers the B note to member T as part of an exchange for T common stock which is intended to qualify for nonrecognition treatment under section 351 but with a view to sell the T stock at a reduced gain. On February 1 of year 4, all of the stock of T is sold at a reduced gain.

(ii) *Deemed satisfaction and reissuance.* Because the assignment of the B note does not occur within 12 months of the sale of T stock, paragraph (g)(3)(i)(B)(1)(vi) of this section does not apply to treat the assignment as a triggering transaction. However, because the assignment of the B note was engaged in with a view to shift built-in loss from the obligation in order to secure a tax benefit that the group or its members would not otherwise enjoy, under paragraph (g)(3)(i)(C) of this section, the assignment of the B note is a triggering transaction to which paragraph (g)(3)(ii) of this section applies. Under paragraph (g)(3)(ii) of this section, B's note is treated as satisfied and reissued for its fair market value, immediately before S's transfer to T. As a result of the deemed satisfaction of the note for less than its adjusted issue price, B takes into account discharge of indebtedness income and S has a corresponding loss which is treated as ordinary loss. B is also treated as reissuing, immediately after the deemed satisfaction, a new note to S with an issue price and basis equal to its fair market value. S is then treated as transferring the new note to T as part of the section 351 exchange. Because S's basis in the T stock received with respect to the transferred B note is equal to its fair market value, S's gain with respect to the T stock will not reflect any of the built-in loss attributable to the B note. (This example does not address common law doctrines or other authorities that might apply to recharacterize the transaction or to otherwise affect the tax treatment of the transaction.)

*Example 9. Issuance at off-market rate of interest.* (i) *Facts.* T is a member with a SRLY loss. T's sole shareholder, P, borrows an amount of cash from T in return for a P note that provides for a materially above market rate of interest. The P note is issued with a view to generate additional interest income to T over the term of the note to facilitate the absorption of T's SRLY loss.

(ii) *With a view.* Because the P note is issued with a view to shift interest income from the off-market obligation in order to secure a tax benefit that the group or its members would not otherwise enjoy, under paragraph (g)(4)(iii) of this section, the intercompany obligation is treated, for all Federal income tax purposes, as originally issued for its fair market value so T is treated as purchasing the note at a premium. The difference between the amount loaned and the fair market value of the obligation is treated as transferred from P to T as a capital contribution at the time the note is issued. Throughout the term of the note, T takes into account interest income and bond premium and P takes into account interest deduction and bond issuance premium under generally applicable Internal Revenue Code sections. The adjustment under paragraph (g)(4)(iii) of this section is made without regard to the application of, and in lieu of any adjustment under, section 482 or 1274.

*Example 10. Nonintercompany obligation becomes intercompany obligation.* (i) *Facts.* On January 1 of year 1, B borrows $100 from X in return for B's note providing for $10 of interest annually at the end of each year, and repayment of $100 at the end of year 5. As of January 1 of year 3, B has fully performed its obligations, but the note's fair market value is $70, reflecting an increase in prevailing market interest rates. On January 1 of year 3, P buys all of X's stock. B is solvent within the meaning of section 108(d)(3).

(ii) *Deemed satisfaction and reissuance.* Under paragraph (g)(5)(ii) of this section, B's note is treated as satisfied for $70 (determined under the principles of § 1.108-2(f)(2)) immediately after it becomes an intercompany obligation. Both X's $30 capital loss (under section 1271(a)(1)) and B's $30 of discharge of indebtedness income (under § 1.61-12) are taken into account in determining consolidated taxable income for year 3. Under paragraph (g)(6)(i)(B) of this section, the attributes of items resulting from the satisfaction are determined on a separate entity basis. But see section 382 and § 1.1502-15 (as appropriate). B is also treated as reissuing a new note to X. The new note is an intercompany obligation, it has a $70 issue price and $100 stated redemption price at maturity, and the $30 of original issue discount will be taken into account by B and X in the same manner as provided in paragraph (iii) of *Example 1* of this paragraph (g)(7).

(iii) *Amortization of repurchase premium.* The facts are the same as in paragraph (i) of this *Example 10,* except that on January 1 of year 3, the B note has a fair market value of $130 and rather than P purchasing the X stock, P purchases the B note from X by issuing its own note. The P note has an issue price, stated redemption price at maturity, stated principal amount, and fair market value of $130. Under paragraph (g)(5)(ii) of this section, B's note is treated as satisfied for $130 (determined under the principles of § 1.108-2(f)(1)) immediately after it becomes an intercompany obligation. As a result of the deemed satisfaction of the note, P has no gain or loss and B has $30 of repurchase premium. Under paragraph (g)(6)(iii) of this section, B's $30 of repurchase premium from the deemed satisfaction is amortized by B over the term of the newly issued P note in the same manner as if it were original issue discount and the newly issued P note had been issued directly by B. B is also treated as reissuing a new note to P. The new note is an intercompany obligation, it has a $130 issue price and $100 stated redemption price at maturity, and the treatment of B's $30 of bond issuance premium under the new B note is determined under § 1.163-13.

(iv) *Election to file consolidated returns.* Assume instead that B borrows $100 from S during year 1, but the P group does not file consolidated returns until year 3. Under paragraph (g)(5)(ii) of this section, B's note is treated as satisfied and reissued as a new note immediately after the note becomes an intercompany obligation. The satisfaction and reissuance are deemed to occur on January 1 of year 3, for the fair market value of the obligation (determined under the principles of § 1.108-2(f)(2)) at that time.

*Example 11. Notional principal contracts.* (i) *Facts.* On April 1 of year 1, M1 enters into a contract with counterparty M2 under which, for a term of five years, M1 is obligated to make a payment to M2 each April 1, beginning in year 2, in an amount equal to the London Interbank Offered Rate (LIBOR), as determined by reference to LIBOR on the day each payment is due, multiplied by a $1,000 notional principal amount. M2 is obligated to make a payment to M1 each April 1, beginning in year 2, in an amount equal to 8 percent multiplied by the same notional principal amount. LIBOR is 7.80 percent on April 1 of year 2, and therefore, M2 owes $2 to M1.

(ii) *Matching rule.* Under § 1.446-3(d), the net income (or net deduction) from a notional principal contract for a taxable year is included in (or deducted from) gross income. Under § 1.446-3(e), the ratable daily portion of M2's obligation to M1 as of December 31 of year 1 is $1.50 ($2 multiplied by 275/365). Under the matching rule, M1's net income for year 1 of $1.50 is taken into account to reflect the difference between M2's net deduction of $1.50 taken into account and the $0 recomputed net deduction. Similarly, the $.50 balance of the $2 of net periodic payments made on April 1 of year 2 is taken into account for year 2 in M1's and M2's net income and net deduction from the contract. In addition, the attributes of M1's intercompany income and M2's corresponding deduction are redetermined to produce the same effect as if the transaction had occurred between divisions of a single corporation. Under paragraph (c)(4)(i) of this section, the attributes of M2's corresponding deduction control the attributes of M1's intercompany income. (Although M1 is the selling member with respect to the payment on April 1 of year 2, it might be the buying member in a subsequent period if it owes the net payment.)

(iii) *Dealer.* The facts are the same as in paragraph (i) of this *Example 11*, except that M2 is a dealer in securities, and the contract with M1 is not inventory in the hands of M2. Under section 475, M2 must mark its securities to fair market value at year-end. Assume that under section 475, M2's loss from marking to fair market value the contract with M1 is $10. Because M2 realizes an amount of loss from the mark to fair market value of the contract, the transaction is a triggering transaction under paragraph (g)(3)(i)(A)(*1*) of this section. Under paragraph (g)(3)(ii) of this section, M2 is treated as making a $10 payment to M1 to terminate the contract immediately before a new contract is treated as reissued with an up-front payment by M1 to M2 of $10. M1's $10 of income from the termination payment is taken into account under the matching rule to reflect M2's deduction under §1.446-3(h). The attributes of M1's intercompany income and M2's corresponding deduction are redetermined to produce the same effect as if the transaction had occurred between divisions of a single corporation. Under paragraph (c)(4)(i) of this section, the attributes of M2's corresponding deduction control the attributes of M1's intercompany income. Accordingly, M1's income is treated as ordinary income. Under §1.446-3(f), the deemed $10 up-front payment by M1 to M2 in connection with the issuance of a new contract is taken into account over the term of the new contract in a manner reflecting the economic substance of the contract (for example, allocating the payment in accordance with the forward rates of a series of cash-settled forward contracts that reflect the specified index and the $1,000 notional principal amount). (The timing of taking items into account is the same if M1, rather than M2, is the dealer subject to the mark-to-market requirement of section 475 at year-end. However in this case, because the attributes of the corresponding deduction control the attributes of the intercompany income, M1's income from the deemed termination payment from M2 might be ordinary or capital). Under paragraph (g)(3)(ii)(A) of this section, section 475 does not apply to mark the notional principal contract to fair market value after its deemed satisfaction and reissuance.

(8) *Effective/applicability date.*—The rules of this paragraph (g) apply to transactions involving intercompany obligations occurring in consolidated return years beginning on or after December 24, 2008.

(h) *Anti-avoidance rules.*—(1) *In general.*—If a transaction is engaged in or structured with a principal purpose to avoid the purposes of this section (including, for example, by avoiding treatment as an intercompany transaction), adjustments must be made to carry out the purposes of this section.

(2) *Examples.*—The anti-avoidance rules of this paragraph (h) are illustrated by the following examples. The examples set forth below do not address common law doctrines or other authorities that might apply to recast a transaction or to otherwise affect the tax treatment of a transaction. Thus, in addition to adjustments under this paragraph (h), the Commissioner can, for example, apply the rules of section 269 or §1.701-2 to disallow a deduction or to recast a transaction.

(i) *Example 1. Sale of a partnership interest.* (A) *Facts.* S owns land with a $10 basis and $100 value. B has net operating losses from separate return limitation years (SRLYs) subject to limitation under §1.1502-21(c). Pursuant to a plan to absorb the losses without limitation by the SRLY rules, S transfers the land to an unrelated, calendar-year partnership in exchange for a 10% interest in the capital and profits of the partnership in a transaction to which section 721 applies. The partnership does not have a section 754 election in effect. S later sells its partnership interest to B for $100. In the following year, the partnership sells the land to X for $100. Because the partnership does not have a section 754 election in effect, its $10 basis in the land does not reflect B's $100 basis in the partnership interest. Under section 704(c), the partnership's $90 built-in gain is allocated to B, and B's basis in the partnership interest increases to $190 under section 705. In a later year, B sells the partnership interest to a nonmember for $100.

(B) *Adjustments.* Under §1.1502-21(c), the partnership's $90 built-in gain allocated to B ordinarily increases the amount of B's SRLY limitation, and B's $90 loss from its sale of the partnership interest ordinarily is not subject to limitation under the SRLY rules. Because the contribution of property to the partnership and the sale of the partnership interest were part of a plan a principal purpose of which was to achieve a reduction in consolidated tax liability by creating offsetting gain and loss for B while deferring S's intercompany gain, B's allocable share of the partnership's gain from its sale of the land is treated under paragraph (h)(1) of this section as not increasing the amount of B's SRLY limitation.

(ii) *Example 2. Transitory status as an intercompany obligation.* (A) *Facts.* P historically has owned 70% of X's stock and the remaining 30% is owned by unrelated shareholders. On January 1 of Year 1, S borrows $100 from X in return for S's note requiring $10 of interest annually at the end of each year, and repayment of $100 at the end of Year 20. As of January 1 of Year 3, the P group has substantial net operating loss carryovers, and the fair market value of S's note falls to $70 due to an increase in prevailing market interest rates. X is not permitted under section 166(a)(2) to take into account a $30 loss with respect to the note. Pursuant to a plan to permit X to take into account its $30 loss without disposing of the note, P acquires an additional 10% of X's stock, causing X to become a member, and P subsequently resells the 10% interest. X's $30 loss with respect to the note is a net unrealized built-in loss within the meaning of §1.1502-15.

(B) *Adjustments.* Under paragraph (g)(4) of this section, X ordinarily would take into account its $30 loss as a result of the note becoming an intercompany obligation, and S would take into account $30 of discharge of indebtedness income. Under §1.1502-22, X's loss is not combined with items of the other members and the loss would be carried to X's separate return years as a result of X becoming a nonmember. However, the transitory status of S's indebtedness to X as an intercompany obligation is structured with a principal purpose to accelerate the recognition of X's loss. Thus, S's note is treated under paragraph (h)(1) of this section as not becoming an intercompany obligation.

(iii) *Example 3. Corporate mixing bowl.* (A) *Facts.* M1 and M2 are subsidiaries of P. M1 operates a manufacturing business on land it leases from M2. The land is the only asset held by M2. P intends to dispose of the M1 business, including the land owned by M2; P's basis in the M1 stock is equal to the stock's fair market value. M2's land has a value of $20 and a basis of $0 and P has a $0 basis in the stock of M2. In Year 1, with a principal purpose of avoiding gain from the sale of the land (by transferring the land to M1 with a carryover basis without affecting P's basis in the stock of M1 or M2), M1 and M2 form corporation T; M1 contributes cash in exchange for 80% of the T stock and M2 contributes the land in exchange for 20% of the stock. In Year 3, T liquidates, distributing $20 cash to M2 and the land (plus $60 cash) to M1. Under §1.1502-34, section 332 applies to both M1 and M2. Under section 337, T recognizes no gain or loss from its liquidating distribution of the land to M1. T has neither gain nor loss on its distribution of cash to M2. In Year 4, P sells all of the stock of M1 to X and liquidates M2.

(B) *Adjustments.* A principal purpose for the formation and liquidation of T was to avoid gain from the sale of M2's land. Thus, under paragraph (h)(1) of this section, M2 must take $20 of gain into account when the stock of M1 is sold to X.

(iv) *Example 4. Partnership mixing bowl.* (A) *Facts.* M1 owns a self-created intangible asset with a $0 basis and a fair market value of $100. M2 owns land with a basis of $100 and a fair market value of $100. In Year 1, with a principal purpose of creating basis in the intangible asset (which would be eligible for amortization under section 197), M1 and M2 form partnership PRS; M1 contributes the intangible asset and M2 contributes the land. X, an unrelated person, contributes cash to PRS in exchange for a substantial interest in the partnership. PRS uses the contributed assets in legitimate business activities. Five years and six months later, PRS liquidates, distributing the land to M1, the intangible to M2, and cash to X. The group reports no gain under sections 707(a)(2)(B) and 737(a) and claims that M2'S basis in the intangible asset is $100 under section 732 and that the asset is eligible for amortization under section 197.

(B) *Adjustments.* A principal purpose of the formation and liquidation of PRS was to create additional amortization without an offsetting increase in consolidated taxable income by avoiding treatment as an intercompany transaction. Thus, under paragraph (h)(1) of this section, appropriate adjustments must be made.

(v) *Example 5. Sale and leaseback.* (A) *Facts.* S operates a factory with a $70 basis and $100 value, and has loss carryovers from SRLYS. Pursuant to a plan to take into account the $30 unrealized gain while continuing to operate the factory, S sells the factory to X for $100 and leases it back on a long-term basis. In the transaction, a substantial interest in the factory is transferred to X. The sale and leaseback are not recharacterized under general principles of Federal income tax law. As a result of S's sale to X, the $30 gain is taken into account and increases S's SRLY limitation.

(B) *No adjustments.* Although S's sale was pursuant to a plan to accelerate the $30 gain, it is not subject to adjustment under paragraph (h)(1) of this section. The sale is not treated as engaged in or structured with a principal purpose to avoid the purposes of this section.

(vi) *Example 6: Section 163(j) interest limitation.* (A) *Facts.* S1 and S2 are members of a consolidated group of which P is the common parent. S1 is engaged in an excepted trade or business, and S2 is engaged in a non-excepted trade or business. If S1 were to lend funds directly to S2 in an intercompany transaction, under § 1.163(j)-10(a)(4)(i), the intercompany obligation of S2 would not be considered an asset of S1 for purposes of § 1.163(j)-10 (concerning allocations of interest and other taxable items between excepted and non-excepted trades or businesses for purposes of section 163(j)). With a principal purpose of avoiding treatment of a lending transaction between S1 and S2 as an intercompany transaction (and increasing the P group's basis in its assets allocable to excepted trades or businesses), S1 lends funds to X (an unrelated third party). X then onlends funds to S2 on substantially similar terms.

(B) *Analysis.* A principal purpose of the steps undertaken was to avoid treatment of a lending transaction between S1 and S2 as an intercompany transaction. Therefore, under paragraph (h)(1) of this section, appropriate adjustments are made, and the X obligation in the hands of S1 is not treated as an asset of S1 for purposes of § 1.163(j)-10, to the extent of the loan from X to S2.

(i) [Reserved]

(j) *Miscellaneous operating rules.*—For purposes of this section—

(1) *Successor assets.*—Any reference to an asset includes, as the context may require, a reference to any other asset the basis of which is determined, directly or indirectly, in whole or in part, by reference to the basis of the first asset.

(2) *Successor persons.*—(i) *In general.*—Any reference to a person includes, as the context may require, a reference to a predecessor or successor. For this purpose, a predecessor is a transferor of assets to a transferee (the successor) in a transaction—

(A) To which section 381(a) applies;

(B) In which substantially all of the assets of the transferor are transferred to members in a complete liquidation;

(C) In which the successor's basis in assets is determined (directly or indirectly, in whole or in part) by reference to the basis of the transferor, but the transferee is a successor only with respect to the assets the basis of which is so determined; or

(D) Which is an intercompany transaction, but only with respect to assets that are being accounted for by the transferor in a prior intercompany transaction.

(ii) *Intercompany items.*—If the assets of a predecessor are acquired by a successor member, the successor succeeds to, and takes into account (under the rules of this section), the predecessor's intercompany items. If two or more successor members acquire assets of the predecessor, the successors take into account the predecessor's intercompany items in a manner that is consistently applied and reasonably carries out the purposes of this section and applicable provisions of law.

(3) *Multiple triggers.*—If more than one corresponding item can cause an intercompany item to be taken into account under the matching rule, the intercompany item is taken into account in connection with the corresponding item most consistent with the treatment of members as divisions of a single corporation. For example, if S sells a truck to B, its intercompany gain from the sale is not taken into account by reference to B's depreciation if the depreciation is capitalized under section 263A as part of B's cost for a building; instead, S's gain relating to the capitalized depreciation is taken into account when the building is sold or as it is depreciated. Similarly, if B purchases appreciated land from S and transfers the land to a lower-tier member in exchange for stock, thereby duplicating the basis of the land in the basis of the stock, items with respect to both the stock and the land can cause S's intercompany gain to be taken into account; if the lower-tier member becomes a nonmember as a result of the sale of its stock, the attributes of S's intercompany gain are determined with respect to the land rather than the stock.

(4) *Multiple or successive intercompany transactions.*—If a member's intercompany item or corresponding item affects the accounting for more than one intercompany transaction, appropriate adjustments are made to treat all of the intercompany transactions as transactions between divisions of a single corporation. For example, if S sells property to M, and M sells the property to B, then S, M, and B are treated as divisions of a single corporation for purposes of applying the rules of this section. Similar principles apply with

respect to intercompany transactions that are part of the same plan or arrangement. For example, if S sells separate properties to different members as part of the same plan or arrangement, all of the participating members are treated as divisions of a single corporation for purposes of determining the attributes (which might also affect timing) of the intercompany items and corresponding items from each of the properties.

(5) *Acquisition of group.*—(i) *Scope.*—This paragraph (j)(5) applies only if a consolidated group (the terminating group) ceases to exist as a result of—

(A) The acquisition of either the assets of the common parent of the terminating group in a reorganization described in section 381(a)(2), or the stock of the common parent of the terminating group; or

(B) The application of the principles of § 1.1502-75(d)(2) or (d)(3).

(ii) *Application.*—If the terminating group ceases to exist under circumstances described in paragraph (j)(5)(i) of this section, the surviving group is treated as the terminating group for purposes of applying this section to the intercompany transactions of the terminating group. For example, intercompany items and corresponding items from intercompany transactions between members of the terminating group are taken into account under the rules of this section by the surviving group. This treatment does not apply, however, to members of the terminating group that are not members of the surviving group immediately after the terminating group ceases to exist (for example, under section 1504(a)(3) relating to reconsolidation, or section 1504(c) relating to includible insurance companies).

(6) *Former common parent treated as continuation of group.*—If a group terminates because the common parent is the only remaining member, the common parent succeeds to the treatment of the terminating group for purposes of applying this section so long as it neither becomes a member of an affiliated group filing separate returns nor becomes a corporation described in section 1504(b). For example, if the only subsidiary of the group liquidates into the common parent in a complete liquidation to which section 332 applies, or the common parent merges into the subsidiary and the subsidiary is treated as the common parent's successor under paragraph (j)(2)(i) of this section, the taxable income of the surviving corporation is treated as the group's consolidated taxable income in which the intercompany and corresponding items must be included. See § 1.267(f)-1 for additional rules applicable to intercompany losses or deductions.

(7) *Becoming a nonmember.*—For purposes of this section, a member is treated as becoming a nonmember if it has a separate return year (including another group's consolidated return year). A member is not treated as having a separate return year if its items are treated as taken into account in computing the group's consolidated taxable income under paragraph (j)(5) or (6) of this section.

(8) *Recordkeeping.*—Intercompany and corresponding items must be reflected on permanent records (including work papers). See also section 6001, requiring records to be maintained. The group must be able to identify from these permanent records the amount, location, timing, and attributes of the items, so as to permit the application of the rules of this section for each year.

(9) *Examples.*—The operating rules of this paragraph (j) are illustrated generally throughout this section, and by the following examples.

*Example 1. Intercompany sale followed by section 351 transfer to member.* (a) *Facts.* S holds land for investment with a basis of $70. On January 1 of Year 1, S sells the land to M for $100. M also holds the land for investment. On July 1 of Year 3, M transfers the land to B in exchange for all of B's stock in a transaction to which section 351 applies. Under section 358, M's basis in the B stock is $100. B holds the land for sale to customers in the ordinary course of business and, under section 362(b), B's basis in the land is $100. On December 1 of Year 5, M sells 20% of the B stock to X for $22. In an unrelated transaction on July 1 of Year 8, B sells 20% of the land for $22.

(b) *Definitions.* Under paragraph (b)(1) of this section, S's sale of the land to M and M's transfer of the land to B are both intercompany transactions. S is the selling member and M is the buying member in the first intercompany transaction, and M is the selling member and B is the buying member in the second intercompany transaction. M has no intercompany items under paragraph (b)(2) of this section. Because B acquired the land in an intercompany transaction, B's items from the land are corresponding items to be taken into account under this section. Under the successor asset rule of paragraph (j)(1) of this section, references to the land include references to M's B stock. Under the successor person rule of paragraph (j)(2) of this section, references to M include references to B with respect to the land.

(c) *Timing and attributes resulting from the stock sale.* Under paragraph (c)(3) of this section, M is treated as owning and selling B's stock for purposes of the matching rule even though, as divisions, M could not own and sell stock in B. Under paragraph (j)(3) of this section, both M's B stock and B's land can cause S's intercompany gain to be taken into account under the matching rule. Thus, S takes $6 of its gain into account in Year 5 to reflect the $6 difference between M's $2 gain taken into account from its sale of B stock and the $8 recomputed gain. Under paragraph (j)(4) of this section, the attributes of this gain are determined by treating S, M, and B as divisions of a single corporation. Under paragraph (c)(1) of this section, S's $6 gain and M's $2 gain are treated as long-term capital gain. The gain would be capital on a separate entity basis (assuming that section 341 does not apply), and this treatment is not inconsistent with treating S, M, and B as divisions of a single corporation because the stock sale and subsequent land sale are unrelated transactions and B remains a member following the sale.

(d) *Timing and attributes resulting from the land sale.* Under paragraph (j)(3) of this section, S takes $6 of its gain into account in Year 8 under the matching rule to reflect the $6 difference between B's $2 gain taken into account from its sale of an interest in the land and the $8 recomputed gain. Under paragraph (j)(4) of this section, the attributes of this gain are determined by treating S, M, and B as divisions of a single corporation and taking into account the activities of S, M, and B with respect to the land. Thus, both S's gain and B's gain might be ordinary income as a result of B's activities. (If B subsequently sells the balance of the land, S's gain taken into account is limited to its remaining $18 of intercompany gain.)

(e) *Sale of successor stock resulting in deconsolidation.* The facts are the same as in paragraph (a) of this *Example 1*, except that M sells 60% of the B stock to X for $66 on December 1 of Year 5 and B becomes a nonmember. Under the matching rule, M's sale of B stock results in $18 of S's gain being taken into account (to reflect the difference between M's $6 gain taken into account and the $24 recomputed gain). Under the acceleration rule, however, the entire $30 gain is taken into account (to reflect B becoming a nonmember, because its basis in the land reflects M's $100 cost basis from the prior intercompany transaction). Under paragraph (j)(4) of this section, the attributes of S's gain are determined by treating S, M, and B as divisions of a single corporation. Because M's cost basis in the land will be reflected by B as a nonmember, all of S's gain is treated as from the land (rather than a portion being from B's stock), and B's activities with respect to the land might therefore result in S's gain being ordinary income.

*Example 2. Intercompany sale of member stock followed by recapitalization.* (a) *Facts.* Before becoming a member of the P group, S owns P stock with a basis of $70. On January 1 of Year 1, P buys all of S's stock. On July 1 of Year 3, S sells the P stock to M for $100. On December 1 of Year 5, P acquires M's original P stock in exchange for new P stock in a recapitalization described in section 368(a)(1)(E).

(b) *Timing and attributes.* Although P's basis in the stock acquired from M is eliminated under paragraph (f)(4) of this section, the new P stock received by M is exchanged basis property (within the meaning of section 7701(a)(44)) having a basis under section 358 equal to M's basis in the original P stock. Under the successor asset rule of paragraph (j)(1) of this section, references to M's original P stock include references to M's new P stock. Because it is still possible to take S's intercompany item into account under the matching rule with respect to the successor asset, S's gain is not taken into account under the acceleration rule as a result of the basis elimination under paragraph (f)(4) of this section. Instead, the gain is taken into account based on subsequent events with respect to M's new P stock (for example, a subsequent distribution or redemption of the new stock).

*Example 3. Back-to-back intercompany transactions—matching.* (a) *Facts.* S holds land for investment with a basis of $70. On January 1 of Year 1, S sells the land to M for $90. M also holds the land for investment. On July 1 of Year 3, M sells the land for $100 to B, and B holds the land for sale to customers in the ordinary course of business. During Year 5, B sells all of the land to customers for $105.

(b) *Timing.* Under paragraph (b)(1) of this section, S's sale of the land to M and M's sale of the land to B are both intercompany transactions. S is the selling member and M is the buying member in the first intercompany transaction, and M is the selling member and B is the buying member in the second intercompany transaction. Under paragraph (j)(4) of this section, S, M and B are treated as divisions of a single corporation for purposes of determining the timing of their items from the intercompany transactions. See also paragraph (j)(2) of this section (B is treated as a successor to M for purposes of taking S's intercompany gain into account). Thus, S's $20 gain and M's $10 gain are both taken into account in Year 5 to reflect the difference between B's $5 gain taken into account with respect to the land and the $35 recomputed gain (the gain that B would have taken into account if the intercompany sales had been transfers between divisions of a single corporation, and B succeeded to S's $70 basis).

(c) *Attributes.* Under paragraphs (j)(4) of this section, the attributes of the intercompany items and corresponding items of S, M, and B are also determined by treating S, M, and B as divisions of a single corporation. For example, the attributes of S's and M's intercompany items are determined by taking B's activities into account.

*Example 4. Back-to-back intercompany transactions—acceleration.* (a) *Facts.* During Year 1, S performs services for M in exchange for $10 from M. S incurs $8 of employee expenses. M capitalizes the $10 cost of S's services under section 263 as part of M's cost to acquire real property from X. Under its separate entity method of accounting, S would take its income and expenses into account in Year 1. M holds the real property for investment and, on July 1 of Year 5, M sells it to B at a gain. B also holds the real property for investment. On December 1 of Year 8, while B still owns the real property, P sells all of M's stock to X and M becomes a nonmember.

(b) *M's items.* M takes its gain into account immediately before it becomes a nonmember. Because the real property stays in the group, the acceleration rule redetermines the attributes of M's gain under the principles of the matching rule as if B sold the real property to an affiliated corporation that is not a member of the group for a cash payment equal to B's adjusted basis in the real property, and S, M, and B were divisions of a single corporation. Thus, M's gain is capital gain.

(c) *S's items.* Under paragraph (b)(2)(ii) of this section, S includes the $8 of expenses in determining its $2 intercompany income. In Year 1, S takes into account $8 of income and $8 of expenses. Under paragraph (j)(4) of this section, appropriate adjustments must be made to treat both S's performance of services for M and M's sale to B as occurring between divisions of a single corporation. Thus, S's $2 of intercompany income is not taken into account as a result of M becoming a nonmember, but instead will be taken into account based on subsequent events (e.g., under the matching rule based on B's sale of the real property to a nonmember, or under the acceleration rule based on P's sale of the stock of S or B to a nonmember). See the successor person rules of paragraph (j)(2) of this section (B is treated as a successor to M for purposes of taking S's intercompany income into account).

(d) *Sale of S's stock.* The facts are the same as in paragraph (a) of this *Example 4*, except that P sells all of S's stock (rather than M's stock) and S becomes a nonmember on July 1 of Year 5. S's remaining $2 of intercompany income is taken into account immediately before S becomes a nonmember. Because S's intercompany income is not from an intercompany sale, exchange, or distribution of property, the attributes of the intercompany income are determined on a separate entity basis. Thus, S's $2 of intercompany income is ordinary income. M does not take any of its intercompany gain into account as a result of S becoming a nonmember.

(e) *Intercompany income followed by intercompany loss.* The facts are the same as in paragraph (a) of this *Example 4*, except that M sells the real property to B at a $1 loss (rather than a gain). M takes its $1 loss into account under the acceleration rule immediately before M becomes a nonmember. But see § 1.267(f)-1 (which might further defer M's loss if M and B remain in a controlled group relationship after M becomes a nonmember). Under paragraph (j)(4) of this section appropriate adjustments must be made to treat the group as if both intercompany transactions occurred between divisions of a single corporation. Accordingly, P's sale of M stock also results in S taking into account $1 of intercompany income as capital gain to offset M's $1 of corresponding capital loss. The remaining $1 of S's intercompany income is taken into account based on subsequent events.

*Example 5. Successor group.* (a) *Facts.* On January 1 of Year 1, B borrows $100 from S in return for B's note providing for $10 of interest annually at the end of each year, and repayment of $100 at the end of Year 20. As of January 1 of Year 3, B has paid the interest accruing under the note. On that date, X acquires all of P's stock and the former P group members become members of the X consolidated group.

(b) *Successor.* Under paragraph (j)(5) of this section; although B's note ceases to be an intercompany obligation of the P group, the note is not treated as satisfied and reissued under paragraph (g) of this section as a result of X's acquisition of P stock. Instead, the X consolidated group succeeds to the treatment of the P group for purposes of paragraph (g) of this section, and B's note is treated as an intercompany obligation of the X consolidated group.

*Example 6. Liquidation—80% distributee.* (a) *Facts.* X has had preferred stock described in section 1504(a)(4) outstanding for several years. On January 1 of Year 1, S buys all of X's common stock for $60, and B buys all of X's preferred stock for $40. X's assets have a $0 basis and $100 value. On July 1 of Year 3, X distributes all of its assets to S and B in a complete liquidation. Under § 1.1502-34, section 332 applies to both S and B. Under section 337, X has no gain or loss from its liquidating distribution to S. Under sections 336 and 337(c), X has a $40 gain from its liquidating distribution to B. B has a $40 basis under section 334(a) in the assets received from X, and S has a $0 basis under section 334(b) in the assets received from X.

(b) *Intercompany items from the liquidation.* Under the matching rule, X's $40 gain from its liquidating distribution to B is not taken into account under this section as a result of the liquidation (and therefore is not yet reflected under §§ 1.1502-32 and 1.1502-33). Under the successor person rule of paragraph (j)(2)(i) of this section, S and B are both successors to X. Under section 337(c), X recognizes gain or loss only with respect to the assets distributed to B. Under paragraph (j)(2)(ii) of this section, to be consistent with the purposes of this section, S succeeds to X's $40 intercompany gain. The gain will be taken into account by S under the matching and acceleration rules of this section based on subsequent events. (The allocation of the intercompany gain to S does not govern the allocation of any other attributes.)

*Example 7. Liquidation—no 80% distributee.* (a) *Facts.* X has only common stock outstanding. On January 1 of Year 1, S buys 60% of X's stock for $60, and B buys 40% of X's stock for $40. X's assets have a $0 basis and $100 value. On July 1 of Year 3, X distributes all of its assets to S and B in a complete liquidation. Under § 1.1502-34, section 332 applies to both S and B. Under sections 336 and 337(c), X has a $100 gain from its liquidating distributions to S and B. Under section 334(b), S has a $60 basis in the assets received from X and B has a $40 basis in the assets received from X.

(b) *Intercompany items from the liquidation.* Under the matching rule, X's $100 intercompany gain from its liquidating distributions to S and B is not taken into account under this section as a result of the liquidation (and therefore is not yet reflected under §§ 1.1502-32 and 1.1502-33). Under the successor person rule of paragraph (j)(2)(i) of this section, S and B are both successors to X. Under paragraph (j)(2)(ii) of this section, to be consistent with the purposes of this section, S succeeds to X's $40 intercompany gain with respect to the assets distributed to B, and B succeeds to X's $60 intercompany gain with respect to the assets distributed to S. The gain will be taken into account by S and B under the matching and acceleration rules of this section based on subsequent events. (The allocation of the intercompany gain does not govern the allocation of any other attributes.)

(k) *Cross references.*—(1) *Section 108.*—See § 1.108-3 for the treatment of intercompany deductions and losses as subject to attribute reduction under section 108(b).

(2) *Section 263A(f).*—See section 263A(f) and § 1.263A9(g)(5) for special rules regarding interest from intercompany transactions.

(3) *Section 267(f).*—See section 267(f) and § 1.267(f)-1 for special rules applicable to certain losses and deductions from transactions between members of a controlled group.

(4) *Section 460.*—See § 1.460-4(j) for special rules regarding the application of section 460 to intercompany transactions.

(5) *Section 469.*—See § 1.469-1(h) for special rules regarding the application of section 469 to intercompany transactions.

(6) *§ 1.1502-80.*—See § 1.1502-80 for the non-application of certain Internal Revenue Code rules.

(l) *Effective/applicability dates.*—(1) *In general.*—This section applies with respect to transactions occurring in years beginning on or after July 12, 1995. If both this section and prior law apply to a transaction, or neither applies, with the result that items may be duplicated, omitted, or eliminated in determining taxable income (or tax liability), or items may be treated inconsistently, prior law (and not this section) applies to the transaction. For example, S's and B's items from S's sale of property to B which occurs in a consolidated return year beginning before July 12, 1995, are taken into account under prior law, even though B may dispose of the property in a consolidated return year beginning on or after July 12, 1995. Similarly, an intercompany distribution to which a shareholder becomes entitled in a consolidated return year beginning before July 12, 1995, but which is distributed in a consolidated return year beginning on or after that date is taken into account under prior law (generally when distributed), because this section generally takes dividends into account when the shareholder becomes entitled to them but this section does not apply at that time. If application of prior law to S's deferred gain or loss from a deferred intercompany transaction (as defined under prior law) occurring in a consolidated return year beginning prior to July 12, 1995, would be affected by an intercompany transaction (as defined under this section) occurring in a consolidated return year beginning on or after July 12, 1995, S's deferred gain or loss continues to be taken into account as provided under prior law, and the items from the subsequent intercompany transaction are taken into account under this section. Appropriate adjustments must be made to prevent items from being duplicated, omitted, or eliminated in determining taxable income as a result of the application of both this section and prior law to the successive transactions, and to

ensure the proper application of prior law. Paragraphs (a)(4), (f)(6)(ii), (f)(6)(iv)(A), (g)(3)(ii)(B)(2), and (j)(5)(i)(A) of this section apply with respect to transactions occurring on or after September 17, 2008. However, taxpayers may apply paragraph (j)(5)(i)(A) of this section to transactions that occurred prior to September 17, 2008.

(2) *Avoidance transactions.*—This paragraph (1)(2) applies if a transaction is engaged in or structured on or after April 8, 1994, with a principal purpose to avoid the rules of this section (and instead to apply prior law). If this paragraph (1)(2) applies, appropriate adjustments must be made in years beginning on or after July 12, 1995, to prevent the avoidance, duplication, omission, or elimination of any item (or tax liability), or any other inconsistency with the rules of this section. For example, if S is a dealer in real property and sells land to B on March 16, 1995 with a principal purpose of converting any future appreciation in the land to capital gain, B's gain from the sale of the land on May 11, 1997 might be characterized as ordinary income under this paragraph (1)(2).

(3) *Election for certain stock elimination transactions.*—(i) *In general.*—A group may elect pursuant to this paragraph (1)(3) to apply this section (including the elections available under paragraph (f)(5)(ii) of this section) to stock elimination transactions to which prior law would otherwise apply. If an election is made, this section, and not prior law, applies to determine the timing and attributes of S's and B's gain or loss from stock with respect to all stock elimination transactions.

(ii) *Stock elimination transactions.*—For purposes of this paragraph (1)(3), a stock elimination transaction is a transaction in which stock transferred from S to B—

(A) Is cancelled or redeemed on or after July 12, 1995;

(B) Is treated as cancelled in a liquidation pursuant to an election under section 338(h)(10) with respect to a qualified stock purchase with an acquisition date on or after July 12, 1995;

(C) Is distributed on or after July 12, 1995; or

(D) Is exchanged on or after July 12, 1995 for stock of a member (determined immediately after the exchange) in a transaction that would cause S's gain or loss from the transfer to be taken into account under prior law.

(iii) *Time and manner of making election.*—An election under this paragraph (1)(3) is made by attaching to a timely filed original return (including extensions) for the consolidated return year including July 12, 1995 a statement entitled "[Insert Name and Employer Identification Number of Common Parent] HEREBY ELECTS THE APPLICATION OF § 1.1502-13(1)(3)." See paragraph (f)(5)(ii)(E) of this section for the manner of electing the relief provisions of paragraph (f)(5)(ii) of this section.

(4) *Prior law.*—For transactions occurring in S's years beginning before July 12, 1995, see the applicable regulations issued under section 1502. See §§ 1.1502-13, 1.1502-13T, 1.1502-14, 1.1502-14T, 1.1502-31, and 1.1502-32 (as contained in the 26 CFR part 1 edition revised as of April 1, 1995).

(5) *Consent to adopt method of accounting.*—For intercompany transactions occurring in a consolidated group's first taxable year beginning on or after July 12, 1995, the Commissioner's consent under section 446(e) is hereby granted for any changes in methods of accounting that are necessary solely by reason of the timing rules of this section. Changes in method of accounting for these transactions are to be effected on a cut-off basis.

(6) *Effective/applicability date.*—(i) In general.—Paragraph (f)(7)(i) Example 4. applies to transactions occurring on or after December 18, 2009.

(ii) [Reserved]

(m) *Effective/applicability date.*—Paragraphs (f)(5)(ii)(E) and (f)(6)(i)(C)(2) of this section apply to any original consolidated Federal income tax return due (without extensions) after June 14, 2007. For original consolidated Federal income tax returns due (without extensions) after May 30, 2006, and on or before June 14, 2007, see § 1.1502-13T as contained in 26 CFR part 1 in effect on April 1, 2007. For original consolidated Federal income tax returns due (without extensions) on or before May 30, 2006, see § 1.1502-13 as contained in 26 CFR part 1 in effect on April 1, 2006. Paragraph (f)(5)(ii)(C) of this section is applicable to any qualified stock disposition (as defined in § 1.336-1(b)(6)) for which the disposition date (as defined in § 1.336-1(b)(8)) is on or after May 15, 2013. [Reg. § 1.1502-13.]

☐ [*T.D.* 6894, 9-7-66. *Amended by T.D.* 7246, 12-29-72; *T.D.* 8131, 3-24-87; *T.D.* 8196, 4-14-88; *T.D.* 8295, 3-9-90; *T.D.* 8478, 3-9-93; *T.D.* 8482, 8-6-93; *T.D.* 8560, 8-12-94; *T.D.* 8584, 12-28-94; *T.D.* 8597, 7-12-95; *T.D.* 8660, 3-13-96; *T.D.* 8677, 6-26-96; *T.D.* 8823, 6-25-99; *T.D.* 8883, 5-11-2000; *T.D.* 9025, 12-13-2002; *T.D.* 9048, 3-11-2003; *T.D.* 9117, 3-12-2004; *T.D.* 9192, 3-21-2005; *T.D.* 9261, 5-5-2006; *T.D.* 9264,

5-26-2006; *T.D. 9329*, 6-13-2007; *T.D. 9383*, 3-6-2008; *T.D. 9424*, 9-9-2008 (*corrected* 10-17-2008); *T.D. 9442*, 12-24-2008 (*corrected* 2-10-2009); *T.D. 9458*, 9-3-2009; *T.D. 9475*, 12-17-2009 (*corrected* 8-9-2011); *T.D. 9515*, 3-3-2011 (*corrected* 3-30-2011); *T.D. 9594*, 6-19-2012; *T.D. 9619*, 5-10-2013 (*corrected* 8-27-2013), *T.D. 9901*, 7-9-2020, *T.D. 9905*, 9-3-2020 *and T.D. 9921*, 12-10-2020.]

⋙→ *Caution: Reg. §1.1502-14Z, below, as adopted by T.D. 9889, generally applies to tax years beginning after March 13, 2020. For exceptions regarding reliance on the proposed regulations, see Reg. §1.1502-14Z(k).*

[Reg. §1.1502-14Z]

**§1.1502-14Z. Application of opportunity zone rules to members of a consolidated group.**—(a) *Scope and definitions.*—(1) *Scope.*—This section provides rules regarding the Federal income tax treatment of QOFs owned by members of a consolidated group (as defined in §1.1502-1(b) and (h), respectively). Rules in the section 1400Z-2 regulations (as defined in §1.1400Z2(a)-1(b)(41)) apply to consolidated groups except as modified in this section. Paragraph (b) of this section generally provides rules regarding the effects of an election under §1.1504-3(b)(2) to treat a subsidiary QOF C corporation as a member of a consolidated group. Paragraph (c) of this section provides rules regarding qualifying investments made by members of a consolidated group (including an election to treat the investment by one member as a qualifying investment by another member) and the application of §1.1502-13 to intercompany transfers of a qualifying investment. Paragraph (d) of this section provides coordinating rules for basis adjustments within a consolidated group. Paragraph (e) of this section provides coordinating rules for §1.1502-36(d). Paragraph (f) of this section provides elective transition relief to taxpayers that consolidated a subsidiary QOF C corporation prior to May 1, 2019. Paragraph (g) of this section provides rules regarding the consequences of a deconsolidation of a QOF C corporation. Paragraph (h) of this section provides instructions for making the elections provided by paragraphs (c) and (f) of this section. Paragraph (i) of this section is reserved. Paragraph (j) of this section provides examples. Paragraph (k) of this section provides the applicability dates.

(2) *Definitions.*—(i) *In general.*—The definitions provided in §§1.1400Z2(a)-1(b) and 1.1400Z2(d)-1 apply for purposes of this section.

(ii) *Definitions for consolidated groups.*—(A) *Day one.*—The term *day one* means the date members of the consolidated group formed or acquired section 1504 control of the pre-existing QOF sub. If a pre-existing QOF sub was a member of the consolidated group prior to becoming a QOF C corporation, day one is the first day of the first month in which the member self-certified as, or is treated as, a QOF C corporation, whichever is earlier.

(B) *Election date.*—The term *election date* means the date on which an election under paragraph (c) or (f) of this section is made.

(C) *Pre-existing QOF sub.*—The term *pre-existing QOF sub* means a subsidiary QOF C corporation that meets the affiliation requirements in section 1504 (without regard to §1.1504-3(b)(1)) as of May 1, 2019.

(D) *QOF investor member.*—The term *QOF investor member* means any member holding a qualifying investment in the QOF member.

(E) *QOF member.*—The term *QOF member* means a subsidiary QOF C corporation that is treated as a member of a consolidated group pursuant to an election in §1.1504-3(b)(2).

(F) *QOF member stock.*—The term *QOF member stock* means the QOF stock of a QOF member.

(G) *QOF SAG.*—The term *QOF SAG* means, with respect to a QOF member, the affiliated group that would be determined under section 1504(a) if the QOF member were the common parent.

(H) *Subsidiary QOF C corporation.*—The term *subsidiary QOF C corporation* means a QOF C corporation that meets the requirements to be a member of an affiliated group (as defined in section 1504(a)(1), and without regard to §1.1504-3(b)(1)) other than the common parent of such consolidated group.

(b) *Subsidiary QOF C corporation treated as member of the consolidated group.*—(1) *Effects of election to treat a subsidiary QOF C corporation as a member.*—(i) *Determining whether a distribution is an inclusion event.*—A distribution of property with respect to qualifying QOF stock by a QOF member to a QOF investor member is an inclusion event to the extent the distribution would create or increase an excess loss account (ELA) in the qualifying QOF stock, without regard to any inclusion resulting from application of this paragraph (b)(1)(i). Solely for purposes of determining whether a distribution creates or increases an ELA during a taxable year, investment adjustments pertaining to a distribution on qualifying QOF stock by a QOF member are made after all other investment adjustments under §1.1502-32 for that year.

(ii) *Determining the amount of deferred gain includible by the QOF investor member.*—The amount of gain included in gross income of a QOF investor member under section 1400Z-2(a)(1)(B) on a date described in §1.1400Z2(b)-1(b) (modified by paragraph (c)(3) of this section, as applicable) is determined under this paragraph (b)(1)(ii). The amount of gain included in gross income of the QOF investor member is the lesser of:

(A) The product of:

(1) The percentage of the qualifying investment that gave rise to the inclusion event; and

(2) The remaining deferred gain (see §1.1400Z2(a)-1(b)(40)), less any basis adjustments pursuant to section 1400Z-2(b)(2)(B)(iii) and (iv); or

(B) The gain that would be recognized on a fully taxable disposition of the qualifying investment that gave rise to the inclusion event.

(iii) *Application of ELA rules on the disposition of QOF member stock.*—When a QOF investor member disposes of a share of qualifying QOF member stock, any ELA in the share is taken into account as income or gain from the disposition under §1.1502-19(b)(1) before the basis of the share is increased under section 1400Z-2(c), if applicable. See paragraph (g)(3)(i) of this section for the general rule regarding the treatment of an ELA upon the deconsolidation of a QOF member.

(iv) *Transactions between the QOF member and other members of the consolidated group.*—(A) *In general.*—This paragraph (b)(1)(iv) governs transactions between a member of a QOF SAG and other members of the consolidated group.

(B) *Sale or exchange of property.*—A sale or exchange of property between a member of a QOF SAG and a member of the consolidated group that is not a member of a single QOF SAG is not treated as an intercompany transaction (as defined in §1.1502-13(b)(1)) and is not subject to the rules in §1.1502-13. In contrast, a sale or exchange of property between members of the QOF SAG is an intercompany transaction that is subject to the rules in §1.1502-13.

(C) *Other transactions.*—Any transaction between a member of a QOF SAG and a member of the consolidated group that is not a member of that QOF SAG that is not a sale or exchange of property is an intercompany transaction subject to the rules in §1.1502-13.

(v) *Separate-entity application of QOF qualifying rules to QOF member.*—A consolidated group is not treated as a single entity for purposes of determining whether a QOF member or a qualified opportunity zone business that is a consolidated group member satisfies the investment standard rules in section 1400Z-2(d) and (f) and §§1.1400Z2(d)-1 and 1.1400Z2(f)-1. Instead, those investment standard rules apply on a separate-entity basis. Therefore, for example, the QOF member's satisfaction of the requirements under section 1400Z-2(d) is determined by taking into account only property (including qualified opportunity zone stock or qualified opportunity zone partnership interests) held by the QOF member, without regard to property transferred by the QOF member to other members of the consolidated group.

(2) *Anti-avoidance rule.*—The purposes of section 1400Z-2 and the section 1400Z-2 regulations are to provide specified tax benefits to owners of QOFs to encourage the making of longer-term investments, through QOFs and qualified opportunity zone businesses, of new capital in one or more qualified opportunity zones and to increase the economic growth of such qualified opportunity zones. If a transaction is engaged in or structured with a view to avoid the application of the rules of section 1400Z-2, the section 1400Z-2 regulations, or the regulations in this part under section 1502 of the Code (including this section), appropriate adjustments will be made to carry out the purposes of section 1400Z-2 and the section 1400Z-2 regulations. For example, if a consolidated group engages in a restructuring (such as a distribution described in section 355) with a view to using stock basis adjustments under §1.1502-32 resulting from increases in the basis of stock under section 1400Z-2(b) in a sale or exchange transaction without disposing of any part of the consolidated group's direct ownership of the relevant qualifying investment, the transaction will be treated as an inclusion event with regard to an appropriate amount of deferred gain.

(c) *Qualifying investments by members of a consolidated group.*—(1) *In general.*—Except as otherwise provided in this section or in §1.1400Z2(b)-1 (see, for example, §1.1400Z2(b)-1(c)(9)(i)(B)(1)), section 1400Z-2 applies separately to each member of a consolidated group. Therefore, for example, the same member of the consolidated group generally must both engage in the sale of a capital asset giving rise to eligible gain and timely invest an amount equal to some or all of such gain in a QOF (as provided in section 1400Z-2(a)(1)) in order to qualify for deferral of such gain under section 1400Z-2.

(2) *Election to treat investment of one member as a qualifying investment by another member.*—(i) *Availability of election.*—If members of a consolidated group satisfy the requirements of this paragraph (c)(2), the consolidated group may elect to treat an investment by one member as a qualifying investment by another member. The election provided by this paragraph (c)(2) is available when a member of a consolidated group (M1) has eligible gain and a second member (M2) makes an investment in a QOF that would be a qualifying investment if M1, rather than M2, had made the investment. For example, if M1 has $100x of eligible gain but M2 has none, and M2 makes a $120x investment in a QOF C corporation, only $100x of M2's investment in the QOF C corporation is eligible for the election under this paragraph (c)(2). See paragraph (h)(2) of this section for the form and manner of making this election. If M2 has its own eligible gain, M2 may make a qualifying investment on its own behalf and defer such eligible gain under section 1400Z-2(a)(1)(A) and § 1.1400Z2(a)-1.

(ii) *Effect of election.*—If a consolidated group makes an election under this paragraph (c)(2), then M1 is treated as having made the investment in the QOF that is actually made by M2. M1 is then treated as having immediately sold such investment to M2 for fair market value. The deemed sale by M1 is subject to the rules in paragraph (c)(3) of this section. The consolidated group must treat the deemed investment by M1 and the deemed sale by M1 to M2 as having occurred for all Federal income tax purposes.

(3) *Intercompany transfers of a qualifying investment.*—(i) *In general.*—Except as otherwise provided in this paragraph (c)(3), when one member (S) transfers its qualifying investment to another member (B), the transaction is not treated as an intercompany transaction within the meaning of § 1.1502-13(b)(1) for purposes of applying the rules of section 1400Z-2 and the section 1400Z-2 regulations. Therefore, § 1.1502-13(c) does not apply to treat S and B as divisions of a single entity for purposes of section 1400Z-2. For example, if S transfers its qualifying investment to B in a section 351 transaction, the transfer is an inclusion event for S under § 1.1400Z2(b)-1(c). In addition, because the transfer is not an intercompany transaction for purposes of section 1400Z-2, § 1.1502-13 does not apply to continue S's deferral under § 1.1400Z2(a)-1(a)(1).

(ii) *Application of § 1.1502-13 to fully taxable intercompany transfers of a qualifying investment.*—(A) *Applicable transactions.*—Notwithstanding paragraph (c)(3)(i) of this section, if S transfers its qualifying investment to B in a fully taxable transaction, the transaction is treated as an intercompany transaction, and § 1.1502-13(c) applies to treat S and B as divisions of a single entity for purposes of applying section 1400Z-2.

(B) *Treatment of S's intercompany gain on its qualifying investment.*—If a transaction is described in paragraph (c)(3)(ii)(A) of this section, § 1.1502-13(c)(6)(ii) is inapplicable in determining the excludability of S's gain (or the treatment of such gain as tax-exempt income) on the application of section 1400Z-2(b) and (c) to S and B as a single entity. Thus, S's gain on the qualifying investment (including the amount includible under § 1.1400Z2(b)-1(e)) may be redetermined to be excluded from gross income (or treated as tax-exempt income), as appropriate, to achieve single-entity treatment between S and B with regard to the ownership and disposal of the qualifying investment. To qualify for benefits under section 1400Z-2, S and B must otherwise satisfy the requirements of section 1400Z-2. See also § 1.1502-13(j)(4) (concerning multiple or successive intercompany transactions).

(C) *Investment adjustments and adjustments to earnings and profits.*—Income of S excluded under section 1400Z-2 by application of paragraphs (c)(3)(ii)(A) and (B) of this section and § 1.1502-13 results in adjustments to S's earnings and profits and is treated as tax-exempt income to S for purposes of § 1.1502-32(b)(2)(ii).

(D) *Election under section 1400Z-2(c).*—To the extent paragraph (c)(3)(ii)(A) of this section applies to S's transfer of its qualifying investment to B, B (and not S) is entitled to make the election under section 1400Z-2(c) at the time when, treating S and B as divisions of a single entity, the single entity would be entitled to make such an election. For example, pursuant to § 1.1502-13(c)(1)(ii), B takes S's holding period into account in determining whether B is treated as holding the transferred qualifying investment for 10 years. In addition, the attributes of S's intercompany item on the transfer of the qualifying investment may be redetermined based on B's election.

(4) *Intercompany transfer as qualifying investment in a QOF member.*—A transfer by a consolidated group member with an eligible gain to a QOF member before January 1, 2027, is not treated as an intercompany transaction within the meaning of § 1.1502-13 and may constitute a qualifying investment. But see § 1.1504-3(b)(2) regarding conditions for consolidating a QOF C corporation.

(5) *Intercompany gain as eligible gain.*—When S sells property to B, § 1.1502-13 applies to determine if, and when, S's intercompany gain and B's corresponding gain constitute eligible gain. S's gain and B's gain are treated as eligible gain only to the extent such gain would be eligible gain if S and B were divisions of a single entity. For example, if S sells a piece of property to B at a gain, B subsequently sells that property to an unrelated party at a further gain, and the gains are treated as capital gain under § 1.1502-13(c)(1) and (4), then both S's gain and B's gain are eligible gains at the time B sells the property to the unrelated party. In contrast, if S sells a piece of property to B at a loss, and B subsequently sells that property to an unrelated party at a gain, then B's corresponding gain on the property is eligible gain only to the extent that S and B, if treated as divisions of a single entity, would have eligible gain on the sale of property to the unrelated party. See § 1.1502-13(a)(1).

(d) *Tiering-up of investment adjustments provided by section 1400Z-2.*—Basis increases in a qualifying investment in a QOF under sections 1400Z-2(b)(2)(B)(iii), 1400Z-2(b)(2)(B)(iv), and 1400Z-2(c) are treated as satisfying the requirements of § 1.1502-32(b)(3)(ii)(A) and thus qualify as tax-exempt income to the QOF owner. Therefore, if the QOF owner is a member of a consolidated group and is owned by other members of the same consolidated group (upper-tier members), the upper-tier members increase their bases in the shares of the QOF owner under § 1.1502-32(b)(2)(ii). However, there is no basis adjustment under § 1.1502-32(b)(2)(ii) or (iii) in shares of upper-tier members with regard to a basis adjustment under section 1400Z-2(c) and § 1.1400Z2(c)-1 unless and until the basis of the qualifying investment is adjusted to its fair market value, as provided in section 1400Z-2(c) and § 1.1400Z2(c)-1.

(e) *Application of § 1.1502-36(d).*—This paragraph (e) clarifies how § 1.1502-36(d) applies if a member (M) transfers a loss share of another member (S) that is a QOF owner that owns a qualifying investment. To determine S's attribute reduction amount under § 1.1502-36(d)(3), S's basis in its qualifying investment is included in S's net inside attribute amount to compute S's aggregate inside loss under § 1.1502-36(d)(3)(iii)(A). However, S's basis in the qualifying investment is not included in S's Category D attributes available for attribute reduction under § 1.1502-36(d)(4). Thus, S's basis in the qualifying investment cannot be reduced under § 1.1502-36(d). If S's attribute reduction amount exceeds S's attributes available for reduction, then to the extent of the lesser of S's basis in the qualifying investment or the remaining attribute reduction amount, the common parent is treated as making the election under § 1.1502-36(d)(6) to reduce M's basis in the transferred loss S shares.

(f) *Transition relief.*—(1) *Overview.*—This paragraph (f) provides options for elective relief to pre-existing QOF subs. An election under this paragraph (f) is made in the manner provided in paragraph (h)(3) of this section. If a timely election under this paragraph (f) is not made, the pre-existing QOF sub is treated as deconsolidating on March 13, 2020.

(2) *Reclassification election.*—(i) *In general.*—For each pre-existing QOF sub of a consolidated group, the consolidated group may make one of the alternative, irrevocable elections provided in paragraphs (f)(2)(ii) through (iv) of this section. All elective relief provided in this paragraph (f)(2) is effective on day one.

(ii) *Treatment as a QOF partnership.*—(A) *Election.*—A consolidated group may elect to treat a pre-existing QOF subs as QOF partnership (electing QOF partnership). To be eligible for the election in this paragraph (f)(2)(ii)(A), a pre-existing QOF sub must have converted to an entity treated as a partnership for Federal income tax purposes as of the election date.

(B) *Effect of the QOF partnership election.*—As a result of making the election under this paragraph (f)(2)(ii), the pre-existing QOF sub is treated as a QOF partnership from day one. Consequently, the consolidated group must file amended or superseding returns, as applicable, to account for the electing QOF partnership's income, gain, deduction, and loss; the electing QOF partnership also must file its own partnership returns for taxable periods beginning on day one, as applicable. The electing QOF partnership must include its self-certification under § 1.1400Z2(d)-1(a) with its own returns, and the self-certification will be treated as timely so long as the consolidated group filed a timely self-certification under § 1.1400Z2(d)-1(a) for the pre-existing QOF sub. In addition, appropriate adjustments must be made to account for the change in status of the electing QOF partnership from day one, including modifications to investment adjustments to the basis in members' stock made under § 1.1502-32 and adjustments to members' earnings and profits made under § 1.1502-33.

(C) *Pre-existing QOF sub with single owner.*—If a pre-existing QOF sub is wholly owned by one member of a consolidated group, then for purposes of making the election under this paragraph (f)(2)(ii), the electing QOF partnership is deemed to have had a nominal partner from day one until the date the electing QOF partnership is treated as a partnership for Federal income tax purposes without regard to this paragraph (f)(2)(ii).

(D) *Example.*—The following example illustrates the election under this paragraph (f)(2)(ii).

(1) *Facts.* P, the common parent of a consolidated group (P group), wholly owns M1 and M2. On July 1, 2018, M1 and M2 each sell an asset to an unrelated party and realize $70x and $30x of eligible gain, respectively. On August 13, 2018, M1 and M2 form Q12 (a QOF C corporation that was formed as a corporation under state law). Also on August 13, 2018, M1 and M2 contribute $70x and $30x, respectively, to Q12 in exchange for stock of Q12 and properly elect to defer their respective eligible gains under section 1400Z-2(a) and § 1.1400Z2(a)-1. The P group also makes a timely self-certification under § 1.1400Z2(d)-1(a) for Q12. Following March 13, 2020, the P group intends to timely elect under this paragraph (f)(2)(ii) to treat Q12 as a QOF partnership.

(2) *Analysis*— (i) *Eligibility to elect.* For the P group to elect to treat Q12 as a QOF partnership under this paragraph (f)(2)(ii), by the date of the election, Q12 must either convert to a state law partnership or another entity treated as a partnership for Federal income tax purposes.

(ii) *Consequences of the election.* As a result of making the election under this paragraph (f)(2)(ii), Q12 is treated as a QOF partnership from August 13, 2018 (day one). The P group must file amended or superseding returns, as applicable and as necessary, to account for Q12's income, gain, deduction, and loss. In addition, Q12 must file its own returns for the taxable period beginning on August 13, 2018, as applicable. The returns must be filed within the time frame provided in paragraph (h)(3)(iii) of this section. Finally, because the P group filed a timely self-certification under § 1.1400Z2(d)-(1)(a) for Q12 as a QOF C corporation, Q12's self-certification as a QOF partnership would be is considered timely filed.

(3) *Deemed nominal partner*—(i) *Facts.* The facts are the same as in paragraph (f)(2)(iii)(D)(1) of this section, except that on July 1, 2018, only M1 sells an asset to an unrelated party and realizes $70x of eligible gain. On August 13, 2018, M1 contributes cash of $70x to Q12 in exchange for stock of Q12 and properly elects to defer the eligible gain under section 1400Z-2(a) and § 1.1400Z2(a)-1. As of the date the election is made to treat Q12 as a partnership from day one, a second party invests in Q12, and Q12 is an entity treated as a partnership for Federal income tax purposes.

(ii) *Analysis.* The analysis is generally the same as in paragraph (f)(2)(iii)(D)(2) of this section. In addition, because Q12 is wholly owned by M1, solely for purposes of treating Q12 as a QOF partnership from August 13, 2018, Q12 is deemed to have a nominal partner from August 13, 2018 until the election date or the date Q12 qualifies as a partnership, if earlier.

(iii) *Treatment as a non-member QOF C corporation.*—(A) *Election.*—A consolidated group may elect to treat a pre-existing QOF sub as a QOF C corporation that is not a member of the consolidated group.

(B) *Effect of the non-member QOF C corporation election.*—As a result of making the election under this paragraph (f)(2)(iii), the pre-existing QOF sub is treated as not being a member of the consolidated group from day one. Consequently, the consolidated group must file amended or superseding returns, as applicable, to exclude all of the pre-existing QOF sub's income, gain, deduction, and loss from the consolidated returns; the pre-existing QOF sub also must file its own returns for taxable periods beginning on day one, as applicable. In addition, all adjustments resulting from the pre-existing QOF sub's operations must be eliminated from the consolidated group, including investment adjustments made under § 1.1502-32 to basis in members' stock (as well as stock in the pre-existing QOF sub) and adjustments made under § 1.1502-33 to members' earnings and profits.

(iv) *Treatment as a non-QOF C corporation.*—(A) *Election.*—A consolidated group may elect to treat a pre-existing QOF sub as if it never self-certified to be a QOF pursuant to § 1.1400Z2(d)-1.

(B) *Effect of the non-QOF C corporation election.*—As a result of making the election under this paragraph (f)(2)(iv), the pre-existing QOF sub is treated from day one as a member of the consolidated group and not as a QOF. Therefore, section 1400Z-2 is not

applicable, and amended returns or superseding returns must be filed, as applicable, to account for the eligible gain that was invested in the pre-existing QOF sub. In addition, appropriate adjustments must be made to account for the non-applicability of section 1400Z-2, including adjustments to members' stock basis and earnings and profits under § § 1.1502-32 and 1.1502-33, respectively.

(3) *Election to continue treating pre-existing QOF sub as a member of the consolidated group.*—(i) *Election.*—A consolidated group may elect to have a pre-existing QOF sub retain its QOF status and remain a member of the consolidated group.

(ii) *Effects of electing to remain a QOF and a member of the consolidated group.*—As a result of making the election under this paragraph (f)(3), the conditions and effects provided in § 1.1504-3(b)(2) and paragraph (b)(1) of this section will apply to the preexisting QOF sub and the consolidated group as of the effective date of this election. See paragraph (h)(1) of this section for the effective date of this election, and see paragraph (h)(3)(iii) of this section regarding the timing for meeting the requirements in § 1.1504-3(b)(2)(ii).

(g) *Deconsolidation rules.*—(1) *In general.*—This paragraph (g) provides rules applicable on any deconsolidation of a QOF C corporation (deconsolidating QOF).

(2) *Deconsolidation and inclusion event.*—A deconsolidation event is not an inclusion event unless the deconsolidation is the result of an actual transfer of the QOF member stock or a worthlessness event within the meaning of § 1.1502-80(c). For example, when a consolidated group fails to meet the conditions in § 1.1504-3(b)(2) of this section and causes a QOF member to deconsolidate, the deconsolidation event is not an inclusion event solely as a result of the consolidated group's failure to meet the requirements in § 1.1504-3(b)(2) of this section.

(3) *Basis in the deconsolidating QOF at time of deconsolidation.*—(i) *ELA in a deconsolidating QOF.*—Any ELA in stock of the deconsolidating QOF at the time of the deconsolidation is taken into account under the rules of § 1.1502-19. See paragraph (b)(1)(iii) of this section for rules coordinating the application of section 1400Z-2(c) with § 1.1502-19.

(ii) *Positive basis in the deconsolidating QOF resulting from § 1.1502-32.*—Consolidated group members retain any positive basis in the deconsolidating QOF resulting from investment adjustments under § 1.1502-32 following its deconsolidation. However, following the deconsolidation, for purposes of determining the amount includible under § 1.1400Z2(b)-1(e), the amount of basis referred to in section 1400Z-2(b)(2)(A)(ii) is computed by applying only those rules applicable to corporations that do not file a consolidated return (that is, the basis rules under subchapter C and section 1400Z-2). Therefore, any positive basis resulting from § 1.1502-32 adjustments is not taken into account in computing the amount includable under § 1.1400Z2(b)-1(e).

(4) *Deconsolidating QOF's earnings and profits.*—(i) *Deconsolidation on or before December 31, 2026.*—Notwithstanding § 1.1502-33(e)(1), if a deconsolidating QOF deconsolidates before December 31, 2026, the deconsolidating QOF retains its earnings and profits under this paragraph (g)(4)(i). Any earnings and profits of the deconsolidating QOF that were taken into account by any other members under § 1.1502-33 are eliminated from those members as of the end of the day on which the deconsolidating QOF deconsolidates.

(ii) *Deconsolidation after December 31, 2026.*—If the deconsolidating QOF deconsolidates after December 31, 2026, the rules under § 1.1502-33(e) apply.

(5) *Consequences under § 1.1502-36.*—See § 1.1502-36(f)(10)(i)(B) for the treatment of a deconsolidation as a transfer of all of the stock in the deconsolidating member held by other members of the consolidated group.

(h) *Form and manner of making an election under this section.*—(1) *In general.*—The elections provided in this section are irrevocable. The information required for each election is provided in this paragraph (h). A reclassification election under paragraph (f)(2) of this section is effective as of day one. All other elections are effective on the election date.

(2) *Election under paragraph (c)(2) of this section to treat investment by M2 as qualifying investment by M1.*—(i) *Form of election.*—The election under paragraph (c)(2) of this section must be made in the form of a statement titled "THIS IS AN ELECTION UNDER § 1.1502-14Z(c)(2) TO TREAT AN INVESTMENT BY [insert name and employer identification number (E.I.N.) of M2] AS A QUALIFYING INVESTMENT BY [insert name and E.I.N. of M1]." The statement must be included with the consolidated group's timely filed

return (original, superseding, or amended return, as applicable, including extensions). In addition, the statement must include the information required under paragraph (h)(2)(ii) of this section.

(ii) *Required information.*—(A) The amount of M1's eligible gain;

(B) The amount of the investment M2 has made in a QOF, including identification of the amount of the investment that is eligible for treatment as a qualifying investment under paragraph (c)(2) of this section and the amount (if any) that is not eligible for such treatment; and

(C) The date on which M1 recognized its eligible gain, and the date on which M2 made the investment in the QOF.

(3) *Elections under paragraph (f) of this section for transition relief.*—(i) *Form of election.*—The elections under paragraph (f) of this section must be made in the form of a statement titled "THIS IS AN ELECTION UNDER §1.1502-14Z(f) FOR [insert name and E.I.N. of pre-existing QOF sub]." All actions necessary to make these elections, including the filing of an amended return (or superseding return, as applicable), or filing an original return, as applicable, must be completed within the time designated in paragraph (h)(3)(iii) of this section. The statement must be included on or with any amended prior-year consolidated return (or superseding or original return, as applicable) and on or with the consolidated group's timely filed return (original or amended if filed by the due date for the return, including extensions) for the election year. In addition, the statement must include the information required in paragraph (h)(3)(ii) of this section.

(ii) *Required information.*—(A) *Reclassification election under paragraph (f)(2)(ii) of this section.*—(1) A statement that the pre-existing QOF sub is electing to be a QOF partnership;

(2) The election date;

(3) The effective date of the election;

(4) Specification of the appropriate adjustments required under paragraph (f)(2)(ii) of this section made by the pre-existing QOF sub and the consolidated group; and

(5) Certification that the appropriate change under state law or the entity classification election under §301.7701-3 of this chapter (as applicable) has been made, and the date of the change or entity classification election.

(B) *Reclassification election under paragraph (f)(2)(iii) or (iv) of this section.*—(1) A statement that the pre-existing QOF sub is changing its status;

(2) The pre-existing QOF sub's new status (either a non-member QOF C corporation, under paragraph (f)(2)(iii) of this section, or a non-QOF C corporation, under paragraph (f)(2)(iv) of this section);

(3) The election date;

(4) The effective date of the election; and

(5) Specification of the appropriate adjustments made by pre-existing QOF sub and the consolidated group pursuant to paragraph (f)(2)(iii) or (iv) of this section, as applicable.

(C) *Election to continue treating the pre-existing QOF sub as a subsidiary member of the consolidated group under paragraph (f)(3) of this section.*—(1) A statement that the pre-existing QOF sub is electing to retain its status as a QOF C corporation and remain a member of the consolidated group;

(2) The election date; and

(3) Certification that the pre-existing QOF sub and the consolidated group are in compliance with the conditions under §1.1504-3(b)(2)(ii) as of the date that the pre-existing QOF sub and the consolidated group are in compliance with the conditions under §1.1504-3(b)(2)(ii).

(iii) *Time for completing the elections under paragraph (f) of this section.*—(A) If the pre-existing QOF sub is making an election under paragraph (f)(2)(ii) or (f)(3) of this section, all actions necessary to make such election must be completed by April 13, 2020. Specifically, if the pre-existing QOF sub is making the election under paragraph (f)(3) of this section, the conditions in §1.1504-3(b)(2)(ii) must be met by April 13, 2020. In addition, the consolidated group's amended return (or superseding return, as applicable), taking into account the relevant changes, if applicable, must be filed by May 12, 2020. Moreover, if the electing QOF partnership had been a QOF partnership on day one and the electing QOF partnership's return would have been due, then such return also must be filed by May 12, 2020.

(B) If the pre-existing QOF sub is making a reclassification election under paragraph (f)(2)(iii) or (iv) of this section, all actions necessary to make such election, including the filing of the pre-existing QOF sub's own return (if the return would have been due had the pre-existing QOF sub not been included in the consolidated group on day one), and the consolidated group's amended return (or

superseding return, as applicable), if applicable, must be completed by April 13, 2020.

(iv) *Extension of statute of limitations.*—If, as a result of making a reclassification election in paragraph (f)(2) of this section, the consolidated group is required to file an amended return, and the electing QOF partnership is required to file a return by May 12, 2020 or the pre-existing QOF sub is required to file a return by April 13, 2020 (collectively, the related returns), then the consolidated group (and the pre-existing QOF sub, if an election under paragraph (f)(2)(iii) of this section is made) also must consent to extend the period of limitations on assessment with respect to any issues arising under section 1400Z-2 in the related returns of the consolidated group (and the pre-existing QOF sub, if applicable). This consent must be effected at such time and in such form and manner as may be prescribed by the Commissioner of Internal Revenue in Internal Revenue Service forms or instructions or in publications or guidance published in the Internal Revenue Bulletin (see §§601.601(d)(2) and 601.602 of this chapter).

(i) [Reserved]

(j) *Examples.*—The following examples illustrate the rules of this section. For purposes of these examples, and unless otherwise stated: P is the common parent of the P consolidated group (P group); S, B, and M are members of the P group; Q is a QOF C corporation that is not a member of the P group; and X is an unrelated party.

(1) *Example 1: Distribution by a QOF member and inclusion events*—(i) *Facts.* P wholly owns S. In 2018, S sells an asset to an unrelated party and realizes $500x of eligible gain. S forms a new QOF C corporation Q2, contributes $500x to Q2 in exchange for stock of Q2, and properly elects to defer the eligible gain under section 1400Z-2(a) and §1.1400Z2(a)-1. The P group elects under §1.1504-3(b)(2) to consolidate Q2. In 2024, Q2 distributes $20x to S when S's basis in Q2 is $50x, the value of Q2 exceeds $500x, and Q2 has no earnings and profits. There are no other events in 2024 that result in investment adjustments to Q2 stock.

(ii) *Analysis.* Under §§1.1502-13(f)(2) and 1.1502-32, the intercompany distribution from Q2 to S of $20x reduces S's basis in Q2 to $30x ($50x - $20x). Under paragraph (b)(1)(i) of this section, because the distribution does not create or increase an ELA in Q2 stock, the distribution is not an inclusion event.

(iii) *Distribution that creates an ELA.* The facts are the same as in paragraph (j)(1)(i) of this section except that in 2024 Q2 distributes $70x to S. Under §§1.1502-13(f)(2) and 1.1502-32, the intercompany distribution from Q2 to S of $70x reduces S's basis in Q2 to $0 and creates an ELA of $20x ($50x - $70x). Under paragraph (b)(1)(i) of this section, because an ELA is created in Q2's stock, the distribution is an inclusion event to the extent of the increase in the ELA. S therefore includes $20x of its deferred gain into income in 2024. See §1.1400Z2(b)-1(e)(2). In addition, under §1.1400Z2(b)-1(g)(1)(ii), the adjustment to S's basis in Q2 under section 1400Z-2(b)(2)(B)(ii) is applied before determining the other Federal income tax consequences of the distribution. Therefore, as a result of the inclusion event, S's basis in Q2 is first increased to $70x ($50x + $20x), and then S's basis in Q2 is reduced by $70x (the amount of the distribution) to $0 under §1.1502-32.

(2) *Example 2: Basis adjustment when member owns qualifying QOF stock*—(i) *Facts.* P wholly owns S. In 2018, S sells an asset to an unrelated party and realizes $500x of eligible gain. S contributes $500x to Q in exchange for stock of Q and properly elects to defer the eligible gain under section 1400Z-2(a) and §1.1400Z2(a)-1. S does not otherwise own stock in Q. In 2026, the fair market value of S's qualifying investment in Q exceeds $500x. In 2029, when S still owns its qualifying investment in Q, P sells all of the stock of S to X. S retains its stock in Q.

(ii) *Analysis*—(A) *Five-year and seven-year basis increase and §1.1502-32 tier-up.* In 2023, when S has held the stock of Q for five years, under section 1400Z-2(b)(2)(B)(iii), S increases its basis in its Q stock by $50x (10 percent of $500x, the amount of gain deferred by reason of section 1400Z-2(a)(1)(A)). The 10-percent basis increase qualifies as tax-exempt income to S under paragraph (d) of this section. Thus, P (an upper-tier member) increases its basis in S's stock by $50x under §1.1502-32(b)(2)(ii). Similarly, in 2025, when S has held the stock of Q for seven years, under section 1400Z-2(b)(2)(B)(iv), S increases its basis in its Q stock by an additional $25x (5 percent of $500x). The 5-percent basis increase also qualifies as tax-exempt income to S under paragraph (d) of this section, and P increases its basis in S's stock by an additional $25x under §1.1502-32(b)(2)(ii).

(B) *S's recognition of deferred capital gain in 2026.* S did not dispose of its Q stock prior to December 31, 2026. Therefore, under section 1400Z-2(b)(1)(B) and §1.1400Z2(b)-1(b)(2), S's remaining deferred gain is included in S's income on December 31, 2026. The amount of gain included under section 1400Z-2(b)(2)(A) and §1.1400Z2(b)-1(e)(3) is $425x ($500x of remaining deferred gain less

S's $75x basis in Q). S's basis in Q is increased by $425x to $500x, and P's basis in S also is increased by $425x under § 1.1502-32(b)(2)(i).

(C) *P's disposition of S.* P's sale of S stock in 2029 results in the deconsolidation of S. S retains its Q stock, and S is not treated as selling or exchanging its Q stock for purposes of section 1400Z-2(c). Therefore, no basis adjustments under section 1400Z-2 are made as a result of P's sale of S stock.

(iii) *S sells the stock of Q after 10 years.* The facts are the same as in paragraph (j)(2)(i) of this section, except that in 2029, instead of P selling all of the stock of S, S sells all of the stock of Q to X for its fair market value of $800x. At the time of the sale, S has owned the Q stock for over 10 years, and S elects under section 1400Z-2(c) to adjust its stock basis in Q from $500x (see the analysis in paragraph (j)(2)(ii)(B) of this section) to $800x, the fair market value of Q on the date of the sale. As a result of the election, S has no gain on the sale of Q stock. Additionally, the $300x basis increase in Q is treated as tax-exempt income to S pursuant to paragraph (d) of this section. Thus, P increases its basis in P's S stock by $300x under § 1.1502-32(b)(2)(ii).

(3) *Example 3: Intercompany sale of qualifying investment*—(i) *Facts.* In 2018, S sells an asset to an unrelated party and realizes $100x of eligible gain. Also in 2018, S contributes $100x to Q in exchange for Q stock and properly elects to defer the eligible gain under section 1400Z-2(a) and § 1.1400Z2(a)-1. S does not otherwise own stock in Q. In 2021, S sells all of its Q stock to B for $250x in a fully taxable transaction. In 2026, the fair market value of Q is $300x. In 2030, B sells the Q stock to X for $800x.

(ii) *Analysis*—(A) *Intercompany sale treated as an inclusion event.* In 2021, S's sale of its Q stock to B is an inclusion event under section 1400Z-2(b)(1) and § 1.1400Z2(b)-1(c). The amount includible pursuant to § 1.1400Z2(b)-1(e)(1) is $100x (the lesser of the remaining deferred gain of $100x and the fair market value of the qualifying investment of $250x, over S's basis in Q, $0). As a result of the inclusion, S's basis in Q increases from $0 to $100x and S also realizes a capital gain of $150x ($250x of amount realized less its $100x basis in the Q stock) from the intercompany sale of Q to B. Because S's sale of its Q stock to B is a fully taxable transaction, paragraph (c)(3)(ii) of this section applies to treat the sale as an intercompany transaction and S's intercompany gains are taken into account under § 1.1502-13(c)(2)(ii). Thus, S defers the inclusion of its $100x of remaining deferred gain and its $150x of capital gain in 2021. B has a $250x basis in its Q stock.

(B) *Five-year basis increase in 2023.* Pursuant to paragraph (c)(3)(ii) of this section, S and B are treated as divisions of a single entity for purposes of applying section 1400Z-2. In 2023, the single entity would have held the QOF investment for five years and its basis in Q would be increased to $10x ($100x × 10%) under section 1400Z-2(b)(2)(B)(iii). To achieve this single entity result, $10x of S's $100x of remaining deferred gain is redetermined to be tax-exempt income. See § 1.1502-13(c)(1); see also paragraph (c)(3)(ii)(B) of this section making § 1.1502-13(c)(6)(ii) inapplicable in determining the excludability of S's intercompany gain. Therefore, in 2023, S is treated as having $10x of tax-exempt income, S's remaining deferred gain is $90x ($100x - $10x), while B's basis in Q remains $250x.

(C) *Seven-year basis increase in 2025.* The same analysis in paragraph (j)(3)(ii)(B) of this section applies for the year 2025. Therefore, in 2025, S is treated as having $5x ($100x × 5%) of tax-exempt income, S's remaining deferred gain is $85x ($90x - $5x), and B's basis in Q remains $250x.

(D) *Inclusion of S's remaining deferred gain in 2026.* B continues to own the Q stock through 2026, and, treating S and B as divisions of a single entity for purposes of section 1400Z-2, the single entity would include its remaining deferred gain in income on December 31, 2026. See section 1400Z-2(b)(1), § 1.1400Z2(b)-1(b). On a single-entity basis, the amount includible pursuant to § 1.1400Z2(b)-1(e) is $85x (the lesser of the remaining deferred gain of $100x and the fair market value of the qualifying investment of $300x, over the single entity's basis in Q, $15x). B does not otherwise have an income event with respect to its Q stock in 2026. Therefore, under § 1.1502-13(c), all $85x of S's remaining deferred gain is taken into account in 2026. In addition, S's $150x of capital gain on its Q stock sale continues to be deferred, and B's basis in Q remains $250x.

(E) *B sells the Q stock in 2030.* In 2030, B sells all its Q stock to X for $800x. Under paragraph (c)(3)(ii)(D) of this section, B is entitled to make the election under section 1400Z-2(c) if, treating S and B as a single entity, the single entity would be eligible to make the election. Taking into account S's holding period, B has held Q for over 10 years, and B is eligible for the election when it sells Q to X in 2030. B makes the section 1400Z-2(c) election at the time of sale. Following the election, if S and B were divisions of a single entity, the single entity's basis in Q would increase from $100x to its fair market value of $800x, causing to be excluded the $700x of gain on the sale of Q stock. To achieve this single entity result, § 1.1502-13(c)(1) redetermines B's $550x ($800x - $250x) of gain and S's deferred $150x of capital gain to be tax-exempt income. See paragraph (c)(3)(ii)(B) of this section making § 1.1502-13(c)(6)(ii) inapplicable in determining

the excludability of S's intercompany gain. Therefore, as a result of the sale of the Q stock and B making the section 1400Z-2(c) election, S has $150x of tax-exempt income, and B has $550x of tax-exempt income.

(4) *Example 4: Intercompany sale of qualifying investment followed by sale of QOF at a loss outside of the consolidated group*—(i) *Facts.* The facts are the same as in paragraph (j)(3)(i) of this section, except that in 2030, B sells the stock of Q for $225x to X.

(ii) *Analysis.* The analysis for tax years prior to 2030 is the same as in paragraphs (j)(3)(ii)(A) through (D) of this section. In addition, applying the analysis in paragraph (j)(3)(ii)(E) of this section, B is entitled to make the election under section 1400Z-2(c) and B makes the election. Following the election, if S and B were divisions of a single entity, the single entity's basis in Q would increase from $100x to $225x, causing to be excluded the $125x of gain on the sale of Q stock. To achieve this single entity result, § 1.1502-13(c)(1) redetermines B's $25x ($225x - $250x) of loss to be a noncapital, nondeductible expense and S's deferred $150x of capital gain to be tax-exempt income. Therefore, as a result of the sale of Q stock and B making the section 1400Z-2 election, S has $150x of tax-exempt income, and B has $25x of noncapital, nondeductible expense.

(5) *Example 5: Intercompany section 351 transfer of qualifying investment*—(i) *Facts.* In 2018, M sells an asset to an unrelated party and realizes $100x of eligible gain. Also in 2018, M contributes $100x to Q in exchange for Q stock and properly elects to defer the eligible gain under section 1400Z-2(a) and § 1.1400Z2(a)-1. M does not otherwise own stock in Q. In 2021, when the value of Q is $200x, M contributes all of its Q stock to S in exchange for S stock in a transaction that qualifies under section 351.

(ii) *Analysis.* In 2021, M's contribution of its Q stock to S is an inclusion event under section 1400Z-2(b)(1) and § 1.1400Z2(b)-1(c). The amount includible pursuant to § 1.1400Z2(b)-1(e) is $100x (the lesser of the remaining deferred gain of $100x and the fair market value of the qualifying investment of $200x, over S's basis in Q, $0). Because M's contribution of its Q stock to S is not a fully taxable transaction, the general rule in paragraph (c)(3)(i) of this section applies to treat the contribution as not an intercompany transaction for purposes of applying section 1400Z-2, and § 1.1502-13 does not apply to treat M and S as a single entity for purposes of section 1400Z-2. Thus, as a result of the transfer, M takes its $100x of remaining deferred gain into account, M's basis in S is $100x, and S's basis in Q is $100x.

(6) *Example 6: Intercompany sale of qualifying investment followed by a tax-free transfer of the qualifying investment*—(i) *Section 351 transfer to another member of the consolidated group*—(A) *Facts.* In 2018, S sells an asset to an unrelated party and realizes $100x of eligible gain. Also in 2018, S contributes $100x to Q in exchange for Q stock and properly elects to defer the eligible gain under section 1400Z-2(a) and § 1.1400Z2(a)-1. S does not otherwise own stock in Q. In 2021, when the fair market value of the Q stock is $250, S sells all of its Q stock to B for $250x in a fully taxable transaction. In 2024, B transfers all its Q stock to another member of the P group, B2, in a section 351 transaction. At such time, the fair market value of the Q stock is $300x.

(B) *Analysis*—(1) *Intercompany sale in 2021.* In 2021, S's sale of its Q stock to B is an inclusion event under section 1400Z-2(b)(1) and § 1.1400Z2(b)-1(c). The amount includible pursuant to § 1.1400Z2(b)-1(e) is $100x (the lesser of the remaining deferred gain of $100x and the fair market value of the qualifying investment of $250x, over S's basis in Q, $0). As a result of the inclusion, S's basis in its Q stock increases from $0 to $100x and S also realizes a capital gain of $150x ($250x of amount realized less its $100x basis in the Q stock) from the intercompany sale of the Q stock to B. Because S's sale of its Q stock to B is a fully taxable transaction, paragraph (c)(3)(ii) of this section applies to treat the sale as an intercompany transaction. Therefore, S's intercompany gains are taken into account under § 1.1502-13(c) and (d). Thus, S defers the inclusion of its $100x of remaining deferred gain and its $150x of capital gain in 2021. B has a $250x basis in its Q stock.

(2) *Five-year basis increase in 2023.* Pursuant to paragraph (c)(3)(ii) of this section, S and B are treated as divisions of a single entity for purposes of applying section 1400Z-2. In 2023, the single entity has held the QOF investment for five years and its basis in the Q stock would be increased to $10x ($100x × 10%) under section 1400Z-2(b)(2)(B)(iii). To achieve this single entity result, $10x of S's $100x of remaining deferred gain is redetermined to be tax-exempt income. See § 1.1502-13(c)(1); see also paragraph (c)(3)(ii)(B) of this section making § 1.1502-13(c)(6)(ii) inapplicable in determining the excludability of S's intercompany gain. Therefore, in 2023, S is treated as having $10x of tax-exempt income, S's remaining deferred gain is $90x ($100x - $10x), and B's basis in the Q stock remains $250x.

(3) *Intercompany transfer in a section 351 transaction.* In 2024, B's contribution of its Q stock to B2, a member of the P group, is an inclusion event under section 1400Z-2(b)(1) and § 1.1400Z2(b)-1(c). The amount includible pursuant to § 1.1400Z2(b)-1(e) is $90x (the

remaining deferred gain as determined in paragraph (j)(6)(i)(B) of this section). Because B's contribution of its Q stock to B2 is not a fully taxable transaction, the general rule in paragraph (c)(3)(i) of this section applies to prevent the contribution from being treated as an intercompany transaction for purposes of section 1400Z-2. As a result, for purposes of section 1400Z-2, §1.1502-13 does not apply to treat B and B2 as a single entity, and the application of §1.1502-13(j) is adjusted accordingly. As a result of the section 351 transfer, S takes its $90x of remaining deferred gain into account. B's basis in its B2 stock is $250x, and B's basis in its Q stock is $250x. However, because S's $150x of capital gain from the intercompany sale of its Q stock to B in 2021 is not an item related to section 1400Z-2, it continues to be deferred under §1.1502-13 because B2 is a member of the P group. See §1.1502-13(j)(4) regarding successive intercompany transactions.

(ii) *Section 351 transfer to a non-member*—(A) *Facts.* The facts are the same as in paragraph (j)(6)(i)(A) of this section, except that B2 is not a member of the P group, and B contributes all its Q stock to B2 in a transaction that qualifies under section 351.

(B) *Analysis*—(1) *Intercompany sale in 2021 and five-year basis increase in 2023.* The analysis for the 2021 and 2023 tax years are the same as in paragraphs (j)(6)(i)(B)(1) and (2) of this section.

(2) *Transfer of Q to a non-member in a section 351 transaction.* In 2024, B's contribution of its Q stock to B2, a non-member of the P group, is an inclusion event under section 1400Z-2(b)(1) and §1.1400Z2(b)-1(c). The amount includible pursuant to §1.1400Z2(b)-1(e) is $90x (the remaining deferred gain as determined in paragraph (j)(6)(ii)(B)(1) of this section). S's deferred capital gain of $150x is taken into account in 2024 under the acceleration rule of §1.1502-13(d) because the Q stock has left the P group. B2's holding period for the qualifying investment does not include the time during which B and S held the qualifying investment.

(iii) *Section 721(a) transfer to a partnership*—(A) *Facts.* The facts are the same as in paragraph (j)(6)(i)(A) of this section, except that B2 is a partnership, and an unrelated party is the other partner in B2. B's transfer of all of its Q stock to B2 qualifies for non-recognition treatment under section 721(a). In 2026, the fair market value of Q is $330x.

(B) *Analysis*—(1) *Intercompany sale in 2021 and five-year basis increase in 2023.* The analysis for the 2021 and 2023 tax years are the same as in paragraphs (j)(6)(i)(B)(1) and (2) of this section.

(2) *Transfer of Q stock to a partnership in a section 721(a) transaction.* In 2024, B transfers its Q stock to B2, a partnership, in a section 721(a) transaction. Although a section 721(a) transaction is not an inclusion event under §1.1400Z2(b)-1(c)(7), under the acceleration rule of §1.1502-13(d), S must take into account its $90x of remaining deferred gain because B2 has benefited from an increased basis in the Q stock as a result of the intercompany sale between S and B such that this is the appropriate time to take the remaining deferred gain into account. S's deferred capital gain of $150x is taken into account in 2024 for the same reason.

(7) *Example 7: Computation and application of the attribute reduction amount under §1.1502-36(d) when S owns a QOF*—(i) *Facts.* In 2018, S sells an asset to an unrelated party and realizes $5,000x of eligible gain. S contributes $5,000x to Q in exchange for stock of Q and properly elects to defer the eligible gain under section 1400Z-2(a) and §1.1400Z2(a)-1. In 2024, M sells all of its S stock to X for its fair market value of $100x, and M's basis in the stock of S is $300x. At the time of sale, S owns the Q stock with a basis of $500x (S's basis in its Q stock was increased under section 1400Z-2(b)(2)(B)(iii) to $500x in 2023), and S has a net operating loss carryover of $50x. M's transfer of the S shares is a transfer of loss shares under §1.1502-36. Assume that no basis redetermination is required under §1.1502-36(b) and no basis reduction is required under §1.1502-36(c).

(ii) *Attribute reduction under §1.1502-36(d).* Under §1.1502-36(d), S's attributes are reduced by S's attribute reduction amount. Section 1.1502-36(d)(3) provides that S's attribute reduction amount is the lesser of the net stock loss and S's aggregate inside loss. The net stock loss is the excess of the $300x aggregate basis of the transferred S shares over the $100x aggregate value of those shares, or $200x. S's aggregate inside loss, which includes the basis of the stock of Q as provided by paragraph (e) of this section, is the excess of S's net inside attribute amount over the value of the S share. S's net inside attribute amount is $550x, computed as the sum of S's $50x loss carryover and its $500x basis in Q. S's aggregate inside loss is therefore $450x ($550x net inside attribute amount over the $100x value of the S share). Accordingly, S's attribute reduction amount is the lesser of the $200x net stock loss and the $450x aggregate inside loss, or $200x. Under §1.1502-36(d)(4), S's $200x attribute reduction is first allocated and applied to reduce S's $50x loss carryover to $0. Under §1.1502-36(d)(4)(i)(D), S generally would be able to reduce the basis of its category D assets (including stock in other corporations) by the remaining attribute reduction amount ($150x). However, paragraph (e) of this section provides that S's basis in the stock of Q is not included in S's Category D attributes that are available for reduction

under §1.1502-36(d)(4), and the remaining $150x of attribute reduction amount cannot be used to reduce the basis of Q shares under §1.1502-36(d). Rather, under paragraph (e) of this section, P is treated as making the election under §1.1502-36(d)(6) to reduce M's basis in the transferred loss S shares by $150x. As a result, P's basis in its M stock is also reduced by $150x.

(k) *Applicability dates.*—(1) *In general.*—This section applies for taxable years beginning after March 13, 2020.

(2) *Prior periods.*—With respect to the portion of a consolidated group's first taxable year ending after December 21, 2017, and for taxable years beginning after December 21, 2017, and on or before March 13, 2020, a consolidated group may choose either—

(i) To apply the section 1400Z-2 regulations, if applied in a consistent manner for all such taxable years; or

(ii) To rely on the rules in proposed §1.1400Z2(g)-1 contained in the notice of proposed rulemaking (REG-120186-18) published on May 1, 2019, but only if applied in a consistent manner for all such taxable years. [Reg. §1.1502-14Z.]

☐ [T.D. 9889, 12-31-2019 (corrected 4-1-2020).]

**[Reg. §1.1502-15]**

**§1.1502-15. SRLY limitation on built-in losses.**—(a) *SRLY limitation.*—Except as provided in paragraph (f) of this section (relating to built-in losses of the common parent) and paragraph (g) of this section (relating to an overlap with section 382), built-in losses are subject to the SRLY limitation under §§1.1502-21(c) and 1.1502-22(c) (including applicable subgroup principles). Built-in losses are treated as deductions or losses in the year recognized, except for the purpose of determining the amount of, and the extent to which the built-in loss is limited by, the SRLY limitation for the year in which it is recognized. Solely for such purpose, a built-in loss is treated as a hypothetical net operating loss carryover or net capital loss carryover arising in a SRLY, instead of as a deduction or loss in the year recognized. To the extent that a built-in loss is allowed as a deduction under this section in the year it is recognized, it offsets any consolidated taxable income for the year before any loss carryovers or carrybacks are allowed as a deduction. To the extent not so allowed, it is treated as a separate net operating loss or net capital loss carryover or carryback arising in the year of recognition and, under §1.1502-21(c) or 1.1502-22(c), the year of recognition is treated as a SRLY.

(b) *Built-in losses.*—(1) *Defined.*—If a corporation has a net unrealized built-in loss under section 382(h)(3) (as modified by this section) on the day it becomes a member of the group (whether or not the group is a consolidated group), its deductions and losses are built-in losses under this section to the extent they are treated as recognized built-in losses under section 382(h)(2)(B) (as modified by this section). This paragraph (b) generally applies separately with respect to each member, but see paragraph (c) of this section for circumstances in which it is applied on a subgroup basis.

(2) *Operating rules.*—Solely for purposes of applying paragraph (b)(1) of this section, the principles of §1.1502-94(c) apply with appropriate adjustments, including the following:

(i) *Stock acquisition.*—A corporation is treated as having an ownership change under section 382(g) on the day the corporation becomes a member of a group, and no other events (e.g., a subsequent ownership change under section 382(g) while it is a member) are treated as causing an ownership change.

(ii) *Asset acquisition.*—In the case of an asset acquisition by a group, the assets and liabilities acquired directly from the same transferor (whether corporate or non-corporate, foreign or domestic) pursuant to the same plan are treated as the assets and liabilities of a corporation that becomes a member of the group (and has an ownership change) on the date of the acquisition.

(iii) *Recognized built-in gain or loss.*—A loss that is included in the determination of net unrealized built-in gain or loss and that is recognized but disallowed or deferred (e.g., under §§1.337(d)-2, 1.1502-35, 1.1502-36, or section 267) is not treated as a built-in loss unless and until the loss would be allowed during the recognition period without regard to the application of this section. Section 382(h)(1)(B)(ii) does not apply to the extent it limits the amount of recognized built-in loss that may be treated as a pre-change loss to the amount of the net unrealized built-in loss.

(c) *Built-in losses of subgroups.*—(1) *In general.*—In the case of a subgroup, the principles of paragraph (b) of this section apply to the subgroup, and not separately to its members. Thus, the net unrealized built-in loss and recognized built-in loss for purposes of paragraph (b) of this section are based on the aggregate amounts for each member of the subgroup.

(2) *Members of subgroups.*—A subgroup is composed of those members that have been continuously affiliated with each other for the 60 consecutive month period ending immediately before they become members of the group in which the loss is recognized. A member remains a member of the subgroup until it ceases to be affiliated with the loss member. For this purpose, the principles of § 1.1502-21(c)(2)(iv) through (vi) apply with appropriate adjustments.

(3) *Coordination of 60 month affiliation requirement with the overlap rule.*—If one or more corporations become members of a group and are included in the determination of a net unrealized built-in loss that is subject to the overlap rule described in paragraph (g)(1) of this section, then for purposes of paragraph (c)(2) of this section, such corporations that become members of the group are treated as having been affiliated for 60 consecutive months with the common parent of the group and are also treated as having been affiliated with any other members who have been affiliated or are treated as having been affiliated with the common parent at such time. The corporations are treated as having been affiliated with such other members for the same period of time that those members have been affiliated or are treated as having been affiliated with the common parent. If two or more corporations become members of the group at the same time, but this paragraph (c)(3) does not apply to every such corporation, then immediately after the corporations become members of the group, and solely for purposes of paragraph (c)(2) of this section, the corporations to which this paragraph (c)(3) applies are treated as having not been previously affiliated with the corporations to which this paragraph (c)(3) does not apply. If the common parent has become the common parent of an existing group within the previous five year period in a transaction described in § 1.1502-75(d)(2)(ii) or (3), the principles of §§ 1.1502-91(g)(6) and 1.1502-96(a)(2)(iii) shall apply.

(4) *Built-in amounts.*—Solely for purposes of determining whether the subgroup has a net unrealized built-in loss or whether it has a recognized built-in loss, the principles of § 1.1502-91(g) and (h) apply with appropriate adjustments.

(d) *Examples.*—For purposes of the examples in this section, unless otherwise stated, all groups file consolidated returns, all corporations have calendar taxable years, the facts set forth the only corporate activity, value means fair market value and the adjusted basis of each asset equals its value, all transactions are with unrelated persons, and the application of any limitation or threshold under section 382 is disregarded. The principles of this section are illustrated by the following examples:

*Example 1. Determination of recognized built-in loss.* (i) Individual A owns all of the stock of P and T. T has two depreciable assets. Asset 1 has an unrealized loss of $55 (basis $75, value $20), and asset 2 has an unrealized gain of $20 (basis $30, value $50). P acquires all the stock of T from Individual A during Year 1, and T becomes a member of the P group. P's acquisition of T is not an ownership change as defined by section 382(g). Paragraph (g) of this section does not apply because there is not an overlap of the application of the rules contained in paragraph (a) of this section and section 382.

(ii) Under paragraph (b)(2)(i) of this section, and solely for purposes of applying paragraph (b)(1) of this section, T is treated as having an ownership change under section 382(g) on becoming a member of the P group. Under paragraph (b)(1) of this section, none of T's $55 of unrealized loss is treated as a built-in loss unless T has a net unrealized built-in loss under section 382(h)(3) on becoming a member of the P group.

(iii) Under section 382(h)(3)(A), T has a $35 net unrealized built-in loss on becoming a member of the P group (($55) + $20 = ($35)). Assume that this amount exceeds the threshold requirement in section 382(h)(3)(B). Under section 382(h)(2)(B), the entire amount of T's $55 unrealized loss is treated as a built-in loss to the extent it is recognized during the 5-year recognition period described in section 382(h)(7). Under paragraph (b)(2)(iii) of this section, the restriction under section 382(h)(1)(B)(ii), which limits the amount of recognized built-in loss that is treated as pre-change loss to the amount of the net unrealized built-in loss, is inapplicable for this purpose. Consequently, the entire $55 of unrealized loss (not just the $35 net unrealized loss) is treated under paragraph (b)(1) of this section as a built-in loss to the extent it is recognized within 5 years of T's becoming a member of the P group. Under paragraph (a) of this section, a built-in loss is subject to the SRLY limitation under § 1.1502-21(c)(1).

(iv) Under paragraph (b)(2)(ii) of this section, the built-in loss would similarly be subject to a SRLY limitation under § 1.1502-21(c)(1) if T transferred all of its assets and liabilities to a subsidiary of the P group in a single transaction described in section 351. To the extent the built-in loss is recognized within 5 years of T's transfer, all of the items contributed by the acquiring subsidiary to consolidated taxable income (and not just the items attributable to the assets and liabilities transferred by T) are included for purposes of determining the SRLY limitation under § 1.1502-21(c)(1).

*Example 2. Actual application of section 382 not relevant.* (i) Individual A owns all of the stock of P, and Individual B owns all of the stock of T. T has two depreciable assets. Asset 1 has an unrealized loss of $25 (basis $75, value $50), and asset 2 has an unrealized gain of $20 (basis $30, value $50). P buys 55 percent of the stock of T in January of Year 1, resulting in an ownership change of T under section 382(g). During March of Year 2, P buys the 45 percent balance of the T stock, and T becomes a member of the P group.

(ii) Although T has an ownership change for purposes of section 382 in Year 1 and not Year 2, T's joining the P group in Year 2 is treated as an ownership change under section 382(g) solely for purposes of this section. Consequently, for purposes of this section, whether T has a net unrealized built-in loss under section 382(h)(3) is determined as if the day T joined the P group were a change date.

*Example 3. Determination of a recognized built-in loss of a subgroup.* (i) Individual A owns all of the stock of P, S, and M. P and M are each the common parent of a consolidated group. During Year 1, P acquires all of the stock of S from Individual A, and S becomes a member of the P group. P's acquisition of S is not an ownership change as defined by section 382(g). At the beginning of Year 7, M acquires all of the stock of P from Individual A, and P and S become members of the M group. M's acquisitions of P and S are also not ownership changes as defined by section 382(g). At the time of M's acquisition of the P stock, P has (disregarding the stock of S) a $10 net unrealized built-in gain (two depreciable assets, asset 1 with a basis of $35 and a value of $55, and asset 2 with a basis of $55 and a value of $45), and S has a $75 net unrealized built-in loss (two depreciable assets, asset 3 with a basis of $95 and a value of $10, and asset 4 with a basis of $10 and a value of $20).

(ii) Under paragraph (c) of this section, P and S compose a subgroup on becoming members of the M group because P and S were continuously affiliated for the 60 month period ending immediately before they became members of the M group. Consequently, paragraph (b) of this section does not apply to P and S separately. Instead, their separately computed unrealized gains and losses are aggregated for purposes of determining whether, and the extent to which, any unrealized loss is treated as built-in loss under this section and is subject to the SRLY limitation under § 1.1502-21(c).

(iii) Under paragraph (c) of this section, the P subgroup has a net unrealized built-in loss on the day P and S become members of the M group, determined by treating the day they become members as a change date. The net unrealized built-in loss is the aggregate of P's net unrealized built-in gain of $10 and S's net unrealized built-in loss of $75, or an aggregate net unrealized built-in loss of $65. (The stock of S owned by P is disregarded for purposes of determining the net unrealized built-in loss. However, any loss allowed on the sale of the stock within the recognition period is taken into account in determining recognized loss.) Assume that the $65 net unrealized built-in loss exceeds the threshold requirement under section 382(h)(3)(B).

(iv) Under paragraphs (b)(1), (b)(2)(iii), and (c) of this section, a loss recognized during the 5-year recognition period on an asset of P or S held on the day that P and S became members of the M group is a built-in loss except to the extent the group establishes that such loss exceeds the amount by which the adjusted basis of such asset on the day the member became a member exceeded the fair market value of such asset on that same day. If P sells asset 2 for $45 in Year 7 and recognizes a $10 loss, the entire $10 loss is treated as a built-in loss under paragraphs (b)(2)(iii) and (c) of this section. If S sells asset 3 for $10 in Year 7 and recognizes an $85 loss, the entire $85 loss is treated as a built-in loss under paragraphs (b)(2)(iii) and (c) of this section (not just the $55 balance of the P subgroup's $65 net unrealized built-in loss).

(v) The determination of whether P and S constitute a SRLY subgroup for purposes of loss carryovers and carrybacks, and the extent to which built-in losses are not allowed under the SRLY limitation, is made under § 1.1502-21(c).

*Example 4. Computation of SRLY limitation.* (i) Individual A owns all of the stock of P, the common parent of a consolidated group. During Year 1, Individual A forms T by contributing $300 and T sustains a $100 net operating loss. During Year 2, T's assets decline in value to $100. At the beginning of Year 3, P acquires all the stock of T from Individual A, and T becomes a member of the P group with a net unrealized built-in loss of $100. P's acquisition of T is not an ownership change as defined by section 382(g). Assume that $100 exceeds the threshold requirements of section 382(h)(3)(B). During Year 3, T recognizes its unrealized built-in loss as a $100 ordinary loss. The members of the P group contribute the following net income to the consolidated taxable income of the P group (disregarding T's recognized built-in loss and any consolidated net operating loss deduction under § 1.1502-21) for Years 3 and 4:

| | Year 3 | Year 4 | Total |
|---|---|---|---|
| P group (without T) | $100 | $100 | $200 |
| T | $60 | $40 | $100 |
| CTI | $160 | $140 | $300 |

(ii) Under paragraph (b) of this section, T's $100 ordinary loss in Year 3 (not taken into account in the consolidated taxable income computations above) is a built-in loss. Under paragraph (a) of this section, the built-in loss is treated as a net operating loss carryover for purposes of determining the SRLY limitation under § 1.1502-21(c).

(iii) For Year 3, § 1.1502-21(c) limits T's $100 built-in loss and $100 net operating loss carryover from Year 1 to the aggregate of the P group's consolidated taxable income through Year 3, determined by reference to only T's items. For this purpose, consolidated taxable income is determined without regard to any consolidated net operating loss deductions under § 1.1502-21(a).

(iv) The P group's consolidated taxable income through Year 3 is $60 when determined by reference to only T's items. Under § 1.1502-21(c), the SRLY limitation for Year 3 is therefore $60.

(v) Under paragraph (a) of this section, the $100 built-in loss is treated as a current deduction for all purposes other than determination of the SRLY limitation under § 1.1502-21(c). Consequently, a deduction for the built-in loss is allowed in Year 3 before T's loss carryover from Year 1 is allowed, but only to the extent of the $60 SRLY limitation. None of T's Year 1 loss carryover is allowed because the built-in loss ($100) exceeds the SRLY limitation for Year 3.

(vi) The $40 balance of the built-in loss that is not allowed in Year 3 because of the SRLY limitation is treated as a $40 net operating loss arising in Year 3 that is carried to other years in accordance with the rules of § 1.1502-21(b). The $40 net operating loss is treated under paragraph (a) of this section and § 1.1502-21(c)(1)(ii) as a loss carryover or carryback from Year 3 that arises in a SRLY, and is subject to the rules of § 1.1502-21 (including § 1.1502-21(c)) rather than this section. See also § 1.1502-21(c)(1)(iii) *Example 4.*

(vii) The facts are the same as in paragraphs (i) through (vi) of this *Example 4,* except that T has an additional built-in loss when it joins the P group which is recognized in Year 4. For purposes of determining the SRLY limitation for this additional loss in Year 4 (or any subsequent year), the $60 of built-in loss allowed as a deduction in Year 3 is treated under paragraph (a) of this section as a deduction in Year 3 that reduces the P group's consolidated taxable income when determined by reference to only T's items.

*Example 5. Built-in loss exceeding consolidated taxable income in the year recognized.* (i) Individual A owns all of the stock of P and T. During Year 1, P acquires all the stock of T from Individual A, and T becomes a member of the P group. P's acquisition of T was not an ownership change as defined by section 382(g). At the time of acquisition, T has a noncapital asset with an unrealized loss of $45 (basis $100, value $55), which exceeds the threshold requirements of section 382(h)(3)(B). During Year 2, T sells its asset for $55 and recognizes the unrealized built-in loss. The P group has $10 of consolidated taxable income in Year 2, computed by disregarding T's recognition of the $45 built-in loss and the consolidated net operating loss deduction, while the consolidated taxable income would be $25 if determined by reference to only T's items (other than the $45 loss).

(ii) T's $45 loss is recognized in Year 2 and, under paragraph (b) of this section, constitutes a built-in loss. Under paragraph (a) of this section and § 1.1502-21(c)(1)(ii), the loss is treated as a net operating loss carryover to Year 2 for purposes of applying the SRLY limitation under § 1.1502-21(c).

(iii) For Year 2, T's SRLY limitation is the aggregate of the P group's consolidated taxable income through Year 2 determined by reference to only T's items. For this purpose, consolidated taxable income is determined by disregarding any built-in loss that is treated as a net operating loss carryover, and any consolidated net operating loss deductions under § 1.1502-21(a). Consolidated taxable income so determined is $25.

(iv) Under § 1.1502-21(c), $25 of the $45 built-in loss could be deducted in Year 2. Because the P group has only $10 of consolidated taxable income (determined without regard to the $45), the $25 loss creates a consolidated net operating loss of $15. This loss is carried back or forward under the rules of § 1.1502-21(b) and absorbed under the rules of § 1.1502-21(a). This loss is not treated as arising in a SRLY (see § 1.1502-21(c)(1)(ii)) and therefore is not subject to the SRLY limitation under § 1.1502-21(c) in any consolidated return year of the group to which it is carried. The remaining $20 is treated as a loss carryover arising in a SRLY and is subject to the limitation of § 1.1502-21(c) in the year to which it is carried.

(e) *Predecessors and successors.*—For purposes of this section, any reference to a corporation or member includes, as the context may require, a reference to a successor or predecessor, as defined in § 1.1502-1(f)(4).

(f) *Built-in losses recognized by common parent of group.*—(1) *General rule.*—Paragraph (a) of this section does not apply to any loss recognized by the group on an asset held by the common parent on the date the group is formed. Following an acquisition described in § 1.1502-75(d)(2) or (3), references to the common parent are to the corporation that was the common parent immediately before the acquisition.

(2) *Anti-avoidance rule.*—If a corporation that becomes a common parent of a group acquires assets with a net unrealized built-in loss in excess of the threshold requirement of section 382(h)(3)(B) (and thereby increases its net unrealized built-in loss or decreases its net unrealized built-in gain) prior to, and in anticipation of, the formation of the group, paragraph (f)(1) of this section does not apply.

(g) *Overlap with section 382.*—(1) *General rule.*—The limitations provided in § § 1.1502-21(c) and 1.1502-22(c) do not apply to recognized built-in losses or to loss carryovers or carrybacks attributable to recognized built-in losses when the application of paragraph (a) of this section results in an overlap with the application of section 382.

(2) *Definitions.*—(i) *Generally.*—For purposes of this paragraph (g), the definitions and nomenclature contained in section 382, the regulations thereunder, and § § 1.1502-90 through 1.1502-99 apply.

(ii) *Overlap.*—(A) An overlap of the application of paragraph (a) of this section and the application of section 382 with respect to built-in losses occurs if a corporation becomes a member of a consolidated group (the SRLY event) within six months of the change date of an ownership change giving rise to a section 382(a) limitation that would apply with respect to the corporation's recognized built-in losses (the section 382 event). Except as provided in paragraph (g)(3) of this section, application of the overlap rule does not require that the size and composition of the corporation's net unrealized built-in loss is the same on the date of the section 382 event and the SRLY event.

(B) For special rules in the event that there is a SRLY subgroup and/or a loss subgroup as defined in § 1.1502-91(d)(2) with respect to built-in losses, see paragraph (g)(4) of this section.

(3) *Operating rules.*—(i) *Section 382 event before SRLY event.*—If a SRLY event occurs on the same date as a section 382 event or within the six month period beginning on the date of the section 382 event, paragraph (g)(1) of this section applies beginning with the tax year that includes the SRLY event. Paragraph (g)(1) of this section does not apply, however, if a corporation that would otherwise be subject to the overlap rule acquires assets from a person other than a member of the group with a net unrealized built-in loss in excess of the threshold requirement of section 382(h)(3)(B) (and thereby increases its net unrealized built-in loss) after the section 382 event, and before the SRLY event.

(ii) *SRLY event before section 382 event.*—If a section 382 event occurs within the period beginning the day after the SRLY event and ending six months after the SRLY event, paragraph (g)(1) of this section applies starting with the first tax year that begins after the section 382 event. However, paragraph (g)(1) of this section does not apply at any time if a corporation that otherwise would be subject to paragraph (g)(1) of this section transfers assets with an unrealized built-in loss to another member of the group after the SRLY event, but before the section 382 event, unless the corporation recognizes the built-in loss upon the transfer.

(4) *Subgroup rules.*—In general, in the case of built-in losses for which there is a SRLY subgroup and the corporations joining the group at the time of the SRLY event also constitute a loss subgroup (as defined in § 1.1502-91(d)(2)), the principles of this paragraph (g) apply to the SRLY subgroup, and not separately to its members. However, paragraph (g)(1) of this section applies with respect to built-in losses only if—

(i) All members of the SRLY subgroup with respect to those built-in losses are also included in a loss subgroup (as defined in § 1.1502-91(d)(2)); and

(ii) All members of a loss subgroup (as defined in § 1.1502-91(d)(2)) are also members of a SRLY subgroup with respect to those built-in losses.

(5) *Asset acquisitions.*—Notwithstanding the application of this paragraph (g), paragraph (a) of this section applies to asset acquisitions by the corporation that occurs after the later of the SRLY event and the section 382 event. See, paragraph (b)(2)(ii) of this section.

(6) *Examples.*—The principles of this paragraph (g) are illustrated by the following examples:

*Example 1. Determination of subgroup.* (i) Individual A owns all of the stock of P, P1, and S. In Year 1, P acquires all of the stock of P1, and they file a consolidated return. In Year 3, P acquires all of the stock of S, and S joins the P group. Individual B, unrelated to Individual A, owns all of the stock of M and K, each the common parent of a consolidated group. Individual C, unrelated to either Individual A or Individual B, owns all of the stock of T.

(ii) At the beginning of Year 7, M acquires all of the stock of P from Individual A, and, as a result, P, P1, and S become members of the M group. At the time of M's acquisition of the P stock, P has a $15 net unrealized built-in loss (disregarding the stock of P1), P1 has a net unrealized built-in gain of $10, and S has a net unrealized built-in gain of $5.

(iii) During Year 8, M acquires all of the stock of T, and T joins the M group. At the time of M's acquisition of the T stock, T had an unrealized built-in loss of $15. At the beginning of Year 9, K acquires all of the stock of M from Individual B, and the members of the M consolidated group including P, P1, S, and T become members of the K group. At the time of K's acquisition of the M stock, M has (disregarding the stock of P and T) a $15 net unrealized built-in loss, P has a $20 net unrealized built-in loss (disregarding the stock of P1), P1 has a net unrealized built-in gain of $5, S has a net unrealized built-in loss of $35, and T has a $15 net unrealized built-in loss.

(iv) M's acquisition of P in Year 7 results in P, P1, and S becoming members of the M group (the SRLY event). Under paragraph (c) of this section, P and P1 compose a SRLY built-in loss subgroup because they have been affiliated for the 60 consecutive month period immediately preceding joining the M group. S is not a member of the subgroup because on becoming a member of the M group it had not been continuously affiliated with P and P1 for the 60 month period ending immediately before it became a member of the M group. Consequently, §1.1502-15 applies to S separately from the P and P1 subgroup.

(v) Assuming that the $5 net unrealized built-in loss of the P/P1 subgroup exceeds the threshold requirement under section 382(h)(3)(B), M's acquisition of P resulted in an ownership change of P and P1 within the meaning of section 382(g) that subjects P and P1 to a limitation under section 382(a) (the section 382 event). Because, with respect to P and P1, the SRLY event and the change date of the section 382 event occur on the same date and because the loss subgroup and SRLY subgroup are coextensive, there is an overlap of the application of the SRLY rules and the application of section 382.

(vi) S was not a loss corporation because it did not have a net operating loss carryover, or a net unrealized built-in loss, and therefore, M's acquisition of P did not result in an ownership change of S within the meaning of section 382(g). S, therefore is not subject to the overlap rule of paragraph (g) of this section.

(vii) M's acquisition of T resulted in T becoming a member of the M group (the SRLY event). Assuming that T's $15 net unrealized built-in loss exceeds the threshold requirement under section 382(h)(3)(B), M's acquisition of T also resulted in an ownership change of T within the meaning of section 382(g) that subjects T to a limitation under section 382(a) (the section 382 event). Because, with respect to T, the SRLY event and the change date of the section 382 event occur on the same date, there is an overlap of the application of the SRLY rules and the application of section 382 within the meaning of paragraph (g) of this section.

(viii) K's acquisition of M results in the members of the M consolidated group, including T, P, P1, and S, becoming members of the K group (the SRLY event). Because T, P, and P1 were each included in the determination of a net unrealized built-in loss that was subject to the overlap rule described in paragraph (g)(1) of this section when they each became members of the M group, they are deemed under paragraph (c)(3) of this section to have been continuously affiliated with M for the 60 month period ending immediately before becoming a member of the M group, notwithstanding their actual affiliation history. As a result, M, T, P, and P1 compose a SRLY built-in loss subgroup under paragraph (c)(2) of this section. K's acquisition of M is not subject to paragraph (g) of this section because it does not result in a section 382 event.

(ix) S, however, is not a member of the subgroup under paragraph (c)(2) of this section. Because S was not included in the determination of a net unrealized built-in loss that was subject to the overlap rule described in paragraph (g)(1) of this section when it joined the M group, S is treated as becoming an affiliate of M on the date it joined the M group. Furthermore, under paragraph (c)(3) of this section, S is deemed to have begun its affiliation with P and P1 on the date it joined the M group. Consequently, §1.1502-15 applies to S separately to the extent its built-in loss is recognized within the recognition period.

*Example 2. Post-overlap acquisition of assets.* (i) Individual A owns all of the stock of P, the common parent of a consolidated group. B,

an individual unrelated to Individual A, owns all of the stock of T. T has two depreciable assets. Asset 1 has an unrealized built-in loss of $25 (basis $75, value $50), and asset 2 has an unrealized built-in gain of $20 (basis $30, value $50). During Year 3, P buys all of the stock of T from Individual B. On January 1, Year 4, P contributes $80 cash and Individual A contributes asset 3, a depreciable asset, with a net unrealized built-in loss of $45 (basis $65, value $20), in exchange for T stock in a transaction that is described in section 351.

(ii) P's acquisition of T results in T becoming a member of the P group (the SRLY event) and also results in an ownership change of T, within the meaning of section 382(g), that gives rise to a limitation under section 382(a) (the section 382 event).

(iii) Because the SRLY event and the change date of the section 382 event occur on the same date, there is an overlap of the application of the SRLY rules and the application of section 382. Consequently, under paragraph (g) of this section, the limitation under paragraph (a) of this section does not apply to T's net unrealized built-in loss when it joined the P group.

(iv) Individual A's Year 4 contribution of a depreciable asset occurred after T was a member of the P group. Assuming that the amount of the net unrealized built-in loss exceeds the threshold requirement of section 382(h)(3)(B), the sale of asset 3 within the recognition period is subject to the SRLY limitation of paragraphs (a) and (b)(2)(ii) of this section.

*Example 3. Overlap rule.* (i) Individual A owns all of the stock of P, the common parent of a consolidated group. B, an individual unrelated to Individual A, owns all of the stock of T. T has two depreciable assets. Asset 1 has an unrealized loss of $55 (basis $75, value $20), and asset 2 has an unrealized gain of $30 (basis $30, value $60). On February 28 of Year 2, P purchases 55% of T from Individual B. On June 30, of Year 2, P purchases an additional 35% of T from Individual B.

(ii) The February 28 purchase of 55% of T is a section 382 event because it results in an ownership change of T that gives rise to a section 382(a) limitation. The June 30 purchase of 35% of T results in T becoming a member of the P group and is therefore a SRLY event.

(iii) Because the SRLY event occurred within six months of the change date of the section 382 event, there is an overlap of the application of the SRLY rules and the application of section 382, and paragraph (a) of this section does not apply. Therefore, the SRLY limitation does not apply to any of the $55 loss in asset 1 recognized by T after T joined the P group. See §1.1502-94 for rules relating to the application of section 382 with respect to T's $25 unrealized built-in loss.

*Example 4. Overlap rule-Fluctuation in value.* (i) The facts are the same as in *Example 3*, except that by June 30, of Year 2, asset 1 had declined in value by a further $10. Thus asset 1 had an unrealized loss of $65 (basis $75, value $10), and asset 2 had an unrealized gain of $30 (basis $30, value $60).

(ii) Because paragraph (a) of this section does not apply, the further decrease in asset 1's value is disregarded. Consequently, the results are the same as in *Example 3*.

(h) *Effective date.*—(1) *In general.*—This section generally applies to built-in losses recognized in taxable years for which the due date (without extensions) of the consolidated return is after June 25, 1999. However—

(i) In the event that paragraphs (f)(1) and (g)(1) of this section do not apply to a particular built-in loss in the current group, then solely for purposes of applying paragraph (a) of this section to determine a limitation with respect to that built-in loss and with respect to which the SRLY register (consolidated taxable income determined by reference to only the member's (or subgroup's) items of income, gain, deduction or loss) began in a taxable year for which the due date of the return was on or before June 25, 1999, paragraph (c)(3) of this section shall not apply; and

(ii) For purposes of paragraph (g) of this section, only an ownership change to which section 382(a) as amended by the Tax Reform Act of 1986 applies shall constitute a section 382 event.

(2) *Prior periods.*—For certain taxable years ending on or before June 25, 1999, see §1.1502-15T in effect prior to June 25, 1999, as contained in 26 CFR part 1 revised April 1, 1999, as applicable. [Reg. §1.1502-15.]

☐ [T.D. 8823, 6-25-99 (*corrected* 7-30-99). *Amended by* T.D. 9048, 3-11-2003 T.D. 9187, 3-2-2005; T.D. 9254, 3-9-2006 *and* T.D. 9424, 9-9-2008.]

### [Reg. §1.1502-15A]

**§1.1502-15A. Limitations on the allowance of built-in deductions for consolidated return years beginning before January 1, 1997.**—(a) *Limitation on built-in deductions.*—(1) *General rule.*—Built-in deductions (as defined in subparagraph (2) of this paragraph) for a taxable year shall be subject to the limitation of §1.1502-21A(c) (determined without regard to such deductions and without regard to net operating loss carryovers to such year) and the limitation of §1.1502-22A(c) (determined without regard to such deductions and without regard to captial loss carryovers to such year). If as a result of applying such limitations, built-in deductions are not allowable in such consolidated return year, such deductions shall be treated as a net operating loss or net capital loss (as the case may be) sustained in such year and shall be carried to those taxable years (consolidated or separate) to which a consolidated net operating loss or a consolidated net capital loss could be carried under §§1.1502-21A, 1.1502-22A, and 1.1502-79A (or §§1.1502-21T and 1.1502-22T, as appropriate), except that such losses shall be treated as losses subject to the limitations contained in §1.1502-21T(c) or §1.1502-22T(c) (or §§1.1502-21A(c) or 1.1502-22A(c), as appropriate), as the case may be. Thus, for example, if member X sells a capital asset during a consolidated return year at a $1,000 loss and such loss is treated as a built-in deduction, then such loss shall be subject to the limitation contained in §1.1502-22(c), which, in general, would allow such loss to be offset only against X's own net capital gain. Assuming X had no capital gain net income (net capital gain for taxable years beginning before January 1, 1977) reflected in such year (after taking into account its capital losses, other than capital loss carryovers and the built-in deduction), such $1,000 loss shall be treated as a net capital loss and shall be carried over for 5 years under §1.1502-22, subject to the limitation contained in §1.1502-22(c) for consolidated return years.

(2) *Built-in deductions.*—(i) For purposes of this paragraph, the term "built-in deductions" for a consolidated return year means those deductions or losses of a corporation which are recognized in such year, or which are recognized in a separate return year and carried over in the form of a net operating or net capital loss to such year, but which are economically accrued in a separate return limitation year (as defined in §1.1502-1(f)). Such term does not include deductions or losses incurred in rehabilitating such corporation. Thus, for example, assume P is the common parent of a group filing consolidated returns on the basis of a calendar year and that P purchases all of the stock of S on December 31, 1966. Assume further that on December 31, 1966, S owns a capital asset with an adjusted basis of $100 and a fair market value of $50. If the group files a consolidated return for 1967, and S sells the asset for $30, $50 of the $70 loss is treated as a built-in deduction, since it was economically accrued in a separate return limitation year. If S sells the asset for $80 instead of $30, the $20 loss is treated as a built-in deduction. On the other hand, if such asset is a depreciable asset and is not sold by S, depreciation deductions attributable to the $50 difference between basis and fair market value are treated as built-in deductions.

(ii) In determining, for purposes of subdivision (i) of this subparagraph, whether a deduction or loss with respect to any asset is economically accrued in a separate return limitation year, the term "predecessor" as used in §1.1502-1(f)(1) shall include any transferor of such asset if the basis of the asset in the hands of the transferee is determined (in whole or in part) by reference to its basis in the hands of such transferor.

(3) *Transitional rule.*—If the assets which produced the built-in deductions were acquired (either directly or by acquiring a new member) by the group on or before January 4, 1973, and the separate return limitation year in which such deductions were economically accrued ended before such date, then at the option of the taxpayer, the provisions of this paragraph before amendment by T.D. 7246 shall apply, and, in addition, if such assets were acquired on or before April 17, 1968, and the separate return limitation year in which the built-in deductions were economically accrued ended on or before such date, then at the option of the taxpayer, the provisions of §1.1502-31A(b)(9) (as contained in the 26 C.F.R. edition revised as of April 1, 1996) shall apply in lieu of this paragraph.

(4) *Exceptions.*—(i) Subparagraphs (1), (2), and (3) of this paragraph shall not limit built-in deductions in a taxable year with respect to assets acquired (either directly or by acquiring a new member) by the group if—

(a) The group acquired the assets more than 10 years before the first day of such taxable year, or

(b) Immediately before the group acquired the assets, the aggregate of the adjusted basis of all assets (other than cash, marketable securities, and goodwill) acquired from the transferor or owned by the new member did not exceed the fair market value of all such assets by more than 15 percent.

(ii) For purposes of subdivision (i)(b) of this subparagraph, a security is not a marketable security if immediately before the group acquired the assets—

(a) The fair market value of the security is less than 95 percent of its adjusted basis, or

(b) The transferor or new member had held the security for at least 24 months, or

(c) The security is stock in a corporation at least 50 percent of the fair market value of the outstanding stock of which is owned by the transferor or new member.

(b) *Effective date.*—This section applies to any consolidated return years to which §1.1502-21T does not apply. See §1.1502-21T(g) for effective dates of that section. [Reg. §1.1502-15A.]

☐ [*T.D. 6894, 9-7-66 and T.D. 6909, 12-29-66. Amended by T.D. 7246, 12-29-72 and T.D. 7728, 10-31-80. Redesignated as Reg. §1.1502-15A and amended by T.D. 8677, 6-26-96.*]

[Reg. §1.1502-16]

**§1.1502-16. Mine exploration expenditures.**—(a) *Section 617.*—(1) *In general.*—If the aggregate amount of the expenditures to which section 617(a) applies, paid or incurred with respect to mines or deposits located outside the United States (as defined in section 638 and the regulations thereunder), does not exceed—

(i) $400,000 minus

(ii) all amounts deducted or deferred during the taxable year and all preceding taxable years under section 617 or section 615 of the Internal Revenue Code of 1954 and section 23(ff) of the Internal Revenue Code of 1939 by corporations which are members of the group during the taxable year (and individuals or corporations which have transferred any mineral property to any such member within the meaning of section 617(g)(2)(B)) for taxable years ending after December 31, 1950 and prior to the taxable year,

then the deduction under section 617 with respect to such foreign expenditures and paragraph (c) of §1.1502-12 for each member shall be no greater than an allocable portion of such amount hereinafter referred to as the "consolidated foreign exploration limitation." Such allocable portion shall be determined under subparagraph (2) of this paragraph. If the amount of such expenditures exceeds the consolidated foreign exploration limitation, no deduction shall be allowed with respect to such excess.

(2) *Allocable portion of limitation.*—A member's allocable portion of the consolidated foreign exploration limitation for a consolidated return year shall be—

(i) The amount allocated by the common parent pursuant to an allocation plan adopted by the consolidated group, but in no event shall a member be allocated more than the amount it could have deducted had it filed a separate return. Such allocation plan must include a statement which also contains the total foreign exploration expenditures of each member which could have been deducted under section 617 if the member had filed a separate return. Such plan must be attached to a consolidated return filed on or before the due date of such return (including extensions of time), and may not be changed after such date, or

(ii) If no plan is filed in accordance with subdivision (i) of this subparagraph, then the portion of the consolidated foreign exploration limitation allocable to each member incurring such expenditures is an amount equal to such limitation multiplied by a fraction, the numerator of which is the amount of foreign exploration expenditures which could have been deducted under section 617 by such member had it filed a separate return and the denominator of which is the aggregate of such amounts for all members of the group.

(b) *Section 615.*—(1) *In general.*—If the aggregate amount of the expenditures, to which section 615(a) applies, which are paid or incurred by the members of the group during any consolidated return year exceeds the lesser of—

(i) $100,000, or

(ii) $400,000 minus all such expenditures deducted (or deferred) by corporations which are members of the group during the taxable year (and individuals or corporations which have transferred any mineral property to any such member within the meaning of section 615(c)(2)(B)) for taxable years ending after December 31, 1950, and prior to the taxable year,

then the deduction (or amount deferrable) under section 615 and paragraph (c) of §1.1502-12 for each member shall be no greater than an allocable portion of such lesser amount, hereinafter referred to as the "consolidated exploration limitation." Such allocable portion shall be determined under subparagraph (2) of this paragraph.

(2) *Allocable portion of limitation.*—A member's allocable portion of the consolidated exploration limitation for a consolidated return year shall be—

(i) The amount allocated by the common parent pursuant to an allocation plan adopted by the consolidated group, but in no event shall a member be allocated more than the amount it could have deducted (or deferred) had it filed a separate return. Such allocation plan must include a statement which also contains the total exploration expenditures of each member for the taxable year, and the expenditures of each member which could have been deducted (or deferred) under section 615 if the member had filed a separate return. Such plan must be attached to a consolidated return filed on or before the due date of such return (including extensions of time), and may not be changed after such date, or

(ii) If no plan is filed in accordance with subdivision (i) of this subparagraph, then the portion of the consolidated exploration limitation allocable to each member incurring such expenditures is an amount equal to such limitation multiplied by a fraction, the numerator of which is the amount which could have been deducted (or deferred) under section 615 by such member had it filed a separate return and the denominator of which is the aggregate of such amounts for all members of the group.

(c) *Examples.*—The provisions of this section may be illustrated by the following examples:

*Example (1).* Corporation X and its wholly-owned subsidiaries, corporations Y and Z, file a consolidated return for the calendar year 1971. None of the corporations have incurred exploration expenditures described in section 617 in previous years. During 1971, X incurred foreign exploration expenditures of $30,000, Y of $20,000

| Corporation | Expenditure |
|---|---|
| X . . . . . . . . . . . . . . . . . . . . . . | $25,000 |
| Y . . . . . . . . . . . . . . . . . . . . . . | $75,000 |
| Z . . . . . . . . . . . . . . . . . . . . . . | $125,000 |

The denominator of $200,000 was calculated as follows:

X = $ 25,000

Y = $ 75,000

Z = $100,000 (maximum amount allowed if filed separately)

Total $200,000

*Example (3).* Assume the same facts as in example (2) and that on January 1, 1971, X acquired all of the stock of corporation T which prior to its taxable year beginning January 1, 1971, had previously deducted (or deferred) $310,000 of exploration expenditures. Assume further that in 1971 X incurred $25,000 of foreign exploration expenditures, Y $50,000, T $50,000 and Z none. A consolidated return is filed for 1971. None of the expenditures may be deducted under section 617 since the consolidated exploration limitation is zero. The limitation is zero since the aggregate amount of previously deducted (or deferred) exploration expenditures by the members of the group exceeds $400,000. (The total of such expenditures is $410,000, of which $310,000 is attributable to T and, assuming the allocation of the limitation in example (2) is made under paragraph (a)(2)(ii) of this section, $12,500 is attributable to X, $37,500 to Y, and $50,000 to Z.)

*Example (4).* Assume the same facts as in example (3) except that on December 31, 1971, X sold all of the stock in Z to an unrelated party. The consolidated exploration limitation for 1972 will be $40,000, computed by subtracting from $400,000 the aggregate amount of previously deducted (or deferred) exploration expenditures incurred by the members of the group prior to 1972. (The total of such expenditures is $360,000, of which $12,500 is attributable to X, $37,500 to Y and $310,000 to T.) Amounts previously deducted (or deferred) by Z are not taken into account since it was not a member of the group at any time during 1972. Amounts previously deducted (or deferred) by Z shall be taken into account by it for subsequent separate return years. [Reg. § 1.1502-16.]

☐ [*T.D. 6894, 9-7-66. Amended by T.D. 7192, 6-29-72.*]

**[Reg. § 1.1502-17]**

**§ 1.1502-17. Methods of accounting.**—(a) *General rule.*—The method of accounting to be used by each member of the group shall be determined in accordance with the provisions of section 446 as if such member filed a separate return. For treatment of depreciable property after a transfer within the group, see paragraph (g) of § 1.1502-12.

(b) *Adjustments required if method of accounting changes.*—(1) *General rule.*—If a member of a group changes its method of accounting for a consolidated return year, the terms and conditions prescribed by the Commissioner under section 446(e), including section 481(a) where applicable, shall apply to the member. If the requirements of section 481(b) are met because applicable adjustments under section 481(a) are substantial, the increase in tax for any prior year shall be computed upon the basis of a consolidated return or a separate return, whichever was filed for such prior year.

and Z of $40,000. The amount of foreign exploration expenditures deductible under section 617 for purposes of computing separate taxable income under § 1.1502-12 will be the amount actually expended by each corporation.

*Example (2).* Assume the same facts as in example (1) except that prior to 1971, X, Y, and Z had deducted (or deferred) under section 615 and 617 a total of $300,000 of exploration expenditures. During 1971, with respect to deposits located outside the United States X incurred exploration expenditures of $25,000, Y of $75,000 and Z of $125,000. The consolidated exploration limitation under paragraph (a) of this section with respect to the foreign deposits (there is no limitation with respect to the domestic expenditures) is $100,000. X may allocate the $100,000 in any manner among the three members, except that X may not be allocated more than $25,000 nor Y more than $75,000, the amount actually expended by X and Y and which they could have deducted had they each filed a separate return. If the allocation is not made in accordance with paragraph (a)(2)(i) of this section, the $100,000 limitation will be allocated under paragraph (a)(2)(ii) of this section as follows:

| Fraction | Limitation | Allocable portion |
|---|---|---|
| $\dfrac{25,000}{200,000}$ | $\times \$100,000 =$ | $12,500 |
| $\dfrac{75,000}{200,000}$ | $\times \$100,000 =$ | $37,500 |
| $\dfrac{100,000}{200,000}$ | $\times \$100,000 =$ | $50,000 |

(2) *Changes in method of accounting for intercompany transactions.*—If a member changes its method of accounting for intercompany transactions for a consolidated return year, the change in method generally will be effected on a cut-off basis.

(c) *Anti-avoidance rules.*—(1) *General rule.*—If one member (B) directly or indirectly acquires an activity of another member (S), or undertakes S's activity, with the principal purpose to avail the group of an accounting method that would be unavailable (or would be unavailable without securing consent from the Commissioner) if S and B were treated as divisions of a single corporation, B must use the accounting method for the acquired or undertaken activity determined under paragraph (c)(2) of this section or must secure consent from the Commissioner under applicable administrative procedures to use a different method.

(2) *Treatment as divisions of a single corporation.*—B must use the method of accounting that would be required if B acquired the activity from S in a transaction to which section 381 applied. Thus, the principles of section 381(c)(4) and (c)(5) apply to resolve any conflicts between the accounting methods of S and B, and the acquired or undertaken activity is treated as having the accounting method used by S. Appropriate adjustments are made to treat all acquisitions or undertakings that are part of the same plan or arrangement as a single acquisition or undertaking.

(d) *Examples.*—The provisions of this section are illustrated by the following examples:

*Example 1. Separate return treatment generally.* X and its wholly owned subsidiary Y filed separate returns for their calendar years ending December 31, 1965. During calendar year 1965, X employed an accrual method of accounting, established a reserve for bad debts, and elected under section 171 to amortize bond premiums with respect to its fully taxable bonds. During calendar year 1965, Y employed the cash receipts and disbursements method, used the specific charge-off method with respect to its bad debts, and did not elect to amortize bond premiums under section 171 with respect to its bonds. X and Y filed a consolidated return for 1966. For 1966 X and Y must continue to compute income under their respective methods of accounting (unless a change in method under section 446 is made).

*Example 2. Adopting methods.* Corporation P is a member of a consolidated group. P provides consulting services to customers under various agreements. For one type of customer, P's agreements require payment only when the contract is completed (payment-on-completion contracts). P uses an overall accrual method of accounting. Accordingly, P takes its income from consulting contracts into account when earned, received, or due, whichever is earlier. With the principal purpose to avoid seeking the consent of the Commissioner to change its method of accounting for the payment-on-completion contracts to the cash method, P forms corporation S, and S begins to render services to those customers subject to the payment-on-completion contracts. P continues to render services to those customers not subject to these contracts.

(b) Under paragraph (c) of this section, S must account for the consulting income under the payment-on-completion contracts on an accrual method rather than adopting the cash method contemplated by P.

*Example 3. Changing inventory sub-method.* (a) Corporation P is a member of a consolidated group. P operates a manufacturing business that uses dollar-value LIFO, and has built up a substantial LIFO reserve. P has historically manufactured all its inventory and has used one natural business unit pool. P begins purchasing goods identical to its own finished goods from a foreign supplier, and is concerned that it must establish a separate resale pool under §1.472-8(c). P anticipates that it will begin to purchase, rather than manufacture, a substantial portion of its inventory, resulting in a recapture of most of its LIFO reserve because of decrements in its manufacturing pool. With the principal purpose to avoid the decrements, P forms corporation S in Year 1. S operates as a distributor to nonmembers, and P sells all of its existing inventories to S. S adopts LIFO, and elects dollar-value LIFO with one resale pool. Thereafter, P continues to manufacture and purchase inventory, and to sell it to S for resale to nonmembers. P's intercompany gain from sales to S is taken into account under §1.1502-13. S maintains its Year 1 base dollar value of inventory so that P will not be required to take its intercompany items (which include the effects of the LIFO reserve recapture) into account.

(b) Under paragraph (c) of this section, S must maintain two pools (manufacturing and resale) to the same extent that P would be required to maintain those pools under §1.472-8 if it had not formed S.

(e) *Effective dates.*—Paragraph (b) of this section applies to changes in method of accounting effective for years beginning on or after July 12, 1995. For changes in method of accounting effective for years beginning before that date, see §1.1502-17 (as contained in the 26 CFR part 1 edition revised as of April 1, 1995). Paragraphs (c) and (d) apply with respect to acquisitions occurring or activities undertaken in years beginning on or after July 12, 1995. [Reg. §1.1502-17.]

☐ [T.D. 6894, 9-7-66. Amended by T.D. 8597, 7-12-95.]

## [Reg. §1.1502-18]

**§1.1502-18. Inventory adjustments.**—(a) *Definition of intercompany profit amount.*—For purposes of this section, the term "intercompany profit amount" for a taxable year means an amount equal to the profits of a corporation (other than those profits which such corporation has elected not to defer pursuant to §1.1502-13(c)(3) or which have been taken into account pursuant to §1.1502-13(f)(1)(viii)) arising in transactions with other members of the group with respect to goods which are, at the close of such corporation's taxable year, included in the inventories of any member of the group. See §1.1502-13(c)(2) with respect to the determination of profits. See the last sentence of §1.1502-13(f)(1)(i) for rules for determining which goods are considered to be disposed of outside the group and therefore not included in inventories of members.

(b) *Addition of initial inventory amount to taxable income.*—If a corporation—

(1) Is a member of a group filing a consolidated return for the taxable year,

(2) Was a member of such group for its immediately preceding taxable year, and

(3) Filed a separate return for such preceding year,

then the intercompany profit amount of such corporation for such separate return year (hereinafter referred to as the "initial inventory amount") shall be added to the income of such corporation for the consolidated return year (or years) in which the goods to which the initial inventory amount is attributable are disposed of outside the group or such corporation becomes a nonmember. Such amount shall be treated as gain from the sale or exchange of property which is neither a capital asset nor property described in section 1231.

(c) *Recovery of initial inventory amount.*—(1) *Unrecovered inventory amount.*—The term "unrecovered inventory amount" for any consolidated return year means the lesser of—

(i) The intercompany profit amount for such year, or

(ii) The initial inventory amount.

However, if a corporation ceases to be a member of the group during a consolidated return year, its unrecovered inventory amount for such year shall be considered to be zero.

(2) *Recovery during consolidated return years.*—(i) To the extent that the unrecovered inventory amount of a corporation for a consolidated return year is less than such amount for its immediately preceding year, such decrease shall be treated for such year by such corporation as a loss from the sale or exchange of property which is neither a capital asset nor property described in section 1231.

(ii) To the extent that the unrecovered inventory amount for a consolidated return year exceeds such amount for the preceding year, such increase shall be treated as gain from the sale or exchange of property which is neither a capital asset nor property described in section 1231.

(3) *Recovery during first separate return year.*—For the first separate return year of a member following a consolidated return year, the unrecovered inventory amount for such consolidated return year (minus any part of the initial inventory amount which has not been added to income pursuant to paragraph (b) of this section) shall be treated as a loss from the sale or exchange of property which is neither a capital asset nor property described in section 1231.

(4) *Acquisition of group.*—For purposes of this section, a member of a group shall not become a nonmember or be considered as filing a separate return solely because of a termination of the group (hereinafter referred to as the "terminating group") resulting from—

(i) The acquisition by a nonmember corporation of (a) the assets of the common parent in a reorganization described in subparagraph (A), (C), or (D) (but only if the requirements of subparagraphs (A) and (B) of section 354(b)(1) are met) of section 368(a)(1), or (b) stock of the common parent, or

(ii) The acquisition (in a transaction to which §1.1502-75(d)(3) applies) by a member of (a) the assets of a nonmember corporation in a reorganization referred to in subdivision (i) of this subparagraph, or (b) stock of a nonmember corporation,

if all the members of the terminating group (other than such common parent if its assets are acquired) immediately before the acquisition are members immediately after the acquisition of another group (hereinafter referred to as the "succeeding group") which files a consolidated return for the first taxable year ending after the date of acquisition. The members of the succeeding group shall succeed to any initial inventory amount and to any unrecovered inventory amount of members of the terminating group. This subparagraph shall not apply with respect to acquisitions occurring before August 25, 1971.

(d) *Examples.*—The provisions of paragraphs (a), (b), and (c) of this section may be illustrated by the following examples:

*Example (1).* Corporations P, S, and T report income on the basis of a calendar year. Such corporations file separate returns for 1965. P manufactures widgets which it sells to both S and T, who act as distributors. The inventories of S and T at the close of 1965 are comprised of widgets which they purchased from P and with respect to which P derived profits of $5,000 and $8,000, respectively. P, S, and T file a consolidated return for 1966. During 1966, P sells widgets to S and T with respect to which it derives profits of $7,000 and $10,000, respectively. The inventories of S and T as of December 31, 1966, are comprised of widgets on which P derived net profits of $4,000 and $8,000, respectively. P's initial inventory amount is $13,000, P's intercompany profit amount for 1965 (such $13,000 amount is the profits of P with respect to goods sold to S and T and included in their inventories at the close of 1965). Assuming that S and T identify their goods on a first-in, first-out basis, the entire opening inventory amount of $13,000 is added to P's income for 1966 as gain from the sale or exchange of property which is neither a capital asset nor property described in section 1231, since the goods to which the initial inventory amount is attributable were disposed of in 1966 outside the group. However, since P's unrecovered inventory amount for 1966, $12,000 (the intercompany profit amount for the year, which is less than the initial inventory amount), is less than the unrecovered inventory amount for 1965, $13,000, this decrease of $1,000 is treated by P for 1966 as a loss from the sale or exchange of property which is neither a capital asset nor property described in section 1231.

*Example (2).* Assume the same facts as in example (1) and that at the close of 1967, a consolidated return year, the inventories of S and T are comprised of widgets on which P derived profits of $5,000 and $3,000, respectively. Since P's unrecovered inventory amount for 1967, $8,000, is less than $12,000, the unrecovered inventory amount for 1966, this decrease of $4,000 is treated by P for 1967 as a loss from the sale or exchange of property which is neither a capital asset nor property described in section 1231.

*Example (3).* Assume the same facts as in examples (1) and (2) and that in 1968, a consolidated return year, P's intercompany profit amount is $11,000. P will report $3,000 (the excess of $11,000, P's unrecovered inventory amount for 1968, over $8,000, P's unrecovered inventory amount for 1967) for 1968 as a gain from the sale or exchange of property which is neither a capital asset nor property described in section 1231.

*Example (4).* Assume the same facts as in examples (1), (2), and (3) and that in 1969 P, S, and T file separate returns. P will report $11,000 (its unrecovered inventory amount for 1968, $11,000, minus the portion of the initial inventory amount which has not been added to income during 1966, 1967, and 1968, zero) as a loss from the sale or exchange of property which is neither a capital asset nor property described in section 1231.

*Example (5).* Corporations P and S file a consolidated return for the first time for the calendar year 1966. P manufactures machines and sells them to S, which sells them to users throughout the country. At the close of 1965, S has on hand 20 machines which it purchased from P and with respect to which P derived profits of $3,500. During 1966, P sells 6 machines to S on which it derives profits of $1,300, and S sells 5 machines which it had on hand at the beginning of the year (S specifically identifies the machines which it sells) and on which P had derived profits of $900. P's initial inventory amount is $3,500, of which $900 is added to P's income in 1966 as gain from the sale or exchange of property which is neither a capital asset nor property described in section 1231, since such $900 amount is attributable to goods disposed of in 1966 outside the group, which goods were included in S's inventory at the close of 1965. If P and S continue to file consolidated returns, the remaining $2,600 of the initial inventory amount will be added to P's income as the machines on which such profits were derived are disposed of outside the group.

*Example (6).* Assume that in example (5) S had elected to inventory its goods under section 472 (relating to last-in, first-out inventories). None of P's initial inventory amount of $3,500 would be added to P's income in 1966, since none of the goods to which such amount is attributable would be considered to be disposed of during such year under the last-in, first-out method of identifying inventories.

(e) *Section 381 transfer.*—If a member of the group is a transferor or distributor of assets to another member of the group within the meaning of section 381(a), then the acquiring corporation shall be treated as succeeding to the initial inventory amount of the transferor or distributor corporation to the extent that as of the date of distribution or transfer such amount has not yet been added to income. Such amount shall then be added to the acquiring corporation's income under the provisions of paragraph (b) of this section. For purposes of applying paragraph (c) of this section—

(1) The initial inventory amount of the transferor or distributor corporation shall be added to such amount of the acquiring corporation as of the close of the acquiring corporation's taxable year in which the date of distribution or transfer occurs, and

(2) The unrecovered inventory amount of the transferor or distributor corporation for its taxable year preceding the taxable year of the group in which the date of distribution or transfer occurs shall be added to such amount of the acquiring corporation.

(f) *Transitional rules for years before 1966.*—(1) *In general.*—If—

(i) A group filed a consolidated return for the taxable year immediately preceding the first taxable year to which this section applies,

(ii) Any member of such group made an opening adjustment to its inventory pursuant to paragraph (b) of § 1.1502-39A (as contained in the 26 C.F.R. edition revised as of April 1, 1996), and

(iii) Paragraph (c) of § 1.1502-39A (as contained in the 26 C.F.R. edition revised as of April 1, 1996) has not been applicable for any taxable year subsequent to the taxable year for which such adjustment was made,

then subparagraphs (2) and (3) of this paragraph shall apply.

(2) *Closing adjustment to inventory.*—(i) For the first consolidated return year to which this section applies, the increase in inventory prescribed in paragraph (c) of § 1.1502-39A (as contained in the 26 C.F.R. edition revised as of April 1, 1996) shall be made as if such year were a separate return year.

(ii) For the first separate return year of a member to which this section applies, the adjustment to inventory (whether an increase or a decrease) prescribed in paragraph (c) of § 1.1502-39A (as contained in the 26 C.F.R. edition revised as of April 1, 1996), minus any adjustment already made pursuant to subdivision (i) of this subparagraph, shall be made to the inventory of such member.

(3) *Addition and recovery of initial inventory amount.*—Each selling member shall treat as an initial inventory amount its share of the net amount by which the inventories of all members are increased pursuant to subparagraph (2)(i) of this paragraph for the first taxable year to which this section applies. A member's share shall be such net amount multiplied by a fraction, the numerator of which is its initial inventory amount (computed under paragraph (b) as if such taxable year were its first consolidated return year), and the denominator of which is the sum of such initial inventory amounts of all members. Such initial inventory amount shall be added to the income of such selling member and shall be recovered at the time and in the manner prescribed in paragraphs (b) and (c) of this section.

(4) *Example.*—The provisions of this paragraph may be illustrated by the following example:

*Example.* (i) Corporations P, S, and T file consolidated returns for calendar 1966, having filed consolidated returns continuously since 1962. P is a wholesale distributor of groceries selling to chains of supermarkets, including those owned by S and T. The opening inventories of S and T for 1962 were reduced by $40,000 and $80,000, respectively, pursuant to paragraph (b) of § 1.1502-39A (as contained in the 26 C.F.R. edition revised as of April 1, 1996). At the close of 1965, S and T have on hand in their inventories goods on which P derived profits of $80,000 and $90,000, respectively. The inventories of S and T at the close of 1966 include goods which they purchased from P during the year on which P derived profits of $85,000 and $105,000, respectively.

(ii) The opening inventories of S and T for 1966, the first year to which this section applies, are increased by $40,000 and $80,000, respectively, pursuant to the provisions of subparagraph (2)(i) of this paragraph. P will take into account (as provided in paragraphs (b) and (c) of this section) an initial inventory amount of $120,000 as of the beginning of 1966, the net amount by which the inventories of S and T were increased in such year. Since the increases in the inventories of S and T are the maximum allowable under paragraph (c) of § 1.1502-39A (as contained in the 26 C.F.R. edition revised as of April 1, 1996) (*i.e.*, the amount by which such inventories were originally decreased), no further adjustments will be made pursuant to subparagraph (2)(ii) of this paragraph to such inventories in the event that separate returns are subsequently filed.

(5) *Election not to eliminate.*—If a group filed a consolidated return for the taxable year immediately preceding the first taxable year to which this section applies, and for such preceding year the members of the group did not eliminate gain or loss on intercompany inventory transactions pursuant to the adoption under § 1.1502-31A(b)(1) (as contained in the 26 C.F.R. edition revised as of April 1, 1996) of a consistent accounting practice taking into account such gain or loss, then for purposes of this section each member shall be treated as if it had filed a separate return for such immediately preceding year.

(g) *Transitional rules for years beginning on or after July 12, 1995.*—Paragraphs (a) through (f) of this section do not apply for taxable years beginning on or after July 12, 1995. Any remaining unrecovered inventory amount of a member under paragraph (c) of this section is recovered in the first taxable year beginning on or after July 12, 1995, under the principles of paragraph (c)(3) of this section by treating the first taxable year as the first separate return year of the member. The unrecovered inventory amount can be recovered only to the extent it was previously included in taxable income. The principles of this section apply, with appropriate adjustments, to comparable amounts under paragraph (f) of this section. [Reg. § 1.1502-18.]

☐ [T.D. 6894, 9-7-66. Amended by T.D. 7246, 12-29-72; T.D. 8597, 7-12-95 and T.D. 8677, 6-26-96.]

## [Reg. § 1.1502-19]

§ 1.1502-19. **Excess loss accounts.**—(a) *In general.*—(1) *Purpose.*—This section provides rules for a member (M) to include in income its excess loss account in the stock of another member (S). The purpose of the excess loss account is to recapture in consolidated taxable income M's negative adjustments with respect to S's stock (e.g., under § 1.1502-32 from S's deductions, losses, and distributions), to the extent the negative adjustments exceed M's basis in the stock. This section also provides rules for eliminating losses and other attributes attributable to S in certain cases in which S stock becomes worthless or S ceases to be a member and does not have a separate return year.

(2) *Excess loss accounts.*—(i) *In general.*—M's basis in S's stock is adjusted under the consolidated return regulations and other rules of law. Negative adjustments may exceed M's basis in S's stock. The resulting negative amount is M's excess loss account in S's stock. For example:

(A) Once M's negative adjustments under § 1.1502-32 exceed its basis in S's stock, the excess is M's excess loss account in the S stock. If M has further adjustments, they first increase or decrease the excess loss account.

(B) If M forms S by transferring property subject to liabilities in excess of basis, § 1.1502-80(d) provides for the nonapplicability of section 357(c) and the resulting negative basis under section 358 is M's excess loss account in the S stock.

(ii) *Treatment as negative basis.*—M's excess loss account is treated for all Federal income tax purposes as basis that is a negative amount, and a reference to M's basis in S's stock includes a reference to M's excess loss account.

(3) *Application of other rules of law, duplicative recapture.*—See § 1.1502-80(a) regarding the general applicability of other rules of law and a limitation on duplicative adjustments and recapture.

(b) *Excess loss account taken into account as income or gain.*—(1) *Operating rules.*—(i) *General rule.*—Except as provided in paragraph (b)(1)(ii) of this section, if M is treated under this section as disposing of a share of S's stock, M takes into account its excess loss account in the share as income or gain from the disposition.

(ii) *Special limitation on amount taken into account.*—Notwithstanding paragraph (b)(1)(i) of this section, if M is treated as disposing of a share of S's stock as a result of the application of paragraph (c)(1)(iii)(B) of this section, the aggregate amount of its excess loss account in the shares of S's stock that M takes into account as income or gain from the disposition shall not exceed the amount of S's indebtedness that is discharged that is neither included in gross income nor treated as tax-exempt income under § 1.1502-32(b)(3)(ii)(C)(*1*). If more than one share of S's stock has an excess loss account, such excess loss accounts shall be taken into account pursuant to the preceding sentence, to the extent possible, in a manner that equalizes the excess loss accounts in S's shares that have an excess loss account.

(iii) *Treatment of disposition.*—Except as provided in paragraph (b)(4) of this section, the disposition is treated as a sale or exchange for purposes of determining the character of the income or gain.

(iv) *Reduction of attributes in the case of certain dispositions by worthlessness or where S ceases to be a member and does not become a nonmember.*—If this paragraph (b)(1)(iv) applies, any net operating or capital loss carryover that is attributable to S, including any losses that would be apportioned to S under the principles of § 1.1502-21(b)(2) if S had a separate return year, any deferred deductions attributable to S, including S's portion of such consolidated tax attributes (for example, consolidated excess charitable contributions that would be apportioned to S under the principles of § 1.1502-79(e) if S had a separate return year), and any credit carryover attributable to S, including any consolidated credits that would be apportioned to S under the principles of § 1.1502-79 if S had a separate return year, are eliminated. Attributes other than consolidated tax attributes (determined as of the disposition) are eliminated under this paragraph (b)(1)(iv) immediately before the disposition resulting in the application of this paragraph (b)(1)(iv). The elimination of attributes under this paragraph (b)(1)(iv) is not a noncapital, nondeductible expense described in § 1.1502-32(b)(2)(iii). This paragraph (b)(1)(iv) applies if—

(A) A share of S stock becomes worthless under section 165, the requirements of paragraph (c)(1)(iii) of this section are satisfied, M does not recognize a net deduction or loss on the S stock, and S is a member of the group on the day following the last day of the group's taxable year during which the share becomes worthless; or

(B) M recognizes any amount that is not a net deduction or loss on the stock of S in a transaction in which S ceases to be a member and does not become a nonmember.

(2) *Nonrecognition or deferral.*—(i) *In general.*—M's income or gain under paragraph (b)(1) of this section is subject to any nonrecognition or deferral rules applicable to the disposition. For example, if S liquidates and the exchange of M's stock in S is subject to section 332, or M transfers all of its assets (including S's stock) to S in a reorganization to which section 361(a) applies, M's income or gain from the excess loss account is not recognized under these rules.

(ii) *Nonrecognition or deferral inapplicable.*—If M's income or gain under paragraph (b)(1) of this section is from a disposition described in paragraph (c)(1)(ii) or (iii) of this section (relating to deconsolidations and worthlessness), the income or gain is taken into account notwithstanding any nonrecognition or deferral rules (even if the disposition is also described in paragraph (c)(1)(i) of this section). For example, if M transfers S's stock to a nonmember in a transaction to which section 351 applies, M's income or gain from the excess loss account is taken into account.

(3) *Tiering up in chains.*—If the stock of more than one subsidiary is disposed of in the same transaction, the income or gain under this section is taken into account in the order of the tiers, from the lowest to the highest.

(4) *Insolvency.*—(i) *In general.*—Gain under this section is treated as ordinary income to the extent of the amount by which S is insolvent (within the meaning of section 108(d)(3)) immediately before the disposition. For this purpose S's liabilities include any amount to which preferred stock would be entitled if S were liquidated immediately before the disposition, and any former liabilities that were discharged to the extent the discharge was treated as tax-exempt income under § 1.1502-32(b)(3)(ii)(C) (special rule for discharges).

(ii) *Reduction for amount of distributions.*—The amount treated as ordinary income under this paragraph (b)(4) is reduced to the

extent it exceeds the amount of M's excess loss account redetermined without taking into account S's distributions to M to which § 1.1502-32(b)(2)(iv) applies.

(c) *Disposition of stock.*—For purposes of this section:

(1) *In general.*—M is treated as disposing of a share of S's stock.

(i) *Transfer, cancellation, etc..*—At the time—

(A) M transfers or otherwise ceases to own the share for Federal income tax purposes, even if no gain or loss is taken into account; or

(B) M takes into account gain or loss (in whole or in part) with respect to the share.

(ii) *Deconsolidation.*—At the time—

(A) M becomes a nonmember, or a nonmember determines its basis in the share (or any other asset) by reference to M's basis in the share, directly or indirectly, in whole or in part (e.g., under section 362); or

(B) S becomes a nonmember, or M's basis in the share is reflected, directly or indirectly, in whole or in part, in the basis of any asset other than member stock (e.g., under section 1071).

(iii) *Worthlessness.*—At the time—

(A) All of S's assets (other than its corporate charter and those assets, if any, necessary to satisfy state law minimum capital requirements to maintain corporate existence) are treated as disposed of, abandoned, or destroyed for Federal income tax purposes (for example, under section 165(a) or § 1.1502-80(c), or, if S's asset is stock of a lower-tier member, the stock is treated as disposed of under this paragraph (c)). An asset of S is not considered to be disposed of or abandoned to the extent the disposition is in complete liquidation of S under section 332 or is in exchange for consideration (other than relief from indebtedness);

(B) An indebtedness of S is discharged, if any part of the amount discharged is not included in gross income and is not treated as tax-exempt income under § 1.1502-32(b)(3)(ii)(C); or

(C) A member takes into account a deduction or loss for the uncollectibility of an indebtedness of S, and the deduction or loss is not matched in the same tax year by S's taking into account a corresponding amount of income or gain from the indebtedness in determining consolidated taxable income.

(2) *Becoming a nonmember.*—A member is treated as becoming a nonmember if it has a separate return year (including another group's consolidated return year). For example, S may become a nonmember if it issues additional stock to nonmembers, but S does not become a nonmember as a result of its complete liquidation. A disposition under paragraph (c)(1)(ii) of this section must be taken into account in the consolidated return of the group. For example, if a group ceases under § 1.1502-75(c) to file a consolidated return as of the close of its consolidated return year, the disposition under paragraph (c)(1)(ii) of this section is treated as occurring immediately before the close of the year. If S becomes a nonmember because M sells S's stock to a nonmember, M's sale is a disposition under both paragraphs (c)(1)(i) and (ii) of this section. If a group terminates under § 1.1502-75(d) because the common parent is the only remaining member, the common parent is not treated as having a deconsolidation event under paragraph (c)(1)(ii) of this section.

(3) *Exception for acquisition of group.*—(i) *Application.*—This paragraph (c)(3) applies only if a consolidated group (the terminating group) ceases to exist as a result of—

(A) The acquisition of either the assets of the common parent of the terminating group in a reorganization described in section 381(a)(2), or the stock of the common parent of the terminating group; or

(B) The application of the principles of § 1.1502-75(d)(2) or (d)(3).

(ii) *General rule.*—Paragraph (c)(1)(ii) of this section does not apply solely by reason of the termination of a group in a transaction to which this paragraph (c)(3) applies, if there is a surviving group that is, immediately thereafter, a consolidated group. Instead, the surviving group is treated as the terminating group for purposes of applying this section to the terminating group. This treatment does not apply, however, to members of the terminating group that are not members of the surviving group immediately after the terminating group ceases to exist (e.g., under section 1504(a)(3) relating to reconsolidation, or section 1504(c) relating to includible insurance companies).

(d) *Special allocation of basis in connection with an adjustment or determination.*—(1) *Excess loss account in original shares.*—If a member has an excess loss account in shares of a class of S's stock at the time of a basis adjustment or determination under the Internal Revenue

Code with respect to shares of the same class of S's stock owned by the member, the adjustment or determination is allocated first to equalize and eliminate that member's excess loss account. See §1.1502-32(c) for similar allocations of investment adjustments to prevent or eliminate excess loss accounts.

(2) *Excess loss account in new S shares.*—If a member would otherwise determine shares of a class of S's stock (new shares) to have an excess loss account and such member owns one or more other shares of the same class of S's stock, the basis of such other shares is allocated to eliminate and equalize any excess loss account that would otherwise be in the new shares.

(e) *Anti-avoidance rule.*—If any person acts with a principal purpose contrary to the purposes of this section, to avoid the effect of the rules of this section or apply the rules of this section to avoid the effect of any other provision of the consolidated return regulations, adjustments must be made as necessary to carry out the purposes of this section.

(f) *Predecessors and successors.*—For purposes of this section, any reference to a corporation (or to a share of the corporation's stock) includes a reference to a successor or predecessor (or to a share of stock of a predecessor or successor), as the context may require.

(g) *Examples.*—For purposes of the examples in this section, unless otherwise stated, M owns all 100 shares of the only class of S's stock and S owns all 100 shares of the only class of T's stock, the stock is owned for the entire year, T owns no stock of lower-tier members, the tax year of all persons is the calendar year, all persons use the accrual method of accounting, the facts set forth the only corporate activity, all transactions are between unrelated persons, and tax liabilities are disregarded. The principles of this section are illustrated by the following examples.

*Example 1. Taxable disposition of stock.* (a) *Facts.* M has a $150 basis in S's stock, and S has a $100 basis in T's stock. For Year 1, M has $500 of ordinary income, S has no income or loss, and T has a $200 ordinary loss. S sells T's stock to a nonmember for $60 at the close of Year 1.

(b) *Analysis.* Under paragraph (c) of this section, the sale is a disposition of T's stock at the close of Year 1 (the day of the sale). Under §1.1502-32(b), T's loss results in S having a $100 excess loss account in T's stock immediately before the sale. Under paragraph (b)(1) of this section, S takes into account the $100 excess loss account as an additional $100 of gain from the sale. Consequently, S takes into account a $160 gain from the sale in determining the group's consolidated taxable income. Under §1.1502-32(b), T's $200 loss and S's $160 gain result in a net $40 decrease in M's basis in S's stock as of the close of Year 1, from $150 to $110.

(c) *Intercompany sale followed by sale to nonmember.* The facts are the same as in paragraph (a) of this *Example 1,* except that S sells T's stock to M for $60 at the close of Year 1, and M sells T's stock to a nonmember at a gain at the beginning of Year 5. Under paragraph (c) of this section, S's sale is treated as a disposition of T's stock at the close of Year 1 (the day of the sale). Under §1.1502-13 and paragraph (b)(2) of this section, S's $160 gain from the sale is deferred and taken into account in Year 5 as a result of M's sale of the T stock. Under §1.1502-32(b), the absorption of T's $200 loss in Year 1 results in M having a $50 excess loss account in S's stock at the close of Year 1. In Year 5, S's $160 gain taken into account eliminates M's excess loss account in S's stock and increases M's basis in the stock to $110.

(d) *Intercompany distribution followed by sale to a nonmember.* The facts are the same as in paragraph (a) of this *Example 1,* except that the value of the T stock is $60 and S declares and distributes a dividend of all of the T stock to M at the close of Year 1, and M sells the T stock to a nonmember at a gain at the beginning of Year 5. Under paragraph (c) of this section, S's distribution is treated as a disposition of T's stock at the close of Year 1 (the day of the distribution). S's $100 excess loss account in T's stock is treated as additional gain under section 311(b) from the distribution. Under section 301(d), M's basis in the T stock is $60. Under §1.1502-13, and paragraph (b)(2) of this section, S's $160 gain from the distribution is deferred and taken into account in Year 5 as a result of M's sale of the T stock. Under §1.1502-32(b), T's $200 loss and S's $60 distribution result in M having a $110 excess loss account in S's stock at the close of Year 1. In Year 5, S's $160 gain taken into account eliminates M's excess loss account in S's stock and increases M's basis in the stock to $50.

*Example 2. Basis determinations under the Internal Revenue Code in intercompany reorganizations—transfer of shares without an excess loss account.* (i) *Facts.* M owns all of the sole class of stock of each of S and T. M has 150 shares of S stock that it acquired on Date 1. Each S share has a $1 basis and a fair market value of $1. M has 100 shares of T stock that it acquired on Date 2. Each T share has a $1.20 excess loss account and a fair market value of $1. M transfers S's stock to T without receiving additional T stock. The transfer is an exchange described in both section 351 and section 354.

(ii) *Analysis.* Under sections 351 and 354, M does not recognize gain in connection with the transfer. Under §1.358-2(a)(2)(iii), M is deemed to receive 150 shares of T stock of the same class. Without regard to the application of paragraph (d) of this section, under section 358 and §1.358-2 (a) (2) (i), M would have a $1 basis in each such share. However, because the basis of the additional shares of T stock will be determined when M has an excess loss account in its original shares of T stock, under paragraph (d)(1) of this section, the basis that M would otherwise have in such additional shares will eliminate the excess loss account in M's original shares of T stock such that each original share of T stock will have a basis of $0 and each share of T stock deemed received will have a basis of $0.20. Then, under §1.358-2(a) (2) (iii), the S stock is deemed to be recapitalized in a reorganization under section 368(a)(1)(E) in which M receives 100 shares of T stock (those shares M actually owns immediately after the transfer) in exchange for those 100 shares of T stock that M held immediately prior to the transfer and those 150 shares of T stock M is deemed to receive in the transfer. Under §1.358-2(a)(2)(i), immediately after the transfer, M holds 100 shares of T stock, 60 of which take a basis of $0.50 each and 40 of which take a basis of $0 each. In addition, T takes a $1 basis in each share of S stock under section 362. (If M had actually received an additional 150 shares of T stock of the same class, paragraph (d)(1) of this section would apply to shift basis from such additional T shares to M's original T shares because the basis of the additional T stock would be determined when M had an excess loss account in its original T shares. M would have a basis of $0 in each of the original T shares and a basis of $0.20 in each of the additional T shares.)

(iii) *Transfer of shares with an excess loss account.* The facts are the same as in paragraph (i) of this *Example 2,* except that M transfers T's stock to S without receiving additional S stock. The transfer is an exchange described in both section 351 and section 354. Under paragraph (c) of this section, M's transfer is treated as a disposition of T's stock. Under sections 351 and 354 and paragraph (b)(2) of this section, M does not recognize gain from the disposition. Under §1.358-2(a)(2)(iii), M is deemed to have received 100 shares of S stock of the same class. Without regard to the application of paragraph (d) of this section, M would have a $1.20 excess loss account in each such share. However, because M will have an excess loss account in such shares and M owns other shares of S stock of the same class, under paragraph (d)(2) of this section, the excess loss account that M would otherwise have in such shares will decrease M's basis in its original shares of S's stock such that each such original share will have a basis of $0.20 and each share deemed received will have a basis of $0. Then, under §1.358-2(a)(2)(iii), the S stock is deemed to be recapitalized in a reorganization under section 368(a)(1)(E) in which M receives 150 shares of S stock (those shares M actually owns immediately after the transfer) in exchange for those 150 shares of S stock that M held immediately prior to the transfer and those 100 shares of S stock that M is deemed to receive in connection with the transfer. Under §1.358-2(a)(2)(i), immediately after the transfer, M holds 150 shares of S stock, 90 of which take a basis of $0.33 each and 60 of which take a basis of $0 each. In addition, S takes an excess loss account of $1.20 in each share of T stock under section 362. (If M had actually received 100 additional shares of S stock of the same class, paragraph (d)(2) of this section would apply to shift basis from M's original S stock because M would have otherwise had an excess loss account in such additional shares and M owned other shares of S stock of the same class. The excess loss account that M would have otherwise had in such additional shares would have decreased M's basis in its original shares of S's stock. M would have had a basis of $0.20 in each of the original shares and a basis of $0 in each of the additional shares.)

(iv) *Intercompany merger—shares with excess loss account retained.* The facts are the same as in paragraph (i) of this *Example 2,* except that S merges into T in a reorganization described in section 368(a)(1)(A) (and in section 368(a)(1)(D)), and M receives 150 additional shares of T stock of the same class in the reorganization. Under section 354, M does not recognize gain. Without regard to the application of paragraph (d) of this section, under section 358 and §1.358-2(a)(2)(i), M would have a $1 basis in each such share. However, because the basis of the additional shares of T stock will be determined when M has an excess loss account in its original shares of T stock, under paragraph (d)(1) of this section, the basis that M would otherwise have in such additional shares eliminates the excess loss account in M's original shares of T stock such that each original share of T stock has a basis of $0 and each additional share of T stock has a basis of $0.20.

(v) *Intercompany merger—shares with excess loss account surrendered.* The facts are the same as in paragraph (i) of this *Example 2,* except that T merges into S in a reorganization described in section 368(a)(1)(A) (and in section 368(a)(1)(D)), and M receives 100 additional shares of S stock of the same class in the reorganization. Under section 354 and paragraph (b)(2) of this section, M does not recognize gain from the disposition. Without regard to the application of paragraph (d) of this section, under section 358 and §1.358-2(a)(2)(i), M

Reg. §1.1502-19(g)

would have a $1.20 excess loss account in each additional share of S stock received. However, because M would have an excess loss account in such shares and M owns other shares of S stock of the same class, under paragraph (d)(2) of this section, the excess loss account that M would otherwise have in such shares decreases M's basis in its original shares of S's stock such that each original share of S stock has a basis of $0.20 and each additional share of S stock has a basis of $0.

*Example 3. Section 355 distribution of stock with an excess loss account.* (a) *Facts.* M has a $30 excess loss account in S's stock, and S has a $90 excess loss account in T's stock. S distributes the T stock to M in a transaction to which section 355 applies, and neither M nor S recognizes any gain or loss. At the time of the distribution, the T stock represents 33% of the value of the S stock. Following the distribution, M's basis in the S stock is allocated under § 1.358-2 in proportion to the fair market values of the S stock and the T stock.

(b) *Analysis.* Under paragraph (c) of this section, S's distribution of the T stock is treated as a disposition. Under section 355(c) and paragraph (b)(2) of this section, S does not recognize any gain from the distribution. Under section 358, S's excess loss account in the T stock is eliminated, and M's $30 excess loss account in the S stock is treated as basis allocated between the S stock and the T stock based on their relative values. Consequently, M has a $20 excess loss account in the S stock and a $10 excess loss account in the T stock. (If M had a $30 basis rather than a $30 excess loss account in the S stock, S would not recognize gain, its excess loss account in the T stock would be eliminated, and M's basis in the stock of S and T would be $20 and $10, respectively.)

(c) *Section 355 distribution to nonmember.* The facts are the same as in paragraph (a) of this *Example 3,* except that M also distributes the T stock to its shareholders in a transaction to which section 355 applies. Under paragraph (c) of this section, M's distribution is treated as a disposition of T's stock. Under paragraph (b)(2) of this section, because M's disposition is described in paragraph (c)(1)(ii) of this section, M's $10 excess loss account in the T stock must be taken into account at the time of the distribution, notwithstanding the nonrecognition rules of section 355(c).

*Example 4. Deconsolidation of a member.* (a) *Facts.* M has a $50 excess loss account in S's stock, and S has a $100 excess loss account in T's stock. T issues additional stock to a nonmember and, as a consequence, T becomes a nonmember.

(b) *Analysis.* Under paragraph (c)(2) of this section, S is treated as disposing of each of its shares of T's stock immediately before T becomes a nonmember. Under paragraph (b)(1) of this section, S takes into account its $100 excess loss account as gain from the sale or exchange of T's stock. Under § 1.1502-32(b) of this section, S's $100 gain eliminates M's excess loss account in S's stock and increases M's basis in S's stock to $50.

(c) *Deconsolidation of a higher-tier member.* The facts are the same as in paragraph (a) of this *Example 4,* except that S (rather than T) issues the stock and, as a consequence, both S and T become nonmembers. Under paragraph (c)(2) of this section, M is treated as disposing of S's stock and S is treated as disposing of T's stock immediately before S and T become nonmembers. Under § 1.1502-32(b) and paragraph (b)(3) of this section, because S and T become nonmembers in the same transaction and T is the lower-tier member, S is first treated under paragraph (b)(1) of this section as taking into account its $100 excess loss account as gain from the sale or exchange of T's stock. Under § 1.1502-32(b), S's $100 gain eliminates M's excess loss account in S's stock and increases M's basis in S's stock to $50 immediately before S becomes a nonmember. Thus, only S's $100 gain is taken into account in the determination of the group's consolidated taxable income.

(d) *Intercompany gain and deconsolidation.* The facts are the same as in paragraph (c) of this *Example 4,* except that T has $30 of gain that is deferred under § 1.1502-13 and taken into account in determining consolidated taxable income immediately before T becomes a nonmember. Under § 1.1502-32(b), T's $30 gain decreases S's excess loss account in T's stock from $100 to $70 immediately before S is treated as disposing of T's stock. Under paragraph (b)(1) of this section, S is treated as taking into account its $70 excess loss account as gain from the disposition of T's stock. Under § 1.1502-32(b), S's $70 gain from the excess loss account and T's $30 deferred gain that is taken into account eliminate M's $50 excess loss account in S's stock and increase M's basis in S's stock to $50 immediately before S becomes a nonmember.

*Example 5. Worthlessness.* (a) *Facts.* M forms S with a $150 contribution, and S borrows $150. For Year 1, S has a $50 ordinary loss that is carried over as part of the group's consolidated net operating loss. For Year 2, M has $160 of ordinary income, and S has a $160 ordinary loss. Under § 1.1502-32(b), S's loss results in M having a $10 excess loss account in S's stock. During Year 3, the value of S's assets (without taking into account S's liabilities into account) continues to decline and S's stock becomes worthless within the meaning of section 165(g)

(without taking into account § 1.1502-80(c)). For Year 4, S has $10 of ordinary income.

(b) *Analysis.* Under paragraph (c)(1)(iii)(A) of this section, M is not treated as disposing of S's stock in Year 3 solely because S's stock becomes worthless within the meaning of section 165(g) (taking S's liabilities into account). In addition, because S's stock is not treated as worthless, section 382(g)(4)(D) does not prevent the Year 1 consolidated net operating loss carryover from offsetting S's $10 of income in Year 4.

(c) *Discharge of indebtedness.* The facts are the same as in paragraph (a) of this *Example 5,* except that, instead of S's stock becoming worthless within the meaning of section 165(g), S's creditor discharges $40 of S's indebtedness during Year 3, S is insolvent by more than $40 before the discharge, the discharge is excluded from the M group's gross income under section 108(a), and $40 of the $50 consolidated net operating loss carryover attributable to S is eliminated under section 108(b). Under § 1.1502-32(b)(3)(ii)(C), S's $40 of discharge income is treated as tax-exempt income because there is a corresponding decrease under § 1.1502-32(b)(3)(iii) for elimination of the loss carryover. Under paragraph (c)(1)(iii)(B) of this section, M is treated as disposing of S's stock if the amount discharged is not included in gross income and is not treated as tax-exempt income under § 1.1502-32(b)(3)(ii)(C). Because the discharge is treated as tax-exempt income, M is not treated as disposing of S's stock by reason of the discharge.

*Example 6. Avoiding worthlessness.* (a) *Facts.* M forms S with a $100 contribution and S borrows $150. For Years 1 through 5, S has a $210 ordinary loss that is absorbed by the group. Under § 1.1502-32(b), S's loss results in M having a $110 excess loss account in S's stock. S defaults on the indebtedness, but the creditor does not discharge the debt (or initiate collection procedures). At the beginning of Year 6, S ceases any substantial operations with respect to the assets, but maintains their ownership with a principal purpose to avoid M's taking into account its excess loss account in S's stock.

(b) *Analysis.* Under paragraph (c)(1)(iii)(A) of this section, M's excess loss account on each of its shares of S's stock ordinarily is taken into account at the time substantially all of S's assets are treated as disposed of, abandoned, or destroyed for Federal income tax purposes. Under paragraph (e) of this section, however, S's assets are not taken into account at the beginning of Year 6 for purposes of applying paragraph (c)(1)(iii)(A) of this section. Consequently, S is treated as worthless at the beginning of Year 6, and M's $110 excess loss account is taken into account.

(h) *Effective/applicability dates.*—(1) *Application.*—This section applies with respect to determinations of the basis of (including an excess loss account in) the stock of a member in consolidated return years beginning on or after January 1, 1995. If this section applies, basis (and excess loss accounts) must be determined or redetermined as if this section were in effect for all years (including, for example, the consolidated return years of another consolidated group to the extent adjustments during those consolidated return years are still reflected). Any such determination or redetermination does not, however, affect any prior period. Paragraphs (a)(3), (c)(1)(iii)(A), and (c)(3)(i)(A) of this section apply with respect to determinations and transactions occurring on or after September 17, 2008. However, taxpayers may apply paragraph (c)(3)(i)(A) of this section to transactions that occurred prior to September 17, 2008. The last sentence of paragraph (a)(1) and paragraph (b)(1)(iv) of this section applies with respect to dispositions on or after December 16, 2008.

(2) *Dispositions of stock.*—(i) *Dispositions of stock before effective date.*—If M was treated as disposing of stock of S in a tax year beginning before January 1, 1995 (including, for example, a deemed disposition because S was worthless) under the rules of this section then in effect, the amount of M's income, gain, deduction, or loss, and the stock basis reflected in that amount, are not redetermined under paragraph (h)(1) of this section. See paragraph (h)(3) of this section for the applicable rules.

(ii) *Application of special limitation.*—If M was treated as disposing of stock of S because S was treated as worthless as a result of the application of paragraph (c)(1)(iii)(B) of this section after August 29, 2003, the amount of M's income, gain, deduction, or loss, and the stock basis reflected in that amount, are determined or redetermined with regard to paragraph (b)(1)(ii) of this section. If M was treated as disposing of stock of S because S was treated as worthless as a result of the application of paragraph (c)(1)(iii)(B) of this section on or before August 29, 2003, the group may determine or redetermine the amount of M's income, gain, deduction, or loss, and the stock basis reflected in that amount with regard to paragraph (b)(1)(ii) of this section.

(iii) *Intercompany amounts.*—For purposes of this paragraph (h)(2), a disposition does not include a transaction to which § 1.1502-13, § 1.1502-13T, § 1.1502-14, or § 1.1502-14T applies. Instead, the transaction is deemed to occur as the income, gain, deduction, or loss (if any) is taken into account.

(iv) *Intercompany reorganizations.*—Paragraphs (d) and (g) *Example 2* of this section apply to transactions occurring on or after July 18, 2007. For transactions occurring on or after January 23, 2006, and before July 18, 2007, see § 1.1502-19T as contained in 26 CFR part 1 in effect April 1, 2007. For transactions occurring before January 23, 2006, see § 1.1502-19 as contained in 26 CFR part 1 in effect April 1, 2005.

(3) *Prior law.*—For prior determinations, see prior regulations under section 1502 as in effect with respect to the determination. See, e.g., § 1.1502-19 as contained in the 26 CFR part 1 edition revised as of April 1, 1994. For guidance regarding determinations of the basis of the stock of a subsidiary acquired in an intercompany reorganization before January 23, 2006, see paragraph (d) and (g) *Example* 2 of § 1.1502-19 as contained in the 26 CFR part 1 edition revised as of April 1, 2005. [Reg. § 1.1502-19.]

☐ [*T.D.* 6909, 12-29-66. *Amended by T.D.* 7246, 12-29-72; *T.D.* 8364, 9-13-91; *T.D.* 8560, 8-12-94 (*corrected* 3-17-97); *T.D.* 9089, 8-29-2003; *T.D.* 9192, 3-21-2005; *T.D.* 9244, 1-23-2006; *T.D.* 9341, 7-17-2007 and *T.D.* 9424, 9-9-2008 (*corrected* 10-17-2008).]

### [Reg. § 1.1502-21]

**§ 1.1502-21. Net operating losses.**—(a) *Consolidated net operating loss deduction.*—(1) *In general.*—Subject to any limitations under the Internal Revenue Code or this chapter (for example, the limitations under section 172(a)(2) and paragraph (a)(2) of this section), the consolidated net operating loss deduction (or CNOL deduction) for any consolidated return year is the aggregate of the net operating loss carryovers and carrybacks to the year. The net operating loss carryovers and carrybacks consist of—

(i) Any CNOLs (as defined in paragraph (e) of this section) of the consolidated group; and

(ii) Any net operating losses (or NOLs) of the members arising in separate return years.

(2) *Application of section 172 for computing net operating loss deductions.*—(i) *Overview.*—For purposes of § 1.1502-11(a)(2) (regarding a CNOL deduction), the rules of section 172 regarding the use of net operating losses are taken into account as provided by this paragraph (a)(2) in calculating the consolidated taxable income of a group for a particular consolidated return year. More specifically, in computing taxable income for taxable years beginning after December 31, 2020, section 172(a) generally limits the deductibility of net operating losses arising in taxable years beginning after December 31, 2017 (post-2017 NOLs). However, these limitations do not apply to net operating losses arising in taxable years beginning before January 1, 2018 (pre-2018 NOLs). Therefore, in any particular consolidated return year beginning after December 31, 2020, the group's CNOL deduction includes CNOLs arising in taxable years beginning before January 1, 2018 (pre-2018 CNOLs), without limitation under section 172(a). Following the deduction of pre-2018 CNOLs, this paragraph (a)(2) applies to compute the maximum amount of CNOLs from taxable years beginning after December 31, 2017 (post-2017 CNOLs), that can be deducted against taxable income in a consolidated return year beginning after December 31, 2020 (post-2017 CNOL deduction limit). See section 172(a)(2)(A) and (B).

(ii) *Computation of the 80-percent limitation and special rule for nonlife insurance companies.*—(A) *Determinations based on status of group members.*—If a portion of a post-2017 CNOL is carried back or carried over to a consolidated return year beginning after December 31, 2020, whether the members of the group include nonlife insurance companies, other types of corporations, or both determines whether section 172(a) (including the limitation described in section 172(a)(2)(B)(ii) (80-percent limitation)), section 172(f) (providing special rules for nonlife insurance companies), or both, apply to the group for the consolidated return year.

(B) *Determination of post-2017 CNOL deduction limit.*—The post-2017 CNOL deduction limit is determined under paragraph (a)(2)(iii) of this section by applying section 172(a)(2)(B)(ii) (that is, the 80-percent limitation), section 172(f) (that is, the special rule for nonlife insurance companies), or both, to the group's consolidated taxable income for that year.

(C) *Inapplicability of 80-percent limitation.*—The 80-percent limitation does not apply to CNOL deductions taken in taxable years beginning before January 1, 2021, or to CNOLs arising in taxable years beginning before January 1, 2018 (that is, pre-2018 CNOLs). See section 172(a).

(iii) *Computations under sections 172(a)(2)(B) and 172(f).*—This paragraph (a)(2)(iii) provides rules for applying sections 172(f) and 172(a)(2)(B) to consolidated return years beginning after December

31, 2020 (that is, for computing the post-2017 CNOL deduction limit). Section 172(f) applies to income of nonlife insurance company members, whereas section 172(a)(2)(B)(ii) applies to income of members that are not nonlife insurance companies. Thus, this paragraph (a)(2)(iii) provides specific rules for groups with no nonlife insurance company members, only nonlife insurance company members, or a combination of nonlife insurance company members and other members. For groups with both nonlife insurance company members and life insurance company members, see paragraph (b)(2)(iv)(E) of this section.

(A) *Groups without nonlife insurance company members.*—If no member of a group is a nonlife insurance company during a particular consolidated return year beginning after December 31, 2020, section 172(a)(2)(B)(ii) (that is, the 80-percent limitation) applies to all income of the group for that year. Therefore, the post-2017 CNOL deduction limit for the group for that year is the lesser of—

(1) The aggregate amount of post-2017 NOLs carried to that year; or

(2) The amount determined by multiplying—

(i) 80 percent, by

(ii) Consolidated taxable income for the group for that year (determined without regard to any deductions under sections 172, 199A, and 250) less the aggregate amount of pre-2018 NOLs carried to that year.

(B) *Groups comprised solely of nonlife insurance companies.*—If a group is comprised solely of nonlife insurance companies during a particular consolidated return year beginning after December 31, 2020, section 172(f) applies to all income of the group for that year. Therefore, the post-2017 CNOL deduction limit for the group for that year equals the lesser of—

(1) The aggregate amount of post-2017 NOLs carried to that year, or

(2) Consolidated taxable income less the aggregate amount of pre-2018 NOLs carried to that year.

(C) *Groups that include both nonlife insurance companies and other corporations.*—(1) *General rule.*—Except as provided in paragraph (a)(2)(iii)(C)(5) of this section, if a group has at least one member that is a nonlife insurance company and at least one member that is not a nonlife insurance company during a particular consolidated return year beginning after December 31, 2020, the post-2017 CNOL deduction limit for the group for that year equals the lesser of—

(i) The aggregate amount of post-2017 NOLs carried to that year, or

(ii) The sum of the amounts in the income pools determined under paragraphs (a)(2)(iii)(C)(2) and (3) of this section.

(2) *Residual income pool.*—The amount determined under this paragraph (a)(2)(iii)(C)(2) (residual income pool) is eighty percent of the excess of—

(i) The consolidated taxable income of the group for a consolidated return year beginning after December 31, 2020, determined without regard to any income, gain, deduction, or loss of members that are nonlife insurance companies and without regard to any deductions under sections 172, 199A, and 250, over

(ii) The aggregate amount of pre-2018 NOLs carried to that year that are allocated to this income pool under paragraph (a)(2)(iii)(C)(4) of this section (that is, by applying the 80-percent limitation). See section 172(a)(2)(B)(ii).

(3) *Nonlife income pool.*—The amount determined under this paragraph (a)(2)(iii)(C)(3) (nonlife income pool) is the consolidated taxable income of the group for a consolidated return year beginning after December 31, 2020, determined without regard to any income, gain, deduction, or loss of members included in the computation under paragraph (a)(2)(iii)(C)(2) of this section, less the aggregate amount of pre-2018 NOLs carried to that year that are allocated to this income pool under paragraph (a)(2)(iii)(C)(4) of this section. See section 172(f).

(4) *Pro rata allocation of pre-2018 NOLs between pools of income.*—For purposes of paragraphs (a)(2)(iii)(C)(2) and (3) of this section, the aggregate amount of pre-2018 NOLs carried to any particular consolidated return year beginning after December 31, 2020, is prorated between the residual income pool and the nonlife income pool based on the relative amounts of positive income of those two pools. For example, if $30 of pre-2018 NOLs is carried over to a consolidated return year in which the residual income pool contains $75 and the nonlife income pool contains $150, the residual income pool is allocated $10 of the pre-2018 NOLs ($30 x $75/($75 + $150), or $30 x 1/3), and the nonlife income pool is allocated the remaining $20 of pre-2018 NOLs ($30 x $150/($75 + $150), or $30 x 2/3).

*(5) Exception.*—The post-2017 CNOL deduction limit for the group for a consolidated return year is determined under this paragraph (a)(2)(iii)(C)(5) if the amounts computed under paragraphs (a)(2)(iii)(C)(2) and (3) of this section for that year are not both positive.

*(i) Positive residual income pool and negative nonlife income pool.*—This paragraph (a)(2)(iii)(C)(5)(i) applies if the amount computed under paragraph (a)(2)(iii)(C)(2) of this section for the residual income pool is positive and the amount computed under paragraph (a)(2)(iii)(C)(3) of this section for the nonlife income pool is negative. If this paragraph (a)(2)(iii)(C)(5)(i) applies, the post-2017 CNOL deduction limit for the group for a consolidated return year equals the lesser of the aggregate amount of post-2017 NOLs carried to that year, or 80 percent of the consolidated taxable income of the entire group (determined without regard to any deductions under sections 172, 199A, and 250) after subtracting the aggregate amount of pre-2018 NOLs carried to that year (that is, by applying the 80-percent limitation). See section 172(a)(2)(B).

*(ii) Positive nonlife income pool and negative residual income pool.*—If the amount computed under paragraph (a)(2)(iii)(C)(3) of this section for the nonlife income pool is positive and the amount computed under paragraph (a)(2)(iii)(C)(2) of this section for the residual income pool is negative, the post-2017 CNOL deduction limit for the group for a consolidated return year equals the lesser of the aggregate amount of post-2017 NOLs carried to that year, or the consolidated taxable income of the entire group less the aggregate amount of pre-2018 NOLs carried to that year. See section 172(f).

*(b) Net operating loss carryovers and carrybacks to consolidated return and separate return years.*—Net operating losses of members arising during a consolidated return year are taken into account in determining the group's CNOL under paragraph (e) of this section for that year. Losses taken into account in determining the CNOL may be carried to other taxable years (whether consolidated or separate) only under this paragraph (b).

*(1) Carryovers and carrybacks generally.*—The net operating loss carryovers and carrybacks to a taxable year are determined under the principles of, and are subject to any limitations under, section 172 and this section. Thus, losses permitted to be absorbed in a consolidated return year generally are absorbed in the order of the taxable years in which they arose, and losses carried from taxable years ending on the same date, and which are available to offset consolidated taxable income for the year, generally are absorbed on a pro rata basis. In addition, except as otherwise provided in this section, the amount of any CNOL absorbed by the group in any year is apportioned among members based on the percentage of the CNOL eligible for carryback or carryover that is attributable to each member as of the beginning of the year. The percentage of the CNOL attributable to a member is determined pursuant to paragraph (b)(2)(iv)(B) of this section. Additional rules provided under the Internal Revenue Code or regulations also apply. See, for example, section 382(l)(2)(B) (if losses are carried from the same taxable year, losses subject to limitation under section 382 are absorbed before losses that are not subject to limitation under section 382). See paragraph (c)(1)(iii)(B) of this section, (Example 2), for an illustration losses subject to a SRLY limitation.

*(2) Carryovers and carrybacks of CNOLs to separate return years.*—(i) *In general.*—If any CNOL that is attributable to a member may be carried to a separate return year of the member, the amount of the CNOL that is attributable to the member is apportioned to the member (apportioned loss) and carried to the separate return year. If carried back to a separate return year, the apportioned loss may not be carried back to an equivalent, or earlier, consolidated return year of the group; if carried over to a separate return year, the apportioned loss may not be carried over to an equivalent, or later, consolidated return year of the group.

*(ii) Special rules.*—(A) *Year of departure from group.*—If a corporation ceases to be a member during a consolidated return year, net operating loss carryovers attributable to the corporation are first carried to the consolidated return year, then are subject to reduction under section 108 and §1.1502-28 (regarding discharge of indebtedness income that is excluded from gross income under section 108(a)), and then are subject to reduction under §1.1502-36 (regarding transfers of loss shares of subsidiary stock). Only the amount that is neither absorbed by the group in that year nor reduced under section 108 and §1.1502-28 or under §1.1502-36 may be carried to the corporation's first separate return year. For rules concerning a member departing a subgroup, see paragraph (c)(2)(vii) of this section.

*(B) Offspring rule.*—In the case of a member that has been a member continuously since its organization (determined without regard to whether the member is a successor to any other corpora-

tion), the CNOL attributable to the member is included in the carrybacks to consolidated return years before the member's existence. If the group did not file a consolidated return for a carryback year, the loss may be carried back to a separate return year of the common parent under paragraph (b)(2)(i) of this section, but only if the common parent was not a member of a different consolidated group or of an affiliated group filing separate returns for the year to which the loss is carried or any subsequent year in the carryback period. Following an acquisition described in §1.1502-75(d)(2) or (3), references to the common parent are to the corporation that was the common parent immediately before the acquisition.

*(iii) Equivalent years.*—Taxable years are equivalent if they bear the same numerical relationship to the consolidated return year in which a CNOL arises, counting forward or backward from the year of the loss. For example, in the case of a member's third taxable year (which was a separate return year) that preceded the consolidated return year in which the loss arose, the equivalent year is the third consolidated return year preceding the consolidated return year in which the loss arose. See paragraph (b)(3)(iii) of this section for certain short taxable years that are disregarded in making this determination.

*(iv) Operating rules.*—(A) *Amount of CNOL attributable to a member.*—The amount of a CNOL that is attributable to a member equals the product obtained by multiplying the CNOL and the percentage of the CNOL attributable to the member.

*(B) Percentage of CNOL attributable to a member.*—(1) *In general.*—Except as provided in paragraph (b)(2)(iv)(B)(2) of this section, the percentage of the CNOL for the consolidated return year attributable to a member equals the separate net operating loss of the member for the consolidated return year divided by the sum of the separate net operating losses for that year of all members having such losses for that year. For this purpose, the separate net operating loss of a member is determined by computing the CNOL by reference to only the member's items of income, gain, deduction, and loss, including the member's losses and deductions actually absorbed by the group in the consolidated return year (whether or not absorbed by the member). The source and section 904(d) separate category of the CNOL attributable to a member is determined under §1.1502-4(c)(1)(iii).

*(2) Recomputed percentage.*—If, for any reason, a member's portion of a CNOL is absorbed or reduced on a non-pro rata basis (for example, under §1.1502-11(b) or (c), paragraph (b)(2)(iv)(C) of this section, §1.1502-28, or 1.1502-36(d), or as the result of a carryback to a separate return year), the percentage of the CNOL attributable to each member is recomputed. In addition, if a member with a separate net operating loss ceases to be a member, the percentage of the CNOL attributable to each remaining member is recomputed. The recomputed percentage of the CNOL attributable to each member equals the remaining CNOL attributable to the member at the time of the recomputation divided by the sum of the remaining CNOL attributable to all of the remaining members at the time of the recomputation. For purposes of this paragraph (b)(2)(iv)(B)(2), a CNOL that is permanently disallowed or eliminated is treated as absorbed.

*(C) Net operating loss carryovers and carrybacks.*—(1) *General rules.*—Subject to the rules regarding allocation of special status losses under paragraph (b)(2)(iv)(D) of this section—

*(i) Nonlife insurance companies.*—The portion of a CNOL attributable to any members of the group that are nonlife insurance companies is carried back or carried over under the rules in section 172(b) applicable to nonlife insurance companies.

*(ii) Corporations other than nonlife insurance companies.*—The portion of a CNOL attributable to any other members of the group is carried back or carried over under the rules in section 172(b) applicable to corporations other than nonlife insurance companies.

*(2) Recomputed percentage.*—For rules governing the recomputation of the percentage of a CNOL attributable to each remaining member if any portion of the CNOL attributable to a member is carried back under section 172(b)(1)(B) or (C) and absorbed on a non-pro rata basis, see paragraph (b)(2)(iv)(B)(2) of this section.

*(D) Allocation of special status losses.*—The amount of the group's CNOL that is determined to constitute a farming loss (as defined in section 172(b)(1)(B)(ii)) or any other net operating loss that is subject to special carryback or carryover rules (special status loss) is allocated to each member separately from the remainder of the CNOL based on the percentage of the CNOL attributable to the member, as determined under paragraph (b)(2)(iv)(B) of this section. This allocation is made without regard to whether a particular mem-

ber actually incurred specific expenses or engaged in specific activities required by the special status loss provisions. This paragraph (b)(2)(iv)(D) applies only with regard to losses for which the special carryback or carryover rules are dependent on the type of expense generating the loss, rather than on the special status of the entity to which the loss is allocable. See section 172(b)(1)(C) and paragraph (b)(2)(iv)(C)(1)(i) of this section (applicable to losses of nonlife insurance companies). This paragraph (b)(2)(iv)(D) does not apply to farming losses incurred by a consolidated group in any taxable year beginning after December 31, 2017, and before January 1, 2021.

(E) *Coordination with rules for life-nonlife groups under § 1.1502-47.*—For groups that include at least one member that is a life insurance company and for which an election is in effect under section 1504(c)(2), any computation of the 80-percent limitation under paragraph (a)(2)(iii)(C) of this section is computed only with respect to items of income, gain, deduction, and loss of the members of the nonlife subgroup (as defined in § 1.1502-47(b)(9)). For rules regarding the use of CNOLs of the nonlife subgroup to offset life insurance company taxable income of the life subgroup (each as defined in § 1.1502-47(b)), or the use of CNOLs of the life subgroup to offset consolidated taxable income of the nonlife subgroup, see generally section 1503(c)(1) and § 1.1502-47.

(v) *Examples.*—For purposes of the examples in this paragraph (b)(2)(v), unless otherwise stated, all groups file consolidated returns, all corporations have calendar taxable years, all losses are farming losses within the meaning of section 172(b)(1)(B)(ii), all taxable years begin after December 31, 2020, the facts set forth the only corporate activity, value means fair market value and the adjusted basis of each asset equals its value, all transactions are with unrelated persons, and the application of any limitation or threshold under section 382 is disregarded. The principles of this paragraph (b) are illustrated by the following examples:

(A) *Example 1: Offspring rule.*—(1) During Year 1, Individual A forms P and T, and they each file a separate return. P forms S on March 15 of Year 2, and P and S file a consolidated return. P acquires all the stock of T from Individual A at the beginning of Year 3, and T becomes a member of the P group. P's acquisition of T is not an ownership change within the meaning of section 382. P, S, and T sustain a $1,100 CNOL in Year 3 and, under paragraph (b)(2)(iv) of this section, the loss is attributable $200 to P, $300 to S, and $600 to T.

(2) Of the $1,100 CNOL in Year 3, the $500 amount of the CNOL that is attributable to P and S ($200 + $300) may be carried to P's separate return in Year 1. Even though S was not in existence in Year 1, the $300 amount of the CNOL attributable to S may be carried back to P's separate return in Year 1 because S (unlike T) has been a member of the P group since its organization and P is a qualified parent under paragraph (b)(2)(ii)(B) of this section. To the extent not absorbed in that year, the loss may then be carried to the P group's return in Year 2. The $600 amount of the CNOL attributable to T is a net operating loss carryback to T's separate return in Year 1, and if not absorbed in Year 1, then to Year 2.

(B) *Example 2: Departing members.*—(1) The facts are the same as in *Example 1*. In addition, on June 15 of Year 4, P sells all the stock of T. The P group's consolidated return for Year 4 includes the income of T through June 15. T files a separate return for the period from June 16 through December 31.

(2) $600 of the Year 3 CNOL attributable to T is apportioned to T and is carried back to its separate return in Year 1. To the extent the $600 is not absorbed in T's separate return in Year 1 or Year 2, it is carried to the consolidated return in Year 4 before being carried to T's separate return in Year 4. Any portion of the loss not absorbed in T's Year 1 or Year 2 or in the P group's Year 4 is then carried to T's separate return in Year 4.

(C) *Example 3: Offspring rule following acquisition.*—(1) Individual A owns all of the stock of P, the common parent of a consolidated group. In Year 1, B, an individual unrelated to Individual A, forms T. P acquires all of the stock of T at the beginning of Year 3, and T becomes a member of the P group. The P group has $200 of consolidated taxable income in Year 2, and $300 of consolidated taxable income in Year 3 (computed without regard to the CNOL deduction). At the beginning of Year 4, T forms a subsidiary, Y, in a transaction described in section 351. The P group has a $300 consolidated net operating loss in Year 4, and under paragraph (b)(2)(iv) of this section, the loss is attributable entirely to Y.

(2) Even though Y was not in existence in Year 2, $300, the amount of the consolidated net operating loss attributable to Y, may be carried back to the P group's Year 2 consolidated return under paragraph (b)(2)(ii)(B) of this section because Y has been a member of the P group since its organization. To the extent not absorbed in that year, the loss may then be carried to the P group's consolidated return in Year 3.

(D) *Example 4: Allocation of a CNOL arising in a consolidated return year beginning after December 31, 2020.*—(1) P is the common parent of a consolidated group that includes S. Neither P nor S is a nonlife insurance company. The P group also includes nonlife insurance companies PC1, PC2, and PC3. In the P group's 2021 consolidated return year, all members except S have separate net operating losses, and the P group's CNOL in that year is $40. No member of the P group engages in farming activities. See section 172(b)(1)(B)(ii).

(2) Under paragraphs (b)(1) and (b)(2)(iv)(B)(1) of this section, for purposes of carrying losses to other taxable years, the P group's $40 CNOL is allocated pro rata among the group members that have separate net operating losses. Under paragraph (b)(2)(iv)(C) of this section, those respective portions of the CNOL attributable to PC1, PC2, and PC3 (that is, members that are nonlife insurance companies) are carried back to each of the two preceding taxable years and then carried over to each of the 20 subsequent taxable years. See section 172(b)(1)(C). The portion attributable to P (which is not a nonlife insurance company) may not be carried back but is carried over to future years. See section 172(b)(1)(A).

(E) *Example 5: Allocation of a CNOL arising in a consolidated return year beginning before January 1, 2021.*—The facts are the same as in paragraph (b)(2)(v)(D)(1) of this section, except that the P group incurred the CNOL during the P group's 2020 consolidated return year. The allocation among the P group members of the CNOL described in paragraph (b)(2)(v)(D)(2) of this section would be the same. However, those respective portions of the CNOL attributable to PC1, PC2, and PC3 (that is, members that are nonlife insurance companies) will be carried back to each of the five preceding taxable years and then carried over to each of the 20 subsequent taxable years. See section 172(b)(1)(C) and section 172(b)(1)(D)(i). The portion attributable to P (which is not a nonlife insurance company) will be carried back to each of the five preceding taxable years and then carried over to future years. See section 172(b)(1)(A) and section 172(b)(1)(D)(i).

(F) *Example 6: CNOL deduction and application of section 172.*—(1) P (a type of corporation other than a nonlife insurance company) is the common parent of a consolidated group that includes PC1 (a nonlife insurance company). P and PC1 were both incorporated in Year 1 (a year beginning after December 31, 2020). In Year 1, P and PC1 have separate taxable income of $20 and $25, respectively. As a result, the P group has Year 1 consolidated taxable income of $45. In Year 2, P has separate taxable income of $24, and PC1 has a separate taxable loss of $40, resulting in a P group CNOL of $16. Additionally, in Year 3, P has separate taxable income of $15, and PC1 has a separate taxable loss of $45, resulting in a P group CNOL of $30. No member of the P group engages in farming activities. See section 172(b)(1)(B)(ii).

(2) Under paragraph (b)(2)(iv)(B) of this section, the P group's Year 2 CNOL and Year 3 CNOL are entirely attributable to PC1, a nonlife insurance company. Therefore, under section 172(b)(1)(C)(i), the entire amount of each of these CNOLs is eligible to be carried back to Year 1.

(3) Under paragraph (a)(2)(ii) of this section, the amount of the Year 2 CNOL that may be used by the P group in Year 1 is determined by taking into account the status (nonlife insurance company or other type of corporation) of the member that has separate taxable income composing in whole or in part the P group's consolidated taxable income. Because the P group includes both a nonlife insurance company member and a member that is not a nonlife insurance company, paragraph (a)(2)(iii)(C) of this section applies to determine the computation of the post-2017 CNOL deduction limit for the group for Year 1. Therefore, the 80-percent limitation is applied to the residual income pool, which consists of the taxable income of P, a type of corporation other than a nonlife insurance company. Under the 80-percent limitation, the maximum amount of P's Year 1 income that may be offset by the P group's post-2017 CNOLs is $16, which equals 80 percent of the excess of P's taxable income for Year 1 ($20) over the aggregate amount of pre-2018 NOLs allocable to P ($0) (80 percent x ($20 - $0)). See paragraph (a)(2)(iii)(C)(2) and (a)(2)(iii)(C)(4) of this section. PC1 is a nonlife insurance company to which section 172(f), rather than the 80-percent limitation in section 172(a)(2)(B)(ii), applies. Therefore, the maximum amount of PC1's Year 1 income that may be offset by the P group's post-2017 CNOLs is $25, which equals the excess of PC1's taxable income for Year 1 ($25) over the aggregate amount of pre-2018 NOLs allocable to PC1 ($0). See paragraph (a)(2)(iii)(C)(3) and (4) of this section.

(4) Based on paragraph (a)(2)(iii)(C) of this section and the analysis set forth in paragraph (b)(2)(v)(F)(3) of this section, at the end of Year 2, the P group's post-2017 CNOL deduction limit for Year 1 is the lesser of the aggregate amount of post-2017 NOLs carried to Year 1 ($16), or $41 ($16 + $25). Therefore, the P group can offset $16 of its Year 1 income with its CNOL carryback from Year 2.

(5) When the Year 3 CNOL is carried back to Year 1, the P group's post-2017 CNOL deduction limit for Year 1 is the lesser of $46 (the aggregate amount of post-2017 NOLs carried to Year 1) or $41 ($16 + $25; see the computation in paragraph (b)(2)(v)(F)(3) of this section). Thus, the total amount of the P group's Year 1 income that may be offset by the P group's Year 2 and Year 3 CNOLs is $41 ($16 from Year 2 + $25 from Year 3). As a result, the P group reports $4 of income ($45 - $41) in Year 1 that is ineligible for offset by any

other NOLs. The P group carries over its remaining $5 CNOL ($46 - $41) to future years.

(G) *Example 7: Pre-2018 and post-2017 CNOLs.*—(1) P is the common parent of a consolidated group. No member of the P group is a nonlife insurance company or is engaged in a farming business, and no member of the P group has a loss that is subject to a SRLY limitation. The P group had the following consolidated taxable income or CNOL for the following taxable years:

Table 1 to paragraph (b)(2)(v)(G)(1)

| 2014 | 2015 | 2016 | 2017 | 2018 | 2019 | 2020 | 2021 |
|------|------|------|------|------|------|------|------|
| $60 | $0 | $0 | ($90) | $30 | ($40) | ($100) | $120 |

(2) Under section 172(a)(1), all $30 of the P group's 2018 consolidated taxable income is offset by the 2017 CNOL carryover without limitation. The remaining $60 of the P group's 2017 CNOL is carried over to 2021 under section 172(b)(1)(A)(ii)(I).

(3) Under section 172(b)(1)(D)(i)(I), the P group's $40 2019 CNOL is carried back to the five taxable years preceding the year of the loss. Thus, the P group's $40 2019 CNOL is carried back to offset $40 of its 2014 consolidated taxable income.

(4) Under section 172(a)(2) and paragraph (a)(2)(i) of this section, the P group's CNOL deduction for 2021 equals the aggregate amount of pre-2018 NOLs carried to 2021 plus the group's post-2017 CNOL deduction limit. The P group has $60 of pre-2018 NOLs carried to 2021 ($90 - $30). Because no member of the P group is a nonlife insurance company, paragraph (a)(2)(iii)(A) of this section applies to determine the computation of the group's post-2017 CNOL deduction limit for 2021. See also section 172(a)(2)(B). Therefore, the post-2017 CNOL deduction limit of the P group for 2021 is $48, which equals the lesser of the aggregate amount of post-2017 NOLs carried to 2021 ($100), or 80 percent of the excess of the P group's consolidated taxable income for that year computed without regard to any deductions under sections 172, 199A, and 250 ($120) over the aggregate amount of pre-2018 NOLs carried to 2021 ($60) (that is, 80 percent x $60). Thus, the P group's CNOL deduction for 2021 equals $108 ($60 pre-2018 NOLs carried to 2021 + $48 post-2017 CNOL deduction limit). See section 172(a)(2) and paragraph (a)(2)(i) of this section. The P group offsets $108 of its $120 of 2021 consolidated taxable income, resulting in $12 of consolidated taxable income in 2021. The remaining $52 of the P group's 2020 CNOL ($100 - $48) is carried over to future taxable years. See section 172(b)(1)(A)(ii)(II).

(3) *Special rules.*—(i) *Election to relinquish carryback.*—A group may make an irrevocable election under section 172(b)(3) to relinquish the entire carryback period with respect to a CNOL for any consolidated return year. Except as provided in § 1.1502-21(b)(3)(ii)(B), the election may not be made separately for any member (whether or not it remains a member), and must be made in a separate statement entitled "THIS IS AN ELECTION UNDER § 1.1502-21(b)(3)(i) TO WAIVE THE ENTIRE CARRYBACK PERIOD PURSUANT TO SECTION 172(b)(3) FOR THE [insert consolidated return year] CNOLs OF THE CONSOLIDATED GROUP OF WHICH [insert name and employer identification number of common parent] IS THE COMMON PARENT." The statement must be filed with the group's income tax return for the consolidated return year in which the loss arises. If the consolidated return year in which the loss arises begins before January 1, 2003, the statement making the election must be signed by the common parent. If the consolidated return year in which the loss arises begins after December 31, 2002, the election may be made in an unsigned statement.

(ii) *Special elections.*—(A) *Groups that include insolvent financial institutions.*—For rules applicable to relinquishing the entire carryback period with respect to losses attributable to insolvent financial institutions, see § 301.6402-7 of this chapter.

(B) *Acquisition of member from another consolidated group.*—If one or more members of a consolidated group becomes a member of another consolidated group, the acquiring group may make an irrevocable election to relinquish, with respect to all consolidated net operating losses attributable to the member, the portion of the carryback period for which the corporation was a member of another group, provided that any other corporation joining the acquiring group that was affiliated with the member immediately before it joined the acquiring group is also included in the waiver. This election is not a yearly election and applies to all losses that would otherwise be subject to a carryback to a former group under section 172. The election must be made in a separate statement entitled "THIS IS AN ELECTION UNDER § 1.1502-21(b)(3)(ii)(B) TO WAIVE THE PRE-[insert first taxable year for which the member (or members) was not a member of another group] CARRYBACK PERIOD FOR THE CNOLs attributable to [insert names and employer identification number of members]." The statement must be filed with the

acquiring consolidated group's original income tax return for the year the corporation (or corporations) became a member. If the year in which the corporation (or corporations) became a member begins before January 1, 2003, the statement must be signed by the common parent and each of the members to which it applies. If the year in which the corporation (or corporations) became a member begins after December 31, 2002, the election may be made in an unsigned statement.

(C) *Waiver of carryback period for losses in taxable years to which statutorily amended carryback rules apply.*—For further information, see § 1.1502-21T(b)(3)(ii)(C).

(D) *Examples.*—For further information, see § 1.1502-21T(b)(3)(ii)(D).

(iii) *Short years in connection with transactions to which section 381(a) applies.*—If a member distributes or transfers assets to a corporation that is a member immediately after the distribution or transfer in a transaction to which section 381(a) applies, the transaction does not cause the distributor or transferor to have a short year within the consolidated return year of the group in which the transaction occurred that is counted as a separate year for purposes of determining the years to which a net operating loss may be carried.

(iv) *Special status losses.*—[Reserved].

(v) [Reserved]. For further guidance, see § 1.1502-21T(b)(3)(v).

(c) *Limitations on net operating loss carryovers and carrybacks from separate return limitation years.*—(1) *SRLY limitation.*—(i) *General rule.*—Except as provided in paragraph (g) of this section (relating to an overlap with section 382), the aggregate of the net operating loss carryovers and carrybacks of a member (SRLY member) arising (or treated as arising) in SRLYs (SRLY NOLs) that are included in the CNOL deductions for all consolidated return years of the group under paragraph (a) of this section may not exceed the aggregate consolidated taxable income for all consolidated return years of the group determined by reference to only the member's items of income, gain, deduction, and loss (cumulative register). For this purpose—

(A) Consolidated taxable income is computed without regard to CNOL deductions;

(B) Consolidated taxable income takes into account the member's losses and deductions (including capital losses) actually absorbed by the group in consolidated return years (whether or not absorbed by the member);

(C) In computing consolidated taxable income, the consolidated return years of the group include only those years, including the year to which the loss is carried, that the member has been continuously included in the group's consolidated return but exclude—

(1) For carryovers, any years ending after the year to which the loss is carried; and

(2) For carrybacks, any years ending after the year in which the loss arose;

(D) The treatment under § 1.1502-15 of a built-in loss as a hypothetical net operating loss carryover in the year recognized is solely for purposes of determining the limitation under this paragraph (c) with respect to the loss in that year and not for any other purpose. Thus, for purposes of determining consolidated taxable income for any other losses, a built-in loss allowed under this section in the year it arises is taken into account; and

(E) If a limitation on the amount of taxable income that may be offset under section 172(a) (see paragraph (a)(2) of this section) applies in a taxable year to a member whose carryovers or carrybacks are subject to a SRLY limitation (SRLY member), the amount of net operating loss subject to a SRLY limitation that is available for use by the group in that year is limited to the percentage of the balance in the cumulative register that would be available for offset under section 172(a) if the SRLY member filed a separate return and reported as taxable income in that year the amount contained in the cumulative register. For example, assume that a consolidated group has a SRLY member that is a corporation other than a nonlife insurance company, and that the SRLY member has a SRLY NOL that arose in a taxable year beginning after December 31, 2017 (post-2017 NOL). The group's consolidated taxable income for a consolidated return year beginning after December 31, 2020 is $200, but the cumulative register has a positive balance of only $120 (and no other net operating loss carryovers or carrybacks are available for the year). Because the SRLY limitation would be $96 ($120 x 80 percent), only $96 of SRLY loss may be used, rather than $160 ($200 x 80 percent). In addition, to the extent that this paragraph (c)(1)(i)(E) applies, the cumulative register is decreased by the full amount of income required under section 172(a) to support the amount of SRLY NOL absorption. See, for example, paragraph (c)(1)(iii)(A) and (B) of this section for examples illustrating the application of this rule.

(ii) *Losses treated as arising in SRLYs.*—If a net operating loss carryover or carryback did not arise in a SRLY but is attributable to a built-in loss (as defined under §1.1502-15), the carryover or carryback is treated for purposes of this paragraph (c) as arising in a SRLY if the built-in loss was not allowed, after application of the SRLY limitation, in the year it arose. For an illustration, see §1.1502-15(d), *Example 5*. But see §1.1502-15(g)(1).

(iii) *Examples.*—For purposes of the examples in this paragraph (c)(1)(iii), no corporation is a nonlife insurance company and, unless otherwise specified, all taxable years begin after December 31, 2020, and all CNOLs arise in taxable years beginning after December 31, 2020. The principles of this paragraph (c)(1) are illustrated by the following examples:

(A) *Example 1: Determination of SRLY limitation.*—(1) Individual A owns P. In Year 1, Individual A forms T, and T sustains a $100 net operating loss that is carried forward. P acquires all the stock of T at the beginning of Year 2, and T becomes a member of the P group. The P group has $300 of consolidated taxable income in Year 2 (computed without regard to the CNOL deduction). Such consolidated taxable income would be $70 if determined by reference to only T's items.

(2) T's $100 net operating loss carryover from Year 1 arose in a SRLY. See §1.1502-1(f)(2)(iii). P's acquisition of T was not an ownership change as defined by section 382(g). Thus, the $100 net operating loss carryover is subject to the SRLY limitation in paragraph (c)(1) of this section. The positive balance of the cumulative register of T for Year 2 equals the consolidated taxable income of the P group determined by reference to only T's items, or $70. However, due to the 80-percent limitation and the application of paragraph (c)(1)(i)(E) of this section, the SRLY limitation is $56 ($70 x 80 percent). No losses from equivalent years are available, and the P group otherwise has sufficient consolidated taxable income to support the CNOL deduction ($300 x 80 percent = $240). Therefore, $56 of the SRLY net operating loss is included under paragraph (a) of this section in the P group's CNOL deduction for Year 2. Although only $56 is absorbed, the cumulative register of T is reduced by $70, the full amount of income necessary to support the $56 deduction after taking into account the 80-percent limitation ($70 x 80 percent = $56).

(3) The facts are the same as in paragraph (i) of this *Example 1*, except that such consolidated taxable income (computed without regard to the CNOL deduction and by reference to only T's items) for Year 2 is a loss (a CNOL) of $370. Because the SRLY limitation may not exceed the consolidated taxable income determined by reference to only T's items, and such items aggregate to a CNOL, T's $100 net operating loss carryover from Year 1 is not allowed under the SRLY limitation in Year 2. Moreover, if consolidated taxable income (computed without regard to the CNOL deduction and by reference to only T's items) did not exceed $370 in Year 3, the carryover would still be restricted under paragraph (c) of this section in Year 3, because the aggregate consolidated taxable income for all consolidated return years of the group computed by reference to only T's items would not be a positive amount.

(B) *Example 2: Net operating loss carryovers.*—(1) In Year 1, Individual A forms P, and P sustains a $40 net operating loss that is carried forward. P has no income in Year 2. Individual A also owns T which sustains a net operating loss of $50 in Year 2 that is carried forward. P acquires the stock of T from Individual A during Year 3, but T is not a member of the P group for each day of the year. P and T file separate returns and sustain net operating losses of $120 and $60, respectively, for Year 3. The P group files consolidated returns beginning in Year 4. During Year 4, the P group has $160 of consolidated taxable income (computed without regard to the CNOL deduction). Such consolidated taxable income would be $70 if determined by reference to only T's items. These results are summarized as follows:

| | Separate Year 1 | Separate Year 2 | Separate/ Affiliated Year 3 | Consolidated Year 4 |
|---|---|---|---|---|
| P | $(40) | $0 | $(120) | $90 |
| T | 0 | (50) | (60) | 70 |
| CTI | | | | 160 |

(2) P's Year 1, Year 2, and Year 3 are not SRLYs with respect to the P group. See §1.1502-1(f)(2)(i). Thus, P's $40 net operating loss arising in Year 1 and $120 net operating loss arising in Year 3 are not subject to the SRLY limitation under paragraph (c) of this section. Although the P group has $160 of taxable income in Year 4, the 80-percent limitation reduces the P group's net operating loss deduction in that year to $128 ($160 x 80 percent). Under the principles of section 172, paragraph (b) of this section requires that P's $40 loss arising in Year 1 be the first loss absorbed by the P group in Year 4. Absorption of this loss leaves $88 ($128 - $40) of the P group's Year 4 consolidated taxable income available for offset by loss carryovers.

(3) T's Year 2 and Year 3 are SRLYs with respect to the P group. See §1.1502-1(f)(2)(ii). P's acquisition of T was not an ownership change as defined by section 382(g). Thus, T's $50 net operating loss arising in Year 2 and $60 net operating loss arising in Year 3 are subject to the SRLY limitation. The positive balance of the cumulative register of T for Year 4 equals the P group's consolidated taxable income determined by reference to only T's items, or $70. Under paragraph (c)(1)(i)(E) of this section, after taking into account the 80-percent limitation, T's SRLY limitation is $56 ($70 x 80 percent). Therefore, the P group can absorb up to $56 of T's SRLY net operating losses in Year 4. Under the principles of section 172, T's $50 SRLY net operating loss from Year 2 is included under paragraph (a) of this section in the P group's CNOL deduction for Year 4. After absorption of this loss, under paragraph (c)(1)(i) of this section, $6 of SRLY limit remains in Year 4 ($56 - $50). Further, the total amount of Year 4 consolidated taxable income available for offset by other loss carryovers under section 172(a) is $38 ($88 - $50).

(4) P and T each carry over net operating losses to Year 4 from a taxable year ending on the same date (that is, Year 3). The losses carried over from Year 3 total $180. However, the remaining Year 4 SRLY limit is $6. Therefore, the total amount of loss available for absorption is $126 ($120 allocable to P and $6 allocable to T). Under paragraph (b) of this section, the losses available for absorption that are carried over from Year 3 are absorbed on a pro rata basis, even though one loss arises in a SRLY and the other loss does not. Thus, $36.19 of P's Year 3 loss is absorbed ($120/($120 + $6)) x $38 = $36.19. In addition, $1.81 of T's Year 3 loss is absorbed ($6/($120 + $6)) x $38 = $1.81.

(5) After deduction of T's SRLY net operating losses in Year 4, the cumulative register of T is adjusted pursuant to paragraph (c)(1)(i)(E) of this section. A total of $51.81 of SRLY net operating losses were absorbed in Year 4 ($50 + $1.81). After taking into account the 80-percent limitation, the amount of income necessary to support this deduction is $64.76 ($64.76 x 80 percent = $51.81). Therefore, the cumulative register of T is decreased by $64.76, and $5.24 remains in the cumulative register ($70 - $64.76).

(6) P carries its remaining $83.81 ($120 - $36.19) Year 3 net operating loss and T carries its remaining $58.19 ($60 - $1.81) Year 3 net operating loss over to Year 5. Assume that, in Year 5, the P group has $90 of consolidated taxable income (computed without regard to the CNOL deduction). The P group's consolidated taxable income determined by reference to only T's items is a CNOL of $4. Therefore, the positive balance of the cumulative register of T in Year 5 equals $1.24 ($5.24 - $4). Under paragraph (c)(1)(i)(E) of this section, after taking into account the 80-percent limitation, T's SRLY limitation is $0.99 ($1.24 x 80 percent). For Year 5, the total amount of Year 5 consolidated taxable income available for offset by loss carryovers as a result of the 80-percent limitation is $72 ($90 x 80 percent). Under paragraph (b) of this section, the losses carried over from Year 3 are absorbed on a pro rata basis, even though one loss arises in a SRLY and the other loss does not. Therefore, $71.16 of P's Year 3 loss is absorbed (($83.81/($83.81 + $0.99)) x $72 = $71.16). In addition, $0.84 of T's Year 3 losses is absorbed (($0.99/($83.81 + $0.99)) x $72 = $0.84).

(C) *Example 3: Net operating loss carrybacks.*—(1) P owns all of the stock of S and T. The members of the P group contribute the following to the consolidated taxable income of the P group for Years 1, 2, and 3:

| | Year 1 | Year 2 | Year 3 | Total |
|---|---|---|---|---|
| P .............. | $100 | $60 | $80 | $240 |
| S ............. | 20 | 20 | 30 | 70 |
| T ............. | 30 | 10 | (50 ) | (10 ) |
| CTI ......... | 150 | 90 | 60 | 300 |

(2) P sells all of the stock of T to Individual A at the beginning of Year 4, a taxable year that begins on January 1, 2021. For its Year 4 separate return year, T has a net operating loss of $30.

(3) T's Year 4 is a SRLY with respect to the P group. See §1.1502-1(f)(1). T's $30 net operating loss carryback to the P group from Year 4 is not allowed under paragraph (c) of this section to be included in the CNOL deduction under paragraph (a) of this section for Year 1, 2, or 3, because the P group's consolidated taxable income would not be a positive amount if determined by reference to only T's items for all consolidated return years through Year 4 (without regard to the $30 net operating loss). The $30 loss is carried forward to T's Year 5 and succeeding taxable years as provided under the Internal Revenue Code.

(D) *Example 4: Computation of SRLY limitation for built-in losses treated as net operating loss carryovers.*—(1) Individual A owns P. In Year 1, Individual A forms T by contributing $300 and T sustains a $100 net operating loss. During Year 2, T's assets decline in value by $100. At the beginning of Year 3, P acquires all the stock of T from Individual A, and T becomes a member of the P group in a transaction that does not result in an ownership change under section 382(g). At the time of the acquisition, T has a $100 net unrealized built-in loss, which exceeds the threshold requirements of section 382(h)(3)(B). During Year 3, T recognizes its unrealized loss as a $100 ordinary loss. The members of the P group contribute the following to the consolidated taxable income of the P group for Years 3 and 4 (computed without regard to T's recognition of its unrealized loss and any CNOL deduction under this section):

| | Year 3 | Year 4 | Total |
|---|---|---|---|
| P group ............. | $100 | $100 | $200 |
| (without T) | | | |
| T ................. | $60 | $40 | $100 |
| CTI ............... | $160 | $140 | $300 |

(2) Under §1.1502-15(a), T's $100 of ordinary loss in Year 3 constitutes a built-in loss that is subject to the SRLY limitation under paragraph (c) of this section. The amount of the limitation is determined by treating the deduction as a net operating loss carryover from a SRLY. The built-in loss is therefore subject to both a SRLY limitation and the 80-percent limitation for Year 3. The built-in loss is treated as a net operating loss carryover solely for purposes of determining the extent to which the loss is not allowed by reason of the SRLY limitation, and for all other purposes the loss remains a loss arising in Year 3. See §1.1502-21(c)(1)(i)(D). Consequently, under paragraph (b) of this section, the built-in loss is absorbed by the P group before the net operating loss carryover from Year 1 is absorbed. The positive balance of the cumulative register of T for Year 3 equals the P group's consolidated taxable income determined by reference to only T's items, or $60. Under paragraph (c)(1)(i)(E) of this section, after taking into account the 80-percent limitation, the SRLY limitation for Year 3 is $48 ($60 x 80 percent). Therefore, $48 of the built-in loss is absorbed by the P group. None of T's $100 SRLY net operating loss carryover from Year 1 is allowed.

(3) After deduction of T's $48 SRLY built-in loss in Year 4, the cumulative register of T is adjusted pursuant to paragraph (c)(1)(i)(E) of this section. After taking into account the 80-percent limitation, the amount of income necessary to support this deduction is $60 ($60 x 80 percent = $48). Therefore, the cumulative register of T is decreased by $60, and zero remains in the cumulative register ($60 - $60).

(4) Under §1.1502-15(a), the $52 balance of the built-in loss that is not allowed in Year 3 because of the SRLY limitation and the 80-percent limitation is treated as a $52 net operating loss arising in Year 3 that is subject to the SRLY limitation because, under paragraph (c)(1)(ii) of this section, Year 3 is treated as a SRLY. The built-in loss is carried to other years in accordance with the rules of paragraph (b) of this section. The positive balance of the cumulative register of T for Year 4 equals $40 (zero from Year 3 + $40). Under paragraph (c)(1)(i)(E) of this section, after taking into account the 80-percent limitation, the SRLY limitation for Year 4 is $32 ($40 x 80 percent). Therefore, under paragraph (c) of this section, $32 of T's $100 net operating loss carryover from Year 1 is included in the CNOL deduction under paragraph (a) of this section in Year 4.

(5) After deduction of T's $32 SRLY net operating loss in Year 4, the cumulative register of T is adjusted pursuant to paragraph (c)(1)(i)(E) of this section. After taking into account the 80-percent limitation, the amount of income necessary to support this deduction is $40 ($40 x 80 percent = $32). Therefore, the cumulative register is decreased by $40, and zero remains in the cumulative register ($40 - $40).

(E) *Example 5: Dual SRLY registers and accounting for SRLY losses actually absorbed.*—(1) In Year 1, T sustains a $100 net operating loss and a $50 net capital loss. At the beginning of Year 2, T becomes a member of the P group in a transaction that does not result in an ownership change under section 382(g). Both of T's carryovers from Year 1 are subject to SRLY limits under this paragraph (c) and §1.1502-22(c). The members of the P group contribute the following to the consolidated taxable income for Years 2 and 3 (computed without regard to T's CNOL deduction under this section or net capital loss carryover under §1.1502-22):

| | P | T |
|---|---|---|
| **Year 1 (SRLY)** | | |
| Ordinary ......................... | | (100 ) |
| Capital ........................... | | (50 ) |
| **Year 2** | | |
| Ordinary ....................... | 30 | 60 |
| Capital ......................... | 0 | (20 ) |
| **Year 3** | | |
| Ordinary ...................... | 10 | 40 |
| Capital ....................... | 0 | 30 |

(2) For Year 2, the P group computes separate SRLY limits for each of T's SRLY carryovers from Year 1. The group determines its ability to use its capital loss carryover before it determines its ability to use its ordinary loss carryover. Under section 1212, because the P group has no Year 2 capital gain, it cannot absorb any capital losses in Year 2. T's Year 1 net capital loss and the P group's Year 2 consolidated net capital loss (all of which is attributable to T) are carried over to Year 3.

(3) The P group's ability to deduct net operating losses in Year 2 is subject to the 80-percent limitation, based on the P group's consolidated taxable income for the year. Thus, the group's limitation for Year 2 is $72 ($90 x 80 percent). However, use of the Year 1 net operating loss also is subject to the SRLY limitation. The positive balance of the cumulative register of T applicable to SRLY net operating losses for Year 2 equals the P group's consolidated taxable income determined by reference to only T's items, or $60. Under paragraph (c)(1)(i)(E) of this section, after taking into account the 80-percent limitation, the SRLY limitation for Year 2 is $48 ($60 x 80 percent). Therefore, only $48 of T's Year 1 SRLY net operating loss is absorbed by the P group in Year 2. T carries over its remaining $52 of its Year 1 loss to Year 3.

(4) After deduction of T's SRLY net operating losses in Year 2, the net operating loss cumulative register is adjusted pursuant to paragraph (c)(1)(i)(E) of this section. The P group deducted $48 of T's SRLY net operating losses in Year 2. After taking into account the 80-percent limitation, the amount of taxable income necessary to support this deduction is $60 ($60 x 80 percent = $48). Therefore, the net operating loss cumulative register of T is decreased by $60, and zero remains in the net operating loss cumulative register ($60 - $60).

(5) For Year 3, the P group again computes separate SRLY limits for each of T's SRLY carryovers from Year 1. The group has consolidated net capital gain (without taking into account a net capital loss carryover deduction) of $30. Under §1.1502-22(c), the aggregate amount of T's $50 capital loss carryover from Year 1 that is included in computing the P group's consolidated net capital gain for all years of the group (in this case, Years 2 and 3) may not exceed $30 (the aggregate consolidated net capital gain computed by reference only to T's items, including losses and deductions actually absorbed (that is, $30 of capital gain in Year 3)). Thus, the P group may include $30 of T's Year 1 capital loss carryover in its computation of consolidated net capital gain for Year 3, which offsets the group's capital gains for Year 3. T carries over its remaining $20 of its Year 1 capital loss to Year 4. Therefore, the capital loss cumulative register of T is decreased by $30, and zero remains in the capital loss cumulative register ($30 - $30). Further, because the net operating loss cumulative register includes all taxable income of T included in the P group, as well as all absorbed losses of T (including capital items), a zero net increase occurs in the net operating loss cumulative register. The P group carries over the Year 2 consolidated net capital loss to Year 4.

(6) The P group's ability to deduct net operating losses in Year 3 is subject to the 80-percent limitation, based on the P group's consolidated taxable income for the year. Thus, the P group's taxable income for Year 3 that can be offset, before use of net operating losses, is $40 (80 percent x the sum of zero capital gain, after use of the capital loss carryover, plus $50 of ordinary income). However,

use of the Year 1 net operating loss also is subject to the SRLY limitation. The positive balance of the cumulative register of T applicable to SRLY net operating losses for Year 3 equals the P group's consolidated taxable income determined by reference only to T's items, or $40. This amount equals the sum obtained by adding the zero carryover from Year 2, a net inclusion of zero from capital items implicated in Year 3 ($30 - $30), and $40 of taxable income in Year 3. Under paragraph (c)(1)(i)(E) of this section, after taking into account the 80-percent limitation, the SRLY limitation for Year 3 is $32 ($40 x 80 percent). Therefore, only $32 of the Year 1 net operating loss is absorbed by the P group in Year 3. T carries over its remaining $20 of its Year 1 loss to Year 4.

(F) *Example 6: Pre-2018 NOLs and post-2017 NOLs.*—(1) Individual A owns P. On January 1, 2017, A forms T. P and T are calendar-year taxpayers. In 2017, T sustains a $100 net operating loss that is carried over. During 2018, 2019, and 2020, T deducts a total of $90 of its 2017 net operating loss against its taxable income, and T carries over the remaining $10 of its 2017 net operating loss. In 2021, T sustains a net operating loss of $50. On December 31, 2021, P acquires all the stock of T, and T becomes a member of the P group. The P group has $300 of consolidated taxable income in 2022 (computed without regard to the CNOL deduction). Such consolidated taxable income would be $70 if determined by reference to only T's items. The P group has no other SRLY net operating loss carryovers or CNOL carryovers.

(2) T's remaining $10 of net operating loss carryover from 2017 and its $50 net operating loss carryover from 2021 are both SRLY losses in the P group. See § 1.1502-1(f)(2)(iii). P's acquisition of T was not an ownership change as defined by section 382(g). Thus, T's net operating loss carryovers are subject to the SRLY limitation in paragraph (c)(1) of this section. The SRLY limitation for the P group's 2022 consolidated return year is consolidated taxable income determined by reference to only T's $70 of items.

(3) Because T's oldest (2017) carryover was sustained in a year beginning before January 1, 2018, its use is not subject to limitation under section 172(a)(2)(B). Therefore, all $10 of T's 2017 SRLY net operating loss (that is, a pre-2018 NOL) is included under paragraph (a) of this section in the P group's CNOL deduction for 2022. After deduction of T's $10 SRLY net operating loss from 2017, the cumulative register of T is reduced on a dollar-for-dollar basis, pursuant to paragraph (c)(1)(i) of this section. Therefore, the cumulative register of T is decreased by $10, and $60 remains in the cumulative register ($70 - $10).

(4) The P group's deduction of T's 2021 net operating loss is subject to both a SRLY limitation and the 80-percent limitation under section 172(a)(2)(B)(ii). Therefore, the total limitation on the use of T's 2021 net operating loss in the P group is $48 (the remaining cumulative register of $60 x 80 percent). No losses from equivalent years are available, and the P group otherwise has sufficient consolidated taxable income to support the CNOL deduction ($290 x 80 percent = $232). Therefore, $48 of T's 2021 SRLY net operating loss is included under paragraph (a) of this section in the P group's CNOL deduction for 2022. The remaining $2 of T's 2021 SRLY net operating loss ($50 - $48) is carried over to the P group's 2023 consolidated return year.

(5) After deduction of T's $48 SRLY NOL in 2022, the cumulative register of T is adjusted pursuant to paragraph (c)(1)(i)(E) of this section. After taking into account the 80-percent limitation, the amount of income necessary to support this deduction is $60 ($60 x 80 percent = $48). Therefore, the cumulative register of T is decreased by $60, and zero remains in the cumulative register ($60 - $60).

(2) *SRLY subgroup limitation.*—In the case of a net operating loss carryover or carryback for which there is a SRLY subgroup, the principles of paragraph (c)(1) of this section apply to the SRLY subgroup, and not separately to its members. Thus, the contribution to consolidated taxable income and the net operating loss carryovers and carrybacks arising (or treated as arising) in SRLYs that are included in the CNOL deductions for all consolidated return years of the group under paragraph (a) of this section are based on the aggregate amounts of income, gain, deduction, and loss of the members of the SRLY subgroup for the relevant consolidated return years (as provided in paragraph (c)(1)(i)(C) of this section). For an illustration of aggregate amounts during the relevant consolidated return years following the year in which a member of a SRLY subgroup ceases to be a member of the group, see paragraph (c)(2)(viii) *Example 4* of this section. A SRLY subgroup may exist only for a carryover or carryback arising in a year that is not a SRLY (and is not treated as a SRLY under paragraph (c)(1)(ii) of this section) with respect to another group (the former group), whether or not the group is a consolidated group, or for a carryover that was subject to the overlap rule described in paragraph (g) of this section or § 1.1502-15(g) with respect to another group (the former group). A separate SRLY subgroup is determined for each such carryover or carryback. A consolidated group may include more than one SRLY subgroup and a member may be a member of more than one SRLY subgroup. Solely for purposes of determining the members of a SRLY subgroup with respect to a loss:

(i) *Carryovers.*—In the case of a carryover, the SRLY subgroup is composed of the member carrying over the loss (the loss member) and each other member that was a member of the former group that becomes a member of the group at the same time as the loss member. A member remains a member of the SRLY subgroup until it ceases to be affiliated with the loss member. The aggregate determination described in paragraph (c)(1) of this section and this paragraph (c)(2) includes the amounts of income, gain, deduction, and loss of each member of the SRLY subgroup for the consolidated return years during which it remains a member of the SRLY subgroup. For an illustration of the aggregate determination of a SRLY subgroup, see paragraph (c)(2)(viii) *Example 2* of this section.

(ii) *Carrybacks.*—In the case of a carryback, the SRLY subgroup is composed of the member carrying back the loss (the loss member) and each other member of the group from which the loss is carried back that has been continuously affiliated with the loss member from the year to which the loss is carried through the year in which the loss arises.

(iii) *Built-in losses.*—In the case of a built-in loss, the SRLY subgroup is composed of the member recognizing the loss (the loss member) and each other member that was part of the subgroup with respect to the loss determined under § 1.1502-15(c)(2) immediately before the members became members of the group. The principles of paragraphs (c)(2)(i) and (ii) of this section apply to determine the SRLY subgroup for the built-in loss that is, under paragraph (c)(1)(ii) of this section, treated as arising in a SRLY with respect to the group in which the loss is recognized. For this purpose and as the context requires, a reference in paragraphs (c)(2)(i) and (ii) of this section to a group or former group is a reference to the subgroup determined under § 1.1502-15(c)(2).

(iv) *Principal purpose of avoiding or increasing a SRLY limitation.*—The members composing a SRLY subgroup are not treated as a SRLY subgroup if any of them is formed, acquired, or availed of with a principal purpose of avoiding the application of, or increasing any limitation under, this paragraph (c). Any member excluded from a SRLY subgroup, if excluded with a principal purpose of so avoiding or increasing any SRLY limitation, is treated as included in the SRLY subgroup.

(v) *Coordination with other limitations.*—This paragraph (c)(2) does not allow a net operating loss to offset income to the extent inconsistent with other limitations or restrictions on the use of losses, such as a limitation based on the nature or activities of members. For example, a net operating loss may not offset income in excess of any limitations under section 172(a) and paragraph (a)(2) of this section. Additionally, any dual consolidated loss may not reduce the taxable income to an extent greater than that allowed under section 1503(d) and § § 1.1503(d)-1 through 1.1503(d)-8. See also § 1.1502-47(k) (relating to preemption of rules for life-nonlife groups).

(vi) *Anti-duplication.*—If the same item of income or deduction could be taken into account more than once in determining a limitation under this paragraph (c), or in a manner inconsistent with any other provision of the Internal Revenue Code or regulations incorporating this paragraph (c), the item of income or deduction is taken into account only once and in such manner that losses are absorbed in accordance with the ordering rules in paragraph (b) of this section and the underlying purposes of this section.

(vii) *Corporations that leave a SRLY subgroup.*—If a loss member ceases to be affiliated with a SRLY subgroup, the amount of the member's remaining SRLY loss from a specific year is determined pursuant to the principles of paragraphs (b)(2)(ii)(A) and (b)(2)(iv) of this section.

(viii) *Examples.*—For purposes of the examples in this paragraph (c)(2)(viii), no corporation is a nonlife insurance company or has any farming losses. The principles of this paragraph (c)(2) are illustrated by the following examples:

(A) *Example 1: Members of SRLY subgroups.*—(1) Individual A owns all of the stock of P, S, T and M. P and M are each the common parent of a consolidated group. During Year 1, P sustains a $50 net operating loss. At the beginning of Year 2, P acquires all the stock of S at a time when the aggregate basis of S's assets exceeds their aggregate value by $70 and S becomes a member of the P group. At the beginning of Year 3, P acquires all the stock of T, T has a $60 net operating loss carryover at the time of the acquisition, and T becomes a member of the P group. During Year 4, S forms S1 and T forms T1, each by contributing assets with built-in gains which are, in the aggregate, material. S1 and T1 become members of the P group.

During Year 7, M acquires all of the stock of P, and the members of the P group become members of the M group for the balance of Year 7. The $50 and $60 loss carryovers of P and T are carried to Year 7 of the M group, and the value and basis of S's assets did not change after it became a member of the former P group. None of the transactions described above resulted in an ownership change under section 382(g).

(2) Under paragraph (c)(2) of this section, a separate SRLY subgroup is determined for each loss carryover and built-in loss. In the P group, P's $50 loss carryover is not treated as arising in a SRLY. See §1.1502-1(f). Consequently, the carryover is not subject to limitation under paragraph (c) of this section in the P group.

(3) In the M group, P's $50 loss carryover is treated as arising in a SRLY and is subject to the limitation under paragraph (c) of this section, including the limitation under paragraph (c)(1)(i)(E) of this section. A SRLY subgroup with respect to that loss is composed of members which were members of the P group, the group as to which the loss was not a SRLY. The SRLY subgroup is composed of P, the member carrying over the loss, and each other member of the P group that became a member of the M group at the same time as P. A member of the SRLY subgroup remains a member until it ceases to be affiliated with P. For Year 7, the SRLY subgroup is composed of P, S, T, S1, and T1.

(4) In the P group, S's $70 unrealized loss, if recognized within the 5-year recognition period after S becomes a member of the P group, is subject to limitation under paragraph (c) of this section, including the limitation under paragraph (c)(1)(i)(E) of this section. See §1.1502-15 and paragraph (c)(1)(ii) of this section. Because S was not continuously affiliated with P, T, or T1 for 60 consecutive months prior to joining the P group, these corporations cannot be included in a SRLY subgroup with respect to S's unrealized loss in the P group. See paragraph (c)(2)(iii) of this section. As a successor to S, S1 is included in a subgroup with S in the P group, and because 100 percent of S1's stock is owned directly by corporations that were members of the SRLY subgroup when the members of the SRLY subgroup became members of the P group, its net positive income is not excluded from the consolidated taxable income of the P group that may be offset by the built-in loss. See paragraph (f) of this section.

(5) In the M group, S's $70 unrealized loss, if recognized within the 5-year recognition period after S becomes a member of the M group, is subject to limitation under paragraph (c) of this section, including the limitation under paragraph (c)(1)(i)(E) of this section. Prior to becoming a member of the M group, S had been continuously affiliated with P (but not T or T1) for 60 consecutive months and S1 is a successor that has remained continuously affiliated with S. Those members had a net unrealized built-in loss immediately before they became members of the group under §1.1502-15(c). Consequently, in Year 7, S, S1, and P compose a subgroup in the M group with respect to S's unrealized loss. Because S1 was a member of the SRLY subgroup when it became a member of the M group and also because 100 percent of S1's stock is owned directly by corporations that were members of the SRLY subgroup when the members of the SRLY subgroup became members of the M group its net positive income is not excluded from the consolidated taxable income of the M group that may be offset by the recognized built-in loss. See paragraph (f) of this section.

(6) In the P group, T's $60 loss carryover arose in a SRLY and is subject to limitation under paragraph (c) of this section, including the limitation under paragraph (c)(1)(i)(E) of this section. P, S, and S1 were not members of the group in which T's loss arose and T's loss carryover was not subject to the overlap rule described in paragraph (g) of this section with respect to the P group (the former group). Thus, P, S, and S1 are not members of a SRLY subgroup with respect to the T carryover in the P group. See paragraph (c)(2)(i) of this section. As a successor to T, T1 is included in a SRLY subgroup with T in the P group; and, because 100 percent of T1's stock is owned directly by corporations that were members of the SRLY subgroup when the members of the SRLY subgroup became members of the P group, its net positive income is not excluded from the consolidated taxable income of the P group that may be offset by the carryover. See paragraph (f) of this section.

(7) In the M group, T's $60 loss carryover arose in a SRLY and is subject to limitation under paragraph (c) of this section, including the limitation under paragraph (c)(1)(i)(E) of this section. T and T1 remain the only members of a SRLY subgroup with respect to the carryover. Because T1 was a member of the SRLY subgroup when it became a member of the M group and also because 100 percent of T1's stock is owned directly by corporations that were members of the SRLY subgroup when the members of the SRLY subgroup became members of the M group, its net positive income is not excluded from the consolidated taxable income of the M group that may be offset by the carryover. See paragraph (f) of this section.

(B) *Example 2: Computation of SRLY subgroup limitation.*—(1) Individual A owns all of the stock of S, T, P and M, none of which is a nonlife insurance company. P and M are each the common parent of a consolidated group. In Year 2, P acquires all the stock of S and T from Individual A, and S and T become members of the P group. For Year 3 (a taxable year beginning after December 31, 2020), the P group has a $45 CNOL, which is attributable to P, and which P carries forward. M is the common parent of another group. At the beginning of Year 4, M acquires all of the stock of P and the former members of the P group become members of the M group. None of the transactions described above resulted in an ownership change under section 382(g).

(2) P's year to which the loss is attributable, Year 3, is a SRLY with respect to the M group. See §1.1502-1(f)(1). However, P, S, and T compose a SRLY subgroup with respect to the Year 3 loss under paragraph (c)(2)(i) of this section because Year 3 is not a SRLY (and is not treated as a SRLY) with respect to the P group. P's loss is carried over to the M group's Year 4 and is therefore subject to the SRLY subgroup limitation in paragraph (c)(2) of this section.

(3) In Year 4, the M group has $10 of consolidated taxable income (computed without regard to the CNOL deduction for Year 4). That consolidated taxable income would be $45 if determined by reference only to the items of P, S, and T, the members included in the SRLY subgroup with respect to P's loss carryover. Therefore, the positive balance of the cumulative register of the P SRLY subgroup for Year 4 equals $45 and, due to the application of the 80-percent limitation under paragraph (c)(2)(v) of this section, the SRLY subgroup limitation under this paragraph (c)(2) is $36 ($45 x 80 percent). However, the M group has only $10 of consolidated taxable income in Year 4. Thus, due to the 80-percent limitation and the application of paragraph (b)(1) of this section, the M group's deduction of all net operating losses in Year 4 is limited to $8 ($10 x 80 percent). As a result, the M group deducts $8 of P's SRLY net operating loss carryover, and the remaining $37 is carried over to Year 5.

(4) After deduction of $8 of P's SRLY net operating loss in Year 4, the cumulative register of the P SRLY subgroup is adjusted pursuant to paragraph (c)(1)(i)(E) of this section. After taking into account the 80-percent limitation, the amount of income necessary to support this deduction is $10 ($10 x 80 percent = $8). Therefore, the cumulative register of the P SRLY subgroup is decreased by $10, and $35 remains in the cumulative register ($45 - $10).

(5) In Year 5, the M group has $100 of consolidated taxable income (computed without regard to the CNOL deduction for Year 5). None of P, S, or T has any items of income, gain, deduction, or loss in Year 5. Although the members of the P SRLY subgroup do not contribute to the $100 of consolidated taxable income in Year 5, the positive balance of the cumulative register of the P SRLY subgroup for Year 5 is $35 and, due to the application of the 80-percent limitation under paragraph (c)(2)(v) of this section, the SRLY subgroup limitation under this paragraph (c)(2) is $28 ($35 x 80 percent). Because of the 80-percent limitation and the application of paragraph (b)(1) of this section, the M group's deduction of net operating losses in Year 5 is limited to $80 ($100 x 80 percent). Because the $28 of net operating loss available to be absorbed is less than 80 percent of the M group's consolidated taxable income, $28 of P's SRLY net operating loss is absorbed in Year 5, and the remaining $9 ($37 - $28) is carried over to Year 6.

(6) After deduction of $28 of P's SRLY net operating loss in Year 5, the cumulative register of the P SRLY subgroup is adjusted pursuant to paragraph (c)(1)(i)(E) of this section. After taking into account the 80-percent limitation, the amount of income necessary to support this deduction is $35 ($35 x 80 percent = $28). Therefore, the cumulative register of the P SRLY subgroup is decreased by $35, and zero remains in the cumulative register ($35 - $35).

(C) *Example 3: Inclusion in more than one SRLY subgroup.*—(1) Individual A owns all of the stock of S, T, P and M. S, P, and M are each the common parent of a consolidated group. At the beginning of Year 1, S acquires all the stock of T from Individual A, and T becomes a member of the S group. For Year 1, the S group has a CNOL of $10, all of which is attributable to S and is carried over to Year 2. At the beginning of Year 2, P acquires all the stock of S, and S and T become members of the P group. For Year 2, the P group has a CNOL of $35, all of which is attributable to P and is carried over to Year 3. At the beginning of Year 3, M acquires all of the stock of P and the former members of the P group become members of the M group. None of the transactions described above resulted in an ownership change under section 382(g).

(2) P's and S's net operating losses arising in SRLYs with respect to the M group are subject to limitation under paragraph (c) of this section. P, S, and T compose a SRLY subgroup for purposes of determining the limitation for P's $35 net operating loss carryover arising in Year 2 because, under paragraph (c)(2)(i) of this section, Year 2 is not a SRLY with respect to the P group. Similarly, S and T compose a SRLY subgroup for purposes of determining the limitation

for S's $10 net operating loss carryover arising in Year 1 because Year 1 is not a SRLY with respect to the S group.

(3) S and T are members of both the SRLY subgroup with respect to P's losses and the SRLY subgroup with respect to S's losses. Under paragraph (c)(2) of this section, S's and T's items cannot be included in the determination of the SRLY subgroup limitation for both SRLY subgroups for the same consolidated return year; paragraph (c)(2)(vi) of this section requires the M group to consider the items of S and T only once so that the losses are absorbed in the order of the taxable years in which they were sustained. Because S's loss was incurred in Year 1, while P's loss was incurred in Year 2, the items will be added in the determination of the consolidated taxable income of the S and T SRLY subgroup to enable S's loss to be absorbed first. The taxable income of the P, S, and T SRLY subgroup is then computed by including the consolidated taxable income for the S and T SRLY subgroup less the amount of any net operating loss carryover of S that is absorbed after applying this section to the S subgroup for the year.

(D) *Example 1: Corporation ceases to be affiliated with a SRLY subgroup.*—(1) Individual A owns all of the stock of P and M. P and S are members of the P group and the P group has a CNOL of $30 in Year 1, all of which is attributable to P and carried over to Year 2. At the beginning of Year 2, M acquires all of the stock of P, and P and S become members of the M group. P and S compose a SRLY subgroup with respect to P's net operating loss carryover. For Year 2, consolidated taxable income of the M group determined by reference to only the items of P (and without regard to the CNOL deduction for Year 2) is $40. However, such consolidated taxable income of the M group determined by reference to the items of both P and S is a loss of $20. Thus, the SRLY subgroup limitation under paragraph (c)(2) of this section prevents the M group from including any of P's net operating loss carryover in the CNOL deduction under paragraph (a) of this section in Year 2, and P carries the Year 1 loss to Year 3.

(2) At the end of Year 2, P sells all of the S stock and S ceases to be a member of the M group and the P subgroup. For Year 3, consolidated taxable income of the M group is $50 (determined without regard to the CNOL deduction for Year 3), and such consolidated taxable income would be $10 if determined by reference to only items of P. However, the limitation under paragraph (c) of this section for Year 3 for P's net operating loss carryover still prevents the M group from including any of P's loss in the CNOL deduction under paragraph (a) of this section. The limitation results from the inclusion of S's items for Year 2 in the determination of the SRLY subgroup limitation for Year 3 even though S ceased to be a member of the M group (and the P subgroup) at the end of Year 2. Thus, the M group's consolidated taxable income determined by reference to only the SRLY subgroup members' items for all consolidated return years of the group through Year 3 (determined without regard to the CNOL deduction) is not a positive amount.

(ix) *Application to other than loss carryovers.*—Paragraph (g) of this section and the phrase "or for a carryover that was subject to the overlap rule described in paragraph (g) of this section or § 1.1502-15(g) with respect to another group (the former group)" in this paragraph (c)(2) apply only to carryovers of net operating losses, net capital losses, and for taxable years for which the due date (without extensions) of the consolidated return is after May 25, 2000, to carryovers of credits described in section 383(a)(2). Accordingly, as the context may require, if another regulation references this section and such other regulation does not concern a carryover of net operating losses, net capital losses, or for taxable years for which the due date (without extensions) of the consolidated return is after May 25, 2000, carryovers of credits described in section 383(a)(2), then such reference does not include a reference to such paragraph or phrase.

(3) *Cross-reference.*—For rules governing the application of a SRLY limitation to business interest expense for which a deduction is disallowed under section 163(j), see § 1.163(j)-5(d) and (f).

(d) *Coordination with consolidated return change of ownership limitation and transactions subject to old section 382.*—(1) *Consolidated return changes of ownership.*—If a consolidated return change of ownership occurred before January 1, 1997, the principles of § 1.1502-21A(d) apply to determine the amount of the aggregate of the net operating losses attributable to old members of the group that may be included in the consolidated net operating loss deduction under paragraph (a) of this section. For this purpose, § 1.1502-1(g) is applied by treating that date as the end of the year of change.

(2) *Old section 382.*—The principles of § 1.1502-21A(e) apply to disallow or reduce the amount of a net operating loss carryover of a member as a result of a transaction subject to old section 382.

(e) *Consolidated net operating loss.*—Any excess of deductions over gross income, as determined under § 1.1502-11(a) (without regard to

any consolidated net operating loss deduction), is also referred to as the consolidated net operating loss (or CNOL).

(f) *Predecessors and successors.*—(1) *In general.*—For purposes of this section, any reference to a corporation, member, common parent, or subsidiary, includes, as the context may require, a reference to a successor or predecessor, as defined in § 1.1502-1(f)(4).

(2) *Limitation on SRLY subgroups.*—(i) *General rule.*—Except as provided in paragraph (f)(2)(ii) of this section, if a successor's items of income and again exceed the successor's items of deduction and loss (net positive income), then the net positive income attributable to the successor is excluded from the computation of the consolidated taxable income of a SRLY subgroup.

(ii) *Exceptions.*—A successor's net positive income is not excluded from the consolidated taxable income of a SRLY subgroup if—

(A) The successor acquires substantially all the assets and liabilities of its predecessor and the predecessor ceases to exist;

(B) The successor was a member of the SRLY subgroup when the SRLY subgroup members became members of the group;

(C) 100 percent of the stock of the successor is owned directly by corporations that were members of the SRLY subgroup when the SRLY subgroup members became members of the group; or

(D) The Commissioner so determines

(g) *Overlap with section 382.*—(1) *General rule.*—The limitation provided in paragraph (c) of this section does not apply to net operating loss carryovers (other than a hypothetical carryover described in paragraph (c)(1)(i)(D) of this section and a carryover described in paragraph (c)(1)(ii) of this section) when the application of paragraph (c) of this section results in an overlap with the application of section 382. For a similar rule applying in the case of net operating loss carryovers described in paragraphs (c)(1)(i)(D) and (c)(1)(ii) of this section, see § 1.1502-15(g).

(2) *Definitions.*—(i) *Generally.*—For purposes of this paragraph (g), the definitions and nomenclature contained in section 382, the regulations thereunder, and § § 1.1502-90 through 1.1502-99 apply.

(ii) *Overlap.*—(A) An overlap of the application of paragraph (c) of this section and the application of section 382 with respect to a net operating loss carryover occurs if a corporation becomes a member of a consolidated group (the SRLY event) within six months of the change date of an ownership change giving rise to a section 382(a) limitation with respect to that carryover (the section 382 event).

(B) If an overlap described in paragraph (g)(2)(ii)(A) of this section occurs with respect to net operating loss carryovers of a corporation whose SRLY event occurs within the six month period beginning on the date of a section 382 event, then an overlap is treated as also occurring with respect to that corporation's net operating loss carryover that arises within the period beginning with the section 382 event and ending with the SRLY event.

(C) For special rules in the event that there is a SRLY subgroup and/or a loss subgroup as defined in § 1.1502-91(d)(1) with respect to a carryover, see paragraph (g)(4) of this section.

(3) *Operating rules.*—(i) *Section 382 event before SRLY event.*—If a SRLY event occurs on the same date as a section 382 event or within the six month period beginning on the date of the section 382 event, paragraph (g)(1) of this section applies beginning with the tax year that includes the SRLY event.

(ii) *SRLY event before section 382 event.*—If a section 382 event occurs within the period beginning the day after the SRLY event and ending six months after the SRLY event, paragraph (g)(1) of this section applies starting with the first tax year that begins after the section 382 event.

(4) *Subgroup rules.*—In general, in the case of a net operating loss carryover for which there is a SRLY subgroup and a loss subgroup (as defined in § 1.1502-91(d)(1)), the principles of this paragraph (g) apply to the SRLY subgroup, and not separately to its members. However, paragraph (g)(1) of this section applies—

(i) With respect to a carryover described in paragraph (g)(2)(ii)(A) of this section only if—

(A) All members of the SRLY subgroup with respect to that carryover are also included in a loss subgroup with respect to that carryover; and

(B) All members of a loss subgroup with respect to that carryover are also members of a SRLY subgroup with respect to that carryover; and

(ii) With respect to a carryover described in paragraph (g)(2)(ii)(B) of this section only if all members of the SRLY subgroup for that carryover are also members of a SRLY subgroup that has net operating loss carryovers described in paragraph (g)(2)(ii)(A) of this section that are subject to the overlap rule of paragraph (g)(1) of this section.

(5) *Examples.*—The principles of this paragraph (g) are illustrated by the following examples:

(i) *Example 1: Overlap—Simultaneous Acquisition.*—(A) Individual A owns all of the stock of P, which in turn owns all of the stock of S. P and S file a consolidated return. In Year 2, B, an individual unrelated to Individual A, forms T which incurs a $100 net operating loss for that year. At the beginning of Year 3, S acquires T.

(B) S's acquisition of T results in T becoming a member of the P group (the SRLY event) and also results in an ownership change of T, within the meaning of section 382(g), that gives rise to a limitation under section 382(a) (the section 382 event) with respect to the T carryover.

(C) Because the SRLY event and the change date of the section 382 event occur on the same date, there is an overlap of the application of the SRLY rules and the application of section 382.

(D) Consequently, under this paragraph (g), in Year 3 the SRLY limitation does not apply to the Year 2 $100 net operating loss.

(ii) *Example 2: Overlap—Section 382 event before SRLY event.*—(A) Individual A owns all of the stock of P, which in turn owns all of the stock of S. P and S file a consolidated return. In Year 1, B, an individual unrelated to Individual A, forms T which incurs a $100 net operating loss for that year. On February 28 of Year 2, S purchases 55% of T from Individual B. On June 30, of Year 2, S purchases an additional 35% of T from Individual B.

(B) The February 28 purchase of 55% of T is a section 382 event because it results in an ownership change of T, under section 382(g), that gives rise to a section 382(a) limitation with respect to the T carryover. The June 30 purchase of 35% of T results in T becoming a member of the P group and is therefore a SRLY event.

(C) Because the SRLY event occurred within six months of the change date of the section 382 event, there is an overlap of the application of the SRLY rules and the application of section 382.

(D) Consequently, under paragraph (g) of this section, in Year 2 the SRLY limitation does not apply to the Year 1 $100 net operating loss.

(iii) *Example 3: No overlap—Section 382 event before SRLY event.*—(A) The facts are the same as in *Example 2* except that Individual B does not sell the additional 35% of T to S until September 30, Year 2.

(B) The February 28 purchase of 55% of T is a section 382 event because it results in an ownership change of T, under section 382(g), that gives rise to a section 382(a) limitation with respect to the T carryover. The September 30 purchase of 35% of T results in T becoming a member of the P group and is therefore a SRLY event.

(C) Because the SRLY event did not occur within six months of the change date of the section 382 event, there is no overlap of the application of the SRLY rules and the application of section 382. Consequently, the Year 1 net operating loss is subject to a SRLY limitation and a section 382 limitation.

(iv) *Example 4: Overlap—SRLY event before section 382 event.*—(A) P and S file a consolidated return. S has owned 40% of T for 6 years. For Year 6, T has a net operating loss of $500 that is carried forward. On March 31, Year 7, S acquires an additional 40% of T, and on August 31, Year 7, S acquires the remaining 20% of T.

(B) The March 31 purchase of 40% of T results in T becoming a member of the P group and is therefore a SRLY event. The August 31 purchase of 20% of T is a section 382 event because it results in an ownership change of T, under section 382(g), that gives rise to a section 382(a) limitation with respect to the T carryover.

(C) Because the SRLY event occurred within six months of the change date of the section 382 event, there is an overlap of the application of the SRLY rules and the application of section 382 within the meaning of this paragraph (g).

(D) Under this paragraph (g), the SRLY rules of paragraph (c) of this section will apply to the Year 7 tax year. Beginning in Year 8 (the year after the section 382 event), any unabsorbed portion of the Year 6 net operating loss will not be subject to a SRLY limitation.

(v) *Example 5: Overlap—Coextensive subgroups.*—(A) Individual A owns all of the stock of S, which in turn owns all of the stock of T. S and T file a consolidated return beginning in Year 1. B, an individual unrelated to Individual A, owns all of the stock of P, the common parent of a consolidated group. In Year 2, the S group has a $200 consolidated net operating loss which is carried forward, of which $100 is attributable to S, and $100 is attributable to T. At the beginning of Year 3, the P group acquires all of the stock of S from Individual A.

(B) P's acquisition of S results in S and T becoming members of the P group (the SRLY event). With respect to the Year 2 net

operating loss carryover, S and T compose a SRLY subgroup under paragraph (c)(2) of this section.

(C) S and T also compose a loss subgroup under §1.1502-91(d)(1) with respect to the Year 2 net operating loss carryover. P's acquisition also results in an ownership change of S, the subgroup parent, within the meaning of section 382(g), that gives rise to a limitation under section 382(a) (the section 382 event) with respect to the Year 2 carryover.

(D) Because the SRLY event and the change date of the section 382 event occur on the same date, there is an overlap of the application of the SRLY rules and the application of section 382 within the meaning of paragraph (g) of this section. Because the SRLY subgroup and the loss subgroup are coextensive, under paragraph (g) of this section, the SRLY limitation does not apply to the Year 2 $200 net operating loss.

(vi) *Example 6: No Overlap—Different subgroups.*—(A) Individual B owns all of the stock of P, the common parent of a consolidated group. P owns all of the stock of S and all of the stock of T. Individual A owns all of the stock of X, the common parent of another consolidated group. In Year 1, the P group has a $200 consolidated net operating loss, of which $100 is attributable to S and $100 is attributable to T. At the beginning of Year 3, the X group acquires all of the stock of S and T from P and does not make an election under §1.1502-91(d)(4) (concerning an election to treat the loss subgroup parent requirement as having been satisfied).

(B) X's acquisition of S and T results in S and T becoming members of the X group (the SRLY event). With respect to the Year 1 net operating loss, S and T compose a SRLY subgrop under paragraph (c)(2) of this section.

(C) S and T do not bear (and are not treated as bearing) a section 1504(a)(1) relationship. Therefore S and T do not qualify as a loss subgroup under §1.1502-91(d)(1). X's acquisition of S and T results in separate ownership changes of S and T, that give rise to separate limitations under section 382(a) (the section 382 events) with respect to each of S and T's Year 1 net operating loss carryovers. See §1.1502-94.

(D) The SRLY event and the change dates of the section 382 events occur on the same date. However, paragraph (g)(1) of this section does not apply because the SRLY subgroup (composed of S and T) is not coextensive with a loss subgroup with respect to the Year 1 carryovers. Consequently, the Year 1 net operating loss is subject to both a SRLY subgroup limitation and also separate section 382 limitations for each of S and T.

(vii) *Example 7: No Overlap—Different subgroups.*—(A) Individual A owns all of the stock of T and all of the stock of S, the common parent of a consolidated group. B, an individual unrelated to Individual A, owns all of the stock of P, the common parent of another consolidated group. In Year 1, T has a net operating loss of $100 that is carried forward. At the end of Year 2, S acquires all of the stock of T from Individual A. In Year 3, the S group sustains a $200 consolidated net operating loss that is carried forward. In Year 8, the P group acquires all of the stock of S from Individual A.

(B) S's acquisition of T in Year 1 results in T becoming a member of the S group. The acquisition, however, did not result in an ownership change under section 382(g). As a result, T's Year 1 net operating loss is subject to SRLY within the S group. At the end of Year 7, §1.1502-96(a) treats T's Year 1 net operating loss as not having arisen in a SRLY with respect to the S group. Section 1.1502-96(a), however, applies only for purposes of §§1.1502-91 through 1.1502-96 and §1.1502-98 but not for purposes of this section. See §1.1502-96(a)(5).

(C) P's acquisition of S in Year 8 results in S and T becoming members of the P group (the SRLY event). With respect to the Year 1 net operating loss, S and T do not compose a SRLY subgroup under paragraph (c)(2) of this section.

(D) S and T compose a loss subgroup under §1.1502-91(d)(1) with respect to the Year 1 net operating loss carryover. P's acquisition of S results in an ownership change of the loss subgroup, within the meaning of section 382(g), that gives rise to a subgroup limitation under section 382(a) (the section 382 event) with respect to that carryover.

(E) The SRLY event and the change date of the section 382 event occur on the same date. However, under paragraph (g)(4) of this section, because the SRLY subgroup and the loss subgroup are not coextensive, T's Year 1 net operating loss carryover is subject to a SRLY limitation.

(F) With respect to the Year 3 net operating loss carryover, S and T compose both a SRLY subgroup and a loss subgroup under $1.1502-91(d)(1). Thus, paragraph (g)(1) of this section applies and the S group's Year 3 net operating loss carryover is not subject to a SRLY limitation.

(viii) *Example 8: SRLY after overlap.*—(A) Individual A owns all of the stock of R and M, each the common parent of a consolidated group. B, an individual unrelated to Individual A, owns all of the stock of D. In Year 1, D incurs a $100 net operating loss that is carried forward. At the beginning of Year 3, R acquires all of the stock of D. In Year 5, M acquires all of the stock of R in a transaction that did not result in an ownership change of R.

(B) R's Year 3 acquisition of D results in D becoming a member of the R group (the SRLY event) and also results in an ownership change of D, that gives rise to a limitation under section 382(a) (the section 382 event) with respect to D's net operating loss carryover.

(C) Because the SRLY event and the change date of the section 382 event occur on the same date, there is an overlap of the application of paragraph (c) of this section and section 382 with respect to D's net operating loss. Consequently, under this paragraph (g), D's Year 1 $100 net operating loss is not subject to a SRLY limitation in the R group.

(D) M's Year 5 acquisition of R results in R and D becoming members of the M group (the SRLY event), but does not result in an ownership change of R or D that gives rise to a limitation under section 382(a). Because there is no section 382 event, the application of the SRLY rules and section 382 do not overlap. Consequently, D's Year 1 $100 net operating loss is subject to a SRLY limitation in the M group.

(E) Because D's Year 1 net operating loss carryover was subject to the overlap rule of paragraph (g) of this section when it joined the R group, under §1.1502-21(c)(2) the SRLY subgroup with respect to that carryover includes all of the members of the R group that joined the M group at the same time as D.

(ix) *Example 9: Overlap—Interim losses.*—(A) Individual A owns all of the stock of P and S, each the common parent of a consolidated group. S owns all of the stock of T, its only subsidiary. B, an individual unrelated to Individual A, owns all of the stock of M, the common parent of a consolidated group. In Year 1, the S group has a $100 consolidated net operating loss. On January 1 of Year 2, P acquires all of the stock of S from Individual A. On December 31 of Year 2, M acquires 51% of the stock of P from Individual A. On May 31 of Year 3, M acquires the remaining 49% of the stock of P from Individual A. The P group, for the Year 3 period prior to June 1 had a $50 consolidated net operating loss, and under paragraph (b)(2)(iv) of this section, the loss is attributable entirely to S. Other than the losses described above, the P group does not have any other consolidated net operating losses.

(B) In the P group, S's $100 loss carryover is treated as arising in a SRLY and is subject to the limitation under paragraph (c) of this section. A SRLY subgroup with respect to that loss is composed of S and T, the members which were members of the S group as to which the loss was not a SRLY.

(C) M's December 31 purchase of 51% of P is a section 382 event because it results in an ownership change of the S loss subgroup that gives rise to a section 382(a) limitation (the section 382 event) with respect to the Year 1 net operating loss carryover. The purchase, however, does not result in an ownership change of P because it is not a loss corporation under section 382(k)(1). M's May 31 purchase of 49% of P results in P, S, and T becoming members of the M group and is therefore a SRLY event.

(D) With respect to the Year 1 net operating loss, S and T compose a SRLY subgroup under paragraph (c)(2) of this section and a loss subgroup under §1.1502-91(d)(1). The loss subgroup does not include P because the only loss at the time of the section 382 event was subject to SRLY with respect to the P group. See §1.1502-91(d)(1).

(E) Because the SRLY event occurred within six months of the change date of the section 382 event and the SRLY subgroup and loss subgroup are coextensive with respect to the Year 1 net operating loss carryover, there is an overlap of the application of the SRLY rules and the application of section 382 within the meaning of paragraph (g) of this section. Thus, the SRLY limitation does not apply to that carryover.

(F) The Year 3 net operating loss, which arose between the section 382 event and the SRLY event, is a net operating loss described in paragraph (g)(2)(ii)(B) of this section because it is the net operating loss of a corporation whose SRLY event occurs within the six month period beginning on the date of a section 382 event.

(G) With respect to the Year 3 net operating loss, P, S, and T compose a SRLY subgroup under paragraph (c)(2) of this section. Because P, a member of the SRLY subgroup for the Year 3 carryover, is not also a member of a SRLY subgroup that has net operating loss carryovers described in paragraph (g)(2)(ii)(A) of this section (the Year 1 net operating loss), the Year 3 carryover is subject to a SRLY limitation in the M group. See paragraph (g)(4)(ii) of this section.

(h) *Effective/applicability dates.*—(1) *In general.*—This section generally applies to taxable years for which the due date (without extensions) of the consolidated return is after June 25, 1999. However—

(i) In the event that paragraph (g)(1) of this section does not apply to a particular net operating loss carryover in the current group, then solely for purposes of applying paragraph (c) of this section to determine a limitation with respect to that carryover and with respect to which the SRLY register (consolidated taxable income determined by reference to only the member's or subgroup's items of income, gain, deduction or loss) began in a taxable year for which the due date of the return was on or before June 25, 1999, paragraph (c)(2) of this section shall be applied without regard to the phrase "or for a carryover that was subject to the overlap rule described in paragraph (g) of this section or §1.1502-15(g) with respect to another group (the former group)"; and

(ii) For purposes of paragraph (g) of this section, only an ownership change to which section 382(a), as amended by the Tax Reform Act of 1986, applies shall constitute a section 382 event.

(iii) Paragraphs (b)(2)(ii)(A) and (b)(2)(iv)(B)(2) of this section apply to taxable years for which the due date of the original return (without regard to extensions) is on or after September 17, 2008.

(2) *SRLY limitation.*—Except in the case of those members (including members of a SRLY subgroup) described in paragraph (h)(3) of this section, a group does not take into account a consolidated taxable year beginning before January 1, 1997, in determining the aggregate of the consolidated taxable income under paragraph (c)(1) of this section (including for purposes of §1.1502-15 and §1.1502-22(c)) for the members (or SRLY subgroups).

(3) *Prior retroactive election.*—A consolidated group that applied the rules of §1.1502-21T(g)(3) in effect prior to June 25, 1999, as contained in 26 CFR part 1 revised April 1, 1999, to all consolidated return years ending on or after January 29, 1991, and beginning before January 1, 1997, does not take into account a consolidated taxable year beginning before January 29, 1991, in determining the aggregate of the consolidated taxable income under paragraph (c)(1) of this section (including for purposes of §1.1502-15 and §1.1502-22(c)) for the members (or SRLY subgroups).

(4) *Offspring rule.*—Paragraph (b)(2)(ii)(B) of this section applies to net operating losses arising in taxable years ending on or after June 25, 1999.

(5) *Waiver of carrybacks.*—Paragraph (b)(3)(ii)(B) of this section (relating to the waiver of carrybacks for acquired members) applies to acquisitions occurring after June 25, 1999.

(6) *Certain prior periods.*—Paragraphs (b)(1), (b)(2)(iv)(A), (b)(2)(iv)(B)(1), and (c)(2)(vii) of this section apply to taxable years for which the due date of the original return (without regard to extensions) is after March 21, 2005. Paragraphs (b)(2)(ii)(A) and (b)(2)(iv)(B)(2) (as contained in 26 CFR part 1 revised as of April 1, 2008) apply to taxable years for which the due date of the original return (without regard to extensions) is on or after March 21, 2005, and before September 17, 2008. Paragraph (b)(2)(ii)(A) of this section and §1.1502-21T(b)(1), (b)(2)(iv), and (c)(2)(vii), as contained in 26 CFR part 1 revised as of April 1, 2004, apply to taxable years for which the due date of the original return (without regard to extensions) is after August 29, 2003, and on or before March 21, 2005. For taxable years for which the due date of the original return (without regard to extensions) is on or before August 29, 2003, see paragraphs (b)(1), (b)(2)(ii)(A), (b)(2)(iv), and (c)(2)(vii) of this section and §1.1502-21T(b)(1) as contained in 26 CFR part 1 revised as of April 1, 2003.

(7) *Prior periods.*—For certain taxable years ending on or before June 25, 1999, see §1.1502-21T in effect prior to June 25, 1999, as contained in 26 CFR part 1 revised April 1, 1999, as applicable.

(8) *Losses treated as expired under §1.1502-35(f)(1).*—For rules regarding losses treated as expired under §1.1502-35(f) on or after March 10, 2006, see §1.1502-21(b)(3)(v) as contained in 26 CFR part 1 in effect on April 1, 2006. For rules regarding losses treated as expired before March 10, 2006, see §1.1502-21T(h)(8) as contained in 26 CFR part 1 in effect on January 1, 2006.

(9) For the applicability dates of paragraphs (b)(3)(ii)(C) and (b)(3)(ii)(D) of this section, see §1.1502-21T(h)(9).

(10) The rules of paragraphs (a), (b)(1), (b)(2)(iv), and (c)(1)(i)(E) of this section apply to taxable years beginning after December 31, 2020. [Reg. §1.1502-21.]

□ [*T.D.* 8823, 6-25-99 (*corrected* 7-30-99). *Amended by T.D.* 8884, 5-24-2000; *T.D.* 8997, 5-30-2002; *T.D.* 9048, 3-11-2003; *T.D.* 9089, 8-29-2003; *T.D.* 9100, 12-18-2003 (*corrected* 2-2-2004) *T.D.* 9192, 3-21-2005; *T.D.* 9254, 3-9-2006; *T.D.* 9300, 12-7-2006; *T.D.* 9315, 3-19-2007; *T.D.* 9424, 9-9-2008, *T.D.* 9490, 6-22-2010, *T.D.* 9905, 9-3-2020, *T.D.* 9922, 11-2-2020 and *T.D.* 9927, 10-23-2020.]

**[Reg. § 1.1502-21A]**

**§ 1.1502-21A. Consolidated net operating loss deduction generally applicable for consolidated return years beginning before January 1, 1997.**—(a) *In general.*—The consolidated net operating loss deduction shall be an amount equal to the aggregate of the consolidated net operating loss carryovers and carrybacks to the taxable year (as determined under paragraph (b) of this section).

(b) *Consolidated net operating loss carryovers and carrybacks.*—(1) *In general.*—The consolidated net operating loss carryovers and carrybacks to the taxable year shall consist of any consolidated net operating losses (as determined under paragraph (f) of this section) of the group, plus any net operating losses sustained by members of the group in separate return years, which may be carried over or back to the taxable year under the principles of section 172(b). However, such consolidated carryovers and carrybacks shall not include any consolidated net operating loss apportioned to a corporation for a separate return year pursuant to § 1.1502-79A, and shall be subject to the limitations contained in paragraphs (c), (d), and (e) of this section and to the limitation contained in § 1.1502-15A (or § 1.1502-11(c), as appropriate).

(2) *Rules for applying section 172(b)(1).*—(i) *Regulated transportation corporations.*—For purposes of applying section 172(b)(1)(C) (relating to net operating losses sustained by regulated transportation corporations), in the case of a consolidated net operating loss sustained in a taxable year for which a member of the group was a regulated transportation corporation (as defined in section 172(j)(1)), the portion, if any, of such consolidated net operating loss which is attributable to such corporation (as determined under this paragraph) shall be a carryover to the sixth taxable year following the loss year only if such corporation is a regulated transportation corporation for such sixth year, and shall be a carryover to the seventh taxable year following the loss year only if such corporation is a regulated transportation corporation for both such sixth and seventh years.

(ii) *Trade expansion losses.*—In the case of a carryback of a consolidated net operating loss from a taxable year for which a member of the group has been issued a certification under section 317 of the Trade Expansion Act of 1962 and with respect to which the requirements of section 172(b)(3)(A) have been met, section 172(b)(1)(A)(ii) shall apply only to the portion of such consolidated net operating loss attributable to such member.

(iii) *Foreign expropriation losses.*—An election under section 172(b)(3)(C) (relating to 10-year carryover of portion of net operating loss attributable to a foreign expropriation loss) may be made for a consolidated return year only if the sum of the foreign expropriation losses (as defined in section 172(k)) of the members of the group for such year equals or exceeds 50 percent of the consolidated net operating loss for such year. If such election is made, the amount which may be carried over under section 172(b)(1)(D) is the smaller of (a) the sum of such foreign expropriation losses, or (b) the consolidated net operating loss.

(3) *Absorption rules.*—For purposes of determining the amount, if any, of a net operating loss (whether consolidated or separate) which can be carried to a taxable year (consolidated or separate), the amount of such net operating loss which is absorbed in a prior consolidated return year under section 172(b)(2) shall be determined by—

(i) Applying all net operating losses which can be carried to such prior year in the order of the taxable years in which such losses were sustained, beginning with the taxable year which ends earliest, and

(ii) Applying all such losses which can be carried to such prior year from taxable years ending on the same date on a pro rata basis, except that any portion of a net operating loss attributable to a foreign expropriation loss to which section 172(b)(1)(D) applies shall be applied last.

(c) *Limitation on net operating loss carryovers and carrybacks from separate return limitation years.*—(1) *General rule.*—In the case of a net operating loss of a member of the group arising in a separate return limitation year (as defined in paragraph (f) of § 1.1502-1) of such member (and in a separate return limitation year of any predecessor of such member), the amount which may be included under paragraph (b) of this section (computed without regard to the limitation contained in paragraph (d) of this section) in the consolidated net operating loss carryovers and carrybacks to a consolidated return year of the group shall not exceed the amount determined under subparagraph (2) of this paragraph.

(2) *Computation of limitation.*—The amount referred to in subparagraph (1) of this paragraph with respect to a member of the group is the excess, if any, of—

(i) Consolidated taxable income (computed without regard to the consolidated net operating loss deduction), minus such consolidated taxable income recomputed by excluding the items of income and deduction of such member, over

(ii) The net operating losses attributable to such member which may be carried to the consolidated return year arising in taxable years ending prior to the particular separate return limitation year.

(3) *Examples.*—The provisions of this paragraph and paragraphs (a) and (b) of this section may be illustrated by the following examples:

*Example (1).* (i) Corporation P formed corporations S and T on January 1, 1965. P, S, and T filed separate returns for the calendar year 1965, a year for which an election under section 1562 was effective. T's return for that year reflected a net operating loss of $10,000. The group filed a consolidated return for 1966 reflecting consolidated taxable income of $30,000 (computed without regard to the consolidated net operating loss deduction). Among the transactions occuring during 1966 were the following:

(a) P sold goods to T deriving deferred profits of $7,000 on such sales, $2,000 of which was restored to consolidated taxable income on the sale of such goods to outsiders:

(b) T sold a machine to S deriving a deferred profit of $5,000, $1,000 of which was restored to consolidated taxable income as a result of S's depreciation deductions;

(c) T distributed a $3,000 dividend to P; and

(d) In addition to the transactions described above, T had other taxable income of $6,000.

(ii) The carryover of T's 1965 net operating loss to 1966 is subject to the limitation contained in this paragraph, since 1965 was a separate return limitation year (an election under section 1562 was effective for such year). Thus, only $7,000 of T's $10,000 net operating loss is a consolidated net operating loss carryover to 1966, since such carryover is limited to consolidated taxable income (computed without regard to the consolidated net operating loss deduction), $30,000, minus such consolidated taxable income recomputed by excluding the items of income and deduction of T, $23,000 (i.e., consolidated taxable income computed without regard to the $1,000 restoration of T's deferred gain and T's $6,000 of other income). In making such recomputation, no change is made in the effect on consolidated taxable income of P's sale to T, or of the dividend from T to P.

*Example (2).* (i) Corporation P was formed on January 1, 1966. P filed separate returns for the calendar years 1966 and 1967 reflecting net operating losses of $4,000 and $12,000, respectively. P purchased corporation S on March 15, 1967. S was formed on February 1, 1966, and filed a separate return for the taxable year ending January 31, 1967. S also filed a short period return for the period from February 1 to December 31, 1967, and joined with P in filing a consolidated return for 1968. S sustained net operating losses of $5,000 and $6,000 for its taxable years ending January 31, 1967 and December 31, 1967, respectively. An election under section 1562 was not effective for P and S during the period involved. Consolidated taxable income for 1968 (computed without regard to the consolidated net operating loss deduction) was $16,000; such consolidated taxable income recomputed by disregarding the items of income and deduction of S was $9,000.

(ii) In order of time, the following losses are absorbed in 1968:

(a) P's $4,000 net operating loss for the calendar year 1966 (such loss is not subject to the limitation contained in this paragraph since P is the common parent corporation for 1968);

(b) S's $5,000 net operating loss for the year ended January 31, 1967. Such loss is subject to the limitation contained in this paragraph, since S was not a member of the group on each day of such year. However, such loss can be carried over and absorbed in full since such limitation is $7,000 (consolidated taxable income computed without regard to the consolidated net operating loss deduction, $16,000, minus such consolidated taxable income recomputed, $9,000); and

(c) $6,000 of P's net operating loss and $1,000 of S's net operating loss for the taxable years ending December 31, 1967. This is determined by applying the losses from such year which can be carried to 1968 (P's $12,000 loss and $2,000 of S's $6,000 loss, since such $6,000 loss is limited under this paragraph) on a pro rata basis against the amount of such losses which can be absorbed in that year, $7,000 (consolidated taxable income of $16,000 less the $9,000 of losses absorbed from prior years). The carryover of S's loss to 1968 is subject to the limitation contained in that paragraph, since S was not a member of the group on each day of its taxable year ending December 31, 1967. Such loss is limited to $2,000, the excess of $7,000 (as determined under (ii)(b)) over $5,000 (S's carryover from the year ended January 31, 1967). If a consolidated return is filed in 1969, the consolidated net operating loss carryovers will consist of P's unabsorbed loss of $6,000 ($12,000 minus $6,000) from 1967 and, subject to the limitation contained in this paragraph, S's unabsorbed loss of $5,000 ($6,000 minus $1,000) from its year ended December 31, 1967.

(d) *Limitations on carryovers where there has been a consolidated return change of ownership.*—(1) *General rule.*—If a consolidated return change of ownership (as defined in paragraph (g) of § 1.1502-1) occurs during the taxable year or an earlier taxable year, the amount which may be included under paragraph (b) of this section in the consolidated net operating loss carryovers to the taxable year with respect to the aggregate of the net operating losses attributable to old member of the group (as defined in paragraph (g)(3) of § 1.1502-1) arising in taxable years (consolidated or separate) ending on the same day and before the taxable year in which the consolidated return change of ownership occurred shall not exceed the amount determined under subparagraph (2) of this paragraph.

(2) *Computation of limitation.*—The amount referred to in subparagraph (1) of this paragraph shall be the excess of—

(i) The consolidated taxable income for the taxable year (determined without regard to the consolidated net operating loss deduction) recomputed by including only the items of income and deduction of the old members of the group, over

(ii) The sum of the net operating losses attributable to the old members of the group which may be carried to the taxable year arising in taxable years ending prior to the particular loss year or years.

(3) *Example.*—The provisions of this paragraph may be illustrated by the following example:

*Example.* (i) Corporation P is formed on January 1, 1967 and on the same day it forms corporation S. P and S file a consolidated return for the calendar year 1967, reflecting a consolidated net operating loss of $500,000. On January 1, 1968, individual X purchases all of the outstanding stock of P. X subsequently contributes $1,000,000 to P and P purchases the stock of corporation T. P, S, and T file a consolidated return for 1968 reflecting consolidated taxable income of $600,000 (computed without regard to the consolidated net operating loss deduction). Such consolidated taxable income recomputed by including only the items of income and deduction of P and S is $350,000.

(ii) Since a consolidated return change of ownership took place in 1968 (there was more than a 50 percent change of ownership of P), the amount of the consolidated net operating loss from 1967 which can be carried over to 1968 is limited to $350,000, the excess of $350,000 (consolidated taxable income recomputed by including only the items of income and deduction of the old members of the group, P and S) over zero (the amount of the consolidated net operating loss carryovers attributable to the old members of the group arising in taxable years ending before 1967).

(4) *Cross-reference.*—See § 1.1502-21T(d)(1) for the rule that applies the principles of this paragraph (d) in consolidated return years beginning on or after January 1, 1997, with respect to a consolidated return change of ownership occurring before January 1, 1997.

(e) *Limitations on net operating loss carryovers under section 382.*—(1) *Section 382(a).*—(i) If at the end of a taxable year (consolidated or separate) there has been an increase in ownership of the stock of the common parent of a group (within the meaning of section 382(a)(1)(A) and (B)), and any member of the group has not continued to carry on a trade or business substantially the same as that conducted before any such increase (within the meaning of section 382(a)(1)(C)), then the portion of any consolidated net operating loss sustained in prior taxable years attributable to such member (as determined under this paragraph) shall not be allowed as a carryover to such taxable year or to any subsequent taxable year.

(ii) If the provisions of section 382(a) disallow the deduction of a net operating loss carryover from a separate return year of a member of the group to a subsequent taxable year, no amount shall be included under paragraph (b) of this section as a consolidated net operating loss carryover to such a subsequent consolidated return year with respect to such separate return year of such member.

(iii) The provisions of this subparagraph may be illustrated by the following example:—*Example.* P, S, and T file a consolidated return for the calendar year 1969, reflecting a consolidated net operating loss attributable in part to each member. P owns 80 percent of S's stock and S owns 80 percent of T's stock. On January 1, 1970, A purchases 50 percent of P's stock. During 1970 T's business is discontinued. Since there has been a 50 percentage point increase in ownership of P, the common parent of the group, and since T has not continued to carry on the same trade or business after such increase, the portion of the 1969 consolidated net operating loss attributable to

T shall not be included in any net operating loss deduction for 1970 or for any subsequent taxable years, whether consolidated or separate.

(2) *Section 382(b).*—If a net operating loss carryover from a separate return year of a predecessor of a member of the group to the taxable year is reduced under the provisions of section 382(b), the amount included under paragraph (b) of this section with respect to such predecessor shall be so reduced.

(3) *Effective date.*—This paragraph (e) disallows or reduces the net operating loss carryovers of a member as a result of a transaction to which old section 382 (as defined in § 1.382-2T(f)(21)) applies. See § 1.1502-21T(d)(2) for the rule that applies the principles of this paragraph (e) in consolidated return years beginning on or after January 1, 1997, with respect to such a transaction.

(f) *Consolidated net operating loss.*—The consolidated net operating loss shall be determined by taking into account the following:

(1) The separate taxable income (as determined under § 1.1502-12) of each member of the group, computed without regard to any deduction under section 242;

(2) Any consolidated capital gain net income (net capital gain for taxable years beginning before January 1, 1977);

(3) Any consolidated section 1231 net loss;

(4) Any consolidated charitable contributions deduction;

(5) Any consolidated dividends received deduction (determined under § 1.1502-26 without regard to paragraph (a)(2) of that section); and

(6) Any consolidated section 247 deduction (determined under § 1.1502-27 without regard to paragraph (a)(1)(ii) of that section).

(g) *Groups that include insolvent financial institutions.*—For rules applicable to relinquishing the entire carryback period with respect to losses attributable to insolvent financial institutions, see § 301.6402-7 of this chapter.

(h) *Effective date.*—Except as provided in § 1.1502-21T(d)(1), (d)(2), and (g)(3), this section applies to consolidated return years beginning before January 1, 1997. [Reg. § 1.1502-21A.]

☐ [*T.D. 6894, 9-7-66. Amended by T.D. 7728, 10-31-80; T.D. 8387, 12-30-91 and T.D. 8446, 11-5-92. Redesignated as Reg. § 1.1502-21A and amended by T.D. 8677, 6-26-96.*]

**[Reg. § 1.1502-21T]**

**§ 1.1502-21T. Net operating losses (temporary).**—(a) For further guidance, see § 1.1502-21(a).

(b) For further guidance, see § 1.1502-21(b) introductory text through (b)(2).

(1) and (2) [Reserved]

(3) For further guidance, see § 1.1502-21(b)(3) introductory text through (b)(3)(ii)(B).

(i) [Reserved]

(ii)(A) [Reserved]

(B) [Reserved]

(C) *Waiver of carryback period for losses in taxable years to which statutorily amended carryback rules apply.*—(1) *In general.*—An acquiring group may make either (but not both) an amended statute split-waiver election or an extended split-waiver election with respect to a particular amended carryback CNOL. (See paragraph (b)(3)(ii)(C)(2) of this section for definitions of terms used in this paragraph (b)(3)(ii)(C) and paragraph (b)(3)(ii)(D) of this section.) These elections are available only if the statutory amendment to the carryback period referred to in paragraph (b)(3)(ii)(C)(2)(*iv*) of this section occurs after the date of acquisition of an acquired member. A separate election is available for each taxable year to which amended carryback rules apply. An acquiring group may make an amended statute split-waiver election or an extended split-waiver election only if the acquiring group, with regard to that election—

(*i*) Satisfies the requirements in paragraph (b)(3)(ii)(C)(3) of this section; and

(*ii*) Follows the procedures in paragraphs (b)(3)(ii)(C)(5) and (6) of this section, as relevant to that election.

(2) *Definitions.*—The definitions provided in this paragraph (b)(3)(ii)(C)(2) apply for purposes of this paragraph (b)(3)(ii)(C) and paragraph (b)(3)(ii)(D) of this section.

(*i*) *Acquired member.*—The term *acquired member* means a member of a consolidated group that joins another consolidated group.

(*ii*) *Acquiring group.*—The term *acquiring group* means a consolidated group that has acquired a former member of another consolidated group (that is, an acquired member).

*(iii) Amended carryback CNOL.*—The term *amended carryback CNOL* means the portion of a CNOL attributable to an acquired member (determined pursuant to §1.1502-21(b)(2)(iv)(B)) arising in a taxable year to which amended carryback rules apply.

*(iv) Amended carryback rules.*—The term *amended carryback rules* means the rules of section 172 of the Code after amendment by statute to extend the carryback period for NOLs attributable to an acquired member (determined pursuant to §1.1502-21(b)(2)(iv)(B)).

*(v) Amended statute split-waiver election.*—The term *amended statute split-waiver election* means, with respect to any amended carryback CNOL, an irrevocable election made by an acquiring group to relinquish the portion of the carryback period (including the default carryback period and the extended carryback period) for that loss during which an acquired member was a member of any former group.

*(vi) Amended statute split-waiver election statement.*—The term *amended statute split-waiver election statement* has the meaning provided in paragraph (b)(3)(ii)(C)(5)(*i*) of this section.

*(vii) Default carryback period.*—The term *default carryback period* means the NOL carryback period existing at the time the acquiring group acquired the acquired member, before the applicability of amended carryback rules.

*(viii) Extended carryback period.*—The term *extended carryback period* means the additional taxable years added to a default carryback period by any amended carryback rules.

*(ix) Extended split-waiver election.*—The term *extended split-waiver election* means, with respect to any amended carryback CNOL, an irrevocable election made by an acquiring group to relinquish solely the portion of the extended carryback period (and no part of the default carryback period) for that loss during which an acquired member was a member of any former group.

*(x) Extended split-waiver election statement.*—The term *extended split-waiver election statement* has the meaning provided in paragraph (b)(3)(ii)(C)(5)(*ii*) of this section.

*(xi) Former group.*—The term *former group* means a consolidated group of which an acquired member previously was a member.

*(3) Conditions for making an amended statute split-waiver election or an extended split-waiver election.*—An acquiring group may make an amended statute split-waiver election or an extended split-waiver election (but not both) with respect to an amended carryback CNOL only if—

*(i)* The acquiring group has not filed a valid election described in §1.1502-21(b)(3)(ii)(B) with respect to the acquired member on or before the effective date of amended carryback rules;

*(ii)* The acquiring group has not filed a valid election described in section 172(b)(3) and §1.1502-21(b)(3)(i) with respect to a CNOL of the acquiring group from which the amended carryback CNOL is attributed to the acquired member;

*(iii)* Any other corporation joining the acquiring group that was affiliated with the acquired member immediately before the acquired member joined the acquiring group is included in the waiver; and

*(iv)* A former group does not claim any carryback (as provided in paragraph (b)(3)(ii)(C)(4) of this section) to any taxable year in the carryback period (in the case of an amended statute split-waiver election) or in the extended carryback period (in the case of an extended split-waiver election) with respect to the amended carryback CNOL on a return or other filing filed on or before the date the acquiring group files the election.

*(4) Claim for a carryback.*—For purposes of paragraph (b)(3)(ii)(C)(3)(*iv*) of this section, a carryback is claimed with respect to an amended carryback CNOL if there is a claim for refund, an amended return, an application for a tentative carryback adjustment, or any other filing that claims the benefit of the NOL in a taxable year prior to the taxable year of the loss, whether or not subsequently revoked in favor of a claim based on the period provided for in the amended carryback rules.

*(5) Procedures for making an amended statute split-waiver election or an extended split-waiver election.*—(*i*) *Amended statute split-waiver election.*—An amended statute split-waiver election **must be** made in a separate statement entitled "THIS IS AN ELECTION UNDER SECTION 1.1502-21T(b)(3)(ii)(C)(*1*) TO WAIVE THE PRE-[insert first day of the first taxable year for which the acquired member was a member of the acquiring group] CARRYBACK PERIOD FOR THE CNOLS ATTRIBUTABLE TO THE [insert taxable

year of losses]TAXABLE YEAR(S) OF [insert names and employer identification numbers of members]" (amended statute split-waiver election statement). This statement must be filed as provided in paragraph (b)(3)(ii)(C)(6) of this section.

*(ii) Extended split-waiver election.*—An extended split-waiver election must be made in a separate statement entitled "THIS IS AN ELECTION UNDER SECTION 1.1502-21T(b)(3)(iii)(C)(*1*) TO WAIVE THE PRE-PRE-[insert first day of the first taxable year for which the acquired member was a member of the acquiring group] EXTENDED CARRYBACK PERIOD FOR THE CNOLS ATTRIBUTABLE TO THE [insert taxable year of losses] TAXABLE YEAR(S) OF [insert names and employer identification numbers of members]" (extended split-waiver election statement). This statement must be filed as provided in paragraph (b)(3)(ii)(C)(6) of this section.

*(6) Time and manner for filing statement.*—(*i*) *In general.*—Except as otherwise provided in paragraph (b)(3)(ii)(C)(6)(*ii*) or (*iii*) of this section, an amended statute split-waiver election statement or extended split-waiver election statement must be filed with the acquiring group's timely filed consolidated return (including extensions) for the year during which the amended carryback CNOL is incurred.

*(ii) Amended returns.*—This paragraph (b)(3)(ii)(C)(6)(*ii*) applies if the date of the filing required under paragraph (b)(3)(ii)(C)(6)(*i*) of this section is not at least 150 days after the date of the statutory amendment to the carryback period referred to in paragraph (b)(3)(ii)(C)(2)(*iv*) of this section. Under this paragraph (b)(3)(ii)(C)(6)(*ii*), an amended statute split-waiver election statement or extended split-waiver election statement may be attached to an amended return filed by the date that is 150 days after the date of the statutory amendment referred to in paragraph (b)(3)(ii)(C)(2)(*iv*) of this section.

*(iii) Certain taxable years beginning before January 1, 2021.*—This paragraph (b)(3)(ii)(C)(6)(*iii*) applies to taxable years beginning before January 1, 2021, for which the date of the filing required under paragraph (b)(3)(ii)(C)(6)(*i*) of this section precedes November 30, 2020. Under this paragraph (b)(3)(ii)(C)(6)(*iii*), an amended statute split-waiver election statement or extended split-waiver election statement may be attached to an amended return filed by November 30, 2020.

*(D) Examples.*—The following examples illustrate the rules of paragraph (b)(3)(ii)(C) of this section. For purposes of these examples: all affiliated groups file consolidated returns; all corporations are includible corporations that have calendar taxable years; each of P, X, and T is a corporation having one class of stock outstanding; each of P and X is the common parent of a consolidated group (P Group and X Group, respectively); neither the P Group nor the X Group includes an insolvent financial institution or an insurance company; no NOL is a farming loss; there are no other relevant NOL carrybacks to the X Group's consolidated taxable years; except as otherwise stated, the X Group has sufficient consolidated taxable income determined under §1.1502-11 (CTI) to absorb the stated NOL carryback by T; T has sufficient SRLY register income within the X Group to absorb the stated NOL carryback by T; all transactions occur between unrelated parties; and the facts set forth the only relevant transactions.

*(1) Example 1: Computation and absorption of amended carrybacks.*—(*i*) *Facts.* In Year 1, T became a member of the X Group. On the last day of Year 5, P acquired all the stock of T from X. At the time of P's acquisition of T stock, the default carryback period was zero taxable years. The P Group did not make an irrevocable split-waiver election under §1.1502-21(b)(3)(ii)(B) to relinquish, with respect to all CNOLs attributable to T while a member of the P Group, the portion of the carryback period for which T was a member of the X Group (that is, a former group). In Year 7, the P Group sustained a $1,000 CNOL, $600 of which was attributable to T pursuant to §1.1502-21(b)(2)(iv)(B). In that year, P did not make an irrevocable general waiver election under section 172(b)(3) and §1.1502-21(b)(3)(i) with respect to the $1,000 CNOL when the P Group filed its consolidated return for Year 7. In Year 8, legislation was enacted that amended section 172 to require a carryback period of five years for NOLs arising in a taxable year beginning after Year 5 and before Year 9.

*(ii) Analysis.* As a result of the amended carryback rules enacted in Year 8, the P Group's $1,000 CNOL in Year 7 must be carried back to Year 2. Therefore, T's $600 attributed portion of the P Group's Year 7 CNOL (that is, T's amended carryback CNOL) must be carried back to taxable years of the X Group. See §§1.1502-21(b)(1) and 1.1502-21(b)(2)(i). To the extent T's amended carryback CNOL is not absorbed in the X Group's Year 2 taxable year, the remaining portion must be carried to the X Group's Year 3, Year 4, and Year 5 taxable years, as appropriate. See id. Any remaining portion of T's

amended carryback CNOL is carried to consolidated return years of the P Group. See § 1.1502-21(b)(1).

(2) *Example 2: Amended statute split-waiver election.*—(*i*) *Facts.* The facts are the same as in paragraph (b)(3)(ii)(D)(*1*)(*i*) of this section (*Example 1*), except that, following the change in statutory carryback period in Year 8, the P Group made a valid amended statute split-waiver election under paragraph (b)(3)(ii)(C) of this section to relinquish solely the carryback of T's amended carryback CNOL.

(*ii*) *Analysis.* Because the P Group made a valid amended statute split-waiver election, T's amended carryback CNOL is not eligible to be carried back to any taxable years of the X Group (that is, a former group). However, the amended statute split-waiver election does not prevent T's Year 7 amended carryback CNOL from being carried back to years of the P group (that is, the acquiring group) during which T was a member. See paragraph (b)(3)(ii)(C)(*2*)(*v*) of this section. As a result, the entire amount of T's amended carryback CNOL is eligible to be carried back to taxable Year 6 of the P Group. Any remaining CNOL may then be carried over within the P Group. See § 1.1502-21(b)(1).

(3) *Example 3: Computation and absorption of extended carrybacks.*—(*i*) *Facts.* The facts are the same as in paragraph (b)(3)(ii)(D)(*1*)(*i*) of this section (*Example 1*), except that the X Group had $300 of CTI in Year 4 and $200 of CTI in Year 5 and, at the time of the P Group's acquisition of T, the default carryback period was two years. Therefore, T's $600 attributed portion of the P Group's Year 7 CNOL was required to be carried back to the X Group's Year 5 taxable year, and the X Group was able to offset $200 of CTI in Year 5.

(*ii*) *Analysis.* As a result of the amended carryback rules, the X Group must offset its $300 of CTI in Year 4 against T's amended carryback CNOL. See §§ 1.1502-21(b)(1) and (b)(2)(i). The remaining $100 ($600 - $300 - $200) of T's amended carryback CNOL is carried to taxable years of the P Group. See § 1.1502-21(b)(1).

(4) *Example 4: Extended split-waiver election.*—(*i*) *Facts.* The facts are the same as in paragraph (b)(3)(ii)(D)(*3*)(*i*) of this section (*Example 3*), except that, following the change in law in Year 8, the P Group made a valid extended split-waiver election under paragraph (b)(3)(ii)(C) of this section to relinquish the extended carryback period for T's amended carryback CNOL for years in which T was a member of the X Group.

(*ii*) *Analysis.* As a result of the P Group's extended split-waiver election, T's amended carryback CNOL is not eligible to be carried back to any portion of the extended carryback period (that is, any taxable year prior to Year 5). See paragraph (b)(3)(ii)(C)(*2*)(*ix*) of this section. As a result, the X Group absorbs $200 of T's $600 loss in Year 5, and the remaining $400 ($600 - $200) is carried to taxable years of the P Group. See § 1.1502-21(b)(1).

(iii) For further guidance, see § 1.1502-21(b)(3)(iii).

(c) For further guidance, see § 1.1502-21(c) through (h)(8).

(d) through (j) [Reserved]

(h)(1) through (8) [Reserved]

(9) *Amended carryback rules.*—(i) *Applicability date.*—Paragraphs (b)(3)(ii)(C) and (D) of this section apply to any CNOLs arising in a taxable year ending after July 2, 2020. However, taxpayers may apply paragraphs (b)(3)(ii)(C) and (D) of this section to any CNOLs arising in a taxable year beginning after December 31, 2017.

(ii) *Expiration date.*—The applicability of paragraphs (b)(3)(ii)(C) and (D) of this section will expire on July 3, 2023. [Temporary Reg. § 1.1502-21T.]

☐ [*T.D. 8997, 5-30-2002. Amended by T.D. 9048, 3-11-2003 (corrected 4-3-2003); T.D. 9089, 8-29-2003; T.D. 9100, 12-18-2003 (corrected 2-2-2004) T.D. 9192, 3-21-2005; T.D. 9254, 3-9-2006; T.D. 9300, 12-7-2006; T.D. 9490, 6-22-2010 (corrected 7-29-2010) and T.D. 9900, 7-2-2020 (corrected 8-27-2020).*]

### [Reg. § 1.1502-22]

**§ 1.1502-22. Consolidated capital gain and loss.**—(a) *Capital gain.*—The determinations under section 1222, including capital gain net income, net long-term capital gain, and net capital gain, with respect to members during consolidated return years are not made separately. Instead, consolidated amounts are determined for the group as a whole. The consolidated capital gain net income for any consolidated return year is determined by reference to—

(1) The aggregate gains and losses of members from sales or exchanges of capital assets for the year (other than gains and losses to which section 1231 applies);

(2) The consolidated net section 1231 gain for the year (determined under § 1.1502-23); and

(3) The net capital loss carryovers or carrybacks to the year.

(b) *Net capital loss carryovers and carrybacks.*—(1) *In general.*—The determinations under section 1222, including net capital loss and net short-term capital loss, with respect to members during consolidated return years are not made separately. Instead, consolidated amounts are determined for the group as a whole. Losses included in the consolidated net capital loss may be carried to consolidated return years, and, after apportionment, may be carried to separate return years. The net capital loss carryovers and carrybacks consist of—

(i) Any consolidated net capital losses of the group; and

(ii) Any net capital losses of the members arising in separate return years.

(2) *Carryovers and carrybacks generally.*—The net capital loss carryovers and carrybacks to a taxable year are determined under the principles of section 1212 and this section. Thus, losses permitted to be absorbed in a consolidated return year generally are absorbed in the order of the taxable years in which they were sustained, and losses carried from taxable years ending on the same date, and which are available to offset consolidated capital gain net income, generally are absorbed on a pro rata basis. Additional rules provided under the Internal Revenue Code or regulations also apply, as well as the SRLY limitation under paragraph (c) of this section. See, e.g., section 382(1)(2)(B).

(3) *Carryovers and carrybacks of consolidated net capital losses to separate return years.*—If any consolidated net capital loss that is attributable to a member may be carried to a separate return year under the principles of § 1.1502-21(b)(2), the amount of the consolidated net capital loss that is attributable to the member is apportioned and carried to the separate return year (apportioned loss).

(4) *Special rules.*—(i) *Short years in connection with transactions to which section 381(a) applies.*—If a member distributes or transfers assets to a corporation that is a member immediately after the distribution or transfer in a transaction to which section 381(a) applies, the transaction does not cause the distributor or transferor to have a short year within the consolidated return year of the group in which the transaction occurred that is counted as a separate year for purposes of determining the years to which a net capital loss may be carried.

(ii) *Special status losses.*—[Reserved]

(c) *Limitations on net capital loss carryovers and carrybacks from separate return limitation years.*—The aggregate of the net capital losses of a member arising (or treated as arising) in SRLYs that are included in the determination of consolidated capital gain net income for all consolidated return years of the group under paragraph (a) of this section may not exceed the aggregate of the consolidated capital gain net income for all consolidated return years of the group determined by reference to only the member's items of gain and loss from capital assets as defined in section 1221 and trade or business assets defined in section 1231(b), including the member's losses actually absorbed by the group in the taxable year (whether or not absorbed by the member). The principles of § 1.1502-21(c) (including the SRLY subgroup principles under § 1.1502-21(c)(2)) apply with appropriate adjustments for purposes of applying this paragraph (c).

(d) *Coordination with respect to consolidated return change of ownership limitation occurring in consolidated return years beginning before January 1, 1997.*—If a consolidated return change of ownership occurred before January 1, 1997, the principles of § 1.1502-22A(d) apply to determine the amount of the aggregate of the net capital loss attributable to old members of the group (as those terms are defined in § 1.1502-1(g)), that may be included in the net capital loss carryover under paragraph (b) of this section. For this purpose, § 1.1502-1(g) is applied by treating that date as the end of the year of change.

(e) *Consolidated net capital loss.*—Any excess of losses over gains, as determined under paragraph (a) of this section (without regard to any carryovers or carrybacks), is also referred to as the consolidated net capital loss.

(f) *Predecessors and successors.*—For purposes of this section, the principles of § 1.1502-21(f) apply with appropriate adjustments.

(g) *Overlap with section 383.*—(1) *General rule.*—The limitation provided in paragraph (c) of this section does not apply to net capital loss carryovers ((other than a hypothetical carryover like those described in § 1.1502-21(c)(1)(i)(D) and a carryover like those described in § 1.1502-21(c)(1)(ii)) when the application of paragraph (c) of this section results in an overlap with the application of section 383. For a similar rule applying in the case of net capital loss carryovers like those described in §§ 1.1502-21(c)(1)(i)(D) and (c)(1)(ii), see § 1.1502-15(g).

(2) *Definitions.*—(i) *Generally.*—For purposes of this paragraph (g), the definitions and nomenclature contained in sections 382 and

383, the regulations thereunder, and §§ 1.1502-90 through 1.1502-99 apply.

(ii) *Overlap.*—(A) An overlap of the application of paragraph (c) of this section and the application of section 383 with respect to a net capital loss carryover occurs if a corporation becomes a member of the consolidated group (the SRLY event) within six months of the change date of an ownership change giving rise to a section 382 limitation with respect to that carryover (the section 383 event).

(B) If an overlap described in paragraph (g)(2)(ii)(A) of this section occurs with respect to net capital loss carryovers of a corporation whose SRLY event occurs within the six month period beginning on the date of a section 383 event, then an overlap is treated as also occurring with respect to that corporation's net capital loss carryover that arises within the period beginning with the section 383 event and ending with the SRLY event.

(C) For special rules in the event that there is a SRLY subgroup and/or a loss subgroup as defined in § 1.1502-91(d)(1) with respect to a carryover, see paragraph (g)(4) of this section.

(3) *Operating rules.*—(i) *Section 383 event before SRLY event.*—If a SRLY event occurs on the same date as a section 383 event or within the six month period beginning on the date of the section 383 event, paragraph (g)(1) of this section applies beginning with the tax year that includes the SRLY event.

(ii) *SRLY event before section 383 event.*—If a section 383 event occurs within the period beginning the day after the SRLY event and ending six months after the SRLY event, paragraph (g)(1) of this section applies starting with the first tax year that begins after the section 383 event.

(4) *Subgroup rules.*—In general, in the case of a net capital loss carryover for which there is a SRLY subgroup and a loss subgroup (as defined in § 1.1502-91(d)(1)), the principles of this paragraph (g) apply to the SRLY subgroup, and not separately to its members. However, paragraph (g)(1) of this section applies—

(i) With respect to a carryover described in paragraph (g)(2)(ii)(A) of this section only if—

(A) All members of the SRLY subgroup with respect to that carryover are also included in a loss subgroup with respect to that carryover; and

(B) All members of a loss subgroup with respect to that carryover are also members of a SRLY subgroup with respect to that carryover; and

(ii) With respect to a carryover described in paragraph (g)(2)(ii)(B) of this section only if all members of the SRLY subgroup for that carryover are also members of a SRLY subgroup that has net capital loss carryovers described in paragraph (g)(2)(ii)(A) of this section that are subject to the overlap rule of paragraph (g)(1) of this section.

(h) *Effective date.*—(1) *In general.*—This section generally applies to taxable years for which the due date (without extensions) of the consolidated return is after June 25, 1999. However—

(i) In the event that paragraph (g)(1) of this section does not apply to a particular net capital loss carryover in the current group, then solely for purposes of applying paragraph (c) of this section to determine a limitation with respect to that carryover and with respect to which the SRLY register (consolidated taxable income determined by reference to only the member's or subgroup's items of income, gain, deduction or loss) began in a taxable year for which the due date of the return was on or before June 25, 1999, the principles of § 1.1502-21(c)(2) shall be applied without regard to the phrase "or for a carryover that was subject to the overlap rule described in paragraph (g) of this section or § 1.1502-15(g) with respect to another group (the former group)"; and

(ii) For purposes of paragraph (g) of this section, only an ownership change to which section 383, as amended by the Tax Reform Act of 1986, applies and which results in a section 382 limitation shall constitute a section 383 event.

(2) *Prior periods.*—For certain taxable years ending on or before June 25, 1999, see § 1.1502-22T in effect prior to June 25, 1999, as contained in 26 CFR part 1 revised April 1, 1999, as applicable. [Reg. § 1.1502-22.]

□ [T.D. 8823, 6-25-99.]

**[Reg. § 1.1502-22A]**

**§ 1.1502-22A. Consolidated net capital gain or loss generally applicable for consolidated return years beginning before January 1, 1997.**—(a) *Computation.*—(1) *Consolidated capital gain net income.*—The consolidated capital gain net income (net capital gain for taxable years beginning before January 1, 1977) for the taxable year shall be determined by taking into account—

(i) The aggregate of the capital gains and losses (determined without regard to gains or losses to which section 1231 applies or net capital loss carryovers or carrybacks) of the members of the group for the consolidated return year.

(ii) The consolidated section 1231 net gain for such year (computed in accordance with §§ 1.1502-23A or 1.1502-23T), and

(iii) The consolidated net capital loss carryovers or carrybacks to such year (as determined under paragraph (b) of this section).

(2) *Consolidated net capital loss.*—The consolidated net capital loss shall be determined under subparagraph (1) of this paragraph but without regard to subdivision (iii) thereof.

(3) *Special rules.*—For purposes of this section, capital gains and losses on intercompany transactions and transactions with respect to stock, bonds, and other obligations of a member of the group shall be reflected as provided in §§ 1.1502-13 and 1.1502-19, and capital losses shall be limited as provided in §§ 1.1502-15A and 1.1502-11(c).

(4) [Reserved]

(5) *Example.*—The provisions of this paragraph may be illustrated by the following example:

*Example.* (i) Corporations P, S, and T file consolidated returns on a calendar year basis for 1966 and 1967. The members had the following transactions involving capital assets during 1967: P sold an asset with a $10,000 basis to S for $17,000 and none of the circumstances of restoration described in § 1.1502-13 occurred by the end of the consolidated return year; S sold an asset to individual A for $7,000 which S had purchased during 1966 from P for $10,000, and with respect to which P had deferred a gain of $2,000; T sold an asset with a basis of $10,000 to individual B for $25,000. The group has a consolidated net capital loss carryover to the taxable year of $10,000.

(ii) The consolidated net capital gain of the group is $4,000, determined as follows: P's net capital gain of $2,000, representing the deferred gain on the sale to S during the taxable year 1966, restored into income during taxable year 1967 (the $7,000 gain on P's deferred intercompany transaction is not taken into account for the current year), plus T's net capital gain of $15,000, minus S's net capital loss of $3,000 and the consolidated net capital loss carryover of $10,000.

(b) *Consolidated net capital loss carryovers and carrybacks.*—(1) *In general.*—The consolidated net capital loss carryovers and carrybacks to the taxable year shall consist of any consolidated net capital losses of the group, plus any net capital losses of members of the group arising in separate return years of such members, which may be carried over or back to the taxable year under the principles of section 1212(a). However, such consolidated carryovers and carrybacks shall not include any consolidated net capital loss apportioned to a corporation for a separate return year pursuant to § 1.1502-79A(b) (or § 1.1502-22T(b), as appropriate) and shall be subject to the limitations contained in paragraphs (c) and (d) of this section. For purposes of section 1212(a)(1), the portion of any consolidated net capital loss for any taxable year attributable to a foreign expropriation capital loss is the amount of the foreign expropriation capital losses of all the members for such year (but not in excess of the consolidated net capital loss for such year).

(2) *Absorption rules.*—For purposes of determining the amount, if any, of a net capital loss (whether consolidated or separate) which can be carried to a taxable year (consolidated or separate), the amount of such net capital loss which is absorbed in a prior consolidated return year under section 1212(a)(1) shall be determined by—

(i) Applying all net capital losses which can be carried to such prior year in the order of the taxable years in which such losses were sustained, beginning with the taxable year which ends earliest, and

(ii) Applying all such losses which can be carried to such prior year from taxable years ending on the same date on a pro rata basis, except that any portion of a net capital loss attributable to a foreign expropriation capital loss to which section 1212(a)(1)(B) applies shall be applied last.

(c) *Limitation on net capital loss carryovers and carrybacks from separate return limitation years.*—(1) *General rule.*—In the case of a net capital loss of a member of the group arising in a separate return limitation year (as defined in paragraph (f) of § 1.1502-1) of such member (and in a separate return limitation year of any predecessor of such member), the amount that may be included under paragraph (b) of this section (computed without regard to the limitation contained in paragraph (d) of this section) shall not exceed the amount determined under subparagraph (2) of this paragraph.

(2) *Computation of limitation.*—The amount referred to in subparagraph (1) of this paragraph with respect to a member of the group is the excess, if any, of—

(i) The consolidated capital gain net income (net capital gain for taxable years beginning before January 1, 1977) for the taxable year (computed without regard to any net capital loss carryovers or carrybacks), minus such consolidated capital gain net income (net capital gain for taxable years beginning before January 1, 1977) for the taxable year recomputed by excluding the capital gains and losses and the gains and losses to which section 1231 applies of such member, over

(ii) The net capital losses attributable to such member which can be carried to the taxable year arising in taxable years ending prior to the particular separate return limitation year.

(d) *Limitation on capital loss carryovers where there has been a consolidated return change of ownership.*—(1) *General rule.*—If a consolidated return change of ownership (as defined in paragraph (g) of § 1.1502-1) occurs during the taxable year or an earlier taxable year, the amount which may be included under paragraph (b) of this section in the consolidated net capital loss carryovers to the taxable year with respect to the aggregate of the net capital losses attributable to old members of the group (as defined in paragraph (g)(3) of § 1.1502-1) arising in taxable years (consolidated or separate) ending on the same day and before the taxable year in which the consolidated return change of ownership occurred shall not exceed the amount determined under subparagraph (2) of this paragraph.

(2) *Computation of limitation.*—The amount referred to in subparagraph (1) of this paragraph shall be the excess of—

(i) The consolidated capital gain net income (net capital gain for taxable years beginning before January 1, 1977) (determined without regard to any net capital loss carryovers for the taxable year) recomputed by including only capital gains and losses and gains and losses to which section 1231 applies of the old members of the group, over

(ii) The aggregate net capital losses attributable to the old members of the group which may be carried to the taxable year

| | P | T |
|---|---|---|
| **Year 1 (SRLY)** | | |
| Ordinary | | |
| Capital | | (20) |
| **Year 2** | | |
| Ordinary | 10 | 20 |
| Capital | 70 | 0 |
| § 1231 | (60) | 30 |

(ii) Under section 1231, if the section 1231 losses for any taxable year exceed the section 1231 gains for such taxable year, such gains and losses are treated as ordinary gains or losses. Because the P group's section 1231 losses, $(60), exceed the section 1231 gains, $30, the P group's net loss is treated as an ordinary loss. T's net section 1231 gain has the same character as the P group's consolidated net section 1231 loss, so T's $30 of section 1231 income is treated as ordinary income for purposes of applying § 1.1502-22(c). Under § 1.1502-22(c), the group's consolidated net capital gain determined by reference only to T's items is $0. None of T's capital loss carryover from Year 1 may be taken into account in Year 2.

(c) *Recapture of ordinary loss.*—[Reserved]

(d) *Effective date.*—(1) *In general.*—This section applies to gains and losses arising in the determination of consolidated net section 1231 gain or loss for taxable years for which the due date (without extensions) of the consolidated return is after June 25, 1999.

(2) *Application to prior periods.*—See § 1.1502-21(h)(3) for rules applicable to groups that applied the rules of this section to consolidated return years ending on or after January 29, 1991, and beginning before January 1, 1997. [Reg. § 1.1502-23.]

☐ [T.D. 8823, 6-25-99 *(corrected 7-30-99).*]

### [Reg. § 1.1502-23A]

**§ 1.1502-23A. Consolidated net section 1231 gain or loss generally applicable for consolidated return years beginning before January 1, 1997.**—(a) The consolidated section 1231 net gain or loss for the taxable year shall be determined by taking into account the aggregate of the gains and losses to which section 1231 applies of the members of the group for the consolidated return year. Section 1231 gains and losses on intercompany transactions shall be reflected as provided in § 1.1502-13. Section 1231 losses that are "built-in deductions" shall be subject to the limitations of §§ 1.1502-21A(c) and 1.1502-22A(c), as provided in § 1.1502-15A(a) (or §§ (1.1502-21T(c) in effect prior to June 25, 1999, as contained in 26 CFR part 1 revised April 1, 1999 and 1.1502-22T(c) in effect prior to June 25, 1999, as contained in 26 CFR part 1 revised April 1, 1999, as provided in 1.1502-15T(a) in effect prior to June 25, 1999, as contained in 26 CFR part 1 revised April 1, 1999) or (1.1502-21(c) and 1.1502-22(c), as provided in 1.1502-15(a), as applicable), as appropriate).

arising in taxable years ending prior to the particular loss year or years.

(3) *Cross-reference.*—See § 1.1502-22T(d) for the rule that applies the principles of this paragraph (d) in consolidated return years beginning on or after January 1, 1997, with respect to a consolidated return change of ownership occurring before January 1, 1997.

(e) *Effective date.*—This section applies to any consolidated return years to which § 1.1502-21T(g) does not apply. See § 1.1502-21T(g) for effective dates of that section. [Reg. § 1.1502-22A.]

☐ [T.D. 6894, 9-7-66. *Amended by T.D. 7637, 8-6-79; T.D. 7728, 10-31-80 and T.D. 8597, 7-12-95. Redesignated as Reg. § 1.1502-22A and amended by T.D. 8677, 6-26-96.*]

### [Reg. § 1.1502-23]

**§ 1.1502-23. Consolidated net section 1231 gain or loss.**—(a) *In general.*—Net section 1231 gains and losses of members arising during consolidated return years are not determined separately. Instead, the consolidated net section 1231 gain or loss is determined under this section for the group as a whole.

(b) Example. The following example illustrates the provisions of this section:

*Example. Use of SRLY registers with net gains and net losses under section 1231.* (i) In Year 1, T sustains a $20 net capital loss. At the beginning of Year 2, T becomes a member of the P group. T's capital loss carryover from Year 1 is subject to SRLY limits under § 1.1502-22(c). The members of the P group contribute the following to the consolidated taxable income for Year 2 (computed without regard to T's net capital loss carryover under § 1.1502-22):

(b) *Effective date.*—This section applies to any consolidated return years to which § 1.1502-21(h) or 1.1502-21T(g) in effect prior to June 25, 1999, as contained in 26 CFR part 1 revised April 1, 1999, as applicable does not apply. See § 1.1502-21(h) or 1.1502-21T(g) in effect prior to June 25, 1999, as contained in 26 CFR part 1 revised April 1, 1999, as applicable for effective dates of these sections. [Reg. § 1.1502-23A.]

☐ [T.D. 6894, 9-7-66. *Amended by T.D. 7246, 12-29-72. Redesignated and amended by T.D. 8677, 6-26-96. Amended by T.D. 8823, 6-25-99.*]

### [Reg. § 1.1502-24]

**§ 1.1502-24. Consolidated charitable contributions deductions.**—(a) *Determination of amount of consolidated charitable contributions deduction.*—The deduction allowed by section 170 for the taxable year shall be the lesser of—

(1) The aggregate deductions of the members of the group allowable under section 170 (determined without regard to section 170(b)(2)), plus the consolidated charitable contribution carryovers to such year, or

(2) Five percent of the adjusted consolidated taxable income as determined under paragraph (c) of this section.

(b) *Carryover of excess charitable contributions.*—The consolidated charitable contribution carryovers to any consolidated return year shall consist of any excess consolidated charitable contributions of the group, plus any excess charitable contributions of members of the group arising in separate return years of such members, which may be carried over to the taxable year under the principles of section 170(b)(2) and (3). However, such consolidated carryovers shall not include any excess charitable contributions apportioned to a corporation for a separate return year pursuant to paragraph (e) of § 1.1502-79.

(c) *Adjusted consolidated taxable income.*—For purposes of this section, the adjusted consolidated taxable income of the group for any consolidated return year shall be the consolidated taxable income computed without regard to this section, section 242, section 243(a)(2) and (3), §§ 1.1502-25, 1.1502-26, and 1.1502-27, and without regard to any consolidated net operating or net capital loss carrybacks to such year. [Reg. § 1.1502-24.]

☐ [T.D. 6894, 9-7-66. *Amended by T.D. 7637, 8-6-79.*]

[Reg. §1.1502-26]

**§1.1502-26. Consolidated dividends received deduction.**—(a) *In general.*—(1) The consolidated dividends received deduction for the taxable year shall be the lesser of—

(i) The aggregate of the deduction of the members of the group allowable under sections 243(a)(1), 244(a) and 245 (computed without regard to the limitation provided in section 246(b)), or

(ii) 85 percent of the consolidated taxable income computed without regard to the consolidated net operating loss deduction, consolidated section 247 deduction, the consolidated dividends received deduction, and any consolidated net capital loss carryback to the taxable year.

Subdivision (ii) of this subparagraph shall not apply for any consolidated return year for which there is a consolidated net operating loss. (See §§1.1502-21(e) or 1.1502-21A(f), as appropriate for the definition of a consolidated net operating loss.)

(2) If any member computes a deduction under section 593(b)(2) for a taxable year beginning after July 11, 1969, and ending before August 30, 1975, the deduction otherwise computed under this section shall be reduced by an amount determined by multiplying the deduction (determined without regard to this sentence and without regard to dividends received by the common parent if such parent does not use the percentage of income method provided by section 593(b)(2)) by the applicable percentage of the member with the highest applicable percentage (determined under subparagraphs (A) and (B) of section 593(b)(2)).

(3) For taxable years ending on or after August 30, 1975, the deduction otherwise computed under this section shall be reduced by the sum of the amounts determined under paragraph (a)(4) of this section for each member that is a thrift institution that computes a deduction under section 593(b)(2).

(4) For each thrift institution, the amount determined under this subparagraph is the product of—

(i) The portion of the deduction determined with regard to the sum of the dividends received by (A) the thrift institution, and (B) any member in which that thrift institution owns, directly and with the application of paragraph (a)(5) of this section, 5 percent or more of the stock on any day during the consolidated return year, and

(ii) The thrift institution's applicable percentage determined under subparagraphs (A) and (B) of section 593(b)(2).

For purposes of this subparagraph, dividends allocated to a thrift institution under §1.596-1(c) shall be considered received by the thrift institution.

(5) For purposes of paragraph (a)(4)(i) of this section, a member owning stock of another member (the "second member") shall be considered as owning its proportionate share of any stock of a member owned by the second member. Stock considered as being owned by reason of the preceding sentence shall, for purposes of applying that sentence, be treated as actually owned. The proportionate share of stock in a member owned by another member is the proportion which the value of the stock so owned bears to the value of all the outstanding stock in the member. For purposes of this paragraph the term "stock" includes nonvoting stock which is limited and preferred as to dividends.

(6) For purposes of paragraph (a)(4)(i) of this section, if two or more thrift institutions that are both members of the group each owns 5 percent or more of the same member's stock, the member's stock will be considered to be owned only by the thrift institution with the highest applicable percentage.

(b) *Intercompany dividends.*—The deduction determined under paragraph (a) of this section is determined without taking into account intercompany dividends to the extent that, under §1.1502-13(f)(2), they are not included in gross income. See §1.1502-13 for additional rules relating to intercompany dividends.

(c) *Examples.*—The provisions of this section may be illustrated by the following examples:

*Example (1).* Corporations P, S, and S-1 filed a consolidated return for the calendar year 1966 showing consolidated taxable income of $100,000 (determined without regard to the consolidated net operating loss deduction, consolidated dividends received deduction, and the consolidated section 247 deduction). Such corporations received dividends during such year from nonmember domestic corporations as follows:

| Corporation | Dividends |
|---|---|
| P | $6,000 |
| S | 10,000 |
| S-1 | 34,000 |
| Total | $50,000 |

The dividends received deduction allowable to each member under section 243(a)(1) (computed without regard to the limitation in section 246(b)) is as follows: P has $5,100 (85 percent of $6,000), S has

$8,500 (85 percent of $10,000), and S-1 has $28,900 (85 percent of $34,000), or a total of $42,500. Since $42,500 is less than $85,000 (85 percent of $100,000), the consolidated dividends received deduction is $42,500.

*Example (2).* Assume the same facts as in example (1) except that consolidated taxable income (computed without regard to the consolidated net operating loss deduction, consolidated dividends received deduction, and the consolidated section 247 deduction) was $40,000. The aggregate of the dividends received deductions, $42,500, computed without regard to section 246(b), results in a consolidated net operating loss of $2,500. See section 172(d)(6). Therefore, paragraph (a)(2) of this section does not apply and the consolidated dividends received deduction is $42,500. [Reg. §1.1502-26.]

☐ [T.D. 6894, 9-7-66. *Amended by* T.D. 7246, 12-29-72; T.D. 7631, 7-10-79; T.D. 8597, 7-12-95; T.D. 8677, 6-26-96 *and* T.D. 8823, 6-25-99.]

[Reg. §1.1502-27]

**§1.1502-27. Consolidated section 247 deduction.**—(a) *Amount of deduction.*—The consolidated section 247 deduction for the taxable year shall be an amount computed as follows:

(1) First, determine the amount which is the lesser of—

(i) The aggregate of the dividends paid (within the meaning of section 247(a)) during such year by members of the group which are public utilities (within the meaning of section 247(b)(1)) on preferred stock (within the meaning of section 247(b)(2)), other than dividends paid to other members of the group, or

(ii) The aggregate of the taxable income (or loss) (as determined under paragraph (b) of this section) of each such member which is a public utility.

(2) Then, multiply the amount determined under subparagraph (1) of this paragraph by the fraction specified in section 247(a)(2).

(b) *Computation of taxable income.*—For purposes of paragraph (a)(1)(ii) of this section, the taxable income (or loss) of a member of the group described in paragraph (a)(1)(i) shall be determined under §1.1502-12, adjusted for the following items taken into account in the computation of consolidated taxable income:

(1) The portion of the consolidated net operating loss deduction, the consolidated charitable contributions deduction, and the consolidated dividends received deduction, attributable to such member;

(2) Such member's capital gain net income (net capital gain for taxable years beginning before January 1, 1977) (determined without regard to any net capital loss carryover or carryback attributable to such member);

(3) Such member's net capital loss and section 1231 net loss, reduced by the portion of the consolidated net capital loss attributable to such member; and

(4) The portion of any consolidated net capital loss carryover or carryback attributable to such member which is absorbed in the taxable year. [Reg. §1.1502-27.]

☐ [T.D. 6894, 9-7-66. *Amended by* T.D. 7637, 8-6-79 *and* T.D. 7728, 10-31-80.]

[Reg. §1.1502-28]

**§1.1502-28. Consolidated section 108.**—(a) *In general.*—This section sets forth rules for the application of section 108(a) and the reduction of tax attributes pursuant to section 108(b) when a member of the group realizes discharge of indebtedness income that is excluded from gross income under section 108(a) (excluded COD income).

(1) *Application of section 108(a).*—Section 108(a)(1)(A) and (B) is applied separately to each member that realizes excluded COD income. Therefore, the limitation of section 108(a)(3) on the amount of discharge of indebtedness income that is treated as excluded COD income is determined based on the assets (including stock and securities of other members) and liabilities (including liabilities to other members) of only the member that realizes excluded COD income.

(2) *Reduction of tax attributes attributable to the debtor.*—(i) *In general.*—With respect to a member that realizes excluded COD income in a taxable year, the tax attributes attributable to that member (and its direct and indirect subsidiaries to the extent required by section 1017(b)(3)(D) and paragraph (a)(3) of this section), including basis of assets and losses and credits arising in separate return limitation years, shall be reduced as provided in sections 108 and 1017 and this section. Basis of subsidiary stock, however, shall not be reduced below zero pursuant to paragraph (a)(2) of this section (including when subsidiary stock is treated as depreciable property under section 1017(b)(3)(D) when there is an election under section 108(b)(5)).

(ii) *Consolidated tax attributes attributable to a member.*—For purposes of this section, the amount of a consolidated tax attribute (e.g., a consolidated net operating loss) that is attributable to a member shall be determined pursuant to the principles of §1.1502-21(b)(2)(iv).

In addition, if the member is a member of a separate return limitation year subgroup, the amount of a tax attribute that arose in a separate return limitation year that is attributable to that member shall also be determined pursuant to the principles of § 1.1502-21(b)(2)(iv).

(3) *Look-through rules.*—(i) *Priority of section 1017(b)(3)(D).*—If a member treats stock of a subsidiary as depreciable property pursuant to section 1017(b)(3)(D), the basis of the depreciable property of such subsidiary shall be reduced pursuant to section 1017(b)(3)(D) prior to the application of paragraph (a)(3)(ii) of this section.

(ii) *Application of additional look-through rule.*—If the basis of stock of a corporation (the lower-tier member) that is owned by another corporation (the higher-tier member) is reduced pursuant to sections 108 and 1017 and paragraph (a)(2) of this section (but not as a result of treating subsidiary stock as depreciable property pursuant to section 1017(b)(3)(D)), and both of such corporations are members of the same consolidated group on the last day of the higher-tier member's taxable year that includes the date on which the excluded COD income is realized or the first day of the higher-tier member's taxable year that follows the taxable year that includes the date on which the excluded COD income is realized, solely for purposes of sections 108 and 1017 and this section other than paragraphs (a)(4) and (b)(1) of this section, the lower-tier member shall be treated as realizing excluded COD income on the last day of the taxable year of the higher-tier member that includes the date on which the higher-tier member realized the excluded COD income. The amount of such excluded COD income shall be the amount of such basis reduction. Accordingly, the tax attributes attributable to such lower-tier member shall be reduced as provided in sections 108 and 1017 and this section. To the extent that the excluded COD income realized by the lower-tier member pursuant to this paragraph (a)(3) does not reduce a tax attribute attributable to the lower-tier member, such excluded COD income shall not be applied to reduce tax attributes attributable to any member under paragraph (a)(4) of this section and shall not cause an excess loss account to be taken into account under § 1.1502-19(b)(1) and (c)(1)(iii)(B).

(4) *Reduction of certain tax attributes attributable to other members.*—To the extent that, pursuant to paragraph (a)(2) of this section, the excluded COD income is not applied to reduce the tax attributes attributable to the member that realizes the excluded COD income, after the application of paragraph (a)(3) of this section, such amount shall be applied to reduce the remaining consolidated tax attributes of the group, other than consolidated tax attributes to which a SRLY limitation applies, as provided in section 108 and this section. Such amount also shall be applied to reduce the tax attributes attributable to members that arose (or are treated as arising) in a separate return limitation year to the extent that the member that realizes excluded COD income is a member of the separate return limitation year subgroup with respect to such attribute if a SRLY limitation applies to the use of such attribute. In addition, such amount shall be applied to reduce the tax attributes attributable to members that arose in a separate return year or that arose (or are treated as arising) in a separate return limitation year if no SRLY limitation applies to the use of such attribute. The reduction of each tax attribute pursuant to the three preceding sentences shall be made in the order prescribed in section 108(b)(2) and pursuant to the principles of § 1.1502-21(b)(1). Except as otherwise provided in this paragraph (a)(4), a tax attribute that arose in a separate return year or that arose (or is treated as arising) in a separate return limitation year is not subject to reduction pursuant to this paragraph (a)(4). Basis in assets is not subject to reduction pursuant to this paragraph (a)(4). Finally, to the extent that the realization of excluded COD income by a member pursuant to paragraph (a)(3) does not reduce a tax attribute attributable to such lower-tier member, such excess shall not be applied to reduce tax attributes attributable to any member pursuant to this paragraph (a)(4).

(b) *Special rules.*—(1) *Multiple debtor members.*—(i) *Reduction of tax attributes attributable to debtor members prior to reduction of consolidated tax attributes.*—If in a single taxable year multiple members realize excluded COD income, paragraphs (a)(2) and (3) of this section shall apply with respect to the excluded COD income of each such member before the application of paragraph (a)(4) of this section.

(ii) *Reduction of higher-tier debtor's tax attributes.*—If in a single taxable year multiple members realize excluded COD income and one such member is a higher-tier member of another such member, paragraphs (a)(2) and (3) of this section shall be applied with respect to the excluded COD income of the higher-tier member before such paragraphs are applied to the excluded COD income of the other such member. In applying the rules of paragraph (a)(2) and (3) of this section with respect to the excluded COD income of the higher-tier member, the liabilities that give rise to the excluded COD income of the other such member shall not be treated as discharged for purposes of computing the limitation on basis reduction under section

1017(b)(2). A member (the first member) is a higher-tier member of another member (the second member) if the first member is the common parent or investment adjustments under § 1.1502-32 with respect to the stock of the second member would affect investment adjustments with respect to the stock of the first member.

(iii) *Reduction of additional tax attributes.*—If more than one member realizes excluded COD income that has not been applied to reduce a tax attribute attributable to such member (the remaining COD amount) and the remaining tax attributes available for reduction under paragraph (a)(4) of this section are less than the aggregate of the remaining COD amounts, after the application of paragraph (a)(2) of this section, each such member's remaining COD amount shall be applied on a pro rata basis (based on the relative remaining COD amounts), pursuant to paragraph (a)(4) of this section, to reduce such remaining available tax attributes.

(iv) *Ownership of lower-tier member by multiple higher-tier members.*—If stock of a corporation is held by more than one higher-tier member of the group and more than one such higher-tier member reduces its basis in such stock, then under paragraph (a)(3) of this section the excluded COD income resulting from the stock basis reductions shall be applied on a pro rata basis (based on the amount of excluded COD income caused by each basis reduction) to reduce the attributes of the corporation.

(v) *Ownership of lower-tier member by multiple higher-tier members in multiple groups.*—If a corporation is a member of one group (the first group) on the last day of the first group's higher-tier member's taxable year that includes the date on which that higher-tier member realizes excluded COD income and is a member of another group (the second group) on the following day and the first group's higher-tier member and the second group's higher-tier member both reduce their basis in the stock of such corporation pursuant to sections 108 and 1017 and this section, paragraph (a)(3) of this section shall first be applied in respect of the excluded COD income that results from the reduction of the basis of the corporation's stock owned by the first group's higher-tier member and then shall be applied in respect of the excluded COD income that results from the reduction of the basis of the corporation's stock owned by the second group's higher-tier member.

(2) *Election under section 108(b)(5).*—(i) *Availability of election.*—The group may make the election described in section 108(b)(5) for any member that realizes excluded COD income. The election is made separately for each member. Therefore, an election may be made for one member that realizes excluded COD income (either actually or pursuant to paragraph (a)(3) of this section) while another election, or no election, may be made for another member that realizes excluded COD income (either actually or pursuant to paragraph (a)(3) of this section). See § 1.108-4 for rules relating to the procedure for making an election under section 108(b)(5).

(ii) *Treatment of shares with an excess loss account.*—For purposes of applying section 108(b)(5)(B), the basis of stock of a subsidiary that has an excess loss account shall be treated as zero.

(3) *Application of section 1017.*—(i) *Timing of basis reduction.*—Basis of property shall be subject to reduction pursuant to the rules of sections 108 and 1017 and this section after the determination of the tax imposed by chapter 1 of the Internal Revenue Code for the taxable year during which the member realizes excluded COD income and any prior years and coincident with the reduction of other attributes pursuant to section 108 and this section. However, only the basis of property held as of the beginning of the taxable year following the taxable year during which the excluded COD income is realized is subject to reduction pursuant to sections 108 and 1017 and this section.

(ii) *Limitation of section 1017(b)(2).*—The limitation of section 1017(b)(2) on the reduction in basis of property shall be applied by reference to the aggregate of the basis of the property held by the member that realizes excluded COD income, not the aggregate of the basis of the property held by all of the members of the group, and the liabilities of such member, not the aggregate liabilities of all of the members of the group.

(iii) *Treatment of shares with an excess loss account.*—For purposes of applying section 1017(b)(2) and § 1.1017-1, the basis of stock of a subsidiary that has an excess loss account shall be treated as zero.

(4) *Application of section 1245.*—Notwithstanding section 1017(d)(1)(B), a reduction of the basis of subsidiary stock is treated as a deduction allowed for depreciation only to the extent that the amount by which the basis of the subsidiary stock is reduced exceeds the total amount of the attributes attributable to such subsidiary that are reduced pursuant to the subsidiary's consent under section

1017(b)(3)(D) or as a result of the application of paragraph (a)(3)(ii) of this section.

(5) *Reduction of basis of intercompany obligations and former intercompany obligations.*—(i) *Intercompany obligations that cease to be intercompany obligations.*—If excluded COD income is realized in a consolidated return year in which an intercompany obligation becomes an obligation that is not an intercompany obligation because the debtor or creditor becomes a nonmember, or because the assets of the debtor or the creditor are acquired by a nonmember in a transaction to which section 381 applies, then the basis of such intercompany obligation (or new obligation if the intercompany obligation is deemed reissued under § 1.1502-13(g)(3)) is available for reduction in respect of such excluded COD income pursuant to sections 108 and 1017 and this section.

(ii) *Intercompany obligations.*—The reduction of the basis of an intercompany obligation pursuant to sections 108 and 1017 and this section shall not result in the satisfaction and reissuance of the obligation under § 1.1502-13(g). Therefore, any income or gain (or reduction of loss or deduction) attributable to a reduction of the basis of an intercompany obligation will be taken into account when § 1.1502-13(g)(3) applies to such obligation. Furthermore, § 1.1502-13(c)(6)(i) (regarding the treatment of intercompany items if corresponding items are excluded or nondeductible) will not apply to exclude any amount of income or gain attributable to a reduction of the basis of an intercompany obligation pursuant to sections 108 and 1017 and this section. See § 1.1502-13(g)(3)(i)(A)(*1*) and (g)(4)(i)(A).

(6) *Taking into account of excess loss account.*—(i) *Determination of inclusion.*—The determination of whether any portion of an excess loss account in a share of stock of a subsidiary that realizes excluded COD income is required to be taken into account as a result of the application of § 1.1502-19(c)(1)(iii)(B) is made after the determination of the tax imposed by chapter 1 of the Internal Revenue Code for the year during which the member realizes excluded COD income (without regard to whether any portion of an excess loss account in a share of stock of the subsidiary is required to be taken into account) and any prior years, after the reduction of tax attributes pursuant to sections 108 and 1017 and this section, and after the adjustment of the basis of the share of stock of the subsidiary pursuant to § 1.1502-32 to reflect the amount of the subsidiary's deductions and losses that are absorbed in the computation of taxable income (or loss) for the year of the disposition and any prior years, and the excluded COD income applied to reduce attributes and the attributes reduced in respect thereof. See § 1.1502-11(c) for special rules related to the computation of tax that apply when an excess loss account is required to be taken into account.

(ii) *Timing of inclusion.*—To the extent an excess loss account in a share of stock of a subsidiary that realizes excluded COD income is required to be taken into account as a result of the application of § 1.1502-19(c)(1)(iii)(B), such amount shall be included on the group's tax return for the taxable year that includes the date on which the subsidiary realizes such excluded COD income.

(7) *Dispositions of stock.*—See § 1.1502-11(c) for limitations on the reduction of tax attributes when a member disposes of stock of another member (including dispositions that result from the application of § 1.1502-19(c)(1)(iii)(B)) during a taxable year in which any member realizes excluded COD income.

(8) *Departure of member.*—If the taxable year of a member (the departing member) during which such member realizes excluded COD income ends on or prior to the last day of the consolidated return year and, on the first day of the taxable year of such member that follows the taxable year during which such member realizes excluded COD income, such member is not a member of the group and does not have a successor member (within the meaning of paragraph (b)(10) of this section), all tax attributes listed in section 108(b)(2) that remain after the determination of the tax imposed that belong to members of the group (including the departing member and subsidiaries of the departing member) shall be subject to reduction as provided in section 108 and the regulations promulgated thereunder (including § 1.108-7(c), if applicable) and this section.

(9) *Intragroup reorganization.*—(i) *In general.*—If the taxable year of a member during which such member realizes excluded COD income ends prior to the last day of the consolidated return year and, on the first day that follows the taxable year of such member during which such member realizes excluded COD income, such member has a successor member, for purposes of applying the rules of sections 108 and 1017 and this section, notwithstanding § 1.108-7, the successor member shall be treated as the member that realized the excluded COD income. Thus, all attributes attributable to the successor member listed in section 108(b)(2) (including attributes that were attributable to the successor member prior to the date such member

became a successor member) are available for reduction under paragraph (a)(2) of this section.

(ii) *Group structure change.*—If a member that realizes excluded COD income acquires the assets of the common parent of the consolidated group in a transaction to which section 381(a) applies and succeeds such common parent under the principles of § 1.1502-75(d)(2) as the common parent of the consolidated group, the member's attributes that remain after the determination of tax for the group for the consolidated return year during which the excluded COD income is realized (and any prior years) (including attributes that were attributable to the former common parent prior to the date of the transaction to which section 381(a) applies) shall be available for reduction under paragraph (a)(2) of this section.

(10) *Definition of successor member.*—A successor member means a person to which the member that realizes excluded COD income (or a successor member) transfers its assets in a transaction to which section 381(a) applies if such transferee is a member of the group immediately after the transaction.

(11) *Non-application of next day rule.*—For purposes of applying the rules of sections 108 and 1017 and this section, the next day rule of § 1.1502-76(b)(1)(ii)(B) shall not apply to treat a member's excluded COD income as realized at the beginning of the day following the day on which such member's status as a member changes.

(c) *Examples.*—The principles of paragraphs (a) and (b) of this section are illustrated by the following examples. Unless otherwise indicated, no election under section 108(b)(5) has been made and the taxable year of all consolidated groups is the calendar year. The examples are as follows:

*Example 1.* (i) *Facts.* P is the common parent of a consolidated group that includes subsidiary S1. P owns 80 percent of the stock of S1. In Year 1, the P group sustained a $250 consolidated net operating loss. Under the principles of § 1.1502-21(b)(2)(iv), of that amount, $125 was attributable to P and $125 was attributable to S1. On Day 1 of Year 2, P acquired 100 percent of the stock of S2, and S2 joined the P group. As of the beginning of Year 2, S2 had a $50 net operating loss carryover from Year 1, a separate return limitation year. In Year 2, the P group sustained a $200 consolidated net operating loss. Under the principles of § 1.1502-21(b)(2)(iv), of that amount, $90 was attributable to P, $70 was attributable to S1, and $40 was attributable to S2. In Year 3, S2 realized $200 of excluded COD income from the discharge of non-intercompany indebtedness. In that same year, the P group sustained a $50 consolidated net operating loss, of which $40 was attributable to S1 and $10 was attributable to S2 under the principles of § 1.1502-21(b)(2)(iv). As of the beginning of Year 4, S2 had Asset A with a fair market value of $10. After the computation of tax imposed for Year 3 and before the application of sections 108 and 1017 and this section, Asset A had a basis of $40 and S2 had no liabilities.

(ii) *Analysis*—(A) *Reduction of tax attributes attributable to debtor.* Pursuant to paragraph (a)(2) of this section, the tax attributes attributable to S2 must first be reduced to take into account its excluded COD income in the amount of $200.

(*1*) *Reduction of net operating losses.* Pursuant to section 108(b)(2)(A) and paragraph (a) of this section, the net operating loss and the net operating loss carryovers attributable to S2 under the principles of § 1.1502-21(b)(2)(iv) are reduced in the order prescribed by section 108(b)(4)(B). Accordingly, the consolidated net operating loss for Year 3 is reduced by $10, the portion of the consolidated net operating loss attributable to S2, to $40. Then, again pursuant to section 108(b)(4)(B), S2's net operating loss carryover of $50 from its separate return limitation year is reduced to $0. Finally, the consolidated net operating loss carryover from Year 2 is reduced by $40, the portion of that consolidated net operating loss carryover attributable to S2, to $160.

(*2*) *Reduction of basis.* Following the reduction of the net operating loss and the net operating loss carryovers attributable to S2, S2 reduces its basis in its assets pursuant to section 1017 and § 1.1017-1. Accordingly, S2 reduces its basis in Asset A by $40, from $40 to $0.

(B) *Reduction of remaining consolidated tax attributes.* The remaining $60 of excluded COD income then reduces consolidated tax attributes pursuant to paragraph (a)(4) of this section. In particular, the remaining $40 consolidated net operating loss for Year 3 is reduced to $0. Then, the consolidated net operating loss carryover from Year 1 is reduced by $20 from $250 to $230. Pursuant to paragraph (a)(4) of this section, a pro rata amount of the consolidated net operating loss carryover from Year 1 that is attributable to each of P and S1 is treated as reduced. Therefore, $10 of the consolidated net operating loss carryover from Year 1 that is attributable to each of P and S1 is treated as reduced.

*Example 2.* (i) *Facts.* P is the common parent of a consolidated group that includes subsidiaries S1 and S2. P owns 100 percent of the stock of S1 and S1 owns 100 percent of the stock of S2. None of P, S1, or S2 has a separate return limitation year. In Year 1, the P group sustained a $50 consolidated net operating loss. Under the principles of §1.1502-21(b)(2)(iv), of that amount, $10 was attributable to P, $20 was attributable to S1, and $20 was attributable to S2. In Year 2, the P group sustained a $70 consolidated net operating loss. Under the principles of §1.1502-21(b)(2)(iv), of that amount, $30 was attributable to P, $30 was attributable to S1, and $10 was attributable to S2. In Year 3, S1 realized $170 of excluded COD income from the discharge of non-intercompany indebtedness. In that same year, the P group sustained a $50 consolidated net operating loss, of which $10 was attributable to S1 and $40 was attributable to S2 under the principles of §1.1502-21(b)(2)(iv). As of the beginning of Year 4, S1's sole asset was the stock of S2, and S2 had Asset A with a $10 value. After the computation of tax imposed for Year 3 and before the application of sections 108 and 1017 and this section, S1 had a $80 basis in the S2 stock, Asset A had a basis of $0, and neither S1 nor S2 had any liabilities.

(ii) *Analysis*—(A) *Reduction of tax attributes attributable to debtor.* Pursuant to paragraph (a)(2) of this section, the tax attributes attributable to S1 must first be reduced to take into account its excluded COD income in the amount of $170.

(1) *Reduction of net operating losses.* Pursuant to section 108(b)(2)(A) and paragraph (a) of this section, the net operating loss and the net operating loss carryovers attributable to S1 under the principles of §1.1502-21(b)(2)(iv) are reduced in the order prescribed by section 108(b)(4)(B). Accordingly, the consolidated net operating loss for Year 3 is reduced by $10, the portion of the consolidated net operating loss for Year 3 attributable to S1, to $40. Then, the consolidated net operating loss carryover from Year 1 is reduced by $20, the portion of that consolidated net operating loss carryover attributable to S1, to $30, and the consolidated net operating loss carryover from Year 2 is reduced by $30, the portion of that consolidated net operating loss carryover attributable to S1, to $40.

(2) *Reduction of basis.* Following the reduction of the net operating loss and the net operating loss carryovers attributable to S1, S1 reduces its basis in its assets pursuant to section 1017 and §1.1017-1. Accordingly, S1 reduces its basis in the stock of S2 by $80, from $80 to $0.

(3) *Tiering down of stock basis reduction.* Pursuant to paragraph (a)(3) of this section, for purposes of sections 108 and 1017 and this section, S2 is treated as realizing $80 of excluded COD income. Pursuant to section 108(b)(2)(A) and paragraph (a) of this section, therefore, the net operating loss and net operating loss carryovers attributable to S2 under the principles of §1.1502-21(b)(2)(iv) are reduced in the order prescribed by section 108(b)(4)(B). Accordingly, the consolidated net operating loss for Year 3 is reduced by an additional $40, the portion of the consolidated net operating loss for Year 3 attributable to S2, to $0. Then, the consolidated net operating loss carryover from Year 1 is reduced by $20, the portion of that consolidated net operating loss carryover attributable to S2, to $10. Then, the consolidated net operating loss carryover from Year 2 is reduced by $10, the portion of that consolidated net operating loss carryover attributable to S2, to $30. S2's remaining $10 of excluded COD income does not reduce consolidated tax attributes attributable to P or S1 under paragraph (a)(4) of this section.

(B) *Reduction of remaining consolidated tax attributes.* Finally, pursuant to paragraph (a)(4) of this section, S1's remaining $30 of excluded COD income reduces the remaining consolidated tax attributes. In particular, the remaining $10 consolidated net operating loss carryover from Year 1 is reduced by $10 to $0, and the remaining $30 consolidated net operating loss carryover from Year 2 is reduced by $20 to $10.

*Example 3.* (i) *Facts.* P is the common parent of a consolidated group that includes subsidiaries S1, S2, and S3. P owns 100 percent of the stock of S1, S1 owns 100 percent of the stock of S2, and S2 owns 100 percent of the stock of S3. None of P, S1, S2, or S3 had a separate return limitation year prior to Year 1. In Year 1, the P group sustained a $150 consolidated net operating loss. Under the principles of §1.1502-21(b)(2)(iv), of that amount, $50 was attributable to S2, and $100 was attributable to S3. In Year 2, the P group sustained a $50 consolidated net operating loss. Under the principles of §1.1502-21(b)(2)(iv), of that amount, $40 was attributable to S1 and $10 was attributable to S2. In Year 3, S1 realized $170 of excluded COD income from the discharge of non-intercompany indebtedness. In that same year, the P group sustained a $50 consolidated net operating loss, of which $10 was attributable to S1, $20 was attributable to S2, and $20 was attributable to S3 under the principles of §1.1502-21(b)(2)(iv). At the beginning of Year 4, S1's only asset was the stock of S2, and S2's only asset was the stock of S3 with a value of $10. After the computation of tax imposed for Year 3 and before the application of sections 108 and 1017 and this section, S1's stock of S2 had a basis of $120 and S2's stock of S3 had a basis of $180. In addition, none of S1, S2, and S3 had any liabilities.

(ii) *Analysis*—(A) *Reduction of tax attributes attributable to debtor.* Pursuant to paragraph (a)(2) of this section, the tax attributes attribu-

table to S1 must first be reduced to take into account its excluded COD income in the amount of $170.

(1) *Reduction of net operating losses.* Pursuant to section 108(b)(2)(A) and paragraph (a) of this section, the net operating loss and the net operating loss carryovers attributable to S1 under the principles of §1.1502-21(b)(2)(iv) are reduced in the order prescribed by section 108(b)(4)(B). Accordingly, the consolidated net operating loss for Year 3 is reduced by $10, the portion of the consolidated net operating loss attributable to S1, to $40. Then, the consolidated net operating loss carryover from Year 2 is reduced by $40, the portion of that consolidated net operating loss carryover attributable to S1, to $10.

(2) *Reduction of basis.* Following the reduction of the net operating loss and the net operating loss carryovers attributable to S1, S1 reduces its basis in its assets pursuant to section 1017 and §1.1017-1. Accordingly, S1 reduces its basis in the stock of S2 by $120, from $120 to $0.

(B) *Tiering down of stock basis reduction to S2.* Pursuant to paragraph (a)(3) of this section, for purposes of sections 108 and 1017 and this section, S2 is treated as realizing $120 of excluded COD income. Pursuant to section 108(b)(2)(A) and paragraph (a) of this section, therefore, the net operating loss and net operating loss carryovers attributable to S2 under the principles of §1.1502-21(b)(2)(iv) are reduced in the order prescribed by section 108(b)(4)(B). Accordingly, the consolidated net operating loss for Year 3 is further reduced by $20, the portion of the consolidated net operating loss attributable to S2, to $20. Then, the consolidated net operating loss carryover from Year 1 is reduced by $50, the portion of that consolidated net operating loss carryover attributable to S2, to $100. Then, the consolidated net operating loss carryover from Year 2 is further reduced by $10, the portion of that consolidated net operating loss carryover attributable to S2, to $0. Following the reduction of the net operating loss and the net operating loss carryovers attributable to S2, S2 reduces its basis in its assets pursuant to section 1017 and §1.1017-1. Accordingly, S2 reduces its basis in its S3 stock by $40 to $140.

(C) *Tiering down of stock basis reduction to S3.* Pursuant to paragraph (a)(3) of this section, for purposes of sections 108 and 1017 and this section, S3 is treated as realizing $40 of excluded COD income. Pursuant to section 108(b)(2)(A) and paragraph (a) of this section, therefore, the net operating loss and the net operating loss carryovers attributable to S3 under the principles of §1.1502-21(b)(2)(iv) are reduced in the order prescribed by section 108(b)(4)(B). Accordingly, the consolidated net operating loss for Year 3 is further reduced by $20, the portion of the consolidated net operating loss attributable to S3, to $0. Then, the consolidated net operating loss carryover from Year 1 is reduced by $20, the lesser of the portion of that consolidated net operating loss carryover attributable to S3 and the remaining excluded COD income, to $80.

*Example 4.* (i) *Facts.* P is the common parent of a consolidated group that includes subsidiaries S1, S2, and S3. P owns 100 percent of the stock of each of S1 and S2. Each of S1 and S2 owns stock of S3 that represents 50 percent of the value of the stock of S3. None of P, S1, S2, or S3 had a separate return limitation year prior to Year 1. In Year 1, the P group sustained a $160 consolidated net operating loss. Under the principles of §1.1502-21(b)(2)(iv), of that amount, $10 was attributable to P, $50 was attributable to S2, and $100 was attributable to S3. In Year 2, the P group sustained a $110 consolidated net operating loss. Under the principles of §1.1502-21(b)(2)(iv), of that amount, $40 was attributable to S1 and $70 was attributable to S2. In Year 3, S1 realized $200 of excluded COD income from the discharge of non-intercompany indebtedness, and S2 realized $270 of excluded COD income from the discharge of non-intercompany indebtedness. In that same year, the P group sustained a $50 consolidated net operating loss, of which $10 was attributable to S1, $20 was attributable to S2, and $20 was attributable to S3 under the principles of §1.1502-21(b)(2)(iv). At the beginning of Year 4, S3 had one asset with a value of $10. After the computation of tax imposed for Year 3 and before the application of sections 108 and 1017 and this section, S1's basis in its S3 stock was $60, S2's basis in its S3 stock was $120, and S3's asset had a basis of $200. In addition, none of S1, S2, and S3 had any liabilities.

(ii) *Analysis*—(A) *Reduction of tax attributes attributable to debtors.* Pursuant to paragraph (b)(1)(i) of this section, the tax attributes attributable to each of S1 and S2 are reduced pursuant to paragraph (a)(2) of this section. Then, pursuant to paragraph (a)(3) of this section, the tax attributes attributable to S3 are reduced so as to reflect a reduction of S1's and S2's basis in the stock of S3. Then, paragraph (a)(4) is applied to reduce additional tax attributes.

(1) *Reduction of net operating losses generally.* Pursuant to section 108(b)(2)(A) and paragraph (a) of this section, the net operating losses and the net operating loss carryovers attributable to S1 and S2 under the principles of §1.1502-21(b)(2)(iv) are reduced in the order prescribed by section 108(b)(4)(B).

(2) *Reduction of net operating losses attributable to S1.* The consolidated net operating loss for Year 3 is reduced by $10, the portion of

the consolidated net operating loss attributable to S1, to $40. Then, the consolidated net operating loss carryover from Year 2 is reduced by $40, the portion of that consolidated net operating loss carryover attributable to S1, to $70.

(3) *Reduction of net operating losses attributable to S2.* The consolidated net operating loss for Year 3 is also reduced by $20, the portion of the consolidated net operating loss attributable to S2, to $20. Then, the consolidated net operating loss carryover from Year 1 is reduced by $50, the portion of that consolidated net operating loss carryover attributable to S2, to $110. Then, the consolidated net operating loss carryover from Year 2 is reduced by $70, the portion of that consolidated net operating loss carryover attributable to S2, to $0.

(4) *Reduction of basis.* Following the reduction of the net operating losses and the net operating loss carryovers attributable to S1 and S2, S1 and S2 must reduce their basis in their assets pursuant to section 1017 and § 1.1017-1. Accordingly, S1 reduces its basis in the stock of S3 by $60, from $60 to $0, and S2 reduces its basis in the stock of S3 by $120, from $120 to $0.

(B) *Tiering down of basis reduction.* Pursuant to paragraph (a)(3) of this section, for purposes of sections 108 and 1017 and this section, S3 is treated as realizing $180 of excluded COD income. Pursuant to section 108(b)(2)(A) and paragraph (a) of this section, therefore, the net operating loss and the net operating loss carryovers attributable to S3 under the principles of § 1.1502-21(b)(2)(iv) are reduced in the order prescribed by section 108(b)(4)(B). Accordingly, the consolidated net operating loss for Year 3 is further reduced by $20, the portion of the consolidated net operating loss attributable to S3, to $0. Then, the consolidated net operating loss carryover from Year 1 is reduced by $100, the portion of that consolidated net operating loss carryover attributable to S3, to $10. Following the reduction of the net operating loss and the net operating loss carryover attributable to S3, S3 reduces its basis in its asset pursuant to section 1017 and § 1.1017-1. Accordingly, S3 reduces its basis in its asset by $60, from $200 to $140.

(C) *Reduction of remaining consolidated tax attributes.* Finally, pursuant to paragraph (a)(4) of this section, the remaining $90 of S1's excluded COD income and the remaining $10 of S2's excluded COD income reduce the remaining consolidated tax attributes. In particular, the remaining $10 consolidated net operating loss carryover from Year 1 is reduced by $10 to $0. Because that amount is less than the aggregate amount of remaining excluded COD income, such income is applied on a pro rata basis to reduce the remaining consolidated tax attributes. Accordingly, $9 of S1's remaining excluded COD income and $1 of S2's remaining excluded COD income is applied to reduce the remaining consolidated net operating loss carryover from Year 1. Consequently, of S1's excluded COD income of $200, only $119 is applied to reduce tax attributes, and, of S2's excluded COD income of $270, only $261 is applied to reduce tax attributes.

*Example 5.* (i) *Facts.* P is the common parent of a consolidated group that includes subsidiaries S1, S2, and S3. P owns 100 percent of the stock of S1 and S2, and S1 owns 100 percent of the stock of S3. None of P, S1, S2, or S3 has a separate return limitation year prior to Year 1. In Year 1, the P group sustained a $90 consolidated net operating loss. Under the principles of § 1.1502-21(b)(2)(iv), of that amount, $10 was attributable to P, $15 was attributable to S1, $20 was attributable to S2, and $45 was attributable to S3. On January 1 of Year 2, P realized $140 of excluded COD income from the discharge of non-intercompany indebtedness. On December 31 of Year 2, S1 issued stock representing 50 percent of the vote and value of its outstanding stock to a person that was not a member of the group. As a result of the issuance of stock, S1 and S3 ceased to be members of the P group. For the consolidated return year of Year 2, the P group sustained a $60 consolidated net operating loss, of which $5 was attributable to S1, $40 was attributable to S2, and $15 was attributable to S3 under the principles of § 1.1502-21(b)(2)(iv). As of the beginning of Year 3, P's only assets were the stock of S1 and S2, S1's sole asset was the stock of S3, S2 had Asset A with a value of $10, and S3 had Asset B with a value of $10. After the computation of tax imposed for Year 2 and before the application of sections 108 and 1017 and this section, P had a $80 basis in the S1 stock and a $50 basis in the S2 stock, S1 had a $80 basis in the S3 stock, and Asset A and B each had a basis of $10. In addition, none of P, S1, S2, and S3 had any liabilities.

(ii) *Analysis.* Pursuant to paragraph (a)(2) of this section, the tax attributes attributable to P must first be reduced to take into account its excluded COD income in the amount of $140.

(A) *Reduction of net operating losses.* Pursuant to section 108(b)(2)(A) and paragraph (a) of this section, the net operating loss and the net operating loss carryover attributable to P under the principles of § 1.1502-21(b)(2)(iv) are reduced in the order prescribed by section 108(b)(4)(B). Accordingly, the consolidated net operating loss carryover from Year 1 is reduced by $10, the portion of that consolidated net operating loss carryover attributable to P, to $80.

(B) *Reduction of basis.* Following the reduction of the net operating loss and the net operating loss carryover attributable to P, P reduces

its basis in its assets pursuant to section 1017 and § 1.1017-1. Accordingly, P reduces its basis in the stock of S1 by $80, from $80 to $0, and its basis in the stock of S2 by $50, from $50 to $0.

(C) *Tiering down of stock basis reduction to S1.* Pursuant to paragraph (a)(3) of this section, for purposes of sections 108 and 1017 and this section, S1 is treated as realizing $80 of excluded COD income, despite the fact that it ceases to be a member of the group at the end of the day on December 31 of Year 2. Pursuant to section 108(b)(2)(A) and paragraph (a) of this section, therefore, the net operating loss and net operating loss carryovers attributable to S1 under the principles of § 1.1502-21(b)(2)(iv) are reduced in the order prescribed by section 108(b)(4)(B). Accordingly, the consolidated net operating loss for Year 2 is reduced by $5, the portion of the consolidated net operating loss for Year 2 attributable to S1, to $55. Then, the consolidated net operating loss carryover from Year 1 is reduced by an additional $15, the portion of that consolidated net operating loss carryover attributable to S1, to $65. Following the reduction of the net operating loss and the net operating loss carryover attributable to S1, S1 reduces its basis in its assets pursuant to section 1017 and § 1.1017-1. Accordingly, S1 reduces its basis in the stock of S3 by $60, from $80 to $20.

(D) *Tiering down of stock basis reduction to S2.* Pursuant to paragraph (a)(3) of this section, for purposes of sections 108 and 1017 and this section, S2 is treated as realizing $50 of excluded COD income. Pursuant to section 108(b)(2)(A) and paragraph (a) of this section, therefore, the net operating loss and net operating loss carryovers attributable to S2 under the principles of § 1.1502-21(b)(2)(iv) are reduced in the order prescribed by section 108(b)(4)(B). Accordingly, the consolidated net operating loss for Year 2 is reduced by an additional $40, the portion of the consolidated net operating loss for Year 2 attributable to S2, to $15. Then, the consolidated net operating loss carryover from Year 1 is reduced by an additional $10, a portion of the consolidated net operating loss carryover attributable to S2, to $55.

(E) *Tiering down of stock basis reduction to S3.* Pursuant to paragraph (a)(3) of this section, for purposes of sections 108 and 1017 and this section, S3 is treated as realizing $60 of excluded COD income (by reason of S1's reduction in its basis of its S3 stock). Pursuant to section 108(b)(2)(A) and paragraph (a) of this section, therefore, the net operating loss and net operating loss carryovers attributable to S3 under the principles of § 1.1502-21(b)(2)(iv) are reduced in the order prescribed by section 108(b)(4)(B). Accordingly, the consolidated net operating loss for Year 2 is reduced by an additional $15, the portion of the consolidated net operating loss for Year 2 attributable to S3, to $0. Then, the consolidated net operating loss carryover from Year 1 is reduced by an additional $45, the portion of that consolidated net operating loss carryover attributable to S3, to $10.

*Example 6.* (i) *Facts.* P1 is the common parent of a consolidated group that includes subsidiaries S1, S2, and S3. P1 owns 100 percent of the stock of S1 and S2. S1 owns 100 percent of the stock of S3. None of P1, S1, S2, or S3 has a separate return limitation year prior to Year 1. In Year 1, the P1 group sustained a $120 consolidated net operating loss. Under the principles of § 1.1502-21(b)(2)(iv), of that amount, $40 was attributable to P1, $35 was attributable to S1, $30 was attributable to S2, and $15 was attributable to S3. On January 1 of Year 2, S3 realized $65 of excluded COD income from the discharge of non-intercompany indebtedness. On June 30 of Year 2, S3 issued stock representing 80 percent of the vote and value of its outstanding stock to P2, the common parent of another group. As a result of the issuance of stock, S3 ceased to be a member of the P1 group and became a member of the P2 group. For the consolidated return year of Year 2, the P1 group sustained a $50 consolidated net operating loss, of which $5 was attributable to S1, $40 was attributable to S2, and $5 was attributable to S3 under the principles of § 1.1502-21(b)(2)(iv). As of the beginning of its taxable year beginning on July 1 of Year 2, S3's sole asset was Asset A with a $10 value. After the computation of tax imposed for Year 2 on the P1 group and before the application of sections 108 and 1017 and this section and the computation of tax imposed for Year 2 on the P2 group, Asset A had a basis of $0. In addition, S3 had no liabilities. On January 1 of Year 3, P1 sold all of its stock of S1.

(ii) *Analysis—(A) Reduction of tax attributes attributable to debtor.* Pursuant to paragraph (a)(2) of this section, the tax attributes attributable to S3 must first be reduced to take into account its excluded COD income in the amount of $65. Pursuant to section 108(b)(2)(A) and paragraph (a) of this section, the net operating loss and the net operating loss carryover attributable to S3 under the principles of § 1.1502-21(b)(2)(iv) are reduced in the order prescribed by section 108(b)(4)(B). Accordingly, the consolidated net operating loss for Year 2 is reduced by $5, the portion of the consolidated net operating loss for Year 2 attributable to S3, to $45. Then, the consolidated net operating loss carryover from Year 1 is reduced by $15, the portion of that consolidated net operating loss carryover attributable to S3, to $105.

(B) *Reduction of remaining consolidated tax attributes.* Pursuant to paragraphs (a)(4) and (b)(8) of this section, S3's remaining $45 of excluded COD income reduces the remaining consolidated tax attributes in the P1 group. In particular, the remaining $45 consolidated net operating loss for Year 2 is reduced by an additional $45 to $0.

(C) *Basis Adjustments.* For purposes of computing P1's gain or loss on the sale of the S1 stock in Year 3, P1's basis in its S1 stock will reflect a net positive adjustment of $40, which is the excess of the amount of S3's excluded COD income that is applied to reduce attributes ($65) over the reduction of S1's and S3's attributes in respect of such excluded COD income ($25).

*Example 7.* (i) *Facts.* P is the common parent of a consolidated group that includes subsidiaries S1 and S2. P owns 100 percent of the stock of S1, and S1 owns 100 percent of the stock of S2. None of P, S1, or S2 has a separate return limitation year prior to Year 1. In Year 1, the P group sustained a $50 consolidated net operating loss. Under the principles of §1.1502-21(b)(2)(iv), of that amount, $10 was attributable to P, $20 was attributable to S1, and $20 was attributable to S2. On January 1 of Year 2, S1 realized $55 of excluded COD income from the discharge of non-intercompany indebtedness. On June 30 of Year 2, P transferred all of its assets to S1 in a transaction to which section 381(a) applied. As a result of that transaction, pursuant to §1.1502-75(d)(2)(ii), S1 succeeded P as the common parent of the group. Pursuant to §1.1502-75(d)(2)(iii), S1's taxable year closed on the date of the acquisition. However, P's taxable year did not close. On the consolidated return for Year 2, the group sustained a $50 consolidated net operating loss. Under the principles of §1.1502-21(b)(2)(iv), of that amount, $10 was attributable to S1 for its taxable year that ended on June 30, $15 was attributable to S1 as the successor of P, and $25 was attributable to S2.

(ii) *Analysis.* Pursuant to paragraph (a)(2) of this section, the tax attributes attributable to S1 must first be reduced to take into account its excluded COD income in the amount of $55. For this purpose, S1's attributes that remain after the determination of tax for the group for Year 2 are subject to reduction. Pursuant to section 108(b)(2)(A) and paragraph (a) of this section, the net operating loss and the net operating loss carryover attributable to S1 under the principles of §1.1502-21(b)(2)(iv) are reduced. Accordingly, the consolidated net operating loss for Year 2 is reduced by $25, the portion of the consolidated net operating loss for Year 2 attributable to S1, to $25. Then, the consolidated net operating loss carryover from Year 1 is reduced by $30, the portion of that consolidated net operating loss carryover attributable to S1 (which includes the portion attributable to P), to $20.

(d) *Effective dates.*—This section applies to discharges of indebtedness that occur after March 21, 2005. Groups, however, may apply this section in whole, but not in part, to discharges of indebtedness that occur on or before March 21, 2005, and after August 29, 2003. For discharges of indebtedness occurring on or before March 21, 2005, and after August 29, 2003, with respect to which a group chooses not to apply this section, see §1.1502-28T as contained in 26 CFR part 1 revised as of April 1, 2004. Furthermore, groups may apply paragraph (b)(4) of this section to discharges of indebtedness that occur on or before August 29, 2003, in cases in which section 1017(b)(3)(D) was applied. Paragraph (b)(5)(i) of this section and the last sentence of paragraph (b)(5)(ii) of this section applies to transactions occurring in consolidated return years beginning on or after December 24, 2008. [Reg. §1.1502-28.]

□ [*T.D. 9192, 3-21-2005. Amended by T.D. 9442, 12-24-2008.*]

**[Reg. §1.1502-30]**

**§1.1502-30. Stock basis after certain triangular reorganizations.**—(a) *Scope.*—This section provides rules for determining the basis of the stock of an acquiring corporation as a result of a triangular reorganization. The definitions and nomenclature contained in §1.358-6 apply to this section.

(b) *General rules.*—(1) *Forward triangular merger. triangular C reorganization, or triangular B reorganization.*—P adjusts its basis in the stock of S as a result of a forward triangular merger, triangular C reorganization, or triangular B reorganization under §1.358-6(c) and (d), except that §1.358-6(c)(1)(ii) and (d)(2) do not apply. Instead, P adjusts such basis by taking into account the full amount of—

(i) T liabilities assumed by S or the amount of liabilities to which the T assets acquired by S are subject, and

(ii) The fair market value of any consideration not provided by P pursuant to the plan of reorganization.

(2) *Reverse triangular merger.*—If P adjusts its basis in the T stock acquired as a result of a reverse triangular merger under §1.358-6(c)(2)(i) and (d), §1.358-6(c)(1)(ii) and (d)(2) do not apply. Instead, P adjusts such basis by taking into account the full amount of—

(i) T liabilities deemed assumed by S or the amount of liabilities to which the T assets deemed acquired by S are subject, and

(ii) The fair market value of any consideration not provided by P pursuant to the plan of reorganization.

(3) *Excess loss accounts.*—Negative adjustments under this section may exceed P's basis in its S or T stock. The resulting negative amount is P's excess loss account in its S or T stock. See §1.1502-19 for rules treating excess loss accounts as negative basis, and treating references to stock basis as including references to excess loss accounts.

(4) *Application of other rules of law.*—If a transaction otherwise subject to this section is also a group structure change subject to §1.1502-31, the provisions of §1.1502-31 and not this section apply to determine stock basis. See §1.1502-80(a) regarding the general applicability of other rules of law and a limitation on duplicative adjustments. See §1.1502-80(d) for the non-application of section 357(c) to P.

(5) *Examples.*—The rules of this paragraph (b) are illustrated by the following examples. For purposes of these examples, P, S, and T are domestic corporations, P and S file consolidated returns P owns all of the only class of S stock, the P stock exchanged in the transaction satisfies the requirements of the applicable triangular reorganization provisions, the facts set forth the only corporate activity, and tax liabilities are disregarded.

*Example 1. Liabilities.* (a) *Facts.* T has assets with an aggregate basis of $60 and fair market value of $100. T's assets are subject to $70 of liabilities. Pursuant to a plan, P forms S with $5 of cash (which S retains), and T merges into S. In the merger, the T shareholders receive P stock worth $30 in exchange for their T stock. The transaction is a reorganization to which sections 368(a)(1)(A) and (a)(2)(D) apply.

(b) *Basis adjustment.* Under §1.358-6, P adjusts its $5 basis in the S stock as if P had acquired the T assets with a carryover basis under section 362 and transferred these assets to S in a transaction in which P determines its basis in the S stock under section 358. Under the rules of this section, the limitation described in §1.358-6(c)(1)(ii) does not apply. Thus, P adjusts its basis in the S stock by –$10 (the aggregate adjusted basis of T's assets decreased by the amount of liabilities to which the T assets are subject). Consequently, as a result of the reorganization, P has an excess loss account of $5 in its S stock.

*Example 2. Consideration not provided by P.* (a) *Facts.* T has assets with an aggregate basis of $10 and fair market value of $100 and no liabilities. S is an operating company with substantial assets that has been in existence for several years. P has a $5 basis in its S stock. Pursuant to a plan, T merges into S and the T shareholders receive $70 of P stock provided by P pursuant to the plan of reorganization and $30 of cash provided by S in exchange for their T stock. The transaction is a reorganization to which sections 368(a)(1)(A) and (a)(2)(D) apply.

(b) *Basis adjustment.* Under §1.358-6, P adjusts its $5 basis in the S stock as if P had acquired the T assets with a carryover basis under section 362 and transferred these assets to S in a transaction in which P determines its basis in the S stock under section 358. Under the rules of this section, the limitation described in §1.358-6(d)(2) does not apply. Thus, P adjusts its basis in the S stock by –$20 (the aggregate adjusted basis of T's assets decreased by the fair market value of the consideration provided by S). As a result of the reorganization, P has an excess loss account of $15 in its S stock.

(c) *Appreciated asset.* The facts are the same as in paragraph (a) of this *Example 2*, except that in the reorganization S provides an asset with a $20 adjusted basis and $30 fair market value instead of $30 cash. The basis is adjusted in the same manner as in paragraph (b) of this *Example 2*. In addition, because S recognizes a $10 gain from the asset under section 1001, P's basis in its S stock is increased under §1.1502-32(b) by S's $10 gain. Consequently, as a result of the reorganization P has an excess loss account of $5 in its S stock. (The results would be the same if the appreciated asset provided by S was P stock with respect to which S recognized gain. See §1.1032-2(c)).

*Example 3. Reverse triangular merger.* (a) *Facts.* T has assets with an aggregate basis of $60 and fair market value of $100. T's assets are subject to $70 of liabilities. P owns all of the only class of S stock. P has a $5 basis in its S stock. Pursuant to a plan, S merges into T with T surviving. In the merger, the T shareholders exchange their T stock for $2 cash from P and $28 worth of P stock provided by P pursuant to the plan. The transaction is a reorganization to which sections 368(a)(1)(A) and (a)(2)(E) apply.

(b) *Basis adjustment.* Under §1.358-6, P's basis in the T stock acquired equals its $5 basis in its S stock immediately before the transaction adjusted by the $60 basis in the T assets deemed transferred, and the $70 of liabilities to which the T assets are subject. Under the rules of this section, the limitation described in §1.358-6(c)(1)(ii) does not apply. Consequently, P has an excess loss account of $5 in its T stock as a result of the transaction.

(c) *Effective/applicability date.*—This section applies to reorganizations occurring on or after December 21, 1995. However, paragraph (b)(4) of this section applies to reorganizations occurring on or after September 17, 2008. [Reg. § 1.1502-30.]

☐ [*T.D. 8648, 12-20-95. Amended by T.D. 9424, 9-9-2008.*]

**[Reg. § 1.1502-31]**

**§ 1.1502-31. Stock basis after a group structure change.**—(a) *In general.*—(1) *Overview.*—If one corporation (P) succeeds another corporation (T) under the principles of § 1.1502-75(d)(2) or (3) as the common parent of a consolidated group in a group structure change, the basis of members in the stock of the former common parent (or the stock of a successor) is adjusted or determined under this section. See § 1.1502-33(f)(1) for the definition of group structure change. For example, if P owns all of the stock of another corporation (S), and T merges into S in a group structure change that is a reorganization described in section 368(a)(2)(D) in which P becomes the common parent of the T group, P's basis in S's stock must be adjusted to reflect the change in S's assets and liabilities. The rules of this section coordinate with the earnings and profits adjustments required under § 1.1502-33(f)(1), generally conforming the results of transactions in which the T group continues under § 1.1502-75 with P as the common parent. By preserving in P the relationship between T's earnings and profits and asset basis, these adjustments limit possible distortions under section 1502 (e.g., in the deconsolidation rules for earnings and profits under § 1.1502-33(e), and the continued filing requirements under § 1.1502-75(a)). This section applies whether or not T continues to exist after the group structure change.

(2) *Application of other rules of law.*—If a transaction subject to this section is also a triangular reorganization otherwise subject to § 1.1502-30, the provisions of this section and not those of § 1.1502-30 apply to determine stock basis. See § 1.1502-80(a) regarding the general applicability of other rules of law and a limitation on duplicative adjustments.

(b) *General rules.*—Except as otherwise provided in this section—

(1) *Asset acquisitions.*—If a corporation acquires the former common parent's assets (and any liabilities assumed or to which the assets are subject) in a group structure change, the basis of members in the stock of the acquiring corporation is adjusted immediately after the group structure change to reflect the acquiring corporation's allocable share of the former common parent's net asset basis as determined under paragraph (c) of this section. For example, if S acquires all of T's assets in a group structure change that is a reorganization described in section 368(a)(2)(D), P's basis in S's stock is adjusted to reflect T's net asset basis. If P owned some of T's stock before the group structure change, the results would be the same because P's basis in the T stock is not taken into account in determining P's basis in S's stock. If T's net asset basis is a negative amount, it reduces P's basis in S's stock and, if the reduction exceeds P's basis in S's stock, the excess is P's excess loss account in S's stock. See § 1.1502-19 for rules treating P's excess loss account as negative basis, and treating a reference to P's basis in S's stock as including an excess loss account.

(2) *Stock acquisitions.*—If a corporation acquires stock of the former common parent in a group structure change, the basis of the members in the former common parent's stock immediately after the group structure change (including any stock of the former common parent owned before the group structure change) that is, or would otherwise be, transferred basis property is redetermined in accordance with the results for an asset acquisition described in paragraph (b)(1) of this section. For example, if all of T's stock is contributed to P in a group structure change to which section 351 applies, P's basis in T's stock is T's net asset basis, rather than the amount determined under section 362. Similarly, if S merges into T in a group structure change described in section 368(a)(2)(E) and P acquires all of the T stock, P's basis in T's stock is the basis that P would have in S's stock under paragraph (b)(1) of this section if T had merged into S in a group structure change described in section 368(a)(2)(D).

(c) *Net asset basis.*—The former common parent's net asset basis is the basis it would have in the stock of a newly formed subsidiary, if—

(1) The former common parent transferred its assets (and any liabilities assumed or to which the assets are subject) to the subsidiary in a transaction to which section 351 applies;

(2) The former common parent and the subsidiary were members of the same consolidated group (see § 1.1502-80(d) for the non-application of section 357(c) to the transfer); and

(3) The asset basis taken into account is each asset's basis immediately after the group structure change (e.g., taking into account any income or gain recognized in the group structure change and reflected in the asset's basis).

(d) *Additional adjustments.*—In addition to the adjustments in paragraph (b) of this section, the following adjustments are made:

(1) *Consideration not provided by P.*—The basis is reduced to reflect the fair market value of any consideration not provided by the member. For example, if S acquires T's assets in a group structure change described in section 368(a)(2)(D), and S provides an appreciated asset (e.g., stock of P) as partial consideration in the transaction, P's basis in S's stock is reduced by the fair market value of the asset.

(2) *Allocable share.*—(i) *Asset acquisitions.*—If a corporation receives less than all of the former common parent's assets and liabilities in the group structure change, the former common parent's net asset basis taken into account under paragraph (b)(1) of this section is adjusted accordingly.

(ii) *Stock acquisitions.*—If less than all of the former common parent's stock is subject to the redetermination described in paragraph (b)(2) of this section, the percentage of the former common parent's net asset basis taken into account in the redetermination equals the percentage (by fair market value) of the former common parent's stock subject to the redetermination. For example, if P owns less than all of the former common parent's stock immediately after the group structure change and such stock would otherwise be transferred basis property, only an allocable part of the basis determined under this section is reflected in the shares owned by P (and the amount allocable to shares owned by nonmembers has no effect on the basis of their shares). Alternatively, if P acquired 10 percent of the former common parent's stock in a transaction in which the stock basis was determined by P's cost, and P later acquires the remaining 90 percent of the former common parent's stock in a separate transaction that is described in paragraph (b)(2) of this section, P retains its cost basis in its original stock and the basis of P's newly acquired shares reflects only an allocable part of the former common parent's net asset basis.

(3) *Allocation among shares of stock.*—The basis determined under this section is allocated among shares under the principles of section 358. For example, if P owns multiple classes of the former common parent's stock immediately after the group structure change, only an allocable part of the basis determined under this section is reflected in the basis of each share. See § 1.1502-19(d), for special allocations with respect to excess loss accounts.

(4) *Higher-tier members.*—To the extent that the former common parent is owned by members other than the new common parent, the basis of members in the stock of all subsidiaries owning, directly or indirectly, in whole or in part, an interest in the former common parent's assets or liabilities is adjusted in accordance with the principles of this section. The adjustments are applied in the order of the tiers, from the lowest to the highest.

(e) *Waiver of loss carryovers of former common parent.*—(1) *General rule.*—An irrevocable election may be made to treat all or any portion of a loss carryover attributable to the common parent as expiring for all Federal income tax purposes immediately before the group structure change. Thus, if the loss carryover is treated as expiring under the election, it will not result in a negative adjustment to the basis of P's stock under § 1.1502-32(b).

(2) *Election.*—The election described in paragraph (e)(1) of this section must be made in a separate statement entitled, "ELECTION TO TREAT LOSS CARRYOVER AS EXPIRING UNDER § 1.1502-31(e)." The election must be filed by including the statement on or with the consolidated group's income tax return for the year that includes the group structure change. The statement must identify the amount of each loss carryover deemed to expire (or the amount of each loss carryover deemed not to expire, with any balance of any loss carryovers being deemed to expire).

(f) *Predecessors and successors.*—For purposes of this section, any reference to a corporation includes a reference to a successor or predecessor as the context may require. See § 1.1502-32(f) for definitions of predecessor and successor.

(g) *Examples.*—For purposes of the examples in this section, unless otherwise stated, all corporations have only one class of stock outstanding, the tax year of all persons is the calendar year, all persons use the accrual method of accounting, the facts set forth the only corporate activity, all transactions are between unrelated persons, and tax liabilities are disregarded. The principles of this section are illustrated by the following examples:

*Example 1. Forward triangular merger.* (i) *Facts.* P is the common parent of one group and T is the common parent of another. T has assets with an aggregate basis of $60 and fair market value of $100 and no liabilities. T's shareholders have an aggregate basis of $50 in T's stock. In Year 1, pursuant to a plan, P forms S and T merges into S with the T shareholders receiving $100 of P stock in exchange for their T stock. The transaction is a reorganization described in section 368(a)(2)(D). The transaction is also a reverse acquisition under §1.1502-75(d)(3) because the T shareholders, as a result of owning T's stock, own more than 50% of the value of P's stock immediately after the transaction. Thus, the transaction is a group structure change under §1.1502-33(f)(1), and P's earnings and profits are adjusted to reflect T's earnings and profits immediately before T ceases to be the common parent of the T group.

(ii) *Analysis.* Under paragraph (b)(1) of this section, P's basis in S's stock is adjusted to reflect T's net asset basis. Under paragraph (c) of this section, T's net asset basis is $60, the basis T would have in the stock of a subsidiary under section 358 if T had transferred all of its assets and liabilities to the subsidiary in a transaction to which section 351 applies. Thus, P has a $60 basis in S's stock.

(iii) *Pre-existing S.* The facts are the same as in paragraph (i) of this *Example 1,* except that P has owned the stock of S for several years and P has a $50 basis in the S stock before the merger with T. Under paragraph (b)(1) of this section, P's $50 basis in S's stock is adjusted to reflect T's net asset basis. Thus, P's basis in S's stock is $110 ($50 plus $60).

(iv) *Excess loss account included in former common parent's net asset basis.* The facts are the same as in paragraph (i) of this *Example 1,* except that T has two assets, an operating asset with an $80 basis and $90 fair market value, and stock of a subsidiary with a $20 excess loss account and $10 fair market value. Under paragraph (c) of this section, T's net asset basis is $60 ($80 minus $20). See sections 351 and 358, and §1.1502-19. Consequently, P has a $60 basis in S's stock. Under section 362 and §1.1502-19, S has an $80 basis in the operating asset and a $20 excess loss account in the stock of the subsidiary.

(v) *Liabilities in excess of basis.* The facts are the same as in paragraph (i) of this *Example 1,* except that T's assets have a fair market value of $170 (and $60 basis) and are subject to $70 of liabilities. Under paragraph (c) of this section, T's net asset basis is negative $10 ($60 minus $70). See sections 351 and 358, and §§1.1502-19 and 1.1502-80(d). Thus, P has a $10 excess loss account in S's stock. Under section 362, S has a $60 basis in its assets (which are subject to $70 of liabilities). (Under paragraph (a)(2) of this section, because the liabilities are taken into account in determining net asset basis under paragraph (c) of this section, the liabilities are not also taken into account as consideration not provided by P under paragraph (d)(1) of this section.)

(vi) *Consideration provided by S.* The facts are the same as in paragraph (i) of this *Example 1,* except that P forms S with a $100 contribution at the beginning of Year 1, and during Year 6, pursuant to a plan, S purchases $100 of P stock and T merges into S with the T shareholders receiving P stock in exchange for their T stock. Under paragraph (b)(1) of this section, P's $100 basis in S's stock is increased by $60 to reflect T's net asset basis. Under paragraph (d)(1) of this section, P's basis in S's stock is decreased by $100 (the fair market value of the P stock) because the P stock purchased by S and used in the transaction is consideration not provided by P.

(vii) *Appreciated asset provided by S.* The facts are the same as in paragraph (i) of this *Example 1,* except that P has owned the stock of S for several years, and the shareholders of T receive $60 of P stock and an asset of S with a $30 adjusted basis and $40 fair market value. S recognizes a $10 gain from the asset under section 1001. Under paragraph (b)(1) of this section, P's basis in S's stock is increased by $60 to reflect T's net asset basis. Under paragraph (d)(1) of this section, P's basis in S's stock is decreased by $40 (the fair market value of the asset provided by S). In addition, P's basis in S's stock is increased under §1.1502-32(b) by S's $10 gain.

(viii) *Depreciated asset provided by S.* The facts are the same as in paragraph (i) of this *Example 1,* except that P has owned the stock of S for several years, and the shareholders of T receive $60 of P stock and an asset of S with a $50 adjusted basis and $40 fair market value. S recognizes a $10 loss from the asset under section 1001. Under paragraph (b)(1) of this section, P's basis in S's stock is increased by $60 to reflect T's net asset basis. Under paragraph (d)(1) of this section, P's basis in S's stock is decreased by $40 (the fair market value of the asset provided by S). In addition, S's $10 loss is taken into account under §1.1502-32(b) in determining P's basis adjustments under that section.

*Example 2. Stock acquisition.* (i) *Facts.* P is the common parent of one group and T is the common parent of another. T has assets with an aggregate basis of $60 and fair market value of $100 and no liabilities. T's shareholders have an aggregate basis of $50 in T's stock. Pursuant to a plan, P forms S and S acquires all of T's stock in exchange for P stock in a transaction described in section 368(a)(1)(B). The transaction is also a reverse acquisition under §1.1502-75(d)(3). Thus, the transaction is a group structure change under §1.1502-33(0)(1), and the earnings and profits of P and S are adjusted to reflect T's earnings and profits immediately before T ceases to be the common parent of the T group.

(ii) *Analysis.* Under paragraph (d)(4) of this section, although S is not the new common parent of the T group, adjustments must be made to S's basis in T's stock in accordance with the principles of this section. Although S's basis in T's stock would ordinarily be determined under section 362 by reference to the basis of T's shareholders in T's stock immediately before the group structure change, under the principles of paragraph (b)(2) of this section, S's basis in T's stock is determined by reference to T's net asset basis. Thus, S's basis in T's stock is $60.

(iii) *Higher-tier adjustments.* Under paragraph (d)(4) of this section, P's basis in S's stock is increased by $60 (to be consistent with the adjustment to S's basis in T's stock).

(iv) *Cross ownership.* The facts are the same as in paragraph (i) of this *Example 2,* except S purchased 10% of T's stock from an unrelated person for cash. in an unrelated transaction, S acquires the remaining 90% of T's stock in exchange for P stock. S's basis in the initial 10% of T's stock is not redetermined under this section. However, S's basis in the additional 90% of T's stock is redetermined under this section. S's basis in that stock is adjusted to $54 (90% of T's net asset basis).

(v) *Allocable share.* The facts are the same as in paragraph (i) of this *Example 2,* except that P owns only 90% of S's stock immediately after the group structure change. S's basis in T's stock is the same as in paragraph (ii) of this *Example 2.* Under paragraph (d)(2) of this section, P's basis in its S stock is increased by $54 (90% of S's $60 adjustment).

*Example 3. Taxable stock acquisition.* (i) *Facts.* P is the common parent of one group and T is the common parent of another. T has assets with an aggregate basis of $60 and fair market value of $100 and no liabilities. T's shareholders have an aggregate basis of $50 in T's stock. Pursuant to a plan, P acquires all of T's stock in exchange for $70 of P's stock and $30 in a transaction that is a group structure change under §1.1502-33(f)(1). P's acquired T stock is not transferred basis property. (Because of P's use of cash, the acquisition is not a transaction described in section 368(a)(1)(B).)

(ii) *Analysis.* The rules of this section do not apply to determine P's basis in T's stock. Therefore, P's basis in T's stock is $100.

(h) *Effective/applicability dates.*—(1) *General rule.*—This section applies to group structure changes that occur after April 26, 2004. However, a group may apply this section to group structure changes that occurred on or before April 26, 2004, and in consolidated return years beginning on or after January 1, 1995. In addition, paragraph (a)(2) of this section applies to group structure changes that occurred on or after September 17, 2008. Paragraph (e)(2) of this section applies to any original consolidated Federal income tax return due (without extensions) after June 14, 2007. For original consolidated Federal income tax returns due (without extensions) after May 30, 2006, and on or before June 14, 2007, see §1.1502-31T as contained in 26 CFR part 1 in effect on April 1, 2007. For original consolidated Federal income tax returns due (without extensions) on or before May 30, 2006, see §1.1502-31 as contained in 26 CFR part 1 in effect on April 1, 2006.

(2) *Prior law.*—For group structure changes that occur on or before April 26, 2004, and in consolidated return years beginning on or after January 1, 1995, with respect to which the group does not elect to apply the provisions of this section, see §1.1502-31 as contained in the 26 CFR part 1 edition revised as of April 1, 2003. For group structure changes that occur in consolidated return years beginning before January 1, 1995, see §1.1502-31T as contained in the 26 CFR part 1 edition revised as of April 1, 1994. [Reg. §1.1502-31.]

☐ [*T.D. 6909,* 12-29-66. *Amended by T.D. 7246,* 12-29-72; *T.D. 8226,* 9-7-88; *T.D. 8560,* 8-12-94; *T.D. 9122,* 4-23-2004; *T.D. 9264,* 5-26-2006; *T.D. 9329,* 6-13-2007 *and T.D. 9424,* 9-9-2008.]

## [Reg. §1.1502-32]

**§1.1502-32. Investment adjustments.**—(a) *In general.*—(1) *Purpose.*—This section provides rules for adjusting the basis of the stock of a subsidiary (S) owned by another member (M). These rules modify the determination of M's basis in S's stock under applicable rules of law by adjusting M's basis to reflect S's distributions and S's items of income, gain, deduction, and loss taken into account for the period that S is a member of the consolidated group. The purpose of the adjustments is to treat M and S as a single entity so that consolidated taxable income reflects the group's income. For example, if M forms S with a $100 contribution, and S takes into account $10 of income, M's $100 basis in S's stock under section 358 is increased by $10 under this section to prevent S's income from being taken into account a second time on M's disposition of S's stock. Comparable adjustments are made for tax-exempt income and noncapital, nondeductible expenses that S takes into account, to preserve their treatment under the Internal Revenue Code.

(2) *Application of other rules of law, duplicative adjustments.*—See §1.1502-80(a) regarding the general applicability of other rules of law

and a limitation on duplicative adjustments. The rules of this section are in addition to other rules of law. See, e.g., section 358 (basis determinations for distributees), section 1016 (adjustments to basis), §1.1502-11(b) (limitations on the use of losses), §1.1502-19 (treatment of excess loss accounts), §1.1502-31 (basis after a group structure change), and §1.1502-35 (additional rules relating to stock loss, including losses attributable to worthlessness and certain dispositions not followed by a separate return year). M's basis in S's stock must not be adjusted under this section and other rules of law in a manner that has the effect of duplicating an adjustment.

(3) *Overview.*—(i) *In general.*—The amount of the stock basis adjustments and their timing are determined under paragraph (b) of this section. Under paragraph (c) of this section, the amount of the adjustment is allocated among the shares of S's stock. Paragraphs (d) through (g) of this section provide definitions, an anti-avoidance rule, successor rules, and recordkeeping requirements.

(ii) *Excess loss account.*—Negative adjustments under this section may exceed M's basis in S's stock. The resulting negative amount is M's excess loss account in S's stock. See §1.1502-19 for rules treating excess loss accounts as negative basis, and treating references to stock basis as including references to excess loss accounts.

(iii) *Tiering up of adjustments.*—The adjustments to S's stock under this section are taken into account in determining adjustments to higher-tier stock. The adjustments are applied in the order of the tiers, from the lowest to the highest. For example, if M is also a subsidiary, M's adjustment to S's stock is taken into account in determining the adjustments to stock of M owned by other members.

(b) *Stock basis adjustments.*—(1) *Timing of adjustments.*—(i) *In general.*—Adjustments under this section are made as of the close of each consolidated return year, and as of any other time (an interim adjustment) if a determination at that time is necessary to determine a tax liability of any person. For example, adjustments are made as of M's sale of S's stock in order to measure M's gain or loss from the sale, and if M's interest in S's stock is not uniform throughout the year (e.g., because M disposes of a portion of its S stock, or S issues additional shares to another person), the adjustments under this section are made by taking into account the varying interests. An interim adjustment may be necessary even if tax liability is not affected until a later time. For example, if M sells only 50% of S's stock and S becomes a nonmember, adjustments must be made for the retained stock as of the disposition (whether or not M has an excess loss account in that stock). Similarly, if S liquidates during a consolidated return year, adjustments must be made as of the liquidation (even if the liquidation is tax free under section 332).

(ii) *Special rule for discharge of indebtedness income.*—Adjustments under this section resulting from the realization of discharge of indebtedness income of a member that is excluded from gross income under section 108(a) (excluded COD income) and from the reduction of attributes in respect thereof pursuant to sections 108 and 1017 and §1.1502-28 (including reductions in the basis of property) when a member (the departing member) ceases to be a member of the group on or prior to the last day of the consolidated return year that includes the date the excluded COD income is realized are made immediately after the determination of tax for the group for the taxable year during which the excluded COD income is realized (and any prior years) and are effective immediately before the beginning of the taxable year of the departing member following the taxable year during which the excluded COD income is realized. Such adjustments when a corporation (the new member) is not a member of the group on the last day of the consolidated return year that includes the date the excluded COD income is realized but is a member of the group at the beginning of the following consolidated return year are also made immediately after the determination of tax for the group for the taxable year during which the excluded COD income is realized (and any prior years) and are effective immediately before the beginning of the taxable year of the new member following the taxable year during which the excluded COD income is realized. If the new member was a member of another group immediately before it became a member of the group, such adjustments are treated as occurring immediately after it ceases to be a member of the prior group.

(iii) *Allocation of items.*—If §1.1502-76(b) applies to S for purposes of an adjustment before the close of the group's consolidated return year, the amount of the adjustment is determined under that section. If §1.1502-76(b) does not apply to the interim adjustment, the adjustment is determined under the principles of §1.1502-76(b), consistently applied, and ratable allocation under the principles of §1.1502-76(b)(2)(ii) or (iii) may be used without filing an election under §1.1502-76(b)(2). The principles would apply, for example, if M becomes a nonmember but S remains a member.

(2) *Amount of adjustments.*—M's basis in S's stock is increased by positive adjustments and decreased by negative adjustments under this paragraph (b)(2). The amount of the adjustment, determined as of the time of the adjustment, is the net amount of S's—

(i) Taxable income or loss;

(ii) Tax-exempt income;

(iii) Noncapital, nondeductible expenses; and

(iv) Distributions with respect to S's stock.

(3) *Operating rules.*—For purposes of determining M's adjustments to the basis of S's stock under paragraph (b)(2) of this section—

(i) *Taxable income or loss.*—S's taxable income or loss is consolidated taxable income (or loss) determined by including only S's items of income, gain, deduction, and loss taken into account in determining consolidated taxable income (or loss), treating S's deductions and losses as taken into account to the extent they are absorbed by S or any other member. For this purpose:

(A) To the extent that S's deduction or loss is absorbed in the year it arises or is carried forward and absorbed in a subsequent year (e.g., under section 172, 465, or 1212), the deduction or loss is taken into account under paragraph (b)(2) of this section in the year in which it is absorbed.

(B) To the extent that S's deduction or loss is carried back and absorbed in a prior year (whether consolidated or separate), the deduction or loss is taken into account under paragraph (b)(2) of this section in the year in which it arises and not in the year in which it is absorbed.

(ii) *Tax-exempt income.*—(A) *In general.*—S's tax-exempt income is its income and gain which is taken into account but permanently excluded from its gross income under applicable law, and which increases, directly or indirectly, the basis of its assets (or an equivalent amount). For example, S's dividend income to which §1.1502-13(f)(2)(ii) applies, and its interest excluded from gross income under section 103, are treated as tax-exempt income. However, S's income not recognized under section 1031 is not treated as tax-exempt income because the corresponding basis adjustments under section 1031(d) prevent S's nonrecognition from being permanent. Similarly, S's tax-exempt income does not include gain not recognized under section 332 from the liquidation of a lower-tier subsidiary, or not recognized under section 118 or section 351 from a transfer of assets to S.

(B) *Equivalent deductions.*—To the extent that S's taxable income or gain is permanently offset by a deduction or loss that does not reduce, directly or indirectly, the basis of S's assets (or an equivalent amount), the income or gain is treated as tax-exempt income and is taken into account under paragraph (b)(3)(ii)(A) of this section. In addition, the income and the offsetting item are taken into account under paragraph (b)(3)(i) of this section. For example, if S receives a $100 dividend with respect to which a $70 dividends received deduction is allowed under section 243, $70 of the dividend is treated as tax-exempt income. Accordingly, M's basis in S's stock increases by $100 because the $100 dividend and $70 deduction are taken into account under paragraph (b)(3)(i) of this section (resulting in $30 of the increase), and $70 of the dividend is also taken into account under paragraph (b)(3)(ii)(A) of this section as tax-exempt income (resulting in $70 of the increase). (See paragraph (b)(3)(iii) of this section if there is a corresponding negative adjustment under section 1059.) Similarly, income from mineral properties is treated as tax-exempt income to the extent it is offset by deductions for depletion in excess of the basis of the property.

(C) *Discharge of indebtedness income.*—(1) *In general.*—Excluded COD income is treated as tax-exempt income only to the extent the discharge is applied to reduce tax attributes attributable to any member of the group under section 108, section 1017 or §1.1502-28. However, if S is treated as realizing excluded COD income pursuant to §1.1502-28(a)(3), S shall not be treated as realizing excluded COD income for purposes of the preceding sentence.

(2) *Expired loss carryovers.*—If the amount of the discharge exceeds the amount of the attribute reduction under sections 108 and 1017, and §1.1502-28, the excess nevertheless is treated as applied to reduce tax attributes to the extent a loss carryover attributable to S expired without tax benefit, the expiration was taken into account as a noncapital, nondeductible expense under paragraph (b)(3)(iii) of this section, and the loss carryover would have been reduced had it not expired.

(D) *Basis shifts.*—An increase in the basis of S's assets (or an equivalent as described in paragraph (b)(3)(iv)(B) of this section) is treated as tax-exempt income to the extent that the increase is not otherwise taken into account in determining stock basis, it corresponds to a negative adjustment that is taken into account by the group under this paragraph (b) (or incurred by the common parent), and it has the effect (viewing the group in the aggregate) of a permanent recovery of the reduction. For example, S's basis increase under section 50(c)(2) is treated as tax-exempt income to the extent the preceding basis reduction under section 50(c)(1) is reflected in the basis of a member's stock. On the other hand, if S increases the basis of an asset as the result of an accounting method change, and the related positive section 481(a) adjustment is taken into account over time, the basis increase is not treated as tax-exempt income.

(E) [Reserved]

(iii) *Noncapital, nondeductible expenses.*—(A) *In general.*—S's noncapital, nondeductible expenses are its deductions and losses that are taken into account but permanently disallowed or eliminated under applicable law in determining its taxable income or loss, and that decrease, directly or indirectly, the basis of its assets (or an equivalent amount). For example, S's Federal taxes described in section 275 and loss not recognized under section 311(a) are noncapital, nondeductible expenses. Similarly, if a loss carryover (e.g., under section 172 or 1212) attributable to S expires or is reduced under section 108(b) and § 1.1502-28, it becomes a noncapital, nondeductible expense at the close of the last tax year to which it may be carried. However, when a tax attribute attributable to S is reduced as required pursuant to § 1.1502-28(a)(3), the reduction of the tax attribute is not treated as a noncapital, nondeductible expense of S. Finally, if S sells and repurchases a security subject to section 1091, the disallowed loss is not a noncapital, nondeductible expense because the corresponding basis adjustments under section 1091(d) prevent the disallowance from being permanent.

(B) *Nondeductible basis recovery.*—Any other decrease in the basis of S's assets (or an equivalent as described in paragraph (b)(3)(iv)(B) of this section) may be a noncapital, nondeductible expense to the extent that the decrease is not otherwise taken into account in determining stock basis and is permanently eliminated for purposes of determining S's taxable income or loss. Whether a decrease is so treated is determined by taking into account both the purposes of the Code or regulatory provision resulting in the decrease and the purposes of this section. For example, S's noncapital, nondeductible expenses include any basis reduction under section 50(c)(1), section 1017, section 1059, § 1.1502-35(b) or (f)(2). Also included as a noncapital, nondeductible expense is the amount of any gross-up for taxes paid by another taxpayer that S is treated as having paid (e.g., income included under section 78, or the portion of an undistributed capital gain dividend that is treated as tax deemed to have been paid by a shareholder under section 852(b)(3)(D)(ii), whether or not any corresponding amount is claimed as a tax credit). In contrast, a decrease generally is not a noncapital, nondeductible expense if it results because S redeems stock in a transaction to which section 302(a) applies, S receives assets in a liquidation to which section 332 applies and its basis in the assets is less than its basis in the stock canceled, or S distributes the stock of a subsidiary in a distribution to which section 355 applies.

(C) [Reserved]

(iv) *Special rules for tax-exempt income and noncapital, nondeductible expenses.*—For purposes of paragraphs (b)(3)(ii) and (iii) of this section:

(A) *Treatment as permanent.*—An amount is permanently excluded from gross income, or permanently disallowed or eliminated, if it is so treated by S even though another person may take a corresponding amount into account. For example, if S sells property to a nonmember at a loss that is disallowed under section 267(a), S's loss is a noncapital, nondeductible expense even though under section 267(d) the nonmember may treat a corresponding amount of gain as not recognized. (If the nonmember is a subsidiary in another consolidated group, its gain not recognized under section 267(d) is tax-exempt income under paragraph (b)(3)(ii)(A) of this section.)

(B) *Amounts equivalent to basis and adjustments to basis.*—Amounts equivalent to basis include the amount of money, the amount of a loss carryover, and the amount of an adjustment to gain or loss under section 475(a) for securities described in section 475(a)(2). An equivalent to a basis increase includes a decrease in an excess loss account, and an equivalent to a basis decrease includes the denial of basis for taxable income.

(C) *Timing.*—An amount is taken into account in the year in which it would be taken into account under paragraph (b)(3)(i) of this section if it were subject to Federal income taxation.

(D) *Tax sharing agreements.*—Taxes are taken into account by applying the principles of section 1552 and the percentage method under § 1.1502-33(d)(3) (and by assuming a 100% allocation of any decreased tax liability). The treatment of amounts allocated under this paragraph (b)(3)(iv)(D) is analogous to the treatment of alloca-

tions under § 1.1552-1(b)(2). For example, if one member owes a payment to a second member, the first member is treated as indebted to the second member. The right to receive payment is treated as a positive adjustment under paragraph (b)(3)(ii) of this section, and the obligation to make payment is treated as a negative adjustment under paragraph (b)(3)(iii) of this section. If the obligation is not paid, the amount not paid generally is treated as a distribution, contribution, or both, depending on the relationship between the members.

(v) *Distributions.*—Distributions taken into account under paragraph (b)(2) of this section are distributions with respect to S's stock to which section 301 applies and all other distributions treated as dividends (e.g., under section 356(a)(2)). See § 1.1502-13(f)(2)(iv) for taking into account distributions to which section 301 applies (but not other distributions treated as dividends) under the entitlement rule.

(4) *Waiver of loss carryovers from separate return limitation years.*—(i) *General rule.*—If S has a loss carryover from a separate return limitation year when it becomes a member of a consolidated group, the group may make an irrevocable election to treat all or any portion of the loss carryover as expiring for all Federal income tax purposes immediately before S becomes a member of the consolidated group (deemed expiration). If S was a member of another group immediately before it became a member of the consolidated group, the expiration is also treated as occurring immediately after it ceases to be a member of the prior group.

(ii) *Stock basis adjustments from a waiver.*—(A) *Qualifying transactions.*—If S becomes a member of the consolidated group in a qualifying cost basis transaction and an election under this paragraph (b)(4) is made, the noncapital, nondeductible expense resulting from the deemed expiration does not result in a corresponding stock basis adjustment for any member under this section. A qualifying cost basis transaction is the purchase (i.e., a transaction in which basis is determined under section 1012) by members of the acquiring consolidated group (while they are members) in a 12-month period of an amount of S's stock satisfying the requirements of section 1504(a)(2).

(B) *Nonqualifying transactions.*—If S becomes a member of the consolidated group other than in a qualifying cost basis transaction and an election under this paragraph (b)(4) is made, the basis of its stock that is owned by members immediately after it becomes a member is subject to reduction under the principles of this section to reflect the deemed expiration. The reduction occurs immediately before S becomes a member, but after it ceases to be a member of any prior group, and it therefore does not result in a corresponding stock basis adjustment for any higher-tier member of the transferring or acquiring consolidated group. Any basis reduction under this paragraph (b)(4)(ii)(B) is taken into account in making determinations of basis under the Code with respect to S's stock (e.g., a determination under section 362 because the stock is acquired in a transaction described in section 368(a)(1)(B)), but it does not result in corresponding stock basis adjustments under this section for any higher-tier member. If the basis reduction exceeds the basis of S's stock, the excess is treated as an excess loss account to which the members owning S's stock succeed.

(C) *Higher-tier corporations.*—If S becomes a member of the consolidated group as a result, in whole or in part, of a higher-tier corporation becoming a member (whether or not in a qualifying cost basis transaction), additional adjustments are required. The highest-tier corporation (T) whose becoming a member resulted in S becoming a member, and T's chain of lower-tier corporations that includes S, are subject to the adjustment. The deemed expiration of S's loss carryover that results in a negative adjustment for the first higher-tier corporation is treated as an expiring loss carryover of that higher-tier corporation for purposes of applying paragraph (b)(4)(ii)(B) of this section to that corporation. For example, if M purchases all of the stock of T, T owns all of the stock of T1, T1 owns all of the stock of S, S becomes a member as a result of T becoming a member, and the election under this paragraph (b)(4) is made, the basis of the S stock is reduced and the reduction tiers up to T1, T1 treats the negative adjustment to its basis in S's stock as an expiring loss carryover of T1, and T then adjusts its basis in T1's stock. In addition, if T becomes a member of the acquiring group in a transaction other than a qualifying cost basis transaction, the amount that tiers up to T also reduces the basis of its stock under paragraph (b)(4)(ii)(B) of this section (but the amount does not tier up to higher-tier members).

(iii) *Net asset basis limitation.*—Basis reduced under this paragraph (b)(4) is restored before S becomes a member (and before the basis of S's stock is taken into account in determining basis under the Code) to the extent necessary to conform a share's basis to its allocable portion of net asset basis. In the case of higher-tier corpora-

**Reg. § 1.1502-32(b)(4)(iii)**

tions under paragraph (b)(4)(ii)(C) of this section, the restoration does not tier up but is instead applied separately to each higher-tier corporation. For purposes of determining each corporation's net asset basis (including the basis of stock in lower-tier corporations), the restoration is applied in the order of tiers, from the lowest to the highest. For purposes of the restoration:

(A) A member's net asset basis is the positive or negative difference between the adjusted basis of its assets (and the amount of any of its loss carryovers that are not deemed to expire) and its liabilities. Appropriate adjustments must be made, for example, to disregard liabilities that subsequently will give rise to deductions (e.g., liabilities to which section 461(h) applies).

(B) Within a class of stock, each share has the same allocable portion of net asset basis. If there is more than one class of common stock, the net asset basis is allocated to each class by taking into account the terms of each class and all other facts and circumstances relating to the overall economic arrangement.

(iv) *Election.*—The election described in paragraph (b)(4) of this section must be made in a separate statement entitled, "ELECTION TO TREAT LOSS CARRYOVER OF [INSERT NAME AND EMPLOYER IDENTIFICATION NUMBER OF S] AS EXPIRING UNDER §1.1502-32(b)(4)." The election must be filed by including a statement on or with the consolidated group's income tax return for the year S becomes a member. A separate statement must be made for each member whose loss carryover is deemed to expire. The statement must identify the amount of each loss carryover deemed to expire (or the amount of each loss carryover deemed not to expire, with any balance of any loss carryovers being deemed to expire) and the basis of any stock reduced as a result of the deemed expiration.

(v) *Special rule for loss carryovers of a subsidiary acquired in a transaction for which an election under §1.1502-20(i)(2) is made.*—(A) *Expired losses.*—Notwithstanding paragraph (b)(4)(iv) of this section, unless a group otherwise chooses, to the extent that S's loss carryovers are increased by reason of an election under §1.1502-20(i)(2) and such loss carryovers expire or would have been properly used to offset income in a taxable year for which the refund of an overpayment is prevented by any law or rule of law as of the date the group files its original return for the taxable year in which S receives the notification described in §1.1502-20(i)(3)(iv) and at all times thereafter, the group will be deemed to have made an election under paragraph (b)(4) of this section to treat all of such loss carryovers as expiring for all Federal income tax purposes immediately before S became a member of the consolidated group. A group may choose not to apply the rule of the previous sentence to all of such loss carryovers of S by taking a position on an original or amended tax return for each relevant taxable year that is consistent with having made such choice.

(B) *Available losses.*—Notwithstanding paragraph (b)(4)(iv) of this section, to the extent that S's loss carryovers are increased by reason of an election under §1.1502-20(i)(2) and such loss carryovers have not expired and would not have been properly used to offset income in a taxable year for which the refund of an overpayment is prevented by any law or rule of law as of the date the group files its original return for the taxable year in which S receives the notification described in §1.1502-20(i)(3)(iv) and at all times thereafter, the group may make an election under paragraph (b)(4) of this section to treat all or a portion of such loss carryovers as expiring for all Federal income tax purposes immediately before S became a member of the consolidated group. Such election must be filed with the group's original return for the taxable year in which S receives the notification described in §1.1502-20(i)(3)(iv).

(C) *Effective dates.*—Paragraph (b)(4)(v) of this section is applicable on and after March 3, 2005. For prior periods, see §1.1502-32T(b)(4)(v) as contained in the 26 CFR part 1 in effect on March 2, 2005.

(vi) *Special rules in the case of certain transactions subject to §1.1502-35.*—If a member of a consolidated group transfers stock of a subsidiary and such stock has a basis that exceeds its value immediately before such transfer or a subsidiary is deconsolidated and any stock of such subsidiary owned by members of the group immediately before such deconsolidation has a basis that exceeds its value, all members of the group are subject to the provisions of §1.1502-35(b), which generally require a redetermination of members' basis in all shares of subsidiary stock.

(vii) *Special rules for amending waiver of loss carryovers from separate return limitation year.*—(A) *Waivers that increased allowable loss or reduced basis reduction required.*—If, in connection with the acquisition of S, the group made an election pursuant to paragraph (b)(4) of this section to treat all or any portion of S's loss carryovers as expiring, and the prior group elected to determine the amount of the allowable loss or the basis reduction required with respect to the stock of S or a higher-tier corporation of S by applying the provisions described in §1.1502-20(i)(2)(i) or (ii), then the group may reduce the amount of any loss carryover deemed to expire (or increase the amount of any loss carryover deemed not to expire) as a result of the election made pursuant to paragraph (b)(4) of this section. The aggregate amount of loss carryovers that may be treated as not expiring as a result of amendments made pursuant to this paragraph (b)(4)(vii)(A) with respect to S and any higher-and lower-tier corporation of S may not exceed the amount described in §1.1502-20(c)(1)(iii) with respect to the acquired stock (computed without regard to the effect of the group's election or elections pursuant to paragraph (b)(4) of this section, but with regard to the effect of the prior group's election pursuant to §1.1502-20(g), if any, prior to the application of §1.1502-20(i)(3)). For purposes of determining the aggregate amount of loss carryovers that may be treated as not expiring as a result of amendments made pursuant to this paragraph (b)(4)(vii)(A) with respect to S and any higher- and lower-tier corporation of S, the group may rely on a written notification provided by the prior group. Nothing in this paragraph shall be construed as permitting a group to increase the amount of any loss carryover deemed to expire (or reduce the amount of any loss carryover deemed not to expire) as a result of the election made pursuant to paragraph (b)(4) of this section.

(B) *Inadvertent waivers of loss carryovers previously subject to an election described in §1.1502-20(g).*—If, in connection with the acquisition of S, the group made an election pursuant to paragraph (b)(4) of this section to waive loss carryovers of S by identifying the amount of each loss carryover deemed not to expire, the prior group elected to determine the amount of the allowable loss or the basis reduction required with respect to the stock of S or a higher-tier corporation of S by applying the provisions described in §1.1502-20(i)(2)(i) or (ii), and the amount of S's loss carryovers treated as reattributed to the prior group pursuant to the election described in §1.1502-20(g) is reduced pursuant to §1.1502-20(i)(3), then the group may amend its election made pursuant to paragraph (b)(4) of this section to provide that all or a portion of the loss carryovers of S that are treated as loss carryovers of S as a result of the prior group's election to apply the provisions described in §1.1502-20(i)(2)(i) or (ii) are deemed not to expire. This paragraph (b)(4)(vii)(B), however, does not permit a group to reduce the amount of any loss carryover deemed not to expire as a result of the election made pursuant to paragraph (b)(4) of this section.

(C) *Time and manner of amending an election under §1.1502-32(b)(4).*—The amendment of an election made pursuant to paragraph (b)(4) of this section must be made in a statement entitled *Amendment of Election to Treat Loss Carryover as Expiring Under §1.1502-32(b)(4) Pursuant to §1.1502-32(b)(4)(vii).* The statement must be filed with or as part of any timely filed (including extensions) original return for the taxable year that includes August 26, 2004, or with or as part of an amended return filed before the date the original return for the taxable year that includes August 26, 2004, is due (with regard to extensions). A separate statement shall be filed for each election made pursuant to paragraph (b)(4) of this section that is being amended pursuant to this paragraph (b)(4)(vii). For purposes of making this statement, the group may rely on the statements set forth in a written notification provided by the prior group. The statement filed under this paragraph must include the following—

(1) The name and employer identification number (E.I.N.) of S;

(2) In the case of an amendment made pursuant to paragraph (b)(4)(vii)(A), a statement that the group has received a written notification from the prior group confirming that the group's prior election or elections pursuant to paragraph (b)(4) of this section had the effect of either increasing the prior group's allowable loss on the disposition of subsidiary stock or reducing the prior group's amount of basis reduction required;

(3) The amount of each loss carryover of S deemed to expire (or the amount of loss carryover deemed not to expire) as set forth in the election made pursuant to paragraph (b)(4) of this section;

(4) The amended amount of each loss carryover of S deemed to expire (or the amended amount of loss carryover deemed not to expire); and

(5) In the case of an amendment made pursuant to paragraph (b)(4)(vii)(A) of this section, a statement that the aggregate amount of loss carryovers of S and any higher- and lower-tier corporation of S that will be treated as not expiring as a result of amendments made pursuant to paragraph (b)(4)(vii)(A) of this section will not exceed the amount described in §1.1502-20(c)(1)(iii) with respect to the acquired stock (computed without regard to the effect of the group's election or elections pursuant to paragraph (b)(4) of this section, but with regard to the effect of the prior group's election

pursuant to § 1.1502-20(g), if any, prior to the application of § 1.1502-20(i)(3)).

(D) *Items taken into account in open years.*—An amendment to an election made pursuant to paragraph (b)(4) of this section affects the group's items of income, gain, deduction, or loss only to the extent that the amendment gives rise, directly or indirectly, to items or amounts that would properly be taken into account in a year for which an assessment of deficiency or a refund for overpayment, as the case may be, is not prevented by any law or rule of law. Under this paragraph, if the year to which a loss previously deemed to expire as a result of an election made pursuant to paragraph (b)(4) of this section is deemed not to expire as a result of an election made pursuant to this paragraph would have been carried back or carried forward is a year for which a refund of overpayment is prevented by law, then to the extent that the absorption of such loss in such year would have affected the tax treatment of another item (e.g., another loss that was absorbed in such year) that has an effect in a year for which a refund of overpayment is not prevented by any law or rule of law, the amendment to the election made pursuant to paragraph (b)(4) of this section will affect the treatment of such other item. Therefore, if the absorption of such loss (the first loss) in a year for which a refund of overpayment is prevented by law would have prevented the absorption of another loss (the second loss) in such year and such second loss would have been carried to and used in a year for which a refund of overpayment is not prevented by any law or rule of law (the other year), the amendment of the election makes the second loss available for use in the other year.

(E) *Higher-and lower-tier corporations of S.*—A *higher-tier corporation of S* is a corporation that was a member of the prior group and, as a result of such higher-tier corporation becoming a member of the group; S became a member of the group. A *lower-tier corporation of S* is a corporation that was a member of the prior group and became a member of the group as a result of S becoming a member of the group.

(F) *Effective date.*—This paragraph (b)(4)(vii) is applicable on and after March 3, 2005. For prior periods, see § 1.1502-32T(b)(4)(vii) as contained in the 26 CFR part 1 in effect on March 2, 2005.

(5) *Examples.*—(i) *In general.*—For purposes of the examples in this section, unless otherwise stated, M owns all of the only class of S's stock, the stock is owned for the entire year, S owns no stock of lower-tier members, the tax year of all persons is the calendar year, all persons use the accrual method of accounting, the facts set forth the only corporate activity, preferred stock is described in section 1504(a)(4), all transactions are between unrelated persons, and tax liabilities are disregarded.

(ii) *Stock basis adjustments.*—The principles of this paragraph (b) are illustrated by the following examples.

*Example 1. Taxable income.* (a) *Current taxable income.* For Year 1, the M group has $100 of taxable income when determined by including only S's items of income, gain, deduction, and loss taken into account. Under paragraph (b)(1) of this section, M's basis in S's stock is adjusted under this section as of the close of Year 1. Under paragraph (b)(2) of this section, M's basis in S's stock is increased by the amount of the M group's taxable income determined by including only S's items taken into account. Thus, M's basis in S's stock is increased by $100 as of the close of Year 1.

(b) *Intercompany gain that is not taken into account.* The facts are the same as in paragraph (a) of this *Example 1,* except that S also sells property to another member at a $25 gain in Year 1, the gain is deferred under § 1.1502-13 and taken into account in Year 3, and M sells 10% of S's stock to nonmembers in Year 2. Under paragraph (b)(3)(i) of this section, S's deferred gain is not additional taxable income for Year 1 or 2 because it is not taken into account in determining the M group's consolidated taxable income for either of those years. The deferred gain is not tax-exempt income under paragraph (b)(3)(ii) of this section because it is not permanently excluded from S's gross income. The deferred gain does not result in a basis adjustment until Year 3, when it is taken into account in determining the M group's consolidated taxable income. Consequently, M's basis in the S shares sold is not increased to reflect S's gain from the intercompany sale of the property. In Year 3, the deferred gain is taken into account, but the amount allocable to the shares sold by M does not increase their basis because these shares are held by nonmembers.

(c) *Intercompany gain taken into account.* The facts are the same as in paragraph (b) of this *Example 1,* except that M sells all of S's stock in Year 2 (rather than only 10%). Under § 1.1502-13, S takes the $25 gain into account immediately before S becomes a nonmember. Thus, M's basis in S's stock is increased to reflect S's gain from the intercompany sale of the property.

*Example 2. Tax loss.* (a) *Current absorption.* For Year 2, the M group has a $50 consolidated net operating loss when determined by taking into account only S's items of income, gain, deduction, and loss. S's loss is absorbed by the M group in Year 2, offsetting M's income for that year. Under paragraph (b)(3)(i)(A) of this section, because S's loss is absorbed in the year it arises, M has a $50 negative adjustment with respect to S's stock. Under paragraph (b)(2) of this section, M reduces its basis in S's stock by $50. Under paragraph (a)(3)(ii) of this section, if the decrease exceeds M's basis in S's stock, the excess is M's excess loss account in S's stock.

(b) *Interim determination from stock sale.* The facts are the same as in paragraph (a) of this *Example 2,* except that S's Year 2 loss arises in the first half of the calendar year, M sells 50% of S's stock on July 1 of Year 2, and M's income for Year 2 does not arise until after the sale of S's stock. M's income for Year 2 (exclusive of the sale of S's stock) is offset by S's loss, even though the income arises after the stock sale, and no loss remains to be apportioned to S. See § § 1.1502-11 and 1.1502-21(b). Under paragraph (b)(3)(i)(A) of this section, because S's $50 loss is absorbed in the year it arises, it reduces M's basis in the S shares sold by $25 immediately before the stock sale. Because S becomes a nonmember, the loss also reduces M's basis in the retained S shares by $25 immediately before S becomes a nonmember.

(c) *Loss carryback.* The facts are the same as in paragraph (a) of this *Example 2,* except that M has no income or loss for Year 2, S's $50 loss is carried back and absorbed by the M group in Year 1 (offsetting the income of M or S), and the M group receives a $17 tax refund in Year 2 that is paid to S. Under paragraph (b)(3)(i)(B) of this section, because the $50 loss is carried back and absorbed in Year 1, it is treated as a tax loss for Year 2 (the year in which it arises). Under paragraph (b)(3)(ii) of this section, the refund is treated as tax-exempt income of S. Under paragraph (b)(3)(iv)(C) of this section, the tax-exempt income is taken into account in Year 2 because that is the year it would be taken into account under S's method of accounting if it were subject to Federal income taxation. Thus, under paragraph (b)(2) of this section, M reduces its basis in S's stock by $33 as of the close of Year 2 (the $50 tax loss, less the $17 tax refund).

(d) *Loss carryforward.* The facts are the same as in paragraph (a) of this *Example 2,* except that M has no income or loss for Year 2, and S's loss is carried forward and absorbed by the M group in Year 3 (offsetting the income of M or S). Under paragraph (b)(3)(i)(A) of this section, the loss is not treated as a tax loss under paragraph (b)(2) of this section until Year 3.

*Example 3. Tax-exempt income and noncapital, nondeductible expenses.* (a) *Facts.* For Year 1, the M group has $500 of consolidated taxable income. However, the M group has a $100 consolidated net operating loss when determined by including only S's items of income, gain, deduction, and loss taken into account. Also for Year 1, S has $80 of interest income that is permanently excluded from gross income under section 103, and S incurs $60 of related expense for which a deduction is permanently disallowed under section 265.

(b) *Analysis.* Under paragraph (b)(3)(i)(A) of this section, S has a $100 tax loss for Year 1. Under paragraph (b)(3)(ii)(A) of this section, S has $80 of tax-exempt income. Under paragraph (b)(3)(iii)(A) of this section, S has $60 of noncapital, nondeductible expense. Under paragraph (b)(3)(iv)(C) of this section, the tax-exempt income and noncapital, nondeductible expense are taken into account in Year 1 because that is the year they would be taken into account under S's method of accounting if they were subject to Federal income taxation. Thus, under paragraph (b) of this section, M reduces its basis in S's stock as of the close of Year 1 by an $80 net amount (the $100 tax loss, less $80 of tax-exempt income, plus $60 of noncapital, nondeductible expenses).

*Example 4. Discharge of indebtedness.* (a) *Facts.* M forms S on January 1 of Year 1 and S borrows $200. During Year 1, S's assets decline in value and the M group has a $100 consolidated net operating loss. Of that amount, $10 is attributable to M and $90 is attributable to S under the principles of § 1.1502-21(b)(2)(iv). None of the loss is absorbed by the group in Year 1, and S is discharged from $100 of indebtedness at the close of Year 1. M has a $0 basis in the S stock. M and S have no attributes other than the consolidated net operating loss. Under section 108(a), S's $100 of discharge of indebtedness income is excluded from gross income because of insolvency. Under section 108(b) and § 1.1502-28, the consolidated net operating loss is reduced to $0.

(b) *Analysis.* Under paragraph (b)(3)(iii)(A) of this section, the reduction of $90 of the consolidated net operating loss attributable to S is treated as a noncapital, nondeductible expense in Year 1 because that loss is permanently disallowed by section 108(b) and § 1.1502-28. Under paragraph (b)(3)(ii)(C)(1) of this section, all $100 of S's discharge of indebtedness income is treated as tax-exempt income in Year 1 because the discharge results in a $100 reduction to the consolidated net operating loss. Consequently, the loss and the cancellation of the indebtedness result in a net positive $10 adjustment to M's basis in its S stock.

(c) *Insufficient attributes*. The facts are the same as in paragraph (a) of this *Example 4*, except that S is discharged from $120 of indebtedness at the close of Year 1. Under section 108(a), S's $120 of discharge of indebtedness income is excluded from gross income because of insolvency. Under section 108(b) and §1.1502-28, the consolidated net operating loss is reduced by $100 to $0 after the determination of tax for Year 1. Under paragraph (b)(3)(iii)(A) of this section, the reduction of $90 of the consolidated net operating loss attributable to S is treated as a noncapital, nondeductible expense. Under paragraph (b)(3)(ii)(C)(*1*) of this section, only $100 of the discharge is treated as tax-exempt income because only that amount is applied to reduce tax attributes. The remaining $20 of discharge of indebtedness income excluded from gross income under section 108(a) has no effect on M's basis in S's stock.

(d) *Purchase price adjustment*. Assume instead that S buys land in Year 1 in exchange for S's $100 purchase money note (bearing interest at a market rate of interest in excess of the applicable Federal rate, and providing for a principal payment at the end of Year 10), and the seller agrees with S in Year 4 to discharge $60 of the note as a purchase price adjustment to which section 108(e)(5) applies. S has no discharge of indebtedness income that is treated as tax-exempt income under paragraph (b)(3)(ii) of this section. In addition, the $60 purchase price adjustment is not a noncapital, nondeductible expense under paragraph (b)(3)(iii) of this section. A purchase price adjustment is not equivalent to a discharge of indebtedness that is offset by a deduction or loss. Consequently, the purchase price adjustment results in no net adjustment to M's basis in S's stock under paragraph (b) of this section.

*Example 5. Distributions.* (a) *Amounts declared and distributed.* For Year 1, the M group has $120 of consolidated taxable income when determined by including only S's items of income, gain, deduction, and loss taken into account. S declares and makes a $10 dividend distribution to M at the close of Year 1. Under paragraph (b) of this section, M increases its basis in S's stock as of the close of Year 1 by a $110 net amount ($120 of taxable income, less a $10 distribution).

(b) *Distributions in later years*. The facts are the same as in paragraph (a) of this *Example 5*, except that S does not declare and distribute the $10 until Year 2. Under paragraph (b) of this section, M increases its basis in S's stock by $120 as of the close of Year 1, and decreases its basis by $10 as of the close of Year 2. (If M were also a subsidiary, the basis of its stock would also be increased in Year 1 to reflect M's $120 adjustment to basis of S's stock; the basis of M's stock would not be changed as a result of S's distribution in Year 2, because M's $10 of tax-exempt dividend income under paragraph (b)(3)(ii) of this section would be offset by the $10 negative adjustment to M's basis in S's stock for the distribution.)

(c) *Amounts declared but not distributed*. The facts are the same as in paragraph (a) of this *Example 5*, except that, during December of Year 1, S declares (and M becomes entitled to) another $70 dividend distribution with respect to its stock, but M does not receive the distribution until after it sells all of S's stock at the close of Year 1. Under §1.1502-13(f)(2)(iv), S is treated as making a $70 distribution to M at the time M becomes entitled to the distribution. (If S is distributing an appreciated asset, its gain under section 311 is also taken into account under paragraph (b)(3)(i) of this section at the time M becomes entitled to the distribution.) Consequently, under paragraph (b) of this section, M increases its basis in S's stock as of the close of Year 1 by only a $40 net amount ($120 of taxable income, less two distributions totalling $80). Any further adjustments after S ceases to be a member and the $70 distribution is made would be duplicative, because the stock basis has already been adjusted for the distribution. Accordingly, the distribution will not result in further adjustments or gain, even if the distribution is a payment to which section 301(c)(2) or (3) applies.

*Example 6. Reorganization with boot.* (i) *Facts.* M owns all the stock of S and T. M owns ten shares of the same class of common stock of S and ten shares of the same class of common stock of T. The fair market value of each share of S stock is $10 and the fair market value of each share of T stock is $10. On January 1 of Year 1, M has a $5 basis in each of its ten shares of S stock and a $10 basis in each of its ten shares of T stock. S and T have no items of income, gain, deduction, or loss for Year 1. S and T each have substantial earnings and profits. At the close of Year 1, T merges into S in a reorganization described in section 368(a)(1)(A) (and in section 368(a)(1)(D)). M receives no additional S stock, but does receive $10 which is treated as a dividend under section 356(a)(2).

(ii) *Analysis*. The merger of T into S is a transaction to which §1.1502-13(f)(3) applies. Under §1.1502-13(f)(3) and §1.358-2(a)(2)(iii), M is deemed to receive ten additional shares of S stock with a total fair market value of $100 (the fair market value of the T stock surrendered by M). Under §1.358-2(a)(2)(i), M will have a basis of $10 in each share of S stock deemed received in the reorganization. Under §1.358-2(a)(2)(iii), M is deemed to surrender all twenty shares of its S stock in a recapitalization under section 368(a)(1)(E) in

exchange for the ten shares of S stock, the number of shares of S stock held by M immediately after the transaction. Thus, under §1.358-2(a)(2)(i), M has five shares of S stock each with a basis of $10 and five shares of S stock each with a basis of $20. The $10 M received is treated as a dividend distribution under section 301 and, under paragraph (b)(3)(v) of this section, the $10 is a distribution to which paragraph (b)(2)(iv) of this section applies. Accordingly, M's total basis in the S stock is decreased by the $10 distribution.

*Example 7. Tiering up of basis adjustments.* M owns all of S's stock, and S owns all of T's stock. For Year 1, the M group has $100 of consolidated taxable income when determined by including only T's items of income, gain, deduction, and loss taken into account, and $50 of consolidated taxable income when determined by including only S's items taken into account. S increases its basis in T's stock by $100 under paragraph (b) of this section. Under paragraph (a)(3) of this section, this $100 basis adjustment is taken into account in determining M's adjustments to its basis in S's stock. Thus, M increases its basis in S's stock by $150 under paragraph (b) of this section.

*Example 8. Allocation of items.* (a) *Acquisition in mid-year.* M is the common parent of a consolidated group, and S is an unaffiliated corporation filing separate returns on a calendar-year basis. M acquires all of S's stock and S becomes a member of the M group on July 1 of Year 1. For the entire calendar Year 1, S has $100 of ordinary income and under §1.1502-76(b) $60 is allocated to the period from January 1 to June 30 and $40 to the period from July 1 to December 31. Under paragraph (b) of this section, M increases its basis in S's stock by $40.

(b) *Sale in mid-year*. The facts are the same as in paragraph (a) of this *Example 8*, except that S is a member of the M group at the beginning of Year 1 but ceases to be a member on June 30 as a result of M's sale of S's stock. Under paragraph (b) of this section, M increases its basis in S's stock by $60 immediately before the stock sale. (M's basis increase would be the same if S became a nonmember because S issued additional shares to nonmembers.)

(c) *Absorption of loss carryovers*. Assume instead that S is a member of the M group at the beginning of Year 1 but ceases to be a member on June 30 as a result of M's sale of S's stock, and a $100 consolidated net operating loss attributable to S is carried over by the M group to Year 1. The consolidated net operating loss may be apportioned to S for its first separate return year only to the extent not absorbed by the M group during Year 1. Under paragraph (b)(3)(i) of this section, if the loss is absorbed by the M group in Year 1, whether the offsetting income arises before or after M's sale of S's stock, the absorption of the loss carryover is included in the determination of S's taxable income or loss for Year 1. Thus, M's basis in S's stock is adjusted under paragraph (b) of this section to reflect any absorption of the loss by the M group.

*Example 9. Gross-ups.* (a) *Facts.* M owns all of the stock of S, and S owns all of the stock of T, a newly formed controlled foreign corporation that is not a passive foreign investment company. In Year 1, T has $100 of subpart F income and pays $34 of foreign income tax, leaving T with $66 of earnings and profits. The M group has $100 of consolidated taxable income when determined by taking into account only S's items (the inclusion under section 951(a), taking into account the section 78 gross-up). As a result of the section 951(a) inclusion, S increases its basis in T's stock by $66 under section 961(a).

(b) *Analysis*. Under paragraph (b)(3)(i) of this section, S has $100 of taxable income. Under paragraph (b)(3)(iii)(B) of this section, the $34 gross-up for taxes paid by T that S is treated as having paid is a noncapital, nondeductible expense (whether or not any corresponding amount is claimed by the M group as a tax credit). Thus, M increases it basis in S's stock under paragraph (b) of this section by the net adjustment of $66.

(c) *Subsequent distribution*. The facts are the same as in paragraph (a) of this *Example 9*, except that T distributes its $66 of earnings and profits in Year 2. The $66 distribution received by S is excluded from S's income under section 959(a) because the distribution represents earnings and profits attributable to amounts that were included in S's income under section 951(a) for Year 1. In addition, S's basis in T's stock is decreased by $66 under section 961(b). The excluded distribution is not tax-exempt income under paragraph (b)(3)(ii) of this section because of the corresponding reduction to S's basis in T's stock. Consequently, M's basis in S's stock is not adjusted under paragraph (b) of this section for Year 2.

*Example 10. Recapture of tax-exempt items.* (a) *Facts.* S is a life insurance company. For Year 1, the M group has $200 of consolidated taxable income, determined by including only S's items of income, gain, deduction, and loss taken into account (including a $300 small company deduction under section 806). In addition, S has $100 of tax-exempt interest income, $60 of which is S's *company share*. The remaining $40 of tax-exempt income is the *policyholders' share* that reduces S's deduction for increase in reserves.

(b) *Tax-exempt items generally*. Under paragraph (b)(3)(i) of this section, S has $200 of taxable income for Year 1. Also for Year 1, S has $100 of tax-exempt income under paragraph (b)(3)(ii)(A) of this section, and another $300 is treated as tax-exempt income under paragraph (b)(3)(ii)(B) of this section because of the deduction under section 806. Under paragraph (b)(3)(iii) of this section, S has $40 of noncapital, nondeductible expenses for Year 1 because S's deduction under section 807 for its increase in reserves has been permanently reduced by the $40 policyholders' share of the tax-exempt interest income. Thus, M increases its basis in S's stock by $560 under paragraph (b) of this section.

(c) *Recapture*. Assume instead that S is a property and casualty company and, for Year 1, S accrues $100 of estimated salvage recoverable under section 832. Of this amount, $87 (87% of $100) is excluded from gross income because of the "fresh start" provisions of Sec. 11305(c) of P.L. 101-508 (the Omnibus Budget Reconciliation Act of 1990). Thus, S has $87 of tax-exempt income under paragraph (b)(3)(ii)(A) of this section that increases M's basis in S's stock for Year 1. (S also has $13 of taxable income over the period of inclusion under section 481.) In Year 5, S determines that the $100 salvage recoverable was overestimated by $30 and deducts $30 for the reduction of the salvage recoverable. However, S has $26.10 (87% of $30) of taxable income in Year 5 due to the partial recapture of its fresh start. Because S has no basis corresponding to this income, S is treated under paragraph (b)(3)(iii)(B) of this section as having a $26.10 noncapital, nondeductible expense in Year 5. This treatment is necessary to reflect the elimination of the erroneous fresh start in S's stock basis and causes a decreases in M's basis in S's stock by $30 for Year 5 (a $3.90 taxable loss and a $26.10 special adjustment).

(c) *Allocation of adjustments among shares of stock*.—(1) *In general*.—(i) *Distributions*.—The adjustment that is described in paragraph (b)(2)(iv) of this section (negative adjustments for distributions) is allocated to the shares of S stock to which the distribution relates.

(ii) *Special rules applicable in the case of certain loss transfers of subsidiary stock*.—(A) *Losses reattributed pursuant to an election under §1.1502-36(d)(6)*.—(1) *General rule*.—If a member transfers loss shares of S stock and the common parent elects under §1.1502-36(d)(6) to reattribute all or a portion of S's attributes, S's resulting noncapital, nondeductible expense is allocated to all loss shares of S stock transferred by members in the transaction. The expense is allocated among those S shares in proportion to the loss in the shares. The tier-up of that expense is included in the remaining adjustment (see paragraph (c)(1)(iii) of this section).

(2) *Reattribution of attributes of a subsidiary that is lower-tier to S*.—If a member transfers loss shares of S stock and the common parent elects under §1.1502-36(d)(6) to reattribute attributes of a subsidiary (S2) that is lower-tier to S, S2's resulting noncapital, nondeductible expense is allocated among S2 shares held by members as of the transaction, other than those transferred in the transaction and with respect to which gain or loss was recognized (recognition transfer), in a manner that permits the full amount of the expense to tier up and be applied to the bases of the loss shares of S stock transferred by members in the transaction. The expense is allocated among those S2 shares with positive basis in a manner that, first, reduces the bases of S2's preferred shares to equalize and then eliminate loss and, second, reduces the bases of S2's common shares in a manner that reduces disparity among the bases of those common shares to the greatest extent possible. The noncapital, nondeductible expense applied to the S2 shares tiers up and is applied to the stock of any subsidiaries that are lower-tier to S (middle-tier subsidiaries) in a manner that will permit the full amount of this expense to be applied to reduce the bases of the loss shares of S stock transferred by members in the transaction. Similar to the allocation among the S2 shares, the tierup of this expense is allocated among the middle-tier subsidiary shares held by members as of the transaction, other than those transferred in a recognition transfer, in a manner that permits the full amount of the expense to tier up and be applied to the bases of the loss shares of S stock transferred by members in the transaction. The tierup of this expense is allocated among those middle-tier subsidiary shares with positive basis in a manner that, first, reduces the bases of the middle-tier subsidiary's preferred shares to equalize and then eliminate loss and, second, reduces the bases of the middle-tier subsidiary's common shares in a manner that reduces disparity among the bases of those common shares to the greatest extent possible. The tier-up of this expense is allocated to the loss shares of S stock transferred by members in the transaction in the same manner as provided in paragraph (c)(1)(ii)(A)(1) of this section, and thereafter the tier-up of that expense is included in the remaining adjustment (see paragraph (c)(1)(iii) of this section).

(3) *Example*.—The following example illustrates the rules of this paragraph (c)(1)(ii)(A).

*Example*. Assume P owns M1, P and M1 own M2, M2 owns S, M1 and S own S1, and M1 and S1 own S2. If S sells a portion of the S1 shares at a gain and M2 sells all of the S stock at a net loss (after adjusting the basis for the gain recognized by S on the sale of the S1 shares), and P elects under §1.1502-36(d)(6) to reattribute attributes of S2, the resulting noncapital, nondeductible expense is allocated entirely to the S2 shares held by S1 with positive basis in a manner that reduces the disparity in those bases to the greatest extent possible. The tier-up of this amount is allocated entirely to the S1 shares held by S (excluding the S1 shares sold) with positive basis in a manner that reduces the disparity in those bases to the greatest extent possible. The tier-up of this amount is allocated to the loss shares of S stock sold by M2 in proportion to the loss in those shares. The tier-up of this amount is then included in the remaining adjustment and tiers up from M2 to M1 and P, and from M1 to P under the general rules of this section.

(B) *Tier-up of reallocated investment adjustments subject to prior use limitation*.—If the reallocation of an investment adjustment under §1.1502-36(b)(2) is subject to the prior use limitation in §1.1502-36(b)(2)(iii)(B)(2), no amount of the tier-up of such reallocated investment adjustment shall be allocated to any share whose prior use resulted in the application of the limitation. Thereafter, the tier-up of this amount is included in the remaining adjustment (see paragraph (c)(1)(iii) of this section).

(iii) *Remaining adjustment*.—The *remaining adjustment* is the adjustment that consists of the items described in paragraphs (b)(2)(i) through (b)(2)(iii) of this section (adjustments for taxable income or loss, tax-exempt income, and noncapital, nondeductible expenses), including adjustments to lower-tier stock basis that tier up under paragraph (a)(3)(iii) of this section, but only to the extent not specially allocated under paragraph (c)(1)(ii) of this section. The remaining adjustment is allocated among the shares of S stock as provided in paragraphs (c)(2) through (c)(4) of this section. If the remaining adjustment is positive, it is allocated first to any preferred stock as provided in paragraph (c)(3) of this section, and then to the common stock as provided in paragraph (c)(2) of this section. If the remaining adjustment is negative, it is allocated only to common stock as provided in paragraph (c)(2) of this section.

(iv) *Nonmember shares*.—No adjustment under this section that is allocated to a share for the period it is owned by a nonmember affects the basis of the share.

(v) *Cross-references*.—See paragraph (c)(4) of this section for the reallocation of adjustments, and paragraph (d) of this section for definitions. See §1.1502-19(d) for special allocations of basis determined or adjusted under the Internal Revenue Code (Code) with respect to excess loss accounts.

(2) *Common stock*.—(i) *Allocation within a class*.—The remaining adjustment described in paragraph (c)(1)(iii) of this section that is allocable to a class of common stock is generally allocated equally to each share within the class. However, if a member has an excess loss account in a share of a class of common stock at the time a positive remaining adjustment is to be allocated, the portion of the positive remaining adjustment allocable to the member with respect to the class is allocated first to equalize and then eliminate that member's excess loss accounts. It is then allocated equally among the members' shares in that class. Similarly, the portion of any negative remaining adjustment allocable to the member with respect to the class is allocated equally to the member's shares with positive bases, eliminating all positive basis in shares of the class before creating or increasing any excess loss accounts. After positive basis is eliminated, any remaining portion of the negative remaining adjustment is allocated to equalize the member's excess loss accounts in the shares of that class to the greatest extent possible. Distributions and any adjustments or determinations under the Internal Revenue Code (for example, under section 358, including any modifications under §1.1502-19(d)) are taken into account before the allocation is made under this paragraph (c)(2)(i).

(ii) *Allocation among classes*.—(A) *General rule*.—If S has more than one class of common stock, the extent to which the remaining adjustment described in paragraph (c)(1)(iii) of this section is allocated to each class is determined, based on consistently applied assumptions, by taking into account the terms of each class and all other facts and circumstances relating to the overall economic arrangement. The allocation generally must reflect the manner in which the classes participate in the economic benefit or burden (if any) corresponding to the items of income, gain, deduction, or loss allocated. In determining participation, any differences in voting rights are not taken into account, and the following factors are among those to be considered—

(1) The interest of each share in economic profits and losses (if different from the interest in taxable income);

(2) The interest of each share in cash flow and other non-liquidating distributions; and

(3) The interest of each share in distributions in liquidation.

(B) *Distributions and Code adjustments.*—Distributions and any adjustments or determinations under the Internal Revenue Code are taken into account before the allocation is made under this paragraph (c)(2)(ii).

(3) *Preferred stock.*—If the remaining adjustment described in paragraph (c)(1)(iii) of this section is positive, it is allocated to preferred stock to the extent required (when aggregated with prior allocations to the preferred stock during the period that S is a member of the consolidated group) to reflect distributions described in section 301 (and all other distributions treated as dividends) to which the preferred stock becomes entitled, and arrearages arising, during the period that S is a member of the consolidated group. For this purpose, the preferred stock is treated as entitled to a distribution no later than the time the distribution is taken into account under the Internal Revenue Code (e.g., under section 305). If the amount of distributions and arrearages exceeds the positive amount (when aggregated with prior allocations), the positive amount is first allocated among classes of preferred stock to reflect their relative priorities, and the amount allocated to each class is then allocated pro rata within the class. An allocation to a share with respect to arrearages and distributions for the period the share is owned by a nonmember is not reflected in the basis of the share under paragraph (b) of this section. However, if M and S cease to be members of one consolidated group and remain affiliated as members of another consolidated group, M's ownership of S's stock during consolidated return years of the prior group is treated for this purpose as ownership by a member to the extent that the the adjustments during the prior consolidated return years are still reflected in the basis of the preferred stock.

(4) *Cumulative redetermination.*—(i) *General rule.*—A member's basis in each share of S preferred and common stock must be redetermined whenever necessary to determine the tax liability of any person. See paragraph (b)(1) of this section. The redetermination is made by reallocating S's adjustments described in paragraphs (c)(1)(ii)(B) (specially allocated adjustments for tier-up of reallocated investment adjustments subject to prior use limitation) and (c)(1)(iii) (remaining adjustments) of this section for each consolidated return year (or other applicable period) of the group by taking into account all of the facts and circumstances affecting allocations under this paragraph (c) as of the redetermination date with respect to all of the S shares. For this purpose:

(A) Amounts may be reallocated from one class of S's stock to another class, but not from one share of a class to another share of the same class.

(B) If there is a change in the equity structure of S (e.g., as the result of S's issuance, redemption, or recapitalization of shares), a cumulative redetermination is made for the period before the change. If a reallocation is required by another redetermination after a change, amounts arising after the change are reallocated before amounts arising before the change.

(C) If S becomes a nonmember as a result of a change in its equity structure, any reallocation is made only among the shares of S's stock immediately before the change. For example, if S issues stock to a nonmember creditor in exchange for its debt, and the exchange results in S becoming a nonmember, any reallocation is only among the shares of S's stock immediately before the exchange.

(D) Any reallocation is treated for all purposes after it is made (including subsequent redeterminations) as the original allocation of an amount under this paragraph (c), but the reallocation does not affect any prior period.

(ii) *Prior use of allocations.*—An amount may not be reallocated under paragraph (c)(4)(i) of this section to the extent that the amount has been used before the reallocation. For this purpose, an amount has been used to the extent it has been taken into account, directly or indirectly, by any member in determining income, gain, deduction, or loss, or in determining the basis of any property that is not subject to this section (e.g., stock of a corporation that has become a nonmember). For example, if M sells a share of S stock, an amount previously allocated to the share cannot be reallocated to another share of S stock, but an amount allocated to another share of S stock can still be reallocated to the sold share because the reallocated amount has not been taken into account; however, any adjustment reallocated to the sold share may effectively be eliminated, because the reallocation was not in effect when the share was previously sold and M's gain or loss from the sale is not redetermined. If, however, M sells the share of S stock to another member, the amount is not used until M's gain or loss is taken into account under § 1.1502-13.

(5) *Examples.*—The principles of this paragraph (c) are illustrated by the following examples.

*Example 1. Ownership of less than all the stock.* (a) *Facts.* M owns 80% of S's only class of stock with an $800 basis. For Year 1, S has $100 of taxable income.

(b) *Analysis.* Under paragraph (c)(1) of this section, the $100 positive adjustment under paragraph (b) of this section for S's taxable income is allocated among the shares of S's stock, including shares owned by nonmembers. Under paragraph (c)(2)(i) of this section, the adjustment is allocated equally to each share of S's stock. Thus, M increases its basis in S's stock under paragraph (b) of this section as of the close of Year 1 by $80. (The basis of the 20% of S's stock owned by nonmembers is not adjusted under this section.)

(c) *Varying interest.* The facts are the same as in paragraph (a) of this *Example 1*, except that M buys the remaining 20% of S's stock at the close of business on June 30 of Year 1 for $208. Under paragraph (b)(1) of this section and the principles of § 1.1502-76(b), S's $100 of taxable income is allocable $40 to the period from January 1 to June 30 and $60 to the period from July 1 to December 31. Thus, for the period ending June 30, M is treated as having a $32 adjustment with respect to the S stock that M has owned since January 1 (80% of $40) and, under paragraph (c)(2)(i) of this section, the adjustment is allocated equally among those shares. For the period ending December 31, M is treated as having a $60 adjustment (100% of $60) that is also allocated equally among M's shares of S's stock owned after June 30. M's basis in the shares owned as of the beginning of the year therefore increases by $80 (the sum of 80% of $40 and 80% of $60), from $800 to $880, and M's basis in the shares purchased on June 30 increases by $12 (20% of $60), from $208 to $220. Thus, M's aggregate basis in S's stock as of the end of Year 1 is $1,100.

(d) *Tax liability.* The facts are the same as in paragraph (a) of this *Example 1*, except that M pays S's $34 share of the group's consolidated tax liability resulting from S's taxable income, and S does not reimburse M. S's $100 of taxable income results in a positive adjustment under paragraph (b)(3)(i) of this section, and S's $34 of tax liability results in a negative adjustment under paragraph (b)(3)(iv)(D) of this section and the principles of section 1552. Because S does not make any payment in recognition of the additional tax liability, by analogy to the treatment under § 1.1552-1(b)(2), S is treated as having made a $34 payment that is described in paragraph (b)(3)(iii) of this section (noncapital, nondeductible expenses) and as having received an equal amount from M as a capital contribution. Thus, M increases its basis in its S stock by $52.80 (80% of the $100 of taxable income, less 80% of the $34 tax payment). In addition, M increases its basis in S's stock by $34 under the Internal Revenue Code and paragraph (a)(2) of this section to reflect the capital contribution. In the aggregate, M increases its basis in S's stock by $86.80. (If, as in paragraph (c) of this *Example 1*, M buys the remaining 20% of S's stock at the close of business on June 30, M increases its basis in S's stock by another $7.90 for the additional 20% interest in S's income after June 30 ($60 multiplied by 20%, less 20% of the $20.40 tax payment on $60); the $34 capital contribution by M is reflected in all of its S shares (not just the original 80%), and M's aggregate basis adjustment under this section is $94.70 ($86.80 plus $7.90).)

*Example 2. Preferred stock.* (a) *Facts.* M owns all of S's common stock with an $800 basis, and nonmembers own all of S's preferred stock. The preferred stock was issued for $200, has a $20 annual, cumulative preference as to dividends, and has an initial liquidation preference of $200. For Year 1, S has $50 of taxable income and no distributions are declared or made.

(b) *Analysis of arrearages.* Under paragraphs (c)(1) and (3) of this section, $20 of the $50 positive adjustment under paragraph (b) of this section is allocated first to the preferred stock to reflect the dividend arrearage arising in Year 1. The remaining $30 of the positive adjustment is allocated to the common stock, increasing M's basis from $800 to $830 as of the close of Year 1. (The basis of the preferred stock owned by nonmembers is not adjusted under this section.)

(c) *Current distribution.* The facts are the same as in paragraph (a) of this *Example 2*, except that S declares and makes a $20 distribution with respect to the preferred stock during Year 1 in satisfaction of its preference. The results are the same as in paragraph (b) of this *Example 2*.

(d) *Varying interest.* The facts are the same as in paragraph (a) of this *Example 2*, except that S has no income or loss for Years 1 and 2, M purchases all of S's preferred stock at the beginning of Year 3 for $240, and S has $70 of taxable income for Year 3. Under paragraph (c)(3) of this section, $60 of the $70 positive adjustment under paragraph (b) of this section is allocated to the preferred stock to reflect the dividends arrearages for Years 1 through 3, but only the $20 for Year 3 is reflected in the basis of the preferred stock under paragraph (b) of this section. (The remaining $40 is not reflected because the preferred stock was owned by nonmembers during Years 1 and 2.) Thus, M increases its basis in S's preferred stock from $240 to $260, and its basis in S's common stock from $800 to $810, as of the close of Year 3. (If M had acquired all of S's preferred stock in a transaction to which section 351 applies, and M's initial basis in S's preferred stock was $200 under section 362, M's basis in S's preferred stock would increase from $200 to $220.)

(e) *Varying interest with current distributions.* The facts are the same as in paragraph (d) of this *Example 2*, except that S declares and makes a $20 distribution with respect to the preferred stock in each of Years 1 and 2 in satisfaction of its preference, and M purchases all of S's preferred stock at the beginning of Year 3 for $200. Under paragraph (c)(3) of this section, $40 of the $70 positive adjustment under paragraph (b) of this section is allocated to the preferred stock to reflect the distributions in Years 1 and 2, and $20 of the $70 is allocated to the preferred stock to reflect the arrearage for Year 3. However, as in paragraph (d) of this *Example 2*, only the $20 attributable to Year 3 is reflected in the basis of the preferred stock under paragraph (b) of this section. Thus, M increases its basis in S's preferred stock from $200 to $220, and M increases its basis in S's common stock from $800 to $810.

*Example 3. Cumulative redetermination.* (a) *Facts.* M owns all of S's common and preferred stock. The preferred stock has a $100 annual, cumulative preference as to dividends. For Year 1, S has $200 of taxable income, the first $100 of which is allocated to the preferred stock and the remaining $100 of which is allocated to the common stock. For Year 2, S has no adjustment under paragraph (b) of this section, and M sells all of S's common stock at the close of Year 2.

(b) *Analysis.* Under paragraph (c)(4) of this section, M's basis in S's common stock must be redetermined as of the sale of the stock. The redetermination is made by reallocating the $200 positive adjustment under paragraph (b) of this section for Year 1 by taking into account all of the facts and circumstances affecting allocations as of the sale. Thus, the $200 positive adjustment for Year 1 is reallocated entirely to the preferred stock to reflect the dividend arrearages for Years 1 and 2. The reallocation away from the common stock reflects the fact that, because of the additional amount of arrearage in Year 2, the common stock is not entitled to any part of the $200 of taxable income from Year 1. Thus, the common stock has no positive or negative adjustment, and the preferred stock has a $200 positive adjustment. These reallocations are treated as the original allocations for Years 1 and 2. (The results for the common stock would be the same if the common and preferred stock were not owned by the same member, or the preferred stock were owned by nonmembers.)

(c) *Preferred stock issued after adjustment arises.* The facts are the same as in paragraph (a) of this *Example 3*, except that S does not issue its preferred stock until the beginning of Year 2, S has no further adjustment under paragraph (b) of this section for Years 2 and 3, and M sells S's common stock at the close of Year 3. Under paragraphs (c)(1) and (2) of this section, the $200 positive adjustment for Year 1 is initially allocated entirely to the common stock. Under paragraph (c)(4) of this section, the $200 adjustment is reallocated to the preferred stock to reflect the arrearages for Years 2 and 3. Thus, the common stock has no positive or negative adjustment.

(d) *Common stock issued after adjustment arises.* The facts are the same as in paragraph (a) of this *Example 3*, except that S has no preferred stock, S issues additional common stock of the same class at the beginning of Year 2, S has no further adjustment under paragraph (b) of this section in Years 2 and 3, and M sells its S common stock at the close of Year 3. Under paragraphs (c)(1) and (2) of this section, the $200 positive adjustment for Year 1 is initially allocated entirely to the original common stock. Under paragraph (c)(4)(i)(A) of this section, the $200 adjustment is not reallocated among the original common stock and the additional stock. Unlike the preferred stock in paragraph (c) of this *Example 3*, the additional common stock is of the same class as the original stock, and there is no reallocation between shares of the same class.

(e) *Positive and negative adjustments.* The facts are the same as in paragraph (a) of this *Example 3*, except that S has a $200 loss for Year 2 that results in a negative adjustment to the common stock before any redetermination. For purposes of the basis redetermination under paragraph (c)(4) of this section, the Year 1 and 2 adjustments under paragraph (b) of this section are not netted. Thus, as in paragraph (b) of this *Example 3*, the redetermination is made by reallocating the $200 positive adjustment for Year 1 entirely to the preferred stock. The $200 negative adjustment for Year 2 is allocated entirely to the common stock. Consequently, the preferred stock has a $200 positive cumulative adjustment, and the common stock has a $200 negative cumulative adjustment. (The results would be the same if there were no other adjustments described in paragraph (b) of this section, M sells S's common stock at the close of Year 3 rather than Year 2, and an additional $100 arrearage arises in Year 3; only adjustments under paragraph (b) of this section may be reallocated, and there is no additional adjustment for Year 3.)

(f) *Current distributions.* The facts are the same as in paragraph (a) of this *Example 3*, except that, during Year 1, S declares and makes a distribution to M of $100 as a dividend on the preferred stock and $100 as a dividend on the common stock. The taxable income and distributions result in no Year 1 adjustment under paragraph (b) of this section for either the common or preferred stock. However, as in paragraph (b) of this *Example 3*, the redetermination under paragraph (c)(4) of this section is made by reallocating a $200 positive adjustment for Year 1 (S's net adjustment described in paragraph (b) of this section, determined without taking distributions into account) to the preferred stock. Consequently, the preferred stock has a $100 positive cumulative adjustment ($200 of taxable income, less a $100 distribution with respect to the preferred stock) and the common stock has a $100 negative cumulative adjustment (for the distribution).

(g) *Convertible preferred stock.* The facts are the same as in paragraph (a) of this *Example 3*, except that the preferred stock is convertible into common stock that is identical to the common stock already outstanding, the holders of the preferred stock convert the stock at the close of Year 2, and no stock is sold until the close of Year 5. Under paragraph (c)(4) of this section, the $200 positive adjustment for Year 1 is reallocated entirely to the preferred stock immediately before the conversion. The newly issued common stock is treated as a second class of S common stock, and adjustments under paragraph (b) of this section are allocated between the original and the new common stock under paragraph (c)(2)(ii) of this section. Although the preferred stock is converted to common stock, the $200 adjustment to the preferred stock is not subsequently reallocated between the original and the new common stock. Because the original and the new stock are equivalent, adjustments under paragraph (b) of this section for subsequent periods are allocated equally to each share.

(h) *Prior use of allocations.* The facts are the same as in paragraph (a) of this *Example 3*, except that M sells 10% of S's common stock at the close of Year 1, and the remaining 90% at the close of Year 2. M's basis in the common stock sold in Year 1 reflects $10 of the adjustment allocated to the common stock for Year 1. Under paragraph (c)(4)(ii) of this section, because $10 of the Year 1 adjustment was used in determining M's gain or loss, only $90 is reallocated to the preferred stock, and $10 remains allocated to the common stock sold.

(i) *Lower-tier members.* The facts are the same as in paragraph (a) of this *Example 3*, except that M owns only S's common stock, and M is also a subsidiary. If there is a redetermination under paragraph (c)(4) of this section by a member owning M's stock, a redetermination with respect to S's stock must be made first, and the effect of that redetermination on M's adjustments is taken into account under paragraph (b) of this section. However, as in paragraph (h) of this *Example 3*, to the extent an amount of the initial adjustments with respect to S's common stock have already been tiered up and used by a member owning M's stock, that amount remains with S's common stock (and the higher-tier member using the adjustment with respect to M's stock), and may not be reallocated to S's preferred stock.

*Example 4. Allocation to preferred stock between groups.* (a) *Facts.* M owns all of S's only class of stock, and S owns all of T's common and preferred stock. The preferred stock has a $100 annual, cumulative preference as to dividends. For Year 1, T has $200 of taxable income, the first $100 of which is allocated to the preferred stock and the remaining $100 of which is allocated to the common stock, and S has no adjustments other than the amounts tiered up from T. S and T have no adjustments under paragraph (b) of this section for Years 2 and 3. X, the common parent of another consolidated group, purchases all of S's stock at the close of Year 3, and S and T become members of the X group. For Year 4, T has $200 of taxable income, and S has no adjustments other than the amounts tiered up from T.

(b) *Analysis for Years 1 through 3.* Under paragraph (c)(4) of this section, the allocation of S's adjustments under paragraph (b) of this section (determined without taking distributions into account) must be redetermined as of the time M sells S's stock. As a result of this redetermination, T's common stock has no positive or negative adjustment and the preferred stock has a $200 positive adjustment.

(c) *Analysis for Year 4.* Under paragraph (c)(3) of this section, the allocation of T's $200 positive adjustment in Year 4 to T's preferred stock with respect to arrearages is made by taking into account the consolidated return years of both the M group and the X group. Thus, the allocation of the $200 positive adjustment for Year 4 to T's preferred stock is not treated as an allocation for a period for which the preferred stock is owned by a nonmember. Thus, the $200 adjustment is reflected in S's basis in T's preferred stock under paragraph (b) of this section.

(d) *Definitions.*—For purposes of this section—

(1) *Class.*—The shares of a member having the same material terms (without taking into account voting rights) are treated as a single class of stock.

(2) *Preferred stock.*—Preferred stock is stock that is limited and preferred as to dividends and has a liquidation preference. A class of stock that is not described in section 1504(a)(4), however, is not treated as preferred stock for purposes of paragraph (c) of this

section if members own less than 80% of each class of common stock (determined without taking this paragraph (d)(2) into account).

(3) *Common stock.*—Common stock is stock that is not preferred stock.

(4) *Becoming a nonmember.*—A member is treated as becoming a nonmember if it has a separate return year (including another group's consolidated return year). For example, S may become a nonmember if it issues additional stock to nonmembers, but S does not become a nonmember as a result of its complete liquidation.

(e) *Anti-avoidance rule.*—(1) *General rule.*—If any person acts with a principal purpose contrary to the purposes of this section, to avoid the effect of the rules of this section or apply the rules of this section to avoid the effect of any other provision of the consolidated return regulations, adjustments must be made as necessary to carry out the purposes of this section.

(2) *Examples.*—The principles of this paragraph (e) are illustrated by the following examples.

*Example 1. Preferred stock treated as common stock.* (a) *Facts.* S has 100 shares of common stock and 100 shares of preferred stock described in section 1504(a)(4). M owns 80 shares of S's common stock and all of S's preferred stock. The shareholders expect that S will have negative adjustments under paragraph (b) of this section for Years 1 and 2 (all of which will be allocable to S's common stock), the negative adjustments will have no significant effect on the value of S's stock, and S will have offsetting positive adjustments thereafter. When the preferred stock was issued, M intended to cause S to recapitalize the preferred stock into additional common stock at the end of Year 2 in a transaction described in section 368(a)(1)(E). M's temporary ownership of the preferred stock is with a principal purpose to limit M's basis reductions under paragraph (b) of this section to 80% of the anticipated negative adjustments. The recapitalization is intended to cause significantly more than 80% of the anticipated positive adjustments to increase M's basis in S's stock because of M's increased ownership of S's common stock immediately after the recapitalization.

(b) *Analysis.* S has established a transitory capital structure with a principal purpose to enhance M's basis in S's stock under this section. Under paragraph (e)(1) of this section, all of S's common and preferred stock is treated as a single class of common stock in Years 1 and 2 for purposes of this section. Thus, S's items are allocated under the principles of paragraph (c)(2)(ii) of this section, and M decreases its basis in both the common and preferred stock accordingly.

*Example 2. Contribution of appreciated property.* (a) *Facts.* M owns all of the stock of S and T, and S and T each own 50% of the stock of U. M's S stock has a $150 basis and $200 value, and M's T stock has a $200 basis and $200 value. With a principal purpose to eliminate M's gain from an anticipated sale of S's stock, T contributes to U an asset with a $100 value and $0 basis, and S contributes $100 cash. U sells T's asset and recognizes a $100 gain that results in a $100 positive adjustment under paragraph (b) of this section.

(b) *Analysis.* Under paragraph (c)(2) of this section, U's adjustment ordinarily would be allocated equally to each share of U's stock. If so allocated, M's basis in S's stock would increase from $150 to $200 and M would recognize no gain from the sale of S's stock for $200. Under paragraph (e)(1) of this section, however, because T transferred an appreciated asset to U with a principal purpose to shift a portion of the stock basis increase from M's stock in T to M's stock in S, the allocation of the $100 positive adjustment under paragraph (c) of this section between the shares of U's stock must take into account the contribution. Consequently, all $100 of the positive adjustment is allocated to the U stock owned by T, rather than $50 to the U stock owned by S and $50 to the U stock owned by T. M's basis in S's stock remains $150, and its basis in T's stock increases to $300. Thus, M recognizes a $50 gain from its sale of S's stock for $200.

*Example 3. Reorganizations.* (a) *Facts.* M forms S with an $800 contribution, $200 of which is in exchange for S's preferred stock described in section 1504(a)(4) and the balance of which is for S's common stock. For Years 1 through 3, S has a total of $160 of ordinary income, $60 of which is distributed with respect to the preferred stock in satisfaction of its $20 annual preference as to dividends. Under this section, M's basis in S's preferred stock is unchanged, and its basis in S's common stock is increased from $600 to $700. To reduce its gain from an anticipated sale of S's preferred stock, M forms T at the close of Year 3 with a contribution of all of S's stock in exchange for corresponding common and preferred stock of T in a transaction to which section 351 applies. At the time of the contribution, the fair market value of the common stock is $700 and the fair market value of the preferred stock is $300 (due to a decrease in prevailing market interest rates). M subsequently sells T's preferred stock for $300.

(b) *Analysis.* Under section 358(b), M ordinarily has a $630 basis in T's common stock (70% of the $900 aggregate stock basis) and a $270 basis in T's preferred stock (30% of the $900 aggregate stock basis). However, because M transferred S's stock to T with a principal purpose to shift the allocation of basis adjustments under this section, adjustments are made under paragraph (e)(1) of this section to preserve the allocation under this section. Thus, M has a $700 basis in T's common stock and a $200 basis in T's preferred stock. Consequently, M recognizes a $100 gain from the sale of T's preferred stock.

*Example 4. Post-deconsolidation basis adjustments.* (a) *Facts.* For Year 1, the M group has $40 of taxable income when determined by including only S's items of income, gain, deduction, and loss taken into account, and M increases its basis in S's stock by $40 under paragraph (b) of this section. M anticipates that S will have a $40 ordinary loss for Year 2 that will be carried back and offset S's income in Year 1 and result in a $40 reduction to M's basis in S's stock for Year 2 under paragraph (b) of this section. With a principal purpose to avoid the reduction, M causes S to issue voting preferred stock that results in S becoming a nonmember at the beginning of Year 2. As anticipated, S has a $40 loss for Year 2, which is carried back to Year 1 and offsets S's income from Year 1.

(b) *Analysis.* Under paragraph (e)(1) of this section, because M caused S to become a nonmember with a principal purpose to absorb S's loss but avoid the corresponding negative adjustment under this section, and M bears a substantial portion of the loss because of its continued ownership of S common stock, the basis of M's common stock in S is decreased by $40 for Year 2. (If M has less than a $40 basis in the retained S stock, M must recognize income for Year 2 to the extent of the excess.) Section 1504(a)(3) limits the ability of S to subsequently rejoin the M group's consolidated return.

(c) *Carryback to pre-consolidation year.* The facts are the same as in paragraph (a) of this *Example 4*, except that M anticipates that S's loss will be carried back and absorbed in a separate return year of S before Year 1 (rather than to the M group's consolidated return for Year 1). Although M causes S to become a nonmember with a principal purpose to avoid the negative adjustment under this section, and M bears a substantial portion of the loss because of its continued ownership of S common stock, both S's income and loss are taken into account under the separate return rules. Consequently, no one has acted with a principal purpose contrary to the purposes of this section, and no adjustments are necessary to carry out the purposes of this section.

*Example 5. Pre-consolidation basis adjustments.* (a) *Facts.* M forms S with a $100 contribution, and S becomes a member of the M affiliated group which does not file consolidated returns. For Years 1 through 3, S earns $300. M anticipates that it will elect under section 1501 for the M group to begin filing consolidated returns in Year 5. In anticipation of filing consolidated returns, and to avoid the negative stock basis adjustment that would result under paragraph (b) of this section from distributing S's earnings after Year 5, M causes S to distribute $300 during Year 4 as a qualifying dividend within the meaning of section 243(b). There is no plan or intention to recontribute the funds to S after the distribution.

(b) *Analysis.* Although S's distribution of $300 is with a principal purpose to avoid a corresponding negative adjustment under this section, the $300 was both earned and distributed entirely under the separate return rules. Consequently, M and S have not acted with a principal purpose contrary to the purposes of this section, and no adjustments are necessary to carry out the purposes of this section.

(f) *Predecessors and successors.*—For purposes of this section, any reference to a corporation or to a share of stock includes a reference to a successor or predecessor as the context may require. A corporation is a successor if the basis of its assets is determined, directly or indirectly, in whole or in part, by reference to the basis of another corporation (the predecessor). For example, if T merges into S, S is treated, as the context may require, as a successor to T and as becoming a member of the group. A share is a successor if its basis is determined, directly or indirectly, in whole or in part, by reference to the basis of another share (the predecessor).

(g) *Recordkeeping.*—Adjustments under this section must be reflected annually on permanent records (including work papers). See also section 6001, requiring records to be maintained. The group must be able to identify from these permanent records the amount and allocation of adjustments, including the nature of any tax-exempt income and noncapital, nondeductible expenses, so as to permit the application of the rules of this section for each year.

(h) *Effective/applicability date.*—(1) *General rule.*—Except as provided in paragraph (h)(8) of this section, this section applies with respect to determinations of the basis of the stock of a subsidiary (e.g., for determining gain or loss from a disposition of stock), in consolidated return years beginning on or after January 1, 1995. If this section applies, basis must be determined or redetermined as if this section were in effect for all years (including, for example, the consolidated return years of another consolidated group to the extent adjustments from those years are still reflected). For example, if the portion of a consolidated net operating loss carryover attributable to S expired in 1990 and is treated as a noncapital, nondeductible expense under paragraph (b) of this section, it is taken into account in tax years beginning on or after January 1, 1995 as a negative adjustment for 1990. Any such determination or redetermination does not, however, affect any prior period. Thus, the negative adjustment for S's noncapital, nondeductible expense is not taken into account for tax years beginning before January 1, 1995.

(2) *Dispositions of stock before effective date.*—(i) *In general.*—If M disposes of stock of S in a consolidated return year beginning before January 1, 1995, the amount of M's income, gain, deduction, or loss, and the basis reflected in that amount, are not redetermined under this section. See § 1.1502-19 as contained in the 26 CFR part 1 edition revised as of April 1, 1994 for the definition of disposition, and paragraph (h)(5) of this section for the rules applicable to such dispositions.

(ii) *Lower-tier members.*—Although M disposes of S's stock in a tax year beginning before January 1, 1995, S's determinations or adjustments with respect to the stock of a lower-tier member with which it continues to file a consolidated return are redetermined in accordance with the rules of this section (even if they were previously taken into account by M and reflected in income, gain, deduction, or loss from the disposition of S's stock). For example, assume that M owns all of S's stock, S owns all of T's stock, and T owns all of U's stock. If S sells 80% of T's stock in a tax year beginning before January 1, 1995 (the effective date), the amount of S's income, gain, deduction, or loss from the sale, and the stock basis adjustments reflected in that amount, are not redetermined if M sells S's stock after the effective date. If S sells the remaining 20% of T's stock after the effective date, S's stock basis adjustments with respect to that T stock are also not redetermined because T became a nonmember before the effective date. However, if T and U continue to file a consolidated return with each other and T sells U's stock after the effective date, T's stock basis adjustments with respect to U's stock are redetermined (even though some of those adjustments may have been taken into account by S in its prior sale of T's stock before the effective date).

(iii) *Deferred amounts.*—For purposes of this paragraph (h)(2), a disposition does not include a transaction to which § 1.1502-13, § 1.1502-13T, § 1.1502-14, or § 1.1502-14T applies. Instead, the transaction is deemed to occur as the income, gain, deduction, or loss (if any) is taken into account.

(3) *Distributions.*—(i) *Deemed dividend elections.*—If there is a deemed distribution and recontribution pursuant to § 1.1502-32(f)(2) as contained in the 26 CFR part 1 edition revised as of April 1, 1994 in a consolidated return year beginning before January 1, 1995, the deemed distribution and recontribution under the election are treated as an actual distribution by S and recontribution by M as provided under the election.

(ii) *Affiliated earnings and profits.*—This section does not apply to reduce the basis in S's stock as a result of a distribution of earnings and profits accumulated in separate return years, if the distribution is made in a consolidated return year beginning before January 1, 1995, and the distribution does not cause a negative adjustment under the investment adjustment rules in effect at the time of the distribution. See paragraph (h)(5) of this section for the rules in effect with respect to the distribution.

(4) *Expiring loss carryovers.*—If S became a member of a consolidated group in a consolidated return year beginning before January 1, 1995, and S had a loss carryover from a separate return limitation year at that time, the group does not treat any expiration of the loss carryover (even if in a tax year beginning on or after January 1, 1995) as a noncapital, nondeductible expense resulting in a negative adjustment under this section. If S becomes a member of a consolidated group in a consolidated return year beginning on or after January 1, 1995, and S has a loss carryover from a separate return limitation year at that time, adjustments with respect to the expiration are determined under this section.

(5) *Prior law.*—(i) *In general.*—For prior determinations, see prior regulations under section 1502 as in effect with respect to the determination. See, e.g., § § 1.1502-32 and 1.1502-32T as contained in the 26 CFR part 1 edition revised as of April 1, 1994.

(ii) *Continuing basis reductions for certain deconsolidated subsidiaries.*—If a subsidiary ceases to be a member of a group in a consolidated return year beginning before January 1, 1995, and its basis was subject to reduction under § 1.1502-32T or § 1.1502-32(g) as contained in the 26 CFR part 1 edition revised as of April 1, 1994, its basis remains subject to reduction under those principles. For example, if S ceased to be a member in 1990, and M's basis in any retained S stock

was subject to a basis reduction account, the basis remains subject to reduction. Similarly, if an election could be made to apply § 1.1502-32T instead of § 1.1502-32(g), the election remains available. However, § § 1.1502-32T and 1.1502-32(g) do not apply as a result of a subsidiary ceasing to be a member in tax years beginning on or after January 1, 1995.

(6) *Loss suspended under § 1.1502-35(c) or disallowed under § 1.1502-35(g)(3)(iii).*—Paragraphs (a)(2), (b)(3)(iii)(C), (b)(3)(iii)(D) and (b)(4)(vi) of this section are applicable on and after March 10, 2006. For rules applicable before March 10, 2006, see § 1.1502-32T(h)(6) as contained in 26 CFR part 1 in effect on January 1, 2006.

(7) *Rules related to discharge of indebtedness income excluded from gross income.*—Paragraphs (b)(1)(ii), (b)(3)(ii)(C)(1), (b)(3)(iii)(A), and (b)(5)(ii), *Example 4*, paragraphs (a), (b), and (c) of this section apply with respect to determinations of the basis of the stock of a subsidiary in consolidated return years the original return for which is due (without regard to extensions) after March 21, 2005. However, groups may apply those provisions with respect to determinations of the basis of the stock of a subsidiary in consolidated return years the original return for which is due (without regard to extensions) on or before March 21, 2005, and after August 29, 2003. For determinations of the basis of the stock of a subsidiary in consolidated return years the original return for which is due (without regard to extensions) on or before March 21, 2005, and after August 29, 2003, with respect to which a group chooses not to apply paragraphs (b)(1)(ii), (b)(3)(ii)(C)(1), (b)(3)(iii)(A), and (b)(5)(ii), *Example 4*, paragraphs (a), (b), and (c) of this section, see § 1.1502-32T(b)(3)(ii)(C)(1), (b)(3)(iii)(A), and (b)(5)(ii), *Example 4*, paragraphs (a), (b), and (c) as contained in 26 CFR part 1 revised as of April 1, 2004.

(8) Paragraph (b)(5)(ii) *Example 6* of this section applies only with respect to determinations of the basis of the stock of a subsidiary on or after January 23, 2006. For determinations of the basis of the stock of a subsidiary before January 23, 2006, see § 1.1502-32(b)(5)(ii) *Example 6* as contained in the 26 CFR part 1 edition revised as of April 1, 2005.

(9) *Allocations of investment adjustments, including adjustments attributable to certain loss transfers; certain conforming amendments.*—Paragraphs (a)(2), (b)(3)(ii)(C)(2), (c)(1), (c)(2)(i), (c)(2)(ii)(A), (c)(3), and (c)(4)(i) of this section are applicable for determinations of the basis of stock of a subsidiary on or after September 17, 2008.

(i) [Reserved]. For further guidance, see § 1.1502-32T(i) through (j)(1).

(j) *Effective/applicability date.*—Paragraph (b)(4)(iv) of this section applies to any original consolidated Federal income tax return due (without extensions) after June 14, 2007. For original consolidated Federal income tax returns due (without extensions) after May 30, 2006, and on or before June 14, 2007, see § 1.1502-32T as contained in 26 CFR part 1 in effect on April 1, 2007. For original consolidated Federal income tax returns due (without extensions) on or before May 30, 2006, see § 1.1502-32 as contained in 26 CFR part 1 in effect on April 1, 2006.

(k) [Reserved]. For further guidance, see § 1.1502-32T(k). [Reg. § 1.1502-32.]

☐ [T.D. 6909, 12-29-66. *Amended by* T.D. 7246, 12-29-72; T.D. 7637, 8-6-79; T.D. 7655, 11-28-79; T.D. 7947, 3-5-84; T.D. 8188, 3-14-88; T.D. 8245, 3-14-89; T.D. 8294, 3-9-90; T.D. 8319, 11-19-90; T.D. 8364, 9-13-91; T.D. 8401, 3-13-92; T.D. 8560, 8-12-94; T.D. 8677, 6-26-96; T.D. 8823, 6-25-99; T.D. 8984, 3-7-2002; T.D. 9048, 3-11-2003; T.D. 9089, 8-29-2003; T.D. 9187, 3-2-2005; T.D. 9192, 3-21-2005 T.D. 9244, 1-23-2006 (corrected 4-12-2006); T.D. 9254, 3-9-2006; T.D. 9264, 5-26-2006 (corrected 10-25-2006); T.D. 9322, 4-9-2007; T.D. 9329, 6-13-2007, T.D. 9424, 9-9-2008 and T.D. 9866, 6-14-2019.]

### [Reg. § 1.1502-33]

**§ 1.1502-33. Earnings and profits.**—(a) *In general.*—(1) *Purpose.*—This section provides rules for adjusting the earnings and profits of a subsidiary (S) and any member (P) owning S's stock. These rules modify the determination of P's earnings and profits under applicable rules of law, including section 312, by adjusting P's earnings and profits to reflect S's earnings and profits for the period that S is a member of the consolidated group. The purpose for modifying the determination of earnings and profits is to treat P and S as a single entity by reflecting the earnings and profits of lower-tier members in the earnings and profits of higher-tier members and consolidating the group's earnings and profits in the common parent. References in this section to earnings and profits include deficits in earnings and profits.

(2) *Application of other rules of law, duplicative adjustments.*—See § 1.1502-80(a) regarding the general applicability of other rules of law and a limitation on duplicative adjustments. The rules of this section

are in addition to other rules of law. For example, the allowance for depreciation is determined in accordance with section 312(k). P's earnings and profits must not be adjusted under this section and other rules of law in a manner that has the effect of duplicating an adjustment. For example, if S's earnings and profits are reflected in P's earnings and profits under paragraph (b) of this section, and S transfers its assets to P in a liquidation to which section 332 applies, S's earnings and profits that P succeeds to under section 381 must be adjusted to prevent duplication.

(b) *Tiering up earnings and profits.*—(1) *General rule.*—P's earnings and profits are adjusted under this section to reflect changes in S's earnings and profits in accordance with the applicable principles of §1.1502-32, consistently applied, and an adjustment to P's earnings and profits for a tax year under this paragraph (b)(1) is treated as earnings and profits of P for the tax year in which the adjustment arises. Under these principles, for example, the adjustments are made as of the close of each consolidated return year, and as of any other time if a determination at that time is necessary to determine the earnings and profits of any person. Similarly, S's earnings and profits are allocated under the principles of §1.1502-32(c), and the adjustments are applied in the order of the tiers, from the lowest to the highest. However, modifications to the principles include:

(i) The amount of P's adjustment is determined by reference to S's earnings and profits, rather than S's taxable and tax-exempt items (and therefore, for example, the deferral of a negative adjustment for S's unabsorbed losses does not apply).

(ii) The tax sharing rules under paragraph (d) of this section apply rather than those of §1.1502-32(b)(3)(iv)(D).

(2) *Affiliated earnings and profits.*—The reduction in S's earnings and profits under section 312 from a distribution of earnings and profits accumulated in separate return years of S that are not separate return limitation years does not tier up to P's earnings and profits. Thus, the increase in P's earnings and profits under section 312 from receipt of the distribution is not offset by a corresponding reduction.

(3) *Examples.*—(i) *In general.*—For purposes of the examples in this section, unless otherwise stated, P owns all of the only class of S's stock, the stock is owned for the entire year, S owns no stock of lower-tier members, the tax year of all persons is the calendar year, all persons use the accrual method of accounting, the facts set forth the only corporate activity, preferred stock is described in section 1504(a)(4), all transactions are between unrelated persons, and tax liabilities are disregarded.

(ii) *Tiering up earnings and profits.*—The principles of this paragraph (b) are illustrated by the following examples.

*Example 1. Tier-up and distribution of earnings and profits.* (a) *Facts.* P forms S in Year 1 with a $100 contribution. S has $100 of earnings and profits for Year 1 and no earnings and profits for Year 2. During Year 2, S declares and distributes a $50 dividend to P.

(b) *Analysis.* Under paragraph (b)(1) of this section, S's $100 of earnings and profits for Year 1 increases P's earnings and profits for Year 1. P has no additional earnings and profits for Year 2 as a result of the $50 distribution in Year 2, because there is a $50 increase in P's earnings and profits as a result of the receipt of the dividend and a corresponding $50 decrease in S's earnings and profits under section 312(a) that is reflected in P's earnings and profits under paragraph (b)(1) of this section.

(c) *Distribution of current earnings and profits.* The facts are the same as in paragraph (a) of this *Example 1*, except that S distributes the $50 dividend at the end of Year 1 rather than during Year 2. Under paragraph (b)(1) of this section, P's earnings and profits are increased by $100 (S's $50 of undistributed earnings and profits, plus P's receipt of the $50 distribution). Thus, S's earnings and profits increase by $50 and P's earnings and profits increase by $100.

(d) *Affiliated earnings and profits.* The facts are the same as in paragraph (a) of this *Example 1*, except that P and S do not begin filing consolidated returns until Year 2. Because P and S file separate returns for Year 1, P's basis in S's stock remains $100 under §1.1502-32 and this section, S has $100 of earnings and profits, and none of S's earnings and profits is reflected in P's earnings and profits under paragraph (b) of this section. S's distribution in Year 2 ordinarily would reduce S's earnings and profits but not increase P's earnings and profits. (P's $50 of earnings and profits from the dividend would be offset by S's $50 reduction in earnings and profits that tiers up under paragraph (b) of this section.) However, under paragraph (b)(2) of this section, the negative adjustment for S's distribution to P does not apply. Thus, S's distribution reduces its earnings and profits by $50 but increases P's earnings and profits by $50. (If S's earnings and profits had been accumulated in a separate return limitation year, paragraph (b)(2) of this section would not apply and the distribution would reduce S's earnings and profits but not increase P's earnings and profits.)

(e) *Earnings and profits deficit.* Assume instead that after P forms S in Year 1 with a $100 contribution, S borrows additional funds and has a $150 deficit in earnings and profits for Year 1. The corresponding loss for tax purposes is not absorbed in Year 1, and is included in the group's consolidated net operating loss carried forward to Year 2. Under paragraph (b)(1) of this section, however, S's $150 deficit in earnings and profits decreases P's earnings and profits for Year 1 by $150. (Absorption of the loss in a later tax year has no effect on the earnings and profits of P and S.)

*Example 2. Section 355 distribution.* (a) *Facts.* P owns all of S's stock and S owns all of T's stock. For Year 1, T has $100 of earnings and profits. Under paragraph (b)(1) of this section, the earnings and profits of T tier up to S and to P. S and P have no other earnings and profits for Year 1. S distributes T's stock to P at the end of Year 1 in a distribution to which section 355 applies.

(b) *Analysis.* Because S's distribution of T's stock is a distribution to which section 355 applies, the applicable principles of §1.1502-32(b)(2)(iv) do not require P's earnings and profits to be adjusted by reason of the distribution. In addition, although S's earnings and profits may be reduced under section 312(h) as a result of the distribution, the applicable principles of §1.1502-32(b)(3)(iii) do not require P's earnings and profits to be adjusted to reflect this reduction in S's earnings and profits.

*Example 3. Allocating earnings and profits among shares.* P owns 80% of S's stock throughout Year 1. For Year 1, S has $100 of earnings and profits. Under paragraph (b)(1) of this section, $80 of S's earnings and profits is allocated to P based on P's ownership of S's stock. Accordingly, $80 of S's earnings and profits for Year 1 is reflected in P's earnings and profits for Year 1.

(c) *Special rules.*—For purposes of this section—

(1) *Stock of members.*—For purposes of determining P's earnings and profits from the disposition of S's stock, P's basis in S's stock is adjusted to reflect S's earnings and profits determined under paragraph (b) of this section, rather than under §1.1502-32. For example, P's basis in S's stock is increased by positive earnings and profits and decreased by deficits in earnings and profits. Similarly, P's basis in S's stock is not reduced for distributions to which paragraph (b)(2) of this section applies (affiliated earnings and profits). P may have an excess loss account in S's stock for earnings and profits purposes (whether or not there is an excess loss account under §1.1502-32), and the excess loss account is determined, adjusted, and taken into account in accordance with the principles of §§1.1502-19 and 1.1502-32.

(2) *Intercompany transactions.*—Intercompany items and corresponding items are not reflected in earnings and profits before they are taken into account under §1.1502-13. See §1.1502-13 for the applicable rules and definitions.

(3) *Example.*—The principles of this paragraph (c) are illustrated by the following example.

*Example. Adjustments to stock basis.* (a) *Facts.* P forms S in Year 1 with a $100 contribution. For Year 1, S has $75 of taxable income and $100 of earnings and profits. For Year 2, S has no taxable income or earnings and profits, and S declares and distributes a $50 dividend to P. P sells all of S's stock for $150 at the end of Year 2.

(b) *Analysis.* Under paragraph (c)(1) of this section, P's basis in S's stock for earnings and profits purposes immediately before the sale is $150 (the $100 initial basis, plus S's $100 of earnings and profits for Year 1, minus the $50 distribution of earnings and profits in Year 2). Thus, P recognizes no gain or loss from the sale of S's stock for earnings and profits purposes.

(c) *Earnings and profits deficit.* Assume instead that S has a $100 tax loss and earnings and profits deficit for Year 1. The tax loss is not absorbed in Year 1 and is included in the group's consolidated net operating loss carried forward to Year 2. Under paragraph (b) of this section, S's $100 deficit in earnings and profits decreases P's earnings and profits for Year 1. Under paragraph (c) of this section, P decreases its basis in S's stock for purposes of determining earnings and profits from $100 to $0. (If S had borrowed an additional $50 that it also lost in Year 1, P would have decreased its earnings and profits for Year 1 by the additional $50, and P would have had a $50 excess loss account in S's stock for earnings and profits purposes, which would be taken into account in determining P's earnings and profits from its sale of S's stock.)

(d) *Affiliated earnings and profits.* Assume instead that P and S do not begin filing consolidated returns until Year 2. Under paragraph (b) of this section, the negative adjustment under §1.1502-32(b) for distributions does not apply to S's distribution of earnings and profits accumulated in a separate return year that is a not separate return limitation year. Thus, P's basis in S's stock for earnings and profits purposes remains $100, and P has $50 of earnings and profits from the sale of S's stock.

(d) *Federal income tax liability.*—(1) *In general.*—(i) *Extension of tax allocations.*—Section 1552 allocates the tax liability of a consolidated group among its members for purposes of determining the amounts by which their earnings and profits are reduced for taxes. Section 1552 does not reflect the absorption by one member of another member's tax attributes (e.g., losses, deductions and credits). For example, if P's $100 of income is offset by S's $100 of deductions, consolidated tax liability is $0 and no amount is allocated under section 1552. However, the group may elect under this paragraph (d) to allocate additional amounts to reflect the absorption by one member of the tax attributes of another member. Permissible methods are set forth in paragraphs (d)(2) through (4) of this section, and election procedures are provided in paragraph (d)(5) of this section. Allocations under this paragraph (d) must be reflected annually on permanent records (including work papers). Any computations of separate return tax liability are subject to the principles of section 1561.

(ii) *Effect of extended tax allocations.*—The amounts allocated under this paragraph (d) are treated as allocations of tax liability for purposes of §1.1552-1(b)(2). For example, if P's taxable income is offset by S's loss, and tax liability is allocated under the percentage method of paragraph (d)(3) of this section, P's earnings and profits are reduced as if its income were subject to tax, P is treated as liable to S for the amount of the tax, and corresponding adjustments are made to S's earnings and profits. If the liability of one member to another is not paid, the amount not paid generally is treated as a distribution, contribution, or both, depending on the relationship between the members.

(2) *Wait-and-see method.*—The wait-and-see method under this paragraph (d)(2) is derived from Securities and Exchange Commission procedures. In the year that a member's tax attribute is absorbed, the group's consolidated tax liability is allocated in accordance with the group's method under section 1552. When, in effect, the member with the tax attribute could have absorbed the attribute on a separate return basis in a later year, a portion of the group's consolidated tax liability for the later year that is otherwise allocated to members under section 1552 is reallocated. The reallocation takes into account all consolidated return years to which this paragraph (d) applies (the computation period), and is determined by comparing the tax allocated to a member during the computation period with the member's tax liability determined as if it had filed separate returns during the computation period.

(i) *Cap on allocation under section 1552.*—A member's allocation under section 1552 for a tax year may not exceed the excess, if any, of—

(A) The total of the tax liabilities of the member for the computation period (including the current year), determined as if the member had filed separate returns; over

(B) The total amount allocated to the member under section 1552 and this paragraph (d) for the computation period (except the current year).

(ii) *Reallocation of capped amounts.*—To the extent that the amount allocated to a member under section 1552 exceeds the limitation under paragraph (d)(2)(i) of this section, the excess is allocated among the remaining members in proportion to (but not to exceed the amount of) each member's excess, if any, of—

(A) The total of the tax liabilities of the member for the computation period (including the current year), determined as if the member had filed separate returns; over

(B) The total amount allocated to the member under section 1552 and this paragraph (d) for the computation period (including for the current year only the amount allocated under section 1552).

(iii) *Reallocation of excess capped amounts.*—If the reductions under paragraph (d)(2)(i) of this section exceed the amounts allocable under paragraph (d)(2)(ii) of this section, the excess is allocated among the members in accordance with the group's method under section 1552 without taking this paragraph (d)(2) into account.

(3) *Percentage method.*—The percentage method under this paragraph (d)(3) allocates tax liability based on the absorption of tax attributes, without taking into account the ability of any member to subsequently absorb its own tax attributes. The allocation under this method is in addition to the allocation under section 1552.

(i) *Decreased earnings and profits.*—A member's allocation under section 1552 for any year is increased, thereby decreasing its earnings and profits, by a fixed percentage (not to exceed 100%) of the excess, if any, of—

(A) The member's separate return tax liability for the consolidated return year as determined under §1.1552-1(a)(2)(ii); over

(B) The amount allocated to the member under section 1552.

(ii) *Increased earnings and profits.*—An amount equal to the total decrease in earnings and profits under paragraph (d)(3)(i) of this section (including amounts allocated as a result of a carryback) increases the earnings and profits of the members whose attributes are absorbed, and is allocated among them in a manner that reasonably reflects the absorption of the tax attributes.

(4) *Additional methods.*—The absorption by one member of the tax attributes of another member may be reflected under any other method approved in writing by the Commissioner.

(5) *Election of allocation method.*—(i) *In general.*—Tax liability may be allocated under this paragraph (d) only if an election is filed with the group's first return. The election must—

(A) Be made in a separate statement entitled "ELECTION TO ALLOCATE TAX LIABILITY UNDER §1.1502-33(d)";

(B) State the allocation method elected under §1.1502-33(d) and under section 1552;

(C) If the percentage method is elected, state the percentage (not to exceed 100%) to be used; and

(D) If a method is permitted under paragraph (d)(4) of this section, provide the date and control number of the private letter ruling issued by the Internal Revenue Service approving such method.

(ii) *Consent.*—(A) *Electing or changing methods.*—An election for a later year, or an election to change methods, may be made only with the written consent of the Commissioner.

(B) *Prior law elections.*—An election in effect for the last tax year beginning before January 1, 1995, remains in effect under this section. However, a group may elect to conform its earnings and profits computations to the method described in §1.1502-32(b)(3)(iv)(D) (the percentage method, using a 100% allocation), whether or not it has previously made an election for earnings and profits purposes. If a conforming election is made, the group must make all adjustments necessary to prevent amounts from being duplicated or omitted. The conforming election is made by attaching a statement entitled "ELECTION TO CONFORM TAX ALLOCATIONS UNDER §§1.1502-32 and 1.1502-33(d)" to the consolidated group's return for its first tax year beginning on or after January 1, 1995. The statement must be signed by the common parent, and must specify whether the method is conformed only for years beginning on or after January 1, 1995 or as if the method were in effect for all prior years. The statement must also describe the adjustments made by reason of the change (e.g., to reflect prior use of earnings and profits).

(6) *Examples.*—The principles of this paragraph (d) are illustrated by the following examples.

*Example 1. Wait-and-see method.* (a) *Facts.* P owns all of the stock of S1 and S2. The P group uses the wait-and-see method of allocation under paragraph (d)(2) of this section in conjunction with §1.1552-1(a)(1). For Year 1, each member's taxable income, both for purposes of §1.1552-1(a)(1) and redetermined as if the member had filed separate returns, is as follows: P $0, S1 $2,000, and S2 ($1,000). Thus, the P group's consolidated tax liability for Year 1 is $340 (assuming a 34% tax rate).

(b) *Analysis.* Under §1.1552-1(a)(1)(i), the tax liability of the P group is allocated among the members in accordance with the portion of the consolidated taxable income attributable to each member having taxable income. Thus, all of the P group's $340 consolidated tax liability is allocated to S1. As a result, S1 decreases its earnings and profits under section 1552 by $340 (even if S1 does not pay the tax liability). No further allocations are made under paragraph (d)(2) of this section because S2 cannot yet absorb its loss on a separate return basis.

(c) *Payment of tax liability.* If S1 pays the $340 tax liability, there is no further effect on the income, earnings and profits, or stock basis of any member. If P pays the $340 tax liability (and the payment is not a loan from P to S1), P is treated as making a $340 contribution to the capital of S1; if S2 pays the $340 tax liability (and the payment is not a loan from S2 to S1), S2 is treated as making a $340 distribution to P with respect to its stock, and P is treated as making a $340 contribution to the capital of S1. See §1.1552-1(b)(2).

(d) *Year 2.* For Year 2, each member's taxable income, under §1.1552-1(a)(1)(ii) and redetermined as if the member had filed separate returns, without taking into account any carryover from Year 1, is as follows: P $0, S1 $1,000, and S2 $3,000. Thus, the P group's consolidated tax liability for Year 2 is $1,360 (assuming a 34% tax rate). Of this amount, section 1552 would allocate $340 to S1 and $1,020 to S2. However, under paragraph (d)(2)(i) of this section, no more than $680 may be allocated to S2. This is because S2 would have had an aggregate tax liability of $680 if it had filed separate returns for Years 1 and 2 (a $0 tax liability for Year 1, and a $680 tax liability for Year 2, taking into account a $1,000 net operating loss

**Reg. §1.1502-33(d)(6)**

carryover from Year 1). Under paragraph (d)(2)(ii) of this section, the entire excess of $340 which would otherwise be allocated to S2 under §1.1552-1(a)(1) is allocated to S1. This is because S1 would have had an additional $340 of aggregate tax liability if it had filed separate returns for Years 1 and 2 (a $680 tax liability for Year 1, and a $340 tax liability for Year 2, not taking into account S2's $1,000 net operating loss for Year 1). The effect of the allocation of $680 to S1 and $680 to S2 is determined under §1.1552-1(b)(2).

*Example 2. Percentage method.* (a) *Facts.* The facts are the same as in *Example 1*, but the P group uses the percentage method of allocation under paragraph (d)(3) of this section, with a percentage of 100%. In addition, the taxable incomes and losses of the members are the same if computed as provided in §1.1552-1(a)(1).

(b) *Analysis.* Under §1.1552-1(a)(2)(ii), $340 of tax liability is allocated to S1 for Year 1. Under paragraph (d)(3)(i) of this section, S1 is allocated another $340 of tax liability because S1 would have had a $680 tax liability if it had filed separate returns but only $340 is allocated to S1 under section 1552. Thus, S1's earnings and profits are decreased by the $680 total. Under paragraph (d)(3)(ii) of this section, S2's earnings and profits are increased by $340 because the additional $340 allocated to S1 under paragraph (d)(3)(i) of this section is attributable to the absorption of S2's losses.

(c) *Payment of tax liability.* If S1 pays the $340 tax liability of the P group and pays $340 to S2, the Year 1 tax liability results in no further adjustments to the income, earnings and profits, or basis of any member's stock. If S1 pays the $340 tax liability of the P group and pays the other $340 to P instead of S2 because, for example, of an agreement among the members, S2 is treated as distributing $340 to P with respect to its stock in the year that S1 makes the payment to P. See §1.1552-1(b)(2).

(d) *Year 2.* For Year 2, $340 is allocated to S1 and $1,020 is allocated to S2 under section 1552. No additional amounts are allocated under paragraph (d)(3) of this section.

(e) *Deconsolidations.*—(1) *In general.*—Immediately before it becomes a nonmember, S's earnings and profits are eliminated to the extent they were taken into account by any member under this section. If S's earnings and profits are eliminated under this paragraph (e)(1), no corresponding adjustment is made to the earnings and profits of P (or any other member) under paragraph (b) of this section or to any basis in a member's stock under paragraph (c) of this section. For this purpose, S is treated as becoming a nonmember on the first day of its first separate return year (including another group's consolidated return year).

(2) *Acquisition of group.*—(i) *Application.*—This paragraph (e)(2) applies only if a consolidated group (the terminating group) ceases to exist as a result of—

(A) The acquisition of either the assets of the common parent of the terminating group in a reorganization described in section 381(a)(2), or the stock of the common parent of the terminating group; or

(B) The application of the principles of §1.1502-75(d)(2) or (d)(3).

(ii) *General rule.*—Paragraph (e)(1) of this section does not apply solely by reason of the termination of a group because it is acquired, if there is a surviving group that is, immediately thereafter, a consolidated group. Instead, the surviving group is treated as the terminating group for purposes of applying this paragraph (e) to the terminating group. This treatment does not apply, however, to members of the terminating group that are not members of the surviving consolidated group immediately after the terminating group ceases to exist (e.g., under section 1504(a)(3) relating to reconsolidation, or section 1504(c) relating to includible insurance companies).

(3) *Certain corporate separations and reorganizations.*—The adjustments under paragraph (e)(1) of this section must be modified to the extent necessary to effectuate the principles of section 312(h). Thus, P's earnings and profits rather than S's earnings and profits may be eliminated immediately before S becomes a nonmember. P's earnings and profits are eliminated to the extent that its earnings and profits reflect S's earnings and profits after applying section 312(h) immediately after S becomes a nonmember (determined without taking this paragraph (e) into account).

(4) *Special uses of earnings and profits.*—Paragraph (e)(1) of this section does not apply for purposes of determining—

(i) The extent to which a distribution is charged to reserve accounts under section 593(e);

(ii) The extent to which a distribution is taxable to the recipient under sections 805(a)(4) and 832; and

(iii) Any other special use identified in guidance published in the Internal Revenue Bulletin.

(5) *Example.*—The principles of this paragraph (e) are illustrated by the following example.

*Example.* (a) *Facts.* Individuals A and B own all of P's stock, and P owns all of the stock of S and T, each with a $500 basis. For Year 1, S has $100 of earnings and profits and T has $50 of earnings and profits. Under paragraph (b)(1) of this section, the earnings and profits of S and T tier up to P, and P has $150 of earnings and profits for Year 1. P sells all of S's stock for $600 at the close of Year 1.

(b) *Analysis.* Under paragraph (e)(1) of this section, S's $100 of earnings and profits is eliminated immediately before S becomes a nonmember because the earnings and profits are taken into account under paragraph (b) of this section in P's earnings and profits. However, no corresponding adjustment is made to P's earnings and profits or to P's basis in S's stock for purposes of earnings and profits. P's earnings and profits for Year 1 remain $150 following the sale of S's stock.

(c) *Forward merger.* The facts are the same as in paragraph (a) of this *Example*, except that, rather than P selling S's stock, S merges into a nonmember in a transaction described in section 368(a)(2)(D). Under paragraph (h) of this section, the nonmember is treated as a successor to S. Thus, as in paragraph (b) of this *Example*, S's $100 of earnings and profits is eliminated immediately before S ceases to be a member.

(d) *Acquisition of entire group.* The facts are the same as in paragraph (a) of this *Example*, except that X, the common parent of another consolidated group, purchases all of P's stock at the close of Year 1, and P sells S's stock during Year 3. Under paragraph (e)(2) of this section, the earnings and profits of S and T are not eliminated as a result of X purchasing P's stock. However, S's earnings and profits from consolidated return years of both the P group and the X group are eliminated immediately before S becomes a nonmember of the X group.

(e) *Earnings and profits deficit.* The facts are the same as in paragraph (d) of this *Example,* except that S has a $550 deficit in earnings and profits for Year 1. The effect of paragraph (e)(1) of this section is the same. Under paragraph (c)(1) of this section, P would have an excess loss account in S's stock for earnings and profits purposes under the principles of §§1.1502-19 and 1.1502-32, and, under the principles of §1.1502-19(c)(2), the excess loss account is not taken into account as a result of X's purchase of P's stock. Under paragraph (e)(2) of this section, S's deficit is not eliminated under paragraph (e)(1) of this section immediately before X's purchase of P's stock. However, S's earnings and profits (or deficit) is eliminated immediately before S becomes a nonmember of the X group.

(f) *Section 355 distribution.* The facts are the same as in paragraph (a) of this *Example,* except that, rather than selling S's stock, P distributes S's stock to A at the close of Year 1 in a distribution to which section 355 applies. Under paragraph (e)(3) of this section, P's earnings and profits may be reduced under section 312(h) as a result of the distribution. To the extent that P's earnings and profits are reduced, S's earnings and profits are not eliminated under paragraph (e)(1) of this section.

(f) *Changes in the structure of the group.*—(1) *Changes in the common parent.*—(i) *General rule.*—If P succeeds another corporation under the principles of §1.1502-75(d)(2) or (3) as the common parent of a consolidated group (a group structure change), the earnings and profits of P are adjusted immediately after P becomes the new common parent to reflect the earnings and profits of the former common parent immediately before the former common parent ceases to be the common parent. The adjustment is made as if P succeeds to the earnings and profits of the former common parent in a transaction described in section 381(a). See §1.1502-31 for the basis of the stock of members following a group structure change.

(ii) *Minority shareholders.*—If the former common parent's stock is not wholly owned by members of the consolidated group immediately after the former common parent ceases to be the common parent, appropriate adjustments must be made to reflect in the new common parent only an allocable part of the former common parent's earnings and profits.

(iii) *Higher-tier members.*—To the extent that earnings and profits are adjusted under this paragraph (f)(1), and the former common parent is owned by members other than P, the earnings and profits of the intermediate subsidiaries must be adjusted in accordance with the principles of this section.

(iv) *Example.*—The principles of this paragraph (f)(1) are illustrated by the following example.

*Example.* (a) *Facts.* X is the common parent of a consolidated group with $100 of earnings and profits, and P is the common parent of another consolidated group with $20 of earnings and profits. P acquires all of X's stock at the close of Year 1 in exchange for 70% of P's stock. The exchange is a reverse acquisition under

§ 1.1502-75(d)(3), and the X group is treated as remaining in existence with P as its new common parent.

(b) *Adjustments for X group earnings and profits.* Under paragraph (f)(1) of this section, P's earnings and profits are adjusted immediately after P becomes the new common parent, to reflect X's $100 of earnings and profits immediately before X ceases to be the common parent. The adjustment is made as if P succeeds to X's earnings and profits in a transaction described in section 381(a). Thus, immediately after the acquisition, P has $120 of accumulated earnings and profits and X continues to have $100 of accumulated earnings and profits.

(c) *Adjustments for P group earnings and profits.* Although the P group terminates on P's acquisition of X's stock, under paragraph (e)(2) of this section, no adjustments are made to the earnings and profits of any subsidiaries in the terminating P group.

(d) *Acquisition of separate return corporation.* The facts are the same as in paragraph (a) of this *Example,* except that, immediately before the acquisition of its stock by P, X is not affiliated with any other corporation. The exchange is a reverse acquisition under § 1.1502-75(d)(3), and P is treated as the common parent of the X group. Consequently, the results are the same as in paragraphs (b) and (c) of this *Example.*

(2) *Change in the location of subsidiaries.*—If the location of a member within a group changes, appropriate adjustments must be made to the earnings and profits of the members to prevent the earnings and profits from being eliminated. For example, if P transfers all of S's stock to another member in a transaction to which section 351 and § 1.1502-13 apply, the transferee's earnings and profits are adjusted immediately after the transfer to reflect S's earnings and profits immediately before the transfer from consolidated return years. On the other hand, if the transferee purchases S's stock from P, the transferee's earnings and profits are not adjusted.

(g) *Anti-avoidance rule.*—If any person acts with a principal purpose contrary to the purposes of this section, to avoid the effect of the rules of this section or apply the rules of this section to avoid the effect of any other provision of the consolidated return regulations, adjustments must be made as necessary to carry out the purposes of this section.

(h) *Predecessors and successors.*—For purposes of this section, any reference to a corporation or to a share includes a reference to a successor or predecessor as the context may require. A corporation is a successor if its earnings and profits are determined, directly or indirectly, in whole or in part, by reference to the earnings and profits of another corporation (the predecessor). A share is a successor if its basis is determined, directly or indirectly, in whole or in part, by reference to the basis of another share (the predecessor).

(i) [Reserved]

(j) *Effective/applicability date.*—(1) *General rule.*—This section applies with respect to determinations of the earnings and profits of a member (e.g., for purposes of a characterizing a distribution to which section 301 applies) in consolidated return years beginning on or after January 1, 1995. If this section applies, earnings and profits must be determined or redetermined as if this section were in effect for all years (including, for example, the consolidated return years of another consolidated group to the extent the earnings and profits from those years are still reflected). For example, if a distribution by P to a nonmember shareholder in 1990 was a dividend because of an unabsorbed loss carryover attributable to S, P's earnings and profits in tax years beginning after January 1, 1995 are redetermined by taking into account a negative adjustment in the tax year S's loss arose and in 1990 for P's distribution, and any subsequent absorption of the loss has no effect on earnings and profits. Any such determination or redetermination does not, however, affect any prior period. Thus, the shareholder's treatment in 1990 of the distribution as a dividend (and the effect of the distribution on stock basis) is not redetermined under this section. Paragraphs (a)(2) and (e)(2)(i)(A) of this section apply with respect to determinations of the earnings and profits of a member in consolidated return years beginning on or after September 17, 2008. However, taxpayers may apply paragraph (e)(2)(i)(A) of this section with respect to determinations of the earnings and profits of a member in consolidated return years beginning prior to September 17, 2008.

(2) *Dispositions of stock before effective date.*—(i) *In general.*—If P disposes of stock of S in a consolidated return year beginning before January 1, 1995, the amount of P's earnings and profits with respect to S are not redetermined under paragraph (j)(1) of this section. See § 1.1502-19 as contained in the 26 CFR part 1 edition revised as of April 1, 1994 for the definition of disposition, and paragraph (j)(5) of this section for the rules applicable to such dispositions.

(ii) *Lower-tier members.*—Although P disposes of S's stock in a tax year beginning before January 1, 1995, S's determinations or

adjustments with respect to lower-tier members with which it continues to file a consolidated return are redetermined in accordance with the rules of this section (even if S's earnings and profits were previously taken into account by P). For example, assume that P owns all of S's stock, S owns all of T's stock, and T owns all of U's stock. If S sells 80% of T's stock in a tax year beginning before January 1, 1995 (the effective date), the amount of S's earnings and profits from the sale, and the adjustments to stock basis for earnings and profits purposes that are reflected in that amount, are not redetermined if P sells S's stock after the effective date. If S sells the remaining 20% of T's stock after the effective date, S's stock basis adjustments with respect to that T stock are also not redetermined because T became a nonmember before the effective date. However, if T and U continue to file a consolidated return with each other, paragraph (e)(1) of this section did not apply, and T sells U's stock after the effective date, T's earnings and profits with respect to U are redetermined (even though some of the earnings and profits may have been taken into account by S in its prior sale of T's stock before the effective date).

(iii) *Deferred amounts.*—For purposes of this paragraph (j)(2), a disposition does not include a transaction to which § 1.1502-13, § 1.1502-13T, § 1.1502-14, or § 1.1502-14T applies. Instead, the transaction is deemed to occur as the earnings and profits (if any) are taken into account.

(3) *Deconsolidations and group structure changes.*—(i) *In general.*— Paragraphs (e) and (f) of this section apply with respect to deconsolidations and group structure changes occurring in consolidated return years beginning on or after January 1, 1995.

(ii) *Prior period group structure changes.*—If there was a group structure change in a consolidated return year beginning before January 1, 1995, and earnings and profits were not determined under § 1.1502-33T(a) as contained in the 26 CFR part 1 edition revised as of April 1, 1994, a distribution in a tax year ending after September 7, 1988, of earnings and profits that are not reflected in the earnings and profits of the distributee member, but would have been so reflected if § 1.1502-33T(a) as contained in the 26 CFR part 1 edition revised as of April 1, 1994 had applied, the negative adjustment under paragraph (b) of this section for distributions does not apply (and there is therefore no offset to the increase in the earnings and profits of the distributee).

(4) *Deemed dividend elections.*—If there is a deemed distribution and recontribution pursuant to § 1.1502-32(f)(2) as contained in the 26 CFR part 1 edition revised as of April 1, 1994 in a consolidated return year beginning before January 1, 1995, the deemed distribution and recontribution under the election are treated as an actual distribution by S and recontribution by P as provided under the election.

(5) *Prior law.*—For prior determinations, see prior regulations under section 1502 as in effect with respect to the determination. See, e.g., §§ 1.1502-33 and 1.1502-33T as contained in the 26 CFR part 1 edition revised as of April 1, 1994.

(k) *Effective/applicability date.*—Paragraph (d)(5)(i)(D) of this section applies to any original consolidated Federal income tax return due (without extensions) after June 14, 2007. For original consolidated Federal income tax returns due (without extensions) after May 30, 2006, and on or before June 14, 2007, see § 1.1502-33T as contained in 26 CFR part 1 in effect on April 1, 2007. For original consolidated Federal income tax returns due (without extensions) on or before May 30, 2006, see § 1.1502-33 as contained in 26 CFR part 1 in effect on April 1, 2006. [Reg. § 1.1502-33.]

☐ [*T.D. 6909, 12-29-66. Amended by T.D. 6943, 1-15-68; T.D. 6962, 7-2-68; T.D. 7246, 12-29-72; T.D. 8226, 9-7-88; T.D. 8294, 3-9-90; T.D. 8319, 11-19-90; T.D. 8364, 9-13-91; T.D. 8560, 8-12-94; T.D. 8597, 7-12-9;5 T.D. 9264, 5-26-2006; T.D. 9329, 6-13-2007 and T.D. 9424, 9-9-2008 (corrected 10-17-2008).*]

### [Reg. § 1.1502-34]

**§ 1.1502-34. Special aggregate stock ownership rules.**—For purposes of §§ 1.1502-1 through 1.1502-80, in determining the stock ownership of a member of the group in another corporation (the "issuing corporation") for purposes of determining the application of section 165(g)(3)(A), 332(b)(1), 333(b), 351(a), 732(f), or 904(f), in a consolidated return year, there shall be included stock owned by all other members of the group in the issuing corporation. Thus, assume that members A, B, and C each own 33⅓ percent of the stock issued by D. In such case, A, B, and C shall each be treated as meeting the 80-percent stock ownership requirement for purposes of section 332, and no member can elect to have section 333 apply. Furthermore, the special rule for minority shareholders in section 337(d) cannot apply with respect to amounts received by A, B, or C in liquidation of D. [Reg. § 1.1502-34.]

☐ [*T.D. 6894, 9-7-66. Amended by T.D. 8949, 6-18-2001.*]

[Reg. § 1.1502-35]

**§ 1.1502-35. Transfers of subsidiary stock and deconsolidations of subsidiaries.**—(a) *In general.*—(1) *Purpose.*—The purpose of this section is to prevent a group from obtaining more than one tax benefit from a single economic loss. The provisions of this section shall be construed in a manner that is consistent with that purpose and in a manner that reasonably carries out that purpose.

(2) *Dates of applicability.*—This section applies if—

(i) On or after March 7, 2002, a member recognizes a loss on the disposition of a share of stock of a subsidiary (or, on or after April 10, 2007, a share of stock of a former subsidiary) or a carryover basis asset (subject to paragraph (c)(6) of this section),

(ii) The member's loss on the share of subsidiary stock or the carryover basis asset is allowed on or before the date that is ten years after the disposition of the share or carryover basis asset, and

(iii) If the disposition is of a share of subsidiary stock, it is not a transfer to which § 1.1502-36 applies.

(b) *Redetermination of basis on certain nondeconsolidating transfers of subsidiary stock and on certain deconsolidations of subsidiaries.*—(1) *Redetermination of basis on certain nondeconsolidating transfers of subsidiary stock.*—Except as provided in paragraph (b)(3)(i) of this section, if, immediately after a transfer of stock of a subsidiary that has a basis that exceeds its value, the subsidiary remains a member of the group, then the basis in each share of subsidiary stock owned by each member of the group shall be redetermined in accordance with the provisions of this paragraph (b)(1) immediately before such transfer. All of the members' bases in the shares of subsidiary stock immediately before such transfer shall be aggregated. Such aggregated basis shall be allocated first to the shares of the subsidiary's preferred stock that are owned by the members of the group immediately before such transfer, in proportion to, but not in excess of, the value of those shares at such time. After allocation of the aggregated basis to all shares of the preferred stock of the subsidiary pursuant to the preceding sentence, any remaining basis shall be allocated among all common shares of subsidiary stock held by members of the group immediately before the transfer, in proportion to the value of such shares at such time.

(2) *Redetermination of basis on certain deconsolidations of subsidiaries.*—(i) *Allocation of reallocable basis amount.*—Except as provided in paragraph (b)(3)(ii) of this section, if, immediately before a deconsolidation of a subsidiary, any share of stock of such subsidiary owned by a member of the group has a basis that exceeds its value, then the basis in each share of the subsidiary's stock owned by each member of the group shall be redetermined in accordance with the provisions of this paragraph (b)(2) immediately before such deconsolidation. The basis in each share of the subsidiary's stock held by members of the group immediately before the deconsolidation that has a basis in excess of value at such time shall be reduced, but not below such share's value, in a manner that, to the greatest extent possible, causes the ratio of the basis to the value of each such share to be the same; provided, however, that the aggregate amount of such reduction shall not exceed the reallocable basis amount (as computed pursuant to paragraph (b)(2)(ii) of this section). Then, to the extent of the reallocable basis amount, the basis of each share of the preferred stock of the subsidiary that are held by members of the group immediately before the deconsolidation shall be increased, but not above such share's value, in a manner that, to the greatest extent possible, causes the ratio of the basis to the value of each such share to be the same. Then, to the extent that the reallocable basis amount does not increase the basis of shares of preferred stock of the subsidiary pursuant to the third sentence of this paragraph (b)(2)(i), such amount shall increase the basis of all common shares of the subsidiary's stock held by members of the group immediately before the deconsolidation in a manner that, to the greatest extent possible, causes the ratio of the basis to the value of each such share to be the same.

(ii) *Calculation of reallocable basis amount.*—The reallocable basis amount shall equal the lesser of—

(A) The aggregate of all amounts by which, immediately before the deconsolidation, the basis exceeds the value of a share of subsidiary stock owned by any member of the group at such time; and

(B) The total of the subsidiary's (and any predecessor's) items of deduction and loss, and the subsidiary's (and any predecessor's) allocable share of items of deduction and loss of all lower-tier subsidiaries, that were taken into account in computing the adjustment under § 1.1502-32 to the bases of shares of stock of the subsidiary (and any predecessor) held by members of the group immediately before the deconsolidation, other than shares that have bases in excess of value immediately before the deconsolidation.

(3) *Exceptions to application of redetermination rules.*—(i) Paragraph (b)(1) of this section shall not apply to a transfer of subsidiary stock if—

(A) During the taxable year of such transfer, in one or more fully taxable transactions, the members of the group dispose of all of the shares of the subsidiary stock that they own immediately before the transfer, other than the shares the transfer of which would otherwise trigger the application of paragraph (b)(1) of this section, to a person or persons that are not members of the group;

(B) During the taxable year of such transfer, the members of the group are allowed a worthless stock loss under section 165(g) (taking into account the provisions of § 1.1502-80(c)) with respect to all of the shares of subsidiary stock that they own immediately before the transfer, other than the shares the transfer of which would otherwise trigger the application of paragraph (b)(1) of this section; or

(C) Such transfer is to a member of the group and section 332 (provided the stock is transferred to an 80-percent distributee), section 351, section 354, or section 361 applies to such transfer.

(ii) Paragraph (b)(2) of this section shall not apply to a deconsolidation of a subsidiary if—

(A) During the taxable year of such deconsolidation, in one or more fully taxable transactions, the members of the group dispose of all of the shares of the subsidiary stock that they own immediately before the deconsolidation to a person or persons that are not members of the group;

(B) Such deconsolidation results from a fully taxable disposition, to a person or persons that are not members of the group, of some of the shares of the subsidiary, and, during the taxable year of such deconsolidation, the members of the group are allowed a worthless stock loss under section 165(g) with respect to all of the shares of the subsidiary stock that they own immediately after the deconsolidation;

(C) The members of the group are allowed a worthless stock loss under section 165(g) with respect to all of the shares of the subsidiary stock that they own immediately before the deconsolidation;

(D) The deconsolidation of the subsidiary results from the deconsolidation of a higher-tier subsidiary and, immediately after the deconsolidation of the subsidiary, none of the stock of the subsidiary is owned by a group member; or

(E) The deconsolidation of the subsidiary results from a termination of the group.

(4) *Special rule for lower-tier subsidiaries.*—If, immediately after a transfer of subsidiary stock or a deconsolidation of a subsidiary, a lower-tier subsidiary some of the stock of which is owned by the subsidiary is a member of the group, then, for purposes of applying this paragraph (b), the subsidiary shall be treated as having transferred its stock of the lower-tier subsidiary. This principle shall apply to stock of subsidiaries that are owned by such lower-tier subsidiary.

(5) *Stock basis adjustments for higher-tier stock.*—The basis adjustments required under this paragraph (b) result in basis adjustments to higher-tier member stock. The adjustments are applied in the order of the tiers, from the lowest to highest. For example, if a common parent owns stock of a subsidiary that owns stock of a lower-tier subsidiary and the subsidiary recognizes a loss on the disposition of a portion of its shares of the lower-tier subsidiary stock, the common parent must adjust its basis in its subsidiary stock under the principles of § 1.1502-32 to reflect the adjustments that the subsidiary must make to its basis in its stock of the lower-tier subsidiary.

(6) *Ordering rules.*—(i) The rules of this paragraph (b) apply after the rules of § 1.1502-32 are applied.

(ii) The rules of this paragraph (b) apply before the rules of § 1.337(d)-2 and paragraphs (c) and (f) of this section are applied.

(iii) This paragraph (b)(and any resulting basis adjustments to higher-tier member stock made pursuant to paragraph (b)(5) of this section) applies to redetermine the basis of stock of a lower-tier subsidiary before this paragraph (b) applies to higher-tier member of such lower-tier subsidiary.

(c) *Loss suspension.*—(1) *General rule.*—Any loss recognized by a member of a consolidated group with respect to the disposition of a share of subsidiary stock shall be suspended to the extent of the duplicated loss with respect to such share of stock if, immediately after the disposition, the subsidiary is a member of the consolidated group of which it was a member immediately prior to the disposition (or any successor group).

(2) *Special rule for lower-tier subsidiaries.*—This paragraph (c)(2) applies if neither paragraph (c)(1) nor (f) of this section applies to a member's disposition of a share of stock of a subsidiary (the departing member), a loss is recognized on the disposition of such share,

and the departing member owns stock of one or more other subsidiaries (a remaining member) that is a member of such group immediately after the disposition. In that case, such loss shall be suspended to the extent the duplicated loss with respect to the departing member stock disposed of is attributable to the remaining member or members.

(3) *Treatment of suspended loss.*—(i) *General rule.*—For purposes of the rules of § 1.1502-32, any loss suspended pursuant to paragraph (c)(1) or (c)(2) of this section is treated as a noncapital, nondeductible expense of the member that disposes of subsidiary stock, incurred during the taxable year that includes the date of the disposition of stock to which paragraph (c)(1) or (c)(2) of this section applies. See § 1.1502-32(b)(3)(iii)(C). Consequently, the basis of a higher-tier member's stock of the member that disposes of subsidiary stock is reduced by the suspended loss in the year it is suspended.

(ii) *Location of suspended loss following deconsolidation of selling member.*—If a member recognizes a loss that is suspended under this paragraph (c) but that member ceases to be a member of the group before the loss is allowable, the common parent is treated as succeeding to the loss in a transaction to which section 381(a) applies.

(4) *Reduction of suspended loss.*—(i) *General rule.*—The amount of any loss suspended pursuant to paragraph (c)(1) or (c)(2) of § 1.1502-35 shall be reduced, but not below zero, by the subsidiary's (and any successor's) items of deduction and loss, and the subsidiary's (and any successor's) allocable share of items of deduction and loss of all lower-tier subsidiaries, that are allocable to the period beginning on the date of the disposition that gave rise to the suspended loss and ending on the day before the first date on which the subsidiary (and any successor) is not a member of the group of which it was a member immediately prior to the disposition (or any successor group), and that are taken into account in determining consolidated taxable income (or loss) of such group for any taxable year that includes any date on or after the date of the disposition and before the first date on which the subsidiary (and any successor) is not a member of such group; provided, however, that such reduction shall not exceed the excess of the amount of such items over the amount of such items that are taken into account in determining the basis adjustments made under § 1.1502-32 to stock of the subsidiary (or any successor) owned by members of the group. The preceding sentence shall not apply to items of deduction and loss to the extent that the group can establish that all or a portion of the duplicated loss with respect to the subsidiary was not reflected in the computation of the duplicated loss with respect to the subsidiary on the date of the disposition of stock that gave rise to the suspended loss.

(ii) *Operating rules.*—(A) *Year in which deduction or loss is taken into account.*—For purposes of paragraph (c)(4)(i) of this section, a subsidiary's (or any successor's) deductions and losses are treated as taken into account when and to the extent they are absorbed by the subsidiary (or any successor) or any other member. To the extent that the subsidiary's (or any successor's) deduction or loss is absorbed in the year it arises or is carried forward and absorbed in a subsequent year (e.g., under section 172, 465, or 1212), the deduction is treated as taken into account in the year in which it is absorbed. To the extent that a subsidiary's (or any successor's) deduction or loss is carried back and absorbed in a prior year (whether consolidated or separate), the deduction or loss is treated as taken into account in the year in which it arises and not in the year in which it is absorbed.

(B) *Determination of items that are allocable to the post-disposition, pre-deconsolidation period.*—For purposes of paragraph (c)(4)(i) of this section, the determination of whether a subsidiary's (or any successor's) items of deduction and loss and allocable share of items of deduction and loss of all lower-tier subsidiaries are allocable to the period beginning on the date of the disposition of subsidiary stock that gave rise to the suspended loss and ending on the day before the first date on which the subsidiary (or any successor) is not a member of the consolidated group of which it was a member immediately prior to the disposition (or any successor group) is determined pursuant to the rules of § 1.1502-76(b)(2), without regard to § 1.1502-76(b)(2)(ii)(D), as if the subsidiary ceased to be a member of the group at the end of the day before the disposition and filed separate returns for the period beginning on the date of the disposition and ending on the day before the first date on which it is not a member of such group.

(5) *Allowable loss.*—(i) *General rule.*—To the extent not reduced under paragraph (c)(4) of this section, any loss suspended pursuant to paragraph (c)(1) or (c)(2) of this section shall be allowed, to the extent otherwise allowable under applicable provisions of the Internal Revenue Code and regulations, on a return filed by the group of which the subsidiary was a member on the date of the disposition of subsidiary stock that gave rise to the suspended loss (or any successor group) for the taxable year that includes the earlier of—

(A) The day before the first date on which the subsidiary (and any successor) is not a member of such group or the date the group is allowed a worthless stock loss under section 165 (taking into account the provisions of § 1.1502-80(c)) with respect to all of the subsidiary stock owned by members and;

(B) The date that is ten years after the date of the disposition of subsidiary stock that gave rise to the suspended loss.

(ii) *No tiering up of certain adjustments.*—No adjustments shall be made to a member's basis of stock of a subsidiary (or any successor) for a suspended loss that is taken into account under paragraph (c)(5)(i) of this section. See § 1.1502-32(a)(2).

(iii) *Statement of allowed loss.*—Paragraph (c)(5)(i) of this section applies only if the separate statement required under this paragraph (c)(5)(iii) is filed with, or as part of, the taxpayer's return for the year in which the loss is allowable. The statement must be entitled "ALLOWED LOSS UNDER § 1.1502-35(c)(5)" and must contain the name and employer identification number of the subsidiary the stock of which gave rise to the loss.

(6) *Special rule for dispositions of certain carryover basis assets.*—If—

(i) A member of a group recognizes a loss on the disposition of an asset other than stock of a subsidiary;

(ii) Such member's basis in the asset disposed of was determined, directly or indirectly, in whole or in part, by reference to the basis of stock of a subsidiary and, at the time of the determination of the member's basis in the asset disposed of, there was a duplicated loss with respect to such stock of the subsidiary; and

(iii) Immediately after the disposition, the subsidiary is a member of such group, then such loss shall be suspended pursuant to the principles of paragraphs (c)(1) and (c)(2) of this section to the extent of the duplicated loss with respect to such stock at the time of the determination of basis of the asset disposed of. Principles similar to those set forth in paragraphs (c)(3), (c)(4), and (c)(5) of this section shall apply to a loss suspended pursuant to this paragraph (c)(6).

(7) *Coordination with loss deferral, loss disallowance, and other rules.*—(i) *In general.*—Loss recognized on the disposition of subsidiary stock or another asset is subject to redetermination, deferral, or disallowance under other applicable provisions of the Internal Revenue Code and regulations thereunder, including sections 267(f) and 482. Paragraphs (c)(1), (c)(2), and (c)(6) of this section do not apply to a loss that is disallowed under any other provision. If loss is deferred under any other provision, paragraphs (c)(1), (c)(2), and (c)(6) of this section apply when the loss would otherwise be taken into account under such other provision. However, if an overriding event described in paragraph (c)(7)(ii) of this section occurs before the deferred loss is taken into account, paragraphs (c)(1), (c)(2), and (c)(6) of this section apply to the loss immediately before the event occurs, even though the loss may not be taken into account until a later time.

(ii) *Overriding events.*—For purposes of paragraph (c)(7)(i) of this section, the following are overriding events—

(A) The stock ceases to be owned by a member of the consolidated group;

(B) The stock is canceled or redeemed (regardless of whether it is retired or held as treasury stock); or

(C) The stock is treated as disposed of under § 1.1502-19(c)(1)(ii)(B) or (c)(1)(iii).

(8) *No elimination of economic loss.*—This paragraph (c) shall not be applied in a manner that permanently disallows a deduction for an economic loss, provided that such deduction is otherwise allowable. If the application of any provision of this paragraph (c) results in such a disallowance, proper adjustment may be made to prevent such a disallowance. Whether a provision of this paragraph (c) has resulted in such a disallowance is determined on the date on which the subsidiary (or any successor) the disposition of the stock of which gave rise to a suspended stock loss is not a member of the group or the date the group is allowed a worthless stock loss under section 165(g) (taking into account the provisions of § 1.1502-80(c)) with respect to all of such subsidiary stock owned by members. Proper adjustment in such cases shall be made by restoring the suspended stock loss immediately before the subsidiary ceases to be a member of the group or the group is allowed a worthless stock loss under section 165(g) (taking into account the provisions of § 1.1502-80(c)) with respect to all of such subsidiary stock owned by members, to the extent that its reduction pursuant to paragraph (c)(4) of this section had the result of permanently disallowing a deduction for an economic loss.

(9) *Ordering rule.*—The rules of this paragraph (c) apply after the rules of paragraph (b) of this section and § 1.337(d)-2 are applied.

(d) *Definitions.*—(1) *Disposition* means any event in which gain or loss is recognized, in whole or in part.

(2) *Deconsolidation* means any event that causes a subsidiary to no longer be a member of the consolidated group.

(3) *Value* means fair market value.

(4) *Duplicated loss.*—(i) *In general.*—Duplicated loss is determined immediately after a disposition and equals the excess, if any, of—

(A) The sum of—

(1) The aggregate adjusted basis of the subsidiary's assets other than any stock that subsidiary owns in another subsidiary;

(2) Any losses attributable to the subsidiary and carried to the subsidiary's first taxable year following the disposition; and

(3) Any deductions of the subsidiary that have been recognized but are deferred under a provision of the Internal Revenue Code (such as deductions deferred under section 469); over

(B) The sum of—

(1) The value of the subsidiary's stock; and

(2) Any liabilities of the subsidiary that have been taken into account for tax purposes.

(ii) *Special rules.*—(A) The amounts determined under paragraph (d)(4)(i) (other than amounts described in paragraph (d)(4)(i)(B)(*1*)) of this section with respect to a subsidiary include its allocable share of corresponding amounts with respect to all lower-tier subsidiaries. If 80 percent or more in value of the stock of a subsidiary is acquired by purchase in a single transaction (or in a series of related transactions during any 12-month period), the value of the subsidiary's stock may not exceed the purchase price of the stock divided by the percentage of the stock (by value) so purchased. For this purpose, stock is acquired by purchase if the transferee is not related to the transferor within the meaning of sections 267(b) and 707(b)(1), using the language "'10 percent'" instead of "'50 percent'" each place that it appears, and the transferee's basis in the stock is determined wholly by reference to the consideration paid for such stock.

(B) The amounts determined under paragraph (d)(4)(i) of this section are not applied more than once to suspend a loss under this section.

(5) *Predecessor and successor.*—A predecessor is a transferor of assets to a transferee (the successor) in a transaction—

(i) To which section 381(a) applies;

(ii) In which substantially all of the assets of the transferor are transferred to members in a complete liquidation;

(iii) In which the successor's basis in assets is determined (directly or indirectly, in whole or in part) by reference to the transferor's basis in such assets, but the transferee is a successor only with respect to the assets the basis of which is so determined; or

(iv) Which is an intercompany transaction, but only with respect to assets that are being accounted for by the transferor in a prior intercompany transaction.

(6) *Successor group.*—A surviving group is treated as a successor group of a consolidated group (the terminating group) that ceases to exist as a result of—

(i) The acquisition by a member of another consolidated group of either the assets of the common parent of the terminating group in a reorganization described in section 381(a)(2), or the stock of the common parent of the terminating group; or

(ii) The application of the principles of § 1.1502-75(d)(2) or (3).

(7) *Preferred stock, common stock.*—Preferred stock and common stock shall have the meanings set forth in § 1.1502-32(d)(2) and (3), respectively.

(8) *Higher-tier.*—A subsidiary is higher-tier with respect to a member if or to the extent investment adjustments under § 1.1502-32 with respect to the stock of the latter member would affect investment adjustments with respect to the stock of the former member.

(9) *Lower-tier.*—A subsidiary is lower-tier with respect to a member if or to the extent investment basis adjustments under § 1.1502-32 with respect to the stock of the former member would affect investment adjustments with respect to the stock of the latter member.

(e) *Examples.*—For purposes of the examples in this section, unless otherwise stated, all groups file consolidated returns on a calendar-year basis, the facts set forth the only corporate activity, all transactions are between unrelated persons, and tax liabilities are disregarded. In addition, all transactions described in section 362(a) are completed before October 22, 2004, and therefore are not subject to section 362(e)(2). The principles of paragraphs (a) through (d) of this section are illustrated by the following examples:

*Example 1. Nondeconsolidating sale of preferred stock of lower-tier subsidiary*— (i) *Facts.* P owns 100 percent of the common stock of each of

S1 and S2. S1 and S2 each have only one class of stock outstanding. P's basis in the stock of S1 is $100 and the value of such stock is $130. P's basis in the stock of S2 is $120 and the value of such stock is $90. P, S1, and S2 are all members of the P group. S1 and S2 form S3. In year 1, in transfers to which section 351 applies, S1 contributes $100 to S3 in exchange for all of the common stock of S3 and S2 contributes an asset with a basis of $50 and a value of $20 to S3 in exchange for all of the preferred stock of S3. S3 becomes a member of the P group. In Year 3, in a transaction that is not part of the plan that includes the contributions to S3, S2 sells the preferred stock of S3 for $20. Immediately after the sale, S3 is a member of the P group.

(ii) *Application of basis redetermination rule.* Because S2's basis in the preferred stock of S3 exceeds its value immediately prior to the sale and S3 is a member of the P group immediately after the sale, all of the P group members' bases in the stock of S3 is redetermined pursuant to paragraph (b)(1) of this section. Of the group members' total basis of $150 in the S3 stock, $20 is allocated to the preferred stock, the fair market value of the preferred stock on the date of the sale, and $130 is allocated to the common stock. S2's sale of the preferred stock results in the recognition of $0 of gain/loss. Pursuant to paragraph (b)(5) of this section, the redetermination of S1's and S2's bases in the stock of S3 results in adjustments to P's basis in the stock of S1 and S2. In particular, P's basis in the stock of S1 is increased by $30 to $130 and its basis in the stock of S2 is decreased by $30 to $90.

*Example 2. Deconsolidating sale of common stock*—(i) *Facts.* In Year 1, in a transfer to which section 351 applies, P contributes Asset A with a basis of $900 and a value of $200 to S in exchange for one share of S common stock (CS1). In Years 2 and 3, in successive but unrelated transfers to which section 351 applies, P transfers $200 to S in exchange for one share of S common stock (CS2), Asset B with a basis of $300 and a value of $200 in exchange for one share of S common stock (CS3), and Asset C with a basis of $1000 and a value of $200 in exchange for one share of S common stock (CS4). In Year 4, S sells Asset A for $200, recognizing $700 of loss that is used to offset income of P recognized during Year 4. As a result of the sale of Asset A, the basis of each of P's four shares of S common stock is reduced by $175. Therefore, the basis of CS1 is $725. The basis of CS2 is $25. The basis of CS3 is $125, and the basis of CS4 is $825. In Year 5 in a transaction that is not part of a plan that includes the Year 1 contribution, P sells CS4 for $200. Immediately after the sale of CS4, S is not a member of the P group.

(ii) *Application of basis redetermination rule.* Because P's basis in each of CS1 and CS4 exceeds its value immediately prior to the deconsolidation of S, P's basis in its shares of S common stock is redetermined pursuant to paragraph (b)(2) of this section. Pursuant to paragraph (b)(2)(ii) of this section, the reallocable basis amount is $350 (the lesser of $1150, the gross loss inherent in the stock of S owned by P immediately before the sale, and $350, the aggregate amount of S's items of deduction and loss that were previously taken into account in the computation of the adjustment to the basis of the stock of S that P did not hold at a loss immediately before the deconsolidation). Pursuant to paragraph (b)(2)(i) of this section, first, P's basis in CS1 is reduced from $725 to $600 and P's basis in CS4 is reduced from $825 to $600. Then, the reallocable basis amount increases P's basis in CS2 from $25 to $250 and P's basis in CS3 from $125 to $250. P recognizes $400 of loss on the sale of CS4. The loss suspension rule does not apply because S is no longer a member of the P group. Thus, the loss is allowable at that time.

*Example 3. Nondeconsolidating sale of common stock*—(i) *Facts.* In Year 1, P forms S with a contribution of $80 in exchange for 80 shares of the common stock of S, which at that time represents all of the outstanding stock of S. S becomes a member of the P group. In Year 2, P contributes Asset A with a basis of $50 and a value of $20 in exchange for 20 shares of the common stock of S in a transfer to which section 351 applies. In Year 4, in a transaction that is not part of the plan that includes the Year 2 contribution, P sells the 20 shares of the common stock of S that it acquired in Year 2 for $20. Immediately after the Year 4 stock sale, S is a member of the P group. At the time of the Year 4 stock sale, S has $80 and Asset A. In Year 5, S sells Asset A, the basis and value of which have not changed since its contribution to S. On the sale of Asset A for $20, S recognizes a $30 loss. The P group cannot establish that all or a portion of the $30 loss was not reflected in the calculation of the duplicated loss of S on the date of the Year 4 stock sale. The $30 loss is used on the P group return to offset income of P. In Year 6, P sells its remaining S common stock for $80.

(ii) *Application of basis redetermination and loss suspension rules.* Because P's basis in the common stock sold exceeds its value immediately prior to the sale and S is a member of the P group immediately after the sale, P's basis in all of the stock of S is redetermined pursuant to paragraph (b)(1) of this section. Of P's total basis of $130 in the S common stock, a proportionate amount is allocated to each of the 100 shares of S common stock. Accordingly, $26 is allocated to the common stock of S that is sold and $104 is allocated to the common stock of S that is retained. On P's sale of the 20 shares of the common stock of S for $20, P recognizes a loss of $6. Because the sale of the 20 shares of common stock of S does not result in the deconsolidation of S, under paragraph (c)(1) of this section, that loss is suspended to the extent of the duplicated loss with respect to the shares sold. The duplicated loss with respect to the shares sold is $6. Therefore, the entire $6 loss is suspended.

(iii) *Effect of subsequent asset sale on stock basis.* Of the $30 loss recognized on the sale of Asset A, $24 is taken into account in determining the basis adjustments made under §1.1502-32 to the stock of S owned by P. Accordingly, P's basis in its S stock is reduced by $24 from $104 to $80.

(iv) *Effect of subsequent asset sale on suspended loss.* Because P cannot establish that all or a portion of the loss recognized on the sale of Asset A was not reflected in the calculation of the duplicated loss of S on the date of the Year 4 stock sale and such loss is allocable to the period beginning on the date of the Year 4 stock sale and ending on the day before the first date on which S is not a member of the P group and is taken into account in determining consolidated taxable income (or loss) of the P group for a taxable year that includes a date on or after the date of the Year 4 disposition and before the first date on which S is not a member of the P group, such asset loss reduces the suspended loss pursuant to paragraph (c)(4) of this section. The amount of such reduction, however, cannot exceed $6, the excess of the amount of such loss, $30, over the amount of such loss that is taken into account in determining the basis adjustment made to the stock of S owned by P, $24. Therefore, the suspended loss is reduced to zero.

(v) *Effect of subsequent stock sale.* P recognizes $0 gain/loss on the Year 6 sale of its remaining S common stock. No amount of suspended loss remains to be allowed under paragraph (c)(5) of this section.

*Example 4. Nondeconsolidating sale of common stock of lower-tier subsidiary*—(i) *Facts.* In Year 1, P forms S1 with a contribution of $200 in exchange for all of the common stock of S1, which represents all of the outstanding stock of S1. In the same year, S1 forms S2 with a contribution of $80 in exchange for 80 shares of the common stock of S2, which at that time represents all of the outstanding stock of S2. S1 and S2 become members of the P group. In the same year, S2 purchases Asset A for $80. In Year 2, S1 contributes Asset B with a basis of $50 and a value of $20 in exchange for 20 shares of the common stock of S2 in a transfer to which section 351 applies. In Year 4, S1 sells the 20 shares of the common stock of S2 that it acquired in Year 2 for $20. Immediately after the Year 4 stock sale, S2 is a member of the P group. At the time of the Year 4 stock sale, the bases and values of Asset A and Asset B are unchanged. In Year 5, S2 sells Asset B for $45, recognizing a $5 loss. The P group cannot establish that all or a portion of the $5 loss was not reflected in the calculation of the duplicated loss of S2 on the date of the Year 4 stock sale. The $5 loss is used on the P group return to offset income of P. In Year 6, S1 sells its remaining S2 common stock for $100.

(ii) *Application of basis redetermination and loss suspension rules.* Because S1's basis in the S2 common stock sold exceeds its value immediately prior to the sale and S2 is a member of the P group immediately after the sale, S1's basis in all of the stock of S2 is redetermined pursuant to paragraph (b)(1) of this section. Of S1's total basis of $130 in the S2 common stock, a proportionate amount is allocated to each of the 100 shares of S2 common stock. Accordingly, a total of $26 is allocated to the common stock of S2 that is sold and $104 is allocated to the common stock of S2 that is retained. On S1's sale of the 20 shares of the common stock of S2 for $20, S1 recognizes a loss of $6. Because the sale of the 20 shares of common stock of S2 does not result in the deconsolidation of S2, under paragraph (c)(1) of this section, that loss is suspended to the extent of the duplicated loss with respect to the shares sold. The duplicated loss with respect to the shares sold is $6. Therefore, the entire $6 loss is suspended. Pursuant to paragraph (c)(3) of this section and §1.1502-32(b)(3)(iii)(C), the suspended loss is treated as a noncapital, nondeductible expense incurred by S1 during the tax year that includes the date of the disposition of stock to which paragraph (c)(1) of this section applies. Accordingly, P's basis in its S1 stock is reduced from $200 to $194.

(iii) *Effect of subsequent asset sale on stock basis.* Of the $5 loss recognized on the sale of Asset B, $4 is taken into account in determining the basis adjustments made under §1.1502-32 to the stock of S2 owned by S1. Accordingly, S1's basis in its S2 stock is reduced by $4 from $104 to $100 and P's basis in its S1 stock is reduced by $4 from $194 to $190.

(iv) *Effect of subsequent asset sale on suspended loss.* Because P cannot establish that all or a portion of the loss recognized on the sale of Asset B was not reflected in the calculation of the duplicated loss of S2 on the date of the Year 4 stock sale and such loss is allocable to the period beginning on the date of the Year 4 disposition of the S2 stock and ending on the day before the first date on which S2 is not a

member of the P group and is taken into account in determining consolidated taxable income (or loss) of the P group for a taxable year that includes a date on or after the date of the Year 4 disposition and before the first date on which S2 is not a member of the P group, such asset loss reduces the suspended loss pursuant to paragraph (c)(4) of this section. The amount of such reduction, however, cannot exceed $1, the excess of the amount of such loss, $5, over the amount of such loss that is taken into account in determining the basis adjustment made to the stock of S2 owned by members of the P group, $4. Therefore, the suspended loss is reduced to $5.

(v) *Effect of subsequent stock sale.* In year 6, when S1 sells its remaining S2 stock for $100, it recognizes $0 gain/loss. Pursuant to paragraph (c)(5) of this section, the remaining $5 of the suspended loss is allowed on the P group's return for Year 6 when S1 sells its remaining S2 stock.

*Example 5. Deconsolidating sale of subsidiary owning stock of another subsidiary that remains in group*—(i) *Facts.* In Year 1, P forms S1 with a contribution of Asset A with a basis of $50 and a value of $20 in exchange for 100 shares of common stock of S1 in a transfer to which section 351 applies. Also in Year 1, P and S1 form S2. P contributes $80 to S2 in exchange for 80 shares of common stock of S2. S1 contributes Asset A to S2 in exchange for 20 shares of common stock of S2 in a transfer to which section 351 applies. In Year 3, in a transaction that is not part of a plan that includes the Year 1 contributions, P sells its 100 shares of S1 common stock for $20. Immediately after the Year 3 stock sale, S2 is a member of the P group. At the time of the Year 3 stock sale, S1 owns 20 shares of common stock of S2, and S2 has $80 and Asset A. In Year 4, S2 sells Asset A, the basis and value of which have not changed since its contribution to S2. On the sale of Asset A for $20, S2 recognizes a $30 loss. That $30 loss is used on the P group return to offset income of P. In Year 5, P sells its S2 common stock for $80.

(ii) *Application of basis redetermination and loss suspension rules.* Pursuant to paragraph (b)(4) of this section, because immediately before P's transfer of S1 stock S1 owns stock of S2 (another subsidiary of the same group) that has a basis that exceeds its value, paragraph (b) of this section applies as if S1 had transferred its stock of S2. Because S2 is a member of the group immediately after the transfer of the S1 stock, the group member's basis in the S2 stock is redetermined pursuant to paragraph (b)(1) of this section immediately prior to the sale of the S1 stock. Of the group members' total basis of $130 in the S2 stock, $26 is allocated to S1's 20 shares of S2 common stock and $104 is allocated to P's 80 shares of S2 common stock. Pursuant to paragraph (b)(5) of this section, the redetermination of S1's basis in the stock of S2 results in an adjustment to P's basis in the stock of S1. In particular, P's basis in the stock of S1 is decreased by $24 to $26. On P's sale of its 100 shares of S1 common stock for $20, P recognizes a loss of $6. Because S1 is not a member of the P group immediately after P's sale of the S1 stock, paragraph (c)(1) of this section does not apply to suspend such loss. However, because P recognizes a loss with respect to the disposition of the S1 stock and S1 owns stock of S2 (which is a member of the P group immediately after the disposition), paragraph (c)(2) of this section does apply to suspend up to $6 of that loss, an amount equal to the amount by which the duplicated loss with respect to the stock of S1 sold is attributable to S2's adjusted basis in its assets, loss carryforwards, and deferred deductions.

(iii) *Effect of subsequent asset sale on stock basis.* Of the $30 loss recognized on the sale of Asset A, $24 is taken into account in determining the basis adjustments made under §1.1502-32 to the stock of S2 owned by P. Accordingly, P's basis in its S2 stock is reduced by $24 from $104 to $80.

(iv) *Effect of subsequent asset sale on suspended loss.* Because P cannot establish that all or a portion of the loss recognized on the sale of Asset A was not reflected in the calculation of the duplicated loss of S2 on the date of the Year 3 stock sale and such loss is allocable to the period beginning on the date of the Year 3 deemed disposition of the S2 stock and ending on the day before the first date on which S2 is not a member of the P group and is taken into account in determining consolidated taxable income (or loss) of the P group for a taxable year that includes a date on or after the date of the Year 3 deemed disposition and before the first date on which S2 is not a member of the P group, such asset loss reduces the suspended loss pursuant to paragraph (c)(4) of this section. The amount of such reduction, however, cannot exceed $6, the excess of the amount of such loss, $30, over the amount of such loss that is taken into account in determining the basis adjustment made to the stock of S2 owned by P, $24. Therefore, the suspended loss is reduced to zero.

(v) *Effect of subsequent stock sale.* P recognizes $0 gain/loss on the Year 5 sale of its remaining S2 common stock. No amount of suspended loss remains to be allowed under paragraph (c)(5) of this section.

*Example 6. Loss recognized on asset with basis determined by reference to stock basis of subsidiary*—(i) *Facts.* In Year 1, P forms S with a contribution of $80 in exchange for 80 shares of common stock of S which at that time represents all of the outstanding stock of S. S becomes a member of the P group. In Year 2, P contributes Asset A with a basis of $50 and a value of $20 in exchange for 20 shares of common stock of S in a transfer to which section 351 applies. In Year 4, in a transaction that is not part of a plan that includes the Year 1 and Year 2 contributions, P contributes the 20 shares of S common stock it acquired in Year 2 to PS, in exchange for a 20 percent capital and profits interest in a transaction described in section 721. Immediately after the contribution to PS, S is a member of the P group. In Year 5, P sells its interest in PS for $20.

(ii) *Application of basis redetermination rule upon nonrecognition transfer.* Because P's basis in the S common stock contributed to PS exceeds its value immediately prior to the transfer and S is a member of the P group immediately after the transfer, P's basis in all of the S stock is redetermined pursuant to paragraph (b)(1) of this section. Of P's total basis of $130 in the common stock of S, a proportionate amount is allocated to each share of S common stock. Accordingly, $26 is allocated to the S common stock that is contributed to PS and, under section 722, P's basis in its interest in PS is $26.

(iii) *Application of loss suspension rule on disposition of asset with basis determined by reference to stock basis of subsidiary.* P recognizes a $6 loss on its disposition of its interest in PS. Because P's basis in its interest in PS was determined by reference to the basis of S stock and at the time of the determination of P's basis in its interest in PS such S stock had a duplicated loss of $6, and, immediately after the disposition, S is a member of the P group, such loss is suspended to the extent of such duplicated loss. Principles similar to those of paragraphs (c)(3), (c)(4), and (c)(5) of this section shall apply to such suspended loss.

(f) *Worthlessness not followed by separate return years.*—Notwithstanding any other provision in the regulations under section 1502, if a member of a group (the claiming group) treats stock of a subsidiary as worthless under section 165 (taking into account the provisions of § 1.1502-80(c)) and, on the day following the last day of the claiming group's taxable year in which the worthless stock deduction is claimed, the subsidiary (or its successor, determined without regard to paragraphs (d)(5)(iii) and (iv) of this section) is a member of a group that includes any corporation that, during that taxable year, was a member of the claiming group (other than a lower-tier subsidiary of the subsidiary) or is a successor (determined without regard to paragraphs (d)(5)(iii) and (iv) of this section) of such a member, then all losses treated as attributable to the subsidiary under the principles of § 1.1502-21(b)(2)(iv) shall be treated as expired as of the beginning of the day following the last day of the claiming group's taxable year in which the worthless stock deduction is claimed. In addition, notwithstanding any other provision in the regulations under section 1502, if a member recognizes a loss with respect to subsidiary stock and on the following day the subsidiary is not a member of the group and does not have a separate return year, then all losses treated as attributable to the subsidiary under the principles of § 1.1502-21(b)(2)(iv) shall be treated as expired as of the beginning of the day following the last day of the group's taxable year in which the stock loss is claimed. For purposes of this paragraph (f), the determination of the losses attributable to the subsidiary shall be made after computing the taxable income of the group for the taxable year in which the group treats the stock of the subsidiary as worthless or the subsidiary liquidates and after computing the taxable income for any taxable year to which such losses may be carried back. The loss treated as expired under this paragraph (f) shall not be treated as a noncapital, nondeductible expense under § 1.1502-32(b)(2)(iii). This paragraph (f) applies to worthlessness determinations and liquidations that occur on or after March 10, 2006. For rules applicable to worthless determinations and liquidations before March 10, 2006, see § 1.1502-35T(f)(1) and (2) as contained in 26 CFR part 1 in effect on January 1, 2006.

(g) *Anti-avoidance rules.*—(1) *Transfer of share without a loss in avoidance.*—If a share of subsidiary stock has a basis that does not exceed its value and the share is transferred with a view to avoiding application of the rules of paragraph (b) of this section prior to the transfer of a share of subsidiary stock that has a basis that does exceed its value or a deconsolidation of a subsidiary, the rules of paragraph (b) of this section shall apply immediately prior to the transfer of stock that has a basis that does not exceed its value.

(2) *Transfers of loss property in avoidance.*—If a member of a consolidated group contributes an asset with a basis that exceeds its value to a partnership in a transaction described in section 721 or a corporation that is not a member of such group in a transfer described in section 351, such partnership or corporation contributes such asset to a subsidiary in a transfer described in section 351, and such contributions are undertaken with a view to avoiding the rules of paragraph (b) or (c) of this section, adjustments must be made to carry out the purposes of this section.

(3) *Anti-loss reimportation rule.*—(i) *Conditions for application.*—This paragraph (g)(3) applies when—

(A) A member of a group (selling group) recognized and was allowed a loss with respect to a share of stock of S, a subsidiary or former subsidiary of the selling group;

(B) That stock loss was duplicated (in whole or in part) in S's attributes (duplicating items) at the earlier of the time that the loss was recognized or that S ceased to be a member; and

(C) Within ten years of the date that S ceased to be a member, there is a reimportation event. For this purpose, a reimportation event is any event after which a duplicating item is a reimported item. A reimported item is any duplicating item that is reflected in the attributes of any member of the selling group, including S, or, if not reflected in the attributes, would be properly taken into account by any member of the selling group (for example as the result of a carryback).

(ii) *Effect of application.*—Immediately before the time that a reimported item (or any portion of a reimported item) would be properly taken into account (but for the application of this paragraph (g)(3)), such item (or such portion of the item) is reduced to zero and no deduction or loss is allowed, directly or indirectly, with respect to that item.

(iii) *Operating rules.*—For purposes of this paragraph (g)(3)—

(A) The terms *member*, *subsidiary*, and *group* include their predecessors and successors to the extent necessary to effectuate the purposes of this section; and

(B) The reduction of a reimported item (other than duplicating items that are carried back to a consolidated return year of the selling group) is a noncapital, nondeductible expense within the meaning of § 1.1502-32(b)(3)(iii).

(4) *Avoidance of recognition of gain.*—(i) If a transaction is structured with a view to, and has the effect of, deferring or avoiding the recognition of gain on a disposition of stock by invoking the application of paragraph (b)(1) of this section to redetermine the basis of stock of a subsidiary, and the stock loss that gives rise to the application of paragraph (b)(1) of this section is not significant, paragraphs (b) and (c) of this section shall not apply.

(ii) If a transaction is structured with a view to, and has the effect of, deferring or avoiding the recognition of gain on a disposition of stock by invoking the application of paragraph (b)(2) of this section to redetermine the basis of stock of a subsidiary, and the duplicated loss of the subsidiary that is reflected in stock of the subsidiary owned by members of the group immediately before the deconsolidation is not significant, paragraphs (b) and (c) of this section shall not apply.

(5) *Examples.*—For purposes of the examples in this section, all transactions described in section 362(a) are completed before October 22, 2004, and therefore are not subject to section 362(e)(2). The principles of this paragraph (g) are illustrated by the following examples:

*Example 1. Transfers of property in avoidance of basis redetermination rule*—(i) *Facts.* In Year 1, P forms S with a contribution of $100 in exchange for 100 shares of common stock of S which at that time represents all of the outstanding stock of S. S becomes a member of the P group. In Year 2, P contributes 20 shares of common stock of S to PS, a partnership, in exchange for a 20 percent capital and profits interest in a transaction described in section 721. In Year 3, P contributes Asset A with a basis of $50 and a value of $20 to PS in exchange for an additional capital and profits interest in PS in a transaction described in section 721. Also in Year 3, PS contributes Asset A to S and P contributes an additional $80 to S in transfers to which section 351 applies. In Year 4, S sells Asset A for $20, recognizing a loss of $30. The P group uses that loss to offset income of P. In Year 5, P sells its entire interest in PS for $40.

(ii) *Analysis.* Pursuant to paragraph (g)(2) of this section, if P's contributions of S stock and Asset A to PS were undertaken with a view to avoiding the application of the basis redetermination or the loss suspension rule, adjustments must be made such that the group does not obtain more than one tax benefit from the $30 loss inherent in Asset A.

*Example 2. Transfers effecting a reimportation of loss*—(i) *Facts.* In Year 1, P forms S with a contribution of Asset A with a value of $100 and a basis of $120, Asset B with a value of $50 and a basis of $70, and Asset C with a value of $90 and a basis of $100 in exchange for all of the common stock of S and S becomes a member of the P group. In Year 2, in a transaction that is not part of a plan that includes the contribution, P sells the stock of S for $240, recognizing a loss of $50. At such time, the bases and values of Assets A, B, and C have not changed since their contribution to S. In Year 3, S sells Asset A, recognizing a $20 loss. In Year 3, S merges into M in a reorganization described in section 368(a)(1)(A). In Year 8, P purchases all of the stock of M for $300. At that time, M has a $10 net operating loss. In addition, M owns Asset D, which was acquired in an exchange described in section 1031 in connection with the surrender of Asset B. Asset C has a value of $80 and a basis of $100. Asset D has a value of $60 and a basis of $70. In Year 9, P has operating income of $100 and M recognizes $20 of loss on the sale of Asset C. In Year 10, P has operating income of $50 and M recognizes $50 of loss on the sale of Asset D.

(ii) *Analysis.* P's $50 loss on the sale of S stock is entirely attributable to duplicated loss. Therefore, pursuant to paragraph (g)(3) of this section, assuming the P group cannot establish otherwise, M's $10 net operating loss is treated as attributable to assets that were owned by S on the date of the disposition and that had bases in excess of value on such date. Without regard to any other limitations on the group's use of M's net operating loss, the P group cannot use M's $10 net operating loss pursuant to paragraph (g)(3)(iii)(D) of this section. Pursuant to paragraph (g)(3)(iv) of this section and §1.1502-32(b)(3)(iii)(D), such loss is treated as a noncapital, nondeductible expense of M incurred during the taxable year that it would otherwise be absorbed, namely in Year 9. In addition, the P group is denied the use of $10 of the loss recognized on the sale of Asset C. Finally, the P group is denied the use of $10 of the loss recognized on the sale of Asset D. Pursuant to paragraph (g)(3)(iv) of this section and §1.1502-32(b)(3)(iii)(D), each such disallowed loss is treated as a noncapital, nondeductible expense of M incurred during the taxable year that includes the date of the disposition of the asset with respect to which such loss was recognized.

*Example 3. Transfers to avoid recognition of gain*—(i) *Facts.* P owns all of the stock of S1 and S2. The S2 stock has a basis of $400 and a value of $500. S1 owns 50% of the S3 common stock with a basis of $150. S2 owns the remaining 50% of the S3 common stock with a basis of $100 and a value of $200 and one share of S3 preferred stock with a basis of $10 and a value of $9. P intends to sell all of its S2 stock to an unrelated buyer. P, therefore, engages in the following steps to dispose of S2 without recognizing a substantial portion of the built-in gain in S2. First, P causes a recapitalization of S3 in which S2's S3 common stock is exchanged for new S3 preferred shares. P then sells all of its S2 stock. Immediately after the sale of the S2 stock, S3 is a member of the P group.

(ii) *Analysis.* Pursuant to paragraph (b)(4) of this section, because S2 owns stock of S3 (another subsidiary of the same group) and, immediately after the sale of the S2 stock, S3 is a member of the group, then for purposes of applying paragraph (b) of this section, S2 is deemed to have transferred its S3 stock. Because S3 is a member of the group immediately after the transfer of the S2 stock and the S3 stock deemed transferred has a basis in excess of value, the group in the S3 stock is redetermined pursuant to paragraph (b)(1) of this section immediately prior to the sale of the S2 stock. Accordingly, P would recognize only $1 of gain on the sale of its S2 stock. However, because the recapitalization of the S3 was structured with a view to, and has the effect of, avoiding the recognition of gain on a disposition of stock by invoking the application of paragraph (b) of this section, paragraph (g)(4)(i) of this section applies. Accordingly, paragraph (b) of this section does not apply upon P's disposition of the S2 stock and P recognizes $100 gain on the disposition of the S2 stock.

(6) *General anti-avoidance rule.*—If a taxpayer acts with a view to avoid the purposes of this section, appropriate adjustments will be made to carry out the purposes of this section.

(h) *Application of other rules of law.*—See §1.1502-80(a) regarding the general applicability of other rules of law.

(i) [Reserved].

(j) *Effective/applicability dates.*—This section applies after September 16, 2008. For prior law, see §§1.1502-35 and 1.1502-35T as contained in 26 CFR part 1 in effect on April 1, 2008 [Reg. §1.1502-35.]

☐ [*T.D. 9254, 3-9-2006. Amended by T.D. 9264, 5-26-2006 (corrected 8-18-2006); T.D. 9322, 4-9-2007; T.D. 9342, 7-19-2007 and T.D. 9424, 9-9-2008 (corrected 3-4-2010).*]

### [Reg. §1.1502-36]

**§1.1502-36. Unified loss rule.**—(a) *In general.*—(1) *Scope.*—This section provides rules for adjusting members' bases in stock of a subsidiary (S) and for reducing S's attributes when a member (M) transfers a loss share of S stock. See paragraph (f) of this section for definitions of the terms used in this section, including *transfer* and *value.*

(2) *Purpose.*—The rules in this section have two principal purposes. The first is to prevent the consolidated return provisions from reducing a group's consolidated taxable income through the creation and recognition of noneconomic loss on S stock. The second is to prevent members (including former members) of the group from collectively obtaining more than one tax benefit from a single economic loss. Additional purposes are set forth in other paragraphs of

this section. The rules of this section must be interpreted and applied in a manner that is consistent with and reasonably carries out the purposes of this section.

(3) *Overview.*—(i) *General application of section.*—This section applies when M transfers a share of S stock and, after taking into account the effects of all applicable rules of law (even if the adjustments required by such provisions are not deemed effective until after the transfer, such as certain adjustments required under sections 108 and 1017 and §1.1502-28), the share is a loss share. When this section applies, paragraph (b) of this section applies first and may redetermine members' bases in their shares of S stock. If the transferred share is a loss share after any basis redetermination under paragraph (b) of this section, paragraph (c) of this section applies and may reduce M's basis in the transferred loss share. If the transferred share is a loss share after any basis reduction required by paragraph (c) of this section, paragraph (d) of this section applies and may reduce attributes of S and subsidiaries that are lower-tier to S. Although the determination of whether there is a transfer of a loss share is made as of the transfer, this section applies, and any adjustments it requires are given effect, immediately before the transfer. Paragraphs (e), (f), and (g) of this section provide general operating rules (including rules for transfers of S stock between members), definitions, and an anti-abuse rule, respectively.

(ii) *Stock of multiple subsidiaries transferred in the transaction.*—(A) *Initial application of section to transferred shares in lowest tier.*—If shares of stock of more than one subsidiary are transferred in a transaction, the application of this section begins at the lowest tier. If no transferred shares of stock of the lowest-tier subsidiary (S2) are loss shares, any gain recognized with respect to the S2 shares immediately tiers up and adjusts members' bases in subsidiary stock under §1.1502-32. However, if any of the transferred S2 shares are loss shares, paragraph (b) of this section applies with respect to those shares. If, after the application of paragraph (b) of this section, any transferred S2 shares are still loss shares, paragraph (c) of this section applies with respect to those shares. If, after the application of paragraph (c) of this section, any transferred S2 shares are still loss shares and P makes an election under paragraph (d)(6) of this section with respect to those S2 shares, then paragraph (d) of this section applies with respect to those shares, but only to the extent necessary to give effect to the election. After taking into account the effects of any adjustments required by this initial application of this section, recognized gain or loss is computed on all transferred S2 shares. Any adjustments under paragraph (b) or (c) of this section, the effect of any election under paragraph (d)(6) of this section, any gain or loss recognized on the transferred S2 shares (whether allowed or disallowed), and any other related or resulting adjustments then tier-up and apply to adjust members' bases in subsidiary stock under §1.1502-32.

(B) *Initial application of section to transferred shares in higher tiers.*—After taking into account the effects of any adjustments described in paragraph (a)(3)(ii)(A) of this section, transferred shares in the next higher tier, and then in each next higher tier successively, other than the transferred loss shares at the highest tier, are treated in the manner described in paragraph (a)(3)(ii)(A) of this section.

(C) *Application of section to transferred shares in highest tier.*—After paragraphs (b) and (c) of this section, and, to the extent necessary to give effect to any election under paragraph (d)(6) of this section, paragraph (d) of this section, have been applied to or with respect to all lower-tier transferred loss shares, and after all lower-tier adjustments have been taken into account (whether resulting from the application of paragraph (b) or (c) of this section, an election under paragraph (d)(6) of this section, the recognition of gain or loss on a transfer, or otherwise), paragraphs (b), then (c), and then (d) of this section apply with respect to the highest-tier shares that are transferred loss shares.

(D) *Final application of section to transferred shares in lower tiers.*—After paragraph (d) of this section has been applied with respect to transferred loss shares in the highest tier, it is applied with respect to transferred shares in each next lower tier, successively, to the extent such shares are loss shares after the application of paragraph (d) of this section.

(4) *Other rules of law and coordination with deferral and disallowance provisions.*—In general, this section applies and has effect immediately upon the transfer of a loss share even if the loss is deferred, disallowed, or otherwise not taken into account under any other applicable rules of law. However, see paragraph (e)(3) of this section for special rules applicable to shares of S stock transferred in an intercompany transaction. See section §1.1502-80(a) for the general applicability of other rules of law and a limitation on duplicative adjustments.

(5) *Nomenclature, factual assumptions adopted in this section.*—Unless otherwise stated, for purposes of this section, the following nomenclature and assumptions are adopted. P is the common parent of a consolidated group of which S, M, and M1 are members. X is not a member of the P group. If a corporation has preferred stock outstanding, it is stock described in section 1504(a)(4). The examples set forth the only facts, elections, and activities relevant to the example. All transactions are between unrelated persons and are independent of each other. Tax liabilities and their effect, and the application of any other loss disallowance or deferral provisions of the Internal Revenue Code (Code) or regulations, including but not limited to section 267, are disregarded. All persons report on a calendar year basis and use the accrual method of accounting. All parties comply with filing and other requirements of this section and all other provisions of the Code and regulations.

(b) *Basis redetermination to reduce disparity.*—(1) *In general.*—(i) *Purpose and scope.*—The rules of this paragraph (b) reduce the extent to which there is disparity in members' bases in shares of S stock. These rules supplement the operation of the investment adjustment system; their purpose is to prevent the realization of noneconomic loss and facilitate the elimination of duplicated loss when members hold S shares with disparate bases. The rules of this paragraph (b) only reallocate investment adjustments previously applied to members' bases in shares of S stock, thus they do not alter the aggregate amount of basis in shares of S stock held by members or the aggregate amount of investment adjustments applied to shares of S stock.

(ii) *Special rules for applicability of redetermination rule.*—Notwithstanding the general rule in paragraph (b)(2) of this section, members' bases in shares of S stock are not redetermined under this paragraph (b) if—

(A) There is no disparity among members' bases in shares of S common stock and no member owns a share of S preferred stock with respect to which there is unrecognized gain or loss; or

(B) All the shares of S stock held by members are transferred to one or more nonmembers, become worthless under section 165 (taking into account the provisions of §1.1502-80(c)), or a combination thereof, in one fully taxable transaction. However, in such a case, P may elect to redetermine such bases under this paragraph (b). Such an election is made in the manner provided in paragraph (e)(5) of this section. If stock of more than one subsidiary is transferred in the transaction, the election may be made with respect to one or more of such subsidiaries.

(iii) *Investment adjustment.*—For purposes of this paragraph (b), the term *investment adjustment* includes adjustments specially allocated under §1.1502-32(c)(1)(ii)(B) and remaining adjustments described in §1.1502-32(c)(1)(iii). In applying any provision of this section, the term includes all such adjustments reflected in the basis of the share as of the application of the provision, whether originally allocated under §1.1502-32 or otherwise. The term therefore includes adjustments previously reallocated to the share, and it does not include adjustments previously reallocated from the share, whether pursuant to this section or any other provision of law. It also includes the proportionate amount of adjustments reflected in the exchanged basis of a share, such as the basis determined under section 358 in connection with a reorganization or a transaction qualifying under section 355.

(2) *Basis redetermination rule.*—If M transfers a loss share of S stock, all members' bases in all their shares of S stock are subject to redetermination under this paragraph (b). The determination of whether a share is a loss share is made as of the transfer, taking into account the effects of all applicable rules of law. The redeterminations are made immediately before applying paragraph (c) of this section and in accordance with the following:

(i) *Decreasing the bases of transferred loss shares.*—(A) *Removing positive investment adjustments from transferred loss shares of common stock.*—M's basis in each of its transferred loss shares of S common stock is first reduced, but not below value, by removing positive investment adjustments previously applied to the basis of the share. The positive investment adjustments removed from transferred loss shares of S common stock are reallocated under paragraph (b)(2)(ii) of this section after negative investment adjustments are reallocated under paragraph (b)(2)(i)(B) of this section.

(B) *Reallocating negative investment adjustments from shares of S common stock.*—If a transferred share is still a loss share after applying paragraph (b)(2)(i)(A) of this section, M's basis in the share is reduced, but not below value, by reallocating negative investment adjustments to the transferred loss share (whether common or preferred stock) from members' shares of S common stock that are not transferred loss shares. The adjustments reallocated under this paragraph (b)(2)(i)(B) are reallocated and applied first to M's bases in

transferred loss shares of S preferred stock and then to M's bases in transferred loss shares of S common stock. Reallocations under this paragraph (b)(2)(i)(B) are made in a manner that, to the greatest extent possible, reduces the disparity among members' bases in all transferred loss shares of S preferred stock, and reduces the disparity among members' bases in all shares of S common stock.

(ii) *Increasing the bases of gain preferred and all common shares.*—(A) *Preferred stock.*—After the application of paragraph (b)(2)(i) of this section, the positive investment adjustments removed from transferred loss shares of S common stock under paragraph (b)(2)(i)(A) of this section are reallocated and applied to increase, but not above value, members' bases in shares of S preferred stock (without regard to whether such shares are transferred in the transaction). Reallocations under this paragraph (b)(2)(ii)(A) are made in a manner that, to the greatest extent possible, reduces the disparity among members' bases in all shares of S preferred stock.

(B) *Common stock.*—Any positive investment adjustments removed from transferred loss shares of S common stock under paragraph (b)(2)(i)(A) of this section and not reallocated and applied to S preferred shares are reallocated and applied to increase members' bases in shares of S common stock. Reallocations are made to shares of S common stock without regard to whether a particular share is a loss share or a transferred share, and without regard to the share's value. Reallocations under this paragraph (b)(2)(ii)(B) are made in a manner that, to the greatest extent possible, reduces the disparity among members' bases in all shares of S common stock.

(iii) *Operating rules.*—(A) *Method.*—In general, reallocations should be made first with respect to the earliest available adjustments. However, the overall application of this paragraph (b) to a transaction must be made in a manner that, to the greatest extent possible, reduces basis disparity (as provided in paragraphs (b)(2)(i)(B) and (b)(2)(ii) of this section). The specific reallocation of an investment adjustment under this paragraph (b) may be made using any reasonable method or formula that is consistent with the provisions of this paragraph (b)(2) and furthers the purposes of this section.

(B) *Limits on reallocation.*—(1) *Restriction to members' outstanding shares.*—Investment adjustments can only be reallocated to shares that were held by members at the time the adjustment was originally applied.

(2) *Limitation by prior use.*—(i) *In general.*—In order to prevent the reallocation of investment adjustments from either increasing or decreasing members' aggregate bases in subsidiary stock, no investment adjustment (positive or negative) may be reallocated under this paragraph (b)(2) to the extent that it was (or would have been) used prior to the time that it would otherwise be reallocated under this paragraph (b)(2). For this purpose, an investment adjustment was used (or would have been used) to the extent that it was reflected in (or would have been reflected in) the basis of a share of subsidiary stock and the basis of that share has already been taken into account, directly or indirectly, in determining income, gain, deduction, or loss (including by affecting the application of this section to a prior transfer of subsidiary stock) or in determining the basis of any property that is not subject to §1.1502-32. However, if the prior use was in an intercompany transaction, an investment adjustment may be reallocated to the extent that §1.1502-13 has prevented the gain or loss on the transaction from being taken into account. (In that case, appropriate adjustments must be made to the intercompany item from the prior intercompany transaction that has not yet been taken into account.) Further, if an investment adjustment was reflected in (or would have been reflected in) the basis of a share that has been taken into account, the limitation on reallocation under this paragraph (b)(2)(iii)(B)(2) does not apply to the extent the basis of that share would not change as a result of the reallocation (for example, because the reallocation is between shares that are both lower-tier to the share with the previously used basis). See §1.1502-32(c)(1)(ii)(B) regarding special allocations applicable to the tier-up of the reallocated investment adjustment if the reallocation is limited under this paragraph (b)(2)(iii)(B)(2) due to prior use at a higher tier.

(ii) *Example.*—The application of this paragraph (b)(2)(iii)(B)(2) is illustrated by the following example:

*Example.* (i) *Facts.* P owns all 20 shares of M stock, and 10 shares of S stock. M owns the remaining 10 shares of S stock. In year 1, S recognizes $200 of income that results in a $10 positive investment adjustment being allocated to each share of S stock. The group does not recognize any other items. The $100 positive adjustment to M's basis in the S stock tiers up, and results in a $5 positive adjustment to each share of M stock. In year 2, P sells one share of M stock and recognizes a gain. In year 3, M sells one loss share of S stock, and this paragraph (b) applies and requires a reallocation of the year 1 positive investment adjustment applied to the basis of the transferred S share.

(ii) *Application of limitation by prior use.* M's basis in the transferred loss share of S stock reflects a $10 positive investment adjustment attributable to S's year 1 income. Under the general rule of this paragraph (b), that $10 would be subject to reallocation to reduce basis disparity. However, that $10 adjustment had originally tiered up to adjust P's basis in its M shares and, as a result, $.50 of that adjustment was reflected in P's basis in each share of M stock. When P sold the share of M stock, the basis of that share (which included the tiered-up $.50) was used in determining the gain on the sale. Thus, $.50 of the $10 investment adjustment originally allocated to the transferred S share that tiered-up to the sold M share was previously used and, as such, cannot be reallocated in a manner that would (if it were the original allocation) affect the basis of the sold M share. Accordingly, no more than $9.50 of the adjustment to M's transferred S share could be reallocated to P's shares of S stock. If so, under the special allocation rule in §1.1502-32(c)(1)(ii)(B), the tier-up of this $9.50 would only be allocated among P's remaining 19 shares of M stock. Alternatively, all $10 of the investment adjustment could be reallocated to M's other S shares (because the tier-up to P's M shares would have been the same regardless which of M's shares of S stock were adjusted).

(iii) *Application of limitation where adjustment would have been used.* The facts are the same as in paragraph (i) of this *Example* except that M does not sell any shares of S stock and, in year 3, P sells a loss share of S stock. As in paragraph (i) of this *Example*, when P sold the share of M stock, the basis of that share was used in determining the gain on the share. When P sells the loss share of S stock, the $10 positive investment adjustment from S's year 1 income cannot be reallocated in a manner that would (if it were the original adjustment) affect the basis of the sold M share. If this $10 positive investment adjustment had originally been allocated to the S shares held by M, $.50 of the $10 investment adjustment would have tiered up to the M share that P sold, would have been reflected in P's basis in that M share, and would have been used in determining P's gain or loss on the sale. Accordingly, up to $9.50 of the $10 investment adjustment applied to the basis of P's transferred S share could be reallocated to M's shares of S stock. If so, under the special allocation rule in §1.1502-32(c)(1)(ii)(B), the tier-up of this $9.50 would only be allocated among P's remaining 19 shares of M stock. Alternatively, all $10 of the investment adjustment could be reallocated to P's other S shares.

(3) *Examples.*—The general application of this paragraph (b) is illustrated by the following examples:

*Example 1. Transfer of stock received in section 351 exchange.* (i) *Redetermination to prevent noneconomic loss.* (A) *Facts.* For many years, M has owned two assets, Asset 1 and Asset 2. On January 1, year 1, M receives the only four outstanding shares of S common stock (Block 1 shares) in exchange for Asset 1, which has a basis and value of $80. Section 351 applies to the exchange and, therefore, under section 358, M's aggregate basis in the Block 1 shares is $80 ($20 per share). On July 1, year 2, M receives another share of S common stock (Block 2 share) in exchange for Asset 2, which has a basis of $0 and value of $20. Section 351 applies to this exchange and, under section 358, M's basis in the Block 2 share is $0. On October 1, year 3, S sells Asset 2 for $20, recognizing a $20 gain. On December 31, year 3, M sells one of its Block 1 shares to X for $20. After taking into account the effects of all applicable rules of law, M's basis in each Block 1 share is $24 (M's original $20 basis increased under §1.1502-32 by $4, the share's allocable portion of the $20 gain recognized on the sale of Asset 2). In addition, M's basis in its Block 2 share is $4 (M's original $0 basis increased under §1.1502-32 by $4 (the share's allocable portion of the $20 gain recognized on the sale of Asset 2)). M's sale of the Block 1 share is a transfer of a loss share and therefore subject to this section.

(B) *Basis redetermination under this paragraph (b).* Under this paragraph (b), M's bases in all its shares of S stock are subject to redetermination. First, paragraph (b)(2)(i)(A) of this section applies to reduce M's basis in the transferred loss share, but not below value, by removing positive investment adjustments applied to the basis of the share. Accordingly, M's basis in the transferred Block 1 share is reduced by $4 (the amount of the positive investment adjustment applied to the share), from $24 to $20. Even if there were negative investment adjustments applied to adjust the bases of nontransferred common shares, no further reduction to the basis of the share would be required under this paragraph (b) because the basis of the transferred share is then equal to the share's value. Under paragraph (b)(2)(ii)(B) of this section, the positive investment adjustment removed from the transferred loss share is reallocated and applied to increase M's bases in its S common shares in a manner that reduces disparity in M's bases in all the S common shares, to the greatest extent possible. Accordingly, the $4 positive investment adjustment

removed from the Block 1 share is reallocated and applied to the basis of the Block 2 share, increasing it from $4 to $8.

(C) *Application of paragraphs (c) and (d) of this section.* Because M's sale of the Block 1 share is not a transfer of a loss share after the application of this paragraph (b), neither paragraph (c) of this section nor paragraph (d) of this section applies to the transfer.

(ii) *Redetermination to eliminate duplicated loss.* (A) *Facts.* The facts are the same as in paragraph (i)(A) of this *Example 1*, except that, at the time of the second contribution, the value of Asset 1 had declined to $20 and so, instead of contributing Asset 2, M contributed Asset 3 to S in exchange for the Block 2 share. At the time of that exchange, Asset 3 had a basis and value of $5. On October 1, year 3, S sells Asset 1 for $20, recognizing a $60 loss that is absorbed by the group. On December 31, year 3, M sells one of its Block 1 shares to X for $5. After taking into account the effects of all applicable rules of law, M's basis in each Block 1 share is $8 (M's original $20 basis decreased under §1.1502-32 by $12 (the share's allocable portion of the $60 loss recognized on the sale of Asset 1)). M's basis in its Block 2 share is an excess loss account of $7 (M's original basis of $5 reduced under §1.1502-32 by $12, the share's allocable portion of the loss recognized on the sale of Asset 1). M's sale of the Block 1 share is a transfer of a loss share and therefore subject to this section.

(B) *Basis redetermination under this paragraph (b).* Under this paragraph (b), M's bases in all its shares of S stock are subject to redetermination. There are no positive investment adjustments and so there is no adjustment under paragraph (b)(2)(i)(A) of this section. However, under paragraph (b)(2)(i)(B) of this section, M's basis in the transferred Block 1 share is reduced, but not below value, by reallocating negative investment adjustments from common shares that are not transferred loss shares. In total, there were $48 of negative investment adjustments applied to common shares that are not transferred loss shares. Accordingly, M's basis in the Block 1 share is reduced by $3, from $8 to its value of $5. Under paragraph (b)(2)(i)(B) of this section, the negative investment adjustments applied to the transferred share are reallocated from (and therefore cause an increase in the basis of) S common shares that are not transferred loss shares in a manner that reduces disparity among members' bases in all S common shares to the greatest extent possible. Accordingly, the $3 negative investment adjustment reallocated and applied to the transferred Block 1 share is reallocated entirely from the Block 2 share, increasing the basis in the Block 2 share from an excess loss account of $7 to an excess loss account of $4.

(C) *Application of paragraphs (c) and (d) of this section.* Because M's sale of the Block 1 share is not a transfer of a loss share after the application of this paragraph (b), neither paragraph (c) of this section nor paragraph (d) of this section applies to the transfer.

(iii) *Nonapplicability of redetermination rule to sale of entire interest.* The facts are the same as in paragraph (ii)(A) of this *Example 1*, except that, on December 31, year 3, M sells all its shares of S stock to X for $25. M's sale of the S stock to X is a transfer of all of the shares of S stock held by members to one or more nonmembers in one fully taxable transaction and, therefore, basis is not redetermined under this paragraph (b). Accordingly, the sale of the Block 1 shares remains a transfer of loss shares and, as such, subject to paragraphs (c) and (d) of this section. However, paragraphs (c)(7) and (d)(3)(i)(A) of this section apply netting principles to prevent adjustments under either paragraph (c) or paragraph (d) of this section, respectively. Alternatively, the group could elect to apply this paragraph (b). In that case, the $12 negative adjustment applied to the Block 2 shares would be reallocated to the Block 1 shares with the result that there would be no loss (or gain) on any of the transferred shares following the application of this paragraph (b). In that case, there would be no further application of this section to the transfer.

(iv) *Transfer of entire interest, partially taxable.* The facts are the same as in paragraph (iii) of this *Example 1*, except that, instead of selling the Block 2 share to X, M contributes the share to a nonmember in a section 351 exchange that is part of the same transaction. Although all the S shares held by members are transferred in the transaction, not all the shares are transferred to one or more nonmembers in one fully taxable transaction. Therefore, paragraph (b)(1)(ii)(B) of this section does not apply and M must redetermine its bases in its shares of S stock under this paragraph (b). In total, there were $12 of negative investment adjustments applied to common shares that are not transferred loss shares (the Block 2 share, a gain share). Accordingly, M's basis in each of the Block 1 shares is reduced by $3, from $8 to its value of $5. Under paragraph (b)(2)(i)(B) of this section, the negative investment adjustments applied to the transferred shares are reallocated from (and therefore cause an increase in the basis of) S shares that are not transferred loss shares in a manner that reduces disparity among members' bases in all S common shares to the greatest extent possible. Accordingly, the $12 negative investment adjustment reallocated and applied to the transferred Block 1 shares is reallocated entirely from the Block 2 share, increasing the basis in the Block 2 share from an excess loss account of $7 to a basis of $5. Because M's transfer is not a transfer of loss shares after the application of this paragraph (b), neither paragraph (c) of this section nor paragraph (d) of this section applies to the transfer.

*Example 2. Redetermination increases basis of transferred loss share.* (i) *Facts.* On January 1, year 1, M owns all 10 outstanding shares of S common stock. Five of the shares have a basis of $20 per share (Block 1 shares) and five of the shares have a basis of $10 per share (Block 2 shares). S's only asset, Asset 1, has a basis of $50. S has no other attributes. On October 1, year 1, S sells Asset 1 for $100, recognizing a $50 gain. On December 31, year 2, M sells one Block 1 share and one Block 2 share to X for $10 per share. After taking into account the effects of all applicable rules of law, M's basis in each Block 1 share is $25 (M's original $20 basis increased under §1.1502-32 by $5, the share's allocable portion of the $50 gain recognized on the sale of Asset 1), and M's basis in each Block 2 share is $15 (M's original $10 basis increased under §1.1502-32 by $5, the share's allocable portion of the $50 gain recognized on the sale of Asset 1). M's sale of the Block 1 and Block 2 shares is a transfer of loss shares and therefore subject to this section.

(ii) *Basis redetermination under this paragraph (b).* Under this paragraph (b), M's bases in all its shares of S stock are subject to redetermination. First, paragraph (b)(2)(i)(A) of this section applies to reduce M's basis in the transferred Block 1 and Block 2 shares, but not below value, by removing the positive investment adjustments applied to the bases of the transferred loss shares. Accordingly, the basis of the transferred Block 1 share is reduced by $5, from $25 to $20. The basis of the transferred Block 2 share is also reduced by $5, from $15 to $10. (Although the transferred Block 1 share is still a loss share, there is no reduction to its basis under paragraph (b)(2)(i)(B) of this section because there were no negative investment adjustments applied to the bases of the S common shares that are not transferred loss shares.) Next, paragraph (b)(2)(ii)(B) of this section applies to reallocate and apply the $10 of positive investment adjustments removed from the transferred loss shares to increase M's bases in its S common shares in a manner that reduces the disparity in its bases in all S common shares to the greatest extent possible. Accordingly, of the $10 of positive investment adjustments to be reallocated, $6 is reallocated and applied to the basis of the transferred Block 2 share (increasing it from $10 to $16) and $4 is reallocated and applied equally to the basis of each of the four retained Block 2 shares (increasing the basis of each from $15 to $16). After giving effect to the reallocations under this paragraph (b), M's basis in each retained Block 1 share is $25, M's basis in the transferred Block 1 share is $20, and M's basis in each Block 2 share is $16.

(iii) *Application of paragraph (c) of this section.* After the application of this paragraph (b), M's sale of the Block 1 and Block 2 shares is still a transfer of loss shares and, accordingly, subject to paragraph (c) of this section. No adjustment is required to the basis of the transferred Block 1 share under paragraph (c) of this section because, after its basis is redetermined under this paragraph (b), the net positive adjustment to the basis of the share is $0. See paragraph (c)(3) of this section. However, under paragraph (c) of this section M's basis in the transferred Block 2 share is reduced by $6 (the lesser of its net positive adjustment, $6, and its disconformity amount, $6), from $16 to $10, its value. See paragraph (c)(2) of this section.

(iv) *Application of paragraph (d) of this section.* After the application of paragraph (c) of this section, M's sale of the Block 1 share is still a transfer of a loss share and, accordingly, subject to paragraph (d) of this section. No adjustment is required under paragraph (d) of this section because there is no aggregate inside loss. See paragraph (d)(3)(iii) of this section. Because M's sale of the Block 2 share is no longer a transfer of a loss share after the application of paragraph (c) of this section, paragraph (d) of this section does not apply to the transfer of the Block 2 share.

*Example 3. Tiered subsidiaries.* (i) *Transfer of all shares of common stock.* (A) *Facts.* P owns the sole outstanding share of S stock with a basis of $100, and the sole outstanding share of M stock with a basis of $300. M has $200 and owns an asset with a basis of $0. S owns one asset, Asset 1, with a basis of $100. At a time when Asset 1 has a value of $200, S issues a second share of common stock to M in exchange for $200. Later S sells Asset 1 for $200, recognizing a $100 gain. After taking into account the effects of all applicable rules of law, P's basis in its S stock is $150 (P's original $100 basis increased under §1.1502-32 by $50, the share's allocable portion of the $100 gain recognized on the sale of Asset 1), M's basis in its S stock is $250 (M's original $200 basis increased under §1.1502-32 by $50, the share's allocable portion of the $100 gain recognized on the sale of Asset 1), and P's basis in its M stock is $350 (P's original $300 basis increased under §1.1502-32 by $50, the tier-up of M's increase in its basis in its S stock). P then sells its M share and its S share to X for $300 and $200, respectively. M and S are not members of the same consolidated group immediately after the sale. Therefore, the M share

and both of the S shares are transferred in the transaction. Regarding P's sale of its share of S stock and its share of M stock, see paragraph (f)(10)(i)(A) of this section (ceasing to own a share in a taxable transaction) and paragraph (f)(10)(i)(C) of this section (nonmember acquires share); regarding M's share of S stock, see paragraph (f)(10)(i)(B) of this section (ceasing to be members of the same group). The application of this section begins with respect to the stock of S, the subsidiary at the lowest tier in which there is a transfer of subsidiary stock. See paragraph (a)(3)(ii) of this section. Although both P and M transfer their S shares, only M's S share is a loss share. Thus, only M's transfer is a transfer of a loss share of S stock and only M's transfer is subject to this section.

(B) *Application of section to transferred S shares.* Although only M's transfer is subject to this section, all members' bases in their shares of S stock are subject to redetermination under this paragraph (b). First, paragraph (b)(2)(i)(A) of this section applies to reduce M's basis in its transferred S share, but not below value, by removing the positive investment adjustment applied to that share. Accordingly, the basis of M's S share is reduced by $50, from $250 to $200 (under §1.1502-32, that redetermination adjustment tiers up to reduce P's basis in its M stock by $50, from $350 to $300). Because there are no negative adjustments to reallocate under paragraph (b)(2)(i)(B) of this section, paragraph (b)(2)(ii)(B) of this section then applies to reallocate and apply the $50 positive investment adjustment removed from the transferred loss S share to increase P's basis in its S share in a manner that reduces disparity among members' bases in all S common shares to the greatest extent possible. Accordingly, all $50 of the positive investment adjustment is reallocated and applied to P's basis in its S share (increasing the basis from $150 to $200). Because M's transfer of its S share is not a transfer of a loss share after the application of this paragraph (b), neither paragraph (c) of this section nor paragraph (d) of this section applies to that transfer.

(C) *Application of section to transfers at next higher tier.* After the adjustments to M's share of S stock are given effect, P's transfer of its share of M stock is not a transfer of a loss share and so this section does not apply to that transfer.

(D) *Result of application of section.* After the application of this section, P recognizes no gain or loss on its sale of either the S share or the M share. In addition, the unrecognized (noneconomic) loss in M's basis in its S share is eliminated. The results would be the same if, in addition to the facts in paragraph (i)(A) of this *Example 3*, M transferred its S share to X in a fully taxable transaction and, as permitted under paragraph (b)(1)(ii)(B) of this section, P elected to redetermine basis under this paragraph (b).

(ii) *Transfer of less than all lower-tier shares of stock.* (A) *Facts.* The facts are the same as in paragraph (i)(A) of this *Example 1*, except that M and S are members of the same consolidated group immediately after the sale. Therefore, in this case, M's S share is not transferred and so this section has no application with respect to M's S share. P's transfer of its S share is not a transfer of a loss share and so is also not subject to this section. However, P's sale of its share of M stock is a transfer of a loss share and is subject to this section.

(B) *Basis redetermination under this paragraph (b).* Although P's transfer of its share of M stock is subject to this section, this paragraph (b) does not apply to the transfer because there is only one share of M stock outstanding (and so there can be no disparity among members' bases in common shares and there are no outstanding preferred shares with respect to which there can be unrecognized gain or loss). Accordingly, after the application of this paragraph (b), P's sale of its M share is still a transfer of a loss share and therefore subject to paragraph (c) of this section.

(C) *Application of paragraphs (c) and (d) of this section.* Under paragraph (c) of this section, P must reduce its basis in its M share by $50, the lesser of its net positive adjustment ($50, see paragraph (c)(3) of this section) and its disconformity amount ($150, see paragraphs (c)(4), (c)(5), and (c)(6) of this section). As a result, the share is no longer a loss share and the transfer is not subject to paragraph (d) of this section.

(D) *Result of application of section.* After the application of this section, P recognizes a $50 gain on its sale of the S share and no loss on its sale of the M share. Although there is unrecognized loss preserved in M's basis in its S share, if M later transfers the share when it is a loss share, that transfer will be subject to this section.

*Example 4. Application to outstanding common and preferred shares.* (i) *Facts.* P owns all the stock of M and all eight outstanding shares of S common stock. S also has two shares of nonvoting preferred stock outstanding; the preferred shares each have a $100 annual, cumulative preference as to dividends. M owns one of the preferred shares (PS1) and P owns the other (PS2). On January 1, year 1, the bases and values of the outstanding S shares are:

| | Preferred | | Common | | | | | | | |
|---|---|---|---|---|---|---|---|---|---|---|
| | PS1 (M) | PS2 (P) | CS1 (P) | CS2 (P) | CS3 (P) | CS4 (P) | CS5 (P) | CS6 (P) | CS7 (P) | CS8 (P) |
| Basis | 1250 | 990 | 1025 | 710 | 550 | 400 | 375 | 250 | 215 | 100 |
| Value | 1000 | 1000 | 375 | 375 | 375 | 375 | 375 | 375 | 375 | 375 |

(A) As of January 1, year 1, there are no arrearages on the preferred stock. In year 1, S has a $1100 capital loss and $100 of ordinary income. The group absorbs the loss and the negative remaining adjustment of $1000 is allocable entirely to the common stock, equally to each common share ($125 per share). See § 1.1502-32(c)(1)(iii) and (c)(2).

(B) In year 2, S has $700 of ordinary income and a $100 ordinary loss. Also, on October 1, year 2, S declares and makes a $200 dividend distribution with respect the preferred stock ($100 per share). Under § 1.1502-32(c)(1)(i), a negative adjustment of $100 is first allocated to each of the preferred shares to reflect the declaration of the dividend. The $600 positive remaining adjustment determined under § 1.1502-32(c)(1)(iii) (reflecting S's net income reduced by the distribution) is then allocated to each of the preferred shares to the extent of its entitlement to dividends accruing in year 1 and year 2 ($200 per share). See § 1.1502-32(c)(1)(iii) and (c)(3). The $200 of the positive remaining adjustment not allocated to the preferred shares is then allocated to the common stock, equally to each common share ($25 per share). See § 1.1502-32(c)(1)(iii) and (c)(2). After taking into account the effects of all applicable rules of law, the adjusted bases and the values of the shares as of January 1, year 3, are:

| | Preferred | | Common | | | | | | | |
|---|---|---|---|---|---|---|---|---|---|---|
| | PS1 (M) | PS2 (P) | CS1 (P) | CS2 (P) | CS3 (P) | CS4 (P) | CS5 (P) | CS6 (P) | CS7 (P) | CS8 (P) |
| Basis | 1250 | 990 | 1025 | 710 | 550 | 400 | 375 | 250 | 215 | 100 |
| Year 1 § 1.1502-32 adjustments | N/A | N/A | -125 | -125 | -125 | -125 | -125 | -125 | -125 | -125 |
| Year 2 § 1.1502-32 adjustments | -100 +200 +100 | -100 +200 +100 | +25 | +25 | +25 | +25 | +25 | +25 | +25 | +25 |
| Adjusted basis | 1350 | 1090 | 925 | 610 | 450 | 300 | 275 | 150 | 115 | 0 |
| Value | 1100 | 1100 | 275 | 275 | 275 | 275 | 275 | 275 | 275 | 275 |
| Unrecognized gain/(loss) | (250) | 10 | (650) | (335) | (175) | (25) | 0 | 125 | 160 | 275 |

(C) On January 1, year 3, M sells PS1 for $1100 and P sells CS2 for $275. The sales of PS1 and CS2 are transfers of loss shares and therefore subject to this section.

(ii) *Basis redetermination under this paragraph (b).* Under this paragraph (b), all members' bases in shares of S stock are subject to redetermination in accordance with the following:

(A) *Removing positive investment adjustments from transferred loss common shares.* First, paragraph (b)(2)(i)(A) of this section applies to reduce P's basis in CS2, but not below value, by removing the positive investment adjustment applied to the basis of the share. Accordingly, P's basis in CS2 is reduced by $25, from $610 to $585.

(B) *Reallocating negative investment adjustments from common shares that are not transferred loss shares.* Because the transferred shares remain loss shares after the removal of positive investment adjustments, their bases are further reduced under paragraph (b)(2)(i)(B) of this section, but not below value, by reallocating negative investment adjustments applied to common shares that are not transferred loss shares. Reallocations are made first to preferred shares and then to the common shares, in a manner that reduces disparity among members' bases in transferred loss preferred shares, and reduces disparity among members' bases in all common shares, to the greatest extent possible. The loss on PS1 is $250, the remaining loss on CS2 is $310, and the total amount of negative investment adjustments applied to shares that are not transferred loss shares is $875 (the sum of the negative adjustments applied to all common shares other than CS2). Thus, $250 of negative investment adjustments are reallocated and applied to the basis of PS1, reducing it to the share's value, $1100. The negative investment adjustments are reallocated from the common shares that are not transferred loss shares in a manner that reduces disparity among members' bases in all common shares to the greatest extent possible. The negative investment adjustments may be reallocated to PS1 from the common shares that are not transferred loss shares as follows: $125 from each of CS7 and CS8. Such reallocations increase the basis of CS7 by $125, from $115 to $240, and increase the basis of CS8 by $125, from $0 to $125. Negative investment adjustments are then reallocated to CS2 from the common shares that are not transferred loss shares in a manner that reduces disparity among members' bases in all common shares to the greatest extent possible. The negative investment adjustments may be reallocated to CS2 from the other common shares as follows: $80 from CS4, $105 from CS5, and $125 from CS6. Such reallocations reduce the basis of CS2 by $310, from $585 to $275, increase the basis of CS4 by $80, from $300 to $380, increase the basis of CS5 by $105, from $275 to $380, and increase the basis of CS6 by $125, from $150 to $275. However, there may be other reasonable reallocations.

(C) *Increasing basis by reallocated positive investment adjustments.* Under paragraph (b)(2)(ii)(A) of this section, the $25 positive investment adjustment removed from CS2 (the transferred loss common share) is then reallocated and applied to increase the basis of preferred shares, but not above value. Accordingly, $10 of that amount is reallocated to PS2, increasing its basis from $1090 to $1100, its value. Under paragraph (b)(2)(ii)(B) of this section, the remaining $15 is reallocated and applied to the common shares in a manner that reduces disparity among members' bases in all common shares to the greatest extent possible. The $15 positive investment adjustment that is reallocated to common shares may be reallocated entirely to CS8, increasing its basis from $125 to $140. However, there may be other reasonable reallocations.

(D) *Summary of the reallocation of adjustments.* The adjustments made under this paragraph (b) are:

| | Preferred | | Common | | | | | | | |
|---|---|---|---|---|---|---|---|---|---|---|
| | PS1 (M) | PS2 (P) | CS1 (P) | CS2 (P) | CS3 (P) | CS4 (P) | CS5 (P) | CS6 (P) | CS7 (P) | CS8 (P) |
| Adjusted basis before redetermination | 1350 | 1090 | 925 | 610 | 450 | 300 | 275 | 150 | 115 | 0 |
| Removing positive adjustments from transferred loss shares | | | | -25 | | | | | | |
| Reallocating negative adjustments | -250 | | | -310 | | +80 | +105 | +125 | +125 | +125 |
| Applying positive adjustments removed from transferred loss shares | | +10 | | | | | | | | +15 |
| Basis after redetermination | 1100 | 1100 | 925 | 275 | 450 | 380 | 380 | 275 | 240 | 140 |
| Value | 1100 | 1100 | 275 | 275 | 275 | 275 | 275 | 275 | 275 | 275 |
| Gain/(loss) | 0 | 0 | (650) | 0 | (175) | (105) | (105) | 0 | 35 | 135 |

(iii) *Application of paragraphs (c) and (d) of this section.* Because M's sale of PS1 and P's sale of CS2 are not transfers of loss shares after the application of this paragraph (b), paragraphs (c) and (d) of this section do not apply.

(iv) *Higher-tier effects.* The $250 reduction in the basis of PS1 under this paragraph (b) is a noncapital, nondeductible expense under § 1.1502-32(b)(3)(iii)(B) that will be included in the year 3 investment adjustment to be applied to P's basis in its M stock.

(c) *Stock basis reduction to prevent noneconomic loss.*—(1) *In general.*—The rules of this paragraph (c) reduce M's basis in a transferred share of S stock to prevent noneconomic stock loss and thus promote the clear reflection of the group's income. These rules limit the reduction to M's basis in the S share to the amount of net unrealized appreciation reflected in the share's basis as of the transfer (the disconformity amount). These rules also limit the reduction to M's basis in the S share to the portion of the share's basis that is attributable to investment adjustments made pursuant to the consolidated return regulations.

(2) *Basis reduction rule.*—This paragraph (c) applies if M transfers a share of S stock and, after taking into account the effects of all applicable rules of law, including any adjustments under paragraph (b) of this section, the share is a loss share. Under this paragraph (c), M's basis in the share is reduced, but not below value, by the lesser of—

(i) The share's net positive adjustment (as defined in paragraph (c)(3) of this section); and

(ii) The share's disconformity amount (as defined in paragraph (c)(4) of this section).

(3) *Net positive adjustment.*—A share's *net positive adjustment* is the greater of—

(i) Zero; and

(ii) The sum of all investment adjustments reflected in the basis of the share. The term *investment adjustment* has the same meaning as in paragraph (b)(1)(iii) of this section, except that it includes all adjustments specially allocated under § 1.1502-32(c)(1)(ii).

(4) *Disconformity amount.*—A share's *disconformity amount* is the excess, if any, of—

(i) M's basis in the share; over

(ii) The share's allocable portion of S's net inside attribute amount (as defined in paragraph (c)(5) of this section).

(5) *Net inside attribute amount.*—S's *net inside attribute amount* is determined as of the transfer, taking into account all applicable rules of law (even if the adjustments required by such rules are not deemed effective until after the transfer, such as certain adjustments required under sections 108 and 1017 and § 1.1502-28). S's net inside attribute amount is the sum of S's net operating and capital loss carryovers, deferred deductions, money, and basis in assets other than money, reduced by the amount of S's liabilities. For this purpose, S's basis in any share of lower-tier subsidiary stock is generally S's basis in that share, adjusted to reflect any gain or loss recognized in the transaction with respect to the share and any other related or resulting adjustments to the basis of the share. However, see paragraph (c)(6) of this section for special rules regarding the computation of S's net inside attribute amount for purposes of this paragraph (c) if S holds stock of a subsidiary that is not transferred in the transaction. See paragraph (f) of this section for definitions of "allocable portion," "deferred deduction," "liability," "loss carryover," and other relevant terms.

(6) *Determination of S's net inside attribute amount if S owns stock of a lowertier subsidiary.*—(i) *Overview.*—If a loss share of S stock is transferred when S holds a share of stock of another subsidiary (S1) and the S1 share is not transferred in the same transaction, S's net inside attribute amount is determined by treating S's basis in its S1 share as tentatively reduced under this paragraph (c)(6). The purpose of this rule is to reduce the extent to which S1's investment adjustments increase noneconomic loss on S stock (as a result of S1's recognition of items that are indirectly reflected in a member's basis in a share of S stock).

(ii) *General rule for nontransferred shares of lower-tier subsidiary stock.*—For purposes of determining the disconformity amount of a share of S stock, S's basis in a nontransferred share of S1 stock is treated as reduced by the share's tentative reduction amount. The tentative reduction amount is the lesser of the S1 share's net positive adjustment and the S1 share's disconformity amount.

(iii) *Multiple tiers of nontransferred shares.*—If S directly or indirectly owns nontransferred shares of stock of subsidiaries in multiple tiers, then, subject to the limitations in paragraph (c)(6)(iv) of this section (regarding nontransferred shares that are lower-tier to transferred shares), the rules of this paragraph (c)(6) first apply to determine the tentatively reduced basis of stock of the subsidiary at the lowest tier. These rules then apply to determine the tentatively reduced basis of nontransferred shares of stock of subsidiaries successively at each next higher tier that is lower-tier to S. The tentative reductions at each tier are treated as noncapital, nondeductible expenses that tier up under the principles of § 1.1502-32, and, as such, result in a tentative reduction of basis and any net positive adjustment of subsidiary shares that are lower-tier to S.

(iv) *Nonapplicability of tentative basis reduction rule to transferred shares.*—The tentative basis reduction rule in this paragraph (c)(6) does not apply to any share of stock of a lower-tier subsidiary (S1) that is transferred in the same transaction in which the S share is transferred. Further, for purposes of determining the S share's disconformity amount, the tentative basis reduction rule in this paragraph (c)(6) only applies with respect to stock of a lower-tier subsidiary if such stock is lower-tier to a nontransferred S1 share. The purpose of this rule is to prevent tentative adjustments to the bases of lower-tier shares if this paragraph (c) has already applied with respect to the shares, without regard to whether such application resulted in the reduction of the basis of any share.

(v) *Example.*—The rules of this paragraph (c)(6) are illustrated by the following example:

*Example.* (i) *Facts.* M owns the sole outstanding share of S stock, S owns the sole outstanding share of S1 stock, S1 owns all five outstanding shares of S2 stock (the bases of which are equal), and S2 owns the sole outstanding share of S3 stock. The basis of each of the shares reflects its allocable portion of a $5 positive investment adjustment attributable to income recognized by S3. The basis of the S share exceeds its value by $10 and the basis of the S1 share exceeds its value by $5. The basis of each S2 share is $1 less than its value. In one transaction, M sells its S share to X, S1 issues new shares in an amount that prevents S and S1 from being members of the same group, and S1 sells one of its S2 shares to an unrelated individual. S1, S2, and S3 elect to file a consolidated return following the transaction.

(ii) *General applicability of section.* As a result of the transaction, there is a transfer of the S share and the S2 share that was sold (because both shares were sold to nonmembers) and of the S1 share (because S and S1 cease to be members of the same group as a result of the stock issuance). The transfer of the S2 share is not a transfer of a loss share, and so this section does not apply to that transfer. The transfers of the S and S1 shares are transfers of loss shares, and so this section applies to those transfers. The S3 share and the four retained S2 shares are not transferred in the transaction. Under paragraph (a)(3)(ii)(A) of this section, this section applies first to the transfer of the S1 share because it is the lowest-tier transferred loss share.

(iii) *Application of paragraph (b) of this section and this paragraph (c) to transfer of S1 stock.* First, the $1 gain recognized on the transfer of the S2 share tiers up to adjust the basis of each upper-tier share. The transferred S1 share is still a loss share (by $4) and is therefore subject to this section. Although the transfer is subject to paragraph (b) of this section, there is no basis redetermination under paragraph (b) of this section because there is only one share of S1 stock outstanding (and so there can be no disparity among members' bases in common shares and there are no outstanding preferred shares with respect to which there can be unrecognized gain or loss). See paragraph (b)(1)(ii)(A) of this section. Therefore, after the application of paragraph (b) of this section, the S1 share is still a loss share and, as such, subject to this paragraph (c). In determining the amount of any basis reduction under this paragraph (c), the disconformity amount of the S1 share is computed by comparing S's basis in its S1 share to S1's net inside attribute amount (because there is only one S1 share outstanding, the entire amount is allocable to that share). In determining S1's net inside attribute amount, the tentative reduction rule in this paragraph (c)(6) applies to nontransferred lower-tier shares (provided they are lower-tier to nontransferred shares). Thus, the rule applies to S1's four retained shares of S2 stock and to S2's share of S3 stock. The tentative reduction begins at the lowest level (S2's share of S3 stock) and any tentative reduction amount tiers up as a noncapital, nondeductible expense under the principles of § 1.1502-32, tentatively reducing the bases of any upper tier nontransferred shares that are lower-tier to the transferred loss share (the S1 share). Accordingly, each of S1s nontransferred share of S2 stock is tentatively reduced by its portion of the tentative reduction to S2's share of S3 stock. S1 then applies the tentative reduction rule to its four nontransferred S2 shares. S1's net inside attribute amount is the sum of its basis in each of its nontransferred S2 shares, as tentatively reduced under this paragraph (c)(6) and S1's actual basis in the transferred S2 share, increased to reflect the gain recognized on the sale of that share. After the application of this paragraph (c) to the transfer of the S1 share, paragraph (b) of this section applies to M's transfer of the S share.

(iv) *Application of section to transfer of S stock.* Because the S share is still a loss share after applying paragraph (b) of this section and this paragraph (c) to the transfer of the S1 stock, this section applies to M's transfer of the S share. Although paragraph (b) of this section applies to the transfer, there is no basis redetermination under paragraph (b) of this section because there is only one share of S stock outstanding (and so there can be no disparity among members' bases in common shares and there are no outstanding preferred shares with respect to which there can be unrecognized gain or loss). See paragraph (b)(1)(ii)(A) of this section. Therefore, after the application of paragraph (b) of this section, the share is still a loss share and, as such, subject to this paragraph (c). In determining the disconformity amount of the S share, S's net inside attribute amount is determined using S's actual basis in the transferred S1 stock (after any reduction under this paragraph (c)), because the tentative reduction rule in this paragraph (c)(6) does not apply to shares that are transferred in the transaction. All other shares are lower-tier to the transferred S1 share and are therefore also not subject to tentative reduction for purposes of determining the disconformity amount of the S share. After the application of this paragraph (c) to the transfer of the S share, paragraph (d) of this section applies with respect to M's transfer of the S share. After the application of paragraph (d) of this section with respect to the transfer of the S share, if the S1 share is still a loss share, paragraph (d) of this section applies with respect to S's transfer of the S1 share.

(7) *Netting of gains and losses taken into account.*—(i) *General rule.*—Solely for purposes of computing the basis reduction required under this paragraph (c), the basis of each transferred loss share of S stock is treated as reduced proportionately (as to loss) by the amount of income or gain taken into account by members with respect to transferred shares of S stock, provided that—

(A) The shares are transferred in one transaction; and

(B) The gain is taken into account as of the transaction.

(ii) *Example.*—The netting rule of this paragraph (c)(7) is illustrated by the following example:

*Example. Disposition of gain and loss shares.* (i) *Facts.* M owns the only three outstanding shares of S stock. Share A has a basis of $54, Share B has a basis of $100, and Share C has a basis of $80. In the same transaction, M sells all three S shares to X for $60 each. M realizes a gain of $6 on Share A, a loss of $40 on Share B, and a loss of $20 on Share C. M's sales of Share B and Share C are transfers of loss shares and therefore subject to this section. M's sale is a transfer of all of the shares of S stock held by members to one or more nonmembers in one fully taxable transaction and, therefore, basis is not redetermined under paragraph (b) of this section. See paragraph (b)(1)(ii)(B) of this section. The transfer is then subject to this paragraph (c). However, for this purpose, M treats its bases in Share B and Share C as reduced by the $6 gain taken into account on Share A. The gain is allocated to Share B and Share C proportionately based on the amount of loss in each share. Thus, $4 of gain ($40/$60 × $6) is treated as allocated to Share B and $2 of gain ($20/$60 × $6) is treated as allocated to Share C. Accordingly, M computes the basis reduction required under this paragraph (c) by treating its basis in Share B as $96 ($100 less $4) and its basis in Share C as $78 ($80 less $2). If, after the application of this paragraph (c), the sales of Share B and Share C are still transfers of loss shares, then the transfers are subject to paragraph (d) of this section. (Although the bases of Share B and Share C are not actually reduced by any portion of the gain, paragraph (d)(3)(i)(A) of this section applies netting principles to limit adjustments under paragraph (d) of this section.)

(ii) *Disposition of stock with deferred gain.* The facts are the same as in paragraph (i) of this *Example,* except that M sells the gain share to another member. Under §1.1502-13, M's gain recognized on Share A is not taken into account in the taxable year of the transfer and therefore cannot be treated as reducing M's loss recognized on Share B and Share C for purposes of this paragraph (c). The applicability of this section to the transfer of Share A is determined as of the time that the intercompany item (the gain on M's sale to the other member) is taken into account, see paragraph (e)(3) of this section. However, if Share B (instead of Share A) were sold to a member, the entire gain on Share A would be treated as reducing the loss on Share C for purposes of applying this paragraph (c), see paragraph (e)(3) of this section.

(8) *Examples.*—The application of this paragraph (c) is illustrated by the following examples.

*Example 1. Appreciation reflected in stock basis at acquisition.* (i) *Appreciation recognized as gain.* (A) *Facts.* On January 1, year 1, M purchases the sole outstanding share of S stock for $100. At that time, S owns two assets, Asset 1 with a basis of $0 and a value of $40, and Asset 2 with a basis and value of $60. In year 1, S sells Asset 1 for $40, recognizing a $40 gain. On December 31, year 1, M sells its S share for $100. After taking into account the effects of all applicable rules of law, M's basis in the S share is $140 (M's original $100 basis increased under §1.1502-32 by $40, the share's allocable portion of the gain recognized on the sale of Asset 1). M's sale of the S share is a transfer of a loss share and therefore subject to this section.

(B) *Application of paragraph (b) of this section.* Although the transfer is subject to this section, there is no basis redetermination under paragraph (b) of this section because there is only one share of S stock outstanding (and so there can be no disparity among members' bases in common shares and there are no outstanding preferred shares with respect to which there can be unrecognized gain or loss). See paragraph (b)(1)(ii)(A) of this section. Therefore, after the application of paragraph (b) of this section, the share is still a loss share and, as such, subject to this paragraph (c).

(C) *Basis reduction under this paragraph (c).* Under this paragraph (c), M's basis in the S share, $140, is reduced, but not below value, $100, by the lesser of the share's net positive adjustment and disconformity amount. The share's net positive adjustment is the greater of zero and the sum of all investment adjustments (as defined in paragraph (b)(1)(iii) of this section) applied to the basis of the share. The only investment adjustment applied to the basis of the share is the $40 adjustment attributable to the gain recognized on the sale of Asset 1. Thus, the share's net positive adjustment is $40. The share's disconformity amount is the excess, if any, of its basis, $140, over its allocable portion of S's net inside attribute amount. S's net inside attribute amount is the sum of S's money ($40 from the sale of Asset 1) and S's basis in Asset 2, $60, or $100. The share is the only outstanding S share and so its allocable portion of the $100 net inside attribute amount is the entire $100. Thus, the share's disconformity amount is $40, the excess of $140 over $100. The lesser of the net positive adjustment, $40, and the share's disconformity amount, $40, is $40. Accordingly, immediately before the application of paragraph (d) of this section, M's basis in the share is reduced by $40, from $140 to $100.

(D) *Application of paragraph (d) of this section.* Because M's sale of the S share is not a transfer of a loss share after the application of this paragraph (c), paragraph (d) of this section does not apply to the transfer.

(ii) *Appreciation recognized as income earned in the consumption of built-in gain.* The facts are the same as in paragraph (i)(A) of this *Example 1,* except that, instead of selling Asset 1, the value of Asset 1 is consumed in the production of $40 of income in year 1 (reducing the value of Asset 1 to $0). Because the net positive adjustment includes items of income as well as items of gain, the results are the same as those described in paragraph (i) of this *Example 1.*

(iii) *Post-acquisition appreciation eliminates stock loss.* The facts are the same as in paragraph (i)(A) of this *Example 1* except that, in addition, the value of Asset 2 increases to $100 before the stock is sold. As a result, M sells the S share for $140. Because M's sale of the S share is not a transfer of a loss share, this section does not apply to the transfer, notwithstanding that P's basis in the S share was increased by the gain recognized on Asset 1.

(iv) *Distributions.* (A) *Facts.* The facts are the same as in paragraph (i)(A) of this *Example 1* except that, in addition, S declares and makes a $10 dividend distribution before the end of year 1. As a result, the value of the share decreases and M sells the share for $90. After taking into account the effects of all applicable rules of law, M's basis in the S share is $130 (M's original $100 basis increased under §1.1502-32 by $30, the $10 distribution on the share reduced by the share's allocable portion of the $40 gain recognized on the sale of Asset 1). M's sale of the S share is a transfer of a loss share and therefore subject to this section.

(B) *Application of paragraph (b) of this section.* Although the transfer is subject to this section, there is no basis redetermination under paragraph (b) of this section for the reasons set forth in paragraph (i)(B) of this *Example 1.* Therefore, after the application of paragraph (b) of this section, the share is still a loss share and, as such, subject to this paragraph (c).

(C) *Basis reduction under this paragraph (c).* Under this paragraph (c), M's basis in the S share, $130, is reduced, but not below value, $90, by the lesser of the share's net positive adjustment and disconformity amount. The share's net positive adjustment is $40 (the sum of all investment adjustments (as defined in paragraph (b)(1)(iii) of this section) applied to the basis of the share). The share's disconformity amount is the excess of its basis, $130, over its allocable portion of S's net inside attribute amount. S's net inside attribute amount is $90, the sum of S's money ($30, the $40 sale proceeds less the $10 distribution) and S's basis in Asset 2, $60. The share is the only outstanding S share and so its allocable portion of the $90 net inside attribute amount is the entire $90. The lesser of the share's net positive adjustment, $40, and its disconformity amount, $40, is $40. Accordingly, immediately before the application of paragraph (d) of this section, the basis in the share is reduced by $40, from $130 to $90.

(D) *Application of paragraph (d) of this section.* Because M's sale of the S share is not a transfer of a loss share after the application of this paragraph (c), paragraph (d) of this section does not apply to the transfer.

*Example 2. Loss of appreciation reflected in basis.* (i) *Facts.* On January 1, year 1, M purchases the sole outstanding share of S stock for $100. At that time, S owns two assets, Asset 1 with a basis of $0 and a value of $40, and Asset 2 with a basis and value of $60. The value of Asset 1 declines to $0 and M sells its S share for $60. After taking into account the effects of all applicable rules of law, M's basis in the S share is $100. M's sale of the S share is a transfer of a loss share and therefore subject to this section.

(ii) *Application of paragraph (b) of this section.* Although the transfer is subject to this section, there is no basis redetermination under paragraph (b) of this section because there is only one share of S stock outstanding (and so there can be no disparity among members' bases in common shares and there are no outstanding preferred shares with respect to which there can be unrecognized gain or loss). See paragraph (b)(1)(ii)(A) of this section. Therefore, after the application of paragraph (b) of this section, the share is still a loss share and, as such, subject to this paragraph (c).

(iii) *Basis reduction under this paragraph (c).* Under this paragraph (c), M's $100 basis in the S share is reduced, but not below its $60 value by the lesser of the share's net positive adjustment and disconformity amount. There were no investment adjustments applied to M's basis in the share and so the share's net positive adjustment is $0. Thus, although the share's disconformity amount is $40 (the excess of M's $100 basis in the share over the share's $60 allocable portion of S's net inside attribute amount), no basis reduction is required under this paragraph (c).

(iv) *Application of paragraph (d) of this section.* After the application of this paragraph (c), M's sale of the S share is still a transfer of a loss share, and, accordingly, subject to paragraph (d) of this section. No adjustment is required under paragraph (d) of this section because there is no aggregate inside loss. See paragraph (d)(3)(iii) of this section.

*Example 3. Items accruing after S becomes a member.* (i) *Recognition of loss accruing after S becomes a member.* (A) *Facts.* On January 1, year 1, M purchases the sole outstanding share of S stock for $100. At that time, S owns two assets, Asset 1, with a basis of $0 and a value of $40, and Asset 2, with a basis and value of $60. In year 1, S sells Asset 1 for $40, recognizing a $40 gain. Also in year 1, the value of Asset 2 declines and S sells Asset 2 for $20, recognizing a $40 loss that is absorbed by the group. On December 31, year 1, M sells its S share for $60. After taking into account the effects of all applicable rules of law, M's basis in the S share is $100 (M's original $100 basis, unadjusted under §1.1502-32 because the $40 gain recognized on the sale of Asset 1 and the $40 loss on the sale of Asset 2 net, resulting in an adjustment of $0). M's sale of the S share is a transfer of a loss share and therefore subject to this section.

(B) *Application of paragraph (b) of this section.* Although the transfer is subject to this section, there is no basis redetermination under paragraph (b) of this section because there is only one share of S stock outstanding (and so there can be no disparity among members' bases in common shares and there are no outstanding preferred shares with respect to which there can be unrecognized gain or loss). See paragraph (b)(1)(ii)(A) of this section. Therefore, after the application of paragraph (b) of this section, the share is still a loss share and, as such, subject to this paragraph (c).

(C) *Basis reduction under this paragraph (c).* Under this paragraph (c), M's basis in the S share is reduced, but not below the share's $60 value, by the lesser of the share's net positive adjustment and disconformity amount. The share's net positive adjustment is $0. Thus, although the share has a disconformity amount of $40 (the excess of M's basis in the share, $100, over the share's allocable portion of S's net inside attribute amount, $60), no basis reduction is required under this paragraph (c).

(D) *Application of paragraph (d) of this section.* After the application of this paragraph (c), M's sale of the S share is still a transfer of a loss share, and, accordingly, subject to paragraph (d) of this section. No adjustment is required under paragraph (d) of this section because there is no aggregate inside loss. See paragraph (d)(3)(iii) of this section.

(ii) *Recognition of gain accruing after S becomes a member.* (A) *Facts.* The facts are the same as in paragraph (i)(A) of this *Example 3*, except that M does not sell the S share and S does not sell either asset in year

1. In addition, in year 2, the value of Asset 1 declines to $0, the value of Asset 2 returns to $60, and S creates Asset 3 (with a basis of $0). In year 3, S sells Asset 3 for $40, recognizing a $40 gain. On December 31, year 3, M sells its S share for $100. After taking into account the effects of all applicable rules of law, M's basis in the S share is $140 (M's original $100 basis increased under §1.1502-32 by $40 (the share's allocable portion of the gain recognized on the sale of Asset 3 in year 3)). M's sale of the S share is a transfer of a loss share and therefore subject to this section.

(B) *Application of paragraph (b) of this section.* Although the transfer is subject to this section, there is no basis redetermination under paragraph (b) of this section for the reasons set forth in paragraph (i)(B) of this *Example 3*. Therefore, after the application of paragraph (b) of this section, the share is still a loss share and, as such, subject to this paragraph (c).

(C) *Basis reduction under this paragraph (c).* Under this paragraph (c), M's basis in the S share, $140, is reduced, but not below value, $100, by the lesser of the share's net positive adjustment and disconformity amount. The share's net positive adjustment is $40 (the year 3 investment adjustment). The share's disconformity amount is the excess of its basis, $140, over its allocable portion of S's net inside attribute amount. S's net inside attribute amount is $100, the sum of S's money ($40 from the sale of Asset 3) and its basis in its assets ($60 (the sum of Asset 1's basis of $0 and Asset 2's basis of $60)). S's $100 net inside attribute amount is allocable entirely to the sole outstanding S share. Thus, the share's disconformity amount is the excess of $140 over $100, or $40. The lesser of the share's net positive adjustment, $40, and its disconformity amount, $40, is $40. Accordingly, the basis in the share is reduced by $40, from $140 to $100.

(D) *Application of paragraph (d) of this section.* Because M's sale of the S share is not a transfer of a loss share after the application of this paragraph (c), paragraph (d) of this section does not apply to the transfer.

(iii) *Recognition of income earned after S becomes a member.* The facts are the same as in paragraph (ii)(A) of this *Example 3*, except that instead of creating Asset 3, S earns $40 of income from services provided in year 3. Because the net positive adjustment includes items of income as well as items of gain, the results are the same as those described in paragraph (ii) of this *Example 3*.

*Example 4. Computing the disconformity amount.* (i) *Unrecognized loss reflected in stock basis.* (A) *Facts.* M owns the sole outstanding share of S stock with a basis of $100. S owns two assets, Asset 1 with a basis of $20 and a value of $60, and Asset 2 with a basis of $60 and a value of $40. In year 1, S sells Asset 1 for $60, recognizing a $40 gain. On December 31, year 1, M sells the S share for $100. After taking into account the effects of all applicable rules of law, M's basis in the S share is $140 (M's original $100 basis increased under §1.1502-32 by $40, the share's allocable portion of the gain recognized on the sale of Asset 1). M's sale of the S share is a transfer of a loss share and therefore subject to this section.

(B) *Application of paragraph (b) of this section.* Although the transfer is subject to this section, there is no basis redetermination under paragraph (b) of this section because there is only one share of S stock outstanding (and so there can be no disparity among members' bases in common shares and there are no outstanding preferred shares with respect to which there can be unrecognized gain or loss). See paragraph (b)(1)(ii)(A) of this section. Therefore, after the application of paragraph (b) of this section, the share is still a loss share and, as such, subject to this paragraph (c).

(C) *Basis reduction under this paragraph (c).* Under this paragraph (c), M's basis in the S share, $140, is reduced, but not below the share's $100 value, by the lesser of the share's net positive adjustment and disconformity amount. The share's net positive adjustment is $40 (the year 1 investment adjustment). The share's disconformity amount is the excess of its basis, $140, over its allocable portion of S's net inside attribute amount. S's net inside attribute amount is $120, the sum of S's money ($60 from the sale of Asset 1) and S's basis in Asset 2, $60. S's net inside attribute amount is allocable entirely to the sole outstanding S share. Thus, the share's disconformity amount is $20, the excess of $140 over $120. The lesser of the share's net positive adjustment, $40, and its disconformity amount, $20, is $20. Accordingly, the basis in the share is reduced by $20, from $140 to $120.

(D) *Application of paragraph (d) of this section.* After the application of this paragraph (c), M's sale of the S share is still a transfer of a loss share, and, accordingly, S's attributes (to the extent of the $20 duplicated loss) are subject to reduction under paragraph (d) of this section.

(ii) *Loss carryover.* The facts are the same as in paragraph (i)(A) of this *Example 4*, except that Asset 2 has a basis of $0 (rather than $60) and S has a $60 loss carryover (as defined in paragraph (f)(6) of this section). The analysis is the same as paragraph (i) of this *Example 4*. Furthermore, the analysis of the application of this paragraph (c) would be the same if the $60 loss carryover were subject to a section 382 limitation from a prior ownership change, or if, instead, the $60 loss carryover were subject to the limitation in §1.1502-21(c) on losses carried from separate return limitation years.

(iii) *Liabilities.* The facts are the same as in paragraph (i)(A) of this *Example 4*, except that S borrows $100 before M sells the S share. S's net inside attribute amount remains $120, computed as the sum of S's money ($160, $60 from the sale of Asset 1 plus the $100 borrowed) and S's basis in Asset 2, $60, less its liabilities, $100. Thus, the S share's disconformity remains the excess of $140 over $120, or $20. The results are the same as in paragraph (i) of this *Example 4*.

*Example 5. Computing the allocable portion of the net inside attribute amount.* (i) *Facts.* On January 1, year 1, M owns all five outstanding shares of S stock with a basis of $20 per share. S owns Asset with a basis of $0. In year 1, S sells Asset for $100, recognizing a $100 gain. On December 31, year 1, M sells one of the S shares, Share 1, for $20. After taking into account the effects of all applicable rules of law, M's basis in Share 1 is $40 (M's original $20 basis increased under §1.1502-32 by $20 (the share's allocable portion of the gain recognized on the sale of Asset)). M's sale of Share 1 is a transfer of a loss share and therefore subject to this section.

(ii) *Application of paragraph (b) of this section.* Although the transfer is subject to this section, basis is not redetermined under paragraph (b) of this section because there is no disparity among M's bases in shares of S common stock and there are no shares of S preferred stock outstanding (so there can be no unrecognized gain or loss with respect to preferred shares). See paragraph (b)(1)(ii)(A) of this section. After the application of paragraph (b) of this section, M's sale of Share 1 is still a transfer of a loss share and therefore subject to this paragraph (c).

(iii) *Basis reduction under this paragraph (c).* Under this paragraph (c), M's $40 basis in Share 1 is reduced, but not below its $20 value by the lesser of the share's net positive adjustment and disconformity amount. Share 1's net positive adjustment is $20 (the year 1 investment adjustment). Share 1's disconformity amount is the excess of its $40 basis over its allocable portion of S's net inside attribute amount. S's net inside attribute amount is equal to the amount of S's money ($100 from the sale of the asset). Share 1's allocable portion of S's $100 net inside attribute amount is $20 (1/5 × $100). Thus, Share 1's disconformity amount is the excess of $40 over $20, or $20. The lesser of the share's $20 net positive adjustment and its $20 disconformity amount is $20. Accordingly, the basis in the share is reduced by $20, from $40 to $20.

(iv) *Application of paragraph (d) of this section.* Because M's sale of Share 1 is not a transfer of a loss share after the application of this paragraph (c), paragraph (d) of this section does not apply to the transfer.

*Example 6. Liabilities.* (i) *In general.* (A) *Facts.* On January 1, year 1, M purchases the sole outstanding share of S stock for $100. At that time, S owns Asset, with a basis of $0 and value of $100, and $100 cash. S also has a $100 liability. In year 1, S declares and makes a $60 dividend distribution to M and recognizes $20 of income. The value of Asset declines to $60 and, on December 31, year 1, M sells the S share for $20. After taking into account the effects of all applicable rules of law, M's basis in the S share is $60 (M's original $100 basis decreased under §1.1502-32 by $40 (the net of the $60 distribution and the $20 income recognized)). M's sale of the S share is a transfer of a loss share and therefore subject to this section.

(B) *Application of paragraph (b) of this section.* Although the transfer is subject to this section, there is no basis redetermination under paragraph (b) of this section because there is only one share of S stock outstanding (and so there can be no disparity among members' bases in common shares and there are no outstanding preferred shares with respect to which there can be unrecognized gain or loss). See paragraph (b)(1)(ii)(A) of this section. Therefore, after the application of paragraph (b) of this section, the share is still a loss share and, as such, subject to this paragraph (c).

(C) *Basis reduction under this paragraph (c).* Under this paragraph (c), M's basis in the S share, $60, is reduced, but not below value, $20, by the lesser of the share's net positive adjustment and disconformity amount. The share's net positive adjustment is $20 (the year 1 investment adjustment, as defined in paragraph (b)(1)(iii) of this section). The share's disconformity amount is the excess of its basis, $60, over its allocable portion of S's net inside attribute amount. S's net inside attribute amount is negative $40, computed as the sum of S's money ($60 ($100 less the $60 distribution plus the $20 income recognized)) and S's basis in Asset, $0, less S's liability, $100. S's net inside attribute amount is allocable entirely to the sole outstanding S share. Thus, the share's disconformity amount is the excess of $60 over negative $40, or $100. The lesser of the share's net positive adjustment, $20, and its disconformity amount, $100, is $20. Accordingly, the basis in the share is reduced by $20, from $60 to $40.

(D) *Application of paragraph (d) of this section.* After the application of this paragraph (c), the S share is still a loss share and, accordingly, S's attributes are subject to reduction under paragraph (d) of this section. No adjustment is required under paragraph (d) of this sec-

tion, however, because there is no aggregate inside loss. See paragraph (d)(3)(iii) of this section.

(ii) *Excluded cancellation of indebtedness income—insufficient attributes available for reduction under sections 108 and 1017, and §1.1502-28.* (A) *Facts.* The facts are the same as in paragraph (i)(A) of this *Example 6*, except that M does not sell the S share. Instead, in year 4, Asset is destroyed in a fire and S spends its $60 on deductible expenses that are not absorbed by the group. S's loss becomes part of the consolidated net operating loss (CNOL). In year 5, S becomes insolvent and S's debt is discharged. Because of S's insolvency, S's discharge of indebtedness income is excluded under section 108 and, as a result, S's attributes are subject to reduction under sections 108 and 1017, and §1.1502-28. S's only attribute is the portion of the CNOL attributable to S, $60, and it is reduced to $0. There are no other consolidated attributes. In year 5, the S stock (which is treated as a capital asset) becomes worthless under section 165, taking into account §1.1502-80(c). After taking into account the effects of all applicable rules of law, M's basis in the S share is $60 (M's original $100 basis decreased under §1.1502-32 by the year 1 investment adjustment of $40 (the net of the $60 distribution and the $20 income recognized). The investment adjustment for year 5 is $0 (the net of the $60 tax exempt income from the excluded COD applied to reduce attributes and the $60 noncapital, nondeductible expense from the reduction of S's portion of the CNOL). Under paragraph (f)(10)(i)(D) of this section, a share is transferred on the last day of the taxable year during which it becomes worthless under section 165 if the share is treated as a capital asset, or the date the share becomes worthless if the share is not treated as a capital asset, taking into account §1.1502-80(c). Accordingly, M transfers the loss share of S stock on December 31, year 5, and the transfer is therefore subject to this section.

(B) *Application of paragraph (b) of this section.* Although the transfer is subject to this section, there is no basis redetermination under paragraph (b) of this section for the reasons set forth in paragraph (i)(B) of this *Example 6*. Therefore, after the application of paragraph (b) of this section, the share is still a loss share and, as such, subject to this paragraph (c).

(C) *Basis reduction under this paragraph (c).* Under this paragraph (c), M's basis in its S share, $60, is reduced, but not below value, $0, by the lesser of the share's net positive adjustment and disconformity amount. The share's net positive adjustment is $20 (the year 1 investment adjustment, as defined in paragraph (b)(1)(iii) of this section). The share's disconformity amount is the excess of its basis, $60, over its allocable portion of S's net inside attribute amount. S's net inside attribute amount is $0. (The effects of the attribute reduction required under sections 108 and 1017 and §1.1502-28 are taken into account in applying this section; therefore, for purposes of this section, S's portion of the CNOL is treated as eliminated under section 108 and §1.1502-28.) S's net inside attribute amount is allocable entirely to the sole outstanding S share. Thus, the share's disconformity amount is the excess of $60 over $0, or $60. The lesser of the share's net positive adjustment, $20, and its disconformity amount, $60, is $20. Accordingly, the basis in the share is reduced by $20, from $60 to $40, immediately before the transfer.

(D) *Application of paragraph (d) of this section.* After the application of this paragraph (c), the S share is still a loss share, and, accordingly, S's attributes are subject to reduction under paragraph (d) of this section. No adjustment is required under paragraph (d) of this section, however, because there is no aggregate inside loss. See paragraph (d)(3)(iii) of this section.

(iii) *Excluded cancellation of indebtedness income—full attribute reduction under sections 108 and 1017, and §1.1502-28 (using attributes attributable to another member).* (A) *Facts.* The facts are the same as in paragraph (ii)(A) of this *Example 6* except that M loses the $60 distributed in year 1 and the group does not absorb the loss. Thus, as of December 31, year 5, the CNOL is $120, attributable $60 to S and $60 to P. As a result, under §1.1502-28(a)(4), after the portion of the CNOL attributable to S is reduced to $0, the remaining $40 of excluded COD applies to the portion of the CNOL attributable to P, reducing it from $60 to $20. After taking into account the effects of all applicable rules of law, M's basis in the S share at the end of year 5 is $100 (M's original $100 basis decreased under §1.1502-32 by $40 at the end of year 1 and then increased under §1.1502-32 by $40 at the end of year 5 (the net of the $100 tax exempt income from the excluded COD applied to reduce attributes and the $60 noncapital, nondeductible expense from the reduction of S's portion of the CNOL)). Under paragraph (f)(10)(i)(D) of this section, a share is transferred on the last day of the taxable year during which it becomes worthless under section 165 if the share is treated as a capital asset, or the date the share becomes worthless if the share is not treated as a capital asset, taking into account §1.1502-80(c). Accordingly, M transfers the loss share of S stock on December 31, year 5, and the transfer is therefore subject to this section.

(B) *Application of paragraph (b) of this section.* Although the transfer is subject to this section, there is no basis redetermination under paragraph (b) of this section for the reasons set forth in paragraph (i)(B) of this *Example 6*. Therefore, after the application of paragraph (b) of this section, the share is still a loss share and, as such, subject to this paragraph (c).

(C) *Basis reduction under this paragraph (c)*. Under this paragraph (c), M's basis in the S share, $100, is reduced, but not below value, $0, by the lesser of the share's net positive adjustment and disconformity amount. The share's net positive adjustment is $60 (the sum of the year 1 investment adjustment, as defined in paragraph (b)(1)(iii) of this section, $20, and the year 5 investment adjustment, $40). The share's disconformity amount is the excess of its basis, $100, over its allocable portion of S's net inside attribute amount. S's net inside attribute amount is $0 (taking into account the effects of the attribute reduction required under sections 108 and 1017 and § 1.1502-28). S's net inside attribute amount is allocable entirely to the sole outstanding S share. The share's disconformity amount is therefore $100. The lesser of the share's net positive adjustment, $60, and its disconformity amount, $100, is $60. Accordingly, M's basis in the share is reduced by $60, from $100 to $40, immediately before the transfer.

(D) *Application of paragraph (d) of this section*. After the application of this paragraph (c), the S share is still a loss share, and, accordingly, S's attributes are subject to reduction under paragraph (d) of this section. No adjustment is required under paragraph (d) of this section, however, because there is no aggregate inside loss. See paragraph (d)(3)(iii) of this section.

*Example 7. Lower-tier subsidiary (no transfer of lower-tier stock)*. (i) *Facts*. M owns the sole outstanding share of S stock with a basis of $160. S owns two assets, Asset 1 with a basis and value of $100, and the sole outstanding share of S1 stock with a basis of $60. S1 owns one asset, Asset 2, with a basis of $20 and value of $60. In year 1, S1 sells Asset 2 to X for $60, recognizing a $40 gain. On December 31, year 1, M sells its S share to Y, a member of another consolidated group, for $160. After taking into account the effects of all applicable rules of law, M's basis in the S share is $200 (M's original $160 basis increased under § 1.1502-32 by $40 (to reflect the tier-up of the adjustment to S's basis in the S1 stock for the gain recognized on S1's sale of Asset 2)). M's sale of the S share is a transfer of a loss share and therefore subject to this section. (S does not transfer the S1 share because S and S1 are members of the same group following the transfer. See paragraph (f)(10) of this section.)

(ii) *Application of paragraph (b) of this section*. Although the transfer is subject to this section, there is no basis redetermination under paragraph (b) of this section because there is only one share of S stock outstanding (and so there can be no disparity among members' bases in common shares and there are no outstanding preferred shares with respect to which there can be unrecognized gain or loss). See paragraph (b)(1)(ii)(A) of this section. Therefore, after the application of paragraph (b) of this section, the share is still a loss share and, as such, subject to this paragraph (c).

(iii) *Basis reduction under this paragraph (c)*. (A) *In general*. Under this paragraph (c), M's basis in the S share, $200, is reduced, but not below value, $160, by the lesser of the share's net positive adjustment and disconformity amount. The S share's net positive adjustment is $40. The share's disconformity amount is the excess of its basis, $200, over the share's allocable portion of S's net inside attribute amount. S's net inside attribute amount is the sum of S's basis in Asset 1, $100, and S's basis in the S1 share.

(B) *S's basis in the S1 share*. Although S's actual basis in the S1 share is $100 (S's original $60 basis increased under § 1.1502-32 by $40 (the share's allocable portion of the gain recognized on the sale of Asset 2)), for purposes of computing the S share's disconformity amount, S's net inside attribute amount is determined by treating S's basis in the S1 share as tentatively reduced by the lesser of the S1 share's net positive adjustment and the S1 share's disconformity amount. The S1 share's net positive adjustment is $40 (the year 1 investment adjustment). The S1 share's disconformity amount is the excess of its basis, $100, over the share's allocable portion of S1's net inside attribute amount. S1's net inside attribute amount is equal to the amount of S1's money ($60 from the sale of Asset 2), and is allocable entirely to the sole outstanding S1 share. Thus, the S1 share's disconformity amount is the excess of $100 over $60, or $40. The lesser of the S1 share's net positive adjustment, $40, and its disconformity amount, $40, is $40. Accordingly, for purposes of computing the disconformity amount of the S share, S's net inside attribute amount is determined by treating S's basis in its S1 share as tentatively reduced by $40, from $100 to $60.

(C) *The disconformity amount of M's S share*. S's net inside attribute amount is treated as the sum of its basis in Asset 1, $100, and its tentatively reduced basis in the S1 share, $60, or $160. S's net inside attribute amount is allocable entirely to the sole outstanding S share. Thus, the S share's disconformity amount is the excess of $200 over $160, or $40.

(D) *Amount of reduction*. M's basis in its S share is reduced by the lesser of the S share's net positive adjustment, $40, and disconformity

amount, $40, or $40. Accordingly, M's basis in the S share is reduced by $40, from $200 to $160.

(E) *Effect on S's basis in its S1 share*. The tentative reduction under this paragraph (c) has no effect on S's actual basis in the S1 share. Thus, after the application of this paragraph (c), S owns the S1 share with a basis of $100 (S's original $60 basis increased under § 1.1502-32 by $40 (the share's allocable portion of the gain recognized on the sale of Asset 2)).

(iv) *Application of paragraph (d) of this section*. Because M's sale of the S share is not a transfer of a loss share after the application of this paragraph (c), paragraph (d) of this section does not apply to the transfer.

(d) *Attribute reduction to prevent duplication of loss*.—(1) *In general*.—The rules of this paragraph (d) reduce attributes of S and its lower-tier subsidiaries to the extent they duplicate a net loss on shares of S stock transferred by members in one transaction. This rule furthers single-entity principles by preventing S (or its lower-tier subsidiaries) from using deductions and losses to the extent that the group or its members (including former members) have either used, or preserved for later use, a corresponding loss in S shares.

(2) *Attribute reduction rule*.—(i) *General rule*.—If a transferred share is a loss share after taking into account the effects of all applicable rules of law, including any adjustments under paragraph (b), (c), or (d)(5)(iii) of this section, S's attributes are reduced by S's attribute reduction amount immediately before the transfer. S's attribute reduction amount is determined under paragraph (d)(3) of this section and applied in accordance with the provisions of paragraphs (d)(4), (d)(5), and (d)(6) of this section. In addition, paragraph (d)(7) of this section provides for additional attribute reduction in the case of certain transfers due to worthlessness and certain transfers not followed by a separate return year.

(ii) *Attribute reduction amount less than five percent of value*.—This paragraph (d) generally does not apply to a transaction if the aggregate attribute reduction amount in the transaction is less than five percent of the aggregate value of the shares transferred by members in the transaction. However, in such a case, P may elect to apply this paragraph (d) to the transaction. If such an election is made, this paragraph (d) will apply with respect to the entire aggregate attribute reduction amount determined in the transaction. Such an election is made in the manner provided in paragraph (e)(5) of this section.

(3) *Attribute reduction amount*.—(i) *In general*.—S's *attribute reduction amount* is the lesser of—

(A) The net stock loss (as defined in paragraph (d)(3)(ii) of this section); and

(B) S's aggregate inside loss (as defined in paragraph (d)(3)(iii) of this section).

(ii) *Net stock loss*.—The *net stock loss* is the excess, if any, of—

(A) The aggregate basis of all shares of S stock transferred by members in the transaction; over

(B) The aggregate value of those shares.

(iii) *Aggregate inside loss*.—(A) *In general*.—S's *aggregate inside loss* is the excess, if any, of—

*(1)* S's net inside attribute amount; over

*(2)* The value of all outstanding shares of S stock.

(B) *Net inside attribute amount*.—S's *net inside attribute amount* generally has the same meaning as in paragraph (c)(5) of this section. However, if S holds stock of a lower-tier subsidiary, the provisions of paragraph (d)(5) of this section (and not the provisions of paragraph (c)(6) of this section) modify the computation of S's net inside attribute amount for purposes of this paragraph (d).

(iv) *Lower-tier subsidiaries*.—See paragraph (d)(5) of this section for special rules relating to the application of this paragraph (d) if S owns shares of stock of a subsidiary.

(4) *Application of attribute reduction amount*.—(i) *Attributes available for reduction*.—S's attributes available for reduction under this paragraph (d) are—

(A) *Category A*.—Capital loss carryovers;

(B) *Category B*.—Net operating loss carryovers;

(C) *Category C*.—Deferred deductions; and

(D) *Category D*.—Basis of assets other than assets identified as Class I assets in § 1.338-6(b)(1).

(ii) *Rules of application*.—(A) *Category A, Category B, and Category C attributes*.—S's attribute reduction amount is first allocated and applied to reduce the attributes in Category A, Category B, and Category C.

*(1) Attribute reduction amount less than total attributes in Category A, Category B, and Category C.*—If S's attribute reduction amount is less than S's total attributes in Category A, Category B, and Category C, all of S's attribute reduction amount will be applied to reduce such attributes. However, P may specify the allocation of S's attribute reduction amount among such attributes. An election to specify the allocation of S's attribute reduction amount is made in the manner provided in paragraph (e)(5) of this section. To the extent that P does not specify an allocation of S's attribute reduction amount, S's attribute reduction amount will be applied to reduce any Category A attributes not reduced as a result of the specific allocation of S's attribute reduction amount, from oldest to newest, until they are eliminated. Then, any remaining attribute reduction amount will be applied to reduce any Category B attributes not reduced as a result of the specific allocation of S's attribute reduction amount, from oldest to newest, until they are eliminated. Finally, any remaining attribute reduction amount will be applied to reduce any Category C attributes not reduced as a result of the specific allocation of S's attribute reduction amount, proportionately.

*(2) Attribute reduction amount not less than the total attributes in Category A, Category B, and Category C.*—If S's attribute reduction amount equals or exceeds S's total attributes in Category A, Category B, and Category C, all such attributes are eliminated and any remaining attribute reduction amount is allocated and applied as provided in paragraphs (d)(4)(ii)(B) and (d)(4)(ii)(C) of this section.

(B) *Category D attributes.*—Any attribute reduction amount not applied to reduce S's Category A, Category B, and Category C attributes is allocated and applied as provided in this paragraph (d)(4)(ii)(B) and, to the extent applicable, paragraph (d)(5) of this section.

*(1) Allocation if S holds stock of another subsidiary.*—If S holds shares of stock of another subsidiary, the attribute reduction amount not applied to reduce S's Category A, Category B, and Category C attributes is first allocated between S's shares of lower-tier subsidiary stock and S's other Category D assets in the manner provided in paragraph (d)(5)(ii) of this section. S's attribute reduction amount allocated to shares of lower-tier subsidiary stock is applied to reduce S's bases in those shares, becomes an attribute reduction amount of the lower-tier subsidiary, and, subject to certain limitations, reduces the lower-tier subsidiary's attributes. See paragraphs (d)(5)(iii) through (d)(5)(vi) of this section.

*(2) Allocation and application of attribute reduction amount not applied to lower-tier subsidiary stock.*—Any portion of S's attribute reduction amount not applied to reduce S's Category A, Category B, and Category C attributes and not allocated to lower-tier subsidiary stock is allocated to S's Category D assets other than lower-tier subsidiary stock in the manner provided in this paragraph (d)(4)(ii)(B)(2). Such amount is first allocated to S's bases (if any) in its assets identified as Class VII assets in § 1.338-6(b)(2)(vii). If the attribute reduction amount allocated to Class VII assets is less than S's aggregate basis in those assets, it is applied proportionately (by basis) to reduce the bases of such assets. If the attribute reduction amount allocated to Class VII assets equals or exceeds S's aggregate basis in those assets, it is applied to reduce the bases of such assets to zero. Any remaining attribute reduction amount is then allocated and applied in the same manner to reduce S's bases (if any) in assets identified as Class VI assets in § 1.338-6(b)(2)(vi), and then to reduce S's bases (if any) in its assets identified in § 1.338-6(b)(2) as Class V, Class IV, Class III, and Class II, successively.

(C) *Attribute reduction amount exceeding attributes available for reduction.*—If the amount to be allocated and applied to attributes in Category D other than lower-tier subsidiary stock exceeds the amount of attributes in that category, then—

*(1)* To the extent of any liabilities of S that are not taken into account for tax purposes before the transfer, such excess amount is suspended. The suspended amount is applied proportionately to reduce any amounts attributable to S that would be deductible or capitalizable as a result of such liabilities being taken into account by S or any other person. Solely for purposes of this paragraph (d)(4)(ii)(C)(1) and paragraph (d)(5)(ii)(B) of this section, the term *liability* means any liability or obligation the satisfaction of which would be required to be capitalized as an assumed liability by a person that purchased all of S's assets and assumed all of S's liabilities in a single transaction.

*(2)* To the extent such excess amount is greater than any amount suspended under paragraph (d)(4)(ii)(C)(1) of this section, it is disregarded and has no further effect.

(iii) *Time and effect of attribute reduction.*—In general, the reduction of attributes is effective immediately before the transfer of a loss share of S stock. If the reduction to a member's basis in a share of lower-tier subsidiary stock exceeds the basis of that share, to the extent the excess is not restored under paragraph (d)(5)(vi) of this section it is an excess loss account in that share (and such excess loss account is not taken into account under §1.1502-19 or otherwise as a result of the transaction). The reductions to attributes required under this paragraph (d)(4), including by reason of paragraph (d)(5)(v) of this section (tier down of attribute reduction amounts to lower-tier subsidiaries), are not noncapital, nondeductible expenses described in §1.1502-32(b)(2)(iii).

(5) *Special rules applicable if S holds stock of another subsidiary.*—If S holds shares of stock of any other subsidiary (S1) as of a transfer of loss shares of S stock, the rules of this paragraph (d)(5) apply with respect to each such subsidiary.

(i) *Treatment of lower-tier subsidiary stock for computation of S's attribute reduction amount.*—For purposes of determining S's net inside attribute amount and attribute reduction amount under paragraph (d)(3) of this section—

(A) *Single share.*—All of S's shares of S1 stock held as of the transfer of S stock (whether or not transferred in, or held by S immediately after, the transaction) are treated as a single share of stock (generally referred to as the S1 stock); and

(B) *Deemed basis.*—S's basis in its S1 stock is treated as its *deemed basis* in the stock, which is equal to the greater of—

*(1)* The sum of S's basis in each share of S1 stock (adjusted to reflect any gain or loss recognized on the transfer of any S1 shares in the transaction, whether allowed or disallowed); and

*(2)* The portion of S1's net inside attribute amount allocable to S's shares of S1 stock.

(C) *Multiple tiers.*—For purposes of computing deemed basis under paragraph (d)(5)(i)(B) of this section, a subsidiary's basis in stock of a lower-tier subsidiary is the deemed basis in that lower-tier subsidiary stock. Thus, if stock is held in multiple tiers, the computation of deemed basis begins at the lowest tier, so that the computation of deemed basis at each tier takes into account the deemed basis of all lower-tier shares.

(ii) *Allocation of S's attribute reduction amount between lower-tier subsidiary stock and other Category D assets.*—The portion of S's attribute reduction amount that is not applied to reduce S's Category A, Category B, and Category C attributes must be allocated between each of S's deemed single shares of S1 stock and all of S's other Category D assets. For this purpose, S's Category D assets other than lower-tier subsidiary stock are treated as one asset with a basis equal to the aggregate bases of all Category D assets other than lower-tier subsidiary stock (non-stock Category D asset). S's attribute reduction amount is allocated proportionately (by basis) between (among) the non-stock Category D asset and S's deemed single share(s) of subsidiary stock. (See paragraphs (d)(4)(ii)(B)(2) and (d)(4)(ii)(C) of this section regarding the portion of S's attribute reduction amount allocated to the Category D assets other than lower-tier subsidiary stock.) For allocation purposes, S's basis in each deemed single share of S1 stock is its deemed basis (determined under paragraphs (d)(5)(i)(B) and (d)(5)(i)(C) of this section), reduced by—

(A) The value of S's transferred shares of S1 stock; and

(B) The nontransferred S1 shares' allocable portion of the excess of S1's nonloss assets over S1's liabilities (including liabilities described in paragraph (d)(4)(ii)(C)(1) of this section). For this purpose, S1's non-loss assets are—

*(1)* S1's assets identified as Class I assets in § 1.338-6(b)(1),

*(2)* The value of S1's transferred shares of lower-tier subsidiary stock, and

*(3)* The nontransferred lower-tier subsidiary shares' allocable portions of lower-tier non-loss assets (net of liabilities, including liabilities described in paragraph (d)(4)(ii)(C)(1) of this section) of all lower-tier subsidiaries.

(iii) *Application of attribute reduction amount to S's S1 stock.*—The portion of S's attribute reduction amount allocated under paragraph (d)(5)(ii) of this section to each deemed single share of S1 stock (allocated attribute reduction amount) is apportioned among, and applied to reduce S's bases in, individual S1 shares in accordance with the following—

(A) No portion of the allocated attribute reduction amount is apportioned to an individual share of transferred S1 stock if gain or loss is recognized on its transfer (recognition transfer);

(B) The allocated attribute reduction amount is apportioned among all of S's other shares of S1 stock in a manner that, first reduces the loss in and disparity among S's bases in loss shares of S1 preferred stock to the greatest extent possible, and then reduces the disparity among S's bases in the shares of S1 common stock (other than those transferred in a recognition transfer) to the greatest extent possible;

(C) The allocated attribute reduction amount apportioned to an individual S1 share is applied to reduce the basis of that share to, but not below, value if the share is either a preferred share or a common share that is transferred other than in a recognition transfer; and

(D) The allocated attribute reduction amount apportioned to an individual S1 share is applied to reduce the basis of that share without regard to value if the share is a common share that is not transferred in the transaction.

(iv) *Unapplied allocated attribute reduction amount.*—Any portion of the allocated attribute reduction amount that is not applied to reduce S's basis in a share of S1 stock has no effect on any other attributes of S, it is not a noncapital, nondeductible expense of S, and it does not cause S to recognize income or gain. However, such amounts continue to be part of the allocated attribute reduction amount for purposes of the tier down rule in paragraph (d)(5)(v) of this section.

(v) *Tier down of attribute reduction amount.*—(A) *General rule.*—The allocated attribute reduction amount of each deemed single share of S1 stock is an attribute reduction amount of S1 (tier-down attribute reduction amount). Accordingly, the tierdown attribute reduction amount, in combination with any attribute reduction amount computed with respect to the transferred S1 shares (if any) (direct S1 attribute reduction amount), applies to reduce S1's attributes under the provisions of this paragraph (d). The tier-down attribute reduction amount is an attribute reduction amount of S1 that must be deemed allocated to S1's assets, and may become an allocated attribute reduction amount of lower-tier subsidiary stock (and thus a tier-down attribute reduction amount of a lower-tier subsidiary), even if its application to S1's attributes is limited under paragraph (d)(5)(v)(B) of this section.

(B) *Conforming limitation on reduction of lower-tier subsidiary's attributes.*—Notwithstanding the general rule in paragraph (d)(5)(v)(A) of this section, and unless P elects otherwise in the manner provided in paragraph (e)(5) of this section, the application of S1's tier-down attribute reduction amount to S1's attributes is limited to an amount equal to the excess of the portion of S1's net inside attribute amount that is allocable to all S1 shares held by members as of the transaction (whether or not transferred in the transaction) over the sum of—

(1) Any direct S1 attribute reduction amount;

(2) The aggregate value of all S1 shares transferred by members in the transaction with respect to which gain or loss was recognized (recognition transfer);

(3) The sum of all members' bases (after any reduction under this section, including this paragraph (d)) in any shares of S1 stock transferred by members in the transaction (other than in a recognition transfer), reduced by any direct S1 attribute reduction amount computed with respect to the transfer of such S1 shares; and

(4) The sum of all members' bases (after any reduction under this section, including this paragraph (d)) in any nontransferred shares of S1 stock held as of the transaction.

(vi) *Stock basis restoration.*—(A) *In general.*—After paragraph (d)(5)(v) of this section has applied with respect to all shares of subsidiary stock transferred in the transaction, lower-tier subsidiary stock basis is restored under this paragraph (d)(5)(vi). Under this paragraph (d)(5)(vi), the reductions to members' bases in shares of lower-tier subsidiary stock under paragraph (d)(5)(iii) of this section are reversed to the extent necessary to restore such bases to an amount that conforms the basis of each such share to its allocable portion of the subsidiary's net inside attribute amount, taking into account any reductions under this paragraph (d). Restoration adjustments are first made at the lowest tier and then at each next higher tier successively. Restoration adjustments do not tier up to affect the bases of higher-tier shares. Rather, restoration is computed and applied separately at each tier. For purposes of this rule, when computing a subsidiary's net inside attribute amount—

(1) The subsidiary's basis in stock of a lower-tier subsidiary is the actual basis of the stock after application of this paragraph (d); and

(2) Any attribute reduction amount allocated to the subsidiary's Category D assets other than lower-tier subsidiary stock that is suspended under paragraph (d)(4)(ii)(C)(1) of this section is treated as reducing the subsidiary's net inside attribute amount.

(B) *Election not to restore basis.*—Notwithstanding paragraph (d)(5)(vi)(A) of this section, P may elect not to restore basis in stock of a lower-tier subsidiary that was reduced under paragraph (d)(5)(iii) of this section. An election not to restore lower-tier subsidiary stock

basis is made in the manner provided in paragraph (e)(5) of this section.

(6) *Elections to reduce the potential for loss duplication.*—(i) *In general.*—Notwithstanding the general operation of this paragraph (d), P may elect to reduce the potential for loss duplication, and thereby reduce or avoid attribute reduction. To the extent of S's attribute reduction amount tentatively computed without regard to any election under this paragraph (d)(6), P may elect—

(A) To reduce all or any portion (including any portion in excess of a specified amount) of members' bases in transferred loss shares of S stock;

(B) To reattribute all or any portion (including any portion in excess of a specified amount) of S's Category A, Category B, and Category C attributes (including such attributes of lower-tier subsidiaries), to the extent they would otherwise be subject to reduction under this paragraph (d); or

(C) Any combination thereof.

(ii) *Manner and effect of election.*—An election to reduce loss duplication under this paragraph (d)(6) is made in the manner provided in paragraph (e)(5) of this section. Although such elections are irrevocable, they have no effect—

(A) If there is no attribute reduction amount; or

(B) To the extent S's attribute reduction amount is less than the amount specified in the election.

(iii) *Order of application.*—(A) *Stock of one subsidiary transferred in the transaction.*—If shares of stock of only one subsidiary are transferred in the transaction, any stock basis reduction and reattribution of attributes (including from lower-tier subsidiaries) is deemed to occur immediately before the application of this paragraph (d). If a transferred share is still a loss share after giving effect to this election, the other provisions of this paragraph (d) then apply with respect to that share.

(B) *Stock of multiple subsidiaries transferred in the transaction.*—If shares of stock of more than one subsidiary are transferred in the transaction and elections under this paragraph (d)(6) are made with respect to transfers of stock of subsidiaries in multiple tiers, effect is given to the elections from the lowest tier to the highest tier in the manner provided in this paragraph (d)(6)(iii)(B). The amount of the election for the transfer at the lowest tier is determined by applying this paragraph (d) with respect to the transferred loss shares of this lowest-tier subsidiary immediately after applying paragraphs (b) and (c) of this section to the stock of such subsidiary. The effect of any stock basis reduction or reattribution of losses immediately tiers up under §1.1502-32 to adjust members' bases in higher-tier shares. Elections and adjustments are then made with respect to transfers at each next higher tier successively.

(iv) *Special rules for reattribution elections.*—(A) *In general.*—Because the reattribution election is intended to provide the group a means to retain certain S attributes, and not to change the location of attributes where S continues to be a member of the same group as P, the election to reattribute attributes may only be made if S becomes a nonmember (within the meaning of §1.1502-19(c)(2)) as a result of the transaction and S does not become a member of any group that includes P. The election to reattribute S's attributes can only be made for attributes in Category A, Category B, and Category C. The attributes that would otherwise be reduced under paragraph (d)(4) of this section may be reattributed to P. Accordingly, P may specify the attributes in Category A, Category B, and Category C to be reattributed. Such an election is made in the manner provided in paragraph (e)(5) of this section. To the extent that P elects to reattribute attributes but does not specify the attributes to be reattributed, any attributes not specifically reattributed will be reattributed in the default amount, order, and category described in paragraph (d)(4)(ii)(A)(1) of this section. P succeeds to reattributed attributes as if such attributes were succeeded to in a transaction to which section 381(a) applies. Any owner shift of the subsidiary (including any deemed owner shift resulting from section 382(g)(4)(D) or section 382(l)(3)) in connection with the transaction is not taken into account under section 382 with respect to the reattributed attributes. (See §1.1502-96(d) for rules relating to section 382 and the reattribution of losses under this paragraph (d)(6)). The reattribution of S's attributes is a noncapital, nondeductible expense described in §1.1502-32(b)(2)(iii). See §1.1502-32(c)(1)(ii)(A) regarding special allocations applicable to such noncapital, nondeductible expense. If P elects to reattribute S attributes (including attributes of a lower-tier subsidiary) and reduce S stock basis, the reattribution is given effect before the stock basis reduction.

(B) *Insolvency limitation.*—If S, or any higher-tier subsidiary, is insolvent within the meaning of section 108(d)(3) at the time of the transfer, S's losses may be reattributed only to the extent they exceed the sum of the separate insolvencies of any subsidiaries (taking into account only S and its higher-tier subsidiaries) that are insolvent. For purposes of determining insolvency, liabilities owed to higher-tier members are not taken into account, and stock of a subsidiary that is limited and preferred as to dividends and that is not owned by higher-tier members is treated as a liability to the extent of the amount of preferred distributions to which the stock would be entitled if the subsidiary were liquidated on the date of the transfer.

(C) *Limitation on reattribution from lower-tier subsidiaries.*—P's ability to reattribute attributes of lower-tier subsidiaries is limited under this paragraph (d)(6)(iv)(C) in order to prevent circular computations of the attribute reduction amount. Accordingly, attributes that would otherwise be reduced as a result of tier-down attribute reduction under paragraph (d)(5)(v) of this section may only be reattributed to the extent that the reduction in the basis of any lower-tier subsidiary stock resulting from the noncapital, nondeductible expense (as allocated under § 1.1502-32(c)(1)(ii)(A)(2)) will not create an excess loss account in any such stock.

(v) *Special rules for stock basis reduction elections.*—(A) *In general.*—An election to reduce basis in S stock is made with respect to all members' bases in loss shares of S stock that are transferred in the transaction. The reduction is allocated among all such shares in proportion to the amount of loss on each share. This reduction in S stock basis is a noncapital, nondeductible expense described in § 1.1502-32(b)(2)(iii) of the transferring member.

(B) *Adjustment to the attribute reduction amount.*—The attribute reduction amount (determined under paragraph (d)(3)(i) of this section) is treated as reduced by the amount of any elective reduction in the basis of the S stock under this paragraph (d)(6). Accordingly, the election to reduce stock basis under this paragraph (d)(6) is treated as reducing or eliminating the duplication even if the shares of S stock are loss shares after giving effect to the election.

(C) *Deemed stock basis reduction election in the case of certain disallowed stock losses.*—If there is a net stock loss in transferred shares after taking into account any actual elections under this paragraph (d)(6), and the stock loss would otherwise be permanently disallowed (for example, under section 311(a)), P will be deemed to have made a stock basis reduction election equal to such net stock loss.

(7) *Additional attribute reduction in the case of certain transfers due to worthlessness and certain transfers not followed by a separate return year.*—(i) *In general.*—Notwithstanding any other provision of this paragraph (d), if a transfer is subject to this paragraph (d)(7) any of S's Category A, Category B, and Category C attributes not otherwise reduced or reattributed under this paragraph (d), and any credit carryover attributable to S, including any consolidated credits that would be apportioned to S under the principles of § 1.1502-79 if S had a separate return year, are eliminated. Attributes other than consolidated tax attributes are eliminated under this paragraph (d)(7)(i) immediately before the transfer subject to this paragraph (d)(7)(i). The elimination of attributes under this paragraph (d)(7)(i) is not a noncapital, nondeductible expense described in § 1.1502-32(b)(2)(iii).

(ii) *Transfers subject to this paragraph (d)(7).*—A transfer is subject to this paragraph (d)(7) if—

(A) M transfers a share of S stock solely by reason of a transfer defined in paragraph (f)(10)(i)(D) of this section (worthlessness where the provisions of § 1.1502-80(c) are satisfied), M recognizes a net deduction or loss on the share, and S is a member of the group on the day following the last day of the group's taxable year during which the share becomes worthless under section 165 (taking into account the provisions of § 1.1502-80(c)), or

(B) M recognizes a net deduction or loss on the stock of S in a transaction in which S ceases to be a member and does not become a nonmember within the meaning of § 1.1502-19(c)(2).

(iii) *Example.*—The application of this paragraph (d) to transfers due to worthlessness and to loss transfers not followed by separate return years is illustrated by the following example.

*Example.* (i) *Worthlessness where S continues as a member.* M owns the sole share of S stock. The share is worthless under section 165. In addition, S has disposed of all its assets within the meaning of § 1.1502-19(c)(1)(iii)(A) and therefore satisfies the provisions of § 1.1502-80(c). M claims a worthless securities deduction with respect to the share. The worthlessness is a transfer of the S share, a loss share, and therefore subject to this section. After the application of paragraphs (b) and (c) of this section, M's basis in the share (and therefore M's net stock loss) is $75. The portion of the consolidated net operating loss attributable to S is $100. Under the general rules of this paragraph (d), S's attribute reduction amount is $75 (the lesser of M's $75 net stock loss and S's $100 aggregate inside loss ($100 net inside attribute amount over $0 value of S share). S's attributes are reduced by $75, from $100 to $25. In addition, if S remains a member of the P group, this paragraph (d)(7) applies to eliminate the remain-

ing $25 of the consolidated net operating loss attributable to S because the S share is worthless, and M recognizes a deduction (taking into account § 1.1502-80(c)) with respect to the share. Accordingly, after the application of this section, M recognizes a $75 worthless securities deduction, S has $0 net inside attributes, and the consolidated net operating loss is reduced by a total of $100.

(ii) *Dissolution of insolvent subsidiary.* The facts are the same as in paragraph (i) of this *Example,* except that S is insolvent, does not dispose of all its assets within the meaning of § 1.1502-19(c)(1)(iii)(A), M causes S to be legally dissolved, and the S share held by M is cancelled without consideration. Under paragraph (d)(7)(ii)(B) of this section, the dissolution of S is subject to this paragraph (d)(7) and the result is the same as in paragraph (i) of this *Example.* The result would also be the same if instead of being legally dissolved, S was converted into an entity that is disregarded as separate from M.

(iii) *Stock cancelled in connection with a section 381(a) transaction with another member.* M owns the sole share of S common stock with a basis of $75. M1 owns the sole share of S preferred stock. The value of S's assets (net of liabilities) is less than the liquidation preference on the S preferred stock. In a reorganization described in section 368(a)(1)(D), S transfers all of its assets to M2 in exchange for M2 common stock and M2's assumption of S's liabilities, S distributes all of the M2 common stock received in the exchange to M1 in exchange for M1's S preferred stock, the S common stock held by M is cancelled without consideration, and S ceases to exist. Notwithstanding that M is not entitled to treat its common share of S stock as worthless until § 1.1502-80(c) is satisfied, M's share is transferred within the meaning of paragraph (f)(10)(i)(A) of this section because M ceases to own the share in a transaction in which, but for this section (and notwithstanding the deferral of any amount recognized on the transfer, other than by reason of § 1.1502-13), M would recognize a loss or deduction with respect to the share. Accordingly, there is a transfer of the S common share and this section applies to the transfer. There are no adjustments under paragraphs (b) or (c) of this section because no investment adjustments have been applied to the bases of the shares. The transfer of the S common stock is subject to the general rules of this paragraph (d), but is not subject to the additional attribute reduction under this paragraph (d)(7) because the transfer was not solely by reason of worthlessness where § 1.1502-80(c) is satisfied, and S did not cease to be a member because M2 is a successor to S.

(iv) *Stock cancelled in connection with a section 381(a) transaction with a nonmember.* The facts are the same as in paragraph (iii) of this *Example,* except that the S preferred share is held by X, instead of M2 acquiring S's assets, S merges into Y in a reorganization described in section 368(a)(1)(A), M1 receives all of the Y stock issued in the merger in exchange for M1's S preferred stock, and Y does not become a member as a result of the transaction. M treats the cancelled S common stock as worthless, and § 1.1502-80(c) is satisfied because S ceases to be a member. In this case, there is a transfer of M's S common share because it becomes worthless (taking into account § 1.1502-80(c)); because M ceases to own the share in a transaction in which, but for this section (and notwithstanding the deferral of any amount recognized on the transfer, other than by reason of § 1.1502-13), M would recognize a loss or deduction with respect to the share; and because M and S cease to be members of the same group. The transfer of the S common stock is subject to the general rules of this paragraph (d), but is not subject to the additional attribute reduction under this paragraph (d)(7) because the transfer was not solely by reason of worthlessness where § 1.1502-80(c) is satisfied and, although S did cease to be a member, S became a nonmember within the meaning of § 1.1502-19(c)(2) because Y is a successor to S.

(8) *Examples.*—The application of this paragraph (d) is illustrated by the following examples:

*Example 1. Computation of attribute reduction amount.* (i) *Transfer of all S shares.* (A) *Facts.* M owns all 100 of the outstanding shares of S stock with a basis of $2 per share. S owns land with a basis of $100, has a $120 loss carryover, and has no liabilities. Each share has a value of $1. M sells 30 of the S shares to X for $30. As a result of the sale, M and S cease to be members of the same group. Accordingly, all 100 of the S shares are transferred. See paragraphs (f)(10)(i)(A), (f)(10)(i)(B), and (f)(10)(i)(C) (with respect to the 30 S shares sold to X) of this section. M's transfer of the S shares is a transfer of loss shares and therefore subject to this section.

(B) *Application of paragraphs (b) and (c) of this section.* Although the transfer is subject to this section, there is no basis redetermination under paragraph (b) of this section because there is no disparity among M's bases in shares of S common stock and there are no shares of S preferred stock outstanding (so there can be no unrecognized gain or loss on preferred stock). See paragraph (b)(1)(ii)(A) of this section. Therefore, after the application of paragraph (b) of this section, the share is still a loss share and, as such, subject to paragraph (c) of this section. No adjustment is required under paragraph

(c) of this section because the net positive adjustment is $0. See paragraph (c)(3) of this section. Thus, after the application of paragraph (c) of this section, M's transfer of the S shares is still a transfer of loss shares and, accordingly, subject to this paragraph (d).

(C) *Attribute reduction under this paragraph (d)*. Under this paragraph (d), S's attributes are reduced by S's attribute reduction amount. Paragraph (d)(3) of this section provides that S's attribute reduction amount is the lesser of the net stock loss and S's aggregate inside loss. The net stock loss is the excess of the $200 aggregate bases of the transferred shares over the $100 aggregate value of the transferred shares, or $100. S's aggregate inside loss is the excess of its $220 net inside attribute amount (the sum of the $100 basis in the land and the $120 loss carryover) over the $100 value of all outstanding S shares, or $120. The attribute reduction amount is therefore the lesser of the $100 net stock loss and the $120 aggregate inside loss, or $100. Under paragraph (d)(4) of this section, S's $100 attribute reduction amount is allocated and applied to reduce S's $120 loss carryover to $20. Under paragraph (d)(4)(iii) of this section, the reduction of the loss carryover is not a noncapital, nondeductible expense and has no effect on M's basis in the S stock.

(ii) *Transfer of less than all S shares*. (A) *Facts*. The facts are the same as in paragraph (i)(A) of this *Example 1*, except that M sells 20 S shares to X. M's sale of the 20 S shares is a transfer of loss shares and therefore subject to this section. See paragraph (f)(10)(i)(A) and (f)(10)(i)(C) of this section. (There is no transfer of the remaining shares because S and M remain members of the same group.)

(B) *Application of paragraphs (b) and (c) of this section*. No adjustment is required under paragraph (b) or paragraph (c) of this section for the reasons set forth in paragraph (i)(B) of this *Example 1*. Thus, after the application of paragraph (c) of this section, M's transfer of the S shares is still a transfer of loss shares and, accordingly, subject to this paragraph (d).

(C) *Attribute reduction under this paragraph (d)*. Under this paragraph (d), S's attributes are reduced by S's attribute reduction amount. Paragraph (d)(3) of this section provides that S's attribute reduction amount is the lesser of the net stock loss and S's aggregate inside loss. The net stock loss is $20, the excess of the $40 aggregate bases of the transferred shares over the $20 aggregate value of the

transferred shares. S's aggregate inside loss is $120, the excess of its $220 net inside attribute amount (the sum of the $100 basis in the land and the $120 loss carryover) over the $100 value of all outstanding S shares. The attribute reduction amount is therefore $20, the lesser of the $20 net stock loss and the $120 aggregate inside loss. Under paragraph (d)(4) of this section, S's $20 attribute reduction amount is allocated and applied to reduce S's $120 loss carryover to $100.

*Example 2. Proportionate allocation of attribute reduction amount*. (i) *Facts*. M owns the sole outstanding share of S stock with a basis of $150. S owns land with a basis of $60, a factory with a basis of $30, publicly traded property with a basis of $30 and goodwill with a basis of $30. M sells its S share for $90. M's sale of the S share is a transfer of a loss share and therefore subject to this section. See paragraphs (f)(10)(i)(A), (f)(10)(i)(B), and (f)(10)(i)(C) of this section.

(ii) *Application of paragraphs (b) and (c) of this section*. Although the transfer is subject to this section, there is no basis redetermination under paragraph (b) of this section because there is only one share of S stock outstanding (and so there can be no disparity among members' bases in common shares and there are no outstanding preferred shares with respect to which there can be unrecognized gain or loss). See paragraph (b)(1)(ii)(A) of this section. Therefore, after the application of paragraph (b) of this section, the share is still a loss share and, as such, subject to paragraph (c) of this section. No adjustment is required under paragraph (c) of this section because both the disconformity amount and the net positive adjustment are $0. See paragraph (c)(3) of this section. Thus, after the application of paragraph (c) of this section, M's sale of the S share is still a transfer of a loss share and, accordingly, subject to this paragraph (d).

(iii) *Attribute reduction under this paragraph (d)*. Under paragraph (d)(3) of this section, S's attribute reduction amount is determined to be $60, the lesser of the $60 net stock loss ($150 basis over $90 value) and S's $60 aggregate inside loss (the excess of S's $150 net inside attribute amount (the $60 basis of the land, plus the $30 basis of the factory, plus the $30 basis of the publicly traded property, plus the $30 basis of the goodwill) over the $90 value of the S share). Under paragraph (d)(4)(ii)(B)(2) of this section, the $60 attribute reduction amount is allocated and applied to reduce S's bases in its Category D assets, S's only attributes available for reduction, as follows:

| Available attributes, Basis in Category D assets | Attribute amount | Allocable portion of attribute reduction amount | Adjusted attribute amount |
| --- | --- | --- | --- |
| Class VII, Goodwill | $30 | $30 | $0 |
| Class V | | | |
| Land | $60 | (60/90 × $60) $40 | $20 |
| Factory | $30 | (30/90 × $60) $20 | $10 |
| Total Class V | $90 | $60 | $30 |
| Class II, publicly traded property | $30 | $0 | $30 |
| Totals | $150 | $60 | $90 |

*Example 3. Attribute reduction amount less than total attributes in Category, A, Category B, and Category C*. (i) *No election to prescribe the allocation of S's attribute reduction amount*. (A) *Facts*. P owns the sole outstanding share of M stock with a basis of $1,000 and M owns the sole outstanding share of S stock with a basis of $210. M sells its S

share to X for $100. M's sale of the S share is a transfer of a loss share and therefore subject to this section. See paragraphs (f)(10)(i)(A), (f)(10)(i)(B), and (f)(10)(i)(C) of this section. At the time of the sale, S has no liabilities and the following attributes:

| Category | Attribute | Attribute amount |
| --- | --- | --- |
| Category A | Capital loss carryover | $10 |
| Category B | NOL carryover | $200 |
| Category C | Deferred deductions | $40 |
| Category D, Class V | Basis in Land | $50 |
| | Total Attributes | $300 |

(B) *Application of paragraphs (b) and (c) of this section*. Although the transfer is subject to this section, there is no basis redetermination under paragraph (b) of this section because there is only one share of S stock outstanding (and so there can be no disparity among members' bases in common shares and there are no outstanding preferred shares with respect to which there can be unrecognized gain or loss). See paragraph (b)(1)(ii)(A) of this section. Therefore, after the application of paragraph (b) of this section, the share is still a loss share and, as such, subject to paragraph (c) of this section. No adjustment is required under paragraph (c) of this section because both the disconformity amount and the net positive adjustment are $0. See paragraph (c)(3) of this section. Thus, after the application of paragraph

(c) of this section, M's transfer of the S share is still a transfer of a loss share and, accordingly, subject to this paragraph (d).

(C) *Attribute reduction under this paragraph (d)*. (1) *Computation of attribute reduction amount*. Under paragraph (d)(3) of this section, S's attribute reduction amount is the lesser of the $110 net stock loss ($210 basis over $100 value) and S's aggregate inside loss. S's aggregate inside loss is $200 (S's $300 net inside attribute amount (the $10 capital loss carryover, plus the $200 NOL carryover, plus the $40 deferred deductions, plus the $50 basis in land) less the $100 value of all outstanding S shares). Thus, the attribute reduction amount is $110, the lesser of the $110 net stock loss and S's $200 aggregate inside loss. Under paragraph (d)(4)(ii)(A)(1) of this section, the $110 attribute reduction amount is allocated and applied to reduce S's attributes as follows:

| Category | Attribute | Attribute amount | Allocation of attribute reduction amount | Adjusted attribute amount |
|---|---|---|---|---|
| Category A | Capital loss carryover | $10 | $10 | $0 |
| Category B | NOL carryover | $200 | $100 | $100 |
| Category C | Deferred deductions | $40 | $0 | $40 |
| Category D, Class V | Basis in land | $50 | $0 | $50 |
| Totals | | $300 | $110 | $190 |

(ii) *Election to prescribe the allocation of attribute reduction amount.* (A) *Facts.* The facts are the same as in paragraph (i)(A) of this *Example 3*, except that, P elects to allocate the attribute reduction amount to eliminate the Category C attributes, preserve the capital loss carryover, and reduce Category B attributes.

(B) *Application of paragraphs (b) and (c) of this section.* No adjustment is required under paragraph (b) or paragraph (c) of this section for the reasons set forth in paragraph (i)(B) of this *Example 3*. Thus,

after the application of paragraph (c) of this section, M's sale of the S share is still a transfer of a loss share, and, accordingly, subject to this paragraph (d).

(C) *Attribute reduction under this paragraph (d).* For the reasons set forth in paragraph (i)(C) of this *Example 3*, under this paragraph (d)(3), S's attribute reduction amount is determined to be $110. M elects to apply S's $110 attribute reduction amount as follows:

| Category | Attribute | Attribute amount | Allocation of attribute reduction amount | Adjusted attribute amount |
|---|---|---|---|---|
| Category A | Capital loss carryover | $10 | $0 | $10 |
| Category B | NOL carryover | $200 | $70 | $130 |
| Category C | Deferred deductions | $40 | $40 | $0 |
| Category D, Class V | Basis of land | $50 | $0 | $50 |
| Totals | | $300 | $110 | $190 |

*Example 4. Attributes attributable to liability not taken into account.* (i) *S operates one business.* (A) *Facts.* On January 1, year 1, M forms S by exchanging $150 for the sole outstanding share of S stock. In year 1, S earns $500, purchases land for $50, spends $100 to build a factory on that land, and then purchases publicly traded property for $250. In year 2, S earns a section 38 general business credit of $50. However, pollution generated by S's business gives rise to an environmental remediation liability under Federal law that would be required to be capitalized if a person purchased S's assets and assumed the liability. Before any amounts have been taken into account with respect to the environmental remediation liability, when the liability has a present value of $500, M sells its S share to X for $150. After giving effect to all other provisions of law, M's basis in the S share is $650 (the original basis of $150 increased under §1.1502-32 by $500 for the income earned). The sale is therefore a transfer of a loss share of subsidiary stock and subject to this section. See paragraphs (f)(10)(i)(A), (f)(10)(i)(B), and (f)(10)(i)(C) of this section.

(B) *Application of paragraphs (b) and (c) of this section.* Although the transfer is subject to this section, there is no basis redetermination under paragraph (b) of this section because there is only one share of S stock outstanding (and so there can be no disparity among mem-

bers' bases in common shares and there are no outstanding preferred shares with respect to which there can be unrecognized gain or loss). See paragraph (b)(1)(ii)(A) of this section. Therefore, after the application of paragraph (b) of this section, the share is still a loss share and, as such, subject to paragraph (c) of this section. No adjustment to basis is made under paragraph (c) of this section because, although the net positive adjustment is $500, the disconformity amount is $0. See paragraph (c)(3) of this section. Thus, after the application of paragraph (c) of this section, M's sale of the S share is still a transfer of a loss share and, accordingly, subject to this paragraph (d).

(C) *Attribute reduction under this paragraph (d).* (1) Under paragraph (d)(3) of this section, S's attribute reduction amount is the lesser of the $500 net stock loss ($650 basis over $150 value) and the aggregate inside loss. The aggregate inside loss is $500, computed as the excess of S's $650 net inside attribute amount (the sum of S's $100 basis in the factory, $50 basis in the land, $250 basis in the publicly traded property, and $250 cash remaining after the purchases) over the $150 value of the S share. Thus, S's attribute reduction amount is $500, the lesser of the $500 net stock loss and the $500 aggregate inside loss. Under paragraph (d)(4)(ii)(B)(2) of this section, S's $500 attribute reduction amount is allocated and applied to reduce S's attributes as follows:

| Available attributes | Attribute amount | Allocable portion of attribute reduction amount | Adjusted attribute amount |
|---|---|---|---|
| Category D | | | |
| Class V Assets | | | |
| Basis of factory | $100 | $100 | $0 |
| Basis of land | $50 | $50 | $0 |
| Class II Assets | | | |
| Publicly traded property | $250 | $250 | $0 |

(2) The remaining $100 attribute reduction amount is not applied to S's $250 cash (Class I asset) or to S's $50 general business tax credit. Under the general rule of this paragraph (d), that remaining $100 attribute reduction amount would have no further effect on S's attributes. However, S has a $500 liability that has not been taken into account. Therefore, under paragraph (d)(4)(ii)(C)(1) of this section, the remaining $100 attribute reduction amount is suspended and will be allocated and applied to reduce any amounts that become deductible or capitalizable as a result of the environmental remediation liability later being taken into account. If the liability is satisfied for an amount that is less than $100, under paragraph (d)(4)(ii)(C)(2) of

this section the remaining portion of that $100 suspended attribute reduction amount is disregarded and has no further effect.

(ii) *Lower-tier subsidiary with additional liability.* (A) *Facts.* The facts are the same as in paragraph (i)(A) of *Example 4*, except that, in addition, S exchanged $50 for the sole outstanding share of stock of S1. S1 has $50 and equipment with an aggregate basis of $0. S1 also has employee medical expense liabilities that have not been taken into account and that would be required to be capitalized if a person purchased S1's assets and assumed the liabilities. At the time of the sale, S's environmental remediation liability had a present value of $475 and S1's employee medical expenses had a present value of $25. For the reasons set forth in paragraph (i)(A) of this *Example 4*, M's sale of the S share is a transfer of a loss share and therefore subject to this section.

(B) *Application of paragraphs (b) and (c) of this section.* No adjustment is made under paragraph (b) or paragraph (c) of this section for the reasons set forth in paragraph (i)(B) of this *Example 4.* Thus, after the application of paragraph (c) of this section, M's sale of the S share is still a transfer of a loss share and, accordingly, subject to this paragraph (d).

(C) *Attribute reduction under this paragraph (d).* (1) *Computation of attribute reduction amount.* Under paragraph (d)(3) of this section, S's attribute reduction amount is the lesser of the $500 net stock loss ($650 basis over $150 value) and the aggregate inside loss. The aggregate inside loss is the excess of S's net inside attribute amount over the value of the S share. Under paragraphs (d)(3)(iii)(B) and (d)(5)(i)(B) of this section, S's net inside attribute amount is determined by using S's $50 deemed basis in the S1 share (the greater of S's $50 actual basis in the share and S1's $50 net inside attribute amount). Accordingly, S's net inside attribute amount is $650 (the sum of its $100 basis in the factory, $50 basis in the land, $250 basis in the publicly traded property, $200 cash, and $50 deemed basis in its S1 share). The aggregate inside loss is $500, the excess of S's $650 net inside attribute amount over the $150 value of the S share. Thus, S's attribute reduction amount is $500, the lesser of the $500 net stock loss and S's $500 aggregate inside loss.

(2) *Allocation, apportionment, and application of attribute reduction amount.* Under paragraphs (d)(4) and (d)(5)(ii) of this section, S's $500 attribute reduction amount is allocated proportionately (by basis) between its S1 share and its non-stock Category D asset (consisting of all S's Category D assets other than its share of S1 stock, with a basis equal to $600, the aggregate basis of S's non-stock assets). However, under paragraph (d)(5)(ii) of this section, for purposes of allocating S's attribute reduction amount between its non-stock Category D asset and the S1 share, S's $50 deemed basis in its S1 share is treated as reduced by S1's $25 net non-loss assets (its Class I asset, $50 cash over S1's liabilities (which, for this purpose include the $25 of employee medical expense liabilities not taken into account as of the transfer)). As a result, S's attribute reduction amount is allocated $480 (600/625 × 500) to S's non-stock Category D asset and $20 (25/625 × 500) to the S1 share. The $480 attribute reduction allocated to S's non-stock Category D asset produces the same reduction in the bases of S's assets (other than the S1 stock) as in paragraph (i)(C) of this *Example 4;* in addition, the $80 attribute reduction amount not applied to reduce S's attributes is suspended and applied to reduce any amounts that become deductible or capitalizable as a result of the environmental remediation liability later being taken into account. If the liability is satisfied for an amount that is less than $80, under paragraph (d)(4)(ii)(C)(2) of this section the remaining portion of that $80 suspended attribute reduction amount is disregarded and has no further effect. Because the S1 share is not transferred within the meaning of paragraph (f)(10) of this section, the allocated attribute reduction amount apportioned to the S1 share is applied fully to reduce the basis of the S1 share to $30. See paragraph (d)(5)(iii) of this section.

(D) *Tier down of S's attribute reduction amount.* The $20 portion of S's attribute reduction amount allocated to the S1 share is an attribute reduction amount of S1. Because S1 holds only cash, it has no attributes available for reduction under this paragraph (d). However, because S1 has a $25 liability not taken into account for tax purposes, paragraph (d)(4)(ii)(C)(1) of this section requires that $20 of the unapplied attribute reduction amount be suspended and then allocated and applied to reduce any amounts that become deductible or capitalizable as a result of the employee medical expense liabilities later being taken into account. If these liabilities are satisfied for an amount that is less than $20, under paragraph (d)(4)(ii)(C)(2) of this section the remaining portion of that $20 suspended attribute reduction amount is disregarded and has no further effect.

*Example 5. Wholly owned lower-tier subsidiary (no lower-tier transfer).* (i) *Application of conforming limitation.* (A) *Facts.* M owns the sole outstanding share of S stock with a basis of $250. S owns Asset with a basis of $100 and the only two outstanding shares of S1 stock (Share A has a basis of $40 and Share B has a basis of $60). S1 owns Asset 1 with a basis of $50. M sells its S share to P1, the common parent of another consolidated group, for $50. The sale is a transfer of a loss share and therefore subject to this section. See paragraphs (f)(10)(i)(A), (f)(10)(i)(B), and (f)(10)(i)(C) of this section.

(B) *Application of paragraphs (b) and (c) of this section.* Although the transfer is subject to this section, there is no basis redetermination under paragraph (b) of this section because there is only one share of S stock outstanding (and so there can be no disparity among members' bases in common shares and there are no outstanding preferred shares with respect to which there can be unrecognized gain or loss). See paragraph (b)(1)(ii)(A) of this section. Therefore, after the application of paragraph (b) of this section, the share is still a loss share and, as such, subject to paragraph (c) of this section. No adjustment is required under paragraph (c) of this section because, although there

is a $50 disconformity amount, the net positive adjustment is $0. See paragraph (c)(3) of this section. Thus, after the application of paragraph (c) of this section, M's sale of the S share is still a transfer of a loss share and, accordingly, subject to this paragraph (d).

(C) *Attribute reduction under this paragraph (d).* (1) *Computation of attribute reduction amount.* Under paragraph (d)(3) of this section, S's attribute reduction amount is the lesser of M's net stock loss and S's aggregate inside loss. M's net stock loss is $200 ($250 basis over $50 value). S's aggregate inside loss is the excess of S's net inside attribute amount over the value of the S share. Under paragraphs (d)(3)(iii)(B) and (d)(5)(i)(B) of this section, S's net inside attribute amount is $200, computed as the sum of S's $100 basis in Asset and its $100 deemed basis in the deemed single share of S1 stock (computed as the greater of S's $100 aggregate basis in the S1 shares and S1's $50 basis in Asset 1). S's aggregate inside loss is therefore $150, $200 net inside attribute amount over the $50 value of the S share. Accordingly, S's attribute reduction amount is $150, the lesser of the $200 net stock loss and the $150 aggregate inside loss.

(2) *Allocation, apportionment, and application of S's attribute reduction amount.* Under paragraphs (d)(4) and (d)(5)(ii) of this section, S's $150 attribute reduction amount is allocated proportionately (by basis) between Asset (non-stock Category D asset) with a basis of $100, and the S1 stock (treated as a single share with a deemed basis of $100). Accordingly, $75 of the attribute reduction amount ($100/$200 × $150) is allocated to Asset and $75 of the attribute reduction amount ($100/$200 × $150) is allocated to the S1 stock. The $75 of the attribute reduction amount allocated to Asset is applied to reduce S's basis in Asset from $100 to $25. The $75 of the attribute reduction amount allocated to the S1 stock is first apportioned between the shares in a manner that reduces disparity to the greatest extent possible. Thus, of the total $75 allocated to the S1 stock, $27.50 is apportioned to Share A and $47.50 is apportioned to Share B. Because neither of the S1 shares is transferred within the meaning of paragraph (f)(10) of this section, the allocated attribute reduction amount apportioned to each of the individual S1 shares is applied fully to reduce the basis of each share to $12.50. See paragraph (d)(5)(iii) of this section. As a result, immediately after the allocation, apportionment, and application of S's attribute reduction amount, S's basis in Asset is $25 and S's basis in each of the S1 shares is $12.50.

(3) *Tier down of S's attribute reduction amount, application of conforming limitation.* Under paragraph (d)(5)(v)(A) of this section, the $75 portion of S's attribute reduction amount allocated to the S1 stock is an attribute reduction amount of S1 (regardless of the extent, if any, to which it is apportioned and applied to reduce the basis of any shares of S1 stock). Under the general rules of this paragraph (d), the $75 tier-down attribute reduction amount would be allocated and applied to reduce S1's basis in Asset 1 from $50 to $0. However, under paragraph (d)(5)(v)(B) of this section, S1's attributes can be reduced by only $25, the excess of the $50 portion of S1's net inside attribute amount that is allocable to all S1 shares held by members as of the transaction over $25, the aggregate amount of members' bases in nontransferred S1 shares after reduction under this paragraph (d). Thus, of S1's $75 tier-down attribute reduction amount, only $25 is applied to reduce S1's basis in Asset 1, from $50 to $25. The $50 unapplied portion of the tier-down attribute reduction amount subject to the conforming limitation has no further effect.

(ii) *Application of basis restoration rule.* (A) *Facts.* The facts are the same as in paragraph (i)(A) of this *Example 5,* except that S's basis in Share A is $15 and S's basis in Share B is $35, and S1's basis in Asset 1 is $100.

(B) *Basis redetermination and basis reduction under paragraphs (b) and (c) of this section.* No adjustment is required under paragraph (b) or paragraph (c) of this section for the reasons set forth in paragraph (i)(B) of this *Example 5.* Thus, after the application of paragraph (c) of this section, M's transfer of the S share is still a transfer of a loss share and, accordingly, subject to this paragraph (d).

(C) *Attribute reduction under this paragraph (d).* (1) *Computation of attribute reduction amount.* Under paragraph (d)(3) of this section, S's attribute reduction amount is the lesser of M's net stock loss and S's aggregate inside loss. M's net stock loss is $200 ($250 basis over $50 value). S's aggregate inside loss is the excess of S's net inside attribute amount over the value of the S share. Under paragraphs (d)(3)(iii)(B) and (d)(5)(i)(B) of this section, S's net inside attribute amount is $200, the sum of S's $100 basis in Asset and its $100 deemed basis in the deemed single share of S1 stock (computed as the greater of S's $50 aggregate basis in the S1 shares and S1's $100 basis in Asset 1). S's aggregate inside loss is therefore $150, $200 net inside attribute amount over the $50 value of the S share. Accordingly, S's attribute reduction amount is $150, the lesser of the $200 net stock loss and the $150 aggregate inside loss.

(2) *Allocation, apportionment, and application of S's attribute reduction amount.* Under paragraphs (d)(4) and (d)(5)(ii) of this section, S's $150 attribute reduction amount is allocated proportionately (by basis) between Asset (non-stock Category D asset) with a basis of

$100, and the S1 stock (treated as a single share with a deemed basis of $100). Accordingly, $75 of the attribute reduction amount ($100/$200 × $150) is allocated to Asset and $75 of the attribute reduction amount ($100/$200 × $150) is allocated to the S1 stock. The $75 of the attribute reduction amount allocated to Asset is applied to reduce S's basis in Asset from $100 to $25. The $75 of the attribute reduction amount allocated to the S1 stock is first apportioned between the shares in a manner that reduces disparity to the greatest extent possible. Thus, of the total $75 allocated to the S1 stock, $27.50 is apportioned to Share A and $47.50 is apportioned to Share B. Because neither of the S1 shares is transferred within the meaning of paragraph (f)(10) of this section, the allocated attribute reduction amount apportioned to each of the individual S1 shares is applied fully to reduce the basis of each share to an excess loss account of $12.50. See paragraph (d)(5)(iii) of this section. As a result, immediately after the allocation, apportionment, and application of S's attribute reduction amount, S's basis in Asset is $25 and S's basis in each of the S1 shares is an excess loss account of $12.50.

(3) *Tier down of S's attribute reduction amount.* Under paragraph (d)(5)(v)(A) of this section, the $75 portion of S's attribute reduction amount allocated to S1 stock is an attribute reduction amount of S1 (regardless of the extent, if any, to which it is apportioned and applied to reduce the basis of any shares of S1 stock). Accordingly, under the general rules of this paragraph (d), the $75 tier-down attribute reduction amount is applied to reduce S1's basis in Asset 1 from $100 to $25.

(4) *Basis restoration.* Under paragraph (d)(5)(vi)(A) of this section, after this paragraph (d) has been applied with respect to all transfers of subsidiary stock, any reduction made to the basis of a share of lower-tier subsidiary stock under paragraph (d)(5)(iii) of this section is reversed to the extent necessary to conform the basis of that share to the share's allocable portion of the subsidiary's net inside attribute amount (after reduction). S1's net inside attribute amount after the application of this paragraph (d) is $25 and thus each of the two S1 share's allocable portion of S1's net inside attribute amount is $12.50. Accordingly, the reductions to Share A and to Share B under paragraph (d)(5)(iii) of this section are reversed to the extent necessary to restore the basis of each share to $12.50. Thus, $25 of the $27.50 of reduction to the basis of Share A, and $25 of the $47.50 of reduction to the basis of share B, is reversed, restoring the basis of each share to $12.50.

*Example 6. Multiple blocks of lower-tier subsidiary stock outstanding.* (i) *Excess loss account taken into account (transfer of upper-tier share causes disposition within the meaning of §1.1502-19(c)(1)(ii)(B)).* (A) *Facts.* M owns the sole outstanding share of S stock with a basis of $200. S holds all five outstanding shares of S1 common stock (Shares A, B, C, D, and E). S has an excess loss account of $20 in Share A and a positive basis of $20 in each of the other shares. The only investment adjustment applied to any S1 share was a negative $20 investment adjustment applied to Share A when it was the only outstanding share, and this amount tiered up and adjusted M's basis in the S share. S1 owns one asset with a basis of $250. M sells its S share to P1, the common parent of a consolidated group, for $20. The sale of the S share is a disposition of Share A under §1.1502-19(c)(1)(ii)(B) (S1 becomes a nonmember because it will have a separate return year as a member of the P1 group). Accordingly, under §1.1502-19(b)(1)(i) and paragraph (a)(3)(i) of this section, before the application of this section, S's excess loss account in Share A is taken into account, increasing S's basis in Share A to $0 and M's basis in its S share to $220. After giving effect to the recognition of the excess loss account, M's sale of the S share is a transfer of a loss share and therefore subject to this section. See paragraphs (f)(10)(i)(A), (f)(10)(i)(B), and (f)(10)(i)(C) of this section.

(B) *Basis redetermination and basis reduction under paragraphs (b) and (c) of this section.* Although the transfer is subject to this section, there is no basis redetermination under paragraph (b) of this section because there is only one share of S stock outstanding (and so there can be no disparity among members' bases in common shares and there are no outstanding preferred shares with respect to which there can be unrecognized gain or loss). See paragraph (b)(1)(ii)(A) of this section. Therefore, after the application of paragraph (b) of this section, the share is still a loss share and, as such, subject to paragraph (c) of this section. No adjustment is made under paragraph (c) of this section because, even though there is a disconformity amount of $140, the net positive adjustment is $0. See paragraph (c)(3) of this section. Thus, after the application of paragraph (c) of this section, M's sale of the S share remains a transfer of a loss share and, accordingly, subject to this paragraph (d).

(C) *Attribute reduction under this paragraph (d).* (1) *Computation of attribute reduction amount.* Under paragraph (d)(3) of this section, S's attribute reduction amount is the lesser of M's net stock loss and S's aggregate inside loss. M's net stock loss is $200 ($220 basis over $20 value). S's aggregate inside loss is the excess of S's net inside attribute amount over the value of the S share. Under paragraphs (d)(3)(iii)(B) and (d)(5)(i)(B) of this section, S's net inside attribute

amount is $250, S's $250 deemed basis in the deemed single share of S1 stock (computed as the greater of S's $80 aggregate basis in the S1 shares ($0 basis in Share A plus $20 basis in each of the four other shares) and S1's $250 basis in its asset). S's aggregate inside loss is therefore $230, $250 net inside attribute amount over the $20 value of the S share. Accordingly, S's attribute reduction amount is $200, the lesser of the $200 net stock loss and the $230 aggregate inside loss.

(2) *Allocation, apportionment, and application of S's attribute reduction amount.* Under paragraphs (d)(4) and (d)(5)(ii) of this section, S's $200 attribute reduction amount is allocated entirely to the S1 stock (treated as a single share) and then apportioned among the shares in a manner that reduces disparity to the greatest extent possible. Thus, $24 is apportioned to Share A and $44 is apportioned to each of the other shares. Because none of the S1 shares are transferred within the meaning of paragraph (f)(10) of this section (notwithstanding that there is a disposition under §1.1502-19(c)(1)(ii)(B)), the allocated attribute reduction amount apportioned to each of the individual S1 shares is applied fully to reduce the basis of each share to an excess loss account of $24. See paragraph (d)(5)(iii) of this section.

(3) *Tier down of S's attribute reduction amount.* Under paragraph (d)(5)(v)(A) of this section, the $200 of S's attribute reduction amount allocated to the S1 shares is an attribute reduction amount of S1 (regardless of the extent, if any, to which it is apportioned and applied to reduce the basis of any shares of S1 stock). Under the general rules of this paragraph (d), S1's $200 tier-down attribute reduction amount is allocated and applied to reduce S1's basis in its asset from $250 to $50.

(4) *Basis restoration.* Under paragraph (d)(5)(vi)(A) of this section, after this paragraph (d) has been applied with respect to all transfers of subsidiary stock, any reduction made to the basis of a share of lower-tier subsidiary stock under paragraph (d)(5)(iii) of this section is reversed to the extent necessary to conform the basis of that share to the share's allocable portion of the subsidiary's net inside attribute amount (after reduction). S1's net inside attribute amount after the application of this paragraph (d) is $50 and thus each of the five S1 share's allocable portion of S1's net inside attribute amount is $10. Accordingly, the reductions to the bases of S1 shares under paragraph (d)(5)(iii) of this section are reversed to the extent necessary to restore (to the extent possible) the basis of each share to $10. Thus, $24 of the $24 of reduction to the basis of Share A is reversed, restoring the basis of Share A to $0, and $34 of the $44 of reduction to the basis of each other share is reversed, restoring the basis of each of those shares to $10.

(ii) *Sale of gain share to member.* (A) *Facts.* The facts are the same as in paragraph (i)(A) of this *Example 6*, except that M owns Shares A, B, C, and D, S owns Share E, S has a liability of $20, and S1's basis in its asset is $500. Also, as part of the transaction, S sells Share E to M for $40. Unlike under the facts of paragraph (i)(A) of this *Example 6*, there is no disposition of Share A within the meaning of §1.1502-19(c)(1)(ii)(B) (S1 continues to be a member of the group, and thus does not have a separate return year). As a result, the Share A excess loss account is not taken into account. Although S's sale of Share E is a transfer of that share, the share is not a loss share and thus the transfer is not subject to this section. M's sale of the S share, however, is a transfer of a loss share and therefore subject to this section. See paragraphs (f)(10)(i)(A), (f)(10)(i)(B), and (f)(10)(i)(C) of this section.

(B) *Transfer in lowest tier (gain share).* S's sale of Share E is the lowest-tier transfer in the transaction. Under paragraph (a)(3)(ii)(A) of this section, because there are no transfers of loss shares at that tier, no adjustments are required under paragraph (b) or (c) of this section. However, S's gain recognized on the transfer of Share E is computed and immediately adjusts members' bases in subsidiary stock under §1.1502-32 (because M and S are not members of the same group immediately after the transaction, the sale is not an intercompany transaction subject to §1.1502-13). Accordingly, M's basis in its S share is increased by $20, from $200 to $220.

(C) *Transfers in next higher tier, application of paragraphs (b) and (c) of this section.* The next higher tier transfer is M's sale of the S stock. The sale is a transfer of a loss share and therefore subject to this section. Although the transfer is subject to this section, there is no basis redetermination under paragraph (b) of this section because there is only one share of S stock outstanding (and so there can be no disparity among members' bases in common shares and there are no outstanding preferred shares with respect to which there can be unrecognized gain or loss). See paragraph (b)(1)(ii)(A) of this section. Therefore, after the application of paragraph (b) of this section, the share is still a loss share and, as such, subject to paragraph (c) of this section. Under paragraph (c) of this section, M's basis in its S share is decreased by $20, the lesser of S's $200 disconformity amount (computed as the excess of M's $220 basis in the S stock over S's $20 net inside attribute amount (computed as the $20 basis in Share E, increased by $20 to reflect the gain recognized with respect to the share, less the $20 liability)), and the $20 net positive adjustment. Thus, after the application of paragraph (c) of this section, M's basis in the S share is $200, and the sale remains a transfer of a loss share. There are no higher tier transfers and, therefore, M's transfer of the S share is then subject to this paragraph (d).

(D) *Attribute reduction under this paragraph (d).* (1) *Computation of attribute reduction amount.* Under paragraph (d)(3) of this section, S's attribute reduction amount is the lesser of M's net stock loss and S's aggregate inside loss. M's net stock loss is $180 ($200 basis over $20 value). S's aggregate inside loss is the excess of S's net inside attribute amount over the value of the S share. Under paragraphs (d)(3)(iii)(B) and (d)(5)(i)(B) of this section, S's net inside attribute amount is $80, computed as $100 (S's deemed basis in Share E (the greater of $40 (S's $20 basis in Share E, adjusted for the $20 gain recognized with respect to the share), and Share E's allocable portion of S1's net inside attribute amount of $100 (1/5 of S1's $500 basis in its asset)), less S's $20 liability. Accordingly, S's aggregate inside loss is $60 ($80 net inside attribute amount over the $20 value of the S stock). S's attribute reduction amount is therefore $60, the lesser of $180 net stock loss and $60 aggregate inside loss.

(2) *Allocation, apportionment, and application of S's attribute reduction amount.* Under paragraphs (d)(4) and (d)(5)(ii) of this section, S's $60 attribute reduction amount is allocated entirely to its S1 stock, Share E. However, because Share E was transferred within the meaning of paragraph (f)(10) of this section and gain was recognized on its transfer, none of the allocated amount is apportioned to, or applied to reduce the basis of Share E. See paragraph (d)(5)(iii)(A) of this section. Under paragraph (d)(5)(iv) of this section, the $60 allocated attribute reduction amount not apportioned or applied to Share E has no effect on S or S's attributes.

(3) *Tier down of S's attribute reduction amount.* Notwithstanding the fact that no portion of the allocated attribute reduction amount was apportioned to or applied to reduce the basis of Share E, the entire $60 allocated attribute reduction amount is an attribute reduction amount of S1. See paragraph (d)(5)(v)(A) of this section. Under the general rules of this paragraph (d), S1's $60 tier-down attribute reduction amount is allocated and applied to reduce S1's basis in its asset from $500 to $440.

(4) *Basis restoration.* Under paragraph (d)(5)(vi)(A) of this section, after this paragraph (d) has been applied with respect to all transfers of subsidiary stock, any reduction made to the basis of a share of subsidiary stock under paragraph (d)(5)(iii) of this section is reversed to the extent necessary to conform the basis of that share to the share's allocable portion of the subsidiary's net inside attribute amount. No reduction was made to the basis of the S1 stock under paragraph (d)(5)(iii) of this section. Therefore, no stock basis is increased under the basis restoration rule in paragraph (d)(5)(vi)(A) of this section.

*Example 7. Allocation of attribute reduction if lower-tier subsidiary has non-loss assets or liabilities.* (i) *S1 holds cash.* (A) *Facts.* M owns the sole outstanding share of S stock with a basis of $800. S owns Asset with a basis of $400 and the sole outstanding share of S1 stock with a basis of $300. S1 holds Asset 1 with a basis of $50, and $100 cash. M sells its S share to P1, the common parent of a consolidated group, for $100. The sale is not a transfer of the S1 share because S and S1 are members of the same group following the transaction. However, the sale is a transfer of the S share, a loss share, and therefore subject to this section. See paragraphs (f)(10)(i)(A), (f)(10)(i)(B), and (f)(10)(i)(C) of this section.

(B) *Application of paragraphs (b) and (c) of this section.* Although the transfer is subject to this section, there is no basis redetermination under paragraph (b) of this section because there is only one share of S stock outstanding (and so there can be no disparity among members' bases in common shares and there are no outstanding preferred shares with respect to which there can be unrecognized gain or loss). See paragraph (b)(1)(ii)(A) of this section. Therefore, after the application of paragraph (b) of this section, the share is still a loss share and, as such, subject to the provisions of this paragraph (c). No adjustment is required under paragraph (c) of this section because, even though there is a disconformity amount of $100, the net positive adjustment is $0. See paragraph (c)(3) of this section. Thus, after the application of paragraph (c) of this section, M's sale of the S share is still a transfer of a loss share and, accordingly, subject to this paragraph (d).

(C) *Attribute reduction under this paragraph (d).* (1) *Computation of attribute reduction amount.* Under paragraph (d)(3) of this section, S's attribute reduction amount is the lesser of M's net stock loss and S's aggregate inside loss. M's net stock loss is $700 ($800 basis over $100 value). S's aggregate inside loss is the excess of S's net inside attribute amount over the value of the S share. Under paragraphs (d)(3)(iii)(B) and (d)(5)(i)(B) of this section, S's net inside attribute amount is $700, the sum of its $400 basis in Asset and its $300 deemed basis in the S1 share (computed as the greater of S's $300 basis in the S1 share and S1's $150 net inside attribute amount (reflecting the sum of S1's $50 basis in Asset 1 and S1's $100 cash)). Therefore, S's aggregate inside loss is $600 ($700 net inside attribute

amount over the $100 value of the S stock). S's attribute reduction amount is $600, the lesser of the $700 net stock loss and the $600 aggregate inside loss.

(2) *Allocation, apportionment, and application of S's attribute reduction amount.* Under paragraphs (d)(4) and (d)(5)(ii) of this section, S's $600 attribute reduction amount is allocated proportionately (by basis) between S's $400 basis in Asset (nonstock Category D asset) and its deemed basis in the S1 share. However, under paragraph (d)(5)(ii) of this section, for purposes of allocating the attribute reduction amount, S's $300 deemed basis in the S1 share is treated as reduced by S1's net nonloss assets (its Class I asset, $100 cash) to $200. Thus, the $600 is allocated $400 to Asset ($400/$600 × $600) and $200 to the S1 share ($200/$600 × $600). The $400 allocated to Asset is applied to reduce S's basis in Asset from $400 to $0. Because the S1 share is not transferred within the meaning of paragraph (f)(10) of this section, the allocated attribute reduction amount apportioned to the S1 share is applied fully to reduce the basis of the S1 share to $100. See paragraph (d)(5)(iii) of this section.

(3) *Tier down of S's attribute reduction amount.* Under paragraph (d)(5)(v)(A) of this section, the $200 portion of S's attribute reduction amount allocated to the S1 stock is an attribute reduction amount of S1 (regardless of the extent, if any, to which it is apportioned and applied to reduce the basis of any shares of S1 stock). Under the general rules of this paragraph (d), S1's $200 tier-down attribute reduction amount is allocated and applied to reduce S1's basis in Asset 1 (S1's only attribute available for reduction) from $50 to $0. The $150 unapplied attribute reduction amount is disregarded and has no further effect.

(4) *Basis restoration.* Under paragraph (d)(5)(vi)(A) of this section, after this paragraph (d) has been applied with respect to all transfers of subsidiary stock, any reduction made to the basis of a share of subsidiary stock under paragraph (d)(5)(iii) of this section is reversed to the extent necessary to conform the basis of that share to the share's allocable portion of the subsidiary's net inside attribute amount. There is only one share of S1 stock outstanding and so S1's entire $100 net inside attribute amount is allocable to that share. Because S's $100 basis in the S1 share (as reduced under this paragraph (d)) is already conformed with its $100 allocable portion of S1's net inside attribute amount, there is no restoration under paragraph (d)(5)(vi)(A) of this section.

(ii) *S1 borrows cash.* The facts are the same as in paragraph (i)(A) of this *Example 7* except that, in addition, S1 borrows $50 from X immediately before M sells the S share. The computation of the attribute reduction amount is the same as in paragraph (i)(C) of this *Example 7* (the $50 cash from the loan proceeds and the $50 liability offset in the computation of S1's net inside attribute amount and so the net amount is unaffected, and the computation of S's deemed basis in the S1 stock is unaffected). Similarly, for purposes of allocating the attribute reduction amount between the non-stock Category D asset and the S1 stock, paragraph (d)(5)(ii) of this section requires S's deemed basis in the S1 share to be treated as reduced by S1's net nonloss assets (S1's non-loss assets over S1's liabilities). Accordingly, the additional $50 cash proceeds is offset by the $50 liability and there is no effect on the allocation of the attribute reduction amount. The results are the same as in paragraph (i) of this *Example 7.*

(iii) *S1 has a liability not taken into account for tax purposes.* (A) *Facts.* The facts are the same as in paragraph (ii) of this *Example 7* except that, in addition, S1 has a $40 liability that is not taken into account for tax purposes as of the transfer and that would be required to be capitalized if a person purchased S1's assets and assumed the liability.

(B) *Application of paragraphs (b) and (c) of this section.* No adjustment is required under paragraph (b) or paragraph (c) of this section for the reasons set forth in paragraph (i)(B) of this *Example 7*. Thus, after the application of paragraph (c) of this section, P's sale of the S share is still a transfer of a loss share and, accordingly, subject to this paragraph (d).

(C) *Attribute reduction under this paragraph (d).* (1) *Computation of attribute reduction amount.* The attribute reduction amount is the same as computed in paragraph (i)(C)(1) of this *Example 7* (under paragraph (f)(5) of this section, the term liability does not include liabilities not taken into account for tax purposes and so the additional $40 liability not yet taken into account for tax purposes does not affect the computation of S's attribute reduction amount).

(2) *Allocation, apportionment, and application of S's attribute reduction amount.* Under paragraphs (d)(4) and (d)(5)(ii) of this section, S's $600 attribute reduction amount is allocated proportionately (by basis) between S's $400 basis in Asset 1 (nonstock Category D asset) and its deemed basis in the S1 share. However, under paragraph (d)(5)(ii) of this section, for purposes of allocating the attribute reduction amount, S's $300 deemed basis in the S1 share is treated as reduced by S1's net nonloss assets (S1's non-loss assets over S1's liabilities). For this purpose, the term liabilities includes liabilities not taken into account for tax purposes, as described in paragraph

(d)(4)(ii)(C)(*1*) of this section (generally, liabilities that, if assumed in a purchase, would give rise to a capitalized amount when satisfied). Thus, for this purpose, S's $300 deemed basis in the S1 share is reduced by S1's $60 net non-loss assets (the excess of S1's $150 non-loss assets (its Class I asset, $150 cash) over S1's $90 liabilities ($50 loan and $40 liability not yet taken into account for tax purposes)), to $240. Accordingly, S's $600 attribute reduction amount is allocated and applied $375 ($400/$640 × $600) to Asset (reducing S's basis in Asset from $400 to $25) and $225 ($240/$640 × $600) to the S1 share. Because the S1 share is not transferred within the meaning of paragraph (f)(10) of this section, the allocated attribute reduction amount apportioned to the S1 share is applied fully to reduce the basis of the S1 share to $75. See paragraph (d)(5)(iii) of this section.

(*3*) *Tier down of S's attribute reduction amount, application of conforming limitation.* Under paragraph (d)(5)(v)(A) of this section, the $225 portion of S's attribute reduction amount allocated to the S1 stock is an attribute reduction amount of S1 (regardless of the extent, if any, to which it is apportioned and applied to reduce the basis of any shares of S1 stock). Under the general rules of this paragraph (d), S1's $225 tier-down attribute reduction amount would be allocated and applied to reduce S1's attributes. However, under paragraph (d)(5)(v)(B) of this section, S1's attributes can be reduced by only $75, the excess of the $150 portion of S1's net inside attribute amount that is allocable to all S1 shares held by members as of the transaction over $75, the aggregate amount of members' bases in nontransferred S1 shares, after reduction under this paragraph (d). Thus, of S1's $225 tier-down attribute reduction amount, $50 is applied to reduce S1's basis in Asset 1, from $50 to $0. Although the $25 unapplied attribute reduction amount not subject to the conforming limitation would generally be disregarded without further effect, because S1 has a $40 liability not taken into account for tax purposes, paragraph (d)(4)(ii)(C)(*1*) of this section requires that the $25 of the unapplied attribute reduction amount not subject to the conforming limitation

be suspended and then allocated and applied to reduce any amounts that become deductible or capitalizable as a result of that liability later being taken into account. If the liability is satisfied for an amount that is less than $25, under paragraph (d)(4)(ii)(C)(*2*) of this section the remaining portion of that $25 suspended attribute reduction amount is disregarded and has no further effect. The $150 unapplied portion of the tier-down attribute reduction amount subject to the conforming limitation has no further effect.

(*4*) *Basis restoration.* Under paragraph (d)(5)(vi)(A) of this section, after this paragraph (d) has been applied with respect to all transfers of subsidiary stock, any reduction made to the basis of a share of lower-tier subsidiary stock under paragraph (d)(5)(iii) of this section is reversed to the extent necessary to conform the basis of that share to the share's allocable portion of the subsidiary's net inside attribute amount. Paragraph (d)(5)(vi)(A) provides that, for this purpose, S1's net inside attribute amount is its net inside attribute amount, taking into account any reductions under this paragraph (d) and treating it as reduced by any attribute reduction amount suspended under paragraph (d)(4)(ii)(C)(*1*) of this section. Because S's $75 basis in its S1 stock (after application of this paragraph (d)) is already conformed with its $75 allocable portion of S1's net inside attribute amount ($100 net inside attributes after reduction, reduced by S1's $25 suspended attribute reduction amount), there is no restoration under paragraph (d)(5)(vi)(A) of this section.

*Example 8. Election to reduce stock basis or reattribute attributes under paragraph (d)(6) of this section.* (i) *Deconsolidating sale.* (A) *Facts.* P owns the sole outstanding share of M stock with a basis of $1,000. M owns all 100 outstanding shares of S stock with a basis of $2.10 per share ($210 total). M sells all its S shares to X for $1 per share ($100 total). M's sale of the S shares is a transfer of loss shares and therefore subject to this section. See paragraphs (f)(10)(i)(A), (f)(10)(i)(B), and (f)(10)(i)(C) of this section. At the time of the sale, S has no liabilities and the following:

| Category | Attribute | Attribute amount |
|---|---|---|
| Category A | Capital loss carryover | $10 |
| Category B | NOL carryover | $90 |
| Category C | Deferred deduction | $40 |
| | Total Category A, Category B, and Category C Attributes | $140 |
| Category D, Class V | Basis in land | $70 |
| | Total Attributes | $210 |

(B) *Application of paragraphs (b) and (c) of this section.* Although the transfer is subject to this section, there is no basis redetermination under paragraph (b) of this section because there is no disparity among M's bases in shares of S common stock and there are no shares of S preferred stock outstanding (so there can be no unrecognized gain or loss with respect to preferred shares). See paragraph (b)(1)(ii)(A) of this section. No adjustment is required under paragraph (c) of this section because both the disconformity amount and the net positive adjustment are $0. See paragraph (c)(3) of this section. Thus, after the application of paragraph (c) of this section, M's transfer of the S shares is still a transfer of loss shares and, accordingly, subject to this paragraph (d).

(C) *Attribute reduction under this paragraph (d).* (1) *Computation of attribute reduction amount.* Under paragraph (d)(3) of this section, S's attribute reduction amount is the lesser of the $110 net stock loss ($210 aggregate basis over the $100 aggregate value) and S's aggregate inside loss. S's aggregate inside loss is $110 (S's $210 net inside attribute amount (the $10 capital loss carryover, plus the $90 NOL carryover, plus the $40 deferred deduction, plus the $70 basis in the land) over the $100 value of all outstanding S shares). S's attribute reduction amount is $110, the lesser of the $110 net stock loss and the $110 aggregate inside loss.

(2) *Application of attribute reduction amount.* (i) S's $110 attribute reduction amount is applied as follows:

| Category | Attribute | Attribute amount | Allocation of attribute reduction amount | Adjusted attribute amount |
|---|---|---|---|---|
| Category A | Capital loss carryover | $10 | $10 | $0 |
| Category B | NOL carryover | $90 | $90 | $0 |
| Category C | Deferred deduction | $40 | $10 | $30 |
| Category D, Class V | Basis in land | $70 | $0 | $70 |
| Totals | | $210 | $110 | $100 |

(*ii*) Alternatively, under paragraph (d)(4)(ii)(A)(*1*) of this section, P could specify the allocation of S's $110 attribute reduction amount among S's $10 capital loss carryover, S's $90 NOL carryover, and S's $40 deferred deduction.

(D) *Results.* The P group recognizes a $110 loss on M's sale of the S shares that is absorbed by the group, which reduces P's basis in the M share under §1.1502-32 from $1,000 to $890. Immediately after the transaction, the entities own the following:

| Entity | Asset | Basis |
|---|---|---|
| P | M share | $890 |
| X | 100 S shares | $100 |
| S | Category C, deferred deduction | $30 |
| | Category D, Class V Asset (land) | $70 |

**Reg. §1.1502-36(d)(8)**

(E) *Election to reduce stock basis.* The facts are the same as in paragraph (i)(A) of this *Example 8* except that P elects under paragraph (d)(6) of this section to reduce M's basis in the S shares by the full attribute reduction amount of $110, in lieu of S reducing its attributes. The election is effective for all transferred loss shares and is allocated to those shares in proportion to the loss in each. See paragraph (d)(6)(v)(A) of this section. Accordingly, the basis of each of the 100 transferred shares is reduced from $2.10 to $1.00. After

giving effect to the election, the S shares are not loss shares and this section has no further application to the transfer. The $110 reduction in M's basis in the S shares pursuant to the election under paragraph (d)(6) of this section is a noncapital, nondeductible expense of M that will reduce P's basis in the M share. See paragraph (d)(6)(v)(A) of this section. Immediately after the transaction, the entities own the following:

| Entity | Asset | Basis/Attribute |
|---|---|---|
| P | M share | $890 |
| X | 100 S shares | $100 |
| S | Category A, capital loss carryover | $10 |
| | Category B, NOL carryover | $90 |
| | Category C, deferred deduction | $40 |
| | Category D, Class V Asset (land) | $70 |

(F) *Election to reattribute losses.* The facts are the same as in paragraph (i)(A) of this *Example 8* except that P elects under paragraph (d)(6) of this section to reattribute S's attributes. S's attribute reduction amount is $110, and P can reattribute all or any portion of the attributes in Category A, Category B, and Category C to the extent of $110. P elects to reattribute the $90 NOL, and, as a result, S's NOL is $0. Under paragraph (d)(6)(iv)(A) of this section, the reattribution of the $90 NOL is a noncapital, nondeductible expense of S. Under § 1.1502-32(c)(1)(ii)(A)(*1*) this $90 expense is allocated to the transferred loss shares of S stock in proportion to the loss in the shares, or $.90 per share. Further, this expense tiers up under § 1.1502-32 and reduces P's basis in the M stock by $90. After giving effect to the election, the P group would recognize a $20 loss on M's sale of the S shares, S would have an aggregate inside loss of $20 (S's $120 net inside attribute amount (the $10 capital loss carryover, plus the $40 deferred deduction, plus the $70 basis in the land) over the $100 value of all outstanding S shares), and S's attribute reduction amount would be $20 (applied $10 to the $10 capital loss carryover and $10 to the $40 deferred deduction). (Alternatively, under paragraph (d)(4)(ii)(A)(*1*) of this section, P could specify the allocation of S's $20 attribute reduction amount between S's $10 capital loss carryover and S's $40 deferred deduction. Further, P could elect to reduce

M's remaining basis in the S shares by any amount up to the $20 attribute reduction amount, thereby reducing or eliminating S's attribute reduction amount.)

(ii) *Nondeconsolidating sale.* (A) *Facts.* The facts are the same as in paragraph (i)(A) of this *Example 8*, except that M only sells 20 S shares ($20 total).

(B) *Application of paragraphs (b) and (c) of this section.* No adjustment is required under paragraph (b) or paragraph (c) of this section for the reasons set forth in paragraph (i)(B) of this *Example 8*. Thus, after the application of paragraph (c) of this section, M's sale of the S shares is still a transfer of loss shares and, accordingly, subject to this paragraph (d).

(C) *Attribute reduction under this paragraph (d).* (1) *Computation of attribute reduction amount.* Under paragraph (d)(3) of this section, S's attribute reduction amount is the lesser of the $22 net stock loss ($42 aggregate basis over $20 aggregate value) and S's $110 aggregate inside loss (as calculated in paragraph (i)(C)(*1*) of this *Example 8*). S's attribute reduction amount is $22, the lesser of the $22 net stock loss and the $110 aggregate inside loss.

(2) *Application of attribute reduction amount.* (i) S's $22 attribute reduction amount is applied as follows:

| Category | Attribute | Attribute amount | Allocation of attribute reduction amount | Adjusted attribute amount |
|---|---|---|---|---|
| Category A | Capital loss carryover | $10 | $10 | $0 |
| Category B | NOL carryover | $90 | $12 | $78 |
| Category C | Deferred deduction | $40 | $0 | $40 |
| Category D, Class V | Land | $70 | $0 | $70 |

(ii) Alternatively, under paragraph (d)(4)(ii)(A)(*1*) of this section, P could specify the allocation of S's $22 attribute reduction amount among S's $10 capital loss carryover, S's $90 NOL carryover, and S's $40 deferred deduction.

(D) *Results.* The P group recognizes a $22 loss on M's sale of the S shares that is absorbed by the group, which reduces P's basis in the M share under § 1.1502-32 from $1,000 to $978. Immediately after the transaction, the entities have the following:

| Entity | Asset | Basis |
|---|---|---|
| P | M share | $978 |
| X | 20 S shares | $20 |
| S | Category B, NOL carryover | $78 |
| | Category C, deferred deduction | $40 |
| | Category D, Class V Asset (land) | $70 |

(E) *Election to reduce stock basis.* The facts are the same as in paragraph (ii)(A) of this *Example 8*, except that P elects under paragraph (d)(6) of this section to reduce M's basis in the S shares by the full attribute reduction amount of $22, in lieu of S reducing its attributes. The election is effective for all transferred loss shares and is allocated to such shares in proportion to the loss in each share. See paragraph (d)(6)(v)(A) of this section. Accordingly, the basis of each of the 20 transferred shares is reduced from $2.10 to $1.00. After

giving effect to the election, the transferred S shares are not loss shares and this section has no further application to the transfer. The $22 reduction in M's basis in the S shares pursuant to the election under paragraph (d)(6) of this section is a noncapital, nondeductible expense of M that will reduce P's basis in the M share. See paragraph (d)(6)(v)(A) of this section. Immediately after the transaction, the entities have the following:

| Entity | | Basis/Attribute |
|---|---|---|
| P | M share | $978 |
| M | 80 S shares | $168 |
| X | 20 S shares | $20 |
| S | Category A, capital loss carryover | $10 |
| | Category B, NOL | $90 |
| | Category C, deferred deduction | $40 |
| | Category D Class V Asset (land) | $70 |

(F) *Election to reattribute attributes.* The facts are the same as in paragraph (ii)(A) of this *Example 8.* Because S remains a member of the same group as P following M's sale of S stock, P cannot elect under paragraph (d)(6) of this section to reattribute any portion of S's attributes in lieu of attribute reduction.

*Example 9. Transfers at multiple tiers, gain and loss shares.* (i) *Facts.* M owns the sole outstanding share of S stock with a basis of $700. S owns Asset 1 (basis of $170) and all ten outstanding shares of S1 common stock ($170 basis in share 1, $10 basis in share 2, and $15 basis in each of share 3 through share 10). S1 owns the sole outstanding share of S2 ($0 basis), the sole outstanding share of S3 ($60 basis), and the sole outstanding share of S4 ($100 basis). S2's sole asset is Asset 2 ($75 basis). S3's sole asset is Asset 3 ($75 basis). S4's sole asset is Asset 4 ($80 basis). In one transaction, M sells its S share to P1 (the common parent of a consolidated group) for $240, S sells S1 share 1 to X for $20, S contributes S1 share 2 to a partnership in a section 721 transaction, and S1 sells its S2 share to Y for $50. M's sale of the S share and S1's sale of the S2 share are transfers under paragraphs (f)(10)(i)(A), (f)(10)(i)(B), and (f)(10)(i)(C) of this section. S's sale of S1 share 1 to X is a transfer under paragraphs (f)(10)(i)(A) and (f)(10)(i)(C) of this section. S's contribution of S1 share 2 to the partnership is a transfer under paragraph (f)(10)(i)(C) of this section.

(ii) *Transfer in lowest tier (gain share).* S1's sale of the S2 share is the lowest tier transfer in the transaction. Under paragraph (a)(3)(ii)(A) of this section, because there are no transfers of loss shares at that tier, no adjustments are required under paragraph (b) or (c) of this section. However, S1's gain recognized on the transfer of the S2 share is computed and immediately adjusts members' bases in subsidiary stock under §1.1502-32. Accordingly, $5 is allocated to each of 10 S1 shares, increasing the basis of share 1 to $175, the basis of share 2 to $15, and the basis of each other share to $20. The $50 applied to S's bases in the S1 shares then tiers up to increase P's basis in the S share from $700 to $750.

(iii) *Transfers in next highest tier (loss share).* S's sale of the S1 share 1 and S's transfer of the S1 share 2 to a partnership are both transfers of stock in the next higher tier. However, only the S1 share 1 is a loss share and so this section only applies with respect to the transfer of that share.

(A) *Basis redetermination under paragraph (b) of this section.* Under paragraph (b)(2)(i)(A) of this section, members' bases in S1 shares are redetermined by first removing the positive investment adjustments applied to the bases of transferred loss common shares. Accordingly, the $5 positive investment adjustment applied to the basis of S1 share 1 is removed, reducing the basis of S1 share 1 from $175 to $170. Because there were no negative adjustments applied to the bases of S1 shares, there are no negative adjustments that can be reallocated to further reduce the basis of S1 share 1 under paragraph (b)(2)(i)(B) of this section. Finally, under paragraph (b)(2)(ii)(B) of this section, the $5 positive investment adjustment removed from S1 share 1 is reallocated and applied to increase the bases of other S1 common shares in a manner that reduces disparity to the greatest extent possible. Accordingly, the entire $5 investment adjustment removed from S1 share 1 is reallocated and applied to increase the basis of S1 share 2, from $15 to $20. After basis is redetermined under paragraph (b) of this section, the S1 share 1 is still a loss share and therefore subject to basis reduction under paragraph (c) of this section. (Because the S1 share 2 is not a loss share, this section does not apply with respect to the transfer of that share.)

(B) *Basis reduction under paragraph (c) of this section.* No adjustment is required to the basis of S1 share 1 under paragraph (c) of this section. The S1 share 1 has a disconformity amount of $149. This $149 disconformity amount is computed as the excess of the $170 basis in the S1 share 1 over the S1 share 1's $21 allocable portion (1/10) of S1's $210 net inside attribute amount. S1's $210 net inside attribute amount is determined under paragraph (c)(5) of this section as the sum of $50 (S1's $0 basis in the S2 share, adjusted for the $50 gain recognized with respect to that share), S1's $60 basis in the S3 stock, and S1's $100 basis in the S4 stock. (In computing the disconformity amount, the basis of the S2 share is not treated as tentatively reduced because that share is transferred in the transaction, and the bases of the S3 and S4 shares are not treated as tentatively reduced because no positive investment adjustments were applied to the bases of those shares.) However, the S1 share 1's net positive adjustment is $0 because the $5 positive investment adjustment originally allocated to S1 share 1 was reallocated to S1 share 2 under paragraph (b) of this section. See paragraph (c)(3) of this section. No adjustment is required to the basis of S1 share 2 under paragraph (c) of this section because S1 share 2 is not a loss share.

(C) *Computation of loss, adjustments to stock basis.* S recognizes a loss of $150 on the sale of the S1 share 1 ($170 basis over $20 amount realized) that is absorbed by the group. Under §1.1502-32, M's basis

in its S share is therefore decreased by $100, the net of the $150 loss recognized by S on the sale of the S1 share, and the $50 gain that tiered up from S1 (as a result of S1's sale of the S2 share). Following these adjustments, M's basis in the S share is $600 and the sale of the S share is still a transfer of a loss share.

(iv) *Transfer in highest tier (loss share).* The sale of the S share is a transfer in the next higher tier, which is the highest tier in this transaction. Because the sale is a transfer of a loss share, it is subject to this section.

(A) *Basis redetermination and basis reduction under paragraphs (b) and (c) of this section.* Although the transfer is subject to this section, there is no basis redetermination under paragraph (b) of this section because there is only one share of S stock outstanding (and so there can be no disparity among members' bases in common shares and there are no outstanding preferred shares with respect to which there can be unrecognized gain or loss). See paragraph (b)(1)(ii)(A) of this section. Therefore, after the application of paragraph (b) of this section, the share is still a loss share and, as such, subject to paragraph (c) of this section. In addition, no adjustment is required under paragraph (c) of this section. The S share has a disconformity amount of $230. This $230 disconformity amount is computed as the excess of the $600 basis in the S share over the S share's $370 allocable portion (1/1) of S's $370 net inside attribute amount. S's $370 net inside attribute amount is determined under paragraph (c)(5) of this section as the sum of $200 (S's $170 basis in the S1 share 1, adjusted for the $150 loss recognized with respect to that share, and S's $20 basis in each of S1 share 2 through share 10), and S's $170 basis in Asset 1. (In computing the disconformity amount, the bases of S1 share 1 and share 2 are not treated as tentatively reduced because those shares are transferred in the transaction, and the bases of S1 share 3 through share 10 are not treated as tentatively reduced because none of those shares have a disconformity amount -each share has a basis of $20 and a $21 allocable portion (1/10) of S1's $210 net inside attribute amount, as determined in paragraph (iii)(B) of this *Example 9.*) However, the S share's net positive adjustment is $0 (the S share's net adjustment is negative $100). See paragraph (c)(3) of this section. Accordingly, the sale of the S share is still a transfer of a loss share. Because there are no higher-tier loss shares transferred in the transaction, this paragraph (d) then applies with respect to the transfer of the S share.

(B) *Attribute reduction under this paragraph (d).* (1) *Computation of S's attribute reduction amount.* Under paragraph (d)(3) of this section, S's attribute reduction amount is the lesser of P's net stock loss and S's aggregate inside loss. P's net stock loss is $360 ($600 basis over $240 amount realized). S's aggregate inside loss is the excess of S's net inside attribute amount over the value of the S share. S's net inside attribute amount is the sum of its bases in its assets, treating its S1 shares as a single share (the S1 stock) and treating S's deemed basis in the S1 stock as its basis in that stock. Under paragraph (d)(5)(i)(C) of this section, when subsidiaries are owned in multiple tiers, deemed basis is first determined for shares at the lowest tier, and then for stock in each next higher tier. Under paragraph (d)(5)(i)(B) of this section, S1's deemed basis in the S2 stock is $75 (computed as the greater of $50 (S1's $0 basis in the S2 share, adjusted for the $50 gain recognized with respect to the share) and $75 (S2's net inside attribute amount, the basis in Asset 2)). S1's deemed basis in the S3 stock is $75 (computed as the greater of $60 (S1's basis in the S3 share) and $75 (S3's net inside attribute amount, the basis in Asset 3)). S1's deemed basis in the S4 stock is $100 (computed as the greater of $100 (S1's basis in the S4 share) and $80 (S4's net inside attribute amount, the basis in Asset 4)). Accordingly, S1's net inside attribute amount is $250 ($75 deemed basis in the S2 stock plus $75 deemed basis in the S3 stock plus $100 deemed basis in the S4 stock). S's deemed basis in the S1 stock is the greater of the sum of S's actual basis in each share of S1 stock (adjusted for any gain or loss recognized) and S1's net inside attribute amount. S's actual basis in the S1 stock, adjusted for the loss recognized, is $200 (the sum of S's $170 basis in the S1 share 1, adjusted by the $150 loss recognized with respect to the share, and S's $20 basis in each of S1 share 2 through share 10). Thus, S's deemed basis in the S1 stock is $250, the greater of $200 (aggregate basis in S1 shares, adjusted for loss recognized) and $250 (S1's net inside attribute amount). As a result, S's net inside attribute amount is $420, the sum of S's $250 deemed basis in the S1 stock and S's $170 basis in Asset 1. Accordingly, the aggregate inside loss is $180, the excess of S's $420 net inside attribute amount over the $240 value of all of the S stock. S's attribute reduction amount is therefore $180, the lesser of the $360 net stock loss and the $180 aggregate inside loss.

(2) *Allocation, apportionment, and application of S's attribute reduction amount.* Under paragraphs (d)(4) and (d)(5)(ii) of this section, S's $180 attribute reduction amount is allocated proportionately (by

basis) between Asset 1 (non-stock Category D asset) and the S1 stock. However, under paragraph (d)(5)(ii) of this section, for purposes of allocating S's $180 attribute reduction amount between S's non-stock Category D asset and the S1 stock, S's $250 deemed basis in the S1 stock is reduced by the $40 value of the transferred S1 shares (S1 share 1 and share 2) and the nontransferred S1 shares' $40 allocable portion (8/10) of S1's $50 net non-loss assets. S1's net non-loss assets is the $50 value of S1's transferred S2 shares. (S1 has no other non-loss assets, and there are no non-loss assets held by lower-tier subsidiaries.) Accordingly, for this purpose, S's deemed basis in the S1 stock is reduced by $80, from $250 to $170. Thus, $90 of the attribute reduction amount ($170/$340 × $180) is allocated to Asset 1 (reducing S's basis in Asset 1 from $170 to $80) and $90 of the attribute reduction amount ($170/$340 × $180) is allocated to the S1 stock. Under paragraph (d)(5)(iii)(A) of this section, none of the $90 allocated attribute reduction amount is apportioned to S1 share 1 because loss is recognized on the transfer of S1 share 1. Under paragraph (d)(5)(iii)(B) of this section, the $90 allocated attribute reduction amount is apportioned among the other nine shares of S1 common stock in a manner that reduces disparity to the greatest extent possible. Accordingly, of the total $90 allocated amount, $10 is apportioned to each of the remaining nine shares of S1 stock. Under paragraph (d)(5)(iii)(C) of this section, the allocated attribute reduction amount apportioned to an individual share cannot be applied to reduce the basis of the share below its value if the share is transferred other than in a recognition transfer. Because the S1 share 2 is transferred (contributed to the partnership) and the basis of S1 share 2 is already equal to its value, none of the $10 allocated attribute reduction amount apportioned to S1 share 2 is applied to reduce its basis. Because none of S1 share 3 through share 10 are transferred within the meaning of paragraph (f)(10) of this section, the $10 allocated attribute reduction amount apportioned to each of S1 share 3 through share 10 is applied fully to reduce the basis of each of those shares from $20 to $10. As a result, immediately after the allocation and application of S's attribute reduction amount, S's basis in Asset 1 is $80 ($170 minus $90), its bases in S1 share 1 and share 2 are not adjusted under paragraph (d)(5)(iii), and its basis in each of S1 share 3 through share 10 is $10. Under paragraph (d)(5)(v)(A) of this section, the entire $90 of S's attribute reduction amount that was allocated to the S1 stock is an attribute reduction amount of S1, regardless of the fact that none of the allocated amount was apportioned to S1 share 1 and none of the amount apportioned to S1 share 2 was applied to reduce the basis of S1 share 2.

(v) *Attribute reduction under this paragraph (d) in next lower tier.* (A) *Computation of S1's attribute reduction amount.* S's sale of S1 share 1 is a transfer of a loss share and it is in the next lower tier. Thus, this paragraph (d) next applies with respect to S's transfer of S1 share 1. S1's attribute reduction amount will include both the $90 attribute reduction amount that tiered down from S and any attribute reduction amount resulting from the application of this paragraph (d) with respect to S's transfer of S1 share 1 and share 2 (S1's direct attribute reduction amount). Under paragraph (d)(3) of this section, S1's direct attribute reduction amount is the lesser of the net stock loss on transferred S1 shares and S1's aggregate inside loss. The net stock loss on transferred S1 shares is $150, computed as the excess of S's $190 adjusted bases in transferred shares of S1 stock ($170 in S1 share 1 plus $20 in S1 share 2) over the $40 aggregate value of those shares. S1's aggregate inside loss is $50, the excess of S1's $250 net inside attribute amount (as calculated in paragraph (iv)(B)(1) of this *Example 9*) over the $200 value of all outstanding S1 shares. Therefore, S1's direct attribute reduction amount is $50, the lesser of the $150 net stock loss and S1's $50 aggregate inside loss. S1's total attribute reduction amount is thus $140, the sum of the $90 tierdown attribute reduction amount and the $50 direct attribute reduction amount.

(B) *Allocation, apportionment, and application of S1's attribute reduction amount.* Under paragraphs (d)(4) and (d)(5)(ii) of this section, S1's $140 attribute reduction amount is allocated proportionately (by basis) among the S2 stock, the S3 stock, and the S4 stock. However, under paragraph (d)(5)(ii) of this section, for purposes of allocating S1's $140 attribute reduction amount among S1's lower-tier subsidiary stock, S1's $75 deemed basis in the S2 stock is reduced by the $50 value of the transferred S2 share. Accordingly, for this purpose, S1's deemed basis in the S2 stock is reduced by $50, from $75 to $25. Thus, $17.50 of S1's attribute reduction amount ($25/$200 × $140) is allocated to the S2 stock, $52.50 of S1's attribute reduction amount ($75/$200 x $140) is allocated to the S3 stock, and $70 of S1's attribute reduction amount ($100/$200 × $140) is allocated to the S4 stock. Under paragraph (d)(5)(iii)(A) of this section, none of the $17.50 of S1's attribute reduction amount allocated to S2 stock is apportioned to the S2 share because gain was recognized on the transfer of the S2 share. Because neither the S3 share nor the S4 share is transferred within the meaning of paragraph (f)(10) of this section, the $52.50 of S1's attribute reduction amount allocated to the S3 stock, and the $70 of S1's attribute reduction amount allocated to the S4 stock, is apportioned to and applied fully to reduce the basis of such shares. Thus,

S1's basis in the S3 share is reduced by $52.50, from $60 to $7.50, and S1's basis in the S4 stock is reduced by $70, from $100 to $30. (Note: The conforming limitation in paragraph (d)(5)(v)(B) of this section limits the application of the $90 tier down attribute reduction amount to $80, the amount by which the portion (10/10) S1's $250 net inside attribute amount attributable to S1 shares held by members exceeds $170 (the sum of the $50 direct attribute reduction amount, the $20 value of the S1 share 1 transferred in a recognition transfer, the $20 basis (after reduction) in the S1 share 2 transferred other than in a recognition transfer, and the $80 aggregate basis (after reduction) in the nontransferred S1 shares held by members). However, the conforming limitation does not limit the application of S1's $90 tier-down attribute reduction amount because none of the $17.50 of S1's total attribute reduction amount allocated to the S2 share was applied to reduce the basis of the share. Accordingly, only $78.75 ($90 - ($17.50 × ($90/$140)) of the $90 tier-down attribute reduction was applied to reduce S1's attributes.) Under paragraph (d)(5)(v)(A) of this section, the attribute reduction amount allocated to the S2 stock, the S3 stock, and the S4 stock becomes an attribute reduction amount of S2, S3, and S4, respectively (even though the amount allocated to S2 stock was not apportioned to or applied to reduce the basis of the S2 share).

(vi) *Attribute reduction under this paragraph (d) in lowest tier.* Although the sale of the S2 share is a transfer of subsidiary stock at the next lower tier, the S2 share is not a loss share. Thus, this paragraph (d) does not apply with respect to that transfer. However, S2, S3, and S4 have attribute reduction amounts that tiered down from S1 and that are applied to reduce attributes under this paragraph (d).

(A) *Tier down of S1's attribute reduction amount to S2.* Under the general rules of this paragraph (d), S2's $17.50 tier-down attribute reduction amount is allocated and applied to reduce S2's basis in Asset 2 from $75 to $57.50.

(B) *Tier down of S1's attribute reduction amount to S3.* Under the general rules of this paragraph (d), S3's $52.50 tier-down attribute reduction amount is allocated and applied to reduce S3's basis in Asset 3 from $75 to $22.50.

(C) *Tier down of S1's attribute reduction amount to S4, application of conforming limitation.* Under the general rules of this paragraph (d), S4's $70 tier-down attribute reduction amount is allocated to, and would be applied to reduce, S4's basis in Asset 4. However, under paragraph (d)(5)(v)(B) of this section, the reduction is limited to the excess of S4's $80 net inside attribute amount over the $30 basis of the S4 share (after reduction under this paragraph (d)). As a result, only $50 (the excess of $80 over $30) of S4's $70 attribute reduction amount is applied to S4's basis in Asset 4, reducing it from $80 to $30. The $20 unapplied portion of S4's tier-down attribute reduction amount subject to the conforming limitation is disregarded and has no further effect.

(vii) *Application of basis restoration rule.* Under paragraph (d)(5)(vi)(A) of this section, after this paragraph (d) has been applied with respect to all transfers of subsidiary stock, any reduction made to the basis of a share of lower-tier subsidiary stock under paragraph (d)(5)(iii) of this section is reversed to the extent necessary to conform the basis of that share to the share's allocable portion of the subsidiary's net inside attribute amount. Restoration adjustments are first made at the lowest tier and then at each next higher tier successively.

(A) *Basis restoration at lowest tier.* The basis of the S2 share was not reduced under paragraph (d)(5)(iii) of this section and so there is no restoration of any basis in the S2 share. S3's $22.50 net inside attribute amount (after reduction under this paragraph (d)) exceeds S1's $7.50 basis in the S3 share (after reduction under this paragraph (d)) by $15. To conform S1's basis in the S3 share to S3's net inside attribute amount, the $52.50 reduction to the basis of the S3 share under paragraph (d)(5)(iii) of this section is reversed by $15 (restoring S1's basis in the S3 share to $22.50). The restoration of S1's basis in the S3 share does not tier up to affect the basis in stock of any other subsidiary. S1's $30 basis in the S4 share (after reduction under this paragraph (d)) is already conformed with S4's $30 net inside attribute amount (after reduction under this paragraph (d)) and so there is no restoration of any basis in the S4 share.

(B) *Basis restoration at next higher tier.* Each share of S1 stock has an allocable portion of S1's net inside attribute amount (after reduction) equal to $10.25 (1/10 x $102.50, the sum of S1's $0 basis in the S2 stock, adjusted for the $50 gain recognized with respect to the share, S1's $22.50 basis in the S3 stock (after restoration), and S1's $30 basis in the S4 stock). Neither S's basis in S1 share 1 nor S's basis in S1 share 2 was reduced under paragraph (d)(5)(iii) of this section. Accordingly, there is no restoration of any basis in either S1 share 1 or share 2. However, S's basis in each of S1 share 3 through share 10 was reduced under paragraph (d)(5)(iii) of this section by $10, from $20 to $10. Accordingly, the $10 reduction to the basis of each of those shares is reversed to the extent of $.25, to restore the basis of each such share to $10.25 (its allocable portion of S1's net inside attribute amount).

(viii) *Results*. After the application of this section, P recognizes a loss of $360 on the sale of the S share, S recognizes a loss of $150 on the sale of S1 share 1, and S1 recognizes a $50 gain on the sale of the S2 share. Immediately after the transaction, the entities each directly own the following:

| Entity | Asset | Basis | Value |
|---|---|---|---|
| P1 | S share | $240 | $240 |
| P | Proceeds of the sale of S share | $240 | $240 |
| S | Proceeds of sale of S1 share 1 | $20 | $20 |
| | Partnership interest received for S1 share 2 | $20 | $20 |
| | S1 share 3 through share 10 | $82 ($10.25 per share) | |
| | Asset 1 | $80 | |
| S1 | Proceeds of sale of S2 share | $50 | $50 |
| | The S3 share | $22.50 | |
| | The S4 share | $30 | |
| S2 | Asset 2 | $57.50 | |
| S3 | Asset 3 | $22.50 | |
| S4 | Asset 4 | $30 | |
| X | S1 share 1 | $20 | $20 |
| Partnership | S1 share 2 | $20 | $20 |
| Y | The S2 share | $50 | $50 |

(e) *Operating rules.*—(1) *Predecessors, successors.*—This section applies to predecessor or successor persons, groups, and assets to the extent necessary to effectuate the purposes of this section.

(2) *Adjustments for prior transactions that altered stock basis or other attributes.*—In certain situations, M's basis in S stock or S's attributes may be adjusted in a manner that alters the relationship between stock basis and inside attributes and prevents that relationship from identifying the extent to which stock basis reflects unrecognized gain and duplicated loss. The provisions of this paragraph (e)(2) modify the computations in paragraphs (c) and (d) of this section to adjust for the effects of such adjustments.

(i) *Prior reductions to S's basis in assets or other attributes pursuant to section 362(e)(2)(A).*—If M transferred loss property to S in an intercompany transaction subject to section 362(e)(2) (for example, if the transfer was prior to September 17, 2008, no election was made to apply §1.1502-80(h), and, as a result, S's attributes were reduced under section 362(e)(2)), then the disconformity amount of the S shares received in the section 362(e)(2) transaction is reduced by the amount that the basis in such shares would have been reduced under section 362(e)(2)(C) had such an election been made. In addition, for purposes of determining the attribute reduction amount under paragraph (d) of this section resulting from the transfer of any S shares received (or deemed received) in such a transfer, and for purposes of applying paragraph (d)(5)(v)(B) of this section (conforming limitation) to S, the bases in such shares is treated as reduced by the amount the bases in such shares would have been reduced under section 362(e)(2)(C) had such an election been made.

(ii) *Prior reductions to the basis of any share of S stock pursuant to an election under section 362(e)(2)(C).*—If M transferred loss property to S in an intercompany transaction subject to section 362(e)(2) and the basis of any share of S stock was reduced as the result of an election under section 362(e)(2)(C) (including in the hands of a predecessor, to the extent that the effect of the election remains reflected in the basis of the S stock), then, for purposes of computing either any S share's disconformity amount or S's aggregate inside loss, and for purposes of applying paragraph (d)(5)(vi)(A) of this section (stock basis restoration) to S, S's net inside attribute amount is treated as reduced by the amount that S's attributes would have been reduced under section 362(e)(2)(A) in the absence of an election under section 362(e)(2)(C). Notwithstanding the general rule of this paragraph (e)(2)(ii), no reduction will be required to the extent that the group can establish that the net loss in the S shares transferred by M is no longer reflected in S's net inside attributes.

(iii) *Other adjustments.*—Appropriate adjustments will be made in any other case in which an adjustment to S's net inside attributes or to M's basis in a share of S stock alters the relationship between such amounts, and the adjustment does not relate to the extent to which loss reflected in M's basis in S stock is noneconomic or duplicated within the meaning of this section.

(3) *Special rules for subsidiary stock transferred in an intercompany transaction.*—(i) *In general.*—This section applies with respect to M's transfer of a share of S stock to another member in an intercompany transaction in which M's intercompany item is deferred under §1.1502-13 (and to any subsequent transfer of that share by a member) as of the time M's intercompany item is taken into account under §1.1502-13. In determining the application of this section, all transferor-members are treated as divisions of a single corporation. Appropriate adjustments will be made to the intercompany item(s), any member's basis in an S share, to S's attributes, or any combination thereof, to further the purposes of this section and §1.1502-13.

(ii) *Certain prior intercompany transactions.*—If M transferred a share of S stock to another member before September 17, 2008 and M's intercompany item related to the transfer is taken into account on or after September 17, 2008, P may elect to apply this paragraph (e)(3) to the transfer. The election is made in the manner provided in paragraph (e)(5) of this section.

(iii) *Examples.*—The application of this paragraph (e)(3) is illustrated by the following examples:

*Example 1. Intercompany sale with duplicated loss.* (i) *Buying member later sells at gain.* (A) *Facts.* M owns the sole outstanding share of stock of S with a basis of $100. S has one asset with a basis of $100. M sells the S share to M1 for $70, recognizing a loss of $30. While owned by M1, S recognizes $10 of depreciation deductions that are absorbed by the group. S's basis in the asset is reduced by $10 (from $100 to $90), and M1's basis in the S stock is reduced under §1.1502-32 by $10 (from $70 to $60). Later, M1 sells the S share to X, an unrelated person, for $80.

(B) *Analysis.* M's sale of its S share to M1 is a transfer of the share, but this section applies as of the time M's intercompany item is taken into account under §1.1502-13, as if M and M1 were divisions of a single corporation. If M and M1 were divisions of a single corporation, the S share's basis would be $90 ($100 reduced by $10 for the depreciation deductions absorbed by the group) and the group would recognize a $10 loss on the sale of the share that is potentially subject to this section. Thus, the sale would be a transfer of a loss share (to the extent of $10) and would be subject to this section (to the extent of that $10). Although the transfer would be subject to this section, there would be no adjustment under paragraph (b) of this section (S has only one share outstanding and so there is no disparity in bases of common shares and no unrecognized gain or loss with respect to preferred) or under paragraph (c) of this section (S has no net positive adjustment). Thus, after the application of paragraph (c) of this section, the share would still be a loss share and would therefore be subject to paragraph (d) of this section. Under paragraph (d) of this section, S would be subject to $10 of attribute reduction (the lesser of the $10 net stock loss and S's $10 aggregate inside loss), allocable to the basis in S's asset. Accordingly, S's basis in its asset is reduced by $10, from $90 to $80, M takes its $30 intercompany stock loss into account, and M1 recognizes a $20 stock gain.

(ii) *Selling member deconsolidates.* Assume the same facts as in paragraph (i)(A) of this *Example 1*, except that M1 does not sell the S share and M ceases to be a member of the group when the value of the S share is $80. Under §1.1502-13, M's deconsolidation causes M's intercompany loss to be taken into account and this section applies at that time. At the time that M deconsolidates, if M and M1 were divisions of a single corporation, the basis in the S share would be $90 ($100 reduced by $10 for the depreciation deductions absorbed by the group) and the group would recognize a $10 loss on the sale of the share that is potentially subject to this section. Such a sale would be a transfer of a loss share (to the extent of $10) and would be subject to this section (to the extent of that $10). The analysis is then

**Reg. §1.1502-36(e)(3)(iii)**

the same as in paragraph (i)(B) of this *Example 1*. As a result, S's basis in its asset is reduced from $90 to $80, M takes its $30 intercompany stock loss into account, and M1 holds the S stock with a basis of $60 (and an unrecognized gain of $20).

(iii) *M1 sells the S share at a loss.* Assume the same facts as in paragraph (i)(A) of this *Example 1*, except that S declines in value and M1 sells the S share to X for $50, realizing a $10 loss. In this case, if M and M1 were divisions of a single corporation, the share's basis would be $90 ($100 reduced by $10 for the depreciation deductions absorbed by the group) and the group would recognize a $40 loss on the sale of the share that is potentially subject to this section. Thus, the sale would be a transfer of a loss share (to the extent of $40) and would be subject to this section (to the extent of that $40). Although the transfer would be subject to this section, for the reasons set forth in paragraph (i)(B) of this *Example 1*, there would be no adjustment under either paragraph (b) or paragraph (c) of this section. Thus, after the application of paragraph (c), the share would still be a loss share and would therefore be subject to paragraph (d) of this section. Under paragraph (d) of this section, S would be subject to $40 of attribute reduction (the lesser of the $40 net stock loss and S's $40 aggregate inside loss), allocable to the basis in S's asset. Accordingly, S's basis in its asset is reduced by $40, from $90 to $50, M takes its $30 intercompany stock loss into account, and M1 recognizes a $10 stock loss.

*Example 2. Intercompany sale of built-in gain stock.* (i) *Facts.* M owns the sole outstanding share of stock of S with a basis of $100. S's sole asset has a basis of $0. S sells its asset for $100 and recognizes a $100 gain that increases M's basis in its S share under § 1.1502-32 to $200. M sells the S share to M1 for $100 and recognizes a $100 intercompany loss. Later, M1 sells the S share to X, an unrelated person, for $120.

(ii) *Analysis.* M's sale of the S share to M1 is a transfer of the share, but this section applies as of the time M's intercompany item is taken into account under § 1.1502-13, as if M and M1 were divisions of a single corporation. If M and M1 were divisions of a single corporation, the S share's basis would be $200 ($100 increased by $100 for the gain recognized on the sale of the asset) and the group would recognize an $80 loss on the sale of the share that is potentially subject to this section. Thus, the sale would be a transfer of a loss share (to the extent of $80) and would be subject to this section (to the extent of that $80). Although the transfer would be subject to this section, there would be no adjustment under paragraph (b) of this section (S has only one share outstanding and so there is no disparity in bases of common shares and no unrecognized gain or loss with respect to preferred). Thus, after the application of paragraph (b), the share would still be a loss share and would therefore be subject to paragraph (c) of this section. Under paragraph (c) of this section, the basis in the S share would be reduced, but not below its $120 value, by the lesser of the $100 disconformity amount and the $100 net positive adjustment that was applied to the share when held by M. Accordingly, the basis in the S share would be reduced by $80, to $120. Because the S share would not be a loss share after the application of paragraph (c) of this section, paragraph (d) of this section would not apply to the transfer. As a result, because the positive adjustment was applied to the share when held by M, M's intercompany item is adjusted to reflect what it would have been had M's basis in its S share been reduced by $80 immediately before its sale to M1. Thus, M's intercompany loss is reduced to $20 and M takes this loss into account, and M1 recognizes a gain of $20.

*Example 3. Intercompany sale creates built-in gain stock.* (i) *Facts.* M owns the sole outstanding share of stock of S with a basis of $0. S's sole asset has a basis of $0. M sells the S share to M1 for $100 and recognizes a $100 intercompany gain. While owned by M1, S sells its asset for $100, recognizing a $100 gain that increases M1's basis in the S share under § 1.1502-32 to $200. Later, M1 sells the S share to X for $120.

(ii) *Analysis.* M's sale of its S share to M1 is a transfer of the share, but this section applies as of the time M's intercompany item is taken into account under § 1.1502-13, as if M and M1 were divisions of a single corporation. If M and M1 were divisions of a single corporation, the S share's basis would be $100 ($0 increased by $100 for the gain recognized on the sale of the asset) and the group would recognize a $20 gain on the sale of the share. Thus, the sale would not be a transfer of a loss share and this section would not apply to the transfer. Accordingly, under this paragraph (e)(3), no portion of M1's $80 loss is subject to this section. M takes its $100 intercompany stock gain into account, and M1 recognizes an $80 loss.

*Example 4. Disparate bases in members' shares.* (i) *Facts.* M holds Share A, one of the two outstanding shares of S stock, with a basis of $50 and M1 holds Share B, the other outstanding share of S stock with a basis of $0. S has $50 cash and an asset with a basis of $0. S sells the asset for $50, recognizing a $50 gain that increases M's basis in its S share under § 1.1502-32 by $25 (from $50 to $75) and increases M1's basis under § 1.1502-32 by $25 (from $0 to $25). Later, M sells its

Share A to M1 for $50 and recognizes a $25 intercompany loss. Later, M1 sells both S shares to X for $100.

(ii) *Analysis.* M's sale of its Share A to M1 is a transfer of the share, but this section applies as of the time M's intercompany item is taken into account under § 1.1502-13, as if M and M1 were divisions of a single corporation. If M and M1 were divisions of a single corporation, the basis of Share A would be $75 ($50 increased by $25 for its share of the gain recognized on the sale of the asset), the basis of Share B would be $25, and the group would recognize a $25 loss on the sale of Share A that is potentially subject to this section and a $25 gain on the sale of Share B. Thus, the sale would be a transfer of a loss share (to the extent of $25) and would be subject to this section (to the extent of $25). Although the transfer is subject to this section, there would be no adjustment under paragraph (b) of this section (all S shares held by members are transferred to a nonmember in one taxable transaction). Thus, after the application of paragraph (b), Share A would still be a loss share and therefore subject to paragraph (c) of this section. Under paragraph (c)(7) of this section, the basis of Share A would be treated as reduced by the gain recognized and taken into account with respect to the transfer of Share B in the same transaction, and so Share A would not be a loss share for purposes of paragraph (c) of this section. Although the share would be a loss share after the application of paragraph (c) of this section, no adjustment would be required under paragraph (d) of this section because there would be no net stock loss in the transaction. Because no adjustment would be made under this section if M and M1 were divisions of a single corporation, M takes its $25 intercompany stock loss into account and M1 recognizes a gain of $25. Alternatively, if the group elects to apply paragraph (b) of this section, M's intercompany item would be adjusted to reflect what it would have been had the $25 investment adjustment applied to Share A been reallocated to Share B, and M1's basis in Share B would be increased by that amount. If so, M's $25 intercompany loss would be reduced to zero, M1's basis in Share B would be increased from $25 to $50, and there would be no gain or loss recognized on either share.

*Example 5. Subsidiary with built-in gain and built-in loss assets.* (i) *Facts.* M owns the sole outstanding share of stock of S with a basis of $100. S has two assets, Asset 1 with a basis of $0 and Asset 2 with a basis of $80. M sells the S share to M1 for $90 and recognizes a $10 intercompany loss. While owned by M1, S sells Asset 1 for $60, recognizing a $60 gain that increases M1's basis in the S share under § 1.1502-32 to $150. Later, M1 sells the S share to X for $90.

(ii) *Analysis.* M's sale of the S share to M1 is a transfer of the share, but this section applies as of the time M's intercompany item is taken into account under § 1.1502-13, as if M and M1 were divisions of a single corporation. If M and M1 were divisions of a single corporation, the S share's basis would be $160 ($100 increased by $60 for the gain recognized on the sale of Asset 1) and the group would recognize a $70 loss on the sale of the share that is potentially subject to this section. Thus, the sale would be a transfer of a loss share (to the extent of $70) and would be subject to this section (to the extent of that $70). Although the transfer is subject to this section, there would be no adjustment under paragraph (b) of this section (S has only one share outstanding and so there is no disparity in bases of common shares and no unrecognized gain or loss with respect to preferred). Thus, after the application of paragraph (b), the share would still be a loss share and would therefore be subject to paragraph (c) of this section. Under paragraph (c) of this section, the basis in the S share would be reduced, but not below its $90 value, by the lesser of the $20 disconformity amount ($160 stock basis over $140 net inside attribute amount) and the $60 net positive adjustment that was applied to the share when held by M1. Accordingly, the basis in the S share would be reduced by $20, to $140. Because the S share would still be a loss share after the application of paragraph (c) of this section, paragraph (d) of this section would apply to the transfer. Under paragraph (d) of this section, S would have an attribute reduction amount of $50, the lesser of the $50 net stock loss ($140 basis over $90 value) and S's $50 aggregate inside loss (the excess of the sum of S's $80 basis in Asset 2 and S's $60 cash from the sale of Asset 1, over the $90 value of the S share). The adjustments required under this section are applied as follows: because the positive adjustment was applied to the share when held by M1, the $20 basis reduction required under paragraph (c) of this section is applied to M1's basis in its S share immediately before its sale to X, reducing it from $150 to $130. In addition, pursuant to paragraph (d) of this section, S's basis in Asset 2 is reduced by $50, from $80 to $30. M takes its $10 intercompany stock loss into account and M1 recognizes a loss of $40.

(iii) *Allocation of basis reduction.* Assume the same facts as in paragraph (i) of this *Example 5*, except that, while S is held by M, S earns $30 (consuming a portion of Asset 1) and, while S is held by M1, S earns $20 (consuming a portion of Asset 1) and sells Asset 1 for $10. Thus, M's basis in the S share immediately before the sale to M1 is $130, and M recognizes a $40 intercompany stock loss, and M1's basis in the S share immediately before the sale to X is $120. The analysis regarding the application of this section is the same as in paragraph (ii) of this *Example 5*. On a separate entity basis, M's basis in the S share would be subject to a $20 reduction under paragraph (c) of this section (at the time M transferred the S share the share had a $30 net positive adjustment and a $20 disconformity amount), and M1's basis in the S share would not be subject to reduction under paragraph (c) of this section (at the time M1 transferred the S share the share had a $30 net positive adjustment and a $20 negative disconformity amount). Therefore, the $20 basis reduction required under paragraph (c) of this section is allocated entirely to M. Accordingly, M's intercompany item is adjusted to reflect what it would have been had the entire $20 basis reduction been applied to the S share while held by M, and M1's basis in the S share is not reduced. Thus, M's intercompany stock loss is reduced by $20 to $20 and M takes this loss into account, and M1 recognizes a $30 loss. S's basis in Asset 2 is reduced by $50, from $80 to $30.

(4) *Limited application to multiple-member section 332 liquidations.*—If more than one member owns shares of S stock, paragraphs (c) and (d) of this section do not apply to any transfer of S shares resulting from a liquidation of S to which section 332 applies.

(5) *Form and manner of election(s) under this section.*—The elections provided in this section are irrevocable and made in the form of a statement titled "Section 1.1502-36 Statement." The statement must be included on or with the group's timely filed return (original or amended, if filed by the due date for the return, including extensions) for the taxable year of the transfer of the subsidiary stock to which the election relates or, in the case of an intercompany transfer, the year in which the intercompany item from the transfer is taken into account. The statement must include—

(i) The name and employer identification number (E.I.N.) of each subsidiary with respect to which an election is being made;

(ii) If P is electing under paragraph (b)(1)(ii) of this section to redetermine basis with respect to the transfer of stock of one or more subsidiaries, a statement that members' bases in shares of [name of subsidiary or subsidiaries] stock are being redetermined notwithstanding that all members' shares of [name of subsidiary or subsidiaries] are being transferred to one or more nonmembers in one fully taxable transaction;

(iii) If P is electing under paragraph (d)(2)(ii) of this section (attribute reduction amount less than five percent of value) to apply the attribute reduction provisions, a statement that paragraph (d) of this section is being applied to the transfer of shares of stock of [names of all subsidiaries whose shares are transferred] notwithstanding that the aggregate attribute reduction amount in the transaction is less than five percent of the aggregate value of the stock of [names of all subsidiaries whose shares are transferred] transferred by members in the transaction;

(iv) If P is electing under paragraph (d)(4)(ii)(A)(*1*) of this section to specify the allocation of the attribute reduction amount, a statement (for each subsidiary for which the election is being made) that the attribute reduction amount of [name of subsidiary] is being applied (or not applied) to reduce [identify the attributes in Category A, Category B, and Category C, and the amount of each, with respect to which the election is being made];

(v) If P is electing under paragraph (d)(5)(v)(B) of this section not to apply the conforming limitation on tier-down attribute reduction with respect to one or more subsidiaries, a statement that the conforming limitation in paragraph (d)(5)(v)(B) of this section is not being applied with respect to [name of subsidiary or subsidiaries];

(vi) If P is electing under paragraph (d)(5)(vi)(B) of this section not to restore lower-tier subsidiary stock basis with respect to one or more subsidiaries, a statement that members' bases in [name of subsidiary or subsidiaries] is not being restored under paragraph (d)(5)(vi)(A) of this section;

(vii) If P is electing under paragraph (d)(6) of this section to reattribute attributes, a statement (for each subsidiary for which the election is being made) that [identify the attributes in Category A, Category B, and Category C, and the amount of each or the amount in excess of an amount, with respect to which the election is being made] of [name of subsidiary] are being reattributed (or not) to P;

(viii) If P is electing under paragraph (d)(6) of this section to reduce stock basis, a statement (for each subsidiary for which the election is being made) that members' bases in shares of stock of [name of subsidiary] are being reduced by [specify amount or the amount in excess of an amount];

(ix) If P is electing under paragraph (e)(3)(ii) of this section to apply paragraph (e)(3) of this section to an intercompany transfer that occurred before September 17, 2008, a statement that paragraph (e)(3) of this section is being elected to apply to the transfer of stock of [name of subsidiary] by [name of transferor subsidiary] to [name of transferee subsidiary] on [date of transfer]; and

(x) If P is electing under §1.1502-96(d)(5) to reattribute to itself all or any part of a section 382 limitation, a statement that P is electing to reattribute a section 382 limitation with respect to losses of [name of subsidiary or, if two or more subsidiaries are members of a loss subgroup, the name of each subsidiary in the loss subgroup]. A separate statement is made for each subsidiary or loss subgroup for which an election is being made. Each statement must include—

(A) The date of the ownership change giving rise to the separate section 382 limitation or subgroup section 382 limitation that is being apportioned;

(B) The amount of the separate (or subgroup) section 382 limitation for the taxable year in which the reattribution occurs (determined without reference to any apportionment under this section or §1.1502-95(c)); and

(C) The amount of each net operating loss carryover, capital loss carryover, or deferred deduction, and the year in which it arose, of the subsidiary (or subsidiaries) that is subject to the separate section 382 limitation or subgroup section 382 limitation that is being apportioned to the common parent, and the amount of the value element and adjustment element of that limitation that is apportioned to the common parent.

(f) *Definitions.*—In addition to the definitions in other paragraphs of this section and in other provisions of the regulations under section 1502, the following definitions apply for purposes of this section.

(1) *Allocable portion* has the same meaning as in §1.1502-32(b)(4)(iii)(B). Thus, for example, within a class of stock, each share has the same allocable portion of the net inside attribute amount and, if there is more than one class of stock, the net inside attribute amount is allocated to each class by taking into account the terms of each class and all other facts and circumstances relating to the overall economic arrangement.

(2) *Deferred deduction* means any deduction for expenses or loss that would be taken into account under general tax accounting principles as of the time of the transfer of the share, but that is nevertheless not taken into account immediately after the transfer by reason of the application of a deferral provision. Such provisions include, for example, sections 163(j), 267(f), and 469, and §1.1502-13. "Deferred deduction" also includes S's portion of such consolidated tax attributes, for example consolidated excess charitable contributions that would be apportioned to S under the principles of §1.1502-79(e) if S had a separate return year. Additionally, it includes amounts equivalent to deductions, such as negative adjustments under section 475 (mark to market accounting method for dealers in securities) and section 481 (adjustments required by changes in method of accounting).

(3) *Distribution* has the same meaning as in §1.1502-32(b)(3)(v).

(4) *Higher-tier, lower-tier.*—A subsidiary (S1) (and its shares of stock) is "highertier" with respect to another subsidiary (S2) (and its shares of stock) if investment adjustments made to the bases of shares of S2 stock under §1.1502-32 affect the investment adjustments made to the bases of shares of S1 stock. A subsidiary (S1) (and its shares of stock) is "lower-tier" with respect to another subsidiary (S) (and its shares of stock) if investment adjustments made to the bases of shares of S1 stock affect the investment adjustments made to the bases of shares of S stock. The term *lowest-tier subsidiary* generally refers to a subsidiary that owns no stock of another subsidiary. The term *highest-tier subsidiary* generally refers to a subsidiary the stock of which is not lower tier to any shares transferred in the transaction.

(5) *Liability* means a liability that has been incurred within the meaning of section 461(h), except to the extent otherwise provided in paragraph (d)(4)(ii)(C)(*1*) of this section.

(6) *Loss carryover* means any net operating or capital loss carryover that is attributable to S, including any losses that would be apportioned to S under the principles of §1.1502-21(b)(2) if S had a separate return year. However, solely for purposes of applying paragraph (d) of this section, loss carryovers do not include the amount of any losses waived under §1.1502-32(b)(4).

(7) *Loss share, gain share.*—A *loss share* is a share of stock with a basis that exceeds its value. A *gain share* is a share of stock with a value that exceeds its basis.

(8) *Preferred stock, common stock.*—*Preferred stock* and *common stock* have the same meanings as in §1.1502-32(d)(2) and (3), respectively.

(9) *Transaction* includes all the steps taken pursuant to the same plan or arrangement.

(10) *Transfer.*—(i) *Definition.*—Except as provided in paragraph (f)(10)(ii) of this section, for purposes of this section, M transfers a share of S stock on the earliest of—

(A) The date that M ceases to own the share as a result of a transaction in which, but for the application of this section (and notwithstanding the deferral of any amount recognized on the transfer, other than by reason of § 1.1502-13), M would recognize income, gain, loss or deduction with respect to the share (see paragraph (e)(3) of this section in the case of a transfer in an intercompany transaction);

(B) The date that M and S cease to be members of the same group;

(C) The date that a nonmember acquires the share from M; and

(D) The last day of the taxable year during which the share becomes worthless under section 165 (taking into account the provisions of § 1.1502-80(c)) if the share is treated as a capital asset, or the date the share becomes worthless (taking into account the provisions of § 1.1502-80(c)) if the share is not treated as a capital asset.

(ii) *Excluded transactions.*—Notwithstanding paragraph (f)(10)(i) of this section, M does not transfer a share of S stock if—

(A) M ceases to own the share as a result of a transaction to which section 381(a) applies and in which either a member acquires assets from S or S acquires assets from M, provided that—

(1) M recognizes no income, gain, loss, or deduction with respect to the share, and

(2) If the transaction is a liquidation to which section 332 applies, M is the only member that owns shares of S stock (if another member owns shares of S stock, see paragraph (e)(4) of this section for a limitation on the application of this section); or

(B) M ceases to own the share as a result of a distribution of the share to a nonmember in a transaction to which section 355 applies, and in which the share is treated as qualified property for purposes of section 355(c) or section 361(c).

(11) *Value* means the amount realized, if any, or otherwise the fair market value.

(g) *Anti-abuse rule.*—(1) *General rule.*—If a taxpayer acts with a view to avoid the purposes of this section or to apply the rules of this section to avoid the purposes of any other rule of law, appropriate adjustments will be made to carry out the purposes of this section or such other rule of law.

(2) *Examples.*—The following examples illustrate the principles of the anti-abuse rule in this paragraph (g). No implication is intended regarding the potential applicability of any other anti-abuse rules:

*Example 1. Loss Trafficking.* (i) *Facts.* M purchases the sole outstanding share of S stock for $100. At that time, S owns Asset 1 with a basis of $0. S sells Asset 1 for $100. Later, S purchases the sole outstanding share of X stock, a corporation with losses, with a view to liquidating X in a transaction to which section 332 applies in order to reduce S's disconformity amount. S purchases the X share for $1, and X has a $100 NOL and an asset with a basis of $1. Subsequently, M sells its S share for $100. After taking into account the effects of all applicable rules of law, M's basis in the S share is $200 (M's original $100 basis, increased under § 1.1502-32 to reflect the $100 gain recognized on the sale of Asset 1). M's sale of the S share is a transfer of a loss share and therefore subject to this section.

(ii) *Analysis.* Although M's transfer of the S share is subject to this section, there is no adjustment under paragraph (b) of this section (S has only one share outstanding and so there is no disparity in bases of common shares and no shares of S preferred stock outstanding (and so there is no unrecognized gain or loss on S preferred stock)). See paragraph (b)(1)(ii)(A) of this section. Accordingly, after the application of paragraph (b) of this section, M's sale of the S share is still a transfer of a loss share and therefore subject to paragraph (c) of this section. Under paragraph (c) of this section, M's $200 basis in the S share is reduced, but not below the share's $100 value, by the lesser of the share's net positive adjustment and disconformity amount. The share's net positive adjustment is $100, the positive adjustment attributable to the gain recognized on the sale of Asset 1. The share's disconformity amount is $0, the excess of M's $200 basis in the S share over S's $200 net inside attribute amount. Thus, the reduction to basis under paragraph (c) of this section would be $0. However, because S purchased the X stock and liquidated X with a view to avoiding the purposes of this section (by using X's attributes to minimize the disconformity amount of the S share), the attributes acquired from X are disregarded for purposes of applying this section. Accordingly, S's net inside attribute amount is limited to the $100 of attributes S would have had absent the purchase of the X stock, S's money ($100 from the sale of Asset 1). The loss share's disconformity amount is therefore the excess of $200 over $100, or $100. The lesser of the share's $100 net positive adjustment and $100 disconformity amount is $100. As a result, M's $200 basis in the S share is reduced by $100, to $100, and M recognizes no gain or loss on the sale of the S share.

*Example 2. Use of a partnership to prevent current attribute reduction.* (i) *Facts.* M owns all 5 outstanding shares of S common stock with a basis of $200 each. S owns Asset 1 with a basis of $1000. In year 1, with a view to preventing a current reduction in the basis of Asset 1, S contributes Asset 1 to a partnership in a transaction in which S recognizes no gain or loss. On December 31, year 2, M sells one S share for $20. After taking into account the effects of all applicable rules of law, M's basis in each S share is $200. M's sale of the S share is a transfer of a loss share and therefore subject to this section.

(ii) *Analysis.* Although M's transfer of the S share is subject to this section, there is no basis redetermination under paragraph (b) of this section because there is no disparity among M's bases in its shares of S common stock and there are no shares of S preferred stock outstanding (and so there is no unrecognized gain or loss on S preferred stock). See paragraph (b)(1)(ii)(A) of this section. Accordingly, after the application of paragraph (b) of this section, M's sale of the S share is still a transfer of a loss share and therefore subject to paragraph (c) of this section. However, no adjustment is required under paragraph (c) of this section because both the disconformity amount and the net positive adjustment are $0. See paragraph (c)(3) of this section. Under paragraph (d) of this section, S's attribute reduction amount is $180 (the lesser of the $180 net stock loss and S's $900 aggregate inside loss ($1000 of attributes over $100 value of all of the S shares)). Absent the application of this paragraph (g), the $180 attribute reduction amount would be applied to reduce S's basis in the partnership interest. However, because S acted with a view to avoiding a current reduction in the basis of Asset 1 under paragraph (d) of this section, this section is applied by treating S as if it held Asset 1 at the time of the stock sale. The basis of Asset 1 is reduced by $180, to $820, effective immediately before the transfer to the partnership and, as a result, S's basis in its partnership interest is $820.

*Example 3. Creation of an intercompany receivable to mitigate attribute reduction.* (i) *Facts.* M owns all five outstanding shares of S common stock each with equal basis that exceeds value. S holds cash and Asset 1 with a basis that exceeds value. In year 1, with a view to mitigating a reduction in the basis of Asset 1, S lends the cash to M1. Asset 1 and the intercompany note received from M1 are assets of the same class under § 1.338-6(b)(2). On December 31, year 2, M sells one of its S shares and, without regard to this section, recognizes a loss. M's sale of the S share is a transfer of a loss share and therefore subject to this section.

(ii) *Analysis.* Although M's transfer of the S share is subject to this section, no adjustment is required under paragraph (b) of this section because there is no disparity among M's bases in shares of S common stock and there are no shares of S preferred stock outstanding (and so there is no unrecognized gain or loss on S preferred stock). See paragraph (b)(1)(ii)(A) of this section. Accordingly, after the application of paragraph (b) of this section, M's sale of the S shares is still a transfer of a loss share and therefore subject to paragraph (c) of this section. However, there is no adjustment under paragraph (c) of this section because the net positive adjustment is $0. See paragraph (c)(3) of this section. Under paragraph (d) of this section, S's attribute reduction amount would be applied to reduce S's basis in Asset 1 and the intercompany receivable in proportion to basis. However, because S acted with a view to mitigating the reduction in the basis of Asset 1 under paragraph (d) of this section, this section is applied without regard to the intercompany receivable. Accordingly, S's basis in Asset 1 is reduced by the full attribute reduction amount.

*Example 4. Use of a partnership to reduce net stock loss.* (i) *Facts.* M owns all ten outstanding shares of S common stock, one share (Share 1) has a basis of $0, and one share (Share 2) has a basis of $160. S has an aggregate inside loss of $80. In one transaction and with a view to mitigating a reduction in S's attributes, M contributes Share 1 to a partnership, recognizing no gain or loss, and sells Share 2 for $80. M's contribution of Share 1 to the partnership is a transfer, but the share is not a loss share and so the transfer is not subject to this section. M's sale of Share 2 is a transfer of a loss share and is therefore subject to this section.

(ii) *Analysis.* Although M's transfer of Share 2 is subject to this section, there is no adjustment under paragraph (b) of this section because there are no investment adjustments that have been applied to the shares. Accordingly, after the application of paragraph (b) of this section, M's sale of Share 2 is still a transfer of a loss share and therefore subject to paragraph (c) of this section. There is no adjustment under paragraph (c) of this section because the net positive adjustment is $0. See paragraph (c)(3) of this section. Accordingly, after the application of paragraph (c) of this section, M's sale of Share 2 is still a transfer of loss shares and therefore subject to paragraph (d) of this section. Under paragraph (d) of this section, the net stock loss would be determined to be $0, the excess of the $160 aggregate basis in all of the transferred shares over the $160 aggregate value of those shares. S's attribute reduction amount would be determined to be $0, the lesser of the $0 net stock loss and S's $80 aggregate inside loss. Thus, there would be no reduction of attributes under this paragraph (d) of this section. However, because M acted with a view to reducing the attribute reduction amount by transferring a gain share to a partnership while avoiding the recognition of the gain on the share, this section is applied without regard to the transfer of the gain share. Accordingly, the net stock loss is determined to be $80, and the attribute reduction amount is determined to be $80.

*Example 5. Stuffing gain asset.* (i) *Facts.* M owns the sole outstanding share of S stock (Share 1) with a basis of $100. S owns Asset 1 with a basis of $100 and a value of $20. With a view to avoid the purposes of this section, M transfers Asset 2 with a basis of $0 and a value of $80 to S in exchange for four additional shares of S stock (Share 2 through Share 5) in a transaction to which section 351 applies. M later sells Share 1 to X for $20. M's sale of Share 1 is a transfer of a loss share and therefore subject to this section.

(ii) *Analysis.* Although M's transfer of the Share 1 is subject to this section, there is no adjustment under paragraph (b) of this section because no investment adjustments have been applied to the basis of any S shares. Thus, after the application of paragraph (b) of this section, M's sale of the S share is still a transfer of a loss share and therefore subject to paragraph (c) of this section. There is no adjustment under paragraph (c) of this section because the net positive adjustment is $0. Accordingly, after the application of paragraph (c) of this section, M's sale of the S share is still a transfer of a loss share and therefore subject to paragraph (d) of this section. Under paragraph (d) of this section, S's attribute reduction amount would be $0, the lesser of the $80 net stock loss and S's $0 aggregate inside loss ($100 of attributes does not exceed the $100 value of all of the S shares). However, because M transferred Asset 2 to S with a view to avoid the purposes of this section, the application of this section to M's transfer of Share 1 is made without regard to the transfer of Asset 2. Accordingly, under paragraph (d) of this section, S's attribute reduction amount is $80, the lesser of the $80 net stock loss and S's $80 aggregate inside loss (computed without regard to Asset 2). S's basis in Asset 1 is therefore reduced by $80, from $100 to $20, under paragraph (d) of this section.

(iii) *Transfer of all S shares.* Assume the same facts as in paragraph (i) of this *Example 5*, except that M sells all five S shares to X, recognizing both the gain and the loss on the S shares. The transfer of Share 1 is still a transfer of a loss share and therefore subject to this section. However, because all the shares are transferred, the group's income is clearly reflected. Therefore, the purposes of this section are not avoided and this section applies without modification. S's attribute reduction amount is $0, the lesser of the $0 net stock loss and S's $0 aggregate inside loss.

(h) *Applicability date.*—(1) *In general.*—This section applies to transfers of shares of subsidiary stock on or after September 17, 2008 unless the transfer was made pursuant to a binding agreement that was in effect prior to September 17, 2008 and at all times thereafter. For transfers of shares of subsidiary stock that are not subject to this section, see §§ 1.337(d)-2 and 1.1502-35.

(2) *Definition in paragraph (f)(2) of this section.*—Paragraph (f)(2) of this section applies to taxable years beginning on or after November 13, 2020. For taxable years beginning before November 13, 2020, see § 1.1502-36 as contained in 26 CFR part 1, revised April 1, 2019. However, taxpayers and their related parties, within the meaning of sections 267(b) and 707(b)(1), may choose to apply the rules of this section to a taxable year beginning after December 31, 2017, and before November 13, 2020, so long as the taxpayers and their related parties consistently apply the rules of this section, the section 163(j) regulations (as defined in § 1.163(j)-1(b)(37)), and, if applicable, §§ 1.263A-9, 1.263A-15, 1.381(c)(20)-1, 1.382-1, 1.382-2, 1.382-5, 1.382-6, 1.382-7, 1.383-0, 1.383-1, 1.469-9, 1.469-11, 1.704-1, 1.882-5, 1.1362-3, 1.1368-1, 1.1377-1, 1.1502-13, 1.1502-21, 1.1502-79, 1.1502-91 through 1.1502-99 (to the extent they effectuate the rules of §§ 1.382-2, 1.382-5, 1.382-6, 1.382-7, and 1.383-1), and 1.1504-4, to that taxable year. [Reg. § 1.1502-36.]

□ [T.D. 9424, 9-9-2008 (corrected 10-17-2008). *Amended by T.D.* 9905, 9-3-2020.]

### [Reg. § 1.1502-41A]

**§ 1.1502-41A. Determination of consolidated net long-term capital gain and consolidated net short-term capital loss generally applicable for consolidated return years beginning before January 1, 1997.**—(a) *Consolidated net long-term capital gain.*—The consolidated net long-term capital gain shall be determined by taking into account (1) those gains and losses to which § 1.1502-22A(a) applies which are treated as long term under section 1222, and (2) the consolidated section 1231 net gain (computed in accordance with § 1.1502-23A).

(b) *Consolidated net short term capital loss.*—The consolidated net short term capital loss shall be determined by taking into account (1) those gains and losses to which § 1.1502-22A(a) applies which are treated as short term under section 1222, and (2) the consolidated net capital loss carryovers and carrybacks to the taxable year (as determined under § 1.1502-22A(b)).

(c) *Effective date.*—This section applies to any consolidated return years to which § 1.1502-21(h) or 1.1502-21T(g) in effect prior to June 25, 1999, as contained in 26 CFR part 1 revised April 1, 1999, as applicable does not apply. See § 1.1502-21(h) or 1.1502-21T(g) in effect prior to June 25, 1999, as contained in 26 CFR part 1 revised April 1, 1999, as applicable for effective dates of these sections. [Reg. § 1.1502-41A.]

□ [T.D. 6984, 9-7-66. *Amended by T.D.* 7637, 8-6-79; T.D. 8677, 6-26-96 *and T.D.* 8823, 6-25-99.]

### [Reg. § 1.1502-42]

**§ 1.1502-42. Mutual savings banks, etc.**—(a) *In general.*—This section applies to mutual savings banks and other institutions described in section 593(a).

(b) *Total deposits.*—In computing for purposes of section 593(b)(1)(B)(ii) total deposits or withdrawable accounts at the close of the taxable year, the total deposits or withdrawable accounts of other members shall be excluded.

(c) *Taxable income; taxable years for which the due date (without extensions) for filing returns is before March 15, 1983.*—For taxable years for which the due date (without extensions) for filing returns is before March 15, 1983, a member's taxable income for purposes of section 593(b)(2) is determined under § 1.1502-27(b) (computed without regard to any deduction under section 593(b)(2)). In addition, for taxable years beginning after July 11, 1969, taxable income as computed under the preceding sentence is subject to the adjustments provided in section 593(b)(2)(E). See § 1.593-6A(b)(5).

(d) *Taxable income; taxable years for which the due date (without extensions) for filing returns is after March 14, 1983.*—(1) *In general.*—For a taxable year for which the due date (without extensions) for filing returns is after March 14, 1983, a thrift's taxable income for purposes of section 593(b)(2) is its tentative taxable income (as defined in paragraph (e)(1) of this section).

(2) *Definitions.*—For purposes of this section—
(i) A "thrift" is a member described in section 593(a).
(ii) A "nonthrift" is a member that is not a thrift.

(e) *Tentative taxable income (or loss).*—(1) *Thrift.*—For purposes of this section, a thrift's tentative taxable income (or loss) is its separate taxable income (determined under § 1.1502-12 without paragraph (q) thereof and without any deduction under section 593(b)), subject to the following adjustments in the following order:

(i) the adjustments described in paragraph (e)(3) of this section;
(ii) the adjustments described in section 593(b)(2)(E) for those thrifts with separate taxable income greater than zero (determined after the adjustments under paragraph (e)(3) of this section); and
(iii) the adjustments described in paragraph (f) of this section.

(2) *Nonthrift.*—For purposes of this section, a nonthrift's tentative taxable income (or loss) is its separate taxable income (determined under § 1.1502-12), adjusted for the portion of the consolidated net operating loss deduction attributable to the member, the portion of the consolidated net capital loss carryover or carryback attributable to the member, and further adjusted as described in paragraph (e)(3) of this section.

(3) *Adjustments for all members.*—For each member, the following adjustments taken into account in the computation of consolidated taxable income are included in determining its tentative taxable income (or loss) in order to adjust separate taxable income of the member to take into account certain consolidated items:

(i) The portions of the consolidated charitable contributions deduction and the consolidated dividends received deduction attributable to the member.
(ii) The member's capital gain net income, determined without any net capital loss carryover or carryback attributable to the member.
(iii) The member's net capital loss and section 1231 net loss, reduced by the portion of the consolidated net capital loss attributable to the member.

(f) *Adjustments for thrifts.*—(1) *Reductions.*—A thrift's separate taxable income (as adjusted under paragraph (e)(3) of this section) is reduced (but not below zero) by losses of thrifts and to the extent attributable to functionally related activities, losses of a nonthrift. Certain operating rules for determining the amount of the reductions are provided in paragraph (f)(4) of this section. The reductions are made in the following amounts in the following order:

(i) The thrift's allocable share (as determined under paragraph (h)(2) of this section) of another thrift's tentative taxable loss. That tentative taxable loss is determined by including a deduction under section 593(b) (other than paragraph (2) thereof) for the year in which the loss arises.

(ii) The thrift's allocable share (as determined under paragraph (h)(3) of this section) of the portion of the consolidated net operating loss deduction attributable to it or another thrift. That consolidated net operating loss deduction is determined by including a deduction under section 593(b) (other than paragraph (2) thereof) for the year in which the loss arose. The portion of a consolidated net operating loss deduction attributable to another thrift is computed by excluding losses arising in taxable years for which the due date (without extensions) for filing returns is before March 15, 1983.

(iii) The thrift's allocable share (as determined under paragraph (h)(4) of this section) of the loss attributable to functionally related activities of a nonthrift (as determined under paragraph (g) of this section). For a rule netting that share against certain income attributable to functionally related activities of that nonthrift, see paragraph (f)(4)(iv) of this section.

(iv) The thrift's allocable share (as determined under paragraph (h)(3) of this section) of the portion of the consolidated net operating loss deduction attributable to functionally related activities of a nonthrift (as determined under paragraph (h)(5) of this section). That consolidated net operating loss deduction is determined by excluding losses arising in taxable years for which the due date (without extensions) for filing returns is before March 15, 1983. For a rule netting that share against certain income attributable to functionally related activities of that nonthrift, see paragraph (f)(4)(iv) of this section.

(2) *Increases.*—(i) A thrift's separate taxable income (as adjusted under paragraphs (e)(3) and (f)(1) of this section) is increased in a subsequent consolidated return year to restore reductions made in a prior consolidated return year to a thrift's separate taxable income by reason of losses of a nonthrift. This increase is the amount of the thrift's allocable share (as determined under paragraph (h)(6) of this section) of the income attributable to functionally related activities of a nonthrift in a consolidated return year and is made only in that year. This increase is made only if both the thrift and the nonthrift were members of the group in the consolidated return years in which both the reduction and increase are made.

(ii) This subdivision (ii) limits the increases to a thrift's separate taxable income to assure that income of a particular nonthrift is used to restore reductions of a thrift only to the extent that such nonthrift's losses reduced the thrift's income. Therefore, as of the end of a consolidated return year, the cumulative increases to a thrift's tentative taxable income (by reason of income attributable to functionally related activities of a nonthrift) may not exceed the cumulative reductions to the thrift's separate taxable income made (by reason of the nonthrift's functionally related activities) under paragraph (f)(1)(iii) and (iv) of this section in the current and all prior consolidated return years during which both the thrift institution and the nonthrift institution were members of the group.

(iii) For a netting rule, see paragraph (f)(4)(iv) of this section.

(3) *Special rule.*—(i) If a carryback to a thrift's separate taxable income diminishes the reduction to a thrift's separate taxable income for a prior consolidated return year otherwise required by paragraph (f)(1)(iii) or (iv) of this section, then any increase to a thrift's separate taxable income under paragraph (f)(2) of this section for an intervening consolidated return year must be recomputed to take into account the effect of such carryback. Thus, if a net operating loss attributable to a thrift is carried back and completely offsets the thrift's separate taxable income (before the reductions under paragraph (f)(1)(iii) or (iv) of this section), any increase to the thrift's separate taxable income under paragraph (f)(2) of this section (attributable to a reduction in the year to which the loss is carried) for an intervening consolidated return year will be eliminated. The recomputation required by this subparagraph (3) must be reflected on an amended return for the intervening consolidated return year for which the increase was previously reported. See example (2) in paragraph (j) of this section.

(ii) If a deficiency for an intervening consolidated return year results from the application of paragraph (f)(3)(i) of this section with respect to an item to which section 6501(h) applies, the deficiency may be assessed at any time within the period described in section 6501(h).

(iii) For purposes of chapter 67 of the Code (relating to interest), the last date prescribed for payment of any tax owed as a result of the application of paragraph (f)(3)(i) of this section is deemed to be the last day of the taxable year for which the item carried back arose.

(4) *Operating rules.*—For purposes of paragraphs (d)-(j) of this section—

(i) The portion of a consolidated net operating loss deduction attributable to a member is determined as follows:

(A) First, determine under §1.1502-21(b) (or §1.1502-79A(a)(3), as appropriate) the portion of each consolidated net operating loss attributable to the member for the particular year in which the loss arose.

(B) Second, apply the anti-double-counting rule in paragraph (h)(3)(iii) of this section so as not to take the same loss into account twice.

(C) Finally, apply the loss absorption limit in paragraph (f)(4)(iii) of this section to the total amount of the consolidated net operating loss deduction from a particular loss year.

(ii) Capital loss carryovers and carrybacks shall be taken into account in a manner consistent with the principles of paragraphs (d)-(j) of this section.

(iii) This subdivision (iii) prescribes a loss absorption limit. The total amount of the consolidated net operating loss deduction from a given year (loss year) taken into account as reductions under paragraph (f)(1) of this section for another year (absorption year) shall not exceed the amount of the consolidated net operating loss deduction attributable to the loss year absorbed in computing consolidated taxable income for the absorption year. For this purpose, consolidated taxable income for the absorption year shall include a deduction under section 593(b) (other than paragraph (2) thereof) for each thrift member.

(iv) This subdivision (iv) prescribes a rule for netting in certain cases income attributable to functionally related activities of a nonthrift in a consolidated return year ("income year") against losses attributable to functionally related activities of that nonthrift which arise in a consolidated return year ("loss year"). That nonthrift's income is netted against the portion of that nonthrift's loss which would otherwise be applied in a consolidated return year ("reduction year") under paragraph (f)(1)(iii) or (iv) of this section to reduce a thrift's tentative taxable income, but—

(A) only if the income year is not later than the loss year and the reduction year, and

(B) only to the extent the income had not previously been taken into account under paragraph (f)(2) of this section or this subdivision (iv) as of the close of the later of the loss year and the reduction year.

(g) *Income (or loss) attributable to functionally related activities of a nonthrift.*—(1) *In general.*—For purposes of this section, the income (or loss) attributable to functionally related activities of a nonthrift is the income (or loss) of the nonthrift

(i) attributable to the provision of assets or the rendition of services to a thrift (such as the leasing of office space or providing computer or financial services), or

(ii) derived from the assets described in section 7701(a)(19)(C)(iii)-(x), but only if such assets comprise 5 percent or more of the gross assets of the nonthrift.

(2) *Amount of income (or loss).*—The amount of income (or loss) from such activities is the excess of (i) gross income from such activities over (ii) the deductions of the nonthrift allocable and apportionable to that gross income under the principles of §1.861-8. The loss attributable to functionally related activities of a nonthrift is the excess (if any) of such deductions over such gross income. That loss, however, may not exceed the amount of the tentative taxable loss of that nonthrift (determined by excluding losses arising in taxable years for which the due date (without extensions) for filing returns is before March 15, 1983).

(h) *Allocation of income and losses.*—(1) *In general.*—Paragraph (h)(2)-(5) of this section provides rules for allocating different losses among thrifts that have tentative taxable income greater than zero. Generally, these allocations are made in the order listed in paragraph (f)(1) of this section and are based upon the relative tentative taxable income of the thrifts to which the particular loss is allocated. For purposes of each allocation under a subdivision of such paragraph (f)(1), the tentative taxable income of the thrifts used in making this allocation is reduced by the thrift's allocable share of losses allocated to the thrift under a prior subdivision of such paragraph (f)(1). Accordingly, for purposes of this paragraph (h), tentative taxable income is determined without regard to paragraph (f) of this section, except as otherwise provided. Paragraph (h)(6) of this section provides rules for allocating income attributable to functionally related activities of a nonthrift based upon the relative reductions to thrift income made on account of that nonthrift.

(2) *Allocation of tentative taxable loss of other thrifts.*—For purposes of paragraph (f)(1)(i) of this section, a thrift's allocable share of another thrift's tentative taxable loss is the loss multiplied by a fraction. The numerator of the fraction is the tentative taxable income (if greater than zero) of the thrift, and the denominator is the aggregate of such tentative taxable income of each thrift.

(3) *Allocation of portions of a consolidated net operating loss deduction.*—(i) For purposes of paragraph (f)(1)(ii) of this section, a first thrift's allocable share of the portion of the consolidated net operating loss deduction attributable to another thrift is determined under paragraph (h)(2) of this section as if that portion were a tentative taxable loss of that other thrift and by computing tentative taxable income under such paragraph (h)(2) by taking into account paragraph (f)(1)(i) of this section. A thrift's allocable share of the portion

of the consolidated net operating loss deduction attributable to that thrift is equal to that entire portion.

(ii) For purposes of paragraph (f)(1)(iv) of this section, a thrift's allocable share of the portion of a consolidated net operating loss deduction attributable to functionally related activities of a nonthrift (determined under paragraph (h)(5) of this section) is determined under paragraph (h)(4) of this section as if that portion were a loss attributable to functionally related activities of the nonthrift and by computing tentative taxable income under such paragraph (h)(4) by taking into account paragraph (f)(1)(i), (ii), and (iii) of this section.

(iii) This subdivision (iii) prevents the "double-counting" of losses. The reduction to the tentative taxable income of a thrift is diminished to the extent the loss that gave rise to the reduction has previously been taken into account in reducing a thrift's tentative taxable income. Thus, any loss taken into account as a reduction to a thrift's separate taxable income under any subdivision of paragraph (f)(1) of this section shall be reduced (but not below zero) to the extent taken into account—

(A) in a prior consolidated return year under any subdivision of such paragraph (f)(1) or

(B) in the current consolidated return year under a previous subdivision of such paragraph (f)(1).

(4) *Allocation of loss attributable to functionally related activities of a nonthrift.*—For purposes of paragraph (f)(1)(iii) of this section, a thrift's allocable share of a loss attributable to functionally related activities of a nonthrift is determined by multiplying the loss by a fraction. The numerator of the fraction is the tentative taxable income (if greater than zero) of the thrift (taking into account paragraph (f)(1)(i) and (ii) of this section) and the denominator is the aggregate of such tentative taxable income (so determined) of each thrift.

(5) *Portion of the consolidated net operating loss deduction attributable to functionally related activities of a particular nonthrift.*—The portion of the consolidated net operating loss deduction attributable to functionally related activities of a particular nonthrift is the lesser of the following two amounts:

(i) The portion of the consolidated net operating loss deduction attributable to that nonthrift.

(ii) The aggregate of the losses attributable to functionally related activities of that nonthrift for the taxable years in which the consolidated net operating loss deduction arose.

(6) *Allocation of income attributable to functionally related activities of a nonthrift.*—For purposes of paragraph (f)(2) of this section, a thrift institution's allocable share of the income attributable to functionally related activities of a nonthrift is determined by multiplying that income by a fraction. The numerator of the fraction is the amount of the cumulative reductions referred to in paragraph (f)(2)(ii) of this section (minus the cumulative increases under paragraph (f)(2) of this section) made on account of that nonthrift for the thrift and the denominator is the sum of such cumulative reductions (minus such cumulative increases) made on account of that nonthrift for all thrifts.

(7) *Proper accounting.*—The provisions of section 482 apply in determining a thrift institution's tentative taxable income, and in determining the gross income and deductions attributable to functionally related activities. For example, an expense such as the salary of an individual who performs services for both a thrift and a nonthrift must be allocated in a manner that fairly reflects the value of the services rendered to each.

(i) [Reserved]

(j) *Examples.*—The provisions of this section may be illustrated by the following examples. In each example the letter "T" for a member denotes a thrift and the letters "NT" denote a nonthrift. Also, in each example, a thrift loss includes a bad debt deduction under section 593(b) (other than paragraph (2) thereof) for such year and a thrift with income would have such a bad debt deduction of zero.

*Example (1).* (a) In 1983, corporations T1, T2, NT1, and NT2 are formed. These corporations constitute an affiliated group that files a consolidated return on the basis of a calendar year. For 1983, 1984, and 1985, the tentative taxable income (or loss) of each member (before the application of paragraph (f) of this section) is as follows:

|     | 1983 | 1984 | 1985 |
|-----|------|------|------|
| NT1 | $(60) | $(140) | $15 |
| T1  | 1,000 | 500 | 750 |
| NT2 | (90) | (220) | 150 |
| T2  | (300) | 400 | 250 |

In 1983, NT1, in addition to its other business activities, acted as a collection agency for T1. Deductions attributable to those collection activities exceeded gross income attributable to those activities by $70. NT1's other activities generated a $10 gain. In 1984 and 1985, NT1 acted as a collection agency for T1 as its sole activity.

(b) The tentative taxable incomes of T1 and T2 for 1983 (determined under paragraph (e) of this section) as of the close of that year are adjusted by paragraph (f) of this section as follows:

(i) T1's tentative taxable income:

| | | |
|---|---|---|
| T1's tentative taxable income (before the application of paragraph (f) of this section) . . . . . . . . . . . . . . . . . . . . | | $1,000 |
| Less: | | |
| T2's tentative taxable loss . . . . . . . . . . | $300 | |
| NT1's functionally related loss (limited by NT1's overall loss) . . . . . . . . . . . . . . | 60 | 360 |
| T1's tentative taxable income for 1983 . . | | 640 |

(ii) T2's tentative taxable income for 1983 is zero.

(c) The tentative taxable incomes of T1 and T2 for 1984 (determined under paragraph (e) of this section as of the close of that year) are adjusted by paragraph (f) of this section as follows:

(i) T1's tentative taxable income:

| | |
|---|---|
| T1's tentative taxable income (before the application of paragraph (f) of this section) . . . . . . . . . . | $500 |
| Less: | |
| T1's allocable portion of NT1's functionally related loss (140 × 500/(500 + 400)) . . . . . . . . . . . . . . | 78 |
| T1's tentative taxable income for 1984 . . . . . . . . . . | 422 |

(ii) T2's tentative taxable income:

| | |
|---|---|
| T2's tentative taxable income (before the application of paragraph (f) of this section . . . . . . . . . . . . . . | 400 |
| Less: | |
| T2's allocable portion of NT1's functionally related loss (140 × 400/(500 + 400)) . . . . . . . . . . . . . . | 62 |
| T2's tentative taxable income for 1984 . . . . . . . . . | $338 |

(d) For 1985, the amount under paragraph (f)(2) of this section for both T1 and T2 is $15 (NT1's tentative taxable income from functionally related activities for 1985). For 1983 and 1984, T1's tentative taxable income was reduced by a total of $138 (*i.e.,* $60 + $78) due to NT1's losses from functionally related activities. For 1984, T2's tentative taxable income was reduced by $62 due to those losses. Accordingly, under paragraph (f)(2) of this section, T1's tentative taxable income for 1983 is increased by $10 (*i.e.,* $15 × $138/($138 + $62)) and T2's tentative taxable income is increased by $5 (*i.e.,* $15 × $62/($138 + $62)).

*Example (2).* (a) In 1983, corporations T, NT1, and NT2 are formed. These corporations constitute an affiliated group. NT2 provides computer services to T as its sole activity. For the calendar years of 1983, 1984, and 1985, the group files a consolidated return. The tentative taxable income of each member (before the application of paragraph (f) of this section) is as follows:

|     | 1983 | 1984 | 1985 |
|-----|------|------|------|
| T   | $100 | $0 | $(200) |
| NT1 | 200 | 0 | 100 |
| NT2 | (20) | 20 | 0 |

(b) Under paragraph (f)(1) of this section, T's tentative taxable income for 1983 (determined at the close of that year) is reduced to $80 (*i.e.,* $100 less NT2's $20 loss). For 1984, under paragraph (f)(2) of this section, T's tentative taxable income is increased by $20. For 1985, the consolidated net operating loss of $100 (all of which is attributable to T) is carried back to 1983. That $100 carryback is not limited by paragraph (f)(4)(iii) of this section, since consolidated taxable income for 1983 available for absorption after a bad debt deduction of $0 under section 593(b) (other than paragraph (2) thereof) for that year is $280. Accordingly, under paragraph (f)(1)(ii) of this section, T's tentative taxable income is reduced by the full $100, which is taken into account before the previous reduction of T's tentative taxable income under paragraph (f)(1)(iii) of this section. In addition, under paragraph (f)(3)(ii) of this section, the group must file an amended return for 1984 to eliminate the increase to T's bad debt deduction for 1984 by reason of the consolidated net operating loss carryback to 1983.

*Example (3).* (a) T and NT are formed in 1983 and are the only members of an affiliated group filing a consolidated return on a calendar year basis. NT provided computer services to T as its sole activity. For 1983, 1984, and 1985, the tentative taxable income of T and NT (before the application of paragraph (f) of this section) is as follows:

|    | 1983 | 1984 | 1985 |
|----|------|------|------|
| T  | $100 | $0 | $0 |
| NT | 0 | 40 | (40) |

(b) At the close of 1983, T's tentative taxable income is $100. For 1985, however, the group has a consolidated net operating loss of $40, all of which is attributable to NT's functionally related activities and which is carried back to 1983. However, T's tentative taxable income for 1983 is not reduced under paragraph (f)(1)(iv) of this section, since, under paragraph (f)(4)(iv) of this section, NT's 1984 income attributable to functionally related activities of $40 is netted against that $40 carryback.

*Example (4).* (a) In 1983, corporations T1, T2, NT1, and NT2 are formed. For calendar years 1983, 1984, and 1985, the affiliated group consisting of T1, T2, NT1, and NT2 filed a consolidated return. NT1 provided computer services to T1 as its sole activity. The tentative taxable income of each member (before the application of paragraph (f) of this section) is as follows:

|       | 1983   | 1984  | 1985  |
|-------|--------|-------|-------|
| T1    | ($50)  | $100  | $30   |
| T2    | (50)   | (80)  | (25)  |
| NT1   | (50)   | (40)  | (99)  |
| NT2   | 120    | 30    | 100   |

(b) For 1983, the group has a consolidated net operating loss of $30, apportioned $10 each to T1, T2, and NT1 under § 1.1502-79A(a)(3). For 1984, the only thrift with tentative taxable income greater than zero (before applying paragraph (f) of this section) is T1. That tentative taxable income of $100 is first reduced to $20 by T2's $80 1984 loss under paragraph (f)(1)(i) of this section. Next, T1's remaining tentative taxable income of $20 is reduced to $10 by the portions attributable to T1 and T2 of the 1983 consolidated net operating loss carryover to 1984 under paragraph (f)(1)(ii) of this section. The sum of those portions is limited to $10 (*i.e.,* $5 each) by paragraph (f)(4)(iii) of this section because 1984 consolidated taxable income available for absorption after a bad debt deduction under section 593(b) (other than paragraph (2) thereof) for each thrift member for that year is $10. For that reason, paragraph (f)(4)(iii) of this section also prevents any further portion of that carryover from being taken into account in 1984 as a reduction under paragraph (f)(1) of this section. T1's remaining tentative taxable income of $10 is reduced to zero, under paragraph (f)(1)(iii) of this section, by NT1's 1984 tentative taxable loss.

(c) For 1985, the only thrift with tentative taxable income greater than zero (before applying paragraph (f) of this section) is T1. T1's tentative taxable income for 1985 of $30 is reduced to $5 by T2's 1985 loss of $25 under paragraph (f)(1)(i) of this section. Next, the portions attributable to T1 and T2 of the consolidated net operating loss carryover from 1983 to 1985 for purposes of paragraph (f)(1)(ii) of this section must be determined. That determination is made without applying the rules for loss absorption in computing consolidated taxable income under § 1.1502-21A(b)(3). Those portions are instead determined in 3 steps under paragraph (f)(4)(i) of this section. The first of those steps is to determine each of T1's and T2's attributable portions of the 1983 consolidated net operating loss which under § 1.1502-79A(a)(3) is $10 or $20 for both thrifts. The second of those steps is to apply the anti-double counting rule under paragraph (h)(3)(iii) of this section to reduce that $20 amount by the $10 total of the two $5 portions attributable to T1 and T2 of the consolidated net operating loss carryover from 1983 to 1984 taken into account as reductions to T1's tentative taxable income for 1984 under paragraph (f)(1)(ii) of this section. That leaves a $10 total amount available to be taken into account as reductions to T1's remaining tentative taxable income of $5 for 1985 under paragraph (f)(1)(ii) of this section. Under the third of those steps that $10 amount, however, is limited, under the loss absorption limit of paragraph (f)(4)(iii) of this section, to the $6 of the 1983 consolidated net operating loss carryover to 1985 which is absorbed in computing consolidated taxable income for 1985 since 1985 consolidated taxable income available for absorption after a bad debt deduction under section 593(b) (other than paragraph (2) thereof) for that year is $6 (*i.e.,* $30 + $100 – $99 – $25). Because separate taxable income cannot be reduced below zero under paragraph (f)(1) of this section, T1's remaining tentative taxable income of $5 if thus reduced to zero by the portions attributable to T1 and T2, respectively, of the consolidated net operating loss carryover from 1983 to 1985 under paragraph (f)(1)(ii) of this section. [Reg. § 1.1502-42.]

☐ [*T.D. 7246, 12-29-72. Amended by T.D. 7637, 8-6-79; T.D. 7815, 3-12-82; T.D. 7876, 3-14-83; T.D. 8677, 6-26-96 and T.D. 8823, 6-25-99.*]

## [Reg. § 1.1502-43]

**§ 1.1502-43. Consolidated accumulated earnings tax.**—(a) *Group subject to tax.*—(1) *General rule.*—For a group filing a consolidated return for the taxable year, the accumulated earnings tax under section 531 is imposed on consolidated accumulated taxable income (as defined in paragraph (b) of this section). This tax applies to any group that is formed or availed of to avoid or prevent the imposition of the individual income tax on the shareholders of either any of its members or any other corporation by permitting earnings and profits to accumulate instead of dividing or distributing them. Section 531

and this section do not apply to a group that is treated as a "personal holding company" under section 542(a)(1) as a result of the application of section 542(b)(1). Special rules are provided in this section for other groups which include one or more personal holding companies.

(2) *Evidence of purpose to avoid income tax.*—(i) Under section 533(a), the fact that the group's earnings and profits are permitted to accumulate beyond the reasonable needs of its business is determinative of the purpose to avoid the income tax with respect to shareholders, unless the group by the preponderance of the evidence proves to the contrary.

(ii) The fact that a group is a mere holding or investment group is prima facie evidence of the group's purpose to avoid the income tax with respect to shareholders. The activities of a member which is a personal holding company are not taken into account in determining if the group is a mere holding or investment group.

(3) *Earnings and profits.*—For purposes of this paragraph (a) and paragraph (d) of this section, the following rules apply:

(i) If no member of the group is a personal holding company, the group's earnings and profits are the aggregate of the earnings and profits (or deficit) of each corporation that is a member at the close of the taxable year, determined in accordance with § 1.1502-33.

(ii) Earnings and profits resulting from the application of § 1.1502-33(b) are not taken into account.

(iii) Earnings and profits resulting from the disposition of a member's stock are determined without regard to the stock basis adjustments under § § 1.1502-32 and 1.1502-33(c)(1).

(4) *Reasonable needs of the business.*—The reasonable needs of the group's business include the reasonable needs of the business of any corporation (other than a personal holding company) that is a member at the close of the taxable year. Thus, the earnings and profits of one member may be accumulated with respect to the reasonable business needs of another member. If under § 1.537-3(b) the business of a nonmember corporation is considered the business of a member, then the earnings and profits of any member may be accumulated with respect to such nonmember's reasonable business needs.

(5) *Burden of proof.*—The notification described in section 534(b) and the statement described in section 534(c) are made to or by the common parent corporation in accordance with § 1.1502-77.

(b) *Consolidated accumulated taxable income.*—(1) *In general.*—"Consolidated accumulated taxable income" is the group's consolidated taxable income determined under § 1.1502-11 adjusted in the manner provided in paragraph (b)(2) of this section, minus the sum of—

(i) The consolidated dividends paid deduction determined under paragraph (c) of this section and

(ii) The consolidated accumulated earnings credit determined under paragraph (d) of this section.

(2) *Adjustments to consolidated taxable income.*—For purposes of paragraph (b)(1) of this section, consolidated taxable income is adjusted as follows:

(i) Under section 535(b)(1), the deduction for taxes is the excess of—

(A) The consolidated liability for tax determined without § 1.1502-2(a)(2) through (4), and without the foreign tax credit provided by section 27, over

(B) The consolidated foreign tax credit determined pursuant to § 1.1502-4.

Foreign taxes deductible under § 1.535-2(a)(2) are also allowed as a deduction under section 535(b)(1).

(ii) The consolidated charitable contributions deduction under § 1.1502-24 does not apply. Under section 535(b)(2), there shall be allowed the aggregate charitable contributions of the members allowable under section 170, determined without section 170(b)(2) and (d)(2).

(iii) Under section 535(b)(3), the deductions provided in § § 1.1502-26 and 1.1502-27 are not allowed.

(iv) Under section 535(b)(4), the consolidated net operating loss deduction described in § § 1.1502-21(a) or 1.1502-21A(a), as appropriate is not allowed.

(v) Under section 535(b)(5), there is allowed as a deduction the consolidated net capital loss, determined under § § 1.1502-22(a) or 1.1502A(a), as appropriate.

(vi) Under section 535(b)(6), there is allowed as a deduction an amount equal to (A) the excess of the consolidated net long-term capital gain (determined under §§1.1502-22(a) or 1.1502-41A, as appropriate) over the consolidated net short-term capital loss (determined under §§1.1502-22(a) or 1.1502-41A, as appropriate), minus (B) the taxes attributable to this excess. This consolidated net short-term capital loss is determined without the consolidated net capital loss carryovers or carrybacks to the taxable year.

(vii) Under section 535(b)(7), the consolidated net capital loss carryovers and carrybacks are not allowed. See §§1.1502-22(b) or 1.1502-22A(b), as appropriate.

(viii) Sections 1.1502-15A (Limitations on built-in deductions not subject to §1.1502-15) and 1.1502-15 do not apply.

(3) *Personal holding company a member.*—If a member is a personal holding company for the taxable year—

(i) [Reserved].

(ii) In applying paragraph (b)(2)(i) of this section, consolidated liability for tax (as determined under that paragraph (b)(2)(i)) is reduced by the portion thereof allocable to that member under section 1552(a)(1), (2), (3), or (4) (or §1.1502-33(d)), whichever is applicable. The consolidated foreign tax credit is computed by excluding the taxable income and any foreign taxes paid or accrued by that member, and foreign taxes deductible under §1.535-2(a)(2) do not include foreign taxes attributable to that member.

(c) *Consolidated dividends paid deduction.*—(1) *General rule.*—For purposes of this section, the consolidated dividends paid deduction is the aggregate of the members' deductions under section 561(a)(1) and (2). This deduction is determined by excluding deductions for dividends paid to other members.

(2) *Exception for certain personal holding companies.*—[Reserved].

(3) *Dividends paid defined.*—For purposes of this paragraph (c), "dividends paid" and "dividend (or portion thereof) paid" include amounts treated as dividends paid during the taxable year under sections 562(b)(1), 563, and 565 (relating respectively to liquidating distributions, dividends paid after year end, and consent dividends).

(4) *Examples.*—This paragraph (c) can be illustrated by the following examples:

*Example (1).* Corporations P and S constitute an affiliated group which files a consolidated return on a calendar year basis for 1984 and 1985. P owns all of S's stock and two individuals own all of P's stock. Neither member of the group is a personal holding company for 1984. Assume that on December 15, 1984, S pays a dividend (as defined in section 316(a)) of $2,000 to P, and P pays a dividend (as so defined) of $3,000 on January 15, 1985 to its individual shareholders. All dividends are paid in cash and are pro rata with no preference as to any shares or class of stock. For purposes of this paragraph (c), the consolidated dividends paid deduction for 1984 is $3,000, *i.e.*, the dividend paid on January 15, 1985, by P to its nonmember shareholders. See section 563(a). The $2,000 dividend paid by S to P is not taken into account in computing the consolidated dividends paid deduction.

*Example (2).* [Reserved].

(d) *Consolidated accumulated earnings credit.*—(1) *In general.*—[Reserved]

(2) *Special rule if a consolidated group is part of a controlled group.*—If a consolidated group is treated collectively as being one component member of a controlled group, or if each member of a consolidated group is treated as being a separate component member of a controlled group, see section 1561 for determining the portion of the accumulated earnings credit to be allocated to such group or to such members.

(e) *Effective/applicability date.*—This section applies to any consolidated Federal income tax return due (without extensions) on or after December 21, 2009. However, a consolidated group may apply this section to any consolidated Federal income tax return filed on or after December 21, 2009. For returns due before December 21, 2009, see §1.1502-43T as contained in 26 CFR part 1 in effect on April 1, 2009. [Reg. §1.1502-43.]

☐ [*T.D. 7937, 1-26-84. Amended by T.D. 8560, 8-12-94; T.D. 8677, 6-26-96; T.D. 8823, 6-25-99; T.D. 9304, 12-21-2006, T.D. 9476, 12-22-2009 and T.D. 9885, 12-2-2019.*]

## [Reg. §1.1502-44]

**§1.1502-44. Percentage depletion for independent producers and royalty owners.**—(a) *In general.*—The sum of the percentage depletion deductions for the taxable year for all oil or gas property owned by all members, plus any carryovers under section 613A(d)(1) or paragraph (d) of this section from a prior taxable year, may not exceed 65 percent of the group's adjusted consolidated taxable income (under paragraph (b) of this section) for the consolidated return year.

(b) *Adjusted consolidated taxable income.*—For purposes of this section, adjusted consolidated taxable income is an amount (not less than zero) equal to the group's consolidated taxable income determined without—

(1) Any depletion with respect to an oil or gas property (other than a gas property with respect to which the depletion allowance for all production is determined pursuant to section 613A(b)) for which percentage depletion would exceed cost depletion in the absence of the depletable quantity limitations contained in section 613A(c)(1) and (6) and the consolidated taxable income limitation contained in paragraph (a) of this section,

(2) Any consolidated net operating loss carryback to the consolidated return year under §§1.1502-21 or 1.1502-21A (as appropriate), and

(3) Any consolidated net capital loss carryback to the consolidated return year under §§1.1502-22 or 1.1502-22A (as appropriate).

(c) *Allocation to oil and gas properties.*—The maximum amount allowable as a deduction under section 613A(c), after the application of paragraph (a) of this section, is allocated to properties held by members in accordance with the regulations under section 613A(d). Those regulations provide for an initial allocation and possible reallocation of the maximum allowable percentage depletion deduction among oil and gas properties. Thus, if, after the initial allocation, cost depletion exceeds the percentage depletion that would be allowable for a particular oil or gas property, cost depletion must be used for that property and the maximum amount of percentage depletion allowable as a deduction for the group is reallocated among only the remaining properties held by all members.

(d) *Carryover for disallowed amounts.*—(1) If any amount is disallowed as a deduction for the taxable year by reason of section 613A(d)(1) or paragraph (a) of this section, the disallowed amount for each oil or gas property is treated as an amount allowed as a deduction under section 613A(c), for the following taxable year for the member that owned the property, in accordance with the regulations under section 613A and paragraphs (a) and (d)(2) of this section.

(2) Any amount that was disallowed as a deduction in a separate return limitation year of a member may be carried to a consolidated return year only to the extent that 65 percent of the excess determined under paragraph (d)(3) of this section exceeds the sum of the otherwise allowable percentage depletion deductions for the member's oil and gas properties for the year.

(3) The excess determined in this subparagraph (3) for a member is the excess, if any, of adjusted consolidated taxable income for the year under paragraph (b) of this section over that income recomputed by excluding the items of income and deductions of the member.

(e) *Effective date.*—This section applies to taxable years for which the due date (without extensions) for filing returns is after September 30, 1980. [Reg. §1.1502-44.]

☐ [*T.D. 7725, 9-30-80. Amended by T.D. 8677, 6-26-96 and T.D. 8823, 6-25-99.*]

## [Reg. §5.1502-45]

**§5.1502-45. Limitation on losses to amount at risk (Temporary).**—(a) *In general.*—(1) *Scope.*—This section applies to a loss of any subsidiary if the common parent's stock meets the stock ownership requirement described in section 465(a)(1)(C).

(2) *Limitation on use of losses.*—Except as provided in paragraph (a)(4) of this section, a loss from an activity of a subsidiary during a consolidated return year is includible in the computation of consolidated taxable income (or consolidated net operating loss) and consolidated capital gain net income (or consolidated net capital loss) only to the extent the loss does not exceed the amount that the parent is at risk in the activity at the close of that subsidiary's taxable year. In addition, the sum of a subsidiary's losses from all its activities is includible only to the extent that the parent is at risk in the subsidiary at the close of that year. Any excess may not be taken into account for the consolidated return year but will be treated as a deduction allocable to that activity of the subsidiary in the first succeeding taxable year.

(3) *Amount parent is at risk in subsidiary's activity.*—The amount the parent is at risk in an activity of a subsidiary is the lesser of (i) the amount the parent is at risk in the subsidiary or (ii) the amount the subsidiary is at risk in the activity. These amounts are determined under paragraph (b) of this section and the principles of section 465. See section 465 and the regulations thereunder and the examples in paragraph (e) of this section.

(4) *Excluded activities.*—The limitation on the use of losses in paragraph (a)(2) of this section does not apply to a loss attributable to an activity described in section 465 (c)(3)(D).

(5) *Substance over form.*—Any transaction or arrangement between members (or between a member and a person that is not a member) which does not cause the parent to be economically at risk in an activity of a subsidiary will be treated in accordance with the substance of the transaction or arrangement notwithstanding any other provision of this section.

(b) *Rules for determining amount at risk.*—(1) *Excluded amounts.*—The amount a parent is at risk in an activity of a subsidiary at the close of the subsidiary's taxable year does not include any amount which would not be taken into account under section 465 were the subsidiary not a separate corporation. Thus, for example, if the amount a parent is at risk in the activity of a subsidiary is attributable to nonrecourse financing, the amount at risk is not more than the fair market value of the property (other than the subsidiary's stock or debt or assets) pledged as security.

(2) *Guarantees.*—If a parent guarantees a loan by a person other than a member to a subsidiary, the loan increases the amount the parent is at risk in the activity of the subsidiary.

(c) *Application of section 465.*—This section applies in a manner consistent with the provisions of section 465. Thus, for example, the recapture of losses provided in section 465(e) applies if the amount the parent is at risk in the activity of a subsidiary is reduced below zero.

(d) *Other consolidated return provisions unaffected.*—This section limits only the extent to which losses of a subsidiary may be used in a consolidated return year. This section does not apply for other purposes, such as § 1.1502-32 and § 1.1502-19, relating to investment in stock of a subsidiary and excess loss accounts, respectively. Thus, a loss which reduces a subsidiary's earnings and profits in a consolidated return year, but is disallowed as a deduction for the year by reason of this section, may nonetheless result in a negative adjustment to the basis of an owning member's stock in the subsidiary or create (or increase) an excess loss account.

(e) *Examples.*—The provisions of this section may be illustrated by the examples in this paragraph (e). In each example, the stock ownership requirement of section 465(a)(1)(C) is met for the stock of the parent (P), and each affiliated group files a consolidated return on a calendar year basis and comprises only the members described.

*Example (1).* In 1979, P forms S with a contribution of $200 in exchange for all of S's stock. During the year, S borrows $400 from a commercial lender and P guarantees $100 of the loan. S uses $500 of its funds to acquire a motion picture film. S incurs a loss of $120 for the year with respect to the film. At the close of 1979, the amount P is at risk in S's activity is $300. If S has no gain or loss in 1980, and there are no contributions from or distributions to P, at the close of 1980 P's amount at risk in S's activity will be $180.

*Example (2).* P forms S-1 with a capital contribution of $1 on January 1, 1980. On February 1, 1980, S-1 borrows $100 with full recourse and contributes all $101 to its newly formed subsidiary S-2. S-2 uses the proceeds to explore for natural oil and gas resources. S-2 incurs neither gain nor loss from its explorations during the taxable year. As of December 31, 1980, P is at risk in the exploration activity of S-2 only to the extent of $1.

(f) *Effective date.*—This section applies to consolidated return years ending on or after December 31, 1979. [Temporary Reg. § 5.1502-45.]

☐ [*T.D. 7685, 3-12-80.*]

**[Reg. § 1.1502-47]**

**§ 1.1502-47. Consolidated returns by life-nonlife groups.**—(a) *Scope.*—(1) *In general.*—Under section 1504(b)(2), insurance companies that are taxed under section 801 (relating to life insurance companies) are not treated as includible corporations for purposes of determining under section 1504(a) the existence of an affiliated group and the composition of its membership. Section 1504(c)(2) provides an election whereby certain life insurance companies may be treated as includible corporations, and thus members, of a group composed of other includible corporations. This section provides regulations for the making of this election and for the determination of an electing group's composition, its consolidated taxable income (or loss), and its consolidated tax liability.

(2) *General method of consolidation.*—(i) *Subgroup method.*—The regulations adopt a subgroup method to determine consolidated taxable income. One subgroup is the group's nonlife companies. The other subgroup is the group's life insurance companies. Initially, the nonlife subgroup computes nonlife consolidated taxable income and the life subgroup computes consolidated LICTI. A subgroup's in-

come may in effect be reduced by a loss of the other subgroup, subject to the limitations in sections 172 and 1503(c). The life subgroup losses consist of life consolidated net operating loss, consolidated operations loss carryovers from taxable years beginning before January 1, 2018 (consolidated operations loss carryovers), and life consolidated net capital loss. The nonlife subgroup losses consist of nonlife consolidated net operating loss and nonlife consolidated net capital loss. Consolidated taxable income is therefore defined in pertinent part as the sum of nonlife consolidated taxable income and consolidated LICTI, reduced by life subgroup losses and/or nonlife subgroup losses.

(ii) *Subgroup loss.*—A subgroup loss does not actually affect the computation of nonlife consolidated taxable income or consolidated LICTI. It merely constitutes a bottom-line adjustment in reaching consolidated taxable income. Furthermore, the amount of a subgroup's loss, if any, that is eligible to be carried back to a prior taxable year first must be carried back against income of the same subgroup before it may be used as a setoff against the other subgroup's income in the taxable year the loss arose. (See sections 172(b)(1) and 1503(c)(1); see also § 1.1502-21(b)). The carryback of losses from one subgroup may not be used to offset income of the other subgroup in the year to which the loss is to be carried. This carryback of one subgroup's loss may "bump" the other subgroup's loss that, in effect, previously reduced the income of the first subgroup. The subgroup's loss that is bumped in appropriate cases may, in effect, reduce a succeeding year's income of either subgroup. This approach gives the group the tax savings of the use of losses, but the bumping rule assures that, insofar as possible, life deductions will be matched against life income and nonlife deductions against nonlife income.

(iii) *Carryover of subgroup loss.*—A subgroup's loss may be used in a succeeding year, but in any particular succeeding year the loss must be used to reduce the income of the same subgroup before it may be used as a setoff against the other subgroup's income.

(3) *Other provisions.*—The provisions of § § 1.1502-0 through 1.1502-100 apply unless this section provides otherwise. Further, unless otherwise indicated in this section, a term used in this section has the same meaning as in sections 801-848.

(b) *Definitions.*—For purposes of this section—

(1) *Life company.*—The term *life company* means a life insurance company as defined in section 816 and subject to tax under section 801. Section 816 applies to each company separately.

(2) *Nonlife insurance company.*—The term *nonlife insurance company* has the meaning provided in § 1.1502-1(k).

(3) *Life insurance company taxable income.*—The term *life insurance company taxable income* or *LICTI* has the meaning provided in section 801(b).

(4) *Group.*—The term *group* has the meaning provided in § 1.1502-1(a). Unless otherwise indicated in this section, a group's composition is determined without regard to section 1504(b)(2).

(5) *Member.*—The term *member* has the meaning provided in § 1.1502-1(b). A life company is tentatively treated as a member for any taxable year for purposes of determining if it is an eligible corporation under paragraph (b)(12) of this section and, therefore, if it is an includible corporation under section 1504(c)(2). If such a company is eligible and includible (under section 1504(c)(2)), it will actually be treated as a member of the group.

(6) *Life member.*—A life member is a member of the group that is a life company.

(7) *Nonlife member.*—A nonlife member is a member of the group that is not a life company.

(8) *Life subgroup.*—A life subgroup is composed of those members that are life members. If the group has only one life member, it constitutes a life subgroup.

(9) *Nonlife subgroup.*—A nonlife subgroup is composed of those members that are nonlife members. If the group has only one nonlife member, it constitutes a nonlife subgroup.

(10) *Separate return year.*—The term *separate return year* has the meaning provided in § 1.1502-1(e). For purposes of this paragraph (b)(10), the term *group* is defined with regard to section 1504(b)(2) for years in which an election under section 1504(c)(2) is not in effect. Thus, a separate return year includes a taxable year for which that election is not in effect.

(11) *Separate return limitation year.*—Section 1.1502-1(f)(2) provides exceptions to the definition of the term separate return limita-

tion year. For purposes of applying those exceptions to this section, the term *group* is defined without regard to section 1504(b)(2), and the definition in this paragraph (b)(11) applies separately to the nonlife subgroup in determining nonlife consolidated taxable income under paragraph (f) of this section and to the life subgroup in determining consolidated LICTI under paragraph (g) of this section. Paragraph (h)(3)(ix) of this section defines the term separate return limitation year for purposes of determining whether the losses of one subgroup may be used against the income of the other subgroup.

(12) *Eligible corporations.*—(i) *In general.*—A corporation is an eligible corporation for a taxable year of a group only if, throughout every day of the base period the corporation—

(A) Was in existence and a member of the group determined without the exclusions in section 1504(b)(2) (see paragraphs (b)(12)iii)-(vi) of this section),

(B) Was engaged in the active conduct of a trade or business ("active business"),

(C) Did not experience a change in tax character (see paragraph (b)(12)(vii) of this section), and

(D) Did not undergo disproportionate asset acquisitions (see paragraph (b)(12)(viii) of this section).

(ii) *Base period.*—The base period consists of the common parent's five taxable years immediately preceding the group's taxable year for which the consolidated return and the determination of eligibility are made. Eligibility is determined for each consolidated return year beginning with the first year for which the election under section 1504(c)(2) is effective.

(iii) *In existence.*—Except as provided in paragraph (b)(12)(v) and (vi) of this section, a corporation organized after the base period begins is not eligible even though it is a member of the group immediately after its organization. For purposes of this paragraph (b)(12)(iii), a corporation that was a party to a reorganization described in section 368(a)(1)(F) shall be treated as the same entity both before and after the reorganization.

(iv) *Membership period.*—Except as provided in paragraph (b)(12)(v) and (vi) of this section, a corporation must have been a member of the group throughout the base period to be eligible. Thus, an ineligible corporation includes one whose stock was acquired from outside the group at any time during the base period or one which was a member of a different group (whether by application of reverse acquisition rules in § 1.1502-75(d)(3) or otherwise) at any time during the base period. For purposes of this paragraph (b)(12)(iv), the common parent of a group is treated as constituting a group (and hence is a member) during any period when it was not a member of an affiliated group within the meaning of section 1504(a) (applied without section 1504(b)(2)).

(v) *Tacking rule.*—The period during which an old corporation is in existence and a member of the group engaged in active business is included in (or tacks onto) the period for the new corporation if the following four conditions listed in this paragraph (b)(12)(v) are met. For purposes of this paragraph (b)(12)(v), a new corporation is a corporation (whether or not newly organized) during the period its eligibility depends upon the tacking rule. The four conditions are as follows—

(A) The first condition is that, at any time, 80 percent or more of the new corporation's assets it acquired (other than in the ordinary course of its trade or business) were acquired from the old corporation in one or more transactions described in section 351(a) or 381(a). This asset test is applied by using the fair market values of assets on the date they were acquired and without regard to liabilities. Assets acquired in the ordinary course of business will be excluded from total assets only if they were acquired after the new corporation became a member of the group (determined without section 1504(b)(2)). In addition, assets that the old corporation acquired from outside the group in transactions not conducted in the ordinary course of its trade or business are not included in the 80 percent (but are included in total assets) if the old corporation acquired those assets within five calendar years before the date of their transfer to the new corporation.

(B) The second condition is that at the end of the taxable year during which the first condition is first met, the old corporation and the new corporation must both have the same tax character. For purposes of this paragraph (b)(12), a corporation's tax character is the section under which it would be taxed (for example, section 11, section 801, or section 831) if it filed a separate return. If the old corporation is not in existence (or adopts a plan of complete liquidation) at the end of that taxable year, this paragraph (b)(12)(v)(B) will apply to the old corporation's taxable year immediately preceding the beginning of the taxable year during which the first condition is first met.

(C) The third condition is that, at the end of the taxable year during which the first condition is first met, the new corporation does not undergo a disproportionate asset acquisition under paragraph (b)(12)(viii) of this section.

(D) The fourth condition is that, if there is more than one old corporation, the first two conditions apply to all of the corporations. Thus, the second condition (tax character) must be met by all of the old corporations transferring assets taken into account in meeting the test in paragraph (b)(12)(v)(A) of this section.

(vi) *Old group remaining in existence.*—If the common parent of a group (or a new common parent) became the common parent in a transaction described in § 1.1502-75(b)(12) or (3) where a group remained in existence, then paragraph (b)(12)(ii)-(iv) of this section apply by treating that common parent as if it were also the previous common parent of the group that remains in existence. If this subdivision (vi) applies to a transaction, the tacking rule in paragraph (b)(12)(v) of this section does not apply to the transaction.

(vii) *Change in tax character.*—A corporation must not experience during the base period a change in tax character (as defined in paragraph (b)(12)(v)(B) of this section) if the change is attributable to an acquisition of assets from outside the group in transactions not conducted in the ordinary course of its trade or business. However, if a new corporation relies on the tacking rules in paragraph (b)(12)(v) of this section, this paragraph (b)(12)(vi) shall apply during the base period and the current consolidated return year even if the change in tax character is attributable to an asset acquisition from within the group.

(viii) *Disproportionate asset acquisition.*—To be eligible, a corporation must not undergo during the base period disproportionate asset acquisitions which are attributable to an acquisition (or a series of acquisitions) of assets from outside the group in transactions not conducted in the ordinary course of its trade or business (special acquisition). Whether special acquisitions are disproportionate is determined at the end of each base period. Whether an acquisition results in a disproportionate asset acquisition depends on all of the facts and circumstances including the following factors and rules:

(A) One factor is the portion of the insurance reserves (that is, total reserves in section 816(c), as modified by section 816(h)) of the acquiring company at the end of the base period which is attributable to special acquisitions.

(B) A second factor is the portion of the fair market value of the assets (without reduction for liabilities) of the acquiring company at the end of the base period that is attributable to special acquisitions.

(C) A third factor is the portion of the premiums generated during the last taxable year of the base period which are attributable to special acquisitions.

(D) A corporation will not experience a disproportionate asset acquisition unless 75 percent of one factor (whether or not listed in this paragraph (b)(12)(viii)) is attributable to special acquisitions.

(E) Money or other property contributed to a corporation by a shareholder that is not a member of the group (without section 1504(b)(2)) is not a special acquisition.

(F) If a new corporation relies on the tacking rules in paragraph (b)(12)(v) of this section, this paragraph (b)(12)(viii) applies to that corporation during a consolidated return year. Thus, if at any time during a consolidated return year, a new corporation undergoes a disproportionate asset acquisition, the corporation becomes ineligible at that time.

(13) *Ineligible corporation.*—A corporation that is not an eligible corporation is ineligible. If a life company is ineligible, it is not treated under section 1504(c)(2) as an includible corporation. Losses of a nonlife member arising in years when it is ineligible may not be used under section 1503(c)(2) and paragraph (g) of this section to set off the income of a life member. If a life company is ineligible and is the common parent of the group (without regard to section 1504(b)(2)), the election under section 1504(c)(2) may not be made.

(14) *Examples.*—The following examples illustrate this paragraph (b). In each example, L indicates a life company, another letter indicates a non-life company, and each corporation uses the calendar year as its taxable year.

(i) *Example 1.*—P has owned all of the stock of S since 2012. On January 1, 2018, P purchased all of the stock of $L_1$ which owns all of the stock of $L_2$ and $S_2$. $L_1$ and $L_2$ are treated as members for purposes of determining if they are eligible for 2020. However, for 2020, $L_1$, $L_2$, and $S_2$ are ineligible because none of them has been a member of the group for P's five taxable years preceding 2020. For 2020, $L_1$ and $L_2$ may elect to file a consolidated return because they constitute an affiliated group under section 1504(c)(1), and P and S may file a consolidated return. $S_2$ must file its own separate return for 2020.

(ii) *Example 2.*—Since 2012, L1 has been a life company owning all the stock of L2. In 2018, L1 transfers assets to S1, a new nonlife insurance company subject to taxation under section 831(a). For 2020, only L1 and L2 are eligible corporations. The tacking rule in paragraph (b)(12)(v) of this section does not apply in 2020 because the old corporation (L1) and the new corporation (S1) do not have the same tax character.

(iii) *Example 3.*—Since 2012, L has owned all the stock of $L_1$ which has owned all the stock of $S_1$, a nonlife insurance company. $L_1$ writes some accident and health insurance business. In 2018, $L_1$ transfers this business, and $S_1$ transfers some of its business, to a new nonlife insurance company, $S_2$, in a transaction described in section 351(a). The property transferred to $S_2$ by $L_1$ had a fair market value of $50 million. The property transferred by $S_1$ had a fair market value of $40 million. $S_2$ is ineligible for 2020 because the tacking rule in paragraph (b)(12)(v) of this section does not apply. The old corporations ($L_1$ and $S_1$) and the new corporation ($S_2$) do not all have the same tax character. See paragraph (b)(12)(v)(B) and (D) of this section. The result would be the same if $L_1$ transferred other property (for example stock and securities) with the same value, rather than accident and health insurance contracts, to $S_2$.

(iv) *Example 4.*—Since 2012, P has owned all the stock of S and $L_1$. $L_1$ is a large life company engaged in active business since 2012. On January 1, 2020, $L_1$ transfers in a section 351(a) transaction assets (not acquired from outside the group) to a new life company, $L_2$. For 2020, $L_2$ is eligible because under paragraph (b)(12)(v) of this section, $L_2$ is considered to have been in existence and a member of the group engaged in the active business since 2012 which is the period $L_1$, the old corporation, was in existence and a member of the group so engaged.

(v) *Example 5.*—The facts are the same as in example (4). Assume that the fair market value of the assets $L_1$ transferred to $L_2$ was $10 million on January 1, 2020 and that $L_2$ acquired no other assets prior to June 30, 2021. Assume further that on January 1, 2021, $L_1$ acquires (other than in the ordinary course of its trade or business) assets having a fair market value of $40 million from $L_3$, an unrelated life company. On June 30, 2021, $L_1$ transfers those assets to $L_2$. $L_2$ becomes ineligible on June 30, 2021. Since by fair market values, 80 percent (in other words, 40/50) of $L_2$'s assets are attributable to special acquisitions, $L_2$ has undergone a disproportionate asset acquisition at that time. See paragraph (b)(12)(viii)(B), (D), and (F) of this section.

(vi) *Example 6.*—The facts are the same as in example (5) except that $L_1$ transfers assets (other than life insurance contracts) having a fair market value of $40 million to $L_2$ and $L_2$ purchases the assets of $L_3$ on June 30, 2021. The result of the 1983 acquisition is the same as in example (5).

(vii) *Example 7.*—The facts are the same as in example (5) except the acquired assets acquired by $L_2$ in 2021 from $L_1$ have a fair market value of $20 million. In 2021, $L_2$ had $1 million of premiums on its pre-existing contracts but premiums generated by the acquired business for the entire year would have been $2 million. $L_2$ is eligible in 2021 because it did not experience a disproportionate asset acquisition on June 30, 2021.

(viii) *Example 8.*—Since 2012, L, a State A corporation, has owned all of the stock of $L_1$ and $S_1$. On January 1, 2020, L merges into $L_3$, a smaller State B corporation, which owns the stock of $S_2$. The transaction is a reverse acquisition described in §1.1502-75(d)(3) and the group of which L was the common parent remains in existence. Under paragraph (b)(12)(vi) of this section, $L_3$ is eligible for 2020. However, $S_2$ is ineligible in 2020 under paragraph (b)(12)(iv) of this section.

(ix) *Example 9.*—The facts are the same as in example (8) except that L acquires the stock of $L_3$. $L_3$ and $S_2$ are both ineligible for 2020. On January 1, 2021, the fair market value of $L_3$'s assets are $5 million (without liabilities) and on that date L transfers assets (not acquired from outside the group) having a fair market value of $95 million (without liabilities) to $L_3$. L and $L_3$ are life companies at the end of 2021. $L_3$ is eligible in 2021 under the tacking rule in paragraph (b)(12)(v) of this section. $S_2$ is ineligible in that year. The result would be the same if $L_3$ was not a life company prior to January 1, 2021. See paragraph (b)(12)(v)(B) of this section.

(x) *Example 10.*—Since 2012, X, a foreign corporation, has owned all the stock of $S_2$ and $S_1$, and $S_1$ has owned all of the stock of $L_1$. On January 1, 2020, X incorporates a new U.S. company P, and transfers the stock of $S_1$ and $S_2$ to P. Assume that under §1.1502-75(d)(3) (relating to reverse acquisitions), the $S_1$-$L_1$ affiliated

group remains in existence. Under paragraph (d)(12)(vi) of this section, P, $S_1$, and $L_1$ are eligible but $S_2$ is ineligible. The result would be the same if X were an individual.

(xi) *Example 11.*—The facts are the same as in *Example (10)* except that X owns all of the stock of $S_1$, $L_1$, and $S_2$. In addition, on January 1, 2020, X transfers the stock of $S_1$ and $S_2$ to $L_1$. $L_1$ is eligible in 2020 under paragraph (d)(12)(iv) of this section. $L_1$ would still be eligible even if it owned a subsidiary during the base period but sold the subsidiary prior to January 1, 2020, $S_1$ and $S_2$ are ineligible in 2020.

(xii) *Example 12.*—Since 2012, $S_1$ has owned all of the stock of $L_1$. $S_2$, an unrelated company, has owned all of the stock of $L_2$ and $S_3$ for 10 years. $S_1$ and $S_2$ are active nonlife insurance companies and not holding companies. On January 1, 2020, $S_1$ and $S_2$ merge into a new nonlife insurance company, S, in a transaction described in §1.1502-75(d)(3) so that the group of which $S_1$ was the common parent remains in existence. S and $L_1$ are eligible in 2020 under paragraph (b)(12)(vi) of this section. $L_2$ and $S_3$ are ineligible.

(xiii) *Example 13.*—The facts are the same as in *Example (12)* except that $S_2$ (the first corporation in §1.1502-75(d)(3)) acquires the stock of $S_1$ in exchange for the stock of $S_2$. The result is that only $S_2$, $S_1$, and $L_1$ are eligible in 2020.

(c) *Election.*—(1) *In general.*—The election under section 1504(c)(2) may not be made if the group's common parent is an ineligible life company. The election under section 1504(c)(2) may only be made by the common parent of the group (as defined in section 1504(c)(2) without the exclusions in section 1504(b)(2)). For example, assume that P owns all of the stock of $L_1$, an eligible life company, which owns the stock of $S_1$. Assume further that P also owns the stock of $L_2$, an ineligible life member, which (for more than five years) has owned the stock of a nonlife company, $S_2$. Only P may make the election and, if it does so, P, $L_1$, and $S_1$ may file a consolidated return under this section. $L_2$ may not make the election under section 1504(c)(2) and may not file a consolidated return with $S_2$.

(2) *How election is made.*—(i) *General rule.*—The election under section 1504(c)(2) is generally made by the group's common parent in the same manner (and it has the same effect) as the election to file a consolidated return is made under §1.1502-75(a) and (b) for a group which did not file a consolidated return for the immediately preceding taxable year. The procedure for making the election under section 1504(c)(2) is the same whether or not a consolidated return was filed by the life members or the nonlife members for the immediately preceding taxable year.

(ii) *Special rule.*—Notwithstanding the general rule, however, if the nonlife members in the group filed a consolidated return for the immediately preceding taxable year and had executed and filed a Form 1122 that is effective for the preceding year, then such members will be treated as if they filed a Form 1122 when they join in the filing of a consolidated return under section 1504(c)(2) and they will be deemed to consent to the regulations under this section. However, an affiliation schedule (Form 851) must be filed by the group and the life members must execute a Form 1122 in the manner prescribed in §1.1502-75(h)(2).

(3) *Irrevocability.*—Except as provided in §1.1502-75(c), the election under section 1504(c)(2) is irrevocable.

(4) *Cross reference.*—If an election is made under section 1504(c)(2), see §1.1502-75(e) and (f) for rules that apply for not including (or including) a member or a nonmember in the consolidated return.

(d) *Effect of election.*—If the common parent makes the election under section 1504(c)(2), the following rules apply:

(1) *Termination of group.*—A mere election under section 1504(c)(2) will not cause the creation of a new group or the termination of an affiliated group that files a consolidated return in the immediately preceding taxable year.

(2) *Effect of eligibility.*—If a life member is eligible after an election under section 1504(c)(2), it may not be included as a member of an affiliated group as defined in section 1504(c)(1).

(3) *Eligible and ineligible life companies.*—If any life company was a member of an affiliated group of life companies (as defined in section 1504(c)(1)) but is ineligible for a taxable year for which the election under section 1504(c)(2) is effective, that year is not a separate return year merely by reason of the election under section 1504(c)(2) in applying §§1.1502-13 and 1.1502-19 to transactions occurring in prior consolidated return years of that affiliated group. In addition, if more than one ineligible life member of the group (as defined in section 1504(c)(1)) joined in the filing of a consolidated

return in the taxable year immediately preceding the year for which the election under section 1504(c)(2) is effective and, solely as a result of the election, one of the ineligible life members becomes the common parent of such a group (section 1504(c)(1)), the group must continue to file a consolidated return. For example, assume that $L_1$ owns all of the stock of $S_1$ and all of the stock of $L_2$. $L_2$ owns the stock of $L_3$. $L_1$, $L_2$, and $L_3$ are life companies and $S_1$ is a nonlife company. Assume further that in 2019, $L_1$, $L_2$, and $L_3$ file a consolidated return but $L_1$ makes the election under section 1504(c)(2) for 2020 and $L_2$ and $L_3$ are ineligible. $L_2$ and $L_3$ must continue to file a consolidated return in 2020. Moreover, $L_2$ could elect in 2020 to file a consolidated return (section 1504(c)(1)) with $L_3$ even if they did not file a consolidated return in 2019 with $L_1$.

(4) *Inclusion of life company.*—If a life company is ineligible in the consolidated return year for which the election is effective, it will be treated as an includible corporation for the common parent's first taxable year in which the company becomes eligible.

(5) *Dividends received deduction.*—(i) *Dividends received by an includible insurance company.*—Dividends received by an includible member insurance company, taxed under either section 801 or section 831, from another includible member of the group are treated for Federal income tax purposes as if the group did not file a consolidated return. See sections 818(e)(2) and 805(a)(4)for rules regarding a member taxed under section 801, and see sections 832(g) and 832(b)(5)(B) through (E) for rules regarding a member taxed under section 831.

(ii) *Other dividends.*—Dividends received from a life company member of the group that are not subject to paragraph (d)(5)(i) of this section are not included in gross income of the distributee member. See section 1504(c)(2)(B)(i). If the distributee corporation is a nonlife insurance company subject to tax under section 831, the rules of section 832(b)(5)(B) through (E) apply.

(6) *Controlled group.*—Sections 1563(a)(4), (b)(2)(D), and (b)(3)(C) (insofar as it applies to corporations described in section 1563(b)(2)(D)) do not apply to any eligible or ineligible life company that is a member of the group for a taxable year during which the election is effective.

(7) *Consolidated tax.*—The tax liability of a group for a consolidated return year (before application of credits against that tax) is computed on a consolidated basis by adding together the following taxes:

(i) The tax imposed under section 11 on consolidated taxable income (as determined under paragraph (e) of this section). The taxes imposed under sections 801(a) and 831(a) will each be treated as a tax imposed under section 11.

(ii) Any taxes described in §1.1502-2 (other than in §1.1502-2(a)(1), (a)(6), and (a)(7)).

(e) *Consolidated taxable income.*—The consolidated taxable income is the sum of the following two amounts:

(1) *Nonlife consolidated taxable income.*—The nonlife consolidated taxable income (as defined in paragraph (f) of this section) of the nonlife subgroup, as set off by the life subgroup losses as provided in paragraph (j) of this section. The amount in this paragraph (e)(1) may not be less than zero.

(2) *Consolidated LICTI.*—The consolidated LICTI (as defined in paragraph (g)(1) of this section) of the life subgroup, as set off by the nonlife subgroup losses as provided in paragraph (h) of this section. The amount in this paragraph (e)(2) may not be less than zero.

(f) *Nonlife consolidated taxable income.*—(1) *In general.*—Nonlife consolidated taxable income is the consolidated taxable income of the nonlife subgroup, computed under §1.1502-11 as modified by this paragraph (f). For this purpose, separate taxable income of a member includes insurance company taxable income (as defined in section 832).

(2) *Nonlife consolidated net operating loss deduction.*—(i) *In general.*—In applying §§1.1502-21, the rules in this paragraph (f)(2) apply in determining for the nonlife subgroup the nonlife net operating loss and the portion of the nonlife net operating loss carryovers and carrybacks to the taxable year.

(ii) *Nonlife CNOL.*—The nonlife consolidated net operating loss is determined under §1.1502-21(e) by treating the nonlife subgroup as the group.

(iii) *Carrybacks.*—The portion of the nonlife consolidated net operating loss for the nonlife subgroup described in paragraph (f)(2)(vi) of this section, if any, that is eligible to be carried back to

prior taxable years under §1.1502-21 is carried back to the appropriate years (whether consolidated or separate) before the nonlife consolidated net operating loss may be used as a nonlife subgroup loss under paragraphs (e)(2) and (h) of this section to set off consolidated LICTI in the year the loss arose. The election under section 172(b)(3) to relinquish the entire carryback period for the net operating loss of the nonlife subgroup may be made by the agent for the group within the meaning of §1.1502-77.

(iv) *Subgroup rule.*—In determining the portion of the nonlife consolidated net operating loss that is absorbed when the loss is carried back to a consolidated return year, §1.1502-21 is applied by treating the nonlife subgroup as the group. Therefore, the absorption is determined without taking into account any life subgroup losses that were previously reported on a consolidated return as setting off nonlife consolidated taxable income for the year to which the nonlife subgroup loss is carried back.

(v) *Carryover.*—The portion of the nonlife consolidated net operating loss that is not absorbed in a prior year as a carryback, or as a nonlife subgroup loss that set off consolidated LICTI for the year the loss arose, constitutes a nonlife carryover under this paragraph (f)(2) to reduce nonlife consolidated taxable income before that portion may constitute a nonlife subgroup loss that sets off consolidated LICTI for a particular year. For limitations on the use of nonlife carryovers to offset nonlife consolidated taxable income or consolidated LICTI, see §1.1502-21.

(vi) *Portion of nonlife consolidated net operating loss that is carried back to prior taxable years.*—The portion of the nonlife consolidated net operating loss that (absent an election to waive carrybacks) is carried back to the two preceding taxable years is the sum of the nonlife subgroup's farming loss (within the meaning of section 172(b)(1)(B)(ii)) and the amount of the subgroup's net operating loss that is attributable to nonlife insurance companies (as determined under §1.1502-21). For rules governing the absorption of net operating loss carrybacks, including limitations on the amount of net operating loss carrybacks that may be absorbed in prior taxable years, see §1.1502-21(b).

(vii) *Example.*—P, a holding company that is not an insurance company, owns all of the stock of S, a nonlife insurance company, and L1, a life insurance company. L1 owns all of the stock of L2, a life insurance company. Both L1 and L2 satisfy the eligibility requirements of §1.1502-47(b)(12). Each corporation uses the calendar year as its taxable year, and no corporation has incurred farming losses (within the meaning of section 172(b)(1)(B)(ii)). For 2021, the group first files a consolidated return for which the election under section 1504(c)(2) is effective. P and S filed consolidated returns for 2019 and 2020. In 2021, the P-S group sustains a nonlife consolidated net operating loss that is attributable entirely to S (see §1.1502-21(b)). The election in 2021 under section 1504(c)(2) does not result under paragraph (d)(1) of this section in the creation of a new group or the termination of the P-S group. The loss is carried back to the consolidated return years 2019 and 2020 of P and S. Pursuant to §1.1502-21(b), the loss may be used to offset S's income in 2019 and 2020 without limitation, and the loss may be used to offset P's income in those years, subject to the limitation in section 172(a) (see §1.1502-21(b)). The portion of the loss not absorbed in 2019 and 2020 may serve as a nonlife subgroup loss in 2021 that may set off the consolidated LICTI of L1 and L2 under paragraphs (e)(2) and (h) of this section.

(3) *Nonlife consolidated capital gain net income or loss.*—(i) *In general.*—In applying §1.1502-22, the rules in this paragraph (f)(3) apply in determining for the nonlife subgroup the nonlife consolidated capital gain net income or loss and the portion of the nonlife net capital loss carryovers and carrybacks to the taxable year. In particular, the nonlife consolidated capital gain net income and nonlife consolidated net capital loss are determined under the principles of §1.1502-22 by treating the nonlife subgroup as the group.

(ii) *Additional principles.*—In applying §1.1502-22 to nonlife consolidated net capital loss carryovers and carrybacks, the principles set forth in paragraph (f)(2)(iii) through (v) of this section for applying §1.1502-21 to nonlife consolidated net operating loss carryovers and carrybacks also apply, without regard to the limitation in paragraph (f)(2)(vi) of this section.

(iii) *Special rules.*—The nonlife consolidated net capital loss is reduced, for purposes of determining the carryovers and carrybacks under §1.1502-22(b), by the lesser of—

(A) The aggregate of the additional capital loss deductions allowed under section 832(c)(5), or

(B) The nonlife consolidated taxable income computed without capital gains and losses.

(g) *Consolidated LICTI.*—(1) *General rule.*—Consolidated LICTI is the consolidated taxable income of the life subgroup, computed under § 1.1502-11 as modified by this paragraph (g).

(2) *Life consolidated net operating loss deduction.*—(i) *In general.*—In applying § 1.1502-21, the rules in this paragraph (g)(2) apply in determining for the life subgroup the life net operating loss and the portion of the life net operating loss carryovers and carrybacks to the taxable year.

(ii) *Life CNOL.*—The life consolidated net operating loss is determined under § 1.1502-21(e) by treating the life subgroup as the group.

(iii) *Carrybacks.*—(A) *General rule.*—The portion of the life consolidated net operating loss for the life subgroup, if any, that is eligible to be carried back under § 1.1502-21 is carried back to the appropriate years (whether consolidated or separate) before the life consolidated net operating loss may be used as a life subgroup loss under paragraphs (e)(1) and (j) of this section to set off nonlife consolidated taxable income in the year the loss arose. The election under section 172(b)(3) to relinquish the entire carryback period for the consolidated net operating loss of the life subgroup may be made by the agent for the group within the meaning of § 1.1502-77.

(B) *Special rule for life consolidated net operating losses arising in 2018, 2019, or 2020.*—If a life consolidated net operating loss arising in a taxable year beginning after December 31, 2017, and before January 1, 2021, is carried back to a life insurance company taxable year beginning before January 1, 2018, then such life consolidated net operating loss is treated as an operations loss carryback (within the meaning of section 810, as in effect prior to its repeal) of such company to such taxable year.

(iv) *Subgroup rule.*—In determining the portion of the life consolidated net operating loss that is absorbed when the loss is carried back to a consolidated return year, § 1.1502-21 is applied by treating the life subgroup as the group. Therefore, the absorption is determined without taking into account any nonlife subgroup losses that were previously reported on a consolidated return as setting off life consolidated taxable income for the year to which the life subgroup loss is carried back.

(v) *Carryovers.*—The portion of the life consolidated net operating loss that is not absorbed in a prior year as a carryback, or as a life subgroup loss that set off nonlife consolidated taxable income for the year the loss arose, constitutes a life carryover under this paragraph (g)(2) to reduce consolidated LICTI before that portion may constitute a life subgroup loss that sets off nonlife consolidated taxable income for that particular year. For limitations on the use of life carryovers to offset nonlife consolidated taxable income or consolidated LICTI, see § 1.1502-21(b).

(3) *Life consolidated capital gain net income or loss.*—(i) [Reserved].

(ii) *Life consolidated net capital loss carryovers and carrybacks.*—The life consolidated net capital loss carryovers and carrybacks for the life subgroup are determined by applying the principles of § 1.1502-22 as modified by the following rules in this paragraph (g)(3)(ii):

(A) Life consolidated net capital loss is first carried back (or apportioned to the life members for separate return years) to be absorbed by life consolidated capital gain net income without regard to any nonlife subgroup capital losses and before the life consolidated net capital loss may serve as a life subgroup capital loss that sets off nonlife consolidated capital gain net income in the year the life consolidated net capital loss arose.

(B) If a life consolidated net capital loss is not carried back or is not a life subgroup loss that sets off nonlife consolidated capital gain net income in the year the life consolidated net capital loss arose, then it is carried over to the particular year under this paragraph (g)(3)(ii) first against life consolidated capital gain net income before it may serve as a life subgroup capital loss that sets off nonlife consolidated capital gain net income in that particular year.

(h) *Consolidated LICTI setoff by nonlife subgroup losses.*—(1) *In general.*—The nonlife subgroup losses consist of the nonlife consolidated net operating loss and the nonlife consolidated net capital loss. Under paragraph (e)(2) of this section, consolidated LICTI is set off by the amounts of these two consolidated losses specified in paragraph (h)(2) of this section. The setoff is subject to the rules and limitations in paragraph (h)(3) of this section.

(2) *Amount of setoff.*—(i) *Current year.*—Consolidated LICTI for the current taxable year is set off by the portion of the nonlife consolidated net operating loss and nonlife consolidated net capital loss arising in that year that cannot be carried back under paragraph

(f) of this section to prior taxable years (whether consolidated or separate return years) of the nonlife subgroup.

(ii) *Carryovers.*—The portion of the offsettable nonlife consolidated net operating loss or nonlife consolidated net capital loss that has not been used as a nonlife subgroup loss setoff against consolidated LICTI in the year it arose may be carried over to succeeding taxable years under the principles of § 1.1502-21 (relating to net operating loss deduction) or § 1.1502-22 (relating to net capital loss carryovers). However, in any particular succeeding year, the losses will be used under paragraph (f) of this section in computing nonlife consolidated taxable income before being used in that year as a nonlife subgroup loss that sets off consolidated LICTI. Additionally, the amount of consolidated LICTI that may be offset by nonlife consolidated net operating loss carryovers may be subject to limitation (see section 172 and § 1.1502-21).

(3) *Nonlife subgroup loss rules and limitations.*—The nonlife subgroup losses are subject to the following operating rules and limitations:

(i) *Separate return years.*—The carryovers in paragraph (h)(2)(ii) of this section may include net operating losses and net capital losses of the nonlife members arising in separate return years that may be carried over to a succeeding year under the principles (including limitations) of §§ 1.1502-21 and 1.1502-22. But see paragraph (h)(3)(ix) of this section.

(ii) *Capital loss.*—Nonlife consolidated net capital loss sets off consolidated LICTI only to the extent of life consolidated capital gain net income (as determined under paragraph (g)(4) of this section) and this setoff applies before any nonlife consolidated net operating loss sets off consolidated LICTI.

(iii) *Capital gain.*—Life consolidated capital gain net income is zero in any taxable year in which the life subgroup has a life consolidated net operating loss and, in any taxable year, it may not exceed consolidated LICTI.

(iv) *Ordering rule.*—Consolidated LICTI for a consolidated return year is set off by nonlife subgroup losses for that year before being set off (under paragraph (h)(2)(ii) of this section) by a carryover of a nonlife subgroup loss to that year. The amount of consolidated LICTI that may be offset by nonlife consolidated net operating loss carryovers may be subject to limitation (see section 172 and § 1.1502-21).

(v) *Setoff at bottom line.*—The setoff of nonlife subgroup losses against consolidated LICTI does not affect life member deductions that depend in whole or in part on taxable income. Thus, the setoff does not affect the amount of consolidated LICTI for any taxable year but it merely constitutes an adjustment in arriving at the group's consolidated taxable income under paragraph (e) of this section.

(vi) *Ineligible nonlife member.*—(A) The offsetable nonlife consolidated net operating loss that arises in any consolidated return year (that may be set off against consolidated LICTI in the current taxable year or in a succeeding taxable year) is the amount computed under paragraph (f)(2)(ii) of this section reduced by the ineligible NOL. For purposes of this paragraph (h)(3), the "ineligible NOL" is in the year the loss arose the amount of the separate net operating loss (determined under §§ 1.1502-21(b)) of any nonlife member that is ineligible in that year (and not the portion of the nonlife consolidated net operating loss attributable under §§ 1.1502-21(b) to such a member).

(B) The carryovers of offsetable nonlife net operating losses under paragraph (h)(2)(ii) of this section do not include an ineligible NOL arising in a consolidated return year or a loss attributable to an ineligible member arising in a separate return year. See section 1503(c)(2).

(C) For absorption within the nonlife subgroup of an ineligible NOL arising in a consolidated return year or a loss of an ineligible member arising in a separate return year which is not a separate return limitation year under paragraph (h)(3)(ix) of this section, see paragraph (h)(3)(vii) of this section.

(vii) *Absorption of ineligible NOL.*—(A) If all or a portion of a nonlife member's ineligible NOL (determined under paragraph (h)(3)(vi)(A) of this section) may be carried back or carried over under paragraph (f)(2) of this section to a particular consolidated return year of the nonlife subgroup (absorption year), then notwithstanding § 1.1502-21(b), the amount carried to the absorption year will be absorbed by that member's contribution (to the extent thereof) to nonlife consolidated taxable income for that year, subject to the limitation in section 172(a).

(B) For purposes of paragraph (h)(3)(vii)(A) of this section, a member's contribution to nonlife consolidated taxable income for an absorption year is the amount of such income (computed without the portion of the nonlife consolidated net operating loss deduction attributable to taxable years subsequent to the year the loss arose), minus such consolidated taxable income recomputed by excluding both that member's items of income and deductions for the absorption year. The deductions of the member include the prior application of this paragraph (h)(3)(vii) to the absorption of the nonlife consolidated net operating loss deduction for losses arising in taxable years prior to the particular loss year.

(viii) *Election to relinquish carryback.*—The offsetable nonlife consolidated net operating loss does not include the amount that could be carried back under paragraph (f)(2) of this section but for the election by the agent for the group (within the meaning of § 1.1502-77) under section 172(b)(3) to relinquish the carryback. See section 1503(c)(1).

(ix) *Separate return limitation year.*—The offsetable nonlife consolidated net operating and capital loss carryovers do not include any losses attributable to a nonlife member that were sustained (A) in a separate return limitation year (determined without section 1504(b)(2)) of that member (or a predecessor), or (B) in a separate return year, in which an election was in effect under neither section 1504(c)(2) nor section 243(b)(3).

(x) *Percentage limitation.*—The offsetable nonlife consolidated net operating losses that may be set off against consolidated LICTI in a particular year may not exceed a percentage limitation. This limitation is the applicable percentage in section 1503(c)(1) of the lesser of two amounts. The first amount is the sum of the offsetable nonlife consolidated net operating losses under paragraph (h)(2) of this section that may serve in the particular year (determined without this limitation) as a setoff against consolidated LICTI. The second amount is consolidated LICTI in the particular year reduced by any nonlife consolidated net capital loss that sets off consolidated LICTI in that year.

(xi) *Further limitation.*—Any offsetable nonlife consolidated net operating loss remaining after applying the percentage limitation that is carried over to a succeeding taxable year may not be set off against the consolidated LICTI attributable to a life member that was not an eligible life member in the year the loss arose. See section 1503(c)(2).

(xii) *Restoration rule.*—The carryback of a life consolidated net operating loss or life consolidated net capital loss under paragraph (g) of this section that reduces consolidated LICTI (or life consolidated capital gain net income) for a prior year may reduce the amount of nonlife subgroup losses that would offset consolidated LICTI in that prior year. Thus, that amount may be carried over under paragraph (f)(2) or (3) of this section from that prior year in determining nonlife consolidated taxable income in a succeeding year or serve as offsetable nonlife subgroup losses in a succeeding year.

(4) *Examples.*—The following examples illustrate the principles of this paragraph (f). In the examples, L indicates a life company, S is a nonlife insurance company, another letter indicates a nonlife company that is not an insurance company, no company has farming losses (within the meaning of section 172(b)(1)(B)(ii)), and each corporation uses the calendar year as its taxable year.

(i) *Example 1.*—P owns all of the stock of L and S. S owns all of the stock of I, a nonlife member that is an ineligible corporation for 2021 under paragraph (b)(13) of this section. For 2021, the group elects under section 1504(c)(2) to file a consolidated return. For 2021, assume that any nonlife consolidated net operating loss may not be carried back to a prior taxable year. Other facts are summarized in the following table.

| | Separate taxable income (loss) |
|---|---|
| P | $100 |
| S | (100) |
| I | (100) |
| Nonlife consolidated net operating loss | (100) |

Under paragraph (h)(3)(vi) of this section, P's separate income is considered to absorb the loss of S, an eligible member, first and the offsetable nonlife consolidated net operating loss is zero, that is the consolidated net operating loss ($100) reduced by I's loss ($100). The consolidated net operating loss ($100) may be carried over, but since it is entirely attributable to I (an ineligible member that is not a nonlife insurance company) its use is subject to the restrictions in paragraph (h)(3)(vi) of this section and section 172(a). The result

would be the same if the group contained two additional members, $S_1$, an eligible member, and $I_1$, an ineligible member, where $S_1$ had a loss of ($100) and $I_1$ had income of $100.

(ii) *Example 2.*—(A) The facts are the same as in paragraph (f)(4)(i) of this section, except that, for 2021, S's separate net operating loss is $200. Assume further that L's consolidated LICTI is $200. Under paragraph (f)(3)(vi) of this section, the offsetable nonlife consolidated net operating loss is $100 (the nonlife consolidated net operating loss computed under paragraph (f)(2)(ii) of this section ($200), reduced by the separate net operating loss of I ($100)). The offsetable nonlife consolidated net operating loss that may be set off against consolidated LICTI in 2021 is $35 (35 percent of the lesser of the offsetable $100 or consolidated LICTI of $200). See section 1503(c)(1) and paragraph (f)(3)(x) of this section. S carries over a loss of $65, and I carries over a loss of $100, to 2022 under paragraph (f)(2) of this section to be used against nonlife consolidated taxable income (consolidated net operating loss ($200) less amount used in 2021 ($35)). Under paragraph (f)(2)(ii) of this section, the offsetable nonlife consolidated net operating loss that may be carried to 2022 is $65 ($100 minus $35). The facts and results are summarized in the following table.

**Table 1 to paragraph (f)(4)(ii)(A)**
(Dollars omitted)

| | | Facts | Offsetable | Limit | Unused Loss |
|---|---|---|---|---|---|
| | | (a) | (b) | (c) | (d) |
| 1 | P | 100 | | | |
| 2 | S | (200) | (100) | | (65) |
| 3 | I | (100) | | | (100) |
| 4 | Nonlife Subgroup | (200) | (100) | (100) | (165) |
| 5 | L | 200 | | 200 | |
| 6 | 35% of lower of line 4(c) or 5(c) | | | 35 | |
| 7 | Unused offsetable loss | | | | (65) |

(B) Accordingly, under paragraph (e) of this section, consolidated taxable income is $165 (line 5(a) minus line 6(c)).

(iii) *Example 3.*—The facts are the same as in paragraph (f)(4)(ii) of this section, with the following additions for 2022. The nonlife subgroup has nonlife consolidated taxable income of $50 (all of which is attributable to I) before the nonlife consolidated net operating loss deduction under paragraph (f)(2) of this section. Consolidated LICTI is $100. Under paragraph (f)(2) of this section, $50 of the nonlife consolidated net operating loss carryover ($165) is used in 2022 and, under paragraph (f)(3)(vi) and (vii) of this section, the portion used in 2022 is attributable to I, the ineligible nonlife member. Accordingly, the offsetable nonlife consolidated net operating loss from 2021 under paragraph (f)(3)(ii) of this section is $65, the unused loss from 2021. The offsetable nonlife consolidated net operating loss in 2022 is $22.75 (35 percent of the lesser of the offsetable loss of $65 or consolidated LICTI of $100). Accordingly, under paragraph (e) of this section, consolidated taxable income is $77.25 (consolidated LICTI of $100 minus the offsetable loss of $22.75).

(iv) *Example 4.*—P owns all of the stock of S and L. For 2021, all corporations are eligible corporations, and the group elects under section 1504(c)(2) to file a consolidated return, the nonlife consolidated net operating loss is $100, and the nonlife consolidated net capital loss is $50. Assume that the losses may not be carried back and the capital losses are not attributable to built-in deductions under paragraph (h)(3)(ix) of this section. Other facts and the results are set forth in the following table:

| | P-S | L |
|---|---|---|
| 1. Nonlife consolidated net operating loss | ($100) | |
| 2. Nonlife consolidated capital loss | (50) | |
| 3. Consolidated LICTI | | $100 |
| 4. Life consolidated capital gain net income included in line 3 | | 50 |
| 5. Offsetable: | | |
| (a) 35% of lower of line (1) or line (3) - (4) | (17.5) | |
| (b) Line 2 | (50) | |
| (c) Total | (67.5) | |
| 6. Unused losses available to be carried over: | | |
| (a) From line 1 (line 1 minus line 5(a)) | (82.5) | |
| (b) From line 2 (line 2 minus line 5(b)) | 0 | |

Accordingly, under paragraph (e) of this section consolidated taxable income is $32.5, that is line 3 minus line 5(c).

(i) [Reserved]

(j) *Nonlife consolidated taxable income set off by life subgroup losses.*—(1) *In general.*—The life subgroup losses consist of the life consolidated net operating loss and consolidated operations loss carryovers and the life consolidated net capital loss. Under paragraph (e)(1) of this section, nonlife consolidated taxable income is set off by the amounts of these two consolidated losses specified in paragraph (j)(2) of this section, subject to the rules and limitations in paragraph (j)(3) of this section.

(2) *Amount of setoff.*—The portion of the life consolidated net operating loss and consolidated operations loss carryovers or life consolidated net capital loss that may be set off against nonlife consolidated taxable income (determined under paragraph (f) of this section) is determined by applying the rules prescribed in paragraphs (h)(2) and (3) of this section in the following manner:

(i) Substitute the term "life" for "nonlife", and vice versa.

(ii) Substitute the term "nonlife consolidated taxable income" for "consolidated LICTI", and vice versa.

(iii) Substitute the term "life consolidated net operating loss and consolidated operations loss carryovers" for "nonlife consolidated net operating loss", and "paragraph (g)" for "paragraph (f)".

(iv) Paragraphs (h)(3)(vi), (vii), (x), and (xi) of this section do not apply to a consolidated LO.

(v) The setoff of life subgroup losses against nonlife consolidated taxable income does not affect nonlife member deductions that depend in whole or in part on taxable income.

(3) *Examples.*—The following examples illustrate the principles of this paragraph (j). In the examples, L indicates a life company, S is a nonlife insurance company, another letter indicates a nonlife company that is not an insurance company, no company has farming losses (within the meaning of section 172(b)(1)(B)(ii)), and each corporation uses the calendar year as its taxable year.

(i) *Example 1.*—P, S, L1 and L2 constitute a group that elects under section 1504(c)(2) to file a consolidated return for 2021. In 2021, the nonlife subgroup consolidated taxable income is $100 and there is $20 of nonlife consolidated net capital loss that cannot be carried back under paragraph (f) of this section to taxable years (whether consolidated or separate) preceding 2021. The nonlife subgroup has no carryover from years prior to 2021. The life consolidated net operating loss is $150, which under paragraph (g) of this section includes life consolidated capital gain net income of $25. Since life consolidated capital gain net income is zero for 2021 (see paragraph (h)(3)(iii) of this section), the nonlife capital loss offset is zero (see paragraph (h)(3)(ii) of this section). However, $100 of life consolidated net operating loss sets off the $100 nonlife consolidated taxable income in 2021. The life subgroup carries under paragraph (g)(2) of this section to 2022 $50 of the life consolidated net operating loss ($150 minus $100). The $50 carryover will be used in 2022 (subject to the limitation in section 172(a)) against life subgroup income before it may be used in 2022 to setoff nonlife consolidated taxable income.

(ii) *Example 2.*—The facts are the same as in paragraph (j)(3)(i) of this section, except that, for 2021, the nonlife consolidated taxable income is $150 (this amount is entirely attributable to S and includes nonlife consolidated capital gain net income of $50), consolidated LICTI is $200, and a life consolidated net capital loss is $50. The $50 life consolidated net capital loss sets off the $50 nonlife consolidated capital gain net income. Consolidated taxable income under paragraph (e) of this section is $300 (nonlife consolidated taxable income ($150) minus the setoff of the life consolidated net capital loss ($50), plus consolidated LICTI ($200)).

(iii) *Example 3.*—The facts are the same as in paragraph (j)(3)(ii) of this section, except that, for 2022, the nonlife consolidated net operating loss is $150. This entire amount is attributable to S; thus, it is eligible to be carried back to 2021 against nonlife consolidated taxable income under paragraph (f)(2) of this section and § 1.1502-21(b). If P, the agent for the group within the meaning of § 1.1502-77, does not elect to relinquish the carryback under section 172(b)(3), the entire $150 will be carried back, reducing 2021 nonlife consolidated taxable income to zero and nonlife consolidated capital gain net income to zero. Under paragraph (h)(3)(xii) of this section, the setoff in 2021 of the nonlife consolidated capital gain net income ($50) by the life consolidated net capital loss ($50) is restored. Accordingly, the 2021 life consolidated net capital loss may be carried over by the life subgroup to 2022. Under paragraph (e) of this section, after the carryback, consolidated taxable income for 2021 is $200 (nonlife consolidated taxable income ($0) plus consolidated LICTI ($200)).

(iv) *Example 4.*—The facts are the same as in paragraph (j)(3)(iii) of this section, except that P elects under section 172(b)(3) to relinquish the carryback of $150 arising in 2022. The setoff in Example 2 is not restored. However, the offsettable nonlife consolidated net operating loss for 2022 (or that may be carried over from 2022) is zero. See paragraph (h)(3)(viii) of this section. Nevertheless, the $150 nonlife consolidated net operating loss may be carried over to be used by the nonlife group.

(v) *Example 5.*—P owns all of the stock of S1 and of L1. On January 1, 2017, L1 purchases all of the stock of L2. For 2021, the group elects under section 1504(c)(2) to file a consolidated return. For 2021, L1 is an eligible corporation under paragraph (b)(12) of this section but L2 is ineligible. Thus, L1 but not L2 is a member for 2021. For 2021, L2 sustains a net operating loss, which cannot be carried back (see section 172(b)). For 2021, L2 is treated under paragraph (d)(6) of this section as a member of a controlled group of corporations under section 1563 with P, S, and L1. For 2022, L2 is eligible and is included on the group's consolidated return. L2's net operating loss for 2021 that may be carried to 2022 is not treated under paragraph (b)(11) of this section as having been sustained in a separate return limitation year for purposes of computing consolidated LICTI of the L1-L2 life subgroup for 2022. Furthermore, the portion of L2's net operating loss not used under paragraph (g)(2) of this section against life subgroup income in 2022 may be included in offsettable life consolidated net operating loss under paragraph (j)(2) and (h)(3)(i) of this section that reduces in 2022 nonlife consolidated taxable income (subject to the limitation in section 172(a)) because L2's loss in 2021 was not sustained in a separate return limitation year under paragraph (j)(2) and (h)(3)(ix)(A) of this section or in a separate return year (2021) when an election was in effect under neither section 1504(c)(2) nor section 243(b)(3).

(k) *Preemption.*—The rules in this section preempt any inconsistent rules in other sections (§§ 1.1502-0 through 1.1502-100) of the consolidated return regulations. For example, the rules in paragraph (h)(3)(vi) apply notwithstanding § 1.1502-21.

(l) *Other consolidation principles.*—The fact that this section treats the life and nonlife members as separate groups in computing, respectively, consolidated LICTI (or life consolidated net operating loss) and nonlife consolidated taxable income (or loss) does not affect the usual rules in §§ 1.1502-0 through 1.1502-100 unless this section provides otherwise. Thus, the usual rules in § 1.1502-13 (relating to intercompany transactions) apply to both the life and nonlife members by treating them as members of one affiliated group.

(m) *Filing requirements.*—(1) *In general.*—To file a consolidated income tax return for a life-nonlife consolidated group, the common parent shall—

(i) File the applicable consolidated corporate income tax return: a Form 1120-L, "U.S. Life Insurance Company Income Tax Return," where the common parent is a life insurance company; a Form 1120-PC, "U.S. Property and Casualty Insurance Company Income Tax Return," where the common parent is an insurance company, other than a life insurance company; or a Form 1120, "U.S. Corporation Income Tax Return," where the common parent is any other type of corporation;

(ii) Indicate clearly on the face of this return that such corporate tax return is a life-nonlife return;

(iii) Show any set offs required by paragraphs (e), (h), and (j) of this section;

(iv) Report separately the nonlife consolidated taxable income or loss, determined under paragraph (f) of this section, on a Form 1120 or 1120-PC (whether filed by the common parent or as an attachment to the consolidated return), as the case may be, of all nonlife members of the consolidated group; and

(v) Report separately the consolidated Life Insurance Company Taxable Income or life consolidated net operating loss on a Form 1120-L (whether filed by the common parent or as an attachment to the consolidated return), of all life members of the consolidated group.

(2) *Cross reference.*—See § 1.1502-75(j), regarding the inclusion in a corporate tax return of the required statements and schedules for subsidiaries.

(n) *Effective/applicability dates.*—The rules of this section apply to taxable years beginning after December 31, 2020. However, a taxpayer may choose to apply the rules of this section to taxable years beginning on or before December 31, 2020. If a taxpayer makes the choice described in the previous sentence, the taxpayer must apply those rules in their entirety and consistently with the provisions of subchapter L of the Internal Revenue Code applicable to the years at issue. [Reg. § 1.1502-47.]

□ [*T.D. 7877, 3-14-83. Amended by T.D. 7912, 9-1-83, T.D. 8560, 8-12-94, T.D. 8597, 7-12-95, T.D. 8677, 6-26-96, T.D. 8823, 6-25-99, T.D. 9258, 4-24-2006, T.D. 9304, 12-21-2006, T.D. 9342, 7-19-2007, T.D. 9476, 12-22-2009, T.D. 9885, 12-2-2019 and T.D. 9927, 10-23-2020.*]

[Reg. §1.1502-50]

**§1.1502-50. Consolidated section 250.**—(a) *In general.*—(1) *Scope.*—This section provides rules for applying section 250 and §§1.250-1 through 1.250(b)-6 (the *section 250 regulations*) to a member of a consolidated group (*member*). Paragraph (b) of this section provides rules for the determination of the amount of the deduction allowed to a member under section 250(a)(1). Paragraph (c) of this section provides rules governing the impact of intercompany transactions on the determination of a member's qualified business asset investment (QBAI) and the effect of intercompany transactions on the determination of a member's foreign-derived deduction eligible income (FDDEI). Paragraph (d) of this section provides rules governing basis adjustments to member stock resulting from the application of paragraph (b)(1) of this section. Paragraph (e) of this section provides definitions. Paragraph (f) of this section provides examples illustrating the rules of this section. Paragraph (g) of this section provides an applicability date.

(2) *Overview.*—The rules of this section ensure that the aggregate amount of deductions allowed under section 250 to members appropriately reflects the income, expenses, gains, losses, and property of all members. Paragraph (b) of this section allocates the consolidated group's overall deduction amount under section 250 to each member on the basis of its contribution to the consolidated foreign-derived deduction eligible income (consolidated FDDEI) and consolidated global intangible low-taxed income (consolidated GILTI). The definitions in paragraph (e) of this section provide for the aggregation of the deduction eligible income (DEI), FDDEI, deemed tangible income return, and global intangible low-taxed income (GILTI) of all members in order to calculate the consolidated group's overall deduction amount under section 250.

(b) *Allowance of deduction.*—(1) *In general.*—A member is allowed a deduction for a consolidated return year under section 250. See §1.250(a)-1(b). The amount of the deduction is equal to the sum of—

(i) The product of the consolidated FDII deduction amount and the member's FDII deduction allocation ratio; and

(ii) The product of the consolidated GILTI deduction amount and the member's GILTI deduction allocation ratio.

(2) *Consolidated taxable income limitation.*—For purposes of applying the limitation described in §1.250(a)-1(b)(2) to the determination of the consolidated FDII deduction amount and the consolidated GILTI deduction amount of a consolidated group for a consolidated return year—

(i) The consolidated foreign-derived intangible income (consolidated FDII) (if any) is reduced (but not below zero) by an amount which bears the same ratio to the consolidated section 250(a)(2) amount that such consolidated FDII bears to the sum of the consolidated FDII and the consolidated GILTI; and

(ii) The consolidated GILTI (if any) is reduced (but not below zero) by the excess of the consolidated section 250(a)(2) amount over the reduction described in paragraph (b)(2)(i) of this section.

(c) *Impact of intercompany transactions.*—(1) *Impact on qualified business asset investment determination.*—(i) *In general.*—For purposes of determining a member's QBAI, the basis of specified tangible property does not include an amount equal to any gain or loss recognized with respect to such property by another member in an intercompany transaction (as defined in §1.1502-13(b)(1)) until the time that such gain or loss is no longer deferred under §1.1502-13. Thus, for example, if a selling member owns specified tangible property with an adjusted basis (within the meaning of section 1011) of $60x and an adjusted basis (for purposes of calculating QBAI) of $80x, and sells it for $50x to the purchasing member (and the intercompany loss remains deferred), the basis of such property for purposes of computing the purchasing member's QBAI is $80x.

(ii) *Partner-specific QBAI basis.*—A member's partner-specific QBAI basis (as defined in §1.250(b)-2(g)(7)) includes a basis adjustment under section 743(b) resulting from an intercompany transaction only at the time, and to the extent, gain or loss, if any, is recognized in the transaction and no longer deferred under §1.1502-13.

(2) *Impact on foreign-derived deduction eligible income characterization.*—For purposes of redetermining attributes of members from an intercompany transaction as FDDEI, see §1.1502-13(c)(1)(i) and (c)(7)(ii)(R) (*Example 18*).

(d) *Adjustments to the basis of a member.*—For adjustments to the basis of a member related to paragraph (b)(1) of this section, see §1.1502-32(b)(3)(ii)(B).

(e) *Definitions.*—The following definitions apply for purposes of this section.

(1) *Consolidated deduction eligible income (consolidated DEI).*—With respect to a consolidated group for a consolidated return year, the term *consolidated deduction eligible income* or *consolidated DEI* means the greater of the sum of the DEI (whether positive or negative) of all members or zero.

(2) *Consolidated deemed intangible income.*—With respect to a consolidated group for a consolidated return year, the term *consolidated deemed intangible income* means the excess (if any) of the consolidated DEI, over the consolidated deemed tangible income return.

(3) *Consolidated deemed tangible income return.*—With respect to a consolidated group for a consolidated return year, the term *consolidated deemed tangible income return* means the sum of the deemed tangible income return of all members.

(4) *Consolidated FDII deduction amount.*—With respect to a consolidated group for a consolidated return year, the term *consolidated FDII deduction amount* means the product of the FDII deduction rate and the consolidated FDII, as adjusted by paragraph (b)(2) of this section.

(5) *Consolidated foreign-derived deduction eligible income (consolidated FDDEI).*—With respect to a consolidated group for a consolidated return year, the term *consolidated foreign-derived deduction eligible income* or *consolidated FDDEI* means the greater of the sum of the FDDEI (whether positive or negative) of all members or zero.

(6) *Consolidated foreign-derived intangible income (consolidated FDII).*—With respect to a consolidated group for a consolidated return year, the term *consolidated foreign-derived intangible income* or *consolidated FDII* means the product of the consolidated deemed intangible income and the consolidated foreign-derived ratio.

(7) *Consolidated foreign-derived ratio.*—With respect to a consolidated group for a consolidated return year, the term *consolidated foreign-derived ratio* means the ratio (not to exceed one) of—

(i) The consolidated FDDEI; to

(ii) The consolidated DEI.

(8) *Consolidated GILTI deduction amount.*—With respect to a consolidated group for a consolidated return year, the term *consolidated GILTI deduction amount* means the product of the GILTI deduction rate and the sum of the consolidated GILTI, as adjusted by paragraph (b)(2) of this section, and the amounts treated as dividends received by the members under section 78 which are attributable to their GILTI for the consolidated return year.

(9) *Consolidated global intangible low-taxed income (consolidated GILTI).*—With respect to a consolidated group for a consolidated return year, the term *consolidated global intangible low-taxed income* or *consolidated GILTI* means the sum of the GILTI of all members.

(10) *Consolidated section 250(a)(2) amount.*—With respect to a consolidated group for a consolidated return year, the term *consolidated section 250(a)(2) amount* means the excess (if any) of the sum of the consolidated FDII and the consolidated GILTI (determined without regard to section 250(a)(2) and paragraph (b)(2) of this section), over the consolidated taxable income of the consolidated group (within the meaning of §1.1502-11).

(11) *Deduction eligible income (DEI).*—With respect to a member for a consolidated return year, the term *deduction eligible income* or *DEI* means the member's gross DEI for the year (within the meaning of §1.250(b)-1(c)(15)) reduced (including below zero) by the deductions properly allocable to gross DEI for the year (as determined under §1.250(b)-1(d)(2)).

(12) *Deemed tangible income return.*—With respect to a member for a consolidated return year, the term *deemed tangible income return* means an amount equal to 10 percent of the member's QBAI, as adjusted by paragraph (c)(1) of this section.

(13) *FDII deduction allocation ratio.*—With respect to a member for a consolidated return year, the term *FDII deduction allocation ratio* means the ratio of—

(i) The member's positive FDDEI (if any); to

(ii) The sum of the positive FDDEI of all members.

(14) *FDII deduction rate.*—The term *FDII deduction rate* means 37.5 percent for consolidated return years beginning before January 1, 2026, and 21.875 percent for consolidated return years beginning after December 31, 2025.

(15) *Foreign-derived deduction eligible income (FDDEI).*—With respect to a member for a consolidated return year, the term *foreign-derived deduction eligible income* or *FDDEI* means the member's gross FDDEI for the year (within the meaning of § 1.250(b)-1(c)(16)) reduced (including below zero) by the deductions properly allocable to gross FDDEI for the year (as determined under § 1.250(b)-1(d)(2)).

(16) *GILTI deduction allocation ratio.*—With respect to a member for a consolidated return year, the term *GILTI deduction allocation ratio* means the ratio of—

(i) The sum of the member's GILTI and the amount treated as a dividend received by the member under section 78 which is attributable to its GILTI for the consolidated return year; to

(ii) The sum of consolidated GILTI and the amounts treated as dividends received by the members under section 78 which are attributable to their GILTI for the consolidated return year.

(17) *GILTI deduction rate.*—The term *GILTI deduction rate* means 50 percent for consolidated return years beginning before January 1, 2026, and 37.5 percent for consolidated return years beginning after December 31, 2025.

(18) *Global intangible low-taxed income (GILTI).*—With respect to a member for a consolidated return year, the term *global intangible low-taxed income* or *GILTI* means the sum of the member's GILTI inclusion amount under § 1.1502-51(b) and the member's distributive share of any domestic partnership's GILTI inclusion amount under § 1.951A-5(b)(2).

(19) *Qualified business asset investment (QBAI).*—The term *qualified business asset investment* or *QBAI* has the meaning provided in § 1.250(b)-2(b).

(20) *Specified tangible property.*—The term *specified tangible property* has the meaning provided in § 1.250(b)-2(c)(1).

(f) *Examples.*—The following examples illustrate the rules of this section.

(1) *Example 1: Calculation of deduction attributable to FDII.*—(i) *Facts.* P is the common parent of the P group and owns all of the only class of stock of subsidiaries USS1 and USS2. The consolidated return year of all persons is the calendar year. In 2018, P has DEI of $400x, FDDEI of $0, and QBAI of $0; USS1 has DEI of $200x, FDDEI of $200x, and QBAI of $600x; and USS2 has DEI of -$100x, FDDEI of $100x, and QBAI of $400x. The P group has consolidated taxable income that is sufficient to make inapplicable the limitation in paragraph (b)(2) of this section. No member of the P group has GILTI.

(ii) *Analysis*—(A) *Consolidated DEI.* Under paragraph (e)(1) of this section, the P group's consolidated DEI is $500x, the greater of the sum of the DEI (whether positive or negative) of all members ($400x + $200x - $100x) or zero.

(B) *Consolidated FDDEI.* Under paragraph (e)(5) of this section, the P group's consolidated FDDEI is $300x, the greater of the sum of the FDDEI (whether positive or negative) of all members ($0 + $200x + $100x) or zero.

(C) *Consolidated deemed tangible income return.* Under paragraph (e)(12) of this section, a member's deemed tangible income return is 10 percent of its QBAI. Therefore, P's deemed tangible income return is $0 (0.10 x $0), USS1's deemed tangible income return is $60x (0.10 x $600x), and USS2's deemed tangible income return is $40x (0.10 x $400x). Under paragraph (e)(3) of this section, the P group's consolidated deemed tangible income return is $100x, the sum of the deemed tangible income return of all members ($0 + $60x + $40x).

(D) *Consolidated deemed intangible income.* Under paragraph (e)(2) of this section, the P group's consolidated deemed intangible income is $400x, the excess of its consolidated DEI over its consolidated deemed tangible income return ($500x - $100x).

(E) *Consolidated FDII.* Under paragraph (e)(7) of this section, the P group's consolidated foreign-derived ratio is 0.60, the ratio of its consolidated FDDEI to its consolidated DEI ($300x / $500x). Under paragraph (e)(6) of this section, the P group's consolidated FDII is $240x, the product of its consolidated deemed intangible income and its consolidated foreign-derived ratio ($400x x 0.60).

(F) *Consolidated FDII deduction amount.* Under paragraph (e)(4) of this section, the P group's consolidated FDII deduction amount is $90x, the product of the FDII deduction rate and the consolidated FDII (0.375 x $240x).

(G) *Member's deduction attributable to consolidated FDII deduction amount.* Under paragraph (b)(1) of this section, a member is allowed a deduction equal, in part, to the product of the consolidated FDII deduction amount of the consolidated group to which the member belongs and the member's FDII deduction allocation ratio. Under paragraph (e)(13) of this section, a member's FDII deduction allocation ratio is the ratio of its positive FDDEI to the sum of each member's positive FDDEI for such consolidated return year. As a result, the FDII deduction allocation ratios of P, USS1, and USS2 are 0

($0 / $300x), 2/3 ($200x / $300x), and 1/3 ($100x / $300x), respectively. Therefore, P, USS1, and USS2 are permitted deductions under paragraph (b)(1) of this section in the amount of $0 (0 x $90x), $60x (2/3 x $90x), and $30x (1/3 x $90x), respectively.

(2) *Example 2: Limitation on consolidated foreign-derived deduction eligible income.*—(i) *Facts.* The facts are the same as in paragraph (f)(1)(i) of this section (the facts in *Example 1*), except that P's FDDEI is $300x.

(ii) *Analysis*—(A) *Consolidated DEI and consolidated deemed tangible income return.* As in paragraphs (f)(1)(ii)(A) and (C) of this section (the analysis in *Example 1*), the P group's consolidated DEI is $500x and the P group's consolidated deemed tangible income return is $100x.

(B) *Consolidated FDDEI.* Under paragraph (e)(5) of this section, the P group's consolidated FDDEI is $600x, the greater of the sum of the FDDEI (whether positive or negative) of all members ($300x + $200x + $100x) or zero.

(C) *Consolidated deemed intangible income and consolidated FDII.* Under paragraph (e)(2) of this section, the P group's consolidated deemed intangible income is $400x ($500x - $100x). Under paragraph (e)(7) of this section, the P group's consolidated foreign-derived ratio is 1.00 ($600x / $500x, but not in excess of one). Under paragraph (e)(6) of this section, the P group's consolidated FDII is $400x ($400x x 1.00).

(D) *Consolidated FDII deduction amount and member's deduction attributable to consolidated FDII deduction amount.* Under paragraph (e)(4) of this section, the P group's consolidated FDII deduction amount is $150x (0.375 x $400x). Under paragraph (e)(13) of this section, the FDII deduction allocation ratios of P, USS1, and USS2 are 1/2 ($300 / $600x), 1/3 ($200x / $600x), and 1/6 ($100x / $600x), respectively. Therefore, P, USS1, and USS2 are permitted deductions under paragraph (b)(1) of this section in the amounts of $75x (1/2 x $150x), $50x (1/3 x $150x), and $25x (1/6 x $150x), respectively.

(3) *Example 3: Member with negative FDDEI.*—(i) *Facts.* The facts are the same as in paragraph (f)(1)(i) of this section (the facts in *Example 1*), except that P's FDDEI is -$100x.

(ii) *Analysis*—(A) *Consolidated DEI and consolidated deemed tangible income return.* As in paragraphs (f)(1)(ii)(A) and (C) of this section (the facts in *Example 1*), the P group's consolidated DEI is $500x and the P group's consolidated deemed tangible income return is $100x.

(B) *Consolidated FDDEI.* Under paragraph (e)(5) of this section, the P group's consolidated FDDEI is $200x, the greater of the sum of the FDDEI (whether positive or negative) of all members (-$100x + $200x + $100x) or zero.

(C) *Consolidated deemed intangible income and consolidated FDII.* Under paragraphs (e)(2) and (6) of this section, the P group's consolidated deemed intangible income is $400x ($500x - $100x), and the P group's consolidated FDII is $160x ($400x x ($200x / $500x)).

(D) *Consolidated FDII deduction amount and member's deduction attributable to consolidated FDII deduction amount.* Under paragraph (e)(4) of this section, the P group's consolidated FDII deduction amount is $60x (0.375 x $160x). Under paragraph (e)(13) of this section, the FDII deduction allocation ratios of P, USS1, and USS2 are 0 ($0 / $300x), 2/3 ($200x / $300x), and 1/3 ($100x / $300x), respectively. Therefore, P, USS1, and USS2 are permitted deductions under paragraph (b)(1) of this section in the amounts of $0 (0 x $60x), $40x (2/3 x $60x), and $20x (1/3 x $60x), respectively.

(4) *Example 4: Calculation of deduction attributable to GILTI.*—(i) *Facts.* The facts are the same as in paragraph (f)(1)(i) of this section (the facts in *Example 1*), except that USS1 owns CFC1 and USS2 owns CFC2. USS1 and USS2 have GILTI of $65x and $20x, respectively, and amounts treated as dividends received under section 78 attributable to their GILTI of $10x and $5x, respectively.

(ii) *Analysis*—(A) *Consolidated GILTI.* Under paragraph (e)(9) of this section, the P group's consolidated GILTI is $85x, the sum of the GILTI of all members ($0 + $65x + $20x).

(B) *Consolidated GILTI deduction amount.* Under paragraph (e)(8) of this section, the P group's consolidated GILTI deduction amount is $50x, the product of the GILTI deduction rate and the sum of its consolidated GILTI and the amounts treated as dividends received by the members under section 78 which are attributable to their GILTI for the consolidated return year (0.50 x ($85x + $10x + $5x)).

(C) *Member's deduction attributable to consolidated GILTI deduction amount.* Under paragraph (b)(1) of this section, a member is allowed a deduction equal, in part, to the product of the consolidated GILTI deduction amount of the consolidated group to which the member belongs and the member's GILTI deduction allocation ratio. Under paragraph (e)(16) of this section, a member's GILTI deduction allocation ratio is the ratio of the sum of its GILTI and the amount treated as a dividend received by the member under section 78 which is attributable to its GILTI for the consolidated return year to the sum of the consolidated GILTI and the amounts treated as dividends received by the members under section 78 which are attributable to their GILTI for the consolidated return year. As a result, the GILTI deduction allocation ratios of P, USS1, and USS2 are 0 ($0 / ($85x + $10x + $5x)), 3/4 (($65x + $10x) / ($85x + $10x + $5x)), and 1/4 (($20x + $5x) / ($85x + $10x + $5x)), respectively. Therefore, P, USS1, and USS2 are permitted deductions of $0 (0 x $50x), $37.50x (3/4 x $50x), and $12.50x (1/4 x $50x), respectively.

(D) *Member's deduction under section 250.* Under paragraph (b)(1) of this section, a member is allowed a deduction equal to the sum of the member's deduction attributable to the consolidated FDII deduction amount and the member's deduction attributable to the consolidated GILTI deduction amount. As a result P, USS1, and USS2 are entitled to deductions under paragraph (b)(1) of this section of $0 ($0 + $0), $97.50x ($60x + $37.50x), and $42.50x ($30x + $12.50x), respectively.

(5) *Example 5: Taxable income limitation.*—(i) *Facts.* The facts are the same as in paragraph (f)(4)(i) of this section (the facts in *Example 4*), except that the P group's consolidated taxable income (within the meaning of paragraph (e)(10) of this section) is $300x.

(ii) *Analysis*—(A) *Determination of whether the limitation described in paragraph (b)(2) of this section applies.* Under paragraph (b)(2) of this section, in the case of a consolidated group with a consolidated section 250(a)(2) amount for a consolidated year, the amount of the consolidated FDII and the consolidated GILTI otherwise taken into account in the determination of the consolidated FDII deduction amount and the consolidated GILTI deduction amount are subject to reduction. As in paragraph (f)(1)(ii)(E) of this section (the facts in *Example 1*), the P group's consolidated FDII is $240x. As in paragraph (f)(4)(ii)(A) of this section (the analysis in *Example 4*), the P group's consolidated GILTI is $85x. The P group's consolidated taxable income is $300x. Under paragraph (e)(10) of this section, the P group's consolidated section 250(a)(2) amount is $25x (($240x + $85x) - $300x), the excess of the sum of the consolidated FDII and the consolidated GILTI, over the P group's consolidated taxable income. Therefore, the limitation described in paragraph (b)(2) of this section applies.

(B) *Allocation of reduction.* Under paragraph (b)(2)(i) of this section, the P group's consolidated FDII is reduced by an amount which bears the same ratio to the consolidated section 250(a)(2) amount as the consolidated FDII bears to the sum of the consolidated FDII and consolidated GILTI, and the P group's consolidated GILTI is reduced by the excess of the consolidated section 250(a)(2) amount over the reduction described in paragraph (b)(2)(i) of this section. Therefore, for purposes of determining the P group's consolidated FDII deduction amount and consolidated GILTI deduction amount, its consolidated FDII is reduced to $221.54x ($240x - ($25x x ($240x / $325x))) and its consolidated GILTI is reduced to $78.46x ($85x -($25x - ($25x x ($240x / $325x)))).

(C) *Calculation of consolidated FDII deduction amount and consolidated GILTI deduction amount.* Under paragraph (e)(4) of this section, the P group's consolidated FDII deduction amount is $83.08x ($221.54x x 0.375). Under paragraph (e)(8) of this section, the P group's consolidated GILTI deduction amount is $46.73x (($78.46x + 10x + 5x) x 0.50).

(D) *Member's deduction attributable to the consolidated FDII deduction amount.* As in paragraph (f)(1)(ii)(G) of this section (the analysis in *Example 1*), the FDII deduction allocation ratios of P, USS1, and USS2 are 0, 2/3, and 1/3, respectively. Therefore, P, USS1, and USS2 are permitted deductions attributable to the consolidated FDII deduction amount of $0 (0 x $83.08x), $55.39x (2/3 x $83.08x), and $27.69x (1/3 x $83.08x), respectively.

(E) *Member's deduction attributable to the consolidated GILTI deduction amount.* As in paragraph (f)(4)(ii)(C) of this section (the analysis in *Example 4*), the GILTI deduction allocation ratios of P, USS1, and USS2 are 0, 3/4, and 1/4, respectively. Therefore, P, USS1, and USS2 are permitted deductions attributable to the consolidated GILTI deduction amount of $0 (0 x $46.73x), $35.05x (3/4 x $46.73x), and $11.68x (1/4 x $46.73x), respectively.

(F) *Member's deduction pursuant section 250.* Under paragraph (b)(1) of this section, a member is allowed a deduction equal to the sum of the member's deduction attributable to the consolidated FDII deduction amount and the member's deduction attributable to the consolidated GILTI deduction amount. As a result, P, USS1, and USS2 are entitled to deductions under paragraph (b)(1) of this section of $0 ($0 + $0), $90.44x ($55.39x + $35.05x), and $39.37x ($27.69x + $11.68x), respectively.

(g) *Applicability date.*—This section applies to consolidated return years beginning on or after January 1, 2021. A taxpayer that chooses to apply the rules in §§ 1.250(a)-1 and 1.250(b)-1 through 1.250(b)-6 to taxable years beginning before January 1, 2021, pursuant to § 1.250-1(b), must also apply the rules of this section in their entirety to consolidated return years beginning after December 31, 2017, and before January 1, 2021. [Reg. § 1.1502-50.]

☐ [*T.D. 9901, 7-9-2020.*]

**[Reg. § 1.1502-51]**

**§ 1.1502-51. Consolidated section 951A.**—(a) *In general.*—This section provides rules for applying section 951A to each member of a consolidated group (each, a *member*) that is a United States shareholder of any controlled foreign corporation. Paragraph (b) of this section describes the inclusion of the GILTI inclusion amount by a member of a consolidated group. Paragraphs (c) and (d) of this section are reserved. Paragraph (e) of this section provides definitions for purposes of this section. Paragraph (f) of this section provides examples illustrating the rules of this section. Paragraph (g) of this section provides an applicability date.

(b) *Calculation of the GILTI inclusion amount for a member of a consolidated group.*—Each member who is a United States shareholder of any controlled foreign corporation includes in gross income in the U.S. shareholder inclusion year the member's GILTI inclusion amount, if any, for the U.S. shareholder inclusion year. See section 951A(a) and § 1.951A-1(b). The GILTI inclusion amount of a member for a U.S. shareholder inclusion year is the excess (if any) of the member's net CFC tested income for the U.S. shareholder inclusion year, over the member's net deemed tangible income return for the U.S. shareholder inclusion year, determined using the definitions provided in paragraph (e) of this section. In addition, see § 1.951A-1(e).

(c) [Reserved]

(d) [Reserved]

(e) *Definitions.*—Any term used but not defined in this section has the meaning set forth in §§ 1.951A-1 through 1.951A-6. In addition, the following definitions apply for purposes of this section.

(1) *Aggregate tested income.*—With respect to a member, the term *aggregate tested income* means the aggregate of the member's pro rata share (determined under § 1.951A-1(d)(2)) of the tested income of each tested income CFC for a CFC inclusion year that ends with or within the U.S. shareholder inclusion year.

(2) *Aggregate tested loss.*—With respect to a member, the term *aggregate tested loss* means the aggregate of the member's pro rata share (determined under § 1.951A-1(d)(4)) of the tested loss of each tested loss CFC for a CFC inclusion year that ends with or within the U.S. shareholder inclusion year.

(3) *Allocable share.*—The term *allocable share* means, with respect to a member that is a United States shareholder and a U.S. shareholder inclusion year—

(i) With respect to consolidated QBAI, the product of the consolidated QBAI of the member's consolidated group and the member's GILTI allocation ratio.

(ii) With respect to consolidated specified interest expense, the product of the consolidated specified interest expense of the member's consolidated group and the member's GILTI allocation ratio.

(iii) With respect to consolidated tested loss, the product of the consolidated tested loss of the member's consolidated group and the member's GILTI allocation ratio.

(4) *Consolidated QBAI.*—With respect to a consolidated group, the term *consolidated QBAI* means the sum of each member's pro rata share (determined under § 1.951A-1(d)(3)) of the qualified business asset investment of each tested income CFC for a CFC inclusion year that ends with or within the U.S. shareholder inclusion year.

(5) *Consolidated specified interest expense.*—With respect to a consolidated group, the term *consolidated specified interest expense* means the excess (if any) of—

(i) The sum of each member's pro rata share (determined under § 1.951A-1(d)(5)) of the tested interest expense of each controlled foreign corporation for a CFC inclusion year that ends with or within the U.S. shareholder inclusion year, over

(ii) The sum of each member's pro rata share (determined under § 1.951A-1(d)(6)) of the tested interest income of each controlled foreign corporation for a CFC inclusion year that ends with or within the U.S. shareholder inclusion year.

(6) *Consolidated tested income.*—With respect to a consolidated group, the term *consolidated tested income* means the sum of each member's aggregate tested income for the U.S. shareholder inclusion year.

(7) *Consolidated tested loss.*—With respect to a consolidated group, the term *consolidated tested loss* means the sum of each member's aggregate tested loss for the U.S. shareholder inclusion year.

(8) *Controlled foreign corporation.*—The term *controlled foreign corporation* has the meaning provided in § 1.951A-1(f)(2).

(9) *Deemed tangible income return.*—With respect to a member, the term *deemed tangible income return* means 10 percent of the member's allocable share of the consolidated QBAI.

(10) *GILTI allocation ratio.*—With respect to a member, the term *GILTI allocation ratio* means the ratio of—

(i) The aggregate tested income of the member for the U.S. shareholder inclusion year, to

(ii) The consolidated tested income of the consolidated group of which the member is a member for the U.S. shareholder inclusion year.

(11) *GILTI inclusion amount.*—With respect to a member, the term *GILTI inclusion amount* has the meaning provided in paragraph (b) of this section.

(12) *Net CFC tested income.*—With respect to a member, the term *net CFC tested income* means the excess (if any) of—

(i) The member's aggregate tested income, over

(ii) The member's allocable share of the consolidated tested loss.

(13) *Net deemed tangible income return.*—With respect to a member, the term *net deemed tangible income return* means the excess (if any) of the member's deemed tangible income return over the member's allocable share of the consolidated specified interest expense.

(14) through (16) [Reserved]

(17) *Qualified business asset investment.*—The term qualified business asset investment has the meaning provided in §1.951A-3(b).

(18) *Tested income.*—The term *tested income* has the meaning provided in §1.951A-2(b)(1).

(19) *Tested income CFC.*—The term *tested income CFC* has the meaning provided in §1.951A-2(b)(1).

(20) *Tested interest expense.*—The term *tested interest expense* has the meaning provided in §1.951A-4(b)(1).

(21) *Tested interest income.*—The term *tested interest income* has the meaning provided in §1.951A-4(b)(2).

(22) *Tested loss.*—The term *tested loss* has the meaning provided in §1.951A-2(b)(2).

(23) *Tested loss CFC.*—The term *tested loss CFC* has the meaning provided in §1.951A-2(b)(2).

(24) *United States shareholder.*—The term *United States shareholder* has the meaning provided in §1.951A-1(f)(6).

(25) *U.S. shareholder inclusion year.*—The term *U.S. shareholder inclusion year* has the meaning provided in §1.951A-1(f)(7).

(f) *Examples.*—The following examples illustrate the rules of this section. For purposes of the examples in this section, unless otherwise stated: P is the common parent of the P consolidated group; P owns all of the single class of stock of subsidiaries USS1, USS2, and USS3, all of whom are members of the P consolidated group; CFC1, CFC2, CFC3, and CFC4 are all controlled foreign corporations (within the meaning of paragraph (e)(8) of this section); and the taxable year of all persons is the calendar year.

(1) *Example 1: Calculation of net CFC tested income within a consolidated group when all CFCs are wholly owned by a member*—(i) *Facts.* USS1 owns all of the single class of stock of CFC1. USS2 owns all of the single class of stock of each of CFC2 and CFC3. USS3 owns all of the single class of stock of CFC4. In Year 1, CFC1 has tested loss of $100x, CFC2 has tested income of $200x, CFC3 has tested loss of $200x, and CFC4 has tested income of $600x. None of CFC1, CFC2, CFC3, or CFC4 has qualified business asset investment in Year 1.

(ii) *Analysis*—(A) *Consolidated tested income and GILTI allocation ratio.* USS1 has no aggregate tested income; USS2's aggregate tested income is $200x, its pro rata share (determined under §1.951A-1(d)(2)) of CFC2's tested income; and USS3's aggregate tested income is $600x, its pro rata share (determined under §1.951A-1(d)(2)) of CFC4's tested income. Therefore, under paragraph (e)(6) of this section, the P consolidated group's consolidated tested income is $800x ($200x + $600x). As a result, the GILTI allocation ratios of USS1, USS2, and USS3 are 0 ($0/$800x), 0.25 ($200x/$800x), and 0.75 ($600x/$800x), respectively.

(B) *Consolidated tested loss.* Under paragraph (e)(7) of this section, the P consolidated group's consolidated tested loss is $300x ($100x + $200x), the sum of USS1's aggregate tested loss, which is equal to its pro rata share (determined under §1.951A-1(d)(4)) of CFC1's tested loss ($100x), and USS2's aggregate tested loss, which is equal to its pro rata share (determined under §1.951A-1(d)(4)) of CFC3's tested loss ($200x). Under paragraph (e)(3)(iii) of this section, a member's

allocable share of the consolidated tested loss is the product of the consolidated tested loss of the member's consolidated group and the member's GILTI allocation ratio. Therefore, the allocable shares of the consolidated tested loss of USS1, USS2, and USS3 are $0 (0 x $300x), $75x (0.25 x $300x), and $225x (0.75 x $300x), respectively.

(C) *Calculation of net CFC tested income.* Under paragraph (e)(12) of this section, a member's net CFC tested income is the excess (if any) of the member's aggregate tested income over the member's allocable share of the consolidated tested loss. As a result, the net CFC tested income of USS1, USS2, and USS3 are $0 ($0 - $0), $125x ($200x - $75x), and $375x ($600x - $225x), respectively.

(2) *Example 2: Calculation of net CFC tested income within a consolidated group when ownership of a tested loss CFC is split between members*—(i) *Facts.* The facts are the same as in paragraph (f)(1)(i) of this section (the facts in *Example 1*), except that USS2 and USS3 each own 50% of the single class of stock of CFC3.

(ii) *Analysis.* As in paragraph (f)(1)(ii)(A) of this section (paragraph (A) of the analysis in *Example 1*), USS1 has no aggregate tested income and a GILTI allocation ratio of 0, USS2 has $200x of aggregate tested income and a GILTI allocation ratio of 0.25, and USS3 has $600x of aggregate tested income and a GILTI allocation ratio of 0.75. Additionally, the P consolidated group's consolidated tested loss is $300x (the aggregate of USS1's aggregate tested loss, which is equal to its pro rata share (determined under §1.951A-1(d)(4)) of CFC1's tested loss ($100x); USS2's aggregate tested loss, which is equal to its pro rata share (determined under §1.951A-1(d)(4)) of CFC3's tested loss ($100x); and USS3's aggregate tested loss, which is equal to its pro rata share (determined under §1.951A-1(d)(4)) of CFC3's tested loss ($100x)). As a result, under paragraph (e)(12) of this section, as in paragraph (f)(1)(ii)(C) of this section (paragraph (C) of the analysis in *Example 1*), the net CFC tested income of USS1, USS2, and USS3 are $0 ($0 - $0), $125x ($200x - $75x), and $375x ($600x - $225x), respectively.

(3) *Example 3: Calculation of GILTI inclusion amount*—(i) *Facts.* The facts are the same as in paragraph (f)(1)(i) of this section (the facts in *Example 1*), except that CFC2 and CFC4 have qualified business asset investment of $500x and $2,000x, respectively, for Year 1. In Year 1, CFC1 and CFC4 each have tested interest expense (within the meaning of §1.951A-4(b)(1)) of $25x, and none of CFC1, CFC2, CFC3, and CFC4 have tested interest income (within the meaning of §1.951A-4(b)(2)). CFC1's tested loss of $100x and CFC4's tested income of $600x take into account the tested interest expense.

(ii) *Analysis*—(A) *GILTI allocation ratio.* As in paragraph (f)(1)(ii)(A) of this section (paragraph (A) of the analysis in *Example 1*), the GILTI allocation ratios of USS1, USS2, and USS3 are 0 ($0/$800x), 0.25 ($200x/$800x), and 0.75 ($600x/$800x), respectively.

(B) *Consolidated QBAI.* Under paragraph (e)(4) of this section, the P consolidated group's consolidated QBAI is $2,500x ($500x + $2,000x), the aggregate of USS2's pro rata share (determined under §1.951A-1(d)(3)) of the qualified business asset investment of CFC2 and USS3's pro rata share (determined under §1.951A-1(d)(3)) of the qualified business asset investment of CFC4. Under paragraph (e)(3)(i) of this section, a member's allocable share of consolidated QBAI is the product of the consolidated QBAI of the member's consolidated group and the member's GILTI allocation ratio. Therefore, the allocable shares of the consolidated QBAI of each of USS1, USS2, and USS3 are $0 (0 x $2,500x), $625x (0.25 x $2,500x), and $1,875x (0.75 x $2,500x), respectively.

(C) *Consolidated specified interest expense*—(1) *Pro rata share of tested interest expense.* USS1's pro rata share (determined under §1.951A-1(d)(5)) of the tested interest expense of CFC1 is $25x, the amount by which the tested interest expense increases USS1's pro rata share of CFC1's tested loss (from $75x to $100x) for Year 1. USS3's pro rata share (determined under §1.951A-1(d)(5)) of the tested interest expense of CFC4 is also $25x, the amount by which the tested interest expense decreases USS3's pro rata share of CFC4's tested income (from $625x to $600x).

(2) *Consolidated specified interest expense.* Under paragraph (e)(5) of this section, the P consolidated group's consolidated specified interest expense is $50x, the excess of the sum of each member's pro rata share of the tested interest expense of each controlled foreign corporation ($50x, $25x from USS1 + $25x from USS3), over the sum of each member's pro rata share of tested interest income ($0). Under paragraph (e)(3)(ii) of this section, a member's allocable share of consolidated specified interest expense is the product of the consolidated specified interest expense of the member's consolidated group and the member's GILTI allocation ratio. Therefore, the allocable shares of consolidated specified interest expense of USS1, USS2, and USS3 are $0 (0 x $50x), $12.50x (0.25 x $50x), and $37.50x (0.75 x $50x), respectively.

(D) *Calculation of deemed tangible income return.* Under paragraph (e)(9) of this section, a member's deemed tangible income return means 10 percent of the member's allocable share of the consolidated QBAI. As a result, the deemed tangible income returns of USS1,

USS2, and USS3 are $0 (0.1 x $0), $62.50x (0.1 x $625x), and $187.50x (0.1 x $1,875x), respectively.

(E) *Calculation of net deemed tangible income return.* Under paragraph (e)(13) of this section, a member's net deemed tangible income return means the excess (if any) of a member's deemed tangible income return over the member's allocable share of the consolidated specified interest expense. As a result, the net deemed tangible income returns of USS1, USS2, and USS3 are $0 ($0 - $0), $50x ($62.50x - $12.50x), and $150x ($187.50x - $37.50x), respectively.

(F) *Calculation of GILTI inclusion amount.* Under paragraph (b) of this section, a member's GILTI inclusion amount for a U.S. shareholder inclusion year is the excess (if any) of the member's net CFC tested income for the U.S. shareholder inclusion year, over the shareholder's net deemed tangible income return for the U.S. shareholder inclusion year. As described in paragraph (f)(1)(ii)(C) of this section (paragraph (C) of the analysis in *Example 1*), the net CFC tested income of USS1, USS2, and USS3 are $0, $125x, and $375x, respectively. As described in paragraph (f)(3)(ii)(E) of this section (paragraph (E) of the analysis in this example), the net deemed tangible income returns of USS1, USS2, and USS3 are $0, $50x, and $150x, respectively. As a result, under paragraph (b) of this section, the GILTI inclusion amounts of USS1, USS2, and USS3 are $0 ($0 - $0), $75x ($125x - $50x), and $225x ($375x - $150x), respectively.

(g) *Applicability date.*—(1) *In general.*—Except as otherwise provided in this paragraph (g), this section applies to taxable years of United States shareholders for which the due date (without extensions) of the consolidated return is after June 21, 2019. However, a consolidated group may apply the rules of this section in their entirety to all taxable years of its members that are described in §1.951A-7(a). In such a case, the consolidated group must apply the rules of this section to all taxable years described in §1.951A-7(a) and with respect to all members.

(2) [Reserved]

[Reg. §1.1502-51.]

☐ [*T.D. 9866, 6-14-2019. Amended by T.D. 9902, 7-20-2020.*]

### [Reg. §1.1502-55]

**§1.1502-55. Computation of alternative minimum tax of consolidated groups.**—(a) through (h)(3) [Reserved].

(h)(4) *Separate return year minimum tax credit.*

(i) and (ii) [Reserved].

(iii)(A) *Limitation on portion of separate return year minimum tax credit arising in separate return limitation years.*—The aggregate of a member's minimum tax credits arising in SRLYs that are included in the consolidated minimum tax credits for all consolidated return years of the group may not exceed—

(1) The aggregate for all consolidated return years of the member's contributions to the consolidated section 53(c) limitation for each consolidated return year; reduced by

(2) The aggregate of the member's minimum tax credits arising and absorbed in all consolidated return years (whether or not absorbed by the member).

(B) *Computational rules.*—(1) *Member's contribution to the consolidated section 53(c) limitation.*—Except as provided in the special rule of paragraph (h)(4)(iii)(B)(2) of this section, a member's contribution to the consolidated section 53(c) limitation for a consolidated return year equals the member's share of the consolidated net regular tax liability minus its share of consolidated tentative minimum tax. The group computes the member's shares by applying to the respective consolidated amounts the principles of section 1552 and the percentage method under §1.1502-33(d)(3), assuming a 100% allocation of any decreased tax liability. The group makes proper adjustments so that taxes and credits not taken into account in computing the limitation under section 53(c) are not taken into account in computing the member's share of the consolidated net regular tax, etc. (See, for example, the taxes described in section 26(b) that are disregarded in computing regular tax liability.)

(2) *Adjustment for year in which alternative minimum tax is paid.*—For a consolidated return year for which consolidated tentative minimum tax is greater than consolidated regular tax liability, the group reduces the member's share of the consolidated tentative minimum tax by the member's share of the consolidated alternative minimum tax for the year. The group determines the member's share of consolidated alternative minimum tax for a year using the same method it uses to determine the member's share of the consolidated minimum tax credits for the year.

(3) *Years included in computation.*—For purposes of computing the limitation under this paragraph (h)(4)(iii), the consolidated return years of the group include only those years, including

the year to which a credit is carried, that the member has been continuously included in the group's consolidated return, but exclude any years after the year to which the credit is carried.

(4) *Subgroup principles.*—The SRLY subgroup principles under §1.1502-21(c)(2) apply for purposes of this paragraph (h)(4)(iii). The predecessor and successor principles under §1.1502-21(f) also apply for purposes of this paragraph (h)(4)(iii).

(5) *Overlap with section 383.*—The principles under §1.1502-21(g) apply for purposes of this paragraph (h)(4)(iii). For example, an overlap of this paragraph (h)(4)(iii) and the application of section 383 with respect to a credit carryover occurs if a corporation becomes a member of a consolidated group (the SRLY event) within six months of the change date of an ownership change giving rise to a section 383 credit limitation with respect to that carryover (the section 383 event), with the result that the limitation of this paragraph (h)(4)(iii) does not apply. See §§1.1502-21(g)(2)(ii)(A) and 1.383-1; see also §1.1502-21(g)(4) (subgroup rules).

(C) *Effective date.*—(1) *In general.*—This paragraph (h)(4)(iii) generally applies to consolidated return years for which the due date of the income tax return (without extensions) is after March 13, 1998. See §1.1502-3(d)(4) for an optional effective date rule (generally making this paragraph (h)(4)(iii) also applicable to a consolidated return year beginning on or after January 1, 1997, if the due date of the income tax return (without extensions) was on or before March 13, 1998).

(i) *Contribution years.*—In general, a group does not take into account a consolidated taxable year for which the due date of the income tax return (without extensions) is on or before March 13, 1998, in determining a member's (or subgroup's) contributions to the consolidated section 53(c) limitation under this paragraph (h)(4)(iii). However, if a consolidated group chooses to apply the optional effective date rule, the consolidated group shall not take into account a consolidated taxable year beginning before January 1, 1997 in determining a member's (or subgroup's) contributions to the consolidated section 53(c) limitation under this paragraph (h)(4)(iii).

(ii) *Special subgroup rule.*—In the event that the principles of §1.1502-21(g)(1) do not apply to a particular credit carryover in the current group, then solely for purposes of applying this paragraph (h)(4)(iii) to determine the limitation with respect to that carryover and with respect to which the SRLY register (the aggregate of the member's or subgroup's contribution to consolidated section 53(c) limitation reduced by the aggregate of the member's or subgroup's minimum tax credits arising and absorbed in all consolidated return years) began in a taxable year for which the due date of the return is on or before May 25, 2000, the principles of §1.1502-21(c)(2) shall be applied without regard to the phrase "or for a carryover that was subject to the overlap rule described in paragraph (g) of this section or §1.1502-15(g) with respect to another group (the former group)."

(2) *Overlap rule.*—Paragraph (h)(4)(iii)(B)(5) of this section (relating to overlap with section 383) applies to taxable years for which the due date (without extensions) of the consolidated return is after May 25, 2000. For purposes of paragraph (h)(4)(iii)(B)(5) of this section, only an ownership change to which section 383, as amended by the Tax Reform Act of 1986 (100 Stat. 2095), applies and which results, in a section 383 credit limitation shall constitute a section 383 event. The optional effective date rule of §1.1502-3(d)(4) (generally making this paragraph (h)(4)(iii) also applicable to a consolidated return year beginning on or after January 1, 1997, if the due date of the income tax return (without extensions) was on or before March 13, 1998) does not apply with respect to paragraph (h)(4)(iii)(B)(5) of this section (relating to the overlap rule). [Reg. §1.1502-55.]

☐ [*T.D. 8884, 5-24-2000.*]

### [Reg. §1.1502-59A]

**§1.1502-59A. Application of section 59A to consolidated groups.**—(a) *Scope.*—This section provides rules for the application of section 59A and the regulations thereunder (the *section 59A regulations*) to consolidated groups and their members (as defined in §1.1502-1(h) and (b), respectively). Rules in the section 59A regulations apply to consolidated groups except as modified in this section. Paragraph (b) of this section provides rules treating a consolidated group (rather than each member of the group) as a single taxpayer, and a single applicable taxpayer, as relevant, for certain purposes. Paragraph (c) of this section coordinates the application of the business interest stacking rule under §1.59A-3(c)(4) to consolidated groups. Paragraph (d) of this section addresses how the base erosion minimum tax amount is allocated among members of the consolidated group. Paragraph (e) of this section coordinates the application of this section and §1.1502-47. Paragraph (f) of this section sets forth definitions. Paragraph (g) of this section provides examples. Paragraph (h) of this section provides the applicability date.

(b) *Consolidated group as the applicable taxpayer.*—(1) *In general.*—For purposes of determining whether the consolidated group is an applicable taxpayer (within the meaning of §1.59A-2(b)) and the amount of tax due pursuant to section 59A(a), all members of a consolidated group are treated as a single taxpayer. Thus, for example, members' deductions are aggregated in making the required computations under section 59A. In addition, to ensure that intercompany transactions (as defined in §1.1502-13(b)(1)(i)) do not affect the consolidated group's base erosion percentage or base erosion minimum tax amount, items resulting from intercompany transactions are not taken into account in making such computations under section 59A. For example, additional depreciation deductions resulting from intercompany asset sales are not taken into account for purposes of applying the base erosion percentage test under §1.59A-2(e).

(2) *Consolidated group as member of the aggregate group.*—The consolidated group is treated as a single member of an aggregate group for purposes of §1.59A-2(c).

(3) *Related party determination.*—For purposes of section 59A and the section 59A regulations, if a person is a related party with respect to any member of a consolidated group, that person is a related party of the group and of each of its members.

(c) *Coordination of section 59A(c)(3) and section 163(j) in a consolidated group.*—(1) *Overview.*—This paragraph (c) provides rules regarding the application of §1.59A-3(c)(4) to a consolidated group's section 163(j) interest deduction. The classification rule in paragraph (c)(3) of this section addresses how to determine if, and to what extent, the group's section 163(j) interest deduction is a base erosion tax benefit. These regulations contain a single-entity classification rule with regard to the deduction of the consolidated group's aggregate current year business interest expense ("BIE"), but a separate-entity classification rule for the deduction of the consolidated group's disallowed BIE carryforwards. Paragraph (c)(3) of this section classifies the group's aggregate current year BIE deduction, in conformity with §1.59A-3(c)(4), as constituting domestic related current year BIE deduction, foreign related current year BIE deduction, or unrelated current year BIE deduction. The allocation rules in paragraph (c)(4) of this section then allocate to specific members of the group the domestic related current year BIE deduction, foreign related current year BIE deduction, and unrelated current year BIE deduction taken in the taxable year. Any member's current year BIE that is carried forward to the succeeding taxable year as a disallowed BIE carryforward is allocated a status as domestic related BIE carryforward, foreign related BIE carryforward, or unrelated BIE carryforward under paragraph (c)(5) of this section. The status of any disallowed BIE carryforward deducted by a member in a later year is classified on a separate-entity basis by the deducting member under paragraph (c)(3) of this section, based on the status allocated to the member's disallowed BIE carryforward under paragraph (c)(5) of this section. This paragraph (c) also provides rules regarding the consequences of the deconsolidation of a corporation that has been allocated a domestic related BIE carryforward status, a foreign related BIE carryforward status, or an unrelated BIE carryforward status; and the consolidation of a corporation with a disallowed BIE carryforward classified as from payments to a domestic related party, foreign related party, or unrelated party.

(2) *Absorption rule for the group's business interest expense.*—To determine the amount of the group's section 163(j) interest deduction, and to determine the year in which the member's business interest expense giving rise to the deduction was incurred or accrued, see §§1.163(j)-4(d) and 1.163(j)-5(b)(3).

(3) *Classification of the group's section 163(j) interest deduction.*—(i) *In general.*—Consistent with §1.59A-3(c)(4)(i) and paragraph (b) of this section, the classification rule of this paragraph (c)(3) determines whether the consolidated group's section 163(j) interest deduction is a base erosion tax benefit. To the extent the consolidated group's business interest expense is permitted as a deduction under section 163(j)(1) in a taxable year, the deduction is classified first as from business interest expense paid or accrued to a foreign related party and business interest expense paid or accrued to a domestic related party (on a pro-rata basis); any remaining deduction is treated as from business interest expense paid or accrued to an unrelated party.

(ii) *Year-by-year application of the classification rule.*—If the consolidated group's section 163(j) interest deduction in any taxable year is attributable to business interest expense paid or accrued in more than one taxable year (for example, the group deducts the group's aggregate current year BIE, the group's disallowed BIE carryforward from year 1, and the group's disallowed BIE carryforward from year

2), the classification rule in paragraph (c)(3)(i) of this section applies separately to each of those years, pursuant to paragraphs (c)(3)(iii) and (iv) of this section.

(iii) *Classification of current year BIE deductions.*—Current year BIE deductions are classified under the section 59A regulations and this paragraph (c) as if the consolidated group were a single taxpayer that had paid or accrued the group's aggregate current year BIE to domestic related parties, foreign related parties, and unrelated parties. The rules of paragraph (c)(4) of this section apply for allocating current year BIE deductions among members of the consolidated group. To the extent the consolidated group's aggregate current year BIE exceeds its section 163(j) limitation, the rules of paragraph (c)(5) of this section apply.

(iv) *Classification of deductions of disallowed BIE carryforwards.*—Each member of the group applies the classification rule in this paragraph (c)(3) to its deduction of any part of a disallowed BIE carryforward from a year, after the group applies paragraph (c)(5) of this section to the consolidated group's disallowed BIE carryforward from that year. Therefore, disallowed BIE carryforward that is actually deducted by a member is classified based on the status of the components of that carryforward, assigned pursuant to paragraph (c)(5) of this section.

(4) *Allocation of domestic related current year BIE deduction status and foreign related current year BIE deduction status among members of the consolidated group.*—(i) *In general.*—This paragraph (c)(4) applies if the group has domestic related current year BIE deductions, foreign related current year BIE deductions, or both, as a result of the application of the classification rule in paragraph (c)(3) of this section. Under this paragraph (c)(4), the domestic related current year BIE, foreign related current year BIE, or both, that is treated as deducted in the current year are deemed to have been incurred pro-rata by all members that have current year BIE deduction in that year, regardless of which member or members actually incurred the current year BIE to a domestic related party or a foreign related party.

(ii) *Domestic related current year BIE deduction.*—(A) *Amount of domestic related current year BIE deduction status allocable to a member.*—The amount of domestic related current year BIE deduction status that is allocated to a member is determined by multiplying the group's domestic related current year BIE deduction (determined pursuant to paragraph (c)(3) of this section) by the percentage of current year BIE deduction allocable to such member in that year.

(B) *Percentage of current year BIE deduction allocable to a member.*—The percentage of current year BIE deduction allocable to a member is equal to the amount of the member's current year BIE deduction divided by the amount of the group's aggregate current year BIE deduction.

(iii) *Amount of foreign related current year BIE deduction status allocable to a member.*—The amount of foreign related current year BIE deduction status that is allocated to a member is determined by multiplying the group's foreign related current year BIE deduction (determined pursuant to paragraph (c)(3) of this section) by the percentage of current year BIE deduction allocable to such member (defined in paragraph (c)(4)(ii)(B) of this section).

(iv) *Treatment of amounts as having unrelated current year BIE deduction status.*—To the extent the amount of a member's current year BIE that is absorbed under paragraph (c)(2) of this section exceeds the domestic related current year BIE deduction status and foreign related current year BIE deduction status allocated to the member under paragraph (c)(4)(ii) and (iii) of this section, such excess amount is treated as from payments or accruals to an unrelated party.

(5) *Allocation of domestic related BIE carryforward status and foreign related BIE carryforward status to members of the group.*—(i) *In general.*—This paragraph (c)(5) applies in any year the consolidated group's aggregate current year BIE exceeds its section 163(j) limitation. After the application of paragraph (c)(4) of this section, any remaining domestic related current year BIE, foreign related current year BIE, and unrelated current year BIE is deemed to have been incurred pro-rata by members of the group pursuant to the rules in paragraph (c)(5)(ii), (iii), and (iv) of this section, regardless of which member or members actually incurred the business interest expense to a domestic related party, foreign related party, or unrelated party.

(ii) *Domestic related BIE carryforward.*—(A) *Amount of domestic related BIE carryforward status allocable to a member.*—The amount of domestic related BIE carryforward status that is allocated to a member equals the group's domestic related BIE carryforward from that year multiplied by the percentage of disallowed BIE carryforward allocable to the member.

(B) *Percentage of disallowed BIE carryforward allocable to a member.*—The percentage of disallowed BIE carryforward allocable to a member for a taxable year equals the member's disallowed BIE carryforward from that year divided by the consolidated group's disallowed BIE carryforwards from that year.

(iii) *Amount of foreign related BIE carryforward status allocable to a member.*—The amount of foreign related BIE carryforward status that is allocated to a member equals the group's foreign related BIE carryforward from that year multiplied by the percentage of disallowed BIE carryforward allocable to the member (as defined in paragraph (c)(5)(ii)(B) of this section).

(iv) *Treatment of amounts as having unrelated BIE carryforward status.*—If a member's disallowed BIE carryforward for a year exceeds the amount of domestic related BIE carryforward status and foreign related BIE carryforward status that is allocated to the member pursuant to paragraphs (c)(5)(ii) and (iii) of this section, respectively, the excess carryforward amount is treated as from payments or accruals to an unrelated party.

(v) *Coordination with section 381.*—If a disallowed BIE carryforward is allocated a status as a domestic related BIE carryforward, foreign related BIE carryforward, or unrelated BIE carryforward under the allocation rule of paragraph (c)(5) of this section, the acquiring corporation in a transaction described in section 381(a) will succeed to and take into account the allocated status of the carryforward for purposes of section 59A. See §1.381(c)(20)-1.

(6) *Member deconsolidates from a consolidated group.*—(i) *General rule.*—When a member deconsolidates from a group (the original group), the member's disallowed BIE carryforwards retain their allocated status, pursuant to paragraph (c)(5) of this section, as a domestic related BIE carryforward, foreign related BIE carryforward, or unrelated BIE carryforward (as applicable). Following the member's deconsolidation, the status of the disallowed BIE carryforwards of the remaining members is not redetermined.

(ii) *Gross receipts exception.*—This paragraph (c)(6)(ii) applies if the original group had insufficient gross receipts to satisfy the gross receipts test under §1.59A-2(d) and thus was not an applicable taxpayer in the year in which the deconsolidating member's disallowed BIE carryforward was incurred. If this paragraph (c)(6)(ii) applies, the deconsolidating member may determine the status of its disallowed BIE carryforward from that year by applying the classification rule of §1.59A-3(c)(4) solely to the interest payments or accruals of the deconsolidating member, rather than by applying §1.1502-59A(c)(3).

(iii) *Failure to substantiate.*—If the deconsolidating member fails to substantiate a disallowed BIE carryforward as a domestic related BIE carryforward, foreign related BIE carryforward, or unrelated BIE carryforward, then the disallowed BIE carryforward is treated as a foreign related BIE carryforward.

(7) *Corporation joins a consolidated group.*—If a corporation joins a consolidated group (the acquiring group), and that corporation was allocated a domestic related BIE carryforward status, foreign related BIE carryforward status, or unrelated BIE carryforward status pursuant to paragraph (c)(5) of this section from another consolidated group (the original group), or separately has a disallowed BIE carryforward that is classified as from payments or accruals to a domestic related party, foreign related party, or unrelated party, the status of the carryforward is taken into account in determining the acquiring group's base erosion tax benefit when the corporation's disallowed BIE carryforward is absorbed.

(d) *Allocation of the base erosion minimum tax amount to members of the consolidated group.*—For rules regarding the allocation of the base erosion minimum tax amount, see section 1552. Allocations under section 1552 take into account the classification and allocation provisions of paragraphs (c)(3) through (5) of this section.

(e) [Reserved].

(f) *Definitions.*—The following definitions apply for purposes of this section—

(1) *Aggregate current year BIE.*—The consolidated group's *aggregate current year BIE* is the aggregate of all members' current year BIE.

(2) *Aggregate current year BIE deduction.*—The consolidated group's *aggregate current year BIE deduction* is the aggregate of all members' current year BIE deductions.

(3) *Applicable taxpayer.*—The term *applicable taxpayer* has the meaning provided in §1.59A-2(b).

(4) *Base erosion minimum tax amount.*—The consolidated group's *base erosion minimum tax amount* is the tax imposed under section 59A.

(5) *Base erosion tax benefit.*—The term *base erosion tax benefit* has the meaning provided in §1.59A-3(c)(1).

(6) *Business interest expense.*—The term *business interest expense*, with respect to a member and a taxable year, has the meaning provided in §1.163(j)-1(b)(3), and with respect to a consolidated group and a taxable year, has the meaning provided in §1.163(j)-4(d)(2)(iii).

(7) *Consolidated group's disallowed BIE carryforwards.*—The term *consolidated group's disallowed BIE carryforwards* has the meaning provided in §1.163(j)-5(b)(3)(i).

(8) *Current year BIE.*—A member's *current year BIE* is the member's business interest expense that would be deductible in the current taxable year without regard to section 163(j) and that is not a disallowed business interest expense carryforward from a prior taxable year.

(9) *Current year BIE deduction.*—A member's *current year BIE deduction* is the member's current year BIE that is permitted as a deduction in the taxable year.

(10) *Domestic related BIE carryforward.*—The consolidated group's *domestic related BIE carryforward* for any taxable year is the excess of the group's domestic related current year BIE over the group's domestic related current year BIE deduction (if any).

(11) *Domestic related current year BIE.*—The consolidated group's *domestic related current year BIE* for any taxable year is the consolidated group's aggregate current year BIE paid or accrued to a domestic related party.

(12) *Domestic related current year BIE deduction.*—The consolidated group's *domestic related current year BIE deduction* for any taxable year is the portion of the group's aggregate current year BIE deduction classified as from interest paid or accrued to a domestic related party under paragraph (c)(3) of this section.

(13) *Domestic related party.*—A *domestic related party* is a related party that is not a foreign related party and is not a member of the same consolidated group.

(14) *Disallowed BIE carryforward.*—The term *disallowed BIE carryforward* has the meaning provided in §1.163(j)-1(b)(11).

(15) *Foreign related BIE carryforward.*—The consolidated group's *foreign related BIE carryforward* for any taxable year, is the excess of the group's foreign related current year BIE over the group's foreign related current year BIE deduction (if any).

(16) *Foreign related current year BIE.*—The consolidated group's *foreign related current year BIE* for any taxable year is the consolidated group's aggregate current year BIE paid or accrued to a foreign related party.

(17) *Foreign related current year BIE deduction.*—The consolidated group's *foreign related current year BIE deduction* for any taxable year is the portion of the consolidated group's aggregate current year BIE deduction classified as from interest paid or accrued to a foreign related party under paragraph (c)(3) of this section.

(18) *Foreign related party.*—A *foreign related party* has the meaning provided in §1.59A-1(b)(12).

(19) *Related party.*—The term *related party* has the meaning provided in §1.59A-1(b)(17), but excludes members of the same consolidated group.

(20) *Section 163(j) interest deduction.*—The term *section 163(j) interest deduction* means, with respect to a taxable year, the amount of the consolidated group's business interest expense permitted as a deduction pursuant to §1.163(j)-5(b)(3) in the taxable year.

(21) *Section 163(j) limitation.*—The term *section 163(j) limitation* has the meaning provided in §1.163(j)-1(b)(36).

(22) *Unrelated BIE carryforward.*—The consolidated group's *unrelated BIE carryforward* for any taxable year is the excess of the group's unrelated current year BIE over the group's unrelated current year BIE deduction.

(23) *Unrelated current year BIE.*—The consolidated group's *unrelated current year BIE* for any taxable year is the consolidated group's aggregate current year BIE paid or accrued to an unrelated party.

(24) *Unrelated current year BIE deduction.*—The consolidated group's *unrelated current year BIE deduction* for any taxable year is the

portion of the group's aggregate current year BIE deduction classified as from interest paid or accrued to an unrelated party under paragraph (c)(3) of this section.

(25) *Unrelated party.*—An *unrelated party* is a party that is not a related party.

(g) *Examples.*—The following examples illustrate the general application of this section. For purposes of the examples, a foreign corporation (FP) wholly owns domestic corporation (P), which in turn wholly owns S1 and S2. P, S1, and S2 are members of a consolidated group. The consolidated group is a calendar year taxpayer.

(1) *Example 1: Computation of the consolidated group's base erosion minimum tax amount.* (i) *The consolidated group is the applicable taxpayer*—(A) *Facts.* The members have never engaged in intercompany transactions. For the 2019 taxable year, P, S1, and S2 were permitted the following amounts of deductions (within the meaning of section 59A(c)(4)), $2,400x, $1,000x, and $2,600x; those deductions include base erosion tax benefits of $180x, $370x, and $230x. The group's consolidated taxable income for the year is $150x. In addition, the group satisfies the gross receipts test in § 1.59A-2(d).

(B) *Analysis.* Pursuant to paragraph (b) of this section, the receipts and deductions of P, S1, and S2 are aggregated for purposes of making the computations under section 59A. The group's base erosion percentage is 13% (($180x + $370x + $230x)/($2,400x + $1,000x + $2,600x)). The consolidated group is an applicable taxpayer under § 1.59A-2(b) because the group satisfies the gross receipts test and the group's base erosion percentage (13%) is higher than 3%. The consolidated group's modified taxable income is computed by adding back the members' base erosion tax benefits (and, when the consolidated group has consolidated net operating loss available for deduction, the consolidated net operating loss allowed multiplied by the base erosion percentage) to the consolidated taxable income, $930x ($150x + $180x + $370x + $230x). The group's base erosion minimum tax amount is then computed as 10 percent of the modified taxable income less the regular tax liability, $61.5x ($930x × 10% - $150x × 21%).

(ii) *The consolidated group engages in intercompany transactions*—(A) *Facts.* The facts are the same as in paragraph (g)(1)(i)(A) of this section (the facts in *Example* 1(i)), except that S1 sold various inventory items to S2 during 2019. Such items are depreciable in the hands of S2 (but would not have been depreciable in the hands of S1) and continued to be owned by S2 during 2019.

(B) *Analysis.* The result is the same as paragraph (g)(1)(i)(A) of this section (the facts in *Example 1*(i)). Pursuant to paragraph (b)(2) of this section, items resulting from the intercompany sale (for example, gross receipts, depreciation deductions) are not taken into account in computing the group's gross receipts under § 1.59A-2(d) and base erosion percentage under § 1.59A-2(e)(3).

(2) *Example 2: Business interest expense subject to section 163(j) and the group's domestic related current year BIE and foreign related current year BIE for the year equals its section 163(j) limitation*—(i) *Facts.* During the current year (Year 1), P incurred $150x of business interest expense to domestic related parties; S1 incurred $150x of business interest expense to foreign related parties; and S2 incurred $150x of business interest expense to unrelated parties. The group's section 163(j) limitation for the year is $300x. After applying the rules in § 1.163(j)-5(b)(3), the group deducts $150x of P's Year 1 business interest expense, and $75x each of S1 and S2's Year 1 business interest expense. Assume the group is an applicable taxpayer for purposes of section 59A.

(ii) *Analysis*—(A) *Application of the absorption rule in paragraph (c)(2) of this section.* Following the rules in section 163(j), the group's section 163(j) interest deduction for Year 1 is $300x, and the entire amount is from members' Year 1 business interest expense.

(B) *Application of the classification rule in paragraph (c)(3) of this section.* Under paragraph (c)(3) of this section, the group's aggregate current year BIE deduction of $300x is first classified as payments or accruals to related parties (pro-rata among domestic related parties and foreign related parties), and second as payments or accruals to unrelated parties. For Year 1, the group has $150x of domestic related current year BIE and $150x of foreign related current year BIE, and the group's aggregate current year BIE deduction will be classified equally among the related party expenses. Therefore, $150x of the group's deduction is classified as domestic related current year BIE deduction and $150x is classified as a foreign related current year BIE deduction.

(C) *Application of the allocation rule in paragraph (c)(4) of this section.* After the application of the classification rule in paragraph (c)(3) of this section, the group has $150x each of domestic related current year BIE deduction and foreign related current year BIE deduction from the group's aggregate current year BIE in Year 1. The domestic related current year BIE deduction and foreign related current year BIE deduction will be allocated to P, S1, and S2 based on each member's deduction of its Year 1 business interest expense.

(1) *Allocations to P.* The percentage of current year BIE deduction attributable to P is 50% (P's deduction of its Year 1 current year BIE, $150x, divided by the group's aggregate current year BIE deduction for Year 1, $300x). Thus, the amount of domestic related current year BIE deduction status allocated to P is $75x (the group's domestic related current year BIE deduction, $150x, multiplied by the percentage of current year BIE deduction allocable to P, 50%); and the amount of foreign related current year BIE deduction status allocated to P is $75x (the group's foreign related current year BIE deduction, $150x, multiplied by the percentage of current year BIE deduction allocable to P, 50%).

(2) *Allocations to S1 and S2.* The percentage of current year BIE deduction attributable to S1 is 25% (S1's deduction of its Year 1 current year BIE, $75x, divided by the group's aggregate current year BIE deduction for Year 1, $300x). Thus, the amount of domestic related current year BIE deduction status allocated to S1 is $37.5x (the group's domestic related current year BIE deduction, $150x, multiplied by the percentage of current year BIE deduction allocable to S1, 25%); and the amount of foreign related current year BIE deduction status allocated to S1 is $37.5x (the group's foreign related current year BIE deduction, $150x, multiplied by the percentage of current year BIE deduction allocable to S1, 25%). Because S2 also deducted $75 of its Year 1 current year BIE, S2's deductions are allocated the same pro-rata status as those of S1 under this paragraph (f)(2)(ii)(C)(2).

(D) *Application of the allocation rule in paragraph (c)(5) of this section.* Although the group will have disallowed BIE carryforwards after Year 1 (the group's aggregate current year BIE of $450x ($150x + $150x + $150x) exceeds the section 163(j) limitation of $300x), all of the domestic related current year BIE and foreign related current year BIE in Year 1 has been taken into account pursuant to the classification rule in paragraph (c)(3) of this section. Thus, under paragraph (c)(5)(iv) of this section, each member's disallowed BIE carryforward is treated as from payments or accruals to unrelated parties.

(3) *Example 3: Business interest expense subject to section 163(j)*—(i) *The group's domestic related current year BIE and foreign related current year BIE for the year exceeds its section 163(j) limitation.* (A) *Facts.* During the current year (Year 1), P incurred $60x of business interest expense to domestic related parties; S1 incurred $40x of business interest expense to foreign related parties; and S2 incurred $80x of business interest expense to unrelated parties. The group's section 163(j) limitation for the year is $60x. After applying the rules in § 1.163(j)-5(b)(3), the group deducts $20x each of P, S1, and S2's current year business interest expense. Assume the group is an applicable taxpayer for purposes of section 59A.

(B) *Analysis*—(1) *Application of the absorption rule in paragraph (c)(2) of this section.* Following the rules in section 163(j), the group's section 163(j) interest deduction is $60x, and the entire amount is from members' Year 1 business interest expense.

(2) *Application of the classification rule in paragraph (c)(3) of this section.* Under paragraph (c)(3) of this section, the group's $60x of aggregate current year BIE deduction is first classified as payments or accruals to related parties (pro-rata among domestic related parties and foreign related parties), and second as payments or accruals from unrelated parties. The group's total related party interest expense in Year 1, $100x (sum of the group's Year 1 domestic related current year BIE, $60x, and the group's Year 1 foreign related current year BIE, $40x), exceeds the group's aggregate current year BIE deduction of $60x. Thus, the group's aggregate current year BIE deduction will be classified, pro-rata, as from payments or accruals to domestic related parties and foreign related parties. Of the group's aggregate current year BIE deduction in Year 1, $36x is classified as a domestic related current year BIE deduction (the group's aggregate current year BIE deduction, $60x, multiplied by the ratio of domestic related current year BIE over the group's total Year 1 related party interest expense ($60x / ($60x+$40x))); and $24x of the group's aggregate current year BIE deduction is classified as a foreign related current year BIE deduction (the group's section 163(j) interest deduction, $60x, multiplied by the ratio of foreign related current year BIE over the group's total Year 1 related party interest expense ($40x / ($60x+$40x))).

(3) *Application of the allocation rule in paragraph (c)(4) of this section.* After the application of the classification rule in paragraph (c)(3) of this section, the group has $36x of domestic related current year BIE deduction and $24x of foreign related current year BIE deduction from the group's aggregate current year BIE in Year 1. The domestic related current year BIE deduction and foreign related current year BIE deduction will be allocated to P, S1, and S2 based on each member's current year BIE deduction in Year 1.

(i) *Allocation of the group's domestic related current year BIE deduction status.* Because each member is deducting $20x of its Year 1 business interest expense, all three members have the same percentage of current year BIE deduction attributable to them. The percentage of current year BIE deduction attributable to each of P, S1, and S2 is

33.33% (each member's current year BIE deduction in Year 1, $20x, divided by the group's aggregate current year BIE deduction for Year 1, $60x). Thus, the amount of domestic related current year BIE deduction status allocable to each member is $12x (the group's domestic related current year BIE deduction, $36x, multiplied by the percentage of current year BIE deduction allocable to each member, 33.33%).

*(ii) Allocations of the group's foreign related current year BIE deduction status.* The amount of foreign related current year BIE deduction status allocable to each member is $8x (the group's foreign related current year BIE deduction, $24x, multiplied by the percentage of current year BIE deduction allocable to each member, 33.33%, as computed earlier in paragraph (f)(3) of this section (*Example 3*).

*(4) Application of the allocation rule in paragraph (c)(5) of this section.* In Year 1 the group has $60x of domestic related current year BIE, of which $36x is deducted in the year (by operation of the classification rule). Therefore, the group has $24x of domestic related BIE carryforward. Similarly, the group has $40x of foreign related current year BIE in Year 1, of which $24x is deducted in the year. Therefore, the group has $16x of foreign related BIE carryforward. The $24x domestic related BIE carryforward status and $16x foreign related BIE carryforward status will be allocated to P, S1, and S2 in proportion to the amount of each member's disallowed BIE carryforward.

*(i) Allocation to P.* The percentage of disallowed BIE carryforward allocable to P is 33.33% (P's Year 1 disallowed BIE carryforward, $40x ($60x - $20x), divided by the group's Year 1 disallowed BIE carryforward, $120x ($60x + $40x + 80x - $60x)). Thus, the amount of domestic related BIE carryforward status allocated to P is $8x (the group's domestic related BIE carryforward, $24x, multiplied by the percentage of disallowed BIE carryforward allocable to P, 33.33%); and the amount of foreign related BIE carryforward status allocated to P is $5.33x (the group's foreign related BIE carryforward, $16x, multiplied by the percentage of disallowed BIE carryforward allocable to P, 33.33%). Under paragraph (c)(5)(iv) of this section, P's disallowed BIE carryforward that has not been allocated a status as either a domestic related BIE carryforward or a foreign related BIE carryforward will be treated as interest paid or accrued to an unrelated party. Therefore, $26.67x ($40x P's disallowed BIE carryforward - $8x domestic related BIE carryforward status allocated to P - $5.33x foreign related BIE carryforward status allocated to P) is treated as interest paid or accrued to an unrelated party.

*(ii) Allocation to S1.* The percentage of disallowed BIE carryforward allocable to S1 is 16.67% (S1's Year 1 disallowed BIE carryforward, $20x ($40x - $20x), divided by the group's Year 1 disallowed BIE carryforward, $120x ($60x + $40x + 80x - $60x)). Thus, the amount of domestic related BIE carryforward status allocated to S1 is $4x (the group's domestic related BIE carryforward, $24x, multiplied by the percentage of disallowed BIE carryforward allocable to S1, 16.67%); and the amount of foreign related BIE carryforward status allocated to S1 is $2.67x (the group's foreign related BIE carryforward, $16x, multiplied by the percentage of disallowed BIE carryforward allocable to S1, 16.67%). Under paragraph (c)(5)(iv) of this section, S1's disallowed BIE that has not been allocated a status as either a domestic related BIE carryforward or a foreign related BIE carryforward will be treated as interest paid or accrued to an unrelated party. Therefore, $13.33x ($20x S1's disallowed BIE carryforward - $4x domestic related BIE carryforward status allocated to S1 - $2.67x foreign related BIE carryforward status allocated to S1) is treated as interest paid or accrued to an unrelated party.

*(iii) Allocation to S2.* The percentage of disallowed BIE carryforward allocable to S2 is 50% (S2's Year 1 disallowed BIE carryforward, $60x ($80x-$20x), divided by the group's Year 1 disallowed BIE carryforward, $120x ($60x+$40x+80x-$60x)). Thus, the amount of domestic related BIE carryforward status allocated to S2 is $12x (the group's domestic related BIE carryforward, $24x, multiplied by the percentage of disallowed BIE carryforward allocable to S2, 50%); and the amount of foreign related BIE carryforward status allocated to S2 is $8x (the group's foreign related BIE carryforward, $16x, multiplied by the percentage of disallowed BIE carryforward allocable to S2, 50%). Under paragraph (c)(5)(iv) of this section, S2's disallowed BIE that has not been allocated a status as either a domestic related BIE carryforward or a foreign related BIE carryforward will be treated as interest paid or accrued to an unrelated party. Therefore, $40x ($60x S2's disallowed BIE carryforward - $12x domestic related BIE carryforward status allocated to S2 - $8x foreign related BIE carryforward status allocated to S2) is treated as interest paid or accrued to an unrelated party.

*(ii) The group deducting its disallowed BIE carryforwards*—(A) *Facts.* The facts are the same as in paragraph (g)(3)(i)(A) of this section (the facts in *Example 3*(i)), and in addition, none of the members incurs any business interest expense in Year 2. The group's section 163(j) limitation for Year 2 is $30x.

(B) *Analysis*—(1) *Application of the absorption rule in paragraph (c)(2) of this section.* Following the rules in section 163(j), each member of the group is deducting $10x of its disallowed BIE carryforward from Year 1. Therefore, the group's section 163(j) deduction for Year 2 is $30x.

(2) *Application of the classification rule in paragraph (c)(3) of this section.* Under paragraph (c)(3)(iv) of this section, to the extent members are deducting their Year 1 disallowed BIE carryforward in Year 2, the classification rule will apply to the deduction in Year 2 after the allocation rule in paragraph (c)(5) of this section has allocated the related and unrelated party status to the member's disallowed BIE carryforward in Year 1. The allocation required under paragraph (c)(5) of this section is described in paragraph (f)(3)(i)(B)(4) of this section.

*(i) Use of P's allocated domestic related BIE carryforward status and foreign related BIE carryforward status.* P has $40x of Year 1 disallowed BIE carryforward, and P was allocated $8x of domestic related BIE carryforward status and $5.33x of foreign related BIE carryforward status. In Year 2, P deducts $10x of its Year 1 disallowed BIE carryforward. Under the classification rule of paragraph (c)(3) of this section, P is treated as deducting pro-rata from its allocated status of domestic related BIE carryforward and foreign related BIE carryforward. Therefore, P is treated as deducting $6x of its allocated domestic related BIE carryforward ($10x × $8x / ($8x + $5.33x)), and $4x of its allocated foreign related BIE carryforward ($10x × $5.33x / $8x + $5.33x)). After Year 2, P has remaining $30x of Year 1 disallowed BIE carryforward, of which $2x has a status of domestic related BIE carryforward, $1.33x has the status of foreign related BIE carryforward, and $26.67x of interest treated as paid or accrued to unrelated parties.

*(ii) Use of S1's allocated domestic related BIE carryforward status and foreign related BIE carryforward status.* S1 has $20x of Year 1 disallowed BIE carryforward, and S1 was allocated $4x of domestic related BIE carryforward status and $2.67x of foreign related BIE carryforward status. In Year 2, S2 deducts $10x of its Year 1 disallowed BIE carryforward. Because S2's deduction of its Year 1 disallowed BIE carryforward, $10x, exceeds its allocated domestic related BIE carryforward status ($4x) and foreign related BIE carryforward status ($2.67x), all of the allocated related party status are used up. After Year 2, all of S1's Year 1 disallowed BIE carryforward, $10x, is treated as interest paid or accrued to an unrelated party.

*(iii) Use of S2's allocated domestic related BIE carryforward status and foreign related BIE carryforward status.* S2 has $60x of Year 1 disallowed BIE carryforward, and S2 was allocated $12x of domestic related BIE carryforward status and $8x of foreign related BIE carryforward status. In Year 2, S2 deducts $10x of its Year 1 disallowed BIE carryforward. Under the classification rule of paragraph (c)(3) of this section, S2 is treated as deducting $6x of its allocated domestic related BIE carryforward ($10x × $12x / ($12x + $8x)), and $4x of its allocated foreign related BIE carryforward ($10x × $8x / $8x + $12x)). After Year 2, P has remaining $50x of Year 1 disallowed BIE carryforward, of which $6x has a status of domestic related BIE carryforward, $4x has the status of foreign related BIE carryforward, and $40x of interest treated as paid or accrued to unrelated parties.

(h) *Applicability date.* This section applies to taxable years for which the original consolidated Federal income tax return is due (without extensions) after December 6, 2019. [Reg. § 1.1502-59A.]

☐ [*T.D.* 9885, 12-2-2019. *Amended by T.D.* 9910, 10-8-2020.]

**[1.1502-68]**

**§ 1.1502-68. Additional first year depreciation deduction for property acquired and placed in service after September 27, 2017.**—(a) *In general.*—(1) *Overview.*—This section provides rules governing the availability of the additional first year depreciation deduction allowable under section 168(k) for qualified property that is acquired and placed in service after September 27, 2017, by a member of a consolidated group. Except as otherwise provided in paragraph (c) of this section, the rules in § 1.168(k)-2 apply to members of a consolidated group in addition to the rules in this section. Paragraph (a)(2) of this section provides definitions of terms used in this section. Paragraph (b) of this section provides rules addressing the application of § 1.168(k)-2(b)(3)(iii)(A)(1) (requiring that a taxpayer claiming the additional first year depreciation deduction for used property not previously have used the property) to members of a consolidated group. Paragraph (c) of this section provides rules addressing certain transfers of eligible property (as defined in paragraph (a)(2)(vii) of this section) between members of a consolidated group if the transferee member (as defined in paragraph (a)(2)(xii) of this section) leaves the group pursuant to the same series of related transactions. Paragraph (d) of this section provides examples illustrating the application of the rules of this section. Paragraph (e) of this section provides the applicability dates.

(2) *Definitions.*—The following definitions apply for purposes of this section.

(i) *Consolidated Asset Acquisition Rule.*—The term *Consolidated Asset Acquisition Rule* refers to the rule set forth in paragraph (c)(1)(i) of this section addressing certain intercompany transfers of eligible property.

(ii) *Consolidated Deemed Acquisition Rule.*—The term *Consolidated Deemed Acquisition Rule* refers to the rule set forth in paragraph (c)(2)(i) of this section addressing certain intercompany transfers of the stock of target (as defined in paragraph (a)(2)(xi) of this section).

(iii) *Deconsolidation date.*—The term *deconsolidation date* means the date on which a transferee member ceases to be a member of a consolidated group.

(iv) *Designated transaction.*—The term *designated transaction* has the meaning provided in paragraph (c)(4)(i) of this section.

(v) *Deemed replacement property.*—The term *deemed replacement property* means used property that is identical to (but is separate and distinct from) the eligible property that the transferee member or target is deemed to sell to an unrelated party under the Consolidated Asset Acquisition Rule or the Consolidated Deemed Acquisition Rule. For all Federal income tax purposes, the deemed purchase of deemed replacement property by the transferee member or target under paragraph (c)(1)(i)(B) or (c)(2)(i)(B) of this section, respectively, does not result in the basis in such property being determined, in whole or in part, by reference to the basis of other property held at any time by the transferee member or target. See section 179(d)(3) and § 1.168(k)-2(b)(3)(iii)(A)(3).

(vi) *Deemed sale amount.*—The term *deemed sale amount* means an amount equal to the transferee member's or the target's adjusted basis in the eligible property immediately before the transferee member or target is deemed to sell the property to an unrelated party under the Consolidated Asset Acquisition Rule or the Consolidated Deemed Acquisition Rule.

(vii) *Eligible property.*—The term *eligible property* means depreciable property (as defined in § 1.168(b)-1(a)(1)) that meets the requirements in § 1.168(k)-2(b)(2), determined without regard to § 1.168(k)-2(b)(2)(ii)(C) (property subject to an election not to claim the additional first year depreciation for a class of property) except on the day after the deconsolidation date.

(viii) *Group Prior Use Rule.*—The term *Group Prior Use Rule* refers to the rule set forth in paragraph (b)(1) of this section addressing when a member of a consolidated group is attributed another member's depreciable interest in property.

(ix) *Lookback Period.*—The term *lookback period* means, with respect to a member of a consolidated group, the period that includes the five calendar years immediately prior to the current calendar year in which the property is placed in service by such member, as well as the portion of such current calendar year before the date on which the member placed the property in service (without taking into account the applicable convention).

(x) *Stock and Asset Acquisition Rule.*—The term *Stock and Asset Acquisition Rule* refers to the rule set forth in paragraph (b)(2) of this section addressing when a member of a consolidated group is attributed a new member's depreciable interest in property.

(xi) *Target.*—The term *target* means the member whose stock is transferred in a transaction that is subject to the Consolidated Deemed Acquisition Rule.

(xii) *Transferee member.*—The term *transferee member* means the member that acquires eligible property or target stock, respectively, in a transaction that is subject to the Consolidated Asset Acquisition Rule or the Consolidated Deemed Acquisition Rule.

(xiii) *Transferor member.*—The term *transferor member* means the member that transfers eligible property or target stock, respectively, in a transaction that is subject to the Consolidated Asset Acquisition Rule or the Consolidated Deemed Acquisition Rule.

(b) *Acquisitions of depreciable property by a member of a consolidated group.*—(1) *General rule (Group Prior Use Rule).*—Solely for purposes of applying § 1.168(k)-2(b)(3)(iii)(A)(1), if a member of a consolidated group acquires depreciable property in which the group had a depreciable interest at any time within the lookback period, the member is treated as having a depreciable interest in the property prior to the acquisition. For purposes of this paragraph (b)(1), a consolidated group is treated as having a depreciable interest in property during the time any current or previous member of the group had a depreciable interest in the property while a member of the group. For special rules that apply when a member of a consolidated group acquires depreciable property in an intercompany transaction (as defined in § 1.1502-13(b)(1)(i)) and then leaves the group pursuant to

the same series of related transactions, see paragraph (c) of this section.

(2) *Certain acquisitions pursuant to a series of related transactions (Stock and Asset Acquisition Rule).*—Solely for purposes of applying § 1.168(k)-2(b)(3)(iii)(A)(1), if a series of related transactions includes one or more transactions in which property is acquired by a member of a consolidated group, and one or more transactions in which a corporation that had a depreciable interest in the property (determined without regard to the application of the Group Prior Use Rule) within the lookback period becomes a member of the group, then the member that acquires the property is treated as having a depreciable interest in the property prior to the acquisition.

(c) *Certain intercompany transfers of eligible property followed by deconsolidation.*—(1) *Acquisition of eligible property by a member that leaves the group.*—(i) *General rule (Consolidated Asset Acquisition Rule).*—This paragraph (c)(1) applies to certain transactions pursuant to which one member of a consolidated group (transferee member) acquires from another member of the same consolidated group (transferor member) eligible property. Except as otherwise provided in paragraph (c)(3) or (4) of this section, if a transaction satisfies the requirements of paragraph (c)(1)(ii) of this section, then § 1.168(k)-2(b)(3)(iii)(C) (providing special rules when depreciable property is acquired as part of a series of related transactions) does not apply to the transaction, and for all Federal income tax purposes—

(A) The transferee member is treated as selling the eligible property to an unrelated person on the day after the deconsolidation date in exchange for an amount of cash equal to the deemed sale amount; and

(B) Immediately after the deemed sale in paragraph (c)(1)(i)(A) of this section, the transferee member is treated as purchasing deemed replacement property from an unrelated person for an amount of cash equal to the deemed sale amount.

(ii) *Requirements.*—A transaction satisfies the requirements of this paragraph (c)(1)(ii) if—

(A) The transferee member's acquisition of the eligible property meets the requirements of § 1.168(k)-2(b)(3)(iii)(A) without regard to section 179(d)(2)(A) or (B) and § 1.179-4(c)(1)(ii) or (iii) or the Group Prior Use Rule;

(B) As part of the same series of related transactions that includes the acquisition, the transferee member ceases to be a member of the consolidated group and ceases to be related, within the meaning of section 179(d)(2)(A) or (B) and § 1.179-4(c)(1)(ii) or (iii), to the transferor member; and

(C) The acquired eligible property continues to be eligible property on the deconsolidation date and the day after the deconsolidation date.

(2) *Deemed acquisition of eligible property pursuant to an election under section 338 or 336(e) by a member that leaves the group.*—(i) *General rule (Consolidated Deemed Acquisition Rule).*—This paragraph (c)(2) applies to certain transactions pursuant to which a transferee member acquires from a transferor member the stock of another member of the same consolidated group that holds eligible property (target) in either a qualified stock purchase for which a section 338 election is made or a qualified stock disposition described in § 1.336-2(b)(1) for which a section 336(e) election is made. Except as otherwise provided in paragraph (c)(3) or (4) of this section, if a transaction satisfies the requirements of paragraph (c)(2)(ii) of this section, then § 1.168(k)-2(b)(3)(iii)(C) does not apply to the transaction, and for all Federal income tax purposes—

(A) The target is treated as selling the eligible property to an unrelated person on the day after the deconsolidation date in exchange for an amount of cash equal to the deemed sale amount; and

(B) Immediately after the deemed sale in paragraph (c)(2)(i)(A) of this section, the target is treated as purchasing deemed replacement property from an unrelated person for an amount of cash equal to the deemed sale amount.

(ii) *Requirements.*—A transaction satisfies the requirements of this paragraph (c)(2)(ii) if:

(A) The target's acquisition of the eligible property meets the requirements of § 1.168(k)-2(b)(3)(iii)(A) without regard to the Group Prior Use Rule;

(B) As part of the same series of related transactions that includes the qualified stock purchase or qualified stock disposition, the transferee member and the target cease to be members of the transferor member's consolidated group and cease to be related, within the meaning of section 179(d)(2)(A) or (B) and § 1.179-4(c)(1)(ii) or (iii), to the transferor member; and

(C) The target's eligible property on the acquisition date (within the meaning of § 1.338-2(c)(1)) or the disposition date (within the meaning of §1.336-1(b)(8)) continues to be eligible property on the deconsolidation date and the day after the deconsolidation date.

(3) *Disposition of depreciable property pursuant to the same series of related transactions.*—Paragraph (c)(1) of this section does not apply if, following the acquisition of eligible property, the transferee member disposes of such property pursuant to the same series of related transactions that includes the property acquisition. Paragraph (c)(2) of this section does not apply if, following the deemed acquisition of eligible property, the target disposes of such property pursuant to the same series of related transactions that includes the qualified stock purchase or qualified stock disposition. See §1.168(k)-2(b)(3)(iii)(C) for rules regarding the transfer of property in a series of related transactions. See also §1.168(k)-2(g)(1) for rules regarding property placed in service and disposed of in the same taxable year. For purposes of this paragraph (c)(3), the deemed sale of eligible property by the transferee member or the target pursuant to paragraph (c)(1)(i)(A) or (c)(2)(i)(A) of this section is not treated as a "disposition" of such property.

(4) *Election to not apply paragraph (c)(1)(i) or (c)(2)(i) of this section.*—(i) *In general.*—If a transaction satisfies the requirements of the Consolidated Asset Acquisition Rule or the Consolidated Deemed Acquisition Rule in paragraph (c)(1)(ii) or (c)(2)(ii) of this section, respectively, the transferee member or the target nonetheless may elect not to apply the Consolidated Asset Acquisition Rule or the Consolidated Deemed Acquisition Rule, respectively, to all eligible property that is acquired or deemed acquired in such transaction. If a transferee member or target makes an election under this paragraph (c)(4) with respect to any transaction (designated transaction), then—

(A) The transferee member or target is deemed to have made such an election for all other transactions—

(1) That satisfy the requirements of the Consolidated Asset Acquisition Rule or the Consolidated Deemed Acquisition Rule;

(2) That are part of the same series of related transactions as the designated transaction; and

(3) In which the transferee member or target either is the same transferee member or target as in the designated transaction or is related, within the meaning of section 179(d)(2)(A) or (B) and §1.179-4(c)(1)(ii) or (iii), to the transferee member or target in the designated transaction immediately after the end of the series of related transactions; and

(B) Any eligible property acquired or deemed acquired in the designated transaction and in any transactions described in paragraph (c)(4)(i)(A) of this section does not satisfy either the original use requirement or the used property acquisition requirements in §1.168(k)-2(b)(3) and, thus, is not "qualified property" within the meaning of §1.168(k)-2(b)(1).

(ii) *Time and manner for making election.*—(A) *Time to make election.*—An election under this paragraph (c)(4) must be made by the due date, including extensions, for the Federal tax return for the taxable year of the transferee member or target that begins on the day after the deconsolidation date.

(B) *Manner of making election.*—A transferee member or target, as applicable, makes the election under this paragraph (c)(4) by attaching a statement to its return for the taxable year that begins on the day after the deconsolidation date. The statement must describe the transaction(s) to which the Consolidated Asset Acquisition Rule or Consolidated Deemed Acquisition Rule otherwise would apply and state that the transferee member or the target, as applicable, is not claiming the additional first year depreciation deduction for any eligible property transferred in such transaction(s). If, at the time the election is made, the transferee member or the target is a member of a consolidated group, the statement is made by the agent for the group (within the meaning of §1.1502-77(a) and (c)) on behalf of the transferee member or the target and is attached to the consolidated return of the group for the taxable year of the group that includes the taxable year of the transferee member or target that begins on the day after the deconsolidation date.

(C) *Additional procedural guidance.*—The IRS may publish procedural guidance in the Internal Revenue Bulletin (see §601.601(d)(2)(ii)(b) of this chapter) that provides alternative procedures for complying with paragraph (c)(4)(ii)(A) or (B) of this section.

(iii) *Revocation of election.*—An election specified in this paragraph (c)(4), once made, may be revoked only by filing a request for a private letter ruling and obtaining the Commissioner of Internal Revenue's written consent to revoke the election. The Commissioner may grant a request to revoke the election if the taxpayer acted reasonably and in good faith, and the revocation will not prejudice the interests of the Government. See generally §301.9100-3 of this chapter. An election specified in this paragraph (c)(4) may not be revoked through a request under section 446(e) to change the taxpayer's method of accounting.

(d) *Examples.*—For purposes of the examples in this section, unless otherwise stated: Parent, S, B, Controlled, and T are members of a consolidated group of which Parent is the common parent (Parent group); Parent owns all of the only class of stock of each of S, B, Controlled, and T; X is the common parent of the X consolidated group (X group); no member of the X group is related, within the meaning of section 179(d)(2)(A) or (B) and §1.179-4(c)(1)(ii) or (iii) (Related), to any member of the Parent group; G and U are corporations that are not Related to each other or to any member of the Parent group or the X group; the Equipment in each example is eligible property; no member of the Parent group or the X group has had a depreciable interest in the Equipment within the lookback period; §1.168(k)-2(b)(3)(iii)(A)(1) is referred to as the No Prior Use Requirement; and §1.168(k)-2(b)(3)(iii)(A)(2) is referred to as the Unrelated Party Requirement. The rules of this section are illustrated by the following examples.

(1) *Example 1: Intercompany sale of eligible property.*—(i) *Facts.* S has a depreciable interest in Equipment #1. In 2018, S sells Equipment #1 to B, and B places Equipment #1 in service in the same year.

(ii) *Analysis.* B's acquisition of Equipment #1 does not satisfy either the No Prior Use Requirement or the Unrelated Party Requirement. Under the Group Prior Use Rule, B is treated as previously having a depreciable interest in Equipment #1 because B (a member of the Parent group) acquired Equipment #1 and S, while a member of the Parent group, had a depreciable interest in Equipment #1 within the lookback period. In addition, B acquires Equipment #1 from S, and B and S are Related at the time of the acquisition. Accordingly, B is not eligible to claim the additional first year depreciation deduction for Equipment #1 in 2018.

(2) *Example 2: Sale outside of the consolidated group followed by a reacquisition within the lookback period.*—(i) *Facts.* S has a depreciable interest in Equipment #2. In 2018, S sells Equipment #2 to G. In 2019, in an unrelated transaction, B acquires Equipment #2 from G and places it in service in the same year.

(ii) *Analysis.* B's acquisition of Equipment #2 does not satisfy the No Prior Use Requirement as a result of the Group Prior Use Rule. Pursuant to the Group Prior Use Rule, B is treated as previously having a depreciable interest in Equipment #2 because B is a member of the Parent group and S, while a member of the Parent group, had a depreciable interest in Equipment #2 within the lookback period. Thus, B is not eligible to claim the additional first year depreciation deduction for Equipment #2 in 2019. The result would be the same if, after selling Equipment #2 to G, S had ceased to be a member of the Parent group prior to B's acquisition of Equipment #2.

(iii) *Sale outside of the consolidated group followed by a reacquisition beyond the lookback period.* The facts are the same as in paragraph (d)(2)(i) of this section, except that B acquires Equipment #2 and places it in service in 2024 instead of 2019. B's acquisition of Equipment #2 satisfies the No Prior Use Requirement. B would not be treated as previously having a depreciable interest in Equipment #2 under the Group Prior Use Rule because the Parent group did not have a depreciable interest in Equipment #2 within the lookback period. Further, B itself did not have a prior depreciable interest in Equipment #2 within the lookback period. Assuming all other requirements in §1.168(k)-2 are satisfied, B is eligible to claim the additional first year depreciation deduction for Equipment #2 in 2024. The result would be the same if S, rather than B, acquired and placed in service Equipment #2 in 2024.

(3) *Example 3: Acquisition of eligible property by the consolidated group followed by a corporation with a prior depreciable interest joining the group as part of the same series of related transactions.*—(i) *Facts.* G has a depreciable interest in Equipment #3. During 2018, G sells Equipment #3 to U. In a series of related transactions that does not include the 2018 sale, Parent acquires all of the stock of G in 2019. Later in 2019, B purchases Equipment #3 from U and places it in service immediately thereafter.

(ii) *Analysis.* B's acquisition of Equipment #3 does not satisfy the No Prior Use Requirement as a result of the Stock and Asset Acquisition Rule. In a series of related transactions, G became a member of the Parent group and B acquired Equipment #3. Because G had a depreciable interest in Equipment #3 within the lookback period, B is treated as having a depreciable interest in Equipment #3 under the Stock and Asset Acquisition Rule. Thus, B is not eligible to claim the additional first year depreciation deduction for Equipment #3 in 2019.

(iii) *B purchases Equipment #3 in 2024.* The facts are the same as in paragraph (d)(3)(i) of this section, except that B acquires and places in service Equipment #3 in 2024 instead of 2019. B is not treated under the Stock and Asset Acquisition Rule as having a prior depreciable interest in Equipment #3 because G (which sold Equipment #3 to U in 2018) did not have a depreciable interest in Equipment #3 within the lookback period. In addition, B is not treated under the Group Prior Use Rule as having a prior depreciable interest in

Equipment #3 at the time of the purchase because neither G nor any other member of the Parent group had a depreciable interest in Equipment #3 while a member of the Parent group within the lookback period. Further, B itself did not have a depreciable interest in Equipment #3 within the lookback period. Accordingly, B's acquisition of Equipment #3 satisfies the No Prior Use Requirement. Assuming all other requirements in § 1.168(k)-2 are satisfied, B is eligible to claim the additional first year depreciation deduction for Equipment #3 in 2024.

(iv) *No series of related transactions.* The facts are the same as in paragraph (d)(3)(i) of this section, except that Parent's acquisition of the G stock and B's purchase of Equipment #3 are not part of the same series of related transactions. Because B's purchase of Equipment #3 and Parent's acquisition of the G stock did not occur pursuant to the same series of related transactions, the Stock and Asset Acquisition Rule does not apply. In addition, B is not treated under the Group Prior Use Rule as having a prior depreciable interest in Equipment #3 at the time of the purchase because neither G nor any other member of the Parent group had a depreciable interest in Equipment #3 while a member of the Parent group within the lookback period. Further, B itself did not have a depreciable interest in Equipment #3 within the lookback period. Accordingly, B's acquisition of Equipment #3 satisfies the No Prior Use Requirement. Assuming all other requirements in § 1.168(k)-2 are satisfied, B is eligible to claim the additional first year depreciation deduction for Equipment #3 in 2019.

(4) *Example 4: Termination of the consolidated group.*—(i) *Facts.* S owns Equipment #4. In 2018, S sells Equipment #4 to U. In 2019, X acquires all of the stock of Parent in a transaction that causes the Parent group to terminate and Parent, B, and S to become members of the X group. In 2020, in a transaction that is not part of a series of related transactions, B purchases Equipment #4 from U and places it in service in the same year.

(ii) *Analysis.* B's acquisition of Equipment #4 satisfies the No Prior Use Requirement. The Group Prior Use Rule does not apply to treat B as having a prior depreciable interest in Equipment #4 because B is a member of the X group and no member of the X group had a depreciable interest in Equipment #4 while a member of the X group within the lookback period. Further, B itself did not have a prior depreciable interest in Equipment #4 within the lookback period. Assuming all other requirements in § 1.168(k)-2 are satisfied, B is eligible to claim the additional first year depreciation deduction for Equipment #4 in 2020.

(iii) *S purchases Equipment #4 in 2020.* The facts are the same as in paragraph (d)(4)(i) of this section, except that S rather than B purchases and places in service Equipment #4 in 2020. S's purchase of Equipment #4 does not satisfy the No Prior Use Requirement because S had a depreciable interest in Equipment #4 within the lookback period. Thus, S is not eligible to claim the additional first year depreciation deduction for Equipment #4 in 2020.

(iv) *Acquisitions are part of the same series of related transactions.* The facts are the same as in paragraph (d)(4)(i) of this section, except that X's acquisition of the Parent stock and B's purchase of Equipment #4 are part of the same series of related transactions. Thus, pursuant to the same series of related transactions, S became a member of the X group and B (another member of the X group) acquired Equipment #4. Because S had a depreciable interest in Equipment #4 within the lookback period, B is treated as having a depreciable interest in Equipment #4 under the Stock and Asset Acquisition Rule. As a result, B's acquisition of Equipment #4 does not satisfy the No Prior Use Requirement, and B is not eligible to claim the additional first year depreciation deduction for Equipment #4 in 2020.

(5) *Example 5: Intercompany sale of eligible property followed by sale of B stock as part of the same series of related transactions.*—(i) *Facts.* S has a depreciable interest in Equipment #5. On January 1, 2019, B purchases Equipment #5 from S and places it in service. On June 1, 2019, as part of the same series of related transactions that includes B's purchase of Equipment #5, Parent sells all of the stock of B to X. Thus, B leaves the Parent group at the end of the day on June 1, 2019, and B is a member of the X group starting June 2, 2019. See § 1.1502-76(b). As of June 1, 2019, Equipment #5 remains eligible property.

(ii) *Analysis*—(A) *Application of the Consolidated Asset Acquisition Rule.* B was a member of the Parent group when it acquired Equipment #5. Because S, another member of the Parent group, had a depreciable interest in Equipment #5 while a member of the group within the lookback period, B would be treated as having a prior depreciable interest in Equipment #5 under the Group Prior Use Rule and B's acquisition of Equipment #5 would not satisfy the No Prior Use Requirement. However, B's acquisition of Equipment #5 satisfies the requirements of the Consolidated Asset Acquisition Rule in paragraph (c)(1)(ii) of this section. First, B's acquisition of Equipment #5 meets the requirements of § 1.168(k)-2(b)(3)(iii)(A) without regard to

the related-party tests under section 179(d)(2)(A) or (B) and § 1.179-4(c)(1)(ii) or (iii) or the Group Prior Use Rule. Second, as part of the same series of related transactions that includes B's acquisition of Equipment #5, B ceases to be a member of the Parent group and ceases to be Related to S. Third, Equipment #5 continues to be eligible property on the deconsolidation date (June 1, 2019).

(B) *Consequences of the Consolidated Asset Acquisition Rule.* Under the Consolidated Asset Acquisition Rule, B is treated for all Federal income tax purposes as transferring Equipment #5 to an unrelated person on June 2, 2019, in exchange for an amount of cash equal to the deemed sale amount and, immediately thereafter, acquiring deemed replacement property (New Equipment #5) from an unrelated person for an amount of cash equal to the deemed sale amount. Accordingly, assuming all other requirements in § 1.168(k)-2 are satisfied, B is eligible to claim the additional first year depreciation for an amount equal to the deemed sale amount for the taxable year in which it places New Equipment #5 in service.

(iii) *Distribution of B.* The facts are the same as in paragraph (d)(5)(i) of this section, except that, on June 1, 2019, Parent distributes the stock of B to its shareholders (which are not Related to S) in a distribution that qualifies for nonrecognition under section 355(a). Accordingly, the Consolidated Asset Acquisition Rule applies. As in paragraph (d)(5)(ii)(B) of this section, assuming all other requirements in § 1.168(k)-2 are satisfied, B is eligible to claim the additional first year depreciation deduction for an amount equal to the deemed sale amount for the taxable year in which it places New Equipment #5 in service.

(iv) *Equipment #5 ceases to be eligible property.* The facts are the same as in paragraph (d)(5)(i) of this section, except that, on June 1, 2019, Equipment #5 is no longer eligible property. The Consolidated Asset Acquisition Rule does not apply because B's acquisition of Equipment #5 fails to satisfy the requirement in paragraph (c)(1)(ii)(C) of this section that the acquired eligible property continue to be eligible property on the deconsolidation date. Therefore, B's acquisition of Equipment #5 on January 1, 2019, fails to satisfy the No Prior Use Requirement. Under the Group Prior Use Rule, B is treated as having a prior depreciable interest in Equipment #5 because B is a member of the Parent group and S, while a member of the Parent group, had a depreciable interest in Equipment #5 within the lookback period. Accordingly, B is not eligible to claim the additional first year depreciation deduction with respect to Equipment #5 in 2019.

(6) *Example 6: Intercompany sale of member stock for which a section 338(h)(10) election is made followed by sale of B stock as part of a series of related transactions.*—(i) *Facts.* S owns all of the stock of T, which has a depreciable interest in Equipment #6. On January 1, 2019, B purchases all of the T stock from S in a qualified stock purchase for which a section 338(h)(10) election is made. On June 1, 2019, as part of the same series of related transactions that includes B's purchase of the T stock, Parent sells all of the stock of B to X. Thus, B and T leave the Parent group at the end of the day on June 1, 2019, and B and T are members of the X group starting June 2, 2019. See § 1.1502-76(b). As of June 1, 2019, Equipment #6 remains eligible property.

(ii) *Analysis*—(A) *Section 338(h)(10) election.* Pursuant to the section 338(h)(10) election, Old T is treated as transferring all of its assets, including Equipment #6, to an unrelated person in a single transaction in exchange for consideration at the close of the acquisition date (January 1, 2019), and New T is treated as acquiring all of its assets, including Equipment #6, from an unrelated person in exchange for consideration. Old T is deemed to liquidate following the deemed asset sale. See § 1.338-1(a)(1).

(B) *Application of the Consolidated Deemed Acquisition Rule.* New T was a member of the Parent group when New T acquired Equipment #6 from an unrelated person. Because Old T, another member of the Parent group, had a depreciable interest in Equipment #6 while a member of the group within the lookback period, New T would be treated as having a prior depreciable interest in Equipment #6 under the Group Prior Use Rule and New T's acquisition of Equipment #6 would not satisfy the No Prior Use Requirement. However, New T's acquisition of Equipment #6 satisfies the requirements of the Consolidated Deemed Acquisition Rule in paragraph (c)(2)(ii) of this section. First, New T's acquisition of Equipment #6 meets the requirements of § 1.168(k)-2(b)(3)(iii)(A) without regard to the Group Prior Use Rule. Second, as part of the same series of related transactions that includes B's qualified stock purchase of the T stock, B and New T cease to be members of the Parent group and cease to be Related to S. Third, Equipment #6 continues to be eligible property on the deconsolidation date (June 1, 2019).

(C) *Consequences of the Consolidated Deemed Acquisition Rule.* Under the Consolidated Deemed Acquisition Rule, New T is treated for all Federal income tax purposes as transferring Equipment #6 to an unrelated person on June 2, 2019, in exchange for an amount of cash equal to the deemed sale amount and, immediately thereafter, acquiring deemed replacement property (New Equipment #6) from an unrelated person for an amount of cash equal to the deemed sale amount. Accordingly, assuming all other requirements in § 1.168(k)-2 are satisfied, New T is eligible to claim the additional first year depreciation deduction for an amount equal to the deemed sale amount for the taxable year in which it places New Equipment #6 in service.

(iii) *T owns multiple assets.* The facts are the same as in paragraph (d)(6)(i) of this section, except that, in addition to Equipment #6, T also owns Asset A (depreciable real estate that is not eligible property). With respect to Equipment #6, the results are the same as in paragraph (d)(6)(ii) of this section. However, the Consolidated Deemed Acquisition Rule does not apply to Asset A because it is not eligible property. Accordingly, New T is not treated as transferring Asset A to an unrelated person on June 2, 2019 and then, immediately thereafter, acquiring deemed replacement property for Asset A. If Equipment #6 had ceased to be eligible property as of June 1, 2019, the Consolidated Deemed Acquisition Rule also would not apply to Equipment #6.

(7) *Example 7: Section 355 transaction following a section 338(h)(10) transaction pursuant to the same series of related transactions.*—(i) *Facts.* T has a depreciable interest in Equipment #7. On January 1, 2019, Parent contributes all of the stock of T to B in exchange for common and non-voting preferred stock of B and sells the non-voting preferred stock of B to U pursuant to a binding commitment entered into prior to the contribution (T Exchange). The non-voting preferred stock is not treated as "stock" for purposes of section 1504(a). See section 1504(a)(4). Parent and B jointly make an election under section 338(h)(10) with respect to the T Exchange. On June 1, 2019, as part of the same series of related transactions that includes the T Exchange, Parent contributes the stock of B and assets comprising an active trade or business (within the meaning of section 355(b)) to Controlled in exchange for Controlled common stock and then distributes the Controlled common stock to Parent's shareholders in a distribution qualifying under section 355(a) (Controlled Distribution). In the Controlled Distribution, T and B cease to be Related to Parent. Equipment #7 remains eligible property on June 1, 2019.

(ii) *Section 338(h)(10) election.* Immediately after the Controlled Distribution, Parent and B are not related as determined under section 338(h)(3)(A)(iii). Further, B's basis in the T stock is not determined, in whole or in part, by reference to the adjusted basis of the T stock in the hands of Parent, and the stock is not acquired in an exchange to which section 351, 354, 355, or 356 applies. Accordingly, the T Exchange qualifies as a "purchase" within the meaning of section 338(h)(3). Pursuant to the section 338(h)(10) election, Old T is treated as transferring all of its assets, including Equipment #7, to an unrelated person in a single transaction in exchange for consideration at the close of the acquisition date (January 1, 2019), and New T is treated as acquiring all of its assets, including Equipment #7, from an unrelated person in exchange for consideration. Old T is deemed to liquidate following the deemed asset sale. See § 1.338-1(a)(1).

(iii) *Application of the Consolidated Deemed Acquisition Rule.* New T was a member of the Parent group when New T acquired Equipment #7 from an unrelated person. Because Old T, another member of the Parent group, had a depreciable interest in Equipment #7 while a member of the group within the lookback period, New T would be treated as having a prior depreciable interest in Equipment #7 under the Group Prior Use Rule and New T's acquisition of Equipment #7 would not satisfy the No Prior Use Requirement. However, New T's acquisition of Equipment #7 satisfies the requirements of the Consolidated Deemed Acquisition Rule in paragraph (c)(2)(ii) of this section. Thus, New T is treated for all Federal income tax purposes as transferring Equipment #7 to an unrelated person on June 2, 2019, in exchange for an amount of cash equal to the deemed sale amount and, immediately thereafter, acquiring deemed replacement property (New Equipment #7) from an unrelated person for an amount of cash equal to the deemed sale amount. Accordingly, assuming all other requirements in § 1.168(k)-2 are satisfied, New T is eligible to claim the additional first year depreciation deduction for an amount equal to the deemed sale amount for the taxable year in which it places New Equipment #7 in service.

(e) *Applicability dates.*—(1) *In general.*—Except as provided in paragraph (e)(2) of this section, this section applies to—

(i) Depreciable property acquired after September 27, 2017, by the taxpayer and placed in service by the taxpayer during or after the taxpayer's taxable year that begins on or after January 1, 2021;

(ii) A specified plant for which the taxpayer properly made an election to apply section 168(k)(5) and that is planted, or grafted to a plant that was previously planted, by the taxpayer during or after the taxpayer's taxable year that begins on or after January 1, 2021; and

(iii) Components acquired or self-constructed after September 27, 2017, of larger self-constructed property described in § 1.168(k)-2(c)(2) and placed in service by the taxpayer during or after the taxpayer's taxable year that begins on or after January 1, 2021.

(2) *Early application of this section and § 1.168(k)-2.*—(i) *In general.*—Subject to paragraphs (e)(2)(ii) and (iii) of this section, and provided that all members of a consolidated group consistently apply the same set of rules, a taxpayer may choose to apply both the rules of this section and the rules of § 1.168(k)-2, in their entirety and in a consistent manner, to—

(A) Depreciable property acquired after September 27, 2017, by the taxpayer and placed in service by the taxpayer during a taxable year ending on or after September 28, 2017;

(B) A specified plant for which the taxpayer properly made an election to apply section 168(k)(5) and that is planted, or grafted to a plant that was previously planted, after September 27, 2017, by the taxpayer during a taxable year ending on or after September 28, 2017; and

(C) Components acquired or self-constructed after September 27, 2017, of larger self-constructed property described in § 1.168(k)-2(c)(2) and placed in service by the taxpayer during a taxable year ending on or after September 28, 2017.

(ii) *Early application to certain transactions.*—In the case of property described in paragraph (e)(2)(i) of this section that is acquired in a transaction that satisfies the requirements of paragraph (c)(1)(ii) or (c)(2)(ii) of this section, the taxpayer may apply the rules of this section and the rules of § 1.168(k)-2, in their entirety and in a consistent manner, to such property only if those rules are applied, in their entirety and in a consistent manner, by all parties to the transaction (including the transferor member, the transferee member, and the target, as applicable) and the consolidated groups of which they are members, for the taxable year(s) in which the transaction occurs and the taxable year(s) that includes the day after the deconsolidation date.

(iii) *Bound by early application.*—Once a taxpayer applies the rules of this section and the rules of § 1.168(k)-2, in their entirety, for a taxable year, the taxpayer must continue to apply the rules of this section and the rules of § 1.168(k)-2, in their entirety, for the taxpayer's subsequent taxable years. [Reg. § 1.1502-68.]

☐ [T.D. 9916, 11-5-2020.]

**[Reg. § 1.1502-75]**

**§ 1.1502-75. Filing of consolidated returns.**—(a) *Privilege of filing consolidated returns.*—(1) *Exercise of privilege for first consolidated return year.*—A group which did not file a consolidated return for the immediately preceding taxable year may file a consolidated return in lieu of separate returns for the taxable year, provided that each corporation which has been a member during any part of the taxable year for which the consolidated return is to be filed consents (in the manner provided in paragraph (b) of this section) to the regulations under section 1502. If a group wishes to exercise its privilege of filing a consolidated return, such consolidated return must be filed not later than the last day prescribed by law (including extensions of time) for the filing of the common parent's return. Such consolidated return may not be withdrawn after such last day (but the group may change the basis of its return at any time prior to such last day).

(2) *Continued filing requirement.*—A group which filed (or was required to file) a consolidated return for the immediately preceding taxable year is required to file a consolidated return for the taxable year unless it has an election to discontinue filing consolidated returns under paragraph (c) of this section.

(b) *How consent for first consolidated year exercised.*—(1) *General rule.*—The consent of a corporation referred to in paragraph (a)(1) of this section shall be made by such corporation joining in the making of the consolidated return for such year. A corporation shall be deemed to have joined in the making of such return for such year if it files a Form 1122 in the manner specified in paragraph (h)(2) of this section.

(2) *Consent under facts and circumstances.*—If a member of the group fails to file Form 1122, the Commissioner may under the facts and circumstances determine that such member has joined in the making of a consolidated return by such group. The following circumstances, among others, will be taken into account in making this determination:

(i) Whether or not the income and deductions of the member were included in the consolidated return;

(ii) Whether or not a separate return was filed by the member for that taxable year; and

(iii) Whether or not the member was included in the affiliations schedule, Form 851.

If the Commissioner determines that the member has joined in the making of the consolidated return, such member shall be treated as if it had filed a Form 1122 for such year for purposes of paragraph (h)(2) of this section.

(3) *Failure to consent due to mistake.*—If any member has failed to join in the making of a consolidated return under either subparagraph (1) or (2) of this paragraph, then the tax liability of each member of the group shall be determined on the basis of separate returns unless the common parent corporation establishes to the satisfaction of the Commissioner that the failure of such member to join in the making of the consolidated return was due to a mistake of law or fact, or to inadvertence. In such case, such member shall be treated as if it had filed a Form 1122 for such year for purposes of paragraph (h)(2) of this section, and thus joined in the making of the consolidated return for such year.

(c) *Election to discontinue filing consolidated returns.*—(1) *Good cause.*—(i) *In general.*—Notwithstanding that a consolidated return is required for a taxable year, the Commissioner, upon application by the common parent, may for good cause shown grant permission to a group to discontinue filing consolidated returns. Any such application shall be made to the Commissioner of Internal Revenue, Washington, D.C. 20224, and shall be made not later than the 90th day before the due date for the filing of the consolidated return (including extensions of time). In addition, if an amendment of the Code, or other law affecting the computation of tax liability, is enacted and the enactment is effective for a taxable year ending before or within 90 days after the date of enactment, then application for such a taxable year may be made not later than the 180th day after the date of enactment, and if the application is approved the permission to discontinue filing consolidated returns will apply to such taxable year notwithstanding that a consolidated return has already been filed for such year.

(ii) *Substantial adverse change in law affecting tax liability.*—Ordinarily, the Commissioner will grant a group permission to discontinue filing consolidated returns if the net result of all amendments to the Code or regulations with effective dates commencing within the taxable year has a substantial adverse effect on the consolidated tax liability of the group for such year relative to what the aggregate tax liability would be if the members of the group filed separate returns for such year. Thus, for example, assume P and S filed a consolidated return for the calendar year 1966 and that the provisions of the Code have been amended by a bill which was enacted by Congress in 1966, but which is first effective for taxable years beginning on or after January 1, 1967. Assume further that P makes a timely application to discontinue filing consolidated returns. In order to determine whether the amendments have a substantial adverse effect on the consolidated tax liability for 1967, relative to what the aggregate tax liability would be if the members of the group filed separate returns for 1967, the difference between the tax liability of the group computed on a consolidated basis and taking into account the changes in the law effective for 1967 and the aggregate tax liability of the members of the group computed as if each such member filed separate returns for such year (also taking into account such changes) shall be compared with the difference between the tax liability of such group for 1967 computed on a consolidated basis without regard to the changes in the law effective in such year and the aggregate tax liability of the members of the group computed as if separate returns had been filed by such members for such year without regard to the changes in the law effective in such year.

(iii) *Other factors.*—In addition, the Commissioner will take into account other factors in determining whether good cause exists for granting permission to discontinue filing consolidated returns beginning with the taxable year, including—

(a) Changes in law or circumstances, including changes which do not affect Federal income tax liability,

(b) Changes in law which are first effective in the taxable year and which result in a substantial reduction in the consolidated net operating loss (or consolidated unused investment credit) for such year relative to what the aggregate net operating losses (or investment credits) would be if the members of the group filed separate returns for such year, and

(c) Changes in the Code or regulations which are effective prior to the taxable year but which first have a substantial adverse effect on the filing of a consolidated return relative to the filing of separate returns by members of the group in such year.

(2) *Discretion of Commissioner to grant blanket permission.*—(i) *Permission to all groups.*—The Commissioner, in his discretion, may grant all groups permission to discontinue filing consolidated returns if any provision of the Code or regulations has been amended and such amendment is of the type which could have a substantial adverse effect on the filing of consolidated returns by substantially all groups, relative to the filing of separate returns. Ordinarily, the permission to discontinue shall apply with respect to the taxable year of each group which includes the effective date of such an amendment.

(ii) *Permission to a class of groups.*—The Commissioner, in his discretion, may grant a particular class of groups permission to discontinue filing consolidated returns if any provision of the Code or regulations has been amended and such amendment is of the type which could have a substantial adverse effect on the filing of consolidated returns by substantially all such groups relative to the filing of separate returns. Ordinarily, the permission to discontinue shall apply with respect to the taxable year of each group within the class which includes the effective date of such an amendment.

(3) *Time and manner for exercising election.*—If, under subparagraph (1) or (2) of this paragraph, a group has an election to discontinue filing consolidated returns for any taxable year and such group wishes to exercise such election, then the common parent must file a separate return for such year on or before the last day prescribed by law (including extensions of time) for the filing of the consolidated return for such year. See section 6081 (relating to extensions of time for filing returns).

(d) *When a group remains in existence.*—(1) *General rule.*—A group remains in existence for a tax year if the common parent remains as the common parent and at least one subsidiary that was affiliated with it at the end of the prior year remains affiliated with it at the beginning of the year, whether or not one or more corporations have ceased to be subsidiaries at any time after the group was formed. Thus, for example, assume that corporation P acquires the sole outstanding share of stock of S on January 1, year 1, and that P and S file a consolidated return for the year 1 calendar year. On May 1, year 2, P acquires the sole outstanding share of stock of S1 and, on July 1, year 2, P sells the S share. The group (consisting originally of P and S) remains in existence in year 2 because P remained the common parent and, S, a subsidiary that was affiliated with P at the end of year 1, remained affiliated with P at the beginning of year 2.

(2) *Common parent no longer in existence.*—(i) *Mere change in identity.*—For purposes of this paragraph, the common parent corporation shall remain as the common parent irrespective of a mere change in identity, form, or place of organization of such common parent corporation (see section 368(a)(1)(F)).

(ii) *Transfer of assets to subsidiary.*—The group shall be considered as remaining in existence notwithstanding that the common parent is no longer in existence if the members of the affiliated group succeed to and become the owners of substantially all of the assets of such former parent and there remains one or more chains of includible corporations connected through stock ownership with a common parent corporation which is an includible corporation and which was a member of the group prior to the date such former parent ceases to exist. For purposes of applying paragraph (f)(2)(i) of § 1.1502-1 to separate return years ending on or before the date on which the former parent ceases to exist, such former parent, and not the new common parent, shall be considered to be the corporation described in such paragraph.

(iii) *Taxable years.*—If a transfer of assets described in subdivision (ii) of this subparagraph is an acquisition to which section 381(a) applies and if the group files a consolidated return for the taxable year in which the acquisition occurs, then for purposes of section 381—

(a) The former common parent shall not close its taxable year merely because of the acquisition, and all taxable years of such former parent ending on or before the date of acquisition shall be treated as taxable years of the acquiring corporation, and

(b) The corporation acquiring the assets shall close its taxable year as of the date of acquisition, and all taxable years of such corporation ending on or before the date of acquisition shall be treated as taxable years of the transferor corporation.

(iv) *Exception.*—With respect to acquisitions occurring before January 1, 1971, subdivision (iii) of this subparagraph shall not apply if the group, in its income tax return, treats the taxable year of the former common parent as having closed as of the date of acquisition.

(3) *Reverse acquisitions.*—(i) *In general.*—If a corporation (hereinafter referred to as the "first corporation") or any member of a group of which the first corporation is the common parent acquires after October 1, 1965—

(a) Stock of another corporation (hereinafter referred to as the second corporation), and as a result the second corporation becomes (or would become but for the application of this subparagraph) a member of a group of which the first corporation is the common parent, or

(b) Substantially all the assets of the second corporation, in exchange (in whole or in part) for stock of the first corporation, and the stockholders (immediately before the acquisition) of the second corporation, as a result of owning stock of the second corporation, own (immediately after the acquisition) more than 50 percent of the fair market value of the outstanding stock of the first corporation, then any group of which the first corporation was the common parent immediately before the acquisition shall cease to exist as of the date of acquisition, and any group of which the second corporation was the common parent immediately before the acquisition shall be treated as remaining in existence (with the first corporation becoming the common parent of the group). Thus, assume that corporations P and S comprised groups PS (P being the common parent), that P was merged into corporation T (the common parent of a group composed of T and corporation U), and that the shareholders of P immediately before the merger, as a result of owning stock in P, own 90 percent of the fair market value of T's stock immediately after the merger. The group of which P was the common parent is treated as continuing in existence with T and U being added as members of the group, and T taking the place of P as the common parent.

For purposes of determining under (a) of this subdivision whether the second corporation becomes (or would become) a member of the group of which the first corporation is the common parent, and for purposes of determining whether the former stockholders of the second corporation own more than 50 percent of the outstanding stock of the first corporation, there shall be taken into account any acquisitions or redemptions of the stock of either corporation which are pursuant to a plan of acquisition described in (a) or (b) of this subdivision.

(ii) *Prior ownership of stock.*—For purposes of subdivision (i) of this subparagraph, if the first corporation, and any members of a group of which the first corporation is the common parent, have continuously owned for a period of at least five years ending on the date of the acquisition an aggregate of at least 25 percent of the fair market value of the outstanding stock of the second corporation, then the first corporation (and any subsidiary which owns stock of the second corporation immediately before the acquisition) shall, as a result of owning such stock, be treated as owning (immediately after the acquisition) a percentage of the fair market value of the first corporation's outstanding stock which bears the same ratio to (a) the percentage of the fair market value of all the stock of the second corporation owned immediately before the acquisition by the first corporation and its subsidiaries as (b) the fair market value of the total outstanding stock of the second corporation immediately before the acquisition bears to (c) the sum of (1) the fair market value, immediately before the acquisition, of the total outstanding stock of the first corporation, and (2) the fair market value, immediately before the acquisition, of the total outstanding stock of the second corporation (other than any such stock owned by the first corporation and any of its subsidiaries). For example, assume that corporation P owns stock in corporation T having a fair market value of $100,000, that P acquires the remaining stock of T from individuals in exchange for stock of P, that immediately before the acquisition the total outstanding stock of T had a fair market value of $150,000, and that immediately before the acquisition the total outstanding stock of P had a fair market value of $200,000. Assuming P owned at least 25 percent of the fair market value of T's stock for five years, then for purposes of this subparagraph, P is treated as owning (immediately after the acquisition) 40 percent of the fair market value of its own outstanding stock, determined as follows:

$$\frac{\$150{,}000}{\$200{,}000 + \$50{,}000} \times 66^2/3\% = 40\%$$

Thus, if the former individual stockholders of T own, immediately after the acquisition more than 10 percent of the fair market value of the outstanding stock of P as a result of owning stock of T, the group of which T was the common parent is treated as continuing in existence with P as the common parent, and the group of which P was the common parent before the acquisition ceases to exist.

(iii) *Election.*—The provisions of subdivision (ii) of this subparagraph shall not apply to any acquisition occurring in a taxable year ending after October 7, 1969, unless the first corporation elects to have such subdivision apply. The election shall be made by means of a statement, signed by any officer who is duly authorized to act on behalf of the first corporation, stating that the corporation elects to have the provisions of §1.1502-75(d)(3)(ii) apply and identifying the acquisition to which such provisions will apply. The statement shall be filed, on or before the due date (including extensions of time) of the return for the group's first consolidated return year ending after the date of the acquisition, with the internal revenue officer with whom such return is required to be filed.

(iv) *Transfer of assets to subsidiary.*—This subparagraph shall not apply to a transaction to which subparagraph (2)(ii) of this paragraph applies.

(v) *Taxable years.*—If, in a transaction described in subdivision (i) of this subparagraph, the first corporation files a consolidated return for the first taxable year ending after the date of acquisition, then—

(a) The first corporation, and each corporation which, immediately before the acquisition, is a member of the group of which the first corporation is the common parent, shall close its taxable year as of the date of acquisition, and each such corporation shall, immediately after the acquisition, change to the taxable year of the second corporation, and

(b) If the acquisition is a transaction described in section 381(a)(2), then for purposes of section 381—

(1) All taxable years ending on or before the date of acquisition, of the first corporation and each corporation which, immediately before the acquisition, is a member of the group of which the first corporation is the common parent, shall be treated as taxable years of the transfer corporation, and

(2) The second corporation shall not close its taxable year merely because of such acquisition, and all taxable years ending on or before the date of acquisition, of the second corporation and each corporation which, immediately before the acquisition, is a member of any group of which the second corporation is the common parent, shall be treated as taxable years of the acquiring corporation.

(vi) *Exception.*—With respect to acquisitions occurring before April 17, 1968, subdivision (v) of this subparagraph shall not apply if the parties to the transaction, in their income tax returns, treat subdivision (i) as not affecting the closing of taxable years or the operation of section 381.

(4) [Reserved.]

(5) *Coordination with section 833.*—(i) *Election to continue old group.*—If, solely by reason of the enactment of section 833 (relating to certain Blue Cross or Blue Shield organizations and certain other health insurers), an organization to which section 833 applies (a "section 833 organization") became the new common parent of an old group on January 1, 1987, the old group may elect to continue in existence with that section 833 organization as its new common parent, provided all the old groups having the same section 833 organization as their new common parent elect to continue in existence. To revoke this election, see paragraph (d)(5)(x) of this section. To file as a new group, see paragraph (d)(5)(v) of this section.

(ii) *Old group.*—For purposes of this paragraph (d)(5), an old group is a group which, for its last taxable year ending in 1986, either filed a consolidated return or was eligible to (but did not) file a consolidated return.

(iii) *Manner of electing to continue.*—(A) *Deemed election.*—If all the members of all the old groups having the same section 833 organization as their new common parent are included for the first taxable year beginning after December 31, 1986, on the same consolidated (or amended consolidated) return and a Form 1122 was not filed, the old groups are deemed to have elected under paragraph (d)(5)(i) of this section to continue in existence.

(B) *Delayed election.*—If a deemed election to continue in existence was not made under paragraph (d)(5)(iii)(A) of this section, all the members of all the old groups having the same section 833 organization as their new common parent may make a delayed election under paragraph (d)(5)(i) of this section to continue in existence by

(1) filing an appropriate consolidated (or amended consolidated) return or returns for each taxable year beginning after December 31, 1986, (notwithstanding §1.1502-75(a)(1)) on or before January 3, 1991 and

(2) on the top of any such return prominently affixing a statement containing the following declaration: "THIS RETURN" (or, if applicable, "AMENDED RETURN") "REFLECTS A DELAYED ELECTION TO CONTINUE UNDER §1.1502-75T(d)(5)(iii)(B)". A delayed election to continue in existence automatically revokes a deemed election to file as a new group which was made under paragraph (d)(5)(vi) of this section.

(iv) *Effects of election to continue in existence.*—If an old group or groups elect to continue in existence under paragraph (d)(5)(i) of this section, the following rules apply:

(A) *Taxable years.*—Each member that filed returns other than on a calendar year basis shall close its taxable year on December 31, 1986, and change to a calendar year beginning on January 1, 1987. See section 843 and §1.1502-76(a)(1).

(B) *Carryovers from separate return limitation years.*—For purposes of applying the separate return limitation year rules to carryovers from taxable years beginning before 1987 to taxable years beginning after 1986, the following rules apply:

*(1)* Any taxable year beginning before 1987 of a corporation that was not a member of an old group (including a section 833 organization) will be treated as a separate return limitation year;

*(2)* Any taxable year beginning before 1987 of a corporation that was a member of an old group that, without regard to this section and the enactment of section 833, was a separate return limitation year will continue to be treated as a separate return limitation year;

*(3)* Any taxable year beginning before 1987 of a member of an old group (other than a separate return limitation year described in paragraph (d)(5)(iv)(B)(2) of this section) will not be treated as a separate return limitation year with respect to any corporation that was a member of such group for each day of that taxable year; and

*(4)* Any taxable year beginning before 1987 of a member of an old group will be treated as a separate return limitation year with respect to any corporation that was not a member of such group for each day of that taxable year (*e.g.*, a corporation that was not a member of an old group, including a section 833 organization, or a corporation that was a member of another old group).

*(C) Five-year rules for life-nonlife groups.*—Any life-nonlife election under section 1504(c)(2) in effect for an old group remains in effect. Any old group which was eligible to make a life-nonlife election will remain eligible to make the election. For purposes of section 1503(c), a nonlife member is treated as ineligible under §1.1502-47(d)(13) with respect to a life member, unless both were members of the same affiliated group (determined without regard to the exclusions in section 1504(b)(1) and (2)) for five taxable years immediately preceding the taxable year in which the loss arose. See paragraph (d)(5)(ix) of this section for a tacking rule.

*(v) Election to file as a new group.*—If, solely by reason of the enactment of section 833, a section 833 organization became the new common parent of an old group on January 1, 1987, the application of the five-year prohibition on reconsolidation in section 1504(a)(3)(A) to the old group is waived and the old group together with the new section 833 organization common parent may elect to file as a new group provided that all includible corporations elect to file a consolidated (or amended consolidated) return as a new group for the first taxable year beginning after December 31, 1986. To revoke this election, see paragraph (d)(5)(x) of this section.

*(vi) Manner of electing to file as a new group.*—(A) *Deemed election.*—The old group or groups and the section 833 organization are deemed to have elected under paragraph (d)(5)(v) of this section to file as a new group by filing, for the first taxable year beginning after December 31, 1986, a Form 1122 and a consolidated (or amended consolidated) tax return.

*(B) Delayed election.*—If a deemed election to file as a new group was not made pursuant to paragraph (d)(5)(vi)(A) of this section, the old group or groups and the section 833 organization may make a delayed election under paragraph (d)(5)(v) of this section to file as a new group by

*(1)* filing an appropriate consolidated (or amended consolidated) return or returns for each taxable year beginning after December 31, 1986, (notwithstanding §1.1502-75(a)(1)) on or before January 3, 1991 and

*(2)* on the top of any such return prominently affixing a statement containing the following declaration: "THIS RETURN" (or, if applicable, "AMENDED RETURN") "REFLECTS A DELAYED ELECTION TO FILE AS A NEW GROUP UNDER §1.1502-75T(d)(5)(vi)(B)". A delayed election to file as a new group automatically revokes any deemed election to continue in existence which was made under paragraph (d)(5)(iii) of this section.

*(vii) Effects of election to file as a new group.*—If an old group or groups elect to file as a new group under paragraph (d)(5)(v) of this section, the following rules apply:

*(A) Termination.*—Each old group is treated as if it terminated on January 1, 1987, and the termination is not treated as resulting from the acquisition by a nonmember of all of the stock of the common parent.

*(B) Taxable years.*—Each member that filed returns other than on a calendar year basis shall close its taxable year on December 31, 1986, and change to a calendar year beginning on January 1, 1987. See section 843 and §1.1502-76(a)(1).

*(C) Separate return limitation year and life-nonlife groups.*—For purposes of §1.1502-1(f), sections 1503(c) and 1504(c), and §1.1502-47, the group is treated as coming into existence as a new group on January 1, 1987. Thus, for example, paragraphs (d)(5)(iv)(B) and (C) of this section do not apply.

*(viii) Earnings and profits.*—All distributions after January 1, 1987 by a corporation, whether or not such corporation was a member of an old group, to an existing Blue Cross or Blue Shield organization (as defined in section 833(c)(2)) out of earnings and profits accumulated before 1987 are deemed made out of earnings and profits accumulated in pre-affiliation years. See §1.1502-32(h)(5).

*(ix) Five-year tacking rules for certain life-nonlife groups.*—For purposes of applying §1.1502-47(d)(5) and (12) to any taxable year ending after 1986 to a corporation, whether or not the corporation was a member of an old group, (A) the determination of whether the corporation was in existence and a member or tentatively treated as a member of a group, for taxable years ending before 1987, is made without regard to the exclusions under section 1504(b)(1) and (2) of any section 833 organization or life insurance company (as the case may be) and (B) a section 833 organization is not treated as having a change in tax character solely by reason of the loss of its tax-exempt status due to the enactment of section 833. This paragraph (d)(5)(ix) does not apply if an election to file as a new group under paragraph (d)(5)(v) of this section is made.

*(x) Time to revoke elections made before September 5, 1990.*—An election by an old group to continue in existence or to file as a new group that was made (or deemed made) before September 5, 1990 may be revoked by filing an appropriate return (or returns) on or before January 3, 1991. For purposes of this paragraph (d)(5)(x), appropriate returns include separate returns filed by each member of the group or consolidated returns filed in accordance with a delayed election either under paragraph (d)(5)(iii)(B) or (vi)(B) of this section.

*(xi) Examples.*—The following examples illustrate this paragraph (d)(5). In these examples, each corporation uses the calendar year as its taxable year.

*Example 1.* B is a section 833 organization. For several years, B has owned all of the outstanding stock of X, Y, and Z. X has owned all the outstanding stock of $X_1$ throughout $X_1$'s existence and Y has owned all of the outstanding stock of $Y_1$ throughout $Y_1$'s existence. For 1986, X and $X_1$ filed a consolidated federal income tax return but Y and $Y_1$ filed separate returns. Under paragraph (d)(5)(ii) of this section, X and $X_1$ and Y and $Y_1$ each constitute an old group because they either filed a consolidated return or were eligible to file a consolidated return for 1986. The X and Y groups may elect under paragraph (d)(5)(i) of this section to continue in existence. If they elect to continue, under paragraph (d)(5)(iv)(B) of this section, the separate return limitation year rules apply as follows: any taxable year of B or Z beginning before 1987 is treated as a separate return limitation year with respect to each other and to all other members of the group; any taxable year of X or $X_1$ beginning before 1987 is treated as a separate return limitation year with respect to B, Z, Y and $Y_1$, but not with respect to each other; and any taxable year of Y or $Y_1$ beginning before 1987 is treated as a separate return limitation year with respect to B, Z, X and $X_1$, but not with respect to each other.

*Example 2.* The facts are the same as in Example 1 except that B is owned by C, another section 833 organization. If the X and Y groups elect to continue, the results are the same as in Example 1, except that, under paragraph (d)(5)(iv)(B)(1) of this section, for purposes of applying the separate return limitation year rules, any taxable year of C beginning before 1987 is also treated as a separate return limitation year with respect to all other members of the group.

*Example 3.* The facts are the same as in Example 1 except that Y purchased $Y_1$ on January 1, 1985. If the X and Y groups elect to continue, the results are the same as in Example 1, except that, under paragraph (d)(5)(iv)(B)(2) of this section, for purposes of applying the separate return limitation year rules, any taxable year of $Y_1$ beginning before 1985 is treated as a separate return limitation year with respect to Y as well as with respect to all other members of the group.

*Example 4.* B, a section 833 organization, has owned all the stock of X since November 1984. X has owned all the stock of L, a life insurance company, throughout L's existence. In 1986, X and L properly filed a life-nonlife consolidated return. Under paragraph (d)(5)(i) of this section, the X group elects to continue in existence. Under paragraph (d)(5)(iv)(C) of this section, the life-nonlife election will remain in effect. However, losses of B which arise before 1990 cannot be used to offset the income of L. See section 1503(c)(2) and §1.1502-47(d)(13) and paragraph (d)(5)(iv)(C) of this section. Under paragraph (d)(5)(iv)(B) of this section, the separate return limitation year rules apply as follows: any taxable year of B beginning before 1987 is treated as a separate return limitation year with respect to all other members of the group; and any taxable year of X or L beginning before 1987 is treated as a separate return limitation year with respect to B, but not with respect to each other.

*Example 5.* The facts are the same as [in] Example 4 except that, on January 1, 1984, B formed $L_1$, a life insurance company. Under paragraph (d)(5)(ix) of this section and section 1504(c), the first year $L_1$ is eligible to join in B's life-nonlife election is 1989.

*Example 6.* The facts are the same as in Example 4 except that B and the X group elect under paragraph (d)(5)(v) of this section to file as a new group. The X group will be considered to have terminated under §1.1502-75(d)(1) on December 31, 1986. X and L are each separately subject to the separate return limitation year rules of §1.1502-1(f). The first year L and L₁ are eligible to join the new group in a life-nonlife election is 1992 (five years after the new group is formed). See section 1504(c)(2) and paragraphs (d)(5)(vii)(C) and (ix) of this section.

(e) *Failure to include subsidiary.*—If a consolidated return is required for the taxable year under the provisions of paragraph (a)(2) of this section, the tax liability of all members of the group for such year shall be computed on a consolidated basis even though—

(1) Separate returns are filed by one or more members of the group, or

(2) There has been a failure to include in the consolidated return the income of any member of the group.

If subparagraph (1) of this paragraph applies, the amounts assessed or paid upon the basis of separate returns shall be considered as having been assessed or paid upon the basis of a consolidated return.

(f) *Inclusion of one or more corporations not members of the group.*—(1) *Method of determining tax liability.*—If a consolidated return includes the income of a corporation which was not a member of the group at any time during the consolidated return year, the tax liability of such corporation will be determined upon the basis of a separate return (or a consolidated return of another group, if paragraph (a)(2) or (b)(3) of this section applies), and the consolidated return will be considered as including only the income of the corporations which were members of the group during that taxable year. If a consolidated return includes the income of two or more corporations which were not members of the group but which constitute another group, the tax liability of such corporations will be computed in the same manner as if separate returns had been made by such corporations unless the Commissioner upon application approves the making of a consolidated return for the other group or unless under paragraph (a)(2) of this section a consolidated return is required for the other group.

(2) *Allocation of tax liability.*—In any case in which amounts have been assessed and paid upon the basis of a consolidated return and the tax liability of one or more of the corporations included in the consolidated return is to be computed in the manner described in subparagraph (1) of this paragraph, the amounts so paid shall be allocated between the group composed of the corporations properly included in the consolidated return and each of the corporations the tax liability of which is to be computed on a separate basis (or on the basis of a consolidated return of another group) in such manner as the corporations which were included in the consolidated return may, subject to the approval of the Commissioner, agree upon or in the absence of an agreement upon the method used in allocating the tax liability of the members of the group under the provisions of section 1552(a).

(g) *Computing periods of limitation.*—(1) *Income incorrectly included in consolidated return.*—If—

(i) A consolidated return is filed by a group for the taxable year, and

(ii) The tax liability of a corporation whose income is included in such return must be computed on the basis of a separate return (or on the basis of a consolidated return with another group),

then for the purpose of computing any period of limitation with respect to such separate return (or such other consolidated return), the filing of such consolidated return by the group shall be considered as the making of a return by such corporation.

(2) *Income incorrectly included in separate returns.*—If a consolidated return is required for the taxable year under the provisions of paragraph (a)(2) of this section, the filing of separate returns by the members of the group for such year shall not be considered as the making of a return for the purpose of computing any period of limitation with respect to such consolidated return unless there is attached to each such separate return a statement setting forth—

(i) The most recent taxable year of the member for which its income was included in a consolidated return, and

(ii) The reasons for the group's belief that a consolidated return is not required for the taxable year.

(h) *Method of filing return and forms.*—(1) *Consolidated return made by common parent corporation.*—The consolidated return shall be made on Form 1120 for the group by the common parent corporation. The consolidated return, with Form 851 (affiliations schedule) attached, shall be filed with the district director with whom the common parent would have filed a separate return.

(2) *Filing of Form 1122 for first year.*—If, under the provisions of paragraph (a)(1) of this section, a group wishes to file a consolidated return for a taxable year, then a Form 1122 ("Authorization and Consent of Subsidiary Corporation To Be Included in a Consolidated Income Tax Return") must be executed by each subsidiary. For taxable years beginning before January 1, 2003, the executed Forms 1122 must be attached to the consolidated return for the taxable year. For taxable years beginning after December 31, 2002, the group must attach either executed Forms 1122 or unsigned copies of the completed Forms 1122 to the consolidated return. If the group submits unsigned Forms 1122 with its return, it must retain the signed originals in its records in the manner required by §1.6001-1(e). Form 1122 is not required for a taxable year if a consolidated return was filed (or was required to be filed) by the group for the immediately preceding taxable year.

(3) *Persons qualified to execute returns and forms.*—Each return or form required to be made or prepared by a corporation must be executed by the person authorized under section 6062 to execute returns of separate corporations.

(i) [Reserved]

(j) *Statements and schedules for subsidiaries.*—The statement of gross income and deductions and the schedules required by the instructions on the return shall be prepared and filed in columnar form so that the details of the items of gross income, deductions, and credits for each member may be readily audited. Such statements and schedules shall include in columnar form a reconciliation of surplus for each corporation, and a reconciliation of consolidated surplus. Consolidated balance sheets as of the beginning and close of the taxable year of the group, taken from the books of the members, shall accompany the consolidated return and shall be prepared in a form similar to that required for reconciliation of surplus.

(k) *Cross-reference.*—See §1.338(h)(10)-1(d)(7) for special rules regarding filing consolidated returns when a section 338(h)(10) election is made for a target acquired from a selling consolidated group.

(l) *Effective/applicability dates.*—Paragraph (d)(1) of this section applies to taxable years for which the due date of the original return (without regard to extensions) is on or after September 17, 2008. [Reg. §1.1502-75.]

☐ [T.D. 6894, 9-7-66. *Amended by* T.D. 7016, 10-6-69; T.D. 7024, 2-9-70; T.D. 7244, 12-29-72; T.D. 7246, 12-29-72; T.D. 8438, 9-24-92; T.D. 8515, 1-12-94; T.D. 8560, 8-12-94; T.D. 8858, 1-5-2000; T.D. 8940, 2-12-2001; T.D. 9100, 12-18-2003; T.D. 9300, 12-7-2006 *and* T.D. 9424, 9-9-2008.]

**[Reg. §1.1502-76]**

**§1.1502-76. Taxable year of members of group.**—(a) *Taxable year of members of group.*—The consolidated return of a group must be filed on the basis of the common parent's taxable year, and each subsidiary must adopt the common parent's annual accounting period for the first consolidated return year for which the subsidiary's income is includible in the consolidated return. If any member is on a 52-53-week taxable year, the rule of the preceding sentence shall, with the advance consent of the Commissioner, be deemed satisfied if the taxable years of all members of the group end within the same 7-day period. Any request for such consent shall be filed with the Commissioner of Internal Revenue, Washington, DC 20224, not later than the 30th day before the due date (not including extensions of time) for the filing of the consolidated return.

(b) *Items included in the consolidated return.*—(1) *General rules.*—(i) *In general.*—A consolidated return must include the common parent's items of income, gain, deduction, loss, and credit for the entire consolidated return year, and each subsidiary's items for the portion of the year for which it is a member. If the consolidated return includes the items of a corporation for only a portion of its tax year determined without taking this section into account, items for the portion of the year not included in the consolidated return must be included in a separate return (including the consolidated return of another group). The rules of this paragraph (b) must be applied to prevent the duplication or elimination of the corporation's items.

(ii) *The day a corporation becomes or ceases to be a member.*—(A) *End of the day rule.*—(1) *In general.*—If a corporation (S), other than one described in paragraph (b)(1)(ii)(A)(2) of this section, becomes or ceases to be a member during a consolidated return year, it becomes or ceases to be a member at the end of the day on which its status as a member changes, and its tax year ends for all Federal income tax purposes at the end of that day. Appropriate adjustments must be made if another provision of the Internal Revenue Code or the regulations thereunder contemplates the event occurring before or after S's change in status. For example, S's items restored under §1.1502-13 immediately before it becomes a nonmember are taken into account in determining the basis of S's stock under § 1.1502-32. On the other hand, if a section 338(g) election is made in connection with S becoming a member, the deemed asset sale under that section takes place before S becomes a member. See § 1.338-10(a)(5) (deemed sale excluded from purchasing corporation's consolidated return.)

*(2) Special rule for former S corporations.*—If S becomes a member in a transaction other than in a qualified stock purchase for which an election under section 338(g) is made, and immediately before becoming a member an election under section 1362(a) was in effect, then S will become a member at the beginning of the day the termination of its S corporation election is effective. S's tax year ends for all Federal income tax purposes at the end of the preceding day. This paragraph (b)(1)(ii)(A)(2) applies to transactions occurring after November 10, 1999.

(B) *Next day rule.*—If, on the day of S's change in status as a member, a transaction occurs that is properly allocable to the portion of S's day after the event resulting in the change, S and all persons related to S under section 267(b) immediately after the event must treat the transaction for all Federal income tax purposes as occurring at the beginning of the following day. A determination as to whether a transaction is properly allocable to the portion of S's day after the event will be respected if it is reasonable and consistently applied by all affected persons. In determining whether an allocation is reasonable, the following factors are among those to be considered—

*(1)* Whether income, gain, deduction, loss, and credit are allocated inconsistently (e.g., to maximize a seller's stock basis adjustments under § 1.1502-32);

*(2)* If the item is from a transaction with respect to S stock, whether it reflects ownership of the stock before or after the event (e.g., if a member transfers encumbered land to nonmember S in exchange for additional S stock in a transaction to which section 351 applies and the exchange results in S becoming a member of the consolidated group, the applicability of section 357(c) to the exchange must be determined under § 1.1502-80(d) by treating the exchange as occurring after the event; on the other hand, if S is a member but has a minority shareholder and becomes a nonmember as a result of its redemption of stock with appreciated property, S's gain under section 311 is treated as from a transaction occurring before the event);

*(3)* Whether the allocation is inconsistent with other requirements under the Internal Revenue Code and regulations promulgated thereunder (e.g., if a section 338(g) election is made in connection with a group's acquisition of S, the deemed asset sale must take place before S becomes a member and S's gain or loss with respect to its assets must be taken into account by S as a nonmember (but see § 1.338-1(d)), or if S realizes discharge of indebtedness income that is excluded from gross income under section 108(a) on the day it becomes a nonmember, the discharge of indebtedness income must be treated as realized by S as a member (see § 1.1502-28(b)(11))); and

*(4)* Whether other facts exist, such as a prearranged transaction or multiples changes in S's status, indicating that the transaction is not properly allocable to the portion of S's day after the event resulting in S's change.

(C) *Successor corporations.*—For purposes of this paragraph (b)(1)(ii), any reference to a corporation includes a reference to a successor or predecessor as the context may require. A corporation is a successor if the basis of its assets is determined, directly or indirectly, in whole or in part, by reference to the basis of the assets of another corporation (the predecessor). For example, if a member forms S, S is treated as a member from the beginning of its existence.

(iii) *Group structure changes.*—If the common parent ceases to be the common parent but the group remains in existence, adjustments must be made in accordance with the principles of § 1.1502-75(d)(2) and (3).

(2) *Determination of items included in separate and consolidated returns.*—(i) *In general.*—The returns for the years that end and begin with S becoming (or ceasing to be) a member are separate tax years for all Federal income tax purposes. The returns are subject to the rules of the Internal Revenue Code applicable to short periods, as if S ceased to exist on becoming a member (or first existed on becoming a nonmember). For example, cost recovery deductions under section 168 must be allocated for short periods. On the other hand, annualization under section 443 is not required of S solely because it has a short year as a result of becoming a member. (Similarly, section 443 applies with respect to a consolidated return only to the extent that the group's return is for a short period and section 443 applies without taking this paragraph (b) into account.)

(ii) *Ratable allocation of a year's items.*—(A) *Application.*—Although the periods ending and beginning with S's change in status are different tax years, items (other than extraordinary items) may be ratably allocated between the periods if—

*(1)* S is not required to change its annual accounting period or its method of accounting as a result of its change in status (e.g., because its stock is sold between consolidated groups that have the same annual accounting periods); and

*(2)* An irrevocable ratable allocation election is made under paragraph (b)(2)(ii)(D) of this section.

(B) *General rule.*—*(1) Allocation within original year.*—Under a ratable allocation election, paragraph (b)(2) of this section applies by allocating to each day of S's original year (S's tax year determined without taking this section into account) an equal portion of S's items taken into account in the original year, except that extraordinary items must be allocated to the day that they are taken into account. All persons affected by the election must take into account S's extraordinary items and the ratable allocation of S's remaining items in a manner consistent with the election.

*(2) Items to be allocated.*—Under ratable allocation, the items to be allocated and their timing, location, character, and source are generally determined by treating the original year as a single tax year, and the items are not subject to the rules of the Internal Revenue Code applicable to short periods (unless the original year is a short period). However, the years ending and beginning with S's change in status are treated as different tax years (and as short periods) with respect to any item carried to or from these years (e.g., a net operating loss carried under section 172) and with respect to the application of section 481.

*(3) Multiple applications.*—If this paragraph (b) applies more than once with respect to an original year, adjustments must be made in accordance with the principles of this paragraph (b). For example, if S becomes a member of two different consolidated groups during the same original year and ratable allocation is elected with respect to both groups, ratable allocation is generally determined for both groups by treating the original year as a single tax year; however, if ratable allocation is elected only with respect to the first group, the ratable allocation is determined by treating the original year as a short period that does not include the period that S is a member of the second group. Ratable allocation is not a method of accounting, and ratable allocation with respect to one application of this paragraph (b) to S does not require ratable allocation to be subsequently applied with respect to S.

(C) *Extraordinary items.*—An extraordinary item is—

*(1)* Any item from the disposition or abandonment of a capital asset as defined in section 1221 (determined without the application of any other rules of law);

*(2)* Any item from the disposition or abandonment of property used in a trade or business as defined in section 1231(b) (determined without the application of any holding period requirement);

*(3)* Any item from the disposition or abandonment of an asset described in section 1221(1), (3), (4), or (5), if substantially all the assets in the same category from the same trade or business are disposed of or abandoned in one transaction (or series of related transactions);

*(4)* Any item from assets disposed of in an applicable asset acquisition under section 1060(c);

*(5)* Any item carried to or from any portion of the original year (e.g., a net operating loss carried under section 172), and any section 481(a) adjustment;

*(6)* The effects of any change in accounting method initiated by the filing of the appropriate form after S's change in status;

*(7)* Any item from the discharge or retirement of indebtedness (e.g., cancellation of indebtedness income or a deduction for retirement at a premium);

*(8)* Any item from the settlement of a tort or similar third-party liability;

*(9)* Any compensation-related deduction in connection with S's change in status (including, for example, deductions from bonus, severance, and option cancellation payments made in connection with S's change in status);

*(10)* Any dividend income from a nonmember that S controls within the meaning of section 304 at the time the dividend is taken into account;

*(11)* Any deemed income inclusion from a foreign corporation, or any deferred tax amount on an excess distribution from a passive foreign investment company under section 1291;

*(12)* Any interest expense allocable under section 172(h) to a corporate equity reduction transaction causing this paragraph (b) to apply;

*(13)* Any credit, to the extent it arises from activities or items that are not ratably allocated (e.g., the rehabilitation credit under section 47, which is based on placement in service); and

*(14)* Any item which, in the opinion of the Commissioner, would, if ratably allocated, result in a substantial distortion of income in any consolidated return or separate return in which the item is included.

(D) *Election.*—(1) *Statement.*—The election to ratably allocate items under this paragraph (b)(2)(ii) must be made in a separate statement entitled, "THIS IS AN ELECTION UNDER § 1.1502-76(b)(2)(ii) TO RATABLY ALLOCATE THE YEAR'S ITEMS OF [INSERT NAME AND EMPLOYER IDENTIFICATION NUMBER OF THE MEMBER]." The election must be filed by including a statement on or with the returns including the items for the years ending and beginning with S's change in status. If two or more members of the same consolidated group, as a consequence of the same plan or arrangement, cease to be members of that group and remain affiliated as members of another consolidated group, an election under this paragraph (b)(2)(ii)(D)(1) may be made only if it is made by each such member. Each statement must also indicate that an agreement, as described in paragraph (b)(2)(ii)(D)(2) of this section, has been entered into. Each party signing the agreement must retain either the original or a copy of the agreement as part of its records. See § 1.6001-1(e).

(2) *Agreement.*—For each election under this paragraph (b)(2)(ii), the member and the common parent of each affected group must sign and date an agreement. The agreement must—

(i) Identify the extraordinary items, their amounts, and the separate or consolidated returns in which they are included;

(ii) Identify the aggregate amount to be ratably allocated, and the portion of the amount included in the separate and consolidated returns; and

(iii) Include the name and employer identification number of the common parent (if any) of each group that must take the items into account.

(iii) *Ratable allocation of a month's items.*—If ratable allocation under paragraph (b)(2)(ii) of this section is not elected (e.g., because S is required to change its annual accounting period), this paragraph (b)(2)(iii) may be applied to ratably allocate only S's items taken into account in the month of its change in status, but only if the allocation is consistently applied by all affected persons. The ratable allocation is made by applying the principles of paragraph (b)(2)(ii) of this section under any reasonable method. For example, S may close its books both at the end of the preceding month and at the end of the month of the change, and allocate only its items (other than extraordinary items) from the month of the change. See paragraph (b)(1)(ii)(B) of this section for factors to be considered in determining whether the method is reasonable.

(iv) *Taxes.*—To the extent properly taken into account during the member's tax year (determined without the application of this paragraph (b)), Federal, state, local, and foreign taxes are allocated under paragraph (b)(2) of this section on the basis of the items or activities to which the taxes relate. Thus, income tax is allocated based on the inclusion of the income (determined under the principles of this paragraph (b)) to which the tax relates. For example, if a calendar-year domestic corporation has $100 of foreign source dividend income (determined in accordance with United States tax accounting principles but without taking this paragraph (b) into account) that is passive income for purposes of section 904, and $60 of the income is allocated under this paragraph (b) to the period of the calendar year after it becomes a member of a consolidated group, then 60% of the corporation's deemed paid foreign tax credit associated with its dividend income for the calendar year is taken into account in computing the group's passive basket consolidated foreign tax credit. Similarly, property taxes relate to the ownership of property and are allocated over the period that the property is owned. This paragraph (b)(2)(iv) applies without regard to any determination or allocation by another taxing jurisdiction.

(v) *Acquisition of S corporation.*—If a corporation is acquired in a transaction to which paragraph (b)(1)(ii)(A)(2) of this section applies, then paragraphs (b)(2)(ii) and (iii) of this section do not apply and items of income, gain, loss, deduction, and credit are assigned to each short taxable year on the basis of the corporation's normal method of accounting as determined under section 446. This paragraph (b)(2)(v) applies to transactions occurring after November 10, 1999.

(vi) *Passthrough entities.*—(A) *In general.*—If S is a partner in a partnership or an owner of a similar interest with respect to which items of the entity are taken into account by S, S is treated, solely for purposes of determining the year to which the entity's items are allocated under paragraph (b)(2) of this section, as selling or exchanging its entire interest in the entity immediately before S's change in status.

(B) *Treatment as a conduit.*—For purposes of this paragraph (b)(2), if a member (together with other members) would be treated under section 318(a)(2) as owning an aggregate of at least 50% of any stock owned by the passthrough entity, the method that is used to determine the inclusion of the entity's items in the consolidated or separate return must be the same method that is used to determine the inclusion of the member's items in the consolidated or separate return.

(C) *Exception for certain foreign entities.*—This paragraph (b)(2)(v) does not apply to any foreign corporation generating the deemed inclusion of income, or to any passive foreign investment company generating a deferred tax amount on an excess distribution under section 1291.

(3) *Anti-avoidance rule.*—If any person acts with a principal purpose contrary to the purposes of this paragraph (b), to substantially reduce the Federal income tax liability of any person, adjustments must be made as necessary to carry out the purposes of this section.

(4) *Determination of due date for separate return.*—Paragraph (c) of this section contains rules for the filing of the separate return referred to in this paragraph (b). In applying paragraph (c) of this section, the due date for the filing of S's separate return shall also be determined without regard to the ending of the tax year under paragraph (b)(1)(ii) of this section or the deemed cessation of its existence under paragraph (b)(2)(i) of this section.

(5) *Examples.*—For purposes of the examples in this paragraph (b), unless otherwise stated, P and X are common parents of calendar-year consolidated groups, P owns all of the only class of T's stock, T owns no stock of lower-tier members, all persons use the accrual method of accounting, the facts set forth the only corporate activity, all transactions are between unrelated persons, tax liabilities are disregarded, and any election required under paragraph (b)(2) of this section is properly made. The principles of this paragraph (b) are illustrated by the following examples.

*Example 1. Items allocated between consolidated and separate returns.* (a) *Facts.* P and S are the only members of the P group. P sells all of S's stock to individual A on June 30, and therefore S becomes a nonmember on July 1 of Year 2.

(b) *Analysis.* Under paragraph (b)(1) of this section, the P group's consolidated return for Year 2 includes P's income for the entire tax year and S's income for the period from January 1 to June 30, and S must file a separate return for the period from July 1 to December 31.

(c) *Acquisition of another subsidiary before end of tax year.* The facts are the same as in paragraph (a) of this *Example 1,* except that on July 31 P acquires all the stock of T (which filed a separate return for its year ending on November 30 of Year 1) and T therefore becomes a member on August 1 of Year 2. Under § 1.1502-75(d) and paragraph (b)(1) of this section, the P group's consolidated return for Year 2 includes P's income for the entire year, S's income from January 1 to June 30, and T's income from August 1 to December 31. S must file a separate return that includes its income from July 1 to December 31, and T must file a separate return that includes its income from December 1 of Year 1 to July 31 of Year 2. (If P had acquired T after December 31, the P group that included S is a different group from the P group that includes T, and, for example, the P group that includes T must make a separate election under section 1501 and § 1.1502-75 if consolidated returns are to be filed.)

*Example 2. Group structure change.* (a) *Facts.* P owns all of the stock of S and T. Shortly after the beginning of Year 1, P merges into T in a reorganization described in section 368(a)(1)(A) (and in section 368(a)(1)(D)), and P's shareholders receive T's stock in exchange for all of P's stock. The P group is treated under § 1.1502-75(d)(2)(ii) as remaining in existence with T as its common parent.

(b) *Analysis.* Under paragraph (b)(1) of this section, the P group's return must include the common parent's items for the entire consolidated return year and, if the common parent ceases to be the common parent but the group remains in existence, appropriate adjustments must be made. Consequently, although P did not exist for all of Year 1, P's items for the portion of Year 1 ending with the merger are treated as the items of the common parent that must be included in the P group's return for Year 1.

(c) *Reverse acquisition.* Assume instead that X acquires all of P's assets in exchange for more than 50% of X's stock in a reorganization described in section 368(a)(1)(D). The reorganization constitutes a reverse acquisition under § 1.1502-75(d)(3), with the X group terminating and the P group surviving with X as its common parent. Consequently, P's items for the portion of Year 1 ending with the acquisition are treated as the items of the common parent that must be included in the P group's return for Year 1, and X's items are treated for purposes of paragraph (b)(1) of this section as the items of a subsidiary included in the P group's return for the portion of Year 1 for which X is a member.

*Example 3. Ratable allocation.* (a) *Facts.* P sells all of T's stock to X, and T becomes a nonmember on July 1 of Year 1. T engages in the production and sale of merchandise throughout Year 1 and is required to use inventories. The sale is treated as causing T's tax year to end on June 30, and the periods beginning and ending with the sale are treated as two tax years for Federal income tax purposes.

(b) *Analysis.* If ratable allocation under paragraph (b)(2)(ii) of this section is not elected, T must perform an inventory valuation as of the acquisition and also as of the end of Year 1. If ratable allocation is elected, T must perform an inventory valuation only as of the close of Year 1, and T's income from inventory is ratably allocated, along with T's other items that are not extraordinary items, between the P and X consolidated returns.

(c) *Merger into nonmember.* Assume instead that T merges into a wholly owned subsidiary of X in a reorganization described in section 368(a)(2)(D), and P receives 10% of X's stock in exchange for all of T's stock. Under paragraph (b)(2)(ii)(B) of this section, because T's tax year ends on June 30 under section 381(b)(1), T's original year determined without taking paragraph (b) of this section into account also ends on June 30. Consequently, a ratable allocation under paragraph (b)(2)(ii) of this section is the same as an allocation based on closing the books.

*Example 4. Net operating loss.* P sells all of T's stock to X, T becomes a nonmember on June 30 of Year 1, and ratable allocation under paragraph (b)(2)(ii) of this section is elected. Under ratable allocation, the X group has a $100 consolidated net operating loss for Year 1, all of which is attributable to T. However, because of extraordinary items, T has $100 of income for the portion of Year 1 that T is a member of the P group. Under paragraph (b)(2)(ii)(B)(2) of this section, T's loss may be carried back from the X group to the portion of Year 1 that T was a member of the P group. See also section 172 and § 1.1502-21(b). Under paragraph (b)(2)(ii)(C)(5) of this section, any item carried to or from any portion of the original year is an extraordinary item, and the loss therefore is not taken into account again in determining the ratable allocation under paragraph (b)(2)(ii) of this section.

*Example 5. Employee benefit plans.* (a) *Facts.* P sells all of T's stock to X, and T becomes a nonmember on June 30 of Year 1. On March 15 of Year 2, T contributes $100 to its retirement plan, which is a qualified plan under section 401(a). T is not required to make quarterly contributions to the plan for Year 1 under section 412(m). The contribution is made on account of T's taxable period beginning on July 1 of Year 1, and is deemed in accordance with section 404(a)(6) to have been made on the last day of T's taxable period beginning on July 1 of Year 1. Ratable allocation under paragraph (b)(2)(ii) of this section is not elected.

(b) *Analysis.* Under paragraph (b) of this section, the sale is treated as causing T's tax year to end on June 30, and the period beginning on July 1 is treated as a separate annual accounting period for all Federal income tax purposes. T's income from January 1 to June 30 is included in the P group's Year 1 return, and T's income from July 1 to December 31 is included in the X group's Year 1 return. Thus, the $100 contribution is deductible by T for the period of Year 1 that it is a member of the X group, subject to the applicable limitations of section 404, if a contribution on the last day of that period would otherwise be deductible.

(c) The facts are the same as in paragraph (a) of this *Example 5*, except that, in accordance with section 404(a)(6), $40 of the $100 contribution is made on account of T's taxable period beginning on January 1 of Year 1 and is deemed to be made on the last day of T's taxable period beginning on January 1 of Year 1. The remaining $60 is made on account of T's taxable period beginning on July 1 of Year 1 and is deemed to be made on the last day of T's taxable period beginning on July 1 of Year 1. As in paragraph (b) of this *Example 5*, under paragraph (b) of this section, the sale is treated as causing T's tax year to end on June 30, and the period beginning on July 1 is treated as a separate annual accounting period for all Federal income tax purposes. The $40 portion of the contribution is deductible by T for the period of Year 1 that it is a member of the P group, subject to the applicable limitations of section 404 and provided that a $40 contribution on the last day of that period would otherwise be deductible for that period, and the $60 portion is deductible by T for the period of Year 1 that it is a member of the X group, subject to the same conditions.

(d) *Ratable allocation.* The facts are the same as in paragraph (a) of this *Example 5*, except that P, T, and X elect ratable allocation under paragraph (b)(2)(ii) of this section and T's deduction for the retirement plan contribution is not an extraordinary item. T's deduction may be ratably allocated, subject to the applicable limitations of section 404, and is allowable only if a contribution on the last day of Year 1 otherwise would be deductible for any period in the year. (The results would be the same if S were an unaffiliated corporation when acquired by X, and the due date of its last separate return (including

extensions) were before the pension contribution was made on March 15 of Year 2.)

*Example 6. Allocation of partnership items.* (a) *Facts.* P sells all of T's stock to X, and T becomes a nonmember on June 30 of Year 1. T has a 10% interest in the capital and profits of a calendar-year partnership.

(b) *Analysis.* Under paragraph (b)(2)(vi)(A) of this section, T is treated, solely for purposes of determining T's tax year in which the partnership's items are included, as selling or exchanging its entire interest in the partnership as of P's sale of T's stock. Thus, the deemed disposition is not taken into account under section 708, it does not result in gain or loss being recognized by T, and T's holding period is unaffected. However, under section 706(a), in determining T's income, T is required to include its distributive share of partnership items for the partnership's year ending within or with T's tax year. Under section 706(c)(2), the partnership's tax year is treated as closing with respect to T for this purpose as of P's sale of T's stock. The allocation of T's distributive share of partnership items must be made under § 1.706-1(c)(2)(ii).

(c) *Controlled partnership.* The facts are the same as in paragraph (a) of this *Example 6*, except that T has a 75% interest in the capital and profits of the partnership. Under paragraph (b)(2)(vi)(B) of this section, T's distributive share of the partnership items is treated as T's items for purposes of paragraph (b)(2) of this section. Thus, if ratable allocation under paragraph (b)(2)(ii) of this section is not elected, T's distributive share of the partnership's items must be determined under § 1.706-1(c)(2)(ii) by an interim closing of the partnership's books. Similarly, if ratable allocation is elected for T's items that are not extraordinary items, T's distributive share of the partnership's nonextraordinary items must also be ratably allocated under § 1.706-1(c)(2)(ii).

*Example 7. Acquisition of S corporation.* (a) *Facts.* Z is a small business corporation for which an election under section 1362(a) was in effect at all times since Year 1. At all times, Z had only 100 shares of stock outstanding, all of which were owned by individual A. On July 1 of Year 3, P acquired all of the Z stock. P does not make an election under section 338(g) with respect to its purchase of the Z stock.

(b) *Analysis.* As a result of P's acquisition of the Z stock, Z's election under section 1362(a) terminates. See sections 1361(b)(1)(B) and 1362(d)(2). Z is required to join in the filing of the P consolidated return. See § 1.1502-75. Z's tax year ends for all Federal income tax purposes on June 30 of Year 3. If no extension of time is sought, Z must file a separate return for the period from January 1 through June 30 of Year 3 on or before March 15 of Year 4. See paragraph (b)(4) of this section. Z will become a member of the P consolidated group as of July 1 of Year 3. See paragraph (b)(1)(ii)(A)(2) of this section. P group's Year 3 consolidated return will include Z's items from July 1 to December 31 of Year 3.

(6) *Effective date.*—(i) *General rule.*—Except as provided in paragraphs (b)(1)(ii)(A)(2) and (b)(2)(v) of this section, this paragraph (b) applies to corporations becoming or ceasing to be members of consolidated groups on or after January 1, 1995.

(ii) *Prior law.*—For prior transactions, see prior regulations under section 1502 as in effect with respect to the transaction. See, e.g., § 1.1502-76(b) and (d) as contained in the 26 CFR part 1 edition revised as of April 1, 1994. However, § 1.1502-76(b)(5) and (6) as contained in the 26 CFR part 1 edition revised as of April 1, 1994 do not apply with respect to corporations becoming or ceasing to be members of consolidated groups on or after January 1, 1995. If both this paragraph (b) and prior law may apply to determine the inclusion of any amount in a return, appropriate adjustments must be made to prevent the omission or duplication of the amount.

(c) *Time for making separate returns for periods not included in consolidated return.*—(1) *Consolidated return filed by due date for separate return.*—If the group has filed a consolidated return on or before the due date for the filing of a subsidiary's separate return (including extensions of time and determined without regard to any change of its taxable year required under paragraph (a) of this section), then the separate return for any portion of the subsidiary's taxable year for which its income is not included in the consolidated return of the group must be filed no later than the due date of such consolidated return (including extensions of time).

(2) *Consolidated return not filed by due date for separate return.*—If the group has not filed a consolidated return on or before the due date for the filing of a subsidiary corporation's separate return (including extensions of time and determined without regard to any change of its taxable year required under paragraph (a) of this section), then on or before such due date such subsidiary shall file a separate return either for the portion of its taxable year for which its income would not be included in a consolidated return if such a return were filed, or for its complete taxable year. However, if a separate return is filed for such portion of its taxable year and the

group subsequently does not file a consolidated return, such subsidiary corporation shall file a substituted return for its complete taxable year not later than the due date (including extensions of time) prescribed for the filing of the common parent's return. On the other hand, if the return is filed for the subsidiary's complete taxable year and the group later files a consolidated return, such subsidiary must file an amended return not later than the due date (including extensions of time) for the filing of the consolidated return of the group. Such amended return shall be for that portion of such subsidiary's taxable year which is not included in the consolidated return. If, under this subparagraph, a substituted return must be filed, then the return previously filed shall not be considered a return within the meaning of section 6011. If, under this subparagraph, a substituted or amended return must be filed, then, for purposes of sections 6513(a) and 6601(a), the last date prescribed for payment of tax shall be the due date (not including extensions of time) for the filing of the subsidiary's separate return (determined without regard to this subparagraph and without regard to any change of its taxable year required under paragraph (a) of this section).

(3) *Examples.*—The provisions of this paragraph may be illustrated by the following examples:

*Example (1).* Corporation P, which filed a separate return for the calendar year 1966, acquires all of the stock of corporation S as of the close of December 31, 1966. Corporation S reports its income on the basis of a fiscal year ending March 31. On June 15, 1967, the due date for the filing of a separate return by S (assuming no extensions of time), a consolidated return has not been filed for the group (P and S). On such date S may either file a return for the period April 1, 1966, through December 31, 1966, or it may file a return for the complete fiscal year ending March 31, 1967. If S files a return for the short period ending December 31, 1966, and if the group elects not to file a consolidated return for the calendar year 1967, S, on or before March 15, 1968 (the due date of P's return, assuming no extensions of time) must file a substituted return for the complete fiscal year ending March 31, 1967, in lieu of the return previously filed for the short period. Interest is computed from June 15, 1967. If, however, S files a return for the complete fiscal year ending March 31, 1967, and the group elects to file a consolidated return for the calendar year 1967, then S must file an amended return covering the period from April 1, 1966, through December 31, 1966, in lieu of the return previously filed for the complete fiscal year. Interest is computed from June 15, 1967.

*Example (2).* Assume the same facts as in example (1) except that corporation P acquires all of the stock of corporation S at the close of September 30, 1967, and that P files a consolidated return for the group for 1967 on March 15, 1968 (not having obtained any extensions of time). Since a consolidated return has been filed on or before the due date (June 15, 1968) for the filing of the separate return for the taxable year ending March 31, 1968, the return of S for the short taxable year beginning April 1, 1967, and ending September 30, 1967, should be filed no later than March 15, 1968.

(d) *Effective/applicability date.*—(1) *Taxable years of members of group effective date.*—(i) *In general.*—Paragraph (a) of this section applies to any original consolidated Federal income tax return due (without extensions) after July 20, 2007.

(ii) *Prior law.*—For original consolidated Federal income tax returns due (without extensions) after April 25, 2006, and on or before July 20, 2007, see § 1.1502-76T as contained in 26 CFR part 1 in effect on April 1, 2007. For original consolidated Federal income tax returns due (without extensions) on or before April 25, 2006, see § 1.1502-76 as contained in 26 CFR part 1 in effect on April 1, 2006.

(2) *Election to ratably allocate items effective date.*—(i) *In general.*—Paragraph (b)(2)(ii)(D) of this section applies to any original consolidated Federal income tax return due (without extensions) after July 20, 2007.

(ii) *Prior law.*—For original consolidated Federal income tax returns due (without extensions) after May 30, 2006, and on or before July 20, 2007, see § 1.1502-76T as contained in 26 CFR part 1 in effect on April 1, 2007. For original consolidated Federal income tax returns due (without extensions) on or before May 30, 2006, see § 1.1502-76 as contained in 26 CFR part 1 in effect on April 1, 2006. [Reg. § 1.1502-76.]

☐ [T.D. 6894, 9-7-66. *Amended by* T.D. 7244, 12-29-72; T.D. 7246, 12-29-72; T.D. 8560, 8-12-94; T.D. 8842, 11-9-99; T.D. 8858, 1-5-2000; T.D. 8940, 2-12-2001; T.D. 9192, 3-21-2005; T.D. 9258, 4-24-2006; T.D. 9264, 5-26-2006 *and* T.D. 9342, 7-19-2007.]

[Reg. § 1.1502-77]

**§ 1.1502-77. Agent for the group.**—(a) *Agent for the group.*—(1) *Sole agent.*—Except as provided in paragraphs (e) and (f)(2) of this section, one entity (the agent) is the sole agent that is authorized to act in its own name regarding all matters relating to the federal income tax liability for the consolidated return year for each member of the group and any successor or transferee of a member (and any subsequent successors and transferees thereof). The identity of that agent is determined under the rules of paragraph (c) of this section.

(2) *Agent for each consolidated return year.*—Agency for the group is established for each consolidated return year and is not affected by the status or membership of the group in later years. Thus, subject to the rules of paragraph (c) of this section, the agent will generally remain agent for that consolidated return year regardless of whether one or more subsidiaries later cease to be members of the group, whether the group files a consolidated return for any subsequent year, whether the agent ceases to be the agent or a member of the group in any subsequent year, or whether the group continues pursuant to § 1.1502-75(d) with a new common parent in any subsequent year.

(3) *Communications under this section.*—Any designation, notification, objection, request, or other communication made to or by the Commissioner pursuant to paragraphs (c) and (f)(2) of this section must be made in accordance with procedures prescribed by the Commissioner in the Internal Revenue Bulletin (see § 601.601(d)(2)(ii) of this chapter), forms, instructions, or other appropriate guidance.

(b) *Definitions.*—The following definitions apply for purposes of this section only—

(1) *Successor.*—A *successor* is an individual or entity (including a disregarded entity as defined in paragraph (b)(3) of this section) that is primarily liable, pursuant to applicable law (including, for example, by operation of a state or federal merger statute), for the tax liability of a corporation that was a member of the group but is no longer in existence under applicable law. The determination of tax liability is made without regard to § 1.1502-1(f)(4) or § 1.1502-6(a). (For inclusion of a successor in references to a subsidiary or member, see paragraph (b)(5)(iii) of this section.)

(2) *Entity.*—The term *entity* includes any corporation, limited liability company, or partnership formed under any state, federal, or foreign jurisdiction. The term entity includes a disregarded entity (as defined in paragraph (b)(3) of this section). The term entity does not include an entity that has terminated even if it is in a winding up period under the law under which it is organized.

(3) *Disregarded entity.*—The term *disregarded entity* includes any of the following types of entities that are disregarded as separate from their owners—

(i) Qualified real estate investment trust subsidiaries (within the meaning of section 856(i)(2));

(ii) Qualified subchapter S subsidiaries (within the meaning of section 1361(b)(3)(B)); and

(iii) Eligible entities with a single owner (within the meaning of § 301.7701-3 of this chapter).

(4) *Default successor.*—A successor to the agent is the *default successor* if it is an entity (whether domestic or foreign) that is the sole successor to the agent. A partnership is treated as a sole successor with primary liability notwithstanding that one or more partners may also be primarily liable by virtue of being partners.

(5) *Member or subsidiary.*—All references to a member or subsidiary for a consolidated return year include—

(i) Each corporation that was a member of the group during any part of such year (except that any reference to a subsidiary does not include the common parent);

(ii) Each corporation whose income was included in the consolidated return for such year, notwithstanding that the tax liability of such corporation should have been computed on the basis of a separate return, or as a member of another consolidated group, under the provisions of § 1.1502-75; and

(iii) Except as indicated otherwise, a successor of any of the foregoing corporations.

(6) *Completed year.*—A *completed year* is a consolidated return year that has ended, or will end at the time of the referenced event.

(7) *Current year.*—A *current year* is a consolidated return year that is not a completed year.

(c) *Identity of the agent.*—(1) *In general.*—Except as otherwise provided in this section, the agent for a current year is the common parent and the agent for a completed year is the common parent at the close of the completed year or its default successor, if any. Except as specifically provided otherwise in this paragraph (c), any entity that is an agent pursuant to paragraph (c)(3) of this section (agent following group structure change), paragraph (c)(5) of this section (agent designated by agent terminating without default successor), paragraph (c)(6) of this section (agent designated by Commissioner), or paragraph (c)(7) of this section (agent designated by resigning agent), or any entity subsequently serving as agent following such agent, acts as an agent for and under the same terms and conditions that apply to a common parent. For example, such an agent would generally be able to designate an agent if it terminates without a default successor; however, an entity that became agent pursuant to a designation by the Commissioner under paragraphs (c)(6)(i)(A)(2), (3), or (4) of this section is not permitted to designate an agent if it terminates without a default successor. Other special rules described in this paragraph (c) apply.

(2) *Purported agent.*—If any entity files a consolidated return, or takes any other action related to the tax liability for the consolidated return year, purporting to be the agent but is subsequently determined not to have been the agent with respect to the claimed group, that entity is treated, to the extent necessary to avoid prejudice to the Commissioner, as if it were the agent.

(3) *New common parent after a group structure change.*—If the group continues in existence after a group structure change (as described in § 1.1502-33(f)(1)), the former common parent is the agent until the group structure change, and the new common parent becomes the agent after the group structure change. Following the group structure change, the new common parent is the agent with respect to the entire current year (including the period before the group structure change) and the former common parent is no longer the agent for that year. However, actions taken by the former common parent as the agent before the group structure change are not nullified when the new common parent becomes the agent with respect to the entire consolidated return year. Following the group structure change, the new common parent continues as the agent for succeeding years subject to the rules of this section.

(4) *Notification by default successor.*—(i) *In general.*—Failure to provide notice to the Commissioner pursuant to this paragraph (c)(4)(i) does not invalidate an entity's status as the default successor. However, until the Commissioner receives notification in writing that an entity is the default successor—

(A) Any notice of deficiency or other communication mailed to the predecessor agent, even if no longer in existence, is considered as having been properly mailed to the agent; and

(B) The Commissioner is not required to act on any communication (including, for example, a claim for refund) submitted on behalf of the group by any person (including the default successor) other than the predecessor agent.

(ii) *Conversions and continuances.*—For purposes of the notice requirements under paragraph (c)(4)(i) of this section, any entity that results from the agent's conversion or continuance by operation of state law and that qualifies as a default successor under paragraph (b)(4) of this section is treated as a default successor for purposes of the notice provisions of paragraph (c)(4)(i) of this section, even if applicable state or local law may treat the converted or continued entity as not ceasing to exist.

(5) *Designation by terminating agent.*—(i) *In general.*—Prior to the termination of its existence without a default successor, an agent may designate an entity described in paragraph (c)(5)(ii) of this section to act as agent for any completed year. This designation is effective upon the termination of the designating agent's existence. However, this paragraph (c)(5) does not apply to, and no designation can be made by, an agent that was designated by the Commissioner under paragraphs (c)(6)(i)(A)(2), (3), or (4) of this section, or any successor of such an agent; in such a case, the terminating agent should request that the Commissioner designate an agent pursuant to paragraph (c)(6)(i)(B) of this section.

(ii) *Permissible agents.*—(A) The terminating agent may designate as agent a member of the group during any part of the completed year, or an entity (whether domestic or foreign) that is a successor of such a member, including an entity that will become a successor at the time the agent's existence terminates.

(B) The terminating agent may not designate as agent any entity that was previously replaced as agent by the Commissioner pursuant to paragraphs (c)(6)(i)(A)(2), (3), or (4) of this section, or any successor of such an agent. However, the terminating agent may submit a request pursuant to paragraph (c)(6)(i)(B) of this section that the Commissioner designate such an entity as agent.

(iii) *Notification of designation.*—The terminating agent must notify the Commissioner in writing of its designation of an entity as agent pursuant to paragraph (c)(5)(i) of this section and provide a statement executed by the designated entity acknowledging that it will serve as the agent for each specified completed year for which it is designated as the agent. If the designated entity was not itself a member of the group during any specified year (because it is a

successor of a member), the notification must include a statement acknowledging that the designated entity is or will be primarily liable for the tax liability for the specified completed year as a successor of a member.

(iv) *Failure to designate an agent.*—If the agent terminates without a default successor, and no agent is designated pursuant to this paragraph (c)(5)—

(A) Any notice of deficiency or other communication mailed to the agent, even if no longer in existence, is considered as having been properly mailed to the agent; and

(B) The Commissioner is not required to act on any communication (including, for example, a claim for refund) submitted on behalf of the group by any person.

(6) *Designation by the Commissioner.*—(i) *In general.*—The Commissioner has the authority to designate an entity to act as the agent under the circumstances prescribed in this paragraph (c)(6)(i). The designated agent for a completed year must be an entity described in paragraph (c)(5)(ii)(A) of this section when the designation becomes effective. The designated agent for a current year must be a member of the group when the designation becomes effective. If, pursuant to this paragraph (c)(6), the Commissioner replaces the common parent or another entity as the agent, the common parent or other entity, or any successor thereof, may not later act as the agent unless so designated by the Commissioner.

(A) *On Commissioner's own accord.*—With or without a request from any member of the group, the Commissioner may designate an entity to act as the agent if—

(1) The agent's existence terminates, other than in a group structure change, without there being a default successor and without any designation made under paragraph (c)(5)(i) of this section;

(2) An agent previously designated by the Commissioner is no longer a member of the group in the current year and does not have a default successor that is a member of the group;

(3) The Commissioner believes that the agent or its default successor exists but such entity has either not timely responded to the Commissioner's notices (sent to the last known address on file for the entity or left at the usual place of business for such entity) or has failed to perform its obligations as agent as prescribed by the Internal Revenue Code (Code) or regulations promulgated thereunder; or

(4) The agent is or becomes a foreign entity as a result of any action or transaction (including, for example, a continuance into a foreign jurisdiction or certain inversion transactions subject to section 7874 in which a foreign parent is treated as a domestic corporation).

(B) *Written request from any member.*—At the request of any member, in a circumstance not described in paragraph (c)(6)(i)(A) of this section, the Commissioner may, but is not required to, replace an agent previously designated under this paragraph (c)(6).

(ii) *Notification by Commissioner.*—The Commissioner will notify the designated entity in writing of the Commissioner's designation of the entity as agent pursuant to paragraph (c)(6)(i) of this section, and the designation will be effective as prescribed by the Commissioner. The designated entity should give notice of the designation by the Commissioner pursuant to paragraph (c)(6)(i) of this section to each member of the group during any part of the consolidated return year. However, a failure by the designated entity to notify any such member of the group does not invalidate the designation by the Commissioner.

(iii) *Term and effect of designation.*—Unless otherwise provided by the Commissioner in the designation, any agent designated by the Commissioner pursuant to paragraph (c)(6)(i) of this section (new agent) is the agent with respect to the entire consolidated return year for which it is designated and successive years, subject to the rules of this section. An agent immediately preceding a new agent (former agent) ceases to be the agent for a particular consolidated return year once the new agent has been designated for that year, but the designation of the new agent does not nullify actions taken on behalf of the group by the former agent while it was agent. If there is more than one new agent designated by the Commissioner for a consolidated return year, the new agent that is designated last in time by the Commissioner is the agent with respect to the entire consolidated return year. A designation pursuant to this paragraph (c)(6) is effective as prescribed by the Commissioner in such designation or the Internal Revenue Bulletin (see § 601.601(d)(2)(ii) of this chapter), forms, instructions, or other appropriate guidance.

(iv) *Request by member of the group where agent previously designated by the Commissioner is no longer a member.*—If an agent at any time after it is designated as agent by the Commissioner pursuant to paragraph (c)(6)(i) of this section is no longer a member of the group for any current year, and its default successor, if any, is not a member of the group at that time, a member of the group, including the agent that will cease to be a member, should request, in writing, that the Commissioner designate a member of the group to be the new agent pursuant to paragraph (c)(6)(i)(A)(2) of this section. Until such a request is made—

(A) Any notice of deficiency or other communication mailed to the agent, even if no longer a member, is considered as having been properly mailed to the agent; and

(B) The Commissioner is not required to act on any communication (including, for example, a claim for refund) submitted on behalf of the group by any person.

(7) *Agent resigns.*—(i) *In general.*—The agent may resign for a completed year if—

(A) It provides written notice to the Commissioner that it no longer intends to be the agent for that completed year;

(B) An entity described in paragraph (c)(5)(ii)(A) of this section consents, in writing, to be the agent with respect to that completed year;

(C) Immediately after its resignation takes effect, the resigning agent will not be the agent for the current year; and

(D) The Commissioner does not object to the agent's resignation.

(iii) *Notification by agent that replaces agent that resigns.*—If the Commissioner does not object to the agent's resignation, the agent that replaces the agent that resigns should give written notice that it is the new agent to each member of the group for any part of the completed year for which it is designated the agent.

(8) *Transactions under the Code.*—Notwithstanding section 338(a)(2), a target corporation for which an election is made under section 338 is not deemed to terminate for purposes of this section.

(d) *Examples of matters subject to agency.*—With respect to any consolidated return year for which it is the agent—

(1) The agent makes any election (or similar choice of a permissible option) that is available to a subsidiary in the computation of its separate taxable income, and any change in an election (or similar choice of a permissible option) previously made by or for a subsidiary, including, for example, a request to change a subsidiary's method or period of accounting;

(2) All correspondence concerning the income tax liability for the consolidated return year is carried on directly with the agent;

(3) The agent files for all extensions of time, including extensions of time for payment of tax under section 6164, and any extension so filed is considered as having been filed by each member;

(4) The agent gives waivers, gives bonds, and executes closing agreements, offers in compromise, and all other documents, and any waiver or bond so given, or agreement, offer in compromise, or any other document so executed, is considered as having also been given or executed by each member;

(5) The agent files claims for refund, and any refund is made directly to and in the name of the agent and discharges any liability of the Government to any member with respect to such refund;

(6) The agent takes any action on behalf of a member of the group with respect to a foreign corporation including, for example, elections by, and changes to the method of accounting of, a controlled foreign corporation in accordance with § 1.964-1(c)(3);

(7) Notices of claim disallowance are mailed only to the agent, and the mailing to the agent is considered as a mailing to each member;

(8) Notices of deficiencies are mailed only to the agent (except as provided in paragraph (f)(3) of this section), and the mailing to the agent is considered as a mailing to each member;

(9) Notices of final partnership administrative adjustment under section 6223 with respect to any partnership in which a member of the group is a partner may be mailed to the agent, and, if so, the mailing to the agent is considered as a mailing to each member that is a partner entitled to receive such notice (for other rules regarding partnership proceedings, see paragraph (f)(2)(iii) of this section);

(10) The agent files petitions and conducts proceedings before the United States Tax Court, and any such petition is considered as also having been filed by each member;

(11) Any assessment of tax may be made in the name of the agent, and an assessment naming the agent is considered as an assessment with respect to each member; and

(12) Notice and demand for payment of taxes is given only to the agent, and such notice and demand is considered as a notice and demand to each member.

(e) *Matters reserved to subsidiaries.*—Except as provided in this paragraph (e) and paragraph (f)(2) of this section, no subsidiary (unless it is or becomes an agent pursuant to paragraph (c) of this section) has authority to act for or to represent itself in any matter related to the tax liability for the consolidated return year. The following matters, however, are reserved exclusively to each subsidiary—

(1) The making of the consent required by § 1.1502-75(a)(1);

(2) Any action with respect to the subsidiary's liability for a federal tax other than the income tax imposed by chapter 1 of the Code (including, for example, employment taxes under chapters 21 through 25 of the Code, and miscellaneous excise taxes under chapters 31 through 47 of the Code); and

(3) The making of an election to be treated as a Domestic International Sales Corporation under § 1.992-2.

(f) *Dealings with members.*—(1) *Identifying members in notice of a lien.*—Notwithstanding any other provisions of this section, any notice of a lien, any levy, or any other proceeding to collect the amount of any assessment, after the assessment has been made, must name the entity from which such collection is to be made.

(2) *Direct dealing with a member.*—(i) *Several liability.*—The Commissioner may, upon issuing to the agent written notice that expressly invokes the authority of this provision, deal directly with any member of the group with respect to its liability under § 1.1502-6 for the consolidated tax of the group, in which event such member has sole authority to act for itself with respect to that liability. However, if the Commissioner believes or has reason to believe that the existence of the agent has terminated without an agent being identified under this section, the Commissioner may, if the Commissioner deems it advisable, deal directly with any member with respect to that member's liability under § 1.1502-6 without issuing notice to any other entity.

(ii) *Information requests.*—The Commissioner may, upon issuing to the agent written notice, request information relevant to the consolidated tax liability from any member of the group. However, if the Commissioner believes or has reason to believe that the existence of the agent has terminated without an agent being identified under this section, the Commissioner may request such information from any member of the group without issuing notice to any other entity.

(iii) *Members as partners in partnerships subject to the provisions of the Code.*—Except as otherwise provided in this paragraph (f)(2)(iii), the general rule of paragraph (a)(1) of this section applies so that the agent is the agent for any subsidiary member that for any part of the consolidated return year is a partner in a partnership subject to the provisions of sections 6221 through 6234 of the Code (as originally enacted by the Tax Equity and Fiscal Responsibility Act of 1982 and subsequently amended) and the accompanying regulations (TEFRA partnership). However—

(A) Any subsidiary or any disregarded entity owned by a subsidiary that is designated as tax matters partner of a TEFRA partnership will act in its own name and perform its responsibilities under sections 6221 through 6234 and the accompanying regulations without requiring any action by the agent (but see paragraph (d)(9) of this section regarding the mailing of a final partnership administrative adjustment to the agent); and

(B) The Commissioner may at any time communicate directly with a subsidiary or a disregarded entity owned by a subsidiary that is a partner in a TEFRA partnership, without having to deal with each member separately pursuant to paragraph (f)(2)(i) of this section, whenever the Commissioner determines that such direct communication will facilitate the conduct of an examination, appeal, or settlement with respect to the partnership.

(3) *Copy of notice of deficiency to entity that has ceased to be a member of the group.*—A subsidiary that ceases to be a member of the group during or after a consolidated return year may file a written notice of that fact with the Commissioner and request a copy of any notice of deficiency with respect to the tax for a consolidated return year during which it was a member, or a copy of any notice and demand for payment of such deficiency, or both. Such filing does not limit the scope of the agency of the agent provided for in this section. Any failure by the Commissioner to comply with such request does not limit the subsidiary's tax liability under § 1.1502-6.

(g) *Examples.*—Unless otherwise indicated, all entities are domestic and have a calendar year taxable year, and each of P, S, S-1, S-2, S-3, T, U, V, W, W-1, Y, Z, and Z-1 is a corporation. For none of the consolidated return years at issue does the Commissioner exercise the authority under paragraph (f)(2) of this section to deal with any member separately. Any surviving entity in a merger is either a successor as described in paragraph (b)(1) of this section, or a default successor as described in paragraph (b)(4) of this section, as the case may be. Except as otherwise indicated, no agent will be replaced under paragraph (c)(6) of this section or will resign under paragraph (c)(7) of this section, and all communications to and from the Commissioner are made in accordance with procedures prescribed by the Commissioner.

*Example 1. Disposition of all group members where the agent remains the agent.* (i) *Facts.* As of January 1 of Year 1, P is the common parent and agent for the P consolidated group, consisting of P and its two subsidiaries, S and S-1. P files consolidated returns for the P group in Years 1 and 2. On December 31 of Year 1, P sells all the stock of S-1 to X. On December 31 of Year 2, P distributes all the stock of S to P's shareholders. P files a separate return for Year 3.

(ii) *Analysis.* Although the consolidated group terminates after Year 2 under § 1.1502-75(d)(1) and P is no longer the common parent nor the agent for years after Year 2, P remains the agent for the P group for Years 1 and 2 under paragraph (a)(2) of this section. Accordingly, for as long as P remains in existence, P is the agent for the P group under paragraphs (a)(1) and (2) and (c)(1) of this section for Years 1 and 2.

*Example 2. Acquisition of the agent by another group where the agent remains the agent.* (i) *Facts.* The facts are the same as in *Example 1*, except on January 1 of Year 3, all of the outstanding stock of P is acquired by Y, which is the common parent and agent of the Y consolidated group. P thereafter joins in the Y group's consolidated return as a member of the Y group.

(ii) *Analysis.* Although P is a member of the Y group in Year 3 and succeeding years, P remains the agent for the P group for Years 1 and 2 under paragraph (a)(2) of this section. Accordingly, for as long as P remains in existence, P is the agent for the P group under paragraphs (a)(1) and (2) and (c)(1) of this section for Years 1 and 2.

*Example 3. Reverse triangular merger of the agent where the agent remains the agent.* (i) *Facts.* As of January 1 of Year 1, P is the common parent and agent for the P consolidated group consisting of P and its two subsidiaries, S and S-1. P files consolidated returns for the P group in Years 1 and 2. On March 1 of Year 3, W-1, a subsidiary of W, merges into P in a reverse triangular merger qualifying as a reorganization under section 368(a)(1)(A) and (a)(2)(E). P survives the merger with W-1. The transaction constitutes a reverse acquisition under § 1.1502-75(d)(3)(i) because P's shareholders receive more than 50 percent of W's stock in exchange for all of P's stock. The transaction is therefore a group structure change as described in paragraph (c)(3) of this section.

(ii) *Analysis.* Because the transaction constitutes a reverse acquisition that results in a group structure change, the P group is treated as remaining in existence with W as its common parent and agent. Under paragraphs (a)(1) and (2) and (c)(1) of this section, P remains the agent for the P group for Years 1 and 2 for as long as P remains in existence, even though the P group continues with W as its new common parent pursuant to § 1.1502-75(d)(3)(i). Until the merger of W-1 and P on March 1 of Year 3, P is the agent for the P group for Year 3. From the time of that merger, W, as common parent of the P group, becomes the agent for the P group with respect to all of Year 3 (including the period through March 1) and succeeding consolidated return years. The actions taken by P before the merger as agent for the P group for Year 3 are not nullified by the fact that W becomes the agent for all of Year 3.

*Example 4. Reverse triangular merger of the agent—subsequent distribution of agent where the agent remains the agent.* (i) *Facts.* The facts are the same as in *Example 3*, except that on April 1 of Year 4, in a transaction unrelated to the March 1, Year 3 reverse acquisition, P distributes the stock of its subsidiaries S and S-1 to W, and W then distributes the stock of P to the W shareholders.

(ii) *Analysis.* Although P is no longer a member of the P group after the Year 4 distribution, P remains the agent for the P group under paragraphs (a)(1) and (2) and (c)(1) of this section for Years 1 and 2 for as long as P remains in existence.

*Example 5. Agent Resigns.* (i) *Facts.* The facts are the same as in *Example 4*, except that on August 1 of Year 4, P provides written notice to the Commissioner that it resigns as the agent for Years 1 and 2. Included with the written notice is a statement executed by either S or S-1 consenting to be the agent for the P group for Years 1 and 2.

(ii) *Analysis.* Pursuant to paragraph (c)(7) of this section, because P is not the agent in Year 4, the current year, it will not be the agent immediately after its resignation takes effect. Accordingly, if the Commissioner does not object to P's resignation, P may resign with respect to Years 1 and 2, both of which are completed years, and either S or S-1, each an entity described in paragraph (c)(5)(ii)(A) of this section, can be the agent for the P group for Years 1 and 2 if it consents in writing. W cannot be the agent for the P group for Years 1 and 2 because it is not an entity described in paragraph (c)(5)(ii)(A) of this section with respect to the P group for Years 1 and 2.

*Example 6. Qualified stock purchase and section 338 election where the agent remains the agent.* (i) *Facts.* As of January 1 of Year 1, P is the common parent and agent for the P consolidated group consisting of P and its two subsidiaries, S and S-1. P files consolidated returns for the P group in Years 1 and 2. On March 31 of Year 2, V purchases the stock of P in a qualified stock purchase (within the meaning of section 338(d)(3)), and V makes a timely election pursuant to section 338(g) with respect to P.

(ii) *Analysis.* Although section 338(a)(2) provides that P is treated as a new corporation as of the beginning of the day after the acquisition date for purposes of subtitle A, paragraph (c)(8) of this section provides that P's existence is not deemed to terminate for purposes of this section notwithstanding the general rule of section 338(a)(2). Accordingly, new P is the agent for the P group for Year 1 and the period ending March 31 of Year 2 regardless of the election under section 338(g).

*Example 7. Change in the agent's federal income tax classification to a partnership and the resulting partnership continues as the agent.* (i) *Facts.* P, a State M limited liability partnership with two partners that is formed on January 1 of Year 1, elects pursuant to § 301.7701-3(c) of this chapter to be an association taxable as a corporation for federal income tax purposes effective on the date of formation. P is the common parent and agent for the P consolidated group consisting of P and its two subsidiaries, S and S-1. P files consolidated returns for the P group in Years 1 through 6. On January 1 of Year 7, P elects pursuant to § 301.7701-3(c) of this chapter to be treated as a partnership. P remains in existence under applicable law.

(ii) *Analysis.* The P group terminates and P is no longer the common parent of a consolidated group after its election to be treated as a partnership for federal income tax purposes. Because P remains in existence under applicable law, P is the agent for the P group under paragraphs (a)(1) and (2) and (c)(1) of this section for Years 1 through 6. If P merged into a foreign partnership instead of converting to a partnership, the foreign partnership would be P's default successor and agent for the P group for Years 1 through 6. See paragraphs (b)(4) and (c)(1) of this section.

*Example 8. Forward triangular merger of agent—successor as default successor.* (i) *Facts.* As of January 1 of Year 1, P is the common parent and agent for the P consolidated group consisting of P and its two subsidiaries, S and S-1. P files a consolidated return for the P group for Year 1. On January 1 of Year 3, P merges with and into Z-1, a subsidiary of Z, in a forward triangular merger qualifying as a reorganization under section 368(a)(1)(A) and (a)(2)(D). The transaction constitutes a reverse acquisition under § 1.1502-75(d)(3)(i) resulting in a group structure change as described in paragraph (c)(3) of this section because P's shareholders receive more than 50 percent of Z's stock in exchange for all of P's stock. Z-1, the corporation that survives the merger and the successor of P, is the default successor for the P group for Years 1 and 2.

(ii) *Analysis.* Although Z is the new common parent for the P group (which continues pursuant to § 1.1502-75(d)(3)(i)) for consolidated return years after the merger, and, as a consequence, Z is the new agent as a result of this group structure change, P may not designate an agent for Years 1 or 2 because Z-1 is P's default successor and the agent for the P group for Years 1 and 2. Z-1 must file the P group's consolidated return for Year 2. See paragraphs (b)(4) and (c)(1) of this section.

*Example 9. Merger of the agent into a disregarded entity in exchange for stock of owner in a transaction qualifying as a reorganization under the Code where successor is the default successor.* (i) *Facts.* As of January 1 of Year 1, P is the common parent and agent for the P consolidated group consisting of P and its two subsidiaries, S and S-1. P files a consolidated return for the P group in Year 1. On January 1 of Year 2, the shareholders of P form Y, a State M corporation. On the same date, Y forms Y-1, a State M limited liability company that is a disregarded entity (as defined in paragraph (b)(3) of this section) for federal income tax purposes, and P merges into Y-1 under State M law. In the merger, the P shareholders receive all of the Y stock. Y (through Y-1) is treated as acquiring the assets of P in a transaction qualifying as a reorganization of P into Y under section 368(a)(1)(F), and the P group continues under § 1.1502-75(d)(2) with Y as the common parent and, as a consequence, the transaction is treated as a group structure change as described in paragraph (c)(3) with Y as the P group's agent for Year 2. In Year 4, the Commissioner seeks to extend the period of limitations on assessment with respect to Year 1 of the P group. In Year 5, the Commissioner seeks to extend the period of limitations on assessment with respect to Year 2 of the Y group (formerly the P group).

(ii) *Analysis.* (A) *Year 1 extension.* As a result of the January 1, Year 2 merger, Y-1 is the default successor of P, and the agent for the P group for Year 1. See paragraphs (b)(4) and (c)(1) of this section. Therefore, Y-1 is the only party that can sign the extension with respect to the P group for Year 1.

(B) *Year 2 extension.* Because the January 1, Year 2 merger qualified as a reorganization under section 368(a)(1)(F), the P group remains in existence with Y as the common parent. Therefore, Y, the common parent of the P group after the merger, is the P group's agent for all of Year 2 (see paragraph (c)(3) of this section) and is the only party that can sign the extension with respect to the P group for that year and in succeeding years. See paragraphs (a)(1) and (2) and (c)(1) of this section.

*Example 10. Designation of agent where there is no default successor.* (i) *Facts.* P is incorporated under the laws of State X. Fifty percent of its stock is owned at all times by A, an individual, and 50 percent by BCD, a partnership. On January 1 of Year 1, P forms two subsidiaries, S and T, and becomes the common parent of the P group. P files consolidated returns for the P group beginning in Year 1 and is the agent for the P consolidated group beginning on January 1 of Year 1. On November 30 of Year 3, P dissolves under X law. Under X law, A and BCD are primarily liable for the federal income tax liability of dissolved corporation P. State X law allows the officers of a dissolved corporation to perform certain actions incident to the winding up of its affairs after its dissolution, including the filing of tax returns.

(ii) *Analysis.* Upon P's dissolution, there is no default successor to P, pursuant to paragraph (b)(4) of this section, because there are two successors. Prior to its dissolution on November 30 of Year 3, pursuant to paragraph (c)(5)(i) of this section, P may designate an agent for the P group for Years 1 and 2 and the short taxable year ending on November 30 of Year 3, to be effective upon P's dissolution. P may designate S or T, pursuant to paragraph (c)(5)(ii)(A) of this section (because they are members of the former group), or BCD (because it is an entity that is a successor to P pursuant to paragraph (b)(1) of this section). P cannot designate A pursuant to paragraph (c)(5)(ii) of this section, because A is not an entity. Under paragraph (b)(2) of this section, the officers of P cannot designate an agent for the P group after P dissolves on November 30 of Year 3, notwithstanding the winding up provisions of State X law. Accordingly, P should designate an agent prior to its dissolution to ensure that there is an agent authorized to file the short Year 3 consolidated return. If P does not designate an agent prior to dissolution under paragraph (c)(5)(i) of this section, the Commissioner may designate an agent under paragraph (c)(6)(i)(A)(1) of this section from among S, T, or BCD, upon their request or otherwise. If any of S, T, A, or BCD realizes that P has dissolved without designating an agent, it should request, in writing, a designation of an agent by the Commissioner as soon as possible.

*Example 11. Commissioner designates a new agent.* (i) *Agent fails to fulfill its obligations.* (A) *Facts.* P is the common parent and agent for the P consolidated group consisting of P and its two subsidiaries, S-1 and S-2, each a State Y corporation. P files a consolidated return for the P group in Year 1. In Year 2, S-3, also a State Y corporation, joins the P group. The P group continues as a consolidated group in Years 2, 3, and 4. As of Year 4, P has failed to file the P group consolidated returns for Years 2 and 3.

(B) *Analysis.* (1) *Scope of designation.* Because P failed to perform its obligations as agent as prescribed by federal tax law, the Commissioner may, under the authority of paragraph (c)(6)(i)(A)(3) of this section, on his own accord, with or without a written request from a member, designate another entity described in paragraph (c)(6)(i) of this section to act as the agent for not just Years 2 and 3, but any of Years 1 through 4.

(2) *Year 1 designation.* The Commissioner may designate either S-1 or S-2, both of which are entities described in paragraphs (c)(6)(i) and (c)(5)(ii)(A) of this section, to act as the agent for the P group for Year 1. Because S-3 was not a member of the group in Year 1, it is not an entity described in paragraphs (c)(6)(i) and (c)(5)(ii)(A) of this section for Year 1 and therefore cannot be the agent for Year 1. Unless otherwise provided in the designation, the designation of either S-1 or S-2 will also be effective for Years 2, 3, and 4 and all succeeding consolidated return years of the group.

(3) *Year 2 designation.* The Commissioner may designate either S-1, S-2, or S-3, all of which are entities described in paragraph (c)(5)(ii)(A) of this section, to act as the agent for the P group for Year 2. Unless otherwise provided in the designation, the designation of either S-1, S-2, or S-3 will also be effective for Years 3 and 4 and all succeeding consolidated return years of the group.

(4) *Year 3 designation.* The Commissioner may designate any of S-1, S-2, or S-3 as the agent for Year 3. Unless otherwise provided in the designation, the designation of either S-1, S-2, or S-3 will also be effective for Year 4 and all succeeding consolidated return years of the group.

(5) *Year 4 designation.* The Commissioner may designate any of S-1, S-2, or S-3 as the agent for Year 4. Unless otherwise provided in the designation, the designation of either S-1, S-2, or S-3 will also be effective for all succeeding consolidated return years of the group.

(ii) *Member requests replacement of designated agent.* (A) *Facts.* The facts are the same as in paragraph (i)(A) of this *Example 11,* except that in Year 4 the Commissioner designates S-1 as agent for Years 1 and succeeding years to replace P for P's failure to fulfill its obligations. After receiving notification that S-1 has been designated, S-3 submits a request in Year 4, pursuant to paragraph (c)(6)(i)(B) of this section, that the Commissioner designate S-2 as the agent because S-1 does not have ready access to the group's books and records, which are located in another state and are in the possession of S-2.

(B) *Analysis.* In light of S-3's request, the Commissioner may, under the authority of paragraph (c)(6)(i)(B) of this section, designate either S-2 (for all or any years) or S-3 (for any year or years other than Year 1) as agent in lieu of the previously designated agent, S-1. However, notwithstanding S-3's request, the Commissioner is not required to replace S-1 as agent for any of the consolidated return years for which S-1 was designated.

*Example 12. Designated agent ceases to be a member of the group.* (i) *Facts.* The facts are the same as in paragraph (ii)(A) of *Example 11,* except that in Year 4 no member requests that the Commissioner replace S-1, which accordingly continues to be the agent for the P group in Year 5 pursuant to paragraph (c)(6)(iii) of this section. On May 2 of Year 5, S-1 converts under State Y law into S-1 LLC, a limited liability company that is an entity that is treated as a disregarded entity (as defined in paragraph (b)(3) of this section) and, as a consequence, is no longer a member of the P group after the conversion.

(ii) *Analysis for completed years.* S-1 LLC, the disregarded entity resulting from the conversion, becomes S-1's default successor. As such, S-1 LLC is the agent for Years 1-4.

(iii) *Analysis for current and succeeding years.* S-1 is an agent designated by the Commissioner pursuant to paragraph (c)(6)(i)(A)(3) of this section. Because S-1 is no longer a member of the P group after May 2 of Year 5, S-1 is the agent for the P group for Year 5 only while it remains a member (see paragraphs (c)(6)(i) and (iii) of this section). According to paragraph (c)(6)(i) of this section, although S-1 LLC is S-1's default successor, it is not a member of the group for the current year and therefore cannot be its agent. Furthermore, S-1 cannot designate an agent for Year 5 under paragraph (c)(5)(i) of this section because that paragraph pertains only to designations for completed years for which there is no default successor. In addition, S-1 cannot designate an agent for Year 5 under paragraph (c)(5)(i) of this section because S-1 was previously designated by the Commissioner under paragraph (c)(6)(i)(A)(3) of this section.

(iv) *Member's notice to Commissioner for Commissioner to designate a member of the group for a current year.* A member of the group in Year 5 should request that the Commissioner designate, pursuant to paragraphs (c)(6)(i)(A)(2) and (c)(6)(iv) of this section, another member of the P group to be the agent of the group for Year 5. The Commissioner may then, pursuant to paragraph (c)(6)(i)(A)(2) of this section, designate either S-2, S-3, or P to be the agent for the P group and, once so designated, that member will be, effective on May 3 of Year 5, the agent for all of Year 5 and for succeeding years (subject to the rules of this section) pursuant to paragraph (c)(6)(iii) of this section. No actions taken by S-1 on behalf of the P group through May 2, Year 5, are nullified by the Commissioner's designation of another agent even though the agent so designated will be the agent for all of Year 5.

*Example 13. Fraudulent conveyance of assets.* (i) *Facts.* As of January 1 of Year 1, P is the common parent and agent for the P consolidated group consisting of P and its two subsidiaries, S and S-1. On March 15 of Year 2, P files a consolidated return that includes the income of S and S-1 for Year 1. On December 1 of Year 2, S-1 transfers assets having a fair market value of $100x to U in exchange for $10x. This transfer of assets for less than fair market value constitutes a fraudulent conveyance under applicable state law. On March 1 of Year 5, P executes a waiver extending to December 31 of Year 6 the period of limitations on assessment with respect to the P group's Year 1 consolidated return. On February 1 of Year 6, the Commissioner issues a notice of deficiency to P asserting a deficiency of $30x for the P group's Year 1 consolidated tax liability. P does not file a petition for redetermination in the Tax Court, and the Commissioner makes a timely assessment against the P group. P, S, and S-1 are all insolvent and are unable to pay the deficiency. On February 1 of Year 8, the Commissioner sends a notice of transferee liability to U, which does not file a petition in the Tax Court. On August 1 of Year 8, the Commissioner assesses the amount of the P group's deficiency against U. Under section 6901(c), the Commissioner may assess U's transferee liability within one year after the expiration of the period of limitations against the transferor, S-1. By operation of section 6213(a) and 6503(a), the issuance of the notice of deficiency to P and the expiration of the 90-day period for filing a petition in the Tax Court have the effect of further extending by 150 days the P group's limitations period on assessment from the previously extended date of December 31 of Year 6 to May 30 of Year 7.

(ii) *Analysis.* Pursuant to paragraph (a)(1) of this section, the waiver executed by P on March 1 of Year 5 to extend the period of limitations on assessment to December 31 of Year 6 and the further extension of the P group's limitations period to May 30 of Year 7 (by operation of sections 6213(a) and 6503(a)) have the derivative effect of extending the period of limitations on assessment of U's transferee liability to May 30 of Year 8. By operation of section 6901(f), the issuance of the notice of transferee liability to U and the expiration of the 90-day period for filing a petition in the Tax Court have the effect of further extending the limitations period on assessment of U's liability as a transferee by 150 days, from May 30 of Year 8 to October 27 of Year 8. Accordingly, the Commissioner may send a notice of transferee liability to U at any time on or before May 30 of Year 8 and assess the unpaid liability against U at any time on or before October 27 of Year 8. The result would be the same even if S-1 ceased to exist before March 1 of Year 5, the date P executed the waiver.

*Example 14. Consent to extend the statute of limitations for a partnership where a member of the consolidated group is a partner of such partnership subject to the provisions of the Code and the tax matters partner is not a member of the group.* (i) *Facts.* P is the common parent and agent for the P consolidated group consisting of P and its two subsidiaries, S and S-1. The P group has a November 30 fiscal year end and P files consolidated returns for the P group for the years ending November 30, Year 1 and November 30, Year 2. S-1 is a partner in the PRS partnership, which is subject to the provisions of sections 6221 through 6234. PRS has a calendar year end and A, an individual, is the tax matters partner of the PRS partnership. PRS files a partnership return for the year ending December 31, Year 1. On January 10, Year 5, A, as the tax matters partner for the PRS partnership, executes a consent to extend the period for assessment of partnership items of PRS for all partners, and the Commissioner co-executes the consent on the same day for the year ending December 31, Year 1.

(ii) *Analysis.* A's consent to extend the statute of limitations for the partnership items of PRS partnership for the year ending December 31, Year 1, extends the statute of limitations with respect to the partnership items for all members of the P group, including P, S, and S-1 for the consolidated return year ending November 30, Year 2. This is because S-1 is a partner in the PRS partnership for which A, the tax matters partner for the PRS partnership, consents, pursuant to section 6229(b)(1)(B), to extend the statute of limitations for the year ending December 31, Year 1. However, under paragraph (f)(2)(iii) of this section, such agreement with respect to the statute of limitations for the PRS partnership for the year ending December 31, Year 1 does not obviate the need to obtain a consent from P, the agent for the P consolidated group, to extend the statute of limitations for the P consolidated group for the P group's consolidated return years ending November 30, Year 1 and November 30, Year 2 regarding any items other than partnership items or affected items of the PRS partnership.

*Example 15. Contacting subsidiary member in order to facilitate the conduct of an examination, appeal, or settlement where a member of the consolidated group is a partner of a partnership subject to the provisions of the Code.* (i) *Facts.* P is the common parent and agent for the P consolidated group consisting of P and its two subsidiaries, S and S-1. The P group has a November 30 fiscal year end, and P files consolidated returns for the P group for the years ending November 30, Year 1 and November 30, Year 2. S-1 is a partner in the PRS partnership, which is subject to the provisions of sections 6221 through 6234. PRS has a calendar year end and A, an individual, is the tax matters partner of the PRS partnership. PRS files a partnership return for the year ending December 31, Year 1. The Commissioner, on January 10, Year 4, in the course of an examination of the PRS partnership for the year ending December 31, Year 1, seeks to obtain information in the course of that examination to resolve the audit.

(ii) *Analysis.* Because the direct contact with a subsidiary member of a consolidated group that is a partner in a partnership subject to the provisions under sections 6221 through 6234 may facilitate the conduct of an examination, appeal, or settlement, the Commissioner, under paragraph (f)(2)(iii) of this section, may communicate directly with either S-1, P, or A regarding the PRS partnership without breaking agency pursuant to paragraph (f)(2)(i) of this section. However, if the Commissioner were instead seeking to execute a settlement agreement with respect to S-1 as a partner with respect to its liability as a partner in PRS partnership, P would need to execute such settlement agreement for all members of the group including the partner subsidiary.

(h) *Cross-reference.*—For further rules applicable to groups that include insolvent financial institutions, see § 301.6402-7 of this chapter.

(i) [*Reserved*]

(j) *Effective/applicability date.*—(1) *In general.*—The rules of this section apply to consolidated return years beginning on or after April 1, 2015. For prior years beginning before June 28, 2002, see § 1.1502-77A. For prior years beginning on or after June 28, 2002, and before April 1, 2015, see § 1.1502-77B.

(2) *Application of this section to prior years.*—Notwithstanding paragraph (j)(1) of this section, an agent may apply the rules of paragraph (c)(7) of this section to resign as agent for a completed year that began before April 1, 2015. [Reg. § 1.1502-77.]

☐ [*T.D.* 9715, 3-31-2015 (*corrected* 4-24-2015).]

**[Reg. § 1.1502-77A]**

**§1.1502-77A. Common parent agent for subsidiaries applicable for consolidated return years beginning before June 28, 2002.—**
(a) *Scope of agency of common parent corporation.*—The common parent, for all purposes other than the making of the consent required by paragraph (a)(1) of §1.1502-75, the making of an election under section 936(e), the making of an election to be treated as a DISC under §1.992-2 and a change of the annual accounting period pursuant to paragraph (b)(3)(ii) of §1.991-1, shall be the sole agent for each subsidiary in the group, duly authorized to act in its own name in all matters relating to the tax liability for the consolidated return year. Except as provided in the preceding sentence, no subsidiary shall have authority to act for or to represent itself in any such matter. For example, any election available to a subsidiary corporation in the computation of its separate taxable income must be made by the common parent, as must any change in an election previously made by the subsidiary corporation; all correspondence will be carried on directly with the common parent; the common parent shall file for all extensions of time including extensions of time for payment of tax under section 6164; notices of deficiencies will be mailed only to the common parent, and the mailing to the common parent shall be considered as a mailing to each subsidiary in the group; notice and demand for payment of taxes will be given only to the common parent and such notice and demand will be considered as a notice and demand to each subsidiary; the common parent will file petitions and conduct proceedings before the Tax Court of the United States, and any such petition shall be considered as also having been filed by each such subsidiary. The common parent will file claims for refund or credit, and any refund will be made directly to and in the name of the common parent and will discharge any liability of the Government in respect thereof to any such subsidiary; and the common parent in its name will give waivers, give bonds, and execute closing agreements, offers in compromise, and all other documents, and any waiver or bond so given, or agreement, offer in compromise, or any other document so executed, shall be considered as having also been given or executed by each such subsidiary. Notwithstanding the provisions of this paragraph, any notice of deficiency, in respect of the tax for a consolidated return year, will name each corporation which was a member of the group during any part of such period (but a failure to include the name of any such member will not affect the validity of the notice of deficiency as to the other members); any notice and demand for payment will name each corporation which was a member of the group during any part of such period (but a failure to include the name of any such member will not affect the validity of the notice and demand as to the other members); and any levy, any notice of a lien, or any other proceeding to collect the amount of any assessment, after the assessment has been made, will name the corporation from which such collection is to be made. The provisions of this paragraph shall apply whether or not a consolidated return is made for any subsequent year, and whether or not one or more subsidiaries have become or have ceased to be members of the group at any time. Notwithstanding the provisions of this paragraph, the Commissioner may, upon notifying the common parent, deal directly with any member of the group in respect of its liability, in which event such member shall have full authority to act for itself.

(b) *Notification of deficiency to corporation which has ceased to be a member of the group.*—If a subsidiary has ceased to be a member of the group and if such subsidiary files written notice of such cessation with the Commissioner, then the Commissioner upon request of such subsidiary will furnish it with a copy of any notice of deficiency in respect of the tax for a consolidated return year for which it was a member and a copy of any notice and demand for payment of such deficiency. The filing of such written notification and request by a corporation shall not have the effect of limiting the scope of the agency of the common parent provided for in paragraph (a) of this section and a failure by the Commissioner to comply with such written request shall not have the effect of limiting the tax liability of such corporation provided for in § 1.1502-6.

(c) *Effect of waiver given by common parent.*—Unless the Commissioner agrees to the contrary, an agreement entered into by the common parent extending the time within which an assessment may be made or levy or proceeding in court begun in respect of the tax for a consolidated return year shall be applicable—

(1) To each corporation which was a member of the group during any part of such taxable year, and

(2) To each corporation the income of which was included in the consolidated return for such taxable year, notwithstanding that the tax liability of any such corporation is subsequently computed on the basis of a separate return under the provisions of §1.1502-75.

(d) *Effect of dissolution of common parent corporation.*—If the common parent corporation contemplates dissolution, or is about to be dissolved, or if for any other reason its existence is about to terminate, it shall forthwith notify the Commissioner of such fact and designate, subject to the approval of the Commissioner, another member to act as agent in its place to the same extent and subject to the same conditions and limitations as are applicable to the common parent. If the notice thus required is not given by the common parent, or the designation is not approved by the Commissioner, the remaining members may, subject to the approval of the Commissioner, designate another member to act as such agent, and notice of such designation shall be given to the Commissioner. Until a notice in writing designating a new agent has been approved by the Commissioner, any notice of deficiency or other communication mailed to the common parent shall be considered as having been properly mailed to the agent of the group; or, if the Commissioner has reason to believe that the existence of the common parent has terminated, he may, if he deems it advisable, deal directly with any member in respect of its liability.

(e) *General rules.*—(1) *Scope.*—This section applies if the corporation that is the common parent of the group ceases to be the common parent, whether or not the group remains in existence under §1.1502-75(d).

(2) *Notice of deficiency.*—A notice of deficiency mailed to any one or more corporations referred to in paragraph (e)(4) of this section is deemed for purposes of §1.1502-77A to be mailed to the agent of the group. If the group has designated an agent that has been approved by the Commissioner under §1.1502-77A(d), a notice of deficiency shall be mailed to that designated agent in addition to any other corporation referred to in paragraph (e)(4) of this section. However, failure by the Commissioner to mail a notice of deficiency to that designated agent shall not invalidate the notice of deficiency mailed to any other corporation referred to in paragraph (e)(4) of this section.

(3) *Waiver of statute of limitations.*—A waiver of the statute of limitations with respect to the group given by any one or more corporations referred to in paragraph (e)(4) of this section is deemed to be given by the agent of the group.

(4) *Alternative agents.*—The corporations referred to in paragraph (e)(2) and (3) of this section are—

(i) The common parent of the group for all or any part of the year to which the notice or waiver applies,

(ii) A successor to the former common parent in a transaction to which section 381(a) applies,

(iii) The agent designated by the group under §1.1502-77A(d), or

(iv) If the group remains in existence under §1.1502-75(d)(2) or (3), the common parent of the group at the time the notice is mailed or the waiver given.

(f) *Cross-reference.*—For further rules applicable to groups that include insolvent financial institutions, see §301.6402-7 of this chapter.

(g) *Effective/applicability dates.*—This section applies to taxable years beginning before June 28, 2002, except paragraph (e) of this section applies to statutory notices and waivers of the statute of limitations for taxable years for which the due date (without extensions) of the consolidated return is after September 7, 1988, and which begin before June 28, 2002. [Reg. §1.1502-77A.]

☐ [*T.D.* 6894, 9-7-66. *Amended by T.D.* 7323, 9-24-74; *T.D.* 7673, 2-7-80; *T.D.* 8226, 9-7-88; *T.D.* 8387, 12-30-91, *T.D.* 8446, 11-5-92. *Redesignated and amended by T.D.* 9002, 6-27-2002. *Amended by T.D.* 9715, 3-31-15.]

### [Reg. §1.1502-77B]

**§1.1502-77B. Agent for the group applicable for consolidated return years beginning on or after June 28, 2002, and before April 1, 2015.**—(a) *Scope of agency.*—(1) *In general.*—(i) *Common parent.*—Except as provided in paragraphs (a)(3) and (6) of this section, the common parent (or a substitute agent described in paragraph (a)(1)(ii) of this section) for a consolidated return year is the sole agent (agent for the group) that is authorized to act in its own name with respect to all matters relating to the tax liability for that consolidated return year, for—

(A) Each member in the group; and

(B) Any successor (see paragraph (a)(1)(iii) of this section) of a member.

(ii) *Substitute agents.*—For purposes of this section, any corporation designated as a substitute agent pursuant to paragraph (d) of this section to replace the common parent or a previously designated substitute agent acts as agent for the group to the same extent and subject to the same limitations as are applicable to the common

parent, and any reference in this section to the common parent includes any such substitute agent.

(iii) *Successor.*—For purposes of this section only, the term *successor* means an individual or entity (including a disregarded entity) that is primarily liable, pursuant to applicable law (including, for example, by operation of a state or Federal merger statute), for the tax liability of a member of the group. Such determination is made without regard to §1.1502-1(f)(4) or 1.1502-6(a). (For inclusion of a successor in references to a subsidiary or member, see paragraph (c)(2) of this section.)

(iv) *Disregarded entity.*—If a subsidiary of a group becomes, or its successor is or becomes, a disregarded entity for Federal tax purposes, the common parent continues to serve as the agent with respect to that subsidiary's tax liability under §1.1502-6 for consolidated return years during which it was included in the group, even though the entity generally is not treated as a person separate from its owner for Federal tax purposes.

(v) *Transferee liability.*—For purposes of assessing, paying and collecting transferee liability, any exercise of or reliance on the common parent's agency authority pursuant to this section is binding on a transferee (or subsequent transferees) of a member, regardless of whether the member's existence terminates prior to such exercise or reliance.

(vi) *Purported common parent.*—If any corporation files a consolidated return purporting to be the common parent of a consolidated group but is subsequently determined not to have been the common parent of the claimed group, that corporation is treated, to the extent necessary to avoid prejudice to the Commissioner, as if it were the common parent.

(2) *Examples of matters subject to agency.*—With respect to any consolidated return year for which it is the common parent—

(i) The common parent makes any election (or similar choice of a permissible option) that is available to a subsidiary in the computation of its separate taxable income, and any change in an election (or similar choice of a permissible option) previously made by or for a subsidiary, including, for example, a request to change a subsidiary's method or period of accounting;

(ii) All correspondence concerning the income tax liability for the consolidated return year is carried on directly with the common parent;

(iii) The common parent files for all extensions of time, including extensions of time for payment of tax under section 6164, and any extension so filed is considered as having been filed by each member;

(iv) The common parent gives waivers, gives bonds, and executes closing agreements, offers in compromise, and all other documents, and any waiver or bond so given, or agreement, offer in compromise, or any other document so executed, is considered as having also been given or executed by each member;

(v) The common parent files claims for refund, and any refund is made directly to and in the name of the common parent and discharges any liability of the Government to any member with respect to such refund;

(vi) The common parent takes any action on behalf of a member of the group with respect to a foreign corporation, for example, elections by, and changes to the method of accounting of, a controlled foreign corporation in accordance with §1.964-1(c)(3);

(vii) Notices of claim disallowance are mailed only to the common parent, and the mailing to the common parent is considered as a mailing to each member;

(viii) Notices of deficiencies are mailed only to the common parent (except as provided in paragraph (b) of this section), and the mailing to the common parent is considered as a mailing to each member;

(ix) Notices of final partnership administrative adjustment under section 6223 with respect to any partnership in which a member of the group is a partner may be mailed to the common parent, and, if so, the mailing to the common parent is considered as a mailing to each member that is a partner entitled to receive such notice (for other rules regarding partnership proceedings, see paragraphs (a)(3)(v) and (a)(6)(iii) of this section);

(x) The common parent files petitions and conducts proceedings before the United States Tax Court, and any such petition is considered as also having been filed by each member;

(xi) Any assessment of tax may be made in the name of the common parent, and an assessment naming the common parent is considered as an assessment with respect to each member; and

(xii) Notice and demand for payment of taxes is given only to the common parent, and such notice and demand is considered as a notice and demand to each member.

(3) *Matters reserved to subsidiaries.*—Except as provided in this paragraph (a)(3) and paragraph (a)(6) of this section, no subsidiary has authority to act for or to represent itself in any matter related to the tax liability for the consolidated return year. The following matters, however, are reserved exclusively to each subsidiary—

(i) The making of the consent required by § 1.1502-75(a)(1);

(ii) Any action with respect to the subsidiary's liability for a federal tax other than the income tax imposed by chapter 1 of the Internal Revenue Code (including, for example, employment taxes under chapters 21 through 25 of the Internal Revenue Code, and miscellaneous excise taxes under chapters 31 through 47 of the Internal Revenue Code);

(iii) The making of an election under section 936(e);

(iv) The making of an election to be treated as a DISC under § 1.992-2; and

(v) Any actions by a subsidiary acting as tax matters partner under sections 6221 through 6234 and the accompanying regulations (but see paragraph (a)(2)(ix) of this section regarding the mailing of a final partnership administrative adjustment to the common parent).

(4) *Term of agency.*—(i) *In general.*—Except as provided in paragraph (a)(4)(iii) of this section, the common parent for the consolidated return year remains the agent for the group with respect to that year until the common parent's existence terminates, regardless of whether one or more subsidiaries in that year cease to be members of the group, whether the group files a consolidated return for any subsequent year, whether the common parent ceases to be the common parent or a member of the group in any subsequent year, or whether the group continues pursuant to § 1.1502-75(d) with a new common parent in any subsequent year.

(ii) *Replacement of substitute agent designated by Commissioner.*—If the Commissioner replaces a previously designated substitute agent pursuant to paragraph (d)(3)(ii) of this section, the replaced substitute agent ceases to be the agent after the Commissioner designates another substitute agent.

(iii) *New common parent after a group structure change.*—If the group continues in existence with a new common parent pursuant to § 1.1502-75(d) during a consolidated return year, the common parent at the beginning of the year is the agent for the group through the date of the § 1.1502-75(d) transaction, and the new common parent becomes the agent for the group beginning the day after the transaction, at which time it becomes the agent for the group with respect to the entire consolidated return year (including the period through the date of the transaction) and the former common parent is no longer the agent for that year.

(5) *Identifying members in notice of a lien.*—Notwithstanding any other provisions of this paragraph (a), any notice of a lien, any levy or any other proceeding to collect the amount of any assessment, after the assessment has been made, must name the entity from which such collection is to be made.

(6) *Direct dealing with a member.*—(i) *Several liability.*—The Commissioner may, upon issuing to the common parent written notice that expressly invokes the authority of this provision, deal directly with any member of the group with respect to its liability under § 1.1502-6 for the consolidated tax of the group, in which event such member has sole authority to act for itself with respect to that liability. However, if the Commissioner believes or has reason to believe that the existence of the common parent has terminated, he may, if he deems it advisable, deal directly with any member with respect to that member's liability under § 1.1502-6 without giving the notice required by this provision.

(ii) *Information requests.*—The Commissioner may, upon informing the common parent, request information relevant to the consolidated tax liability from any member of the group. However, if the Commissioner believes or has reason to believe that the existence of the common parent has terminated, he may request such information from any member of the group without informing the common parent.

(iii) *Members as partners in partnerships.*—The Commissioner generally will deal directly with any member in its capacity as a partner of a partnership that is subject to the provisions of sections 6221 through 6234 and the accompanying regulations (but see paragraph (a)(2)(ix) of this section regarding the mailing of a final partnership administrative adjustment to the common parent). However, if requested to do so in accordance with the provisions of § 301.6223(c)-1(b) of this chapter, the Commissioner may deal with the common parent as agent for such member on any matter related to the partnership, except in regards to a settlement under section 6224(c) and except to the extent the member acts as tax matters partner of the partnership.

(b) *Copy of notice of deficiency to entity that has ceased to be a member of the group.*—An entity that ceases to be a member of the group during or after a consolidated return year may file a written notice of that fact with the Commissioner and request a copy of any notice of deficiency with respect to the tax for a consolidated return year during which the entity was a member, or a copy of any notice and demand for payment of such deficiency, or both. Such filing does not limit the scope of the agency of the common parent provided for in paragraph (a) of this section. Any failure by the Commissioner to comply with such request does not limit an entity's tax liability under § 1.1502-6. For purposes of this paragraph (b), references to an entity include a successor of such entity.

(c) *References to member or subsidiary.*—For purposes of this section, all references to a member or subsidiary for a consolidated return year include—

(1) Each corporation that was a member of the group during any part of such year (except that any reference to a subsidiary does not include the common parent);

(2) Except as indicated otherwise, a successor (as defined in paragraph (a)(1)(iii) of this section) of any corporation described in paragraph (c)(1) of this section; and

(3) Each corporation whose income was included in the consolidated return for such year, notwithstanding that the tax liability of such corporation should have been computed on the basis of a separate return, or as a member of another consolidated group, under the provisions of § 1.1502-75.

(d) *Termination of common parent.*—(1) *Designation of substitute agent by common parent.*—(i) If the common parent's existence terminates, it may designate a substitute agent for the group and notify the Commissioner, as provided in this paragraph (d)(1).

(A) Subject to the Commissioner's approval under paragraph (d)(1)(ii) of this section, before the common parent's existence terminates, the common parent may designate, for each consolidated return year for which it is the common parent and for which the period of limitations either for assessment, for collection after assessment, or for claiming a credit or refund has not expired, one of the following to act as substitute agent in its place—

*(1)* Any corporation that was a member of the group during any part of the consolidated return year and, except as provided in paragraph (e)(3)(ii) of this section, has not subsequently been disregarded as an entity separate from its owner or reclassified as a partnership for Federal tax purposes; or

*(2)* Any successor (as defined in paragraph (a)(1)(iii) of this section) of such a corporation or of the common parent that is a domestic corporation (and, except as provided in paragraph (e)(3)(ii) of this section, is not disregarded as an entity separate from its owner or classified as a partnership for Federal tax purposes), including a corporation that will become a successor at the time that the common parent's existence terminates.

(B) The common parent must notify the Commissioner in writing (under procedures prescribed by the Commissioner) of the designation and provide the following—

*(1)* An agreement executed by the designated corporation agreeing to serve as the group's substitute agent; and

*(2)* If the designated corporation was not itself a member of the group during the consolidated return year (because the designated corporation is a successor of a member of the group for the consolidated return year), a statement by the designated corporation acknowledging that it is or will be primarily liable for the consolidated tax as a successor of a member.

(ii) A designation under paragraph (d)(1)(i)(A) of this section does not apply unless and until it is approved by the Commissioner. The Commissioner's approval of such a designation is not effective before the existence of the common parent terminates.

(2) *Default substitute agent.*—If the common parent fails to designate a substitute agent for the group before its existence terminates and if the common parent has a single successor that is a domestic corporation, such successor becomes the substitute agent for the group upon termination of the common parent's existence. However, see paragraph (d)(4) of this section regarding the consequences of the successor's failure to notify the Commissioner of its status as default substitute agent in accordance with procedures established by the Commissioner.

(3) *Designation by the Commissioner.*—(i) In the event the common parent's existence terminates and no designation is made and approved under paragraph (d)(1) of this section and the Commissioner believes or has reason to believe that there is no successor of the common parent that satisfies the requirements of paragraph (d)(2) of this section (or the Commissioner believes or has reason to believe there is such a successor but has no last known address on file for such successor), the Commissioner may, at any time, with or without a request from any member of the group, designate a corpo-

ration described in paragraph (d)(1)(i)(A) of this section to act as the substitute agent. The Commissioner will notify the designated substitute agent in writing of its designation, and the designation is effective upon receipt by the designated substitute agent of such notice. The designated substitute agent must give notice of the designation to each corporation that was a member of the group during any part of the consolidated return year, but a failure by the designated substitute agent to notify any such member of the group does not invalidate the designation.

(ii) At the request of any member, the Commissioner may, but is not required to, replace a substitute agent previously designated under paragraph (d)(3)(i) of this section with another corporation described in paragraph (d)(1)(i)(A) of this section.

(4) *Absence of designation or notification of default substitute agent.*—Until a designation of a substitute agent for the group under paragraph (d)(1) of this section has become effective, the Commissioner has received notification in accordance with procedures established by the Commissioner that a successor qualifying under paragraph (d)(2) of this section has become the substitute agent by default, or the Commissioner has designated a substitute agent under paragraph (d)(3) of this section—

(i) Any notice of deficiency or other communication mailed to the common parent, even if no longer in existence, is considered as having been properly mailed to the agent for the group; and

(ii) The Commissioner is not required to act on any communication (including, for example, a claim for refund) submitted on behalf of the group by any person other than the common parent (including a successor of the common parent qualifying as a default substitute agent under paragraph (d)(2) of this section).

(e) *Termination of a corporation's existence.*—(1) *In general.*—For purposes of paragraphs (a)(1)(v), (a)(4)(i), (d), and (j) of this section, the existence of a corporation is deemed to terminate if—

(i) Its existence terminates under applicable law; or

(ii) Except as provided in paragraph (e)(3) of this section, it becomes, for Federal tax purposes, either—

(A) An entity that is disregarded as an entity separate from its owner; or

(B) An entity that is reclassified as a partnership.

(2) *Purported agency.*—If the existence of the agent for the group terminates under circumstances described in paragraph (e)(1)(ii) of this section, until the Commissioner has approved the designation of a substitute agent for the group pursuant to paragraph (d)(1) of this section or the Commissioner designates a substitute agent and notifies the designated substitute agent pursuant to paragraph (d)(3) of this section, any post-termination action by that purported agent on behalf of the group has the same effect, to the extent necessary to avoid prejudice to the Commissioner, as if the agent's corporate existence had not terminated.

(3) *Exceptions where no eligible corporation exists.*—(i) For purposes of the common parent's term as agent under paragraph (a)(4)(i) of this section and the term as agent of the substitute agent designated under paragraph (d) of this section, if a corporation either becomes disregarded as an entity separate from its owner or is reclassified as a partnership for Federal tax purposes, its existence is not deemed to terminate if the effect of such termination would be that no corporation remains eligible to serve as the substitute agent for the group's consolidated return year.

(ii) Similarly, for purposes of paragraph (d) of this section, an entity that is either disregarded as an entity separate from its owner or reclassified as a partnership for Federal tax purposes is not precluded from designation as a substitute agent merely because of such classification if the effect of the inability to make such designation would be that no corporation remains eligible to serve as the substitute agent for the group's consolidated return year.

(iii) Any entity described in paragraphs (e)(3)(i) or (ii) of this section that remains or becomes the agent for the group is treated as a corporation for purposes of this section.

(4) *Exception for section 338 transactions.*—Notwithstanding section 338(a)(2), a target corporation for which an election is made under section 338 is not deemed to terminate for purposes of this section.

(f) *Examples.*—The following examples illustrate the principles of this section. Unless otherwise indicated, each example addresses the question of which corporation is the proper party to execute a consent to waive the statute of limitations for Years 1 and 2 or the more general question of which corporation may be designated as a substitute agent for the group for Years 1 and 2. In each example, as of January 1 of Year 1, the P group consists of P and its two subsidiaries, S and S-1. P, as the common parent of the P group, files consolidated returns for the P group in Years 1 and 2. On January 1 of

Year 1, domestic corporations S-2, U, V, W, W-1, X, Y, Z and Z-1 are not related to P or the members of the P group. All corporations are calendar year taxpayers. For none of the tax years at issue does the Commissioner exercise the authority under paragraph (a)(6) of this section to deal with any member separately. Any surviving corporation in a merger is a successor as described in paragraph (a)(1)(iii) of this section. Any notification to the Commissioner of the designation of the P group's substitute agent also contains a statement signed on behalf of the designated agent that it agrees to act as the group's substitute agent and, in the case of a successor, that it is primarily liable as a successor of a member. The examples are as follows:

*Example 1. Disposition of all group members.* On December 31 of Year 1, P sells all the stock of S-1 to X. On December 31 of Year 2, P distributes all the stock of S to P's shareholders. P files a separate return for Year 3. Although P is no longer a common parent after Year 2, P remains the agent for the P group for Years 1 and 2. For as long as P remains in existence, only P may execute a waiver of the period of limitations on assessment on behalf of the group for Years 1 and 2.

*Example 2. Acquisition of common parent by another group.* The facts are the same as in *Example 1*, except on January 1 of Year 3, all of the outstanding stock of P is acquired by Y. P thereafter joins in the Y group consolidated return as a member of Y group. Although P is a member of Y group in Year 3, P remains the agent for the P group for Years 1 and 2. For as long as P remains in existence, only P may execute a waiver of the period of limitations on assessment on behalf of the P group for Years 1 and 2.

*Example 3. Merger of common parent—designation of remaining member as substitute agent.* On December 31 of Year 1, P sells all the stock of S-1 to X. On July 1 of Year 2, P acquires all the stock of S-2. On November 30 of Year 2, P distributes all the stock of S to P's shareholders. On January 1 of Year 3, P merges into Y corporation. Just before the merger, P notifies the Commissioner in writing of the planned merger and of its designation of S as the substitute agent for the P group for Years 1 and 2. S is the only member that P can designate as the substitute agent for both Years 1 and 2 because it is the only subsidiary that was a member of the P group during part of both years. Although S-2 is the only remaining subsidiary of the P group when P merges into Y, S-2 was a member of the P group only in Year 2. For that reason, S-2 cannot be the substitute agent for the P group for Year 1. Alternatively, P could designate a different substitute agent for each year, selecting S or S-1 as the substitute agent for Year 1, and S or S-2 as the substitute agent for Year 2. P could also designate its successor Y as the substitute agent for both Years 1 and 2.

*Example 4. Forward triangular merger of common parent.* On January 1 of Year 3, P merges with and into Z-1, a subsidiary of Z, in a forward triangular merger described in section 368(a)(1)(A) and (a)(2)(D). The transaction constitutes a reverse acquisition under §1.1502-75(d)(3)(i) because P's shareholders receive more than 50% of Z's stock in exchange for all of P's stock. Just before the merger, P notifies the Commissioner in writing of the planned merger and its designation of Z-1, the corporation that will survive the planned merger, as the substitute agent of the P group for Years 1 and 2. Because Z-1 will be P's successor (within the meaning of paragraph (a)(1) of this section) after the planned merger, P may designate Z-1 as the substitute agent for the P group for Years 1 and 2, pursuant to paragraph (d)(1) of this section. Alternatively, P could have designated S or S-1 as the substitute agent for the P group for Years 1 and 2. Although Z is the new common parent of the P group, which continues pursuant to §1.1502-75(d)(3)(i), P may not designate Z as the substitute agent for Years 1 and 2 because Z was not a member of the group during any part of Years 1 or 2 and is not a successor of P or any other member of P group.

*Example 5. Reverse triangular merger of common parent.* On March 1 of Year 3, W-1, a subsidiary of W, merges into P, in a reverse triangular merger described in section 368(a)(1)(A) and (a)(2)(E). P survives the merger with W-1. The transaction constitutes a reverse acquisition under §1.1502-75(d)(3)(i) because P's shareholders receive more than 50% of W's stock in exchange for all of P's stock. Under paragraph (a) of this section, P remains the agent for the P group for Years 1 and 2, even though the P group continues with W as its new common parent pursuant to §1.1502-75(d)(3)(i). Because the transaction constitutes a reverse acquisition, the P group is treated as remaining in existence with W as its common parent. Before March 2 of Year 3, P is the agent for the P group for Year 3. Beginning on March 2 of Year 3, W becomes the agent for the P group with respect to all of Year 3 (including the period through March 1) and subsequent consolidated return years. For as long as P remains in existence, P remains the agent of the P group under paragraph (a) of this section for Years 1 and 2, and therefore only P may execute a waiver of the period of limitations on assessment on behalf of the P group for Years 1 and 2.

*Example 6. Reverse triangular merger of common parent—subsequent spinoff of common parent.* The facts are the same as in *Example 5*, except that on April 1 of Year 4, in a transaction unrelated to the Year 3

reverse acquisition, P distributes the stock of its subsidiaries S and S-1 to W, and W then distributes the stock of P to the W shareholders. Beginning on March 2 of Year 3, W becomes the agent for the P group with respect to Year 3 (including the period through March 1) and subsequent consolidated return years. Although P is no longer a member of the P group after the Year 4 spinoff, P remains the agent for the P group under paragraph (a) of this section for Years 1 and 2. Thus, for as long as P remains in existence, only P may execute a waiver of the period of limitations on assessment on behalf of the P group for Years 1 and 2.

*Example 7. Qualified stock purchase and section 338 election.* On March 31 of Year 2, V purchases the stock of P in a qualified stock purchase (within the meaning of section 338(d)(3)), and V makes a timely election pursuant to section 338(g) with respect to P. Although section 338(a)(2) provides that P is treated as a new corporation as of the beginning of the day after the acquisition date for purposes of subtitle A, paragraph (e)(4) of this section provides that P's existence is not deemed to terminate for purposes of this section notwithstanding the general rule of section 338(a)(2). Therefore, the election under section 338(g) does not result in a termination of P under paragraph (e) of this section, and new P remains the agent of the P group for Year 1 and the period ending March 31 of Year 2 (short Year 2). For as long as new P remains in existence, only new P may execute a waiver of the period of limitations on assessment on behalf of the P group for Year 1 and short Year 2.

*Example 8. Fraudulent conveyance of assets.* On March 15 of Year 2, P files a consolidated return that includes the income of S and S-1 for Year 1. On December 1 of Year 2, S-1 transfers assets having a fair market value of $100x to U in exchange for $10x. This transfer of assets for less than fair market value constitutes a fraudulent conveyance under applicable state law. On March 1 of Year 5, P executes a waiver extending to December 31 of Year 6 the period of limitations on assessment with respect to the group's Year 1 consolidated return. On February 1 of Year 6, the Commissioner issues a notice of deficiency to P asserting a deficiency of $30x for the P group's Year 1 consolidated tax liability. P does not file a petition for redetermination in the Tax Court, and the Commissioner makes a timely assessment against the P group. P, S and S-1 are all insolvent and are unable to pay the deficiency. On February 1 of Year 8, the Commissioner sends a notice of transferee liability to U, which does not file a petition in the Tax Court. On August 1 of Year 8, the Commissioner assesses the amount of the P group's deficiency against U. Under section 6901(c), the Commissioner may assess U's transferee liability within one year after the expiration of the period of limitations against the transferor S-1. By operation of sections 6213(a) and 6503(a), the issuance of the notice of deficiency to P and the expiration of the 90-day period for filing a petition in the Tax Court have the effect of further extending by 150 days the P group's limitations period on assessment from the previously extended date of December 31 of Year 6 to May 30 of Year 7. Pursuant to paragraph (a)(1)(v) of this section, the waiver executed by P on March 1 of Year 5 to extend the period of limitations on assessment to December 31 of Year 6 and the further extension of the P group's limitations period to May 30 of Year 7 (by operation of sections 6213(a) and 6503(a)) have the derivative effect of extending the period of limitations on assessment of U's transferee liability to May 30 of Year 8. By operation of section 6901(f), the issuance of the notice of transferee liability to U and the expiration of the 90-day period for filing a petition in the Tax Court have the effect of further extending the limitations period on assessment of U's liability as a transferee by 150 days, from May 30 of Year 8 to October 27 of Year 8. Accordingly, the Commissioner may send a notice of transferee liability to U at any time on or before May 30 of Year 8 and assess the unpaid liability against U at any time on or before October 27 of Year 8. The result would be the same even if S-1 ceased to exist before March 1 of Year 5, the date P executed the waiver.

(g) *Cross-reference.*—For further rules applicable to groups that include insolvent financial institutions, see §301.6402-7 of this chapter.

(h) *Effective/applicability date.*—(1) *Application.*—(i) *In general.*—This section applies to consolidated return years beginning on or after June 28, 2002, and before April 1, 2015. For instructions regarding communications relating to the determination of a substitute agent and other matters under this section, see Rev. Proc. 2002-43, 2002-2 CB 99 (see §601.601(d)(2)(ii)(*b*) of this chapter). For rules governing the resignation of certain agents for the group subject to this section, see §1.1502-77(c)(7) and (j)(2).

(ii) *Election to apply for prior taxable years.*—Notwithstanding paragraphs (h)(1)(i) and (h)(2) of this section, the common parent may elect to apply paragraph (d)(1) of this section in lieu of §1.1502-77A(d) in designating a substitute agent for taxable years beginning before June 28, 2002. The common parent makes such an election by expressly referring to the election under this paragraph

(h)(1)(ii) in notifying the Commissioner of the designation of the substitute agent. Once made, such election applies to any subsequent designation of a substitute agent for the consolidated return year(s) subject to the election.

(2) *Prior law.*—For taxable years beginning before June 28, 2002, see §1.1502-77A.

(3) *Designation of a domestic substitute agent.*—(i) *In general.*—The provisions of paragraphs (e)(1) and (j) of this section apply to taxable years for which the consolidated Federal income tax return is due (without extensions) after July 23, 2007.

(ii) *Prior law.*—For taxable years for which the consolidated Federal income tax return is due (without extensions) on or before July 23, 2007, see Sec. 1.1502-77(e)(1) as contained in the 26 CFR part 1 edition revised as of April 1, 2007. For taxable years for which the consolidated Federal income tax return is due (without extensions) after March 14, 2006, and on or before July 23, 2007, see Sec. 1.1502-77T as contained in the 26 CFR part 1 edition revised as of April 1, 2007.

(i) [Reserved].

(j) *Designation by Commissioner if common parent is treated as a domestic corporation under section 7874 or section 953(d).*—(1) *In general.*—If the common parent is an entity created or organized under the law of a foreign country and is treated as a domestic corporation by reason of section 7874 (or regulations under that section) or a section 953(d) election (a foreign common parent), the Commissioner may at any time, with or without a request from any member of the group, designate another member of the group to act as the agent for the group (a domestic substitute agent) for any taxable year for which the consolidated Federal income tax return is due (without extensions) after July 23, 2007, and the foreign common parent would otherwise be the agent for the group. For each such year, the domestic substitute agent will be the sole agent for the group even though the foreign common parent remains in existence. The foreign common parent ceases to be the agent for the group when the Commissioner's designation of a domestic substitute agent becomes effective. The Commissioner may designate a domestic substitute agent for the term of a single taxable year, multiple years, or on a continuing basis.

(2) *Domestic substitute agent.*—The domestic substitute agent, by designation or by succession, shall be a domestic corporation described in paragraph (d)(1)(i)(A) of this section (determined without regard to section 7874, a section 953(d) election or section 1504(d)).

(3) *Designation by the Commissioner.*—The Commissioner will notify the domestic substitute agent in writing by mail or faxed transmission of the designation. The domestic substitute agent's designation is effective on the earliest of the 14th day following the date of a mailing, the 4th day following a faxed transmission, or the date the Commissioner receives written confirmation of the designation by a duly authorized officer of the domestic substitute agent (within the meaning of section 6062). The domestic substitute agent must give notice of its designation to the foreign common parent and each corporation that was a member of the group during any part of any consolidated return year for which the domestic substitute agent will be the agent. A failure of the domestic substitute agent to notify the foreign common parent or any member of the group does not invalidate the designation. The Commissioner will send a copy of the notification to the foreign common parent, and if applicable, to any domestic substitute agent the designation replaces; a failure to send a copy of the notification does not invalidate the designation.

(4) *Term of agency.*—(i) *Taxable years for which domestic substitute agent is the agent.*—If the Commissioner designates a domestic substitute agent for one or more taxable years, unless the designation is expressly limited to such term, such domestic substitute agent will continue as the group's sole agent for subsequent taxable years until the domestic substitute agent ceases to be a member of the continuing group, is replaced by a new domestic common parent (as provided in paragraph (j)(4)(iv)(A) of this section), is replaced by the Commissioner, or is replaced by a default substitute agent (as provided in paragraph (j)(5)(ii) of this section). If during the course of a consolidated return year the domestic substitute agent ceases to be a member of the continuing group or is replaced, it shall no longer act as agent for such taxable year or subsequent taxable years in any matter.

(ii) *Continuing agency for prior taxable years.*—Unless replaced by a default substitute agent (as provided in paragraph (j)(5)(ii) of this section) or by the Commissioner, the domestic substitute agent at the end of a taxable year of the group will remain the agent for such year until its existence terminates, even if the group subsequently ceases to exist or the domestic substitute agent subsequently ceases to be a member of the group.

(iii) *Replacement of a Sec. 1.1502-77(d)(1) agent.*—If, pursuant to paragraph (d)(1) of this section, the common parent of the group designates a foreign common parent as the agent for the group for any taxable year, the Commissioner may, at any time, designate a domestic substitute agent to replace the foreign common parent, even if the Commissioner approved the terminating common parent's designation.

(iv) *Group continues with a new common parent.*—(A) *Year the new common parent becomes the common parent.*—If the group has a domestic substitute agent and the group continues in existence with a new common parent during a consolidated return year, and such new common parent is a domestic corporation (determined without regard to section 7874 or a section 953(d) election), the domestic substitute agent at the beginning of the year is the agent for the group through the date of the transaction in which the new common parent becomes the common parent, and the new common parent becomes the agent for the group beginning the day after the transaction, at which time it becomes the agent for the group with respect to the entire consolidated return year (including the period through the date of the transaction) and the former domestic substitute agent will no longer be the agent for the group for that year.

(B) *Years preceding the year the new common parent becomes the common parent.*—If after the Commissioner's designation of a domestic substitute agent the group remains in existence with a new common parent, and such new common parent is a domestic corporation (determined without regard to section 7874 or a section 953(d) election), the Commissioner may designate the new common parent as the sole agent for the group for any of the group's prior taxable years (for which the consolidated Federal income tax return is due (without extensions) after July 23, 2007) in which the new common parent was a member of the group. For this purpose, the new common parent is treated as having been a member of the group for any taxable year it is primarily liable for the group's income tax liability.

(v) *Replacement of domestic substitute agent by the Commissioner.*—The Commissioner may at any time, with or without a request from any member of the group, designate a replacement for a domestic substitute agent (or a successor to such agent).

(5) *Deemed Sec. 1.1502-77(d) designation.*—(i) *In general.*—If the Commissioner designates a domestic substitute agent under this paragraph (j), it will be treated as a designation of a substitute agent under paragraph (d) of this section.

(ii) *Default substitute agent.*—If the domestic substitute agent's existence terminates and it has a single successor that is a domestic corporation (without regard to section 269B) that is eligible to be a domestic substitute agent, such successor becomes the domestic substitute agent and is treated as a default substitute agent under paragraph (d)(2) of this section. See paragraph (d)(4) of this section regarding the consequences of the successor's failure to notify the Commissioner of its status as a default substitute agent. The default substitute agent shall use procedures in section 9 of Rev. Proc. 2002-43 (2002-2 CB 99) or a corresponding provision of a successor revenue procedure for notification. (See Sec. 601.601(d)(2)(ii)(b) of this chapter.)

(6) *Request that IRS designate a domestic substitute agent.*—(i) *Original designation.*—If the common parent of the group is a foreign common parent, and the IRS has not designated a domestic substitute agent, one or more members of the group may request the IRS to make a designation for taxable years for which the consolidated Federal income tax return is due (without extensions) after July 23, 2007. Such request is deemed to be a request under paragraph (d)(3)(i) of this section. Members of the group shall use the procedures in section 10 of Rev. Proc. 2002-43 (2002-2 CB 99) or a corresponding provision of a successor revenue procedure for this purpose. (See Sec. 601.601(d)(2)(ii)(b) of this chapter.)

(ii) *Request that IRS replace a previously designated substitute agent.*—If the IRS designates a domestic substitute agent pursuant to this paragraph (j), one or more members of the group may request that the IRS replace the designated domestic substitute agent with another member (or successor to another member). Such a request is deemed to be a request pursuant to paragraph (d)(3)(ii) of this section. Members of the group shall use the procedures in section 11 of Rev. Proc. 2002-43 (2002-2 CB 99) or a corresponding provision of a successor revenue procedure for this purpose. (See Sec. 601.601(d)(2)(ii)(b) of this chapter.) [Reg. §1.1502-77B.]

☐ [T.D. 9002, 6-27-2002. *Amended by T.D. 9255, 3-9-2006, T.D. 9343, 7-23-2007. Redesignated and amended by T.D. 9715, 3-31-2015.*]

**[Reg. §1.1502-78]**

**§1.1502-78. Tentative carryback adjustments.**—(a) *General rule.*—If a group has a consolidated net operating loss, a consolidated net capital loss, or a consolidated unused business credit for any taxable year, then any application under section 6411 for a tentative carryback adjustment of the taxes for a consolidated return year or years preceding such year shall be made by the common parent corporation for the carryback year (or the agent determined under §1.1502-77(c) or §1.1502-77B(d) for the carryback year) to the extent such loss or unused business credit is not apportioned to a corporation for a separate return year pursuant to §1.1502-21(b), 1.1502-22(b), or 1.1502-79(c). In the case of the portion of a consolidated net operating loss or consolidated net capital loss or consolidated unused business credit to which the preceding sentence does not apply and that is to be carried back to a corporation that was not a member of a consolidated group in the carryback year, the corporation to which such loss or credit is attributable shall make any application under section 6411. In the case of a net capital loss or net operating loss or unused business credit arising in a separate return year that may be carried back to a consolidated return year, after taking into account the application of §1.1502-21(b)(3)(ii)(B) with respect to any net operating loss arising in another consolidated group, the common parent for the carryback year (or the agent determined under §1.1502-77(c) or §1.1502-77B(d) for the carryback year) shall make any application under section 6411.

(b) *Special rules.*—(1) *Payment of refund.*—Any refund allowable under an application referred to in paragraph (a) of this section shall be made directly to and in the name of the corporation filing the application, except that in all cases where a loss is deducted from the consolidated taxable income or a credit is allowed in computing the consolidated tax liability for a consolidated return year, any refund shall be made directly to and in the name of the common parent corporation for the carryback year (or the agent determined under §1.1502-77(c) or §1.1502-77B(d) for the carryback year). The payment of any such refund shall discharge any liability of the Government with respect to such refund.

(2) *Several liability.*—If a group filed a consolidated return for a taxable year for which there was an adjustment by reason of an application under section 6411, and if a deficiency is assessed against such group under section 6213(b)(3), then each member of such group shall be severally liable for such deficiency including any interest or penalty assessed in connection with such deficiency.

(3) *Groups that include insolvent financial institutions.*—For further rules applicable to groups that include insolvent financial institutions, see §301.6402-7 of this chapter.

(c) *Examples.*—The provisions of paragraphs (a) and (b) of this section may be illustrated by the following examples:

*Example (1).* Corporations P, S, and S-1 filed a consolidated return for the calendar year 2003. P, S, and S-1 also filed a consolidated return for the calendar year 2006. The group incurred a consolidated net operating loss in 2006 attributable to S-1 which may be carried back to 2003 as a consolidated net operating loss carryback. If a tentative carryback adjustment is desired, P, the common parent for the carryback year, must file an application under section 6411 and any refund will be made to P.

*Example (2).* Assume the same facts as in example (1) except that P, S, and S-1 filed separate returns for the calendar year 2006, even though they were members of the same group for such year. S-1 incurred a net operating loss in 2006 which may be carried back to 2003. If a tentative carryback adjustment is desired, P must file an application under section 6411 and any refund from such application will be made to P.

*Example (3).* Corporations X, Y, and Z filed a consolidated return for the calendar year 2003. Z ceased to be a member of the group in 2004. Z filed a separate return for 2005 while X and Y filed a consolidated return for such year. The group incurred a consolidated net operating loss in 2005 attributable to Y, which may be carried back to 2003. Z also incurred a net operating loss for 2005 which may be carried back to 2003. If a tentative carryback adjustment is claimed with respect to the consolidated net operating loss, X, the common parent, must file an application under section 6411. If a tentative carryback adjustment is desired with respect to Z's loss, X must file an application. Any refunds attributable to either application will be made to X. If an assessment is made under section 6213(b)(3) to recover an excessive tentative allowance made with respect to calendar year 2003, X, Y, and Z are severally liable for such assessment.

*Example (4).* Corporations L and M filed a consolidated return for the calendar year 2003. Corporation N filed a separate return for such year. Later, N became a member of the group and filed a consolidated return with the group for the calendar year 2005. The group incurred a consolidated net operating loss in 2005 attributable to N which may be carried back to N's separate return for 2003. If a tentative carryback adjustment is desired, N must file an application under section 6411 and any refund will be made directly to N.

(d) *Adjustments of overpayments of estimated income tax.*—If a group paid its estimated income tax on a consolidated basis, then any application under section 6425 for an adjustment of overpayment of estimated income tax shall be made by the common parent corporation. If the members of a group paid estimated income taxes on a separate basis, then any application under section 6425 shall be made by the member of the group which claims an overpayment on a separate basis. Any refund allowable under an application under section 6425 shall be made directly to and in the name of the corporation filing the application.

(e) *Time for filing application.*—(1) *General rule.*—The provisions of section 6411(a) apply to the filing of an application for a tentative carryback adjustment by a consolidated group.

(2) *Special rule for new members.*—(i) *New member.*—A new member is a corporation that, in the preceding taxable year, did not qualify as a member, as defined in §1.1502-1(b), of the consolidated group that it now joins.

(ii) *End of taxable year.*—Solely for the purpose of complying with the twelve-month requirement for making an application for a tentative carryback adjustment under section 6411(a), the separate return year of a qualified new member shall be treated as ending on the same date as the end of the current taxable year of the consolidated group that the qualified new member joins.

(iii) *Qualified new member.*—A new member of a consolidated group qualifies for purposes of the provisions of this paragraph (e)(2) if, immediately prior to becoming a new member, either—

(A) It was the common parent of a consolidated group; or

(B) It was not required to join in the filing of a consolidated return.

(iv) *Examples.*—The provisions of this paragraph (e)(2) may be illustrated by the following examples:

*Example 1.* Individual A owns 100 percent of the stock of X, a corporation that is not a member of a consolidated group and files separate tax returns on a calendar year basis. On January 31 of year 1, X becomes a member of the Y consolidated group, which also files returns on a calendar year basis. X is a qualified new member as defined in paragraph (e)(2)(iii)(B) of this section because, immediately prior to becoming a new member of the Y consolidated group, X was not required to join in the filing of a consolidated return. As a result of its becoming a new member of Group Y, X's separate return for the short taxable year (January 1 of year 1 through January 31 of year 1) is due September 15 of year 2 (with extensions). See §1.1502-76(c). Group Y's consolidated return is also due September 15 of year 2 (with extensions). See '1.1502-76(c). Solely for the purpose of complying with the twelve-month requirement for making an application for a tentative carryback adjustment under section 6411(a), X's taxable year for the separate return year is treated as ending on December 31 of year 1. X's application for a tentative carryback adjustment is therefore due on or before December 31 of year 2.

*Example 2.* Assume the same facts as in *Example 1* except that immediately prior to becoming a new member of Group Y, X was a member of the Z consolidated group. Because X was required to join in the filing of the consolidated return for Group Z, X is not a qualified new member as defined in paragraph (e)(2)(iii) of this section. X's items for the one-month period will be included in the consolidated return for Group Z. Group Z's application for a tentative carryback adjustment, if any, continues to be due within 12 months of the end of its taxable year, which is not affected by X's change in status as a new member of Group Y.

(f) *Effective date.*—(1) *In general.*—This section applies to taxable years to which a loss or credit may be carried back and for which the due date (without extensions) of the original return is after June 28, 2002, except that the provisions of paragraph (e)(2) apply for applications by new members of consolidated groups for tentative carryback adjustments resulting from net operating losses, net capital losses, or unused business credits arising in separate return years of new members that begin on or after January 1, 2001.

(2) *Prior law.*—For taxable years to which a loss or credit may be carried back and for which the due date (without extensions) of the original return is on or before June 28, 2002, see §1.1502-78 in effect prior to June 28, 2002, as contained in 26 CFR part 1 revised April 1, 2002. [Reg. §1.1502-78.]

☐ [*T.D. 6894,* 9-7-66. *Amended by T.D. 7059,* 7-16-70; *T.D. 7246,* 12-29-72; *T.D. 8387,* 12-30-91; *T.D. 8446,* 11-5-92; *T.D. 8677,* 6-26-96;

*T.D. 8823,* 6-25-99; *T.D. 8950,* 6-21-2001, *T.D. 9002,* 6-27-2002 (*corrected* 12-18-2002) *and T.D. 9715,* 3-31-2015.]

**[Reg. §1.1502-79]**

**§1.1502-79. Separate return years.**—(a) *Carryover and carryback of consolidated net operating losses to separate return years.*—For losses arising in consolidated return years beginning before January 1, 1997, see §1.1502-79A(a). For later years, see §1.1502-21(b).

(b) *Carryover and carryback of consolidated net capital loss to separate return years.*—For losses arising in consolidated return years beginning before January 1, 1997, see §1.1502-79A(b). For later years, see §1.1502-22(b).

(c) *Carryover and carryback of consolidated unused investment credit to separate return years.*—(1) *In general.*—If a consolidated unused investment credit can be carried under the principles of section 46(b) and paragraph (b) of §1.1502-3 to a separate return year of a corporation (or could have been so carried if such corporation were in existence) which was a member of the group in the year in which such unused credit arose, then the portion of such consolidated unused credit attributable to such corporation (as determined under subparagraph (2) of this paragraph) shall be apportioned to such corporation (and any successor to such corporation in a transaction to which section 381(a) applies) under the principles of §1.1502-21(b) (or §§1.1502-79A(a)(1) and (2), as appropriate) and shall be an investment credit carryover or carryback to such separate return year.

(2) *Portion of consolidated unused investment credit attributable to a member.*—(i) *Investment credit carryback.*—In the case of a consolidated unused credit which is an investment credit carryback, the portion of such consolidated unused credit attributable to a member of the group is an amount equal to such consolidated unused credit multiplied by a fraction, the numerator of which is the credit earned of such member for the consolidated unused credit year, and the denominator of which is the consolidated credit earned for such unused credit year.

(ii) *Investment credit carryover.*—In the case of a consolidated unused credit which is an investment credit carryover, the portion of such consolidated unused credit attributable to a member of the group is an amount equal to such consolidated unused credit multiplied by a fraction, the numerator of which is the credit earned with respect to any section 38 property placed in service in the consolidated unused credit year and owned by such member (whether or not placed in service by such member) at the close of the last day as of which the taxable income of such member is included in a consolidated return filed by the group, and the denominator of which is the consolidated credit earned for such unused credit year.

(d) *Carryover and carryback of consolidated unused foreign tax.*—(1) *In general.*—If a consolidated unused foreign tax can be carried under the principles of section 904(d) and paragraph (e) of §1.1502-4 to a separate return year of a corporation (or could have been so carried if such corporation were in existence) which was a member of the group in the year in which such unused foreign tax arose, then the portion of such consolidated unused foreign tax attributable to such corporation (as determined under subparagraph (2) of this paragraph) shall be apportioned to such corporation (and any successor to such corporation in a transaction to which section 381(a) applies) under the principles of §1.1502-21(b) (or §§1.1502-79A(a)(1) and (2), as appropriate) and shall be deemed paid or accrued in such separate return year to the extent provided in section 904(d).

(2) *Portion of consolidated unused foreign tax attributable to a member.*—The portion of a consolidated unused foreign tax for any year attributable to a member of a group is an amount equal to such consolidated unused foreign tax multiplied by a fraction, the numerator of which is the foreign taxes paid or accrued for such year (including those taxes deemed paid or accrued, other than by reason of section 904(d)) to each foreign country or possession (or to all foreign countries or possessions if the overall limitation is effective) by such member, and the denominator of which is the aggregate of all such taxes paid or accrued for such year (including those taxes deemed paid or accrued, other than by reason of section 904(d)) to each such foreign country or possession (or to all foreign countries or possessions if the overall limitation is effective) by all the members of the group.

(e) *Carryover of consolidated excess charitable contributions to separate return years.*—(1) *In general.*—If the consolidated excess charitable contributions for any taxable year can be carried under the principles of section 170(b)(2) and paragraph (b) of §1.1502-24 to a separate return year of a corporation (or could have been so carried if such corporation were in existence) which was a member of the group in the year in which such excess contributions arose, then the portion of such consolidated excess charitable contributions attributable to such corporation (as determined under subparagraph (2) of this paragraph) shall be apportioned to such corporation (and any successor to such corporation in a transaction to which section 381(a) applies) under the principles of §1.1502-21(b) (or §§1.1502-79A(a)(1) and (2), as appropriate) and shall be a charitable contribution carryover to such separate return year.

(2) *Portion of consolidated excess charitable contributions attributable to a member.*—The portion of the consolidated excess charitable contributions attributable to a member of a group is an amount equal to such consolidated excess contributions multiplied by a fraction, the numerator of which is the charitable contributions paid by such member for the taxable year, and the denominator of which is the aggregate of all such charitable contributions paid for such year by all the members of the group.

(f) *Disallowed business interest expense carryforwards.*—For the treatment of disallowed business interest expense carryforwards (as defined in §1.163(j)-1(b)(11)) of a member arising in a separate return limitation year, see §1.163(j)-5(d) and (f). [Reg. §1.1502-79.]

☐ [T.D. 6894, 9-7-66. *Amended by T.D. 7637, 8-6-79; T.D. 7728, 10-31-80; T.D. 8294, 3-9-90; T.D. 8319, 11-19-90; T.D. 8364, 9-13-91; T.D. 8597, 7-12-95; T.D. 8677, 6-26-96, T.D. 8823, 6-25-99 and T.D. 9905, 9-3-2020.]*

### [Reg. §1.1502-79A]

**§1.1502-79A. Separate return years generally applicable for consolidated return years beginning before January 1, 1997.**—
(a) *Carryover and carryback of consolidated net operating losses to separate return years.*—(1) *In general.*—(i) If a consolidated net operating loss can be carried under the principles of section 172(b) and paragraph (b) of §1.1502-21A to a separate return year of a corporation (or could have been so carried if such corporation were in existence) which was a member in the year in which such loss arose, then the portion of such consolidated net operating loss attributable to such corporation (as determined under subparagraph (3) of this paragraph) shall be apportioned to such corporation (and any successor to such corporation in a transaction to which section 381(a) applies) and shall be a net operating loss carryover or carryback to such separate return year; accordingly, such portion shall not be included in the consolidated net operating loss carryovers or carrybacks to the equivalent consolidated return year. Thus, for example, if a member filed a separate return for the third year preceding a consolidated return year in which a consolidated net operating loss was sustained and if any portion of such loss is apportioned to such member for such separate return year, such portion may not be carried back by the group to its third year preceding such consolidated return year.

(ii) If a corporation ceases to be a member during a consolidated return year, any consolidated net operating loss carryover from a prior consolidated return year must first be carried to such consolidated return year, notwithstanding that all or a portion of the consolidated net operating loss giving rise to the carryover is attributable to the corporation which ceases to be a member. To the extent not absorbed in such consolidated return year, the portion of the consolidated net operating loss attributable to the corporation ceasing to be a member shall then be carried to such corporation's first separate return year.

(iii) For rules permitting the reattribution of losses of a subsidiary to the common parent in the case of loss disallowance or basis reduction on the disposition or deconsolidation of stock of the subsidiary, see §1.1502-20.

(2) *Nonapportionment to certain members not in existence.*—Notwithstanding subparagraph (1) of this paragraph, the portion of a consolidated net operating loss attributable to a member shall not be apportioned to a prior separate return year for which such member was not in existence and shall be included in the consolidated net operating loss carrybacks to the equivalent consolidated return year of the group (or, if such equivalent year is a separate return year, then to such separate return year), provided that such member was a member of the group immediately after its organization.

(3) *Portion of consolidated net operating loss attributable to a member.*—The portion of a consolidated net operating loss attributable to a member of a group is an amount equal to the consolidated net operating loss multiplied by a fraction, the numerator of which is the separate net operating loss of such corporation, and the denominator of which is the sum of the separate net operating losses of all members of the group in such year having such losses. For purposes of this subparagraph, the separate net operating loss of a member of the group shall be determined under §1.1502-12 (except that no deduction shall be allowed under section 242), adjusted for the following items taken into account in the computation of the consolidated net operating loss:

(i) The portion of the consolidated dividends received deduction, the consolidated charitable contributions deductions, and the consolidated section 247 deduction, attributable to such member;

(ii) Such member's capital gain net income (net capital gain for taxable years beginning before January 1, 1977) (determined without regard to any net capital loss carryover attributable to such member);

(iii) Such member's net capital loss and section 1231 net loss, reduced by the portion of the consolidated net capital loss attributable to such member (as determined under paragraph (b)(2) of this section); and

(iv) The portion of any consolidated net capital loss carryover attributable to such member which is absorbed in the taxable year.

(4) *Examples.*—The provisions of this paragraph may be illustrated by the following examples:

*Example (1).* (i) Corporation P was formed on January 1, 1966. P filed a separate return for the calendar year 1966. On March 15, 1967, P formed corporation S. P and S filed a consolidated return for 1967. On January 1, 1968, P purchased all the stock of corporation T, which had been formed in 1967 and had filed a separate return for its taxable year ending December 31, 1967.

(ii) P, S, and T join in the filing of a consolidated return for 1968, which return reflects a consolidated net operating loss of $11,000. $2,000 of such consolidated net operating loss is attributable to P, $3,000 to S, and $6,000 to T. Such apportionment of the consolidated net operating loss was made on the basis of the separate net operating losses of each member as determined under subparagraph (3) of this paragraph.

(iii) $5,000 of the 1968 consolidated net operating loss can be carried back to P's separate return for 1966. Such amount is the portion of the consolidated net operating loss attributable to P and S. Even though S was not in existence in 1966, the portion attributable to S can be carried back to P's separate return year, since S (unlike T) was a member of the group immediately after its organization. The 1968 consolidated net operating loss can be carried back against the group's income in 1967 except to the extent (*i.e.*, $6,000) that it is apportioned to T for its 1967 separate return year and to the extent that it was absorbed in P's 1966 separate return year. The portion of the 1968 consolidated net operating loss attributable to T ($6,000) is a net operating loss carryback to its 1967 separate return.

*Example (2).* (i) Assume the same facts as in example (1). Assume further that on June 15, 1969, P sells all the stock of T to an outsider, that P and S file a consolidated return for 1969 (which includes the income of T for the period January 1 through June 15, and that T files a separate return for the period June 16 through December 31, 1969.

(ii) The 1968 consolidated net operating loss, to the extent not absorbed in prior years, must first be carried to the consolidated return year 1969. Any portion of the $6,000 amount attributable to T which is not absorbed in T's 1967 separate return year or in the 1969 consolidated return year shall then be carried to T's separate return year ending December 31, 1969.

(b) *Carryover and carryback of consolidated net capital loss to separate return years.*—(1) *In general.*—If a consolidated net capital loss can be carried under the principles of section 1212(a) and paragraph (b) of §1.1502-22A to a separate return year of a corporation (or could have been so carried if such corporation were in existence) which was a member of the group in the year in which such consolidated net capital loss arose, then the portion of such consolidated net capital loss attributable to such corporation (as determined under subparagraph (2) of this paragraph) shall be apportioned to such corporation (and any successor to such corporation in a transaction to which section 381(a) applies) under the principles of paragraph (a)(1), (2), and (3) of this section and shall be a net capital loss carryback or carryover to such separate return year.

(2) *Portion of consolidated net capital loss attributable to a member.*—The portion of a consolidated net capital loss attributable to a member of a group is an amount equal to such consolidated net capital loss multiplied by a fraction, the numerator of which is the net capital loss of such member, and the denominator of which is the sum of the net capital losses of those members of the group having net capital losses. For purposes of this subparagraph, the net capital loss of a member of the group shall be determined by taking into account the following:

(i) Such member's capital gain net income (net capital gain for taxable years beginning before January 1, 1977) or loss (determined without regard to any net capital loss carryover or carryback); and

(ii) Such member's section 1231 net loss, reduced by the portion of the consolidated section 1231 net loss attributable to such member.

(a)[(c)]through (e). [Reserved]

(f) *Effective date.*—Paragraphs (a) and (b) of this section apply to losses arising in consolidated return years to which §1.1502-21T(g) does not apply for this purpose net operating loss deductions, carryovers, and carrybacks arise in the year from which they are carried.

See §1.1502-21T(g) for effective dates of that section. [Reg. §1.1502-79A.]

☐ [*T.D. 8677, 6-26-96.*]

**[Reg. §1.1502-80]**

**§1.1502-80. Applicability of other provisions of law.**—(a) *In general.*—(1) *Application of other provisions.*—The Internal Revenue Code (Code), or other law, shall be applicable to the group to the extent the regulations do not exclude its application. To the extent not excluded, other rules operate in addition to, and may be modified by, these regulations. Thus, for example, in a transaction to which section 381(a) applies, the acquiring corporation will succeed to the tax attributes described in section 381(c). Furthermore, sections 269 and 482 apply for any consolidated return year. However, in a recognition transaction otherwise subject to section 1001, for example, the rules of section 1001 continue to apply, but may be modified by the intercompany transaction regulations under §1.1502-13.

(2) *No duplicative adjustments.*—Nothing in these regulations shall be interpreted or applied to require an adjustment, inclusion, or other item to the extent it would have the effect of duplicating any other adjustment, inclusion, or other item required under the Code or other rule of law, including other provisions of these regulations.

(3) *Application of single-entity principles.*—If two or more adjustments, inclusions, or other items are subject to paragraph (a)(2) of this section, the determination of which adjustment, inclusion, or other item is treated as applied or taken into account is made by taking into account the purposes of the provisions and applying single-entity principles as appropriate.

(4) *Effective/applicability dates.*—This paragraph (a) is applicable with respect to transactions and determinations on or after September 17, 2008.

(b) *Non-applicability of section 304.*—Section 304 does not apply to any acquisition of stock of a corporation in an intercompany transaction or to any intercompany item from such transaction occurring on or after July 24, 1991.

(c) *Deferral of section 165.*—(1) *General rule.*—Subsidiary stock is not treated as worthless under section 165 until immediately before the earlier of the time—

(i) The stock is worthless within the meaning of §1.1502-19(c)(1)(iii); or

(ii) The subsidiary for any reason ceases to be a member of the group.

(2) *Cross reference.*—See §1.1502-36 for additional rules relating to worthlessness of subsidiary stock on or after September 17, 2008.

(3) *Effective/applicability date.*—This paragraph (c) applies to taxable years for which the original consolidated Federal income tax return is due (without extensions) after July 18, 2007. However, taxpayers may apply this paragraph (c) to taxable years beginning on or after January 1, 1995.

(d) *Non-applicability of section 357(c).*—(1) *In general.*—Section 357(c) does not apply to any transaction to which §1.1502-13, §1.1502-13T, §1.1502-14, or §1.1502-14T applies, if it occurs in a consolidated return year beginning on or after January 1, 1995. For example, P, S, and T are members of a consolidated group, P owns all of the stock of S and T with bases of $30 and $20, respectively, S has a $30 basis in its assets and $40 of liabilities, S merges into T in a transaction described in section 368(a)(1)(A) (and in section 368(a)(1)(D)); section 357(c) does not apply to the merger, P's basis in T's stock increases to $50 ($30 plus $20), and T succeeds to S's $30 basis in the assets transferred subject to the $40 liability. Similarly, if S instead transferred its assets and liabilities to a newly formed subsidiary in a transaction to which section 351 applies, section 357(c) does not apply and S's basis in the subsidiary's stock is a $10 excess loss account. This paragraph (d) does not apply to a transaction if the transferor or transferee becomes a nonmember as part of the same plan or arrangement. The transferor (or transferee) is treated as becoming a nonmember once it is no longer a member of a consolidated group that includes the transferee (or transferor). For purposes of this paragraph (d), any reference to a transferor or transferee includes, as the context may require, a reference to a successor or predecessor.

(2) *Prior period transactions.*—If, in a tax year beginning before January 1, 1995, a member's stock with an excess loss account is transferred in a transaction to which §1.1502-13, §1.1502-13T, §1.1502-14, or §1.1502-14T applies, paragraph (d)(1) of this section applies to the stock transfer to the extent that the income, gain, deduction, or loss (if any) is not taken into account in a tax year beginning before January 1, 1995. For example, if P, S, and T, are

members of a consolidated group, T's stock has a excess loss account, and P transfers the T stock to S in 1993 in a transaction to which section 351 and §1.1502-13 apply, section 357(c) applies to the transfer only to the extent P's gain is taken into account in tax years beginning before January 1, 1995.

(e) *Non-applicability of section 163(e)(5).*—Section 163(e)(5) does not apply to any intercompany obligation (within the meaning of §1.1502-13(g)) issued in a consolidated return year beginning on or after July 12, 1995.

(f) *Non-applicability of section 1031.*—Section 1031 does not apply to any intercompany transaction occurring in consolidated return years beginning on or after July 12, 1995.

(g) *Special rules for liquidations to which section 332 applies.*—Notwithstanding the general rule of section 381, if multiple members (distributee members) acquire assets of a corporation in a liquidation to which section 332 applies (regardless of whether any single member owns stock in the liquidating corporation meeting the requirements of section 1504(a)(2)), such members succeed to and take into account the items of the liquidating corporation (including items described in section 381(c), but excluding intercompany items under §1.1502-13) as provided in this paragraph (g) to the extent not otherwise prohibited by any applicable provision of law. This paragraph (g) does not apply to the intercompany items of the liquidating corporation. See §1.1502-13(j)(2)(ii).

(1) *Income offset items and deferred income.*—Except as otherwise provided in this paragraph (g)(1), each distributee member succeeds to and takes into account the items of the liquidating corporation that could be used to offset the income of the group or any member (including deferred deductions, net operating loss carryovers, and capital loss carryovers) (income offset items) to the extent that such items would have been reflected in investment adjustments to the stock of the liquidating corporation owned by such distributee member under §1.1502-32(c) if, immediately prior to the liquidation, any stock of the liquidating corporation owned by nonmembers had been redeemed and then such items had been taken into account. However, each distributee member succeeds to the full amount of any deferred deduction or deferred income item attributable to the particular property or business operations distributed to such distributee in the liquidation to the extent that such item is not taken into account in the determination of the income or loss of the liquidating corporation with regard to the liquidation under chapter 1 of the Internal Revenue Code (Code). If the liquidating corporation is not a member of the group at the time of the liquidation, the rules of this paragraph (g)(1) are applied as if the liquidating corporation had been a member of the group.

(2) *Accounting for deferred income items.*—Solely for the purpose of determining whether deferred income items of a liquidating corporation are taken into account under applicable principles of law as a result of a liquidation to which section 332 applies, the transfer of property to, and the assumption of liabilities by, a distributee member that does not own stock in the liquidating corporation meeting the requirements of section 1504(a)(2) without regard to the application of §1.1502-34 immediately prior to the liquidation is not treated as part of a transaction to which section 381(a) applies. In addition, section 332(a) does not apply in determining the recognition or nonrecognition of any income realized by the distributee member under applicable principles of law on account of consideration received (or deemed received) on the assumption of the liquidating corporation's obligation or liability attributable to any deferred income item.

(3) *Credits and earnings and profits.*—Each distributee member succeeds to and takes into account a percentage of each credit of the liquidating corporation equal to the value of the stock of the liquidating corporation owned by such distributee at the time of the liquidation divided by the total value of all the stock of the liquidating corporation owned by members of the group at the time of the liquidation. Except to the extent that the distributee member's earnings and profits already reflect the liquidating corporation's earnings and profits, each distributee member succeeds to and takes into account under the principles of §1.1502-32(c) the earnings and profits, or deficit in earnings and profits, of the liquidating corporation (determined after taking into account the amount of earnings and profits properly applicable to distributions to non-member shareholders under §1.381(c)(2)-1(c)(2)). If the liquidating corporation is not a member of the group at the time of the liquidation, the rules of this paragraph (g)(3) are applied as if the liquidating corporation had been a member of the group.

(4) *Other items.*—With regard to items to which neither paragraph (g)(1) nor (g)(3) of this section applies, a distributee member that, immediately prior to the liquidation, owns stock in the liquidat-

ing corporation meeting the requirements of section 1504(a)(2) without regard to the application of §1.1502-34 succeeds to the items of the liquidating corporation in accordance with section 381 and other applicable principles. A distributee member that, immediately prior to the liquidation, does not own stock in the liquidating corporation meeting the requirements of section 1504(a)(2) without regard to the application of §1.1502-34 succeeds to the items of the liquidating corporation to the extent that it would have succeeded to those items if it had purchased, in a taxable transaction, the assets or businesses of the liquidating corporation that it received in the liquidation and had assumed the liabilities that it assumed in the liquidation.

(5) *Determination of the items of a liquidating subsidiary.*—For purposes of this section, the items of a liquidating subsidiary include the amount of any consolidated tax attribute attributable to the liquidating subsidiary that is determined pursuant to the principles of §1.1502-21(b)(2)(iv). In addition, if the liquidating subsidiary is a member of a separate return limitation year subgroup, the amount of a tax attribute that arose in a separate return limitation year that is attributable to that member shall also be determined pursuant to the principles of §1.1502-21(b)(2)(iv).

(6) *Examples.*—The following examples illustrate the application of this paragraph (g):

*Example 1. Liquidation-80 percent distributee.* (i) *Facts.* X has only common stock outstanding. On January 1 of year 1, X acquired equipment with a 10-year recovery period and elected to depreciate the equipment using the straight-line method of depreciation. On January 1 of year 7, M1 and M2 own 80 percent and 20 percent, respectively, of X's stock. X is a domestic corporation but is not a member of the group that includes M1 and M2. On that date, X distributes all of its assets to M1 and M2 in complete liquidation. The equipment is distributed to M1. Under section 334(b), M1's basis in the equipment is the same as it would be in X's hands. After computing its tax liability for the taxable year that includes the liquidation, X has net operating losses of $100, business credits of $40, and earnings and profits of $80.

(ii) *Succession to items described in section 381(c).* (A) *Losses.* Under paragraph (g)(1) of this section, each distributee member succeeds to X's items that could be used to offset the income of the group or any member to the extent that such items would have been reflected in investment adjustments to the stock of X it owned under §1.1502-32(c) if, immediately prior to the liquidation, such items had been taken into account. Accordingly, M1 and M2 succeed to $80 and $20, respectively, of X's net operating loss.

(B) *Credits and earnings and profits.* Under paragraph (g)(3) of this section, because, immediately prior to the liquidation, M1 and M2 hold 80 percent and 20 percent, respectively, of the value of the stock of X, M1 and M2 succeed to $32 and $8, respectively, of X's $40 of business credits. In addition, because M1's and M2's earnings and profits do not reflect X's earnings and profits, X's earnings and profits are allocated to M1 and M2 under the principles of §1.1502-32(c). Therefore, M1 and M2 succeed to $64 and $16, respectively, of X's earnings and profits.

(C) *Depreciation of equipment's basis.* Under paragraph (g)(4) of this section, because M1 owns stock in X meeting the requirements of section 1504(a)(2) without regard to the application of §1.1502-34, M1 is required to continue to depreciate the equipment using the straight-line method of depreciation over the remaining recovery period of 4.5 years (assuming X used a half-year convention).

*Example 2. Liquidation-no 80 percent distributee.* (i) *Facts.* The facts are the same as in *Example 1* except that M1 and M2 own 60 percent and 40 percent, respectively, of X's stock. In addition, on January 1 of year 6, X entered into a long-term contract with Y, an unrelated party. The total contract price is $1000, and X estimates the total allocable contract costs to be $500. At the time of the liquidation, X had received $250 in progress payments under the contract and incurred costs of $125. X accounted for the contract under the percentage of completion method described in section 460(b). In the liquidation, M1 assumes X's contract obligations and rights.

(ii) *Succession to items described in section 381(c).* (A) *Losses.* Under paragraph (g)(1) of this section, each distributee member succeeds to X's items that could be used to offset the income of the group or any member to the extent that such items would have been reflected in investment adjustments to the stock of X it owned under §1.1502-32(c) if, immediately prior to the liquidation, such items had been taken into account. Accordingly, M1 and M2 succeed to $60 and $40, respectively, of X's net operating loss.

(B) *Credits and earnings and profits.* Under paragraph (g)(3) of this section, because, immediately prior to the liquidation, M1 and M2 hold 60 percent and 40 percent, respectively, of the value of the stock of X, M1 and M2 succeed to $24 and $16, respectively, of X's $40 of business credits. In addition, because M1's and M2's earnings and profits do not reflect X's earnings and profits, X's earnings and profits are allocated to M1 and M2 under the principles of

§1.1502-32(c). Therefore, M1 and M2 succeed to $48 and $32, respectively, of X's earnings and profits.

(C) *Depreciation of equipment's basis.* Under section 334(a), M1's basis in the equipment is its fair market value at the time of the distribution. Pursuant to section 168(i)(7), to the extent that M1's basis in the equipment does not exceed X's adjusted basis in the equipment at the time of the transfer, M1 is required to continue to depreciate the equipment using the straight-line method of depreciation over the remaining recovery period of 4.5 years (assuming X used a half-year convention). Any portion of M1's basis in the equipment that exceeds X's adjusted basis in the equipment at the time of the transfer is treated as being placed in service by M1 in the year of the transfer. Thus, M1 may choose any applicable depreciation method, recovery period, and convention under section 168 for such excess basis.

(D) *Method of accounting for long-term contract.* Under paragraph (g)(4) of this section, M1 does not succeed to X's method of accounting for the contract. Rather, under §1.460-4(k)(2), M1 is treated as having entered into a new contract on the date of the liquidation. Under §1.460-4(k)(2)(iii), M1 must evaluate whether the new contract should be classified as a long-term contract within the meaning of §1.460-1(b) and account for the contract under a permissible method of accounting.

*Example 3. Liquidation—deferred items.* (i) *Facts.* X has only common stock outstanding, and M1 and M2 (who are members of the same group) own 80 percent and 20 percent, respectively, of X's stock. X operates two divisions, each of which defers prepaid subscription income pursuant to an election under section 455. X distributes all of its assets in complete liquidation. M1 receives all of the assets of Division 1, including prepaid subscription income, and assumes X's liability to furnish or deliver the newspaper, magazine, or other periodical to which the prepaid subscription income received by M1 relates. M2 receives all of the assets of Division 2, including prepaid subscription income, and assumes X's liability to furnish or deliver the newspaper, magazine, or other periodical to which the prepaid subscription income received by M2 relates.

(ii) *Acceleration of deferred income items and succession to other deferred items.* Under paragraph (g)(1) of this section, M1 succeeds to the full amount of the deferred prepaid subscription income of X attributable to Division 1. Under applicable law, X does not recognize the deferred prepaid subscription income attributable to Division 1 because X's liability to furnish or deliver the newspaper, magazine, or other periodical ends as a result of a transaction to which section 381(a) applies. Under paragraph (g)(2) of this section, solely for purposes of determining whether the deferred income items of X attributable to Division 2 are taken into account as a result of the liquidation, the distribution of property to M2 is not treated as a transaction to which section 381(a) applies. Therefore, under applicable law, X's deferred prepaid subscription income attributable to Division 2 is taken into account in the determination of X's income or loss with regard to the liquidation. Further, under paragraph (g)(2) of this section, section 332(a) does not apply in determining the recognition or nonrecognition of any income that M2 realizes on account of consideration received (or deemed received) on its assumption of X's liability to furnish or deliver the newspaper, magazine, or other periodical to which the prepaid subscription income relates.

(7) *Effective/applicability date.*—This paragraph (g) applies to transactions occurring after April 14, 2008.

(h) *Non-applicability of section 362(e)(2).*—(1) *General rule.*—Section 362(e)(2) does not apply to any intercompany transaction occurring on or after September 17, 2008. Taxpayers may apply this paragraph (h) to intercompany transactions occurring on or after October 22, 2004, and in such case, any election made under section 362(e)(2)(C) will have no effect. The purpose of this paragraph (h) is to facilitate the application of the consolidated return provisions addressing the duplication of loss between members of a consolidated group.

(2) *Anti-abuse rule.*—(i) *General rule.*—If a taxpayer engages in a transaction to which section 362(e)(2) would apply but for the application of paragraph (h)(1) of this section, and acts with a view to prevent the consolidated return provisions from properly addressing loss duplication, appropriate adjustments will be made to clearly reflect the income of the group.

(ii) *Example.*—The following example illustrates the principle of the anti-abuse rule in this paragraph (h)(2).

*Example.* (A) *Facts.* P, the common parent of a consolidated group, owns the four outstanding shares of S stock (Share 1 through Share 4) with an aggregate basis of $0 and value of $80. S owns Asset 1 with a basis of $0 and a value of $80. With a view to prevent the consolidated return provisions from addressing the duplication of loss, P transfers Asset 2 with a basis of $100 and a value of $20 to S in exchange for an additional share of S stock (Share 5) in a transaction to which section 351 applies. P later sells Share 5 to X, an unrelated person, for $20 at a time when S's basis in Asset 2 was still $100. The sale is a transfer of a loss share and therefore subject to § 1.1502-36.

(B) *Analysis.* Although the sale would be subject to § 1.1502-36, that section would not prevent the stock loss or reduce S's attributes (to prevent duplication of the stock loss) because neither § 1.1502-36(b) nor § 1.1502-36(c) would adjust the basis of the transferred share (because there are no investment adjustments) and § 1.1502-36(d) would not reduce S's attributes (because S's aggregate inside loss is $0). However, because P acted with a view to prevent the consolidated return provisions from addressing the duplication of the loss on Asset 2, P's transfer of Asset 2 to S is subject to the anti-abuse rule in this paragraph (h)(2). Accordingly, effective immediately before the transfer of Share 5 to X, either P's basis in Share 5 or S's basis in Asset 2 must be adjusted to reflect what it would have been had section 362(e)(2) been applied at the time P transferred Asset 2 to S (taking into account the interim facts and circumstances). Accordingly, S must either reduce its basis in Asset 2 by $80 to $20 (eliminating the duplicated loss) or P must reduce its basis in Share 5 by $80 to $20 (eliminating the duplicated loss).

(C) *Transfer of all S shares.* Assume the same facts as those in paragraph (A) of this *Example*, except that P sells all five S shares to X. Although P's transfer of Asset 2 to S results in the duplication of an $80 loss, because all the shares are transferred, the transaction does not prevent the consolidated return provisions from properly addressing loss duplication. P's $80 duplicated loss is offset by an $80 duplicated gain, and the group recognizes the offsetting stock gain and loss. Accordingly, this paragraph (h)(2) does not apply to P's transfer of Asset 2 to S.

[Reg. § 1.1502-80.]

☐ [*T.D.* 6894, 9-7-66. *Amended by T.D.* 8402, 3-13-92; *T.D.* 8560, 8-12-94; *T.D.* 8597, 7-12-95; *T.D.* 8677, 6-26-96; *T.D.* 9048, 3-11-2003; *T.D.* 9118, 3-17-2004 *T.D.* 9192, 3-21-2005; *T.D.* 9254, 3-9-2006; *T.D.* 9341, 7-17-2007; *T.D.* 9376, 1-14-2008 *and T.D.* 9424, 9-9-2008.]

## [Reg. § 1.1502-81T]

**§ 1.1502-81T. Alaska Native Corporations (Temporary).—** (a) *General Rule.*—The application of section 60(b)(5) of the Tax Reform Act of 1984 and section 1804(e)(4) of the Tax Reform Act of 1986 (relating to Native Corporations established under the Alaska Native Claims Settlement Act (43 U.S.C. 1601 *et seq.*)) is limited to the use on a consolidated return of losses and credits of a Native Corporation, and of a corporation all of whose stock is owned directly by a Native Corporation, during any taxable year (beginning after the effective date of such sections and before 1992), or any part thereof, against the income and tax liability of a corporation affiliated with the Native Corporation. Thus, no other tax saving, tax benefit, or tax loss is intended to result from the application of section 60(b)(5) of the Tax Reform Act of 1984 and section 1804(e)(4) of the Tax Reform Act of 1986 to any person (whether or not such person is a member of an affiliated group of which a Native Corporation is the common parent). In particular, except as approved by the Secretary, no positive adjustment under § 1.1502-32(b) will be made with respect to the basis of stock of a corporation that is affiliated with a Native Corporation through application of section 60(b)(5) of the Tax Reform Act of 1984 and section 1804(e)(4) of the Tax Reform Act of 1986.

(b) *Effective dates.*—This section applies to taxable years beginning after December 31, 1984. [Temporary Reg. § 1.1502-81T.]

☐ [*T.D.* 8130, 3-13-87. *Amended by T.D.* 8560, 8-12-94.]

## [Reg. § 1.1502-90]

**§ 1.1502-90. Table of contents.**—The following list contains the major headings in §§ 1.1502-91 through 1.1502-99:

☐ [*T.D.* 8824, 6-25-99. *Amended by T.D.* 9304, 12-21-2006; *T.D.* 9329, 6-13-2007, *T.D.* 9424, 9-9-2008 and *T.D.* 9905, 9-3-2020.]

### [Reg. §1.1502-90A]

**§1.1502-90A. Table of contents.**—The following list contains the major headings in §§1.1502-91A through 1.1502-99A:

(2) Special rule for post-change year that includes the change date.

    (3) Cross reference.

  (b) Definitions and nomenclature.

  (c) Loss group.

    (1) Defined.

    (2) Coordination with rule that ends separate tracking.

    (3) Example.

  (d) Loss subgroup.

    (1) Net operating loss carryovers.

    (2) Net unrealized built-in loss.

    (3) Loss subgroup parent.

    (4) Principal purpose of avoiding a limitation.

    (5) Special rules.

    (6) Examples.

  (e) Pre-change consolidated attribute.

    (1) Defined.

    (2) Example.

  (f) Pre-change subgroup attribute.

    (1) Defined.

    (2) Example.

  (g) Net unrealized built-in gain and loss.

    (1) In general.

    (2) Members included.

      (i) Consolidated group.

      (ii) Loss subgroup.

    (3) Acquisitions of built-in gain or loss assets.

    (4) Indirect ownership.

  (h) Recognized built-in gain or loss.

    (1) In general. [Reserved]

    (2) Disposition of stock or an intercompany obligation of a member.

    (3) Deferred gain or loss.

    (4) Exchanged basis property.

  (i) [Reserved]

  (j) Predecessor and successor corporations.

*§1.1502-92A Ownership change of a loss group or a loss subgroup generally applicable for testing dates before June 25, 1999.*

  (a) Scope.

  (b) Determination of an ownership change.

    (1) Parent change method.

      (i) Loss group.

      (ii) Loss subgroup.

    (2) Examples.

    (3) Special adjustments.

      (i) Common parent succeeded by a new common parent.

      (ii) Newly created loss subgroup parent.

      (iii) Examples.

    (4) End of separate tracking of certain losses.

  (c) Supplemental rules for determining ownership change.

    (1) Scope.

    (2) Cause for applying supplemental rule.

    (3) Operating rules.

    (4) Supplemental ownership change rules.

      (i) Additional testing dates for the common parent (or loss subgroup parent).

      (ii) Treatment of subsidiary stock as stock of the common parent (or loss subgroup parent).

      (iii) 5-percent shareholder of the common parent (or loss subgroup parent).

    (5) Examples.

  (d) Testing period following ownership change under this section.

  (e) Information statements.

    (1) Common parent of a loss group.

    (2) Abbreviated statement with respect to loss subgroups.

*§1.1502-93A Consolidated section 382 limitation (or subgroup section 382 limitation) generally applicable for testing dates before June 25, 1999.*

  (a) Determination of the consolidated section 382 limitation (or subgroup section 382 limitation).

    (1) In general.

    (2) Coordination with apportionment rule.

  (b) Value of the loss group (or loss subgroup).

    (1) Stock value immediately before ownership change.

    (2) Adjustment to value.

    (3) Examples.

  (c) Recognized built-in gain of a loss group or loss subgroup.

  (d) Continuity of business.

    (1) In general.

    (2) Example.

  (e) Limitations of losses under other rules.

*§1.1502-94A Coordination with section 382 and the regulations thereunder when a corporation becomes a member of a consolidated group generally applicable for corporations becoming members of a group before June 25, 1999.*

  (a) Scope.

    (1) In general.

    (2) Successor corporation as new loss member.

    (3) Coordination in the case of a loss subgroup.

    (4) End of separate tracking of certain losses.

    (5) Cross-reference.

  (b) Application of section 382 to a new loss member.

    (1) In general.

    (2) Adjustment to value.

    (3) Pre-change separate attribute defined.

    (4) Examples.

  (c) Built-in gains and losses.

  (d) Information statements.

*§1.1502-95A Rules on ceasing to be a member of a consolidated group (or loss subgroup) generally applicable for corporations ceasing to be members before June 25, 1999.*

  (a) In general.

    (1) Consolidated group.

    (2) Election by common parent.

    (3) Coordination with §§1.1502-91T through 1.1502-93T.

  (b) Separate application of section 382 when a member leaves a consolidated group.

    (1) In general.

    (2) Effect of a prior ownership change of the group.

    (3) Application in the case of a loss subgroup.

    (4) Examples.

  (c) Apportionment of a consolidated section 382 limitation.

    (1) In general.

    (2) Amount of apportionment.

    (3) Effect of apportionment on the consolidated section 382 limitation.

    (4) Effect on corporations to which the consolidated section 382 limitation is apportioned.

    (5) Deemed apportionment when loss group terminates.

    (6) Appropriate adjustments when former member leaves during the year.

    (7) Examples.

  (d) Rules pertaining to ceasing to be a member of a loss subgroup.

    (1) In general.

    (2) Examples.

  (e) Filing the election to apportion.

    (1) Form of the election to apportion.

    (2) Signing of the election.

    (3) Filing of the election.

    (4) Revocation of election.

*§1.1502-96A Miscellaneous rules generally applicable for testing dates before June 25, 1999.*

  (a) End of separate tracking of losses.

    (1) Application.

    (2) Effect of end of separate tracking.

    (3) Continuing effect of end of separate tracking.

    (4) Special rule for testing period.

    (5) Limits on effects of end of separate tracking.

  (b) Ownership change of subsidiary.

    (1) Ownership change of a subsidiary because of options or plan or arrangement.

    (2) Effect of the ownership change.

      (i) In general.

      (ii) Pre-change losses.

    (3) Coordination with §§1.1502-91T, 1.1502-92T, and 1.1502-94T.

    (4) Example.

  (c) Continuing effect of an ownership change.

*§1.1502-97A Special rules under section 382 for members under the jurisdiction of a court in a title 11 or similar case*

  [Reserved]

*§1.1502-98A Coordination with section 383 generally applicable for testing dates (or members joining or leaving a group) before June 25, 1999.*

*§1.1502-99A Effective dates.*

  (a) Effective date.

(1) In general.

(2) Anti-duplication rules for recognized built-in gain.

(b) Testing period may include a period beginning before January 1, 1997.

(c) Transition rules.

(1) Methods permitted.

(i) In general.

(ii) Adjustments to offset excess limitation.

(iii) Coordination with effective date.

(2) Permitted methods.

(d) Amended returns.

(e) Section 383.

[Reg. § 1.1502-90A.]

☐ [*T.D. 8678, 6-26-96. Amended and redesignated by T.D. 8824, 6-25-99.*]

### [Reg. § 1.1502-91]

**§ 1.1502-91. Application of section 382 with respect to a consolidated group.**—(a) *Determination and effect of an ownership change.*—(1) *In general.*—This section and § § 1.1502-92 and 1.1502-93 set forth the rules for determining an ownership change under section 382 for members of consolidated groups and the section 382 limitations with respect to attributes described in paragraphs (e) and (f) of this section. These rules generally provide that an ownership change and the section 382 limitation are determined with respect to these attributes for the group (or loss subgroup) on a single entity basis and not for its members separately. Following an ownership change of a loss group (or a loss subgroup) under § 1.1502-92, the amount of consolidated taxable income for any post-change year which may be offset by pre-change consolidated attributes (or pre-change subgroup attributes) shall not exceed the consolidated section 382 limitation (or subgroup section 382 limitation) for such year as determined under § 1.1502-93.

(2) *Special rule for post-change year that includes the change date.*—If the post-change year includes the change date, section 382(b)(3)(A) is applied so that the consolidated section 382 limitation (or subgroup section 382 limitation) does not apply to the portion of consolidated taxable income that is allocable to the period in the year on or before the change date. See generally § 1.382-6 (relating to the allocation of income and loss). The allocation of consolidated taxable income for the post-change year that includes the change date must be made before taking into account any consolidated net operating loss deduction (as defined in § 1.1502-21(a)).

(3) *Cross-reference.*—See § § 1.1502-94 and 1.1502-95 for rules that apply section 382 to a corporation that becomes or ceases to be a member of a group or loss subgroup.

(b) *Definitions and nomenclature.*—For purposes of this section and § § 1.1502-92 through 1.1502-99, unless otherwise stated:

(1) The definitions and nomenclature contained in section 382 and the regulations thereunder (including the nomenclature and assumptions relating to the examples in § 1.382-2T(b)) and this section and § § 1.1502-92 through 1.1502-99 apply.

(2) In all examples, all groups file consolidated returns, all corporations file their income tax returns on a calendar year basis, the only 5-percent shareholder of a corporation is a public group, the facts set forth the only owner shifts during the testing period, no election is made under paragraph (d)(4) of this section, and each asset of a corporation has a value equal to its adjusted basis.

(3) As the context requires, references to § § 1.1502-91 through 1.1502-96 include references to corresponding provisions of § § 1.1502-91A through 1.1502-96A. For example, a reference to an ownership change under § 1.1502-92 in § 1.1502-95(b) can include a reference to an ownership change under § 1.1502-92A.

(c) *Loss group.*—(1) *Defined.*—A loss group is a consolidated group that—

(i) Is entitled to use a net operating loss carryover to the taxable year that did not arise (and is not treated under § 1.1502-21(c) as arising) in a SRLY;

(ii) Has a consolidated net operating loss for the taxable year in which a testing date of the common parent occurs (determined by treating the common parent as a loss corporation); or

(iii) Has a net unrealized built-in loss (determined under paragraph (g) of this section by treating the date on which the determination is made as though it were a change date).

(2) *Coordination with rule that ends separate tracking.*—A consolidated group may be a loss group because a member's losses that arose in (or are treated as arising in) a SRLY are treated as described in paragraph (c)(1)(i) of this section. See § 1.1502-96(a).

(3) *Example.*—The following example illustrates the principles of this paragraph (c):

*Example. Loss group.* (i) L and L1 file separate returns and each has a net operating loss carryover arising in Year 1 that is carried over to Year 2. A owns 40 shares and L owns 60 shares of the 100 outstanding shares of L1 stock. At the close of Year 1, L buys the 40 shares of L1 stock from A. For Year 2, L and L1 file a consolidated return. The following is a graphic illustration of these facts:

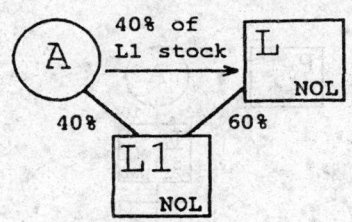

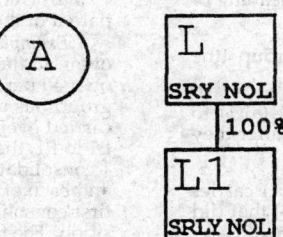

(ii) L and L1 become a loss group at the beginning of Year 2 because the group is entitled to use the Year 1 net operating loss carryover of L, the common parent, which did not arise (and is not treated under § 1.1502-21(c) as arising) in a SRLY. See § 1.1502-94 for rules relating to the application of section 382 with respect to L1's net operating loss carryover from Year 1 which did arise in a SRLY.

(d) *Loss subgroup.*—(1) *Net operating loss carryovers.*—Two or more corporations that become members of a consolidated group (the current group) compose a loss subgroup if—

(i) They were affiliated with each other in another group (the former group), whether or not the group was a consolidated group;

(ii) They bear the relationship described in section 1504(a)(1) to each other through a loss subgroup parent immediately after they become members of the current group (or are deemed to bear that relationship as a result of an election described in paragraph (d)(4) of this section); and

(iii) At least one of the members carries over a net operating loss that did not arise (and is not treated under § 1.1502-21(c) as arising) in a SRLY with respect to the former group.

(2) *Net unrealized built-in loss.*—Two or more corporations that become members of a consolidated group compose a loss subgroup if they—

(i) Have been continuously affiliated with each other for the 5 consecutive year period ending immediately before they become members of the group;

(ii) Bear the relationship described in section 1504(a)(1) to each other through a loss subgroup parent immediately after they become members of the current group (or are deemed to bear that relationship as a result of an election described in paragraph (d)(4) of this section); and

(iii) Have a net unrealized built-in loss (determined under paragraph (g) of this section on the day they become members of the group by treating that day as though it were a change date).

(3) *Loss subgroup parent.*—A loss subgroup parent is the corporation that bears the same relationship to the other members of the loss subgroup as a common parent bears to the members of a group.

(4) *Election to treat loss subgroup parent requirement as satisfied.*— (i) *In general.*—Solely for purposes of paragraphs (d)(1)(i) and (2)(ii) of this section, two or more corporations that become members of a consolidated group at the same time and that were affiliated with each other immediately before becoming members of the group are deemed to bear a section 1504(a)(1) relationship to each other immediately after they become members of the group if the common parent of that group makes an election under this paragraph (d)(4) with respect to those members. See §1.1502-96(e) for the time and manner of making the election.

(ii) *Members included.*—An election under this paragraph (d)(4) includes all corporations that become members of the current group at the same time and that were affiliated with each other immediately before they become members of the current group.

(iii) *Each member included treated as loss subgroup parent.*—If the members to which this election applies are a loss subgroup described in paragraph (d)(1) or (2) of this section, then each member is treated as a loss subgroup parent. See §1.1502-92(b)(1)(iii) for special rules relating to an ownership change of a loss subgroup if the election under this paragraph (d)(4) is made.

(5) *Principal purpose of avoiding a limitation.*—The corporations described in paragraphs (d)(1) or (2) of this section do not compose a loss subgroup if any one of them is formed, acquired, or availed of with a principal purpose of avoiding the application of, or increasing any limitation under, section 382. Instead, §1.1502-94 applies with respect to the attributes of each such corporation. Any member excluded from a loss subgroup, if excluded with a principal purpose of so avoiding or increasing any section 382 limitation, is treated as included in the loss subgroup. This paragraph (d)(5) does not apply solely because, in connection with becoming members of the group, the members of a group (or loss subgroup) are rearranged (or, in the case of the preceding sentence, are not rearranged) to bear a relationship to the other members described in section 1504(a)(1).

(6) *Special rules.*—See §1.1502-95(d) for rules concerning when a corporation ceases to be a member of a loss subgroup, and for certain exceptions that may apply if a member does not continue to satisfy the loss subgroup parent requirement within the current group. See also §1.1502-96(a) for a special rule regarding the end of separate tracking of SRLY losses of a member that has an ownership change or that has been a member of a group for at least 5 consecutive years.

(7) *Examples.*—The following examples illustrate the principles of this paragraph (d):

*Example 1. Loss subgroup.* (i) P owns all the L stock and L owns all the L1 stock. The P group has a consolidated net operating loss arising in Year 1 that is carried to Year 2. On May 2, Year 2, P sells all the stock of L to A, and L and L1 thereafter file consolidated returns. A portion of the Year 1 consolidated net operating loss is apportioned under §1.1502-21(b) to each of L and L1, which they carry over to Year 2. The following is a graphic illustration of these facts:

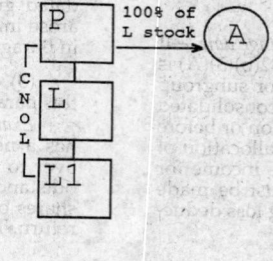

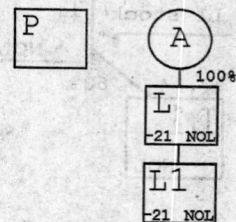

(ii) (a) L and L1 compose a loss subgroup within the meaning of paragraph (d)(1) of this section because—

(A) They were affiliated with each other in the P group (the former group);

(B) They bear a relationship described in section 1504(a)(1) to each other through a loss subgroup parent (L) immediately after they became members of the L group; and

(C) At least one of the members (here, both L and L1) carries over a net operating loss to the L group (the current group) that did not arise in a SRLY with respect to the P group.

(b) Under paragraph (d)(3) of this section, L is the loss subgroup parent of the L loss subgroup.

*Example 2. Loss subgroup—section 1504(a)(1) relationship.* (i) P owns all the stock of L and L1. L owns all the stock of L2. L1 and L2 own 40 percent and 60 percent of the stock of L3, respectively. The P group has a consolidated net operating loss arising in Year 1 that is carried over to Year 2. On May 22, Year 2, P sells all the stock of L and L1 to P1, the common parent of another consolidated group. The Year 1 consolidated net operating loss is apportioned under §1.1502-21(b), and each of L, L2, L2, and L3 carries over a portion of such loss to the first consolidated return year of the P1 group ending after the acquisition. The following is a graphic illustration of these facts:

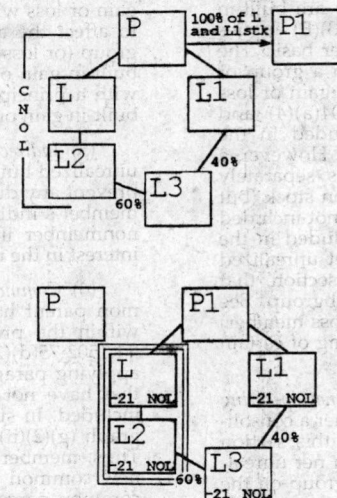

(ii) L and L2 compose a loss subgroup within the meaning of paragraph (d)(1) of this section. Neither L1 nor L3 is included in a loss subgroup because neither bears a relationship described in section 1504(a)(1) through a loss subgroup parent to any other member of the former group immediately after becoming members of the P1 group.

*Example 3. Loss subgroup—section 1504(a)(1) relationship.* The facts are the same as in *Example 2*, except that the stock of L1 is transferred to L in connection with the sale of the L stock to P1. L, L1, L2, and L3 compose a loss subgroup within the meaning of paragraph (d)(1) of this section because—

(i) They were affiliated with each other in the P group (the former group);

(ii) They bear a relationship described in section 1504(a)(1) to each other through a loss subgroup parent (L) immediately after they become members of the P1 group; and

(iii) At least one of the members (here, each of L, L1, L2, and L3) carries over a net operating loss to the P1 group (the current group).

*Example 4. Loss subgroup—elective section 1504(a)(1) relationship.* The facts are the same as in *Example 2*, except that P1 makes the election under paragraph (d)(4) of this section. The election includes L, L1, L2, and L3 (even though L and L2 would compose a loss subgroup without regard to the election) because they become members of the current group (the P1 group) at the same time and were affiliated with each other in the P group immediately before they became members of the P1 group. As a result of the election, L, L1, L2, and L3 are treated as satisfying the requirement that they bear a relationship described in section 1504(a)(1) to each other through a loss subgroup parent immediately after they become members of the P1 group. L, L1, L2, and L3 compose a loss subgroup within the meaning of paragraph (d)(1) of this section.

(e) *Pre-change consolidated attribute.*—(1) *Defined.*—A pre-change consolidated attribute of a loss group is—

(i) Any loss described in paragraph (c)(1)(i) or (ii) of this section (relating to the definition of loss group) that is allocable to the period ending on or before the change date; and

(ii) Any recognized built-in loss of the loss group.

(2) *Example.*—(i) *Facts.* The L group has a consolidated net operating loss arising in Year 1 that is carried over to Year 2. The L loss group has an ownership change at the beginning of Year 2.

(ii) *Analysis.* The net operating loss carryover of the L loss group from Year 1 is a pre-change consolidated attribute because the L group was entitled to use the loss in Year 2 and therefore the loss was described in paragraph (c)(1)(i) of this section. Under paragraph (a)(2)(i) of this section, the amount of consolidated taxable income of the L group for Year 2 that may be offset by this loss carryover may not exceed the consolidated section 382 limitation of the L group for that year. See §1.1502-93 for rules relating to the computation of the consolidated section 382 limitation.

(iii) *Business interest expense.* The facts are the same as in the *Example* in paragraph (e)(2)(i) of this section, except that, rather than a consolidated net operating loss, a member of the L group pays or accrues a business interest expense in Year 1 for which a deduction is disallowed in that year under section 163(j) and §1.163(j)-2(b). The disallowed business interest expense is carried over to Year 2 under section 163(j)(2) and §1.163(j)-2(c). Thus, the disallowed business interest expense carryforward is a pre-change loss. Under section 163(j), the L loss group is entitled to deduct the carryforward in Year

2; however, the amount of consolidated taxable income of the L group for Year 2 that may be offset by this carryforward may not exceed the consolidated section 382 limitation of the L group for that year. See §1.1502-98(b) (providing that §§1.1502-91 through 1.1502-96 apply section 382 to business interest expense, with appropriate adjustments).

(f) *Pre-change subgroup attribute.*—(1) *Defined.*—A pre-change subgroup attribute of a loss subgroup is—

(i) Any net operating loss carryover described in paragraph (d)(1)(iii) of this section (relating to the definition of loss subgroup); and

(ii) Any recognized built-in loss of the loss subgroup.

(2) *Example.*—The following example illustrates the principle of this paragraph (f):

*Pre-change subgroup attribute.* (i) P is the common parent of a consolidated group. P owns all the stock of L, and L owns all the stock of L1. L2 is not a member of an affiliated group, and has a net operating loss arising in Year 1 that is carried over to Year 2. On December 11, Year 2, L1 acquires all the stock of L2, causing an ownership change of L2. During Year 2, the P group has a consolidated net operating loss that is carried over to Year 3. On November 2, Year 3, M acquires all the L stock from P. M, L, L1, and L2 thereafter file consolidated returns. All of the P group Year 2 consolidated net operating loss is apportioned under §1.1502-21(b) to L and L2, which they carry over to the M group.

(ii)(a) L, L1, and L2 compose a loss subgroup because—

(1) They were affiliated with each other in the P group (the former group);

(2) They bear a relationship described in section 1504(a)(1) to each other through a loss subgroup parent (L) immediately after they became members of the L group; and

(3) At least one of the members (here, both L and L2) carries over a net operating loss to the M group (the current group) that is described in paragraph (d)(1)(iii) of this section.

(b) For this purpose, L2's loss from Year 1 that was a SRLY loss with respect to the P group (the former group) is described in paragraph (d)(1)(iii) of this section because L2 had an ownership change on becoming a member of the P group (see §1.1502-96(a)) on December 11, Year 2. Starting on December 12, Year 2, the P group no longer separately tracked owner shifts of the stock of L1 with respect to the Year 1 loss. M's acquisition results in an ownership change of L, and therefore the L loss subgroup under §1.1502-92(a)(2). See §1.1502-93 for rules governing the computation of the subgroup section 382 limitation.

(iii) In the M group, L2's Year 1 loss continues to be subject to a section 382 limitation resulting from the ownership change that occurred on December 11, Year 2. See §1.1502-96(c).

(g) *Net unrealized built-in gain and loss.*—(1) *In general.*—The determination whether a consolidated group (or loss subgroup) has a net unrealized built-in gain or loss under section 382(h)(3) is based on the aggregate amount of the separately computed net unrealized built-in gains or losses of each member that is included in the group (or loss subgroup) under paragraph (g)(2) of this section, including items of built-in income and deduction described in section 382(h)(6). Thus, for example, amounts deferred under section 267, or under §1.1502-13 (other than amounts deferred with respect to the stock of a member (or an intercompany obligation) included in the group (or

**Reg. §1.1502-91(g)(1)**

loss subgroup) under paragraph (g)(2) of this section) are built-in items. The threshold requirement under section 382(h)(3)(B) applies on an aggregate basis and not on a member-by-member basis. The separately computed amount of a member included in a group or loss subgroup does not include any unrealized built-in gain or loss on stock (including stock described in section 1504(a)(4) and § 1.382-2T(f)(18)(ii) and (iii)) of another member included in the group or loss subgroup (or an intercompany obligation). However, a member of a group or loss subgroup includes in its separately computed amount the unrealized built-in gain or loss on stock (but not on an intercompany obligation) of another member not included in the group or loss subgroup. If a member is not included in the determination whether a group (or subgroup) has a net unrealized built-in loss under paragraph (g)(2)(ii) or (iv) of this section, that member is not included in the loss group or loss subgroup. See § 1.1502-94(c) (relating to built-in gain or loss of a new loss member) and § 1.1502-96(a) (relating to the end of separate tracking of certain losses).

(2) *Members included.*—(i) *Consolidated group with a net operating loss.*—The members included in the determination whether a consolidated group described in paragraph (c)(1)(i) or (ii) of this section (relating to loss groups with net operating losses) has a net unrealized built-in gain are all members of the consolidated group on the day that the determination is made.

(ii) *Determination whether a consolidated group has a net unrealized built-in loss.*—The members included in the determination whether a consolidated group is a loss group described in paragraph (c)(1)(iii) of this section are—

(A) The common parent and all other members that have been affiliated with the common parent for the 5 consecutive year period ending on the day that the determination is made;

(B) Any other member that has a net unrealized built-in loss determined under paragraph (g)(1) of this section on the date that the determination is made, and that is neither a new loss member described in § 1.1502-94(a)(1)(ii) nor a member of a loss subgroup described in paragraph (d)(2) of this section;

(C) Any new loss member described in § 1.1502-94(a)(1)(ii) that has a net unrealized built-in gain determined under paragraph (g)(1) of this section on the day that the determination is made; and

(D) The members of a loss subgroup described in paragraph (d)(2) of this section if the members of the subgroup have, in the aggregate, a net unrealized built-in gain on the day that the determination is made.

(iii) *Loss subgroup with net operating loss carryovers.*—The members included in the determination whether a loss subgroup described in paragraph (d)(1) of this section (relating to loss subgroups with net operating loss carryovers) has a net unrealized built-in gain are all members of the loss subgroup on the day that the determination is made.

(iv) *Determination whether subgroup has a net unrealized built-in loss.*—The members included in the determination whether a subgroup has a net unrealized built-in loss are those members described in paragraphs (d)(2)(i) and (ii) of this section.

(v) *Separate determination of section 382 limitation for recognized built-in losses and net operating losses.*—In determining whether a loss group described in paragraph (c)(1)(i) or (ii) of this section (relating to loss groups that have net operating loss carryovers) has a net unrealized built-in gain which, if recognized, increases the consolidated section 382 limitation, the group includes, under paragraph (g)(2)(i) of this section, all of its members on the day the determination is made. Under paragraph (g)(2)(ii) of this section, however, for purposes of determining whether a group has a net unrealized built-in loss described in paragraph (c)(1)(iii) of this section, not all members of the consolidated group may be included. Thus, a consolidated group may have recognized built-in gains that increase the amount of consolidated taxable income that may be offset by its pre-change net operating loss carryovers that did not arise (and are not treated as arising) in a SRLY, and also may have recognized built-in losses the absorption of which is limited. Similar results may obtain for loss subgroups under paragraphs (g)(2)(iii) and (iv) of this section. See § 1.1502-93(c)(2) for rules prohibiting the use of recognized built-in gains to increase the amount of consolidated taxable income that can be offset by recognized built-in losses.

(3) *Coordination with rule that ends separate tracking.*—See § 1.1502-96(a) for special rules relating to members (or loss subgroups) that have an ownership change within six months before, on, or after becoming a member of the group.

(4) *Acquisitions of built-in gain or loss assets.*—A member of a consolidated group (or loss subgroup) may not, in determining its separately computed net unrealized built-in gain or loss, include any

gain or loss with respect to assets acquired with a principal purpose to affect the amount of its net unrealized built-in gain or loss. A group (or loss subgroup) may not, in determining its net unrealized built-in gain or loss, include any gain or loss of a member acquired with a principal purpose to affect the amount of its net unrealized built-in gain or loss.

(5) *Indirect ownership.*—A member's separately computed net unrealized built-in gain or loss is adjusted to the extent necessary to prevent any duplication of unrealized gain or loss attributable to the member's indirect ownership interest in another member through a nonmember if the member has a 5-percent or greater ownership interest in the nonmember.

(6) *Common parent not common parent for five years.*—If the common parent has become the common parent of an existing group within the previous 5 year period in a transaction described in § 1.1502-75(d)(2)(ii) or (3), appropriate adjustments must be made in applying paragraph (g)(2)(ii)(A) of this section so that corporations that have not been members of the group for five years are not included. In such a case, references to the common parent in paragraph (g)(2)(ii)(A) of this section are to the former common parent. Thus, members of the group remaining in existence (including the new common parent) that have not been affiliated with the former common parent (or that have not been members of that group) for the five consecutive year period ending on the day that the determination is made are not included under paragraph (g)(2)(ii)(A) of this section. See, however, § 1.1502-96(a)(2) for special rules relating to members (or loss subgroups) that have an ownership change within six months before, on, or after the time that the member becomes a member of the group.

(h) *Recognized built-in gain or loss.*—(1) *In general.*—[Reserved].

(2) *Disposition of stock or an intercompany obligation of a member.*—Gain or loss recognized by a member on the disposition of stock (including stock described in section 1504(a)(4) and § 1.382-2T(f)(18)(ii) and (iii)) of another member is treated as a recognized gain or loss for purposes of section 382(h)(2) (unless disallowed) even though gain or loss on such stock was not included in the determination of a net unrealized built-in gain or loss under paragraph (g)(1) of this section. Gain or loss recognized by a member with respect to an intercompany obligation is treated as recognized gain or loss only to the extent (if any) the transaction gives rise to aggregate income or loss within the consolidated group. The first sentence of this paragraph (h)(2) is applicable on or after September 17, 2008.

(3) *Intercompany transactions.*—Gain or loss that is deferred under provisions such as section 267 and § 1.1502-13 is treated as recognized built-in gain or loss only to the extent taken into account by the group during the recognition period. See also § 1.1502-13(c)(7) *Example 10.*

(4) *Exchanged basis property.*—If the adjusted basis of any asset is determined, directly or indirectly, in whole or in part, by reference to the adjusted basis of another asset held by the member a: the beginning of the recognition period, the asset is treated, with appropriate adjustments, as held by the member at the beginning of the recognition period.

(i) [Reserved]

(j) *Predecessor and successor corporations.*—A reference in this section and §§ 1.1502-92 through 1.1502-99 to a corporation, member, common parent, loss subgroup parent, or subsidiary includes, as the context may require, a reference to a predecessor or successor corporation as defined in § 1.1502-1(f)(4). For example, the determination whether a successor satisfies the continuous affiliation requirement of paragraph (d)(2)(i) or (g)(2)(ii) of this section is made by reference to its predecessor. [Reg. § 1.1502-91.]

☐ [T.D. 8824, 6-25-99. *Amended by T.D. 9048, 3-11-2003 T.D. 9187,* 3-2-2005; *T.D. 9254, 3-9-2006, T.D. 9424, 9-9-2008 and T.D. 9905,* 9-3-2020.]

### [Reg. § 1.1502-91A]

**§ 1.1502-91A. Application of section 382 with respect to a consolidated group generally applicable for testing dates before June 25, 1999.**—(a) *Determination and effect of an ownership change.*—(1) *In general.*—This section and §§ 1.1502-92A and 1.1502-93A set forth the rules for determining an ownership change under section 382 for members of consolidated groups and the section 382 limitations with respect to attributes described in paragraphs (e) and (f) of this section. These rules generally provide that an ownership change and the section 382 limitation are determined with respect to these attributes for the group (or loss subgroup) on a single entity basis and not for its members separately. Following an ownership change of a loss group (or a loss subgroup) under § 1.1502-92A, the amount of consolidated taxable income for any post-change year which may be offset by pre-change consolidated attributes (or pre-change subgroup attributes) shall not exceed the consolidated section 382 limitation (or subgroup section 382 limitation) for such year as determined under §1.1502-93A.

(2) *Special rule for post-change year that includes the change date.*—If the post-change year includes the change date, section 382(b)(3)(A) is applied so that the consolidated section 382 limitation (or subgroup section 382 limitation) does not apply to the portion of consolidated taxable income that is allocable to the period in the year on or before the change date. See generally §1.382-6 (relating to the allocation of income and loss). The allocation of consolidated taxable income for the post-change year that includes the change date must be made before taking into account any consolidated net operating loss deduction (as defined in §1.1502-21(a) or 1.1502-21T(a) in effect prior to June 25, 1999, as contained in 26 CFR part 1 revised April 1, 1999, as applicable).

(3) *Cross reference.*—See §§1.1502-94A and 1.1502-95A for rules that apply section 382 to a corporation that becomes or ceases to be a member of a group or loss subgroup.

(b) *Definitions and nomenclature.*—For purposes of this section and §§1.1502-92A through 1.1502-99A, unless otherwise stated:

(1) The definitions and nomenclature contained in section 382 and the regulations thereunder (including the nomenclature and assumptions relating to the examples in §1.382-2T(b)) and this section and §§1.1502-92A through 1.1502-99A apply; and

(2) In all examples, all groups file consolidated returns, all corporations file their income tax returns on a calendar year basis, the

only 5-percent shareholder of a corporation is a public group, the facts set forth the only owner shifts during the testing period, and each asset of a corporation has a value equal to its adjusted basis.

(c) *Loss group.*—(1) *Defined.*—A loss group is a consolidated group that:

(i) Is entitled to use a net operating loss carryover to the taxable year that did not arise (and is not treated under §1.1502-21T(c) as arising) in a SRLY;

(ii) Has a consolidated net operating loss for the taxable year in which a testing date of the common parent occurs (determined by treating the common parent as a loss corporation); or

(iii) Has a net unrealized built-in loss (determined under paragraph (g) of this section by treating the date on which the determination is made as though it were a change date).

(2) *Coordination with rule that ends separate tracking.*—A consolidated group may be a loss group because a member's losses that arose in (or are treated as arising in) a SRLY are treated as described in paragraph (c)(1)(i) of this section. See §1.1502-96A(a).

(3) *Example.*—The following example illustrates the principles of this paragraph (c).

*Example. Loss group.* (a) L and L1 file separate returns and each has a net operating loss carryover arising in Year 1 that is carried over to Year 2. A owns 40 shares and L owns 60 shares of the 100 outstanding shares of L1 stock. At the close of Year 1, L buys the 40 shares of L1 stock from A. For Year 2, L and L1 file a consolidated return. The following is a graphic illustration of these facts:

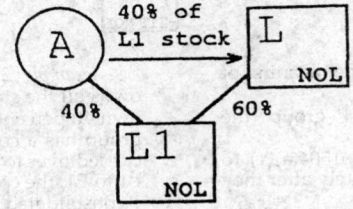

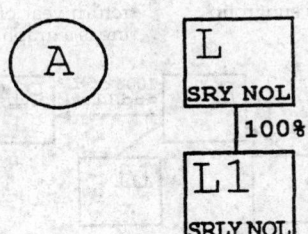

(b) L and L1 become a loss group at the beginning of Year 2 because the group is entitled to use the Year 1 net operating loss carryover of L, the common parent, which did not arise (and is not treated under §1.1502-21(c) or 1.1502-21T(c) in effect prior to June 25, 1999, as contained in 26 CFR part 1 revised April 1, 1999, as applicable as arising) in a SRLY. See §1.1502-94A for rules relating to the application of section 382 with respect to L1's net operating loss carryover from Year 1 which did arise in a SRLY.

(d) *Loss subgroup.*—(1) *Net operating loss carryovers.*—Two or more corporations that become members of a consolidated group (the current group) compose a loss subgroup if:

(i) They were affiliated with each other in another group (the former group), whether or not the group was a consolidated group;

(ii) They bear the relationship described in section 1504(a)(1) to each other through a loss subgroup parent immediately after they become members of the current group; and

(iii) At least one of the members carries over a net operating loss that did not arise (and is not treated under §1.1502-21(c) or 1.1502-21T(c) in effect prior to June 25, 1999, as contained in 26 CFR part 1 revised April 1, 1999, as applicable as arising) in a SRLY with respect to the former group.

(2) *Net unrealized built-in loss.*—Two or more corporations that become members of a consolidated group compose a loss subgroup if they:

(i) Have been continuously affiliated with each other for the 5 consecutive year period ending immediately before they become members of the group;

(ii) Bear the relationship described in section 1504(a)(1) to each other through a loss subgroup parent immediately after they become members of the current group; and

(iii) Have a net unrealized built-in loss (determined under paragraph (g) of this section on the day they become members of the group by treating that day as though it were a change date).

(3) *Loss subgroup parent.*—A loss subgroup parent is the corporation that bears the same relationship to the other members of the loss subgroup as a common parent bears to the members of a group.

(4) *Principal purpose of avoiding a limitation.*—The corporations described in paragraph (d)(1) or (2) of this section do not compose a loss subgroup if any one of them is formed, acquired, or availed of with a principal purpose of avoiding the application of, or increasing any limitation under, section 382. Instead, §1.1502-94A applies with respect to the attributes of each such corporation. This paragraph (d)(4) does not apply solely because, in connection with becoming members of the group, the members of a group (or loss subgroup) are rearranged to bear a relationship to the other members described in section 1504(a)(1).

(5) *Special rules.*—See §1.1502-95A(d) for rules concerning when a corporation ceases to be a member of a loss subgroup. See also §1.1502-96A(a) for a special rule regarding the end of separate track-

Reg. §1.1502-91A(d)(5)

ing of SRLY losses of a member that has an ownership change or that has been a member of a group for at least 5 consecutive years.

(6) *Examples.*—The following examples illustrate the principles of this paragraph (d).

*Example 1. Loss subgroup.* (a) P owns all the L stock and L owns all the L1 stock. The P group has a consolidated net operating loss

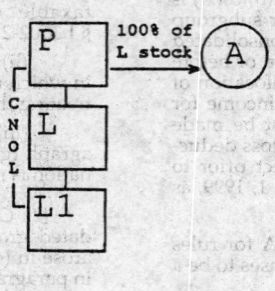

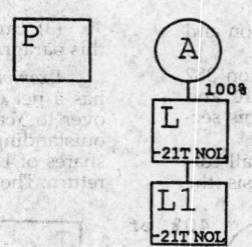

(b) (1) L and L1 compose a loss subgroup within the meaning of paragraph (d)(1) of this section because—

(i) They were affiliated with each other in the P group (the former group);

(ii) They bear a relationship described in section 1504(a)(1) to each other through a loss subgroup parent (L) immediately after they became members of the L group; and

(iii) At least one of the members (here, both L and L1) carries over a net operating loss to the L group (the current group) that did not arise in a SRLY with respect to the P group.

(2) Under paragraph (d)(3) of this section, L is the loss subgroup parent of the L loss subgroup.

arising in Year 1 that is carried to Year 2. On May 2, Year 2, P sells all the stock of L to A, and L and L1 thereafter file consolidated returns. A portion of the Year 1 consolidated net operating loss is apportioned under § 1.1502-21(b) or 1.1502-21T(b) in effect prior to June 25, 1999, as contained in 26 CFR part 1 revised April 1, 1999, as applicable to each of L and L1, which they carry over to Year 2. The following is a graphic illustration of these facts:

*Example 2. Loss subgroup—section 1504(a)(1) relationship.* (a) P owns all the stock of L and L1. L owns all the stock of L2. L1 and L2 own 40 percent and 60 percent of the stock of L3, respectively. The P group has a consolidated net operating loss arising in Year 1 that is carried over to Year 2. On May 22, Year 2, P sells all the stock of L and L1 to P1, the common parent of another consolidated group. The Year 1 consolidated net operating loss is apportioned under § 1.1502-21(b) or 1.1502-21T(b) in effect prior to June 25, 1999, as contained in 26 CFR part 1 revised April 1, 1999, as applicable, and each of L, L1, L2, and L3 carries over a portion of such loss to the first consolidated return year of the P1 group ending after the acquisition. The following is a graphic illustration of these facts:

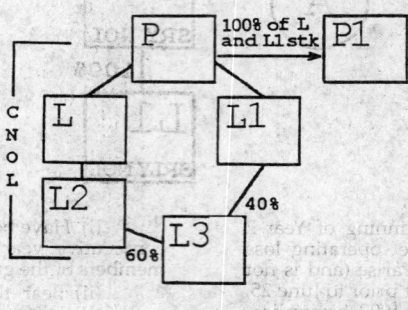

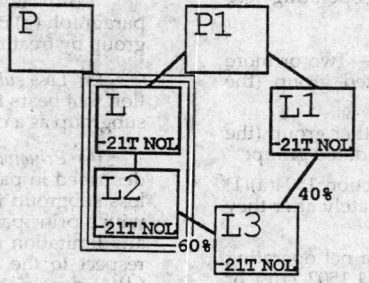

(b) L and L2 compose a loss subgroup within the meaning of paragraph (d)(1) of this section. Neither L1 nor L3 is included in a loss subgroup because neither bears a relationship described in section 1504(a)(1) through a loss subgroup parent to any other member of the former group immediately after becoming members of the P1 group.

*Example 3. Loss subgroup—section 1504(a)(1) relationship.* The facts are the same as in *Example 2*, except that the stock of L1 is transferred to L in connection with the sale of the L stock to P1. L, L1, L2, and L3 compose a loss subgroup within the meaning of paragraph (d)(1) of this section because—

(1) They were affiliated with each other in the P group (the former group);

(2) They bear a relationship described in section 1504(a)(1) to each other through a loss subgroup parent (L) immediately after they become members of the P1 group; and

(3) At least one of the members (here, each of L, L1, L2, and L3) carries over to the P1 group (the current group) a net operating loss that did not arise in a SRLY with respect to the P group (the former group).

(e) *Pre-change consolidated attribute.*—(1) *Defined.*—A pre-change consolidated attribute of a loss group is—

(i) Any loss described in paragraph (c)(1)(i) or (ii) of this section (relating to the definition of loss group) that is allocable to the period ending on or before the change date; and

(ii) Any recognized built-in loss of the loss group.

(2) *Example.*—The following example illustrates the principle of this paragraph (e).

*Example. Pre-change consolidated attribute.* (a) The L group has a consolidated net operating loss arising in Year 1 that is carried over to Year 2. The L loss group has an ownership change at the beginning of Year 2.

(b) The net operating loss carryover of the L loss group from Year 1 is a pre-change consolidated attribute because the L group was entitled to use the loss in Year 2, the loss did not arise in a SRLY with respect to the L group, and therefore the loss was described in paragraph (c)(1)(i) of this section. Under paragraph (a) of this section, the amount of consolidated taxable income of the L group for Year 2 that may be offset by this loss carryover may not exceed the consolidated section 382 limitation of the L group for that year. See § 1.1502-93A for rules relating to the computation of the consolidated section 382 limitation.

(f) *Pre-change subgroup attribute.*—(1) *Defined.*—A pre-change subgroup attribute of a loss subgroup is—

(i) Any net operating loss carryover described in paragraph (d)(1)(iii) of this section (relating to the definition of loss subgroup); and

(ii) Any recognized built-in loss of the loss subgroup.

(2) *Example.*—The following example illustrates the principle of this paragraph (f).

*Example. Pre-change subgroup attribute.* (a) P is the common parent of a consolidated group. P owns all the stock of L, and L owns all the stock of L1. L2 is not a member of an affiliated group, and has a net operating loss arising in Year 1 that is carried over to Year 2. On December 11, Year 2, L1 acquires all the stock of L2, causing an ownership change of L2. During Year 2, the P group has a consolidated net operating loss that is carried over to Year 3. On November 2, Year 3, M acquires all the L stock from P. M, L, L1, and L2 thereafter file consolidated returns. All of the P group Year 2 consolidated net operating loss is apportioned under § 1.1502-21(b) or 1.1502-21T(b) in effect prior to June 25, 1999, as contained in 26 CFR part 1 revised April 1, 1999, as applicable to L and L2, which they carry over to the M group.

(b)(1) L, L1, and L2 compose a loss subgroup because—

(i) They were affiliated with each other in the P group (the former group);

(ii) They bore a relationship described in section 1504(a)(1) to each other through a loss subgroup parent (L) immediately after they became members of the L group; and

(iii) At least one of the members (here, both L and L2) carries over a net operating loss to the M group (the current group) that is described in paragraph (d)(1)(iii) of this section.

(2) For this purpose, L2's loss from Year 1 that was a SRLY loss with respect to the P group (the former group) is treated as described in paragraph (d)(1)(iii) of this section because of the application of the principles of § 1.1502-96A(a). See paragraph (d)(5) of this section. M's acquisition results in an ownership change of L, and therefore the L loss subgroup under § 1.1502-92A(a)(2). See § 1.1502-93A for rules governing the computation of the subgroup section 382 limitation.

(c) In the M group, L2's Year 1 loss continues to be subject to a section 382 limitation resulting from the ownership change that occurred on December 11, Year 2. See § 1.1502-96A(c).

(g) *Net unrealized built-in gain and loss.*—(1) *In general.*—The determination whether a consolidated group (or loss subgroup) has a net unrealized built-in gain or loss under section 382(h)(3) is based on the aggregate amount of the separately computed net unrealized built-in gains or losses of each member that is included in the group (or loss subgroup) under paragraph (g)(2) of this section, including items of built-in income and deduction described in section 382(h)(6). Thus, for example, amounts deferred under section 267, or under

§ 1.1502-13 (other than amounts deferred with respect to the stock of a member (or an intercompany obligation) included in the group (or loss subgroup) under paragraph (g)(2) of this section) are built-in items. The threshold requirement under section 382(h)(3)(B) applies on an aggregate basis and not on a member-by-member basis. The separately computed amount of a member included in a group or loss subgroup does not include any unrealized built-in gain or loss on stock (including stock described in section 1504(a)(4) and § 1.382-2T(f)(18)(ii) and (iii)) of another member included in the group or loss subgroup (or on an intercompany obligation). However, a member of a group or loss subgroup includes in its separately computed amount the unrealized built-in gain or loss on stock of another member (or on an intercompany obligation) not included in the group or loss subgroup. If a member is not included in a group (or loss subgroup) under paragraph (g)(2) of this section, the determination of whether the member has a net unrealized built-in gain or loss under section 382(h)(3) is made on a separate entity basis. See § 1.1502-94A(c) (relating to built-in gain or loss of a new loss member) and § 1.1502-96A(a) (relating to the end of separate tracking of certain losses).

(2) *Members included.*—(i) *Consolidated group.*—The members included in the determination whether a consolidated group has a net unrealized built-in gain or loss are all members of the group on the day that the determination is made other than—

(A) A new loss member with a net unrealized built-in loss described in § 1.1502-94A(a)(1)(ii); and

(B) Members included in a loss subgroup described in § 1.1502-91A(d)(2).

(ii) *Loss subgroup.*—The members included in the determination whether a loss subgroup has a net unrealized built-in gain or loss are those members described in paragraphs (d)(2)(i) and (ii) of this section.

(3) *Acquisitions of built-in gain or loss assets.*—A member of a consolidated group (or loss subgroup) may not, in determining its separately computed net unrealized built-in gain or loss, include any gain or loss with respect to assets acquired with a principal purpose to affect the amount of its net unrealized built-in gain or loss. A group (or loss subgroup) may not, in determining its net unrealized built-in gain or loss, include any gain or loss of a member acquired with a principal purpose to affect the amount of its net unrealized built-in gain or loss.

(4) *Indirect ownership.*—A member's separately computed net unrealized built-in gain or loss is adjusted to the extent necessary to prevent any duplication of unrealized gain or loss attributable to the member's indirect ownership interest in another member through a nonmember if the member has a 5-percent or greater ownership interest in the nonmember.

(h) *Recognized built-in gain or loss.*—(1) *In general.*—[Reserved]

(2) *Disposition of stock or an intercompany obligation of a member.*— Gain or loss recognized by a member on the disposition of stock (including stock described in section 1504(a)(4) and § 1.382-2T(f)(18)(ii) and (iii)) of another member (or an intercompany obligation disposed of before June 25, 1999) is treated as a recognized built-in gain or loss under section 382(h)(2) (unless disallowed under § 1.1502-20 or otherwise), even though gain or loss on such stock or obligation was not included in the determination of a net unrealized built-in gain or loss under paragraph (g)(1) of this section.

(3) *Deferred gain or loss.*—Gain or loss that is deferred under provisions such as section 267 and § 1.1502-13 is treated as recognized built-in gain or loss only to the extent taken into account by the group during the recognition period.

(4) *Exchanged basis property.*—If the adjusted basis of any asset is determined, directly or indirectly, in whole or in part, by reference to the adjusted basis of another asset held by the member at the beginning of the recognition period, the asset is treated, with appropriate adjustments, as held by the member at the beginning of the recognition period.

(i) [Reserved]

(j) *Predecessor and successor corporations.*—A reference in this section and §§ 1.1502-92A through 1.1502-99A to a corporation, member, common parent, loss subgroup parent, or subsidiary includes, as the context may require, a reference to a predecessor or successor corporation. For example, the determination whether a successor satisfies the continuous affiliation requirement of paragraph (d)(2)(i) of this section is made by reference to its predecessor. [Reg. § 1.1502-91A.]

□ [*T.D. 8678, 6-26-96. Amended by T.D. 8823, 6-25-99 and amended and redesignated by T.D. 8824, 6-25-99.*]

[Reg. §1.1502-92]

**§1.1502-92. Ownership change of a loss group or a loss subgroup.**—(a) *Scope.*—This section provides rules for determining if there is an ownership change for purposes of section 382 with respect to a loss group or a loss subgroup. See §1.1502-94 for special rules for determining if there is an ownership change with respect to a new loss member and §1.1502-96(b) for special rules for determining if there is an ownership change of a subsidiary.

(b) *Determination of an ownership change.*—(1) *Parent change method.*—(i) *Loss group.*—A loss group has an ownership change if the loss group's common parent has an ownership change under section 382 and the regulations thereunder. Solely for purposes of determining whether the common parent has an ownership change—

(A) The losses described in §1.1502-91(c) are treated as net operating losses (or a net unrealized built-in loss) of the common parent; and

(B) The common parent determines the earliest day that its testing period can begin by reference to only the attributes that make the group a loss group under §1.1502-91(c).

(ii) *Loss subgroup.*—A loss subgroup has an ownership change if the loss subgroup parent has an ownership change under section 382 and the regulations thereunder. The principles of §1.1502-95(b) (relating to ceasing to be a member of a consolidated group) apply in determining whether the loss subgroup parent has an ownership change. Solely for purposes of determining whether the loss subgroup parent has an ownership change—

(A) The losses described in §1.1502-91(d) are treated as net operating losses (or a net unrealized built-in loss) of the loss subgroup parent;

(B) The day that the members of the loss subgroup become members of the group (or a loss subgroup) is treated as a testing date within the meaning of §1.382-2(a)(4); and

(C) The loss subgroup parent determines the earliest day that its testing period can begin under §1.382-2T(d)(3) by reference to only the attributes that make the members a loss subgroup under §1.1502-91(d).

(iii) *Special rule if election regarding section 1504(a)(1) relationship is made.*—(A) *Ownership change of deemed loss subgroup parent is an ownership change of loss subgroup.*—If the common parent makes an election under §1.1502-91(d)(4), each of the members in the loss subgroup is treated as the loss subgroup parent for purposes of determining whether the loss subgroup has an ownership change under section 382 and the regulations thereunder on or after the day the members become members of the group.

(B) *Exception.*—Paragraph (b)(1)(iii)(A) of this section does not apply to cause an ownership change of a loss subgroup if a deemed loss subgroup parent has an ownership change upon (or after) ceasing to be a member of the current group.

(2) *Examples.*—The following examples illustrate the principles of this paragraph (b):

*Example 1. Loss group—ownership change of the common parent.* (i) A owns all the L stock. L owns 80 percent and B owns 20 percent of the L1 stock. For Year 1, the L group has a consolidated net operating loss that resulted from the operations of L1 and that is carried over to Year 2. The value of the L stock is $1000. The total value of the L1 stock is $600 and the value of the L1 stock held by B is $120. The L group is a loss group under §1.1502-91(c)(1) because it is entitled to use its net operating loss carryover from Year 1. On August 15, Year 2, A sells 51 percent of the L stock to C. The following is a graphic illustration of these facts:

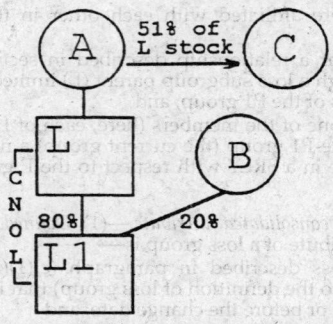

(ii) Under paragraph (b)(1)(i) of this section, section 382 and the regulations thereunder are applied to L to determine whether it (and therefore the L loss group) has an ownership change with respect to its net operating loss carryover from Year 1 attributable to L1 on August 15, Year 2. The sale of the L stock to C causes an ownership change of L under §1.382-2T and of the L loss group under paragraph (b)(1)(i) of this section. The amount of consolidated taxable income of the L loss group for any post-change taxable year that may be offset by its pre-change consolidated attributes (that is, the net operating loss carryover from Year 1 attributable to L1) may not exceed the consolidated section 382 limitation for the L loss group for the taxable year.

*Example 2. Loss group—owner shifts of subsidiaries disregarded.* (i) The facts are the same as in *Example 1,* except that on August 15, Year 2, A sells only 49 percent of the L stock to C and, on December 12, Year 3, in an unrelated transaction, B sells the 20 percent of the L1 stock to D. A's sale of the L stock to C does not cause an ownership change of L under §1.382-2T nor of the L loss group under paragraph (b)(1)(i) of this section. The following is a graphic illustration of these facts:

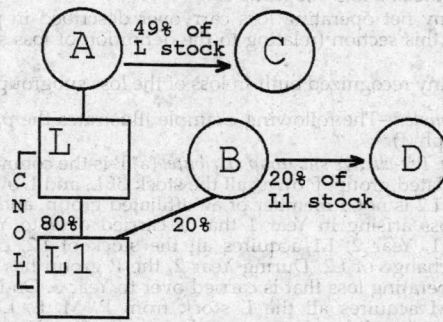

(ii) B's subsequent sale of L1 stock is not taken into account for purposes of determining whether the L loss group has an ownership change under paragraph (b)(1)(i) of this section, and, accordingly, there is no ownership change of the L loss group. See paragraph (c) of this section, however, for a supplemental ownership change method that would apply to cause an ownership change if the purchases by C and D were pursuant to a plan or arrangement and certain other conditions are satisfied.

*Example 3. Loss subgroup—ownership change of loss subgroup parent controls.* (i) P owns all the L stock. L owns 80 percent and A owns 20 percent of the L1 stock. The P group has a consolidated net operating loss arising in Year 1 that is carried over to Year 2. On September 9, Year 2, P sells 51 percent of the L stock to B, and L1 is apportioned a portion of the Year 1 consolidated net operating loss under §1.1502-21(b), which it carries over to its next taxable year. L and L1 file a consolidated return for their first taxable year ending after the sale to B. The following is a graphic illustration of these facts:

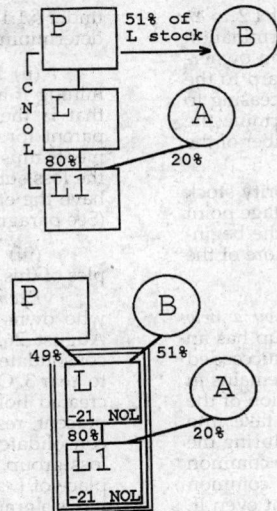

(ii) Under § 1.1502-91(d)(1), L and L1 compose a loss subgroup on September 9, Year 2, the day that they become members of the L group. Under paragraph (b)(1)(ii) of this section, section 382 and the regulations thereunder are applied to L to determine whether it (and therefore the L loss subgroup) has an ownership change with respect to the portion of the Year 1 consolidated net operating loss that is apportioned to L1 on September 9, Year 2. L has an ownership change resulting from P's sale of 51 percent of the L stock to A. Therefore, the L loss subgroup has an ownership change with respect to that loss.

*Example 4. Loss group and loss subgroup—contemporaneous ownership changes.* (i) A owns all the stock of corporation M, M owns 35 percent and B owns 65 percent of the L stock, and L owns all the L1 stock. The L group has a consolidated net operating loss arising in Year 1 that is carried over to Year 2. On May 19, Year 2, B sells 45 percent of the L stock to M for cash. M, L, and L1 thereafter file consolidated returns. L and L1 are each apportioned a portion of the Year 1 consolidated net operating loss, which they carry over to the M group's Year 2 and Year 3 consolidated return years. The M group has a consolidated net operating loss arising in Year 2 that is carried over to Year 3. On June 9, Year 3, A sells 70 percent of the M stock to C. The following is a graphic illustration of these facts:

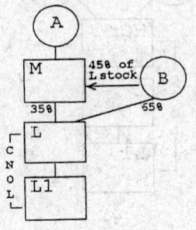

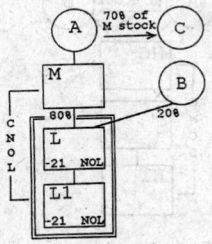

(ii) Under § 1.1502-91(d)(1), L and L1 compose a loss subgroup on May 19, Year 2, the day they become members of the M group. Under paragraph (b)(1)(ii) of this section, section 382 and the regulations thereunder are applied to L to determine whether L (and therefore the L loss subgroup) has an ownership change with respect to the loss carryovers from Year 1 on May 19, Year 2, a testing date because of B's sale of L stock to M. The sale of L stock to M results in only a 45 percentage point increase in A's ownership of L stock. Thus, there is no ownership change of L (or the L loss subgroup) with respect to those loss carryovers under paragraph (b)(1)(ii) of this section on that day.

(iii) June 9, Year 3, is also a testing date with respect to the L loss subgroup because of A's sale of M stock to C. The sale results in a 56 percentage point increase in C's ownership of L stock, and L has an ownership change. Therefore, the L loss subgroup has an ownership change on that day with respect to the loss carryovers from Year 1.

(iv) Paragraph (b)(1)(i) of this section requires that section 382 and the regulations thereunder be applied to M to determine whether M (and therefore the M loss group) has an ownership change with respect to the net operating loss carryover from Year 2 on June 9, Year 3, a testing date because of A's sale of M stock to C.

The sale results in a 70 percentage point increase in C's ownership of M stock, and M has an ownership change. Therefore, the M loss group has an ownership change on that day with respect to that loss carryover.

*Example 5—Deemed subgroup parent.* (i) P owns all the stock of L and L1 and 80 percent of the stock of T. A owns the remaining 20 percent of the stock of T. L1 owns all the stock of L2. P1, which owns 60 percent of the stock of P, acquires, at the beginning of Year 2, the T, L, and L1 stock owned by P, and T, L, L1, and L2 become members of the P1 group. The P group has a consolidated net operating loss arising in Year 1 that is carried over to Year 2. L, L1, and L2 are each apportioned a portion of the Year 1 consolidated net operating loss under § 1.1502-21(b), which they carry over to the P1 group's Year 2 and Year 3 consolidated return years. P1 makes the election described in § 1.1502-91(d)(4) to treat T, L, L1 and L2 as meeting the section 1504(a)(1) requirement of § 1.1502-91(d)(1)(ii). As a result of the election, T, L, L1 and L2 compose a loss subgroup and T, L, L1, and L2 are each treated as the loss subgroup parent for purposes of this paragraph (b). Because of P1's indirect ownership of T, L, L1, and L2 prior to Pi's acquisition of the T, L, and L1 stock, P1's acquisition does not cause an ownership change of the loss subgroup.

(ii) On February 2, Year 3, L1 sells all of the stock of L2 to B. Although L2 is treated as a loss subgroup parent, the determination whether the loss subgroup comprised of T, L, and L1 has an ownership change under this paragraph (b) is made without regard to the sale of L2 because L2's ownership change occurred upon ceasing to be a member of the P1 group. See § 1.1502-95(b) to determine the application of section 382 to L2 when L2 ceases to be a member of the P1 group and the T, L, L1 and L2 loss subgroup.

(iii) On March 26, Year 3, A sells her 20 percent minority stock interest in T to C. C's purchase, together with the 32 percentage point owner shift effected by P1's acquisition of the T stock at the beginning of Year 2, causes an ownership change of T, and therefore of the loss subgroup comprised of T, L, and L1.

(3) *Special adjustments.*—(i) *Common parent succeeded by a new common parent.*—For purposes of determining if a loss group has an ownership change, if the common parent of a loss group is succeeded or acquired by a new common parent and the loss group remains in existence, the new common parent is treated as a continuation of the former common parent with appropriate adjustments to take into account shifts in ownership of the former common parent during the testing period (including shifts that occur incident to the common parent's becoming the former common parent). A new common parent may be a continuation of the former common parent even if,

under § 1.1502-91(g)(2)(ii), the new common parent is not included in determining whether the group has a net unrealized built-in loss.

(ii) *Newly created loss subgroup parent.*—For purposes of determining if a loss subgroup has an ownership change, if the member that is the loss subgroup parent has not been the loss subgroup parent for at least 3 years as of a testing date, appropriate adjustments must be made to take into account owner shifts of members of the loss subgroup so that the structure of the loss subgroup does not have the effect of avoiding an ownership change under section 382. (See paragraph (b)(3)(iii), *Example 3* of this section.)

(iii) *Examples.*—The following examples illustrate the principles of this paragraph (b)(3):

*Example 1. New common parent acquires old common parent.* (i) A, who owns all the L stock, sells 30 percent of the L stock to B on August 26, Year 1. L owns all the L1 stock. The L group has a consolidated net operating loss arising in Year 1 that is carried over to Year 3. On July 16, Year 2, A and B transfer their L stock to a newly created holding company, HC, in exchange for 70 percent and 30 percent, respectively, of the HC stock. HC, L, and L1 thereafter file consolidated returns. Under the principles of § 1.1502-75(d), the L loss group is treated as remaining in existence, with HC taking the place of L as the new common parent of the loss group. The following is a graphic illustration of these facts:

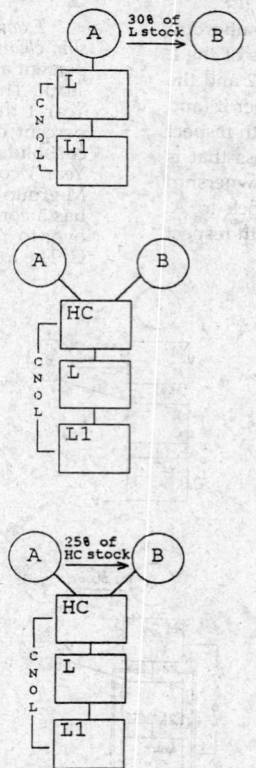

(ii) On November 11, Year 3, A sells 25 percent of the HC stock to B. For purposes of determining if the L loss group has an ownership change under paragraph (b)(1)(i) of this section on November 11, Year 3, HC is treated as a continuation of L under paragraph (b)(4)(i) of this section because it acquired L and became the common parent without terminating the L loss group. Accordingly, HC's testing period commences on January 1, Year 1, the first day of the taxable year of the L loss group in which the consolidated net operating loss that is carried over to Year 3 arose (see § 1.382-2T(d)(3)(i)). Immediately after the close of November 11, Year 3, B's percentage ownership interest in the common parent of the loss group (HC) has increased by 55 percentage points over its lowest percentage ownership during the testing period (zero percent). Ac

cordingly, HC and the L loss group have an ownership change on that day.

*Example 2. New common parent in case in which common parent ceases to exist.* (i) A, B, and C each own one-third of the L stock. L owns all the L1 stock. The L group has a consolidated net operating loss arising in Year 2 that is carried over to Year 3. On November 22, Year 3, L is merged into P, a corporation owned by D, and L1 thereafter files consolidated returns with P. A, B, and C, as a result of owning stock of L, own 90 percent of P's stock after the merger. D owns the remaining 10 percent of P's stock. The merger of L into P qualifies as a reverse acquisition of the L group under § 1.1502-75(d)(3)(i), and the L loss group is treated as remaining in existence, with P taking the place of L as the new common parent of the L group. The following is a graphic illustration of these facts:

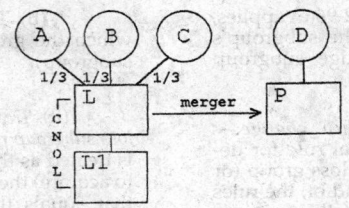

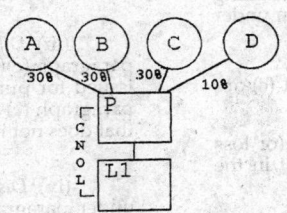

(ii) For purposes of determining if the L loss group has an ownership change on November 22, Year 3, the day of the merger, P is treated as a continuation of L so that the testing period for P begins on January 1, Year 2, the first day of the taxable year of the L loss group in which the consolidated net operating loss that is carried over to Year 3 arose. Immediately after the close of November 22, Year 3, D is the only 5-percent shareholder that has increased his ownership interest in P during the testing period (from zero to 10 percentage points).

(iii) The facts are the same as in paragraph (i) of this *Example 2*, except that A has held 23 $^1/_3$ shares (23 $^1/_3$ percent) of L's stock for five years, and A purchased an additional 10 shares of L stock from E two years before the merger. Immediately after the close of the day of the merger (a testing date), A's ownership interest in P, the common parent of the L loss group, has increased by 6 $^2/_3$ percentage points over A's lowest percentage ownership during the testing period (23 $^1/_3$ percent to 30 percent).

(iv) The facts are the same as in (i) of this *Example 2*, except that P has a net operating loss arising in Year 1 that is carried to the first consolidated return year ending after the day of the merger.

Solely for purposes of determining whether the L loss group has an ownership change under paragraph (b)(1)(i) of this section, the testing period for P commences on January 1, Year 2. P does not determine the earliest day for its testing period by reference to its net operating loss carryover from Year 1, which §§ 1.1502-1(f)(3) and 1.1502-75(d)(3)(i) treat as arising in a SRLY. See § 1.1502-94 to determine the application of section 382 with respect to P's net operating loss carryover.

*Example 3. Newly acquired loss subgroup parent.* (i) P owns all the L stock and L owns all the L1 stock. The P group has a consolidated net operating loss arising in Year 1 that is carried over to Year 3. On January 19, Year 2, L issues a 20 percent stock interest to B. On February 5, Year 3, P contributes its L stock to a newly formed subsidiary, HC, in exchange for all the HC stock, and distributes the HC stock to its sole shareholder A. HC, L, and L1 thereafter file consolidated returns. A portion of the P group's Year 1 consolidated net operating loss is apportioned to L and L1 under § 1.1502-21(b) and is carried over to the HC group's year ending after February 5, Year 3. HC, L, and L1 compose a loss subgroup within the meaning of § 1.1502-91(d) with respect to the net operating loss carryovers from Year 1. The following is a graphic illustration of these facts:

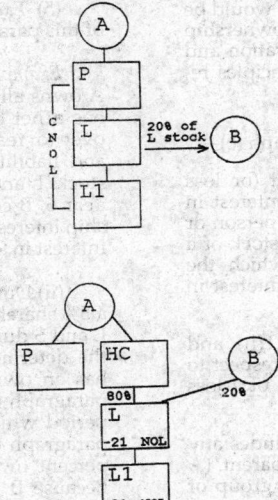

(ii) February 5, Year 3, is a testing date for HC as the loss subgroup parent with respect to the net operating loss carryovers of L and L1 from Year 1. See paragraph (b)(1)(ii)(B) of this section. For purposes of determining whether HC has an ownership change on the testing date, appropriate adjustments must be made with respect to the changes in the percentage ownership of the stock of HC because HC was not the loss subgroup parent for at least 3 years prior to the day on which it became a member of the HC loss subgroup (a testing date). The appropriate adjustments include adjustments so that HC succeeds to the owner shifts of other members of the former group. Thus, HC succeeds to the owner shift of L that resulted from the sale of the 20 percent interest to B in determining

whether the HC loss subgroup has an ownership change on February 5, Year 3, and on any subsequent testing date that includes January 19, Year 2.

(4) *End of separate tracking of certain losses.*—If § 1.1502-96(a) (relating to the end of separate tracking of attributes) applies to a loss subgroup, then, while one or more members that were included in the loss subgroup remain members of the consolidated group, there is an ownership change with respect to their attributes described in § 1.1502-96(a)(2) only if the consolidated group is a loss group and has an ownership change under paragraph (b)(1)(i) of this section (or such a member has an ownership change under § 1.1502-96(b) (relating to ownership changes of subsidiaries)). If, however, the loss

subgroup has had an ownership change before § 1.1502-96(a) applies, see § 1.1502-96(c) for the continuing application of the subgroup's section 382 limitation with respect to its pre-change subgroup attributes.

(c) *Supplemental rules for determining ownership change.*— (1) *Scope.*—This paragraph (c) contains a supplemental rule for determining whether there is an ownership change of a loss group (or loss subgroup). It applies in addition to, and not instead of, the rules of paragraph (b) of this section. Thus, for example, if the common parent of the loss group has an ownership change under paragraph (b) of this section, the loss group has an ownership change even if, by applying this paragraph (c), the common parent would not have an ownership change. This paragraph (c) does not apply in determining an ownership change of a loss subgroup for which an election under § 1.1502-91(d)(4) is made.

(2) *Cause for applying supplemental rule.*—This paragraph (c) applies to a loss group (or loss subgroup) if—

(i) Any 5-percent shareholder of the common parent (or loss subgroup parent) increases its percentage ownership interest in the stock of both—

(A) A subsidiary of the loss group (or loss subgroup) other than by a direct or indirect acquisition of stock of the common parent (or loss subgroup parent); and

(B) The common parent (or loss subgroup parent);

(ii) Those increases occur within a 3 year period ending on any day of a consolidated return year or, if shorter, the period beginning on the first day following the most recent ownership change of the loss group (or loss subgroup); and

(iii) Either—

(A) The common parent (or loss subgroup parent) has actual knowledge of the increase in the 5-percent shareholder's ownership interest in the stock of the subsidiary (or has actual knowledge of the plan or arrangement described in paragraph (c)(3)(i) of this section) before the date that the group's income tax return is filed for the taxable year that includes the date of that increase; or

(B) At any time during the period described in paragraph (c)(2)(ii) of this section, the 5-percent shareholder of the common parent is also a 5-percent shareholder of the subsidiary (determined without regard to paragraph (c)(3)(i) of this section) whose percentage increase in the ownership of the stock of the subsidiary would be taken into account in determining if the subsidiary has an ownership change (determined as if the subsidiary was a loss corporation and applying the principles of § 1.382-2T(k), including the principles relating to duty to inquire).

(3) *Operating rules.*—Solely for purposes of this paragraph (c)—

(i) A 5-percent shareholder of the common parent (or loss subgroup, parent) is treated as increasing its ownership interest in the stock of a subsidiary to the extent, if any, that another person or persons increases its percentage ownership interest in the stock of a subsidiary pursuant to a plan or arrangement under which the 5-percent shareholder increases its percentage ownership interest in the common parent (or loss subgroup parent);

(ii) The rules in section 382(l)(3) and § § 1.382-2T(h) and 1.382-4(d) (relating to constructive ownership) apply with respect to the stock of the subsidiary by treating such stock as stock of a loss corporation; and

(iii) In the case of a loss subgroup, a subsidiary includes any member of the loss subgroup other than the loss subgroup parent. (A loss subgroup parent is, however, a subsidiary of the loss group of which it is a member.)

(4) *Supplemental ownership change rules.*—The determination whether the common parent (or loss subgroup parent) has an ownership change is made by applying paragraph (b)(1) of this section as modified by the following additional rules:

(i) *Additional testing dates for the common parent (or loss subgroup parent).*—A testing date for the common parent (or loss subgroup parent) also includes—

(A) Each day on which there is an increase in the percentage ownership of stock of a subsidiary as described in paragraph (c)(2) of this section; and

(B) The first day of the first consolidated return year for which the group is a loss group (or the members compose a loss subgroup).

(ii) *Treatment of subsidiary stock as stock of the common parent (or loss subgroup parent).*—The common parent (or loss subgroup parent) is treated as though it had issued to the person acquiring (or deemed to acquire) the subsidiary stock an amount of its own stock (by value) that equals the value of the subsidiary stock represented by the percentage increase in that person's ownership of the subsidiary (determined on a separate entity basis). Similar principles apply if the increase in percentage ownership interest is effected by a redemption or similar transaction.

(iii) *Different testing periods.*—Stock treated as issued under paragraph (c)(4)(ii) of this section on a testing date is not treated as so issued for purposes of applying the ownership change rules of this paragraph (c) and paragraph (b) (1) of this section in a testing period that does not include that testing date.

(iv) *Disaffiliation of a subsidiary.*—If a deemed issuance of stock under paragraph (c)(4)(ii) of this section would not cause the loss group (or loss subgroup) to have an ownership change before the day (if any) on which the subsidiary ceases to be a member of the loss group (or subgroup), then paragraph (c)(4) of this section shall not apply.

(v) *Subsidiary stock acquired first.*—If an increase of subsidiary stock described in paragraph (c)(2)(i)(A) of this section occurs before the date that the 5-percent shareholder increases its percentage ownership interest in the stock of the common parent (or loss subgroup parent), then the deemed issuance of stock is treated as occurring on that later date, but in an amount equal to the value of the subsidiary stock on the date it was acquired.

(vi) *Anti-duplication rule.*—If two or more 5-percent shareholders are treated as increasing their percentage ownership interests pursuant to the same plan or arrangement described in paragraph (c)(3)(i) of this section, appropriate adjustments must be made so that the amount of stock treated as issued is not taken into account more than once.

(5) *Examples.*—The following examples illustrate the principles of this paragraph (c):

*Example 1. Stock of the common parent under supplemental rules.* (i) A owns all the L stock. L is not a member of an affiliated group and has a net operating loss carryover arising in Year 1 that is carried over to Year 6. On September 20, Year 6, L transfers all of its assets and liabilities to a newly created subsidiary, S, in exchange for S stock. L and S thereafter file consolidated returns. On November 23, Year 6, B contributes cash to L in exchange for a 45 percent ownership interest in L and contributes cash to S for a 20 percent ownership interest in S.

(ii) During the 3 year period ending on November 23, Year 6, B is a 5% shareholder of L and of S that increases its ownership interest in L and S during that period. Under paragraph (c)(4)(ii) of this section, the determination whether L (the common parent of a loss group) has an ownership change on November 23, Year 6 (or, subject to paragraph (c)(4)(iv) of this section, on any testing date in the testing period which includes November 23, Year 6), is made by applying paragraph (b)(1)(i) of this section and by treating the value of B's 20 percent ownership interest in S as if it were L stock issued to B. Because B is a 5% shareholder of both L and S during the 3 year period ending on November 23, Year 6, and B's increase in its percentage ownership in the stock of S would be taken into account in determining if S (if it were a loss corporation) had an ownership change, it is not relevant whether L has actual knowledge of B's acquisition of S stock.

*Example 2. Plan or arrangement—public offering of subsidiary stock.* (i) A owns all the stock of L and L owns all the stock of L1. The L group has a consolidated net operating loss arising in Year 1 that resulted from the operations of L1 and that is carried over to Year 2. On October 7, Year 2, A sells 49 percent of the L stock to B. As part of a plan that includes the sale of L stock, A causes a public offering of L1 stock on November 6, Year 2. L has actual knowledge of the plan. The following is a graphic illustration of these facts:

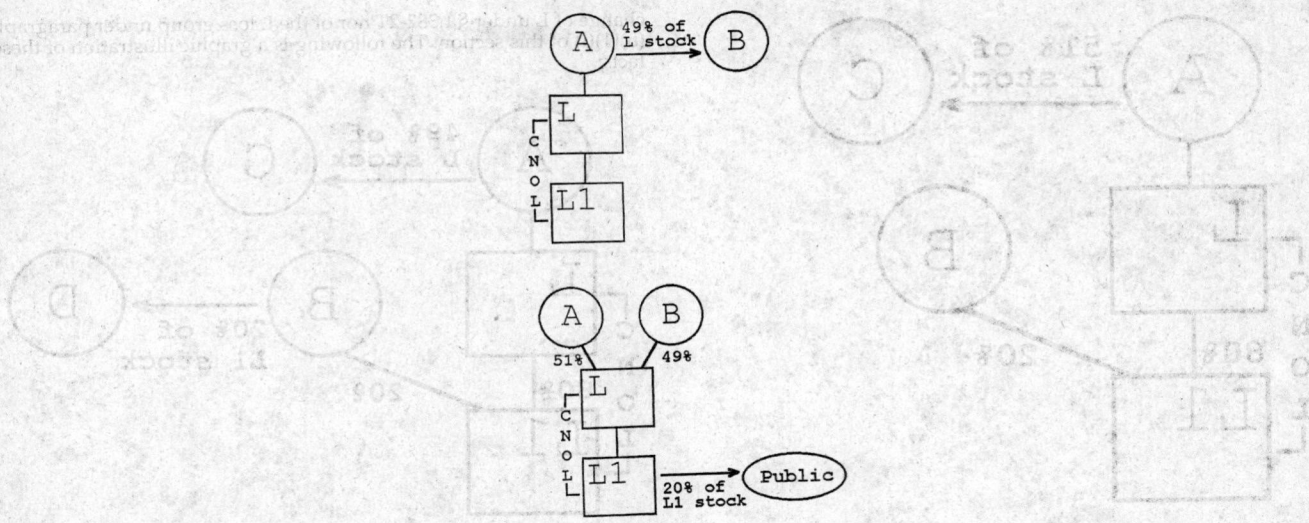

(ii) A's sale of the L stock to B does not cause an ownership change of the L loss group on October 7, Year 2, under the rules of § 1.382-2T and paragraph (b)(1)(i) of this section.

(iii) Because the issuance of L1 stock to the public occurs as part of the same plan as B's acquisition of L stock, and L has knowledge of the plan, paragraph (c)(4) of this section applies to determine whether the L loss group has an ownership change on November 6, Year 2 (or, subject to paragraph (c)(4)(iv) of this section, on any testing date for which the testing period includes November 6, Year 2).

(d) *Testing period following ownership change under this section.*—If a loss group (or a loss subgroup) has had an ownership change under this section, the testing period for determining a subsequent ownership change with respect to pre-change consolidated attributes (or pre-change subgroup attributes) begins no earlier than the first day following the loss group's (or loss subgroup's) most recent change date.

(e) *Information statements.*—(1) *Common parent of a loss group.*—The common parent of a loss group must file the information statement required by § 1.382-11(a) for a consolidated return year because of any owner shift, equity structure shift, or other transaction described in § 1.382-2T(a)(2)(i)—

(i) With respect to the common parent and with respect to any subsidiary stock subject to paragraph (c) of this section; and

(ii) With respect to an ownership change described in § 1.1502-96(b) (relating to ownership changes of subsidiaries).

(2) *Abbreviated statement with respect to loss subgroups.*—The common parent of a consolidated group that has a loss subgroup during a consolidated return year must file the information statement required by § 1.382-11(a) because of any owner shift, equity structure shift, or other transaction described in § 1.382-2T(a)(2)(i) with respect to the loss subgroup parent and with respect to any subsidiary stock subject to paragraph (c) of this section. Instead of filing a separate statement for each loss subgroup parent, the common parent (which is treated as a loss corporation) may file the single statement described in paragraph (e)(1) of this section. In addition to the information concerning stock ownership of the common parent, the single statement must identify each loss subgroup parent and state which loss subgroups, if any, have had ownership changes during the consolidated return year. The loss subgroup parent is, however, still required to maintain the records necessary to determine if the loss subgroup has an ownership change. This paragraph (e)(2) applies with respect to the attributes of a loss subgroup until, under § 1.1502-96(a), the attributes are no longer treated as described in § 1.1502-91(d) (relating to the definition of loss subgroup). After that time, the information statement described in paragraph (e)(1) of this section must be filed with respect to those attributes. [Reg. § 1.1502-92.]

☐ [*T.D. 8824, 6-25-99. Amended by T.D. 9264, 5-26-2006 and T.D. 9329, 6-13-2007.*]

**[Reg. § 1.1502-92A]**

**§ 1.1502-92A. Ownership change of a loss group or a loss subgroup generally applicable for testing dates before June 25, 1999.**— (a) *Scope.*—This section provides rules for determining if there is an ownership change for purposes of section 382 with respect to a loss group or a loss subgroup. See § 1.1502-94A for special rules for determining if there is an ownership change with respect to a new loss member and § 1.1502-96A(b) for special rules for determining if there is an ownership change of a subsidiary.

(b) *Determination of an ownership change.*—(1) *Parent change method.*—(i) *Loss group.*—A loss group has an ownership change if the loss group's common parent has an ownership change under section 382 and the regulations thereunder. Solely for purposes of determining whether the common parent has an ownership change—

(A) The losses described in § 1.1502-91A(c) are treated as net operating losses (or a net unrealized built-in loss) of the common parent; and

(B) The common parent determines the earliest day that its testing period can begin by reference to only the attributes that make the group a loss group under § 1.1502-91A(c).

(ii) *Loss subgroup.*—A loss subgroup has an ownership change if the loss subgroup parent has an ownership change under section 382 and the regulations thereunder. The principles of § 1.1502-95A(b) (relating to ceasing to be a member of a consolidated group) apply in determining whether the loss subgroup parent has an ownership change. Solely for purposes of determining whether the loss subgroup parent has an ownership change—

(A) The losses described in § 1.1502-91A(d) are treated as net operating losses (or a net unrealized built-in loss) of the loss subgroup parent;

(B) The day that the members of the loss subgroup become members of the group (or a loss subgroup) is treated as a testing date within the meaning of § 1.382-2(a)(4); and

(C) The loss subgroup parent determines the earliest day that its testing period can begin under § 1.382-2T(d)(3) by reference to only the attributes that make the members a loss subgroup under § 1.1502-91A(d).

(2) *Examples.*—The following examples illustrate the principles of this paragraph (b).

*Example 1. Loss group—ownership change of the common parent.* (a) A owns all the L stock. L owns 80 percent and B owns 20 percent of the L1 stock. For Year 1, the L group has a consolidated net operating loss that resulted from the operations of L1 and that is carried over to Year 2. The value of the L stock is $1000. The total value of the L1 stock is $600 and the value of the L1 stock held by B is $120. The L group is a loss group under § 1.1502-91A(c)(1) because it is entitled to use its net operating loss carryover from Year 1. On August 15, Year 2, A sells 51 percent of the L stock to C. The following is a graphic illustration of these facts:

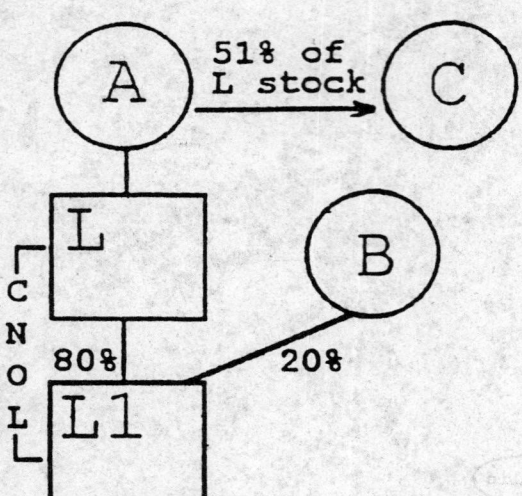

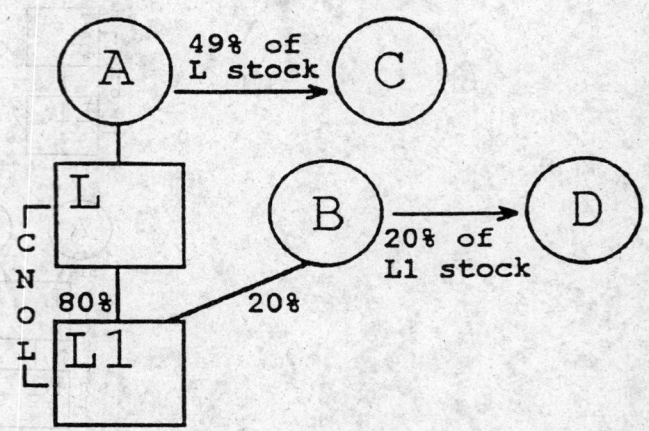

change of L under §1.382-2T nor of the L loss group under paragraph (b)(1)(i) of this section. The following is a graphic illustration of these facts:

(b) Under paragraph (b)(1)(i) of this section, section 382 and the regulations thereunder are applied to L to determine whether it (and therefore the L loss group) has an ownership change with respect to its net operating loss carryover from Year 1 attributable to L1 on August 15, Year 2. The sale of the L stock to C causes an ownership change of L under §1.382-2T and of the L loss group under paragraph (b)(1)(i) of this section. The amount of consolidated taxable income of the L loss group for any post-change taxable year that may be offset by its pre-change consolidated attributes (that is, the net operating loss carryover from Year 1 attributable to L1) may not exceed the consolidated section 382 limitation for the L loss group for the taxable year.

*Example 2. Loss group—owner shifts of subsidiaries disregarded.* (a) The facts are the same as in *Example 1*, except that on August 15, Year 2, A sells only 49 percent of the L stock to C and, on December 12, Year 3, in an unrelated transaction, B sells the 20 percent of the L1 stock to D. A's sale of the L stock to C does not cause an ownership

(b) B's subsequent sale of L1 stock is not taken into account for purposes of determining whether the L loss group has an ownership change under paragraph (b)(1)(i) of this section, and, accordingly, there is no ownership change of the L loss group. See paragraph (c) of this section, however, for a supplemental ownership change method that would apply to cause an ownership change if the purchases by C and D were pursuant to a plan or arrangement.

*Example 3. Loss subgroup—ownership change of loss subgroup parent controls.* (a) P owns all the L stock. L owns 80 percent and A owns 20 percent of the L1 stock. The P group has a consolidated net operating loss arising in Year 1 that is carried over to Year 2. On September 9, Year 2, P sells 51 percent of the L stock to B, and L1 is apportioned a portion of the Year 1 consolidated net operating loss under §1.1502-21(b) or 1.1502-21T(b) in effect prior to June 25, 1999, as contained in 26 CFR part 1 revised April 1, 1999, as applicable, which it carries over to its next taxable year. L and L1 file a consolidated return for their first taxable year ending after the sale to B. The following is a graphic illustration of these facts:

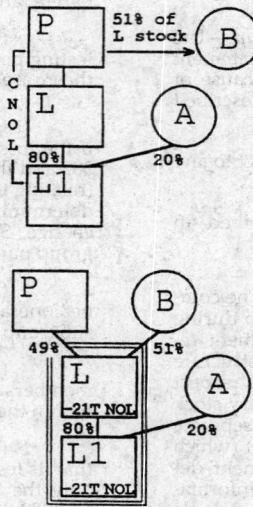

(b) Under §1.1502-91A(d)(1), L and L1 compose a loss subgroup on September 9, Year 2, the day that they become members of the L group. Under paragraph (b)(1)(ii) of this section, section 382 and the regulations thereunder are applied to L to determine whether it (and therefore the L loss subgroup) has an ownership change with respect to the portion of the Year 1 consolidated net operating loss that is apportioned to L1 on September 9, Year 2. L has an ownership change resulting from P's sale of 51 percent of the L stock to A. Therefore, the L loss subgroup has an ownership change with respect to that loss.

*Example 4. Loss group and loss subgroup—contemporaneous ownership changes.* (a) A owns all the stock of corporation M, M owns 35 percent and B owns 65 percent of the L stock, and L owns all the L1 stock. The L group has a consolidated net operating loss arising in Year 1 that is carried over to Year 2. On May 19, Year 2, B sells 45 percent of the L stock to M for cash. M, L, and L1 thereafter file consolidated returns. L and L1 are each apportioned a portion of the Year 1 consolidated net operating loss, which they carry over to the M group's Year 2 and Year 3 consolidated return years. The M group has a consolidated net operating loss arising in Year 2 that is carried over to Year 3. On June 9, Year 3, A sells 70 percent of the M stock to C. The following is a graphic illustration of these facts:

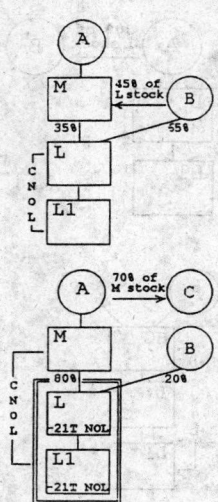

(b) Under §1.1502-91A(d)(1), L and L1 compose a loss subgroup on May 19, Year 2, the day they become members of the M group. Under paragraph (b)(1)(ii) of this section, section 382 and the regulations thereunder are applied to L to determine whether L (and therefore the L loss subgroup) has an ownership change with respect to the loss carryovers from Year 1 on May 19, Year 2, a testing date because of B's sale of L stock to M. The sale of L stock to M results in only a 45 percentage point increase in A's ownership of L stock. Thus, there is no ownership change of L (or the L loss subgroup) with respect to those loss carryovers under paragraph (b)(1)(ii) of this section on that day.

(c) June 9, Year 3, is also a testing date with respect to the L loss subgroup because of A's sale of M stock to C. The sale results in a 56 percentage point increase in C's ownership of L stock, and L has an ownership change. Therefore, the L loss subgroup has an ownership change on that day with respect to the loss carryovers from Year 1.

(d) Paragraph (b)(1)(i) of this section requires that section 382 and the regulations thereunder be applied to M to determine whether M (and therefore the M loss group) has an ownership change with respect to the net operating loss carryover from Year 2 on June 9, Year 3, a testing date because of A's sale of M stock to C. The sale results in a 70 percentage point increase in C's ownership of M stock, and M has an ownership change. Therefore, the M loss group has an ownership change on that day with respect to that loss carryover.

(3) *Special adjustments.*—(i) *Common parent succeeded by a new common parent.*—For purposes of determining if a loss group has an ownership change, if the common parent of a loss group is succeeded

or acquired by a new common parent and the loss group remains in existence, the new common parent is treated as a continuation of the former common parent with appropriate adjustments to take into account shifts in ownership of the former common parent during the testing period (including shifts that occur incident to the common parent's becoming the former common parent).

(ii) *Newly created loss subgroup parent.*—For purposes of determining if a loss subgroup has an ownership change, if the member that is the loss subgroup parent has not been the loss subgroup parent for at least 3 years as of a testing date, appropriate adjustments must be made to take into account owner shifts of members of the loss subgroup so that the structure of the loss subgroup does not have the effect of avoiding an ownership change under section 382. (See paragraph (b)(3)(iii) *Example 3* of this section.)

(iii) *Examples.*—The following examples illustrate the principles of this paragraph (b)(3).

*Example 1. New common parent acquires old common parent.* (a) A, who owns all the L stock, sells 30 percent of the L stock to B on August 26, Year 1. L owns all the L1 stock. The L group has a consolidated net operating loss arising in Year 1 that is carried over to Year 3. On July 16, Year 2, A and B transfer their L stock to a newly created holding company, HC, in exchange for 70 percent and 30 percent, respectively, of the HC stock. HC, L, and L1 thereafter file consolidated returns. Under the principles of §1.1502-75(d), the L loss group is treated as remaining in existence, with HC taking the place of L as the new common parent of the loss group. The following is a graphic illustration of these facts:

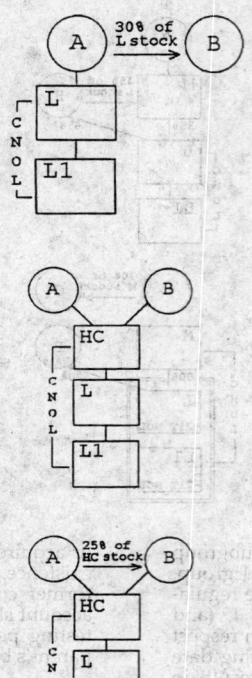

(b) On November 11, Year 3, A sells 25 percent of the HC stock to B. For purposes of determining if the L loss group has an ownership change under paragraph (b)(1)(i) of this section on November 11, Year 3, HC is treated as a continuation of L under paragraph (b)(3)(i) of this section because it acquired L and became the common parent without terminating the L loss group. Accordingly, HC's testing period commences on January 1, Year 1, the first day of the taxable year of the L loss group in which the consolidated net operating loss that is carried over to Year 3 arose (see §1.382-2T(d)(3)(i)). Immediately after the close of November 11, Year 3, B's percentage ownership interest in the common parent of the loss group (HC) has increased by 55 percentage points over its lowest percentage ownership during the testing period (zero percent). Ac-

cordingly, HC and the L loss group have an ownership change on that day.

*Example 2. New common parent in case in which common parent ceases to exist.* (a) A, B, and C each own one-third of the L stock. L owns all the L1 stock. The L group has a consolidated net operating loss arising in Year 2 that is carried over to Year 3. On November 22, Year 3, L is merged into P, a corporation owned by D, and L1 thereafter files consolidated returns with P. A, B, and C, as a result of owning stock of L, own 90 percent of P's stock after the merger. D owns the remaining 10 percent of P's stock. The merger of L into P qualifies as a reverse acquisition of the L group under §1.1502-75(d)(3)(i), and the L loss group is treated as remaining in existence, with P taking the place of L as the new common parent of the L group. The following is a graphic illustration of these facts:

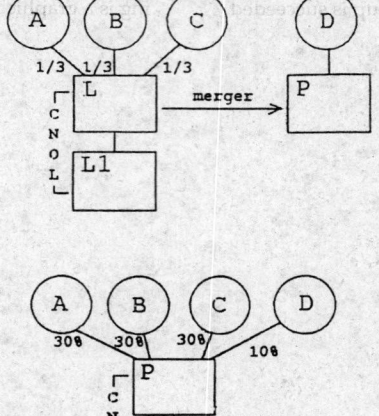

(b) For purposes of determining if the L loss group has an ownership change on November 22, Year 3, the day of the merger, P is treated as a continuation of L so that the testing period for P begins on January 1, Year 2, the first day of the taxable year of the L loss group in which the consolidated net operating loss that is carried over to Year 3 arose. Immediately after the close of November 22, Year 3, D is the only 5-percent shareholder that has increased his

ownership interest in P during the testing period (from zero to 10 percentage points).

(c) The facts are the same as in paragraph (a) of this *Example 2*, except that A has held 23$^{1}/_{3}$ shares (23$^{1}/_{3}$ percent) of L's stock for five years, and A purchased an additional 10 shares of L stock from E two years before the merger. Immediately after the close of the day of the merger (a testing date), A's ownership interest in P, the common parent of the L loss group, has increased by $6^2/3$ percentage points over her lowest percentage ownership during the testing period ($23^1/3$ percent to 30 percent).

(d) The facts are the same as in (a) of this *Example 2*, except that P has a net operating loss arising in Year 1 that is carried to the first consolidated return year ending after the day of the merger. Solely for purposes of determining whether the L loss group has an ownership change under paragraph (b)(1)(i) of this section, the testing period for P commences on January 1, Year 2. P does not determine the earliest day for its testing period by reference to its net operating loss carryover from Year 1, which §§ 1502-1(f)(3) and 1.1502-75(d)(3)(i) treat as arising in a SRLY. See § 1.1502-94A to determine the application of section 382 with respect to P's net operating loss carryover.

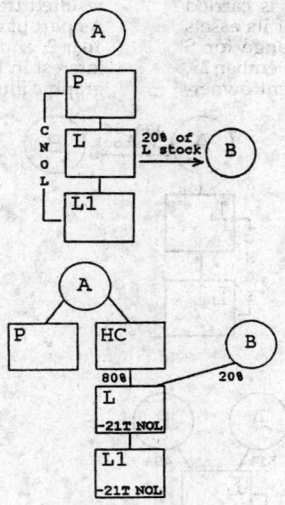

(b) February 5, Year 3, is a testing date for HC as the loss subgroup parent with respect to the net operating loss carryovers of L and L1 from Year 1. See paragraph (b)(1)(ii)(B) of this section. For purposes of determining whether HC has an ownership change on the testing date, appropriate adjustments must be made with respect to the changes in the percentage ownership of the stock of HC because HC was not the loss subgroup parent for at least 3 years prior to the day on which it became a member of the HC loss subgroup (a testing date). The appropriate adjustments include adjustments so that HC succeeds to the owner shifts of other members of the former group. Thus, HC succeeds to the owner shift of L that resulted from the sale of the 20 percent interest to B in determining whether the HC loss subgroup has an ownership change on February 5, Year 3, and on any subsequent testing date that includes January 19, Year 2.

(4) *End of separate tracking of certain losses.*—If § 1.1502-96A(a) (relating to the end of separate tracking of attributes) applies to a loss subgroup, then, while one or more members that were included in the loss subgroup remain members of the consolidated group, there is an ownership change with respect to their attributes described in § 1.1502-96A(a)(2) only if the consolidated group is a loss group and has an ownership change under paragraph (b)(1)(i) of this section (or such a member has an ownership change under § 1.1502-96A(b) (relating to ownership changes of subsidiaries)). If, however, the loss subgroup has had an ownership change before § 1.1502-96A(a) applies, see § 1.1502-96A(c) for the continuing application of the subgroup's section 382 limitation with respect to its pre-change subgroup attributes.

(c) *Supplemental rules for determining ownership change.*—(1) *Scope.*—This paragraph (c) contains a supplemental rule for determining whether there is an ownership change of a loss group (or loss subgroup). It applies in addition to, and not instead of, the rules of paragraph (b) of this section. Thus, for example, if the common parent of the loss group has an ownership change under paragraph (b) of this section, the loss group has an ownership change even if, by applying this paragraph (c), the common parent would not have an ownership change.

(2) *Cause for applying supplemental rule.*—This paragraph (c) applies to a loss group (or loss subgroup) if—

(i) Any 5-percent shareholder of the common parent (or loss subgroup parent) increases its percentage ownership interest in the stock of both—

*Example 3. Newly acquired loss subgroup parent.* (a) P owns all the L stock and L owns all the L1 stock. The P group has a consolidated net operating loss arising in Year 1 that is carried over to Year 3. On January 19, Year 2, L issues a 20 percent stock interest to B. On February 5, Year 3, P contributes its L stock to a newly formed subsidiary, HC, in exchange for all the HC stock, and distributes the HC stock to its sole shareholder A. HC, L, and L1 thereafter file consolidated returns. A portion of the P group's Year 1 consolidated net operating loss is apportioned to L and L1 under § 1.1502-21T(b) and is carried over to the HC group's year ending after February 5, Year 3. HC, L, and L1 compose a loss subgroup within the meaning of § 1.1502-91A(d) with respect to the net operating loss carryovers from Year 1. The following is a graphic illustration of these facts:

(A) A subsidiary of the loss group (or loss subgroup) other than by a direct or indirect acquisition of stock of the common parent (or loss subgroup parent); and

(B) The common parent (or loss subgroup parent); and

(ii) Those increases occur within a 3 year period ending on any day of a consolidated return year or, if shorter, the period beginning on the first day following the most recent ownership change of the loss group (or loss subgroup).

(3) *Operating rules.*—Solely for purposes of this paragraph (c)—

(i) A 5-percent shareholder of the common parent (or loss subgroup parent) is treated as increasing its percentage ownership interest in the common parent (or loss subgroup parent) or a subsidiary to the extent, if any, that any person acting pursuant to a plan or arrangement with the 5-percent shareholder increases its percentage ownership interest in the stock of that entity;

(ii) The rules in section 382(l)(3) and §§ 1.382-2T(h) and 1.382-4(d) (relating to constructive ownership) apply with respect to the stock of the subsidiary by treating such stock as stock of a loss corporation; and

(iii) In the case of a loss subgroup, a subsidiary includes any member of the loss subgroup other than the loss subgroup parent. (The loss subgroup parent is, however, a subsidiary of the loss group of which it is a member.)

(4) *Supplemental ownership change rules.*—The determination whether the common parent (or loss subgroup parent) has an ownership change is made by applying paragraph (b)(1) of this section as modified by the following additional rules—

(i) *Additional testing dates for the common parent (or loss subgroup parent).*—A testing date for the common parent (or loss subgroup parent) also includes—

(A) Each day on which there is an increase in the percentage ownership of stock of a subsidiary as described in paragraph (c)(2) of this section; and

(B) The first day of the first consolidated return year for which the group is a loss group (or the members compose a loss subgroup);

(ii) *Treatment of subsidiary stock as stock of the common parent (or loss subgroup parent).*—The common parent (or loss subgroup parent) is treated as though it had issued to the person acquiring (or deemed to acquire) the subsidiary stock an amount of its own stock (by value) that equals the value of the subsidiary stock represented by the percentage increase in that person's ownership of the subsidiary (determined on a separate entity basis). A similar principle applies if the increase in percentage ownership interest is effected by a redemption or similar transaction; and

(iii) *5-percent shareholder of the common parent (or loss subgroup parent).*—Any person described in paragraph (c)(3)(i) of this section who is acting pursuant to the plan or arrangement is treated as a 5-percent shareholder of the common parent (or loss subgroup parent).

(5) *Examples.*—The following examples illustrate the principles of this paragraph (c).

*Example 1. Stock of the common parent under supplemental rules.* (a) A owns all the L stock. L is not a member of an affiliated group and has a net operating loss carryover arising in Year 1 that is carried over to Year 6. On September 20, Year 6, L transfers all of its assets and liabilities to a newly created subsidiary, S, in exchange for S stock. L and S thereafter file consolidated returns. On November 23, Year 6, B contributes cash to L in exchange for a 45 percent owner-

ship interest in L and contributes cash to S for a 20 percent ownership interest in S.

(b) B is a 5-percent shareholder of L who increases his percentage ownership interest in L and S during the 3 year period ending on November 23, Year 6. Under paragraph (c)(4)(ii) of this section, the determination whether L (the common parent of a loss group) has an ownership change on November 23, Year 6 (or on any testing date in the testing period which includes November 23, Year 6), is made by applying paragraph (b)(1)(i) of this section and by treating the value of B's 20 percent ownership interest in S as if it were L stock issued to B.

*Example 2. Plan or arrangement—public offering of subsidiary stock.* (a) A owns all the stock of L and L owns all the stock of L1. The L group has a consolidated net operating loss arising in Year 1 that resulted from the operations of L1 and that is carried over to Year 2. As part of a plan, A sells 49 percent of the L stock to B on October 7, Year 2, and L1 issues new stock representing a 20 percent ownership interest in L1 to the public on November 6, Year 2. The following is a graphic illustration of these facts:

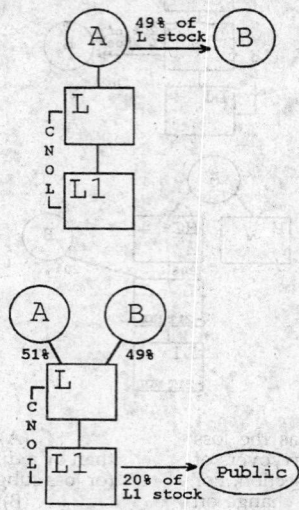

(b) A's sale of the L stock to B does not cause an ownership change of the L loss group on October 7, Year 2, under the rules of § 1.382-2T and paragraph (b)(1)(i) of this section.

(c) Because the issuance of L1 stock to the public occurs in connection with B's acquisition of L stock pursuant to a plan, paragraph (c)(4) of this section applies to determine whether the L loss group has an ownership change on November 6, Year 2 (or on any testing date for which the testing period includes November 6, Year 2).

(d) *Testing period following ownership change under this section.*—If a loss group (or a loss subgroup) has had an ownership change under this section, the testing period for determining a subsequent ownership change with respect to pre-change consolidated attributes (or pre-change subgroup attributes) begins no earlier than the first day following the loss group's (or loss subgroup's) most recent change date.

(e) *Information statements.*—(1) *Common parent of a loss group.*—The common parent of a loss group must file the information statement required by § 1.382-2T(a)(2)(ii) for a consolidated return year because of any owner shift, equity structure shift, or the issuance or transfer of an option—

(i) With respect to the common parent and with respect to any subsidiary stock subject to paragraph (c) of this section; and

(ii) With respect to an ownership change described in § 1.1502-96A(b) (relating to ownership changes of subsidiaries).

(2) *Abbreviated statement with respect to loss subgroups.*—The common parent of a consolidated group that has a loss subgroup during a consolidated return year must file the information statement required by § 1.382-2T(a)(2)(ii) because of any owner shift, equity structure shift, or issuance or transfer of an option with respect to the loss subgroup parent and with respect to any subsidiary stock subject to paragraph (c) of this section. Instead of filing a separate statement for each loss subgroup parent, the common parent (which is treated as a loss corporation) may file the single statement described in paragraph (e)(1) of this section. In addition to the information concerning stock ownership of the common parent, the single statement must identify each loss subgroup parent and state which loss subgroups, if

any, have had ownership changes during the consolidated return year. The loss subgroup parent is, however, still required to maintain the records necessary to determine if the loss subgroup has an ownership change. This paragraph (e)(2) applies with respect to the attributes of a loss subgroup until, under § 1.1502-96A(a), the attributes are no longer treated as described in § 1.1502-91A(d) (relating to the definition of loss subgroup). After that time, the information statement described in paragraph (e)(1) of this section must be filed with respect to those attributes. [Reg. § 1.1502-92A.]

☐ [*T.D. 8678, 6-26-96. Amended by T.D. 8823, 6-25-99 and amended and redesignated by T.D. 8824, 6-25-99.*]

**[Reg. § 1.1502-93]**

**§ 1.1502-93. Consolidated section 382 limitation (or subgroup section 382 limitation).**—(a) *Determination of the consolidated section 382 limitation (or subgroup section 382 limitation).*—(1) *In general.*—Following an ownership change, the consolidated section 382 limitation (or subgroup section 382 limitation) for any post-change year is an amount equal to the value of the loss group (or loss subgroup), as defined in paragraph (b) of this section, multiplied by the long-term tax-exempt rate that applies with respect to the ownership change, and adjusted as required by section 382 and the regulations thereunder. See, for example, section 382(b)(2) (relating to the carryforward of unused section 382 limitation), section 382(b)(3)(B) (relating to the section 382 limitation for the post-change year that includes the change date), section 382(h) (relating to recognized built-in gains and section 338 gains), and section 382(m)(2) (relating to short taxable years). For special rules relating to the recognized built-in gains of a loss group (or loss subgroup), see paragraph (c)(2) of this section.

(2) *Coordination with apportionment rule.*—For special rules relating to apportionment of a consolidated section 382 limitation (or a subgroup section 382 limitation) or net unrealized built-in gain when one or more corporations cease to be members of a loss group (or a loss subgroup) and to aggregation of amounts so apportioned, see § 1.1502-95(c).

(b) *Value of the loss group (or loss subgroup).*—(1) *Stock value immediately before ownership change.*—Subject to any adjustment under paragraph (b)(2) of this section, the value of the loss group (or loss subgroup) is the value, immediately before the ownership change, of the stock of each member, other than stock that is owned directly or indirectly by another member. For this purpose—

(i) Ownership is determined under §1.382-2T;

(ii) A member is considered to indirectly own stock of another member through a nonmember only if the member has a 5-percent or greater ownership interest in the nonmember; and

(iii) Stock includes stock described in section 1504(a)(4) and §1.382-2T(f)(18)(ii) and (iii).

(2) *Adjustment to value.*—(i) *In general.*—The value of the loss group (or loss subgroup), as determined under paragraph (b)(1) of this section, is adjusted under any rule in section 382 or the regulations thereunder requiring an adjustment to such value for purposes of computing the amount of the section 382 limitation. See, for example, section 382(e)(2) (redemptions and corporate contractions), section 382(l)(1) (certain capital contributions) and section 382(l)(4) (ownership of substantial nonbusiness assets). For purposes of section 382(e)(2), redemptions and corporate contractions that do not effect a transfer of value outside of the loss group (or loss subgroup) are disregarded. For purposes of section 382(l)(1), capital contributions between members of the loss group (or loss subgroup) (or a contribution of stock to a member made solely to satisfy the loss subgroup parent requirement of paragraph (d)(1)(ii) or (2)(ii) of this section), are not taken into account. Also, the substantial nonbusiness asset test of section 382(l)(4) is applied on a group (or subgroup) basis, and is not applied separately to its members.

(ii) *Anti-duplication.*—Appropriate adjustments must be made to the extent necessary to prevent any duplication of the value of the stock of a member, even though corporations that do not file consolidated returns may not be required to make such an adjustment. In making these adjustments, the group (or loss subgroup) may apply the principles of §1.382-8 (relating to controlled groups of corporations) in determining the value of a loss group (or loss subgroup) even if that section would not apply if separate returns were filed. Also, the principles of §1.382-5(d) (relating to successive ownership changes and absorption of a section 382 limitation) may apply to adjust the consolidated section 382 limitation (or subgroup section 382 limitation) of a loss group (or loss subgroup) to avoid a duplication of value if there are simultaneous (rather than successive) ownership changes.

(3) *Examples.*—The following examples illustrate the principles of this paragraph (b):

*Example 1. Basic case.* (i) L, L1, and L2 compose a loss group. L has outstanding common stock, the value of which is $100. L1 has outstanding common stock and preferred stock that is described in section 1504(a)(4). L owns 90 percent of the L1 common stock, and A owns the remaining 10 percent of the L1 common stock plus all the preferred stock. The value of the L1 common stock is $40, and the value of the L1 preferred stock is $30. L2 has outstanding common stock, 50 percent of which is owned by L and 50 percent by L1. The L group has an ownership change. The following is a graphic illustration of these facts:

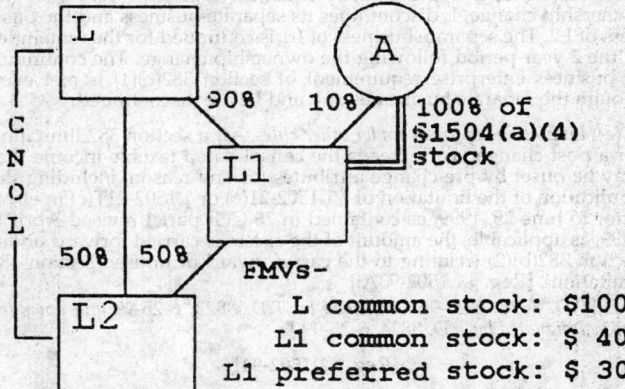

FMVs—
L common stock: $100
L1 common stock: $ 40
L1 preferred stock: $ 30

(ii) Under paragraph (b)(1) of this section, the L group does not include the value of the stock of any member that is owned directly or indirectly by another member in computing its consolidated section 382 limitation. Accordingly, the value of the stock of the loss group is $134, the sum of the value of—

(a) The common stock of L ($100);

(b) The 10 percent of the L1 common stock ($4) owned by A; and

(c) The L1 preferred stock ($30) owned by A.

*Example 2—Indirect ownership.* (i) L and L1 compose a consolidated group. L's stock has a value of $100. L owns 80 shares (worth $80) and corporation M owns 20 shares (worth $20) of the L1 stock. L

also owns 79 percent of the stock of corporation M. The L group has an ownership change. The following is a graphic illustration of these facts:

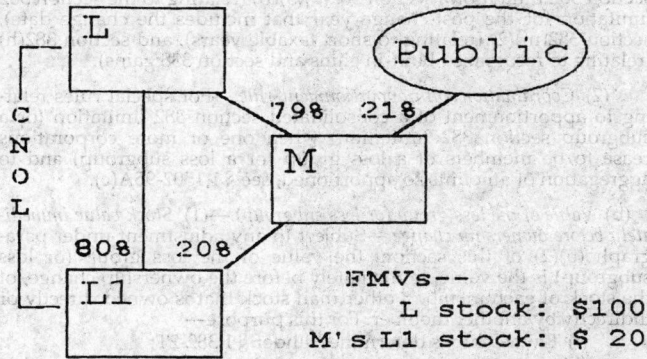

FMVs—
L stock: $100
M's L1 stock: $ 20

(ii) Under paragraph (b)(1) of this section, because of L's more than 5 percent ownership interest in M, a nonmember, L is considered to indirectly own 15.8 shares of the L1 stock held by M (79%×20 shares). The value of the L loss group is $104.20, the sum of the values of—

(a) The L stock ($100); and

(b) The L1 stock not owned directly or indirectly by L (21%×$20, or $4.20).

(c) *Recognized built-in gain of a loss group or loss subgroup.*—(1) *In general.*—If a loss group (or loss subgroup) has a net unrealized built-in gain, any recognized built-in gain of the loss group (or loss subgroup) is taken into account under section 382(h) in determining the consolidated section 382 limitation (or subgroup section 382 limitation).

(2) *Adjustments.*—Appropriate adjustments must be made so that any recognized built-in gain of a member that increases more than one section 382 limitation (whether consolidated, subgroup, or separate) does not effect a duplication in the amount of consolidated taxable income that can be offset by pre-change net operating losses. For example, a consolidated section 382 limitation that is increased by recognized built-in gains is reduced to the extent that pre-change net operating losses of a loss subgroup absorb additional consolidated taxable income because the same recognized built-in gains caused an increase in that loss subgroup's section 382 limitation. In addition, recognized built-in gain may not increase the amount of consolidated taxable income that can be offset by recognized built-in losses.

(d) *Continuity of business.*—(1) *In general.*—A loss group (or a loss subgroup) is treated as a single entity for purposes of determining whether it satisfies the continuity of business enterprise requirement of section 382(c)(1).

(2) *Example.*—The following example illustrates the principle of this paragraph (d):

*Example. Continuity of business enterprise.* L owns all the stock of two subsidiaries, L1 and L2. The L group has an ownership change. It has pre-change consolidated attributes attributable to L2. Each of the members has historically conducted a separate line of business. Each line of business is approximately equal in value. One year after the ownership change, L discontinues its separate business and the business of L2. The separate business of L1 is continued for the remainder of the 2 year period following the ownership change. The continuity of business enterprise requirement of section 382(c)(1) is met even though the separate businesses of L and L2 are discontinued.

(e) *Limitations of losses under other rules.*—If a section 382 limitation for a post-change year exceeds the consolidated taxable income that may be offset by pre-change attributes for any reason, including the application of the limitation of §1.1502-21(c), the amount of the excess is carried forward under section 382(b)(2) (relating to the carryforward of unused section 382 limitation). [Reg. §1.1502-93.]

☐ [*T.D.* 8824, 6-25-99.]

### [Reg. §1.1502-93A]

§1.1502-93A. Consolidated section 382 limitation (or subgroup section 382 limitation) generally applicable for testing dates before June 25, 1999.—(a) *Determination of the consolidated section 382 limitation (or subgroup section 382 limitation).*—(1) *In general.*—Following an ownership change, the consolidated section 382 limitation (or subgroup section 382 limitation) for any post-change year is an amount equal to the value of the loss group (or loss subgroup), as defined in paragraph (b) of this section, multiplied by the long-term tax-exempt rate that applies with respect to the ownership change, and adjusted as required by section 382 and the regulations thereunder. See, for example, section 382(b)(2) (relating to the carryforward of unused section 382 limitation), section 382(b)(3)(B) (relating to the section 382 limitation for the post-change year that includes the change date), section 382(m)(2) (relating to short taxable years), and section 382(h) (relating to recognized built-in gains and section 338 gains).

(2) *Coordination with apportionment rule.*—For special rules relating to apportionment of a consolidated section 382 limitation (or a subgroup section 382 limitation) when one or more corporations cease to be members of a loss group (or a loss subgroup) and to aggregation of amounts so apportioned, see § 1.1502-95A(c).

(b) *Value of the loss group (or loss subgroup).*—(1) *Stock value immediately before ownership change.*—Subject to any adjustment under paragraph (b)(2) of this section, the value of the loss group (or loss subgroup) is the value, immediately before the ownership change, of the stock of each member, other than stock that is owned directly or indirectly by another member. For this purpose—

(i) Ownership is determined under § 1.382-2T;

(ii) A member is considered to indirectly own stock of another member through a nonmember only if the member has a 5-percent or greater ownership interest in the nonmember; and

(iii) Stock includes stock described in section 1504(a)(4) and § 1.382-2T(f)(18)(ii) and (iii).

(2) *Adjustment to value.*—The value of the loss group (or loss subgroup), as determined under paragraph (b)(1) of this section, is adjusted under any rule in section 382 or the regulations thereunder requiring an adjustment to such value for purposes of computing the amount of the section 382 limitation. See, for example, section 382(e)(2) (redemptions and corporate contractions), section 382(l)(1) (certain capital contributions) and section 382(l)(4) (ownership of substantial nonbusiness assets). The value of the loss group (or loss subgroup) determined under this paragraph (b) is also adjusted to the extent necessary to prevent any duplication of the value of the stock of a member. For example, the principles of § 1.382-8 (relating to controlled groups of corporations) apply in determining the value of a loss group (or loss subgroup) if, under § 1.1502-91A(g)(2), members are not included in the determination whether the group (or loss subgroup) has a net unrealized built-in loss.

(3) *Examples.*—The following examples illustrate the principles of this paragraph (b).

*Example 1. Basic case.* (a) L, L1, and L2 compose a loss group. L has outstanding common stock, the value of which is $100. L1 has outstanding common stock and preferred stock that is described in section 1504(a)(4). L owns 90 percent of the L1 common stock, and A owns the remaining 10 percent of the L1 common stock plus all the preferred stock. The value of the L1 common stock is $40, and the value of the L1 preferred stock is $30. L2 has outstanding common stock, 50 percent of which is owned by L and 50 percent by L1. The L group has an ownership change. The following is a graphic illustration of these facts:

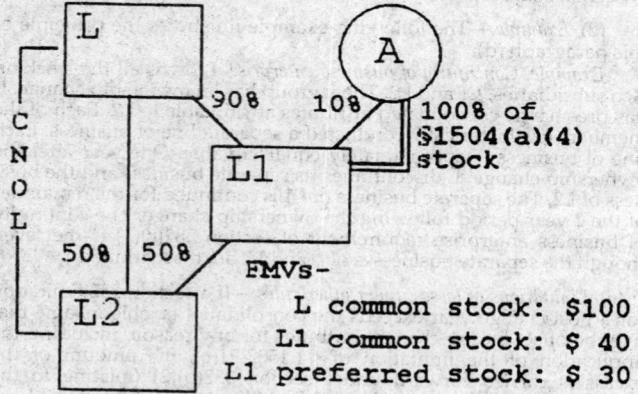

(b) Under paragraph (b)(1) of this section, the L group does not include the value of the stock of any member that is owned directly or indirectly by another member in computing its consolidated section 382 limitation. Accordingly, the value of the stock of the loss group is $134, the sum of the value of—

(1) The common stock of L ($100);

(2) the 10 percent of the L1 common stock ($4) owned by A; and

(3) The L1 preferred stock ($30) owned by A.

*Example 2. Indirect ownership.* (a) L and L1 compose a consolidated group. L's stock has a value of $100. L owns 80 shares (worth $80) and corporation M owns 20 shares (worth $20) of the L1 stock. L

also owns 79 percent of the stock of corporation M. The L group has an ownership change. The following is a graphic illustration of these facts:

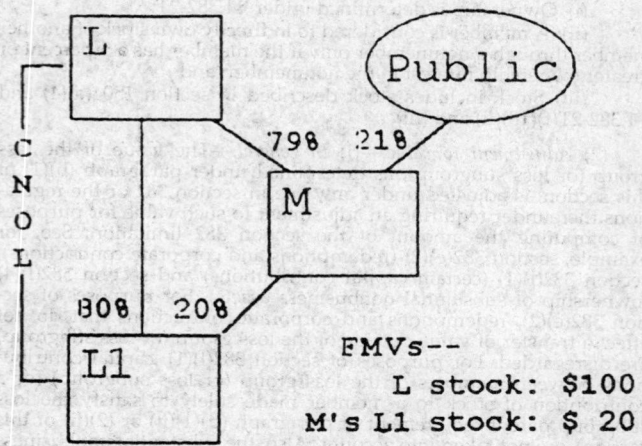

(b) Under paragraph (b)(1) of this section, because of L's more than 5 percent ownership interest in M, a nonmember, L is considered to indirectly own 15.8 shares of the L1 stock held by M (79% × 20 shares). The value of the L loss group is $104.20, the sum of the values of—

(1) The L stock ($100); and

(2) The L1 stock not owned directly or indirectly by L (21% × $20, or $4.20).

(c) *Recognized built-in gain of a loss group or loss subgroup.*—If a loss group (or loss subgroup) has a net unrealized built-in gain, any recognized built-in gain of the loss group (or loss subgroup) is taken into account under section 382(h) in determining the consolidated section 382 limitation (or subgroup section 382 limitation). See § 1.1502-99A(a)(2) for a special rule relating to the application of § 1.502-93(c)(2) to consolidated return years for which the due date of the return is after June 25, 1999.

(d) *Continuity of business.*—(1) *In general.*—A loss group (or a loss subgroup) is treated as a single entity for purposes of determining whether it satisfies the continuity of business enterprise requirement of section 382(c)(1).

(2) *Example.*—The following example illustrates the principle of this paragraph (d).

*Example. Continuity of business enterprise.* L owns all the stock of two subsidiaries, L1 and L2. The L group has an ownership change. It has pre-change consolidated attributes attributable to L2. Each of the members has historically conducted a separate line of business. Each line of business is approximately equal in value. One year after the ownership change, L discontinues its separate business and the business of L2. The separate business of L1 is continued for the remainder of the 2 year period following the ownership change. The continuity of business enterprise requirement of section 382(c)(1) is met even though the separate businesses of L and L2 are discontinued.

(e) *Limitations of losses under other rules.*—If a section 382 limitation for a post-change year exceeds the consolidated taxable income that may be offset by pre-change attributes for any reason, including the application of the limitation of § 1.1502-21(c) or 1.1502-21T(c) in effect prior to June 25, 1999, as contained in 26 CFR part 1 revised April 1, 1999, as applicable, the amount of the excess is carried forward under section 382(b)(2) (relating to the carryforward of unused section 382 limitation). [Reg. § 1.1502-93A.]

☐ [T.D. 8678, 6-26-96. *Amended by T.D. 8823, 6-25-99 and amended and redesignated by T.D. 8824, 6-25-99.*]

**[Reg. § 1.1502-94]**

**§ 1.1502-94. Coordination with section 382 and the regulations thereunder when a corporation becomes a member of a consolidated group.**—(a) *Scope.*—(1) *In general.*—This section applies section 382 and the regulations thereunder to a corporation that is a new loss member of a consolidated group. A corporation is a new loss member if it—

(i) Carries over a net operating loss that arose (or is treated under § 1.1502-21(c) as arising) in a SRLY with respect to the current group, and that is not described in § 1.1502-91(d)(1); or

(ii) Has a net unrealized built-in loss (determined under paragraph (c) of this section immediately before it becomes a member of the current group by treating that day as a change date) that is not taken into account under §1.1502-91(d)(2) in determining whether two or more corporations compose a loss subgroup.

(2) *Successor corporation as new loss member.*—A new loss member also includes any successor to a corporation that has a net operating loss carryover arising in a SRLY and that is treated as remaining in existence under §1.382-2(a)(1)(ii) following a transaction described in section 381(a).

(3) *Coordination in the case of a loss subgroup.*—For rules regarding the determination of whether there is an ownership change of a loss subgroup with respect to a net operating loss or a net unrealized built-in loss described in §1.1502-91(d) (relating to the definition of loss subgroup) and the computation of a subgroup section 382 limitation following such an ownership change, see §§1.1502-92 and 1.1502-93.

(4) *End of separate tracking of certain losses.*—If §1.1502-96(a) (relating to the end of separate tracking of attributes) applies to a new loss member, then, while that member remains a member of the consolidated group, there is an ownership change with respect to its attributes described in §1.1502-96(a)(2) only if the consolidated group is a loss group and has an ownership change under §1.1502-92(b)(1)(i) (or that member has an ownership change under §1.1502-96(b) (relating to ownership changes of subsidiaries)). If, however, the new loss member has had an ownership change before §1.1502-96(a) applies, see §1.1502-96(c) for the continuing application of the section 382 limitation with respect to the member's pre-change losses.

(5) *Cross-reference.*—See section 382(a) and §1.1502-96(c) for the continuing effect of an ownership change after a corporation becomes or ceases to be a member.

(b) *Application of section 382 to a new loss member.*—(1) *In general.*—Section 382 and the regulations thereunder apply to a new loss member to determine, on a separate entity basis, whether and to

what extent a section 382 limitation applies to limit the amount of consolidated taxable income that may be offset by the new loss member's pre-change separate attributes. For example, if an ownership change with respect to the new loss member occurs under section 382 and the regulations thereunder, the amount of consolidated taxable income for any post-change year that may be offset by the new loss member's pre-change separate attributes shall not exceed the section 382 limitation as determined separately under section 382(b) with respect to that member for such year. If the post-change year includes the change date, section 382(b)(3)(A) is applied so that the section 382 limitation of the new loss member does not apply to the portion of the taxable income for such year that is allocable to the period in such year on or before the change date. See generally §1.382-6 (relating to the allocation of income and loss).

(2) *Adjustment to value.*—Appropriate adjustments must be made to the extent necessary to prevent any duplication of the value of the stock of a member, even though corporations that do not file consolidated returns may not be required to make such an adjustment. For example, the principles of §1.1502-93(b)(2)(ii) (relating to adjustments to value) apply in determining the value of a new loss member.

(3) *Pre-change separate attribute defined.*—A pre-change separate attribute of a new loss member is—

(i) Any net operating loss carryover of the new loss member described in paragraph (a)(1) of this section; and

(ii) Any recognized built-in loss of the new loss member.

(4) *Examples.*—The following examples illustrate the principles of this paragraph (b):

*Example 1. Basic case.* (i) A and P each own 50 percent of the L stock. On December 19, Year 6, P purchases 30 percent of the L stock from A for cash. L has net operating losses arising in Year 1 and Year 2 that it carries over to Year 6 and Year 7. The following is a graphic illustration of these facts:

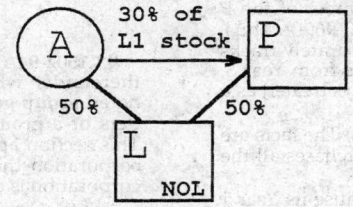

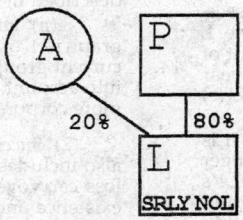

(ii) L is a new loss member because it has net operating loss carryovers that arose in a SRLY with respect to the P group and L is not a member of a loss subgroup under §1.1502-91(d). Under section 382 and the regulations thereunder, L is a loss corporation on December 19, Year 6, that day is a testing date for L, and the testing period for L commences on December 20, Year 3.

(iii) P's purchase of L stock does not cause an ownership change of L on December 19, Year 6, with respect to the net operating loss

carryovers from Year 1 and Year 2 under section 382 and §1.382-2T. The use of the loss carryovers, however, is subject to limitation under §1.1502-21(c).

*Example 2. Multiple new loss members.* (i) The facts are the same as in *Example 1*, and, on December 31, Year 6, L purchases all the stock of L1 from B for cash. L1 has a net operating loss of $40 arising in Year 3 that it carries over to Year 7. The following is a graphic illustration of these facts:

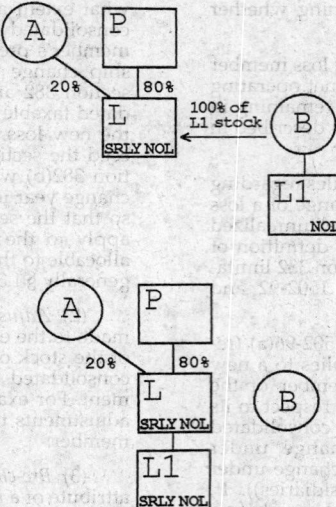

(ii) L1 is a new loss member because it has a net operating loss carryover from Year 3 that arose in a SRLY with respect to the P group and L1 is not a member of a loss subgroup under § 1.1502-91(d)(1).

(iii) L's purchase of all the stock of L1 causes an ownership change of L1 on December 31, Year 6, under section 382 and § 1.382-2T. Accordingly, a section 382 limitation based on the value of the L1 stock immediately before the ownership change limits the amount of consolidated taxable income of the P group for any post-change year that may be offset by L1's loss from Year 3.

(iv) L1's ownership change upon becoming a member of the P group is an ownership change described in § 1.1502-96(a). Thus, starting on January 1, Year 7, the P group no longer separately tracks owner shifts of the stock of L1 with respect to L1's loss from Year 3, and the P group is a loss group because L1's Year 3 loss is treated as a loss described in § 1.1502-91(c).

*Example 3. Ownership changes of new loss members.* (i) The facts are the same as in *Example 2*, and, on July 30, Year 7, C purchases all the stock of P for cash.

(ii) L is a new loss member on July 30, Year 7, because its Year 1 and Year 2 losses arose in SRLYs with respect to the P group and it is not a member of a loss subgroup under § 1.1502-91(d)(1). The testing period for L commences on August 1, Year 4. C's purchase of all the P stock causes an ownership change of L on July 30, Year 7, under section 382 and § 1.382-2T with respect to its Year 1 and Year 2 losses. Accordingly, a section 382 limitation based on the value of the L stock immediately before the ownership change limits the amount of consolidated taxable income of the P group for any post-change year that may be offset by L's Year 1 and Year 2 losses. See § 1.1502-21(c) for rules relating to an additional limitation.

(iii) The P group is a loss group on July 30, Year 7, because it is entitled to use L1's loss from Year 3, and such loss is no longer treated as a loss of a new loss member starting the day after L1's ownership change on December 31, Year 6. See §§ 1.1502-96(a) and 1.1502-91(c)(2). C's purchase of all the P stock causes an ownership change of P, and therefore the P loss group, on July 30, Year 7, with respect to L1's Year 3 loss. Accordingly, a consolidated section 382 limitation based on the value of the P stock immediately before the ownership change limits the amount of consolidated taxable income of the P group for any post-change year that may be offset by L1's Year 3 loss.

(c) *Built-in gains and losses.*—As the context may require, the principles of §§ 1.1502-91(g) and (h) and 1.1502-93(c) (relating to built-in gains and losses) apply to a new loss member on a separate entity basis. See § 1.1502-91(g)(4). See § 1.1502-13 (including *Example 10* of § 1.1502-13(c)(7)) for rules relating to the treatment of intercompany transactions.

(d) *Information statements.*—The common parent of a consolidated group that has a new loss member subject to paragraph (b)(1) of this section during a consolidated return year must file the information statement required by § 1.382-11(a) because of any owner shift, equity structure shift, or other transaction described in § 1.382-2T(a)(2)(i). Instead of filing a separate statement for each new loss member, the common parent may file a single statement described in § 1.382-11(a) with respect to the stock ownership of the common parent (which is treated as a loss corporation). In addition to the information concerning stock ownership of the common parent, the single statement must identify each new loss member and state which new loss

members, if any, have had ownership changes during the consolidated return year. The new loss member is, however, required to maintain the records necessary to determine if it has an ownership change. This paragraph (d) applies with respect to the attributes of a new loss member until an event occurs which ends separate tracking under § 1.1502-96(a). After that time, the information statement described in § 1.1502-92(e)(1) must be filed with respect to these attributes. [Reg. § 1.1502-94.]

☐ [*T.D.* 8824, 6-25-99. *Amended by T.D.* 9264, 5-26-2006 *and T.D.* 9329, 6-13-2007.]

[Reg. § 1.1502-94A]

**§ 1.1502-94A. Coordination with section 382 and the regulations thereunder when a corporation becomes a member of a consolidated group generally applicable for corporations becoming members of a group before June 25, 1999.**—(a) *Scope.*—(1) *In general.*— This section applies section 382 and the regulations thereunder to a corporation that is a new loss member of a consolidated group. A corporation is a new loss member if it—

(i) Carries over a net operating loss that arose (or is treated under § 1.1502-21(c) or 1.1502-21T(c) in effect prior to June 25, 1999, as contained in 26 CFR part 1 revised April 1, 1999, as applicable as arising) in a SRLY with respect to the current group, and that is not described in § 1.1502-91A(d)(1); or

(ii) Has a net unrealized built-in loss (determined under paragraph (c) of this section on the day it becomes a member of the current group by treating that day as a change date) that is not taken into account under § 1.1502-91A(d)(2) in determining whether two or more corporations compose a loss subgroup.

(2) *Successor corporation as new loss member.*—A new loss member also includes any successor to a corporation that has a net operating loss carryover arising in a SRLY and that is treated as remaining in existence under § 1.382-2(a)(1)(ii) following a transaction described in section 381(a).

(3) *Coordination in the case of a loss subgroup.*—For rules regarding the determination of whether there is an ownership change of a loss subgroup with respect to a net operating loss or a net unrealized built-in loss described in § 1.1502-91A(d) (relating to the definition of loss subgroup) and the computation of a subgroup section 382 limitation following such an ownership change, see §§ 1.1502-92A and 1.1502-93A.

(4) *End of separate tracking of certain losses.*—If § 1.1502-96A(a) (relating to the end of separate tracking of attributes) applies to a new loss member, then, while that member remains a member of the consolidated group, there is an ownership change with respect to its attributes described in § 1.1502-96A(a)(2) only if the consolidated group is a loss group and has an ownership change under § 1.1502-92A(b)(1)(i) (or that member has an ownership change under § 1.1502-96A(b) (relating to ownership changes of subsidiaries)). If, however, the new loss member has had an ownership change before § 1.1502-96A(a) applies, see § 1.1502-96A(c) for the continuing application of the section 382 limitation with respect to the member's pre-change losses.

(5) *Cross-reference.*—See section 382(a) and § 1.1502-96A(c) for the continuing effect of an ownership change after a corporation becomes or ceases to be a member.

(b) *Application of section 382 to a new loss member.*—(1) *In general.*— Section 382 and the regulations thereunder apply to a new loss member to determine, on a separate entity basis, whether and to what extent a section 382 limitation applies to limit the amount of consolidated taxable income that may be offset by the new loss member's pre-change separate attributes. For example, if an owner-ship change with respect to the new loss member occurs under section 382 and the regulations thereunder, the amount of consoli-dated taxable income for any post-change year that may be offset by the new loss member's pre-change separate attributes shall not ex-ceed the section 382 limitation as determined separately under sec-tion 382(b) with respect to that member for such year. If the post-change year includes the change date, section 382(b)(3)(A) is applied so that the section 382 limitation of the new loss member does not apply to the portion of the taxable income for such year that is allocable to the period in such year on or before the change date. See generally § 1.382-6 (relating to the allocation of income and loss).

(2) *Adjustment to value.*—The value of the new loss member is adjusted to the extent necessary to prevent any duplication of the value of the stock of a member. For example, the principles of § 1.382-8T (relating to controlled groups of corporations) apply in determining the value of a new loss member.

(3) *Pre-change separate attribute defined.*—A pre-change separate attribute of a new loss member is—

(i) Any net operating loss carryover of the new loss member described in paragraph (a)(1) of this section; and

(ii) Any recognized built-in loss of the new loss member.

(4) *Examples.*—The following examples illustrate the principles of this paragraph (b).

*Example 1. Basic case.* (a) A and P each own 50 percent of the L stock. On December 19, Year 6, P purchases 30 percent of the L stock from A for cash. L has net operating losses arising in Year 1 and Year 2 that it carries over to Year 6 and Year 7. The following is a graphic illustration of these facts:

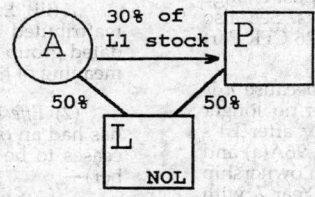

(b) L is a new loss member because it has net operating loss carryovers that arose in a SRLY with respect to the P group and L is not a member of a loss subgroup under § 1.1502-91A(d). Under section 382 and the regulations thereunder, L is a loss corporation on December 19, Year 6, that day is a testing date for L, and the testing period for L commences on December 20, Year 3.

(c) P's purchase of L stock does not cause an ownership change of L on December 19, Year 6, with respect to the net operating loss carryovers from Year 1 and Year 2 under section 382 and § 1.382-2T.

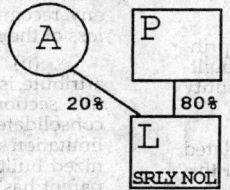

The use of the loss carryovers, however, is subject to limitation under § 1.1502-21(c) or 1.1502-21T(c) in effect prior to June 25, 1999, as contained in 26 CFR part 1 revised April 1, 1999, as applicable.

*Example 2. Multiple new loss members.* (a) The facts are the same as in *Example 1,* and, on December 31, Year 6, L purchases all the stock of L1 from B for cash. L1 has a net operating loss of $40 arising in Year 3 that it carries over to Year 7. The following is a graphic illustration of these facts:

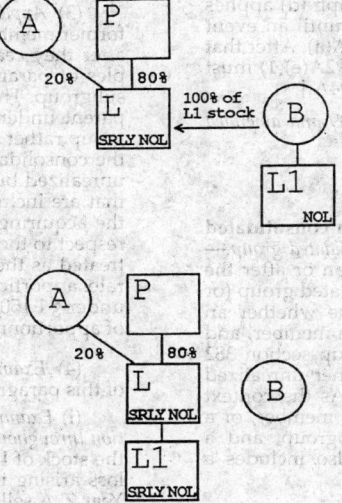

(b) L1 is a new loss member because it has a net operating loss carryover from Year 3 that arose in a SRLY with respect to the P group and L1 is not a member of a loss subgroup under § 1.1502-91A(d)(1).

(c) L's purchase of all the stock of L1 causes an ownership change of L1 on December 31, Year 6, under section 382 and § 1.382-2T. Accordingly, a section 382 limitation based on the value of the L1 stock immediately before the ownership change limits the amount of consolidated taxable income of the P group for any post-change year that may be offset by L1's loss from Year 3.

(d) L1's ownership change in connection with its becoming a member of the P group is an ownership change described in §1.1502-96A(a). Thus, starting on January 1, Year 7, the P group no longer separately tracks owner shifts of the stock of L1 with respect to L1's loss from Year 3. Instead, the P group is a loss group because of such loss under §1.1502-91A(c).

*Example 3. Ownership changes of new loss members.* (a) The facts are the same as in *Example 2*, and, on April 30, Year 7, C purchases all the stock of P for cash.

(b) L is a new loss member on April 30, Year 7, because its Year 1 and Year 2 losses arose in SRLYs with respect to the P group and it is not a member of a loss subgroup under §1.1502-91A(d)(1). The testing period for L commences on May 1, Year 4. C's purchase of all the P stock causes an ownership change of L on April 30, Year 7, under section 382 and §1.382-2T with respect to its Year 1 and Year 2 losses. Accordingly, a section 382 limitation based on the value of the L stock immediately before the ownership change limits the amount of consolidated taxable income of the P group for any post-change year that may be offset by L's Year 1 and Year 2 losses. See also §1.1502-21T in effect prior to June 25, 1999, contained in 26 CFR Part 1, revised April 1, 1999, or §1.1502-21, as applicable.

(c) The P group is a loss group on April 30, Year 7, because it is entitled to use L1's loss from Year 3, and such loss is no longer treated as a loss of a new loss member starting the day after L1's ownership change on December 31, Year 6. See §§1.1502-96A(a) and 1.1502-91A(c)(2). C's purchase of all the P stock causes an ownership change of P, and therefore the P loss group, on April 30, Year 7, with respect to L1's Year 3 loss. Accordingly, a consolidated section 382 limitation based on the value of the P stock immediately before the ownership change limits the amount of consolidated taxable income of the P group for any post-change year that may be offset by L1's Year 3 loss.

(c) *Built-in gains and losses.*—As the context may require, the principles of §§1.1502-91A(g) and (h) and 1.1502-93A(c) (relating to built-in gains and losses) apply to a new loss member on a separate entity basis. See §1.1502-91A(g)(3).

(d) *Information statements.*—The common parent of a consolidated group that has a new loss member subject to paragraph (b)(1) of this section during a consolidated return year must file the information statement required by §1.382-2T(a)(2)(ii) because of any owner shift, equity structure shift, or issuance or transfer of an option with respect to the new loss member. Instead of filing a separate statement for each new loss member the common parent may file a single statement described in §1.382-2T(a)(2)(ii) with respect to the stock ownership of the common parent (which is treated as a loss corporation). In addition to the information concerning stock ownership of the common parent, the single statement must identify each new loss member and state which new loss members, if any, have had ownership changes during the consolidated return year. The new loss member is, however, required to maintain the records necessary to determine if it has an ownership change. This paragraph (d) applies with respect to the attributes of a new loss member until an event occurs which ends separate tracking under §1.1502-96A(a). After that time, the information statement described in §1.1502-92A(e)(1) must be filed with respect to these attributes. [Reg. §1.1502-94A.]

☐ [*T.D. 8678, 6-26-96. Amended by T.D. 8823, 6-25-99 and amended and redesignated by T.D. 8824, 6-25-99.*]

**[Reg. §1.1502-95]**

**§1.1502-95. Rules on ceasing to be a member of a consolidated group (or loss subgroup).**—(a) *In general.*—(1) *Consolidated group.*—This section provides rules for applying section 382 on or after the day that a member ceases to be a member of a consolidated group (or loss subgroup). The rules concern how to determine whether an ownership change occurs with respect to losses of the member, and how a consolidated section 382 limitation (or subgroup section 382 limitation) and a loss group's (or loss subgroup's) net unrealized built-in gain or loss is apportioned to the member. As the context requires, a reference in this section to a loss group, a member, or a corporation also includes a reference to a loss subgroup, and a reference to a consolidated section 382 limitation also includes a reference to a subgroup section 382 limitation.

(2) *Election by common parent.*—Only the common parent (not the loss subgroup parent) may make the election under paragraph (c) of this section to apportion a consolidated section 382 limitation (or subgroup section 382 limitation) or a loss group's (or loss subgroup's) net unrealized built-in gain.

(3) *Coordination with §§1.1502-91 through 1.1502-93.*—For rules regarding the determination of whether there is an ownership change of a loss subgroup and the computation of a subgroup section 382 limitation following such an ownership change, see §§1.1502-91 through 1.1502-93.

(b) *Separate application of section 382 when a member leaves a consolidated group.*—(1) *In general.*—Except as provided in §§1.1502-91 through 1.1502-93 (relating to rules applicable to loss groups and loss subgroups), section 382 and the regulations thereunder apply to a corporation on a separate entity basis after it ceases to be a member of a consolidated group (or loss subgroup). Solely for purposes of determining whether a corporation has an ownership change—

(i) Any portion of a consolidated net operating loss that is apportioned to the corporation under §1.1502-21(b) is treated as a net operating loss of the corporation beginning on the first day of the taxable year in which the loss arose;

(ii) The testing period may include the period during which (or before which) the corporation was a member of the group (or loss subgroup); and

(iii) Except to the extent provided in §1.1502-96(d) (relating to reattributed losses), the day it ceases to be a member of a consolidated group is treated as a testing date of the corporation within the meaning of §1.382-2(a)(4).

(2) *Effect of a prior ownership change of the group.*—If a loss group has had an ownership change under §1.1502-92 before a corporation ceases to be a member of a consolidated group (the former member)—

(i) Any pre-change consolidated attribute that is subject to a consolidated section 382 limitation continues to be treated as a pre-change loss with respect to the former member after it is apportioned to the former member and, if any net unrealized built-in loss is allocated to the former member under paragraph (e) of this section, any recognized built-in loss of the former member is a pre-change loss of the member;

(ii) The section 382 limitation with respect to such pre-change attribute is zero unless the common parent, under paragraph (c) of this section, apportions to the former member all or part of the consolidated section 382 limitation applicable to such attribute. The limitation applicable to a pre-change attribute other than a recognized built-in loss may be increased to the extent that the common parent has apportioned all or part of the loss group's net unrealized built-in gain to the former member, and the former member recognizes built-in gain during the recognition period;

(iii) The testing period for determining a subsequent ownership change with respect to such pre-change attribute (or such net unrealized built-in loss, if any) begins no earlier than the first day following the loss group's most recent change date; and

(iv) As generally provided under section 382, an ownership change of the former member that occurs on or after the day it ceases to be a member of a loss group may result in an additional, lesser limitation amount with respect to such losses.

(3) *Application in the case of a loss subgroup.*—If two or more former members are included in the same loss subgroup immediately after they cease to be members of a consolidated group, the principles of paragraphs (b), (c) and (e) of this section apply to the loss subgroup. Therefore, for example, an apportionment by the common parent under paragraph (c) of this section is made to the loss subgroup rather than separately to its members. If the common parent of the consolidated group apportions all or part of a limitation (or net unrealized built-in gain) separately to one or more former members that are included in a loss subgroup because the common parent of the acquiring group makes an election under §1.1502-91(d)(4) with respect to those members, the aggregate of those separate amounts is treated as the amount apportioned to the loss subgroup. Such separate apportionment may occur, for example, because the election under §1.1502-91(d)(4) has not been filed at the time that the election of apportionment is made under paragraph (f) of this section.

(4) *Examples.*—The following examples illustrate the principles of this paragraph (b):

(i) *Example 1. Treatment of departing member as a separate corporation throughout the testing period.* (A) A owns all the L stock. L owns all the stock of L1 and L2. The L group has a consolidated net operating loss arising in Year 1 that is carried over to Year 3. On January 12, Year 2, A sells 30 percent of the L stock to B. On February 7, Year 3, L sells 40 percent of the L2 stock to C, and L2 ceases to be a member of the group. A portion of the Year 1 consolidated net operating loss is apportioned to L2 under §1.1502-21(b) and is carried to L2's first separate return year, which ends December 31, Year 3. The following is a graphic illustration of these facts:

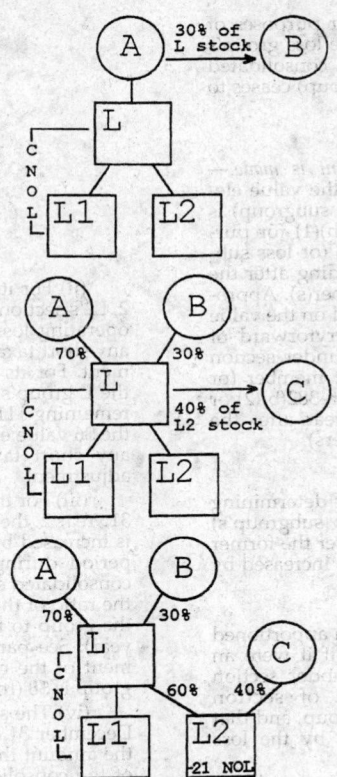

(B) Under paragraph (b)(1) of this section, L2 is a loss corporation on February 7, Year 3. Under paragraph (b)(1)(iii) of this section, February 7, Year 3, is a testing date. Under paragraph (b)(1)(ii) of this section, the testing period for L2 with respect to this testing date commences on January 1, Year 1, the first day of the taxable year in which the portion of the consolidated net operating loss apportioned to L2 arose. Therefore, in determining whether L2 has an ownership change on February 7, Year 3, B's purchase of 30 percent of the L stock and C's purchase of 40 percent of the L2 stock are each owner shifts. L2 has an ownership change under section 382(g) and § 1.382-2T because B and C have increased their ownership interests in L2 by 18 and 40 percentage points, respectively, during the testing period.

(ii) *Example 2. Effect of prior ownership change of loss group.* (A) L owns all the L1 stock and L1 owns all the L2 stock. The L loss group had an ownership change under § 1.1502-92 in Year 2 with respect to a consolidated net operating loss arising in Year 1 and carried over to Year 2 and Year 3. The consolidated section 382 limitation computed solely on the basis of the value of the stock of L is $100. On December 31, Year 2, L1 sells 25 percent of the stock of L2 to B. L2 is apportioned a portion of the Year 1 consolidated net operating loss which it carries over to its first separate return year ending after December 31, Year 2. L2's separate section 382 limitation with respect to this loss is zero unless L elects to apportion all or a part of the consolidated section 382 limitation to L2. (See paragraph (c) of this section for rules regarding the apportionment of a consolidated section 382 limitation.) L apportions $50 of the consolidated section 382 limitation to L2, and the remaining $50 of the consolidated section 382 limitation stays with the loss group composed of L and L1.

(B) On December 31, Year 3, L1 sells its remaining 75 percent stock interest in L2 to C, resulting in an ownership change of L2. L2's section 382 limitation computed on the change date with respect to the value of its stock is $30. Accordingly, L2's section 382 limitation for post-change years ending after December 31, Year 3, with respect to its pre-change losses, including the consolidated net operating losses apportioned to it from the L group, is $30, adjusted for a short taxable year, carryforward of unused limitation, or any other adjustment required under section 382. The analysis would be similar if the L loss group had an ownership change under § 1.1502-92 in Year 2 with respect to disallowed business interest expense paid or accrued by L2 in Year 1 and carried forward under section 163(j)(2) to Year 2 and Year 3. See § 1.1502-98(b) (providing that § § 1.1502-91 through 1.1502-96 apply section 382 to business interest expense, with appropriate adjustments).

(c) *Apportionment of a consolidated section 382 limitation.*—(1) *In general.*—The common parent may elect to apportion all or any part of a consolidated section 382 limitation to a former member (or loss subgroup). The common parent also may elect to apportion all or any part of the loss group's net unrealized built-in gain to a former member (or loss subgroup).

(2) *Amount which may be apportioned.*—(i) *Consolidated section 382 limitation.*—The common parent may apportion all or part of each element of the consolidated section 382 limitation determined under § 1-1502-93. For this purpose, the consolidated section 382 limitation consists of two elements—

(A) The value element, which is the element of the limitation determined under section 382(b)(1) (relating to value multiplied by the long-term tax-exempt rate) without regard to such adjustments as those described in section 382(b)(2) (relating to the carryforward of unused section 382 limitation), section 382(b)(3)(B) (relating to the section 382 limitation for the post-change year that includes the change date), section 382(h) (relating to built-in gains and section 338 gains), and section 382(m)(2) (relating to short taxable years); and

(B) The adjustment element, which is so much (if any) of the limitation for the taxable year during which the former member ceases to be a member of the consolidated group that is attributable to a carryover of unused limitation under section 382(b)(2) or to recognized built-in gains under 382(h).

(ii) *Net unrealized built-in gain.*—The aggregate amount of the loss group's net unrealized built-in gain that may be apportioned to one or more former members that cease to be members during the same consolidated return year cannot exceed the loss group's excess, immediately after the close of that year, of net unrealized built-in gain over recognized built-in gain, determined under section 382(h)(1)(A)(ii) (relating to a limitation on recognized built-in gain). For this purpose, net unrealized built-in gain apportioned to former members in prior consolidated return years is treated as recognized built-in gain in those years.

(3) *Effect of apportionment on the consolidated group.*—(i) *Consolidated section 382 limitation.*—The value element of the consolidated section 382 limitation for any post-change year ending after the day that a former member (or loss subgroup) ceases to be a member(s) is reduced to the extent that it is apportioned under this paragraph (c). The consolidated section 382 limitation for the post-change year in which the former member (or loss subgroup) ceases to be a member(s) is also reduced to the extent that the adjustment element for that year is apportioned under this paragraph (c).

(ii) *Net unrealized built-in gain.*—The amount of the loss group's net unrealized built-in gain that is apportioned to the former member (or loss subgroup) is treated as recognized built-in gain for a

Reg. § 1.1502-95(c)(3)(ii)

prior taxable year ending in the recognition period for purposes of applying the limitation of section 382(h)(1)(A)(ii) to the loss group's recognition period taxable years beginning after the consolidated return year in which the former member (or loss subgroup) ceases to be a member.

(4) *Effect on corporations to which an apportionment is made.*—(i) *Consolidated section 382 limitation.*—The amount of the value element that is apportioned to a former member (or loss subgroup) is treated as the amount determined under section 382(b)(1) for purposes of determining the amount of that corporation's (or loss subgroup's) section 382 limitation for any taxable year ending after the former member (or loss subgroup) ceases to be a member(s). Appropriate adjustments must be made to the limitation based on the value element so apportioned for a short taxable year, carryforward of unused limitation, or any other adjustment required under section 382. The adjustment element apportioned to a former member (or loss subgroup) is treated as an adjustment under section 382(b)(2) or section 382(h), as appropriate, for the first taxable year after the member (or members) ceases to be a member (or members).

(ii) *Net unrealized built-in gain.*—For purposes of determining the amount by which the former member's (or loss subgroup's) section 382 limitation for any taxable year beginning after the former member (or loss subgroup), ceases to be a member(s) is increased by its recognized built-in gain—

(A) The amount of net unrealized built-in gain apportioned to a former member (or loss subgroup) is treated as if it were an amount of net unrealized built-in gain determined under section 382(h)(1)(A)(i) (without regard to the threshold of section 382(h)(3)(B)) with respect to such member or loss subgroup, and that amount is not reduced under section 382(h)(1)(A)(ii) by the loss group's recognized built-in gain;

(B) The former member's (or loss subgroup's) 5 year recognition period begins on the loss group's change date;

(C) In applying section 382(h)(1)(A)(ii), the former member (or loss subgroup) takes into account only its prior taxable years that begin after it ceases to be a member of the loss group; and

(D) The former member's (or loss subgroup's) recognized built-in gain on the disposition of an asset is determined under section 382(h)(2)(A), treating references to the change date in that section as references to the loss group's change date.

(5) *Deemed apportionment when loss group terminates.*—If a loss group terminates, to the extent the consolidated section 382 limitation or net unrealized built-in gain is not apportioned under paragraph (c)(1) of this section, the consolidated section 382 limitation or net unrealized built-in gain is deemed to be apportioned to the loss subgroup that includes the common parent, or, if there is no loss subgroup that includes the common parent immediately after the loss group terminates, to the common parent. A loss group terminates on the first day of the first taxable year that is a separate return year with respect to each member of the former loss group.

(6) *Appropriate adjustments when former member leaves during the year.*—Appropriate adjustments are made to the consolidated section 382 limitation for the consolidated return year during which the former member (or loss subgroup) ceases to be a member(s) to reflect the inclusion of the former member in the loss group for a portion of that year.

(7) *Examples.*—The following examples illustrate the principles of this paragraph (c):

*Example 1. Consequence of apportionment.* (i) L owns all the L1 stock and L1 owns all the L2 stock. The L group has a $200 consolidated net operating loss arising in Year 1 that is carried over to Year 2. At the close of December 31, Year 1, the group has an ownership change under § 1.1502-92. The ownership change results in a consolidated section 382 limitation of $10 based on the value of the stock of the group. On August 29, Year 2, L1 sells 30 percent of the stock of L2 to A. L2 is apportioned $90 of the group's $200 consolidated net operating loss under § 1.1502-21(b). L, the common parent, elects to apportion $6 of the consolidated section 382 limitation to L2. The following is a graphic illustration of these facts:

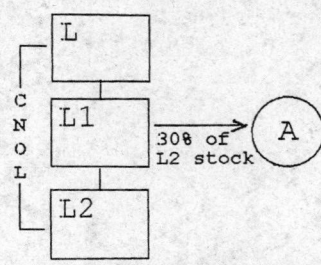

(ii) For its separate return years ending after December 31, Year 2, L2's section 382 limitation with respect to the $90 of the group's net operating loss apportioned to it is $6, adjusted, as appropriate, for any short taxable year, unused section 382 limitation, or other adjustment. For its consolidated return year ending December 31, Year 2 the L group's consolidated section 382 limitation with respect to the remaining $110 of pre-change consolidated attribute is $4 ($10 minus the $6 value element apportioned to L2), adjusted, as appropriate, for any short taxable year, unused section 382 limitation, or other adjustment.

(iii) For the L group's consolidated return year ending December 31, Year 2, the value element of its consolidated section 382 limitation is increased by $4 (rounded to the nearest dollar), to account for the period during which L2 was a member of the L group ($6, the consolidated section 382 limitation apportioned to L2, times 241/365, the ratio of the number of days during Year 2 that L2 is a member of the group to the number of days in the group's consolidated return year). See paragraph (c)(6) of this section. Therefore, the value element of the consolidated section 382 limitation for Year 2 of the L group is $8 (rounded to the nearest dollar).

(iv) The section 382 limitation for L2's short taxable year ending December 31, Year 2, is $2 (rounded to the nearest dollar), which is the amount that bears the same relationship to $6, the value element of the consolidated section 382 limitation apportioned to L2, as the number of days during that short taxable year, 124 days, bears to 365. See § 1.382-5(c).

*Example 2. Consequence of no apportionment.* The facts are the same as in *Example 1*, except that L does not elect to apportion any portion of the consolidated section 382 limitation to L2. For its separate return years ending after August 29, Year 2, L2's section 382 limitation with respect to the $90 of the group's pre-change consolidated attribute apportioned to L2 is zero under paragraph (b)(2)(ii) of this section. Thus, the $90 consolidated net operating loss apportioned to L2 cannot offset L2's taxable income in any of its separate return years ending after August 29, Year 2. For its consolidated return years ending after August 29, Year 2, the L group's consolidated section 382 limitation with respect to the remaining $110 of pre-change consolidated attribute is $10, adjusted, as appropriate, for any short taxable year, unused section 382 limitation, or other adjustment.

*Example 3. Apportionment of adjustment element.* The facts are the same as in *Example 1*, except that L2 ceases to be a member of the L group on August 29, Year 3, and the L group has a $4 carryforward of an unused consolidated section 382 limitation (under section 382(b)(2)) to the Year 3 consolidated return year. The carryover of unused limitation increases the consolidated section 382 limitation for the Year 3 consolidated return year from $10 to $14. L may elect to apportion all or any portion of the $10 value element and all or any portion of the $4 adjustment element to L2.

(d) *Rules pertaining to ceasing to be a member of a loss subgroup.*—(1) *In general.*—A corporation ceases to be a member of a loss subgroup on the earlier of—

(i) The first day of the first taxable year for which it files a separate return; or

(ii) The first day that it ceases to bear a relationship described in section 1504(a)(1) to the loss subgroup parent (treating for this purpose the loss subgroup parent as the common parent described in section 1504(a)(1)(A)).

(2) *Exceptions.*—Paragraph (d)(1)(ii) of this section does not apply to a member of a loss subgroup while that member remains a member of the current group—

(i) If an election under § 1.1502-91(d)(4)(relating to treating the subgroup parent requirement as satisfied) applies to the members of the loss subgroup;

(ii) Starting on the day after the change date (but not earlier than the date the loss subgroup becomes a member of the group), if there is an ownership change of the loss subgroup within six months before, on, or after becoming members of the group; or

(iii) Starting the day after the period of 5 consecutive years following the day that the loss subgroup become members of the group during which the loss subgroup has not had an ownership change.

(3) *Examples.*—The principles of this paragraph (d) are illustrated by the following examples:

*Example 1. Basic case.* (i) P owns all the L stock, L owns all the L1 stock and L1 owns all the L2 stock. The P group has a consolidated net operating loss arising in Year 1 that is carried over to Year 2. On

December 11, Year 2, P sells all the stock of L to corporation M. Each of L, L1, and L2 is apportioned a portion of the Year 1 consolidated net operating loss, and thereafter each joins with M in filing consolidated returns. Under §1.1502-92, the L loss subgroup has an ownership change on December 11, Year 2. The L loss subgroup has a subgroup section 382 limitation of $100. The following is a graphic illustration of these facts:

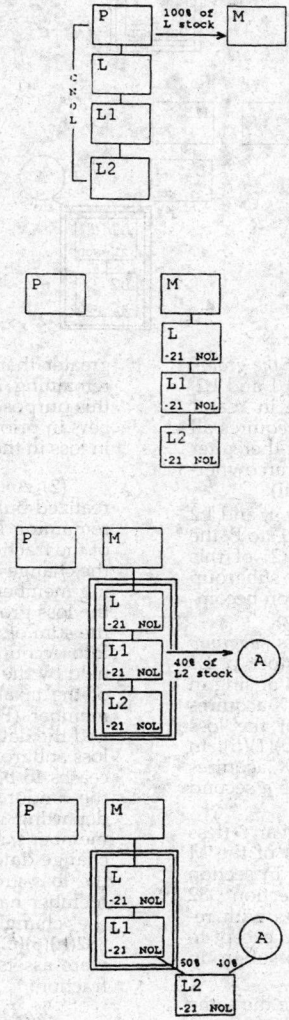

(ii) On May 22, Year 3, L1 sells 40 percent of the L2 stock to A. L2 carries over a portion of the P group's net operating loss from Year 1 to its separate return year ending December 31, Year 3. Under paragraph (d)(1) of this section, L2 ceases to be a member of the L loss subgroup on May 22, Year 3, which is both (1) the first day of the first taxable year for which it files a separate return and (2) the day it ceases to bear a relationship described in section 1504(a)(1) to the loss subgroup parent, L. The net operating loss of L2 that is carried over from the P group is treated as a pre-change loss of L2 for its separate return years ending after May 22, Year 3. Under paragraphs (a)(2) and (b)(2) of this section, the separate section 382 limitation with respect to this loss is zero unless M elects to apportion all or a part of the subgroup section 382 limitation of the L loss subgroup to L2.

*Example 2. Formation of a new loss subgroup.* The facts are the same as in *Example 1*, except that A purchases 40 percent of the L1 stock from L rather than purchasing L2 stock from L1. L1 and L2 file a consolidated return for their first taxable year ending after May 22, Year 3, and each of L1 and L2 carries over a part of the net operating loss of the P group that arose in Year 1. Under paragraph (d)(1) of this section, L1 and L2 cease to be members of the L loss subgroup on May 22, Year 3. The net operating losses carried over from the P group are treated as pre-change subgroup attributes of the loss subgroup composed of L1 and L2. The subgroup section 382 limitation with respect to those losses is zero unless M elects to apportion all or part of the subgroup section 382 limitation of the L loss subgroup to the L1 loss subgroup. The following is a graphic illustration of these facts:

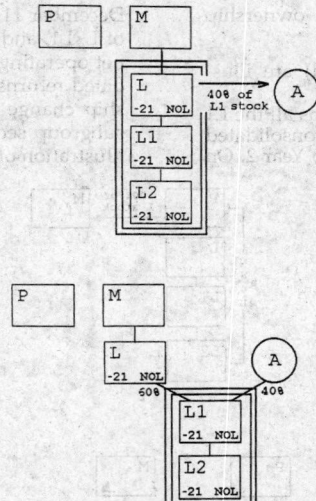

*Example 3. Ownership change upon becoming members of the group.* (i) A owns all the stock of P, and P owns all the stock of L1 and L2. The P group has a consolidated net operating loss arising in Year 1 that is carried over to Year 3 and Year 4. Corporation M acquires all the stock of P on November 11, Year 3, and P, L1, and L2 thereafter file consolidated returns with M. M's acquisition results in an ownership change of the P loss subgroup under § 1.1502-92(b)(1)(ii).

(ii) P distributes the L2 stock to M on October 7, Year 4, and L2 ceases to bear the relationship described in section 1504(a)(1) to P, the P loss subgroup parent. However, under paragraph (d)(2) of this section, L2 does not cease to be a member of the P loss subgroup because the P loss subgroup had an ownership change upon becoming members of the M group and L2 remains in the M group.

*Example 4. Ceasing to bear a section 1504(a)(1) to the loss subgroup parent.* (i) A owns all the stock of P, and, P owns all the stock of L1 and L2. The P group has a consolidated net operating loss arising in Year 1 that is carried over to Year 7. At the close of Year 2, X acquires all of the stock of P, causing an ownership change of the loss subgroup composed of P, L1 and L2 under § 1.1502-92(b)(1)(ii). In Year 4, M, which is owned by the same person that owns X, acquires all of the stock of P, and the M acquisition does not cause a second ownership change of the P loss subgroup.

(ii) P distributes the L2 stock to M on February 3, Year 6 (less than 5 years after the P loss subgroup became members of the M group) and L2 ceases to bear the relationship described in section 1504(a)(1) to P, the loss subgroup parent. Thus, the section 382 limitation from the Year 2 ownership change that applies with respect to the pre-change attributes attributable to L2 is zero except to the extent M elects to apportion all or part of the P loss subgroup section 382 limitation to L2.

*Example 5. Relationship through a successor.* The facts are the same as in *Example 3*, except that M's acquisition of the P stock does not result in an ownership change of the P loss subgroup, and, instead of P's distributing the stock of L2, L2 merges into L1 on October 7, Year 4. L1 (as successor to L2 in the merger within the meaning of § 1.1502-1(f)(4)) continues to bear a relationship described in section 1504(a)(1) to P, the loss subgroup parent. Thus, L2 does not cease to be a member of the P loss subgroup as a result of the merger.

*Example 6. Reattribution of net operating loss carryover under § 1.1502-36(d)(6).* The facts are the same as in *Example 3*, except that, instead of distributing the L2 stock to M, P sells that stock to B, and, under § 1.1502-36(d)(6), M reattributes $10 of L2's net operating loss carryover to itself. Under § 1.1502-36(d)(6)(iv)(A), M succeeds to the reattributed loss as if the loss were succeeded to in a transaction to which section 381(a) applies. M, as successor to L2, does not cease to be a member of the P loss subgroup.

(e) *Allocation of net unrealized built-in loss.*—(1) *In general.*—This paragraph (e) provides rules for the allocation of a loss group's (or loss subgroup's) net unrealized built-in loss if a member ceases to be a member of a loss group (or loss subgroup). This paragraph (e) applies if—

(i) A loss group (or loss subgroup) has a net unrealized built-in loss on a change date; and

(ii) Immediately after the close of the consolidated return year in which the departing member ceases to be a member, the amount of the loss group's (or loss subgroup's) excess of net unrealized built-in loss over recognized built-in loss, determined under section 382(h)(1)(B)(ii) (relating to a limitation on recognized built-in loss), is

greater than zero. (The amount of such excess is referred to as the remaining NUBIL balance.) In applying section 382(h)(1)(B)(ii) for this purpose, net unrealized built-in loss allocated to departing members in prior consolidated return years is treated as recognized built-in loss in those years.

(2) *Amount of allocation.*—(i) *In general.*—The amount of net unrealized built-in loss allocated to a departing member is equal to the remaining NUBIL balance, multiplied by a fraction. The numerator of the fraction is the amount of the built-in loss, taken into account on the change date under § 1.1502-91(g), in the assets held by the departing member immediately after the member ceases to be a member of the loss group (or loss subgroup). The denominator of the fraction is the sum of the numerator, plus the amount of the built-in loss, taken into account under § 1.1502-91(g) on the change date, in the assets held by the loss group (or loss subgroup) immediately after the close of the taxable year in which the departing member ceases to be a member. (Fluctuations in value of the assets between the change date and the date that the member ceases to be a member of the group (or loss subgroup), or the close of the taxable year in which the member ceases to be a member of the loss group, are disregarded.) Because the amount of built-in loss on the change date with respect to a departing member's assets is taken into account (rather than that member's separately computed net unrealized built-in loss on the change date), a departing member can be apportioned all or part of the loss group's net unrealized built-in loss, even if the departing member had a separately computed net unrealized built-in gain on the change date. Amounts taken into account under section 382(h)(6)(C) (relating to certain deduction items) are treated as if they were assets in determining the numerator and denominator of the fraction.

(ii) *Transferred basis property and deferred gain or loss.*—For purposes of paragraph (b)(2)(i) of this section, assets held by the departing member immediately after it ceases to be a member of the group (or by other members immediately after the close of the taxable year) include—

(A) Assets held at that time that are transferred basis property that was held by any member of the group (or loss subgroup) on the change date; and

(B) Assets held at that time by any member of the consolidated group with respect to which gain or loss of the group member or loss subgroup member at issue has been deferred in an intercompany transaction and has not been taken into account.

(iii) *Assets for which gain or loss has been recognized.*—For purposes of paragraph (b)(2)(i) of this section, assets held by the departing member immediately after it ceases to be a member of the group (or by other members immediately after the close of the taxable year) do not include assets with respect to which gain or loss has previously been recognized and taken into account during the recognition period (including gain or loss recognized in an intercompany transaction and taken into account immediately before the member leaves the group). Appropriate adjustments must be made if gain or loss on an asset has been only partially recognized and taken into account.

(iv) *Exchanged basis property.*—The rules of § 1.1502-91(h) apply for purposes of this paragraph (e) (disregarding stock received from the departing member or another member that is a member immediately after the close of the taxable year).

(v) *Two or more members depart during the same year.*—If two or more members cease to be members during the same consolidated return year, appropriate adjustments must be made to the denominator of the fraction for each departing member by treating the other departing members as if they had not ceased to be members during that year and as if the assets held by those other departing members immediately after they cease to be members of the group (or loss subgroup) are assets held by the group immediately after the close of the taxable year.

(vi) *Anti-abuse rule.*—If assets are transferred between members or a member ceases to be a member with a principal purpose of causing or affecting the allocation of amounts under this paragraph (e), appropriate adjustments must be made to eliminate any benefit of such acquisition, disposition, or allocation.

(3) *Effect of allocation on the consolidated group.*—The amount of the net unrealized built-in loss that is allocated to the former member is treated as recognized built-in loss for a prior taxable year ending in the recognition period for purposes applying the limitation of section 382(h)(1)(B)(ii) to a loss group's (or loss subgroup's) recognition period taxable years beginning after the consolidated return year in which the former member ceases to be a member.

(4) *Effect on corporations to which the allocation is made.*—For purposes of determining the amount of the former member's recognized built-in losses in any taxable year beginning after the former member ceases to be a member—

(i) The amount of the loss group's (or loss subgroup's) net unrealized built-in loss that is allocated to the former member is treated as if it were an amount of net unrealized built-in loss determined under section 382(h)(1)(B)(i)(without regard to the threshold of section 382(h)(3)(B)) with respect to such member or loss subgroup, and that amount is not reduced under section 382(h)(1)(B)(ii) by the loss group's (or loss subgroup's) recognized built-in losses;

(ii) The former member's 5 year recognition period begins on the loss group's (or loss subgroup's) change date;

(iii) In applying section 382(h)(1)(B)(ii), the former member takes into account only its prior taxable years that begin after it ceases to be a member of the loss group (or loss subgroup); and

(iv) The former member's recognized built-in loss on the disposition of an asset is determined under section 382(h)(2)(B), treating references to the change date in that section as references to the loss group's (or loss subgroup's) change date.

(5) *Subgroup principles.*—If two or more former members are members of the same consolidated group (the second group) immediately after they cease to be members of the current group, the principles of paragraphs (e)(1), (2) and (4) of this section apply to those former members on an aggregate basis. Thus, for example, the amount of net unrealized built-in loss allocated to those members is based on the assets held by those members immediately after they cease to be members of the current group and the limitation of section 382(h)(1)(B)(ii) on recognized built-in losses is applied by taking into account the aggregate amount of net unrealized built-in loss allocated to the former members and the aggregate recognized losses of those members in taxable years beginning after they cease to be members of the current group. If one or more of such members cease to be members of the second group, the principles of this paragraph (e) are applied with respect to those members to allocate to them all or part of any remaining unrecognized amount of net unrealized built-in loss allocated to the members that became members of the second group.

(6) *Apportionment of consolidated section 382 limitation (or subgroup section 382 limitation).*—(i) *In general.*—For rules relating to the apportionment of a consolidated section 382 limitation (or subgroup section 382 limitation) to a former member, see paragraph (c) of this section.

(ii) *Special rule for former members that become members of the same consolidated group.*—If recognized built-in losses of one or more former members would be subject to a consolidated section 382 limitation (or subgroup section 382 limitation) if recognized immediately before the member (or members) cease to be members of the group, an apportionment of that limitation may be made, under paragraph (c) of this section, to a loss subgroup that includes such member (or members), and the recognized built-in losses (if any) of that member (or members) will be subject to that apportioned limitation. If two or more of such former members are not included in a loss subgroup immediately after they cease to be members of the group (for example, because they do not have net operating loss carryovers or, in the aggregate, a net unrealized built-in loss), but are members of the same consolidated group, an apportionment of the consolidated section 382 limitation (or subgroup section 382 limitation) may be made to them as if they were a loss subgroup.

(7) *Examples.*—The following examples illustrate the principles of this paragraph (e):

*Example 1. Basic allocation case.* (i) P owns all of the stock of L1 and L2. On September 4, Year 1, A purchases all of the P stock, causing an ownership change of the P group. On that date P has two assets (other than the L1 and L2 stock), asset 1 with an adjusted basis of $40 and a fair market value of $15 and asset 2 with an adjusted basis of $50 and a fair market value of $100. L1 has two assets, asset 3, with a fair market value of $50 and an adjusted basis of $100, and asset 4, with an adjusted basis of $125 and a fair market value of $75. L2 has two assets, asset 5, with a fair market value of $150 and an adjusted basis of $100, and asset 6, with an adjusted basis of $90 and a fair market value of $40. Thus, the P loss group has a net unrealized built-in loss of $75.

(ii) On March 19, Year 3, P sells all of the L2 stock to M. At that time, asset 5, which has appreciated in value, has a fair market value of $250 and an adjusted basis of $100. Asset 6, which has declined in value, has an adjusted basis of $90 and a fair market value of $10.

(iii) On April 8, Year 3, P sells asset 1, and has a recognized built-in loss of $25 that is subject to the P group's section 382 limitation. On November 11, Year 4, L2 sells asset 6 for its then fair market value, $10, recognizing a loss of $80. On June 3, Year 5, L1 sells asset 4, recognizing a loss of $50.

(iv) Immediately after the close of Year 3, the P loss group's remaining NUBIL balance is $50 ($75 net unrealized built-in loss reduced by the $25 recognized built-in loss of P). The portion of the remaining NUBIL balance that is allocated to L2 is $17 (rounded to the nearest dollar). Seventeen dollars is the product obtained by multiplying $50 (the remaining NUBIL balance) by $50/$150. The numerator of the fraction ($50) is the amount of built-in loss in asset 6, taken into account on the change date under §1.1502-91(g). The denominator ($150) is the sum of the numerator ($50) and the amount of built-in loss in assets 3 and 4, taken into account on the change date under §1.1502-91(g) ($100). The built-in loss in asset 1 is not included in the denominator of the fraction because it is not held by the P group immediately after the close of Year 3.

(v) Seventeen dollars of L2's $80 loss on the sale of asset 6 is a recognized built-in loss and subject to a section 382 limitation of zero, unless P apportions some or all of the P group's consolidated section 382 limitation to L2 (adjusted for a short taxable year, carryover of unused limitation, or any other adjustment required under section 382).

(vi) Thirty-three dollars of L1's $50 loss on the sale of asset 4 is subject to the P group's consolidated section 382 limitation, reduced by the amount of such limitation apportioned to L2, and adjusted for any short taxable year, a carryforward of unused limitation, or other adjustment. (In applying section 382(h)(1)(B)(ii) with respect to Year 5, the P group's net unrealized built-in loss is reduced by P's $25 recognized built-in loss in Year 3 and the $17 of net unrealized built-in loss allocated to L2, thus limiting the P group's recognized built-in loss in Year 5 to $33.)

*Example 2. Two members depart in the same year.* The facts are the same as in *Example 1*, except that P sells all of the stock of L1 to C on November 1, Year 3. The amount of net unrealized built-in loss apportioned to L2 (rounded to the nearest dollar) is $17 ($50 remaining NUBIL balance × $50/$150). The amount of net unrealized built-in loss apportioned to L1 (rounded to the nearest dollar) is $33 ($50 remaining NUBIL balance × $100/$150).

(8) *Reporting requirements.*—(i) *Common Parent.*—Except as provided in paragraph (e)(8)(iii) of this section, if a net unrealized built-in loss is allocated under paragraph (e) of this section, the common parent must include a statement entitled, "STATEMENT OF NET UNREALIZED BUILT-IN LOSS ALLOCATION PURSUANT TO §1.1502-95(e)," on or with its income tax return for the taxable year in which the former member(s) (or a new loss subgroup that includes that member) ceases to be a member. The statement must include—

(A) The name and employer identification number of the departing member;

(B) The amount of the remaining NUBIL balance for the taxable year in which the member departs;

(C) The amount of the net unrealized built-in loss allocated to the departing member; and

(D) A representation that the common parent has delivered a copy of the statement to the former member (or the common parent of the group of which the former member is a member) on or before the day the group files its income tax return for the consolidated return year that the former member ceases to be a member.

(ii) *Former Member.*—Except as provided in paragraph (e)(8)(iii) of this section, the former member must include a statement on or with its first income tax return (or the first return in which the former member joins) that is filed after the close of the consolidated return year of the group of which the former member (or a new loss subgroup that includes that member) ceases to be a member. The statement will be identical to the statement filed by the common parent under paragraph (e)(8)(i) of this section except that instead of including the information described in paragraph (e)(8)(i)(A) of this section the former member must provide the name, employer identification number and tax year of the former common parent, and instead of the representation described in paragraph (e)(8)(i)(D) of this section the former member must represent that it has received and retained the copy of the statement delivered by the common parent as part of its records. See § 1.6001-1(e).

(iii) *Exception.*—This paragraph (e)(8) does not apply if the required information (other than the amount of the remaining NUBIL balance) is included in a statement of election under paragraph (f) of this section (relating to apportioning a section 382 limitation).

(f) *Filing the election to apportion the section 382 limitation and net unrealized built-in gain.*—(1) *Form of the election to apportion.*—(i) *Statement.*—An election under paragraph (c) of this section must be made in the form set forth in this paragraph (f)(1)(i). The election must be made by the common parent and the party described in paragraph (f)(2) of this section. It must be filed in accordance with paragraph (f)(3) of this section and be entitled, "THIS IS AN ELECTION UNDER § 1.1502-95 TO APPORTION ALL OR PART OF THE [INSERT THE CONSOLIDATED SECTION 382 LIMITATION, THE SUBGROUP SECTION 382 LIMITATION, THE LOSS GROUP'S NET UNREALIZED BUILT-IN GAIN, OR THE LOSS SUBGROUP'S NET UNREALIZED BUILT-IN GAIN, AS APPROPRIATE] IN THE AMOUNT OF [INSERT THE AMOUNT OF THE LOSS LIMITATION OR NET UNREALIZED BUILT-IN GAIN] TO [INSERT NAME(S) AND EMPLOYER IDENTIFICATION NUMBER(S) OF THE CORPORATION (OR THE CORPORATIONS THAT COMPOSE A NEW LOSS SUBGROUP) TO WHICH ALLOCATION IS MADE]." The statement must also indicate that an agreement, as described in paragraph (f)(1)(ii) of this section, has been entered into.

(ii) *Agreement.*—Both the common parent and the party described in paragraph (f)(2) of this section must sign and date the agreement. The agreement must include, as appropriate—

(A) The date of the ownership change that resulted in the consolidated section 382 limitation (or subgroup section 382 limitation) or the loss group's (or loss subgroup's) net unrealized built-in gain;

(B) The amount of the departing member's (or loss subgroup's) pre-change net operating loss carryovers and the taxable years in which they arose that will be subject to the limitation that is being apportioned to that member (or loss subgroup);

(C) The amount of any net unrealized built-in loss allocated to the departing member (or loss subgroup) under paragraph (e) of this section, which, if recognized, can be a pre-change attribute subject to the limitation that is being apportioned;

(D) If a consolidated section 382 limitation (or subgroup section 382 limitation) is being apportioned, the amount of the consolidated section 382 limitation (or subgroup section 382 limitation) for the taxable year during which the former member (or new loss subgroup) ceases to be a member of the consolidated group (determined without regard to any apportionment under this section);

(E) If any net unrealized built-in gain is being apportioned, the amount of the loss group's (or loss subgroup's) net unrealized built-in gain (as determined under paragraph (c)(2)(ii) of this section) that may be apportioned to members that ceased to be members during the consolidated return year;

(F) The amount of the value element and adjustment element of the consolidated section 382 limitation (or subgroup section 382 limitation) that is apportioned to the former member (or new loss subgroup) pursuant to paragraph (c) of this section;

(G) The amount of the loss group's (or loss subgroup's) net unrealized built-in gain that is apportioned to the former member (or new loss subgroup) pursuant to paragraph (c) of this section;

(H) If the former member is allocated any net unrealized built-in loss under paragraph (e) of this section, the amount of any adjustment element apportioned to the former member that is attributable to recognized built-in gains (determined in a manner that will enable both the group and the former member to apply the principles of § 1.1502-93(c)); and

(I) The name and employer identification number of the common parent making the apportionment.

(2) *Signing the agreement.*—The agreement must be signed by both the common parent and the former member (or, in the case of a loss subgroup, the common parent and the loss subgroup parent) by persons authorized to sign their respective income tax returns. If the allocation is made to a loss subgroup for which an election under § 1.1502-91(d)(4) is made, and not separately to its members, the agreement under this paragraph (f) must be signed by the common parent and any member of the new loss subgroup by persons author-

ized to sign their respective income tax returns. Each party signing the agreement must retain either the original or a copy of the agreement as part of its records. See § 1.6001-1(e).

(3) *Filing of the election.*—(i) *Filing by the common parent.*—The election must be filed by the common parent of the group that is apportioning the consolidated section 382 limitation (or the subgroup section 382 limitation) or the loss group's net unrealized built-in gain (or loss subgroup's net unrealized built-in gain) by including the statement on or with its income tax return for the taxable year in which the former member (or new loss subgroup) ceases to be a member.

(ii) *Filing by the former member.*—An identical statement must be included on or with the first return of the former member (or the first return in which the former member, or the members of a new loss subgroup, join) that is filed after the close of the consolidated return year of the group of which the former member (or the members of a new loss subgroup) ceases to be a member.

(4) *Revocation of election.*—An election statement made under paragraph (c) of this section is revocable only with the consent of the Commissioner.

(g) *Effective/applicability date.*—Paragraphs (e)(8) and (f) of this section apply to any original consolidated Federal income tax return due (without extensions) after June 14, 2007. For original consolidated Federal income tax returns due (without extensions) after May 30, 2006, and on or before June 14, 2007, see § 1.1502-95T as contained in 26 CFR part 1 in effect on April 1, 2007. For original consolidated Federal income tax returns due (without extensions) on or before May 30, 2006, see § 1.1502-95 as contained in 26 CFR part 1 in effect on April 1, 2006. [Reg. § 1.1502-95.]

□ [*T.D.* 8824, 6-25-99. *Amended by T.D.* 9264, 5-26-2006; *T.D.* 9329, 6-13-2007, *T.D.* 9424, 9-9-2008 *and T.D.* 9905, 9-3-2020.]

**[Reg. § 1.1502-95A]**

**§ 1.1502-95A. Rules on ceasing to be a member of a consolidated group generally applicable for corporations ceasing to be members before June 25, 1999.**—(a) *In general.*—(1) *Consolidated group.*—This section provides rules for applying section 382 on or after the day that a member ceases to be a member of a consolidated group (or loss subgroup). The rules concern how to determine whether an ownership change occurs with respect to losses of the member, and how a consolidated section 382 limitation (or subgroup section 382 limitation) is apportioned to the member. As the context requires, a reference in this section to a loss group, a member, or a corporation also includes a reference to a loss subgroup, and a reference to a consolidated section 382 limitation also includes a reference to a subgroup section 382 limitation.

(2) *Election by common parent.*—Only the common parent (not the loss subgroup parent) may make the election under paragraph (c) of this section to apportion either a consolidated section 382 limitation or a subgroup section 382 limitation.

(3) *Coordination with §§ 1.1502-91A through 1.1502-93A.*—For rules regarding the determination of whether there is an ownership change of a loss subgroup and the computation of a subgroup section 382 limitation following such an ownership change, see §§ 1.1502-91A through 1.1502-93A.

(b) *Separate application of section 382 when a member leaves a consolidated group.*—(1) *In general.*—Except as provided in §§ 1.1502-91A through 1.1502-93A (relating to rules applicable to loss groups and loss subgroups), section 382 and the regulations thereunder apply to a corporation on a separate entity basis after it ceases to be a member of a consolidated group (or loss subgroup). Solely for purposes of determining whether a corporation has an ownership change—

(i) Any portion of a consolidated net operating loss that is apportioned to the corporation under § 1.1502-21(b) or 1.1502-21T(b) in effect prior to June 25, 1999, as contained in 26 CFR part 1 revised April 1, 1999, as applicable is treated as a net operating loss of the corporation beginning on the first day of the taxable year in which the loss arose;

(ii) The testing period may include the period during which (or before which) the corporation was a member of the group (or loss subgroup); and

(iii) Except to the extent provided in § 1.1502-20(g) (relating to reattributed losses), the day it ceases to be a member of a consolidated group is treated as a testing date of the corporation within the meaning of § 1.382-2(a)(4).

(2) *Effect of a prior ownership change of the group.*—If a loss group has had an ownership change under § 1.1502-92A before a corporation ceases to be a member of a consolidated group (the former member)—

(i) Any pre-change consolidated attribute that is subject to a consolidated section 382 limitation continues to be treated as a pre-change loss with respect to the former member after the attribute is apportioned to the former member;

(ii) The former member's section 382 limitation with respect to such attribute is zero except to the extent the common parent apportions under paragraph (c) of this section all or a part of the consolidated section 382 limitation to the former member;

(iii) The testing period for determining a subsequent ownership change with respect to such attribute begins no earlier than the first day following the loss group's most recent change date; and

(iv) As generally provided under section 382, an ownership change of the former member that occurs on or after the day it ceases to be a member of a loss group may result in an additional, lesser limitation amount with respect to such loss.

(3) *Application in the case of a loss subgroup.*—If two or more former members are included in the same loss subgroup immediately after they cease to be members of a consolidated group, the princi-

ples of paragraphs (b) and (c) of this section apply to the loss subgroup. Therefore, for example, an apportionment by the common parent under paragraph (c) of this section is made to the loss subgroup rather than separately to its members.

(4) *Examples.*—The following examples illustrate the principles of this paragraph (b).

*Example 1. Treatment of departing member as a separate corporation throughout the testing period.* (a) A owns all the L stock. L owns all the stock of L1 and L2. The L group has a consolidated net operating loss arising in Year 1 that is carried over to Year 3. On January 12, Year 2, A sells 30 percent of the L stock to B. On February 7, Year 3, L sells 40 percent of the L2 stock to C, and L2 ceases to be a member of the group. A portion of the Year 1 consolidated net operating loss is apportioned to L2 under § 1.1502-21(b) or 1.1502-21T(b) in effect prior to June 25, 1999, as contained in 26 CFR part 1 revised April 1, 1999, as applicable and is carried to L2's first separate return year, which ends December 31, Year 3. The following is a graphic illustration of these facts:

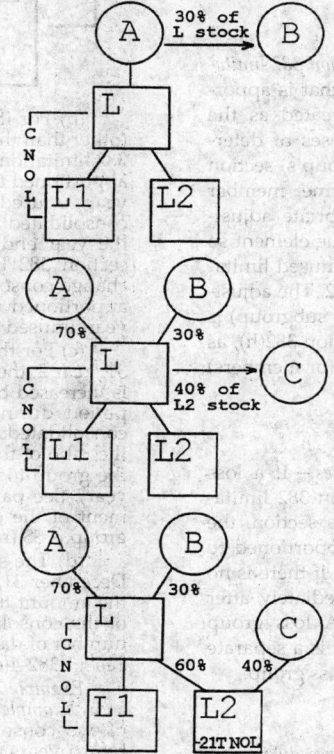

(b) Under paragraph (b)(1) of this section, L2 is a loss corporation on February 7, Year 3. Under paragraph (b)(1)(iii) of this section, February 7, Year 3, is a testing date. Under paragraph (b)(1)(ii) of this section, the testing period for L2 with respect to this testing date commences on January 1, the first day of the taxable year in which the portion of the consolidated net operating loss apportioned to L2 arose. Therefore, in determining whether L2 has an ownership change on February 7, Year 3, B's purchase of 30 percent of the L stock and C's purchase of 40 percent of the L2 stock are each owner shifts. L2 has an ownership change under section 382(g) and § 1.382-2T because B and C have increased their ownership interests in L2 by 18 and 40 percentage points, respectively, during the testing period.

*Example 2. Effect of prior ownership change of loss group.* (a) L owns all the L1 stock and L1 owns all the L2 stock. The L loss group had an ownership change under § 1.1502-92A in Year 2 with respect to a consolidated net operating loss arising in Year 1 and carried over to Year 2 and Year 3. The consolidated section 382 limitation computed solely on the basis of the value of the stock of L is $100. On December 31, Year 2, L1 sells 25 percent of the stock of L2 to B. L2 is apportioned a portion of the Year 1 consolidated net operating loss which it carries over to its first separate return year ending after December 31, Year 2. L2's separate section 382 limitation with respect to this loss is zero unless L elects to apportion all or a part of the consolidated section 382 limitation to L2. (See paragraph (c) of this section for rules regarding the apportionment of a consolidated section 382 limitation.) L apportions $50 of the consolidated section 382 limitation to L2.

(b) On December 31, Year 3, L1 sells its remaining 75 percent stock interest in L2 to C, resulting in an ownership change of L2. L2's section 382 limitation computed on the change date with respect to the value of its stock is $30. Accordingly, L2's section 382 limitation for post-change years ending after December 31, Year 3, with respect to its pre-change losses, including the consolidated net operating losses apportioned to it from the L group, is $30, adjusted as required by section 382 and the regulations thereunder.

(c) *Apportionment of a consolidated section 382 limitation.*—(1) *In general.*—The common parent may elect to apportion all or any part of a consolidated section 382 limitation to a former member (or loss subgroup). See paragraph (e) of this section for the time and manner of making the election to apportion.

(2) *Amount of apportionment.*—The common parent may apportion all or part of each element of the consolidated section 382 limitation determined under § 1.1502-93A. For this purpose, the consolidated section 382 limitation consists of two elements —

(i) The value element, which is the element of the limitation determined under section 382(b)(1) (relating to value multiplied by the long-term tax-exempt rate) without regard to such adjustments as those described in section 382(b)(2) (relating to the carryforward of unused section 382 limitation), section 382(b)(3)(B) (relating to the section 382 limitation for the post-change year that includes the change date), section 382(h) (relating to built-in gains and section 338 gains), and section 382(m)(2) (relating to short taxable years); and

(ii) The adjustment element, which is so much (if any) of the limitation for the taxable year during which the former member ceases to be a member of the consolidated group that is attributable to a carryover of unused limitation under section 382(b)(2) or to recognized built-in gains under 382(h).

(3) *Effect of apportionment on the consolidated section 382 limitation.*—The value element of the consolidated section 382 limitation for any post-change year ending after the day that a former member (or loss subgroup) ceases to be a member(s) is reduced to the extent that it is apportioned under this paragraph (c). The consolidated section 382 limitation for the post-change year in which the former member (or loss subgroup) ceases to be a member(s) is also reduced to the extent that the adjustment element for that year is apportioned under this paragraph (c).

(4) *Effect on corporations to which the consolidated section 382 limitation is apportioned.*—The amount of the value element that is apportioned to a former member (or loss subgroup) is treated as the amount determined under section 382(b)(1) for purposes of determining the amount of that corporation's (or loss subgroup's) section 382 limitation for any taxable year ending after the former member (or loss subgroup) ceases to be a member(s). Appropriate adjustments must be made to the limitation based on the value element so apportioned for a short taxable year, carryforward of unused limitation, or any other adjustment required under section 382. The adjustment element apportioned to a former member (or loss subgroup) is treated as an adjustment under section 382(b)(2) or section 382(h), as appropriate, for the first taxable year after the member (or members) ceases to be a member (or members).

(5) *Deemed apportionment when loss group terminates.*—If a loss group terminates, to the extent the consolidated section 382 limitation is not apportioned under paragraph (c)(1) of this section, the consolidated section 382 limitation is deemed to be apportioned to the loss subgroup that includes the common parent, or, if there is no loss subgroup that includes the common parent immediately after the loss group terminates, to the common parent. A loss group terminates on the first day of the first taxable year that is a separate return year with respect to each member of the former loss group.

(6) *Appropriate adjustments when former member leaves during the year.*—Appropriate adjustments are made to the consolidated section 382 limitation for the consolidated return year during which the former member (or loss subgroup) ceases to be a member(s) to reflect the inclusion of the former member in the loss group for a portion of that year.

(7) *Examples.*—The following examples illustrate the principles of this paragraph (c).

*Example 1. Consequence of apportionment.* (a) L owns all the L1 stock and L1 owns all the L2 stock. The L group has a $200 consolidated net operating loss arising in Year 1 that is carried over to Year 2. At the close of December 31, Year 1, the group has an ownership change under § 1.1502-92A. The ownership change results in a consolidated section 382 limitation of $10 based on the value of the stock of the group. On August 29, Year 2, L1 sells 30 percent of the stock of L2 to A. L2 is apportioned $90 of the group's $200 consolidated net operating loss under § 1.1502-21(b) or 1.1502-21T(b) in effect prior to June 25, 1999, as contained in 26 CFR part 1 revised April 1, 1999, as applicable. L, the common parent, elects to apportion $6 of the consolidated section 382 limitation to L2. The following is a graphic illustration of these facts:

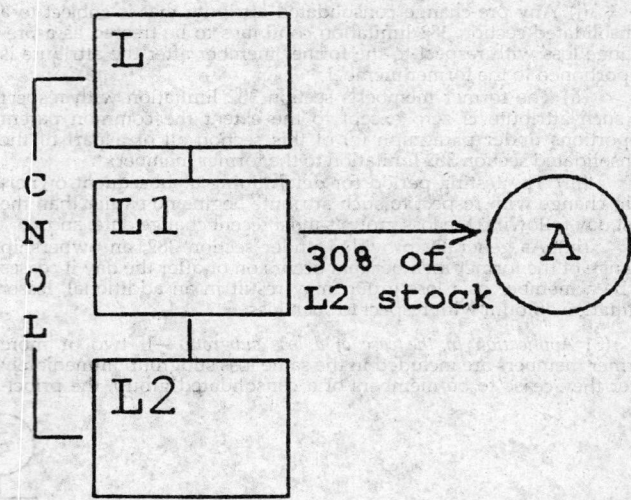

(b) For its separate return years ending after August 29, Year 2 (other than the taxable year ending December 31, Year 2), L2's section 382 limitation with respect to the $90 of the group's net operating loss apportioned to it is $6, adjusted, as appropriate, for any short taxable year, unused section 382 limitation, or other adjustment. For its consolidated return years ending after August 29, Year 2, (other than the year ending December 31, Year 2) the L group's consolidated section 382 limitation with respect to the remaining $110 of pre-change consolidated attribute is $4 ($10 minus the $6 value element apportioned to L2), adjusted, as appropriate, for any short taxable year, unused section 382 limitation, or other adjustment.

(c) For the L group's consolidated return year ending December 31, Year 2, the value element of its consolidated section 382 limitation is increased by $4 (rounded to the nearest dollar), to account for the period during which L2 was a member of the L group ($6, the consolidated section 382 limitation apportioned to L2, times 241/365, the ratio of the number of days during Year 2 that L2 is a member of the group to the number of days in the group's consolidated return year). See paragraph (c)(6) of this section. Therefore, the value element of the consolidated section 382 limitation for Year 2 of the L group is $8 (rounded to the nearest dollar).

(d) The section 382 limitation for L2's short taxable year ending December 31, Year 2, is $2 (rounded to the nearest dollar), which is the amount that bears the same relationship to $6, the value element of the consolidated section 382 limitation apportioned to L2, as the number of days during that short taxable year, 124 days, bears to 365. See § 1.382-4(c).

*Example 2. Consequence of no apportionment.* The facts are the same as in *Example 1*, except that L does not elect to apportion any portion of the consolidated section 382 limitation to L2. For its separate return years ending after August 29, Year 2, L2's section 382 limitation with respect to the $90 of the group's pre-change consolidated attribute apportioned to L2 is zero under paragraph (b)(2)(ii) of this section. Thus, the $90 consolidated net operating loss apportioned to L2 cannot offset L2's taxable income in any of its separate return years ending after August 29, Year 2. For its consolidated return years ending after August 29, Year 2, the L group's consolidated section 382 limitation with respect to the remaining $110 of pre-change consolidated attribute is $10, adjusted, as appropriate, for any short taxable year, unused section 382 limitation, or other adjustment.

*Example 3. Apportionment of adjustment element.* The facts are the same as in *Example 1*, except that L2 ceases to be a member of the L group on August 29, Year 3, and the L group has a $4 carryforward of an unused consolidated section 382 limitation (under section 382(b)(2)) to the 1993 consolidated return year. The carryover of unused limitation increases the consolidated section 382 limitation for the Year 3 consolidated return year from $10 to $14. L may elect to apportion all or any portion of the $10 value element and all or any portion of the $4 adjustment element to L2.

(d) *Rules pertaining to ceasing to be a member of a loss subgroup.*—(1) *In general.*—A corporation ceases to be a member of a loss subgroup—

(i) On the first day of the first taxable year for which it files a separate return; or

(ii) The first day that it ceases to bear a relationship described in section 1504(a)(1) to the loss subgroup parent (treating for this purpose the loss subgroup parent as the common parent described in section 1504(a)(1)(A)).

(2) *Examples.*—The principles of this paragraph (d) are illustrated by the following examples.

*Example 1. Basic case.* (a) P owns all the L stock, L owns all the L1 stock and L1 owns all the L2 stock. The P group has a consolidated net operating loss arising in Year 1 that is carried over to Year 2. On December 11, Year 2, P sells all the stock of L to corporation M. Each

of L, L1, and L2 is apportioned a portion of the Year 1 consolidated net operating loss, and thereafter each joins with M in filing consolidated returns. Under §1.1502-92A, the L loss subgroup has an ownership change on December 11, Year 2. The L loss subgroup has a subgroup section 382 limitation of $100. The following is a graphic illustration of these facts:

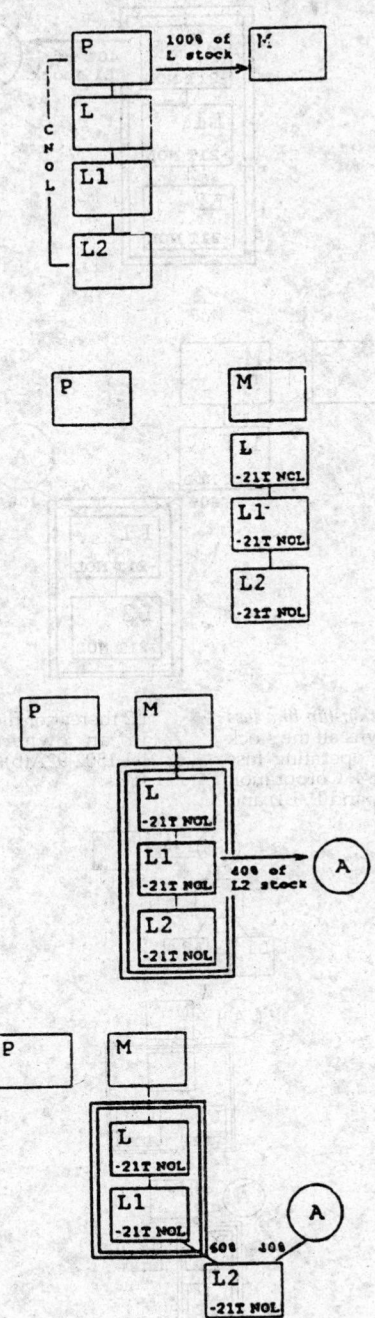

(b) On May 22, Year 3, L1 sells 40 percent of the L2 stock to A. L2 carries over a portion of the P group's net operating loss from Year 1 to its separate return year ending December 31, Year 3. Under paragraph (d)(1) of this section, L2 ceases to be a member of the L loss subgroup on May 22, Year 3, which is both (1) the first day of the first taxable year for which it files a separate return and (2) the day it ceases to bear a relationship described in section 1504(a)(1) to the loss subgroup parent, L. The net operating loss of L2 that is carried over from the P group is treated as a pre-change loss of L2 for its separate return years ending after May 22, Year 3. Under paragraphs (a)(2) and (b)(2) of this section, the separate section 382 limitation with respect to this loss is zero unless M elects to apportion all or a part of the subgroup section 382 limitation of the L loss subgroup to L2.

*Example 2. Formation of a new loss subgroup.* The facts are the same as in *Example 1,* except that A purchases 40 percent of the L1 stock from L rather than purchasing L2 stock from L1. L1 and L2 file a consolidated return for their first taxable year ending after May 22, Year 3, and each of L1 and L2 carries over a part of the net operating loss of the P group that arose in Year 1. Under paragraph (d)(1) of this section, L1 and L2 cease to be members of the L loss subgroup on May 22, Year 3. The net operating losses carried over from the P group are treated as pre-change subgroup attributes of the loss subgroup composed of L1 and L2. The subgroup section 382 limitation with respect to those losses is zero unless M elects to apportion all or part of the subgroup section 382 limitation of the L loss subgroup to the L1 loss subgroup. The following is a graphic illustration of these facts:

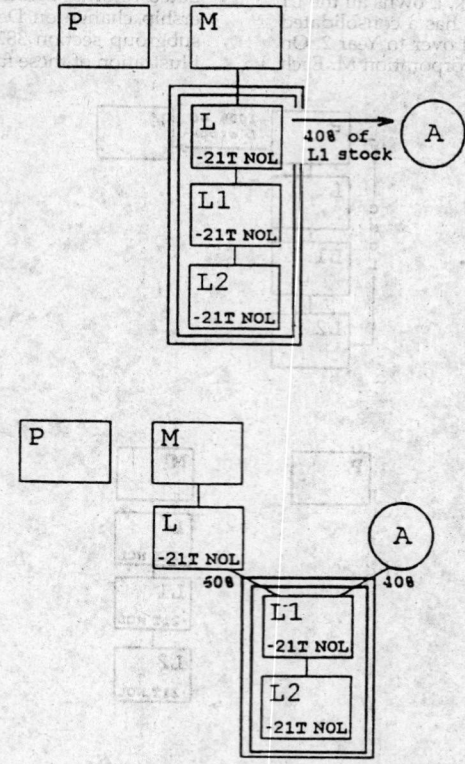

*Example 3. Ceasing to bear a section 1504(a)(1) relationship to a loss subgroup parent.* (a) A owns all the stock of P, and P owns all the stock of L1 and L2. The P group has a consolidated net operating loss arising in Year 1 that is carried over to Year 3 and Year 4. Corporation M acquires all the stock of P on November 11, Year 3, and P, L1, and

L2 thereafter file consolidated returns with M. M's acquisition results in an ownership change of the P loss subgroup under §1.1502-92A(b)(1)(ii). The following is a graphic illustration of these facts:

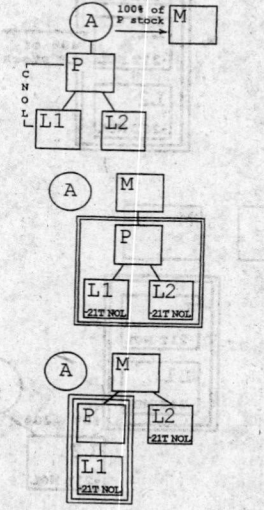

(b) P distributes the L2 stock to M on October 7, Year 4. L2 ceases to be a member of the P loss subgroup on October 7, Year 4, the first day that it ceases to bear the relationship described in section 1504(a)(1) to P, the P loss subgroup parent. See paragraph (d)(1)(ii) of this section. Thus, the section 382 limitation with respect to the pre-change subgroup attributes attributable to L2 is zero except to the extent M elects to apportion all or a part of the subgroup section 382 limitation of the P loss subgroup to L2.

*Example 4. Relationship through a successor.* The facts are the same as in *Example 3*, except that, instead of P's distributing the stock of L2, L2 merges into L1 on October 7, Year 4. L1 (as successor to L2 in the merger within the meaning of §1.382-2T(f)(4)) continues to bear a relationship described in section 1504(a)(1) to P, the loss subgroup

parent. Thus, L2 does not cease to be a member of the P loss subgroup as a result of the merger.

(e) *Filing the election to apportion.*—(1) *Form of the election to apportion.*—An election under paragraph (c) of this section must be made by the common parent. The election must be made in the form of the following statement: "THIS IS AN ELECTION UNDER §1.1502-95A OF THE INCOME TAX REGULATIONS TO APPORTION ALL OR PART OF THE [insert either CONSOLIDATED SECTION 382 LIMITATION or SUBGROUP SECTION 382 LIMITATION, as appropriate] TO [insert name and E.I.N. of the corporation (or the corporations that compose a new loss subgroup) to which allocation is made]. The declaration must also include the following information, as appropriate—

(i) The date of the ownership change that resulted in the consolidated section 382 limitation (or subgroup section 382 limitation);

(ii) The amount of the consolidated section 382 limitation (or subgroup section 382 limitation) for the taxable year during which the former member (or new loss subgroup) ceases to be a member of the consolidated group (determined without regard to any apportionment under this section;

(iii) The amount of the value element and adjustment element of the consolidated section 382 limitation (or subgroup section 382 limitation) that is apportioned to the former member (or new loss subgroup) pursuant to paragraph (c) of this section; and

(iv) The name and E.I.N. of the common parent making the apportionment.

(2) *Signing of the election.*—The election statement must be signed by both the common parent and the former member (or, in the case of a loss subgroup, the common parent and the loss group parent) by persons authorized to sign their respective income tax returns.

(3) *Filing of the election.*—The election statement must be filed by the common parent of the group that is apportioning the consolidated section 382 limitation (or the subgroup section 382 limitation) with its income tax return for the taxable year in which the former member (or new loss subgroup) ceases to be a member. The common parent must also deliver a copy of the statement to the former member (or the members of the new loss subgroup) on or before the day the group files its income tax return for the consolidated return year that the former member (or new loss subgroup) ceases to be a member. A copy of the statement must be attached to the first return of the former member (or the first return in which the members of a new loss subgroup join) that is filed after the close of the consolidated return year of the group of which the former member (or the members of a new loss subgroup) ceases to be a member.

(4) *Revocation of election.*—An election statement made under paragraph (c) of this section is revocable only with the consent of the Commissioner. [Reg. § 1.1502-95A.]

☐ [T.D. 8678, 6-26-96. *Amended by T.D. 8823, 6-25-99 and amended and redesignated by T.D. 8824, 6-25-99.*]

### [Reg. § 1.1502-96]

**§1.1502-96. Miscellaneous rules.**—(a) *End of separate tracking of losses.*—(1) *Application.*—This paragraph (a) applies to a member (or a loss subgroup) with a net operating loss carryover that arose (or is treated under § 1.1502-21(c) as arising) in a SRLY, or a member (or loss subgroup) with a net unrealized built-in loss determined at the time that the member (or loss subgroup) becomes a member of the consolidated group if there is—

(i) An ownership change of the member (or loss subgroup) within six months before, on, or after becoming a member of the group; or

(ii) A period of 5 consecutive years following the day that the member (or loss subgroup) becomes a member of a group during which the member (or loss subgroup) has not had an ownership change.

(2) *Effect of end of separate tracking.*—(i) *Net operating loss carryovers.*—If this paragraph (a) applies with respect to a member (or loss subgroup) with a net operating loss carryover, then, starting on the day after the earlier of the change date (but not earlier than the day the member (or loss subgroup) becomes a member of the consolidated group) or the last day of the 5 consecutive year period described in paragraph (a)(1)(ii) of this section, such loss carryover is treated as described in § 1.1502-91(c)(1)(i). The preceding sentence also applies for purposes of determining whether there is an ownership change with respect to such loss carryover following such change date or 5 consecutive year period. Thus, for example, starting the day after the change date (but not earlier than the day the member (or loss subgroup) becomes a member of the consolidated group) or the end of the 5 consecutive year period—

(A) The consolidated group which includes the new loss member or loss subgroup is no longer required to separately track owner shifts of the stock of the new loss member or subgroup parent to determine if an ownership change occurs with respect to the loss carryover of the new loss member or members included in the loss subgroup;

(B) The group is a loss group because the member's loss carryover is treated as a loss described in § 1.1502-91(c)(1)(i);

(C) There is an ownership change with respect to such loss carryover only if the group has an ownership change; and

(D) If the group has an ownership change, such loss carryover is a pre-change consolidated attribute subject to the loss group's consolidated section 382 limitation.

(ii) *Net unrealized built-in losses.*—If this paragraph (a) applies with respect to a new loss member described in § 1.1502-94(a)(1)(ii) (or a loss subgroup described in § 1.1502-91(d)(2)) then, starting on the day after the earlier of the change date (but not earlier than the day the member (or loss subgroup) becomes a member of the group) or the last day of the 5 consecutive year period described in paragraph (a)(1)(ii) of this section, the member (or members of the loss subgroup) are treated, for purposes of applying § 1.1502-91(g)(2)(ii), as if they have been affiliated with the common parent for 5 consecutive years. Starting on that day, the member's (or the members of the loss subgroup's) separately computed net unrealized built-in loss is included in the determination whether the group has a net unrealized built-in loss, and there is an ownership change with respect to the member's separately computed net unrealized built-in loss only if the group (including the member) has a net unrealized built-in loss and has an ownership change. Thus, for example, starting the day after the change date (but not earlier than the day the member (or loss subgroup) becomes a member of the consolidated group), or the end of the 5 consecutive period—

(A) The consolidated group which includes the new loss member or loss subgroup is no longer required to separately track owner shifts of the stock of the new loss member or subgroup parent to determine if an ownership change occurs with respect to the net unrealized built-in loss of the new loss member or members of the loss subgroup;

(B) The group includes the member's (or the loss subgroup members') separately computed net unrealized built-in loss in determining whether it is a loss group under § 1.1502-91(c)(1)(iii);

(C) There is an ownership change with respect to such net unrealized built-in loss only if the group is a loss group and has an ownership change; and

(D) If the group has an ownership change, the member's separately computed net unrealized built-in loss and its assets are taken into account in determining the group's pre-change consolidated attributes described in § 1.1502-91(e)(1) (relating to recognized built-in losses) that are subject to the group's consolidated section 382 limitation.

(iii) *Common parent not common parent for five years.*—If the common parent has become the common parent of an existing group within the previous 5-year period in a transaction described in § 1.1502-75(d)(2)(ii) or (3), appropriate adjustments must be made in applying paragraphs (a)(2)(ii) and (3) of this section. In such a case, as the context requires, references to the common parent are to the former common parent.

(3) *Continuing effect of end of separate tracking.*—(i) *In general.*—As the context may require, a current group determines which of its members are included in a loss subgroup on any testing date by taking into account the application of this section in the former group. See the example in § 1.1502-91(f)(2). For this purpose, corporations that are treated under paragraph (a)(2)(ii) of this section as having been affiliated with the common parent of the former group for 5 consecutive years are also treated as having been affiliated with any other members that have been (or are treated as having been) affiliated with the common parent. The corporations are treated as having been affiliated with such other members for the same period of time that those members have been (or are treated as having been) affiliated with the common parent. If two or more corporations become members of the group at the same time, but paragraph (a)(1) of this section does not apply to every such corporation, then immediately after the corporations become members of the group, the corporations to which paragraph (a)(1) of this section applied are treated as not having been previously affiliated, for purposes of applying this paragraph (a)(3), with the corporations to which paragraph (a)(2)(ii) of this section did not apply.

(ii) *Example.*—The following example illustrates the principles of this paragraph (a)(3):

*Example.* (i) L has owned all the stock of L1 for three years. At the close of December 31, Year 1, the M group purchases all the L stock, and L and L1 become members of the M group. Other than the stock of L1, L has one asset (the L loss asset) with a net unrealized built-in loss of $200 on this date. L1 has one asset with a net unrealized built-in gain of $50 (the L1 gain asset). L and L1 do not compose a loss subgroup because they do not meet the five year affiliation requirement of § 1.1502-91(d)(2)(i). L is a new loss member, and M's purchase of L causes an ownership change of L. At the close of December 31, Year 4, at a time when L1 has been affiliated with the M group for three years and has been affiliated with L for six years, the S group purchases all the M stock. On this date, the L loss asset has a net unrealized built-in loss of $300, the L1 gain asset has a net unrealized built-in gain of $80, and M, the common parent of the M group, has one asset with a net unrealized built-in gain of $200.

(ii) Paragraph (a)(1) of this section applies to L because L is a new loss member described in § 1.1502-94(a)(1)(ii) that has an ownership change upon becoming a member of the M group on December 31, Year 1. Accordingly, L is treated as having been affiliated with M for 5 consecutive years, and the L loss asset with a net unrealized built-in loss of $300 is included in the determination whether the M group has a net unrealized built-in loss.

(iii) The S group determines which of its members are included in a loss subgroup by taking into account application of paragraph (a) of this section in the M group. For this purpose, application of paragraph (a) of this section causes L to be treated as having been affiliated with M (or as having been a member of the M group) for 5 consecutive years as of January 1, Year 2. Therefore, the S group includes L in the determination whether the M subgroup acquired by S on December 31, Year 4, has a net unrealized built-in loss.

(iv) Because paragraph (a)(1) of this section applied to L when L became a member of the M group, but did not apply to L1, L is treated as not having been affiliated with L1 before L and L1 joined the M group. Also, L1 is not included in the determination whether the M subgroup has a net unrealized built-in loss because L1 has not been continuously affiliated with members of the M group for the five consecutive year period ending immediately before they become members of the S group. See § 1.1502-91(g)(2).

(4) *Special rule for testing period.*—For purposes of determining the beginning of the testing period for a loss group, the member's (or loss subgroup's) net operating loss carryovers (or net unrealized built-in loss) described in paragraph (a)(2) of this section are considered to arise—

(i) In a case described in paragraph (a)(1)(i) of this section, in a taxable year that begins not earlier than the later of the day following the change date or the day that the member becomes a member of the group; and

(ii) In a case described in paragraph (a)(1)(ii) of this section, in a taxable year that begins 3 years before the end of the 5 consecutive year period.

(5) *Limits on effects of end of separate tracking.*—The rule contained in this paragraph (a) applies solely for purposes of §§ 1.1502-91 through 1.1502-95 and this section (other than paragraph (b)(2)(ii)(B) of this section (relating to the definition of pre-change attributes of a subsidiary)) and § 1.1502-98, and not for purposes of other provisions of the consolidated return regulations. However, the rule contained in this paragraph (a) does apply in §§ 1.1502-15(g), 1.1502-21(g) and 1.1502-22(g) for purposes of determining the composition of loss subgroups defined in § 1.1502-91(d). See also paragraph (c) of this section for the continuing effect of an ownership change with respect to pre-change attributes.

(b) *Ownership change of subsidiary.*—(1) *Ownership change of a subsidiary because of options or plan or arrangement.*—Notwithstanding § 1.1502-92, a subsidiary may have an ownership change for purposes of section 382 with respect to its attributes which a group or loss subgroup includes in making a determination under § 1.1502-91(c)(1) (relating to the definition of loss group) or § 1.1502-91(d) (relating to the definition of loss subgroup). The subsidiary has such an ownership change if it has an ownership change under the principles of § 1.1502-95(b) and section 382 and the regulations thereunder (determined on a separate entity basis by treating the subsidiary as not being a member of a consolidated group) in the event of—

(i) The deemed exercise under § 1.382-4(d) of an option or options (other than an option with respect to stock of the common parent) held by a person (or persons acting pursuant to a plan or arrangement) to acquire more than 20 percent of the stock of the subsidiary; or

(ii) An increase by 1 or more 5-percent shareholders, acting pursuant to a plan or arrangement to avoid an ownership change of a subsidiary, in their percentage ownership interest in the subsidiary by more than 50 percentage points during the testing period of the subsidiary through the acquisition (or deemed acquisition pursuant to § 1.382-4(d)) of ownership interests in the subsidiary and in higher-tier members with respect to the subsidiary.

(2) *Effect of the ownership change.*—(i) *In general.*—If a subsidiary has an ownership change under paragraph (b)(1) of this section, the amount of consolidated taxable income for any post-change year that may be offset by the pre-change losses of the subsidiary shall not exceed the section 382 limitation for the subsidiary. For purposes of this limitation, the value of the subsidiary is determined solely by reference to the value of the subsidiary's stock.

(ii) *Pre-change losses.*—The pre-change losses of a subsidiary are—

(A) Its allocable part of any consolidated net operating loss which is attributable to it under § 1.1502-21(b) (determined on the last day of the consolidated return year that includes the change date)

that is not carried back and absorbed in a taxable year prior to the year including the change date;

(B) Its net operating loss carryovers that arose (or are treated under § 1.1502-21(c) as having arisen) in a SRLY; and

(C) Its recognized built-in loss with respect to its separately computed net unrealized built-in loss, if any, determined on the change date.

(3) *Coordination with §§ 1.1502-91, 1.1502-92, and 1.1502-94.*—If an increase in percentage ownership interest causes an ownership change with respect to an attribute under this paragraph (b) and under § 1.1502-92 on the same day, the ownership change is considered to occur only under § 1.1502-92 and not under this paragraph (b). See § 1.1502-94 for anti-duplication rules relating to value.

(4) *Example.*—The following example illustrates paragraph (b)(1)(ii) of this section:

*Example. Plan to avoid an ownership change of a subsidiary.* (i) L owns all the stock of L1, L1 owns all the stock of L2, L2 owns all the stock of L3, and L3 owns all the stock of L4. The L group has a consolidated net operating loss arising in Year 1 that is carried over to Year 2. L has assets other than its L1 stock with a value of $900. L1, L2, and L3 own no assets other than their L2, L3, and L4 stock. L4 has assets with a value of $100. During Year 2, A, B, C, and D, acting pursuant to a plan to avoid an ownership change of L4, acquire the following ownership interests in the members of the L loss group: (A) on September 11, Year 2, A acquires 20 percent of the L1 stock from L and B acquires 20 percent of the L2 stock from L1; and (B) on September 20, Year 2, C acquires 20 percent of the stock of L3 from L2 and D acquires 20 percent of the stock of L4 from L3.

(ii) The acquisitions by A, B, C, and D pursuant to the plan have increased their respective percentage ownership interests in L4 by approximately 10, 13, 16, and 20 percentage points, for a total of approximately 59 percentage points during the testing period. This more than 50 percentage point increase in the percentage ownership interest in L4 causes an ownership change of L4 under paragraph (b)(2) of this section.

(c) *Continuing effect of an ownership change.*—A loss corporation (or loss subgroup) that is subject to a limitation under section 382 with respect to its pre-change losses continues to be subject to the limitation regardless of whether it becomes a member or ceases to be a member of a consolidated group. See § 1.382-5(d) (relating to successive ownership changes and absorption of a section 382 limitation).

(d) *Losses reattributed under § 1.1502-36(d)(6).*—(1) *In general.*—This paragraph (d) contains rules relating to net operating carryovers, capital loss carryovers, and deferred deductions (collectively, loss or losses) that are reattributed to the common parent under § 1.1502-36(d)(6). References in this paragraph (d) to a subsidiary are references to the subsidiary (or lower-tier subsidiary) whose loss is reattributed to the common parent.

(2) *Deemed section 381(a) transaction.*—Under § 1.1502-36(d)(6)(iv)(A), the common parent succeeds to the reattributed losses as if the losses were succeeded to in a transaction to which section 381(a) applies. In general, §§ 1.1502-91 through 1.1502-95, this section, and § 1.1502-98 are applied to the reattributed losses in accordance with that characterization. See generally, § 1.382-2(a)(1)(ii) (relating to distributor or transferor loss corporations in transactions under section 381), § 1.1502-1(f)(4) (relating to the definition of predecessor and successor) and § 1.1502-91(j) (relating to predecessor and successor corporations). For example, if the reattributed loss is a pre-change attribute subject to a section 382 limitation, it remains subject to that limitation following the reattribution. In certain cases, the limitation applicable to the reattributed loss is zero unless the common parent apportions all or part of the limitation to itself. (See paragraph (d)(4) of this section.)

(3) *Rules relating to owner shifts.*—(i) *In general.*—Any owner shift of the subsidiary (including any deemed owner shift resulting from section 382(g)(4)(D) or 382(l)(3)) in connection with the disposition of the stock of the subsidiary is not taken into account in determining whether there is an ownership change with respect to the reattributed loss. However, any owner shift with respect to the successor corporation that is treated as continuing in existence under § 1.382-2(a)(1)(ii) must be taken into account for such purpose if such owner shift is effected by the reattribution and an owner shift of the stock of the subsidiary not held directly or indirectly by the common parent would have been taken into account if such shift had occurred immediately before the reattribution. See paragraph (d)(3)(ii) *Example* 2 of this section.

(ii) *Examples.*—The following examples illustrate the principles of this paragraph (d)(3):

*Example 1. No owner shift for reattributed loss.* (i) *Facts.* P, the common parent of a consolidated group, owns 60% of the stock of L, and B owns the remaining 40%. L has a net operating loss carryover of $100 from year 1 that it carries over to years 2, 3, and 4. At the beginning of year 2, P purchases 40% of the L stock from B, which does not cause an ownership change of L. On December 31, year 3, P sells all of the L stock to M. Pursuant to §1.1502-36(d)(6), P reattributes $10 of L's $100 net operating loss carryover to itself, and L carries $90 of its net operating loss carryover to its year 4.

(ii) *Analysis.* The sale of the L stock to M does not cause an owner shift that is taken into account in determining if there is an ownership change with respect to the $10 reattributed loss. Following the reattribution, §1.1502-94(b) continues to apply to determine if there is an ownership change with respect to the $10 reattributed loss, until, under paragraph (a) of this section, the loss is treated as described in §1.1502-91(c)(1)(i). In applying §1.1502-94(b), the 40 percentage point increase by the P shareholders prior to the reattribution is taken into account. The sale of the L stock to M does cause an ownership change of L with respect to the $90 of its net operating loss that it carries over to year 4.

*Example 2. Owner shift for reattributed loss.* The facts are the same as in Example 1, except that P only purchases 20% of the L stock from B and sells 80% of the L stock to M. L is a new loss member, and, under §1.1502-94(b)(1), an owner shift of the stock of L not held directly or indirectly by the common parent (the 20% of L stock still held by B) would have been taken into account if such shift had occurred immediately before the reattribution. Following the reattribution, §1.1502-94(b) continues to apply to determine if there is an ownership change with respect to the $10 reattributed loss, until, under paragraph (a) of this section, the loss is treated as described in §1.1502-91(c)(1)(i). With respect to the $10 reattributed loss, the P shareholders have increased their percentage ownership interest by 40 percentage points. The P shareholders have increased their ownership interests by 20 percentage points as a result of P's purchase of stock from B, and, under §1.382-2(a)(1)(ii), are treated as increasing their interests by an additional 20 percentage points as a result of the reattribution. (The acquisition of the L stock by M does not, however, effect an owner shift for the $10 of reattributed loss.) The sale of the L stock to M causes an ownership change of L with respect to the $90 of net operating loss that L carries over to Year 4.

(4) *Rules relating to the section 382 limitation.*—(i) *Reattributed loss is a prechange separate attribute of a new loss member.*—If the reattributed loss is a prechange separate attribute of a new loss member that is subject to a separate section 382 limitation prior to the disposition of subsidiary stock, the common parent's limitation with respect to that loss is zero, except to the extent that the common parent apportions to itself, under paragraph (d)(5) of this section, all or part of such limitation. A separate section 382 limitation is the limitation described in §1.1502-94(b) that applies to a prechange separate attribute.

(ii) *Reattributed loss is a pre-change subgroup attribute.*—If the reattributed loss is a pre-change subgroup attribute subject to a subgroup section 382 limitation prior to the disposition of subsidiary stock, and, immediately after the reattribution, the common parent is not a member of the loss subgroup, the section 382 limitation with respect to that loss is zero, except to the extent that the common parent apportions to itself, under paragraph (d)(5) of this section, all or part of the subgroup section 382 limitation. See, however, §1.1502-95(d)(3) *Example 6,* for an illustration of a case where the common parent, as successor to the subsidiary, is a member of the loss subgroup immediately after the reattribution.

(iii) *Potential application of section 382(l)(1).*—In general, the value of the stock of the common parent is used to determine the section 382 limitation for an ownership change with respect to the reattributed loss that occurs at the time of, or after, the reattribution. For example, if the loss is a pre-change consolidated attribute, the value of the stock of the common parent is used to determine the section 382 limitation, and no adjustment to that value is required because of the deemed section 381(a) transaction. However, if the loss is a pre-change separate attribute of a new loss member (or is a pre-change attribute of a loss subgroup member and the common parent was not the loss subgroup parent immediately before the reattribution), the deemed section 381(a) transaction is considered to constitute a capital contribution with respect to the new loss member (or loss subgroup member) for purposes of section 382(l)(1). Accordingly, if that section applies because the deemed capital contribution is (or is considered under section 382(l)(1)(B) to be) part of a plan described in section 382(l)(1)(A), the value of the stock of the common parent after the deemed section 381(a) transaction must be adjusted to reflect the capital contribution. Ordinarily, this will require the value of the stock of the common parent to be reduced to an amount that represents the value of the stock of the subsidiary (or loss subgroup of which the subsidiary was a member) when the reattribution occurred.

(iv) *Duplication or omission of value.*—In determining any section 382 limitation with respect to the reattributed loss and with respect to other pre-change losses, appropriate adjustments must be made so that value is not improperly omitted or duplicated as a result of the reattribution. For example, if the subsidiary has an ownership change upon its departure, and the common parent (as successor) has an ownership change with respect to the reattributed pre-change separate attribute upon its reattribution under paragraph (d)(3)(i) of this section, proper adjustments must be made so that the value of the subsidiary is not taken into account more than once in determining the section 382 limitation for the reattributed loss and the loss that is not reattributed.

(v) *Special rule for continuity of business requirement.*—If the reattributed loss is a pre-change attribute of new loss member and the reattribution occurs within the two-year period beginning on the change date, then, starting immediately after the reattribution, the continuity of business requirement of section 382(c)(1) is applied with respect to the business enterprise of the common parent. Similar principles apply if the reattributed loss is a pre-change subgroup attribute and, on the day after the reattribution, the common parent is not a member of the loss subgroup.

(5) *Election to reattribute section 382 limitation.*—(i) *Effect of election.*—The common parent may elect to apportion to itself all or part of any separate section 382 limitation or subgroup section 382 limitation to which the loss is subject immediately before the reattribution. However, no net unrealized built-in gain of the member (or loss subgroup) whose loss is reattributed can be apportioned to the common parent. The principles of §1.1502-95(c) apply to the apportionment, treating, as the context requires, references to the former member as references to the common parent, and references to the consolidated section 382 limitation as references to the separate section 382 limitation (or subgroup section 382 limitation) that is being apportioned. Thus, for example, the common parent can reattribute to itself all or part of the value element or adjustment element of the limitation, and any part of such element that is apportioned requires a corresponding reduction in such element of the separate section 382 limitation of the subsidiary whose loss is reattributed (or in the subgroup section 382 limitation if the reattributed loss is a pre-change subgroup attribute). Appropriate adjustments must be made to the separate section 382 limitation (or subgroup section 382 limitation) for the consolidated return year in which the reattribution is made to reflect that the reattributed loss is an attribute acquired by the common parent during the year in a transaction to which section 381(a) applies. The election is made by the common parent as part of the election to reattribute the loss. See §1.1502-36(e)(5)(x) for the time and manner of making the election.

(ii) *Examples.*—The following examples illustrate the principles of this paragraph (d)(5):

*Example 1. Consequence of apportionment.* (i) *Facts.* P, the common parent of a consolidated group, purchases all of the stock of L on December 31, year 1. L carries over a net operating loss arising in year 1 to each of the next 5 taxable years. The purchase of the L stock causes an ownership change of L, and results in a separate section 382 limitation of $10 for L's net operating loss carryover based on the value of the L stock. On July 2, year 3, P sells 30% of the L stock to A. Under §1.1502-36(d)(6), P elects to reattribute to itself $110 of L's $200 net operating loss carryover. P also elects to apportion to itself $6 of the $10 value element of the separate section 382 limitation.

(ii) *Analysis.* (A) *P's separate section 382 limitation.* For the consolidated return years ending after December 31, year 3, P's separate section 382 limitation with respect to the reattributed net operating loss carryover is $6, adjusted as appropriate for any short taxable year, unused section 382 limitation, or other adjustment. For the P group's consolidated return year ending December 31, year 3, the separate section 382 limitation for L's net operating loss carryover is $8, the sum of $5 and $3. Five dollars of the limitation is the amount that bears the same relationship to $10 as the number of days in the period ending with the deemed section 381(a) transaction, 183 days, bears to 365. Three dollars of the limitation is the amount that bears the same relationship to $6 as the number of days in the period between July 3 and December 31, 182, bears to 365.

(B) *L's separate section 382 limitation.* For L's taxable years ending after December 31, year 3, L's separate section 382 limitation for its $90 of net operating loss carryover that was not reattributed to P is $4, adjusted as appropriate for any short taxable year, unused section 382 limitation, or other adjustment. For L's short taxable year ending December 31, year 3, the section 382 limitation for its $90 of net operating loss carryover is $2, the amount that bears the same relationship to $4 (the portion of the value element that was not apportioned to P), as the number of days during the short taxable year, 182 days, bears to 365. See §1.382-5(c).

*Example 2. No apportionment required for consolidated pre-change attribute.* (i) *Facts.* P, the common parent of a consolidated group, forms L. For year 1, L has an operating loss of $70 that is not absorbed and is included in the group's consolidated net operating loss that is carried over to subsequent years. On January 1 of year 3, A buys all of the P stock and the P group has an ownership change. The consolidated section 382 limitation based on the value of the P stock is $10.

(ii) *Analysis.* On April 13 of year 4, P sells all of the stock of L to B and, under §1.1502-36(d)(6), elects to reattribute to itself $45 of L's net operating loss carryover. Following the reattribution, the $45 portion of the year 1 net operating loss carryover retains its character as a pre-change consolidated attribute, and remains subject to so much of the $10 consolidated section 382 limitation as P does not elect to apportion to L under §1.1502-95(c).

(e) *Time and manner of making election under §1.1502-91(d)(4).*—(1) *In general.*—This paragraph (e) prescribes the time and manner of making the election under §1.1502-91(d)(4), relating to treating two or more corporations as treating the section 1504(a)(1) requirement of §1.1502-91(d)(1)(ii) and (d)(2)(ii) as satisfied.

(2) *Election statement.*—An election under §1.1502-91(d)(4) must be made by the common parent. The election must be made in the form of the following statement: "THIS IS AN ELECTION UNDER §1.1502-91(d)(4) TO TREAT THE FOLLOWING CORPORATIONS AS MEETING THE REQUIREMENTS OF §1.1502-91(d)(1)(ii) AND (d)(2)(ii) IMMEDIATELY AFTER THEY BECAME MEMBERS OF THE GROUP." [List separately the name of each corporation, its E.I.N., and the date that it became a member of the group]. If separate elections are being made for corporations that became members at different times or that were acquired from different affiliated groups, provide a separate statement and list for each election.

(3) The election statement must be filed by the common parent with its income tax return for the consolidated return year in which the members with respect to which the election is made become members of the group. Such election must be filed on or before the due date for such income tax return, including extensions.

(4) An election made under this paragraph (e) is irrevocable. [Reg. §1.1502-96.]

☐ [*T.D. 8824, 6-25-99. Amended by T.D. 9424, 9-9-2008.*]

**[Reg. §1.1502-96A]**

**§1.1502-96A. Miscellaneous rules generally applicable for testing dates before June 25, 1999.**—(a) *End of separate tracking of losses.*—(1) *Application.*—This paragraph (a) applies to a member (or a loss subgroup) with a net operating loss carryover that arose (or is treated under §1.1502-21(c) or 1.1502-21T(c) in effect prior to June 25, 1999, as contained in 26 CFR part 1 revised April 1, 1999, as applicable as arising) in a SRLY (or a net unrealized built-in gain or loss determined at the time that the member (or loss subgroup) becomes a member of the consolidated group if there is—

(i) An ownership change of the member (or loss subgroup in connection with, or after, becoming a member of the group; or

(ii) A period of 5 consecutive years following the day that the member (or loss subgroup) becomes a member of a group during which the member (or loss subgroup) has not had an ownership change.

(2) *Effect of end of separate tracking.*—If this paragraph (a) applies with respect to a member (or loss subgroup), then, starting on the day after the earlier of the change date (but not earlier than the day the member (or loss subgroup) becomes a member of the consolidated group) or the last day of the 5 consecutive year period described in paragraph (a)(1)(ii) of this section, the member's net operating loss carryover that arose (or is treated under §1.1502-21(c) or 1.1502-21T(c) in effect prior to June 25, 1999, as contained in 26 CFR part 1 revised April 1, 1999, as applicable as arising) in a SRLY, is treated as described in §1.1502-91A(c)(1)(i). Also, the member's separately computed net unrealized built-in gain or loss is included in the determination whether the group has a net unrealized built-in gain or loss. The preceding sentences also apply for purposes of determining whether there is an ownership change with respect to such attributes following such change date (or earlier day) or 5 consecutive year period. Thus, for example, starting the day after the change date or the end of the 5 consecutive year period—

(i) The consolidated group which includes the new loss member or loss subgroup is no longer required to separately track owner shifts of the stock of the new loss member or loss subgroup parent to determine if an ownership change occurs with respect to the attributes of the new loss member or members included in the loss subgroup;

(ii) The group includes the member's attributes in determining whether it is a loss group under §1.1502-91A(c);

(iii) There is an ownership change with respect to such attributes only if the group is a loss group and has an ownership change; and

(iv) If the group has an ownership change, such attributes are pre-change consolidated attributes subject to the loss group's consolidated section 382 limitation.

(3) *Continuing effect of end of separate tracking.*—As the context may require, a current group determines which of its members are included in a loss subgroup on any testing date by taking into account the application of this section in the former group. See the example in §1.1502-91A(f)(2).

(4) *Special rule for testing period.*—For purposes of determining the beginning of the testing period for a loss group, the member's (or loss subgroup's) net operating loss carryovers (or net unrealized built-in gain or loss) described in paragraph (a)(2) of this section are considered to arise—

(i) in a case described in paragraph (a)(1)(i) of this section, in a taxable year that begins not earlier than the later of the day following the change date or the day that the member becomes a member of the group; and

(ii) in a case described in paragraph (a)(1)(ii) of this section, in a taxable year that begins 3 years before the end of the 5 consecutive year period.

(5) *Limits on effects of end of separate tracking.*—The rule contained in this paragraph (a) applies solely for purposes of §§1.1502-91A through 1.1502-95A and this section (other than paragraph (b)(2)(ii)(B) of this section (relating to the definition of pre-change attributes of a subsidiary)) and §1.1502-98A, and not for purposes of other provisions of the consolidated return regulations, including, for example, §§1.1502-15 and 1.1502-21 (or §1.1502-15T in effect prior to June 25, 1999, as contained in 26 CFR part 1 revised April 1, 1999 and 1.1502-21T in effect prior to June 25, 1999, as contained in 26 CFR part 1 revised April 1, 1999, as applicable) (relating to the consolidated net operating loss deduction). See also paragraph (c) of this section for the continuing effect of an ownership change with respect to pre-change attributes.

(b) *Ownership change of subsidiary.*—(1) *Ownership change of a subsidiary because of options or plan or arrangement.*—Notwithstanding §1.1502-92A, a subsidiary may have an ownership change for purposes of section 382 with respect to its attributes which a group or loss subgroup includes in making a determination under §1.1502-91A(c)(1) (relating to the definition of loss group) or §1.1502-91A(d) (relating to the definition of loss subgroup). The subsidiary has such an ownership change if it has an ownership change under the principles of §1.1502-95A(b) and section 382 and the regulations thereunder (determined on a separate entity basis by treating the subsidiary as not being a member of a consolidated group) in the event of—

(i) The deemed exercise under §1.382-4(d) of an option or options (other than an option with respect to stock of the common parent) held by a person (or persons acting pursuant to a plan or arrangement) to acquire more than 20 percent of the stock of the subsidiary; or

(ii) An increase by 1 or more 5-percent shareholders, acting pursuant to a plan or arrangement to avoid an ownership change of a subsidiary, in their percentage ownership interest in the subsidiary by more than 50 percentage points during the testing period of the subsidiary through the acquisition (or deemed acquisition pursuant to §1.382-4(d)) of ownership interests in the subsidiary and in higher-tier members with respect to the subsidiary.

(2) *Effect of the ownership change.*—(i) *In general.*—If a subsidiary has an ownership change under paragraph (b)(1) of this section, the amount of consolidated taxable income for any post-change year that may be offset by the pre-change losses of the subsidiary shall not exceed the section 382 limitation for the subsidiary. For purposes of this limitation, the value of the subsidiary is determined solely by reference to the value of the subsidiary's stock.

(ii) *Pre-change losses.*—The pre-change losses of a subsidiary are—

(A) Its allocable part of any consolidated net operating loss which is attributable to it under §1.1502-21(b) or 1.1502-21T(b) in effect prior to June 25, 1999, as contained in 26 CFR part 1 revised April 1, 1999, as applicable (determined on the last day of the consolidated return year that includes the change date) that is not carried back and absorbed in a taxable year prior to the year including the change date;

(B) Its net operating loss carryovers that arose (or are treated under §1.1502-21(c) or 1.1502-21T(c) in effect prior to June 25, 1999, as contained in 26 CFR part 1 revised April 1, 1999, as applicable as having arisen) in a SRLY; and

(C) Its recognized built-in loss with respect to its separately computed net unrealized built-in loss, if any, determined on the change date.

(3) *Coordination with §§1.1502-91A, 1.1502-92A, and 1.1502-94A.*—If an increase in percentage ownership interest causes an ownership change with respect to an attribute under this paragraph (b) and under §1.1502-92A on the same day, the ownership change is considered to occur only under §1.1502-92A and not under this paragraph (b). See §1.1502-94A for anti-duplication rules relating to value.

(4) *Example.*—The following example illustrates paragraph (b)(1)(ii) of this section.

*Example. Plan to avoid an ownership change of a subsidiary.* (a) L owns all the stock of L1, L1 owns all the stock of L2, L2 owns all the

stock of L3, and L3 owns all the stock of L4. The L group has a consolidated net operating loss arising in Year 1 that is carried over to Year 2. L has assets other than its L1 stock with a value of $900. L1, L2, and L3 own no assets other than their L2, L3, and L4 stock. L4 has assets with a value of $100. During Year 2, A, B, C, and D, acting pursuant to a plan to avoid an ownership change of L4, acquire the following ownership interests in the members of the L loss group: (A) on September 11, Year 2, A acquires 20 percent of the L1 stock from L and B acquires 20 percent of the L2 stock from L1; and (B) on September 20, Year 2, C acquires 20 percent of the stock of L3 from L2 and D acquires 20 percent of the stock of L4 from L3. The following is a graphic illustration of these facts:

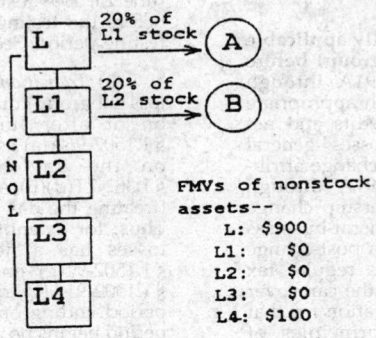

FMVs of nonstock
assets--
  L: $900
  L1: $0
  L2: $0
  L3: $0
  L4: $100

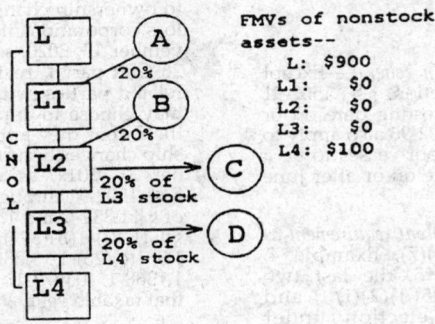

FMVs of nonstock
assets--
  L: $900
  L1: $0
  L2: $0
  L3: $0
  L4: $100

(b) The acquisitions by A, B, C, and D pursuant to the plan have increased their respective percentage ownership interests in L4 by approximately 10, 13, 16, and 20 percentage points, for a total of approximately 59 percentage points during the testing period. This more than 50 percentage point increase in the percentage ownership interest in L4 causes an ownership change of L4 under paragraph (b)(2) of this section.

(c) *Continuing effect of an ownership change.*—A loss corporation (or loss subgroup) that is subject to a limitation under section 382 with respect to its pre-change losses continues to be subject to the limitation regardless of whether it becomes a member or ceases to be a member of a consolidated group. See §1.382-5(d) (relating to successive ownership changes and absorption of a section 382 limitation). [Reg. §1.1502-96A.]

☐ [*T.D.* 8678, 6-26-96. *Amended by T.D.* 8823, 6-25-99 *and amended and redesignated by T.D.* 8824, 6-25-99.]

### [Reg. §1.1502-97]

**§1.1502-97. Special rules under section 382 for members under the jurisdiction of a court in a title 11 or similar case.**—[Reserved]

☐ [*T.D.* 8824, 6-25-99.]

### [Reg. §1.1502-97A]

**§1.1502-97A. Special rules under section 382 for members under the jurisdiction of a court in a title 11 or similar case.**—[Reserved]

☐ [*T.D.* 8678, 6-26-96. *Amended and redesignated by T.D.* 8824, 6-25-99.]

### [Reg. §1.1502-98]

**§1.1502-98. Coordination with sections 383 and 163(j).**—
(a) *Coordination with section 383.*—The rules contained in §§1.1502-91 through 1.1502-96 also apply for purposes of section 383, with appro-

priate adjustments to reflect that section 383 applies to credits and net capital losses. For example, subgroups with respect to the carryover of general business credits, minimum tax credits, unused foreign tax, and net capital loss are determined by applying the principles of §1.1502-91(d)(1). Similarly, in the case of net capital losses, general business credits, and excess foreign taxes that are pre-change attributes, §1.383-1 applies the principles of §§1.1502-91 through 1.1502-96. For example, if a loss group has an ownership change under §1.1502-92 and has a carryover of unused general business credits from a pre-change consolidated return year to a post-change consolidated return year, the amount of the group's regular tax liability for the post-change year that can be offset by the carryover cannot exceed the consolidated section 383 credit limitation for that post-change year, determined by applying the principles of §§1.383-1(c)(6) and 1.1502-93 (relating to the computation of the consolidated section 382 limitation).

(b) *Application to section 163(j).*—(1) *In general.*—The regulations in this part under sections 163(j), 382, and 383 of the Code contain rules governing the application of section 382 to interest expense governed by section 163(j) and the regulations in this part under section 163(j) of the Code. See, for example, §§1.163(j)-11(c), 1.382-2, 1.382-6, 1.382-7, and 1.383-1. The rules contained in §§1.1502-91 through 1.1502-96 apply these rules to members of a consolidated group, or corporations that join or leave a consolidated group, with appropriate adjustments. For example, for purposes of §§1.1502-91 through 1.1502-96, the term *loss group* includes a consolidated group in which any member is entitled to use a disallowed business interest expense carryforward, as defined in §1.163(j)-1(b)(11), that did not arise, and is not treated as arising, in a SRLY with regard to that group. Additionally, a reference to net operating loss carryovers in §§1.1502-91 through 1.1502-96 generally includes a reference to disallowed business interest expense carryforwards. References to a loss or losses in §§1.1502-91 through 1.1502-96 include references to disallowed business interest expense carryforwards or section 382 disallowed business interest carryforwards, within the meaning of §1.382-2(a)(7), as appropriate.

(2) *Appropriate adjustments.*—For purposes of applying the rules in §§1.1502-91 through 1.1502-96 to current-year business interest expense (as defined in §1.163(j)-1(b)(9)), disallowed business interest expense carryforwards, and section 382 disallowed business interest carryforwards, appropriate adjustments are required. [Reg. §1.1502-98.]

☐ [*T.D. 8824, 6-25-99. Amended by T.D. 8884, 5-24-2000 and T.D. 9905, 9-3-2020.*]

### [Reg. §1.1502-98A]

**§1.1502-98A. Coordination with section 383 generally applicable for testing dates (or members joining or leaving a group) before June 25, 1999.**—The rules contained in §§1.1502-91A through 1.1502-96A also apply for purposes of section 383, with appropriate adjustments to reflect that section 383 applies to credits and net capital losses. Similarly, in the case of net capital losses, general business credits, and excess foreign taxes that are pre-change attributes, §1.383-1 applies the principles of §§1.1502-91A through 1.1502-96A. For example, if a loss group has an ownership change under §1.1502-92A and has a carryover of unused general business credits from a pre-change consolidated return year to a post-change consolidated return year, the amount of the group's regular tax liability for the post-change year that can be offset by the carryover cannot exceed the consolidated section 383 credit limitation for that post-change year, determined by applying the principles of §§1.3831(c)(6) and 1.1502-93A (relating to the computation of the consolidated section 382 limitation). [Reg. §1.1502-98A.]

☐ [*T.D. 8678, 6-26-96. Amended and redesignated by T.D. 8824, 6-25-99.*]

### [Reg. §1.1502-99]

**§1.1502-99. Effective/applicability dates.**—(a) *In general.*—Except as provided in paragraphs (b) and (c) of this section, §§1.1502-91 through 1.1502-96 and §1.1502-98 apply to any testing date on or after June 25, 1999. Sections 1.1502-94 through 1.1502-96 also apply to a corporation that becomes a member of a group or ceases to be a member of a group (or loss subgroup) on any date on or after June 25, 1999.

(b) *Special rules.*—(1) *Election to treat subgroup parent requirement as satisfied.*—Section 1.1502-91(d)(4), §1.1502-91(d)(7), Example 4, §1.1502-92(b)(1)(iii), §1.1502-92(b)(2), Example 5, the last two sentences of §1.1502-95(b)(3), §1.1502-95(d)(2)(i), and §1.1502-96(e)(all of which relate to the election under §1.1502-91(d)(4) to treat the loss subgroup parent requirement as satisfied) apply to corporations that become members of a consolidated group in taxable years for which the due date of the income tax return (without extensions) is after June 25, 1999.

(2) *Principal purpose of avoiding a limitation.*—The third sentence of §1.1502-91(d)(5) (relating to members excluded from a loss subgroup) applies to corporations that become members of a consolidated group on or after June 25, 1999.

(3) *Ceasing to be a member of a loss subgroup.*—(i) *Ownership change of a loss subgroup.*—Section 1.1502-95(d)(2)(ii) and §1.1502-95(d)(3), Example 3 apply to corporations that cease to bear a relationship described in section 1504(a)(1) to a loss subgroup parent in taxable years for which the due date of the income tax return (without extensions) is after June 25, 1999.

(ii) *Expiration of 5-year period.*—Section 1.1502-95(d)(2)(iii) applies with respect to the day after the last day of any 5 consecutive year period described in that section that ends in a taxable year for which the due date of the income tax return (without extensions) is after June 25, 1999.

(4) *Reattribution of losses under §1.1502-36(d)(6).*—Section 1.1502-96(d) applies to reattributions of net operating loss carryovers, capital loss carryovers, and deferred deductions in connection with a transfer of stock to which §1.1502-36 applies, and the election under §1.1502-96(d)(5) (relating to an election to reattribute section 382 limitation) can be made with an election under §1.1502-36(d)(6) to reattribute a loss to the common parent that is filed at the time and in the manner provided in §1.1502-36(e)(5)(x).

(5) *Election to apportion net unrealized built-in gain.*—In the case of corporations that cease to be members of a loss group (or loss subgroup) before June 25, 1999 in a taxable year for which the due date of the income tax return (without extensions) is after June 25, 1999, §1.1502-95(a), (b), (c), and (f) apply to those corporations if the common parent makes the election described in the second sentence

of paragraph (c)(1) of §1.1502-95 in the time and manner prescribed in paragraph (f) of §1.1502-95.

(c) *Testing period may include a period beginning before June 25, 1999.*—(1) *In general.*—A testing period for purposes of §§1.1502-91 through 1.1502-96 and 1.1502-98 may include a period beginning before June 25, 1999. Thus, for example, in applying §1.1502-92(b)(1)(i)(relating to the determination of an ownership change of a loss group), the determination of the lowest percentage of ownership interest of any 5-percent shareholder of the common parent during a testing period ending on a testing date occurring on or after June 25, 1999 takes into account the period beginning before June 25, 1999, except the extent that the period is more than 3 years before the testing date or is otherwise before the beginning of the testing period. See §1.1502-92(b)(1).

(2) *Transition rule for net unrealized built-in loss.*—A loss group (or loss subgroup) that has a net unrealized built-in loss on a testing date on or after June 25, 1999 may apply §1.1502-91A(g) (and §1.1502-96A(a) as it relates to §1.1502-91A(g)) for the period ending on the day before June 25, 1999 to determine under §1.382-2T(d)(ii)(A) the earliest date that its testing period begins (treating the day before June 25, 1999 as the end of a taxable year.) Thus, for example, if a consolidated group with no net operating losses has a net unrealized built-in loss determined under §1.1502-91(g) on a testing date after June 25, 1999, but, under §1.1502-91A(g), does not have a net unrealized built-in loss for the period ending on the day before June 25, 1999, the group's testing period begins no earlier than June 25, 1999.

(d) *Application to section 163(j).*—(1) *Sections 1.382-2 and 1.382-5.*—To the extent the rules of §§1.1502-91 through 1.1502-99 effectuate the rules of §§1.382-2 and 1.382-5, the provisions apply with respect to ownership changes occurring on or after November 13, 2020. For loss corporations that have ownership changes occurring before November 13, 2020, see §§1.1502-91 through 1.1502-99 as contained in 26 CFR part 1, revised April 1, 2019. However, taxpayers and their related parties, within the meaning of sections 267(b) and 707(b)(1), may choose to apply the rules of §§1.1502-91 through 1.1502-99 to the extent they apply the rules of §§1.382-2 and 1.382-5, to ownership changes occurring during a taxable year beginning after December 31, 2017, as well as consistently applying the rules of the §§1.1502-91 through 1.1502-99 (to the extent they effectuate the rules of §§1.382-6 and 1.383-1), the section 163(j) regulations (as defined in §1.163(j)-1(b)(37)), and, if applicable, §§1.263A-9, 1.263A-15, 1.381(c)(20)-1, 1.382-7, 1.469-9, 1.469-11, 1.704-1, 1.882-5, 1.1362-3, 1.1368-1, 1.1377-1, 1.1502-13, 1.1502-21, 1.1502-79, and 1.1504-4, to that taxable year.

(2) *Sections 1.382-6 and 1.383-1.*—To the extent the rules of §§1.1502-91 through 1.1502-98 effectuate the rules of §§1.382-6 and 1.383-1, the provisions apply with respect to ownership changes occurring during a taxable year beginning on or after November 13, 2020. For the application of these rules to an ownership change with respect to an ownership change occurring during a taxable year beginning before November 13, 2020, see §§1.1502-91 through 1.1502-99 as contained in 26 CFR part 1, revised April 1, 2019. However, taxpayers and their related parties, within the meaning of sections 267(b) and 707(b)(1), may choose to apply the rules of §§1.1502-91 through 1.1502-99 (to the extent that those rules effectuate the rules of §§1.382-6 and 1.383-1), to ownership changes occurring during a taxable year beginning after December 31, 2017, so long as the taxpayers and their related parties consistently apply the rules of 1.1502-91 through 1.1502-99 (to the extent that those rules effectuate the rules of §§1.382-2 and 1.382-5), the section 163(j) regulations (as defined in §1.163(j)-1(b)(37)), and, if applicable, §§1.263A-9, 1.263A-15, 1.381(c)(20)-1, 1.382-7, 1.469-9, 1.469-11, 1.704-1, 1.882-5, 1.1362-3, 1.1368-1, 1.1377-1, 1.1502-13, 1.1502-21, 1.1502-36, 1.1502-79, and 1.1504-4, to a taxable year beginning after December 31, 2017. [Reg. §1.1502-99.]

☐ [*T.D. 8824, 6-25-99. Amended by T.D. 9424, 9-9-2008 and T.D. 9905, 9-3-2020.*]

### [Reg. §1.1502-99A]

**§1.1502-99A. Effective dates.**—(a) *Effective date.*—(1) *In general.*—Except as provided in §1.1502-99(b), §§1.1502-91A through 1.1502-96A and 1.1502-98A apply to any testing date on or after January 1, 1997, and before June 25, 1999. Sections 1.1502-94A through 1.1502-96A also apply on any date on or after January 1, 1997, and before June 25, 1999, on which a corporation becomes a member of a group or on which a corporation ceases to be a member of a loss group (or a loss subgroup).

(2) *Anti-duplication rules for recognized built-in gain.*—Section 1.1502-93(c)(2) (relating to recognized built-in gain of a loss group or

loss subgroup) applies to taxable years for which the due date for income tax returns (without extensions) is after June 25, 1999.

(b) *Testing period may include a period beginning before January 1, 1997.*—A testing period for purposes of §§1.1502-91A through 1.1502-96A and 1.1502-98A may include a period beginning before January 1, 1997. Thus, for example, in applying §1.1502-92A(b)(1)(i) (relating to the determination of an ownership change of a loss group), the determination of the lowest percentage ownership interest of any 5-percent shareholder of the common parent during a testing period ending on a testing date occurring on or after January 1, 1997, takes into account the period beginning before January 1, 1997, except to the extent that the period is more than 3 years before the testing date or is otherwise before the beginning of the testing period. See §1.1502-92A(b)(1).

(c) *Transition rules.*—(1) *Methods permitted.*—(i) *In general.*—For the period ending before January 1, 1997, a consolidated group is permitted to use any method described in paragraph (c)(2) of this section which is consistently applied to determine if an ownership change occurred with respect to a consolidated net operating loss, a net operating loss carryover (including net operating loss carryovers arising in SRLYs), or a net unrealized built-in loss. If an ownership change occurred during that period, the group is also permitted to use any method described in paragraph (c)(2) of this section which is consistently applied to compute the amount of the section 382 limitation that applies to limit the use of taxable income in any post-change year ending before, on, or after January 1, 1997. The preceding sentence does not preclude the imposition of an additional, lesser limitation due to a subsequent ownership change nor, except as provided in paragraph (c)(1)(iii) of this section, does it permit the beginning of a new testing period for the loss group.

(ii) *Adjustments to offset excess limitation.*—If an ownership change occurred during the period ending before January 1, 1997, and a method described in paragraph (c)(2) of this section was not used for a post-change year, the members (or group) must reduce the section 382 limitation for post-change years for which an income tax return is filed after January 1, 1997, to offset, as quickly as possible, the effects of any section 382 limitation that members took into account in excess of the amount that would have been allowable under §§1.1502-91A through 1.1502-96A and 1.1502-98A.

(iii) *Coordination with effective date.*—Notwithstanding that a group may have used a method described in paragraph (c)(2)(ii) or (iii) of this section for the period before January 1, 1997, §§1.1502-91A through 1.1502-96A and 1.1502-98A apply to any testing date occurring on or after January 1, 1997, for purposes of determining whether there is an ownership change with respect to any losses and, if so, the collateral consequences. Any ownership change of a member other than the common parent pursuant to a method described in paragraph (c)(2)(ii) or (iii) of this section does not cause a new testing period of the loss group to begin for purposes of applying §1.1502-92A on or after January 1, 1997.

(2) *Permitted methods.*—The methods described in this paragraph (c)(2) are:

(i) A method that does not materially differ from the rules in §§1.1502-91A through 1.1502-96A and 1.1502-98A (other than those in §1.1502-95A(c) and (b)(2)(ii) (relating to the apportionment of a section 382 limitation) as they would apply to a corporation that ceases to be a member of the group before January 1, 1997). As the context requires, the method must treat references to rules in current regulations as references to rules in regulations generally effective for taxable years before January 1, 1997. Thus, for example, the taxpayer must treat a reference to §1.382-4(d) (relating to options) as a reference to §1.382-2T(h)(4) for any testing date to which §1.382-2T(h)(4) applies. Similarly, a reference to §1.1502-21(c) or 1.1502-21T(c) in effect prior to June 25, 1999, as contained in 26 CFR part 1 revised April 1, 1999, as applicable may be a reference to §1.1502-21A(c), as appropriate. Furthermore, the method must treat all corporations that were affiliated on January 1, 1987, and continuously thereafter as having met the 5 consecutive year requirement of §1.1502-91A(d)(2)(i) on any day before January 1, 1992, on which the determination of net unrealized built-in gain or loss of a loss subgroup is made; or

(ii) A reasonable application of the rules in section 382 and the regulations thereunder applied to each member on a separate entity basis, treating each member's allocable part of a consolidated net operating loss which is attributable to it under §1.1502-21(b) or 1.1502-21T(b) in effect prior to June 25, 1999, as contained in 26 CFR part 1 revised April 1, 1999, as applicable as a net operating loss of that member and applying rules similar to §1.382-8 to avoid duplication of value in computing the section 382 limitation for the member (see §1.382-8(h) (relating to the effective date and transition rules regarding controlled groups)); or

(iii) A method approved by the Commissioner upon application by the common parent.

(d) *Amended returns.*—A group may file an amended return in connection with an ownership change occurring before January 1, 1997, to modify the amount of a section 382 limitation with respect to a consolidated net operating loss, a net operating loss carryover (including net operating loss carryovers arising in SRLYs), or a recognized built-in loss (or gain) only if it files amended returns:

(1) For the earliest taxable year ending after December 31, 1986, in which it had an ownership change, if any, under §1.1502-92A;

(2) For all subsequent taxable years for which returns have already been filed as of the date of the amended return;

(3) The modification with respect to all members for all taxable years ending in 1987 and thereafter complies with §§1.1502-91A through 1.1502-96A and 1.1502-98A; and

(4) The amended return(s) permitted by the applicable statute of limitations is/are filed before March 26, 1997.

(e) *Section 383.*—This section also applies for the purposes of section 383, with appropriate adjustments to reflect that section 383 applies to credits and net capital losses. [Reg. §1.1502-99A.]

☐ [T.D. 8678, 6-26-96. *Amended by T.D. 8823, 6-25-99 and amended and redesignated by T.D. 8824, 6-25-99.*]

**[Reg. §1.1502-100]**

**§1.1502-100. Corporations exempt from tax.**—(a) *In general.*—(1) *Computation of tax liability.*—The tax liability for a consolidated return year of a group of two or more corporations described in section 1504(e) which are exempt from taxation under section 501 (hereinafter referred to in this section as "exempt group") shall be determined on a consolidated basis by applying the provisions of subchapter F of chapter 1 of the Code in the manner provided in this section. See section 1504(e) for tax-exempt corporations eligible to file a consolidated return.

(2) *Applicability of other consolidated return provisions.*—The provisions of §1.1502-1 through §1.1502-80 shall be applicable to an exempt group to the extent they are not inconsistent with the provisions of this section or the provisions of subchapter F of chapter 1 of the Code. For purposes of applying the provisions of §1.1502-1 through §1.1502-80 to an exempt group, the following substitutions shall be made—

(i) The term "exempt group" shall be substituted for the term "group",

(ii) The terms "unrelated business taxable income", "separate unrelated business taxable income", and "consolidated unrelated business taxable income" shall be substituted for the terms"taxable income", "separate taxable income", and "consolidated taxable income", and

(iii) The term "consolidated liability for tax determined under §1.1502-2" (or an equivalent term) shall mean the consolidated liability for tax of an exempt group determined under paragraph (b) of this section.

(b) *Consolidated liability for tax.*—The tax liability for a consolidated return year of an exempt group is the tax imposed by section 511(a) on the consolidated unrelated taxable income for the year (determined under paragraph (c) of this section), and by allowing the credits provided in §1.1502-2(b).

(c) *Consolidated unrelated business taxable income.*—The consolidated unrelated business taxable income for a consolidated return year shall be determined by taking into account—

(1) The separate unrelated business taxable income of each member of the exempt group (determined under paragraph (d) of this section);

(2) Any consolidated net operating loss deduction (determined under §1.1502-21A or 1.1502-21 (as appropriate)) subject to the limitations provided in section 512(b)(6);

(3) Any consolidated charitable contribution deduction (determined under §1.1502-24) subject to the limitations provided in section 512(b)(10); and

(4) Any consolidated net gain or net loss from the disposition of debt-financed property (as defined in section 514(b)) taken into account as provided by section 514(a), or from the cutting of timber to which section 631 applies.

(d) *Separate unrelated business taxable income.*—The separate unrelated business taxable income of a member of an exempt group shall be computed in accordance with the provisions of section 512 covering the determination of unrelated business taxable income of separate corporations, except that—

(1) The provisions of paragraphs (a) through (k) and (o) of §1.1502-12 shall apply; and

(2) No charitable contributions deduction shall be taken into account under section 512(b)(10).

See sections 511(c) and 512(a)(3)(C) for special rules applicable to organizations described in section 501(c)(2). [Reg. § 1.1502-100.]

☐ *T.D. 7183, 4-30-72. Amended by T.D. 2-16-79; T.D. 8677, 6-26-96, T.D. 8823, 6-25-99 and T.D. 9885, 12-2-2019.]*

### [Reg. § 1.1503-1]

**§1.1503-1. Computation and payment of tax.**—(a) *General rule.*—In any case in which a consolidated return is filed or required to be filed, the tax shall be determined, computed, assessed, collected, and adjusted in accordance with the regulations prescribed under section 1502 promulgated prior to the last date prescribed by law for the filing of such return.

(b) *Limitation.*—If the affiliated group includes one or more Western Hemisphere trade corporations (as defined in section 921) or one or more regulated public utilities (as defined in section 1503(c)) the increase in tax described in section 1503(a) shall be applied in a manner provided in the regulations under section 1502. [Reg. § 1.1503-1.]

☐ *T.D. 6140, 8-29-55. Amended by T.D. 7244, 12-29-72.]*

⟫⟫→ *Caution: Reg. §1.1503-2, below, applies to dual consolidated losses incurred in tax years beginning before April 18, 2007 (January 1, 2007, in certain cases). For dual consolidated losses incurred in tax years beginning on or after April 18, 2007 (January 1, 2007, in certain cases), see Reg. §§1.1503(d)-1 through 1.1503(d)-7. For further details and special/transition rules, see Reg. §1.1503(d)-8.*

### [Reg. § 1.1503-2]

**§1.1503-2. Dual consolidated loss.**—(a) *Purpose and scope.*—This section provides rules for the application of section 1503(d), concerning the determination and use of dual consolidated losses. Paragraph (b) of this section provides a general rule prohibiting a dual consolidated loss from offsetting the taxable income of a domestic affiliate. Paragraph (c) of this section provides definitions of the terms used in this section. Paragraph (d) of this section provides rules for calculating the amount of a dual consolidated loss and for adjusting the basis of stock of a dual resident corporation. Paragraph (e) of this section contains an anti-avoidance provision. Paragraph (f) of this section applies the rules of paragraph (d) of this section to the computation of foreign tax credit limitations. Paragraph (g) of this section provides certain exceptions to the limitation rule of paragraph (b) of this section. Finally, paragraph (h) of this section provides the effective date of the regulations and a provision for the retroactive application of the regulations to qualifying taxpayers.

(b) *In general.*—(1) *Limitation on the use of a dual consolidated loss to offset income of a domestic affiliate.*—Except as otherwise provided in this section, a dual consolidated loss of a dual resident corporation cannot offset the taxable income of any domestic affiliate in the taxable year in which the loss is recognized or in any other taxable year, regardless of whether the loss offsets income of another person under the income tax laws of a foreign country and regardless of whether the income that the loss may offset in the foreign country is, has been, or will be subject to tax in the United States. Pursuant to paragraph (c)(1) and (2) of this section, the same limitation shall apply to a dual consolidated loss of a separate unit of a domestic corporation as if the separate unit were a wholly owned subsidiary of such corporation.

(2) *Limitation on the use of a dual consolidated loss to offset income of a successor-in-interest.*—A dual consolidated loss of a dual resident corporation also cannot be used to offset the taxable income of another corporation by means of a transaction in which the other corporation succeeds to the tax attributes of the dual resident corporation under section 381 of the Code. Similarly, a dual consolidated loss of a separate unit of a domestic corporation cannot be used to offset income of the domestic corporation following the termination, liquidation, sale, or other disposition of the separate unit. However, if a dual resident corporation transfers its assets to another corporation in a transaction subject to section 381, and the acquiring corporation is a dual resident corporation of the same foreign country of which the transferor dual resident corporation is a resident, or a domestic corporation that carries on the business activities of the transferor dual resident corporation as a separate unit, then income generated by the transferee dual resident corporation, or separate unit, may be offset by the carryover losses of the transferor dual resident corporation. In addition, if a domestic corporation transfers a separate unit to another domestic corporation in a transaction subject to section 381, the income generated by the separate unit following the transfer may be offset by the carryover losses of the separate unit.

(3) *Application of rules to multiple tiers of separate units.*—If a separate unit of a domestic corporation is owned indirectly through another separate unit, the principles of paragraph (b)(1) and (2) of this section shall apply as if the upper-tier separate unit were a subsidiary of the domestic corporation and the lower-tier separate unit were a lower-tier subsidiary.

(4) *Examples.*—The following examples illustrate the application of this paragraph (b).

*Example 1.* P, a domestic corporation, owns all of the outstanding stock of DRC, a domestic corporation. P and DRC file a consolidated U.S. income tax return. DRC is managed and controlled in Country W, a country that determines the tax residence of corporations according to their place of management and control. Therefore, DRC is a dual resident corporation and any net operating loss it incurs is a dual consolidated loss. In Years 1 through 3, DRC incurs dual consolidated losses. Under this paragraph (b), the dual consolidated losses may not be used to offset P's income on the group's consolidated U.S. income tax return. At the end of Year 3, DRC sells all of its assets and discontinues its business operations. DRC is then liquidated into P, pursuant to the provisions of section 332. Normally, under section 381, P would succeed to, and be permitted to utilize, DRC's net operating loss carryovers. However, this paragraph (b) prohibits the dual consolidated losses of DRC from reducing P's income for U.S. tax purposes. Therefore, DRC's net operating loss carryovers will not be available to offset P's income.

*Example 2.* The facts are the same as in *Example 1*, except that DRC does not sell its assets and, following the liquidation of DRC, P continues to operate DRC's business as a separate unit (*e.g.*, a branch). DRC's loss carryovers are available to offset P's income generated by the assets previously owned by DRC and now held by the separate unit.

(c) *Definitions.*—The following definitions shall apply for purposes of this section.

(1) *Domestic corporation.*—The term "domestic corporation" has the meaning assigned to it by section 7701(a)(3) and (4). The term also includes any corporation otherwise treated as a domestic corporation by the Code, including, but not limited to, sections 269B, 953(d), and 1504(d). For purposes of this section, any separate unit of a domestic corporation, as defined in paragraph (c)(3) and (4) of this section, shall be treated as a separate domestic corporation.

(2) *Dual resident corporation.*—A dual resident corporation is a domestic corporation that is subject to the income tax of a foreign country on its worldwide income or on a residence basis. A corporation is taxed on a residence basis if it is taxed as a resident under the laws of the foreign country. An S corporation, as defined in section 1361, is not a dual resident corporation. For purposes of this section, any separate unit of a domestic corporation, as defined in paragraph (c)(3) and (4) of this section, shall be treated as a dual resident corporation. Unless otherwise indicated, any reference in this section to a dual resident corporation refers also to a separate unit.

(3) *Separate unit.*—(i) The term "separate unit" shall mean any of the following:

(A) A foreign branch, as defined in §1.367(a)-6T(g) (or a successor regulation), that is owned either directly by a domestic corporation or indirectly by a domestic corporation through ownership of a partnership or trust interest (regardless of whether the partnership or trust is a United States person);

(B) an interest in a partnership; or

(C) an interest in a trust.

(ii) If two or more foreign branches located in the same foreign country are owned by a single domestic corporation and the losses of each branch are made available to offset the income of the other branches under the tax laws of the foreign country, within the meaning of paragraph (c)(15)(ii) of this section, then the branches shall be treated as one separate unit.

(4) *Hybrid entity separate unit.*—The term "separate unit" includes an interest in an entity that is not taxable as an association for U.S. income tax purposes but is subject to income tax in a foreign country as a corporation (or otherwise at the entity level) either on its worldwide income or on a residence basis.

(5) *Dual consolidated loss.*—(i) *In general.*—The term "dual consolidated loss" means the net operating loss (as defined in section 172(c) and the regulations thereunder) of a domestic corporation incurred in a year in which the corporation is a dual resident corporation. The dual consolidated loss shall be computed under paragraph (d)(1) of this section. The fact that a particular item taken into account in computing a dual resident corporation's net operating loss is not taken into account in computing income subject to a foreign

country's income tax shall not cause such item to be excluded from the calculation of the dual consolidated loss.

(ii) *Exceptions.*—A dual consolidated loss shall not include the following—

(A) A net operating loss incurred by a dual resident corporation in a foreign country whose income tax laws—

*(1)* Do not permit the dual resident corporation to use its losses, expenses or deductions to offset the income of any other person that is recognized in the same taxable year in which the losses, expenses or deductions are incurred; and

*(2)* Do not permit the losses, expenses or deductions of the dual resident corporation to be carried over or back to be used, by any means, to offset the income of any other person in other taxable years; or

(B) A net operating loss incurred during that portion of the taxable year prior to the date on which the domestic corporation becomes a dual resident corporation or subsequent to the date on which the domestic corporation ceases to be a dual resident corporation. For purposes of determining the amount of the net operating loss incurred in that portion of the taxable year prior to the date on which the domestic corporation becomes a dual resident corporation or subsequent to the date on which the domestic corporation ceases to be a dual resident corporation, in no event shall more than the aggregate of the equal daily portion of the net operating loss commensurate with the portion of the taxable year during which the domestic corporation was not a dual resident corporation be allocated to that portion of the taxable year in which the domestic corporation was not a dual resident corporation.

(iii) *Dual consolidated losses of separate units that are partnership interests, including interests in hybrid entities.*—[Reserved]

(6) *Subject to tax.*—For purposes of determining whether a domestic corporation is subject to the income tax of a foreign country on its income, the fact that the corporation has no actual income tax liability to the foreign country for a particular taxable year shall not be taken into account.

(7) *Foreign country.*—For purposes of this section, possessions of the United States shall be considered foreign countries.

(8) *Consolidated group.*—The term "consolidated group" means an affiliated group, as defined in section 1504(a), with which a dual resident corporation or domestic owner files a consolidated U.S. income tax return.

(9) *Domestic owner.*—The term "domestic owner" means a domestic corporation that owns one or more separate units.

(10) *Affiliated dual resident corporation or affiliated domestic owner.*—The term "affiliated dual resident corporation" or "affiliated domestic owner" means a dual resident corporation or domestic owner that is a member of a consolidated group.

(11) *Unaffiliated dual resident corporation or unaffiliated domestic owner.*—The term "unaffiliated dual resident corporation" or "unaffiliated domestic owner" means a dual resident corporation or domestic owner that is an unaffiliated domestic corporation.

(12) *Successor-in-interest.*—The term "successor-in-interest" means an acquiring corporation that succeeds to the tax attributes of an acquired corporation by means of a transaction subject to section 381.

(13) *Domestic affiliate.*—The term "domestic affiliate" means any member of an affiliated group, without regard to the exceptions contained in section 1504(b) (other than section 1504(b)(3)) relating to includible corporations.

(14) *Unaffiliated domestic corporation.*—The term "unaffiliated domestic corporation" means a domestic corporation that is not a member of an affiliated group.

(15) *Use of loss to offset income of a domestic affiliate or another person.*—(i) A dual consolidated loss shall be deemed to offset income of a domestic affiliate in the year it is included in the computation of the consolidated taxable income of a consolidated group. The fact that no tax benefit results from the inclusion of the dual consolidated loss in the computation of the group's consolidated taxable income in the taxable year shall not be taken into account.

(ii) Except as provided in paragraph (c)(15)(iii) of this section, a loss, expense, or deduction taken into account in computing a dual consolidated loss shall be deemed to offset income of another person under the income tax laws of a foreign country in the year it is made available for such offset. The fact that the other person does not have sufficient income in that year to benefit from such an offset shall not be taken into account. However, where the laws of a foreign country provide an election that would enable a dual resident corporation or

separate unit to use its losses, expenses, or deductions to offset income of another person, the losses, expenses, or deductions shall be considered to offset such income only if the election is made.

(iii) The losses, expenses, or deductions taken into account in computing a dual resident corporation's or separate unit's dual consolidated loss shall not be deemed to offset income of another person under the income tax laws of a foreign country for purposes of this section, if under the laws of the foreign country the losses, expenses, or deductions of the dual resident corporation or separate unit are used to offset the income of another dual resident corporation or separate unit within the same consolidated group (or income of another separate unit that is owned by the unaffiliated domestic owner of the first separate unit). If the losses, expenses, or deductions of a dual resident corporation or separate unit are made available under the laws of a foreign country to offset the income of other dual resident corporations or separate units within the same consolidated group (or other separate units owned by the unaffiliated domestic owner of the first separate unit), as well as the income of another person, and the laws of the foreign country do not provide applicable rules for determining which person's income is offset by the losses, expenses, or deductions, then for purposes of this section, the losses, expenses or deductions shall be deemed to offset the income of the other dual resident corporations or separate units, to the extent of such income, before being considered to offset the income of the other person.

(iv) Except to the extent paragraph (g)(1) of this section applies, where the income tax laws of a foreign country deny the use of losses, expenses, or deductions of a dual resident corporation to offset the income of another person because the dual resident corporation is also subject to income taxation by another country on its worldwide income or on a residence basis, the dual resident corporation shall be treated as if it actually had offset its dual consolidated loss against the income of another person in such foreign country.

(16) *Examples.*—The following examples illustrate this paragraph (c).

*Example 1.* X, a member of a consolidated group, conducts business through a branch in Country Y. Under Country Y's income tax laws, the branch is taxed as a permanent establishment and its losses may be used under the Country Y form of consolidation to offset the income of Z, a Country Y affiliate of X. In Year 1, the branch of X incurs an overall loss that would be treated as a net operating loss if the branch were a separate domestic corporation. Under paragraph (c)(3) of this section, the branch of X is treated as a separate domestic corporation and a dual resident corporation. Thus, under paragraph (c)(5), its loss constitutes a dual consolidated loss. Unless X qualifies for an exception under paragraph (g) of this section, paragraph (b) of this section precludes the use of the branch's loss to offset any income of X not derived from the branch operations or any income of a domestic affiliate of X.

*Example 2.* A and B are members of a consolidated group. FC is a Country X corporation that is wholly owned by B. A and B organize a partnership, P, under the laws of Country X. P conducts business in Country X and its business activity constitutes a foreign branch within the meaning of paragraph (c)(3)(i)(A) of this section. P also earns U.S. source income that is unconnected with the branch operations and, therefore, is not subject to tax by Country X. Under the laws of Country X, the branch can consolidate with FC. The interests in P held by A and B are each treated as a dual resident corporation. The branch is also treated as a separate dual resident corporation. Unless an exception under paragraph (g) of this section applies, any dual consolidated loss incurred by P's branch cannot offset the U.S. source income earned by P or any other income of A or B.

*Example 3.* X is classified as a partnership for U.S. income tax purposes. A, B and C are the sole partners of X. A and B are domestic corporations and C is a Country Y corporation. For U.S. income tax purposes, each partner has an equal interest in each item of partnership profit or loss. Under Country Y's law, X is classified as a corporation and its income and losses may be used under the Country Y form of consolidation to offset the income of companies that are affiliates of X. Under paragraph (c)(3) and (4) of this section, the partnership interests held by A and B are treated as separate domestic corporations and as dual resident corporations. Unless an exception under paragraph (g) of this section applies, losses allocated to A and B can only be used to offset profits of X allocated to A and B, respectively.

*Example 4.* P, a domestic corporation, files a consolidated U.S. income tax return with its two wholly-owned domestic subsidiaries, DRC1 and DRC2. Each subsidiary is also treated as a Country Y resident for Country Y tax purposes. Thus, DRC1 and DRC2 are dual resident corporations. DRC1 owns FC, a Country Y corporation. Country Y's tax laws permit affiliated resident corporations to file a form of consolidated return. In Year 1, DRC1 incurs a $200 net operating loss for both U.S. and Country Y tax purposes, while DRC2 recognizes $200 of income under the tax laws of each country. FC also earns $200 of income for Country Y tax purposes. DRC1, DRC2, and FC file a Country Y consolidated return. However, Country Y has no applicable rules for determining which income is offset by DRC1's $200 loss. Under paragraph (c)(15)(iii) of this section, the loss shall be treated as offsetting DRC2's $200 of income. Because DRC1 and DRC2 are members of the same consolidated group, for purposes of this section, the offset of DRC1's loss against the income of DRC2 is not considered a use of the loss against the income of another person under the laws of a foreign country.

*Example 5.* DRC, a domestic corporation, files a consolidated U.S. income tax return with its parent, P. DRC is also subject to tax in Country Y on its worldwide income. Therefore, DRC is a dual resident corporation and any net operating loss incurred by DRC is a dual consolidated loss. Country Y's tax laws permit corporations that are subject to tax on their worldwide income to use the Country Y form of consolidation, thus enabling eligible corporations to use their losses to offset income of affiliates. However, to prevent corporations like DRC from offsetting losses against income of affiliates in Country Y and then again offsetting the losses against income of foreign affiliates under the tax laws of another country, Country Y prevents a corporation that is also subject to the income tax of another country on its worldwide income or on a residence basis from using the Country Y form of consolidation. There is no agreement, as described in paragraph (g)(1) of this section, between the United States and Country Y. Because of Country Y's statute, DRC will be treated as having actually offset its losses against the income of affiliates in Country Y under paragraph (c)(15)(iv) of this section. Therefore, DRC will not be able to file an agreement described in paragraph (g)(2) of this section and offset its losses against the income of P or any other domestic affiliate.

(d) *Special rules for accounting for dual consolidated losses.*—(1) *Determination of amount of dual consolidated loss.*—(i) *Dual resident corporation that is a member of a consolidated group.*—For purposes of determining whether a dual resident corporation that is a member of a consolidated group has a dual consolidated loss for the taxable year, the dual resident corporation shall compute its taxable income (or loss) in accordance with the rules set forth in the regulations under section 1502 governing the computation of consolidated taxable income, taking into account only the dual resident corporation's items of income, gain, deduction, and loss for the year. However, for purposes of this computation, the following items shall not be taken into account:

(A) Any net capital loss of the dual resident corporation; and

(B) Any carryover or carryback losses.

(ii) *Dual resident corporation that is a separate unit of a domestic corporation.*—For purposes of determining whether a separate unit has a dual consolidated loss for the taxable year, the separate unit shall compute its taxable income (or loss) as if it were a separate domestic corporation and a dual resident corporation in accordance with the provisions of paragraph (d)(1)(i) of this section, using only those items of income, expense, deduction, and loss that are otherwise attributable to such separate unit.

(2) *Effect of a dual consolidated loss.*—For any taxable year in which a dual resident corporation or separate unit has a dual consolidated loss to which paragraph (b) of this section applies, the following rules shall apply.

(i) If the dual resident corporation is a member of a consolidated group, the group shall compute its consolidated taxable income without taking into account the items of income, loss, or deduction taken into account in computing the dual consolidated loss. The dual consolidated loss may be carried over or back for use in other taxable years as a separate net operating loss carryover or carryback of the dual resident corporation arising in the year incurred. It shall be treated as a loss incurred by the dual resident corporation in a separate return limitation year and (without regard to whether the dual resident corporation is a common parent) shall be subject to all of the limitations of § 1.1502-21A(c) or 1.1502-21(c), as appropriate (relating to limitations on net operating loss carryovers and carrybacks from separate return limitation years).

(ii) The unaffiliated domestic owner of a separate unit, or the consolidated group of an affiliated domestic owner, shall compute its taxable income without taking into account the items of income, loss or deduction taken into account in computing the separate unit's dual consolidated loss. The dual consolidated loss shall be treated as a loss incurred by a separate corporation and its use shall be subject to all of the limitations of § 1.1502-21A(c) or 1.1502-21(c), as appropriate, as if the separate unit were filing a consolidated return with the unaffiliated domestic owner or with the consolidated group of the affiliated domestic owner.

(3) *Basis adjustments for dual consolidated losses.*—(i) *Dual resident corporation that is a member of an affiliated group.*—When a dual resi-

dent corporation is a member of a consolidated group, each other member owning stock in the dual resident corporation shall adjust the basis of the stock in the following manner.

(A) *Positive adjustments.*—Positive adjustments shall be made in accordance with the principles of § 1.1502-32(b)(1), except that there shall be no positive adjustment under § 1.1502-32(b)(1)(ii) for any amount of the dual consolidated loss that is not absorbed as a result of the application of paragraph (b) of this section. In addition, there shall be no positive adjustment for any amount included in income pursuant to paragraph (g)(2)(vii) of this section.

(B) *Negative adjustments.*—Negative adjustments shall be made in accordance with the principles of § 1.1502-32(b)(2), except that there shall be no negative adjustment under § 1.1502-32(b)(2)(ii) for the amount of the dual consolidated loss subject to paragraph (b) of this section that is absorbed in a carryover year.

(ii) *Dual resident corporation that is a separate unit arising from an interest in a partnership.*—Where a separate unit is an interest in a partnership, the domestic owner shall adjust its basis in the separate unit in accordance with section 705, except that no increase in basis shall be permitted for any amount included as income pursuant to paragraph (g)(2)(vii) of this section.

(4) *Examples.*—The following examples illustrate this paragraph (d).

*Example 1.* (i) P, S1, S2, and T are domestic corporations. P owns all of the stock of S1 and S2. S2 owns all of the stock of T. T is a resident of Country FC for Country FC income tax purposes. Therefore, T is a dual resident corporation. P, S1, S2, and T file a consolidated U.S. income tax return. X and Y are corporations that are not members of the consolidated group.

(ii) At the beginning of Year 1, P has a basis of $1,000 in the stock of S2. S2 has a $500 basis in the stock of T.

(iii) In Year 1, T incurs interest expense in the amount of $100. In addition, T sells a noncapital asset, *u*, in which it has a basis of $10, to S1 for $50. T also sells a noncapital asset, *v*, in which it has a basis of $200, to S1 for $100. The sales of *u* and *v* are intercompany transactions described in § 1.1502-13. T also sells a capital asset, *z*, in which it has a basis of $180, to Y for $90. In Year 1, S1 earns $200 of separate taxable income, calculated in accordance with § 1.1502-12, as well as $90 of capital gain from a sale of an asset to X. P and S2 have no items of income, loss, or deduction for Year 1.

(iv) In Year 1, T has a dual consolidated loss of $100 (attributable to its interest expense). T's $90 capital loss is not included in the computation of the dual consolidated loss. Instead, T's capital loss is included in the computation of the consolidated group's capital gain net income under § 1.1502-22(c) and is used to offset S1's $90 capital gain.

(v) No elective agreement, as described in paragraph (g)(1) of this section, exists between the United States and Country FC. For Country FC tax purposes, T's $100 loss is offset against the income of a Country FC affiliate. Therefore, T is not eligible for the exception provided in paragraph (g)(2) of this section.

(vi) Because T has a dual consolidated loss for the year, the consolidated taxable income of the consolidated group is calculated without regard to T's items of income, loss or deduction taken into account in computing the dual consolidated loss. Therefore, the consolidated taxable income of the consolidated group is $200 (the sum of $200 of separate taxable income earned by S1 plus $90 of capital gain earned by S1 minus $90 of capital loss incurred by T). The $40 gain recognized by T upon the sale of item *u* to S1 and the $100 loss recognized by T upon the sale of Item *v* to S1 are deferred pursuant to § 1.1502-13(c)(1).

(vii) S2 may not make the positive adjustment provided for in § 1.1502-32(b)(1)(ii) to its basis in the stock of T for the $100 dual consolidated loss incurred by T. In addition, no positive adjustment in the basis of the stock is required for T's $90 capital loss because the loss has been absorbed by the consolidated group. S2, however, must make the negative adjustment provided for in § 1.1502-32(b)(2)(i) for its allocable part of T's deficit in earnings and profits for the taxable year attributable to both T's $100 dual consolidated loss and T's $90 capital loss. Thus, as provided in § 1.1502-32(e)(1), S2 must make a $190 net negative adjustment to its basis in the stock of T, reducing its basis to $310. As provided in § 1.1502-33(c)(4)(ii) (a), S2's earnings and profits for Year 1 will reflect S2's decrease in its basis in T stock for the taxable year. Since S2 has no other earnings and profits for the taxable year, S2 has a $190 deficit in earnings and profits for the year. As provided in § 1.1502-32(b)(2)(i), P must make a negative adjustment to its basis in the stock of S2 for its allocable part of S2's deficit in earnings and profits for the taxable year. Thus, P must make a $190 net negative adjustment to its basis in S2 stock, reducing its basis to $810.

*Example 2.* (i) The facts are the same as in *Example 1*, except that in Year 2, S1 sells items *u* and *v* to X for no gain or loss. The disposition of items *u* and *v* outside of the consolidated group restores the deferred loss and gain to T. T also incurs $100 of interest expense in Year 2. In addition, T sells a noncapital asset, *r*, in which it has a basis of $100, to Y for $300. P and S2 have no items of income, loss, or deduction for Year 2.

(ii) T has $40 of separate taxable income in Year 2, computed as follows:

| | |
|---|---|
| ($100) | interest expense |
| ($100) | sale of item *v* to S1 |
| $40 | sale of item *u* to S1 |
| $200 | sale of item *r* to Y |
| $40 | |

Thus, T has no dual consolidated loss for the year.

(iii) Since T does not have a dual consolidated loss for the taxable year, the group's consolidated taxable income is calculated in accordance with the general rule of §1.1502-11 and not in accordance with paragraph (d)(2) of this section. T is the only member of the consolidated group that has any income or loss for the taxable year. Thus, the consolidated taxable income of the group, computed without regard to T's dual consolidated loss carryover, is $40.

(iv) As provided by §1.1502-21A(c), the amount of the dual consolidated loss arising in Year 1 that is included in the group's consolidated net operating loss deduction for Year 2 is $40 (that is, the consolidated taxable income computed without regard to the consolidated net operating loss deduction minus such consolidated taxable income recomputed by excluding the items of income and deduction of T). Thus, the group has no consolidated taxable income for the year.

(v) S2 must make the positive adjustment provided for in §1.1502-32(b)(1)(i) to its basis in T stock for its allocable part of T's undistributed earnings and profits for the taxable year. S2 cannot make the negative adjustment provided for in §1.1502-32(b)(2)(ii) for the dual consolidated loss of T incurred in Year 1 and absorbed in Year 2. Thus, as provided in §1.1502-32(e)(2), S2 must make a $40 net positive adjustment to its basis in T stock, increasing its basis to $350. As provided in §1.1502-33(c)(4)(ii)(a), S2's earnings and profits for Year 2 will reflect S2's increase in its basis in T stock for the taxable year. Since S2 has no other earnings and profits for the taxable year, S2 has $40 of earnings and profits for the year. As provided in §1.1502-32(b)(1)(i), P must make a positive adjustment to its basis in the stock of S2 for its allocable part of the undistributed earnings and profits of S2 for the taxable year. Thus, P must make a $40 net positive adjustment to its basis in S2 stock, increasing its basis to $850.

(e) *Special rule for use of dual consolidated loss to offset tainted income.*—(1) *In general.*—The dual consolidated loss of any dual resident corporation that ceases to be a dual resident corporation shall not be used to offset income of such corporation to the extent that such income is tainted income, as defined in paragraph (e)(2) of this section.

(2) *Tainted income defined.*—Tainted income is any income derived from tainted assets, as defined in paragraph (e)(3) of this section, beginning on the date such assets are acquired by the dual resident corporation. In the absence of evidence establishing the actual amount of income that is attributable to the tainted assets, the portion of a corporation's income in a particular taxable year that is treated as tainted income shall be an amount equal to the corporation's taxable income for the year multiplied by a fraction, the numerator of which is the fair market value of the tainted asset at the end of the taxable year and the denominator of which is the fair market value of the total assets owned by the corporation at the end of the taxable year. Documentation submitted to establish the actual amount of income that is attributable to the tainted assets must be attached to the consolidated group's or unaffiliated dual resident corporation's timely filed tax return for the taxable year in which the income is recognized.

(3) *Tainted assets defined.*—Tainted assets are any assets acquired by a dual resident corporation in a nonrecognition transaction, as defined in section 7701(a)(45), or any assets otherwise transferred to the corporation as a contribution to capital, at any time during the three taxable years immediately preceding the taxable year in which the corporation ceases to be a dual resident corporation or at any time thereafter. Tainted assets shall not include assets that were acquired by such dual resident corporation on or before December 31, 1986.

(4) *Exceptions.*—Income derived from assets acquired by a dual resident corporation shall not be subject to the limitation described in paragraph (e)(1) of this section, if—

(i) For the taxable year in which the assets were acquired, the corporation did not have a dual consolidated loss (or a carry forward of a dual consolidated loss to such year); or

(ii) The assets were acquired as replacement property in the ordinary course of business.

(f) *Computation of foreign tax credit limitations.*—If a dual resident corporation or separate unit is subject to paragraph (d)(2) of this section, the consolidated group or unaffiliated domestic owner shall compute its foreign tax credit limitation by applying the limitations of paragraph (d)(2). Thus, the dual consolidated loss is not taken into account until the year in which it is absorbed.

(g) *Exception.*—(1) *Elective agreement in place between the United States and a foreign country.*—Paragraph (b) of this section shall not apply to a dual consolidated loss to the extent the dual resident corporation, or domestic owner of a separate unit, elects to deduct the loss in the United States pursuant to an agreement entered into between the United States and a foreign country that puts into place an elective procedure through which losses offset income in only one country.

(2) *Elective relief provision.*—(i) *In general.*—Paragraph (b) of this section shall not apply to a dual consolidated loss if the consolidated group, unaffiliated dual resident corporation, or unaffiliated domestic owner elects to be bound by the provisions of this paragraph (g)(2). In order to elect relief under this paragraph (g)(2), the consolidated group, unaffiliated dual resident corporation, or unaffiliated domestic owner must attach to its timely filed (including extensions) U.S. income tax return for the taxable year in which the dual consolidated loss is incurred an agreement described in paragraph (g)(2)(i)(A) of this section. The agreement must be signed under penalties of perjury by the person who signs the return. For taxable years beginning after December 31, 2002, the agreement attached to the income tax return of the consolidated group, unaffiliated dual resident corporation or unaffiliated domestic owner pursuant to the preceding sentence may be an unsigned copy. If an unsigned copy is attached to the return, the consolidated group, unaffiliated dual resident corporation, or unaffiliated domestic owner must retain the original in its records in the manner specified by §1.6001-1(e). The agreement must include the following items, in paragraphs labeled to correspond with the items set forth in paragraph (g)(2)(i)(A) through (F) of this section.

(A) A statement that the document submitted is an election and an agreement under the provisions of paragraph (g)(2) of this section.

(B) The name, address, identifying number, and place and date of incorporation of the dual resident corporation, and the country or countries that tax the dual resident corporation on its worldwide income or on a residence basis, or, in the case of a separate unit, identification of the separate unit, including the name under which it conducts business, its principal activity, and the country in which its principal place of business is located.

(C) An agreement by the consolidated group, unaffiliated dual resident corporation, or unaffiliated domestic owner to comply with all of the provisions of §1.1503-2(g)(2)(iii)-(vii).

(D) A statement of the amount of the dual consolidated loss covered by the agreement.

(E) A certification that no portion of the dual resident corporation's or separate unit's losses, expenses, or deductions taken into account in computing the dual consolidated loss has been, or will be, used to offset the income of any other person under the income tax laws of a foreign country.

(F) A certification that arrangements have been made to ensure that no portion of the dual consolidated loss will be used to offset the income of another person under the laws of a foreign country and that the consolidated group, unaffiliated dual resident corporation, or unaffiliated domestic owner will be informed of any such foreign use of any portion of the dual consolidated loss.

(ii) *Consistency rule.*—(A) If any loss, expense, or deduction taken into account in computing the dual consolidated loss of a dual resident corporation or separate unit is used under the laws of a foreign country to offset the income of another person, then the following other dual consolidated losses (if any) shall be treated as also having been used to offset income of another person under the laws of such foreign country, but only if the income tax laws of the foreign country permit any loss, expense, or deduction taken into account in computing the other dual consolidated loss to be used to offset the income of another person in the same taxable year:

(1) Any dual consolidated loss of a dual resident corporation that is a member of the same consolidated group of which the first dual resident corporation or domestic owner is a member, if any loss, expense, or deduction taken into account in computing such dual consolidated loss is recognized under the income tax laws of such country in the same taxable year; and

(2) Any dual consolidated loss of a separate unit that is owned by the same domestic owner that owns the first separate unit, or that is owned by any member of the same consolidated group of

which the first dual resident corporation or domestic owner is a member, if any loss, expense, or deduction taken into account in computing such dual consolidated loss is recognized under the income tax laws of such country in the same taxable year.

(B) The following examples illustrate the application of this paragraph (g)(2)(ii).

*Example 1.* P, a domestic corporation, owns A and B, which are domestic corporations, and C, a Country X corporation. A is subject to the income tax laws of Country X on a residence basis and, thus, is a dual resident corporation. B conducts business in Country X through a branch, which is a separate unit under paragraph (c)(3) of this section. The income tax laws of Country X permit branches of foreign corporations to elect to file consolidated returns with Country X affiliates. In Year 1, A incurs a dual consolidated loss, which is used to offset the income of C under the Country X form of consolidation. The branch of B also incurs a net operating loss. However, B elects not to use the loss on a Country X consolidated return to offset the income of foreign affiliates. The use of A's loss to offset the income of C in Country X will cause the separate unit of B to be treated as if it too had used its dual consolidated loss to offset the income of an affiliate in Country X. Therefore, an election and agreement under this paragraph (g)(2) cannot be made with respect to the separate unit's dual consolidated loss.

*Example 2.* The facts are the same as in *Example 1*, except that the income tax laws of Country X do not permit branches of foreign corporations to file consolidated income tax returns with Country X affiliates. Therefore, an election and agreement described in this paragraph (g)(2) may be made for the dual consolidated loss incurred by the separate unit of B.

(iii) *Triggering events requiring the recapture of dual consolidated losses.*—(A) The consolidated group, unaffiliated dual resident corporation, or unaffiliated domestic owner must agree that, if there is a triggering event described in this paragraph (g)(2)(iii), and no exception applies under paragraph (g)(2)(iv) of this section, the consolidated group, unaffiliated dual resident corporation, or unaffiliated domestic owner will recapture and report as income the amount of the dual consolidated loss provided in paragraph (g)(2)(vii) of this section on its tax return for the taxable year in which the triggering event occurs (or, when the triggering event is a use of the loss for foreign purposes, the taxable year that includes the last day of the foreign tax year during which such use occurs). In addition, the consolidated group, unaffiliated dual resident corporation, or unaffiliated domestic owner must pay any applicable interest charge required by paragraph (g)(2)(vii) of this section. For purposes of this section, any of the following events shall constitute a triggering event:

(1) In any taxable year up to and including the 15th taxable year following the year in which the dual consolidated loss that is the subject of the agreement filed under this paragraph (g)(2) was incurred, any portion of the losses, expenses, or deductions taken into account in computing the dual consolidated loss is used by any means to offset the income of any other person under the income tax laws of a foreign country;

(2) An affiliated dual resident corporation or affiliated domestic owner ceases to be a member of the consolidated group that filed the election. For purposes of this paragraph (g)(2)(iii)(A)(2), a dual resident corporation or domestic owner shall be considered to cease to be a member of the consolidated group if it is no longer a member of the group within the meaning of § 1.1502-1(b), or if the group ceases to exist because the common parent is no longer in existence or is no longer a common parent or the group no longer files on the basis of a consolidated return. Such disaffiliation, however, shall not constitute a triggering event if the taxpayer demonstrates, to the satisfaction of the Commissioner, that the dual resident corporation's or separate unit's losses, expenses, or deductions cannot be used to offset income of another person under the laws of a foreign country at any time after the affiliated dual resident corporation or affiliated domestic owner ceases to be a member of the consolidated group;

(3) An unaffiliated dual resident corporation or unaffiliated domestic owner becomes a member of a consolidated group. Such affiliation of the dual resident corporation or domestic owner, however, shall not constitute a triggering event if the taxpayer demonstrates, to the satisfaction of the Commissioner, that the losses, expenses, or deductions of the dual resident corporation or separate unit cannot be used to offset the income of another person under the laws of a foreign country at any time after the dual resident corporation or domestic owner becomes a member of the consolidated group;

(4) A dual resident corporation transfers assets in a transaction that results, under the laws of a foreign country, in a carryover of its losses, expenses, or deductions. For purposes of this paragraph (g)(2)(iii) (A)(4), a transfer, either in a single transaction or a series of transactions within a twelve-month period, of 50% or more of the

dual resident corporation's assets (measured by the fair market value of the assets at the time of such transfer (or for multiple transactions, at the time of the first transfer)) shall be deemed a triggering event, unless the taxpayer demonstrates, to the satisfaction of the Commissioner, that the transfer of assets did not result in a carryover under foreign law of the dual resident corporation's losses, expenses, or deductions to the transferee of the assets;

(5) A domestic owner of a separate unit transfers assets of the separate unit in a transaction that results, under the laws of a foreign country, in a carryover of the separate unit's losses, expenses, or deductions. For purposes of this paragraph (g)(2)(iii)(A)(5), a transfer, either in a single transaction or a series of transactions over a twelve-month period, of 50% or more of the separate unit's assets (measured by the fair market value of the assets at the time of the transfer (or for multiple transfers, at the time of the first transfer)), shall be deemed a triggering event, unless the taxpayer demonstrates, to the satisfaction of the Commissioner, that the transfer of assets did not result in a carryover under foreign law of the separate unit's losses, expenses, or deductions to the transferee of the assets;

(6) An unaffiliated dual resident corporation or unaffiliated domestic owner becomes a foreign corporation by means of a transaction (*e.g.*, a reorganization) that, for foreign tax purposes, is not treated as involving a transfer of assets (and carryover of losses) to a new entity. Such a transaction, however, shall not constitute a triggering event if the taxpayer demonstrates, to the satisfaction of the Commissioner, that the dual resident corporation's or separate unit's losses, expenses, or deductions cannot be used to offset income of another person under the laws of the foreign country at any time after the unaffiliated dual resident corporation or unaffiliated domestic owner becomes a foreign corporation.

(7) A domestic owner of a separate unit, either in a single transaction or a series of transactions within a twelve-month period, sells, or otherwise disposes of, 50% or more of the interest in the separate unit (measured by voting power or value) owned by the domestic owner on the last day of the taxable year in which the dual consolidated loss was incurred. For purposes of this paragraph (g)(2)(iii)(A)(7), the domestic owner shall be deemed to have disposed of its entire interest in a hybrid entity separate unit if such hybrid entity becomes classified as a foreign corporation for U.S. tax purposes. The disposition of 50% or more of the interest in a separate unit, however, shall not constitute a triggering event if the taxpayer demonstrates, to the satisfaction of the Commissioner, that the losses, expenses, or deductions of the separate unit cannot be used to offset income of another person under the laws of the foreign country at any time after the disposition of the interest in the separate unit; or

(8) The consolidated group, unaffiliated dual resident corporation, or unaffiliated domestic owner fails to file a certification required under paragraph (g)(2)(vi)(B) of this section.

(B) A taxpayer wishing to rebut the presumption of a triggering event described in paragraphs (g)(2)(iii)(A) (2) through (7) of this section, by demonstrating that the losses, expenses, or deductions of the dual resident corporation or separate unit cannot be carried over or otherwise used under the laws of the foreign country, must attach documents demonstrating such facts to its timely filed U.S. income tax return for the year in which the presumed triggering event occurs.

(C) The following example illustrates this paragraph (g)(2)(iii).

*Example.* DRC, a domestic corporation, is a member of CG, a consolidated group. DRC is a resident of Country Y for Country Y income tax purposes. Therefore, DRC is a dual resident corporation. In Year 1, DRC incurs a dual consolidated loss of $100. CG files an agreement described in paragraph (g)(2) of this section and, thus, the $100 dual consolidated loss is included in the computation of CG's consolidated taxable income. In Year 6, all of the stock of DRC is sold to P, a domestic corporation that is a member of NG, another consolidated group. The sale of DRC to P is a triggering event under paragraph (g)(2)(iii)(A) of this section, requiring the recapture of the dual consolidated loss. However, the laws of Country Y provide for a five-year carryover period for losses. At the time of DRC's disaffiliation from CG, the losses, expenses and deductions that were included in the computation of the dual consolidated loss had expired for Country Y purposes. Therefore, upon adequate documentation that the losses, expenses, or deductions have expired for Country Y purposes, CG can rebut the presumption that a triggering event has occurred.

(iv) *Exceptions.*—(A) *Acquisition by a member of the consolidated group.*—The following events shall not constitute triggering events, requiring the recapture of the dual consolidated loss under paragraph (g)(2)(vii) of this section:

(1) An affiliated dual resident corporation or affiliated domestic owner ceases to be a member of a consolidated group solely by reason of a transaction in which a member of the same consoli-

dated group succeeds to the tax attributes of the dual resident corporation or domestic owner under the provisions of section 381;

(2) Assets of an affiliated dual resident corporation or assets of a separate unit of an affiliated domestic owner are acquired by a member of its consolidated group in any other transaction; or

(3) An affiliated domestic owner of a separate unit transfers its interest in the separate unit to another member of its consolidated group.

(B) *Acquisition by an unaffiliated domestic corporation or a new consolidated group.*—(1) If all the requirements of paragraph (g)(2)(iv)(B)(3) of this section are met, the following events shall not constitute triggering events requiring the recapture of the dual consolidated loss under paragraph (g)(2)(vii) of this section:

(i) An affiliated dual resident corporation or affiliated domestic owner becomes an unaffiliated domestic corporation or a member of a new consolidated group (other than in a transaction described in paragraph (g)(2)(iv)(B)(2)(ii) of this section);

(ii) Assets of a dual resident corporation or a separate unit are acquired by an unaffiliated domestic corporation or a member of a new consolidated group; or

(iii) A domestic owner of a separate unit transfers its interest in the separate unit to an unaffiliated domestic corporation or to a member of a new consolidated group.

(2) If the requirements of paragraph (g)(2)(iv)(B)(3)(iii) of this section are met, the following events shall not constitute triggering events requiring the recapture of the dual consolidated loss under paragraph (g)(2)(vii) of this section—

(i) An unaffiliated dual resident corporation or unaffiliated domestic owner becomes a member of a consolidated group;

(ii) A consolidated group that filed an agreement under this paragraph (g)(2) ceases to exist as a result of a transaction described in §1.1502-13(j)(5)(i) (other than a transaction in which any member of the terminating group, or the successor-in-interest of such member, is not a member of the surviving group immediately after the terminating group ceases to exist).

(3) If the following requirements (as applicable) are satisfied, the events listed in paragraphs (g)(2)(iv)(B)(1) and (2) of this section shall not constitute triggering events requiring recapture under paragraph (g)(2)(vii) of this section.

(i) The consolidated group, unaffiliated dual resident corporation, or unaffiliated domestic owner that filed the agreement under this paragraph (g)(2) and the unaffiliated domestic corporation or new consolidated group must enter into a closing agreement with the Internal Revenue Service providing that the consolidated group, unaffiliated dual resident corporation, or unaffiliated domestic owner and the unaffiliated domestic corporation or new consolidated group will be jointly and severally liable for the total amount of the recapture of dual consolidated loss and interest charge required in paragraph (g)(2)(vii) of this section, if there is a triggering event described in paragraph (g)(2)(iii) of this section;

(ii) The unaffiliated domestic corporation or new consolidated group must agree to treat any potential recapture amount under paragraph (g)(2)(vii) of this section as unrealized built-in gain for purposes of section 384(a), subject to any applicable exceptions thereunder;

(iii) The unaffiliated domestic corporation or new consolidated group must file, with its timely filed (including extensions) income tax return for the taxable year in which the event described in paragraph (g)(2)(iv)(B)(1) or (2) of this section occurs, an agreement described in paragraph (g)(2)(i) of this section (new (g)(2)(i) agreement), whereby it assumes the same obligations with respect to the dual consolidated loss as the corporation or consolidated group that filed the original (g)(2)(i) agreement with respect to that loss. The new (g)(2)(i) agreement must be signed under penalties of perjury by the person who signs the return and must include a reference to this paragraph (g)(2)(iv)(B)(3)(iii). For taxable years beginning after December 31, 2002, the agreement attached to the return pursuant to the preceding sentence may be an unsigned copy. If an unsigned copy is attached to the return, the corporation or consolidated group must retain the original in its records in the manner specified by §1.6001-1(e).

(C) *Subsequent triggering events.*—Any triggering event described in paragraph (g)(2)(iii) of this section that occurs subsequent to one of the transactions described in paragraph (g)(2)(iv)(A) or (B) of this section and does not fall within the exceptions provided in paragraph (g)(2)(iv)(A) or (B) of this section shall require recapture under paragraph (g)(2)(vii) of this section.

(D) Example. The following example illustrates the application of paragraph (g)(2)(iv)(B)(2)(ii) of this section:

*Example.* (i) Facts. C is the common parent of a consolidated group (the C Group) that includes DRC, a domestic corporation. DRC is a dual resident corporation and incurs a dual consolidated loss in its taxable year ending December 31, Year 1. The C Group

elects to be bound by the provisions of this paragraph (g)(2) with respect to the Year 1 dual consolidated loss. No member of the C Group incurs a dual consolidated loss in Year 2. On December 31, Year 2, stock of C is acquired by D in a transaction described in §1.1502-13(j)(5)(i). As a result of the acquisition, all the C Group members, including DRC, become members of a consolidated group of which D is the common parent (the D Group).

(ii) Acquisition not a triggering event. Under paragraph (g)(2)(iv)(B)(2)(ii) of this section, the acquisition by D of the C Group is not an event requiring the recapture of the Year 1 dual consolidated loss of DRC, or the payment of an interest charge, as described in paragraph (g)(2)(vii) of this section, provided that the D Group files the new (g)(2)(i) agreement described in paragraph (g)(2)(iv)(B)(3)(iii) of this section.

(iii) Subsequent event. A triggering event occurs on December 31, Year 3, that requires recapture by the D Group of the dual consolidated loss that DRC incurred in Year 1, as well as the payment of an interest charge, as provided in paragraph (g)(2)(vii) of this section. Each member of the D Group, including DRC and the other former members of the C Group, is severally liable for the additional tax (and the interest charge) due upon the recapture of the dual consolidated loss of DRC.

(v) *Ordering rules for determining the foreign use of losses.*—If the laws of a foreign country provide for the use of losses of a dual resident corporation to offset the income of another person but do not provide applicable rules for determining the order in which such losses are used to offset the income of another person in a taxable year, then for purposes of this section, the following rules shall govern:

(A) If under the laws of the foreign country the dual resident corporation has losses from different taxable years, the dual resident corporation shall be deemed to use first the losses from the earliest taxable year from which a loss may be carried forward or back for foreign law purposes.

(B) Any net loss, or income, that the dual resident corporation has in a taxable year shall first be used to offset net income, or loss, recognized by affiliates of the dual resident corporation in the same taxable year before any carryover of the dual resident corporation's losses is considered to be used to offset any income from the taxable year.

(C) Where different losses, expenses, or deductions (*e.g.*, capital losses and ordinary losses) of a dual resident corporation incurred in the same taxable year are available to offset the income of another person, the different losses shall be deemed to offset such income on a pro rata basis.

*Example.* DRC, a domestic corporation, is taxed as a resident under the tax laws of Country Y. Therefore, DRC is a dual resident corporation. FA is a Country Y affiliate of DRC. Country Y's tax laws permit affiliated corporations to file a form of consolidated return. In Year 1, DRC incurs a capital loss of $80 which, for Country Y purposes, offsets completely $30 of capital gain recognized by FA. Neither corporation has any other taxable income or loss for the year. In Year 1 (and in other years), DRC recognizes the same amount of income for U.S. purposes as it does for Country Y purposes. Under paragraph (d)(1)(i) of this section, however, DRC's $80 capital loss is not a dual consolidated loss. In Year 2, DRC incurs a net operating loss of $100, while FA incurs a net operating loss of $50. DRC's $100 loss is a dual consolidated loss. Since the dual consolidated loss is not used to offset the income of another person under Country Y law, DRC is permitted to file an agreement described in this paragraph (g)(2). In Year 3, DRC has a net operating loss of $10 and FA has capital gains of $60. For Country Y purposes, DRC's $10 net operating loss is used to offset $10 of FA's $60 capital gain. DRC's $10 loss is a dual consolidated loss. Because the loss is used to offset FA's income, DRC will not be able to file an agreement under this paragraph (g)(2) with respect to the loss. Country Y permits FA's remaining $50 of Year 3 income to be offset by carryover losses. However, Country Y has no applicable rules for determining which carryover losses from Years 1 and 2 are used to offset such income. Under the ordering rules of paragraph (g)(2)(v)(A) of this section, none of DRC's $100 Year 2 loss will be deemed to offset FA's remaining $50 of Year 3 income. Instead, the $50 of capital loss carryover from Year 1 will be considered to offset the income.

(vi) *Reporting requirements.*—(A) *In general.*—The consolidated group, unaffiliated dual resident corporation, or unaffiliated domestic owner must answer the applicable questions regarding dual consolidated losses on its U.S. income tax return filed for the year in which the dual consolidated loss is incurred and for each of the following fifteen taxable years.

(B) *Annual certification.*—Except as provided in §1.1503-2(g)(2)(vi)(C), until and unless Form 1120 or the Schedules thereto contain questions pertaining to dual consolidated losses, the consolidated group, unaffiliated dual resident corporation, or unaffiliated domestic owner must file with its income tax return for each of the 15 taxable years following the taxable year in which the dual consolidated loss is incurred a certification that the losses, expenses, or deductions that make up the dual consolidated loss have not been used to offset the income of another person under the tax laws of a foreign country. For taxable years beginning before January 1, 2003, the annual certification must be signed under penalties of perjury by a person authorized to sign the agreement described in §1.1503-2(g)(2)(i). For taxable years beginning after December 31, 2002, the certification is verified by signing the return with which the certification is filed. The certification for a taxable year must identify the dual consolidated loss to which it pertains by setting forth the taxpayer's year in which the loss was incurred and the amount of such loss. In addition, the certification must warrant that arrangements have been made to ensure that the loss will not be used to offset the income of another person under the laws of a foreign country and that the taxpayer will be informed of any such foreign use of any portion of the loss. If dual consolidated losses of more than one taxable year are subject to the rules of this paragraph (g)(2)(vi)(B), the certifications for those years may be combined in a single document but each dual consolidated loss must be separately identified.

(C) *Exception.*—A consolidated group or unaffiliated domestic owner is not required to file annual certifications under paragraph (g)(2)(vi)(B) of this section with respect to a dual consolidated loss of any separate unit other than a hybrid entity separate unit.

(vii) *Recapture of loss and interest charge.*—(A) *Presumptive rule.*—(1) *Amount of recapture.*—Except as otherwise provided in this paragraph (g)(2)(vii), upon the occurrence of a triggering event described in paragraph (g)(2)(iii) of this section, the taxpayer shall recapture and report as gross income the total amount of the dual consolidated loss to which the triggering event applies on its income tax return for the taxable year in which the triggering event occurs (or, when the triggering event is a use of the loss for foreign tax purposes, the taxable year that includes the last day of the foreign tax year during which such use occurs).

(2) *Interest charge.*—In connection with the recapture, the taxpayer shall pay an interest charge. Except as otherwise provided in this paragraph (g)(2)(vii), such interest shall be determined under the rules of section 6601(a) as if the additional tax owed as a result of the recapture had accrued and been due and owing for the taxable year in which the losses, expenses, or deductions taken into account in computing the dual consolidated loss gave rise to a tax benefit for U.S. income tax purposes. For purposes of this paragraph (g)(2)(vii)(A)(2), a tax benefit shall be considered to have arisen in a taxable year in which such losses, expenses or deductions reduced U.S. taxable income.

(B) *Rebuttal of presumptive rule.*—(1) *Amount of recapture.*—The amount of dual consolidated loss that must be recaptured under this paragraph (g)(2)(vii) may be reduced if the taxpayer demonstrates, to the satisfaction of the Commissioner, the offset permitted by this paragraph (g)(2)(vii)(B). The reduction in the amount of recapture is the amount by which the dual consolidated loss would have offset other taxable income reported on a timely filed U.S. income tax return for any taxable year up to and including the year of the triggering event if such loss had been subject to the restrictions of paragraph (b) of this section (and therefore had been subject to the separate return limitation year restrictions of §1.1502-21A(c) or 1.1502-21(c) (as appropriate)) commencing in the taxable year in which the loss was incurred. A taxpayer utilizing this rebuttal rule must attach to its timely filed U.S. income tax return a separate accounting showing that the income for each year that offsets the dual resident corporation's or separate unit's recapture amount is attributable only to the dual resident corporation or separate unit.

(2) *Interest charge.*—The interest charge imposed under this paragraph (g)(2)(vii) may be appropriately reduced if the taxpayer demonstrates, to the satisfaction of the Commissioner, that the net interest owed would have been less than that provided in paragraph (g)(2)(vii)(A)(2) of this section if the taxpayer had filed an amended return for the year in which the loss was incurred, and for any other affected years up to and including the year of recapture, treating the dual consolidated loss as a loss subject to the restrictions of paragraph (b) of this section (and therefore subject to the separate return limitation year restrictions of §1.1502-21A(c) or 1.1502-21(c) (as appropriate)). A taxpayer utilizing this rebuttal rule must attach to its timely filed U.S. income tax return a computation demonstrating the reduction in the net interest owed as a result of treating the dual consolidated loss as a loss subject to the restrictions of paragraph (b) of this section.

(C) *Computation of taxable income in year of recapture.*—(1) *Presumptive rule.*—Except as otherwise provided in paragraph (g)(2)(vii)(C)(2) of this section, for purposes of computing the taxable income for the year of recapture, no current, carryover or carryback losses of the dual resident corporation or separate unit, of other members of the consolidated group, or of the domestic owner that are not attributable to the separate unit, may offset and absorb the recapture amount.

(2) *Rebuttal of presumptive rule.*—The recapture amount included in gross income may be offset and absorbed by that portion of the taxpayer's (consolidated or separate) net operating loss carryover that is attributable to the dual consolidated loss being recaptured, if the taxpayer demonstrates, to the satisfaction of the Commissioner, the amount of such portion of the carryover. A taxpayer utilizing this rebuttal rule must attach to its timely filed U.S. income tax return a computation demonstrating the amount of net operating loss carryover that, under this paragraph (g)(2)(vii)(C)(2), may absorb the recapture amount included in gross income.

(D) *Character and source of recapture income.*—The amount recaptured under this paragraph (g)(2)(vii) shall be treated as ordinary income in the year of recapture. The amount recaptured shall be treated as income having the same source and falling within the same separate category for purposes of section 904 as the dual consolidated loss being recaptured.

(E) *Reconstituted net operating loss.*—Commencing in the taxable year immediately following the year in which the dual consolidated loss is recaptured, the dual resident corporation or separate unit shall be treated as having a net operating loss in an amount equal to the amount actually recaptured under paragraph (g)(2)(vii)(A) or (B) of this section. This reconstituted net operating loss shall be subject to the restrictions of paragraph (b) of this section (and therefore, the separate return limitation year restrictions of §§1.1502-21A(c) or 1.1502-21T(c) (as appropriate)). The net operating loss shall be available only for carryover, under section 172(b), to taxable years following the taxable year of recapture. For purposes of determining the remaining carryover period, the loss shall be treated as if it had been recognized in the taxable year in which the dual consolidated loss that is the basis of the recapture amount was incurred.

(F) *Consequences of failing to comply with recapture provisions.*—(1) *In general.*—If the taxpayer fails to comply with the recapture provisions of this paragraph (g)(2)(vii) upon the occurrence of a triggering event, then the dual resident corporation or separate unit that incurred the dual consolidated loss (or a successor-in-interest) shall not be eligible for the relief provided in paragraph (g)(2) of this section with respect to any dual consolidated losses incurred in the five taxable years beginning with the taxable year in which recapture is required.

(2) *Exceptions.*—In the case of a triggering event other than a use of the losses, expenses, or deductions taken into account in computing the dual consolidated loss to offset income of another person under the income tax laws of a foreign country, this rule shall not apply in the following circumstances:

(i) The failure to recapture is due to reasonable cause; or

(ii) A taxpayer seeking to rebut the presumption of a triggering event satisfies the filing requirements of paragraph (g)(2)(iii)(B) of this section.

(G) *Examples.*—The following examples illustrate this paragraph (g)(2)(vii).

*Example 1.* P, a domestic corporation, files a consolidated return with DRC, a dual resident corporation. In Year 1, DRC incurs a dual consolidated loss of $100 and P earns $100. P files an agreement under this paragraph (g)(2). Therefore, the consolidated group is permitted to offset P's $100 of income with DRC's $100 loss. In Year 2, DRC earns $30, which is completely offset by a $30 net operating loss incurred by P. In Year 3, DRC earns income of $25 while P recognizes no income or loss. In addition, there is a triggering event in Year 3. Therefore, under the presumptive rule of paragraph (g)(2)(vii)(A) of this section, DRC must recapture $100. However, the $100 recapture amount may be reduced by $25 (the amount by which the dual consolidated loss would have offset other taxable income if it had been subject to the separate return limitation year restrictions from Year 1) upon adequate documentation of such offset under paragraph (g)(2)(vii)(B)(1) of this section. Commencing in Year 4, the $100 (or $75) recapture amount is treated as a loss incurred by DRC in a separate return limitation year, subject to the restrictions of §1.1502-21A(c) or 1.1502-21(c), as appropriate. The carryover period of the loss, for purposes of section 172(b), will start from Year 1, when the dual consolidated loss was incurred.

*Example 2.* The facts are the same as in *Example 1*, except that in Year 2, DRC earns $75 and P earns $50. In Year 3, DRC earns $25 while P earns $30. A triggering event occurs in Year 3. The $100 presumptive amount of recapture can be reduced to zero by the $75 and $25 earned by DRC in Years 2 and 3, respectively, upon adequate documentation of such offset under paragraph (g)(2)(vii)(B)(1) of this section. Nevertheless, an interest charge will be owed. Under the presumptive rule of paragraph (g)(2)(vii)(A)(2) of this section, interest will be charged on the additional tax owed on the $100 of recapture income as if the tax had accrued in Year 1 (the year in which the dual consolidated loss reduced the income of P). However, the net interest will be reduced to the amount that would have been owed if the consolidated group had filed amended returns, treating the dual consolidated loss as a loss subject to the separate return limitation year restrictions of § 1.1502-21A(c) or 1.1502-21(c), as appropriate, upon adequate documentation of such reduction of interest under paragraph (g)(2)(vii)(B)(2) of this section.

*Example 3.* P, a domestic corporation, owns DRC, a domestic corporation that is subject to the income tax laws of Country Z on a residence basis. DRC owns FE, a Country Z corporation. In Year 1, DRC incurs a net operating loss for U.S. tax purposes. Under the tax laws of Country Z, the loss is not recognized until Year 3. The Year 1 net operating loss is a dual consolidated loss under paragraph (c)(5) of this section. The consolidated group elects relief under paragraph (g)(2) of this section by filing the appropriate agreement and uses the dual consolidated loss on its U.S. income tax return. In Year 3, the dual consolidated loss is used under the laws of Country Z to offset the income of FE, which is a triggering event under paragraph (g)(2)(iii) of this section. However, the consolidated group does not recapture the dual consolidated loss. The consolidated group's failure to comply with the recapture provisions of this paragraph (g)(2)(vii) prevents DRC from being eligible for the relief provided under paragraph (g)(2) of this section for any dual consolidated losses incurred in Years 3 through 7, inclusive.

(h) *Effective date.*—(1) *In general.*—These regulations are effective for taxable years beginning on or after October 1, 1992. Section 1.1503-3A is effective for taxable years beginning after December 31, 1986, and before October 1, 1992. Paragraph (g)(2)(iv)(B)(2) of this section shall apply with respect to transactions otherwise constituting triggering events occurring on or after January 1, 2002.

(2) *Taxpayers that have filed for relief under § 1.1503-2A.*—(i) *In general.*—Except as provided in paragraph (h)(ii)(b) of this section, taxpayers that have filed agreements described in § 1.1503-2A(c)(3) or certifications described in § 1.1503-2A(d)(3) shall continue to be subject to the provisions of such agreements or certifications, including the amended return or recapture requirements applicable in the event of a triggering event, for the remaining term of such agreements or certifications.

(ii) *Special transition rule.*—A taxpayer that has filed an agreement described in § 1.1503-2A(c)(3) or a certification described in § 1.1503-2A(d)(3) and that is in compliance with the provisions of § 1.1503-2A may elect to replace such agreement or certification with an agreement described in paragraph (g)(2)(i) of this section. However, a taxpayer making this election must replace all agreements and certifications filed under § 1.1503-2A. If the taxpayer is a consolidated group, the election must be made with respect to all dual resident corporations or separate units within the group. Likewise, if the taxpayer is an unaffiliated domestic owner, the election must be made with respect to all separate units of the domestic owner. The taxpayer must file the replacement agreement with its timely filed income tax return for its first taxable year commencing on or after October 1, 1992, stating that such agreement is a replacement for the agreement filed under § 1.1503-2A(c)(3) or the certification filed under § 1.1503-2A(d)(3) and identifying the taxable year for which the original agreement or certification was filed. A single agreement described in paragraph (g)(2)(i) of this section may be filed to replace more than one agreement or certification filed under § 1.1503-2A; however, each dual consolidated loss must be separately identified. A taxpayer may also elect to apply § 1.1503-2 for all open years, with respect to agreements filed under § 1.1503-2A(c)(3) or certifications filed under § 1.1503-2A(d)(3), in cases where the agreement or certification is no longer in effect and the taxpayer has complied with the provisions of § 1.1503-2A. For example, a taxpayer may have had a triggering event under § 1.1503-2A that is not a triggering event under § 1.1503-2. If the taxpayer fully complied with the requirements of the agreement entered into under § 1.1503-2A(c)(3) and filed amended U.S. income tax returns within the time required under § 1.1503-2A(c)(3), the taxpayer may file amended U.S. income tax returns consistent with the position that the earlier triggering event is no longer a triggering event.

(3) *Taxpayers that are in compliance with § 1.1503-2A but have not filed for relief thereunder.*—A taxpayer that is in compliance with the provisions of § 1.1503-2A but has not filed an agreement described in § 1.1503-2A(c)(3) or a certification described in § 1.1503-2A(d)(3) may elect to have the provisions of § 1.1503-2 apply for any open year. In particular, a taxpayer may elect to apply the provisions of § 1.1503-2 in a case where the dual consolidated loss has been subjected to the separate return limitation year restrictions of § 1.1502-21A(c) or 1.1502-21(c) (as appropriate) but the losses, expenses, or deductions taken into account in computing the dual consolidated loss have not been used to offset the income of another person for foreign tax purposes. However, if a taxpayer is a consolidated group, the election must be made with respect to all dual resident corporations or separate units within the group. Likewise, if the taxpayer is an unaffiliated domestic owner, the election must be made with respect to all separate units of the domestic owner. [Reg. § 1.1503-2.]

☐ [*T.D. 8434, 9-4-92. Amended by T.D. 8597, 7-12-95; T.D. 8677, 6-26-96; T.D. 8823, 6-25-99; T.D. 9084, 7-29-2003; T.D. 9100, 12-18-2003 and T.D. 9300, 12-7-2006.*]

### [Reg. § 1.1503(d)-0]

**§ 1.1503(d)-0. Table of contents.**—This section lists the captions contained in §§ 1.1503(d)-1 through 1.1503(d)-8.

(iii) Reduction in interest.

(5) De minimis reduction of an interest in a separate unit.

(i) General rule.

(ii) Limitations.

(iii) Reduction in interest.

(iv) Examples and coordination with exceptions to other triggering events.

(6) Certain asset basis carryovers.

(7) Assumption of certain liabilities.

(i) In general.

(ii) Ordinary course limitation.

(8) Multiple-party events.

(9) Additional guidance.

(d) Ordering rules for determining the foreign use of losses.

(e) Mirror legislation rule.

(1) In general.

(2) Stand-alone exception.

(i) In general.

(ii) Stand-alone domestic use agreement.

(iii) Termination of stand-alone domestic use agreement.

*§1.1503(d)-4. Domestic use limitation and related operating rules.*

(a) Scope.

(b) Limitation on domestic use of a dual consolidated loss.

(c) Effect of a dual consolidated loss on a consolidated group, unaffiliated dual resident corporation, or unaffiliated domestic owner.

(1) Dual resident corporation.

(2) Separate unit.

(3) SRLY limitation.

(4) Items of a dual consolidated loss used in other taxable years.

(5) Reconstituted net operating losses.

(d) Elimination of a dual consolidated loss after certain transactions.

(1) General rule.

(i) Transactions described in section 381(a).

(ii) Cessation of separate unit status.

(2) Exceptions.

(i) Certain section 368(a)(1)(F) reorganizations.

(ii) Acquisition of a dual resident corporation by another dual resident corporation.

(iii) Acquisition of a separate unit by a domestic corporation.

(A) Acquisition by a corporation that is not a member of the same consolidated group.

(B) Acquisition by a member of the same consolidated group.

(iv) Special rules for foreign insurance companies.

(e) Special rule denying the use of a dual consolidated loss to offset tainted income.

(1) In general.

(2) Tainted income.

(i) Definition.

(ii) Income presumed to be derived from holding tainted assets.

(3) Tainted assets defined.

(4) Exceptions.

(f) Computation of foreign tax credit limitation.

*§1.1503(d)-5. Attribution of items and basis adjustments.*

(a) In general.

(b) Determination of amount of income or dual consolidated loss of a dual resident corporation.

(1) In general.

(2) Exceptions.

(c) Determination of amount of income or dual consolidated loss attributable to a separate unit, and income or loss attributable to an interest in a transparent entity.

(1) In general.

(i) Scope and purpose.

(ii) Only items of domestic owner taken into account.

(iii) Separate application.

(2) Foreign branch separate unit.

(i) In general.

(ii) Principles of §1.882-5.

(iii) Exception where foreign country attributes interest expense solely by reference to books and records.

(3) Hybrid entity separate unit and an interest in a transparent entity.

(i) General rule.

(ii) Interests in certain disregarded entities, partnerships, and grantor trusts owned by a hybrid entity or transparent entity.

(4) Special rules.

(i) Allocation of items between certain tiered separate units and interests in transparent entities.

(A) Foreign branch separate unit.

(B) Hybrid entity separate unit or interest in a transparent entity.

(ii) Combined separate unit.

(iii) Gain or loss on the direct or indirect disposition of a separate unit or an interest in a transparent entity.

(A) In general.

(B) Multiple separate units or interests in transparent entities.

(iv) Inclusions on stock.

(v) Foreign currency gain or loss recognized under section 987.

(vi) Recapture of dual consolidated loss.

(d) Foreign tax treatment disregarded.

(e) Items generated or incurred while a dual resident corporation, a separate unit, or a transparent entity.

(f) Assets and liabilities of a separate unit or an interest in a transparent entity.

(g) Basis adjustments.

(1) Affiliated dual resident corporation or affiliated domestic owner.

(2) Interests in hybrid entities that are partnerships or interests in partnerships through which a separate unit is owned indirectly.

(i) Scope.

(ii) Determination of basis of partner's interest.

(3) Combined separate units.

*§1.1503(d)-6. Exceptions to the domestic use limitation rule.*

(a) In general.

(1) Scope and purpose.

(2) Absence of foreign affiliate or foreign consolidation regime.

(3) Foreign insurance companies treated as domestic corporations.

(b) Elective agreement in place between the United States and a foreign country.

(1) In general.

(2) Application to combined separate units.

(c) No possibility of foreign use.

(1) In general.

(2) Statement.

(d) Domestic use election.

(1) In general.

(2) No domestic use election available if there is a triggering event in the year the dual consolidated loss is incurred.

(e) Triggering events requiring the recapture of a dual consolidated loss.

(1) Events.

(i) Foreign use.

(ii) Disaffiliation.

(iii) Affiliation.

(iv) Transfer of assets.

(v) Transfer of an interest in a separate unit.

(vi) Conversion to a foreign corporation.

(vii) Conversion to a regulated investment company, a real estate investment trust, or an S corporation.

(viii) Failure to certify.

(ix) Cessation of stand-alone status.

(2) Rebuttal.

(i) General rule.

(ii) Certain asset transfers.

(iii) Reporting.

(iv) Examples.

(f) Triggering event exceptions.

(1) Continuing ownership of assets or interests.

(i) Disaffiliation as a result of a transaction described in section 381.

(ii) Continuing ownership by consolidated group.

(iii) Continuing ownership by unaffiliated dual resident corporation or unaffiliated domestic owner.

(2) Transactions requiring a new domestic use agreement.

(i) Multiple-party events.

(ii) Events resulting in a single consolidated group.

(iii) Requirements.

(A) New domestic use agreement.

(B) Statement filed by original elector.

(3) Certain transfers qualifying for the de minimis exception to foreign use.

(4) Deemed transactions as a result of certain transfers that do not result in a foreign use.

(5) Compulsory transfers.

(6) Subsequent triggering events.

(g) Annual certification reporting requirement.

(h) Recapture of dual consolidated loss and interest charge.

(1) Presumptive rules.

(i) Amount of recapture.

(ii) Interest charge.

(2) Reduction of presumptive recapture amount and presumptive interest charge.

(i) Amount of recapture.

(ii) Interest charge.

(3) Rules regarding multiple-party event exceptions to triggering events.

(i) Scope.

(ii) Original elector and prior subsequent electors not subject to recapture or interest charge.

(iii) Recapture tax amount and required statement.

(A) In general.

(B) Recapture tax amount.

(iv) Tax assessment and collection procedures.

(A) In general.

(B) Collection from original elector and prior subsequent electors; joint and several liability.

(C) Allocation of partial payments of tax.

(D) Refund.

(v) Definition of income tax liability.

(vi) Example.

(4) Computation of taxable income in year of recapture.

(i) Presumptive rule.

(ii) Exception to presumptive rule.

(5) Character and source of recapture income.

(6) Reconstituted net operating loss.

(i) General rule.

(ii) Exception.

(iii) Special rule for recapture following multiple-party event exception to a triggering event.

(i) [Reserved]

(j) Termination of domestic use agreement and annual certifications.

(1) Rebuttals, exceptions to triggering events, and recapture.

(2) Termination of ability for foreign use.

(i) In general.

(ii) Statement.

(3) Agreements filed in connection with stand-alone exception.

*§ 1.1503(d)-7. Examples.*

(a) In general.

(b) Presumed facts for examples.

(c) Examples.

*§ 1.1503(d)-8. Effective dates.*

(a) General rule.

(b) Special rules.

(1) Reduction of term of agreements filed under §§ 1.1503-2A(c)(3), 1.1503-2A(d)(3), 1.1503-2(g)(2)(i), or 1.1503-2T(g)(2)(i).

(2) Reduction of term of agreements filed under §§ 1.1503-2(g)(2)(iv)(B)(2)(i) (1992), 1.1503-2(g)(2)(iv)(B)(3)(i), or Rev. Proc. 2000-42.

(3) Relief for untimely filings.

(i) General rule.

(ii) Closing agreements.

(iii) Pending requests for relief.

(4) Multiple-party event exception to triggering events.

(5) Basis adjustment rules.

[Reg. § 1.1503(d)-0.]

☐ [*T.D. 9315, 3-16-2007 (corrected 4–24–2007).*]

**[Reg. § 1.1503(d)-1]**

**§ 1.1503(d)-1. Definitions and special rules for filings under section 1503(d).**—(a) *In general.*—This section and §§ 1.1503(d)-2 through 1.1503(d)-8 provide rules concerning the determination and use of dual consolidated losses pursuant to section 1503(d). Paragraph (b) of this section provides definitions that apply for purposes of this section and §§ 1.1503(d)-2 through 1.1503(d)-8. Paragraph (c)

of this section provides a reasonable cause exception and a signature requirement for filings.

(b) *Definitions.*—The following definitions apply for purposes of this section and §§ 1.1503(d)-2 through 1.1503(d)-8:

(1) Domestic corporation means an entity classified as a domestic corporation under section 7701(a)(3) and (4) or otherwise treated as a domestic corporation by the Internal Revenue Code, including, but not limited to, sections 269B, 953(d), 1504(d), and 7874. However, solely for purposes of section 1503(d), the term domestic corporation shall not include a regulated investment company as defined in section 851, a real estate investment trust as defined in section 856, or an S corporation as defined in section 1361.

(2) Dual resident corporation means—

(i) A domestic corporation that is subject to an income tax of a foreign country on its worldwide income or on a residence basis. A corporation is taxed on a residence basis if it is taxed as a resident under the laws of the foreign country;

(ii) A foreign insurance company that makes an election to be treated as a domestic corporation pursuant to section 953(d) and is treated as a member of an affiliated group for purposes of chapter 6, even if such company is not subject to an income tax of a foreign country on its worldwide income or on a residence basis. See section 953(d)(3); and

(iii) A domestic consenting corporation (as defined in § 301.7701-3(c)(3)(i) of this chapter), as provided in paragraph (c)(1) of this section. See § 1.1503(d)-7(c)(41) for an example illustrating the application of section 1503(d) to a domestic consenting corporation.

(3) Hybrid entity means an entity that is not taxable as an association for Federal tax purposes, but is subject to an income tax of a foreign country as a corporation (or otherwise at the entity level) either on its worldwide income or on a residence basis.

(4) *Separate unit.*—(i) *In general.*—The term separate unit means either of the following that is carried on or owned, as applicable, directly or indirectly, by a domestic corporation (including a dual resident corporation):

(A) Except to the extent provided in paragraph (b)(4)(iii) of this section, a business operation outside the United States that, if carried on by a U.S. person, would constitute a foreign branch as defined in § 1.367(a)-6T(g)(1) (foreign branch separate unit).

(B) An interest in a hybrid entity (hybrid entity separate unit).

(ii) *Separate unit combination rule.*.—Except as otherwise provided in this paragraph, if a domestic owner, or two or more domestic owners that are members of the same consolidated group, have two or more separate units (individual separate units), then all such individual separate units that are located (in the case of a foreign branch separate unit) or subject to an income tax either on their worldwide income or on a residence basis (in the case of a hybrid entity an interest in which is a hybrid entity separate unit) in the same foreign country shall be treated as one separate unit (combined separate unit). See § 1.1503(d)-7(c) *Example 1.* Separate units of a foreign insurance company that is a dual resident corporation under paragraph (b)(2)(ii) of this section, however, shall not be combined with separate units of any other domestic corporation. Except as specifically provided in this section or §§ 1.1503(d)-2 through 1.1503(d)-8, any individual separate unit composing a combined separate unit loses its character as an individual separate unit.

(iii) Business operations that do not constitute a permanent establishment. A business operation carried on by a domestic corporation that is not a dual resident corporation shall not constitute a foreign branch separate unit, provided the business operation:

(A) Is not carried on indirectly through a hybrid entity or a transparent entity; and

(B) Is conducted in a country with which the United States has entered into an income tax convention and is not treated as a permanent establishment pursuant to that convention, or is not otherwise subject to tax on a net basis under that convention. See § 1.1503(d)-7(c) *Example 2.*

(iv) Foreign branch separate units held by dual resident corporations or hybrid entities in the same foreign country. A foreign branch separate unit may be owned by a dual resident corporation, or through a hybrid entity (an interest in which is a separate unit), even where the foreign branch is located in the same foreign country that subjects such dual resident corporation or hybrid entity to tax on its worldwide income or on a residence basis. But see the rule under paragraph (b)(4)(ii) of this section that combines certain same-country hybrid entity separate units and foreign branch separate units. See also § 1.1503(d)-7(c) *Example 1.*

(5) Dual consolidated loss means—

(i) In the case of a dual resident corporation, and except to the extent provided in § 1.1503(d)-5(b), the net operating loss (as defined in section 172(c) and the related regulations) incurred in a year in which the corporation is a dual resident corporation; and

(ii) In the case of a separate unit, the net loss attributable to the separate unit under §1.1503(d)-5(c) through (e).

(6) *Subject to tax.*—For purposes of determining whether a domestic corporation or another entity is subject to an income tax of a foreign country on its income, the fact that it has no actual income tax liability to the foreign country for a particular taxable year shall not be taken into account.

(7) Foreign country includes any possession of the United States.

(8) Consolidated group has the meaning provided in §1.1502-1(h).

(9) Domestic owner means—

(i) A domestic corporation (including a dual resident corporation) that has one or more separate units or interests in a transparent entity; and

(ii) In the case of a combined separate unit, a domestic corporation (including a dual resident corporation) that has one or more individual separate units that are treated as part of the combined separate unit under paragraph (b)(4)(ii) of this section.

(10) Affiliated dual resident corporation and affiliated domestic owner mean a dual resident corporation and a domestic owner, respectively, that is a member of a consolidated group.

(11) Unaffiliated dual resident corporation, unaffiliated domestic corporation, and unaffiliated domestic owner mean a dual resident corporation, domestic corporation, and domestic owner, respectively, that is not a member of a consolidated group.

(12) Domestic affiliate means—

(i) A member of an affiliated group, without regard to the exceptions contained in section 1504(b) (other than section 1504(b)(3)) relating to includible corporations;

(ii) A domestic owner;

(iii) A separate unit; or

(iv) An interest in a transparent entity, as defined in paragraph (b)(16) of this section.

(13) *Domestic use.*—See §1.1503(d)-2.

(14) *Foreign use.*—See §1.1503(d)-3.

(15) Grantor trust means a trust, any portion of which is treated as being owned by the grantor or another person under subpart E of subchapter J of this chapter.

(16) *Transparent entity.*—(i) *In general.*—The term transparent entity means an entity described in this paragraph (b)(16) where all or a portion of its interests are owned, directly or indirectly, by a domestic corporation. An entity is described in this paragraph (b)(16) if the entity—

(A) Is not taxable as an association for Federal tax purposes;

(B) Is not subject to income tax in a foreign country as a corporation (or otherwise at the entity level) either on its worldwide income or on a residence basis; and

(C) Is not a pass-through entity under the laws of the applicable foreign country. For purposes of applying the preceding sentence, the applicable foreign country is the foreign country in which the relevant foreign branch separate unit is located, or the foreign country that subjects the relevant hybrid entity (an interest in which is a separate unit) or dual resident corporation to an income tax either on its worldwide income or on a residence basis.

(ii) *Example.*—A U.S. limited liability company (LLC) does not elect to be taxed as an association for Federal tax purposes and is not subject to income tax in a foreign country as a corporation (or otherwise at the entity level) either on its worldwide income or on a residence basis. The LLC is owned by a hybrid entity (an interest in which is a separate unit) that is the relevant hybrid entity. Provided the LLC is not treated as a pass-through entity by the applicable foreign country that subjects the relevant hybrid entity to an income tax either on its worldwide income or on a residence basis, the LLC would qualify as a transparent entity. See also §1.1503(d)-7(c) *Example 26.*

(17) Disregarded entity means an entity that is disregarded as an entity separate from its owner, under §§301.7701-1 through 301.7701-3 of this chapter, for Federal tax purposes.

(18) Partnership means an entity that is classified as a partnership, under §§301.7701-1 through 301.7701-3 of this chapter, for Federal tax purposes.

(19) Indirectly, when used in reference to ownership, means ownership through a partnership, a disregarded entity, or a grantor trust, regardless of whether the partnership, disregarded entity, or grantor trust is a U.S. person.

(20) Certification period means the period of time up to and including the fifth taxable year following the year in which the dual

consolidated loss that is the subject of a domestic use agreement (as described in §1.1503(d)-6(d)(1)) was incurred.

(c) *Treatment of domestic consenting corporation as a dual resident corporation.*—(1) *Rule.*—A domestic consenting corporation is treated as a dual resident corporation under paragraph (b)(2)(iii) of this section for a taxable year if, on any day during the taxable year, the following requirements are satisfied:

(i) Under the tax law of a foreign country where a specified foreign tax resident is tax resident, the specified foreign tax resident derives or incurs (or would derive or incur) items of income, gain, deduction, or loss of the domestic consenting corporation (because, for example, the domestic consenting corporation is fiscally transparent under such tax law).

(ii) The specified foreign tax resident bears a relationship to the domestic consenting corporation that is described in section 267(b) or 707(b). See §1.1503(d)-7(c)(41) for an example illustrating the application of paragraph (c) of this section.

(2) *Definitions.*—The following definitions apply for purposes of this paragraph (c).

(i) The term *fiscally transparent* means, with respect to a domestic consenting corporation or an intermediate entity, fiscally transparent as determined under the principles of §1.894-1(d)(3)(ii) and (iii), without regard to whether a specified foreign tax resident is a resident of a country that has an income tax treaty with the United States.

(ii) The term *specified foreign tax resident* means a body corporate or other entity or body of persons liable to tax under the tax law of a foreign country as a resident.

(d) *Special rules for filings under section 1503(d).*—(1) *Reasonable cause exception.*—A person that is permitted or required to file an election, agreement, statement, rebuttal, computation, or other information pursuant to section 1503(d) and these regulations, that fails to make such filing in a timely manner, shall be considered to have satisfied the timeliness requirement with respect to such filing if the person is able to demonstrate, to the Area Director, Field Examination, Small Business/Self Employed or the Director of Field Operations, Large and Mid-Size Business (Director) having jurisdiction of the taxpayer's tax return for the taxable year, that such failure was due to reasonable cause and not willful neglect. In determining whether the taxpayer has reasonable cause, the Director shall consider whether the taxpayer acted reasonably and in good faith. In general, the taxpayer must demonstrate that it exercised ordinary care and prudence in meeting its tax obligations but nonetheless did not comply with the prescribed duty within the prescribed time. Whether the taxpayer acted reasonably and in good faith will be determined after considering all the facts and circumstances. The Director shall notify the person in writing within 120 days of the filing if it is determined that the failure to comply was not due to reasonable cause, or if additional time will be needed to make such determination. For this purpose, the 120-day period shall begin on the date the taxpayer is notified in writing that the request has been received and assigned for review. If, once such period commences, the taxpayer is not again notified within 120 days, then the taxpayer shall be deemed to have established reasonable cause. The reasonable cause exception of this paragraph (d) shall only apply if, once the person becomes aware of its failure to file the election, agreement, statement, rebuttal, computation or other information in a timely manner, the person complies with the requirements of paragraph (d)(2) of this section.

(2) *Requirements for reasonable cause relief.*—(i) *Time of submission.*—Requests for reasonable cause relief will only be considered if once the person becomes aware of the failure to file the election, agreement, statement, rebuttal, computation or other information, the person attaches all the documents that should have been filed, as well as a written statement setting forth the reasons for the failure to timely comply, to an amended return that amends the return to which the documents should have been attached pursuant to the rules of section 1503(d) and these regulations.

(ii) *Notice requirement.*—In addition to the requirements of paragraph (d)(2)(i) of this section, the taxpayer must provide a copy of the amended return and all required attachments to the Director as follows:

(A) If the taxpayer is under examination for any taxable year when the taxpayer requests relief, the taxpayer must provide a copy of the amended return and attachments to the personnel conducting the examination.

(B) If the taxpayer is not under examination for any taxable year when the taxpayer requests relief, the taxpayer must provide a copy of the amended return and attachments to the Director having jurisdiction of the taxpayer's return.

(3) *Signature requirement.*—When an election, agreement, statement, rebuttal, computation, or other information is required pursuant to section 1503(d) and these regulations to be attached to and filed by the due date (including extensions) of a U.S. tax return and signed under penalties of perjury by the person who signs the return, the attachment and filing of an unsigned copy is considered to satisfy such requirement, provided the taxpayer retains the original in its records in the manner specified by § 1.6001-1(e). [Reg. § 1.1503(d)-1.]

☐ [*T.D. 9315, 3-16-2007. Amended by T.D. 9896, 4-7-2020.*]

### [Reg. § 1.1503(d)-2]

**§ 1.1503(d)-2. Domestic use.**—A domestic use of a dual consolidated loss shall be deemed to occur when the dual consolidated loss is made available to offset, directly or indirectly, the income of a domestic affiliate (other than the dual resident corporation or separate unit that, in each case, incurred the dual consolidated loss) in the taxable year in which the dual consolidated loss is recognized, or in any other taxable year, regardless of whether the dual consolidated loss offsets income under the income tax laws of a foreign country and regardless of whether any income that the dual consolidated loss may offset in the foreign country is, has been, or will be subject to tax in the United States. A domestic use shall be deemed to occur in the year the dual consolidated loss is included in the computation of the taxable income of a consolidated group, unaffiliated dual resident corporation, or an unaffiliated domestic owner, as applicable, even if no tax benefit results from such inclusion in that year. See § 1.1503(d)-7(c) *Examples 2 through 4.* [Reg. § 1.1503(d)-2.]

☐ [*T.D. 9315, 3-16-2007.*]

### [Reg. § 1.1503(d)-3]

**§ 1.1503(d)-3. Foreign use.**—(a) *Foreign use.*—(1) *In general.*—Except as provided in paragraph (c) of this section, a foreign use of a dual consolidated loss shall be deemed to occur when any portion of a deduction or loss taken into account in computing the dual consolidated loss is made available under the income tax laws of a foreign country to offset or reduce, directly or indirectly, any item that is recognized as income or gain under such laws and that is, or would be, considered under U.S. tax principles to be an item of—

(i) A foreign corporation as defined in section 7701(a)(3) and (a)(5); or

(ii) A direct or indirect owner of an interest in a hybrid entity, provided such interest is not a separate unit. See § 1.1503(d)-7(c) *Examples 5 through 10 and 37.*

(2) *Indirect use.*—(i) *General rule.*—Except to the extent provided in paragraph (a)(2)(ii) of this section, an item of deduction or loss shall be deemed to be made available indirectly if—

(A) One or more items are taken into account as deductions or losses for foreign tax purposes, but do not give rise to corresponding items of income or gain for U.S. tax purposes; and

(B) The item or items described in paragraph (a)(2)(i)(A) of this section have the effect of making an item of deduction or loss composing the dual consolidated loss available for a foreign use as described in paragraph (a)(1) of this section.

(ii) *Exception.*—The general rule provided in paragraph (a)(2)(i) of this section shall not apply if the consolidated group, unaffiliated domestic owner, or unaffiliated dual resident corporation demonstrates, to the satisfaction of the Commissioner, that the item or items described in paragraph (a)(2)(i)(A) of this section that gave rise to the indirect foreign use—

(A) Were not incurred, or taken into account, with a principal purpose of avoiding the provisions of section 1503(d). For purposes of this paragraph (a)(2)(ii), an item incurred or taken into account as interest for foreign tax purposes, but disregarded for U.S. tax purposes, shall be deemed to have been incurred, or taken into account, with a principal purpose of avoiding the provisions of section 1503(d). Similarly, for purposes of this paragraph (a)(2)(ii), an item incurred or taken into account as the result of an instrument that is treated as debt for foreign tax purposes and equity for U.S. tax purposes, shall be deemed to have been incurred, or taken into account, with a principal purpose of avoiding the provisions of section 1503(d); and

(B) Were incurred, or taken into account, in the ordinary course of the dual resident corporation's or separate unit's trade or business.

(iii) *Examples.*—See § 1.1503(d)-7(c) *Examples 6 through 8.*

(3) *Deemed use.*—See paragraph (e) of this section for a deemed foreign use pursuant to the mirror legislation rule.

(b) *Available for use.*—A foreign use shall be deemed to occur in the year in which any portion of a deduction or loss taken into account in computing the dual consolidated loss is made available for an offset described in paragraph (a) of this section, regardless of whether it actually offsets or reduces any items of income or gain under the income tax laws of the foreign country in such year, and regardless of whether any of the items that may be so offset or reduced are regarded as income under U.S. tax principles.

(c) *Exceptions.*—(1) *In general.*—Paragraphs (c)(2) through (9) of this section provide exceptions to the general definition of foreign use set forth in paragraphs (a) and (b) of this section. These exceptions only apply to a foreign use that occurs solely as a result of the conditions or circumstances described therein, and do not apply if a foreign use occurs in any other case or by any other means. For example, the exception under paragraph (c)(4) of this section (regarding certain interests in partnerships or grantor trusts) shall not apply where the item of deduction or loss is made available through a foreign consolidation regime (or similar method). In addition, these exceptions do not apply when attempting to demonstrate that no foreign use of a dual consolidated loss can occur in any other year by any means under § 1.1503(d)-6(c), (e)(2)(i), or (j)(2). But see § 1.1503(d)-6(e)(2)(ii), which takes into account the exception under paragraph (c)(7) of this section for purposes of rebutting certain asset transfers.

(2) *Election or merger required to enable foreign use.*—Where the laws of a foreign country provide an election that would enable a foreign use, a foreign use shall be considered to occur only if the election is made. Similarly, where the laws of a foreign country would enable a foreign use through a sale, merger, or similar transaction, a foreign use shall be considered to occur only if the sale, merger, or similar transaction occurs.

(3) *Presumed use where no foreign country rule for determining use.*—This paragraph (c)(3) applies if the losses or deductions composing the dual consolidated loss are made available under the laws of a foreign country both to offset income that would constitute a foreign use and to offset income that would not constitute a foreign use, and the laws of the foreign country do not provide applicable rules for determining which income is offset by the losses or deductions. In such a case, the losses or deductions shall be deemed to be made available to offset the income that does not constitute a foreign use, to the extent of such income, before being considered to be made available to offset the income that does constitute a foreign use. See § 1.1503(d)-7(c) *Example 11.*

(4) *Certain interests in partnerships or grantor trusts.*—(i) *General rule.*—Except to the extent provided in paragraph (c)(4)(iii) of this section, this paragraph (c)(4)(i) applies to a dual consolidated loss attributable to an interest in a hybrid entity partnership or a hybrid entity grantor trust, or to a separate unit owned indirectly through a partnership or grantor trust. In such a case, a foreign use will not be considered to occur if the foreign use is solely the result of another person's ownership of an interest in the partnership or grantor trust, as applicable, and the allocation or carry forward of an item of deduction or loss composing such dual consolidated loss as a result of such ownership. See § 1.1503(d)-7(c) *Example 13.*

(ii) *Combined separate unit.*—This paragraph applies to a dual consolidated loss attributable to a combined separate unit that includes an individual separate unit to which paragraph (c)(4)(i) of this section would apply, but for the application of the separate unit combination rule provided under § 1.1503(d)-1(b)(4)(ii). In such a case, paragraph (c)(4)(i) of this section shall apply to the portion of the dual consolidated loss of such combined separate unit that is attributable, as provided under § 1.1503(d)-5(c) through (e), to the individual separate unit (otherwise described in paragraph (c)(4)(i) of this section) that is a component of the combined separate unit. See § 1.1503(d)-7(c) *Example 14.*

(iii) *Reduction in interest.*—The exception under paragraph (c)(4)(i) of this section shall not apply if, at any time following the year in which the dual consolidated loss is incurred, there is more than a de minimis reduction in the domestic owner's percentage interest in the partnership or grantor trust, as applicable, as described in paragraph (c)(5) of this section. In such a case, a foreign use shall be deemed to occur at the time the reduction in interest exceeds the de minimis amount. See § 1.1503(d)-7(c) *Example 13.*

(5) *De minimis reduction of an interest in a separate unit.*—(i) *General rule.*—This paragraph applies to a de minimis reduction of a domestic owner's interest in a separate unit (including an interest described in paragraph (c)(4)(i) of this section). Except to the extent provided in paragraph (c)(5)(ii) of this section, no foreign use shall be considered to occur with respect to a dual consolidated loss as a result of an item of deduction or loss composing such dual consolidated loss being made available solely as a result of a reduction in the domestic owner's interest in the separate unit, as provided under paragraph (c)(5)(iii) of this section. See § 1.1503(d)-7(c) *Example 5.*

(ii) *Limitations.*—The exception provided in paragraph (c)(5)(i) of this section shall not apply if—

(A) During any 12-month period the domestic owner's percentage interest in the separate unit is reduced by 10 percent or more, as determined by reference to the domestic owner's interest at the beginning of the 12-month period; or

(B) At any time the domestic owner's percentage interest in the separate unit is reduced by 30 percent or more, as determined by reference to the domestic owner's interest at the end of the taxable year in which the dual consolidated loss was incurred.

(iii) *Reduction in interest.*—The following rules apply for purposes of paragraphs (c)(4) and (5) of this section. A reduction of a domestic owner's interest in a separate unit shall include a reduction resulting from another person acquiring through sale, exchange, contribution, or other means, an interest in the foreign branch or hybrid entity, as applicable. A reduction may occur either directly or indirectly, including through an interest in a partnership, a disregarded entity, or a grantor trust through which a separate unit is carried on or owned. In the case of an interest in a hybrid entity partnership or a separate unit all or a portion of which is carried on or owned through a partnership, an interest in such separate unit (or portion of such separate unit) is determined by reference to the owner's interest in the profits or the capital in the separate unit. In the case of an interest in a hybrid entity grantor trust or a separate unit all or a portion of which is carried on or owned through a grantor trust, an interest in such separate unit (or portion of such separate unit) is determined by reference to the domestic owner's share of the assets and liabilities of the separate unit.

(iv) *Examples and coordination with exceptions to other triggering events.*—See §1.1503(d)-7(c) *Examples 5, 13,* and *14.* See also §1.1503(d)-6(f)(3) and (f)(5) for rules that coordinate the de minimis exception to foreign use with exceptions to other triggering events described in §1.1503(d)-6(e)(1), and provide an exception to foreign use following certain compulsory transfers.

(6) *Certain asset basis carryovers.*—No foreign use shall be considered to occur with respect to a dual consolidated loss solely as a result of items of deduction or loss composing such dual consolidated loss being made available as a result of the transfer of assets of a dual resident corporation or separate unit, provided—

(i) Such items of loss and deduction are made available solely as a result of the basis of the transferred assets being determined, under foreign law, in whole or in part by reference to the basis of the assets in the hands of the dual resident corporation or separate unit;

(ii) The aggregate adjusted basis, as determined under U.S. tax principles, of all the assets so transferred during any 12-month period is less than 10 percent of the aggregate adjusted basis, as determined under U.S. tax principles, of all the dual resident corporation's or separate unit's assets, determined by reference to the assets held at the beginning of such 12-month period; and

(iii) The aggregate adjusted basis, as determined under U.S. tax principles, of all the assets so transferred at any time is less than 30 percent of the aggregate adjusted basis, as determined under U.S. tax principles, of all the dual resident corporation's or separate unit's assets, determined by reference to the assets held at the end of the taxable year in which the dual consolidated loss was generated. See §1.1503(d)-7(c) *Example 15.*

(7) *Assumption of certain liabilities.*—(i) *In general.*—Except to the extent provided in paragraph (c)(7)(ii) of this section, no foreign use shall be considered to occur with respect to any dual consolidated loss solely as a result of an item of deduction or loss composing such dual consolidated loss being made available following the assumption of liabilities of a dual resident corporation or separate unit, provided such availability arises solely as the result of an item of deduction or loss incurred with respect to, or as a result of, such liabilities. See §1.1503(d)-7(c) *Example 16.*

(ii) *Ordinary course limitation.*—Paragraph (c)(7)(i) of this section shall apply only to the extent the liabilities assumed were incurred in the ordinary course of the dual resident corporation's, or separate unit's, trade or business. For purposes of this paragraph, liabilities incurred in the ordinary course of a trade or business shall include debt incurred to finance the trade or business of the dual resident corporation or separate unit.

(8) *Multiple-party events.*—This paragraph applies to a transaction that qualifies for the triggering event exception described in §1.1503(d)-6(f)(2)(i)(B) where the acquiring unaffiliated domestic corporation or consolidated group owns, directly or indirectly, more than 90 percent, but less than 100 percent, of the transferred assets or interests immediately after the transaction. In such a case, no foreign use shall be considered to occur with respect to a dual consolidated loss of the dual resident corporation or separate unit whose assets or

interests were acquired, solely as a result of the less than 10 percent direct or indirect ownership of the acquired assets or interests by persons other than the acquiring unaffiliated domestic corporation or consolidated group, as applicable, immediately after the transaction. See §1.1503(d)-7(c) *Example 37.*

(9) *Additional guidance.*—The Commissioner may provide, by guidance published in the Internal Revenue Bulletin, that certain events or transactions do or do not result in a foreign use. Such guidance may also modify the triggering events and rebuttals described in §1.1503(d)-6(e), and the exceptions thereto under §1.1503(d)-6(f), as appropriate.

(d) *Ordering rules for determining the foreign use of losses.*—If the laws of a foreign country provide for the foreign use of losses of a dual resident corporation or a separate unit, but do not provide applicable rules for determining the order in which such losses are used in a taxable year, the following rules shall apply:

(1) Any net loss, or net income, that the dual resident corporation or separate unit has in a taxable year shall first be used to offset net income, or loss, recognized by its affiliates in the same taxable year before any carry over of its losses is considered to be used to offset any income from the taxable year.

(2) If under the laws of the foreign country the dual resident corporation or separate unit has losses from different taxable years, it shall be deemed to use first the losses which would not constitute a triggering event that would result in the recapture of a dual consolidated loss pursuant to §1.1503(d)-6(h). Thereafter, it shall be deemed to use first the losses from the most recent taxable year from which a loss may be carried forward or back for foreign law purposes.

(3) Where different losses or deductions (for example, capital losses and ordinary losses) of a dual resident corporation or separate unit incurred in the same taxable year are available for foreign use, the different losses shall be deemed to be used on a pro rata basis. See §1.1503(d)-7(c) *Example 12.*

(e) *Mirror legislation rule.*—(1) *In general.*—Except as provided in paragraph (e)(2) or (3) of this section and §1.1503(d)-6(b) (relating to agreements entered into between the United States and a foreign country), a foreign use shall be deemed to occur if the income tax laws of a foreign country would deny any opportunity for the foreign use of the dual consolidated loss in the year in which the dual consolidated loss is incurred (mirror legislation), determined by assuming that such foreign country had recognized the dual consolidated loss in such year, for any of the following reasons:

(i) The dual resident corporation or separate unit that incurred the loss is subject to income taxation by another country (for example, the United States) on its worldwide income or on a residence basis.

(ii) The loss may be available to offset income (other than income of the dual resident corporation or separate unit) under the laws of another country (for example, the United States).

(iii) The deductibility of any portion of a deduction or loss taken into account in computing the dual consolidated loss depends on whether such amount is deductible under the laws of another country (for example, the United States). See §1.1503(d)-7(c) *Examples 17* through *19.*

(2) *Stand-alone exception.*—(i) *In general.*—This paragraph (e)(2) applies if, in the absence of the mirror legislation described in paragraph (e)(1) of this section, no item of deduction or loss composing the dual consolidated loss of such dual resident corporation or separate unit would otherwise be available for a foreign use in the taxable year in which such dual consolidated loss is incurred. This determination is made without regard to whether such availability is limited by election (or other similar procedure). However, for purposes of this paragraph (e)(2)(i), no item of deduction or loss composing the dual consolidated loss of a dual resident corporation or separate unit is considered to be made available for foreign use solely because the laws of a foreign country would enable a foreign use through a sale, merger, or similar transaction (provided no such sale, merger, or similar transaction actually occurs). In such a case, no foreign use shall be considered to occur pursuant to paragraph (e)(1) of this section with respect to the dual consolidated loss, provided the requirements of paragraph (e)(2)(ii) of this section are satisfied. See §1.1503(d)-7(c) *Examples 17* through *19.*

(ii) *Stand-alone domestic use agreement.*—In order to qualify for the exception under paragraph (e)(2)(i) of this section, the consolidated group, unaffiliated dual resident corporation, or unaffiliated domestic owner, as the case may be, must enter into a domestic use agreement in accordance with the provisions of §1.1503(d)-6(d) and, in addition, must include the following items in such domestic use agreement:

(A) A statement that the document is also being submitted under the provisions of paragraph (e)(2) of this section.

(B) A certification that the conditions of paragraph (e)(2)(i) of this section are satisfied during the taxable year in which the dual consolidated loss is incurred.

(C) An agreement to include with each annual certification required under § 1.1503(d)-6(g), a certification that the conditions described in paragraph (e)(2)(i) of this section are satisfied during the taxable year of each such certification.

(iii) *Termination of stand-alone domestic use agreement.*—This paragraph (e)(2)(iii) applies to a consolidated group, unaffiliated dual resident corporation, or unaffiliated domestic owner, as the case may be, that entered into a domestic use agreement pursuant to paragraph (e)(2)(ii) of this section, with respect to a dual consolidated loss, and which subsequently makes an election pursuant to § 1.1503(d)-6(b) (relating to agreements entered into between the United States and a foreign country) with respect to such dual consolidated loss. In such a case, the dual consolidated loss shall be subject to the election under § 1.1503(d)-6(b) (and any related agreements, representations and conditions), and the domestic use agreement entered into pursuant to paragraph (e)(2)(ii) of this section shall terminate and have no further effect.

(3) *Exception for domestic consenting corporations.*—Paragraph (e)(1) of this section will not apply so as to deem a foreign use of a dual consolidated loss incurred by a domestic consenting corporation that is a dual resident corporation under § 1.1503(d)-1(b)(2)(iii). [Reg. § 1.1503(d)-3.]

☐ [*T.D. 9315, 3-16-2007. Amended by T.D. 9896, 4-7-2020.*]

### [Reg. § 1.1503(d)-4]

**§ 1.1503(d)-4. Domestic use limitation and related operating rules.**—(a) *Scope.*—This section prescribes rules that apply when the general limitation on the domestic use of a dual consolidated loss under paragraph (b) of this section applies. Thus, the rules of this section do not apply when an exception to the domestic use limitation applies (for example, as a result of a domestic use election under § 1.1503(d)-6(d)). In general, when the domestic use limitation applies, the dual consolidated loss of a dual resident corporation or separate unit is subject to the separate return limitation year (SRLY) provisions of § 1.1502-21(c), as modified under this section. Paragraph (c) of this section provides rules that determine the effect of a dual consolidated loss on a consolidated group, an unaffiliated dual resident corporation, or an unaffiliated domestic owner. Paragraph (d) of this section provides rules that eliminate dual consolidated losses following certain transactions or events. Paragraph (e) of this section contains provisions that prevent dual consolidated losses from offsetting tainted income. Finally, paragraph (f) of this section provides rules for computing foreign tax credits.

(b) *Limitation on domestic use of a dual consolidated loss.*—Except as provided in § 1.1503(d)-6, the domestic use of a dual consolidated loss is not permitted. See § 1.1503(d)-2 for the definition of a domestic use. See also § 1.1503(d)-7(c) *Examples* 2 through 4.

(c) Effect of a dual consolidated loss on a consolidated group, unaffiliated dual resident corporation, or unaffiliated domestic owner. For any taxable year in which a dual resident corporation or separate unit has a dual consolidated loss that is subject to the domestic use limitation of paragraph (b) of this section, the following rules shall apply:

(1) *Dual resident corporation.*—This paragraph (c)(1) applies to a dual consolidated loss of a dual resident corporation. The unaffiliated dual resident corporation, or consolidated group that includes the dual resident corporation, shall compute its taxable income (or loss), or consolidated taxable income (or loss), respectively, without taking into account those items of deduction and loss that compose the dual resident corporation's dual consolidated loss. For this purpose, the dual consolidated loss shall be treated as composed of a pro rata portion of each item of deduction and loss of the dual resident corporation taken into account in calculating the dual consolidated loss. The dual consolidated loss is subject to the limitations on its use contained in paragraph (c)(3) of this section and, subject to such limitations, may be carried over or back for use in other taxable years as a separate net operating loss carryover or carryback of the dual resident corporation arising in the year incurred. If the dual resident corporation owns a separate unit or an interest in a transparent entity, the limitations contained in paragraph (c)(3) of this section shall apply to the dual resident corporation as if the separate unit or interest in a transparent entity were a separate domestic corporation that filed a consolidated return with the unaffiliated dual resident corporation, or with the consolidated group of the affiliated dual resident corporation, as applicable.

(2) *Separate unit.*—This paragraph (c)(2) applies to a dual consolidated loss that is attributable to a separate unit. The unaffiliated domestic owner of a separate unit, or the consolidated group of an affiliated domestic owner of a separate unit, shall compute its taxable income (or loss) or consolidated taxable income (or loss), respectively, without taking into account those items of deduction and loss that compose the separate unit's dual consolidated loss. For this purpose, the dual consolidated loss shall be treated as composed of a pro rata portion of each item of deduction and loss of the separate unit taken into account in calculating the dual consolidated loss. The dual consolidated loss is subject to the limitations contained in paragraph (c)(3) of this section as if the separate unit to which the dual consolidated loss is attributable were a separate domestic corporation that filed a consolidated return with its unaffiliated domestic owner or with the consolidated group of its affiliated domestic owner, as applicable. Subject to such limitations, the dual consolidated loss may be carried over or back for use in other taxable years as a separate net operating loss carryover or carryback of the separate unit arising in the year incurred. See § 1.1503(d)-7(c) *Examples 29 and 38.*

(3) *SRLY limitation.*—The dual consolidated loss shall be treated as a loss incurred by the dual resident corporation or separate unit in a separate return limitation year and shall be subject to all of the limitations of § 1.1502-21(c) (SRLY limitation), subject to the following modifications—

(i) Notwithstanding § 1.1502-1(f)(2)(i), the SRLY limitation is applied to any dual consolidated loss of a common parent that is a dual resident corporation, or any dual consolidated loss attributable to a separate unit of a common parent;

(ii) The SRLY limitation is applied without regard to § 1.1502-21(c)(2) (SRLY subgroup limitation) and 1.1502-21(g) (overlap with section 382);

(iii) For purposes of calculating the general SRLY limitation under § 1.1502-21(c)(1)(i), the calculation of aggregate consolidated taxable income shall only include items of income, gain, deduction, and loss generated—

(A) In the case of a hybrid entity separate unit, in years in which the hybrid entity (an interest in which is a separate unit) is taxed as a corporation (or otherwise at the entity level) either on its worldwide income or as a resident in the same foreign country in which it was so taxed during the year in which the dual consolidated loss was generated; and

(B) In the case of a foreign branch separate unit, in years in which the foreign branch qualified as a separate unit in the same foreign country in which it so qualified during the year in which the dual consolidated loss was generated;

(iv) For purposes of calculating the general SRLY limitation under § 1.1502-21(c)(1)(i), the calculation of aggregate consolidated taxable income shall not include any amount included in income pursuant to § 1.1503(d)-6(h) (relating to the recapture of a dual consolidated loss); and

(v) The SRLY limitation is applied without regard to § 1.1502-21(c)(1)(i)(E) (section 172(a) limitation applicable to a SRLY member).

(4) *Items of a dual consolidated loss used in other taxable years.*—A pro rata portion of each item of deduction or loss that composes the dual consolidated loss shall be considered to be used when the dual consolidated loss is used in other taxable years. See § 1.1503(d)-7(c) *Examples 29 and 38.*

(5) *Reconstituted net operating losses.*—For additional rules and limitations that apply to reconstituted net operating losses, see § 1.1503(d)-6(h)(6).

(d) *Elimination of a dual consolidated loss after certain transactions.*—(1) *General rule.*—In general, a dual resident corporation has a net operating loss (and, therefore, a dual consolidated loss) only if it sustains such loss, or succeeds to such loss as a result of acquiring the assets of a corporation that sustained the loss in a transaction described in section 381(a). Similarly, a net operating loss generally is attributable to a separate unit of a domestic owner (and therefore is a dual consolidated loss) only if the domestic owner incurs the deductions or losses, or succeeds to such deductions or losses in a transaction described in section 381(a). Except as provided in § 1.1503(d)-6(h)(6)(iii), section 1503(d) and these regulations do not alter these general rules. Thus, the provisions of §§ 1.1503(d)-1 through 1.1503(d)-8 generally do not cause a corporation to have a dual consolidated loss if it did not sustain (or inherit) the loss. Instead, these regulations either eliminate a dual consolidated loss that a corporation sustained (or inherited), or prevent the carryover of a dual consolidated loss under section 381 that would ordinarily occur, as a result of certain transactions.

(i) *Transactions described in section 381(a).*—This paragraph (d)(1)(i) applies to a dual consolidated loss of a dual resident corporation, or of a domestic owner attributable to a separate unit, that is subject to the domestic use limitation rule of paragraph (b) of this section. In such a case, and except as provided in paragraph (d)(2) of this section, the dual consolidated loss shall not carry over to another corporation in a transaction described in section 381(a) and, as a result, shall be eliminated. See § 1.1503(d)-7(c) *Example 20*.

(ii) *Cessation of separate unit status.*—This paragraph (d)(1)(ii) applies when a separate unit of an unaffiliated domestic owner ceases to be a separate unit of its domestic owner, or when a separate unit of an affiliated domestic owner ceases to be a separate unit with respect to its domestic owner and all other members of the affiliated domestic owner's consolidated group. In such a case, and except as provided in paragraph (d)(2)(iii) of this section, a dual consolidated loss of the domestic owner attributable to such separate unit, that is subject to the domestic use limitation of paragraph (b) of this section, shall be eliminated. For purposes of this paragraph (d)(1)(ii), a separate unit may cease to be a separate unit if, for example, such separate unit is terminated, dissolved, liquidated, sold, or otherwise disposed of. See § 1.1503(d)-7(c) *Example 21*.

(2) *Exceptions.*—(i) *Certain section 368(a)(1)(F) reorganizations.*.—Paragraph (d)(1)(i) of this section (relating to transactions described in section 381(a)) shall not apply to a dual consolidated loss of a dual resident corporation that undergoes a reorganization described in section 368(a)(1)(F) in which the resulting corporation is a domestic corporation. In such a case, the dual consolidated loss of the resulting corporation continues to be subject to the limitations of paragraphs (b) and (c) of this section, applied as if the resulting corporation incurred the dual consolidated loss.

(ii) *Acquisition of a dual resident corporation by another dual resident corporation.*—If a dual resident corporation transfers its assets to another dual resident corporation in a transaction described in section 381(a), and the transferee corporation is a resident of (or is taxed on its worldwide income by) the same foreign country of which the transferor was a resident (or was taxed on its worldwide income), then paragraph (d)(1)(i) of this section shall not apply with respect to dual consolidated losses of the dual resident corporation, and income generated by the transferee may be offset by the carryover dual consolidated losses of the transferor, subject to the limitations of paragraphs (b) and (c) of this section applied as if the transferee incurred the dual consolidated loss. Dual consolidated losses of the transferor dual resident corporation may not, however, be used to offset income attributable to separate units or interests in transparent entities owned by the transferee because they constitute domestic affiliates under § 1.1503(d)-1(b)(12)(iii) and (iv), respectively.

(iii) *Acquisition of a separate unit by a domestic corporation.*—This paragraph (d)(2)(iii) provides exceptions to the general rules in paragraphs (d)(1)(i) and (ii) of this section that eliminate the dual consolidated loss of a domestic owner that is attributable to a separate unit following certain transactions or events. The exceptions set forth in this paragraph (d)(2)(iii) shall only apply where a domestic owner transfers its assets to a domestic corporation (transferee corporation) in a transaction described in section 381(a).

(A) *Acquisition by a corporation that is not a member of the same consolidated group.*—(1) *General rule.*—If a domestic owner transfers either an individual separate unit or a combined separate unit to a transferee corporation that is not a member of its consolidated group in a transaction described in section 381(a), and the transferee corporation, or a member of the transferee's consolidated group, is a domestic owner of the transferred separate unit immediately after the transaction, then paragraphs (d)(1)(i) and (ii) of this section shall not apply to such transfer. In addition, income of the transferee, or a member of the transferee's consolidated group, that is attributable to the transferred separate unit may be offset by the carryover dual consolidated losses of the transferor domestic owner that were attributable to the transferred separate unit, subject to the limitations of paragraphs (b) and (c) of this section applied as if the transferee incurred the dual consolidated losses and such losses were attributable to the separate unit. See § 1.1503(d)-7(c) *Example 21*.

(2) *Combination with separate units of the transferee.*—This paragraph (d)(2)(iii)(A)(2) applies to a transaction described in paragraph (d)(2)(iii)(A)(1) of this section where the transferred separate unit is combined with another separate unit of the transferee, or another member of the transferee's consolidated group, immediately after the transfer as provided under § 1.1503(d)-1(b)(4)(ii). In such a case, income generated by the transferee, or another member of the transferee's consolidated group, that is attributable to the combined separate unit may be offset by the carryover dual consolidated losses that were attributable to the transferred separate unit, subject to the limitations of paragraphs (b) and (c) of this section, applied as if the transferee incurred the dual consolidated losses and such losses were attributable to the combined separate unit.

(B) *Acquisition by a member of the same consolidated group.*—If an affiliated domestic owner transfers its assets to another member of its consolidated group in a transaction described in section 381(a), and the transferee corporation or another member of such consolidated group is a domestic owner of the separate unit to which the dual consolidated loss was attributable, then paragraphs (d)(1)(i) and (ii) of this section shall not apply. In addition, income generated by the transferee that is attributable to the transferred separate unit may be offset by the carryover dual consolidated losses that were attributable to the transferred separate unit, subject to the limitations of paragraphs (b) and (c) of this section, applied as if the transferee incurred the dual consolidated losses and such losses were attributable to the separate unit. See § 1.1503(d)-7(c) *Example 21*.

(iv) *Special rules for foreign insurance companies.*—See § 1.1503(d)-6(a) for additional limitations that apply where the transferor is a foreign insurance company that is a dual resident corporation under § 1.1503(d)-1(b)(2)(ii).

(e) *Special rule denying the use of a dual consolidated loss to offset tainted income.*—(1) *In general.*—Dual consolidated losses incurred by a dual resident corporation that are subject to the domestic use limitation rule under paragraph (b) of this section shall not be used to offset income it earns after it ceases to be a dual resident corporation to the extent that such income is tainted income.

(2) *Tainted income.*—(i) *Definition.*—For purposes of paragraph (e)(1) of this section, the term tainted income means—

(A) Income or gain recognized on the sale or other disposition of tainted assets; and

(B) Income derived as a result of holding tainted assets.

(ii) *Income presumed to be derived from holding tainted assets.*—In the absence of evidence establishing the actual amount of income that is attributable to holding tainted assets, the portion of a corporation's income in a particular taxable year that is treated as tainted income derived as a result of holding tainted assets shall be an amount equal to the corporation's taxable income for the year (other than income described in paragraph (e)(2)(i)(A) of this section) multiplied by a fraction, the numerator of which is the fair market value of all tainted assets acquired by the corporation (determined at the time such assets were so acquired) and the denominator of which is the fair market value of the total assets owned by the corporation at the end of such taxable year. To establish the actual amount of income that is attributable to holding tainted assets, documentation must be attached to, and filed by the due date (including extensions) of, the domestic corporation's tax return or the consolidated tax return of an affiliated group of which it is a member, as the case may be, for the taxable year in which the income is generated. See § 1.1503(d)-7(c) *Example 22*.

(3) *Tainted assets defined.*—For purposes of paragraph (e)(2) of this section, tainted assets are any assets acquired by a domestic corporation in a nonrecognition transaction, as defined in section 7701(a)(45), any assets otherwise transferred to the corporation as a contribution to capital, or any assets otherwise received from a separate unit or a transparent entity owned by such domestic corporation, at any time during the three taxable years immediately preceding the taxable year in which the corporation ceases to be a dual resident corporation or at any time thereafter.

(4) *Exceptions.*—Income derived from assets acquired by a domestic corporation shall not be subject to the limitation described in paragraph (e)(1) of this section, and in addition shall not be treated as tainted assets as defined in paragraph (e)(3) of this section, if—

(i) For the taxable year in which the assets were acquired, the corporation did not have a dual consolidated loss (or a carryforward of a dual consolidated loss to such year); or

(ii) The assets were acquired as replacement property in the ordinary course of business.

(f) *Computation of foreign tax credit limitation.*—If a dual consolidated loss is subject to the domestic use limitation rule under paragraph (b) of this section, the consolidated group, unaffiliated dual resident corporation, or unaffiliated domestic owner shall compute its foreign tax credit limitation by applying the limitations of paragraph (c) of this section. Thus, the items constituting the dual consolidated loss are not taken into account until the year in which such items are absorbed. [Reg. § 1.1503(d)-4.]

□ [*T.D. 9315, 3-16-2007. Amended by T.D. 9927, 10-23-2020.*]

**[Reg. § 1.1503(d)-5]**

§1.1503(d)-5. **Attribution of items and basis adjustments.**—(a) *In general.*—This section provides rules for determining the amount of income or dual consolidated loss of a dual resident corporation. This section also provides rules for determining the income or dual consolidated loss attributable to a separate unit, as well as the income or loss attributable to an interest in a transparent entity. Paragraph (b) of this section provides rules with respect to dual resident corporations. Paragraph (c) of this section provides rules with respect to separate units and interests in transparent entities. These determinations are required for various purposes under section 1503(d). For example, it is necessary for purposes of applying the domestic use limitation rule under §1.1503(d)-4(b) to a dual consolidated loss, and for determining the extent to which a dual consolidated loss is available to offset income as provided under §1.1503(d)-4(c). These determinations are also necessary for purposes of determining whether the amount subject to recapture may be reduced pursuant to §1.1503(d)-6(h)(2). Paragraph (d) of this section provides rules with respect to the foreign tax treatment of items. Paragraph (e) of this section provides rules regarding the treatment of items where a dual resident corporation, separate unit, or transparent entity only qualified as such during a portion of a taxable year. Paragraph (f) of this section provides rules for determining the assets and liabilities of a separate unit. Finally, paragraph (g) of this section provides rules for making basis adjustments to stock of certain members of a consolidated group and to certain interests in partnerships. The rules in this section apply for purposes of §§1.1503(d)-1 through 1.1503(d)-7.

(b) *Determination of amount of income or dual consolidated loss of a dual resident corporation.*—(1) *In general.*—For purposes of determining whether a dual resident corporation has income or a dual consolidated loss for the taxable year, and except as provided in paragraph (b)(2) of this section, the dual resident corporation shall compute its income or dual consolidated loss taking into account only those items of income, gain, deduction, and loss from such year (including any items recognized by such corporation as a result of an election under section 338). In the case of an affiliated dual resident corporation, such calculation shall be made in accordance with the rules set forth in the regulations under section 1502 governing the computation of consolidated taxable income. See also paragraphs (d) and (e) of this section.

(2) *Exceptions.*—For purposes of determining the income or dual consolidated loss of a dual resident corporation, the following shall not be taken into account—

(i) Any net capital loss of the dual resident corporation;

(ii) Any carryover or carryback losses; or

(iii) Any items of income, gain, deduction, and loss that are attributable to a separate unit or an interest in a transparent entity of the dual resident corporation.

(c) *Determination of amount of income or dual consolidated loss attributable to a separate unit, and income or loss attributable to an interest in a transparent entity.*—(1) *In general.*—(i) *Scope and purpose.*— Paragraphs (c) through (e) of this section apply for purposes of determining the income or dual consolidated loss attributable to a separate unit, and the income or loss attributable to an interest in a transparent entity, for the taxable year. In the case of an affiliated domestic owner, this determination shall be made in accordance with the rules set forth in the regulations under section 1502 governing the computation of consolidated taxable income. These rules apply solely for purposes of section 1503(d).

(ii) *Only items of domestic owner taken into account.*—The computation made under paragraphs (c) through (e) of this section shall be made using only those existing items of income, gain, deduction, and loss of the separate unit's or transparent entity's domestic owner (or owners, in the case of certain combined separate units), as determined for U.S. tax purposes. These items must be translated into U.S. dollars (if necessary) at the appropriate exchange rate provided under section 989(b), as modified by regulations. The computation shall be made as if the separate unit or interest in a transparent entity were a domestic corporation, using items that are attributable to the separate unit or interest in a transparent entity. However, for purposes of making this computation, net capital losses, and carryover or carryback losses, of the domestic owner shall not be taken into account. Items of income, gain, deduction, and loss that are otherwise disregarded for U.S. tax purposes shall not be regarded or taken into account for purposes of this section. See §1.1503(d)-7(c) *Examples 6 and 23 through 25.*

(iii) *Separate application.*—The attribution rules of this section shall apply separately to each separate unit or interest in a transparent entity. Thus, an item of income, gain, deduction, or loss shall not be considered attributable to more than one separate unit or interest in a transparent entity. In addition, for purposes of this section items of income, gain, deduction, and loss attributable to a separate unit or an interest in a transparent entity shall not offset items of income, gain, deduction, and loss of another separate unit or interest in a transparent entity. See §1.1503(d)-7(c) *Example 24.* See also the separate unit combination rule in §1.1503(d)-1(b)(4)(ii).

(2) *Foreign branch separate unit.*—(i) *In general.*—Except to the extent provided in paragraph (c)(4) of this section, for purposes of determining the items of income, gain, deduction (other than interest), and loss of a domestic owner that are attributable to the domestic owner's foreign branch separate unit, the principles of section 864(c)(2), (c)(4), and (c)(5), as set forth in §1.864-4(c), and §§1.864-5 through 1.864-7, shall apply. The principles apply without regard to limitations imposed on the effectively connected treatment of income, gain, or loss under the trade or business safe harbors in section 864(b) and the limitations for treating foreign source income as effectively connected under section 864(c)(4)(D). Except as provided in paragraph (c)(2)(iii) of this section, for purposes of determining the domestic owner's interest expense that is attributable to a foreign branch separate unit, the principles of §1.882-5, as modified in paragraph (c)(2)(ii) of this section, shall apply. When applying the principles of section 864(c) (as modified by this paragraph) and §1.882-5 (as modified in paragraph (c)(2)(ii) of this section), the foreign branch separate unit's domestic owner shall be treated as a foreign corporation, the foreign branch separate unit shall be treated as a trade or business within the United States, and the other assets of the domestic owner shall be treated as assets that are not U.S. assets.

(ii) *Principles of §1.882-5.*—For purposes of paragraph (c)(2)(i) of this section, the principles of §1.882-5 shall be applied, subject to the following modifications—

(A) Except as otherwise provided in this section, only the assets, liabilities, and interest expense of the domestic owner shall be taken into account in the §1.882-5 formula;

(B) Except as provided under paragraph (c)(2)(ii)(C) of this section, a taxpayer may use the alternative tax book value method under §1.861-9(i) for purposes of determining the value of its U.S. assets pursuant to §1.882-5(b)(2) and its worldwide assets pursuant to §1.882-5(c)(2);

(C) For purposes of determining the value of a U.S. asset pursuant to §1.882-5(b)(2), and worldwide assets pursuant to §1.882-5(c)(2), the taxpayer must use the same methodology under §1.861-9T(g) (that is, tax book value, alternative tax book value, or fair market value) that the taxpayer uses for purposes of allocating and apportioning interest expense for the taxable year under section 864(e);

(D) Asset values shall be determined pursuant to §1.861-9T(g)(2); and

(E) For purposes of determining the step-two U.S. connected liabilities, the amounts of worldwide assets and liabilities under §1.882-5(c)(2)(iii) and (iv) must be determined in accordance with U.S. tax principles, rather than substantially in accordance with U.S. tax principles.

(iii) *Exception where foreign country attributes interest expense solely by reference to books and records.*—The principles of §1.882-5 shall not apply if the foreign country in which the foreign branch separate unit is located determines, for purposes of computing taxable income (or loss) of a permanent establishment or branch of a nonresident corporation under the laws of the foreign country, the interest expense of the foreign branch separate unit by taking into account only the items of interest expense reflected on the foreign branch separate unit's books and records. In such a case, only those items of the domestic owner's interest expense reflected on the foreign branch separate unit's books and records (as provided in paragraph (c)(3)(i) of this section), adjusted to conform to U.S. tax principles, shall be attributable to the foreign branch separate unit. This paragraph shall not apply where the foreign country does not use a method of attributing interest based solely on the interest that is reflected on the books and records. For example, this paragraph does not apply if the foreign country uses a method for attributing interest expense similar to §1.882-5 or that set forth in the Organization for Economic Cooperation and Development Report on the Attribution of Profits to Permanent Establishments, Part II (Banks), December 2006. See http://www.oecd.org.

(3) *Hybrid entity separate unit and an interest in a transparent entity.*—(i) *General rule.*—This paragraph (c)(3) applies to determine the items of income, gain, deduction, and loss of a domestic owner that are attributable to a hybrid entity separate unit, or an interest in a transparent entity, of such domestic owner. Except to the extent provided in paragraph (c)(4) of this section, the domestic owner's items of income, gain, deduction, and loss are attributable to the extent they are reflected on the books and records of the hybrid entity or transparent entity, as applicable, as adjusted to conform to U.S. tax principles. See §1.1503(d)-7(c) *Examples 23 through 26.* For purposes of this paragraph (c)(3), the term "books and records" has the meaning provided under §1.989(a)-1(d). The treatment of items for foreign tax purposes, including under any type of foreign anti-deferral regime, is not relevant for purposes of determining whether items are reflected on the books and records of the entity, or for purposes of making adjustments to such items to conform to U.S. tax principles.

The method described in the second sentence of this paragraph shall not apply to the extent that the Commissioner determines that booking practices are employed with a principal purpose of avoiding the principles of section 1503(d), including inconsistently treating the same or similar items of income, gain, deduction, and loss. In such a case, the Commissioner may reallocate the items of income, gain, deduction, and loss between or among a domestic owner, its hybrid entities, its transparent entities (and interests therein), its separate units, or any other entity, as applicable, in a manner consistent with the principles of section 1503(d) and which properly reflects income (or loss).

(ii) *Interests in certain disregarded entities, partnerships, and grantor trusts owned by a hybrid entity or transparent entity.*—This paragraph (c)(3)(ii) applies if a hybrid entity or transparent entity to which paragraph (c)(3)(i) of this section applies owns, directly or indirectly (other than through a hybrid entity or transparent entity), an interest in an entity that is treated as a disregarded entity, partnership, or grantor trust for U.S. tax purposes, but is not a hybrid entity or a transparent entity. For example, the rules of this paragraph would apply when a hybrid entity holds an interest in a limited partnership created in the United States and, for both U.S. and foreign tax purposes the entity is considered a partnership. In such a case, and except to the extent provided in paragraph (c)(4) of this section, items of income, gain, deduction, and loss that are reflected on the books and records of such disregarded entity, partnership or grantor trust, as determined under paragraph (c)(3)(i) of this section, shall be treated as being reflected on the books and records of the hybrid entity or transparent entity for purposes of applying paragraph (c)(3)(i) of this section. See § 1.1503(d)-7(c) *Example 26.*

(4) *Special rules.*—The following special rules shall apply for purposes of attributing items to separate units or interests in transparent entities under this section:

(i) *Allocation of items between certain tiered separate units and interests in transparent entities.*—(A) *Foreign branch separate unit.*—This paragraph (c)(4)(i) applies where a hybrid entity or transparent entity owns directly or indirectly (other than through a hybrid entity or a transparent entity), a foreign branch separate unit. For purposes of determining items of income, gain, deduction, and loss of the domestic owner that are attributable to the domestic owner's foreign branch separate unit described in the preceding sentence, only items of income, gain, deduction, and loss that are attributable to the domestic owner's interest in the hybrid entity, or transparent entity, as provided in paragraph (c)(3) of this section, shall be taken into account. Further, only assets, liabilities, and activities of the domestic owner's interest in the hybrid entity or the transparent entity shall be taken into account under paragraph (c)(2) of this section when applying the principles of 864(c)(2), (c)(4), (c)(5) (as set forth in § 1.864-4(c), and §§ 1.864-5 through 1.864-7), and § 1.882-5 (as modified in paragraph (c)(2)(ii) of this section). See § 1.1503(d)-7(c) *Examples 25 and 26.*

(B) *Hybrid entity separate unit or interest in a transparent entity.*—For purposes of determining items of income, gain, deduction, and loss that are attributable to a hybrid entity separate unit or an interest in a transparent entity described in paragraph (c)(3) of this section, such items shall not be taken into account to the extent they are attributable to a foreign branch separate unit pursuant to paragraph (c)(4)(i)(A) of this section. See § 1.1503(d)-7(c) *Examples 25 and 26.*

(ii) *Combined separate unit.*—If two or more individual separate units defined in § 1.1503(d)-1(b)(4)(i) are treated as one combined separate unit pursuant to § 1.1503(d)-1(b)(4)(ii), the items of income, gain, deduction, and loss that are attributable to the combined separate unit shall be determined as follows:

(A) Items of income, gain, deduction, and loss are first attributed to each individual separate unit without regard to § 1.1503(d)-1(b)(4)(ii), pursuant to the rules of paragraphs (c) through (e) of this section.

(B) The combined separate unit then takes into account all of the items of income, gain, deduction, and loss attributable to its individual separate units pursuant to paragraph (c)(4)(ii)(A) of this section. See § 1.1503(d)-7(c) *Examples 25 and 26.*

(iii) *Gain or loss on the direct or indirect disposition of a separate unit or an interest in a transparent entity.*—(A) *In general.*—This paragraph (c)(4)(iii) applies for purposes of attributing items of income, gain, deduction, and loss that are recognized on the sale, exchange, or other disposition of a separate unit or an interest in a transparent entity (or an interest in a disregarded entity, partnership, or grantor trust that owns, directly or indirectly, a separate unit or an interest in a transparent entity). For purposes of this paragraph (c)(4)(iii), items taken into account on the sale, exchange, or other disposition include loss recapture income or gain under section 367(a)(3)(C) or 904(f)(3), and gain or loss recognized by the domestic owner as the result of an

election under section 338. In cases where this paragraph (c)(4)(iii)(A) applies, items taken into account on the sale, exchange, or other disposition shall be attributable to the separate unit or the interest in the transparent entity to the extent of gain or loss that would have been recognized had the separate unit or transparent entity sold all its assets (as determined in paragraph (f) of this section) in a taxable exchange, immediately before the sale, exchange, or other disposition (deemed sale). For purposes of a deemed sale described in this paragraph (c)(4)(iii), the assets are treated as being sold for an amount equal to their fair market value, plus the assumption of the liabilities of the separate unit or interest in a transparent entity (as determined in paragraph (f) of this section). See § 1.1503(d)-7(c) *Example 27.*

(B) *Multiple separate units or interests in transparent entities.*—This paragraph (c)(4)(iii)(B) applies to a sale, exchange, or other disposition described in paragraph (c)(4)(iii)(A) of this section that results in more than one separate unit or interest in a transparent entity being, directly or indirectly, disposed of. In such a case, items of income, gain, deduction, and loss recognized on such sale, exchange, or other disposition are allocated and attributed to each separate unit or interest in a transparent entity, based on the relative gain or loss that would have been recognized by each separate unit or interest in a transparent entity pursuant to a deemed sale of their assets. See § 1.1503(d)-7(c) *Example 28.*

(iv) *Inclusions on stock.*—Any amount included in income of a domestic owner arising from ownership of stock in a foreign corporation (for example, under sections 78, 951, or 986(c)) through a separate unit, or interest in a transparent entity, shall be attributable to the separate unit or interest in a transparent entity, if an actual dividend from such foreign corporation would have been so attributed. See § 1.1503(d)-7(c) *Example 24.*

(v) *Foreign currency gain or loss recognized under section 987.*—Foreign currency gain or loss of a domestic owner recognized under section 987 as a result of a transfer or remittance shall not be attributable to a separate unit or an interest in a transparent entity.

(vi) *Recapture of dual consolidated loss.*—If all or a portion of a dual consolidated loss that was attributable to a separate unit is included in the gross income of a domestic owner under the recapture provisions of § 1.1503(d)-6(h), such amount shall be attributable to the separate unit that incurred the dual consolidated loss being recaptured. See § 1.1503(d)-7(c) *Examples 38 and 40.*

(d) *Foreign tax treatment disregarded.*—The fact that a particular item taken into account in computing the income or dual consolidated loss of a dual resident corporation or a separate unit, or the income or loss of an interest in a transparent entity, is not taken into account in computing income (or loss) subject to a foreign country's income tax shall not cause such item to be excluded from being taken into account under paragraph (b), (c), or (e) of this section.

(e) *Items generated or incurred while a dual resident corporation, a separate unit, or a transparent entity.*—For purposes of determining the amount of the dual consolidated loss of a dual resident corporation for the taxable year, only the items of income, gain, deduction, and loss generated or incurred during the period the dual resident corporation qualified as such shall be taken into account. For purposes of determining the amount of income of a dual resident corporation for the taxable year, all the items of income, gain, deduction, and loss generated or incurred during the year shall be taken into account. For purposes of determining the amount of the income or dual consolidated loss attributable to a separate unit, or the income or loss attributable to an interest in a transparent entity, for the taxable year, only the items of income, gain, deduction, and loss generated or incurred during the period the separate unit or the interest in the transparent entity qualified as such shall be taken into account. For purposes of this paragraph (e), the allocation of items to periods shall be made under the principles of § 1.1502-76(b).

(f) *Assets and liabilities of a separate unit or an interest in a transparent entity.*—A separate unit or an interest in a transparent entity shall be treated as owning assets to the extent items of income, gain, deduction, and loss from such assets would be attributable to the separate unit or interest in the transparent entity under paragraphs (c) through (e) of this section. Similarly, liabilities shall be treated as liabilities of a separate unit, or an interest in a transparent entity, to the extent interest expense incurred on such liabilities would be attributable to the separate unit, or the interest in a transparent entity, under paragraphs (c) through (e) of this section.

(g) *Basis adjustments.*—(1) *Affiliated dual resident corporation or affiliated domestic owner.*—If a member of a consolidated group owns stock in an affiliated dual resident corporation or an affiliated domestic owner that is a member of the same consolidated group, the member shall adjust the basis of the stock in accordance with the provisions of

§1.1502-32. Corresponding adjustments shall be made to the stock of other members in accordance with the provisions of §1.1502-32. In the case where two or more individual separate units are treated as a combined separate unit pursuant to §1.1503(d)-1(b)(4)(ii), see paragraph (g)(3) of this section.

(2) *Interests in hybrid entities that are partnerships or interests in partnerships through which a separate unit is owned indirectly.—* (i) *Scope.—*This paragraph (g)(2) applies for purposes of determining the adjusted basis of an interest in—

(A) A hybrid entity that is a partnership; and

(B) A partnership through which a domestic owner indirectly owns a separate unit.

(ii) *Determination of basis of partner's interest.—*The adjusted basis of an interest described in paragraph (g)(2)(i) of this section shall be adjusted in accordance with section 705 and this paragraph (g)(2). The adjusted basis shall not be decreased for any amount of a dual consolidated loss that is attributable to the partnership interest, or separate unit owned indirectly through the partnership interest, as applicable, that is not absorbed as a result of the application of §1.1503(d)-4(b) and (c). The adjusted basis shall, however, be decreased for the amount of such dual consolidated loss that is absorbed in a carryover or carryback taxable year. The adjusted basis shall be increased for any amount included in income pursuant to §1.1503(d)-6(h) as a result of the recapture of a dual consolidated loss that was attributable to the interest in the hybrid partnership, or separate unit owned indirectly through the partnership interest, as applicable.

(3) *Combined separate units.—*This paragraph (g)(3) applies where two or more individual separate units of one or more affiliated domestic owners are treated as one combined separate unit pursuant to §1.1503(d)-1(b)(4)(ii). In such a case, a member owning stock in an affiliated domestic owner of the combined separate unit shall adjust the basis in the stock of such domestic owner as provided in paragraph (g)(1) of this section, and an affiliated domestic owner shall adjust its basis in a partnership, as provided in paragraph (g)(2) of this section, taking into account only those items of income, gain, deduction, or loss attributable to each individual separate unit, prior to combination. For purposes of this rule, if the dual consolidated loss attributable to a combined separate unit is subject to the domestic use limitation of §1.1503(d)-4(b), then for purposes of this paragraph (g) and §1.1502-32, the dual consolidated loss shall be allocated to an individual separate unit to the extent such individual separate unit contributed items of deduction or loss giving rise to the dual consolidated loss. In addition, if one or more affiliated domestic owners are required to recapture all or a portion of a dual consolidated loss pursuant to paragraph (h) of this section, such recapture amount shall be allocated to the affiliated domestic owner of the individual separate units composing the combined separate unit, to the extent such individual separate units contributed items of deduction or loss giving rise to the recaptured dual consolidated loss. [Reg. §1.1503(d)-5.]

☐ [*T.D. 9315, 3-16-2007 (corrected 4-24-2007).*]

### [Reg. §1.1503(d)-6]

§1.1503(d)-6. Exceptions to the domestic use limitation rule.—
(a) *In general.—*(1) *Scope and purpose.—*This section provides certain exceptions to the domestic use limitation rule of §1.1503(d)-4(b). Paragraph (b) of this section provides an exception for bilateral elective agreements. Paragraph (c) of this section provides rules regarding an exception that applies when there is no possibility of a foreign use. Paragraphs (d) through (h) of this section provide rules for an exception where a domestic use election is made. Paragraph (e) of this section provides rules with respect to triggering events, and paragraph (f) of this section provides rules regarding exceptions to triggering events. Paragraph (g) of this section provides rules with respect to the annual certification reporting requirement. Paragraph (h) of this section provides rules regarding the recapture of dual consolidated losses. Finally, paragraph (j) of this section provides rules regarding the termination of domestic use agreements and the annual certification requirement.

(2) *Absence of foreign affiliate or foreign consolidation regime.—*The absence of a foreign affiliate or a foreign consolidation regime alone does not constitute an exception to the domestic use limitation rule. This is the case because it is still possible that all or a portion of the dual consolidated loss may be put to a foreign use. For example, there may be a foreign use with respect to an affiliate acquired in a year subsequent to the year in which the dual consolidated loss was incurred. In addition, a foreign use may occur in the absence of a foreign consolidation regime through a sale, merger, or similar transaction. See §1.1503(d)-7(c) *Example 2.*

(3) *Foreign insurance companies treated as domestic corporations.—*The exceptions contained in this section shall not apply to losses of a foreign insurance company that is a dual resident corporation under §1.1503(d)-1(b)(2)(ii), or to losses attributable to any separate unit of such foreign insurance company. In addition, these exceptions shall not apply to losses described in the preceding sentence that, subject to the rules of §1.1503(d)-4(d), carry over to a domestic corporation pursuant to a transaction described in section 381(a).

(b) *Elective agreement in place between the United States and a foreign country.—*(1) *In general.—*The domestic use limitation rule of §1.1503(d)-4(b) shall not apply to a dual consolidated loss to the extent the consolidated group, unaffiliated dual resident corporation, or unaffiliated domestic owner, as the case may be, elects to deduct the loss in the United States pursuant to an agreement entered into between the United States and a foreign country that puts into place an elective procedure through which losses in a particular year may be used to offset income in only one country. This exception shall apply only if all the terms and conditions required under such agreement are satisfied, including any reporting or filing requirements. See §1.1503(d)-3(e)(2)(iii) for the effect of an agreement described in this paragraph on a stand-alone domestic use agreement.

(2) *Application to combined separate units.—*This paragraph (b)(2) applies where two or more individual separate units are treated as one combined separate unit pursuant to §1.1503(d)-1(b)(4)(ii), and an agreement described in paragraph (b)(1) of this section would apply to at least one of the individual separate units. In such a case, and except to the extent provided in the agreement, the consolidated group, unaffiliated dual resident corporation, or unaffiliated domestic owner, as the case may be, may apply the agreement to the individual separate units, as applicable, provided the terms and conditions of the agreement are otherwise satisfied. See §1.1503(d)-7(c) *Example 19.*

(c) *No possibility of foreign use.—*(1) *In general.—*The domestic use limitation rule of §1.1503(d)-4(b) shall not apply to a dual consolidated loss if the consolidated group, unaffiliated dual resident corporation, or unaffiliated domestic owner, as the case may be—

(i) Demonstrates, to the satisfaction of the Commissioner, that no foreign use (as defined in §1.1503(d)-3) of the dual consolidated loss occurred in the year in which it was incurred, and that no foreign use can occur in any other year by any means; and

(ii) Prepares a statement described in paragraph (c)(2) of this section that is attached to, and filed by the due date (including extensions) of, its U.S. income tax return for the taxable year in which the dual consolidated loss is incurred. See §1.1503(d)-7(c) *Examples 2, 30, and 31.*

(2) *Statement.—*The statement described in this paragraph (c)(2) must be signed under penalties of perjury by the person who signs the tax return. The statement must be labeled "No Possibility of Foreign Use of Dual Consolidated Loss Statement" at the top of the page and must include the following items, in paragraphs labeled to correspond with the items set forth in paragraphs (c)(2)(i) through (iv) of this section:

(i) A statement that the document is submitted under the provisions of paragraph (c) of this section.

(ii) The name, address, taxpayer identification number, and place and date of incorporation of the dual resident corporation, and the country or countries that tax the dual resident corporation on its worldwide income or on a residence basis, or, in the case of a separate unit, identification of the separate unit, including the name under which it conducts business, its principal activity, and the country in which its principal place of business is located. In the case of a combined separate unit, such information must be provided for each individual separate unit that is treated as part of the combined separate unit under §1.1503(d)-1(b)(4)(ii).

(iii) A statement of the amount of the dual consolidated loss at issue.

(iv) An analysis, in reasonable detail and specificity, of the treatment of the losses and deductions composing the dual consolidated loss under the relevant facts. The analysis must include the reasons supporting the conclusion that no foreign use of the dual consolidated loss can occur as described in paragraph (c)(1)(i) of this section. The analysis must be supported with official or certified English translations of the relevant provisions of foreign law. The analysis may, for example, be based on the taxpayer's interpretation of foreign law, on advice received from local tax advisers in an opinion, or on a ruling from local country tax authorities. In all cases, however, the determination must be made to the satisfaction of the Commissioner.

(d) *Domestic use election.—*(1) *In general.—*The domestic use limitation rule of §1.1503(d)-4(b) shall not apply to a dual consolidated loss if an election to be bound by the provisions of paragraphs (d) through (j) of this section is made by the consolidated group, unaffiliated dual resident corporation, or unaffiliated domestic owner, as the case may be (elector). In order to elect such relief, an agreement described in this paragraph (d)(1) (domestic use agreement) must be attached to, and filed by the due date (including extensions) of, the U.S. income tax return of the elector for the taxable year in which the dual consolidated loss is incurred. The domestic use agreement must be signed under penalties of perjury by the person who signs the return. If dual consolidated losses of more than one dual resident corporation or separate unit requires the filing of domestic use agreements by the same elector, the agreements may be combined in a single document, but the information required by paragraphs (d)(1)(ii) and (iv) of this section must be provided separately with respect to each dual consolidated loss. The domestic use agreement must be labeled "Domestic Use Election and Agreement" at the top of the page and must include the following items, in paragraphs labeled to correspond with the following:

(i) A statement that the document submitted is an election and an agreement under the provisions of paragraph (d) of this section.

(ii) The information required by paragraph (c)(2)(ii) of this section.

(iii) An agreement by the elector to comply with all of the provisions of paragraphs (d) through (j) of this section, as applicable.

(iv) A statement of the amount of the dual consolidated loss at issue.

(v) A certification that there has not been, and will not be, a foreign use (as defined in §1.1503(d)-3) during the certification period (as defined in §1.1503(d)-1(b)(20)).

(vi) A certification that arrangements have been made to ensure that there will be no foreign use of the dual consolidated loss during the certification period, and that the elector will be informed of any such foreign use of the dual consolidated loss during such period.

(vii) If applicable, a notification that an excepted triggering event under paragraph (f)(2) of this section has occurred with respect to the dual consolidated loss within the taxable year in which the loss is incurred. See paragraph (g) of this section for notification of excepted triggering events occurring during the certification period.

(2) *No domestic use election available if there is a triggering event in the year the dual consolidated loss is incurred.*—Except as otherwise provided in this section, if a dual resident corporation or separate unit incurs a dual consolidated loss in a taxable year and a triggering event, as described in paragraph (e)(1) of this section, occurs (and no exception applies) with respect to the dual consolidated loss in such taxable year, then the consolidated group, unaffiliated dual resident corporation, or unaffiliated domestic owner, as the case may be, may not make a domestic use election with respect to such dual consolidated loss and the loss will be subject to the domestic use limitation rule of §1.1503(d)-4(b). See §1.1503(d)-7(c) *Examples 5* through 7. See also §1.1503(d)-4(d) for rules that eliminate a dual consolidated loss after certain transactions.

(e) *Triggering events requiring the recapture of a dual consolidated loss.*—(1) *Events.*—Except as provided under paragraphs (e)(2) (rebuttal of triggering events) and (f) (exceptions to triggering events) of this section, if there is a triggering event described in this paragraph (e)(1) with respect to a dual consolidated loss of a dual resident corporation or a separate unit during the certification period (as defined in §1.1503(d)-1(b)(20)), the elector will recapture and report as ordinary income the amount of such dual consolidated loss as provided in paragraph (h) of this section on its tax return for the taxable year in which the triggering event occurs (or, when the triggering event is a foreign use of the dual consolidated loss, the taxable year that includes the last day of the foreign taxable year during which such use occurs). In addition, the elector must pay any applicable interest charge required by paragraph (h) of this section. For purposes of this section, any of the following events shall constitute a triggering event:

(i) *Foreign use.*—A foreign use (as defined in §1.1503(d)-3) of the dual consolidated loss. See §1.1503(d)-3(c) for exceptions to foreign use.

(ii) *Disaffiliation.*—An affiliated dual resident corporation or affiliated domestic owner that incurred directly or through a separate unit, respectively, a dual consolidated loss that is subject to a domestic use election, ceases to be a member of the consolidated group that made the domestic use election. For purposes of this paragraph (e)(1)(ii), an affiliated dual resident corporation or affiliated domestic owner shall be considered to cease to be a member of the consolidated group if it is no longer a member of the group within the meaning of §1.1502-1(b), or if the group ceases to exist (for example, when the group no longer files a consolidated return). See §1.1503(d)-7(c) *Example 34.* Any consequences resulting from this

triggering event (for example, recapture of a dual consolidated loss) shall be taken into account on the tax return of the consolidated group for the taxable year that includes the date on which the affiliated dual resident corporation or affiliated domestic owner ceases to be a member of the consolidated group. This paragraph (e)(1)(ii) shall not apply to an acquisition described in §1.1502-75(d)(3) where the consolidated group that includes the affiliated dual resident corporation or affiliated domestic owner, as applicable, is treated as remaining in existence.

(iii) *Affiliation.*—An unaffiliated dual resident corporation or unaffiliated domestic owner becomes a member of a consolidated group. Any consequences resulting from this triggering event (for example, recapture of a dual consolidated loss) shall be taken into account on the tax return of the unaffiliated dual resident corporation or unaffiliated domestic owner for the taxable year that ends at the end of the day on which such corporation becomes a member of the consolidated group.

(iv) *Transfer of assets.*—Fifty percent or more of the dual resident corporation's or separate unit's gross assets (measured by the fair market value of the assets at the time of such transaction or, for multiple transactions, at the time of the first transaction) is sold or otherwise disposed of in either a single transaction or a series of transactions within a twelve-month period. See §1.1503(d)-7(c) *Examples 5* and *35* through *37*. In determining whether fifty percent or more of such assets is sold or otherwise disposed of, any dispositions occurring in the ordinary course of the dual resident corporation's or separate unit's trade or business shall be disregarded. In addition, for purposes of this paragraph (e)(1)(iv), an interest in another separate unit and the shares of a dual resident corporation shall not be treated as assets of a separate unit or a dual resident corporation.

(v) *Transfer of an interest in a separate unit.*—Fifty percent or more of the interest in a separate unit (measured by voting power or value at the time of such transaction, or for multiple transactions, at the time of the first transaction) of the domestic owner, as determined by reference to such domestic owner's percentage interest on the last day of the taxable year in which the dual consolidated loss was incurred, is sold or otherwise disposed of either in a single transaction or a series of transactions within a twelve-month period. See §1.1503(d)-7(c) *Examples 5* and *35* through *37*.

(vi) *Conversion to a foreign corporation.*—An unaffiliated dual resident corporation, unaffiliated domestic owner, or hybrid entity an interest in which is a separate unit, that incurred the dual consolidated loss, becomes a foreign corporation (for example, as a result of a reorganization or an election to be classified as a corporation under §301.7701-3(c) of this chapter).

(vii) *Conversion to a regulated investment company, a real estate investment trust, or an S corporation.*—An unaffiliated dual resident corporation or unaffiliated domestic owner elects to be a regulated investment company pursuant to section 851(b)(1), a real estate investment trust pursuant to section 856(c)(1), or an S corporation pursuant to section 1362(a).

(viii) *Failure to certify.*—The elector fails to file a certification with respect to a dual consolidated loss as required under paragraph (g) of this section.

(ix) *Cessation of stand-alone status.*—In the case of a dual consolidated loss that is subject to the stand-alone exception described in §1.1503(d)-3(e)(2), the conditions described in §1.1503(d)-3(e)(2)(i) are no longer satisfied. See §1.1503(d)-7(c) *Example 18.*

(2) *Rebuttal.*—(i) *General rule.*—An event described in paragraph (e)(1) of this section shall not constitute a triggering event if the elector demonstrates, to the satisfaction of the Commissioner, that there can be no foreign use (as defined in §1.1503(d)-3) of the dual consolidated loss during the remaining certification period by any means. See paragraph (j)(1) of this section for rules regarding the termination of domestic use agreements and annual certifications following rebuttals under this general rule.

(ii) *Certain asset transfers.*—An event described in paragraph (e)(1)(iv) of this section shall not constitute a triggering event if the elector demonstrates, to the satisfaction of the Commissioner, that the transfer of assets did not result in a carryover under foreign law of the dual resident corporation's, or separate unit's, losses, expenses, or deductions to the transferee of the assets. For purposes of this determination, the exception to foreign use in §1.1503(d)-3(c)(7) shall be taken into account. Following rebuttal under this paragraph (e)(2)(ii), the domestic use agreement continues in effect.

(iii) *Reporting.*—In order to satisfy the requirements of paragraph (e)(2)(i) or (ii) of this section, the elector must prepare a statement, labeled "Rebuttal of Triggering Event" at the top of the page, that indicates that it is submitted under the provisions of this paragraph (e)(2). The statement must include the information described in paragraphs (c)(2)(ii) and (iii) of this section. The statement must also include the information described in paragraph (c)(2)(iv) of this section that supports the conclusions under paragraph (e)(2)(i) or (ii) of this section, as applicable. The statement must be attached to, and filed by the due date (including extensions) of, the elector's income tax return for the taxable year in which the presumed triggering event occurs.

(iv) *Examples.*—See § 1.1503(d)-7(c) *Examples 32 and 33.*

(f) *Triggering event exceptions.*—(1) *Continuing ownership of assets or interests.*—The following events shall not constitute triggering events, requiring the recapture of the dual consolidated loss under paragraph (h) of this section:

(i) *Disaffiliation as a result of a transaction described in section 381.*—An affiliated dual resident corporation or affiliated domestic owner ceases to be a member of a consolidated group solely by reason of a transaction in which a member of the same consolidated group succeeds to the tax attributes of the dual resident corporation or domestic owner under the provisions of section 381.

(ii) *Continuing ownership by consolidated group.*—This paragraph (f)(1)(ii) applies when assets of an affiliated dual resident corporation, or assets of, or interests in, a separate unit of an affiliated domestic owner are sold or otherwise disposed of. In such a case, the sale or disposition shall not be treated as a triggering event to the extent the assets or interests are acquired by one or more members of the consolidated group that includes the affiliated dual resident corporation or affiliated domestic owner, or by a partnership or a grantor trust, but only if immediately after the acquisition more than 90 percent of the partnership's or grantor trust's interests is owned, directly or indirectly, by members of such consolidated group.

(iii) *Continuing ownership by unaffiliated dual resident corporation or unaffiliated domestic owner.*—This paragraph (f)(1)(iii) applies when assets of an unaffiliated dual resident corporation, or assets of, or interests in, a separate unit of an unaffiliated domestic owner, are sold or otherwise disposed of. In such a case, the sale or disposition shall not be a triggering event to the extent such assets or interests are acquired by the unaffiliated dual resident corporation, or unaffiliated domestic owner, as applicable, or by a partnership or grantor trust, but only if immediately after the acquisition more than 90 percent of the partnership's or grantor trust's interests is owned, directly or indirectly, by the unaffiliated dual resident corporation or unaffiliated domestic owner. For example, this paragraph (f)(1)(iii) applies when an unaffiliated domestic owner acquires direct ownership of the assets of a separate unit that it had immediately before owned indirectly through a partnership.

(2) *Transactions requiring a new domestic use agreement.*—(i) *Multiple-party events.*—If all the requirements of paragraph (f)(2)(iii) of this section are satisfied, the following events shall not constitute triggering events requiring the recapture of the dual consolidated loss under paragraph (h) of this section:

(A) An affiliated dual resident corporation or affiliated domestic owner becomes an unaffiliated domestic corporation or a member of a new consolidated group (other than in a transaction described in paragraph (f)(2)(ii)(B) of this section).

(B) Assets of a dual resident corporation or assets of, or interests in, a separate unit, are sold or otherwise disposed of in a transaction in which such assets or interests are acquired by an unaffiliated domestic corporation, one or more members of a new consolidated group, or by a partnership or grantor trust, but only if immediately after the sale or disposition more than 90 percent of the partnership's or grantor trust's interests is owned, directly or indirectly, by the unaffiliated domestic owner or by members of a new consolidated group, as applicable. See the related exception to foreign use provided under § 1.1503(d)-3(c)(8). See also § 1.1503(d)-7(c) *Examples 36 and 37.*

(ii) *Events resulting in a single consolidated group.*—If the requirements of paragraph (f)(2)(iii)(A) of this section are satisfied, the following events shall not constitute triggering events requiring the recapture of the dual consolidated loss under paragraph (h) of this section:

(A) An unaffiliated dual resident corporation or unaffiliated domestic owner becomes a member of a consolidated group.

(B) A consolidated group ceases to exist as a result of a transaction described in § 1.1502-13(j)(5)(i) (relating to acquisitions of the common parent of the consolidated group), other than a transaction in which any member of the terminating group, or the successor-in-interest of such member, is not a member of the surviving group immediately after the terminating group ceases to exist. See § 1.1503(d)-7(c) *Example 34.*

(iii) *Requirements.*—(A) *New domestic use agreement.*—The unaffiliated domestic corporation or new consolidated group (subsequent elector) must file an agreement described in paragraph (d)(1) of this section (new domestic use agreement). The new domestic use agreement must be labeled "New Domestic Use Agreement" at the top of the page, and must be attached to and filed by the due date (including extensions) of, the subsequent elector's income tax return for the taxable year in which the event described in paragraph (f)(2)(i) or (f)(2)(ii) of this section occurs. The new domestic use agreement must be signed under penalties of perjury by the person who signs the return and must include the following items:

(1) A statement that the document submitted is an election and agreement under the provisions of paragraph (f)(2) of this section.

(2) An agreement to assume the same obligations with respect to the dual consolidated loss as the unaffiliated dual resident corporation, unaffiliated domestic owner, or consolidated group, as applicable, that filed the original domestic use agreement (original elector) with respect to that loss. In such a case, obligations of an elector provided under this section shall also be considered to be obligations of a subsequent elector.

(3) In the event of a transaction described in section 384(a) involving the subsequent elector, an agreement to treat any potential recapture amount under paragraph (h) of this section with respect to the dual consolidated loss as unrealized built-in gain for purposes of section 384(a), subject to any applicable exceptions (for example, the threshold requirements under section 382(h)(3)(B)). The potential recapture amount treated as unrealized built-in gain under this paragraph (f)(2)(iii)(A)(3) may be reduced to the extent permitted by paragraph (h)(2)(i) of this section.

(4) In the case of a multiple-party event described in paragraph (f)(2)(i) of this section, an agreement to be subject to the rules provided in paragraph (h)(3) of this section.

(5) The name, U.S. taxpayer identification number, and address of the original elector and prior subsequent electors, if any, with respect to the dual consolidated loss.

(B) *Statement filed by original elector.*—In the case of a multiple-party event described in paragraph (f)(2)(i) of this section, the original elector must file a statement that is attached to and filed by the due date (including extensions) of its income tax return for the taxable year in which the event occurs. The statement must be labeled "Original Elector Statement" at the top of the page, must be signed under penalties of perjury by the person who signs the tax return, and must include the following items:

(1) A statement that the document submitted is an election and agreement under the provisions of paragraph (f)(2) of this section.

(2) An agreement to be subject to the rules provided in paragraph (h)(3) of this section.

(3) The name, U.S. taxpayer identification number, and address of the subsequent elector.

(3) *Certain transfers qualifying for the de minimis exception to foreign use.*—If a transaction or event qualifies for the de minimis exception to foreign use described in § 1.1503(d)-3(c)(5), the transaction or event shall not constitute a triggering event under paragraph (e)(1)(iv) (transfers of assets) or (v) (transfers of an interest in a separate unit) of this section. For purposes of the preceding sentence, the transaction or event shall include deemed transfers that occur as a result of the transaction or event. See, for example, deemed transfers occurring pursuant to Rev. Rul. 99-5 (1999-1 CB 434), see § 601.601(d)(2)(ii)(b), and section 708 and the related regulations. See also § 1.1503(d)-7 *Example 5.* This paragraph (f)(3) only applies if the entire transaction or event qualifies for the de minimis exception to foreign use. For example, if a domestic owner sells five percent of a separate unit to a foreign corporation, which would qualify for the de minimis exception to foreign use if it were the only transfer, but pursuant to the same transaction also sells 70 percent of the same separate unit to another corporation in a manner that results in a triggering event under paragraph (e)(1)(v) of this section, this paragraph shall not apply to prevent the transaction from resulting in a triggering event.

(4) *Deemed transactions as a result of certain transfers that do not result in a foreign use.*—The rules in this paragraph (f)(4) apply where the assets of, or the interests in, a separate unit are transferred in a transaction that would not result in a foreign use and, but for resulting deemed transactions or events, would not result in a triggering event described in paragraph (e)(1) of this section. For purposes of this paragraph (f)(4), deemed transactions or events shall include transactions or events that are deemed to occur pursuant to Rev. Rul. 99-5 and section 708 and the related regulations. In such a case, the deemed transactions shall not result in a triggering event under paragraph (e)(1)(iv) (transfers of assets) or (v) (transfers of an

interest in a separate unit) of this section. See also § 1.1503(d)-7 *Example 35.*

(5) *Compulsory transfers.*—Transfers of the assets or stock of a dual resident corporation, or of the assets or interests in a separate unit, shall not constitute a triggering event (including a foreign use that occurs as a result of, or following, the transfer) if such transfers are—

(i) Legally required by a government of a country as a necessary condition of doing business in the country;

(ii) Compelled by a genuine threat of immediate expropriation by a government of a country; or

(iii) The result of the expropriation of assets by a government of a country.

(6) *Subsequent triggering events.*—Any triggering event described in paragraph (e) of this section that occurs subsequent to one of the transactions described in this paragraph (f), and that itself does not meet any of the exceptions provided in this paragraph (f), shall require recapture under paragraph (h) of this section by the elector or subsequent elector, as applicable.

(g) *Annual certification reporting requirement.*—Unless and until the domestic use agreement is terminated pursuant to paragraph (j) of this section, the elector must file a certification, labeled "Certification of Dual Consolidated Loss" at the top of the page, that is attached to, and filed by the due date (including extensions) of, its income tax return for each taxable year during the certification period. The certification must provide that there has been no foreign use of the dual consolidated loss. The certification must identify the dual consolidated loss to which it pertains by setting forth the elector's year in which the loss was incurred and the amount of such loss. In addition, the certification must warrant that arrangements have been made to ensure that there will be no foreign use of the dual consolidated loss and that the elector will be informed of any such foreign use. If applicable, the certification must include a notification that an excepted triggering event under paragraph (f)(2) of this section has occurred with respect to the dual consolidated loss within the taxable year being certified. If dual consolidated losses of more than one taxable year are subject to the rules of this paragraph (g), the certification for those years may be combined in a single document, but each dual consolidated loss must be separately identified. See § 1.1503(d)-3(e)(2)(ii) for additional certifications required where taxpayers elect the stand-alone exception of § 1.1503(d)-3(e)(2).

(h) *Recapture of dual consolidated loss and interest charge.*—(1) *Presumptive rules.*—(i) *Amount of recapture.*—Except as otherwise provided in this section, upon the occurrence of a triggering event described in paragraph (e) of this section that does not meet any of the exceptions provided in paragraph (f) of this section, the dual resident corporation or domestic owner of the separate unit shall recapture as gross income the total amount of the dual consolidated loss to which the triggering event applies on its income tax return for the taxable year in which the triggering event occurs (or, when the triggering event is a foreign use of the dual consolidated loss, the taxable year that includes the last day of the foreign taxable year during which such foreign use occurs). See § 1.1503(d)-5(c)(4)(vi) for rules with respect to the attribution of recapture income to a separate unit. See also § 1.1503(d)-7 *Examples 38* through *40.*

(ii) *Interest charge.*—In connection with the recapture, the elector shall pay an interest charge. An interest charge may be due even if the amount of recapture income is reduced to zero pursuant to paragraph (h)(2)(i) of this section. See § 1.1503(d)-7(c) *Example 39.* Except as otherwise provided in this section, the amount of the interest shall be computed under the rules of section 6601(a) by treating the additional tax resulting from the recapture as though it had been due and unpaid as of the date for payment of the tax for the taxable year in which the taxpayer received a tax benefit from the dual consolidated loss. For purposes of this paragraph (h)(1)(ii), a tax benefit shall be considered to have arisen in a taxable year in which the losses or deductions taken into account in computing the dual consolidated loss reduced U.S. taxable income. For the purpose of computing the interest charge, the additional tax resulting from the recapture is determined by treating the recapture income as the last income earned in the year of recapture. The interest shall be computed to the date for payment of the tax for the year of recapture and the interest thus computed becomes a part of the tax liability for that taxable year. See section 6601 for the computation of interest on a tax liability that it is not paid timely. The recapture interest charge shall be deductible to the same extent as interest under section 6601.

(2) *Reduction of presumptive recapture amount and presumptive interest charge.*—(i) *Amount of recapture.*—The dual resident corporation or domestic owner may recapture an amount less than the total dual consolidated loss if the elector demonstrates, to the satisfaction of the Commissioner, the lesser amount described in this paragraph

(h)(2)(i). The reduction in the amount of recapture is the amount by which the dual consolidated loss would have offset other taxable income reported on a timely filed U.S. income tax return for any taxable year up to and including the taxable year of the triggering event (or, when the triggering event is a foreign use of the dual consolidated loss, the taxable year that includes the last day of the foreign taxable year during which such foreign use occurs) if no domestic use election had been made for the loss such that it was subject to the domestic use limitation of § 1.1503(d)-4(b) (and therefore subject to the limitation under § 1.1503(d)-4(c)). For this purpose, the rules for attributing items of income, gain, deduction, and loss under § 1.1503(d)-5 shall apply. An elector using this rebuttal rule must prepare a separate accounting showing the income for each year that would have offset the dual resident corporation's or separate unit's recapture amount if no domestic use election had been made for the dual consolidated loss. The separate accounting must be signed under penalties of perjury by the person who signs the elector's tax return, must be labeled "Reduction of Recapture Amount" at the top of the page, and must indicate that it is submitted under the provisions of this paragraph (h)(2)(i). The accounting must be attached to, and filed by the due date (including extensions) of, the elector's income tax return for the taxable year in which the triggering event occurs. See § 1.1503(d)-7(c) *Examples 38* through *40.*

(ii) *Interest charge.*—The interest charge imposed under this section may be reduced if the elector demonstrates, to the satisfaction of the Commissioner, that the net interest owed would have been less than that provided in paragraph (h)(1)(ii) of this section if the elector had filed an amended return for the taxable year in which the recaptured dual consolidated loss was incurred, and for any other affected taxable years up to and including the taxable year of recapture, if no domestic use election had been made for the dual consolidated loss such that it had been subject to the restrictions of § 1.1503(d)-4(b) (and therefore subject to the limitations under § 1.1503(d)-4(c)). An elector using this rebuttal rule must prepare a computation demonstrating the reduction in the net interest owed as a result of treating the dual consolidated loss as a loss subject to the restrictions of § 1.1503(d)-4(b) (and therefore subject to the limitations under § 1.1503(d)-4(c)). The computation must be labeled "Reduction of Interest Charge" at the top of the page and must indicate that it is submitted under the provisions of this paragraph (h)(2)(ii). The computation must be signed under penalties of perjury by the person who signs the elector's tax return, and must be attached to, and filed by the due date (including extensions) of, the elector's income tax return for the taxable year in which the triggering event occurs. See § 1.1503(d)-7(c) *Examples 39* and *40.*

(3) *Rules regarding multiple-party event exceptions to triggering events.*—(i) *Scope.*—The rules of this paragraph (h)(3) apply when, after a triggering event described in paragraph (e) of this section with respect to which the requirements of paragraph (f)(2)(i) of this section were met (excepted event), a triggering event under paragraph (e) of this section occurs, and no exception applies to such triggering event under paragraph (f) of this section (subsequent triggering event). See § 1.1503(d)-7(c) *Examples 36* and *37.*

(ii) *Original elector and prior subsequent electors not subject to recapture or interest charge.*—(A) Except to the extent otherwise provided in this paragraph (h)(3), neither the original elector nor any prior subsequent elector shall be subject to the rules of this paragraph (h) with respect to dual consolidated losses subject to the original domestic use agreement.

(B) In the case of a dual consolidated loss with respect to which multiple excepted events have occurred, only the subsequent elector that owns the dual resident corporation or separate unit at the time of the subsequent triggering event shall be subject to the recapture rules of this paragraph (h). For purposes of this paragraph (h), the term *prior subsequent elector* refers to all other subsequent electors.

(iii) *Recapture tax amount and required statement.*—(A) *In general.*—If a subsequent triggering event occurs, the subsequent elector shall take into account the recapture tax amount as determined under paragraph (h)(3)(iii)(B) of this section. The subsequent elector must prepare a statement that computes the recapture tax amount, as provided under paragraph (h)(3)(iii)(B) of this section, with respect to the dual consolidated loss subject to the new domestic use agreement. This statement must be attached to, and filed by the due date (including extensions) of, the subsequent elector's income tax return for the taxable year in which the subsequent triggering event occurs (or, when the subsequent triggering event is a foreign use of the dual consolidated loss, the taxable year that includes the last day of the foreign taxable year during which such foreign use occurs). The statement must be signed under penalties of perjury by the person who signs the return. The statement must be labeled "Statement Identifying Liability" at the top and, in addition to the calculation of the recapture tax amount, must include the following items, in paragraphs labeled to correspond with the items set forth in paragraphs (h)(3)(iii)(A)(1) through (3) of this section:

(1) A statement that the document is submitted under the provisions of §1.1503(d)-6(h)(3)(iii).

(2) A statement identifying the amount of the dual consolidated losses at issue and the taxable years in which they were used.

(3) The name, address, and taxpayer identification number of the original elector and all prior subsequent electors.

(B) *Recapture tax amount.*—The recapture tax amount equals the excess (if any) of—

(1) The income tax liability of the subsequent elector for the taxable year that includes the amount of recapture and related interest charge with respect to the dual consolidated losses that are recaptured as a result of the subsequent triggering event, as provided under paragraphs (h)(1) and (h)(2) of this section; over

(2) The income tax liability of the subsequent elector for such taxable year, computed by excluding the amount of recapture and related interest charge described in paragraph (h)(3)(iii)(B)(1) of this section.

(iv) *Tax assessment and collection procedures.*—(A) *In general.*—(1) *Subsequent elector.*—An assessment identifying an income tax liability of the subsequent elector is considered an assessment of the recapture tax amount where the recapture tax amount is part of the income tax liability being assessed and the recapture tax amount is reflected in a statement attached to the subsequent elector's income tax return as provided under paragraph (h)(3)(iii) of this section.

(2) *Original elector and prior subsequent electors.*—The assessment of the recapture tax amount as set forth in paragraph (h)(3)(iv)(A)(1) of this section shall be considered as having been properly assessed as an income tax liability of the original elector and of each prior subsequent elector, if any. The date of such assessment shall be the date the income tax liability of the subsequent elector was properly assessed. The Commissioner may collect all or a portion of such recapture tax amount from the original elector and/or the prior subsequent electors under the circumstances set forth in paragraph (h)(3)(iv)(B) of this section.

(B) *Collection from original elector and prior subsequent electors; joint and several liability.*—(1) *In general.*—If the subsequent elector does not pay in full the income tax liability that includes a recapture tax amount, the Commissioner may collect that portion of the unpaid balance of such income tax liability attributable to the recapture tax amount in full or in part from the original elector and/or from any prior subsequent elector, provided that the following conditions are satisfied with respect to such elector:

(i) The Commissioner properly has assessed the recapture tax amount pursuant to paragraph (h)(3)(iv)(A)(1) of this section.

(ii) The Commissioner has issued a notice and demand for payment of the recapture tax amount to the subsequent elector in accordance with §301.6303-1 of this chapter.

(iii) The subsequent elector has failed to pay all of the recapture tax amount by the date specified in such notice and demand.

(iv) The Commissioner has issued a notice and demand for payment of the unpaid portion of the recapture tax amount to the original elector, or prior subsequent elector (as the case may be), in accordance with §301.6303-1 of this chapter.

(2) *Joint and several liability.*—The liability imposed under this paragraph (h)(3)(iv)(B) on the original elector and each prior subsequent elector shall be joint and several.

(C) *Allocation of partial payments of tax.*—If the subsequent elector's income tax liability for a taxable period includes a recapture tax amount, and if such income tax liability is satisfied in part by payment, credit, or offset, such payment, credit or offset shall be allocated first to that portion of the income tax liability that is not attributable to the recapture tax amount, and then to that portion of the income tax liability that is attributable to the recapture tax amount.

(D) *Refund.*—If the Commissioner makes a refund of any income tax liability that includes a recapture tax amount, the Commissioner shall allocate and pay the refund to each elector who paid a portion of such income tax liability as follows:

(1) The Commissioner shall first determine the total amount of recapture tax paid by and/or collected from the original elector and from any prior subsequent electors. The Commissioner shall then allocate and pay such refund to the original elector and prior subsequent electors, with each such elector receiving an amount of such refund on a pro rata basis, not to exceed the amount of recapture tax paid by and/or collected from such elector.

(2) The Commissioner shall pay the balance of such refund, if any, to the subsequent elector.

(v) *Definition of income tax liability.*—Solely for purposes of paragraph (h)(3) of this section, the term income tax liability means the income tax liability imposed on a domestic corporation under Title 26 of the United States Code for a taxable year, including additions to tax, additional amounts, penalties, and any interest charge related to such income tax liability.

(vi) *Example.*—See §1.1503(d)-7(c) *Example 36.*

(4) *Computation of taxable income in year of recapture.*—(i) *Presumptive rule.*—Except to the extent provided in paragraph (h)(4)(ii) of this section, for purposes of computing the taxable income for the year of recapture, no current, carryover or carryback losses may offset and absorb the recapture amount.

(ii) *Exception to presumptive rule.*—The recapture amount included in gross income may be offset and absorbed by that portion of the elector's net operating loss carryover that is attributable to the dual resident corporation or separate unit that incurred the dual consolidated loss being recaptured, if the elector demonstrates, to the satisfaction of the Commissioner, the amount of such portion of the carryover. The principles of §1.1502-21(b)(2)(iv) shall apply for purposes of determining whether any portion of a net operating loss carryover is attributable to the dual resident corporation or separate unit. In the case of a separate unit, such determination shall be made by treating the separate unit as a domestic corporation and a member of the consolidated group composing its unaffiliated domestic owner, or members of the consolidated group of which its affiliated domestic owner is a member, as appropriate. An elector utilizing this rebuttal rule must prepare a computation demonstrating the amount of net operating loss carryover that, under this paragraph (h)(4)(ii), may absorb the recapture amount included in gross income. Such computation must be signed under penalties of perjury and attached to and filed by the due date (including extensions) of, the income tax return for the taxable year in which the triggering event occurs (or, when the triggering event is a foreign use of the dual consolidated loss, the taxable year that includes the last day of the foreign taxable year during which such foreign use occurs).

(5) *Character and source of recapture income.*—The amount recaptured under this paragraph (h) shall be treated as ordinary income. Except as provided in the prior sentence, such income shall be treated, as applicable, as income from the same source, having the same character, and falling within the same separate category, for all purposes, including sections 904(d) and 907, to which the items of deduction or loss composing the dual consolidated loss were allocated and apportioned, as provided under sections 861(b), 862(b), 863(a), 864(e), 865, and the related regulations. For this determination, the pro rata computation of the items of deduction or loss composing the dual consolidated loss as described in §1.1503(d)-4(c)(4) shall apply. See §1.1503(d)-7(c) *Example 38.*

(6) *Reconstituted net operating loss.*—(i) *General rule.*—Except as provided in paragraphs (h)(6)(ii) and (iii) of this section, commencing in the taxable year immediately following the year in which the dual consolidated loss is recaptured, the dual resident corporation, or the domestic owner of the separate unit, that incurred the dual consolidated loss that is recaptured shall be treated as having a net operating loss (reconstituted net operating loss) in an amount equal to the amount actually recaptured under this paragraph (h). If a domestic corporation (transferee) acquires the assets of the dual resident corporation or domestic owner in a transaction described in section 381(a), the preceding sentence shall be applied by treating the transferee as the dual resident corporation or domestic owner, as applicable. In a case to which this paragraph (h)(6) applies, the transferee corporation shall be treated as having a reconstituted net operating loss in an amount equal to the amount actually recaptured under this paragraph (h). In no event, however, shall more than one corporation be treated as having a reconstituted net operating loss as a result of a single dual consolidated loss being recaptured. A reconstituted net operating loss of a domestic owner shall be attributable under §1.1503(d)-5 to the separate unit that incurred the dual consolidated loss that was recaptured. Moreover, a reconstituted net operating loss shall be subject to the domestic use limitation of §1.1503(d)-4(b) (and therefore subject to the limitation under §1.1503(d)-4(c)), without regard to the exceptions contained in paragraphs (b) through (d) of this section (relating to elective agreements in place between the United States and a foreign country, the ability to demonstrate no possibility of a foreign use, and a domestic use election, respectively). The reconstituted net operating loss shall be available only for carryover, under section 172(b), to taxable years following the taxable year of recapture. For purposes of determining the remaining carryover period, the reconstituted net operating loss shall be treated as if it had been recognized in the taxable year in which the dual consoli-

dated loss that is the basis of the recapture amount was incurred. See § 1.1503(d)-7(c) *Examples 36, 38, and 40*.

(ii) *Exception.*—Paragraph (h)(6)(i) of this section shall not apply to the extent the dual consolidated loss that is the basis of the recapture amount would have been eliminated pursuant to § 1.1503(d)-4(d) if no domestic use election had been made for such loss. See § 1.1503(d)-7(c) *Example 40*.

(iii) *Special rule for recapture following multiple-party event exception to a triggering event.*—This paragraph applies to an excepted event described in paragraph (f)(2)(i)(B) of this section that is followed by a subsequent triggering event requiring recapture as described in paragraph (f)(6) of this section. In such a case, the domestic corporation that owns, directly or indirectly, the assets of the dual resident corporation, or the assets of or the interests in a separate unit, immediately following the excepted event shall be treated as if it incurred the dual consolidated loss that is recaptured for purposes of applying paragraph (h)(6)(i) of this section. See § 1.1503(d)-7(c) *Example 36*.

(i) *[Reserved].*

(j) *Termination of domestic use agreement and annual certifications.*—(1) *Rebuttals, exceptions to triggering events, and recapture.*—The domestic use agreement filed with respect to a dual consolidated loss shall terminate prior to the end of the certification period and have no further effect if—

(i) An elector is able to rebut the presumption of a triggering event pursuant to the general rule in paragraph (e)(2)(i) of this section;

(ii) An event described in paragraph (e)(1) of this section is not a triggering event as a result of the application of paragraphs (f)(2)(i) or (ii) (relating to events requiring a new domestic use agreement) of this section; this paragraph (j)(1)(ii) does not, however, apply to terminate the new domestic use agreement filed in connection with the event pursuant to paragraph (f)(2)(iii)(A) of this section. See also paragraph (h)(3)(iv) of this section regarding collection from the original elector and prior subsequent electors in certain cases; or

(iii) A dual consolidated loss is recaptured pursuant to paragraph (h) of this section. See § 1.1503(d)-7(c) *Examples 32* through *34*.

(2) *Termination of ability for foreign use.*—(i) *In general.*—A domestic use agreement filed with respect to a dual consolidated loss shall terminate and have no further effect as of the end of a taxable year if the elector—

(A) Demonstrates, to the satisfaction of the Commissioner, that as of the end of such taxable year no foreign use (as defined in § 1.1503(d)-3) of the dual consolidated loss can occur in any other year by any means; and

(B) Prepares a statement described in paragraph (j)(2)(ii) of this section that is attached to, and filed by the due date (including extensions) of, its U.S. income tax return for such taxable year.

(ii) *Statement.*—The statement described in this paragraph (j)(2)(ii) must be signed under penalties of perjury by the person who signs the return. The statement must be labeled "Termination of Ability for Foreign Use" at the top of the page and must include the following information, in paragraphs labeled to correspond with the following:

(A) A statement that the document is submitted under the provisions of paragraph (j)(2) of this section.

(B) The information required by paragraph (c)(2)(ii) of this section.

(C) A statement of the amount of the dual consolidated loss at issue and the year in which such dual consolidated loss was incurred.

(D) The information described in paragraph (c)(2)(iv) of this section that supports the conclusion that no foreign use can occur as provided in paragraph (j)(2)(i)(A) of this section.

(3) *Agreements filed in connection with stand-alone exception.*—See § 1.1503(d)-3(e)(2)(iii) for the termination of domestic use agreements filed in connection with the stand-alone exception to the mirror legislation rule when a subsequent election is made under paragraph (b) of this section (relating to agreements entered into between the United States and a foreign country). [Reg. § 1.1503(d)-6.]

☐ [*T.D. 9315, 3-16-2007. Amended by T.D. 9896, 4-7-2020.*]

## [Reg. § 1.1503(d)-7]

**§ 1.1503(d)-7. Examples.**—(a) *In general.*—This section provides examples that illustrate the application of §§ 1.1503(d)-1 through 1.1503(d)-6. This section also provides facts that are presumed for such examples.

(b) *Presumed facts for examples.*—For purposes of the examples in this section, unless otherwise indicated, the following facts are presumed:

(1) Each entity has only a single class of equity outstanding, all of which is held by a single owner.

(2) P, a domestic corporation and the common parent of the P consolidated group, owns S, a domestic corporation and a member of the P consolidated group.

(3) DRCX, a domestic corporation, is subject to Country X tax on its worldwide income or on a residence basis, and is a dual resident corporation.

(4) DE1X and DE2X are both Country X entities, subject to Country X tax on their worldwide income or on a residence basis, and disregarded as entities separate from their owners for U.S. tax purposes. DE3Y is a Country Y entity, subject to Country Y tax on its worldwide income or on a residence basis, and disregarded as an entity separate from its owner for U.S. tax purposes. All the interests in DE1X, DE2X, and DE3Y constitute hybrid entity separate units.

(5) FBX is a Country X business operation that, if carried on by a U.S. person, would constitute a foreign branch, as defined in § 1.367(a)-6T(g)(1), and is a Country X foreign branch separate unit.

(6) Neither the assets nor the activities of an entity constitute a foreign branch separate unit.

(7) FSX is a Country X entity that is subject to Country X tax on its worldwide income or on a residence basis and is classified as a foreign corporation for U.S. tax purposes.

(8) The applicable foreign country has a consolidation regime that—

(i) Includes as members of a consolidated group any commonly controlled branches and permanent establishments in such jurisdiction, and entities that are subject to tax in such jurisdiction on their worldwide income or on a residence basis; and

(ii) Allows the losses of members of consolidated groups to offset income of other members.

(9) There is no mirror legislation, within the meaning of § 1.1503(d)-3(e)(1), in the applicable foreign country.

(10) There is no elective agreement described in § 1.1503(d)-6(b) between the United States and the applicable foreign country.

(11) There is no income tax convention between the United States and the applicable foreign country.

(12) If a domestic use election, within the meaning of § 1.1503(d)-6(d), is made, all the necessary filings related to such election are properly completed on a timely basis.

(13) If there is a triggering event requiring recapture of a dual consolidated loss, the amount of recapture is not reduced pursuant to § 1.1503(d)-6(h)(2).

(14) There are no other items of income, gain, deduction, and loss. In addition, the United States and the applicable foreign country recognize the same items of income, gain, deduction, and loss in each taxable year.

(15) All taxpayers use the calendar year as their taxable year.

(c) *Examples.*—The following examples illustrate the application of §§ 1.1503(d)-1 through 1.1503(d)-6:

(1) *Example 1. Separate unit combination rule.* (i) *Facts.* P owns DE3Y which, in turn, owns DE1X. DE1X owns FBX. PRS, an entity treated as a partnership for both U.S. and Country X tax purposes, is owned 50 percent by P and 50 percent by an unrelated foreign person. PRS carries on a business operation in Country X that, if carried on by a U.S. person, would constitute a foreign branch within the meaning of § 1.367(a)-6T(g)(1). In addition, P owns DRCX, a member of the consolidated group of which P is the parent, which carries on business operations in Country X that constitute a foreign branch within the meaning of § 1.367(a)-6T(g)(1). S owns DE2X.

(ii) *Result.* Pursuant to § 1.1503(d)-1(b)(4)(ii), the interest in DE1X, the interest in DE2X, FBX, P's share of the Country X business operations carried on by PRS (which is owned by P indirectly through its interest in PRS), and DRCX's Country X business operations are combined and treated as a single separate unit of the consolidated group of which P is the parent. This is the case regardless of whether the losses of each individual separate unit are made available to offset the income of the other individual separate units under Country X tax laws. Because DRCX is a dual resident corporation, it is not combined and treated as part of this combined separate unit and, as a result, DRCx's income or dual consolidated loss is not taken into account in determining the income or dual consolidated loss of the combined separate unit. In addition, P's interest in DE3Y is not combined and is another separate unit because it is subject to tax in Country Y, rather than Country X.

(2) *Example 2. Definition of a separate unit and application of domestic use limitation—foreign branch separate unit.* (i) *Facts.* P carries on business operations in Country X that constitute a permanent establishment under the U.S.-Country X income tax convention. In year 1,

a loss is attributable to P's Country X permanent establishment, as determined under §1.1503(d)-5.

(ii) *Result.* Under §§1.1503(d)-1(b)(4)(i)(A) and 1.367(a)-6T(g)(1), P's Country X permanent establishment constitutes a foreign branch separate unit. Therefore, the year 1 loss attributable to the foreign branch separate unit constitutes a dual consolidated loss pursuant to §1.1503(d)-1(b)(5)(ii). The dual consolidated loss rules apply to the dual consolidated loss even though there is no affiliate of the foreign branch separate unit in Country X, because it is still possible that all or a portion of the dual consolidated loss can be put to a foreign use. For example, there may be a foreign use with respect to a Country X affiliate acquired in a year subsequent to the year in which the dual consolidated loss was incurred. See §1.1503(d)-6(a)(2). Accordingly, unless an exception under §1.1503(d)-6 applies (such as a domestic use election), the year 1 dual consolidated loss attributable to P's Country X permanent establishment is subject to the domestic use limitation rule of §1.1503(d)-4(b). As a result, pursuant to §1.1503(d)-4(c), the year 1 dual consolidated loss cannot offset income of P that is not attributable to its Country X foreign branch separate unit, nor can it offset income of any other domestic affiliate. The loss can, however, offset income of the Country X foreign branch separate unit, subject to the application of §1.1503(d)-4(c). The result would be the same even if Country X did not have a consolidation regime that includes as members of consolidated groups Country X branches or permanent establishments of nonresident corporations. The dual consolidated loss rules apply even in the absence of a consolidation regime in the foreign country because it is possible that all or a portion of a dual consolidated loss can be put to a foreign use by other means, such as through a sale, merger, or similar transaction. See §1.1503(d)-6(a)(2).

(iii) *Alternative facts.* The facts are the same as in paragraph (c)(2)(i) of this section, except that P's Country X business operations constitute a foreign branch as defined in §1.367(a)-6T(g)(1), but do not constitute a permanent establishment under the U.S.-Country X income tax convention. Although the activities carried on by P in Country X would otherwise constitute a foreign branch separate unit as described in §1.1503(d)-1(b)(4)(i)(A), the exception under §1.1503(d)-1(b)(4)(iii) applies because the activities do not constitute a permanent establishment under the U.S.-Country X income tax convention. Thus, the Country X business operations do not constitute a foreign branch separate unit, and the year 1 loss is not subject to the dual consolidated loss rules. If P instead carried on its Country X business operations through DE1X, then the exception under §1.1503(d)-1(b)(4)(iii) would not apply because P carries on the business operations through a hybrid entity and, as a result, the business operations would constitute a foreign branch separate unit. Thus, in such a case the year 1 loss would be subject to the dual consolidated loss rules.

(3) *Example 3. Domestic use limitation—foreign branch separate unit owned through a partnership.* (i) *Facts.* P and S organize a partnership, PRSX, under the laws of Country X. PRSX is treated as a partnership for both U.S. and Country X tax purposes. PRSX owns FBX. PRSX earns U.S. source income that is unconnected with its FBX branch operations, and such income is not subject to tax by Country X. In addition, such U.S. source income is not attributable to FBX under §1.1503(d)-5.

(ii) *Result.* Under §1.1503(d)-1(b)(4)(i)(A), P's and S's shares of FBX owned indirectly through their interests in PRSX are individual foreign branch separate units. Pursuant to §1.1503(b)-1(b)(4)(ii), these individual separate units are combined and treated as a single separate unit of the consolidated group of which P is the parent. Unless an exception under §1.1503(d)-6 applies, any dual consolidated loss attributable to FBX cannot offset income of P or S (other than income attributable to FBX, subject to the application of §1.1503(d)-4(c)), including their distributive share of the U.S. source income earned through their interests in PRSX, nor can it offset income of any other domestic affiliates.

(4) *Example 4. Definition of a separate unit and domestic use limitation—interest in hybrid entity partnership and indirectly owned foreign branch separate unit.* (i) *Facts.* HPSX is a Country X entity that is subject to Country X tax on its worldwide income. HPSX is classified as a partnership for Federal tax purposes. P, S, and FSX, are the sole partners of HPSX. For U.S. tax purposes, P, S, and FSX each has an equal interest in each item of HPSX's profit or loss. HPSX carries on operations in Country Y that, if carried on by a U.S. person, would constitute a foreign branch within the meaning of §1.367(a)-6T(g)(1).

(ii) *Result.* Under §1.1503(d)-1(b)(4)(i)(B), the partnership interests in HPSX held by P and S are individual hybrid entity separate units. These individual separate units are combined into a single separate unit under §1.1503(d)-1(b)(4)(ii). In addition, P's and S's share of the Country Y operations owned indirectly through their interests in HPSX are individual foreign branch separate units under §1.1503(d)-1(b)(4)(i)(B). These individual separate units are also combined into a single separate unit §1.1503(d)-1(b)(4)(ii). Unless an exception under §1.1503(d)-6 applies, dual consolidated losses

attributable to P's and S's combined interests in HPSX can only be used to offset income attributable to their combined interests in HPSX (other than income attributable to P's and S's combined interests in the Country Y foreign branch separate unit), subject to the application of §1.1503(d)-4(c). Similarly, dual consolidated losses attributable to P's and S's combined interests in the Country Y operations of HPSX can only be used to offset income attributable to their combined interests in such Country Y operations, subject to the application of §1.1503(d)-4(c). Neither FSX's interest in HPSX, nor its share of the Country Y operations owned by HPSX, is a separate unit because FSX is not a domestic corporation.

(5) *Example 5. Foreign use—general rule and de minimis reduction exception.* (i) *Facts.* P owns DE1X. DE1X owns FSX. In year 1, there is a $100x loss attributable to P's interest in DE1X that is a dual consolidated loss. Also in year 1, FSX earns $200x of income. DE1X and FSX file a Country X consolidated tax return. For Country X tax purposes, the year 1 $100x loss of DE1X is used to offset $100x of year 1 income generated by FSX. Under Country X tax law, unused losses are carried forward and available to offset income in subsequent taxable years.

(ii) *Result.* The $100x loss attributable to P's interest in DE1X is available to, and in fact does, offset FSX's income under the laws of Country X. In addition, under U.S. tax principles, such income is considered to be an item of FSX, a foreign corporation. As a result, under §1.1503(d)-3(a), there has been a foreign use of the year 1 dual consolidated loss attributable to P's interest in DE1X. Therefore, P cannot make a domestic use election with respect to the loss as provided under §1.1503(d)-6(d)(2), and such loss will be subject to the domestic use limitation rule of §1.1503(d)-4(b). The result would be the same even if FSX, under Country X tax law, had no income against which the dual consolidated loss of DE1X could be offset (unless FSX's ability to use the loss under Country X tax law requires an election, and no such election is made).

(iii) *Alternative facts.* The facts are the same as in paragraph (c)(5)(i) of this section, except that FSX cannot use the loss of DE1X under Country X tax law without an election, and no such election is made. Pursuant to the exception in §1.1503(d)-3(c)(2), there is no foreign use of the year 1 dual consolidated loss attributable to P's interest in DE1X. In addition, P files a domestic use election with respect to the year 1 dual consolidated loss attributable to its interest in DE1X and, at the beginning of year 3, P sells its interest in DE1X to F, a Country Y entity that is a foreign corporation. The sale of the interest in DE1X to F results in a foreign use triggering event pursuant to §1.1503(d)-6(e)(1)(i) because, immediately after the sale, the loss attributable to the interest in DE1X carries over under Country X law and, therefore, is available under U.S. tax principles to offset income of the owner of the interest in DE1X which, in the hands of F, is not a separate unit. It is also a foreign use because the loss is available under U.S. tax principles to offset the income of F, a foreign corporation. See §1.1503(d)-3(a)(1). Finally, the transfer is a triggering event pursuant to §1.1503(d)-6(e)(1)(iv) and (v).

(iv) *Alternative facts.* The facts are the same as in paragraph (c)(5)(iii) of this section, except that P only sells 5 percent of its interest in DE1X to F. Pursuant to Rev. Rul. 99-5 (1999-1 CB 434), see §601.601(d)(2)(ii)(b) of this chapter, the transaction is treated as if P sold 5 percent of its interest in each of DE1X's assets to F, and then immediately thereafter P and F transferred their interests in the assets of DE1X to a partnership in exchange for an ownership interest therein. The sale of the 5 percent interest in DE1X generally results in a foreign use triggering event because a portion of the dual consolidated loss carries over under Country X tax law and is available under U.S. tax principles to offset income of the owner of the interest in DE1X, a hybrid entity, which in the hands of F is not a separate unit. It is also a foreign use because the loss is available under U.S. tax principles to offset the income of F, a foreign corporation. See §1.1503(d)-3(a)(1). However, pursuant to the exception under §1.1503(d)-3(c)(5) (relating to a de minimis reduction of an interest in a separate unit), such availability does not result in a foreign use. In addition, pursuant to §1.1503(d)-6(f)(1) and (3), the deemed transfers pursuant to Rev. Rul. 99-5 as a result of the sale are not treated as triggering events described in §1.1503(d)-6(e)(1)(iv) or (v).

(6) *Example 6. Foreign use and indirect foreign use—foreign reverse hybrid structure and disregarded payments.* (i) *Facts.* P owns DE1X. DE1X owns 99 percent and S owns 1 percent of FRHX, a Country X partnership that elected to be treated as a corporation for U.S. tax purposes. FRHX conducts a trade or business in Country X. In year 1, DE1X incurs interest expense on a third-party loan, which constitutes a dual consolidated loss attributable to P's interest in DE1X. In year 1, for Country X tax purposes, DE1X takes into account its distributive share of income generated by FRHX and offsets such income with its interest expense.

(ii) *Result.* In year 1, the dual consolidated loss attributable to P's interest in DE1X is available to, and in fact does, offset income recognized in Country X and, under U.S. tax principles, the income is considered to be income of FRHX, a foreign corporation. Accordingly, pursuant to §1.1503(d)-3(a)(1), there is a foreign use of the dual consolidated loss. Therefore, P cannot make a domestic use election with respect to the year 1 dual consolidated loss attributable to its interest in DE1X, as provided under §1.1503(d)-6(d)(2), and such loss will be subject to the domestic use limitation rule of §1.1503(d)-4(b).

(iii) *Alternative facts.* (A) The facts are the same as in paragraph (c)(6)(i) of this section, except as follows. Instead of owning DE1X, P owns DE3Y which, in turn, owns DE1X. In addition, DE3Y, rather than DE1X, is the obligor on the third-party loan and therefore incurs the interest expense on such loan. Finally, DE3Y on-lends the loan proceeds from the third-party loan to DE1X, and DE1X pays interest to DE3Y on such loan that is generally disregarded for U.S. tax purposes.

(B) Pursuant to §1.1503(d)-5(c)(1)(ii), for purposes of calculating income or a dual consolidated loss, DE3Y and DE1X do not take into account interest income or interest expense, respectively, with respect to amounts paid on the disregarded loan from DE3Y to DE1X. As a result, such items neither create a dual consolidated loss with respect to the interest in DE1X, nor do they reduce (or eliminate) the dual consolidated loss attributable to the interest in DE3Y. Thus, in year 1, there is a dual consolidated loss attributable to P's interest in DE3Y, but not to P's indirect interest in DE1X.

(C) In year 1, interest expense paid by DE1X to DE3Y on the disregarded loan is taken into account as a deduction in computing DE1X's taxable income for Country X tax purposes, but does not give rise to a corresponding item of income or gain for U.S. tax purposes (because it is generally disregarded). In addition, such interest has the effect of making an item of deduction or loss composing the dual consolidated loss attributable to P's interest in DE3Y available for a foreign use. This is the case because it may reduce or offset items of deduction or loss composing the dual consolidated loss for foreign tax purposes, and creates another deduction or loss that may reduce or offset income of DE1X for foreign tax purposes that, under U.S. tax principles, is treated as income of FRHX, a foreign corporation. Moreover, because the disregarded item is incurred or taken into account as interest for foreign tax purposes, it is deemed to have been incurred or taken into account with a principal purpose of avoiding the provisions of section 1503(d). Accordingly, there is an indirect foreign use of the year 1 dual consolidated loss attributable to P's interest in DE3Y, and P cannot make a domestic use election with respect to such loss as provided under §1.1503(d)-6(d)(2). Thus, the loss will be subject to the domestic use limitation rule of §1.1503(d)-4(b).

(7) *Example 7. Indirect foreign use—hybrid instrument.* (i) *Facts.* P owns DE1X which, in turn, owns FSX. DE1X borrows cash from an unrelated lender and transfers the cash to FSX in exchange for an instrument (hybrid instrument). The hybrid instrument is treated as equity for U.S. tax purposes and debt for Country X tax purposes. Interest expense on the loan from the unrelated lender results in a dual consolidated loss being attributable to P's interest in DE1X in year 1. DE1X does not elect under Country X law to consolidate with FSX. In year 1, FSX distributes its stock as a payment on the hybrid instrument to DE1X. For U.S. tax purposes, such payment is excluded from P's gross income under section 305. However, for Country X tax purposes, such payment is treated as interest and gives rise to a deduction taken into account in computing FSX's Country X tax liability; the payment also gives rise to interest income to DE1X for Country X tax purposes.

(ii) *Result.* The payment on the hybrid instrument does not give rise to an item of income or gain for U.S. tax purposes and therefore does not reduce (or eliminate) the dual consolidated loss attributable to P's interest in DE1X. In addition, such payment is taken into account as a deduction in computing FSX's taxable income for Country X tax purposes. Moreover, such payment has the effect of making an item of deduction or loss composing the dual consolidated loss attributable to P's interest in DE1X available for a foreign use. This is the case because it may reduce or offset items of deduction or loss composing the dual consolidated loss for foreign tax purposes, and creates a deduction that reduces or offsets income of FSX for foreign tax purposes that, under U.S. tax principles, is income of a foreign corporation. Further, because the item is incurred, or taken into account, using an instrument that is treated as equity for U.S. tax purposes and debt for foreign tax purposes, it is deemed to have been engaged in with the principal purpose of avoiding the provisions of section 1503(d). As a result, there has been an indirect foreign use of the year 1 dual consolidated loss, and P cannot make a domestic use election with respect to such loss, as provided under §1.1503(d)-6(d)(2). Thus, the year 1 dual consolidated loss will be subject to the domestic use limitation rule of §1.1503(d)-4(b).

(8) *Example 8. No indirect foreign use—transaction entered into in the ordinary course of business.* (i) *Facts.* P owns DE1X and FBY. FBY is a foreign branch separate unit located in Country Y. DE1X owns FBX and FSX. P's interest in DE1X and FBX are combined and treated as a single separate unit (Country X separate unit) pursuant to §1.1503(d)-1(b)(4)(ii). Under Country X tax laws, DE1X elects to consolidate with FSX. FBY engages in the business of providing services and, in connection with its ordinary course of business, provides services to unrelated third parties and to DE1X. As compensation for services, DE1X makes a payment to FBY. Under Country X tax law, the payment is deductible. However, the payment is generally disregarded for U.S. tax purposes and, pursuant to §1.1503(d)-5(c)(1)(ii), is not taken into account in calculating the income or dual consolidated loss attributable to the Country X separate unit or FBY. In year 1, the Country X separate unit and FBY each has a dual consolidated loss. The dual consolidated loss attributable to the Country X separate unit is subject to the domestic use limitation under §1.1503(d)-4(b) because DE1X and FSX elect to consolidate and, as a result, the dual consolidated loss is put to a foreign use.

(ii) *Result.* The payment made by DE1X to FBY in connection with the performance of services is taken into account as a deduction in computing DE1X's taxable income for Country X tax purposes, but does not give rise to an item of income or gain for U.S. tax purposes. In addition, such payment has the effect of making an item of deduction or loss composing the dual consolidated loss attributable to FBY available for a foreign use. This is the case because it may reduce or offset items of deduction or loss composing the dual consolidated loss of FBY for foreign tax purposes, and creates another deduction that reduces or offsets income of FSX for foreign tax purposes (because DE1X and FSX elect to file a consolidated return) that, under U.S. tax principles, is income of a foreign corporation. However, the transaction between DE1X and FBY was entered into in the ordinary course of FBY's trade or business. As a result, if P can demonstrate to the satisfaction of the Commissioner that the transaction was not entered into with a principal purpose of avoiding the provisions of section 1503(d), FBY's year 1 dual consolidated loss will not be treated as having been made available for an indirect foreign use. In such a case, P would be entitled to make a domestic use election with respect to such loss.

(9) *Example 9. Foreign use—dual resident corporation with hybrid entity joint venture.* (i) *Facts.* P owns DRCX, a member of the P consolidated group. DRCX owns 80 percent of HPSX, a Country X entity that is subject to Country X tax on its worldwide income. HPSX is classified as a partnership for U.S. tax purposes. FSX owns the remaining 20 percent of HPSX. In year 1, DRCX generates a $100x net operating loss (without regard to items attributable to DRCX's interest in HPSX). Also in year 1, HPSX generates $100x of income, $80x of which is attributable to DRCX's interest in HPSX. DRCX and HPSX file a consolidated tax return for Country X tax purposes, and HPSX offsets its $100x of income with the $100x loss generated by DRCX.

(ii) *Result.* DRCX and its interest in HPSX are not combined because DRCX is a dual resident corporation and the combination rule under §1.1503(d)-1(b)(4)(ii) only applies to separate units. The $100x year 1 net operating loss incurred by DRCX (without regard to items attributable to DRCX's interest in HPSX) is a dual consolidated loss. In addition, HPSX is a hybrid entity and DRCX's interest in HPSX is a hybrid entity separate unit; however, there is no dual consolidated loss attributable to such separate unit in year 1 (instead, there is $80x of income attributable to such separate unit). DRCX's year 1 dual consolidated loss offsets $100x of income for Country X purposes, and $20x of such income is, under U.S. tax principles, income of FSX, which owns an interest in HPSX that is not a separate unit (in addition, FSX is a foreign corporation). As a result, pursuant to §1.1503(d)-3(a), there is a foreign use of the year 1 dual consolidated loss of DRCX, and P cannot make a domestic use election with respect to such loss pursuant to §1.1503(d)-6(d)(2). Therefore, such loss will be subject to the domestic use limitation rule of §1.1503(d)-4(b). The result would be the same even if HPSX, under Country X laws, had no income against which the dual consolidated loss could be offset (unless the ability to use the loss under Country X laws required an election, and no such election is made).

(10) *Example 10. Foreign use—foreign parent corporation.* (i) *Facts.* F1 and F2, nonresident alien individuals, each owns 50 percent of FPX, a Country X entity that is subject to Country X tax on its worldwide income. FPX is classified as a foreign corporation for U.S. tax purposes. FPX owns DRCX. DRCX is the parent of a consolidated group that includes as a member DS, a domestic corporation. In year 1, DRCX incurs a dual consolidated loss of $100x and, for Country X tax purposes, FPX generates $100x of income. In year 1, FPX elects to consolidate with DRCX for Country X tax purposes, and the $100x year 1 loss of DRCX is used to offset the income of FPX under the laws of Country X. For U.S. tax purposes, the items of FPX do not constitute items of income in year 1.

(ii) *Result.* The year 1 dual consolidated loss of DRCX offsets the income of FPX under the laws of Country X. Pursuant to §1.1503(d)-3(a), the offset constitutes a foreign use because the items constituting such income are considered under U.S. tax principles to be items of a foreign corporation. This is the case even though the United States does not recognize such items as income in year 1.

Therefore, DRCX cannot make a domestic use election with respect to its year 1 dual consolidated loss pursuant to §1.1503(d)-6(d)(2). As a result, such loss will be subject to the domestic use limitation rule of §1.1503(d)-4(b).

(iii) *Alternative facts.* The facts are the same as in paragraph (c)(10)(i) of this section, except that FPX is classified as a partnership for U.S. tax purposes. The result would be the same as in paragraph (c)(10)(ii) of this section, because the offset of the income generated by FPX is a foreign use pursuant to §1.1503(d)-3(a). This is the case because the items constituting such income are considered under U.S. tax principles to be items of F1 and F2, the owners of interests in FPX (a hybrid entity), that are not separate units. Moreover, the result would be the same if F1 and F2 owned their interests in FPX indirectly through another partnership.

(11) *Example 11. No foreign use—absence of foreign loss allocation rules.* (i) *Facts.* P owns DE1X and DRCX. DRCX is a member of the P consolidated group and owns FSX. DE1X owns FBX. P's interest in DE1X and P's indirect interest in FBX are individual separate units that are combined into a single separate unit (Country X separate unit) pursuant to §1.1503(d)-1(b)(4)(ii). In year 1, DRCX incurs a $200x net operating loss and $200x of income is attributable to P's Country X separate unit. The $200x net operating loss incurred by DRCX is a dual consolidated loss. FSX also earns $200x of income in year 1. DRCX, DE1X, and FSX file a Country X consolidated tax return. However, Country X has no applicable rules for determining which income is offset by DRCX's year 1 $200x loss.

(ii) *Result.* Under §1.1503(d)-3(c)(3), DRCX's $200x loss shall be treated as having been made available to offset the $200x of income attributable to P's Country X separate unit. P's Country X separate unit is not, under U.S. tax principles, a foreign corporation, and there is no interest in DE1X (which is a hybrid entity) that is not a separate unit. As a result, DRCX's loss being made available to offset the income attributable to P's Country X separate unit is not considered a foreign use of such loss. Therefore, P can make a domestic use election with respect to DRCX's year 1 dual consolidated loss.

(iii) *Alternative facts.* The facts are the same as in paragraph (c)(11)(i) of this section, except that in year 1 only $150x of income is attributable to P's Country X separate unit. Because only $150x of income is attributed to P's Country X separate unit, $50x of DRCX's year 1 dual consolidated loss is treated as being made available to offset the income of FSX, a foreign corporation, and therefore constitutes a foreign use. As a result, DRCX cannot make a domestic use election with respect to its year 1 dual consolidated loss pursuant to §1.1503(d)-6(d)(2), and such loss will be subject to the domestic use limitation rule of §1.1503(d)-4(b).

(12) *Example 12. No foreign use—absence of foreign loss usage ordering rules.* (i) *Facts.* (A) P owns DRCX, a member of the P consolidated group. DRCX owns FSX. Under the Country X consolidation regime, a consolidated group may elect in any given year to use all or a portion of the losses of one consolidated group member to offset income of other consolidated group members. If no such election is made in a year in which losses are generated by a consolidated member, such losses carry forward and are available, at the election of the consolidated group, to offset income of consolidated group members in subsequent taxable years. Country X law does not provide ordering rules for determining when a loss from a particular taxable year is used because, under Country X law, losses never expire. In addition, Country X law does not provide ordering rules for determining when a particular type of loss (for example, capital or ordinary) is used.

(B) In year 1, DRCX incurs a capital loss of $80x which, under §1.1503(d)-5(b)(2), is not a dual consolidated loss. DRCX also incurs a net operating loss of $80x in year 1 which is a dual consolidated loss. FSX generates $60x of capital gain in year 1 which, for Country X purposes, can be offset by capital losses and net operating losses. Under the laws of Country X, DRCX elects to use $60x of its total year 1 loss of $160x to offset the $60x of capital gain generated by FSX in year 1; the remaining $100x of year 1 loss carries forward. In both year 2 and year 3, DRCX incurs a net operating loss of $100x, while FSX incurs no income or loss in years 2 and 3. DRCX's $100x losses incurred in year 2 and year 3 are dual consolidated losses. Because DRCX does not elect under the laws of Country X to use all or a portion of its year 2 or year 3 net operating losses of $100x to offset the income of other members of the Country X consolidated group, P is permitted to make (and in fact does make) a domestic use election with respect to both the year 2 and year 3 dual consolidated losses of DRCX. In year 4, DRCX has a net operating loss of $10x and FSX generates $125x of income. Country X law permits, upon an election, FSX's $125x of income generated in year 4 to be offset by losses (including carryover losses from prior years) of other group members. Accordingly, in year 4, DRCX elects to use $125x of its accumulated losses to offset the $125x of year 4 income generated by FSX.

(ii) *Result.* (A) Under the ordering rules of §1.1503(d)-3(d)(3), a pro rata amount of DRCX's year 1 net operating loss ($30x) and

capital loss ($30x) is considered to be used to offset FSX's year 1 $60x capital gain. As a result, P cannot make a domestic use election with respect to DRCX's year 1 $80x dual consolidated loss because a portion of such loss is put to a foreign use.

(B) DRCX's $10x year 4 net operating loss is also a dual consolidated loss. Under the ordering rules of §1.1503(d)-3(d)(1), such loss is considered to be used to offset $10x of FSX's year 4 $125x of income. Consequently, P cannot make a domestic use election with respect to such loss. Under the ordering rules of §1.1503(d)-3(d)(2), $50x of capital loss carryover and $50x of ordinary loss from year 1 will be considered to offset $100x of FSX's year 4 income because the income is first deemed to have been offset by losses the use of which would not constitute a triggering event that would result in the recapture of a dual consolidated loss. The remaining $15x of FSX's year 4 income is considered to be offset by losses from year 3 because it is the most recent taxable year from which a loss may be carried forward. Thus, a portion of the year 3 dual consolidated loss has been put to a foreign use and the entire year 3 dual consolidated loss is recaptured. However, none of DRCX's $100x year 2 net operating loss will be deemed to offset FSX's year 4 income. As a result, DRCX's year 2 dual consolidated loss will not be recaptured.

(13) *Example 13. Exception to foreign use through partnership interest.* (i) *Facts.* (A) P owns 80 percent of HPSX, a Country X entity subject to Country X tax on its worldwide income. FSZ, an unrelated foreign corporation, owns the remaining 20 percent of HPSX. HPSX is classified as a partnership for Federal tax purposes and carries on operations in Country X that, if carried on by a U.S. person, would constitute a foreign branch within the meaning of §1.367(a)-6T(g)(1). P's interest in HPSX and P's indirect interest in the Country X branch are individual separate units that are combined into a single separate unit (Country X separate unit) pursuant to §1.1503(d)-1(b)(4)(ii).

(B) In year 1, HPSX incurs a loss of $100x, $80x of which is attributable to P's Country X separate unit. The $80x of loss attributable to P's Country X separate unit constitutes a dual consolidated loss and P makes a domestic use election with respect to such loss. In year 2, HPSX generates $50x of income, $40x of which is attributable to P's interest in the Country X separate unit. Under Country X income tax laws, the $100x of year 1 loss incurred by HPSX is carried forward and offsets the $50x of income generated by HPSX in year 2; the remaining $50x of loss is carried forward and is available to offset income generated by HPSX in subsequent years. P and FSZ maintain their ownership interests in HPSX throughout years 1 and 2.

(ii) *Result.* In year 2, under the laws of Country X, the $100x of year 1 loss, which includes the $80x dual consolidated loss attributable to P's Country X separate unit, is made available to offset income of HPSX. Such income is attributable to P's interest in HPSX, which is a separate unit. Such income also is income of FSZ, a foreign corporation that is an owner of an interest in HPSX, which is not a separate unit. However, pursuant to §1.1503(d)-3(c)(4), there is no foreign use of the year 1 dual consolidated loss in year 2. This is the case because P's interest in HPSX as of the end of year 1 has not been reduced by more than a de minimis amount, and the portion of the $80x dual consolidated loss was made available for a foreign use in year 2 solely as a result of FSZ's ownership in HPSX and the allocation or carry forward of the dual consolidated loss as a result of such ownership.

(iii) *Alternative facts.* The facts are the same as in paragraph (c)(13)(i) of this section, except that P also owns FSX. In addition, FSX and HPSX elect to file a consolidated return under Country X law. The exception to foreign use under §1.1503(d)-3(c)(4) does not apply because there is a foreign use other than by reason of the dual consolidated loss being made available as a result of FSZ's ownership in HPSX and the allocation or carry forward of the dual consolidated loss as a result of such ownership. That is, the exception does not apply because there is also a foreign use of the dual consolidated loss as a result of FSX and HPSX filing a consolidated return under Country X law.

(iv) *Alternative facts.* The facts are the same as in paragraph (c)(13)(i) of this section, except that at the end of year 2, FSZ contributes cash to HPSX in exchange for additional equity of HPSX. As a result of the contribution, FSZ's interest in HPSX increases from 20 percent to 30 percent, and P's interest in HPSX decreases from 80 percent to 70 percent. P's interest in HPSX is reduced within a single 12-month period by 12.5 percent (10/80), as compared to P's interest in HPSX as of the beginning of such 12-month period. Accordingly, pursuant to §1.1503(d)-3(c)(4)(iii), the exception to foreign use provided under §1.1503(d)-3(c)(4)(i) does not apply. Therefore, in year 2 there is a foreign use of the $80x year 1 dual consolidated loss attributable to P's Country X separate unit. Such foreign use constitutes a triggering event in year 2 and the $80x year 1 dual consolidated loss is recaptured. Alternatively, if FSZ were a domestic corporation, there would not be a foreign use of the $80x year 1 dual consolidated loss because the loss would not be available to offset income that, under U.S. tax principles, is income of a foreign corporation or a direct or indirect owner of an interest in a hybrid entity that is not a separate unit.

(14) *Example 14. Exception to foreign use through partnership interest—combination rule.* (i) *Facts.* (A) P and FSX form PRSX. P and FSX each own 50 percent of PRSX throughout years 1 and 2. PRSX is treated as a partnership for both U.S. and Country X tax purposes. PRSX owns DEY. DEY is a Country Y entity subject to Country Y tax on its worldwide income and disregarded as an entity separate from its owner for U.S. tax purposes. DEY conducts business operations in Country Y that, if carried on by a U.S. person, would constitute a foreign branch as defined in §1.367(a)-6T(g)(1). P's interest in the Country Y operations conducted by DEY is an individual foreign branch separate unit. P's interest in DEY, owned indirectly through PRSX, is a hybrid entity individual separate unit. P also owns FBY, a Country Y foreign branch individual separate unit. Under §1.1503(d)-1(b)(4)(ii), FBY and P's indirect interests in DEY and DEY's Country Y business operations are treated as a combined separate unit (Country Y separate unit).

(B) In year 1, there is a $100x loss attributable to the Country Y business operations conducted by DEY. Thus, there is a $50x loss attributable to P's interest in DEY's Country Y business operations in year 1. Also in year 1, there is a $200x loss attributable to FBY. No income or loss is attributable to P's interest in DEY in year 1. Under §1.1503(d)-5(c)(4)(ii), the dual consolidated loss attributable to P's combined Country Y separate unit is $250x ($50x loss attributable to P's indirect interest in DEY's Country Y operations, plus $200x loss attributable to FBY). In year 2, neither DEY nor DEY's Country Y operations generates income or loss. Under Country Y law, the $100x of year 1 loss incurred by DEY is carried forward and is available to offset income of DEY in year 2.

(ii) *Result.* As a result of the carryover of the year 1 $100x loss (which includes $50x of the year 1 dual consolidated loss) under Country Y law, a portion of such loss will be available to offset income of DEY that is attributable to P's interest in DEY owned indirectly through PRSX. A portion of such loss will also be available to offset income of DEY that is attributable to FSX's indirect ownership of DEY. Accordingly, under §1.1503(d)-3(a), there would be a foreign use of a portion of P's $250x year 1 dual consolidated loss because it is available to offset an item of income of the owner of an interest in a hybrid entity, which is not a separate unit (there would also be a foreign use in this case because FSX is a foreign corporation). However, there has not been a reduction of P's interest in DEY, DEY has not consolidated under the laws of Country Y, and there has not been any other foreign use of the dual consolidated losses. As a result, no foreign use occurs as a result of the carryforward pursuant to §1.1503(d)-3(c)(4)(i) and (ii).

(15) *Example 15. No foreign use—asset basis carryover exception.* (i) *Facts.* P owns FBX and FSX. In year 1, there is a dual consolidated loss attributable to FBX. P's items of income, gain, deduction, and loss that are taken into account in calculating FBX's dual consolidated loss include depreciation deductions attributable to FBX's assets. P makes a domestic use election under §1.1503(d)-6(d) with respect to the year 1 dual consolidated loss of FBX. At the end of year 2, P contributes a portion of FBX's assets to FSX, in exchange for stock in FSX. The aggregate adjusted basis of the assets transferred by P to FSX is less than 10 percent of the aggregate adjusted basis of all of FBX's assets held at the beginning of year 2. In addition, no other assets of FBX are transferred during the certification period. Under Country X law, FSX's basis in the transferred assets is determined by reference to P's basis in such assets. In addition, under Country X law, a portion of the depreciation deductions that were taken into account in year 1 for U.S. tax purposes, are taken into account in year 2 for Country X tax purposes.

(ii) *Result.* As a result of the transfer of assets from P to FSX, a portion of the year 1 dual consolidated loss is available for a foreign use. This is the case because a portion of the basis in FBX's assets, which gave rise to depreciation deductions that were taken into account in computing the year 1 dual consolidated loss, will give rise to a depreciation deduction under Country X laws that will be available, under U.S. tax principles, to offset the income of FSX, a foreign corporation, in year 2. However, the aggregate adjusted basis of all the assets transferred by P to FSX, within the 12-month period ending at the end of year 2, is less than 10 percent of the aggregate adjusted basis of all of FBX's assets at the beginning of such 12-month period. Moreover, the aggregate adjusted basis of the assets transferred by P to FSX at any time during the certification period is less than 30 percent of the aggregate adjusted basis of FBX's assets held at the end of year 1. In addition, the item of deduction giving rise to the foreign use is being made available solely as a result of the adjusted basis of the transferred assets being determined in whole, or in part, by reference to the adjusted basis of such transferred assets in the hands of FBX. As a result, this transfer will not result in a foreign use pursuant to §1.1503(d)-3(c)(6).

(16) *Example 16. No foreign use—liability assumption exception.* (i) *Facts.* P owns FBX. In year 1, there is a dual consolidated loss

attributable to FBX for which P makes a domestic use election under §1.1503(d)-6(d). The dual consolidated loss includes a deduction for salary expense that was deductible for U.S. tax purposes at the end of year 1, even though it was not paid until year 2. The deduction was incurred in the ordinary course of FBX's trade or business. During year 2, and before the accrued salary expense liability was paid, P sells all the assets of FBX to FSX in exchange for cash and FSX's assumption of the liabilities of the FBX trade or business, including the obligation to pay the accrued salary expense. Under Country X law, the accrued salary expense of FBX is deductible, and is taken into account for purposes of computing the taxable income of FBX, when paid. FBX pays the accrued salary expense after the sale of FBX to FSX.

(ii) *Result.* (A) As a result of FSX's assumption of the FBX liabilities, including the accrued salary expense, a portion of the dual consolidated loss is available for a foreign use in year 2. This is the case because the deduction that was taken into account in year 1 in computing the dual consolidated loss under U.S. tax principles will, under Country X tax law, be taken into account and will be available to offset the income of FSX, a foreign corporation, in year 2. However, because this item of expense is made available solely as a result of the assumption of a liability of FBX, and such liability was incurred in the ordinary course of FBX's trade or business, there will not be a foreign use of the year 1 dual consolidated loss pursuant to §1.1503(d)-3(c)(7).

(B) The transfer of all the assets of FBX to FSX is a triggering event under §1.1503(d)-6(e)(1)(iv), unless P can rebut the triggering event under §1.1503(d)-6(e)(2). For purposes of determining whether, under §1.1503(d)-6(e)(2)(ii), the transfer of assets resulted in a carryover under foreign law of FBX's losses, expenses, or deductions, the exception to foreign use for the assumption of liabilities is taken into account. However, the other exceptions to foreign use do not apply for this purpose (or for purposes of demonstrating that no foreign use of a dual consolidated loss can occur in any other year under §1.1503(d)-6(c), (e)(2)(i) or (j)(2)). See §1.1503(d)-3(c)(1). Provided the other requirements of §1.1503(d)-6(e)(2)(ii) and (iii) are satisfied, P may be able to rebut the occurrence of a triggering event upon the transfer of FBX's assets to FSX.

(17) *Example 17. Mirror legislation rule—dual resident corporation and hybrid entity separate unit.* (i) *Facts.* P owns DRCX, a member of the P consolidated group. DRCX owns FSX. In year 1, DRCX incurs a $100x net operating loss that is a dual consolidated loss. To prevent corporations like DRCX from offsetting losses both against income of affiliates in Country X and against income of foreign affiliates under the tax laws of another country, Country X mirror legislation prevents a corporation that is subject to the income tax of another country on its worldwide income or on a residence basis from using the Country X form of consolidation. Accordingly, the Country X mirror legislation prevents the loss of DRCX from being made available to offset income of FSX.

(ii) *Result.* Under §1.1503(d)-3(e), because the losses of DRCX are subject to Country X's mirror legislation, there is a deemed foreign use of DRCX's year 1 dual consolidated loss. The stand-alone exception to the mirror rule in §1.1503(d)-3(e)(2) does not apply because, absent the mirror legislation, DRCX's year 1 dual consolidated loss would be available for a foreign use (as defined in §1.1503(d)-3), without regard to whether such availability is limited by election or similar procedure. That is, absent the mirror legislation, all or a portion of the dual consolidated loss would be available to offset the income of FSX under the Country X consolidation regime. This is the case even if Country X did not recognize DRCX as having a loss in year 1. Therefore, P may not make a domestic use election with respect to DRCX's year 1 dual consolidated loss pursuant to §1.1503(d)-6(d)(2).

(iii) *Alternative facts.* The facts are the same as in paragraph (c)(17)(i) of this section, except that P owns DE1X (rather than DRCX) and, in year 1, there is a $100 dual consolidated loss attributable to P's interest in DE1X (rather than of DRCX). The Country X mirror legislation only applies to Country X dual resident corporations and, therefore, does not apply to losses attributable to P's interest in DE1X. As a result, the mirror legislation rule under §1.1503(d)-3(e) would not deny the opportunity of such loss from being put to a foreign use (for example, by offsetting the income of FSX through the Country X consolidation regime). Therefore, a domestic use election can be made with respect to the dual consolidated loss (provided the conditions for such an election are otherwise satisfied).

(18) *Example 18. Mirror legislation rule—standalone foreign branch separate unit.* (i) *Facts.* P owns FBX. In year 1, there is a $100x dual consolidated loss attributable to FBX. Country X enacted mirror legislation to prevent Country X branches and permanent establishments of nonresident corporations from offsetting losses both against income of Country X affiliates and against other income of its owner (or foreign affiliates thereof) under the tax laws of another country. The Country X mirror legislation prevents a Country X branch or permanent establishment of a nonresident corporation from offset-

ting its losses against the income of Country X affiliates if such losses may be deductible against income (other than income of the Country X branch or permanent establishment) under the laws of another country.

(ii) *Result*. In general, under § 1.1503(d)-3(e), because the losses of FBX are subject to Country X's mirror legislation, there is a deemed foreign use of FBX's year 1 dual consolidated loss. However, in the absence of the Country X mirror legislation, no item of deduction or loss composing FBX's year 1 dual consolidated loss would be available in the year incurred for a foreign use (as defined in § 1.1503(d)-3), without regard to whether such availability is limited by election or otherwise. This is the case because there is no Country X entity through which the dual consolidated loss could be put to a foreign use (absent a sale, merger, or similar transaction involving FBX). As a result, the stand-alone exception in § 1.1503(d)-3(e)(2) may apply, provided P complies with the requirements of § 1.1503(d)-3(e)(2)(ii). Accordingly, P may make a domestic use election with respect to the year 1 dual consolidated loss of FBX pursuant to § 1.1503(d)-6(d). If, however, any item of the dual consolidated loss would otherwise be available for a foreign use during the certification period (for example, as a result of P acquiring a foreign corporation that is organized under the laws of Country X such that losses of FBX could be put to a foreign use through consolidation or similar means), then such loss would be recaptured pursuant to § 1.1503(d)-6(e)(1)(ix).

(iii) *Alternative facts*. The facts are the same as in paragraph (c)(18)(i) of this section, except that the Country X mirror legislation operates in a manner similar to the rules under section 1503(d). That is, it allows the taxpayer to elect to use the loss to either offset income of an affiliate in Country X, or income of an affiliate (or other income of the owner of the Country X branch or permanent establishment) in the other country, but not both. Because the Country X mirror legislation permits the taxpayer to choose to put the dual consolidated loss to a foreign use, it does not deny the opportunity to put the loss to a foreign use. Therefore, there is no deemed foreign use of the dual consolidated loss pursuant to § 1.1503(d)-4(e) and a domestic use election can be made for such loss.

(19) *Example 19. Application of mirror legislation rule to combined separate unit*. (i) *Facts*. P owns FBX, FSX, and DE1X. In year 1, there is a $50x dual consolidated loss attributable to FBX and $10x of income attributable to P's interest in DE1X. FSX has income of $100x. Pursuant to § 1.1503(d)-1(b)(4)(ii), FBX and P's interest in DE1X are combined and treated as a single separate unit (Country X separate unit) which has a year 1 dual consolidated loss of $40x. Country X enacted mirror legislation to prevent Country X branches or permanent establishments of nonresident corporations from offsetting losses both against income of Country X affiliates and against other income of its owner (or foreign affiliates thereof) under the tax laws of another country. The Country X mirror legislation prevents a Country X branch or permanent establishment of a nonresident corporation from offsetting its losses against the income of Country X affiliates if such losses may be deductible against income (other than income of the Country X branch or permanent establishment) under the laws of another country. However, the United States and Country X have entered into an agreement described in § 1.1503(d)-6(b) pursuant to the U.S.-Country X income tax convention (mirror agreement). The mirror agreement applies to Country X foreign branch separate units of domestic corporations, but not to Country X hybrid entity separate units. The mirror agreement provides that neither the Country X mirror legislation nor the mirror legislation rule under § 1.1503(d)-3(e) will apply to losses attributable to Country X foreign branch separate units, provided certain conditions and reporting requirements are satisfied (including a domestic use election, if the loss is to be used to offset income of a domestic affiliate). Thus, losses attributable to Country X foreign branch separate units can, subject to the requirements of the mirror agreement, be used to offset income of a domestic affiliate or a Country X affiliate (but not both).

(ii) *Result*. The Country X mirror legislation only applies to Country X foreign branch separate units and does not apply to hybrid entity separate units. In addition, if P complies with the terms and conditions of the mirror agreement, the Country X mirror legislation would not apply to FBX. As a result, the income tax laws of Country X would not deny the opportunity of a loss of either individual separate unit that composes P's combined Country X separate unit from being put to a foreign use. Therefore, notwithstanding § 1.1503(d)-3(e), a domestic use election can be made with respect to the dual consolidated loss attributable to P's Country X separate unit, provided the terms and conditions of the mirror agreement are satisfied. See § 1.1503(d)-6(b)(2).

(iii) *Alternative facts*. The facts are the same as in paragraph (c)(19)(i) of this section, except that the Country X mirror legislation also applies to losses attributable to DE1X, but the mirror agreement does not apply to such losses. The mirror legislation rule would apply with respect to P's interest in DE1X and, as a result, there is a deemed foreign use of the dual consolidated loss attributable to the Country X separate unit and a domestic use election cannot be made

for such loss. This is the case even though, pursuant to § 1.1503(d)-5(c)(4)(ii)(A), P's interest in DE1X (which is subject to the Country X mirror legislation) does not, as an individual separate unit, have a dual consolidated loss in year 1. Further, the stand-alone exception to the mirror legislation rule in § 1.1503(d)-3(e)(2) does not apply because, absent the mirror legislation, the Country X combined separate unit's dual consolidated loss would be available in the year incurred for a foreign use (as defined in § 1.1503(d)-3) because it could be used to offset income of FSX under the Country X consolidation regime. This is the case even if Country X requires an election to consolidate and no such election is made. The result would be the same even if Country X did not recognize DE1X as having a loss.

(20) *Example 20. Dual consolidated loss limitation after section 381 transaction—disposition of assets and subsequent liquidation of dual resident corporation*. (i) *Facts*. P owns DRCX, a member of the P consolidated group. In year 1, DRCX incurs a dual consolidated loss and P does not make a domestic use election with respect to such loss. Under § 1.1503(d)-4(b), DRCX's year 1 dual consolidated loss is subject to the limitations under § 1.1503(d)-4(c) and, therefore, may not be used to offset the income of P or S (or any other domestic affiliate) on the group's U.S. income tax return. At the beginning of year 2, DRCX sells all of its assets for cash and distributes the cash to P pursuant to a liquidation that qualifies under section 332.

(ii) *Result*. In general, under section 381, P would succeed to, and be permitted to use, DRCX's net operating loss carryover. However, § 1.1503(d)-4(d)(1)(i) prohibits the dual consolidated loss of DRCX from carrying over to P. Therefore, DRCX's year 1 net operating loss carryover is eliminated.

(21) *Example 21. Dual consolidated loss limitation applied to a separate unit transferred in a section 381 transaction*. (i) *Facts*. S owns DE1X which, in turn, owns FBX. S's interest in DE1X and its indirect interest in FBX are combined and treated as a single separate unit (Country X separate unit) pursuant to § 1.1503(d)-1(b)(4)(ii). In year 1, a dual consolidated loss is attributable to the Country X separate unit, and P does not make a domestic use election with respect to such loss. Under § 1.1503(d)-4(b), the year 1 dual consolidated loss attributable to the Country X separate unit may not be used to offset the income of P or S (other than income attributable to the Country X separate unit, subject to the application of § 1.1503(d)-4(c)) on the group's consolidated U.S. income tax return (nor may it be used to offset the income of any other domestic affiliates). At the beginning of year 2, S transfers its entire interest in DE1X, and thus its entire indirect interest in FBX, to FSX in a transaction described in section 381.

(ii) *Result*. Section 1.1503(d)-4(d)(1)(ii) provides that the dual consolidated loss attributable to a separate unit that is subject to the domestic use limitation of § 1.1503(d)-4(b) is eliminated if the separate unit ceases to be a separate unit of its affiliated domestic owner and all other members of the affiliated domestic owner's separate group. As a result of the transfer of the Country X separate unit to FSx, the Country X separate unit ceases to be a separate unit of S, and is not a separate unit of any other member of the P consolidated group. In addition, the exceptions in § 1.1503(d)-4(d)(2)(iii) do not apply because FSX is not a domestic corporation. Thus, the year 1 dual consolidated loss attributable to the Country X separate unit is eliminated.

(iii) *Alternative facts*. Assume the same facts as in paragraph (c)(21)(i) of this section, except S transfers its assets to DC, a domestic corporation that is not a member of the P consolidated group, in a transaction described in section 381(a). Immediately after the transaction, the Country X separate unit is a separate unit of DC. Under § 1.1503(d)-4(d)(1)(ii), the year 1 dual consolidated loss of the Country X separate unit would be eliminated because it ceases to be a separate unit of S, and is not a separate unit of any other member of the P consolidated group. However, because the transferee is a domestic corporation and the Country X separate unit is a separate unit in the hands of DC immediately after the transaction, the exception under § 1.1503(d)-4(d)(2)(iii)(A) applies. As a result, the year 1 dual consolidated loss of the Country X separate unit is not eliminated and any income generated by DC that is attributable to the Country X separate unit following the transfer may be offset by the carryover dual consolidated losses attributable to the Country X separate unit, subject to the limitations of § 1.1503(d)-4(b) and (c) applied as if DC generated the dual consolidated loss and such loss was attributable to the Country X separate unit.

(iv) *Alternative facts*. Assume the same facts as in paragraph (c)(21)(iii) of this section, except that P owns DE2X and the interest in DE2X is combined with and therefore included in the Country X separate unit. In addition, a portion of the dual consolidated loss of the Country X separate unit is attributable to P's interest in DE2X. Pursuant to § 1.1503(d)-4(d)(2)(iii)(A), the result would be the same as in paragraph (iii) of this *Example 21*, with respect to the portion of the dual consolidated loss attributable to the combined separate unit that is succeeded to and taken into account by DC pursuant to section 381. The portion of the dual consolidated loss attributable to

P's interest in DE2X, however, does not carry over to DC but is retained by P and continues to be subject to the limitations of §1.1503(d)-4(b) and (c) with respect to P's interest in DE2X.

(v) *Alternative facts.* Assume the same facts as in paragraph (c)(21)(iv) of this section, except that DC is a member of the P consolidated group. Pursuant to §1.1503(d)-4(d)(2)(iii)(B), the dual consolidated loss of the Country X separate unit is not eliminated and income attributable to the Country X separate unit may continue to be offset by the dual consolidated loss that is succeeded to and taken into account by DC pursuant to section 381, subject to the limitations of §1.1503(d)-4(b) and (c). The result would be the same even if the interest in DE1X ceased to be a separate unit in the hands of DC (for example, because it dissolved under Country X law in connection with the transaction), provided P, or another member of the P consolidated group, continued to own a portion of the Country X separate unit.

(22) *Example 22. Tainted income.* (i) *Facts.* P owns 100 percent of DRCZ, a domestic corporation that is included as a member of the P consolidated group. DRCZ conducts a business in the United States. During year 1, DRCZ was managed and controlled in Country Z and therefore was subject to tax as a resident of Country Z and was a dual resident corporation. In year 1, DRCZ incurred a dual consolidated loss of $200x, and P did not make a domestic use election with respect to such loss. As a result, such loss is subject to the domestic use limitation rule of §1.1503(d)-4(b). At the end of year 1, DRCZ moved its management and control to the United States and, as a result, ceased being a dual resident corporation. At the beginning of year 2, P transferred asset A, a non-depreciable asset, to DRCZ in exchange for common stock in a transaction that qualified for nonrecognition under section 351. At the time of the transfer, P's tax basis in asset A equaled $50x and the fair market value of asset A equaled $100x. The tax basis of asset A in the hands of DRCZ immediately after the transfer equaled $50x pursuant to section 362. Asset A did not constitute replacement property acquired in the ordinary course of business. DRCZ did not generate income or gain during years 2, 3, or 4. On June 30, year 5, DRCZ sold asset A to a third party for $100x, its fair market value at the time of the sale, and recognized $50x of income on such sale. In addition to the $50x income generated on the sale of asset A, DRCZ generated $100x of operating income in year 5. At the end of year 5, the fair market value of all the assets of DRCZ was $400x.

(ii) *Result.* DRCZ ceased being a dual resident corporation at the end of year 1. Therefore, its year 1 dual consolidated loss cannot be offset by tainted income. Asset A is a tainted asset because it was acquired in a nonrecognition transaction after DRCZ ceased being a dual resident corporation (and was not replacement property acquired in the ordinary course of business). As a result, the $50x of income recognized by DRCZ on the disposition of asset A is tainted income and cannot be offset by the year 1 dual consolidated loss of DRCZ. In addition, absent evidence establishing the actual amount of tainted income, $25x of the $100x year 5 operating income of DRCZ (($100x/$400x) × $100x) also is treated as tainted income and cannot be offset by the year 1 dual consolidated loss of DRCZ under §1.1503(d)-4(e)(2)(ii). Therefore, $75x of the $150x year 5 income of DRCZ constitutes tainted income and may not be offset by the year 1 dual consolidated loss of DRCZ; however, the remaining $75x of year 5 income of DRCZ may be offset by such dual consolidated loss. The result would be the same if, instead of P transferring asset A to DRCZ, such asset was received from a separate unit or a transparent entity of DRCZ.

(23) *Example 23. Treatment of disregarded item and books and records of a hybrid entity.* (i) *Facts.* P owns DE1X which, in turn, owns FSX. In year 1, P borrows from a third party and on-lends the proceeds to DE1X. In year 1, P incurs interest expense attributable to the third-party loan. Also in year 1, DE1X incurs interest expense attributable to its loan from P, but such expense is generally disregarded for U.S. tax purposes because DE1X is disregarded as an entity separate from P. The third-party loan and related interest expense are reflected on the books and records of P (and not on the books and records of DE1X). The loan from P to DE1X and related interest expense are reflected on the books and records of DE1X. There are no other items of income, gain, deduction, or loss reflected on the books and records of DE1X in year 1.

(ii) *Result.* Because the interest expense on P's third-party loan is not reflected on the books and records of DE1X, no portion of such expense is attributable to P's interest in DE1X pursuant to §1.1503(d)-5(c)(3) for purposes of calculating the year 1 dual consolidated loss, if any, attributable to such interest. In addition, even though P's interest in DE1X is treated as a separate domestic corporation for purposes of determining the amount of income or dual consolidated loss attributable to it pursuant to §1.1503(d)-5(c)(1)(ii), such treatment does not cause the interest expense incurred on the loan from P to DE1X that is generally disregarded for U.S. tax purposes to be regarded for purposes of calculating the year 1 dual consolidated loss, if any, attributable to P's interest in DE1X. As a

result, even though the disregarded interest expense is reflected on the books and records of DE1X, it is not taken into account for purposes of calculating income or a dual consolidated loss. Therefore, there is no dual consolidated loss attributable to P's interest in DE1X in year 1.

(24) *Example 24. Dividend income attributable to a separate unit.* (i) *Facts.* P owns DE1X which, in turn, owns FBX. P's interest in DE1X and its indirect interest in FBX are combined and treated as a single separate unit (Country X separate unit) pursuant to §1.1503(d)-1(b)(4)(ii). DE1X owns DE3Y. DE3Y owns the stock of FSX. P's Country X separate unit would, without regard to year 1 dividend income (or related section 78 gross-up) received from FSX, have a dual consolidated loss of $75x in year 1. In year 1, FSX distributes $50x to DE3Y that is taxable as a dividend. DE3Y distributes the same amount to DE1X. P computes foreign taxes deemed paid on the dividend under section 902 of $25x and includes that amount in gross income under section 78.

(ii) *Result.* The $50x dividend is reflected on the books and records of DE3Y and, therefore, is attributable to P's interest in DE3Y pursuant to §1.1503(d)-5(c)(3)(i). In addition, the $25x section 78 gross-up is attributable to P's interest in DE3Y pursuant to §1.1503(d)-5(c)(4)(iv). The distribution of $50x from DE3Y to DE1X is generally disregarded for U.S. tax purposes and, therefore, does not give rise to an item that is taken into account for purposes of calculating income or a dual consolidated loss. This is the case even though the item would be reflected on the books and records of DE1X. In addition, pursuant to §1.1503(d)-5(c)(1)(iii), each separate unit must calculate its own income or dual consolidated loss, and each item of income, gain, deduction, and loss must be taken into account only once. As a result, the dual consolidated loss of $75x attributable to P's Country X separate unit in year 1 is not reduced by the amount of dividend income attributable to P's indirect interest in DE3Y.

(25) *Example 25. Items reflected on books and records of a combined separate unit.* (i) *Facts.* P owns DE1X which, in turn, owns FBX. P's interest in DE1X and its indirect interest in FBX are combined and treated as a single separate unit (Country X separate unit) pursuant to §1.1503(d)-1(b)(4)(ii). The following items are reflected on the books and records of DE1X in year 1: sales, depreciation expense, a political contribution, royalty expense paid to P, repairs and maintenance expense paid to a third party, and Country X income tax expense. The amount of sales under U.S. tax principles equals the amount of sales reported for accounting purposes. The depreciation expense is calculated on a straight-line basis over the useful life of the asset for accounting purposes, but is subject to accelerated depreciation for U.S. tax purposes. In addition, the repairs and maintenance expense, which is deducted when paid for accounting purposes, is properly capitalized and amortized over five years for U.S. tax purposes. Finally, P elects to claim as a credit under section 901 the Country X income tax expense that was paid in year 1.

(ii) *Result.* (A) For purposes of determining the income or dual consolidated loss attributable to P's Country X separate unit, items of income, gain, deduction, and loss must first be attributed to the individual separate units (that is, P's interest in DE1X and its indirect interest in FBX). For purposes of attributing items to P's interest in DE1X, P's items that are reflected on DE1X's books and records, as adjusted to conform to U.S. tax principles, are taken into account. See §1.1503(d)-5(c)(3)(i). For purposes of attributing items (other than interest expense) to FBX, the principles of section 864(c)(2), (c)(4), and (c)(5) (as set forth in §1.864-4(c) and §§1.864-5 through 1.864-7) must be applied and, for interest expense, the principles of §1.882-5, as modified under §1.1503(d)-5(c)(2)(ii), must be applied; however, for these purposes, pursuant to §1.1503(d)-5(c)(4)(i)(A), FBX only takes into account items attributable to P's interest in DE1X and the assets, liabilities, and activities of such interest. In addition, to the extent such items are taken into account by FBX, they are not taken into account in determining the items attributable to P's interest in DE1X. §1.1503(d)-5(c)(4)(i)(B). Because P's interest in DE1X has no assets or liabilities, and conducts no activities, other than through its ownership of FBX, all of the items that are reflected on the books and records of DE1X, as adjusted to conform to U.S. tax principles, are attributable to FBX; no items are attributable to P's interest in DE1X.

(B) The items reflected on the books and records of DE1X must be adjusted to conform to U.S. tax principles. No adjustment is required to sales because the amount of sales under U.S. tax principles equals the amount of sales for accounting purposes. The amount of straight-line depreciation expense reflected on DE1X's books and records must be adjusted to reflect the amount of depreciation on the asset that is allowable for U.S. tax purposes. The political contribution is not taken into account because it is not deductible for U.S. tax purposes. Similarly, because the royalty expense is paid to P, and therefore is generally disregarded for U.S. tax purposes, it is not taken into account. The repair and maintenance expense that is deducted in year 1 for accounting purposes also must be adjusted to conform to U.S. tax principles. Thus, the repair and maintenance expense will be taken into account in computing the income or dual consolidated loss attributable to P's Country X separate unit over five years (even though no item related to such expense would be reflected on the books and records of DE1X for years 2 through 5). Finally, because P elected to claim as a credit the Country X foreign taxes paid during year 1, no deduction is allowed for such amount pursuant to section 275(a)(4) and, therefore, the Country X tax expense is not taken into account.

(C) Pursuant to § 1.1503(d)-5(c)(4)(ii)(B), the combined Country X separate unit of P calculates its income or dual consolidated loss by taking into account all the items of income, gain, deduction, and loss that were separately attributable to P's interest in DE1X and FBX. However, in this case, there are no items attributable to P's interest in DE1X. Therefore, the items attributable to the Country X separate unit are the items attributable to FBX.

(26) *Example 26. Items attributable to a combined separate unit.* (i) *Facts.* P owns DE1X. DE1X owns a 50 percent interest in PRSZ, a Country Z entity that is classified as a partnership both for Country Z tax purposes and for U.S. tax purposes. FSX, which is unrelated to P, owns the remaining 50 percent interest in PRSZ. PRSZ carries on operations in Country X that, if carried on by a U.S. person, would constitute a foreign branch as defined in § 1.367(a)-6T(g)(1). Therefore, P's share of the Country X operations carried on by PRSZ constitutes a foreign branch separate unit. PRSZ also owns assets that do not constitute a part of its Country X branch, including all of the interests in TET, a disregarded entity. TET is an entity incorporated under the laws of Country T, a country that does not have an income tax. Under the laws of Country X, an interest holder of TET does not take into account on a current basis the interest holder's share of items of income, gain, deduction, and loss of TET.

(ii) *Result.* (A) Pursuant to § 1.1503(d)-1(b)(4)(ii), P's interest in DE1X, and P's indirect ownership of a portion of the Country X operations carried on by PRSZ, are combined and treated as a single separate unit (Country X separate unit). Pursuant to § 1.1503(d)-5(c)(4)(ii)(A), for purposes of determining P's items of income, gain, deduction, and loss attributable to the Country X separate unit, the items of P are first attributed to each separate unit that composes the Country X separate unit.

(B) Pursuant to § 1.1503(d)-5(c)(2)(i), the principles of section 864(c)(2), (c)(4), and (c)(5) (as set forth in § 1.864-4(c) and §§ 1.864-5 through 1.864-7), apply for purposes of determining P's items of income, gain, deduction (other than interest expense), and loss that are attributable to P's indirect interest in the Country X operations carried on by PRSZ. For purposes of determining P's interest expense that is attributable to P's indirect interest in the Country X operations carried on by PRSZ, the principles of § 1.882-5, as modified under § 1.1503(d)-5(c)(2)(ii), shall apply. For purposes of applying these rules, P is treated as a foreign corporation, the Country X operations carried on by PRSZ are treated as a trade or business within the United States, and the assets of P (including its share of the PRSZ assets, other than those of the Country X operations) are treated as assets that are not U.S. assets. In addition, because P carries on its share of the Country X operations through DE1X, a hybrid entity, § 1.1503(d)-5(c)(4)(i)(A) provides that only the items attributable to P's interest in DE1X, and only the assets, liabilities, and activities of P's interest in DE1X, are taken into account for purposes of this determination.

(C) TET is a transparent entity as defined in § 1.1503(d)-1(b)(16) because it is not taxable as an association for Federal tax purposes, is not subject to income tax in a foreign country as a corporation (or otherwise at the entity level) either on its worldwide income or on a residence basis, and is not treated as a pass-through entity under the laws of Country X (the applicable foreign country). TET is not a pass-through entity under the laws of Country X because a Country X holder of an interest in TET does not take into account on a current basis the interest holder's share of items of income, gain, deduction, and loss of TET. For purposes of determining P's items of income, gain, deduction, and loss that are attributable to P's interest in TET, only those items of P that are reflected on the books and records of TET, as adjusted to conform to U.S. tax principles, are taken into account. § 1.1503(d)-5(c)(3)(i). Because the interest in TET is not a separate unit, a loss attributable to such interest is not a dual consolidated loss and is not subject to section 1503(d) and these regulations. Items must nevertheless be attributed to the interests in TET. For example, such attribution is required for purposes of calculating the income or dual consolidated loss attributable to the Country X separate unit, and for purposes of applying the domestic use limitation under § 1.1503(d)-4(b) to a dual consolidated loss attributable to the Country X separate unit.

(D) For purposes of determining P's items of income, gain, deduction, and loss that are attributable to P's interest in DE1X, only those items of P that are reflected on the books and records of DE1X, as adjusted to conform to U.S. tax principles, are taken into account. § 1.1503(d)-5(c)(3)(i). For this purpose, DE1X's distributive share of the items of income, gain, deduction, and loss that are reflected on the books and records of PRSZ, as adjusted to conform to U.S. tax principles, are treated as being reflected on the books and records of DE1X, except to the extent such items are taken into account by the Country X operations of PRSZ. See § 1.1503(d)-5(c)(3)(ii) and (4)(i)(B). Because TET is a transparent entity, the items reflected on its books and records are not treated as being reflected on the books and records of DE1X.

(E) Pursuant to § 1.1503(d)-5(c)(4)(ii)(B), the combined Country X separate unit of P calculates its income or dual consolidated loss by taking into account all the items of income, gain, deduction, and loss that were separately attributable to P's interest in DE1X and the Country X operations of PRSZ owned indirectly by P.

(27) *Example 27. Sale of separate unit by another separate unit.* (i) *Facts.* P owns DE3Y which, in turn, owns DE1X. DE3Y also owns other assets that do not constitute a foreign branch separate unit. DE1X owns FBX. Pursuant to § 1.1503(d)-1(b)(4)(ii), P's indirect interests in DE1X and FBX are combined and treated as one Country X separate unit (Country X separate unit). DE3Y sells its interest in DE1X at the end of year 1 to an unrelated foreign person for cash. The sale results in an ordinary loss of $30x. Items of income, gain, deduction, and loss derived from the assets that gave rise to the $30x loss would be attributable to the Country X separate unit under § 1.1503(d)-5(c) through (e). Without regard to the sale of DE1X, no items of income, gain, deduction, and loss are attributable to P's Country X separate unit in year 1.

(ii) *Result.* Pursuant to § 1.1503(d)-5(c)(4)(iii)(A), the $30x ordinary loss recognized on the sale is attributable to the Country X separate unit, and not P's interest in DE3Y. This is the case because the Country X separate unit is treated as owning the assets that gave rise to the loss under § 1.1503(d)-5(f). Thus, the loss attributable to the sale creates a year 1 dual consolidated loss attributable to the Country X separate unit. In addition, pursuant to § 1.1503(d)-6(d)(2), P cannot make a domestic use election with respect to the dual consolidated loss because the sale of the interest in DE1X is a triggering event described in § 1.1503(d)-6(e)(1)(iv) and (v). Further, although the year 1 dual consolidated loss would otherwise be subject to the domestic use limitation rule of § 1.1503(d)-4(b), it is eliminated pursuant to § 1.1503(d)-4(d)(1)(ii). Finally, if there were a dual consolidated loss attributable to P's interest in DE3Y, the sale of the interest in DE1X would not be taken into account for purposes of determining whether there is an asset triggering event with respect to such dual consolidated loss under § 1.1503(d)-6(e)(1)(iv).

(28) *Example 28. Gain on sale of tiered separate units.* (i) *Facts.* P owns 75 percent of HPSX, a Country X entity subject to Country X tax on its worldwide income. FSX owns the remaining 25 percent of HPSX. HPSX is classified as a partnership for Federal tax purposes. HPSX carries on operations in Country Y that, if carried on by a U.S. person, would constitute a foreign branch within the meaning of § 1.367(a)-6T(g)(1). HPSX also owns assets that do not constitute a part of its Country Y operations and would not themselves constitute a foreign branch within the meaning of § 1.367(a)-6T(g)(1) if owned by a U.S. person. Neither HPSX nor the Country Y operations has liabilities. P's indirect interest in the Country Y operations carried on by HPSX, and P's interest in HPSX, are each separate units. P sells its interest in HPSX and recognizes a gain of $150x on such sale. Immediately prior to P's sale of its interest in HPSX, P's portion of the assets of the Country Y operations (that is, assets the income, gain, deduction and loss from which would be attributable to P's Country Y foreign branch separate unit) had a built-in gain of $200x, and P's portion of HPSX's other assets (that is, assets the income, gain, deduction and loss from which would be attributable to P's interest in HPSX) had a built-in gain of $100x.

(ii) *Result.* Pursuant to § 1.1503(d)-5(c)(4)(iii)(B), $100x of the total $150x of gain recognized ($200x/$300x × $150x) is attributable to P's indirect interest in its share of the Country Y operations carried on by HPSX. Similarly, $50x of such gain ($100x/$300x × $150x) is attributable to P's interest in HPSX.

(29) *Example 29. Effect on domestic affiliate.* (i) *Facts.* (A) P owns DE1X which, in turn, owns FBX. P's interest in DE1X and its indirect interest in FBX are combined and treated as a single separate unit (Country X separate unit) pursuant to § 1.1503(d)-1(b)(4)(ii). In years 1 and 2, the items of income, gain, deduction, and loss that are attributable to P's Country X separate unit pursuant to § 1.1503(d)-5 are as follows:

Table 1 to paragraph (c)(29)(i)(A)

| Item | Year 1 | Year 2 |
|---|---|---|
| Sales Income | $100x | $160x |
| Salary expense | ($75x) | ($75x) |
| Research and experimental expense | ($50x) | ($50x) |
| Interest expense | ($25x) | ($25x) |
| Income/(dual consolidated loss) | ($50x) | $10x |

(B) P does not make a domestic use election with respect to the year 1 dual consolidated loss attributable to its Country X separate unit. Pursuant to § 1.1503(d)-4(b) and (c)(2), the year 1 dual consolidated loss of $50x is treated as a loss incurred by a separate domestic corporation and is subject to the limitations under § 1.1503(d)-4(c)(3). The P consolidated group has $100x of consolidated taxable income in year 2.

(ii) *Result.* (A) P must compute its taxable income for year 1 without taking into account the $50x dual consolidated loss, pursuant to § 1.1503(d)-4(c)(2). Such amount consists of a pro rata portion of the expenses that were taken into account in calculating the year 1 dual consolidated loss. Thus, the items of the dual consolidated loss that are not taken into account by P in computing its taxable income are as follows: $25x of salary expense ($75x/$150x × $50x); $16.67x of research and experimental expense ($50x/$150x × $50x); and $8.33x of interest expense ($25x/$150x × $50x). The remaining amounts of each of these items, together with the $100x of sales income, are taken into account by P in computing its taxable income for year 1 as follows: $50x of salary expense ($75x − $25x); $33.33x of research and experimental expense ($50x − $16.67x); and $16.67x of interest expense ($25x − $8.33x).

(B) Subject to the limitations provided under § 1.1503(d)-4(c), the year 1 $50x dual consolidated loss is carried forward and is available to offset the $10x of income attributable to the Country X separate unit in year 2. Pursuant to § 1.1503(d)-4(c)(4), a pro rata portion of each item of deduction or loss included in such dual consolidated loss is considered to be used to offset the $10x of income, as follows: $5x of salary expense ($25x/$50x × $10x); $3.33x of research and experimental expense ($16.67x/$50x × $10x); and $1.67x of interest expense ($8.33x/$50x × $10x). The remaining amount of each item shall continue to be subject to the limitations under § 1.1503(d)-4(c).

(30) *Example 30.* Exception to domestic use limitation—no possibility of foreign use because items are not deducted or capitalized under foreign law. (i) Facts. P owns DE1X which, in turn, owns FSX. In year 1, the sole item of income, gain, deduction, and loss attributable to P's interest in DE1X, as provided under § 1.1503(d)-5, is $100x of interest expense paid on a loan to an unrelated lender. For Country X tax purposes, the $100x interest expense attributable to P's interest in DE1X in year 1 is treated as a repayment of principal and therefore cannot be deducted (at any time) or capitalized.

(ii) *Result.* The $100x of interest expense attributable to P's interest in DE1X constitutes a dual consolidated loss. However, because the sole item constituting the dual consolidated loss cannot be deducted or capitalized (at any time) for Country X tax purposes, P can demonstrate that there can be no foreign use of the dual consolidated loss at any time. As a result, pursuant to § 1.1503(d)-6(c)(1), if P prepares a statement described in § 1.1503(d)-6(c)(2) and attaches it to its timely filed tax return, the year 1 dual consolidated loss attributable to P's interest in DE1X will not be subject to the domestic use limitation rule of § 1.1503(d)-4(b).

(31) *Example 31.* No exception to domestic use limitation—inability to demonstrate no possibility of foreign use. (i) Facts. P owns DE1X which, in turn, owns FBX. P's interest in DE1X and its indirect interest in FBX are combined and treated as a single separate unit (Country X separate unit) pursuant to § 1.1503(d)-1(b)(4)(ii). In year 1, the sole items of income, gain, deduction, and loss attributable to P's Country X separate unit, as provided under § 1.1503(d)-5, are $75x of sales income and $100x of depreciation expense. For Country X tax purposes, DE1X also generates $75x of sales income in year 1, but the $100x of depreciation expense is not deductible until year 2.

(ii) *Result.* The year 1 $25x net loss attributable to P's interest in the Country X separate unit constitutes a dual consolidated loss. In addition, even though DE1X has positive income in year 1 for Country X tax purposes, P cannot demonstrate that there is no possibility of foreign use with respect to the Country X separate unit's dual consolidated loss as provided under § 1.1503(d)-6(c)(1)(i). P cannot make such a demonstration because the depreciation expense, an item composing the year 1 dual consolidated loss, is deductible (in a later year) for Country X tax purposes and, therefore, may be available to offset or reduce income for Country X purposes that would constitute a foreign use. For example, if DE1X elected to be classified as a corporation pursuant to § 301.7701-3(c) of this chapter effective as of the end of year 1, and the deferred depreciation expense were available for Country X tax purposes to offset year 2 income of DE1X, an entity treated as a foreign corporation in year 2 for U.S. tax purposes, there would be a foreign use.

(iii) *Alternative facts.* (A) The facts are the same as in paragraph (c)(31)(i) of this section, except as follows. In year 1, the sole items of income, gain, deduction, and loss attributable to P's Country X separate unit, as provided in § 1.1503(d)-5, are $75x of sales income,

$100x of interest expense, and $25x of depreciation expense. For Country X tax purposes, DE1X generates $75x of sales income in year 1; the $100x interest expense is treated as a repayment of principal and therefore cannot be deducted or capitalized (at any time); and the $25x of depreciation expense is not deductible in year 1, but is deductible in year 2.

(B) In year 1, the $50x net loss attributable to P's Country X separate unit constitutes a dual consolidated loss. Even though the $100x interest expense, a nondeductible and noncapital item for Country X tax purposes, exceeds the $50x year 1 dual consolidated loss attributable to P's Country X separate unit, P cannot demonstrate that there is no possibility of foreign use of the dual consolidated loss as provided under § 1.1503(d)-6(c)(1)(i). P cannot make such a demonstration because the $25x depreciation expense, an item of deduction or loss composing the year 1 dual consolidated loss, is deductible under Country X law (in year 2) and, therefore, may be available to offset or reduce income for Country X tax purposes that would constitute a foreign use.

(32) *Example 32. Triggering event rebuttal—expiration of losses in foreign country.* (i) Facts. P owns DRCX, a member of the P consolidated group. In year 1, DRCX incurs a dual consolidated loss of $100x. P makes a domestic use election with respect to DRCX's year 1 dual consolidated loss and such loss therefore is included in the computation of the P group's consolidated taxable income. DRCX has no income or loss in year 2 through year 5. In year 5, P sells the stock of DRCX to FSX. At the time of the sale of the stock of DRCX, all of the losses and deductions that were included in the computation of the year 1 dual consolidated loss of DRCX had expired for Country X tax purposes because the laws of Country X only provide for a three-year carryover period for such items.

(ii) *Result.* The sale of DRCX to FSX generally would be a triggering event under § 1.1503(d)-6(e)(1)(ii), which would require DRCX to recapture the year 1 dual consolidated loss (and pay an applicable interest charge) on the P consolidated group's tax return for the year that includes the date on which DRCX ceases to be a member of the P consolidated group. However, upon adequate documentation that the losses and deductions have expired for Country X tax purposes, P can rebut the presumption that a triggering event has occurred pursuant to § 1.1503(d)-6(e)(2)(i). If the triggering event presumption is rebutted, the domestic use agreement filed by the P consolidated group with respect to the year 1 dual consolidated loss of DRCX is terminated and has no further effect pursuant to § 1.1503(d)-6(j)(1)(i). If the presumptive triggering event is not rebutted, the domestic use agreement would terminate and have no further effect pursuant to § 1.1503(d)-6(j)(1)(iii) because the dual consolidated loss would be recaptured.

(33) *Example 33. Triggering events and rebuttals—tax basis carryover transaction.* (i) Facts. (A) P owns DE1X. DE1X's sole asset is A, which it acquired at the beginning of year 1 for $100x. DE1X does not have any liabilities. For U.S. tax purposes, DE1X's tax basis in A at the beginning of year 1 is $100x and DE1X's sole item of income, gain, deduction, and loss for year 1 is a $20x depreciation deduction attributable to A. As a result, the $20x depreciation deduction constitutes a dual consolidated loss attributable to P's interest in DE1X. P makes a domestic use election with respect to the year 1 dual consolidated loss.

(B) For Country X tax purposes, DE1X has a $100x tax basis in A at the beginning of year 1, but A is not a depreciable asset. As a result, DE1X does not have any items of income, gain, deduction, and loss in year 1 for Country X tax purposes.

(C) During year 2, P sells its interest in DE1X to FSX for $80x. P's disposition of its interest in DE1X constitutes a presumptive triggering event under § 1.1503(d)-6(e)(1)(iv) and (v) requiring the recapture of the year 1 $20x dual consolidated loss (plus the applicable interest charge). For Country X tax purposes, DE1X retains its tax basis of $100x in A following the sale.

(ii) *Result.* The year 1 dual consolidated loss is a result of the $20x depreciation deduction attributable to A. Although no item of deduction or loss was recognized by DE1X at the time of the sale for Country X tax purposes, the deduction composing the dual consolidated loss was retained by DE1X after the sale in the form of tax basis in A. As a result, a portion of the dual consolidated loss may be available to offset income for Country X tax purposes in a manner that would constitute a foreign use. For example, if DE1X were to dispose of A, the amount of gain recognized by DE1X would be reduced (or an amount of loss recognized by DE1X would be increased) and, therefore, an item composing the dual consolidated loss would be available, under U.S. tax principles, to reduce income of a foreign corporation (and an owner of an interest in a hybrid entity that is not a separate unit). Thus, P cannot demonstrate pursuant to

§ 1.1503(d)-6(e)(2)(i) that there can be no foreign use of the year 1 dual consolidated loss following the triggering event, and must recapture the year 1 dual consolidated loss. Pursuant to § 1.1503(d)-6(j)(1)(iii), the domestic use agreement filed by the P consolidated group with respect to the year 1 dual consolidated loss is terminated and has no further effect.

(iii) *Alternative facts.* The facts are the same as paragraph (c)(33)(i) of this section, except that instead of P selling its interest in DE1X to FSX, DE1X sells asset A to FSX for $80x and, for Country X tax purposes, FSX's tax basis in A immediately after the sale is $80x. P's disposition of Asset A constitutes a presumptive triggering event under § 1.1503(d)-6(e)(1)(iv) requiring the recapture of the year 1 $20x dual consolidated loss (plus the applicable interest charge). For Country X tax purposes, FSX's tax basis in A was not determined, in whole or in part, by reference to the basis of A in the hands of DE1X. As a result, the deduction composing the dual consolidated loss will not give rise to an item of deduction or loss in the form of tax basis for Country X tax purposes (for example, when FSX disposes of A). Therefore, P may be able to demonstrate (for example, by obtaining the opinion of a Country X tax advisor) pursuant to § 1.1503(d)-6(e)(2)(i) that there can be no foreign use of the year 1 dual consolidated loss and, thus, would not be required to recapture the year 1 dual consolidated loss.

(34) *Example 34. Triggering event resulting in a single consolidated group where acquirer files a new domestic use agreement.* (i) *Facts.* P owns DRCX, a member of the P consolidated group. In year 1, DRCX incurs a dual consolidated loss and P makes a domestic use election with respect to such loss. No member of the P consolidated group incurs a dual consolidated loss in year 2. At the end of year 2, T, the parent of the T consolidated group, acquires all the stock of P, and all the members of the P group, including DRCX, become members of a consolidated group of which T is the common parent.

(ii) *Result.* (A) Under § 1.1503(d)-6(f)(2)(ii)(B), the acquisition by T of the P consolidated group is not an event described in § 1.1503(d)-6(e)(1)(ii) requiring the recapture of the year 1 dual consolidated loss of DRCX (and the payment of an interest charge), provided that the T consolidated group files a new domestic use agreement described in § 1.1503(d)-6(f)(2)(iii)(A). If a new domestic use agreement is filed, then pursuant to § 1.1503(d)-6(j)(1)(ii), the domestic use agreement filed by the P consolidated group with respect to the year 1 dual consolidated loss of DRCX is terminated and has no further effect.

(B) Assume that T files a new domestic use agreement and a triggering event occurs at the end of year 3. As a result, the T consolidated group must recapture the dual consolidated loss that DRCX incurred in year 1 (and pay an interest charge), as provided in § 1.1503(d)-6(h). Each member of the T consolidated group, including DRCX and any former members of the P consolidated group, is severally liable for the additional tax (and the interest charge) due upon the recapture of the dual consolidated loss of DRCX. In addition, pursuant to § 1.1503(d)-6(j)(1)(iii), the new domestic use agreement filed by the T group with respect to the year 1 dual consolidated loss of DRCX is terminated and has no further effect.

(35) *Example 35.* Triggering event exceptions for certain deemed transfers. (i) Facts. P owns DE1X. In year 1, there is a $100x dual consolidated loss attributable to P's interest in DE1X. P files a domestic use agreement under § 1.1503(d)-6(d) with respect to such loss. During year 2, P sells 33 percent of its interest in DE1X to T, an unrelated domestic corporation.

(ii) *Result.* Pursuant to Rev. Rul. 99-5, the transaction is treated as if P sold 33 percent of its interest in each of DE1X's assets to T and then immediately thereafter P and T transferred their interests in the assets of DE1X to a partnership in exchange for an ownership interest therein. Upon the transfer of 33 percent of P's interest to T, a domestic corporation, no foreign use occurs and, therefore, there is no foreign use triggering event. However, P's deemed transfer of 67 percent of its interest in the assets of DE1X to a partnership is nominally a triggering event under § 1.1503(d)-6(e)(1)(iv). Because the initial transfer of 33 percent of DE1X's interest was to a domestic corporation and there is only a triggering event because of the deemed transfer under Rev. Rul. 99-5, the deemed asset transfer is not treated as resulting in a triggering event pursuant to § 1.1503(d)-6(f)(4).

(iii) *Alternative facts.* The facts are the same as in paragraph (c)(35)(i) of this section, except that P sells 60 percent (rather than 33 percent) of its interest in DE1X to T. The sale is a triggering event under § 1.1503(d)-6(e)(1)(iv) and (v) without regard to the occurrence of a deemed transaction. Therefore, § 1.1503(d)-6(f)(4) does not apply.

(36) *Example 36. Triggering event exception involving multiple parties.* (i) *Facts.* P owns DE1X which, in turn, owns FBX. P's interest in DE1X and its indirect interest in FBX are combined and treated as a single separate unit (Country X separate unit) pursuant to

§ 1.1503(d)-1(b)(4)(ii). In year 1, there is a $100x dual consolidated loss attributable to P's Country X separate unit and P makes a domestic use election with respect to such loss. No member of the P consolidated group incurs a dual consolidated loss in year 2. At the end of year 2, T, the parent of the T consolidated group, acquires all of P's interest in DE1X for cash.

(ii) *Result.* (A) Under § 1.1503(d)-6(f)(2)(i)(B), the acquisition by T of the interest in DE1X is not an event described in § 1.1503(d)-6(e)(1)(iv) or (v) requiring the recapture of the year 1 dual consolidated loss attributable to the Country X separate unit (and the payment of an interest charge), provided: (1) the T consolidated group files a new domestic use agreement described in § 1.1503(d)-6(f)(2)(iii)(A) with respect to the year 1 dual consolidated loss of the Country X separate unit; and (2) the P consolidated group files a statement described in § 1.1503(d)-6(f)(2)(iii)(B) with respect to the year 1 dual consolidated loss. If these requirements are satisfied, then pursuant to § 1.1503(d)-6(j)(1)(ii) the domestic use agreement filed by the P consolidated group with respect to the year 1 dual consolidated loss is terminated and has no further effect (if these requirements are not satisfied such that the P consolidated group recaptures the dual consolidated loss, the domestic use agreement would terminate pursuant to § 1.1503(d)-6(j)(1)(iii)).

(B) Assume a triggering event occurs at the end of year 3 that requires recapture by the T consolidated group of the year 1 dual consolidated loss, as well as the payment of an interest charge, as provided in § 1.1503(d)-6(h). T continues to own the Country X separate unit after the triggering event. In that case, each member of the T consolidated group is severally liable for the additional tax (and the interest charge) due upon the recapture of the year 1 dual consolidated loss. The T consolidated group must prepare a statement that computes the recapture tax amount as provided under § 1.1503(d)-6(h)(3)(iii). Pursuant to § 1.1503(d)-6(h)(3)(iv)(A), the recapture tax amount is assessed as an income tax liability of the T consolidated group and is considered as having been properly assessed as an income tax liability of the P consolidated group. If the T consolidated group does not pay in full the income tax liability attributable to the recapture tax amount, the unpaid balance of such recapture tax amount may be collected from the P consolidated group in accordance with the provisions of § 1.1503(d)-6(h)(3)(iv)(B). Pursuant to § 1.1503(d)-6(j)(1)(iii), the new domestic use agreement filed by the T consolidated group is terminated and has no further effect. Finally, pursuant to § 1.1503(d)-6(h)(6)(iii), T is treated as if it incurred the dual consolidated loss that is recaptured for purposes of applying § 1.1503(d)-6(h)(6)(i). Thus, T has a reconstituted net operating loss equal to the amount of the year 1 dual consolidated loss that was recaptured, and such loss is attributable to the Country X separate unit (and subject to the rules and limitations under § 1.1503(d)-6(h)(6)(i)). Because T is treated as if it incurred the year 1 dual consolidated loss, P shall not be treated as having a net operating loss under § 1.1503(d)-6(h)(6)(i).

(37) *Example 37. No foreign use following multiple-party event exception to triggering event.* (i) *Facts.* P owns DE1X which, in turn, owns FBX. P's interest in DE1X and its indirect interest in FBX are combined and treated as a single separate unit (Country X separate unit) pursuant to § 1.1503(d)-1(b)(4)(ii). In year 1, there is a $100x dual consolidated loss attributable to P's Country X separate unit and P makes a domestic use election with respect to such loss. T, a domestic corporation unrelated to P, owns 95 percent of PRS, a partnership. FSX owns the remaining 5 percent of PRS. At the beginning of year 3, PRS purchases 100 percent of the interest in DE1X from P for cash. For Country X tax purposes, the $100x loss incurred by DE1X in year 1 carries forward and is available to offset income of DE1X in subsequent years.

(ii) *Result.* P's sale of its interest in DE1X is a triggering event under § 1.1503(d)-6(e)(1)(iv) and (v). However, if P and T comply with the requirements under § 1.1503(d)-6(f)(2)(iii), the sale would qualify for the multiple-party event exception under § 1.1503(d)-6(f)(2)(i). In addition, because the $100x loss of DE1X carries forward to subsequent years for Country X purposes and is available to offset income of DE1X, there would be a foreign use of the dual consolidated loss immediately after the sale pursuant to § 1.1503(d)-3(a)(1). This is the case because the dual consolidated loss would be available to offset or reduce income that is considered, under U.S. tax principles, to be an item of FSX, a foreign corporation (it would also be a foreign use because FSX is an indirect owner of an interest in a hybrid entity that is not a separate unit). However, there is no foreign use in this case as a result of FSX's 5 percent interest in DE1X pursuant to § 1.1503(d)-3(c)(8).

(38) *Example 38. Character and source of recapture income.* (i) *Facts.* (A) P owns FBX. In year 1, the items of income, gain, deduction, and loss that are attributable to FBX for purposes of determining whether it has a dual consolidated loss are as follows:

Table 2 to paragraph (c)(38)(i)(A)

| | |
|---|---|
| Sales Income | . . . . . . . . . . . . . . . . . . . . . . . . . . $100x |
| Salary Expense | . . . . . . . . . . . . . . . . . . . . . . . . . . ($75x) |
| Interest expense | . . . . . . . . . . . . . . . . . . . . . . . . . . ($50x) |
| Dual consolidated loss | . . . . . . . . . . . . . . . . . . . . . . . . . . ($25x) |

(B) P makes a domestic use election with respect to the year 1 dual consolidated loss attributable to FBX and, thus, the $25x dual consolidated loss is used to offset the P group's consolidated taxable income.

(C) Pursuant to §1.861-8, the $75x of salary expense incurred by FBX is allocated and apportioned entirely to foreign source general limitation income. Pursuant to §1.861-9T, $25x of the $50x interest expense attributable to FBX is allocated and apportioned to domestic source income, $15x of such interest expense is allocated and apportioned to foreign source general limitation income, and the remaining $10x of such interest expense is allocated and apportioned to foreign source passive income.

(D) During year 2, $5x of income is attributable to FBX under the rules of §1.1503(d)-5, and the P consolidated group has $100x of consolidated taxable income. At the end of year 2, FBX undergoes a triggering event described in §1.1503(d)-6(e)(1), and P continues to own FBX following the triggering event. Pursuant to §1.1503(d)-6(h)(2)(i), P is able to demonstrate to the satisfaction of the Commissioner that the $25x dual consolidated loss attributable to FBX in year 1 would have offset the $5x of income attributable to FBX in year 2, if no domestic use election were made with respect to the year 1 loss such that it was subject to the limitations of §1.1503(d)-4(b) and (c).

(ii) *Result.* P must recapture and report as ordinary income $20x ($25x - $5x) of FBX's year 1 dual consolidated loss, plus applicable interest. The $20x recapture income is attributable to FBX pursuant to §1.1503(d)-5(c)(4)(vi). Pursuant to §1.1503(d)-6(h)(5), the recapture income is treated as ordinary income whose source and character (including section 904 separate limitation character) is determined by reference to the manner in which the recaptured items of expense or loss taken into account in calculating the dual consolidated loss were allocated and apportioned. Further, pursuant to §1.1503(d)-6(h)(5), the pro rata computation described in §1.1503(d)-4(c)(4) shall apply. Thus, the character and source of the recapture income is determined in the same proportion as each item of deduction or loss that contributed to the dual consolidated loss being recaptured. Accordingly, P's $20x of recapture income is characterized and sourced as follows: $4x of domestic source income (($25x/$125x) x $20x); $14.4x of foreign source general limitation income (($75x + $15x)/$125x) x $20x); and $1.6x of foreign source passive income (($10x/$125x) x $20x). Pursuant to §1.1503(d)-6(h)(6)(i), commencing in year 3, the $20x recapture amount is reconstituted and treated as a net operating loss incurred by FBX in a separate return limitation year, subject to the limitation under §1.1503(d)-4(b) (and therefore subject to the restrictions of §1.1503(d)-4(c)). Pursuant to §1.1503(d)-6(j)(1)(iii), the domestic use agreement filed by the P consolidated group with respect to the year 1 dual consolidated loss of FBX is terminated and has no further effect.

(39) *Example 39. Interest charge without recapture.* (i) *Facts.* P owns DE1X which, in turn, owns FBX. P's interest in DE1X and its indirect interest in FBX are combined and treated as a single separate unit (Country X separate unit) pursuant to §1.1503(d)-1(b)(4)(ii). In year 1, a dual consolidated loss of $100x is attributable to P's Country X separate unit. P makes a domestic use election with respect to such loss and uses the loss to offset the P group's consolidated taxable income. In year 2, there is $100x of income attributable to P's Country X separate unit and the P consolidated group has $200x of consolidated taxable income. At the end of year 2, the Country X separate unit undergoes a triggering event within the meaning of §1.1503(d)-6(e)(1). P demonstrates, to the satisfaction of the Commissioner, that if no domestic use election were made with respect to the year 1 dual consolidated loss such that it was subject to the limitations of §1.1503(d)-4(b) and (c), the year 1 $100x dual consolidated loss would have been offset by the $100x of year 2 income.

(ii) *Result.* There is no recapture of the year 1 dual consolidated loss attributable to P's Country X separate unit because it is reduced to zero under §1.1503(d)-6(h)(2)(i). However, P is liable for one year of interest charge under §1.1503(d)-6(h)(1)(ii), even though P's recapture amount is zero. This is the case because the P consolidated group had the benefit of the dual consolidated loss in year 1, and the income that offset the recapture income was not recognized until year 2. Pursuant to §1.1503(d)-6(j)(1)(iii), the domestic use agreement filed by the P consolidated group with respect to the year 1 dual consolidated loss is terminated and has no further effect.

(40) *Example 40. Reduced recapture and interest charge, and reconstituted dual consolidated loss.* (i) *Facts.* S owns DE1X which, in turn, owns FBX. S's interest in DE1X and its indirect interest in FBX are combined and treated as a single separate unit (Country X separate

unit) pursuant to §1.1503(d)-1(b)(4)(ii). In year 1, there is a $100x dual consolidated loss attributable to S's Country X separate unit, and P earns $100x. P makes a domestic use election with respect to the Country X separate unit's year 1 dual consolidated loss. Therefore, the consolidated group is permitted to offset P's $100x of income with the Country X separate unit's $100x dual consolidated loss. In year 2, $30x of income is attributable to the Country X separate unit under the rules of §1.1503(d)-5 and such income is offset by a $30x net operating loss incurred by P in such year. In year 3, $25x of income is attributable to the Country X separate unit under the rules of §1.1503(d)-5, and P earns $15x of income. In addition, at the end of year 3 there is a foreign use of the year 1 dual consolidated loss that constitutes a triggering event. S continues to own the Country X separate unit after the triggering event.

(ii) *Result.* (A) Under the presumptive rule of §1.1503(d)-6(h)(1)(i), S must recapture $100x (plus applicable interest). However, under §1.1503(d)-6(h)(2)(i), S may be able to demonstrate that a lesser amount is subject to recapture. The lesser amount is the amount of the $100x dual consolidated loss that would have remained subject to §1.1503(d)-4(c) at the time of the foreign use triggering event if a domestic use election had not been made for such loss.

(B) Although the combined separate unit earned $30x of income in year 2, there was no consolidated taxable income in such year. As a result, as of the end of year 2 the $100x dual consolidated loss would continue to be subject to §1.1503(d)-4(c) if a domestic use election had not been made for such loss. However, the $30x earned in year 2 can be carried forward to subsequent taxable years and may reduce the recapture income to the extent of consolidated taxable income generated in subsequent years. In year 3, $25x of income was attributable to the Country X separate unit and P earns $15x of income. Thus, the P consolidated group has $40x of consolidated taxable income in year 3. As a result, the $100x of recapture income can be reduced by $40x. This is the case because if a domestic use election had not been made for the $100x year 1 dual consolidated loss such that it was subject to the limitations of §1.1503(d)-4(b) and (c), only $60x of the loss would have remained subject to such limitations at the time of the foreign use triggering event. Accordingly, if S can adequately document the lesser amount, the amount of recapture income is $60x ($100x - $40x). The $60x recapture income is attributable to the Country X separate unit pursuant to §1.1503(d)-5(c)(4)(vi).

(C) Pursuant to §1.1503(d)-6(h)(6)(i), commencing in year 4, the $60x recapture amount is reconstituted and treated as a net operating loss incurred by the Country X separate unit of S in a separate return limitation year, subject to the limitation under §1.1503(d)-4(b) (and therefore subject to the restrictions of §1.1503(d)-4(c)). The loss is only available for carryover to taxable years after year 3 (and is not available for carryback). The carryover period of the loss, for purposes of section 172(b), will start from year 1, when the dual consolidated loss that was subject to recapture was incurred. In addition, such reconstituted net operating loss is not eligible for the exceptions contained in §1.1503(d)-6(b) through (d). Pursuant to §1.1503(d)-6(j)(1)(iii), the domestic use agreement filed by the P consolidated group with respect to the year 1 dual consolidated loss of the Country X separate unit is terminated and has no further effect.

(iii) *Alternative facts.* The facts are the same as in paragraph (c)(40)(i) of this section, except that the triggering event that occurs at the end of year 3 is a sale by S of its entire interest in DE1X to B, an unrelated domestic corporation. The sale does not qualify as a transaction described in section 381. The results are the same as in paragraph (c)(40)(ii) of this section, except that pursuant to §1.1503(d)-6(h)(6)(ii) the $60x net operating loss is not reconstituted (with respect to either S or B). The loss is not reconstituted with respect to S because the Country X separate unit ceases to be a separate unit of S (or any other member of the consolidated group that includes S) and therefore would have been eliminated pursuant to §1.1503(d)-4(d)(1)(ii) if no domestic use election had been made with respect to such loss. The loss is not reconstituted with respect to B because B was not the domestic owner of the combined separate unit when the dual consolidated loss that is recaptured was incurred, and B did not acquire the Country X separate unit in a section 381 transaction.

(41) *Example 41. Domestic consenting corporation—treated as dual resident corporation.*—(i) *Facts.* FSZ1, a Country Z entity that is subject to Country Z tax on its worldwide income or on a residence basis and

is classified as a foreign corporation for U.S. tax purposes, owns all the interests in DCC, a domestic eligible entity that has filed an election to be classified as an association. Under Country Z tax law, DCC is fiscally transparent. For taxable year 1, DCC's only item of income, gain, deduction, or loss is a $100x deduction and such deduction comprises a $100x net operating loss of DCC. For Country Z tax purposes, FSZ1's only item of income, gain, deduction, or loss, other than the $100x loss attributable to DCC, is $60x of operating income.

(ii) *Result.* DCC is a domestic consenting corporation because by electing to be classified as an association, it consents to be treated as a dual resident corporation for purposes of section 1503(d). *See* §301.7701-3(c)(3) of this chapter. For taxable year 1, DCC is treated as a dual resident corporation under §1.1503(d)-1(b)(2)(iii) because FSZ1 (a specified foreign tax resident that bears a relationship to DCC that is described in section 267(b) or 707(b)) derives or incurs items of income, gain, deduction, or loss of DCC. *See* §1.1503(d)-1(c). FSZ1 derives or incurs items of income, gain, deduction, or loss of DCC because, under Country Z tax law, DCC is fiscally transparent. Thus, DCC has a $100x dual consolidated loss for taxable year 1. *See* §1.1503(d)-1(b)(5). Because the loss is available to, and in fact does, offset income of FSZ1 under Country Z tax law, there is a foreign use of the dual consolidated loss in year 1. Accordingly, the dual consolidated loss is subject to the domestic use limitation rule of §1.1503(d)-4(b). The result would be the same if FSZ1 were to indirectly own its DCC stock through an intermediate entity that is fiscally transparent under Country Z tax law, or if an individual were to wholly own FSZ1 and FSZ1 were a disregarded entity. In addition, the result would be the same if FSZ1 had no items of income, gain, deduction, or loss, other than the $100x loss attributable to DCC.

(iii) *Alternative facts – DCC not treated as a dual resident corporation.* The facts are the same as in paragraph (c)(41)(i) of this section, except that DCC is not fiscally transparent under Country Z tax law and thus under Country Z tax law FSZ1 does not derive or incur items of income, gain, deduction, or loss of DCC. Accordingly, DCC is not treated as a dual resident corporation under §1.1503(d)-1(b)(2)(iii) for year 1 and, consequently, its $100x net operating loss in that year is not a dual consolidated loss.

(iv) *Alternative facts – mirror legislation.* The facts are the same as in paragraph (c)(41)(i) of this section, except that, under provisions of Country Z tax law that constitute mirror legislation under §1.1503(d)-3(e)(1) and that are substantially similar to the recommendations in Chapter 6 of OECD/G-20, *Neutralising the Effects of Hybrid Mismatch Arrangements, Action 2: 2015 Final Report* (October 2015), Country Z tax law prohibits the $100x loss attributable to DCC from offsetting FSZ1's income that is not also subject to U.S. tax. As is the case in paragraph (c)(41)(ii) of this section, DCC is treated as a dual resident corporation under §1.1503(d)-1(b)(2)(iii) for year 1 and its $100x net operating loss is a dual consolidated loss. Pursuant to §1.1503(d)-3(e)(3), however, the dual consolidated loss is not deemed to be put to a foreign use by virtue of the Country Z mirror legislation. Therefore, DCC is eligible to make a domestic use election for the dual consolidated loss. [Reg. §1.1503(d)-7.]

☐ [*T.D.* 9315, 3-16-2007 (*corrected* 4-24-2007). *Amended by T.D.* 9896, 4-7-2020 (*corrected* 8-11-2020).]

## [Reg. §1.1503(d)-8]

**§1.1503(d)-8. Effective dates.**—(a) *General rule.*—Except as provided in paragraph (b) of this section, this paragraph (a) provides the dates of applicability of §§1.1503(d)-1 through 1.1503(d)-7. Sections 1.1503(d)-1 through 1.1503(d)-7 shall apply to dual consolidated losses incurred in taxable years beginning on or after April 18, 2007. However, a taxpayer may apply §§1.1503(d)-1 through 1.1503(d)-7, in their entirety, to dual consolidated losses incurred in taxable years beginning on or after January 1, 2007, by filing its return and attaching to such return the domestic use agreements, certifications, or other information in accordance with these regulations. For purposes of this section, the term application date means either April 18, 2007, or, if the taxpayer applies these regulations pursuant to the preceding sentence, January 1, 2007. Section 1.1503-2 applies for dual consolidated losses incurred in taxable years beginning on or after October 1, 1992, and before the application date.

(b) *Special rules.*—(1) *Reduction of term of agreements filed under §§1.1503-2A(c)(3), 1.1503-2A(d)(3), 1.1503-2(g)(2)(i), or 1.1503-2T(g)(i).*—If an agreement is filed in accordance with §§1.1503-2A(c)(3), 1.1503-2A(d)(3), 1.1503-2(g)(2)(i), or 1.1503-2T(g)(2)(i) with respect to a dual consolidated loss incurred in a taxable year beginning prior to the application date and an event requiring recapture with respect to the dual consolidated loss subject to the agreement has not occurred as of the application date, then such agreement will be considered by the Internal Revenue Service to apply only for any taxable year up to and including the fifth taxable year following the year in which the dual consolidated loss that is the

subject of the agreement was incurred and thereafter will have no effect.

(2) *Reduction of term of agreements filed under §§1.1503-2(g)(2)(iv)(B)(2)(i)* (1992), *1.1503-2(g)(2)(iv)(B)(3)(i), or Rev. Proc. 2000-42.*—Taxpayers subject to the terms of a closing agreement entered into with the Internal Revenue Service pursuant to §§1.1503-2(g)(2)(iv)(B)(2)(i) (1992), 1.1503-2(g)(2)(iv)(B)(3)(i), or Rev. Proc. 2000-42 (2000-2 CB 394), see §601.601(d)(2)(ii)(b) of this chapter, will be deemed to have satisfied the closing agreement's fifteen-year certification period requirement if the five-year certification period specified in §1.1503(d)-1(b)(20) has elapsed, provided such closing agreement is still in effect as of the application date, and provided the dual consolidated losses have not been recaptured. For example, if a calendar year taxpayer that has a January 1, 2007, application date entered into a closing agreement with respect to a dual consolidated loss incurred in 2003 and, as of January 1, 2007, the closing agreement is still in effect and the dual consolidated loss subject to the closing agreement has not been recaptured, then the closing agreement's fifteen-year certification period will be deemed satisfied when the five-year certification period described in §1.1503(d)-1(b)(20) has elapsed. Thus, the dual consolidated loss will be subject to the recapture and certification provisions of the closing agreement in such a case only through December 31, 2008. Alternatively, if a calendar year taxpayer that has a January 1, 2007, application date entered into a closing agreement with respect to a dual consolidated loss incurred in 2000 and, as of January 1, 2007, the closing agreement is still in effect and the dual consolidated loss subject to the closing agreement has not been recaptured, then the certification period is deemed to be satisfied.

(3) Relief for untimely filings.— Paragraphs (b)(3)(i) through (iii) of this section set forth the effective dates for rules that provide relief for the failure to make timely filings of an election, agreement, statement, rebuttal, computation, closing agreement, or other information, pursuant to section 1503(d) and these regulations.

(i) *General rule.*—Except as provided in paragraphs (b)(3)(ii) and (iii) of this section, the reasonable cause relief standard of §1.1503(d)-1(d) applies for all untimely filings with respect to dual consolidated losses, including with respect to dual consolidated losses incurred in taxable years beginning before the application date.

(ii) *Closing agreements.*—Solely with respect to closing agreements described in §1.1503-2(g)(2)(iv)(B)(3)(i) and Rev. Proc. 2000-42, taxpayers must request relief for untimely requests through the process provided under §§301.9100-1 through 301.9100-3 of this chapter. See paragraph (b)(4) of this section for rules that permit the multiple-party event exception, rather than closing agreements, for certain triggering events.

(iii) *Pending requests for relief.*—Taxpayers that have letter ruling requests under §§301.9100-1 through 301.9100-3 of this chapter pending as of March 19, 2007 (other than requests under paragraph (b)(3)(ii) of this section) are not required to use the reasonable cause procedure under §1.1503(d)-1(d); however, if such taxpayers have not yet received a determination of their request, they may withdraw their request consistent with the procedures contained in Rev. Proc. 2007-1 (2007-1 IRB 1), see §601.601(d)(2)(ii)(b) of this chapter, (or any succeeding document) and use the reasonable cause procedure set forth in §1.1503(d)-1(d). In that event, the Internal Revenue Service will refund the taxpayer's user fee.

(4) *Multiple-party event exception to triggering events.*—This paragraph (b)(4) applies to events described in §1.1503-2(g)(2)(iv)(B)(1)(i) through (iii) that occur after April 18, 2007 and that are with respect to dual consolidated losses that were incurred in taxable years beginning on or after October 1, 1992, and before the application date. The events described in the previous sentence are not eligible for the exception described in §1.1503-2(g)(2)(iv)(B)(1), but instead are eligible for the multiple-party event exception described in §1.1503(d)-6(f)(2)(i), as modified by this paragraph (b)(4). Thus, such events are not eligible for a closing agreement described in §1.1503-2(g)(2)(iv)(B)(3)(i) and Rev. Proc. 2000-42. For purposes of applying §1.1503(d)-6(f)(2)(i) to transactions covered by this paragraph, agreements described in §1.1503-2(g)(2)(i) (rather than domestic use agreements) shall be filed, and subsequent triggering events and exceptions thereto have the meaning provided in §1.1503-2(g)(2)(iii)(A) and (iv) (other than the exception provided under §1.1503-2(g)(2)(iv)(B)(1)). For example, if a calendar year taxpayer that has a January 1, 2007, application date filed an election under §1.1503-2(g)(2)(i) with respect to a dual consolidated loss that was incurred in 2004, and a triggering event described in §1.1503-2(g)(2)(iv)(B)(1)(ii) occurs with respect to such dual consolidated loss after April 18, 2007, then the event is eligible for the multiple-party event exception under §1.1503(d)-6(f)(2)(i) (and not

the exception under §1.1503-2(g)(2)(iv)(B)(1)). However, in order to comply with §1.1503(d)-6(f)(2)(iii)(A), the subsequent elector must file a new agreement described in §1.1503-2(g)(2)(i) (rather than a new domestic use agreement). In addition, for purposes of determining whether there is a subsequent triggering event, and exceptions thereto, pursuant to such new agreement, §1.1503-2(g)(2)(iii)(A) and (iv) (other than the exception provided under §1.1503-2(g)(2)(iv)(B)(1)) shall apply. Notwithstanding the general application of this paragraph (b)(4) to events described in §1.1503-2(g)(2)(iv)(B)(1)(i) through (iii) that occur after April 18, 2007, a taxpayer may choose to apply this paragraph (b)(4) to events described in §1.1503-2(g)(2)(iv)(B)(1)(i) through (iii) that occur after March 19, 2007 and on or before April 18, 2007.

(5) *Basis adjustment rules.*—Taxpayers may apply the basis adjustment rules of §1.1503(d)-5(g) for all open years in which such basis is relevant, even if the basis adjustment is attributable to a dual consolidated loss incurred (or recaptured) in a closed taxable year. Taxpayers applying the provisions of §1.1503(d)-5(g), however, must do so consistently for all open years.

(6) *Rules regarding domestic consenting corporations.*—Section 1.1503(d)-1(b)(2)(iii) and (c), as well §1.1503(d)-3(e)(1) and (3), apply to determinations under §§1.1503(d)-1 through 1.1503(d)-7 relating to taxable years ending on or after December 20, 2018. For taxable years ending before December 20, 2018, see §1.1503(d)-3(e)(1) as contained in 26 CFR part 1 revised as of April 1, 2018.

(7) *Compulsory transfer triggering event exception.*—Section 1.1503(d)-6(f)(5)(i) through (iii) applies to transfers that occur on or after December 20, 2018. For transfers occurring before December 20, 2018, see §1.1503(d)-6(f)(5)(i) through (iii) as contained in 26 CFR part 1 revised as of April 1, 2018. However, taxpayers may consistently apply §1.1503(d)-6(f)(5)(i) through (iii) to transfers occurring before December 20, 2018.

(8) *Rule providing that SRLY limitation applies without regard to §1.1502-21(c)(1)(i)(E).*—Section 1.1503(d)-4(c)(3)(v) applies to any period to which §1.1502-21(c)(1)(i)(E) applies. [Reg. §1.1503(d)-8.]

□ [*T.D.* 9315, 3-16-2007 (*corrected* 4-24-2007). *Amended by T.D.* 9896, 4-7-2020 *and T.D.* 9927, 10-23-2020.]

### [Reg. §1.1504-0]

**§1.1504-0. Outline of provisions.**—In order to facilitate the use of §§1.1504-1 through 1.1504-4, this section lists the captions contained in §§1.1504-1 through 1.1504-4.

*§1.1504-1. Definitions.*

*§1.1504-2.* [Reserved].

*§1.1504-3.* [Reserved].

*§1.1504-4. Treatment of warrants, options, convertible obligations, and other similar interests.*—

(a) Introduction.
　(1) General rule.
　(2) Exceptions.
(b) Options not treated as stock or as exercised.
　(1) General rule.
　(2) Options treated as exercised.
　　(i) In general.
　　(ii) Aggregation of options.
　　(iii) Effect of treating option as exercised.
　　　(A) In general.
　　　(B) Cash settlement options, phantom stock, stock appreciation rights, or similar interests.
　　(iv) Valuation.
　(3) Example.
(c) Definitions.
　(1) Issuing corporation.

(2) Related or sequential option.
(3) Related persons.
(4) Measurement date.
　(i) General rule.
　(ii) Issuances, transfers, or adjustments not treated as measurement dates.
　(iii) Transactions increasing likelihood of exercise.
　(iv) Measurement date for options issued pursuant to a plan.
　(v) Measurement date for related or sequential options.
　(vi) Example.
(5) In-the-money.
(d) Options.
　(1) Instruments treated as options.
　(2) Instruments generally not treated as options.
　　(i) Options on section 1504(a)(4) stock.
　　(ii) Certain publicly traded options.
　　　(A) General rule.
　　　(B) Exception.
　　(iii) Stock purchase agreements.
　　(iv) Escrow, pledge, or other security agreements.
　　(v) Compensatory options.
　　　(A) General rule.
　　　(B) Exceptions.
　　(vi) Options granted in connection with a loan.
　　(vii) Options created pursuant to a title 11 or similar case.
　　(viii) Convertible preferred stock.
　　(ix) Other enumerated instruments.
(e) Elimination of federal income tax liability.
(f) Substantial amount of federal income tax liability.
(g) Reasonable certainty of exercise.
　(1) Generally.
　　(i) Purchase price.
　　(ii) In-the-money option.
　　(iii) Not in-the-money option.
　　(iv) Exercise price.
　　(v) Time of exercise.
　　(vi) Related or sequential options.
　　(vii) Stockholder rights.
　　(viii) Restrictive covenants.
　　(ix) Intention to alter value.
　　(x) Contingencies.
　(2) Cash settlement options, phantom stock, stock appreciation rights, or similar interests.
　(3) Safe harbors.
　　(i) Options to acquire stock.
　　(ii) Options to sell stock.
　　(iii) Options exercisable at fair market value.
　　(iv) Exceptions.
　　(v) Failure to satisfy safe harbor.
(h) Examples.
(i) Effective date.
[Reg. §1.1504-0.]

□ [*T.D.* 8462, 12-28-92.]

### [Reg. §1.1504-1]

**§1.1504-1. Definitions.**—The privilege of filing consolidated returns is extended to all includible corporations constituting affiliated groups as defined in section 1504. See the regulations under §1.1502 for a description of an affiliated group and the corporations which may be considered as includible corporations. [Reg. §1.1504-1.]

□ [*T.D.* 6140, 8-29-55.]

### [Reg. §1.1504-2]

**§1.1504-2.** [Reserved].

≫→ *Caution: Reg. §1.1504-3, below, as adopted by T.D. 9889, generally applies to tax years beginning after March 13, 2020. For exceptions regarding reliance on the proposed regulations, see Reg. §1.1504-3(e).*

### [Reg. §1.1504-3]

**§1.1504-3. Treatment of stock in a QOF C corporation for purposes of consolidation.**—(a) *Scope and definitions.*—(1) *Scope.*—This section provides rules regarding the treatment of stock in a QOF C corporation for purposes of determining whether such corporation can join in the filing of a consolidated return. Paragraph (b) of this section generally prevents a subsidiary QOF C corporation from joining in the filing of a consolidated return, but it provides an election to consolidate a subsidiary QOF C corporation (subject to certain conditions). Paragraph (c) of this section provides instructions for making the election provided by paragraph (b) of this section.

Paragraph (d) of this section provides an example. Paragraph (e) of this section provides the applicability dates.

(2) *Definitions.*—The definitions provided in §§1.1400Z2(a)-1(b) and 1.1502-14Z(a)(2)(ii) apply for purposes of this section.

(b) *QOF stock not stock for purposes of consolidation.*—(1) *In general.*—Except as otherwise provided in paragraph (b)(2) of this section, stock in a QOF C corporation (whether qualifying QOF stock or otherwise) is not treated as stock under section 1504 for purposes of determining whether any corporation may join in the filing of a consolidated return under section 1501. Therefore, a QOF C corporation can be the common parent of a consolidated group, and a QOF C corporation generally can be a member of an affiliated group for purposes of section 1504, but a QOF C corporation cannot join in the filing of a consolidated return as a subsidiary member (except as provided in paragraph (b)(2) of this section).

(2) *Election to consolidate a subsidiary QOF C corporation.*—(i) *In general.*—Notwithstanding paragraph (b)(1) of this section, a consolidated group may elect to consolidate a subsidiary QOF C corporation that was formed, or section 1504 control of which was acquired, by the consolidated group after May 1, 2019, and that otherwise meets the affiliation requirements under section 1504. If a pre-existing corporation was a member of the consolidated group prior to becoming a QOF C corporation, a consolidated group may elect to continue to consolidate such pre-existing corporation if it self-certified to be a QOF after May 1, 2019. The consolidated group must make the election under this paragraph (b)(2) with regard to the first taxable year during which the subsidiary QOF C corporation otherwise meets the section 1504 affiliation requirements (without regard to paragraph (b)(1) of this section). See § 1.1502-14Z(f)(3) for an election available with regard to a subsidiary QOF C corporation that met the section 1504 affiliation requirements as of May 1, 2019. The election under this paragraph (b)(2) is effective on the later of May 1, 2019, or the first date on which the QOF C corporation otherwise meets the requirements of section 1504. If a consolidated group makes the election under this paragraph (b)(2), then the conditions in paragraph (b)(2)(ii) of this section apply to the consolidated group and to the QOF member. See paragraph (c) of this section for the form and manner of making this election.

(ii) *Conditions to consolidate a subsidiary QOF C corporation.*—(A) *Ownership status of QOF investor member.*—On and at all times after the date of the investment, the common parent must directly or indirectly own all shares of all classes of stock (including nonqualified preferred stock) issued by any QOF investor member.

(B) *Direct investment.*—Except as provided in § 1.1502-14Z(c), each QOF investor member must maintain direct ownership of its qualifying investment (see, for example, § 1.1400Z2(b)-1(c), which generally treats transfers of a qualifying investment as an inclusion event). See § 1.1502-14Z(c)(4) for rules regarding the treatment of intercompany transfers as qualifying investments in a QOF member. See also § 1.1502-14Z(c)(2) and (c)(3)(ii) for rules regarding actual and deemed intercompany transfers of qualifying investments.

(3) *Failure of continued qualification.*—Consolidation of a subsidiary QOF C corporation is contingent upon continued satisfaction of all of the conditions of paragraph (b)(2)(ii) of this section. The requirements of paragraph (b)(2) of this section continue to apply (with appropriate modifications to reflect single-entity treatment) following any intercompany transfer of the QOF member stock that is subject to § 1.1502-14Z(c)(3)(ii). For example, following an intercompany transfer of the QOF member stock that is subject to § 1.1502-14Z(c)(3)(ii), the buying member must maintain a direct investment in the QOF member. On the failure to satisfy any condition of paragraph (b)(2), the QOF member will deconsolidate, and § 1.1502-14Z(g) will apply with respect to such deconsolidation.

(c) *Election under paragraph (b)(2) of this section to consolidate a subsidiary QOF C corporation.*—(1) *In general.*—The election under paragraph (b)(2) of this section is irrevocable and is made in the form provided in paragraph (c)(2) of this section.

(2) *Form of election.*—The election under paragraph (b)(2) of this section must be made in the form of a statement titled "THIS IS AN ELECTION UNDER § 1.1504-3(b)(2) TO CONSOLIDATE [insert name and employer identification number (E.I.N.) of subsidiary QOF C corporation] as of [insert date]." The statement must be included with the consolidated group's timely filed return (original, superseding, or amended return, as applicable, including extensions) for the year the election under § 1.1504-3(b)(2) is made.

(d) *Example.*—The following example illustrates the treatment of QOF stock as not stock for purposes of affiliation as described in paragraph (b)(1) of this section.

(1) *QOF stock as not stock for purposes of affiliation to join in the filing of a consolidated return*—(i) *Facts.* P wholly owns S, which wholly owns corporation Q1. P, S, and Q1 are members of the P group. In 2021, S sells an asset to an unrelated party and realizes $500x of eligible gain. S contributes $500x to Q1 and properly elects to defer the eligible gain under section 1400Z-2(a) and § 1.1400Z2(a)-1. At such time, Q1 qualifies and elects to be treated as a QOF, but the P group does not elect to consolidate Q1 under paragraph (b)(2) of this section.

(ii) *Analysis.* Under paragraph (b)(1) of this section, stock of a QOF C corporation (qualifying or otherwise) is not treated as stock for purposes of determining whether the QOF C corporation may join in

the filing of a consolidated return. Thus, because no election has been made under paragraph (b)(2) of this section, once Q1 becomes a QOF, Q1 ceases to be affiliated with the P group members for purposes of section 1501, and it deconsolidates from the P group. See §§ 1.1502-1 through 1.1502-100 generally for the consequences of deconsolidation.

(2) [Reserved]

(e) *Applicability dates.*—(1) *In general.*—This section applies for taxable years beginning after March 13, 2020.

(2) *Prior periods.*—With respect to the portion of a consolidated group's first taxable year ending after December 21, 2017, and for taxable years beginning after December 21, 2017, and on or before March 13, 2020, a consolidated group may choose either—

(i) To apply the section 1400Z-2 regulations, if applied in a consistent manner for all such taxable years; or

(ii) To rely on the rules in proposed § 1.1400Z2(g)-1 contained in the notice of proposed rulemaking (REG-120186-18) published on May 1, 2019, but only if applied in a consistent manner for all such taxable years. [Reg. § 1.1504-3.]

☐ [*T.D. 9889, 12-31-2019 (corrected 4-1-2020).*]

### [Reg. § 1.1504-4]

**§ 1.1504-4. Treatment of warrants, options, convertible obligations, and other similar interests.**—(a) *Introduction.*—(1) *General rule.*—This section provides regulations under section 1504(a)(5)(A) and (B) regarding the circumstances in which warrants, options, obligations convertible into stock, and other similar interests are treated as exercised for purposes of determining whether a corporation is a member of an affiliated group. The fact that an instrument may be treated as an option under these regulations does not prevent such instrument from being treated as stock under general principles of law. Except as provided in paragraph (a)(2) of this section, this section applies to all provisions under the Internal Revenue Code and the regulations to which affiliation within the meaning of section 1504(a) (with or without the exceptions in section 1504(b)) is relevant, including those provisions that refer to section 1504(a)(2) (with or without the exceptions in section 1504(b)) without referring to affiliation, provided that the 80 percent voting power and 80 percent value requirements of section 1504(a)(2) are not modified therein.

(2) *Exceptions.*—This section does not apply to sections 864(e) or 904(i) or to the regulations thereunder. This section also does not apply to any other provision specified by the Internal Revenue Service in regulations, a revenue ruling, or revenue procedure. See § 601.601(d)(2)(ii)(*b*) of this chapter.

(b) *Options not treated as stock or as exercised.*—(1) *General rule.*—Except as provided in paragraph (b)(2) of this section, an option is not considered either as stock or as exercised. Thus, options are disregarded in determining whether a corporation is a member of an affiliated group unless they are described in paragraph (b)(2) of this section.

(2) *Options treated as exercised.*—(i) *In general.*—Solely for purposes of determining whether a corporation is a member of an affiliated group, an option is treated as exercised if, on a measurement date with respect to such option—

(A) It could reasonably be anticipated that, if not for this section, the issuance or transfer of the option in lieu of the issuance, redemption, or transfer of the underlying stock would result in the elimination of a substantial amount of federal income tax liability (as described in paragraphs (e) and (f) of this section); and

(B) It is reasonably certain that the option will be exercised (as described in paragraph (g) of this section).

(ii) *Aggregation of options.*—All options with the same measurement date are aggregated in determining whether the issuance or transfer of an option in lieu of the issuance, redemption, or transfer of the underlying stock would result in the elimination of a substantial amount of federal income tax liability.

(iii) *Effect of treating option as exercised.*—(A) *In general.*—An option that is treated as exercised is treated as exercised for purposes of determining the percentage of the value of stock owned by the holder and other parties, but is not treated as exercised for purposes of determining the percentage of the voting power of stock owned by the holder and other parties.

(B) *Cash settlement options, phantom stock, stock appreciation rights, or similar interests.*—If a cash settlement option, phantom stock, stock appreciation right, or similar interest is treated as exercised, the option is treated as having been converted into stock of the issuing corporation. If the amount to be received upon the exercise of such an option is determined by reference to a multiple of the increase in the value of a share of the issuing corporation's stock on the exercise date over the value of a share of the stock on the date the option is issued, the option is treated as converted into a corresponding number of shares of such stock. Appropriate adjustments must be made in any situation in which the amount to be received upon exercise of the option is determined in another manner.

(iv) *Valuation.*—For purposes of section 1504(a)(2)(B) and this section, all shares of stock within a single class are considered to have the same value. Thus, control premiums and minority and blockage discounts within a single class are not taken into account.

(3) *Example.*—The provisions of paragraph (b)(2) of this section may be illustrated by the following example:

*Example.* (i) Corporation P owns all 100 shares of the common stock of Corporation S, the only class of S stock outstanding. Each share of S stock has a fair market value of $10 and has one vote. On June 30, 1992, P issues to Corporation X an option to acquire 80 shares of the S stock from P.

(ii) If, under the provisions of this section, the option is treated as exercised, then, solely for purposes of determining affiliation, P is treated as owning only 20 percent of the value of the outstanding S stock and X is treated as owing the remaining 80 percent of the value of the S stock. P is still treated as owning all of the voting power of S. Accordingly, because P is treated as owning less than 80 percent of the value of the outstanding S stock, P and S are no longer affiliated. However, because X is not treated as owning any of the voting power of S, X and S are also not affiliated.

(c) *Definitions.*—For purposes of this section—

(1) *Issuing corporation.*—"Issuing corporation" means the corporation whose stock is subject to an option.

(2) *Related or sequential option.*—"Related or sequential option" means an option that is one of a series of options issued to the same or related persons. For purposes of this section, any options issued to the same person or related persons within a two year period are presumed to be part of a series of options. This presumption may be rebutted if the facts and circumstances clearly establish that the options are not part of a series of options. Any options issued to the same person or related persons more than two years apart are presumed not to be part of a series of options. This presumption may be rebutted if the facts and circumstances clearly establish that the options are part of a series of options.

(3) *Related persons.*—Persons are related if they are related within the meaning of section 267(b) (without the application of sections 267(c) and 1563(e)(1)) or 707(b)(1), substituting "10 percent" for "50 percent" wherever it appears.

(4) *Measurement date.*—(i) *General rule.*—"Measurement date" means a date on which an option is issued or transferred or on which the terms of an existing option or the underlying stock are adjusted (including an adjustment pursuant to the terms of the option or the underlying stock).

(ii) *Issuances, transfers, or adjustments not treated as measurement dates.*—A measurement date does not include a date on which—

(A) An option is issued or transferred by gift, at death, or between spouses or former spouses under section 1041;

(B) An option is issued or transferred—

*(1)* Between members of an affiliated group (determined with the exceptions in section 1504(b) and without the application of this section); or

*(2)* Between persons none of which is a member of the affiliated group (determined without the exceptions in section 1504(b) and without the application of this section), if any, of which the issuing corporation is a member, unless—

*(i)* Any such person is related to (or acting in concert with) the issuing corporation or any member of its affiliated group; and

*(ii)* The issuance or transfer is pursuant to a plan a principal purpose of which is to avoid the application of section 1504 and this section;

(C) An adjustment occurs in the terms or pursuant to the terms of an option or the underlying stock that does not materially increase the likelihood that the option will be exercised; or

(D) A change occurs in the exercise price of an option or in the number of shares that may be issued or transferred pursuant to the option as determined by a bona fide, reasonable, adjustment formula that has the effect of preventing dilution of the interests of the holders of the options.

(iii) *Transactions increasing likelihood of exercise.*—If a change or alteration referred to in this paragraph (c)(4)(iii) is made for a principal purpose of increasing the likelihood that an option will be exercised, a measurement date also includes any date on which—

(A) The capital structure of the issuing corporation is changed; or

(B) The fair market value of the stock of the issuing corporation is altered through a transfer of assets to or from the issuing corporation (other than regular, ordinary dividends) or by any other means.

(iv) *Measurement date for options issued pursuant to a plan.*—In the case of options issued pursuant to a plan, a measurement date for any of the options constitutes a measurement date for all options issued pursuant to the plan that are outstanding on the measurement date.

(v) *Measurement date for related or sequential options.*—In the case of related or sequential options, a measurement date for any of the options constitutes a measurement date for all related or sequential options that are outstanding on the measurement date.

(vi) *Example.*—The provisions of paragraph (c)(4)(v) of this section may be illustrated by the following example.

*Example.* (i) Corporation P owns all 80 shares of the common stock of Corporation S, the only class of S stock outstanding. On January 1, 1992, S issues a warrant, exercisable within 3 years, to U, an unrelated corporation, to acquire 10 newly issued shares of S common stock. On July 1, 1992, S issues a second warrant to U to acquire 10 additional newly issued shares of S common stock. On January 1, 1993, S issues a third warrant to T, a wholly owned subsidiary of U, to acquire 10 newly issued shares of S common stock. Assume that the facts and circumstances do not clearly establish that the options are not part of a series of options.

(ii) January 1, 1992, July 1, 1992, and January 1, 1993, constitute measurement dates for the first warrant, the second warrant, and the third warrant, respectively, because the warrants were issued on those dates.

(iii) Because the first and second warrants were issued within two years of each other, and both warrants were issued to U, the warrants constitute related or sequential options. Accordingly, July 1, 1992, constitutes a measurement date for the first warrant as well as for the second warrant.

(iv) Because the first, second, and third warrants were all issued within two years of each other, and were all issued to the same or related persons, the warrants constitute related or sequential options. Accordingly, January 1, 1993, constitutes a measurement date for the first and second warrants, as well as for the third warrant.

(5) *In-the-money.*—"In-the-money" means the exercise price of the option is less than (or in the case of an option to sell stock, greater than) the fair market value of the underlying stock.

(d) *Options.*—(1) *Instruments treated as options.*—For purposes of this section, except to the extent otherwise provided in this paragraph (d), the following are treated as options:

(i) A call option, warrant, convertible obligation, put option, redemption agreement (including a right to cause the redemption of stock), or any other instrument that provides for the right to issue, redeem, or transfer stock (including an option on an option); and

(ii) A cash settlement option, phantom stock, stock appreciation right, or any other similar interest (except for stock).

(2) *Instruments generally not treated as options.*—For purposes of this section, the following will not be treated as options:

(i) *Options on section 1504(a)(4) stock.*—Options on stock described in section 1504(a)(4);

(ii) *Certain publicly traded options.*—(A) *General rule.*—Options which on the measurement date are traded on (or subject to the rules of) a qualified board or exchange as defined in section 1256(g)(7), or on any other exchange, board of trade, or market specified by the Internal Revenue Service in regulations, a revenue ruling, or revenue procedure. See § 601.601(d)(2)(ii)(*b*) of this chapter;

(B) *Exception.*—Paragraph (d)(2)(ii)(A) of this section does not apply to options issued, transferred, or listed with a principal purpose of avoiding the application of section 1504 and this section. For example, a principal purpose of avoiding the application of section 1504 and this section may exist if warrants, convertible or exchangeable debt instruments, or other similar instruments have an exercise price (or, in the case of convertible or exchangeable instruments, a conversion or exchange premium) that is materially less than, or a term that is materially longer than, those that are customary for publicly traded instruments of their type. A principal purpose may also exist if a large percentage of an issuance of an instrument is placed with one investor (or group of investors) and a very small percentage of the issuance is traded on a qualified board or exchange;

(iii) *Stock purchase agreements.*—Stock purchase agreements or similar arrangements whose terms are commercially reasonable and in which the parties' obligations to complete the transaction are subject only to reasonable closing conditions;

(iv) *Escrow, pledge, or other security agreements.*—Agreements for holding stock in escrow or under a pledge or other security agreement that are part of a typical commercial transaction and that are subject to customary commercial conditions;

(v) *Compensatory options.*—(A) *General rule.*—Stock appreciation rights, warrants, stock options, phantom stock, or other similar instruments provided to employees, directors, or independent contractors in connection with the performance of services for the corporation or a related corporation (and that is not excessive by reference to the services performed) and which—

(1) Are nontransferable within the meaning of § 1.83-3(d); and

(2) Do not have a readily ascertainable fair market value as defined in § 1.83-7(b) on the measurement date;

(B) *Exceptions.*—(1) Paragraph (d)(2)(v)(A) of this section does not apply to options issued or transferred with a principal purpose of avoiding the application of section 1504 and this section; and

(2) Paragraph (d)(2)(v)(A) of this section ceases to apply to options that become transferable;

(vi) *Options granted in connection with a loan.*—Options granted in connection with a loan if the lender is actively and regularly engaged in the business of lending and the options are issued in connection with a loan to the issuing corporation that is commercially reasonable. This paragraph (d)(2)(vi) continues to apply if the option is transferred with the loan (or if a portion of the option is transferred with a corresponding portion of the loan). However, if the option is transferred without a corresponding portion of the loan, this paragraph (d)(2)(vi) ceases to apply;

(vii) *Options created pursuant to a title 11 or similar case.*—Options created by the solicitation or receipt of acceptances to a plan of reorganization in a title 11 or similar case (within the meaning of section 368(a)(3)(A)), the option created by the confirmation of the plan, and any option created under the plan prior to the time the plan becomes effective;

(viii) *Convertible preferred stock.*—Convertible preferred stock, provided the terms of the conversion feature do not permit or require the tender of any consideration other than the stock being converted; and

(ix) *Other enumerated instruments.*—Any other instruments specified by the Internal Revenue Service in regulations, a revenue ruling, or revenue procedure. See § 601.601(d)(2)(ii)(b) of this chapter.

(e) *Elimination of federal income tax liability.*—For purposes of this section, the elimination of federal income tax liability includes the elimination or deferral of federal income tax liability. In determining whether there is an elimination of federal income tax liability, the tax consequences to all involved parties are considered. Examples of elimination of federal income tax liability include the use of a loss or deduction that would not otherwise be utilized, the acceleration of a loss or deduction to a year earlier than the year in which the loss or deduction would otherwise be utilized, the deferral of gain or income to a year later than the year in which the gain or income would otherwise be reported, and the acceleration of gain or income to a year earlier than the year in which the gain or income would otherwise be reported, if such gain or income is offset by a net operating loss or net capital loss that would otherwise expire unused. The elimination of federal income tax liability does not include the deferral of gain with respect to the stock subject to the option that would be recognized if such stock were sold on a measurement date.

(f) *Substantial amount of federal income tax liability.*—The determination of what constitutes a substantial amount of federal income tax liability is based on all the facts and circumstances, including the absolute amount of the elimination, the amount of the elimination relative to overall tax liability, and the timing of items of income and deductions, taking into account present value concepts.

(g) *Reasonable certainty of exercise.*—(1) *Generally.*—The determination of whether, as of a measurement date, an option is reasonably certain to be exercised is based on all the facts and circumstances, including:

(i) *Purchase price.*—The purchase price of the option in absolute terms and in relation to the fair market value of the stock and the exercise price of the option;

(ii) *In-the-money option.*—Whether and to what extent the option is in-the-money on the measurement date;

(iii) *Not in-the-money option.*—If the option is not in-the-money on the measurement date, the amount or percentage by which the exercise price of the option is greater than (or in the case of an option to sell stock, is less than) the fair market value of the underlying stock;

(iv) *Exercise price.*—Whether the exercise price of the option is fixed or fluctuates depending on the earnings, value, or other indication of economic performance of the issuing corporation;

(v) *Time of exercise.*—The time at which, or the period of time during which, the option can be exercised;

(vi) *Related or sequential options.*—Whether the option is one in a series of related or sequential options;

(vii) *Stockholder rights.*—The existence of an arrangement (either within the option agreement or in a related agreement) that, directly or indirectly, affords managerial or economic rights in the issuing corporation that ordinarily would be afforded to owners of the issuing corporation's stock (*e.g.*, voting rights, dividend rights, or rights to proceeds on liquidation) to the person who would acquire the stock upon exercise of the option or a person related to such person. For this purpose, managerial or economic rights in the issuing corporation possessed because of actual stock ownership in the issuing corporation are not taken into account;

(viii) *Restrictive covenants.*—The existence of restrictive covenants or similar arrangements (either within the option agreement or in a related agreement) that, directly or indirectly, prevent or limit the ability of the issuing corporation to undertake certain activities while the option is outstanding (*e.g.*, covenants limiting the payment of dividends or borrowing of funds);

(ix) *Intention to alter value.*—Whether it was intended that through a change in the capital structure of the issuing corporation or a transfer of assets to or from the issuing corporation (other than regular, ordinary dividends) or by any other means, the fair market value of the stock of the issuing corporation would be altered for a principal purpose of increasing the likelihood that the option would be exercised; and

(x) *Contingencies.*—Any contingency (other than the mere passage of time) to which the exercise of the option is subject (*e.g.*, a public offering of the issuing corporation's stock or reaching a certain level of earnings).

(2) *Cash settlement options, phantom stock, stock appreciation rights, or similar interests.*—A cash settlement option, phantom stock, stock appreciation right, or similar interest is treated as reasonably certain to be exercised if it is reasonably certain that the option will have value at some time during the period in which the option may be exercised.

(3) *Safe harbors.*—(i) *Options to acquire stock.*—Except as provided in paragraph (g)(3)(iv) of this section, an option to acquire stock is not considered reasonably certain, as of a measurement date, to be exercised if—

(A) The option may be exercised no more than 24 months after the measurement date and the exercise price is equal to or greater than 90 percent of the fair market value of the underlying stock on the measurement date; or

(B) The terms of the option provide that the exercise price of the option is equal to or greater than the fair market value of the underlying stock on the exercise date.

(ii) *Options to sell stock.*—Except as provided in paragraph (g)(3)(iv) of this section, an option to sell stock is not considered reasonably certain, as of a measurement date, to be exercised if—

(A) The option may be exercised no more than 24 months after the measurement date and the exercise price is equal to or less than 110 percent of the fair market value of the underlying stock on the measurement date; or

(B) The terms of the option provide that the exercise price of the option is equal to or less than the fair market value of the underlying stock on the exercise date.

(iii) *Options exercisable at fair market value.*—For purposes of paragraphs (g)(3)(i)(B) and (g)(3)(ii)(B) of this section, an option whose exercise price is determined by a formula is considered to have an exercise price equal to the fair market value of the underlying stock on the exercise date if the formula is agreed upon by the parties when the option is issued in a bona fide attempt to arrive at fair market value on the exercise date and is to be applied based upon the facts in existence on the exercise date.

(iv) *Exceptions.*—The safe harbors of this paragraph (g)(3) do not apply if—

(A) An arrangement exists that provides the holder or a related party with stockholder rights described in paragraph (g)(1)(vii) of this section (except for rights arising upon a default under the option or a related agreement);

(B) It is intended that through a change in the capital structure of the issuing corporation or a transfer of assets to or from the issuing corporation (other than regular, ordinary dividends) or by any other means, the fair market value of the stock of the issuing corporation will be altered for a principal purpose of increasing the likelihood that the option will be exercised; or

(C) The option is one in a series of related or sequential options, unless all such options satisfy paragraph (g)(3)(i) or (ii) of this section.

(v) *Failure to satisfy safe harbor.*—Failure of an option to satisfy one of the safe harbors of this paragraph (g)(3) does not affect the determination of whether an option is treated as reasonably certain to be exercised.

(h) *Examples.*—The provisions of this section may be illustrated by the following examples. These examples assume that the measurement dates set forth in the examples are the only measurement dates that have taken place or will take place.

*Example 1.* (i) P is the common parent of a consolidated group, consisting of P, S, and T. P owns all 100 shares of S's only class of stock, which is voting common stock. P also owns all the stock of T. On June 30, 1992, when the fair market value of the S stock is $40 per share, P sells to U, an unrelated corporation, an option to acquire 40 shares of the S stock that P owns at an exercise price of $30 per share, exercisable at any time within 3 years after the granting of the option. P and T have had substantial losses for 5 consecutive years while S has had substantial income during the same period. Because P, S, and T have been filing consolidated returns, P and T have been able to use all of their losses to offset S's income. It is anticipated that P, S, and T will continue their earnings histories for several more years. On July 31, 1992, S declares and pays a dividend of $1 per share to P.

(ii) If P, S, and T continue to file consolidated returns after June 30, 1992, it could reasonably be anticipated that P, S, and T would eliminate a substantial amount of federal income tax liability by using P's and T's future losses to offset S's income in consolidated returns. Furthermore, based on the difference between the exercise price of the option and the fair market value of the S stock, it is reasonably certain, on June 30, 1992, a measurement date, that the option will be exercised. Therefore, the option held by U is treated as exercised. As a result, for purposes of determining whether P and S are affiliated, P is treated as owning only 60 percent of the value of outstanding shares of S stock and U is treated as owning the remaining 40 percent. P is still treated as owning 100 percent of the voting power. Because members of the P group are no longer treated as owning stock possessing 80 percent of the total value of the S stock as of June 30, 1992, S is no longer a member of the P group. Additionally, P is not entitled to a 100 percent dividends received deduction under section 243(a)(3) because P and S are also treated as not affiliated for purposes of section 243. P is only entitled to an 80 percent dividends received deduction under section 243(c).

*Example 2.* (i) The facts are the same as in *Example 1* except that rather than P issuing an option to acquire 40 shares of S stock to U on June 30, 1992, P, pursuant to a plan, issues an option to U1 on July 1, 1992, to acquire 20 shares of S stock, and issues an option to U2 on July 2, 1992, to acquire 20 shares of S stock.

(ii) Because the options issued to U1 and U2 were issued pursuant to a plan, July 2, 1992, constitutes a measurement date for both options. Therefore, both options are aggregated in determining whether the issuance of the options, rather than the sale of the S stock, would result in the elimination of a substantial amount of federal income tax liability. Accordingly, as in *Example 1*, because the continued affiliation of P, S, and T could reasonably be anticipated to result in the elimination of a substantial amount of federal tax liability and the options are reasonably certain to be exercised, the options are treated as exercised for purposes of determining whether P and S are affiliated, and P and S are no longer affiliated as of July 2, 1992.

*Example 3.* (i) The facts are the same as in *Example 1* except that the option gives U the right to acquire all 100 shares of the S stock, and U is the common parent of a consolidated group. The U group has had substantial losses for 5 consecutive years and it is anticipated that the U group will continue its earnings history for several more years.

(ii) If P sold the S stock, in lieu of the option, to U, S would become a member of the U group. Because the U group files consolidated returns, if P sold the S stock to U, U would be able to use its future losses to offset future income of S. When viewing the transaction from the effect on all parties, the sale of the option, in lieu of the underlying S stock, does not result in the elimination of federal income tax liability because S's income would be offset by the losses of members of either the P or U group. Accordingly, the option is disregarded and S remains a member of the P group.

*Example 4.* (i) P is the common parent of a consolidated group, consisting of P and S. P owns 90 of the 100 outstanding shares of S's only class of stock, which is voting common stock, and U, an unrelated corporation, owns the remaining 10 shares. On August 31, 1992, when the fair market value of the S stock is $100 per share, P sells a call option to U that entitles U to purchase 20 shares of S stock from P, at any time before August 31, 1993, at an exercise price of $115 per share. The call option does not provide U with any voting rights, dividend rights, or any other managerial or economic rights ordinarily afforded to owners of the S stock. There is no intention on August 31, 1992, to alter the value of S to increase the likelihood of the exercise of the call option.

(ii) Because the exercise price of the call option is equal to or greater than 90 percent of the fair market value of the S stock on August 31, 1992, a measurement date, the option may be exercised no more than 24 months after the measurement date, and none of the items described in paragraph (g)(3)(iv) of this section that preclude application of the safe harbor are present, the safe harbor of paragraph (g)(3)(i) of this section applies and the call option is treated as if it is not reasonably certain to be exercised. Therefore, regardless of whether the continued affiliation of P and S would result in the elimination of a substantial amount of federal income tax liability, the call option is disregarded in determining whether S remains a member of the P group.

*Example 5.* (i) The facts are the same as in *Example 4* except that the call option gives U the right to vote similar to that of a shareholder.

(ii) Under paragraph (g)(3)(iv) of this section, the safe harbor of paragraph (g)(3)(i) of this section does not apply because the call option entitles U to voting rights equivalent to that of a shareholder. Accordingly, all of the facts and circumstances surrounding the sale of the call option must be taken into consideration in determining whether it is reasonably certain that the call option will be exercised.

*Example 6.* (i) In 1992, two unrelated corporations, X and Y, decide to engage jointly in a new business venture. To accomplish this purpose, X organizes a new corporation, S, on September 30, 1992. X acquires 100 shares of the voting common stock of S, which are the only shares of S stock outstanding. Y acquires a debenture of S which is convertible, on September 30, 1995, into 100 shares of S common stock. If the conversion right is not exercised, X will have the right, on September 30, 1995, to put 50 shares of its S stock to Y in exchange for 50 percent of the debenture held by Y. The likelihood of the success of the venture is uncertain. It is anticipated that S will generate substantial losses in its early years of operation. X expects to have substantial taxable income during the three years following the organization of S.

(ii) Under the terms of this arrangement, it is reasonably certain, on September 30, 1992, a measurement date, that on September 30, 1995, either through Y's exercise of its conversion right or X's right to put S stock to Y, that Y will own 50 percent of the S stock. Additionally, it could reasonably be anticipated, on September 30, 1992, a measurement date, that the affiliation of X and S would result in the elimination of a substantial amount of federal income tax liability. Accordingly, for purposes of determining whether X and S are affiliated, X is treated as owning only 50 percent of the value of the S stock as of September 30, 1992, a measurement date, and S is not a member of the X affiliated group.

*Example 7.* (i) The facts are the same as in *Example 6* except that rather than acquiring 100 percent of the S stock and the right to put S stock to Y, X acquires only 80 percent of the S stock, while S, rather than acquiring a convertible debenture, acquires 20 percent of the S stock, and an option to acquire an additional 30 percent of the S stock. The terms of the option are such that the option will only be exercised if the new business venture succeeds.

(ii) In contrast to *Example 6*, because of the true business risks involved in the start-up of S and whether the business venture will ultimately succeed, along with the fact that X does not have an option to put S stock to Y, it is not reasonably certain on September 30, 1992, a measurement date, that the option will be exercised and that X will only own 50 percent of the S stock on September 30, 1995. Accordingly, the option is disregarded in determining whether S is a member of the X group.

(i) *Effective date.*—This section applies, generally, to options with a measurement date on or after February 28, 1992. This section does not apply to options issued prior to February 28, 1992, which have a measurement date on or after February 28, 1992, if the measurement date for the option occurs solely because of an adjustment in the terms of the option pursuant to the terms of the option as it existed on February 28, 1992. Paragraph (b)(2)(iv) of this section applies to stock outstanding on or after February 28, 1992. Paragraph (a)(2) of this section applies with respect to taxable years beginning on or after November 13, 2020. However, taxpayers and their related parties, within the meaning of sections 267(b) and 707(b)(1), may choose to apply the rules of this section to a taxable year beginning after December 31, 2017, so long as the taxpayers and their related parties consistently apply the rules of this section, the section 163(j) regulations (as defined in §1.163(j)-1(b)(37)), and, if applicable, §§1.263A-9, 1.263A-15, 1.381(c)(20)-1, 1.382-1, 1.382-2, 1.382-5, 1.382-6, 1.382-7,

1.383-0, 1.383-1, 1.469-9, 1.469-11, 1.704-1, 1.882-5, 1.1362-3, 1.1368-1, 1.1377-1, 1.1502-13, 1.1502-21, 1.1502-36, 1.1502-79, 1.1502-91 through 1.1502-99 (to the extent they effectuate the rules of §§1.382-2, 1.382-5, 1.382-6, 1.382-7, and 1.383-1), to that taxable year. [Reg. §1.1504-4.]

□ [T.D. 8462, 12-28-92. Amended by T.D. 9905, 9-3-2020.]

# RELATED RULES

## In General

### [Reg. §1.1551-1]

**§1.1551-1. Disallowance of surtax exemption and accumulated earnings credit.**—(a) *In general.*—If—

(1) Any corporation transfers, on or after January 1, 1951, and before June 13, 1963, all or part of its property (other than money) to a transferee corporation,

(2) Any corporation transfers, directly or indirectly, after June 12, 1963, all or part of its property (other than money) to a transferee corporation, or

(3) Five or fewer individuals are in control of a corporation and one or more of them transfer, directly or indirectly, after June 12, 1963, property (other than money) to a transferee corporation,

and the transferee was created for the purpose of acquiring such property or was not actively engaged in business at the time of such acquisition, and if after such transfer the transferor or transferors are in control of the transferee during any part of the taxable year of the transferee, then for such taxable year of the transferee the Secretary or his delegate may disallow the surtax exemption defined in section 11(d) or the accumulated earnings credit of $150,000 ($100,000 in the case of taxable years beginning before January 1, 1975) provided in paragraph (2) or (3) of section 535(c), unless the transferee establishes by the clear preponderance of the evidence that the securing of such exemption or credit was not a major purpose of the transfer.

(b) *Purpose of section 1551.*—The purpose of section 1551 is to prevent avoidance or evasion of the surtax imposed by section 11(c) or of the accumulated earnings tax imposed by section 531. It is not intended, however, that section 1551 be interpreted as delimiting or abrogating any principle of law established by judicial decision, or any existing provisions of the Code, such as sections 269 and 482, which have the effect of preventing the avoidance or evasion of income taxes. Such principles of law and such provisions of the Code, including section 1551, are not mutually exclusive, and in appropriate cases they may operate together or they may operate separately.

(c) *Application of section 269(b) to cases covered by section 1551.*—The provisions of section 269(b) and the authority of the district director thereunder, to the extent not inconsistent with the provisions of section 1551, are applicable to cases covered by section 1551. Pursuant to the authority provided in section 269(b) the district director may allow to the transferee any part of a surtax exemption or accumulated earnings credit for a taxable year for which such exemption or credit would otherwise be disallowed under section 1551(a); or he may apportion such exemption or credit among the corporations involved. For example, corporation A transfers on January 1, 1955, all of its property to corporations B and C in exchange for all of the stock of such corporations. Immediately thereafter, corporation A is dissolved and its stockholders become the sole stockholders of corporations B and C. Assuming that corporations B and C are unable to establish by the clear preponderance of the evidence that the securing of the surtax exemption defined in section 11(d) or the accumulated earnings credit provided in section 535, or both, was not a major purpose of the transfer, the district director is authorized under sections 1551(c) and 269(b) to allow one such exemption and credit and to apportion such exemption and credit between corporations B and C.

(d) *Actively engaged in business.*—For purposes of this section, a corporation maintaining an office for the purpose of preserving its corporate existence is not considered to be "actively engaged in business" even though such corporation may be deemed to be "doing business" for other purposes. Similarly, for purposes of this section, a corporation engaged in winding up its affairs, prior to an acquisition to which section 1551 is applicable, is not considered to be "actively engaged in business."

(e) *Meaning and application of the term "control".*—(1) *In general.*— For purposes of this section, the term "control" means—

(i) With respect to a transferee corporation described in paragraph (a)(1) or (2) of this section, the ownership by the transferor corporation, its shareholders, or both, of stock possessing either (a) at least 80 percent of the total combined voting power of all classes of stock entitled to vote, or (b) at least 80 percent of the total value of shares of all classes of stock.

(ii) With respect to each corporation described in paragraph (a)(3) of this section, the ownership by five or fewer individuals of stock possessing (a) at least 80 percent of the total combined voting power of all classes of stock entitled to vote or at least 80 percent of the total value of shares of all classes of the stock of each corporation, and (b) more than 50 percent of the total combined voting power of all classes of stock entitled to vote or more than 50 percent of the total value of shares of all classes of stock of each corporation, taking into account the stock ownership of each such individual only to the extent such stock ownership is identical with respect to each such corporation.

(2) *Special rules.*—In determining for purposes of this section whether stock possessing at least 80 percent (or more than 50 percent in the case of subparagraph (1)(ii)(b) of this paragraph) of the total combined voting power of all classes of stock entitled to vote is owned, all classes of such stock shall be considered together; it is not necessary that at least 80 percent (or more than 50 percent) of each class of voting stock be owned. Likewise, in determining for purposes of this section whether stock possessing at least 80 percent (or more than 50 percent) of the total value of shares of all classes of stock is owned, all classes of stock of the corporation shall be considered together; it is not necessary that at least 80 percent (or more than 50 percent) of the value of shares of each class be owned. The fair market value of a share shall be considered as the value to be used for purposes of this computation. With respect to transfers described in paragraph (a)(2) or (3) of this section, the ownership of stock shall be determined in accordance with the provisions of section 1563(e) and the regulations thereunder. With respect to transfers described in paragraph (a)(1) of this section, the ownership of stock shall be determined in accordance with the provisions of section 544 and the regulations thereunder, except that constructive ownership under section 544(a)(2) shall be determined only with respect to the individual's spouse and minor children. In determining control, no stock shall be excluded because such stock was acquired before January 1, 1951 (the effective date of section 1551(a)(1)), or June 13, 1963 (the effective date of section 1551(a)(2) and (3)).

(3) *Example.*—This paragraph may be illustrated by the following example:

*Example.* On January 1, 1964, individual A, who owns 50 percent of the voting stock of corporation X, and individual B, who owns 30 percent of such voting stock, transfer property (other than money) to corporation Y (newly created for the purpose of acquiring such property) in exchange for all of Y's voting stock. After the transfer, A and B own the voting stock of corporations X and Y in the following proportions:

| Individual | Corporation X | Corporation Y | Identical Ownership |
|---|---|---|---|
| A | 50 | 30 | 30 |
| B | 30 | 50 | 30 |
| Total | 80 | 80 | 60 |

The transfer of property by A and B to corporation Y is a transfer described in paragraph (a)(3) of this section since (i) A and B own at least 80 percent of the voting stock of corporations X and Y, and (ii) taking into account each such individual's stock ownership only to the extent such ownership is identical with respect to each such corporation, A and B own more than 50 percent of the voting stock of corporations X and Y.

(f) *Taxable year of allowance or disallowance.*—(1) *In general.*—The district director's authority with respect to cases covered by section 1551 is not limited to the taxable year of the transferee corporation in which the transfer of property occurs. Such authority extends to the taxable year in which the transfer occurs or any subsequent taxable year of the transferee corporation if, during any part of such year, the transferor or transferors are in control of the transferee.

(2) *Examples.*—This paragraph may be illustrated by the following examples:

**Reg. §1.1551-1(f)(2)**

*Example (1).* On January 1, 1955, corporation D transfers property (other than money) to corporation E, a corporation not actively engaged in business at the time of the acquisition of such property, in exchange for 60 percent of the voting stock of E. During a later taxable year of E, corporation D acquires an additional 20 percent of such voting stock. As a result of such additional acquisition, D owns 80 percent of the voting stock of E. Accordingly, section 1551(a)(1) is applicable for the taxable year in which the later acquisition of stock occurred and for each taxable year thereafter in which the requisite control continues.

*Example (2).* On June 20, 1963, individual A, who owns all of the stock of corporation X, transfers property (other than money) to corporation Y, a corporation not actively engaged in business at the time of the acquisition of such property, in exchange for 60 percent of the voting stock of Y. During a later taxable year of Y, A acquires an additional 20 percent of such voting stock. After such acquisition A owns at least 80 percent of the voting stock of corporations X and Y. Accordingly, section 1551(a)(3) is applicable for the taxable year in which the later acquisition of stock occurred and for each taxable year thereafter in which the requisite control continues.

*Example (3).* Individuals A and B each owns 50 percent of the stock of corporation X. On January 15, 1964, A transfers property (other than money) to corporation Y (newly created by A for the purpose of acquiring such property) in exchange for all the stock of Y. In a subsequent taxable year of Y, individual B buys 50 percent of the stock which A owns in Y (or he transfers money to Y in exchange for its stock, as a result of which he owns 50 percent of Y's stock). Immediately thereafter the stock ownership of A and B in corporation Y is identical to their stock ownership in corporation X. Accordingly, section 1551(a)(3) is applicable for the taxable year in which B acquires stock in corporation Y (see paragraph (g)(3) of this section) and for each taxable year thereafter in which the requisite control continues. Moreover, if B's acquisition of stock in Y is pursuant to a preexisting agreement with A, A's transfer to Y and B's acquisition of Y's stock are considered a single transaction and section 1551(a)(3) also would be applicable for the taxable year in which A's transfer to Y took place and for each taxable year thereafter in which the requisite control continues.

(g) *Nature of transfer.*—(1) *Corporate transfers before June 13, 1963.*—A transfer made before June 13, 1963, by any corporation of all or part of its assets, whether or not such transfer qualifies as a reorganization under section 368, is within the scope of section 1551(a)(1), except that section 1551(a)(1) does not apply to a transfer of money only. For example, the transfer of cash for the purpose of expanding the business of the transferor corporation through the formation of a new corporation is not a transfer within the scope of section 1551(a)(1), irrespective of whether the new corporation uses the cash to purchase from the transferor corporation stock in trade or similar property.

(2) *Corporate transfers after June 12, 1963.*—A direct or indirect transfer made after June 12, 1963, by any corporation of all or part of its assets to a transferee corporation, whether or not such transfer qualifies as a reorganization under section 368, is within the scope of section 1551(a)(2) except that section 1551(a)(2) does not apply to a transfer of money only. For example, if a transferor corporation transfers property to its shareholders or to a subsidiary, the transfer of that property by the shareholders or the subsidiary to a transferee corporation as part of the same transaction is a transfer of property by the transferor corporation to which section 1551(a)(2) applies. A transfer of property pursuant to a purchase by a transferee corporation from a transferor corporation controlling the transferee is within the scope of section 1551(a)(2), whether or not the purchase follows a transfer of cash from the controlling corporation.

(3) *Other transfers after June 12, 1963.*—A direct or indirect transfer made after June 12, 1963, by five or fewer individuals to a transferee corporation, whether or not such transfer qualifies under one or more other provisions of the Code (for example, section 351), is within the scope of section 1551(a)(3) except that section 1551(a)(3) does not apply to a transfer of money only. Thus, if one of five or fewer individuals who are in control of a corporation transfers property (other than money) to a controlled transferee corporation, the transfer is within the scope of section 1551(a)(3) notwithstanding that the other individuals transfer nothing or transfer only money.

(4) *Examples.*—This paragraph may be illustrated by the following examples:

*Example (1).* Individuals A and B each owns 50 percent of the voting stock of corporation X. On January 15, 1964, A and B each acquires property (other than money) from X and, as part of the same transaction, each transfers such property to his wholly owned corporation (newly created for the purpose of acquiring such property). A and B retain substantial continuing interests in corporation X. The transfers to the two newly created corporations are within the scope of section 1551(a)(2).

*Example (2).* Corporation W organizes corporation X, a wholly owned subsidiary, for the purpose of acquiring the properties of corporation Y. Pursuant to a reorganization qualifying under section 368(a)(1)(C), substantially all of the properties of corporation Y are transferred on June 15, 1963, to corporation X solely in exchange for voting stock of corporation W. There is a transfer of property from W to X within the meaning of section 1551(a)(2).

*Example (3).* Individuals A and B, each owning 50 percent of the voting stock of corporation X, organize corporation Y to which each transfers money only in exchange for 50 percent of the stock of Y. Subsequently, Y uses such money to acquire other property from A and B after June 12, 1963. Such acquisition is within the scope of section 1551(a)(3).

*Example (4).* Individual A owns 55 percent of the stock of corporation X. Another 25 percent of corporation X's stock is owned in the aggregate by individuals B, C, D, and E. On June 15, 1963, individual A transfers property to corporation Y (newly created for the purpose of acquiring such property) in exchange for 60 percent of the stock of Y, and B, C, and D acquire all of the remaining stock of Y. The transfer is within the scope of section 1551(a)(3).

(h) *Purpose of transfer.*—In determining, for purposes of this section, whether the securing of the surtax exemption or accumulated earnings credit constituted "a major purpose" of the transfer, all circumstances relevant to the transfer shall be considered. "A major purpose" will not be inferred from the mere purchase of inventory by a subsidiary from a centralized warehouse maintained by its parent corporation or by another subsidiary of the parent corporation. For disallowance of the surtax exemption and accumulated earnings credit under section 1551, it is not necessary that the obtaining of either such credit or exemption, or both, have been the sole or principal purpose of the transfer of the property. It is sufficient if it appears, in the light of all the facts and circumstances, that the obtaining of such exemption or credit, or both, was one of the major considerations that prompted the transfer. Thus, the securing of the surtax exemption or the accumulated earnings credit may constitute "a major purpose" of the transfer, notwithstanding that such transfer was effected for a valid business purpose and qualified as a reorganization within the meaning of section 368. The taxpayer's burden of establishing by the clear preponderance of the evidence that the securing of either such exemption or credit or both was not "a major purpose" of the transfer may be met, for example, by showing that the obtaining of such exemption, or credit, or both, was not a major factor in relationship to the other consideration or considerations which prompted the transfer. [Reg. § 1.1551-1.]

☐ [*T.D. 6140,* 8-29-55. *Amended by T.D. 6377,* 5-12-59; *T.D. 6412,* 9-10-59; *T.D. 6911,* 2-23-67 *and T.D. 7376,* 9-15-75.]

### [Reg. § 1.1552-1]

**§ 1.1552-1. Earnings and profits.**—(a) *General rule.*—For the purpose of determining the earnings and profits of each member of an affiliated group which is required to be included in a consolidated return for such group filed for a taxable year beginning after December 31, 1953, and ending after August 16, 1954, the tax liability of the group shall be allocated among the members of the group in accordance with one of the following methods, pursuant to an election under paragraph (c) of this section:

(1)(i) The tax liability of the group shall be apportioned among the members of the group in accordance with the ratio which that portion of the consolidated taxable income attributable to each member of the group having taxable income bears to the consolidated taxable income.

(ii) For consolidated return years beginning after December 31, 1965, a member's portion of the tax liability of the group under the method of allocation provided by subdivision (i) of this subparagraph is an amount equal to the tax liability of the group multiplied by a fraction, the numerator of which is the taxable income of such member, and the denominator of which is the sum of the taxable incomes of all the members. For purposes of this subdivision the taxable income of a member shall be the separate taxable income determined under § 1.1502-12, adjusted for the following items taken into account in the computation of consolidated taxable income:

(*a*) The portion of the consolidated net operating loss deduction, the consolidated charitable contributions deduction, the consolidated dividends received deduction, the consolidated section 247 deduction, the consolidated section 582(c) net loss, and the consolidated section 922 deduction, attributable to such member;

(*b*) Such member's capital gain net income (net capital gain for taxable years beginning before January 1, 1977) (determined without regard to any net capital loss carryover attributable to such member);

(c) Such member's net capital loss and section 1231 net loss, reduced by the portion of the consolidated net capital loss attributable to such member; and

(d) The portion of any consolidated net capital loss carryover attributable to such member which is absorbed in the taxable year.

If the computation of the taxable income of a member under this subdivision results in an excess of deductions over gross income, then for purposes of this subdivision such member's taxable income shall be zero.

(2)(i) The tax liability of the group shall be allocated to the several members of the group on the basis of the percentage of the total tax which the tax of such member if computed on a separate return would bear to the total amount of the taxes for all members of the group so computed.

(ii) For consolidated return years beginning after December 31, 1965, a member's portion of the tax liability of the group under the method of allocation provided by subdivision (i) of this subparagraph is an amount equal to the tax liability of the group multiplied by a fraction, the numerator of which is the separate return tax liability of such member, and the denominator of which is the sum of the separate return tax liabilities of all the members. For purposes of this subdivision the separate return tax liability of a member is its tax liability computed as if it has filed a separate return for the year except that—

(a) Gains and losses on intercompany transactions shall be taken into account as provided in §1.1502-13 as if a consolidated return had been filed for the year;

(b) Gains and losses relating to inventory adjustments shall be taken into account as provided in §1.1502-18 as if a consolidated return had been filed for the year;

(c) Transactions with respect to stock, bonds, or other obligations of members shall be reflected as provided in §1.1502-13(f) and (g) as if a consolidated return had been filed for the year;

(d) Excess losses shall be included in income as provided in §1.1502-19 as if a consolidated return had been filed for the year;

(e) In the computation of the deduction under section 167, property shall not lose its character as new property as a result of a transfer from one member to another member during the year;

(f) A dividend distributed by one member to another member during the year shall not be taken into account in computing the deductions under section 243(a)(1), 244(a), 245, or 247 (relating to deductions with respect to dividends received and dividends paid);

(g) Basis shall be determined under §§1.1502-31 and 1.1502-32, and earnings and profits shall be determined under §1.1502-33, as if a consolidated return had been filed for the year;

(h) Subparagraph (2) of §1.1502-3(f) shall apply as if a consolidated return had been filed for the year; and

(i) For purposes of subtitle A of the Code, the surtax exemption of the member shall be an amount equal to $25,000 ($50,000 in the case of a taxable year ending in 1975), divided by the number of members (or such portion of $25,000 or $50,000 which is apportioned to the member pursuant to a schedule attached to the consolidated return for the taxable year). (However, if for the taxable year some or all of the members are component members of a controlled group of corporations (within the meaning of section 1563) and if there are other such component members which do not join in filing the consolidated return for such year, the amount to be divided among the members filing the consolidated return shall be (in lieu of $25,000 or $50,000) the sum of the amounts apportioned to the component members which join in filing the consolidated return (as determined for taxable years beginning after December 31, 1974, under §1.1561-2(a)(2) or §1.1561-3, whichever is applicable, and for taxable years beginning before January 1, 1975, under §1.1561-2A(a)(2) or §1.1561-3A, whichever is applicable).)

If the computation of the separate return tax liability of a member under this subdivision does not result in a positive tax liability, then for purposes of this subdivision such member's separate return tax liability shall be zero.

(3)(i) The tax liability of the group (excluding the tax increases arising from the consolidation) shall be allocated on the basis of the contribution of each member of the group to the consolidated taxable income of the group. Any tax increases arising from the consolidation shall be distributed to the several members in direct proportion to the reduction in tax liability resulting to such members from the filing of the consolidated return as measured by the difference between their tax liabilities determined on a separate return basis and their tax liabilities (determined without regard to the 2-percent increase provided by section 1503(a) and paragraph (a) of §1.1502-30A (as contained in the 26 C.F.R. edition revised as of April 1, 1996) for taxable years beginning before Jan. 1, 1964) based on their contributions to the consolidated taxable income.

(ii) For consolidated return years beginning after December 31, 1965, a member's portion of the tax liability of the group under the method of allocation provided by subdivision (i) of this subparagraph shall be determined by—

(a) Allocating the tax liability of the group in accordance with subparagraph (1)(ii) of this paragraph, but

(b) The amount of tax liability allocated to any member shall not exceed the separate return tax liability of such member, determined in accordance with subparagraph (2)(ii) of this paragraph, and

(c) The sum of the amounts which would be allocated to the members but for (b) of this subdivision (ii) shall be apportioned among the other members in direct proportion to, but limited to, the reduction in tax liability resulting to such other members. Such reduction for any member shall be the excess, if any, of

(1) its separate return tax liability determined in accordance with subparagraph (2)(ii) of this paragraph, over

(2) the amount allocated to such member under (a) of this subdivision (ii).

If any amount remains after being apportioned among members with a reduction in tax liability to the extent of such reduction, as provided in (c) of this subdivision (ii), such remaining amount shall, notwithstanding (b) of this subdivision (ii), be allocated to the members in accordance with the fractions determined under subparagraph (1)(ii) of this paragraph.

(4) The tax liability of the group shall be allocated in accordance with any other method selected by the group with the approval of the Commissioner. No method of allocation may be approved under this subparagraph which may result in the allocation of a positive tax liability for a taxable year, among the members who are allocated a positive tax liability for such year, in a total amount which is more or less than the tax liability of the group for such year. (However, see paragraph (d) of §1.1502-33.)

(b) *Application of rules.*—(1) *Tax liability of the group.*—For purposes of section 1552 and this section, the tax liability of the group for a taxable year shall consist of the Federal income tax liability of the group for such year determined in accordance with §1.1502-2 or §1.1502-30A (as contained in the 26 C.F.R. edition revised as of April 1, 1996), whichever is applicable. Thus, in the case of a carryback of a loss or credit to such year, although the earnings and profits of the members of the group may not be adjusted until the subsequent taxable year from which the loss or credit was carried back, the effect of the carryback, for purposes of this section, shall be determined by allocating the amount of the adjustment as a part of the tax liability of the group for the taxable year to which the loss or credit is carried. For example, if a consolidated net operating loss is carried back from 1969 to 1967, the allocation of the tax liability of the group for 1967 shall be recomputed in accordance with the method of allocation used for 1967, and the changes resulting from such recomputation shall, for accrual method taxpayers, be reflected in the earnings and profits of the appropriate members in 1969.

(2) *Effect of allocation.*—The amount of tax liability allocated to a corporation as its share of the tax liability of the group, pursuant to this section, shall (i) result in a decrease in the earnings and profits of such corporation in such amount, and (ii) be treated as a liability of such corporation for such amount. If the full amount of such liability is not paid by such corporation, pursuant to an agreement among the members of the group or otherwise, the amount which is not paid will generally be treated as a distribution with respect to stock, a contribution to capital, or a combination thereof, as the case may be.

(c) *Method of election.*—(1) The election under paragraph (a)(1), (2), or (3) of this section shall be made not later than the time prescribed by law for filing the first consolidated return of the group for a taxable year beginning after December 31, 1953, and ending after August 16, 1954 (including extensions thereof). If the group elects to allocate its tax liability in accordance with the method prescribed in paragraph (a)(1), (2), or (3) of this section, a statement shall be attached to the return stating which method is elected. Such statement shall be made by the common parent corporation and shall be binding upon all members of the group. In the event that the group desires to allocate its tax liability in accordance with any other method pursuant to paragraph (a)(4) of this section, approval of such method by the Commissioner must be obtained within the time prescribed above. If such approval is not obtained in such time, the group shall allocate in accordance with the method prescribed in paragraph (a)(1) of this section. The request shall state fully the method which the group wishes to apply in apportioning the tax liability. Except as provided in subparagraph (2) of this paragraph, an election once made shall be irrevocable and shall be binding upon the group with respect to the year for which made and for all future years for which a consolidated return is filed or required to be filed unless the Commissioner authorizes a change to another method prior to the time prescribed by law for filing the return for the year in which such change is to be effective.

(2) Each group may make a new election to use any one of the methods prescribed in paragraph (a)(1), (2), or (3) of this section for its first consolidated return year beginning after December 31, 1965, or in conjunction with an election under paragraph (d) of §1.1502-33, or may request the Commissioner's approval of a method under paragraph (a)(4) of this section for its first consolidated return year beginning after December 31, 1965, irrespective of its previous method of allocation under this section. If such new election is not made in conjunction with an election under paragraph (d) of §1.1502-33, it shall be effective for the first consolidated return year beginning after December 31, 1965, and all succeeding years. (See §1.1502-33 for the method of making such new election in conjunction with an election under paragraph (d) of §1.1502-33.) Any other such new election (or request for the Commissioner's approval of a method under paragraph (a)(4) of this section) shall be made within the time prescribed by law for filing the consolidated return for the first taxable year beginning after December 31, 1965 (including extensions thereof), or within 60 days after July 3, 1968, whichever is later. Such new election shall be made by attaching a statement to the consolidated return for the first taxable year beginning after December 31, 1965, or if such election is made within the time prescribed above but after such return is filed, by filing a statement with the internal revenue officer with whom such return was filed.

(d) *Failure to elect.*—If a group fails to make an election in its first consolidated return, or any other election, in accordance with paragraph (c) of this section, the method prescribed under paragraph (a)(1) of this section shall be applicable and shall be binding upon the group in the same manner as if an election had been made to so allocate.

(e) *Definitions.*—Except as otherwise provided in this section, the terms used in this section shall have the same meaning as provided in the regulations under section 1502.

(f) *Example.*—The provisions of this section may be illustrated by the following example:

*Example.* Corporation P is the common parent owning all of the stock of corporations S1 and S2, members of an affiliated group. A consolidated return is filed for the taxable year ending December 31, 1966, by P, S1, and S2. For 1966 such corporations had the following taxable incomes or losses computed in accordance with paragraph (a)(1)(ii) of this section:

| | |
|---|---:|
| P . . . . . . . . . . . . . . . . . . . . . . . . . . . . . . . . . . . . . . . . | $0 |
| S1 . . . . . . . . . . . . . . . . . . . . . . . . . . . . . . . . . . . . . . . | 2,000 |
| S2 . . . . . . . . . . . . . . . . . . . . . . . . . . . . . . . . . . . . . . . | (1,000) |

The group has not made an election under paragraph (c) of this section or paragraph (d) of §1.1502-33. Accordingly, the method of allocation provided by paragraph (a)(1) of this section is in effect for the group. Assuming that the consolidated taxable income is equal to the sum of the members' taxable income and losses, or $1,000, the tax liability of the group for the year (assuming a 22-percent rate) is $220, all of which is allocated to S1. S1 accordingly reduces its earnings and profits in the amount of $220, irrespective of who actually pays the tax liability. If S1 pays the $220 tax liability there will be no further effect upon the income, earnings and profits, or the basis of stock of any member. If, however, P pays the $220 tax liability (and such payment is not in fact a loan from P to S1), then P shall be treated as having made a contribution to the capital of S1 in the amount of $220. On the other hand, if S2 pays the $220 tax liability (and such payment is not in fact a loan from S2), then S2 shall be treated as having made a distribution with respect to its stock to P in the amount of $220, and P shall be treated as having made a contribution to the capital of S1 in the amount of $220. [Reg. §1.1552-1.]

☐ [*T.D. 6140, 8-29-55. Amended by T.D. 6962, 7-2-68; T.D. 7528, 12-27-77; T.D. 7728, 10-31-80; T.D. 8560, 8-12-94; T.D. 8597, 7-12-95 and T.D. 8677, 6-26-96.*]

# Certain Controlled Corporations

### [Reg. §1.1561-0]

**§1.1561-0. Table of contents.**—This section lists the table of contents for §§1.1561-1 through 1.1561-3.

☐ [*T.D. 9476, 12-22-2009.*]

### [Reg. §1.1561-1]

**§1.1561-1. General rules regarding certain tax benefits available to the component members of a controlled group of corporations.**—(a) *In general.*—(1) *Limitation.*—Part II (section 1561 and following) of subchapter B of chapter 6 of the Internal Revenue Code (Code) (part II) provides rules to limit the amounts of certain specified tax benefit items of component members of a controlled group of corporations for their tax years which include a particular December 31st date, or, in the case of a short taxable year member (see section 1561(b) and §1.1561-2(e)), the date substituted for that December 31st date. The amount of the tax items enumerated in section 1561(a) available to any of the component members of a controlled group shall be determined for purposes of subtitle A of the Code as if the component members were a single corporation. Certain other tax items also set forth in section 1561(a) (for example, the additional tax imposed by section 11(b)(1) and the section 55(d)(3) phase out of the alternative minimum tax exemption amount) will be determined by combining the positive taxable income or positive alternative minimum taxable income of the component members of such a group and then allocating the amount of such items among those members.

(2) *Definitions.*—For certain definitions (including the definition of a *controlled group of corporations* and a *component member*) and special rules for purposes of this part II see section 1563.

(b) *Special rules.*—(1) *S Corporation.*—For purposes of this part II, the term *corporation* includes a small business corporation (as defined in section 1361). However, for the treatment of such a corporation as an *excluded member* of a controlled group of corporations see §1.1563-1(b)(2)(ii)(C).

(2) *52-53-week taxable year.*—In the case of corporations electing a 52-53-week taxable year under section 441(f)(1), the provisions of this part II shall be applied in accordance with the special rule of section 441(f)(2)(A). See §1.441-2.

(c) *Tax avoidance.*—The provisions of this part II do not delimit or abrogate any principle of law established by judicial decision, or any existing provisions of the Code, such as sections 269, 482, and 1551, which serve to prevent any avoidance or evasion of income taxes.

(d) *Effective/applicability date.*—This section applies to any tax year beginning on or after December 21, 2009. However, taxpayers may apply this section to any Federal income tax return filed on or after December 21, 2009. For tax years beginning before December 21, 2009, see §1.1561-1T as contained in 26 CFR part 1 in effect on April 1, 2009. [Reg. §1.1561-1.]

☐ [*T.D. 9476, 12-22-2009.*]

### [Reg. §1.1561-2]

**§1.1561-2. Special rules for allocating reductions of certain section 1561(a) tax-benefit items.**—(a) *Additional tax.*—(1) *Calculation.*—(i) *In general.*—For the purpose of determining the amount, if any, of the additional tax imposed by section 11(b)(1) (the additional tax), the taxable incomes of all of the component members of a controlled group of corporations shall be combined to determine whether either of the income thresholds for imposing the additional tax have been attained.

(ii) *Special rules.*—For purposes of paragraph (a)(1)(i) of this section—

(A) *Component member* means a corporation that is apportioned some part of any applicable tax bracket amount; and

(B) *Taxable income* means the positive taxable income of a component member for its entire tax year (even if it was not a member of the group for each day of that tax year) that includes the same December 31st testing date, which is also applicable to the other component members of that same controlled group.

(2) *Apportionment.*—(i) *General rule.*—Any additional tax determined under paragraph (a)(1) of this section shall be apportioned among such members in the same manner as the corresponding tax bracket of section 11(b)(1) is apportioned. For rules to apportion the section 11(b)(1) tax brackets among the component members of a controlled group, see § 1.1561-3(b) or (c).

(ii) *Apportionment methods.*—Unless the component members of a controlled group elect to use the first-in-first-out (FIFO) method described in paragraph (a)(2)(ii)(B) of this section, such members are required to apportion the amount of the additional tax using the proportionate method described in paragraph (a)(2)(ii)(A) of this section. These component members may elect the FIFO method by specifically adopting such method in their apportionment plan.

(A) *Proportionate method.*—Under the proportionate method, the additional tax is allocated to each component member in the same proportion as the portion of the taxbenefit amount that inured to a member from utilizing lower tax brackets bears to the amount of the group's total tax-benefit amount inuring to it from utilizing those lower tax brackets. The tax-benefit amount that inures to a corporation from using a particular tax bracket is the tax savings that such corporation realizes from having a portion of its taxable income taxed at the lower rate attributed to that tax bracket instead of the high tax rates to which it would otherwise be subject. The steps for applying the proportionate method of allocation are as follows:

(1) *Step 1.*—The regular tax (not including the additional tax) owed by a component member under a particular tax bracket is divided by the total tax owed by all component members under that tax bracket;

(2) *Step 2.*—The percentage calculated under *Step 1* is multiplied by the total taxbenefit amount inuring to all the members of the group from their use of this tax bracket. This computed amount equals the portion of the group's tax-benefit amount that inured to such member from using its portion of this tax bracket;

(3) *Step 3.*—The amount determined under *Step 2* is divided by the total taxbenefit amount, inuring to all the component members of the group from using all the tax brackets to which any component member's income was subject;

(4) *Step 4.*—The percentage calculated under *Step 3* is multiplied by the amount of the group's additional tax. The amount determined under this *Step 4* equals the amount of the additional tax apportioned to such member for that tax bracket; and

(5) *Step 5.*—If a component member is liable for regular tax (not including the additional tax) under more than one tax bracket, that member must calculate the amount of the additional tax apportioned to it with respect to each tax bracket. Accordingly, steps 1 through 4 must be applied for each tax bracket applicable to that member. The sum of all the apportioned amounts of additional tax from each tax bracket for which the member is subject is the total amount of the additional tax apportioned to that member.

(B) *FIFO method.*—Under the FIFO method, the first dollars of the additional tax are to be allocated proportionately to the members starting with the lowest tax bracket (that is, the first tax bracket), up to the amount of the tax benefit inuring to those members from using that tax bracket. Any remaining amount of additional tax is then allocated proportionately among the component members who use the next higher tax bracket, and so on, until the entire amount of the additional tax has been fully apportioned among the members. For example, the first $9,500 of the additional tax liability of a controlled group is apportioned entirely to the member(s) that availed themselves of the benefit of the 15 percent tax bracket.

(3) *Examples.*—The provisions of this paragraph (a) may be illustrated by the following examples:

*Example 1.* (i) *Facts.* A controlled group of corporations consists of three members: X, Y and Z. X owns all the stock of Y and Z. Each corporation files its separate return on a calendar year basis. For calendar year 2007, the component members of the controlled group have an apportionment plan in effect. The members apportioned 80% of the 15 percent tax-bracket amount ($40,000) to X and the remaining 10% ($10,000) to Y. The members apportioned 100% of the 25 percent taxbracket amount ($25,000) to Y. However, these members have not adopted the FIFO method for apportioning the additional taxes. Therefore, they must follow the proportionate method. For 2007, X had taxable income (TI) of $40,000, Y had TI of $60,000 and Z had TI of $100,000. Thus the total TI of the group is $200,000.

(ii) *Calculating the tax from the tax brackets and the tax benefit derived from such tax.* (A) *Regular tax of group subject to a 15 percent tax rate.* (1) *Calculating the group's tax which resulted from applying a 15 percent tax rate.* The amount of tax under the 15 percent tax bracket is $7,500 (15% × $50,000).

(2) *The tax-benefit amount inuring to the group from using the 15 percent tax bracket.* A tax benefit inures to those members of the group who avail themselves of the 15 percent tax bracket. That tax benefit results from having the first $50,000 of its income taxed at the 15 percent tax rate, instead of at the 34 percent tax rate. Thus, the tax-benefit amount inuring to this group from using the 15 percent tax bracket is $9,500 ($17,000 (34% × $50,000) minus $7,500 (15% × $50,000).

(B) *Regular tax of group subject to a 25 percent tax rate.* (1) *Calculating the group's tax which resulted from applying a 25 percent tax rate.* The amount of tax under the 25 percent tax bracket is $6,250 (25% × $25,000 ($75,000 - $50,000)).

(2) *The tax-benefit amount inuring to the group from using the 25 percent tax bracket.* A tax benefit inures to those members of the group who avail themselves of the 25 percent tax bracket. That tax benefit results from having $25,000 of its income taxed at the 25 percent tax rate, instead of at the 34 percent tax rate. Thus, the taxbenefit amount inuring to this group from using the 25 percent tax bracket is $2,250 ($8,500 (34% × $25,000) minus $6,250 (25% × $25,000)).

(C) *Regular tax of group subject to a 34 percent tax rate.* (1) *Calculating the group's tax which resulted from applying a 34 percent tax rate.* The amount of tax under the 34 percent tax bracket is $42,500 (34% × $125,000 ($200,000 (total TI) - $75,000) (amount taxed at lower rates)).

(2) *The tax-benefit amount inuring to the group from using the 34 percent tax bracket.* The group's total TI of $200,000 is less than the $15,000,000 income threshold for imposing any 3 percent additional tax on the group. Therefore, there is no tax benefit inuring to the members of this group for using the 34 percent tax bracket.

(D) *The computation of the additional tax.* Since the combined TI of the group exceeds $100,000, a 5 percent additional tax is imposed on the group. That 5 percent additional tax is the lesser amount of 5 percent of the group's taxable income exceeding $100,000 or $11,750. Five percent of that excess amount of taxable income is $5,000 (5% × $100,000 ($200,000 - $100,000)). Since $5,000 is less than $11,750, the group's 5 percent additional tax is $5,000.

(iii) *Apportioning the amount of additional tax to each applicable tax bracket.* (A) *The apportioned tax under each bracket.* The amount of tax owed by each member under each tax bracket pursuant to the apportionment plan is as follows:

| Name of Component Member | Amount of tax owed under the 15% tax bracket | Amount of tax owed under the 25% tax bracket | Amount of tax owed under the 34% tax bracket |
|---|---|---|---|
| X | $6,000 | 0 | 0 |
| Y | $1,500 | $6,250 | $8,500 |
| Z | 0 | 0 | $34,000 |

(B) *Apportioning the 5 percent additional tax among the component members of the controlled group.* Since the group did not elect to adopt the FIFO method of apportionment, it is required to apportion the $5,000 of its 5 percent additional tax pursuant to the proportionate method in the following manner:

*(1) Amount of the additional tax apportioned to X.* Pursuant to the plan, X was liable for $6,000 of the group's $7,500 regular tax (80%) owed under the 15 percent tax bracket (and X is not liable for any regular tax under any higher tax bracket). See *Step 1* of paragraph (a)(2)(ii)(A) of this section. X's portion of the group's tax benefit which it derived from using the 15 percent tax rate is $7,600 (0.8 × $9,500). See *Step 2.* The tax benefit inuring to the entire group from using the 15 percent and 25 percent tax brackets is $11,750 ($9,500 (from the 15 percent tax bracket) + $2,250 (from the 25 percent tax bracket)). So, X's percentage portion of the group's total tax benefit is $7,600/$11,750 (64.68%). See *Step 3.* Thus, X's allocated portion of the 5 percent additional tax from using the 15 percent tax bracket is $3,234 (0.6468 x $5,000). See *Step 4.*

*(2) Amount of the additional tax apportioned to Y. (i) Regular tax apportioned to Y from using the 15 percent tax bracket.* Pursuant to the plan, Y was liable for the remaining $1,500 of the group's $7,500 regular tax (20%) owed under the 15 percent tax bracket. See *Step 1.* Y's portion of the group's tax benefit which it derived from using the 15 percent tax rate is $1,900 ($9,500 - $7,600, or 0.2 × $9,500). See *Step 2.* So, Y's percentage portion of the group's total tax benefit is $1,900/$11,750 (16.17%). See *Step 3.* Thus, Y's allocated portion of the 5 percent additional tax from using the 15 percent tax bracket is $809 (0.1617 × $5,000). See *Step 4.*

*(ii) Regular tax apportioned to Y from using the 25 percent tax bracket.* Pursuant to the plan, Y was liable for 100% of the group's regular tax owed under the 25 percent tax bracket, an amount of $6,250. See *Step 1.* Y is, therefore, entitled to 100% of the group's tax benefit which it derived from using this tax bracket, an amount of $2,250. See *Step 2.* So, Y's percentage portion of the group's total tax benefit is $2,250/$11,750 (19.15%). See *Step 3.* Thus, Y's allocated portion of the 5 percent additional tax from using the 25 percent tax bracket is $957 (0.1915 × $5,000). See *Step 4.* Y's total allocated portion of the additional tax is $1,766 ($809 + $957). See *Step 5.*

*Example 2.* (i) *Facts.* The facts are the same as in *Example 1*, except that on August 31, 2007, X of the X-Y-Z controlled group sold all of the stock of Z to M of the MN controlled group, a pair of corporations unrelated to the X-Y group. Pursuant to the terms of the sales agreement, the members of the M-N group properly notified the members of the X-Y group on a timely basis that Z's taxable income for its 2007 tax year, as based on the group's December 31st testing date, was $100,000.

(ii) *Controlled group analysis.* On December 31st, 2007, X and Y are members of the selling controlled group and M, N and Z are members of the buying controlled group. However, pursuant to section 1563(b)(3), Z is treated as an additional member of the X-Y group on December 31st 2007, since it was a member for at least one-half the number of days (243 out of 364) during the period beginning on January 1 and ending on December 30, 2007. Conversely, pursuant to section 1563(b)(2)(A), Z is treated as an excluded member of the M-N controlled group. Therefore, on December 31st, 2007, X, Y and Z qualify as component members of the selling group, and only M and N qualify as component members of the buying group.

(iii) *Additional tax analysis.* With regard to X and Y's 2007 tax years, X and Y together owed $5,000 of additional tax, as calculated in *Example 1.* X's allocated portion of the additional tax is $3,234, as calculated in the manner set forth in *Example 1.* Y's allocated portion of the additional tax is $1,766, also as calculated in the manner set forth in *Example 1.*

*Example 3.* (i) *Facts.* The facts are the same as in *Example 2*, except that in 2012, pursuant to an IRS audit, Z's 2007 taxable income was re-determined. It was adjusted by an income increase of $10,000. Pursuant to the terms of the sales agreement, the members of the M-N group timely notified the members of the X-Y group of Z's income adjustment.

(ii) *Additional tax analysis.* For 2007 the X-Y-Z group owed a revised additional tax in the amount of $5,500, allocated as follows: $3,557.40 to X and $1,942.60 to Y. X and Y each filed an amended 2007 tax return to report their portions of the $500 increase to the group's additional tax. Pursuant to their apportionment plan for allocating their regular tax, and as a result of defaulting to the proportionate method for allocating the group's additional tax, X reported $323.40 as its share of the group's increase to its additional tax and Y reported $176.60 as its share of the group's increase to its additional tax.

*Example 4.* The facts are the same as in *Example 1*, except that the members elected in their apportionment plan to adopt the FIFO method for apportioning the additional tax. Under the FIFO method, the 5 percent additional tax amount of $5,000 will be apportioned entirely to those members who would benefit from using the 15 percent tax bracket, by reason that $5,000 of the group's additional tax is less than $9,500, which is the full tax-benefit amount inuring to a controlled group from having a 15 percent tax rate applied to the full income bracket subject to that rate. Since X derived 80 percent of the group's tax benefit by its use of the 15 percent tax bracket, its

share of the group's 5 percent additional tax is $4,000 (80% × $5,000), and Y's share of the group's 5 percent additional tax is, therefore, $1,000, which is the remaining amount of the group's 5 percent additional tax, attributable to the 15 percent tax bracket.

*(b) Reduction to the amount exempted from the alternative minimum tax.—(1) Calculation.—*The alternative minimum taxable incomes of the component members of a controlled group of corporations shall be taken into account in calculating the reduction set forth in section 55(d)(3) to the amount exempted from the alternative minimum tax (the exemption amount). For purposes of the preceding sentence, *alternative minimum taxable income* means the positive alternative minimum taxable income of a component member for its entire tax year (even if it was not a member of the group for each day of that tax year) that includes the same December 31st testing date, which is also applicable to the other component members of that same controlled group.

*(2) Apportionment.—*Any reduction to the exemption amount shall be apportioned to the component members of a controlled group in the same manner that the amount of the exemption (provided in section 55(d)(2)) to the alternative minimum tax was allocated under section 1561(a). For rules to apportion the section 55(d)(2) exemption amount among the component members of a controlled group, see § 1.1561-3(b) or (c).

*(3) Examples.—*The provisions of this paragraph (b) may be illustrated by the following example:

*Example.* (i) *Facts.* A controlled group of corporations consists of three members: X, Y and Z. X owns all of the stock of Y and Z. Each corporation files its separate return on a calendar year basis. For calendar year 2007, the component members of this controlled group have an apportionment plan in effect. The group has chosen to apportion the entire section 55(d)(2) exemption amount of $40,000 to Z. For 2007, X had alternative minimum taxable income (AMTI) of $40,000, Y had AMTI of $60,000 and Z had AMTI of $100,000. Thus the total AMTI of the group is $200,000.

(ii) *Calculating the reduction to the exemption amount.* Section 55(d)(3)(A) provides that the section 55(d)(2) exemption amount shall be reduced (but not below zero) by an amount equal to 25 percent of the amount by which the AMTI of a corporation exceeds $150,000. For the purpose of computing the group's AMTI, the AMTI of each of the component members, for their tax years that have the same December 31st testing date, shall be taken into account. In accordance with these provisions, the $40,000 exemption amount is reduced by $12,500 (25% x $50,000 ($200,000 - $150,000)). Pursuant to the group's allocation plan, the entire $12,500 reduction to the exemption amount is allocated to Z. Thus, after such allocation, Z's $40,000 exemption amount is reduced to $27,500 ($40,000 - $12,500).

*(c) Accumulated earnings credit.—*The component members of a controlled group of corporations are permitted to allocate the amount of the accumulated earnings credit unequally if they have an apportionment plan in effect.

(d) [Reserved].

*(e) Short taxable years not including a December 31st date.—(1) General rule.—*If a corporation has a short taxable year not including a December 31st date and, after applying the rules of section 1561(b) and paragraph (e)(2)(i) of this section, it qualifies as a component member of the group with respect to its short taxable year (short-year member), then, for purposes of subtitle A of the Internal Revenue Code, the amount of any tax-benefit item described in section 1561(b) allocated to that component member's short taxable year shall be the amount specified in section 1561(a) for that item, divided by the number of corporations which are component members of that group on the last day of that component member's short taxable year. The component members of such group may not apportion, by an apportionment plan, an amount of such tax-benefit item to any short-year member that differs from equal apportionment of that item.

*(2) Additional rules.—*For purposes of paragraph (e)(1) of this section—

(i) Section 1563(b) shall be applied as if the last day of the taxable year of a short-year member were substituted for December 31st; and

(ii) The term *short taxable year* does not refer to any portion of a tax year of a corporation for which its income is required to be included in a consolidated return pursuant to § 1.1502-76(b).

*(3) Calculation of the additional tax.—*A short-year member (as defined in paragraph (e)(1) of this section) for its short taxable year calculates its additional tax liability imposed by section 11(b)(1) only on its own income, and therefore the subsequent calculation of the additional tax liability with regard to the remaining members of the group will not include the income of this short-year member.

(4) *Calculation of the alternative minimum tax.*—If a component member has a tax year of less than 12 months, whether or not such tax year includes a December 31st date, see section 443(d) for the annualization method required for calculating the alternative minimum tax.

(5) *Examples.*—The provisions of this paragraph (e) may be illustrated by the following examples:

*Example 1. Formation of a new member of a controlled group.* (i) *Facts.* On January 2, 2007, corporation X transfers cash to newly formed corporation Y (which begins business on that date) and receives all of the stock of Y in return. X also owns all of the stock of corporation Z on each day of 2006 and 2007. X, Y and Z have an apportionment plan in effect, apportioning the 15 percent tax-bracket amount as follows: 40% ($20,000) to each of X and Y and 20% ($10,000) to Z. X, Y and Z each file a separate return with respect to the group's December 31st 2007 testing date. X is on a calendar tax year and Z is on a fiscal tax year ending on March 31. Y adopts a fiscal year ending on June 30 and timely files a tax return for its short taxable year beginning on January 2, 2007, and ending on June 30, 2007.

(ii) *Y's short taxable year.* On June 30, 2007, Y is a component member of a parent-subsidiary controlled group of corporations composed of X, Y and Z. Pursuant to paragraph (e)(1) of this section, the group may not apportion any amount of the 15 percent tax bracket to Y's short taxable year ending on June 30, 2007. Rather, Y is entitled to exactly $1/3$ of such bracket amount, or $16,667.

(iii) *The members' subsequent tax years.* On December 31st, 2007, X, Y and Z are component members of a parent-subsidiary controlled group of corporations. For their tax years that include December 31st, 2007 (X's calendar year ending December 31st, 2007, Z's fiscal year ending March 31, 2008 and Y's fiscal year ending June 30, 2008), X, Y and Z apportion among themselves the full amount of all of the applicable tax brackets pursuant to their apportionment plan. For example, 40% of the 15 percent tax-bracket amount, or $20,000, was apportioned to each of X and Y, and the remaining 10%, or $10,000, was apportioned to Z.

*Example 2. Allocating a tax bracket to the short taxable year of a liquidated member of a controlled group* (i) *Facts.* On January 1, 2007, corporation P owns all of the stock of corporations $S_1$, $S_2$ and $S_3$ (the P group). Each of these four component members of the P group, with respect to the group's December 31st, 2007 testing date, files its separate return on a calendar year basis. These members have an apportionment plan in effect (the P group plan) under which $S_1$ and $S_2$ are each entitled to 40% of the 15 percent tax-bracket amount ($20,000), and P and $S_3$ are each entitled to 10% of the 15 percent tax-bracket amount ($5,000). On May 31, 2007, $S_1$ liquidates and therefore files a return for the short taxable year beginning on January 1, 2007, and ending on May 31, 2007. On July 31, 2007, $S_2$ liquidates and therefore files a return for the short taxable year beginning on January 1, 2007 and ending on July 31, 2007. P and $S_3$ each file a return for their 2007 calendar tax years.

(ii) *Apportionment of the 15 percent tax bracket to S₁ for its short taxable year.* On May 31, 2007, $S_1$ is a component member of the P group composed of P, $S_1$, $S_2$ and $S_3$. Pursuant to paragraph (e)(1) of this section, the group may not apportion any amount of the 15 percent tax bracket to $S_1$'s short taxable year ending on June 30, 2007. Rather, $S_1$ is entitled to exactly $1/4$ of such bracket amount, or $12,500.

(iii) *Apportionment of the 15 percent tax bracket to S₂ for its short taxable year.* On July 31, 2007, $S_2$ is a component member of the P group composed of P, $S_2$ and $S_3$. Pursuant to paragraph (e)(1) of this section, the group may not apportion any amount of the 15 percent tax bracket to $S_2$'s short taxable year ending on June 30, 2007. Rather, $S_2$ is entitled to exactly $1/3$ of such bracket amount, or $16,667.

(iv) *Apportionment of the 15 percent tax bracket to P and S₃ for each of their calendar tax years.* On December 31st, 2007, P and $S_3$ are component members of the P group. Accordingly, for P and $S_3$'s 2007 calendar tax year, they are each apportioned $25,000 of the 15 percent tax bracket, pursuant to the applicable P group plan.

*Example 3. Liquidation of member after its transfer to another controlled group.* (i) *Facts.* The facts are the same as in *Example 2*, except that P, on April 30, 2007, sold all of the stock of $S_2$ to the M-N controlled group. At the time of the sale, M and N are both unrelated to any members of the P group. As in *Example 2*, $S_2$ liquidates on July 31, 2007, and therefore files a tax return for its short taxable year beginning on January 1, 2007, and ending on July 31, 2007. Pursuant to the sales agreement, the N-M group timely notified P that $S_2$ had liquidated.

(ii) *Controlled group analysis.* On April 30, 2007, the date of the sale of $S_2$, the P group reasonably expected that $S_2$ would be treated as an excluded member with respect to its December 31st, 2007 testing date. On that April 30th date, $S_2$ had been a member of the P group for less than one-half the number of days of what it expected would be a full 2007 calendar tax year preceding December 31st, 2007 (120 days (January 1-April 30) out of 364 days (January 1-December 30)). Yet, as a result of $S_2$'s subsequent liquidation by the M-N group

prior to December 31st, 2007, $S_2$ became a component member of the P group with respect to the P group's December 31st testing date. With respect to that December 31st testing date, $S_2$ thus was a member of the P group for more than one-half of the number of days of its tax year ending on July 31, 2007, which days proceeded December 31st, 2007 (120 days (January 1-April 30 of 2007) out of 211 days (January 1-July 30 of 2007)). The allocation of the 15 percent tax-bracket amount to the P group members is determined in the same manner as in *Example 2* and, therefore, the bracket amounts allocated to P, $S_1$, $S_2$ and $S_3$ are the same as determined in *Example 2*. The allocation of the bracket amounts would be the same if, at the time P sold all of the $S_2$ stock, the parties had made a section 338(h)(10) election.

*Example 4. Short tax year including a December 31st date.* Corporation X owns all of the stock of corporations Y and Z. X, Y and Z each file separate returns. X and Y are on a calendar tax year and Z is on a fiscal tax year beginning October 1 and ending September 30. On January 2, 2007, Z liquidates. Because Z's final tax year (beginning on October 1, 2006 and ending on January 2, 2007) includes a December 31st date, that is, December 31, 2006, it is therefore not subject to the short taxable year rule provided by section 1561(b) and paragraph (e) of this section. Accordingly, Z is a component member of the X-Y-Z group, for the group's December 31st, 2006 testing date. Thus, the rules of this paragraph (e) do not limit the amount of any of the tax-benefit items of section 1561(a) available to Z or to this controlled group.

(f) *Effective/applicability date.*—This section applies to any tax year beginning on or after December 21, 2009. However, taxpayers may apply this section to any Federal income tax return filed on or after December 21, 2009. For tax years beginning before December 21, 2009, see §1.1561-2T as contained in 26 CFR part 1 in effect on April 1, 2009. [Reg. §1.1561-2.]

☐ [T.D. 9476, 12-22-2009.]

## [Reg. §1.1561-3]

**§1.1561-3. Allocation of the section 1561(a) tax items.**—(a) *Filing of form.*—(1) *In general.*—For each tax year that a corporation is a component member of the same controlled group of corporations on a December 31st (its testing date), or, in the case of a short-year member (see section 1561(b) and §1.1561-2(e)), the date substituted for that December 31st date (its testing date), such corporation and all the other component members of such group each must file the required form (that is, Schedule O or any successor form) with the Federal income tax return for that component member's tax year that includes a particular testing date. Each such corporation must file that form with its return whether or not—

(i) An apportionment plan is in effect; or

(ii) Any change is made to the group's apportionment of its section 1561(a) tax benefit items from the previous year.

(2) *Exception for component members that are members of a consolidated group.*—If any of the component members of a controlled group of corporations are also members of a consolidated group, the parent of such consolidated group shall file only one form on behalf of all such members. Such form shall contain the information required for each such member.

(b) *No apportionment plan in effect.*—If the component members of a controlled group of corporations do not have an apportionment plan in effect, the amounts of the section 1561(a) items must be divided equally among all such members. For purposes of the preceding sentence, if any of the component members of a controlled group of corporations are also members of a consolidated group, such members will each be treated as a separate component member of the controlled group.

(c) *Apportionment plan in effect.*—(1) *Adoption of plan.*—The component members of a controlled group of corporations consent to the adoption (or amendment) of an apportionment plan by checking the box to that effect on such form. For purposes of this paragraph (c)—

(i) An apportionment plan that is adopted (including a plan that has been amended) continues in effect until it is terminated;

(ii) A consolidated group is treated collectively as one component member of such group. This treatment occurs even where a member of that consolidated group has joined or left the group, if after such corporation joins or leaves the consolidated group, that group remains in existence, pursuant to §1.1502-75(d); and

(iii) The members must allocate the amounts of the section 1561(a) items between/among themselves as described in the plan.

(2) *Limitation on adopting a plan.*—(i) *Sufficient statute of limitations period for making an assessment of tax.*—The members may only adopt or amend such a plan if there is at least one year remaining in the statutory period (including any extensions thereof) for the assess-

ment of a deficiency against every member the tax liability of which would be increased by the adoption of such a plan.

(ii) *Insufficient statute of limitations period for making an assessment of tax.*—If any member cannot satisfy the requirement of paragraph (c)(2)(i) of this section, the members may not adopt or amend such a plan unless the member not satisfying such requirement has entered into an agreement with the Internal Revenue Service to extend the statute of limitations for the limited purpose of assessing any deficiency against such member attributable to the adoption of such a plan.

(3) *Termination of plan.*—An apportionment plan that is in effect for the component members of a controlled group with respect to a preceding December 31st is terminated with respect to the current December 31st if—

(i) Each member of such group consents to the termination of such a plan for the current December 31st by checking the box to that effect on its form;

(ii) The controlled group ceases to remain in existence (within the meaning of section 1563(a)) during the calendar year ending on the current December 31st;

(iii) Any corporation which was a component member of such group on the preceding December 31st is not a component member of such group on the current December 31st; or

(iv) Any corporation which was not a component member of such group on the preceding December 31st is a component member of such group on the current December 31st.

(d) *Effective/applicability date.*—This section applies to any tax year beginning on or after December 21, 2009. However, taxpayers may apply this section to any Federal income tax return filed on or after December 21, 2009. For tax years beginning before December 21, 2009, see § 1.1561-3T as contained in 26 CFR part 1 in effect on April 1, 2009. [Reg. § 1.1561-3.]

☐ [T.D. 9476, 12-22-2009.]

**[Reg. § 1.1563-1]**

**§ 1.1563-1. Definition of controlled group of corporations and component members and related concepts.**—(a) *Controlled group of corporations.*—(1) *In general.*—(i) *Types of controlled groups.*—For purposes of sections 1561 through 1563, the term *controlled group of corporations* means any group of corporations which is—

(A) A *parent-subsidiary controlled group* (as defined in paragraph (a)(2) of this section);

(B) A *brother-sister controlled group* (as defined in paragraph (a)(3)(i) of this section);

(C) A *combined group* (as defined in paragraph (a)(4) of this section); or

(D) A *life insurance controlled group* (as defined in paragraph (a)(5) of this section).

(ii) *Special rules.*—In determining whether a corporation is included in a controlled group of corporations, section 1563(b) and paragraph (b) of this section shall not be taken into account. For rules defining a component member of a controlled group of corporations, including rules defining an excluded member and an additional member, see section 1563(b) and paragraph (b) of this section.

(iii) *Cross reference.*—For the exclusion of certain stock for purposes of applying the definitions contained in this paragraph, see section 1563(c) and § 1.1563-2.

(2) *Parent-subsidiary controlled group.*—(i) *Definition.*—The term *parent-subsidiary controlled group* means one or more chains of corporations connected through stock ownership with a common parent corporation if—

(A) Stock possessing at least 80 percent of the total combined voting power of all classes of stock entitled to vote or at least 80 percent of the total value of shares of all classes of stock of each of the corporations, except the common parent corporation, is owned (directly and with the application of § 1.1563-3(b)(1), relating to options) by one or more of the other corporations; and

(B) The common parent corporation owns (directly and with the application of § 1.1563-3(b)(1), relating to options) stock possessing at least 80 percent of the total combined voting power of all classes of stock entitled to vote or at least 80 percent of the total value of shares of all classes of stock of at least one of the other corporations, excluding, in computing such voting power or value, stock owned directly by such other corporations.

(ii) *Examples.*—The definition of a parent-subsidiary controlled group of corporations may be illustrated by the following examples:

*Example 1.* P Corporation owns stock possessing 80 percent of the total combined voting power of all classes of stock entitled to vote of S Corporation. P is the common parent of a parent-subsidiary controlled group consisting of member corporations P and S.

*Example 2.* Assume the same facts as in *Example 1*. Assume further that S owns stock possessing 80 percent of the total value of shares of all classes of stock of X Corporation. P is the common parent of a parent-subsidiary controlled group consisting of member corporations P, S, and X. The result would be the same if P, rather than S, owned the X stock.

*Example 3.* P Corporation owns 80 percent of the only class of stock of S Corporation and S, in turn, owns 40 percent of the only class of stock of X Corporation. P also owns 80 percent of the only class of stock of Y Corporation and Y, in turn, owns 40 percent of the only class of stock of X. P is the common parent of a parent-subsidiary controlled group consisting of member corporations P, S, X, and Y.

*Example 4.* P Corporation owns 75 percent of the only class of stock of Y and Z Corporations; Y owns all the remaining stock of Z; and Z owns all the remaining stock of Y. Since intercompany stockholdings are excluded (that is, are not treated as outstanding) for purposes of determining whether P owns stock possessing at least 80 percent of the voting power or value of at least one of the other corporations, P is treated as the owner of stock possessing 100 percent of the voting power and value of Y and Z for purposes of paragraph (a)(2)(i)(B) of this section. Also, stock possessing 100 percent of the voting power and value of Y and Z is owned by the other corporations in the group within the meaning of paragraph (a)(2)(i)(A) of this section. (P and Y together own stock possessing 100 percent of the voting power and value of Z, and P and Z together own stock possessing 100 percent of the voting power and value of Y.) Therefore, P is the common parent of a parent-subsidiary controlled group of corporations consisting of member corporations P, Y, and Z.

(3) *Brother-sister controlled group.*—(i) *Definition.*—The term *brother-sister controlled group* means two or more corporations if the same five or fewer persons who are individuals, estates, or trusts own (directly and with the application of the rules contained in § 1.1563-3(b)) stock possessing more than 50 percent of the total combined voting power of all classes of stock entitled to vote or more than 50 percent of the total value of shares of all classes of stock of each corporation, taking into account the stock ownership of each such person only to the extent such stock ownership is identical with respect to each such corporation.

(ii) *Additional stock ownership requirement for purposes of certain other provisions of law.*—For purposes of any provision of law (other than sections 1561 through 1563) that incorporates the section 1563(a) definition of a controlled group, the term *brother-sister controlled group* means two or more corporations if the same five or fewer persons who are individuals, estates, or trusts own (directly and with the application of the rules contained in § 1.1563-3(b)) stock possessing—

(A) At least 80 percent of the total combined voting power of all classes of stock entitled to vote or at least 80 percent of the total value of shares of all classes of stock of each corporation (the 80 percent requirement);

(B) More than 50 percent of the total combined voting power of all classes of stock entitled to vote or more than 50 percent of the total value of shares of all classes of stock of each corporation, taking into account the stock ownership of each such person only to the extent such stock ownership is identical with respect to each such corporation (the more-than-50 percent identical ownership requirement); and

(C) The five or fewer persons whose stock ownership is considered for purposes of the 80 percent requirement must be the same persons whose stock ownership is considered for purposes of the more-than-50 percent identical ownership requirement.

(iii) *Examples.*—The principles of paragraph (a)(3)(ii) of this section may be illustrated by the following examples:

*Example 1.* (i) The outstanding stock of corporations P, W, X, Y, and Z, which have only one class of stock outstanding, is owned by the following unrelated individuals:

| Individuals | P (%) | W (%) | X (%) | Y (%) | Z (%) | Identical Ownership |
|---|---|---|---|---|---|---|
| A | 55 | 51 | 55 | 55 | 55 | 51 |
| B | 45 | 49 | | | | (45% in P and W) |
| C | | | 45 | | | |

| Individuals | P (%) | W (%) | X (%) | Y (%) | Z (%) | Identical Ownership |
|---|---|---|---|---|---|---|
| D | | | | 45 | | |
| E | | | | | 45 | |
| Total | 100 | 100 | 100 | 100 | 100 | |

(ii) Corporations P and W are members of a brother-sister controlled group of corporations. Although the more-than-50 percent identical ownership requirement is met for all 5 corporations, corporations X, Y, and Z are not members because at least 80 percent of the stock of each of those corporations is not owned by the same 5 or fewer persons whose stock ownership is considered for purposes of the more-than-50 percent identical ownership requirement.

*Example 2.* (i) The outstanding stock of corporations X and Y, which have only one class of stock outstanding, is owned by the following unrelated individuals:

| Individuals | Corporations | |
|---|---|---|
| | X (%) | Y (%) |
| A | 12 | 12 |
| B | 12 | 12 |
| C | 12 | 12 |
| D | 12 | 12 |
| E | 13 | 13 |
| F | 13 | 13 |
| G | 13 | 13 |
| H | 13 | 13 |
| Total | 100 | 100 |

(ii) Any group of five of the shareholders will own more than 50 percent of the stock in each corporation, in identical holdings. However, X and Y are not members of a brother-sister controlled group because at least 80 percent of the stock of each corporation is not owned by the same five or fewer persons.

*Example 3.* (i) Corporation X and Y each have two classes of stock outstanding, voting common and non-voting common. (None of this stock is excluded from the definition of stock under section 1563(c).) Unrelated individuals A and B own the following percentages of the class of stock entitled to vote (voting) and of the total value of shares of all classes of stock (value) in each of corporations X and Y:

| Individuals | Corporations | |
|---|---|---|
| | X | Y |
| A | 100% voting; 60% value | 75% voting; 60% value |
| B | 0% voting; 10% value | 25% voting; 10% value |

(ii) No other shareholder of X owns (or is considered to own) any stock in Y. X and Y are a brother-sister controlled group of corporations. The group meets the more-than-50 percent identical ownership requirement because A and B own more than 50 percent of the total value of shares of all classes of stock of X and Y in identical holdings. (The group also meets the more-than-50 percent identical ownership requirement because of A's voting stock ownership.) The group meets the 80 percent requirement because A and B own at least 80 percent of the total combined voting power of all classes of stock entitled to vote.

*Example 4.* Assume the same facts as in *Example 3* except that the value of the stock owned by A and B is not more than 50 percent of the total value of shares of all classes of stock of each corporation in identical holdings. X and Y are not a brother-sister controlled group of corporations. The group meets the more-than-50 percent identical ownership requirement because A owns more than 50 percent of the total combined voting power of the voting stock of each corporation. For purposes of the 80 percent requirement, B's voting stock in Y cannot be combined with A's voting stock in Y since B, who does not own any voting stock in X, is not a person whose ownership is considered for purposes of the more-than-50 percent identical ownership requirement. Because no other shareholder owns stock in both X and Y, these other shareholders' stock ownership is not counted towards meeting either the more-than-50 percent identical ownership requirement or the 80 percent ownership requirement.

(iv) *Special rule if prior law applies.*—Paragraph (a)(3)(ii) of this section, as amended by TD 8179, applies to taxable years ending on or after December 31, 1970. See, however, the transitional rule in paragraph (d) of this section.

(4) *Combined group.*—(i) *Definition.*—The term *combined group* means any group of three or more corporations if—

(A) Each such corporation is a member of either a parent-subsidiary controlled group of corporations or a brother-sister controlled group of corporations; and

(B) At least one of such corporations is the common parent of a parent-subsidiary controlled group and also is a member of a brother-sister controlled group.

(ii) *Examples.*—The definition of a combined group of corporations may be illustrated by the following examples:

*Example 1.* A, an individual, owns stock possessing 80 percent of the total combined voting power of all classes of the stock of corporations X and Y. Y, in turn, owns stock possessing 80 percent of the total combined voting power of all classes of the stock of corporation Z. X, Y, and Z are members of the same combined group since—

(i) X, Y, and Z are each members of either a parent-subsidiary or brother-sister controlled group of corporations; and

(ii) Y is the common parent of a parent-subsidiary controlled group of corporations consisting of Y and Z, and also is a member of a brother-sister controlled group of corporations consisting of X and Y.

*Example 2.* Assume the same facts as in *Example 1,* and further assume that corporation X owns 80 percent of the total value of shares of all classes of stock of corporation S. X, Y, Z, and S are members of the same combined group.

(5) *Life insurance controlled group.*—(i) *Definition.*—The term *life insurance controlled group* means two or more life insurance companies each of which is a member of a controlled group of corporations described in paragraph (a)(2), (a)(3)(i), or (a)(4) of this section and to which §1.1502-47(f)(6) does not apply. Such insurance companies shall be treated as a controlled group of corporations separate from any other corporations which are members of a controlled group described in such paragraph (a)(2), (a)(3)(i), or (a)(4) of this section. For purposes of this section, the common parent of the controlled group described in paragraph (a)(2) of this section shall be referred to as the common parent of the life insurance controlled group.

(ii) *Examples.*—The following examples illustrate the definition of a *life insurance controlled group.* In these examples, L indicates a life company, another letter indicates a nonlife company and each corporation uses the calendar year as its taxable year:

*Example 1.* Since January 1, 1999, corporation P has owned all the stock of corporations $L_1$ and Y, and $L_1$ has owned all the stock of corporation X. On January 1, 2005, Y acquired all of the stock of corporation $L_2$. Since $L_1$ and $L_2$ are members of a parent-subsidiary controlled group of corporations, such companies are treated as

Reg. §1.1563-1(a)(5)(ii)

members of a life insurance controlled group separate from the parent-subsidiary controlled group consisting of P, X and Y. For purposes of this section, P is referred to as the common parent of the life insurance controlled group even though P is not a member of such group.

*Example 2.* The facts are the same as in *Example 1*, except that, beginning with the 2005 tax year, the P affiliated group elected to file a consolidated return and P made a section 1504(c)(2) election. Pursuant to paragraph (a)(5)(i) of this section, $L_1$ and $L_2$ are not members of a separate life insurance controlled group. Instead, P, X, Y, $L_1$ and $L_2$ constitute one controlled group. See § 1.1502-47(f)(6).

(6) *Voting power of stock.*—For purposes of this section, and §§ 1.1563-2 and 1.1563-3, in determining whether the stock owned by a person (or persons) possesses a certain percentage of the total combined voting power of all classes of stock entitled to vote of a corporation, consideration will be given to all the facts and circumstances of each case. A share of stock will generally be considered as possessing the voting power accorded to such share by the corporate charter, by-laws, or share certificate. On the other hand, if there is any agreement, whether express or implied, that a shareholder will not vote his stock in a corporation, the formal voting rights possessed by his stock may be disregarded in determining the percentage of the total combined voting power possessed by the stock owned by other shareholders in the corporation, if the result is that the corporation becomes a component member of a controlled group of corporations. Moreover, if a shareholder agrees to vote his stock in a corporation in the manner specified by another shareholder in the corporation, the voting rights possessed by the stock owned by the first shareholder may be considered to be possessed by the stock owned by such other shareholder if the result is that the corporation becomes a component member of a controlled group of corporations.

(b) *Component members.*—(1) *In general.*—(i) *Definition.*—For purposes of sections 1561 through 1563, a corporation is with respect to its taxable year a component member of a controlled group of corporations for the group's testing date if such corporation—

(A) Is a member of such controlled group on such testing date and is not treated as an excluded member under paragraph (b)(2) of this section; or

(B) Is not a member of such controlled group on such testing date but is treated as an additional member under paragraph (b)(3) of this section.

(ii) *Member of a controlled group of corporations.*—For purposes of sections 1561 through 1563, a member of a controlled group is a corporation connected with other member(s) of a controlled group under the stock ownership rules and the stock qualification rules set forth in section 1563. Under these rules, for a corporation to qualify as a component member of the group with respect to a group's December 31st testing date (or the short-year testing date for a short-year member), that corporation does not have to be a member of that group on that group's testing date. In addition, a corporation that is a member of a controlled group on the group's testing date does not necessarily qualify as a component member of that group with respect to that testing date.

(iii) *Additional concepts used in applying the controlled group rules.*

(A) The term *testing date* means the date used for determining the status of controlled group members as either component members or excluded members. That testing date is then also used to determine which taxable years of those component members are to be subjected to the controlled group rules. Generally, a member's testing date is the December 31st date included within that member's taxable year, whether such member is on a calendar or fiscal taxable year. However, if a component member of a controlled group has a short taxable year that does not include a December 31st date, then the last day of that short taxable year becomes that member's testing date.

(B) The term *testing period* means the time period used for determining the status of controlled group members as either component members or excluded members. The testing period begins on the first day of a member's taxable year and ends on the day before its testing date. (Generally, the testing date is December 31st, but for a component member having a short taxable year not ending on December 31st, the testing date for the short taxable year of that member (and only that member) becomes the last day of that member's short taxable year.) Thus, for a member on a fiscal taxable year, the portion of its taxable year beginning on December 31st and ending on the last day of its taxable year is not taken into account for determining its status as a component member or an excluded member.

(2) *Excluded members.*—(i) *Temporal test.*—A corporation, which is a member of a controlled group of corporations on the group's testing date, a date included within that member's taxable year, but

who was a member of such group for less than one-half of the number of days of its testing period, shall be treated as an excluded member of such group for that group's testing date.

(ii) *Qualification test.*—A corporation which is a member of a controlled group of corporations on a testing date shall be treated as an excluded member of such group on such date if, for its taxable year including such date, such corporation is—

(A) Exempt from taxation under section 501(a) (except a corporation which is subject to tax on its unrelated business taxable income under section 511) or 521 for such taxable year;

(B) A foreign corporation not subject to taxation under section 882(a) for the taxable year;

(C) An S corporation (as defined in section 1361) for purposes of any tax benefit item described in section 1561(a) to which it is not subject;

(D) A franchised corporation (as defined in section 1563(f)(4) and § 1.1563-4); or

(E) An insurance company subject to taxation under section 801, unless such insurance company (without regard to this paragraph (b)(2)(ii)(E)) is a component member of a life insurance controlled group described in paragraph (a)(5)(i) of this section or unless § 1.1502-47(f)(6) applies (which treats a life insurance company, for which a section 1504(c)(2) election is effective, as a member (whether eligible or ineligible) of a life-nonlife affiliated group).

(3) *Additional members.*—A corporation shall be treated as an additional member of a controlled group of corporations, that is, an additional component member, on the group's testing date if it—

(i) Is not a member of such group on such date;

(ii) Is not described, with respect to such taxable year, in paragraph (b)(2)(ii)(A), (b)(2)(ii)(B), (b)(2)(ii)(C), (b)(2)(ii)(D), or (b)(2)(ii)(E) of this section; and

(iii) Was a member of such group for one-half (or more) of the number of days in its testing period.

(4) *Examples.*—The provisions of this paragraph (b) may be illustrated by the following examples:

*Example 1.* B, an individual, owns all of the stock of corporations W and X on each day of 1964. W and X each use the calendar year as their taxable year. On January 1, 1964, B also owns all the stock of corporation Y (a fiscal year corporation with a taxable year beginning on July 1, 1964, and ending on June 30, 1965), which stock he sells on October 15, 1964. On December 1, 1964, B purchases all the stock of corporation Z (a fiscal year corporation with a taxable year beginning on September 1, 1964, and ending on August 31, 1965). On December 31, 1964, W, X, and Z are members of the same controlled group. However, the component members of the group on such December 31st are W, X, and Y. Under paragraph (b)(2)(i) of this section, Z is treated as an excluded member of the group on December 31, 1964, since Z was a member of the group for less than one-half of the number of days (29 out of 121 days) during the period beginning on September 1, 1964 (the first day of its taxable year) and ending on December 30, 1964. Under paragraph (b)(3) of this section, Y is treated as an additional member of the group on December 31, 1964, since Y was a member of the group for at least one-half of the number of days (107 out of 183 days) during the period beginning on July 1, 1964 (the first day of its taxable year) and ending on December 30, 1964.

*Example 2.* On January 1, 1964, corporation P owns all the stock of corporation S, which in turn owns all the stock of corporation S-1. On November 1, 1964, P purchases all of the stock of corporation X from the public and sells all of the stock of S to the public. Corporation X owns all the stock of corporation Y during 1964. P, S, S-1, X, and Y file their returns on the basis of the calendar year. On December 31, 1964, P, X, and Y are members of a parent-subsidiary controlled group of corporations; also, corporations S and S-1 are members of a different parent-subsidiary controlled group on such date. However, since X and Y have been members of the parent-subsidiary controlled group of which P is the common parent for less than one-half the number of days during the period January 1 through December 30, 1964, they are not component members of such group on such date. On the other hand, X and Y have been members of a parent-subsidiary controlled group of which X is the common parent for at least one-half the number of days during the period January 1 through December 30, 1964, and therefore they are component members of such group on December 31, 1964. Also since S and S-1 were members of the parent-subsidiary controlled group of which P is the common parent for at least one-half the number of days in the taxable years of each such corporation during the period January 1 through December 30, 1964, P, S, and S-1 are component members of such group on December 31, 1964.

*Example 3.* Throughout 1964, corporation M owns all the stock of corporation F which, in turn, owns all the stock of corporations $L_1$, $L_2$, X, and Y. M is a domestic mutual insurance company subject to taxation under section 821, F is a foreign corporation not engaged in a trade or business within the United States, $L_1$ and $L_2$ are domestic life insurance companies subject to taxation under section 802, and X and Y are domestic corporations subject to tax under section 11 of the Code. Each corporation uses the calendar year as its taxable year. On December 31, 1964, M, F, $L_1$, $L_2$, X, and Y are members of a parent-subsidiary controlled group of corporations. However, under paragraph (b)(2)(ii) of this section, M, F, $L_1$, $L_2$, X, and Y are treated as excluded members of the group on December 31, 1964. Thus, on December 31, 1964, the component members of the parent-subsidiary controlled group of which M is the common parent include only X and Y. Furthermore, since paragraph (b)(2)(ii)(E) of this section does not result in $L_1$ and $L_2$ being treated as excluded members of a life insurance controlled group, $L_1$ and $L_2$ are component members of a life insurance controlled group on December 31, 1964.

*Example 4.* Individual A owns all of the stock of corporations X, Y and Z. Each of these corporations is an S corporation. X, Y, and Z are each members of a brother-sister controlled group, even though each such corporation is treated as an excluded member of such group. See § 1.1563-1(b)(2)(ii)(C).

(5) *Application of constructive ownership rules.*—For purposes of paragraphs (b)(2)(i) and (b)(3)(iii) of this section, it is necessary to determine whether a corporation was a member of a controlled group of corporations for one-half (or more) of the number of days in its taxable year which precede the December 31st falling within such taxable year. Therefore, the constructive ownership rules contained in § 1.1563-3(b) (to the extent applicable in making such determination) must be applied on a day-by-day basis. For example, if P Corporation owns all the stock of X Corporation on each day of 1964, and on December 30, 1964, acquires an option to purchase all the stock of Y Corporation (a calendar-year taxpayer which has been in existence on each day of 1964), the application of § 1.1563-3(b)(1) on a day-by-day basis results in Y being a member of the brother- sister controlled group on only one day of Y's 1964 year which precedes December 31, 1964. Accordingly, since Y is not a member of such group for one-half or more of the number of days in its 1964 year preceding December 31, 1964, Y is treated as an excluded member of such group on December 31, 1964.

(c) *Overlapping groups.*—(1) *In general.*—If on a December 31st a corporation is a component member of a controlled group of corporations by reason of ownership of stock possessing at least 80 percent of the total value of shares of all classes of stock of the corporation, and if on such December 31st such corporation is also a component member of another controlled group of corporations by reason of ownership of other stock (that is, stock not used to satisfy the at-least-80 percent total value test) possessing at least 80 percent of the total combined voting power of all classes of stock of the corporation entitled to vote, then such corporation shall be treated as a component member only of the controlled group of which it is a component member by reason of the ownership of at least 80 percent of the total value of its shares.

(2) *Brother-sister controlled groups.*—(i) *One corporation.*—If on a December 31st, a corporation would, without the application of this

paragraph (c)(2), be a component member of more than one brother-sister controlled group on such date, the corporation will be treated as a component member of only one such group on such date. Such corporation may elect the group in which it is to be included by including on or with its income tax return for the taxable year that includes such date a statement entitled, "STATEMENT TO ELECT CONTROLLED GROUP PURSUANT TO § 1.1563-1(c)(2)." This statement must include—

(A) A description of each of the controlled groups in which the corporation could be included. The description must include the name and employer identification number of each component member of each such group and the stock ownership of the component members of each such group; and

(B) The following representation: [INSERT NAME AND EMPLOYER IDENTIFICATION NUMBER OF CORPORATION] ELECTS TO BE TREATED AS A COMPONENT MEMBER OF THE [INSERT DESIGNATION OF GROUP].

(ii) *Multiple corporations.*—If more than one corporation would, without the application of this paragraph (c)(2), be a component member of more than one controlled group, those corporations electing to be component members of the same group must file a single statement. The statement must contain the information described in paragraph (c)(2)(i) of this section, plus the names and employer identification numbers of all other corporations designating the same group. The original statement must be included on or with the original Federal income tax return (including any amended return filed on or before the due date (including extensions) of such return) of the corporation that, among those corporations which would (without the application of this paragraph (c)(2)) belong to more than one group, has the taxable year including such December 31st which ends on the earliest date. That corporation must provide a copy of the statement to each other corporation included in the statement and represent in its statement that it has done so. Either the original or a copy of the statement must be retained by each corporation as part of its records. See § 1.6001-1(e) of this chapter.

(iii) *Election.*—(A) An election filed under this paragraph (c)(2) is irrevocable and effective until a change in the stock ownership of the corporation results in termination of membership in the controlled group in which such corporation has been included.

(B) In the event no election is filed in accordance with the provisions of this paragraph (c)(2), then the Internal Revenue Service will determine the group in which such corporation is to be included. Such determination will be binding for all subsequent years unless the corporation files a valid election with respect to any such subsequent year or until a change in the stock ownership of the corporation results in termination of membership in the controlled group in which such corporation has been included.

(iv) *Examples.*—The provisions of this paragraph (c)(2) may be illustrated by the following examples (in which it is assumed that all the individuals are unrelated):

*Example 1.* (i) On each day of 1970 all the outstanding stock of corporations X, Y, and Z is held in the following manner:

| Individuals | Corporations | | |
| --- | --- | --- | --- |
| | X (%) | Y (%) | Z (%) |
| A | 55 | 40 | 5 |
| B | 40 | 20 | 40 |
| C | 5 | 40 | 55 |

(ii) Since the more-than-50 percent identical ownership requirement of section 1563(a)(2) is met with respect to corporations X and Y and with respect to corporations Y and Z, but not with respect to corporations X, Y, and Z, corporation Y would, without the application of this paragraph (c)(2), be a component member on December 31, 1970, of overlapping groups consisting of X and Y and

of Y and Z. If Y does not file an election in accordance with paragraph (c)(2)(i) of this section, the Internal Revenue Service will determine the group in which Y is to be included.

*Example 2.* (i) On each day of 1970, all the outstanding stock of corporations V, W, X, Y, and Z is held in the following manner:

| Individuals | Corporations | | | | |
| --- | --- | --- | --- | --- | --- |
| | V | W | X | Y | Z |
| D | 52 | 52 | 52 | 52 | 52 |
| E | 40 | 2 | 2 | 2 | 2 |
| F | 2 | 40 | 2 | 2 | 2 |
| G | 2 | 2 | 40 | 2 | 2 |
| H | 2 | 2 | 2 | 40 | 2 |
| I | 2 | 2 | 2 | 2 | 40 |

(ii) On December 31, 1970, the more-than-50 percent identical ownership requirement of section 1563(a)(2) may be met with regard

to any combination of the corporations but all five corporations cannot be included as component members of a single controlled group because the inclusion of all the corporations in a single group would be dependent upon taking into account the stock ownership of more than five persons. Therefore, if the corporations do not file a statement in accordance with paragraph (c)(2)(ii) of this section, the Internal Revenue Service will determine the group in which each corporation is to be included. The corporations or the Internal Revenue Service, as the case may be, may designate that three corporations be included in one group and two corporations in another, or that any four corporations be included in one group and that the remaining corporation not be included in any group.

(d) *Transitional rules.*—(1) *In general.*—Treasury decision 8179 amended paragraph (a)(3)(ii) of this section to revise the definition of a brother-sister controlled group of corporations. In general, those amendments are effective for taxable years ending on or after December 31, 1970.

(2) *Limited nonretroactivity.*—(i) *Old group.*—Under the authority of section 7805(b), the Internal Revenue Service will treat an old group as a brother-sister controlled group corporations for purposes of applying sections 401, 404(a), 408(k), 409A, 410, 411, 412, 414, 415, and 4971 of the Internal Revenue Code (Code) and sections 202, 203, 204, and 302 of the Employment Retirement Income Security Act of 1974 (ERISA) in a plan year or taxable year beginning before March 2, 1988, to the extent necessary to prevent an adverse effect on any old member (or any other corporation), or on any plan or other entity described in such sections (including plans, etc., of corporations not part of such old group), that would result solely from the retroactive effect of the amendment to this section by TD 8179. An adverse effect includes the disqualification of a plan or the disallowance of a deduction or credit for a contribution to a plan. The Internal Revenue Service, however, will not treat an old member as a member of an old group to the extent that such treatment will have an adverse effect on that old member.

(ii) *Old member of old group.*—Section 7805(b) will not be applied pursuant to paragraph (d)(2)(i) of this section to treat an old member of an old group as a member of a brother-sister controlled group to prevent an adverse effect for a taxable year if, for that taxable year, that old member treats or has treated itself as not being a member of that old group for purposes of sections 401, 404(a), 408(k), 409A, 410, 411, 412, 414, 415, and 4971 of the Code and sections 202, 203, 204, and 302 and Title IV of ERISA for such taxable year (such as by filing, with respect to such taxable year, a return, amended return, or claim for credit or refund in which the amount of any deduction, credit, limitation, or tax due is determined by treating itself as not being a member of the old group for purposes of those sections). However, the fact that one or more (but not all) of the old members do not qualify for section 7805(b) treatment because of the preceding sentence will not preclude that old member (or members) from being treated as a member of the old group under paragraph (d)(2)(i) of this section in order to prevent the disallowance of a deduction or credit of another old member (or other corporation) or to prevent the disqualification of, or other adverse effect on, another old member's plan (or other entity) described in the sections of the Code and ERISA enumerated in such paragraph.

(3) *Election of general nonretroactivity.*—In the case of a taxable year ending on or after December 31, 1970, and before March 2, 1988, an old group will be treated as a brother-sister controlled group of corporations for all purposes of the Code for such taxable year if—

(i) Each old member files a statement consenting to such treatment for such taxable year with the District Director having audit jurisdiction over its return within six months after March 2, 1988; and

(ii) No old member—

(A) Files or has filed, with respect to such taxable year, a return, amended return, or claim for credit or refund in which the amount of any deduction, credit, limitation, or tax due is determined by treating any old member as not a member of the old group; or

(B) Treats the employees of all members of the old group as not being employed by a single employer for purposes of sections 401, 404(a), 408(k), 409A, 410, 411, 412, 414, 415, and 4971 of the Code and sections 202, 203, 204, and 302 of ERISA for such taxable year.

(4) *Definitions.*—For purposes of this paragraph (d)—

(i) An *old group* is a brother-sister controlled group of corporations, determined by applying paragraph (a)(3)(ii) of this section as in effect before the amendments made by TD 8179, that is not a brother-sister controlled group of corporations, determined by applying paragraph (a)(3)(ii) of this section as amended by such Treasury decision; and

(ii) An *old member* is any corporation that is a member of an old group.

(5) *Election to choose between membership in more than one controlled group.*—(i) *In general.*—A corporation may make an election under

paragraph (c)(2) of this section by filing an amended return on or before September 2, 1988 if—

(A) An old member has filed an election under paragraph (c)(2) of this section to be treated as a component member of an old group for a December 31st before March 2, 1988; and

(B) That corporation would (without regard to such paragraph (c)(2)) be a component member of more than one brother-sister controlled group (not including an old group) on the December 31st.

(ii) *Exception.*—This paragraph (d)(5) does not apply to a corporation that is treated as a member of an old group under paragraph (d)(3) of this section.

(6) *Refunds.*—See section 6511(a) for period of limitation on filing claims for credit or refund.

(e) *Effective/applicability date.*—This section applies to taxable years beginning on or after May 26, 2009. However, taxpayers may apply this section to taxable years beginning before May 26, 2009. For taxable years beginning before May 26, 2009, see §1.1563-1T as contained in 26 CFR part 1 in effect on April 1, 2009. Paragraph (a)(1)(ii) of this section applies to taxable years beginning on or after April 11, 2011. [Reg. §1.1563-1.]

☐ [T.D. 9451, 5-26-2009. Amended by T.D. 9522, 4-8-2011.]

## [Reg. §1.1563-2]

**§1.1563-2. Excluded stock.**—(a) *Certain stock excluded.*—For purposes of sections 1561 through 1563 and the regulations thereunder, the term "stock" does not include—

(1) Nonvoting stock which is limited and preferred as to dividends, and

(2) Treasury stock.

(b) *Stock treated as excluded stock.*—(1) *Parent-subsidiary controlled group.*—If a corporation (hereinafter in this paragraph referred to as "parent corporation") owns 50 percent or more of the total combined voting power of all classes of stock entitled to vote or 50 percent or more of the total value of shares of all classes of stock in another corporation (hereinafter in this paragraph referred to as "subsidiary corporation"), the provisions of subparagraph (2) of this paragraph shall apply. For purposes of this subparagraph, stock owned by a corporation means stock owned directly plus stock owned with the application of the constructive ownership rules of paragraph (b)(1) and (4) of §1.1563-3, relating to options and attribution from corporations. In determining whether the stock owned by a corporation possesses the requisite percentage of the total combined voting power of all classes of stock entitled to vote of another corporation, see paragraph (a)(6) of §1.1563-1.

(2) *Stock treated as not outstanding.*—If the provisions of this subparagraph apply, then for purposes of determining whether the parent corporation or the subsidiary corporation is a member of a parent-subsidiary controlled group of corporations within the meaning of paragraph (a)(2) of §1.1563-1, the following stock of the subsidiary corporation shall, except as otherwise provided in paragraph (c) of this section, be treated as if it were not outstanding:

(i) *Plan of deferred compensation.*—Stock in the subsidiary corporation held by a trust which is part of a plan of deferred compensation for the benefit of the employees of the parent corporation or the subsidiary corporation. The term "plan of deferred compensation" shall have the same meaning such term has in section 406(a)(3) and the regulations thereunder.

(ii) *Principal stockholders and officers.*—Stock in the subsidiary corporation owned (directly and with the application of the rules contained in paragraph (b) of §1.1563-3) by an individual who is a principal stockholder or officer of the parent corporation. A principal stockholder of the parent corporation is an individual who owns (directly and with the application of the rules contained in paragraph (b) of §1.1563-3) 5 percent or more of the total combined voting power of all classes of stock entitled to vote or 5 percent or more of the total value of shares of all classes of stock of the parent corporation. An officer of the parent corporation includes the president, vice-presidents, general manager, treasurer, secretary, and comptroller of such corporation, and any other person who performs duties corresponding to those normally performed by persons occupying such positions.

(iii) *Employees.*—Stock in the subsidiary corporation owned (directly and with the application of the rules contained in paragraph (b) of §1.1563-3) by an employee of the subsidiary corporation if such stock is subject to conditions which substantially restrict or limit the employee's right (or if the employee constructively owns such stock, the direct owner's right) to dispose of such stock and which run in favor of the parent or subsidiary corporation. In general, any condition which extends, directly or indirectly, to the parent corporation or the subsidiary corporation preferential rights with respect to the acquisition of the employee's (or direct owner's) stock will be considered to be a condition described in the preceding sentence. It is not necessary, in order for a condition to be considered to be in favor of the parent corporation or the subsidiary corporation, that the parent or subsidiary be extended a discriminatory concession with respect to the price of the stock. For example, a condition whereby the parent corporation is given a right of first refusal with respect to any stock of the subsidiary corporation offered by an employee for sale is a condition which substantially restricts or limits the employee's right to dispose of such stock and runs in favor of the parent corporation. Moreover, any legally enforceable condition which prohibits the employee from disposing of his stock without the consent of the parent (or a subsidiary of the parent) will be considered to be a substantial limitation running in favor of the parent corporation.

(iv) *Controlled exempt organization.*—Stock in the subsidiary corporation owned (directly and with the application of the rules contained in paragraph (b) of §1.1563-3) by an organization (other than the parent corporation)—

(a) To which section 501 (relating to certain educational and charitable organizations which are exempt from tax) applies, and

(b) Which is controlled directly or indirectly by the parent corporation or subsidiary corporation, by an individual, estate, or trust that is a principal stockholder of the parent corporation, by an officer of the parent corporation, or by any combination thereof.

The terms "principal stockholder of the parent corporation" and "officer of the parent corporation" shall have the same meanings in this subdivision as in subdivision (ii) of this subparagraph. The term "control" as used in this subdivision means control in fact and the determination of whether the control requirement of (b) of this subdivision is met will depend upon all the facts and circumstances of each case, without regard to whether such control is legally enforceable and irrespective of the method by which such control is exercised or exercisable.

(3) *Brother-sister controlled group.*—If 5 or fewer persons (hereinafter referred to as common owners) who are individuals, estates, or trusts own (directly and with the application of the rules contained in paragraph (b) of §1.1563-3) stock possessing 50 percent or more of the total combined voting power of all classes of stock entitled to vote or 50 percent or more of the total value of shares of all classes of stock in a corporation, the provisions of subparagraph (4) of this paragraph shall apply. In determining whether the stock owned by such person or persons possesses the requisite percentage of the total combined voting power of all classes of stock entitled to vote of a corporation, see paragraph (a)(6) of §1.1563-1.

(4) *Stock treated as not outstanding.*—If the provisions of this subparagraph apply, then for purposes of determining whether a corporation is a member of a brother-sister controlled group of corporations within the meaning of paragraph (a)(3) of §1.1563-1, the following stock of such corporation shall, except as otherwise provided in paragraph (c) of this section, be treated as if it were not outstanding:

(i) *Exempt employees' trust.*—Stock in such corporation held by an employees' trust described in section 401(a) which is exempt from tax under section 501(a), if such trust is for the benefit of the employees of such corporation.

(ii) *Employees.*—Stock in such corporation owned (directly and with the application of the rules contained in paragraph (b) of §1.1563-3) by an employee of such corporation if such stock is subject to conditions which run in favor of a common owner of such corporation (or in favor of such corporation) and which substantially restrict or limit the employee's right (or if the employee constructively owns such stock, the record owner's right) to dispose of such stock. The principles of subparagraph (2)(iii) of this paragraph shall apply in determining whether a condition satisfies the requirements of the preceding sentence. Thus, in general, a condition which extends, directly or indirectly, to a common owner or such corporation preferential rights with respect to the acquisition of the employee's (or record owner's) stock will be considered to be a condition which satisfies such requirements. For purposes of this subdivision, if a condition which restricts or limits an employee's right (or record owner's right) to dispose of his stock also applies to the stock in such corporation held by such common owner pursuant to a bona fide reciprocal stock purchase arrangement, such condition shall not be treated as one which restricts or limits the employee's (or record owner's) right to dispose of such stock. An example of a reciprocal stock purchase arrangement is an agreement whereby a common owner and the employee are given a right of first refusal with respect to stock of the employer corporation owned by the other party. If, however, the agreement also provides that the common owner has the right to purchase the stock of the employer corporation owned by

the employee in the event that the corporation should discharge the employee for reasonable cause, the purchase arrangement would not be reciprocal within the meaning of this subdivision.

(iii) *Controlled exempt organization.*—Stock in such corporation owned (directly and with the application of the rules contained in paragraph (b) of §1.1563-3) by an organization—

(a) To which section 501(c)(3) (relating to certain educational and charitable organizations which are exempt from tax) applies, and

(b) Which is controlled directly or indirectly by such corporation, by an individual, estate, or trust that is a principal stockholder of such corporation, by an officer of such corporation, or by any combination thereof. The terms "principal stockholder" and "officer" shall have the same meanings in this subdivision as in subparagraph (2)(ii) of this paragraph. The term "control" as used in this subdivision means control in fact and the determination of whether the control requirement of (b) of this subdivision is met will depend upon all the facts and circumstances of each case, without regard to whether such control is legally enforceable and irrespective of the method by which such control is exercised or exercisable.

(5) *Other controlled groups.*—The provisions of subparagraphs (1), (2), (3), and (4) of this paragraph shall apply in determining whether a corporation is a member of a combined group (within the meaning of paragraph (a)(4) of §1.1563-1) or an insurance group (within the meaning of paragraph (a)(5) of §1.1563-1). For example, under paragraph (a)(4) of §1.1563-1, in order for a corporation to be a member of a combined group such corporation must be a member of a parent-subsidiary group or a brother-sister group. Accordingly, the excluded stock rules provided by this paragraph are applicable in determining whether the corporation is a member of such group.

(6) *Meaning of employee.*—For purposes of this section, §§1.1563-3 and 1.1563-4, the term "employee" has the same meaning such term is given in section 3306(i) of the Code (relating to definitions for purposes of the Federal Unemployment Tax Act). Accordingly, the term employee as used in such sections includes an officer of a corporation.

(7) *Examples.*—The provisions of this paragraph may be illustrated by the following examples:

*Example (1).* Corporation P owns 70 of the 100 shares of the only class of stock of corporation S. The remaining shares of S are owned as follows: 4 shares by Jones (the general manager of P), and 26 shares by Smith (who also owns 5 percent of the total combined voting power of the stock of P). P satisfies the 50 percent stock ownership requirement of subparagraph (1) of this paragraph with respect to S. Since Jones is an officer of P and Smith is a principal stockholder of P, under subparagraph (2)(ii) of this paragraph the S stock owned by Jones and Smith is treated as not outstanding for purposes of determining whether P and S are members of a parent-subsidiary controlled group of corporations within the meaning of paragraph (a)(2) of §1.1563-1. Thus, P is considered to own stock possessing 100 percent (70 ÷ 70) of the total voting power and value of all the S stock. Accordingly, P and S are members of a parent-subsidiary controlled group of corporations.

*Example (2).* Assume the same facts as in example (1) and further assume that Jones owns 15 shares of the 100 shares of the only class of stock of corporation S-1, and corporation S owns 75 shares of such stock. P satisfies the 50 percent stock ownership requirement of subparagraph (1) of this paragraph with respect to S-1 since P is considered as owning 52.5 percent (70 percent × 75 percent) of the S-1 stock with the application of paragraph (b)(4) of §1.1563-3. Since Jones is an officer of P, under subparagraph (2)(ii) of this paragraph, the S-1 stock owned by Jones is treated as not outstanding for purposes of determining whether S-1 is a member of the parent-subsidiary controlled group of corporations. Thus, S is considered to own stock possessing 88.2 percent (75 ÷ 85) of the voting power and value of the S-1 stock. Accordingly, P, S, and S-1 are members of a parent-subsidiary controlled group of corporations.

*Example (3).* Corporation X owns 60 percent of the only class of stock of corporation Y. Davis, the president of Y, owns the remaining 40 percent of the stock of Y. Davis has agreed that if he offers his stock in Y for sale he will first offer the stock to X at a price equal to the fair market value of the stock on the first date the stock is offered for sale. Since Davis is an employee of Y within the meaning of section 3306(i) of the Code, and his stock in Y is subject to a condition which substantially restricts or limits his right to dispose of such stock and runs in favor of X, under subparagraph (2)(iii) of this paragraph such stock is treated as if it were not outstanding for purposes of determining whether X and Y are members of a parent subsidiary controlled group of corporations. Thus, X is considered to own stock possessing 100 percent of the voting power and value of the stock of Y. Accordingly, X and Y are members of a parent-subsidiary controlled group of corporations. The result would be the same if Davis's wife, instead of Davis, owned directly the 40 percent stock interest in Y and such stock was subject to a right of first refusal running in favor of X.

(c) *Exception.*—(1) *General.*—If stock of a corporation is owned by a person directly or with the application of the rules contained in paragraph (b) of § 1.1563-3 and such ownership results in the corporation being a component member of a controlled group of corporations on a December 31, then the stock shall not be treated as excluded stock under the provisions of paragraph (b) of this section if the result of applying such provisions is that such corporation is not a component member of a controlled group of corporations on such December 31.

(2) *Illustration.*—The provisions of this paragraph may be illustrated by the following example:

*Example.* On each day of 1965, corporation P owns directly 50 of the 100 shares of the only class of stock of corporation S. Jones, an officer of P, owns directly 30 shares of S stock and P has an option to acquire such 30 shares from Jones. The remaining shares of S are owned by unrelated persons. If, pursuant to the provisions of paragraph (b)(2)(ii) of this section, the 30 shares of S stock owned directly by Jones is treated as not outstanding, the result is that P would be treated as owning stock possessing only 71 percent (50 ÷ 70) of the total voting power and value of S stock, and S would not be a component member of a controlled group of corporations on December 31, 1965. However, since P is considered as owning the 30 shares of S stock with the application of paragraph (b)(1) of this section, and such ownership plus the S stock directly owned by P (50 shares) results in S being a component member of a controlled group of corporations on December 31, 1965, the provisions of this paragraph apply. Therefore, the provisions of paragraph (b)(2)(ii) of this section do not apply with respect to the 30 shares of S stock, and on December 31, 1965, S is a component member of a controlled group of corporations consisting of P and S. [Reg. § 1.1563-2.]

☐ [*T.D. 6845, 8-4-65. Amended by T.D. 7181, 4-24-72.*]

### [Reg. § 1.1563-3]

**§ 1.1563-3. Rules for determining stock ownership.**—(a) *In general.*—In determining stock ownership for purposes of § § 1.1562-5, 1.1563-1, 1.1563-2, and this section, the constructive ownership rules of paragraph (b) of this section apply to the extent such rules are referred to in such sections. The application of such rules shall be subject to the operating rules and special rules contained in paragraphs (c) and (d) of this section.

(b) *Constructive ownership.*—(1) *Options.*—If a person has an option to acquire any outstanding stock of a corporation, such stock shall be considered as owned by such person. For purposes of this subparagraph, an option to acquire such an option, and each one of a series of such options, shall be considered as an option to acquire such stock. For example, assume Smith owns an option to purchase 100 shares of the outstanding stock of M Corporation. Under this subparagraph, Smith is considered to own such 100 shares. The result would be the same if Smith owned an option to acquire the option (or one of a series of options) to purchase 100 shares of M stock.

(2) *Attribution from partnerships.*—(i) Stock owned, directly or indirectly, by or for a partnership shall be considered as owned by any partner having an interest of 5 percent or more in either the capital or profits of the partnership in proportion to his interest in capital or profits, whichever such proportion is the greater.

(ii) The provisions of this subparagraph may be illustrated by the following example:

*Example.* Green, Jones, and White, unrelated individuals, are partners in the GJW partnership. The partners' interests in the capital and profits of the partnership are as follows:

| Partner | Capital | Profits |
|---|---|---|
| Green | 36 % | 25 % |
| Jones | 60 | 71 |
| White | 4 | 4 |

The GJW partnership owns the entire outstanding stock (100 shares) of X Corporation. Under this subparagraph, Green is considered to own the X stock owned by the partnership in proportion to his interest in capital (36 percent) or profits (25 percent), whichever such proportion is the greater. Therefore, Green is considered to own 36 shares of the X stock. However, since Jones has a greater interest in the profits of the partnership, he is considered to own the X stock in proportion to his interest in such profits. Therefore, Jones is considered to own 71 shares of the X stock. Since White does not have an interest of 5 percent or more in either the capital or profits of the partnership, he is not considered to own any shares of the X stock.

(3) *Attribution from estates or trusts.*—(i) Stock owned, directly or indirectly, by or for an estate or trust shall be considered as owned by

any beneficiary who has an actuarial interest of 5 percent or more in such stock, to the extent of such actuarial interest. For purposes of this subparagraph, the actuarial interest of each beneficiary shall be determined by assuming the maximum exercise of discretion by the fiduciary in favor of such beneficiary and the maximum use of such stock to satisfy his rights as a beneficiary. A beneficiary of an estate or trust who cannot under any circumstances receive any interest in stock held by the estate or trust, including the proceeds from the disposition thereof, or the income therefrom, does not have an actuarial interest in such stock. Thus, where stock owned by a decedent's estate has been specifically bequeathed to certain beneficiaries and the remainder of the estate is bequeathed to other beneficiaries, the stock is attributable only to the beneficiaries to whom it is specifically bequeathed. Similarly, a remainderman of a trust who cannot under any circumstances receive any interest in the stock of a corporation which is a part of the corpus of the trust (including any accumulated income therefrom or the proceeds from a disposition thereof) does not have an actuarial interest in such stock. However, an income beneficiary of a trust does have an actuarial interest in stock if he has any right to the income from such stock even though under the terms of the trust instrument such stock can never be distributed to him. The factors and methods prescribed in § 20.2031-7 of this chapter (Estate Tax Regulations) [Reg. § 20.2031-7 of this chapter is reproduced at ¶ 2391.05.—CCH.] for use in ascertaining the value of an interest in property for estate tax purposes shall be used for purposes of this subdivision in determining a beneficiary's actuarial interest in stock owned directly or indirectly by or for a trust.

(ii) For the purposes of this subparagraph, property of a decedent shall be considered as owned by his estate if such property is subject to administration by the executor or administrator for the purposes of paying claims against the estate and expenses of administration notwithstanding that, under local law, legal title to such property vests in the decedent's heirs, legatees or devisees immediately upon death. With respect to an estate, the term "beneficiary" includes any person entitled to receive property of the decedent pursuant to a will or pursuant to laws of descent and distribution. A person shall no longer be considered a beneficiary of an estate when all the property to which he is entitled has been received by him, when he no longer has a claim against the estate arising out of having been a beneficiary, and when there is only a remote possibility that it will be necessary for the estate to seek the return of property or to seek payment from him by contribution or otherwise to satisfy claims against the estate or expenses of administration. When pursuant to the preceding sentence, a person ceases to be a beneficiary, stock owned by the estate shall not thereafter be considered owned by him.

(iii) Stock owned, directly or indirectly, by or for any portion of a trust of which a person is considered the owner under subpart E, part I, subchapter J of the Code (relating to grantors and others treated as substantial owners) is considered as owned by such person.

(iv) This subparagraph does not apply to stock owned by any employees' trust described in section 401(a) which is exempt from tax under section 501(a).

(4) *Attribution from corporations.*—(i) Stock owned, directly or indirectly, by or for a corporation shall be considered as owned by any person who owns (within the meaning of section 1563(d)) 5 percent or more in value of its stock in that proportion which the value of the stock which such person so owns bears to the value of all the stock in such corporation.

(ii) The provisions of this subparagraph may be illustrated by the following example:

*Example.* Brown, an individual, owns 60 shares of the 100 shares of the only class of outstanding stock of corporation P. Smith, an individual, owns 4 shares of the P stock, and corporation X owns 36 shares of the P stock. Corporation P owns, directly and indirectly, 50 shares of the stock of corporation S. Under this subparagraph, Brown is considered to own 30 shares of the S stock (60/100 × 50), and X is considered to own 18 shares of the S stock (36/100 × 50). Since Smith does not own 5 percent or more in value of the P stock, he is not considered as owning any of the S stock owned by P. If, in this example, Smith's wife had owned directly 1 share of the P stock, Smith (and his wife) would each own 5 shares of the P stock, and therefore Smith (and his wife) would be considered as owning 2.5 shares of the S stock (5/100 × 50).

(5) *Spouse.*—(i) Except as provided in subdivision (ii) of this subparagraph, an individual shall be considered to own the stock owned, directly or indirectly, by or for his spouse, other than a spouse who is legally separated from the individual under a decree of divorce, whether interlocutory or final, or a decree of separate maintenance.

(ii) An individual shall not be considered to own stock in a corporation owned, directly or indirectly, by or for his spouse on any day of a taxable year of such corporation, provided that each of the following conditions are satisfied with respect to such taxable year:

(a) Such individual does not, at any time during such taxable year, own directly any stock in such corporation.

(b) Such individual is not a member of the board of directors or an employee of such corporation and does not participate in the management of such corporation at any time during such taxable year.

(c) Not more than 50 percent of such corporation's gross income for such taxable year was derived from royalties, rents, dividends, interest, and annuities.

(d) Such stock in such corporation is not, at any time during such taxable year, subject to conditions which substantially restrict or limit the spouse's right to dispose of such stock and which run in favor of the individual or his children who have not attained the age of 21 years. The principles of paragraph (b)(2)(iii) of § 1.1563-2 shall apply in determining whether a condition is a condition described in the preceding sentence.

(iii) For purposes of subdivision (ii)(c) of this subparagraph, the gross income of a corporation for a taxable year shall be determined under section 61 and the regulations thereunder. The terms "royalties", "rents", "dividends", "interest", and "annuities" shall have the same meanings such terms are given for purposes of section 1244(c). See paragraph (e)(1)(ii), (iii), (iv), (v), and (vi) of § 1.1244(c)-1.

(6) *Children, grandchildren, parents, and grandparents.*—(i) An individual shall be considered to own the stock owned, directly or indirectly, by or for his children who have not attained the age of 21 years, and, if the individual has not attained the age of 21 years, the stock owned, directly or indirectly, by or for his parents.

(ii) If an individual owns (directly, and with the application of the rules of this paragraph but without regard to this subdivision) stock possessing more than 50 percent of the total combined voting power of all classes of stock entitled to vote or more than 50 percent of the total value of shares of all classes of stock in a corporation, then such individual shall be considered to own the stock in such corporation owned, directly or indirectly, by or for his parents, grandparents, grandchildren, and children who have attained the age of 21 years. In determining whether the stock owned by an individual possesses the requisite percentage of the total combined voting power of all classes of stock entitled to vote of a corporation, see paragraph (a)(6) of § 1.1563-1.

(iii) For purposes of section 1563, and §§ 1.1563-1 through 1.1563-4, a legally adopted child of an individual shall be treated as a child of such individual by blood.

(iv) The provisions of this subparagraph may be illustrated by the following example:

*Example*—(a) *Facts.* Individual F owns directly 40 shares of the 100 shares of the only class of stock of Z Corporation. His son, M (20 years of age), owns directly 30 shares of such stock, and his son, A (30 years of age), owns directly 20 shares of such stock. The remaining 10 shares of the Z stock are owned by an unrelated person.

(b) *F's ownership.* Individual F owns 40 shares of the Z stock directly and is considered to own the 30 shares of Z stock owned directly by M. Since, for purposes of the more-than-50-percent stock ownership test contained in subdivision (ii) of this subparagraph, F is treated as owning 70 shares or 70 percent of the total voting power and value of the Z stock, he is also considered as owning the 20 shares owned by his adult son, A. Accordingly, F is considered as owning a total of 90 shares of the Z stock.

(c) *M's ownership.* Minor son, M, owns 30 shares of the Z stock directly, and is considered to own the 40 shares of Z stock owned directly by his father, F. However, M is not considered to own the 20 shares of Z stock owned directly by his brother, A, and constructively by F, because stock constructively owned by F by reason of family attribution is not considered as owned by him for purposes of making another member of his family the constructive owner of such stock. See paragraph (c)(2) of this section. Accordingly, M owns and is considered as owning a total of 70 shares of the Z stock.

(d) *A's ownership.* Adult son, A, owns 20 shares of the Z stock directly. Since, for purposes of the more-than-50-percent stock ownership test contained in subdivision (ii) of this subparagraph, A is treated as owning only the Z stock which he owns directly, he does not satisfy the condition precedent for the attribution of Z stock from his father. Accordingly, A is treated as owning only the 20 shares of Z stock which he owns directly.

(c) *Operating rules and special rules.*—(1) *In general.*—Except as provided in subparagraph (2) of this paragraph, stock constructively owned by a person by reason of the application of subparagraph (1), (2), (3), (4), (5), or (6) of paragraph (b) of this section shall, for purposes of applying such subparagraphs, be treated as actually owned by such person.

(2) *Members of family.*—Stock constructively owned by an individual by reason of the application of subparagraph (5) or (6) of paragraph (b) of this section shall not be treated as owned by him for purposes of again applying such subparagraphs in order to make another the constructive owner of such stock.

(3) *Precedence of option attribution.*—For purposes of this section, if stock may be considered as owned by a person under subparagraph (1) of paragraph (b) of this section (relating to option attribution) and under any other subparagraph of such paragraph, such stock shall be considered as owned by such person under subparagraph (1) of such paragraph.

(4) *Examples.*—The provisions of this paragraph may be illustrated by the following examples:

*Example (1).* A, 30 years of age, has a 90 percent interest in the capital and profits of a partnership. The partnership owns all the outstanding stock of corporation X and X owns 60 shares of the 100 outstanding shares of corporation Y. Under subparagraph (1) of this paragraph, the 60 shares of Y constructively owned by the partnership by reason of subparagraph (4) of paragraph (b) of this section is treated as actually owned by the partnership for purposes of applying subparagraph (2) of paragraph (b) of this section. Therefore, A is considered as owning 54 shares of the Y stock (90 percent of 60 shares).

*Example (2).* Assume the same facts as in example (1). Assume further that B, who is 20 years of age and the brother of A, directly owns 40 shares of Y stock. Although the stock of Y owned by B is considered as owned by C (the father of A and B) under paragraph (b)(6)(i) of this section, under subparagraph (2) of this paragraph such stock may not be treated as owned by C for purposes of applying paragraph (b)(6)(ii) of this section in order to make A the constructive owner of such stock.

*Example (3).* Assume the same facts assumed for purposes of example (2), and further assume that C has an option to acquire the 40 shares of Y stock owned by his son, B. The rule contained in subparagraph (2) of this paragraph does not prevent the reattribution of such 40 shares to A because, under subparagraph (3) of this paragraph, C is considered as owning the 40 shares by reason of option attribution and not by reason of family attribution. Therefore, since A satisfies the more-than-50-percent stock ownership test contained in paragraph (b)(6)(ii) of this section with respect to Y, the 40 shares of Y stock constructively owned by C are reattributed to A, and A is considered as owning a total of 94 shares of Y stock.

(d) *Special rule of section 1563(f)(3)(B).*—(1) *In general.*—If the same stock of a corporation is owned (within the meaning of section 1563(d)) by two or more persons, then such stock shall be treated as owned by the person whose ownership of such stock results in the corporation being a component member of a controlled group on a December 31 which has at least one other component member on such date.

(2) *Component member of more than one group.*—(i) If, by reason of subparagraph (1) of this paragraph, a corporation would (but for this subparagraph) become a component member of more than one controlled group on a December 31, such corporation shall be treated as a component member of only one such controlled group on such date. The determination as to which group such corporation is treated as a component member of shall be made in accordance with the rules contained in paragraphs (d)(2)(ii), (iii) and (iv) of this section.

(ii) In any case in which a corporation is a component member of a controlled group of corporations on a December 31 as a result of treating each share of its stock as owned only by the person who owns such share directly, then each such share shall be treated as owned by the person who owns such share directly.

(iii) If the application of subdivision (ii) of this subparagraph does not result in a corporation being treated as a component member of only one controlled group on a December 31, then the stock of such corporation described in subparagraph (1) of this paragraph shall be treated as owned by the one person described in such subparagraph who owns, directly and with the application of the rules contained in paragraph (b)(1), (2), (3), and (4) of this section, the stock possessing the greatest percentage of the total value of shares of all classes of stock of the corporation.

(iv) *Statement.*—If the application of paragraph (d)(2)(ii) or (iii) of this section does not result in a corporation being treated as a component member of only one controlled group of corporations on a December 31, then such corporation will be treated as a component member of only one such group on such date. Such corporation may elect the group in which it is to be included by including on or with its income tax return a statement entitled, "STATEMENT TO ELECT CONTROLLED GROUP PURSUANT TO § 1.1563-3(d)(2)(iv)." The statement must include—

Reg. § 1.1563-3(d)(2)(iv)

(A) A description of each of the controlled groups in which the corporation could be included. The description must include the name and employer identification number of each component member of each such group and the stock ownership of the component members of each such group; and

(B) The following representation: [INSERT NAME AND EMPLOYER IDENTIFICATION NUMBER OF CORPORATION] ELECTS TO BE TREATED AS A COMPONENT MEMBER OF THE [INSERT DESIGNATION OF GROUP].

(v) *Election.*—(A) *Election filed.*—An election filed under paragraph (d)(2)(iv) of this section is irrevocable and effective until paragraph (d)(2)(ii) or (iii) of this section applies or until a change in the stock ownership of the corporation results in termination of membership in the controlled group in which such corporation has been included.

(B) *Election not filed.*—In the event no election is filed in accordance with the provisions of paragraph (d)(2)(iv) of this section, then the Internal Revenue Service will determine the group in which such corporation is to be included. Such determination will be binding for all subsequent years unless the corporation files a valid election with respect to any such subsequent year or until a change in the stock ownership of the corporation results in termination of membership in the controlled group in which such corporation has been included.

(3) *Examples.*—The provisions of this paragraph may be illustrated by the following examples, in which each corporation referred to uses the calendar year as its taxable year and the stated facts are assumed to exist on each day of 1970 (unless otherwise provided in the example):

*Example (1).* Jones owns all the stock of corporation X and has an option to purchase from Smith all the outstanding stock of corporation Y. Smith owns all the outstanding stock of corporation Z. Since the Y stock is considered as owned by two or more persons, under subparagraph (2)(ii) of this paragraph the Y stock is treated as owned only by Smith since he has direct ownership of such stock. Therefore, on December 31, 1970, Y and Z are component members of the same brother-sister controlled group. If, however, Smith had owned his stock in corporation Z for less than one-half of the number of days of Z's 1970 taxable year, then under subparagraph (1) of this paragraph the Y stock would be treated as owned only by Jones since his ownership results in Y being a component member of a controlled group on December 31, 1970.

*Example (2).* Individual H owns directly all the outstanding stock of corporation M. W (the wife of H) owns directly all the outstanding stock of corporation N. Neither spouse is considered as owning the stock directly owned by the other because each of the conditions prescribed in paragraph (b)(5)(ii) of this section is satisfied with respect to each corporation's 1970 taxable year. H owns directly 60 percent of the only class of stock of corporation P and W owns the remaining 40 percent of the P stock. Under subparagraph (2)(iii) of this paragraph, the stock of P is treated as owned only by H since H owns (directly and with the application of the rules contained in paragraph (b)(1), (2), (3), and (4) of this section) the stock possessing the greatest percentage of the total value of shares of all classes of stock of P. Accordingly, on December 31, 1970, P is treated as a component member of a brother-sister group consisting of M and P.

*Example (3).* Unrelated individuals A and B each own 49 percent of all the outstanding stock of corporation R, which in turn owns 70 percent of the only class of outstanding stock of corporation S. The remaining 30 percent of the stock of corporation S is owned by unrelated individual C. C also owns the remaining 2 percent of the stock of corporation R. Under the attribution rule of paragraph (b)(4) of this section A and B are each considered to own 34.3 percent of the stock of corporation S. Accordingly, since five or fewer persons own at least 80 percent of the stock of corporations R and S and also own more than 50 percent identically (A's and B's identical ownership each is 34.3 percent, C's identical ownership is 2 percent), on December 31, 1970, corporations R and S are treated as component members of the same brother-sister controlled group for purposes of paragraph (a)(3)(ii) of §1.1563-1.

(e) *Effective/applicability date.*—Paragraph (d)(2)(iv) and (v) of this section apply to any taxable year beginning on or after May 30, 2006. However, taxpayers may apply paragraph (d)(2)(iv) and (v) of this section to any original Federal income tax return (including any amended return filed on or before the due date (including extensions) of such original return) timely filed on or after May 30, 2006. For taxable years beginning before May 30, 2006, see §1.1563-3 as contained in 26 CFR part 1 in effect on April 1, 2006. [Reg. §1.1563-3.]

☐ [*T.D.* 6845, 8-4-65. *Amended by T.D.* 7181, 4-24-72; *T.D.* 7779, 6-1-81; *T.D.* 8179, 3-1-88; *T.D.* 9264, 5-26-2006; *T.D.* 9304, 12-21-2006; *T.D.* 9329, 6-13-2007 *and T.D.* 9451, 5-26-2009.]

[Reg. §1.1563-4]

§1.1563-4. **Franchised corporations.**—(a) *In general.*—For purposes of paragraph (b)(2)(ii)(*d*) of §1.1563-1, a member of a controlled group of corporations shall be considered to be a franchised corporation for a taxable year if each of the following conditions is satisfied for one-half (or more) of the number of days preceding the December 31 included within such taxable year (or, if such taxable year does not include a December 31, for one-half or more of the number of days in such taxable year preceding the last day of such year):

(1) Such member is franchised to sell the products of another member, or the common owner, of such controlled group.

(2) More than 50 percent (determined on the basis of cost) of all the goods held by such member primarily for sale to its customers are acquired from members or the common owner of the controlled group, or both.

(3) The stock of such member is to be sold to an employee (or employees) of such member pursuant to a bona fide plan designed to eliminate the stock ownership of the parent corporation (as defined in paragraph (b)(1) of §1.1563-2) or of the common owner (as defined in paragraph (b)(3) of §1.1563-2) in such member.

(4) Such employee owns (or such employees in the aggregate own) directly more than 20 percent of the total value of shares of all classes of stock of such member. For purposes of this subparagraph, the determination of whether an employee (or employees) owns the requisite percentage of the total value of the stock of the member shall be made without regard to paragraph (b) of §1.1563-2, relating to certain stock treated as excluded stock. Furthermore, if the corporation has more than one class of stock outstanding, the relative voting rights as between each such class of stock shall be disregarded in making such determination.

(b) *Plan for elimination of stock ownership.*—(1) A plan referred to in paragraph (a)(3) of this section must—

(i) Provide a reasonable selling price for the stock of the member, and

(ii) Require that a portion of the employee's compensation or dividends, or both, from such member be applied to the purchase of such stock (or to the purchase of notes, bonds, debentures, or similar evidences of indebtedness of such member held by the parent corporation or the common owner).

It is not necessary, in order to satisfy the requirements of subdivision (ii) of this subparagraph, that the plan require that a percentage of every dollar of the compensation and dividends be applied to the purchase of the stock (or the indebtedness). The requirements of such subdivision are satisfied if an otherwise qualified plan provides that under certain specified conditions (such as a requirement that the member earn a specified profit) no portion of the compensation and/or dividends need be applied to the purchase of the stock (or indebtedness), provided such conditions are reasonable.

(2) A plan for the elimination of the stock ownership of the parent corporation or of the common owner will satisfy the requirements of paragraph (a)(3) of this section and subparagraph (1) of this paragraph even though it does not require that the stock of the member be sold to an employee (or employees) if it provides for the redemption of the stock of the member held by the parent or common owner and under the plan the amount of such stock to be redeemed during any period is calculated by reference to the profits of such member during such period. [Reg. §1.1563-4.]

☐ [*T.D.* 6845, 8-4-65.]

[The next page is 58,501.]

# ESTATE AND GIFT TAXES

## Estate Tax

## ESTATES OF CITIZENS OR RESIDENTS

## Tax Imposed

See p. 20,601 for regulations not amended to reflect law changes

[Reg. § 20.0-1]

§ 20.0-1. **Introduction.**—(a) *In general.*—(1) The regulations in this part (Part 20, Subchapter B, Chapter I, Title 26, Code of Federal Regulations) are designated "Estate Tax Regulations". These regulations pertain to (i) the Federal estate tax imposed by chapter 11 of subtitle B of the Internal Revenue Code on the transfer of estates of decedents dying after August 16, 1954, and (ii) certain related administrative provisions of subtitle F of the Code. It should be noted that the application of many of the provisions of these regulations may be affected by the provisions of an applicable death tax convention with a foreign country. Unless otherwise indicated, references in the regulations to the "Internal Revenue Code" or the "Code" are references to the Internal Revenue Code of 1954, as amended, and references to a section or other provision of law are references to a section or other provision of the Internal Revenue Code of 1954, as amended. Unless otherwise provided, the Estate Tax Regulations are applicable to the estates of decedents dying after August 16, 1954, and supersede the regulations contained in Part 81 of this chapter (1939) (Regulations 105, Estate Tax), as prescribed and made applicable to the Internal Revenue Code of 1954 by Treasury Decision 6091, signed August 16, 1954 (19 F.R. 5167, August 17, 1954).

(2) Section 2208 makes the provisions of chapter 11 of the Code apply to the transfer of the estates of certain decedents dying after September 2, 1958, who were citizens of the United States and residents of a possession thereof at the time of death. Section 2209 makes the provisions of chapter 11 apply to the transfer of the estates of certain other decedents dying after September 14, 1960, who were citizens of the United States and residents of a possession thereof at the time of death. See § § 20.2208-1 and 20.2209-1. Except as otherwise provided in § § 20.2208-1 and 20.2209-1, the provisions of these regulations do not apply to the estates of such decedents.

(b) *Scope of regulations.*—(1) *Estates of citizens or residents.*—Subchapter A of chapter 11 of the Code pertains to the taxation of the estate of a person who was a citizen or a resident of the United States at the time of his death. A "resident" decedent is a decedent who, at the time of his death, had his domicile in the United States. The term "United States," as used in the Estate Tax Regulations, includes only the States and the District of Columbia. The term also includes the Territories of Alaska and Hawaii prior to their admission as States. See section 7701(a)(9). A person acquires a domicile in a place by living there, for even a brief period of time, with no definite present intention of later removing therefrom. Residence without the requisite intention to remain indefinitely will not suffice to constitute domicile, nor will intention to change domicile effect such a change unless accompanied by actual removal. For the meaning of the term "citizen of the United States" as applied in a case where the decedent was a resident of a possession of the United States, see § 20.2208-1. The regulations pursuant to subchapter A are set forth in § § 20.2001 to 20.2056(d)-1.

(2) *Estates of nonresidents not citizens.*—Subchapter B of Chapter 11 of the Code pertains to the taxation of the estate of a person who was a nonresident not a citizen of the United States at the time of his death. A "nonresident" decedent is a decedent who, at the time of his death, had his domicile outside the United States under the principles set forth in subparagraph (1) of this paragraph. (See, however, section 2202 with respect to missionaries in foreign service.) The regulations pursuant to subchapter B are set forth in § § 20.2101 to 20.2108.

(3) *Miscellaneous substantive provisions.*—Subchapter C of chapter 11 of the Code contains a number of miscellaneous substantive provisions. The regulations pursuant to subchapter C are set forth in § § 20.2203-1 through 20.2209-1.

(4) *Procedure and administration provisions.*—Subtitle F of the Internal Revenue Code contains some sections which are applicable to the Federal estate tax. The regulations pursuant to those sections are set forth in § § 20.6001 to 20.7404. Such regulations do not purport to be all the regulations on procedure and administration which are pertinent to estate tax matters. For the remainder of the regulations on procedure and administration which are pertinent to estate tax matters, see Part 301 (Procedure and Administration Regulations) of this chapter.

(c) *Arrangement and numbering.*—Each section of the regulations in this part (other than this section and § 20.0-2) is designated by a number composed of the part number followed by a decimal point (20.); the section of the Internal Revenue Code which it interprets; a hyphen (-); and a number identifying the section. By use of these designations one can ascertain the sections of the regulations relating to a provision of the Code. For example, the regulations pertaining to section 2012 of the Code are designated § 20.2012-1. [Reg. § 20.0-1.]

☐ [T.D. 6296, 6-23-58. *Amended by T.D. 6526, 1-18-61; T.D. 7238, 12-28-72; T.D. 7296, 12-11-73; T.D. 7665, 1-24-80, T.D. 8522, 2-28-94 and T.D. 9849, 3-11-2019.]*

[Reg. § 20.0-2]

§ 20.0-2. **General description of tax.**—(a) *Nature of tax.*—The Federal estate tax is neither a property tax nor an inheritance tax. It is a tax imposed upon the transfer of the entire taxable estate and not upon any particular legacy, devise, or distributive share. Escheat of a decedent's property to the State for lack of heirs is a transfer which causes the property to be included in the decedent's gross estate.

(b) *Method of determining tax; estate of citizen or resident.*—(1) *In general.*—Subparagraphs (2) to (5) of this paragraph contain a general description of the method to be used in determining the Federal estate tax imposed upon the transfer of the estate of a decedent who was a citizen or resident of the United States at the time of his death.

(2) *Gross estate.*—The first step in determining the tax is to ascertain the total value of the decedent's gross estate. The value of the gross estate includes the value of all property to the extent of the interest therein of the decedent at the time of his death. (For certain exceptions in the case of real property situated outside the United States, see paragraphs (a) and (c) of § 20.2031-1.) In addition, the gross estate may include property in which the decedent did not have an interest at the time of his death. A decedent's gross estate for Federal estate tax purposes may therefore be very different from the decedent's estate for local probate purposes. Examples of items which may be included in a decedent's gross estate and not in his probate estate are the following: certain property transferred by the decedent during his lifetime without adequate consideration; property held jointly by the decedent and others; property over which the decedent had a general power of appointment; proceeds of certain policies of insurance on the decedent's life; annuities; and dower or curtesy of a surviving spouse or a statutory estate in lieu thereof. For a detailed explanation of the method of ascertaining the value of the gross estate, see sections 2031 through 2044, and the regulations thereunder.

(3) *Taxable estate.*—The second step in determining the tax is to ascertain the value of the decedent's taxable estate. The value of the taxable estate is determined by subtracting from the value of the gross estate the authorized exemption and deductions. Under various conditions and limitations, deductions are allowable for expenses, indebtedness, taxes, losses, charitable transfers, and transfers to a surviving spouse. For a detailed explanation of the method of ascertaining the value of the taxable estate, see sections 2051 through 2056, and the regulations thereunder.

(4) *Gross estate tax.*—The third step is the determination of the gross estate tax. This is accomplished by the application of certain rates to the value of the decedent's taxable estate. In this connection, see section 2001 and the regulations thereunder.

(5) *Net estate tax payable.*—The final step is the determination of the net estate tax payable. This is done by subtracting from the gross estate tax the authorized credits against tax. Under certain conditions and limitations, credits are allowable for the following (computed in the order stated below):

(i) State death taxes paid in connection with the decedent's estate (section 2011);

(ii) Gift taxes paid on inter-vivos transfers by the decedent of property included in his gross estate (section 2012);

(iii) Foreign death taxes paid in connection with the decedent's estate (section 2014); and

(iv) Federal estate taxes paid on transfers of property to the decedent (section 2013).

Sections 2015 and 2016 contain certain further rules for the application of the credits for State and foreign death taxes.

Sections 25.2701-5 and 25.2702-6 of this chapter contain rules that provide additional adjustments to mitigate double taxation in cases where the amount of the decedent's gift was previously determined under the special valuation provisions of section 2701 and 2702. For a detailed explanation of the credits against tax, see sections 2011 through 2016 and the regulations thereunder.

(c) *Method of determining tax; estate of nonresident not a citizen.*—In general, the method to be used in determining the Federal estate tax imposed upon the transfer of an estate of a decedent who was a nonresident not a citizen of the United States is similar to that described in paragraph (b) of this section with respect to the estate of a citizen or resident. Briefly stated, the steps are as follows: First, ascertain the sum of the value of that part of the decedent's "entire gross estate" which at the time of his death was situated in the United States (see §§ 20.2103-1 and 20.2014-1) and, in the case of an estate of an expatriate to which section 2107 applies, any amounts includible in his gross estate under section 2107(b) (see paragraph (b) of § 20.2107-1); second, determine the value of the taxable estate by subtracting from the amount determined under the first step the amount of the allowable deductions (see § 20.2106-1); third, compute the gross estate tax on the taxable estate (see § 20.2106-1); and fourth, subtract from the gross estate tax the total amount of any allowable credits in order to arrive at the net estate tax payable (see § 20.2102-1 and paragraph (c) of § 20.2107-1). [Reg. § 20.0-2.]

□ [*T.D. 6296, 6-23-58. Amended by T.D. 6684, 10-23-63; T.D. 7296, 12-11-73 and T.D. 8395, 1-28-92.*]

### [Reg. § 20.2001-1]

**§ 20.2001-1. Valuation of adjusted taxable gifts and section 2701(d)taxable events.**—(a) *Adjusted taxable gifts made prior to August 6, 1997.*—For purposes of determining the value of adjusted taxable gifts as defined in section 2001(b), if the gift was made prior to August 6, 1997, the value of the gift may be adjusted at any time, even if the time within which a gift tax may be assessed has expired under section 6501. This paragraph (a) also applies to adjustments involving issues other than valuation for gifts made prior to August 6, 1997.

(b) *Adjusted taxable gifts and section 2701(d) taxable events occurring after August 5, 1997.*—For purposes of determining the amount of adjusted taxable gifts as defined in section 2001(b), if, under section 6501, the time has expired within which a gift tax may be assessed under chapter 12 of the Internal Revenue Code (or under corresponding provisions of prior laws) with respect to a gift made after August 5, 1997, or with respect to an increase in taxable gifts required under section 2701(d) and § 25.2701-4 of this chapter, then the amount of the taxable gift will be the amount as finally determined for gift tax purposes under chapter 12 of the Internal Revenue Code and the amount of the taxable gift may not thereafter be adjusted. The rule of this paragraph (b) applies to adjustments involving all issues relating to the gift, including valuation issues and legal issues involving the interpretation of the gift tax law.

(c) *Finally determined.*—For purposes of paragraph (b) of this section, the amount of a taxable gift as finally determined for gift tax purposes is—

(1) The amount of the taxable gift as shown on a gift tax return, or on a statement attached to the return, if the Internal Revenue Service does not contest such amount before the time has expired under section 6501 within which gift taxes may be assessed;

(2) The amount as specified by the Internal Revenue Service before the time has expired under section 6501 within which gift taxes may be assessed on the gift, if such specified amount is not timely contested by the taxpayer;

(3) The amount as finally determined by a court of competent jurisdiction; or

(4) The amount as determined pursuant to a settlement agreement entered into between the taxpayer and the Internal Revenue Service.

(d) *Definitions.*—For purposes of paragraph (b) of this section, the amount is finally determined by a court of competent jurisdiction when the court enters a final decision, judgment, decree or other order with respect to the amount of the taxable gift that is not subject to appeal. See, for example, section 7481 regarding the finality of a decision by the U.S. Tax Court. Also, for purposes of paragraph (b) of this section, a settlement agreement means any agreement entered into by the Internal Revenue Service and the taxpayer that is binding

on both. The term includes a closing agreement under section 7121, a compromise under section 7122, and an agreement entered into in settlement of litigation involving the amount of the taxable gift.

(e) *Expiration of period of assessment.*—For purposes of determining if the time has expired within which a tax may be assessed under chapter 12 of the Internal Revenue Code, see § 301.6501(c)-1(e) and (f) of this chapter.

(f) *Effective dates.*—Paragraph (a) of this section applies to transfers of property by gift made prior to August 6, 1997, if the estate tax return for the donor/decedent's estate is filed after December 3, 1999. Paragraphs (b) through (e) of this section apply to transfers of property by gift made after August 5, 1997, if the gift tax return for the calendar period in which the gift is made is filed after December 3, 1999. [Reg. § 20.2001-1.]

□ [*T.D. 6296, 6-23-58. Amended by T.D. 8845, 12-2-99.*]

### [Reg. § 20.2001-2]

**§ 20.2001-2. Valuation of adjusted taxable gifts for purposes of determining the deceased spousal unused exclusion amount of last deceased spouse.**—(a) *General rule.*—Notwithstanding § 20.2001-1(b), §§ 20.2010-2(d) and 20.2010-3(d) provide additional rules regarding the authority of the Internal Revenue Service to examine any gift or other tax return(s), even if the time within which a tax may be assessed under section 6501 has expired, for the purpose of determining the deceased spousal unused exclusion amount available under section 2010(c) of the Internal Revenue Code.

(b) *Effective/applicability date.*—Paragraph (a) of this section applies to the estates of decedents dying on or after June 12, 2015. See 26 CFR 20.2001-2T(a), as contained in 26 CFR part 20, revised as of April 1, 2015, for the rules applicable to estates of decedents dying on or after January 1, 2011, and before June 12, 2015. [Reg. § 20.2001-2.]

□ [*T.D. 9725, 6-12-2015.*]

### [Reg. § 20.2002-1]

**§ 20.2002-1. Liability for payment of tax.**—The Federal estate tax imposed both with respect to the estates of citizens or residents and with respect to estates of nonresidents not citizens is payable by the executor or administrator of the decedent's estate. This duty applies to the entire tax, regardless of the fact that the gross estate consists in part of property which does not come within the possession of the executor or administrator. If there is no executor or administrator appointed, qualified, and acting in the United States, any person in actual or constructive possession of any property of the decedent is required to pay the entire tax to the extent of the value of the property in his possession. See section 2203, defining the term "executor". The personal liability of the executor or such other person is described in section 3467 of the Revised Statutes (31 U.S.C. 192) as follows:

> Every executor, administrator, or assignee, or other person, who pays, in whole or in part, any debt due by the person or estate for whom or for which he acts before he satisfies and pays the debts due to the United States from such person or estate, shall become answerable in his own person and estate to the extent of such payments for the debts so due to the United States, or for so much thereof as may remain due and unpaid.

As used in said section, the word "debt" includes a beneficiary's distributive share of an estate. Thus, if the executor pays a debt due by the decedent's estate or distributes any portion of the estate before all the estate tax is paid, he is personally liable, to the extent of the payment or distribution, for so much of the estate tax as remains due and unpaid. In addition, section 6324(a)(2) provides that if the estate tax is not paid when due, then the spouse, transferee, trustee (except the trustee of an employee's trust which meets the requirements of section 401(a)), surviving tenant, person in possession of the property by reason of the exercise, nonexercise, or release of a power of appointment, or beneficiary, who receives, or has on the date of the decedent's death, property included in the gross estate under sections 2034 through 2042, is personally liable for the tax to the extent of the value, at the time of the decedent's death, of such property. See also the following related sections of the Internal Revenue Code: section 2204, discharge of executor from personal liability; section 2205, reimbursement out of estate; sections 2206 and 2207, liability of life insurance beneficiaries and recipients of property over which decedent had power of appointment; sections 6321 through 6325, concerning liens for taxes; and section 6901(a)(1), concerning the liabilities of transferees and fiduciaries. [Reg. § 20.2002-1.]

□ [*T.D. 6296, 6-23-58.*]

## Credits Against Tax

### [Reg. § 20.2010-0]

**§ 20.2010-0. Table of contents.**—This section lists the table of contents for §§ 20.2010-1 through 20.2010-3.

(c) Special rule in the case of a difference between the basic exclusion amount applicable to gifts and that applicable at the donor's date of death.

(d) Credit limitation.

(e) Explanation of terms.

(1) Applicable credit amount.

(2) Applicable exclusion amount.

(3) Basic exclusion amount.

(4) Deceased spousal unused exclusion (DSUE) amount.

(5) Last deceased spouse.

(f) Effective/applicability date.

§ 20.2010-2 *Portability provisions applicable to estate of a decedent survived by a spouse.*

(a) Election required for portability.

(1) Timely filing required.

(2) Portability election upon filing of estate tax return.

(3) Portability election not made; requirements for election not to apply.

(4) Election irrevocable.

(5) Estates eligible to make the election.

(6) Persons permitted to make the election.

(7) Requirements of return.

(b) Requirement for DSUE computation on estate tax return.

(c) Computation of the DSUE amount.

(1) General rule.

(2) Special rule to consider gift taxes paid by decedent.

(3) Impact of applicable credits.

(4) Special rule in case of property passing to qualified domestic trust.

(5) Examples.

(d) Authority to examine returns of decedent.

(e) Effective/applicability date.

§ 20.2010-3 *Portability provisions applicable to the surviving spouse's estate.*

(a) Surviving spouse's estate limited to DSUE amount of last deceased spouse.

(1) In general.

(2) No DSUE amount available from last deceased spouse.

(3) Identity of last deceased spouse unchanged by subsequent marriage or divorce.

(b) Special rule in case of multiple deceased spouses and previously-applied DSUE amount.

(1) In general.

(2) Example.

(c) Date DSUE amount taken into consideration by surviving spouse's estate.

(1) General rule.

(2) Exception when surviving spouse not a U.S. citizen on date of deceased spouse's death.

(3) Special rule when property passes to surviving spouse in a qualified domestic trust.

(d) Authority to examine returns of deceased spouses.

(e) Availability of DSUE amount for estates of nonresidents who are not citizens.

(f) Effective/applicability date.

[Reg. § 20.2010-0.]

☐ [T.D. 9725, 6-12-2015. *Amended by* T.D. 9884, 11-22-2019.]

**[Reg. § 20.2010-1]**

**§ 20.2010-1. Unified credit against estate tax; in general.—**(a) *General rule.—*Section 2010(a) allows the estate of every decedent a credit against the estate tax imposed by section 2001. The allowable credit is the applicable credit amount. See paragraph (e)(1) of this section for an explanation of the term *applicable credit amount.*

(b) *Special rule in case of certain gifts made before 1977.—*The applicable credit amount allowable under paragraph (a) of this section must be reduced by an amount equal to 20 percent of the aggregate amount allowed as a specific exemption under section 2521 (as in effect before its repeal by the Tax Reform Act of 1976) for gifts made by the decedent after September 8, 1976, and before January 1, 1977.

(c) *Special rule in the case of a difference between the basic exclusion amount applicable to gifts and that applicable at the donor's date of death.—*Changes in the basic exclusion amount that occur between the date of a donor's gift and the date of the donor's death may cause the basic exclusion amount allowable on the date of a gift to exceed that allowable on the date of death. If the total of the amounts allowable as a credit in computing the gift tax payable on the decedent's

post-1976 gifts, within the meaning of section 2001(b)(2), to the extent such credits are based solely on the basic exclusion amount as defined and adjusted in section 2010(c)(3), exceeds the credit allowable within the meaning of section 2010(a) in computing the estate tax, again only to the extent such credit is based solely on such basic exclusion amount, in each case by applying the tax rates in effect at the decedent's death, then the portion of the credit allowable in computing the estate tax on the decedent's taxable estate that is attributable to the basic exclusion amount is the sum of the amounts attributable to the basic exclusion amount allowable as a credit in computing the gift tax payable on the decedent's post-1976 gifts.

(1) *Computational rules.—*For purposes of this paragraph (c):

(i) In determining the amounts allowable as a credit:

(A) The amount allowable as a credit in computing gift tax payable for any calendar period may not exceed the tentative tax on the gifts made during that period (section 2505(c)); and

(B) The amount allowable as a credit in computing the estate tax may not exceed the net tentative tax on the taxable estate (section 2010(d)).

(ii) In determining the extent to which an amount allowable as a credit in computing gift tax payable is based solely on the basic exclusion amount:

(A) Any deceased spousal unused exclusion (DSUE) amount available to the decedent is deemed to be applied to gifts made by the decedent before the decedent's basic exclusion amount is applied to those gifts (see § § 20.2010-3(b) and 25.2505-2(b));

(B) In a calendar period in which the applicable exclusion amount allowable with regard to gifts made during that period includes amounts other than the basic exclusion amount, the allowable basic exclusion amount may not exceed that necessary to reduce the tentative gift tax to zero; and

(C) In a calendar period in which the applicable exclusion amount allowable with regard to gifts made during that period includes amounts other than the basic exclusion amount, the portion of the credit based solely on the basic exclusion amount is that which corresponds to the result of dividing the basic exclusion amount allocable to those gifts by the applicable exclusion amount allocable to those gifts.

(iii) In determining the extent to which an amount allowable as a credit in computing the estate tax is based solely on the basic exclusion amount, the credit is computed as if the applicable exclusion amount were limited to the basic exclusion amount.

(2) *Examples.—*All basic exclusion amounts include hypothetical inflation adjustments. Unless otherwise stated, in each example the decedent's date of death is after 2025.

(i) *Example 1.* Individual A (never married) made cumulative post-1976 taxable gifts of $9 million, all of which were sheltered from gift tax by the cumulative total of $11.4 million in basic exclusion amount allowable on the dates of the gifts. The basic exclusion amount on A's date of death is $6.8 million. A was not eligible for any restored exclusion amount pursuant to Notice 2017-15. Because the total of the amounts allowable as a credit in computing the gift tax payable on A's post-1976 gifts (based on the $9 million of basic exclusion amount used to determine those credits) exceeds the credit based on the $6.8 million basic exclusion amount allowable on A's date of death, this paragraph (c) applies, and the credit for purposes of computing A's estate tax is based on a basic exclusion amount of $9 million, the amount used to determine the credits allowable in computing the gift tax payable on A's post-1976 gifts.

(ii) *Example 2.* Assume that the facts are the same as in *Example 1* of paragraph (c)(2)(i) of this section except that A made cumulative post-1976 taxable gifts of $4 million. Because the total of the amounts allowable as a credit in computing the gift tax payable on A's post-1976 gifts is less than the credit based on the $6.8 million basic exclusion amount allowable on A's date of death, this paragraph (c) does not apply. The credit to be applied for purposes of computing A's estate tax is based on the $6.8 million basic exclusion amount as of A's date of death, subject to the limitation of section 2010(d).

(iii) *Example 3.* Individual B's predeceased spouse, C, died before 2026, at a time when the basic exclusion amount was $11.4 million. C had made no taxable gifts and had no taxable estate. C's executor elected, pursuant to § 20.2010-2, to allow B to take into account C's $11.4 million DSUE amount. B made no taxable gifts and did not remarry. The basic exclusion amount on B's date of death is $6.8 million. Because the total of the amounts allowable as a credit in computing the gift tax payable on B's post-1976 gifts attributable to the basic exclusion amount (zero) is less than the credit based on the basic exclusion amount allowable on B's date of death, this paragraph (c) does not apply. The credit to be applied for purposes of computing B's estate tax is based on B's $18.2 million applicable exclusion amount, consisting of the $6.8 million basic exclusion amount on B's date of death plus the $11.4 million DSUE amount, subject to the limitation of section 2010(d).

(iv) *Example 4.* Assume the facts are the same as in *Example 3* of paragraph (c)(2)(iii) of this section except that, after C's death and before 2026, B makes taxable gifts of $14 million in a year when the basic exclusion amount is $12 million. B is considered to apply the DSUE amount to the gifts before applying B's basic exclusion amount. The amount allowable as a credit in computing the gift tax payable on B's post-1976 gifts for that year ($5,545,800) is the tax on $14 million, consisting of $11.4 million in DSUE amount and $2.6 million in basic exclusion amount. This basic exclusion amount is 18.6 percent of the $14 million exclusion amount allocable to those gifts, with the result that $1,031,519 (0.186 x $5,545,800) of the amount allowable as a credit for that year in computing gift tax payable is based solely on the basic exclusion amount. The amount allowable as a credit based solely on the basic exclusion amount for purposes of computing B's estate tax ($2,665,800) is the tax on the $6.8 million basic exclusion amount on B's date of death. Because the portion of the credit allowable in computing the gift tax payable on B's post-1976 gifts based solely on the basic exclusion amount ($1,031,519) is less than the credit based solely on the basic exclusion amount ($2,665,800) allowable on B's date of death, this paragraph (c) does not apply. The credit to be applied for purposes of computing B's estate tax is based on B's $18.2 million applicable exclusion amount, consisting of the $6.8 million basic exclusion amount on B's date of death plus the $11.4 million DSUE amount, subject to the limitation of section 2010(d).

(3) [Reserved]

(d) *Credit limitation.*—The applicable credit amount allowed under paragraph (a) of this section cannot exceed the amount of the estate tax imposed by section 2001.

(e) *Explanation of terms.*—The explanation of terms in this section applies to this section and to §§ 20.2010-2 and 20.2010-3.

(1) *Applicable credit amount.*—The term *applicable credit amount* refers to the allowable credit against estate tax imposed by section 2001 and gift tax imposed by section 2501. The applicable credit amount equals the amount of the tentative tax that would be determined under section 2001(c) if the amount on which such tentative tax is to be computed were equal to the applicable exclusion amount. The applicable credit amount is determined by applying the unified rate schedule in section 2001(c) to the applicable exclusion amount.

(2) *Applicable exclusion amount.*—The *applicable exclusion amount* equals the sum of the basic exclusion amount and, in the case of a surviving spouse, the deceased spousal unused exclusion (DSUE) amount.

(3) *Basic exclusion amount.*—Except to the extent provided in paragraph (e)(3)(iii) of this section, the *basic exclusion amount* is the sum of the amounts described in paragraphs (e)(3)(i) and (ii) of this section.

(i) For any decedent dying in calendar year 2011 or thereafter, $5,000,000; and

(ii) For any decedent dying after calendar year 2011 and before calendar year 2018, $5,000,000 multiplied by the cost-of-living adjustment determined under section 1(f)(3) for the calendar year of the decedent's death by substituting "calendar year 2010" for "calendar year 1992" in section 1(f)(3)(B) and by rounding to the nearest multiple of $10,000. For any decedent dying after calendar year 2017, $5,000,000 multiplied by the cost-of-living adjustment determined under section 1(f)(3) for the calendar year of the decedent's death by substituting "calendar year 2010" for "calendar year 2016" in section 1(f)(3)(A)(ii) and rounded to the nearest multiple of $10,000.

(iii) For any decedent dying after calendar year 2017, and before calendar year 2026, paragraphs (e)(3)(i) and (ii) of this section will be applied by substituting "$10,000,000" for "$5,000,000."

(4) *Deceased spousal unused exclusion (DSUE) amount.*—The term *DSUE amount* refers, generally, to the unused portion of a decedent's applicable exclusion amount to the extent this amount does not exceed the basic exclusion amount in effect in the year of the decedent's death. For the rules on computing the DSUE amount, see §§ 20.2010-2(c) and 20.2010-3(b).

(5) *Last deceased spouse.*—The term *last deceased spouse* means the most recently deceased individual who, at that individual's death after December 31, 2010, was married to the surviving spouse. See §§ 20.2010-3(a) and 25.2505-2(a) for additional rules pertaining to the identity of the last deceased spouse for purposes of determining the applicable exclusion amount of the surviving spouse.

(f) *Applicability dates.*—(1) *In general.*—Except as provided in paragraph (f)(2) of this section, this section applies to the estates of decedents dying after June 11, 2015. For the rules applicable to estates of decedents dying after December 31, 2010, and before June 12, 2015, see § 20.2010-1T, as contained in 26 CFR part 20, revised as of April 1, 2015.

(2) *Exceptions.*—Paragraphs (c) and (e)(3) of this section apply to estates of decedents dying on and after November 26, 2019. However, paragraph (e)(3) of this section may be applied by estates of decedents dying after December 31, 2017, and before November 26, 2019. For the explanation of the basic exclusion amount applicable to estates of decedents dying after June 11, 2015, and before January 1, 2018, see § 20.2010-1(d)(3), as contained in 26 CFR part 20, revised as of April 1, 2019. [Reg. § 20.2010-1.]

☐ [*T.D. 9725, 6-12-2015. Amended by T.D. 9884, 11-22-2019.*]

**[Reg. § 20.2010-2]**

**§ 20.2010-2. Portability provisions applicable to estate of a decedent survived by a spouse.**—(a) *Election required for portability.*—To allow a decedent's surviving spouse to take into account that decedent's deceased spousal unused exclusion (DSUE) amount, the executor of the decedent's estate must elect portability of the DSUE amount on a timely filed Form 706, "United States Estate (and Generation-Skipping Transfer) Tax Return" (estate tax return). This election is referred to in this section and in § 20.2010-3 as the portability election.

(1) *Timely filing required.*—An estate that elects portability will be considered, for purposes of subtitle B and subtitle F of the Internal Revenue Code (Code), to be required to file a return under section 6018(a). Accordingly, the due date of an estate tax return required to elect portability is nine months after the decedent's date of death or the last day of the period covered by an extension (if an extension of time for filing has been obtained). See §§ 20.6075-1 and 20.6081-1 for additional rules relating to the time for filing estate tax returns. An extension of time to elect portability under this paragraph (a) will not be granted under § 301.9100-3 of this chapter to an estate that is required to file an estate tax return under section 6018(a), as determined without regard to this paragraph (a). Such an extension, however, may be available under the procedures applicable under §§ 301.9100-1 and 301.9100-3 of this chapter to an estate that is not required to file a return under section 6018(a), as determined without regard to this paragraph (a).

(2) *Portability election upon filing of estate tax return.*—Upon the timely filing of a complete and properly prepared estate tax return, an executor of an estate of a decedent survived by a spouse will have elected portability of the decedent's DSUE amount unless the executor chooses not to elect portability and satisfies the requirement in paragraph (a)(3)(i) of this section. See paragraph (a)(7) of this section for the return requirements related to the portability election.

(3) *Portability election not made; requirements for election not to apply.*—The executor of the estate of a decedent survived by a spouse will not make or be considered to make the portability election if either of the following applies:

(i) The executor states affirmatively on a timely filed estate tax return, or in an attachment to that estate tax return, that the estate is not electing portability under section 2010(c)(5). The manner in which the executor may make this affirmative statement on the estate tax return is as set forth in the instructions issued with respect to such form ("Instructions for Form 706").

(ii) The executor does not timely file an estate tax return in accordance with paragraph (a)(1) of this section.

(4) *Election irrevocable.*—An executor of the estate of a decedent survived by a spouse who timely files an estate tax return may make or may supersede a portability election previously made, provided that the estate tax return reporting the election or the superseding election is filed on or before the due date of the return, including extensions actually granted. However, see paragraph (a)(6) of this section when contrary elections are made by more than one person permitted to make the election. The portability election, once made, becomes irrevocable once the due date of the estate tax return, including extensions actually granted, has passed.

(5) *Estates eligible to make the election.*—An executor may elect portability on behalf of the estate of a decedent survived by a spouse if the decedent dies on or after January 1, 2011. However, an executor of the estate of a nonresident decedent who was not a citizen of the United States at the time of death may not elect portability on behalf of that decedent, and the timely filing of such a decedent's estate tax return will not constitute the making of a portability election.

(6) *Persons permitted to make the election.*—(i) *Appointed executor.*—An executor or administrator of the estate of a decedent sur-

vived by a spouse that is appointed, qualified, and acting within the United States, within the meaning of section 2203 (an appointed executor), may timely file the estate tax return on behalf of the estate of the decedent and, in so doing, elect portability of the decedent's DSUE amount. An appointed executor also may elect not to have portability apply pursuant to paragraph (a)(3) of this section.

(ii) *Non-appointed executor.*—If there is no appointed executor, any person in actual or constructive possession of any property of the decedent (a non-appointed executor) may timely file the estate tax return on behalf of the estate of the decedent and, in so doing, elect portability of the decedent's DSUE amount, or, by complying with paragraph (a)(3) of this section, may elect not to have portability apply. A portability election made by a non-appointed executor when there is no appointed executor for that decedent's estate can be superseded by a subsequent contrary election made by an appointed executor of that same decedent's estate on an estate tax return filed on or before the due date of the return, including extensions actually granted. An election to allow portability made by a non-appointed executor cannot be superseded by a contrary election to have portability not apply made by another non-appointed executor of that same decedent's estate (unless such other non-appointed executor is the successor of the non-appointed executor who made the election). See § 20.6018-2 for additional rules relating to persons permitted to file the estate tax return.

(7) *Requirements of return.*—(i) *General rule.*—An estate tax return will be considered complete and properly prepared for purposes of this section if it is prepared in accordance with the instructions issued for the estate tax return (Instructions for Form 706) and if the requirements of §§ 20.6018-2, 20.6018-3, and 20.6018-4 are satisfied. However, see paragraph (a)(7)(ii) of this section for reduced requirements applicable to certain property of certain estates.

(ii) *Reporting of value not required for certain property.*—(A) *In general.*—A special rule applies with respect to certain property of estates in which the executor is not required to file an estate tax return under section 6018(a), as determined without regard to paragraph (a)(1) of this section. With respect to such an estate, for bequests, devises, or transfers of property included in the gross estate, the value of which is deductible under section 2056 or 2056A (marital deduction property) or under section 2055(a) (charitable deduction property), an executor is not required to report a value for such property on the estate tax return (except to the extent provided in this paragraph (a)(7)(ii)(A)) and will be required to report only the description, ownership, and/or beneficiary of such property, along with all other information necessary to establish the right of the estate to the deduction in accordance with §§ 20.2056(a)-1(b)(i) through (iii) and 20.2055-1(c), as applicable. However, this rule does not apply in certain circumstances as provided in this paragraph (a) and as may be further described in guidance issued from time to time by publication in the Internal Revenue Bulletin (see § 601.601(d)(2)(ii)(b) of this chapter). In particular, this rule does not apply to marital deduction property or charitable deduction property if—

(1) The value of such property relates to, affects, or is needed to determine, the value passing from the decedent to a recipient other than the recipient of the marital or charitable deduction property;

(2) The value of such property is needed to determine the estate's eligibility for the provisions of sections 2032, 2032A, or another estate or generation-skipping transfer tax provision of the Code for which the value of such property or the value of the gross estate or adjusted gross estate must be known (not including section 1014 of the Code);

(3) Less than the entire value of an interest in property includible in the decedent's gross estate is marital deduction property or charitable deduction property; or

(4) A partial disclaimer or partial qualified terminable interest property (QTIP) election is made with respect to a bequest, devise, or transfer of property includible in the gross estate, part of which is marital deduction property or charitable deduction property.

(B) *Return requirements when reporting of value not required for certain property.*—Paragraph (a)(7)(ii)(A) of this section applies only if the executor exercises due diligence to estimate the fair market value of the gross estate, including the property described in paragraph (a)(7)(ii)(A) of this section. Using the executor's best estimate of the value of properties to which paragraph (a)(7)(ii)(A) of this section applies, the executor must report on the estate tax return, under penalties of perjury, the amount corresponding to the particular range within which falls the executor's best estimate of the total gross estate, in accordance with the Instructions for Form 706.

(C) *Examples.*—The following examples illustrate the application of paragraph (a)(7)(ii) of this section. In each example, assume that Husband (H) dies in 2015, survived by his wife (W), that both H and W are U.S. citizens, that H's gross estate does not exceed the excess of the applicable exclusion amount for the year of his death over the total amount of H's adjusted taxable gifts and any specific exemption under section 2521, and that H's executor (E) timely files Form 706 solely to make the portability election.

*Example 1.* (i) *Facts.* The assets includible in H's gross estate consist of a parcel of real property and bank accounts held jointly with W with rights of survivorship, a life insurance policy payable to W, and a survivor annuity payable to W for her life. H made no taxable gifts during his lifetime.

(ii) *Application.* E files an estate tax return on which these assets are identified on the proper schedule, but E provides no information on the return with regard to the date of death value of these assets in accordance with paragraph (a)(7)(ii)(A) of this section. To establish the estate's entitlement to the marital deduction in accordance with § 20.2056(a)-1(b) (except with regard to establishing the value of the property) and the instructions for the estate tax return, E includes with the estate tax return evidence to verify the title of each jointly held asset, to confirm that W is the sole beneficiary of both the life insurance policy and the survivor annuity, and to verify that the annuity is exclusively for W's life. Finally, E reports on the estate return E's best estimate, determined by exercising due diligence, of the fair market value of the gross estate in accordance with paragraph (a)(7)(ii)(B) of this section. The estate tax return is considered complete and properly prepared and E has elected portability.

*Example 2.* (i) *Facts.* H's will, duly admitted to probate and not subject to any proceeding to challenge its validity, provides that H's entire estate is to be distributed outright to W. The non-probate assets includible in H's gross estate consist of a life insurance policy payable to H's children from a prior marriage, and H's individual retirement account (IRA) payable to W. H made no taxable gifts during his lifetime.

(ii) *Application.* E files an estate tax return on which all of the assets includible in the gross estate are identified on the proper schedule. In the case of the probate assets and the IRA, no information is provided with regard to date of death value in accordance with paragraph (a)(7)(ii)(A) of this section. However, E attaches a copy of H's will and describes each such asset and its ownership to establish the estate's entitlement to the marital deduction in accordance with the instructions for the estate tax return and § 20.2056(a)-1(b) (except with regard to establishing the value of the property). In the case of the life insurance policy payable to H's children, all of the regular return requirements, including reporting and establishing the fair market value of such asset, apply. Finally, E reports on the estate return E's best estimate, determined by exercising due diligence, of the fair market value of the gross estate in accordance with paragraph (a)(7)(ii)(B) of this section. The estate tax return is considered complete and properly prepared and E has elected portability.

*Example 3.* (i) *Facts.* H's will, duly admitted to probate and not subject to any proceeding to challenge its validity, provides that 50 percent of the property passing under the terms of H's will is to be paid to a marital trust for W and 50 percent is to be paid to a trust for W and their descendants.

(ii) *Application.* The amount passing to the non-marital trust cannot be verified without knowledge of the full value of the property passing under the will. Therefore, the value of the property of the marital trust relates to or affects the value passing to the trust for W and the descendants of H and W. Accordingly, the general return requirements apply to all of the property includible in the gross estate and the provisions of paragraph (a)(7)(ii) of this section do not apply.

(b) *Requirement for DSUE computation on estate tax return.*—Section 2010(c)(5)(A) requires an executor of a decedent's estate to include a computation of the DSUE amount on the estate tax return to elect portability and thereby allow the decedent's surviving spouse to take into account that decedent's DSUE amount. This requirement is satisfied by the timely filing of a complete and properly prepared estate tax return, as long as the executor has not elected out of portability as described in paragraph (a)(3)(i) of this section. See paragraph (a)(7) of this section for the requirements for a return to be considered complete and properly prepared.

(c) *Computation of the DSUE amount.*—(1) *General rule.*—Subject to paragraphs (c)(2) through (4) of this section, the DSUE amount of a decedent with a surviving spouse is the lesser of the following amounts—

(i) The basic exclusion amount in effect in the year of the death of the decedent; or

(ii) The excess of—

(A) The decedent's applicable exclusion amount; over

(B) The sum of the amount of the taxable estate and the amount of the adjusted taxable gifts of the decedent, which together is the amount on which the tentative tax on the decedent's estate is determined under section 2001(b)(1).

(2) *Special rule to consider gift taxes paid by decedent.*—Solely for purposes of computing the decedent's DSUE amount, the amount of the adjusted taxable gifts of the decedent referred to in paragraph (c)(1)(ii)(B) of this section is reduced by the amount, if any, on which gift taxes were paid for the calendar year of the gift(s).

(3) *Impact of applicable credits.*—An estate's eligibility under sections 2012 through 2015 for credits against the tax imposed by section 2001 does not impact the computation of the DSUE amount.

(4) *Special rule in case of property passing to qualified domestic trust.*—(i) *In general.*—When property passes for the benefit of a surviving spouse in a qualified domestic trust (QDOT) as defined in section 2056A(a), the DSUE amount of the decedent is computed on the decedent's estate tax return for the purpose of electing portability in the same manner as this amount is computed under paragraph (c)(1) of this section, but this DSUE amount is subject to subsequent adjustments. The DSUE amount of the decedent must be redetermined upon the occurrence of the final distribution or other event (generally, the termination of all QDOTs created by or funded with assets passing from the decedent or the death of the surviving spouse) on which estate tax is imposed under section 2056A. See § 20.2056A-6 for the rules on determining the estate tax under section 2056A. See § 20.2010-3(c)(3) regarding the timing of the availability of the decedent's DSUE amount to the surviving spouse.

(ii) *Surviving spouse becomes a U.S. citizen.*—If the surviving spouse becomes a U.S. citizen and if the requirements of section 2056A(b)(12) and the corresponding regulations are satisfied, the estate tax imposed under section 2056A(b)(1) ceases to apply. Accordingly, no estate tax will be imposed under section 2056A either on subsequent QDOT distributions or on the property remaining in the QDOT on the surviving spouse's death and the decedent's DSUE amount is no longer subject to adjustment.

(5) *Examples.*—The following examples illustrate the application of this paragraph (c):

*Example 1. Computation of DSUE amount.* (i) *Facts.* In 2002, having made no prior taxable gift, Husband (H) makes a taxable gift valued at $1,000,000 and reports the gift on a timely filed gift tax return. Because the amount of the gift is equal to the applicable exclusion amount for that year ($1,000,000), $345,800 is allowed as a credit against the tax, reducing the gift tax liability to zero. H dies in 2015, survived by Wife (W). H and W are U.S. citizens and neither has any prior marriage. H's taxable estate is $1,000,000. The executor of H's estate timely files H's estate tax return and elects portability, thereby allowing W to benefit from H's DSUE amount.

(ii) *Application.* The executor of H's estate computes H's DSUE amount to be $3,430,000 (the lesser of the $5,430,000 basic exclusion amount in 2015, or the excess of H's $5,430,000 applicable exclusion amount over the sum of the $1,000,000 taxable estate and the $1,000,000 amount of adjusted taxable gifts).

*Example 2. Computation of DSUE amount when gift tax paid.* (i) *Facts.* The facts are the same as in *Example 1* of this paragraph (c)(5) except that the value of H's taxable gift in 2002 is $2,000,000. After application of the applicable credit amount, H owes gift tax on $1,000,000, the amount of the gift in excess of the applicable exclusion amount for that year. H pays the gift tax owed on the 2002 transfer.

(ii) *Application.* On H's death, the executor of H's estate computes the DSUE amount to be $3,430,000 (the lesser of the $5,430,000 basic exclusion amount in 2015, or the excess of H's $5,430,000 applicable exclusion amount over the sum of the $1,000,000 taxable estate and $1,000,000 of adjusted taxable gifts sheltered from tax by H's applicable credit amount). H's adjusted taxable gifts of $2,000,000 were reduced for purposes of this computation by $1,000,000, the amount of taxable gifts on which gift taxes were paid.

*Example 3. Computation of DSUE amount when QDOT created.* (i) *Facts.* Husband (H), a U.S. citizen, makes his first taxable gift in 2002, valued at $1,000,000, and reports the gift on a timely filed gift tax return. No gift tax is due because the applicable exclusion amount for that year ($1,000,000) equals the fair market value of the gift. H dies in 2015 with a gross estate of $2,000,000. H's surviving spouse (W) is a resident, but not a citizen, of the United States and, under H's will, a pecuniary bequest of $1,500,000 passes to a QDOT for the benefit of W. H's executor timely files an estate tax return and makes the QDOT election for the property passing to the QDOT, and H's estate is allowed a marital deduction of $1,500,000 under section 2056(d) for the value of that property. H's taxable estate is $500,000. On H's estate tax return, H's executor computes H's preliminary DSUE amount to be $3,930,000 (the lesser of the $5,430,000 basic exclusion

amount in 2015, or the excess of H's $5,430,000 applicable exclusion amount over the sum of the $500,000 taxable estate and the $1,000,000 adjusted taxable gifts). No taxable events within the meaning of section 2056A occur during W's lifetime with respect to the QDOT, and W makes no taxable gifts. At all times since H's death, W has been a U.S. resident. In 2017, W dies and the value of the assets of the QDOT is $1,800,000.

(ii) *Application.* H's DSUE amount is redetermined to be $2,130,000 (the lesser of the $5,430,000 basic exclusion amount in 2015, or the excess of H's $5,430,000 applicable exclusion amount over $3,300,000 (the sum of the $500,000 taxable estate augmented by the $1,800,000 of QDOT assets and the $1,000,000 adjusted taxable gifts)).

*Example 4. Computation of DSUE amount when surviving spouse with QDOT becomes a U.S. citizen.* (i) *Facts.* The facts are the same as in *Example 3* of this paragraph (c)(5) except that W becomes a U.S. citizen in 2016 and dies in 2018. The U.S. Trustee of the QDOT notifies the IRS that W has become a U.S. citizen by timely filing a final estate tax return (Form 706-QDT). Pursuant to section 2056A(b)(12), the estate tax under section 2056A no longer applies to the QDOT property.

(ii) *Application.* Because H's DSUE amount no longer is subject to adjustment once W becomes a citizen of the United States, H's DSUE amount is $3,930,000, as it was preliminarily determined as of H's death. Upon W's death in 2018, the value of the QDOT property is includible in W's gross estate.

(d) *Authority to examine returns of decedent.*—The IRS may examine returns of a decedent in determining the decedent's DSUE amount, regardless of whether the period of limitations on assessment has expired for that return. See § 20.2010-3(d) for additional rules relating to the IRS's authority to examine returns. See also section 7602 for the IRS's authority, when ascertaining the correctness of any return, to examine any returns that may be relevant or material to such inquiry.

(e) *Effective/applicability date.*—This section applies to the estates of decedents dying on or after June 12, 2015. See 26 CFR 20.2010-2T, as contained in 26 CFR part 20, revised as of April 1, 2015, for the rule applicable to estates of decedents dying on or after January 1, 2011, and before June 12, 2015. [Reg. § 20.2010-2.]

☐ [T.D. 9725, 6-12-2015.]

**[Reg. § 20.2010-3]**

**§ 20.2010-3. Portability provisions applicable to the surviving spouse's estate.**—(a) *Surviving spouse's estate limited to DSUE amount of last deceased spouse.*—(1) *In general.*—The deceased spousal unused exclusion (DSUE) amount of a decedent, computed under § 20.2010-2(c), is included in determining the surviving spouse's applicable exclusion amount under section 2010(c)(2), provided—

(i) Such decedent is the last deceased spouse of such surviving spouse within the meaning of § 20.2010-1(e)(5) on the date of the death of the surviving spouse; and

(ii) The executor of the decedent's estate elected portability (see § 20.2010-2(a) and (b) for applicable requirements).

(2) *No DSUE amount available from last deceased spouse.*—If the last deceased spouse of such surviving spouse had no DSUE amount, or if the executor of such a decedent's estate did not make a portability election, the surviving spouse's estate has no DSUE amount (except as provided in paragraph (b)(1)(ii) of this section) to be included in determining the applicable exclusion amount, even if the surviving spouse previously had a DSUE amount available from another decedent who, prior to the death of the last deceased spouse, was the last deceased spouse of such surviving spouse. See paragraph (b) of this section for a special rule in the case of multiple deceased spouses and a previously applied DSUE amount.

(3) *Identity of last deceased spouse unchanged by subsequent marriage or divorce.*—A decedent is the last deceased spouse (as defined in § 20.2010-1(e)(5)) of a surviving spouse even if, on the date of the death of the surviving spouse, the surviving spouse is married to another (then-living) individual. If a surviving spouse marries again and that marriage ends in divorce or an annulment, the subsequent death of the divorced spouse does not end the status of the prior deceased spouse as the last deceased spouse of the surviving spouse. The divorced spouse, not being married to the surviving spouse at death, is not the last deceased spouse as that term is defined in § 20.2010-1(e)(5).

(b) *Special rule in case of multiple deceased spouses and previously-applied DSUE amount.*—(1) *In general.*—A special rule applies to compute the DSUE amount included in the applicable exclusion amount of a surviving spouse who previously has applied the DSUE amount of one or more deceased spouses to taxable gifts in accordance with § 25.2505-2(b) and (c). If a surviving spouse has applied the DSUE amount of one or more (successive) last deceased spouses to the surviving spouse's transfers during life, and if any of those last deceased spouses is different from the surviving spouse's last deceased spouse as defined in §20.2010-1(e)(5) at the time of the surviving spouse's death, then the DSUE amount to be included in determining the applicable exclusion amount of the surviving spouse at the time of the surviving spouse's death is the sum of—

(i) The DSUE amount of the surviving spouse's last deceased spouse as described in paragraph (a)(1) of this section; and

(ii) The DSUE amount of each other deceased spouse of the surviving spouse, to the extent that such amount was applied to one or more taxable gifts of the surviving spouse.

(2) *Example.*—The following example, in which all described individuals are U.S. citizens, illustrates the application of this paragraph (b):

*Example.* (i) *Facts.* Husband 1 (H1) dies in 2011, survived by Wife (W). Neither has made any taxable gifts during H1's lifetime. H1's executor elects portability of H1's DSUE amount. The DSUE amount of H1 as computed on the estate tax return filed on behalf of H1's estate is $5,000,000. In 2012, W makes taxable gifts to her children valued at $2,000,000. W reports the gifts on a timely filed gift tax return. W is considered to have applied $2,000,000 of H1's DSUE amount to the amount of taxable gifts, in accordance with §25.2505-2(c), and, therefore, W owes no gift tax. W has an applicable exclusion amount remaining in the amount of $8,120,000 ($3,000,000 of H1's remaining DSUE amount plus W's own $5,120,000 basic exclusion amount). W marries Husband 2 (H2) in 2013. H2 dies in 2014. H2's executor elects portability of H2's DSUE amount, which is properly computed on H2's estate tax return to be $2,000,000. W dies in 2015.

(ii) *Application.* The DSUE amount to be included in determining the applicable exclusion amount available to W's estate is $4,000,000, determined by adding the $2,000,000 DSUE amount of H2 and the $2,000,000 DSUE amount of H1 that was applied by W to W's 2012 taxable gifts. The $4,000,000 DSUE amount added to W's $5,430,000 basic exclusion amount (for 2015), causes W's applicable exclusion amount to be $9,430,000.

(c) *Date DSUE amount taken into consideration by surviving spouse's estate.*—(1) *General rule.*—A portability election made by an executor of a decedent's estate (see §20.2010-2(a) and (b) for applicable requirements) generally applies as of the date of the decedent's death. Thus, such decedent's DSUE amount is included in the applicable exclusion amount of the decedent's surviving spouse under section 2010(c)(2) and will be applicable to transfers made by the surviving spouse after the decedent's death (subject to the limitations in paragraph (a) of this section). However, such decedent's DSUE amount will not be included in the applicable exclusion amount of the surviving spouse, even if the surviving spouse had made a transfer in reliance on the availability or computation of the decedent's DSUE amount:

(i) If the executor of the decedent's estate supersedes the portability election by filing a subsequent estate tax return in accordance with §20.2010-2(a)(4);

(ii) To the extent that the DSUE amount subsequently is reduced by a valuation adjustment or the correction of an error in calculation; or

(iii) To the extent that the surviving spouse cannot substantiate the DSUE amount claimed on the surviving spouse's return.

(2) *Exception when surviving spouse not a U.S. citizen on date of deceased spouse's death.*—If a surviving spouse becomes a citizen of the United States after the death of the surviving spouse's last deceased spouse, the DSUE amount of the surviving spouse's last deceased spouse becomes available to the surviving spouse on the date the surviving spouse becomes a citizen of the United States (subject to the limitations in paragraph (a) of this section). However, when the special rule regarding qualified domestic trusts in paragraph (c)(3) of this section applies, the earliest date on which a decedent's DSUE amount may be included in the applicable exclusion amount of such decedent's surviving spouse who becomes a U.S. citizen is as provided in paragraph (c)(3) of this section.

(3) *Special rule when property passes to surviving spouse in a qualified domestic trust.*—(i) *In general.*—When property passes from a decedent for the benefit of the decedent's surviving spouse in one or more qualified domestic trusts (QDOT) as defined in section 2056A(a) and the decedent's executor elects portability, the DSUE amount available to be included in the applicable exclusion amount of the surviving spouse under section 2010(c)(2) is the DSUE amount of the decedent as redetermined in accordance with §20.2010-2(c)(4)

(subject to the limitations in paragraph (a) of this section). The earliest date on which such decedent's DSUE amount may be included in the applicable exclusion amount of the surviving spouse under section 2010(c)(2) is the date of the occurrence of the final QDOT distribution or final other event (generally, the termination of all QDOTs created by or funded with assets passing from the decedent or the death of the surviving spouse) on which tax under section 2056A is imposed. However, the decedent's DSUE amount as redetermined in accordance with §20.2010-2(c)(4) may be applied to certain taxable gifts of the surviving spouse. See §25.2505-2(d)(3)(i).

(ii) *Surviving spouse becomes a U.S. citizen.*—If a surviving spouse for whom property has passed from a decedent in one or more QDOTs becomes a citizen of the United States and the requirements in section 2056A(b)(12) and the corresponding regulations are satisfied, then the date on which such decedent's DSUE amount may be included in the applicable exclusion amount of the surviving spouse under section 2010(c)(2) (subject the limitations in paragraph (a) of this section) is the date on which the surviving spouse becomes a citizen of the United States. See §20.2010-2(c)(4) for the rules for computing the decedent's DSUE amount in the case of a qualified domestic trust.

(d) *Authority to examine returns of deceased spouses.*—For the purpose of determining the DSUE amount to be included in the applicable exclusion amount of a surviving spouse, the Internal Revenue Service (IRS) may examine returns of each of the surviving spouse's deceased spouses whose DSUE amount is claimed to be included in the surviving spouse's applicable exclusion amount, regardless of whether the period of limitations on assessment has expired for any such return. The IRS's authority to examine returns of a deceased spouse applies with respect to each transfer by the surviving spouse to which a DSUE amount is or has been applied. Upon examination, the IRS may adjust or eliminate the DSUE amount reported on such a return of a deceased spouse; however, the IRS may assess additional tax on that return only if that tax is assessed within the period of limitations on assessment under section 6501 applicable to the tax shown on that return. See also section 7602 for the IRS's authority, when ascertaining the correctness of any return, to examine any returns that may be relevant or material to such inquiry. For purposes of these examinations to determine the DSUE amount, the surviving spouse is considered to have a material interest that is affected by the return information of the deceased spouse within the meaning of section 6103(e)(3).

(e) *Availability of DSUE amount for estates of nonresidents who are not citizens.*—The estate of a nonresident surviving spouse who is not a citizen of the United States at the time of such surviving spouse's death shall not take into account the DSUE amount of any deceased spouse of such surviving spouse within the meaning of §20.2010-1(e)(5) except to the extent allowed under any applicable treaty obligation of the United States. See section 2102(b)(3).

(f) *Effective/applicability date.*—This section applies to the estates of decedents dying on or after June 12, 2015. See 26 CFR 20.2010-3T, as contained in 26 CFR part 20, revised as of April 1, 2015, for the rules applicable to estates of decedents dying on or after January 1, 2011, and before June 12, 2015. [Reg. §20.2010-3.]

□ [*T.D.* 9725, 6-12-2015. *Amended by T.D.* 9884, 11-22-2019.]

**[Reg. §20.2011-1]**

**§20.2011-1. Credit for State death taxes.**—(a) *In general.*—A credit is allowed under section 2011 against the Federal estate tax for estate, inheritance, legacy or succession taxes actually paid to any State, Territory, or the District of Columbia, or in the case of decedents dying before September 3, 1958, any possession of the United States (hereafter referred to as "State death taxes"). The credit, however, is allowed only for State death taxes paid (1) with respect to property included in the decedent's gross estate, and (2) with respect to the decedent's estate. The amount of the credit is subject to the limitation described in paragraph (b) of this section. It is subject to further limitations described in §20.2011-2 if a deduction is allowed under section 2053(d) for State death taxes paid with respect to a charitable gift. See paragraph (a) of §20.2014-1 as to the allowance of a credit for death taxes paid to a possession of the United States in a case where the decedent died after September 2, 1958.

(b) *Amount of credit.*—(1) If the decedent's taxable estate does not exceed $40,000, the credit for State death taxes is zero. If the decedent's taxable estate does exceed $40,000, the credit for State death taxes is limited to an amount computed in accordance with the following table:

### TABLE FOR COMPUTATION OF MAXIMUM CREDIT FOR STATE DEATH TAXES

| (A) Taxable estate equal to or more than— | (B) Taxable estate less than— | (C) Credit on amount in column (A) | (D) Rates of credit on excess over amount in column (A) |
|---|---|---|---|
| | | | Percent |
| $40,000 | $90,000 | . . . . . | .8 |
| 90,000 | 140,000 | $400 | 1.6 |
| 140,000 | 240,000 | 1,200 | 2.4 |

| (A) Taxable estate equal to or more than— | (B) Taxable estate less than— | (C) Credit on amount in column (A) | (D) Rates of credit on excess over amount in column (A) |
|---|---|---|---|
| 240,000 | 440,000 | 3,600 | 3.2 |
| 440,000 | 640,000 | 10,000 | 4.0 |
| 640,000 | 840,000 | 18,000 | 4.8 |
| 840,000 | 1,040,000 | 27,600 | 5.6 |
| 1,040,000 | 1,540,000 | 38,800 | 6.4 |
| 1,540,000 | 2,040,000 | 70,800 | 7.2 |
| 2,040,000 | 2,540,000 | 106,800 | 8.0 |
| 2,540,000 | 3,040,000 | 146,800 | 8.8 |
| 3,040,000 | 3,540,000 | 190,800 | 9.6 |
| 3,540,000 | 4,040,000 | 238,800 | 10.4 |
| 4,040,000 | 5,040,000 | 290,800 | 11.2 |
| 5,040,000 | 6,040,000 | 402,800 | 12.0 |
| 6,040,000 | 7,040,000 | 522,800 | 12.8 |
| 7,040,000 | 8,040,000 | 650,800 | 13.6 |
| 8,040,000 | 9,040,000 | 786,800 | 14.4 |
| 9,040,000 | 10,040,000 | 930,800 | 15.2 |
| 10,040,000 | . . . . . . . . | 1,082,800 | 16.0 |

(2) Subparagraph (1) of this paragraph may be illustrated by the following example:

*Example.* (i) The decedent died January 1, 1955, leaving a taxable estate of $150,000. On January 1, 1956, inheritance taxes totaling $2,500 were actually paid to a State with respect to property included in the decedent's gross estate. Reference to the table discloses that the specified amount in column (A) nearest to but less than the value of the decedent's taxable estate is $140,000. The maximum credit in respect of this amount, as indicated in column (C), is $1,200. The amount by which the taxable estate exceeds the same specified amount is $10,000. The maximum credit in respect of this amount, computed at the rate of 2.4 percent indicated in column (D), is $240. Thus, the maximum credit in respect of the decedent's taxable estate of $150,000 is $1,440, even though $2,500 in inheritance taxes was actually paid to the State.

(ii) If, in subdivision (i) of this example, the amount actually paid to the State was $950, the credit for State death taxes would be limited to $950. If, in subdivision (i) of this example, the decedent's taxable estate was $35,000, no credit for State death taxes would be allowed.

(c) *Miscellaneous limitations and conditions to credit.*—(1) *Period of limitations.*—The credit for State death taxes is limited under section 2011(c) to those taxes which were actually paid and for which a credit was claimed within four years after the filing of the estate tax return for the decedent's estate. If, however, a petition has been filed with the Tax Court of the United States for the redetermination of a deficiency within the time prescribed in section 6213(a), the credit is limited to those taxes which were actually paid and for which a credit was claimed within four years after the filing of the return or within 60 days after the decision of the Tax Court becomes final, whichever period is the last to expire. Similarly, if an extension of time has been granted under section 6161 for payment of the tax shown on the return, or of a deficiency, the credit is limited to those taxes which were actually paid and for which a credit was claimed within four years after the filing of the return, or before the date of the expiration of the period of the extension, whichever period is last to expire. If a claim for refund or credit of an overpayment of the Federal estate tax is filed within the time prescribed in section 6511, the credit for State death taxes is limited to such taxes as were actually paid and credit therefor claimed within four years after the filing of the return or before the expiration of 60 days from the date of mailing by certified or registered mail by the district director to the taxpayer of a notice of disallowance of any part of the claim, or before the expiration of 60 days after a decision by any court of competent jurisdiction becomes final with respect to a timely suit instituted upon the claim, whichever period is the last to expire. See section 2015 for the applicable period of limitations for credit for State death taxes on reversionary or remainder interests if an election is made under section 6163(a) to postpone payment of the estate tax attributable to reversionary or remainder interests. If a claim for refund based on the credit for State death taxes is filed within the applicable period described in this subparagraph, a refund may be made despite the general limitation provisions of sections 6511 and 6512. Any refund based on the credit described in this section shall be made without interest.

(2) *Submission of evidence.*—Before the credit for State death taxes is allowed, evidence that such taxes have been paid must be submit-

ted to the district director. The district director may require the submission of a certificate from the proper officer of the taxing State, Territory, or possession of the United States, or the District of Columbia, showing: (i) the total amount of tax imposed (before adding interest and penalties and before allowing discount); (ii) the amount of any discount allowed; (iii) the amount of any penalties and interest imposed or charged; (iv) the total amount actually paid in cash; and (v) the date or dates of payment. If the amount of these taxes has been redetermined, the amount finally determined should be stated. The required evidence should be filed with the return, but if that is not convenient or possible, then it should be submitted as soon thereafter as practicable. The district director may require the submission of such additional proof as is deemed necessary to establish the right to the credit. For example, he may require the submission of a certificate of the proper officer of the taxing jurisdiction showing (vi) whether a claim for refund of any part of the State death tax is pending and (vii) whether a refund of any part thereof has been authorized, and if a refund has been made, its date and amount, and a description of the property or interest in respect of which the refund was made. The district director may also require an itemized list of the property in respect of which State death taxes were imposed certified by the officer having custody of the records pertaining to those taxes. In addition, he may require the executor to submit a written statement (containing a declaration that it is made under penalties of perjury) stating whether, to his knowledge, any person has instituted litigation or taken an appeal (or contemplates doing so), the final determination of which may affect the amount of those taxes. See section 2016 concerning the redetermination of the estate tax if State death taxes claimed as credit are refunded.

(d) *Definition of "basic estate tax".*—Section 2011(d) provides definitions of the terms "basic estate tax" and "additional estate tax", used in the Internal Revenue Code of 1939, and "estate tax imposed by the Revenue Act of 1926", for the purpose of supplying a means of computing State death taxes under local statutes using those terms, and for use in determining the exemption provided for in section 2201 for estates of certain members of the Armed Forces. See section 2011(e)(3) for a modification of these definitions if a deduction is allowed under section 2053(d) for State death taxes paid with respect to a charitable gift. [Reg. § 20.2011-1.]

☐ [*T.D. 6296, 6-23-58. Amended by T.D. 6526, 1-18-61.*]

**[Reg. § 20.2011-2]**

**§ 20.2011-2. Limitation on credit if a deduction for State death taxes is allowed under section 2053(d).**—If a deduction is allowed under section 2053(d) for State death taxes paid with respect to a charitable gift, the credit for State death taxes is subject to special limitations. Under these limitations, the credit cannot exceed the least of the following:

(a) The amount of State death taxes paid other than those for which a deduction is allowed under section 2053(d);

(b) The amount indicated in section 2011(b) to be the maximum credit allowable with respect to the decedent's taxable estate; or

(c) An amount, A, which bears the same ratio to B (the amount which would be the maximum credit allowable under section 2011(b) if the deduction under section 2053(d) for State death taxes were not allowed in computing the decedent's taxable estate) as C (the amount of State death taxes paid other than those for which a deduction is allowed under section 2053(d)) bears to D (the total amount of State death taxes paid). For the purpose of this computation, in determining what the decedent's taxable estate would be if the deduction for State death taxes under section 2053(d) were not allowed, adjustment must be made for the decrease in the deduction for charitable gifts under section 2055 or 2106(a)(2) (for estates of nonresidents not citizens) by reason of any increase in Federal estate tax which would be charged against the charitable gifts.

The application of this section may be illustrated by the following example:

| | | | | |
|---|---:|---:|---:|---:|
| Gross estate | | | | $925,000.00 |
|   Expenses, indebtedness, etc. | | $25,000.00 | | |
|   Exemption | | 60,000.00 | | |
|   Deduction under section 2053(d) | | 75,000.00 | | |
| Charitable deduction: | | | | |
|   Gross estate | | $925,000.00 | | |
|     Expenses, etc. | $25,000.00 | | | |
|     Bequest to son | 400,000.00 | | | |
|     State death tax paid from residue | 75,000.00 | | | |
|     Federal estate tax paid from residue | 122,916.67 | 622,916.67 | 302,083.33 | 462,083.33 |
| Taxable estate | | | | $462,916.67 |

If the deduction under section 2053(d) were not allowed, the decedent's taxable estate would be computed as follows:

| | | | | |
|---|---:|---:|---:|---:|
| Gross estate | | | | $925,000.00 |
|   Expenses, indebtedness, etc. | | | $25,000.00 | |
|   Exemption | | | $60,000.00 | |
| Charitable deduction: | | | | |
|   Gross estate | | $925,000.00 | | |
|     Expenses, etc. | $25,000.00 | | | |
|     Bequest to son | 400,000.00 | | | |
|     State death tax paid from residue | 75,000.00 | | | |
|     Federal estate tax paid from residue | 155,000.00 | 655,000.00 | 270,000.00 | $355,000.00 |
| Taxable estate | | | | $570,000.00 |

On a taxable estate of $570,000, the maximum credit allowable under section 2011(b) would be $15,200. Under these facts, the credit for State death taxes is determined as follows:

(1) Amount of State death taxes paid other than those for which a deduction is allowed under section 2053(d) ($135,000 – $75,000) .................... $60,000.00

(2) Amount indicated in section 2011(b) to be the maximum credit allowable with respect to the decedent's taxable estate of $462,916.67 ............ 10,916.67

(3) Amount determined by use of the ratio described in paragraph (c) above

$$\frac{\$60,000}{\$135,000} \times \$15,200 \quad\ldots\ldots\ldots\ldots\ldots\ldots\ldots\ldots\quad 6,755.56$$

(4) Credit for State death taxes (least of subparagraphs (1) through (3) above) ............ 6,755.56

[Reg. §20.2011-2]

☐ [T.D. 6296, 6-23-58. Amended by T.D. 6600, 5-28-62.]

### [Reg. §20.2012-1]

**§20.2012-1. Credit for gift tax.**—(a) *In general.*—With respect to gifts made before 1977, a credit is allowed under section 2012 against the Federal estate tax for gift tax paid under chapter 12 of the Internal Revenue Code, or corresponding provisions of prior law, on a gift by the decedent of property subsequently included in the decedent's gross estate. The credit is allowable even though the gift tax is paid after the decedent's death and the amount of the gift tax is deductible from the gross estate as a debt of the decedent.

(b) *Limitations on credit.*—The credit for gift tax is limited to the smaller of the following amounts:

(1) The amount of gift tax paid on the gift, computed as set forth in paragraph (c) of this section, or

(2) The amount of the estate tax attributable to the inclusion of the gift in the gross estate, computed as set forth in paragraph (d) of this section.

When more than one gift is included in the gross estate, a separate computation of the two limitations on the credit is to be made for each gift.

*Example.* The decedent died January 1, 1955, leaving a gross estate of $925,000. Expenses, indebtedness, etc., amounted to $25,000. The decedent bequeathed $400,000 to his son with the direction that the son bear the State death taxes on the bequest. The residuary estate was left to a charitable organization. Except as noted above, all Federal and State death taxes were payable out of the residuary estate. The State imposed death taxes of $60,000 on the son's bequest and death taxes of $75,000 on the bequest to charity. No death taxes were imposed by a foreign country with respect to any property in the gross estate. The decedent's taxable estate (determined without regard to the limitation imposed by section 2011(e)(2)(B)) is computed as follows:

(c) *"First limitation".*—The amount of the gift tax paid on the gift is the "first limitation." Thus, if only one gift was made during a certain calendar quarter or calendar year if the gift was made before January 1, 1971, and the gift is wholly included in the decedent's gross estate for the purpose of the estate tax, the credit with respect to the gift is limited to the amount of the gift tax paid for that calendar quarter or calendar year. On the other hand, if more than one gift was made during a certain calendar quarter or calendar year, the credit with respect to any such gift which is included in the decedent's gross estate is limited under section 2012(d) to an amount, A, which bears the same ratio to B (the total gift tax paid for that calendar quarter or calendar year) as C (the "amount of the gift," computed as described below) bears to D (the total taxable gifts for the calendar quarter or the calendar year, computed without deduction of the gift tax specific exemption). Stated algebraically, the "first limitation" (A) equals

$$\frac{\text{"amount of the gift" (C)}}{\substack{\text{total taxable gifts, plus} \\ \text{specific exemption allowed} \\ \text{(D)}}} \times \substack{\text{total gift} \\ \text{tax paid} \\ \text{(B)}.}$$

For purposes of the ratio stated above, the "amount of the gift" referred to as factor "C" is the value of the gift reduced by any portion excluded or deducted under section 2503(b) (annual exclusion), 2522 (charitable deduction), or 2523 (marital deduction) of the Internal Revenue Code or corresponding provisions of prior law. In making the computations described in this paragraph, the values to be used are those finally determined for the purpose of the gift tax, irrespective of the values determined for the purpose of the estate tax. A similar computation is made in case only a portion of any gift is included in the decedent's gross estate. The application of this paragraph may be illustrated by the following example:

*Example.* The donor made gifts during the calendar year 1955 on which a gift tax was determined as shown below:

Gift of property to son on February 1 . . . . . . . . . . . . . . . $13,000
Gift of property to wife on May 1 . . . . . . . . . . . . . . . . . . 86,000
Gift of property to charitable organization on May 15 . . . . . . 10,000

| | |
|---|---|
| Total gifts . . . . . . . . . . . . . . . . . . . . . . . . . . . . . | 109,000 |
| Less exclusions ($3,000 for each gift) . . . . . . . . . . . . | 9,000 |
| Total included amount of gifts . . . . . . . . . . . . . . . . | 100,000 |
| Marital deduction (for gift to wife) . . . . . . . . $43,000 | |
| Charitable deduction . . . . . . . . . . . . . . . . . 7,000 | |
| Specific exemption ($30,000 less $20,000 used in prior years) . . . . . . . . . . . . . . . . . 10,000 | |
| Total deductions . . . . . . . . . . . . . . . . . . . . . . . . | 60,000 |
| Taxable gifts . . . . . . . . . . . . . . . . . . . . . . . . . . | 40,000 |
| Total gift tax paid for calendar year 1955 . . . . . . . . . . . | $ 3,600 |

The donor's gift to his wife was made in contemplation of death and was thereafter included in his gross estate. Under the "first limitation," the credit with respect to that gift cannot exceed

$$\frac{\$86{,}000 - \$3{,}000 - \$43{,}000 \text{ (gift to wife, less annual exclusion and marital deduction)}}{\$40{,}000 + \$10{,}000 \text{ (taxable gifts, plus spe- cific exemption allowed)}} \times \$3{,}600 \text{ (total gift tax paid)} = \$2{,}880.$$

(d) *"Second limitation".*—(1) The amount of the estate tax attributable to the inclusion of the gift in the gross estate is the "second limitation". Thus, the credit with respect to any gift of property included in the gross estate is limited to an amount, E, which bears the same ratio to F (the gross estate tax, reduced by any credit for State death taxes under section 2011) as G (the "value of the gift,"

$$(E) \text{ equals } \frac{\text{"value of the gift" (G)}}{\text{value of gross estate, less marital and charitable deductions (H)}} \times$$

(2) For purposes of the ratio stated in subparagraph (1) of this paragraph, the "value of the gift" referred to as factor "G" is the value of the property transferred by gift and included in the gross estate, as determined for the purpose of the gift tax or for the purpose of the estate tax, whichever is lower, and adjusted as follows:

(i) The appropriate value is reduced by all or a portion of any annual exclusion allowed for gift tax purposes under section 2503(b) of the Internal Revenue Code or corresponding provisions of prior law. If the gift tax value is lower than the estate tax value, it is

$$\frac{\$15{,}000 \quad \text{(annual exclusions allowed)}}{\$300{,}000 \quad \text{(value of transferred property for the purpose of the gift tax)}} \times \$270{,}000$$

(ii) The appropriate value is further reduced if any portion of the value of the property is allowed as a marital deduction under section 2056 or as a charitable deduction under section 2055 or section 2106(a)(2) (for estates of nonresidents not citizens). The amount of the reduction is an amount which bears the same ratio to the value determined under subdivision (i) of this subparagraph as the portion of the property allowed as a marital deduction or as a charitable deduction bears to the total value of the property as determined for the purpose of the estate tax. Thus, if a gift is made solely to the decedent's surviving spouse and is subsequently included in the decedent's gross estate as having been made in contemplation of death, but a marital deduction is allowed under section 2056 for the full value of the gift, no credit for gift tax on the gift will be allowed since the reduction under this subdivision together with the reduction under subdivision (i) of this subparagraph will have the effect of reducing the factor "G" of the ratio in subparagraph (1) of this paragraph to zero.

(e) *Credit for "split gifts".*—If a decedent made a gift of property which is thereafter included in his gross estate, and, under the provisions of section 2513 of the Internal Revenue Code of 1954 or section 1000(f) of the Internal Revenue Code of 1939, the gift was considered as made one-half by the decedent and one-half by his spouse, credit against the estate tax is allowed for the gift tax paid with respect to both halves of the gift. The "first limitation" is to be separately computed with respect to each half of the gift in accordance with the principles stated in paragraph (c) of this section. The "second limitation" is to be computed with respect to the entire gift in accordance with the principles stated in paragraph (d) of this section. To illustrate: A donor, in contemplation of death, transferred property valued at $106,000 to his son on January 1, 1955, and he and his wife consented that the gift should be considered as made one-half by him and one-half by her. The property was thereafter included in the donor's gross estate. Under the "first limitation", the amount of the gift tax of the donor paid with respect to the one-half of the gift considered as made by him is determined to be $11,250, and the amount of the gift tax of his wife paid with respect to the

computed as described in subparagraph (2) of this paragraph) bears to H (the value of the entire gross estate, reduced by the total deductions allowed under sections 2055 or 2106(a)(2) (charitable deduction) and 2056 (marital deduction)). Stated algebraically, the "second limitation"

$$\times \quad \text{gross estate tax, less credit for State death taxes (F).}$$

reduced by the entire amount of the exclusion. If the estate tax value is lower than the gift tax value, it is reduced by an amount which bears the same ratio to the estate tax value as the annual exclusion bears to the total value of the property as determined for gift tax purposes. To illustrate: In 1955, a donor, in contemplation of death, transferred certain property to his five children which was valued at $300,000 for the purpose of gift tax. Thereafter, the same property was included in his gross estate at a value of $270,000. In computing his gift tax, the donor was allowed annual exclusions totalling $15,000. The reduction provided for in this subdivision is

$$\begin{array}{l}\text{(value of transferred property} \\ \text{for the purpose of the estate} \\ \text{tax)} = \$13{,}500.\end{array}$$

one-half of the gift considered as made by her is determined to be $1,200. Under the "second limitation", the amount of the estate tax attributable to the property is determined to be $28,914. Therefore, the credit for gift tax allowed is $12,450 ($11,250 plus $1,200). [Reg. § 20.2012-1.]

☐ [*T.D. 6296, 6-23-58. Amended by T.D. 7238, 12-28-72 and T.D. 8522, 2-28-94.*]

### [Reg. § 20.2013-1]

**§ 20.2013-1. Credit for tax on prior transfers.**—(a) *In general.*—A credit is allowed under section 2013 against the Federal estate tax imposed on the present decedent's estate for Federal estate tax paid on the transfer of property to the present decedent from a transferor who died within ten years before, or within two years after, the present decedent's death. See § 20.2013-5 for definition of the terms "property" and "transfer." There is no requirement that the transferred property be identified in the estate of the present decedent or that the property be in existence at the time of the decedent's death. It is sufficient that the transfer of the property was subjected to Federal estate tax in the estate of the transferor and that the transferor died within the prescribed period of time. The executor must submit such proof as may be requested by the district director in order to establish the right of the estate to the credit.

(b) *Limitations on credit.*—The credit for tax on prior transfers is limited to the smaller of the following amounts:

(1) The amount of the Federal estate tax attributable to the transferred property in the transferor's estate, computed as set forth in § 20.2013-2; or

(2) The amount of the Federal estate tax attributable to the transferred property in the decedent's estate, computed as set forth in § 20.2013-3. Rules for valuing property for purposes of the credit are contained in § 20.2013-4.

(c) *Percentage reduction.*—If the transferor died within the two years before, or within the two years after, the present decedent's death, the credit is the smaller of the two limitations described in paragraph (b) of this section. If the transferor predeceased the present decedent by more than two years, the credit is a certain percentage of the smaller of the two limitations described in paragraph (b) of this section, determined as follows:

(1) 80 percent, if the transferor died within the third or fourth years preceding the present decedent's death;

(2) 60 percent, if the transferor died within the fifth or sixth years preceding the present decedent's death;

(3) 40 percent, if the transferor died within the seventh or eighth years preceding the present decedent's death; and

(4) 20 percent, if the transferor died within the ninth or tenth years preceding the present decedent's death.

The word "within" as used in this paragraph means "during". Therefore, if a death occurs on the second anniversary of another death, the first death is considered to have occurred within the two years before the second death. If the credit for tax on prior transfers relates to property received from two or more transferors, the provisions of

$$\frac{\text{value of transferred property (C)}}{\text{"transferor's adjusted taxable estate" (D)}} \times \text{"transferor's adjusted Federal estate tax" (B)}.$$

(b) For purposes of the ratio stated in paragraph (a) of this section, the "transferor's adjusted Federal estate tax" referred to as factor "B" is the amount of the Federal estate tax paid with respect to the transferor's estate plus:

(1) Any credit allowed the transferor's estate for gift tax under section 2012, or the corresponding provisions of prior law; and

(2) Any credit allowed the transferor's estate, under section 2013, for tax on prior transfers, but only if the transferor acquired property from a person who died within 10 years before the death of the present decedent.

(c)(1) For purposes of the ratio stated in paragraph (a) of this section, the "transferor's adjusted taxable estate" referred to as factor "D" is the amount of the transferor's taxable estate (or net estate) decreased by the amount of any "death taxes" paid with respect to his gross estate and increased by the amount of the exemption allowed in computing his taxable estate (or net estate). The amount of the transferor's taxable estate (or net estate) is determined in accordance with the provisions of § 20.2051-1 in the case of a citizen or resident of the United States or of § 20.2106-1 in the case of a nonresident not a citizen of the United States (or the corresponding provisions of prior regulations). The term "death taxes" means the Federal estate tax plus all other estate, inheritance, legacy, succession, or similar death taxes imposed by, and paid to, any taxing authority, whether within or without the United States. However, only the net amount of such taxes paid is taken into consideration.

(2) The amount of the exemption depends upon the citizenship and residence of the transferor at the time of his death. Except in the case of a decedent described in section 2209 (relating to certain residents of possessions of the United States who are considered nonresidents not citizens), if the decedent was a citizen or resident of the United States, the exemption is the $60,000 authorized by section 2052 (or the corresponding provisions of prior law). If the decedent was a nonresident not a citizen of the United States, or is considered under section 2209 to have been such a nonresident, the exemption is the $30,000 or $2,000, as the case may be, authorized by section 2106(a)(3) (or the corresponding provisions of prior law), or such larger amount as is authorized by section 2106(a)(3)(B) or may have been allowed as an exemption pursuant to the prorated exemption provisions of an applicable death tax convention. See § 20.2052-1 and paragraph (a)(3) of § 20.2106-1.

(d) If the credit for tax on prior transfers relates to property received from two or more transferors, the provisions of this section are to be applied separately with respect to the property received from each transferor. See paragraph (b) of example (2) in § 20.2013-6.

(e) For illustrations of the application of this section, see examples (1) and (2) set forth in § 20.2013-6. [Reg. § 20.2013-2.]

☐ [*T.D. 6296, 6-23-58. Amended by T.D. 7296, 12-11-73.*]

### [Reg. § 20.2013-3]

**§ 20.2013-3. "Second limitation."**—(a) The amount of the Federal estate tax attributable to the transferred property in the present decedent's estate is the "second limitation." Thus, the credit is limited to the difference between—

(1) The net estate tax payable (see paragraph (b)(5) or (c)) of § 20.0-2) with respect to the present decedent's estate, determined without regard to any credit for tax on prior transfers under section 2013 or any credit for foreign death taxes claimed under the provisions of a death tax convention, and

(2) The net estate tax determined as provided in paragraph (1) of this section, but computed by subtracting from the present decedent's gross estate the value of the property transferred (see

this paragraph are to be applied separately with respect to the property received from each transferor. See paragraph (d) of example (2) in § 20.2013-6.

(d) *Examples.*—For illustrations of the application of this section, see examples (1) and (2) set forth in § 20.2013-6. [Reg. § 20.2013-1.]

☐ [*T.D. 6296, 6-23-58.*]

### [Reg. § 20.2013-2]

**§ 20.2013-2. "First limitation."**—(a) The amount of the Federal estate tax attributable to the transferred property in the transferor's estate is the "first limitation." Thus, the credit is limited to an amount, A, which bears the same ratio to B (the "transferor's adjusted Federal estate tax," computed as described in paragraph (b) of this section) as C (the value of the property transferred (see § 20.2013-4)) bears to D (the "transferor's adjusted taxable estate," computed as described in paragraph (c) of this section). Stated algebraically, the "first limitation" (A) equals

§ 20.2013-4), and by making only the adjustment indicated in paragraph (b) of this section if a charitable deduction is allowable to the estate of the present decedent.

(b) If a charitable deduction is allowable to the estate of the present decedent under the provisions of section 2055 or section 2106(a)(2) (for estates of nonresidents not citizens), for purposes of determining the tax described in paragraph (a)(2) of this section, the charitable deduction otherwise allowable is reduced by an amount, E, which bears the same ratio to F (the charitable deduction otherwise allowable) as G (the value of the transferred property (see § 20.2013-4)) bears to H (the value of the present decedent's gross estate reduced by the amount of the deductions for expenses, indebtedness, taxes, losses, etc., allowed under the provisions of sections 2053 and 2054 or section 2106(a)(1) (for estates of nonresidents not citizens)). See paragraph (c)(2) of example (1) and paragraph (c)(2) of example (2) in § 20.2013-6.

(c) If the credit for tax on prior transfers relates to property received from two or more transferors, the property received from all transferors is aggregated in determining the limitation on credit under this section (the "second limitation"). However, the limitation so determined is apportioned to the property received from each transferor in the ratio that the property received from each transferor bears to the total property received from all transferors. See paragraph (c) of example (2) in § 20.2013-6.

(d) For illustrations of the application of this section, see examples (1) and (2) set forth in § 20.2013-6. [Reg. § 20.2013-3.]

☐ [*T.D. 6296, 6-23-58. Amended by T.D. 7296, 12-11-73.*]

### [Reg. § 20.2013-4]

**§ 20.2013-4. Valuation of property transferred.**—(a) For purposes of section 2013 and §§ 20.2013-1 to 20.2013-6, the value of the property transferred to the decedent is the value at which the property was included in the transferor's gross estate for the purpose of the Federal estate tax (see sections 2031, 2032, 2103, and 2107, and the regulations thereunder) reduced as indicated in paragraph (b) of this section. If the decedent received a life estate or a remainder or other limited interest in property that was included in a transferor decedent's gross estate, the value of the interest is determined as of the date of the transferor's death on the basis of recognized valuation principles (see §§ 20.2031-7 (or, for certain prior periods, § 20.2031-7A) and 20.7520-1 through 20.7520-4). The application of this paragraph may be illustrated by the following examples:

*Example (1).* A died on January 1, 1953, leaving Blackacre to B. The property was included in A's gross estate at a value of $100,000. On January 1, 1955, B sold Blackacre to C for $150,000. B died on February 1, 1955. For purposes of computing the credit against the tax imposed on B's estate, the value of the property transferred to B is $100,000.

*Example (2).* A died on January 1, 1953, leaving Blackacre to B for life and, upon B's death, remainder to C. At the time of A's death, B was 56 years of age. The property was included in A's gross estate at a value of $100,000. The part of that value attributable to the life estate is $44,688 and the part of that value attributable to the remainder is $55,312 (see § 20.2031-7A(b)). B died on January 1, 1955, and C died on January 1, 1956. For purposes of computing the credit against the tax imposed on B's estate, the value of the property transferred to B is $44,688. For purposes of computing the credit against the tax imposed on C's estate, the value of the property transferred to C is $55,312.

(b) In arriving at the value of the property transferred to the decedent, the value at which the property was included in the transferor's gross estate (see paragraph (a) of this section) is reduced as follows:

(1) By the amount of the Federal estate tax and any other estate, inheritance, legacy, or succession taxes which were payable out of the property transferred to the decedent or which were payable by the decedent in connection with the property transferred to him. For example, if under the transferor's will or local law all death taxes are to be paid out of other property with the result that the decedent receives a bequest free and clear of all death taxes, no reduction is to be made under this subparagraph;

(2) By the amount of any marital deduction allowed the transferor's estate under section 2056 (or under section 812(e) of the Internal Revenue Code of 1939) if the decedent was the spouse of the transferor at the time of the transferor's death;

(3)(i) By the amount of administration expenses in accordance with the principles of § 20.2056(b)-4(d).

(ii) This paragraph (b)(3) applies to transfers from estates of decedents dying on or after December 3, 1999; and

(4)(i) By the amount of any encumbrance on the property or by the amount of any obligation imposed by the transferor and incurred by the decedent with respect to the property, to the extent such charges would be taken into account if the amount of a gift to the decedent of such property were being determined.

(ii) For purposes of this subparagraph, an obligation imposed by the transferor and incurred by the decedent with respect to the property includes a bequest, etc., in lieu of the interest of the surviving spouse under community property laws, unless the interest was, immediately prior to the transferor's death, a mere expectancy. However, an obligation imposed by the transferor and incurred by the decedent with respect to the property does not include a bequest, devise, or other transfer in lieu of dower, curtesy, or of a statutory estate created in lieu of dower or curtesy, or of other marital rights in the transferor's property or estate.

(iii) The application of this subparagraph may be illustrated by the following examples:

*Example (1).* The transferor devised to the decedent real estate subject to a mortgage. The value of the property transferred to the decedent does not include the amount of the mortgage. If, however, the transferor by his will directs the executor to pay off the mortgage, such payment constitutes an additional amount transferred to the decedent.

*Example (2).* The transferor bequeathed certain property to the decedent with a direction that the decedent pay $1,000 to X. The value of the property transferred to the decedent is the value of the property reduced by $1,000.

*Example (3).* The transferor bequeathed certain property to his wife, the decedent, in lieu of her interest in property held by them as community property under the law of the State of their residence. The wife elected to relinquish her community property interest and to take the bequest. The value of the property transferred to the decedent is the value of the property reduced by the value of the community property interest relinquished by the wife.

*Example (4).* The transferor bequeathed to the decedent his entire residuary estate, out of which certain claims were to be satisfied. The entire distributable income of the transferor's estate (during the period of its administration) was applied toward the satisfaction of these claims and the remaining portion of the claims was satisfied by the decedent out of his own funds. Thus, the decedent received a larger sum upon settlement of the transferor's estate than he was actually bequeathed. The value of the property transferred to the decedent is the value at which such property was included in the transferor's gross estate, reduced by the amount of the estate income and the decedent's own funds paid out in satisfaction of the claims. [Reg. § 20.2013-4.]

□ [T.D. 6296, 6-23-58. *Amended by* T.D. 7077, 12-1-70; T.D. 7296, 12-11-73; T.D. 8522, 2-28-94; T.D. 8540, 6-9-94 *and* T.D. 8846, 12-2-99.]

## [Reg. § 20.2013-5]

**§ 20.2013-5. "Property" and "transfer" defined.**—(a) For purposes of section 2013 and §§ 20.2013-1 through 20.2013-6, the term "property" means any beneficial interest in property, including a general power of appointment (as defined in section 2041) over property. Thus, the term does not include an interest in property consisting merely of a bare legal title, such as that of a trustee. Nor does the term include a power of appointment over property which is not a general power of appointment (as defined in section 2041). Examples of property, as described in this paragraph, are annuities, life estates, estates for terms of years, vested or contingent remainders and other future interests.

(b) In order to obtain the credit for tax on prior transfers, there must be a transfer of property described in paragraph (a) of this section by or from the transferor to the decedent. The term "transfer" of property by or from a transferor means any passing of property or an interest in property under circumstances which were such that the property or interest was included in the gross estate of the transferor. In this connection, if the decedent receives property as a result of the exercise or nonexercise of a power of appointment, the donee of the power (and not the creator) is deemed to be the transferor of the property if the property subject to the power is includible in the donee's gross estate under section 2041 (relating to powers of appointment). Thus, notwithstanding the designation by local law of the capacity in which the decedent takes, property received from the transferor includes interests in property held by or devolving upon the decedent: (1) as spouse under dower or curtesy laws or laws creating an estate in lieu of dower or curtesy; (2) as surviving tenant of a tenancy by the entirety or joint tenancy with survivorship rights; (3) as beneficiary of the proceeds of life insurance; (4) as survivor under an annuity contract; (5) as donee (possessor) of a general power of appointment (as defined in section 2041); (6) as appointee under the exercise of a general power of appointment (as defined in section 2041); or (7) as remainderman under the release or nonexercise of a power of appointment by reason of which the property is included in the gross estate of the donee of the power under section 2041.

(c) The application of this section may be illustrated by the following example:

*Example.* A devises Blackacre to B, as trustee, with directions to pay the income therefrom to C, his son, for life. Upon C's death, Blackacre is to be sold. C is given a general testamentary power to appoint one-third of the proceeds, and a testamentary power, which is not a general power, to appoint the remaining two-thirds of the proceeds, to such of the issue of his sister D as he should choose. D has a daughter, E, and a son, F. Upon his death, C exercised his general power by appointing one-third of the proceeds to D and his special power by appointing two-thirds of the proceeds to E. Since B's interest in Blackacre as a trustee is not a beneficial interest, no part of it is "property" for purpose of the credit in B's estate. On the other hand, C's life estate and his testamentary power over the one-third interest in the remainder constitute "property" received from A for purpose of the credit in C's estate. Likewise, D's one-third interest in the remainder received through the exercise of C's general power of appointment is "property" received from C for purpose of the credit in D's estate. No credit is allowed E's estate for the property which passed to her from C since the property was not included in C's gross estate. On the other hand, no credit is allowed in E's estate for property passing to her from A since her interest was not susceptible of valuation at the time of A's death (see § 20.2013-4). [Reg. § 20.2013-5.]

□ [T.D. 6296, 6-23-58.]

## [Reg. § 20.2013-6]

**§ 20.2013-6. Examples.**—The application of §§ 20.2013-1 through 20.2013-5 may be further illustrated by the following examples:

*Example (1).* (a) A died December 1, 1953, leaving a gross estate of $1,000,000. Expenses, indebtedness, etc., amounted to $90,000. A bequeathed $200,000 to B, his wife, $100,000 of which qualifies for the marital deduction. B died November 1, 1954, leaving a gross estate of $500,000. Expenses, indebtedness, etc., amounted to $40,000. B bequeathed $150,000 to charity. A and B were both citizens of the United States. The estates of A and B both paid State death taxes equal to the maximum credit allowable for State death taxes. Death taxes were not a charge on the bequest to B.

(b) "First limitation" on credit for B's estate (§ 20.2013-2):

| | | |
|---|---:|---:|
| A's gross estate | | $1,000,000.00 |
| Expenses, indebtedness, etc. | | 90,000.00 |
| A's adjusted gross estate | | $910,000.00 |
| Marital deduction | $100,000.00 | |
| Exemption | 60,000.00 | 160,000.00 |
| A's taxable estate | | 750,000.00 |
| A's gross estate tax | | 233,200.00 |
| Credit for State death taxes | | 23,280.00 |
| A's net estate tax payable | | $209,920.00 |

"First limitation" = $209,920.00 (§ 20.2013-2(b)) ×
[($200,000.00 − $100,000.00) (§ 20.2013-4) ÷
($750,000.00 − $209,920.00 − $23,280.00 + $60,000.00)
(§ 20.2013-2(c))]

= $36,393.90

(c) "Second limitation" on credit for B's estate (§ 20.2013-3):

(1) B's net estate tax payable as described in § 20.2013-3(a)(1)
(previously taxed transfer included):

| | | |
|---|---|---|
| B's gross estate | $500,000.00 | |
| Expenses, indebtedness, etc. | $40,000.00 | |
| Charitable deduction | 150,000.00 | |
| Exemption | 60,000.00 | 250,000.00 |
| B's taxable estate | | $250,000.00 |
| B's gross estate tax | | $65,700.00 |
| Credit for State death taxes | | 3,920.00 |
| B's net estate tax payable | | $61,780.00 |

(2) B's net estate tax payable as described in § 20.2013-3(a)(2)
(previously taxed transfer excluded):

| | | |
|---|---|---|
| B's gross estate | | $400,000.00 |
| Expenses, indebtedness, etc. | $ 40,000.00 | |
| Charitable deduction (§ 20.2013-3(b)) = | | |
| $150,000.00 − [$150,000.00 × | | |
| ($200,000.00 − $100,000.00 ÷ | | |
| $500,000.00 − $ 40,000.00)] = | $117,391.30 | |
| Exemption | 60,000.00 | 217,391.30 |
| B's taxable estate | | $182,608.70 |
| B's gross estate tax | | $45,482.61 |
| Credit for State death taxes | | 2,221.61 |
| B's net estate tax payable | | $43,260.00 |

(3) "Second limitation":

| | | |
|---|---|---|
| Subparagraph (1) | $61,780.00 | |
| Less: Subparagraph (2) | 43,260.00 | $18,520.00 |

(d) Credit of B's estate for tax on prior transfers (§ 20.2013-1(c)):

Credit for tax on prior transfers = $18,520.00 (lower of paragraphs (b) and (c)) × 100% (percentage to be taken into
account under § 20.2013-1(c)) ............ $18,520.00

*Example (2).* (a) The facts are the same as those contained in
example (1) of this paragraph with the following additions. C died
December 1, 1950, leaving a gross estate of $250,000. Expenses,
indebtedness, etc., amounted to $50,000. C bequeathed $50,000 to B.
C was a citizen of the United States. His estate paid State death taxes
equal to the maximum credit allowable for State death taxes. Death
taxes were not a charge on the bequest to B.

| | | |
|---|---|---|
| C's gross estate | | $250,000.00 |
| Expenses, indebtedness, etc. | $50,000.00 | |
| Exemption | 60,000.00 | 110,000.00 |
| C's taxable estate | | $140,000.00 |
| C's gross estate tax | | $32,700.00 |
| Credit for State death taxes | | 1,200.00 |
| C's net estate tax payable | | $31,500.00 |

"First limitation" = $31,500.00 (§ 20.2013-2(b)) ×
[$50,000.00 (§ 20.2013-4) ÷
($140,000.00 − $31,500.00 − $1,200.00 + $60,000.00)
(§ 20.2013-2(c))]

= $9,414.23

(c) "Second limitation" on credit for B's estate (§ 20.2013-3(c)):

(1) B's net estate tax payable as described in § 20.2013-3(a)(1)
(previously taxed transfers included) = $61,780.00 (this computation
is identical with the one contained in paragraph (c)(1) of example (1)
of this section.

(2) B's net estate tax payable as described in § 20.2013-3(a)(2)
(previously taxed transfers excluded):

| | | |
|---|---|---|
| B's gross estate | | $350,000.00 |
| Expenses, indebtedness, etc. | $40,000.00 | |
| Charitable deduction (§ 20.2013-3(b)) = | | |
| $150,000.00 − [$150,000.00 × | | |
| ($200,000.00 − $100,000.00 + $50,000.00) ÷ | | |
| ($500,000.00 − $40,000.00)] = | 101,086.96 | |
| Exemption | 60,000.00 | 201,086.96 |
| B's taxable estate | | $148,913.04 |
| B's gross estate tax | | $35,373.91 |
| Credit for State death taxes | | 1,413.91 |
| B's net estate tax payable | | $33,960.00 |

(3) "Second limitation":

| | | |
|---|---|---|
| Subparagraph (1) | $61,780.00 | |
| Less: Subparagraph (2) | 33,960.00 | $27,820.00 |

(4) Apportionment of "second limitation" on credit:

| | |
|---|---|
| Transfer from A (§ 20.2013-4) | $100,000.00 |
| Transfer from C (§ 20.2013-4) | 50,000.00 |

(b) "First limitation" on credit for B's estate (§ 20.2013-2(d))—

(1) With respect to the property received from A:

"First limitation" = $36,393.90 (this computation is identical with
the one contained in paragraph (b) of example (1) of this section).

(2) With respect to the property received from C:

| | |
|---|---|
| | $250,000.00 |
| | 110,000.00 |
| | $140,000.00 |
| | $32,700.00 |
| | 1,200.00 |
| | $31,500.00 |

is identical with the one contained in paragraph (c)(1) of example (1)
of this section.

| | |
|---|---:|
| Total . . . . . . . . . . . . . . . . . . . . . . . . . | $150,000.00 |
| Portion of "second limitation" attributable to transfer from A (100/150 of $27,820.00) . . . . . . . . . . . . . . . | 18,546.67 |
| Portion of "second limitation" attributable to transfer from C (50/150 of $27,820.00) . . . . . . . . . . . . | 9,273.33 |

(d) Credit of B's estate for tax on prior transfers (§ 20.2013-1(c)):

| | |
|---|---:|
| Credit for tax on transfer from A = $18,546.67 (lower of "first limitation" computed in paragraph (b)(1) and "second limitation" apportioned to A's transfer in paragraph (c)(4)) × 100% (percentage to be taken into account under § 20.2013-1(c)) . . . . . . . . . . . . . . . . | $18,546.67 |
| Credit for tax on transfer from C = $9,273.33 (lower of "first limitation" computed in paragraph (b)(2) and "second limitation" apportioned to B's transfer in paragraph (c)(4)) × 80% (percentage to be taken into account under § 20.2013-1(c)) . . . . . . . . . . . . . . . | 7,418.66 |
| Total credit for tax on prior transfers . . . . . . . . . . . . . . . | $ 25,965.33 |

[Reg. § 20.2013-6.]

☐ [*T.D. 6296, 6-23-58.*]

**[Reg. § 20.2014-1]**

**§ 20.2014-1. Credit for foreign death taxes.**—(a) *In general.*—(1) A credit is allowed under section 2014 against the Federal estate tax for any estate, inheritance, legacy, or succession taxes actually paid to any foreign country (hereinafter referred to as "foreign death taxes"). The credit is allowed only for foreign death taxes paid (i) with respect to property situated within the country to which the tax is paid, (ii) with respect to property included in the decedent's gross estate, and (iii) with respect to the decedent's estate. The credit is allowable to the estate of a decedent who was a citizen of the United States at the time of his death. The credit is also allowable, as provided in paragraph (c) of this section, to the estate of a decedent who was a resident but not a citizen of the United States at the time of his death. The credit is not allowable to the estate of a decedent who was neither a citizen nor a resident of the United States at the time of his death. See paragraph(b)(1) of § 20.0-1 for the meaning of the term "resident" as applied to a decedent. The credit is allowable not only for death taxes paid to foreign countries which are states in the international sense, but also for death taxes paid to possessions or political subdivisions of foreign states. With respect to the estate of a decedent dying after September 2, 1958, the term "foreign country", as used in this section and §§ 20.2014-2 to 20.2014-6, includes a possession of the United States. See §§ 20.2011-1 and 20.2011-2 for the allowance of a credit for death taxes paid to a possession of the United States in the case of a decedent dying before September 3, 1958. No credit is allowable for interest or penalties paid in connection with foreign death taxes.

(2) In addition to the credit for foreign death taxes under section 2014, similar credits are allowed under death tax conventions with certain foreign countries. If credits against the Federal estate tax are allowable under section 2014, or under section 2014 and one or more death tax conventions, for death taxes paid to more than one country, the credits are combined and the aggregate amount is credited against the Federal estate tax, subject to the limitation provided for in paragraph (c) of § 20.2014-4. For application of the credit in cases involving a death tax convention, see § 20.2014-4.

(3) No credit is allowable under section 2014 in connection with property situated outside of the foreign country imposing the tax for which credit is claimed. However, such a credit may be allowable under certain death tax conventions. In the case of a tax imposed by a political subdivision of a foreign country, credit for the tax shall be allowed with respect to property having a situs in that foreign country, even though, under the principles described in this subparagraph, the property has a situs in a political subdivision different from the one imposing the tax. Whether or not particular property of a decedent is situated in the foreign country imposing the tax is determined in accordance with the same principles that would be applied in determining whether or not similar property of a nonresident decedent not a citizen of the United States is situated within the United States for Federal estate tax purposes. See §§ 20.2104-1 and 20.2105-1. For example, under § 20.2104-1 shares of stock are deemed to be situated in the United States only if issued by a domestic corporation. Thus, a share of corporate stock is regarded as situated in the foreign country imposing the tax only if the issuing corporation is incorporated in that country. Further, under § 20.2105-1 amounts receivable as insurance on the life of a nonresident not a citizen of the United States at the time of his death are not deemed situated in the United States. Therefore, in determining the credit under section 2014 in the case of a decedent who was a citizen or resident of the United States, amounts receivable as insurance on the life of the decedent and payable under a policy issued by a corporation incorporated in a foreign country are not deemed situated in such foreign country. In addition, under § 20.2105-1 in the case of an estate of a nonresident not a citizen of the United States who died on or after November 14, 1966, a debt obligation of a domestic corporation is not considered to be situated in the United States if any interest thereon would be treated under section 862(a)(1) as income from sources without the United States by reason of section 861(a)(1)(B) (relating to interest received from a domestic corporation

less than 20 percent of whose gross income for a 3-year period was derived from sources within the United States). Accordingly, a debt obligation the primary obligor on which is a corporation incorporated in the foreign country imposing the tax is not considered to be situated in that country if, under circumstances corresponding to those described in § 20.2105-1 less than 20 percent of the gross income of the corporation for the 3-year period was derived from sources within that country. Further, under § 20.2104-1 in the case of an estate of a nonresident not a citizen of the United States who died before November 14, 1966, a bond for the payment of money is not situated within the United States unless it is physically located in the United States. Accordingly, in the case of the estate of a decedent dying before November 14, 1966, a bond is deemed situated in the foreign country imposing the tax only if it is physically located in that country. Finally, under § 20.2105-1 moneys deposited in the United States with any person carrying on the banking business by or for a nonresident not a citizen of the United States who died before November 14, 1966, and who was not engaged in business in the United States at the time of death are not deemed situated in the United States. Therefore, an account with a foreign bank in the foreign country imposing the tax is not considered to be situated in that country under corresponding circumstances.

(4) Where a deduction is allowed under section 2053(d) for foreign death taxes paid with respect to a charitable gift, the credit for foreign death taxes is subject to further limitations as explained in § 20.2014-7.

(b) *Limitations on credit.*—The credit for foreign death taxes is limited to the smaller of the following amounts:

(1) The amount of a particular foreign death tax attributable to property situated in the country imposing the tax and included in the decedent's gross estate for Federal estate tax purposes, computed as set forth in § 20.2014-2; or

(2) The amount of the Federal estate tax attributable to particular property situated in a foreign country, subjected to foreign death tax in that country, and included in the decedent's gross estate for Federal estate tax purposes, computed as set forth in § 20.2014-3.

(c) *Credit allowable to estate of resident not a citizen.*—(1) In the case of an estate of a decedent dying before November 14, 1966, who was a resident but not a citizen of the United States, a credit is allowed to the estate under section 2014 only if the foreign country of which the decedent was a citizen or subject, in imposing foreign death taxes, allows a similar credit to the estates of citizens of the United States who were resident in that foreign country at the time of death.

(2) In the case of an estate of a decedent dying on or after November 14, 1966, who was a resident but not a citizen of the United States, a credit is allowed to the estate under section 2014 without regard to the similar credit requirement of subparagraph (1) of this paragraph unless the decedent was a citizen or subject of a foreign country to which there is in effect at the time of the decedent's death a Presidential proclamation, as authorized by section 2014(h), reinstating the similar credit requirement. In the case of an estate of a decedent who was a resident of the United States and a citizen or subject of a foreign country with respect to which such a proclamation has been made, and who dies while the proclamation is in effect, a credit is allowed under section 2014 only if that foreign country, in imposing foreign death taxes, allows a similar credit to the estates of citizens of the United States who were resident in that foreign country at the time of death. The proclamation authorized by section 2014(h) for the reinstatement of the similar credit requirement with respect to the estates of citizens or subjects of a specific foreign country may be made by the President whenever he finds that—

(i) The foreign country, in imposing foreign death taxes, does not allow a similar credit to the estates of citizens of the United States who were resident in the foreign country at the time of death,

(ii) The foreign country, after having been requested to do so, has not acted to provide a similar credit to the estates of such citizens, and

(iii) It is in the public interest to allow the credit under section 2014 to the estates of citizens or subjects of the foreign country only if the foreign country allows a similar credit to the estates of citizens of the United States who were resident in the foreign country at the time of death. The proclamation for the reinstatement of the similar credit requirement with respect to the estates of citizens or subjects of a specific foreign country may be revoked by the President. In that case, a credit is allowed under section 2014, to the estate of a decedent who was a citizen or subject of that foreign country and a resident of the United States at the time of death, without regard to the similar credit requirement if the decedent dies after the proclamation reinstating the similar credit requirement has been revoked. [Reg. § 20.2014-1.]

□ [T.D. 6296, 6-23-58. *Amended by T.D. 6526, 1-18-61, T.D. 6600, 5-28-62 and T.D. 7296, 12-11-73.]*

$$\frac{\text{Value of property in foreign country subjected to foreign death tax, included in gross estate and for which a deduction is not allowed under section 2053(d) (C)}}{\text{Value of all property subjected to foreign death tax (D)}} \times \text{Amount of foreign death tax (B)}$$

The values used in this proportion are the values determined for the purpose of the foreign death tax. The amount of the foreign death tax for which credit is allowable must be converted into United States money. The application of this paragraph may be illustrated by the following example:

*Example.* At the time of his death on June 1, 1966, the decedent, a citizen of the United States, owned stock in X Corp. (a corporation organized under the laws of Country Y) valued at $80,000. In addition, he owned bonds issued by Country Y valued at $80,000. The

## [Reg. § 20.2014-2]

**§ 20.2014-2. "First limitation".**—(a) The amount of a particular foreign death tax attributable to property situated in the country imposing the tax and included in the decedent's gross estate for Federal estate tax purposes is the "first limitation." Thus, the credit for any foreign death tax is limited to an amount, A, which bears the same ratio to B (the amount of the foreign death tax without allowance of credit, if any, for Federal estate tax) as C (the value of the property situated in the country imposing the foreign death tax, subjected to the foreign death tax, included in the gross estate and for which a deduction is not allowed under section 2053(d)) bears to D (the value of all property subjected to the foreign death tax). Stated algebraically, the "first limitation"(A) equals

stock and bond certificates were in the United States. Decedent left by will $20,000 of the stock and $50,000 of the Country Y bonds to his surviving spouse. He left the rest of the stock and bonds to his son. Under the situs rules referred to in paragraph (a)(3) of § 20.2014-1 the stock is deemed situated in Country Y while the bonds are deemed to have their situs in the United States. (The bonds would be deemed to have their situs in Country Y if the decedent had died on or after November 14, 1966.) There is no death tax convention in existence between the United States and Country Y. The laws of Country Y provide for inheritance taxes computed as follows:

| Inheritance tax of surviving spouse: | |
|---|---:|
| Value of stock | $20,000 |
| Value of bonds | 50,000 |
| Total value | 70,000 |
| Tax (16 percent rate) | $11,200 |
| Inheritance tax of son: | |
| Value of stock | $60,000 |
| Value of bonds | 30,000 |
| Total value | $90,000 |
| Tax (16 percent rate) | $14,400 |

The "first limitation" on the credit for foreign death taxes is:

$$\frac{\$20,000 + \$60,000 \text{ (factor C of the ratio stated at § 20.2014-2(a))}}{\$70,000 + \$90,000 \text{ (factor D of the ratio stated at § 20.2014-2(a))}} \times (\$11,200 + \$14,400) \text{ (factor B of the ratio stated at § 20.2014-2(a))} = \$12,800$$

(b) If a foreign country imposes more than one kind of death tax or imposes taxes at different rates upon the several shares of an estate, or if a foreign country and a political subdivision or possession thereof each imposes a death tax, a "first limitation" is to be computed separately for each tax or rate and the results added in order to determine the total "first limitation." The application of this paragraph may be illustrated by the following example:

*Example.* The facts are the same as those contained in the example set forth in paragraph (a) of this section, except that the tax of the surviving spouse was computed at a 10-percent rate and amounted to $7,000, and the tax of the son was computed at a 20-percent rate and amounted to $18,000. In this case, the "first limitation" on the credit for foreign death taxes is computed as follows:

"First limitation" with respect to inheritance tax of surviving spouse =

$$\frac{\$20,000 \text{ (factor C of the ratio stated at § 20.2014-2(a))}}{\$70,000 \text{ (factor D of the ratio stated at § 20.2014-2(a))}} \times \$7,000 \text{ (factor B of the ratio stated at § 20.2014-2(a))} = \$2,000$$

"First limitation" with respect to inheritance tax of son =

$$\frac{\$60,000 \text{ (factor C of the ratio stated at § 20.2014-2(a))}}{\$90,000 \text{ (factor D of the ratio stated at § 20.2014-2(a))}} \times \$18,000 \text{ (factor B of the ratio stated at § 20.2014-2(a))} = \$12,000$$

Total "first limitation" on the credit for foreign death taxes . . . . . . . . . . . . . . . . . . . . . . . . . . . . $14,000

[Reg. § 20.2014-2.]

☐ [*T.D.* 6296, 6-23-58. *Amended by T.D.* 6600, 5-28-62; *T.D.* 6684, 10-23-63 *and T.D.* 7296, 12-11-73.]

**[Reg. § 20.2014-3]**

**§ 20.2014-3. "Second limitation".**—(a) The amount of the Federal estate tax attributable to particular property situated in a foreign country, subjected to foreign death tax in that country, and included in the decedent's gross estate for Federal estate tax purposes is the "second limitation." Thus, the credit is limited to an amount, E,

$$\frac{\text{"adjusted value of the property situated in the foreign country, subjected to foreign death taxes, and included in the gross estate" (G)}}{\text{value of entire gross estate, less charitable and marital deductions (H)}}$$

The values used in this proportion are the values determined for the purpose of the Federal estate tax.

(b) Adjustment is required to factor "G" of the ratio stated in paragraph (a) of this section if a deduction for foreign death taxes under section 2053(d), a charitable deduction under section 2055, or a marital deduction under section 2056 is allowed with respect to the foreign property. If a deduction for foreign death taxes is allowed, the value of the property situated in the foreign country, subjected to foreign death tax, and included in the gross estate does not include the value of any property in respect of which the deduction for foreign death taxes is allowed. See § 20.2014-7. If a charitable deduction or a marital deduction is allowed, the value of such foreign property (after exclusion of the value of any property in respect of which the deduction for foreign death taxes is allowed) is reduced as follows:

(1) If a charitable deduction or a marital deduction is allowed to a decedent's estate with respect to any part of the foreign property, except foreign property in respect of which a deduction for foreign death taxes is allowed, specifically bequeathed, devised, or otherwise specifically passing to a charitable organization or to the decedent's spouse, the value of the foreign property is reduced by the amount of the charitable deduction or marital deduction allowed with respect to such specific transfer. See example (1) of paragraph (c) of this section.

(2) If a charitable deduction or a marital deduction is allowed to a decedent's estate with respect to a bequest, devise or other transfer of an interest in a group of assets including both the foreign property and other property, the value of the foreign property is reduced by an amount, I, which bears the same ratio to J (the amount of the charitable deduction or marital deduction allowed with respect to such transfer of an interest in a group of assets) as K (the value of the foreign property, except foreign property in respect of which a deduction for foreign death taxes is allowed, included in the group of assets) bears to L (the value of the entire group of assets). As used in

$$\frac{\$200{,}000 - \$40{,}000}{\text{(factor G of the ratio stated at § 20.2014-3(a);}}{\text{see also § 20.2014-3(b)(1))}}$$
$$\frac{}{\frac{\$1{,}000{,}000 - \$40{,}000}{\text{(factor H of the ratio stated at § 20.2014-3(a))}}} \times$$

The lesser of this amount and the amount of the "first limitation" (computed under § 20.2014-2) is the credit for foreign death taxes.

*Example (2).* (i) Decedent, a citizen and resident of the United States at the time of his death, left a gross estate of $1,000,000 which includes: shares of stock issued by a United States corporation, valued at $650,000; shares of stock issued by a Country X corporation, valued at $200,000; and life insurance, in the amount of $150,000, payable to a son. Expenses, indebtedness, etc., amounted to $40,000. The decedent made a specific bequest of $25,000 of the Country X corporation stock to Charity A and a general bequest of $100,000 to Charity B. The residue of his estate was left to his

which bears the same ratio to F (the gross Federal estate tax, reduced by any credit for State death taxes under section 2011 and by any credit for gift tax under section 2012) as G (the "adjusted value of the property situated in the foreign country, subjected to foreign death tax, and included in the gross estate," computed as described in paragraph (b) of this section) bears to H (the value of the entire gross estate, reduced by the total amount of the deductions allowed under sections 2055 (charitable deduction) and 2056 (marital deduction)). Stated algebraically, the "second limitation" (E) equals

$$\times \quad \frac{\text{gross Federal estate tax, less credits for State death taxes and gift tax (F).}}{}$$

this subparagraph, the term "group of assets" has reference to those assets which, under applicable law, are chargeable with the charitable or marital transfer. See example (2) of paragraph (c) of this section.

Any reduction described in paragraph (b)(1) or (b)(2) of this section on account of the marital deduction must proportionately take into account, if applicable, the limitation on the aggregate amount of the marital deduction contained in § 20.2056(a)-1(c). See § 20.2014-3(c), *Example 3.*

(c) The application of paragraphs (a) and (b) of this section may be illustrated by the following examples. In each case, the computations relate to the amount of credit under section 2014 without regard to the amount of credit which may be allowable under an applicable death tax convention.

*Example (1).* (i) Decedent, a citizen and resident of the United States at the time of his death on February 1, 1967, left a gross estate of $1,000,000 which includes the following: shares of stock issued by a domestic corporation, valued at $750,000; bonds issued in 1960 by the United States and physically located in foreign Country X, valued at $50,000; and shares of stock issued by a Country X corporation, valued at $200,000, with respect to which death taxes were paid to Country X. Expenses, indebtedness, etc., amounted to $60,000. Decedent specifically bequeathed $40,000 of the stock issued by the Country X corporation to a U. S. charity and left the residue of his estate, in equal shares, to his son and daughter. The gross Federal estate tax is $266,500, and the credit for State death taxes is $27,600. Under the situs rules referred to in paragraph (a)(3) of § 20.2014-1, the shares of stock issued by the Country X corporation comprise the only property deemed to be situated in Country X. (The bonds also would be deemed to have their situs in Country X if the decedent had died before November 14, 1966.)

(ii) The "second limitation" on the credit for foreign death taxes is

$$(\$266{,}500 - \$27{,}600) = \$39{,}816.67$$
(factor F of the ratio stated at § 20.2014-3(a))

daughter. The gross Federal estate tax is $242,450 and the credit for State death taxes is $24,480. Under these facts and applicable law, neither the stock of the Country X corporation specifically bequeathed to Charity A nor the insurance payable to the son could be charged with satisfying the bequest to Charity B. Therefore, the "group of assets" which could be so charged is limited to stock of the Country X corporation valued at $175,000 and stock of the United States corporation valued at $650,000.

(ii) Factor "G" of the ratio which is used in determining the "second limitation" is computed as follows:

| | | | |
|---|---|---|---|
| Value of property situated in Country X . . . . . . . . . . . . . . . . . . | | | $200,000.00 |
| Less: Reduction described in § 20.2014-3(b)(1) . . . . . . . . . . . . . . . . . . . . . . | | $25,000.00 | |
| $\qquad$ Reduction described in § 20.2014-3(b)(2) = | | | |

$$\frac{\$175{,}000}{\underset{\text{(factor L of the ratio stated at § 20.2014-3(b)(2))}}{\$175{,}000 + \$650{,}000}} \times \frac{\$100{,}000 =}{\underset{\text{(factor J of the ratio stated at § 20.2014-3(b)(2))}}{}}$$

| | | |
|---|---|---|
| . . . . . . . . . . | 21,212.12 | 46,212.12 |
| Factor "G" of the ratio . . . . . . . . . . . . . . . . . . . . . . . . . . . . . | | $153,787.88 |

(iii) In this case, the "second limitation" on the credit for foreign death taxes is

$$\frac{\$153,787.88}{\$1,000,000 - \$125,000} \times (\$242,450 - \$24,480) = \$38,309.88$$

(factor G of the ratio stated at §20.2014-3(a); see also subdivision (ii) above) / (factor H of the ratio stated at §20.2014-3(a))

(factor F of the ratio stated at §20.2014-3(a))

*Example (3).* (i) Decedent, a citizen and resident of the United States at the time of his death, left a gross estate of $850,000 which includes: shares of stock issued by United States corporations, valued at $440,000; real estate located in the United States, valued at $110,000; and shares of stock issued by Country X corporations, valued at $300,000. Expenses, indebtedness, etc., amounted to $50,000. Decedent devised $40,000 in real estate to a United States charity. In addition, he bequeathed to his wife $200,000 in United States stocks and $300,000 in Country X stocks. The residue of his estate passed to his children. The gross Federal estate tax is $81,700 and the credit for State death taxes is $5,520.

(ii) Decedent's adjusted gross estate is $800,000 (i.e., $850,000, gross estate less $50,000, expenses, indebtedness, etc.). Assume that the limitation imposed by section 2056(c), as in effect before 1982, is applicable so that the aggregate allowable marital deduction is limited to one-half the adjusted gross estate, or $400,000 (which is 50 percent of $800,000). Factor "G" of the ratio which is used in determining the "second limitation" is computed as follows:

| | | |
|---|---|---:|
| Value of property situated in Country X | | $300,000 |
| Less: | Reduction described in §20.2014-3(b)(1) determined as follows (see also end of §20.2014-3(b))— | |
| | Total amount of bequests which qualify for the marital deduction: | |
| | Specific bequest of Country X stock | $300,000 |
| | Specific bequest of United States stock | 200,000 |
| | | 500,000 |
| | Limitation on aggregate marital deduction under section 2056(c) | $400,000 |
| | Part of specific bequest of Country X stock with respect to which the marital deduction is allowed— | |
| | $\frac{\$400,000}{\$500,000} \times \$300,000$ | $240,000 |
| Factor "G" of the ratio | | 60,000 |

(iii) Thus, the "second limitation" on the credit for foreign death taxes is

$$\frac{\$60,000}{\$850,000 - \$40,000 - \$400,000} \times (\$81,700 - \$5,520) = \$11,148.29$$

(factor G of the ratio stated at §20.2014-3(a); see also subdivision (ii) above) / (factor H of the ratio stated at §20.2014-3(a))

(factor F of the ratio stated at §20.2014-3(a))

(d) If the foreign country imposes more than one kind of death tax or imposes taxes at different rates upon the several shares of an estate, or if the foreign country and a political subdivision or possession thereof each imposes a death tax the "second limitation" is still computed by applying the ratio set forth in paragraph (a) of §20.2014-3. Factor "G" of the ratio is determined by taking into consideration the combined value of the foreign property which is subjected to each different tax or different rate. The combined value, however, cannot exceed the value at which such property was included in the gross estate for Federal estate tax purposes. Thus, if Country X imposes a tax on the inheritance of a surviving spouse at a 10-percent rate and on the inheritance of a son at a 20-percent rate, the combined value of their inheritances is taken into consideration in determining factor "G" of the ratio, which is then used in computing the "second limitation." However, the "first limitation" is computed as provided in paragraph (b) of §20.2014-2. The lesser of the "first limitation" and the "second limitation" is the credit for foreign death taxes. [Reg. §20.2014-3.]

☐ [*T.D.* 6296, 6-23-58. *Amended by T.D.* 6600, 5-28-62; *T.D.* 7296, 12-11-73 *and T.D.* 8522, 2-28-94.]

**[Reg. §20.2014-4]**

**§20.2014-4. Application of credit in cases involving a death tax convention.**—(a) *In general.*—(1) If credit for a particular foreign death tax is authorized by a death tax convention, there is allowed either the credit provided for by the convention or the credit provided for by section 2014, whichever is the more beneficial to the estate. For cases where credit may be taken under both the death tax convention and section 2014, see paragraph (b) of this section. The application of this paragraph may be illustrated by the following example:

*Example.* (i) Decedent, a citizen of the United States and a domiciliary of foreign Country X at the time of his death on December 1, 1966, left a gross estate of $1,000,000 which includes the following: shares of stock issued by a Country X corporation, valued at $400,000; bonds issued in 1962 by the United States and physically located in Country X, valued at $350,000; and real estate located in the United States, valued at $250,000. Expenses, indebtedness, etc., amounted to $50,000. Decedent left his entire estate to his son. There is in effect a death tax convention between the United States and Country X which provides for the allowance of credit by the United States for succession duties imposed by the national government of Country X. The gross Federal estate tax is $307,200, and the credit for State death taxes is $33,760. Country X imposed a net succession duty on the stocks and bonds of $180,000. Under the situs rules referred to in paragraph (a)(3) of §20.2014-1, the shares of stock comprise the only property deemed to be situated in Country X. (If the decedent had died before November 14, 1966, the bonds also would be deemed to have their situs in Country X.) Under the convention, both the stocks and the bonds are deemed to be situated in Country X. In this example all figures are rounded to the nearest dollar.

(ii)(*a*) The credit authorized by the convention for death taxes imposed by Country X is computed as follows:

| | | |
|---|---|---:|
| (1) | Country X tax attributable to property situated in Country X and subjected to tax by both countries | |
| | $\frac{(\$750,000}{(\$750,000} \times \$180,000)$ | $180,000 |
| (2) | Federal estate tax attributable to property situated in Country X and subjected to tax by both countries | |
| | $\frac{(\$750,000}{(\$1,000,000} \times \$273,440)$ | 205,080 |
| (3) | Credit (subdivision *(1)* or *(2)*, whichever is less) | $180,000 |

(b) The credit authorized by section 2014 for death taxes imposed by Country X is computed as follows:

(1) "First limitation" computed under § 20.2014-2

$$\frac{(\$400,000}{(\$750,000} \times \$180,000) \dots\dots\dots\dots \qquad \$96,000$$

(2) "Second limitation" computed under § 20.2014-3

$$\frac{(\$400,000}{(\$1,000,000} \times \$273,440) \dots\dots\dots\dots \qquad 109,376$$

(3) Credit (subdivision (1) or (2), whichever is less) . . . . . . . . . . . . . . . . . . . $96,000

(iii) On the basis of the facts contained in this example, the credit of $180,000 authorized by the convention is the more beneficial to the estate.

(2) It should be noted that the greater of the treaty credit and the statutory credit is not necessarily the more beneficial to the estate. Such is the situation, for example, in those cases which involve both a foreign death tax credit and a credit under section 2013 for tax on prior transfers. The reason is that the amount of the credit for tax on prior transfers may differ depending upon whether the credit for foreign death tax is taken under the treaty or under the statute. Therefore, under certain circumstances, the advantage of taking the greater of the treaty credit and the statutory credit may be more than offset by a resultant smaller credit for tax on prior transfers. The solution is to compute the net estate tax payable first on the assumption that the treaty credit will be taken and then on the assumption that the statutory credit will be taken. Such computations will indicate whether the treaty credit or the statutory credit is in fact the more beneficial to the estate.

(b) *Taxes imposed by both a foreign country and a political subdivision thereof.*—If death taxes are imposed by both a foreign country with which the United States has entered into a death tax convention and one or more of its possessions or political subdivisions, there is allowed, against the tax imposed by section 2001—

(1) A credit for the combined death taxes paid to the foreign country and its political subdivisions or possessions as provided for by the convention, or

(2) A credit for the combined death taxes paid to the foreign country and its political subdivisions or possessions as determined under section 2014, or

(3)(i) A credit for that amount of the combined death taxes paid to the foreign country and its political subdivisions or possessions as is allowable under the convention, and

(ii) A credit under section 2014 for the death taxes paid to each political subdivision or possession, but only to the extent such death taxes are not directly or indirectly creditable under the convention, whichever is the most beneficial to the estate. The application of this paragraph may be illustrated by the following example:

*Example.* (1) Decedent, a citizen of the United States and a domiciliary of Province Y of foreign Country X at the time of his death on February 1, 1966, left a gross estate of $250,000 which includes the following: bonds issued by Country X physically located in Province Y, valued at $75,000; bonds issued by Province Z of Country X and physically located in the United States, valued at $50,000; and shares of stock issued by a domestic corporation, valued at $125,000. Decedent left his entire estate to his son. Expenses, indebtedness, etc., amounted to $26,000. The Federal estate tax after allowance of the credit for State death taxes is $38,124. Province Y imposed a death tax of 8 percent on the Country X bonds located therein which amounted to $6,000. No death tax was imposed by Province Z. Country X imposed a death tax of 15 percent on the Country X bonds and the Province Z bonds which amounted to $18,750 before allowance of any credit for the death tax of Province Y. Country X allows against its death taxes a credit for death taxes paid to any of its provinces on property which it also taxes, but only to the extent of one-half of the Country X death tax attributable to the property, or the amount of death taxes paid to its province, whichever is less. Country X, therefore, allowed a credit of $5,625 for the death taxes paid to Province Y. There is in effect a death tax convention between the United States and Country X which provides for allowance of credit by the United States for death taxes imposed by the national government of Country X. The death tax convention provides that in computing the "first limitation" for the credit under the convention, the tax of Country X is not to be reduced by the amount of the credit allowed for provincial taxes. Under the situs rules described in paragraph (a)(3) of § 20.2014-1, only the Country X

bonds located in Province Y are deemed situated in Country X. (The bonds issued by Province Z also would be deemed to have their situs in Country X if the decedent had died on or after November 14, 1966.) Under the convention, both the Country X bonds and the Province Z bonds are deemed to be situated in Country X. In this example all figures are rounded to the nearest dollar.

(2)(i) The credit authorized by section 2014 for death taxes imposed by Country X (which includes death taxes imposed by Province Y according to § 20.2014-1(a)(1)) is computed as follows:

(a) "First limitation" with respect to tax imposed by national government of Country X (computed under paragraph (b) of § 20.2014-2)

(1) Gross Country X death tax attributable to Country X bonds (before allowance of provincial death taxes)

$$\frac{\$75,000}{\$125,000} \times \$18,750 \dots\dots\dots\dots \qquad \$11,250$$

(2) Less credit for Province Y death taxes on such bonds . . . . . . . . . . . . . . . . . 5,625

(3) Net Country X death tax attributable to such bonds . . . . . . . . . . . . . . . . . 5,625

(b) "First limitation" with respect to tax imposed by Province Y (computed under paragraph (b) of § 20.2014-2)

$$\frac{\$75,000}{\$75,000} \times \$6,000 \dots\dots\dots\dots \qquad \$6,000$$

(c) Total "first limitation" . . . . . . . . . . 11,625

(d) "Second limitation" (computed under paragraph (d) of § 20.2014-3)

$$\frac{\$75,000}{\$250,000} \times \$38,124 \dots\dots\dots\dots \qquad \$11,437$$

(e) Credit (subdivision (c) or (d), whichever is less) . . . . . . . . . . . . . . . . . . . . 11,437

(ii) The credit authorized under the death tax convention between the United States and Country X is computed as follows:

(a) Country X tax attributable to property situated in Country X and subject to tax by both countries

$$\frac{\$125,000}{\$125,000} \times \$18,750 \dots\dots\dots\dots \qquad \$18,750$$

(b) Federal estate tax attributable to property situated in Country X and subjected to tax by both countries:

$$\frac{\$125,000}{\$250,000} \times \$38,124 \dots\dots\dots\dots \qquad \$19,062$$

(c) Credit (subdivision (a) or (b), whichever is less) . . . . . . . . . . . . . . . . . . . . $18,750

(3) If the estate takes a credit for death taxes under the convention, it would receive a credit of $18,750 which would include an indirect credit of $5,625 for death taxes paid to Province Y. The death tax of Province Y which was not directly or indirectly creditable under the convention is $375 ($6,000–$5,625). A credit for this tax would also be allowed under section 2014 but only to the extent of $187, as the amount of credit for the combined foreign death taxes is limited to the amount of Federal estate tax attributable to the property, determined in accordance with the rules prescribed for computing the "second limitation" under section 2014. In this case, the

"second limitation" under section 2014 on the taxes attributable to the Country X bonds is $11,437 (see computation set forth in (2)(i)(*d*) of this example). The amount of credit under the convention for taxes attributable to Country X bonds is $11,250 ($75,000 ÷ $125,000 × $18,750). Inasmuch as the "second limitation" under section 2014 in respect of the Country X bonds ($11,437) exceeds the amount of the credit allowed under the convention in respect of the Country X bonds ($11,250) by $187, the additional credit allowable under section 2014 for the death taxes paid to Province Y not directly or indirectly creditable under the convention is limited to $187.

(c) *Taxes imposed by two foreign countries with respect to the same property.*—It is stated as a general rule in paragraph (a)(2) of §20.2014-1 that if credits against the Federal estate tax are allowable under section 2014, or under section 2014 and one or more death tax conventions, for death taxes paid to more than one country, the credits are combined and the aggregate amount is credited against the Federal estate tax. This rule may result in credit being allowed for taxes imposed by two different countries upon the same item of property. If such is the case, the total amount of the credits with respect to such property is limited to the amount of the Federal estate tax attributable to the property, determined in accordance with the rules prescribed for computing the "second limitation" set forth in §20.2014-3. The application of this section may be illustrated by the following example:

*Example.* The decedent, a citizen of the United States and a domiciliary of Country X at the time of his death on May 1, 1967, left a taxable estate which included bonds issued by Country Z and physically located in Country X. Each of the three countries involved imposed death taxes on the Country Z bonds. Assume that under the provisions of a treaty between the United States and Country X the estate is entitled to a credit against the Federal estate tax for death taxes imposed by Country X on the bonds in the maximum amount of $20,000. Assume, also, that since the decedent died after November 13, 1966, so that under the situs rules referred to in paragraph (a)(3) of §20.2014-1 the bonds are deemed to have their situs in Country Z, the estate is entitled to a credit against the Federal estate tax for death taxes imposed by Country Z on the bonds in the maximum amount of $10,000. Finally, assume that the Federal estate tax attributable to the bonds is $25,000. Under these circumstances, the credit allowed the estate with respect to the bonds would be limited to $25,000. [Reg. §20.2014-4.]

☐ [*T.D. 6296, 6-23-58. Amended by T.D. 6742, 6-22-64 and T.D. 7296,* 12-11-73.]

**[Reg. §20.2014-5]**

**§20.2014-5. Proof of credit.**—(a) If the foreign death tax has not been determined and paid by the time the Federal estate tax return required by section 6018 is filed, credit may be claimed on the return in an estimated amount. However, before credit for the foreign death tax is finally allowed, satisfactory evidence, such as a statement by an authorized official of each country, possession or political subdivision thereof imposing the tax, must be submitted on Form 706CE certifying: (1) the full amount of the tax (exclusive of any interest or penalties), as computed before allowance of any credit, remission, or relief; (2) the amount of any credit, allowance, remission, or relief, and other pertinent information, including the nature of the allowance and a description of the property to which it pertains; (3) the net foreign death tax payable after any such allowance; (4) the date on which the death tax was paid, or if not all paid at one time, the date and amount of each partial payment; and (5) a list of the property situated in the foreign country and subjected to its tax, showing a description and the value of the property. Satisfactory evidence must also be submitted showing that no refund of the death tax is pending and none is authorized or, if any refund is pending or has been authorized, its amount and other pertinent information. See also section 2016 and §20.2016-1 for requirements if foreign death taxes claimed as a credit are subsequently recovered.

(b) The following information must also be submitted whenever applicable:

(1) If any of the property subjected to the foreign death tax was situated outside of the country imposing the tax, the description of each item of such property and its value.

(2) If more than one inheritance or succession is involved with respect to which credit is claimed, or if the foreign country, possession or political subdivision thereof imposes more than one kind of death tax, or if both the foreign country and a possession or political subdivision thereof each imposes a death tax, a separate computation with respect to each inheritance or succession tax.

(c) In addition to the information required under paragraphs (a) and (b) of this section, the district director may require the submission of any further proof deemed necessary to establish the right to the credit. [Reg. §20.2014-5.]

☐ [*T.D. 6296, 6-23-58.*]

**[Reg. §20.2014-6]**

**§20.2014-6. Period of limitations on credit.**—The credit for foreign death taxes under section 2014 is limited to those taxes which were actually paid and for which a credit was claimed within four years after the filing of the estate tax return for the decedent's estate. If, however, a petition has been filed with the The Tax Court of the United States for the redetermination of a deficiency within the time prescribed in section 6213(a), the credit is limited to those taxes which were actually paid and for which a credit was claimed within four years after the filing of the return, or before the expiration of 60 days after the decision of The Tax Court becomes final, whichever period is the last to expire. Similarly, if an extension of time has been granted under section 6161 for payment of the tax shown on the return, or of a deficiency, the credit is limited to those taxes which were actually paid and for which a credit was claimed within four years after the filing of the return, or before the date of the expiration of the period of the extension, whichever period is the last to expire. See section 2015 for the applicable period of limitations for credit for foreign death taxes on reversionary or remainder interests if an election is made under section 6163(a) to postpone payment of the estate tax attributable to reversionary or remainder interests. If a claim for refund based on the credit for foreign death taxes is filed within the applicable period described in this section, a refund may be made despite the general limitation provisions of sections 6511 and 6512. Any refund based on the credit for foreign death taxes shall be made without interest. [Reg. §20.2014-6.]

☐ [*T.D. 6296, 6-23-58.*]

**[Reg. §20.2014-7]**

**§20.2014-7. Limitation on credit if a deduction for foreign death taxes is allowed under section 2053(d).**—If a deduction is allowed under section 2053(d) for foreign death taxes paid with respect to a charitable gift, the credit for foreign death taxes is subject to special limitations. In such a case the property described in subparagraphs(A), (B), and (C) of paragraphs (1) and (2) of section 2014(b) shall not include any property with respect to which a deduction is allowed under section 2053(d). The application of this section may be illustrated by the following example:

*Example.* The decedent, a citizen of the United States, died July 1, 1955, leaving a gross estate of $1,200,000 consisting of: Shares of stock issued by United States corporations, valued at $600,000; bonds issued by the United States Government physically located in the United States, valued at $300,000; and shares of stock issued by a Country X corporation, valued at $300,000. Expenses, indebtedness, etc., amounted to $40,000. The decedent made specific bequests of $400,000 of the United States corporation stock to a niece and $100,000 of the Country X corporation stock to a nephew. The residue of his estate was left to charity. There is no death tax convention in existence between the United States and Country X. The Country X tax imposed was at a 50-percent rate on all beneficiaries. A State inheritance tax of $20,000 was imposed on the niece and nephew. The decedent did not provide in his will for the payment of the death taxes, and under local law the Federal estate tax is payable from the general estate, the same as administration expenses.

*Distribution of the Estate*

| | | |
|---|---:|---:|
| Gross estate | | $1,200,000.00 |
| Debts and charges | $40,000.00 | |
| Bequest of United States corporation stock to niece | 400,000.00 | |
| Bequest of Country X corporation stock to nephew | 100,000.00 | |
| Net Federal estate tax | 136,917.88 | $676,917.88 |
| Residue before Country X tax | | 523,082.12 |
| Country X succession tax on charity | | 100,000.00 |
| Charitable deduction | | $423,082.12 |

### Taxable Estate and Federal Estate Tax

| | | |
|---|---:|---:|
| Gross estate | | $1,200,000.00 |
| Debts and charges | $40,000.00 | |
| Deduction of foreign death tax under section 2053(d) | 100,000.00 | |
| Charitable deduction | 423,082.12 | |
| Exemption | 60,000.00 | 623,082.12 |
| Taxable estate | | $576,917.88 |
| Gross estate tax | | $172,621.26 |
| Credit for State death taxes | | 15,476.72 |
| Gross estate tax less credit for State death taxes | | $157,144.54 |
| Credit for foreign death taxes | | 20,226.66 |
| Net Federal estate tax | | $136,917.88 |

### Credit for Foreign Death Taxes

| | |
|---|---:|
| Country X tax | |
| Succession tax on nephew: | |
| Value of stock of Country X corporation | $100,000.00 |
| Tax (50% rate) | 50,000.00 |
| Succession tax on charity: | |
| Value of stock of Country X corporation | 200,000.00 |
| Tax (50% rate) | 100,000.00 |

### Computation of exclusion under section 2014(b)

| | |
|---|---:|
| Value of property situated in Country X | $300,000.00 |
| Value of property in respect of which a deduction is allowed under section 2053(d) | 200,000.00 |
| Value of property situated within Country X, subjected to tax, and included in gross estate as limited by section 2014(f) | $100,000.00 |

First limitation, §20.2014-2(a)

$$\frac{\$100{,}000 \text{ (factor C of the ratio stated at §20.2014-2(a))}}{\$100{,}000 + \$200{,}000 \text{ (factor D of the ratio stated at §20.2014-2(a))}} \times \frac{(\$50{,}000.00 + \$100{,}000.00)}{\text{(factor B of the ratio stated at §20.2014-2(a))} = \$50{,}000.00}$$

Second limitation, §20.2014-3(a)

$$\frac{\$100{,}000 \text{ (factor G of the ratio stated at §20.2014-3(a)) (as limited by section 2014(f))}}{\$1{,}200{,}000 - \$423{,}082.12 \text{ (factor H of the ratio stated at §20.2014-3(a))}} \times \frac{(\$172{,}621.26 - \$15{,}476.72)}{\text{(factor F of the ratio stated at §20.2014-3(a))} = \$20{,}226.66}$$

[Reg. §20.2014-7.]

☐ [T.D. 6600, 5-28-62.]

### [Reg. §20.2015-1]

**§20.2015-1. Credit for death taxes on remainders.**—(a) If the executor of an estate elects under section 6163(a) to postpone the time for payment of any portion of the Federal estate tax attributable to a reversionary or remainder interest in property, credit is allowed under sections 2011 and 2014 against that portion of the Federal estate tax for State death taxes and foreign death taxes attributable to the reversionary or remainder interest if the State death taxes or foreign death taxes are paid and if credit therefor is claimed either—

(1) Within the time provided for in sections 2011 and 2014, or

(2) Within the time for payment of the tax imposed by section 2001 or 2101 as postponed under section 6163(a) and as extended under section 6163(b) (on account of undue hardship) or, if the precedent interest terminated before July 5, 1958, within 60 days after the termination of the preceding interest or interests in the property. The allowance of credit, however, is subject to the other limitations contained in sections 2011 and 2014 and, in the case of the estate of a decedent who was a nonresident not a citizen of the United States, in section 2102(b).

(b) In applying the rule stated in paragraph (a) of this section, credit for State death taxes or foreign death taxes paid within the time provided in sections 2011 and 2014 is applied first to the portion of the Federal estate tax payment of which is not postponed, and any excess is applied to the balance of the Federal estate tax. However, credit for State death taxes or foreign death taxes not paid within the time provided in sections 2011 and 2014 is allowable only against the portion of the Federal estate tax attributable to the reversionary or remainder interest, and only for State or foreign death taxes attributable to that interest. If a State death tax or a foreign death tax is imposed upon both a reversionary or remainder interest and upon other property, without a definite apportionment of the tax, the amount of the tax deemed attributable to the reversionary or remainder interest is an amount which bears the same ratio to the total tax as the value of the reversionary or remainder interest bears to the value of the entire property with respect to which the tax was imposed. In applying this ratio, adjustments consistent with those required under paragraph (c) of §20.6163-1 must be made.

(c) The application of this section may be illustrated by the following examples:

*Example (1).* One-third of the Federal estate tax was attributable to a remainder interest in real property located in State Y, and two-thirds of the Federal estate tax was attributable to other property located in State X. The payment of the tax attributable to the remainder interest was postponed under the provisions of section 6163(a). The maximum credit allowable for State death taxes under the provisions of section 2011 is $12,000. Therefore, of the maximum credit allowable, $4,000 is attributable to the remainder interest and $8,000 is attributable to the other property. Within the 4-year period provided for in section 2011, inheritance tax in the amount of $9,000 was paid to State X in connection with the other property. With respect to this $9,000, $8,000 (the maximum amount allowable) is allowed as a credit against the Federal estate tax attributable to the other property, and $1,000 is allowed as a credit against the postponed tax. The life estate or other precedent interest expired after July 4, 1958. After the expiration of the 4-year period but before the expiration of the period of postponement elected under section 6163(a) and of the period of extension granted under section 6163(b) for payment of the tax, inheritance tax in the amount of $5,000 was paid to State Y in connection with the remainder interest. As the maximum credit allowable with respect to the remainder interest is $4,000 and $1,000 has already been allowed as a credit, an additional $3,000 will be credited against the Federal estate tax attributable to the remainder interest. It should be noted that if the life estate or other precedent interest had expired after the expiration of the 4-year period but before July 5, 1958, the same result would be reached only if the inheritance tax had been paid to State Y before the expiration of 60 days after the termination of the life estate or other precedent interest.

*Example (2).* The facts are the same as in example (1), except that within the 4-year period inheritance tax in the amount of $2,500 was paid to State Y with respect to the remainder interest and inheritance tax in the amount of $7,500 was paid to State X with respect to the other property. The amount of $8,000 is allowed as a credit against the Federal estate tax attributable to the other property and the amount of $2,000 is allowed as a credit against the postponed tax. The life estate or other precedent interest expired after July 4, 1958. After the expiration of the 4-year period but before the expiration of the period of postponement elected under section 6163(a) and of the period of extension granted under section 6163(b) for payment of the tax, inheritance tax in the amount of $5,000 was paid to State Y in connection with the remainder interest. As the maximum credit allowable with respect to the remainder interest is $4,000 and $2,000 already has been allowed as a credit, an additional $2,000 will be credited against the Federal estate tax attributable to the remainder interest. It should be noted that if the life estate or other precedent interest had expired after the expiration of the 4-year period but before July 5, 1958, the same result would be reached only if the inheritance tax had been paid to State Y before the expiration of 60 days after the termination of the life estate or other precedent interest.

*Example (3).* The facts are the same as in example (2), except that no payment was made to State Y within the 4-year period. The amount of $7,500 is allowed as a credit against the Federal estate tax attributable to the other property. After termination of the life interest additional credit will be allowed in the amount of $4,000 against the Federal estate tax attributable to the remainder interest. Since the payment of $5,000 was made to State Y following the expiration of the 4-year period, no part of the payment may be allowed as a credit against the Federal estate tax attributable to the other property. [Reg. § 20.2015-1.]

☐ [T.D. 6296, 6-23-58. *Amended by T.D. 6526, 1-18-61 and T.D. 7296, 12-11-73.*]

**[Reg. § 20.2016-1]**

**§ 20.2016-1. Recovery of death taxes claimed as credit.**—In accordance with the provisions of section 2016, the executor (or any other person) receiving a refund of any State death taxes or foreign death taxes claimed as a credit under section 2011 or section 2014 shall notify the district director of the refund within 30 days of its receipt. The notice shall contain the following information:

(a) The name of the decedent;

(b) The date of the decedent's death;

(c) The property with respect to which the refund was made;

(d) The amount of the refund, exclusive of interest;

(e) The date of the refund; and

(f) The name and address of the person receiving the refund.

If the refund was in connection with foreign death taxes claimed as a credit under section 2014, the notice shall also contain a statement showing the amount of interest, if any, paid by the foreign country on the refund. Finally, the person filing the notice shall furnish the district director such additional information as he may request. Any Federal estate tax found to be due by reason of the refund is payable by the person or persons receiving it, upon notice and demand, even though the refund is received after the expiration of the period of limitations set forth in section 6501 (see section 6501(c)(5)). If the tax found to be due results from a refund of foreign death tax claimed as a credit under section 2014, such tax shall not bear interest for any period before the receipt of the refund, except to the extent that interest was paid by the foreign country on the refund. [Reg. § 20.2016-1.]

☐ [T.D. 6296, 6-23-58.]

# Gross Estate

**[Reg. § 20.2031-0]**

**§ 20.2031-0. Table of contents.**—This section lists the section headings and undesignated center headings that appear in the regulations under section 2031.

[Reg. § 20.2031-0.]

☐ [T.D. 8540, 6-9-94. *Amended by T.D. 8819, 4-29-99; T.D. 8886, 6-9-2000; T.D. 9448, 5-1-2009 and T.D. 9540, 8-9-2011.*]

**[Reg. § 20.2031-1]**

**§ 20.2031-1. Definition of gross estate; valuation of property.**— (a) *Definition of gross estate.*—Except as otherwise provided in this paragraph the value of the gross estate of a decedent who was a citizen or resident of the United States at the time of his death is the total value of the interests described in sections 2033 through 2044. The gross estate of a decedent who died before October 17, 1962, does not include real property situated outside the United States (as defined in paragraph (b)(1) of § 20.0-1). Except as provided in paragraph (c) of this section (relating to the estates of decedents dying after October 16, 1962, and before July 1, 1964), in the case of a decedent dying after October 16, 1962, real property situated outside the United States which comes within the scope of sections 2033 through 2044 is included in the gross estate to the same extent as any other property coming within the scope of those sections. In arriving at the value of the gross estate the interests described in sections 2033 through 2044 are valued as described in this section, § § 20.2031-2

through 20.2031-9 and § 20.2032-1. The contents of sections 2033 through 2044 are, in general, as follows:

(1) Sections 2033 and 2034 are concerned mainly with interests in property passing through the decedent's probate estate. Section 2033 includes in the decedent's gross estate any interest that the decedent has in property at the time of his death. Section 2034 provides that any interest of the decedent's surviving spouse in the decedent's property, such as dower or curtesy, does not prevent the inclusion of such property in the decedent's gross estate.

(2) Sections 2035 through 2038 deal with interests in property transferred by the decedent during his life under such circumstances as to bring the interests within the decedent's gross estate. Section 2035 includes in the decedent's gross estate property transferred in contemplation of death, even though the decedent had no interest in, or control over, the property at the time of his death. Section 2036 provides for the inclusion of transferred property with respect to which the decedent retained the income or the power to designate who shall enjoy the income. Section 2037 includes in the decedent's gross estate certain transfers under which the beneficial enjoyment of the property could be obtained only by surviving the decedent. Section 2038 provides for the inclusion of transferred property if the decedent had at the time of his death the power to change the beneficial enjoyment of the property. It should be noted that there is a considerable overlap in the application of sections 2036 through 2038 with respect to reserved powers, so that transferred property may be includible in the decedent's gross estate in varying degrees under more than one of those sections.

(3) Sections 2039 through 2042 deal with special kinds of property and powers. Sections 2039 and 2040 concern annuities and jointly held property, respectively. Section 2041 deals with powers held by the decedent over the beneficial enjoyment of property not originating with the decedent. Section 2042 concerns insurance under policies on the life of the decedent.

(4) Section 2043 concerns the sufficiency of consideration for transfers made by the decedent during his life. This has a bearing on the amount to be included in the decedent's gross estate under sections 2035 through 2038, and 2041. Section 2044 deals with retroactivity.

(b) *Valuation of property in general.*—The value of every item of property includible in a decedent's gross estate under sections 2031 through 2044 is its fair market value at the time of the decedent's death, except that if the executor elects the alternate valuation method under section 2032, it is the fair market value thereof at the date, and with the adjustments, prescribed in that section. The fair market value is the price at which the property would change hands between a willing buyer and a willing seller, neither being under any compulsion to buy or to sell and both having reasonable knowledge of relevant facts. The fair market value of a particular item of property includible in the decedent's gross estate is not to be determined by a forced sale price. Nor is the fair market value of an item of property to be determined by the sale price of the item in a market other than that in which such item is most commonly sold to the public, taking into account the location of the item wherever appropriate. Thus, in the case of an item of property includible in the decedent's gross estate, which is generally obtained by the public in the retail market, the fair market value of such an item of property is the price at which the item or a comparable item would be sold at retail. For example, the fair market value of an automobile (an article generally obtained by the public in the retail market) includible in the decedent's gross estate is the price for which an automobile of the same or approximately the same description, make, model, age, condition, etc., could be purchased by a member of the general public and not the price for which the particular automobile of the decedent would be purchased by a dealer in used automobiles. Examples of items of property which are generally sold to the public at retail may be found in §§ 20.2031-6 and 20.2031-8. The value is generally to be determined by ascertaining as a basis the fair market value as of the applicable valuation date of each unit of property. For example, in the case of shares of stock or bonds, such unit of property is generally a share of stock or a bond. Livestock, farm machinery, harvested and growing crops must generally be itemized and the value of each item separately returned. Property shall not be returned at the value at which it is assessed for local tax purposes unless that value represents the fair market value as of the applicable valuation date. All relevant facts and elements of value as of the applicable valuation date shall be considered in every case. The value of items of property which were held by the decedent for sale in the course of a business generally should be reflected in the value of the business. For valuation of interests in businesses, see § 20.2031-3. See § 20.2031-2 and §§ 20.2031-4 through 20.2031-8 for further information concerning the valuation of other particular kinds of property. For certain circumstances under which the sale of an item of property at a price below its fair market value may result in a deduction for the estate, see paragraph (d)(2) of § 20.2053-3.

(c) *Real property situated outside the United States; gross estate of decedent dying after October 16, 1962, and before July 1, 1964.*—(1) *In general.*—In the case of a decedent dying after October 16, 1962, and before July 1, 1964, the value of real property situated outside the United States (as defined in paragraph (b)(1) of § 20.0-1) is not included in the gross estate of the decedent—

(i) Under section 2033, 2034, 2035(a), 2036(a), 2037(a), or 2038(a) to the extent the real property, or the decedent's interest in it, was acquired by the decedent before February 1, 1962;

(ii) Under section 2040 to the extent such property or interest was acquired by the decedent before February 1, 1962, or was held by the decedent and the survivor in a joint tenancy or tenancy by the entirety before February 1, 1962; or

(iii) Under section 2041(a) to the extent that before February 1, 1962, such property or interest was subject to a general power of appointment (as defined in section 2041) possessed by the decedent.

(2) *Certain property treated as acquired before February 1, 1962.*—For purposes of this paragraph real property situated outside the United States (including property held by the decedent and the survivor in a joint tenancy or tenancy by the entirety), or an interest in such property or a general power of appointment in respect of such property, which was acquired by the decedent after January 31, 1962, is treated as acquired by the decedent before February 1, 1962, if—

(i) Such property, interest, or power was acquired by the decedent by gift within the meaning of section 2511, or from a prior decedent by devise or inheritance, or by reason of death, form of ownership, or other conditions (including the exercise or nonexercise of a power of appointment); and

(ii) Before February 1, 1962, the donor or prior decedent had acquired the property or his interest therein or had possessed a power of appointment in respect thereof.

(3) *Certain property treated as acquired after January 31, 1962.*—For purposes of this paragraph that portion of capital additions or improvements made after January 31, 1962, to real property situated outside the United States is, to the extent that it materially increases the value of the property, treated as real property acquired after January 31, 1962. Accordingly, the gross estate may include the value of improvements on unimproved real property, such as office buildings, factories, houses, fences, drainage ditches, and other capital items, and the value of capital additions and improvements to existing improvements, placed on real property after January 31, 1962, whether or not the value of such real property or existing improvements is included in the gross estate. [Reg. § 20.2031-1.]

☐ [T.D. 6296, 6-23-58. Amended by T.D. 6684, 10-23-63 and T.D. 6826, 6-14-65.]

**Reg. § 20.2031-1(c)**

[Reg. § 20.2031-2]

**§ 20.2031-2. Valuation of stocks and bonds.**—(a) *In general.*—The value of stocks and bonds is the fair market value per share or bond on the applicable valuation date.

(b) *Based on selling prices.*—(1) In general, if there is a market for stocks or bonds, on a stock exchange, in an over-the-counter market, or otherwise, the mean between the highest and lowest quoted selling prices on the valuation date is the fair market value per share or bond. If there were no sales on the valuation date but there were sales on dates within a reasonable period both before and after the valuation date, the fair market value is determined by taking a weighted average of the means between the highest and lowest sales on the nearest date before and the nearest date after the valuation date. The average is to be weighted inversely by the respective numbers of trading days between the selling dates and the valuation date. If the stocks or bonds are listed on more than one exchange, the records of the exchange where the stocks or bonds are principally dealt in should be employed if such records are available in a generally available listing or publication of general circulation. In the event that such records are not so available and such stocks or bonds are listed on a composite listing of combined exchanges in a generally available listing or publication of general circulation, the records of such combined exchanges should be employed. In valuing listed securities, the executor should be careful to consult accurate records to obtain values as of the applicable valuation date. If quotations of unlisted securities are obtained from brokers, or evidence as to their sale is obtained from officers of the issuing companies, copies of the letters furnishing such quotations or evidence of sale should be attached to the return.

(2) If it is established with respect to bonds for which there is a market on a stock exchange, that the highest and lowest selling prices are not available for the valuation date in a generally available listing or publication of general circulation but that closing selling prices are so available, the fair market value per bond is the mean between the quoted closing selling price on the valuation date and the quoted closing selling price on the trading day before the valuation date. If there were no sales on the trading day before the valuation date but there were sales on a date within a reasonable period before the valuation date, the fair market value is determined by taking a weighted average of the quoted closing selling price on the valuation date and the quoted closing selling price on the nearest date before the valuation date. The closing selling price for the valuation date is to be weighted by the number of trading days between the previous selling date and the valuation date. If there were no sales within a reasonable period before the valuation date but there were sales on the valuation date, the fair market value is the closing selling price on such valuation date. If there were no sales on the valuation date but there were sales on dates within a reasonable period both before and after the valuation date, the fair market value is determined by taking a weighted average of the quoted closing selling prices on the nearest date before and the nearest date after the valuation date. The average is to be weighted inversely by the respective numbers of trading days between the selling dates and the valuation date. If the bonds are listed on more than one exchange, the records of the exchange where the bonds are principally dealt in should be employed. In valuing listed securities, the executor should be careful to consult accurate records to obtain values as of the applicable valuation date.

(3) The application of this paragraph may be illustrated by the following examples:

*Example (1).* Assume that sales of X Company common stock nearest the valuation date (Friday, June 15) occurred two trading days before (Wednesday, June 13) and three trading days after (Wednesday, June 20) and on these days the mean sale prices per share were $10 and $15, respectively. The price of $12 is taken as representing the fair market value of a share of X Company common stock as of the valuation date

$$\frac{(3 \times 10) + (2 \times 15)}{5}$$

*Example (2).* Assume the same facts as in example (1) except that the mean sale prices per share on June 13 and June 20 were $15 and $10, respectively. The price of $13 is taken as representing the fair market value of a share of X Company common stock as of the valuation date

$$\frac{(3 \times 15) + (2 \times 10)}{5}$$

*Example (3).* Assume the decedent died on Sunday, October 7, and that Saturday and Sunday were not trading days. If sales of X Company common stock occurred on Friday, October 5, at mean sale prices per share of $20 and on Monday, October 8, at mean sale prices per share of $23, the price of $21.50 is taken as representing the fair market value of a share of X Company common stock as of the valuation date

$$\frac{(1 \times 20) + (23 \times 1)}{2}$$

*Example (4).* Assume that on the valuation date (Tuesday, April 3, 1973) the closing selling price of a listed bond was $25 per bond and that the highest and lowest selling prices are not available in a generally available listing or publication of general circulation for that date. Assume further, that the closing selling price of the same listed bond was $21 per bond on the day before the valuation date (Monday, April 2, 1973). Thus, under paragraph (b)(2) of this section the price of $23 is taken as representing the fair market value per bond as of the valuation date

$$\frac{(25 + 21)}{2}$$

*Example (5).* Assume the same facts as in example (4) except that there were no sales on the day before the valuation date. Assume further, that there were sales on Thursday, March 29, 1973 and that the closing selling price on that day was $23. The price of $24.50 is taken as representing the fair market value per bond as of the valuation date

$$\frac{((1 \times 23) + (3 \times 25))}{4}$$

*Example (6).* Assume that no bonds were traded on the valuation date (Friday, April 20). Assume further, that sales of bonds nearest the valuation date occurred two trading days before (Wednesday, April 18) and three trading days after (Wednesday, April 25) the valuation date and that on these two days the closing selling prices per bond were $29 and $22, respectively. The highest and lowest selling prices are not available for these dates in a generally available listing or publication of general circulation. Thus, under paragraph (b)(2) of this section, the price of $26.20 is taken as representing the fair market value of a bond as of the valuation date

$$\frac{((3 \times 29) + (2 \times 22))}{5}$$

(c) *Based on bid and asked prices.*—If the provisions of paragraph (b) of this section are inapplicable because actual sales are not available during a reasonable period beginning before and ending after the valuation date, the fair market value may be determined by taking the mean between the bona fide bid and asked prices on the valuation date, or if none, by taking a weighted average of the means between the bona fide bid and asked prices on the nearest trading date before and the nearest trading date after the valuation date, if both such nearest dates are within a reasonable period. The average is to be determined in the manner described in paragraph (b) of this section.

(d) *Based on incomplete selling prices or bid and asked prices.*—If the provisions of paragraphs (b) and (c) of this section are inapplicable because no actual sale prices or bona fide bid and asked prices are available on a date within a reasonable period before the valuation date, but such prices are available on a date within a reasonable period after the valuation date, or vice versa, then the mean between the highest and lowest available sale prices or bid and asked prices may be taken as the value.

(e) *Where selling prices or bid and asked prices do not reflect fair market value.*—If it is established that the value of any bond or share of stock determined on the basis of selling or bid and asked prices as provided under paragraphs (b), (c), and (d) of this section does not reflect the fair market value thereof, then some reasonable modification of that basis or other relevant facts and elements of value are considered in determining the fair market value.

Where sales at or near the date of death are few or of a sporadic nature, such sales alone may not indicate fair market value. In certain exceptional cases, the size of the block of stock to be valued in relation to the number of shares changing hands in sales may be relevant in determining whether selling prices reflect the fair market value of the block of stock to be valued. If the executor can show that the block of stock to be valued is so large in relation to the actual sales on the existing market that it could not be liquidated in a reasonable time without depressing the market, the price at which the block could be sold as such outside the usual market, as through an underwriter, may be a more accurate indication of value than market quotations. Complete data in support of any allowance claimed due to the size of the block of stock being valued shall be submitted with the return. On the other hand, if the block of stock to be valued represents a controlling interest, either actual or effective, in a going business, the price at which other lots change hands may have little relation to its true value.

(f) *Where selling prices or bid and asked prices are unavailable.*—If the provisions of paragraphs (b), (c), and (d) of this section are inapplicable because actual sale prices and bona fide bid and asked prices are lacking, then the fair market value is to be determined by taking the following factors into consideration:

(1) In the case of corporate or other bonds, the soundness of the security, the interest yield, the date of maturity, and other relevant factors; and

(2) In the case of shares of stock, the company's net worth, prospective earning power and dividend-paying capacity, and other relevant factors.

Some of the "other relevant factors" referred to in subparagraphs (1) and (2) of this paragraph are: the good will of the business; the economic outlook in the particular industry; the company's position in the industry and its management; the degree of control of the business represented by the block of stock to be valued; and the values of securities of corporations engaged in the same or similar lines of business which are listed on a stock exchange. However, the weight to be accorded such comparisons or any other evidentiary factors considered in the determination of a value depends upon the facts of each case. In addition to the relevant factors described above, consideration shall also be given to nonoperating assets, including proceeds of life insurance policies payable to or for the benefit of the company, to the extent such nonoperating assets have not been taken into account in the determination of net worth, prospective earning power and dividend-earning capacity. Complete financial and other data upon which the valuation is based should be submitted with the return, including copies of reports of any examinations of the company made by accountants, engineers, or any technical experts as of or near the applicable valuation date.

(g) *Pledged securities.*—The full value of securities pledged to secure an indebtedness of the decedent is included in the gross estate. If the decedent had a trading account with a broker, all securities belonging to the decedent and held by the broker at the date of death must be included at their fair market value as of the applicable valuation date. Securities purchased on margin for the decedent's account and held by a broker must also be returned at their fair market value as of the applicable valuation date. The amount of the decedent's indebtedness to a broker or other person with whom securities were pledged is allowed as a deduction from the gross estate in accordance with the provisions of § 20.2053-1 or § 20.2106-1 (for estates of nonresidents not citizens).

(h) *Securities subject to an option or contract to purchase.*—Another person may hold an option or a contract to purchase securities owned by a decedent at the time of his death. The effect, if any, that is given to the option or contract price in determining the value of the securities for estate tax purposes depends upon the circumstances of the particular case. Little weight will be accorded a price contained in an option or contract under which the decedent is free to dispose of the underlying securities at any price he chooses during his lifetime. Such is the effect, for example, of an agreement on the part of a shareholder to purchase whatever shares of stock the decedent may own at the time of his death. Even if the decedent is not free to dispose of the underlying securities at other than the option or contract price, such price will be disregarded in determining the value of the securities unless it is determined under the circumstances of the particular case that the agreement represents a bona fide business arrangement and not a device to pass the decedent's shares to the natural objects of his bounty for less than an adequate and full consideration in money or money's worth. See section 2703 and the regulations at § 25.2703 of this chapter for special rules involving options and agreements (including contracts to purchase) entered into (or substantially modified after) October 8, 1990.

(i) *Stock sold "ex-dividend.".*—In any case where a dividend is declared on a share of stock before the decedent's death but payable to stockholders of record on a date after his death and the stock is selling "ex-dividend" on the date of the decedent's death, the amount of the dividend is added to the ex-dividend quotation in determining the fair market value of the stock as of the date of the decedent's death.

(j) *Application of chapter 14.*—See section 2701 and the regulations at § 25.2701 of this chapter for special rules for valuing the transfer of an interest in a corporation and for the treatment of unpaid qualified payments at the death of the transferor or an applicable family member. See section 2704(b) and the regulations at § 25.2704-2 of this chapter for special valuation rules involving certain restrictions on liquidation rights created after October 8, 1990. [Reg. § 20.2031-2]

☐ [*T.D. 6296, 6-23-58. Amended by T.D. 6826, 6-14-65; T.D. 7312, 4-26-74; T.D. 7327, 9-30-74; T.D. 7432, 9-13-76 and T.D. 8395, 1-28-92.*]

[Reg. §20.2031-3]

**§20.2031-3. Valuation of interests in businesses.**—The fair market value of any interest of a decedent in a business, whether a partnership or a proprietorship, is the net amount which a willing purchaser, whether an individual or a corporation, would pay for the interest to a willing seller, neither being under any compulsion to buy or to sell and both having reasonable knowledge of relevant facts. The net value is determined on the basis of all relevant factors including—

(a) A fair appraisal as of the applicable valuation date of all the assets of the business, tangible and intangible, including good will;

(b) The demonstrated earning capacity of the business; and

(c) The other factors set forth in paragraphs (f) and (h) of §20.2031-2 relating to the valuation of corporate stock, to the extent applicable.

Special attention should be given to determining an adequate value of the good will of the business in all cases in which the decedent has not agreed, for an adequate and full consideration in money or money's worth, that his interest passes at his death to, for example, his surviving partner or partners. Complete financial and other data upon which the valuation is based should be submitted with the return, including copies of reports of examinations of the business made by accountants, engineers, or any technical experts as of or near the applicable valuation date. See section 2701 and the regulations at §25.2701 of this chapter for special rules for valuing the transfer of an interest in a partnership and for the treatment of unpaid qualified payments at the death of the transferor or an applicable family member. See section 2703 and the regulations at §25.2703 of this chapter for special rules involving options and agreements (including contracts to purchase) entered into (or substantially modified after) October 8, 1990. See section 2704(b) and the regulations at §25.2704-2 of this chapter for special valuation rules involving certain restrictions on liquidation rights created after October 8, 1990. [Reg. §20.2031-3.]

☐ [*T.D. 6296, 6-23-58. Amended by T.D. 8395, 1-28-92.*]

### [Reg. §20.2031-4]

**§20.2031-4. Valuation of notes.**—The fair market value of notes, secured or unsecured, is presumed to be the amount of unpaid principal, plus interest accrued to the date of death, unless the executor establishes that the value is lower or that the notes are worthless. However, items of interest shall be separately stated on the estate tax return. If not returned at face value, plus accrued interest, satisfactory evidence must be submitted that the note is worth less than the unpaid amount (because of the interest rate, date of maturity, or other cause), or that the note is uncollectible, either in whole or in part (by reason of the insolvency of the party or parties liable, or for other cause), and that any property pledged or mortgaged as security is insufficient to satisfy the obligation. [Reg. §20.2031-4.]

☐ [*T.D. 6296, 6-23-58.*]

### [Reg. §20.2031-5]

**§20.2031-5. Valuation of cash on hand or on deposit.**—The amount of cash belonging to the decedent at the date of his death, whether in his possession or in the possession of another, or deposited with a bank, is included in the decedent's gross estate. If bank checks outstanding at the time of the decedent's death and given in discharge of bona fide legal obligations of the decedent incurred for an adequate and full consideration in money or money's worth are subsequently honored by the bank and charged to the decedent's account, the balance remaining in the account may be returned, but only if the obligations are not claimed as deductions from the gross estate. [Reg. §20.2031-5.]

☐ [*T.D. 6926, 6-23-58.*]

### [Reg. §20.2031-6]

**§20.2031-6. Valuation of household and personal effects.**—(a) *General rule.*—The fair market value of the decedent's household and personal effects is the price which a willing buyer would pay to a willing seller, neither being under any compulsion to buy or to sell and both having reasonable knowledge of relevant facts. A room by room itemization of household and personal effects is desirable. All the articles should be named specifically, except that a number of articles contained in the same room, none of which has a value in excess of $100, may be grouped. A separate value should be given for each article named. In lieu of an itemized list, the executor may furnish a written statement, containing a declaration that it is made under penalties of perjury, setting forth the aggregate value as appraised by a competent appraiser or appraisers of recognized standing and ability, or by a dealer or dealers in the class of personalty involved.

(b) *Special rule in cases involving a substantial amount of valuable articles.*—Notwithstanding the provisions of paragraph (a) of this section, if there are included among the household and personal effects articles having marked artistic or intrinsic value of a total value in excess of $3,000 (e.g., jewelry, furs, silverware, paintings, etchings, engravings, antiques, books, statuary, vases, oriental rugs, coin or stamp collections), the appraisal of an expert or experts, under oath, shall be filed with the return. The appraisal shall be accompanied by a written statement of the executor containing a declaration that it is made under the penalties of perjury as to the completeness of the itemized list of such property and as to the disinterested character and the qualifications of the appraiser or appraisers.

(c) *Disposition of household effects prior to investigation.*—If it is desired to effect distribution or sale of any portion of the household or personal effects of the decedent in advance of an investigation by an officer of the Internal Revenue Service, information to that effect shall be given to the district director. The statement to the district director shall be accompanied by an appraisal of such property, under oath, and by a written statement of the executor, containing a declaration that it is made under the penalties of perjury, regarding the completeness of the list of such property and the qualifications of the appraiser, as heretofore described. If a personal inspection by an officer of the Internal Revenue Service is not deemed necessary, the executor will be so advised. This procedure is designed to facilitate disposition of such property and to obviate future expense and inconvenience to the estate by affording the district director an opportunity to make an investigation should one be deemed necessary prior to sale or distribution.

(d) *Additional rules if an appraisal involved.*—If, pursuant to paragraphs (a), (b), and (c) of this section, expert appraisers are employed, care shall be taken to see that they are reputable and of recognized competency to appraise the particular class of property involved. In the appraisal, books in sets by standard authors shall be listed in separate groups. In listing paintings having artistic value, the size, subject, and artist's name shall be stated. In the case of oriental rugs, the size, make, and general condition shall be given. Sets of silverware shall be listed in separate groups. Groups or individual pieces of silverware shall be weighed and the weights given in troy ounces. In arriving at the value of silverware, the appraisers shall take into consideration its antiquity, utility, desirability, condition, and obsolescence. [Reg. §20.2031-6.]

☐ [*T.D. 6296, 6-23-58.*]

### [Reg. §20.2031-7]

**§20.2031-7. Valuation of annuities, interests for life or term of years, and remainder or reversionary interests.**—(a) *In general.*—Except as otherwise provided in paragraph (b) of this section and §20.7520-3(b) (pertaining to certain limitations on the use of prescribed tables), the fair market value of annuities, life estates, terms of years, remainders, and reversionary interests for estates of decedents is the present value of such interests, determined under paragraph (d) of this section. The regulations in this and in related sections provide tables with standard actuarial factors and examples that illustrate how to use the tables to compute the present value of ordinary annuity, life, and remainder interests in property. These sections also refer to standard and special actuarial factors that may be necessary to compute the present value of similar interests in more unusual fact situations.

(b) *Commercial annuities and insurance contracts.*—The value of annuities issued by companies regularly engaged in their sale, and of insurance policies on the lives of persons other than the decedent, is determined under §20.2031-8. See §20.2042-1 with respect to insurance policies on the decedent's life.

(c) *Actuarial valuations.*—The present value of annuities, life estates, terms of years, remainders, and reversions for estates of decedents for which the valuation date of the gross estate is on or after May 1, 2009, is determined under paragraph (d) of this section. The present value of annuities, life estates, terms of years, remainders, and reversions for estates of decedents for which the valuation date of the gross estate is before May 1, 2009, is determined under the following sections:

| Valuation Date | | Applicable |
|---|---|---|
| *After* | *Before* | *Regulations* |
| - | 01-01-52 | 20.2031-7A(a) |
| 12-31-51 | 01-01-71 | 20.2031-7A(b) |
| 12-31-70 | 12-01-83 | 20.2031-7A(c) |
| 11-30-83 | 05-01-89 | 20.2031-7A(d) |
| 04-30-89 | 05-01-99 | 20.2031-7A(e) |
| 04-30-99 | 05-01-09 | 20.2031-7A(f) |

(d) *Actuarial valuations on or after May 1, 2009.*—(1) *In general.*—Except as otherwise provided in paragraph (b) of this section and §20.7520-3(b) (pertaining to certain limitations on the use of prescribed tables), if the valuation date for the gross estate of the decedent is on or after May 1, 2009, the fair market value of annuities, life estates, terms of years, remainders, and reversionary interests is the present value determined by use of standard or special section 7520 actuarial factors. These factors are derived by using the appropriate section 7520 interest rate and, if applicable, the mortality component for the valuation date of the interest that is being valued. For purposes of the computations described in this section, the age of an individual is the age of that individual at the individual's nearest birthday. See §§20.7520-1 through 20.7520-4.

(2) *Specific interests.*—(i) *Charitable remainder trusts.*—The fair market value of a remainder interest in a pooled income fund, as defined in §1.642(c)-5 of this chapter, is its value determined under §1.642(c)-6(e). The fair market value of a remainder interest in a charitable remainder annuity trust, as defined in §1.664-2(a), is the present value determined under §1.664-2(c). The fair market value of a remainder interest in a charitable remainder unitrust, as defined in §1.664-3, is its present value determined under §1.664-4(e). The fair market value of a life interest or term of years in a charitable remainder unitrust is the fair market value of the property as of the date of valuation less the fair market value of the remainder interest on that date determined under §1.664-4(e)(4) and (5).

(ii) *Ordinary remainder and reversionary interests.*—If the interest to be valued is to take effect after a definite number of years or after the death of one individual, the present value of the interest is computed by multiplying the value of the property by the appropriate remainder interest actuarial factor (that corresponds to the applicable section 7520 interest rate and remainder interest period) in Table B (for a term certain) or in Table S (for one measuring life), as the case may be. Table B is contained in paragraph (d)(6) of this section and Table S (for one measuring life when the valuation date is on or after May 1, 2009) is contained in paragraph (d)(7) of this section and in Internal Revenue Service Publication 1457. See §20.2031-7A containing Table S for valuation of interests before May 1, 2009. For information about obtaining actuarial factors for other types of remainder interests, see paragraph (d)(4) of this section.

(iii) *Ordinary term-of-years and life interests.*—If the interest to be valued is the right of a person to receive the income of certain property, or to use certain nonincome-producing property, for a term of years or for the life of one individual, the present value of the interest is computed by multiplying the value of the property by the appropriate term-of-years or life interest actuarial factor (that corresponds to the applicable section 7520 interest rate and term-of-years or life interest period). Internal Revenue Service Publication 1457 includes actuarial factors for a remainder interest after a term of years in Table B and after the life of one individual in Table S (for one measuring life when the valuation date is on or after May 1, 2009). However, term-of-years and life interest actuarial factors are not included in Table B in paragraph (d)(6) of this section or Table S in paragraph (d)(7) of this section (or in §20.2031-7A). If Internal Revenue Service Publication 1457 (or any other reliable source of term-of-years and life interest actuarial factors) is not conveniently available, an actuarial factor for the interest may be derived mathematically. This actuarial factor may be derived by subtracting the correlative remainder factor (that corresponds to the applicable section 7520 interest rate and the term of years or the life) in Table B (for a term of years) in paragraph (d)(6) of this section or in Table S (for the life of one individual) in paragraph (d)(7) of this section, as the case may be, from 1.000000. For information about obtaining actuarial factors for other types of term-of-years and life interests, see paragraph (d)(4) of this section.

(iv) *Annuities.*—(A) If the interest to be valued is the right of a person to receive an annuity that is payable at the end of each year for a term of years or for the life of one individual, the present value of the interest is computed by multiplying the aggregate amount payable annually by the appropriate annuity actuarial factor (that corresponds to the applicable section 7520 interest rate and annuity period). Internal Revenue Publication 1457 includes actuarial factors for a remainder interest in Table B (after an annuity payable for a term of years) and in Table S (after an annuity payable for the life of one individual when the valuation date is on or after May 1, 2009). However, annuity actuarial factors are not included in Table B in paragraph (d)(6) of this section or Table S in paragraph (d)(7) of this section (or in §20.2031-7A). If Internal Revenue Service Publication 1457 (or any other reliable source of annuity actuarial factors) is not conveniently available, a required annuity factor for a term of years or for one life may be mathematically derived. This annuity factor may be derived by subtracting the applicable remainder factor (that corresponds to the applicable section 7520 interest rate and annuity

period) in Table B (in the case of a term-of-years annuity) in paragraph (d)(6) of this section or in Table S (in the case of a one-life annuity when the valuation date is on or after May 1, 2009) in paragraph (d)(7) of this section, as the case may be, from 1.000000 and then dividing the result by the applicable section 7520 interest rate expressed as a decimal number.

(B) If the annuity is payable at the end of semiannual, quarterly, monthly, or weekly periods, the product obtained by multiplying the annuity factor by the aggregate amount payable annually is then multiplied by the applicable adjustment factor as contained in Table K in paragraph (d)(6) of this section for payments made at the end of the specified periods. The provisions of this paragraph (d)(2)(iv)(B) are illustrated by the following example:

*Example.* At the time of the decedent's death, the survivor/annuitant, age 72, is entitled to receive an annuity of $15,000 a year for life payable in equal monthly installments at the end of each period. The section 7520 rate for the month in which the decedent died is 5.6 percent. Under Table S in paragraph (d)(7) of this section, the remainder factor at 5.6 percent for an individual aged 72 is .53243. By converting the remainder factor to an annuity factor, as described above, the annuity factor at 5.6 percent for an individual aged 72 is 8.3495 (1.000000 minus .53243, divided by .056). Under Table K in paragraph (d)(6) of this section, the adjustment factor under the column for payments made at the end of each monthly period at the rate of 5.6 percent is 1.0254. The aggregate annual amount, $15,000, is multiplied by the factor 8.3495 and the product is multiplied by 1.0254. The present value of the annuity at the date of the decedent's death is, therefore, $128,423.66 ($15,000 × 8.3495 × 1.0254).

(C) If an annuity is payable at the beginning of annual, semiannual, quarterly, monthly, or weekly periods for a term of years, the value of the annuity is computed by multiplying the aggregate amount payable annually by the annuity factor described in paragraph (d)(2)(iv)(A) of this section, and the product so obtained is then multiplied by the adjustment factor in Table J in paragraph (d)(6) of this section at the appropriate interest rate component for payments made at the beginning of specified periods. If an annuity is payable at the beginning of annual, semiannual, quarterly, monthly, or weekly periods for one or more lives, the value of the annuity is the sum of the first payment plus the present value of a similar annuity, the first payment of which is not to be made until the end of the payment period, determined as provided in this paragraph (d)(2)(iv).

(v) *Annuity and unitrust interests for a term of years or until the prior death of an individual.*—See §25.2512-5(d)(2)(v) of this chapter for examples explaining how to compute the present value of an annuity or unitrust interest that is payable until the earlier of the lapse of a specific number of years or the death of an individual.

(3) *Transitional rule.*—(i) If a decedent dies on or after May 1, 2009, and if on May 1, 2009, the decedent was mentally incompetent so that the disposition of the decedent's property could not be changed, and the decedent dies without having regained competency to dispose of the decedent's property or dies within 90 days of the date on which the decedent first regains competency, the fair market value of annuities, life estates, terms for years, remainders, and reversions included in the gross estate of the decedent is their present value determined either under this section or under the corresponding section applicable at the time the decedent became mentally incompetent, at the option of the decedent's executor. For examples, see §20.2031-7A(d).

(ii) If a decedent dies on or after May 1, 2009, and before July 1, 2009, the fair market value of annuities, life estates, remainders, and reversions based on one or more measuring lives included in the gross estate of the decedent is their present value determined under this section by use of the section 7520 interest rate for the month in which the valuation date occurs (see §§20.7520-1(b) and 20.7520-2(a)(2)) and the appropriate actuarial tables under either paragraph (d)(7) of this section or §20.2031-7A(f)(4), at the option of the decedent's executor.

(iii) For purposes of paragraphs (d)(3)(i) and (d)(3)(ii) of this section, where the decedent's executor is given the option to use the appropriate actuarial tables under either paragraph (d)(7) of this section or §20.2031-7A(f)(4), the decedent's executor must use the same actuarial table with respect to each individual transaction and with respect to all transfers occurring on the valuation date. For example, gift and income tax charitable deductions with respect to the same transfer must be determined based on the same tables, and all assets includible in the gross estate and/or estate tax deductions claimed must be valued based on the same tables.

(4) *Publications and actuarial computations by the Internal Revenue Service.*—Many standard actuarial factors not included in paragraph (d)(6) or (d)(7) of this section are included in Internal Revenue Service Publication 1457, "Actuarial Valuations Version 3A" (2009). Publication 1457 also includes examples that illustrate how to com-

pute many special factors for more unusual situations. This publication is available, at no charge, electronically via the Internal Revenue Service Internet site at *www.irs.gov*. If a special factor is required in the case of an actual decedent, the Internal Revenue Service may furnish the factor to the executor upon a request for a ruling. The request for a ruling must be accompanied by a recitation of the facts including a statement of the date of birth for each measuring life, the date of the decedent's death, any other applicable dates, and a copy of the will, trust, or other relevant documents. A request for a ruling must comply with the instructions for requesting a ruling published periodically in the Internal Revenue Bulletin (see §§601.201 and 601.601(d)(2)(ii)(b) of this chapter) and must include payment of the required user fee.

(5) *Examples.*—The provisions of this section are illustrated by the following examples:

*Example 1. Remainder payable at an individual's death.* The decedent, or the decedent's estate, was entitled to receive certain property worth $50,000 upon the death of A, to whom the income was bequeathed for life. At the time of the decedent's death, A was 47 years and 5 months old. In the month in which the decedent died, the section 7520 rate was 6.2 percent. Under Table S in paragraph (d)(7) of this section, the remainder factor at 6.2 percent for determining the present value of the remainder interest due at the death of a person aged 47, the number of years nearest A's actual age at the decedent's death, is .18672. The present value of the remainder interest at the date of the decedent's death is, therefore, $9,336.00 ($50,000 X .18672).

*Example 2. Income payable for an individual's life.* A's parent bequeathed an income interest in property to A for life, with the remainder interest passing to B at A's death. At the time of the parent's death, the value of the property was $50,000 and A was 30 years and 10 months old. The section 7520 rate at the time of the parent's death was 6.2 percent. Under Table S in paragraph (d)(7) of this section, the remainder factor at 6.2 percent for determining the present value of the remainder interest due at the death of a person aged 31, the number of years closest to A's age at the decedent's death, is .08697. Converting this remainder factor to an income factor, as described in paragraph (d)(2)(iii) of this section, the factor for determining the present value of an income interest for the life of a person aged 31 is .91303. The present value of A's interest at the time of the parent's death is, therefore, $45,651.50 ($50,000 X .91303).

*Example 3. Annuity payable for an individual's life.* A purchased an annuity for the benefit of both A and B. Under the terms of the annuity contract, at A's death, a survivor annuity of $10,000 per year payable in equal semiannual installments made at the end of each interval is payable to B for life. At A's death, B was 45 years and 7 months old. Also, at A's death, the section 7520 rate was 4.8 percent. Under Table S in paragraph (d)(7) of this section, the factor at 4.8 percent for determining the present value of the remainder interest at the death of a person age 46 (the number of years nearest B's actual age) is .24774. By converting the factor to an annuity factor, as described in paragraph (d)(2)(iv)(A) of this section, the factor for the present value of an annuity payable until the death of a person age 46 is 15.6721 (1.000000 minus .24774, divided by .048). The adjustment factor from Table K in paragraph (d)(6) of this section at an interest rate of 4.8 percent for semiannual annuity payments made at the end of the period is 1.0119. The present value of the annuity at the date of A's death is, therefore, $158,585.98 ($10,000 X 15.6721 X 1.0119).

*Example 4. Annuity payable for a term of years.* The decedent, or the decedent's estate, was entitled to receive an annuity of $10,000 per year payable in equal quarterly installments at the end of each quarter throughout a term certain. At the time of the decedent's death, the section 7520 rate was 9.8 percent. A quarterly payment had been made immediately prior to the decedent's death and payments were to continue for 5 more years. Under Table B in paragraph (d)(6) of this section for the interest rate of 9.8 percent, the factor for the present value of a remainder interest due after a term of 5 years is .626597. Converting the factor to an annuity factor, as described in paragraph (d)(2)(iv)(A) of this section, the factor for the present value of an annuity for a term of 5 years is 3.8102 (1.000000 minus .626597, divided by .098). The adjustment factor from Table K in paragraph (d)(6) of this section at an interest rate of 9.8 percent for quarterly annuity payments made at the end of the period is 1.0360. The present value of the annuity is, therefore, $39,473.67 ($10,000 X 3.8102 X 1.0360).

(6) *Actuarial Table B, Table J, and Table K where the valuation date is after April 30, 1989.*—Except as provided in §20.7520-3(b) (pertaining to certain limitations on prescribed tables), for determination of the present value of an interest that is dependent on a term of years, the tables in this paragraph (d)(6) must be used in the application of the provisions of this section when the section 7520 interest rate component is between 4.2 and 14 percent.

**TABLE B**
**TERM CERTAIN REMAINDER FACTORS**
**APPLICABLE AFTER APRIL 30, 1989**

**INTEREST RATE**

| YEARS | 4.2% | 4.4% | 4.6% | 4.8% | 5.0% | 5.2% | 5.4% | 5.6% | 5.8% | 6.0% |
|---|---|---|---|---|---|---|---|---|---|---|
| 1 | .959693 | .957854 | .956023 | .954198 | .952381 | .950570 | .948767 | .946970 | .945180 | .943396 |
| 2 | .921010 | .917485 | .913980 | .910495 | .907029 | .903584 | .900158 | .896752 | .893364 | .889996 |
| 3 | .883887 | .878817 | .873786 | .868793 | .863838 | .858920 | .854040 | .849197 | .844390 | .839619 |
| 4 | .848260 | .841779 | .835359 | .829001 | .822702 | .816464 | .810285 | .804163 | .798100 | .792094 |
| 5 | .814069 | .806302 | .798623 | .791031 | .783526 | .776106 | .768771 | .761518 | .754348 | .747258 |
| 6 | .781257 | .772320 | .763501 | .754801 | .746215 | .737744 | .729384 | .721135 | .712994 | .704961 |
| 7 | .749766 | .739770 | .729925 | .720230 | .710681 | .701277 | .692015 | .682893 | .673908 | .665057 |
| 8 | .719545 | .708592 | .697825 | .687242 | .676839 | .666613 | .656561 | .646679 | .636964 | .627412 |
| 9 | .690543 | .678728 | .667137 | .655765 | .644609 | .633663 | .622923 | .612385 | .602045 | .591898 |
| 10 | .662709 | .650122 | .637798 | .625730 | .613913 | .602341 | .591009 | .579910 | .569041 | .558395 |
| 11 | .635997 | .622722 | .609750 | .597071 | .584679 | .572568 | .560729 | .549157 | .537846 | .526788 |
| 12 | .610362 | .596477 | .582935 | .569724 | .556837 | .544266 | .532001 | .520035 | .508361 | .496969 |
| 13 | .585760 | .571339 | .557299 | .543630 | .530321 | .517363 | .504745 | .492458 | .480492 | .468839 |
| 14 | .562150 | .547259 | .532790 | .518731 | .505068 | .491790 | .478885 | .466343 | .454151 | .442301 |
| 15 | .539491 | .524195 | .509360 | .494972 | .481017 | .467481 | .454350 | .441612 | .429255 | .417265 |
| 16 | .517746 | .502102 | .486960 | .472302 | .458112 | .444374 | .431072 | .418194 | .405723 | .393646 |
| 17 | .496877 | .480941 | .465545 | .450670 | .436297 | .422408 | .408987 | .396017 | .383481 | .371364 |
| 18 | .476849 | .460671 | .445071 | .430028 | .415521 | .401529 | .388033 | .375016 | .362458 | .350344 |
| 19 | .457629 | .441256 | .425498 | .410332 | .395734 | .381681 | .368153 | .355129 | .342588 | .330513 |
| 20 | .439183 | .422659 | .406786 | .391538 | .376889 | .362815 | .349291 | .336296 | .323807 | .311805 |
| 21 | .421481 | .404846 | .388897 | .373605 | .358942 | .344881 | .331396 | .318462 | .306056 | .294155 |
| 22 | .404492 | .387783 | .371794 | .356494 | .341850 | .327834 | .314417 | .301574 | .289278 | .277505 |
| 23 | .388188 | .371440 | .355444 | .340166 | .325571 | .311629 | .298309 | .285581 | .273420 | .261797 |
| 24 | .372542 | .355785 | .339813 | .324586 | .310068 | .296225 | .283025 | .270437 | .258431 | .246979 |
| 25 | .357526 | .340791 | .324869 | .309719 | .295303 | .281583 | .268525 | .256096 | .244263 | .232999 |
| 26 | .343115 | .326428 | .310582 | .295533 | .281241 | .267664 | .254768 | .242515 | .230873 | .219810 |
| 27 | .329285 | .312670 | .296923 | .281998 | .267848 | .254434 | .241715 | .229654 | .218216 | .207368 |
| 28 | .316012 | .299493 | .283866 | .269082 | .255094 | .241857 | .229331 | .217475 | .206253 | .195630 |
| 29 | .303275 | .286870 | .271382 | .256757 | .242946 | .229902 | .217582 | .205943 | .194947 | .184557 |
| 30 | .291051 | .274780 | .259447 | .244997 | .231377 | .218538 | .206434 | .195021 | .184260 | .174110 |

| YEARS | 4.2% | 4.4% | 4.6% | 4.8% | 5.0% | 5.2% | 5.4% | 5.6% | 5.8% | 6.0% |
|---|---|---|---|---|---|---|---|---|---|---|
| 31 | .279319 | .263199 | .248038 | .233776 | .220359 | .207736 | .195858 | .184679 | .174158 | .164255 |
| 32 | .268061 | .252106 | .237130 | .223069 | .209866 | .197468 | .185823 | .174886 | .164611 | .154957 |
| 33 | .257256 | .241481 | .226702 | .212852 | .199873 | .187707 | .176303 | .165612 | .155587 | .146186 |
| 34 | .246887 | .231304 | .216732 | .203103 | .190355 | .178429 | .167270 | .156829 | .147058 | .137912 |
| 35 | .236935 | .221556 | .207201 | .193801 | .181290 | .169609 | .158701 | .148512 | .138996 | .130105 |
| 36 | .227385 | .212218 | .198089 | .184924 | .172657 | .161225 | .150570 | .140637 | .131376 | .122741 |
| 37 | .218220 | .203274 | .189377 | .176454 | .164436 | .153256 | .142856 | .133179 | .124174 | .115793 |
| 38 | .209424 | .194707 | .181049 | .168373 | .156605 | .145681 | .135537 | .126116 | .117367 | .109239 |
| 39 | .200983 | .186501 | .173087 | .160661 | .149148 | .138480 | .128593 | .119428 | .110933 | .103056 |
| 40 | .192882 | .178641 | .165475 | .153302 | .142046 | .131635 | .122004 | .113095 | .104851 | .097222 |
| 41 | .185107 | .171112 | .158198 | .146281 | .135282 | .125128 | .115754 | .107098 | .099103 | .091719 |
| 42 | .177646 | .163900 | .151241 | .139581 | .128840 | .118943 | .109823 | .101418 | .093670 | .086527 |
| 43 | .170486 | .156992 | .144590 | .133188 | .122704 | .113064 | .104197 | .096040 | .088535 | .081630 |
| 44 | .163614 | .150376 | .138231 | .127088 | .116861 | .107475 | .098858 | .090947 | .083682 | .077009 |
| 45 | .157019 | .144038 | .132152 | .121267 | .111297 | .102163 | .093793 | .086124 | .079094 | .072650 |
| 46 | .150690 | .137968 | .126340 | .115713 | .105997 | .097113 | .088988 | .081557 | .074758 | .068538 |
| 47 | .144616 | .132153 | .120784 | .110413 | .100949 | .092312 | .084429 | .077232 | .070660 | .064658 |
| 48 | .138787 | .126583 | .115473 | .105356 | .096142 | .087749 | .080103 | .073136 | .066786 | .060998 |
| 49 | .133193 | .121248 | .110395 | .100530 | .091564 | .083412 | .075999 | .069258 | .063125 | .057546 |
| 50 | .127824 | .116138 | .105540 | .095926 | .087204 | .079289 | .072106 | .065585 | .059665 | .054288 |
| 51 | .122672 | .111243 | .100898 | .091532 | .083051 | .075370 | .068411 | .062107 | .056394 | .051215 |
| 52 | .117728 | .106555 | .096461 | .087340 | .079096 | .071644 | .064907 | .058813 | .053302 | .048316 |
| 53 | .112982 | .102064 | .092219 | .083340 | .075330 | .068103 | .061581 | .055695 | .050380 | .045582 |
| 54 | .108428 | .097763 | .088164 | .079523 | .071743 | .064737 | .058426 | .052741 | .047618 | .043001 |
| 55 | .104058 | .093642 | .084286 | .075880 | .068326 | .061537 | .055433 | .049944 | .045008 | .040567 |
| 56 | .099864 | .089696 | .080580 | .072405 | .065073 | .058495 | .052593 | .047296 | .042541 | .038271 |
| 57 | .095839 | .085916 | .077036 | .069089 | .061974 | .055604 | .049898 | .044787 | .040208 | .036105 |
| 58 | .091976 | .082295 | .073648 | .065924 | .059023 | .052855 | .047342 | .042412 | .038004 | .034061 |
| 59 | .088268 | .078826 | .070409 | .062905 | .056212 | .050243 | .044916 | .040163 | .035921 | .032133 |
| 60 | .084710 | .075504 | .067313 | .060024 | .053536 | .047759 | .042615 | .038033 | .033952 | .030314 |

**TABLE B**
**TERM CERTAIN REMAINDER FACTORS**
**APPLICABLE AFTER APRIL 30, 1989**

**INTEREST RATE**

| YEARS | 6.2% | 6.4% | 6.6% | 6.8% | 7.0% | 7.2% | 7.4% | 7.6% | 7.8% | 8.0% |
|---|---|---|---|---|---|---|---|---|---|---|
| 1 | .941620 | .939850 | .938086 | .936330 | .934579 | .932836 | .931099 | .929368 | .927644 | .925926 |
| 2 | .886647 | .883317 | .880006 | .876713 | .873439 | .870183 | .866945 | .863725 | .860523 | .857339 |
| 3 | .834885 | .830185 | .825521 | .820892 | .816298 | .811738 | .807211 | .802718 | .798259 | .793832 |
| 4 | .786144 | .780249 | .774410 | .768626 | .762895 | .757218 | .751593 | .746021 | .740500 | .735030 |
| 5 | .740248 | .733317 | .726464 | .719687 | .712986 | .706360 | .699808 | .693328 | .686920 | .680583 |
| 6 | .697032 | .689208 | .681486 | .673864 | .666342 | .658918 | .651590 | .644357 | .637217 | .630170 |
| 7 | .656339 | .647752 | .639292 | .630959 | .622750 | .614662 | .606694 | .598845 | .591111 | .583490 |
| 8 | .618022 | .608789 | .599711 | .590786 | .582009 | .573379 | .564892 | .556547 | .548340 | .540269 |
| 9 | .581942 | .572170 | .562581 | .553170 | .543934 | .534868 | .525971 | .517237 | .508664 | .500249 |
| 10 | .547968 | .537754 | .527750 | .517950 | .508349 | .498944 | .489731 | .480704 | .471859 | .463193 |
| 11 | .515977 | .505408 | .495075 | .484972 | .475093 | .465433 | .455987 | .446750 | .437717 | .428883 |
| 12 | .485854 | .475007 | .464423 | .454093 | .444012 | .434173 | .424569 | .415196 | .406046 | .397114 |
| 13 | .457490 | .446436 | .435669 | .425181 | .414964 | .405012 | .395316 | .385870 | .376666 | .367698 |
| 14 | .430781 | .419582 | .408695 | .398109 | .387817 | .377810 | .368078 | .358615 | .349412 | .340461 |
| 15 | .405632 | .394344 | .383391 | .372762 | .362446 | .352434 | .342717 | .333285 | .324130 | .315242 |
| 16 | .381951 | .370624 | .359654 | .349028 | .338735 | .328763 | .319103 | .309745 | .300677 | .291890 |
| 17 | .359653 | .348331 | .337386 | .326805 | .316574 | .306682 | .297117 | .287867 | .278921 | .270269 |
| 18 | .338656 | .327379 | .316498 | .305997 | .295864 | .286084 | .276645 | .267534 | .258739 | .250249 |
| 19 | .318885 | .307687 | .296902 | .286514 | .276508 | .266870 | .257584 | .248638 | .240018 | .231712 |
| 20 | .300268 | .289179 | .278520 | .268272 | .258419 | .248946 | .239836 | .231076 | .222651 | .214548 |
| 21 | .282739 | .271785 | .261276 | .251191 | .241513 | .232225 | .223311 | .214755 | .206541 | .198656 |
| 22 | .266232 | .255437 | .245099 | .235197 | .225713 | .216628 | .207925 | .199586 | .191596 | .183941 |
| 23 | .250689 | .240073 | .229924 | .220222 | .210947 | .202078 | .193598 | .185489 | .177733 | .170315 |
| 24 | .236054 | .225632 | .215689 | .206201 | .197147 | .188506 | .180259 | .172387 | .164873 | .157699 |
| 25 | .222273 | .212060 | .202334 | .193072 | .184249 | .175845 | .167839 | .160211 | .152943 | .146018 |
| 26 | .209297 | .199305 | .189807 | .180779 | .172195 | .164035 | .156275 | .148895 | .141877 | .135202 |
| 27 | .197078 | .187317 | .178056 | .169269 | .160930 | .153017 | .145507 | .138379 | .131611 | .125187 |
| 28 | .185572 | .176049 | .167031 | .158491 | .150402 | .142740 | .135482 | .128605 | .122088 | .115914 |
| 29 | .174739 | .165460 | .156690 | .148400 | .140563 | .133153 | .126147 | .119521 | .113255 | .107328 |
| 30 | .164537 | .155507 | .146989 | .138951 | .131367 | .124210 | .117455 | .111079 | .105060 | .099377 |
| 31 | .154932 | .146154 | .137888 | .130104 | .122773 | .115868 | .109362 | .103233 | .097458 | .092016 |
| 32 | .145887 | .137362 | .129351 | .121820 | .114741 | .108085 | .101827 | .095942 | .090406 | .085200 |
| 33 | .137370 | .129100 | .121342 | .114064 | .107235 | .100826 | .094811 | .089165 | .083865 | .078889 |
| 34 | .129350 | .121335 | .113830 | .106802 | .100219 | .094054 | .088278 | .082867 | .077797 | .073045 |
| 35 | .121798 | .114036 | .106782 | .100001 | .093663 | .087737 | .082196 | .077014 | .072168 | .067635 |
| 36 | .114688 | .107177 | .100171 | .093634 | .087535 | .081844 | .076532 | .071574 | .066946 | .062625 |
| 37 | .107992 | .100730 | .093969 | .087673 | .081809 | .076347 | .071259 | .066519 | .062102 | .057986 |
| 38 | .101688 | .094671 | .088151 | .082090 | .076457 | .071219 | .066349 | .061821 | .057609 | .053690 |
| 39 | .095751 | .088977 | .082693 | .076864 | .071455 | .066436 | .061778 | .057454 | .053440 | .049713 |
| 40 | .090161 | .083625 | .077573 | .071970 | .066780 | .061974 | .057521 | .053396 | .049573 | .046031 |
| 41 | .084897 | .078595 | .072770 | .067387 | .062412 | .057811 | .053558 | .049625 | .045987 | .042621 |
| 42 | .079941 | .073867 | .068265 | .063097 | .058329 | .053929 | .049868 | .046120 | .042659 | .039464 |
| 43 | .075274 | .069424 | .064038 | .059079 | .054513 | .050307 | .046432 | .042862 | .039572 | .036541 |
| 44 | .070880 | .065248 | .060074 | .055318 | .050946 | .046928 | .043233 | .039835 | .036709 | .033834 |
| 45 | .066742 | .061323 | .056354 | .051796 | .047613 | .043776 | .040254 | .037021 | .034053 | .031328 |
| 46 | .062845 | .057635 | .052865 | .048498 | .044499 | .040836 | .037480 | .034406 | .031589 | .029007 |
| 47 | .059176 | .054168 | .049592 | .045410 | .041587 | .038093 | .034898 | .031976 | .029303 | .026859 |
| 48 | .055722 | .050910 | .046522 | .042519 | .038867 | .035535 | .032493 | .029717 | .027183 | .024869 |
| 49 | .052469 | .047848 | .043641 | .039812 | .036324 | .033148 | .030255 | .027618 | .025216 | .023027 |
| 50 | .049405 | .044970 | .040939 | .037277 | .033948 | .030922 | .028170 | .025668 | .023392 | .021321 |
| 51 | .046521 | .042265 | .038405 | .034903 | .031727 | .028845 | .026229 | .023855 | .021699 | .019742 |
| 52 | .043805 | .039722 | .036027 | .032681 | .029651 | .026907 | .024422 | .022170 | .020129 | .018280 |
| 53 | .041248 | .037333 | .033796 | .030600 | .027711 | .025100 | .022739 | .020604 | .018673 | .016925 |
| 54 | .038840 | .035087 | .031704 | .028652 | .025899 | .023414 | .021172 | .019149 | .017322 | .015672 |
| 55 | .036572 | .032977 | .029741 | .026828 | .024204 | .021842 | .019714 | .017796 | .016068 | .014511 |
| 56 | .034437 | .030993 | .027900 | .025119 | .022621 | .020375 | .018355 | .016539 | .014906 | .013436 |
| 57 | .032427 | .029129 | .026172 | .023520 | .021141 | .019006 | .017091 | .015371 | .013827 | .012441 |
| 58 | .030534 | .027377 | .024552 | .022023 | .019758 | .017730 | .015913 | .014285 | .012827 | .011519 |
| 59 | .028751 | .025730 | .023032 | .020620 | .018465 | .016539 | .014817 | .013276 | .011899 | .010666 |
| 60 | .027073 | .024183 | .021606 | .019307 | .017257 | .015428 | .013796 | .012339 | .011038 | .009876 |

**TABLE B**
**TERM CERTAIN REMAINDER FACTORS**
**APPLICABLE AFTER APRIL 30, 1989**

**INTEREST RATE**

| YEARS | 8.2% | 8.4% | 8.6% | 8.8% | 9.0% | 9.2% | 9.4% | 9.6% | 9.8% | 10.0% |
|---|---|---|---|---|---|---|---|---|---|---|
| 1 | .924214 | .922509 | .920810 | .919118 | .917431 | .915751 | .914077 | .912409 | .910747 | .909091 |
| 2 | .854172 | .851023 | .847892 | .844777 | .841680 | .838600 | .835536 | .832490 | .829460 | .826446 |
| 3 | .789438 | .785077 | .780747 | .776450 | .772183 | .767948 | .763744 | .759571 | .755428 | .751315 |
| 4 | .729610 | .724241 | .718920 | .713649 | .708425 | .703250 | .698121 | .693039 | .688003 | .683013 |
| 5 | .674316 | .668119 | .661989 | .655927 | .649931 | .644001 | .638136 | .632335 | .626597 | .620921 |
| 6 | .623213 | .616346 | .609566 | .602874 | .596267 | .589745 | .583305 | .576948 | .570671 | .564474 |
| 7 | .575982 | .568585 | .561295 | .554112 | .547034 | .540059 | .533186 | .526412 | .519737 | .513158 |
| 8 | .532331 | .524524 | .516846 | .509294 | .501866 | .494560 | .487373 | .480303 | .473349 | .466507 |
| 9 | .491988 | .483879 | .475917 | .468101 | .460428 | .452894 | .445496 | .438233 | .431101 | .424098 |
| 10 | .454703 | .446383 | .438230 | .430240 | .422411 | .414738 | .407218 | .399848 | .392624 | .385543 |
| 11 | .420243 | .411792 | .403526 | .395441 | .387533 | .379797 | .372228 | .364824 | .357581 | .350494 |
| 12 | .388394 | .379882 | .371571 | .363457 | .355535 | .347799 | .340245 | .332869 | .325666 | .318631 |
| 13 | .358960 | .350445 | .342147 | .334060 | .326179 | .318497 | .311010 | .303713 | .296599 | .289664 |
| 14 | .331756 | .323288 | .315052 | .307040 | .299246 | .291664 | .284287 | .277110 | .270127 | .263331 |
| 15 | .306613 | .298236 | .290103 | .282206 | .274538 | .267092 | .259860 | .252838 | .246017 | .239392 |
| 16 | .283376 | .275126 | .267130 | .259381 | .251870 | .244589 | .237532 | .230691 | .224059 | .217629 |
| 17 | .261901 | .253806 | .245976 | .238401 | .231073 | .223983 | .217123 | .210485 | .204061 | .197845 |
| 18 | .242052 | .234139 | .226497 | .219119 | .211994 | .205113 | .198467 | .192048 | .185848 | .179859 |
| 19 | .223708 | .215995 | .208561 | .201396 | .194490 | .187832 | .181414 | .175226 | .169260 | .163508 |
| 20 | .206754 | .199257 | .192045 | .185107 | .178431 | .172007 | .165826 | .159878 | .154153 | .148644 |
| 21 | .191085 | .183817 | .176837 | .170135 | .163698 | .157516 | .151578 | .145874 | .140395 | .135131 |
| 22 | .176604 | .169573 | .162834 | .156374 | .150182 | .144245 | .138554 | .133097 | .127864 | .122846 |
| 23 | .163220 | .156432 | .149939 | .143726 | .137781 | .132093 | .126649 | .121439 | .116452 | .111678 |
| 24 | .150850 | .144310 | .138065 | .132101 | .126405 | .120964 | .115767 | .110802 | .106058 | .101526 |
| 25 | .139418 | .133128 | .127132 | .121416 | .115968 | .110773 | .105820 | .101097 | .096592 | .092296 |
| 26 | .128852 | .122811 | .117064 | .111596 | .106393 | .101441 | .096727 | .092241 | .087971 | .083905 |
| 27 | .119087 | .113295 | .107794 | .102570 | .097608 | .092894 | .088416 | .084162 | .080119 | .076278 |
| 28 | .110062 | .104515 | .099258 | .094274 | .089548 | .085068 | .080819 | .076790 | .072968 | .069343 |
| 29 | .101721 | .096416 | .091398 | .086649 | .082155 | .077901 | .073875 | .070064 | .066456 | .063039 |
| 30 | .094012 | .088945 | .084160 | .079640 | .075371 | .071338 | .067527 | .063927 | .060524 | .057309 |
| 31 | .086887 | .082053 | .077495 | .073199 | .069148 | .065328 | .061725 | .058327 | .055122 | .052099 |
| 32 | .080302 | .075694 | .071358 | .067278 | .063438 | .059824 | .056422 | .053218 | .050202 | .047362 |
| 33 | .074216 | .069829 | .065708 | .061837 | .058200 | .054784 | .051574 | .048557 | .045722 | .043057 |
| 34 | .068592 | .064418 | .060504 | .056835 | .053395 | .050168 | .047142 | .044304 | .041641 | .039143 |
| 35 | .063394 | .059426 | .055713 | .052238 | .048986 | .045942 | .043092 | .040423 | .037924 | .035584 |
| 36 | .058589 | .054821 | .051301 | .048013 | .044941 | .042071 | .039389 | .036882 | .034539 | .032349 |
| 37 | .054149 | .050573 | .047239 | .044130 | .041231 | .038527 | .036005 | .033652 | .031457 | .029408 |
| 38 | .050045 | .046654 | .043498 | .040560 | .037826 | .035281 | .032911 | .030704 | .028649 | .026735 |
| 39 | .046253 | .043039 | .040053 | .037280 | .034703 | .032309 | .030083 | .028015 | .026092 | .024304 |
| 40 | .042747 | .039703 | .036881 | .034264 | .031838 | .029587 | .027498 | .025561 | .023763 | .022095 |
| 41 | .039508 | .036627 | .033961 | .031493 | .029209 | .027094 | .025136 | .023322 | .021642 | .020086 |
| 42 | .036514 | .033789 | .031271 | .028946 | .026797 | .024811 | .022976 | .021279 | .019711 | .018260 |
| 43 | .033746 | .031170 | .028795 | .026605 | .024584 | .022721 | .020807 | .019197 | .017715 | .016600 |
| 44 | .031189 | .028755 | .026515 | .024453 | .022555 | .020807 | .019197 | .017715 | .016349 | .015091 |
| 45 | .028825 | .026527 | .024415 | .022475 | .020692 | .019054 | .017548 | .016163 | .014890 | .013719 |
| 46 | .026641 | .024471 | .022482 | .020657 | .018984 | .017449 | .016040 | .014747 | .013561 | .012472 |
| 47 | .024622 | .022575 | .020701 | .018986 | .017416 | .015978 | .014662 | .013456 | .012351 | .011338 |
| 48 | .022756 | .020825 | .019062 | .017451 | .015978 | .014632 | .013402 | .012277 | .011248 | .010307 |
| 49 | .021031 | .019212 | .017552 | .016039 | .014659 | .013400 | .012250 | .011202 | .010244 | .009370 |
| 50 | .019437 | .017723 | .016163 | .014742 | .013449 | .012271 | .011198 | .010221 | .009330 | .008519 |
| 51 | .017964 | .016350 | .014883 | .013550 | .012338 | .011237 | .010236 | .009325 | .008497 | .007744 |
| 52 | .016603 | .015083 | .013704 | .012454 | .011319 | .010290 | .009356 | .008508 | .007739 | .007040 |
| 53 | .015345 | .013914 | .012619 | .011446 | .010385 | .009423 | .008552 | .007763 | .007048 | .006400 |
| 54 | .014182 | .012836 | .011620 | .010521 | .009527 | .008629 | .007817 | .007083 | .006419 | .005818 |
| 55 | .013107 | .011841 | .010699 | .009670 | .008741 | .007902 | .007146 | .006463 | .005846 | .005289 |
| 56 | .012114 | .010923 | .009852 | .008888 | .008019 | .007237 | .006532 | .005897 | .005324 | .004809 |
| 57 | .011196 | .010077 | .009072 | .008169 | .007357 | .006627 | .005971 | .005380 | .004849 | .004371 |
| 58 | .010347 | .009296 | .008354 | .007508 | .006749 | .006069 | .005458 | .004909 | .004416 | .003974 |
| 59 | .009563 | .008576 | .007692 | .006901 | .006192 | .005557 | .004989 | .004479 | .004022 | .003613 |
| 60 | .008838 | .007911 | .007083 | .006343 | .005681 | .005089 | .004560 | .004087 | .003663 | .003284 |

**TABLE B**
**TERM CERTAIN REMAINDER FACTORS**
**APPLICABLE AFTER APRIL 30, 1989**

**INTEREST RATE**

| YEARS | 10.2% | 10.4% | 10.6% | 10.8% | 11.0% | 11.2% | 11.4% | 11.6% | 11.8% | 12.0% |
|---|---|---|---|---|---|---|---|---|---|---|
| 1 | .907441 | .905797 | .904159 | .902527 | .900901 | .899281 | .897666 | .896057 | .894454 | .892857 |
| 2 | .823449 | .820468 | .817504 | .814555 | .811622 | .808706 | .805804 | .802919 | .800049 | .797194 |
| 3 | .747232 | .743178 | .739153 | .735158 | .731191 | .727253 | .723343 | .719461 | .715607 | .711780 |
| 4 | .678069 | .673168 | .668312 | .663500 | .658731 | .654005 | .649321 | .644679 | .640078 | .635518 |
| 5 | .615307 | .609754 | .604261 | .598827 | .593451 | .588134 | .582873 | .577669 | .572520 | .567427 |
| 6 | .558355 | .552313 | .546348 | .540457 | .534641 | .528897 | .523225 | .517625 | .512093 | .506631 |
| 7 | .506674 | .500284 | .493985 | .487777 | .481658 | .475627 | .469682 | .463821 | .458044 | .452349 |
| 8 | .459777 | .453156 | .446641 | .440232 | .433926 | .427722 | .421617 | .415610 | .409700 | .403883 |
| 9 | .417221 | .410467 | .403835 | .397322 | .390925 | .384642 | .378472 | .372411 | .366458 | .360610 |
| 10 | .378603 | .371800 | .365131 | .358593 | .352184 | .345901 | .339741 | .333701 | .327780 | .321973 |
| 11 | .343560 | .336775 | .330137 | .323640 | .317283 | .311062 | .304974 | .299016 | .293184 | .287476 |
| 12 | .311760 | .305050 | .298496 | .292094 | .285841 | .279732 | .273765 | .267935 | .262240 | .256675 |
| 13 | .282904 | .276313 | .269888 | .263623 | .257514 | .251558 | .245749 | .240085 | .234561 | .229174 |
| 14 | .256719 | .250284 | .244022 | .237927 | .231995 | .226221 | .220601 | .215130 | .209804 | .204620 |
| 15 | .232957 | .226706 | .220634 | .214735 | .209004 | .203436 | .198026 | .192769 | .187661 | .182696 |
| 16 | .211395 | .205350 | .199489 | .193804 | .188292 | .182946 | .177761 | .172732 | .167854 | .163122 |
| 17 | .191828 | .186005 | .180369 | .174914 | .169633 | .164520 | .159570 | .154778 | .150138 | .145644 |
| 18 | .174073 | .168483 | .163083 | .157864 | .152822 | .147950 | .143241 | .138690 | .134291 | .130040 |
| 19 | .157961 | .152612 | .147453 | .142477 | .137678 | .133048 | .128582 | .124274 | .120117 | .116107 |
| 20 | .143340 | .138235 | .133321 | .128589 | .124034 | .119648 | .115424 | .111357 | .107439 | .103667 |
| 21 | .130073 | .125213 | .120543 | .116055 | .111742 | .107597 | .103612 | .099782 | .096100 | .092560 |
| 22 | .118033 | .113418 | .108990 | .104743 | .100669 | .096760 | .093009 | .089410 | .085957 | .082643 |
| 23 | .107108 | .102733 | .098544 | .094533 | .090693 | .087014 | .083491 | .080117 | .076884 | .073788 |
| 24 | .097195 | .093056 | .089100 | .085319 | .081705 | .078250 | .074947 | .071789 | .068770 | .065882 |
| 25 | .088198 | .084289 | .080560 | .077003 | .073608 | .070369 | .067278 | .064327 | .061511 | .058823 |
| 26 | .080035 | .076349 | .072839 | .069497 | .066314 | .063281 | .060393 | .057641 | .055019 | .052521 |
| 27 | .072627 | .069157 | .065858 | .062723 | .059742 | .056908 | .054213 | .051650 | .049212 | .046894 |
| 28 | .065905 | .062642 | .059547 | .056609 | .053822 | .051176 | .048665 | .046281 | .044018 | .041869 |
| 29 | .059804 | .056741 | .053840 | .051091 | .048488 | .046022 | .043685 | .041470 | .039372 | .037383 |
| 30 | .054269 | .051396 | .048680 | .046111 | .043683 | .041386 | .039214 | .037160 | .035216 | .033378 |
| 31 | .049246 | .046554 | .044014 | .041617 | .039354 | .037218 | .035201 | .033297 | .031500 | .029802 |
| 32 | .044688 | .042169 | .039796 | .037560 | .035454 | .033469 | .031599 | .029836 | .028175 | .026609 |
| 33 | .040552 | .038196 | .035982 | .033899 | .031940 | .030098 | .028365 | .026735 | .025201 | .023758 |
| 34 | .036798 | .034598 | .032533 | .030595 | .028775 | .027067 | .025463 | .023956 | .022541 | .021212 |
| 35 | .033392 | .031339 | .029415 | .027613 | .025924 | .024341 | .022857 | .021466 | .020162 | .018940 |
| 36 | .030301 | .028387 | .026596 | .024921 | .023355 | .021889 | .020518 | .019235 | .018034 | .016910 |
| 37 | .027497 | .025712 | .024047 | .022492 | .021040 | .019684 | .018418 | .017236 | .016131 | .015098 |
| 38 | .024952 | .023290 | .021742 | .020300 | .018955 | .017702 | .016533 | .015444 | .014428 | .013481 |
| 39 | .022642 | .021096 | .019658 | .018321 | .017077 | .015919 | .014841 | .013839 | .012905 | .012036 |
| 40 | .020546 | .019109 | .017774 | .016535 | .015384 | .014316 | .013323 | .012400 | .011543 | .010747 |
| 41 | .018645 | .017309 | .016071 | .014923 | .013860 | .012874 | .011959 | .011111 | .010325 | .009595 |
| 42 | .016919 | .015678 | .014531 | .013469 | .012486 | .011577 | .010735 | .009956 | .009235 | .008567 |
| 43 | .015353 | .014201 | .013138 | .012156 | .011249 | .010411 | .009637 | .008922 | .008260 | .007649 |
| 44 | .013932 | .012864 | .011879 | .010971 | .010134 | .009362 | .008651 | .007994 | .007389 | .006830 |
| 45 | .012642 | .011652 | .010740 | .009902 | .009130 | .008419 | .007765 | .007163 | .006609 | .006098 |
| 46 | .011472 | .010554 | .009711 | .008937 | .008225 | .007571 | .006971 | .006419 | .005911 | .005445 |
| 47 | .010410 | .009560 | .008780 | .008065 | .007410 | .006809 | .006257 | .005752 | .005287 | .004861 |
| 48 | .009447 | .008659 | .007939 | .007279 | .006676 | .006123 | .005617 | .005154 | .004729 | .004340 |
| 49 | .008572 | .007844 | .007178 | .006570 | .006014 | .005506 | .005042 | .004618 | .004230 | .003875 |
| 50 | .007779 | .007105 | .006490 | .005929 | .005418 | .004952 | .004526 | .004138 | .003784 | .003460 |
| 51 | .007059 | .006435 | .005868 | .005351 | .004881 | .004453 | .004063 | .003708 | .003384 | .003089 |
| 52 | .006406 | .005829 | .005306 | .004830 | .004397 | .004005 | .003647 | .003322 | .003027 | .002758 |
| 53 | .005813 | .005280 | .004797 | .004359 | .003962 | .003601 | .003274 | .002977 | .002708 | .002463 |
| 54 | .005275 | .004783 | .004337 | .003934 | .003569 | .003238 | .002939 | .002668 | .002422 | .002199 |
| 55 | .004786 | .004332 | .003922 | .003551 | .003215 | .002912 | .002638 | .002390 | .002166 | .001963 |
| 56 | .004343 | .003924 | .003546 | .003205 | .002897 | .002619 | .002368 | .002142 | .001938 | .001753 |
| 57 | .003941 | .003554 | .003206 | .002892 | .002610 | .002355 | .002126 | .001919 | .001733 | .001565 |
| 58 | .003577 | .003220 | .002899 | .002610 | .002351 | .002118 | .001908 | .001720 | .001550 | .001398 |
| 59 | .003246 | .002916 | .002621 | .002356 | .002118 | .001905 | .001713 | .001541 | .001387 | .001248 |
| 60 | .002945 | .002642 | .002370 | .002126 | .001908 | .001713 | .001538 | .001381 | .001240 | .001114 |

Reg. § 20.2031-7(d)(6)

## TABLE B
### TERM CERTAIN REMAINDER FACTORS
### APPLICABLE AFTER APRIL 30, 1989

**INTEREST RATE**

| YEARS | 12.2% | 12.4% | 12.6% | 12.8% | 13.0% | 13.2% | 13.4% | 13.6% | 13.8% | 14.0% |
|---|---|---|---|---|---|---|---|---|---|---|
| 1 | .891266 | .889680 | .888099 | .886525 | .884956 | .883392 | .881834 | .880282 | .878735 | .877193 |
| 2 | .794354 | .791530 | .788721 | .785926 | .783147 | .780382 | .777632 | .774896 | .772175 | .769468 |
| 3 | .707981 | .704208 | .700462 | .696743 | .693050 | .689383 | .685742 | .682127 | .678536 | .674972 |
| 4 | .630999 | .626520 | .622080 | .617680 | .613319 | .608996 | .604711 | .600464 | .596254 | .592080 |
| 5 | .562388 | .557402 | .552469 | .547589 | .542760 | .537982 | .533255 | .528577 | .523949 | .519369 |
| 6 | .501237 | .495909 | .490648 | .485451 | .480319 | .475249 | .470242 | .465297 | .460412 | .455587 |
| 7 | .446735 | .441200 | .435744 | .430364 | .425061 | .419831 | .414676 | .409592 | .404580 | .399637 |
| 8 | .398160 | .392527 | .386984 | .381529 | .376160 | .370876 | .365675 | .360557 | .355518 | .350559 |
| 9 | .354866 | .349223 | .343680 | .338235 | .332885 | .327629 | .322465 | .317391 | .312406 | .307508 |
| 10 | .316280 | .310697 | .305222 | .299853 | .294588 | .289425 | .284361 | .279394 | .274522 | .269744 |
| 11 | .281889 | .276421 | .271068 | .265827 | .260698 | .255676 | .250759 | .245945 | .241232 | .236617 |
| 12 | .251238 | .245926 | .240735 | .235663 | .230706 | .225862 | .221128 | .216501 | .211979 | .207559 |
| 13 | .223920 | .218795 | .213797 | .208921 | .204165 | .199525 | .194998 | .190582 | .186273 | .182069 |
| 14 | .199572 | .194658 | .189873 | .185213 | .180677 | .176258 | .171956 | .167766 | .163685 | .159710 |
| 15 | .177872 | .173183 | .168626 | .164196 | .159891 | .155705 | .151637 | .147681 | .143835 | .140096 |
| 16 | .158531 | .154077 | .149757 | .145564 | .141496 | .137549 | .133718 | .130001 | .126393 | .122892 |
| 17 | .141293 | .137080 | .132999 | .129046 | .125218 | .121510 | .117917 | .114438 | .111066 | .107800 |
| 18 | .125930 | .121957 | .118116 | .114403 | .110812 | .107341 | .103984 | .100737 | .097598 | .094561 |
| 19 | .112237 | .108503 | .104899 | .101421 | .098064 | .094824 | .091696 | .088677 | .085762 | .082948 |
| 20 | .100033 | .096533 | .093161 | .089912 | .086782 | .083767 | .080861 | .078061 | .075362 | .072762 |
| 21 | .089156 | .085883 | .082736 | .079709 | .076798 | .073999 | .071306 | .068716 | .066224 | .063826 |
| 22 | .079462 | .076408 | .073478 | .070664 | .067963 | .065370 | .062880 | .060489 | .058193 | .055988 |
| 23 | .070821 | .067979 | .065255 | .062646 | .060144 | .057747 | .055450 | .053247 | .051136 | .049112 |
| 24 | .063121 | .060480 | .057953 | .055537 | .053225 | .051014 | .048898 | .046873 | .044935 | .043081 |
| 25 | .056257 | .053807 | .051468 | .049235 | .047102 | .045065 | .043119 | .041261 | .039486 | .037790 |
| 26 | .050140 | .047871 | .045709 | .043648 | .041683 | .039810 | .038024 | .036321 | .034698 | .033149 |
| 27 | .044688 | .042590 | .040594 | .038695 | .036888 | .035168 | .033531 | .031973 | .030490 | .029078 |
| 28 | .039829 | .037892 | .036052 | .034304 | .032644 | .031067 | .029569 | .028145 | .026793 | .025507 |
| 29 | .035498 | .033711 | .032017 | .030411 | .028889 | .027444 | .026075 | .024776 | .023544 | .022375 |
| 30 | .031638 | .029992 | .028435 | .026960 | .025565 | .024244 | .022994 | .021810 | .020689 | .019627 |
| 31 | .028198 | .026684 | .025253 | .023901 | .022624 | .021417 | .020277 | .019199 | .018180 | .017217 |
| 32 | .025132 | .023740 | .022427 | .021189 | .020021 | .018920 | .017881 | .016900 | .015975 | .015102 |
| 33 | .022399 | .021121 | .019917 | .018785 | .017718 | .016714 | .015768 | .014877 | .014038 | .013248 |
| 34 | .019964 | .018791 | .017689 | .016653 | .015680 | .014765 | .013905 | .013096 | .012336 | .011621 |
| 35 | .017793 | .016718 | .015709 | .014763 | .013876 | .013043 | .012261 | .011528 | .010840 | .010194 |
| 36 | .015858 | .014873 | .013951 | .013088 | .012279 | .011522 | .010813 | .010148 | .009525 | .008942 |
| 37 | .014134 | .013233 | .012390 | .011603 | .010867 | .010178 | .009535 | .008933 | .008370 | .007844 |
| 38 | .012597 | .011773 | .011004 | .010286 | .009617 | .008992 | .008408 | .007864 | .007355 | .006880 |
| 39 | .011227 | .010474 | .009772 | .009119 | .008510 | .007943 | .007415 | .006922 | .006463 | .006035 |
| 40 | .010007 | .009319 | .008679 | .008084 | .007531 | .007017 | .006538 | .006093 | .005679 | .005294 |
| 41 | .008919 | .008291 | .007708 | .007167 | .006665 | .006199 | .005766 | .005364 | .004991 | .004644 |
| 42 | .007949 | .007376 | .006845 | .006354 | .005898 | .005476 | .005085 | .004722 | .004386 | .004074 |
| 43 | .007084 | .006562 | .006079 | .005633 | .005219 | .004837 | .004484 | .004157 | .003854 | .003573 |
| 44 | .006314 | .005838 | .005399 | .004993 | .004619 | .004273 | .003954 | .003659 | .003386 | .003135 |
| 45 | .005628 | .005194 | .004795 | .004427 | .004088 | .003775 | .003487 | .003221 | .002976 | .002750 |
| 46 | .005016 | .004621 | .004258 | .003924 | .003617 | .003335 | .003075 | .002835 | .002615 | .002412 |
| 47 | .004470 | .004111 | .003782 | .003479 | .003201 | .002946 | .002711 | .002496 | .002298 | .002116 |
| 48 | .003984 | .003658 | .003359 | .003084 | .002833 | .002602 | .002391 | .002197 | .002019 | .001856 |
| 49 | .003551 | .003254 | .002983 | .002734 | .002507 | .002299 | .002108 | .001934 | .001774 | .001628 |
| 50 | .003165 | .002895 | .002649 | .002424 | .002219 | .002031 | .001859 | .001702 | .001559 | .001428 |
| 51 | .002821 | .002576 | .002353 | .002149 | .001963 | .001794 | .001640 | .001499 | .001370 | .001253 |
| 52 | .002514 | .002292 | .002089 | .001905 | .001737 | .001585 | .001446 | .001319 | .001204 | .001099 |
| 53 | .002241 | .002039 | .001856 | .001689 | .001538 | .001400 | .001275 | .001161 | .001058 | .000964 |
| 54 | .001997 | .001814 | .001648 | .001497 | .001361 | .001237 | .001124 | .001022 | .000930 | .000846 |
| 55 | .001780 | .001614 | .001463 | .001327 | .001204 | .001093 | .000991 | .000900 | .000817 | .000742 |
| 56 | .001586 | .001436 | .001300 | .001177 | .001066 | .000965 | .000874 | .000792 | .000718 | .000651 |
| 57 | .001414 | .001277 | .001154 | .001043 | .000943 | .000853 | .000771 | .000697 | .000631 | .000571 |
| 58 | .001260 | .001136 | .001025 | .000925 | .000835 | .000753 | .000680 | .000614 | .000554 | .000501 |
| 59 | .001123 | .001011 | .000910 | .000820 | .000739 | .000665 | .000600 | .000540 | .000487 | .000439 |
| 60 | .001001 | .000900 | .000809 | .000727 | .000654 | .000588 | .000529 | .000476 | .000428 | .000385 |

**TABLE J**
**ADJUSTMENT FACTORS FOR TERM CERTAIN ANNUITIES**
**PAYABLE AT THE BEGINNING OF EACH INTERVAL**
**APPLICABLE AFTER APRIL 30, 1989**
**FREQUENCY OF PAYMENTS**

| INTEREST RATE | ANNUALLY | SEMI ANNUALLY | QUARTERLY | MONTHLY | WEEKLY |
|---|---|---|---|---|---|
| 4.2 | 1.0420 | 1.0314 | 1.0261 | 1.0226 | 1.0213 |
| 4.4 | 1.0440 | 1.0329 | 1.0274 | 1.0237 | 1.0223 |
| 4.6 | 1.0460 | 1.0344 | 1.0286 | 1.0247 | 1.0233 |
| 4.8 | 1.0480 | 1.0359 | 1.0298 | 1.0258 | 1.0243 |
| 5.0 | 1.0500 | 1.0373 | 1.0311 | 1.0269 | 1.0253 |
| 5.2 | 1.0520 | 1.0388 | 1.0323 | 1.0279 | 1.0263 |
| 5.4 | 1.0540 | 1.0403 | 1.0335 | 1.0290 | 1.0273 |
| 5.6 | 1.0560 | 1.0418 | 1.0348 | 1.0301 | 1.0283 |
| 5.8 | 1.0580 | 1.0433 | 1.0360 | 1.0311 | 1.0293 |
| 6.0 | 1.0600 | 1.0448 | 1.0372 | 1.0322 | 1.0303 |
| 6.2 | 1.0620 | 1.0463 | 1.0385 | 1.0333 | 1.0313 |
| 6.4 | 1.0640 | 1.0478 | 1.0397 | 1.0343 | 1.0323 |
| 6.6 | 1.0660 | 1.0492 | 1.0409 | 1.0354 | 1.0333 |
| 6.8 | 1.0680 | 1.0507 | 1.0422 | 1.0365 | 1.0343 |
| 7.0 | 1.0700 | 1.0522 | 1.0434 | 1.0375 | 1.0353 |
| 7.2 | 1.0720 | 1.0537 | 1.0446 | 1.0386 | 1.0363 |
| 7.4 | 1.0740 | 1.0552 | 1.0458 | 1.0396 | 1.0373 |
| 7.6 | 1.0760 | 1.0567 | 1.0471 | 1.0407 | 1.0383 |
| 7.8 | 1.0780 | 1.0581 | 1.0483 | 1.0418 | 1.0393 |
| 8.0 | 1.0800 | 1.0596 | 1.0495 | 1.0428 | 1.0403 |
| 8.2 | 1.0820 | 1.0611 | 1.0507 | 1.0439 | 1.0413 |
| 8.4 | 1.0840 | 1.0626 | 1.0520 | 1.0449 | 1.0422 |
| 8.6 | 1.0860 | 1.0641 | 1.0532 | 1.0460 | 1.0432 |
| 8.8 | 1.0880 | 1.0655 | 1.0544 | 1.0471 | 1.0442 |
| 9.0 | 1.0900 | 1.0670 | 1.0556 | 1.0481 | 1.0452 |
| 9.2 | 1.0920 | 1.0685 | 1.0569 | 1.0492 | 1.0462 |
| 9.4 | 1.0940 | 1.0700 | 1.0581 | 1.0502 | 1.0472 |
| 9.6 | 1.0960 | 1.0715 | 1.0593 | 1.0513 | 1.0482 |
| 9.8 | 1.0980 | 1.0729 | 1.0605 | 1.0523 | 1.0492 |
| 10.0 | 1.1000 | 1.0744 | 1.0618 | 1.0534 | 1.0502 |
| 10.2 | 1.1020 | 1.0759 | 1.0630 | 1.0544 | 1.0512 |
| 10.4 | 1.1040 | 1.0774 | 1.0642 | 1.0555 | 1.0521 |
| 10.6 | 1.1060 | 1.0788 | 1.0654 | 1.0565 | 1.0531 |
| 10.8 | 1.1080 | 1.0803 | 1.0666 | 1.0576 | 1.0541 |
| 11.0 | 1.1100 | 1.0818 | 1.0679 | 1.0586 | 1.0551 |
| 11.2 | 1.1120 | 1.0833 | 1.0691 | 1.0597 | 1.0561 |
| 11.4 | 1.1140 | 1.0847 | 1.0703 | 1.0607 | 1.0571 |
| 11.6 | 1.1160 | 1.0862 | 1.0715 | 1.0618 | 1.0581 |
| 11.8 | 1.1180 | 1.0877 | 1.0727 | 1.0628 | 1.0590 |
| 12.0 | 1.1200 | 1.0892 | 1.0739 | 1.0639 | 1.0600 |
| 12.2 | 1.1220 | 1.0906 | 1.0752 | 1.0649 | 1.0610 |
| 12.4 | 1.1240 | 1.0921 | 1.0764 | 1.0660 | 1.0620 |
| 12.6 | 1.1260 | 1.0936 | 1.0776 | 1.0670 | 1.0630 |
| 12.8 | 1.1280 | 1.0950 | 1.0788 | 1.0681 | 1.0639 |
| 13.0 | 1.1300 | 1.0965 | 1.0800 | 1.0691 | 1.0649 |
| 13.2 | 1.1320 | 1.0980 | 1.0812 | 1.0701 | 1.0659 |
| 13.4 | 1.1340 | 1.0994 | 1.0824 | 1.0712 | 1.0669 |
| 13.6 | 1.1360 | 1.1009 | 1.0836 | 1.0722 | 1.0679 |
| 13.8 | 1.1380 | 1.1024 | 1.0849 | 1.0733 | 1.0688 |
| 14.0 | 1.1400 | 1.1039 | 1.0861 | 1.0743 | 1.0698 |

**TABLE K**
**ADJUSTMENT FACTORS FOR ANNUITIES**
**PAYABLE AT THE END OF EACH INTERVAL**
**APPLICABLE AFTER APRIL 30, 1989**
**FREQUENCY OF PAYMENTS**

| INTEREST RATE | ANNUALLY | SEMI ANNUALLY | QUARTERLY | MONTHLY | WEEKLY |
|---|---|---|---|---|---|
| 4.2 | 1.0000 | 1.0104 | 1.0156 | 1.0191 | 1.0205 |
| 4.4 | 1.0000 | 1.0109 | 1.0164 | 1.0200 | 1.0214 |
| 4.6 | 1.0000 | 1.0114 | 1.0171 | 1.0209 | 1.0224 |
| 4.8 | 1.0000 | 1.0119 | 1.0178 | 1.0218 | 1.0234 |
| 5.0 | 1.0000 | 1.0123 | 1.0186 | 1.0227 | 1.0243 |
| 5.2 | 1.0000 | 1.0128 | 1.0193 | 1.0236 | 1.0253 |
| 5.4 | 1.0000 | 1.0133 | 1.0200 | 1.0245 | 1.0262 |
| 5.6 | 1.0000 | 1.0138 | 1.0208 | 1.0254 | 1.0272 |

| INTEREST RATE | ANNUALLY | SEMI ANNUALLY | QUARTERLY | MONTHLY | WEEKLY |
|---|---|---|---|---|---|
| 5.8 | 1.0000 | 1.0143 | 1.0215 | 1.0263 | 1.0282 |
| 6.0 | 1.0000 | 1.0148 | 1.0222 | 1.0272 | 1.0291 |
| 6.2 | 1.0000 | 1.0153 | 1.0230 | 1.0281 | 1.0301 |
| 6.4 | 1.0000 | 1.0158 | 1.0237 | 1.0290 | 1.0311 |
| 6.6 | 1.0000 | 1.0162 | 1.0244 | 1.0299 | 1.0320 |
| 6.8 | 1.0000 | 1.0167 | 1.0252 | 1.0308 | 1.0330 |
| 7.0 | 1.0000 | 1.0172 | 1.0259 | 1.0317 | 1.0339 |
| 7.2 | 1.0000 | 1.0177 | 1.0266 | 1.0326 | 1.0349 |
| 7.4 | 1.0000 | 1.0182 | 1.0273 | 1.0335 | 1.0358 |
| 7.6 | 1.0000 | 1.0187 | 1.0281 | 1.0344 | 1.0368 |
| 7.8 | 1.0000 | 1.0191 | 1.0288 | 1.0353 | 1.0378 |
| 8.0 | 1.0000 | 1.0196 | 1.0295 | 1.0362 | 1.0387 |
| 8.2 | 1.0000 | 1.0201 | 1.0302 | 1.0370 | 1.0397 |
| 8.4 | 1.0000 | 1.0206 | 1.0310 | 1.0379 | 1.0406 |
| 8.6 | 1.0000 | 1.0211 | 1.0317 | 1.0388 | 1.0416 |
| 8.8 | 1.0000 | 1.0215 | 1.0324 | 1.0397 | 1.0425 |
| 9.0 | 1.0000 | 1.0220 | 1.0331 | 1.0406 | 1.0435 |
| 9.2 | 1.0000 | 1.0225 | 1.0339 | 1.0415 | 1.0444 |
| 9.4 | 1.0000 | 1.0230 | 1.0346 | 1.0424 | 1.0454 |
| 9.6 | 1.0000 | 1.0235 | 1.0353 | 1.0433 | 1.0463 |
| 9.8 | 1.0000 | 1.0239 | 1.0360 | 1.0442 | 1.0473 |
| 10.0 | 1.0000 | 1.0244 | 1.0368 | 1.0450 | 1.0482 |
| 10.2 | 1.0000 | 1.0249 | 1.0375 | 1.0459 | 1.0492 |
| 10.4 | 1.0000 | 1.0254 | 1.0382 | 1.0468 | 1.0501 |
| 10.6 | 1.0000 | 1.0258 | 1.0389 | 1.0477 | 1.0511 |
| 10.8 | 1.0000 | 1.0263 | 1.0396 | 1.0486 | 1.0520 |
| 11.0 | 1.0000 | 1.0268 | 1.0404 | 1.0495 | 1.0530 |
| 11.2 | 1.0000 | 1.0273 | 1.0411 | 1.0503 | 1.0539 |
| 11.4 | 1.0000 | 1.0277 | 1.0418 | 1.0512 | 1.0549 |
| 11.6 | 1.0000 | 1.0282 | 1.0425 | 1.0521 | 1.0558 |
| 11.8 | 1.0000 | 1.0287 | 1.0432 | 1.0530 | 1.0568 |
| 12.0 | 1.0000 | 1.0292 | 1.0439 | 1.0539 | 1.0577 |
| 12.2 | 1.0000 | 1.0296 | 1.0447 | 1.0548 | 1.0587 |
| 12.4 | 1.0000 | 1.0301 | 1.0454 | 1.0556 | 1.0596 |
| 12.6 | 1.0000 | 1.0306 | 1.0461 | 1.0565 | 1.0605 |
| 12.8 | 1.0000 | 1.0310 | 1.0468 | 1.0574 | 1.0615 |
| 13.0 | 1.0000 | 1.0315 | 1.0475 | 1.0583 | 1.0624 |
| 13.2 | 1.0000 | 1.0320 | 1.0482 | 1.0591 | 1.0634 |
| 13.4 | 1.0000 | 1.0324 | 1.0489 | 1.0600 | 1.0643 |
| 13.6 | 1.0000 | 1.0329 | 1.0496 | 1.0609 | 1.0652 |
| 13.8 | 1.0000 | 1.0334 | 1.0504 | 1.0618 | 1.0662 |
| 14.0 | 1.0000 | 1.0339 | 1.0511 | 1.0626 | 1.0671 |

(7) *Actuarial Table S and Table 2000CM where the valuation date is on or after May 1, 2009.*—Except as provided in § 20.7520-2(b) (pertaining to certain limitations on the use of prescribed tables), for determination of the present value of an interest that is dependent on the termination of a life interest, Table 2000CM and Table S (single life remainder factors applicable where the valuation date is on or after May 1, 2009) contained in this paragraph (d)(7) and Table J and Table K contained in paragraph (d)(6) of this section, must be used in the application of the provisions of this section when the section 7520 interest rate component is between 0.2 and 14 percent.

**Table S**
**Based on Life Table 2000CM**
**Single Life Remainder Factors**
**Applicable On or After May 1, 2009**

| | | | | | Interest Rate | | | | | |
|---|---|---|---|---|---|---|---|---|---|---|
| AGE | 0.2% | 0.4% | 0.6% | 0.8% | 1.0% | 1.2% | 1.4% | 1.6% | 1.8% | 2.0% |
| 0 | .85816 | .73751 | .63478 | .54723 | .47252 | .40872 | .35416 | .30747 | .26745 | .23313 |
| 1 | .85889 | .73863 | .63604 | .54844 | .47355 | .40948 | .35459 | .30752 | .26711 | .23239 |
| 2 | .86054 | .74145 | .63968 | .55260 | .47802 | .41409 | .35922 | .31209 | .27155 | .23664 |
| 3 | .86221 | .74433 | .64339 | .55687 | .48263 | .41887 | .36404 | .31685 | .27619 | .24112 |
| 4 | .86390 | .74725 | .64716 | .56121 | .48733 | .42374 | .36898 | .32175 | .28098 | .24575 |
| 5 | .86560 | .75018 | .65097 | .56561 | .49209 | .42871 | .37401 | .32675 | .28588 | .25050 |
| 6 | .86731 | .75314 | .65482 | .57006 | .49692 | .43375 | .37913 | .33186 | .29090 | .25538 |
| 7 | .86902 | .75611 | .65868 | .57454 | .50180 | .43885 | .38432 | .33704 | .29601 | .26035 |
| 8 | .87073 | .75909 | .66258 | .57907 | .50674 | .44403 | .38960 | .34233 | .30122 | .26544 |
| 9 | .87246 | .76209 | .66651 | .58364 | .51173 | .44928 | .39497 | .34771 | .30654 | .27064 |
| 10 | .87419 | .76511 | .67046 | .58826 | .51679 | .45459 | .40042 | .35319 | .31197 | .27596 |
| 11 | .87592 | .76814 | .67445 | .59291 | .52190 | .45998 | .40596 | .35876 | .31750 | .28139 |
| 12 | .87766 | .77119 | .67845 | .59761 | .52706 | .46544 | .41157 | .36443 | .32313 | .28693 |
| 13 | .87939 | .77424 | .68247 | .60232 | .53225 | .47094 | .41723 | .37015 | .32884 | .29255 |
| 14 | .88112 | .77728 | .68649 | .60704 | .53746 | .47646 | .42293 | .37592 | .33460 | .29823 |
| 15 | .88284 | .78031 | .69050 | .61176 | .54267 | .48199 | .42865 | .38172 | .34038 | .30394 |

**Gross Estate**
See p. 20,601 for regulations not amended to reflect law changes

| AGE | 0.2% | 0.4% | 0.6% | 0.8% | 1.0% | 1.2% | 1.4% | 1.6% | 1.8% | 2.0% |
|---|---|---|---|---|---|---|---|---|---|---|
| 16 | .88455 | .78333 | .69449 | .61647 | .54788 | .48752 | .43437 | .38752 | .34619 | .30968 |
| 17 | .88625 | .78633 | .69848 | .62117 | .55309 | .49307 | .44012 | .39336 | .35203 | .31546 |
| 18 | .88795 | .78933 | .70246 | .62588 | .55830 | .49863 | .44589 | .39923 | .35791 | .32129 |
| 19 | .88964 | .79232 | .70644 | .63059 | .56354 | .50422 | .45170 | .40514 | .36385 | .32719 |
| 20 | .89132 | .79532 | .71044 | .63534 | .56882 | .50987 | .45757 | .41114 | .36987 | .33317 |
| 21 | .89301 | .79832 | .71445 | .64010 | .57413 | .51555 | .46350 | .41719 | .37597 | .33925 |
| 22 | .89470 | .80133 | .71847 | .64488 | .57947 | .52129 | .46948 | .42332 | .38216 | .34541 |
| 23 | .89639 | .80434 | .72251 | .64970 | .58486 | .52708 | .47554 | .42954 | .38844 | .35168 |
| 24 | .89808 | .80737 | .72658 | .65456 | .59031 | .53295 | .48169 | .43586 | .39484 | .35809 |
| 25 | .89978 | .81042 | .73068 | .65947 | .59583 | .53890 | .48795 | .44230 | .40137 | .36464 |
| 26 | .90149 | .81349 | .73482 | .66443 | .60141 | .54494 | .49430 | .44886 | .40804 | .37134 |
| 27 | .90320 | .81657 | .73899 | .66944 | .60707 | .55107 | .50076 | .45554 | .41484 | .37819 |
| 28 | .90492 | .81968 | .74319 | .67450 | .61278 | .55728 | .50733 | .46233 | .42178 | .38520 |
| 29 | .90665 | .82279 | .74741 | .67960 | .61856 | .56356 | .51398 | .46924 | .42884 | .39233 |
| 30 | .90837 | .82591 | .75165 | .68473 | .62438 | .56990 | .52070 | .47623 | .43601 | .39959 |
| 31 | .91010 | .82904 | .75592 | .68989 | .63024 | .57631 | .52751 | .48333 | .44329 | .40698 |
| 32 | .91182 | .83218 | .76020 | .69509 | .63616 | .58278 | .53440 | .49052 | .45068 | .41449 |
| 33 | .91355 | .83532 | .76449 | .70031 | .64212 | .58931 | .54137 | .49780 | .45818 | .42213 |
| 34 | .91527 | .83847 | .76880 | .70556 | .64811 | .59589 | .54839 | .50516 | .46578 | .42988 |
| 35 | .91700 | .84162 | .77312 | .71082 | .65414 | .60253 | .55549 | .51261 | .47347 | .43774 |
| 36 | .91872 | .84477 | .77744 | .71611 | .66021 | .60921 | .56266 | .52014 | .48127 | .44572 |
| 37 | .92043 | .84792 | .78178 | .72142 | .66631 | .61594 | .56989 | .52774 | .48916 | .45381 |
| 38 | .92215 | .85107 | .78613 | .72675 | .67244 | .62272 | .57718 | .53544 | .49715 | .46201 |
| 39 | .92386 | .85422 | .79048 | .73210 | .67860 | .62955 | .58453 | .54320 | .50523 | .47032 |
| 40 | .92557 | .85736 | .79483 | .73746 | .68479 | .63641 | .59194 | .55104 | .51340 | .47873 |
| 41 | .92727 | .86050 | .79918 | .74283 | .69100 | .64331 | .59940 | .55894 | .52165 | .48724 |
| 42 | .92896 | .86364 | .80354 | .74820 | .69723 | .65024 | .60690 | .56691 | .52998 | .49585 |
| 43 | .93065 | .86677 | .80789 | .75359 | .70348 | .65721 | .61447 | .57495 | .53840 | .50457 |
| 44 | .93234 | .86990 | .81225 | .75899 | .70976 | .66422 | .62208 | .58305 | .54690 | .51338 |
| 45 | .93402 | .87302 | .81660 | .76439 | .71605 | .67125 | .62973 | .59122 | .55547 | .52228 |
| 46 | .93569 | .87613 | .82095 | .76980 | .72236 | .67832 | .63743 | .59945 | .56413 | .53129 |
| 47 | .93735 | .87924 | .82530 | .77521 | .72867 | .68541 | .64517 | .60773 | .57286 | .54037 |
| 48 | .93901 | .88233 | .82964 | .78062 | .73501 | .69253 | .65295 | .61606 | .58166 | .54955 |
| 49 | .94065 | .88541 | .83397 | .78604 | .74135 | .69967 | .66077 | .62446 | .59053 | .55882 |
| 50 | .94229 | .88849 | .83830 | .79145 | .74771 | .70684 | .66864 | .63292 | .59949 | .56819 |
| 51 | .94393 | .89156 | .84263 | .79688 | .75409 | .71404 | .67655 | .64143 | .60852 | .57766 |
| 52 | .94556 | .89462 | .84695 | .80230 | .76048 | .72127 | .68450 | .65001 | .61763 | .58722 |
| 53 | .94717 | .89767 | .85126 | .80772 | .76687 | .72852 | .69249 | .65863 | .62680 | .59687 |
| 54 | .94878 | .90070 | .85555 | .81313 | .77326 | .73577 | .70050 | .66730 | .63603 | .60658 |
| 55 | .95037 | .90371 | .85983 | .81853 | .77964 | .74302 | .70851 | .67598 | .64530 | .61635 |
| 56 | .95195 | .90670 | .86406 | .82388 | .78599 | .75024 | .71651 | .68465 | .65457 | .62613 |
| 57 | .95351 | .90965 | .86827 | .82920 | .79230 | .75744 | .72448 | .69332 | .66384 | .63593 |
| 58 | .95505 | .91257 | .87243 | .83447 | .79857 | .76459 | .73242 | .70195 | .67309 | .64573 |
| 59 | .95657 | .91546 | .87655 | .83970 | .80479 | .77170 | .74033 | .71057 | .68233 | .65553 |
| 60 | .95807 | .91832 | .88064 | .84490 | .81098 | .77879 | .74822 | .71918 | .69158 | .66534 |
| 61 | .95955 | .92115 | .88469 | .85005 | .81713 | .78584 | .75608 | .72776 | .70081 | .67515 |
| 62 | .96101 | .92395 | .88869 | .85515 | .82323 | .79283 | .76388 | .73630 | .71001 | .68494 |
| 63 | .96245 | .92670 | .89265 | .86020 | .82926 | .79977 | .77164 | .74479 | .71917 | .69470 |
| 64 | .96387 | .92942 | .89655 | .86518 | .83524 | .80665 | .77933 | .75323 | .72828 | .70443 |
| 65 | .96527 | .93210 | .90040 | .87011 | .84116 | .81346 | .78697 | .76162 | .73735 | .71411 |
| 66 | .96665 | .93476 | .90423 | .87502 | .84706 | .82027 | .79461 | .77002 | .74645 | .72385 |
| 67 | .96802 | .93739 | .90803 | .87990 | .85292 | .82705 | .80223 | .77841 | .75554 | .73359 |
| 68 | .96937 | .93999 | .91179 | .88472 | .85874 | .83378 | .80980 | .78676 | .76461 | .74331 |
| 69 | .97070 | .94255 | .91549 | .88949 | .86449 | .84044 | .81731 | .79504 | .77362 | .75299 |
| 70 | .97200 | .94506 | .91914 | .89419 | .87016 | .84702 | .82473 | .80326 | .78256 | .76260 |
| 71 | .97328 | .94754 | .92273 | .89882 | .87577 | .85353 | .83209 | .81140 | .79143 | .77215 |
| 72 | .97453 | .94997 | .92626 | .90338 | .88129 | .85996 | .83935 | .81945 | .80021 | .78162 |
| 73 | .97576 | .95234 | .92972 | .90785 | .88671 | .86627 | .84651 | .82739 | .80888 | .79098 |
| 74 | .97695 | .95466 | .93310 | .91223 | .89202 | .87247 | .85353 | .83518 | .81741 | .80019 |
| 75 | .97811 | .95692 | .93638 | .91649 | .89720 | .87851 | .86039 | .84281 | .82577 | .80923 |
| 76 | .97924 | .95910 | .93957 | .92063 | .90224 | .88440 | .86708 | .85026 | .83393 | .81807 |
| 77 | .98033 | .96122 | .94267 | .92465 | .90715 | .89013 | .87360 | .85753 | .84191 | .82671 |
| 78 | .98138 | .96327 | .94567 | .92855 | .91190 | .89571 | .87995 | .86461 | .84968 | .83515 |
| 79 | .98239 | .96526 | .94857 | .93233 | .91652 | .90112 | .88611 | .87149 | .85725 | .84337 |
| 80 | .98337 | .96717 | .95138 | .93598 | .92098 | .90635 | .89208 | .87817 | .86460 | .85135 |
| 81 | .98431 | .96901 | .95408 | .93951 | .92529 | .91141 | .89786 | .88463 | .87172 | .85910 |
| 82 | .98521 | .97077 | .95667 | .94290 | .92944 | .91629 | .90344 | .89088 | .87861 | .86660 |
| 83 | .98608 | .97247 | .95917 | .94616 | .93343 | .92099 | .90882 | .89691 | .88526 | .87385 |
| 84 | .98691 | .97409 | .96156 | .94928 | .93727 | .92551 | .91399 | .90271 | .89166 | .88084 |

| AGE | 0.2% | 0.4% | 0.6% | 0.8% | 1.0% | 1.2% | 1.4% | 1.6% | 1.8% | 2.0% |
|---|---|---|---|---|---|---|---|---|---|---|
| 85 | .98770 | .97565 | .96384 | .95228 | .94094 | .92984 | .91895 | .90828 | .89782 | .88757 |
| 86 | .98845 | .97713 | .96602 | .95514 | .94446 | .93398 | .92371 | .91362 | .90373 | .89402 |
| 87 | .98917 | .97854 | .96810 | .95786 | .94781 | .93794 | .92825 | .91873 | .90939 | .90021 |
| 88 | .98985 | .97988 | .97008 | .96046 | .95100 | .94171 | .93258 | .92361 | .91479 | .90612 |
| 89 | .99049 | .98115 | .97196 | .96292 | .95404 | .94530 | .93671 | .92826 | .91994 | .91176 |
| | | | | | | | | | | |
| 90 | .99110 | .98235 | .97373 | .96526 | .95691 | .94871 | .94062 | .93267 | .92484 | .91713 |
| 91 | .99168 | .98348 | .97541 | .96747 | .95964 | .95193 | .94434 | .93686 | .92949 | .92223 |
| 92 | .99222 | .98455 | .97700 | .96955 | .96222 | .95498 | .94785 | .94083 | .93390 | .92707 |
| 93 | .99273 | .98556 | .97849 | .97152 | .96464 | .95786 | .95117 | .94457 | .93806 | .93163 |
| 94 | .99321 | .98651 | .97989 | .97337 | .96692 | .96057 | .95429 | .94810 | .94199 | .93595 |
| | | | | | | | | | | |
| 95 | .99366 | .98739 | .98121 | .97510 | .96907 | .96312 | .95724 | .95143 | .94569 | .94002 |
| 96 | .99408 | .98822 | .98244 | .97673 | .97108 | .96551 | .95999 | .95454 | .94916 | .94384 |
| 97 | .99447 | .98900 | .98359 | .97825 | .97297 | .96774 | .96258 | .95747 | .95242 | .94742 |
| 98 | .99483 | .98973 | .98467 | .97967 | .97473 | .96984 | .96500 | .96021 | .95547 | .95078 |
| 99 | .99518 | .99040 | .98568 | .98101 | .97638 | .97180 | .96727 | .96278 | .95834 | .95394 |
| | | | | | | | | | | |
| 100 | .99549 | .99103 | .98661 | .98224 | .97791 | .97362 | .96937 | .96516 | .96100 | .95687 |
| 101 | .99579 | .99162 | .98750 | .98340 | .97935 | .97534 | .97136 | .96742 | .96351 | .95964 |
| 102 | .99607 | .99217 | .98831 | .98448 | .98068 | .97692 | .97319 | .96950 | .96583 | .96220 |
| 103 | .99634 | .99271 | .98911 | .98553 | .98199 | .97848 | .97500 | .97155 | .96812 | .96473 |
| 104 | .99659 | .99320 | .98984 | .98651 | .98320 | .97992 | .97666 | .97344 | .97023 | .96705 |
| | | | | | | | | | | |
| 105 | .99683 | .99369 | .99056 | .98747 | .98439 | .98134 | .97830 | .97530 | .97231 | .96934 |
| 106 | .99713 | .99429 | .99146 | .98865 | .98586 | .98309 | .98033 | .97760 | .97488 | .97218 |
| 107 | .99747 | .99496 | .99246 | .98998 | .98751 | .98506 | .98262 | .98020 | .97779 | .97539 |
| 108 | .99800 | .99602 | .99404 | .99208 | .99012 | .98818 | .98624 | .98431 | .98240 | .98049 |
| 109 | .99900 | .99801 | .99702 | .99603 | .99505 | .99407 | .99310 | .99213 | .99116 | .99020 |

**Table S**
**Based on Life Table 2000CM**
**Single Life Remainder Factors**
**Applicable On or After May 1, 2009**

**Interest Rate**

| AGE | 2.2% | 2.4% | 2.6% | 2.8% | 3.0% | 3.2% | 3.4% | 3.6% | 3.8% | 4.0% |
|---|---|---|---|---|---|---|---|---|---|---|
| 0 | .20365 | .17830 | .15648 | .13767 | .12144 | .10741 | .09528 | .08476 | .07564 | .06772 |
| 1 | .20251 | .17677 | .15458 | .13542 | .11885 | .10451 | .09209 | .08131 | .07194 | .06379 |
| 2 | .20656 | .18060 | .15817 | .13877 | .12197 | .10740 | .09476 | .08376 | .07420 | .06586 |
| 3 | .21084 | .18466 | .16200 | .14236 | .12533 | .11054 | .09767 | .08647 | .07670 | .06817 |
| 4 | .21527 | .18888 | .16600 | .14613 | .12887 | .11385 | .10076 | .08935 | .07938 | .07066 |
| | | | | | | | | | | |
| 5 | .21984 | .19324 | .17013 | .15004 | .13255 | .11730 | .10399 | .09237 | .08220 | .07329 |
| 6 | .22454 | .19773 | .17440 | .15408 | .13636 | .12089 | .10736 | .09553 | .08515 | .07605 |
| 7 | .22933 | .20233 | .17879 | .15824 | .14030 | .12460 | .11085 | .09880 | .08822 | .07892 |
| 8 | .23425 | .20705 | .18330 | .16254 | .14436 | .12844 | .11447 | .10221 | .09142 | .08193 |
| 9 | .23930 | .21191 | .18795 | .16697 | .14857 | .13243 | .11824 | .10576 | .09476 | .08507 |
| | | | | | | | | | | |
| 10 | .24446 | .21689 | .19273 | .17153 | .15292 | .13655 | .12214 | .10945 | .09824 | .08835 |
| 11 | .24975 | .22200 | .19764 | .17623 | .15740 | .14081 | .12619 | .11328 | .10187 | .09177 |
| 12 | .25515 | .22724 | .20268 | .18107 | .16202 | .14521 | .13037 | .11724 | .10563 | .09533 |
| 13 | .26064 | .23256 | .20782 | .18600 | .16674 | .14972 | .13466 | .12132 | .10949 | .09900 |
| 14 | .26620 | .23796 | .21303 | .19101 | .17154 | .15430 | .13903 | .12547 | .11344 | .10273 |
| | | | | | | | | | | |
| 15 | .27179 | .24340 | .21829 | .19607 | .17639 | .15894 | .14344 | .12968 | .11743 | .10652 |
| 16 | .27742 | .24887 | .22358 | .20117 | .18128 | .16361 | .14790 | .13391 | .12145 | .11034 |
| 17 | .28309 | .25439 | .22893 | .20632 | .18622 | .16834 | .15241 | .13821 | .12554 | .11421 |
| 18 | .28881 | .25997 | .23434 | .21154 | .19123 | .17314 | .15699 | .14258 | .12969 | .11815 |
| 19 | .29461 | .26563 | .23983 | .21684 | .19633 | .17803 | .16167 | .14703 | .13393 | .12218 |
| | | | | | | | | | | |
| 20 | .30050 | .27139 | .24543 | .22226 | .20156 | .18304 | .16646 | .15161 | .13829 | .12633 |
| 21 | .30649 | .27726 | .25114 | .22779 | .20689 | .18817 | .17138 | .15631 | .14277 | .13060 |
| 22 | .31259 | .28323 | .25697 | .23344 | .21235 | .19342 | .17642 | .16114 | .14739 | .13500 |
| 23 | .31879 | .28934 | .26293 | .23923 | .21795 | .19882 | .18161 | .16612 | .15215 | .13955 |
| 24 | .32515 | .29559 | .26904 | .24519 | .22372 | .20440 | .18699 | .17128 | .15710 | .14429 |
| | | | | | | | | | | |
| 25 | .33166 | .30201 | .27534 | .25133 | .22969 | .21018 | .19256 | .17665 | .16226 | .14924 |
| 26 | .33833 | .30861 | .28182 | .25767 | .23586 | .21616 | .19835 | .18224 | .16764 | .15440 |
| 27 | .34517 | .31538 | .28849 | .26420 | .24224 | .22236 | .20436 | .18804 | .17324 | .15980 |
| 28 | .35217 | .32233 | .29535 | .27093 | .24882 | .22877 | .21058 | .19407 | .17907 | .16542 |
| 29 | .35932 | .32944 | .30237 | .27784 | .25558 | .23537 | .21701 | .20031 | .18511 | .17126 |
| | | | | | | | | | | |
| 30 | .36661 | .33670 | .30956 | .28492 | .26253 | .24216 | .22362 | .20674 | .19135 | .17730 |
| 31 | .37403 | .34411 | .31691 | .29217 | .26965 | .24914 | .23044 | .21338 | .19779 | .18355 |
| 32 | .38160 | .35167 | .32442 | .29960 | .27697 | .25631 | .23745 | .22022 | .20445 | .19002 |
| 33 | .38930 | .35939 | .33211 | .30721 | .28447 | .26368 | .24467 | .22727 | .21133 | .19671 |
| 34 | .39713 | .36724 | .33993 | .31497 | .29213 | .27123 | .25207 | .23451 | .21839 | .20360 |
| | | | | | | | | | | |
| 35 | .40509 | .37523 | .34792 | .32290 | .29998 | .27896 | .25967 | .24195 | .22567 | .21070 |
| 36 | .41318 | .38337 | .35606 | .33100 | .30800 | .28688 | .26746 | .24961 | .23317 | .21803 |
| 37 | .42139 | .39165 | .36435 | .33927 | .31621 | .29499 | .27546 | .25746 | .24087 | .22557 |
| 38 | .42974 | .40008 | .37281 | .34771 | .32460 | .30330 | .28366 | .26554 | .24880 | .23334 |

| AGE | 2.2% | 2.4% | 2.6% | 2.8% | 3.0% | 3.2% | 3.4% | 3.6% | 3.8% | 4.0% |
|---|---|---|---|---|---|---|---|---|---|---|
| 39 | .43821 | .40864 | .38141 | .35631 | .33316 | .31179 | .29205 | .27381 | .25694 | .24133 |
| 40 | .44679 | .41734 | .39016 | .36507 | .34189 | .32046 | .30064 | .28229 | .26529 | .24954 |
| 41 | .45549 | .42616 | .39906 | .37399 | .35080 | .32932 | .30942 | .29097 | .27386 | .25797 |
| 42 | .46430 | .43511 | .40809 | .38307 | .35987 | .33836 | .31840 | .29986 | .28264 | .26662 |
| 43 | .47324 | .44421 | .41729 | .39232 | .36913 | .34760 | .32758 | .30897 | .29165 | .27552 |
| 44 | .48229 | .45343 | .42663 | .40172 | .37857 | .35702 | .33697 | .31829 | .30088 | .28465 |
| 45 | .49144 | .46277 | .43611 | .41128 | .38817 | .36663 | .34655 | .32782 | .31033 | .29400 |
| 46 | .50072 | .47225 | .44574 | .42101 | .39796 | .37644 | .35634 | .33757 | .32002 | .30360 |
| 47 | .51009 | .48185 | .45550 | .43089 | .40791 | .38642 | .36633 | .34753 | .32992 | .31343 |
| 48 | .51958 | .49158 | .46540 | .44093 | .41803 | .39660 | .37652 | .35770 | .34006 | .32351 |
| 49 | .52917 | .50143 | .47545 | .45113 | .42833 | .40696 | .38691 | .36810 | .35043 | .33383 |
| 50 | .53888 | .51141 | .48566 | .46150 | .43883 | .41754 | .39754 | .37874 | .36106 | .34442 |
| 51 | .54871 | .52153 | .49602 | .47204 | .44951 | .42832 | .40838 | .38961 | .37194 | .35528 |
| 52 | .55865 | .53179 | .50653 | .48276 | .46038 | .43931 | .41945 | .40073 | .38307 | .36641 |
| 53 | .56869 | .54217 | .51718 | .49363 | .47143 | .45050 | .43074 | .41208 | .39446 | .37781 |
| 54 | .57882 | .55265 | .52796 | .50465 | .48265 | .46186 | .44222 | .42364 | .40607 | .38945 |
| 55 | .58902 | .56322 | .53884 | .51579 | .49400 | .47338 | .45387 | .43540 | .41789 | .40131 |
| 56 | .59926 | .57383 | .54978 | .52701 | .50544 | .48501 | .46565 | .44729 | .42987 | .41335 |
| 57 | .60951 | .58449 | .56078 | .53830 | .51698 | .49675 | .47755 | .45932 | .44201 | .42555 |
| 58 | .61978 | .59517 | .57182 | .54964 | .52858 | .50858 | .48956 | .47147 | .45427 | .43790 |
| 59 | .63007 | .60589 | .58290 | .56105 | .54027 | .52050 | .50167 | .48375 | .46668 | .45041 |
| 60 | .64039 | .61665 | .59405 | .57254 | .55205 | .53253 | .51392 | .49617 | .47925 | .46310 |
| 61 | .65072 | .62743 | .60524 | .58409 | .56390 | .54465 | .52627 | .50872 | .49196 | .47595 |
| 62 | .66104 | .63822 | .61645 | .59566 | .57581 | .55683 | .53870 | .52136 | .50478 | .48892 |
| 63 | .67133 | .64900 | .62766 | .60726 | .58774 | .56907 | .55120 | .53409 | .51770 | .50200 |
| 64 | .68161 | .65977 | .63887 | .61887 | .59970 | .58134 | .56375 | .54688 | .53071 | .51519 |
| 65 | .69186 | .67053 | .65009 | .63049 | .61170 | .59367 | .57637 | .55976 | .54381 | .52849 |
| 66 | .70216 | .68136 | .66140 | .64223 | .62383 | .60615 | .58916 | .57283 | .55713 | .54203 |
| 67 | .71250 | .69224 | .67277 | .65405 | .63605 | .61874 | .60208 | .58605 | .57062 | .55575 |
| 68 | .72283 | .70312 | .68416 | .66590 | .64833 | .63140 | .61509 | .59938 | .58423 | .56963 |
| 69 | .73312 | .71398 | .69553 | .67776 | .66062 | .64409 | .62815 | .61277 | .59793 | .58360 |
| 70 | .74335 | .72479 | .70688 | .68959 | .67291 | .65680 | .64124 | .62621 | .61168 | .59764 |
| 71 | .75353 | .73556 | .71819 | .70141 | .68519 | .66951 | .65434 | .63968 | .62549 | .61176 |
| 72 | .76364 | .74626 | .72945 | .71318 | .69744 | .68220 | .66745 | .65317 | .63933 | .62593 |
| 73 | .77365 | .75686 | .74061 | .72487 | .70962 | .69484 | .68051 | .66662 | .65315 | .64009 |
| 74 | .78350 | .76733 | .75164 | .73643 | .72167 | .70735 | .69346 | .67997 | .66688 | .65417 |
| 75 | .79318 | .77761 | .76249 | .74781 | .73355 | .71971 | .70625 | .69318 | .68048 | .66813 |
| 76 | .80266 | .78769 | .77314 | .75899 | .74524 | .73187 | .71886 | .70621 | .69390 | .68192 |
| 77 | .81194 | .79756 | .78358 | .76997 | .75672 | .74382 | .73127 | .71904 | .70713 | .69553 |
| 78 | .82100 | .80722 | .79380 | .78072 | .76798 | .75556 | .74346 | .73166 | .72016 | .70894 |
| 79 | .82984 | .81664 | .80378 | .79124 | .77900 | .76706 | .75542 | .74405 | .73296 | .72213 |
| 80 | .83843 | .82582 | .81351 | .80149 | .78976 | .77830 | .76711 | .75618 | .74550 | .73507 |
| 81 | .84678 | .83474 | .82298 | .81148 | .80025 | .78927 | .77853 | .76803 | .75777 | .74773 |
| 82 | .85487 | .84339 | .83217 | .82119 | .81045 | .79994 | .78966 | .77959 | .76974 | .76009 |
| 83 | .86269 | .85177 | .84107 | .83060 | .82035 | .81030 | .80047 | .79083 | .78139 | .77214 |
| 84 | .87024 | .85986 | .84968 | .83970 | .82993 | .82035 | .81095 | .80174 | .79271 | .78385 |
| 85 | .87751 | .86765 | .85798 | .84849 | .83919 | .83005 | .82110 | .81230 | .80368 | .79521 |
| 86 | .88450 | .87515 | .86597 | .85696 | .84811 | .83942 | .83089 | .82251 | .81428 | .80619 |
| 87 | .89119 | .88234 | .87363 | .86508 | .85668 | .84843 | .84031 | .83234 | .82450 | .81679 |
| 88 | .89760 | .88922 | .88099 | .87289 | .86492 | .85708 | .84938 | .84180 | .83434 | .82700 |
| 89 | .90372 | .89580 | .88801 | .88034 | .87280 | .86537 | .85806 | .85087 | .84378 | .83681 |
| 90 | .90954 | .90207 | .89471 | .88746 | .88032 | .87329 | .86637 | .85954 | .85282 | .84620 |
| 91 | .91508 | .90803 | .90109 | .89424 | .88750 | .88085 | .87429 | .86783 | .86146 | .85518 |
| 92 | .92033 | .91369 | .90714 | .90068 | .89432 | .88803 | .88184 | .87572 | .86969 | .86374 |
| 93 | .92530 | .91904 | .91287 | .90678 | .90078 | .89484 | .88899 | .88321 | .87751 | .87188 |
| 94 | .92999 | .92411 | .91830 | .91256 | .90690 | .90130 | .89578 | .89032 | .88493 | .87961 |
| 95 | .93442 | .92889 | .92342 | .91802 | .91269 | .90741 | .90220 | .89706 | .89197 | .88694 |
| 96 | .93858 | .93338 | .92824 | .92316 | .91813 | .91316 | .90825 | .90340 | .89859 | .89385 |
| 97 | .94248 | .93759 | .93276 | .92798 | .92325 | .91857 | .91395 | .90937 | .90484 | .90036 |
| 98 | .94614 | .94155 | .93701 | .93252 | .92807 | .92367 | .91931 | .91500 | .91073 | .90650 |
| 99 | .94959 | .94528 | .94101 | .93679 | .93260 | .92846 | .92436 | .92030 | .91628 | .91229 |
| 100 | .95278 | .94874 | .94473 | .94075 | .93682 | .93292 | .92906 | .92523 | .92144 | .91769 |
| 101 | .95581 | .95201 | .94824 | .94451 | .94081 | .93715 | .93352 | .92992 | .92635 | .92281 |
| 102 | .95860 | .95503 | .95149 | .94798 | .94450 | .94105 | .93763 | .93424 | .93088 | .92754 |
| 103 | .96136 | .95802 | .95470 | .95142 | .94816 | .94492 | .94171 | .93853 | .93538 | .93224 |
| 104 | .96390 | .96077 | .95766 | .95458 | .95152 | .94848 | .94547 | .94248 | .93951 | .93657 |
| 105 | .96640 | .96347 | .96057 | .95769 | .95483 | .95199 | .94917 | .94637 | .94359 | .94083 |
| 106 | .96950 | .96684 | .96420 | .96157 | .95896 | .95636 | .95379 | .95123 | .94868 | .94616 |
| 107 | .97301 | .97064 | .96829 | .96595 | .96362 | .96131 | .95901 | .95672 | .95445 | .95219 |

| AGE | 2.2% | 2.4% | 2.6% | 2.8% | 3.0% | 3.2% | 3.4% | 3.6% | 3.8% | 4.0% |
|---|---|---|---|---|---|---|---|---|---|---|
| 108 | .97859 | .97670 | .97482 | .97295 | .97109 | .96923 | .96739 | .96555 | .96373 | .96191 |
| 109 | .98924 | .98828 | .98733 | .98638 | .98544 | .98450 | .98356 | .98263 | .98170 | .98077 |

## Table S
### Based on Life Table 2000CM
### Single Life Remainder Factors
### Applicable On or After May 1, 2009

**Interest Rate**

| AGE | 4.2% | 4.4% | 4.6% | 4.8% | 5.0% | 5.2% | 5.4% | 5.6% | 5.8% | 6.0% |
|---|---|---|---|---|---|---|---|---|---|---|
| 0 | .06083 | .05483 | .04959 | .04501 | .04101 | .03749 | .03441 | .03170 | .02931 | .02721 |
| 1 | .05668 | .05049 | .04507 | .04034 | .03618 | .03254 | .02934 | .02652 | .02403 | .02183 |
| 2 | .05858 | .05222 | .04665 | .04178 | .03750 | .03373 | .03042 | .02750 | .02492 | .02264 |
| 3 | .06072 | .05420 | .04848 | .04346 | .03904 | .03516 | .03173 | .02871 | .02603 | .02366 |
| 4 | .06303 | .05634 | .05046 | .04530 | .04075 | .03674 | .03319 | .03006 | .02729 | .02483 |
| 5 | .06547 | .05861 | .05258 | .04726 | .04258 | .03844 | .03478 | .03153 | .02866 | .02610 |
| 6 | .06805 | .06102 | .05482 | .04935 | .04453 | .04026 | .03647 | .03312 | .03014 | .02749 |
| 7 | .07074 | .06353 | .05717 | .05155 | .04658 | .04217 | .03826 | .03479 | .03171 | .02895 |
| 8 | .07356 | .06617 | .05964 | .05386 | .04875 | .04421 | .04017 | .03658 | .03338 | .03053 |
| 9 | .07651 | .06895 | .06225 | .05631 | .05105 | .04637 | .04220 | .03849 | .03518 | .03222 |
| 10 | .07960 | .07185 | .06499 | .05889 | .05347 | .04865 | .04435 | .04052 | .03709 | .03402 |
| 11 | .08283 | .07490 | .06786 | .06160 | .05603 | .05106 | .04663 | .04267 | .03912 | .03594 |
| 12 | .08620 | .07808 | .07087 | .06444 | .05871 | .05360 | .04903 | .04494 | .04127 | .03798 |
| 13 | .08967 | .08137 | .07397 | .06738 | .06149 | .05623 | .05152 | .04729 | .04351 | .04010 |
| 14 | .09321 | .08472 | .07715 | .07038 | .06433 | .05892 | .05406 | .04971 | .04579 | .04227 |
| 15 | .09680 | .08812 | .08036 | .07342 | .06721 | .06164 | .05664 | .05214 | .04810 | .04445 |
| 16 | .10041 | .09154 | .08360 | .07649 | .07011 | .06438 | .05923 | .05459 | .05041 | .04664 |
| 17 | .10409 | .09502 | .08689 | .07960 | .07305 | .06716 | .06185 | .05707 | .05276 | .04886 |
| 18 | .10782 | .09855 | .09024 | .08276 | .07604 | .06998 | .06452 | .05959 | .05514 | .05111 |
| 19 | .11164 | .10217 | .09366 | .08600 | .07910 | .07288 | .06726 | .06218 | .05758 | .05341 |
| 20 | .11559 | .10592 | .09721 | .08937 | .08228 | .07589 | .07010 | .06487 | .06012 | .05582 |
| 21 | .11965 | .10977 | .10087 | .09283 | .08557 | .07900 | .07305 | .06765 | .06276 | .05831 |
| 22 | .12383 | .11376 | .10465 | .09642 | .08897 | .08223 | .07610 | .07055 | .06550 | .06090 |
| 23 | .12817 | .11789 | .10859 | .10016 | .09252 | .08559 | .07930 | .07358 | .06837 | .06363 |
| 24 | .13270 | .12221 | .11270 | .10408 | .09625 | .08914 | .08267 | .07678 | .07141 | .06651 |
| 25 | .13744 | .12674 | .11703 | .10821 | .10019 | .09289 | .08625 | .08018 | .07465 | .06960 |
| 26 | .14239 | .13149 | .12158 | .11256 | .10435 | .09686 | .09003 | .08380 | .07810 | .07288 |
| 27 | .14758 | .13647 | .12636 | .11714 | .10873 | .10106 | .09405 | .08764 | .08177 | .07639 |
| 28 | .15300 | .14169 | .13137 | .12195 | .11335 | .10549 | .09829 | .09171 | .08567 | .08012 |
| 29 | .15864 | .14712 | .13660 | .12698 | .11819 | .11013 | .10275 | .09598 | .08977 | .08406 |
| 30 | .16448 | .15275 | .14203 | .13222 | .12323 | .11498 | .10742 | .10047 | .09408 | .08820 |
| 31 | .17053 | .15861 | .14769 | .13768 | .12849 | .12006 | .11230 | .10517 | .09860 | .09255 |
| 32 | .17680 | .16468 | .15357 | .14336 | .13398 | .12535 | .11741 | .11009 | .10335 | .09712 |
| 33 | .18330 | .17099 | .15968 | .14927 | .13970 | .13088 | .12275 | .11525 | .10832 | .10192 |
| 34 | .19000 | .17750 | .16599 | .15539 | .14562 | .13661 | .12829 | .12061 | .11350 | .10693 |
| 35 | .19692 | .18423 | .17253 | .16174 | .15178 | .14258 | .13408 | .12621 | .11892 | .11217 |
| 36 | .20407 | .19119 | .17931 | .16833 | .15818 | .14879 | .14009 | .13204 | .12457 | .11764 |
| 37 | .21144 | .19838 | .18631 | .17515 | .16481 | .15523 | .14635 | .13811 | .13046 | .12335 |
| 38 | .21904 | .20582 | .19357 | .18222 | .17170 | .16193 | .15287 | .14444 | .13661 | .12932 |
| 39 | .22687 | .21348 | .20105 | .18952 | .17882 | .16887 | .15962 | .15102 | .14300 | .13554 |
| 40 | .23493 | .22137 | .20878 | .19707 | .18619 | .17606 | .16663 | .15784 | .14965 | .14201 |
| 41 | .24322 | .22950 | .21674 | .20487 | .19381 | .18350 | .17390 | .16493 | .15656 | .14873 |
| 42 | .25173 | .23786 | .22494 | .21290 | .20168 | .19120 | .18141 | .17227 | .16372 | .15572 |
| 43 | .26049 | .24648 | .23342 | .22122 | .20982 | .19918 | .18922 | .17990 | .17118 | .16301 |
| 44 | .26950 | .25535 | .24214 | .22979 | .21824 | .20742 | .19730 | .18781 | .17892 | .17057 |
| 45 | .27874 | .26447 | .25112 | .23862 | .22692 | .21595 | .20566 | .19600 | .18694 | .17843 |
| 46 | .28824 | .27385 | .26038 | .24774 | .23589 | .22476 | .21431 | .20450 | .19527 | .18659 |
| 47 | .29798 | .28349 | .26989 | .25712 | .24513 | .23386 | .22326 | .21328 | .20390 | .19505 |
| 48 | .30797 | .29338 | .27967 | .26678 | .25466 | .24325 | .23250 | .22238 | .21283 | .20383 |
| 49 | .31822 | .30355 | .28974 | .27674 | .26449 | .25294 | .24206 | .23179 | .22210 | .21294 |
| 50 | .32876 | .31401 | .30011 | .28701 | .27465 | .26298 | .25196 | .24156 | .23172 | .22242 |
| 51 | .33958 | .32477 | .31079 | .29759 | .28513 | .27335 | .26221 | .25168 | .24170 | .23226 |
| 52 | .35068 | .33582 | .32178 | .30851 | .29595 | .28407 | .27282 | .26216 | .25206 | .24249 |
| 53 | .36206 | .34717 | .33308 | .31974 | .30710 | .29513 | .28378 | .27301 | .26279 | .25309 |
| 54 | .37371 | .35880 | .34467 | .33127 | .31857 | .30651 | .29507 | .28420 | .27388 | .26406 |
| 55 | .38559 | .37067 | .35652 | .34308 | .33032 | .31820 | .30668 | .29572 | .28529 | .27537 |
| 56 | .39765 | .38275 | .36859 | .35512 | .34232 | .33014 | .31855 | .30751 | .29699 | .28697 |
| 57 | .40990 | .39502 | .38086 | .36739 | .35455 | .34233 | .33068 | .31957 | .30898 | .29887 |
| 58 | .42231 | .40747 | .39333 | .37985 | .36700 | .35474 | .34304 | .33188 | .32121 | .31103 |
| 59 | .43490 | .42011 | .40600 | .39253 | .37968 | .36740 | .35567 | .34446 | .33374 | .32348 |
| 60 | .44768 | .43296 | .41890 | .40546 | .39261 | .38033 | .36858 | .35733 | .34656 | .33625 |

Reg. §20.2031-7(d)(7)

| AGE | 4.2% | 4.4% | 4.6% | 4.8% | 5.0% | 5.2% | 5.4% | 5.6% | 5.8% | 6.0% |
|---|---|---|---|---|---|---|---|---|---|---|
| 61 | .46064 | .44600 | .43200 | .41860 | .40578 | .39351 | .38175 | .37048 | .35968 | .34933 |
| 62 | .47373 | .45920 | .44527 | .43194 | .41915 | .40690 | .39514 | .38387 | .37305 | .36267 |
| 63 | .48696 | .47253 | .45870 | .44544 | .43271 | .42049 | .40876 | .39749 | .38666 | .37625 |
| 64 | .50030 | .48601 | .47229 | .45911 | .44645 | .43428 | .42258 | .41133 | .40051 | .39010 |
| 65 | .51377 | .49963 | .48603 | .47295 | .46037 | .44827 | .43662 | .42540 | .41460 | .40420 |
| 66 | .52750 | .51352 | .50007 | .48711 | .47464 | .46262 | .45103 | .43987 | .42911 | .41872 |
| 67 | .54144 | .52765 | .51436 | .50154 | .48919 | .47727 | .46578 | .45468 | .44397 | .43363 |
| 68 | .55554 | .54196 | .52885 | .51619 | .50398 | .49218 | .48079 | .46978 | .45915 | .44887 |
| 69 | .56976 | .55640 | .54349 | .53102 | .51896 | .50731 | .49603 | .48513 | .47458 | .46438 |
| 70 | .58407 | .57095 | .55826 | .54598 | .53410 | .52260 | .51147 | .50069 | .49025 | .48013 |
| 71 | .59848 | .58561 | .57316 | .56109 | .54940 | .53808 | .52710 | .51646 | .50615 | .49614 |
| 72 | .61294 | .60035 | .58815 | .57632 | .56484 | .55371 | .54291 | .53243 | .52225 | .51237 |
| 73 | .62741 | .61512 | .60318 | .59160 | .58035 | .56943 | .55882 | .54851 | .53849 | .52876 |
| 74 | .64183 | .62983 | .61818 | .60686 | .59586 | .58516 | .57476 | .56464 | .55480 | .54523 |
| 75 | .65612 | .64444 | .63309 | .62204 | .61129 | .60083 | .59065 | .58074 | .57109 | .56169 |
| 76 | .67026 | .65891 | .64786 | .63710 | .62661 | .61640 | .60646 | .59676 | .58731 | .57810 |
| 77 | .68423 | .67321 | .66248 | .65201 | .64181 | .63186 | .62215 | .61269 | .60345 | .59444 |
| 78 | .69800 | .68733 | .67692 | .66676 | .65684 | .64717 | .63772 | .62849 | .61948 | .61068 |
| 79 | .71156 | .70124 | .69116 | .68132 | .67170 | .66230 | .65312 | .64414 | .63537 | .62680 |
| 80 | .72487 | .71490 | .70516 | .69563 | .68632 | .67721 | .66830 | .65959 | .65106 | .64272 |
| 81 | .73791 | .72830 | .71890 | .70970 | .70069 | .69188 | .68325 | .67481 | .66654 | .65844 |
| 82 | .75065 | .74140 | .73235 | .72348 | .71479 | .70628 | .69794 | .68977 | .68176 | .67391 |
| 83 | .76308 | .75419 | .74548 | .73695 | .72858 | .72037 | .71232 | .70443 | .69669 | .68909 |
| 84 | .77516 | .76664 | .75828 | .75008 | .74203 | .73413 | .72638 | .71877 | .71130 | .70396 |
| 85 | .78689 | .77873 | .77072 | .76285 | .75512 | .74753 | .74008 | .73275 | .72556 | .71849 |
| 86 | .79825 | .79044 | .78278 | .77524 | .76783 | .76055 | .75340 | .74636 | .73944 | .73264 |
| 87 | .80921 | .80176 | .79443 | .78722 | .78014 | .77316 | .76630 | .75956 | .75292 | .74638 |
| 88 | .81978 | .81268 | .80569 | .79880 | .79203 | .78536 | .77880 | .77234 | .76598 | .75971 |
| 89 | .82994 | .82317 | .81651 | .80995 | .80349 | .79712 | .79085 | .78467 | .77859 | .77259 |
| 90 | .83967 | .83324 | .82690 | .82065 | .81450 | .80843 | .80244 | .79655 | .79073 | .78500 |
| 91 | .84898 | .84288 | .83685 | .83091 | .82505 | .81928 | .81358 | .80795 | .80241 | .79693 |
| 92 | .85787 | .85208 | .84636 | .84072 | .83515 | .82966 | .82423 | .81888 | .81360 | .80838 |
| 93 | .86632 | .86083 | .85541 | .85006 | .84477 | .83955 | .83440 | .82931 | .82428 | .81931 |
| 94 | .87435 | .86915 | .86402 | .85894 | .85393 | .84898 | .84409 | .83925 | .83447 | .82975 |
| 95 | .88197 | .87705 | .87219 | .86739 | .86265 | .85795 | .85331 | .84872 | .84419 | .83970 |
| 96 | .88915 | .88451 | .87991 | .87537 | .87088 | .86643 | .86203 | .85768 | .85338 | .84912 |
| 97 | .89593 | .89154 | .88720 | .88290 | .87865 | .87444 | .87028 | .86616 | .86208 | .85804 |
| 98 | .90232 | .89818 | .89408 | .89002 | .88600 | .88202 | .87808 | .87418 | .87031 | .86649 |
| 99 | .90835 | .90444 | .90057 | .89674 | .89294 | .88918 | .88546 | .88177 | .87811 | .87449 |
| 100 | .91397 | .91028 | .90663 | .90301 | .89942 | .89587 | .89234 | .88885 | .88539 | .88196 |
| 101 | .91930 | .91583 | .91238 | .90897 | .90558 | .90223 | .89890 | .89560 | .89233 | .88908 |
| 102 | .92424 | .92096 | .91771 | .91448 | .91128 | .90811 | .90496 | .90184 | .89875 | .89568 |
| 103 | .92914 | .92605 | .92300 | .91996 | .91695 | .91397 | .91100 | .90806 | .90514 | .90225 |
| 104 | .93364 | .93074 | .92786 | .92501 | .92217 | .91935 | .91656 | .91379 | .91103 | .90830 |
| 105 | .93809 | .93537 | .93266 | .92998 | .92731 | .92467 | .92204 | .91943 | .91683 | .91426 |
| 106 | .94365 | .94115 | .93867 | .93621 | .93376 | .93133 | .92892 | .92651 | .92413 | .92176 |
| 107 | .94994 | .94771 | .94549 | .94328 | .94108 | .93890 | .93673 | .93457 | .93242 | .93028 |
| 108 | .96010 | .95830 | .95651 | .95472 | .95295 | .95118 | .94942 | .94767 | .94593 | .94420 |
| 109 | .97985 | .97893 | .97801 | .97710 | .97619 | .97529 | .97438 | .97348 | .97259 | .97170 |

**Table S**
**Based on Life Table 2000CM**
**Single Life Remainder Factors**
**Applicable On or After May 1, 2009**

**Interest Rate**

| AGE | 6.2% | 6.4% | 6.6% | 6.8% | 7.0% | 7.2% | 7.4% | 7.6% | 7.8% | 8.0% |
|---|---|---|---|---|---|---|---|---|---|---|
| 0 | .02534 | .02370 | .02223 | .02093 | .01978 | .01874 | .01782 | .01699 | .01625 | .01559 |
| 1 | .01989 | .01817 | .01664 | .01528 | .01406 | .01298 | .01202 | .01115 | .01037 | .00967 |
| 2 | .02061 | .01882 | .01722 | .01580 | .01454 | .01340 | .01239 | .01148 | .01066 | .00993 |
| 3 | .02156 | .01969 | .01802 | .01654 | .01521 | .01403 | .01297 | .01201 | .01115 | .01038 |
| 4 | .02264 | .02069 | .01896 | .01741 | .01602 | .01478 | .01367 | .01267 | .01176 | .01095 |
| 5 | .02383 | .02180 | .01999 | .01838 | .01693 | .01563 | .01446 | .01341 | .01246 | .01161 |
| 6 | .02512 | .02301 | .02113 | .01944 | .01793 | .01657 | .01535 | .01424 | .01325 | .01235 |
| 7 | .02650 | .02430 | .02234 | .02058 | .01900 | .01758 | .01630 | .01514 | .01410 | .01315 |
| 8 | .02798 | .02570 | .02365 | .02182 | .02017 | .01868 | .01734 | .01613 | .01503 | .01404 |
| 9 | .02957 | .02720 | .02507 | .02316 | .02143 | .01988 | .01848 | .01721 | .01606 | .01502 |
| 10 | .03128 | .02881 | .02659 | .02460 | .02280 | .02118 | .01971 | .01838 | .01718 | .01608 |
| 11 | .03309 | .03053 | .02823 | .02615 | .02428 | .02258 | .02105 | .01966 | .01839 | .01725 |
| 12 | .03503 | .03237 | .02997 | .02781 | .02585 | .02408 | .02248 | .02103 | .01971 | .01850 |
| 13 | .03704 | .03428 | .03179 | .02954 | .02750 | .02565 | .02398 | .02246 | .02108 | .01982 |
| 14 | .03909 | .03623 | .03364 | .03130 | .02918 | .02726 | .02551 | .02392 | .02248 | .02116 |

| AGE | 6.2% | 6.4% | 6.6% | 6.8% | 7.0% | 7.2% | 7.4% | 7.6% | 7.8% | 8.0% |
|---|---|---|---|---|---|---|---|---|---|---|
| 15 | .04117 | .03820 | .03551 | .03308 | .03087 | .02886 | .02704 | .02538 | .02387 | .02249 |
| 16 | .04324 | .04016 | .03737 | .03484 | .03254 | .03046 | .02855 | .02682 | .02524 | .02379 |
| 17 | .04533 | .04214 | .03924 | .03661 | .03422 | .03205 | .03007 | .02826 | .02661 | .02509 |
| 18 | .04746 | .04415 | .04114 | .03841 | .03592 | .03366 | .03159 | .02970 | .02798 | .02639 |
| 19 | .04963 | .04620 | .04309 | .04025 | .03766 | .03530 | .03315 | .03117 | .02937 | .02772 |
| 20 | .05191 | .04835 | .04512 | .04217 | .03948 | .03702 | .03478 | .03272 | .03083 | .02910 |
| 21 | .05427 | .05058 | .04723 | .04416 | .04137 | .03881 | .03647 | .03432 | .03235 | .03054 |
| 22 | .05672 | .05291 | .04943 | .04625 | .04334 | .04067 | .03823 | .03599 | .03394 | .03205 |
| 23 | .05930 | .05535 | .05174 | .04844 | .04542 | .04265 | .04010 | .03777 | .03562 | .03364 |
| 24 | .06204 | .05795 | .05421 | .05078 | .04764 | .04476 | .04211 | .03967 | .03743 | .03536 |
| 25 | .06497 | .06074 | .05687 | .05331 | .05005 | .04705 | .04429 | .04174 | .03940 | .03724 |
| 26 | .06811 | .06373 | .05972 | .05603 | .05264 | .04952 | .04665 | .04400 | .04155 | .03929 |
| 27 | .07146 | .06694 | .06278 | .05895 | .05543 | .05219 | .04920 | .04644 | .04389 | .04153 |
| 28 | .07503 | .07036 | .06605 | .06209 | .05844 | .05507 | .05196 | .04908 | .04642 | .04396 |
| 29 | .07881 | .07398 | .06953 | .06542 | .06163 | .05814 | .05490 | .05191 | .04913 | .04656 |
| 30 | .08279 | .07780 | .07319 | .06894 | .06502 | .06138 | .05802 | .05491 | .05202 | .04933 |
| 31 | .08697 | .08182 | .07707 | .07267 | .06860 | .06483 | .06134 | .05810 | .05509 | .05229 |
| 32 | .09137 | .08606 | .08115 | .07660 | .07239 | .06848 | .06485 | .06148 | .05835 | .05543 |
| 33 | .09601 | .09053 | .08546 | .08075 | .07639 | .07234 | .06858 | .06508 | .06182 | .05878 |
| 34 | .10084 | .09520 | .08996 | .08511 | .08059 | .07640 | .07249 | .06886 | .06547 | .06231 |
| 35 | .10590 | .10009 | .09470 | .08968 | .08501 | .08067 | .07662 | .07285 | .06933 | .06605 |
| 36 | .11120 | .10522 | .09966 | .09448 | .08966 | .08517 | .08098 | .07706 | .07341 | .06999 |
| 37 | .11674 | .11059 | .10486 | .09952 | .09454 | .08990 | .08556 | .08150 | .07771 | .07416 |
| 38 | .12254 | .11621 | .11032 | .10481 | .09968 | .09487 | .09039 | .08618 | .08225 | .07856 |
| 39 | .12857 | .12208 | .11601 | .11035 | .10505 | .10009 | .09545 | .09110 | .08702 | .08320 |
| 40 | .13487 | .12820 | .12196 | .11613 | .11067 | .10555 | .10076 | .09626 | .09204 | .08807 |
| 41 | .14142 | .13458 | .12817 | .12217 | .11655 | .11127 | .10632 | .10167 | .09730 | .09319 |
| 42 | .14823 | .14122 | .13464 | .12848 | .12269 | .11725 | .11214 | .10734 | .10282 | .09856 |
| 43 | .15535 | .14816 | .14141 | .13508 | .12913 | .12353 | .11826 | .11330 | .10863 | .10422 |
| 44 | .16274 | .15538 | .14847 | .14196 | .13585 | .13008 | .12466 | .11954 | .11472 | .11016 |
| 45 | .17042 | .16290 | .15581 | .14914 | .14286 | .13694 | .13135 | .12608 | .12110 | .11640 |
| 46 | .17842 | .17073 | .16348 | .15664 | .15020 | .14411 | .13836 | .13293 | .12780 | .12294 |
| 47 | .18672 | .17886 | .17145 | .16445 | .15784 | .15159 | .14568 | .14010 | .13481 | .12980 |
| 48 | .19534 | .18732 | .17974 | .17258 | .16581 | .15940 | .15334 | .14759 | .14215 | .13699 |
| 49 | .20429 | .19612 | .18838 | .18106 | .17413 | .16757 | .16134 | .15544 | .14984 | .14453 |
| 50 | .21362 | .20529 | .19740 | .18993 | .18284 | .17612 | .16974 | .16368 | .15793 | .15247 |
| 51 | .22332 | .21484 | .20680 | .19917 | .19194 | .18506 | .17853 | .17232 | .16642 | .16080 |
| 52 | .23341 | .22479 | .21660 | .20883 | .20144 | .19442 | .18774 | .18138 | .17533 | .16957 |
| 53 | .24388 | .23513 | .22681 | .21889 | .21136 | .20419 | .19737 | .19087 | .18467 | .17876 |
| 54 | .25473 | .24585 | .23739 | .22935 | .22168 | .21437 | .20741 | .20076 | .19442 | .18837 |
| 55 | .26593 | .25693 | .24835 | .24017 | .23238 | .22494 | .21784 | .21105 | .20458 | .19838 |
| 56 | .27742 | .26831 | .25962 | .25132 | .24340 | .23583 | .22860 | .22169 | .21508 | .20875 |
| 57 | .28922 | .28001 | .27121 | .26280 | .25476 | .24707 | .23971 | .23267 | .22593 | .21947 |
| 58 | .30129 | .29199 | .28309 | .27457 | .26642 | .25862 | .25114 | .24398 | .23712 | .23053 |
| 59 | .31367 | .30428 | .29529 | .28667 | .27842 | .27051 | .26293 | .25565 | .24867 | .24197 |
| 60 | .32638 | .31691 | .30784 | .29914 | .29079 | .28278 | .27509 | .26771 | .26062 | .25380 |
| 61 | .33940 | .32987 | .32073 | .31195 | .30352 | .29542 | .28763 | .28015 | .27295 | .26603 |
| 62 | .35269 | .34311 | .33391 | .32506 | .31656 | .30837 | .30050 | .29293 | .28564 | .27862 |
| 63 | .36625 | .35663 | .34738 | .33847 | .32990 | .32165 | .31370 | .30604 | .29867 | .29155 |
| 64 | .38007 | .37043 | .36113 | .35218 | .34356 | .33524 | .32723 | .31950 | .31204 | .30484 |
| 65 | .39417 | .38451 | .37519 | .36620 | .35753 | .34917 | .34110 | .33330 | .32577 | .31850 |
| 66 | .40871 | .39905 | .38972 | .38071 | .37201 | .36361 | .35550 | .34765 | .34006 | .33273 |
| 67 | .42365 | .41400 | .40468 | .39567 | .38696 | .37853 | .37038 | .36250 | .35487 | .34749 |
| 68 | .43892 | .42931 | .42001 | .41101 | .40230 | .39387 | .38570 | .37780 | .37014 | .36272 |
| 69 | .45450 | .44493 | .43567 | .42670 | .41800 | .40958 | .40141 | .39350 | .38582 | .37837 |
| 70 | .47033 | .46083 | .45162 | .44269 | .43403 | .42563 | .41748 | .40957 | .40189 | .39443 |
| 71 | .48644 | .47702 | .46788 | .45901 | .45040 | .44203 | .43391 | .42602 | .41835 | .41090 |
| 72 | .50278 | .49347 | .48441 | .47562 | .46707 | .45877 | .45069 | .44284 | .43520 | .42776 |
| 73 | .51930 | .51010 | .50115 | .49245 | .48399 | .47575 | .46774 | .45994 | .45234 | .44494 |
| 74 | .53591 | .52684 | .51802 | .50943 | .50106 | .49291 | .48497 | .47724 | .46970 | .46235 |
| 75 | .55253 | .54361 | .53492 | .52645 | .51820 | .51015 | .50230 | .49465 | .48719 | .47991 |
| 76 | .56912 | .56036 | .55182 | .54349 | .53536 | .52742 | .51968 | .51213 | .50475 | .49754 |
| 77 | .58565 | .57706 | .56868 | .56050 | .55251 | .54471 | .53708 | .52964 | .52236 | .51525 |
| 78 | .60209 | .59369 | .58549 | .57747 | .56963 | .56197 | .55448 | .54715 | .53999 | .53298 |
| 79 | .61841 | .61021 | .60219 | .59435 | .58668 | .57917 | .57182 | .56463 | .55760 | .55071 |
| 80 | .63456 | .62657 | .61875 | .61109 | .60359 | .59625 | .58906 | .58202 | .57512 | .56836 |
| 81 | .65050 | .64273 | .63512 | .62766 | .62034 | .61318 | .60616 | .59927 | .59252 | .58590 |
| 82 | .66621 | .65867 | .65127 | .64401 | .63690 | .62992 | .62308 | .61636 | .60977 | .60330 |
| 83 | .68164 | .67433 | .66716 | .66012 | .65321 | .64642 | .63976 | .63322 | .62680 | .62050 |

Reg. §20.2031-7(d)(7)

| AGE | 6.2% | 6.4% | 6.6% | 6.8% | 7.0% | 7.2% | 7.4% | 7.6% | 7.8% | 8.0% |
|---|---|---|---|---|---|---|---|---|---|---|
| 84 | .69676 | .68969 | .68275 | .67593 | .66923 | .66265 | .65618 | .64983 | .64358 | .63745 |
| 85 | .71154 | .70472 | .69801 | .69141 | .68493 | .67856 | .67229 | .66613 | .66007 | .65412 |
| 86 | .72595 | .71937 | .71290 | .70654 | .70028 | .69412 | .68806 | .68210 | .67623 | .67046 |
| 87 | .73995 | .73362 | .72740 | .72127 | .71523 | .70929 | .70344 | .69768 | .69201 | .68642 |
| 88 | .75354 | .74746 | .74148 | .73558 | .72978 | .72406 | .71842 | .71287 | .70739 | .70200 |
| 89 | .76668 | .76085 | .75511 | .74945 | .74387 | .73837 | .73295 | .72761 | .72234 | .71714 |
| 90 | .77934 | .77377 | .76827 | .76284 | .75749 | .75222 | .74701 | .74188 | .73681 | .73181 |
| 91 | .79153 | .78620 | .78094 | .77575 | .77063 | .76558 | .76059 | .75566 | .75080 | .74600 |
| 92 | .80323 | .79814 | .79312 | .78816 | .78326 | .77843 | .77365 | .76894 | .76428 | .75967 |
| 93 | .81440 | .80956 | .80477 | .80004 | .79536 | .79074 | .78618 | .78166 | .77721 | .77280 |
| 94 | .82508 | .82047 | .81591 | .81140 | .80694 | .80253 | .79817 | .79387 | .78961 | .78539 |
| 95 | .83526 | .83088 | .82654 | .82225 | .81800 | .81380 | .80965 | .80554 | .80148 | .79746 |
| 96 | .84491 | .84074 | .83662 | .83254 | .82850 | .82450 | .82055 | .81663 | .81276 | .80892 |
| 97 | .85405 | .85009 | .84617 | .84230 | .83846 | .83466 | .83089 | .82717 | .82348 | .81982 |
| 98 | .86270 | .85895 | .85523 | .85155 | .84791 | .84430 | .84072 | .83718 | .83367 | .83019 |
| 99 | .87090 | .86735 | .86382 | .86033 | .85687 | .85345 | .85005 | .84668 | .84335 | .84004 |
| 100 | .87856 | .87519 | .87185 | .86854 | .86526 | .86201 | .85878 | .85559 | .85242 | .84927 |
| 101 | .88587 | .88268 | .87952 | .87638 | .87327 | .87019 | .86713 | .86409 | .86109 | .85810 |
| 102 | .89263 | .88961 | .88662 | .88364 | .88069 | .87777 | .87487 | .87199 | .86913 | .86629 |
| 103 | .89938 | .89653 | .89370 | .89089 | .88810 | .88534 | .88259 | .87987 | .87717 | .87448 |
| 104 | .90558 | .90289 | .90021 | .89756 | .89492 | .89231 | .88971 | .88713 | .88456 | .88202 |
| 105 | .91170 | .90916 | .90664 | .90413 | .90164 | .89917 | .89672 | .89428 | .89186 | .88945 |
| 106 | .91940 | .91706 | .91474 | .91242 | .91013 | .90784 | .90558 | .90332 | .90108 | .89885 |
| 107 | .92816 | .92605 | .92395 | .92186 | .91978 | .91772 | .91567 | .91362 | .91159 | .90957 |
| 108 | .94247 | .94075 | .93904 | .93734 | .93565 | .93396 | .93229 | .93062 | .92895 | .92730 |
| 109 | .97081 | .96992 | .96904 | .96816 | .96729 | .96642 | .96555 | .96468 | .96382 | .96296 |

**Table S**
**Based on Life Table 2000CM**
**Single Life Remainder Factors**
**Applicable On or After May 1, 2009**

**Interest Rate**

| AGE | 8.2% | 8.4% | 8.6% | 8.8% | 9.0% | 9.2% | 9.4% | 9.6% | 9.8% | 10.0% |
|---|---|---|---|---|---|---|---|---|---|---|
| 0 | .01498 | .01444 | .01395 | .01351 | .01310 | .01273 | .01240 | .01209 | .01181 | .01155 |
| 1 | .00904 | .00847 | .00796 | .00749 | .00707 | .00668 | .00633 | .00601 | .00572 | .00545 |
| 2 | .00926 | .00866 | .00812 | .00763 | .00718 | .00677 | .00640 | .00606 | .00575 | .00547 |
| 3 | .00968 | .00905 | .00848 | .00796 | .00748 | .00705 | .00666 | .00630 | .00597 | .00567 |
| 4 | .01021 | .00955 | .00894 | .00839 | .00789 | .00744 | .00702 | .00664 | .00629 | .00597 |
| 5 | .01083 | .01013 | .00949 | .00891 | .00839 | .00790 | .00746 | .00706 | .00669 | .00635 |
| 6 | .01153 | .01080 | .01012 | .00951 | .00895 | .00844 | .00798 | .00755 | .00715 | .00679 |
| 7 | .01229 | .01151 | .01081 | .01016 | .00957 | .00903 | .00854 | .00808 | .00767 | .00728 |
| 8 | .01314 | .01232 | .01157 | .01089 | .01026 | .00969 | .00917 | .00869 | .00825 | .00784 |
| 9 | .01407 | .01321 | .01242 | .01170 | .01104 | .01044 | .00989 | .00938 | .00891 | .00848 |
| 10 | .01509 | .01418 | .01335 | .01259 | .01190 | .01126 | .01068 | .01014 | .00965 | .00919 |
| 11 | .01620 | .01525 | .01437 | .01358 | .01285 | .01218 | .01156 | .01099 | .01047 | .00998 |
| 12 | .01740 | .01640 | .01549 | .01465 | .01388 | .01317 | .01252 | .01192 | .01137 | .01086 |
| 13 | .01867 | .01762 | .01665 | .01577 | .01496 | .01422 | .01353 | .01290 | .01231 | .01177 |
| 14 | .01995 | .01885 | .01784 | .01691 | .01606 | .01527 | .01455 | .01389 | .01327 | .01270 |
| 15 | .02123 | .02007 | .01901 | .01803 | .01714 | .01632 | .01556 | .01485 | .01420 | .01360 |
| 16 | .02247 | .02126 | .02015 | .01913 | .01818 | .01732 | .01652 | .01578 | .01509 | .01446 |
| 17 | .02371 | .02244 | .02127 | .02020 | .01921 | .01830 | .01746 | .01668 | .01596 | .01529 |
| 18 | .02494 | .02361 | .02239 | .02126 | .02022 | .01926 | .01838 | .01756 | .01680 | .01610 |
| 19 | .02620 | .02480 | .02352 | .02234 | .02125 | .02024 | .01931 | .01844 | .01764 | .01690 |
| 20 | .02751 | .02605 | .02471 | .02346 | .02232 | .02126 | .02028 | .01937 | .01853 | .01775 |
| 21 | .02888 | .02735 | .02593 | .02463 | .02343 | .02231 | .02128 | .02032 | .01944 | .01861 |
| 22 | .03030 | .02870 | .02722 | .02585 | .02458 | .02341 | .02233 | .02132 | .02038 | .01951 |
| 23 | .03181 | .03013 | .02858 | .02714 | .02581 | .02458 | .02344 | .02237 | .02139 | .02047 |
| 24 | .03345 | .03169 | .03006 | .02855 | .02715 | .02586 | .02465 | .02353 | .02249 | .02152 |
| 25 | .03524 | .03340 | .03169 | .03010 | .02863 | .02727 | .02600 | .02482 | .02373 | .02270 |
| 26 | .03720 | .03527 | .03348 | .03181 | .03027 | .02884 | .02750 | .02626 | .02510 | .02402 |
| 27 | .03934 | .03732 | .03544 | .03370 | .03208 | .03057 | .02916 | .02786 | .02664 | .02549 |
| 28 | .04167 | .03955 | .03759 | .03576 | .03406 | .03247 | .03099 | .02962 | .02833 | .02713 |
| 29 | .04417 | .04196 | .03990 | .03798 | .03619 | .03453 | .03298 | .03153 | .03017 | .02890 |
| 30 | .04684 | .04452 | .04237 | .04036 | .03848 | .03674 | .03510 | .03358 | .03215 | .03081 |
| 31 | .04969 | .04727 | .04501 | .04291 | .04094 | .03911 | .03739 | .03579 | .03428 | .03287 |
| 32 | .05272 | .05019 | .04783 | .04563 | .04357 | .04165 | .03984 | .03816 | .03657 | .03509 |
| 33 | .05595 | .05331 | .05085 | .04854 | .04639 | .04437 | .04248 | .04070 | .03904 | .03748 |
| 34 | .05936 | .05661 | .05403 | .05162 | .04936 | .04725 | .04527 | .04341 | .04166 | .04001 |
| 35 | .06297 | .06010 | .05741 | .05489 | .05253 | .05032 | .04824 | .04629 | .04445 | .04272 |
| 36 | .06679 | .06380 | .06100 | .05837 | .05590 | .05358 | .05140 | .04935 | .04742 | .04561 |

| AGE | 8.2% | 8.4% | 8.6% | 8.8% | 9.0% | 9.2% | 9.4% | 9.6% | 9.8% | 10.0% |
|-----|------|------|------|------|------|------|------|------|------|-------|
| 37 | .07083 | .06771 | .06479 | .06204 | .05947 | .05704 | .05476 | .05261 | .05059 | .04868 |
| 38 | .07511 | .07186 | .06881 | .06595 | .06326 | .06072 | .05834 | .05609 | .05397 | .05196 |
| 39 | .07961 | .07623 | .07306 | .07007 | .06726 | .06462 | .06212 | .05977 | .05754 | .05544 |
| 40 | .08434 | .08083 | .07753 | .07442 | .07149 | .06873 | .06612 | .06366 | .06133 | .05913 |
| 41 | .08932 | .08568 | .08225 | .07901 | .07596 | .07308 | .07035 | .06778 | .06534 | .06304 |
| 42 | .09455 | .09077 | .08720 | .08384 | .08066 | .07766 | .07481 | .07213 | .06958 | .06717 |
| 43 | .10007 | .09615 | .09245 | .08895 | .08564 | .08251 | .07955 | .07674 | .07408 | .07156 |
| 44 | .10586 | .10180 | .09796 | .09433 | .09089 | .08763 | .08454 | .08162 | .07884 | .07621 |
| 45 | .11195 | .10774 | .10376 | .09999 | .09642 | .09303 | .08982 | .08677 | .08387 | .08112 |
| 46 | .11835 | .11400 | .10987 | .10596 | .10225 | .09873 | .09539 | .09222 | .08920 | .08633 |
| 47 | .12505 | .12055 | .11629 | .11224 | .10839 | .10474 | .10126 | .09796 | .09482 | .09182 |
| 48 | .13209 | .12745 | .12303 | .11884 | .11485 | .11106 | .10746 | .10402 | .10075 | .09764 |
| 49 | .13948 | .13469 | .13013 | .12579 | .12167 | .11774 | .11400 | .11043 | .10703 | .10379 |
| 50 | .14727 | .14233 | .13762 | .13314 | .12887 | .12481 | .12093 | .11723 | .11370 | .11033 |
| 51 | .15546 | .15037 | .14551 | .14089 | .13648 | .13228 | .12826 | .12443 | .12077 | .11726 |
| 52 | .16407 | .15884 | .15384 | .14907 | .14452 | .14018 | .13603 | .13206 | .12826 | .12463 |
| 53 | .17312 | .16774 | .16260 | .15769 | .15300 | .14852 | .14423 | .14012 | .13620 | .13243 |
| 54 | .18259 | .17707 | .17179 | .16674 | .16191 | .15729 | .15286 | .14862 | .14456 | .14067 |
| 55 | .19247 | .18680 | .18139 | .17620 | .17123 | .16648 | .16192 | .15755 | .15335 | .14933 |
| 56 | .20270 | .19690 | .19135 | .18602 | .18092 | .17603 | .17134 | .16684 | .16251 | .15836 |
| 57 | .21329 | .20736 | .20167 | .19622 | .19099 | .18596 | .18114 | .17650 | .17205 | .16777 |
| 58 | .22422 | .21816 | .21235 | .20677 | .20140 | .19625 | .19130 | .18653 | .18195 | .17754 |
| 59 | .23553 | .22935 | .22341 | .21770 | .21221 | .20693 | .20185 | .19696 | .19225 | .18772 |
| 60 | .24725 | .24095 | .23489 | .22906 | .22345 | .21805 | .21285 | .20783 | .20300 | .19834 |
| 61 | .25937 | .25296 | .24679 | .24084 | .23511 | .22959 | .22427 | .21914 | .21419 | .20941 |
| 62 | .27185 | .26534 | .25906 | .25300 | .24716 | .24153 | .23609 | .23084 | .22577 | .22088 |
| 63 | .28469 | .27808 | .27169 | .26553 | .25959 | .25384 | .24830 | .24294 | .23776 | .23275 |
| 64 | .29789 | .29119 | .28471 | .27845 | .27240 | .26656 | .26091 | .25544 | .25016 | .24504 |
| 65 | .31148 | .30468 | .29812 | .29177 | .28563 | .27969 | .27394 | .26837 | .26299 | .25777 |
| 66 | .32564 | .31877 | .31213 | .30570 | .29948 | .29345 | .28761 | .28195 | .27647 | .27115 |
| 67 | .34034 | .33341 | .32671 | .32021 | .31391 | .30780 | .30188 | .29614 | .29057 | .28517 |
| 68 | .35552 | .34855 | .34179 | .33523 | .32887 | .32270 | .31671 | .31089 | .30524 | .29976 |
| 69 | .37115 | .36414 | .35734 | .35073 | .34432 | .33809 | .33204 | .32616 | .32045 | .31489 |
| 70 | .38719 | .38016 | .37332 | .36668 | .36023 | .35396 | .34786 | .34193 | .33616 | .33054 |
| 71 | .40366 | .39662 | .38977 | .38311 | .37663 | .37032 | .36419 | .35821 | .35240 | .34674 |
| 72 | .42053 | .41350 | .40665 | .39998 | .39349 | .38716 | .38100 | .37500 | .36916 | .36346 |
| 73 | .43774 | .43073 | .42389 | .41723 | .41074 | .40441 | .39824 | .39222 | .38636 | .38063 |
| 74 | .45519 | .44821 | .44140 | .43476 | .42829 | .42197 | .41580 | .40979 | .40391 | .39818 |
| 75 | .47280 | .46587 | .45910 | .45250 | .44605 | .43975 | .43360 | .42759 | .42173 | .41599 |
| 76 | .49051 | .48364 | .47693 | .47037 | .46396 | .45770 | .45158 | .44560 | .43975 | .43403 |
| 77 | .50830 | .50150 | .49486 | .48836 | .48201 | .47580 | .46972 | .46377 | .45795 | .45225 |
| 78 | .52613 | .51942 | .51286 | .50644 | .50015 | .49400 | .48797 | .48208 | .47630 | .47064 |
| 79 | .54396 | .53736 | .53089 | .52456 | .51835 | .51227 | .50632 | .50048 | .49476 | .48915 |
| 80 | .56174 | .55525 | .54888 | .54265 | .53653 | .53054 | .52466 | .51890 | .51325 | .50770 |
| 81 | .57941 | .57305 | .56681 | .56068 | .55467 | .54878 | .54299 | .53731 | .53174 | .52627 |
| 82 | .59696 | .59073 | .58461 | .57861 | .57272 | .56693 | .56125 | .55566 | .55018 | .54480 |
| 83 | .61430 | .60822 | .60224 | .59637 | .59061 | .58494 | .57937 | .57389 | .56851 | .56322 |
| 84 | .63142 | .62549 | .61966 | .61393 | .60830 | .60276 | .59731 | .59196 | .58669 | .58150 |
| 85 | .64825 | .64249 | .63682 | .63124 | .62575 | .62035 | .61503 | .60980 | .60465 | .59958 |
| 86 | .66477 | .65918 | .65367 | .64825 | .64291 | .63765 | .63248 | .62738 | .62236 | .61741 |
| 87 | .68092 | .67550 | .67016 | .66490 | .65972 | .65462 | .64959 | .64463 | .63975 | .63493 |
| 88 | .69669 | .69145 | .68628 | .68119 | .67618 | .67123 | .66635 | .66154 | .65680 | .65212 |
| 89 | .71201 | .70696 | .70198 | .69706 | .69221 | .68742 | .68270 | .67805 | .67345 | .66892 |
| 90 | .72688 | .72201 | .71721 | .71246 | .70779 | .70317 | .69861 | .69411 | .68966 | .68528 |
| 91 | .74126 | .73658 | .73196 | .72739 | .72289 | .71844 | .71404 | .70970 | .70541 | .70117 |
| 92 | .75513 | .75063 | .74620 | .74181 | .73748 | .73320 | .72897 | .72479 | .72066 | .71657 |
| 93 | .76844 | .76414 | .75988 | .75568 | .75152 | .74741 | .74334 | .73932 | .73535 | .73142 |
| 94 | .78123 | .77711 | .77303 | .76901 | .76502 | .76108 | .75718 | .75332 | .74951 | .74573 |
| 95 | .79348 | .78954 | .78565 | .78179 | .77798 | .77421 | .77047 | .76677 | .76312 | .75950 |
| 96 | .80513 | .80137 | .79765 | .79397 | .79032 | .78671 | .78314 | .77960 | .77610 | .77263 |
| 97 | .81621 | .81262 | .80908 | .80556 | .80208 | .79864 | .79522 | .79184 | .78849 | .78517 |
| 98 | .82674 | .82333 | .81995 | .81660 | .81328 | .80999 | .80673 | .80351 | .80031 | .79713 |
| 99 | .83677 | .83352 | .83030 | .82711 | .82395 | .82082 | .81771 | .81463 | .81158 | .80855 |
| 100 | .84616 | .84307 | .84001 | .83697 | .83396 | .83097 | .82801 | .82507 | .82216 | .81927 |
| 101 | .85514 | .85221 | .84930 | .84641 | .84355 | .84070 | .83788 | .83509 | .83231 | .82956 |
| 102 | .86348 | .86069 | .85792 | .85517 | .85245 | .84974 | .84706 | .84439 | .84175 | .83912 |
| 103 | .87182 | .86918 | .86655 | .86395 | .86136 | .85880 | .85625 | .85372 | .85121 | .84872 |
| 104 | .87950 | .87699 | .87450 | .87203 | .86957 | .86713 | .86471 | .86231 | .85992 | .85755 |
| 105 | .88706 | .88468 | .88232 | .87998 | .87765 | .87534 | .87304 | .87076 | .86849 | .86624 |

## Gross Estate
### See p. 20,601 for regulations not amended to reflect law changes

| AGE | 8.2% | 8.4% | 8.6% | 8.8% | 9.0% | 9.2% | 9.4% | 9.6% | 9.8% | 10.0% |
|---|---|---|---|---|---|---|---|---|---|---|
| 106 | .89664 | .89444 | .89225 | .89008 | .88792 | .88577 | .88364 | .88152 | .87941 | .87731 |
| 107 | .90756 | .90557 | .90358 | .90160 | .89964 | .89768 | .89574 | .89380 | .89188 | .88997 |
| 108 | .92565 | .92401 | .92238 | .92075 | .91914 | .91753 | .91592 | .91433 | .91274 | .91116 |
| 109 | .96211 | .96125 | .96041 | .95956 | .95872 | .95788 | .95704 | .95620 | .95537 | .95455 |

## Table S
### Based on Life Table 2000CM
### Single Life Remainder Factors
### Applicable On or After May 1, 2009

**Interest Rate**

| AGE | 10.2% | 10.4% | 10.6% | 10.8% | 11.0% | 11.2% | 11.4% | 11.6% | 11.8% | 12.0% |
|---|---|---|---|---|---|---|---|---|---|---|
| 0 | .01132 | .01110 | .01089 | .01071 | .01053 | .01037 | .01022 | .01008 | .00995 | .00983 |
| 1 | .00520 | .00497 | .00476 | .00457 | .00439 | .00423 | .00407 | .00393 | .00379 | .00367 |
| 2 | .00521 | .00496 | .00474 | .00454 | .00435 | .00417 | .00401 | .00385 | .00371 | .00358 |
| 3 | .00539 | .00513 | .00490 | .00468 | .00447 | .00429 | .00411 | .00395 | .00380 | .00366 |
| 4 | .00567 | .00540 | .00515 | .00492 | .00470 | .00450 | .00432 | .00414 | .00398 | .00383 |
| 5 | .00603 | .00574 | .00547 | .00523 | .00500 | .00478 | .00459 | .00440 | .00423 | .00407 |
| 6 | .00646 | .00615 | .00587 | .00560 | .00536 | .00513 | .00492 | .00472 | .00453 | .00436 |
| 7 | .00693 | .00660 | .00630 | .00602 | .00576 | .00551 | .00529 | .00508 | .00488 | .00469 |
| 8 | .00747 | .00712 | .00680 | .00650 | .00622 | .00596 | .00572 | .00549 | .00528 | .00509 |
| 9 | .00808 | .00771 | .00737 | .00705 | .00675 | .00648 | .00622 | .00598 | .00576 | .00555 |
| 10 | .00877 | .00838 | .00801 | .00767 | .00736 | .00707 | .00679 | .00654 | .00630 | .00608 |
| 11 | .00954 | .00912 | .00873 | .00838 | .00804 | .00773 | .00744 | .00717 | .00692 | .00668 |
| 12 | .01038 | .00994 | .00953 | .00915 | .00880 | .00847 | .00816 | .00788 | .00761 | .00735 |
| 13 | .01127 | .01081 | .01038 | .00998 | .00960 | .00925 | .00893 | .00862 | .00833 | .00806 |
| 14 | .01217 | .01168 | .01122 | .01080 | .01040 | .01003 | .00969 | .00937 | .00906 | .00878 |
| 15 | .01305 | .01253 | .01205 | .01160 | .01118 | .01079 | .01042 | .01008 | .00976 | .00946 |
| 16 | .01387 | .01333 | .01282 | .01234 | .01190 | .01149 | .01110 | .01074 | .01040 | .01009 |
| 17 | .01467 | .01409 | .01356 | .01306 | .01259 | .01216 | .01175 | .01137 | .01101 | .01067 |
| 18 | .01544 | .01484 | .01427 | .01374 | .01325 | .01279 | .01236 | .01195 | .01157 | .01122 |
| 19 | .01621 | .01557 | .01497 | .01442 | .01390 | .01341 | .01295 | .01253 | .01213 | .01175 |
| 20 | .01702 | .01634 | .01571 | .01512 | .01457 | .01406 | .01357 | .01312 | .01270 | .01230 |
| 21 | .01784 | .01713 | .01646 | .01584 | .01526 | .01471 | .01420 | .01372 | .01327 | .01285 |
| 22 | .01870 | .01794 | .01724 | .01658 | .01596 | .01539 | .01485 | .01434 | .01386 | .01342 |
| 23 | .01961 | .01881 | .01807 | .01737 | .01672 | .01611 | .01554 | .01500 | .01449 | .01402 |
| 24 | .02062 | .01977 | .01899 | .01825 | .01756 | .01691 | .01630 | .01573 | .01520 | .01469 |
| 25 | .02175 | .02085 | .02002 | .01924 | .01851 | .01782 | .01718 | .01657 | .01600 | .01547 |
| 26 | .02301 | .02207 | .02119 | .02036 | .01958 | .01886 | .01817 | .01753 | .01692 | .01635 |
| 27 | .02443 | .02343 | .02250 | .02162 | .02080 | .02003 | .01930 | .01862 | .01798 | .01737 |
| 28 | .02600 | .02495 | .02396 | .02303 | .02216 | .02134 | .02057 | .01985 | .01916 | .01852 |
| 29 | .02771 | .02660 | .02555 | .02457 | .02365 | .02278 | .02197 | .02120 | .02047 | .01979 |
| 30 | .02956 | .02838 | .02728 | .02624 | .02526 | .02434 | .02348 | .02266 | .02189 | .02116 |
| 31 | .03155 | .03031 | .02914 | .02804 | .02701 | .02604 | .02512 | .02425 | .02344 | .02266 |
| 32 | .03370 | .03239 | .03115 | .02999 | .02890 | .02787 | .02690 | .02598 | .02511 | .02429 |
| 33 | .03601 | .03463 | .03333 | .03210 | .03095 | .02985 | .02883 | .02785 | .02693 | .02606 |
| 34 | .03847 | .03701 | .03564 | .03434 | .03312 | .03197 | .03088 | .02985 | .02887 | .02795 |
| 35 | .04109 | .03956 | .03811 | .03675 | .03546 | .03424 | .03308 | .03199 | .03096 | .02998 |
| 36 | .04390 | .04228 | .04076 | .03932 | .03795 | .03667 | .03545 | .03429 | .03320 | .03216 |
| 37 | .04688 | .04518 | .04358 | .04206 | .04062 | .03926 | .03798 | .03676 | .03560 | .03450 |
| 38 | .05007 | .04829 | .04660 | .04500 | .04349 | .04205 | .04069 | .03940 | .03818 | .03701 |
| 39 | .05346 | .05158 | .04981 | .04812 | .04653 | .04502 | .04358 | .04222 | .04092 | .03969 |
| 40 | .05705 | .05508 | .05321 | .05144 | .04976 | .04817 | .04666 | .04522 | .04385 | .04255 |
| 41 | .06086 | .05879 | .05683 | .05497 | .05320 | .05152 | .04993 | .04841 | .04697 | .04559 |
| 42 | .06488 | .06271 | .06066 | .05870 | .05684 | .05508 | .05340 | .05180 | .05028 | .04882 |
| 43 | .06917 | .06690 | .06474 | .06269 | .06074 | .05888 | .05711 | .05543 | .05382 | .05229 |
| 44 | .07370 | .07132 | .06906 | .06691 | .06486 | .06291 | .06105 | .05928 | .05759 | .05598 |
| 45 | .07850 | .07602 | .07365 | .07139 | .06924 | .06719 | .06524 | .06338 | .06160 | .05990 |
| 46 | .08360 | .08100 | .07852 | .07616 | .07390 | .07176 | .06970 | .06775 | .06587 | .06409 |
| 47 | .08897 | .08626 | .08367 | .08120 | .07884 | .07659 | .07443 | .07238 | .07041 | .06853 |
| 48 | .09466 | .09183 | .08912 | .08654 | .08407 | .08172 | .07946 | .07730 | .07524 | .07326 |
| 49 | .10069 | .09774 | .09492 | .09222 | .08964 | .08717 | .08481 | .08255 | .08038 | .07831 |
| 50 | .10711 | .10403 | .10109 | .09827 | .09558 | .09300 | .09053 | .08816 | .08589 | .08371 |
| 51 | .11392 | .11072 | .10765 | .10472 | .10191 | .09921 | .09663 | .09415 | .09178 | .08950 |
| 52 | .12116 | .11783 | .11464 | .11159 | .10866 | .10585 | .10315 | .10057 | .09808 | .09569 |
| 53 | .12883 | .12538 | .12206 | .11889 | .11584 | .11291 | .11010 | .10740 | .10481 | .10231 |
| 54 | .13694 | .13336 | .12992 | .12662 | .12345 | .12041 | .11748 | .11467 | .11196 | .10936 |
| 55 | .14547 | .14176 | .13820 | .13478 | .13149 | .12832 | .12528 | .12235 | .11953 | .11682 |
| 56 | .15437 | .15054 | .14685 | .14330 | .13989 | .13661 | .13345 | .13040 | .12747 | .12464 |
| 57 | .16365 | .15969 | .15588 | .15221 | .14868 | .14527 | .14199 | .13883 | .13578 | .13284 |
| 58 | .17330 | .16921 | .16528 | .16149 | .15783 | .15431 | .15091 | .14763 | .14447 | .14141 |
| 59 | .18335 | .17914 | .17508 | .17117 | .16739 | .16375 | .16023 | .15684 | .15356 | .15039 |

| AGE | 10.2% | 10.4% | 10.6% | 10.8% | 11.0% | 11.2% | 11.4% | 11.6% | 11.8% | 12.0% |
|---|---|---|---|---|---|---|---|---|---|---|
| 60 | .19385 | .18952 | .18534 | .18131 | .17741 | .17365 | .17001 | .16650 | .16311 | .15982 |
| 61 | .20480 | .20035 | .19605 | .19189 | .18788 | .18400 | .18025 | .17662 | .17311 | .16971 |
| 62 | .21615 | .21158 | .20717 | .20290 | .19877 | .19477 | .19090 | .18716 | .18354 | .18003 |
| 63 | .22791 | .22323 | .21870 | .21431 | .21007 | .20596 | .20198 | .19812 | .19439 | .19077 |
| 64 | .24009 | .23530 | .23066 | .22616 | .22181 | .21758 | .21349 | .20953 | .20568 | .20195 |
| 65 | .25271 | .24781 | .24306 | .23846 | .23400 | .22967 | .22547 | .22139 | .21744 | .21360 |
| 66 | .26600 | .26100 | .25615 | .25145 | .24688 | .24245 | .23814 | .23396 | .22990 | .22596 |
| 67 | .27992 | .27483 | .26989 | .26509 | .26043 | .25590 | .25150 | .24722 | .24306 | .23901 |
| 68 | .29443 | .28926 | .28423 | .27934 | .27459 | .26997 | .26548 | .26110 | .25685 | .25271 |
| 69 | .30950 | .30424 | .29914 | .29417 | .28934 | .28463 | .28005 | .27559 | .27125 | .26703 |
| 70 | .32508 | .31976 | .31459 | .30955 | .30464 | .29986 | .29520 | .29067 | .28625 | .28194 |
| 71 | .34122 | .33585 | .33062 | .32552 | .32054 | .31570 | .31097 | .30637 | .30187 | .29749 |
| 72 | .35790 | .35249 | .34721 | .34205 | .33703 | .33213 | .32734 | .32268 | .31812 | .31367 |
| 73 | .37505 | .36960 | .36428 | .35909 | .35403 | .34908 | .34425 | .33953 | .33492 | .33042 |
| 74 | .39258 | .38711 | .38177 | .37655 | .37145 | .36647 | .36160 | .35684 | .35219 | .34764 |
| 75 | .41039 | .40491 | .39956 | .39432 | .38921 | .38420 | .37931 | .37452 | .36983 | .36525 |
| 76 | .42843 | .42296 | .41760 | .41236 | .40724 | .40222 | .39731 | .39250 | .38779 | .38318 |
| 77 | .44668 | .44122 | .43588 | .43065 | .42552 | .42050 | .41559 | .41077 | .40605 | .40143 |
| 78 | .46510 | .45967 | .45435 | .44914 | .44403 | .43902 | .43411 | .42930 | .42458 | .41995 |
| 79 | .48365 | .47826 | .47298 | .46780 | .46271 | .45773 | .45284 | .44804 | .44333 | .43871 |
| 80 | .50226 | .49693 | .49169 | .48655 | .48150 | .47655 | .47169 | .46692 | .46224 | .45763 |
| 81 | .52090 | .51562 | .51044 | .50536 | .50036 | .49546 | .49064 | .48590 | .48125 | .47668 |
| 82 | .53951 | .53431 | .52920 | .52418 | .51924 | .51439 | .50963 | .50494 | .50033 | .49580 |
| 83 | .55802 | .55291 | .54788 | .54294 | .53808 | .53329 | .52859 | .52396 | .51941 | .51493 |
| 84 | .57640 | .57139 | .56645 | .56159 | .55681 | .55210 | .54747 | .54291 | .53843 | .53401 |
| 85 | .59459 | .58968 | .58484 | .58008 | .57539 | .57077 | .56623 | .56175 | .55733 | .55298 |
| 86 | .61254 | .60774 | .60302 | .59836 | .59377 | .58925 | .58479 | .58040 | .57607 | .57180 |
| 87 | .63019 | .62551 | .62090 | .61635 | .61187 | .60745 | .60309 | .59880 | .59456 | .59038 |
| 88 | .64751 | .64296 | .63847 | .63405 | .62968 | .62537 | .62112 | .61693 | .61279 | .60871 |
| 89 | .66444 | .66003 | .65567 | .65137 | .64712 | .64293 | .63880 | .63471 | .63068 | .62670 |
| 90 | .68094 | .67667 | .67244 | .66827 | .66415 | .66009 | .65607 | .65210 | .64818 | .64431 |
| 91 | .69699 | .69285 | .68877 | .68473 | .68074 | .67680 | .67291 | .66906 | .66526 | .66150 |
| 92 | .71254 | .70855 | .70460 | .70071 | .69685 | .69304 | .68928 | .68555 | .68187 | .67823 |
| 93 | .72753 | .72369 | .71989 | .71613 | .71242 | .70874 | .70510 | .70150 | .69794 | .69442 |
| 94 | .74200 | .73830 | .73464 | .73103 | .72745 | .72390 | .72040 | .71693 | .71350 | .71010 |
| 95 | .75591 | .75236 | .74885 | .74538 | .74194 | .73853 | .73516 | .73182 | .72851 | .72524 |
| 96 | .76920 | .76580 | .76243 | .75909 | .75579 | .75252 | .74928 | .74607 | .74289 | .73974 |
| 97 | .78188 | .77863 | .77540 | .77220 | .76904 | .76590 | .76279 | .75971 | .75665 | .75363 |
| 98 | .79399 | .79088 | .78779 | .78473 | .78170 | .77869 | .77571 | .77276 | .76983 | .76693 |
| 99 | .80555 | .80257 | .79962 | .79670 | .79380 | .79092 | .78807 | .78525 | .78244 | .77966 |
| 100 | .81641 | .81357 | .81075 | .80796 | .80518 | .80243 | .79971 | .79700 | .79432 | .79165 |
| 101 | .82683 | .82412 | .82144 | .81877 | .81612 | .81350 | .81089 | .80831 | .80574 | .80320 |
| 102 | .83652 | .83394 | .83137 | .82882 | .82630 | .82379 | .82130 | .81883 | .81637 | .81394 |
| 103 | .84624 | .84379 | .84135 | .83892 | .83652 | .83413 | .83176 | .82941 | .82707 | .82475 |
| 104 | .85519 | .85285 | .85053 | .84822 | .84593 | .84365 | .84139 | .83915 | .83692 | .83470 |
| 105 | .86400 | .86178 | .85957 | .85737 | .85519 | .85302 | .85087 | .84873 | .84660 | .84449 |
| 106 | .87523 | .87316 | .87110 | .86905 | .86702 | .86500 | .86299 | .86099 | .85900 | .85703 |
| 107 | .88806 | .88617 | .88429 | .88242 | .88055 | .87870 | .87686 | .87502 | .87320 | .87139 |
| 108 | .90958 | .90802 | .90646 | .90490 | .90336 | .90182 | .90028 | .89876 | .89724 | .89573 |
| 109 | .95372 | .95290 | .95208 | .95126 | .95045 | .94964 | .94883 | .94803 | .94723 | .94643 |

### Table S
### Based on Life Table 2000CM
### Single Life Remainder Factors
### Applicable On or After May 1, 2009

### Interest Rate

| AGE | 12.2% | 12.4% | 12.6% | 12.8% | 13.0% | 13.2% | 13.4% | 13.6% | 13.8% | 14.0% |
|---|---|---|---|---|---|---|---|---|---|---|
| 0 | .00972 | .00961 | .00951 | .00941 | .00932 | .00924 | .00916 | .00908 | .00901 | .00894 |
| 1 | .00355 | .00345 | .00334 | .00325 | .00316 | .00307 | .00299 | .00292 | .00285 | .00278 |
| 2 | .00346 | .00334 | .00323 | .00313 | .00303 | .00294 | .00286 | .00278 | .00270 | .00263 |
| 3 | .00353 | .00340 | .00329 | .00318 | .00307 | .00298 | .00289 | .00280 | .00272 | .00264 |
| 4 | .00369 | .00356 | .00343 | .00332 | .00321 | .00310 | .00300 | .00291 | .00283 | .00274 |
| 5 | .00392 | .00377 | .00364 | .00352 | .00340 | .00329 | .00318 | .00308 | .00299 | .00290 |
| 6 | .00420 | .00405 | .00391 | .00377 | .00365 | .00353 | .00342 | .00331 | .00321 | .00311 |
| 7 | .00452 | .00436 | .00421 | .00406 | .00393 | .00380 | .00368 | .00357 | .00346 | .00336 |
| 8 | .00490 | .00473 | .00457 | .00441 | .00427 | .00413 | .00400 | .00388 | .00376 | .00365 |
| 9 | .00535 | .00517 | .00499 | .00483 | .00467 | .00453 | .00439 | .00426 | .00413 | .00402 |
| 10 | .00587 | .00567 | .00548 | .00531 | .00514 | .00499 | .00484 | .00470 | .00456 | .00444 |
| 11 | .00645 | .00624 | .00605 | .00586 | .00568 | .00551 | .00536 | .00521 | .00506 | .00493 |
| 12 | .00711 | .00689 | .00668 | .00648 | .00629 | .00611 | .00595 | .00579 | .00563 | .00549 |

| AGE | 12.2% | 12.4% | 12.6% | 12.8% | 13.0% | 13.2% | 13.4% | 13.6% | 13.8% | 14.0% |
|---|---|---|---|---|---|---|---|---|---|---|
| 13 | .00781 | .00757 | .00735 | .00714 | .00694 | .00675 | .00657 | .00640 | .00624 | .00609 |
| 14 | .00851 | .00826 | .00802 | .00780 | .00759 | .00739 | .00720 | .00702 | .00684 | .00668 |
| 15 | .00918 | .00891 | .00866 | .00842 | .00820 | .00799 | .00779 | .00759 | .00741 | .00724 |
| 16 | .00979 | .00950 | .00924 | .00899 | .00875 | .00853 | .00832 | .00811 | .00792 | .00774 |
| 17 | .01035 | .01006 | .00978 | .00951 | .00926 | .00902 | .00880 | .00859 | .00838 | .00819 |
| 18 | .01088 | .01057 | .01027 | .00999 | .00973 | .00948 | .00924 | .00901 | .00880 | .00860 |
| 19 | .01139 | .01106 | .01075 | .01045 | .01017 | .00990 | .00965 | .00942 | .00919 | .00898 |
| 20 | .01192 | .01157 | .01124 | .01092 | .01063 | .01035 | .01008 | .00983 | .00959 | .00936 |
| 21 | .01245 | .01208 | .01173 | .01139 | .01108 | .01078 | .01050 | .01023 | .00998 | .00974 |
| 22 | .01300 | .01260 | .01222 | .01187 | .01154 | .01122 | .01092 | .01064 | .01037 | .01011 |
| 23 | .01357 | .01315 | .01275 | .01238 | .01202 | .01168 | .01137 | .01106 | .01078 | .01051 |
| 24 | .01422 | .01377 | .01334 | .01294 | .01257 | .01221 | .01187 | .01155 | .01124 | .01095 |
| 25 | .01496 | .01448 | .01403 | .01361 | .01320 | .01282 | .01246 | .01212 | .01180 | .01149 |
| 26 | .01582 | .01531 | .01483 | .01438 | .01395 | .01354 | .01316 | .01279 | .01244 | .01211 |
| 27 | .01680 | .01626 | .01575 | .01527 | .01481 | .01437 | .01396 | .01357 | .01320 | .01285 |
| 28 | .01791 | .01734 | .01679 | .01628 | .01579 | .01533 | .01489 | .01447 | .01408 | .01370 |
| 29 | .01914 | .01853 | .01795 | .01740 | .01688 | .01639 | .01592 | .01548 | .01505 | .01465 |
| 30 | .02048 | .01982 | .01921 | .01862 | .01807 | .01754 | .01704 | .01657 | .01612 | .01569 |
| 31 | .02193 | .02124 | .02058 | .01996 | .01937 | .01881 | .01828 | .01777 | .01729 | .01683 |
| 32 | .02351 | .02278 | .02208 | .02142 | .02079 | .02019 | .01962 | .01908 | .01857 | .01808 |
| 33 | .02523 | .02445 | .02371 | .02300 | .02234 | .02170 | .02109 | .02052 | .01997 | .01944 |
| 34 | .02707 | .02624 | .02545 | .02470 | .02399 | .02331 | .02267 | .02205 | .02146 | .02091 |
| 35 | .02905 | .02817 | .02733 | .02653 | .02577 | .02505 | .02436 | .02371 | .02308 | .02249 |
| 36 | .03117 | .03024 | .02935 | .02850 | .02769 | .02693 | .02619 | .02550 | .02483 | .02419 |
| 37 | .03345 | .03246 | .03151 | .03061 | .02976 | .02894 | .02816 | .02742 | .02671 | .02603 |
| 38 | .03590 | .03485 | .03385 | .03289 | .03198 | .03112 | .03029 | .02950 | .02874 | .02802 |
| 39 | .03852 | .03740 | .03634 | .03533 | .03436 | .03344 | .03256 | .03172 | .03092 | .03015 |
| 40 | .04131 | .04013 | .03900 | .03793 | .03690 | .03593 | .03499 | .03410 | .03324 | .03242 |
| 41 | .04428 | .04303 | .04184 | .04070 | .03962 | .03858 | .03759 | .03664 | .03573 | .03486 |
| 42 | .04744 | .04612 | .04486 | .04366 | .04250 | .04140 | .04035 | .03934 | .03838 | .03745 |
| 43 | .05083 | .04943 | .04810 | .04683 | .04561 | .04444 | .04333 | .04226 | .04123 | .04025 |
| 44 | .05443 | .05296 | .05155 | .05021 | .04892 | .04768 | .04650 | .04537 | .04428 | .04324 |
| 45 | .05827 | .05672 | .05523 | .05381 | .05245 | .05114 | .04989 | .04869 | .04754 | .04643 |
| 46 | .06237 | .06074 | .05917 | .05767 | .05623 | .05485 | .05352 | .05225 | .05103 | .04986 |
| 47 | .06673 | .06500 | .06335 | .06177 | .06025 | .05879 | .05739 | .05605 | .05475 | .05351 |
| 48 | .07137 | .06955 | .06781 | .06614 | .06454 | .06300 | .06152 | .06010 | .05874 | .05742 |
| 49 | .07632 | .07441 | .07258 | .07082 | .06913 | .06750 | .06595 | .06444 | .06300 | .06161 |
| 50 | .08162 | .07962 | .07769 | .07584 | .07407 | .07236 | .07071 | .06913 | .06760 | .06614 |
| 51 | .08731 | .08520 | .08318 | .08124 | .07937 | .07757 | .07583 | .07416 | .07256 | .07101 |
| 52 | .09340 | .09119 | .08907 | .08703 | .08507 | .08317 | .08135 | .07959 | .07790 | .07627 |
| 53 | .09991 | .09760 | .09538 | .09324 | .09118 | .08919 | .08728 | .08543 | .08365 | .08193 |
| 54 | .10685 | .10443 | .10211 | .09987 | .09771 | .09562 | .09361 | .09167 | .08980 | .08799 |
| 55 | .11420 | .11168 | .10925 | .10690 | .10464 | .10246 | .10035 | .09832 | .09635 | .09445 |
| 56 | .12191 | .11928 | .11675 | .11430 | .11193 | .10965 | .10745 | .10531 | .10325 | .10126 |
| 57 | .13001 | .12727 | .12462 | .12207 | .11960 | .11721 | .11491 | .11268 | .11052 | .10843 |
| 58 | .13846 | .13561 | .13286 | .13020 | .12762 | .12513 | .12273 | .12040 | .11814 | .11595 |
| 59 | .14732 | .14436 | .14150 | .13873 | .13605 | .13346 | .13095 | .12851 | .12616 | .12388 |
| 60 | .15665 | .15358 | .15060 | .14772 | .14494 | .14224 | .13962 | .13709 | .13463 | .13225 |
| 61 | .16642 | .16324 | .16016 | .15717 | .15428 | .15147 | .14875 | .14611 | .14355 | .14107 |
| 62 | .17663 | .17333 | .17014 | .16704 | .16404 | .16113 | .15830 | .15556 | .15290 | .15031 |
| 63 | .18726 | .18385 | .18055 | .17734 | .17423 | .17121 | .16828 | .16544 | .16267 | .15999 |
| 64 | .19833 | .19481 | .19140 | .18809 | .18487 | .18175 | .17871 | .17576 | .17289 | .17010 |
| 65 | .20987 | .20624 | .20273 | .19931 | .19598 | .19275 | .18961 | .18656 | .18358 | .18069 |
| 66 | .22213 | .21840 | .21478 | .21125 | .20783 | .20449 | .20125 | .19809 | .19501 | .19202 |
| 67 | .23508 | .23125 | .22753 | .22390 | .22037 | .21694 | .21360 | .21034 | .20716 | .20407 |
| 68 | .24868 | .24476 | .24094 | .23722 | .23359 | .23006 | .22662 | .22327 | .22000 | .21681 |
| 69 | .26291 | .25889 | .25498 | .25117 | .24745 | .24383 | .24030 | .23685 | .23349 | .23020 |
| 70 | .27773 | .27364 | .26964 | .26574 | .26194 | .25823 | .25461 | .25107 | .24762 | .24425 |
| 71 | .29321 | .28904 | .28496 | .28099 | .27710 | .27331 | .26961 | .26599 | .26246 | .25900 |
| 72 | .30933 | .30508 | .30094 | .29689 | .29294 | .28907 | .28530 | .28160 | .27799 | .27446 |
| 73 | .32602 | .32171 | .31751 | .31340 | .30938 | .30545 | .30160 | .29784 | .29416 | .29056 |
| 74 | .34319 | .33884 | .33458 | .33042 | .32634 | .32236 | .31845 | .31463 | .31089 | .30723 |
| 75 | .36076 | .35637 | .35207 | .34786 | .34374 | .33970 | .33575 | .33188 | .32808 | .32437 |
| 76 | .37867 | .37425 | .36991 | .36567 | .36151 | .35744 | .35344 | .34953 | .34569 | .34192 |
| 77 | .39690 | .39245 | .38810 | .38383 | .37964 | .37554 | .37151 | .36756 | .36369 | .35989 |
| 78 | .41541 | .41096 | .40659 | .40231 | .39811 | .39398 | .38993 | .38596 | .38206 | .37823 |
| 79 | .43418 | .42973 | .42536 | .42107 | .41686 | .41272 | .40866 | .40467 | .40075 | .39691 |
| 80 | .45311 | .44868 | .44432 | .44003 | .43582 | .43169 | .42763 | .42363 | .41971 | .41585 |
| 81 | .47219 | .46777 | .46343 | .45916 | .45497 | .45084 | .44679 | .44280 | .43888 | .43502 |

Reg. § 20.2031-7(d)(7)

| AGE | 12.2% | 12.4% | 12.6% | 12.8% | 13.0% | 13.2% | 13.4% | 13.6% | 13.8% | 14.0% |
|---|---|---|---|---|---|---|---|---|---|---|
| 82 | .49135 | .48696 | .48265 | .47841 | .47424 | .47014 | .46610 | .46213 | .45822 | .45437 |
| 83 | .51052 | .50618 | .50191 | .49771 | .49357 | .48950 | .48549 | .48154 | .47766 | .47383 |
| 84 | .52966 | .52537 | .52115 | .51700 | .51291 | .50887 | .50490 | .50099 | .49714 | .49334 |
| 85 | .54870 | .54448 | .54032 | .53622 | .53218 | .52820 | .52428 | .52041 | .51660 | .51284 |
| 86 | .56759 | .56344 | .55935 | .55532 | .55135 | .54742 | .54356 | .53974 | .53598 | .53227 |
| 87 | .58626 | .58219 | .57818 | .57422 | .57031 | .56646 | .56266 | .55891 | .55521 | .55155 |
| 88 | .60468 | .60070 | .59677 | .59290 | .58907 | .58529 | .58157 | .57788 | .57425 | .57066 |
| 89 | .62277 | .61888 | .61505 | .61126 | .60753 | .60383 | .60018 | .59658 | .59302 | .58950 |
| 90 | .64048 | .63670 | .63296 | .62927 | .62563 | .62202 | .61846 | .61494 | .61146 | .60803 |
| 91 | .65778 | .65411 | .65048 | .64689 | .64334 | .63983 | .63636 | .63293 | .62954 | .62619 |
| 92 | .67462 | .67106 | .66754 | .66406 | .66061 | .65720 | .65383 | .65050 | .64720 | .64393 |
| 93 | .69094 | .68749 | .68408 | .68071 | .67737 | .67406 | .67079 | .66756 | .66435 | .66118 |
| 94 | .70673 | .70340 | .70011 | .69685 | .69362 | .69042 | .68725 | .68412 | .68102 | .67794 |
| 95 | .72199 | .71878 | .71560 | .71246 | .70934 | .70625 | .70319 | .70016 | .69716 | .69419 |
| 96 | .73662 | .73353 | .73047 | .72743 | .72443 | .72145 | .71850 | .71557 | .71268 | .70981 |
| 97 | .75063 | .74766 | .74471 | .74180 | .73890 | .73604 | .73319 | .73038 | .72758 | .72482 |
| 98 | .76405 | .76120 | .75837 | .75557 | .75279 | .75003 | .74730 | .74459 | .74190 | .73923 |
| 99 | .77690 | .77417 | .77146 | .76877 | .76610 | .76345 | .76083 | .75822 | .75564 | .75308 |
| 100 | .78901 | .78639 | .78379 | .78121 | .77866 | .77612 | .77360 | .77110 | .76862 | .76616 |
| 101 | .80067 | .79816 | .79568 | .79321 | .79076 | .78832 | .78591 | .78351 | .78114 | .77877 |
| 102 | .81152 | .80912 | .80674 | .80438 | .80203 | .79970 | .79738 | .79508 | .79280 | .79054 |
| 103 | .82245 | .82016 | .81789 | .81563 | .81339 | .81116 | .80895 | .80676 | .80458 | .80241 |
| 104 | .83250 | .83031 | .82814 | .82599 | .82384 | .82171 | .81960 | .81750 | .81541 | .81334 |
| 105 | .84239 | .84030 | .83823 | .83617 | .83412 | .83209 | .83006 | .82806 | .82606 | .82407 |
| 106 | .85507 | .85311 | .85117 | .84924 | .84733 | .84542 | .84352 | .84164 | .83976 | .83790 |
| 107 | .86958 | .86779 | .86600 | .86422 | .86246 | .86070 | .85895 | .85721 | .85548 | .85376 |
| 108 | .89422 | .89272 | .89123 | .88974 | .88826 | .88679 | .88533 | .88386 | .88241 | .88096 |
| 109 | .94563 | .94484 | .94405 | .94326 | .94248 | .94170 | .94092 | .94014 | .93937 | .93860 |

## Table 2000CM

| Age x | $l_x$ | Age x | Age x | $l_x$ |
|---|---|---|---|---|
| 0 | 100000 | 37 | 74 | 66882 |
| 1 | 99305 | 38 | 75 | 64561 |
| 2 | 99255 | 39 | 76 | 62091 |
| 3 | 99222 | 40 | 77 | 59476 |
| 4 | 99197 | 41 | 78 | 56721 |
| 5 | 99176 | 42 | 79 | 53833 |
| 6 | 99158 | 43 | 80 | 50819 |
| 7 | 99140 | 44 | 81 | 47694 |
| 8 | 99124 | 45 | 82 | 44475 |
| 9 | 99110 | 46 | 83 | 41181 |
| 10 | 99097 | 47 | 84 | 37837 |
| 11 | 99085 | 48 | 85 | 34471 |
| 12 | 99073 | 49 | 86 | 31114 |
| 13 | 99057 | 50 | 87 | 27799 |
| 14 | 99033 | 51 | 88 | 24564 |
| 15 | 98998 | 52 | 89 | 21443 |
| 16 | 98950 | 53 | 90 | 18472 |
| 17 | 98891 | 54 | 91 | 15685 |
| 18 | 98822 | 55 | 92 | 13111 |
| 19 | 98745 | 56 | 93 | 10773 |
| 20 | 98664 | 57 | 94 | 8690 |
| 21 | 98577 | 58 | 95 | 6871 |
| 22 | 98485 | 59 | 96 | 5315 |
| 23 | 98390 | 60 | 97 | 4016 |
| 24 | 98295 | 61 | 98 | 2959 |
| 25 | 98202 | 62 | 99 | 2122 |
| 26 | 98111 | 63 | 100 | 1477 |
| 27 | 98022 | 64 | 101 | 997 |
| 28 | 97934 | 65 | 102 | 650 |
| 29 | 97844 | 66 | 103 | 410 |
| 30 | 97750 | 67 | 104 | 248 |
| 31 | 97652 | 68 | 105 | 144 |
| 32 | 97549 | 69 | 106 | 81 |
| 33 | 97441 | 70 | 107 | 43 |
| 34 | 97324 | 71 | 108 | 22 |
| 35 | 97199 | 72 | 109 | 11 |
| 36 | 97065 | 73 | 110 | 0 |

(e) *Effective/applicability dates.*—This section applies on and after May 1, 2009. [Reg. § 20.2031-7.]

☐ [T.D. 8540, 6-10-94. *Amended by* T.D. 8819, 4-29-99; T.D. 8886, 6-9-2000; *T.D. 9448, 5-1-2009 and T.D. 9540, 8-9-2011.*]

### [Reg. § 20.2031-7A]

**§ 20.2031-7A. Valuation of annuities, interests for life or term of years, and remainder or reversionary interests for estates of decedents for which the valuation date of the gross estate is before May 1, 2009.**—(a) *Valuation of annuities, interests for life or term of years, and remainder or reversionary interests for estates of decedents for which the valuation date of the gross estate is before January 1, 1952.*—Except as otherwise provided in § 20.2031-7(b), if the valuation date of the decedent's gross estate is before January 1, 1952, the present value of annuities, life estates, terms for years, remainders, and reversions is their present value determined under this section. If the valuation of the interest involved is dependent upon the continuation or termination of one or more lives or upon a term certain concurrent with one or more lives, the factor for the present value is computed on the basis of interest at the rate of 4 percent a year, compounded annually, and life contingencies as to each life involved from values that are based on the Actuaries' or Combined Experience Table of Mortality, as extended. This table and related factors are described in former § 81.10 (as contained in the 26 CFR Part 81 edition revised as of April 1, 1958). The present value of an interest measured by a term of years is computed on the basis of interest at the rate of 4 percent a year.

(b) *Valuation of annuities, interests for life or term of years, and remainder or reversionary interests for estates of decedents for which the valuation date of the gross estate is after December 31, 1951, and before January 1, 1971.*—Except as otherwise provided in § 20.2031-7(b), if the valuation date for the decedent's gross estate is after December 31, 1951, and before January 1, 1971, the present value of annuities, life estates, terms of years, remainders, and reversions is their present value determined under this section. If the valuation of the interest involved is dependent upon the continuation or termination of one or

more lives, or upon a term certain concurrent with one or more lives, the factor for the present value is computed on the basis of interest at the rate of 3 1/2 percent a year, compounded annually, and life contingencies as to each life involved are taken from U.S. Life Table 38. This table and related factors are set forth in former § 20.2031-7 (as contained in the 26 CFR Part 20 edition revised as of April 1, 1984). Special factors involving one and two lives may be found in or computed with the use of tables contained in the publication entitled "Actuarial Values for Estate and Gift Tax," Internal Revenue Service Publication Number 11 (Rev. 5-59). This publication is no longer available for purchase from the Superintendent of Documents. However, it may be obtained by requesting a copy from: CC:DOM:CORP:T:R (IRS Publication 11), room 5228, Internal Revenue Service, POB 7604, Ben Franklin Station, Washington, DC 20044. The present value of an interest measured by a term of years is computed on the basis of interest at the rate of 3 1/2 percent a year.

(c) *Valuation of annuities, interests for life or term of years, and remainder or reversionary interests for estates of decedents for which the valuation date of the gross estate is after December 31, 1970, and before December 1, 1983.*—Except as otherwise provided in § 20.2031-7(b), if the valuation date of the decedent's gross estate is after December 31, 1970, and before December 1, 1983, the present value of annuities, life estates, terms of years, remainders, and reversions is their present value determined under this section. If the valuation of the interest involved is dependent upon the continuation of or termination of one or more lives or upon a term certain concurrent with one or more lives, the factor for the present value is computed on the basis of interest at the rate of 6 percent a year, compounded annually, and life contingencies are determined as to each male and female life involved, from values that are set forth in Table LN. Table LN contains values that are taken from the life table for total males and the life table for total females appearing as Tables 2 and 3, respectively, in United States Life Tables: 1959-1960, published by the Department of Health and Human Services, Public Health Service. Table LN and related factors are set forth in former § 20.2031-10 (as contained in the 26 CFR Part 20 edition revised as of April 1, 1994 (see FEGT ¶ 6435)).

Special factors involving one and two lives may be found in or computed with the use of tables contained in Internal Revenue Service Publication 723, "Actuarial Values I: Valuation of Last Survivor Charitable Remainders," (12-70), and Internal Revenue Service Publication 723A, "Actuarial Values II: Factors at 6 Percent Involving One and Two Lives," (12-70). These publications are no longer available for purchase from the Superintendent of Documents. However, a copy of each may be obtained from: CC:DOM:CORP:T:R (IRS Publication 723/723A), room 5228, Internal Revenue Service, POB 7604, Ben Franklin Station, Washington, DC 20044.

(d) *Valuation of annuities, interests for life or term of years, and remainder or reversionary interests for estates of decedents for which the valuation date of the gross estate is after November 30, 1983, and before May 1, 1989.*—(1) MDULIn general.—(i) Except as otherwise provided in §20.2031-7(b), if the decedent died after November 30, 1983, and the valuation date for the gross estate is before May 1, 1989, the fair market value of annuities, life estates, terms of years, remainders, and reversions is their present value determined under this section. If the decedent died after November 30, 1983, and before August 9, 1984, or, in cases where the valuation date of the decedent's gross estate is before May 1, 1989, if, on December 1, 1983, the decedent was mentally incompetent so that the disposition of the decedent's property could not be changed, and the decedent died on or after December 1, 1983, without having regained competency to dispose of the decedent's property, or if the decedent died within 90 days of the date on which the decedent first regained competency, the fair market value of annuities, life estates, terms for years, remainders, and reversions included in the gross estate of such decedent is their present value determined under either this section or §20.2031-7A(c), at the option of the taxpayer. The value of annuities issued by companies regularly engaged in their sale, and of insurance policies on the lives of persons other than the decedent, is determined under §20.2031-8. The fair market value of a remainder interest in a charitable remainder unitrust, as defined in §1.664-3 of this chapter, is its present value determined under §1.664-4 of this chapter. The fair market value of a life interest or term for years in a charitable remainder unitrust is the fair market value of the property as of the date of valuation less the fair market value of the remainder interest on such date determined under §1.664-4 of this chapter. The fair market value of the interests in a pooled income fund, as defined in §1.642(c)-5 of this chapter, is their value determined under §1.642(c)-6 of this chapter.

(ii) The present value of an annuity, life estate, remainder, or reversion determined under this section which is dependent on the continuation or termination of the life of one person is computed by the use of Table A in paragraph (d)(6) of this section. The present value of an annuity, term for years, remainder, or reversion dependent on a term certain is computed by the use of Table B in paragraph (d)(6) of this section. If the interest is to be valued is dependent upon more than one life or there is a term certain concurrent with one or more lives, see paragraph (d)(5) of this section. For purposes of the computations described in this section, the age of a person is to be taken as the age of that person at his or her nearest birthday.

(iii) In all examples set forth in this section, the decedent is assumed to have died on or after August 9, 1984, with the valuation date of the decedent's gross estate before May 1, 1989, and to have been competent to change the disposition of the property on December 1, 1983.

(2) *Annuities.*—(i) If an annuity is payable annually at the end of each year during the life of an individual (as for example if the first payment is due one year after the decedent's death), the amount payable annually is multiplied by the figure in column 2 of Table A opposite the number of years in column 1 nearest the age of the individual whose life measures the duration of the annuity. If the annuity is payable annually at the end of each year for a definite number of years, the amount payable annually is multiplied by the figure in column 2 of Table B opposite the number of years in column 1 representing the duration of the annuity. The application of this paragraph (d)(2)(i) may be illustrated by the following examples:

*Example (1).* The decedent received, under the terms of the decedent's father's will an annuity of $10,000 a year payable annually for the life of the decedent's elder brother. At the time the decedent died, an annual payment had just been made. The brother at the decedent's death was 40 years eight months old. By reference to Table A, the figure in column 2 opposite 41 years, the number nearest to the brother's actual age, is found to be 9.1030. The present value of the annuity at the date of the decedent's death is, therefore, $91,030 ($10,000 × 9.1030).

*Example (2).* The decedent was entitled to receive an annuity of $10,000 a year payable annually throughout a term certain. At the time the decedent died, the annual payment had just been made and five more annual payments were still to be made. By reference to Table B, it is found that the figure in column 2 opposite five years is

3.7908. The present value of the annuity is, therefore, $37,908 ($10,000 × 3.7908).

(ii) If an annuity is payable at the end of semiannual, quarterly, monthly, or weekly periods during the life of an individual (as for example if the first payment is due one month after the decedent's death), the aggregate amount to be paid within a year is first multiplied by the figure in column 2 of Table A opposite the number of years in column 1 nearest the age of the individual whose life measures the duration of the annuity. The product so obtained is then multiplied by whichever of the following factors is appropriate:

1.0244 for semiannual payments,
1.0368 for quarterly payments,
1.0450 for monthly payments,
1.0482 for weekly payments.

If the annuity is payable at the end of semiannual, quarterly, monthly or weekly periods for a definite number of years, the aggregate amount to be paid within a year is first multiplied by the figure in column 2 of Table B opposite the number of years in column 1 representing the duration of the annuity. The product so obtained is then multiplied by whichever of the above factors is appropriate. The application of this paragraph (d)(2)(ii) may be illustrated by the following example.

*Example.* The facts are the same as those contained in example (1) set forth in paragraph (d)(2)(i) of this section, except that the annuity is payable semiannually. The aggregate annual amount, $10,000, is multiplied by the factor 9.1030 and the product multiplied by 1.0244. The present value of the annuity at the date of the decedent's death is, therefore, $93,251.13 ($10,000 × 9.1030 × 1.0244).

(iii)(A) If the first payment of an annuity for the life of an individual is due at the beginning of the annual or other payment period rather than at the end (as for example if the first payment is to be made immediately after the decedent's death), the value of the annuity is the sum of (A) the first payment plus (B) the present value of a similar annuity, the first payment of which is not to be made until the end of the payment period, determined as provided in paragraphs (d)(2)(i) or (ii) of this section, the application of this paragraph (d)(2)(iii)(A) may be illustrated by the following example:

*Example.* The decedent was entitled to receive an annuity of $50 a month during the life of another person. The decedent died on the date the payment was due. At the date of the decedent's death, the person whose life measures the duration of the annuity was 50 years of age. The value of the annuity at the date of the decedent's death is $50 plus the product of $50 × 12 × 8.4743 (see Table A) × 1.0450 (See paragraph (d)(2)(ii) of this section). That is $50 plus $5,313.39, or $5,363.39.

(B) If the first payment of an annuity for a definite number of years is due at the beginning of the annual or other payment period, the applicable factor is the product of the factor shown in Table B multiplied by whichever of the following factors is appropriate:

1.1000 for annual payments,
1.0744 for semiannual payments,
1.0618 for quarterly payments,
1.0534 for monthly payments,
1.0502 for weekly payments.

The application of this paragraph (d)(2)(iii)(B) may be illustrated by the following example:

*Example.* The decedent was the beneficiary of an annuity of $50 a month. On the day a payment was due, the decedent died. There were 300 payments to be made, including the payment due. The value of the annuity as of the date of decedent's death is the product of $50 × 12 × 9.0770 (see Table B) × 1.0534, or $5,737.03.

(3) *Life estates and terms for years.*—If the interest to be valued is the right of a person for his or her life, or for the life of another person, to receive the income of certain property or to use nonincome-producing property, the value of the interest is the value of the property multiplied by the figure in column 3 of Table A opposite the number of years nearest to the actual age of the measuring life. If the interest to be valued is the right to receive income of property or to use noncome-producing property for a term of years, column 3 of Table B is used. The application of this paragraph (d)(3) may be illustrated by the following example:

*Example.* The decedent or the decedent's estate was entitled to receive the income from a fund of $50,000 during the life of the decedent's elder brother. Upon the brother's death, the remainder is to go to B. The brother was 31 years, five months old at the time of the decedent's death. By reference to Table A the figure in column 3 opposite 31 years is found to be 0.95254. The present value of the decedent's interest is, therefore, $47,627 ($50,000 × 0.95254).

(4) *Remainders or reversionary interests.*—If a decedent had, at the time of the decedent's death, a remainder or a reversionary interest in property to take effect after an estate for the life of another, the

present value of the decedent's interest is obtained by multiplying the value of the property by the figure in column 4 of Table A opposite the number of years nearest to the actual age of the person whose life measures the preceding estate. If the remainder or reversion is to take effect at the end of the term for years, column 4 of Table B is used. The application of this paragraph (d)(4) may be illustrated by the following example:

*Example.* The decedent was entitled to receive certain property worth $50,000 upon the death of the decedent's elder sister, to whom the income was bequeathed for life. At the time of the decedent's death, the elder sister was 31 years five months old. By reference to Table A the figure in column 4 opposite 31 years is found to be .04746. The present value of the remainder interest at the date of the decedent's death is, therefore, $2,373 ($50,000 × .04746).

(5) *Actuarial computation by the Internal Revenue Service.*—If the valuation of the interest involved is dependent upon the continuation or the termination of more than one life or upon a term certain concurrent with one or more lives a special factor must be used. The factor is to be computed on the basis of interest at the rate of 10 percent a year, compounded annually, and life contingencies deter-

mined, as to each person involved, from the values of 1x that are set forth in column 2 of Table LN of paragraph (d)(6). Table LN contains values of *lx* taken from the life table for the total population appearing as Table 1 of United States Life Tables: 1969-71, published by the Department of Health and Human Services, Public Health Service. Many special factors involving one and two lives may be found in or computed with the use of the tables contained in Internal Revenue Service Publication 723E, "Actuarial Values II: Factors at 10 Percent Involving One and Two Lives," (12-83). This publication is no longer available for purchase from the Superintendent of Documents. However, it may be obtained by requesting a copy from: CC:DOM:CORP:T:R (IRS Publication 723E), room 5228, Internal Revenue Service, POB 7604, Ben Franklin Station, Washington, DC 20044. However, if a special factor is required in the case of an actual decedent, the Commission will furnish the factor to the executor upon request. The request must be accompanied by a statement of the date of birth of each person, the duration of whose life may affect the value of the interest, and by copies of the relevant instruments. Special factors are not furnished for prospective transfers.

(6) *Tables.*—The following tables shall be used in the application of the provisions of this section:

## TABLE A

**TABLE A**—SINGLE LIFE, UNISEX, 10 PERCENT—TABLE SHOWING THE PRESENT WORTH OF AN ANNUITY, OF A LIFE ESTATE, AND A REMAINDER INTEREST—APPLICABLE FOR TRANSFERS AFTER NOVEMBER 30, 1983, AND BEFORE MAY 1, 1989

| Age (1) | Annuity (2) | Life Estate (3) | Remainder (4) | Age (1) | Annuity (2) | Life Estate (3) | Remainder (4) |
|---|---|---|---|---|---|---|---|
| 0 | 9.7188 | .97188 | .02812 | 55 | 8.0046 | .80046 | .19954 |
| 1 | 9.8988 | .98988 | .01012 | 56 | 7.9006 | .79006 | .20994 |
| 2 | 9.9017 | .99017 | .00983 | 57 | 7.7931 | .77931 | .22069 |
| 3 | 9.9008 | .99008 | .00992 | 58 | 7.6822 | .76822 | .23178 |
| 4 | 9.8981 | .98981 | .01019 | 59 | 7.5675 | .75675 | .24325 |
| 5 | 9.8938 | .98938 | .01062 | 60 | 7.4491 | .74491 | .25509 |
| 6 | 9.8884 | .98884 | .01116 | 61 | 7.3267 | .73267 | .26733 |
| 7 | 9.8822 | .98822 | .01178 | 62 | 7.2002 | .72002 | .27998 |
| 8 | 9.8748 | .98748 | .01252 | 63 | 7.0696 | .70696 | .29304 |
| 9 | 9.8663 | .98663 | .01337 | 64 | 6.9352 | .69352 | .30648 |
| 10 | 9.8565 | .98565 | .01435 | 65 | 6.7970 | .67970 | .32030 |
| 11 | 9.8453 | .98453 | .01547 | 66 | 6.6551 | .66551 | .33449 |
| 12 | 9.8329 | .98329 | .01671 | 67 | 6.5098 | .65098 | .34902 |
| 13 | 9.8198 | .98198 | .01802 | 68 | 6.3610 | .63610 | .36390 |
| 14 | 9.8066 | .98066 | .01934 | 69 | 6.2086 | .62086 | .37914 |
| 15 | 9.7937 | .97937 | .02063 | 70 | 6.0522 | .60522 | .39478 |
| 16 | 9.7815 | .97815 | .02185 | 71 | 5.8914 | .58914 | .41086 |
| 17 | 9.7700 | .97700 | .02300 | 72 | 5.7261 | .57261 | .42739 |
| 18 | 9.7590 | .97590 | .02410 | 73 | 5.5571 | .55571 | .44429 |
| 19 | 9.7480 | .97480 | .02520 | 74 | 5.3862 | .53862 | .46138 |
| 20 | 9.7365 | .97365 | .02635 | 75 | 5.2149 | .52149 | .47851 |
| 21 | 9.7245 | .97245 | .02755 | 76 | 5.0441 | .50441 | .49559 |
| 22 | 9.7120 | .97120 | .02880 | 77 | 4.8742 | .48742 | .51258 |
| 23 | 9.6986 | .96986 | .03014 | 78 | 4.7049 | .47049 | .52951 |
| 24 | 9.6841 | .96841 | .03159 | 79 | 4.5357 | .45357 | .54643 |
| 25 | 9.6678 | .96678 | .03322 | 80 | 4.3659 | .43659 | .56341 |
| 26 | 9.6495 | .96495 | .03505 | 81 | 4.1967 | .41967 | .58033 |
| 27 | 9.6290 | .96290 | .03710 | 82 | 4.0295 | .40295 | .59705 |
| 28 | 9.6062 | .96062 | .03938 | 83 | 3.8642 | .38642 | .61358 |
| 29 | 9.5813 | .95813 | .04187 | 84 | 3.6998 | .36998 | .63002 |
| 30 | 9.5543 | .95543 | .04457 | 85 | 3.5359 | .35359 | .64641 |
| 31 | 9.5254 | .95254 | .04746 | 86 | 3.3764 | .33764 | .66236 |
| 32 | 9.4942 | .94942 | .05058 | 87 | 3.2262 | .32262 | .67738 |
| 33 | 9.4608 | .94608 | .05392 | 88 | 3.0859 | .30859 | .69141 |
| 34 | 9.4250 | .94250 | .05750 | 89 | 2.9526 | .29526 | .70474 |
| 35 | 9.3868 | .93868 | .06132 | 90 | 2.8221 | .28221 | .71779 |
| 36 | 9.3460 | .93460 | .06540 | 91 | 2.6955 | .26955 | .73045 |
| 37 | 9.3026 | .93026 | .06974 | 92 | 2.5771 | .25771 | .74229 |
| 38 | 9.2567 | .92567 | .07433 | 93 | 2.4692 | .24692 | .75308 |
| 39 | 9.2083 | .92083 | .07917 | 94 | 2.3728 | .23728 | .76272 |
| 40 | 9.1571 | .91571 | .08429 | 95 | 2.2887 | .22887 | .77113 |
| 41 | 9.1030 | .91030 | .08970 | 96 | 2.2181 | .22181 | .77819 |
| 42 | 9.0457 | .90457 | .09543 | 97 | 2.1550 | .21550 | .78450 |
| 43 | 8.9855 | .89855 | .10145 | 98 | 2.1000 | .21000 | .79000 |
| 44 | 8.9221 | .89221 | .10779 | 99 | 2.0486 | .20486 | .79514 |
| 45 | 8.8558 | .88558 | .11442 | 100 | 1.9975 | .19975 | .80025 |
| 46 | 8.7863 | .87863 | .12137 | 101 | 1.9532 | .19532 | .80468 |
| 47 | 8.7137 | .87137 | .12863 | 102 | 1.9054 | .19054 | .80946 |
| 48 | 8.6374 | .86374 | .13626 | 103 | 1.8437 | .18437 | .81563 |
| 49 | 8.5578 | .85578 | .14422 | 104 | 1.7856 | .17856 | .82144 |
| 50 | 8.4743 | .84743 | .15257 | 105 | 1.6962 | .16962 | .83038 |
| 51 | 8.3874 | .83874 | .16126 | 106 | 1.5488 | .15488 | .84512 |
| 52 | 8.2969 | .82969 | .17031 | 107 | 1.3409 | .13409 | .86591 |
| 53 | 8.2028 | .82028 | .17972 | 108 | 1.0068 | .10068 | .89932 |
| 54 | 8.1054 | .81054 | .18946 | 109 | 0.4545 | .04545 | .95455 |

**TABLE B**
**TABLE B—TERM CERTAIN, UNISEX, 10 PERCENT—TABLE SHOWING THE PRESENT WORTH OF AN ANNUITY FOR A TERM CERTAIN, OF AN INCOME INTEREST FOR A TERM CERTAIN, AND OF A REMAINDER INTEREST POSTPONED FOR A TERM CERTAIN—APPLICABLE FOR TRANSFERS AFTER NOVEMBER 30, 1983, AND BEFORE MAY 1, 1989**

| (1) Number of Years | (2) Annuity | (3) Term Certain | (4) Remainder | (1) Number of Years | (2) Annuity | (3) Term Certain | (4) Remainder |
|---|---|---|---|---|---|---|---|
| 1 | 0.9091 | .090909 | .909091 | 31 | 9.4790 | .947901 | .052099 |
| 2 | 1.7355 | .173554 | .826446 | 32 | 9.5264 | .952638 | .047362 |
| 3 | 2.4869 | .248685 | .751315 | 33 | 9.5694 | .956943 | .043057 |
| 4 | 3.1699 | .316987 | .683013 | 34 | 9.6086 | .960857 | .039143 |
| 5 | 3.7908 | .379079 | .620921 | 35 | 9.6442 | .964416 | .035584 |
| 6 | 4.3553 | .435526 | .564474 | 36 | 9.6765 | .967651 | .032349 |
| 7 | 4.8684 | .486842 | .513158 | 37 | 9.7059 | .970592 | .029408 |
| 8 | 5.3349 | .533493 | .466507 | 38 | 9.7327 | .973265 | .026735 |
| 9 | 5.7590 | .575902 | .424098 | 39 | 9.7570 | .975686 | .024304 |
| 10 | 6.1446 | .614457 | .385543 | 40 | 9.7791 | .977905 | .022095 |
| 11 | 6.4951 | .649506 | .350494 | 41 | 9.7991 | .979914 | .020096 |
| 12 | 6.8137 | .681369 | .318631 | 42 | 9.8174 | .981740 | .018260 |
| 13 | 7.1034 | .710336 | .289664 | 43 | 9.8340 | .983400 | .016600 |
| 14 | 7.3667 | .736669 | .263331 | 44 | 9.8491 | .984909 | .015091 |
| 15 | 7.6061 | .760608 | .239392 | 45 | 9.8628 | .986281 | .013718 |
| 16 | 7.8237 | .782371 | .217629 | 46 | 9.8753 | .987528 | .012472 |
| 17 | 8.0216 | .802155 | .197845 | 47 | 9.8866 | .988662 | .011338 |
| 18 | 8.2014 | .820141 | .179859 | 48 | 9.8969 | .989693 | .010307 |
| 19 | 8.3649 | .836492 | .163508 | 49 | 9.9063 | .990630 | .009370 |
| 20 | 8.5136 | .851356 | .148644 | 50 | 9.9148 | .991481 | .008519 |
| 21 | 8.6487 | .864869 | .135131 | 51 | 9.9226 | .992256 | .007744 |
| 22 | 8.7715 | .877154 | .122846 | 52 | 9.9296 | .992960 | .007040 |
| 23 | 8.8832 | .888322 | .111678 | 53 | 9.9360 | .993600 | .006400 |
| 24 | 8.9847 | .898474 | .101526 | 54 | 9.9418 | .994182 | .005818 |
| 25 | 9.0770 | .907704 | .092296 | 55 | 9.9471 | .994711 | .005289 |
| 26 | 9.1609 | .916095 | .083900 | 56 | 9.9519 | .995191 | .004809 |
| 27 | 9.2372 | .923722 | .076278 | 57 | 9.9563 | .995629 | .004371 |
| 28 | 9.3066 | .930657 | .069343 | 58 | 9.9603 | .996026 | .003974 |
| 29 | 9.3696 | .936961 | .063039 | 59 | 9.9639 | .996387 | .003613 |
| 30 | 9.4269 | .942691 | .057309 | 60 | 9.9672 | .996716 | .003284 |

**TABLE LN**
TABLE LN—APPLICABLE FOR TRANSFERS AFTER NOVEMBER 30, 1983, AND BEFORE MAY 1, 1989

| Age X (1) | lx (2) | Age X (1) | lx (2) | Age X (1) | lx (2) | Age X (1) | lx (2) | Age X (1) | lx (2) | Age X (1) | lx (2) |
|---|---|---|---|---|---|---|---|---|---|---|---|
| 0 | 100000 | 19 | 96846 | 38 | 93843 | 57 | 83103 | 76 | 46946 | 95 | 2786 |
| 1 | 97998 | 20 | 96716 | 39 | 93593 | 58 | 81988 | 77 | 44101 | 96 | 2068 |
| 2 | 97876 | 21 | 96580 | 40 | 93322 | 59 | 80798 | 78 | 41192 | 97 | 1511 |
| 3 | 97792 | 22 | 96438 | 41 | 93028 | 60 | 79529 | 79 | 38245 | 98 | 1087 |
| 4 | 97724 | 23 | 96292 | 42 | 92712 | 61 | 78181 | 80 | 35285 | 99 | 772 |
| 5 | 97668 | 24 | 96145 | 43 | 92368 | 62 | 76751 | 81 | 32323 | 100 | 542 |
| 6 | 97619 | 25 | 96000 | 44 | 91995 | 63 | 75236 | 82 | 29375 | 101 | 375 |
| 7 | 97573 | 26 | 95859 | 45 | 91587 | 64 | 73631 | 83 | 26469 | 102 | 257 |
| 8 | 97531 | 27 | 95721 | 46 | 91144 | 65 | 71933 | 84 | 23638 | 103 | 175 |
| 9 | 97494 | 28 | 95586 | 47 | 90662 | 66 | 70139 | 85 | 20908 | 104 | 117 |
| 10 | 97460 | 29 | 95448 | 48 | 90142 | 67 | 68246 | 86 | 18282 | 105 | 78 |
| 11 | 97430 | 30 | 95307 | 49 | 89579 | 68 | 66254 | 87 | 15769 | 106 | 52 |
| 12 | 97401 | 31 | 95158 | 50 | 88972 | 69 | 64166 | 88 | 13407 | 107 | 34 |
| 13 | 97367 | 32 | 95003 | 51 | 88315 | 70 | 61984 | 89 | 11240 | 108 | 22 |
| 14 | 97322 | 33 | 94840 | 52 | 87605 | 71 | 59715 | 90 | 9297 | 109 | 14 |
| 15 | 97261 | 34 | 94666 | 53 | 86838 | 72 | 57360 | 91 | 7577 | 110 | 0 |
| 16 | 97181 | 35 | 94482 | 54 | 86007 | 73 | 54913 | 92 | 6070 | | |
| 17 | 97083 | 36 | 94285 | 55 | 85110 | 74 | 52363 | 93 | 4773 | | |
| 18 | 96970 | 37 | 94073 | 56 | 84142 | 75 | 49705 | 94 | 3682 | | |

(e) *Valuation of annuities, interests for life or term of years, and remainder or reversionary interests for estates of decedents for which the valuation date of the gross estate is after April 30, 1989, and before May 1, 1999.*—(1) *In general.*—Except as otherwise provided in § 20.2031-7(b) and § 20.7520-3(b) (pertaining to certain limitations on the use of prescribed tables), if the valuation date for the gross estate of the decedent is after April 30, 1989, and before May 1, 1999, the fair market value of annuities, life estates, terms of years, remainders, and reversionary interests is the present value of the interests determined by use of standard or special section 7520 actuarial factors and the valuation methodology described in § 20.2031-7(d). These factors are derived by using the appropriate section 7520 interest rate and, if applicable, the mortality component for the valuation date of the interest that is being valued. See § § 20.7520-1 through 20.7520-4. See paragraph (e)(4) of this section for determination of the appropriate table for use in valuing these interests.

(2) *Transitional rule.*—(i) If the valuation date is after April 30, 1989, and before June 10, 1994, a taxpayer can rely on Notice 89-24 (1989-1 C.B. 660), or Notice 89-60 (1989-1 C.B. 700). See § 601.601(d)(2)(ii)(*b*) of this chapter.

(ii) If a decedent dies after April 30, 1989, and if on May 1, 1989, the decedent was mentally incompetent so that the disposition of the decedent's property could not be changed, and the decedent dies without having regained competency to dispose of the decedent's property or dies within 90 days of the date on which the decedent first regains competency, the fair market value of annuities, life estates, terms for years, remainders, and reversions included in the gross estate of the decedent is their present value determined either under this section or under the corresponding section applicable at the time the decedent became mentally incompetent, at the option of the decedent's executor. For example, see paragraph (d) of this section.

(3) *Publications and actuarial computations by the Internal Revenue Service.*—Many standard actuarial factors not included in paragraph (e)(4) of this section or in § 20.2031-7(d)(6) are included in Internal Revenue Service Publication 1457, "Actuarial Values, Alpha Volume," (8-89). Publication 1457 also includes examples that illustrate how to compute many special factors for more unusual situations. Publication 1457 is no longer available for purchase from the Superintendent of Documents, United States Government Printing Office, Washington, DC 20402. However, pertinent factors in this publication may be obtained from: CC:DOM:CORP:R (IRS Publication 1457), room 5226, Internal Revenue Service, POB 7604, Ben Franklin Station, Washington, DC 20044. If a special factor is required in the case of an actual decedent, the Internal Revenue Service may furnish the factor to the executor upon a request for a ruling. The request for a ruling must be accompanied by a recitation of the facts including a statement of the date of birth for each measuring life, the date of the decedent's death, any other applicable dates, and a copy of the will, trust, or other relevant documents. A request for a ruling must comply with the instructions for requesting a ruling published periodically in the Internal Revenue Bulletin (see § § 601.201 and 601.601(d)(2)(ii)(*b*) of this chapter) and include payment of the required user fee.

(4) *Actuarial tables.*—Except as provided in § 20.7520-3(b) (pertaining to certain limitations on the use of prescribed tables), Life Table 80CNSMT and Table S (Single life remainder factors applicable where the valuation date is after April 30, 1989, and before May 1, 1999), contained in this paragraph (e)(4), and Table B, Table J, and Table K set forth in § 20.2031-7(d)(6) must be used in the application of the provisions of this section when the section 7520 interest rate component is between 4.2 and 14 percent. Table S and Table 80CNSMT are as follows:

TABLE S
BASED ON LIFE TABLE 80CNSMT
SINGLE LIFE REMAINDER FACTORS
APPLICABLE AFTER APRIL 30, 1989,
AND BEFORE MAY 1, 1999
INTEREST RATE

| AGE | 4.2% | 4.4% | 4.6% | 4.8% | 5.0% | 5.2% | 5.4% | 5.6% | 5.8% | 6.0% |
|---|---|---|---|---|---|---|---|---|---|---|
| 0 | .07389 | .06749 | .06188 | .05695 | .05261 | .04879 | .04541 | .04243 | .03978 | .03744 |
| 1 | .06494 | .05832 | .05250 | .04738 | .04287 | .03889 | .03537 | .03226 | .02950 | .02705 |
| 2 | .06678 | .05999 | .05401 | .04874 | .04410 | .03999 | .03636 | .03314 | .03028 | .02773 |
| 3 | .06897 | .06200 | .05587 | .05045 | .04567 | .04143 | .03768 | .03435 | .03139 | .02875 |
| 4 | .07139 | .06425 | .05796 | .05239 | .04746 | .04310 | .03922 | .03578 | .03271 | .02998 |
| 5 | .07401 | .06669 | .06023 | .05451 | .04944 | .04494 | .04094 | .03738 | .03421 | .03137 |
| 6 | .07677 | .06928 | .06265 | .05677 | .05156 | .04692 | .04279 | .03911 | .03583 | .03289 |
| 7 | .07968 | .07201 | .06521 | .05918 | .05381 | .04903 | .04477 | .04097 | .03757 | .03453 |
| 8 | .08274 | .07489 | .06792 | .06172 | .05621 | .05129 | .04689 | .04297 | .03945 | .03630 |
| 9 | .08597 | .07794 | .07079 | .06443 | .05876 | .05370 | .04917 | .04511 | .04148 | .03821 |
| 10 | .08936 | .08115 | .07383 | .06730 | .06147 | .05626 | .05159 | .04741 | .04365 | .04027 |
| 11 | .09293 | .08453 | .07704 | .07035 | .06436 | .05900 | .05419 | .04988 | .04599 | .04250 |
| 12 | .09666 | .08807 | .08040 | .07354 | .06739 | .06188 | .05693 | .05248 | .04847 | .04486 |
| 13 | .10049 | .09172 | .08387 | .07684 | .07053 | .06487 | .05977 | .05518 | .05104 | .04731 |
| 14 | .10437 | .09541 | .08738 | .08017 | .07370 | .06788 | .06263 | .05791 | .05364 | .04978 |
| 15 | .10827 | .09912 | .09090 | .08352 | .07688 | .07090 | .06551 | .06064 | .05623 | .05225 |
| 16 | .11220 | .10285 | .09445 | .08689 | .08008 | .07394 | .06839 | .06337 | .05883 | .05472 |
| 17 | .11615 | .10661 | .09802 | .09028 | .08330 | .07699 | .07129 | .06612 | .06144 | .05719 |

| AGE | 4.2% | 4.4% | 4.6% | 4.8% | 5.0% | 5.2% | 5.4% | 5.6% | 5.8% | 6.0% |
|---|---|---|---|---|---|---|---|---|---|---|
| 18 | .12017 | .11043 | .10165 | .09373 | .08656 | .08009 | .07422 | .06890 | .06408 | .05969 |
| 19 | .12428 | .11434 | .10537 | .09726 | .08992 | .08327 | .07724 | .07177 | .06679 | .06226 |
| 20 | .12850 | .11836 | .10919 | .10089 | .09337 | .08654 | .08035 | .07471 | .06959 | .06492 |
| 21 | .13282 | .12248 | .11311 | .10462 | .09692 | .08991 | .08355 | .07775 | .07247 | .06765 |
| 22 | .13728 | .12673 | .11717 | .10848 | .10059 | .09341 | .08686 | .08090 | .07546 | .07049 |
| 23 | .14188 | .13113 | .12136 | .11248 | .10440 | .09703 | .09032 | .08418 | .07858 | .07345 |
| 24 | .14667 | .13572 | .12575 | .11667 | .10839 | .10084 | .09395 | .08764 | .08187 | .07659 |
| 25 | .15167 | .14051 | .13034 | .12106 | .11259 | .10486 | .09778 | .09130 | .08536 | .07991 |
| 26 | .15690 | .14554 | .13517 | .12569 | .11703 | .10910 | .10184 | .09518 | .08907 | .08346 |
| 27 | .16237 | .15081 | .14024 | .13056 | .12171 | .11359 | .10614 | .09930 | .09302 | .08724 |
| 28 | .16808 | .15632 | .14555 | .13567 | .12662 | .11831 | .11068 | .10366 | .09720 | .09125 |
| 29 | .17404 | .16208 | .15110 | .14104 | .13179 | .12329 | .11547 | .10827 | .10163 | .09551 |
| 30 | .18025 | .16808 | .15692 | .14665 | .13721 | .12852 | .12051 | .11313 | .10631 | .10002 |
| 31 | .18672 | .17436 | .16300 | .15255 | .14291 | .13403 | .12584 | .11827 | .11127 | .10480 |
| 32 | .19344 | .18090 | .16935 | .15870 | .14888 | .13980 | .13142 | .12367 | .11650 | .10985 |
| 33 | .20044 | .18772 | .17598 | .16514 | .15513 | .14587 | .13730 | .12936 | .12201 | .11519 |
| 34 | .20770 | .19480 | .18287 | .17185 | .16165 | .15221 | .14345 | .13533 | .12780 | .12080 |
| 35 | .21522 | .20215 | .19005 | .17884 | .16846 | .15883 | .14989 | .14159 | .13388 | .12670 |
| 36 | .22299 | .20974 | .19747 | .18609 | .17552 | .16571 | .15660 | .14812 | .14022 | .13287 |
| 37 | .23101 | .21760 | .20516 | .19360 | .18286 | .17288 | .16358 | .15492 | .14685 | .13933 |
| 38 | .23928 | .22572 | .21311 | .20139 | .19048 | .18032 | .17085 | .16201 | .15377 | .14607 |
| 39 | .24780 | .23409 | .22133 | .20945 | .19837 | .18804 | .17840 | .16939 | .16097 | .15310 |
| 40 | .25658 | .24273 | .22982 | .21778 | .20654 | .19605 | .18624 | .17706 | .16847 | .16043 |
| 41 | .26560 | .25163 | .23858 | .22639 | .21499 | .20434 | .19436 | .18502 | .17627 | .16806 |
| 42 | .27486 | .26076 | .24758 | .23525 | .22370 | .21289 | .20276 | .19326 | .18434 | .17597 |
| 43 | .28435 | .27013 | .25683 | .24436 | .23268 | .22172 | .21143 | .20177 | .19270 | .18416 |
| 44 | .29407 | .27975 | .26633 | .25373 | .24191 | .23081 | .22038 | .21057 | .20134 | .19265 |
| 45 | .30402 | .28961 | .27608 | .26337 | .25142 | .24019 | .22962 | .21966 | .21028 | .20144 |
| 46 | .31420 | .29970 | .28608 | .27326 | .26120 | .24983 | .23913 | .22904 | .21951 | .21053 |
| 47 | .32460 | .31004 | .29632 | .28341 | .27123 | .25975 | .24892 | .23870 | .22904 | .21991 |
| 48 | .33521 | .32058 | .30679 | .29379 | .28151 | .26992 | .25897 | .24862 | .23883 | .22957 |
| 49 | .34599 | .33132 | .31746 | .30438 | .29201 | .28032 | .26926 | .25879 | .24888 | .23949 |
| 50 | .35695 | .34224 | .32833 | .31518 | .30273 | .29094 | .27978 | .26921 | .25918 | .24966 |
| 51 | .36809 | .35335 | .33940 | .32619 | .31367 | .30180 | .29055 | .27987 | .26973 | .26010 |
| 52 | .37944 | .36468 | .35070 | .33744 | .32486 | .31292 | .30158 | .29081 | .28057 | .27083 |
| 53 | .39098 | .37622 | .36222 | .34892 | .33629 | .32429 | .31288 | .30203 | .29170 | .28186 |
| 54 | .40269 | .38794 | .37393 | .36062 | .34795 | .33590 | .32442 | .31349 | .30308 | .29316 |
| 55 | .41457 | .39985 | .38585 | .37252 | .35983 | .34774 | .33621 | .32522 | .31474 | .30473 |
| 56 | .42662 | .41194 | .39796 | .38464 | .37193 | .35981 | .34824 | .33720 | .32666 | .31658 |
| 57 | .43884 | .42422 | .41028 | .39697 | .38426 | .37213 | .36053 | .34945 | .33885 | .32872 |
| 58 | .45123 | .43668 | .42279 | .40951 | .39682 | .38468 | .37307 | .36196 | .35132 | .34114 |
| 59 | .46377 | .44931 | .43547 | .42224 | .40958 | .39745 | .38584 | .37471 | .36405 | .35383 |
| 60 | .47643 | .46206 | .44830 | .43513 | .42250 | .41040 | .39880 | .38767 | .37699 | .36674 |
| 61 | .48916 | .47491 | .46124 | .44814 | .43556 | .42350 | .41192 | .40080 | .39012 | .37985 |
| 62 | .50196 | .48783 | .47427 | .46124 | .44874 | .43672 | .42518 | .41408 | .40340 | .39314 |
| 63 | .51480 | .50081 | .48736 | .47444 | .46201 | .45006 | .43856 | .42749 | .41684 | .40658 |
| 64 | .52770 | .51386 | .50054 | .48773 | .47540 | .46352 | .45208 | .44105 | .43043 | .42019 |
| 65 | .54069 | .52701 | .51384 | .50115 | .48892 | .47713 | .46577 | .45480 | .44422 | .43401 |
| 66 | .55378 | .54029 | .52727 | .51472 | .50262 | .49093 | .47965 | .46876 | .45824 | .44808 |
| 67 | .56697 | .55368 | .54084 | .52845 | .51648 | .50491 | .49373 | .48293 | .47248 | .46238 |
| 68 | .58026 | .56717 | .55453 | .54231 | .53049 | .51905 | .50800 | .49729 | .48694 | .47691 |
| 69 | .59358 | .58072 | .56828 | .55624 | .54459 | .53330 | .52238 | .51179 | .50154 | .49160 |
| 70 | .60689 | .59427 | .58205 | .57021 | .55874 | .54762 | .53683 | .52638 | .51624 | .50641 |
| 71 | .62014 | .60778 | .59578 | .58415 | .57287 | .56193 | .55131 | .54100 | .53099 | .52126 |
| 72 | .63334 | .62123 | .60948 | .59808 | .58700 | .57624 | .56579 | .55563 | .54577 | .53617 |
| 73 | .64648 | .63465 | .62315 | .61198 | .60112 | .59056 | .58029 | .57030 | .56059 | .55113 |
| 74 | .65961 | .64806 | .63682 | .62590 | .61527 | .60492 | .59485 | .58504 | .57550 | .56620 |
| 75 | .67274 | .66149 | .65054 | .63987 | .62948 | .61936 | .60950 | .59990 | .59053 | .58140 |
| 76 | .68589 | .67495 | .66429 | .65390 | .64377 | .63390 | .62427 | .61487 | .60570 | .59676 |
| 77 | .69903 | .68841 | .67806 | .66796 | .65811 | .64849 | .63910 | .62993 | .62097 | .61223 |
| 78 | .71209 | .70182 | .69179 | .68199 | .67242 | .66307 | .65393 | .64501 | .63628 | .62775 |
| 79 | .72500 | .71507 | .70537 | .69588 | .68660 | .67754 | .66867 | .65999 | .65151 | .64321 |
| 80 | .73768 | .72809 | .71872 | .70955 | .70058 | .69180 | .68320 | .67479 | .66655 | .65849 |
| 81 | .75001 | .74077 | .73173 | .72288 | .71422 | .70573 | .69741 | .68926 | .68128 | .67345 |
| 82 | .76195 | .75306 | .74435 | .73582 | .72746 | .71926 | .71123 | .70335 | .69562 | .68804 |
| 83 | .77346 | .76491 | .75654 | .74832 | .74026 | .73236 | .72460 | .71699 | .70952 | .70219 |
| 84 | .78456 | .77636 | .76831 | .76041 | .75265 | .74503 | .73756 | .73021 | .72300 | .71592 |
| 85 | .79530 | .78743 | .77971 | .77212 | .76466 | .75733 | .75014 | .74306 | .73611 | .72928 |
| 86 | .80560 | .79806 | .79065 | .78337 | .77621 | .76917 | .76225 | .75544 | .74875 | .74216 |
| 87 | .81535 | .80813 | .80103 | .79404 | .78717 | .78041 | .77375 | .76720 | .76076 | .75442 |
| 88 | .82462 | .81771 | .81090 | .80420 | .79760 | .79111 | .78472 | .77842 | .77223 | .76612 |
| 89 | .83356 | .82694 | .82043 | .81401 | .80769 | .80147 | .79533 | .78929 | .78334 | .77747 |
| 90 | .84225 | .83593 | .82971 | .82357 | .81753 | .81157 | .80570 | .79991 | .79420 | .78857 |
| 91 | .85058 | .84455 | .83861 | .83276 | .82698 | .82129 | .81567 | .81013 | .80466 | .79927 |
| 92 | .85838 | .85263 | .84696 | .84137 | .83585 | .83040 | .82503 | .81973 | .81449 | .80933 |
| 93 | .86557 | .86009 | .85467 | .84932 | .84405 | .83884 | .83370 | .82862 | .82360 | .81865 |
| 94 | .87212 | .86687 | .86169 | .85657 | .85152 | .84653 | .84160 | .83673 | .83192 | .82717 |
| 95 | .87801 | .87298 | .86801 | .86310 | .85825 | .85345 | .84872 | .84404 | .83941 | .83484 |
| 96 | .88322 | .87838 | .87360 | .86888 | .86420 | .85959 | .85502 | .85051 | .84605 | .84165 |
| 97 | .88795 | .88328 | .87867 | .87411 | .86961 | .86515 | .86074 | .85639 | .85208 | .84782 |
| 98 | .89220 | .88769 | .88323 | .87883 | .87447 | .87016 | .86589 | .86167 | .85750 | .85337 |
| 99 | .89612 | .89176 | .88745 | .88318 | .87895 | .87478 | .87064 | .86656 | .86251 | .85850 |
| 100 | .89977 | .89555 | .89136 | .88722 | .88313 | .87908 | .87506 | .87109 | .86716 | .86327 |

| AGE | 4.2% | 4.4% | 4.6% | 4.8% | 5.0% | 5.2% | 5.4% | 5.6% | 5.8% | 6.0% |
|---|---|---|---|---|---|---|---|---|---|---|
| 101 | .90326 | .89917 | .89511 | .89110 | .88712 | .88318 | .87929 | .87543 | .87161 | .86783 |
| 102 | .90690 | .90294 | .89901 | .89513 | .89128 | .88746 | .88369 | .87995 | .87624 | .87257 |
| 103 | .91076 | .90694 | .90315 | .89940 | .89569 | .89200 | .88835 | .88474 | .88116 | .87760 |
| 104 | .91504 | .91138 | .90775 | .90415 | .90058 | .89704 | .89354 | .89006 | .88661 | .88319 |
| 105 | .92027 | .91681 | .91337 | .90996 | .90658 | .90322 | .89989 | .89659 | .89331 | .89006 |
| 106 | .92763 | .92445 | .92130 | .91816 | .91506 | .91197 | .90890 | .90586 | .90284 | .89983 |
| 107 | .93799 | .93523 | .93249 | .92977 | .92707 | .92438 | .92170 | .91905 | .91641 | .91378 |
| 108 | .95429 | .95223 | .95018 | .94814 | .94611 | .94409 | .94208 | .94008 | .93809 | .93611 |
| 109 | .97985 | .97893 | .97801 | .97710 | .97619 | .97529 | .97438 | .97348 | .97259 | .97170 |

## TABLE S
### BASED ON LIFE TABLE 80CNSMT
#### SINGLE LIFE REMAINDER FACTORS
#### APPLICABLE AFTER APRIL 30, 1989,
#### AND BEFORE MAY 1, 1999
#### INTEREST RATE

| AGE | 6.2% | 6.4% | 6.6% | 6.8% | 7.0% | 7.2% | 7.4% | 7.6% | 7.8% | 8.0% |
|---|---|---|---|---|---|---|---|---|---|---|
| 0 | .03535 | .03349 | .03183 | .03035 | .02902 | .02783 | .02676 | .02579 | .02492 | .02413 |
| 1 | .02486 | .02292 | .02119 | .01963 | .01824 | .01699 | .01587 | .01486 | .01395 | .01312 |
| 2 | .02547 | .02345 | .02164 | .02002 | .01857 | .01727 | .01609 | .01504 | .01408 | .01321 |
| 3 | .02640 | .02429 | .02241 | .02073 | .01921 | .01785 | .01662 | .01552 | .01451 | .01361 |
| 4 | .02753 | .02535 | .02339 | .02163 | .02005 | .01863 | .01735 | .01619 | .01514 | .01418 |
| 5 | .02883 | .02656 | .02453 | .02269 | .02105 | .01956 | .01822 | .01700 | .01590 | .01490 |
| 6 | .03026 | .02790 | .02578 | .02387 | .02215 | .02060 | .01919 | .01792 | .01677 | .01572 |
| 7 | .03180 | .02935 | .02714 | .02515 | .02336 | .02174 | .02027 | .01894 | .01773 | .01664 |
| 8 | .03347 | .03092 | .02863 | .02656 | .02469 | .02300 | .02146 | .02007 | .01881 | .01766 |
| 9 | .03528 | .03263 | .03025 | .02810 | .02615 | .02438 | .02278 | .02133 | .02000 | .01880 |
| 10 | .03723 | .03449 | .03201 | .02977 | .02774 | .02590 | .02423 | .02271 | .02133 | .02006 |
| 11 | .03935 | .03650 | .03393 | .03160 | .02949 | .02757 | .02583 | .02424 | .02279 | .02147 |
| 12 | .04160 | .03865 | .03598 | .03356 | .03136 | .02936 | .02755 | .02589 | .02438 | .02299 |
| 13 | .04394 | .04088 | .03811 | .03560 | .03331 | .03123 | .02934 | .02761 | .02603 | .02458 |
| 14 | .04629 | .04312 | .04025 | .03764 | .03527 | .03311 | .03113 | .02933 | .02768 | .02617 |
| 15 | .04864 | .04536 | .04238 | .03968 | .03721 | .03496 | .03290 | .03103 | .02930 | .02773 |
| 16 | .05099 | .04759 | .04451 | .04170 | .03913 | .03679 | .03466 | .03270 | .03090 | .02926 |
| 17 | .05333 | .04982 | .04662 | .04370 | .04104 | .03861 | .03638 | .03434 | .03247 | .03075 |
| 18 | .05570 | .05207 | .04875 | .04573 | .04296 | .04044 | .03812 | .03599 | .03404 | .03225 |
| 19 | .05814 | .05438 | .05095 | .04781 | .04494 | .04231 | .03990 | .03769 | .03565 | .03378 |
| 20 | .06065 | .05677 | .05321 | .04996 | .04698 | .04424 | .04173 | .03943 | .03731 | .03535 |
| 21 | .06325 | .05922 | .05554 | .05217 | .04907 | .04623 | .04362 | .04122 | .03901 | .03697 |
| 22 | .06594 | .06178 | .05797 | .05447 | .05126 | .04831 | .04559 | .04309 | .04078 | .03865 |
| 23 | .06876 | .06446 | .06051 | .05688 | .05355 | .05048 | .04766 | .04505 | .04265 | .04042 |
| 24 | .07174 | .06729 | .06321 | .05945 | .05599 | .05281 | .04987 | .04715 | .04465 | .04233 |
| 25 | .07491 | .07031 | .06609 | .06219 | .05861 | .05530 | .05224 | .04941 | .04680 | .04438 |
| 26 | .07830 | .07355 | .06918 | .06515 | .06142 | .05799 | .05481 | .05187 | .04915 | .04662 |
| 27 | .08192 | .07702 | .07250 | .06832 | .06446 | .06090 | .05759 | .05454 | .05170 | .04906 |
| 28 | .08577 | .08071 | .07603 | .07171 | .06772 | .06402 | .06059 | .05740 | .05445 | .05170 |
| 29 | .08986 | .08464 | .07981 | .07534 | .07120 | .06736 | .06380 | .06049 | .05742 | .05456 |
| 30 | .09420 | .08882 | .08383 | .07921 | .07492 | .07095 | .06725 | .06381 | .06061 | .05763 |
| 31 | .09881 | .09327 | .08812 | .08335 | .07891 | .07479 | .07095 | .06738 | .06405 | .06095 |
| 32 | .10369 | .09797 | .09267 | .08774 | .08315 | .07888 | .07491 | .07120 | .06774 | .06451 |
| 33 | .10885 | .10297 | .09750 | .09241 | .08767 | .08325 | .07913 | .07529 | .07170 | .06834 |
| 34 | .11430 | .10824 | .10261 | .09736 | .09246 | .08790 | .08363 | .07964 | .07592 | .07243 |
| 35 | .12002 | .11380 | .10800 | .10259 | .09754 | .09282 | .08841 | .08428 | .08041 | .07679 |
| 36 | .12602 | .11963 | .11366 | .10809 | .10288 | .09800 | .09344 | .08917 | .08516 | .08140 |
| 37 | .13230 | .12574 | .11961 | .11387 | .10850 | .10347 | .09876 | .09433 | .09018 | .08628 |
| 38 | .13887 | .13214 | .12584 | .11994 | .11441 | .10922 | .10436 | .09978 | .09549 | .09145 |
| 39 | .14573 | .13883 | .13237 | .12630 | .12061 | .11527 | .11025 | .10553 | .10109 | .09690 |
| 40 | .15290 | .14583 | .13920 | .13297 | .12712 | .12162 | .11644 | .11157 | .10698 | .10266 |
| 41 | .16036 | .15312 | .14633 | .13994 | .13393 | .12827 | .12294 | .11792 | .11318 | .10871 |
| 42 | .16810 | .16071 | .15375 | .14720 | .14103 | .13522 | .12973 | .12456 | .11967 | .11505 |
| 43 | .17614 | .16858 | .16146 | .15475 | .14842 | .14245 | .13682 | .13149 | .12645 | .12169 |
| 44 | .18447 | .17675 | .16948 | .16261 | .15613 | .15000 | .14421 | .13873 | .13355 | .12864 |
| 45 | .19310 | .18524 | .17780 | .17078 | .16414 | .15787 | .15192 | .14630 | .14096 | .13591 |
| 46 | .20204 | .19402 | .18644 | .17926 | .17247 | .16604 | .15995 | .15418 | .14870 | .14350 |
| 47 | .21128 | .20311 | .19538 | .18806 | .18112 | .17454 | .16830 | .16238 | .15676 | .15141 |
| 48 | .22080 | .21249 | .20462 | .19716 | .19007 | .18335 | .17696 | .17090 | .16513 | .15964 |
| 49 | .23059 | .22214 | .21413 | .20653 | .19930 | .19244 | .18591 | .17970 | .17379 | .16816 |
| 50 | .24063 | .23206 | .22391 | .21617 | .20881 | .20180 | .19514 | .18879 | .18274 | .17697 |
| 51 | .25095 | .24225 | .23398 | .22610 | .21861 | .21147 | .20466 | .19818 | .19199 | .18609 |
| 52 | .26157 | .25275 | .24436 | .23636 | .22874 | .22147 | .21453 | .20791 | .20159 | .19556 |
| 53 | .27249 | .26357 | .25505 | .24694 | .23919 | .23180 | .22474 | .21799 | .21154 | .20537 |
| 54 | .28369 | .27466 | .26604 | .25782 | .24995 | .24244 | .23526 | .22839 | .22181 | .21552 |
| 55 | .29518 | .28605 | .27734 | .26900 | .26103 | .25341 | .24611 | .23912 | .23243 | .22601 |
| 56 | .30695 | .29774 | .28893 | .28050 | .27242 | .26469 | .25728 | .25019 | .24338 | .23685 |
| 57 | .31902 | .30973 | .30084 | .29232 | .28415 | .27632 | .26881 | .26161 | .25469 | .24805 |
| 58 | .33138 | .32203 | .31306 | .30446 | .29621 | .28829 | .28069 | .27339 | .26637 | .25962 |
| 59 | .34402 | .33461 | .32558 | .31691 | .30859 | .30059 | .29290 | .28550 | .27839 | .27155 |
| 60 | .35690 | .34745 | .33836 | .32963 | .32124 | .31317 | .30540 | .29792 | .29073 | .28379 |
| 61 | .36999 | .36050 | .35137 | .34259 | .33414 | .32601 | .31817 | .31062 | .30334 | .29633 |
| 62 | .38325 | .37374 | .36458 | .35576 | .34726 | .33907 | .33117 | .32356 | .31621 | .30912 |
| 63 | .39669 | .38717 | .37799 | .36913 | .36060 | .35236 | .34441 | .33674 | .32933 | .32217 |
| 64 | .41031 | .40078 | .39159 | .38272 | .37415 | .36588 | .35789 | .35016 | .34270 | .33548 |
| 65 | .42416 | .41464 | .40545 | .39656 | .38798 | .37968 | .37166 | .36390 | .35639 | .34912 |
| 66 | .43825 | .42876 | .41958 | .41070 | .40211 | .39380 | .38576 | .37797 | .37043 | .36312 |
| 67 | .45260 | .44315 | .43399 | .42513 | .41655 | .40824 | .40019 | .39238 | .38482 | .37749 |
| 68 | .46720 | .45779 | .44868 | .43985 | .43129 | .42299 | .41494 | .40713 | .39956 | .39221 |
| 69 | .48197 | .47263 | .46357 | .45478 | .44625 | .43798 | .42995 | .42215 | .41458 | .40722 |
| 70 | .49686 | .48760 | .47861 | .46988 | .46140 | .45316 | .44516 | .43738 | .42983 | .42248 |
| 71 | .51182 | .50265 | .49374 | .48508 | .47666 | .46847 | .46051 | .45276 | .44523 | .43790 |
| 72 | .52685 | .51778 | .50896 | .50038 | .49203 | .48390 | .47599 | .46829 | .46079 | .45349 |
| 73 | .54194 | .53298 | .52426 | .51578 | .50751 | .49946 | .49161 | .48397 | .47652 | .46926 |
| 74 | .55714 | .54832 | .53972 | .53134 | .52317 | .51520 | .50744 | .49986 | .49247 | .48527 |
| 75 | .57250 | .56382 | .55536 | .54710 | .53904 | .53118 | .52351 | .51601 | .50870 | .50156 |
| 76 | .58803 | .57951 | .57120 | .56308 | .55515 | .54740 | .53984 | .53245 | .52522 | .51817 |

| AGE | 6.2% | 6.4% | 6.6% | 6.8% | 7.0% | 7.2% | 7.4% | 7.6% | 7.8% | 8.0% |
|-----|------|------|------|------|------|------|------|------|------|------|
| 77 | .60369 | .59535 | .58720 | .57923 | .57144 | .56383 | .55639 | .54912 | .54200 | .53504 |
| 78 | .61942 | .61126 | .60329 | .59549 | .58787 | .58040 | .57310 | .56596 | .55896 | .55212 |
| 79 | .63508 | .62713 | .61935 | .61174 | .60428 | .59698 | .58983 | .58283 | .57597 | .56925 |
| 80 | .65059 | .64285 | .63527 | .62785 | .62058 | .61345 | .60646 | .59961 | .59290 | .58632 |
| 81 | .66579 | .65827 | .65090 | .64368 | .63659 | .62965 | .62283 | .61615 | .60959 | .60316 |
| 82 | .68061 | .67332 | .66616 | .65914 | .65226 | .64550 | .63886 | .63235 | .62595 | .61968 |
| 83 | .69499 | .68793 | .68099 | .67418 | .66749 | .66092 | .65447 | .64813 | .64191 | .63579 |
| 84 | .70896 | .70213 | .69541 | .68881 | .68233 | .67595 | .66969 | .66353 | .65748 | .65153 |
| 85 | .72256 | .71596 | .70947 | .70308 | .69681 | .69063 | .68456 | .67859 | .67271 | .66693 |
| 86 | .73569 | .72931 | .72305 | .71688 | .71081 | .70484 | .69896 | .69318 | .68748 | .68188 |
| 87 | .74818 | .74204 | .73599 | .73003 | .72417 | .71839 | .71271 | .70711 | .70159 | .69616 |
| 88 | .76011 | .75419 | .74836 | .74261 | .73695 | .73137 | .72588 | .72046 | .71512 | .70986 |
| 89 | .77169 | .76599 | .76037 | .75484 | .74938 | .74400 | .73870 | .73347 | .72831 | .72323 |
| 90 | .78302 | .77755 | .77215 | .76683 | .76158 | .75640 | .75129 | .74625 | .74128 | .73638 |
| 91 | .79395 | .78870 | .78352 | .77842 | .77337 | .76840 | .76349 | .75864 | .75385 | .74913 |
| 92 | .80423 | .79920 | .79423 | .78933 | .78449 | .77971 | .77499 | .77033 | .76572 | .76118 |
| 93 | .81377 | .80894 | .80417 | .79946 | .79481 | .79022 | .78568 | .78120 | .77677 | .77239 |
| 94 | .82247 | .81784 | .81325 | .80873 | .80425 | .79983 | .79547 | .79115 | .78688 | .78266 |
| 95 | .83033 | .82586 | .82145 | .81709 | .81278 | .80852 | .80431 | .80014 | .79602 | .79195 |
| 96 | .83729 | .83298 | .82872 | .82451 | .82034 | .81622 | .81215 | .80812 | .80414 | .80019 |
| 97 | .84361 | .83944 | .83532 | .83124 | .82721 | .82322 | .81927 | .81537 | .81151 | .80769 |
| 98 | .84929 | .84525 | .84126 | .83730 | .83339 | .82952 | .82569 | .82190 | .81815 | .81443 |
| 99 | .85454 | .85062 | .84674 | .84290 | .83910 | .83534 | .83161 | .82792 | .82427 | .82066 |
| 100 | .85942 | .85561 | .85184 | .84810 | .84440 | .84074 | .83711 | .83352 | .82997 | .82644 |
| 101 | .86408 | .86037 | .85670 | .85306 | .84946 | .84589 | .84236 | .83886 | .83539 | .83196 |
| 102 | .86894 | .86534 | .86177 | .85823 | .85473 | .85126 | .84782 | .84442 | .84104 | .83770 |
| 103 | .87408 | .87060 | .86714 | .86371 | .86032 | .85695 | .85362 | .85031 | .84703 | .84378 |
| 104 | .87980 | .87644 | .87311 | .86980 | .86653 | .86328 | .86005 | .85686 | .85369 | .85054 |
| 105 | .88684 | .88363 | .88046 | .87731 | .87418 | .87108 | .86800 | .86494 | .86191 | .85890 |
| 106 | .89685 | .89389 | .89095 | .88804 | .88514 | .88226 | .87940 | .87656 | .87374 | .87094 |
| 107 | .91117 | .90858 | .90600 | .90344 | .90089 | .89836 | .89584 | .89334 | .89085 | .88838 |
| 108 | .93414 | .93217 | .93022 | .92828 | .92634 | .92442 | .92250 | .92060 | .91870 | .91681 |
| 109 | .97081 | .96992 | .96904 | .96816 | .96729 | .96642 | .96555 | .96468 | .96382 | .96296 |

TABLE S
BASED ON LIFE TABLE 80CNSMT
SINGLE LIFE REMAINDER FACTORS
APPLICABLE AFTER APRIL 30, 1989,
AND BEFORE MAY 1, 1999
INTEREST RATE

| AGE | 8.2% | 8.4% | 8.6% | 8.8% | 9.0% | 9.2% | 9.4% | 9.6% | 9.8% | 10.0% |
|---|---|---|---|---|---|---|---|---|---|---|
| 0 | .02341 | .02276 | .02217 | .02163 | .02114 | .02069 | .02027 | .01989 | .01954 | .01922 |
| 1 | .01237 | .01170 | .01108 | .01052 | .01000 | .00953 | .00910 | .00871 | .00834 | .00801 |
| 2 | .01243 | .01172 | .01107 | .01048 | .00994 | .00944 | .00899 | .00857 | .00819 | .00784 |
| 3 | .01278 | .01203 | .01135 | .01073 | .01016 | .00964 | .00916 | .00872 | .00832 | .00795 |
| 4 | .01332 | .01253 | .01182 | .01116 | .01056 | .01001 | .00951 | .00904 | .00862 | .00822 |
| 5 | .01400 | .01317 | .01241 | .01172 | .01109 | .01051 | .00998 | .00949 | .00904 | .00862 |
| 6 | .01477 | .01390 | .01310 | .01238 | .01171 | .01110 | .01054 | .01002 | .00954 | .00910 |
| 7 | .01563 | .01472 | .01389 | .01312 | .01242 | .01178 | .01118 | .01064 | .01013 | .00966 |
| 8 | .01660 | .01564 | .01477 | .01396 | .01322 | .01254 | .01192 | .01134 | .01081 | .01031 |
| 9 | .01770 | .01669 | .01577 | .01492 | .01414 | .01342 | .01276 | .01216 | .01159 | .01107 |
| 10 | .01891 | .01785 | .01688 | .01599 | .01517 | .01442 | .01372 | .01308 | .01249 | .01194 |
| 11 | .02026 | .01915 | .01814 | .01720 | .01634 | .01555 | .01481 | .01414 | .01351 | .01293 |
| 12 | .02173 | .02056 | .01950 | .01852 | .01761 | .01678 | .01601 | .01529 | .01463 | .01402 |
| 13 | .02326 | .02204 | .02092 | .01989 | .01895 | .01807 | .01726 | .01651 | .01582 | .01517 |
| 14 | .02478 | .02351 | .02234 | .02126 | .02027 | .01935 | .01850 | .01771 | .01698 | .01630 |
| 15 | .02628 | .02495 | .02372 | .02259 | .02155 | .02058 | .01969 | .01886 | .01810 | .01738 |
| 16 | .02774 | .02635 | .02507 | .02388 | .02279 | .02178 | .02084 | .01997 | .01917 | .01842 |
| 17 | .02917 | .02772 | .02637 | .02513 | .02399 | .02293 | .02194 | .02103 | .02018 | .01940 |
| 18 | .03059 | .02907 | .02767 | .02637 | .02517 | .02406 | .02302 | .02207 | .02118 | .02035 |
| 19 | .03205 | .03046 | .02899 | .02763 | .02637 | .02521 | .02412 | .02312 | .02218 | .02131 |
| 20 | .03355 | .03188 | .03035 | .02892 | .02760 | .02638 | .02524 | .02419 | .02320 | .02229 |
| 21 | .03509 | .03334 | .03173 | .03024 | .02886 | .02758 | .02638 | .02527 | .02424 | .02328 |
| 22 | .03669 | .03487 | .03318 | .03162 | .03017 | .02882 | .02757 | .02640 | .02532 | .02430 |
| 23 | .03837 | .03646 | .03470 | .03306 | .03154 | .03013 | .02881 | .02759 | .02644 | .02538 |
| 24 | .04018 | .03819 | .03634 | .03463 | .03303 | .03155 | .03016 | .02888 | .02767 | .02655 |
| 25 | .04214 | .04006 | .03812 | .03633 | .03465 | .03309 | .03164 | .03029 | .02902 | .02784 |
| 26 | .04428 | .04210 | .04008 | .03820 | .03644 | .03481 | .03328 | .03186 | .03052 | .02928 |
| 27 | .04662 | .04434 | .04223 | .04025 | .03841 | .03670 | .03509 | .03360 | .03219 | .03088 |
| 28 | .04915 | .04677 | .04456 | .04249 | .04056 | .03876 | .03708 | .03550 | .03403 | .03264 |
| 29 | .05189 | .04941 | .04709 | .04493 | .04291 | .04102 | .03925 | .03760 | .03604 | .03458 |
| 30 | .05485 | .05226 | .04984 | .04757 | .04546 | .04348 | .04162 | .03988 | .03825 | .03671 |
| 31 | .05805 | .05535 | .05282 | .05045 | .04824 | .04616 | .04421 | .04238 | .04067 | .03905 |
| 32 | .06149 | .05867 | .05603 | .05356 | .05124 | .04906 | .04702 | .04510 | .04329 | .04160 |
| 33 | .06520 | .06226 | .05950 | .05692 | .05449 | .05221 | .05007 | .04806 | .04616 | .04438 |
| 34 | .06916 | .06609 | .06322 | .06052 | .05799 | .05560 | .05336 | .05125 | .04926 | .04738 |
| 35 | .07339 | .07020 | .06720 | .06439 | .06174 | .05925 | .05690 | .05469 | .05260 | .05063 |
| 36 | .07787 | .07455 | .07143 | .06850 | .06573 | .06313 | .06068 | .05836 | .05617 | .05411 |
| 37 | .08262 | .07917 | .07593 | .07287 | .06999 | .06727 | .06470 | .06228 | .05999 | .05783 |
| 38 | .08765 | .08407 | .08069 | .07751 | .07451 | .07167 | .06899 | .06646 | .06407 | .06180 |
| 39 | .09296 | .08925 | .08574 | .08243 | .07931 | .07635 | .07356 | .07092 | .06841 | .06604 |
| 40 | .09858 | .09472 | .09109 | .08765 | .08440 | .08132 | .07841 | .07565 | .07303 | .07055 |
| 41 | .10449 | .10050 | .09673 | .09316 | .08978 | .08658 | .08355 | .08067 | .07794 | .07535 |
| 42 | .11069 | .10656 | .10265 | .09895 | .09544 | .09212 | .08896 | .08596 | .08312 | .08041 |
| 43 | .11718 | .11291 | .10887 | .10503 | .10140 | .09794 | .09466 | .09154 | .08858 | .08576 |
| 44 | .12399 | .11958 | .11540 | .11143 | .10766 | .10407 | .10067 | .09743 | .09434 | .09141 |
| 45 | .13111 | .12656 | .12224 | .11814 | .11423 | .11052 | .10699 | .10362 | .10042 | .09736 |
| 46 | .13856 | .13387 | .12941 | .12516 | .12113 | .11728 | .11362 | .11013 | .10680 | .10363 |
| 47 | .14633 | .14150 | .13690 | .13252 | .12835 | .12438 | .12059 | .11697 | .11352 | .11022 |
| 48 | .15442 | .14945 | .14471 | .14020 | .13589 | .13179 | .12787 | .12412 | .12055 | .11713 |
| 49 | .16280 | .15769 | .15281 | .14816 | .14373 | .13949 | .13544 | .13157 | .12787 | .12433 |
| 50 | .17147 | .16622 | .16121 | .15643 | .15186 | .14749 | .14331 | .13931 | .13548 | .13182 |
| 51 | .18045 | .17507 | .16993 | .16501 | .16030 | .15580 | .15150 | .14737 | .14342 | .13963 |
| 52 | .18979 | .18427 | .17899 | .17394 | .16911 | .16448 | .16004 | .15579 | .15172 | .14780 |
| 53 | .19947 | .19383 | .18842 | .18324 | .17828 | .17352 | .16896 | .16458 | .16038 | .15635 |
| 54 | .20950 | .20372 | .19819 | .19288 | .18779 | .18291 | .17822 | .17372 | .16940 | .16524 |
| 55 | .21986 | .21397 | .20831 | .20288 | .19767 | .19266 | .18785 | .18322 | .17878 | .17450 |
| 56 | .23058 | .22457 | .21879 | .21324 | .20791 | .20278 | .19785 | .19310 | .18854 | .18414 |
| 57 | .24167 | .23554 | .22965 | .22399 | .21854 | .21329 | .20824 | .20338 | .19870 | .19419 |
| 58 | .25314 | .24690 | .24090 | .23512 | .22956 | .22420 | .21904 | .21407 | .20927 | .20464 |
| 59 | .26497 | .25863 | .25252 | .24664 | .24097 | .23550 | .23023 | .22515 | .22024 | .21551 |
| 60 | .27712 | .27068 | .26448 | .25849 | .25272 | .24716 | .24178 | .23659 | .23158 | .22674 |
| 61 | .28956 | .28304 | .27674 | .27067 | .26480 | .25913 | .25366 | .24837 | .24325 | .23831 |
| 62 | .30228 | .29567 | .28929 | .28312 | .27717 | .27141 | .26584 | .26045 | .25524 | .25020 |
| 63 | .31525 | .30857 | .30211 | .29586 | .28982 | .28397 | .27832 | .27284 | .26754 | .26240 |
| 64 | .32851 | .32176 | .31522 | .30890 | .30278 | .29685 | .29111 | .28555 | .28016 | .27493 |
| 65 | .34209 | .33528 | .32868 | .32229 | .31610 | .31010 | .30429 | .29865 | .29317 | .28787 |
| 66 | .35604 | .34918 | .34253 | .33609 | .32983 | .32377 | .31788 | .31217 | .30663 | .30124 |
| 67 | .37037 | .36347 | .35678 | .35028 | .34398 | .33786 | .33191 | .32614 | .32053 | .31508 |
| 68 | .38508 | .37815 | .37142 | .36489 | .35854 | .35237 | .34638 | .34055 | .33488 | .32937 |
| 69 | .40008 | .39313 | .38638 | .37982 | .37344 | .36724 | .36120 | .35533 | .34961 | .34405 |
| 70 | .41533 | .40838 | .40162 | .39504 | .38864 | .38241 | .37634 | .37043 | .36468 | .35907 |
| 71 | .43076 | .42382 | .41705 | .41047 | .40405 | .39780 | .39171 | .38578 | .38000 | .37436 |
| 72 | .44638 | .43945 | .43269 | .42611 | .41969 | .41344 | .40733 | .40138 | .39558 | .38991 |
| 73 | .46218 | .45527 | .44854 | .44197 | .43556 | .42931 | .42321 | .41725 | .41143 | .40575 |
| 74 | .47823 | .47137 | .46466 | .45812 | .45173 | .44549 | .43940 | .43345 | .42763 | .42195 |
| 75 | .49459 | .48777 | .48112 | .47462 | .46826 | .46205 | .45598 | .45004 | .44424 | .43856 |
| 76 | .51127 | .50452 | .49793 | .49148 | .48517 | .47900 | .47297 | .46706 | .46129 | .45563 |

Reg. §20.2031-7A(e)(4)

| AGE | 8.2% | 8.4% | 8.6% | 8.8% | 9.0% | 9.2% | 9.4% | 9.6% | 9.8% | 10.0% |
|-----|------|------|------|------|------|------|------|------|------|-------|
| 77 | .52823 | .52157 | .51505 | .50867 | .50243 | .49632 | .49033 | .48447 | .47873 | .47311 |
| 78 | .54541 | .53885 | .53242 | .52613 | .51996 | .51392 | .50800 | .50220 | .49652 | .49094 |
| 79 | .56267 | .55621 | .54989 | .54369 | .53762 | .53166 | .52582 | .52009 | .51448 | .50897 |
| 80 | .57987 | .57354 | .56733 | .56125 | .55527 | .54941 | .54366 | .53802 | .53248 | .52705 |
| 81 | .59685 | .59065 | .58457 | .57860 | .57274 | .56699 | .56134 | .55579 | .55035 | .54499 |
| 82 | .61351 | .60746 | .60151 | .59567 | .58993 | .58429 | .57875 | .57331 | .56796 | .56270 |
| 83 | .62978 | .62387 | .61806 | .61236 | .60675 | .60123 | .59581 | .59047 | .58523 | .58007 |
| 84 | .64567 | .63992 | .63426 | .62869 | .62321 | .61783 | .61253 | .60731 | .60218 | .59713 |
| 85 | .66125 | .65565 | .65014 | .64472 | .63938 | .63413 | .62896 | .62387 | .61886 | .61392 |
| 86 | .67636 | .67092 | .66557 | .66030 | .65511 | .65000 | .64496 | .64000 | .63511 | .63030 |
| 87 | .69081 | .68554 | .68034 | .67522 | .67018 | .66520 | .66031 | .65548 | .65071 | .64602 |
| 88 | .70468 | .69957 | .69453 | .68956 | .68466 | .67983 | .67507 | .67037 | .66574 | .66117 |
| 89 | .71821 | .71326 | .70838 | .70357 | .69882 | .69414 | .68952 | .68495 | .68045 | .67601 |
| 90 | .73153 | .72676 | .72204 | .71739 | .71280 | .70827 | .70379 | .69938 | .69502 | .69071 |
| 91 | .74447 | .73986 | .73532 | .73083 | .72640 | .72202 | .71770 | .71343 | .70921 | .70504 |
| 92 | .75669 | .75225 | .74787 | .74354 | .73927 | .73504 | .73087 | .72674 | .72267 | .71864 |
| 93 | .76807 | .76379 | .75957 | .75540 | .75127 | .74719 | .74317 | .73918 | .73524 | .73135 |
| 94 | .77849 | .77437 | .77030 | .76627 | .76229 | .75835 | .75446 | .75061 | .74680 | .74303 |
| 95 | .78792 | .78394 | .78001 | .77611 | .77226 | .76845 | .76468 | .76096 | .75727 | .75362 |
| 96 | .79630 | .79244 | .78863 | .78485 | .78112 | .77742 | .77377 | .77015 | .76657 | .76303 |
| 97 | .80391 | .80016 | .79646 | .79280 | .78917 | .78559 | .78203 | .77852 | .77504 | .77160 |
| 98 | .81076 | .80712 | .80352 | .79996 | .79643 | .79294 | .78948 | .78606 | .78267 | .77931 |
| 99 | .81709 | .81354 | .81004 | .80657 | .80313 | .79972 | .79635 | .79302 | .78971 | .78644 |
| 100 | .82296 | .81950 | .81609 | .81270 | .80934 | .80602 | .80273 | .79947 | .79624 | .79304 |
| 101 | .82855 | .82518 | .82185 | .81854 | .81526 | .81201 | .80880 | .80561 | .80245 | .79932 |
| 102 | .83438 | .83110 | .82785 | .82462 | .82142 | .81826 | .81512 | .81200 | .80892 | .80586 |
| 103 | .84056 | .83737 | .83420 | .83106 | .82795 | .82487 | .82181 | .81878 | .81577 | .81279 |
| 104 | .84743 | .84433 | .84127 | .83822 | .83521 | .83221 | .82924 | .82630 | .82338 | .82048 |
| 105 | .85591 | .85295 | .85001 | .84709 | .84419 | .84132 | .83846 | .83563 | .83282 | .83003 |
| 106 | .86816 | .86540 | .86266 | .85993 | .85723 | .85454 | .85187 | .84922 | .84659 | .84397 |
| 107 | .88592 | .88348 | .88105 | .87863 | .87623 | .87384 | .87147 | .86911 | .86676 | .86443 |
| 108 | .91493 | .91306 | .91119 | .90934 | .90749 | .90566 | .90383 | .90201 | .90020 | .89840 |
| 109 | .96211 | .96125 | .96041 | .95956 | .95872 | .95788 | .95704 | .95620 | .95537 | .95455 |

TABLE S
BASED ON LIFE TABLE 80CNSMT
SINGLE LIFE REMAINDER FACTORS
APPLICABLE AFTER APRIL 30, 1989,
AND BEFORE MAY 1, 1999
INTEREST RATE

| AGE | 10.2% | 10.4% | 10.6% | 10.8% | 11.0% | 11.2% | 11.4% | 11.6% | 11.8% | 12.0% |
|---|---|---|---|---|---|---|---|---|---|---|
| 0 | .01891 | .01864 | .01838 | .01814 | .01791 | .01770 | .01750 | .01732 | .01715 | .01698 |
| 1 | .00770 | .00741 | .00715 | .00690 | .00667 | .00646 | .00626 | .00608 | .00590 | .00574 |
| 2 | .00751 | .00721 | .00693 | .00667 | .00643 | .00620 | .00600 | .00580 | .00562 | .00544 |
| 3 | .00760 | .00728 | .00699 | .00671 | .00646 | .00622 | .00600 | .00579 | .00560 | .00541 |
| 4 | .00786 | .00752 | .00721 | .00692 | .00665 | .00639 | .00616 | .00594 | .00573 | .00554 |
| 5 | .00824 | .00788 | .00755 | .00724 | .00695 | .00668 | .00643 | .00620 | .00598 | .00578 |
| 6 | .00869 | .00832 | .00796 | .00764 | .00733 | .00705 | .00678 | .00654 | .00630 | .00608 |
| 7 | .00923 | .00883 | .00846 | .00811 | .00779 | .00749 | .00720 | .00694 | .00669 | .00646 |
| 8 | .00986 | .00943 | .00904 | .00867 | .00833 | .00801 | .00771 | .00743 | .00716 | .00692 |
| 9 | .01059 | .01014 | .00972 | .00933 | .00897 | .00863 | .00831 | .00801 | .00773 | .00747 |
| 10 | .01142 | .01095 | .01051 | .01009 | .00971 | .00935 | .00901 | .00869 | .00840 | .00812 |
| 11 | .01239 | .01189 | .01142 | .01098 | .01057 | .01019 | .00983 | .00950 | .00918 | .00889 |
| 12 | .01345 | .01292 | .01243 | .01197 | .01154 | .01113 | .01075 | .01040 | .01007 | .00975 |
| 13 | .01457 | .01401 | .01349 | .01300 | .01255 | .01212 | .01172 | .01135 | .01100 | .01067 |
| 14 | .01567 | .01508 | .01453 | .01402 | .01354 | .01309 | .01267 | .01227 | .01190 | .01155 |
| 15 | .01672 | .01610 | .01552 | .01498 | .01448 | .01400 | .01356 | .01314 | .01275 | .01238 |
| 16 | .01772 | .01707 | .01646 | .01589 | .01536 | .01486 | .01439 | .01396 | .01354 | .01315 |
| 17 | .01866 | .01798 | .01734 | .01674 | .01618 | .01566 | .01516 | .01470 | .01427 | .01386 |
| 18 | .01958 | .01886 | .01818 | .01755 | .01697 | .01641 | .01590 | .01541 | .01495 | .01452 |
| 19 | .02050 | .01974 | .01903 | .01837 | .01775 | .01717 | .01662 | .01611 | .01563 | .01517 |
| 20 | .02143 | .02064 | .01989 | .01919 | .01854 | .01793 | .01735 | .01681 | .01630 | .01582 |
| 21 | .02238 | .02154 | .02075 | .02002 | .01933 | .01868 | .01807 | .01750 | .01696 | .01646 |
| 22 | .02336 | .02247 | .02164 | .02087 | .02014 | .01946 | .01882 | .01821 | .01764 | .01711 |
| 23 | .02438 | .02345 | .02257 | .02176 | .02099 | .02027 | .01959 | .01895 | .01835 | .01778 |
| 24 | .02550 | .02451 | .02359 | .02273 | .02192 | .02115 | .02044 | .01976 | .01913 | .01853 |
| 25 | .02673 | .02569 | .02472 | .02381 | .02295 | .02214 | .02138 | .02067 | .01999 | .01936 |
| 26 | .02811 | .02701 | .02598 | .02502 | .02411 | .02326 | .02246 | .02170 | .02098 | .02031 |
| 27 | .02965 | .02849 | .02741 | .02639 | .02543 | .02452 | .02367 | .02287 | .02211 | .02140 |
| 28 | .03134 | .03013 | .02898 | .02790 | .02689 | .02593 | .02503 | .02418 | .02338 | .02262 |
| 29 | .03322 | .03193 | .03072 | .02958 | .02851 | .02750 | .02654 | .02564 | .02479 | .02398 |
| 30 | .03527 | .03391 | .03264 | .03143 | .03030 | .02923 | .02821 | .02726 | .02635 | .02550 |
| 31 | .03753 | .03610 | .03475 | .03348 | .03228 | .03115 | .03008 | .02907 | .02811 | .02720 |
| 32 | .04000 | .03849 | .03707 | .03573 | .03446 | .03326 | .03213 | .03105 | .03004 | .02907 |
| 33 | .04269 | .04111 | .03961 | .03819 | .03685 | .03558 | .03438 | .03325 | .03217 | .03115 |
| 34 | .04561 | .04394 | .04236 | .04087 | .03946 | .03812 | .03685 | .03565 | .03451 | .03342 |
| 35 | .04877 | .04702 | .04535 | .04378 | .04229 | .04087 | .03953 | .03826 | .03706 | .03591 |
| 36 | .05215 | .05031 | .04856 | .04690 | .04533 | .04384 | .04242 | .04108 | .03980 | .03859 |
| 37 | .05578 | .05384 | .05200 | .05025 | .04860 | .04703 | .04553 | .04411 | .04276 | .04148 |
| 38 | .05965 | .05761 | .05568 | .05385 | .05211 | .05045 | .04888 | .04738 | .04595 | .04460 |
| 39 | .06379 | .06165 | .05962 | .05770 | .05587 | .05412 | .05247 | .05089 | .04939 | .04795 |
| 40 | .06820 | .06596 | .06383 | .06181 | .05989 | .05806 | .05631 | .05465 | .05307 | .05155 |
| 41 | .07288 | .07054 | .06832 | .06620 | .06418 | .06226 | .06042 | .05868 | .05701 | .05541 |
| 42 | .07784 | .07539 | .07306 | .07085 | .06873 | .06671 | .06479 | .06295 | .06119 | .05952 |
| 43 | .08308 | .08052 | .07808 | .07576 | .07355 | .07143 | .06941 | .06748 | .06564 | .06387 |
| 44 | .08861 | .08594 | .08340 | .08097 | .07865 | .07644 | .07432 | .07230 | .07036 | .06851 |
| 45 | .09445 | .09167 | .08901 | .08648 | .08406 | .08174 | .07953 | .07741 | .07538 | .07343 |
| 46 | .10060 | .09770 | .09494 | .09230 | .08977 | .08735 | .08503 | .08281 | .08068 | .07865 |
| 47 | .10707 | .10406 | .10119 | .09843 | .09579 | .09327 | .09085 | .08853 | .08630 | .08417 |
| 48 | .11386 | .11073 | .10774 | .10487 | .10213 | .09949 | .09697 | .09455 | .09222 | .08999 |
| 49 | .12094 | .11769 | .11458 | .11160 | .10874 | .10600 | .10337 | .10084 | .09842 | .09609 |
| 50 | .12831 | .12494 | .12172 | .11862 | .11565 | .11280 | .11006 | .10743 | .10490 | .10247 |
| 51 | .13600 | .13251 | .12917 | .12596 | .12288 | .11991 | .11706 | .11432 | .11169 | .10915 |
| 52 | .14405 | .14044 | .13698 | .13366 | .13046 | .12738 | .12442 | .12157 | .11883 | .11619 |
| 53 | .15247 | .14875 | .14517 | .14172 | .13841 | .13522 | .13215 | .12919 | .12635 | .12360 |
| 54 | .16124 | .15740 | .15370 | .15014 | .14671 | .14341 | .14023 | .13717 | .13421 | .13136 |
| 55 | .17039 | .16642 | .16261 | .15893 | .15539 | .15198 | .14868 | .14551 | .14244 | .13948 |
| 56 | .17991 | .17583 | .17190 | .16811 | .16445 | .16092 | .15752 | .15423 | .15106 | .14799 |
| 57 | .18984 | .18564 | .18160 | .17769 | .17392 | .17029 | .16677 | .16338 | .16010 | .15692 |
| 58 | .20018 | .19587 | .19172 | .18770 | .18382 | .18007 | .17645 | .17295 | .16956 | .16628 |
| 59 | .21093 | .20652 | .20225 | .19812 | .19414 | .19028 | .18655 | .18294 | .17945 | .17606 |
| 60 | .22206 | .21753 | .21316 | .20893 | .20483 | .20087 | .19703 | .19332 | .18972 | .18624 |
| 61 | .23353 | .22890 | .22442 | .22009 | .21589 | .21182 | .20788 | .20407 | .20037 | .19678 |
| 62 | .24532 | .24059 | .23601 | .23158 | .22728 | .22311 | .21907 | .21515 | .21135 | .20767 |
| 63 | .25742 | .25260 | .24793 | .24339 | .23900 | .23473 | .23060 | .22658 | .22268 | .21890 |
| 64 | .26987 | .26495 | .26019 | .25556 | .25107 | .24671 | .24248 | .23837 | .23438 | .23050 |
| 65 | .28271 | .27771 | .27286 | .26815 | .26357 | .25912 | .25480 | .25059 | .24651 | .24254 |
| 66 | .29601 | .29093 | .28600 | .28120 | .27654 | .27200 | .26760 | .26331 | .25913 | .25507 |
| 67 | .30978 | .30462 | .29961 | .29474 | .29000 | .28539 | .28090 | .27653 | .27227 | .26813 |
| 68 | .32401 | .31879 | .31371 | .30877 | .30396 | .29927 | .29471 | .29027 | .28593 | .28171 |
| 69 | .33863 | .33336 | .32822 | .32322 | .31835 | .31359 | .30896 | .30445 | .30005 | .29576 |
| 70 | .35361 | .34829 | .34310 | .33804 | .33311 | .32830 | .32361 | .31903 | .31457 | .31021 |
| 71 | .36886 | .36349 | .35826 | .35316 | .34818 | .34332 | .33858 | .33394 | .32942 | .32500 |
| 72 | .38439 | .37899 | .37373 | .36858 | .36356 | .35866 | .35387 | .34919 | .34461 | .34015 |
| 73 | .40021 | .39479 | .38950 | .38432 | .37927 | .37433 | .36950 | .36478 | .36016 | .35565 |
| 74 | .41639 | .41096 | .40565 | .40046 | .39538 | .39042 | .38556 | .38081 | .37616 | .37161 |
| 75 | .43301 | .42758 | .42226 | .41706 | .41198 | .40699 | .40212 | .39734 | .39267 | .38809 |
| 76 | .45009 | .44467 | .43937 | .43417 | .42908 | .42410 | .41921 | .41443 | .40974 | .40514 |

Reg. §20.2031-7A(e)(4)

| AGE | 10.2% | 10.4% | 10.6% | 10.8% | 11.0% | 11.2% | 11.4% | 11.6% | 11.8% | 12.0% |
|---|---|---|---|---|---|---|---|---|---|---|
| 77 | .46761 | .46221 | .45693 | .45175 | .44667 | .44170 | .43682 | .43203 | .42734 | .42274 |
| 78 | .48548 | .48013 | .47488 | .46973 | .46468 | .45972 | .45486 | .45009 | .44541 | .44082 |
| 79 | .50356 | .49826 | .49306 | .48795 | .48294 | .47802 | .47319 | .46845 | .46379 | .45922 |
| 80 | .52171 | .51647 | .51133 | .50628 | .50132 | .49644 | .49166 | .48695 | .48233 | .47779 |
| 81 | .53974 | .53457 | .52950 | .52451 | .51961 | .51479 | .51006 | .50541 | .50083 | .49633 |
| 82 | .55753 | .55245 | .54745 | .54254 | .53771 | .53296 | .52828 | .52369 | .51917 | .51472 |
| 83 | .57500 | .57001 | .56510 | .56026 | .55551 | .55083 | .54623 | .54170 | .53724 | .53285 |
| 84 | .59216 | .58726 | .58245 | .57770 | .57304 | .56844 | .56391 | .55945 | .55506 | .55074 |
| 85 | .60906 | .60428 | .59956 | .59492 | .59034 | .58583 | .58139 | .57702 | .57270 | .56845 |
| 86 | .62555 | .62088 | .61627 | .61173 | .60725 | .60284 | .59849 | .59420 | .58997 | .58580 |
| 87 | .64139 | .63683 | .63233 | .62790 | .62352 | .61921 | .61495 | .61076 | .60661 | .60253 |
| 88 | .65666 | .65221 | .64783 | .64350 | .63923 | .63502 | .63086 | .62675 | .62270 | .61871 |
| 89 | .67163 | .66730 | .66304 | .65882 | .65466 | .65055 | .64650 | .64249 | .63854 | .63463 |
| 90 | .68646 | .68226 | .67812 | .67402 | .66998 | .66599 | .66204 | .65814 | .65430 | .65049 |
| 91 | .70093 | .69686 | .69285 | .68888 | .68496 | .68108 | .67725 | .67347 | .66973 | .66604 |
| 92 | .71466 | .71073 | .70684 | .70300 | .69920 | .69545 | .69173 | .68806 | .68444 | .68085 |
| 93 | .72750 | .72370 | .71994 | .71622 | .71254 | .70890 | .70530 | .70174 | .69822 | .69474 |
| 94 | .73931 | .73562 | .73198 | .72838 | .72481 | .72129 | .71780 | .71434 | .71093 | .70755 |
| 95 | .75001 | .74644 | .74291 | .73941 | .73595 | .73253 | .72914 | .72579 | .72247 | .71919 |
| 96 | .75953 | .75606 | .75262 | .74923 | .74586 | .74253 | .73924 | .73598 | .73275 | .72955 |
| 97 | .76819 | .76481 | .76147 | .75816 | .75489 | .75165 | .74844 | .74526 | .74211 | .73899 |
| 98 | .77599 | .77270 | .76944 | .76621 | .76302 | .75986 | .75672 | .75362 | .75054 | .74750 |
| 99 | .78319 | .77998 | .77680 | .77365 | .77053 | .76744 | .76437 | .76134 | .75833 | .75535 |
| 100 | .78987 | .78673 | .78362 | .78054 | .77748 | .77446 | .77146 | .76849 | .76555 | .76263 |
| 101 | .79622 | .79315 | .79010 | .78708 | .78409 | .78113 | .77819 | .77528 | .77239 | .76953 |
| 102 | .80283 | .79983 | .79685 | .79390 | .79097 | .78807 | .78519 | .78234 | .77951 | .77671 |
| 103 | .80983 | .80690 | .80399 | .80111 | .79825 | .79541 | .79260 | .78981 | .78705 | .78430 |
| 104 | .81760 | .81475 | .81192 | .80912 | .80633 | .80357 | .80083 | .79810 | .79541 | .79273 |
| 105 | .82726 | .82451 | .82178 | .81907 | .81638 | .81371 | .81106 | .80843 | .80582 | .80322 |
| 106 | .84137 | .83879 | .83623 | .83368 | .83115 | .82863 | .82614 | .82366 | .82119 | .81874 |
| 107 | .86211 | .85981 | .85751 | .85523 | .85297 | .85071 | .84847 | .84624 | .84403 | .84182 |
| 108 | .89660 | .89481 | .89304 | .89127 | .88950 | .88775 | .88601 | .88427 | .88254 | .88081 |
| 109 | .95372 | .95290 | .95208 | .95126 | .95045 | .94964 | .94883 | .94803 | .94723 | .94643 |

TABLE S
BASED ON LIFE TABLE 80CNSMT
SINGLE LIFE REMAINDER FACTORS
APPLICABLE AFTER APRIL 30, 1989,
AND BEFORE MAY 1, 1999
INTEREST RATE

| AGE | 12.2% | 12.4% | 12.6% | 12.8% | 13.0% | 13.2% | 13.4% | 13.6% | 13.8% | 14.0% |
|---|---|---|---|---|---|---|---|---|---|---|
| 0 | .01683 | .01669 | .01655 | .01642 | .01630 | .01618 | .01607 | .01596 | .01586 | .01576 |
| 1 | .00559 | .00544 | .00531 | .00518 | .00506 | .00494 | .00484 | .00473 | .00464 | .00454 |
| 2 | .00528 | .00513 | .00499 | .00485 | .00473 | .00461 | .00449 | .00439 | .00428 | .00419 |
| 3 | .00524 | .00508 | .00493 | .00479 | .00465 | .00453 | .00441 | .00429 | .00419 | .00408 |
| 4 | .00536 | .00519 | .00503 | .00488 | .00473 | .00460 | .00447 | .00435 | .00423 | .00412 |
| 5 | .00558 | .00540 | .00523 | .00507 | .00492 | .00477 | .00464 | .00451 | .00439 | .00427 |
| 6 | .00588 | .00569 | .00550 | .00533 | .00517 | .00502 | .00487 | .00473 | .00460 | .00448 |
| 7 | .00624 | .00604 | .00584 | .00566 | .00549 | .00532 | .00517 | .00502 | .00488 | .00475 |
| 8 | .00668 | .00646 | .00626 | .00606 | .00588 | .00570 | .00554 | .00538 | .00523 | .00509 |
| 9 | .00722 | .00699 | .00677 | .00656. | .00636 | .00617 | .00600 | .00583 | .00567 | .00552 |
| 10 | .00785 | .00761 | .00737 | .00715 | .00694 | .00674 | .00655 | .00637 | .00620 | .00604 |
| 11 | .00861 | .00835 | .00810 | .00786 | .00764 | .00743 | .00723 | .00704 | .00686 | .00668 |
| 12 | .00946 | .00918 | .00891 | .00866 | .00843 | .00820 | .00799 | .00779 | .00760 | .00741 |
| 13 | .01035 | .01006 | .00978 | .00951 | .00927 | .00903 | .00880 | .00859 | .00839 | .00819 |
| 14 | .01122 | .01091 | .01061 | .01034 | .01007 | .00982 | .00958 | .00936 | .00914 | .00894 |
| 15 | .01203 | .01171 | .01140 | .01110 | .01082 | .01056 | .01031 | .01007 | .00985 | .00963 |
| 16 | .01279 | .01244 | .01211 | .01181 | .01151 | .01123 | .01097 | .01072 | .01048 | .01025 |
| 17 | .01347 | .01311 | .01276 | .01244 | .01213 | .01184 | .01156 | .01130 | .01104 | .01081 |
| 18 | .01411 | .01373 | .01336 | .01302 | .01270 | .01239 | .01210 | .01182 | .01155 | .01130 |
| 19 | .01474 | .01434 | .01396 | .01359 | .01325 | .01293 | .01262 | .01233 | .01205 | .01178 |
| 20 | .01537 | .01494 | .01454 | .01415 | .01379 | .01345 | .01313 | .01282 | .01252 | .01224 |
| 21 | .01598 | .01553 | .01510 | .01470 | .01432 | .01396 | .01361 | .01329 | .01298 | .01268 |
| 22 | .01660 | .01613 | .01568 | .01525 | .01485 | .01446 | .01410 | .01375 | .01343 | .01312 |
| 23 | .01725 | .01674 | .01627 | .01581 | .01539 | .01498 | .01460 | .01423 | .01388 | .01355 |
| 24 | .01796 | .01742 | .01692 | .01644 | .01599 | .01556 | .01515 | .01476 | .01439 | .01404 |
| 25 | .01876 | .01819 | .01765 | .01714 | .01666 | .01621 | .01577 | .01536 | .01497 | .01460 |
| 26 | .01967 | .01907 | .01850 | .01796 | .01745 | .01696 | .01650 | .01606 | .01565 | .01525 |
| 27 | .02072 | .02008 | .01948 | .01890 | .01836 | .01784 | .01735 | .01688 | .01644 | .01601 |
| 28 | .02190 | .02122 | .02057 | .01996 | .01938 | .01883 | .01831 | .01781 | .01734 | .01689 |
| 29 | .02322 | .02249 | .02181 | .02116 | .02054 | .01996 | .01940 | .01887 | .01836 | .01788 |
| 30 | .02469 | .02392 | .02319 | .02250 | .02184 | .02122 | .02062 | .02006 | .01952 | .01900 |
| 31 | .02634 | .02552 | .02475 | .02401 | .02331 | .02264 | .02201 | .02140 | .02083 | .02028 |
| 32 | .02816 | .02729 | .02647 | .02568 | .02494 | .02423 | .02355 | .02291 | .02229 | .02170 |
| 33 | .03018 | .02926 | .02838 | .02755 | .02675 | .02600 | .02528 | .02459 | .02393 | .02331 |
| 34 | .03239 | .03142 | .03048 | .02960 | .02875 | .02795 | .02718 | .02645 | .02575 | .02508 |
| 35 | .03482 | .03378 | .03279 | .03185 | .03095 | .03009 | .02928 | .02850 | .02775 | .02704 |
| 36 | .03743 | .03633 | .03528 | .03428 | .03333 | .03242 | .03155 | .03072 | .02992 | .02916 |
| 37 | .04026 | .03909 | .03798 | .03692 | .03591 | .03494 | .03401 | .03313 | .03228 | .03147 |
| 38 | .04330 | .04207 | .04089 | .03977 | .03869 | .03767 | .03668 | .03574 | .03484 | .03398 |
| 39 | .04658 | .04528 | .04403 | .04284 | .04170 | .04061 | .03957 | .03857 | .03762 | .03670 |
| 40 | .05011 | .04873 | .04741 | .04615 | .04495 | .04379 | .04269 | .04163 | .04061 | .03964 |
| 41 | .05389 | .05244 | .05104 | .04971 | .04844 | .04721 | .04604 | .04492 | .04384 | .04281 |
| 42 | .05791 | .05638 | .05491 | .05350 | .05216 | .05086 | .04962 | .04844 | .04729 | .04620 |
| 43 | .06219 | .06057 | .05902 | .05754 | .05612 | .05475 | .05344 | .05218 | .05098 | .04981 |
| 44 | .06673 | .06503 | .06340 | .06184 | .06034 | .05890 | .05752 | .05619 | .05491 | .05368 |
| 45 | .07157 | .06978 | .06806 | .06642 | .06484 | .06332 | .06186 | .06046 | .05911 | .05781 |
| 46 | .07669 | .07481 | .07301 | .07128 | .06962 | .06802 | .06649 | .06501 | .06358 | .06221 |
| 47 | .08212 | .08015 | .07826 | .07645 | .07470 | .07302 | .07140 | .06984 | .06834 | .06690 |
| 48 | .08784 | .08578 | .08380 | .08190 | .08006 | .07830 | .07660 | .07496 | .07338 | .07186 |
| 49 | .09384 | .09169 | .08961 | .08762 | .08570 | .08384 | .08206 | .08034 | .07868 | .07708 |
| 50 | .10013 | .09787 | .09570 | .09361 | .09160 | .08966 | .08779 | .08598 | .08424 | .08256 |
| 51 | .10671 | .10436 | .10209 | .09991 | .09780 | .09577 | .09381 | .09192 | .09009 | .08832 |
| 52 | .11365 | .11120 | .10883 | .10655 | .10435 | .10222 | .10017 | .09819 | .09628 | .09442 |
| 53 | .12095 | .11840 | .11593 | .11355 | .11126 | .10904 | .10689 | .10482 | .10282 | .10088 |
| 54 | .12860 | .12595 | .12338 | .12090 | .11851 | .11619 | .11396 | .11179 | .10970 | .10767 |
| 55 | .13663 | .13386 | .13120 | .12862 | .12613 | .12372 | .12138 | .11912 | .11694 | .11482 |
| 56 | .14503 | .14217 | .13940 | .13672 | .13413 | .13162 | .12919 | .12683 | .12456 | .12235 |
| 57 | .15385 | .15089 | .14801 | .14523 | .14254 | .13994 | .13741 | .13496 | .13259 | .13029 |
| 58 | .16311 | .16004 | .15706 | .15418 | .15139 | .14868 | .14606 | .14352 | .14105 | .13866 |
| 59 | .17279 | .16961 | .16654 | .16355 | .16066 | .15786 | .15514 | .15250 | .14994 | .14745 |
| 60 | .18286 | .17958 | .17640 | .17332 | .17033 | .16743 | .16462 | .16188 | .15922 | .15664 |
| 61 | .19330 | .18992 | .18665 | .18347 | .18038 | .17738 | .17447 | .17164 | .16889 | .16622 |
| 62 | .20409 | .20061 | .19724 | .19396 | .19078 | .18768 | .18467 | .18175 | .17891 | .17614 |
| 63 | .21522 | .21165 | .20818 | .20480 | .20152 | .19833 | .19523 | .19221 | .18928 | .18642 |
| 64 | .22672 | .22306 | .21949 | .21602 | .21265 | .20937 | .20617 | .20306 | .20003 | .19708 |
| 65 | .23867 | .23491 | .23125 | .22769 | .22423 | .22085 | .21757 | .21437 | .21125 | .20821 |
| 66 | .25112 | .24727 | .24353 | .23988 | .23632 | .23286 | .22948 | .22619 | .22299 | .21986 |
| 67 | .26409 | .26016 | .25633 | .25260 | .24896 | .24541 | .24195 | .23857 | .23528 | .23206 |
| 68 | .27760 | .27359 | .26968 | .26586 | .26214 | .25851 | .25497 | .25151 | .24814 | .24484 |
| 69 | .29157 | .28748 | .28350 | .27961 | .27581 | .27211 | .26849 | .26495 | .26150 | .25812 |
| 70 | .30596 | .30181 | .29775 | .29379 | .28992 | .28614 | .28245 | .27884 | .27532 | .27187 |
| 71 | .32069 | .31648 | .31236 | .30833 | .30440 | .30055 | .29679 | .29312 | .28952 | .28600 |
| 72 | .33578 | .33151 | .32733 | .32325 | .31925 | .31535 | .31152 | .30778 | .30412 | .30054 |
| 73 | .35123 | .34691 | .34269 | .33855 | .33450 | .33054 | .32666 | .32286 | .31914 | .31550 |
| 74 | .36715 | .36279 | .35852 | .35434 | .35024 | .34623 | .34230 | .33845 | .33468 | .33098 |
| 75 | .38360 | .37921 | .37491 | .37069 | .36656 | .36250 | .35853 | .35464 | .35082 | .34708 |
| 76 | .40064 | .39623 | .39190 | .38765 | .38349 | .37941 | .37540 | .37148 | .36762 | .36384 |

Reg. § 20.2031-7A(e)(4)

| AGE | 12.2% | 12.4% | 12.6% | 12.8% | 13.0% | 13.2% | 13.4% | 13.6% | 13.8% | 14.0% |
|---|---|---|---|---|---|---|---|---|---|---|
| 77 | .41823 | .41381 | .40947 | .40521 | .40103 | .39692 | .39290 | .38895 | .38507 | .38126 |
| 78 | .43632 | .43189 | .42755 | .42329 | .41910 | .41499 | .41095 | .40698 | .40309 | .39926 |
| 79 | .45473 | .45032 | .44599 | .44173 | .43755 | .43344 | .42940 | .42543 | .42153 | .41770 |
| 80 | .47333 | .46894 | .46463 | .46040 | .45623 | .45213 | .44811 | .44414 | .44025 | .43642 |
| 81 | .49191 | .48755 | .48328 | .47907 | .47493 | .47085 | .46684 | .46290 | .45902 | .45520 |
| 82 | .51034 | .50603 | .50179 | .49762 | .49351 | .48947 | .48549 | .48157 | .47772 | .47392 |
| 83 | .52852 | .52427 | .52008 | .51595 | .51189 | .50788 | .50394 | .50006 | .49623 | .49246 |
| 84 | .54648 | .54228 | .53815 | .53407 | .53006 | .52610 | .52221 | .51836 | .51458 | .51084 |
| 85 | .56426 | .56013 | .55606 | .55205 | .54810 | .54420 | .54035 | .53656 | .53282 | .52913 |
| 86 | .58169 | .57764 | .57364 | .56970 | .56581 | .56197 | .55818 | .55445 | .55076 | .54713 |
| 87 | .59850 | .59452 | .59060 | .58673 | .58291 | .57913 | .57541 | .57174 | .56811 | .56453 |
| 88 | .61476 | .61086 | .60702 | .60322 | .59947 | .59577 | .59212 | .58851 | .58494 | .58142 |
| 89 | .63078 | .62697 | .62321 | .61950 | .61583 | .61220 | .60862 | .60508 | .60159 | .59813 |
| 90 | .64674 | .64302 | .63935 | .63573 | .63215 | .62861 | .62511 | .62165 | .61823 | .61485 |
| 91 | .66238 | .65877 | .65520 | .65167 | .64819 | .64474 | .64133 | .63795 | .63462 | .63132 |
| 92 | .67730 | .67379 | .67032 | .66689 | .66350 | .66014 | .65682 | .65354 | .65029 | .64708 |
| 93 | .69130 | .68789 | .68452 | .68119 | .67789 | .67463 | .67140 | .66820 | .66504 | .66191 |
| 94 | .70421 | .70090 | .69762 | .69438 | .69118 | .68800 | .68486 | .68175 | .67867 | .67563 |
| 95 | .71594 | .71272 | .70954 | .70639 | .70326 | .70017 | .69712 | .69409 | .69109 | .68812 |
| 96 | .72638 | .72325 | .72014 | .71707 | .71403 | .71101 | .70803 | .70507 | .70215 | .69925 |
| 97 | .73590 | .73285 | .72982 | .72682 | .72385 | .72090 | .71799 | .71510 | .71224 | .70941 |
| 98 | .74448 | .74149 | .73853 | .73560 | .73269 | .72981 | .72696 | .72414 | .72134 | .71856 |
| 99 | .75240 | .74948 | .74658 | .74371 | .74086 | .73805 | .73525 | .73248 | .72974 | .72702 |
| 100 | .75974 | .75687 | .75403 | .75121 | .74842 | .74566 | .74292 | .74020 | .73751 | .73484 |
| 101 | .76669 | .76388 | .76109 | .75833 | .75559 | .75287 | .75018 | .74751 | .74486 | .74223 |
| 102 | .77393 | .77117 | .76844 | .76573 | .76304 | .76037 | .75773 | .75511 | .75251 | .74993 |
| 103 | .78158 | .77888 | .77620 | .77355 | .77091 | .76830 | .76571 | .76313 | .76058 | .75805 |
| 104 | .79007 | .78743 | .78482 | .78222 | .77964 | .77709 | .77455 | .77203 | .76953 | .76705 |
| 105 | .80065 | .79809 | .79556 | .79304 | .79054 | .78805 | .78559 | .78314 | .78071 | .77829 |
| 106 | .81631 | .81389 | .81149 | .80911 | .80674 | .80438 | .80204 | .79972 | .79741 | .79511 |
| 107 | .83963 | .83745 | .83529 | .83313 | .83099 | .82886 | .82674 | .82463 | .82254 | .82045 |
| 108 | .87910 | .87739 | .87569 | .87400 | .87232 | .87064 | .86897 | .86731 | .86566 | .86401 |
| 109 | .94563 | .94484 | .94405 | .94326 | .94248 | .94170 | .94092 | .94014 | .93937 | .93860 |

TABLE 80CNSMT
APPLICABLE AFTER APRIL 30, 1989,
AND BEFORE MAY 1, 1999

| Age x | l(x) | Age x | l(x) | Age x | l(x) |
|-------|------|-------|------|-------|------|
| (1) | (2) | (1) | (2) | (1) | (2) |
| 0 | 100000 | 37 | 95492 | 74 | 59279 |
| 1 | 98740 | 38 | 95317 | 75 | 56799 |
| 2 | 98648 | 39 | 95129 | 76 | 54239 |
| 3 | 98584 | 40 | 94926 | 77 | 51599 |
| 4 | 98535 | 41 | 94706 | 78 | 48878 |
| 5 | 98495 | 42 | 94465 | 79 | 46071 |
| 6 | 98459 | 43 | 94201 | 80 | 43180 |
| 7 | 98426 | 44 | 93913 | 81 | 40208 |
| 8 | 98396 | 45 | 93599 | 82 | 37172 |
| 9 | 98370 | 46 | 93256 | 83 | 34095 |
| 10 | 98347 | 47 | 92882 | 84 | 31012 |
| 11 | 98328 | 48 | 92472 | 85 | 27960 |
| 12 | 98309 | 49 | 92021 | 86 | 24961 |
| 13 | 98285 | 50 | 91526 | 87 | 22038 |
| 14 | 98248 | 51 | 90986 | 88 | 19235 |
| 15 | 98196 | 52 | 90402 | 89 | 16598 |
| 16 | 98129 | 53 | 89771 | 90 | 14154 |
| 17 | 98047 | 54 | 89087 | 91 | 11908 |
| 18 | 97953 | 55 | 88348 | 92 | 9863 |
| 19 | 97851 | 56 | 87551 | 93 | 8032 |
| 20 | 97741 | 57 | 86695 | 94 | 6424 |
| 21 | 97623 | 58 | 85776 | 95 | 5043 |
| 22 | 97499 | 59 | 84789 | 96 | 3884 |
| 23 | 97370 | 60 | 83726 | 97 | 2939 |
| 24 | 97240 | 61 | 82581 | 98 | 2185 |
| 25 | 97110 | 62 | 81348 | 99 | 1598 |
| 26 | 96982 | 63 | 80024 | 100 | 1150 |
| 27 | 96856 | 64 | 78609 | 101 | 815 |
| 28 | 96730 | 65 | 77107 | 102 | 570 |
| 29 | 96604 | 66 | 75520 | 103 | 393 |
| 30 | 96477 | 67 | 73846 | 104 | 267 |
| 31 | 96350 | 68 | 72082 | 105 | 179 |
| 32 | 96220 | 69 | 70218 | 106 | 119 |
| 33 | 96088 | 70 | 68248 | 107 | 78 |
| 34 | 95951 | 71 | 66165 | 108 | 51 |
| 35 | 95808 | 72 | 63972 | 109 | 33 |
| 36 | 95655 | 73 | 61673 | 110 | 0 |

(f) *Valuation of annuities, interests for life or term of years, and remainder or reversionary interests for estates of decedents for which the valuation date of the gross estate is after April 30,1999, and before May 1, 2009.*—(1) *In general.*—Except as otherwise provided in §20.2031-7(b) and §20.7520-3(b) (pertaining to certain limitations on the use of prescribed tables), if the valuation date for the gross estate of the decedent is after April 30, 1999, and before May 1, 2009, the fair market value of annuities, life estates, terms of years, remainders, and reversionary interests is the present value of the interests determined by use of standard or special section 7520 actuarial factors and the valuation methodology described in §20.2031-7(d). These factors are derived by using the appropriate section 7520 interest rate and, if applicable, the mortality component for the valuation date of the interest that is being valued. See §§20.7520-1 through 20.7520-4. See paragraph (f)(4) of this section for determination of the appropriate table for use in valuing these interests.

(2) *Transitional rule.*—(i) If a decedent dies after April 30, 1999, and if on May 1, 1999, the decedent was mentally incompetent so that the disposition of the decedent's property could not be changed, and the decedent dies without having regained competency to dispose of the decedent's property or dies within 90 days of the date on which the decedent first regains competency, the fair market value of annuities, life estates, terms for years, remainders, and reversions included in the gross estate of the decedent is their present value determined either under this section or under the corresponding section applicable at the time the decedent became mentally incompetent, at the option of the decedent's executor. For example, see paragraph (d) of this section.

(ii) If a decedent dies after April 30, 1999, and before July 1, 1999, the fair market value of annuities, life estates, remainders, and reversions based on one or more measuring lives included in the gross estate of the decedent is their present value determined under this section by use of the section 7520 interest rate for the month in which the valuation date occurs (see §§20.7520-1(b) and 20.7520-2(a)(2) and the appropriate actuarial tables under either paragraph (e)(4) or paragraph (f)(4) of this section, at the option of the decedent's executor.

(iii) For purposes of paragraphs (f)(2)(i) and (f)(2)(ii) of this section, where the decedent's executor is given the option to use the appropriate actuarial tables under either paragraph (e)(4) or paragraph (f)(4) of this section, the decedent's executor must use the same actuarial table with respect to each individual transaction and with respect to all transfers occurring on the valuation date (for example, gift and income tax charitable deductions with respect to the same transfer must be determined based on the same tables, and all assets includible in the gross estate and/or estate tax deductions claimed must be valued based on the same tables).

(3) *Publications and actuarial computations by the Internal Revenue Service.*—Many standard actuarial factors not included in paragraph (f)(4) of this section or in §20.2031-7(d)(6) are included in Internal Revenue Service Publication 1457, "Actuarial Values, Book Aleph," (7-99). Publication 1457 also includes examples that illustrate how to compute many special factors for more unusual situations. Publication 1457 is no longer available for purchase from the Superintendent of Documents, United States Government Printing Office. However, pertinent factors in this publication may be obtained from: CC:PA:LPD:PR (IRS Publication 1457), Room 5205, Internal Revenue Service, P.O.Box 7604, Ben Franklin Station, Washington, DC 20044. If a special factor is required in the case of an actual decedent, the Internal Revenue Service may furnish the factor to the executor upon a request for a ruling. The request for a ruling must be accompanied by a recitation of the facts including a statement of the date of birth for each measuring life, the date of the decedent's death, any other applicable dates, and a copy of the will, trust, or other relevant documents. A request for a ruling must comply with the instructions for requesting a ruling published periodically in the Internal Revenue Bulletin (see §§601.201 and 601.601(d)(2)(ii)(*b*)) and include payment of the required user fee.

(4) *Actuarial tables.*—Except as provided in §20.7520-3(b) (pertaining to certain limitations on the use of prescribed tables), Life Table 90CM and Table S (Single life remainder factors applicable where the valuation date is after April 30, 1999, and before May 1, 2009), contained in this paragraph (f)(4), and Table B, Table J, and Table K set forth in §20.2031-7(d)(6) must be used in the application of the provisions of this section when the section 7520 interest rate component is between 4.2 and 14 percent. Table S and Table 90CM are as follows:

**TABLE S**
**BASED ON LIFE TABLE 90CM**
**SINGLE LIFE REMAINDER FACTORS**
**[APPLICABLE AFTER APRIL 30, 1999, AND BEFORE MAY 1, 2009]**

**INTEREST RATE**

| AGE | 4.2% | 4.4% | 4.6% | 4.8% | 5.0% | 5.2% | 5.4% | 5.6% | 5.8% | 6.0% |
|---|---|---|---|---|---|---|---|---|---|---|
| 0 | .06752 | .06130 | .05586 | .05109 | .04691 | .04322 | .03998 | .03711 | .03458 | .03233 |
| 1 | .06137 | .05495 | .04932 | .04438 | .04003 | .03620 | .03283 | .02985 | .02721 | .02487 |
| 2 | .06325 | .05667 | .05088 | .04580 | .04132 | .03737 | .03388 | .03079 | .02806 | .02563 |
| 3 | .06545 | .05869 | .05275 | .04752 | .04291 | .03883 | .03523 | .03203 | .02920 | .02668 |
| 4 | .06784 | .06092 | .05482 | .04944 | .04469 | .04048 | .03676 | .03346 | .03052 | .02791 |
| 5 | .07040 | .06331 | .05705 | .05152 | .04662 | .04229 | .03845 | .03503 | .03199 | .02928 |
| 6 | .07310 | .06583 | .05941 | .05372 | .04869 | .04422 | .04025 | .03672 | .03357 | .03076 |
| 7 | .07594 | .06849 | .06191 | .05607 | .05089 | .04628 | .04219 | .03854 | .03528 | .03236 |
| 8 | .07891 | .07129 | .06453 | .05853 | .05321 | .04846 | .04424 | .04046 | .03709 | .03407 |
| 9 | .08203 | .07423 | .06731 | .06115 | .05567 | .05079 | .04643 | .04253 | .03904 | .03592 |
| 10 | .08532 | .07734 | .07024 | .06392 | .05829 | .05326 | .04877 | .04474 | .04114 | .03790 |
| 11 | .08875 | .08059 | .07331 | .06683 | .06104 | .05587 | .05124 | .04709 | .04336 | .04002 |
| 12 | .09233 | .08398 | .07653 | .06989 | .06394 | .05862 | .05385 | .04957 | .04572 | .04226 |
| 13 | .09601 | .08748 | .07985 | .07304 | .06693 | .06146 | .05655 | .05214 | .04816 | .04458 |
| 14 | .09974 | .09102 | .08322 | .07624 | .06997 | .06435 | .05929 | .05474 | .05064 | .04694 |
| 15 | .10350 | .09460 | .08661 | .07946 | .07303 | .06725 | .06204 | .05735 | .05312 | .04930 |
| 16 | .10728 | .09818 | .09001 | .08268 | .07608 | .07014 | .06479 | .05996 | .05559 | .05164 |
| 17 | .11108 | .10179 | .09344 | .08592 | .07916 | .07306 | .06755 | .06257 | .05807 | .05399 |
| 18 | .11494 | .10545 | .09691 | .08921 | .08227 | .07601 | .07034 | .06521 | .06057 | .05636 |
| 19 | .11889 | .10921 | .10047 | .09259 | .08548 | .07904 | .07322 | .06794 | .06315 | .05880 |
| 20 | .12298 | .11310 | .10417 | .09610 | .08881 | .08220 | .07622 | .07078 | .06584 | .06135 |
| 21 | .12722 | .11713 | .10801 | .09976 | .09228 | .08550 | .07935 | .07375 | .06866 | .06403 |
| 22 | .13159 | .12130 | .11199 | .10354 | .09588 | .08893 | .08260 | .07685 | .07160 | .06682 |
| 23 | .13613 | .12563 | .11612 | .10748 | .09964 | .09250 | .08601 | .08009 | .07468 | .06975 |
| 24 | .14084 | .13014 | .12043 | .11160 | .10357 | .09625 | .08958 | .08349 | .07793 | .07284 |
| 25 | .14574 | .13484 | .12493 | .11591 | .10768 | .10018 | .09334 | .08708 | .08135 | .07611 |
| 26 | .15084 | .13974 | .12963 | .12041 | .11199 | .10431 | .09728 | .09085 | .08496 | .07956 |
| 27 | .15615 | .14485 | .13454 | .12513 | .11652 | .10865 | .10144 | .09484 | .08878 | .08322 |
| 28 | .16166 | .15016 | .13965 | .13004 | .12124 | .11319 | .10580 | .09901 | .09279 | .08706 |
| 29 | .16737 | .15567 | .14497 | .13516 | .12617 | .11792 | .11035 | .10339 | .09699 | .09109 |
| 30 | .17328 | .16138 | .15048 | .14047 | .13129 | .12286 | .11510 | .10796 | .10138 | .09532 |
| 31 | .17938 | .16728 | .15618 | .14599 | .13661 | .12799 | .12004 | .11272 | .10597 | .09974 |
| 32 | .18568 | .17339 | .16210 | .15171 | .14214 | .13333 | .12520 | .11769 | .11076 | .10435 |
| 33 | .19220 | .17972 | .16824 | .15766 | .14790 | .13889 | .13058 | .12289 | .11578 | .10920 |
| 34 | .19894 | .18627 | .17460 | .16383 | .15388 | .14468 | .13618 | .12831 | .12102 | .11426 |
| 35 | .20592 | .19307 | .18121 | .17025 | .16011 | .15073 | .14204 | .13399 | .12652 | .11958 |
| 36 | .21312 | .20010 | .18805 | .17691 | .16658 | .15701 | .14814 | .13990 | .13225 | .12514 |
| 37 | .22057 | .20737 | .19514 | .18382 | .17331 | .16356 | .15450 | .14608 | .13825 | .13096 |
| 38 | .22827 | .21490 | .20251 | .19100 | .18031 | .17038 | .16113 | .15253 | .14452 | .13705 |
| 39 | .23623 | .22270 | .21013 | .19845 | .18759 | .17747 | .16805 | .15927 | .15108 | .14344 |
| 40 | .24446 | .23078 | .21805 | .20620 | .19516 | .18487 | .17527 | .16631 | .15795 | .15013 |
| 41 | .25298 | .23915 | .22626 | .21425 | .20305 | .19259 | .18282 | .17368 | .16514 | .15715 |
| 42 | .26178 | .24782 | .23478 | .22262 | .21125 | .20062 | .19069 | .18138 | .17267 | .16450 |
| 43 | .27087 | .25678 | .24360 | .23129 | .21977 | .20898 | .19888 | .18941 | .18053 | .17220 |
| 44 | .28025 | .26603 | .25273 | .24027 | .22860 | .21766 | .20740 | .19777 | .18873 | .18023 |
| 45 | .28987 | .27555 | .26212 | .24953 | .23772 | .22664 | .21622 | .20644 | .19724 | .18858 |
| 46 | .29976 | .28533 | .27179 | .25908 | .24714 | .23591 | .22536 | .21542 | .20606 | .19725 |
| 47 | .30987 | .29535 | .28171 | .26889 | .25682 | .24546 | .23476 | .22468 | .21518 | .20621 |
| 48 | .32023 | .30563 | .29190 | .27897 | .26678 | .25530 | .24447 | .23425 | .22460 | .21549 |
| 49 | .33082 | .31615 | .30234 | .28931 | .27702 | .26543 | .25447 | .24412 | .23434 | .22509 |
| 50 | .34166 | .32694 | .31306 | .29995 | .28756 | .27586 | .26479 | .25432 | .24441 | .23502 |
| 51 | .35274 | .33798 | .32404 | .31085 | .29838 | .28658 | .27541 | .26482 | .25479 | .24528 |
| 52 | .36402 | .34924 | .33525 | .32200 | .30946 | .29757 | .28630 | .27561 | .26547 | .25584 |
| 53 | .37550 | .36070 | .34668 | .33339 | .32078 | .30882 | .29746 | .28667 | .27643 | .26669 |
| 54 | .38717 | .37237 | .35833 | .34500 | .33234 | .32031 | .30888 | .29801 | .28766 | .27782 |
| 55 | .39903 | .38424 | .37019 | .35683 | .34413 | .33205 | .32056 | .30961 | .29918 | .28925 |
| 56 | .41108 | .39631 | .38227 | .36890 | .35617 | .34405 | .33250 | .32149 | .31099 | .30097 |
| 57 | .42330 | .40857 | .39455 | .38118 | .36844 | .35629 | .34469 | .33363 | .32306 | .31297 |
| 58 | .43566 | .42098 | .40699 | .39364 | .38089 | .36873 | .35710 | .34600 | .33538 | .32522 |
| 59 | .44811 | .43351 | .41956 | .40623 | .39350 | .38133 | .36968 | .35855 | .34789 | .33768 |
| 60 | .46066 | .44613 | .43224 | .41896 | .40624 | .39408 | .38243 | .37127 | .36058 | .35033 |
| 61 | .47330 | .45887 | .44505 | .43182 | .41914 | .40699 | .39535 | .38418 | .37347 | .36318 |
| 62 | .48608 | .47175 | .45802 | .44485 | .43223 | .42011 | .40848 | .39732 | .38660 | .37629 |
| 63 | .49898 | .48478 | .47115 | .45807 | .44550 | .43343 | .42184 | .41069 | .39997 | .38966 |

| AGE | 4.2% | 4.4% | 4.6% | 4.8% | 5.0% | 5.2% | 5.4% | 5.6% | 5.8% | 6.0% |
|-----|------|------|------|------|------|------|------|------|------|------|
| 64 | .51200 | .49793 | .48442 | .47143 | .45895 | .44694 | .43539 | .42427 | .41357 | .40326 |
| 65 | .52512 | .51121 | .49782 | .48495 | .47255 | .46062 | .44912 | .43805 | .42738 | .41709 |
| 66 | .53835 | .52461 | .51137 | .49862 | .48634 | .47449 | .46307 | .45206 | .44143 | .43118 |
| 67 | .55174 | .53818 | .52511 | .51250 | .50034 | .48860 | .47727 | .46633 | .45576 | .44556 |
| 68 | .56524 | .55188 | .53899 | .52654 | .51452 | .50291 | .49168 | .48083 | .47034 | .46020 |
| 69 | .57882 | .56568 | .55299 | .54071 | .52885 | .51737 | .50627 | .49552 | .48513 | .47506 |
| 70 | .59242 | .57951 | .56703 | .55495 | .54325 | .53193 | .52096 | .51034 | .50004 | .49007 |
| 71 | .60598 | .59332 | .58106 | .56918 | .55767 | .54651 | .53569 | .52520 | .51503 | .50516 |
| 72 | .61948 | .60707 | .59504 | .58338 | .57206 | .56108 | .55043 | .54009 | .53004 | .52029 |
| 73 | .63287 | .62073 | .60895 | .59751 | .58640 | .57561 | .56513 | .55495 | .54505 | .53543 |
| 74 | .64621 | .63435 | .62282 | .61162 | .60073 | .59015 | .57985 | .56984 | .56009 | .55061 |
| 75 | .65953 | .64796 | .63671 | .62575 | .61510 | .60473 | .59463 | .58480 | .57523 | .56591 |
| 76 | .67287 | .66160 | .65063 | .63995 | .62954 | .61940 | .60952 | .59989 | .59050 | .58135 |
| 77 | .68622 | .67526 | .66459 | .65419 | .64404 | .63415 | .62450 | .61509 | .60590 | .59694 |
| 78 | .69954 | .68892 | .67856 | .66845 | .65858 | .64895 | .63955 | .63036 | .62140 | .61264 |
| 79 | .71278 | .70250 | .69246 | .68265 | .67308 | .66372 | .65457 | .64563 | .63690 | .62836 |
| 80 | .72581 | .71588 | .70618 | .69668 | .68740 | .67833 | .66945 | .66077 | .65227 | .64396 |
| 81 | .73857 | .72899 | .71962 | .71045 | .70147 | .69268 | .68408 | .67566 | .66741 | .65933 |
| 82 | .75101 | .74178 | .73274 | .72389 | .71522 | .70672 | .69840 | .69024 | .68225 | .67441 |
| 83 | .76311 | .75423 | .74553 | .73700 | .72864 | .72044 | .71240 | .70451 | .69678 | .68919 |
| 84 | .77497 | .76645 | .75809 | .74988 | .74183 | .73393 | .72618 | .71857 | .71110 | .70377 |
| 85 | .78665 | .77848 | .77047 | .76260 | .75487 | .74728 | .73982 | .73250 | .72530 | .71823 |
| 86 | .79805 | .79025 | .78258 | .77504 | .76764 | .76036 | .75320 | .74617 | .73925 | .73245 |
| 87 | .80904 | .80159 | .79427 | .78706 | .77998 | .77301 | .76615 | .75940 | .75277 | .74624 |
| 88 | .81962 | .81251 | .80552 | .79865 | .79188 | .78521 | .77865 | .77220 | .76584 | .75958 |
| 89 | .82978 | .82302 | .81636 | .80980 | .80335 | .79699 | .79072 | .78455 | .77847 | .77248 |
| 90 | .83952 | .83309 | .82676 | .82052 | .81437 | .80831 | .80234 | .79645 | .79064 | .78492 |
| 91 | .84870 | .84260 | .83658 | .83064 | .82479 | .81902 | .81332 | .80771 | .80217 | .79671 |
| 92 | .85716 | .85136 | .84563 | .83998 | .83441 | .82891 | .82348 | .81812 | .81283 | .80761 |
| 93 | .86494 | .85942 | .85396 | .84858 | .84326 | .83801 | .83283 | .82771 | .82266 | .81767 |
| 94 | .87216 | .86690 | .86170 | .85657 | .85149 | .84648 | .84153 | .83664 | .83181 | .82704 |
| 95 | .87898 | .87397 | .86902 | .86412 | .85928 | .85450 | .84977 | .84510 | .84049 | .83592 |
| 96 | .88537 | .88060 | .87587 | .87121 | .86659 | .86203 | .85751 | .85305 | .84864 | .84427 |
| 97 | .89127 | .88672 | .88221 | .87775 | .87335 | .86898 | .86467 | .86040 | .85618 | .85200 |
| 98 | .89680 | .89245 | .88815 | .88389 | .87968 | .87551 | .87138 | .86730 | .86326 | .85926 |
| 99 | .90217 | .89803 | .89393 | .88987 | .88585 | .88187 | .87793 | .87402 | .87016 | .86633 |
| 100 | .90738 | .90344 | .89953 | .89567 | .89183 | .88804 | .88428 | .88056 | .87687 | .87322 |
| 101 | .91250 | .90876 | .90504 | .90137 | .89772 | .89412 | .89054 | .88699 | .88348 | .88000 |
| 102 | .91751 | .91396 | .91045 | .90696 | .90350 | .90007 | .89668 | .89331 | .88997 | .88666 |
| 103 | .92247 | .91912 | .91579 | .91249 | .90922 | .90598 | .90276 | .89957 | .89640 | .89326 |
| 104 | .92775 | .92460 | .92148 | .91839 | .91532 | .91227 | .90924 | .90624 | .90326 | .90031 |
| 105 | .93290 | .92996 | .92704 | .92415 | .92127 | .91841 | .91558 | .91276 | .90997 | .90719 |
| 106 | .93948 | .93680 | .93415 | .93151 | .92889 | .92628 | .92370 | .92113 | .91857 | .91604 |
| 107 | .94739 | .94504 | .94271 | .94039 | .93808 | .93579 | .93351 | .93124 | .92899 | .92675 |
| 108 | .95950 | .95767 | .95585 | .95404 | .95224 | .95045 | .94867 | .94689 | .94512 | .94336 |
| 109 | .97985 | .97893 | .97801 | .97710 | .97619 | .97529 | .97438 | .97348 | .97259 | .97170 |

## TABLE S
### BASED ON LIFE TABLE 90CM
### SINGLE LIFE REMAINDER FACTORS
### [APPLICABLE AFTER APRIL 30, 1999, AND BEFORE MAY 1, 2009]

**INTEREST RATE**

| AGE | 6.2% | 6.4% | 6.6% | 6.8% | 7.0% | 7.2% | 7.4% | 7.6% | 7.8% | 8.0% |
|---|---|---|---|---|---|---|---|---|---|---|
| 0 | .03034 | .02857 | .02700 | .02559 | .02433 | .02321 | .02220 | .02129 | .02047 | .01973 |
| 1 | .02279 | .02094 | .01929 | .01782 | .01650 | .01533 | .01427 | .01331 | .01246 | .01168 |
| 2 | .02347 | .02155 | .01983 | .01829 | .01692 | .01569 | .01458 | .01358 | .01268 | .01187 |
| 3 | .02444 | .02243 | .02065 | .01905 | .01761 | .01632 | .01516 | .01412 | .01317 | .01232 |
| 4 | .02558 | .02349 | .02163 | .01996 | .01846 | .01712 | .01590 | .01481 | .01382 | .01292 |
| 5 | .02686 | .02469 | .02275 | .02101 | .01945 | .01804 | .01677 | .01562 | .01458 | .01364 |
| 6 | .02825 | .02600 | .02398 | .02217 | .02053 | .01906 | .01773 | .01653 | .01544 | .01445 |
| 7 | .02976 | .02742 | .02532 | .02343 | .02172 | .02019 | .01880 | .01754 | .01640 | .01536 |
| 8 | .03137 | .02894 | .02675 | .02479 | .02301 | .02140 | .01995 | .01864 | .01744 | .01635 |
| 9 | .03311 | .03059 | .02832 | .02627 | .02442 | .02274 | .02122 | .01985 | .01859 | .01745 |
| 10 | .03499 | .03237 | .03001 | .02788 | .02595 | .02420 | .02262 | .02118 | .01987 | .01867 |
| 11 | .03700 | .03428 | .03183 | .02961 | .02760 | .02578 | .02413 | .02262 | .02125 | .02000 |
| 12 | .03913 | .03632 | .03377 | .03146 | .02937 | .02748 | .02575 | .02418 | .02275 | .02144 |
| 13 | .04135 | .03843 | .03579 | .03339 | .03122 | .02924 | .02744 | .02580 | .02431 | .02294 |
| 14 | .04359 | .04057 | .03783 | .03534 | .03308 | .03102 | .02915 | .02744 | .02587 | .02444 |
| 15 | .04584 | .04270 | .03986 | .03728 | .03493 | .03279 | .03083 | .02905 | .02742 | .02593 |
| 16 | .04806 | .04482 | .04187 | .03919 | .03674 | .03452 | .03248 | .03063 | .02892 | .02736 |
| 17 | .05029 | .04692 | .04387 | .04108 | .03855 | .03623 | .03411 | .03218 | .03040 | .02877 |
| 18 | .05253 | .04905 | .04588 | .04299 | .04036 | .03795 | .03574 | .03373 | .03187 | .03017 |
| 19 | .05484 | .05124 | .04796 | .04496 | .04222 | .03972 | .03742 | .03532 | .03339 | .03161 |
| 20 | .05726 | .05354 | .05013 | .04702 | .04418 | .04158 | .03919 | .03700 | .03498 | .03313 |
| 21 | .05980 | .05595 | .05242 | .04920 | .04625 | .04354 | .04105 | .03877 | .03667 | .03473 |
| 22 | .06246 | .05847 | .05482 | .05147 | .04841 | .04559 | .04301 | .04063 | .03844 | .03642 |
| 23 | .06524 | .06112 | .05734 | .05387 | .05069 | .04777 | .04508 | .04260 | .04032 | .03821 |
| 24 | .06819 | .06392 | .06001 | .05642 | .05312 | .05008 | .04728 | .04470 | .04232 | .04012 |
| 25 | .07131 | .06690 | .06285 | .05913 | .05570 | .05255 | .04964 | .04695 | .04447 | .04218 |
| 26 | .07460 | .07005 | .06586 | .06200 | .05845 | .05518 | .05215 | .04936 | .04677 | .04438 |
| 27 | .07810 | .07340 | .06907 | .06508 | .06140 | .05800 | .05485 | .05195 | .04925 | .04676 |
| 28 | .08179 | .07693 | .07246 | .06833 | .06451 | .06098 | .05772 | .05469 | .05189 | .04929 |
| 29 | .08566 | .08065 | .07603 | .07176 | .06780 | .06414 | .06075 | .05761 | .05469 | .05198 |
| 30 | .08973 | .08456 | .07978 | .07536 | .07127 | .06748 | .06396 | .06069 | .05766 | .05483 |
| 31 | .09398 | .08865 | .08372 | .07915 | .07491 | .07098 | .06733 | .06394 | .06078 | .05785 |
| 32 | .09843 | .09294 | .08785 | .08313 | .07875 | .07468 | .07089 | .06737 | .06409 | .06103 |
| 33 | .10310 | .09745 | .09220 | .08732 | .08279 | .07858 | .07466 | .07100 | .06759 | .06441 |
| 34 | .10799 | .10217 | .09676 | .09173 | .08705 | .08269 | .07862 | .07483 | .07129 | .06798 |
| 35 | .11314 | .10715 | .10157 | .09638 | .09155 | .08704 | .08283 | .07890 | .07522 | .07179 |
| 36 | .11852 | .11236 | .10662 | .10127 | .09628 | .09162 | .08726 | .08319 | .07938 | .07581 |
| 37 | .12416 | .11783 | .11193 | .10641 | .10126 | .09645 | .09194 | .08772 | .08377 | .08006 |
| 38 | .13009 | .12359 | .11751 | .11183 | .10652 | .10155 | .09689 | .09253 | .08843 | .08459 |
| 39 | .13629 | .12962 | .12338 | .11753 | .11206 | .10693 | .10212 | .09761 | .09337 | .08938 |
| 40 | .14281 | .13597 | .12955 | .12355 | .11791 | .11262 | .10766 | .10299 | .09860 | .09447 |
| 41 | .14966 | .14264 | .13606 | .12989 | .12409 | .11864 | .11352 | .10870 | .10417 | .09989 |
| 42 | .15685 | .14966 | .14291 | .13657 | .13061 | .12500 | .11972 | .11475 | .11006 | .10564 |
| 43 | .16437 | .15702 | .15010 | .14360 | .13747 | .13171 | .12627 | .12115 | .11631 | .11174 |
| 44 | .17224 | .16472 | .15764 | .15098 | .14469 | .13876 | .13317 | .12789 | .12290 | .11819 |
| 45 | .18042 | .17274 | .16550 | .15867 | .15223 | .14615 | .14040 | .13496 | .12982 | .12496 |
| 46 | .18893 | .18110 | .17370 | .16671 | .16011 | .15387 | .14796 | .14238 | .13708 | .13207 |
| 47 | .19775 | .18975 | .18220 | .17505 | .16830 | .16190 | .15584 | .15010 | .14466 | .13950 |
| 48 | .20688 | .19873 | .19102 | .18373 | .17682 | .17027 | .16406 | .15817 | .15258 | .14727 |
| 49 | .21633 | .20804 | .20018 | .19274 | .18568 | .17898 | .17262 | .16658 | .16084 | .15539 |
| 50 | .22612 | .21769 | .20969 | .20210 | .19490 | .18805 | .18155 | .17536 | .16948 | .16388 |
| 51 | .23625 | .22769 | .21955 | .21182 | .20448 | .19749 | .19084 | .18452 | .17849 | .17275 |
| 52 | .24669 | .23799 | .22973 | .22186 | .21438 | .20726 | .20047 | .19400 | .18784 | .18196 |
| 53 | .25742 | .24861 | .24022 | .23222 | .22461 | .21735 | .21043 | .20383 | .19753 | .19151 |
| 54 | .26845 | .25952 | .25101 | .24290 | .23516 | .22777 | .22072 | .21399 | .20756 | .20140 |
| 55 | .27978 | .27074 | .26212 | .25389 | .24604 | .23853 | .23136 | .22450 | .21793 | .21166 |
| 56 | .29140 | .28227 | .27355 | .26522 | .25725 | .24963 | .24233 | .23535 | .22867 | .22227 |
| 57 | .30333 | .29411 | .28529 | .27686 | .26879 | .26106 | .25365 | .24656 | .23976 | .23324 |
| 58 | .31551 | .30621 | .29731 | .28878 | .28061 | .27278 | .26528 | .25807 | .25116 | .24453 |
| 59 | .32790 | .31854 | .30956 | .30095 | .29269 | .28477 | .27716 | .26986 | .26284 | .25610 |
| 60 | .34050 | .33107 | .32202 | .31334 | .30500 | .29699 | .28929 | .28190 | .27478 | .26794 |
| 61 | .35331 | .34384 | .33473 | .32598 | .31757 | .30948 | .30170 | .29422 | .28701 | .28007 |
| 62 | .36639 | .35688 | .34772 | .33892 | .33044 | .32229 | .31443 | .30687 | .29958 | .29255 |
| 63 | .37974 | .37020 | .36101 | .35216 | .34363 | .33542 | .32750 | .31986 | .31250 | .30539 |
| 64 | .39334 | .38378 | .37456 | .36568 | .35711 | .34884 | .34087 | .33317 | .32574 | .31857 |

Reg. §20.2031-7A(f)(4)

| AGE | 6.2% | 6.4% | 6.6% | 6.8% | 7.0% | 7.2% | 7.4% | 7.6% | 7.8% | 8.0% |
|-----|------|------|------|------|------|------|------|------|------|------|
| 65 | .40718 | .39761 | .38838 | .37947 | .37087 | .36257 | .35455 | .34681 | .33932 | .33208 |
| 66 | .42128 | .41172 | .40249 | .39357 | .38496 | .37663 | .36858 | .36079 | .35326 | .34597 |
| 67 | .43569 | .42616 | .41694 | .40803 | .39941 | .39107 | .38299 | .37518 | .36761 | .36028 |
| 68 | .45038 | .44089 | .43170 | .42281 | .41419 | .40585 | .39777 | .38994 | .38235 | .37499 |
| 69 | .46531 | .45587 | .44672 | .43786 | .42927 | .42094 | .41286 | .40503 | .39743 | .39006 |
| 70 | .48040 | .47103 | .46194 | .45312 | .44456 | .43626 | .42820 | .42038 | .41278 | .40540 |
| 71 | .49558 | .48629 | .47727 | .46851 | .46000 | .45174 | .44371 | .43591 | .42832 | .42095 |
| 72 | .51082 | .50162 | .49268 | .48399 | .47554 | .46733 | .45934 | .45157 | .44401 | .43666 |
| 73 | .52607 | .51697 | .50813 | .49952 | .49114 | .48299 | .47506 | .46733 | .45981 | .45249 |
| 74 | .54139 | .53241 | .52367 | .51515 | .50686 | .49879 | .49092 | .48325 | .47578 | .46849 |
| 75 | .55683 | .54798 | .53936 | .53095 | .52276 | .51477 | .50698 | .49938 | .49197 | .48474 |
| 76 | .57243 | .56373 | .55524 | .54696 | .53888 | .53100 | .52330 | .51579 | .50846 | .50130 |
| 77 | .58819 | .57965 | .57132 | .56318 | .55523 | .54747 | .53988 | .53247 | .52523 | .51815 |
| 78 | .60408 | .59572 | .58755 | .57957 | .57177 | .56414 | .55668 | .54939 | .54225 | .53527 |
| 79 | .62001 | .61184 | .60385 | .59604 | .58840 | .58092 | .57360 | .56644 | .55943 | .55256 |
| 80 | .63582 | .62786 | .62007 | .61244 | .60497 | .59765 | .59048 | .58347 | .57659 | .56985 |
| 81 | .65142 | .64367 | .63608 | .62864 | .62135 | .61421 | .60721 | .60034 | .59361 | .58701 |
| 82 | .66673 | .65920 | .65182 | .64458 | .63748 | .63052 | .62368 | .61698 | .61041 | .60395 |
| 83 | .68175 | .67444 | .66728 | .66024 | .65334 | .64656 | .63991 | .63338 | .62696 | .62066 |
| 84 | .69657 | .68950 | .68256 | .67574 | .66904 | .66246 | .65599 | .64964 | .64340 | .63727 |
| 85 | .71128 | .70446 | .69775 | .69116 | .68467 | .67830 | .67204 | .66587 | .65982 | .65386 |
| 86 | .72576 | .71919 | .71272 | .70636 | .70010 | .69394 | .68789 | .68193 | .67606 | .67029 |
| 87 | .73981 | .73349 | .72726 | .72114 | .71511 | .70917 | .70333 | .69757 | .69190 | .68632 |
| 88 | .75342 | .74735 | .74137 | .73548 | .72968 | .72396 | .71833 | .71279 | .70732 | .70194 |
| 89 | .76658 | .76076 | .75503 | .74938 | .74381 | .73832 | .73290 | .72757 | .72231 | .71712 |
| 90 | .77928 | .77371 | .76823 | .76281 | .75748 | .75221 | .74702 | .74190 | .73684 | .73186 |
| 91 | .79131 | .78600 | .78075 | .77557 | .77046 | .76542 | .76044 | .75553 | .75068 | .74589 |
| 92 | .80246 | .79737 | .79235 | .78740 | .78250 | .77767 | .77290 | .76818 | .76353 | .75893 |
| 93 | .81274 | .80788 | .80307 | .79832 | .79363 | .78899 | .78441 | .77989 | .77542 | .77100 |
| 94 | .82232 | .81766 | .81306 | .80850 | .80401 | .79956 | .79517 | .79082 | .78653 | .78228 |
| 95 | .83141 | .82695 | .82254 | .81818 | .81387 | .80961 | .80539 | .80122 | .79710 | .79302 |
| 96 | .83996 | .83569 | .83147 | .82729 | .82316 | .81907 | .81503 | .81103 | .80707 | .80315 |
| 97 | .84787 | .84378 | .83973 | .83573 | .83176 | .82784 | .82396 | .82012 | .81632 | .81255 |
| 98 | .85530 | .85138 | .84750 | .84366 | .83985 | .83609 | .83236 | .82867 | .82502 | .82140 |
| 99 | .86255 | .85880 | .85508 | .85140 | .84776 | .84415 | .84057 | .83703 | .83353 | .83005 |
| 100 | .86960 | .86601 | .86246 | .85894 | .85546 | .85200 | .84858 | .84519 | .84183 | .83849 |
| 101 | .87655 | .87313 | .86974 | .86638 | .86305 | .85975 | .85648 | .85324 | .85003 | .84684 |
| 102 | .88338 | .88012 | .87689 | .87369 | .87052 | .86738 | .86426 | .86116 | .85809 | .85505 |
| 103 | .89015 | .88706 | .88399 | .88095 | .87793 | .87494 | .87197 | .86903 | .86611 | .86321 |
| 104 | .89737 | .89446 | .89157 | .88871 | .88586 | .88304 | .88024 | .87745 | .87469 | .87195 |
| 105 | .90443 | .90170 | .89898 | .89628 | .89360 | .89094 | .88830 | .88568 | .88307 | .88049 |
| 106 | .91351 | .91101 | .90852 | .90605 | .90359 | .90115 | .89873 | .89632 | .89392 | .89154 |
| 107 | .92452 | .92230 | .92010 | .91791 | .91573 | .91356 | .91141 | .90927 | .90714 | .90502 |
| 108 | .94161 | .93987 | .93814 | .93641 | .93469 | .93298 | .93128 | .92958 | .92790 | .92622 |
| 109 | .97081 | .96992 | .96904 | .96816 | .96729 | .96642 | .96555 | .96468 | .96382 | .96296 |

## TABLE S
### BASED ON LIFE TABLE 90CM
### SINGLE LIFE REMAINDER FACTORS
### [APPLICABLE AFTER APRIL 30, 1999, AND BEFORE MAY 1, 2009]

#### INTEREST RATE

| AGE | 8.2% | 8.4% | 8.6% | 8.8% | 9.0% | 9.2% | 9.4% | 9.6% | 9.8% | 10.0% |
|---|---|---|---|---|---|---|---|---|---|---|
| 0 | .01906 | .01845 | .01790 | .01740 | .01694 | .01652 | .01613 | .01578 | .01546 | .01516 |
| 1 | .01098 | .01034 | .00977 | .00924 | .00876 | .00833 | .00793 | .00756 | .00722 | .00691 |
| 2 | .01113 | .01046 | .00986 | .00930 | .00880 | .00834 | .00791 | .00753 | .00717 | .00684 |
| 3 | .01155 | .01084 | .01020 | .00962 | .00909 | .00860 | .00816 | .00775 | .00737 | .00702 |
| 4 | .01211 | .01137 | .01069 | .01008 | .00952 | .00900 | .00853 | .00810 | .00770 | .00733 |
| 5 | .01279 | .01201 | .01130 | .01065 | .01006 | .00952 | .00902 | .00856 | .00814 | .00775 |
| 6 | .01356 | .01274 | .01199 | .01131 | .01068 | .01011 | .00959 | .00910 | .00865 | .00824 |
| 7 | .01442 | .01356 | .01277 | .01205 | .01140 | .01079 | .01023 | .00972 | .00925 | .00881 |
| 8 | .01536 | .01446 | .01363 | .01287 | .01218 | .01154 | .01096 | .01041 | .00991 | .00945 |
| 9 | .01641 | .01546 | .01460 | .01380 | .01307 | .01240 | .01178 | .01120 | .01068 | .01019 |
| 10 | .01758 | .01659 | .01567 | .01484 | .01407 | .01336 | .01270 | .01210 | .01154 | .01103 |
| 11 | .01886 | .01781 | .01686 | .01598 | .01517 | .01442 | .01373 | .01310 | .01251 | .01196 |
| 12 | .02024 | .01915 | .01814 | .01721 | .01636 | .01558 | .01485 | .01419 | .01357 | .01299 |
| 13 | .02168 | .02054 | .01948 | .01851 | .01762 | .01679 | .01603 | .01533 | .01467 | .01407 |
| 14 | .02313 | .02193 | .02083 | .01981 | .01887 | .01801 | .01721 | .01646 | .01578 | .01514 |
| 15 | .02456 | .02330 | .02214 | .02107 | .02009 | .01918 | .01834 | .01756 | .01684 | .01617 |
| 16 | .02593 | .02462 | .02340 | .02229 | .02126 | .02030 | .01942 | .01860 | .01785 | .01714 |
| 17 | .02728 | .02590 | .02463 | .02346 | .02238 | .02138 | .02046 | .01960 | .01880 | .01806 |
| 18 | .02861 | .02717 | .02584 | .02462 | .02348 | .02243 | .02146 | .02056 | .01972 | .01894 |
| 19 | .02998 | .02847 | .02708 | .02580 | .02461 | .02351 | .02249 | .02154 | .02066 | .01984 |
| 20 | .03142 | .02984 | .02839 | .02704 | .02580 | .02465 | .02357 | .02258 | .02165 | .02079 |
| 21 | .03295 | .03130 | .02978 | .02837 | .02706 | .02585 | .02473 | .02368 | .02271 | .02180 |
| 22 | .03455 | .03283 | .03124 | .02976 | .02839 | .02712 | .02594 | .02484 | .02382 | .02286 |
| 23 | .03626 | .03446 | .03279 | .03124 | .02981 | .02847 | .02723 | .02608 | .02500 | .02400 |
| 24 | .03809 | .03620 | .03446 | .03283 | .03133 | .02993 | .02863 | .02741 | .02628 | .02522 |
| 25 | .04005 | .03808 | .03625 | .03456 | .03298 | .03151 | .03014 | .02887 | .02768 | .02656 |
| 26 | .04216 | .04010 | .03819 | .03641 | .03476 | .03322 | .03178 | .03044 | .02919 | .02802 |
| 27 | .04444 | .04229 | .04029 | .03843 | .03670 | .03508 | .03357 | .03217 | .03085 | .02962 |
| 28 | .04687 | .04463 | .04254 | .04059 | .03877 | .03708 | .03550 | .03402 | .03263 | .03133 |
| 29 | .04946 | .04712 | .04493 | .04289 | .04099 | .03922 | .03756 | .03600 | .03455 | .03318 |
| 30 | .05221 | .04976 | .04748 | .04534 | .04335 | .04149 | .03975 | .03812 | .03659 | .03515 |
| 31 | .05511 | .05255 | .05017 | .04794 | .04585 | .04390 | .04208 | .04037 | .03876 | .03725 |
| 32 | .05818 | .05551 | .05302 | .05069 | .04851 | .04647 | .04455 | .04276 | .04107 | .03948 |
| 33 | .06144 | .05866 | .05606 | .05363 | .05135 | .04921 | .04720 | .04532 | .04355 | .04188 |
| 34 | .06489 | .06200 | .05928 | .05674 | .05436 | .05212 | .05002 | .04805 | .04619 | .04444 |
| 35 | .06857 | .06555 | .06273 | .06007 | .05758 | .05524 | .05304 | .05097 | .04902 | .04718 |
| 36 | .07246 | .06932 | .06638 | .06361 | .06101 | .05856 | .05626 | .05409 | .05205 | .05012 |
| 37 | .07659 | .07332 | .07025 | .06737 | .06466 | .06210 | .05969 | .05742 | .05528 | .05325 |
| 38 | .08098 | .07758 | .07439 | .07138 | .06855 | .06588 | .06336 | .06099 | .05874 | .05662 |
| 39 | .08563 | .08210 | .07878 | .07565 | .07270 | .06992 | .06729 | .06480 | .06245 | .06023 |
| 40 | .09059 | .08692 | .08347 | .08021 | .07714 | .07423 | .07149 | .06889 | .06643 | .06411 |
| 41 | .09586 | .09206 | .08848 | .08509 | .08189 | .07886 | .07600 | .07329 | .07072 | .06828 |
| 42 | .10147 | .09753 | .09381 | .09029 | .08696 | .08381 | .08083 | .07800 | .07531 | .07277 |
| 43 | .10742 | .10334 | .09948 | .09583 | .09237 | .08909 | .08598 | .08304 | .08024 | .07758 |
| 44 | .11373 | .10950 | .10551 | .10172 | .09813 | .09472 | .09148 | .08841 | .08549 | .08272 |
| 45 | .12035 | .11599 | .11185 | .10792 | .10420 | .10066 | .09730 | .09410 | .09106 | .08817 |
| 46 | .12732 | .12281 | .11853 | .11447 | .11061 | .10694 | .10345 | .10013 | .09696 | .09395 |
| 47 | .13460 | .12995 | .12553 | .12133 | .11733 | .11353 | .10991 | .10646 | .10317 | .10004 |
| 48 | .14223 | .13743 | .13287 | .12853 | .12439 | .12046 | .11671 | .11313 | .10972 | .10646 |
| 49 | .15020 | .14526 | .14056 | .13608 | .13181 | .12774 | .12385 | .12015 | .11661 | .11322 |
| 50 | .15855 | .15347 | .14862 | .14401 | .13960 | .13540 | .13138 | .12754 | .12388 | .12037 |
| 51 | .16727 | .16205 | .15707 | .15232 | .14777 | .14344 | .13929 | .13532 | .13153 | .12789 |
| 52 | .17634 | .17098 | .16587 | .16097 | .15630 | .15183 | .14755 | .14345 | .13953 | .13577 |
| 53 | .18576 | .18027 | .17501 | .16999 | .16518 | .16057 | .15616 | .15194 | .14789 | .14400 |
| 54 | .19552 | .18990 | .18451 | .17935 | .17441 | .16968 | .16514 | .16078 | .15661 | .15260 |
| 55 | .20564 | .19989 | .19437 | .18908 | .18402 | .17915 | .17449 | .17001 | .16571 | .16157 |
| 56 | .21613 | .21025 | .20461 | .19919 | .19400 | .18901 | .18422 | .17962 | .17519 | .17093 |
| 57 | .22698 | .22098 | .21522 | .20968 | .20436 | .19925 | .19434 | .18961 | .18507 | .18069 |
| 58 | .23816 | .23204 | .22616 | .22051 | .21507 | .20984 | .20481 | .19996 | .19530 | .19080 |
| 59 | .24962 | .24339 | .23740 | .23163 | .22608 | .22073 | .21558 | .21062 | .20584 | .20123 |
| 60 | .26136 | .25502 | .24892 | .24304 | .23738 | .23192 | .22666 | .22158 | .21669 | .21196 |
| 61 | .27339 | .26695 | .26075 | .25477 | .24900 | .24343 | .23806 | .23288 | .22787 | .22304 |
| 62 | .28578 | .27925 | .27295 | .26687 | .26100 | .25533 | .24985 | .24456 | .23945 | .23451 |
| 63 | .29854 | .29192 | .28553 | .27935 | .27339 | .26762 | .26205 | .25666 | .25145 | .24641 |
| 64 | .31164 | .30494 | .29846 | .29221 | .28615 | .28030 | .27463 | .26915 | .26384 | .25870 |

Reg. §20.2031-7A(f)(4)

| AGE | 8.2% | 8.4% | 8.6% | 8.8% | 9.0% | 9.2% | 9.4% | 9.6% | 9.8% | 10.0% |
|---|---|---|---|---|---|---|---|---|---|---|
| 65 | .32508 | .31831 | .31177 | .30543 | .29930 | .29336 | .28761 | .28203 | .27663 | .27140 |
| 66 | .33891 | .33208 | .32547 | .31906 | .31285 | .30684 | .30101 | .29536 | .28987 | .28456 |
| 67 | .35318 | .34630 | .33963 | .33316 | .32689 | .32081 | .31491 | .30918 | .30363 | .29823 |
| 68 | .36785 | .36093 | .35422 | .34770 | .34138 | .33524 | .32928 | .32349 | .31787 | .31240 |
| 69 | .38290 | .37595 | .36920 | .36265 | .35628 | .35009 | .34408 | .33824 | .33256 | .32703 |
| 70 | .39823 | .39127 | .38450 | .37791 | .37151 | .36529 | .35924 | .35335 | .34762 | .34204 |
| 71 | .41378 | .40681 | .40003 | .39343 | .38701 | .38076 | .37467 | .36875 | .36298 | .35736 |
| 72 | .42950 | .42253 | .41575 | .40914 | .40271 | .39644 | .39034 | .38438 | .37858 | .37293 |
| 73 | .44535 | .43840 | .43162 | .42502 | .41858 | .41231 | .40619 | .40022 | .39440 | .38872 |
| 74 | .46139 | .45446 | .44771 | .44112 | .43469 | .42842 | .42230 | .41632 | .41049 | .40479 |
| 75 | .47769 | .47080 | .46408 | .45752 | .45111 | .44485 | .43874 | .43277 | .42693 | .42123 |
| 76 | .49430 | .48747 | .48079 | .47427 | .46790 | .46167 | .45558 | .44963 | .44380 | .43811 |
| 77 | .51123 | .50447 | .49786 | .49139 | .48506 | .47888 | .47282 | .46690 | .46111 | .45543 |
| 78 | .52845 | .52177 | .51523 | .50884 | .50257 | .49645 | .49044 | .48457 | .47881 | .47317 |
| 79 | .54584 | .53926 | .53282 | .52650 | .52032 | .51426 | .50833 | .50251 | .49681 | .49122 |
| 80 | .56325 | .55678 | .55044 | .54423 | .53813 | .53216 | .52630 | .52056 | .51492 | .50939 |
| 81 | .58054 | .57419 | .56797 | .56186 | .55587 | .54999 | .54422 | .53856 | .53300 | .52754 |
| 82 | .59762 | .59140 | .58530 | .57931 | .57343 | .56766 | .56198 | .55641 | .55094 | .54557 |
| 83 | .61448 | .60840 | .60243 | .59657 | .59081 | .58515 | .57958 | .57411 | .56874 | .56346 |
| 84 | .63124 | .62531 | .61949 | .61376 | .60813 | .60259 | .59715 | .59179 | .58652 | .58134 |
| 85 | .64800 | .64224 | .63657 | .63099 | .62550 | .62010 | .61478 | .60955 | .60441 | .59934 |
| 86 | .66461 | .65902 | .65351 | .64810 | .64276 | .63751 | .63233 | .62724 | .62222 | .61728 |
| 87 | .68083 | .67541 | .67008 | .66483 | .65965 | .65455 | .64953 | .64458 | .63970 | .63489 |
| 88 | .69663 | .69140 | .68624 | .68116 | .67615 | .67121 | .66634 | .66154 | .65680 | .65213 |
| 89 | .71201 | .70696 | .70199 | .69708 | .69224 | .68747 | .68276 | .67811 | .67353 | .66900 |
| 90 | .72694 | .72209 | .71730 | .71257 | .70791 | .70330 | .69876 | .69427 | .68984 | .68547 |
| 91 | .74117 | .73650 | .73190 | .72735 | .72286 | .71842 | .71404 | .70972 | .70545 | .70123 |
| 92 | .75439 | .74991 | .74548 | .74110 | .73678 | .73251 | .72829 | .72412 | .72000 | .71593 |
| 93 | .76664 | .76233 | .75806 | .75385 | .74969 | .74557 | .74150 | .73748 | .73350 | .72957 |
| 94 | .77809 | .77394 | .76983 | .76578 | .76177 | .75780 | .75388 | .75000 | .74616 | .74237 |
| 95 | .78899 | .78500 | .78106 | .77715 | .77329 | .76947 | .76569 | .76195 | .75826 | .75460 |
| 96 | .79928 | .79544 | .79165 | .78790 | .78418 | .78050 | .77686 | .77326 | .76970 | .76617 |
| 97 | .80883 | .80514 | .80149 | .79787 | .79430 | .79075 | .78725 | .78377 | .78033 | .77693 |
| 98 | .81781 | .81427 | .81075 | .80727 | .80382 | .80041 | .79703 | .79368 | .79036 | .78708 |
| 99 | .82661 | .82320 | .81982 | .81648 | .81316 | .80988 | .80662 | .80340 | .80020 | .79704 |
| 100 | .83519 | .83192 | .82868 | .82547 | .82228 | .81913 | .81600 | .81290 | .80982 | .80678 |
| 101 | .84368 | .84055 | .83744 | .83437 | .83131 | .82829 | .82529 | .82231 | .81936 | .81643 |
| 102 | .85203 | .84904 | .84607 | .84313 | .84021 | .83731 | .83444 | .83159 | .82876 | .82596 |
| 103 | .86034 | .85748 | .85465 | .85184 | .84906 | .84629 | .84355 | .84082 | .83812 | .83544 |
| 104 | .86923 | .86653 | .86385 | .86119 | .85855 | .85593 | .85333 | .85074 | .84818 | .84563 |
| 105 | .87792 | .87537 | .87283 | .87032 | .86782 | .86534 | .86287 | .86042 | .85799 | .85557 |
| 106 | .88918 | .88683 | .88450 | .88218 | .87987 | .87758 | .87530 | .87304 | .87079 | .86855 |
| 107 | .90291 | .90082 | .89873 | .89666 | .89460 | .89255 | .89051 | .88849 | .88647 | .88447 |
| 108 | .92455 | .92288 | .92123 | .91958 | .91794 | .91630 | .91468 | .91306 | .91145 | .90984 |
| 109 | .96211 | .96125 | .96041 | .95956 | .95872 | .95788 | .95704 | .95620 | .95537 | .95455 |

**TABLE S**
**BASED ON LIFE TABLE 90CM**
**SINGLE LIFE REMAINDER FACTORS**
**[APPLICABLE AFTER APRIL 30, 1999, AND BEFORE MAY 1, 2009]**

**INTEREST RATE**

| AGE | 10.2% | 10.4% | 10.6% | 10.8% | 11.0% | 11.2% | 11.4% | 11.6% | 11.8% | 12.0% |
|-----|-------|-------|-------|-------|-------|-------|-------|-------|-------|-------|
| 0 | .01488 | .01463 | .01439 | .01417 | .01396 | .01377 | .01359 | .01343 | .01327 | .01312 |
| 1 | .00662 | .00636 | .00612 | .00589 | .00568 | .00548 | .00530 | .00513 | .00497 | .00482 |
| 2 | .00654 | .00626 | .00600 | .00576 | .00554 | .00533 | .00514 | .00496 | .00479 | .00463 |
| 3 | .00670 | .00641 | .00613 | .00588 | .00564 | .00542 | .00522 | .00502 | .00484 | .00468 |
| 4 | .00699 | .00668 | .00639 | .00612 | .00587 | .00563 | .00542 | .00521 | .00502 | .00484 |
| 5 | .00739 | .00706 | .00675 | .00646 | .00620 | .00595 | .00571 | .00550 | .00529 | .00510 |
| 6 | .00786 | .00751 | .00718 | .00687 | .00659 | .00633 | .00608 | .00585 | .00563 | .00543 |
| 7 | .00841 | .00803 | .00769 | .00736 | .00706 | .00678 | .00652 | .00627 | .00604 | .00582 |
| 8 | .00902 | .00863 | .00826 | .00791 | .00759 | .00730 | .00702 | .00675 | .00651 | .00628 |
| 9 | .00973 | .00931 | .00892 | .00856 | .00822 | .00790 | .00760 | .00733 | .00706 | .00682 |
| 10 | .01055 | .01010 | .00969 | .00930 | .00894 | .00861 | .00829 | .00799 | .00772 | .00746 |
| 11 | .01146 | .01099 | .01055 | .01014 | .00976 | .00940 | .00907 | .00875 | .00846 | .00818 |
| 12 | .01246 | .01196 | .01150 | .01106 | .01066 | .01028 | .00993 | .00960 | .00928 | .00899 |
| 13 | .01351 | .01298 | .01249 | .01204 | .01161 | .01121 | .01084 | .01049 | .01016 | .00985 |
| 14 | .01455 | .01400 | .01348 | .01300 | .01255 | .01213 | .01173 | .01136 | .01102 | .01069 |
| 15 | .01555 | .01497 | .01443 | .01392 | .01345 | .01300 | .01259 | .01220 | .01183 | .01148 |
| 16 | .01648 | .01587 | .01530 | .01477 | .01427 | .01380 | .01336 | .01295 | .01257 | .01220 |
| 17 | .01737 | .01673 | .01612 | .01556 | .01504 | .01455 | .01408 | .01365 | .01324 | .01286 |
| 18 | .01822 | .01754 | .01691 | .01632 | .01576 | .01525 | .01476 | .01430 | .01387 | .01347 |
| 19 | .01908 | .01837 | .01770 | .01708 | .01650 | .01595 | .01544 | .01495 | .01450 | .01407 |
| 20 | .01999 | .01924 | .01854 | .01788 | .01726 | .01669 | .01615 | .01564 | .01516 | .01471 |
| 21 | .02096 | .02017 | .01943 | .01874 | .01809 | .01748 | .01691 | .01637 | .01586 | .01539 |
| 22 | .02197 | .02114 | .02036 | .01963 | .01895 | .01830 | .01770 | .01713 | .01660 | .01610 |
| 23 | .02306 | .02218 | .02136 | .02059 | .01987 | .01919 | .01855 | .01795 | .01739 | .01686 |
| 24 | .02424 | .02331 | .02245 | .02163 | .02087 | .02016 | .01948 | .01885 | .01825 | .01769 |
| 25 | .02552 | .02455 | .02364 | .02278 | .02197 | .02122 | .02051 | .01984 | .01920 | .01861 |
| 26 | .02692 | .02589 | .02493 | .02403 | .02318 | .02238 | .02162 | .02091 | .02025 | .01961 |
| 27 | .02846 | .02738 | .02636 | .02541 | .02451 | .02367 | .02287 | .02212 | .02141 | .02074 |
| 28 | .03012 | .02898 | .02791 | .02690 | .02595 | .02506 | .02422 | .02342 | .02267 | .02196 |
| 29 | .03190 | .03070 | .02957 | .02851 | .02751 | .02656 | .02567 | .02483 | .02404 | .02329 |
| 30 | .03381 | .03254 | .03135 | .03023 | .02917 | .02817 | .02723 | .02634 | .02551 | .02471 |
| 31 | .03583 | .03450 | .03324 | .03206 | .03094 | .02989 | .02890 | .02796 | .02707 | .02623 |
| 32 | .03799 | .03659 | .03527 | .03402 | .03284 | .03173 | .03068 | .02968 | .02874 | .02785 |
| 33 | .04031 | .03883 | .03744 | .03612 | .03488 | .03371 | .03260 | .03155 | .03055 | .02961 |
| 34 | .04279 | .04123 | .03976 | .03838 | .03707 | .03583 | .03465 | .03354 | .03249 | .03149 |
| 35 | .04545 | .04382 | .04227 | .04081 | .03943 | .03812 | .03688 | .03571 | .03459 | .03354 |
| 36 | .04830 | .04658 | .04495 | .04341 | .04196 | .04058 | .03927 | .03803 | .03685 | .03573 |
| 37 | .05134 | .04953 | .04782 | .04620 | .04467 | .04321 | .04183 | .04052 | .03928 | .03809 |
| 38 | .05462 | .05272 | .05092 | .04921 | .04760 | .04606 | .04461 | .04322 | .04191 | .04066 |
| 39 | .05812 | .05613 | .05424 | .05245 | .05075 | .04913 | .04760 | .04614 | .04475 | .04343 |
| 40 | .06190 | .05981 | .05782 | .05594 | .05415 | .05245 | .05083 | .04929 | .04783 | .04643 |
| 41 | .06597 | .06378 | .06170 | .05972 | .05784 | .05605 | .05435 | .05272 | .05118 | .04970 |
| 42 | .07035 | .06806 | .06587 | .06380 | .06182 | .05994 | .05815 | .05644 | .05481 | .05326 |
| 43 | .07505 | .07265 | .07036 | .06818 | .06611 | .06414 | .06225 | .06045 | .05874 | .05710 |
| 44 | .08008 | .07757 | .07518 | .07290 | .07072 | .06865 | .06667 | .06478 | .06298 | .06125 |
| 45 | .08542 | .08279 | .08029 | .07791 | .07563 | .07346 | .07138 | .06940 | .06750 | .06569 |
| 46 | .09108 | .08834 | .08573 | .08324 | .08085 | .07858 | .07640 | .07432 | .07233 | .07043 |
| 47 | .09705 | .09419 | .09147 | .08886 | .08637 | .08399 | .08172 | .07954 | .07745 | .07545 |
| 48 | .10335 | .10038 | .09754 | .09482 | .09222 | .08973 | .08735 | .08507 | .08288 | .08078 |
| 49 | .10999 | .10690 | .10394 | .10111 | .09840 | .09581 | .09332 | .09093 | .08864 | .08644 |
| 50 | .11701 | .11380 | .11073 | .10778 | .10496 | .10225 | .09965 | .09716 | .09477 | .09247 |
| 51 | .12441 | .12108 | .11789 | .11482 | .11189 | .10907 | .10636 | .10376 | .10126 | .09886 |
| 52 | .13217 | .12871 | .12540 | .12222 | .11916 | .11623 | .11341 | .11071 | .10810 | .10560 |
| 53 | .14028 | .13670 | .13327 | .12997 | .12680 | .12375 | .12082 | .11801 | .11529 | .11268 |
| 54 | .14875 | .14505 | .14150 | .13808 | .13480 | .13163 | .12859 | .12566 | .12284 | .12012 |
| 55 | .15760 | .15378 | .15011 | .14657 | .14317 | .13989 | .13674 | .13370 | .13077 | .12794 |
| 56 | .16684 | .16290 | .15911 | .15546 | .15194 | .14855 | .14528 | .14213 | .13909 | .13615 |
| 57 | .17648 | .17242 | .16851 | .16474 | .16111 | .15760 | .15422 | .15096 | .14781 | .14477 |
| 58 | .18647 | .18229 | .17827 | .17438 | .17064 | .16702 | .16353 | .16015 | .15689 | .15374 |
| 59 | .19678 | .19249 | .18835 | .18435 | .18049 | .17676 | .17316 | .16968 | .16631 | .16305 |
| 60 | .20740 | .20300 | .19875 | .19464 | .19066 | .18682 | .18311 | .17952 | .17604 | .17268 |
| 61 | .21837 | .21385 | .20949 | .20527 | .20119 | .19724 | .19341 | .18971 | .18613 | .18266 |
| 62 | .22973 | .22511 | .22064 | .21631 | .21212 | .20807 | .20414 | .20033 | .19664 | .19306 |
| 63 | .24152 | .23680 | .23222 | .22779 | .22350 | .21934 | .21530 | .21139 | .20760 | .20392 |
| 64 | .25372 | .24890 | .24422 | .23969 | .23529 | .23103 | .22690 | .22289 | .21899 | .21521 |

Reg. §20.2031-7A(f)(4)

| AGE | 10.2% | 10.4% | 10.6% | 10.8% | 11.0% | 11.2% | 11.4% | 11.6% | 11.8% | 12.0% |
|-----|-------|-------|-------|-------|-------|-------|-------|-------|-------|-------|
| 65 | .26633 | .26141 | .25664 | .25201 | .24752 | .24316 | .23893 | .23482 | .23083 | .22695 |
| 66 | .27940 | .27439 | .26953 | .26481 | .26023 | .25577 | .25145 | .24724 | .24316 | .23918 |
| 67 | .29299 | .28790 | .28296 | .27815 | .27348 | .26894 | .26453 | .26024 | .25606 | .25200 |
| 68 | .30709 | .30193 | .29691 | .29202 | .28728 | .28265 | .27816 | .27378 | .26952 | .26537 |
| 69 | .32166 | .31643 | .31134 | .30639 | .30157 | .29687 | .29230 | .28785 | .28351 | .27928 |
| 70 | .33661 | .33133 | .32618 | .32116 | .31628 | .31152 | .30688 | .30235 | .29794 | .29364 |
| 71 | .35188 | .34654 | .34134 | .33627 | .33133 | .32651 | .32181 | .31722 | .31275 | .30838 |
| 72 | .36742 | .36204 | .35679 | .35168 | .34668 | .34181 | .33706 | .33241 | .32788 | .32345 |
| 73 | .38317 | .37776 | .37248 | .36733 | .36229 | .35738 | .35257 | .34788 | .34330 | .33882 |
| 74 | .39923 | .39380 | .38849 | .38330 | .37823 | .37328 | .36844 | .36370 | .35908 | .35455 |
| 75 | .41566 | .41021 | .40489 | .39968 | .39459 | .38961 | .38474 | .37997 | .37531 | .37074 |
| 76 | .43254 | .42709 | .42176 | .41655 | .41144 | .40645 | .40156 | .39677 | .39208 | .38749 |
| 77 | .44988 | .44444 | .43912 | .43391 | .42880 | .42380 | .41891 | .41411 | .40940 | .40479 |
| 78 | .46765 | .46224 | .45694 | .45174 | .44665 | .44166 | .43677 | .43197 | .42726 | .42265 |
| 79 | .48574 | .48037 | .47510 | .46993 | .46487 | .45990 | .45502 | .45024 | .44554 | .44094 |
| 80 | .50397 | .49865 | .49343 | .48830 | .48327 | .47834 | .47349 | .46873 | .46406 | .45947 |
| 81 | .52219 | .51693 | .51176 | .50669 | .50171 | .49682 | .49201 | .48729 | .48265 | .47809 |
| 82 | .54029 | .53510 | .53000 | .52499 | .52007 | .51523 | .51047 | .50580 | .50120 | .49667 |
| 83 | .55826 | .55315 | .54813 | .54319 | .53834 | .53356 | .52886 | .52424 | .51969 | .51522 |
| 84 | .57624 | .57123 | .56629 | .56144 | .55666 | .55195 | .54732 | .54277 | .53828 | .53386 |
| 85 | .59435 | .58944 | .58460 | .57984 | .57516 | .57054 | .56599 | .56151 | .55710 | .55275 |
| 86 | .61241 | .60762 | .60289 | .59824 | .59365 | .58913 | .58468 | .58029 | .57596 | .57170 |
| 87 | .63015 | .62548 | .62087 | .61633 | .61185 | .60744 | .60309 | .59880 | .59456 | .59039 |
| 88 | .64753 | .64299 | .63851 | .63409 | .62973 | .62543 | .62118 | .61700 | .61287 | .60879 |
| 89 | .66454 | .66013 | .65579 | .65150 | .64726 | .64308 | .63895 | .63488 | .63086 | .62689 |
| 90 | .68115 | .67689 | .67268 | .66853 | .66442 | .66037 | .65637 | .65241 | .64851 | .64465 |
| 91 | .69706 | .69294 | .68887 | .68486 | .68089 | .67696 | .67309 | .66925 | .66547 | .66173 |
| 92 | .71190 | .70792 | .70399 | .70011 | .69627 | .69247 | .68872 | .68501 | .68134 | .67771 |
| 93 | .72569 | .72184 | .71804 | .71429 | .71057 | .70689 | .70326 | .69967 | .69611 | .69259 |
| 94 | .73861 | .73490 | .73123 | .72759 | .72400 | .72044 | .71692 | .71344 | .71000 | .70659 |
| 95 | .75097 | .74739 | .74384 | .74033 | .73686 | .73342 | .73002 | .72665 | .72331 | .72001 |
| 96 | .76267 | .75922 | .75579 | .75240 | .74905 | .74572 | .74243 | .73917 | .73595 | .73275 |
| 97 | .77356 | .77022 | .76691 | .76363 | .76039 | .75718 | .75399 | .75084 | .74772 | .74463 |
| 98 | .78382 | .78059 | .77740 | .77423 | .77110 | .76799 | .76491 | .76186 | .75884 | .75584 |
| 99 | .79390 | .79079 | .78771 | .78465 | .78162 | .77862 | .77565 | .77270 | .76978 | .76688 |
| 100 | .80376 | .80076 | .79779 | .79485 | .79193 | .78904 | .78617 | .78333 | .78051 | .77771 |
| 101 | .81353 | .81066 | .80780 | .80497 | .80217 | .79938 | .79662 | .79388 | .79117 | .78847 |
| 102 | .82318 | .82042 | .81768 | .81496 | .81227 | .80960 | .80694 | .80431 | .80170 | .79911 |
| 103 | .83278 | .83014 | .82752 | .82491 | .82233 | .81977 | .81723 | .81470 | .81220 | .80971 |
| 104 | .84310 | .84059 | .83810 | .83563 | .83317 | .83073 | .82831 | .82591 | .82352 | .82115 |
| 105 | .85318 | .85079 | .84843 | .84607 | .84374 | .84142 | .83911 | .83682 | .83455 | .83229 |
| 106 | .86633 | .86413 | .86193 | .85975 | .85758 | .85543 | .85329 | .85116 | .84904 | .84694 |
| 107 | .88247 | .88049 | .87852 | .87656 | .87460 | .87266 | .87073 | .86881 | .86690 | .86500 |
| 108 | .90825 | .90666 | .90507 | .90350 | .90193 | .90037 | .89881 | .89727 | .89572 | .89419 |
| 109 | .95372 | .95290 | .95208 | .95126 | .95045 | .94964 | .94883 | .94803 | .94723 | .94643 |

**TABLE S**
**BASED ON LIFE TABLE 90CM**
**SINGLE LIFE REMAINDER FACTORS**
**[APPLICABLE AFTER APRIL 30, 1999, AND BEFORE MAY 1, 2009]**

**INTEREST RATE**

| AGE | 12.2% | 12.4% | 12.6% | 12.8% | 13.0% | 13.2% | 13.4% | 13.6% | 13.8% | 14.0% |
|---|---|---|---|---|---|---|---|---|---|---|
| 0 | .01298 | .01285 | .01273 | .01261 | .01250 | .01240 | .01230 | .01221 | .01212 | .01203 |
| 1 | .00468 | .00455 | .00443 | .00431 | .00420 | .00410 | .00400 | .00391 | .00382 | .00374 |
| 2 | .00448 | .00435 | .00421 | .00409 | .00398 | .00387 | .00376 | .00366 | .00357 | .00348 |
| 3 | .00452 | .00437 | .00423 | .00410 | .00398 | .00386 | .00375 | .00365 | .00355 | .00345 |
| 4 | .00468 | .00452 | .00437 | .00423 | .00410 | .00397 | .00386 | .00375 | .00364 | .00354 |
| 5 | .00493 | .00476 | .00460 | .00445 | .00431 | .00418 | .00405 | .00393 | .00382 | .00371 |
| 6 | .00524 | .00506 | .00489 | .00473 | .00458 | .00444 | .00430 | .00418 | .00406 | .00394 |
| 7 | .00562 | .00543 | .00525 | .00508 | .00492 | .00477 | .00462 | .00449 | .00436 | .00423 |
| 8 | .00606 | .00586 | .00566 | .00548 | .00531 | .00515 | .00499 | .00485 | .00471 | .00458 |
| 9 | .00659 | .00637 | .00616 | .00597 | .00579 | .00561 | .00545 | .00529 | .00514 | .00500 |
| 10 | .00721 | .00698 | .00676 | .00655 | .00636 | .00617 | .00600 | .00583 | .00567 | .00552 |
| 11 | .00792 | .00767 | .00744 | .00722 | .00701 | .00682 | .00663 | .00645 | .00628 | .00612 |
| 12 | .00871 | .00845 | .00821 | .00797 | .00775 | .00754 | .00735 | .00716 | .00698 | .00681 |
| 13 | .00955 | .00928 | .00902 | .00877 | .00854 | .00831 | .00810 | .00790 | .00771 | .00753 |
| 14 | .01038 | .01009 | .00981 | .00955 | .00930 | .00907 | .00885 | .00864 | .00843 | .00824 |
| 15 | .01116 | .01085 | .01056 | .01028 | .01002 | .00977 | .00954 | .00932 | .00910 | .00890 |
| 16 | .01186 | .01153 | .01123 | .01094 | .01066 | .01040 | .01015 | .00992 | .00969 | .00948 |
| 17 | .01250 | .01215 | .01183 | .01152 | .01124 | .01096 | .01070 | .01045 | .01022 | .00999 |
| 18 | .01308 | .01272 | .01238 | .01206 | .01175 | .01147 | .01119 | .01093 | .01068 | .01044 |
| 19 | .01367 | .01329 | .01293 | .01259 | .01227 | .01196 | .01167 | .01140 | .01113 | .01088 |
| 20 | .01428 | .01388 | .01350 | .01314 | .01280 | .01248 | .01217 | .01188 | .01161 | .01134 |
| 21 | .01494 | .01451 | .01411 | .01373 | .01337 | .01303 | .01271 | .01240 | .01211 | .01183 |
| 22 | .01562 | .01517 | .01475 | .01435 | .01397 | .01361 | .01326 | .01294 | .01263 | .01233 |
| 23 | .01635 | .01588 | .01543 | .01501 | .01460 | .01422 | .01386 | .01351 | .01319 | .01287 |
| 24 | .01716 | .01665 | .01618 | .01573 | .01530 | .01489 | .01451 | .01415 | .01380 | .01347 |
| 25 | .01804 | .01751 | .01701 | .01653 | .01608 | .01565 | .01524 | .01485 | .01448 | .01413 |
| 26 | .01902 | .01845 | .01792 | .01741 | .01693 | .01648 | .01604 | .01563 | .01524 | .01487 |
| 27 | .02011 | .01951 | .01895 | .01841 | .01790 | .01742 | .01696 | .01652 | .01610 | .01571 |
| 28 | .02129 | .02066 | .02006 | .01949 | .01895 | .01844 | .01795 | .01748 | .01704 | .01662 |
| 29 | .02258 | .02191 | .02127 | .02067 | .02009 | .01955 | .01903 | .01853 | .01806 | .01762 |
| 30 | .02396 | .02325 | .02257 | .02193 | .02132 | .02074 | .02019 | .01966 | .01916 | .01869 |
| 31 | .02543 | .02467 | .02396 | .02328 | .02263 | .02201 | .02143 | .02087 | .02034 | .01983 |
| 32 | .02701 | .02621 | .02545 | .02472 | .02404 | .02338 | .02276 | .02217 | .02160 | .02106 |
| 33 | .02871 | .02786 | .02706 | .02629 | .02556 | .02487 | .02420 | .02357 | .02297 | .02240 |
| 34 | .03054 | .02964 | .02879 | .02797 | .02720 | .02646 | .02576 | .02509 | .02445 | .02383 |
| 35 | .03253 | .03158 | .03067 | .02981 | .02898 | .02820 | .02745 | .02674 | .02606 | .02541 |
| 36 | .03467 | .03366 | .03269 | .03178 | .03090 | .03007 | .02928 | .02852 | .02779 | .02710 |
| 37 | .03697 | .03590 | .03488 | .03391 | .03298 | .03209 | .03125 | .03044 | .02967 | .02893 |
| 38 | .03947 | .03833 | .03725 | .03622 | .03524 | .03430 | .03340 | .03254 | .03172 | .03094 |
| 39 | .04217 | .04096 | .03982 | .03873 | .03768 | .03669 | .03573 | .03482 | .03395 | .03312 |
| 40 | .04510 | .04383 | .04262 | .04146 | .04035 | .03930 | .03828 | .03732 | .03639 | .03550 |
| 41 | .04830 | .04695 | .04567 | .04445 | .04327 | .04215 | .04108 | .04005 | .03907 | .03812 |
| 42 | .05177 | .05035 | .04900 | .04770 | .04646 | .04527 | .04413 | .04304 | .04200 | .04100 |
| 43 | .05553 | .05404 | .05261 | .05123 | .04992 | .04866 | .04746 | .04630 | .04520 | .04413 |
| 44 | .05960 | .05802 | .05651 | .05506 | .05368 | .05235 | .05107 | .04985 | .04867 | .04754 |
| 45 | .06395 | .06229 | .06069 | .05917 | .05770 | .05630 | .05495 | .05365 | .05241 | .05121 |
| 46 | .06860 | .06685 | .06517 | .06356 | .06202 | .06053 | .05911 | .05774 | .05643 | .05516 |
| 47 | .07353 | .07169 | .06992 | .06823 | .06660 | .06504 | .06353 | .06209 | .06070 | .05936 |
| 48 | .07877 | .07684 | .07498 | .07320 | .07149 | .06984 | .06826 | .06673 | .06527 | .06385 |
| 49 | .08433 | .08231 | .08036 | .07849 | .07669 | .07495 | .07329 | .07168 | .07013 | .06864 |
| 50 | .09026 | .08814 | .08609 | .08413 | .08224 | .08042 | .07867 | .07698 | .07535 | .07378 |
| 51 | .09655 | .09433 | .09219 | .09013 | .08815 | .08624 | .08440 | .08262 | .08091 | .07926 |
| 52 | .10318 | .10086 | .09863 | .09647 | .09439 | .09239 | .09046 | .08860 | .08680 | .08506 |
| 53 | .11017 | .10774 | .10541 | .10315 | .10098 | .09888 | .09686 | .09491 | .09302 | .09120 |
| 54 | .11750 | .11498 | .11254 | .11019 | .10792 | .10572 | .10361 | .10156 | .09958 | .09767 |
| 55 | .12522 | .12258 | .12005 | .11759 | .11522 | .11294 | .11072 | .10859 | .10652 | .10451 |
| 56 | .13332 | .13059 | .12794 | .12539 | .12292 | .12054 | .11823 | .11599 | .11383 | .11174 |
| 57 | .14183 | .13899 | .13624 | .13359 | .13102 | .12853 | .12613 | .12380 | .12154 | .11936 |
| 58 | .15070 | .14775 | .14490 | .14215 | .13948 | .13689 | .13439 | .13197 | .12962 | .12734 |
| 59 | .15990 | .15685 | .15389 | .15103 | .14826 | .14558 | .14298 | .14046 | .13801 | .13564 |
| 60 | .16942 | .16626 | .16321 | .16024 | .15737 | .15459 | .15189 | .14927 | .14673 | .14426 |
| 61 | .17929 | .17603 | .17287 | .16981 | .16684 | .16395 | .16115 | .15844 | .15580 | .15324 |
| 62 | .18960 | .18623 | .18297 | .17980 | .17673 | .17375 | .17085 | .16803 | .16530 | .16264 |
| 63 | .20035 | .19688 | .19352 | .19025 | .18708 | .18400 | .18100 | .17809 | .17525 | .17250 |
| 64 | .21154 | .20797 | .20451 | .20114 | .19787 | .19469 | .19159 | .18859 | .18566 | .18281 |

| AGE | 12.2% | 12.4% | 12.6% | 12.8% | 13.0% | 13.2% | 13.4% | 13.6% | 13.8% | 14.0% |
|---|---|---|---|---|---|---|---|---|---|---|
| 65 | .22318 | .21951 | .21595 | .21249 | .20912 | .20584 | .20265 | .19955 | .19652 | .19358 |
| 66 | .23532 | .23156 | .22790 | .22434 | .22088 | .21751 | .21422 | .21102 | .20791 | .20487 |
| 67 | .24804 | .24419 | .24044 | .23679 | .23324 | .22977 | .22640 | .22311 | .21990 | .21678 |
| 68 | .26133 | .25740 | .25356 | .24983 | .24618 | .24263 | .23917 | .23579 | .23250 | .22929 |
| 69 | .27516 | .27114 | .26723 | .26341 | .25969 | .25605 | .25251 | .24905 | .24567 | .24237 |
| 70 | .28945 | .28536 | .28137 | .27747 | .27367 | .26996 | .26633 | .26279 | .25934 | .25596 |
| 71 | .30412 | .29996 | .29590 | .29193 | .28806 | .28427 | .28057 | .27696 | .27343 | .26998 |
| 72 | .31913 | .31491 | .31078 | .30675 | .30281 | .29895 | .29519 | .29150 | .28790 | .28438 |
| 73 | .33444 | .33016 | .32597 | .32188 | .31788 | .31396 | .31013 | .30638 | .30271 | .29913 |
| 74 | .35012 | .34579 | .34155 | .33741 | .33335 | .32938 | .32549 | .32168 | .31795 | .31430 |
| 75 | .36628 | .36190 | .35762 | .35343 | .34932 | .34530 | .34136 | .33750 | .33372 | .33001 |
| 76 | .38299 | .37858 | .37427 | .37004 | .36589 | .36183 | .35784 | .35394 | .35011 | .34636 |
| 77 | .40028 | .39585 | .39151 | .38725 | .38307 | .37898 | .37496 | .37103 | .36716 | .36337 |
| 78 | .41812 | .41368 | .40933 | .40506 | .40086 | .39675 | .39271 | .38874 | .38485 | .38103 |
| 79 | .43641 | .43198 | .42762 | .42334 | .41914 | .41502 | .41096 | .40698 | .40308 | .39924 |
| 80 | .45496 | .45054 | .44619 | .44192 | .43772 | .43360 | .42954 | .42556 | .42164 | .41779 |
| 81 | .47360 | .46920 | .46487 | .46061 | .45643 | .45231 | .44827 | .44429 | .44038 | .43653 |
| 82 | .49223 | .48785 | .48355 | .47932 | .47516 | .47106 | .46703 | .46307 | .45916 | .45532 |
| 83 | .51081 | .50648 | .50221 | .49802 | .49388 | .48982 | .48581 | .48187 | .47799 | .47416 |
| 84 | .52951 | .52523 | .52101 | .51686 | .51277 | .50874 | .50477 | .50086 | .49701 | .49321 |
| 85 | .54847 | .54425 | .54009 | .53600 | .53196 | .52798 | .52406 | .52019 | .51638 | .51262 |
| 86 | .56749 | .56335 | .55926 | .55523 | .55126 | .54734 | .54348 | .53966 | .53591 | .53220 |
| 87 | .58627 | .58221 | .57820 | .57425 | .57035 | .56650 | .56270 | .55895 | .55526 | .55161 |
| 88 | .60477 | .60079 | .59688 | .59301 | .58919 | .58542 | .58170 | .57802 | .57439 | .57081 |
| 89 | .62297 | .61909 | .61527 | .61149 | .60776 | .60408 | .60044 | .59685 | .59330 | .58979 |
| 90 | .64084 | .63707 | .63335 | .62968 | .62604 | .62246 | .61891 | .61540 | .61194 | .60851 |
| 91 | .65803 | .65437 | .65076 | .64719 | .64366 | .64017 | .63672 | .63330 | .62993 | .62659 |
| 92 | .67412 | .67058 | .66707 | .66360 | .66017 | .65678 | .65342 | .65010 | .64682 | .64357 |
| 93 | .68911 | .68567 | .68227 | .67890 | .67557 | .67227 | .66901 | .66578 | .66258 | .65942 |
| 94 | .70321 | .69988 | .69657 | .69330 | .69006 | .68686 | .68369 | .68055 | .67744 | .67437 |
| 95 | .71674 | .71351 | .71031 | .70713 | .70399 | .70088 | .69781 | .69476 | .69174 | .68875 |
| 96 | .72959 | .72646 | .72335 | .72028 | .71724 | .71422 | .71123 | .70828 | .70534 | .70244 |
| 97 | .74156 | .73853 | .73552 | .73254 | .72959 | .72666 | .72376 | .72089 | .71804 | .71522 |
| 98 | .75287 | .74993 | .74702 | .74413 | .74126 | .73842 | .73561 | .73282 | .73006 | .72732 |
| 99 | .76401 | .76117 | .75834 | .75555 | .75277 | .75002 | .74730 | .74459 | .74191 | .73926 |
| 100 | .77494 | .77219 | .76946 | .76676 | .76408 | .76142 | .75878 | .75616 | .75357 | .75099 |
| 101 | .78580 | .78315 | .78052 | .77791 | .77532 | .77275 | .77021 | .76768 | .76517 | .76268 |
| 102 | .79654 | .79399 | .79146 | .78894 | .78645 | .78397 | .78152 | .77908 | .77666 | .77426 |
| 103 | .80724 | .80479 | .80236 | .79994 | .79755 | .79517 | .79280 | .79046 | .78813 | .78582 |
| 104 | .81879 | .81646 | .81413 | .81183 | .80954 | .80726 | .80501 | .80276 | .80054 | .79832 |
| 105 | .83005 | .82782 | .82560 | .82340 | .82121 | .81904 | .81688 | .81474 | .81260 | .81049 |
| 106 | .84485 | .84277 | .84071 | .83866 | .83662 | .83459 | .83257 | .83057 | .82857 | .82659 |
| 107 | .86311 | .86124 | .85937 | .85751 | .85566 | .85382 | .85199 | .85017 | .84835 | .84655 |
| 108 | .89266 | .89114 | .88963 | .88812 | .88662 | .88513 | .88364 | .88216 | .88068 | .87922 |
| 109 | .94563 | .94484 | .94405 | .94326 | .94248 | .94170 | .94092 | .94014 | .93937 | .93860 |

## LIFE TABLE
### TABLE 90CM
#### APPLICABLE AFTER APRIL 30, 1999, AND BEFORE MAY 1, 2009

| Age x | l(x) | Age x | l(x) | Age x | l(x) |
|---|---|---|---|---|---|
| (1) | (2) | (1) | (2) | (1) | (2) |
| 0 | 100000 | 37 | 95969 | 74 | 62852 |
| 1 | 99064 | 38 | 95780 | 75 | 60449 |
| 2 | 98992 | 39 | 95581 | 76 | 57955 |
| 3 | 98944 | 40 | 95373 | 77 | 55373 |
| 4 | 98907 | 41 | 95156 | 78 | 52704 |
| 5 | 98877 | 42 | 94928 | 79 | 49943 |
| 6 | 98850 | 43 | 94687 | 80 | 47084 |
| 7 | 98826 | 44 | 94431 | 81 | 44129 |
| 8 | 98803 | 45 | 94154 | 82 | 41091 |
| 9 | 98783 | 46 | 93855 | 83 | 37994 |
| 10 | 98766 | 47 | 93528 | 84 | 34876 |
| 11 | 98750 | 48 | 93173 | 85 | 31770 |
| 12 | 98734 | 49 | 92787 | 86 | 28687 |
| 13 | 98713 | 50 | 92370 | 87 | 25638 |
| 14 | 98681 | 51 | 91918 | 88 | 22658 |
| 15 | 98635 | 52 | 91424 | 89 | 19783 |
| 16 | 98573 | 53 | 90885 | 90 | 17046 |
| 17 | 98497 | 54 | 90297 | 91 | 14466 |
| 18 | 98409 | 55 | 89658 | 92 | 12066 |
| 19 | 98314 | 56 | 88965 | 93 | 9884 |
| 20 | 98215 | 57 | 88214 | 94 | 7951 |
| 21 | 98113 | 58 | 87397 | 95 | 6282 |
| 22 | 98006 | 59 | 86506 | 96 | 4868 |
| 23 | 97896 | 60 | 85537 | 97 | 3694 |
| 24 | 97784 | 61 | 84490 | 98 | 2745 |
| 25 | 97671 | 62 | 83368 | 99 | 1999 |
| 26 | 97556 | 63 | 82169 | 100 | 1424 |
| 27 | 97441 | 64 | 80887 | 101 | 991 |
| 28 | 97322 | 65 | 79519 | 102 | 672 |
| 29 | 97199 | 66 | 78066 | 103 | 443 |
| 30 | 97070 | 67 | 76531 | 104 | 284 |
| 31 | 96934 | 68 | 74907 | 105 | 175 |
| 32 | 96791 | 69 | 73186 | 106 | 105 |
| 33 | 96642 | 70 | 71357 | 107 | 60 |
| 34 | 96485 | 71 | 69411 | 108 | 33 |
| 35 | 96322 | 72 | 67344 | 109 | 17 |
| 36 | 96150 | 73 | 65154 | 110 | 0 |

(5) *Effective/applicability dates.*—Paragraphs (f)(1) through (f)(4) apply after April 30, 1999, and before May 1, 2009. [Reg. §20.2031-7A.]

☐ [T.D. 6296, 6-23-58. Amended by T.D. 7077, 12-1-70 and T.D. 7955, 5-10-84. *Reg. §20.2031-7 was redesignated Reg. §20.2031-7A(d) and amended by T.D. 8540, 6-9-94. Amended by T.D. 8819, 4-29-99 (corrected 6-21-99); T.D. 8886, 6-9-2000; T.D. 9448, 5-1-2009 and T.D. 9540, 8-9-2011.*]

### [Reg. §20.2031-8]

**§20.2031-8. Valuation of certain life insurance and annuity contracts; valuation of shares in an open-end investment company.—** (a) *Valuation of certain life insurance and annuity contracts.*—(1) The value of a contract for the payment of an annuity, or an insurance policy on the life of a person other than the decedent, issued by a company regularly engaged in the selling of contracts of that character is established through the sale by that company of comparable contracts. An annuity payable under a combination annuity contract and life insurance policy on the decedent's life (e.g., a "retirement income" policy with death benefit) under which there was no insurance element at the time of the decedent's death (see paragraph (d) of §20.2039-1) is treated like a contract for the payment of an annuity for purposes of this section.

(2) As valuation of an insurance policy through sale of comparable contracts is not readily ascertainable when, at the date of the decedent's death, the contract has been in force for some time and further premium payments are to be made, the value may be approximated by adding to the interpolated terminal reserve at the date of the decedent's death the proportionate part of the gross premium last paid before the date of the decedent's death which covers the period extending beyond that date. If, however, because of the unusual nature of the contract such an approximation is not reasonably close to the full value of the contract, this method may not be used.

(3) The application of this section may be illustrated by the following examples. In each case involving an insurance contract, it is assumed that there are no accrued dividends or outstanding indebtedness on the contract.

*Example (1).* X purchased from a life insurance company a joint and survivor annuity contract under the terms of which X was to receive payments of $1,200 annually for his life and, upon X's death, his wife was to receive payments of $1,200 annually for her life. Five years after such purchase, when his wife was 50 years of age, X died. The value of the annuity contract at the date of X's death is the amount which the company would charge for an annuity providing for the payment of $1,200 annually for the life of a female 50 years of age.

*Example (2).* Y died holding the incidents of ownership in a life insurance policy on the life of his wife. The policy was one on which no further payments were to be made to the company (e.g., a single premium policy or a paid-up policy). The value of the insurance policy at the date of Y's death is the amount which the company would charge for a single premium contract of the same specified amount on the life of a person of the age of the insured.

*Example (3).* Z died holding the incidents of ownership in a life insurance policy on the life of his wife. The policy was an ordinary life policy issued nine years and four months prior to Z's death and at a time when Z's wife was 35 years of age. The gross annual premium is $2,811 and the decedent died four months after the last premium due date. The value of the insurance policy at the date of Z's death is computed as follows:

| | |
|---|---|
| Terminal reserve at end of tenth year | $14,601.00 |
| Terminal reserve at end of ninth year | 12,965.00 |
| Increase | $1,636.00 |
| One-third of such increase (Z having died four months following the last preceding premium due date) is | $545.33 |
| Terminal reserve at end of ninth year | 12,965.00 |
| Interpolated terminal reserve at date of Z's death | 13,510.33 |
| Two-thirds of gross premium ($2/3 \times \$2,811$) | 1,874.00 |
| Value of the insurance policy | $15,384.33 |

(b) *Valuation of shares in an open-end investment company.*—(1) The fair market value of a share in an open-end investment company (commonly known as a "mutual fund") is the public redemption price of a share. In the absence of an affirmative showing of the public redemption price in effect at the time of death, the last public redemption price quoted by the company for the date of death shall be presumed to be the applicable public redemption price. If the alternate valuation method under 2032 is elected, the last public redemption price quoted by the company for the alternate valuation date shall be the applicable redemption price. If there is no public redemption price quoted by the company for the applicable valuation date (e.g., the valuation date is a Saturday, Sunday, or holiday), the fair market value of the mutual fund share is the last public redemption price quoted by the company for the first day preceding the applicable valuation date for which there is a quotation. In any case where a dividend is declared on a share in an open-end investment company before the decedent's death but payable to shareholders of record on a date after his death and the share is quoted "ex-dividend" on the date of the decedent's death, the amount of the dividend is added to the ex-dividend quotation in determining the fair market value of the share as of the date of the decedent's death. As used in this paragraph, the term "open-end investment company" includes only a company which on the applicable valuation date was engaged in offering its shares to the public in the capacity of an open-end investment company.

(2) The provisions of this paragraph shall apply with respect to estates of decedents dying after August 16, 1954. [Reg. § 20.2031-8.]

☐ [*T.D. 6296, 6-23-58. Amended by T.D. 6680, 10-9-63 and T.D. 7319, 7-22-74.*]

### [Reg. § 20.2031-9]

**§ 20.2031-9. Valuation of other property.**—The valuation of any property not specifically described in §§ 20.2031-2 through 20.2031-8 is made in accordance with the general principles set forth in § 20.2031-1. For example, a future interest in property not subject to valuation in accordance with the actuarial principles set forth in § 20.2031-7 is to be valued in accordance with the general principles set forth in § 20.2031-1. [Reg. § 20.2031-9.]

☐ [*T.D. 6296, 6-23-58.*]

### [Reg. § 20.2032-1]

**§ 20.2032-1. Alternate valuation.**—(a) *In general.*—In general, section 2032 provides for the valuation of a decedent's gross estate at a date other than the date of the decedent's death. More specifically, if an executor elects the alternate valuation method under section 2032, the property included in the decedent's gross estate on the date of his death is valued as of whichever of the following dates is applicable:

(1) Any property distributed, sold, exchanged, or otherwise disposed of within 6 months (1 year, if the decedent died on or before December 31, 1970) after the decedent's death is valued as of the date on which it is first distributed, sold, exchanged, or otherwise disposed of;

(2) Any property not distributed, sold, exchanged, or otherwise disposed of within 6 months (1 year, if the decedent died on or before December 31, 1970) after the decedent's death is valued as of the date 6 months (1 year, if the decedent died on or before December 31, 1970) after the date of the decedent's death;

(3) Any property, interest, or estate which is affected by mere lapse of time is valued as of the date of the decedent's death, but adjusted for any difference in its value not due to mere lapse of time as of the date 6 months (1 year, if the decedent died on or before December 31, 1970) after the decedent's death, or as of the date of its distribution, sale, exchange, or other disposition, whichever date first occurs.

(b) *Method and effect of election.*—(1) *In general.*—The election to use the alternate valuation method is made on the return of tax imposed by section 2001. For purposes of this paragraph (b), the term *return of tax imposed by section 2001* means the last estate tax return filed by the executor on or before the due date of the return (including extensions of time to file actually granted) or, if a timely return is not filed, the first estate tax return filed by the executor after the due date, provided the return is filed no later than 1 year after the due date (including extensions of time to file actually granted). Once the election is made, it is irrevocable, provided that an election may be revoked on a subsequent return filed on or before the due date of the return (including extensions of time to file actually granted). The election may be made only if it will decrease both the value of the gross estate and the sum (reduced by allowable credits) of the estate tax and the generation-skipping transfer tax payable by reason of the decedent's death with respect to the property includible in the decedent's gross estate. If the election is made, the alternate valuation method applies to all property included in the gross estate and cannot be applied to only a portion of the property.

(2) *Protective election.*—If, based on the return of tax as filed, use of the alternate valuation method would not result in a decrease in both the value of the gross estate and the sum (reduced by allowable credits) of the estate tax and the generation-skipping transfer tax liability payable by reason of the decedent's death with respect to the property includible in the decedent's gross estate, a protective election may be made to use the alternate valuation method if it is subsequently determined that such a decrease would occur. A protective election is made on the return of tax imposed by section 2001. The protective election is irrevocable as of the due date of the return (including extensions of time actually granted). The protective election becomes effective on the date on which it is determined that use of the alternate valuation method would result in a decrease in both the value of the gross estate and in the sum (reduced by allowable credits) of the estate tax and generation-skipping transfer tax liability payable by reason of the decedent's death with respect to the property includible in the decedent's gross estate.

(3) *Requests for extension of time to make the election.*—A request for an extension of time to make the election or protective election pursuant to §§ 301.9100-1 and 301.9100-3 of this chapter will not be granted unless the return of tax imposed by section 2001 is filed no later than 1 year after the due date of the return (including extensions of time actually granted).

(c) *Meaning of "distributed, sold, exchanged, or otherwise disposed of".*—(1) The phrase "distributed, sold, exchanged, or otherwise disposed of" comprehends all possible ways by which property ceases to form a part of the gross estate. For example, money on hand at the date of the decedent's death which is thereafter used in the payment of funeral expenses, or which is thereafter invested, falls within the term "otherwise disposed of." The term also includes the surrender of a stock certificate for corporate assets in complete or partial liquidation of a corporation pursuant to section 331. The term does not, however, extend to transactions which are mere changes in form. Thus, it does not include a transfer of assets to a corporation in exchange for its stock in a transaction with respect to which no gain or loss would be recognizable for income tax purposes under section 351. Nor does it include an exchange of stock or securities in a corporation for stock or securities in the same corporation or another corporation in a transaction, such as a merger, recapitalization, reorganization or other transaction described in section 368(a) or 355, with respect to which no gain or loss is recognizable for income tax purposes under section 354 or 355.

(2) Property may be "distributed" either by the executor, or by a trustee of property included in the gross estate under sections 2035 through 2038, or section 2041. Property is considered as "distributed" upon the first to occur of the following:

(i) The entry of an order or decree of distribution, if the order or decree subsequently becomes final;

(ii) The segregation or separation of the property from the estate or trust so that it becomes unqualifiedly subject to the demand or disposition of the distributee; or

(iii) The actual paying over or delivery of the property to the distributee.

(3) Property may be "sold, exchanged, or otherwise disposed of" by:

(i) The executor;

(ii) A trustee or other donee to whom the decedent during his lifetime transferred property included in his gross estate under sections 2035 through 2038, or section 2041;

(iii) An heir or devisee to whom title to property passes directly under local law;

(iv) A surviving joint tenant or tenant by the entirety; or

(v) Any other person.

If a binding contract for the sale, exchange, or other disposition of property is entered into, the property is considered as sold, exchanged, or otherwise disposed of on the effective date of the contract, unless the contract is not subsequently carried out substantially in accordance with its terms. The effective date of a contract is normally the date it is entered into (and not the date it is consummated, or the date legal title to the property passes) unless the contract specifies a different effective date.

(d) *"Included property" and "excluded property".*—If the executor elects the alternate valuation method under section 2032, all property interests existing at the date of decedent's death which form a part of his gross estate as determined under sections 2033 through 2044 are valued in accordance with the provisions of this section. Such property interests are referred to in this section as "included property". Furthermore, such property interests remain "included property" for the purpose of valuing the gross estate under the alternate valuation method even though they change in form during the alternate valuation period by being actually received, or disposed of, in whole or in part, by the estate. On the other hand, property earned or accrued

**58,574**

(whether received or not) after the date of the decedent's death and during the alternate valuation period with respect to any property interest existing at the date of the decedent's death, which does not represent a form of "included property" itself or the receipt of "included property" is excluded in valuing the gross estate under the alternate valuation method. Such property is referred to in this section as "excluded property". Illustrations of "included property" and "excluded property" are contained in the subparagraphs (1) to (4) of this paragraph:

(1) *Interest-bearing obligations.*—Interest-bearing obligations, such as bonds or notes, may comprise two elements of "included property" at the date of the decedent's death, namely, (i) the principal of the obligation itself, and (ii) interest accrued to the date of death. Each of these elements is to be separately valued as of the applicable valuation date. Interest accrued after the date of death and before the subsequent valuation date constitutes "excluded property". However, any part payment of principal made between the date of death and the subsequent valuation date, or any advance payment of interest for a period after the subsequent valuation date made during the alternate valuation period which has the effect of reducing the value of the principal obligation as of the subsequent valuation date, will be included in the gross estate, and valued as of the date of such payment.

(2) *Leased property.*—The principles set forth in subparagraph (1) of this paragraph with respect to interest-bearing obligations also apply to leased realty or personalty which is included in the gross estate and with respect to which an obligation to pay rent has been reserved. Both the realty or personalty itself and the rents accrued to the date of death constitute "included property", and each is to be separately valued as of the applicable valuation date. Any rent accrued after the date of death and before the subsequent valuation date is "excluded property". Similarly, the principle applicable with respect to interest paid in advance is equally applicable with respect to advance payments of rent.

(3) *Noninterest-bearing obligations.*—In the case of noninterest-bearing obligations sold at a discount, such as savings bonds, the principal obligation and the discount amortized to the date of death are property interests existing at the date of death and constitute "included property". The obligation itself is to be valued at the subsequent valuation date without regard to any further increase in value due to amortized discount. The additional discount amortized after death and during the alternate valuation period is the equivalent of interest accruing during that period and is, therefore, not to be included in the gross estate under the alternate valuation method.

(4) *Stock of a corporation.*—Shares of stock in a corporation and dividends declared to stockholders of record on or before the date of the decedent's death and not collected at the date of death constitute "included property" of the estate. On the other hand, ordinary dividends out of earnings and profits (whether in cash, shares of the corporation, or other property) declared to stockholders of record after the date of the decedent's death are "excluded property" and are not to be valued under the alternate valuation method. If, however, dividends are declared to stockholders of record after the date of the decedent's death with the effect that the shares of stock at the subsequent valuation date do not reasonably represent the same "included property" of the gross estate as existed at the date of the decedent's death, the dividends are "included property", except to the extent that they are out of earnings of the corporation after the date of the decedent's death. For example, if a corporation makes a distribution in partial liquidation to stockholders of record during the alternate valuation period which is not accompanied by a surrender of a stock certificate for cancellation, the amount of the distribution received on stock included in the gross estate is itself "included property", except to the extent that the distribution was out of earnings and profits since the date of the decedent's death. Similarly, if a corporation, in which the decedent owned a substantial interest and which possessed at the date of the decedent's death accumulated earnings and profits equal to its paid-in capital, distributed all of its accumulated earnings and profits as a cash dividend to shareholders of record during the alternate valuation period, the amount of the dividends received on stock includible in the gross estate will be included in the gross estate under the alternate valuation method. Likewise, a stock dividend distributed under such circumstances is "included property".

(e) *Illustrations of "included property" and "excluded property".*—The application of paragraph (d) of this section may be further illustrated by the following example in which it is assumed that the decedent died on January 1, 1955:

| Description | Subsequent valuation date | Alternate value | Value at date of death |
|---|---|---|---|
| Bond, par value $1,000, bearing interest at 4% payable quarterly on Feb. 1, May 1, Aug. 1, and Nov. 1. Bond distributed to legatee on Mar. 1, 1955 | Mar. 1, 1955 | $1,000.00 | $1,000.00 |
| Interest coupon of $10 attached to bond and not cashed at date of death although due and payable Nov. 1, 1954. Cashed by executor on Feb. 1, 1955 | Feb. 1, 1955 | 10.00 | 10.00 |
| Interest accrued from Nov. 1, 1954, to Jan. 1, 1955, collected on Feb. 1, 1955 | Feb. 1, 1955 | 6.67 | 6.67 |
| Real estate, not disposed of within year following death. Rent of $300 due at the end of each quarter, Feb. 1, May 1, Aug. 1, and Nov. 1 | Jan. 1, 1956 | 11,000.00 | 12,000.00 |
| Rent due for quarter ending Nov. 1, 1954, but not collected until Feb. 1, 1955 | Feb. 1, 1955 | 300.00 | 300.00 |
| Rent accrued for November and December 1954, collected on Feb. 1, 1955 | Feb. 1, 1955 | 200.00 | 200.00 |
| Common stock, X Corporation, 500 shares, not disposed of within year following decedent's death | Jan. 1, 1956 | 47,500.00 | 50,000.00 |
| Dividend of $2 per share declared Dec. 10, 1954, and paid on Jan. 10, 1955, to holders of record on Dec. 30, 1954 | Jan. 10, 1955 | $1,000.00 | $1,000.00 |

(f) *Mere lapse of time.*—In order to eliminate changes in value due only to mere lapse of time, section 2032(a)(3) provides that any interest or estate "affected by mere lapse of time" is included in a decedent's gross estate under the alternate valuation method at its value as of the date of the decedent's death, but with adjustment for any difference in its value as of the subsequent valuation date not due to mere lapse of time. Properties, interests, or estates which are "affected by mere lapse of time" include patents, estates for the life of a person other than the decedent, remainders, reversions, and other like properties, interests, or estates. The phrase "affected by mere lapse of time" has no reference to obligations for the payment of money, whether or not interest-bearing, the value of which changes with the passing of time. However, such an obligation, like any other property, may become affected by lapse of time when made the subject of a bequest or transfer which itself is creative of an interest or estate so affected. The application of this paragraph is illustrated in subparagraphs (1) and (2) of this paragraph:

(1) [Reserved]. For guidance, see § 20.2032-1T(f)(1).

(2) *Patents.*—To illustrate the alternate valuation of a patent, assume that the decedent owned a patent which, on the date of the decedent's death, had an unexpired term of ten years and a value of $78,000. Six months after the date of the decedent's death, the patent was sold, because of lapse of time and other causes, for $60,000. The alternate value thereof would be obtained by dividing $60,000 by 0.95 (ratio of the remaining life of the patent at the alternate date to the remaining life of the patent at the date of the decedent's death), and would, therefore, be $63,157.89.

(g) *Effect of election on deductions.*—If the executor elects the alternate valuation method under section 2032, any deduction for administration expenses under section 2053(b) (pertaining to property not subject to claims) or losses under section 2054 (or section 2106(a)(1), relating to estates of nonresidents not citizens) is allowed only to the extent that it is not otherwise in effect allowed in determining the value of the gross estate. Furthermore, the amount of any charitable deduction under section 2055 (or section 2106(a)(2), relating to the estates of nonresidents not citizens) or the amount of any marital deduction under section 2056 is determined by the value of the property with respect to which the deduction is allowed as of the date of the decedent's death, adjusted, however, for any difference in its value as of the date 6 months (1 year, if the decedent died on or before December 31, 1970) after death, or as of the date of its distribution, sale, exchange, or other disposition, whichever first occurs. However, no such adjustment may take into account any difference in value due to lapse of time or to the occurrence or nonoccurrence of a contingency.

(h) *Effective date.*—Paragraph (b) of this section is applicable to decedents dying on or after January 4, 2005. However, pursuant to section 7805(b)(7), taxpayers may elect to apply paragraph (b) of this section retroactively if the period of limitations for filing a claim for a credit or refund of Federal estate or generation-skipping transfer tax under section 6511 has not expired. [Reg. § 20.2032-1.]

☐ [T.D. 6296, 6-23-58. *Amended by T.D. 7238, 12-28-72, T.D. 7955,* 5-10-84; T.D. 8540, 6-9-94; T.D. 8819, 4-29-99; T.D. 9172, 1-3-2005 *and* T.D. 9448, 5-1-2009 *(corrected 6-5-2009).*]

### [Reg. § 20.2032-1T]

**§ 20.2032-1T. Alternate Valuation (temporary).**—(a) through (e) [Reserved]. For further guidance, see § 20.2032-1(a) through (e).

(f) [Reserved]. For further guidance, see § 20.2032-1(f).

(1) *Life estates, remainders, and similar interests.*—The values of life estates, remainders, and similar interests are to be obtained by applying the methods prescribed in § 20.2031-7, using (i) the age of each person, the duration of whose life may affect the value of the interest, as of the date of the decedent's death, and (ii) the value of the property as of the alternate valuation date. For example, assume that the decedent, or the decedent's estate, was entitled to receive certain property worth $50,000 upon the death of A, who was entitled to the income for life. At the time of the decedent's death, on or after May 1, 2009, A was 47 years and 5 months old. In the month in which the decedent died, the section 7520 rate was 6.2 percent. The value of the decedent's remainder interest at the date of the decedent's death would, as illustrated in *Example 1* of § 20.2031-7T(d)(5), be $9,336.00 ($50,000 × .18672). If, because of economic conditions, the property declined in value and was worth only $40,000 on the date that was 6 months after the date of the decedent's death, the value of the remainder interest would be $7,468.80 ($40,000 × .18672), even though A would be 48 years old on the alternate valuation date.

(f)(2) through (g) [Reserved]. For further guidance, see § 20.2032-1(f)(2) through (g).

(h) *Effective/applicability date.*—Paragraph (f)(1) applies on or after May 1, 2009.

(i) *Expiration date.*—Paragraph (f)(1) expires on or before May 1, 2012. [Temporary Reg. § 20.2032-1T.]

☐ [T.D. 9448, 5-1-2009.]

### [Reg. § 20.2032A-3]

**§ 20.2032A-3. Material participation requirements for valuation of certain farm and closely-held business real property.**—(a) *In general.*—Under section 2032A, an executor may, for estate tax purposes, make a special election concerning valuation of qualified real property (as defined in section 2032A(b)) used as a farm for farming purposes or in another trade or business. If this election is made, the property will be valued on the basis of its value for its qualified use in farming or the other trade or business, rather than its fair market value determined on the basis of highest and best use (irrespective of whether its highest and best use is the use in farming or other business). For the special valuation rules of section 2032A to apply, the deceased owner and/or a member of the owner's family (as defined in section 2032A(e)(2)) must materially participate in the operation of the farm or other business. Whether the required material participation occurs is a factual determination, and the types of activities and financial risks which will support such a finding will vary with the mode of ownership of both the property itself and of any business in which it is used. Passively collecting rents, salaries, draws, dividends, or other income from the farm or other business is not sufficient for material participation, nor is merely advancing capital and reviewing a crop plan or other business proposal and financial reports each season or business year.

(b) *Types of qualified property.*—(1) *In general.*—Real property valued under section 2032A must pass from the decedent to a qualified heir or be acquired from the decedent by a qualified heir. The real property may be owned directly or may be owned indirectly through ownership of an interest in a corporation, a partnership, or a trust. Where the ownership is indirect, however, the decedent's interest in the business must, in addition to meeting the tests for qualification under section 2032A, qualify under the tests of section 6166(b)(1) as

an interest in a closely-held business on the date of the decedent's death and for sufficient other time (combined with periods of direct ownership) to equal at least 5 years of the 8 year period preceding the death. All specially valued property must be used in a trade or business. Directly owned real property that is leased by a decedent to a separate closely held business is considered to be qualified real property, but only if the separate business qualifies as a closely held business under section 6166(b)(1) with respect to the decedent on the date of his or her death and for sufficient other time (combined with periods during which the property was operated as a proprietorship) to equal at least 5 years of the 8 year period preceding the death. For example, real property owned by the decedent and leased to a farming corporation or partnership owned and operated entirely by the decedent and fewer than 15 members of the decedent's family is eligible for special valuation. Under section 2032A, the term trade or business applies only to an active business such as a manufacturing, mercantile, or service enterprise, or to the raising of agricultural or horticultural commodities, as distinguished from passive investment activities. The mere passive rental of property to a party other than a member of the decedent's family will not qualify. The decedent or a member of the decedent's family must own an equity interest in the farm operation. A trade or business is not necessarily present even though an office and regular hours are maintained for management of income producing assets, as the term "business" is not as broad under section 2032A as under section 162. Additionally, no trade or business is present in the case of activities not engaged in for profit. *See* section 183.

(2) *Structures and other real property improvements.*—Qualified real property includes residential buildings and other structures and real property improvements occupied or used on a regular basis by the owner or lessee of real property (or by employees of the owner or lessee) for the purpose of operating the farm or other closely held business. A farm residence occupied by the decedent owner of the specially valued property is considered to be occupied for the purpose of operating the farm even though a family member (not the decedent) was the person materially participating in the operation of the farm as required under section 2032A(b)(1)(C).

(c) *Period material participation must last.*—The required participation must last—

(1) For periods totalling 5 years or more during the 8 years immediately preceding the date of the decedent's death; and

(2) For periods totalling 5 years or more during any 8 year period ending after the date of the decedent's death (up to a maximum of 15 years after decedent's death, when the additional estate tax provisions of section 2032A(c) cease to apply).

In determining whether the material participation requirement is satisfied, no exception is made for periods during which real property is held by the decedent's estate. Additionally, contemporaneous material participation by 2 or more family members during a period totalling a year will not result in that year being counted as 2 or more years for purposes of satisfying the requirements of this paragraph (c). Death of a qualified heir (as defined in section 2032A(e)(1)) before the requisite time has passed ends any material participation requirement for that heir's portion of the property as to the original decedent's estate if the heir received a separate, joint or other undivided property interest from the decedent. If qualified heirs receive successive interests in specially valued property (e.g., life estate and remainder interests) from the decedent, the material participation requirement does not end with respect to any part of the property until the death of the last qualified heir (or, if earlier, the expiration of 15 years from the date of the decedent's death). The requirements of section 2032A will fully apply to an heir's estate if an election under this section is made for the same property by the heir's executor. In general, to determine whether the required participation has occurred, brief periods (e. g., periods of 30 days or less) during which there was no material participation may be disregarded. This is so only if these periods were both preceded and followed by substantial periods (e. g., periods of more than 120 days) in which there was uninterrupted material participation. *See* paragraph (e)(1) of this section which provides a special rule for periods when little or no activity is necessary to manage fully a farm.

(d) *Period property must be owned by decedent and family members.*— Only real property which is actually owned by any combination of the decedent, members of the decedent's family, and qualified closely held businesses for periods totalling at least 5 of the 8 years preceding the date of decedent's death may be valued under section 2032A. For example, replacement property acquired in [a] like-kind exchange under section 1031 is considered to be owned only from the date on which the replacement property is actually acquired. On the other hand, replacement property acquired as a result of an involuntary conversion in a transfer that would meet the requirements of section 2032A(h) if it occurred after the date of the decedent's death is considered to have been owned from the date in which the involuntarily converted property was acquired. Property transferred from a proprietorship to a corporation or a partnership during the 8-year period ending on the date of the decedent's death is considered to be continuously owned to the extent of the decedent's equity interest in the corporation or partnership if, (1) the transfer meets the requirements of section 351 or 721, respectively, and (2) the decedent's interest in the corporation or partnership meets the requirements for indirectly held property contained in paragraph (b)(1) of this section. Likewise, property transferred to a trust is considered to be continuously owned if the beneficial ownership of the trust property is such that the requirements of section 6166(b)(1)(C) would be so satisfied if the property were owned by a corporation and all beneficiaries having vested interests in the trust were shareholders in the corporation. Any periods following the transfer during which the interest in the corporation, partnership, or trust does not meet the requirements of section 6166(b)(1) may not be counted for purposes of satisfying the ownership requirement of this paragraph (d).

(e) *Required activities.*—(1) *In general.*—Actual employment of the decedent (or of a member of the decedent's family) on a substantially full-time basis (35 hours a week or more) or to any lesser extent necessary personally to manage fully the farm or business in which the real property to be valued under section 2032A is used constitutes material participation. For example, many farming operations require only seasonal activity. Material participation is present as long as all necessary functions are performed even though little or no actual activity occurs during nonproducing seasons. In the absence of this direct involvement in the farm or other business, the activities of either the decedent or family members must meet the standards prescribed in this paragraph and those prescribed in the regulations issued under section 1402(a)(1). Therefore, if the participant (or participants) is self-employed with respect to the farm or other trade or business, his or her income from the farm or other business must be earned income for purposes of the tax on self-employment income before the participant is considered to be materially participating under section 2032A. Payment of the self-employment tax is not conclusive as to the presence of material participation. If no self-employment taxes have been paid, however, material participation is presumed not to have occurred unless the executor demonstrates to the satisfaction of the Internal Revenue Service that material participation did in fact occur and informs the Service of the reason no such tax was paid. In addition, all such taxes (including interest and penalties) determined to be due must be paid. In determining whether the material participation requirement is satisfied, the activities of each participant are viewed separately from the activities of all other participants, and at any given time, the activities of at least one participant must be material. If the involvement is less than full-time, it must be pursuant to an arrangement providing for actual participation in the production or management of production where the land is used by any nonfamily member, or any trust or business entity, in farming or another business. The arrangement may be oral or written, but must be formalized in some manner capable of proof. Activities not contemplated by the arrangement will not support a finding of material participation under section 2032A, and activities of any agent or employee other than a family member may not be considered in determining the presence of material participation. Activities of family members are considered only if the family relationship existed at the time the activities occurred.

(2) *Factors considered.*—No single factor is determinative of the presence of material participation, but physical work and participation in management decisions are the principal factors to be considered. As a minimum, the decedent and/or a family member must regularly advise or consult with the other managing party on the operation of the business. While they need not make all final management decisions alone, the decedent and/or family members must participate in making a substantial number of these decisions. Additionally, production activities on the land should be inspected regularly by the family participant, and funds should be advanced and financial responsibility assumed for a substantial portion of the expense involved in the operation of the farm or other business in which the real property is used. In the case of a farm, the furnishing by the owner or other family members of a substantial portion of the machinery, implements, and livestock used in the production activities is an important factor to consider in finding material participation. With farms, hotels, or apartment buildings, the operation of which qualifies as a trade or business, the participating decedent or heir's maintaining his or her principal place of residence on the premises is a factor to consider in determining whether the overall participation is material. Retention of a professional farm manager will not by itself prevent satisfaction of the material participation requirement by the decedent and family members. However, the decedent and/or a family member must personally materially participate under the terms of arrangement with the professional farm manager to satisfy this requirement.

(f) *Special rules for corporations, partnerships, and trusts.*—(1) *Required arrangement.*—With indirectly owned property as with property that is directly owned, there must be an arrangement calling for material participation in the business by the decedent owner or a family member. Where the real property is indirectly owned, however, even full-time involvement must be pursuant to an arrangement between the entity and the decedent or family member specifying the services to be performed. Holding an office in which certain material functions are inherent may constitute the necessary arrangement for material participation. Where property is owned by a trust, the arrangement will generally be found in one or more of four situations. First, the arrangement may result from appointment as a trustee. Second, the arrangement may result from an employer-employee relationship in which the participant is employed by a qualified closely held business owned by the trust in a position requiring his or her material participation in its activities. Third, the participants may enter into a contract with the trustees to manage, or take part in managing, the real property for the trust. Fourth, where the trust agreement expressly grants the management rights to the beneficial owner, that grant is sufficient to constitute the arrangement required under this section.

(2) *Required activities.*—The same participation standards apply under section 2032A where property is owned by a qualified closely held business as where the property is directly owned. In the case of a corporation, a partnership, or a trust where the participating decedent and/or family members are employees and thereby not subject to self-employment income taxes, they are to be viewed as if they were self-employed, and their activities must be activities that would subject them to self-employment income taxes were they so. Where property is owned by a corporation, a partnership or a trust, participation in the management and operation of the real property itself as a component of the closely held business is the determinative factor. Nominally holding positions as a corporate officer or director and receiving a salary therefrom or merely being listed as a partner and sharing in profits and losses will not alone support a finding of material participation. This is so even though, as partners, the participants pay self-employment income taxes on their distributive shares of partnership earnings under § 1.1402(a)-2. Further, it is especially true for corporate directors in states where the board of directors need not be an actively functioning entity or need only act informally. Corporate offices held by an owner are, however, factors to be considered with all other relevant facts in judging the degree of participation. When real property is directly owned and is leased to a corporation or partnership in which the decedent owns an interest which qualifies as an interest in a trade or business within the meaning of section 6166(b)(1), the presence of material participation is determined by looking at the activities of the participant with regard to the property in whatever capacity rendered. During any periods when qualified real property is held by an estate, material participation is to be determined in the same manner as if the property were owned by a trust.

(g) *Examples.*—The rules for determining material participation may be illustrated by the following examples. Additional illustrations may be found in examples (1) through (6) in § 1.1402(a)-4.

*Example (1).* A, the decedent, actively operated his 100-acre farm on a full-time basis for 20 years. He then leased it to B for the 10 years immediately preceding his death. By the terms of the lease, A was to consult with B on where crops were to be planted, to supervise marketing of the crop, and to share equally with B in expenses and earnings. A was present on the farm each spring for consultation; however, once planting was complete, he left for his retirement cottage where he remained until late summer, at which time he returned to the farm to supervise the marketing operations. A at all times maintained the farm home in which he had lived for the time he had owned the farm and lived there when at the farm. In light of his activities, assumption of risks, and valuable knowledge of proper techniques for the particular land gained over 20 years of full-time farming on the land involved, A is deemed to have materially participated in the farming business.

*Example (2).* D is the 70-year old widow of farmer C. She lives on a farm for which special valuation has been elected and has lived there for 20 years. D leases the land to E under an arrangement calling for her participation in the operation of the farm. D annually raises a vegetable garden, chickens, and hogs. She also inspects the tobacco fields (which produce approximately 50 percent of farm income) weekly and informs E if she finds any work that needs to be done. D and E share expenses and income equally. Other decisions such as what fields to plant and when to plant and harvest crops are left to E, but D does occasionally make suggestions. During the harvest season, D prepares and serves meals for all temporary farm help. D is deemed to participate materially in the farm operation based on her farm residence and her involvement with the main money crop.

*Example (3).* Assume that D in example (2) moved to a nursing home 1 year after her husband's death. E completely operated the farm for her for 6 years following her move. If E is not a member of D's family, material participation ceases when D moves; however, if E is a member of D's family, E's material participation will prevent disqualification even if D owns the property. Further, upon D's death, the section 2032A valuation could be elected for her estate if E were a member of her family and the other requirements of section 2032A were satisfied.

*Example (4).* F, a qualified heir, owned a specially valued farm. He contracted with G to manage the farm for him as F, a lawyer, lived and worked 15 miles away in a nearby town. F supplied all machinery and equipment and assumed financial responsibility for the expenses of the farm operation. The contract specified that G was to submit a crop plan and a list of expenses and earnings for F's approval. It also called for F to inspect the farm regularly and to approve all expenditures over $100. In practice, F visited the farm weekly during the growing season to inspect and discuss operations. He actively participated in making important management decisions such as what fields to plant or pasture and how to utilize the subsidy program. F is deemed to have materially participated in the farm operation as his personal involvement amounted to more than managing an investment. Had F not regularly inspected the farm and participated in management decisions, however, he would not be considered to be materially participating. This would be true even though F did assume financial responsibility for the operation and did review annual crop plans.

*Example (5).* Decedent I owned 90 percent of all outstanding stock of X Corporation, a qualified closely-held business which owns real property to be specially valued. I held no formal position in the corporation and there was no arrangement for him to participate in daily business operations. I regularly spent several hours each day at the corporate offices and made decisions on many routine matters. I is not deemed to have materially participated in the X Corporation despite his activity because there was no arrangement requiring him to act in the manner in which he did.

*Example (6).* Decedent J was a senior partner in the law firm of X, Y and Z, which is a qualified closely held business owning the building in which its offices are located. J ceased to practice law actively 5 years before his death in 1977; however, he remained a full partner and annually received a share of firm profits. J is not deemed to have materially participated under section 2032A even though he still may have reported his distributive share of partnership income for self-employment income tax purposes if the payments were not made pursuant to any retirement agreement. This is so because J does not meet the requirement of actual personal material participation.

*Example (7).* K, the decedent, owned a tree farm. He contracted with L, a professional forester, to manage the property for him as K, a doctor, lived and worked in a town 50 miles away. The activities of L are not considered in determining whether K materially participated in the tree farm operation. During the 5 years preceding K's death, there was no need for frequent inspections of the property or consultation concerning it, inasmuch as most of the land had been reforested and the trees were in the beginning stages of their growing cycle. However, once every year, L submitted for K's approval a proposed plan for the management of the property over the next year. K actively participated in making important management decisions, such as where and whether a pre-commercial thinning should be conducted, whether the timber was adequately protected from fire and disease, whether fire lines needed to be plowed around the new trees, and whether boundary lines were properly maintained around the property. K inspected the property at least twice every year and assumed financial responsibility for the expenses of the tree farm. K also reported his income from the tree farm as earned income for purposes of the tax on self-employment income. Over a period of several years, K had harvested and marketed timber from certain tracts of the tree farm and had supervised replanting of the areas where trees were removed. K's history of harvesting, marketing, and replanting of trees showed him to be in the business of tree farming rather than merely passively investing in timber land. If the history of K's tree farm did not show such an active business operation, however, the tree farm would not qualify for special use valuation. In light of all these facts, K is deemed to have materially participated in the farm as his personal involvement amounted to more than managing an investment.

*Example (8).* Decedent M died on January 1, 1978, owning a farm for which special use valuation under section 2032A has been elected. M owned the farm real property for 15 years before his death. During the 4 years preceding M's death (January 1, 1974 through December 31, 1977), the farm was rented to N, a non-family member, and neither M nor any member of his family materially participated in the farming operation. From January 1, 1970, until December 31, 1973, both M and his daughter, O, materially participated in the farming operation. The material participation requirement of section

2032A(b)(1)(C)(ii) is not satisfied because material participation did not occur for periods aggregating at least 5 different years of the 8 years preceding M's death. [Reg. § 20.2032A-3.]

☐ *[T.D. 7710, 7-28-80. Amended by T.D. 7786, 8-25-81.]*

## [Reg. § 20.2032A-4]

**§ 20.2032A-4. Method of valuing farm real property.**—(a) *In general.*—Unless the executor of the decedent's estate elects otherwise under section 2032A(e)(7)(B)(ii) or fails to document comparable rented farm property meeting the requirements of this section, the value of the property which is used for farming purposes and which is subject to an election under section 2032A is determined by—

(1) Subtracting the average annual state and local real estate taxes on actual tracts of comparable real property in the same locality from the average annual gross cash rental for that same comparable property, and

(2) Dividing the results so obtained by the average annual effective interest rate charged on new Federal land bank loans.

The computation of each average annual amount is to be based on the 5 most recent calendar years ending before the date of the decedent's death.

(b) *Gross cash rental.*—(1) *Generally.*—Gross cash rental is the total amount of cash received for the use of actual tracts of comparable farm real property in the same locality as the property being specially valued during the period of one calendar year. This amount is not diminished by the amount of any expenses or liabilities associated with the farm operation or the lease. *See,* paragraph (d) of this section for a definition of comparable property and rules for property on which buildings or other improvements are located and farms including multiple property types. Only rentals from tracts of comparable farm property which are rented solely for an amount of cash which is not contingent upon production are acceptable for use in valuing real property under section 2032A(e)(7). The rentals considered must result from an arm's-length transaction as defined in this section. Additionally, rentals received under leases which provide for payment solely in cash are not acceptable as accurate measures of cash rental value if involvement by the lessor (or a member of the lessor's family who is other than a lessee) in the management or operation of the farm to an extent which amounts to material participation under the rules of section 2032A is contemplated or actually occurs. In general, therefore, rentals for any property which qualifies for special use valuation cannot be used to compute gross cash rentals under this section because the total amount received by the lessor does not reflect the true cash rental value of the real property.

(2) *Special rules.*—(i) *Documentation required of executor.*—The executor must identify to the Internal Revenue Service actual comparable property for all specially valued property and cash rentals from that property if the decedent's real property is valued under section 2032A(e)(7). If the executor does not identify such property and cash rentals, all specially valued real property must be valued under the rules of section 2032A(e)(8) if special use valuation has been elected. *See,* however, § 20.2032A-8(d) for a special rule for estates electing section 2032A treatment on or before August 30, 1980.

(ii) *Arm's-length transaction required.*—Only those cash rentals which result from a lease entered into in an arm's-length transaction are acceptable under section 2032A(e)(7). For these purposes, lands leased from the Federal government, or any state or local government, which are leased for less than the amount that would be demanded by a private individual leasing for profit are not leased in an arm's-length transaction. Additionally, leases between family members (as defined in section 2032A(e)(2)) which do not provide a return on the property commensurate with that received under leases between unrelated parties in the locality are not acceptable under this section.

(iii) *In-kind rents, statements of appraised rental value, and area averages.*—Rents which are paid wholly or partly in kind (*e.g.,* crop shares) may not be used to determine the value of real property under section 2032A(e)(7). Likewise, appraisals or other statements regarding rental value as well as area-wide averages of rentals (*i.e.,* those compiled by the United States Department of Agriculture) may not be used under section 2032A(e)(7) because they are not true measures of the actual cash rental value of comparable property in the same locality as the specially valued property.

(iv) *Period for which comparable real property must have been rented solely for cash.*—Comparable real property rented solely for cash must be identified for each of the five calendar years preceding the year of the decedent's death if section 2032A(e)(7) is used to value the decedent's real property. Rentals from the same tract of comparable property need not be used for each of these 5 years, however, provided an actual tract of property meeting the requirements of this section is identified for each year.

(v) *Leases under which rental of personal property is included.*—No adjustment to the rents actually received by the lessor is made for the use of any farm equipment or other personal property the use of which is included under a lease for comparable real property unless the lease specifies the amount of the total rental attributable to the personal property and that amount is reasonable under the circumstances.

(c) *State and local real estate taxes.*—For purposes of the farm valuation formula under section 2032A(e)(7) state and local taxes are taxes which are assessed by a state or local government and which are allowable deductions under section 164. However, only those taxes on the comparable real property from which cash rentals are determined may be used in the formula valuation.

(d) *Comparable real property defined.*—Comparable real property must be situated in the same locality as the specially valued property. This requirement is not to be viewed in terms of mileage or political divisions alone, but rather is to be judged according to generally accepted real property valuation rules. The determination of properties which are comparable is a factual one and must be based on numerous factors, no one of which is determinative. It will, therefore, frequently be necessary to value farm property in segments where there are different uses or land characteristics included in the specially valued farm. For example, if section 2032A(e)(7) is used, rented property on which comparable buildings or improvements are located must be identified for specially valued property on which buildings or other real property improvements are located. In cases involving multiple areas or land characteristics, actual comparable property for each segment must be used, and the rentals and taxes from all such properties combined (using generally accepted real property valuation rules) for use in the valuation formula given in this section. However, any premium or discount resulting from the presence of multiple uses or other characteristics in one farm is also to be reflected. All factors generally considered in real estate valuation are to be considered in determining comparability under section 2032A. While not intended as an exclusive list, the following factors are among those to be considered in determining comparability—

(1) Similarity of soil as determined by any objective means, including an official soil survey reflected in a soil productivity index;

(2) Whether the crops grown are such as would deplete the soil in a similar manner;

(3) The types of soil conservation techniques that have been practiced on the two properties;

(4) Whether the two properties are subject to flooding;

(5) The slope of the land;

(6) In the case of livestock operations, the carrying capacity of the land;

(7) Where the land is timbered, whether the timber is comparable to that on the subject property;

(8) Whether the property as a whole is unified or whether it is segmented, and where segmented, the availability of the means necessary for movement among the different segments;

(9) The number, types, and conditions of all buildings and other fixed improvements located on the properties and their location as it affects efficient management and use of property and value per se; and

(10) Availability of, and type of, transportation facilities in terms of costs and of proximity of the properties to local markets.

(e) *Effective interest rate defined.*—(1) *Generally.*—The annual effective interest rate on new Federal land bank loans is the average billing rate charged on new agricultural loans to farmers and ranchers in the farm credit district in which the real property to be valued under section 2032A is located, adjusted as provided in paragraph (e)(2) of this section. This rate is to be a single rate for each district covering the period of one calendar year and is to be computed to the nearest one-hundredth of one percent. In the event that the district billing rates of interest on such new agricultural loans change during a year, the rate for that year is to be weighted to reflect the portion of the year during which each such rate was charged. If a district's billing rate on such new agricultural loans varies according to the amount of the loan, the rate applicable to a loan in an amount resulting from dividing the total dollar amount of such loans closed during the year by the total number of the loans closed is to be used under section 2032A. Applicable rates may be obtained from the district director of internal revenue.

(2) *Adjustment to billing rate of interest.*—The billing rate of interest determined under this paragraph is to be adjusted to reflect the increased cost of borrowing resulting from the required purchase of land bank association stock. For section 2032A purposes, the rate of required stock investment is the average of the percentages of the face amount of new agricultural loans to farmers and ranchers required to be invested in such stock by the applicable district bank

during the year. If this percentage changes during a year, the average is to be adjusted to reflect the period when each percentage requirement was effective. The percentage is viewed as a reduction in the loan proceeds actually received from the amount upon which interest is charged.

(3) *Example.*—The determination of the effective interest rate for any year may be illustrated as follows:

*Example.* District X of the Federal land bank system charged an 8 percent billed interest rate on new agricultural loans for 8 months of the year, 1976, and an 8.75 percent rate for 4 months of the year. The average billing rate was, therefore, 8.25 percent [(1.08 × $^{8}/_{12}$) + (1.0875 × $^{4}/_{12}$) = 1.0825]. The district required stock equal to 5 percent of the face amount of the loan to be purchased as a precondition to receiving a loan. Thus, the borrower only received 95 percent of the funds upon which he paid interest. The applicable annual interest rate for 1976 of 8.68 percent is computed as follows:

8.25 percent × 1.00 (total loan amount) = 8.25 percent (billed interest rate) divided by 0.95 (percent of loan proceeds received by borrower) = 8.68 percent (effective interest rate for 1976).

[Reg. § 20.2032A-4.]

☐ [*T.D.* 7710, 7-28-80.]

### [Reg. § 20.2032A-8]

**§ 20.2032A-8. Election and agreement to have certain property valued under section 2032A for estate tax purposes.**—(a) *Election of special use valuation.*—(1) *In general.*—An election under section 2032A is made as prescribed in paragraph (a)(3) of this section and on Form 706, United States Estate Tax Return. Once made, this election is irrevocable; however, see paragraph(d) of this section for a special rule for estates for which elections are made on or before August 30, 1980. Under section 2032A(a)(2), special use valuation may not reduce the value of the decedent's estate by more than $500,000. This election is available only if, at the time of death, the decedent was a citizen or resident of the United States.

(2) *Elections to specially value less than all qualified real property included in an estate.*—An election under section 2032A need not include all real property included in an estate which is eligible for special use valuation, but sufficient property to satisfy the threshold requirements of section 2032A(b)(1)(B) must be specially valued under the election. If joint or undivided interests (e.g. interests as joint tenants or tenants in common) in the same property are received from a decedent by qualified heirs, an election with respect to one heir's joint or undivided interest need not include any other heir's interest in the same property if the electing heir's interest plus other property to be specially valued satisfy the requirements of section 2032A(b)(1)(B). If successive interests (e.g. life estates and remainder interests) are created by a decedent in otherwise qualified property, an election under section 2032A is available only with respect to that property (or portion thereof) in which qualified heirs of the decedent receive all of the successive interests, and such an election must include the interests of all of those heirs. For example, if a surviving spouse receives a life estate in otherwise qualified property and the spouse's brother receives a remainder interest in fee, no part of the property may be valued pursuant to an election under section 2032A. Where successive interests in specially valued property are created, remainder interests are treated as being received by qualified heirs only if such remainder interests are not contingent upon surviving a nonfamily member or are not subject to divestment in favor of a nonfamily member.

(3) *Time and manner of making election.*—An election under this section is made by attaching to a timely filed estate tax return the agreement described in paragraph (c)(1) of this section and a notice of election which contains the following information:

(i) The decedent's name and taxpayer identification number as they appear on the estate tax return;

(ii) The relevant qualified use;

(iii) The items of real property shown on the estate tax return to be specially valued pursuant to the election (identified by schedule and item number);

(iv) The fair market value of the real property to be specially valued under section 2032A and its value based on its qualified use (both values determined without regard to the adjustments provided by section 2032A(b)(3)(B));

(v) The adjusted value (as defined in section 2032A(b)(3)(B)) of all real property which is used in a qualified use and which passes from the decedent to a qualified heir and the adjusted value of all real property to be specially valued;

(vi) The items of personal property shown on the estate tax return that pass from the decedent to a qualified heir and are used in a qualified use under section 2032A (identified by schedule and item number) and the total value of such personal property adjusted as provided under section 2032A(b)(3)(B);

(vii) The adjusted value of the gross estate, as defined in section 2032A(b)(3)(A);

(viii) The method used in determining the special value based on use;

(ix) Copies of written appraisals of the fair market value of the real property;

(x) A statement that the decedent and/or a member of his or her family has owned all specially valued real property for at least 5 years of the 8 years immediately preceding the date of the decedent's death;

(xi) Any periods during the 8-year period preceding the date of the decedent's death during which the decedent or a member of his or her family did not own the property, use it in a qualified use, or materially participate in the operation of the farm or other business within the meaning of section 2032A(e)(6);

(xii) The name, address, taxpayer identification number, and relationship to the decedent of each person taking an interest in each item of specially valued property, and the value of the property interests passing to each such person based on both fair market value and qualified use;

(xiii) Affidavits describing the activities constituting material participation and the identity of the material participant or participants; and

(xiv) A legal description of the specially valued property.

If neither an election nor a protective election is timely made, special use valuation is not available to the estate. *See* sections 2032A(d)(1), 6075(a), and 6081(a).

(b) *Protective election.*—A protective election may be made to specially value qualified real property. The availability of special use valuation pursuant to this election is contingent upon values as finally determined (or agreed to following examination of a return) meeting the requirements of section 2032A. A protective election does not, however, extend the time for payment of any amount of tax. Rules for such extensions are contained in sections 6161, 6163, 6166, and 6166A. The protective election is to be made by a notice of election filed with a timely estate tax return stating that a protective election under section 2032A is being made pending final determination of values. This notice is to include the following information:

(1) The decedent's name and taxpayer identification number as they appear on the estate tax return;

(2) The relevant qualified use; and

(3) The items of real and personal property shown on the estate tax return which are used in a qualified use, and which pass to qualified heirs (identified by schedule and item number).

If it is found that the estate qualifies for special use valuation based upon values as finally determined (or agreed to following examination of a return), an additional notice of election must be filed within 60 days after the date of such determination. This notice must set forth the information required under paragraph (a)(3) of this section and is to be attached, together with the agreement described in paragraph (c)(1) of this section, to an amended estate tax return. The new return is to be filed with the Internal Revenue Service office where the original return was filed.

(c) *Agreement to special valuation by persons with an interest in property.*—(1) *In general.*—The agreement required under section 2032A(a)(1)(B) and (d)(2) must be executed by all parties who have any interest in the property being valued based on its qualified use as of the date of the decedent's death. In the case of a qualified heir, the agreement must express consent to personal liability under section 2032A(c) in the event of certain early dispositions of the property or early cessation of the qualified use. See section 2032A(c)(6). In the case of parties (other than qualified heirs) with interests in the property, the agreement must express consent to collection of any additional estate tax imposed under section 2032A(c) from the qualified property. The agreement is to be in a form that is binding on all parties having an interest in the property. It must designate an agent with satisfactory evidence of authority to act for the parties to the agreement in all dealings with the Internal Revenue Service on matters arising under section 2032A and must indicate the address of that agent.

(2) *Persons having an interest in designated property.*—An interest in property is an interest which, as of the date of the decedent's death, can be asserted under applicable local law so as to affect the disposition of the specially valued property by the estate. Any person in being at the death of the decedent who has any such interest in the property, whether present or future, or vested or contingent, must enter into the agreement. Included among such persons are owners of remainder and executory interests, the holders of general or special powers of appointment, beneficiaries of a gift over in default of exercise of any such power, co-tenants, joint tenants and holders of other undivided interests when the decedent held only a joint or undivided interest in the property or when only an undivided inter-

est is specially valued, and trustees of trusts holding any interest in the property. An heir who has the power under local law to caveat (challenge) a will and thereby affect disposition of the property is not, however, considered to be a person with an interest in property under section 2032A solely by reason of that right. Likewise, creditors of an estate are not such persons solely by reason of their status as creditors.

(3) *Consent on behalf of interested party.*—If any person required to enter into the agreement provided for by paragraph (c)(1) either desires that an agent act for him or her or cannot legally bind himself or herself due to infancy or other incompetency, or to death before the election under section 2032A is timely exercised, a representative authorized under local law to bind such person in an agreement of this nature is permitted to sign the agreement on his or her behalf.

(4) *Duties of agent designated in agreement.*—The Internal Revenue Service will contact the agent designated in the agreement under paragraph (c)(1) on all matters relating to continued qualification under section 2032A of the specially valued real property and on all matters relating to the special lien arising under section 6324B. It is the duty of the agent as attorney-in-fact for the parties with interests in the specially valued property to furnish the Service with any requested information and to notify the Service of any disposition or cessation of qualified use of any part of the property.

(d) *Special rule for estates for which elections under section 2032A are made on or before August 30, 1980.*—An election to specially value real property under section 2032A that is made on or before August 30, 1980, may be revoked. To revoke an election, the executor must file a notice of revocation with the Internal Revenue Service office where the original estate tax return was filed on or before January 31, 1981 (or if earlier, the date on which the period of limitation for assessment expires). This notice of revocation must contain the decedent's name, date of death, and taxpayer identification number, and is to be accompanied by remittance of any additional amount of estate tax and interest determined to be due as a result of valuation of the qualified property based upon its fair market value. Elections that are made on or before August 30, 1980, that do not comply with this section as proposed on July 13, 1978 (43 FR 30070), and amended on December 21, 1978 (43 FR 59517), must be conformed to this final regulation by means of an amended return before the original estate tax return can be finally accepted by the Internal Revenue Service. [Reg. § 20.2032A-8.]

☐ [*T.D. 7710, 7-28-80. Amended by T.D. 7786, 8-25-81.*]

**[Reg. § 22.0]**

**§ 22.0. Certain elections under the Economic Recovery Tax Act of 1981.**—(a) *Election of special rules for woodlands.*

(1) *In general.*—This paragraph applies to the election of special rules for woodlands under section 2032A(e)(13) of the Code, as added by section 421(h) of the Economic Recovery Tax Act of 1981. The executor shall make this election for an estate by attaching to the estate tax return a statement that—

(i) Contains the decedent's name and taxpayer identification number as they appear on the estate tax return,

(ii) Identifies the election as an election under section 2032A(e)(13) of the Code,

(iii) Specifies the property with respect to which the election is made, and

(iv) Provides all information necessary to show that the executor is entitled to make the election.

(2) *Additional information required.*—If later regulations issued under section 2032A(e)(13) require the executor to furnish information in addition to that required under paragraph (a)(1) of this section and an office of the Internal Revenue Service requests the executor to furnish the additional information, the executor shall furnish the additional information in a statement filed with that office of the Internal Revenue Service within 60 days after the request is made. The statement shall also contain the information required by paragraph (a)(1)(i), (ii), and (iii) of this section. If the additional information is not provided within 60 days after the request is made, the election may, at the discretion of the Commissioner, be held invalid.

(b) *Election of special use valuation for qualified real property.*—This paragraph applies to the election of special use valuation for qualified real property under section 2032A(d)(1) of the Code, as amended by section 421(j)(3) of the Economic Recovery Tax Act of 1981. This election shall be made in the manner prescribed in § 20.2032A-8(a)(3), except that the election shall be valid even if the estate tax return is not timely filed.

(c) *Elections irrevocable.*—Elections to which this section applies may not be revoked.

(d) *Effective date.*—The elections described in this section are available with respect to the estate of decedents dying after 1981. [Temporary Reg. § 22.0.]

☐ [*T.D. 7793,* 10-29-81.]

**[Reg. § 20.2033-1]**

**§ 20.2033-1. Property in which the decedent had an interest.—**
(a) *In general.*—The gross estate of a decedent who was a citizen or resident of the United States at the time of his death includes under section 2033 the value of all property, whether real or personal, tangible or intangible, and wherever situated, beneficially owned by the decedent at the time of his death. (For certain exceptions in the case of real property situated outside the United States, see paragraphs (a) and (c) of § 20.2031-1.) Real property is included whether it came into the possession and control of the executor or administrator or passed directly to heirs or devisees. Various statutory provisions which exempt bonds, notes, bills, and certificates of indebtedness of the Federal Government or its agencies and the interest thereon from taxation are generally not applicable to the estate tax, since such tax is an excise tax on the transfer of property at death and is not a tax on the property transferred.

(b) *Miscellaneous examples.*—A cemetery lot owned by the decedent is part of his gross estate, but its value is limited to the salable value of that part of the lot which is not designed for the interment of the decedent and the members of his family. Property subject to homestead or other exemptions under local law is included in the gross estate. Notes or other claims held by the decedent are likewise included even though they are cancelled by the decedent's will. Interest and rents accrued at the date of the decedent's death constitute a part of the gross estate. Similarly, dividends which are payable to the decedent or his estate by reason of the fact that on or before the date of the decedent's death he was a stockholder of record (but which have not been collected at death) constitute a part of the gross estate. [Reg. § 20.2033-1.]

☐ [*T.D. 6296,* 6-23-58. *Amended by T.D. 6684,* 10-23-63.]

**[Reg. § 20.2034-1]**

**§ 20.2034-1. Dower or curtesy interests.—**A decedent's gross estate includes under section 2034 any interest in property of the decedent's surviving spouse existing at the time of the decedent's death as dower or curtesy, or any interest created by statute in lieu thereof (although such other interest may differ in character from dower or curtesy). Thus, the full value of property is included in the decedent's gross estate, without deduction of such an interest of the surviving husband or wife, and without regard to when the right to such an interest arose. [Reg. § 20.2034-1.]

☐ [*T.D. 6296,* 6-23-58.]

**[Reg. § 20.2036-1]**

**§ 20.2036-1. Transfers with retained life estate.—**(a) *In general.*—A decedent's gross estate includes under section 2036 the value of any interest in property transferred by the decedent after March 3, 1931, whether in trust or otherwise, except to the extent that the transfer was for an adequate and full consideration in money or money's worth (see § 20.2043-1), if the decedent retained or reserved—

(1) For his life;

(2) For any period not ascertainable without reference to his death (if the transfer was made after June 6, 1932); or

(3) For any period which does not in fact end before his death:

(i) The use, possession, right to income, or other enjoyment of the transferred property.

(ii) The right, either alone or in conjunction with any other person or persons, to designate the person or persons who shall possess or enjoy the transferred property or its income (except that, if the transfer was made before June 7, 1932, the right to designate must be retained by or reserved to the decedent alone).

(b) *Meaning of terms.*—(1) A reservation by the decedent "for any period not ascertainable without reference to his death" may be illustrated by the following examples:

(i) A decedent reserved the right to receive the income from transferred property in quarterly payments, with the proviso that no part of the income between the last quarterly payment and the date of the decedent's death was to be received by the decedent or his estate; and

(ii) A decedent reserved the right to receive the income, annuity, or other payment from transferred property after the death of another person who was in fact enjoying the income, annuity, or other payment at the time of the decedent's death. In such a case, the amount to be included in the decedent's gross estate under this section does not include the value of the outstanding interest of the

other person as determined in paragraphs (c)(1)(i) and (c)(2)(ii) of this section. See also, paragraphs (c)(1)(ii) *Example 1* and (c)(2)(iv) *Example 8* of this section. If the other person predeceased the decedent, the reservation by the decedent may be considered to be either for life, or for a period that does not in fact end before death.

(2) The "use, possession, right to the income, or other enjoyment of the transferred property" is considered as having been retained by or reserved to the decedent to the extent that the use, possession, right to the income, or other enjoyment is to be applied toward the discharge of a legal obligation of the decedent, or otherwise for his pecuniary benefit. The term "legal obligation" includes a legal obligation to support a dependent during the decedent's lifetime.

(3) The phrase "right . . . to designate the person or persons who shall possess or enjoy the transferred property or the income therefrom" includes a reserved power to designate the person or persons to receive the income from the transferred property, or to possess or enjoy nonincome-producing property, during the decedent's life or during any other period described in paragraph (a) of this section. With respect to such a power, it is immaterial (i) whether the power was exercisable alone or only in conjunction with another person or persons, whether or not having an adverse interest; (ii) in what capacity the power was exercisable by the decedent or by another person or persons in conjunction with the decedent; and (iii) whether the exercise of the power was subject to a contingency beyond the decedent's control which did not occur before his death (e.g., the death of another person during the decedent's lifetime). The phrase, however, does not include a power over the transferred property itself which does not affect the enjoyment of the income received or earned during the decedent's life. (See, however, section 2038 for the inclusion of property in the gross estate on account of such a power.) Nor does the phrase apply to a power held solely by a person other than the decedent. But, for example, if the decedent reserved the unrestricted power to remove or discharge a trustee at any time and appoint himself as trustee, the decedent is considered as having the powers of the trustee.

(c) *Retained or reserved interest.*—(1) *Amount included in gross estate.*—(i) *In general.*—If the decedent retained or reserved an interest or right with respect to all of the property transferred by him, the amount to be included in his gross estate under section 2036 is the value of the entire property, less only the value of any outstanding income interest which is not subject to the decedent's interest or right and which is actually being enjoyed by another person at the time of the decedent's death. If the decedent retained or reserved an interest or right with respect to a part only of the property transferred by him, the amount to be included in his gross estate under section 2036 is only a corresponding proportion of the amount described in the preceding sentence. An interest or right is treated as having been retained or reserved if at the time of the transfer there was an understanding, express or implied, that the interest or right would later be conferred. If this section applies to an interest retained by the decedent in a trust or otherwise and the terms of the trust or other governing instrument provide that, after the decedent's death, payments the decedent was receiving during life are to continue to be made to the decedent's estate for a specified period (as opposed to payments that were payable to the decedent prior to the decedent's death but were not actually paid until after the decedent's death), such payments that become payable after the decedent's death are not includible in the decedent's gross estate under section 2033 because they are properly reflected in the value of the trust corpus included under this section. Payments that become payable to the decedent prior to the decedent's date of death, but are not paid until after the decedent's date of death, are includible in the decedent's gross estate under section 2033.

(ii) *Examples.*—The application of paragraph (c)(1)(i) of this section is illustrated in the following examples:

*Example 1.* Decedent (D) creates an irrevocable inter vivos trust. The terms of the trust provide that all of the trust income is to be paid to D and D's child, C, in equal shares during their joint lives and, on the death of the first to die of D and C, all of the trust income is to be paid to the survivor. On the death of the survivor of D and C, the remainder is to be paid to another individual, F. Subsequently, D dies survived by C. Fifty percent of the value of the trust corpus is includible in D's gross estate under section 2036(a)(1) because, under the terms of the trust, D retained the right to receive one-half of the trust income for D's life. In addition, the excess (if any) of the value of the remaining 50 percent of the trust corpus, over the present value of C's outstanding life estate in that 50 percent of trust corpus, also is includible in D's gross estate under section 2036(a)(1), because D retained the right to receive all of the trust income for such time as D survived C. If C had predeceased D, then 100 percent of the trust corpus would have been includible in D's gross estate.

*Example 2.* D transferred D's personal residence to D's child (C), but retained the right to use the residence for a term of years. D dies during the term. At D's death, the fair market value of the personal residence is includible in D's gross estate under section 2036(a)(1) because D retained the right to use the residence for a period that did not in fact end before D's death.

(2) *Retained annuity, unitrust, and other income interests in trusts.*—(i) *In general.*—This paragraph (c)(2) applies to a grantor's retained use of an asset held in trust or a retained annuity, unitrust, or other interest in any trust (other than a trust constituting an employee benefit) including without limitation the following (collectively referred to in this paragraph (c)(2) as "trusts"): certain charitable remainder trusts (collectively CRTs) such as a charitable remainder annuity trust (CRAT) within the meaning of section 664(d)(1), a charitable remainder unitrust (CRUT) within the meaning of section 664(d)(2) or (d)(3), and any charitable remainder trust that does not qualify under section 664(d), whether because the CRT was created prior to 1969, there was a defect in the drafting of the CRT, there was no intention to qualify the CRT for the charitable deduction, or otherwise; other trusts established by a grantor (collectively GRTs) such as a grantor retained annuity trust (GRAT) paying out a qualified annuity interest within the meaning of § 25.2702-3(b) of this chapter, a grantor retained unitrust (GRUT) paying out a qualified unitrust interest within the meaning of § 25.2702-3(c) of this chapter; and various other forms of grantor retained income trusts (GRITs) whether or not the grantor's retained interest is a qualified interest as defined in section 2702(b), including without limitation a qualified personal residence trust (QPRT) within the meaning of § 25.2702-5(c) of this chapter and a personal residence trust (PRT) within the meaning of § 25.2702-5(b) of this chapter. If a decedent transferred property into such a trust and retained or reserved the right to use such property, or the right to an annuity, unitrust, or other interest in such trust with respect to the property decedent so transferred for decedent's life, any period not ascertainable without reference to the decedent's death, or for a period that does not in fact end before decedent's death, then the decedent's right to use the property or the retained annuity, unitrust, or other interest (whether payable from income and/or principal) constitutes the retention of the possession or enjoyment of, or the right to the income from, the property for purposes of section 2036. The portion of the trust's corpus includible in the decedent's gross estate for Federal estate tax purposes is that portion of the trust corpus necessary to provide the decedent's retained use or retained annuity, unitrust, or other payment (without reducing or invading principal). In the case of a retained annuity or unitrust, the portion of the trust's corpus includible in the decedent's gross estate is that portion of the trust corpus necessary to generate sufficient income to satisfy the retained annuity or unitrust (without reducing or invading principal), using the interest rates provided in section 7520 and the adjustment factors prescribed in § 20.2031-7 (or § 20.2031-7A), if applicable. The computation is illustrated in paragraph (c)(2)(iv), *Examples 1, 2,* and *3* of this section. The portion of the trust's corpus includible in the decedent's gross estate under section 2036, however, shall not exceed the fair market value of the trust's corpus at the decedent's date of death.

(ii) *Decedent's retained annuity following a current annuity interest of another person.*—If the decedent retained the right to receive an annuity or other payment (rather than income) after the death of the current recipient of that interest, then the amount includible in the decedent's gross estate under this section is the amount of trust corpus required to produce sufficient income to satisfy the entire annuity or other payment the decedent would have been entitled to receive if the decedent had survived the current recipient (thus, also

including the portion of that entire amount payable to the decedent before the current recipient's death), reduced by the present value of the current recipient's interest. However, the amount includible shall not be less than the amount of corpus required to produce sufficient income to satisfy the annuity or other payment the decedent was entitled, at the time of the decedent's death, to receive for each year. In addition, in no event shall the amount includible exceed the value of the trust corpus on the date of death. Finally, in calculating the present value of the current recipient's interest, the exhaustion of trust corpus test described in § 20.7520-3(b)(2) (exhaustion test) is not to be applied, even in cases where § 20.7520-3(b)(2) would otherwise require it to be applied. The following steps implement this computation.

(A) *Step 1:* Determine the fair market value of the trust corpus on the decedent's date of death.

(B) *Step 2:* Determine, in accordance with paragraph (c)(2)(i) of this section, the amount of corpus required to generate sufficient income to pay the annuity, unitrust, or other payment (determined on the date of the decedent's death) payable to the decedent for the trust year in which the decedent's death occurred.

(C) *Step 3:* Determine, in accordance with paragraph (c)(2)(i) of this section, the amount of corpus required to generate sufficient income to pay the annuity, unitrust, or other payment that the decedent would have been entitled to receive for each trust year if the decedent had survived the current recipient.

(D) *Step 4:* Determine the present value of the current recipient's annuity, unitrust, or other payment (without applying the exhaustion test).

(E) *Step 5:* Reduce the amount determined in Step 3 by the amount determined in Step 4, but not to below the amount determined in Step 2.

(F) *Step 6:* The amount includible in the decedent's gross estate under this section is the lesser of the amounts determined in Step 5 and Step 1.

(iii) *Graduated retained interests.*—(A) *In general.*—For purposes of this section, a *graduated retained interest* is the grantor's reservation of a right to receive an annuity, unitrust, or other payment as described in paragraph (c)(2)(i) of this section, payable at least annually, that increases (but does not decrease) over a period of time, not more often than annually.

(B) *Other definitions.*—(1) *Base amount.*—The *base amount* is the amount of corpus required to generate the annuity, unitrust, or other payment payable for the trust year in which the decedent's death occurs. See paragraph (c)(2)(i) of this section for the calculation of the base amount.

(2) *Periodic addition.*—The *periodic addition* in a graduated retained interest for each year after the year in which decedent's death occurs is the amount (if any) by which the annuity, unitrust, or other payment that would have been payable for that year if the decedent had survived exceeds the total amount of payments that would have been payable for the year immediately preceding that year. For example, assume the trust instrument provides that the grantor is to receive an annual annuity payable to the grantor or the grantor's estate for a 5-year term. The initial annual payment is $100,000, and each succeeding annual payment is to be 120 percent of the amount payable for the preceding year. Assuming the grantor dies in the second year of the trust (whether before or after the due date of the second annual payment), the periodic additions for years 3, 4, and 5 of the trust are as follows:

| | (1)<br>Annual<br>Payment | (2)<br>Prior Year<br>Payment | (1 - 2)<br>Periodic<br>Addition |
|---|---|---|---|
| Year 3 | 144,000 | 120,000 | 24,000 |
| Year 4 | 172,800 | 144,000 | 28,800 |
| Year 5 | 207,360 | 172,800 | 34,560 |

(3) *Corpus amount.*—For each trust year in which a periodic addition occurs (increase year), the *corpus amount* is the amount of trust corpus which, starting from the decedent's date of death, is necessary to generate an amount of income sufficient to pay the periodic addition, beginning in the increase year and continuing in perpetuity, without reducing or invading principal. For each year with a periodic addition, the corpus amount required as of the decedent's date of death is the product of two factors: the first is the result of dividing the periodic addition (adjusted for payments made more frequently than annually, if applicable, and for payments due

at the beginning, rather than the end, of a payment period (see Table K or J of § 20.2031-7(d)(6)) by the section 7520 rate (periodic addition / rate)); and the second is 1 divided by the sum of 1 and the section 7520 rate raised to the T power (1 / (1 + rate)^T). The second factor applies a present value discount to reflect the period beginning with the date of death and ending on the last day of the trust year immediately before the year for which the periodic addition is first payable.

(i) The corpus amount is determined as follows:

$$\frac{\text{(Periodic Addition)} \times \text{(Adjustment Factor)}}{\text{Section 7520 Rate}}$$

(ii) The adjustment factor, if applicable, is the factor for payments made more frequently than annually and for payments

$$\times \quad \frac{1}{(1 + \text{Section 7520 Rate})^T}$$

due at the beginning, rather than the end, of a calendar period (see Table K or J of § 20.2031-7(d)(6)). T equals the time period in years

**Reg. § 20.2036-1(c)(2)(iii)(B)(3)(ii)**

from the decedent's date of death through the last day of the trust year immediately before the year for which the periodic addition is first payable.

(C) *Amount includible.*—The amount includible in the gross estate in the case of a graduated retained interest is the sum of the base amount and the corpus amount for each year for which a periodic addition is first payable. The sum of these amounts represents the amount of trust principal that would be necessary to generate the annual payments that would have been paid to the decedent if the decedent had survived and had continued to receive the graduated retained interest. The amount of trust corpus includible in a decedent's gross estate under this section, however, shall not exceed the fair market value of the trust corpus on the decedent's date of death. The provisions of this section also apply to graduated retained interests in transferred property not held in trust.

(iv) *Examples.*—The application of paragraphs (c)(2)(i), (c)(2)(ii), and (c)(2)(iii) of this section is illustrated in the following examples:

*Example 1.* (i) Decedent (D) transferred $100,000 to an inter vivos trust that qualifies as a CRAT under section 664(d)(1). The trust agreement provides for an annuity of $7,500 to be paid each year to D for D's life, then to D's child (C) for C's life, with the remainder to be distributed upon the survivor's death to N, a charitable organization described in sections 170(c), 2055(a), and 2522(a). The annuity is payable to D or C, as the case may be, annually on each December 31st. D dies in September 2006, survived by C who was then age 40. On D's death, the value of the trust assets was $300,000 and the section 7520 interest rate was 6 percent. D's executor does not elect to use the alternate valuation date.

(ii) The amount of corpus with respect to which D retained the right to the income, and thus the amount includible in D's gross estate under section 2036, is that amount of corpus necessary to yield the annual annuity payment to D (without reducing or invading principal). In this case, the formula for determining the amount of corpus necessary to yield the annual annuity payment to D is: annual annuity / section 7520 interest rate = amount includible under section 2036. The amount of corpus necessary to yield the annual annuity is $7,500 / .06 = $125,000. Therefore, $125,000 is includible in D's gross estate under section 2036(a)(1). (The result would be the same if D had retained an interest in the CRAT for a term of years and had died during the term. The result also would be the same if D had irrevocably relinquished D's annuity interest less than 3 years prior to D's death because of the application of section 2035.) If, instead, the trust agreement had provided that D could revoke C's annuity interest or change the identity of the charitable remainderman, see section 2038 with regard to the portion of the trust to be included in the gross estate on account of such a retained power to revoke. Under the facts presented, section 2039 does not apply to include any amount in D's gross estate by reason of this retained annuity. See § 20.2039-1(e).

*Example 2.* (i) D transferred $100,000 to a GRAT in which D's annuity is a qualified interest described in section 2702(b). The trust agreement provides for an annuity of $12,000 per year to be paid to D for a term of ten years or until D's earlier death. The annuity amount is payable in twelve equal installments at the end of each month. At the expiration of the term of years or on D's earlier death, the remainder is to be distributed to D's child (C). D dies prior to the expiration of the ten-year term. On the date of D's death, the value of the trust assets is $300,000 and the section 7520 interest rate is 6 percent. D's executor does not elect to use the alternate valuation date.

(ii) The amount of corpus with respect to which D retained the right to the income, and thus the amount includible in D's gross estate under section 2036, is that amount of corpus necessary to yield the annual annuity payment to D (without reducing or invading principal). In this case, the formula for determining the amount of corpus necessary to yield the annual annuity payment to D is: annual annuity (adjusted for monthly payments) / section 7520 interest rate = amount includible under section 2036. The Table K adjustment factor for monthly annuity payments in this case is 1.0272. Thus, the amount of corpus necessary to yield the annual annuity is ($12,000 × 1.0272) / .06 = $205,440. Therefore, $205,440 is includible in D's gross estate under section 2036(a)(1). If, instead, the trust agreement had provided that the annuity was to be paid to D during D's life and to D's estate for the balance of the 10-year term if D died during that term, then the portion of trust corpus includible in D's gross estate would still be as calculated in this paragraph. It is not material whether payments are made to D's estate after D's death. Under the facts presented, section 2039 does not apply to include any amount in D's gross estate by reason of this retained annuity. See § 20.2039-1(e).

*Example 3.* (i) In 2000, D created a CRUT within the meaning of section 664(d)(2). The trust instrument directs the trustee to hold, invest, and reinvest the corpus of the trust and to pay to D for D's

life, and then to D's child (C) for C's life, in equal quarterly installments payable at the end of each calendar quarter, an amount equal to 6 percent of the fair market value of the trust as valued on December 15 of the prior taxable year of the trust. At the termination of the trust, the then-remaining corpus, together with any and all accrued income, is to be distributed to N, a charitable organization described in sections 170(c), 2055(a), and 2522(a). D dies in 2006, survived by C, who was then age 55. The value of the trust assets on D's death was $300,000. D's executor does not elect to use the alternate valuation date and, as a result, D's executor does not choose to use the section 7520 interest rate for either of the two months prior to D's death.

(ii) The amount of the corpus with respect to which D retained the right to the income, and thus the amount includible in D's gross estate under section 2036(a)(1), is that amount of corpus necessary to yield the unitrust payments. In this case, such amount of corpus is determined by dividing the trust's equivalent income interest rate by the section 7520 rate (which was 6 percent at the time of D's death). The equivalent income interest rate is determined by dividing the trust's adjusted payout rate by the excess of 1 over the adjusted payout rate. Based on § 1.664-4(e)(3) of this chapter, the appropriate adjusted payout rate for the trust at D's death is 5.786 percent (6 percent × .964365). Thus, the equivalent income interest rate is 6.141 percent (5.786 percent / (1 - 5.786 percent)). The ratio of the equivalent interest rate to the assumed interest rate under section 7520 is 102.35 percent (6.141 percent / 6 percent). Because this exceeds 100 percent, D's retained payout interest exceeds a full income interest in the trust, and D effectively retained the income from all the assets transferred to the trust. Accordingly, because D retained for life an interest at least equal to the right to all income from all the property transferred by D to the CRUT, the entire value of the corpus of the CRUT is includible in D's gross estate under section 2036(a)(1). (The result would be the same if D had retained, instead, an interest in the CRUT for a term of years and had died during the term.) Under the facts presented, section 2039 does not apply to include any amount in D's gross estate by reason of D's retained unitrust interest. See § 20.2039-1(e).

(iii) If, instead, D had retained the right to a unitrust amount having an adjusted payout for which the corresponding equivalent interest rate would have been less than the 6 percent assumed interest rate of section 7520, then a correspondingly reduced proportion of the trust corpus would be includible in D's gross estate under section 2036(a)(1). Alternatively, if the interest retained by D was instead only one-half of the 6 percent unitrust interest, then the amount included in D's estate would be the amount needed to produce a 3 percent unitrust interest. All of the results in this *Example* 3 would be the same if the trust had been a GRUT instead of a CRUT.

*Example 4.* During life, D established a 15-year GRIT for the benefit of individuals who are not members of D's family within the meaning of section 2704(c)(2). D retained the right to receive all of the net income from the GRIT, payable annually, during the GRIT's term. D dies during the GRIT's term. D's executor does not elect to use the alternate valuation date. In this case, the GRIT's corpus is includible in D's gross estate under section 2036(a)(1) because D retained the right to receive all of the income from the GRIT for a period that did not in fact end before D's death. If, instead, D had retained the right to receive 60 percent of the GRIT's net income, then 60 percent of the GRIT's corpus would have been includible in D's gross estate under section 2036. Under the facts presented, section 2039 does not apply to include any amount in D's gross estate by reason of D's retained interest. See § 20.2039-1(e).

*Example 5.* In 2003, D transferred $10X to a pooled income fund that conforms to Rev. Proc. 88-53,1988-2 CB 712 (1988) in exchange for 1 unit in the fund. D is to receive all of the income from that 1 unit during D's life. Upon D's death, D's child (C), is to receive D's income interest for C's life. In 2008, D dies. D's executor does not elect to use the alternate valuation date. In this case, the fair market value of D's 1 unit in the pooled income fund is includible in D's gross estate under section 2036(a)(1) because D retained the right to receive all of the income from that unit for a period that did not in fact end before D's death. See § 601.601(d)(2)(ii)(b) of this chapter.

*Example 6.* D transferred D's personal residence to a trust that met the requirements of a qualified personal residence trust (QPRT) as set forth in § 25.2702- 5(c) of this chapter. Pursuant to the terms of the QPRT, D retained the right to use the residence for 10 years or until D's prior death. D dies before the end of the term. D's executor does not elect to use the alternate valuation date. In this case, the fair market value of the QPRT's assets on the date of D's death are includible in D's gross estate under section 2036(a)(1) because D retained the right to use the residence for a period that did not in fact end before D's death.

*Example 7.* (i) On November 1, year N, D transfers assets valued at $2,000,000 to a GRAT. Under the terms of the GRAT, the trustee is to pay to D an annuity for a 5-year term that is a qualified interest described in section 2702(b). The annuity amount is to be paid annually at the end of each trust year, on October 31st. The first annual payment is to be $100,000. Each succeeding payment is to be 120 percent of the amount paid in the preceding year. Income not distributed in any year is to be added to principal. If D dies during the 5-year term, the payments are to be made to D's estate for the balance of the GRAT term. At the end of the 5-year term, the trust is to terminate and the corpus is to be distributed to C, D's child. D dies on January 31st of the third year of the GRAT term. On the date of D's death, the value of the trust corpus is $3,200,000, the section 7520 interest rate is 6.8 percent, and the adjustment factor from Table K of §20.2031-7 is 1.0000. D's executor does not elect to value the gross estate as of the alternate valuation date pursuant to section 2032.

(ii) The amount includible in D's gross estate under section 2036(a)(1) as described in paragraph (c)(2)(iii)(C) of this section is determined and illustrated as follows:

| A | B | C | D | E | F | G |
|---|---|---|---|---|---|---|
| GRAT Year | Annual Annuity Payment | Periodic Addition | Required Principal: C × Adj. Factor / 0.068 | Deferral Period: Death to GRAT Year | Present Value Factor: 1/(1+.068) E | Corpus or Base Amount At Death: D × F |
| 3 | 144,000 | n/a | 2,117,647 | n/a | n/a | 2,117,647 |
| 4 | 172,800 | 28,800 | 423,529 | 0.747945 | 0.951985 | 403,193 |
| 5 | 207,360 | 34,560 | 508,235 | 1.747945 | 0.891372 | 453,026 |
| | | | | | Total: | 2,973,866 |

(iii) Specifically:

(A) *Column A.* First, determine the year of the trust term during which the decedent's death occurs, and the number of subsequent years remaining in the trust term for which the decedent retained or reserved an interest. In this example, D dies during year 3, with two additional years remaining in the term.

(B) *Column B.* Under the formula specified in the trust, the annuity payment to be made on October 31st of the 3rd year of the trust term is $144,000. Using that same formula, determine the annuity amounts for years 4 and 5.

(C) *Column C.* Determine the periodic addition for year 4 and year 5 by subtracting the annuity amount for the preceding year from the annuity amount for that year; the periodic addition for that year is the amount of the increase in the annuity amount for that year.

(D) *Columns D through G for year 3.* For the year of the decedent's death (year 3), determine the principal required to produce the annuity amount (Column D) by multiplying the annuity amount (Column B) by the adjustment factor (in this case 1.0000) and by dividing the product by the applicable interest rate under section 7520. Because this is the year of decedent's death and reflects the annuity amount payable to the decedent in that year, there is no

deferral, so this is also the Base Amount (the amount of corpus required to produce the annuity for year 3) (Column G).

(E) *Columns D through G for years 4 and 5.* For each succeeding year of the trust term during which the periodic addition will not be payable until a year subsequent to the year of the decedent's death, determine the principal required to produce the periodic addition payable for that year (Column D) by multiplying the periodic addition (Column C) by the adjustment factor and by dividing the product by the applicable interest rate under section 7520. Compute the factors to reflect the length of the deferral period (Column E) and the present value (Column F) as described in paragraph (c)(2)(iii)(B)(3) of this section. Multiply the amount of corpus in Column D by the factors in Columns E and F to determine the Corpus Amount for that year (Column G).

(F) *Column G total.* The sum of the amounts in Column G represents the total amount includable in the gross estate (but not in excess of the fair market value of the trust on the decedent's date of death).

(iv) An illustration of the amount of trust corpus (as of the decedent's death) necessary to produce the scheduled payments is as follows:

| | Year 3 | Year 4 | Year 5 | Corpus Amount |
|---|---|---|---|---|
| 2nd Periodic Addition | $34,560 | Deferral Period | $453,026 | $453,026 |
| 1st Periodic Addition | $28,800 | Deferral Period | $403,193 | $403,193 |
| Annuity in year of death | $144,000 | $2,117,647 | | $2,117,647 |
| | | | | $2,973,866 |

Total amount (sum) included in gross estate

(v) A total corpus amount (as defined in paragraph (c)(2)(iii)(B)(3) of this section) of $2,973,866 constitutes the principal required as of decedent's date of death to produce (without reducing or invading principal) the annual payments that D would have received if D had survived and had continued to receive the retained annuity. Therefore, $2,973,866 of the trust corpus is includible in D's gross estate under section 2036(a)(1). The remaining $226,134 of the trust corpus is not includible in D's gross estate under section 2036(a)(1). The result would be the same if D's retained annuity instead had been payable to D for a term of 5 years, or until D's prior death, at which time the GRAT would have terminated and the trust corpus would have become payable to another.

(vi) If, instead, D's annuity was to have been paid on a monthly or quarterly basis, then the periodic addition would have to be adjusted as provided in paragraph (c)(2)(iii)(B)(3) of this section. Specifically, in Column D of the Table for years 4 and 5 in this example, the amount of the principal required would be computed by multiplying the periodic addition by the appropriate factor from Table K or J of §20.2031-7(d)(6) before dividing as indicated and

computing the amounts in Columns E through G. In addition, Column D in year 3 also would have to be so adjusted. Under the facts presented, section 2039 does not apply to include any amount in D's gross estate by reason of this retained interest. See §20.2039-1(e).

*Example 8.* (i) D creates an irrevocable inter vivos trust. The terms of the trust provide that an annuity of $10,000 per year is to be paid to D and C, D's child, in equal shares during their joint lives. On the death of the first to die of D and C, the entire $10,000 annuity is to be paid to the survivor for life. On the death of the survivor of D and C, the remainder is to be paid to another individual, F. Subsequently, D dies survived by C. On D's date of death, the fair market value of the trust is $120,000 and the section 7520 rate is 7 percent. At the date of D's death, the amount of trust corpus needed to produce D's annuity interest ($5,000 per year) is $71,429 ($5,000/0.07). In addition, assume the present value of C's right to receive $5,000 annually for the remainder of C's life is $40,000. The portion of the trust corpus includible in D's gross estate under section 2036(a)(1) is $102,857, determined as follows:

(ii) *Step 1:* Fair market value of corpus. — $120,000

(iii) *Step 2:* Corpus required to produce D's date of death annuity ($5,000/0.07). — $71,429

(iv) *Step 3:* Corpus required to produce D's annuity if D had survived C ($10,000/0.07). — $142,857

(v) *Step 4:* Present value of C's interest. — $40,000

(vi) *Step 5:* The amount determined in Step 3, reduced by the amount determined in Step 4, but not to below the amount determined in Step 2 ($142,857 - $40,000, but not less than $71,429). — $102,857

(vii) *Step 6:* The lesser of the amounts determined in Steps 5 and 1 ($102,857 or $120,000). — $102,857.

(3) *Effective/applicability dates.*—Paragraphs (a) and (c)(1)(i) of this section are applicable to the estates of decedents dying after August 16, 1954. Paragraphs (c)(1)(ii) and (c)(2) of this section apply to the estates of decedents dying on or after July 14, 2008. All but the last two sentences at the end of paragraph (c)(1)(i) of this section are applicable to the estates of decedents dying after August 16, 1954.

The first, second, and sixth sentences in paragraph (c)(2)(i) of this section and all but the introductory text, *Example 7*, and *Example 8* of paragraph (c)(2)(iv) of this section are applicable to the estates of decedent's dying on or after July 14, 2008. Paragraph (b)(1)(ii) of this section, the last two sentences at the end of paragraph (c)(1)(i) of this section, *Example 1* of paragraph (c)(1)(ii) of this section, the third, fourth, and fifth sentences in paragraph (c)(2)(i) of this section; paragraph (c)(2)(ii) of this section; paragraph (c)(2)(iii) of this section; and the introductory text, *Example 7*, and *Example 8* of paragraph (c)(2)(iv) of this section are applicable to the estates of decedents dying on or after November 8, 2011. [Reg. § 20.2036-1.]

☐ [*T.D. 6296, 6-23-58. Amended by T.D. 6501, 11-15-60; T.D. 9414, 7-11-2008 (corrected 7-30-2008) and T.D. 9555, 11-7-2011.*]

### [Reg. § 20.2037-1]

§ 20.2037-1. **Transfers taking effect at death.**—(a) *In general.*—A decedent's gross estate includes under section 2037 the value of any interest in property transferred by the decedent after September 7, 1916, whether in trust or otherwise, except to the extent that the transfer was for an adequate and full consideration in money or money's worth (see § 20.2043-1), if—

(1) Possession or enjoyment of the property could, through ownership of the interest, have been obtained only by surviving the decedent,

(2) The decedent had retained a possibility (hereinafter referred to as a "reversionary interest") that the property, other than the income alone, would return to the decedent or his estate or would be subject to a power of disposition by him, and

(3) The value of the reversionary interest immediately before the decedent's death exceeded 5 percent of the value of the entire property.

However, if the transfer was made before October 8, 1949, section 2037 is applicable only if the reversionary interest arose by the express terms of the instrument of transfer and not by operation of law (see paragraph (f) of this section). See also paragraph (g) of this section with respect to transfers made between November 11, 1935, and January 29, 1940. The provisions of section 2037 do not apply to transfers made before September 8, 1916.

(b) *Condition of survivorship.*—As indicated in paragraph (a) of this section, the value of an interest in transferred property is not included in a decedent's gross estate under section 2037 unless possession or enjoyment of the property could, through ownership of such interest, have been obtained only by surviving the decedent. Thus, property is not included in the decedent's gross estate if, immediately before the decedent's death, possession or enjoyment of the property could have been obtained by any beneficiary either by surviving the decedent or through the occurrence of some other event such as the expiration of a term of years. However, if a consideration of the terms and circumstances of the transfer as a whole indicates that the "other event" is unreal and if the death of the decedent does, in fact, occur before the "other event," the beneficiary will be considered able to possess or enjoy the property only by surviving the decedent. Notwithstanding the foregoing, an interest in transferred property is not includible in a decedent's gross estate under section 2037 if possession or enjoyment of the property could have been obtained by any beneficiary during the decedent's life through the exercise of a general power of appointment (as defined in section 2041) which in fact was exercisable immediately before the decedent's death. See examples (5) and (6) in paragraph (e) of this section.

(c) *Retention of reversionary interest.*—(1) As indicated in paragraph (a) of this section, the value of an interest in transferred property is not included in a decedent's gross estate under section 2037 unless the decedent had retained a reversionary interest in the property, and the value of the reversionary interest immediately before the death of the decedent exceeded 5 percent of the value of the property.

(2) For purposes of section 2037, the term "reversionary interest" includes a possibility that property transferred by the decedent may return to him or his estate and a possibility that property transferred by the decedent may become subject to a power of disposition by him. The term is not used in a technical sense, but has reference to any reserved right under which the transferred property shall or may be returned to the grantor. Thus, it encompasses an interest arising either by the express terms of the instrument of transfer or by operation of law. (See, however, paragraph (f) of this section with respect to transfers made before October 8, 1949.) The term "reversionary interest" does not include rights to income only, such as the right to receive the income from a trust after the death of another person. (However, see section 2036 for the inclusion of property in the gross estate on account of such rights.) Nor does the term "reversionary interest" include the possibility that the decedent during his lifetime might have received back an interest in transferred property by inheritance through the estate of another person. Similarly, a statutory right of a spouse to receive a portion of whatever estate a decedent may leave at the time of his death is not a "reversionary interest".

(3) For purposes of this section, the value of the decedent's reversionary interest is computed as of the moment immediately before his death, without regard to whether or not the executor elects the alternate valuation method under section 2032 and without regard to the fact of the decedent's death. The value is ascertained in accordance with recognized valuation principles for determining the value for estate tax purposes of future or conditional interests in property. (See §§ 20.2031-1, 20.2031-7, and 20.2031-9.) For example, if the decedent's reversionary interest was subject to an outstanding life estate in his wife, his interest is valued according to the actuarial rules set forth in § 20.2031-7. On the other hand, if the decedent's reversionary interest was contingent on the death of his wife without issue surviving and if it cannot be shown that his wife is incapable of having issue (so that his interest is not subject to valuation according to the actuarial rules in § 20.2031-7), his interest is valued according to the general rules set forth in § 20.2031-1. A possibility that the decedent may be able to dispose of property under certain conditions is considered to have the same value as a right of the decedent to the return of the property under those same conditions.

(4) In order to determine whether or not the decedent retained a reversionary interest in transferred property of a value in excess of 5 percent, the value of the reversionary interest is compared with the value of the transferred property, including interests therein which are not dependent upon survivorship of the decedent. For example, assume that the decedent, A, transferred property in trust with the income payable to B for life and with the remainder payable to C if A predeceases B, but with the property to revert to A if B predeceases A. Assume further that A does, in fact, predecease B. The value of A's reversionary interest immediately before his death is compared with the value of the trust corpus, without deduction of the value of B's outstanding life estate. If, in the above example, A had retained a reversionary interest in one-half only of the trust corpus, the value of his reversionary interest would be compared with the value of one-half of the trust corpus, again without deduction of any part of the value of B's outstanding life estate.

(d) *Transfers partly taking effect at death.*—If separate interests in property are transferred to one or more beneficiaries, paragraphs (a) through (c) of this section are to be separately applied with respect to each interest. For example, assume that the decedent transferred an interest in Blackacre to A which could be possessed or enjoyed only by surviving the decedent, and that the decedent transferred an interest in Blackacre to B which could be possessed or enjoyed only on the occurrence of some event unrelated to the decedent's death. Assume further that the decedent retained a reversionary interest in Blackacre of a value in excess of 5 percent. Only the value of the interest transferred to A is includible in the decedent's gross estate. Similar results would obtain if possession or enjoyment of the entire property could have been obtained only by surviving the decedent, but the decedent had retained a reversionary interest in a part only of such property.

(e) *Examples.*—The provisions of paragraphs (a) through (d) of this section may be further illustrated by the following examples. It is assumed that the transfers were made on or after October 8, 1949; for the significance of this date, see paragraphs (f) and (g) of this section:

*Example (1).* The decedent transferred property in trust with the income payable to his wife for life and, at her death, remainder to the decedent's then surviving children, or if none, to the decedent or his estate. Since each beneficiary can possess or enjoy the property without surviving the decedent, no part of the property is includible in the decedent's gross estate under section 2037, regardless of the value of the decedent's reversionary interest. (However, see section 2033 for inclusion of the value of the reversionary interest in the decedent's gross estate.)

*Example (2).* The decedent transferred property in trust with the income to be accumulated for the decedent's life, and at his death, principal and accumulated income to be paid to the decedent's then surviving issue, or, if none, to A or A's estate. Since the decedent retained no reversionary interest in the property, no part of the property is includible in the decedent's gross estate, even though possession or enjoyment of the property could be obtained by the issue only by surviving the decedent.

*Example (3).* The decedent transferred property in trust with the income payable to his wife for life and with the remainder payable to the decedent or, if he is not living at his wife's death, to his daughter or her estate. The daughter cannot obtain possession or enjoyment of the property without surviving the decedent. Therefore, if the decedent's reversionary interest immediately before his death exceeded 5 percent of the value of the property, the value of the property, less the value of the wife's outstanding life estate, is includible in the decedent's gross estate.

*Example (4).* The decedent transferred property in trust with the income payable to his wife for life and with the remainder payable to his son or, if the son is not living at the wife's death, to the decedent or, if the decedent is not then living, to X or X's estate. Assume that the decedent was survived by his wife, his son, and X. Only X cannot obtain possession or enjoyment of the property without surviving the decedent. Therefore, if the decedent's reversionary interest immediately before his death exceeded 5 percent of the value of the property, the value of X's remainder interest (with reference to the time immediately after the decedent's death) is includible in the decedent's gross estate.

*Example (5).* The decedent transferred property in trust with the income to be accumulated for a period of 20 years or until the decedent's prior death, at which time the principal and accumulated income was to be paid to the decedent's son if then surviving. Assume that the decedent does, in fact, die before the expiration of the 20-year period. If, at the time of the transfer, the decedent was 30 years of age, in good health, etc., the son will be considered able to possess or enjoy the property without surviving the decedent. If, on the other hand, the decedent was 70 years of age at the time of the transfer, the son will not be considered able to possess or enjoy the property without surviving the decedent. In this latter case, if the value of the decedent's reversionary interest (arising by operation of law) immediately before his death exceeded 5 percent of the value of the property, the value of the property is includible in the decedent's gross estate.

*Example (6).* The decedent transferred property in trust with the income to be accumulated for his life and, at his death, the principal and accumulated income to be paid to the decedent's then surviving children. The decedent's wife was given the unrestricted power to alter, amend, or revoke the trust. Assume that the wife survived the decedent but did not, in fact, exercise her power during the decedent's lifetime. Since possession or enjoyment of the property could have been obtained by the wife during the decedent's lifetime under the exercise of a general power of appointment, which was, in fact, exercisable immediately before the decedent's death, no part of the property is includible in the decedent's gross estate.

(f) *Transfers made before October 8, 1949.*—(1) Notwithstanding any provisions to the contrary contained in paragraphs (a) to (e) of this section, the value of an interest in property transferred by a decedent before October 8, 1949, is included in his gross estate under section 2037 only if the decedent's reversionary interest arose by the express terms of the instrument and not by operation of law. For example, assume that the decedent, on January 1, 1947, transferred property in trust with the income payable to his wife for the decedent's life and, at his death, remainder to his then surviving descendants. Since no provision was made for the contingency that no descendants of the decedent might survive him, a reversion to the decedent's estate existed by operation of law. The descendants cannot obtain possession or enjoyment of the property without surviving the decedent. However, since the decedent's reversionary interest arose by operation of law, no part of the property is includible in the decedent's gross estate under section 2037. If, in the above example, the transfer had been made on or after October 8, 1949, and if the decedent's reversionary interest immediately before his death exceeded 5 percent of the value of the property, the value of the property would be includible in the decedent's gross estate.

(2) The decedent's reversionary interest will be considered to have arisen by the express terms of the instrument of transfer and not by operation of law if the instrument contains an express disposition which affirmatively creates the reversionary interest, even though the terms of the disposition do not refer to the decedent or his estate, as such. For example, where the disposition is, in its terms, to the next of kin of the decedent and such a disposition, under applicable local law, constitutes a reversionary interest in the decedent's estate, the decedent's reversionary interest will be considered to have arisen by the express terms of the instrument of transfer and not by operation of law.

(g) *Transfers made after November 11, 1935, and before January 29, 1940.*—The provisions of paragraphs (a) to (f) of this section are fully applicable to transfers made after November 11, 1935 (the date on which the Supreme Court decided *Helvering v. St. Louis Union Trust Co.* (296 U. S. 39) and *Becker v. St. Louis Union Trust Co.* (296 U. S. 48)), and before January 29, 1940 (the date on which the Supreme Court decided *Helvering v. Hallock* and companion cases (309 U. S. 106)), except that the value of an interest in property transferred between these dates is not included in a decedent's gross estate under section 2037 if—

(1) The Commissioner, whose determination shall be final, determines that the transfer is classifiable with the transfers involved in the *St. Louis Union Trust Co.* cases, rather than with the transfer involved in the case of *Klein v. United States* (283 U. S. 231), previously decided by the Supreme Court, and

(2) The transfer shall have been finally treated for all gift tax purposes, both as to the calendar year of the transfer and as to subsequent calendar years, as a gift in an amount measured by the value of the property undiminished by reason of a provision in the instrument of transfer by which the property, in whole or in part, is to revert to the decedent should he survive the donee or another

person, or the reversion is conditioned upon some other contingency terminable by the decedent's death. [Reg. § 20.2037-1.]

☐ [T.D. 6296, 6-23-58.]

**[Reg. § 20.2038-1]**

**§ 20.2038-1. Revocable transfers.**—(a) *In general.*—A decedent's gross estate includes under section 2038 the value of any interest in property transferred by the decedent, whether in trust or otherwise, if the enjoyment of the interest was subject at the date of the decedent's death to any change through the exercise of a power by the decedent to alter, amend revoke, or terminate, or if the decedent relinquished such a power in contemplation of death. However, section 2038 does not apply—

(1) To the extent that the transfer was for an adequate and full consideration in money or money's worth (see § 20.2043-1);

(2) If the decedent's power could be exercised only with the consent of all parties having an interest (vested or contingent) in the transferred property, and if the power adds nothing to the rights of the parties under local law; or

(3) To a power held solely by a person other than the decedent. But, for example, if the decedent had the unrestricted power to remove or discharge a trustee at any time and appoint himself trustee, the decedent is considered as having the powers of the trustee. However, this result would not follow if he only had the power to appoint himself trustee under limited conditions which did not exist at the time of his death. (See last two sentences of paragraph (b) of this section.)

Except as provided in this paragraph, it is immaterial in what capacity the power was exercisable by the decedent or by another person or persons in conjunction with the decedent; whether the power was exercisable alone or only in conjunction with another person or persons, whether or not having an adverse interest (unless the transfer was made before June 2, 1924; see paragraph (d) of this section); and at what time or from what source the decedent acquired his power (unless the transfer was made before June 23, 1936; see paragraph (c) of this section). Section 2038 is applicable to any power affecting the time or manner of enjoyment of property or its income, even though the identity of the beneficiary is not affected. For example, section 2038 is applicable to a power reserved by the grantor of a trust to accumulate income or distribute it to A, and to distribute corpus to A, even though the remainder is vested in A or his estate, and no other person has any beneficial interest in the trust. However, only the value of an interest in property subject to a power to which section 2038 applies is included in the decedent's gross estate under section 2038.

(b) *Date of existence of power.*—A power to alter, amend, revoke, or terminate will be considered to have existed at the date of the decedent's death even though the exercise of the power was subject to a precedent giving of notice or even though the alteration, amendment, revocation, or termination would have taken effect only on the expiration of a stated period after the exercise of the power, whether or not on or before the date of the decedent's death notice had been given or the power had been exercised. In determining the value of the gross estate in such cases, the full value of the property transferred subject to the power is discounted for the period required to elapse between the date of the decedent's death and the date upon which the alteration, amendment, revocation, or termination could take effect. In this connection, see especially § 20.2031-7. However, section 2038 is not applicable to a power the exercise of which was subject to a contingency beyond the decedent's control which did not occur before his death (e.g., the death of another person during the decedent's life). See, however, section 2036(a)(2) for the inclusion of property in the decedent's gross estate on account of such a power.

(c) *Transfers made before June 23, 1936.*—Notwithstanding anything to the contrary in paragraphs (a) and (b) of this section, the value of an interest in property transferred by a decedent before June 23, 1936, is not included in his gross estate under section 2038 unless the power to alter, amend, revoke, or terminate was reserved at the time of the transfer. For purposes of this paragraph, the phrase "reserved at the time of the transfer" has reference to a power (arising either by the express terms of the instrument of transfer or by operation of law) to which the transfer was subject when made and which continued to the date of the decedent's death (see paragraph (b) of this section) to be exercisable by the decedent alone or by the decedent in conjunction with any other person or persons. The phrase also has reference to any understanding, express or implied, had in connection with the making of the transfer that the power would later be created or conferred.

(d) *Transfers made before June 2, 1924.*—Notwithstanding anything to the contrary in paragraphs (a) to (c) of this section, if an interest in property was transferred by a decedent before the enactment of the Revenue Act of 1924 (June 2, 1924, 4:01 p.m., eastern standard time), and if a power reserved by the decedent to alter, amend, revoke, or terminate was exercisable by the decedent only in conjunction with a person having a substantial adverse interest in the transferred property, or in conjunction with several persons some or all of whom held such an adverse interest, there is included in the decedent's gross estate only the value of any interest or interests held by a person or persons not required to join in the exercise of the power plus the value of any insubstantial adverse interest or interests of a person or persons required to join in the exercise of the power.

(e) *Powers relinquished in contemplation of death.*—(1) *In general.*—If a power to alter, amend, revoke, or terminate would have resulted in the inclusion of an interest in property in a decedent's gross estate under section 2038 if it had been held until the decedent's death, the relinquishment of the power in contemplation of the decedent's death within 3 years before his death results in the inclusion of the same interest in property in the decedent's gross estate, except to the extent that the power was relinquished for an adequate and full consideration in money or money's worth (see § 20.2043-1). For the meaning of the phrase "in contemplation of death", see paragraph (c) of § 20.2035-1.

(2) *Transfers before June 23, 1936.*—In the case of a transfer made before June 23, 1936, section 2038 applies only to a relinquishment made by the decedent. However, in the case of a transfer made after June 22, 1936, section 2038 also applies to a relinquishment made by a person or persons holding the power in conjunction with the decedent, if the relinquishment was made in contemplation of the decedent's death and had the effect of extinguishing the power.

(f) *Effect of disability to relinquish power in certain cases.*—Notwithstanding anything to the contrary in paragraphs (a) through (e) of this section the provisions of this section do not apply to a transfer if—

(1) The relinquishment on or after January 1, 1940, and on or before December 31, 1947, of the power would, by reason of section 1000(e), of the Internal Revenue Code of 1939, be deemed not a transfer of property for the purpose of the gift tax under chapter 4 of the Internal Revenue Code of 1939, and

(2) The decedent was, for a continuous period beginning on or before September 30, 1947, and ending with his death, after August 16, 1954, under a mental disability to relinquish a power.

For the purpose of the foregoing provision, the term "mental disability" means mental incompetence, in fact, to release the power whether or not there was an adjudication of incompetence. Such provision shall apply even though a guardian could have released the power for the decedent. No interest shall be allowed or paid on any overpayment allowable under section 2038(c) with respect to amounts paid before August 7, 1959. [Reg. § 20.2038-1.]

☐ [*T.D. 6296, 6-23-58. Amended by T.D. 6600, 5-28-62.*]

### [Reg. § 20.2039-1]

§ 20.2039-1. Annuities.—(a) In general.—A decedent's gross estate includes under section 2039(a) and (b) the value of an annuity or other payment receivable by any beneficiary by reason of surviving the decedent under certain agreements or plans to the extent that the value of the annuity or other payment is attributable to contributions made by the decedent or his employer. Sections 2039(a) and (b), however, have no application to an amount which constitutes the proceeds of insurance under a policy on the decedent's life. Paragraph (b) of this section describes the agreements or plans to which section 2039(a) and (b) applies; paragraph (c) of this section provides rules for determining the amount includible in the decedent's gross estate; paragraph (d) of this section distinguishes proceeds of life insurance; and paragraph (e) of this section distinguishes annuity, unitrust, and other interests retained by a decedent in certain trusts. The fact that an annuity or other payment is not includible in a decedent's gross estate under section 2039(a) and (b) does not mean that it is not includible under some other section of part III of subchapter A of chapter 11. However, see section 2039(c) and (d) and § 20.2039-2 for rules relating to the exclusion from a decedent's gross estate of annuities and other payments under certain "qualified plans." Further, the fact that an annuity or other payment may be includible under section 2039(a) will not preclude the application of another section of chapter 11 with regard to that interest. For annuity interests in trust, see paragraph (e)(1) of this section.

(b) *Agreements or plans to which section 2039(a) and (b) applies.*—(1) Section 2039(a) and (b) applies to the value of an annuity or other payment receivable by any beneficiary under any form of contract or agreement entered into after March 3, 1931, under which—

(i) An annuity or other payment was payable to the decedent, either alone or in conjunction with another person or persons, for his life or for any period not ascertainable without reference to his death or for any period which does not in fact end before his death, or

(ii) The decedent possessed, for his life or for any period not ascertainable without reference to his death or for any period which does not in fact end before his death, the right to receive such an annuity or other payment, either alone or in conjunction with another person or persons.

The term "annuity or other payment" as used with respect to both the decedent and the beneficiary has reference to one or more payments extending over any period of time. The payments may be equal or unequal, conditional or unconditional, periodic or sporadic. The term "contract or agreement" includes any arrangement, understanding or plan, or any combination of arrangements, understandings or plans arising by reason of the decedent's employment. An annuity or other payment "was payable" to the decedent if, at the time of his death, the decedent was in fact receiving an annuity or other payment, whether or not he had an enforceable right to have payments continued. The decedent "possessed the right to receive" an annuity or other payment if, immediately before his death, the decedent had an enforceable right to receive payments at some time in the future, whether or not, at the time of his death, he had a present right to receive payments. In connection with the preceding sentence, the decedent will be regarded as having had "an enforceable right to receive payments at some time in the future" so long as he had complied with his obligations under the contract or agreement up to the time of his death. For the meaning of the phrase "for his life or for any period not ascertainable without reference to his death or for any period which does not in fact end before his death", see section 2036 and § 20.2036-1.

(2) The application of this paragraph is illustrated and more fully explained in the following examples. In each example: (i) It is assumed that all transactions occurred after March 3, 1931, and (ii) the amount stated to be includible in the decedent's gross estate is determined in accordance with the provisions of paragraph (c) of this section.

*Example (1).* The decedent purchased an annuity contract under the terms of which the issuing company agreed to pay an annuity to the decedent for his life and, upon his death, to pay a specified lump sum to his designated beneficiary. The decedent was drawing his annuity at the time of his death. The amount of the lump sum payment to the beneficiary is includible in the decedent's gross estate under section 2039(a) and (b).

*Example (2).* Pursuant to a retirement plan, the employer made contributions to a fund which was to provide the employee, upon his retirement at age 60, with an annuity for life, and which was to provide the employee's wife, upon his death after retirement, with a similar annuity for life. The benefits under the plan were completely forfeitable during the employee's life, but, upon his death after retirement, the benefits to the wife were forfeitable only upon her remarriage. The employee had no right originally to designate or ever to change the employer's designation of the surviving beneficiary. The retirement plan at no time met the requirements of section 401(a) (relating to qualified plans). Assume that the employee died at age 61 after the employer started payment of his annuity as described above. The value of the wife's annuity is includible in the decedent's gross estate under section 2039(a) and (b). Includibility in this case is based on the fact that the annuity to the decedent "was payable" at the time of his death. The fact that the decedent's annuity was forfeitable is of no consequence since, at the time of his death, he was in fact receiving payments under the plan. Nor is it important that the decedent had no right to choose the surviving beneficiary. The element of forfeitability in the wife's annuity may be taken into account only with respect to the valuation of the annuity in the decedent's gross estate.

*Example (3).* Pursuant to a retirement plan, the employer made contributions to a fund which was to provide the employee, upon his retirement at age 60, with an annuity of $100 per month for life, and which was to provide his designated beneficiary, upon the employee's death after retirement, with a similar annuity for life. The plan also provided that (a) upon the employee's separation from service before retirement, he would have a nonforfeitable right to receive a reduced annuity starting at age 60, and (b) upon the employee's death before retirement, a lump sum payment representing the amount of the employer's contributions credited to the employee's account would be paid to the designated beneficiary. The plan at no time met the requirements of section 401(a) (relating to qualified plans). Assume that the employee died at age 49 and that the designated beneficiary was paid the specified lump sum payment. Such amount is includible in the decedent's gross estate under section 2039(a) and (b). Since, immediately before his death, the employee had an enforceable right to receive an annuity commencing at age 60, he is considered to have "possessed the right to receive" an annuity as that term is used in section 2039(a). If, in this example, the employee would not be entitled to any benefits in the event of his separation from service before retirement for any reason other than death, the result would be the same so long as the decedent had complied with his obligations under the contract up to the time of his death. In such case, he is considered to have had, immediatley before his death, an enforceable right to receive an annuity commencing at age 60.

*Example (4).* Pursuant to a retirement plan, the employer made contributions to a fund which was to provide the employee, upon his retirement at age 60, with an annuity for life, and which was to provide his designated beneficiary, upon the employee's death after retirement, with a similar annuity for life. The plan provided, however, that no benefits were payable in the event of the employee's death before retirement. The retirement plan at no time met the requirements of section 401(a) (relating to qualified plans). Assume that the employee died at age 59 but that the employer nevertheless started payment of an annuity in a slightly reduced amount to the designated beneficiary. The value of the annuity is not includible in the decedent's gross estate under section 2039(a) and (b). Since the employee died before reaching the retirement age, the employer was under no obligation to pay the annuity to the employee's designated beneficiary. Therefore, the annuity was not paid under a "contract or agreement" as that term is used in section 2039(a). If, however, it can be established that the employer has consistently paid an annuity under such circumstances, the annuity will be considered as having been paid under a "contract or agreement."

*Example (5).* The employer made contributions to a retirement fund which were credited to the employee's individual account. Under the plan, the employee was to receive one-half the amount credited to his account upon his retirement at age 60, and his designated beneficiary was to receive the other one-half upon the employee's death after retirement. If the employee should die before reaching the retirement age, the entire amount credited to his account at such time was to be paid to the designated beneficiary. The retirement plan at no time met the requirements of section 401(a) (relating to qualified plans). Assume that the employee received one-half the amount credited to his account upon reaching the retirement age and that he died shortly thereafter. Since the employee received all that he was entitled to receive under the plan before his death, no amount was payable to him for his life or for any period not ascertainable without reference to his death, or for any period which did not in fact end before his death. Thus, the amount of the payment to the designated beneficiary is not includible in the decedent's gross estate under section 2039(a) and (b). If, in this example, the employee died before reaching the retirement age, the amount of the payment to the designated beneficiary would be includible in the decedent's gross estate under section 2039(a) and (b). In this latter case, the decedent possessed the right to receive a lump sum payment for a period which did not in fact end before his death.

*Example (6).* The employer made contributions to two different funds set up under two different plans. One plan was to provide the employee, upon his retirement at age 60, with an annuity for life, and the other plan was to provide the employee's designated beneficiary, upon the employee's death, with a similar annuity for life. Each plan was established at a different time and each plan was administered separately in every respect. Neither plan at any time met the requirements of section 401(a) (relating to qualified plans). The value of the designated beneficiary's annuity is includible in the employee's gross estate. All rights and benefits accruing to an employee and to others by reason of the employment (except rights and benefits accruing under certain plans meeting the requirements of section 401(a) (see § 20.2039-2)) are considered together in determining whether or not section 2039(a) and (b) applies. The scope of section 2039(a) and (b) cannot be limited by indirection.

(c) *Amount includible in the gross estate.*—The amount to be included in a decedent's gross estate under section 2039(a) and (b) is an amount which bears the same ratio to the value at the decedent's death of the annuity or other payment receivable by the beneficiary as the contribution made by the decedent, or made by his employer (or former employer) for any reason connected with his employment, to the cost of the contract or agreement bears to its total cost. In applying this ratio, the value at the decedent's death of the annuity or other payment is determined in accordance with the rules set forth in § § 20.2031-1, 20.2031-7, 20.2031-8, and 20.2031-9. The application of this paragraph may be illustrated by the following examples:

*Example (1).* On January 1, 1945, the decedent and his wife each contributed $15,000 to the purchase price of an annuity contract under the terms of which the issuing company agreed to pay an annuity to the decedent and his wife for their joint lives and to continue the annuity to the survivor for his life. Assume that the value of the survivor's annuity at the decedent's death (computed under § 20.2031-8) is $20,000. Since the decedent contributed one-half of the cost of the contract, the amount to be included in his gross estate under section 2039(a) and (b) is $10,000.

*Example (2).* Under the terms of an employment contract entered into on January 1, 1945, the employer and the employee made contributions to a fund which was to provide the employee, upon his retirement at age 60, with an annuity for life, and which was to

provide his designated beneficiary, upon the employee's death after retirement, with a similar annuity for life. The retirement fund at no time formed part of a plan meeting the requirements of section 401(a) (relating to qualified plans). Assume that the employer and the employee each contributed $5,000 to the retirement fund. Assume, further, that the employee died after retirement at which time the value of the survivor's annuity was $8,000. Since the employer's contributions were made by reason of the decedent's employment, the amount to be included in his gross estate under section 2039(a) and (b) is the entire $8,000. If, in the above example, only the employer made contributions to the fund, the amount to be included in the gross estate would still be $8,000.

(d) *Insurance under policies on the life of the decedent.*—If an annuity or other payment receivable by a beneficiary under a contract or agreement is in substance the proceeds of insurance under a policy on the life of the decedent, section 2039(a) and (b) does not apply. For the extent to which such an annuity or other payment is includible in a decedent's gross estate, see section 2042 and § 20.2042-1. A combination annuity contract and life insurance policy on the decedent's life (e. g., a "retirement income" policy with death benefits) which matured during the decedent's lifetime so that there was no longer an insurance element under the contract at the time of the decedent's death is subject to the provisions of section 2039(a) and (b). On the other hand, the treatment of a combination annuity contract and life insurance policy on the decedent's life which did not mature during the decedent's lifetime depends upon the nature of the contract at the time of the decedent's death. The nature of the contract is generally determined by the relation of the reserve value of the policy to the value of the death benefit at the time of the decedent's death. If the decedent dies before the reserve value equals the death benefit, there is still an insurance element under the contract. The contract is therefore considered, for estate tax purposes, to be an insurance policy subject to the provisions of section 2042. However, if the decedent dies after the reserve value equals the death benefit, there is no longer an insurance element under the contract. The contract is therefore considered to be a contract for an annuity or other payment subject to the provisions of section 2039(a) and (b) or some other section of part III of subchapter A of chapter 11. Notwithstanding the relation of the reserve value to the value of the death benefit, a contract under which the death benefit could never exceed the total premiums paid, plus interest, contains no insurance element.

*Example.* Pursuant to a retirement plan established January 1, 1945, the employer purchased a contract from an insurance company which was to provide the employee, upon his retirement at age 65, with an annuity of $100 per month for life, and which was to provide his designated beneficiary, upon the employee's death after retirement, with a similar annuity for life. The contract further provided that if the employee should die before reaching the retirement age, a lump sum payment of $20,000 would be paid to his designated beneficiary in lieu of the annuity described above. The plan at no time met the requirements of section 401(a) (relating to qualified plans). Assume that the reserve value of the contract at the retirement age would be $20,000. If the employee died after reaching the retirement age, the death benefit to the designated beneficiary would constitute an annuity, the value of which would be includible in the employee's gross estate under section 2039(a) and (b). If, on the other hand, the employee died before reaching his retirement age, the death benefit to the designated beneficiary would constitute insurance under a policy on the life of the decedent since the reserve value would be less than the death benefit. Accordingly, its includibility would depend upon section 2042 and § 20.2042-1.

(e) *No application to certain trusts.*—Section 2039 shall not be applied to include in a decedent's gross estate all or any portion of a trust (other than a trust constituting an employee benefit, but including those described in the following sentence) if the decedent retained a right to use property of the trust or retained an annuity, unitrust, or other interest in the trust, in either case as described in section 2036. Such trusts include without limitation the following (collectively referred to in this paragraph (e) as "trusts"): certain charitable remainder trusts (collectively CRTs) such as a charitable remainder annuity trust (CRAT) within the meaning of section 664(d)(1), a charitable remainder unitrust (CRUT) within the meaning of section 664(d)(2) or (d)(3), and any other charitable remainder trust that does not qualify under section 664(d), whether because the CRT was created prior to 1969, there was a defect in the drafting of the CRT, there was no intention to qualify the CRT for the charitable deduction, or otherwise; other trusts established by a grantor (collectively GRTs) such as a grantor retained annuity trust (GRAT) paying out a qualified annuity interest within the meaning of § 25.2702-3(b) of this chapter, a grantor retained unitrust (GRUT) paying out a qualified unitrust interest within the meaning of § 25.2702-3(c) of this chapter; and various forms of grantor retained income trusts (GRITs) whether or not the grantor's retained interest is a qualified interest as defined in section 2702(b), including without limitation a qualified personal residence trust (QPRT) within the meaning of § 25.2702-5(c) of this chapter and a personal residence trust (PRT) within the meaning of § 25.2702-5(b) of this chapter. For purposes of determining the extent to which a retained interest causes all or a portion of a trust to be included in a decedent's gross estate, see § 20.2036-1(c)(1), (2), and (3).

(f) *Effective/applicability dates.*—The first, second, and fourth sentences in paragraph (a) of this section are applicable to the estates of decedents dying after August 16, 1954. The fifth sentence of paragraph (a) of this section is applicable to the estates of decedents dying on or after October 27, 1972, and to the estates of decedents for which the period for filing a claim for credit or refund of an estate tax overpayment ends on or after October 27, 1972. The third, sixth, and seventh sentences of paragraph (a) of this section and all of paragraph (e) of this section are applicable to the estates of decedents dying on or after July 14, 2008. [Reg. § 20.2039-1.]

☐ *[T.D. 6296, 6-23-58. Amended by T.D. 7416, 4-5-76 and T.D. 9414, 7-11-2008*

### [Reg. § 20.2039-1T]

**§ 20.2039-1T. Limitations and repeal of estate tax exclusion for qualified plans and individual retirement plans (IRAs) (Temporary).**

Q-1: Are there any exceptions to the general effective dates of the $100,000 limitation and the repeal of the estate tax exclusion for the value of interests under qualified plans and IRAs described in section 2039(c) and (e)?

A-1: (a) Yes. Section 245 of the Tax Equity and Fiscal Responsibility Act of 1982 (TEFRA) limited the estate tax exclusion to $100,000 for estates of decedents dying after December 31, 1982. Section 525 of the Tax Reform Act of 1984 (TRA of 1984) repealed the exclusion for estates of decedents dying after December 31, 1984.

(b) Section 525(b)(3) of the TRA of 1984 amended section 245 of TEFRA to provide that the $100,000 limitation on the exclusion for the value of a decedent's interest in a plan or IRA will not apply to the estate of any decedent dying after December 31, 1982, to the extent that the decedent-participant was in pay status on December 31, 1982, with respect to such interest and irrevocably elected the form of benefit payable under the plan or IRA (including the form of any survivor benefits) with respect to such interest before January 1, 1983.

(c) Similarly, the TRA of 1984 provides that the repeal of the estate tax exclusion for the value of a decedent's interest in a plan or IRA will not apply to the estate of a decedent dying after December 31, 1984, to the extent that the decedent-participant was in pay status on December 31, 1984, with respect to such interest and irrevocably elected the form of benefit payable under the plan or IRA (including the form of any survivor benefits) with respect to such interest before July 18, 1984.

Q-2: What is the meaning of "in pay status" on the applicable date?

A-2: A participant was in pay status on the applicable date with respect to a portion of his or her interest in a plan or IRA if such portion is to be paid in a benefit form that has been elected on or before such date and the participant has received, on or before such date, at least one payment under such benefit form.

Q-3: What is required for an election of the form of benefit payable under the plan to have been irrevocable as of any applicable date?

A-3: As of any applicable date, an election of the form of benefit payable under a plan is irrevocable if, as of such date, it was a written irrevocable election that, with respect to all payments to be received after such date, specified the form of distribution (e.g., lump sum, level dollar annuity, formula annuity) and the period over which the distribution would be made (e.g., single life, joint and survivor, term certain). An election is not irrevocable as of any applicable date if, on or after such date, the form or period of the distribution could be determined or altered by any person or persons. An election does not fail to be irrevocable as of an applicable date merely because the beneficiaries were not designated as of such date or could be changed after such date. If any interest in any IRA may not, by law or contract, be subject to an irrevocable election described in this section, any election of the form of benefit payable under the IRA does not satisfy the requirement that an irrevocable election have been made. [Temporary Reg. § 20.2039-1T.]

☐ *[T.D. 8073, 1-29-86.]*

### [Reg. § 20.2039-2]

**§ 20.2039-2. Annuities under "qualified plans" and section 403(b) annuity contracts.**—(a) *Section 2039(c) exclusion.*—In general, in the case of a decedent dying after December 31, 1953, the value of an annuity or other payment receivable under a plan or annuity contract described in paragraph (b) of this section is excluded from the decedent's gross estate to the extent provided in paragraph (c) of this section. In the case of a plan described in paragraph (b) (1) or (2) of

this section(a "qualified plan"), the exclusion is subject to the limitation described in § 20.2039-3 (relating to lump sum distributions paid with respect to a decedent dying after December 31, 1976, and before January 1, 1979) or § 20.2039-4 (relating to lump sum distributions paid with respect to a decedent dying after December 31, 1978).

(b) *Plans and annuity contracts to which section 2039(c) applies.*—Section 2039(c) excludes from a decedent's gross estate, to the extent provided in paragraph (c) of this section, the value of an annuity or other payment receivable by any beneficiary (except the value of an annuity or other payment receivable by or for the benefit of the decedent's estate) under—

(1) An employees' trust (or under a contract purchased by an employees' trust) forming part of a pension, stock bonus, or profit-sharing plan which, at the time of the decedent's separation from employment (whether by death or otherwise), or at the time of the earlier termination of the plan, met the requirements of section 401(a);

(2) A retirement annuity contract purchased by an employer (and not by an employees' trust) pursuant to a plan which, at the time of decedent's separation from employment (by death or otherwise), or at the time of the earlier termination of the plan, was described in section 403(a);

(3) In the case of a decedent dying after December 31, 1957, a retirement annuity contract purchased for an employee by an employer which, for its taxable year in which the purchase occurred, is an organization referred to in section 170(b)(1)(A)(ii) or (vi) or which is a religious organization (other than a trust), and is exempt from tax under section 501(a);

(4) In the case of a decedent dying after December 31, 1965, an annuity under chapter 73 of title 10 of the United States Code, (10 U. S. C. 1431, *et seq.*); or

(5) In the case of a decedent dying after December 31, 1962, a bond purchase plan described in section 405.

For the meaning of the term "annuity or other payment", see paragraph (b) of § 20.2039-1. For the meaning of the phrase "receivable by or for the benefit of the decedent's estate", see paragraph (b) of § 20.2042-1. The application of this paragraph may be illustrated by the following examples in each of which it is assumed that the amount stated to be excludable from the decedent's gross estate is determined in accordance with paragraph (c) of this section:

*Example (1).* Pursuant to a pension plan, the employer made contributions to a trust which was to provide the employee, upon his retirement at age 60, with an annuity for life, and which was to provide his wife, upon the employee's death after retirement, with a similar annuity for life. At the time of the employee's retirement, the pension trust formed part of a plan meeting the requirements of section 401(a). Assume that the employee died at age 61 after the trustee started payment of his annuity as described above. Since the wife's annuity was receivable under a qualified pension plan, no part of the value of such annuity is includible in the decedent's gross estate by reason of the provisions of section 2039(c). If, in this example, the employer provided other benefits under nonqualified plans, the result would be the same since the exclusion under section 2039(c) is confined to the benefits provided for under the qualified plan.

*Example (2).* Pursuant to a profit-sharing plan, the employer made contributions to a trust which were allocated to the employee's individual account. Under the plan, the employee would, upon retirement at age 60, receive a distribution of the entire amount credited to the account. If the employee should die before reaching retirement age, the amount credited to the account would be distributed to the employee's designated beneficiary. Assume that the employee died before reaching the retirement age and that at such time the plan met the requirements of section 401(a). Since the payment to the designated beneficiary is receivable under a qualified profit-sharing plan, the provisions of section 2039(c) apply. However, if the payment is a lump sum distribution to which § 20.2039-3 or § 20.2039-4 applies, the payment is excludable from the decedent's gross estate only as provided in such section.

*Example (3).* Pursuant to a pension plan, the employer made contributions to a trust which were used by the trustee to purchase a contract from an insurance company for the benefit of an employee. The contract was to provide the employee, upon retirement at age 65, with an annuity of $100 per month for life, and was to provide the employee's designated beneficiary upon the employee's death after retirement, with a similar annuity for life. The contract further provided that if the employee should die before reaching retirement age, a lump sum payment equal to the greater of (a) $10,000 or (b) the reserve value of the policy would be paid to the designated beneficiary in lieu of the annuity. Assume that the employee died before reaching the retirement age and that at such time the plan met the requirements of section 401(a). Since the payment to the designated beneficiary is receivable under a qualified pension plan, the provisions of section 2039(c) apply. However, if the payment is a lump sum distribution to which §20.2039-3 or §20.2039-4 applies, the payment is excludable from decedent's gross estate only as provided in such section. It should be noted that for purposes of the exclusion under section 2039(c) it is immaterial whether or not the payment constitutes the proceeds of life insurance under the principles set forth in §20.2039-1(d).

*Example (4).* Pursuant to a profit-sharing plan, the employer made contributions to a trust which were allocated to the employee's individual account. Under the plan, the employee would, upon his retirement at age 60, be given the option to have the amount credited to his account (a) paid to him in a lump sum, (b) used to purchase a joint and survivor annuity for him and his designated beneficiary, or (c) left with the trustee under an arrangement whereby interest would be paid to him for his lifetime with the principal to be paid, at his death, to his designated beneficiary. The plan further provided that, if the third method of settlement were selected, the employee would retain the right to have the principal paid to himself in a lump sum up to the time of his death. At the time of the employee's retirement, the profit-sharing plan met the requirements of section 401(a). Assume that the employee, upon reaching his retirement age, elected to have the amount credited to his account left with the trustee under the interest arrangement. Assume, further, that the employee did not exercise his right to have such amount paid to him before his death. Under such circumstances, the employee is considered as having constructively received the amount credited to his account upon his retirement. Thus, such amount is not considered as receivable by the designated beneficiary under the profit-sharing plan and the exclusion of section 2039(c) is not applicable.

*Example (5).* An employer purchased a retirement annuity contract for an employee which was to provide the employee, upon his retirement at age 60, with an annuity for life and which was to provide his wife, upon the employee's death after retirement, with a similar annuity for life. The employer, for its taxable year in which the annuity contract was purchased, was an organization referred to in section 170(b)(1)(A)(ii), and was exempt from tax under section 501(a). The entire amount of the purchase price of the annuity contract was excluded from the employee's gross income under section 403(b). No part of the value of the survivor annuity payable after the employee's death is includible in the decedent's gross estate by reason of the provisions of section 2039(c).

(c) *Amounts excludable from the gross estate.*—(1) The amount to be excluded from a decedent's gross estate under section 2039(c) is an amount which bears the same ratio to the value at the decedent's death of an annuity or other payment receivable by the beneficiary as the employer's contribution (or a contribution made on the employer's behalf) on the employee's account to the plan or towards the purchase of the annuity contract bears to the total contributions on the employee's account to the plan or towards the purchase of the annuity contract. In applying this ratio—

(i) Payments or contributions made by or on behalf of the employer towards the purchase of an annuity contract described in paragraph (b)(3) of this section are considered to include only such payments or contributions as are, or were, excludable from the employee's gross income under section 403(b).

(ii) In the case of a decedent dying before January 1, 1977, payments or contributions made under a plan described in paragraph (b)(1), (2) or (5) of this section on behalf of the decedent for a period for which the decedent was self-employed, within the meaning of section 401(c)(1), with respect to the plan are considered payments or contributions made by the decedent and not by the employer.

(iii) In the case of a decedent dying after December 31, 1976, however, payments or contributions made under a plan described in

paragraph (b)(1), (2) or (5) of this section on behalf of the decedent for a period for which the decedent was self-employed, within the meaning of section 401(c)(1), with respect to the plan are considered payments or contributions made by the employer to the extent the payments or contributions are, or were, deductible under section 404 or 405(c). Contributions or payments attributable to that period which are not, or were not, so deductible are considered made by the decedent.

(iv) In the case of a plan described in paragraph (b)(1) or (2) of this section, a rollover contribution described in section 402(a)(5), 403(a)(4), 408(d)(3)(A)(ii) or 409(b)(3)(C) is considered an amount contributed by the employer.

(v) In the case of an annuity contract described in paragraph (b)(3) of this section, a rollover contribution described in section 403(b)(8) is considered an amount contributed by the employer.

(vi) In the case of a plan described in paragraph (b)(1), (2) or (5) of this section, an amount includable in the gross income of an employer under section 1379(b) (relating to shareholder-employee beneficiaries under certain qualified plans) is considered an amount paid or contributed by the decedent.

(vii) Amounts payable under paragraph (b)(4) of this section are attributable to payments or contributions made by the decedent only to the extent of amounts deposited by the decedent pursuant to section 1438 or 1452(d) of Title 10 of the United States Code.

(viii) The value at the decedent's death of the annuity or other payment is determined under the rules of §§20.2031-1 and 20.2031-7 or, for certain prior periods, §20.2031-7A.

(2) In certain cases, the employer's contribution (or a contribution made on his behalf) to a plan on the employee's account and thus the total contributions to the plan on the employee's account cannot be readily ascertained. In order to apply the ratio stated in subparagraph (1) of this paragraph in such a case, the method outlined in the following two sentences must be used unless a more precise method is presented. In such a case, the total contributions to the plan on the employee's account is the value of any annuity or other payment payable to the decedent and his survivor computed as of the time the decedent's rights first mature (or as of the time the survivor's rights first mature if the decedent's rights never mature) and computed in accordance with the rules set forth in §§20.2031-1, 20.2031-7, 20.2031-8, and 20.2031-9. By subtracting from such value the amount of the employee's contribution to the plan, the amount of the employer's contribution to the plan on the employee's account may be obtained. The application of this paragraph may be illustrated by the following example:

*Example.* Pursuant to a pension plan, the employer and the employee contributed to a trust which was to provide the employee, upon his retirement at age 60, with an annuity for life, and which was to provide his wife, upon the employee's death after retirement, with a similar annuity for life. At the time of the employee's retirement, the pension trust formed part of a plan meeting the requirements of section 401(a). Assume the following: (i) that the employer's contributions to the fund were not credited to the accounts of individual employees; (ii) that the value of the employee's annuity and his wife's annuity, computed as of the time of the decedent's retirement, was $40,000; (iii) that the employee contributed $10,000 to the plan; and (iv) that the value at the decedent's death of the wife's annuity was $16,000. On the basis of these facts, the total contributions to the fund on the employee's account are presumed to be $40,000 and the employer's contribution to the plan on the employee's account is presumed to be $30,000 ($40,000 less $10,000). Since the wife's annuity was receivable under a qualified pension plan, that part of the value of such annuity which is attributable to the

$$\text{employer's contributions } \left( \frac{\$30,000}{\$40,000} \times \$16,000, \text{ or } \$12,000 \right) \text{ is excludable from}$$

the decedent's gross estate by reason of the provisions of section 2039(c). Compare this result with the results reached in the examples set forth in paragraph (b) of this section in which all contributions to the plans were made by the employer.

(d) *Exclusion of certain annuity interests created by community property laws.*—(1) In the case of an employee on whose behalf contributions or payments were made by his employer or former employer under an employees' trust forming part of a pension, stock bonus, or profit-sharing plan described in section 2039(c)(1), under an employee's retirement annuity contract described in section 2039(c)(2), or toward the purchase of an employee's retirement annuity contract described in section 2039(c)(3), which under section 2039(c) are not considered as contributed by the employee, if the spouse of such employee predeceases him, then, notwithstanding the provisions of section 2039 or of any other provision of law, there shall be excluded from the gross estate of such spouse the value of any interest of such

spouse in such plan or trust or such contract, to the extent such interest—

(i) Is attributable to such contributions or payments, and

(ii) Arises solely by reason of such spouse's interest in community income under the community property laws of a State.

(2) Section 2039(d) and this paragraph do not provide any exclusion for such spouse's property interest in the plan, trust or contract to the extent it is attributable to the contributions of the employee spouse. Thus, the decedent's community property interest in the plan, trust, or contract which is attributable to contributions made by the employee spouse are includible in the decedent's gross estate. See paragraph (c) of this section.

(3) Section 2039(d) and this paragraph apply to the estate of a decedent who dies on or after October 27, 1972, and to the estate of a decedent who died before October 27, 1972, if the period for filing a claim for credit or refund of an overpayment of the estate tax ends on

or after October 27, 1972. Interest will not be allowed or paid on any overpayment of tax resulting from the application of section 2039(d) and this paragraph for any period prior to April 26, 1973. [Reg. §20.2039-2.]

□ [*T.D. 6296, 6-23-58. Amended by T.D. 6526, 1-18-61, T.D. 6666, 7-15-63, T.D. 7043, 6-1-70, T.D. 7416, 4-5-76, T.D. 7428, 8-13-76, T.D. 7761, 1-21-81 and T.D. 8540, 6-9-94.*]

### [Reg. §20.2039-3]

**§20.2039-3. Lump sum distributions under "qualified plans"; decedents dying after December 31, 1976, and before January 1, 1979.**—(a) *Limitation of section 2039(c) exclusion.*—This section applies in the case of a decedent dying after December 31, 1976, and before January 1, 1979. If a lump sum distribution is paid with respect to the decedent under a plan described in §20.2039-2(b)(1) or (2) (a "qualified plan"), no amount payable with respect to the decedent under the plan is excludable from the decedent's gross estate under §20.2039-2.

(b) *"Lump sum distribution" defined.*—For purposes of this section the term "lump sum distribution" means a lump sum distribution defined in section 402(e)(4)(A) that satisfies the requirements of section 402(e)(4)(C), relating to the aggregation of certain trusts and plans. The distribution of an annuity contract is not a lump sum distribution for purposes of this section, and §20.2039-2 will apply with respect to the distribution of an annuity contract without regard to whether the contract is included in a distribution that is otherwise a lump sum distribution under this paragraph (b). A distribution is a lump sum distribution for purposes of this section without regard to the election described in section 402(e)(4)(B).

(c) *Amounts payable as a lump sum distribution.*—If on the date the estate tax return is filed, an amount under a qualified plan is payable with respect to the decedent as a lump sum distribution (whether at the election of a beneficiary or otherwise), for purposes of this section the amount is deemed paid as a lump sum distribution no later than on such date. Accordingly, no portion of the amount payable under the plan is excludable from the value of the decedent's gross estate under §20.2039-2. If, however, the amount payable as a lump sum distribution is not, in fact, thereafter paid as a lump sum distribution, there shall be allowed a credit or refund of any tax paid which is attributable to treating such amount as a lump sum distribution under this paragraph. Any claim for credit or refund filed under this paragraph must be filed within the time prescribed by section 6511, and must provide satisfactory evidence that the amount originally payable as a lump sum distribution is no longer payable in such form.

(d) *Filing date.*—For purposes of paragraph (c) of this section, "the date the estate tax return is filed" means the earlier of—

(1) The date the estate tax return is actually filed, or

(2) The date nine months after the decedent's death, plus any extension of time for filing the estate tax return granted under section 6081. [Reg. §20.2039-3.]

□ [*T.D. 7761, 1-21-81.*]

### [Reg. §20.2039-4]

**§20.2039-4. Lump sum distributions from "qualified plans"; decedents dying after December 31, 1978.**—(a) *Limitation on section 2039(c) exclusion.*—This section applies in the case of a decedent dying after December 31, 1978. If a lump sum distribution is paid or payable with respect to a decedent under a plan described in §20.2039-2(b)(1) or (2) (a "qualified plan"), no amount paid or payable with respect to the decedent under the plan is excludable from the decedent's gross estate under §20.2039-2, unless the recipient of the distribution makes the section 402(a)/403(a) taxation election described in paragraph(c) of this section. For purposes of this section, an amount is payable as a lump sum distribution under a plan if, as of the date the estate tax return is filed (as determined under §20.2039-3(d)), it is payable as a lump sum distribution at the election of the recipient or otherwise.

(b) *"Lump sum distribution" defined; treatment of annuity contracts.*—For purposes of this section the term "lump sum distribution" means a lump sum distribution defined in section 402(e)(4)(A) that satisfies the requirements of section 402(e)(4)(C), relating to the aggregation of certain trusts and plans. A distribution is a lump sum distribution for purposes of this section without regard to the election described in section 402(e)(4)(B). The distribution of an annuity contract is not a lump sum distribution for purposes of this section, and the limitation described in this section does not apply to an annuity contract distributed under a plan. Accordingly, if the amount payable with respect to a decedent under a plan is paid to a recipient partly by the distribution of an annuity contract, and partly by the distribution of an amount that is a lump sum distribution within the meaning of this paragraph (b), §20.2039-2 shall apply with respect to the annuity contract without regard to whether the recipient makes the section 402(a)/403(a) taxation election with respect to the remainder of the distribution.

(c) *Recipient's section 402(a)/403(a) taxation election.*—The section 402(a)/403(a) taxation election is the election by the recipient of a lump sum distribution to treat the distribution as—

(1) Taxable under section 402(a), without regard to section 402(a)(2), to the extent includable in gross income (in the case of a distribution under a qualified plan described in §20.2039-2(b)(1)),

(2) Taxable under section 403(a), without regard to section 403(a)(2), to the extent includable in gross income (in the case of a distribution under a qualified annuity contract described in §20.2039-2(b)(2)), or

(3) A rollover contribution, in whole or in part, under section 402(a)(7) (relating to rollovers by a decedent's surviving spouse).

Accordingly, if a recipient makes the election, no portion of the distribution is taxable to the recipient under the 10-year averaging provisions of section 402(e) or as long-term capital gain under section 402(a)(2). However, a recipient's election under this paragraph (c) does not preclude the application of section 402(e)(4)(J) to any securities of the employer corporation included in the distribution.

(d) *Method of election.*—(1) *General rule.*—The recipient of a lump sum distribution shall make the section 402(a)/403(a) taxation election by:

(i) Determining the income tax liability on the income tax return (or amended return) for the taxable year of the distribution in a manner consistent with paragraph (c)(1) or (2) of this section,

(ii) Rolling over all or any part of the distribution under section 402(a)(7), or

(iii) Filing a section 2039(f)(2) election statement described in paragraph (d)(2) of this section.

(2) *Election statement.*—A recipient may file a section 2039(f)(2) election statement indicating that the recipient elects to treat a lump sum distribution in the manner described in paragraph (c) of this section. The statement must be filed where the recipient would file the income tax return for the taxable year of the distribution. The statement must be signed by the recipient and include the individual's name, address, social security number, the name of the decedent, and a statement indicating the election is being made. A section 2039(f)(2) election statement may be filed at any time prior to making the election under paragraph (d)(1)(i) or (ii) of this section.

(3) *Effect on estate tax return.*—If the date the estate tax return is filed precedes the date on which the recipient makes the section 402(a)/403(a) taxation election with respect to a lump sum distribution, the estate tax return may not reflect the election. However, if after the estate tax return is filed, the recipient makes the section 402(a)/403(a) taxation election, the executor of the estate may file a claim for refund or credit of an overpayment of the Federal estate tax within the time prescribed in section 6511. See also, §20.6081-1 for rules relating to obtaining an extension of time for filing the estate tax return.

(e) *Election irrevocable.*—If a recipient of a lump sum distribution files a section 2039(f)(2) election statement, an income tax return (or amended return) or makes a rollover contribution that constitutes the section 402(a)/403(a) taxation election described in paragraphs (c) and (d), the election may not be revoked. Accordingly, a subsequent and amended income tax return filed by the recipient that is inconsistent with the prior election will not be given effect for purposes of section 2039 and section 402 or 403.

(f) *Lump sum distribution to multiple recipients.*—In the case of a lump sum distribution paid or payable under a qualified plan with respect to the decedent to more than one recipient, the exclusion under §20.2039-2 applies to so much of the distribution as is paid or payable to a recipient who makes the section 402(a)/403(a) taxation election.

(g) *Distributions of annuity contracts included multiple distributions.*—Notwithstanding that a recipient makes the section 402(a)/403(a) taxation election with respect to a lump sum distribution that includes the distribution of an annuity contract, the distribution of an annuity contract is to be taken into account by the recipient for purposes of the multiple distribution rules under section 402(e). [Reg. §20.2039-4.]

□ [*T.D. 7761, 1-21-81. Amended by T.D. 7956, 5-11-84.*]

### [Reg. §20.2039-5]

**§20.2039-5. Annuities under individual retirement plans.**—(a) *Section 2039(e) exclusion.*—(1) *In general.*—In the case of a decedent dying after December 31, 1976, section 2039(e) excludes from the decedent's gross estate, to the extent provided in paragraph (c) of this section, the value of a "qualifying annuity" receivable by a beneficiary under an individual retirement plan. The term "individual retirement plan" means—

(i) An individual retirement account described in section 408(a),

(ii) An individual retirement annuity described in section 408(b), or

(iii) A retirement bond described in section 409(a).

(2) *Limitations.*—(i) Section 2039(e) applies only with respect to the gross estate of a decedent on whose behalf the individual retirement plan was established. Accordingly, section 2039(e) does not apply with respect to the estate of a decedent who was only a beneficiary under the plan.

(ii) Section 2039(e) does not apply to an annuity receivable by or for the benefit of the decedent's estate. For the meaning of the term "receivable by or for the benefit of the decedent's estate," see §20.2042-1(b).

(b) *Qualifying annuity.*—For purposes of this section, the term "qualifying annuity" means an annuity contract or other arrangement providing for a series of substantially equal periodic payments to be made to a beneficiary for the beneficiary's life or over a period ending at least 36 months after the decedent's death. The term "annuity contract" includes an annuity purchased for a beneficiary and distributed to the beneficiary, if under section 408 the contract is not included in the gross income of the beneficiary upon distribution. The term "other arrangement" includes any arrangement arising by reason of the decedent's participation in the program providing the individual retirement plan. Payments shall be considered "periodic" if under the arrangement or contract (including a distributed contract) payments are to be made to the beneficiary at regular intervals. If the contract or arrangement provides optional payment provisions, not all of which provide for periodic payments, payments shall be considered periodic only if an option providing periodic payments is elected not later than the date the estate tax return is filed (as determined under §20.2039-3(d)). For this purpose, the right to surrender a contract (including a distributed contract) for a cash surrender value will not be considered an optional payment provision. Payments shall be considered "substantially equal" even though the amounts receivable by the beneficiary may vary. Payments shall not be considered substantially equal, however, if more than 40% of the total amount payable to the beneficiary under the individual retirement plan, determined as of the date of the decedent's death and excluding any postmortem increase, is payable to the beneficiary in any 12-month period.

(c) *Amount excludible from gross estate.*—(1) *In general.*—Except as otherwise described in this paragraph (c), the amount excluded from the decedent's gross estate under section 2039(e) is the entire value of the qualifying annuity (as determined under §§20.2031-1 and 20.2031-7 or, for certain prior periods, §20.2031-7A) payable under the individual retirement plan.

(2) *Excess contribution.*—In any case in which there exists, on the date of the decedent's death, an excess contribution (as defined in section 4973(b)) with respect to the individual retirement plan, the amount excluded from the value of the decedent's gross estate is determined under the following formula:

$$E = A - A \left( \frac{X}{C - R} \right)$$

Where:

E = the amount excluded from the decedent's gross estate under section 2039(e),

A = the value of the qualifying annuity at the decedent's death (as determined under §§20.2031-1 and 20.2031-7 or, for certain prior periods, §20.2031-7A),

X = the amount which is an excess contribution at the decedent's death (as determined under section 4973(b)),

C = the total amount contributed by or on behalf of the decedent to the individual retirement plan, and

R = the total of amounts paid or distributed from the individual retirement plan before the death of the decedent which were either includable in the gross income of the recipient under section 408(d)(1) and represented the payment or distribution of an excess contribution, or were payments or distributions described in section 408(d)(4) or (5) (relating to returned excess contributions).

(3) *Certain section 403(b)(8) rollover contributions.*—This subparagraph (3) applies if the decedent made a rollover contribution to the individual retirement plan under section 403(b)(8), and the contribution was attributable to a distribution under an annuity contract other than an annuity contract described in §20.2039-2(b)(3). If such a

rollover contribution was the only contribution made to the plan, no part of the value of the qualifying annuity payable under the plan is excluded from the decedent's gross estate under section 2039(e). If a contribution other than such a rollover contribution was made to the plan, the amount excluded from the decedent's gross estate is determined under the formula described in subparagraph (2) of this paragraph, except that for purposes of that formula, X includes the amount that was a rollover contribution under section 403(b)(8) attributable to a distribution under an annuity contract not described in §20.2039-2(b)(3).

(4) *Surviving spouse's rollover contribution.*—This subparagraph (4) applies if the decedent made a rollover contribution to the individual retirement plan under section 402(a)(7), relating to rollovers by a surviving spouse. If the rollover contribution under section 402(a)(7) was the only contribution made by the decedent to the plan, no part of the value of the qualifying annuity payable under the plan is excluded from the decedent's gross estate under section 2039(e). If a contribution other than a rollover contribution under section 402(a)(7) was made by the decedent to the plan, the amount excluded from the decedent's gross estate is determined under the formula described in subparagraph (2) of this paragraph, except that for purposes of that formula, X includes the amount that was a rollover contribution under section 402(a)(7).

(5) *Election under §1.408-2(b)(7)(ii).*—This subparagraph (5) applies if the decedent at any time made the election described in §1.408-2(b)(7)(ii) with respect to an amount in the individual retirement plan. If this subparagraph (5) applies, the amount excluded from the decedent's gross estate is determined under the formula described in subparagraph (2), except that for purposes of that formula, X and C include the amount with respect to which the election was made.

(6) *Plan-to-plan rollovers.*—(i) This subparagraph (6) applies if the individual retirement plan is a transferee plan. A "transferee plan" is a plan that was the recipient of a contribution described in section 408(d)(3)(A)(i) or 409(b)(3)(C) (relating to rollovers from one individual retirement plan to another) made by the decedent. The amount of the contribution described in section 408(d)(3)(A)(i) or 409(b)(3)(C) is the "rollover amount." The plan from which the rollover amount was paid or distributed to the decedent is the "transferor plan."

(ii) If the decedent made a contribution described in subparagraph (3) or (4) to the transferor plan, the amount excluded from the decedent's gross estate with respect to the transferee plan is determined under the formula described in subparagraph (2), except that for purposes of that formula, X includes so much of the rollover amount as was attributable to the contribution to the transferor plan that was described in subparagraph (3) or (4). The extent to which a rollover amount is attributable to a contribution described in subparagraph (3) or (4) that was made to the transferor plan is determined by multiplying the rollover amount by a fraction, the numerator of which is the amount of such contribution, and the denominator of which is the sum of all amounts contributed by the decedent to the transferor plan (if not returned as described under R in subparagraph (2)), and any amount in the transferor plan to which the election described in subparagraph (5) applied.

(iii) If the decedent made the election described in subparagraph (5) with respect to an amount in the transferor plan, the amount excluded from the decedent's gross estate with respect to the transferee plan is determined under the formula described in subparagraph (2), except that for purposes of that formula, X includes so much of the rollover amount as was attributable to the amount in the transferor plan to which the election applied. The extent to which a rollover amount is attributable to an amount in the transferor plan to which the election applied is determined by multiplying the rollover amount by a fraction, the numerator of which is the amount to which the election applied, and the denominator of which is the sum of all amounts contributed by the decedent to the transferor plan (if not returned as described under R in subparagraph (2)), and the amount in the transferor plan to which the election applied.

(iv) If a transferor plan described in this subparagraph (6) was also a transferee plan, then the rules described in this subparagraph (6) are to be applied with respect to both the rollover amount paid to the plan and the rollover amount thereafter paid from the plan.

(d) *Examples.*—The provisions of this section are illustrated by the following examples:

*Example (1).* (1) A establishes an individual retirement account described in section 408(a) on January 1, 1976, when A is age 65. A's only contribution to the account is a rollover contribution described in section 402(a)(5). The trust agreement provides that A may at any time elect to have the balance in the account distributed in one of the following methods:

(i) A single sum payment of the account,

(ii) Equal or substantially equal semiannual payments over a period equal to A's life expectancy, or

(iii) Equal or substantially equal semiannual payments over a period equal to the life expectancy of A and A's spouse.

(2) The trust agreement further provides that although semiannual payments have commenced under option (ii) or (iii), A (or A's surviving spouse) may, by written notice to the trustee, receive all or a part of the balance remaining in the account. In addition, under option (ii), any balance remaining in the account at A's death is payable in a single sum to A's designated beneficiary. Under option (iii), any balance remaining in the account at the death of the survivor of A or A's spouse is payable in a single sum to a beneficiary designated by A or A's surviving spouse.

(3) A elects option (iii), and the first semiannual payment is made to A on July 1, 1976. On that date, A's life expectancy is 15 years, and that of A's spouse is 22 years. Under option (iii), the semiannual payments to A or A's surviving spouse will continue until July 1, 1998.

(4) A dies on November 20, 1978. On December 15, 1978, the trust agreement is modified so that A's surviving spouse no longer may elect to receive all or part of the balance remaining in the account. The value of the semiannual payments payable to A's spouse is excluded from A's gross estate under section 2039(e).

(5) A's spouse dies July 12, 1981, and the single sum payment payable on account of the death of A's spouse is paid to the designated beneficiary on August 1, 1981. Notwithstanding that the balance in the account was paid to the designated beneficiary within 36 months after A's death, the value of the semiannual payments payable to A's spouse are excluded from A's gross estate, since at A's death those semiannual payments were to be paid over a period extending beyond 36 months. Section 2039(e) does not apply to exclude any amount from the estate of A's spouse, because A's spouse was only a beneficiary and not the individual on whose behalf the account was established.

*Example (2).* Assume the same facts as in example (1), except that the trust agreement is not modified so that A's surviving spouse no longer may elect to receive all or part of the balance remaining in the account (see (2) and (4) in example (1)). Instead, the balance of the account is applied toward the purchase of a contract providing an immediate annuity, the contract is distributed to A's surviving spouse on December 15, 1978, and under section 408 the contract is not included in the gross income of the spouse upon its distribution. The value of the annuity contract is excluded from A's gross estate, if the contract provides for a series of substantially equal periodic payments (within the meaning of paragraph (b) of this section) to be made over the life of A's surviving spouse or over a period not ending before the date 36 months after A's death.

*Example (3).* (1) B establishes an individual retirement plan described in section 408(a) ("IRA B") on February 6, 1981, in order to receive a $220,000 rollover contribution from a qualified plan, as described in section 402(a)(5). B dies August 14, 1981. C, an individual, is the sole beneficiary under IRA B. The amount in IRA B ($238,000) is payable to C in whole or part as C may elect. Because the amount in IRA B is payable to C as other than a qualifying annuity, within the meaning of paragraph (b) of this section, no amount is excluded from B's gross estate under section 2039(e).

(2) On October 17, 1981, C contributes $1,500 on C's own behalf to IRA B. Under § 1.408-2(b)(7)(ii), C's contribution will cause IRA B to be treated as being maintained by and on behalf of C ("IRA C") and C's making the contribution constitutes an election to which paragraph (c)(5) of this section applies. The balance in IRA C immediately before C's contribution is $240,000. Accordingly, the amount with respect to which C made the election is $240,000.

(3) C dies January 19, 1982. E, an individual, is the sole beneficiary under the plan, and the amounts payable to E ($242,000) are payable as a qualifying annuity, within the meaning of paragraph (b) of this section.

(4) The rules described in section 2039(e) and this section are applied with respect to the gross estate of C without regard to whether amounts now payable under IRA C were or were not excluded from B's gross estate. Under paragraph (c) of this section, the amount not excluded from C's gross estate is the value of the qualifying annuity payable to E ($242,000), multiplied by the fraction $240,000/($240,000 + $1,500). Thus, the amount not excluded from C's gross estate is $240,497. [($242,000) ($240,000 ÷ ($240,000 + $1,500)) = $240,497.]The amount excluded is therefore $1,503 ($242,000 – $240,497).

*Example (4).* (1) F, an individual, establishes an individual retirement plan ("IRA F1") in 1977 and makes $1,250 annual contributions for 1977, 1978, 1979 and 1980 (4 × $1,250 = $5,000), each of which is deducted by F under section 219. In February 1980, F receives an $85,000 distribution on account of the death of G, F's spouse, from the qualified plan of G's former employer, and rolls it over into IRA F1, under section 402(a)(7). Because IRA F1 includes a rollover contri-

bution under section 402(a)(7), paragraph (c)(4) of this section applies. In 1981, F's entire interest in IRA F1, $100,000, is paid to F and contributed to another individual retirement plan ("IRA F2") under section 408(d)(3)(A)(i). IRA F2 is a transferee plan to which paragraph (c)(6) of this section applies because of the rollover. F makes a $1,500 deductible contribution to IRA F2 for 1981.

(2) F dies in 1984. The balance in IRA F2 ($146,000) is payable to G, an individual, as a qualifying annuity, within the meaning of paragraph (b) of this section.

(3) Under paragraph (c) of this section, the amount *not* excluded from F's gross estate is the value of the qualifying annuity payable under IRA F2 multiplied by the fraction $96,700/$101,500. Accordingly, the amount not excluded is $139,096. [($146,000) ($96,700/$101,500) = $139,096.] The amount excluded is $6,904 ($146,000 – $139,096).

(4) The numerator of the fraction ($96,700) is determined by multiplying the amount rolled over from IRA F1 to IRA F2 ($100,000) by a fraction, the numerator of which is the amount of the rollover contribution to IRA F1 ($85,000), and the denominator of which is the total contributions to IRA F1 ($85,000 + $5,000 = $90,000). [($100,000) ($85,000/$90,000) = $96,700.]

(5) The denominator of the fraction ($101,500) is the sum of the contributions to IRA F2 (the $100,000 rollover contribution from IRA F1, and the $1,500 annual contribution to IRA F2). [Reg. § 20.2039-5.]

☐ [*T.D. 7761,* 1-21-81. *Amended by T.D. 8540,* 6-9-94.]

### [Reg. § 20.2040-1]

**§ 20.2040-1. Joint interests.**—(a) *In general.*—A decedent's gross estate includes under section 2040 the value of property held jointly at the time of the decedent's death by the decedent and another person or persons with right of survivorship, as follows:

(1) To the extent that the property was acquired by the decedent and the other joint owner or owners by gift, devise, bequest, or inheritance, the decedent's fractional share of the property is included.

(2) In all other cases, the entire value of the property is included except such part of the entire value as is attributable to the amount of the consideration in money or money's worth furnished by the other joint owner or owners. See § 20.2043-1 with respect to adequacy of consideration. Such part of the entire value is that portion of the entire value of the property at the decedent's death (or at the alternate valuation date described in section 2032) which the consideration in money or money's worth furnished by the other joint owner or owners bears to the total cost of acquisition and capital additions. In determining the consideration furnished by the other joint owner or owners, there is taken into account only that portion of such consideration which is shown not to be attributable to money or other property acquired by the other joint owner or owners from the decedent for less than a full and adequate consideration in money or money's worth.

The entire value of jointly held property is included in a decedent's gross estate unless the executor submits facts sufficient to show that property was not acquired entirely with consideration furnished by the decedent, or was acquired by the decedent and the other joint owner or owners by gift, bequest, devise, or inheritance.

(b) *Meaning of "property held jointly."*—Section 2040 specifically covers property held jointly by the decedent and any other person (or persons), property held by the decedent and spouse as tenants by the entirety, and a deposit of money, or a bond or other instrument, in the name of the decedent and any other person and payable to either or the survivor. The section applies to all classes of property, whether real or personal, and regardless of when the joint interests were created. Furthermore, it makes no difference that the survivor takes the entire interest in the property by right of survivorship and that no interest therein forms a part of the decedent's estate for purposes of administration. The section has no application to property held by the decedent and any other person (or persons) as tenants in common.

(c) *Examples.*—The application of this section may be explained in the following examples in each of which it is assumed that the other joint owner or owners survived the decedent:

(1) If the decedent furnished the entire purchase price of the jointly held property, the value of the entire property is included in his gross estate;

(2) If the decedent furnished only a part of the purchase price, only a corresponding portion of the value of the property is so included;

(3) If the decedent furnished no part of the purchase price, no part of the value of the property is so included;

(4) If the decedent, before the acquisition of the property by himself and the other joint owner, gave the latter a sum of money or other property which thereafter became the other joint owner's entire

contribution to the purchase price then the value of the entire property is so included, notwithstanding the fact that the other property may have appreciated in value due to market conditions between the time of the gift and the time of the acquisition of the jointly held property;

(5) If the decedent, before the acquisition of the property by himself and the other joint owner, transferred to the latter for less than an adequate and full consideration in money or money's worth other income-producing property, the income from which belonged to and became the other joint owner's entire contribution to the purchase price, then the value of the jointly held property less that portion attributable to the income which the other joint owner did furnish is included in the decedent's gross estate;

(6) If the property originally belonged to the other joint owner and the decedent purchased his interest from the other joint owner, only that portion of the value of the property attributable to the consideration paid by the decedent is included;

(7) If the decedent and his spouse acquired the property by will or gift as tenants by the entirety, one-half of the value of the property is included in the decedent's gross estate; and

(8) If the decedent and his two brothers acquired the property by will or gift as joint tenants, one-third of the value of the property is so included. [Reg. § 20.2040-1.]

☐ [T.D. 6296, 6-23-58.]

### [Reg. § 20.2041-1]

**§ 20.2041-1. Powers of appointment; in general.**—(a) *Introduction.*—A decedent's gross estate includes under section 2041 the value of property in respect of which the decedent possessed, exercised, or released certain powers of appointment. This section contains rules of general application; § 20.2041-2 contains rules specifically applicable to general powers of appointment created on or before October 21, 1942; and § 20.2041-3 sets forth specific rules applicable to powers of appointment created after October 21, 1942.

(b) *Definition of "power of appointment".*—(1) *In general.*—The term "power of appointment" includes all powers which are in substance and effect powers of appointment regardless of the nomenclature used in creating the power and regardless of local property law connotations. For example, if a trust instrument provides that the beneficiary may appropriate or consume the principal of the trust, the power to consume or appropriate is a power of appointment. Similarly, a power given to a decedent to affect the beneficial enjoyment of trust property or its income by altering, amending, or revoking the trust instrument or terminating the trust is a power of appointment. If the community property laws of a State confer upon the wife a power of testamentary disposition over property in which she does not have a vested interest she is considered as having a power of appointment. A power in a donee to remove or discharge a trustee and appoint himself may be a power of appointment. For example, if under the terms of a trust instrument, the trustee or his successor has the power to appoint the principal of the trust for the benefit of individuals including himself, and the decedent has the unrestricted power to remove or discharge the trustee at any time and appoint any other person including himself, the decedent is considered as having a power of appointment. However, the decedent is not considered to have a power of appointment if he only had the power to appoint a successor, including himself, under limited conditions which did not exist at the time of his death, without an accompanying unrestricted power of removal. Similarly, a power to amend only the administrative provisions of a trust instrument, which cannot substantially affect the beneficial enjoyment of the trust property or income, is not a power of appointment. The mere power of management, investment, custody of assets, or the power to allocate receipts and disbursements as between income and principal, exercisable in a fiduciary capacity, whereby the holder has no power to enlarge or shift any of the beneficial interests therein except as an incidental consequence of the discharge of such fiduciary duties is not a power of appointment. Further, the right in a beneficiary of a trust to assent to a periodic accounting, thereby relieving the trustee from further accountability, is not a power of appointment if the right of assent does not consist of any power or right to enlarge or shift the beneficial interest of any beneficiary therein.

(2) *Relation to other sections.*—For purposes of § § 20.2041-1 to 20.2041-3, the term "power of appointment" does not include powers reserved by the decedent to himself within the concept of sections 2036 to 2038. (See § § 20.2036-1 to 20.2038-1.) No provision of section 2041 or of § § 20.2041-1 to 20.2041-3 is to be construed as in any way limiting the application of any other section of the Internal Revenue Code or of these regulations. The power of the owner of a property interest already possessed by him to dispose of his interest, and nothing more, is not a power of appointment, and the interest is includible in his gross estate to the extent it would be includible

under section 2033 or some other provision of part III of subchapter A of chapter 11. For example, if a trust created by S provides for payment of the income to A for life with power in A to appoint the remainder by will and, in default of such appointment for payment of the income to A's widow, W, for her life and for payment of the remainder to A's estate, the value of A's interest in the remainder is includible in his gross estate under section 2033 regardless of its includibility under section 2041.

(3) *Powers over a portion of property.*—If a power of appointment exists as to part of an entire group of assets or only over a limited interest in property, section 2041 applies only to such part or interest. For example, if a trust created by S provides for the payment of income to A for life, then to W for life, with power in A to appoint the remainder by will and in default of appointment for payment of the remainder to B or his estate, and if A dies before W, section 2041 applies only to the value of the remainder interest excluding W's life estate. If A dies after W, section 2041 would apply to the value of the entire property. If the power were only over one-half the remainder interest, section 2041 would apply only to one-half the value of the amounts described above.

(c) *Definition of "general power of appointment".*—(1) *In general.*—The term "general power of appointment" as defined in section 2041(b)(1) means any power of appointment exercisable in favor of the decedent, his estate, his creditors, or the creditors of his estate, except (i) joint powers, to the extent provided in § § 20.2041-2 and 20.2041-3, and (ii) certain powers limited by an ascertainable standard, to the extent provided in subparagraph (2) of this paragraph. A power of appointment exercisable to meet the estate tax, or any other taxes, debts, or charges which are enforceable against the estate, is included within the meaning of a power of appointment exercisable in favor of the decedent's estate, his creditors, or the creditors of his estate. A power of appointment exercisable for the purpose of discharging a legal obligation of the decedent or for his pecuniary benefit is considered a power of appointment exercisable in favor of the decedent or his creditors. However, for purposes of § § 20.2041-1 to 20.2041-3, a power of appointment not otherwise considered to be a general power of appointment is not treated as a general power of appointment merely by reason of the fact that an appointee may, in fact, be a creditor of the decedent or his estate. A power of appointment is not a general power if by its terms it is either—

(a) Exercisable only in favor of one or more designated persons or classes other than the decedent or his creditors, or the decedent's estate or the creditors of his estate, or

(b) Expressly not exercisable in favor of the decedent or his creditors, or the decedent's estate or the creditors of his estate.
A decedent may have two powers under the same instrument, one of which is a general power of appointment and the other of which is not. For example, a beneficiary may have a power to withdraw trust corpus during his life, and a testamentary power to appoint the corpus among his descendants. The testamentary power is not a general power of appointment.

(2) *Powers limited by an ascertainable standard.*—A power to consume, invade, or appropriate income or corpus, or both, for the benefit of the decedent which is limited by an ascertainable standard relating to the health, education, support, or maintenance of the decedent is, by reason of section 2041(b)(1)(A), not a general power of appointment. A power is limited by such a standard if the extent of the holder's duty to exercise and not to exercise the power is reasonably measurable in terms of his needs for health, education, or support (or any combination of them). As used in this subparagraph, the words "support" and "maintenance" are synonymous and their meaning is not limited to the bare necessities of life. A power to use property for the comfort, welfare, or happiness of the holder of the power is not limited by the requisite standard. Examples of powers which are limited by the requisite standard are powers exercisable for the holder's "support," "support in reasonable comfort," "maintenance in health and reasonable comfort" "support in his accustomed manner of living," "education, including college and professional education," "health," and "medical, dental, hospital and nursing expenses and expenses of invalidism." In determining whether a power is limited by an ascertainable standard, it is immaterial whether the beneficiary is required to exhaust his other income before the power can be exercised.

(3) *Certain powers under wills of decedents dying between January 1 and April 2, 1948.*—Section 210 of the Technical Changes Act of 1953 provides that if a decedent died after December 31, 1947, but before April 3, 1948, certain property interests described therein may, if the decedent's surviving spouse so elects, be accorded special treatment in the determination of the marital deduction to be allowed the decedent's estate under the provisions of section 812(e) of the Internal Revenue Code of 1939. See § 81.47a(h) of Regulations 105 (26 CFR (1939) 81.47a(h)). The section further provides that property affected

by the election shall, for the purpose of inclusion in the surviving spouse's gross estate, be considered property with respect to which she has a general power of appointment. Therefore, notwithstanding any other provision of law or of §§ 20.2041-1 to 20.2041-3, if the present decedent (in her capacity as surviving spouse of a prior decedent) has made an election under section 210 of the Technical Changes Act of 1953, the property which was the subject of the election shall be considered as property with respect to which the present decedent has a general power of appointment created after October 21, 1942, exercisable by deed or will, to the extent it was treated as an interest passing to the surviving spouse and not passing to any other person for the purpose of the marital deduction in the prior decedent's estate.

(d) *Definition of "exercise.".*—Whether a power of appointment is in fact exercised may depend upon local law. For example, the residuary clause of a will may be considered under local law as an exercise of a testamentary power of appointment in the absence of evidence of a contrary intention drawn from the whole of the testator's will. However, regardless of local law, a power of appointment is considered as exercised for purposes of section 2041 even though the exercise is in favor of the taker in default of appointment, and irrespective of whether the appointed interest and the interest in default of appointment are identical or whether the appointee renounces any right to take under the appointment. A power of appointment is also considered as exercised even though the disposition cannot take effect until the occurrence of an event after the exercise takes place, if the exercise is irrevocable and, as of the time of the exercise, the condition was not impossible of occurrence. For example, if property is left in trust to A for life, with a power in B to appoint the remainder by will, and B dies before A, exercising his power by appointing the remainder to C if C survives A, B is considered to have exercised his power if C is living at B's death. On the other hand, a testamentary power of appointment is not considered as exercised if it is exercised subject to the occurrence during the decedent's life of an express or implied condition which did not in fact occur. Thus, if in the preceding example, C dies before B, B's power of appointment would not be considered to have been exercised. Similarly, if a trust provides for income to A for life, remainder as A appoints by will, and A appoints a life estate in the property to B and does not otherwise exercise his power, but B dies before A, A's power is not considered to have been exercised.

(e) *Time of creation of power.*—A power of appointment created by will is, in general, considered as created on the date of the testator's death. However, section 2041(b)(3) provides that a power of appointment created by a will executed on or before October 21, 1942, is considered a power created on or before that date if the testator dies before July 1, 1949, without having republished the will, by codicil or otherwise, after October 21, 1942. A power of appointment created by an inter vivos instrument is considered as created on the date the instrument takes effect. Such a power is not considered as created at some future date merely because it is not exercisable on the date the instrument takes effect, or because it is revocable, or because the identity of its holders is not ascertainable until after the date the instrument takes effect. However, if the holder of a power exercises it by creating a second power, the second power is considered as created at the time of the exercise of the first. The application of this paragraph may be illustrated by the following examples:

*Example (1).* A created a revocable trust before October 22, 1942, providing for payment of income to B for life with remainder as B shall appoint by will. Even though A dies after October 21, 1942, without having exercised his power of revocation, B's power of appointment is considered a power created before October 22, 1942.

*Example (2).* C created an irrevocable inter vivos trust before October 22, 1942, naming T as trustee and providing for payment of income to D for life with remainder to E. T was given the power to pay corpus to D and the power to appoint a successor trustee. If T resigns after October 21, 1942, and appoints D as successor trustee, D is considered to have a power of appointment created before October 22, 1942.

*Example (3).* F created an irrevocable inter vivos trust before October 22, 1942, providing for payment of income to G for life with remainder as G shall appoint by will, but in default of appointment income to H for life with remainder as H shall appoint by will. If G died after October 21, 1942, without having exercised his power of appointment, H's power of appointment is considered a power created before October 22, 1942, even though it was only a contingent interest until G's death.

*Example (4).* If in example (3) above G had exercised his power of appointment by creating a similar power in J, J's power of appointment would be considered a power created after October 21, 1942. [Reg. § 20.2041-1.]

☐ [*T.D.* 6296, 6-23-58. *Amended by T.D.* 6582, 12/11/61.]

[Reg. § 20.2041-2]

§ 20.2041-2. Powers of appointment created on or before October 21, 1942.—(a) *In general.*—Property subject to a general power of appointment created on or before October 21, 1942, is includible in the gross estate of the holder of the power under section 2041 only if he exercised the power under specified circumstances. Section 2041(a)(1) requires that there be included in the gross estate of a decedent the value of property subject to such a power only if the power is exercised by the decedent either (1) by will, or (2) by a disposition which is of such nature that if it were a transfer of property owned by the decedent, the property would be includible in the decedent's gross estate under section 2035 (relating to transfers in contemplation of death), 2036 (relating to transfers with retained estate), 2037 (relating to transfers taking effect at death), or 2038 (relating to revocable transfers). See paragraphs (b), (c), and (d) of § 20.2041-1 for the definition of various terms used in this section.

(b) *Joint powers created on or before October 21, 1942.*—Section 2041(b)(1)(B) provides that a power created on or before October 21, 1942, which at the time of the exercise is not exercisable by the decedent except in conjunction with another person, is not deemed a general power of appointment.

(c) *Exercise during life.*—The circumstances under which section 2041 applies to the exercise other than by will of a general power of appointment created on or before October 21, 1942, are set forth in paragraph (a) of this section. In this connection, the rules of sections 2035 through 2038 which are to be applied are those in effect on the date of the decedent's death which are applicable to transfers made on the date when the exercise of the power occurred. Those rules are to be applied in determining the extent to which and the conditions under which a disposition is considered a transfer of property. The application of this paragraph may be illustrated by the following examples:

*Example (1).* A decedent in 1951 exercised a general power of appointment created in 1940, reserving no interest in or power over the property subject to the general power. The decedent died in 1956. Since the exercise was not made within three years before the decedent's death, no part of the property is includible in his gross estate. See section 2035(b), relating to transfers in contemplation of death.

*Example (2).* S created a trust in 1930 to pay the income to A for life, remainder as B appoints by an instrument filed with the trustee during B's lifetime, and in default of appointment remainder to C. B exercised the power in 1955 by directing that after A's death the income be paid to himself for life with remainder to C. If B dies after A, the entire value of the trust property would be included in B's gross estate, since such a disposition if it were a transfer of property owned by B would cause the property to be included in his gross estate under section 2036(a)(1). If B dies before A, the value of the trust property less the value of A's life estate would be included in B's gross estate for the same reason.

*Example (3).* S created a trust in 1940 to pay the income to A for life, remainder as A appoints by an instrument filed with the trustee during A's lifetime. A exercised the power in 1955, five years before his death, reserving the right of revocation. The exercise, if not revoked before death, will cause the property subject to the power to be included in A's gross estate under section 2041(a)(1), since such a disposition if it were a transfer of property owned by A would cause the property to be included in his gross estate under section 2038. However, if the exercise were completely revoked, so that A died still possessed of the power, the property would not be included in A's gross estate for the reason that the power will not be treated as having been exercised.

*Example (4).* A decedent exercised a general power of appointment created in 1940 by making a disposition in trust under which possession or enjoyment of the property subject to the exercise could be obtained only by surviving the decedent and under which the decedent retained a reversionary interest in the property of a value of more than five percent. The exercise will cause the property subject to the power to be included in the decedent's gross estate, since such a disposition if it were a transfer of property owned by the decedent would cause the property to be included in his gross estate under section 2037.

(d) *Release or lapse.*—A failure to exercise a general power of appointment created on or before October 21, 1942, or a complete release of such a power is not considered to be an exercise of a general power of appointment. The phrase "a complete release" means a release of all powers over all or a portion of the property subject to a power of appointment, as distinguished from the reduction of a power of appointment to a lesser power. Thus, if the decedent completely relinquished all powers over one-half of the property subject to a power of appointment, the power is completely released as to that one-half. If at or before the time a power of appointment is relinquished, the holder of the power exercises the power in such a manner or to such an extent that the relinquishment results in the reduction, enlargement, or shift in a beneficial interest in property, the relinquishment will be considered to be an exercise and not a release of the power. For example, assume that A created a trust in 1940 providing for payment of the income to B for life and, upon B's death, remainder to C. Assume further that B was given the unlimited power to amend the trust instrument during his lifetime. If B amended the trust in 1948 by providing that upon his death the remainder was to be paid to D, and if he further amended the trust in 1950 by deleting his power to amend the trust, such relinquishment will be considered an exercise and not a release of a general power of appointment. On the other hand, if the 1948 amendment became ineffective before or at the time of the 1950 amendment, or if B in 1948 merely amended the trust by changing the purely ministerial powers of the trustee, his relinquishment of the power in 1950 will be considered as a release of a power of appointment.

(e) *Partial release.*—If a general power of appointment created on or before October 21, 1942, is partially released so that it is not thereafter a general power of appointment, a subsequent exercise of the partially released power is not an exercise of a general power of appointment if the partial release occurs before whichever is the later of the following dates:

(1) November 1, 1951, or

(2) If the decedent was under a legal disability to release the power on October 21, 1942, the day after the expiration of 6 months following the termination of such legal disability.

However, if a general power created on or before October 21, 1942, is partially released on or after the later of these dates, a subsequent exercise of the power will cause the property subject to the power to be included in the holder's gross estate, if the exercise is such that if it were a disposition of property owned by the decedent it would cause the property to be included in his gross estate. The legal disability referred to in this paragraph is determined under local law and may include the disability of an insane person, a minor, or an unborn child. The fact that the type of general power of appointment possessed by the decedent actually was not generally releasable under the local law does not place the decedent under a legal disability within the meaning of this paragraph. In general, however, it is assumed that all general powers of appointment are releasable, unless the local law on the subject is to the contrary, and it is presumed that the method employed to release the power is effective, unless it is not in accordance with the local law relating specifically to releases or, in the absence of such local law, is not in accordance with the local law relating to similar transactions.

(f) *Partial exercise.*—If a general power of appointment created on or before October 21, 1942, is exercised only as to a portion of the property subject to the power, section 2041 is applicable only to the value of that portion. For example, if a decedent had a general power of appointment exercisable by will created on or before October 21, 1942, over a trust fund valued at $200,000 at the date of his death, and if the decedent exercised his power either to the extent of directing the distribution of one-half of the trust property to B or of directing the payment of $100,000 to B, the trust property would be includible in the decedent's gross estate only to the extent of $100,000. [Reg. § 20.2041-2.]

☐ [*T. D. 6296, 6/23/58.*]

**[Reg. § 20.2041-3]**

**§ 20.2041-3. Powers of appointment created after October 21, 1942.**—(a) *In general.*—(1) Property subject to a power of appointment created after October 21, 1942, is includible in the gross estate of the holder of the power under varying conditions depending on whether the power is (i) general in nature, (ii) possessed at death, or (iii) exercised or released. See paragraphs (b), (c), and (d) of § 20.2041-1 for the definition of various terms used in this section. See paragraph (c) of this section for the rules applicable to determine the extent to which joint powers created after October 21, 1942, are to be treated as general powers of appointment.

(2) If the power is a general power of appointment, the value of an interest in property subject to such a power is includible in a decedent's gross estate under section 2041(a)(2) if either—

(i) The decedent has the power at the time of his death (and the interest exists at the time of his death), or

(ii) The decedent exercised or released the power, or the power lapsed, under the circumstances and to the extent described in paragraph (d) of this section.

(3) If the power is not a general power of appointment, the value of property subject to the power is includible in the holder's gross estate under section 2041(a)(3) only if it is exercised to create a further power under certain circumstances (see paragraph (e) of this section).

(b) *Existence of power at death.*—For purposes of section 2041(a)(2), a power of appointment is considered to exist on the date of a decedent's death even though the exercise of the power is subject to the precedent giving of notice, or even though the exercise of the power takes effect only on the expiration of a stated period after its exercise, whether or not on or before the decedent's death notice has been given or the power has been exercised. However, a power which by its terms is exercisable only upon the occurrence during the decedent's lifetime of an event or a contingency which did not in fact take place or occur during such time is not a power in existence on the date of the decedent's death. For example, if a decedent was given a general power of appointment exercisable only after he reached a certain age, only if he survived another person, or only if he died without descendants, the power would not be in existence on the date of the decedent's death if the condition precedent to its exercise had not occurred.

(c) *Joint powers created after October 21, 1942.*—The treatment of a power of appointment created after October 21, 1942, which is exercisable only in conjunction with another person is governed by section 2041(b)(1)(C), which provides as follows:

(1) Such a power is not considered a general power of appointment if it is not exercisable by the decedent except with the consent or joinder of the creator of the power.

(2) Such power is not considered a general power of appointment if it is not exercisable by the decedent except with the consent or joinder of a person having a substantial interest in the property subject to the power which is adverse to the exercise of the power in favor of the decedent, his estate, his creditors, or the creditors of his estate. An interest adverse to the exercise of a power is considered as substantial if its value in relation to the total value of the property subject to the power is not insignificant. For this purpose, the interest is to be valued in accordance with the actuarial principles set forth in § 20.2031-7 or, if it is not susceptible to valuation under those provisions, in accordance with the general principles set forth in § 20.2031-1. A taker in default of appointment under a power has an interest which is adverse to an exercise of the power. A coholder of the power has no adverse interest merely because of his joint possession of the power nor merely because he is a permissible appointee under a power. However, a coholder of a power is considered as having an adverse interest where he may possess the power after the decedent's death and may exercise it at that time in favor of himself, his estate, his creditors, or the creditors of his estate. Thus, for example, if X, Y, and Z held a power jointly to appoint among a group of persons which includes themselves and if on the death of X the power will pass to Y and Z jointly, then Y and Z are considered to have interests adverse to the exercise of the power in favor of X. Similarly, if on Y's death the power will pass to Z, Z is considered to have an interest adverse to the exercise of the power in favor of Y. The application of this subparagraph may be further illustrated by the following additional examples in each of which it is assumed that the value of the interest in question is substantial:

*Example (1).* The decedent and R were trustees of a trust under the terms of which the income was to be paid to the decedent for life and then to M for life, and the remainder was to be paid to R. The trustees had power to distribute corpus to the decedent. Since R's interest was substantially adverse to an exercise of the power in favor of the decedent the latter did not have a general power of appointment. If M and the decedent were the trustees, M's interest would likewise have been adverse.

*Example (2).* The decedent and L were trustees of a trust under the terms of which the income was to be paid to L for life and then to M for life, and the remainder was to be paid to the decedent. The trustees had power to distribute corpus to the decedent during L's life. Since L's interest was adverse to an exercise of the power in favor of the decedent, the decedent did not have a general power of appointment. If the decedent and M were the trustees, M's interest would likewise have been adverse.

*Example (3).* The decedent and L were trustees of a trust under the terms of which the income was to be paid to L for life. The trustees could designate whether corpus was to be distributed to the decedent or to A after L's death. L's interest was not adverse to an exercise of the power in favor of the decedent, and the decedent therefore had a general power of appointment.

(3) A power which is exercisable only in conjunction with another person, and which after application of the rules set forth in subparagraphs (1) and (2) of this paragraph constitutes a general power of appointment, will be treated as though the holders of the power who are permissible appointees of the property were joint owners of property subject to the power. The decedent, under this rule, will be treated as possessed of a general power of appointment over an aliquot share of the property to be determined with reference to the number of joint holders, including the decedent, who (or whose estates or creditors) are permissible appointees. Thus, for example, if X, Y, and Z hold an unlimited power jointly to appoint

among a group of persons, including themselves, but on the death of X the power does not pass to Y and Z jointly, then Y and Z are not considered to have interests adverse to the exercise of the power in favor of X. In this case X is considered to possess a general power of appointment as to one-third of the property subject to the power.

(d) *Releases, lapses, and disclaimers of general powers of appointment.*— (1) Property subject to a general power of appointment created after October 21, 1942, is includible in the gross estate of a decedent under section 2041(a)(2) even though he does not have the power at the date of his death, if during his life he exercised or released the power under circumstances such that, if the property subject to the power had been owned and transferred by the decedent, the property would be includible in the decedent's gross estate under section 2035, 2036, 2037, or 2038. Further, section 2041(b)(2) provides that the lapse of a power of appointment is considered to be a release of the power to the extent set forth in subparagraph (3) of this paragraph. A release of a power of appointment need not be formal or express in character. The principles set forth in §20.2041-2 for determining the application of the pertinent provisions of sections 2035 through 2038 to a particular exercise of a power of appointment are applicable for purposes of determining whether or not an exercise or release of a power of appointment created after October 21, 1942, causes the property to be included in a decedent's gross estate under section 2041(a)(2). If a general power of appointment created after October 21, 1942, is partially released, a subsequent exercise or release of the power under circumstances described in the first sentence of this subparagraph, or its possession at death, will nevertheless cause the property subject to the power to be included in the gross estate of the holder of the power.

(2) Section 2041(a)(2) is not applicable to the complete release of a general power of appointment created after October 21, 1942, whether exercisable during life or by will, if the release was not made in contemplation of death within the meaning of section 2035, and if after the release the holder of the power retained no interest in or control over the property subject to the power which would cause the property to be included in his gross estate under sections 2036 through 2038 if the property had been transferred by the holder.

(3) The failure to exercise a power of appointment created after October 21, 1942, within a specified time, so that the power lapses, constitutes a release of the power. However, section 2041(b)(2) provides that such a lapse of a power of appointment during any calendar year during the decedent's life is treated as a release for purposes of inclusion of property in the gross estate under section 2041(a)(2) only to the extent that the property which could have been appointed by exercise of the lapsed power exceeds the greater of (i) $5,000 or (ii) 5 percent of the aggregate value, at the time of the lapse, of the assets out of which, or the proceeds of which, the exercise of the lapsed power could have been satisfied. For example, assume that A transferred $200,000 worth of securities in trust providing for payment of income to B for life with remainder to B's issue. Assume further that B was given a non-cumulative right to withdraw $10,000 a year from the principal of the trust fund (which neither increased nor decreased in value prior to B's death). In such case, the failure of B to exercise his right of withdrawal will not result in estate tax with respect to the power to withdraw $10,000 which lapses each year before the year of B's death. At B's death there will be included in his gross estate the $10,000 which he was entitled to withdraw for the year in which his death occurs less any amount which he may have taken during that year. However, if in the above example B had possessed the right to withdraw $15,000 of the principal annually, the failure to exercise such power in any year will be considered a release of the power to the extent of the excess of the amount subject to withdrawal over 5 percent of the trust fund (in this example, $5,000, assuming that the trust fund is worth $200,000 at the time of the lapse). Since each lapse is treated as though B had exercised dominion over the trust property by making a transfer of principal reserving the income therefrom for his life, the value of the trust property (but only to the extent of the excess of the amount subject to withdrawal over 5 percent of the trust fund) is includible in B's gross estate (unless before B's death he has disposed of his right to the income under circumstances to which sections 2035 through 2038 would not be applicable). The extent to which the value of the trust property is included in the decedent's gross estate is determined as provided in subparagraph (4) of this paragraph.

(4) The purpose of section 2041(b)(2) is to provide a determination, as of the date of the lapse of the power, of the proportion of the property over which the power lapsed which is an exempt disposition for estate tax purposes and the proportion which, if the other requirements of sections 2035 through 2038 are satisfied, will be considered as a taxable disposition. Once the taxable proportion of any disposition at the date of lapse has been determined, the valuation of that proportion as of the date of the decedent's death (or, if the executor has elected the alternate valuation method under section 2032, the value as of the date therein provided), is to be ascertained in

accordance with the principles which are applicable to the valuation of transfers of property by the decedent under the corresponding provisions of sections 2035 through 2038. For example, if the life beneficiary of a trust had a right exercisable only during one calendar year to draw down $50,000 from the corpus of a trust, which he did not exercise, and if at the end of the year the corpus was worth $800,000, the taxable portion over which the power lapsed is $10,000 (the excess of $50,000 over 5 percent of the corpus), or $1/80$ of the total value. On the decedent's death, if the total value of the corpus of the trust (excluding income accumulated after the lapse of the power) on the applicable valuation date was $1,200,000, $15,000 ($1/80$ of $1,200,000) would be includible in the decedent's gross estate. However, if the total value was then $600,000, only $7,500 ($1/80$ of $600,000) would be includible.

(5) If the failure to exercise a power, such as a right of withdrawal, occurs in more than a single year, the proportion of the property over which the power lapsed which is treated as a taxable disposition will be determined separately for each such year. The aggregate of the taxable proportions for all such years, valued in accordance with the above principles, will be includible in the gross estate by reason of the lapse. The includible amount, however, shall not exceed the aggregate value of the assets out of which, or the proceeds of which, the exercise of the power could have been satisfied, valued as of the date of the decedent's death (or, if the executor has elected the alternate valuation method under section 2032, the value as of the date therein provided).

(6)(i) A disclaimer or renunciation of a general power of appointment created in a transfer made after December 31, 1976, is not considered to be the release of the power if the disclaimer or renunciation is a qualified disclaimer as described in section 2518 and the corresponding regulations, For rules relating to when the transfer creating the power occurs, see §25.2518-2(c)(3) of this chapter. If the disclaimer or renunciation is not a qualified disclaimer, it is considered a release of the power by the disclaimant.

(ii) The disclaimer or renunciation of a general power of appointment created in a taxable transfer before January 1, 1977, in the person disclaiming is not considered to be a release of the power. The disclaimer or renunciation must be unequivocal and effective under local law. A disclaimer is a complete and unqualified refusal to accept the rights to which one is entitled. There can be no disclaimer or renunciation of a power after its acceptance. In the absence of facts to the contrary, the failure to renounce or disclaim within a reasonable time after learning of its existence will be presumed to constitute an acceptance of the power. In any case where a power is purported to be disclaimed or renounced as to only a portion of the property subject to the power, the determination as to whether or not there has been a complete and unqualified refusal to accept the rights to which one is entitled will depend on all the facts and circumstances of the particular case, taking into account the recognition and effectiveness of such a disclaimer under local law. Such rights refer to the incidents of the power and not to other interests of the decedent in the property. If effective under local law, the power may be disclaimed or renounced without disclaiming or renouncing such other interests.

(iii) The first and second sentences of paragraph (d)(6)(i) of this section are applicable for transfers creating the power to be disclaimed made on or after December 31, 1997.

(e) *Successive powers.*—(1) Property subject to a power of appointment created after October 21, 1942, which is not a general power, is includible in the gross estate of the holder of the power under section 2041(a)(3) if the power is exercised, and if both of the following conditions are met:

(i) If the exercise is *(a)* by will, or *(b)* by a disposition which is of such nature that if it were a transfer of property owned by the decedent, the property would be includible in the decedent's gross estate under sections 2035 through 2037; and

(ii) If the power is exercised by creating another power of appointment which, under the terms of the instruments creating and exercising the first power and under applicable local law, can be validly exercised so as to *(a)* postpone the vesting of any estate or interest in the property for a period ascertainable without regard to the date of the creation of the first power, or *(b)* (if the applicable rule against perpetuities is stated in terms of suspension of ownership or of the power of alienation, rather than of vesting) suspend the absolute ownership or the power of alienation of the property for a period ascertainable without regard to the date of the creation of the first power.

(2) For purposes of the application of section 2041(a)(3), the value of the property subject to the second power of appointment is considered to be its value unreduced by any precedent or subsequent interest which is not subject to the second power. Thus, if a decedent has a power to appoint by will $100,000 to a group of persons consisting of his children and grandchildren and exercises the power by making an outright appointment of $75,000 and by giving one appointee a power to appoint $25,000, no more than $25,000 will be

includible in the decedent's gross estate under section 2041(a)(3). If, however, the decedent appoints the income from the entire fund to a beneficiary for life with power in the beneficiary to appoint the remainder by will, the entire $100,000 will be includible in the decedent's gross estate under section 2041(a)(3) if the exercise of the second power can validly postpone the vesting of any estate or interest in the property or can suspend the absolute ownership or power of alienation of the property for a period ascertainable without regard to the date of the creation of the first power.

(f) *Examples.*—The application of this section may be further illustrated by the following examples, in each of which it is assumed, unless otherwise stated, that S has transferred property in trust after October 21, 1942, with the remainder payable to R at L's death, and that neither L nor R has any interest in or power over the enjoyment of the trust property except as is indicated separately in each example:

*Example (1).* Income is directed to be paid to L during his lifetime at the end of each year, if living. L has an unrestricted power during his lifetime to cause the income to be distributed to any other person, but no power to cause it to be accumulated. At L's death, no part of the trust property is includible in L's gross estate since L had a power to dispose of only his income interest, a right otherwise possessed by him.

*Example (2).* Income is directed to be accumulated during L's life but L has a noncumulative power to distribute $10,000 of each year's income to himself. Unless L's power is limited by an ascertainable standard (relating to his health, etc.), as defined in paragraph (c)(2) of §20.2041-1, he has a general power of appointment over $10,000 of each year's income, the lapse of which may cause a portion of any income not distributed to be included in his gross estate under section 2041. See subparagraphs (3), (4), and (5) of paragraph (d) of this section. Thus, if the trust income during the year amounts to $20,000, L's failure to distribute any of the income to himself constitutes a lapse as to $5,000 (i.e., the amount by which $10,000 exceeds $5,000). If L's power were cumulative (i.e., if the power did not lapse at the end of each year but lapsed only by reason of L's death), the total accumulations which L chose not to distribute to himself immediately before his death would be includible in his gross estate under section 2041.

*Example (3).* L is entitled to all the income during his lifetime and has an unrestricted power to cause corpus to be distributed to himself. L had a general power of appointment over the corpus of the trust, and the entire corpus as of the time of his death is includible in his gross estate under section 2041.

*Example (4).* Income was payable to L during his lifetime. R has an unrestricted power to cause corpus to be distributed to L. R dies before L. In such case, R has only a power to dispose of his remainder interest, the value of which is includible in his gross estate under section 2033, and nothing in addition would be includible under section 2041. If in this example R's remainder were contingent on his surviving L, nothing would be includible in his gross estate under either section 2033 or 2041. While R would have a power of appointment, it would not be a general power.

*Example (5).* Income was payable to L during his lifetime. R has an unrestricted power to cause corpus to be distributed to himself. R dies before L. While the value of R's remainder interest is includible in his gross estate under section 2033, R also has a general power of appointment over the entire trust corpus. Under such circumstances, the entire value of the trust corpus is includible in R's gross estate under section 2041. [Reg. §20.2041-3.]

☐ [*T.D. 6296, 6-23-58. Amended by T.D. 8095, 8-6-86 and T.D. 8744, 12-30-97.*]

### [Reg. §20.2042-1]

**§20.2042-1. Proceeds of life insurance.**—(a) *In general.*—(1) Section 2042 provides for the inclusion in a decedent's gross estate of the proceeds of insurance on the decedent's life (i) receivable by or for the benefit of the estate (see paragraph (b) of this section), and (ii) receivable by other beneficiaries(see paragraph (c) of this section). The term "insurance" refers to life insurance of every description, including death benefits paid by fraternal beneficial societies operating under the lodge system.

(2) Proceeds of life insurance which are not includible in the gross estate under section 2042 may, depending upon the facts of the particular case, be includible under some other section of part III of subchapter A of chapter 11. For example, if the decedent possessed incidents of ownership in an insurance policy on his life but gratuitously transferred all rights in the policy in contemplation of death, the proceeds would be includible under section 2035. Section 2042 has no application to the inclusion in the gross estate of the value of rights in an insurance policy on the life of a person other than the decedent, or the value of rights in a combination annuity contract and life insurance policy on the decedent's life (i.e., a "retirement

income" policy with death benefit or an "endowment" policy) under which there was no insurance element at the time of the decedent's death (see paragraph (d) of §20.2039-1).

(3) Except as provided in paragraph (c)(6), the amount to be included in the gross estate under section 2042 is the full amount receivable under the policy. If the proceeds of the policy are made payable to a beneficiary in the form of an annuity for life or for a term of years, the amount to be included in the gross estate is the one sum payable at death under an option which could have been exercised either by the insured or by the beneficiary, or if no option was granted, the sum used by the insurance company in determining the amount of the annuity.

(b) *Receivable by or for the benefit of the estate.*—(1) Section 2042 requires the inclusion in the gross estate of the proceeds of insurance on the decedent's life receivable by the executor or administrator, or payable to the decedent's estate. It makes no difference whether or not the estate is specifically named as the beneficiary under the terms of the policy. Thus, if under the terms of an insurance policy the proceeds are receivable by another beneficiary but are subject to an obligation, legally binding upon the other beneficiary, to pay taxes, debts, or other charges enforceable against the estate, then the amount of such proceeds required for the payment in full (to the extent of the beneficiary's obligation) of such taxes, debts, or other charges is includible in the gross estate. Similarly, if the decedent purchased an insurance policy in favor of another person or a corporation as collateral security for a loan or other accommodation, its proceeds are considered to be receivable for the benefit of the estate. The amount of the loan outstanding at the date of the decedent's death, with interest accrued to that date, will be deductible in determining the taxable estate. See §20.2053-4.

(2) If the proceeds of an insurance policy made payable to the decedent's estate are community assets under the local community property law and, as a result, one-half of the proceeds belongs to the decedent's spouse, then only one-half of the proceeds is considered to be receivable by or for the benefit of the decedent's estate.

(c) *Receivable by other beneficiaries.*—(1) Section 2042 requires the inclusion in the gross estate of the proceeds of insurance on the decedent's life not receivable by or for the benefit of the estate if the decedent possessed at the date of his death any of the incidents of ownership in the policy, exercisable either alone or in conjunction with any other person. However, if the decedent did not possess any of such incidents of ownership at the time of his death nor transfer them in contemplation of death, no part of the proceeds would be includible in his gross estate under section 2042. Thus, if the decedent owned a policy of insurance on his life and, 4 years before his death, irrevocably assigned his entire interest in the policy to his wife retaining no reversionary interest therein (see subparagraph (3) of this paragraph), the proceeds of the policy would not be includible in his gross estate under section 2042.

(2) For purposes of this paragraph, the term "incidents of ownership" is not limited in its meaning to ownership of the policy in the technical legal sense. Generally speaking, the term has reference to the right of the insured or his estate to the economic benefits of the policy. Thus, it includes the power to change the beneficiary, to surrender or cancel the policy, to assign the policy, to revoke an assignment, to pledge the policy for a loan, or to obtain from the insurer a loan against the surrender value of the policy, etc. See subparagraph (6) of this paragraph for rules relating to the circumstances under which incidents of ownership held by a corporation are attributable to a decedent through his stock ownership.

(3) The term "incidents of ownership" also includes a reversionary interest in the policy or its proceeds, whether arising by the express terms of the policy or other instrument or by operation of law, but only if the value of the reversionary interest immediately before the death of the decedent exceeded 5 percent of the value of the policy. As used in this subparagraph, the term "reversionary interest" includes a possibility that the policy or its proceeds may return to the decedent or his estate and a possibility that the policy or its proceeds may become subject to a power of disposition by him. In order to determine whether or not the value of a reversionary interest immediately before the death of the decedent exceeded 5 percent of the value of the policy, the principles contained in paragraph (c)(3) and (4) of §20.2037-1 insofar as applicable, shall be followed under this subparagraph. In that connection, there must be specifically taken into consideration any incidents of ownership held by others immediately before the decedent's death which would affect the value of the reversionary interest. For example, the decedent would not be considered to have a reversionary interest in the policy of a value in excess of 5 percent if the power to obtain the cash surrender value existed in some other person immediately before the decedent's death and was exercisable by such other person alone and in all events. The terms "reversionary interest" and "incidents of ownership" do not include the possibility that the decedent might receive

a policy or its proceeds by inheritance through the estate of another person, or as a surviving spouse under a statutory right of election or a similar right.

(4) A decedent is considered to have an "incident of ownership" in an insurance policy on his life held in trust if, under the terms of the policy, the decedent (either alone or in conjunction with another person or persons) has the power (as trustee or otherwise) to change the beneficial ownership in the policy or its proceeds, or the time or manner of enjoyment thereof, even though the decedent has no beneficial interest in the trust. Moreover, assuming the decedent created the trust, such a power may result in the inclusion in the decedent's gross estate under section 2036 or 2038 of other property transferred by the decedent to the trust if, for example, the decedent has the power to surrender the insurance policy and if the income otherwise used to pay premiums on the policy would become currently payable to a beneficiary of the trust in the event that the policy were surrendered.

(5) As an additional step in determining whether or not a decedent possessed any incidents of ownership in a policy or any part of a policy, regard must be given to the effect of the State or other applicable law upon the terms of the policy. For example, assume that the decedent purchased a policy of insurance on his life with funds held by him and his surviving wife as community property, designating their son as beneficiary but retaining the right to surrender the policy. Under the local law, the proceeds upon surrender would have inured to the marital community. Assuming that the policy is not surrendered and that the son receives the proceeds on the decedent's death, the wife's transfer of her one-half interest in the policy was not considered absolute before the decedent's death. Upon the wife's prior death, one-half of the value of the policy would have been included in her gross estate. Under these circumstances, the power of surrender possessed by the decedent as agent for his wife with respect to one-half of the policy is not, for purposes of this section, an "incident of ownership", and the decedent is, therefore, deemed to possess an incident of ownership in only one-half of the policy.

(6) In the case of economic benefits of a life insurance policy on the decedent's life that are reserved to a corporation of which the decedent is the sole or controlling stockholder, the corporation's incidents of ownership will not be attributed to the decedent through his stock ownership to the extent the proceeds of the policy are payable to the corporation. Any proceeds payable to a third party for a valid business purpose, such as in satisfaction of a business debt of the corporation, so that the net worth of the corporation is increased by the amount of such proceeds, shall be deemed to be payable to the corporation for purposes of the preceding sentence. See §20.2031-2(f) for a rule providing that the proceeds of certain life insurance policies shall be considered in determining the value of the decedent's stock. Except as hereinafter provided with respect to a group-term life insurance policy, if any part of the proceeds of the policy are not payable to or for the benefit of the corporation, and thus are not taken into account in valuing the decedent's stock holdings in the corporation for purposes of section 2031, any incidents of ownership held by the corporation as to that part of the proceeds will be attributed to the decedent through his stock ownership where the decedent is the sole or controlling stockholder. Thus, for example, if the decedent is the controlling stockholder in a corporation, and the corporation owns a life insurance policy on his life, the proceeds of which are payable to the decedent's spouse, the incidents of ownership held by the corporation will be attributed to the decedent through his stock ownership and the proceeds will be included in his gross estate under section 2042. If in this example the policy proceeds had been payable 40 percent to decedent's spouse and 60 percent to the corporation, only 40 percent of the proceeds would be included in decedent's gross estate under section 2042. For purposes of this subparagraph, the decedent will not be deemed to be the controlling stockholder of a corporation unless, at the time of his death, he owned stock possessing more than 50 percent of the total combined voting power of the corporation. Solely for purposes of the preceding sentence, a decedent shall be considered to be the owner of only the stock with respect to which legal title was held, at the time of his death, by (i) the decedent (or his agent or nominee); [(ii)] the decedent and another person jointly (but only the proportionate number of shares which corresponds to the portion of the total consideration which is considered to be furnished by the decedent for purposes of section 2040 and the regulations thereunder); and (iii) by a trustee of a voting trust (to the extent of the decedent's beneficial interest therein) or any other trust with respect to which the decedent was treated as an owner under subpart E, part I, subchapter J, chapter 1 of the Code immediately prior to his death. In the case of group-term life insurance, as defined the regulations under section 79, the power to surrender or cancel a policy held by a corporation shall not be attributed to any decedent through his stock ownership. [Reg. §20.2042-1.]

[T.D. 6296, 6-23-58. Amended by T.D. 7312, 4-26-74 and T.D. 7623, 5-14-79.]

### [Reg. §20.2043-1]

§20.2043-1. Transfers for insufficient consideration.—(a) In general.—The transfers, trusts, interests, rights or powers enumerated and described in sections 2035 through 2038 and section 2041 are not subject to the Federal estate tax if made, created, exercised, or relinquished in a transaction which constituted a bona fide sale for an adequate and full consideration in money or money's worth. To constitute a bona fide sale for an adequate and full consideration in money or money's worth, the transfer must have been made in good faith, and the price must have been an adequate and full equivalent reducible to a money value. If the price was less than such a consideration, only the excess of the fair market value of the property (as of the applicable valuation date) over the price received by the decedent is included in ascertaining the value of his gross estate.

(b) Marital rights and support obligations.—For purposes of chapter 11, a relinquishment or promised relinquishment of dower, curtesy, or of a statutory estate created in lieu of dower or curtesy, or of other marital rights in the decedent's property or estate, is not to support obligations. For purposes of chapter 11, a relinquishment or promised relinquishment of dower, curtesy, or of a statutory estate created in lieu of dower or curtesy, or of other marital rights in the decedent's property or estate, is not to any extent a consideration in "money or money's worth." [Reg. §20.2043-1.]

[T.D. 6296, 6-23-58.]

### [Reg. §20.2044-1]

§20.2044-1. Certain property for which marital deduction was previously allowed.—(a) In general.—Section 2044 generally provides for the inclusion in the gross estate of property in which the decedent had a qualifying income interest for life and for which a deduction was allowed under section 2056(b)(7) or 2523(f). The value of the property included in the gross estate under section 2044 is not reduced by the amount of any section 2503(b) exclusion that applied to the transfer creating the interest. See section 2207A, regarding the right of recovery against the persons receiving the property that is applicable in certain cases.

(b) Passed from.—For purposes of section 1014 and chapters 11 and 13 of subtitle B of the Internal Revenue Code, property included in a decedent's gross estate under section 2044 is considered to have been acquired from or to have passed from the decedent to the person receiving the property upon the decedent's death. Thus, for example, the property is treated as passing from the decedent for purposes of determining the availability of the charitable deduction under section 2055, the marital deduction under section 2056, and special use valuation under section 2032A. In addition, the tax imposed on property includible under section 2044 is eligible for the installment payment of estate tax under section 6166.

(c) Presumption.—Unless established to the contrary, section 2044 applies to the entire value of the trust at the surviving spouse's death. If a marital deduction is taken on either the estate or gift tax return with respect to the transfer which created the qualifying income interest, it is presumed that the deduction was allowed for purposes of section 2044. To avoid the inclusion of property in the decedent-spouse's gross estate under this section, the executor of the spouse's estate must establish that a deduction was not taken for the transfer which created the qualifying income interest. For example, to establish that a deduction was not taken, the executor may produce a copy of the estate or gift tax return filed with respect to the transfer by the first spouse or the first spouse's estate establishing that no deduction was taken under section 2523(f) or section 2056(b)(7). In addition, the executor may establish that no return was filed on the original transfer by the decedent because the value of the first spouse's gross estate was below the threshold requirement for filing under section 6018. Similarly, the executor could establish that the transfer creating the decedent's qualifying income interest for life was made before the effective date of section 2056(b)(7) or section 2523(f).

(d) Amount included.—(1) In general.—The amount included under this section is the value of the entire interest in which the decedent had a qualifying income interest for life, determined as of the date of the decedent's death (or the alternate valuation date, if applicable). If, in connection with the transfer of property that created the decedent's qualifying income interest for life, a deduction was allowed under section 2056(b)(7) or section 2523(f) for less than the entire interest in the property (i.e., for a fractional or percentage share of the entire interest in the transferred property), the amount includible in the decedent's gross estate under this section is equal to the fair market value of the entire interest in the property on the date of the decedent's death (or the alternate valuation date, if applicable) multiplied by the fractional or percentage share of the interest for which the deduction was taken.

(2) *Inclusion of income.*—If any income from the property for the period between the date of the transfer creating the decedent-spouse's interest and the date of the decedent-spouse's death has not been distributed before the decedent-spouse's death, the undistributed income is included in the decedent-spouse's gross estate under this section to the extent that the income is not so included under any other section of the Internal Revenue Code.

(3) *Reduction of includible share in certain cases.*—If only a fractional or percentage share is includible under this section, the includible share is appropriately reduced if—

(i) The decedent-spouse's interest was in a trust and distributions of principal were made to the spouse during the spouse's lifetime;

(ii) The trust provides that the distributions are to be made from the qualified terminable interest share of the trust; and

(iii) The executor of the decedent-spouse's estate can establish the reduction in that share based on the fair market value of the trust assets at the time of each distribution.

(4) *Interest in previously severed trust.*—If the decedent-spouse's interest was in a trust consisting of only qualified terminable interest property and the trust was severed (in compliance with §20.2056(b)-7(b) or §25.2523(f)-1(b) of this chapter) from a trust that, after the severance, held only property that was not qualified terminable interest property, only the value of the property in the severed portion of the trust is includible in the decedent-spouse's gross estate.

(e) *Examples.*—The following examples illustrate the principles in paragraphs (a) through (d) of this section, where the decedent, D, was survived by spouse, S.

*Example 1. Inclusion of trust subject to election.* Under D's will, assets valued at $800,000 in D's gross estate (net of debts, expenses and other charges, including death taxes, payable from the property) passed in trust with income payable to S for life. Upon S's death, the trust principal is to be distributed to D's children. D's executor elected under section 2056(b)(7) to treat the entire trust property as qualified terminable interest property and claimed a marital deduction of $800,000. S made no disposition of the income interest during S's lifetime under section 2519. On the date of S's death, the fair market value of the trust property was $740,000. S's executor did not elect the alternate valuation date. The amount included in S's gross estate pursuant to section 2044 is $740,000.

*Example 2. Inclusion of trust subject to partial election.* The facts are the same as in *Example 1*, except that D's executor elected under section 2056(b)(7) with respect to only 50 percent of the value of the trust ($400,000). Consequently, only the equivalent portion of the trust is included in S's gross estate; i.e., $370,000 (50 percent of $740,000).

*Example 3. Spouse receives qualifying income interest in a fraction of trust income.* Under D's will, assets valued at $800,000 in D's gross estate (net of debts, expenses and other charges, including death taxes, payable from the property) passed in trust with 20 percent of the trust income payable to S for S's life. The will provides that the trust principal is to be distributed to D's children upon S's death. D's executor elected to deduct, pursuant to section 2056(b)(7), 50 percent of the amount for which the election could be made; i.e., $80,000 (50 percent of 20 percent of $800,000). Consequently, on the death of S, only the equivalent portion of the trust is included in S's gross estate; i.e., $74,000 (50 percent of 20 percent of $740,000).

*Example 4. Distribution of corpus during spouse's lifetime.* The facts are the same as in *Example 3*, except that S was entitled to receive all the trust income but the executor of D's estate elected under section 2056(b)(7) with respect to only 50 percent of the value of the trust ($400,000). Pursuant to authority in the will, the trustee made a discretionary distribution of $100,000 of principal to S in 1995 and charged the entire distribution to the qualified terminable interest share. Immediately prior to the distribution, the fair market value of the trust property was $1,100,000 and the qualified terminable interest portion of the trust was 50 percent. Immediately after the distribution, the qualified terminable interest portion of the trust was 45 percent ($450,000 divided by $1,000,000). Provided S's executor can establish the relevant facts, the amount included in S's gross estate is $333,000 (45 percent of $740,000).

*Example 5. Spouse assigns a portion of income interest during life.* Under D's will, assets valued at $800,000 in D's gross estate (net of debts, expenses and other charges, including death taxes, payable from the property) passed in trust with all the income payable to S, for S's life. The will provides that the trust principal is to be distributed to D's children upon S's death. D's executor elected under section 2056(b)(7) to treat the entire trust property as qualified termi-

nable interest property and claimed a marital deduction of $800,000. During the term of the trust, S transfers to C the right to 40 percent of the income from the trust for S's life. Because S is treated as transferring the entire remainder interest in the trust corpus under section 2519 (as well as 40 percent of the income interest under section 2511), no part of the trust is includible in S's gross estate under section 2044. However, if S retains until death an income interest in 60 percent of the trust corpus (which corpus is treated pursuant to section 2519 as having been transferred by S for both gift and estate tax purposes), 60 percent of the property will be includible in S's gross estate under section 2036(a) and a corresponding adjustment is made in S's adjusted taxable gifts.

*Example 6. Inter vivos trust subject to election under section 2523(f).* D transferred $800,000 to a trust providing that trust income is to be paid annually to S, for S's life. The trust provides that upon S's death, $100,000 of principal is to be paid to X charity and the remaining principal distributed to D's children. D elected to treat all of the property transferred to the trust as qualified terminable interest property under section 2523(f). At the time of S's death, the fair market value of the trust is $1,000,000. S's executor does not elect the alternate valuation date. The amount included in S's gross estate is $1,000,000; i.e., the fair market value at S's death of the entire trust property. The $100,000 that passes to X charity on S's death is treated as a transfer by S to X charity for purposes of section 2055. Therefore, S's estate is allowed a charitable deduction for the $100,000 transferred from the trust to the charity to the same extent that a deduction would be allowed by section 2055 for a bequest by S to X charity.

*Example 7. Spousal interest in the form of an annuity.* D died prior to October 24, 1992, the effective date of the Energy Policy Act of 1992 (Pub. L. 102-486). See §20.2056(b)-7(e). Under D's will, assets valued at $500,000 in D's gross estate (net of debts, expenses and other charges, including death taxes, payable from the property) passed in trust pursuant to which an annuity of $20,000 a year was payable to S for S's life. Trust income not paid to S as an annuity is to be accumulated in the trust and may not be distributed during S's lifetime. D's estate deducted $200,000 under section 2056(b)(7) and §20.2056(b)-7(e)(2). S did not assign any portion of S's interest during S's life. At the time of S's death, the value of the trust property is $800,000. S's executor does not elect the alternate valuation date. The amount included in S's gross estate pursuant to section 2044 is $320,000 ([$200,000/$500,000] × $800,000).

*Example 8. Inclusion of trust property when surviving spouse dies before first decedent's estate tax return is filed.* D dies on July 1, 1997. Under the terms of D's will, a trust is established for the benefit of D's spouse, S. The will provides that S is entitled to receive the income from that portion of the trust that the executor elects to treat as qualified terminable interest property. The remaining portion of the trust passes as of D's date of death to a trust for the benefit of C, D's child. The trust terms otherwise provide S with a qualifying income interest for life under section 2056(b)(7)(B)(ii). S dies on February 10, 1998. On April 1, 1998, D's executor files D's estate tax return on which an election is made to treat a portion of the trust as qualified terminable interest property under section 2056(b)(7). S's estate tax return is filed on November 10, 1998. The value on the date of S's death of the portion of the trust for which D's executor made a QTIP election is includible in S's gross estate under section 2044. [Reg. §20.2044-1.]

☐ [*T.D. 8522, 2-28-94. Amended by T.D. 8779, 8-18-98.*]

### [Reg. §20.2044-2]

§20.2044-2. **Effective dates.**—Except as specifically provided in *Example 7* of §20.2044-1(e), the provisions of §20.2044-1 are effective with respect to estates of a decedent-spouse dying after March 1, 1994. With respect to estates of decedent-spouses dying on or before such date, taxpayers may rely on any reasonable interpretation of the statutory provisions. For these purposes, the provisions of §20.2044-1 (as well as project LR-211-76, 1984-1 C.B., page 598, see §601.601(d)(2)(ii)(b) of this chapter) are considered a reasonable interpretation of the statutory provisions. [Reg. §20.2044-2.]

☐ [*T.D. 8522, 2-28-94.*]

### [Reg. §20.2045-1]

§20.2045-1. **Applicability to pre-existing transfers or interests.**—Sections 2034 through 2042 are applicable regardless of when the interests and events referred to in those sections were created or took place, except as otherwise provided in those sections and the regulations thereunder. [Reg. §20.2045-1.]

☐ [*T.D. 6296, 6-23-58. Redesignated by T.D. 8522, 2-28-94.*]

### [Reg. §20.2046-1]

§20.2046-1. **Disclaimed property.**—(a) This section shall apply to the disclaimer or renunciation of an interest in the person disclaiming by a transfer made after December 31, 1976. For rules relating to when the transfer creating the interest occurs, see § 25.2518-2(c)(3) and (c)(4) of this chapter. If a qualified disclaimer is made with respect to such a transfer, the Federal estate tax provisions are to apply with respect to the property interest disclaimed as if the interest had never been transferred to the person making the disclaimer. See section 2518 and the corresponding regulations for rules relating to a qualified disclaimer.

(b) The first and second sentences of this section are applicable for transfers creating the interest to be disclaimed made on or after December 31, 1997. [Reg. § 20.2046-1.]

☐ [*T.D. 8095, 8-6-86. Amended by T.D. 8744, 12-30-97.*]

# Taxable Estate

## [Reg. § 20.2051-1]

**§ 20.2051-1. Definition of taxable estate.**—(a) *General rule.*—The taxable estate of a decedent who was a citizen or resident (see § 20.0-1(b)(1)) of the United States at death is determined by subtracting the total amount of the deductions authorized by sections 2053 through 2058 from the total amount which must be included in the gross estate under sections 2031 through 2044. These deductions are in general as follows—

(1) Funeral and administration expenses and claims against the estate (including certain taxes and charitable pledges) (section 2053).

(2) Losses from casualty or theft during the administration of the estate (section 2054).

(3) Charitable transfers (section 2055).

(4) The marital deduction (section 2056).

(5) Qualified domestic trusts (section 2056A).

(6) Family-owned business interests (section 2057) to the extent applicable to estates of decedents.

(7) State death taxes (section 2058) to the extent applicable to estates of decedents.

(b) *Special rules.*—See section 2106 and the corresponding regulations for special rules regarding the computation of the taxable estate of a decedent who was not a citizen or resident of the United States. See also § 1.642(g)-1 of this chapter concerning the disallowance for income tax purposes of certain deductions allowed for estate tax purposes.

(c) *Effective/applicability date.*—This section applies to the estates of decedents dying on or after October 20, 2009. [Reg. § 20.2051-1.]

☐ [*T.D. 6296, 6-23-58. Amended by T.D. 9468, 10-16-2009.*]

## [Reg. § 20.2053-1]

**§ 20.2053-1. Deductions for expenses, indebtedness, and taxes; in general.**—(a) *General rule.*—In determining the taxable estate of a decedent who was a citizen or resident of the United States at death, there are allowed as deductions under section 2053(a) and (b) amounts falling within the following two categories (subject to the limitations contained in this section and in §§ 20.2053-2 through 20.2053-10)—

(1) *First category.*—Amounts which are payable out of property subject to claims and which are allowable by the law of the jurisdiction, whether within or without the United States, under which the estate is being administered for—

(i) Funeral expenses;

(ii) Administration expenses;

(iii) Claims against the estate (including taxes to the extent set forth in § 20.2053-6 and charitable pledges to the extent set forth in § 20.2053-5); and

(iv) Unpaid mortgages on, or any indebtedness in respect of, property, the value of the decedent's interest in which is included in the value of the gross estate undiminished by the mortgage or indebtedness.

As used in this subparagraph, the phrase "allowable by the law of the jurisdiction" means allowable by the law governing the administration of decedents' estates. The phrase has no reference to amounts allowable as deductions under a law which imposes a State death tax. See further §§ 20.2053-2 through 20.2053-7.

(2) *Second category.*—Amounts representing expenses incurred in administering property which is included in the gross estate but which is not subject to claims and which—

(i) Would be allowed as deductions in the first category if the property being administered were subject to claims; and

(ii) Were paid before the expiration of the period of limitation for assessment provided in section 6501.

See further § 20.2053-8.

(b) *Provisions applicable to both categories.*—(1) *In general.*—If the item is not one of those described in paragraph (a) of this section, it is not deductible merely because payment is allowed by the local law. If the amount which may be expended for the particular purpose is limited by the local law, no deduction in excess of that limitation is permissible.

(2) *Bona fide requirement.*—(i) *In general.*—Amounts allowed as deductions under section 2053(a) and (b) must be expenses and claims that are bona fide in nature. No deduction is permissible to the extent it is founded on a transfer that is essentially donative in character (a mere cloak for a gift or bequest) except to the extent the deduction is for a claim that would be allowable as a deduction under section 2055 as a charitable bequest.

(ii) *Claims and expenses involving family members.*—Factors indicative (but not necessarily determinative) of the bona fide nature of a claim or expense involving a family member of a decedent, a related entity, or a beneficiary of a decedent's estate or revocable trust, in relevant instances, may include, but are not limited to, the following—

(A) The transaction underlying the claim or expense occurs in the ordinary course of business, is negotiated at arm's length, and is free from donative intent.

(B) The nature of the claim or expense is not related to an expectation or claim of inheritance.

(C) The claim or expense originates pursuant to an agreement between the decedent and the family member, related entity, or beneficiary, and the agreement is substantiated with contemporaneous evidence.

(D) Performance by the claimant is pursuant to the terms of an agreement between the decedent and the family member, related entity, or beneficiary and the performance and the agreement can be substantiated.

(E) All amounts paid in satisfaction or settlement of a claim or expense are reported by each party for Federal income and employment tax purposes, to the extent appropriate, in a manner that is consistent with the reported nature of the claim or expense.

(iii) *Definitions.*—The following definitions apply for purposes of this paragraph (b)(2):

(A) *Family members* include the spouse of the decedent; the grandparents, parents, siblings, and lineal descendants of the decedent or of the decedent's spouse; and the spouse and lineal descendants of any such grandparent, parent, and sibling. Family members include adopted individuals.

(B) A *related entity* is an entity in which the decedent, either directly or indirectly, had a beneficial ownership interest at the time of the decedent's death or at any time during the three-year period ending on the decedent's date of death. Such an entity, however, shall not include a publicly-traded entity nor shall it include a closely-held entity in which the combined beneficial interest, either direct or indirect, of the decedent and the decedent's family members, collectively, is less than 30 percent of the beneficial ownership interests (whether voting or non-voting and whether an interest in stock, capital and/or profits), as determined at the time a claim described in this section is being asserted. Notwithstanding the foregoing, an entity in which the decedent, directly or indirectly, had any managing interest (for example, as a general partner of a partnership or as a managing member of a limited liability company) at the time of the decedent's death shall be considered a related entity.

(C) *Beneficiaries* of a decedent's estate include beneficiaries of a trust of the decedent.

(3) *Court decrees and settlements.*—(i) *Court decree.*—If a court of competent jurisdiction over the administration of an estate reviews and approves expenditures for funeral expenses, administration expenses, claims against the estate, or unpaid mortgages (referred to in this section as a "claim or expense"), a final judicial decision in that matter may be relied upon to establish the amount of a claim or expense that is otherwise deductible under section 2053 and these regulations provided that the court actually passes upon the facts on which deductibility depends. If the court does not pass upon those facts, its decree may not be relied upon to establish the amount of the claim or expense that is otherwise deductible under section 2053. It must appear that the court actually passed upon the merits of the claim. This will be presumed in all cases of an active and genuine contest. If the result reached appears to be unreasonable, this is some evidence that there was not such a contest, but it may be rebutted by proof to the contrary. Any amount meeting the requirements of this paragraph (b)(3)(i) is deductible to the extent it actually has been

paid or will be paid, subject to any applicable limitations in this section.

(ii) *Claims and expenses where court approval not required under local law.*—A deduction for the amount of a claim or expense that is otherwise deductible under section 2053 and these regulations will not be denied under section 2053 solely because a local court decree has not been entered with respect to such amount, provided that no court decree is required under applicable law to determine the amount or allowability of the claim or expense.

(iii) *Consent decree.*—A local court decree rendered by consent may be relied on to establish the amount of a claim or expense that is otherwise deductible under section 2053 and these regulations provided that the consent resolves a bona fide issue in a genuine contest. Consent given by all parties having interests adverse to that of the claimant will be presumed to resolve a bona fide issue in a genuine contest. Any amount meeting the requirements of this paragraph (b)(3)(iii) is deductible to the extent it actually has been paid or will be paid, subject to any applicable limitations in this section.

(iv) *Settlements.*—A settlement may be relied on to establish the amount of a claim or expense (whether contingent or noncontingent) that is otherwise deductible under section 2053 and these regulations, provided that the settlement resolves a bona fide issue in a genuine contest and is the product of arm's-length negotiations by parties having adverse interests with respect to the claim or expense. A deduction will not be denied for a settlement amount paid by an estate if the estate can establish that the cost of defending or contesting the claim or expense, or the delay associated with litigating the claim or expense, would impose a higher burden on the estate than the payment of the amount paid to settle the claim or expense. Nevertheless, no deduction will be allowed for amounts paid in settlement of an unenforceable claim. For this purpose, to the extent a claim exceeds an applicable limit under local law, the claim is deemed to be unenforceable. However, as long as the enforceability of the claim is at issue in a bona fide dispute, the claim will not be deemed to be unenforceable for this purpose. Any amount meeting the requirements of this paragraph (b)(3)(iv) is deductible to the extent it actually has been paid or will be paid, subject to any applicable limitations in this section.

(v) *Additional rules.*—Notwithstanding paragraph (b)(3)(i) through (iv) of this section, additional rules may apply to the deductibility of certain claims and expenses. See § 20.2053-2 for additional rules regarding the deductibility of funeral expenses. See § 20.2053-3 for additional rules regarding the deductibility of administration expenses. See § 20.2053-4 for additional rules regarding the deductibility of claims against the estate. See § 20.2053-7 for additional rules regarding the deductibility of unpaid mortgages.

(4) *Examples.*—Unless otherwise provided, assume that the amount of any claim or expense is paid out of property subject to claims and is paid within the time prescribed for filing the "United States Estate (and Generation-Skipping Transfer) Tax Return," Form 706. The following examples illustrate the application of this paragraph (b):

*Example 1. Consent decree at variance with the law of the State.* Decedent's (D's) estate is probated in State. D's probate estate is valued at $100x. State law provides that the executor's commission shall not exceed 3 percent of the probate estate. A consent decree is entered allowing the executor's commission in the amount of $5x. The estate pays the executor's commission in the amount of $5x. For purposes of section 2053, the executor may deduct only $3x of the $5x expense paid for the executor's commission because the amount approved by the consent decree in excess of $3x is in excess of the applicable limit for executor's commissions under local law. Therefore, for purposes of section 2053, the consent decree may not be relied upon to establish the amount of the expense for the executor's commission.

*Example 2. Decedent's (D's) estate is probated in State.* State law grants authority to an executor to administer an estate without court approval, so long as notice of and a right to object to a proposed action is provided to interested persons. The executor of D's estate (E) proposes to sell property of the estate in order to pay the debts of D. E gives requisite notice to all interested parties and no interested person objects. E sells the real estate and pays a real estate commission of $20x to a professional real estate agent. The amount of the real estate commission paid does not exceed the applicable limit under State law. Provided that the sale of the property was necessary to pay D's debts, expenses of administration, or taxes, to preserve the estate, or to effect distribution, the executor may deduct the $20x expense for the real estate commission under section 2053 even though no court decree was entered approving the expense.

*Example 3. Claim by family member.* For a period of three years prior to D's death, D's niece (N) provides accounting and bookkeep-ing services on D's behalf. N is a CPA and provides similar accounting and bookkeeping services to unrelated clients. At the end of each month, N presents an itemized bill to D for services rendered. The fees charged by N conform to the prevailing market rate for the services rendered and are comparable to the fees N charges other clients for similar services. The amount due is timely paid each month by D and is properly reported for Federal income and employment tax purposes by N. In the six months prior to D's death, D's poor health prevents D from making payments to N for the amount due. After D's death, N asserts a claim against the estate for $25x, an amount representing the amount due for the sixmonth period prior to D's death. D's estate pays $25x to N in satisfaction of the claim before the return is timely filed and N properly reports the $25x received by E for income tax purposes. Barring any other relevant facts or circumstances, E may rely on the following factors to establish that the claim is bona fide: (1) N's claim for services rendered arose in the ordinary course of business, as N is a CPA performing similar services for other clients; (2) the fees charged were deemed to be negotiated at arm's length, as the fees were consistent with the fees N charged for similar services to unrelated clients; (3) the billing records and the records of D's timely payments to N constitute contemporaneous evidence of an agreement between D and N for N's bookkeeping services; and (4) the amount of the payments to N is properly reported by N for Federal income and employment tax purposes. E may deduct the amount paid to N in satisfaction of the claim.

(c) *Provision applicable to first category only.*—Deductions of the first category (described in paragraph (a)(1) of this section) are limited under section 2053(a) to amounts which would be properly allowable out of property subject to claims by the law of the jurisdiction under which the decedent's estate is being administered. Further, the total allowable amount of deductions of the first category is limited by section 2053(c)(2) to the sum of—

(1) The value of property included in the decedent's gross estate and subject to claims, plus

(2) Amounts paid, out of property not subject to claims against the decedent's estate, within 9 months (15 months in the case of the estate of a decedent dying before January 1, 1971) after the decedent's death (the period within which the estate tax return must be filed under section 6075), or within any extension of time for filing the return granted under section 6081. The term "property subject to claims" is defined in section 2053(c)(2) as meaning the property includible in the gross estate which, or the avails of which, under the applicable law, would bear the burden of the payment of these deductions in the final adjustment and settlement of the decedent's estate. However, for the purposes of this definition, the value of property subject to claims is first reduced by the amount of any deduction allowed under section 2054 for any losses from casualty or theft incurred during the settlement of the estate attributable to such property. The application of this paragraph may be illustrated by the following examples:

*Example (1).* The only item in the gross estate is real property valued at $250,000 which the decedent and his surviving spouse held as tenants by the entirety. Under the local law, this real property is not subject to claims. Funeral expenses of $1,200 and debts of the decedent in the amount of $1,500 are allowable under local law. Before the prescribed date for filing the estate tax return, the surviving spouse paid the funeral expenses and $1,000 of the debts. The remaining $500 of the debts was paid by her after the prescribed date for filing the return. The total amount allowable as deductions under section 2053 is limited to $2,200, the amount paid prior to the prescribed date for filing the return.

*Example (2).* The only two items in the gross estate were a bank deposit of $20,000 and insurance in the amount of $150,000. The insurance was payable to the decedent's surviving spouse and under local law was not subject to claims. Funeral expenses of $1,000 and debts in the amount of $29,000 were allowable under local law. A son was executor of the estate and before the prescribed date for filing the estate tax return he paid the funeral expenses and $9,000 of the debts, using therefor $5,000 of the bank deposit and $5,000 supplied by the surviving spouse. After the prescribed date for filing the return, the executor paid the remaining $20,000 of the debts, using for that purpose the $15,000 left in the bank account plus an additional $5,000 supplied by the surviving spouse. The total amount allowable as deductions under section 2053 is limited to $25,000 ($20,000 of property subject to claims plus the $5,000 additional amount which, before the prescribed date for filing the return, was paid out of property not subject to claims).

(d) *Amount deductible.*—(1) *General rule.*—To take into account properly events occurring after the date of a decedent's death in determining the amount deductible under section 2053 and these regulations, the deduction for any claim or expense described in paragraph (a) of this section is limited to the total amount actually paid in settlement or satisfaction of that item (subject to any applicable limitations in this section). However, see paragraph (d)(4) of this section for the rules for deducting certain ascertainable amounts; see § 20.2053-4(b) and (c) for the rules regarding the deductibility of certain claims against the estate; and see § 20.2053-7 for the rules regarding the deductibility of unpaid mortgages and other indebtedness.

(2) *Application of post-death events.*—In determining whether and to what extent a deduction under section 2053 is allowable, events occurring after the date of a decedent's death will be taken into consideration—

(i) Until the expiration of the applicable period of limitations on assessment prescribed in section 6501 (including without limitation at all times during which the running of the period of limitations is suspended); and

(ii) During subsequent periods, in determining the amount (if any) of an overpayment of estate tax due in connection with a claim for refund filed within the time prescribed in section 6511(a).

(3) *Reimbursements.*—A deduction is not allowed to the extent that a claim or expense described in paragraph (a) of this section is or could be compensated for by insurance or otherwise could be reimbursed. If the executor is able to establish that only a partial reimbursement could be collected, then only that portion of the potential reimbursement that reasonably could have been expected to be collected will reduce the estate's deductible portion of the total claim or expense. An executor may certify that the executor neither knows nor reasonably should have known of any available reimbursement for a claim or expense described in section 2053(a) or (b) on the estate's United States Estate (and Generation-Skipping Transfer) Tax Return (Form 706), in accordance with the instructions for that form. A potential reimbursement will not reduce the deductible amount of a claim or expense to the extent that the executor, on Form 706 and in accordance with the instructions for that form, provides a reasonable explanation for his or her reasonable determination that the burden of necessary collection efforts in pursuit of a right of reimbursement would outweigh the anticipated benefit from those efforts. Nevertheless, even if a reasonable explanation is provided, subsequent events (including without limitation an actual reimbursement) occurring within the period described in § 20.2053-1(d)(2) will be considered in determining the amount (if any) of a reduction under this paragraph (d)(3) in the deductible amount of a claim or expense.

(4) *Exception for certain ascertainable amounts.*—(i) *General rule.*—A deduction will be allowed for a claim or expense that satisfies all applicable requirements even though it is not yet paid, provided that the amount to be paid is ascertainable with reasonable certainty and will be paid. For example, executors' commissions and attorneys' fees that are not yet paid, and that meet the requirements for deductibility under § 20.2053-3(b) and (c), respectively, are deemed to be ascertainable with reasonable certainty and may be deducted if such expenses will be paid. However, no deduction may be taken upon the basis of a vague or uncertain estimate. To the extent a claim or expense is contested or contingent, such a claim or expense cannot be ascertained with reasonable certainty.

(ii) *Effect of post-death events.*—A deduction under this paragraph (d)(4) will be allowed to the extent the Commissioner is reasonably satisfied that the amount to be paid is ascertainable with reasonable certainty and will be paid. In making this determination, the Commissioner will take into account events occurring after the date of a decedent's death. To the extent the amount for which a deduction was claimed does not satisfy the requirements of this paragraph (d)(4), and is not otherwise deductible, the deduction will be disallowed by the Commissioner. If a deduction is claimed on Form 706 for an amount that is not yet paid and the deduction is disallowed in whole or in part (or if no deduction is claimed on Form 706), then if the claim or expense subsequently satisfies the requirements of this paragraph (d)(4) or is paid, relief may be sought by filing a claim for refund. To preserve the estate's right to claim a refund for amounts becoming deductible after the expiration of the period of limitation for the filing of a claim for refund, a protective claim for refund may be filed in accordance with paragraph (d)(5) of this section.

(5) *Protective claim for refund.*—(i) *In general.*—A protective claim for refund under this section may be filed at any time before the expiration of the period of limitation prescribed in section 6511(a) for the filing of a claim for refund to preserve the estate's right to claim a refund by reason of claims or expenses that are not paid or do not otherwise meet the requirements of deductibility under section 2053 and these regulations until after the expiration of the period of limitation for filing a claim for refund. Such a protective claim shall be made in accordance with guidance that may be provided from time to time by publication in the Internal Revenue Bulletin (see

§ 601.601(d)(2)(ii)(*b*)). Although the protective claim need not state a particular dollar amount or demand an immediate refund, a protective claim must identify each outstanding claim or expense that would have been deductible under section 2053(a) or (b) if such item already had been paid and must describe the reasons and contingencies delaying the actual payment of the claim or expense. Action on protective claims will proceed after the executor has notified the Commissioner within a reasonable period that the contingency has been resolved and that the amount deductible under § 20.2053-1 has been established.

(ii) *Effect on marital and charitable deduction.*—To the extent that a protective claim for refund is filed with respect to a claim or expense that would have been deductible under section 2053(a) or (b) if such item already had been paid and that is payable out of a share that meets the requirements for a charitable deduction under section 2055 or a marital deduction under section 2056 or section 2056A, or from a combination thereof, neither the charitable deduction nor the marital deduction shall be reduced by the amount of such claim or expense until the amount is actually paid or meets the requirements of paragraph (d)(4) of this section for deducting certain ascertainable amounts or the requirements of § 20.2053-4(b) or (c) for deducting certain claims against the estate.

(6) [Reserved].

(7) *Examples.*—Assume that the amounts described in section 2053(a) are payable out of property subject to claims and are allowable by the law of the jurisdiction governing the administration of the estate, whether the applicable jurisdiction is within or outside of the United States. Assume that the claims against the estate are not deductible under § 20.2053-4(b) or (c). Also assume, unless otherwise provided, that none of the limitations on the amount of the deduction described in this section apply to the deduction claimed under section 2053. The following examples illustrate the application of this paragraph (d):

*Example 1. Amount of expense ascertainable.* Decedent's (D's) estate was probated in State. State law provides that the personal representative shall receive compensation equal to 2.5 percent of the value of the probate estate. The executor (E) may claim a deduction for estimated fees equal to 2.5 percent of D's probate estate on the Form 706 filed for D's estate under the rule for deducting certain ascertainable amounts set forth in paragraph (d)(4) of this section, provided that the estimated amount will be paid. However, the Commissioner will disallow the deduction upon examination of the estate's Form 706 to the extent that the amount for which a deduction was claimed no longer satisfies the requirements of paragraph (d)(4) of this section. If this occurs, E may file a protective claim for refund in accordance with paragraph (d)(5) of this section in order to preserve the estate's right to claim a refund for the amount of the fee that is subsequently paid or that subsequently meets the requirements of paragraph (d)(4) of this section for deducting certain ascertainable amounts.

*Example 2. Amount of claim not ascertainable.* Prior to death, Decedent (D) is sued by Claimant (C) for $100x in a tort proceeding and responds asserting affirmative defenses available to D under applicable local law. C and D are unrelated. D subsequently dies and D's Form 706 is due before a final judgment is entered in the case. The executor of D's estate (E) may not claim a deduction with respect to C's claim on D's Form 706 under the special rule contained in paragraph (d)(4) of this section because the deductible amount cannot be ascertained with reasonable certainty. However, E may file a timely protective claim for refund in accordance with paragraph (d)(5) of this section in order to preserve the estate's right to subsequently claim a refund at the time a final judgment is entered in the case and the claim is either paid or meets the requirements of paragraph (d)(4) of this section for deducting certain ascertainable amounts.

*Example 3. Amount of claim payable out of property qualifying for marital deduction.* The facts are the same as in *Example 2* except that the applicable credit amount, under section 2010, against the estate tax was fully consumed by D's lifetime gifts, D is survived by Spouse (S), and D's estate passes entirely to S in a bequest that qualifies for the marital deduction under section 2056. Even though any amount D's estate ultimately pays with respect to C's claim will be paid from the assets qualifying for the marital deduction, in filing Form 706, E need not reduce the amount of the marital deduction claimed on D's Form 706. Instead, pursuant to the protective claim for refund filed by E, the marital deduction will be reduced by the claim once a final judgment is entered in the case. At that time, a deduction will be allowed for the amount that is either paid or meets the requirements of paragraph (d)(4) of this section for deducting certain ascertainable amounts.

(e) *Disallowance of double deductions.*—See section 642(g) and § 1.642(g)-1 with respect to the disallowance for income tax purposes of certain deductions unless the right to take such deductions for estate tax purposes is waived.

(f) *Effective/applicability date.*—This section applies to the estates of decedents dying on or after October 20, 2009. [Reg. § 20.2053-1.]

☐ [*T.D. 6296, 6-23-58. Amended by T.D. 7238, 12-28-72 and T.D. 9468, 10-16-2009 (corrected 11-24-2009).*]

### [Reg. § 20.2053-2]

**§ 20.2053-2. Deduction for funeral expenses.**—Such amounts for funeral expenses are allowed as deductions from a decedent's gross estate as (a) are actually expended, (b) would be properly allowable out of property subject to claims under the laws of the local jurisdiction, and (c) satisfy the requirements of paragraph (c) of § 20.2053-1. A reasonable expenditure for a tombstone, monument, or mausoleum, or for a burial lot, either for the decedent or his family, including a reasonable expenditure for its future care, may be deducted under this heading, provided such an expenditure is allowable by the local law. Included in funeral expenses is the cost of transportation of the person bringing the body to the place of burial. [Reg. § 20.2053-2.]

☐ [*T.D. 6296, 6-23-58.*]

### [Reg. § 20.2053-3]

**§ 20.2053-3. Deduction for expenses of administering estate.**—(a) *In general.*—The amounts deductible from a decedent's gross estate as "administration expenses" of the first category (see paragraphs (a) and (c) of § 20.2053-1) are limited to such expenses as are actually and necessarily incurred in the administration of the decedent's estate; that is, in the collection of assets, payment of debts, and distribution of property to the persons entitled to it. The expenses contemplated in the law are such only as attend the settlement of an estate and the transfer of the property of the estate to individual beneficiaries or to a trustee, whether the trustee is the executor or some other person. Expenditures not essential to the proper settlement of the estate, but incurred for the individual benefit of the heirs, legatees, or devisees, may not be taken as deductions. Administration expenses include (1) executor's commissions; (2) attorney's fees; and (3) miscellaneous expenses. Each of these classes is considered separately in paragraphs (b) through (d) of this section.

(b) *Executor's commissions.*—(1) Executors' commissions are deductible to the extent permitted by § 20.2053-1 and this section, but no deduction may be taken if no commissions are to be paid. In addition, the amount of the commissions claimed as a deduction must be in accordance with the usually accepted standards and practice of allowing such an amount in estates of similar size and character in the jurisdiction in which the estate is being administered, or any deviation from the usually accepted standards or range of amounts (permissible under applicable local law) must be justified to the satisfaction of the Commissioner.

(2) A bequest or devise to the executor in lieu of commissions is not deductible. If, however, the terms of the will set forth the compensation payable to the executor for services to be rendered in the administration of the estate, a deduction may be taken to the extent that the amount so fixed does not exceed the compensation allowable by the local law or practice and to the extent permitted by § 20.2053-1.

(3) Except to the extent that a trustee is in fact performing services with respect to property subject to claims which would normally be performed by an executor, amounts paid as trustees' commissions do not constitute expenses of administration under the first category, and are only deductible as expenses of the second category to the extent provided in § 20.2053-8.

(c) *Attorney's fees.*—(1) Attorney's fees are deductible to the extent permitted by § 20.2053-1 and this section. Further, the amount of the fees claimed as a deduction may not exceed a reasonable remuneration for the services rendered, taking into account the size and character of the estate, the law and practice in the jurisdiction in which the estate is being administered, and the skill and expertise of the attorneys.

(2) A deduction for attorneys' fees incurred in contesting an asserted deficiency or in prosecuting a claim for refund should be claimed at the time the deficiency is contested or the refund claim is prosecuted. A deduction for reasonable attorney's fees actually incurred in contesting an asserted deficiency or in prosecuting a claim for refund will be allowed to the extent permitted by § 20.2053-1 even though the deduction, as such, was not claimed on the estate tax return or in the claim for refund. A deduction for these fees shall not be denied, and the sufficiency of a claim for refund shall not be questioned, solely by reason of the fact that the amount of the fees to be paid was not established at the time that the right to the deduction was claimed.

(3) Attorneys' fees incurred by beneficiaries incident to litigation as to their respective interests are not deductible if the litigation is not essential to the proper settlement of the estate within the meaning of paragraph (a) of this section. An attorney's fee not meeting this test is not deductible as an administration expense under section 2053 and this section, even if it is approved by a probate court as an expense payable or reimbursable by the estate.

(d) *Miscellaneous administration expenses.*—(1) Miscellaneous administration expenses include such expenses as court costs, surrogates' fees, accountants' fees, appraisers' fees, clerk hire, etc. Expenses necessarily incurred in preserving and distributing the estate, including the cost of storing or maintaining property of the estate, if it is impossible to effect immediate distribution to the beneficiaries, are deductible to the extent permitted by § 20.2053-1. Expenses for preserving and caring for the property may not include outlays for additions or improvements; nor will such expenses be allowed for a longer period than the executor is reasonably required to retain the property.

(2) Expenses for selling property of the estate are deductible to the extent permitted by § 20.2053-1 if the sale is necessary in order to pay the decedent's debts, expenses of administration, or taxes, to preserve the estate, or to effect distribution. The phrase "expenses for selling property" includes brokerage fees and other expenses attending the sale, such as the fees of an auctioneer if it is reasonably necessary to employ one. Where an item included in the gross estate is disposed of in a bona fide sale (including a redemption) to a dealer in such items at a price below its fair market value, for purposes of this paragraph there shall be treated as an expense for selling the item whichever of the following amounts is the lesser: (i) the amount by which the fair market value of the property on the applicable valuation date exceeds the proceeds of the sale, or (ii) the amount by which the fair market value of the property on the date of the sale exceeds the proceeds of the sale. The principles used in determining the value at which an item of property is included in the gross estate shall be followed in arriving at the fair market value of the property for purposes of this paragraph. See §§ 20.2031-1 through 20.2031-9.

(3) Expenses incurred in defending the estate against claims described in section 2053(a)(3) are deductible to the extent permitted by § 20.2053-1 if the expenses are incurred incident to the assertion of defenses to the claim available under the applicable law, even if the estate ultimately does not prevail. For purposes of this paragraph (d)(3), "expenses incurred in defending the estate against claims" include costs relating to the arbitration and mediation of contested issues, costs associated with defending the estate against claims (whether or not enforceable), and costs associated with reaching a negotiated settlement of the issues.

(e) *Effective/applicability date.*—This section applies to the estates of decedents dying on or after October 20, 2009. [Reg. § 20.2053-3.]

☐ [*T.D. 6296, 6-23-58. Amended by T.D. 6826, 6-14-65; T.D. 7612, 4-19-79 and T.D. 9468, 10-16-2009.*]

### [Reg. § 20.2053-4]

**§ 20.2053-4. Deduction for claims against the estate.**—(a) *In general.*—(1) *General rule.*—For purposes of this section, liabilities imposed by law or arising out of contracts or torts are deductible if they meet the applicable requirements set forth in § 20.2053-1 and this section. To be deductible, a claim against a decedent's estate must represent a personal obligation of the decedent existing at the time of the decedent's death. Except as otherwise provided in paragraphs (b) and (c) of this section and to the extent permitted by § 20.2053-1, the amounts that may be deducted as claims against a decedent's estate are limited to the amounts of bona fide claims that are enforceable against the decedent's estate (and are not unenforceable when paid) and claims that—

(i) Are actually paid by the estate in satisfaction of the claim; or

(ii) Meet the requirements of § 20.2053-1(d)(4) for deducting certain ascertainable amounts.

(2) *Effect of post-death events.*—Events occurring after the date of a decedent's death shall be considered in determining whether and to what extent a deduction is allowable under section 2053. See § 20.2053-1(d)(2).

(b) *Exception for claims and counterclaims in related matter.*—(1) *General rule.*—If a decedent's gross estate includes one or more claims or causes of action and there are one or more claims against the decedent's estate in the same or a substantially related matter, or, if a decedent's gross estate includes a particular asset and there are one or more claims against the decedent's estate integrally related to that particular asset, the executor may deduct on the estate's United States Estate (and Generation-Skipping Transfer) Tax Return (Form

706) the current value of the claim or claims against the estate, even though payment has not been made, provided that—

(i) Each such claim against the estate otherwise satisfies the applicable requirements set forth in § 20.2053-1;

(ii) Each such claim against the estate represents a personal obligation of the decedent existing at the time of the decedent's death;

(iii) Each such claim is enforceable against the decedent's estate (and is not unenforceable when paid);

(iv) The value of each such claim against the estate is determined from a "qualified appraisal" performed by a "qualified appraiser" within the meaning of section 170 of the Internal Revenue Code and the corresponding regulations;

(v) The value of each such claim against the estate is subject to adjustment for post-death events; and

(vi) The aggregate value of the related claims or assets included in the decedent's gross estate exceeds 10 percent of the decedent's gross estate.

(2) *Limitation on deduction.*—The deduction under this paragraph (b) is limited to the value of the related claims or particular assets included in decedent's gross estate.

(3) *Effect of post-death events.*—If, under this paragraph (b), a deduction is claimed on Form 706 for a claim against the estate and, during the period described in § 20.2053-1(d)(2), the claim is paid or meets the requirements of § 20.2053-1(d)(4) for deducting certain ascertainable amounts, the claimed deduction is subject to adjustment to reflect, and may not exceed, the amount paid on the claim or the amount meeting the requirements of § 20.2053-1(d)(4). If, under this paragraph (b), a deduction is claimed on Form 706 for a claim against the estate and, during the period described in § 20.2053-1(d)(2), the claim remains unpaid (and does not meet the requirements of § 20.2053-1(d)(4) for deducting certain ascertainable amounts), the claimed deduction is subject to adjustment to reflect, and may not exceed, the current valuation of the claim. A valuation of the claim will be considered current if it reflects events occurring after the decedent's death. With regard to any amount in excess of the amount deductible under this paragraph (b), an estate may preserve the estate's right to claim a refund for claims that are paid or that meet the requirements of § 20.2053-(1)(d)(4) after the expiration of the period of limitation for filing a claim for refund by filing a protective claim for refund in accordance with the rules in § 20.2053-1(d)(5).

(c) *Exception for claims totaling not more than $500,000.*—(1) *General rule.*—An executor may deduct on Form 706 the current value of one or more claims against the estate even though payment has not been made on the claim or claims to the extent that—

(i) Each such claim against the estate otherwise satisfies the applicable requirements for deductibility set forth in § 20.2053-1;

(ii) Each such claim against the estate represents a personal obligation of the decedent existing at the time of the decedent's death;

(iii) Each such claim is enforceable against the decedent's estate (and is not unenforceable when paid);

(iv) The value of each such claim against the estate is determined from a "qualified appraisal" performed by a "qualified appraiser" within the meaning of section 170 of the Internal Revenue Code and the corresponding regulations;

(v) The total amount deducted by the estate under this paragraph (c) does not exceed $500,000;

(vi) The full value of each claim, rather than just a portion of that amount, must be deductible under this paragraph (c) and, for this purpose, the full value of each such claim is deemed to be the unpaid amount of that claim that is not deductible after the application of § § 20.2053-1 and 20.2053-4(b); and

(vii) The value of each claim deducted under this paragraph (c) is subject to adjustment for post-death events.

(2) *Effect of post-death events.*—If, under this paragraph (c), a deduction is claimed for a claim against the estate and, during the period described in § 20.2053-1(d)(2), the claim is paid or meets the requirements of § 20.2053-1(d)(4) for deducting certain ascertainable amounts, the amount of the allowable deduction for that claim is subject to adjustment to reflect, and may not exceed, the amount paid on the claim or the amount meeting the requirements of § 20.2053-1(d)(4). If, under this paragraph (c), a deduction is claimed for a claim against the estate and, during the period described in § 20.2053-1(d)(2), the claim remains unpaid (and does not meet the requirements of § 20.2053-1(d)(4) for deducting certain ascertainable amounts), the amount of the allowable deduction for that claim is subject to adjustment to reflect, and may not exceed, the current value of the claim. The value of the claim will be considered current if it reflects events occurring after the decedent's death. To claim a

deduction for amounts in excess of the amount deductible under this paragraph (c), the estate may preserve the estate's right to claim a refund for claims that are not paid or that do not meet the requirements of § 20.2053-1(d)(4) until after the expiration of the period of limitation for the filing of a claim for refund by filing a protective claim for refund in accordance with the rules in § 20.2053-1(d)(5).

(3) *Examples.*—The following examples illustrate the application of this paragraph (c). Assume that the value of each claim is determined from a "qualified appraisal" performed by a "qualified appraiser" and reflects events occurring after the death of the decedent (D). Also assume that each claim represents a personal obligation of D that existed at D's death, that each claim is enforceable against the decedent's estate (and is not unenforceable when paid), and that each claim otherwise satisfies the requirements for deductibility of § 20.2053-1.

*Example 1.* There are three claims against the estate of the decedent (D) that are not paid and are not deductible under § 20.2053-1(d)(4) or paragraph (b) of this section: $25,000 of Claimant A, $35,000 of Claimant B, and $1,000,000 of Claimant C. The executor of D's estate (E) may not claim a deduction under this paragraph with respect to any portion of the claim of Claimant C because the value of that claim exceeds $500,000. E may claim a deduction under this paragraph for the total amount of the claims filed by Claimant A and Claimant B ($60,000) because the aggregate value of the full amount of those claims does not exceed $500,000.

*Example 2.* There are three claims against the estate of the decedent (D) that are not paid and are not deductible under § 20.2053-1(d)(4) or paragraph (b) of this section; specifically, a separate $200,000 claim of each of three claimants, A, B and C. The executor of D's estate (E) may claim a deduction under this paragraph for any two of these three claims because the aggregate value of the full amount of any two of the claims does not exceed $500,000. E may not deduct any part of the value of the remaining claim under this paragraph because the aggregate value of the full amount of all three claims would exceed $500,000.

*Example 3.* As a result of an automobile accident involving the decedent (D) and A, D's gross estate includes a claim against A that is valued at $750,000. In the same matter, A files a counterclaim against D's estate that is valued at $1,000,000. A's claim against D's estate is not paid and is not deductible under § 20.2053-1(d)(4). All other section 2053 claims and expenses of D's estate have been paid and are deductible. The executor of D's estate (E) deducts $750,000 of A's claim against the estate under § 20.2053-4(b). E may claim a deduction under this paragraph (c) for the total value of A's claim not deducted under § 20.2053-4(b), or $250,000. If, instead, the value of A's claim against D's estate is $1,500,000, so that the amount not deductible under § 20.2053-4(b) exceeds $500,000, no deduction is available under this paragraph (c).

(d) *Special rules.*—(1) *Potential and unmatured claims.*—Except as provided in § 20.2053-1(d)(4) and in paragraphs (b) and (c) of this section, no estate tax deduction may be taken for a claim against the decedent's estate while it remains a potential or unmatured claim. Claims that later mature may be deducted (to the extent permitted by § 20.2053-1) in connection with a timely claim for refund. To preserve the estate's right to claim a refund for claims that mature and become deductible after the expiration of the period of limitation for filing a claim for refund, a protective claim for refund may be filed in accordance with § 20.2053-1(d)(5). See § 20.2053-1(b)(3) for rules relating to the treatment of court decrees and settlements.

(2) *Contested claims.*—Except as provided in paragraphs (b) and (c) of this section, no estate tax deduction may be taken for a claim against the decedent's estate to the extent the estate is contesting the decedent's liability. Contested claims that later mature may be deducted (to the extent permitted by § 20.2053-1) in connection with a claim for refund filed within the time prescribed in section 6511(a). To preserve the estate's right to claim a refund for claims that mature and become deductible after the expiration of the period of limitation for the filing a claim for refund, a protective claim for refund may be filed in accordance with § 20.2053-1(d)(5). See § 20.2053-1(b)(3) for rules relating to the treatment of court decrees and settlements.

(3) *Claims against multiple parties.*—If the decedent or the decedent's estate is one of two or more parties against whom the claim is being asserted, the estate may deduct only the portion of the total claim due from and paid by the estate, reduced by the total of any reimbursement received from another party, insurance, or otherwise. The estate's deductible portion also will be reduced by the contribution or other amount the estate could have collected from another party or an insurer but which the estate declines or fails to attempt to collect. See further § 20.2053-1(d)(3).

(4) *Unenforceable claims.*—Claims that are unenforceable prior to or at the decedent's death are not deductible, even if they are actually

paid. Claims that become unenforceable during the administration of the estate are not deductible to the extent that they are paid (or will be paid) after they become unenforceable. However, see § 20.2053-1(b)(3)(iv) regarding a claim whose enforceability is at issue.

(5) *Claims founded upon a promise.*—Except with regard to pledges or subscriptions (see § 20.2053-5), section 2053(c)(1)(A) provides that the deduction for a claim founded upon a promise or agreement is limited to the extent that the promise or agreement was bona fide and in exchange for adequate and full consideration in money or money's worth; that is, the promise or agreement must have been bargained for at arm's length and the price must have been an adequate and full equivalent reducible to a money value.

(6) *Recurring payments.*—(i) *Noncontingent obligations.*—If a decedent is obligated to make recurring payments on an enforceable and certain claim that satisfies the requirements for deductibility under this section and the payments are not subject to a contingency, the amount of the claim will be deemed ascertainable with reasonable certainty for purposes of the rule for deducting certain ascertainable amounts set forth in § 20.2053-1(d)(4). If the recurring payments will be paid, a deduction will be allowed under the rule for deducting certain ascertainable amounts set forth in § 20.2053-1(d)(4) (subject to any applicable limitations in § 20.2053-1). Recurring payments for purposes of this section exclude those payments made in connection with a mortgage or indebtedness described in and governed by § 20.2053-7. If a decedent's obligation to make a recurring payment is contingent on the death or remarriage of the claimant and otherwise satisfies the requirements of this paragraph (d)(6)(i), the amount of the claim (measured according to actuarial principles, using factors set forth in the transfer tax regulations or otherwise provided by the IRS) will be deemed ascertainable with reasonable certainty for purposes of the rule for deducting certain ascertainable amounts set forth in § 20.2053-1(d)(4).

(ii) *Contingent obligations.*—If a decedent has a recurring obligation to pay an enforceable and certain claim but the decedent's obligation is subject to a contingency or is not otherwise described in paragraph (d)(6)(i) of this section, the amount of the claim is not ascertainable with reasonable certainty for purposes of the rule for deducting certain ascertainable amounts set forth in § 20.2053-1(d)(4). Accordingly, the amount deductible is limited to amounts actually paid by the estate in satisfaction of the claim in accordance with § 20.2053-1(d)(1) (subject to any applicable limitations in § 20.2053-1).

(iii) *Purchase of commercial annuity to satisfy recurring obligation to pay.*—If a decedent has a recurring obligation (whether or not contingent) to pay an enforceable and certain claim and the estate purchases a commercial annuity from an unrelated dealer in commercial annuities in an arm's-length transaction to satisfy the obligation, the amount deductible by the estate (subject to any applicable limitations in § 20.2053-1) is the sum of—

(A) The amount paid for the commercial annuity, to the extent that the amount paid is not refunded, or expected to be refunded, to the estate;

(B) Any amount actually paid to the claimant by the estate prior to the purchase of the commercial annuity; and

(C) Any amount actually paid to the claimant by the estate in excess of the annuity amount as is necessary to satisfy the recurring obligation.

(7) *Examples.*—The following examples illustrate the application of paragraph (d) of this section. Except as is otherwise provided in the examples, assume—

(i) A claim satisfies the applicable requirements set forth in § 20.2053-1 and paragraph (a) of this section, is payable from property subject to claims, and the amount of the claim is not subject to any other applicable limitations in § 20.2053-1;

(ii) A claim is not deductible under paragraphs (b) or (c) of this section as an exception to the general rule contained in paragraph (a) of this section; and

(iii) The claimant (C) is not a family member, related entity or beneficiary of the estate of decedent (D) and is not the executor (E).

*Example 1. Contested claim, single defendant, no decision.* D is sued by C for $100x in a tort proceeding and responds asserting affirmative defenses available to D under applicable local law. D dies and E is substituted as defendant in the suit. D's Form 706 is due before a judgment is reached in the case. D's gross estate exceeds $100x. E may not take a deduction on Form 706 for the claim against the estate. However, E may claim a deduction under § 20.2053-3(c) or § 20.2053-3(d)(3) for expenses incurred in defending the estate against the claim if the expenses have been paid in accordance with § 20.2053-1(d)(1) or if the expenses meet the requirements of § 20.2053-1(d)(4) for deducting certain ascertainable amounts. E may file a protective claim for refund before the expiration of the period of

limitation prescribed in section 6511(a) in order to preserve the estate's right to claim a refund, if the amount of the claim will not be paid or cannot be ascertained with reasonable certainty by the expiration of this limitation period. If payment is subsequently made pursuant to a court decision or a settlement, the payment, as well as expenses incurred incident to the claim and not previously deducted, may be deducted and relief may be sought in connection with a timely-filed claim for refund.

*Example 2. Contested claim, single defendant, final court decree and payment.* The facts are the same as in *Example 1* except that, before the Form 706 is timely filed, the court enters a decision in favor of C, no timely appeal is filed, and payment is made. E may claim a deduction on Form 706 for the amount paid in satisfaction of the claim against the estate pursuant to the final decision of the local court, including any interest accrued prior to D's death. In addition, E may claim a deduction under § 20.2053-3(c) or § 20.2053-3(d)(3) for expenses incurred in defending the estate against the claim and in processing payment of the claim if the expenses have been paid in accordance with § 20.2053-1(d)(1) or if the expenses meet the requirements of § 20.2053-1(d)(4) for deducting certain ascertainable amounts.

*Example 3. Contested claim, single defendant, settlement and payment.* The facts are the same as in *Example 1* except that a settlement is reached between E and C for $80x and payment is made before Form 706 is timely filed. E may claim a deduction on Form 706 for the amount paid to C ($80x) in satisfaction of the claim against the estate. In addition, E may claim a deduction under § 20.2053-3(c) or § 20.2053-3(d)(3) for expenses incurred in defending the estate, reaching a settlement, and processing payment of the claim if the expenses have been paid in accordance with § 20.2053-1(d)(1) or if the expenses meet the requirements of § 20.2053-1(d)(4) for deducting certain ascertainable amounts.

*Example 4. Contested claim, multiple defendants.* The facts are the same as in *Example 1* except that the suit filed by C lists D and an unrelated third-party (K) as defendants. If the claim against the estate is not resolved prior to the time the Form 706 is filed, E may not take a deduction for the claim on Form 706. If payment is subsequently made of D's share of the claim pursuant to a court decision holding D liable for 40 percent of the amount due and K liable for 60 percent of the amount due, then E may claim a deduction for the amount paid in satisfaction of the claim against the estate representing D's share of the liability as assigned by the court decree ($40x), plus any interest on that share accrued prior to D's death. If the court decision finds D and K jointly and severally liable for the entire $100x and D's estate pays the entire $100x but could have reasonably collected $50x from K in reimbursement, E may claim a deduction of $50x together with the interest on $50x accrued prior to D's death. In both instances, E also may claim a deduction under § 20.2053-3(c) or § 20.2053-3(d)(3) for expenses incurred and not previously deducted in defending the estate against the claim and processing payment of the amount due from D if the expenses have been paid in accordance with § 20.2053-1(d)(1) or if the expenses meet the requirements of § 20.2053-1(d)(4) for deducting certain ascertainable amounts.

*Example 5. Contested claim, multiple defendants, settlement and payment.* The facts are the same as in *Example 1* except that the suit filed by C lists D and an unrelated third-party (K) as defendants. D's estate settles with C for $10x and payment is made before Form 706 is timely filed. E may take a deduction on Form 706 for the amount paid to C ($10x) in satisfaction of the claim against the estate. In addition, E may claim a deduction under § 20.2053-3(c) or § 20.2053-3(d)(3) for expenses incurred in defending the estate, reaching a settlement, and processing payment of the claim if the expenses have been paid in accordance with § 20.2053-1(d)(1) or if the expenses meet the requirements of § 20.2053-1(d)(4) for deducting certain ascertainable amounts.

*Example 6. Mixed claims.* During life, D contracts with C to perform specific work on D's home for $75x. Under the contract, additional work must be approved in advance by D. C performs additional work and sues D for $100x for work completed including the $75x agreed to in the contract. D dies and D's Form 706 is due before a judgment is reached in the case. E accepts liability of $75x but contests liability of $25x. E may take a deduction of $75x on Form 706 if the amount has been paid or meets the requirements of § 20.2053-1(d)(4) for deducting certain ascertainable amounts. In addition, E may claim a deduction under § 20.2053-3(c) or § 20.2053-3(d)(3) for expenses incurred in defending the estate against the claim if the expenses have been paid or if the expenses meet the requirements of § 20.2053-1(d)(4) for deducting certain ascertainable amounts. E may file a protective claim for refund before the expiration of the period of limitation prescribed in section 6511(a) in order to preserve the estate's right to claim a refund for any amount in excess of $75x that is subsequently paid to resolve the claim against the estate. To the extent that any unpaid expenses incurred in defending the estate against the claim are not deducted as an ascertainable amount pursuant to §20.2053-1(d)(4), they may be included in the protective claim for refund.

*Example 7. Claim having issue of enforceability.* D is sued by C for $100x in a tort proceeding in which there is an issue as to whether the claim is barred by the applicable period of limitations. After D's death but prior to the decision of the court, a settlement meeting the requirements of §20.2053-1(b)(3)(iv) is reached between E and C in the amount of $50x. E pays C this amount before the Form 706 is timely filed. E may take a deduction on Form 706 for the amount paid to C ($50x) in satisfaction of the claim. If, subsequent to E's payment to C, facts develop to indicate that the claim was, in fact, unenforceable, the deduction will not be denied provided the enforceability of the claim was at issue in a bona dispute at the time of the payment. See §20.2053-1(b)(3)(iv). A deduction may be available under §20.2053-3(d)(3) for expenses incurred in defending the estate, reaching a settlement, and processing payment of the claim if the expenses have been paid in accordance with §20.2053-1(d)(1) or if the expenses meet the requirements of §20.2053-1(d)(4) for deducting certain ascertainable amounts.

*Example 8. Noncontingent and recurring obligation to pay, binding on estate.* D's property settlement agreement incident to D's divorce, signed three years prior to D's death, obligates D or D's estate to pay to S, D's former spouse, $20x per year until S's death or remarriage. Prior to D's death, D made payments in accordance with the agreement and, after D's death, E continues to make the payments in accordance with the agreement. D's obligation to pay S under the property settlement agreement is deemed to be a claim against the estate that is ascertainable with reasonable certainty for purposes of §20.2053-1(d)(4). To the extent the obligation to make the recurring payment is a claim that will be paid, E may deduct the amount of the claim (measured according to actuarial principles, using factors set forth in the transfer tax regulations or otherwise provided by the IRS) under the rule for deducting certain ascertainable amounts set forth in §20.2053-1(d)(4).

*Example 9. Recurring obligation to pay, estate purchases a commercial annuity in satisfaction.* D's settlement agreement with T, the claimant in a suit against D, signed three years prior to D's death, obligates D or D's estate to pay to T $20x per year for 10 years, provided that T does not reveal the details of the claim or of the settlement during that period. D dies in Year 1. In Year 2, D's estate purchases a commercial annuity from an unrelated issuer of commercial annuities, XYZ, to fund the obligation to T. E may deduct the entire amount paid to XYZ to obtain the annuity, even though the obligation to T was contingent.

(e) *Interest on claim.*—(1) Subject to any applicable limitations in §20.2053-1, the interest on a deductible claim is itself deductible as a claim under section 2053 to the extent of the amount of interest accrued at the decedent's death (even if the executor elects the alternate valuation method under section 2032), but only to the extent of the amount of interest actually paid or meeting the requirements of §20.2053-1(d)(4) for deducting certain ascertainable amounts.

(2) Post-death accrued interest may be deductible in appropriate circumstances either as an estate tax administration expense under section 2053 or as an income tax deduction.

(f) *Effective/applicability date.*—This section applies to the estates of decedents dying on or after October 20, 2009. [Reg. §20.2053-4.]

□ [*T.D.* 6296, 6-23-58. *Amended by T.D.* 9468, 10-16-2009 (*corrected* 11-24-2009).]

### [Reg. §20.2053-5]

**§20.2053-5. Deductions for charitable, etc., pledges or subscriptions.**—(a) A pledge or a subscription, evidenced by a promissory note or otherwise, even though enforceable against the estate, is deductible (subject to any applicable limitations in §20.2053-1) only to the extent that—

(1) Liability therefore was contracted bona fide and for an adequate and full consideration in cash or its equivalent, or

(2) It would have constituted an allowable deduction under section 2055 (relating to charitable, etc., deductions) if it had been a bequest.

(b) *Effective/applicability date.*—This section applies to the estates of decedents dying on or after October 20, 2009. [Reg. §20.2053-5.]

□ [*T.D.* 6296, 6-23-58. *Amended by T.D.* 9468, 10-16-2009.]

### [Reg. §20.2053-6]

**§20.2053-6. Deduction for taxes.**—(a) *In general.*—(1) Taxes are deductible in computing a decedent's gross estate—

(i) Only as claims against the estate (except to the extent that excise taxes may be allowable as administration expenses);

(ii) Only to the extent not disallowed by section 2053(c)(1)(B) and this section; and

(iii) Subject to any applicable limitations in §20.2053-1.

(2) See §§20.2053-9 and 20.2053-10 with respect to the deduction allowed for certain state and foreign death taxes.

(b) *Property taxes.*—Property taxes are not deductible unless they accrued before the decedent's death. However, they are not deductible merely because they have accrued in an accounting sense. Property taxes in order to be deductible must be an enforceable obligation of the decedent at the time of his death.

(c) *Death taxes.*—(1) For the estates of decedents dying on or before December 31, 2004, no estate, succession, legacy or inheritance tax payable by reason of the decedent's death is deductible, except as provided in §§20.2053-9 and 20.2053-10 with respect to certain state and foreign death taxes on transfers for charitable, etc., uses. However, see sections 2011 and 2014 and the corresponding regulations with respect to credits for death taxes.

(2) For the estates of decedents dying after December 31, 2004, see section 2058 to determine the deductibility of state death taxes.

(d) *Gift taxes.*—Unpaid gift taxes on gifts made by a decedent before his death are deductible. If a gift is considered as made one-half by the decedent and one-half by his spouse under section 2513, the entire amount of the gift tax, unpaid at the decedent's death, attributable to a gift in fact made by the decedent is deductible. No portion of the tax attributable to a gift in fact made by the decedent's spouse is deductible except to the extent that the obligation is enforced against the decedent's estate and his estate has no effective right of contribution against his spouse. (See section 2012 and §20.2012-1 with respect to credit for gift taxes paid upon gifts of property included in a decedent's gross estate.)

(e) *Excise taxes.*—Excise taxes incurred in selling property of a decedent's estate are deductible as an expense of administration if the sale is necessary in order to (1) pay the decedent's debts, expenses of administration, or taxes, (2) preserve the estate, or (3) effect distribution. Excise taxes incurred in distributing property of the estate in kind are also deductible.

(f) *Income taxes.*—Unpaid income taxes are deductible if they are on income properly includible in an income tax return of the decedent for a period before his death. Taxes on income received after the decedent's death are not deductible. If income received by a decedent during his lifetime is included in a joint income tax return filed by the decedent and his spouse, or by the decedent's estate and his surviving spouse, the portion of the joint liability for the period covered by the return for which a deduction would be allowed is the amount for which the decedent's estate would be liable under local law, as between the decedent and his spouse, after enforcement of any effective right of reimbursement or contribution. In the absence of evidence to the contrary, the deductible amount is presumed to be an amount bearing the same ratio to the total joint tax liability for the period covered by the return that the amount of income tax for which the decedent would have been liable if he had filed a separate return for that period bears to the total of the amounts for which the decedent and his spouse would have been liable if they had both filed separate returns for that period. Thus, in the absence of evidence to the contrary, the deductible amount equals

$$\frac{decedent's\ separate\ tax}{both\ separate\ taxes} \times joint\ tax.$$

However, the deduction cannot in any event exceed the lesser of—

(1) The decedent's liability for the period (as determined in this paragraph) reduced by the amounts already contributed by the decedent toward payment of the joint liability, or

(2) If there is an enforceable agreement between the decedent and his spouse or between the executor and the spouse relative to the payment of the joint liability, the amount which pursuant to the agreement is to be contributed by the estate toward payment of the joint liability.

If the decedent's estate and his surviving spouse are entitled to a refund on account of an overpayment of a joint income tax liability, the overpayment is an asset includible in the decedent's gross estate under section 2033 in the amount to which the estate would be entitled under local law, as between the estate and the surviving spouse. In the absence of evidence to the contrary, the includible amount is presumed to be the amount by which the decedent's contributions toward payment of the joint tax exceeds his liability determined in accordance with the principles set forth in this paragraph (other than subparagraph (1) of this paragraph).

(g) *Post-death adjustments of deductible tax liability.*—Post-death adjustments increasing a tax liability accrued prior to the decedent's death, including increases of taxes deducted under this section, will increase the amount of the deduction available under section 2053(a)(3) for that tax liability. Similarly, any refund subsequently determined to be due to and received by the estate or its successor in interest with respect to taxes deducted by the estate under this section reduce the amount of the deduction taken for that tax liability under section 2053(a)(3). Expenses associated with defending the estate against the increase in tax liability or with obtaining the refund may be deductible under § 20.2053-3(d)(3). A protective claim for refund of estate taxes may be filed before the expiration of the period of limitation for filing a claim for refund in order to preserve the estate's right to claim a refund if the amount of a deductible tax liability may be affected by such an adjustment or refund. The application of this section may be illustrated by the following examples:

*Example 1. Increase in tax due.* After the decedent's death, the Internal Revenue Service examines the gift tax return filed by the decedent in the year before the decedent's death and asserts a deficiency of $100x. The estate pays attorney's fees of $30x in a nonfrivolous defense against the increased deficiency. The final determination of the deficiency, in the amount of $90x, is paid by the estate prior to the expiration of the limitation period for filing a claim for refund. The estate may deduct $90x under section 2053(a)(3) and $30x under § 20.2053-3(c)(2) or (d)(3) in connection with a timely claim for refund.

*Example 2. Refund of taxes paid.* Decedent's estate timely files D's individual income tax return for the year in which the decedent died. The estate timely pays the entire amount of the tax due, $50x, as shown on that return. The entire $50x was attributable to income received prior to the decedent's death. Decedent's estate subsequently discovers an error on the income tax return and timely files a claim for refund of income tax. Decedent's estate receives a refund of $10x. The estate is allowed a deduction of only $40x under section 2053(a)(3) for the income tax liability accrued prior to the decedent's death. If D's estate had claimed a deduction of $50x on D's United States Estate (and Generation-Skipping Transfer) Tax Return (Form 706), the deduction claimed under section 2053(a)(3) will be allowed only to the extent of $40x upon examination by the Commissioner.

(h) *Effective/applicability date.*—This section applies to the estates of decedents dying on or after October 20, 2009. [Reg. § 20.2053-6.]

☐ [*T.D. 6296, 6-23-58. Amended by T.D. 9468, 10-16-2009.*]

### [Reg. § 20.2053-7]

**§ 20.2053-7. Deduction for unpaid mortgages.**—A deduction is allowed from a decedent's gross estate of the full unpaid amount of a mortgage upon, or of any other indebtedness in respect of, any property of the gross estate, including interest which had accrued thereon to the date of death, provided the value of the property, undiminished by the amount of the mortgage or indebtedness, is included in the value of the gross estate. If the decedent's estate is liable for the amount of the mortgage or indebtedness, the full value of the property subject to the mortgage or indebtedness must be included as part of the value of the gross estate; the amount of the mortgage or indebtedness being in such case allowed as a deduction. But if the decedent's estate is not so liable, only the value of the equity of redemption (or the value of the property, less the mortgage or indebtedness) need be returned as part of the value of the gross estate. In no case may the deduction on account of the mortgage or indebtedness exceed the liability therefor contracted bona fide and for an adequate and full consideration in money or money's worth. See § 20.2043-1. Only interest accrued to the date of the decedent's death is allowable even though the alternate valuation method under section 2032 is selected. In any case where real property situated outside the United States does not form a part of the gross estate, no deduction may be taken of any mortgage thereon or any other indebtedness in respect thereof. [Reg. § 20.2053-7.]

☐ [*T.D. 6296, 6-23-58. Amended by T.D. 6684, 10-23-63.*]

### [Reg. § 20.2053-8]

**§ 20.2053-8. Deduction for expenses in administering property not subject to claims.**—(a) Expenses incurred in administering property included in a decedent's gross estate but not subject to claims fall within the second category of deductions set forth in § 20.2053-1, and may be allowed as deductions if they—

(1) Would be allowed as deductions in the first category if the property being administered were subject to claims; and

(2) Were paid before the expiration of the period of limitation for assessment provided in section 6501.

Usually, these expenses are incurred in connection with the administration of a trust established by a decedent during his lifetime. They may also be incurred in connection with the collection of other assets or the transfer or clearance of title to other property included in a decedent's gross estate for estate tax purposes but not included in his probate estate.

(b) These expenses may be allowed as deductions only to the extent that they would be allowed as deductions under the first category if the property were subject to claims. See § 20.2053-3. The only expenses in administering property not subject to claims which are allowed as deductions are those occasioned by the decedent's death and incurred in settling the decedent's interest in the property or vesting good title to the property in the beneficiaries. Expenses not coming within the description in the preceding sentence but incurred on behalf of the transferees are not deductible.

(c) The principles set forth in paragraphs (b), (c), and (d) of § 20.2053-3 (relating to the allowance of executor's commissions, attorney's fees, and miscellaneous administration expenses of the first category) are applied in determining the extent to which trustee's commissions, attorney's and accountant's fees, and miscellaneous administration expenses are allowed in connection with the administration of property not subject to claims.

(d) The application of this section may be illustrated by the following examples:

*Example (1).* In 1940, the decedent made an irrevocable transfer of property to the X Trust Company, as trustee. The instrument of transfer provided that the trustee should pay the income from the property to the decedent for the duration of his life and, upon his death, distribute the corpus of the trust among designated beneficiaries. The property was included in the decedent's gross estate under the provisions of section 2036. Three months after the date of death, the trustee distributed the trust corpus among the beneficiaries, except for $6,000 which it withheld. The amount withheld represented $5,000 which it retained as trustee's commissions in connection with the termination of the trust and $1,000 which it had paid to an attorney for representing it in connection with the termination. Both the trustee's commissions and the attorney's fees were allowable under the law of the jurisdiction in which the trust was being administered, were reasonable in amount, and were in accord with local custom. Under these circumstances, the estate is allowed a deduction of $6,000.

*Example (2).* In 1945, the decedent made an irrevocable transfer of property to Y Trust Company, as trustee. The instrument of transfer provided that the trustee should pay the income from the property to the decedent during his life. If the decedent's wife survived him, the trust was to continue for the duration of her life, with Y Trust Company and the decedent's son as co-trustees, and with income payable to the decedent's wife for the duration of her life. Upon the death of both the decedent and his wife, the corpus is to be distributed among designated remaindermen. The decedent was survived by his wife. The property was included in the decedent's gross estate under the provisions of section 2036. In accordance with local custom, the trustee made an accounting to the court as of the date of the decedent's death. Following the death of the decedent, a controversy arose among the remaindermen as to their respective rights under the instrument of transfer, and a suit was brought in court to which the trustee was made a party. As a part of the accounting, the court approved the following expenses which the trustee had paid within 3 years following the date of death: $10,000, trustee's commissions; $5,000, accountant's fees; $25,000, attorney's fees; and $2,500, representing fees paid to the guardian of a remainderman who was a minor. The trustee's commissions and accountant's fees were for services in connection with the usual issues involved in a trust accounting as also were one-half of the attorney's and guardian's fees. The remainder of the attorney's and guardian's fees were for services performed in connection with the suit brought by the remaindermen. The amount allowed as a deduction is the $28,750 ($10,000, trustee's commissions; $5,000, accountant's fees; $12,500, attorney's fees; and $1,250, guardian's fees) incurred as expenses in connection with the usual issues involved in a trust accounting. The remaining expenses are not allowed as deductions since they were incurred on behalf of the transferees.

*Example (3).* Decedent in 1950 made an irrevocable transfer of property to the Z Trust Company, as trustee. The instrument of transfer provided that the trustee should pay the income from the property to the decedent's wife for the duration of her life. If the decedent survived his wife the trust corpus was to be returned to him but if he did not survive her, then upon the death of the wife, the trust corpus was to be distributed among their children. The decedent predeceased his wife and the transferred property, less the value of the wife's outstanding life estate, was included in his gross estate under the provisions of section 2037 since his reversionary interest therein immediately before his death was in excess of 5 percent of the value of the property. At the wife's request, the court ordered the trustee to render an accounting of the trust property as of the date of the decedent's death. No deduction will be allowed the decedent's estate for any of the expenses incurred in connection with the trust accounting, since the expenses were incurred on behalf of the wife.

*Example (4).* If, in the preceding example, the decedent died without other property and no executor or administrator of his estate was appointed, so that it was necessary for the trustee to prepare an estate tax return and participate in its audit, or if the trustee required accounting proceedings for its own protection in accordance with local custom, trustees', attorneys', and guardians' fees in connection with the estate tax or accounting proceedings would be deductible to the same extent that they would be deductible if the property were subject to claims. Deductions incurred under similar circumstances by a surviving joint tenant or the recipient of life insurance proceeds would also be deductible. [Reg. §20.2053-8.]

☐ [*T.D.* 6296, 6-23-58.]

**[Reg. §20.2053-9]**

**§20.2053-9. Deduction for certain State death taxes.**—(a) *General rule.*—A deduction is allowed a decedent's estate under section 2053(d) for the amount of any estate, succession, legacy, or inheritance tax imposed by a State, Territory, or the District of Columbia, or, in the case of a decedent dying before September 3, 1958, a possession of the United States upon a transfer by the decedent for charitable, etc., uses described in section 2055 or 2106(a)(2) (relating to the estates of nonresidents not citizens), but only if (1) the conditions stated in paragraph (b) of this section are met, and (2) an election is made in accordance with the provisions of paragraph (c) of this section. See section 2011(e) and §20.2011-2 for the effect which the allowance of this deduction has upon the credit for State death taxes. However, see section 2058 to determine the deductibility of state death taxes by estates to which section 2058 is applicable.

(b) *Condition for allowance of deduction.*—(1) The deduction is not allowed unless either—

    (i) The entire decrease in the Federal estate tax resulting from the allowance of the deduction inures solely to the benefit of a charitable, etc., transferee described in section 2055 or 2106(a)(2), or

    (ii) The Federal estate tax is equitably apportioned among all the transferees (including the decedent's surviving spouse and the charitable, etc., transferees) of property included in the decedent's gross estate.

For allowance of the credit, it is sufficient if either of these conditions is satisfied. Thus, in a case where the entire decrease in Federal estate tax inures to the benefit of a charitable transferee, the deduction is allowable even though the Federal estate tax is not equitably apportioned among all the transferees of property included in the decedent's gross estate. Similarly, if the Federal estate tax is equitably apportioned among all the transferees of property included in the decedent's gross estate, the deduction is allowable even though a noncharitable transferee receives some benefit from the allowance of the deduction.

    (2) For purposes of this paragraph, the Federal estate tax is considered to be equitably apportioned among all the transferees (including the decedent's surviving spouse and the charitable, etc., transferees) of property included in the decedent's gross estate only if each transferee's share of the tax is based upon the net amount of his transfer subjected to the tax (taking into account any exemptions, credits, or deductions allowed by chapter 11). See examples (2) through (5) of paragraph (e) of this section.

(c) *Exercise of election.*—The election to take a deduction for a state death tax imposed upon a transfer for charitable, etc., uses shall be exercised by the executor by the filing of a written notification to that effect with the Commissioner. The notification shall be filed before the expiration of the period of limitation for assessment provided in section 6501 (usually 3 years from the last day for filing the return). The election may be revoked by the executor by the filing of a written notification to that effect with the Commissioner at any time before the expiration of such period.

(d) *Amount of State death tax imposed upon a transfer.*—If a State death tax is imposed upon the transfer of the decedent's entire estate and not upon the transfer of a particular share thereof, the State death tax imposed upon a transfer for charitable, etc., uses is deemed to be an amount, E, which bears the same ratio to F (the amount of the State death tax imposed with respect to the transfer of the entire estate) as G (the value of the charitable, etc., transfer, reduced as provided in the next sentence) bears to H (the total value of the properties, interests, and benefits subjected to the State death tax received by all persons interested in the estate, reduced as provided in the last sentence of this paragraph). In arriving at amount G of the ratio, the value of the charitable, etc., transfer is reduced by the amount of any deduction or exclusion allowed with respect to such property in determining the amount of the State death tax. In arriving at amount H of the ratio, the total value of the properties, interests, and benefits subjected to State death tax received by all persons interested in the estate is reduced by the amount of all deductions and exclusions allowed in determining the amount of the State death tax on account of the nature of a beneficiary or a beneficiary's relationship to the decedent.

(e) *Examples.*—The application of this section may be illustrated by the following examples:

    *Example (1).* The decedent's gross estate was valued at $200,000. He bequeathed $90,000 to a newphew, $10,000 to Charity A, and the remainder of his estate to Charity B. State inheritance tax in the amount of $13,500 was imposed upon the bequest to the nephew, $1,500 upon the bequest to Charity A, and $15,000 upon the bequest to Charity B. Under the will and local law, each legatee is required to pay the State inheritance tax on his bequest, and the Federal estate tax is to be paid out of the residuary estate. Since the entire burden of paying the Federal estate tax falls on Charity B, it follows that the decrease in the Federal estate tax resulting from the allowance of deductions for State death taxes in the amounts of $1,500 and $15,000 would inure solely for the benefit of Charity B. Therefore, deductions of $1,500 and $15,000 are allowable under section 2053(d). If, in this example, the State death taxes as well as the Federal estate tax were to be paid out of the residuary estate, the result would be the same.

    *Example (2).* The decedent's gross estate was valued at $350,000. Expenses, indebtedness, etc., amounted to $50,000. The entire estate was bequeathed in equal shares to a son, a daughter, and Charity C. State inheritance tax in the amount of $2,000 was imposed upon the bequest to the son, $2,000 upon the bequest to the daughter, and $5,000 upon the bequest to Charity C. Under the will and local law, each legatee is required to pay his own State inheritance tax and his proportionate share of the Federal estate tax determined by taking into consideration the net amount of his bequest subjected to the tax. Since each legatee's share of the Federal estate tax is based upon the net amount of his bequest subjected to the tax (note that the deductions under sections 2053(d) and 2055 will have the effect of reducing Charity C's proportionate share of the tax), the tax is considered to be equitably apportioned. Thus, a deduction of $5,000 is allowable under section 2053(d). This deduction together with a deduction of $95,000 under section 2055 (charitable deduction) will mean that none of Charity C's bequest is subjected to Federal estate tax. Hence, the son and the daughter will bear the entire estate tax.

    *Example (3).* The decedent bequeathed his property in equal shares, after payment of all expenses, to a son, a daughter, and a charity. State inheritance tax of $2,000 was imposed upon the bequest to the son, $2,000 upon the bequest to the daughter, and $15,000 upon the bequest to the charity. Under the will and local law, each beneficiary pays the State inheritance tax on his bequest and the Federal estate tax is to be paid out of the estate as an administration expense. If the deduction for State death tax on the charitable bequest is allowed in this case, some portion of the decrease in the Federal estate tax would inure to the benefit of the son and the daughter. The Federal estate tax is not considered to be equitably apportioned in this case since each legatee's share of the Federal estate tax is not based upon the net amount of his bequest subjected to the tax (note that the deductions under sections 2053(d) and 2055 will not have the effect of reducing the charity's proportionate share of the tax). Inasmuch as some of the decrease in the Federal estate tax payable would inure to the benefit of the son and the daughter, and inasmuch as there is no equitable apportionment of the tax, no deduction is allowable under section 2053(d).

    *Example (4).* The decedent bequeathed his entire residuary estate in trust to pay the income to X for life with remainder to charity. The State imposed inheritance taxes of $2,000 upon the bequest to X and $10,000 upon the bequest to charity. Under the will and local law, all State and Federal taxes are payable out of the residuary estate and therefore they would reduce the amount which would become the corpus of the trust. If the deduction for the State death tax on the charitable bequest is allowed in this case, some portion of the decrease in the Federal estate tax would inure to the benefit of X since the allowance of the deduction would increase the size of the corpus from which X is to receive the income for life. Also, the Federal estate tax is not considered to be equitably apportioned in this case since each legatee's share of the Federal estate tax is not based upon the net amount of his bequest subjected to the tax (note that the deductions under sections 2053(d) and 2055 will not have the effect of reducing the charity's proportionate share of the tax). Inasmuch as some of the decrease in the Federal estate tax payable would inure to the benefit of X, and inasmuch as there is no equitable apportionment of the tax, no deduction is allowable under section 2053(d).

    *Example (5).* The decedent's gross estate was valued at $750,000. Expenses, indebtedness, etc., amounted to $50,000. The decedent bequeathed $350,000 of his estate to his surviving spouse and the remainder of his estate equally to his son and Charity D. State inheritance tax in the amount of $7,000 was imposed upon the bequest to the surviving spouse, $26,250 upon the bequest to the son, and $26,250 upon the bequest to Charity D. The will was silent concerning the payment of taxes. In such a case, the local law provides that each legatee shall pay his own State inheritance tax. The local law further provides for an apportionment of the Federal estate tax among the legatees of the estate. Under the apportionment provisions, the surviving spouse is not required to bear any part of the Federal estate tax with respect to her $350,000 bequest. It should be noted, however, that the marital deduction allowed to the decedent's estate by reason of the bequest to the surviving spouse is limited to $343,000 ($350,000 bequest less $7,000 State inheritance tax payable by the surviving spouse). Thus, the bequest to the surviving spouse is subjected to the Federal estate tax in the net amount of $7,000. If the deduction for State death tax on the charitable bequest is allowed in this case, some portion of the decrease in the Federal estate tax would inure to the benefit of the son. The Federal estate tax is not considered to be equitably apportioned in this case since each legatee's share of the Federal estate tax is not based upon the net amount of his bequest subjected to the tax (note that the surviving spouse is to pay no tax). Inasmuch as some of the decrease in the Federal estate tax payable would inure to the benefit of the son, and inasmuch as there is no equitable apportionment of the tax, no deduction is allowable under section 2053(d).

(f) *Effective/applicability date.*—(1) The last sentence of paragraph (a) of this section applies to the estates of decedents dying on or after October 20, 2009, to which section 2058 is applicable.

(2) The other provisions of this section apply to the estates of decedents dying on or after October 20, 2009, to which section 2058 is not applicable. [Reg. § 20.2053-9.]

☐ [T.D. 6296, 6-23-58. *Amended by T.D.* 6526, 1-18-61 *and T.D.* 9468, 10-16-2009.]

### [Reg. § 20.2053-10]

**§ 20.2053-10. Deduction for certain foreign death taxes.**— (a) *General rule.*—A deduction is allowed the estate of a decedent dying on or after July 1, 1955, under section 2053(d) for the amount of any estate, succession, legacy, or inheritance tax imposed by and actually paid to any foreign country, in respect of any property situated within such foreign country and included in the gross estate of a citizen or resident of the United States, upon a transfer by the decedent for charitable, etc., uses described in section 2055, but only if (1) the conditions stated in paragraph (b) of this section are met, and (2) an election is made in accordance with the provisions of paragraph(c) of this section. The determination of the country within which property is situated is made in accordance with the rules contained in sections 2104 and 2105 in determining whether property is situated within or without the United States. See section 2014(f) and § 20.2014-7 for the effect which the allowance of this deduction has upon the credit for foreign death taxes.

(b) *Condition for allowance of deduction.*—(1) The deduction is not allowed unless either—

(i) The entire decrease in the Federal estate tax resulting from the allowance of the deduction inures solely to the benefit of a charitable, etc., transferee described in section 2055, or

(ii) The Federal estate tax is equitably apportioned among all the transferees (including the decedent's surviving spouse and the charitable, etc., transferees) of property included in the decedent's gross estate.

For allowance of the deduction, it is sufficient if either of these conditions is satisfied. Thus, in a case where the entire decrease in Federal estate tax inures to the benefit of a charitable transferee, the deduction is allowable even though the Federal estate tax is not equitably apportioned among all the transferees of property included in the decedent's gross estate. Similarly, if the Federal estate tax is equitably apportioned among all the transferees of property included in the decedent's gross estate, the deduction is allowable even though a noncharitable transferee receives some benefit from the allowance of the deduction.

(2) For purposes of this paragraph, the Federal estate tax is considered to be equitably apportioned among all the transferees (including the decedent's surviving spouse and the charitable, etc., transferees) of property included in the decedent's gross estate only if each transferee's share of the tax is based upon the net amount of his transfer subjected to the tax (taking into account any exemptions, credits, or deductions allowed by chapter 11). See examples (2) through (5) of paragraph (e) of § 20.2053-9.

(c) *Exercise of election.*—The election to take a deduction for a foreign death tax imposed upon a transfer for charitable, etc., uses shall be exercised by the executor by the filing of a written notification to that effect with the Commissioner of internal revenue in whose district the estate tax return for the decedent's estate was filed. An election to take the deduction for foreign death taxes is deemed to be a waiver of the right to claim a credit under a treaty with any foreign country for any tax or portion thereof claimed as a deduction under this section. The notification shall be filed before the expiration of the period of limitation for assessment provided in section 6501 (usually 3 years from the last day for filing the return). The election

may be revoked by the executor by the filing of a written notification to that effect with the Commissioner at any time before the expiration of such period.

(d) *Amount of foreign death tax imposed upon a transfer.*—If a foreign death tax is imposed upon the transfer of the entire part of the decedent's estate subject to such tax and not upon the transfer of a particular share thereof, the foreign death tax imposed upon a transfer for charitable, etc., uses is deemed to be an amount, J, which bears the same ratio to K (the amount of the foreign death tax imposed with respect to the transfer of the entire part of the decedent's estate subject to such tax) as M (the value of the charitable, etc., transfer, reduced as provided in the next sentence) bears to N (the total value of the properties, interests, and benefits subjected to the foreign death tax received by all persons interested in the estate, reduced as provided in the last sentence of this paragraph). In arriving at amount M of the ratio, the value of the charitable, etc., transfer is reduced by the amount of any deduction or exclusion allowed with respect to such property in determining the amount of the foreign death tax. In arriving at amount N of the ratio, the total value of the properties, interests, and benefits subjected to foreign death tax received by all persons interested in the estate is reduced by the amount of all deductions and exclusions allowed in determining the amount of the foreign death tax on account of the nature of a beneficiary or a beneficiary's relationship to the decedent.

(e) *Effective/applicability date.*—This section applies to the estates of decedents dying on or after October 20, 2009. [Reg. § 20.2053-10.]

☐ [T.D. 6600, 5-28-62. *Amended by T.D.* 9468, 10-16-2009.]

### [Reg. § 20.2054-1]

**§ 20.2054-1. Deduction for losses from casualties or theft.**—A deduction is allowed for losses incurred during the settlement of the estate arising from fires, storms, shipwrecks, or other casualties, or from theft, if the losses are not compensated for by insurance or otherwise. If the loss is partly compensated for, the excess of the loss over the compensation may be deducted. Losses which are not of the nature described are not deductible. In order to be deductible a loss must occur during the settlement of the estate. If a loss with respect to an asset occurs after its distribution to the distributee it may not be deducted. Notwithstanding the foregoing, no deduction is allowed under this section if the estate has waived its right to take such a deduction pursuant to the provisions of section 642(g) in order to permit its allowance for income tax purposes. See further § 1.642(g)-1. [Reg. § 20.2054-1.]

☐ [T.D. 6296, 6-23-58.]

### [Reg. § 20.2055-1]

**§ 20.2055-1. Deduction for transfers for public, charitable, and religious uses; in general.**—(a) *General rule.*—A deduction is allowed under section 2055(a) from the gross estate of a decedent who was a citizen or resident of the United States at the time of his death for the value of property included in the decedent's gross estate and transferred by the decedent during his lifetime or by will—

(1) To or for the use of the United States, any State, Territory, any political subdivision thereof, or the District of Columbia, for exclusively public purposes;

(2) To or for the use of any corporation or association organized and operated exclusively for religious, charitable, scientific, literary, or educational purposes (including the encouragement of art and the prevention of cruelty to children or animals), if no part of the net earnings of the corporation or association inures to the benefit of any private stockholder or individual (other than as a legitimate object of such purposes), if the organization is not disqualified for tax exemption under section 501(c)(3) by reason of attempting to influence legislation, and if, in the case of transfers made after December 31, 1969, it does not participate in, or intervene in (including the publishing or distributing of statements), any political campaign on behalf of or in opposition to any candidate for public office;

(3) To a trustee or trustees, or a fraternal society, order, or association operating under the lodge system, if the transferred property is to be used exclusively for religious, charitable, scientific, literary, or educational purposes (or for the prevention of cruelty to children or animals), if no substantial part of the activities of such transferee is carrying on propaganda, or otherwise attempting, to influence legislation, and if, in the case of transfers made after December 31, 1969, such transferee does not participate in, or intervene in (including the publishing or distributing of statements), any political campaign on behalf of any candidate for public office; or

(4) To or for the use of any veterans' organization incorporated by act of Congress, or of any of its departments, local chapters, or posts, no part of the net earnings of which inures to the benefit of any private shareholder or individual.

The deduction is not limited, in the case of estates of citizens or residents of the United States, to transfers to domestic corporations or associations, or to trustees for use within the United States.

Nor is the deduction subject to percentage limitations such as are applicable to the charitable deduction under the income tax. An organization will not be considered to meet the requirements of subparagraph (2) or (3) of this paragraph if such organization engages in any activity which would cause it to be classified as an "action" organization under paragraph (c)(3) of § 1.501(c)(3)-1 of this chapter (Income Tax Regulations). See § 20.2055-4 and § 20.2055-5 for rules relating to the disallowance of deductions to trusts and organizations which engage in certain prohibited transactions or whose governing instruments do not contain certain specified requirements.

(b) *Powers of appointment.*—(1) *General rule.*—A deduction is allowable under section 2055(b) for the value of property passing to or for the use of a transferee described in paragraph (a) of this section by the exercise, failure to exercise, release or lapse of a power of appointment by reason of which the property is includible in the decedent's gross estate under section 2041.

(2) *Certain bequests subject to power of appointment.*—For the allowance of a deduction in the case of a bequest in trust where the decedent's surviving spouse (i) was over 80 years of age at the date of decedent's death, (ii) was entitled for life to all of the net income from the trust, and (iii) had a power of appointment over the corpus of the trust exercisable by will in favor of, among others, a charitable organization, see section 2055(b)(2). See also section 6503(e) for suspension of the period of limitations for assessment or collection of any deficiency attributable to the allowance of the deduction.

(c) *Submission of evidence.*—In establishing the right of the estate to the deduction authorized by section 2055, the executor should submit the following with the return:

(1) A copy of any instrument in writing by which the decedent made a transfer of property in his lifetime the value of which is required by statute to be included in his gross estate, for which a deduction under section 2055 is claimed. If the instrument is of record the copy should be certified, and if not of record, the copy should be verified.

(2) A written statement by the executor containing a declaration that it is made under penalties of perjury and stating whether any action has been instituted to construe or to contest the decedent's will or any provision thereof affecting the charitable deduction claimed and whether, according to his information and belief, any such action is designed or contemplated.

The executor shall also submit such other documents or evidence as may be requested by the district director.

(d) *Cross references.*—(1) See section 2055(f) for certain cross references relating to section 2055.

(2) For treatment of bequests accepted by the Secretary of State or the Secretary of Commerce, for the purpose of organizing and holding an international conference to negotiate a Patent Corporation Treaty, as bequests to or for the use of the United States, see section 3 of Joint Resolution of December 24, 1969 (P.L. 91-160, 83 Stat. 443).

(3) For treatment of bequests accepted by the Secretary of the Department of Housing and Urban Development, for the purpose of aiding or facilitating the work of the Department, as bequests to or for the use of the United States, see section 7(k) of the Department of Housing and Urban Development Act (42 U.S.C. 3535), as added by section 905 of P.L. 91-609 (84 Stat. 1809).

(4) For treatment of certain property accepted by the Chairman of the Administrative Conference of the United States, for the purpose of aiding and facilitating the work of the Conference, as a devise or bequest to the United States, see 5 U.S.C. 575(c)(12), as added by section 1(b) of the Act of October 21, 1972 (Public Law 92-526, 86 Stat. 1048).

(5) For treatment of the Board for International Broadcasting as a corporation described in section 2055(a)(2), see section 7 of the Board for International Broadcasting Act of 1973 (Public Law 93-129, 87 Stat. 459). [Reg. § 20.2055-1.]

☐ [T.D. 6296, 6-23-58. *Amended by* T.D. 7318, 7-10-74 *and* T.D. 8308, 8-30-90.]

### [Reg. § 20.2055-2]

**§ 20.2055-2. Transfers not exclusively for charitable purposes.**—(a) *Remainders and similar interests.*—If a trust is created or property is transferred for both a charitable and a private purpose, deduction may be taken of the value of the charitable beneficial interest only insofar as that interest is presently ascertainable, and hence severable from the noncharitable interest. Thus, in the case of decedents dying before January 1, 1970, if money or property is placed in trust to pay the income to an individual during his life, or for a term of years, and then to pay the principal to a charitable organization, the present

value of the remainder is deductible. See paragraph (e) of this section for limitations applicable to decedents dying after December 31, 1969. See paragraph (f) of this section for rules relating to valuation of partial interests in property passing for charitable purposes.

(b) *Transfers subject to a condition or a power.*—(1) If, as of the date of a decedent's death, a transfer for charitable purposes is dependent upon the performance of some act or the happening of a precedent event in order that it might become effective, no deduction is allowable unless the possibility that the charitable transfer will not become effective is so remote as to be negligible. If an estate or interest has passed to, or is vested in, charity at the time of a decedent's death and the estate or interest would be defeated by the subsequent performance of some act or the happening of some event, the possibility of occurrence of which appeared at the time of the decedent's death to be so remote as to be negligible, the deduction is allowable. If the legatee, devisee, donee, or trustee is empowered to divert the property or fund, in whole or in part, to a use or purpose which would have rendered it, to the extent that it is subject to such power, not deductible had it been directly so bequeathed, devised, or given by the decedent, the deduction will be limited to that portion, if any, of the property or fund which is exempt from an exercise of the power.

(2) The application of this paragraph may be illustrated by the following examples:

*Example (1).* In 1965, A dies leaving certain property in trust in which charity is to receive the income for the life of his widow. The assets placed in trust by the decedent consist of stock in a corporation the fiscal policies of which are controlled by the decedent and his family. The trustees of the trust and the remaindermen are members of the decedent's family, and the governing instrument contains no adequate guarantee of the requisite income to the charitable organization. Under such circumstances, no deduction will be allowed. Similarly, if the trustees are not members of the decedent's family but have no power to sell or otherwise dispose of the closely held stock, or otherwise insure the requisite enjoyment of income to the charitable organization, no deduction will be allowed.

*Example (2).* C dies leaving a tract of land to a city government for as long as the land is used by the city for a public park. If the city accepts the tract and if, on the date of C's death, the possibility that the city will not use the land for a public park is so remote as to be negligible, a deduction will be allowed.

(c) *Disclaimers.*—(1) *Decedents dying after December 31, 1976.*—In the case of a bequest, devise, or transfer made by a decedent dying after December 31, 1976, the amount of a bequest, devise or transfer for which a deduction is allowable under section 2055 includes an interest which falls into the bequest, devise or transfer as the result of either—

(i) A qualified disclaimer (see section 2518 and the corresponding regulations for rules relating to a qualified disclaimer), or

(ii) The complete termination of a power to consume, invade, or appropriate property for the benefit of an individual by reason of the death of such individual or for any other reason, if the termination occurs within the period of time (including extensions) for filing the decedent's Federal estate tax return and before such power has been exercised.

(2) *Decedents dying before January 1, 1977.*—In the case of a bequest, devise or transfer made by a decedent dying before January 1, 1977, the amount of a bequest, devise or transfer for which a deduction is allowable under section 2055 includes an interest which falls into the bequest, devise or transfer as a result of either—

(i) A disclaimer of a bequest, devise, transfer, or power, if the disclaimer is made within 9 months (15 months if the decedent died on or before December 31, 1970) after the decedent's death (the period of time within which the estate tax return must be filed under section 6075) or within any extension of time for filing the return granted pursuant to section 6081, and the disclaimer is irrevocable at the time the deduction is allowed, or

(ii) The complete termination of a power to consume, invade, or appropriate property for the benefit of an individual (whether the termination occurs by reason of the death of the individual, or otherwise) if the termination occurs within the period described in paragraph (c)(2)(i) of this section and before the power has been exercised. Ordinarily, a disclaimer made by a person not under any legal disability will be considered irrevocable when filed with the probate court. A disclaimer is a complete and unqualified refusal to accept the rights to which one is entitled. Thus, if a beneficiary uses these rights for his own purposes, as by receiving a consideration for his formal disclaimer, he has not refused the rights to which he was entitled. There can be no disclaimer after an acceptance of these rights, expressly or impliedly. The disclaimer of a power is to be distinguished from the release or exercise of a power. The release or exercise of a power by the donee of the power in favor of a person or object described in paragraph (a) of §20.2055-1 does not result in any deduction under section 2055 in the estate of the donor of a power (but see paragraph (b)(1) of §20.2055-1 with respect to the donee's estate).

(d) *Payments in compromise.*—If a charitable organization assigns or surrenders a part of a transfer to it pursuant to a compromise agreement in settlement of a controversy, the amount so assigned or surrendered is not deductible as a transfer to that charitable organization.

(e) *Limitation applicable to decedents dying after December 31, 1969.*— (1) *Disallowance of deduction.*—(i) *In general.*—In the case of decedents dying after December 31, 1969, where an interest in property passes or has passed from the decedent for charitable purposes and an interest (other than an interest which is extinguished upon the decedent's death) in the same property passes or has passed from the decedent for private purposes (for less than an adequate and full consideration in money or money's worth) after October 9, 1969, no deduction is allowed under section 2055 for the value of the interest which passes or has passed for charitable purposes unless the interest in property is a deductible interest described in subparagraph (2) of this paragraph. The principles of section 2056 and the regulations thereunder shall apply for purposes of determining under this subparagraph whether an interest in property passes or has passed from the decedent. If however, as of the date of a decedent's death, a transfer for a private purpose is dependent upon the performance of some act or the happening of a precedent event in order that it might become effective, an interest in property will be considered to pass for a private purpose unless the possibility of occurrence of such act or event is so remote as to be negligible. The application of this subparagraph may be illustrated by the following examples, in each of which it is assumed that the interest in property which passes for private purposes does not pass for an adequate and full consideration in money or money's worth:

*Example (1).* In 1973, H creates a trust which is to pay the income of the trust to W for her life, the reversionary interest in the trust being retained by H. H predeceases W in 1975. H's will provides that the residue of his estate (including the reversionary interest in the trust) is to be transferred to charity. For purposes of this paragraph (e)(1)(i), interests in the same property have passed from H for charitable purposes and for private purposes.

*Example (2).* In 1973, H creates a trust which is to pay the income of the trust to W for her life and upon termination of the life estate to transfer the remainder to S. S predeceases W in 1975. S's will provides that the residue of his estate (including the remainder interest in the trust) is to be transferred to charity. For purposes of this paragraph (e)(1)(i), interests in the same property have not passed from H or S for charitable purposes and for private purposes.

*Example (3).* H transfers Blackacre to A by gift, reserving the right to the rentals of Blackacre for a term of 20 years. H dies within the 20-year term, bequeathing the right to the remaining rentals to charity. For purposes of this paragraph (e)(1)(i) the term "property" refers to Blackacre, and the right to rentals from Blackacre consist of an interest in Blackacre. An interest in Blackacre has passed from H for charitable purposes and for private purposes.

*Example (4).* H bequeaths the residue of his estate in trust for the benefit of A and a charity. An annuity of $5,000 a year is to be paid to charity for 20 years. Upon termination of the 20-year term the corpus is to be distributed to A if living. However, if A should die during the 20-year term, the corpus is to be distributed to charity upon termination of the term. An interest in the residue of the estate has passed from H for charitable purposes. In addition, an interest in the residue of the estate has passed from H for private purposes, unless the possibility that A will survive the 20-year term is so remote as to be negligible.

*Example (5).* H bequeaths the residue of his estate in trust. Under the terms of the trust an annuity of $5,000 a year is to be paid to charity for 20 years. Upon termination of the term, the corpus is to pass to such of A's children and their issue as A may appoint. However, if A should die during the 20-year term without exercising the power of appointment, the corpus is to be distributed to charity upon termination of the term. Since the possible appointees include private persons, an interest in the residue of the estate is considered to have passed from H for private purposes.

*Example (6).* H devises Blackacre to X Charity. Under applicable local law, W, H's widow, is entitled to elect a dower interest in Blackacre. W elects to take her dower interest in Blackacre. For purposes of this paragraph (e)(1)(i), interests in the same property have passed from H for charitable purposes and for private purposes. If, however, W does not elect to take her dower interest in Blackacre, then, for purposes of this paragraph (e)(1)(i), interests in the same property have not passed from H for charitable purposes and for private purposes.

(ii) *Works of art and copyrights treated as separate properties.*— (a) *In general.*—For purposes of paragraphs (e)(1)(i) and (e)(2) of this section, in the case of decedents dying after December 31, 1981, if a decedent makes a qualified contribution of a work of art, the work of art and the copyright on such work of art shall be treated as separate properties. Thus, a deduction is allowable under section 2055 for a qualified contribution of a work of art, whether or not the related copyright is simultaneously transferred to a charitable organization.

(b) *Work of art defined.*—For purposes of paragraph (e)(1)(ii)(a) of this section, the term "work of art" means any tangible personal property with respect to which a copyright exists under Federal law.

(c) *Qualified contribution defined.*—For purposes of paragraph (e)(1)(ii)(a) of this section, the term "qualified contribution" means any transfer of property to a qualified organization (as defined in paragraph (e)(1)(ii)(d) of this section) if the use of the property by the organization is related to the purpose or function constituting the basis for its exemption under section 501. The rules contained in §1.170A-4 (b) (3) shall apply in determining if the use of property by an organization is related to such purpose or function.

(d) *Qualified organization defined.*—For purposes of paragraph (e)(1)(ii)(c) of this section, the term "qualified organization" means any organization described in section 501(c)(3) other than a private foundation (as defined in section 509). A private operating foundation (as defined in section 4042(j)(3)) shall be considered a qualified organization under this paragraph.

(e) *Examples.*—The application of paragraphs (e)(1)(i) and (e)(1)(ii)(a) through (d) of this section may be illustrated by the following examples:

*Example (1).* A, an artist, died in 1983. A work of art created by A and the copyright interest in that work of art were included in A's estate. Under the terms of A's will, the work of art is transferred to X charity, the only charitable beneficiary under A's will. X has no suitable use for the work of art and sells it. It is determined under the rules of §1.170A-4 (b)(3) that the property is put to an unrelated use by X charity. Therefore, the rule of paragraph (e)(1)(ii)(a), which treats works of art and their copyrights as separate properties, does not apply because the transfer of the work of art to X is not a qualified contribution. To determine whether paragraph (e)(1)(i) of this section applies to disallow a deduction under section 2055, it must be determined which interests are treated as passing to X under local law.

(i) If under local law A's will is treated as fully transferring both the work of art and the copyright interest to X, then paragraph (e)(1)(i) of this section does not apply to disallow a deduction under section 2055 for the value of the work of art and the copyright interest.

(ii) If under local law A's will is treated as transferring only the work of art to X, and the copyright interest is treated as part of the residue of the estate, no deduction is allowable under section 2055 to A's estate for the value of the work of art because the transfer of the work of art is not a qualified contribution and paragraph (e)(1)(i) of this section applies to disallow the deduction.

*Example (2).* B, a collector of art, purchased a work of art from an artist who retained the copyright interest. B died in 1983. Under the terms of B's will the work of art is given to Y charity. Since B did not own the copyright interest, paragraph (e)(1)(i) of this section does not apply to disallow a deduction under section 2055 for the value of the work of art, regardless of whether or not the contribution is a qualified contribution under paragraph (e)(1)(ii)(c) of this section.

(2) *Deductible interests.*—A deductible interest for purposes of subparagraph (1) of this paragraph is a charitable interest in property where—

(i) *Undivided portion of decedent's entire interest.*—The charitable interest is an undivided portion, not in trust, of the decedent's entire interest in property. An undivided portion of a decedent's entire interest in property must consist of a fraction or percentage of each and every substantial interest or right owned by the decedent in such property and must extend over the entire term of the decedent's interest in such property and in other property into which such property is converted. For example, if the decedent transferred a life estate in an office building to his wife for her life and retained a reversionary interest in the office building, the devise by the decedent of one-half of that reversionary interest to charity while his wife is still alive will not be considered the transfer of a deductible interest; because an interest in the same property has already passed from the decedent for private purposes, the reversionary interest will not be considered the decedent's entire interest in the property. If, on the other hand, the decedent had been given a life estate in Blackacre for the life of his wife and the decedent had no other interest in

Blackacre at any time during his life, the devise by the decedent of one-half of that life estate to charity would be considered the transfer of a deductible interest; because the life estate would be considered the decedent's entire interest in the property, the devise would be of an undivided portion of such entire interest. An undivided portion of a decedent's entire interest in the property includes an interest in property whereby the charity is given the right, as a tenant in common with the decedent's devisee or legatee, to possession, dominion, and control of the property for a portion of each year appropriate to its interest in such property. However, except as provided in paragraphs (e)(2)(ii), (iii), and (iv) of this section, for purposes of this subdivision a charitable contribution of an interest in property not in trust where the decedent transfers some specific rights to one party and transfers other substantial rights to another party will not be considered a contribution of an undivided portion of the decedent's entire interest in property. A bequest to charity made on or before December 17, 1980, of an open space easement in gross in perpetuity shall be considered the transfer to charity of an undivided portion of the decedent's entire interest in the property. For the definition of an open space easement in gross in perpetuity, see § 1.170A-7(b)(1)(ii) of this chapter (Income Tax Regulations).

(ii) *Remainder interest in personal residence.*—The charitable interest is a remainder interest, not in trust, in a personal residence. Thus, for example, if the decedent devises to charity a remainder interest in a personal residence and bequeaths to his surviving spouse a life estate in such property, the value of the remainder interest is deductible under section 2055. For purposes of this subdivision, the term "personal residence" means any property which was used by the decedent as his personal residence even though it was not used as his principal residence. For example, a decedent's vacation home may be a personal residence for purposes of this subdivision. The term "personal residence" also includes stock owned by the decedent as a tenant-stockholder in a cooperative housing corporation (as those terms are defined in section 216(b)(1) and (2)) if the dwelling which the decedent was entitled to occupy as such stockholder was used by him as his personal residence.

(iii) *Remainder interest in a farm.*—The charitable interest is a remainder interest, not in trust, in a farm. Thus, for example, if the decedent devises to charity a remainder interest in a farm and bequeaths to his daughter a life estate in such property, the value of the remainder interest is deductible under section 2055. For purposes of this subdivision, the term "farm" means any land used by the decedent or his tenant for the production of crops, fruits, or other agricultural products or for the sustenance of livestock. The term "livestock" includes cattle, hogs, horses, mules, donkeys, sheep, goats, captive fur-bearing animals, chickens, turkeys, pigeons, and other poultry. A farm includes the improvements thereon.

(iv) *Qualified conservation contribution.*—The charitable interest is a qualified conservation contribution. For the definition of a qualified conservation contribution, see § 1.170A-14.

(v) *Charitable remainder trusts and pooled income funds.*—The charitable interest is a remainder interest in a trust which is a charitable remainder annuity trust, as defined in section 664(d)(1) and § 1.664-2 of this chapter; a charitable remainder unitrust, as defined in section 664(d)(2) and (3) and § 1.664-3 of this chapter; or a pooled income fund, as defined in section 642(c)(5) and § 1.642(c)-5 of this chapter. The charitable organization to or for the use of which the remainder interest passes must meet the requirements of both section 2055(a) and section 642(c)(5)(A), section 664(d)(1)(C), or section 664(d)(2)(C), whichever applies. For example, the charitable organization to which the remainder interest in a charitable remainder annuity trust passes may not be a foreign corporation.

(vi) *Guaranteed annuity interest.*—(a) The charitable interest is a guaranteed annuity interest, whether or not such interest is in trust. For purposes of this subdivision (vi), the term "guaranteed annuity interest" means the right pursuant to the instrument of transfer to receive a guaranteed annuity. A guaranteed annuity is an arrangement under which a determinable amount is paid periodically, but not less often than annually, for a specified term of years or for the life or lives of certain individuals, each of whom must be living at the date of death of the decedent and can be ascertained at such date. Only one or more of the following individuals may be used as measuring lives: the decedent's spouse, and an individual who, with respect to all remainder beneficiaries (other than charitable organizations described in section 170, 2055, or 2522), is either a lineal ancestor or the spouse of a lineal ancestor of those beneficiaries. A trust will satisfy the requirement that all noncharitable remainder beneficiaries are lineal descendants of the individual who is the measuring life, or that individual's spouse, if there is less than a 15% probability that individuals who are not lineal descendants will receive any trust corpus. This probability must be computed, based on the current

applicable Life Table contained in § 20.2031-7, as of the date of the decedent's death taking into account the interests of all primary and contingent remainder beneficiaries who are living at that time. An interest payable for a specified term of years can qualify as a guaranteed annuity interest even if the governing instrument contains a savings clause intended to ensure compliance with a rule against perpetuities. The savings clause must utilize a period for vesting of 21 years after the deaths of measuring lives who are selected to maximize, rather than limit, the term of the trust. The rule in this paragraph that a charitable interest may be payable for the life or lives of only certain specified individuals does not apply in the case of a charitable guaranteed annuity interest payable under a charitable remainder trust described in section 664. An amount is determinable if the exact amount which must be paid under the conditions specified in the instrument of transfer can be ascertained as of the appropriate valuation date. For example, the amount to be paid may be a stated sum for a term of years, or for the life of the decedent's spouse, at the expiration of which it may be changed by a specified amount, but it may not be redetermined by reference to a fluctuating index such as the cost of living index. In further illustration, the amount to be paid may be expressed in terms of a fraction or a percentage of the net fair market value, as finally determined for Federal estate tax purposes, of the residue of the estate on the appropriate valuation date, or it may be expressed in terms of a fraction or percentage of the cost of living index on the appropriate valuation date.

(b) A charitable interest is a guaranteed annuity interest only if it is a guaranteed annuity interest in every respect. For example, if the charitable interest is the right to receive from a trust each year a payment equal to the lesser of a sum certain or a fixed percentage of the net fair market value of the trust assets, determined annually, such interest is not a guaranteed annuity interest.

(c) Where a charitable interest in the form of a guaranteed annuity interest is not in trust, the interest will be considered a guaranteed annuity interest only if it is to be paid by an insurance company or by an organization regularly engaged in issuing annuity contracts.

(d) Where a charitable interest in the form of a guaranteed annuity interest is in trust, the governing instrument of the trust may provide that income of the trust which is in excess of the amount required to pay the guaranteed annuity interest shall be paid to or for the use of a charity. Nevertheless, the amount of the deduction under section 2055 shall be limited to the fair market value of the guaranteed annuity interest as determined under paragraph (f)(2)(iv) of this section.

(e) Where a charitable interest in the form of a guaranteed annuity interest is in trust and the present value, on the appropriate valuation date, of all the income interests for a charitable purpose exceeds 60 percent of the aggregate fair market value of all amounts in such trust (after the payment of estate taxes and all other liabilities), the charitable interest will not be considered a guaranteed annuity interest unless the governing instrument of the trust prohibits both the acquisition and the retention of assets which would give rise to a tax under section 4944 if the trustee had acquired such assets.

(f) Where a charitable interest in the form of a guaranteed annuity interest is in trust, the charitable interest generally is not a guaranteed annuity interest if any amount may be paid by the trust for a private purpose before the expiration of all the charitable annuity interests. There are two exceptions to this general rule. First, the charitable interest is a guaranteed annuity interest if the amount payable for a private purpose is in the form of a guaranteed annuity interest and the trust's governing instrument does not provide for any preference or priority in the payment of the private annuity as opposed to the charitable annuity. Second, the charitable interest is a guaranteed annuity interest if under the trust's governing instrument the amount that may be paid for a private purpose is payable only from a group of assets that are devoted exclusively to private purposes and to which section 4947(a)(2) is inapplicable by reason of section 4947(a)(2)(B). For purposes of this paragraph (e)(2)(vi)(f), an amount is not paid for a private purpose if it is paid for an adequate and full consideration in money or money's worth. See § 53.4947-1(c) of this chapter for rules relating to the inapplicability of section 4947(a)(2) to segregated amounts in a split-interest trust.

(g) Neither the requirement in (e) of this subdivision (v) for a prohibition in the governing instrument against the retention of assets which would give rise to a tax under section 4944 if the trustee had acquired the assets nor the provisions of (f) of this subdivision (vi) shall apply to—

(1) A trust executed on or before May 21, 1972, if—

(i) The trust is irrevocable on such date,

(ii) The trust is revocable on such date and the decedent dies within 3 years after such date without having amended any dispositive provision of the trust after such date, or

(iii) The trust is revocable on such date and no dispositive provision of the trust is amended within a period ending 3 years after such date and the decedent is, at the end of such 3-year period and at all times thereafter, under a mental disability (as defined in § 1.642(c)-2(b)(3)(ii) of this chapter) to amend the trust, or

(2) A will executed on or before May 21, 1972, if—

(i) The testator dies within 3 years after such date without having amended any dispositive provision of the will after such date, by codicil or otherwise,

(ii) The testator at no time after such date has the right to change the provisions of the will which pertain to the trust, or

(iii) No dispositive provision of the will is amended by the decedent, by codicil or otherwise, within a period ending 3 years after such date and the decedent is, at the end of such 3-year period and at all times thereafter, under a mental disability (as defined in § 1.642(c)-2(b)(3)(ii) of this chapter) to amend the will by codicil or otherwise.

(h) For purposes of this subdivision (vi) and paragraph (f) of this section, the term "appropriate valuation date" means the date of death or the alternate valuation date determined pursuant to an election under section 2032.

(i) For rules relating to certain governing instrument requirements and to the imposition of certain excise taxes where the guaranteed annuity interest is in trust and for rules governing payment of private income interests by split-interest trusts, see section 4947(a)(2) and (b)(3)(A), and the regulations thereunder.

(vii) *Unitrust interest.*—(a) The charitable interest is a unitrust interest, whether or not such interest is in trust. For purposes of this subdivision (vii), the term "unitrust interest" means the right pursuant to the instrument of transfer to receive payment, not less often than annually, of a fixed percentage of the net fair market value, determined annually, of the property which funds the unitrust interest. In computing the net fair market value of the property which funds the unitrust interest, all assets and liabilities shall be taken into account without regard to whether particular items are taken into account in determining the income from the property. The net fair market value of the property which funds the unitrust interest may be determined on any one date during the year or by taking the average of valuations made on more than one date during the year, provided that the same valuation date or dates and valuation methods are used each year. Where the charitable interest is a unitrust interest to be paid by a trust and the governing instrument of the trust does not specify the valuation date or dates, the trustee shall select such date or dates and shall indicate his selection on the first return on Form 1041 which the trust is required to file. Payments under a unitrust interest may be paid for a specified term of years or for the life or lives of certain individuals, each of whom must be living at the date of death of the decedent and can be ascertained at such date. Only one or more of the following individuals may be used as measuring lives: the decedent's spouse, and an individual who, with respect to all remainder beneficiaries (other than charitable organizations described in section 170, 2055, or 2522), is either a lineal ancestor or the spouse of a lineal ancestor of those beneficiaries. A trust will satisfy the requirement that all noncharitable remainder beneficiaries are lineal descendants of the individual who is the measuring life, or that individual's spouse, if there is less than a 15% probability that individuals who are not lineal descendants will receive any trust corpus. This probability must be computed, based on the current applicable Life Table contained in § 20.2031-7, as of the date of the decedent's death taking into account the interests of all primary and contingent remainder beneficiaries who are living at that time. An interest payable for a specified term of years can qualify as a unitrust interest even if the governing instrument contains a savings clause intended to ensure compliance with a rule against perpetuities. The savings clause must utilize a period for vesting of 21 years after the deaths of measuring lives who are selected to maximize, rather than limit, the term of the trust. The rule in this paragraph that a charitable interest may be payable for the life or lives of only certain specified individuals does not apply in the case of a charitable unitrust interest payable under a charitable remainder trust described in section 664.

(b) A charitable interest is a unitrust interest only if it is a unitrust interest in every respect. For example, if the charitable interest is the right to receive from a trust each year a payment equal to the lesser of a sum certain or a fixed percentage of the net fair market value of the trust assets, determined annually, such interest is not a unitrust interest.

(c) Where a charitable interest in the form of a unitrust interest is not in trust, the interest will be considered a unitrust interest only if it is to be paid by an insurance company or by an organization regularly engaged in issuing interests otherwise meeting the requirements of a unitrust interest.

(d) Where a charitable interest in the form of a unitrust interest is in trust, the governing instrument of the trust may provide that income of the trust which is in excess of the amount required to pay the unitrust interest shall be paid to or for the use of a charity. Nevertheless, the amount of the deduction under section 2055 shall be limited to the fair market value of the unitrust interest as determined under paragraph (f)(2)(v) of this section.

(e) Where a charitable interest in the form of a unitrust interest is in trust, the charitable interest generally is not a unitrust interest if any amount may be paid by the trust for a private purpose before the expiration of all the charitable unitrust interests. There are two exceptions to this general rule. First, the charitable interest is a unitrust interest if the amount payable for a private purpose is in the form of a unitrust interest and the trust's governing instrument does not provide for any preference or priority in the payment of the private unitrust interest as opposed to the charitable unitrust interest. Second, the charitable interest is a unitrust interest if under the trust's governing instrument the amount that may be paid for a private purpose is payable only from a group of assets that are devoted exclusively to private purposes and to which section 4947(a)(2) is inapplicable by reason of section 4947(a)(2)(B). For purposes of this paragraph (e)(2)(vii)(e), an amount is not paid for a private purpose if it is paid for an adequate and full consideration in money or money's worth. See § 53.4947-1(c) of this chapter for rules relating to the inapplicability of section 4947(a)(2) to segregated amounts in a split-interest trust.

(f) For rules relating to certain governing instrument requirements and to the imposition of certain excise taxes where the unitrust interest is in trust and for rules governing payment of private income interests by a split-interest trust, see section 4947(a)(2) and (b)(3)(A), and the regulations thereunder.

(3) *Effective/applicability date.*—The provisions of this paragraph apply only in the case of decedents dying after December 31, 1969, except that they do not apply—

(i) In the case of property passing under the terms of a will executed on or before October 9, 1969—

(a) If the decedent dies after October 9, 1969, but before October 9, 1972, without having amended any dispositive provision of the will after October 9, 1969, by codicil or otherwise,

(b) If the decedent dies after October 9, 1969, and at no time after that date had the right to change the portions of the will which pertain to the passing of the property to, or for the use of, an organization described in section 2055(a), or

(c) If no dispositive provision of the will is amended by the decedent, by codicil or otherwise, after October 9, 1969, and before October 9, 1972, and the decedent is on October 9, 1972, and at all times thereafter under a mental disability (as defined in § 1.642(c)-2(b)(3)(ii) of this chapter (Income Tax Regulations)) to amend the will by codicil or otherwise, or

(ii) In the case of property transferred in trust on or before October 9, 1969—

(a) If the decedent dies after October 9, 1969, but before October 9, 1972, without having amended, after October 9, 1969, any dispositive provision of the instrument governing the disposition of the property,

(b) If the property transferred was an irrevocable interest to, or for the use of, an organization described in section 2055(a), or

(c) If no dispositive provision of the instrument governing the disposition of the property is amended by the decedent after October 9, 1969, and before October 9, 1972, and the decedent is on October 9, 1972, and at all times thereafter under a mental disability (as defined in § 1.642(c)-2(b)(3)(ii) of this chapter) to change the disposition of the property, and

(iii) The rule in paragraphs (e)(2)(vi)(a) and (e)(2)(vii)(a) of this section that guaranteed annuity interests or unitrust interests, respectively, may be payable for a specified term of years or for the life or lives of only certain individuals is generally effective in the case of transfers pursuant to wills and revocable trusts when the decedent dies on or after April 4, 2000. Two exceptions from the application of this rule in paragraphs (e)(2)(vi)(a) and(e)(2)(vii)(a) of this section are provided in the case of transfers pursuant to a will or revocable trust executed before April 4, 2000. One exception is for a decedent who dies on or before July 5, 2001, without having republished the will (or amended the trust) by codicil or otherwise. The other exception is for a decedent who was on April 4, 2000, under a mental disability that prevented a change in the disposition of the decedent's property, and who either does not regain competence to dispose of such property before the date of death, or dies prior to the later of 90 days after the date on which the decedent first regains competence, or July 5, 2001, without having republished the will (or amended the trust) by codicil or otherwise. If a guaranteed annuity interest or unitrust interest created pursuant to a will or revocable trust of a decedent dying on or after April 4, 2000, uses an individual other than one permitted in paragraphs (e)(2)(vi)(a) and (e)(2)(vii)(a) of this section, and the interest does not qualify for this transitional relief, the interest may be reformed into a lead interest payable for a specified term of years. The term of years is determined by taking the factor for valuing the annuity or unitrust interest for the named individual measuring life and identifying the term of years (rounded up to the next whole year) that corresponds to the equivalent term of years factor for an annuity or unitrust interest. For example, in the case of an annuity interest payable for the life of an individual age 40 at the time of the transfer on or after May 1, 2009, assuming an interest rate of 7.4 percent under section 7520, the annuity factor from column 1 of Table S(7.4), contained in IRS Publication 1457, "Actuarial Valuations Version 3A", for the life of an individual age 40 is 12.1519 (1.000000 minus .10076, divided by .074). Based on Table B(7.4), contained in Publication 1457, "Actuarial Valuations Version 3A", the factor 12.1519 corresponds to a term of years between 32 and 33 years. Accordingly, the annuity interest must be reformed into an interest payable for a term of 33 years. A judicial reformation must be commenced prior to the later of July 5, 2001, or the date prescribed by section 2055(e)(3)(C)(iii). Any judicial reformation must be completed within a reasonable time after it is commenced. A non-judicial reformation is permitted if effective under state law, provided it is completed by the date on which a judicial reformation must be commenced. In the alternative, if a court, in a proceeding that is commenced on or before July 5, 2001, declares any transfer made pursuant to a will or revocable trust where the decedent dies on or after April 4, 2000, and on or before March 6, 2001, null and void ab initio, the Internal Revenue Service will treat such transfers in a manner similar to that described in section 2055(e)(3)(J).

(4) *Amendment of dispositive provisions.*—For purposes of subparagraphs (2) and (3) of this paragraph, an amendment shall generally be considered as one which amends the dispositive provisions of a will or trust if it results in a change in the persons to whom the funds are to be given or makes changes in the conditions under which the funds are given. Examples of amendments which do not amend the dispositive provisions of a will or trust include the substitution of one fiduciary for another to act in the capacity of executor or trustee and the change in the name of a legatee or beneficiary by reason of the legatee's or beneficiary's marriage. On the other hand, examples of amendments which do amend the dispositive provisions of a will or trust include an increase or decrease in the amount of a general bequest, an amendment which increases or decreases the power of a trustee to determine an allocation of income or corpus in such a way as to change the beneficiaries of the funds or a beneficiary's share of the funds, or a change in the allocation of, or in the right to allocate, receipts and expenditures between income and principal in such a way as to change the beneficiaries of the funds or a beneficiary's share of the funds.

(5) *Amendment of wills providing for pour-over into trusts.*—For purposes of subparagraphs (2) and (3) of this paragraph, an amendment of a dispositive provision of a trust to which assets are to be transferred under a will shall be considered a dispositive amendment of such will.

(f) *Valuation of charitable interest.*—(1) *In general.*—The amount of the deduction in the case of a contribution of a partial interest in property to which this section applies is the fair market value of the partial interest at the appropriate valuation date, as defined in paragraph (e)(2)(vi)(h) of this section. The fair market value of an annuity, life estate, term for years, remainder, reversion, or unitrust interest is its present value.

(2) *Certain decedents dying after July 31, 1969.*—In the case of a transfer of an interest described in subdivision (v), (vi), or (vii) of paragraph (e)(2) of this section by decedents dying after July 31, 1969, the present value of such interest is to be determined under the following rules:

(i) The present value of a remainder interest in a charitable remainder annuity trust is to be determined under § 1.664-2(c) of this chapter (Income Tax Regulations).

(ii) The present value of a remainder interest in a charitable remainder unitrust is to be determined under § 1.664-4 of this chapter.

(iii) The present value of a remainder interest in a pooled income fund is to be determined under § 1.642(c)-6 of this chapter.

(iv) The present value of a guaranteed annuity interest described in paragraph (e)(2)(vi) of this section is to be determined under § 20.2031-7 or, for certain prior periods, § 20.2031-7A, except that, if the annuity is issued by a company regularly engaged in the sale of annuities, the present value is to be determined under § 20.2031-8. If by reason of all the conditions and circumstances surrounding a transfer of an income interest in property in trust it appears that the charity may not receive the beneficial enjoyment of the interest, a deduction will be allowed under section 2055 only for the minimum amount it is evident the charity will receive.

*Example (1).* In 1975, B dies bequeathing $20,000 in trust with the requirement that a designated charity be paid a guaranteed annuity interest (as defined in paragraph (e)(2)(vi) of this section) of $4,100 a year, payable annually at the end of each year, for a period of 6 years and that the remainder be paid to his children. The fair market value of an annuity of $4,100 a year for a period of 6 years is $20,160.93 ($4,100 × 4.9173), as determined under Table B in § 20.2031-7A(d). The deduction with respect to the guaranteed annuity interest will be limited to $20,000, which is the minimum amount it is evident the charity will receive.

*Example (2).* In 1975, C dies bequeathing $40,000 in trust with the requirement that D, an individual, and X Charity be paid simultaneously guaranteed annuity interests (as defined in paragraph (e)(2)(vi) of this section) of $5,000 a year each, payable annually at the end of each year, for a period of 5 years and that the remainder be paid to C's children. The fair market value of two annuities of $5,000 each a year for a period of 5 years is $42,124 ([$5,000 × 4.2124] × 2), as determined under Table B in § 20.2031-7A(d). The trust instrument provides that in the event the trust fund is insufficient to pay both annuities in a given year, the trust fund will be evenly divided between the charitable and private annuitants. The deduction with respect to the charitable annuity will be limited to $20,000, which is the minimum amount it is evident the charity will receive.

*Example (3).* In 1975, D dies bequeathing $65,000 in trust with the requirement that a guaranteed annuity interest (as defined in paragraph (e)(2)(vi) of this section) of $5,000 a year, payable annually at the end of each year, be paid to Y Charity for a period of 10 years and that a guaranteed annuity interest (as defined in paragraph (e)(2)(vi) of this section) of $5,000 a year, payable annually at the end of each year, be paid to W, his widow, aged 62, for 10 years or until her prior death. The annuities are to be paid simultaneously, and the remainder is to be paid to D's children. The fair market value of the private annuity is $33,877 ($5,000 × 6.7754), as determined pursuant to § 20.2031-7A(c) and by the use of factors involving one life and a term of years as published in Publication 723A (12-70). The fair market value of the charitable annuity is $36,800.50 ($5,000 × 7.3601), as determined under Table B in § 20.2031-7A(d). It is not evident from the governing instrument of the trust or from local law that the trustee would be required to apportion the trust fund between the widow and charity in the event the fund were insufficient to pay both annuities in a given year. Accordingly, the deduction with respect to the charitable annuity will be limited to $31,123 ($65,000 less $33,877 [the value of the private annuity]), which is the minimum amount it is evident the charity will receive.

(v) The present value of a unitrust interest described in paragraph (e)(2)(vii) of this section is to be determined by subtracting the present value of all interests in the transferred property other than the unitrust interest from the fair market value of the transferred property.

(3) *Certain decedents dying before August 1, 1969.*—In the case of decedents dying before August 1, 1969, the present value of an interest described in subparagraph (2) of this paragraph is to be determined under § 20.2031-7 except that, if the interest is an annuity issued by a company regularly engaged in the sale of annuities, the present value is to be determined under § 20.2031-8.

(4) *Other decedents.*—The present value of an interest not described in paragraph (f)(2) of this section is to be determined under § 20.2031-7(d) in the case of decedents where the valuation date of the gross estate is on or after May 1, 2009, or under § 20.2031-7A in the case of decedents where the valuation date of the gross estate is before May 1, 2009.

(5) *Special computations.*—If the interest transferred is such that its present value is to be determined by a special computation, a request for a special factor, accompanied by a statement of the date of birth and sex of each individual the duration of whose life may affect the value of the interest, and by copies of the relevant instruments, may be submitted by the fiduciary to the Commissioner who may, if conditions permit, supply the factor requested. If the Commissioner furnishes the factor, a copy of the letter supplying the factor must be attached to the tax return in which the deduction is claimed. If the Commissioner does not furnish the factor, the claim for deduction must be supported by a full statement of the computation of the present value made in accordance with the principles set forth in this paragraph.

(6) *Effective/applicability date.*—Paragraphs (e)(3)(iii) and (f)(4) of this section apply on and after May 1, 2009. [Reg. § 20.2055-2.]

☐ [*T.D. 6296, 6-23-58. Amended by T.D. 7238, 12-28-72; T.D. 7318, 7-10-74; T.D. 7340, 1-6-75; T.D. 7955, 5-10-84; T.D. 7957, 5-16-84; T.D. 8069, 1-13-86; T.D. 8095, 8-6-86; T.D. 8540, 6-9-94; T.D. 8819, 4-29-99; T.D. 8886, 6-9-2000; T.D. 8923, 1-4-2001; T.D. 9068, 7-3-2003; T.D. 9448, 5-1-2009 and T.D. 9540, 8-9-2011.*]

[Reg. § 20.2055-3]

**§ 20.2055-3. Effect of death taxes and administration expenses.—** (a) *Death taxes.*—(1) If under the terms of the will or other governing instrument, the law of the jurisdiction under which the estate is administered, or the law of the jurisdiction imposing the particular tax, the Federal estate tax, or any estate, succession, legacy, or inheritance tax is payable in whole or in part out of any property transfer of which would otherwise be allowable as a deduction under section 2055, section 2055(c) provides that the sum deductible is the amount of the transferred property reduced by the amount of the tax. Section 2055(c) in effect provides that the deduction is based on the amount actually available for charitable uses, that is, the amount of the fund remaining after the payment of all death taxes. Thus, if $50,000 is bequeathed for a charitable purpose and is subjected to a State inheritance tax of $5,000, payable out of the $50,000, the amount deductible is $45,000. If a life estate is bequeathed to an individual with remainder over to a charitable organization, and by the local law the inheritance tax upon the life estate is paid out of the corpus with the result that the charitable organization will be entitled to receive only the amount of the fund less the tax, the deduction is limited to the present value, as of the date of the testator's death, of the remainder of the fund so reduced. If a testator bequeaths his residuary estate, or a portion of it, to charity, and his will contains a direction that certain inheritance taxes, otherwise payable from legacies upon which they were imposed, shall be payable out of the residuary estate, the deduction may not exceed the bequest to charity thus reduced pursuant to the direction of the will. If a residuary estate, or a portion of it, is bequeathed to charity, and by the local law the Federal estate tax is payable out of the residuary estate, the deduction may not exceed that portion of the residuary estate bequeathed to charity as reduced by the Federal estate tax. The return should fully disclose the computation of the amount to be deducted. If the amount to be deducted is dependent upon the amount of any death tax which has not been paid before the filing of the return, there should be submitted with the return a computation of that tax.

(2) It should be noted that if the Federal estate tax is payable out of a charitable transfer so that the amount of the transfer otherwise passing to charity is reduced by the amount of the tax, the resultant decrease in the amount passing to charity will further reduce the allowable deduction. In such a case, the amount of the charitable deduction can be obtained only by a series of trial-and-error computations, or by a formula. If, in addition, interdependent State and Federal taxes are involved, the computation becomes highly complicated. Examples of methods of computation of the charitable deduction and the marital deduction (with which similar problems are encountered) in various situations are contained in supplemental instructions to the estate tax return.

(3) For the allowance of a deduction to a decedent's estate for certain State death taxes imposed upon charitable transfers, see section 2053(d) and § 20.2053-9.

(b) *Administration expenses.*—(1) *Definitions.*—(i) *Management expenses.*—Estate management expenses are expenses that are incurred in connection with the investment of estate assets or with their preservation or maintenance during a reasonable period of administration. Examples of these expenses could include investment advisory fees, stock brokerage commissions, custodial fees, and interest.

(ii) *Transmission expenses.*—Estate transmission expenses are expenses that would not have been incurred but for the decedent's death and the consequent necessity of collecting the decedent's assets, paying the decedent's debts and death taxes, and distributing the decedent's property to those who are entitled to receive it. Estate transmission expenses include any administration expense that is not a management expense. Examples of these expenses could include executor commissions and attorney fees (except to the extent of commissions or fees specifically related to investment, preservation, or maintenance of the assets), probate fees, expenses incurred in construction proceedings and defending against will contests, and appraisal fees.

(iii) *Charitable share.*—The charitable share is the property or interest in property that passed from the decedent for which a deduction is allowable under section 2055(a) with respect to all or part of the property interest. The charitable share includes, for example, bequests to charitable organizations and bequests to a charitable lead unitrust or annuity trust, a charitable remainder unitrust or annuity trust, and a pooled income fund, described in section 2055(e)(2). The charitable share also includes the income produced by the property or interest in property during the period of administration if the income, under the terms of the governing instrument or applicable local law, is payable to the charitable organization or is to be added to the principal of the property interest passing in whole or in part to the charitable organization.

(2) *Effect of transmission expenses.*—For purposes of determining the charitable deduction, the value of the charitable share shall be reduced by the amount of the estate transmission expenses paid from the charitable share.

(3) *Effect of management expenses attributable to the charitable share.*—For purposes of determining the charitable deduction, the value of the charitable share shall not be reduced by the amount of the estate management expenses attributable to and paid from the charitable share. Pursuant to section 2056(b)(9), however, the amount of the allowable charitable deduction shall be reduced by the amount of any such management expenses that are deducted under section 2053 on the decedent's federal estate tax return.

(4) *Effect of management expenses not attributable to the charitable share.*—For purposes of determining the charitable deduction, the value of the charitable share shall be reduced by the amount of estate management expenses paid from the charitable share but attributable to a property interest not included in the charitable share.

(5) *Example.*—The following example illustrates the application of this paragraph (b):

*Example.* The decedent, who dies in 2000, leaves his residuary estate, after the payment of debts, expenses, and estate taxes, to a charitable remainder unitrust that satisfies the requirements of section 664(d). During the period of administration, the estate incurs estate transmission expenses of $400,000. The residue of the estate (the charitable share) must be reduced by the $400,000 of transmission expenses and by the Federal and State estate taxes before the present value of the remainder interest passing to charity can be determined in accordance with the provisions of § 1.664-4 of this chapter. Because the estate taxes are payable out of the residue, the computation of the estate taxes and the allowable charitable deduction are interrelated. See paragraph (a)(2) of this section.

(6) *Cross reference.*—See § 20.2056(b)-4(d) for additional examples applicable to the treatment of administration expenses under this paragraph (b).

(7) *Effective date.*—The provisions of this paragraph (b) apply to estates of decedents dying on or after December 3, 1999. [Reg. § 20.2055-3.]

☐ [*T.D. 6296, 6-23-58. Amended by T.D. 8846, 12-2-99 (corrected 12-17-99).]*

[Reg. § 20.2055-4]

**§ 20.2055-4. Disallowance of charitable, etc., deductions because of "prohibited transactions" in the case of decedents dying before January 1, 1970.—**(a) Sections 503(e) and 681(b)(5) provide that no deduction which would otherwise be allowable under section 2055 for the value of property transferred by the decedent during his lifetime or by will for religious, charitable, scientific, literary, or educational purposes (including the encouragement of art and the prevention of cruelty to children or animals) is allowed if (1) the transfer is made in trust, and, for income tax purposes for the taxable year of the trust in which the transfer is made, the deduction otherwise allowable to the trust under section 642(c) is limited by section 681(b)(1) by reason of the trust having engaged in a prohibited transaction described in section 681(b)(2), or (2) the transfer is made to a corporation, community chest, fund or foundation which, for its taxable year in which the transfer is made, is not exempt from income tax under section 501(a) by reason of having engaged in a prohibited transaction described in section 503(c).

(b) For purposes of section 681(b)(5) and section 503(e), the term "transfer" includes any gift, contribution, bequest, devise, legacy, or other disposition. In applying such sections for estate tax purposes, a transfer, whether made during the decedent's lifetime or by will, is considered as having been made at the moment of the decedent's death.

(c) The income tax regulations contain the rules for the determination of the taxable year of the trust for which the deduction under section 642(c) is limited by section 681(b) and for the determination of the taxable year of the organization for which an exemption is denied under section 503(a). Generally, such taxable year is a taxable year subsequent to the taxable year during which the trust or organization has been notified by the Commissioner of Internal Revenue that it has engaged in a prohibited transaction. However, if the trust or organization during or prior to the taxable year entered into the prohibited transaction for the purpose of diverting its corpus or income from the charitable or other purposes by reason of which it is entitled to a deduction or exemption, and the transaction involves a substantial part of the income or corpus, then the deduction of the trust under section 642(c) for such taxable year is limited by section 681(b), or exemption of the organization for such taxable year is denied under section 503(a), whether or not the organization has previously received notification by the Commissioner of Internal Revenue that it is engaged in a prohibited transaction. In certain cases, the limitation of sections 681 or 503 may be removed or the exemption may be reinstated for certain subsequent taxable years under the rules set forth in the income tax regulations under sections 681 and 503. In cases in which prior notification by the Commissioner of Internal Revenue is not required in order to limit the deduction of the trust under section 681(b) or to deny exemption of the organization under section 503, the deduction otherwise allowable under section 2055 is not disallowed in respect of transfers made during the same taxable year of the trust or organization in which a prohibited transaction occurred or in a prior taxable year unless the decedent or a member of his family was a party to the prohibited transaction. For the purpose of the preceding sentence, the members of the decedent's family include only his brothers and sisters, whether by whole or half blood, spouse, ancestors, and lineal descendants.

(d) This section applies only in the case of decedents dying before January 1, 1970. In the case of decedents dying after December 31, 1969, see §20.2055-5. [Reg. §20.2055-4.]

☐ [*T.D. 6296, 6-23-58. Amended by T.D. 7318, 7-10-74.*]

### [Reg. §20.2055-5]

**§20.2055-5. Disallowance of charitable, etc., deductions in the case of decedents dying after December 31, 1969.**—(a) *Organizations subject to section 507(c) tax.*—Section 508(d)(1) provides that, in the case of decedents dying after December 31, 1969, a deduction which would otherwise be allowable under section 2055 for the value of property transferred by the decedent to or for the use of an organization upon which the tax provided by section 507(c) has been imposed shall not be allowed if the transfer is made by the decedent after notification is made under section 507(a) or if the decedent is a substantial contributor (as defined in section 507(d)(2)) who dies on or after the first day on which action is taken by such organization that culminates in the imposition of the tax under section 507(c). This paragraph does not apply if the entire amount of the unpaid portion of the tax imposed by section 507(c) is abated under section 507(g) by the Commissioner or his delegate.

(b) *Taxable private foundations, section 4947 trusts, etc.*—(1) *In general.*—Section 508(d)(2) provides that, in the case of decedents dying after December 31, 1969, a deduction which would otherwise be allowable under section 2055 for the value of property transferred by the decedent shall not be allowed if the transfer is made to or for the use of—

(i) A private foundation or a trust described in section 4947(a)(2) in a taxable year of such organization for which such organization fails to meet the governing instrument requirements of section 508(e) (determined without regard to section 508(e)(2)(B) and (C)), or

(ii) Any organization in a period for which it is not treated as an organization described in section 501(c)(3) by reason of its failure to give notification under section 508(a) of its status to the Commissioner.

For additional rules, see §1.508-2(b)(1) of this chapter (Income Tax Regulations).

(2) *Transfers not covered by section 508(d)(2)(A).*—(i) *In general.*—Any deduction which would otherwise be allowable under section 2055 for the value of property transferred by a decedent dying after December 31, 1969, will not be disallowed under section 508(d)(2)(A) and subparagraph (1)(i) of this paragraph—

(*a*) In the case of property passing under the terms of a will executed on or before October 9, 1969—

(*1*) If the decedent dies after October 9, 1969, but before October 9, 1972, without having amended any dispositive provision of the will after October 9, 1969, by codicil or otherwise,

(*2*) If the decedent dies after October 9, 1969, and at no time after that date had the right to change the portions of the will which pertain to the passing of the property to, or for the use of, an organization described in section 2055(a), or

(*3*) If no dispositive provision of the will is amended by the decedent, by codicil or otherwise, after October 9, 1969, and before October 9, 1972, and the decedent is on October 9, 1972, and at all times thereafter under a mental disability (as defined in §1.642(c)-2(b)(3)(ii) of this chapter) to amend the will by codicil or otherwise, or

(*b*) In the case of property transferred in trust on or before October 9, 1969—

(*1*) If the decedent dies after October 9, 1969, but before October 9, 1972, without having amended, after October 9, 1969, any dispositive provision of the instrument governing the disposition of the property,

(*2*) If the property transferred was an irrevocable interest to, or for the use of, an organization described in section 2055(a), or

(*3*) If no dispositive provision of the instrument governing the disposition of the property is amended by the decedent after October 9, 1969, and before October 9, 1972, and the decedent is on October 9, 1972, and at all times thereafter under a mental disability (as defined in §1.642(c)-2(b)(3)(ii) of this chapter) to change the disposition of the property.

(ii) *Amendment of dispositive provisions.*—For purposes of subdivision (i) of this subparagraph, the provisions of paragraph (e)(4) and (5) of §20.2055-2 shall apply in determining whether an amendment will be considered as one which amends the dispositive provisions of a will or trust.

(c) *Foreign organization with substantial support from foreign sources.*—Section 4948(c)(4) provides that, in the case of decedents dying after December 31, 1969, a deduction which would otherwise be allowable under section 2055 for the value of property transferred by the decedent to or for the use of a foreign organization which has received substantially all of its support (other than gross investment income) from sources without the United States shall not be allowed if the transfer is made (1) after the date on which the Commissioner has published notice that he has notified such organization that it has engaged in a prohibited transaction, or (2) in a taxable year of such organization for which it is not exempt from taxation under section 501(a) because it has engaged in a prohibited transaction after December 31, 1969. [Reg. §20.2055-5.]

☐ [*T.D. 7318, 7-10-74.*]

### [Reg. §20.2055-6]

**§20.2055-6. Disallowance of double deduction in the case of qualified terminable interest property.**—No deduction is allowed from the decedent's gross estate under section 2055 for property with respect to which a deduction is allowed by reason of section 2056(b)(7). See section 2056(b)(9) and §20.2056(b)-9. [Reg. §20.2055-6.]

☐ [*T.D. 8522, 2-28-94.*]

### [Reg. §20.2056-0]

**§20.2056-0. Table of contents.**—This section lists the captions that appear in the regulations under §§20.2056(a)-1 through 20.2056(d)-2.

(c) Effect of death taxes.

(d) Remainder interests.

*§ 20.2056(b)-5. Marital deduction; life estate with power of appointment in surviving spouse.*

(a) In general.

(b) Specific portion; deductible amount.

(c) Meaning of specific portion.

(1) In general.

(2) Fraction or percentage share.

(3) Special rule in the case of estates of decedents dying on or before October 24, 1992, and certain decedents dying after October 24, 1992, with wills or revocable trusts executed on or prior to that date.

(4) Local law.

(5) Examples.

(d) Meaning of entire interest.

(e) Application of local law.

(f) Right to income.

(g) Power of appointment in surviving spouse.

(h) Requirement of survival for a limited period.

(j) Existence of power in another.

*§ 20.2056(b)-6. Marital deduction; life insurance or annuity payments with power of appointment in surviving spouse.*

(a) In general.

(b) Specific portion; deductible interest.

(c) Applicable principles.

(d) Payments of installments or interest.

(e) Powers of appointment.

*§ 20.2056(b)-7. Election with respect to life estate for surviving spouse.*

(a) In general.

(b) Qualified terminable interest property.

(1) In general.

(2) Property for which an election may be made.

(3) Persons permitted to make the election.

(4) Manner and time of making the election.

(c) Protective elections.

(1) In general.

(2) Protective election irrevocable.

(d) Qualifying income interest for life.

(1) In general.

(2) Entitled for life to all income.

(3) Contingent income interests.

(4) Income between last distribution date and spouse's date of death.

(5) Pooled income funds.

(6) Power to distribute principal to spouse.

(e) Annuities payable from trusts in the case of estates of decedents dying on or before October 24,1992, and certain decedents dying after October 24, 1992, with wills or revocable trusts executed on or prior to that date.

(1) In general.

(2) Deductible interest.

(3) Distributions permissible only to surviving spouse.

(4) Applicable interest rate.

(5) Effective dates.

(f) Joint and survivor annuities. [Reserved]

(g) Application of local law.

(h) Examples.

*§ 20.2056(b)-8. Special rule for charitable remainder trusts.*

(a) In general.

(1) Surviving spouse only noncharitable beneficiary.

(2) Interest for life or term of years.

(3) Payment of state death taxes.

(b) Charitable trusts where surviving spouse is not the only noncharitable beneficiary.

*§ 20.2056(b)-9. Denial of double deduction.*

*§ 20.2056(b)-10. Effective dates.*

*§ 20.2056(c)-1. Marital deduction; definition of passed from the decedent.*

(a) In general.

(b) Expectant interest in property under community property laws.

*§ 20.2056(c)-2. Marital deduction; definition of "passed from the decedent to his surviving spouse."*

(a) In general.

(b) Examples.

(c) Effect of election by surviving spouse.

(d) Will contests.

(e) Survivorship.

*§ 20.2056(c)-3. Marital deduction; definition of passed from the decedent to a person other than his surviving spouse.*

*§ 20.2056(d)-1. Marital deduction; special rules for marital deduction if surviving spouse is not a United States citizen.*

*§ 20.2056(d)-2. Marital deduction; effect of disclaimers of post-December 31,1976 transfers.*

(a) Disclaimer by a surviving spouse.

(b) Disclaimer by a person other than a surviving spouse.

*§ 20.2056(d)-3. Marital deduction; effect of disclaimers of pre-January 1, 1977 transfers.*

(a) Disclaimers by a surviving spouse.

(b) Disclaimer by a person other than a surviving spouse.

(1) Decedents dying after October 3, 1966, and before January 1, 1977.

(2) Decedents dying after September 30, 1963, and before October 4, 1966.

(3) Decedents dying before October 4, 1966.

[Reg. § 20.2056-0.]

☐ [*T.D. 8522, 2-28-94. Amended by T.D. 8612, 8-21-95.*]

**[Reg. § 20.2056(a)-1]**

**§ 20.2056(a)-1. Marital deduction; in general.**—(a) *In general.*—A deduction is allowed under section 2056 from the gross estate of a decedent for the value of any property interest which passes from the decedent to the decedent's surviving spouse if the interest is a *deductible interest* as defined in § 20.2056(a)-2. With respect to decedents dying in certain years, a deduction is allowed under section 2056 only to the extent that the total of the deductible interests does not exceed the applicable limitations set forth in paragraph(c) of this section. The deduction allowed under section 2056 is referred to as the *marital deduction*. See also sections 2056(d) and 2056A for special rules applicable in the case of decedents dying after November 10, 1988, if the decedent's surviving spouse is not a citizen of the United States at the time of the decedent's death. In such cases, the marital deduction may not be allowed unless the property passes to a qualified domestic trust as described in section 2056A(a).

(b) *Requirements for marital deduction.*—(1) *In general.*—To obtain the marital deduction with respect to any property interest, the executor must establish the following facts—

(i) The decedent was survived by a spouse (see § 20.2056(c)-2(e));

(ii) The property interest passed from the decedent to the spouse (see § § 20.2056(b)-5 through 20.2056(b)-8 and 20.2056(c)-1 through 20.2056(c)-3);

(iii) The property interest is a *deductible interest* (see § 20.2056(a)-2); and

(iv) The value of the property interest (see § 20.2056(b)-4).

(2) *Burden of establishing requisite facts.*—The executor must provide the facts relating to any applicable limitation on the amount of the allowable marital deduction under § 20.2056(a)-1(c), and must submit proof necessary to establish any fact required under paragraph (b)(1), including any evidence requested by the district director.

(c) *Marital deduction; limitation on aggregate deductions.*—(1) *Estates of decedents dying before 1977.*—In the case of estates of decedents dying before January 1, 1977, the marital deduction is limited to one-half of the value of the *adjusted gross estate*, as that term was defined under section 2056(c)(2) prior to repeal by the Economic Recovery Tax Act of 1981.

(2) *Estates of decedents dying after December 31, 1976, and before January 1, 1982.*—Except as provided in § 2002(d)(1) of the Tax Reform Act of 1976 (Pub. L. 94-455), in the case of decedents dying after December 31, 1976, and before January 1, 1982, the marital deduction is limited to the greater of—

(i) $250,000; or

(ii) One-half of the value of the decedent's adjusted gross estate, adjusted for intervivos gifts to the spouse as prescribed by section 2056(c)(1)(B) prior to repeal by the Economic Recovery Tax Act of 1981 (Pub. L. 97-34).

(3) *Estates of decedents dying after December 31, 1981.*—In the case of estates of decedents dying after December 31, 1981, the marital deduction is limited as prescribed in paragraph (c)(2) of this section if the provisions of section 403(e)(3) of Pub. L. 97-34 are satisfied. [Reg. § 20.2056(a)-1.]

☐ [*T.D. 6296, 6-23-58. Amended by T.D. 8095, 8-6-86 and T.D. 8522, 2-28-94.*]

### [Reg. § 20.2056(a)-2]

**§ 20.2056(a)-2. Marital deduction; deductible interests and nondeductible interests.**—(a) *In general.*—Property interests which passed from a decedent to his surviving spouse fall within two general categories: (1) those with respect to which the marital deduction is authorized, and (2) those with respect to which the marital deduction is not authorized. These categories are referred to in this section and other sections of the regulations under section 2056 as "deductible interests" and "nondeductible interests," respectively (see paragraph (b) of this section). Subject to any applicable limitations set forth in § 20.2056(a)-1(c), the amount of the marital deduction is the aggregate value of the *deductible interests*.

(b) *Deductible interests.*—An interest passing to a decedent's surviving spouse is a "deductible interest" if it does not fall within one of the following categories of "nondeductible interests":

(1) Any property interest which passed from the decedent to his surviving spouse is a "nondeductible interest" to the extent it is not included in the decedent's gross estate.

(2) If a deduction is allowed under section 2053 (relating to deductions for expenses and indebtedness) by reason of the passing of a property interest from the decedent to his surviving spouse, such interest is, to the extent of the deduction under section 2053, a "nondeductible interest." Thus, a property interest which passed from the decedent to his surviving spouse in satisfaction of a deductible claim of the spouse against the estate is, to the extent of the claim, a "nondeductible interest" (see § 20.2056(b)-4). Similarly, amounts deducted under section 2053(a)(2) for commissions allowed to the surviving spouse as executor are "nondeductible interests." As to the valuation, for the purpose of the marital deduction, of any property interest which passed from the decedent to his surviving spouse subject to a mortgage or other encumbrance, see § 20.2056(b)-4.

(3) If during settlement of the estate a loss deductible under section 2054 occurs with respect to a property interest, then that interest is, to the extent of the deductible loss, a "nondeductible interest" for the purpose of the marital deduction.

(4) A property interest passing to a decedent's surviving spouse which is a "terminable interest," as defined in § 20.2056(b)-1, is a "nondeductible interest" to the extent specified in that section. [Reg. § 20.2056(a)-2.]

☐ [*T.D. 6296, 6-23-58. Amended by T.D. 8522, 2-28-94.*]

### [Reg. § 20.2056(b)-1]

**§ 20.2056(b)-1. Marital deduction; limitation in case of life estate or other terminable interest.**—(a) *In general.*—Section 2056(b) provides that no marital deduction is allowed with respect to certain property interests, referred to generally as "terminable interests," passing from a decedent to his surviving spouse. The phrase "terminable interest" is defined in paragraph (b) of this section. However, the fact that an interest in property passing to a decedent's surviving spouse is a "terminable interest" makes it nondeductible only (1) under the circumstances described in paragraph (c) of this section, and (2) if it does not come within one of the exceptions referred to in paragraph (d) of this section.

(b) *"Terminable interests.".*—A "terminable interest" in property is an interest which will terminate or fail on the lapse of time or on the occurrence or the failure to occur of some contingency. Life estates, terms for years, annuities, patents, and copyrights are therefore terminable interests. However, a bond, note, or similar contractual obligation, the discharge of which would not have the effect of an annuity or a term for years, is not a terminable interest.

(c) *Nondeductible terminable interests.*—(1) A property interest which constitutes a terminable interest, as defined in paragraph (b) of this section, is nondeductible if—

(i) Another interest in the same property passed from the decedent to some other person for less than an adequate and full consideration in money or money's worth, and

(ii) By reason of its passing, the other person or his heirs or assigns may possess or enjoy any part of the property after the termination or failure of the spouse's interest.

(2) Even though a property interest which constitutes a terminable interest is not nondeductible by reason of the rules stated in subparagraph (1) of this paragraph, such an interest is nondeductible if—

(i) The decedent has directed his executor or a trustee to acquire such an interest for the decedent's surviving spouse (see further paragraph (f) of this section), or

(ii) Such an interest passing to the decedent's surviving spouse may be satisfied out of a group of assets which includes a

nondeductible interest (see further § 20.2056(b)-2). In this case, however, full nondeductibility may not result.

(d) *Exceptions.*—A property interest passing to a decedent's surviving spouse is deductible (if it is not otherwise disqualified under § 20.2056(a)-2) even though it is a terminable interest, and even though an interest therein passed from the decedent to another person, if it is a terminable interest only because—

(1) It is conditioned on the spouse's surviving for a limited period, in the manner described in § 20.2056(b)-3;

(2) It is a right to income for life with a general power of appointment, meeting the requirements set forth in § 20.2056(b)-5;

(3) It consists of life insurance or annuity payments held by the insurer with a general power of appointment in the spouse, meeting the requirements set forth in § 20.2056(b)-6;

(4) It is qualified terminable interest property, meeting the requirements set forth in § 20.2056(b)-7; or

(5) It is an interest in a qualified charitable remainder trust in which the spouse is the only noncharitable beneficiary, meeting the requirements set forth in § 20.2056(b)-8.

(e) *Miscellaneous principles.*—(1) In determining whether an interest passed from the decedent to some other person, it is immaterial whether interests in the same property passed to the decedent's spouse and another person at the same time, or under the same instrument.

(2) In determining whether an interest in the same property passed from the decedent both to his surviving spouse and to some other person, a distinction is to be drawn between "property," as such term is used in section 2056, and an "interest in property." The term "property" refers to the underlying property in which various interests exist; each such interest is not for this purpose to be considered as "property."

(3) Whether or not an interest is nondeductible because it is a terminable interest is to be determined by reference to the property interests which actually passed from the decedent. Subsequent conversions of the property are immaterial for this purpose. Thus, where a decedent bequeathed his estate to his wife for life with remainder to his children, the interest which passed to his wife is a nondeductible interest, even though the wife agrees with the children to take a fractional share of the estate in fee in lieu of the life interest in the whole, or sells the life estate for cash, or acquires the remainder interest of the children either by purchase or gift.

(4) The terms *passed from the decedent, passed from the decedent to his surviving spouse,* and *passed from the decedent to a person other than his surviving spouse* are defined in § § 20.2056(c)-1 through 20.2056(c)-3.

(f) *Direction to acquire a terminable interest.*—No marital deduction is allowed with respect to a property interest which a decedent directs his executor or a trustee to convert after his death into a terminable interest for his surviving spouse. The marital deduction is not allowed even though no interest in the property subject to the terminable interest passes to another person and even though the interest would otherwise come within the exceptions described in § § 20.2056(b)-5 and 20.2056(b)-6 (relating to life estates and life insurance and annuity payments with powers of appointment). However, a general investment power, authorizing investments in both terminable interests and other property, is not a direction to invest in a terminable interest.

(g) *Examples.*—The application of this section may be illustrated by the following examples. In each example, it is assumed that the executor made no election under section 2056(b)(7) (even if under the specific facts the election would have been available), that any property interest passing from the decedent to a person other than the surviving spouse passed for less than full and adequate consideration in money or money's worth, and that section 2056(b)(8) is inapplicable.

*Example (1).* H (the decedent) devised real property to W (his surviving wife) for life, with remainder to A and his heirs. The interest which passed from H to W is a nondeductible interest since it will terminate upon her death and A (or his heirs or assigns) will thereafter possess or enjoy the property.

*Example (2).* H bequeathed the residue of his estate in trust for the benefit of W and A. The trust income is to be paid to W for life, and upon her death the corpus is to be distributed to A or his issue. However, if A should die without issue, leaving W surviving, the corpus is then to be distributed to W. The interest which passed from H to W is a nondeductible interest since it will terminate in the event of her death if A or his issue survive, and A or his issue will thereafter possess or enjoy the property.

*Example (3).* H during his lifetime purchased an annuity contract providing for payments to himself for life and then to W for life if she should survive him. Upon the death of the survivor of H and W, the excess, if any, of the cost of the contract over the annuity payments theretofore made was to be refunded to A. The interest which passed from H to W is a nondeductible interest since A may possess or enjoy a part of the property following the termination of the interest of W. If, however, the contract provided for no refund upon the death of the survivor of H and W, or provided that any refund was to go to the estate of the survivor, then the interest which passed from H to W is (to the extent it is included in H's gross estate) a deductible interest.

*Example (4)*. H, in contemplation of death, transferred a residence to A for life with remainder to W provided W survives A, but if W predeceases A, the property is to pass to B and his heirs. If it is assumed that H died during A's lifetime, and the value of the residence was included in determining the value of his gross estate, the interest which passed from H to W is a nondeductible interest since it will terminate if W predeceases A and the property will thereafter be possessed or enjoyed by B (or his heirs or assigns). This result is not affected by B's assignment of his interest during H's lifetime, whether made in favor of W or another person, since the term "assigns" (as used in section 2056(b)(1)(B)) includes such an assignee. However, if it is assumed that A predeceased H, the interest of B in the property was extinguished, and, viewed as of the time of the subsequent death of H, the interest which passed from him to W is the entire interest in the property and, therefore, a deductible interest.

*Example (5)*. H transferred real property to A by gift, reserving the right to the rentals of the property for a term of 20 years. H died within the 20-year term, bequeathing the right to the remaining rentals to a trust for the benefit of W. The terms of the trust satisfy the five conditions stated in §20.2056(b)-5, so that the property interest which passed in trust is considered to have passed from H to W. However, the interest is a nondeductible interest since it will terminate upon the expiration of the term and A will thereafter possess or enjoy the property.

*Example (6)*. H bequeathed a patent to W and A as tenants in common. In this case, the interest of W will terminate upon the expiration of the term of the patent, but possession or enjoyment of the property by A must necessarily cease at the same time. Therefore, since A's possession or enjoyment cannot outlast the termination of W's interest, the latter is a deductible interest.

*Example (7)*. A decedent bequeathed $100,000 to his wife, subject to a direction to his executor to use the bequest for the purchase of an annuity for the wife. The bequest is a nondeductible interest.

*Example (8)*. Assume that pursuant to local law an allowance for support is payable to the decedent's surviving spouse during the period of the administration of the decedent's estate, but that upon her death or remarriage during such period her right to any further allowance will terminate. Assume further that the surviving spouse is sole beneficiary of the decedent's estate. Under such circumstances, the allowance constitutes a deductible interest since any part of the allowance not receivable by the surviving spouse during her lifetime will pass to her estate under the terms of the decedent's will. If, in this example, the decedent bequeathed only one-third of his residuary estate to his surviving spouse, then two-thirds of the allowance for support would constitute a nondeductible terminable interest. [Reg. §20.2056(b)-1.]

☐ [*T.D. 6296, 6-23-58. Amended by T.D. 8522, 2-28-94.*]

### [Reg. §20.2056(b)-2]

**§20.2056(b)-2. Marital deduction; interest in unidentified assets.**—(a) *In general.*—Section 2056(b)(2) provides that if an interest passing to a decedent's surviving spouse may be satisfied out of assets (or their proceeds) which include a particular asset that would be a nondeductible interest if it passed from the decedent to his spouse, the value of the interest passing to the spouse is reduced, for the purpose of the marital deduction, by the value of the particular asset.

(b) *Application of section 2056(b)(2).*—In order for section 2056(b)(2) to apply, two circumstances must coexist, as follows:

(1) The property interest which passed from the decedent to his surviving spouse must be payable out of a group of assets included in the gross estate. Examples of property interests payable out of a group of assets are a general legacy, a bequest of the residue of the decedent's estate or of a portion of the residue, and a right to a share of the corpus of a trust upon its termination.

(2) The group of assets out of which the property interest is payable must include one or more particular assets which, if passing specifically to the surviving spouse, would be nondeductible interests. Therefore, section 2056(b)(2) is not applicable merely because the group of assets includes a terminable interest, but would only be applicable if the terminable interest were nondeductible under the provisions of §20.2056(b)-1.

(c) *Interest nondeductible if circumstances present.*—If both of the circumstances set forth in paragraph (b) of this section are present, the property interest payable out of the group of assets is (except as to any excess of its value over the aggregate value of the particular asset or assets which would not be deductible if passing specifically to the surviving spouse) a nondeductible interest.

(d) The application of this section may be illustrated by the following example:

*Example*. A decedent bequeathed one-third of the residue of his estate to his wife. The property passing under the decedent's will included a right to the rentals of an office building for a term of years, reserved by the decedent under a deed of the building by way of gift to his son. The decedent did not make a specific bequest of the right to such rentals. Such right, if passing specifically to the wife, would be a nondeductible interest (see example (5) of paragraph (g) of §20.2056(b)-1). It is assumed that the value of the bequest of one-third of the residue of the estate to the wife was $85,000, and that the right to the rentals was included in the gross estate at a value of $60,000. If the decedent's executor had the right under the decedent's will or local law to assign the entire lease in satisfaction of the bequest, the bequest is a nondeductible interest to the extent of $60,000. If the executor could only assign a one-third interest in the lease in satisfaction of the bequest, the bequest is a nondeductible interest to the extent of $20,000. If the decedent's will provided that his wife's bequest could not be satisfied with a nondeductible interest, the entire bequest is a deductible interest. If, in this example, the asset in question had been foreign real estate not included in the decedent's gross estate, the results would be the same. [Reg. §20.2056(b)-2.]

☐ [*T.D. 6296, 6-23-58. Amended by T.D. 8522, 2-28-94.*]

### [Reg. §20.2056(b)-3]

**§20.2056(b)-3. Marital deduction; interest of spouse conditioned on survival for limited period.**—(a) *In general.*—Generally, no marital deduction is allowable if the interest passing to the surviving spouse is a terminable interest as defined in paragraph (b) of §20.2056(b)-1. However, section 2056(b)(3) provides an exception to this rule so as to allow a deduction if (1) the only condition under which it will terminate is the death of the surviving spouse within 6 months after the decedent's death, or her death as a result of a common disaster which also resulted in the decedent's death, and (2) the condition does not in fact occur.

(b) *Six months' survival.*—If the only condition which will cause the interest taken by the surviving spouse to terminate is the death of the surviving spouse and the condition is of such nature that it can occur only within 6 months following the decedent's death, the exception provided by section 2056(b)(3) will apply, provided the condition does not in fact occur. However, if the condition (unless it relates to death as a result of a common disaster) is one which may occur either within the 6-month period or thereafter, the exception provided by section 2056(b)(3) will not apply.

(c) *Common disaster.*—If a property interest passed from the decedent to his surviving spouse subject to the condition that she does not die as a result of a common disaster which also resulted in the decedent's death, the exception provided by section 2056(b)(3) will not be applied in the final audit of the return if there is still a possibility that the surviving spouse may be deprived of the property interest by operation of the common disaster provision as given effect by the local law.

(d) *Examples.*—The application of this section may be illustrated by the following examples:

*Example (1)*. A decedent bequeathed his entire estate to his spouse on condition that she survive him by 6 months. In the event his spouse failed to survive him by 6 months, his estate was to go to his niece and her heirs. The decedent was survived by his spouse. It will be observed that, as of the time of the decedent's death, it was possible that the niece would, by reason of the interest which passed to her from the decedent, possess or enjoy the estate after the termination of the interest which passed to the spouse. Hence, under the general rule set forth in §20.2056(b)-1, the interest which passed to the spouse would be regarded as a nondeductible interest. If the surviving spouse in fact died within 6 months after the decedent's death, that general rule is to be applied, and the interest which passed to the spouse is a nondeductible interest. However, if the spouse in fact survived the decedent by 6 months, thus extinguishing the interest of the niece, the case comes within the exception provided by section 2056(b)(3), and the interest which passed to the spouse is a deductible interest. (It is assumed for the purpose of this example that no other factor which would cause the interest to be nondeductible is present.)

*Example (2)*. The facts are the same as in example (1) except that the will provided that the estate was to go to the niece either in case the decedent and his spouse should both die as a result of a common disaster, or in case the spouse should fail to survive the decedent by 3 months. It is assumed that the decedent was survived by his spouse. In this example, the interest which passed from the decedent to his surviving spouse is to be regarded as a nondeductible interest if the surviving spouse in fact died either within 3 months after the decedent's death or as a result of a common disaster which also resulted in the decedent's death. However, if the spouse in fact survived the decedent by 3 months, and did not thereafter die as a result of a common disaster which also resulted in the decedent's death, the exception provided under section 2056(b)(3) will apply and the interest will be deductible.

*Example (3).* The facts are the same as in example (1) except that the will provided that the estate was to go to the niece if the decedent and his spouse should both die as a result of a common disaster and if the spouse failed to survive the decedent by 3 months. If the spouse in fact survived the decedent by 3 months, the interest of the niece is extinguished, and the interest passing to the spouse is a deductible interest.

*Example (4).* A decedent devised and bequeathed his residuary estate to his wife if she was living on the date of distribution of his estate. The devise and bequest is a nondeductible interest even though distribution took place within 6 months after the decedent's death and the surviving spouse in fact survived the date of distribution. [Reg. § 20.2056(b)-3.]

☐ [T.D. 6296, 6-23-58.]

### [Reg. § 20.2056(b)-4]

**§ 20.2056(b)-4. Marital deduction; valuation of interest passing to surviving spouse.**—(a) *In general.*—The value, for the purpose of the marital deduction, of any deductible interest which passed from the decedent to his surviving spouse is to be determined as of the date of the decedent's death, except that if the executor elects the alternate valuation method under section 2032 the valuation is to be determined as of the date of the decedent's death but with the adjustment described in paragraph (a)(3) of § 20.2032-1. The marital deduction may be taken only with respect to the net value of any deductible interest which passed from the decedent to his surviving spouse, the same principles being applicable as if the amount of a gift to the spouse were being determined.

(b) *Property interest subject to an encumbrance or obligation.*—If a property interest passed from the decedent to his surviving spouse subject to a mortgage or other encumbrance, or if an obligation is imposed upon the surviving spouse by the decedent in connection with the passing of a property interest, the value of the property interest is to be reduced by the amount of the mortgage, other encumbrance, or obligation. However, if under the terms of the decedent's will or under local law the executor is required to discharge, out of other assets of the decedent's estate, a mortgage or other encumbrance on property passing from the decedent to his surviving spouse, or is required to reimburse the surviving spouse for the amount of the mortgage or other encumbrance, the payment or reimbursement constitutes an additional interest passing to the surviving spouse. The passing of a property interest subject to the imposition of an obligation by the decedent does not include a bequest, devise, or transfer in lieu of dower, curtesy, or of a statutory estate created in lieu of dower or curtesy, or of other marital rights in the decedent's property or estate. The passing of a property interest subject to the imposition of an obligation by the decedent does, however, include a bequest, etc., in lieu of the interest of his surviving spouse under community property laws unless such interest was, immediately prior to the decedent's death, a mere expectancy. The following examples are illustrative of property interests which passed from the decedent to his surviving spouse subject to the imposition of an obligation by the decedent:

*Example (1).* A decedent devised a residence valued at $25,000 to his wife, with a direction that she pay $5,000 to his sister. For the purpose of the marital deduction, the value of the property interest passing to the wife is only $20,000.

*Example (2).* A decedent devised real property to his wife in satisfaction of a debt owing to her. The debt is a deductible claim under section 2053. Since the wife is obligated to relinquish the claim as a condition to acceptance of the devise, the value of the devise is, for the purpose of the marital deduction, to be reduced by the amount of the claim.

*Example (3).* A decedent bequeathed certain securities to his wife in lieu of her interest in property held by them as community property under the law of the State of their residence. The wife elected to relinquish her community property interest and to take the bequest. For the purpose of the marital deduction, the value of the bequest is to be reduced by the value of the community property interest relinquished by the wife.

(c) *Effect of death taxes.*—(1) In the determination of the value of any property interest which passed from the decedent to his surviving spouse, there must be taken into account the effect which the Federal estate tax, or any estate, succession, legacy, or inheritance tax, has upon the net value to the surviving spouse of the property interest.

(2) For example, assume that the only bequest to the surviving spouse is $100,000 and the spouse is required to pay a State inheritance tax in the amount of $1,500. If no other death taxes affect the net value of the bequest, the value, for the purpose of the marital deduction, is $98,500.

(3) As another example, assume that a decedent devised real property to his wife having a value for Federal estate tax purposes of $100,000 and also bequeathed to her a nondeductible interest for life under a trust. The State of residence valued the real property at $90,000 and the life interest at $30,000, and imposed an inheritance tax (at graduated rates) of $4,800 with respect to the two interests. If it is assumed that the inheritance tax on the devise is required to be paid by the wife, the amount of tax to be ascribed to the devise is

$$\frac{90,000}{120,000} \times \$4,800 = \$3,600.$$

Accordingly, if no other death taxes affect the net value of the bequest, the value, for the purpose of the marital deduction, is $100,000 less $3,600, or $96,400.

(4) If the decedent bequeaths his residuary estate, or a portion of it, to his surviving spouse, and his will contains a direction that all death taxes shall be payable out of the residuary estate, the value of the bequest, for the purpose of the marital deduction, is based upon the amount of the residue as reduced pursuant to such direction. If the residuary estate, or a portion of it, is bequeathed to the surviving spouse, and by the local law the Federal estate tax is payable out of the residuary estate, the value of the bequest, for the purpose of the marital deduction, may not exceed its value as reduced by the Federal estate tax. Methods of computing the deduction, under such circumstances, are set forth in supplemental instructions to the estate tax return.

(d) *Effect of administration expenses.*—(1) *Definitions.*—(i) *Management expenses.*—Estate management expenses are expenses that are incurred in connection with the investment of estate assets or with their preservation or maintenance during a reasonable period of administration. Examples of these expenses could include investment advisory fees, stock brokerage commissions, custodial fees, and interest.

(ii) *Transmission expenses.*—Estate transmission expenses are expenses that would not have been incurred but for the decedent's death and the consequent necessity of collecting the decedent's assets, paying the decedent's debts and death taxes, and distributing the decedent's property to those who are entitled to receive it. Estate transmission expenses include any administration expense that is not a management expense. Examples of these expenses could include executor commissions and attorney fees (except to the extent of commissions or fees specifically related to investment, preservation, or maintenance of the assets), probate fees, expenses incurred in construction proceedings and defending against will contests, and appraisal fees.

(iii) *Marital share.*—The marital share is the property or interest in property that passed from the decedent for which a deduction is allowable under section 2056(a). The marital share includes the income produced by the property or interest in property during the period of administration if the income, under the terms of the governing instrument or applicable local law, is payable to the surviving spouse or is to be added to the principal of the property interest passing to, or for the benefit of, the surviving spouse.

(2) *Effect of transmission expenses.*—For purposes of determining the marital deduction, the value of the marital share shall be reduced by the amount of the estate transmission expenses paid from the marital share.

(3) *Effect of management expenses attributable to the marital share.*—For purposes of determining the marital deduction, the value of the marital share shall not be reduced by the amount of the estate management expenses attributable to and paid from the marital share. Pursuant to section 2056(b)(9), however, the amount of the allowable marital deduction shall be reduced by the amount of any such management expenses that are deducted under section 2053 on the decedent's Federal estate tax return.

(4) *Effect of management expenses not attributable to the marital share.*—For purposes of determining the marital deduction, the value of the marital share shall be reduced by the amount of the estate

management expenses paid from the marital share but attributable to a property interest not included in the marital share.

(5) *Examples.*—The following examples illustrate the application of this paragraph (d):

*Example 1.* The decedent dies after 2006 having made no lifetime gifts. The decedent makes a bequest of shares of ABC Corporation stock to the decedent's child. The bequest provides that the child is to receive the income from the shares from the date of the decedent's death. The value of the bequeathed shares on the decedent's date of death is $3,000,000. The residue of the estate is bequeathed to a trust for which the executor properly makes an election under section 2056(b)(7) to treat as qualified terminable interest property. The value of the residue on the decedent's date of death, before the payment of administration expenses and Federal and State estate taxes, is $6,000,000. Under applicable local law, the executor has the discretion to pay administration expenses from the income or principal of the residuary estate. All estate taxes are to be paid from the residue. The State estate tax equals the State death tax credit available under section 2011. During the period of administration, the estate incurs estate transmission expenses of $400,000, which the executor charges to the residue. For purposes of determining the marital deduction, the value of the residue is reduced by the Federal and State estate taxes and by the estate transmission expenses. If the transmission expenses are deducted on the Federal estate tax return, the marital deduction is $3,500,000 ($6,000,000 minus $400,000 transmission expenses and minus $2,100,000 Federal and State estate taxes). If the transmission expenses are deducted on the estate's Federal income tax return rather than on the estate tax return, the marital deduction is $3,011,111 ($6,000,000 minus $400,000 transmission expenses and minus $2,588,889 Federal and State estate taxes).

*Example 2.* The facts are the same as in *Example 1,* except that, instead of incurring estate transmission expenses, the estate incurs estate management expenses of $400,000 in connection with the residue property passing for the benefit of the spouse. The executor charges these management expenses to the residue. In determining the value of the residue passing to the spouse for marital deduction purposes, a reduction is made for Federal and State estate taxes payable from the residue but no reduction is made for the estate management expenses. If the management expenses are deducted on the estate's income tax return, the net value of the property passing to the spouse is $3,900,000 ($6,000,000 minus $2,100,000 Federal and State estate taxes). A marital deduction is claimed for that amount, and the taxable estate is $5,100,000.

*Example 3.* The facts are the same as in *Example 1,* except that the estate management expenses of $400,000 are incurred in connection with the bequest of ABC Corporation stock to the decedent's child. The executor charges these management expenses to the residue. For purposes of determining the marital deduction, the value of the residue is reduced by the Federal and State estate taxes and by the management expenses. The management expenses reduce the value of the residue because they are charged to the property passing to the spouse even though they were incurred with respect to stock passing to the child. If the management expenses are deducted on the estate's Federal income tax return, the marital deduction is $3,011,111 ($6,000,000 minus $400,000 management expenses and minus $2,588,889 Federal and State estate taxes). If the management expenses are deducted on the estate's Federal estate tax return, rather than on the estate's Federal income tax return, the marital deduction is $3,500,000 ($6,000,000 minus $400,000 management expenses and minus $2,100,000 in Federal and State estate taxes).

*Example 4.* The decedent, who dies in 2000, has a gross estate of $3,000,000. Included in the gross estate are proceeds of $150,000 from a policy insuring the decedent's life and payable to the decedent's child as beneficiary. The applicable credit amount against the tax was fully consumed by the decedent's lifetime gifts. Applicable State law requires the child to pay any estate taxes attributable to the life insurance policy. Pursuant to the decedent's will, the rest of the decedent's estate passes outright to the surviving spouse. During the period of administration, the estate incurs estate management expenses of $150,000 in connection with the property passing to the spouse. The value of the property passing to the spouse is $2,850,000 ($3,000,000 less the insurance proceeds of $150,000 passing to the child). For purposes of determining the marital deduction, if the management expenses are deducted on the estate's income tax return, the marital deduction is $2,850,000 ($3,000,000 less $150,000) and there is a resulting taxable estate of $150,000 ($3,000,000 less a marital deduction of $2,850,000). Suppose, instead, the management expenses of $150,000 are deducted on the estate's estate tax return under section 2053 as expenses of administration. In such a situation, claiming a marital deduction of $2,850,000 would be taking a deduction for the same $150,000 in property under both sections 2053 and 2056 and would shield from estate taxes the $150,000 in insurance proceeds passing to the decedent's child. Therefore, in accordance

with section 2056(b)(9), the marital deduction is limited to $2,700,000, and the resulting taxable estate is $150,000.

*Example 5.* The decedent dies after 2006 having made no lifetime gifts. The value of the decedent's residuary estate on the decedent's date of death is $3,000,000, before the payment of administration expenses and Federal and State estate taxes. The decedent's will provides a formula for dividing the decedent's residuary estate between two trusts to reduce the estate's Federal estate taxes to zero. Under the formula, one trust, for the benefit of the decedent's child, is to be funded with that amount of property equal in value to so much of the applicable exclusion amount under section 2010 that would reduce the estate's Federal estate tax to zero. The other trust, for the benefit of the surviving spouse, satisfies the requirements of section 2056(b)(7) and is to be funded with the remaining property in the estate. The State estate tax equals the State death tax credit available under section 2011. During the period of administration, the estate incurs transmission expenses of $200,000. The transmission expenses of $200,000 reduce the value of the residue to $2,800,000. If the transmission expenses are deducted on the Federal estate tax return, then the formula divides the residue so that the value of the property passing to the child's trust is $1,000,000 and the value of the property passing to the marital trust is $1,800,000. The allowable marital deduction is $1,800,000. The applicable exclusion amount shields from Federal estate tax the entire $1,000,000 passing to the child's trust so that the amount of Federal and State estate taxes is zero. Alternatively, if the transmission expenses are deducted on the estate's Federal income tax return, the formula divides the residue so that the value of the property passing to the child's trust is $800,000 and the value of the property passing to the marital trust is $2,000,000. The allowable marital deduction is $2,000,000. The applicable exclusion amount shields from Federal estate tax the entire $800,000 passing to the child's trust so that the amount of Federal and State estate taxes remains zero.

*Example 6.* The facts are the same as in *Example 5,* except that the decedent's will provides that the child's trust is to be funded with that amount of property equal in value to the applicable exclusion amount under section 2010 allowable to the decedent's estate. The residue of the estate, after the payment of any debts, expenses, and Federal and State estate taxes, is to pass to the marital trust. The applicable exclusion amount in this case is $1,000,000, so the value of the property passing to the child's trust is $1,000,000. After deducting the $200,000 of transmission expenses, the residue of the estate is $1,800,000 less any estate taxes. If the transmission expenses are deducted on the Federal estate tax return, the allowable marital deduction is $1,800,000, the taxable estate is zero, and the Federal and State estate taxes are zero. Alternatively, if the transmission expenses are deducted on the estate's Federal income tax return, the net value of the property passing to the spouse is $1,657,874 ($1,800,000 minus $142,106 estate taxes). A marital deduction is claimed for that amount, the taxable estate is $1,342,106, and the Federal and State estate taxes total $142,106.

*Example 7.* The decedent, who dies in 2000, makes an outright pecuniary bequest of $3,000,000 to the decedent's surviving spouse, and the residue of the estate, after the payment of all debts, expenses, and Federal and State estate taxes, passes to the decedent's child. Under the terms of the governing instrument and applicable local law, a beneficiary of a pecuniary bequest is not entitled to any income on the bequest. During the period of administration, the estate pays estate transmission expenses from the income earned by the property that will be distributed to the surviving spouse in satisfaction of the pecuniary bequest. The income earned on this property is not part of the marital share. Therefore, the allowable marital deduction is $3,000,000, unreduced by the amount of the estate transmission expenses.

(6) *Effective date.*—The provisions of this paragraph (d) apply to estates of decedents dying on or after December 3, 1999.

(e) *Remainder interests.*—If the income from property is made payable to another individual for life, or for a term of years, with remainder absolutely to the surviving spouse or to her estate, the marital deduction is based upon the present value of the remainder. The present value of the remainder is to be determined in accordance with the rules stated in § 20.2031-7. For example, if the surviving spouse is to receive $50,000 upon the death of a person aged 31 years, the present value of the remainder is $14,466. If the remainder is such that its value is to be determined by a special computation (see paragraph (b) of § 20.2031-7), a request for a specific factor may be submitted to the Commissioner. The request should be accompanied by a statement of the date of birth of each person, the duration of whose life may affect the value of the remainder, and copies of the relevant instruments. The Commissioner may, if conditions permit, supply the factor requested. If the Commissioner does not furnish the factor, the claim for deduction must be supported by a full statement of the computation of the present value made in accordance with the

**Reg. § 20.2056(b)-4(e)**

principles set forth in the applicable paragraphs of §20.2031-7. [Reg. §20.2056(b)-4.]

☐ [*T.D. 6296, 6-23-58. Amended by T.D. 8522, 2-28-94; T.D. 8540, 6-9-94 and T.D. 8846, 12-2-99 (corrected 12-17-99).]*

### [Reg. §20.2056(b)-5]

**§20.2056(b)-5. Marital deduction; life estate with power of appointment in surviving spouse.**—(a) *In general.*—Section 2056(b)(5) provides that if an interest in property passes from the decedent to his surviving spouse (whether or not in trust) and the spouse is entitled for life to all the income from the entire interest or all the income from a specific portion of the entire interest, with a power in her to appoint the entire interest or the specific portion, the interest which passes to her is a deductible interest, to the extent that it satisfies all five of the conditions set forth below (see paragraph (b) of this section if one or more of the conditions is satisfied as to only a portion of the interest):

(1) The surviving spouse must be entitled for life to all of the income from the entire interest or a specific portion of the entire interest, or to a specific portion of all the income from the entire interest.

(2) The income payable to the surviving spouse must be payable annually or at more frequent intervals.

(3) The surviving spouse must have the power to appoint the entire interest or the specific portion to either herself or her estate.

(4) The power in the surviving spouse must be exercisable by her alone and (whether exercisable by will or during life) must be exercisable in all events.

(5) The entire interest or the specific portion must not be subject to a power in any other person to appoint any part to any person other than the surviving spouse.

(b) *Specific portion; deductible amount.*—If either the right to income or the power of appointment passing to the surviving spouse pertains only to a specific portion of a property interest passing from the decedent, the marital deduction is allowed only to the extent that the rights in the surviving spouse meet all of the five conditions described in paragraph (a) of this section. While the rights over the income and the power must coexist as to the same interest in property, it is not necessary that the rights over the income or the power as to such interest be in the same proportion. However, if the rights over income meeting the required conditions set forth in paragraph (a)(1) and (2) of this section extend over a smaller share of the property interest than the share with respect to which the power of appointment requirements set forth in paragraph (a)(3) through (5) of this section are satisfied, the deductible interest is limited to the smaller share. Correspondingly, if a power of appointment meeting all the requirements extends to a smaller portion of the property interest than the portion over which the income rights pertain, the deductible interest cannot exceed the value of the portion to which such power of appointment applies. Thus, if the decedent leaves to his surviving spouse the right to receive annually all of the income from a particular property interest and a power of appointment meeting the specifications prescribed in paragraph (a)(3) through (5) of this section as to only one-half of the property interest, then only one-half of the property interest is treated as a deductible interest. Correspondingly, if the income interest of the spouse satisfying the requirements extends to only one-fourth of the property interest and a testamentary power of appointment satisfying the requirements extends to all of the property interest, then only one-fourth of the interest in the spouse qualifies as a deductible interest. Further, if the surviving spouse has no right to income from a specific portion of a property interest but a testamentary power of appointment which meets the necessary conditions over the entire interest, then none of the interest qualifies for the deduction. In addition, if, from the time of the decedent's death, the surviving spouse has a power of appointment meeting all of the required conditions over three-fourths of the entire property interest and the prescribed income rights over the entire interest, but with a power in another person to appoint one-half of the entire interest, the value of the interest in the surviving spouse over only one-half of the property interest will qualify as a deductible interest.

(c) *Meaning of specific portion.*—(1) *In general.*—Except as provided in paragraphs (c)(2) and (c)(3) of this section, a partial interest in property is not treated as a specific portion of the entire interest. In addition, any specific portion of an entire interest in property is nondeductible to the extent the specific portion is subject to invasion for the benefit of any person other than the surviving spouse, except in the case of a deduction allowable under section 2056(b)(5), relating to the exercise of a general power of appointment by the surviving spouse.

(2) *Fraction or percentage share.*—Under section 2056(b)(10), a partial interest in property is treated as a specific portion of the entire

interest if the rights of the surviving spouse in income, and the required rights as to the power described in §20.2056(b)-5(a), constitute a fractional or percentage share of the entire property interest, so that the surviving spouse's interest reflects its proportionate share of the increase or decrease in the value of the entire property interest to which the income rights and the power relate. Thus, if the spouse's right to income and the spouse's power extend to a specified fraction or percentage of the property, or the equivalent, the interest is in a specific portion of the property. In accordance with paragraph (b) of this section, if the spouse has the right to receive the income from a specific portion of the trust property (after applying paragraph (c)(3) of this section) but has a power of appointment over a different specific portion of the property (after applying paragraph (c)(3) of this section), the marital deduction is limited to the lesser specific portion.

(3) *Special rule in the case of estates of decedents dying on or before October 24, 1992, and certain decedents dying after October 24, 1992, with wills or revocable trusts executed on or prior to that date.*

(i) In the case of estates of decedents within the purview of the effective date and transitional rules contained in paragraphs (c)(3)(ii) and (iii) of this section:

(A) A specific sum payable annually, or at more frequent intervals, out of the property and its income that is not limited by the income of the property is treated as the right to receive the income from a specific portion of the property. The specific portion, for purposes of paragraph (c)(2) of this section, is the portion of the property that, assuming the interest rate generally applicable for the valuation of annuities at the time of the decedent's death, would produce income equal to such payments. However, a pecuniary amount payable annually to a surviving spouse is not treated as a right to the income to a specific portion of the trust property for purposes of this paragraph (c)(3)(i)(A) if any person other than the surviving spouse may receive, during the surviving spouse's lifetime, any distribution of the property. To determine the applicable interest rate for valuing annuities, see sections 2031 and 7520 and the regulations under those sections.

(B) The right to appoint a pecuniary amount out of a larger fund (or trust corpus) is considered the right to appoint a specific portion of such fund or trust for purposes of paragraph (c)(2) in an amount equal to such pecuniary amount.

(ii) The rules contained in paragraphs (c)(3)(i)(A) and (B) of this section apply with respect to estates of decedents dying on or before October 24, 1992.

(iii) The rules contained in paragraphs (c)(3)(i)(A) and (B) of this section apply in the case of decedents dying after October 24, 1992, if property passes to the spouse pursuant to a will or revocable trust agreement executed on or before October 24, 1992, and either—

(A) On that date, the decedent was under a mental disability to change the disposition of the property and did not regain competence to dispose of such property before the date of death; or

(B) The decedent dies prior to October 24, 1995.

(iv) Notwithstanding paragraph (c)(3)(iii) of this section, paragraphs (c)(3)(i)(A) and (B) of this section do not apply if the will or revocable trust is amended after October 24, 1992, in any respect that increases the amount of the transfer qualifying for the marital deduction or alters the terms by which the interest so passes to the surviving spouse of the decedent.

(4) *Local law.*—A partial interest in property is treated as a specific portion of the entire interest if it is shown that the surviving spouse has rights under local law that are identical to those the surviving spouse would have acquired had the partial interest been expressed in terms satisfying the requirements of paragraph (c)(2) (or paragraph (c)(3) if applicable) of this section.

(5) *Examples.*—The following examples illustrate the application of paragraphs (a) through (c)(4) of this section:

*Example 1. Spouse entitled to the lesser of an annuity or a fraction of trust income.* The decedent, D, died prior to October 24, 1992. D bequeathed in trust 500 identical shares of X company stock, valued for estate tax purposes at $500,000. The trust provides that during the lifetime of D's spouse, S, the trustee is to pay annually to S the lesser of one-half of the trust income or $20,000. Any trust income not paid to S is to be accumulated in the trust and may not be distributed during S's lifetime. S has a testamentary general power of appointment over the entire trust principal. The applicable interest rate for valuing annuities as of D's date of death under section 7520 is 10 percent. For purposes of paragraphs (a) through (c) of this section, S is treated as receiving all of the income from the lesser of—

(i) One half of the stock ($250,000); or

(ii) $200,000, the specific portion of the stock which, as determined in accordance with §20.2056(b)-5(c)(3)(i)(A), would produce annual income of $20,000 (20,000/.10). Accordingly, the marital deduction is limited to $200,000 (200,000/500,000 or 2/5th of the value of the trust).

*Example 2. Spouse possesses power and income interest over different specific portions of trust.* The facts are the same as in *Example 1* except that S's testamentary general power of appointment is exercisable over only 1/4th of the trust principal. Consequently, under section 2056(b)(5), the marital deduction is allowable only for the value of 1/4th of the trust ($125,000); i.e., the lesser of the value of the portion with respect to which S is deemed to be entitled to all of the income (2/5th of the trust or $200,000), or the value of the portion with respect to which S possesses the requisite power of appointment (1/4th of the trust or $125,000).

*Example 3. Power of appointment over pecuniary amount.* The decedent, D, died prior to October 24, 1992. D bequeathed property valued at $400,000 for estate tax purposes in trust. The trustee is to pay annually to D's spouse, S, one-fourth of the trust income. Any trust income not paid to S is to be accumulated in the trust and may not be distributed during S's lifetime. The will gives S a testamentary general power of appointment over the sum of $160,000. Because D died prior to October 24, 1992, S's power of appointment over $160,000 is treated as a power of appointment over a specific portion of the entire trust interest. The marital deduction allowable under section 2056(b)(5) is limited to $100,000; that is, the lesser of—

(1) The value of the trust corpus ($400,000);

(2) The value of the trust corpus over which S has a power of appointment ($160,000); or

(3) That specific portion of the trust with respect to which S is entitled to all the income ($100,000).

*Example 4. Power of appointment over shares of stock constitutes a power over a specific portion.* Under D's will, 250 shares of Y company stock were bequeathed in trust pursuant to which all trust income was payable annually to S, D's spouse, for life. S was given a testamentary general power of appointment over 100 shares of stock. The trust provides that if the trustee sells the Y company stock, S's general power of appointment is exercisable with respect to the sale proceeds or the property in which the proceeds are reinvested. Because the amount of property represented by a single share of stock would be altered if the corporation split its stock, issued stock dividends, made a distribution of capital, etc., a power to appoint 100 shares at the time of S's death is not necessarily a power to appoint the entire interest that the 100 shares represented on the date of D's death. If it is shown that, under local law, S has a general power to appoint not only the 100 shares designated by D but also 100/250 of any distributions by the corporation that are included in trust principal, the requirements of paragraph (c)(2) of this section are satisfied and S is treated as having a general power to appoint 100/250 of the entire interest in the 250 shares. In that case, the marital deduction is limited to 40 percent of the trust principal. If local law does not give S that power, the 100 shares would not constitute a specific portion under § 20.2056(b)-5(c) (including § 20.2056(b)-5(c)(3)(i)(B)). The nature of the asset is such that a change in the capitalization of the corporation could cause an alteration in the original value represented by the shares at the time of D's death and, thus, it does not represent a specific portion of the trust.

(d) *Meaning of entire interest.*—Because a marital deduction is allowed for each separate qualifying interest in property passing from the decedent to the decedent's surviving spouse (subject to any applicable limitations in § 20.2056(a)-1(c)), for purposes of paragraphs (a) and (b) of this section, each property interest with respect to which the surviving spouse received any rights is considered separately in determining whether the surviving spouse's rights extend to the entire interest or to a specific portion of the entire interest. A property interest which consists of several identical units of property (such as a block of 250 shares of stock, whether the ownership is evidenced by one or several certificates) is considered one property interest, unless certain of the units are to be segregated and accorded different treatment, in which case each segregated group of items is considered a separate property interest. The bequest of a specified sum of money constitutes the bequest of a separate property interest if immediately following distribution by the executor and thenceforth it, and the investments made with it, must be so segregated or accounted for as to permit its identification as a separate item of property. The application of this paragraph may be illustrated by the following examples:

*Example (1).* The decedent transferred to a trustee three adjoining farms, Blackacre, Whiteacre, and Greenacre. His will provided that during the lifetime of the surviving spouse the trustee should pay her all of the income from the trust. Upon her death, all of Blackacre, a one-half interest in Whiteacre, and a one-third interest in Greenacre were to be distributed to the person or persons appointed by her in her will. The surviving spouse is considered as being entitled to all of the income from the entire interest in Blackacre, all of the income from the entire interest in Whiteacre, and all of the income from the entire interest in Greenacre. She also is considered as having a power

of appointment over the entire interest in Blackacre, over one-half of the entire interest in Whiteacre, and over one-third of the entire interest in Greenacre.

*Example (2).* The decedent bequeathed $250,000 to C, as trustee. C is to invest the money and pay all of the income from the investments to W, the decedent's surviving spouse, annually. W was given a general power, exercisable by will, to appoint one-half of the corpus of the trust. Here, immediately following distribution by the executor the $250,000 will be sufficiently segregated to permit its identification as a separate item, and the $250,000 will constitute an entire property interest. Therefore, W has a right to income and a power of appointment such that one-half of the entire interest is a deductible interest.

*Example (3).* The decedent bequeathed 100 shares of Z Corporation stock to D, as trustee. W, the decedent's surviving spouse, is to receive all of the income of the trust annually and is given a general power, exercisable by will, to appoint out of the trust corpus the sum of $25,000. In this case the $25,000 is not, immediately following distribution, sufficiently segregated to permit its identification as a separate item of property in which the surviving spouse has the entire interest. Therefore, the $25,000 does not constitute the entire interest in a property for the purpose of paragraphs (a) and (b) of this section.

(e) *Application of local law.*—In determining whether or not the conditions set forth in paragraph (a)(1) through (5) of this section are satisfied by the instrument of transfer, regard is to be had to the applicable provisions of the law of the jurisdiction under which the interest passes and, if the transfer is in trust, the applicable provisions of the law governing the administration of the trust. For example, silence of a trust instrument as to the frequency of payment will not be regarded as a failure to satisfy the condition set forth in paragraph (a)(2) of this section that income must be payable to the surviving spouse annually or more frequently unless the applicable law permits payment to be made less frequently than annually. The principles outlined in this paragraph and paragraphs (f) and (g) of this section which are applied in determining whether transfers in trust meet such conditions are equally applicable in ascertaining whether, in the case of interests not in trust, the surviving spouse has the equivalent in rights over income and over the property.

(f) *Right to income.*—(1) If an interest is transferred in trust, the surviving spouse is "entitled for life to all of the income from the entire interest or a specific portion of the entire interest," for the purpose of the condition set forth in paragraph (a)(1) of this section, if the effect of the trust is to give her substantially that degree of beneficial enjoyment of the trust property during her life which the principles of the law of trusts accord to a person who is unqualifiedly designated as the life beneficiary of a trust. Such degree of enjoyment is given only if it was the decedent's intention, as manifested by the terms of the trust instrument and the surrounding circumstances, that the trust should produce for the surviving spouse during her life such an income, or that the spouse should have such use of the trust property as is consistent with the value of the trust corpus and with its preservation. The designation of the spouse as sole income beneficiary for life of the entire interest or a specific portion of the entire interest will be sufficient to qualify the trust unless the terms of the trust and the surrounding circumstances considered as a whole evidence an intention to deprive the spouse of the requisite degree of enjoyment. In determining whether a trust evidences that intention, the treatment required or permitted with respect to individual items must be considered in relation to the entire system provided for the administration of the trust. In addition, the surviving spouse's interest shall meet the condition set forth in paragraph (a)(1) of this section if the spouse is entitled to income as determined by applicable local law that provides for a reasonable apportionment between the income and remainder beneficiaries of the total return of the trust and that meets the requirements of § 1.643(b)-1 of this chapter.

(2) If the over-all effect of a trust is to give to the surviving spouse such enforceable rights as will preserve to her the requisite degree of enjoyment, it is immaterial whether that result is effected by rules specifically stated in the trust instrument, or, in their absence, by the rules for the management of the trust property and the allocation of receipts and expenditures supplied by the State law. For example, a provision in the trust instrument for amortization of bond premium by appropriate periodic charges to interest will not disqualify the interest passing in trust even though there is no State law specifically authorizing amortization, or there is a State law denying amortization which is applicable only in the absence of such a provision in the trust instrument.

(3) In the case of a trust, the rules to be applied by the trustee in allocation of receipts and expenses between income and corpus must be considered in relation to the nature and expected productivity of the assets passing in trust, the nature and frequency of occurrence of the expected receipts, and any provisions as to change in the form of investments. If it is evident from the nature of the trust assets and the

rules provided for management of the trust that the allocation to income of such receipts as rents, ordinary cash dividends, and interest will give to the spouse the substantial enjoyment during life required by the statute, provisions that such receipts as stock dividends and proceeds from the conversion of trust assets shall be treated as corpus will not disqualify the interest passing in trust. Similarly, provision for a depletion charge against income in the case of trust assets which are subject to depletion will not disqualify the interest passing in trust, unless the effect is to deprive the spouse of the requisite beneficial enjoyment. The same principle is applicable in the case of deprecia tion, trustees' commissions, and other charges.

(4) Provisions granting administrative powers to the trustee will not have the effect of disqualifying an interest passing in trust unless the grant of powers evidences the intention to deprive the surviving spouse of the beneficial enjoyment required by the statute. Such an intention will not be considered to exist if the entire terms of the instrument are such that the local courts will impose reasonable limitations upon the exercise of the powers. Among the powers which if subject to reasonable limitations will not disqualify the interest passing in trust are the power to determine the allocation or apportionment of receipts and disbursements between income and corpus, the power to apply the income or corpus for the benefit of the spouse, and the power to retain the assets passing to the trust. For example, a power to retain trust assets which consist substantially of unproductive property will not disqualify the interest if the applicable rules for the administration of the trust require, or permit the spouse to require, that the trustee either make the property productive or convert it within a reasonable time. Nor will such a power disqualify the interest if the applicable rules for administration of the trust require the trustee to use the degree of judgment and care in the exercise of the power which a prudent man would use if he were owner of the trust assets. Further, a power to retain a residence or other property for the personal use of the spouse will not disqualify the interest passing in trust.

(5) An interest passing in trust will not satisfy the condition set forth in paragraph (a)(1) of this section that the surviving spouse be entitled to all the income if the primary purpose of the trust is to safeguard property without providing the spouse with the required beneficial enjoyment. Such trusts include not only trusts which expressly provide for the accumulation of the income but also trusts which indirectly accomplish a similar purpose. For example, assume that the corpus of a trust consists substantially of property which is not likely to be income producing during the life of the surviving spouse and that the spouse cannot compel the trustee to convert or otherwise deal with the property as described in subparagraph (4) of this paragraph. An interest passing to such a trust will not qualify unless the applicable rules for the administration require, or permit the spouse to require, that the trustee provide the required beneficial enjoyment, such as by payments to the spouse out of other assets of the trust.

(6) If a trust is created during the decedent's life, it is immaterial whether or not the interest passing in trust satisfied the conditions set forth in paragraph (a)(1) through (5) of this section prior to the decedent's death. If a trust may be terminated during the life of the surviving spouse, under her exercise of a power of appointment or by distribution of the corpus to her, the interest passing in trust satisfies the condition set forth in paragraph (a)(1) of this section (that the spouse be entitled to all the income) if she (i) is entitled to the income until the trust terminates, or (ii) has the right, exercisable in all events, to have the corpus distributed to her at any time during her life.

(7) An interest passing in trust fails to satisfy the condition set forth in paragraph (a)(1) of this section, that the spouse be entitled to all the income, to the extent that the income is required to be accumulated in whole or in part or may be accumulated in the discretion of any person other than the surviving spouse; to the extent that the consent of any person other than the surviving spouse is required as a condition precedent to distribution of the income; or to the extent that any person other than the surviving spouse has the power to alter the terms of the trust so as to deprive her of her right to the income. An interest passing in trust will not fail to satisfy the condition that the spouse be entitled to all the income merely because its terms provide that the right of the surviving spouse to the income shall not be subject to assignment, alienation, pledge, attachment or claims of creditors.

(8) In the case of an interest passing in trust, the terms "entitled for life" and "payable annually or at more frequent intervals", as used in the conditions set forth in paragraph (a)(1) and (2) of this section, require that under the terms of the trust the income referred to must be currently (at least annually; see paragraph (e) of this section) distributable to the spouse or that she must have such command over the income that it is virtually hers. Thus, the conditions in paragraph (a)(1) and (2) of this section are satisfied in this respect if, under the terms of the trust instrument, the spouse has the right exercisable annually (or more frequently) to require distribution

to herself of the trust income, and otherwise the trust income is to be accumulated and added to corpus. Similarly, as respects the income for the period between the last distribution date and the date of the spouse's death, it is sufficient if that income is subject to the spouse's power to appoint. Thus, if the trust instrument provides that income accrued or undistributed on the date of the spouse's death is to be disposed of as if it had been received after her death, and if the spouse has a power of appointment over the trust corpus, the power necessarily extends to the undistributed income.

(9) An interest is not to be regarded as failing to satisfy the conditions set forth in paragraph (a)(1) and (2) of this section (that the spouse be entitled to all the income and that it be payable annually or more frequently) merely because the spouse is not entitled to the income from estate assets for the period before distribution of those assets by the executor, unless the executor is, by the decedent's will, authorized or directed to delay distribution beyond the period reasonably required for administration of the decedent's estate. As to the valuation of the property interest passing to the spouse in trust where the right to income is expressly postponed, see § 20.2056(b)-4.

(g) *Power of appointment in surviving spouse.*—(1) The conditions set forth in paragraph (a)(3) and (4) of this section, that is, that the surviving spouse must have a power of appointment exercisable in favor of herself or her estate and exercisable alone and in all events, are not met unless the power of the surviving spouse to appoint the entire interest or a specific portion of it falls within one of the following categories:

(i) A power so to appoint fully exercisable in her own favor at any time following the decedent's death (as, for example, an unlimited power to invade); or

(ii) A power so to appoint exercisable in favor of her estate. Such a power, if exercisable during life, must be fully exercisable at any time during life, or, if exercisable by will, must be fully exercisable irrespective of the time of her death (subject in either case to the provisions of § 20.2056(b)-3, relating to interests condi tioned on survival for a limited period); or

(iii) A combination of the powers described under subparagraphs (i) and (ii) of this subparagraph. For example, the surviving spouse may, until she attains the age of 50 years, have a power to appoint to herself and thereafter have a power to appoint to her estate. However, the condition that the spouse's power must be exercisable in all events is not satisfied unless irrespective of when the surviving spouse may die the entire interest or a specific portion of it will at the time of her death be subject to one power or the other (subject to the exception in § 20.2056(b)-3, relating to interests contingent on survival for a limited period).

(2) The power of the surviving spouse must be a power to appoint the entire interest or a specific portion of it as unqualified owner (and free of the trust if a trust is involved, or free of the joint tenancy if a joint tenancy is involved) or to appoint the entire interest or a specific portion of it as a part of her estate (and free of the trust if a trust is involved), that is, in effect, to dispose of it to whomsoever she pleases. Thus, if the decedent devised property to a son and the surviving spouse as joint tenants with right of survivorship and under local law the surviving spouse has a power of severance exercisable without consent of the other joint tenant, and by exercising this power could acquire a one-half interest in the property as a tenant in common, her power of severance will satisfy the condition set forth in paragraph (a)(3) of this section that she have a power of appointment in favor of herself or her estate. However, if the surviving spouse entered into a binding agreement with the decedent to exercise the power only in favor of their issue, that condition is not met. An interest passing in trust will not be regarded as failing to satisfy the condition merely because takers in default of the surviving spouse's exercise of the power are designated by the decedent. The decedent may provide that, in default of exercise of the power, the trust shall continue for an additional period.

(3) A power is not considered to be a power exercisable by a surviving spouse alone and in all events as required by paragraph (a)(4) of this section if the exercise of the power in the surviving spouse to appoint the entire interest or a specific portion of it to herself or to her estate requires the joinder or consent of any other person. The power is not "exercisable in all events", if it can be terminated during the life of the surviving spouse by any event other than her complete exercise or release of it. Further, a power is not "exercisable in all events" if it may be exercised for a limited purpose only. For example, a power which is not exercisable in the event of the spouse's remarriage is not exercisable in all events. Likewise, if there are any restrictions, either by the terms of the instrument or under applicable local law, on the exercise of a power to consume property (whether or not held in trust) for the benefit of the spouse, the power is not exercisable in all events. Thus, if a power of invasion is exercisable only for the spouse's support, or only for her limited use, the power is not exercisable in all events. In order for a power of

invasion to be exercisable in all events, the surviving spouse must have the unrestricted power exercisable at any time during her life to use all or any part of the property subject to the power, and to dispose of it in any manner, including the power to dispose of it by gift (whether or not she has power to dispose of it by will).

(4) The power in the surviving spouse is exercisable in all events only if it exists immediately following the decedent's death. For example, if the power given to the surviving spouse is exercisable during life, but cannot be effectively exercised before distribution of the assets by the executor, the power is not exercisable in all events. Similarly, if the power is exercisable by will, but cannot be effectively exercised in the event the surviving spouse dies before distribution of the assets by the executor, the power is not exercisable in all events. However, an interest will not be disqualified by the mere fact that, in the event the power is exercised during administration of the estate, distribution of the property to the appointee will be delayed for the period of administration. If the power is in existence at all times following the decedent's death, limitations of a formal nature will not disqualify an interest. Examples of formal limitations on a power exercisable during life are requirements that an exercise must be in a particular form, that it must be filed with a trustee during the spouse's life, that reasonable notice must be given, or that reasonable intervals must elapse between successive partial exercises. Examples of formal limitations on a power exercisable by will are that it must be exercised by a will executed by the surviving spouse after the decedent's death or that exercise must be by specific reference to the power.

(5) If the surviving spouse has the requisite power to appoint to herself or her estate, it is immaterial that she also has one or more lesser powers. Thus, if she has a testamentary power to appoint to her estate, she may also have a limited power of withdrawal or of appointment during her life. Similarly, if she has an unlimited power of withdrawal, she may have a limited testamentary power.

(h) *Requirement of survival for a limited period.*—A power of appointment in the surviving spouse will not be treated as failing to meet the requirements of paragraph (a)(3) of this section even though the power may terminate, if the only conditions which would cause the termination are those described in paragraph (a) of §20.2056(b)-3, and if those conditions do not in fact occur. Thus, the entire interest or a specific portion of it will not be disqualified by reason of the fact that the exercise of the power in the spouse is subject to a condition of survivorship described in §20.2056(b)-3 if the terms of the condition, that is, the survivorship of the surviving spouse, or the failure to die in a common disaster, are fulfilled.

(i) [Reserved].

(j) *Existence of a power in another.*—Paragraph (a)(5) of this section provides that a transfer described in paragraph (a) is nondeductible to the extent that the decedent created a power in the trustee or in any other person to appoint a part of the interest to any person other than the surviving spouse. However, only powers in other persons which are in opposition to that of the surviving spouse will cause a portion of the interest to fail to satisfy the condition set forth in paragraph (a)(5) of this section. Thus, a power in a trustee to distribute corpus to or for the benefit of a surviving spouse will not disqualify the trust. Similarly, a power to distribute corpus to the spouse for the support of minor children will not disqualify the trust if she is legally obligated to support such children. The application of this paragraph may be illustrated by the following examples:

*Example (1).* Assume that a decedent created a trust, designating his surviving spouse as income beneficiary for life with an unrestricted power in the spouse to appoint the corpus during her life. The decedent further provided that in the event the surviving spouse should die without having exercised the power, the trust should continue for the life of his son with a power in the son to appoint the corpus. Since the power in the son could become exercisable only after the death of the surviving spouse, the interest is not regarded as failing to satisfy the condition set forth in paragraph (a)(5) of this section.

*Example (2).* Assume that the decedent created a trust, designating his surviving spouse as income beneficiary for life and as donee of a power to appoint by will the entire corpus. The decedent further provided that the trustee could distribute 30 percent of the corpus to the decedent's son when he reached the age of 35 years. Since the trustee has a power to appoint 30 percent of the entire interest for the benefit of a person other than the surviving spouse, only 70 percent of the interest placed in trust satisfied the condition set forth in paragraph (a)(5) of this section. If, in this case, the surviving spouse had a power, exercisable by her will, to appoint only one-half of the corpus as it was constituted at the time of her death, it should be noted that only 35 percent of the interest placed in the trust would satisfy the condition set forth in paragraph (a)(3) of this section. [Reg. §20.2056(b)-5.]

☐ [*T.D.* 6296, 6-23-58. *Amended by T.D.* 8522, 2-28-94 *and T.D.* 9102, 12-30-2003.]

**[Reg. §20.2056(b)-6]**

**§20.2056(b)-6. Marital deduction; life insurance or annuity payments with power of appointment in surviving spouse.**—(a) *In general.*—Section 2056(b)(6) provides that an interest in property passing from a decedent to his surviving spouse, which consists of proceeds held by an insurer under the terms of a life insurance, endowment, or annuity contract, is a "deductible interest" to the extent that it satisfied all five of the following conditions (see paragraph (b) of this section if one or more of the conditions is satisfied as to only a portion of the proceeds):

(1) The proceeds, or a specific portion of the proceeds, must be held by the insurer subject to an agreement either to pay the entire proceeds or a specific portion thereof in installments, or to pay interest thereon, and all or a specific portion of the installments or interest payable during the life of the surviving spouse must be payable only to her.

(2) The installments or interest payable to the surviving spouse must be payable annually, or more frequently, commencing not later than 13 months after the decedent's death.

(3) The surviving spouse must have the power to appoint all or a specific portion of the amounts so held by the insurer to either herself or her estate.

(4) The power in the surviving spouse must be exercisable by her alone and (whether exercisable by will or during life) must be exercisable in all events.

(5) The amounts or the specific portion of the amounts payable under such contract must not be subject to a power in any other person to appoint any part thereof to any person other than the surviving spouse.

(b) *Specific portion; deductible interest.*—If the right to receive interest or installment payments or the power of appointment passing to the surviving spouse pertains only to a specific portion of the proceeds held by the insurer, the marital deduction is allowed only to the extent that the rights of the surviving spouse in the specific portion meet the five conditions described in paragraph (a) of this section. While the rights to interest, or to receive payment in installments, and the power must coexist as to the proceeds of the same contract, it is not necessary that the rights to each be in the same proportion. If the rights to interest meeting the required conditions set forth in paragraph (a)(1) and (2) of this section extend over a smaller share of the proceeds than the share with respect to which the power of appointment requirements set forth in paragraph (a)(3) through (5) of this section are satisfied, the deductible interest is limited to the smaller share. Similarly, if the portion of the proceeds payable in installments is a smaller portion of the proceeds than the portion to which the power of appointment meeting such requirements relates, the deduction is limited to the smaller portion. In addition, if a power of appointment meeting all the requirements extends to a smaller portion of the proceeds than the portion over which the interest or installment rights pertain, the deductible interest cannot exceed the value of the portion to which such power of appointment applies. Thus, if the contract provides that the insurer is to retain the entire proceeds and pay all of the interest thereon annually to the surviving spouse and if the surviving spouse has a power of appointment meeting the specifications prescribed in paragraph (a)(3) through (5) of this section, as to only one-half of the proceeds held, then only one-half of the proceeds may be treated as a deductible interest. Correspondingly, if the rights of the spouse to receive installment payments or interest satisfying the requirements extend to only one-fourth of the proceeds and a testamentary power of appointment satisfying the requirements of paragraph (a)(3) through (5) of this section extends to all of the proceeds, then only one-fourth of the proceeds qualifies as a deductible interest. Further, if the surviving spouse has no right to installment payments (or interest) over any portion of the proceeds but a testamentary power of appointment which meets the necessary conditions over the entire remaining proceeds, then none of the proceeds qualifies for the deduction. In addition, if, from the time of the decedent's death, the surviving spouse has a power of appointment meeting all of the required conditions over three-fourths of the proceeds and the right to receive interest from the entire proceeds, but with a power in another person to appoint one-half of the entire proceeds, the value of the interest in the surviving spouse over only one-half of the proceeds will qualify as a deductible interest.

(c) *Applicable principles.*—(1) The principles set forth in paragraph (c) of §20.2056(b)-5 for determining what constitutes a "specific portion of the entire interest" for the purpose of section 2056(b)(5) are applicable in determining what constitutes a "specific portion of all such amounts" for the purpose of section 2056(b)(6). However, the interest in the proceeds passing to the surviving spouse will not be disqualified by the fact that the installment payments or interest to which the spouse is entitled or the amount of the proceeds over which the power of appointment is exercisable may be expressed in terms of a specific sum rather than a fraction or a percentage of the proceeds provided it is shown that such sums are a definite or fixed percentage or fraction of the total proceeds.

(2) The provisions of paragraph (a) of this section are applicable with respect to a property interest which passed from the decedent in the form of proceeds of a policy of insurance upon the decedent's life, a policy of insurance upon the life of a person who predeceased the decedent, a matured endowment policy, or an annuity contract, but only in case the proceeds are to be held by the insurer. With respect to proceeds under any such contract which are to be held by a trustee, with power of appointment in the surviving spouse, see §20.2056(b)-5. As to the treatment of proceeds not meeting the requirements of §20.2056(b)-5 or of this section, see §20.2056(a)-2.

(3) In the case of a contract under which payments by the insurer commenced during the decedent's life, it is immaterial whether or not the conditions in subparagraphs (1) through (5) of paragraph (a) of this section were satisfied prior to the decedent's death.

(d) *Payments of installments or interest.*—The conditions in subparagraphs (1) and (2) of paragraph (a) of this section relative to the payments of installments or interest to the surviving spouse are satisfied if, under the terms of the contract, the spouse has the right exercisable annually (or more frequently) to require distribution to herself of installments of the proceeds or a specific portion thereof, as the case may be, and otherwise such proceeds or interest are to be accumulated and held by the insurer pursuant to the terms of the contract. A contract which otherwise requires the insurer to make annual or more frequent payments to the surviving spouse following the decedent's death, will not be disqualified merely because the surviving spouse must comply with certain formalities in order to obtain the first payment. For example, the contract may satisfy the conditions in subparagraphs (1) and (2) of paragraph (a) of this section even though it requires the surviving spouse to furnish proof of death before the first payment is made. The condition in paragraph (a)(1) of this section is satisfied where interest on the proceeds or a specific portion thereof is payable, annually or more frequently, for a term, or until the occurrence of a specified event, following which the proceeds or a specific portion thereof are to be paid in annual or more frequent installments.

(e) *Powers of appointment.*—(1) In determining whether the terms of the contract satisfy the conditions in subparagraph (3), (4), or (5) of paragraph (a) of this section relating to a power of appointment in the surviving spouse or any other person, the principles stated in §20.2056(b)-5 are applicable. As stated in §20.2056(b)-5, the surviving spouse's power to appoint is "exercisable in all events" only if it is in existence immediately following the decedent's death, subject, however, to the operation of §20.2056(b)-3 relating to interests conditioned on survival for a limited period.

(2) For examples of formal limitations on the power which will not disqualify the contract, see paragraph (g)(4) of §20.2056(b)-5. If the power is exercisable from the moment of the decedent's death, the contract is not disqualified merely because the insurer may require proof of the decedent's death as a condition to making payment to the appointee. If the submission of proof of the decedent's death is a condition to the exercise of the power, the power will not be considered "exercisable in all events" unless in the event the surviving spouse had died immediately following the decedent, her power to appoint would have been considered to exist at the time of her death, within the meaning of section 2041(a)(2). See paragraph (b) of §20.2041-3.

(3) It is sufficient for the purposes of the condition in paragraph (a)(3) of this section that the surviving spouse have the power to appoint amounts held by the insurer to herself or her estate if the surviving spouse has the unqualified power, exercisable in favor of herself or her estate, to appoint amounts held by the insurer which are payable after her death. Such power to appoint need not extend to installments or interest which will be paid to the spouse during her life. Further, the power to appoint need not be a power to require payment in a single sum. For example, if the proceeds of a policy are payable in installments, and if the surviving spouse has the power to direct that all installments payable after her death be paid to her estate, she has the requisite power.

(4) It is not necessary that the phrase "power to appoint" be used in the contract. For example, the condition in paragraph (a)(3) of this section that the surviving spouse have the power to appoint amounts held by the insurer to herself or her estate is satisfied by terms of a contract which give the surviving spouse a right which is, in substance and effect, a power to appoint to herself or her estate, such as a right to withdraw the amount remaining in the fund held by the insurer, or a right to direct that any amount held by the

insurer under the contract at her death shall be paid to her estate. [Reg. §20.2056(b)-6.]

☐ [*T.D.* 6296, 6-23-58.]

**[Reg. §20.2056(b)-7]**

**§20.2056(b)-7. Election with respect to life estate for surviving spouse.**—(a) *In general.*—Subject to section 2056(d), a marital deduction is allowed under section 2056(b)(7) with respect to estates of decedents dying after December 31, 1981, for qualified terminable interest property as defined in paragraph (b) of this section. All of the property for which a deduction is allowed under this paragraph (a) is treated as passing to the surviving spouse (for purposes of §20.2056(a)-1), and no part of the property is treated as passing to any person other than the surviving spouse (for purposes of §20.2056(b)-1).

(b) *Qualified terminable interest property.*—(1) *In general.*—Section 2056(b)(7)(B)(i) provides the definition of *qualified terminable interest property.*

(i) Terminable interests described in section 2056(b)(1)(C) cannot qualify as qualified terminable interest property. Thus, if the decedent directs the executor to purchase a terminable interest with estate assets, the terminable interest acquired will not qualify as qualified terminable interest property.

(ii) For purposes of section 2056(b)(7)(B)(i), the term *property* generally means the *entire interest in property* (within the meaning of §20.2056(b)-5(d)) or a *specific portion of the entire interest* (within the meaning of §20.2056(b)-5(c)).

(2) *Property for which an election may be made.*—(i) *In general.*—The election may relate to all or any part of property that meets the requirements of section 2056(b)(7)(B)(i), provided that any partial election must be made with respect to a fractional or percentage share of the property so that the elective portion reflects its proportionate share of the increase or decrease in value of the entire property for purposes of applying sections 2044 or 2519. The fraction or percentage may be defined by formula.

(ii) *Division of trusts.*—(A) *In general.*—A trust may be divided into separate trusts to reflect a partial election that has been made, or is to be made, if authorized under the governing instrument or otherwise permissible under local law. Any such division must be accomplished no later than the end of the period of estate administration. If, at the time of the filing of the estate tax return, the trust has not yet been divided, the intent to divide the trust must be unequivocally signified on the estate tax return.

(B) *Manner of dividing and funding trust.*—The division of the trust must be done on a fractional or percentage basis to reflect the partial election. However, the separate trusts do not have to be funded with a pro rata portion of each asset held by the undivided trust.

(C) *Local law.*—A trust may be divided only if the fiduciary is required, either by applicable local law or by the express or implied provisions of the governing instrument, to divide the trust on the basis of the fair market value of the assets of the trust at the time of the division.

(3) *Persons permitted to make the election.*—The election referred to in section 2056(b)(7)(B)(i)(III) must be made by the executor that is appointed, qualified, and acting within the United States, within the meaning of section 2203, regardless of whether the property with respect to which the election is to be made is in the executor's possession. If there is no executor appointed, qualified, and acting within the United States, the election may be made by any person with respect to property in the actual or constructive possession of that person and may also be made by that person with respect to other property not in the actual or constructive possession of that person if the person in actual or constructive possession of such other property does not make the election. For example, in the absence of an appointed executor, the trustee of an intervivos trust (that is included in the gross estate of the decedent) can make the election.

(4) *Manner and time of making the election.*—(i) *In general.*—The election referred to in section 2056(b)(7)(B)(i)(III) and (v) is made on the return of tax imposed by section 2001 (or section 2101). For purposes of this paragraph, the term *return of tax imposed by section 2001* means the last estate tax return filed by the executor on or before the due date of the return, including extensions or, if a timely return is not filed, the first estate tax return filed by the executor after the due date.

(ii) *Election irrevocable.*—The election, once made, is irrevocable, provided that an election may be revoked or modified on a subsequent return filed on or before the due date of the return, including extensions actually granted. If an executor appointed under local law has made an election on the return of tax imposed by section 2001 (or section 2101) with respect to one or more properties, no subsequent election may be made with respect to other properties included in the gross estate after the return of tax imposed by section 2001 is filed. An election under section 2056(b)(7)(B)(v) is separate from any elections made under section 2056A(a)(3).

(c) *Protective elections.*—(1) *In general.*—A protective election may be made to treat property as qualified terminable interest property only if, at the time the federal estate tax return is filed, the executor of the decedent's estate reasonably believes that there is a bona fide issue that concerns whether an asset is includible in the decedent's gross estate, or the amount or nature of the property the surviving spouse is entitled to receive, i.e., whether property that is includible is eligible for the qualified terminable interest property election. The protective election must identify either the specific asset, group of assets, or trust to which the election applies and the specific basis for the protective election.

(2) *Protective election irrevocable.*—The protective election, once made on the return of tax imposed by section 2001, cannot be revoked. For example, if a protective election is made on the basis that a bona fide question exists regarding the inclusion of a trust corpus in the gross estate and it is later determined that the trust corpus is so includible, the protective election becomes effective with respect to the trust corpus and cannot thereafter be revoked.

(d) *Qualifying income interest for life.*—(1) *In general.*—Section 2056(b)(7)(B)(ii) provides the definition of *qualifying income interest for life.* For purposes of section 2056(b)(7)(B)(ii)(II), the surviving spouse is included within the prohibited class of powerholders referred to therein. A power under applicable local law that permits the trustee to adjust between income and principal to fulfill the trustee's duty of impartiality between the income and remainder beneficiaries that meets the requirements of §1.643(b)-1 of this chapter will not be considered a power to appoint trust property to a person other than the surviving spouse.

(2) *Entitled for life to all income.*—The principles of §20.2056(b)-5(f), relating to whether the spouse is entitled for life to all of the income from the entire interest, or a specific portion of the entire interest, apply in determining whether the surviving spouse is entitled for life to all of the income from the property regardless of whether the interest passing to the spouse is in trust.

(3) *Contingent income interests.*—(i) An income interest for a term of years, or a life estate subject to termination upon the occurrence of a specified event (e.g., remarriage), is not a qualifying income interest for life. However, a qualifying income interest for life that is contingent upon the executor's election under section 2056(b)(7)(B)(v) will not fail to be a qualifying income interest for life because of such contingency or because the portion of the property for which the election is not made passes to or for the benefit of persons other than the surviving spouse. This paragraph (d)(3)(i) applies with respect to estates of decedents whose estate tax returns are due after February 18, 1997. This paragraph (d)(3)(i) also applies to estates of decedents whose estate tax returns were due on or before February 18, 1997, that meet the requirements of paragraph (d)(3)(ii) of this section.

(ii) Estates of decedents whose estate tax returns were due on or before February 18, 1997, that did not make the election under section 2056(b)(7)(B)(v) because the surviving spouse's income interest in the property was contingent upon the election or because the nonelected portion of the property was to pass to a beneficiary other than the surviving spouse are granted an extension of time to make the QTIP election if the following requirements are satisfied:

(A) The period of limitations on filing a claim for credit or refund under section 6511(a) has not expired.

(B) A claim for credit or refund is filed on Form 843 with a revised Recapitulation and Schedule M, Form 706 (or 706NA) that signifies the QTIP election. Reference to this section should be made on the Form 843.

(C) The following statement is included with the Form 843: "The undersigned certifies that the property with respect to which the QTIP election is being made will be included in the gross estate of the surviving spouse as provided in section 2044 of the Internal Revenue Code, in determining the federal estate tax liability on the spouse's death." The statement must be signed, under penalties of perjury, by the surviving spouse, the surviving spouse's legal representative (if the surviving spouse is legally incompetent), or the surviving spouse's executor (if the surviving spouse is deceased).

(4) *Income between last distribution date and date of spouse's death.*—An income interest does not fail to constitute a qualifying income interest for life solely because income between the last distribution date and the date of the surviving spouse's death is not required to be distributed to the surviving spouse or to the estate of the surviv-

ing spouse. See §20.2044-1 relating to the inclusion of such undistributed income in the gross estate of the surviving spouse.

(5) *Pooled income funds.*—An income interest in a pooled income fund described in section 642(c)(5) constitutes a qualifying income interest for life for purposes of section 2056(b)(7)(B)(ii).

(6) *Power to distribute principal to spouse.*—An income interest in a trust will not fail to constitute a qualifying income interest for life solely because the trustee has a power to distribute principal to or for the benefit of the surviving spouse. The fact that property distributed to a surviving spouse may be transferred by the spouse to another person does not result in a failure to satisfy the requirement of section 2056(b)(7)(B)(ii)(II). However, if the surviving spouse is legally bound to transfer the distributed property to another person without full and adequate consideration in money or money's worth, the requirement of section 2056(b)(7)(B)(ii)(II) is not satisfied.

(e) *Annuities payable from trusts in the case of estates of decedents dying on or before October 24, 1992, and certain decedents dying after October 24, 1992, with wills or revocable trusts executed on or prior to that date.*—(1) *In general.*—In the case of estates of decedents within the purview of the effective date and transitional rules contained in §20.2056(b)-7(e)(5), a surviving spouse's lifetime annuity interest payable from a trust or other group of assets passing from the decedent is treated as a qualifying income interest for life for purposes of section 2056(b)(7)(B)(ii).

(2) *Deductible interest.*—The deductible interest, for purposes of §20.2056(a)-2(b), is the specific portion of the property that, assuming the applicable interest rate for valuing annuities, would produce income equal to the minimum amount payable annually to the surviving spouse. If, based on the applicable interest rate, the entire property from which the annuity may be satisfied is insufficient to produce income equal to the minimum annual payment, the value of the deductible interest is the entire value of the property. The value of the deductible interest may not exceed the value of the property from which the annuity is payable. If the annual payment may increase, the increased amount is not taken into account in valuing the deductible interest.

(3) *Distributions permissible only to surviving spouse.*—An annuity interest is not treated as a qualifying income interest for life for purposes of section 2056(b)(7)(B)(ii) if any person other than the surviving spouse may receive, during the surviving spouse's lifetime, any distribution of the property or its income (including any distribution under an annuity contract) from which the annuity is payable.

(4) *Applicable interest rate.*—To determine the applicable interest rate for valuing annuities, see sections 2031 and 7520 and the regulations under those sections.

(5) *Effective dates.*—(i) The rules contained in §20.2056(b)-7(e) apply with respect to estates of decedents dying on or before October 24, 1992.

(ii) The rules contained in §20.2056(b)-7(e) apply in the case of decedents dying after October 24, 1992, if property passes to the spouse pursuant to a will or revocable trust executed on or before October 24, 1992, and either—

(A) On that date, the decedent was under a mental disability to change the disposition of his property and did not regain his competence to dispose of such property before the date of death; or

(B) The decedent dies prior to October 24, 1995.

(iii) Notwithstanding the foregoing, the rules contained in §20.2056(b)-7(e) do not apply if the will or revocable trust is amended after October 24, 1992, in any respect that increases the amount of the transfer qualifying for the marital deduction or alters the terms by which the interest so passes to the surviving spouse.

(f) *Joint and survivor annuities.*—[Reserved]

(g) *Application of local law.*—The provisions of local law are taken into account in determining whether the conditions of section 2056(b)(7)(B)(ii)(I) are satisfied. For example, silence of a trust instrument as to the frequency of payment is not regarded as a failure to satisfy the requirement that the income must be payable to the surviving spouse annually or more frequently unless applicable local law permits payments less frequently.

(h) *Examples.*—The following examples illustrate the application of paragraphs (a) through (g) of this section. In each example, it is assumed that the decedent, D, was survived by S, D's spouse and that, unless stated otherwise, S is not the trustee of any trust established for S's benefit.

*Example 1. Life estate in residence.* D owned a personal residence valued at $250,000 for estate tax purposes. Under D's will, the exclusive and unrestricted right to use the residence (including the right to continue to occupy the property as a personal residence or to rent the property and receive the income) passes to S for life. At S's death, the property passes to D's children. Under applicable local law, S must consent to any sale of the property. If the executor elects to treat all of the personal residence as qualified terminable interest property, the deductible interest is $250,000, the value of the residence for estate tax purposes.

*Example 2. Power to make property productive.* D's will established a trust funded with property valued for estate tax purposes at $500,000. The assets include both income producing assets and non-productive assets. S was given the power, exercisable annually, to require distribution of all of the trust income to herself. No trust property may be distributed during S's lifetime to any person other than S. Applicable local law permits S to require that the trustee either make the trust property productive or sell the property and reinvest in productive property within a reasonable time after D's death. If the executor elects to treat all of the trust as qualified terminable interest property, the deductible interest is $500,000. If the executor elects to treat only 20 percent of the trust as qualified terminable interest property, the deductible interest is $100,000, i.e., 20 percent of $500,000.

*Example 3. Power of distribution over fraction of trust income.* The facts are the same as in *Example 2* except that S is given the right exercisable annually for S's lifetime to require distribution to herself of only 50 percent of the trust income for life. The remaining trust income is to be accumulated or distributed among S and the decedent's children in the trustee's discretion. The maximum amount that D's executor may elect to treat as qualified terminable interest property is $250,000; i.e., the estate tax value of the trust ($500,000) multiplied by the percentage of the trust in which S has a qualifying income interest for life (50 percent). If D's executor elects to treat only 20 percent of the portion of the trust in which S has a qualifying income interest as qualified terminable interest property, the deductible interest is $50,000, i.e., 20 percent of $250,000.

*Example 4. Power to distribute trust corpus to other beneficiaries.* D's will established a trust providing that S is entitled to receive at least annually all the trust income. The trustee is given the power to use annually during S's lifetime $5,000 from the trust for the maintenance and support of S's minor child, C. Any such distribution does not necessarily relieve S of S's obligation to support and maintain C. S does not have a qualifying income interest for life in any portion of the trust because the bequest fails to satisfy the condition that no person have a power, other than a power the exercise of which takes effect only at or after S's death, to appoint any part of the property to any person other than S. The trust would also be nondeductible under section 2056(b)(7) if S, rather than the trustee, held the power to appoint a portion of the principal to C. However, in the latter case, if S made a qualified disclaimer (within the meaning of section 2518) of the power to appoint to C, the trust could qualify for the marital deduction pursuant to section 2056(b)(7), assuming that the power is personal to S and S's disclaimer terminates the power. Similarly, in either case, if C made a qualified disclaimer of C's right to receive distributions from the trust, the trust would qualify under section 2056(b)(7), assuming that C's disclaimer effectively negates the trustee's power under local law.

*Example 5. Spouse's income interest terminable on remarriage.* D's will established a trust providing that all of the trust income is payable at least annually to S for S's lifetime, provided that, if S remarries, S's interest in the trust will pass to X. The trust is not deductible under section 2056(b)(7). S's income interest is not a *qualifying income interest for life* because it is not for life but, rather, is terminable upon S's remarriage.

*Example 6. Spouse's qualifying income interest for life contingent on executor's election.* D's will established a trust providing that S is entitled to receive the income, payable at least annually, from that portion of the trust that the executor elects to treat as qualified terminable interest property. The portion of the trust which the executor does not elect to treat as qualified terminable interest property passes as of D's date of death to a trust for the benefit of C, D's child. Under these facts, the executor is not considered to have a power to appoint any part of the trust property to any person other than S during S's life.

*Example 7. Formula partial election.* D's will established a trust funded with the residue of D's estate. Trust income is to be paid annually to S for life, and the principal is to be distributed to D's children upon S's death. S has the power to require that all the trust property be made productive. There is no power to distribute trust property during S's lifetime to any person other than S. D's executor elects to deduct a fractional share of the residuary estate under section 2056(b)(7). The election specifies that the numerator of the fraction is the amount of deduction necessary to reduce the Federal estate tax to zero (taking into account final estate tax values) and the denominator of the fraction is the final estate tax value of the residuary estate (taking into account any specific bequests or liabilities of the estate paid out of the residuary estate). The formula election is of a fractional share. The value of the share qualifies for the marital

deduction even though the executor's determinations to claim administration expenses as estate or income tax deductions and the final estate tax values will affect the size of the fractional share.

*Example 8. Formula partial election.* The facts are the same as in *Example 7* except that, rather than defining a fraction, the executor's formula states: "I elect to treat as qualified terminable interest property that portion of the residuary trust, up to 100 percent, necessary to reduce the Federal estate tax to zero, after taking into account the available unified credit, final estate tax values and any liabilities and specific bequests paid from the residuary estate." The formula election is of a fractional share. The share is equivalent to the fractional share determined in *Example 7*.

*Example 9. Severance of QTIP trust.* D's will established a trust funded with the residue of D's estate. Trust income is to be paid annually to S for life, and the principal is to be distributed to D's children upon S's death. S has the power to require that all of the trust property be made productive. There is no power to distribute trust property during S's lifetime to any person other than S. D's will authorizes the executor to make the election under section 2056(b)(7) only with respect to the minimum amount of property necessary to reduce estate taxes on D's estate to zero, authorizes the executor to divide the residuary estate into two separate trusts to reflect the election, and authorizes the executor to charge any payment of principal to S to the qualified terminable interest trust. S is the sole beneficiary of both trusts during S's lifetime. The authorizations in the will do not adversely affect the allowance of the marital deduction. Only the property remaining in the marital deduction trust, after payment of principal to S, is subject to inclusion in S's gross estate under section 2044 or subject to gift tax under section 2519.

*Example 10. Payments to spouse from individual retirement account.* S is the life beneficiary of sixteen remaining annual installments payable from D's individual retirement account. The terms of the account provide for the payment of the account balance in nineteen annual installments that commenced when D reached age 70½. Each installment is equal to all the income earned on the remaining principal in the account plus a share of the remaining principal equal to 1/19 in the first year, 1/18 in the second year, 1/17 in the third year, etc. Under the terms of the account, S has no right to withdraw any other amounts from the account. Any payments remaining after S's death pass to D's children. S's interest in the account qualifies as a qualifying income interest for life under section 2056(b)(7)(B)(ii), without regard to the provisions of section 2056(b)(7)(C).

*Example 11. Spouse's interest in trust in the form of an annuity.* D died prior to October 24, 1992. D's will established a trust funded with income producing property valued at $500,000 for estate tax purposes. The trustee is required by the trust instrument to pay $20,000 a year to S for life. Trust income in excess of the annuity amount is to be accumulated in the trust and may not be distributed during S's lifetime. S's lifetime annuity interest is treated as a qualifying income interest for life. If the executor elects to treat the entire portion of the trust in which S has a qualifying income interest as qualified terminable interest property, the value of the deductible interest is (assuming that 10 percent is the applicable interest rate under section 7520 for valuing annuities on the appropriate valuation date) $200,000, because that amount would yield an income to S of $20,000 a year.

*Example 12. Value of spouse's annuity exceeds value of trust corpus.* The facts are the same as in *Example 11* except that the trustee is required to pay S $70,000 a year for life. If the executor elects to treat the entire portion of the trust in which S has a qualifying income interest as qualified terminable interest property, the value of the deductible interest is $500,000, which is the lesser of the entire value of the property ($500,000), or the amount of property that (assuming a 10 percent interest rate) would yield an income to S of $70,000 a year ($700,000).

*Example 13. Pooled income fund.* D's will provides for a bequest of $200,000 to a pooled income fund described in section 642(c)(5), designating S as the income beneficiary for life. If D's executor elects to treat the entire $200,000 as qualified terminable interest property, the deductible interest is $200,000.

*Example 14. Funding severed QTIP trusts.* D's will established a trust satisfying the requirements of section 2056(b)(7). Pursuant to the authority in D's will and §20.2056(b)-7(b)(2)(ii), D's executor indicates on the Federal estate tax return that an election under section 2056(b)(7) is being made with respect to 50 percent of the trust, and that the trust will subsequently be divided to reflect the partial election on the basis of the fair market value of the property at the time of the division. D's executor funds the trust at the end of the period of estate administration. At that time, the property available to fund the trusts consists of 100 shares of X Corporation stock with a current value of $400,000 and 200 shares of Y Corporation stock with a current value of $400,000. D may fund each trust with the stock of either or both corporations, in any combination, provided that the aggregate value of the stock allocated to each trust is $400,000. [Reg. §20.2056(b)-7.]

☐ [*T.D. 8522, 2-28-94. Amended by T.D. 8779, 8-18-98 and T.D. 9102, 12-30-2003.*]

### [Reg. §20.2056(b)-8]

**§20.2056(b)-8. Special rule for charitable remainder trusts.—** (a) *In general.—*(1) *Surviving spouse only noncharitable beneficiary.—* With respect to estates of decedents dying after December 31, 1981, subject to section 2056(d), if the surviving spouse of the decedent is the only noncharitable beneficiary of a charitable remainder annuity trust or a charitable remainder unitrust described in section 664 (qualified charitable remainder trust), section 2056(b)(1) does not apply to the interest in the trust that is transferred to the surviving spouse. Thus, the value of the annuity or unitrust interest passing to the spouse qualifies for a marital deduction under section 2056(b)(8) and the value of the remainder interest qualifies for a charitable deduction under section 2055. If an interest in property qualifies for a marital deduction under section 2056(b)(8), no election may be made with respect to the property under section 2056(b)(7). For purposes of this section, the term *noncharitable beneficiary* means any beneficiary of the qualified charitable remainder trust other than an organization described in section 170(c).

(2) *Interest for life or term of years.—*The surviving spouse's interest need not be an interest for life to qualify for a marital deduction under section 2056(b)(8). However, for purposes of section 664, an annuity or unitrust interest payable to the spouse for a term of years cannot be payable for a term that exceeds 20 years.

(3) *Payment of state death taxes.—*A deduction is allowed under section 2056(b)(8) even if the transfer to the surviving spouse is conditioned on the spouse's payment of state death taxes, if any, attributable to the qualified charitable remainder trust. See §20.2056(b)-4(c) for the effect of such a condition on the amount of the deduction allowable.

(b) *Charitable remainder trusts where the surviving spouse is not the only noncharitable beneficiary.—*In the case of a charitable remainder trust where the decedent's spouse is not the only noncharitable beneficiary (for example, where the noncharitable interest is payable to the decedent's spouse for life and then to another individual for life), the qualification of the interest as qualified terminable interest property is determined solely under section 2056(b)(7) and not under section 2056(b)(8). Accordingly, if the decedent died on or before October 24, 1992, or the trust otherwise comes within the purview of the transitional rules contained in §20.2056(b)-7(e)(5), the spousal annuity or unitrust interest may qualify under §20.2056(b)-(7)(e) as a qualifying income interest for life. [Reg. §20.2056(b)-8.]

☐ [*T.D. 8522, 2-28-94.*]

### [Reg. §20.2056(b)-9]

**§20.2056(b)-9. Denial of double deduction.—**The value of an interest in property may not be deducted for Federal estate tax purposes more than once with respect to the same decedent. For example, where a decedent transfers a life estate in a farm to the spouse with a remainder to charity, the entire property is, pursuant to the executor's election under section 2056(b)(7), treated as passing to the spouse. The entire value of the property qualifies for the marital deduction. No part of the value of the property qualifies for a charitable deduction under section 2055 in the decedent's estate. [Reg. §20.2056(b)-9.]

☐ [*T.D. 8522, 2-28-94.*]

### [Reg. §20.2056(b)-10]

**§20.2056(b)-10. Effective dates.—**Except as specifically provided in §§20.2056(b)-5(c)(3)(ii) and (iii), 20.2056(b)-7(d)(3), 20.2056(b)-7(e)(5), and 20.2056(b)-8(b), the provisions of §§20.2056(b)-5(c), 20.2056(b)-7, 20.2056(b)-8, and 20.2056(b)-9 are applicable with respect to estates of decedents dying after March 1, 1994. With respect to decedents dying on or before such date, the executor of the decedent's estate may rely on any reasonable interpretation of the statutory provisions. In addition, the rule in the last sentence of §20.2056(b)-5(f)(1) and the rule in the last sentence of §20.2056(b)-7(d)(1) regarding the effect on the spouse's right to income if applicable local law provides for the reasonable apportionment between the income and remainder beneficiaries of the total return of the trust are applicable with respect to trusts for taxable years ending after January 2, 2004. [Reg. §20.2056(b)-10.]

☐ [*T.D. 8522, 2-28-94. Amended by T.D. 8779, 8-18-98 and T.D. 9102, 12-30-2003.*]

### [Reg. §20.2056(c)-1]

**§20.2056(c)-1. Marital deduction; definition of "passed from the decedent".—**(a) *In general.—*The following rules are applicable in determining the person to whom any property interest "passed from the decedent":

(1) Property interests devolving upon any person (or persons) as surviving co-owner with the decedent under any form of joint ownership under which the right of survivorship existed are considered as having passed from the decedent to such person (or persons).

(2) Property interests at any time subject to the decedent's power to appoint (whether alone or in conjunction with any person) are considered as having passed from the decedent to the appointee under his exercise of the power, or, in case of the lapse, release or nonexercise of the power, as having passed from the decedent to the taker in default of exercise.

(3) The dower or curtesy interest (or statutory interest in lieu thereof) of the decedent's surviving spouse is considered as having passed from the decedent to his spouse.

(4) The proceeds of insurance upon the life of the decedent are considered as having passed from the decedent to the person who, at the time of the decedent's death, was entitled to receive the proceeds.

(5) Any property interest transferred during life, bequeathed or devised by the decedent, or inherited from the decedent, is considered as having passed to the person to whom he transferred, bequeathed, or devised the interest, or to the person who inherited the interest from him.

(6) The survivor's interest in an annuity or other payment described in section 2039 (see §§20.2039-1 and 20.2039-2) is considered as having passed from the decedent to the survivor only to the extent that the value of such interest is included in the decedent's gross estate under that section. If only a portion of the entire annuity or other payment is included in the decedent's gross estate and the annuity or other payment is payable to more than one beneficiary, then the value of the interest considered to have passed to each beneficiary is that portion of the amount payable to each beneficiary that the amount of the annuity or other payment included in the decedent's gross estate bears to the total value of the annuity or other payment payable to all beneficiaries.

(b) *Expectant interest in property under community property laws.—*If before the decedent's death the decedent's surviving spouse had merely an expectant interest in property held by her and the decedent under community property laws, that interest is considered as having passed from the decedent to the spouse. [Reg. §20.2056(c)-1.]

☐ [*T.D. 6296, 6-23-58. Redesignated and amended by T.D. 8522, 2-28-94.*]

### [Reg. §20.2056(c)-2]

**§20.2056(c)-2. Marital deduction; definition of "passed from the decedent to his surviving spouse".—**(a) *In general.—*In general, the definition stated in §20.2056(c)-1 is applicable in determining the property interests which "passed from the decedent to his surviving spouse." Special rules are provided, however, for the following:

(1) In the case of certain interests with income for life to the surviving spouse with power of appointment in her (see §20.2056(b)-5);

(2) In the case of certain interests with income for life to the surviving spouse that the executor elects to treat as qualified terminable interest property (see §20.2056(b)-7);

(3) In the case of proceeds held by the insurer under a life insurance, endowment, or annuity contract with power of appointment in the surviving spouse (see §20.2056(b)-6);

(4) In case of the disclaimer of an interest by the surviving spouse or by any other person (see §20.2056(d)-1);

(5) In case of an election by the surviving spouse (see paragraph (c) of this section); and

(6) In case of a controversy involving the decedent's will, see paragraph (d) of this section.

A property interest is considered as passing to the surviving spouse only if it passes to the spouse as beneficial owner, except to the extent otherwise provided in §§20.2056(b)-5 through 20.2056(b)-7 in the case of certain life estates and insurance and annuity contracts with powers of appointment. For this purpose, where a property interest passed from the decedent in trust, such interest is considered to have passed from him to his surviving spouse to the extent of her beneficial interest therein. The deduction may not be taken with respect to a property interest which passed to such spouse merely as trustee, or subject to a binding agreement by the spouse to dispose of the interest in favor of a third person. An allowance or award paid to a surviving spouse pursuant to local law for her support during the administration of the decedent's estate constitutes a property interest passing from the decedent to his surviving spouse. In determining whether or not such an interest is deductible, however, see generally the terminable interest rules of §20.2056(b)-1 and especially example (8) of paragraph (g) of that section.

(b) *Examples.*—The following illustrate the provisions of paragraph (a) of this section:

(1) A property interest bequeathed in trust by H (the decedent) is considered as having passed from him to W (his surviving spouse)—

(i) If the trust income is payable to W for life and upon her death the corpus is distributable to her executors or administrators;

(ii) If W is entitled to the trust income for a term of years following which the corpus is to be paid to W or her estate;

(iii) If the trust income is to be accumulated for a term of years or for W's life and the augmented fund paid to W or her estate; or

(iv) If the terms of the transfer satisfy the requirements of §20.2056(b)-5 or 20.2056(b)-7.

(2) If H devised property—

(i) To A for life with remainder absolutely to W or her estate, the remainder interest is considered to have passed from H to W;

(ii) To W for life with remainder to her estate, the entire property is considered as having passed from H to W; or

(iii) Under conditions which satisfy the provisions of §20.2056(b)-5 or 20.2056(b)-7, the entire property is considered as having passed from H to W.

(3) Proceeds of insurance upon the life of H are considered as having passed from H to W if the terms of the contract—

(i) Meet the requirements of §20.2056(b)-6;

(ii) Provide that the proceeds are payable to W in a lump sum;

(iii) Provide that the proceeds are payable in installments to W for life and after her death any remaining installments are payable to her estate;

(iv) Provide that interest on the proceeds is payable to W for life and upon her death the principal amount is payable to her estate; or

(v) Provide that the proceeds are payable to a trustee under an arrangement whereby the requirements of §2056 (b)(5) or 20.2056(b)-7 are satisfied.

(c) *Effect of election by surviving spouse.*—This paragraph contains rules applicable if the surviving spouse may elect between a property interest offered to her under the decedent's will or other instrument and a property interest to which she is otherwise entitled (such as dower, a right in the decedent's estate, or her interest under community property laws) of which adverse disposition was attempted by the decedent under the will or other instrument. If the surviving spouse elects to take against the will or other instrument, then the property interests offered thereunder are not considered as having "passed from the decedent to his surviving spouse" and the dower or other property interest retained by her is considered as having so passed (if it otherwise so qualifies under this section). If the surviving spouse elects to take under the will or other instrument, then the dower or other property interest relinquished by her is not considered as having "passed from the decedent to his surviving spouse" (irrespective of whether it otherwise comes within the definition stated in paragraph (a) of this section) and the interest taken under the will or other instrument is considered as having so passed (if it otherwise so qualifies). As to the valuation of the property interest taken under the will or other instrument, see paragraph (b) of §20.2056(b)-4.

(d) *Will contests.*—(1) If as a result of a controversy involving the decedent's will, or involving any bequest or devise thereunder, his surviving spouse assigns or surrenders a property interest in settlement of the controversy, the interest so assigned or surrendered is not considered as having "passed from the decedent to his surviving spouse."

(2) If as a result of the controversy involving the decedent's will, or involving any bequest or devise thereunder, a property interest is assigned or surrendered to the surviving spouse, the interest so acquired will be regarded as having "passed from the decedent to his surviving spouse" only if the assignment or surrender was a bona fide recognition of enforceable rights of the surviving spouse in the decedent's estate. Such a bona fide recognition will be presumed where the assignment or surrender was pursuant to a decision of a local court upon the merits in an adversary proceeding following a genuine and active contest. However, such a decree will be accepted only to the extent that the court passed upon the facts upon which deductibility of the property interests depends. If the assignment or surrender was pursuant to a decree rendered by consent, or pursuant to an agreement not to contest the will or not to probate the will, it will not necessarily be accepted as a bona fide evaluation of the rights of the spouse.

(e) *Survivorship.*—If the order of deaths of the decedent and his spouse cannot be established by proof, a presumption (whether supplied by local law, the decedent's will, or otherwise) that the

decedent was survived by his spouse will be recognized as satisfying paragraph (b)(1) of §20.2056(a)-1, but only to the extent that it has the effect of giving to the spouse an interest in property includible in her gross estate under part III of subchapter A of chapter 11. Under these circumstances, if an estate tax return is required to be filed for the estate of the decedent's spouse, the marital deduction will not be allowed in the final audit of the estate tax return of the decedent's estate with respect to any property interest which has not been finally determined to be includible in the gross estate of his spouse. [Reg. §20.2056(c)-2.]

☐ [*T.D.* 6296, 6-23-58. *Redesignated and amended by T.D.* 8522, 2-28-94.]

### [Reg. §20.2056(c)-3]

**§20.2056(c)-3. Marital deduction; definition of "passed from the decedent to a person other than his surviving spouse".**—The expression "passed from the decedent to a person other than his surviving spouse" refers to any property interest which, under the definition stated in §20.2056(c)-1 is considered as having "passed from the decedent" and which under the rules referred to in §20.2056(c)-2 is not considered as having "passed from the decedent to his surviving spouse." Interests which passed to a person other than the surviving spouse include interests so passing under the decedent's exercise, release, or nonexercise of a nontaxable power to appoint. It is immaterial whether the property interest which passed from the decedent to a person other than his surviving spouse is included in the decedent's gross estate. The term "person other than his surviving spouse" includes the possible unascertained takers of a property interest, as, for example, the members of a class to be ascertained in the future. As another example, assume that the decedent created a power of appointment over a property interest, which does not come within the purview of §20.2056(b)-5 or §20.2056(b)-6. In such a case, the term "person other than his surviving spouse" refers to the possible appointees and possible takers in default (other than the spouse) of such property interest. Whether or not there is a possibility that the "person other than his surviving spouse" (or the heirs or assigns of such person) may possess or enjoy the property following termination or failure of the interest therein which passed from the decedent to his surviving spouse is to be determined as of the time of the decedent's death. [Reg. §20.2056(c)-3.]

☐ [*T.D.* 6296, 6-23-58. *Redesignated and amended by T.D.* 8522, 2-28-94.]

### [Reg. §20.2056(d)-1]

**§20.2056(d)-1. Marital deduction; special rules for marital deduction if surviving spouse is not a United States citizen.**—Rules pertaining to the application of section 2056(d), including certain transition rules, are contained in §§20.2056A-1 through 20.2056A-13. [Reg. §20.2056(d)-1.]

☐ [*T.D.* 8612, 8-21-95.]

### [Reg. §20.2056(d)-2]

**§20.2056(d)-2. Marital deduction; effect of disclaimers of post-December 31, 1976 transfers.**—(a) *Disclaimer by a surviving spouse.*—If a surviving spouse disclaims an interest in property passing to such spouse from the decedent, which interest was created in a transfer made after December 31, 1976, the effectiveness of the disclaimer will be determined by section 2518 and the corresponding regulations. For rules relating to when the transfer creating the interest occurs, see §25.2518-2(c)(3) and (c)(4) of this chapter. If a qualified disclaimer is determined to have been made by the surviving spouse, the property interest disclaimed is treated as if such interest had never been transferred to the surviving spouse.

(b) *Disclaimer by a person other than a surviving spouse.*—If an interest in property passes from a decedent to a person other than the surviving spouse, and the interest is created in a transfer made after December 31, 1976, and—

(1) The person other than the surviving spouse makes a qualified disclaimer with respect to such interest; and

(2) The surviving spouse is entitled to such interest in property as a result of such disclaimer, the disclaimed interest is treated as passing directly from the decedent to the surviving spouse. For rules relating to when the transfer creating the interest occurs, see §25.2518-2(c)(3) and (c)(4) of this chapter.

(c) *Effective date.*—The first and second sentences of paragraphs (a) and (b) of this section are applicable for transfers creating the interest to be disclaimed made on or after December 31, 1997. [Reg. §20.2056(d)-2.]

☐ [*T.D.* 6296, 6-23-58. *Amended by T.D.* 8095, 8-6-86. *Redesignated by T.D.* 8612, 8-21-95. *Amended by T.D.* 8744, 12-30-97.]

**[Reg. §20.2056(d)-3]**

**§20.2056(d)-3. Marital deduction; effect of disclaimers of pre-January 1, 1977 transfers.—(a)** *Disclaimer by a surviving spouse.*—If an interest in property passes to a decedent's surviving spouse in a taxable transfer made by a decedent dying before January 1, 1977, and the decedent's surviving spouse makes a disclaimer of this property interest, the disclaimed interest is considered as passing from the decedent to the person or persons entitled to receive the interest as a result of the disclaimer. A disclaimer is a complete and unqualified refusal to accept the rights to which one is entitled. It is, therefore, necessary to distinguish between the surviving spouse's disclaimer of a property interest and such surviving spouse's acceptance and subsequent disposal of a property interest. For example, if proceeds of insurance are payable to the surviving spouse and the proceeds are refused so that they consequently pass to an alternate beneficiary designated by the decedent, the proceeds are considered as having passed from the decedent to the alternate beneficiary. On the other hand, if the insurance company is directed by the surviving spouse to hold the proceeds at interest during such spouse's life and, upon this spouse's death, to pay the principal sum to another person designated by the surviving spouse, thus effecting a transfer of a remainder interest, the proceeds are considered as having passed from the decedent to the surviving spouse. See paragraph(c) of §20.2056(e)-2 with respect to a spouse's exercise or failure to exercise a right to take against a decedent's will.

**(b)** *Disclaimer by a person other than a surviving spouse.*—(1) *Decedents dying after October 3, 1966 and before January 1, 1977.*—This paragraph (b)(1) applies in the case of a disclaimer of property passing to one other than the surviving spouse from a decedent dying after October 3, 1966 and before January 1, 1977. If a surviving spouse is entitled to receive property from the decedent as a result of the timely disclaimer made by the disclaimant, the property received by the surviving spouse is to be treated as passing to the surviving spouse from the decedent. Both a disclaimer of property passing by the laws of intestacy or otherwise, as by insurance or by trust, and a disclaimer of bequests and devises under the will of a decedent are to be fully effective for purposes of computing the marital deduction under section 2056. A disclaimer is a complete and unqualified refusal to accept some or all of the rights to which one is entitled. It must be a valid refusal under State law and must be made without consideration. For example, a disclaimer for the benefit of a surviving spouse who promises to give or bequeath property to a child of the person who disclaims is not a disclaimer within the meaning of this paragraph (b)(1). The disclaimer must be made before the person disclaiming accepts any property under the disclaimed interest. In the case of property transferred by a decedent dying after December 31, 1970, and before January 1, 1977, the disclaimer must be made within 9 months after the decedent's death (or within any extension of time for filing the estate tax return granted pursuant to section 6081). In the case of property transferred by a decedent dying after October 3, 1966, and before January 1, 1971, the disclaimer must be made within 15 months after the decedent's death (or within any extension of time for filing the estate's tax return granted pursuant to section 6081). If the disclaimer does not satisfy the requirements of this paragraph (b)(1), for the purpose of the marital deduction, the property is considered as passing from the decedent to the person who made the disclaimer as if the disclaimer had not been made.

**(2)** *Decedents dying after September 30, 1963 and before October 4, 1966.*—This paragraph (b)(2) applies in the case of a disclaimer of property passing to one other than the surviving spouse from a decedent dying after September 30, 1963 and before October 4, 1966. If, as a result of the disclaimer by the disclaimant, the surviving spouse is entitled to receive the disclaimed property interest, then such interest shall, for the purposes of this paragraph (b)(2), be considered as passing from the decedent to the surviving spouse if the following conditions are met. First, the interest disclaimed was bequeathed or devised to the disclaimant. Second, the disclaimant disclaimed all bequests and devises under the will before the date prescribed for the filing of the estate tax return. Third, the disclaimant did not accept any property under the bequest or devise before making the disclaimer. The interests passing by disclaimer to the surviving spouse under this paragraph (b)(2) are to qualify for the marital deduction only to the extent that, when added to any other allowable marital deduction without regard to this paragraph (b)(2), they do not exceed the greater of the deductions which would be allowable for the marital deduction without regard to the disclaimer if the surviving spouse exercised the election under State law to take against the will, or an amount equal to one-third of the decedent's adjusted gross estate. If the disclaimer does not satisfy the requirements of this paragraph (b)(2), the property is treated as passing from the decedent to the person who made the disclaimer, in the same manner as if the disclaimer had not been made.

**(3)** *Decedents dying before October 4, 1966.*—Unless the rule of paragraph (b)(2) of this section applies, this paragraph (b)(3) applies in the case of a disclaimer of property passing to one other than the surviving spouse from a decedent dying before October 4, 1966. For the purpose of these transfers, it is unnecessary to distinguish for the purpose of the marital deduction between a disclaimer by a person other than the surviving spouse and a transfer by such person. If the surviving spouse becomes entitled to receive an interest in property from the decedent as a result of a disclaimer made by some other person, the interest is, nevertheless, considered as having passed from the decedent, not to the surviving spouse, but to the person who made the disclaimer, as though the disclaimer had not been made. If, as a result of a disclaimer made by a person other than the surviving spouse, a property interest passes to the surviving spouse under circumstances which meet the conditions set forth in §20.2056(b)-5 (relating to a life estate with a power of appointment), the rule stated in the preceding sentence applies, not only with respect to the portion of the interest which beneficially vests in the surviving spouse, but also with respect to the portion over which such spouse acquires a power to appoint. The rule applies also in the case of proceeds under a life insurance, endowment, or annuity contract which, as a result of a disclaimer made by a person other than the surviving spouse, are held by the insurer subject to the conditions set forth in §20.2056(b)-6. [Reg. §20.2056(d)-3.]

☐ [*T.D. 8095, 8-6-86. Redesignated by T.D. 8612, 8-21-95.*]

**[Reg. §20.2056A-0]**

**§20.2056A-0. Table of contents.**—This section lists the captions that appear in the final regulations under §§20.2056A-1 through 20.2056A-13.

*§20.2056A-1. Restrictions on allowance of marital deduction if surviving spouse is not a United States citizen.*

(a) General rule.

(b) Marital deduction allowed if resident spouse becomes citizen.

(c) Special rules in the case of certain transfers subject to estate and gift tax treaties.

*§20.2056A-2. Requirements for qualified domestic trust.*

(a) In general.

(b) Qualified marital interest requirements.

(1) Property passing to QDOT.

(2) Property passing outright to spouse.

(3) Property passing under a nontransferable plan or arrangement.

(c) Statutory requirements.

(d) Additional requirements to ensure collection of the section 2056A estate tax.

(1) Security and other arrangements for payment of estate tax imposed under section 2056A(b)(1).

(2) Individual trustees.

(3) Annual reporting requirements.

(4) Request for alternate arrangement or waiver.

(5) Adjustment of dollar threshold and exclusion.

(6) Effective date and special rules.

*§20.2056A-3. QDOT election.*

(a) General rule.

(b) No partial elections.

(c) Protective elections.

(d) Manner of election.

*§20.2056A-4. Procedures for conforming marital trusts and nontrust marital transfers to the requirements of a qualified domestic trust.*

(a) Marital trusts.

(1) In general.

(2) Judicial reformations.

(3) Tolling of statutory assessment period.

(b) Nontrust marital transfers.

(1) In general.

(2) Form of transfer or assignment.

(3) Assets eligible for transfer or assignment.

(4) Pecuniary assignment - special rules.

(5) Transfer tax treatment of transfer or assignment.

(6) Period for completion of transfer.

(7) Retirement accounts and annuities.

(8) Protective assignment.

(c) Nonassignable annuities and other arrangements.

(1) Definition and general rule.

(2) Agreement to remit section 2056A estate tax on corpus portion of each annuity payment.

(3) Agreement to roll over corpus portion of annuity payment to QDOT.

(4) Determination of corpus portion.

(5) Information Statement.

(6) Agreement to pay section 2056A estate tax.

(7) Agreement to roll over annuity payments.

(d) Examples.

§ 20.2056A-5. *Imposition of section 2056A estate tax.*

(a) In general.

(b) Amounts subject to tax.

(1) Distribution of principal during the spouse's lifetime.

(2) Death of surviving spouse.

(3) Trust ceases to qualify as QDOT.

(c) Distributions and dispositions not subject to tax.

(1) Distributions of principal on account of hardship.

(2) Distributions of income to the surviving spouse.

(3) Certain miscellaneous distributions and dispositions.

§ 20.2056A-6. *Amount of tax.*

(a) Definition of tax.

(b) Benefits allowed in determining amount of section 2056A estate tax.

(1) General rule.

(2) Treatment as resident.

(3) Special rule in the case of trusts described in section 2056(b)(8).

(4) Credit for state and foreign death taxes.

(5) Alternate valuation and special use valuation.

(c) Miscellaneous rules.

(d) Examples.

§ 20.2056A-7. *Allowance of prior transfer credit under section 2013.*

(a) Property subject to QDOT election.

(b) Property not subject to QDOT election.

(c) Example.

§ 20.2056A-8. *Special rules for joint property.*

(a) Inclusion in gross estate.

(1) General rule.

(2) Consideration furnished by surviving spouse.

(3) Amount allowed to be transferred to QDOT.

(b) Surviving spouse becomes citizen.

(c) Examples.

§ 20.2056A-9. *Designated Filer.*

§ 20.2056A-10. *Surviving spouse becomes citizen after QDOT established.*

(a) Section 2056A estate tax no longer imposed under certain circumstances.

(b) Special election by spouse.

§ 20.2056A-11. *Filing requirements and payment of the section 2056A estate tax.*

(a) Distributions during surviving spouse's life.

(b) Tax at death of surviving spouse.

(c) Extension of time for paying section 2056A estate tax.

(1) Extension of time for paying tax under section 6161(a)(2).

(2) Extension of time for paying tax under section 6161(a)(1).

(d) Liability for tax.

§ 20.2056A-12. *Increased basis for section 2056A estate tax paid with respect to distribution from a QDOT.*

§ 20.2056A-13. *Effective date.*
[Reg. § 20.2056A-0.]

□ [*T.D. 8612, 8-21-95. Amended by T.D. 8686, 11-27-96.*]

**[Reg. § 20.2056A-1]**

**§ 20.2056A-1. Restrictions on allowance of marital deduction if surviving spouse is not a United States citizen.**—(a) *General rule.*—Subject to the special rules provided in section 7815(d)(14) of the Omnibus Budget Reconciliation Act of 1989 (Pub. L. 101-239; 103 Stat. 2106), in the case of a decedent dying after November 10, 1988, the federal estate tax marital deduction is not allowed for property passing to or for the benefit of a surviving spouse who is not a United States citizen at the date of the decedent's death (whether or not the surviving spouse is a resident of the United States) unless—

(1) The property passes from the decedent to (or pursuant to)—

(i) A qualified domestic trust (QDOT) described in section 2056A and § 20.2056A-2;

(ii) A trust that, although not meeting all of the requirements for a QDOT, is reformed after the decedent's death to meet the requirements of a QDOT (see § 20.2056A-4(a));

(iii) The surviving spouse not in trust (e.g., by outright bequest or devise, by operation of law, or pursuant to the terms of an annuity or other similar plan or arrangement) and, prior to the date that the estate tax return is filed and on or before the last date prescribed by law that the QDOT election may be made (no more than one year after the time prescribed by law, including extensions, for filing the return), the surviving spouse either actually transfers the property to a QDOT or irrevocably assigns the property to a QDOT (see § 20.2056A-4(b)); or

(iv) A plan or other arrangement that would have qualified for the marital deduction but for section 2056(d)(1)(A), and whose payments are not assignable or transferable to a QDOT, if the requirements of § 20.2056A-4(c) are met; and

(2) The executor makes a timely QDOT election under § 20.2056A-3.

(b) *Marital deduction allowed if resident spouse becomes citizen.*—For purposes of section 2056(d)(1) and paragraph (a) of this section, the surviving spouse is treated as a citizen of the United States at the date of the decedent's death if the requirements of section 2056(d)(4) are satisfied. For purposes of section 2056(d)(4)(A) and notwithstanding § 20.2056A-3(a), a return filed prior to the due date (including extensions) is considered filed on the last date that the return is required to be filed (including extensions), and a late return filed at any time after the due date is considered filed on the date that it is actually filed. A surviving spouse is a resident only if the spouse is a resident under chapter 11 of the Internal Revenue Code. See § 20.0-1(b)(1). The status of the spouse as a resident under section 7701(b) is not relevant to this determination except to the extent that the income tax residency of the spouse is pertinent in applying § 20.0-1(b)(1).

(c) *Special rules in the case of certain transfers subject to estate and gift tax treaties.*—Under section 7815(d)(14) of the Omnibus Budget Reconciliation Act of 1989 (Pub. L. 101-239, 103 Stat. 2106) certain special rules apply in the case of transfers governed by certain estate and gift tax treaties to which the United States is a party. In the case of the estate of, or gift by, an individual who was not a citizen or resident of the United States but was a resident of a foreign country with which the United States has a tax treaty with respect to estate, inheritance, or gift taxes, the amendments made by section 5033 of the Technical and Miscellaneous Revenue Act of 1988 (Pub. L. 100-647, 102 Stat. 3342) do not apply to the extent such amendments would be inconsistent with the provisions of such treaty relating to estate, inheritance, or gift tax marital deductions. Under this rule, the estate may choose either the statutory deduction under section 2056A or the marital deduction allowed under the treaty. Thus, the estate may not avail itself of both the marital deduction under the treaty and the marital deduction under the QDOT provisions of section 2056A and chapter 11 of the Internal Revenue Code with respect to the remainder of the marital property that is not deductible under the treaty. [Reg. § 20.2056A-1.]

□ [*T.D. 8612, 8-21-95.*]

**[Reg. § 20.2056A-2]**

**§ 20.2056A-2. Requirements for qualified domestic trust.**—(a) *In general.*—In order to qualify as a qualified domestic trust (QDOT), the requirements of paragraphs (b) and (c) of this section, and the requirements of § 20.2056A-2T(d), must be satisfied. The executor of the decedent's estate and the U.S. Trustee shall establish in such manner as may be prescribed by the Commissioner on the estate tax return and applicable instructions that these requirements have been satisfied or are being complied with. In order to constitute a QDOT, the trust must be maintained under the laws of a state of the United States or the District of Columbia, and the administration of the trust must be governed by the laws of a particular state of the United States or the District of Columbia. For purposes of this paragraph, a trust is maintained under the laws of a state of the United States or the District of Columbia if the records of the trust (or copies thereof) are kept in that state (or the District of Columbia). The trust may be established pursuant to an instrument executed under either the laws of a state of the United States or the District of Columbia or pursuant to an instrument executed under the laws of a foreign jurisdiction, such as a foreign will or trust, provided that such foreign instrument designates the law of a particular state of the United States or the District of Columbia as governing the administration of the trust, and such designation is effective under the law of the designated jurisdiction. In addition, the trust must constitute an ordinary trust, as defined in § 301.7701-4(a) of this chapter, and not any other type of entity. For purposes of this paragraph (a), a trust will not fail to constitute an ordinary trust solely because of the nature of the assets transferred to that trust, regardless of its classification under §§ 301.7701-2 through 301.7701-4 of this chapter.

(b) *Qualified marital interest requirements.*—(1) *Property passing to QDOT.*—If property passes from a decedent to a QDOT, the trust must qualify for the federal estate tax marital deduction under section 2056(b)(5) (life estate with power of appointment), section 2056(b)(7) (qualified terminable interest property, including joint and survivor annuities under section 2056(b)(7)(C)), or section 2056(b)(8) (surviving spouse is the only noncharitable beneficiary of a charitable remainder trust), or meet the requirements of an estate trust as defined in § 20.2056(c)-2(b)(1)(i) through (iii).

(2) *Property passing outright to spouse.*—If property does not pass from a decedent to a QDOT, but passes to a noncitizen surviving spouse in a form that meets the requirements for a marital deduction without regard to section 2056(d)(1)(A), and that is not described in paragraph (b)(1) of this section, the surviving spouse must either actually transfer the property, or irrevocably assign the property, to a trust (whether created by the decedent, the decedent's executor or by the surviving spouse) that meets the requirements of paragraph (c) of this section and the requirements of § 20.2056A-2T(d) (pertaining, respectively, to statutory requirements and regulatory requirements imposed to ensure collection of tax) prior to the filing of the estate tax return for the decedent's estate and on or before the last date prescribed by law that the QDOT election may be made (see § 20.2056A-3(a)).

(3) *Property passing under a nontransferable plan or arrangement.*— If property does not pass from a decedent to a QDOT, but passes under a plan or other arrangement that meets the requirements for a marital deduction without regard to section 2056(d)(1)(A) and whose payments are not assignable or transferable (see § 20.2056A-4(c)), the property is treated as meeting the requirements of this section, and the requirements of § 20.2056A-2T(d), if the requirements of § 20.2056A-4(c) are satisfied. In addition, where an annuity or similar arrangement is described above except that it is assignable or transferable, see § 20.2056A-4(b)(7).

(c) *Statutory requirements.*—The requirements of section 2056A(a)(1)(A) and (B) must be satisfied. For purposes of that section, a domestic corporation is a corporation that is created or organized under the laws of the United States or under the laws of any state of the United States or the District of Columbia. The trustee required under that section is referred to herein as the "U.S. Trustee".

(d) *Additional requirements to ensure collection of the section 2056A estate tax.*—(1) *Security and other arrangements for payment of estate tax imposed under section 2056A(b)(1).*—(i) *QDOTs with assets in excess of $2 million.*—If the fair market value of the assets passing, treated, or deemed to have passed to the QDOT (or in the form of a QDOT), determined without reduction for any indebtedness with respect to the assets, as finally determined for federal estate tax purposes, exceeds $2 million as of the date of the decedent's death or, if applicable, the alternate valuation date (adjusted as provided in paragraph (d)(1)(iii) of this section), the trust instrument must meet the requirements of either paragraph (d)(1)(i)(A), (B), or (C) of this section at all times during the term of the QDOT. The QDOT may alternate between any of the arrangements provided in paragraphs (d)(1)(i)(A), (B), and (C) of this section provided that, at any given time, one of the arrangements must be operative. See paragraph (d)(1)(iii) of this section for the definition of finally determined. The QDOT may provide that the trustee has the discretion to use any one of the security arrangements or may provide that the trustee is limited to using only one or two of the arrangements specified in the trust instrument. A trust instrument that specifically states that the trust must be administered in compliance with paragraph (d)(1)(i)(A), (B), or (C) of this section is treated as meeting the requirements of paragraphs (d)(1)(i)(A), (B), or (C) for purposes of paragraphs (d)(1)(i) and, if applicable, (d)(1)(ii) of this section.

(A) *Bank Trustee.*—Except as otherwise provided in paragraph (d)(6)(ii) or (iii) of this section, the trust instrument must provide that whenever the Bank Trustee security alternative is used for the QDOT, at least one U.S. Trustee must be a bank as defined in section 581. Alternatively, except as otherwise provided in paragraph (d)(6)(ii) or (iii) of this section, at least one trustee must be a United States branch of a foreign bank, provided that, in such cases, during the entire term of the QDOT a U.S. Trustee must act as a trustee with the foreign bank trustee.

(B) *Bond.*—Except as otherwise provided in paragraph (d)(6)(ii) or (iii) of this section, the trust instrument must provide that whenever the bond security arrangement alternative is used for the QDOT, the U.S. Trustee must furnish a bond in favor of the Internal Revenue Service in an amount equal to 65 percent of the fair market value of the trust assets (determined without regard to any indebted-

ness with respect to the assets) as of the date of the decedent's death (or alternate valuation date, if applicable), as finally determined for federal estate tax purposes (and as further adjusted as provided in paragraph (d)(1)(iv) of this section). If, after examination of the estate tax return, the fair market value of the trust assets, as originally reported on the estate tax return, is adjusted (pursuant to a judicial proceeding or otherwise) resulting in a final determination of the value of the assets as reported on the return, the U.S. Trustee has a reasonable period of time (not exceeding sixty days after the conclusion of the proceeding or other action resulting in a final determination of the value of the assets) to adjust the amount of the bond accordingly. But see, paragraph (d)(1)(i)(D) of this section for a special rule in the case of a substantial undervaluation of QDOT assets. Unless an alternate arrangement under paragraph (d)(1)(i)(A), (B), or (C) of this section, or an arrangement prescribed under paragraph (d)(4) of this section, is provided, or the trust is otherwise no longer subject to the requirements of section 2056A pursuant to section 2056A(b)(12), the bond must remain in effect until the trust ceases to function as a QDOT and any tax liability finally determined to be due under section 2056A(b) is paid, or is finally determined to be zero.

(1) *Requirements for the bond.*—The bond must be with a satisfactory surety, as prescribed under section 7101 and § 301.7101-1 of this chapter (Regulations on Procedure and Administration), and is subject to Internal Revenue Service review as may be prescribed by the Commissioner. The bond may not be cancelled. The bond must be for a term of at least one year and must be automatically renewable at the end of that term, on an annual basis thereafter, unless notice of failure to renew is mailed to the U.S. Trustee and the Internal Revenue Service at least 60 days prior to the end of the term, including periods of automatic extensions. Any notice of failure to renew required to be sent to the Internal Revenue Service must be sent to the Estate and Gift Tax Group in the District Office of the Internal Revenue Service that has examination jurisdiction over the decedent's estate (Internal Revenue Service, District Director, *[specify location]* District Office, Estate and Gift Tax Examination Group, [specify Street Address, City, State, Zip Code]) (or in the case of noncitizen decedents and United States citizens who die domiciled outside the United States, Estate Tax Group, Assistant Commissioner (International), 950 L'Enfant Plaza, CP:IN:D:C:EX:HQ:1114, Washington, DC 20024). The Internal Revenue Service will not draw on the bond if, within 30 days of receipt of the notice of failure to renew, the U.S. Trustee notifies the Internal Revenue Service (at the same address to which notice of failure to renew is to be sent) that an alternate arrangement under paragraph (d)(1)(i)(A), (B), or (C) or (d)(4) of this section, has been secured and that the arrangement will take effect immediately prior to or upon expiration of the bond.

(2) *Form of bond.*—The bond must be in the following form (or in a form that is the same as the following form in all material respects), or in such alternative form as the Commissioner may prescribe by guidance published in the Internal Revenue Bulletin (see § 601.601(d)(2) of this chapter):

Bond in Favor of the Internal Revenue Service To Secure Payment of Section 2056A Estate Tax Imposed Under Section 2056A(b) of the Internal Revenue Code.

**KNOW ALL PERSONS BY THESE PRESENTS**, That the undersigned, _____, the SURETY, and _____, the PRINCIPAL, are irrevocably held and firmly bound to pay the Internal Revenue Service upon written demand that amount of any tax up to $*[amount determined under paragraph (d)(1)(i)(B) of this section]*, imposed under section 2056A(b)(1) of the Internal Revenue Code (including penalties and interest on said tax) determined by the Internal Revenue Service to be payable with respect to the principal as trustee for: *[Identify trust and governing instrument, name and address of trustee]*, a qualified domestic trust as defined in section 2056A(a) of the Internal Revenue Code, for the payment of which the said Principal and said Surety, bind themselves, their heirs, executors, administrators, successors and assigns, jointly and severally, firmly by these presents.

**WHEREAS,** The Internal Revenue Service may demand payment under this bond at any time if the Internal Revenue Service in its sole discretion determines that a taxable event with respect to the trust has occurred; the trust no longer qualifies as a qualified domestic trust as described in section 2056A(a) of the Internal Revenue Code and the regulations promulgated thereunder, or a distribution subject to the tax imposed under section 2056A(b)(1) has been made. Demand by the Internal Revenue Service for payment may be made whether or not the tax and tax return (Form 706-QDT) with respect to the taxable event is due at the time of such demand, or an assessment has been made by the Internal Revenue Service with respect to the tax.

**NOW THEREFORE,** The condition of this obligation is such that it must not be cancelled and, if payment of all tax liability finally determined to be imposed under section 2056A(b) is made, then this obligation is null and void; otherwise, this obligation is to remain in full force and effect for one year from its effective date and is to be automatically renewable on an annual basis unless, at least 60 days prior to the expiration date, including periods of automatic renewals, the surety mails to the U.S. Trustee and the Internal Revenue Service by Registered or Certified Mail, return receipt requested, notice of the failure to renew. Receipt of this notice of failure to renew by the Internal Revenue Service may be considered a taxable event. The Internal Revenue Service will not draw upon the bond if, within 30 days of receipt of the notice of failure to renew, the trustee notifies the Internal Revenue Service that an alternate security arrangement has been secured and that the arrangement will take effect immediately prior to or upon expiration of the bond. The surety remains liable for all taxable events occurring prior to the date of expiration. All notices required to be sent to the Internal Revenue Service under this instrument should be sent to District Director, *[specify location]* District Office, Estate and Gift Tax Examination Group, Street Address, City, State, Zip Code. (In the case of nonresident noncitizen decedents and United States citizens who die domiciled outside the United States, all notices should be sent to Estate Tax Group, Assistant Commissioner (International), 950 L'Enfant Plaza, CP:IN:D:C:EX:HQ:1114, Washington, DC 20024).

This bond shall be effective as of _____.

Principal _____

Date _____

Surety _____

Date _____

*(3) Additional governing instrument requirements.*—The trust instrument must provide that in the event the Internal Revenue Service draws on the bond, in accordance with its terms, neither the U.S. Trustee nor any other person will seek a return of any part of the remittance until after April 15th of the calendar year following the year in which the bond is drawn upon. After that date, any such remittance will be treated as a deposit and returned (without interest) upon request of the U.S. Trustee, unless it is determined that assessment or collection of the tax imposed by section 2056A(b)(1) is in jeopardy, within the meaning of section 6861. If an assessment under section 6861 is made, the remittance will first be credited to any tax liability reported on the Form 706-QDT, then to any unpaid balance of a section 2056A(b)(1)(A) tax liability (plus interest and penalties) for any prior taxable years, and any balance will then be returned to the U.S. Trustee.

*(4) Procedure.*—The bond is to be filed with the decedent's federal estate tax return, Form 706 or 706NA (unless an extension for filing the bond is granted under §301.9100 of this chapter). The U.S. Trustee must provide a written statement with the bond that provides a list of the assets that will be used to fund the QDOT and the respective values of the assets. The written statement must also indicate whether any exclusions under paragraph (d)(1)(iv) of this section are claimed.

(C) *Letter of credit.*—Except as otherwise provided in paragraph (d)(6)(ii) or (iii) of this section, the trust instrument must provide that whenever the letter of credit security arrangement is used for the QDOT, the U.S. Trustee must furnish an irrevocable letter of credit issued by a bank as defined in section 581, a United States branch of a foreign bank, or a foreign bank with a confirmation by a bank as defined in section 581. The letter of credit must be for an amount equal to 65 percent of the fair market value of the trust assets (determined without regard to any indebtedness with respect to the assets) as of the date of the decedent's death (or alternate valuation date, if applicable), as finally determined for federal estate tax purposes (and as further adjusted as provided in paragraph (d)(1)(iv) of this section). If, after examination of the estate tax return, the fair market value of the trust assets, as originally reported on the estate tax return, is adjusted (pursuant to a judicial proceeding or otherwise) resulting in a final determination of the value of the assets as reported on the return, the U.S. Trustee has a reasonable period of time (not exceeding 60 days after the conclusion of the proceeding or other action resulting in a final determination of the value of the assets) to adjust the amount of the letter of credit accordingly. But see, paragraph (d)(1)(i)(D) of this section for a special rule in the case of a substantial undervaluation of QDOT assets. Unless an alternate arrangement under paragraph (d)(1)(i)(A), (B), or (C) of this section, or an arrangement prescribed under paragraph (d)(4) of this section, is provided, or the trust is otherwise no longer subject to the requirements of section 2056A pursuant to section 2056A(b)(12), the letter of credit must remain in effect until the trust ceases to function as a QDOT and any tax liability finally determined to be due under section 2056A(b) is paid or is finally determined to be zero.

*(1) Requirements for the letter of credit.*—The letter of credit must be irrevocable and provide for sight payment. The letter of credit must have a term of at least one year and must be automati-

cally renewable at the end of the term, at least on an annual basis, unless notice of failure to renew is mailed to the U.S. Trustee and the Internal Revenue Service at least sixty days prior to the end of the term, including periods of automatic renewals. If the letter of credit is issued by the U.S. branch of a foreign bank and the U.S. branch is closing, the branch (or foreign bank) must notify the U.S. Trustee and the Internal Revenue Service of the closure and the notice of closure must be mailed at least 60 days prior to the date of closure. Any notice of failure to renew or closure of a U.S. branch of a foreign bank required to be sent to the Internal Revenue Service must be sent to the Estate and Gift Tax Group in the District Office of the Internal Revenue Service that has examination jurisdiction over the decedent's estate (Internal Revenue Service, District Director, *[specify location]* District Office, Estate and Gift Tax Examination Group, [Street Address, City State, Zip Code]) (or in the case of noncitizen decedents and United States citizens who die domiciled outside the United States, Estate Tax, Assistant Commissioner (International), 950 L'Enfant Plaza, CP:IN:D:C:EX:HQ:1114, Washington, DC 20024). The Internal Revenue Service will not draw on the letter of credit if, within 30 days of receipt of the notice of failure to renew or closure of the U.S. branch of a foreign bank, the U.S. Trustee notifies the Internal Revenue Service (at the same address to which notice is to be sent) that an alternate arrangement under paragraph (d)(1)(i)(A), (B), or (C), or (d)(4) of this section, has been secured and that the arrangement will take effect immediately prior to or upon expiration of the letter of credit or closure of the U.S. branch of the foreign bank.

*(2) Form of letter of credit.*—The letter of credit must be made in the following form (or in a form that is the same as the following form in all material respects), or an alternative form that the Commissioner prescribes by guidance published in the Internal Revenue Bulletin (see § 601.601(d)(2) of this chapter):

[Issue Date]

To: Internal Revenue Service

Attention: District Director, *[specify location]* District Office

Estate and Gift Tax Examination Group

[Street Address, City, State, ZIP Code]

[Or in the case of nonresident noncitizen decedents and United States citizens who die domiciled outside the United States,

To: Estate Tax Group,

Assistant Commissioner (International)

950 L'Enfant Plaza

CP:IN:D:C:EX:HQ:1114

Washington, DC 20024].

Dear Sirs:

We hereby establish our irrevocable Letter of Credit No.—in your favor for drawings up to U.S. $*[Applicant should provide bank with amount which Applicant determined under paragraph (d)(1)(i)(C)]* effective immediately. This Letter of Credit is issued, presentable and payable at our office at _____ and expires at 3:00 p.m. [EDT, EST, CDT, CST, MDT, MST, PDT, PST] on at said office.

For information and reference only, we are informed that this Letter of Credit relates to *[Applicant should provide bank with the identity of qualified domestic trust and governing instrument]*, and the name, address, and identifying number of the trustee is *[Applicant should provide bank with the trustee name, address and the QDOT's TIN number, if any]*.

Drawings on this Letter of Credit are available upon presentation of the following documents:

1. Your draft drawn at sight on us bearing our Letter of Credit No. _____; and

2. Your signed statement as follows:

The amount of the accompanying draft is payable under *[identify bank]* irrevocable Letter of Credit No. _____ pursuant to section 2056A of the Internal Revenue Code and the regulations promulgated thereunder, because the Internal Revenue Service in its sole discretion has determined that a "taxable event" with respect to the trust has occurred; e.g., the trust no longer qualifies as a qualified domestic trust as described in section 2056A of the Internal Revenue Code and regulations promulgated thereunder, or a distribution subject to the tax imposed under section 2056A(b)(1) of the Internal Revenue Code has been made.

Except as expressly stated herein, this undertaking is not subject to any agreement, requirement or qualification. The obligation of *[Name of Issuing Bank]* under this Letter of Credit is the individual obligation of *[Name of Issuing Bank]* and is in no way contingent upon reimbursement with respect thereto.

It is a condition of this Letter of Credit that it is deemed to be automatically extended without amendment for a period of one year from the expiration date hereof, or any future expiration date, unless at least 60 days prior to any expiration date, we mail to you and to the U.S. Trustee notice by Registered Mail or Certified Mail, return receipt requested, or by courier to your and the trustee's address indicated above, that we elect not to consider this Letter of Credit renewed for any such additional period. Upon receipt of this notice, you may draw hereunder on or before the then current expiration date, by presentation of your draft and statement as stipulated above.

[In the case of a letter of credit issued by a U.S. branch of a foreign bank the following language must be added]. It is a further condition of this Letter of Credit that if the U.S. branch of [name of foreign bank] is to be closed, that at least sixty days prior to closing, we mail to you and the U.S. Trustee notice by Registered Mail or Certified Mail, return receipt requested, or by courier to your and the U.S. Trustee's address indicated above, that this branch will be closing. This notice will specify the actual date of closing. Upon receipt of the notice, you may draw hereunder on or before the date of closure, by presentation of your draft and statement as stipulated above.

Except where otherwise stated herein, this Letter of Credit is subject to the Uniform Customs and Practice for Documentary Credits, 1993 Revision, ICC Publication No. 500. If we notify you of our election not to consider this Letter of Credit renewed and the expiration date occurs during an interruption of business described in Article 17 of said Publication 500, unless you had consented to cancellation prior to the expiration date, the bank hereby specifically agrees to effect payment if this Letter of Credit is drawn against within 30 days after the resumption of business.

Except as stated herein, this Letter of Credit cannot be modified or revoked without your consent.

Authorized Signature _____

Date _____

*(3) Form of confirmation.*—If the requirements of this paragraph (d)(1)(i)(C) are satisfied by the issuance of a letter of credit by a foreign bank with confirmation by a bank as defined in section 581, the confirmation must be made in the following form (or in a form that is the same as the following form in all material respects), or an alternative form as the Commissioner prescribes by guidance published in the Internal Revenue Bulletin (see § 602.101(d)(2) of this chapter):

[Issue Date]

To: Internal Revenue Service

Attention: District Director, [specify location] District Office

Estate and Gift Tax Examination Group

[State Address, City, State, ZIP Code]

[or in the case of nonresident noncitizen decedents and United States citizens who die domiciled outside the United States,

To: Estate Tax Group,
Assistant Commissioner (International)
950 L'Enfant Plaza
CP:IN:D:C:EX:HQ:1114
Washington, DC 20024].

Dear Sirs:

We hereby confirm the enclosed irrevocable Letter of Credit No. _____, and amendments thereto, if any, in your favor by _____[Issuing Bank] for drawings up to U.S. $_____[same amount as in initial Letter of Credit] effective immediately. This confirmation is issued, presentable and payable at our office at _____and expires at 3:00 p.m. [EDT, EST, CDT, CST, MDT, MST, PDT, PST]on _____ at said office.

For information and reference only, we are informed that this Confirmation relates to [Applicant should provide bank with the identity of qualified domestic trust and governing instrument], and the name, address, and identifying number of the trustee is [Applicant should provide bank with the trustee name, address and the QDOT's TIN number, if any].

We hereby undertake to honor your sight draft(s) drawn as specified in the Letter of Credit.

Except as expressly stated herein, this undertaking is not subject to any agreement, condition or qualification. The obligation of [Name of Confirming Bank] under this Confirmation is the individual obligation of [Name of Confirming Bank] and is in no way contingent upon reimbursement with respect thereto.

It is a condition of this Confirmation that it is deemed to be automatically extended without amendment for a period of one year from the expiry date hereof, or any future expiration date, unless at least sixty days prior to the expiration date, we send to you and to the U.S. Trustee notice by Registered Mail or Certified Mail, return receipt requested, or by courier to your and the trustee's addresses, respectively, indicated above, that we elect not to consider this Confirmation renewed for any additional period. Upon receipt of this notice by you, you may draw hereunder on or before the then current expiration date, by presentation of your draft and statement as stipulated above.

Except where otherwise stated herein, this Confirmation is subject to the Uniform Customs and Practice for Documentary

Credits, 1993 Revision, ICC Publication No. 500. If we notify you of our election not to consider this Confirmation renewed and the expiration date occurs during an interruption of business described in Article 17 of said Publication 500, unless you had consented to cancellation prior to the expiration date, the bank hereby specifically agrees to effect payment if this Confirmation is drawn against within 30 days after the resumption of business.

Except as stated herein, this Confirmation cannot be modified or revoked without your consent.

Authorized Signature _____

Date _____

*(4) Additional governing instrument requirements.*—The trust instrument must provide that if the Internal Revenue Service draws on the letter of credit (or confirmation) in accordance with its terms, neither the U.S. Trustee nor any other person will seek a return of any part of the remittance until April 15th of the calendar year following the year in which the letter of credit (or confirmation) is drawn upon. After that date, any such remittance will be treated as a deposit and returned (without interest) upon request of the U.S. Trustee after the date specified above, unless it is determined that assessment or collection of the tax imposed by section 2056A(b)(1) is in jeopardy, within the meaning of section 6861. If an assessment under section 6861 is made, the remittance will first be credited to any tax liability reported on the Form 706-QDT, then to any unpaid balance of a section 2056A(b)(1)(A) tax liability (plus interest and penalties) for any prior taxable years, and any balance will then be returned to the U.S. Trustee.

*(5) Procedure.*—The letter of credit (and confirmation, if applicable) is to be filed with the decedent's federal estate tax return, Form 706 or 706NA (unless an extension for filing the letter of credit is granted under § 301.9100 of this chapter). The U.S. Trustee must provide a written statement with the letter of credit that provides a list of the assets that will be used to fund the QDOT and the respective values of the assets. The written statement must also indicate whether any exclusions under paragraph (d)(1)(iv) of this section are claimed.

(D) *Disallowance of marital deduction for substantial undervaluation of QDOT property in certain situations.*—*(1)* If either—

*(i)* The bond or letter of credit security arrangement under paragraph (d)(1)(i)(B) or (C) of this section is chosen by the U.S. Trustee; or

*(ii)* The QDOT property as originally reported on the decedent's estate tax return is valued at $2 million or less but, as finally determined for federal estate tax purposes, the QDOT property is determined to be in excess of $2 million, then the marital deduction will be disallowed in its entirety for failure to comply with the requirements of section 2056A if the value of the QDOT property reported on the estate tax return is 50 percent or less of the amount finally determined to be the correct value of the property for federal estate tax purposes.

*(2)* The preceding sentence does not apply if—

*(i)* There was reasonable cause for the undervaluation; and

*(ii)* The fiduciary of the estate acted in good faith with respect to the undervaluation. For this purpose, § 1.6664-4(b) of this chapter applies, to the extent applicable, with respect to the facts and circumstances to be taken into account in making this determination.

(ii) *QDOTs with assets of $2 million or less.*—If the fair market value of the assets passing, treated, or deemed to have passed to the QDOT (or in the form of a QDOT), determined without reduction for any indebtedness with respect to the assets, as finally determined for federal estate tax purposes, is $2 million or less as of the date of the decedent's death or, if applicable, the alternate valuation date (adjusted as provided in paragraph (d)(1)(iv) of this section), the trust instrument must provide that either no more than 35 percent of the fair market value of the trust assets, determined annually on the last day of the taxable year of the trust (or on the last day of the calendar year if the QDOT does not have a taxable year), will consist of real property located outside of the United States, or the trust will meet the requirements prescribed by paragraph (d)(1)(i)(A), (B), or (C) of this section. See paragraph (d)(1)(ii)(D) of this section for special rules in the case of principal distributions from a QDOT, fluctuations in the value of foreign real property held by a QDOT due to changes in value of foreign currency, and fluctuations in the fair market value of assets held by the QDOT. See paragraph (d)(1)(iv) of this section for a special rule for personal residences. If the fair market value, as originally reported on the decedent's estate tax return, of the assets passing or deemed to have passed to the QDOT (determined without reduction for any indebtedness with respect to the assets) is $2 million or less, but the fair market value of the assets as finally determined for federal estate tax purposes is more than $2 million, the U.S. Trustee has a reasonable period of time (not exceeding sixty days after the conclusion of the proceeding or other action resulting in a final determination of the value of the assets) to meet the requirements prescribed by paragraph (d)(1)(i)(A), (B), or (C) of this section. However, see paragraph (d)(1)(i)(D) of this section in the case of a substantial undervaluation of QDOT assets. See § 20.2056A-2(d)(1)(iii) for the definition of finally determined.

(A) *Multiple QDOTs.*—For purposes of this paragraph (d)(1)(ii), if more than one QDOT is established for the benefit of the surviving spouse, the fair market value of all the QDOTs are aggregated in determining whether the $2 million threshold under this paragraph (d)(1)(ii) is exceeded.

(B) *Look-through rule.*—For purposes of determining whether no more than 35 percent of the fair market value of the QDOT assets consists of foreign real property, if the QDOT owns more than 20% of the voting stock or value in a corporation with 15 or fewer shareholders, or more than 20% of the capital interest of a partnership with 15 or fewer partners, then all assets owned by the corporation or partnership are deemed to be owned directly by the QDOT to the extent of the QDOT's pro rata share of the assets of that corporation or partnership. For a partnership, the QDOT partner's pro rata share is based on the greater of its interest in the capital or profits of the partnership. For purposes of this paragraph, all stock in the corporation, or interests in the partnership, as the case may be, owned by or held for the benefit of the surviving spouse, or any members of the surviving spouse's family (within the meaning of section 267(c)(4)), are treated as owned by the QDOT solely for purposes of determining the number of partners or shareholders in the entity and the QDOT's percentage voting interest or value in the corporation or capital interest in the partnership, but not for the purpose of determining the QDOT's pro rata share of the assets of the entity.

(C) *Interests in other entities.*—Interests owned by the QDOT in other entities (such as an interest in a trust) are accorded treatment consistent with that described in paragraph (d)(1)(ii)(B) of this section.

(D) *Special rule for foreign real property.*—For purposes of this paragraph (d)(1)(ii), if, on the last day of any taxable year during the term of the QDOT (or the last day of the calendar year if the QDOT does not have a taxable year), the value of foreign real property owned by the QDOT exceeds 35 percent of the fair market value of the trust assets due to: distributions of QDOT principal during that year; fluctuations in the value of the foreign currency in the jurisdiction where the real estate is located; or fluctuations in the fair market value of any assets held in the QDOT, then the QDOT will not be treated as failing to meet the requirements of this paragraph (d)(1). Accordingly, the QDOT will not cease to be a QDOT within the meaning of § 20.2056A-5(b)(3) if, by the end of the taxable year (or the last day of the calendar year if the QDOT does not have a taxable year) of the QDOT immediately following the year in which the 35 percent limit was exceeded, the value of the foreign real property held by the QDOT does not exceed 35 percent of the fair market value of the trust assets or, alternatively, the QDOT meets the requirements of either paragraph (d)(1)(i)(A), (B), or (C) of this section on or before the close of that succeeding year.

(iii) *Definition of finally determined.*—For purposes of § 20.2056A-2(d)(1)(i) and (ii), the fair market value of assets will be treated as finally determined on the earliest to occur of—

(A) The entry of a decision, judgment, decree, or other order by any court of competent jurisdiction that has become final;

(B) The execution of a closing agreement made under section 7121;

(C) Any final disposition by the Internal Revenue Service of a claim for refund;

(D) The issuance of an estate tax closing letter (Form L-154 or equivalent) if no claim for refund is filed; or

(E) The expiration of the period of assessment.

(iv) *Special rules for personal residence and related personal effects.*—(A) *Two million dollar threshold.*—For purposes of determining whether the $2 million threshold under paragraphs (d)(1)(i) and (ii) of this section has been exceeded, the executor of the estate may elect to exclude up to $600,000 in value attributable to real property (and related furnishings) owned directly by the QDOT that is used by, or held for the use of the surviving spouse as a personal residence and that passes, or is treated as passing, to the QDOT under section 2056(d). The election may be made regardless of whether the real property is situated within or without the United States. The election is made by attaching to the estate tax return on which the QDOT election is made a written statement claiming the exclusion. The statement must clearly identify the property or properties (i.e. address and location) for which the election is being made.

(B) *Security requirement.*—For purposes of determining the amount of the bond or letter of credit required when paragraph (d)(1)(i)(B) or (C) of this section applies, the executor of the estate may elect to exclude, during the term of the QDOT, up to $600,000 in value attributable to real property (and related furnishings) owned directly by the QDOT that is used by, or held for the use of the surviving spouse as a personal residence and that passes, or is treated as passing, to the QDOT under section 2056(d). The election may be made regardless of whether the real property is situated within or without the United States. The election is made by attaching to the estate tax return on which the QDOT election is made a written statement claiming the exclusion. If an election is not made on the decedent's estate tax return, the election may be made, prospectively, at any time, during the term of the QDOT, by attaching to the Form 706-QDT a written statement claiming the exclusion. A statement may also be attached to the Form 706-QDT that cancels a prior election of the personal residence exclusion that was made under this paragraph, either on the decedent's estate tax return or on a Form 706-QDT.

(C) *Foreign real property limitation.*—The special rules of this paragraph (d)(1)(iv) do not apply for purposes of determining whether more than 35 percent of the QDOT assets consist of foreign real property under paragraph (d)(1)(ii) of this section.

(D) *Personal residence.*—For purposes of this paragraph (d)(1)(iv), a *personal residence* is either the principal residence of the surviving spouse within the meaning of section 1034 or one other residence of the surviving spouse. In order to be used by or held for the use of the spouse as a personal residence, the residence must be available at all times for use by the surviving spouse. The residence may not be rented to another party, even when not occupied by the spouse. A personal residence may include appurtenant structures used by the surviving spouse for residential purposes and adjacent land not in excess of that which is reasonably appropriate for residential purposes (taking into account the residence's size and location).

(E) *Related furnishings.*—The term *related furnishings* means furniture and commonly included items such as appliances, fixtures, decorative items and china, that are not beyond the value associated with normal household and decorative use. Rare artwork, valuable antiques, and automobiles of any kind or class are not within the meaning of this term.

(F) *Required statement.*—If one or both of the exclusions provided in paragraph (d)(1)(iv)(A) or (B) of this section are elected by the executor of the estate and the personal residence is later sold or ceases to be used, or held for use as a personal residence, the U.S. Trustee must file the statement that is required under paragraph (d)(3) of this section at the time and in the manner provided in paragraphs (d)(3)(ii) and (iii) of this section.

(G) *Cessation of use.*—Except as provided in this paragraph (d)(1)(iv)(G), if the residence ceases to be used by, or held for the use of, the spouse as a personal residence of the spouse, or if the residence is sold during the term of the QDOT, the exclusions provided in paragraphs (d)(1)(iv)(A) and (B) of this section cease to apply. However, if the residence is sold, the exclusion continues to apply if, within 12 months of the date of sale, the amount of the adjusted sales price (as defined in section 1034(b)(1)) is reinvested to purchase a new personal residence for the spouse. If less than the amount of the adjusted sales price is reinvested, the amount of the exclusion equals the amount reinvested in the new residence plus any amount previously allocated to a residence that continues to qualify for the exclusion, up to a total of $600,000. If the QDOT ceases to qualify for all or any portion of the initially claimed exclusions, paragraph (d)(1)(i) of this section, if applicable (determined as if the portion of the exclusions disallowed had not been initially claimed by the QDOT), must be complied with no later than 120 days after the effective date of the cessation. In addition, if a residence ceases to be used by, or held for the use of the spouse as a personal residence of the spouse or if the personal residence is sold during the term of the QDOT, the personal residence exclusion may be allocated to another residence that is held in either the same QDOT or in another QDOT that is established for the surviving spouse, if the other residence qualifies as being used by, or held for the use of the spouse as a personal residence. The trustee may allocate up to $600,000 to the new personal residence (less the amount previously allocated to a residence that continues to qualify for the exclusion) even if the entire $600,000 exclusion was not previously utilized with respect to the original personal residence(s).

(v) *Anti-abuse rule.*—Regardless of whether the QDOT designates a bank as the U.S. Trustee under paragraph (d)(1)(i)(A) of this section (or otherwise complies with paragraph (d)(1)(i)(A) of this section by naming a foreign bank with a United States branch as a trustee to serve with the U.S. Trustee), complies with paragraph (d)(1)(i)(B) or (C) of this section, or is subject to and complies with the foreign real property requirements of paragraph (d)(1)(ii) of this section, the trust immediately ceases to qualify as a QDOT if the trust utilizes any device or arrangement that has, as a principal purpose, the avoidance of liability for the estate tax imposed under section 2056A(b)(1), or the prevention of the collection of the tax. For example, the trust may become subject to this paragraph (d)(1)(v) if the U.S. Trustee that is selected is a domestic corporation established with insubstantial capitalization by the surviving spouse or members of the spouse's family.

(2) *Individual trustees.*—If the U.S. Trustee is an individual United States citizen, the individual must have a tax home (as defined in section 911(d)(3)) in the United States.

(3) *Annual reporting requirements.*—(i) *In general.*—The U.S. Trustee must file a written statement described in paragraph (d)(3)(iii) of this section, if the QDOT satisfies any one of the following criteria for the applicable reporting years—

(A) The QDOT directly owns any foreign real property on the last day of its taxable year (or the last day of the calendar year if it has no taxable year), and the QDOT does not satisfy the requirements of paragraph (d)(1)(i)(A), (B), or (C) or (d)(4) of this section by employing a bank as trustee or providing security; or

(B) The personal residence previously subject to the exclusion under paragraph (d)(1)(iv) of this section is sold, or that personal residence ceases to be used, or held for use, as a personal residence, during the taxable year (or during the calendar year if the QDOT does not have a taxable year); or

(C) After the application of the look-through rule contained in paragraph (d)(1)(ii)(B) of this section, the QDOT is treated as owning any foreign real property on the last day of the taxable year (or the last day of the calendar year if the QDOT has no taxable year), and the QDOT does not satisfy the requirements of paragraph (d)(1)(A), (B), (C) or (d)(4) of this section by employing a bank as trustee or providing security.

(ii) *Time and manner of filing.*—The written statement, containing the information described in paragraph (d)(3)(iii) of this section, is to be filed for the taxable year of the QDOT (calendar year if the QDOT does not have a taxable year) for which any of the events or conditions requiring the filing of a statement under paragraph (d)(3)(i) of this section have occurred or have been satisfied. The written statement is to be submitted to the Internal Revenue Service by filing a Form 706-QDT, with the statement attached, no later than April 15th of the calendar year following the calendar year in which or with which the taxable year of the QDOT ends (or by April 15th of the following year if the QDOT has no taxable year), unless an extension of time is obtained under §20.2056A-11(a). The Form 706-QDT, with attached statement, must be filed regardless of whether the Form 706-QDT is otherwise required to be filed under the provisions of this chapter. Failure to file timely the statement may subject the QDOT to the rules of paragraph (d)(1)(v) of this section.

(iii) *Contents of statement.*—The written statement must contain the following information—

(A) The name, address, and taxpayer identification number, if any, of the U.S. Trustee and the QDOT; and

(B) A list summarizing the assets held by the QDOT, together with the fair market value of each listed QDOT asset, determined as of the last day of the taxable year (December 31 if the QDOT does not have a taxable year) for which the written statement is filed. If the look-through rule contained in paragraph (d)(1)(ii)(B) of this section applies, then the partnership, corporation, trust or other entity must be identified and the QDOT's pro rata share of the foreign real property and other assets owned by that entity must be listed on the statement as if directly owned by the QDOT; and

(C) If a personal residence previously subject to the exclusion under paragraph (d)(1)(iv) of this section is sold during the taxable year (or during the calendar year if the QDOT does not have a taxable year), the statement must provide the date of sale, the adjusted sales price (as defined in section 1034(b)(1)), the extent to which the amount of the adjusted sales price has been or will be used to purchase a new personal residence and, if not timely reinvested, the steps that will or have been taken to comply with paragraph (d)(1)(i) of this section, if applicable; and

(D) If the personal residence ceases to be used, or held for use, as a personal residence by the surviving spouse during the taxable year (or during the calendar year if the QDOT does not have a taxable year), the written statement must describe the steps that will or have been taken to comply with paragraph (d)(1)(i) of this section, if applicable.

(4) *Request for alternate arrangement or waiver.*—If the Commissioner provides guidance published in the Internal Revenue Bulletin

(see §601.601(d)(2) of this chapter) pursuant to which a testator, executor, or the U.S. Trustee may adopt an alternate plan or arrangement to assure collection of the section 2056A estate tax, and if the alternate plan or arrangement is adopted in accordance with the published guidance, then the QDOT will be treated, subject to paragraph (d)(1)(v) of this section, as meeting the requirements of paragraph (d)(1) of this section. Until this guidance is published in the Internal Revenue Bulletin (see §601.601(d)(2) of this chapter), taxpayers may submit a request for a private letter ruling for the approval of an alternate plan or arrangement proposed to be adopted to assure collection of the section 2056A estate tax in lieu of the requirements prescribed in this paragraph (d)(4).

(5) *Adjustment of dollar threshold and exclusion.*—The Commissioner may increase or decrease the dollar amounts referred to in paragraph (d)(1)(i), (ii) or (iv) of this section in accordance with guidance published in the Internal Revenue Bulletin (see §601.601(d)(2) of this chapter).

(6) *Effective date and special rules.*—(i) This paragraph (d) is effective for estates of decedents dying after February 19, 1996.

(ii) *Special rule in the case of incompetency.*—A revocable trust or a trust created under the terms of a will is deemed to meet the governing instrument requirements of this paragraph (d) notwithstanding that the requirements are not contained in the governing instrument (or otherwise incorporated by reference) if the trust instrument (or will) was executed on or before November 20, 1995, and—

(A) The testator or settlor dies after February 19, 1996;

(B) The testator or settlor is, on November 20, 1995, and at all times thereafter, under a legal disability to amend the will or trust instrument;

(C) The will or trust instrument does not provide the executor or the U.S. Trustee with a power to amend the instrument in order to meet the requirements of section 2056A; and

(D) The U.S. Trustee provides a written statement with the federal estate tax return (Form 706 or 706NA) that the trust is being administered (or will be administered) so as to be in actual compliance with the requirements of this paragraph (d) and will continue to be administered so as to be in actual compliance with this paragraph (d) for the duration of the trust. This statement must be binding on all successor trustees.

(iii) *Special rule in the case of certain irrevocable trusts.*—An irrevocable trust is deemed to meet the governing instrument requirements of this paragraph (d) notwithstanding that the requirements are not contained in the governing instrument (or otherwise incorporated by reference) if the trust was executed on or before November 20, 1995, and:

(A) The settlor dies after February 19, 1996;

(B) The trust instrument does not provide the U.S. Trustee with a power to amend the trust instrument in order to meet the requirements of section 2056A; and

(C) The U.S. Trustee provides a written statement with the decedent's federal estate tax return (Form 706 or 706NA) that the trust is being administered in actual compliance with the requirements of this paragraph (d) and will continue to be administered so as to be in actual compliance with this paragraph (d) for the duration of the trust. This statement must be binding on all successor trustees. [Reg. §20.2056A-2.]

☐ [*T.D. 8612, 8-21-95. Amended by T.D. 8686, 11-27-96.*]

## [Reg. §20.2056A-3]

§20.2056A-3. QDOT election.—(a) *General rule.*—Subject to the time period prescribed in section 2056A(d), the election to treat a trust as a QDOT must be made on the last federal estate tax return filed before the due date (including extensions of time to file actually granted) or, if a timely return is not filed, on the first federal estate tax return filed after the due date. The election, once made, is irrevocable.

(b) *No partial elections.*—An election to treat a trust as a QDOT may not be made with respect to a specific portion of an entire trust that would otherwise qualify for the marital deduction but for the application of section 2056(d). However, if the trust is actually severed in accordance with the applicable requirements of §20.2056(b)-7(b)(2)(ii) prior to the due date for the election, a QDOT election may be made for any one or more of the severed trusts.

(c) *Protective elections.*—A protective election may be made to treat a trust as a QDOT only if at the time the federal estate tax return is filed, the executor of the decedent's estate reasonably believes that there is a bona fide issue that concerns either the residency or citizenship of the decedent, the citizenship of the surviving spouse, whether an asset is includible in the decedent's gross estate, or the amount or nature of the property the surviving spouse is entitled to receive. For example, if at the time the federal estate tax return is filed either the estate is involved in a bona fide will contest, there is uncertainty regarding the inclusion in the gross estate of an asset which, if includible, would be eligible for the QDOT election, or there is uncertainty regarding the status of the decedent as a resident alien or a nonresident alien for estate tax purposes, or a similar uncertainty regarding the citizenship status of the surviving spouse, a protective QDOT election may be made. The protective election is in addition to, and is not in lieu of, the requirements set forth in §20.2056A-4. The protective QDOT election must be made on a written statement signed by the executor under penalties of perjury and must be attached to the return described in paragraph (a) of this section, and must identify the specific assets to which the protective election refers and the specific basis for the protective election. However, the protective election may otherwise be defined by means of a formula (such as the minimum amount necessary to reduce the estate tax to zero). Once made, the protective election is irrevocable. For example, if a protective election is made because a bona fide question exists as to the includibility of an asset in the decedent's gross estate and it is later finally determined that the asset is so includible, the protective election becomes effective with respect to the asset and cannot thereafter be revoked.

(d) *Manner of election.*—The QDOT election under paragraph (a) of this section is made in the form and manner set forth in the decedent's estate tax return, including applicable instructions. [Reg. §20.2056A-3.]

☐ [*T.D. 8612, 8-21-95.*]

**[Reg. §20.2056A-4]**

**§20.2056A-4. Procedures for conforming marital trusts and nontrust marital transfers to the requirements of a qualified domestic trust.**—(a) *Marital trusts.*—(1) *In general.*—If an interest in property passes from the decedent to a trust for the benefit of a noncitizen surviving spouse and if the trust otherwise qualifies for a marital deduction but for the provisions of section 2056(d)(1)(A), the property interest is treated as passing to the surviving spouse in a QDOT if the trust is reformed, either in accordance with the terms of the decedent's will or trust agreement or pursuant to a judicial proceeding, to meet the requirements of a QDOT. For this purpose, the requirements of a QDOT include all of the applicable requirements set forth in §20.2056A-2, and the requirements of §20.2056A-2T(d). A reformation pursuant to the terms of the decedent's will or trust instrument must be completed by the time prescribed (including extensions) for filing the decedent's estate tax return. For purposes of this paragraph (a), a return filed prior to the due date (including extensions) is considered filed on the last date that the return is required to be filed (including extensions), and a late return filed at any time after the due date is considered filed on the date that it is actually filed.

(2) *Judicial reformations.*—In general, a reformation pursuant to a judicial proceeding is permitted under this section if the reformation is commenced on or before the due date (determined with regard to extensions actually granted) for filing the return of tax imposed by chapter 11 of the Internal Revenue Code, regardless of the date that the return is actually filed. The reformation (either pursuant to a judicial proceeding or otherwise) must result in a trust that is effective under local law. The reformed trust may be revocable by the spouse, or otherwise be subject to the spouse's general power of appointment, provided that no person (including the spouse) has the power to amend the trust during the continued existence of the trust such that it would no longer qualify as a QDOT. Prior to the time that the judicial reformation is completed, the trust must be treated as a QDOT. Thus, the trustee of the trust is responsible for filing the Form 706-QDT, paying any section 2056A estate tax that becomes due, and filing the annual statement required under §20.2056A-2T(d)(3), if applicable. Failure to comply with these requirements may cause the trust to be subject to the anti-abuse rule under §20.2056A-2T(d)(1)(iv). In addition, if the judicial reformation is terminated prior to the time that the reformation is completed, the estate of the decedent is required to pay the increased estate tax imposed on the decedent's estate (plus interest and any applicable penalties) that becomes due at the time of such termination as a result of the failure of the trust to comply with section 2056(d). See section 6511 as to applicable time periods for credit or refund of tax.

(3) *Tolling of statutory assessment period.*—For the tolling of the statute of limitations in the case of a judicial reformation, see section 2056(d)(5)(B).

(b) *Nontrust marital transfers.*—(1) *In general.*—Under section 2056(d)(2)(B), if an interest in property passes outright from a decedent to a noncitizen surviving spouse either by testamentary bequest or devise, by operation of law, or pursuant to an annuity or other

similar plan or arrangement, and such property interest otherwise qualifies for a marital deduction except that it does not pass in a QDOT, solely for purposes of section 2056(d)(2)(A), the property is treated as passing to the surviving spouse in a QDOT if the property interest is either actually transferred to a QDOT before the estate tax return is filed and on or before the last date prescribed by law that the QDOT election may be made, or is assigned to a QDOT under an enforceable and irrevocable written assignment made on or before the date on which the return is filed and on or before the last date prescribed by law that the QDOT election may be made. The transfer or assignment of property to a QDOT may be made by the surviving spouse, the surviving spouse's legal representative (if the surviving spouse is incompetent), or the personal representative of the surviving spouse's estate (if the surviving spouse has died). The QDOT to which the property is transferred may be created by the decedent (during life or by will), by the surviving spouse, or by the executor. For purposes of section 2056(d)(2)(B), if no property other than the property passing to the surviving spouse from the decedent is transferred to the QDOT, the transferee QDOT need not be in a form such that the property transferred to the QDOT would qualify for a marital deduction under section 2056(a). However, if other property is or has been transferred to the QDOT, 100 percent of the value of the transferee QDOT must qualify for the marital deduction under section 2056. For example, if the decedent, a U.S. citizen, bequeaths property to a trust that does not satisfy the requirements of section 2056(b)(5) or (7), or to a trust that does not qualify as an estate trust under §20.2056(c)-2(b)(1)(i)-(iii), that trust cannot be used as a transferee QDOT by the surviving spouse, since after that trust is fully funded the portion of the value of the trust attributable to property bequeathed to the trust by the decedent will not qualify for a marital deduction under section 2056. Similarly, if the decedent, a nonresident not a citizen of the United States, bequeaths foreign situs assets to a trust created under his will, the surviving spouse may not transfer U.S. situs assets passing to the spouse outside of the will to that trust under this paragraph. See §20.2056A-3(c) with respect to protective elections. See §20.2056A-3(a) with respect to the time limitations for making the QDOT election.

(2) *Form of transfer or assignment.*—A transfer or assignment of property to a QDOT must be in writing and otherwise be in accordance with all local law requirements for such assignment or transfer. The transfer or assignment may be of a specific asset or a group of assets, or a fractional share of either, or may be of a pecuniary amount. A transfer or assignment of less than an entire interest in an asset or a group of assets may be expressed by means of a formula (such as the minimum amount necessary to reduce the estate tax to zero). In the case of a transfer, a copy of the trust instrument evidencing the transfer must be submitted with the decedent's estate tax return. In the case of an assignment, a copy of the assignment must be submitted with the decedent's estate tax return.

(3) *Assets eligible for transfer or assignment.*—If a transfer or assignment is of a specific asset or group of assets, only assets included in the decedent's gross estate and passing from the decedent to the spouse (or the proceeds from the sale, exchange or conversion of such assets) may be transferred or assigned to the QDOT. The noncitizen surviving spouse may not transfer or assign to the QDOT property owned by the surviving spouse at the time of the decedent's death in lieu of property included in the decedent's gross estate that passes to the spouse (or in lieu of the proceeds from the sale, exchange or conversion of such includible assets). In addition, if only a portion of an asset is includible in the decedent's gross estate, the spouse may only transfer the portion that is so includible to the transferee trust under this paragraph (b)(3).

(4) *Pecuniary assignment—special rules.*—If the assignment is expressed in the form of a pecuniary amount (such as a fixed dollar amount or a formula designed to reduce the decedent's estate tax to zero), the assignment must specify that—

(i) Assets actually transferred to the QDOT in satisfaction of the assignment have an aggregate fair market value on the date of actual transfer to the QDOT amounting to no less than the amount of the pecuniary transfer or assignment; or

(ii) The assets actually transferred to the QDOT be fairly representative of appreciation or depreciation in the value of all property available for transfer to the QDOT between the valuation date and the date of actual transfer to the QDOT, if the assignment is to be satisfied by accounting for the assets on the basis of their fair market value as of some date before the date of actual transfer to the QDOT.

(5) *Transfer tax treatment of transfer or assignment.*—Property assigned or transferred to a QDOT pursuant to section 2056(d)(2)(B) is treated as passing from the decedent to a QDOT solely for purposes of section 2056(d)(2)(A). For all other purposes (e.g., income, gift, estate, generation-skipping transfer tax, and section 1491 excise tax),

the surviving spouse is treated as the transferor of the property to the QDOT. However, the spouse is not considered the transferor of property to a QDOT if the transfer by the spouse constitutes a transfer that satisfies the requirements of section 2518(c)(3). For a special exception to the valuation rules of section 2702 in the case of a transfer by the surviving spouse to a QDOT, see § 25.2702-1(c)(8) of this chapter.

(6) *Period for completion of transfer.*—Property irrevocably assigned but not actually transferred to the QDOT before the estate tax return is filed must actually be conveyed and transferred to the QDOT under applicable local law before the administration of the decedent's estate is completed. If there is no administration of the decedent's estate (because for example, none of the decedent's assets are subject to probate under local law), the conveyance must be made on or before the date that is one year after the due date (including extensions) for filing the decedent's estate tax return. If an actual transfer to the QDOT is not timely made, section 2056(d)(1)(A) applies and the marital deduction is not allowed. The executor of the decedent's estate (or other authorized legal representative) may request a private letter ruling from the Internal Revenue Service requesting an extension of the time for completing the conveyance or waiving the actual conveyance under specified circumstances under § 301.9100-1(a) of this chapter.

(7) *Retirement accounts and annuities.*—(i) *In general.*—An assignment otherwise in compliance with this paragraph (b) of rights under annuities or other similar arrangements that are assignable and thus, are not described in paragraph (c) of this section, is treated as a transfer of such property to the QDOT regardless of the method of payment actually elected under such annuity or plan.

(ii) *Individual retirement annuities.*—Individual retirement annuities described in section 408(b) are not assignable pursuant to section 408(b)(1) and thus, do not come within the purview of this paragraph (b)(7). See the procedures provided in paragragh (c) of this section.

(iii) *Individual retirement accounts.*—Unless the terms of the account provide otherwise, individual retirement accounts described in section 408(a) are assignable and subject to the provisions of this paragraph (b)(7). However, under paragraph (c) of this section, the surviving spouse may treat an individual retirement account as nonassignable and, therefore, eligible for the procedures in paragraph (c) of this section if the spouse timely complies with the requirements in paragraph (c) of this section.

(iv) *Other effects of assignment.*—The provisions of this paragraph (b)(7) apply solely for purposes of qualifying the annuity or account under the rules of § 20.2056A-2 and this section. See, for example, section 408(d) and 4980A regarding the consequences of an assignment for purposes other than this paragraph (b)(7).

(8) *Protective assignment.*—A protective assignment of property to a QDOT may be made only if, at the time the federal estate tax return is filed, the executor of the decedent's estate reasonably believes that there is a bona fide issue that concerns either the residency or citizenship of the decedent, the citizenship of the surviving spouse, whether all or a portion of an asset is includible in the decedent's gross estate, or the amount or nature of the property the surviving spouse is entitled to receive. For example, if at the time the federal estate tax return is filed, either the estate is involved in a bona fide will contest, there is uncertainty regarding the inclusion in the gross estate of an asset which, if includible, would be eligible for the QDOT election, or there is uncertainty regarding the status of the decedent as a resident alien or a nonresident alien for estate tax purposes, or a similar uncertainty regarding the citizenship status of the surviving spouse, a protective assignment may be made. The protective assignment must be made on a written statement signed by the assignor under penalties of perjury on or before the date prescribed under paragraph (b)(1) of this section, and must identify the specific assets to which the assignment refers and the specific basis for the protective assignment. However, the protective assignment may otherwise be defined by means of a formula (such as the minimum amount necessary to reduce the estate tax to zero). Once made, the protective assignment cannot be revoked. For example, if a protective assignment is made because a bona fide question exists as to the includibility of an asset in the decedent's gross estate and it is later finally determined that the asset is so includible, the protective assignment becomes effective with respect to the asset and cannot thereafter be revoked. Protective assignments are, in all events, subject to paragraph (b)(6) of this section. A copy of the protective assignment must be submitted with the decedent's estate tax return.

(c) *Nonassignable annuities and other arrangements.*—(1) *Definition and general rule.*—For purposes of this section, a *nonassignable annuity or other arrangement* means a plan, annuity, or other arrangement (whether qualified or not qualified under part I of subchapter D of chapter 1 of subtitle A of the Internal Revenue Code) that qualifies for the marital deduction but for section 2056(d)(1)(A), and whose payments are not assignable or transferable to the QDOT under either federal law (see, e.g., section 401(a)(13)), state law, foreign law, or the terms of the plan or arrangement itself. For purposes of this paragraph (c), a surviving spouse's interest as beneficiary of an individual retirement annuity described in section 408(b) is a nonassignable annuity or other arrangement. See section 408(b)(1). For purposes of this paragraph (c), a surviving spouse's interest as beneficiary of an individual retirement account described in section 408(a), although assignable under that section, is considered to be a nonassignable annuity or other arrangement eligible for the procedures contained in this paragraph (c), at the option of the surviving spouse, if the requirements of this paragraph are otherwise satisfied. See paragraph (b)(7) of this section if the spouse elects to treat the account as assignable. In the case of a plan, annuity, or other arrangement which is not assignable or transferable (or is treated as such), the property passing under the plan from the decedent is treated as meeting the requirements § 20.2056A-2, and the requirements of § 20.2056A-2T(d) (pertaining, respectively, to general requirements, qualified marital interest requirements, statutory requirements, and requirements to ensure collection of the tax) if the requirements of either paragraph (c)(2) or (3) of this section are satisfied. Thus, the property will be treated as passing in the form of a QDOT, notwithstanding that the spouse does not irrevocably transfer or assign the annuity or other payment to the QDOT as provided in paragraph (b) of this section. The Commissioner will prescribe by administrative guidance the extent, if any, to which the provisions of this paragraph (c) apply to a rollover from a qualified trust to an eligible retirement plan within the meaning of section 402(c) or a distribution from an individual retirement account or an individual retirement annuity that is paid into an individual retirement account or an individual retirement annuity within the meaning of section 408(d)(3).

(2) *Agreement to remit section 2056A estate tax on corpus portion of each annuity payment.*—The requirements of this paragraph (c)(2) are satisfied if—

(i) The noncitizen surviving spouse agrees to pay on an annual basis, as described in paragraph (c)(6)(i) of this section, the estate tax imposed under section 2056A(b)(1) due on the corpus portion, as defined in paragraph (c)(4) of this section, of each nonassignable annuity or other payment received under the plan or arrangement. However, for purposes of this paragraph (c)(2), if the financial circumstances of the spouse are such that an amount equal to all or a portion of the corpus portion of a nonassignable annuity payment received by the spouse would be subject to a hardship exemption (as defined in § 20.2056A-5(c)) if paid from a QDOT, then all or a corresponding part of the corpus portion will be exempt from the tax payment requirement under this paragraph (c)(2);

(ii) The executor of the decedent's estate files with the estate tax return the Information Statement described in paragraph (c)(5) of this section;

(iii) The executor files with the estate tax return the Agreement To Pay Section 2056A Estate Tax described in paragraph (c)(6) of this section; and

(iv) The executor makes the election under § 20.2056A-3 with respect to the nonassignable annuity or other payment.

(3) *Agreement to roll over corpus portion of annuity payment to QDOT.*—The requirements of this paragraph (c)(3) are satisfied if—

(i) The noncitizen surviving spouse agrees to roll over and transfer, within the time prescribed under paragraph (c)(7)(i) of this section, the corpus portion of each annuity payment to a QDOT, whether the QDOT is created by the decedent's will, the executor of the decedent's estate, or the surviving spouse. However, for purposes of this section, if the financial circumstances of the spouse are such that an amount equal to all or a portion of the corpus portion of a nonassignable annuity payment received by the spouse would be subject to a hardship exemption (as defined in § 20.2056A-5(c)) if paid from a QDOT, then all or a corresponding part of the corpus portion will be exempt from the rollover requirement under this paragraph (c)(3);

(ii) A QDOT for the benefit of the surviving spouse is established prior to the date that the estate tax return is filed and on or prior to the last date prescribed by law that the QDOT election may be made;

(iii) The executor of the decedent's estate files with the estate tax return the Information Statement described in paragraph (c)(5) of this section;

(iv) The executor files with the estate tax return the Agreement To Roll Over Annuity Payments described in paragraph (c)(7) of this section; and

(v) The executor makes the election under § 20.2056A-3 with respect to the nonassignable annuity or other payment. See

§ 20.2056A-5(c)(3)(iv)(A), regarding distributions from the QDOT reimbursing the spouse for income taxes paid (either by actual payment or withholding) by the spouse with respect to amounts transferred to the QDOT pursuant to this paragraph (c)(3).

(4) *Determination of corpus portion.*—(i) *Corpus portion.*—For purposes of this paragraph (c), the corpus portion of each nonassignable

$$\text{Corpus Amount} = \frac{\text{Total present value of annuity or other payment}}{\text{Expected annuity term}}$$

(B) The total present value of the annuity or other payment is the present value of the nonassignable annuity or other payment as of the date of the decedent's death, determined in accordance with the interest rates and mortality data prescribed by section 7520. The expected annuity term is the number of years that would be required for the scheduled payments to exhaust a hypothetical fund equal to the present value of the scheduled payments. This is determined by first dividing the total present value of the payments by the annual payment. From the quotient so obtained, the expected annuity term is derived by identifying the term of years that corresponds to the annuity factor equal to the quotient. This is determined by using column 1 of Table B, for the applicable interest rate, contained in Publication 1457, "Actuarial Valuations Version 3A". A copy of this publication is available, at no charge, electronically via the IRS Internet site at *www.irs.gov*. If the quotient obtained falls between two terms, the longer term is used.

(5) *Information Statement.*—(i) *In general.*—In order for a nonassignable annuity or other payment described in this paragraph (c) to qualify under either paragraph (c)(2) or (3) of this section, the Information Statement described in paragraph (c)(5)(ii) of this section must be filed with the decedent's federal estate tax return. The Information Statement must be signed under penalties of perjury by both the executor of the decedent's estate and by the surviving spouse of the decedent (or by the legal representative of the surviving spouse if the surviving spouse is legally incompetent to sign the statement). The Statement must contain all of the information prescribed by this paragraph (c)(5).

(ii) *Annuity source information.*—(A) *Employment-related annuity.*—If the nonassignable annuity or other payment is employment-related, the following information must be provided—

*(1)* The name and address of the employer;

*(2)* The date of retirement or other separation from employment of the decedent;

*(3)* The name and address of the pension fund, insurance company, or other obligor that is paying the annuity (or similar payment); and

*(4)* The identification number, if any, that the obligor has assigned to the annuity or other payment.

(B) *Annuity not employment-related.*—If the nonassignable annuity or other payment is not employment-related, the following information must be provided—

*(1)* The name and address of the person or entity paying the nonassignable annuity or other payment;

*(2)* The date of acquisition of the nonassignable annuity contract by the decedent or by the decedent and the surviving spouse; and

*(3)* The identification number, if any, that the obligor has assigned to the nonassignable annuity or other payment.

(iii) *The total annuity amount payable each year.*—The total amount payable annually under the nonassignable annuity or other arrangement, including a description of whether the annuity is payable monthly, quarterly, or at some other interval, and a description of any scheduled changes in the annuity payout amount.

(iv) *The duration of the annuity.*—A description of the term of the nonassignable annuity or other payment in years, if it is determined by a term certain, and the name, address, and birthdate of any measuring life if the nonassignable annuity or other payment is determined by one or more lives.

(v) *The market interest rate under section 7520.*—The applicable interest rate as determined under section 7520.

(vi) *Determination of corpus portion of each payment (in accordance with paragraph (c)(4) of this section).*—The following items are required in order to determine the corpus portion of each payment—

(A) The present value of the nonassignable annuity or other payment as of the decedent's death;

(B) The expected annuity term;

annuity or other payment is the corpus amount of the annual payment divided by the total annual payment.

(ii) *Corpus amount.*—(A) The corpus amount of the annual payment is determined in accordance with the following formula:

(C) The corpus amount of the annual annuity payments (paragraph (c)(5)(vi)(A) of this section divided by paragraph (c)(5)(vi)(B) of this section); and

(D) The corpus portion of the annual payments (paragraph (c)(5)(vi)(C) of this section divided by the total amount payable annually).

(vii) *Recipient QDOT.*—In the case of an agreement to rollover under paragraph (c)(3) of this section, the following must be provided—

(A) The name and address of the trustee of the QDOT who is the U.S. Trustee; and

(B) The name and taxpayer identification number of the QDOT.

(viii) *Certification statement.*—The executor of the decedent's estate and the surviving spouse of the decedent (or the legal representative of the surviving spouse if the surviving spouse is legally incompetent to so certify) must each sign a Certification Statement as follows:

Under penalties of perjury, I hereby certify that, to the best of my knowledge and belief, the information reported in this Information Statement is true, correct and complete.

(6) *Agreement to pay section 2056A estate tax.*—(i) *Payment of section 2056A estate tax.*—The tax payable under paragraph (c)(2) of this section is payable on an annual basis, commencing in the calendar year following the calendar year of the receipt by the surviving spouse of the spouse's first annuity payment. Form 706QDT and the payment are due on April 15th of each year following the calendar year in which an annuity payment is received except that, in the year of the deceased spouse's death, the Form 706-QDT and the payment are not due prior to the due date, including extensions, for filing the deceased spouse's estate tax return, or if no return is filed, no later than 9 months from the date of the deceased spouse's death; and, in the year of the surviving spouse's death, the Form 706-QDT must be filed and the payment made no later than 9 months from the date of the surviving spouse's death. See § 20.2056A-11 for extensions of time for filing Form 706-QDT and paying the section 2056A estate tax.

(ii) *Agreement.*—In order for a nonassignable annuity or other payment described in this paragraph (c) to qualify under paragraph (c)(2) of this section, the executor of the decedent's estate must file with the estate tax return the following Agreement To Pay Section 2056A Estate Tax, which must be signed by the surviving spouse of the decedent (or by the surviving spouse's legal representative if the surviving spouse is legally incompetent to sign the agreement):

I [*name* ] hereby agree that I will report all annuity payments received under the [*name of plan or arrangement* ]on Form 706-QDT for the calendar year and remit, on an annual basis, to the Internal Revenue Service the estate tax that is imposed under section 2056A(b)(1) of the Internal Revenue Code on the corpus portion of each annuity payment (as defined in § 20.2056A-4(c)(4) of the Estate Tax Regulations) received under the plan during the calendar year. I also agree that Form 706-QDT is to be filed no later than April 15th of the year following the calendar year in which any annuity payments are received except that: in the case of annuity payments received in the year of my spouse's death, Form 706-QDT and the payment shall not be due prior to the due date, including extensions, for filing my spouse's estate tax return or, if no return is filed, no later than 9 months from the date of my spouse's death (except if I am granted an extension of time to file Form 706-QDT under the provisions of § 20.2056A-11); and in the year of my death, the Form 706-QDT must be filed and the payment made no later than the date my estate tax return is filed (or if no return is filed, no later than 9 months from the date of my death). I further agree that if I fail to timely file Form 706-QDT or to timely pay the tax imposed on the corpus portion of any annuity payment (determined after any extensions of time to pay granted to me under the provisions of § 20.2056A-11), I may become immediately liable to pay the amount of the tax determined by application of section 2056A(b)(1) on the entire remaining present value of the annuity, calculated as of the beginning of the year in which the payment was received with respect to which I failed to timely pay the tax or failed to timely file the return. However, I may make an application for relief under § 301.9100-1 of the Procedure and Administration Regualations, from the consequences of failing to timely file the Form 706-QDT or failing to timely pay the tax on the corpus portion. [The following sentence is applicable only in cases where the plan or arrangement is established and administered by a person or an entity that is located outside of the United States.]I agree, at the request of the District Director, [or the Assistant Commissioner (International) in the case of a surviving spouse of a nonresident noncitizen decedent or a surviving spouse of a United States citizen who died domiciled outside the United States] to enter into a security agreement to secure my undertakings under this agreement.

(7) *Agreement to roll over annuity payments.*—(i) *Roll over of corpus portion.*—Beginning in the calendar year of the receipt by the surviving spouse of the spouse's first annuity payment, the corpus portion of each annuity payment, as determined under paragraph (c)(4) of this section, must, within 60 days of receipt, be transferred to a QDOT. In addition, all annuity payments received during the calendar year must be reported on Form 706-QDT no later than April 15th of the year following the year in which the annuity payments are received, except that in the year of the surviving spouse's death, the Form 706-QDT must be filed no later than the date the estate tax return is filed (or if no return is filed, no later than 9 months from the date of the surviving spouse's death). See § 20.2056A-11 for extensions of time for filing Form 706-QDT.

(ii) *Agreement.*—In order for a nonassignable annuity or other payment described in this paragraph (c) to qualify under paragraph (c)(3) of this section, the executor of the decedent's estate must file with the estate tax return the following Agreement To Roll Over Annuity Payments, which must be signed by the surviving spouse of the decedent (or by the legal representative of the surviving spouse if the surviving spouse is legally incompetent to sign the agreement):

I [ *name* ] hereby agree that within 60 days of receipt of each annuity payment paid under the [*name of plan or arrangement* ], I will transfer an amount equal to percent (the corpus portion determined under § 20.2056A-4(c)(4) of the Estate Tax Regulations) of each annuity payment to [*identify the QDOT* ]. Further, I will report all annuity payments received during the calendar year under the [*name of plan or arrangement* ]on Form 706-QDT including a schedule of transfers to the [*identify the QDOT* ]. I also agree that Form 706-QDT is to be filed

no later than April 15th of the year following the year in which any annuity payments are received except that: in the case of annuity payments received in the year of my spouse's death, Form 706-QDT shall not be due prior to the due date, including extensions, for filing my spouse's estate tax return, or, if no return is filed, no later than 9 months from the date of my spouse's death (except if I am granted an extension of time to file Form 706-QDT under the provisions of § 20.2056A-11); and in the year of my death, the Form 706-QDT must be filed no later than the date my estate tax return is filed (or if no return is filed, no later than 9 months from the date of my death), and except if I am granted an extension of time to file Form 706-QDT under the provisions of § 20.2056A-11. I further agree that if I fail to timely transfer any required amount with respect to any annuity payment, or fail to timely file Form 706-QDT reporting the transfers for any year, I may become immediately liable to pay the amount of the tax determined by application of section 2056A(b)(1) on the entire remaining present value of the annuity, calculated as of the beginning of the year in which the payment was received with respect to which I failed to make the timely transfer or timely file a return. However, I may make an application for relief under § 301.9100-1 of the Procedure and Administration Regulations, from the consequences of failing to timely file Form 706-QDT or failing to timely transfer the corpus portion of any annuity payment to the QDOT. [The following sentence is applicable only in cases where the plan or arrangement is established and administered by a person or an entity that is located outside of the United States.] I agree, at the request of the District Director [or the Assistant Commissioner (International) in the case of a surviving spouse of a nonresident noncitizen decedent or a surviving spouse of a United States citizen who died domiciled outside the United States] to enter into a security agreement to secure my undertakings under this agreement.

(d) *Examples.*—The provisions of this section are illustrated by the following examples. In each of the following examples the decedent, D, a citizen of the United States, died after August 22, 1995, and D's surviving spouse, S, is not a United States citizen at the time of D's death.

*Example 1. Transfer and assignment of probate and nonprobate property to QDOT.*—(i) S is the beneficiary of the following probate and nonprobate assets included in D's gross estate:

| | |
|---|---:|
| Pecuniary bequest under will | $400,000 |
| Proceeds of life insurance | 200,000 |
| D's interest in property owned jointly with S includible in the gross estate under § 2040(a) | 300,000 |
| Devise of real property under will | 100,000 |
| Total | $1,000,000 |

(ii) Before the estate tax return for D's estate is filed and before the date that the QDOT election must be made, S creates a QDOT pursuant to which all income is payable to S for life and the remainder is distributable to S's children. S retains a power of appointment over the disposition of the remainder to ensure that S does not make an immediate gift of the remainder of the trust. Also, before the estate tax return is filed and before the date that the QDOT election must be made, S transfers the life insurance proceeds and the specifically devised real property to the QDOT. S decides not to transfer the property that had been jointly owned to the QDOT. Because S has not received distribution of the pecuniary bequest before D's estate tax return is filed and before the date that the QDOT election must be made, S irrevocably assigns the interest in the pecuniary bequest to the QDOT. Assume that the pecuniary bequest is in fact transferred by S to the QDOT before the estate administration is concluded. D's executor makes a QDOT election on the estate tax return for the $700,000 in property that S has transferred and assigned to the QDOT. A marital deduction of $700,000 is allowed to D's estate assuming the estate tax return is filed and the QDOT election is made within the time limitation prescribed in § 20.2056A-3(a). No marital deduction is allowed for the $300,000 interest in jointly-owned property not transferred to the QDOT.

*Example 2. Formula assignment.* Under the terms of D's will, the entire probate estate passes outright to S. Prior to the date D's estate tax return is filed and before the date that the QDOT election must be made, S establishes a QDOT and S executes an irrevocable assignment in which S assigns to the QDOT, "that portion of the gross estate necessary to reduce the estate tax to zero, taking into account all available credits and deductions." The assignment meets the requirements of paragraph (b) of this section, assuming that the QDOT is funded by the time that administration of D's estate is completed.

*Example 3. Jointly owned property.* At the time of D's death, D and S hold real property as joint tenants with right of survivorship. In accordance with section 2056(d)(1)(B), section 2040(a), and § 20.2056A-8(a), 60 percent of the value of the property is included in D's gross estate. S establishes a QDOT and, prior to the date the

estate tax return is filed and before the date that the QDOT election must be made, S transfers a 60 percent interest in the real property to the QDOT. The transfer satisfies the requirements of paragraph (b) of this section.

*Example 4. Computation of corpus portion of annuity payment.* (i) At the time of D's death on or after May 1, 2009, D is a participant in an employees' pension plan described in section 401(a). On D's death, D's spouse S, a resident of the United States, becomes entitled to receive a survivor's annuity of $72,000 per year, payable monthly, for life. At the time of D's death, S is age 60. Assume that under section 7520, the appropriate discount rate to be used for valuing annuities in the case of this decedent is 6.0 percent. The annuity factor at 6.0 percent for a person age 60 is 11.0625 (1.000000 minus .33625, divided by .06). The adjustment factor at 6.0 percent in Table K for monthly payments is 1.0272. Accordingly, the right to receive $72,000 per year on a monthly basis is equal to the right to receive $73,958.40 ($72,000 × 1.0272) on an annual basis.

(ii) The corpus portion of each annuity payment received by S is determined as follows. The first step is to determine the annuity factor for the number of years that would be required to exhaust a hypothetical fund that has a present value and a payout corresponding to S's interest in the payments under the plan, determined as follows:

(A) Present value of S's annuity: $73,958.40 × 11.0625 = $818,164.80.

(B) Annuity Factor for Expected Annuity Term: $818,164.80 / $73,958.40 = 11.0625.

(iii) The second step is to determine the number of years that would be required for S 's annuity to exhaust a hypothetical fund of $818,164.80. The term certain annuity factor of 11.0625 falls between the annuity factors for 18 and 19 years in a 6.0 percent term certain annuity table (Column 1 of Table B, Publication 1457 Actuarial Valuations Version 3A, which may be obtained on the IRS Internet site). Accordingly, the expected annuity term is 19 years.

(iv) The third step is to determine the corpus amount by dividing the expected term of 19 years into the present value of the hypothetical fund as follows:

(A) Corpus amount of annual payment: $818,164.80/19 = $43,061.31.

(B) [Reserved].

(v) In the fourth step, the corpus portion of each annuity payment is determined by dividing the corpus amount of each annual payment by the annual annuity payment (adjusted for payments more frequently than annually as in (i) of this *Example 4*) as follows:

(A) Corpus portion of each annuity payment: $43,061.31/$73,958.40 = .58.

(B) [Reserved].

(vi) Accordingly, 58 percent of each payment to S is deemed to be a distribution of corpus. A marital deduction is allowed for $818,164.80, the present value of the annuity as of D's date of death, if either: S agrees to roll over the corpus portion of each payment to a QDOT and the executor files the Information Statement described in paragraph (c)(5) of this section and the Roll Over Agreement described in paragraph (c)(7) of this section; or S agrees to pay the tax due on the corpus portion of each payment and the executor files the Information Statement described in paragraph (c)(5) of this section and the Payment Agreement described in paragraph (c)(6) of this section.

*Example 5. Transfer to QDOT subject to gift tax.* D's will bequeaths $700,000 outright to S. The bequest qualifies for a marital deduction under section 2056(a) except that it does not pass in a QDOT. S creates an irrevocable trust that meets the requirements for a QDOT and transfers the $700,000 to the QDOT. The QDOT instrument provides that S is entitled to all the income from the QDOT payable at least annually and that, upon the death of S, the property remaining in the QDOT is to be distributed to the grandchildren of D and S in equal shares. The trust instrument contains all other provisions required to qualify as a QDOT. On D's estate tax return, D's executor makes a QDOT election under section 2056A(a)(3). Solely for purposes of the marital deduction, the property is deemed to pass from D to the QDOT. D's estate is entitled to a marital deduction for the $700,000 value of the property passing from D to S. S's transfer of property to the QDOT is treated as a gift of the remainder interest for gift tax purposes because S's transfer creates a vested remainder interest in the grandchildren of D and S. Accordingly, as of the date that S transfers the property to the QDOT, a gift tax is imposed on the present value of the remainder interest. See § 25.2702-1(c)(8) of this chapter exempting S's transfer from the special valuation rules contained in section 2702. At S's death, S is treated as the transferor of the property into the trust for estate tax and generation-skipping transfer tax purposes. See, e.g., sections 2036 and 2652(a)(1). The trust is not eligible for a reverse QTIP election by D's estate under section 2652(a)(3) because a QTIP election cannot be made for the QDOT. This is so because the marital deduction is allowed under section 2056(a) for the outright bequest to the spouse and the spouse is then separately treated as the transferor of the property to the QDOT.

(e) *Effective/applicability date.*—Paragraph (c)(4)(ii)(B) and *Example 4* in paragraph (d) of this section are applicable with respect to decedents dying on or after May 1, 2009. [Reg. § 20.2056A-4.]

□ [T.D. 8612, 8-21-95. *Amended by T.D. 8819, 4-29-99; T.D. 9448, 5-1-2009; and T.D. 9540, 8-9-2011.*]

[Reg. § 20.2056A-5]

**§ 20.2056A-5. Imposition of section 2056A estate tax.**—(a) *In general.*—An estate tax is imposed under section 2056A(b)(1) on the occurrence of a taxable event, as defined in section 2056A(b)(9). The tax is generally equal to the amount of estate tax that would have been imposed if the amount involved in the taxable event had been included in the decedent's taxable estate and had not been deductible under section 2056. See section 2056A(b)(3) and paragraph (c) of this section for certain exceptions from taxable events.

(b) *Amounts subject to tax.*—(1) *Distribution of principal during the spouse's lifetime.*—If a taxable event occurs during the noncitizen surviving spouse's lifetime, the amount on which the section 2056A estate tax is imposed is the amount of money and the fair market value of the property that is the subject of the distribution (including property distributed from the trust pursuant to the exercise of a power of appointment), including any amount withheld from the distribution by the U.S. Trustee to pay the tax. If, however, the tax is not withheld by the U.S. Trustee but is paid by the U.S. Trustee out of other assets of the QDOT, an amount equal to the tax so paid is treated as an additional distribution to the spouse in the year that the tax is paid.

(2) *Death of surviving spouse.*—If a taxable event occurs as a result of the death of the surviving spouse, the amount subject to tax is the fair market value of the trust assets on the date of the spouse's death (or alternate valuation date if applicable). See also section 2032A. Any corpus portion amounts, within the meaning of § 20.2056A-4(c)(4)(i), remaining in a QDOT upon the surviving

spouse's death, are subject to tax under section 2056A(b)(1)(B), as well as any residual payments resulting from a nonassignable plan or arrangement that, upon the surviving spouse's death, are payable to the spouse's estate or to successor beneficiaries.

(3) *Trust ceases to qualify as QDOT.*—If a taxable event occurs as a result of the trust ceasing to qualify as a QDOT (for example, the trust ceases to have at least one U.S. Trustee), the amount subject to tax is the fair market value of the trust assets on the date of disqualification.

(c) *Distributions and dispositions not subject to tax.*—(1) *Distributions of principal on account of hardship.*—Section 2056A(b)(3)(B) provides an exemption from the section 2056A estate tax for distributions to the surviving spouse on account of hardship. A distribution of principal is treated as made on account of hardship if the distribution is made to the spouse from the QDOT in response to an immediate and substantial financial need relating to the spouse's health, maintenance, education, or support, or the health, maintenance, education, or support of any person that the surviving spouse is legally obligated to support. A distribution is not treated as made on account of hardship if the amount distributed may be obtained from other sources that are reasonably available to the surviving spouse; e.g., the sale by the surviving spouse of personally owned, publicly traded stock or the cashing in of a certificate of deposit owned by the surviving spouse. Assets such as closely held business interests, real estate and tangible personalty are not considered sources that are reasonably available to the surviving spouse. Although a hardship distribution of principal is exempt from the section 2056A estate tax, it must be reported on Form 706-QDT even if it is the only distribution that occurred during the filing period. See § 20.2056A-11 regarding filing requirements for Form 706-QDT.

(2) *Distributions of income to the surviving spouse.*—Section 2056A(b)(3)(A) provides an exemption from the section 2056A estate tax for distributions of income to the surviving spouse. In general, for purposes of section 2056A(b)(3)(A), the term *income* has the same meaning as is provided in section 643(b), except that income does not include capital gains. In addition, income does not include any other item that would be allocated to corpus under applicable local law governing the administration of trusts irrespective of any specific trust provision to the contrary. However, distributions made to the surviving spouse as the income beneficiary in conformance with applicable local law that defines the term income as a unitrust amount (or permits a right to income to be satisfied by such an amount), or that permits the trustee to adjust between principal and income to fulfill the trustee's duty of impartiality between income and principal beneficiaries, will be considered distributions of trust income if applicable local law provides for a reasonable apportionment between the income and remainder beneficiaries of the total return of the trust and meets the requirements of § 1.643(b)-1 of this chapter. In cases where there is no specific statutory or case law regarding the allocation of such items under the law governing the administration of the QDOT, the allocation under this paragraph (c)(2) will be governed by general principles of law (including but not limited to any uniform state acts, such as the Uniform Principal and Income Act, or any Restatements of applicable law). Further, except as provided in this paragraph (c)(2) or in administrative guidance published by the Internal Revenue Service, income does not include items constituting income in respect of a decedent (IRD) under section 691. However, in cases where a QDOT is designated by the decedent as a beneficiary of a pension or profit sharing plan described in section 401(a) or an individual retirement account or annuity described in section 408, the proceeds of which are payable to the QDOT in the form of an annuity, any payments received by the QDOT may be allocated between income and corpus using the method prescribed under § 20.2056A-4(c) for determining the corpus and income portion of an annuity payment.

(3) *Certain miscellaneous distributions and dispositions.*—Certain miscellaneous distributions and dispositions of trust assets are exempt from the section 2056A estate tax, including but not limited to the following—

(i) Payments for ordinary and necessary expenses of the QDOT (including bond premiums and letter of credit fees);

(ii) Payments to applicable governmental authorities for income tax or any other applicable tax imposed on the QDOT (other than a payment of the section 2056A estate tax due on the occurrence of a taxable event as described in paragraph (b) of this section);

(iii) Dispositions of trust assets by the trustees (such as sales, exchanges, or pledging as collateral) for full and adequate consideration in money or money's worth; and

(iv) Pursuant to section 2056A(b)(15), amounts paid from the QDOT to reimburse the surviving spouse for any tax imposed on the spouse under Subtitle A of the Internal Revenue Code on any item of income of the QDOT to which the surviving spouse is not entitled under the terms of the trust. Such distributions include (but are not limited to) amounts paid from the QDOT to reimburse the spouse for income taxes paid by the spouse (either by actual payment or through withholding) with respect to amounts received from a non-assignable annuity or other arrangement that are transferred by the spouse to a QDOT pursuant to §20.2056A-4(c)(3); and income taxes paid by the spouse (either by actual payment or through withholding) with respect to amounts received in a lump sum distribution from a qualified plan if the lump sum distribution is assigned by the surviving spouse to a QDOT. For purposes of this paragraph (c)(3)(iv), the amount of attributable tax eligible for reimbursement is the difference between the actual income tax liability of the spouse and the spouse's income tax liability determined as if the item had not been included in the spouse's gross income in the applicable taxable year. [Reg. §20.2056A-5.]

☐ [*T.D. 8612, 8-21-95. Amended by T.D. 9102, 12-30-2003.*]

### [Reg. §20.2056A-6]

**§20.2056A-6. Amount of tax.—(a)** *Definition of tax.*—Section 2056A(b)(2) provides for the computation of the section 2056A estate tax. For purposes of sections 2056A(b)(2)(A)(i) and (ii), in determining the tax that would have been imposed under section 2001 on the estate of the first decedent, the rates in effect on the date of the first decedent's death are used. For this purpose, the provisions of section 2001(c)(2) (pertaining to phaseout of graduated rates and unified credit) apply. In addition, for purposes of sections 2056A(b)(2)(A)(i) and (ii), *the tax which would have been imposed by section 2001 on the estate of the decedent* means the net tax determined under section 2001 or 2101, as the case may be, after allowance of any allowable credits, including the unified credit allowable under section 2010, the credit for state death taxes under section 2011, the credit for tax on prior transfers under section 2013, and the credit for foreign death taxes under section 2014. See paragraph (b)(4) of this section regarding the application of the credits under sections 2011 and 2014. In the case of a decedent nonresident not a citizen of the United States, the applicable credits are determined under section 2102. The estate tax (net of any applicable credits) imposed under section 2056A(b)(1) constitutes an estate tax for purposes of section 691(c)(2)(A).

**(b)** *Benefits allowed in determining amount of section 2056A estate tax.*—**(1)** *General rule.*—Section 2056A(b)(10) provides for the allowance of certain benefits in computing the section 2056A estate tax. Except as provided in this section, the rules of each of the credit, deduction and deferral provisions, as provided in the Internal Revenue Code must be complied with.

**(2)** *Treatment as resident.*—For purposes of section 2056A(b)(10)(A), a noncitizen spouse is treated as a resident of the United States for purposes of determining whether the QDOT property is includible in the spouse's gross estate under chapter 11 of the Internal Revenue Code, and for purposes of determining whether any of the credits, deductions or deferral provisions are allowable with respect to the QDOT property to the estate of the spouse.

**(3)** *Special rule in the case of trusts described in section 2056(b)(8).*— In the case of a QDOT in which the spouse's interest qualifies for a marital deduction under section 2056(b)(8), the provisions of section 2056A(b)(10)(A) apply in determining the allowance of a charitable deduction in computing the section 2056A estate tax, notwithstanding that the QDOT is not includible in the spouse's gross estate.

**(4)** *Credit for state and foreign death taxes.*—If the assets of the QDOT are included in the surviving spouse's gross estate for federal estate tax purposes, or would have been so includible if the spouse had been a United States resident, and state or foreign death taxes are

paid by the spouse's estate with respect to the QDOT, the taxes paid by the spouse's estate with respect to the QDOT are creditable, to the extent allowable under section 2011 or 2014, as applicable, in computing the section 2056A estate tax. In addition, state or foreign death taxes previously paid by the decedent/transferor's estate are also creditable in computing the section 2056A estate tax to the extent allowable under sections 2011 and 2014. Specifically, the tax that would have been imposed on the decedent's estate if the taxable estate had been increased by the value of the QDOT assets on the spouse's death plus the amount involved in prior taxable events (section 2056A(b)(2)(A)(i)), is determined after allowance of a credit equal to the lesser of the state or foreign death tax previously paid by the decedent's estate, or the amount prescribed under section 2011(b) or 2014(b) computed based on a taxable estate increased by such amounts. Similarly, the tax that would have been imposed on the decedent's estate if the taxable estate had been increased only by the amount involved in prior taxable events (section 2056A(b)(2)(A)(ii)) is determined after allowance of a credit equal to the lesser of the state or foreign death tax previously paid by the decedent's estate, or the amount prescribed under section 2011(b) or 2014(b) computed based on a taxable estate increased by the amount involved in such prior taxable events. See paragraph (d), *Example 2*, of this section.

**(5)** *Alternate valuation and special use valuation.*—**(i)** *In general.*— In order to claim the benefits of alternate valuation under section 2032, or special use valuation under section 2032A, for purposes of computing the section 2056A estate tax, an election must be made on the Form 706-QDT that is filed with respect to the balance remaining in the QDOT upon the death of the surviving spouse. In addition, the separate requirements for making the section 2032 and/or section 2032A elections under those sections and the regulations thereunder must be complied with except that, for this purpose, the surviving spouse is treated as a resident of the United States regardless of the surviving spouse's actual residency status. Solely for purposes of this paragraph (b)(5), the citizenship of the first decedent is immaterial.

**(ii)** *Alternate valuation.*—For purposes of the alternate valuation election under section 2032, the election may not be made unless the election decreases both the value of the property remaining in the QDOT upon the death of the surviving spouse and the net amount of section 2056A estate tax due. Once made, the election is irrevocable.

**(iii)** *Special use valuation.*—For purposes of section 2032A, the Designated Filer (in the case of multiple QDOTs) or the U.S. Trustee may elect to value certain farm and closely held business real property at its farm or business use value, rather than its fair market value, if all of the requirements under section 2032A and the applicable regulations are met, except that, for this purpose, the surviving spouse is treated as a resident of the United States regardless of the spouse's actual residency status. The total value of property valued under section 2032A in the QDOT cannot be decreased from fair market value by more than $750,000.

**(c)** *Miscellaneous rules.*—See sections 2056A(b)(2)(B)(i) and 2056A(b)(2)(C) for special rules regarding the appropriate rate of tax. See section 2056A(b)(2)(B)(ii) for provisions regarding a credit or refund with respect to the section 2056A estate tax.

**(d)** *Examples.*—The rules of this section are illustrated by the following examples.

*Example 1.* (i) *D*, a United States citizen, dies in 1995 a resident of State X, with a gross estate of $1,200,000. Under *D*'s will, a pecuniary bequest of $700,000 passes to a QDOT for the benefit of *D*'s spouse *S*, who is a resident but not a citizen of the United States. *D*'s estate tax is computed as follows:

| | | |
|---|---|---|
| Gross estate | $1,200,000 | |
| Marital Deduction | (700,000 ) | |
| Taxable Estate | $500,000 | |
| Gross Tax | | $155,800 |
| Less: Unified Credit | | ( 155,800 ) |
| Net Tax | | 0 |

(ii) *S* dies in 1997 at which time *S* is still a resident of the United States and the value of the assets of the QDOT is $700,000. Assuming there were no taxable events during *S*'s lifetime with respect to the QDOT, the estate tax imposed under section 2056A(b)(1)(B) is $235,000, computed as follows:

| | | |
|---|---|---|
| *D*'s actual taxable estate | $500,000 | |
| QDOT property | 700,000 | |
| Total | $1,200,000 | |
| Gross Tax | | $427,800 |
| Less: Unified Credit | | ( 192,800 ) |
| Net Tax | | $235,000 |

| Less: Tax that would have been imposed on D's actual taxable estate of $500,000 . . . . . . . . . . . . . . . . . . . . . . . . . . . . . . . . . . . . . . | | 0 |
|---|---|---|
| Section 2056A Estate Tax . . . . . . . . . . . . . . . . . . . . . . . . . . . . . . . . | | $235,000 |

*Example 2.* (i) The facts are the same as in *Example 1*, except that D's gross estate was $2,000,000 and D's estate paid $70,000 in state death taxes to State X. D's estate tax is computed as follows:

| | | |
|---|---|---|
| Gross Estate . . . . . . . . . . . . . . . . . . . . . . . . . . . . . . . . . | $2,000,000 | |
| Marital Deduction . . . . . . . . . . . . . . . . . . . . . . . . . . . . . . | ( 700,000 ) | |
| Taxable Estate . . . . . . . . . . . . . . . . . . . . . . . . . . . . . | $1,300,000 | |
| Gross Tax . . . . . . . . . . . . . . . . . . . . . . . . . . . . . . . . . . | | $469,800 |
| Less: Unified Credit . . . . . . . . . . . . . . . . . . . . . . . . . . | 192,800 | |
| State Death Tax Credit Limitation (lesser of $51,600 or $70,000 tax paid) . | 51,600 | ( 244,400 ) |
| Estate Tax . . . . . . . . . . . . . . . . . . . . . . . . . . . . . . | | $225,400 |

(ii) S dies in 1997 at which time S is still a resident of the United States and the value of the assets of the QDOT is $800,000. S's estate pays $40,000 in State X death taxes with respect to the inclusion of the QDOT in S's gross estate for state death tax purposes. Assuming there were no taxable events during S's lifetime with respect to the QDOT, the estate tax imposed under section 2056A(b)(1)(B) is $304,800 computed as follows:

| | | |
|---|---|---|
| D's Actual Taxable Estate . . . . . . . . . . . . . . . . . . . . . . . . | $1,300,000 | |
| QDOT Property . . . . . . . . . . . . . . . . . . . . . . . . . . . . . . | 800,000 | |
| Total . . . . . . . . . . . . . . . . . . . . . . . . . . . . . . . . . . . . | $2,100,000 | |
| Gross Tax . . . . . . . . . . . . . . . . . . . . . . . . . . . . . . . . . . | | $829,800 |
| Less: Unified Credit . . . . . . . . . . . . . . . . . . . . . . . . . . . | | ( 192,800 ) |
| Pre-2011 section 2056A estate tax . . . . . . . . . . . . . . . . . . . | | $637,000 |

(A) State Death Tax Credit Computation:

(1) State death tax paid by S's estate with respect to the QDOT [$40,000] plus state death tax previously paid by D's estate [$70,000] = $110,000.

(2) Credit limit under section 2011(b) (based on D's adjusted taxable estate of $2,040,000 under sections 2056A(b)(2)(A) and 2011(b)) = $106,800.

(B) State death tax credit allowable against section 2056A estate tax (lesser of paragraph (ii)(A)(1) or (2) of this *Example 2*

| | |
|---|---|
| | ( 106,800 ) |
| Net Tax . . . . . . . . . . . . . . . . . . . . . . . . . . . . . . . . . . . . . . . . . . . . | $530,200 |
| Less: Tax that would have been imposed on D's taxable estate of $1,300,000 . . . . . . | 225,400 |
| Section 2056A Estate Tax . . . . . . . . . . . . . . . . . . . . . . . . . . . . . . . . . . . | $304,800 |

[Reg. § 20.2056A-6.]

☐ [T.D. 8612, 8-21-95.]

## [Reg. § 20.2056A-7]

**§ 20.2056A-7. Allowance of prior transfer credit under section 2013.**—(a) *Property subject to QDOT election.*—Section 2056(d)(3) provides special rules for computing the section 2013 credit allowed with respect to property subject to a QDOT election. In computing the credit under section 2013, the amount of the credit is determined under section 2013 and the regulations thereunder, except that—

(1) The first limitation as described in section 2013(b) and § 20.2013-2 is the amount of the estate tax imposed under section 2056A(b)(1)(A), with respect to distributions during the spouse's life, and under section 2056A(b)(1)(B), with respect to the value of the QDOT assets on the spouse's death;

(2) In computing the second limitation as described in section 2013(c) and § 20.2013-3, the value of the property transferred to the decedent (as defined in section 2013(d) and § 20.2013-4) is deemed to be the value of the QDOT assets on the date of death of the surviving spouse. The value as so determined is not reduced by the section 2056A estate tax imposed at the time of the spouse's death; and

(3) The amount of the credit is determined without regard to the percentage limitations contained in section 2013(a).

(b) *Property not subject to QDOT election.*—If property includible in a decedent's gross estate passes to a noncitizen surviving spouse (the transferee) and no deduction is allowed to the decedent's estate for that interest in property under section 2056(a) solely because the requirements of section 2056(d)(2) are not satisfied, and the transferee spouse dies with an estate that is subject to tax under section 2001 or 2101, as the case may be, any credit for tax on prior transfers allowable to the estate of the transferee spouse under section 2013 with respect to such interest in property is determined in accordance with the rules of section 2013 and the regulations thereunder, except that the amount of the credit is determined without regard to the percentage limitations contained in section 2013(a).

(c) *Example.*—The application of this section may be illustrated by the following example:

*Example.* The facts are the same as in § 20.2056A-6, *Example* 2(ii). D, a United States citizen, dies in 1994, a resident of State X, with a gross estate of $2,000,000. Under D's will, a pecuniary bequest of $700,000 passes to a QDOT for the benefit of D's spouse S, who is a resident but not a citizen of the United States. S dies in 1997 at which time S is still a resident of the United States and the value of the assets of the QDOT is $800,000. There were no taxable events during S's lifetime. An estate tax of $304,800 is imposed under section 2056A(b)(1)(B). S's taxable estate, including the value of the QDOT ($800,000), is $1,500,000.

(i) Under paragraph (a)(1) of this section, the first limitation for purposes of section 2013(b) is $304,800, the amount of the section 2056A estate tax.

(ii) Under paragraph (a)(2) of this section, the second limitation for purposes of section 2013(c) is computed as follows:

(A) S's net estate tax payable under § 20.2013-3(a)(1), as modified under paragraph (a)(2) of this section, is computed as follows:

| | | |
|---|---|---|
| Taxable estate . . . . . . . . . . . . . . . . . . . . . . . . . . . . . . . . . . . . . . | | $1,500,000 |
| Gross estate tax . . . . . . . . . . . . . . . . . . . . . . . . . . . . . . . . . . . . . | | 555,800 |
| Less: Unified credit . . . . . . . . . . . . . . . . . . . . . . . . . . . . . . . . . . | $192,800 | |
| Credit for state death taxes . . . . . . . . . . . . . . . . . . . . . . . . . . . . | 64,400 | 257,200 |
| Pre-2013 net estate tax payable . . . . . . . . . . . . . . . . . . . . . . . . . . | | $298,600 |

(B) S's net estate tax payable under § 20.2013-3(a)(2), as modified under paragraph (a)(2) of this section, is computed as follows:

| | | |
|---|---|---|
| Taxable estate . . . . . . . . . . . . . . . . . . . . . . . . . . . . . . . . . . . . . . | | $700,000 |
| Gross estate tax . . . . . . . . . . . . . . . . . . . . . . . . . . . . . . . . . . . . . | | 229,800 |
| Less: Unified credit . . . . . . . . . . . . . . . . . . . . . . . . . . . . . . . . . . | $192,800 | |
| Credit for state death taxes . . . . . . . . . . . . . . . . . . . . . . . . . . . . | 18,000 | 210,800 |
| Net tax payable . . . . . . . . . . . . . . . . . . . . . . . . . . . . . . . . . . . . . | | $19,000 |

(C) *Second Limitation:*

| | | |
|---|---|---|
| Paragraph (ii)(A) of this *Example* . . . . . . . . . . . . . . . . . . . . . . . . . . | $298,600 | |
| Less: Paragraph (ii)(B) of this *Example* . . . . . . . . . . . . . . . . . . . . . . | 19,000 | $279,600 |

(iii) Credit for tax on prior transfers = $279,600 (lesser of paragraphs (i) or (ii) of this *Example*. [Reg. § 20.2056A-7.]

☐ [*T.D.* 8612, 8-21-95.]

## [Reg. § 20.2056A-8]

**§ 20.2056A-8. Special rules for joint property.**—(a) *Inclusion in gross estate.*—(1) *General rule.*—If property is held by the decedent and the surviving spouse of the decedent as joint tenants with right of survivorship, or as tenants by the entirety, and the surviving spouse is not a United States citizen (or treated as a United States citizen) at the time of the decedent's death, the property is subject to inclusion in the decedent's gross estate in accordance with the rules of section 2040(a) (general rule for includibility of joint interests), and section 2040(b) (special rule for includibility of certain joint interests of husbands and wives) does not apply. Accordingly, the rules contained in section 2040(a) and § 20.2040-1 govern the extent to which such joint interests are includible in the gross estate of a decedent who was a citizen or resident of the United States. Under § 20.2040-1(a)(2), the entire value of jointly held property is included in the decedent's gross estate unless the executor submits facts sufficient to show that property was not entirely acquired with consideration furnished by the decedent, or was acquired by the decedent and the other joint owner by gift, bequest, devise or inheritance. If the decedent is a nonresident not a citizen of the United States, the rules of this paragraph (a)(1) apply pursuant to sections 2103, 2031, 2040(a), and 2056(d)(1)(B).

(2) *Consideration furnished by surviving spouse.*—For purposes of applying section 2040(a), in determining the amount of consideration furnished by the surviving spouse, any consideration furnished by the decedent with respect to the property before July 14, 1988, is treated as consideration furnished by the surviving spouse to the extent that the consideration was treated as a gift to the spouse under section 2511, or to the extent that the decedent elected to treat the transfer as a gift to the spouse under section 2515 (to the extent applicable). For purposes of determining whether the consideration was a gift by the decedent under section 2511, it is presumed that the decedent was a citizen of the United States at the time the consideration was so furnished to the spouse. The special rule of this paragraph (a)(2) is applicable only if the donor spouse predeceases the donee spouse and not if the donee spouse predeceases the donor spouse. In cases where the donee spouse predeceases the donor spouse, any portion of the consideration treated as a gift to the donee spouse/decedent on the creation of the tenancy (or subsequently thereafter), regardless of the date the tenancy was created, is not treated as consideration furnished by the donee spouse/decedent for purposes of section 2040(a).

(3) *Amount allowed to be transferred to QDOT.*—If, as a result of the application of the rules described above, only a portion of the value of a jointly-held property interest is includible in a decedent's gross estate, only that portion that is so includible may be transferred to a QDOT under section 2056(d)(2). See § 20.2056A-4(b)(1) and (d), *Example 3*.

(b) *Surviving spouse becomes citizen.*—Paragraph (a) of this section does not apply if the surviving spouse meets the requirements of section 2056(d)(4). For the definition of resident in applying section 2056(d)(4), see § 20.0-1(b).

(c) *Examples.*—The provisions of this section are illustrated by the following examples:

*Example 1.* In 1987, *D*, a United States citizen, purchases real property and takes title in the names of *D* and *S*, *D*'s spouse (a noncitizen, but a United States resident), as joint tenants with right of survivorship. In accordance with § 25.2511-1(h)(5) of this chapter, one-half of the value of the property is a gift to *S*. *D* dies in 1995. Because *S* is not a United States citizen, the provisions of section 2040(a) are determinative of the extent to which the real property is includible in *D*'s gross estate. Because the joint tenancy was established before July 14, 1988, and under the applicable provisions of the Internal Revenue Code and regulations the transfer was treated as a gift of one-half of the property, one-half of the value of the property is deemed attributable to consideration furnished by *S* for purposes of section 2040(a). Accordingly, only one-half of the value of the property is includible in *D*'s gross estate under section 2040(a).

*Example 2.* The facts are the same as in *Example 1*, except that *S* dies in 1995 survived by *D* who is not a citizen of the United States. For purposes of applying section 2040(a), *D*'s gift to *S* on the creation of the tenancy is not treated as consideration furnished by *S* toward the acquisition of the property. Accordingly, since *S* made no other contributions with respect to the property, no portion of the property is includible in *S*'s gross estate.

*Example 3.* The facts are the same as in *Example 1*, except that *D* and *S* purchase real property in 1990 making the down payment with funds from a joint bank account. All subsequent mortgage payments and improvements are paid from the joint bank account. The only funds deposited in the joint bank account are the earnings of *D* and *S*. It is established that *D* earned approximately 60% of the funds and *S* earned approximately 40% of the funds. *D* dies in 1995. The establishment of *S*'s contribution to the joint bank account is sufficient to show that *S* contributed 40% of the consideration for the property. Thus, under paragraph § 20.2040-1(a)(2), 60% of the value of the property is includible in *D*'s gross estate. [Reg. § 20.2056A-8.]

☐ [*T.D.* 8612, 8-21-95.]

## [Reg. § 20.2056A-9]

**§ 20.2056A-9. Designated Filer.**—Section 2056A(b)(2)(C) provides special rules where more than one QDOT is established with respect to a decedent. The designation of a person responsible for filing a return under section 2056A(b)(2)(C)(i) (the Designated Filer) must be made on the decedent's federal estate tax return, or on the first Form 706-QDT that is due and is filed by its prescribed date, including extensions. The Designated Filer must be a U.S. Trustee. If the U.S. Trustee is an individual, that individual must have a tax home (as defined in section 911(d)(3)) in the United States. At least sixty days before the due date for filing the tax returns for all of the QDOTs, the U.S. Trustee(s) of each of the QDOTs must provide to the Designated Filer all of the necessary information relating to distributions from their respective QDOTs. The section 2056A estate tax due from each QDOT is allocated on a pro rata basis (based on the ratio of the amount of each respective distribution constituting a taxable event to the amount of all such distributions), unless a different allocation is required under the terms of the governing instrument or under local law. Unless the decedent has provided for a successor Designated Filer, if the Designated Filer ceases to qualify as a U.S. Trustee, or otherwise becomes unable to serve as the Designated Filer, the remaining trustees of each QDOT must select a qualifying successor Designated Filer (who is also a U.S. Trustee) prior to the due date for the filing of Form 706-QDT (including extensions). The selection is to be indicated on the Form 706-QDT. Failure to select a successor Designated Filer will result in the application of section 2056A(b)(2)(C). [Reg. § 20.2056A-9.]

☐ [*T.D.* 8612, 8-21-95.]

## [Reg. § 20.2056A-10]

**§ 20.2056A-10. Surviving spouse becomes citizen after QDOT established.**—(a) *Section 2056A estate tax no longer imposed under certain circumstances.*—Section 2056A(b)(12) provides that a QDOT is no longer subject to the imposition of the section 2056A estate tax if the surviving spouse becomes a citizen of the United States and the following conditions are satisfied—

(1) The spouse either was a United States resident (for the definition of resident for this purpose, see § 20.2056A-1(b)) at all times after the death of the decedent and before becoming a United States citizen, or no taxable distributions are made from the QDOT before the spouse becomes a United States citizen (regardless of the residency status of the spouse); and

(2) The U.S. Trustee(s) of the QDOT notifies the Internal Revenue Service and certifies in writing that the surviving spouse has become a United States citizen. Notice is to be made by filing a final Form 706-QDT on or before April 15th of the calendar year following the year in which the surviving spouse becomes a United States citizen, unless an extension of time for filing is granted under section 6081.

(b) *Special election by spouse.*—If the surviving spouse becomes a United States citizen and the spouse is not a United States resident at all times after the death of the decedent and before becoming a United States citizen, and a tax was previously imposed under section 2056A(b)(1)(A) with respect to any distribution from the QDOT before the surviving spouse becomes a United States citizen, the estate tax imposed under section 2056A(b)(1) does not apply to distributions after the spouse becomes a citizen if—

(1) The spouse elects to treat any taxable distribution from the QDOT prior to the spouse's election as a taxable gift made by the spouse for purposes of section 2001(b)(1)(B) (referring to adjusted taxable gifts), and for purposes of determining the amount of the tax imposed by section 2501 on actual taxable gifts made by the spouse during the year in which the spouse becomes a citizen or in any subsequent year;

(2) The spouse elects to treat any previous reduction in the section 2056A estate tax by reason of the decedent's unified credit (under either section 2010 or section 2102(c)) as a reduction in the

spouse's unified credit under section 2505 for purposes of determining the amount of the credit allowable with respect to taxable gifts made by the surviving spouse during the taxable year in which the spouse becomes a citizen, or in any subsequent year; and

(3) The elections referred to in this paragraph (b) are made by timely filing a Form 706-QDT on or before April 15th of the year following the year in which the surviving spouse becomes a citizen (unless an extension of time for filing is granted under section 6081) and attaching notification of the election to the return. [Reg. § 20.2056A-10.]

☐ [*T.D.* 8612, 8-21-95.]

### [Reg. § 20.2056A-11]

**§ 20.2056A-11. Filing requirements and payment of the section 2056A estate tax.**—(a) *Distributions during surviving spouse's life.*—Section 2056A(b)(5)(A) provides the due date for payment of the section 2056A estate tax imposed on distributions during the spouse's lifetime. An extension of not more than 6 months may be obtained for the filing of Form 706-QDT under section 6081(a) if the conditions specified therein are satisfied. See also § 20.2056A-5(c)(1) regarding the requirements for filing a Form 706-QDT in the case of a distribution to the surviving spouse on account of hardship, and § 20.2056A-2T(d)(3) regarding the requirements for filing Form 706-QDT in the case of the required annual statement.

(b) *Tax at death of surviving spouse.*—Section 2056A(b)(5)(B) provides the due date for payment of the section 2056A estate tax imposed on the death of the spouse under section 2056A(b)(1)(B). An extension of not more than 6 months may be obtained for the filing of the Form 706-QDT under section 6081(a), if the conditions specified therein are satisfied. The obtaining of an extension of time to file under section 6081(a) does not extend the time to pay the section 2056A estate tax as prescribed under section 2056A(b)(5)(B).

(c) *Extension of time for paying section 2056A estate tax.*—(1) *Extension of time for paying tax under section 6161(a)(2).*—Pursuant to sections 2056A(b)(10)(C) and 6161(a)(2), upon a showing of reasonable cause, an extension of time for a reasonable period beyond the due date may be granted to pay any part of the estate tax that is imposed upon the surviving spouse's death under section 2056A(b)(1)(B) and shown on the final Form 706-QDT, or any part of any installments of such tax payable under section 6166 (including any part of a deficiency prorated to any installment under such section). The extension may not exceed 10 years from the date prescribed for payment of the tax (or in the case of an installment or part of a deficiency prorated to an installment, if later, not beyond the date that is 12 months after the due date for the last installment). Such extension may be granted by the district director or the director of the service center where the Form 706-QDT is filed.

(2) *Extension of time for paying tax under section 6161(a)(1).*—An extension of time beyond the due date to pay any part of the estate tax imposed on lifetime distributions under section 2056A(b)(1)(A), or imposed at the death of the surviving spouse under section 2056A(b)(1)(B), may be granted for a reasonable period of time, not to exceed 6 months (12 months in the case of the estate tax imposed under section 2056A(b)(1)(B) at the surviving spouse's death), by the district director or the director of the service center where the Form 706-QDT is filed.

(d) *Liability for tax.*—Under section 2056A(b)(6), each trustee (and not solely the U.S. Trustee(s)) of a QDOT is personally liable for the amount of the estate tax imposed in the case of any taxable event under section 2056A(b)(1). In the case of multiple QDOTs with respect to the same decedent, each trustee of a QDOT is personally liable for the amount of the section 2056A estate tax imposed on any taxable event with respect to that trustee's QDOT, but is not personally liable for tax imposed with respect to taxable events involving QDOTs of which that person is not a trustee. However, the assets of any QDOT are subject to collection by the Internal Revenue Service for any tax resulting from a taxable event with respect to any other QDOT established with respect to the same decedent. The trustee may also be personally liable as a withholding agent under section 1461 or other applicable provisions of the Internal Revenue Code. [Reg. § 20.2056A-11.]

☐ [*T.D.* 8612, 8-21-95.]

### [Reg. § 20.2056A-12]

**§ 20.2056A-12. Increased basis for section 2056A estate tax paid with respect to distribution from a QDOT.**—Under section 2056A(b)(13), in the case of any distribution from a QDOT on which an estate tax is imposed under section 2056A(b)(1)(A), the distribution is treated as a transfer by gift for purposes of section 1015, and any estate tax paid under section 2056A(b)(1)(A) is treated as a gift tax. See § 1.1015-5(c)(4) and (5) of this chapter for rules for determining the amount by which the basis of the distributed property is increased. [Reg. § 20.2056A-12.]

☐ [*T.D.* 8612, 8-21-95.]

### [Reg. § 20.2056A-13]

**§ 20.2056A-13. Effective date.**—Except as provided in this section, the provisions of § § 20.2056A-1 through 20.2056A-12 are applicable with respect to estates of decedents dying after August 22, 1995. The rule in the fourth sentence of § 20.2056A-5(c)(2) regarding unitrusts and distributions of income to the surviving spouse in conformance with applicable local law is applicable to trusts for taxable years ending after January 2, 2004. [Reg. § 20.2056A-13.]

☐ [*T.D.* 8612, 8-21-95. *Amended by T.D.* 9102, 12-30-2003.]

## Estates of Nonresidents Not Citizens

See p. 20,601 for regulations not amended to reflect law changes

### [Reg. § 20.2101-1]

**§ 20.2101-1. Estates of nonresidents not citizens; tax imposed.**—(a) *Imposition of tax.*—Section 2101 imposes a tax on the transfer of the taxable estate of a nonresident who is not a citizen of the United States at the time of death. In the case of estates of decedents dying after November 10, 1988, the tax is computed at the same rates as the tax that is imposed on the transfer of the taxable estate of a citizen or resident of the United States in accordance with the provisions of sections 2101(b) and (c). For the meaning of the terms *resident*, *nonresident*, and *United States*, as applied to a decedent for purposes of the estate tax, see § 20.0-1(b)(1) and (2). For the liability of the executor for the payment of the tax, see section 2002. For special rules

as to the phaseout of the graduated rates and unified credit, see sections 2001(c)(2) and 2101(b).

(b) *Special rates in the case of certain decedents.*—In the case of an estate of a nonresident who was not a citizen of the United States and who died after December 31, 1976, and on or before November 10, 1988, the tax on the nonresident's taxable estate is computed using the formula provided under section 2101(b), except that the rate schedule in paragraph (c) of this section is to be used in lieu of the rate schedule in section 2001(c).

(c) *Rate schedule for decedents dying after December 31, 1976 and on or before November 10, 1988.*

| If the amount for which the tentative tax to be computed is: | The tentative tax is: |
|---|---|
| Not over $100,000 | 6% of such amount. |
| Over $100,000 but not over $500,000 | $6,000, plus 12% of excess over $100,000. |
| Over $500,000 but not over $1,000,000 | $54,000, plus 18% of excess over $500,000. |
| Over $1,000,000 but not over $2,000,000 | $144,000, plus 24% of excess over $1,000,000 |
| Over $2,000,000 | $384,000, plus 30% of excess over $2,000,000. |

[Reg. § 20.2101-1.]

☐ [*T.D.* 6296, 6-23-58. *Amended by T.D.* 7296, 12-11-73 *and T.D.* 8612, 8-21-95.]

### [Reg. § 20.2102-1]

**§ 20.2102-1. Estates of nonresidents not citizens; credits against tax.**—(a) *In general.*—In arriving at the net estate tax payable with respect to the transfer of an estate of a nonresident who was not a citizen of the United States at the time of his death, the following credits are subtracted from the tax imposed by section 2101:

(1) The State death tax credit under section 2011, to the extent permitted by section 2102(b) and paragraph (b) of this section;

(2) The gift tax credit under section 2012; and

(3) The credit under section 2013 for tax on prior transfers.

Except as provided in section 2102(b) and paragraph (b) of this section (relating to a special limitation on the amount of the credit for State death taxes), the amount of each of these credits is determined in the same manner as that prescribed for its determination in the case of estates of citizens or residents of the United States. See §§ 20.2011 through 20.2013-6. Subject to the additional special limitation contained in section 2102(b) in the case of section 2015, the provisions of sections 2015 and 2016, relating respectively to the credit for death taxes on remainders and the recovery of taxes claimed as a credit, are applicable with respect to the credit for State death taxes in the case of the estates of nonresidents not citizens. However, no credit is allowed under section 2014 for foreign death taxes.

(b) *Special limitation.*—(1) *In general.*—In the case of estates of decedents dying on or after November 14, 1966, other than estates the estate tax treatment of which is subject to a Presidential proclamation made pursuant to section 2108(a), the maximum credit allowable under section 2011 for State death taxes against the tax imposed by section 2101 on the transfer of estates of nonresidents not citizens of the United States is an amount which bears the same ratio to the maximum credit computed as provided in section 2011(b) (and without regard to this special limitation) as the value of the property (determined in the same manner as that prescribed in paragraph (b) of § 20.2031-1 for the estates of citizens or residents of the United States) in respect of which a State death tax was actually paid and which is included in the gross estate under section 2103 or, if applicable, section 2107(b) bears to the value (as so determined) of the total gross estate under section 2103 or 2107(b). For purposes of this special limitation, the term "State death taxes" means the taxes described in section 2011(a) and paragraph (a) of § 20.2011-1.

(2) *Illustrations.*—The application of this paragraph may be illustrated by the following examples:

*Example (1).* A, a nonresident not a citizen of the United States, died on February 15, 1967, owning real property in State Z valued at $50,000 and stock in various domestic corporations valued at $100,000 and not subject to death taxes in any State. State Z's inheritance tax actually paid with respect to the real property in State Z is $2,000. A's taxable estate for Federal estate tax purposes is $110,000, in respect of which the maximum credit under section 2011 would be $720 in the absence of the special limitation contained in section 2102(b). However, under section 2102(b) and this paragraph the amount of the maximum credit allowable in respect to A's estate for State death taxes is limited to the amount which bears the same ratio to $720 (the maximum credit computed as provided in section 2011(b)) as $50,000 (the value of the property in respect of which a State death tax was actually paid and which is included in A's gross estate under section 2103) bears to $150,000 (the value of A's total gross estate under section 2103). Accordingly, the maximum credit allowable under section 2102 and this section for all State death taxes actually paid is $240 ($720 × $50,000/$150,000).

*Example (2).* B, a nonresident not a citizen of the United States, died on January 15, 1967, owning real property in State X valued at $100,000, real property in State Y valued at $200,000, and stock in various domestic corporations valued at $300,000 and not subject to death taxes in any State. States X and Y both impose inheritance taxes. State X has, in addition to its inheritance tax, an estate tax equal to the amount by which the maximum State death tax credit allowable to an estate against its Federal estate tax exceeds the amount of the inheritance tax imposed by State X plus the amount of death taxes paid to other States. State Y has no estate tax. The amount of the inheritance tax actually paid to State X with respect to the real property situated in State X is $4,000; the amount of the inheritance tax actually paid to State Y with respect to the real property situated in State Y is $9,000. B's taxable estate for Federal estate tax purposes is $550,000, in respect of which the maximum credit under section 2011 would be $14,400 in the absence of the special limitation contained in section 2102(b). However, under section 2102(b) and this paragraph the amount of the maximum credit allowable in respect of B's estate for State death taxes is limited to the amount which bears the same ratio to $14,400 (the maximum credit computed as provided in section 2011(b)) as $300,000 (the value of the property in respect of which a State death tax was actually paid and which is included in B's gross estate under section 2103) bears to $600,000 (the value of B's total gross estate under section 2103). Accordingly, the maximum credit allowable under section 2102 and this section for all State death taxes actually paid is $7,200 ($14,400 × $300,000/$600,000), and the estate tax of State X is not applicable to B's estate.

(c) *Unified credit.*—(1) *In general.*—Subject to paragraph (c)(2) of this section, in the case of estates of decedents dying after November 10, 1988, a unified credit of $13,000 is allowed against the tax imposed by section 2101 subject to the limitations of section 2102(c).

(2) *When treaty is applicable.*—To the extent required under any treaty obligation of the United States, the estate of a nonresident not a citizen of the United States is allowed the unified credit permitted to a United States citizen or resident of $192,800, multiplied by the proportion that the total gross estate of the decedent situated in the United States bears to the decedent's total gross estate wherever situated.

(3) *Certain residents of possessions.*—In the case of a decedent who is considered to be a nonresident not a citizen of the United States under section 2209, there is allowed a unified credit equal to the greater of $13,000, or $46,800 multiplied by the proportion that the decedent's gross estate situated in the United States bears to the total gross estate of the decedent wherever situated. [Reg. § 20.2102-1.]

☐ [*T.D.* 6296, 6-23-58. *Amended by T.D.* 7296, 12-11-73 *and T.D.* 8612, 8-21-95.]

### [Reg. § 20.2103-1]

**§ 20.2103-1. Estates of nonresidents not citizens; "entire gross estate".**—The "entire gross estate" wherever situated of a nonresident who was not a citizen of the United States at the time of his death is made up in the same way as the "gross estate" of a citizen or resident of the United States. See §§ 20.2031 through 20.2044-1. See paragraphs (a) and (c) of § 20.2031-1 for the circumstances under which real property situated outside the United States is excluded from the gross estate of a citizen or resident of the United States. However, except as provided in section 2107(b) with respect to the estates of certain expatriates, in the case of a nonresident not a citizen, only that part of the entire gross estate which on the date of the decedent's death is situated in the United States is included in his taxable estate. In fact, property situated outside the United States need not be disclosed on the return unless section 2107 is applicable, certain deductions are claimed, or information is specifically requested. See §§ 20.2106-1, 20.2106-2, and 20.2107-1. For a description of property considered to be situated in the United States, see § 20.2104-1. For a description of property considered to be situated outside the United States, see § 20.2105-1. [Reg. § 20.2103-1.]

☐ [*T.D.* 6296, 6-23-58. *Amended by T.D.* 6684, 10-23-63 *and T.D.* 7296, 12-11-73.]

### [Reg. § 20.2104-1]

**§ 20.2104-1. Estates of nonresidents not citizens; property within the United States.**—(a) *In general.*—Property of a nonresident who was not a citizen of the United States at the time of his death is considered to be situated in the United States if it is—

(1) Real property located in the United States.

(2) Tangible personal property located in the United States, except certain works of art on loan for exhibition (see paragraph (b) of § 20.2105-1).

(3) In the case of an estate of a decedent dying before November 14, 1966, written evidence of intangible personal property which is treated as being the property itself, such as a bond for the payment of money, if it is physically located in the United States; except that this subparagraph shall not apply to obligations of the United States (but not its instrumentalities) issued before March 1, 1941, if the decedent was not engaged in business in the United States at the time of his death. See section 2106(c).

(4) Except as specifically provided otherwise in this section or in § 20.2105-1 (which specific exceptions, in the case of estates of decedents dying on or after November 14, 1966, cause this subparagraph to have relatively limited applicability), intangible personal property the written evidence of which is not treated as being the property itself, if it is issued by or enforceable against a resident of the United States or a domestic corporation or governmental unit.

(5) Shares of stock issued by a domestic corporation, irrespective of the location of the certificates (see, however, paragraph (i) of § 20.2105-1 for a special rule with respect to certain withdrawable accounts in savings and loan or similar associations).

(6) In the case of an estate of a decedent dying before November 14, 1966, moneys deposited in the United States by or for the decedent with any person carrying on the banking business, if the decedent was engaged in business in the United States at the time of his death.

(7) In the case of an estate of a decedent dying on or after November 14, 1966, except as specifically provided otherwise in paragraph (d), (i), (j), (l), or (m) of § 20.2105-1, any debt obligation, including a bank deposit, the primary obligor of which is—

(i) A United States person (as defined in section 7701(a)(30)), or

(ii) The United States, a State or any political subdivision thereof, the District of Columbia, or any agency or instrumentality of any such government.

This subparagraph applies irrespective of whether the written evidence of the debt obligation is treated as being the property itself or whether the decedent was engaged in business in the United States at the time of his death. For purposes of this subparagraph and paragraphs (k), (l), and (m) of § 20.2105-1, a debt obligation on which there are two or more primary obligors shall be apportioned among such obligors, taking into account to the extent appropriate under all the facts and circumstances any choate or inchoate rights of contribution existing among such obligors with respect to the indebtedness. The term "agency or instrumentality", as used in subdivision (ii) of this subparagraph, does not include a possession of the United States or an agency or instrumentality of a possession. Currency is not a debt obligation for purposes of this subparagraph.

(8) In the case of an estate of a decedent dying on or after January 1, 1970, except as specifically provided otherwise in paragraph (i) or (l) of § 20.2105-1, deposits with a branch in the United States of a foreign corporation, if the branch is engaged in the commercial banking business, whether or not the decedent was engaged in business in the United States at the time of his death.

(b) *Transfers.*—Property of which the decedent has made a transfer taxable under sections 2035 through 2038 is deemed to be situated in the United States if it is determined, under the provisions of paragraph (a) of this section, to be so situated either at the time of the transfer or at the time of the decedent's death. See § § 20.2035-1 through 20.2038-1.

(c) *Death tax convention.*—It should be noted that the situs rules described in this section may be modified for various purposes under the provisions of an applicable death tax convention with a foreign country. [Reg. § 20.2104-1.]

☐ [*T.D. 6296, 6-23-58. Amended by T.D. 7296, 12-11-73 and T.D. 7321, 8-15-74.*]

## [Reg. § 20.2105-1]

**§ 20.2105-1. Estates of nonresidents not citizens; property without the United States.**—Property of a nonresident who was not a citizen of the United States at the time of his death is considered to be situated outside the United States if it is—

(a)(1) Real property located outside the United States, except to the extent excludable from the entire gross estate wherever situated under § 20.2103-1.

(2) Tangible personal property located outside the United States.

(b) Works of art owned by the decedent if they were—

(1) Imported into the United States solely for exhibition purposes,

(2) Loaned for those purposes to a public gallery or museum, no part of the net earnings of which inures to the benefit of any private shareholder or individual, and

(3) At the time of the death of the owner, on exhibition, or en route to or from exhibition, in such a public gallery or museum.

(c) In the case of an estate of a decedent dying before November 14, 1966, written evidence of intangible personal property which is treated as being the property itself, such as a bond for the payment of money, if it is not physically located in the United States.

(d) Obligations of the United States issued before March 1, 1941, even though physically located in the United States, if the decedent was not engaged in business in the United States at the time of his death.

(e) Except as specifically provided otherwise in this section or in § 20.2104-1, intangible personal property the written evidence of which is not treated as being the property itself, if it is not issued by or enforceable against a resident of the United States or a domestic corporation or governmental unit.

(f) Shares of stock issued by a corporation which is not a domestic corporation, regardless of the location of the certificates.

(g) Amounts receivable as insurance on the decedent's life.

(h) In the case of an estate of a decedent dying before November 14, 1966, moneys deposited in the United States by or for the decedent with any person carrying on the banking business, if the decedent was not engaged in business in the United States at the time of his death.

(i) In the case of an estate of a decedent dying on or after November 14, 1966, and before January 1, 1976, any amount deposited in the United States which is described in section 861(c) (relating to certain bank deposits, withdrawable accounts, and amounts held by an insurance company under an agreement to pay interest), if any interest thereon, were such interest received by the decedent at the time of his death, would be treated under section 862(a)(1) as income from sources without the United States by reason of section 861(a)(1)(A) (relating to interest on amounts described in section

861(c) which is not effectively connected with the conduct of a trade or business within the United States) and the regulations thereunder. If such interest would be treated by reason of those provisions as income from sources without the United States only in part, the amount described in section 861(c) shall be considered situated outside the United States in the same proportion as the part of the interest which would be treated as income from sources without the United States bears to the total amount of the interest. This paragraph applies whether or not the decedent was engaged in business in the United States at the time of his death, and, except with respect to amounts described in section 861(c)(3) (relating to amounts held by an insurance company under an agreement to pay interest), whether or not the deposit or other amount is in fact interest bearing.

(j) In the case of an estate of a decedent dying on or after November 14, 1966, deposits with a branch outside of the United States of a domestic corporation or domestic partnership, if the branch is engaged in the commercial banking business. This paragraph applies whether or not the decedent was engaged in business in the United States at the time of his death, and whether or not the deposits, upon withdrawal, are payable in currency of the United States.

(k) In the case of an estate of a decedent dying on or after November 14, 1966, except as specifically provided otherwise in paragraph (a)(8) of § 20.2104-1 with respect to estates of decedents dying on or after January 1, 1970, any debt obligation, including a bank deposit, the primary obligor of which is neither—

(1) A United States person (as defined in section 7701(a)(30)), nor

(2) The United States, a State or any political subdivision thereof, the District of Columbia, or any agency or instrumentality of any such government.

This paragraph applies irrespective of whether the written evidence of the debt obligation is treated as being the property itself or whether the decedent was engaged in business in the United States at the time of his death. See paragraph (a)(7) of § 20.2104-1 for the treatment of a debt obligation on which there are two or more primary obligors. The term "agency or instrumentality", as used in subparagraph (2) of this paragraph, does not include a possession of the United States or an agency or instrumentality of a possession. Currency is not a debt obligation for purposes of this paragraph.

(l) In the case of an estate of a decedent dying on or after November 14, 1966, any debt obligation to the extent that the primary obligor on the debt obligation is a domestic corporation, if any interest thereon, were the interest received from such obligor by the decedent at the time of his death, would be treated under section 862(a)(1) as income from sources without the United States by reason of section 861(a)(1)(B) (relating to interest received from a domestic corporation less than 20 percent of whose gross income for a 3-year period was derived from sources within the United States) and the regulations thereunder. For such purposes the 3-year period referred to in section 861(a)(1)(B) is the period of 3 years ending with the close of the domestic corporation's last taxable year terminating before the decedent's death. This paragraph applies whether or not (1) the obligation is in fact interest-bearing, (2) the written evidence of the debt obligation is treated as being the property itself, or (3) the decedent was engaged in business in the United States at the time of his death. See paragraph (a)(7) of § 20.2104-1 for the treatment of a debt obligation on which there are two or more primary obligors.

(m)(1) In the case of an estate of a decedent dying after December 31, 1972, except as otherwise provided in subparagraph (2) of this paragraph, any debt obligation to the extent that the primary obligor on the debt obligation is a domestic corporation or domestic partnership, if any interest thereon, were the interest received from such obligor by the decedent at the time of his death, would be treated under section 862(a)(1) as income from sources without the United States by reason of section 861(a)(1)(G) (relating to interest received on certain debt obligations with respect to which elections have been made under section 4912(c)) and the regulations thereunder. This paragraph applies whether or not (i) the obligation is in fact interest bearing, (ii) the written evidence of the debt obligation is treated as being the property itself, or (iii) the decedent was engaged in business in the United States at the time of his death. See paragraph (a)(7) of § 20.2104-1 for the treatment of a debt obligation on which there are two or more primary obligors.

(2) In the case of an estate of a decedent dying before January 1, 1974, this paragraph does not apply to any debt obligation of a foreign corporation assumed by a domestic corporation which is treated under section 4912(c)(2) as issued by such domestic corporation during 1973. [Reg. § 20.2105-1.]

☐ [*T.D. 6296, 6-23-58. Amended by T.D. 6684, 10-23-63; T.D. 7296, 12-11-73; and T.D. 7321, 8-15-74.*]

## [Reg. § 20.2106-1]

**§ 20.2106-1. Estates of nonresidents not citizens; taxable estate; deductions in general.**—(a) The taxable estate of a nonresident who was not a citizen of the United States at the time of his death is determined by adding the value of that part of his gross estate which, at the time of his death, is situated in the United States and, in the case of an estate to which section 2107 (relating to expatriation to avoid taxes) applies, any amounts includible in his gross estate under section 2107(b), and then subtracting from the sum thereof the total amount of the following deductions:

(1) The deductions allowed in the case of estates of decedents who were citizens or residents of the United States under sections 2053 and 2054 (see §§20.2053-1 through 20.2053-9 and §20.2054-1) for expenses, indebtedness and taxes, and for losses, to the extent provided in §20.2106-2.

(2) A deduction computed in the same manner as the one allowed under section 2055 (see §§20.2055-1 through 20.2055-5) for charitable, etc., transfers, except—

(i) That the deduction is allowed only for transfers to corporations and associations created or organized in the United States, and to trustees for use within the United States, and

(ii) That the provisions contained in paragraph (c)(2) of §20.2055-2 relating to termination of a power to consume are not applicable.

(3) Subject to the special rules set forth at §20.2056A-1(c), the amount which would be deductible with respect to property situated in the United States at the time of the decedent's death under the principles of section 2056. Thus, if the surviving spouse of the decedent is a citizen of the United States at the time of the decedent's death, a marital deduction is allowed with respect to the estate of the decedent if all other applicable requirements of section 2056 are satisfied. If the surviving spouse of the decedent is not a citizen of the United States at the time of the decedent's death, the provisions of section 2056, including specifically the provisions of section 2056(d) and (unless section 2056(d)(4) applies) the provisions of section 2056A (QDOTs) must be satisfied.

(b) Section 2106(b) provides that no deduction is allowed under paragraph (a)(1) or (2) of this section unless the executor discloses in the estate tax return the value of that part of the gross estate not situated in the United States. See §20.2105-1. Such part must be valued as of the date of the decedent's death, or if the alternate valuation method under section 2032 is elected, as of the applicable valuation date. [Reg. §20.2106-1.]

☐ [T.D. 6296, 6-23-58. *Amended by T.D. 6526, 1-18-61; T.D. 7296, 12-11-73; T.D. 7318, 7-10-74 and T.D. 8612, 8-21-95.*]

**[Reg. §20.2106-2]**

**§20.2106-2. Estates of nonresidents not citizens; deductions for expenses, losses, etc.**—(a) In computing the taxable estate of a nonresident who was not a citizen of the United States at the time of his death, deductions are allowed under sections 2053 and 2054 for expenses, indebtedness and taxes, and for losses, to the following extent:

(1) A pledge or subscription is deductible if it is an enforceable claim against the estate and if it would constitute an allowable deduction under paragraph (a)(2) of §20.2106-1, relating to charitable, etc., transfers, if it had been a bequest.

(2) That proportion of other deductions under sections 2053 and 2054 is allowed which the value of that part of the decedent's gross estate situated in the United States at the time of his death bears to the value of the decedent's entire gross estate wherever situated. It is immaterial whether the amounts to be deducted were incurred or expended within or without the United States. For purposes of this subparagraph, an amount which is includible in the decedent's gross estate under section 2107(b) with respect to stock in a foreign corporation shall be included in the value of the decedent's gross estate situated in the United States.

No deduction is allowed under this paragraph unless the value of the decedent's entire gross estate is disclosed in the estate tax return. See paragraph (b) of §20.2106-1.

(b) In order that the Internal Revenue Service may properly pass upon the items claimed as deductions, the executor should submit a certified copy of the schedule of liabilities, claims against the estate, and expenses of administration filed under any applicable foreign death duty act. If no such schedule was filed, the executor should submit a certified copy of the schedule of these liabilities, claims and expenses filed with the foreign court in which administration was had. If the items of deduction allowable under section 2106(a)(1) were not included in either such schedule, or if no such schedules were filed, then there should be submitted a written statement of the foreign executor containing a declaration that it is made under the penalties of perjury setting forth the facts relied upon as entitling the estate to the benefit of the particular deduction or deductions.

(c) [Reserved][Reg. §20.2106-2.]

☐ [T.D. 6296, 6-23-58. *Amended by T.D. 7296, 12-11-73 and T.D. 8612, 8-21-95.*]

**[Reg. §20.2107-1]**

**§20.2107-1. Expatriation to avoid tax.**—(a) *Rate of tax.*—The tax imposed by section 2107(a) on the transfer of the taxable estates of certain nonresident expatriate decedents who were formerly citizens of the United States is computed in accordance with the table contained in section 2001, relating to the rate of the tax imposed on the transfer of the taxable estates of decedents who were citizens or residents of the United States. Except for any amounts included in the gross estate solely by reason of section 2107(b) and paragraph (b)(1)(ii) and (iii) of this section, the value of the taxable estate to be used in this computation is determined as provided in section 2106 and §20.2106-1. The decedents to which section 2107(a) and this section apply are described in paragraph (d) of this section.

(b) *Gross estate.*—(1) *Determination of value.*—(i) *General rule.*—Except as provided in subdivision (i) of this subparagraph with respect to stock in certain foreign corporations, for purposes of the tax imposed by section 2107(a) the value of the gross estate of every estate the transfer of which is subject to the tax imposed by that section is determined as provided in section 2103 and §20.2103-1.

(ii) *Amount includible with respect to stock in certain foreign corporations.*—If at the time of his death a nonresident expatriate decedent the transfer of whose estate is subject to the tax imposed by section 2107(a)—

(a) Owned (within the meaning of section 958(a) and the regulations thereunder) 10 percent or more of the total combined voting power of all classes of stock entitled to vote in a foreign corporation, and

(b) Owned (within the meaning of section 958(a) and the regulations thereunder), or is considered to have owned (by applying the ownership rules of section 958(b) and the regulations thereunder), more than 50 percent of the total combined voting power of all classes of stock entitled to vote in such foreign corporation, then section 2107(b) requires the inclusion in the decedent's gross estate, in addition to amounts otherwise includible therein under subdivision (i) of this subparagraph, of an amount equal to that proportion of the fair market value (determined at the time of the decedent's death or, if so elected by the executor of the decedent's estate, on the alternate valuation date as provided in section 2032) of the stock in such foreign corporation owned (within the meaning of section 958(a) and the regulations thereunder) by the decedent at the time of his death, which the fair market value of any assets owned by such foreign corporation and situated in the United States, at the time of his death, bears to the total fair market value of all assets owned by such foreign corporation at the time of his death.

(iii) *Rules of application.*—(a) In determining the proportion of the fair market value of the stock which is includible in the gross estate under subdivision (ii) of this subparagraph, the fair market value of the foreign corporation's assets situated in the United States and of its total assets shall be determined without reduction for any outstanding liabilities of the corporation.

(b) For purposes of subdivision (ii) of this subparagraph, the foreign corporation's assets which are situated in the United States shall be all its property which, by applying the provisions of sections 2104, 2105, and §§20.2104-1 and 20.2105-1, would be considered to be situated in the United States if such property were property of a nonresident who was not a citizen of the United States.

(c) For purposes of subdivision (ii)(a) of this subparagraph, a decedent is treated as owning stock in a foreign corporation at the time of his death to the extent he owned (within the meaning of section 958(a) and the regulations thereunder) the stock at the time he made a transfer of the stock in a transfer described in sections 2035 to 2038, inclusive (relating respectively to transfers made in contemplation of death, transfers with a retained life estate, transfers taking effect at death, and revocable transfers). For purposes of subdivision (ii)(b) of this subparagraph, a decedent is treated as owning stock in a foreign corporation at the time of his death to the extent he owned (within the meaning of section 958(a) and the regulations thereunder), or is considered to have owned (by applying the ownership rules of section 958(b) and the regulations thereunder), the stock at the time he made a transfer of the stock in a transfer described in sections 2035 to 2038, inclusive. In applying the proportion rule of section 2107(b) and subdivision (ii) of this subparagraph where a decedent is treated as owning stock in a foreign corporation at the time of his death by reason of having transferred his interest in such stock in a transfer described in sections 2035 to 2038, inclusive, the proportionate value of the interest includible in his gross estate is based upon the value as of the applicable valuation date described in section 2031 or 2032 of the amount, determined as of the date of transfer, of his interest in the stock. See example (2) in subparagraph (2) of this paragraph.

(d) For purposes of applying subdivision (ii) (b) of this subparagraph, the same shares of stock may not be counted more than once. See example (2) in subparagraph (2) of this paragraph.

(e) The principles applied in paragraph (b) of § 1.957-1 of this chapter (Income Tax Regulations) for determining what constitutes total combined voting power of all classes of stock entitled to vote in a foreign corporation for purposes of section 957(a) shall be applied in determining what constitutes total combined voting power of all classes of stock entitled to vote in a foreign corporation for purposes of section 2107(b) and subdivision (ii) of this subparagraph. In applying such principles under this paragraph changes in language shall be made, where necessary, in order to treat the nonresident expatriate decedent, rather than U. S. shareholders, as owning such total combined voting power.

(2) *Illustrations.*—The application of this paragraph may be illustrated by the following examples:

*Example (1).* (a) At the time of his death, H, a nonresident expatriate decedent the transfer of whose estate is subject to the tax imposed by section 2107(a), owned a 60-percent interest in M Company, a foreign partnership, which in turn owned stock issued by N Corporation, a foreign corporation. The stock in N Corporation held by M Company, which constituted 50 percent of the total combined voting power of all classes of stock entitled to vote in N Corporation, was valued at $50,000 at the time of H's death. In addition, W, H's wife, also a nonresident not a citizen of the United States, owned at the time of H's death stock in N Corporation constituting 25 percent of the total combined voting power of all classes of stock entitled to vote in that corporation. The fair market value of the assets of N Corporation which, at the time of H's death, were situated in the United States constituted 40 percent of the fair market value of all assets of that corporation. It is assumed for purposes of this example that the executor of H's estate has not elected to value the estate on the alternate valuation date provided in section 2032.

(b) The test contained in subparagraph (1)(ii)(a) of this paragraph is met since at the time of his death H indirectly owned (within the meaning of section 958(a) and the regulations thereunder) 30 percent (60% of 50%) of the total combined voting power of all classes of stock entitled to vote in N Corporation; and the test contained in subparagraph (1)(ii)(b) of this paragraph is met since at such time H owned or is considered to have owned (within the meaning of section 958(a) and (b) and the regulations thereunder) 55 percent of the total combined voting power of all classes of stock entitled to vote in N Corporation (having constructive ownership of his wife's 25 percent, in addition to his own indirect ownership of 30 percent, of the total combined voting power). Accordingly, $12,000 is included in H's gross estate by reason of section 2107(b) and this paragraph. This $12,000 is the amount which is equal to 40 percent (the percentage of the fair market value of N Corporation's assets which were situated within the United States at H's death) of $30,000 (the fair market value of the stock then owned by H within the meaning of section 958(a) and the regulations thereunder, *i. e.*, H's 60-percent interest in the $50,000 fair market value of stock held by M Company).

*Example (2).* (a) Assume the same facts as those given in example (1) except that H made a transfer to W in contemplation of his death (within the meaning of section 2035) of his 60-percent interest in M Company, that on the date of the transfer M Company held stock in N Corporation constituting 80 percent of the total combined voting power of all classes of stock entitled to vote in that corporation (rather than the 50 percent of total combined voting power held by M Company on the date of H's death), and that the 80 percent of total combined voting power owned by M Company on the date of the transfer is valued at $70,000 on that date and at $85,000 at the time of H's death. It is assumed for purposes of this example that the 60-percent interest in M Company was held by W at the time of H's death.

(b) The test contained in subparagraph (1)(ii)(a) of this paragraph is met since, under subparagraph (1)(iii)(c) of this paragraph, H is treated as owning (within the meaning of section 958(a) and the regulations thereunder), at the time of his death, the 48 percent (60% of 80%) of the total combined voting power of all classes of stock entitled to vote in N Corporation represented by his transferred interest in M Company; and the test contained in subparagraph (1)(ii)(b) of this paragraph is met since, under that subparagraph and subparagraph (1)(iii)(c) of this paragraph, H is treated as owning (within the meaning of section 958(a) or (b)), at the time of his death, 73 percent (48% plus 25%) of the total combined voting power of all classes of stock entitled to vote in N Corporation. Accordingly, $20,400 is included in H's gross estate by reason of section 2107(b) and this paragraph. This $20,400 is the amount which is equal to 40 percent (the percentage of the fair market value of N Corporation's assets which were situated within the United States at H's death) of $51,000 (the fair market value at the time of H's death of the transferred interest which under subparagraph (1)(iii)(c) of this paragraph

H is considered to own within the meaning of section 958(a) and the regulations thereunder at that time, *i. e.*, the 60-percent interest in the $85,000 fair market value at that time of the 80-percent total combined voting power held by M Company on the date of transfer).

(c) The fact that the stock in N Corporation owned by M Company is considered under subparagraph (1)(ii)(b) of this paragraph to be owned by H for two independent reasons (*i. e.*, under section 958(a) and the regulations thereunder, because H transferred his 60-percent interest in M Company to W in contemplation of death, and under section 958(b) and the regulations thereunder, because H is considered to own the stock in N Corporation indirectly owned by his wife, W, by reason of her ownership of such transferred interest) does not cause the shares of stock represented by the transferred interest in M Company to be counted twice in determining whether the test contained in that subparagraph is met. See subparagraph (1)(iii)(d) of this paragraph.

*Example (3).* (a) At the time of his death, H, a nonresident expatriate decedent the transfer of whose estate is subject to the tax imposed by section 2107(a), owned a 40-percent beneficial interest in a domestic trust; at that time he also directly owned stock in P Corporation, a foreign corporation, constituting 15 percent of the total combined voting power of all classes of stock entitled to vote in that corporation. The trust owned stock in P Corporation constituting 51 percent of the total combined voting power of all classes of stock entitled to vote in that corporation. The stock in P Corporation owned directly by H was valued at $20,000 on the alternate valuation date determined pursuant to an election under section 2032. The fair market value of the assets of P Corporation which, at the time of H's death, were situated in the United States constituted 20 percent of the fair market value of all assets of that corporation.

(b) By reason of section 958(b)(2) and the regulations thereunder, the trust is considered to own all the stock entitled to vote in P Corporation since it owns more than 50 percent of the total combined voting power of all classes of stock entitled to vote in that corporation. The test contained in subparagraph (1)(ii)(a) of this paragraph is met since at the time of his death H owned (within the meaning of section 958(a) and the regulations thereunder) 15 percent of the total combined voting power of all classes of stock entitled to vote in P Corporation; the stock in P Corporation owned by the trust is not considered to have been owned by H under section 958(a)(2) since the trust is not a foreign trust. In addition, the test contained in subparagraph (1)(ii)(b) of this paragraph is met since at the time of his death H owned or is considered to have owned (within the meaning of section 958(a) and (b) and the regulations thereunder) 55 percent of the total combined voting power of all classes of stock entitled to vote in that corporation (his 15 percent directly owned plus his 40 percent (40% of 100%) considered to be owned). Accordingly, $4,000 is included in H's gross estate by reason of section 2107(b) of this paragraph. This $4,000 is the amount which is equal to 20 percent (the percentage of the fair market value of P Corporation's assets which were situated within the United States at H's death) of $20,000 (the fair market value of the stock then owned by H within the meaning of section 958(a) and the regulations thereunder). In addition, the value of H's interest in the domestic trust is included in his gross estate under section 2103 to the extent it constitutes property having a situs in the United States.

(c) *Credits.*—Credits against the tax imposed by section 2107(a) are allowed for any amounts determined in accordance with section 2102 and § 20.2102-1 (relating to credits against the estate tax for State death taxes, gift tax, and tax on prior transfers). In computing the special limitation on the credit for State death taxes contained in section 2102(b) and paragraph (b) of § 20.2102-1, amounts included in the gross estate under section 2107(b) and paragraph (b)(1) of this section are to be taken into account.

(d) *Decedents to whom the tax imposed by section 2107(a) applies.*—(1) *General rule.*—The tax imposed by section 2107(a) applies to the transfer of the taxable estate of every decedent nonresident not a citizen of the United States dying on or after November 14, 1966, who lost his U. S. citizenship after March 8, 1965, and within the 10-year period ending with the date of his death, except in the case of the estate of a decedent whose loss of U. S. citizenship either—

(i) Resulted from the application of section 301(b), 350, or 355 of the Immigration and Nationality Act, as amended (8 U. S. C. 1401(b), 1482, or 1487); or

(ii) Did not have for one of its principal purposes (but not necessarily its only principal purpose) the avoidance of Federal income, estate, or gift tax.

Section 301(b) of the Immigration and Nationality Act provides generally that a U. S. citizen, who is born outside the United States of parents one of whom is an alien and the other is a U. S. citizen who was physically present in the United States for a specified period, shall lose his U. S. citizenship if, within a specified period preceding the age of 28 years, he fails to be continuously physically present in the United States for at least 5 years. Section 350 of that Act provides that under certain circumstances a person, who at birth acquired the nationality of the United States and of a foreign country and who has voluntarily sought or claimed benefits of the nationality of any foreign country, shall lose his U. S. nationality if, after attaining the age of 22 years, he has a continuous residence for 3 years in the foreign country of which he is a national by birth. Section 355 of that Act provides that a person having U. S. nationality, who is under 21 years of age and whose residence is in a foreign country with or under the legal custody of a parent who loses his U. S. nationality under specified circumstances, shall lose his U. S. nationality if he has or acquires the nationality of that foreign country and attains the age of 25 years without having established his residence in the United States. Section 2107 and this section do not apply to the transfer of any estate the estate tax treatment of which is subject to a Presidential proclamation made pursuant to section 2108(a) (relating to the application of pre-1967 estate tax provisions in the case of a foreign country which imposes a more burdensome tax than the United States).

(2) *Burden of proof.*—(i) *General rule.*—In determining for purposes of subparagraph (1)(ii) of this paragraph whether a principal purpose for the loss of U. S. citizenship by a decedent was the avoidance of Federal income, estate, or gift tax, the Commissioner must first establish that it is reasonable to believe that the decedent's loss of U. S. citizenship would, but for section 2107 and this section, result in a substantial reduction in the sum of (a) the Federal estate tax and (b) all estate, inheritance, legacy, and succession taxes imposed by foreign countries and political subdivisions thereof, in respect of the transfer of the decedent's estate. Once the Commis-

sioner has so established, the burden of proving that the loss of citizenship by the decedent did not have for one of its principal purposes the avoidance of Federal income, estate, or gift tax shall be on the executor of the decedent's estate.

(ii) *Tentative determination of substantial reduction in Federal and foreign death taxes.*—In the absence of complete factual information, the Commissioner may make a tentative determination, based on the information available, that the decedent's loss of U. S. citizenship would, but for section 2107 and this section, result in a substantial reduction in the sum of the Federal and foreign death taxes described in subdivision (i)(a) and (b) of this subparagraph. This tentative determination may be based upon the fact that the laws of the foreign country of which the decedent became a citizen and the laws of the foreign country of which the decedent was a resident at the time of his death, including the laws of any political subdivisions of those foreign countries, would ordinarily result, in the case of an estate of a nonexpatriate decedent having the same citizenship and residence as the decedent, in liability for total death taxes under such laws substantially lower than the amount of the Federal estate tax which would be imposed on the transfer of a comparable estate of a citizen of the United States. In the absence of a preponderance of evidence to the contrary, this tentative determination shall be sufficient to establish that it is reasonable to believe that the decedent's loss of U. S. citizenship would, but for section 2107 and this section, result in a substantial reduction in the sum of the Federal and foreign death taxes described in subdivision (i)(a) and (b) of this subparagraph. [Reg. § 20.2107-1.]

☐ [*T.D. 7296, 12-11-73.*]

## Miscellaneous

[Reg. § 20.2203-1]

**§ 20.2203-1. Definition of executor.**—The term "executor" means the executor or administrator of the decedent's estate. However, if there is no executor or administrator appointed, qualified and acting within the United States, the term means any person in actual or constructive possession of any property of the decedent. The term "person in actual or constructive possession of any property of the decedent" includes, among others, the decedent's agents and representatives; safe-deposit companies, warehouse companies, and other custodians of property in this country; brokers holding, as collateral, securities belonging to the decedent; and debtors of the decedent in this country. [Reg. § 20.2203-1.]

☐ [*T.D. 6296, 6-23-58.*]

[Reg. § 20.2204-1]

**§ 20.2204-1. Discharge of executor from personal liability.**—(a) *General rule.*—The executor of a decedent's estate may make written application to the applicable internal revenue officer with whom the estate tax return is required to be filed, as provided in § 20.6091-1, for a determination of the Federal estate tax and for a discharge of personal liability therefrom. Within 9 months after receipt of the application, or if the application is made before the return is filed then within 9 months after the return is filed, the executor will be notified of the amount of the tax and, upon payment thereof, he will be discharged from personal liability for any deficiency in the tax thereafter found to be due. If no such notification is received, the executor is discharged at the end of such 9-month period from personal liability for any deficiency thereafter found to be due. The discharge of the executor from personal liability under this section applies only to him in his personal capacity and to his personal assets. The discharge is not applicable to his liability as executor to the extent of the assets of the estate in his possession or control. Further, the discharge is not to operate as a release of any part of the gross estate from the lien for estate tax for any deficiency that may thereafter be determined to be due.

(b) *Special rule in the case of extension of time for payment of tax.*—In addition to the provisions of paragraph (a) of this section, an executor of the estate of a decedent dying after December 31, 1970, may make written application to be discharged from personal liability for the amount of Federal estate tax for which the time for payment has been extended under section 6161, 6163, or 6166. In such a case, the executor will be notified of the amount of bond, if any, to be furnished within 9 months after receipt of the application, or, if the application is made before the return is filed, within 9 months after the return is filed. The amount of any bond required under the provisions of this paragraph shall not exceed the amount of tax the payment of which has been extended. Upon furnishing the bond in

the form required under § 301.7101-1 of this chapter (Regulations on Procedure and Administration), or upon receipt of the notification that no bond is required, the executor will be discharged from personal liability for the tax the payment of which has been extended. If no notification is received, the executor is discharged at the end of such 9-month period from personal liability for the tax the payment of which has been extended. [Reg. § 20.2204-1.]

☐ [*T.D. 6296, 6-23-58. Amended by T.D. 7238, 12-28-72, and T.D. 7941, 2-6-84.*]

[Reg. § 20.2204-2]

**§ 20.2204-2. Discharge of fiduciary other than executor from personal liability.**—(a) A fiduciary (not including a fiduciary of the estate of a nonresident decedent), other than the executor, who as a fiduciary holds, or has held at any time since the decedent's death, property transferred to the fiduciary from a decedent dying after December 31, 1970, or his estate, may make written application to the applicable internal revenue officer with whom the estate tax return is required to be filed, as provided in § 20.6091-1, for a determination of the Federal estate tax liability with respect to such property and for a discharge of personal liability therefrom. The application must be accompanied by a copy of the instrument, if any, under which the fiduciary is acting, a description of all the property transferred to the fiduciary from the decedent or his estate, and any other information that would be relevant to a determination of the fiduciary's tax liability.

(b) Upon the discharge of the executor from personal liability under § 20.2204-1, or, if later, within 6 months after the receipt of the application filed by a fiduciary pursuant to the provisions of paragraph (a) of this section, such fiduciary will be notified either (1) of the amount of tax for which it has been determined the fiduciary is liable, or (2) that it has been determined that the fiduciary is not liable for any such tax. The fiduciary will also be notified of the amount of bond, if any, to be furnished for any Federal estate tax for which the time for payment has been extended under section 6161, 6163, or 6166. The amount of any bond required under the provisions of this paragraph shall not exceed the amount of tax the payment of which has been so extended. Upon payment of the amount for which it has been determined the fiduciary is liable, and upon furnishing any bond required under this paragraph in the form specified under § 301.7101-1 of this chapter (Regulations on Procedure and Administration), or upon receipt by the fiduciary of notification of a determination that he is not liable for such tax or that a bond is not required, the fiduciary will be discharged from personal liability for any deficiency in the tax thereafter found to be due. If no such notification is received, the fiduciary is discharged at the end of such 6 months (or upon discharge of the executor, if later) from personal liability for any deficiency thereafter found to be due. The discharge of the fiduciary from personal liability under this section applies only to him in his personal capacity and to his personal assets. The discharge is not applicable to his liability as a fiduciary (such as a trustee) to the extent of the assets of the estate in his possession or control. Further, the discharge is not to operate as a release of any part of the gross estate from the lien for estate tax for any deficiency that may thereafter be determined to be due. [Reg. § 20.2204-2.]

☐ [*T.D.* 7238, 12-28-72.]

### [Reg. § 20.2204-3]

**§ 20.2204-3. Special rules for estates of decedents dying after December 31, 1976; special lien under section 6324A.**—For purposes of §§ 20.2204-1(b) and 20.2204-2(b), in the case of a decedent dying after December 31, 1976, if the executor elects a special lien in favor of the United States under section 6324A, relating to special lien for estate taxes deferred under section 6166 or 6166A (as in effect prior to its repeal by the Economic Recovery Tax Act of 1981), such lien shall be treated as the furnishing of a bond with respect to the amount for which the time for payment has been extended under section 6166. If an election has been made under section 6324A, the executor may not thereafter substitute a bond pursuant to section 2204 in lieu of that lien. If a bond has been supplied under section 2204, however, the executor may, by filing a proper notice of election and agreement, substitute a lien under section 6324A for any part or all of such bond. See §§ 20.6324A-1 and 301.6324A-1 for rules relating to a special lien under section 6324A. [Reg. § 20.2204-3.]

☐ [*T.D.* 7941, 2-6-84.]

### [Reg. § 20.2205-1]

**§ 20.2205-1. Reimbursement out of estate.**—If any portion of the tax is paid by or collected out of that part of the estate passing to, or in the possession of, any person other than the duly qualified executor or administrator, that person may be entitled to reimbursement, either out of the undistributed estate or by contribution from other beneficiaries whose shares or interests in the estate would have been reduced had the tax been paid before distribution of the estate, or whose shares or interests are subject either to an equal or prior liability for the payment of taxes, debts, or other charges against the estate. For specific provisions giving the executor the right to reimbursement from life insurance beneficiaries and from recipients of property over which the decedent had a power of appointment, see sections 2206 and 2207. These provisions, however, are not designed to curtail the right of the district director to collect the tax from any person, or out of any property, liable for its payment. The district director cannot be required to apportion the tax among the persons liable nor to enforce any right of reimbursement or contribution. [Reg. § 20.2205-1.]

☐ [*T.D.* 6296, 6-23-58.]

### [Reg. § 20.2206-1]

**§ 20.2206-1. Liability of life insurance beneficiaries.**—With respect to the right of the district director to collect the tax without regard to the provisions of section 2206, see § 20.2205-1. [Reg. § 20.2206-1.]

☐ [*T.D.* 6296, 6-23-58.]

### [Reg. § 20.2207-1]

**§ 20.2207-1. Liability of recipient of property over which decedent had power of appointment.**—With respect to the right of the district director to collect the tax without regard to the provisions of section 2207, see § 20.2205-1. [Reg. § 20.2207-1.]

☐ [*T.D.* 6296, 6-23-58.]

### [Reg. § 20.2207A-1]

**§ 20.2207A-1. Right of recovery of estate taxes in the case of certain marital deduction property.**—(a) *In general.*—(1) *Right of recovery from person receiving the property.*—If the gross estate includes the value of property that is includible by reason of section 2044 (relating to certain property in which the decedent had a qualifying income interest for life under sections 2056(b)(7) or 2523(f)), the estate of the surviving spouse is entitled to recover from the *person receiving the property* (as defined in paragraph (d) of this section) the amount of Federal estate tax attributable to that property. The right of recovery arises when the Federal estate tax with respect to the property includible in the gross estate by reason of section 2044 is paid by the estate. There is no right of recovery from any person for the property received by that person for which a deduction was allowed from the gross estate if no tax is attributable to that property.

(2) *Failure to exercise right of recovery.*—Failure of an estate to exercise a right of recovery under this section upon a transfer subject to section 2044 is treated as a transfer for Federal gift tax purposes of the unrecovered amounts from the persons who would benefit from

the recovery to the persons from whom the recovery could have been obtained. See § 25.2511-1 of this chapter. The transfer is considered made when the right of recovery is no longer enforceable under applicable law. A delay in the exercise of the right of recovery without payment of sufficient interest is a below-market loan. Section 1.7872-5T of the Temporary Income Tax regulations describes factors that are used to determine, based on the facts and circumstances of a particular case, whether a loan otherwise subject to imputation under section 7872 (relating to the treatment of below-market loans) is exempted from its provisions.

(3) *Waiver of right of recovery.*—The provisions of § 20.2207A-1(a)(2) do not apply to the extent that the surviving spouse's will provides that a recovery shall not be made or to the extent that the beneficiaries cannot otherwise compel recovery. Thus, e.g., if the surviving spouse gives the executor of the estate discretion to waive the right of recovery and the executor waives the right, no gift occurs under § 25.2511-1 of this chapter if the persons who would benefit from the recovery cannot compel the executor to exercise the right of recovery.

(b) *Amount of estate tax attributable to property includible under section 2044.*—The amount of Federal estate tax attributable to property includible in the gross estate under section 2044 is the amount by which the total Federal estate tax (including penalties and interest attributable to the tax) under chapter 11 of the Internal Revenue Code that has been paid, exceeds the total Federal estate tax (including penalties and interest attributable to the tax) under chapter 11 of the Internal Revenue Code that would have been paid if the value of the property includible in the gross estate by reason of section 2044 had not been so included.

(c) *Amount of estate tax attributable to a particular property.*—An estate's right of recovery with respect to a particular property is an amount equal to the amount determined in paragraph (b) of this section multiplied by a fraction. The numerator of the fraction is the value for Federal estate tax purposes of the particular property included in the gross estate by reason of section 2044, less any deduction allowed with respect to the property. The denominator of the fraction is the total value of all properties included in the gross estate by reason of section 2044, less any deductions allowed with respect to those properties.

(d) *Person receiving the property.*—If the property is in a trust at the time of the decedent's death, the *person receiving the property* is the trustee and any person who has received a distribution of the property prior to the expiration of the right of recovery if the property does not remain in trust. This paragraph (d) does not affect the right, if any, under local law, of any person with an interest in property to reimbursement or contribution from another person with an interest in the property.

(e) *Example.*—The following example illustrates the application of paragraphs (a) through (d) of this section.

*Example.* D died in 1994. D's will created a trust funded with certain income producing assets included in D's gross estate at $1,000,000. The trust provides that all the income is payable to D's wife, S, for life, remainder to be divided equally among their four children. In computing D's taxable estate, D's executor deducted, pursuant to section 2056(b)(7), $1,000,000. Assume that S received no other property from D and that S died in 1996. Assume further that S made no section 2519 disposition of the property, that the property was included in S's gross estate at a value of $1,080,000, and that S's will contained no provision regarding section 2207A(a). The tax attributable to the property is equal to the amount by which the total Federal estate tax (including penalties and interest) paid by S's estate exceeds the Federal estate tax (including penalties and interest) that would have been paid if S's gross estate had been reduced by $1,080,000. That amount of tax may be recovered by S's estate from the trust. If, at the time S's estate seeks reimbursement, the trust has been distributed to the four children, S's estate is also entitled to recover the tax from the children. [Reg. § 20.2207A-1.]

☐ [*T.D.* 8522, 2-28-94. *Amended by T.D.* 9077, 7-17-2003.]

### [Reg. § 20.2207A-2]

**§ 20.2207A-2. Effective date.**—The provisions of § 20.2207A-1 are effective with respect to estates of decedents dying after March 1, 1994. With respect to estates of decedent dying on or before such date, the executor of the decedent's estate may rely on any reasonable interpretation of the statutory provisions. For these purposes, the provisions of § 20.2207A-1 (as well as project LR-211-76, 1984-1 C.B., page 598, see § 601.601(d)(2)(ii)(*b*) of this chapter), are considered a reasonable interpretation of the statutory provisions. [Reg. § 20.2207A-2.]

☐ [*T.D.* 8522, 2-28-94.]

[Reg. §20.2208-1]

**§20.2208-1. Certain residents of possessions considered citizens of the United States.**—As used in this part, the term "citizen of the United States" is considered to include a decedent dying after September 2, 1958, who, at the time of his death, was domiciled in a possession of the United States and was a United States citizen, and who did not acquire his United States citizenship solely by reason of his being a citizen of such possession or by reason of his birth or residence within such possession. The estate of such a decedent is, therefore, subject to the tax imposed by section 2001. See paragraph (a)(2) of §20.0-1 and §20.2209-1 for further information relating to the application of the Federal estate tax to the estates of decedents who were residents of possessions of the United States. The application of this section may be illustrated by the following example and the examples set forth in §20.2209-1:

*Example.* A, a citizen of the United States by reason of his birth in the United States at San Francisco, established residence in Puerto Rico and acquired a Puerto Rican citizenship. A died on September 4, 1958, while a citizen and domiciliary of Puerto Rico. A's estate is, by reason of the provisions of section 2208, subject to the tax imposed by section 2001 inasmuch as his United States citizenship is based on birth in the United States and is not based solely on being a citizen of a possession or solely on birth or residence in a possession. [Reg. §20.2208-1.]

□ [*T.D.* 6526, 1-18-61.]

[Reg. §20.2209-1]

**§20.2209-1. Certain residents of possessions considered nonresidents not citizens of the United States.**—As used in this part, the term "nonresident not a citizen of the United States" is considered to include a decedent dying after September 14, 1960, who, at the time of his death, was domiciled in a possession of the United States and was a United States citizen, and who acquired his United States citizenship solely by reason of his being a citizen of such possession or by reason of his birth or residence within such possession. The estate of such a decedent is, therefore, subject to the tax imposed by section 2101 which is the tax applicable in the case of a "nonresident not a citizen of the United States." See paragraph (a)(2) of §20.0-1 and §20.2208-1 for further information relating to the application of the Federal estate tax to the estates of decedents who were residents of possessions of the United States. The application of this section may be illustrated by the following examples and the example set

forth in §20.2208-1. In each of the following examples the decedent is deemed a "nonresident not a citizen of the United States" and his estate is subject to the tax imposed by section 2101 since the decedent died after September 14, 1960, but would not have been so deemed and subject to such tax if the decedent had died on or before September 14, 1960.

*Example (1).* C, who acquired his United States citizenship under section 5 of the Act of March 2, 1917 (39 Stat. 953), by reason of being a citizen of Puerto Rico, died in Puerto Rico on October 1, 1960, while domiciled therein. C is considered to have acquired his United States citizenship solely by reason of his being a citizen of Puerto Rico.

*Example (2).* E, whose parents were United States citizens by reason of their birth in Boston, was born in the Virgin Islands on March 1, 1927. On September 30, 1960, he died in the Virgin Islands while domiciled therein. E is considered to have acquired his United States citizenship solely by reason of his birth in the Virgin Islands (section 306 of the Immigration and Nationality Act (66 Stat. 237, 8 U. S. C. 1406)).

*Example (3).* N, who acquired United States citizenship by reason of being a native of the Virgin Islands and a resident thereof on June 28, 1932 (section 306 of the Immigration and Nationality Act (66 Stat. 237, 8 U. S. C. 1406)), died on October 1, 1960, while domiciled in the Virgin Islands. N is considered to have acquired his United States citizenship solely by reason of his birth or residence in the Virgin Islands.

*Example (4).* P, a former Danish citizen, who on January 17, 1917, resided in the Virgin Islands, made the declaration to preserve his Danish citizenship required by Article 6 of the treaty entered into on August 4, 1916, between the United States and Denmark. Subsequently P acquired United States citizenship when he renounced such declaration before a court of record (section 306 of the Immigration and Nationality Act (66 Stat. 237, 8 U. S. C. 1406)). P died on October 1, 1960, while domiciled in the Virgin Islands. P is considered to have acquired his United States citizenship solely by reason of his birth or residence in the Virgin Islands.

*Example (5).* R, a former French citizen, acquired his United States citizenship through naturalization proceedings in a court located in the Virgin Islands after having qualified for citizenship by residing in the Virgin Islands for 5 years. R died on October 1, 1960, while domiciled in the Virgin Islands. R is considered to have acquired his United States citizenship solely by reason of his birth or residence within the Virgin Islands. [Reg. §20.2209-1.]

□ [*T.D.* 6526, 1-18-61.]

→ *Caution: Reg. §§20.6001-1, 20.6011-1, 20.6018-1—20.6018-4, 20.6036-1—20.6036-2, 20.6061-1, 20.6065-1, 20.6071-1, 20.6075-1, 20.6081-1, 20.6091-1—20.6091-2, 20.6151-1, 20.6161-1—20.6161-2, 20.6163-1, 20.6165-1, 20.6166-1—20.6166A-4, 20.6314-1, 20.6321-1, 20.6323-1, 20.6324-1, 20.6324A-1—20.6324B-1, 20.6325-1, 20.6601-1, 20.6905-1, and 20.7101-1, dealing with administration of the estate tax, are reproduced in Code section numerical order.*

# Gift Tax

# DETERMINATION OF TAX LIABILITY

See p. 20,601 for regulations not amended to reflect law changes

[Reg. §25.0-1]

**§25.0-1. Introduction.**—(a) *In general.*—(1) The regulations in this part are designated "Gift Tax Regulations." These regulations pertain to (i) the gift tax imposed by chapter 12 of subtitle B of the Internal Revenue Code on the transfer of property by gift by individuals in the calendar year 1955, in subsequent calendar years beginning before the calendar year 1971, in calendar quarters beginning with the first calendar quarter of calendar year 1971 through the last calendar quarter of the calendar year 1981, and in calendar years beginning with the calendar year 1982, and (ii) certain related administrative provisions of subtitle F of the Code. It should be noted that the application of some of the provisions of these regulations may be affected by the provisions of an applicable gift tax convention with a foreign country. Unless otherwise indicated, references in these regulations to the "Internal Revenue Code" or the "Code" are references to the Internal Revenue Code of 1954, as amended, and references to a section or other provision of law are references to a section or other provision of the Internal Revenue Code of 1954, as amended. The Gift Tax Regulations are applicable to the transfer of property by gift by individuals in calendar years 1955 through 1970, in calendar quarters beginning with the first calendar quarter of calendar year 1971 through the last calendar quarter of the calendar year 1981, and in calendar years beginning with the calendar year 1982, and supersede the regulations contained in Part 86, Subchapter B, Chapter 1, Title 26, Code of Federal Regulations (1939) (Regulations 108, Gift Tax (8 F. R. 10858)), as prescribed and made applicable to the Internal Revenue Code of 1954 by Treasury Decision 6091, signed August 16, 1954 (19 F. R. 5167, Aug. 17, 1954).

(2) Section 2501(b) makes the provisions of chapter 12 of the Code apply in the case of gifts made after September 2, 1958, by certain citizens of the United States who were residents of a possession thereof at the time the gifts were made. Section 2501(c) makes the provisions of chapter 12 apply in the case of gifts made after September 14, 1960, by certain other citizens of the United States who were residents of a possession thereof at the time the gifts were made. See paragraphs (c) and (d) of §25.2501-1. Except as otherwise provided in paragraphs (c) and (d) of §25.2501-1, the provisions of these regulations do not apply to the making of gifts by such citizens.

(b) *Nature of tax.*—The gift tax is not a property tax. It is a tax imposed upon the transfer of property by individuals. It is not applicable to transfers by corporations or persons other than individuals. However, see paragraph (h)(1) of §25.2511-1 with respect to the extent to which a transfer by or to a corporation is considered a transfer by or to its shareholders.

(c) *Scope of regulations.*—(1) *Determination of tax liability.*—Subchapter A of chapter 12 of the Code pertains to the determination of tax liability. The regulations pursuant to subchapter A are set forth in §§25.2501-1 through 25.2504-2 of this part. Sections 25.2701-5 and 25.2702-6 contain rules that provide additional adjustments to mitigate double taxation where the amount of the transferor's property was previously determined under the special valuation provisions of sections 2701 and 2702.

(2) *Transfer.*—Subchapter B of chapter 12 and chapter 14 of the Internal Revenue Code pertain to the transfers which constitute the

making of gifts and the valuation of those transfers. The regulations pursuant to subchapter B are set forth in §§25.2511-1 through 25.2518-3. The regulations pursuant to chapter 14 are set forth in §§25.2701-1 through 25.2704-3.

(3) *Deductions.*—Subchapter C of chapter 12 of the Code pertains to the deductions which are allowed in determining the amount of taxable gifts. The regulations pursuant to subchapter C are set forth in §§25.2521-1 through 25.2524-1 of this part.

(4) *Procedure and administration provisions.*—Subtitle F of the Internal Revenue Code contains some sections which are applicable to the gift tax. The regulations pursuant to those sections are set forth in §§25.6001-1 through 25.7101-1. Such regulations do not purport to be all the regulations on procedure and administration which are pertinent to gift tax matters. For the remainder of the regulations on procedure and administration which are pertinent to gift tax matters, see part 301 of this chapter (Regulations on Procedure and Administration).

(d) *Arrangement and numbering.*—Each section of the regulations in this part (other than this section) is designated by a number composed of the part number followed by a decimal point (25.); the section of the Internal Revenue Code which it interprets; a hyphen (-); and a number identifying the section. By use of these designations one can ascertain the sections of the regulations relating to a provision of the Code. For example, the regulations pertaining to section 2521 of the Code are designated §25.2521-1. [Reg. §25.0-1.]

☐ [*T.D.* 6334, 11-14-58. *Amended by T.D.* 6542, 1-19-61; *T.D.* 7238, 12-28-72; *T.D.* 7296, 12-11-73; *T.D.* 7665, 1-24-80; *T.D.* 7910, 9-6-83 *and T.D.* 8395, 1-28-92.]

**[Reg. §25.2207A-1]**

**§25.2207A-1. Right of recovery of gift taxes in the case of certain marital deduction property.**—(a) *In general.*—If an individual is treated as transferring an interest in property by reason of section 2519, the individual or the individual's estate is entitled to recover from the *person receiving the property* (as defined in paragraph (e) of this section) the amount of gift tax attributable to that property. The value of property to which this paragraph (a) applies is the value of all interests in the property other than the qualifying income interest. There is no right of recovery from any person for the property received by that person for which a deduction was allowed from the total amount of gifts, if no Federal gift tax is attributable to the property. The right of recovery arises at the time the Federal gift tax is actually paid by the transferor subject to section 2519.

(b) *Failure of a person to exercise the right of recovery.*—(1) The failure of a person to exercise a right of recovery provided by section 2207A(b) upon a lifetime transfer subject to section 2519 is treated as a transfer for Federal gift tax purposes of the unrecovered amounts to the person(s) from whom the recovery could have been obtained. See §25.2511-1. The transfer is considered to be made when the right to recovery is no longer enforceable under applicable law and is treated as a gift even if recovery is impossible. A delay in the exercise of the right of recovery without payment of sufficient interest is a below-market loan. Section 1.7872-5T of this chapter describes factors that are used to determine, based on the facts and circumstances of a particular case, whether a loan otherwise subject to imputation under section 7872 (relating to the treatment of below-market loans) is exempted from its provisions.

(2) The transferor subject to section 2519 may execute a written waiver of the right of recovery arising under section 2207A before that right of recovery becomes unenforceable. If a waiver is executed, the transfer of the unrecovered amounts by the transferor is considered to be made on the later of—

(i) The date of the valid and irrevocable waiver rendering the right of recovery no longer enforceable; or

(ii) The date of the payment of the tax by the transferor.

(c) *Amount of gift tax attributable to all properties.*—The amount of Federal gift tax attributable to all properties includible in the total amount of gifts under section 2519 made during the calendar year is the amount by which the total Federal gift tax for the calendar year (including penalties and interest attributable to the tax) under chapter 12 of the Internal Revenue Code which has been paid, exceeds the total Federal gift tax for the calendar year (including penalties and interest attributable to the tax) under chapter 12 of the Internal Revenue Code which would have been paid if the value of the properties includible in the total amount of gifts by reason of section 2519 had not been included.

(d) *Amount of gift tax attributable to a particular property.*—A person's right of recovery with respect to a particular property is an amount equal to the amount determined in paragraph (c) of this section multiplied by a fraction. The numerator of the fraction is the value of the particular property included in the total amount of gifts made during the calendar year by reason of section 2519, less any deduction allowed with respect to the property. The denominator of the fraction is the total value of all properties included in the total amount of gifts made during the calendar year by reason of section 2519, less any deductions allowed with respect to those properties.

(e) *Person receiving the property.*—If the property is in a trust at the time of the transfer, the *person receiving the property* is the trustee, and any person who has received a distribution of the property prior to the expiration of the right of recovery if the property does not remain in trust. This paragraph (e) does not affect the right, if any, under local law, of any person with an interest in property to reimbursement or contribution from another person with an interest in the property.

(f) *Example.*—The following example illustrates the application of paragraphs (a) through (e) of this section.

*Example.* D created an inter vivos trust during 1994 with certain income producing assets valued at $1,000,000. The trust provides that all income is payable to D's wife, S, for S's life, with the remainder at S's death to be divided equally among their four children. In computing taxable gifts during calendar year 1994, D deducted, pursuant to section 2523(f), $1,000,000 from the total amount of gifts made. In addition, assume that S received no other transfers from D and that S made a gift during 1996 of the entire life interest to one of the children, at which time the value of trust assets was $1,080,000 and the value of S's life interest was $400,000. Although the entire value of the trust assets ($1,080,000) is, pursuant to sections 2511 and 2519, included in the total amount of S's gifts for calendar year 1996, S is only entitled to reimbursement for the Federal gift tax attributable to the value of the remainder interest, that is, the Federal gift tax attributable to $680,000 ($1,080,000 less $400,000). The Federal gift tax attributable to $680,000 is equal to the amount by which the total Federal gift tax (including penalties and interest) paid for the calendar year exceeds the federal gift tax (including penalties and interest) that would have been paid if the total amount of gifts during 1996 had been reduced by $680,000. That amount of tax may be recovered by S from the trust. [Reg. §25.2207A-1.]

☐ [*T.D.* 8522, 2-28-94, *Amended by T.D.* 9077, 7-17-2003.]

**[Reg. §25.2207A-2]**

**§25.2207A-2. Effective date.**—The provisions of §25.2207A-1 are effective with respect to dispositions made after March 1, 1994. With respect to gifts made on or before such date, the donor may rely on any reasonable interpretation of the statutory provisions. For these purposes, the provisions of §25.2207A-1 (as well as project LR-211-76, 1984-1 C.B., page 598, see §601.601(d)(2)(ii)(*b*) of this chapter), are considered a reasonable interpretation of the statutory provisions. [Reg. §25.2207A-2.]

☐ [*T.D.* 8522, 2-28-94.]

**[Reg. §25.2501-1]**

**§25.2501-1. Imposition of tax.**—(a) *In general.*—(1) The tax applies to all transfers by gift of property, wherever situated, by an individual who is a citizen or resident of the United States, to the extent the value of the transfers exceeds the amount of the exclusions authorized by section 2503 and the deductions authorized by sections 2521 (as in effect prior to its repeal by the Tax Reform Act of 1976), 2522, and 2523. For each "calendar period" (as defined in §25.2502-1(c)(1)), the tax described in this paragraph (a) is imposed on the transfer of property by gift during such calendar quarter. For calendar years after 1954 and before 1971, the tax described in this subparagraph is imposed on the transfer of property by gift during such calendar period. For gift tax rules related to an ABLE account established under section 529A, see §1.529A-4 of this chapter.

(2) The tax does not apply to a transfer by gift of intangible property before January 1, 1967, by a nonresident not a citizen of the United States, unless the donor was engaged in business in the United States during the calendar year in which the transfer was made.

(3)(i) The tax does not apply to any transfer by gift of intangible property on or after January 1, 1967, by a nonresident not a citizen of the United States (whether or not he was engaged in business in the United States), unless the donor is an expatriate who lost his U. S. citizenship after March 8, 1965, and within the 10-year period ending with the date of transfer, and the loss of citizenship—

(*a*) Did not result from the application of section 301(b), 350, or 355 of the Immigration and Nationality Act, as amended (8 U. S. C. 1401(b), 1482, or 1487) (For a summary of these sections, see paragraph (d)(1) of §20.2107-1 of this chapter (Estate Tax Regulations)), and

(b) Had for one of its principal purposes (but not necessarily its only principal purpose) the avoidance of Federal income, estate, or gift tax.

(ii) In determining for purposes of subdivision (i)(b) of this subparagraph whether a principal purpose for the loss of U. S. citizenship by a donor was the avoidance of Federal income, estate, or gift tax, the Commissioner must first establish that it is reasonable to believe that the donor's loss of U. S. citizenship would, but for section 2501(a)(3) and this subparagraph, result in a substantial reduction for the "calendar period" (as defined in §25.2502-1(c)(1)), in the sum of (a) the Federal gift tax and (b) all gift taxes imposed by foreign countries and political subdivisions thereof, in respect of the transfer of property by gift. Once the Commissioner has so established, the burden of proving that the loss of citizenship by the donor did not have for one of its principal purposes the avoidance of Federal income, estate, or gift tax shall be on the donor. In the absence of complete factual information, the Commissioner may make a tentative determination, based on the information available, that the donor's loss of U. S. citizenship would, but for section 2501(a)(3) and this subparagraph, result in a substantial reduction for the calendar period in the sum of the Federal and foreign gift taxes described in (a) and (b) of this subdivision on the transfer of property by gift. This tentative determination may be based upon the fact that the laws of the foreign country of which the donor became a citizen and the laws of the foreign country of which the donor was a resident at the time of the transfer, including the laws of any political subdivision of those foreign countries, would ordinarily result, in the case of a nonexpatriate donor having the same citizenship and residence as the donor, in liability for total gift taxes under such laws for the calendar period substantially lower than the amount of the Federal gift tax which would be imposed for such period on an amount of comparable gifts by a citizen of the United States. In the absence of a preponderance of evidence to the contrary, this tentative determination shall be sufficient to establish that it is reasonable to believe that the donor's loss of U. S. citizenship would, but for section 2501(a)(3) and this subparagraph, result in a substantial reduction for the calendar period in the sum of the Federal and foreign gift taxes described in (a) and (b) of this subdivision on the transfer of property by gift.

(4) For additional rules relating to the application of the tax to transfers by nonresidents not citizens of the United States, see section 2511 and §25.2511-3.

(5) The general rule of this paragraph (a) shall not apply to a transfer after May 7, 1974, of money or other property to a political organization for the use of that organization. However, this exception to the general rule applies solely to a transfer to a political organization as defined in section 527(e)(1) and including a newsletter fund to the extent provided under section 527(g). The general rule governs a transfer of property to an organization other than a political organization as so defined.

(b) *Resident.*—A resident is an individual who has his domicile in the United States at the time of the gift. For this purpose the United States includes the States and the District of Columbia. The term also includes the Territories of Alaska and Hawaii prior to admission as a State. See section 7701(a)(9). All other individuals are nonresidents. A person acquires a domicile in a place by living there, for even a brief period of time, with no definite present intention of moving therefrom. Residence without the requisite intention to remain indefinitely will not constitute domicile, nor will intention to change domicile effect such a change unless accompanied by actual removal.

(c) *Certain residents of possessions considered citizens of the United States.*—As used in this part, the term "citizen of the United States" includes a person who makes a gift after September 2, 1958 and who, at the time of making the gift, was domiciled in a possession of the United States and was a United States citizen, and who did not acquire his United States citizenship solely by reason of his being a citizen of such possession or by reason of his birth or residence within such possession. The gift of such a person is, therefore, subject to the tax imposed by section 2501 in the same manner in which a gift made by a resident of the United States is subject to the tax. See paragraph (a) of §25.01 and paragraph (d) of this section for further information relating to the application of the Federal gift tax to gifts made by persons who were residents of possessions of the United States. The application of this paragraph may be illustrated by the following example and the examples set forth in paragraph (d) of this section:

*Example.* A, a citizen of the United States by reason of his birth in the United States at San Francisco, established residence in Puerto Rico and acquired Puerto Rican citizenship. A makes a gift of stock of a Spanish corporation on September 4, 1958, while a citizen and domiciliary of Puerto Rico. A's gift is, by reason of the provisions of section 2501(b) subject to the tax imposed by section 2501 inasmuch

as his United States citizenship is based on birth in the United States and is not based solely on being a citizen of a possession or solely on birth or residence in a possession.

(d) *Certain residents of possessions considered nonresidents not citizens of the United States.*—As used in this part, the term "nonresident not a citizen of the United States" includes a person who makes a gift after September 14, 1960, and who at the time of making the gift, was domiciled in a possession of the United States and was a United States citizen, and who acquired his United States citizenship solely by reason of his being a citizen of such possession or by reason of his birth or residence within such possession. The gift of such a person is, therefore, subject to the tax imposed by section 2501 in the same manner in which a gift is subject to the tax when made by a donor who is a "nonresident not a citizen of the United States." See paragraph (a) of §25.01 and paragraph (c) of this section for further information relating to the application of the Federal gift tax to gifts made by persons who were residents of possessions of the United States. The application of this paragraph may be illustrated by the following examples and the example set forth in paragraph (c) of this section. In each of the following examples the person who makes the gift is deemed a "nonresident not a citizen of the United States" and his gift is subject to the tax imposed by section 2501 in the same manner in which a gift is subject to the tax when made by a donor who is a nonresident not a citizen of the United States, since he made the gift after September 14, 1960, but would not have been so deemed and subject to such tax if the person who made the gift had made it on or before September 14, 1960.

*Example (1).* C, who acquired his United States citizenship under section 5 of the Act of March 2, 1917 (39 Stat. 953), by reason of being a citizen of Puerto Rico, while domiciled in Puerto Rico makes a gift on October 1, 1960, of real estate located in New York. C is considered to have acquired his United States citizenship solely by reason of his being a citizen of Puerto Rico.

*Example (2).* E, whose parents were United States citizens by reason of their birth in Boston, was born in the Virgin Islands on March 1, 1927. On September 30, 1960, while domiciled in the Virgin Islands, he made a gift of tangible personal property situated in Kansas. E is considered to have acquired his United States citizenship solely by reason of his birth in the Virgin Islands (section 306 of the Immigration and Nationality Act (66 Stat. 237, 8 U. S. C. 1406)).

*Example (3).* N, who acquired United States citizenship by reason of being a native of the Virgin Islands and a resident thereof on June 28, 1932 (section 306 of the Immigration and Nationality Act (66 Stat. 237, 8 U. S. C. 1406)), made a gift on October 1, 1960, at which time he was domiciled in the Virgin Islands, of tangible personal property situated in Wisconsin. N is considered to have acquired his United States citizenship solely by reason of his birth or residence in the Virgin Islands.

*Example (4).* P, a former Danish citizen, who on January 17, 1917 resided in the Virgin Islands, made the declaration to preserve his Danish citizenship required by Article 6 of the treaty entered into on August 14, 1916, between the United States and Denmark. Subsequently P acquired United States citizenship when he renounced such declaration before a court of record (section 306 of the Immigration and Nationality Act (66 Stat. 237, 8 U. S. C. 1406)). P, while domiciled in the Virgin Islands, made a gift on October 1, 1960, of tangible personal property situated in California. P is considered to have acquired his United States citizenship solely by reason of his birth or residence in the Virgin Islands.

*Example (5).* R, a former French citizen, acquired his United States citizenship through naturalization proceedings in a court located in the Virgin Islands after having qualified for citizenship by residing in the Virgin Islands for 5 years. R, while domiciled in the Virgin Islands, made a gift of tangible personal property situated in Hawaii on October 1, 1960. R is considered to have acquired his United States citizenship solely by reason of his birth or residence within the Virgin Islands. [Reg. §25.2501-1.]

☐ [*T.D. 6334*, 11-14-58. *Amended by T.D. 6542*, 1-19-61; *T.D. 7238*, 12-28-72; *T.D. 7296*, 12-11-73; *T.D. 7671*, 2-5-80, *T.D. 7910*, 9-6-83 *and T.D. 9923*, 11-18-2020.]

**[Reg. §25.2502-1]**

**§25.2502-1. Rate of tax.**—(a) *Computation of tax.*—The rate of tax is determined by the total of all gifts made by the donor during the calendar period and all the preceding calendar periods since June 6, 1932. See §25.2502-1(c)(1) for the definition of "calendar period" and §25.2502-1(c)(2) for the definition of "preceding calendar periods." The following six steps are to be followed in computing the tax:

(1) *First step.*—Ascertain the amount of the "taxable gifts" (as defined in §25.2503-1) for the calendar period for which the return is being prepared.

(2) *Second step.*—Ascertain "the aggregate sum of the taxable gifts for each of the preceding "calendar periods" (as defined in §25.2504-1), considering only those gifts made after June 6, 1932.

(3) *Third step.*—Ascertain the total amount of the taxable gifts, which is the sum of the amounts determined in the first and second steps. See §25.2702-6 for an adjustment to the total amount of an individual's taxable gifts where the individual's current taxable gifts include the transfer of certain interests in trust that were previously valued under the provisions of section 2702.

(4) *Fourth step.*—Compute the tentative tax on the total amount of taxable gifts (as determined in the third step) using the rate schedule in effect at the time the gift (for which the return is being filed) is made.

(5) *Fifth step.*—Compute the tentative tax on the aggregate sum of the taxable gifts for each of the preceding calendar periods (as determined in the second step), using the same rate schedule set forth in the fourth step of this paragraph (a).

(6) *Sixth step.*—Subtract the amount determined in the fifth step from the amount determined in the fourth step. The amount remaining is the gift tax for the calendar period for which the return is being prepared.

(b) *Rate of tax.*—The tax is computed in accordance with the rate schedule in effect at the time the gift was made as set forth in section 2001(c) or corresponding provisions of prior law.

(c) *Definitions.*—(1) The term "calendar period" means:

(i) Each calendar year for the calendar years 1932 (but only that portion of such year after June 6, 1932) through 1970;

(ii) Each calendar quarter for the first calendar quarter of the calendar year 1971 through the last calendar quarter of calendar year 1981; or

(iii) Each calendar year for the calendar year 1982 and each succeeding calendar year.

(2) The term "preceding calendar periods" means all calendar periods ending prior to the calendar period for which the tax is being computed.

| | | |
|---|---|---:|
| (1) | Amount of taxable gifts for year | $57,000 |
| (2) | Total amount of taxable gifts for preceding years | $115,000 |
| (3) | Total taxable gifts | $172,000 |
| (4) | Tax computed on item 3 in accordance with the rate schedule in effect for the year 1955 | $31,725 |
| (5) | Tax computed on item 2 (using same rate schedule) | 18,900 |
| (6) | Tax for year 1955 (item 4 minus item 5) | $12,825 |

*Example (3).* (i) *Facts.* During the calendar year 1955, H makes the following gifts of present interests:

| | |
|---|---:|
| To his daughter | $ 40,000 |
| To his son | 5,000 |
| To W, his wife | 5,000 |
| To a charitable organization | 10,000 |

The gifts to W qualify for the marital deduction, and, pursuant to the provisions of section 2513 (see §25.2513-1), H and W consent to treat the gifts to third parties as having been made one-half by each

(d) *Examples.*—The following examples illustrate the application of this section with respect to gifts made by citizens or residents of the United States:

*Example (1).* Assume that in 1955 the donor made taxable gifts, as ascertained under the first step (paragraph (a)(2) of this section), of $62,500 and that there were no taxable gifts for prior years, with the result that the amount ascertainable under the third step is $62,500. Under the fourth step a tax is computed on this amount. Reference to the tax rate schedule in effect in the year 1955 discloses that the tax on this amount is $7,650.

*Example (2).* A donor makes gifts (other than gifts of future interests in property) during the calendar year 1955 of $30,000 to A and $33,000 to B. Two exclusions of $3,000 each are allowable, in accordance with the provisions of section 2503(b), which results in included gifts for 1955 of $57,000. Specific exemption was claimed and allowed in a total amount of $50,000 in the donor's gift tax returns for the calendar years 1934 and 1935 so there remains no specific exemption available for the donor to claim for 1955. The total amount of gifts made by the donor during preceding years, after excluding $5,000 for each donee for each calendar year in accordance with the provisions of section 1003(b)(1) of the 1939 Code, is computed as follows:

| | |
|---|---:|
| Calendar year 1934 | $120,000 |
| Calendar year 1935 | 25,000 |
| Total amount of included gifts for preceding calendar years | $145,000 |

The aggregate sum of the taxable gifts for preceding calendar years is $115,000, which is determined by deducting a specific exemption of $30,000 from $145,000, the total amount of included gifts for preceding calendar years. The deduction from the 1934 and 1935 gifts for the specific exemption cannot exceed $30,000 for purposes of computing the tax on the 1955 gifts even though a specific exemption in a total amount of $50,000 was allowed in computing the donor's gift tax liability for 1934 and 1935. See paragraph (b) of §25.2504-1. The computation of the tax for the calendar year 1955 (following the steps set forth in paragraph (a) of this section) is shown below:

spouse. The amount of H's taxable gifts for preceding years is $50,000. Only $25,000 of H's specific exemption provided under section 2521, which was in effect at the time, was claimed and allowed in preceding years. H's remaining specific exemption of $5,000 is claimed for the calendar year 1955. See §25.2521-1. W made no gifts during the calendar year 1955 nor during any preceding calendar year. W claims sufficient specific exemption on her return to eliminate tax liability.

(ii) *Computation of H's tax for the calendar year 1955—(a) H's taxable gifts for year*

| | | |
|---|---:|---:|
| Total gifts of H | | $60,000 |
| Less: Portion of items to be reported by spouse (one-half of total gifts to daughter, son and charity) | | 27,500 |
| Balance | | $32,500 |
| Less: Exclusions (three of $3,000 each for daughter, wife and charity and one of $2,500 for son) | | 11,500 |
| Total included amount of gifts for year | | $21,000 |
| Less: Deductions: | | |
| Charity | $2,000 | |
| Marital | 2,000 | |
| Specific exemption | 5,000 | |
| Total deductions | | 9,000 |
| Amount of taxable gifts for year | | $12,000 |

(b) *Computation of tax.* The steps set forth in paragraph (a) of this section are followed.

| | | |
|---|---|---:|
| (1) | Amount of taxable gifts for year | $12,000 |
| (2) | Total taxable gifts for preceding years | 50,000 |
| (3) | Total taxable gifts (item (1) plus item (2)) | $62,000 |
| (4) | Tax computed on item 3 in accordance with the rate schedule in effect for the year 1955 | $7,545 |
| (5) | Tax computed on item 2 in accordance with the rate schedule in effect for the year 1955 | 5,250 |
| (6) | Tax for calendar year (item (4) minus item (5)) | $2,295 |

(iii) *Computation of W's tax for calendar year 1955—(a) W's taxable gifts for year*

| | |
|---|---:|
| Total gifts of W . . . . . . . . . . . . | $0 |
| Less: Portion of items to be reported by spouse . . . . . . . . . . . . | 0 |
| Balance . . . . . . . . . . . . | $0 |
| Gifts of spouse to be included . . . . . . . . . . . . | 27,500 |
| Total gifts for year . . . . . . . . . . . . | $27,500 |
| Less: Exclusions (two of $3,000 each for daughter and charity and one of $2,500 for son) . . . . . . . . . . . . | 8,500 |
| Balance . . . . . . . . . . . . | $19,000 |

Less: Deductions:

| | | |
|---|---:|---:|
| Charity . . . . . . . . . . . . | $ 2,000 | |
| Marital . . . . . . . . . . . . | 0 | |
| Specific exemption . . . . . . . . . . . . | 17,000 | |
| Total deductions . . . . . . . . . . . . | | 19,000 |
| Amount of taxable gifts for year . . . . . . . . . . . . | | $ 0 |

*(b) Computation of tax.*—Since W had no "taxable gifts" during the year, there is no tax.

*Example (4). (i) Facts.* The facts are the same as in example (3) except that W made outright gifts of $10,000 to her niece and $20,000 to H at various times during the year. The amount of taxable gifts made by W in preceding calendar years is $75,000, and only $20,000 of her specific exemption provided under section 2521, which was in effect at the time, was claimed and allowed for preceding years. See § 25.2521-1. The remaining specific exemption of $10,000 is claimed for the calendar year 1955.

*(ii) Computation of H's tax for the calendar year 1955—(a) H's taxable gifts for year.*

| | |
|---|---:|
| Total gifts of H . . . . . . . . . . . . | $60,000 |
| Less: Portion of items to be reported by spouse . . . . . . . . . . . . | 27,500 |
| Balance . . . . . . . . . . . . | $32,500 |
| Gifts of spouse to be included . . . . . . . . . . . . | 5,000 |
| Total gifts for year . . . . . . . . . . . . | $37,500 |
| Less: Exclusions ($11,500) as shown in example (3) plus $3,000 exclusion for gift to niece) . . . . . . . . . . . . | 14,500 |
| Total included amount of gifts for year . . . . . . . . . . . . | $23,000 |

Deductions:

| | | |
|---|---:|---:|
| Charity . . . . . . . . . . . . | $2,000 | |
| Marital . . . . . . . . . . . . | 2,000 | |
| Specific exemption . . . . . . . . . . . . | 5,000 | |
| Total deductions . . . . . . . . . . . . | | 9,000 |
| Amount of taxable gifts for year . . . . . . . . . . . . | | $14,000 |

*(b) Computation of tax.*

| | | |
|---|---|---:|
| (1) | Amount of taxable gifts for year . . . . . . . . . . . . | $14,000 |
| (2) | Total taxable gifts for preceding years . . . . . . . . . . . . | 50,000 |
| (3) | Total taxable gifts (item (1) plus item (2)) . . . . . . . . . . . . | $64,000 |
| (4) | Tax computed on item 3 . . . . . . . . . . . . | $7,965 |
| (5) | Tax computed on item 2 . . . . . . . . . . . . | $5,250 |
| (6) | Tax for year (item (4) minus item (5)) . . . . . . . . . . . . | $2,715 |

*(iii) Computation of W's tax for the calendar year 1955—(a) W's taxable gifts for year*

| | |
|---|---:|
| Total gifts of W . . . . . . . . . . . . | $30,000 |
| Less: Portion of items to be reported by spouse (one-half of gift to niece) . . . . . . . . . . . . | 5,000 |
| Balance . . . . . . . . . . . . | $25,000 |
| Gifts of spouse to be included . . . . . . . . . . . . | 27,500 |
| Total gifts for year . . . . . . . . . . . . | $52,500 |
| Less: Exclusions (four of $3,000 each for daughter, husband, niece and charity, and one of $2,500 for son) . . . . | 14,500 |
| Total included amount of gifts for year . . . . . . . . . . . . | $38,000 |

Deductions:

| | | |
|---|---:|---:|
| Charity . . . . . . . . . . . . | $2,000 | |
| Marital . . . . . . . . . . . . | 10,000 | |
| Specific exemption . . . . . . . . . . . . | 10,000 | |
| Total deductions . . . . . . . . . . . . | | 22,000 |
| Amount of taxable gifts for year . . . . . . . . . . . . | | $16,000 |

*(b) Computation of tax.*

| | | |
|---|---|---:|
| (1) | Amount of taxable gifts for year . . . . . . . . . . . . | $16,000 |
| (2) | Total taxable gifts for preceding years . . . . . . . . . . . . | 75,000 |
| (3) | Total taxable gifts . . . . . . . . . . . . | $91,000 |
| (4) | Tax computed on item 3 . . . . . . . . . . . . | 13,635 |
| (5) | Tax computed on item 2 . . . . . . . . . . . . | 10,275 |
| (6) | Tax for year (item 4 minus item 5) . . . . . . . . . . . . | $ 3,360 |

*Example (5).* A makes gifts (other than gifts of future interests in property) to B in the first quarter of 1971 of $43,000 and in the second quarter of 1971 of $60,000. A gave to C in the second quarter of 1971 land valued at $11,000. The full amount of A's specific exemption provided under section 2521 was claimed and allowed in 1956. In 1966, A made taxable gifts totaling $21,000 on which gift tax was timely paid and no other taxable gifts were made by A in any other year preceding 1971. The gift tax return due for the first calendar quarter of 1971 was timely filed and the tax paid. With respect to the gifts made to B in 1971, the $3,000 annual gift tax exclusion provided by section 2503(b) is applied in its entirety against the $43,000 gift made to B in the first quarter and therefore is not available to offset the $60,000 gift made to B in the second quarter. (See §25.2503-2(b).) A further $3,000 annual gift tax exclusion is available, however, to offset the $11,000 gift made to C in the second quarter of 1971. The

| | | |
|---|---|---:|
| (1) | Amount of taxable gifts for the second calendar quarter of 1971 ($60,000 + $11,000 − $3,000) . . . . . . . . . . . . . . . . . . . . . . . . . . . . . . . . | $ 68,000 |
| (2) | Total amount of taxable gifts for preceding calendar periods ($43,000 − $3,000 + $21,000) . . . . . . . . . . . . . . . . . . . . . . . . . . . . . | 61,000 |
| (3) | Total taxable gifts . . . . . . . . . . . . . . . . . . . . . . . . . . . . . . . . . . . . . . . . | $129,000 |
| (4) | Tax computed on item 3 in accordance with rate schedule in effect for the year 1971 . . . . . . . . . . . . . . . . . . . . . . . . . . . . . . . . | $ 22,050 |
| (5) | Tax computed on item 2 (using same rate schedule) . . . . . . . . . . . | $ 7,335 |
| (6) | Tax for second calendar quarter of 1971 (item 4 minus item 5) . . . . . . . . . . . . . . . . . . . . . . . . . . . . . . . . . . . | $ 14,715 |

*Example (6).* A makes gifts (other than gifts of future interests in property) during the calendar year 1982 of $160,000 to B and $100,000 to C. Two exclusions of $10,000 each are allowable, in accordance with the provisions of section 2503(b), which results in taxable gifts for 1982 of $240,000. In the first calendar quarter of 1978, A made taxable gifts totaling $100,000 on which gift tax was paid. For the calendar year 1969, A made taxable gifts totaling $50,000. The full amount of A's specific exemption provided under section 2521, which was in effect at the time, was claimed and allowed in 1968. The computation of the gift tax for the calendar period 1982 (following the steps set forth in paragraph (a) of this section) is shown below.

(1) Amount of taxable gifts for the calendar year 1982, $240,000.

(2) Total amount of taxable gifts for preceding calendar periods ($100,000 + $50,000), $150,000.

(3) Total taxable gifts, $390,000.

(4) Tax computed on item 3 (in accordance with the rate schedule in effect for the year 1982), $118,400.

(5) Tax computed on item 2 (using same rate schedule), $38,800.

(6) Tax for year 1982 (Item 4 minus item 5), $79,600.
[Reg. §25.2502-1.]

☐ [*T.D. 6334, 11-14-58. Amended by T.D. 7238, 12-28-72; T.D. 7910, 9-6-83 and T.D. 8395, 1-28-92.*]

### [Reg. §25.2502-2]

**§25.2502-2. Donor primarily liable for tax.**—Section 2502(d) provides that the donor shall pay the tax. If the donor dies before the tax is paid the amount of the tax is a debt due the United States from the decedent's estate and his executor or administrator is responsible for its payment out of the estate. (See §25.6151-1 for the time and place for paying the tax.) If there is no duly qualified executor or administrator, the heirs, legatees, devisees and distributees are liable for and required to pay the tax to the extent of the value of their inheritances, bequests, devises or distributive shares of the donor's estate. If a husband and wife effectively signify consent, under section 2513, to have gifts made to a third party during any "calendar period" (as defined in §25.2502-1(c)(1)) considered as made one-half by each, the liability with respect to the gift tax of each spouse for that calendar period is joint and several (see §25.2513-4). As to the personal liability of the donee, see paragraph (b) of §301.6324-1 of this chapter (Regulations on Procedure and Administration). As to the personal liability of the executor or administrator, see section 3467 of the Revised Statutes (31 U. S. C. 192), which reads as follows:

Every executor, administrator, or assignee, or other person, who pays, in whole or in part, any debt due by the person or estate for whom or for which he acts before he satisfies and pays the debts due to the United States from such person or estate, shall become answerable in his own person and estate to the extent of such payments for the debts so due to the United States, or for so much thereof as may remain due and unpaid.

As used in such section 3467, the word "debt" includes a beneficiary's distributive share of an estate. Thus if an executor pays a debt due by the estate which is being administered by him or distributes any portion of the estate before there is paid all of the gift tax which he has a duty to pay, the executor is personally liable, to the extent of the payment or distribution, for so much of the gift tax as remains due and unpaid. [Reg. §25.2502-2.]

☐ [*T.D. 6334, 11-14-58. Amended by T.D. 7238, 12-38-72 and T.D. 7910, 9-6-83.*]

### [Reg. §25.2503-1]

**§25.2503-1. General definitions of "taxable gifts" and of "total amount of gifts.".**—The term "taxable gifts" means the "total amount of gifts" made by the donor during the "calendar period" (as defined in §25.2502-1(c)(1)) less the deductions provided for in sections 2521 (as in effect before its repeal by the Tax Reform Act of 1976), 2522, and 2523 (specific exemption, charitable, etc., gifts and the marital deduction, respectively). The term "total amount of gifts"

computation of the gift tax for the second calendar quarter of 1971 due on August 15, 1971 (following the steps set forth in paragraph (a) of this section) is shown below:

means the sum of the values of the gifts made during the calendar period less the amounts excludable under section 2503(b). See §25.2503-2. The entire value of any gift of a future interest in property must be included in the total amount of gifts for the calendar period in which the gift is made. See §25.2503-3. [Reg. §25.2503-1.]

☐ [*T.D. 6334, 11-14-58. Amended by T.D. 7238, 12-28-72 and T.D. 7910, 9-6-83.*]

### [Reg. §25.2503-2]

**§25.2503-2. Exclusions from gifts.**—(a) *Gifts made after December 31, 1981.*—Except as provided in paragraph (f) of this section (involving gifts to a noncitizen spouse), the first $10,000 of gifts made to any one donee during the calendar year 1982 or any calendar year thereafter, except gifts of future interests in property as defined in §§25.2503-3 and 25.2503-4, is excluded in determining the total amount of gifts for the calendar year. In the case of a gift in trust the beneficiary of the trust is the donee.

(b) *Gifts made after December 31, 1970 and before January 1, 1982.*—In computing taxable gifts for the calendar quarter, in the case of gifts (other than gifts of future interests in property) made to any person by the donor during any calendar quarter of the calendar year 1971 or any subsequent calendar year, $3,000 of such gifts to such person less the aggregate of the amounts of such gifts to such person during all preceding calendar quarters of any such calendar year shall not be included in the total amount of gifts made during such quarter. Thus, the first $3,000 of gifts made to any one donee during the calendar year 1971 or any calendar year thereafter, except gifts of future interests in property as defined in §§25.2503-3 and 25.2503-4, is excluded in determining the total amount of gifts for a calendar quarter. In the case of a gift in trust the beneficiary of the trust is the donee. The application of this paragraph may be illustrated by the following examples:

*Example (1).* A made a gift of $3,000 to B on January 8, 1971, and on April 20, 1971, gave B an additional gift of $10,000. A made no other gifts in 1971. The total amount of gifts made by A during the second quarter of 1971 is $10,000 because the $3,000 exclusion provided by section 2503(b) is first applied to the January 8 gift.

*Example (2).* A gave $2,000 to B on January 8, 1971, and on April 20, 1971, gave him $10,000. The total amount of gifts made by A during the second quarter of 1971 is $9,000 because only $2,000 of the $3,000 exclusion provided by section 2503(b) was applied against the January 8 gift; $1,000 was available to offset other gifts (except gifts of a future interest) made to B during 1971.

(c) *Gifts made before January 1, 1971.*—The first $3,000 of gifts made to any one donee during the calendar year 1955, or 1970, or any calendar year intervening between calendar year 1955 and calendar year 1970, except gifts of future interests in property as defined in §§25.2503-3 and 25.2503-4, is excluded in determining the total amount of gifts for the calendar year. In the case of a gift in trust the beneficiary of the trust is the donee.

(d) *Transitional rule.*—The increased annual gift tax exclusion as defined in section 2503(b) shall not apply to any gift subject to a power of appointment granted under an instrument executed before September 12, 1981, and not amended on or after that date, provided that: (1) The power is exercisable after December 31, 1981, (2) the power is expressly defined in terms of, or by reference to, the amount of the gift tax exclusion under section 2503(b) (or the corresponding provision of prior law), and (3) there is not enacted a State law applicable to such instrument which construes the power of appointment as referring to the increased annual gift tax exclusion provided by the Economic Recovery Tax Act of 1981.

(e) *Examples.*—The provisions of paragraph (d) of this section may be illustrated by the following examples:

*Example (1).* A executed an instrument to create a trust for the benefit of B on July 2, 1981. The trust granted to B the power, for a period of 90 days after any transfer of cash to the trust, to withdraw from the trust the lesser of the amount of the transferred cash or the amount equal to the section 2503(b) annual gift tax exclusion. The trust was not amended on or after September 12, 1981. No state statute has been enacted which construes the power of appointment as referring to the increased annual gift tax exclusion provided by the Economic Recovery Tax Act of 1981. Accordingly, the maximum annual gift tax exclusion applicable to any gift subject to the exercise of the power of appointment is $3,000.

*Example (2).* Assume the same facts as in example (1) except that the power of appointment granted in the trust refers to section 2503(b) as amended at any time. The maximum annual gift tax exclusion applicable to any gift subject to the exercise of the power of appointment is $10,000.

(f) *Special rule in the case of gifts made on or after July 14, 1988, to a spouse who is not a United States citizen.*—(1) *In general.*—Subject to the special rules set forth at §20.2056A-1(c) of this chapter, in the case of gifts made on or after July 14, 1988, if the donee of the gift is the donor's spouse and the donee spouse is not a citizen of the United States at the time of the gift, the first $100,000 of gifts made during the calendar year to the donee spouse (except gifts of future interests) is excluded in determining the total amount of gifts for the calendar year. The rule of this paragraph (f) applies regardless of whether the donor is a citizen or resident of the United States for purposes of chapter 12 of the Internal Revenue Code.

(2) *Gifts made after June 29, 1989.*—In the case of gifts made after June 29, 1989, the $100,000 exclusion provided in paragraph (f)(1) of this section applies only if the gift in excess of the otherwise applicable annual exclusion is in a form that qualifies for the gift tax marital deduction under section 2523(a) but for the provisions of section 2523(i)(1) (disallowing the marital deduction if the donee spouse is not a United States citizen.) See §25.2523(i)-1(d), *Example 4.*

(3) *Effective date.*—This paragraph (f) is effective with respect to gifts made after August 22, 1995. [Reg. §25.2503-2.]

☐ [*T.D. 6334*, 11-14-58. *Amended by T.D. 7238*, 12-28-72; *T.D. 7910*, 9-6-83; *T.D. 7978*, 9-28-84 *and T.D. 8612*, 8-21-95.]

## [Reg. §25.2503-3]

**§25.2503-3. Future interests in property.**—(a) No part of the value of a gift of a future interest may be excluded in determining the total amount of gifts made during the "calendar period"(as defined §25.2502-1(c)(1)). "Future interest" is a legal term, and includes reversions, remainders, and other interests or estates, whether vested or contingent, and whether or not supported by a particular interest or estate, which are limited to commence in use, possession, or enjoyment at some future date or time. The term has no reference to such contractual rights as exist in a bond, note (though bearing no interest until maturity), or in a policy of life insurance, the obligations of which are to be discharged by payments in the future. But a future interest or interests in such contractual obligations may be created by the limitations contained in a trust or other instrument of transfer used in effecting a gift. A contribution to an ABLE account established under section 529A is not a future interest.

(b) An unrestricted right to the immediate use, possession, or enjoyment of property or the income from property (such as a life estate or term certain) is a present interest in property. An exclusion is allowable with respect to a gift of such an interest (but not in excess of the value of the interest). If a donee has received a present interest in property, the possibility that such interest may be diminished by the transfer of a greater interest in the same property to the donee through the exercise of a power is disregarded in computing the value of the present interest, to the extent that no part of such interest will at any time pass to any other person (see example (4) of paragraph (c) of this section). For an exception to the rule disallowing an exclusion for gifts of future interests in the case of certain gifts to minors, see §25.2503-4.

(c) The operation of this section may be illustrated by the following examples:

*Example (1).* Under the terms of a trust created by A the trustee is directed to pay the net income to B, so long as B shall live. The trustee is authorized in his discretion to withhold payments of income during any period he deems advisable and add such income to the trust corpus. Since B's right to receive the income payments is subject to the trustee's discretion, it is not a present interest and no exclusion is allowable with respect to the transfer in trust.

*Example (2).* C transfers certain insurance policies on his own life to a trust created for the benefit of D. Upon C's death the proceeds of the policies are to be invested and the net income therefrom paid to D during his lifetime. Since the income payments to D will not begin until after C's death the transfer in trust represents a gift of a future interest in property against which no exclusion is allowable.

*Example (3).* Under the terms of a trust created by E the net income is to be distributed to E's three children in such shares as the trustee, in his uncontrolled discretion, deems advisable. While the terms of the trust provide that all of the net income is to be distributed, the amount of income any one of the three beneficiaries will receive rests entirely within the trustee's discretion and cannot be presently ascertained. Accordingly, no exclusions are allowable with respect to the transfers to the trust.

*Example (4).* Under the terms of a trust the net income is to be paid to F for life, with the remainder payable to G on F's death. The trustee has the uncontrolled power to pay over the corpus to F at any time. Although F's present right to receive the income may be terminated, no other person has the right to such income interest. Accordingly, the power in the trustee is disregarded in determining the value of F's present interest. The power would not be disregarded to the extent that the trustee during F's life could distribute corpus to persons other than F.

*Example (5).* The corpus of a trust created by J consists of certain real property, subject to a mortgage. The terms of the trust provide that the net income from the property is to be used to pay the mortgage. After the mortgage is paid in full the net income is to be paid to K during his lifetime. Since K's right to receive the income payments will not begin until after the mortgage is paid in full the transfer in trust represents a gift of a future interest in property against which no exclusion is allowable.

*Example (6).* L pays premiums on a policy of insurance on his life. All the incidents of ownership in the policy (including the right to surrender the policy) are vested in M. The payment of premiums by L constitutes a gift of a present interest in property. [Reg. §25.2503-3.]

☐ [*T.D. 6334*, 11-14-58. *Amended by T.D. 7238*, 12-28-72, *T.D. 7910*, 9-6-83 *and T.D. 9923*, 11-18-2020.]

## [Reg. §25.2503-4]

**§25.2503-4. Transfer for the benefit of a minor.**—(a) Section 2503(c) provides that no part of a transfer for the benefit of a donee who has not attained the age of 21 years on the date of the gift will be considered a gift of a future interest in property if the terms of the transfer satisfy all of the following conditions:

(1) Both the property itself and its income may be expended by or for the benefit of the donee before he attains the age of 21 years;

(2) Any portion of the property and its income not disposed of under (1) will pass to the donee when he attains the age of 21 years; and

(3) Any portion of the property and its income not disposed of under (1) will be payable either to the estate of the donee or as he may appoint under a general power of appointment as defined in section 2514(c) if he dies before attaining the age of 21 years.

(b) Either a power of appointment exercisable by the donee by will or a power of appointment exercisable by the donee during his lifetime will satisfy the conditions set forth in paragraph (a)(3) of this section. However, if the transfer is to qualify for the exclusion under this section, there must be no restrictions of substance (as distinguished from formal restrictions of the type described in paragraph (g)(4) of §25.2523(e)-1) by the terms of the instrument of transfer on the exercise of the power by the donee. However, if the minor is given a power of appointment exercisable during lifetime or is given a power of appointment exercisable by will, the fact that under the local law a minor is under a disability to exercise an inter vivos power or to execute a will does not cause the transfer to fail to satisfy the conditions of section 2503(c). Further, a transfer does not fail to satisfy the conditions of section 2503(c) by reason of the mere fact that—

(1) There is left to the discretion of a trustee the determination of the amounts, if any, of the income or property to be expended for the benefit of the minor and the purpose for which the expenditure is to be made, provided there are no substantial restrictions under the terms of the trust instrument on the exercise of such discretion;

(2) The donee, upon reaching age 21, has the right to extend the term of the trust; or

(3) The governing instrument contains a disposition of the property or income not expended during the donee's minority to persons other than the donee's estate in the event of the default of appointment by the donee.

(c) A gift to a minor which does not satisfy the requirements of section 2503(c) may be either a present or a future interest under the general rules of §25.2503-3. Thus, for example, a transfer of property in trust with income required to be paid annually to a minor beneficiary and corpus to be distributed to him upon his attaining the age of 25 is a gift of a present interest with respect to the right to income but is a gift of a future interest with respect to the right to corpus. [Reg. §25.2503-4.]

☐ [*T.D. 6334*, 11-14-58.]

[Reg. § 25.2503-6]

### § 25.2503-6. Exclusion for certain qualified transfer for tuition or medical expenses.

—(a) *In general.*—Section 2503(e) provides that any qualified transfer after December 31, 1981, shall not be treated as a transfer of property by gift for purposes of chapter 12 of subtitle B of the Code. Thus, a qualified transfer on behalf of any individual is excluded in determining the total amount of gifts in calendar year 1982 and subsequent years. This exclusion is available in addition to the $10,000 annual gift tax exclusion. Furthermore, an exclusion for a qualified transfer is permitted without regard to the relationship between the donor and the donee. A contribution to an ABLE account established under section 529A is not a qualified transfer.

(b) *Qualified transfers.*—(1) *Definition.*—For purposes of this paragraph, the term "qualified transfer" means any amount paid on behalf of an individual—

    (i) As tuition to a qualifying educational organization for the education or training of that individual, or

    (ii) To any person who provides medical care with respect to that individual as payment for the qualifying medical expenses arising from such medical care.

(2) *Tuition expenses.*—For purposes of paragraph (b)(1)(i) of this section, a qualifying educational organization is one which normally maintains a regular faculty and curriculum and normally has a regularly enrolled body of pupils or students in attendance at the place where its educational activities are regularly carried on. See section 170(b)(1)(A)(ii) and the regulations thereunder. The unlimited exclusion is permitted for tuition expenses of full-time or part-time students paid directly to the qualifying educational organization providing the education. No unlimited exclusion is permitted for amounts paid for books, supplies, dormitory fees, board, or other similar expenses which do not constitute direct tuition costs.

(3) *Medical expenses.*—For purposes of paragraph (b)(1)(ii) of this section, qualifying medical expenses are limited to those expenses defined in section 213(d) (section 213(e) prior to January 1, 1984) and include expenses incurred for the diagnosis, cure, mitigation, treatment or prevention of disease, or for the purpose of affecting any structure or function of the body or for transportation primarily for and essential to medical care. In addition, the unlimited exclusion from the gift tax includes amounts paid for medical insurance on behalf of any individual. The unlimited exclusion from the gift tax does not apply to amounts paid for medical care that are reimbursed by the donee's insurance. Thus, if payment for a medical expense is reimbursed by the donee's insurance company, the donor's payment for that expense, to the extent of the reimbursed amount, is not eligible for the unlimited exclusion from the gift tax and the gift is treated as having been made on the date the reimbursement is received by the donee.

(c) *Examples.*—The provisions of paragraph (b) of this section may be illustrated by the following examples.

*Example (1).* In 1982, A made a tuition payment directly to a foreign univerity on behalf of B. A had no legal obligation to make this payment. The foreign university is described in section 170(b)(1)(A)(ii) of the Code. A's tuition payment is exempt from the gift tax under section 2503(e) of the Code.

*Example (2).* A transfers $100,000 to a trust the provisions of which state that the funds are to be used for tuition expenses incurred by A's grandchildren. A's transfer to the trust is a completed gift for Federal gift tax purposes and is not a direct transfer to an educational organization as provided in paragraph (b)(2) of this section and does not qualify for the unlimited exclusion from gift tax under section 2503(e).

*Example (3).* C was seriously injured in an automobile accident in 1982. D, who is unrelated to C, paid C's various medical expenses by checks made payable to the physician. D also paid the hospital for C's hospital bills. These medical and hospital expenses were types described in section 213 of the Code and were not reimbursed by insurance or otherwise. Because the medical and hospital bills paid in 1982 for C were medical expenses within the meaning of section 213 of the Code, and since they were paid directly by D to the person rendering the medical care, they are not treated as transfers subject to the gift tax.

*Example (4).* Assume the same facts as in example (2) except that instead of making the payments directly to the medical service provider, D reimbursed C for the medical expenses which C had previously paid. The payments made by D to C do not qualify for the exclusion under section 2503(e) of the Code and are subject to the gift tax on the date the reimbursement is received by C to the extent the reimbursement and all other gifts from D to C during the year of the reimbursement exceed the $10,000 annual exclusion provided in section 2503(b). [Reg. § 25.2503-6.]

   ☐ [*T.D.* 7978, 9-28-84. *Amended by T.D.* 9923, 11-18-2020.]

[Reg. § 25.2504-1]

### § 25.2504-1. Taxable gifts for preceding calendar periods.

—(a) In order to determine the correct gift tax liability for any calendar period it is necessary to ascertain the correct amount, if any, of the aggregate sum of the taxable gifts for each of the "preceding calendar periods" (as defined in § 25.2502-1(c)(2)). See paragraph (a) of § 25.2502-1. The term aggregate sum of the taxable gifts for each of the preceding calendar periods means the correct aggregate of such gifts, not necessarily that returned for those calendar periods and in respect of which tax was paid. All transfers that constituted gifts in prior calendar periods under the laws, including the provisions of law relating to exclusions from gifts, in effect at the time the transfers were made are included in determining the amount of taxable gifts for preceding calendar periods. The deductions other than for the specific exemption (see paragraph (b) of this section) allowed by the laws in effect at the time the transfers were made also are taken into account in determining the aggregate sum of the taxable gifts for preceding calendar periods. (The allowable exclusion from a gift is $5,000 for years before 1939, $4,000 for the calendar years 1939 through 1942, $3,000 for the calendar years 1943 through 1981, and $10,000 thereafter.)

(b) In determining the aggregate sum of the taxable gifts for the "preceding calendar periods" (as defined in § 25.2502-1(c)(2)), the total of the amounts allowed as deductions for the specific exemption, under section 2521 (as in effect prior to its repeal by the Tax Reform Act of 1976) and the corresponding provisions of prior laws, shall not exceed $30,000. Thus, if the only prior gifts by a donor were made in 1940 and 1941 (at which time the specific exemption allowable was $40,000), and if in the donor's returns for those years the donor claimed deductions totaling $40,000 for the specific exemption and reported taxable gifts totaling $110,000, then in determining the aggregate sum of the taxable gifts for the preceding calendar period: the deductions for the specific exemption cannot exceed $30,000, and the donor's taxable gifts for such periods will be $120,000 (instead of the $110,000 reported on his returns). (The allowable deduction for the specific exemption was $50,000 for calendar years before 1936, $40,000 for calendar years 1936 through 1942, and $30,000 for 1943 through 1976.)

(c) If the donor and the donor's spouse consented to have gifts made to third parties considered as made one-half by each spouse, pursuant to the provisions of section 2513 or section 1000(f) of the Internal Revenue Code of 1939 (which corresponds to section 2513), these provisions shall be taken into account in determining the aggregate sum of the taxable gifts for the preceding calendar periods (under paragraph (a) of this section).

(d) If interpretations of the gift tax law in preceding calendar periods resulted in the erroneous inclusion of property for gift tax purposes that should have been excluded, or the erroneous exclusion of property that should have been included, adjustments must be made in order to arrive at the correct aggregate of taxable gifts for the preceding calendar periods (under paragraph (a) of this section). However, see § 25.2504-2(b) regarding certain gifts made after August 5, 1997. [Reg. § 25.2504-1.]

   ☐ [*T.D.* 6334, 11-14-58. *Amended by T.D.* 7238, 12-28-72; *T.D.* 7910, 9-6-83 *and T.D.* 8845, 12-2-99.]

[Reg. § 25.2504-2]

### § 25.2504-2. Determination of gifts for preceding calendar periods.

—(a) *Gifts made before August 6, 1997.*—If the time has expired within which a tax may be assessed under chapter 12 of the Internal Revenue Code (or under corresponding provisions of prior laws) on the transfer of property by gift made during a preceding calendar period, as defined in § 25.2502-1(c)(2), the gift was made prior to August 6, 1997, and a tax has been assessed or paid for such prior calendar period, the value of the gift, for purposes of arriving at the correct amount of the taxable gifts for the preceding calendar periods (as defined under § 25.2504-1(a)), is the value used in computing the tax for the last preceding calendar period for which a tax was assessed or paid under chapter 12 of the Internal Revenue Code or the corresponding provisions of prior laws. However, this rule does not apply where no tax was paid or assessed for the prior calendar period. Furthermore, this rule does not apply to adjustments involving issues other than valuation. See § 25.2504-1(d).

(b) *Gifts made or section 2701(d) taxable events occurring after August 5, 1997.*—If the time has expired under section 6501 within which a gift tax may be assessed under chapter 12 of the Internal Revenue Code (or under corresponding provisions of prior laws) on the transfer of property by gift made during a preceding calendar period, as defined in § 25.2502-1(c)(2), or with respect to an increase in taxable gifts required under section 2701(d) and § 25.2701-4, and the gift was made, or the section 2701(d) taxable event occurred, after August 5, 1997, the amount of the taxable gift or the amount of the increase in taxable gifts, for purposes of determining the correct amount of taxable gifts for the preceding calendar periods (as defined in § 25.2504-1(a)), is the amount that is finally determined for gift tax purposes (within the meaning of § 20.2001-1(c) of this chapter) and such amount may not be thereafter adjusted. The rule of this paragraph (b) applies to adjustments involving all issues relating to the gift including valuation issues and legal issues involving the interpretation of the gift tax law. For purposes of determining if the time has expired within which a gift tax may be assessed, see § 301.6501(c)-1(e) and (f) of this chapter.

(c) *Examples.*—The following examples illustrate the rules of paragraphs (a) and (b) of this section:

*Example 1.* (i) *Facts.* In 1996, A transferred closely-held stock in trust for the benefit of B, A's child. A timely filed a Federal gift tax return reporting the 1996 transfer to B. No gift tax was assessed or paid as a result of the gift tax annual exclusion and the application of A's available unified credit. In 2001, A transferred additional closely-held stock to the trust. A's Federal gift tax return reporting the 2001 transfer was timely filed and the transfer was adequately disclosed under § 301.6501(c)-1(f)(2) of this chapter. In computing the amount of taxable gifts, A claimed annual exclusions with respect to the transfers in 1996 and 2001. In 2003, A transfers additional property to B and timely files a Federal gift tax return reporting the gift.

(ii) *Application of the rule limiting adjustments to prior gifts.* Under section 2504(c), in determining A's 2003 gift tax liability, the amount of A's 1996 gift can be adjusted for purposes of computing prior taxable gifts, since that gift was made prior to August 6, 1997, and therefore, the provisions of paragraph (a) of this section apply. Adjustments can be made with respect to the valuation of the gift and legal issues presented (for example, the availability of the annual exclusion with respect to the gift). However, A's 2001 transfer was adequately disclosed on a timely filed gift tax return and, thus, under paragraph (b) of this section, the amount of the 2001 taxable gift by A may not be adjusted (either with respect to the valuation of the gift or any legal issue) for purposes of computing prior taxable gifts in determining A's 2003 gift tax liability.

*Example 2.* (i) *Facts.* In 1996, A transferred closely-held stock to B, A's child. A timely filed a Federal gift tax return reporting the 1996 transfer to B and paid gift tax on the value of the gift reported on the return. On August 1, 1997, A transferred additional closely-held stock to B in exchange for a promissory note signed by B. Also, on September 10, 1997, A transferred closely-held stock to C, A's other child. On April 15, 1998, A timely filed a gift tax return for 1997 reporting the September 10, 1997, transfer to C and, under § 301.6501(c)-1(f)(2) of this chapter, adequately disclosed that transfer and paid gift tax with respect to the transfer. However, A believed that the transfer to B on August 1, 1997, was for full and adequate consideration and A did not report the transfer to B on the 1997 Federal gift tax return. In 2002, A transfers additional property to B and timely files a Federal gift tax return reporting the gift.

(ii) *Application of the rule limiting adjustments to prior gifts.* Under section 2504(c), in determining A's 2002 gift tax liability, the value of A's 1996 gift cannot be adjusted for purposes of computing the value of prior taxable gifts, since that gift was made prior to August 6, 1997, and a timely filed Federal gift tax return was filed on which a gift tax was assessed and paid. However, A's prior taxable gifts can be adjusted to reflect the August 1, 1997, transfer because, although a gift tax return for 1997 was timely filed and gift tax was paid, under § 301.6501(c)-1(f) of this chapter the period for assessing gift tax with respect to the August 1, 1997, transfer did not commence to run since that transfer was not adequately disclosed on the 1997 gift tax return. Accordingly, a gift tax may be assessed with respect to the August 1, 1997, transfer and the amount of the gift would be reflected in prior taxable gifts for purposes of computing A's gift tax liability for 2002. A's September 10, 1997, transfer to C was adequately disclosed on a timely filed gift tax return and, thus, under paragraph (b) of this section, the amount of the September 10, 1997, taxable gift by A may not be adjusted for purposes of computing prior taxable gifts in determining A's 2002 gift tax liability.

*Example 3.* (i) *Facts.* In 1994, A transferred closely-held stock to B and C, A's children. A timely filed a Federal gift tax return reporting the 1994 transfers to B and C and paid gift tax on the value of the gifts reported on the return. Also in 1994, A transferred closely-held stock to B in exchange for a bona fide promissory note signed by B. A believed that the transfer to B in exchange for the promissory note was for full and adequate consideration and A did not report that transfer to B on the 1994 Federal gift tax return. In 2002, A transfers additional property to B and timely files a Federal gift tax return reporting the gift.

(ii) *Application of the rule limiting adjustments to prior gifts.* Under section 2504(c), in determining A's 2002 gift tax liability, the value of A's 1994 gift cannot be adjusted for purposes of computing prior taxable gifts because those gifts were made prior to August 6, 1997, and a timely filed Federal gift tax return was filed with respect to which a gift tax was assessed and paid, and the period of limitations

on assessment has expired. The provisions of paragraph (a) of this section apply to the 1994 transfers. However, for purposes of determining A's adjusted taxable gifts in computing A's estate tax liability, the gifts may be adjusted. See § 20.2001-1(a) of this chapter.

(d) *Effective dates.*—Paragraph (a) of this section applies to transfers of property by gift made prior to August 6, 1997. Paragraphs (b) and (c) of this section apply to transfers of property by gift made after August 5, 1997, if the gift tax return for the calendar period in which the transfer is reported is filed after December 3, 1999. [Reg. § 25.2504-2.]

☐ [*T.D. 6334,* 11-14-58. *Amended by T.D. 7238,* 12-28-72; *T.D. 7910,* 9-6-83 *and T.D. 8845,* 12-2-99.]

## [Reg. § 25.2505-0]

**§ 25.2505-0. Table of contents.**—This section lists the table of contents for § § 25.2505-1 and 25.2505-2.

[Reg. § 25.2505-0.]

☐ [*T.D. 9725,* 6-12-2015.]

## [Reg. § 25.2505-1]

**§ 25.2505-1. Unified credit against gift tax; in general.**—(a) *General rule.*—Section 2505(a) allows a citizen or resident of the United States a credit against the tax imposed by section 2501 for each calendar year. The allowable credit is the applicable credit amount in effect under section 2010(c) that would apply if the donor died as of the end of the calendar year, reduced by the sum of the amounts allowable as a credit against the gift tax due for all preceding calendar periods. See § § 25.2505-2, 20.2010-1, and 20.2010-2 for additional rules and definitions related to determining the applicable credit amount in effect under section 2010(c).

(b) *Applicable rate of tax.*—In determining the amounts allowable as a credit against the gift tax due for all preceding calendar periods, the unified rate schedule under section 2001(c) in effect for such calendar year applies instead of the rates of tax actually in effect for preceding calendar periods. See sections 2505(a) and 2502(a)(2).

(c) *Special rule in case of certain gifts made before 1977.*—The applicable credit amount allowable under paragraph (a) of this section must be reduced by an amount equal to 20 percent of the aggregate amount allowed as a specific exemption under section 2521 (as in effect before its repeal by the Tax Reform Act of 1976) for gifts made by the decedent after September 8, 1976, and before January 1, 1977.

(d) *Credit limitation.*—The applicable credit amount allowed under paragraph (a) of this section for any calendar year shall not exceed the amount of the tax imposed by section 2501 for such calendar year.

(e) *Effective/applicability date.*—This section applies to gifts made on or after June 12, 2015. See 26 CFR 25.2505-1T, as contained in 26 CFR part 25, revised as of April 1, 2015, for the rules applicable to gifts made on or after January 1, 2011, and before June 12, 2015. [Reg. §25.2505-1.]

☐ [*T.D. 9725, 6-12-2015.*]

### [Reg. §25.2505-2]

**§25.2505-2. Gifts made by a surviving spouse having a DSUE amount available.**—(a) *Donor who is surviving spouse is limited to DSUE amount of last deceased spouse.*—(1) *In general.*—In computing a surviving spouse's gift tax liability with regard to a transfer subject to the tax imposed by section 2501 (taxable gift), a deceased spousal unused exclusion (DSUE) amount of a decedent, computed under §20.2010-2(c), is included in determining the surviving spouse's applicable exclusion amount under section 2010(c)(2), provided:

(i) Such decedent is the last deceased spouse of such surviving spouse within the meaning of §20.2010-1(e)(5) at the time of the surviving spouse's taxable gift; and

(ii) The executor of the decedent's estate elected portability (see §20.2010-2(a) and (b) for applicable requirements).

(2) *No DSUE amount available from last deceased spouse.*—If on the date of the surviving spouse's taxable gift the last deceased spouse of such surviving spouse had no DSUE amount or if the executor of the estate of such last deceased spouse did not elect portability, the surviving spouse has no DSUE amount (except as and to the extent provided in paragraph (c)(1)(ii) of this section) to be included in determining his or her applicable exclusion amount, even if the surviving spouse previously had a DSUE amount available from another decedent who, prior to the death of the last deceased spouse, was the last deceased spouse of such surviving spouse. See paragraph (c) of this section for a special rule in the case of multiple deceased spouses.

(3) *Identity of last deceased spouse unchanged by subsequent marriage or divorce.*—A decedent is the last deceased spouse (as defined in §20.2010-1(e)(5)) of a surviving spouse even if, on the date of the surviving spouse's taxable gift, the surviving spouse is married to another (then-living) individual. If a surviving spouse marries again and that marriage ends in divorce or an annulment, the subsequent death of the divorced spouse does not end the status of the prior deceased spouse as the last deceased spouse of the surviving spouse. The divorced spouse, not being married to the surviving spouse at death, is not the last deceased spouse as that term is defined in §20.2010-1(e)(5).

(b) *Manner in which DSUE amount is applied.*—If a donor who is a surviving spouse makes a taxable gift and a DSUE amount is included in determining the surviving spouse's applicable exclusion amount under section 2010(c)(2), such surviving spouse will be considered to apply such DSUE amount to the taxable gift before the surviving spouse's own basic exclusion amount.

(c) *Special rule in case of multiple deceased spouses and previously-applied DSUE amount.*—(1) *In general.*—A special rule applies to compute the DSUE amount included in the applicable exclusion amount of a surviving spouse who previously has applied the DSUE amount of one or more deceased spouses. If a surviving spouse applied the DSUE amount of one or more (successive) last deceased spouses to the surviving spouse's previous lifetime transfers, and if any of those last deceased spouses is different from the surviving spouse's last deceased spouse as defined in §20.2010-1(e)(5) at the time of the current taxable gift by the surviving spouse, then the DSUE amount to be included in determining the applicable exclusion amount of the surviving spouse that will be applicable at the time of the current taxable gift is the sum of—

(i) The DSUE amount of the surviving spouse's last deceased spouse as described in paragraph (a)(1) of this section; and

(ii) The DSUE amount of each other deceased spouse of the surviving spouse to the extent that such amount was applied to one or more previous taxable gifts of the surviving spouse.

(2) *Example.*—The following example, in which all described individuals are U.S. citizens, illustrates the application of this paragraph (c):

*Example.* (i) *Facts.* Husband 1 (H1) dies in 2011, survived by Wife (W). Neither has made any taxable gifts during H1's lifetime. H1's executor elects portability of H1's deceased spousal unused exclusion (DSUE) amount. The DSUE amount of H1 as computed on the estate tax return filed on behalf of H1's estate is $5,000,000. In 2012, W makes taxable gifts to her children valued at $2,000,000. W reports the gifts on a timely filed gift tax return. W is considered to have applied $2,000,000 of H1's DSUE amount to the 2012 taxable gifts, in accordance with paragraph (b) of this section, and, therefore, W owes no gift tax. W is considered to have an applicable exclusion amount remaining in the amount of $8,120,000 ($3,000,000 of H1's remaining DSUE amount plus W's own $5,120,000 basic exclusion amount). In 2013, W marries Husband 2 (H2). H2 dies on June 30, 2015. H2's

executor elects portability of H2's DSUE amount, which is properly computed on H2's estate tax return to be $2,000,000.

(ii) *Application.* The DSUE amount to be included in determining the applicable exclusion amount available to W for gifts during the second half of 2015 is $4,000,000, determined by adding the $2,000,000 DSUE amount of H2 and the $2,000,000 DSUE amount of H1 that was applied by W to W's 2012 taxable gifts. Thus, W's applicable exclusion amount during the balance of 2015 is $9,430,000 ($4,000,000 DSUE plus $5,430,000 basic exclusion amount for 2015).

(d) *Date DSUE amount taken into consideration by donor who is a surviving spouse.*—(1) *General rule.*—A portability election made by an executor of a decedent's estate (see §20.2010-2(a) and (b) for applicable requirements) generally applies as of the date of such decedent's death. Thus, the decedent's DSUE amount is included in the applicable exclusion amount of the decedent's surviving spouse under section 2010(c)(2) and will be applicable to transfers made by the surviving spouse after the decedent's death (subject to the limitations in paragraph (a) of this section). However, such decedent's DSUE amount will not be included in the applicable exclusion amount of the surviving spouse, even if the surviving spouse had made a taxable gift in reliance on the availability or computation of the decedent's DSUE amount:

(i) If the executor of the decedent's estate supersedes the portability election by filing a subsequent estate tax return in accordance with §20.2010-2(a)(4);

(ii) To the extent that the DSUE amount subsequently is reduced by a valuation adjustment or the correction of an error in calculation; or

(iii) To the extent that the DSUE amount claimed on the decedent's return cannot be determined.

(2) *Exception when surviving spouse not a U.S. citizen on date of deceased spouse's death.*—If a surviving spouse becomes a citizen of the United States after the death of the surviving spouse's last deceased spouse, the DSUE amount of the surviving spouse's last deceased spouse becomes available to the surviving spouse on the date the surviving spouse becomes a citizen of the United States (subject to the limitations in paragraph (a) of this section). However, when the special rule regarding qualified domestic trusts in paragraph (d)(3) of this section applies, the earliest date on which a decedent's DSUE amount may be included in the applicable exclusion amount of such decedent's surviving spouse who becomes a U.S. citizen is as provided in paragraph (d)(3) of this section.

(3) *Special rule when property passes to surviving spouse in a qualified domestic trust.*—(i) *In general.*—When property passes from a decedent for the benefit of the decedent's surviving spouse in one or more qualified domestic trusts (QDOT) as defined in section 2056A(a) and the decedent's executor elects portability, the DSUE amount available to be included in the applicable exclusion amount of the surviving spouse under section 2010(c)(2) is the DSUE amount of the decedent as redetermined in accordance with §20.2010-2(c)(4) (subject to the limitations in paragraph (a) of this section). The earliest date on which such decedent's DSUE amount may be included in the applicable exclusion amount of the surviving spouse under section 2010(c)(2) is the date of the occurrence of the final QDOT distribution or final other event (generally, the termination of all QDOTs created by or funded with assets passing from the decedent or the death of the surviving spouse) on which tax under section 2056A is imposed. However, the decedent's DSUE amount as redetermined in accordance with §20.2010-2(c)(4) may be applied to the surviving spouse's taxable gifts made in the year of the surviving spouse's death or, if the terminating event occurs prior to the surviving spouse's death, then in the year of that terminating event and/or in any subsequent year during the surviving spouse's life.

(ii) *Surviving spouse becomes a U.S. citizen.*—If a surviving spouse for whom property has passed from a decedent in one or more QDOTs becomes a citizen of the United States and the requirements in section 2056A(b)(12) and the corresponding regulations are satisfied, then the date on which such decedent's DSUE amount may be included in the applicable exclusion amount of the surviving spouse under section 2010(c)(2) (subject to the limitations in paragraph (a) of this section) is the date on which the surviving spouse becomes a citizen of the United States. See §20.2010-2(c)(4) for the rules for computing the decedent's DSUE amount in the case of a qualified domestic trust.

(iii) *Example.*—The following example illustrates the application of this paragraph (d)(3):

*Example.* (i) *Facts.* Husband (H), a U.S. citizen, dies in 2011 having made no taxable gifts during his lifetime. H's gross estate is $3,000,000. H's wife (W) is not a citizen of the United States and, under H's will, a pecuniary bequest of $2,000,000 passes to a QDOT for the benefit of W. H's executor timely files an estate tax return and makes the QDOT election for the property passing to the QDOT, and H's estate is allowed a marital deduction of $2,000,000 under section 2056(d) for the value of that property. H's taxable estate is $1,000,000. On H's estate tax return, H's executor computes H's preliminary DSUE amount to be $4,000,000. No taxable events within the meaning of section 2056A occur during W's lifetime with respect to the QDOT, and W resides in the United States at all times after H's death. W makes a taxable gift of $1,000,000 to X in 2012 and a taxable gift of $1,000,000 to Y in January 2015, in each case from W's own assets rather than from the QDOT. W dies in September 2015, not having married again, when the value of the assets of the QDOT is $2,200,000.

(ii) *Application.* H's DSUE amount is redetermined to be $1,800,000 (the lesser of the $5,000,000 basic exclusion amount for 2011, or the excess of H's $5,000,000 applicable exclusion amount over $3,200,000 (the sum of the $1,000,000 taxable estate augmented by the $2,200,000 of QDOT assets)). On W's gift tax return filed for 2012, W cannot apply any DSUE amount to the gift made to X. However, because W's gift to Y was made in the year that W died, W's executor will apply $1,000,000 of H's redetermined DSUE amount to the gift on W's gift tax return filed for 2015. The remaining $800,000 of H's redetermined DSUE amount is included in W's applicable exclusion amount to be used in computing W's estate tax liability.

(e) *Authority to examine returns of deceased spouses.*—For the purpose of determining the DSUE amount to be included in the applicable exclusion amount of a surviving spouse, the Internal Revenue Service (IRS) may examine returns of each of the surviving spouse's deceased spouses whose DSUE amount is claimed to be included in the surviving spouse's applicable exclusion amount, regardless of whether the period of limitations on assessment has expired for any such return. The IRS's authority to examine returns of a deceased spouse applies with respect to each transfer by the surviving spouse to which a DSUE amount is or has been applied. Upon examination, the IRS may adjust or eliminate the DSUE amount reported on such a return of a deceased spouse; however, the IRS may assess additional tax on that return only if that tax is assessed within the period of limitations on assessment under section 6501 applicable to the tax shown on that return. See also section 7602 for the IRS's authority, when ascertaining the correctness of any return, to examine any returns that may be relevant or material to such inquiry.

(f) *Availability of DSUE amount for nonresidents who are not citizens.*—A nonresident surviving spouse who was not a citizen of the United States at the time of making a transfer subject to tax under chapter 12 of the Internal Revenue Code shall not take into account the DSUE amount of any deceased spouse except to the extent allowed under any applicable treaty obligation of the United States. See section 2102(b)(3).

(g) *Effective/applicability date.*—This section applies to gifts made on or after June 12, 2015. See 26 CFR 25.2505-2T, as contained in 26 CFR part 25, revised as of April 1, 2015, for the rules applicable to gifts made on or after January 1, 2011, and before June 12, 2015. [Reg. §25.2505-2.]

☐ [*T.D. 9725,* 6-12-2015 (*corrected* 2-5-2020).]

# TRANSFERS

## [Reg. §25.2511-1]

**§25.2511-1. Transfers in general.**—(a) The gift tax applies to a transfer by way of gift whether the transfer is in trust or otherwise, whether the gift is direct or indirect, and whether the property is real or personal, tangible or intangible. For example, a taxable transfer may be effected by the creation of a trust, the forgiving of a debt, the assignment of a judgment, the assignment of the benefits of an insurance policy, or the transfer of cash, certificates of deposit, or Federal, State or municipal bonds. Statutory provisions which exempt bonds, notes, bills and certificates of indebtedness of the Federal Government or its agencies and the interest thereon from taxation are not applicable to the gift tax, since the gift tax is an excise tax on the transfer, and is not a tax on the subject of the gift.

(b) In the case of a gift by a nonresident not a citizen of the United States—

(1) If the gift was made on or after January 1, 1967, by a donor who was not an expatriate to whom section 2501(a)(2) was inapplicable on the date of the gift by reason of section 2501(a)(3) and paragraph (a)(3) of §25.2501-1, or

(2) If the gift was made before January 1, 1967, by a donor who was not engaged in business in the United States during the calendar year in which the gift was made,

the gift tax applies only if the gift consisted of real property or tangible personal property situated within the United States at the time of the transfer. See §§25.2501-1 and 25.2511-3.

(c)(1) The gift tax also applies to gifts indirectly made. Thus, any transaction in which an interest in property is gratuitously passed or conferred upon another, regardless of the means or device employed, constitutes a gift subject to tax. See further §25.2512-8 relating to transfers for insufficient consideration. However, in the case of a transfer creating an interest in property (within the meaning of §25.2518-2(c)(3) and (c)(4)) made after December 31, 1976, this paragraph (c)(1) shall not apply to the donee if, as a result of a qualified disclaimer by the donee, the interest passes to a different donee. Nor shall it apply to a donor if, as a result of a qualified disclaimer by the donee, a completed transfer of an interest in property is not effected. See section 2518 and the corresponding regulations for rules relating to a qualified disclaimer.

(2) In the case of taxable transfers creating an interest in the person disclaiming made before January 1, 1977, where the law governing the administration of the decedent's estate gives a beneficiary, heir, or next-of-kin a right completely and unqualifiedly to refuse to accept ownership of property transferred from a decedent (whether the transfer is effected by the decedent's will or by the law of descent and distribution), a refusal to accept ownership does not constitute the making of a gift if the refusal is made within a reasonable time after knowledge of the existence of the transfer. The refusal must be unequivocal and effective under the local law. There can be no refusal of ownership of property after its acceptance. In the absence of the facts to the contrary, if a person fails to refuse to accept a transfer to him of ownership of a decedent's property within a reasonable time after learning of the existence of the transfer, he will be presumed to have accepted the property. Where the local law does not permit such a refusal, any disposition by the beneficiary, heir, or next-of-kin whereby ownership is transferred gratuitously to another constitutes the making of a gift by the beneficiary, heir, or next-of-kin. In any case where a refusal is purported to relate to only a part of the property, the determination of whether or not there has been a complete and unqualified refusal to accept ownership will depend on all of the facts and circumstances in each particular case, taking into account the recognition and effectiveness of such a purported refusal under the local law. In illustration, if Blackacre was devised to A under the decedent's will (which also provided that all lapsed legacies and devises shall go to B, the residuary beneficiary), and under the local law A could refuse to accept ownership in which case title would be considered as never having passed to A, A's refusal to accept Blackacre within a reasonable time of learning of the devise will not constitute the making of a gift by A to B. However, if a decedent who owned Greenacre died intestate with C and D as his only heirs, and under local law the heir of a decedent cannot, by refusal to accept, prevent himself from becoming an owner of intestate property, any gratuitous disposition by C (by whatever term it is known) whereby he gives up his ownership of a portion of Greenacre and D acquires the whole thereof constitutes the making of a gift by C to D.

(3) The fourth sentence of paragraph (c)(1) of this section is applicable for transfers creating an interest to be disclaimed made on or after December 31, 1997.

(d) If a joint income tax return is filed by a husband and wife for a taxable year, the payment by one spouse of all or part of the income tax liability for such year is not treated as resulting in a transfer which is subject to gift tax. The same rule is applicable to the payment of gift tax for a "calendar period" (as defined in §25.2502-1(c)(1)) in the case of a husband and wife who have consented to have the gifts made considered as made half by each of them in accordance with the provisions of section 2513.

(e) If a donor transfers by gift less than his entire interest in property, the gift tax is applicable to the interest transferred. The tax is applicable, for example, to the transfer of an undivided half interest in property, or to the transfer of a life estate when the grantor retains the remainder interest, or vice versa. However, if the donor's retained interest is not susceptible of measurement on the basis of generally accepted valuation principles, the gift tax is applicable to the entire value of the property subject to the gift. Thus, if a donor, aged 65 years, transfers a life estate in property to A, aged 25 years, with remainder to A's issue, or in default of issue, with reversion to the donor, the gift tax will normally be applicable to the entire value of the property.

(f) If a donor is the owner of only a limited interest in property, and transfers his entire interest, the interest is in every case to be valued by the rules set forth in §§25.2512-1 through 25.2512-7. If the interest is a remainder or reversion or other future interest, it is to be valued on the basis of actuarial principles set forth in §25.2512-5, or if it is not susceptible of valuation in that manner, in accordance with the principles set forth in §25.2512-1.

(g)(1) Donative intent on the part of the transferor is not an essential element in the application of the gift tax to the transfer. The application of the tax is based on the objective facts of the transfer and the circumstances under which it is made, rather than on the subjective motives of the donor. However, there are certain types of transfers to which the tax is not applicable. It is applicable only to a transfer of a beneficial interest in property. It is not applicable to a transfer of bare legal title to a trustee. A transfer by a trustee of trust property in which he has no beneficial interest does not constitute a gift by the trustee (but such a transfer may constitute a gift by the creator of the trust, if until the transfer he had the power to change the beneficiaries by amending or revoking the trust). The gift tax is not applicable to a transfer for a full and adequate consideration in money or money's worth, or to ordinary business transactions, described in §25.2512-8.

(2) If a trustee has a beneficial interest in trust property, a transfer of the property by the trustee is not a taxable transfer if it is made pursuant to a fiduciary power the exercise or nonexercise of which is limited by a reasonably fixed or ascertainable standard which is set forth in the trust instrument. A clearly measurable standard under which the holder of a power is legally accountable is such a standard for this purpose. For instance, a power to distribute corpus for the education, support, maintenance, or health of the beneficiary; for his reasonable support and comfort; to enable him to maintain his accustomed standard of living; or to meet an emergency, would be such a standard. However, a power to distribute corpus for the pleasure, desire, or happiness of a beneficiary is not such a standard. The entire context of a provision of a trust instrument granting a power must be considered in determining whether the power is limited by a reasonably definite standard. For example, if a trust instrument provides that the determination of the trustee shall be conclusive with respect to the exercise or nonexercise of a power, the power is not limited by a reasonably definite standard. However, the fact that the governing instrument is phrased in discretionary terms is not in itself an indication that no such a standard exists.

(h) The following are examples of transactions resulting in taxable gifts and in each case it is assumed that the transfers were not made for an adequate and full consideration in money or money's worth:

(1) A transfer of property by a corporation to B is a gift to B from the stockholders of the corporation. If B himself is a stockholder, the transfer is a gift to him from the other stockholders but only to the extent it exceeds B's own interest in such amount as a shareholder. A transfer of property by B to a corporation generally represents gifts by B to the other individual shareholders of the corporation to the extent of their proportionate interests in the corporation. However, there may be an exception to this rule, such as a transfer made by an individual to a charitable, public, political or similar organization which may constitute a gift to the organization as a single entity, depending upon the facts and circumstances in the particular case.

(2) The transfer of property to B if there is imposed upon B the obligation of paying a commensurate annuity to C is a gift to C.

(3) The payment of money or the transfer of property to B in consideration of B's promise to render a service to C is a gift to C, or to both B and C, depending on whether the service to be rendered to C is or is not an adequate and full consideration in money or money's worth for that which is received by B. See section 2512(b) and the regulations thereunder.

(4) If A creates a joint bank account for himself and B (or a similar type of ownership by which A can regain the entire fund without B's consent), there is a gift to B when B draws upon the account for his own benefit, to the extent of the amount drawn without any obligation to account for a part of the proceeds to A. Similarly, if A purchases a United States savings bond, registered as payable to "A or B," there is a gift to B when B surrenders the bond for cash without any obligation to account for a part of the proceeds to A.

(5) If A with his own funds purchases property and has the title conveyed to himself and B as joint owners, with rights of survivorship (other than a joint ownership described in example (4)) but which rights may be defeated by either party severing his interest, there is a gift to B in the amount of half the value of the property. However, see §25.2515-1 relative to the creation of a joint tenancy (or tenancy by the entirety) between husband and wife in real property with rights of survivorship which, unless the donor elects otherwise, is not considered as a transfer includible for Federal gift tax purposes at the time of the creation of the joint tenancy. See §25.2515-2 with respect to determining the extent to which the creation of a tenancy by the entirety constitutes a taxable gift if the donor elects to have the creation of the tenancy so treated. See also §25.2523(d)-1 with respect to the marital deduction allowed in the case of the creation of a joint tenancy or a tenancy by the entirety.

(6) If A is possessed of a vested remainder interest in property, subject to being divested only in the event he should fail to survive one or more individuals or the happening of some other event, an irrevocable assignment of all or any part of his interest would result in a transfer includible for Federal gift tax purposes. See especially §25.2512-5 for the valuation of an interest of this type.

(7) If A, without retaining a power to revoke the trust or to change the beneficial interests therein, transfers property in trust whereby B is to receive the income for life and at his death the trust is to terminate and the corpus is to be returned to A, provided A survives, but if A predeceases B the corpus is to pass to C, A has made a gift equal to the total value of the property less the value of his retained interest. See §25.2512-5 for the valuation of the donor's retained interest.

(8) If the insured purchases a life insurance policy, or pays a premium on a previously issued policy, the proceeds of which are payable to a beneficiary or beneficiaries other than his estate, and with respect to which the insured retains no reversionary interest in himself or his estate and no power to revest the economic benefits in himself or his estate or to change the beneficiaries or their proportionate benefits (or if the insured relinquishes by assignment, by designation of a new beneficiary or otherwise, every such power that was retained in a previously issued policy), the insured has made a gift of the value of the policy, or to the extent of the premium paid, even though the right of the assignee or beneficiary to receive the benefits is conditioned upon his surviving the insured. For the valuation of life insurance policies see §25.2512-6.

(9) Where property held by a husband and wife as community property is used to purchase insurance upon the husband's life and a third person is revocably designated as beneficiary and under the State law the husband's death is considered to make absolute the transfer by the wife, there is a gift by the wife at the time of the husband's death of half the amount of the proceeds of such insurance.

(10) If under a pension plan (pursuant to which he has an unqualified right to an annuity) an employee has an option to take either a retirement annuity for himself alone or a smaller annuity for himself with a survivorship annuity payable to his wife, an irrevocable election by the employee to take the reduced annuity in order that an annuity may be paid, after the employee's death, to his wife results in the making of a gift. However, see section 2517 and the regulations thereunder for the exemption from gift tax of amounts attributable to employers' contributions under qualified plans and certain other contracts. [Reg. §25.2511-1.]

☐ [*T.D. 6334*, 11-14-58. Amended by *T.D. 6542*, 1-19-61; *T.D. 7150*, 12-1-71; *T.D. 7238*, 12-28-72; *T.D. 7296*, 12-11-73; *T.D. 7910*, 9-6-83; *T.D. 8095*, 8-6-86; *T.D. 8540*, 6-9-94 and *T.D. 8744*, 12-30-97.]

### [Reg. §25.2511-2]

**§25.2511-2. Cessation of donor's dominion and control.**—(a) The gift tax is not imposed upon the receipt of the property by the donee, nor is it necessarily determined by the measure of enrichment resulting to the donee from the transfer, nor is it conditioned upon ability to identify the donee at the time of the transfer. On the contrary, the tax is a primary and personal liability of the donor, is an excise upon his act of making the transfer, is measured by the value of the property passing from the donor, and attaches regardless of the fact that the identity of the donee may not then be known or ascertainable. For gift tax rules related to an ABLE account established under section 529A, see §1.529A-4 of this chapter.

(b) As to any property, or part thereof or interest therein, of which the donor has so parted with dominion and control as to leave in him no power to change its disposition, whether for his own benefit or for the benefit of another, the gift is complete. But if upon a transfer of property (whether in trust or otherwise) the donor reserves any power over its disposition, the gift may be wholly incomplete, or may be partially complete and partially incomplete, depending upon all the facts in the particular case. Accordingly, in every case of a transfer of property subject to a reserved power, the terms of the power must be examined and its scope determined. For example, if a donor transfers property to another in trust to pay the income to the donor or accumulate it in the discretion of the trustee, and the donor retains a testamentary power to appoint the remainder among his descendants, no portion of the transfer is a completed gift. On the other hand, if the donor had not retained the testamentary power of appointment, but instead provided that the remainder should go to X or his heirs, the entire transfer would be a completed gift. However, if the exercise of the trustee's power in favor of the grantor is limited by a fixed or ascertainable standard (see paragraph (g)(2) of §25.2511-1), enforceable by or on behalf of the grantor, then the gift is incomplete to the extent of the ascertainable value of any rights thus retained by the grantor.

(c) A gift is incomplete in every instance in which a donor reserves the power to revest the beneficial title to the property in himself. A gift is also incomplete if and to the extent that a reserved power gives the donor the power to name new beneficiaries or to change the interests of the beneficiaries as between themselves unless the power is a fiduciary power limited by a fixed or ascertainable standard. Thus, if an estate for life is transferred but, by an exercise of a power, the estate may be terminated or cut down by the donor to one of less value, and without restriction upon the extent to which the estate may be so cut down, the transfer constitutes an incomplete gift. If in this example the power was confined to the right to cut down the estate for life to one for a term of five years, the certainty of an estate for life for not less than that term results in a gift to that extent complete.

(d) A gift is not considered incomplete, however, merely because the donor reserves the power to change the manner or time of enjoyment. Thus, the creation of a trust the income of which is to be paid annually to the donee for a period of years, the corpus being distributable to him at the end of the period, and the power reserved by the donor being limited to a right to require that, instead of the income being so payable, it should be accumulated and distributed with the corpus to the donee at the termination of the period, constitutes a completed gift.

(e) A donor is considered as himself having a power if it is exercisable by him in conjunction with any person not having a substantial adverse interest in the disposition of the transferred property or the income therefrom. A trustee, as such, is not a person having an adverse interest in the disposition of the trust property or its income.

(f) The relinquishment or termination of a power to change the beneficiaries of transferred property, occurring otherwise than by the death of the donor (the statute being confined to transfers by living donors), is regarded as the event which completes the gift and causes the tax to apply. For example, if A transfers property in trust for the benefit of B and C but reserves the power as trustee to change the proportionate interests of B and C, and if A thereafter has another person appointed trustee in place of himself, such later relinquishment of the power by A to the new trustee completes the gift of the transferred property, whether or not the new trustee has a substantial adverse interest. The receipt of income or of other enjoyment of the transferred property by the transferee or by the beneficiary (other than by the donor himself) during the interim between the making of the initial transfer and the relinquishment or termination of the power operates to free such income or other enjoyment from the power, and constitutes a gift of such income or of such other enjoyment taxable as of the "calendar period" (as defined in §25.2502-1(c)(1). If property is transferred in trust to pay the income to A for life with remainder to B, powers to distribute corpus to A, and to withhold income from A for future distribution to B, are powers to change the beneficiaries of the transferred property.

(g) If a donor transfers property to himself as trustee (or to himself and some other person, not possessing a substantial adverse interest, as trustees), and retains no beneficial interest in the trust property and no power over it except fiduciary powers, the exercise or nonexercise of which is limited by a fixed or ascertainable standard, to change the beneficiaries of the transferred property, the donor has made a completed gift and the entire value of the transferred property is subject to the gift tax.

(h) If a donor delivers a properly indorsed stock certificate to the donee or the donee's agent, the gift is completed for gift tax purposes on the date of delivery. If the donor delivers the certificate to his bank or broker as his agent, or to the issuing corporation or its transfer agent, for transfer into the name of the donee, the gift is completed on the date the stock is transferred on the books of the corporation.

(i) [Reserved]

(j) If the donor contends that a power is of such nature as to render the gift incomplete, and hence not subject to the tax as of the calendar period (as defined in §25.2502-1(c)(1)) of the initial transfer, see §301.6501(c)-1(f)(5) of this chapter. [Reg. §25.2511-2.]

☐ [T.D. 6334, 11-14-58. *Amended by T.D. 7238, 12-28-72; T.D. 7910, 9-6-83, T.D. 8845, 12-2-99 and T.D. 9923, 11-18-2020.*]

## [Reg. §25.2511-3]

**§25.2511-3. Transfers by nonresidents not citizens.**—(a) *In general.*—Sections 2501 and 2511 contain rules relating to the taxation of transfers of property by gift by a donor who is a nonresident not a citizen of the United States. (See paragraph(b) of §25.2501-1 for the definition of the term "resident" for purposes of the gift tax.) As combined these rules are:

(1) The gift tax applies only to the transfer of real property and tangible personal property situated in the United States at the time of the transfer if either—

(i) The gift was made on or after January 1, 1967, by a nonresident not a citizen of the United States who was not an expatriate to whom section 2501(a)(2) was inapplicable on the date of the gift by reason of section 2501(a)(3) and paragraph (a)(3) of §25.2501-1, or

(ii) The gift was made before January 1, 1967, by a nonresident not a citizen of the United States who was not engaged in business in the United States during the calendar year in which the gift was made.

(2) The gift tax applies to the transfer of all property (whether real or personal, tangible or intangible) situated in the United States at the time of the transfer if either—

(i) The gift was made on or after January 1, 1967, by a nonresident not a citizen of the United States who was an expatriate to whom section 2501(a)(2) was inapplicable on the date of the gift by reason of section 2501(a)(3) and paragraph (a)(3) of §25.2501-1, or

(ii) The gift was made before January 1, 1967, by a nonresident not a citizen of the United States who was engaged in business in the United States during the calendar year in which the gift was made.

(b) *Situs of property.*—For purposes of applying the gift tax to the transfer of property owned and held by a nonresident not a citizen of the United States at the time of the transfer—

(1) *Real property and tangible personal property.*—Real property and tangible personal property constitute property within the United States only if they are physically situated therein.

(2) *Intangible personal property.*—Except as provided otherwise in subparagraphs (3) and (4) of this paragraph, intangible personal property constitutes property within the United States if it consists of a property right issued by or enforceable against a resident of the United States or a domestic corporation (public or private), irrespective of where the written evidence of the property is physically located at the time of the transfer.

(3) *Shares of stock.*—Irrespective of where the stock certificates are physically located at the time of the transfer—

(i) Shares of stock issued by a domestic corporation constitute property within the United States, and

(ii) Shares of stock issued by a corporation which is not a domestic corporation constitute property situated outside the United States.

(4) *Debt obligations.*—(i) In the case of gifts made on or after January 1, 1967, a debt obligation, including a bank deposit, the primary obligor of which is a United States person (as defined in section 7701(a)(30)), the United States, a State, or any political subdivision thereof, the District of Columbia, or any agency or instrumentality of any such government constitutes property situated within the United States. This subdivision applies—

(a) In the case of a debt obligation of a domestic corporation, whether or not any interest on the obligation would be treated under section 862(a)(1) as income from sources without the United States by reason of section 861(a)(1)(B) (relating to interest received from a domestic corporation less than 20 percent of whose gross income for a 3-year period was derived from sources within the United States) and the regulations thereunder;

(b) In the case of an amount described in section 861(c) (relating to certain bank deposits, withdrawable accounts, and amounts held by an insurance company under an agreement to pay interest), whether or not any interest thereon would be treated under section 862(a)(1) as income from sources without the United States, by reason of section 861(a)(1)(A) (relating to interest on amounts described in section 861(c) which is not effectively connected with the conduct of a trade or business within the United States) and the regulations thereunder;

(c) In the case of a deposit with a domestic corporation or domestic partnership, whether or not the deposit is with a foreign branch thereof engaged in the commercial banking business; and

(d) Irrespective of where the written evidence of the debt obligation is physically located at the time of the transfer.

For purposes of this subdivision, a debt obligation on which there are two or more primary obligors shall be apportioned among such obligors, taking into account to the extent appropriate under all the facts and circumstances any choate or inchoate rights of contribution existing among such obligors with respect to the indebtedness. The term "agency or instrumentality," as used in this subdivision, does not include a possession of the United States or an agency or instrumentality of a possession.

(ii) In the case of gifts made on or after January 1, 1967, a debt obligation, including a bank deposit, not deemed under subdivision (i) of this subparagraph to be situated within the United States, constitutes property situated outside the United States.

(iii) In the case of gifts made before January 1, 1967, a debt obligation the written evidence of which is treated as being the property itself constitutes property situated within the United States if the written evidence of the obligation is physically located in the United States at the time of the transfer, irrespective of who is the primary obligor on the debt. If the written evidence of the obligation is physically located outside the United States, the debt obligation constitutes property situated outside the United States.

(iv) Currency is not a debt obligation for purposes of this subparagraph. [Reg. § 25.2511-3.]

☐ [*T.D. 6334, 11-14-58. Amended by T.D. 6542, 1-19-61; T.D. 7238, 12-28-72 and T.D. 7296, 12-11-73.*]

### [Reg. § 25.2512-0]

**§ 25.2512-0. Table of contents.**—This section lists the section headings that appear in the regulations under section 2512.

*§ 25.2512-1 Valuation of property; in general.*

*§ 25.2512-2 Stocks and bonds.*

*§ 25.2512-3 Valuation of interest in businesses.*

*§ 25.2512-4 Valuation of notes.*

*§ 25.2512-5 Valuation of annuities, unitrust interests, interests for life or term of years, and remainder or reversionary interests.*

*§ 25.2512-6 Valuation of certain life insurance and annuity contracts; valuation of shares in an open-end investment company.*

*§ 25.2512-7 Effect of excise tax.*

*§ 25.2512-8 Transfers for insufficient consideration.*

### Actuarial Tables Applicable Before May 1, 2009

*§ 25.2512-5A Valuation of annuities, unitrust interests, interests for life or term of years, and remainder or reversionary interests transferred before May 1, 2009.*
[Reg. § 25.2512-0.]

☐ [*T.D. 8540, 6-9-94. Amended by T.D. 8819, 4-29-99; T.D. 8886, 6-9-2000; T.D. 9448, 5-1-2009 and T.D. 9540, 8-9-2011.*]

### [Reg. § 25.2512-1]

**§ 25.2512-1. Valuation of property; in general.**—Section 2512 provides that if a gift is made in property, its value at the date of the gift shall be considered the amount of the gift. The value of the property is the price at which such property would change hands between a willing buyer and a willing seller, neither being under any compulsion to buy or to sell, and both having reasonable knowledge of relevant facts. The value of a particular kind of property is not the price that a forced sale of the property would produce. Nor is the fair market value of an item of property the sale price in a market other than that in which such item is most commonly sold to the public, taking into account, the location of the item wherever appropriate. Thus, in the case of an item of property made the subject of a gift, which is generally obtained by the public in the retail market, the fair market value of such an item of property is the price at which the item or a comparable item would be sold at retail. For example, the value of an automobile (an article generally obtained by the public in the retail market) which is the subject of a gift, is the price for which an automobile of the same or approximately the same description, make, model, age, condition, etc., could be purchased by a member of the general public and not the price for which the particular automobile of the donor would be purchased by a dealer in used automobiles. Examples of items of property which are generally sold to the public at retail may be found in § 25.2512-6. The value is generally to be determined by ascertaining as a basis the fair market value at the time of the gift of each unit of the property. For example, in the case of shares of stocks or bonds, such unit of property is generally a share or a bond. Property shall not be returned at the value at which it is assessed for local tax purposes unless that value represents the fair market value thereof on the date of the gift. All relevant facts and elements of value as of the time of the gift shall be considered. Where the subject of a gift is an interest in a business, the value of items of property in the inventory of the business generally should be reflected in the value of the business. For valuation of interests in businesses, see § 25.2512-3. See § 25.2512-2 and §§ 25.2512-4 through 25.2512-6 for further information concerning the valuation of other particular kinds of property. See section 2701 and the regulations at § 25.2701 for special rules for valuing transfers of an interest in a corporation or a partnership and for the treatment of unpaid qualified payments at the subsequent transfer of an applicable retained interest by the transferor or by an applicable family member. See section 2704(b) and the regulations at § 25.2704-2 for special valuation rules where an interest in property is subject to an applicable restriction. [Reg. § 25.2512-1.]

☐ [*T.D. 6334, 11-14-58. Amended by T.D. 6826, 6-14-65 and T.D. 8395, 1-28-92.*]

### [Reg. § 25.2512-2]

**§ 25.2512-2. Stocks and bonds.**—(a) *In general.*—The value of stocks and bonds is the fair market value per share or bond on the date of the gift.

(b) *Based on selling prices.*—(1) In general, if there is a market for stocks or bonds, on a stock exchange, in an over-the-counter market or otherwise, the mean between the highest and lowest quoted selling prices on the date of the gift is the fair market value per share or bond. If there were no sales on the date of the gift but there were sales on dates within a reasonable period both before and after the date of the gift, the fair market value is determined by taking a weighted average of the means between the highest and lowest sales on the nearest date before and the nearest date after the date of the gift. The average is to be weighted inversely by the respective numbers of trading days between the selling dates and the date of the gift. If the stocks or bonds are listed on more than one exchange, the records of the exchange where the stocks or bonds are principally dealt in should be employed if such records are available in a generally available listing or publication of general circulation. In the event such records are not so available and such stocks or bonds are listed on a composite listing of combined exchanges available in a generally available listing or publication of general circulation, the records of such combined exchanges should be employed. In valuing listed securities, the donor should be careful to consult accurate records to obtain values as of the date of the gift. If quotations of unlisted securities are obtained from brokers, or evidence as to their sale is obtained from the officers of the issuing companies, copies of letters furnishing such quotations or evidence of sale should be attached to the return.

(2) If it is established with respect to bonds for which there is a market on a stock exchange, that the highest and lowest selling prices are not available for the date of the gift in a generally available listing or publication of general circulation but that closing prices are so available, the fair market value per bond is the mean between the quoted closing selling price on the date of the gift and the quoted closing selling price on the trading day before the date of the gift. If there were no sales on the trading day before the date of the gift but there were sales on dates within a reasonable period before the date of the gift, the fair market value is determined by taking a weighted average of the quoted closing selling prices on the date of the gift and the nearest date before the date of the gift. The closing selling price for the date of the gift is to be weighted by the respective number of trading days between the previous selling date and the date of the gift. If there were no sales within a reasonable period before the date of the gift but there were sales on the date of the gift, the fair market value is the closing selling price on the date of the gift. If there were no sales on the date of the gift but there were sales within a reasonable period both before and after the date of the gift, the fair market value is determined by taking a weighted average of the quoted closing selling prices on the nearest date before and the nearest date after the date of the gift. The average is to be weighted inversely by the respective numbers of trading days between the selling dates and the date of the gift. If the bonds are listed on more than one exchange, the records of the exchange where the bonds are principally dealt in should be employed. In valuing listed securities, the donor should be careful to consult accurate records to obtain values as of the date of the gift.

(3) The application of this paragraph may be illustrated by the following examples:

*Example (1).* Assume that sales of stock nearest the date of the gift (Friday, June 15) occurred two trading days before (Wednesday, June 13) and three trading days after (Wednesday, June 20) and on these days the mean sale prices per share were $10 and $15, respectively. The price of $12 is taken as representing the fair market value of a share of stock as of the date of the gift

$$\frac{((3 \times 10) + (2 \times 15)).}{5}$$

*Example (2).* Assume the same facts as in example 1 except that the mean sale prices per share on June 13 and June 20 were $15 and $10 respectively. The price of $13 is taken as representing the fair market value of a share of stock as of the date of the gift

$$\frac{(3 \times 15) + (2 \times 10).}{5}$$

*Example (3).* Assume that on the date of the gift (Tuesday, April 3, 1973) the closing selling price of certain listed bonds was $25 per bond and that the highest and lowest selling prices are not available in a generally available listing or publication of general circulation for that date. Assume further, that the closing selling price of such bonds was $21 per bond on the day before the date of the gift (Monday, April 2, 1973). Thus, under paragraph (b)(2) of this section, the price of $23 is taken as representing the fair market value per bond as of the date of the gift

$$\frac{(25 + 21)}{2}.$$

*Example (4).* Assume the same facts as in example 3 except that there were no sales on the day before the date of the gift. Assume further, that there were sales on Thursday, March 29, 1973, and that the closing selling price on that day was $23. The price of $24.50 is taken as representing the fair market value per bond as of the date of the gift

$$\frac{((1 \times 23) + (3 \times 25))}{4}.$$

*Example (5).* Assume that no bonds were traded on the date of the gift (Friday, April 20). Assume further, that sales of bonds nearest the date of the gift occurred two trading days before (Wednesday, April 18) and three trading days after (Wednesday, April 25) the date of the gift and that on these two days the closing selling prices per bond were $29 and $22, respectively. The highest and lowest selling prices are not available for these dates in a generally available listing or publication of general circulation. Thus, under paragraph (b)(2) of this section the price of $26.20 is taken as representing the fair market value of a bond as of the date of the gift

$$\frac{((3 \times 29) + (2 \times 22))}{5}.$$

(c) *Based on bid and asked prices.*—If the provisions of paragraph (b) of this section are inapplicable because actual sales are not available during a reasonable period beginning before and ending after the date of the gift, the fair market value may be determined by taking the mean between the bona fide bid and asked prices on the date of the gift, or if none, by taking a weighted average of the means between the bona fide bid and asked prices on the nearest trading date before and the nearest trading date after the date of the gift, if both such nearest dates are within a reasonable period. The average is to be determined in the manner described in paragraph (b) of this section.

(d) *Where selling prices and bid and asked prices are not available for dates both before and after the date of gift.*—If the provisions of paragraphs (b) and (c) of this section are inapplicable because no actual sale prices or quoted bona fide bid and asked prices are available on a date within a reasonable period before the date of the gift, but such prices are available on a date within a reasonable period after the date of the gift, or vice versa, then the mean between the highest and lowest available sale prices or bid and asked prices may be taken as the value.

(e) *Where selling prices or bid and asked prices do not represent fair market value.*—In cases in which it is established that the value per bond or share of any security determined on the basis of the selling or bid and asked prices as provided under paragraphs (b), (c), and (d) of this section does not represent the fair market value thereof, then some reasonable modification of the value determined on that basis or other relevant facts and elements of value shall be considered in determining fair market value. Where sales at or near the date of the gift are few or of a sporadic nature, such sales alone may not indicate fair market value. In certain exceptional cases, the size of the block of securities made the subject of each separate gift in relation to the number of shares changing hands in sales may be relevant in determining whether selling prices reflect the fair market value of the block of stock to be valued. If the donor can show that the block of stock to be valued, with reference to each separate gift, is so large in relation to the actual sales on the existing market that it could not be liquidated in a reasonable time without depressing the market, the price at which the block could be sold as such outside the usual market, as through an underwriter, may be a more accurate indication of value than market quotations. Complete data in support of any allowance claimed due to the size of the block of stock being valued should be submitted with the return. On the other hand, if the block of stock to be valued represents a controlling interest, either actual or effective, in a going business, the price at which other lots change hands may have little relation to its true value.

(f) *Where selling prices or bid and asked prices are unavailable.*—If the provisions of paragraphs (b), (c), and (d) of this section are inapplicable because actual sale prices and bona fide bid and asked prices are lacking, then the fair market value is to be determined by taking the following factors into consideration:

(1) In the case of corporate or other bonds, the soundness of the security, the interest yield, the date of maturity, and other relevant factors; and

(2) In the case of shares of stock, the company's net worth, prospective earning power and dividend-paying capacity, and other relevant factors.

Some of the "other relevant factors" referred to in subparagraphs (1) and (2) of this paragraph are: the good will of the business; the economic outlook in the particular industry; the company's position in the industry and its management; the degree of control of the business represented by the block of stock to be valued; and the values of securities of corporations engaged in the same or similar lines of business which are listed on a stock exchange. However, the weight to be accorded such comparisons or any other evidentiary factors considered in the determination of a value depends upon the facts of each case. Complete financial and other data upon which the valuation is based should be submitted with the return, including copies of reports of any examinations of the company have been made by accountants, engineers, or any technical experts as of or near the date of the gift. [Reg. § 25.2512-2.]

☐ [*T.D.* 6334, 11-14-58. *Amended by T.D.* 7327, 9-30-74 *and by T.D.* 7432, 9-10-76.]

### [Reg. § 25.2512-3]

**§ 25.2512-3. Valuation of interests in businesses.**—(a) Care should be taken to arrive at an accurate valuation of any interest in a business which the donor transfers without an adequate and full consideration in money or money's worth. The fair market value of any interest in a business, whether a partnership or a proprietorship, is the net amount which a willing purchaser, whether an individual or a corporation, would pay for the interest to a willing seller, neither being under any compulsion to buy or to sell and both having reasonable knowledge of the relevant facts. The net value is determined on the basis of all relevant factors including—

(1) A fair appraisal as of the date of the gift of all the assets of the business, tangible and intangible, including good will;

(2) The demonstrated earning capacity of the business; and

(3) The other factors set forth in paragraph (f) of § 25.2512-2 relating to the valuation of corporate stock, to the extent applicable. Special attention should be given to determining an adequate value of the good will of the business. Complete financial and other data upon which the valuation is based should be submitted with the return, including copies of reports of examinations of the business made by accountants, engineers, or any technical experts as of or near the date of the gift. [Reg. § 25.2512-3.]

☐ [*T.D.* 6334, 11-14-58.]

### [Reg. § 25.2512-4]

**§ 25.2512-4. Valuation of notes.**—The fair market value of notes, secured or unsecured, is presumed to be the amount of unpaid principal, plus accrued interest to the date of the gift, unless the donor establishes a lower value. Unless returned at face value, plus accrued interest, it must be shown by satisfactory evidence that the note is worth less than the unpaid amount (because of the interest rate, or date of maturity, or other cause), or that the note is uncollectible in part (by reason of the insolvency of the party or parties liable, or for other cause), and that the property, if any, pledged or mortgaged as security is insufficient to satisfy it. [Reg. § 25.2512-4.]

☐ [*T.D.* 6334, 11-14-58.]

### [Reg. § 25.2512-5]

**§ 25.2512-5. Valuation of annuities, unitrust interests, interests for life or term of years, and remainder or reversionary interests.**—(a) *In general.*—Except as otherwise provided in paragraph(b) of this section and § 25.7520-3(b), the fair market value of annuities, unitrust interests, life estates, terms of years, remainders, and reversions transferred by gift is the present value of the interests determined under paragraph (d) of this section. Section 20.2031-7 of this chapter (Estate Tax Regulations) and related sections provide tables with standard actuarial factors and examples that illustrate how to use the tables to compute the present value of ordinary annuity, life, and remainder interests in property. These sections also refer to standard and special actuarial factors that may be necessary to compute the present value of similar interests in more unusual fact situations. These factors and examples are also generally applicable for gift tax purposes in computing the values of taxable gifts.

(b) *Commercial annuities and insurance contracts.*—The value of life insurance contracts and contracts for the payment of annuities issued by companies regularly engaged in their sale is determined under § 25.2512-6.

(c) *Actuarial valuations.*—The present value of annuities, unitrust interests, life estates, terms of years, remainders, and reversions transferred by gift on or after May 1, 2009, is determined under paragraph (d) of this section. The present value of annuities, unitrust interests, life estates, terms of years, remainders, and reversions transferred by gift before May 1, 2009, is determined under the following sections:

| | Transfers | | Applicable |
|---|---|---|---|
| After | | Before | Regulations |
| - | | 01-01-52 | 25.2512-5A(a) |
| 12-31-51 | | 01-01-71 | 25.2512-5A(b) |
| 12-31-70 | | 12-01-83 | 25.2512-5A(c) |
| 11-30-83 | | 05-01-89 | 25.2512-5A(d) |
| 04-30-89 | | 05-01-99 | 25.2512-5A(e) |
| 04-30-99 | | 05-01-09 | 25.2512-5A(f) |

(d) *Actuarial valuations on or after May 1, 2009.*—(1) *In general.*—Except as otherwise provided in paragraph (b) of this section and §25.7520-3(b) (relating to exceptions to the use of prescribed tables under certain circumstances), if the valuation date for the gift is on or after May 1, 2009, the fair market value of annuities, life estates, terms of years, remainders, and reversions transferred on or after May 1, 2009, is the present value of such interests determined under paragraph (d)(2) of this section and by use of standard or special section 7520 actuarial factors. These factors are derived by using the appropriate section 7520 interest rate and, if applicable, the mortality component for the valuation date of the interest that is being valued. See §§25.7520-1 through 25.7520-4. The fair market value of a qualified annuity interest described in section 2702(b)(1) and a qualified unitrust interest described in section 2702(b)(2) is the present value of such interests determined under §25.7520-1(c).

(2) *Specific interests.*—When the donor transfers property in trust or otherwise and retains an interest therein, generally, the value of the gift is the value of the property transferred less the value of the donor's retained interest. However, if the donor transfers property after October 8, 1990, to or for the benefit of a member of the donor's family, the value of the gift is the value of the property transferred less the value of the donor's retained interest as determined under section 2702. If the donor assigns or relinquishes an annuity, life estate, remainder, or reversion that the donor holds by virtue of a transfer previously made by the donor or another, the value of the gift is the value of the interest transferred. However, see section 2519 for a special rule in the case of the assignment of an income interest by a person who received the interest from a spouse.

(i) *Charitable remainder trusts.*—The fair market value of a remainder interest in a pooled income fund, as defined in §1.642(c)-5 of this chapter, is its value determined under §1.642(c)-6(e) (see §1.642(c)-6A for certain prior periods). The fair market value of a remainder interest in a charitable remainder annuity trust, as described in §1.664-2(a), is its present value determined under §1.664-2(c). The fair market value of a remainder interest in a charitable remainder unitrust, as defined in §1.664-3, is its present value determined under §1.664-4(e). The fair market value of a life interest or term for years in a charitable remainder unitrust is the fair market value of the property as of the date of transfer less the fair market value of the remainder interest, determined under §1.664-4(e)(4) and (e)(5).

(ii) *Ordinary remainder and reversionary interests.*—If the interest to be valued is to take effect after a definite number of years or after the death of one individual, the present value of the interest is computed by multiplying the value of the property by the appropriate remainder interest actuarial factor (that corresponds to the applicable section 7520 interest rate and remainder interest period) in Table B (for a term certain) or in Table S (for one measuring life), as the case may be. Table B is contained in §20.2031-7(d)(6) of this chapter and Table S (for one measuring life when the valuation date is on or after May 1, 2009) is included in §20.2031-7(d)(7) and Internal Revenue Service Publication 1457. See §20.2031-7A containing Table S for valuation of interests before May 1, 2009. For information about obtaining actuarial factors for other types of remainder interests, see paragraph (d)(4) of this section.

(iii) *Ordinary term-of-years and life interests.*—If the interest to be valued is the right of a person to receive the income of certain property, or to use certain nonincome-producing property, for a term of years or for the life of one individual, the present value of the interest is computed by multiplying the value of the property by the appropriate term-of-years or life interest actuarial factor (that corresponds to the applicable section 7520 interest rate and term-of-years or life interest period). Internal Revenue Service Publication 1457 includes actuarial factors for a remainder interest after a term of years in Table B and after the life of one individual in Table S (for one measuring life when the valuation date is on or after May 1, 2009). However, term-of-years and life interest actuarial factors are not included in Table B in §20.2031-7(d)(6) of this chapter or Table S in §20.2031-7(d)(7) (or in §20.2031-7A). If Internal Revenue Service Publication 1457 (or any other reliable source of term-of-years and life interest actuarial factors) is not conveniently available, an actua-

rial factor for the interest may be derived mathematically. This actuarial factor may be derived by subtracting the correlative remainder factor (that corresponds to the applicable section 7520 interest rate) in Table B (for a term of years) in §20.2031-7(d)(6) or in Table S (for the life of one individual) in §20.2031-7(d)(7), as the case may be, from 1.000000. For information about obtaining actuarial factors for other types of term-of-years and life interests, see paragraph (d)(4) of this section.

(iv) *Annuities.*—(A) If the interest to be valued is the right of a person to receive an annuity that is payable at the end of each year for a term of years or for the life of one individual, the present value of the interest is computed by multiplying the aggregate amount payable annually by the appropriate annuity actuarial factor (that corresponds to the applicable section 7520 interest rate and annuity period). Internal Revenue Service Publication 1457 includes actuarial factors in Table B (for a remainder interest after an annuity payable for a term of years) and in Table S (for a remainder interest after an annuity payable for the life of one individual when the valuation date is on or after May 1, 2009). However, annuity actuarial factors are not included in Table B in §20.2031-7(d)(6) of this chapter or Table S in §20.2031-7(d)(7) (or in §20.2031-7A). If Internal Revenue Service Publication 1457 (or any other reliable source of annuity actuarial factors) is not conveniently available, an annuity factor for a term of years or for one life may be derived mathematically. This annuity factor may be derived by subtracting the applicable remainder factor (that corresponds to the applicable section 7520 interest rate and annuity period) in Table B (in the case of a term-of-years annuity) in §20.2031-7(d)(6) or in Table S (in the case of a one-life annuity) in §20.2031-7(d)(7), as the case may be, from 1.000000 and then dividing the result by the applicable section 7520 interest rate expressed as a decimal number. See §20.2031-7(d)(2)(iv) for an example that illustrates the computation of the present value of an annuity.

(B) If the annuity is payable at the end of semiannual, quarterly, monthly, or weekly periods, the product obtained by multiplying the annuity factor by the aggregate amount payable annually is then multiplied by the applicable adjustment factor set forth in Table K in §20.2031-7(d)(6) at the appropriate interest rate component for payments made at the end of the specified periods. The provisions of this paragraph (d)(2)(iv)(B) are illustrated by the following example:

*Example.* In July of a year after 2009 but before 2019, the donor agreed to pay the annuitant the sum of $10,000 per year, payable in equal semiannual installments at the end of each period. The semiannual installments are to be made on each December 31st and June 30th. The annuity is payable until the annuitant's death. On the date of the agreement, the annuitant is 68 years and 5 months old. The donee annuitant's age is treated as 68 for purposes of computing the present value of the annuity. The section 7520 rate on the date of the agreement is 6.6 percent. Under Table S in §20.2031-7(d)(7), the factor at 6.6 percent for determining the present value of a remainder interest payable at the death of an individual aged 68 is .42001. Converting the remainder factor to an annuity factor, as described above, the annuity factor for determining the present value of an annuity transferred to an individual age 68 is 8.7877 (1.000000 minus .42001 divided by .066). The adjustment factor from Table K in §20.2031-7(d)(6) in the column for payments made at the end of each semiannual period at the rate of 6.6 percent is 1.0162. The aggregate annual amount of the annuity, $10,000, is multiplied by the factor 8.7877 and the product is multiplied by 1.0162. The present value of the donee's annuity is, therefore, $89,300.61 ($10,000 × 8.7877 × 1.0162).

(C) If an annuity is payable at the beginning of annual, semiannual, quarterly, monthly, or weekly periods for a term of years, the value of the annuity is computed by multiplying the aggregate amount payable annually by the annuity factor described in paragraph (d)(2)(iv)(A) of this section; and the product so obtained is then multiplied by the adjustment factor in Table J in §20.2031-7(d)(6) of this chapter at the appropriate interest rate component for payments made at the beginning of specified periods. If an annuity is payable at the beginning of annual, semiannual, quarterly, monthly, or weekly periods for one or more lives, the value of the annuity is the sum of the first payment and the present value of a similar annuity, the first payment of which is not to be made until the end of the payment period, determined as provided in paragraph (d)(2)(iv)(B) of this section.

(v) *Annuity and unitrust interests for a term of years or until the prior death of an individual.*—(A) *Annuity interests.*—The present value of an annuity interest that is payable until the earlier to occur of the lapse of a specific number of years or the death of an individual may be computed with values from the tables in § § 20.2031-7(d)(6) and 20.2031-7(d)(7) of this chapter as described in the following example:

*Example.* The donor transfers $100,000 into a trust early in 2010, and retains the right to receive an annuity from the trust in the amount of $6,000 per year, payable in equal semiannual installments at the end of each period. The semiannual installments are to be made on each June 30th and December 31st.

The annuity is payable for 10 years or until the donor's prior death. At the time of the transfer, the donor is 59 years and 6 months old. The donor's age is deemed to be 60 for purposes of computing the present value of the retained annuity. If the section 7520 rate for the month in which the transfer occurs is 5.8 percent, the present value of the donor's retained interest would be $42,575.65, determined as follows:

| | |
|---|---|
| TABLE S value at 5.8 percent, age 60 | .34656 |
| TABLE S value at 5.8 percent, age 70 | .49025 |
| TABLE 2000CM value at age 70 | 74794 |
| TABLE 2000CM value at age 60 | 87595 |
| TABLE B value at 5.8 percent, 10 years | .569041 |
| TABLE K value at 5.8 percent | 1.0143 |

Factor for donor's retained interest at 5.8 percent:

$$\frac{(1.00000 - .34656) - (.569041 \times (74794/87595) \times (1.00000 - .49025))}{.058} = 6.9959$$

Present value of donor's retained interest:

($6,000 × 6.9959 × 1.0143) ............................................. $42,575.65

(B) *Unitrust interests.*—The present value of a unitrust interest that is payable until the earlier to occur of the lapse of a specific number of years or the death of an individual may be computed with values from the tables in § § 1.664-4(e)(6) and 1.664-4(e)(7) of this chapter as described in the following example:

*Example.* The donor who, as of the nearest birthday, is 60 years old, transfers $100,000 to a unitrust on January 1st of a year after 2009 but before 2019. The trust instrument requires that each year the trust pay to the donor, in equal semiannual installments on June 30th and December 31st, 6 percent of the fair market value of the trust assets, valued as of January 1st each year, for 10 years or until the prior death of the donor. The section 7520 rate for the January in which the transfer occurs is 6.6 percent. Under Table F(6.6) in § 1.664-4(e)(6), the appropriate adjustment factor is .953317 for semiannual payments payable at the end of the semiannual period. The adjusted payout rate is 5.720 percent (6% × .953317). The present value of the donor's retained interest is $41,920.00 determined as follows:

| | |
|---|---|
| TABLE U(1) value at 5.6 percent, age 60 | .33970 |
| TABLE U(1) value at 5.6 percent, age 70 | .48352 |
| TABLE 2000CM value at age 70 | 74794 |
| TABLE 2000CM value at age 60 | 87595 |
| TABLE D value at 5.6 percent, 10 years | .561979 |

Factor for donor's retained interest at 5.6 percent:

(1.000000 −.33970) − (.561979 × (74794/87595) × (1.000000 − .48352)) = .41247

| | |
|---|---|
| TABLE U(1) value at 5.8 percent, age 60 | .32846 |
| TABLE U(1) value at 5.8 percent, age 70 | .47241 |
| TABLE 2000CM value at age 70 | 74794 |
| TABLE 2000CM value at age 60 | 87595 |
| TABLE D value at 5.8 percent, 10 years | .550185 |

Factor for donor's retained interest at 5.8 percent:

(1.000000 − .32846) − (.550185 × (74974/87595) × (1.000000 − .47241)) = .42369

Difference ........................................................... .01122

Interpolation adjustment:

$$\frac{5.720\% - 5.6\%}{0.2\%} = \frac{\times}{.01122}$$

x = .00673

| | |
|---|---|
| Factor at 5.6 percent, age 60 | .41247 |
| Plus: Interpolation adjustment | .00673 |
| Interpolated Factor | .41920 |

Present value of donor's retained interest:

($100,000 × .41920) ................................................. $41,920.00

(3) *Transitional rule.*—If the valuation date of a transfer of property by gift is on or after May 1, 2009, and before July 1, 2009, the fair market value of the interest transferred is determined by use of the section 7520 interest rate for the month in which the valuation date occurs (see § § 25.7520-1(b) and 25.7520-2(a)(2)) and the appropriate actuarial tables under either § 20.2031-7(d)(7) or § 20.2031-7A(f)(4) of this chapter, at the option of the donor. However, with respect to each individual transaction and with respect to all transfers occurring on the valuation date, the donor must use the same actuarial tables (for example, gift and income tax charitable deductions with respect to the same transfer must be determined based on the same tables, and all transfers made on the same date must be valued based on the same tables).

(4) *Publications and actuarial computations by the Internal Revenue Service.*—Many standard actuarial factors not included in §20.2031-7(d)(6) or §20.2031-7(d)(7) of this chapter are included in Internal Revenue Service Publication 1457, "Actuarial Valuations Version 3A" (2009). Internal Revenue Service Publication 1457 also includes examples that illustrate how to compute many special factors for more unusual situations. A copy of this publication is available, at no charge, electronically via the IRS Internet site at *www.irs.gov.* If a special factor is required in the case of a completed gift, the Internal Revenue Service may furnish the factor to the donor upon a request for a ruling. The request for a ruling must be accompanied by a recitation of the facts including a statement of the date of birth for each measuring life, the date of the gift, any other applicable dates, and a copy of the will, trust, or other relevant documents. A request for a ruling must comply with the instructions for requesting a ruling published periodically in the Internal Revenue Bulletin (see §§601.201 and 601.601(d)(2)(ii)(b) of this chapter) and include payment of the required user fee.

(e) *Effective/applicability dates.*—This section applies on and after May 1, 2009. [Reg. §25.2512-5.]

☐ [*T.D.* 8540, 6-9-94. *Amended by T.D.* 8819, 4-29-99; *T.D.* 8886, 6-9-2000 (*corrected* 9-27-2000); *T.D.* 9448-5-1-2009 *and T.D.* 9540, 8-9-2011.]

## [Reg. §25.2512-5A]

**§25.2512-5A. Valuation of annuities, unitrust interests, interests for life or term of years, and remainder or reversionary interests transferred before May 1, 2009.**—(a) *Valuation of annuities, interests for life or term of years, and remainder or reversionary interests transferred before January 1, 1952.*—Except as otherwise provided in §25.2512-5(b), if the transfer was made before January 1, 1952, the present value of annuities, life estates, terms of years, remainders, and reversions is their present value determined under this section. If the valuation of the interest involved is dependent upon the continuation or termination of one or more lives or upon a term certain concurrent with one or more lives, the factor for the present value is computed on the basis of interest at the rate of 4 percent a year, compounded annually, and life contingencies for each life involved from values that are based upon the "Actuaries' or Combined Experience Table of Mortality, as extended." This table and many additional factors are described in former §86.19 (as contained in the 26 CFR Part 81 edition revised as of April 1, 1958). The present value of an interest measured by a term of years is computed on the basis of interest at the rate of 4 percent a year.

(b) *Valuation of annuities, interests for life or term of years, and remainder or reversionary interests transferred after December 31, 1951, and before January 1, 1971.*—Except as otherwise provided in §25.2512-5(b), the present value of annuities, life estates, terms of years, remainders, and reversions transferred after December 31, 1951, and before January 1, 1971, is the present value of such interests determined under this section. If the value of the interest involved is dependent upon the continuation or termination of one or more lives, the factor for the present value is computed on the basis of interest at the rate of 3½ percent a year, compounded annually, and life contingencies for each life involved from U.S. Life Table 38. This table and many accompanying factors are set forth in former §25.2512-5 (as contained in the 26 CFR Part 25 edition revised as of April 1, 1984). Special factors involving one and two lives may be found in or computed with the use of tables contained in Internal Revenue Service Publication Number 11, "Actuarial Values for Estate and Gift Tax," (Rev. 5-59). This publication is no longer available for purchase from the Superintendent of Documents. However, it may be obtained by requesting a copy from: CC:DOM:CORP:T:R (IRS Publication 11), room 5228, Internal Revenue Service, POB 7604, Ben Franklin Station, Washington, DC 20044. The present value of an interest measured by a term of years is computed on the basis of interest at the rate of 3½ percent a year.

(c) *Valuation of annuities, interests for life or term of years, and remainder or reversionary interests transferred after December 31, 1970, and before December 1, 1983.*—Except as otherwise provided in §25.2512-5(b), the present value of annuities, life estates, terms of years, remainders, and reversions transferred after December 31, 1970, and before December 1, 1983, is the present value of such interests determined under this section. If the interest to be valued is dependent upon the continuation or termination of one or more lives or upon a term certain concurrent with one or more lives, the factor for the present value is computed on the basis of interest at the rate of 6 percent a year, compounded annually, and life contingencies determined for each male and female life involved, from the values that are set forth in Table LN. Table LN contains values that are taken from the life table for total males and the life table for total females appearing as Tables 2 and 3, respectively, in United States Life Tables: 1959-61,

published by the Department of Health and Human Services, Public Health Service. Table LN and accompanying factors are set forth in former §25.2512-9 (as contained in the 26 CFR Part 25 edition revised as of April 1, 1994). Special factors involving one and two lives may be found in or computed with the use of tables contained in Internal Revenue Service Publication 723, entitled "Actuarial Values I: Valuation of Last Survivor Charitable Remainders" (12-70), and Internal Revenue Service Publication 723A, entitled "Actuarial Values II: Factors at 6 Percent Involving One and Two Lives" (12-70). These publications are no longer available for purchase from the Superintendent of Documents. However, a copy of each may be obtained from: CC:DOM:CORP:T:R (IRS Publication 723/723A), room 5228, Internal Revenue Service, POB 7604, Ben Franklin Station, Washington, DC 20044. The present value of an interest measured by a term of years is computed on the basis of interest at the rate of 6 percent a year.

(d) *Valuation of annuities, interests for life or term of years, and remainder or reversionary interests transferred after November 30, 1983, and before May 1, 1989.*—(1) *In general.*—(i)(A) Except as otherwise provided in §25.2512-5(b) and in this paragraph (d)(1)(i)(A), the fair market value of annuities, life estates, terms of years, remainders, and reversions transferred after November 30, 1983, and before May 1, 1989, is the present value of such interests determined under this section. The value of annuities issued by companies regularly engaged in their sale and of insurance policies issued by companies regularly engaged in their sale is determined under §25.2512-6. The fair market value of a remainder interest in a charitable remainder unitrust, as defined in §1.664-3, is its present value determined under §1.664-4. The fair market value of a life interest or term for years in a charitable remainder unitrust is the fair market value of the property as of the date of transfer less the fair market value of the remainder interest on such date determined under §1.664-4. The fair market value of interests in a pooled income fund, as defined in §1.642(c)-5, is their value determined under §1.642(c)-6. Where the donor transfers property in trust or otherwise and retains an interest therein, the value of the gift is the value of the property transferred less the value of the donor's retained interest. See section 2702 and the regulations at §25.2702 for special rules for valuing transfers of interests in trust after October 8, 1990. See §25.2512-9 with respect to the valuation of annuities, life estates, terms for years, remainders, and reversions transferred after December 31, 1970, and before December 1, 1983.

(B) If the donor transfers in December of 1983, either—

(1) A remainder or a reversion subject to a life interest or a term for years where the life interest or term for years was transferred by the donor after December 31, 1982, and before December 1, 1983, or

(2) A life interest or term for years, the remainder interest of which was transferred by the donor after December 31, 1982, and before December 1, 1983,

the donor shall make an election. The donor may elect to value both interests transferred in 1983 under §25.2512-5A(c) as if such section applied to all transfers made before January 1, 1984, or the donor may elect to have both interests transferred valued under this section. The donor shall indicate the election being made in a statement attached to the donor's gift tax return for 1983.

(C) If the donor transfers in calendar year 1984, either—

(1) A remainder on [or] a reversion subject to a life interest or a term for years where the life interest or term for years was transferred by the donor in the first eleven months of 1983, or

(2) A life interest or term for years, the remainder interest of which was transferred by the donor in the first eleven months of 1983,

the donor shall make an election. The donor may elect to value the interest transferred in 1984 under §25.2512-5A(c) as if such section applied to all transfers made before January 1, 1985, or the donor may elect to have the transfer valued under this section. If the donor elects to value the interest transferred in 1984 under §25.2512-5A(c), the donor shall indicate that the election is being made by attaching a statement to the donor's gift tax return for 1984. If the donor elects to value the interest transferred in 1984 under this section the election shall not be effective unless the donor declares, in a statement attached to the donor's gift tax return for 1984, that the donor has filed an amended gift tax return for 1983, in which the donor has revalued the transfers made in the first eleven months of 1983 under this section as if this section applied to transfers made after December 31, 1982.

(ii) The present value of an annuity, life estate, remainder, or reversion determined under this section which is dependent on the continuation or termination of the life of one person is computed by the use of Table A in paragraph (d)(6) of this section. The present value of an annuity, term for years, remainder, or reversion dependent on a term certain is computed by the use of Table B in paragraph (d)(6) of this section. If the interest to be valued is dependent upon more than one life or there is a term certain concurrent with one or more lives, see paragraph (d)(5) of this section. For purposes of the computations described in this section, the age of the person is to be taken at his or her nearest birthday.

(iii) In all examples set forth in this section, the interest is assumed to have been transferred after November 30, 1983 and before May 1, 1989.

(2) *Annuities.*—(i) If an annuity is payable annually at the end of each year during the life of an individual (as for example if the first payment is due one year after the date of the gift), the amount payable annually is multiplied by the figure in column 2 of Table A opposite the number of years in column 1 nearest the age of the individual whose life measures the duration of the annuity. If the annuity is payable annually at the end of each year for a definite number of years, the amount payable annually is multiplied by the figure in column 2 of Table B opposite the number of years in column 1 representing the duration of the annuity.

The application of this paragraph (d)(2)(i) may be illustrated by the following examples:

*Example (1).* The donor assigns an annuity of $10,000 a year payable annually during the donor's life immediately after an annual payment has been made. The age of the donor on the date of assignment is 40 years and eight months. By reference to Table A, it is found that the figure in column 2 opposite 41 years is 9.1030. The value of the gift is, therefore, $91,030 ($10,000 multiplied by 9.1030).

*Example (2).* The donor was entitled to receive an annuity of $10,000 a year payable annually at the end of annual periods throughout a term of 20 years. The donor, when 15 years have elapsed, makes a gift thereof to the donor's son. By reference to Table B, it is found that the figure in column 2 opposite five years, the unexpired portion of the 20-year period, is 3.7906. The present value of the annuity is, therefore, $37,908 ($10,000 multiplied by 3.7908).

(ii) If an annuity is payable at the end of semiannual, quarterly, monthly, or weekly periods during the life of an individual (as for example if the first payment is due one month after the date of the gift), the aggregate amount to be paid within a year is first multiplied by the figure in column 2 of Table A opposite the number of years in column 1 nearest the age of the individual whose life measures the duration of the annuity. The product so obtained is then multiplied by whichever of the following factors is appropriate:

1.0244 for semiannual payments,
1.0368 for quarterly payments,
1.0450 for monthly payments,
1.0482 for weekly payments.

If the annuity is payable at the end of semiannual, quarterly, monthly, or weekly periods for a definite number of years the aggregate amount to be paid within a year is first multiplied by the figure in column 2 of Table B opposite the number of years in column 1 representing the duration of the annuity. The product so obtained is then multiplied by whichever of the above factors is appropriate. The application of this paragraph (d)(2)(ii) may be illustrated by the following example:

*Example.* The facts are the same as those contained in example (1) set forth in paragraph (d)(2)(i) above, except that the annuity is payable semiannually. The aggregate annual amount, $10,000[,] is multiplied by the factor 9.1030, and the product multiplied by 1.0244. The value of the gift is, therefore, $93,251.13 ($10,000 × 9.1030 × 1.0244).

(iii)(A) If the first payment of an annuity for the life of an individual is due at the beginning of the annual or other payment period rather than at the end (as for example if the first payment is to be made immediately after the date of the gift), the value of the annuity is the sum of (A) the first payment plus (B) the present value of a similar annuity, the first payment of which is not to be made until the end of the payment period, determined as provided in paragraphs (d)(2)(i) or (ii) of this section. The application of this paragraph (d)(2)(iii)(A) may be illustrated by the following example:

*Example.* The donee is made the beneficiary for life of an annuity of $50 a month from the income of a trust, subject to the right reserved by the donor to cause the annuity to be paid for the donor's own benefit or for the benefit of another. On the day a payment is due, the donor relinquishes the reserved power. The donee is then 50 years of age. The value of the gift is $50 plus the product of $50 × 12 × 8.4743 (see Table A) × 1.0450. That is, $50 plus $5,313.39, or $5,363.39.

(B) If the first payment of an annuity for a definite number of years is due at the beginning of the annual or other payment period, the applicable factor is the product of the factor shown in Table B multiplied by whichever of the following factors is appropriate:

1.1000 for annual payments,
1.0744 for semiannual payments,
1.0618 for quarterly payments,
1.0534 for monthly payments,or

1.0502 for weekly payments.

The application of this paragraph (d)(2)(iii)(B) may be illustrated by the following example:

*Example.* The donee is the beneficiary of an annuity of $50 a month, subject to a reserved right in the donor to cause the annuity or the cash value thereof to be paid for the donor's own benefit or the benefit of another. On the day a payment is due, the donor relinquishes the power. There are 308 payments to be made covering a period of 25 years, including the payment due. The value of the gift is the product of $50 × 12 × 9.0770 (factor for 25 years Table B) × 1.0534, or $5,737.03.

(3) *Life estates and terms for years.*—If the interest to be valued is the right of a person for his or her life, or for the life of another person, to receive the income of certain property or to use non-income-producing property, the value of the interest is the value of the property multiplied by the figure in column 3 of Table A opposite the number of years nearest to the actual age of the measuring life. If the interest to be valued is the right to receive income of property or to use non-income-producing property for a term of years, column 3 of Table B is used. The application of this paragraph (c) may be illustrated by the following example:

*Example.* The donor who during the donor's life is entitled to receive the income from property worth $50,000, makes a gift of such interest. The donor is 31 years old on the date of the gift. The value of the gift is $47,627 ($50,000 × .95254).

(4) *Remainders or reversionary interests.*—If the interest to be valued is a remainder or reversionary interest subject to a life estate, the value of the interest should be obtained by multiplying the value of the property at the date of the gift by the figure in column 4 of Table A opposite the number of years nearest the age of the life tenant. If the remainder or reversion is to take effect at the end of a term for years, column 4 of Table B should be used. The application of this paragraph (d) may be illustrated by the following example:

*Example.* The donor transfers by gift a remainder interest in property worth $50,000, subject to the donor's sister's right to receive the income therefrom for her life. The sister at the date of the gift is 31 years of age. By reference to Table A it is found that the figure in column 4 opposite age 31 is .04746. The value of the gift is, therefore, $2,373 ($50,000 × .04746).

(5) *Actuarial computations by the Internal Revenue Service.*—If the interest to be valued is dependent upon the continuation or termination of more than one life, or there is a term certain concurrent with one or more lives, or if the retained interest of the donor is conditioned upon survivorship, a special factor is necessary. The factor is to be computed on the basis of interest at the rate of 10 percent a year, compounded annually, and life contingencies are determined for each person involved from the values of *lx* that are set forth in column 2 of Table LN in §20.2031-7A(d)(6) of this chapter. Table LN contains values of *lx* taken from the life table for the total population appearing as Table 1 in United States Life Tables: 1969-71, published by the Department of Health and Human Services, Public Health Service. A copy of the publication containing many such special factors, may be purchased from the Superintendent of Documents, United States Government Printing Office, Washington, D.C. 20402. However, if a special factor is required in the case of an actual gift, the Commissioner will furnish the factor to the donor upon request. The request must be accompanied by a statement of the date of birth of each person the duration of whose life may affect the value of the interest, and by copies of the relevant instruments. Special factors are not furnished for prospective transfers.

(6) *Tables.*—(i) For actuarial factors showing the present worth at 10 percent of a single life annuity, a life interest, and a remainder interest postponed for a single life, see §20.2031-7A(d)(6) of this chapter, Table A, of the Estate Tax Regulations.

(ii) For actuarial factors showing the present worth at 10 percent of an annuity for a term certain, an income interest for a term certain, and a remainder interest postponed for a term certain, see §20.2031-7A(d)(6) of this chapter, Table B, of the Estate Tax Regulations.

(e) *Valuation of annuities, unitrust interests, interests for life or term of years, and remainder or reversionary interests transferred after April 30, 1989, and before May 1, 1999.*—(1) *In general.*—Except as otherwise provided in §§25.2512-5(b) and 25.7520-3(b) (pertaining to certain limitations on the use of prescribed tables), if the valuation date of the transferred interest is after April 30, 1989, and before May 1, 1999, the fair market value of annuities, unitrust interests, life estates, terms of years, remainders, and reversions transferred by gift is the present value of the interests determined by use of standard or special section 7520 actuarial factors and the valuation methodology described in §25.2512-5(d). Sections 20.2031-7(d)(6) and 20.2031-7A(e)(4) of this chapter and related sections provide tables with standard actuarial factors and examples that illustrate how to use the tables to compute the present value of ordinary annuity, life, and remainder interests in property. These sections also refer to standard and special actuarial factors that may be necessary to compute the present value of similar interests in more unusual fact situations. These factors and examples are also generally applicable for gift tax purposes in computing the values of taxable gifts.

(2) *Transitional rule.*—(i) If the valuation date of a transfer of an interest in property by gift is after April 30, 1989, and before June 10, 1994, a donor can rely on Notice 89-24 (1989-1 C.B. 660), or Notice 89-60 (1989-1 C.B. 700), in valuing the transferred interest. (See §601.601(d)(2)(ii) (*b*) of this chapter.)

(ii) If a donor transferred an interest in property by gift after December 31, 1988, and before May 1, 1989, retaining an interest in the same property, and after April 30, 1989, and before January 1, 1990, transferred the retained interest in property, the donor may, at the option of the donor, value the transfer of the retained interest under this paragraph (e) or paragraph (d) of this section.

(3) *Publications and actuarial computations by the Internal Revenue Service.*—Many standard actuarial factors not included in §§20.2031-7(d)(6) and 20.2031-7A(e)(4) of this chapter are included in Internal Revenue Service Publication 1457, "Actuarial Values, Alpha Volume," (8-89). Internal Revenue Service Publication 1457 also includes examples that illustrate how to compute many special factors for more unusual situations. Publication 1457 is no longer available for purchase from the Superintendent of Documents, United States Government Printing Office, Washington, DC 20402. However, pertinent factors in this publication may be obtained from: CC:DOM:CORP:R (IRS Publication 1457), room 5226, Internal Revenue Service, POB 7604, Ben Franklin Station, Washington, DC 20044. If a special factor is required in the case of a completed gift, the Internal Revenue Service may furnish the factor to the donor upon a request for a ruling. The request for a ruling must be accompanied by a recitation of the facts including a statement of the date of birth for each measuring life, the date of the gift, any other applicable dates, and a copy of the will, trust, or other relevant documents. A request for a ruling must comply with the instructions for requesting a ruling published periodically in the Internal Revenue Bulletin (see §§601.201 and 601.601(d)(2)(ii) (*b*) of this chapter) and include payment of the required user fee.

(f) *Valuation of annuities, unitrust interests, interests for life or term of years, and remainder or reversionary interests transferred after April 30, 1999, and before May 1, 2009.*—(1) *In general.*—Except as otherwise provided in §§25.2512-5(b) and 25.7520-3(b) (pertaining to certain limitations on the use of prescribed tables), if the valuation date of the transferred interest is after April 30, 1999, and before May 1, 2009, the fair market value of annuities, unitrust interests, life estates, terms of years, remainders, and reversions transferred by gift is the present value of the interests determined by use of standard or special section 7520 actuarial factors and the valuation methodology described in §25.2512-5(d). Sections 20.2031-7(d)(6) and 20.2031-7A(f)(4) and related sections provide tables with standard actuarial factors and examples that illustrate how to use the tables to compute the present value of ordinary annuity, life, and remainder interests in property. These sections also refer to standard and special actuarial factors that may be necessary to compute the present value of similar interests in more unusual fact situations. These factors and examples are also generally applicable for gift tax purposes in computing the values of taxable gifts.

(2) *Transitional rule.*—If the valuation date of a transfer of property by gift is after April 30, 1999, and before July 1, 1999, the fair market value of the interest transferred is determined by use of the section 7520 interest rate for the month in which the valuation date occurs (see §§25.7520-1(b) and 25.7520-2(a)(2) and the appropriate actuarial tables under either §20.2031-7A(e)(4) or §20.2031-7A(f)(4), at the option of the donor. However, with respect to each individual transaction and with respect to all transfers occurring on the valuation date, the donor must use the same actuarial tables (for example, gift and income tax charitable deductions with respect to the same transfer must be determined based on the same tables, and all transfers made on the same date must be valued based on the same tables).

(3) *Publications and actuarial computations by the Internal Revenue Service.*—Many standard actuarial factors not included in §§20.2031-7(d)(6) and 20.2031-7A(f)(4) are included in Internal Revenue Service Publication 1457, "Actuarial Values, Book Aleph," (7-99). Internal Revenue Service Publication 1457 also includes examples that illustrate how to compute many special factors for more unusual situations. Publication 1457 is no longer available for purchase from the Superintendent of Documents, United States Government Printing Office. However, pertinent factors in this publication may be obtained from: CC:PA:LPD:PR (IRS Publication 1457), Room 5205, Internal Revenue Service, P.O.Box 7604, Ben Franklin Station, Washington, DC 20044. If a special factor is required in the case of a completed gift, the Internal Revenue Service may furnish the factor to the donor upon a request for a ruling. The request for a ruling must be accompanied by a recitation of the facts including a statement of the date of birth for each measuring life, the date of the gift, any other applicable dates, and a copy of the will, trust, or other relevant documents. A request for a ruling must comply with the instructions for requesting a ruling published periodically in the Internal Revenue Bulletin (see §§601.201 and 601.601(d)(2)(ii) (*b*)) and include payment of the required user fee.

(4) *Effective/applicability dates.*—Paragraphs (f)(1) through (f)(3) apply after April 30, 1999, and before May 1, 2009. [Reg. §25.2512-5A.]

☐ [*T.D.* 6334, 11-14-58. *Amended by T.D.* 7955, 5-10-84, *T.D.* 8395, 1-28-92. *Reg.* §25.2512-5 *was redesignated Reg.* §25.2512-5A(d) *and amended by T.D.* 8540, 6-9-94. *Amended by T.D.* 8819, 4-29-99; *T.D.* 8886, 6-9-2000; *T.D.* 9448, 5-1-2009 *and T.D.* 9540, 8-9-2011.]

## [Reg. §25.2512-6]

**§25.2512-6. Valuation of certain life insurance and annuity contracts; valuation of shares in an open-end investment company.**—(a) *Valuation of certain life insurance and annuity contracts.*—The value of a life insurance contract or of a contract for the payment of an annuity issued by a company regularly engaged in the selling of contracts of that character is established through the sale of the particular contract by the company, or through the sale by the company of comparable contracts. As valuation of an insurance policy through sale of comparable contracts is not readily ascertainable when the gift is of a contract which has been in force for some time and on which further premium payments are to be made, the value may be approximated by adding to the interpolated terminal reserve at the date of the gift the proportionate part of the gross premium last paid before the date of the gift which covers the period extending beyond that date. If, however, because of the unusual nature of the contract such approximation is not reasonably close to the full value, this method may not be used.

The following examples, so far as relating to life insurance contracts, are of gifts of such contracts on which there are no accrued dividends or outstanding indebtedness.

*Example (1).* A donor purchases from a life insurance company for the benefit of another a life insurance contract or a contract for the payment of an annuity. The value of the gift is the cost of the contract.

*Example (2).* An annuitant purchased from a life insurance company a single payment annuity contract by the terms of which he was entitled to receive payments of $1,200 annually for the duration of his life. Five years subsequent to such purchase, and when the age of 50 years, he gratuitously assigns the contract. The value of the gift is the amount which the company would charge for an annuity contract providing for the payment of $1,200 annually for the life of a person 50 years of age.

*Example (3).* A donor owning a life insurance policy on which no further payments are to be made to the company (e.g., a single premium policy or paid-up policy) makes a gift of the contract. The value of the gift is the amount which the company would charge for a single premium contract of the same specified amount on the life of a person of the age of the insured.

*Example (4).* A gift is made four months after the last premium due date of an ordinary life insurance policy issued nine years and four months prior to the gift thereof by the insured, who was 35 years of age at date of issue. The gross annual premium is $2,811. The computation follows:

| | |
|---|---:|
| Terminal reserve at end of tenth year | $14,601.00 |
| Terminal reserve at end of ninth year | 12,965.00 |
| Increase | $1,636.00 |
| One-third of such increase (the gift having been made four months following the last preceding premium due date), is | $545.33 |
| Terminal reserve at end of ninth year | 12,965.00 |
| Interpolated terminal reserve at the date of gift | $13,510.33 |
| Two-thirds of gross premium ($2,811) | 1,874.00 |
| Value of the gift | $15,384.33 |

*Example (5).* A donor purchases from a life insurance company for $15,198 a joint and survivor annuity contract which provides for the payment of $60 a month to the donor during his lifetime, and then to his sister for such time as she may survive him. The premium which would have been charged by the company for an annuity of $60 monthly payable during the life of the donor alone is $10,690. The value of the gift is $4,508 ($15,198 less $10,690).

(b) *Valuation of shares in an open-end investment company.*—(1) The fair market value of a share in an open-end investment company (commonly known as a "mutual fund") is the public redemption price of a share. In the absence of an affirmative showing of the public redemption price in effect at the time of the gift, the last public redemption price quoted by the company for the date of the gift shall be presumed to be the applicable public redemption price. If there is no public redemption price quoted by the company for the date of the gift (e.g., the date of the gift is a Saturday, Sunday, or holiday), the fair market value of the mutual fund share is the last public redemption price quoted by the company for the first day preceding the date of the gift for which there is a quotation. As used in this paragraph the term "open-end investment company" includes only a company which on the date of the gift was engaged in offering its shares to the public in the capacity of an open-end investment company.

(2) The provisions of this paragraph shall apply with respect to gifts made after December 31, 1954. [Reg. § 25.2512-6.]

☐ [*T.D. 6334, 11-14-58. Amended by T.D. 6542, 1-19-61; T.D. 6680, 10-9-63 and T.D. 7319, 7-22-74.*]

### [Reg. § 25.2512-7]

**§ 25.2512-7. Effect of excise tax.**—If jewelry, furs or other property, the purchase of which is subject to an excise tax, is purchased at retail by a taxpayer and made the subject of gifts within a reasonable time after purchase, the purchase price, including the excise tax, is considered to be the fair market value of the property on the date of the gift, in the absence of evidence that the market price of similar articles has increased or decreased in the meantime. Under other circumstances, the excise tax is taken into account in determining the fair market value of property to the extent, and only to the extent, that it affects the price at which the property would change hands between a willing buyer and a willing seller, as provided in § 25.2512-1. [Reg. § 25.2512-7.]

☐ [*T.D. 6334, 11-14-58.*]

### [Reg. § 25.2512-8]

**§ 25.2512-8. Transfers for insufficient consideration.**—Transfers reached by the gift tax are not confined to those only which, being without a valuable consideration, accord with the common law concept of gifts, but embrace as well sales, exchanges, and other dispositions of property for a consideration to the extent that the value of the property transferred by the donor exceeds the value in money or money's worth of the consideration given therefor. However, a sale, exchange, or other transfer of property made in the ordinary course of business (a transaction which is bona fide, at arm's length, and free from any donative intent), will be considered as made for an adequate and full consideration in money or money's worth. A consideration not reducible to a value in money or money's worth, as love and affection, promise of marriage, etc., is to be wholly disregarded, and the entire value of the property transferred constitutes the amount of the gift. Similarly, a relinquishment or promised relinquishment of dower or curtesy, or of a statutory estate created in lieu of dower or curtesy, or of other marital rights in the spouse's property or estate, shall not be considered to any extent a consideration "in money or money's worth." See, however, section 2516 and the regulations thereunder with respect to certain transfers incident to a divorce. See also sections 2701, 2702, 2703 and 2704 and the regulations at §§ 25.2701-0 through 25.2704-3 for special rules for valuing transfers of business interests, transfers in trust, and transfers pursuant to options and purchase agreements. [Reg. § 25.2512-8.]

☐ [*T.D. 6334, 11-14-58. Amended by T.D. 8395, 1-28-92.*]

### [Reg. § 25.2513-1]

**§ 25.2513-1. Gifts by husband or wife to third party considered as made one-half by each.**—(a) A gift made by one spouse to a person other than his (or her) spouse may, for the purpose of the gift tax, be considered as made one-half by him and one-half by his spouse, but only if at the time of the gift each spouse was a citizen or resident of the United States. For purposes of this section, an individual is to be considered as the spouse of another individual only if he was married to such individual at the time of the gift and does not remarry during the remainder of the "calendar period" (as defined in § 25.2502-1(c)(1)).

(b) The provisions of this section will apply to gifts made during a particular "calendar period" (as defined in § 25.2502-1(c)(1)) only if both spouses signify their consent to treat all gifts made to third parties during that calendar period by both spouses while married to each other as having been made one-half by each spouse. As to the manner and time for signifying consent, see § 25.2513-2. Such consent, if signified with respect to any calendar period, is effective with respect to all gifts made to third parties during such calendar period except as follows:

(1) If the consenting spouses were not married to each other during a portion of the calendar period, the consent is not effective with respect to any gifts made during such portion of the calendar period. Where the consent is signified by an executor or administrator of a deceased spouse, the consent is not effective with respect to gifts made by the surviving spouse during the portion of the calendar period that his spouse was deceased.

(2) If either spouse was a nonresident not a citizen of the United States during any portion of the calendar period, the consent is not effective with respect to any gift made during that portion of the calendar year.

(3) The consent is not effective with respect to a gift by one spouse of a property interest over which he created in his spouse a general power of appointment (as defined in section 2514(c)).

(4) If one spouse transferred property in part to his spouse and in part to third parties, the consent is effective with respect to the interest transferred to third parties only insofar as such interest is ascertainable at the time of the gift and hence severable from the interest transferred to his spouse. See § 25.2512-5 for the principles to be applied in the valuation of annuities, life estates, terms for years, remainders and reversions.

(5) The consent applies alike to gifts made by one spouse alone and to gifts made partly by each spouse, provided such gifts were to third parties and do not fall within any of the exceptions set forth in subparagraphs (1) through (4) of this paragraph. The consent may not be applied only to a portion of the property interest constituting such gifts. For example, a wife may not treat gifts made by her spouse from his separate property to third parties as having been made one-half by her if her spouse does not consent to treat gifts made by her to third parties during the same calendar period as having been made one-half by him. If the consent is effectively signified on either the husband's return or the wife's return, all gifts made by the spouses to third parties (except as described in subparagraphs (1) through (4) of this paragraph), during the calendar period will be treated as having been made one-half by each spouse.

(c) If a husband and wife consent to have the gifts made to third party donees considered as made one-half by each spouse, and only one spouse makes gifts during the "calendar period" (as defined in § 25.2502-1(c)(1)), the other spouse is not required to file a gift tax return provided: (1) The total value of the gifts made to each third party donee since the beginning of the calendar year is not in excess of $20,000 ($6,000 for calendar years prior to 1982), and (2) no portion of the property transferred constitutes a gift of a future interest. If a transfer made by either spouse during the calendar period to a third party represents a gift of a future interest in property and the spouses consent to have the gifts considered as made one-half by each, a gift tax return for such calendar period must be filed by each spouse regardless of the value of the transfer. (See § 25.2503-3 for the definition of a future interest.)

(d) The following examples illustrate the application of this section relative to the requirements for the filing of a return, assuming that a consent was effectively signified:

(1) A husband made gifts valued at $7,000 during the second quarter of 1971 to a third party and his wife made no gifts during this time. Each spouse is required to file a return for the second calendar quarter of 1971.

(2) A husband made gifts valued at $5,000 to each of two third parties during the year 1970 and his wife made no gifts. Only the husband is required to file a return. (See § 25.6019-2.)

(3) During the third quarter of 1971, a husband made gifts valued at $5,000 to a third party, and his wife made gifts valued at $2,000 to the same third party. Each spouse is required to file a return for the third calendar quarter of 1971.

(4) A husband made gifts valued at $5,000 to a third party and his wife made gifts valued at $3,000 to another third party during the year 1970. Only the husband is required to file a return for the calendar year 1970. (See § 25.6019-2.)

(5) A husband made gifts valued at $2,000 during the first quarter of 1971 to third parties which represented gifts of future interests in property (see § 25.2503-3), and his wife made no gifts during such calendar quarter. Each spouse is required to file a return for the first calendar quarter of 1971. [Reg. § 25.2513-1.]

☐ *[T.D. 6334, 11-14-58. Amended by T.D. 7238, 12-28-72 and T.D. 7910, 9-6-83.]*

### [Reg. §25.2513-2]

**§25.2513-2. Manner and time of signifying consent.—** (a)(1) Consent to the application of the provisions of section 2513 with respect to a "calendar period" (as defined in §25.2502-1(c)(1)) shall, in order to be effective, be signified by both spouses. If both spouses file gift tax returns within the time for signifying consent, it is sufficient if—

(i) The consent of the husband is signified on the wife's return, and the consent of the wife is signified on the husband's return;

(ii) The consent of each spouse is signified on his own return; or

(iii) The consent of both spouses is signified on one of the returns.

If only one spouse files a gift tax return within the time provided for signifying consent, the consent of both spouses shall be signified on that return. However, wherever possible, the notice of the consent is to be shown on both returns and it is preferred that the notice be executed in the manner described in subdivision (i) of this subparagraph. The consent may be revoked only as provided in §25.2513-3. If one spouse files more than one gift tax return for a calendar period on or before the due date of the return, the last return so filed shall, for the purpose of determining whether a consent has been signified, be considered as the return. (See §§25.6075-1 and 25.6075-2 for the due date of a gift tax return.)

(2) For gifts made after December 31, 1970, and before January 1, 1982, subject to the limitations of paragraph (b) of this section, the consent signified on a return filed for a calendar quarter will be effective for a previous calendar quarter of the same calendar year for which no return was filed because the gifts made during such previous calendar quarter did not exceed the annual exclusion provided by section 2503(b), if the gifts in such previous calendar quarter are listed on that return. Thus, for example, if A gave $2,000 to his son in the first quarter of 1972 (and filed no return because of section 2503(b)) and gave a further $4,000 to such son in the last quarter of the year, A and his spouse could signify consent to the application of section 2513 on the return filed for the fourth quarter and have it apply to the first quarter as well, provided that the $2,000 gift is listed on such return.

(b)(1) With respect to gifts made after December 31, 1981, or before January 1, 1971, the consent may be signified at any time following the close of the calendar year, subject to the following limitations:

(i) The consent may not be signified after the 15th day of April following the close of the calendar year, unless before such 15th day, no return has been filed for the year by either spouse, in which case the consent may not be signified after a return for the year is filed by either spouse; and

(ii) The consent may not be signified for a calendar year after a notice of deficiency in gift tax for that year has been sent to either spouse in accordance with section 6212(a).

(2) With respect to gifts made after December 31, 1970 and before January 1, 1982, the consent may be signified at any time following the close of the calendar quarter in which the gift was made, subject to the following limitations:

(i) The consent may not be signified after the 15th day of the second month following the close of the calendar quarter, unless before such 15th day, no return has been filed for such quarter by either spouse, in which case the consent may not be signified after a return for such calendar quarter is filed by either spouse; and

(ii) The consent may not be signified after a notice of deficiency with respect to the tax for such calendar quarter has been sent to either spouse in accordance with section 6212(a).

(c) The executor or administrator of a deceased spouse, or the guardian or committee of a legally incompetent spouse, as the case may be, may signify the consent.

(d) If the donor and spouse consent to the application of section 2513, the return or returns for the "calendar period" [as defined in §25.2502-1(c)(1)]must set forth, to the extent provided thereon, information relative to the transfers made by each spouse. [Reg. §25.2513-2.]

☐ *[T.D. 6334, 11-14-58. Amended by T.D. 7238, 12-28-72 and T.D. 7910, 9-6-83.]*

### [Reg. §25.2513-3]

**§25.2513-3. Revocation of consent.—**(a)(1) With respect to gifts made after December 31, 1981, or before January 1, 1971, if the consent to the application of the provisions of section 2513 for a calendar year was effectively signified on or before the 15th day of April following the close of the calendar year, either spouse may revoke the consent by filing in duplicate a signed statement of

revocation, but only if the statement is filed on or before such 15th day of April. Therefore, a consent that was not effectively signified until after the 15th day of April following the close of the calendar year to which it applies may not be revoked.

(2) With respect to gifts made after December 31, 1970, and before January 1, 1982, if the consent to the application of the provisions of section 2513 for a calendar quarter was effectively signified on or before the 15th day of the second month following the close of such calendar quarter, either spouse may revoke the consent by filing in duplicate a signed statement of revocation, but only if the statement is filed on or before such 15th day of the second month following the close of such calendar quarter. Therefore, a consent that was not effectively signified until after the 15th day of the second month following the close of the calendar quarter to which it applies may not be revoked.

(b) Except as provided in paragraph (b) of §301.6091-1 of this chapter (relating to hand-carried documents), the statement referred to in paragraph (a) of this section shall be filed with the internal revenue officer with whom the gift tax return is required to be filed, or with whom the gift tax return would be required to be filed if a return were required. [Reg. §25.2513-3.]

☐ *[T.D. 6334, 11-14-58. Amended by T.D. 7012, 5-14-64; T.D. 7238, 12-28-72 and T.D. 7910, 9-6-83.]*

### [Reg. §25.2513-4]

**§25.2513-4. Joint and several liability for tax.—**If consent to the application of the provisions of section 2513 is signified as provided in §25.2513-2, and not revoked as provided in §25.2513-3, the liability with respect to the entire gift tax of each spouse for such "calendar period" (as defined in §25.2502-1(c)(1)) is joint and several. See paragraph (d) of §25.2511-1. [Reg. §25.2513-4.]

☐ *[T.D. 6334, 11-14-58. Amended by T.D. 7238, 12-28-72 and T.D. 7910, 9-6-83.]*

### [Reg. §25.2514-1]

**§25.2514-1. Transfers under power of appointment.—** (a) *Introductory.*—(1) Section 2514 treats the exercise of a general power of appointment created on or before October 21, 1942, as a transfer of property for purposes of the gift tax. The section also treats as a transfer of property the exercise or complete release of a general power of appointment created after October 21, 1942, and under certain circumstances the exercise of a power of appointment (not a general power of appointment) created after October 21, 1942, by the creation of another power of appointment. See paragraph (d) of §25.2514-3. Under certain circumstances, also, the failure to exercise a power of appointment created after October 21, 1942, within a specified time, so that the power lapses, constitutes a transfer of property. Paragraphs (b) through (e) of this section contain definitions of certain terms used in §§25.2514-2 and 25.2514-3. See §25.2514-2 for specific rules applicable to certain powers created on or before October 21, 1942. See §25.2514-3 for specific rules applicable to powers created after October 21, 1942.

(b) *Definition of "power of appointment".*—(1) *In general.*—The term "power of appointment" includes all powers which are in substance and effect powers of appointment received by the donee of the power from another person, regardless of the nomenclature used in creating the power and regardless of local property law connotations. For example, if a trust instrument provides that the beneficiary may appropriate or consume the principal of the trust, the power to consume or appropriate is a power of appointment. Similarly, a power given to a donee to affect the beneficial enjoyment of a trust property or its income by altering, amending or revoking the trust instrument or terminating the trust is a power of appointment. A power in a donee to remove or discharge a trustee and appoint himself may be a power of appointment. For example, if under the terms of a trust instrument, the trustee or his successor has the power to appoint the principal of the trust for the benefit of individuals including himself, and A, another person, has the unrestricted power to remove or discharge the trustee at any time and appoint any other person including himself, A is considered as having a power of appointment. However, he would not be considered to have a power of appointment if he only had the power to appoint a successor, including himself, under limited conditions which did not exist at the time of exercise, release or lapse of the trustee's power, without an accompanying unrestricted power of removal. Similarly, a power to amend only the administrative provisions of a trust instrument, which cannot substantially affect the beneficial enjoyment of the trust property or income, is not a power of appointment. The mere power of management, investment, custody of assets, or the power to allocate receipts and disbursements as between income and principal, exercisable in a fiduciary capacity, whereby the holder has no power to enlarge or shift any of the beneficial interests therein except as an incidental consequence of the discharge of such fiduciary duties is not a power of appointment. Further, the right in a beneficiary of a trust to assent to a periodic accounting, thereby relieving the trustee from further accountability, is not a power of appointment if the right of assent does not consist of any power or right to enlarge or shift the beneficial interest of any beneficiary therein.

(2) *Relation to other sections.*—For purposes of §§25.2514-1 through 25.2514-3, the term "power of appointment" does not include powers reserved by a donor to himself. No provision of section 2514 or of §§25.2514-1 through 25.2514-3 is to be construed as in any way limiting the application of any other section of the Internal Revenue Code or of these regulations. The power of the owner of a property interest already possessed by him to dispose of his interest, and nothing more, is not a power of appointment, and the interest is includible in the amount of his gifts to the extent it would be includible under section 2511 or other provisions of the Internal Revenue Code. For example, if a trust created by S provides for payment of the income to A for life with power in A to appoint the entire trust property by deed during her lifetime to a class consisting of her children, and a further power to dispose of the entire corpus by will to anyone, including her estate, and A exercises the inter vivos power in favor of her children, she has necessarily made a transfer of her income interest which constitutes a taxable gift under section 2511(a), without regard to section 2514. This transfer also results in a relinquishment of her general power to appoint by will, which constitutes a transfer under section 2514 if the power was created after October 21, 1942.

(3) *Powers over a portion of property.*—If a power of appointment exists as to part of an entire group of assets or only over a limited interest in property, section 2514 applies only to such part or interest.

(c) *Definition of "general power of appointment".*—(1) *In general.*— The term "general power of appointment" as defined in section 2514(c) means any power of appointment exercisable in favor of the person possessing the power (referred to as the "possessor"), his estate, his creditors, or the creditors of his estate, except (i) joint powers, to the extent provided in §§25.2514-2 and 25.2514-3 and (ii) certain powers limited by an ascertainable standard, to the extent provided in subparagraph (2) of this paragraph. A power of appointment exercisable to meet the estate tax, or any other taxes, debts, or charges which are enforceable against the possessor or his estate, is included within the meaning of a power of appointment exercisable in favor of the possessor, his estate, his creditors, or the creditors of his estate. A power of appointment exercisable for the purpose of discharging a legal obligation of the possessor for his pecuniary benefit is considered a power of appointment exercisable in favor of the possessor or his creditors. However, for purposes of §§25.2514-1 through 25.2514-3, a power of appointment not otherwise considered to be a general power of appointment is not treated as a general power of appointment merely by reason of the fact that an appointee may, in fact, be a creditor of the possessor or his estate. A power of appointment is not a general power if by its terms it is either—

(a) Exercisable only in favor of one or more designated persons or classes other than the possessor or his creditors, or the possessor's estate or the creditors of his estate, or

(b) Expressly not exercisable in favor of the possessor or his creditors, the possessor's estate or the creditors of his estate.

A beneficiary may have two powers under the same instrument, one of which is a general power of appointment and the other of which is not. For example, a beneficiary may have a general power to withdraw a limited portion of trust corpus during his life, and a further power exercisable during his lifetime to appoint the corpus among his children. The latter power is not a general power of appointment (but its exercise may result in the exercise of the former power; see paragraph (d) of this section).

(2) *Powers limited by an ascertainable standard.*—A power to consume, invade, or appropriate income or corpus, or both, for the benefit of the possessor which is limited by an ascertainable standard relating to the health, education, support, or maintenance of the possessor is, by reason of section 2514(c)(1), not a general power of appointment. A power is limited by such a standard if the extent of the possessor's duty to exercise and not to exercise the power is reasonably measurable in terms of his needs for health, education, or support (or any combination of them). As used in this subparagraph, the words "support" and "maintenance" are synonymous and their meaning is not limited to the bare necessities of life. A power to use property for the comfort, welfare, or happiness of the holder of the power is not limited by the requisite standard. Examples of powers which are limited by the requisite standard are powers exercisable for the holder's "support," "support in reasonable comfort," "maintenance in health and reasonable comfort," "support in his accustomed manner of living," "education, including college and professional education," "health," and "medical, dental, hospital and nursing expenses and expenses of invalidism." In determining whether a

power is limited by an ascertainable standard, it is immaterial whether the beneficiary is required to exhaust his other income before the power can be exercised.

(3) *Certain powers under wills of decedents dying between January 1 and April 2, 1948.*—Section 210 of the Technical Changes Act of 1953 provides that if a decedent died after December 31, 1947, but before April 3, 1948, certain property interests described therein may, if the decedent's surviving spouse so elects, be accorded special treatment in the determination of the marital deduction to be allowed the decedent's estate under the provisions of section 812(e) of the Internal Revenue Code of 1939. See paragraph (h) of §81.47a of Regulations 105 (26 CFR (1939) 81.47a(h)). The section further provides that property affected by the election shall be considered property with respect to which the surviving spouse has a general power of appointment. Therefore, notwithstanding any other provision of law or of §§25.2514-1 through 25.2514-3, if the surviving spouse has made an election under section 210 of the Technical Changes Act of 1953, the property which was the subject of the election shall be considered as property with respect to which she has a general power of appointment created after October 21, 1942, exercisable by deed or will, to the extent it was treated as an interest passing to the surviving spouse and not passing to any other person for the purpose of the marital deduction in the prior decedent's estate.

(d) *Definition of "exercise".*—Whether a power of appointment is in fact exercised may depend upon local law. However, regardless of local law, a power of appointment is considered as exercised for purposes of section 2514 even though the exercise is in favor of the taker in default of appointment, and irrespective of whether the appointed interest and the interest in default of appointment are identical or whether the appointee renounces any right to take under the appointment. A power of appointment is also considered as exercised even though the disposition cannot take effect until the occurrence of an event after the exercise takes place, if the exercise is irrevocable and, as of the time of the exercise, the condition was not impossible of occurrence. For example, if property is left in trust to A for life, with a power in A to appoint the remainder by an instrument filed with the trustee during his life, and A exercises his power by appointing the remainder to B in the event that B survives A, A is considered to have exercised his power if the exercise was irrevocable. Furthermore, if a person holds both a presently exercisable general power of appointment and a presently exercisable nongeneral power of appointment over the same property, the exercise of the nongeneral power is considered the exercise of the general power only to the extent that immediately after the exercise of the nongeneral power the amount of money or property subject to being transferred by the exercise of the general power is decreased. For example, assume A has a noncumulative annual power to withdraw the greater of $5,000 or 5 percent of the value of a trust having a value of $300,000 and a lifetime nongeneral power to appoint all or a portion of the trust corpus to A's child or grandchildren. If A exercises the nongeneral power by appointing $150,000 to A's child, the exercise of the nongeneral power is treated as the exercise of the general power to the extent of $7,500 (maximum exercise of general power before the exercise of the nongeneral power, 5% of $300,000 or $15,000, less maximum exercise of the general power after the exercise of the nongeneral power, 5% of $150,000 or $7,500).

(e) *Time of creation of power.*—A power of appointment created by will is, in general, considered as created on the date of the testator's death. However, section 2514(f) provides that a power of appointment created by a will executed on or before October 21, 1942, is considered a power created on or before that date if the testator dies before July 1, 1949, without having republished the will, by codicil or otherwise, after October 21, 1942. A power of appointment created by an inter vivos instrument is considered as created on the date the instrument takes effect. Such a power is not considered as created at some future date merely because it is not exercisable on the date the instrument takes effect, or because it is revocable, or because the identity of its holders is not ascertainable until after the date the instrument takes effect. However, if the holder of a power exercises it by creating a second power, the second power is considered as created at the time of the exercise of the first. The application of this paragraph may be illustrated by the following examples:

*Example (1).* A created a revocable trust before October 22, 1942, providing for payment of income to B for life with remainder as B shall appoint by deed or will. Even though A dies after October 21, 1942, without having exercised his power of revocation, B's power of appointment is considered a power created before October 22, 1942.

*Example (2).* C created an irrevocable inter vivos trust before October 22, 1942, naming T as trustee and providing for payment of income to D for life with remainder to E. T was given the power to pay corpus to D and the power to appoint a successor trustee. If T resigns after October 21, 1942, and appoints D as successor trustee, D is considered to have a power of appointment created before October 22, 1942.

*Example (3).* F created an irrevocable inter vivos trust before October 22, 1942, providing for payment of income to G for life with remainder as G shall appoint by deed or will, but in default of appointment income to H for life with remainder as H shall appoint by deed or will. If G died after October 21, 1942, without having exercised his power of appointment, H's power of appointment is considered a power created before October 22, 1942, even though it was only a contingent interest until G's death.

*Example (4).* If in example (3) above G had exercised by will his power of appointment, by creating a similar power in J, J's power of appointment would be considered a power created after October 21, 1942. [Reg. § 25.2514-1.]

☐ [*T.D. 6334, 11-14-58. Amended by T.D. 6582, 12-11-61 and T.D. 7757, 1-16-81.*]

### [Reg. § 25.2514-2]

**§ 25.2514-2. Powers of appointment created on or before October 21, 1942.**—(a) *In general.*—The exercise of a general power of appointment created on or before October 21, 1942, is deemed to be a transfer of property by the individual possessing the power.

(b) *Joint powers created on or before October 21, 1942.*—Section 2514(c)(2) provides that a power created on or before October 21, 1942, which at the time of the exercise is not exercisable by the possessor except in conjunction with another person, is not deemed a general power of appointment.

(c) *Release or lapse.*—A failure to exercise a general power of appointment created on or before October 21, 1942, or a complete release of such a power is not considered to be an exercise of a general power of appointment. The phrase "a complete release" means a release of all powers over all or a portion of the property subject to a power of appointment, as distinguished from the reduction of a power of appointment to a lesser power. Thus, if the possessor completely relinquished all powers over one-half of the property subject to a power of appointment, the power is completely released as to that one-half. If at or before the time a power of appointment is relinquished, the holder of the power exercises the power in such a manner or to such an extent that the relinquishment results in the reduction, enlargement, or shift in a beneficial interest in property, the relinquishment will be considered to be an exercise and not a release of the power. For example, assume that A created a trust in 1940 providing for payment of the income to B for life with the power in B to amend the trust, and for payment of the remainder to such persons as B shall appoint or, upon default of appointment, to C. If B amended the trust in 1948 by providing that upon his death the remainder was to be paid to D, and if he further amended the trust in 1955 by deleting his power to amend the trust, such relinquishment will be considered an exercise and not a release of a general power of appointment. On the other hand, if the 1948 amendment became ineffective before or at the time of the 1955 amendment, or if B in 1948 merely amended the trust by changing the purely ministerial powers of the trustee, his relinquishment of the power in 1955 will be considered as release of a power of appointment.

(d) *Partial release.*—If a general power of appointment created on or before October 21, 1942, is partially released so that it is not thereafter a general power of appointment, a subsequent exercise of the partially released power is not an exercise of a general power of appointment if the partial release occurs before whichever is the later of the following dates:

(1) November 1, 1951; or

(2) If the possessor was under a legal disability to release the power on October 21, 1942, the day after the expiration of 6 months following the termination of such legal disability.

However, if a general power created on or before October 21, 1942, is partially released on or after the later of those dates, a subsequent exercise of the power will constitute an exercise of a general power of appointment. The legal disability referred to in this paragraph is determined under local law and may include the disability of an insane person, a minor, or an unborn child. The fact that the type of general power of appointment possessed by the holder actually was not generally releasable under the local law does not place the holder under a legal disability within the meaning of this paragraph. In general, however, it is assumed that all general powers of appointment are releasable, unless the local law on the subject is to the contrary, and it is presumed that the method employed to release the power is effective, unless it is not in accordance with the local law relating specifically to releases or, in the absence of such local law, is not in accordance with the local law relating to similar transactions.

(e) *Partial exercise.*—If a general power of appointment created on or before October 21, 1942, is exercised only as to a portion of the property subject to the power, the exercise is considered to be a transfer only as to the value of that portion. [Reg. § 25.2514-2.]

☐ [*T.D. 6334, 11-14-58.*]

### [Reg. § 25.2514-3]

**§ 25.2514-3. Powers of appointment created after October 21, 1942.**—(a) *In general.*—The exercise, release, or lapse (except as provided in paragraph (c) of this section) of a general power of appointment created after October 21, 1942, is deemed to be a transfer of property by the individual possessing the power. The exercise of a power of appointment that is not a general power is considered to be a transfer if it is exercised to create a further power under certain circumstances (see paragraph (d) of this section). See paragraph (c) of § 25.2514-1 for the definition of various terms used in this section. See paragraph (b) of this section for the rules applicable to determine the extent to which joint powers created after October 21, 1942, are to be treated as general powers of appointment.

(b) *Joint powers created after October 21, 1942.*—The treatment of a power of appointment created after October 21, 1942, which is exercisable only in conjunction with another person, is governed by section 2514(c)(3), which provides as follows:

(1) Such a power is not considered as a general power of appointment if it is not exercisable by the possessor except with the consent or joinder of the creator of the power.

(2) Such power is not considered as a general power of appointment if it is not exercisable by the possessor except with the consent or joinder of a person having a substantial interest in the property subject to the power which is adverse to the exercise of the power in favor of the possessor, his estate, his creditors, or the creditors of his estate. An interest adverse to the exercise of a power is considered as substantial if its value in relation to the total value of the property subject to the power is not insignificant. For this purpose, the interest is to be valued in accordance with the actuarial principles set forth in § 25.2512-5 or, if it is not susceptible to valuation under those provisions, in accordance with the general principles set forth in § 25.2512-1. A taker in default of appointment under a power has an interest which is adverse to an exercise of the power. A coholder of the power has no adverse interest merely because of his joint possession of the power nor merely because he is a permissible appointee under a power. However, a coholder of a power is considered as having an adverse interest where he may possess the power after the possessor's death and may exercise it at that time in favor of himself, his estate, his creditors, or the creditors of his estate. Thus, for example, if X, Y, and Z held a power jointly to appoint among a group of persons which includes themselves and if on the death of X the power will pass to Y and Z jointly, then Y and Z are considered to have interests adverse to the exercise of the power in favor of X. Similarly, if on Y's death the power will pass to Z, Z is considered to have an interest adverse to the exercise of the power in favor of Y. The application of this subparagraph may be further illustrated by the following examples in each of which it is assumed that the value of the interest in question is substantial:

*Example (1).* The taxpayer and R are trustees of a trust under which the income is to be paid to the taxpayer for life and then to M for life, and R is remainderman. The trustees have power to distribute corpus to the taxpayer. Since R's interest is substantially adverse to an exercise of the power in favor of the taxpayer, the latter does not have a general power of appointment. If M and the taxpayer were trustees, M's interest would likewise be adverse.

*Example (2).* The taxpayer and L are trustees of a trust under which the income is to be paid to L for life and then to M for life, and the taxpayer is remainderman. The trustees have power to distribute corpus to the taxpayer during L's life. Since L's interest is adverse to an exercise of the power in favor of the taxpayer, the taxpayer does not have a general power of appointment. If the taxpayer and M were trustees, M's interest would likewise be adverse.

*Example (3).* The taxpayer and L are trustees of a trust under which the income is to be paid to L for life. The trustees can designate whether corpus is to be distributed to the taxpayer or to A after L's death. L's interest is not adverse to an exercise of the power in favor of the taxpayer, and the taxpayer therefore has a general power of appointment.

(3) A power which is exercisable only in conjunction with another person, and which after application of the rules set forth in subparagraphs (1) and (2) of this paragraph, constitutes a general power of appointment, will be treated as though the holders of the power who are permissible appointees of the property were joint owners of property subject to the power. The possessor, under this rule, will be treated as possessed of a general power of appointment over an aliquot share of the property to be determined with reference to the number of joint holders, including the possessor, who (or whose estates or creditors) are permissible appointees. Thus, for example, if X, Y, and Z hold an unlimited power jointly to appoint

among a group of persons, including themselves, but on the death of X the power does not pass to Y and Z jointly, then Y and Z are not considered to have interests adverse to the exercise of the power in favor of X. In this case, X is considered to possess a general power of appointment as to one-third of the property subject to the power.

(c) *Partial releases, lapses and disclaimers of general powers of appointment created after October 21, 1942.*—(1) *Partial release of power.*—The general principles set forth in § 25.2511-2 for determining whether a donor of property (or of a property right or interest) has divested himself of all or any portion of his interest therein to the extent necessary to effect a completed gift are applicable in determining whether a partial release of a power of appointment constitutes a taxable gift. Thus, if a general power of appointment is partially released so that thereafter the donor may still appoint among a limited class of persons not including himself the partial release does not effect a complete gift, since the possessor of the power has retained the right to designate the ultimate beneficiaries of the property over which he holds the power and since it is only the termination of such control which completes a gift.

(2) *Power partially released before June 1, 1951.*—If a general power of appointment created after October 21, 1942, was partially released prior to June 1, 1951, so that it no longer represented a general power of appointment, as defined in paragraph (c) of § 25.2514-1, the subsequent exercise, release, or lapse of the partially released power at any time thereafter will not constitute the exercise or release of a general power of appointment. For example, assume that A created a trust in 1943 under which B possessed a general power of appointment. By an instrument executed in 1948 such general power of appointment was reduced in scope by B to an excepted power. The inter vivos exercise in 1955, or in any "calendar period" (as defined in § 25.2502-1(c)(1)) thereafter, of such excepted power is not considered an exercise or release of a general power of appointment for purposes of the gift tax.

(3) *Power partially released after May 31, 1951.*—If a general power of appointment created after October 21, 1942, was partially released after May 31, 1951, the subsequent exercise, release or a lapse of the power at any time thereafter, will constitute the exercise or release of a general power of appointment for gift tax purposes.

(4) *Release or lapse of power.*—A release of a power of appointment need not be formal or express in character. For example, the failure to exercise a general power of appointment created after October 21, 1942, within a specified time so that the power lapses, constitutes a release of the power. In any case where the possessor of a general power of appointment is incapable of validly exercising or releasing a power, by reason of minority, or otherwise, and the power may not be validly exercised or released on his behalf, the failure to exercise or release the power is not a lapse of the power. If a trustee has in his capacity as trustee a power which is considered as a general power of appointment, his resignation or removal as trustee will cause a lapse of his power. However, section 2514(e) provides that a lapse during any calendar year is considered as a release so as to be subject to the gift tax only to the extent that the property which could have been appointed by exercise of the lapsed power of appointment exceeds the greater of (i) $5,000, or (ii) 5 percent of the aggregate value, at the time of the lapse, of the assets out of which, or the proceeds of which, the exercise of the lapsed power could be satisfied. For example, if an individual has a noncumulative right to withdraw $10,000 a year from the principal of a trust fund, the failure to exercise this right of withdrawal in a particular year will not constitute a gift if the fund at the end of the year equals or exceeds $200,000. If, however, at the end of the particular year the fund should be worth only $100,000, the failure to exercise the power will be considered a gift to the extent of $5,000, the excess of $10,000 over 5 percent of a fund of $100,000. Where the failure to exercise the power, such as the right of withdrawal, occurs in more than a single year, the value of the taxable transfer will be determined separately for each year.

(5) *Disclaimer of power created after December 31, 1976.*—A disclaimer or renunciation of a general power of appointment created in a transfer made after December 31, 1976, is not considered a release of the power for gift tax purposes if the disclaimer or renunciation is a qualified disclaimer as described in section 2518 and the corresponding regulations. For rules relating to when a transfer creating the power occurs, see § 25.2518-2(c)(3). If the disclaimer or renunciation is not a qualified disclaimer, it is considered a release of the power.

(6) *Disclaimer of power created before January 1, 1977.*—A disclaimer or renunciation of a general power of appointment created in a taxable transfer before January 1, 1977, in the person disclaiming is not considered a release of the power. The disclaimer or renunciation must be unequivocal and effective under local law. A disclaimer is a

complete and unqualified refusal to accept the rights to which one is entitled. There can be no disclaimer or renunciation of a power after its acceptance. In the absence of facts to the contrary, the failure to renounce or disclaim within a reasonable time after learning of the existence of a power shall be presumed to constitute an acceptance of the power. In any case where a power is purported to be disclaimed or renounced as to only a portion of the property subject to the power, the determination as to whether there has been a complete and unqualified refusal to accept the rights to which one is entitled will depend on all the facts and circumstances of the particular case, taking into account the recognition and effectiveness of such a disclaimer under local law. Such rights refer to the incidents of the power and not to other interests of the possessor of the power in the property. If effective under local law, the power may be disclaimed or renounced without disclaiming or renouncing such other interests.

(7) The first and second sentences of paragraph (c)(5) of this section are applicable for transfers creating the power to be disclaimed made on or after December 31, 1997.

(d) *Creation of another power in certain cases.*—Paragraph (d) of section 2514 provides that there is a transfer for purposes of the gift tax of the value of property (or of property rights or interests) with respect to which a power of appointment, which is not a general power of appointment, created after October 21, 1942, is exercised by creating another power of appointment, which under the terms of the instruments creating and exercising the first power and under applicable local law, can be validly exercised so as to (1) postpone the vesting of any estate or interest in the property for a period ascertainable without regard to the date of the creation of the first power, or (2) (if the applicable rule against perpetuities is stated in terms of suspension of ownership or of the power of alienation, rather than of vesting) suspend the absolute ownership or the power of alienation of the property for a period ascertainable without regard to the date of the creation of the first power. For the purpose of section 2514(d), the value of the property subject to the second power of appointment is considered to be its value unreduced by any precedent or subsequent interest which is not subject to the second power. Thus, if a donor has a power to appoint $100,000 among a group consisting of his children or grandchildren and during his lifetime exercises the power by making an outright appointment of $75,000 and by giving one appointee a power to appoint $25,000, no more than $25,000 will be considered a gift under section 2514(d). If, however, the donor appoints the income from the entire fund to a beneficiary for life with power in the beneficiary to appoint the remainder, the entire $100,000 will be considered a gift under section 2514(d), if the exercise of the second power can validly postpone the vesting of any estate or interest in the property or can suspend the absolute ownership or power of alienation of the property for a period ascertainable without regard to the date of the creation of the first power.

(e) *Examples.*—The application of this section may be further illustrated by the following examples in each of which it is assumed, unless otherwise stated, that S has transferred property in trust after October 21, 1942, with the remainder payable to R at L's death, and that neither L nor R has any interest in or power over the enjoyment of the trust property except as is indicated separately in each example:

*Example (1).* The income is payable to L for life. L has the power to cause the income to be paid to R. The exercise of the right constitutes the making of a transfer of property under section 2511. L's power does not constitute a power of appointment since it is only a power to dispose of his income interest, a right otherwise possessed by him.

*Example (2).* The income is to be accumulated during L's life. L has the power to have the income distributed to himself. If L's power is limited by an ascertainable standard (relating to health, etc.) as defined in paragraph (c)(2) of § 25.2514-1, the lapse of such power will not constitute a transfer of property for gift tax purposes. If L's power is not so limited, its lapse or release during L's lifetime may constitute a transfer of property for gift tax purposes. See especially paragraph (c)(4) of § 25.2514-3.

*Example (3).* The income is to be paid to L for life. L has a power, exercisable at any time, to cause corpus to be distributed to himself. L has a general power of appointment over the remainder interest, the release of which constitutes a transfer for gift tax purposes of the remainder interest. If in this example L had a power to cause the corpus to be distributed only to X, L would have a power of appointment which is not a general power of appointment, the exercise or release of which would not constitute a transfer of property for purposes of the gift tax. Although the exercise or release of the nongeneral power is not taxable under this section, see § 25.2514-1(b)(2) for the gift tax consequences of the transfer of the life income interest.

*Example (4).* The income is payable to L for life. R has the right to cause the corpus to be distributed to L at any time. R's power is not a power of appointment, but merely a right to dispose of his remainder

Reg. § 25.2514-3(e)

interest, a right already possessed by him. In such a case, the exercise of the right constitutes the making of a transfer of property under section 2511 of the value, if any, of his remainder interest. See paragraph (e) of § 25.2511-1.

*Example (5).* The income is to be paid to L. R has the right to appoint the corpus to himself at any time. R's general power of appointment over the corpus includes a general power to dispose of L's income interest therein. The lapse or release of R's general power over the income interest during his life may constitute the making of a transfer of property. See especially paragraph (c)(4) of § 25.2514-3. [Reg. § 25.2514-3.]

☐ [*T.D.* 6334, 11-14-68. *Amended by T.D.* 7238, 12-28-72, *T.D.* 7776, 5-20-81; *T.D.* 7910, 9-6-83; *T.D.* 8095, 8-6-86 *and T.D.* 8744, 12-30-97.]

**[Reg. § 25.2515-1]**

**§ 25.2515-1. Tenancies by the entirety; in general.**—(a) *Scope.*—(1) *In general.*—This section and § § 25.2515-2 through 25.2515-4 do not apply to the creation of a tenancy by the entirety after December 31, 1981, and do not reflect changes made to the Internal Revenue Code by sections 702(k)(1)(A) of the Revenue Act of 1978, or section 2002(c)(2) of the Tax Reform Act of 1976.

(2) *Special rule in the case of tenancies created after July 13, 1988, if the donee spouse is not a United States citizen.*—Under section 2523(i)(3), applicable (subject to the special treaty rule contained in Pub. L. 101-239, section 7815(d)(14)) in the case of tenancies by the entirety and joint tenancies created between spouses after July 13, 1988, if the donee spouse is not a citizen of the United States, the principles contained in section 2515 and § § 25.2515-1 through 25.2515-4 apply in determining the gift tax consequences with respect to the creation and termination of the tenancy, except that the election provided in section 2515(a) (prior to repeal by the Economic Recovery Tax Act of 1981) and § 25.2515-2 (relating to the donor's election to treat the creation of the tenancy as a transfer for gift tax purposes) does not apply.

(3) *Nature of.*—An estate by the entirety in real property is essentially a joint tenancy between husband and wife with the right of survivorship. As used in this section and § § 25.2515-2 through 25.2515-4, the term "tenancy by the entirety" includes a joint tenancy between husband and wife in real property with right of survivorship, or a tenancy which accords to the spouses rights equivalent thereto regardless of the term by which such a tenancy is described in local property law.

(b) *Gift upon creation of tenancy by the entirety; in general.*—During calendar years prior to 1955 the contribution made by a husband or wife in the creation of a tenancy by the entirety constituted a gift to the extent that the consideration furnished by either spouse exceeded the value of the rights retained by that spouse. The contribution made by either or both spouses in the creation of such a tenancy during the calendar year 1955, any calendar year beginning before January 1, 1971, or any calendar quarter beginning after December 31, 1970, is not deemed a gift by either spouse, regardless of the proportion of the total consideration furnished by either spouse, unless the donor spouse elects (see § 25.2515-2) under section 2515(c) to treat such transaction as a gift in the calendar quarter or calendar year in which the transaction is effected. See § 25.2502-1(c)(1) for the definition of calendar quarter. However, there is a gift upon the termination of such a tenancy, other than by the death of a spouse, if the proceeds received by one spouse on termination of the tenancy are larger than the proceeds allocable to the consideration furnished by that spouse to the tenancy. The creation of a tenancy by the entirety takes place if (1) a husband or his wife purchases property and causes the title thereto to be conveyed to themselves as tenants by the entirety, (2) both join in such a purchase, or (3) either or both cause to be created such a tenancy in property already owned by either or both of them. The rule prescribed herein with respect to the creation of a tenancy by the entirety applies also to contributions made in the making of additions to the value of such a tenancy (in the form of improvements, reductions in the indebtedness, or otherwise), regardless of the proportion of the consideration furnished by each spouse. See § 25.2516-1 for transfers made pursuant to a property settlement agreement incident to divorce.

(c) *Consideration.*—(1) *In general.*—(i) The consideration furnished by a person in the creation of a tenancy by the entirety or the making of additions to the value thereof is the amount contributed by him in connection therewith. The contribution may be made by either spouse or by a third party. It may be furnished in the form of money, other property, or an interest in property. If it is furnished in the form of other property or an interest in property, the amount of the contribution is the fair market value of the property or interest at the time it was transferred to the tenancy or was exchanged for the property which became the subject of the tenancy. For example, if a

decedent devised real property to the spouses as tenants by the entirety and the fair market value of the property was $30,000 at the time of the decedent's death, the amount of the decedent's contribution to the creation of the tenancy was $30,000. As another example, assume that in 1950 the husband purchased real property for $25,000, taking it in his own name as sole owner, and that in 1956 when the property had a fair market value of $40,000 he caused it to be transferred to himself and his wife as tenants by the entirety. Here, the amount of the husband's contribution to the creation of the tenancy was $40,000 (the fair market value of the property at the time it was transferred to the tenancy). Similarly, assume that in 1950 the husband purchased, as sole owner, corporate shares for $25,000 and in 1956, when the shares had a fair market value of $35,000, he exchanged them for real property which was transferred to the husband and his wife as tenants by the entirety. The amount of the husband's contribution to the creation of the tenancy was $35,000 (the fair market value of the shares at the time he exchanged them for the real property which became the subject of the tenancy).

(ii) Whether consideration derived from third-party sources is deemed to have been furnished by a third party or to have been furnished by the spouses will depend upon the terms under which the transfer is made. If a decedent devises real property to the spouses as tenants by the entirety, the decedent, and not the spouses, is the person who furnished the consideration for the creation of the tenancy. Likewise, if a decedent in his will directs his executor to discharge an indebtedness of the tenancy, the decedent, and not the spouses, is the person who furnished the consideration for the addition to the value of the tenancy. However, if the decedent bequeathed a general legacy to the husband and the wife and they used the legacy to discharge an indebtedness of the tenancy, the spouses, and not the decedent, are the persons who furnished the consideration for the addition to the value of the tenancy. The principles set forth in this subdivision with respect to transfers by decedents apply equally well to inter vivos transfers by third parties.

(iii) Where a tenancy is terminated in part (*e.g.*, where a portion of the property subject to the tenancy is sold to a third party, or where the original property is disposed of and in its place there is substituted other property of lesser value acquired through reinvestment under circumstances which satisfy the requirements of paragraph (d)(2)(ii) of this section), the proportionate contribution of each person to the remaining tenancy is in general the same as his proportionate contribution to the original tenancy, and the character of his contribution remains the same. These proportions are applied to the cost of the remaining or substituted property. Thus, if the total contribution to the cost of the property was $20,000 and a fourth of the property was sold, the contribution to the remaining portion of the tenancy is normally $15,000. However, if it is shown that at the time of the contribution more or less than one-fourth thereof was attributable to the portion sold, the contribution is divided between the portion sold and the portion retained in the proper proportion. If the portion sold was acquired as a separate tract, it is treated as a separate tenancy. As another example of the application of this subdivision, assume that in 1950 X (a third party) gave to H and W (H's wife), as tenants by the entirety, real property then having a value of $15,000. In 1955, H spent $5,000 thereon in improvements and under section 2515(c) elected to treat his contribution as a gift. In 1956, W spent $10,000 in improving the property but did not elect to treat her contribution as a gift. Between 1957 and 1960 the property appreciated in value by $30,000. In 1960, the property was sold for $60,000, and $45,000 of the proceeds of the sale were, under circumstances that satisfy the requirements of paragraph (d)(2)(ii) of this section, reinvested in other real property. Since X contributed one-half of the total consideration for the original property and the additions to its value, he is considered as having furnished $22,500 (one-half of $45,000) toward the creation of the remaining portion of the tenancy and the making of additions to the value thereof. Similarly, H is considered as having furnished $7,500 (one-sixth of $45,000) which was treated as a gift in the year furnished, and W is considered as having furnished $15,000 (one-third of $45,000) which was not treated as a gift in the year furnished.

(2) *Proportion of consideration attributable to appreciation.*—Any general appreciation (appreciation due to fluctuations in market value) in the value of the property occurring between two successive contribution dates which can readily be measured and which can be determined with reasonable certainty to be allocable to any particular contribution or contributions previously furnished is to be treated, for the purpose of the computations in § § 25.2515-3 and 25.2515-4, as though it were additional consideration furnished by the person who furnished the prior consideration. Any general depreciation in value is treated in a comparable manner. For the purpose of the first sentence of this subparagraph, successive contribution dates are the two consecutive dates on which any contributions to the tenancy are made, not necessarily by the same party. Further, appreciation allocable to the prior consideration falls in the same class as the prior

consideration to which it relates. The application of this subparagraph may be illustrated by the following examples:

*Example (1).* In 1940, H purchased real property for $15,000 which he caused to be transferred to himself and W (his wife) as tenants by the entirety. In 1956 when the fair market value of the property was $30,000, W made $5,000 improvements to the property. In 1957 the property was sold for $35,000. The general appreciation of $15,000 which occurred between the date of purchase and the date of W's improvements to the property constitutes an additional contribution by H, having the same characteristics as his original contribution of $15,000.

*Example (2).* In 1955 real property was purchased by H and W and conveyed to them as tenants by the entirety. The purchase price of the property was $15,000 of which H contributed $10,000 and W, $5,000. In 1960 when the fair market value of the property is $21,000, W makes improvements thereto of $5,000. The property then is sold for $26,000. The appreciation in value of $6,000 results in an additional contribution of $4,000 (10,000/15,000 × $6,000) by H, and an additional contribution by W of $2,000 (5,000/15,000 × $6,000). H's total contribution to the tenancy is $14,000 ($10,000 + $4,000) and W's total contribution is $12,000 ($5,000 + $2,000 + $5,000).

*Example (3).* In 1956 real property was purchased by H and W and conveyed to them as tenants by the entirety. The purchase price of the property was $15,000, on which a down payment of $3,000 was made. The remaining $12,000 was to be paid in monthly installments over a period of 15 years. H furnished $2,000 of the down payment and W, $1,000. H paid all the monthly installments. During the period 1956 to 1971 the property gradually appreciates in value to $24,000. Here, the appreciation is so gradual and the contributions so numerous that the amount allocable to any particular contribution cannot be ascertained with any reasonable certainty. Accordingly, in such a case the appreciation in value may be disregarded in determining the amount of consideration furnished in making the computations provided for in §§ 25.2515-3 and 25.2515-4.

(d) *Gift upon termination of tenancy by the entirety.*—(1) *In general.*— Upon the termination of the tenancy, whether created before, during, or subsequent to the calendar year 1955, a gift may result, depending upon the disposition made of the proceeds of the termination (whether the proceeds be in the form of cash, property, or interests in property). A gift may result notwithstanding the fact that the contribution of either spouse to the tenancy was treated as a gift. See § 25.2515-3 for the method of determining the amount of any gift that may result from the termination of the tenancy in those cases in which no portion of the consideration contributed was treated as a gift by the spouses in the calendar quarter or calendar year in which it was furnished. See § 25.2515-4 for the method of determining the amount of any gift that may result from the termination of the tenancy in those cases in which all or a portion of the consideration contributed was treated as constituting a gift by the spouses in the calendar quarter or calendar year in which it was furnished. See § 25.2515-2 for the procedure to be followed by a donor who elects under section 2515(c) to treat the creation of a tenancy by the entirety (or the making of additions to its value) as a transfer subject to the gift tax in the calendar quarter (calendar year with respect to such transfers made before January 1, 1971) in which the transfer is made, and for the method of determining the amount of the gift. See § 25.2502-1(c)(1) for the definition of calendar quarter.

(2) *Termination.*—(i) *In general.*—Except as indicated in subdivision (ii) of this subparagraph, a termination of a tenancy is effected when all or a portion of the property so held by the spouses is sold, exchanged, or otherwise disposed of, by gift or in any other manner, or when the spouses through any form of conveyance or agreement become tenants in common of the property or otherwise alter the nature of their respective interests in the property formerly held by them as tenants by the entirety. In general, any increase in the indebtedness on a tenancy constitutes a termination of the tenancy to the extent of the increase in the indebtedness. However, such an increase will not constitute a termination of the tenancy to the extent that the increase is offset by additions to the tenancy within a reasonable time after such increase. Such additions (to the extent of the increase in the indebtedness) shall not be treated by the spouses as contributions within the meaning of paragraph (c) of this section.

(ii) *Exchange or reinvestment.*—A termination is not considered as effected to the extent that the property subject to the tenancy is exchanged for other real property, the title of which is held by the spouses in an identical tenancy. For this purpose, a tenancy is considered identical if the proportionate values of the spouses' respective rights (other than any change in the proportionate values resulting solely from the passing of time) are identical to those held in the property which was sold. In addition the sale, exchange (other than an exchange described above), or other disposition of property held as tenants by the entirety is not considered as a termination if all three of the following conditions are satisfied:

(a) There is no division of the proceeds of the sale, exchange or other disposition of the property held as tenants by the entirety;

(b) On or before the due date for the filing of a gift tax return for the calendar quarter or calendar year (see § 25.6075-1 for the time for filing gift tax returns) in which the property held as tenants by the entirety was sold, exchanged, or otherwise disposed of, the spouses enter into a binding contract for the purchase of other real property; and

(c) After the sale, exchange or other disposition of the former property and within a reasonable time after the date of the contract referred to in (b) of this subdivision, such other real property actually is acquired by the spouses and held by them in an identical tenancy.

To the extent that all three of the conditions set forth in this subdivision are not met (whether by reason of the death of one of the spouses or for any other reason), the provisions of the preceding sentence shall not apply, and the sale, exchange or other disposition of the property will constitute a termination of the tenancy. As used in subdivision (c) the expression "a reasonable time" means the time which, under the particular facts in each case, is needed for those matters which are incident to the acquisition of the other property (*i.e.*, perfecting of title, arranging for financing, construction, etc.). The fact that proceeds of a sale are deposited in the name of one tenant or of both tenants separately or jointly as a convenience does not constitute a division within the meaning of subdivision (a) if the other requirements of this subdivision are met. The proceeds of a sale, exchange or other disposition of the property held as tenants by the entirety will be deemed to have been used for the purchase of other real property if applied to the purchase or construction of improvements which themselves constitute real property and which are additions to other real property held by the spouses in a tenancy identical to that in which they held the property which was sold, exchanged, or otherwise disposed of.

(3) *Proceeds of termination.*—(i) The proceeds of termination may be received by a spouse in the form of money, property, or an interest in property. Where the proceeds are received in the form of property (other than money) or an interest in property, the value of the proceeds received by that spouse is the fair market value, on the date of termination of the tenancy by the entirety, of the property or interest received. Thus, if a tenancy by the entirety is terminated so that thereafter each spouse owns an undivided half interest in the property as tenant in common, the value of the proceeds of termination received by each spouse is one-half the value of the property at the time of the termination of the tenancy by the entirety. If under local law one spouse, without the consent of the other, can bring about a severance of his or her interest in a tenancy by the entirety and does so by making a gift of his or her interest to a third party, that spouse is considered as having received proceeds of termination in the amount of the fair market value, at the time of the termination, of his severable interest determined in accordance with the rules prescribed in § 25.2512-5. He has, in addition, made a gift to the third party of the fair market value of the interest conveyed to the third party. In such a case, the other spouse also is considered as having received as proceeds of termination the fair market value, at the time of termination, of the interest which she thereafter holds in the property as tenant in common with the third party. However, since section 2515(b) contemplates that the spouses may divide the proceeds of termination in some proportion other than that represented by the values of their respective legal interests in the property, if both spouses join together in making a gift to a third party of property held by them as tenants by the entirety, the value of the proceeds of termination which will be treated as received by each is the amount which each reports (on his or her gift tax return filed for the calendar quarter or calendar year in which the termination occurs) as the value of his or her gift to the third party. This amount is the amount which each reports without regard to whether the spouses elect under section 2513 to treat the gifts as made one-half by each. For example, assume that H and W (his wife) hold real property as tenants by the entirety; that in the first calendar quarter of 1972, when the property has a fair market value of $60,000, they give it to their son; and that on their gift tax returns for such calendar quarter, H reports himself as having made a gift to the son of $36,000 and W reports herself as having made a gift to the son of $24,000. Under these circumstances, H is considered as having received proceeds of termination valued at $36,000, and W is considered as having received proceeds of termination valued at $24,000.

(ii) Except as provided otherwise in subparagraph (2)(ii) of this paragraph (under which certain tenancies by the entirety are considered not to be terminated), where the proceeds of a sale, exchange, or other disposition of the property are not actually divided between the spouses but are held (whether in a bank account or otherwise) in their joint names or in the name of one spouse as custodian or trustee for their joint interests, each spouse is presumed, in the absence of a showing to the contrary, to have received, as of the date of termination, proceeds of termination equal in value to the value of his or her enforceable property rights in respect of the proceeds. [Reg. § 25.2515-1.]

☐ *[T.D. 6334, 11-15-58. Amended by T.D. 7238, 12-29-72 and T.D. 8522, 2-28-94.]*

### [Reg. § 25.2515-2]

**§25.2515-2. Tenancies by the entirety; transfers treated as gifts; manner of election and valuation.**—(a) The election to treat the creation of a tenancy by the entirety in real property, or additions made to its value, as constituting a gift in the calendar quarter or calendar year in which effected, shall be exercised by including the value of such gifts in the gift tax return of the donor for such calendar quarter or calendar year in which the tenancy was created, or the additions in value were made to the property. See section 6019 and the regulations thereunder. The election may be exercised only in a return filed within the time prescribed by law, or before the expiration of any extension of time granted pursuant to law for the filing of the return. See section 6075 for the time for filing the gift tax return and section 6081 for extensions of time for filing the return, together with the regulations thereunder. In order to make the election, a gift tax return must be filed for the calendar quarter or calendar year in which the tenancy was created, or additions in value thereto made, even though the value of the gift involved does not exceed the amount of the exclusion provided by section 2503(b). See § 25.2502-1(c)(1) for the definition of calendar quarter.

(b) If the donor spouse exercises the election as provided in paragraph (a) of this section, the amount of the gift at the creation of the tenancy is the amount of his contribution to the tenancy less the value of his retained interest in it, determined as follows:

(1) If under the law of the jurisdiction governing the rights of the spouses, either spouse, acting alone, can bring about a severance of his or her interest in the property, the value of the donor's retained interest is one-half the value of the property.

(2) If, under the law of the jurisdiction governing the rights of the spouses each is entitled to share in the income or other enjoyment of the property but neither, acting alone, may defeat the right of the survivor of them to the whole of the property, the amount of retained interest of the donor is determined by use of the appropriate actuarial factors for the spouses at their respective attained ages at the time the transaction is effected.

(c) Factors representing the respective interests of the spouses, under a tenancy by the entirety, at their attained ages at the time of the transaction may be readily computed based on the method described in § 25.2512-5. State law may provide that the husband only is entitled to all of the income or other enjoyment of the real property held as tenants by the entirety, and the wife's interest consists only of the right of survivorship with no right of severance. In such a case, a special factor may be needed to determine the value of the interests of the respective spouses. See § 25.2512-5(d)(4) for the procedure for obtaining special factors from the Internal Revenue Service in appropriate cases.

(d) The application of this paragraph may be illustrated by the following example:

*Example.* A husband with his own funds acquires real property valued at $10,000 and has it conveyed to himself and his wife as tenants by the entirety. Under the law of the jurisdiction governing the rights of the parties, each spouse is entitled to share in the income from the property but neither spouse acting alone could bring about a severance of his or her interest. The husband elects to treat the transfer as a gift in the year in which effected. At the time of transfer, the ages of the husband and wife are 45 and 40, respectively, on their birthdays nearest to the date of transfer. The value of the gift to the wife is $5,502.90, computed as follows:

Value of property transferred . . . . . . . . . . . . . . . . . $10,000.00
Less $10,000 × 0.44971 (factor for value of donor's retained rights) . . . . . . . . . . . . . . . . . . . . . . . . . .     4,497.10
Value of gift . . . . . . . . . . . . . . . . . . . . . . . . . .     5,502.90
[Reg. § 25.2515-2.]

☐ *[T.D. 6334, 11-15-58. Amended by T.D. 7150, 12-2-71, T.D. 7238, 12-29-72 and T.D. 8540, 6-9-94.]*

### [Reg. § 25.2515-3]

**§25.2515-3. Termination of tenancy by the entirety; cases in which entire value of gift is determined under section 2515(b).**— (a) *In any case in which.*—(1) The creation of a tenancy by the entirety (including additions in value thereto) was not treated as a gift, and

(2) The entire consideration for the creation of the tenancy, and any additions in value thereto, was furnished solely by the spouses (see paragraph (c)(1)(ii) of § 25.2515-1),

the termination of the tenancy (other than by the death of a spouse) always results in the making of a gift by a spouse who receives a smaller share of the proceeds of the termination (whether received in cash, property or interests in property) than the share of the proceeds attributable to the total consideration furnished by him. See paragraph (c) of § 25.2515-1 for a discussion of what constitutes consideration and the value thereof. Thus, a gift is effected at the time of termination of the tenancy by the spouse receiving less than one-half of the proceeds of termination if such spouse (regardless of age) furnished one-half or more of the total consideration for the purchase and improvements, if any, of the property held in the tenancy. Also, if one spouse furnished the entire consideration, a gift is made by such spouse to the extent that the other spouse receives any portion of the proceeds of termination. See § 25.2515-4 for determination of the amount of the gift, if any, in cases in which the creation of the tenancy was treated as a gift or a portion of the consideration was furnished by a third person. See paragraph (d)(2) of § 25.2515-1 as to the acts which effect a termination of the tenancy.

(b) In computing the value of the gift under the circumstances described in paragraph (a) of this section, it is first necessary to determine the spouse's share of the proceeds attributable to the consideration furnished by him. This share is computed by multiplying the total value of the proceeds of the termination by a fraction, the numerator of which is the total consideration furnished by the donor spouse and the denominator of which is the total consideration furnished by both spouses. From this amount there is subtracted the value of the proceeds of termination received by the donor spouse. The amount remaining is the value of the gift. In arriving at the "total consideration furnished by the donor spouse" and the "total consideration furnished by both spouses", for purposes of the computation provided for in this paragraph, the consideration furnished (see paragraph (c) of § 25.2515-1) is not reduced by any amounts which otherwise would have been excludable under section 2503(b) in determining the amounts of taxable gifts for calendar quarters or calendar years in which the consideration was furnished. (See § 25.2502-1(c)(1) for the definition of calendar quarter.) As an example assume that in 1955, real property was purchased for $30,000, the husband and wife each contributing $12,000 and the remaining $6,000 being obtained through a mortgage on the property. In each of the years 1956 and 1957, the husband paid $3,000 on the principal of the indebtedness, but did not disclose the value of these transfers on his gift tax returns for those years. The total consideration furnished by the husband is $18,000, the total consideration furnished by the wife is $12,000, and the total consideration furnished by both spouses is $30,000.

(c) The application of this section may be illustrated by the following examples:

*Example (1).* In 1956 the husband furnished $30,000 and his wife furnished $10,000 of the consideration for the purchase and subsequent improvement of real property held by them as tenants by the entirety. The husband did not elect to treat the consideration furnished as a gift. The property later is sold for $60,000, the husband receiving $35,000 and his wife receiving $25,000 of the proceeds of the termination. The termination of the tenancy results in a gift of $10,000 by the husband to his wife, computed as follows:

[$30,000 (consideration furnished by husband) ÷ $40,000 (total consideration furnished by both spouses)] × $60,000 (proceeds of termination) = $45,000
$45,000 − $35,000 (proceeds received by husband) = $10,000 gift by husband to wife.

*Example (2).* In 1950 the husband purchased shares of X Company for $10,000. In 1955 when those shares had a fair market value of $30,000, he and his wife purchased real property from A and had it conveyed to them as tenants by the entirety. In payment for the real property, the husband transferred his shares of X Company to A and the wife paid A the sum of $10,000. They later sold the real property for $60,000, divided $24,000 (each taking $12,000) and reinvested the remaining $36,000 in other real property under circumstances that satisfied the conditions set forth in paragraph (d)(2)(ii) of § 25.2515-1. The tenancy was terminated only with respect to the $24,000 divided between them. This termination of the tenancy resulted in a gift of $6,000 by the husband to the wife, computed as follows:

[$30,000 (consideration furnished by husband) ÷ $40,000 (total consideration furnished by both spouses)] × $24,000 (proceeds of termination) = $18,000
$18,000 − $12,000 (proceeds received by husband) = $6,000 gift by husband to wife.

Since the tenancy was terminated only in part, with respect to the remaining portion of the tenancy each spouse is considered as having furnished that proportion of the total consideration for the remaining portion of the tenancy as the consideration furnished by him before the sale bears to the total consideration furnished by both spouses before the sale. See paragraph (c) of § 25.2515-1. The consideration furnished by the husband for the reduced tenancy is $27,000, computed as follows:

[$30,000 (consideration furnished by husband before sale) ÷ $40,000 (total consideration furnished by both spouses before sale)]× $36,000 (consideration for reduced tenancy) = $27,000

The consideration furnished by the wife is $9,000, computed in a similar manner. [Reg. § 25.2515-3.]

☐ [*T.D. 6334, 11-15-58. Amended by T.D. 7238, 12-29-72.*]

### [Reg. § 25.2515-4]

**§ 25.2515-4. Termination of tenancy by entirety; cases in which none, or a portion only, of value of gift is determined under section 2515(b).**—(a) *In general.*—The rules provided in section 2515(b) (see § 25.2515-3) are not applied in determining whether a gift has been made at the termination of a tenancy to the extent that the consideration furnished for the creation of the tenancy was treated as a gift or if the consideration for the creation of the tenancy was furnished by a third party. Consideration furnished for the creation of the tenancy was treated as a gift if it was furnished either (1) during calendar years prior to 1955, or (2) during the calendar year 1955 and subsequent calendar years and calendar quarters and the donor spouse exercised the election to treat the furnishing of consideration as a gift. (For the definition of calendar quarter see § 25.2502-1(c)(1).) See paragraph (b) of this section for the manner of computing the value of gifts resulting from the termination of the tenancy under these circumstances. See paragraph (c) of this section for the rules to be applied where part of the total consideration for the creation of the tenancy and additions to the value thereof was not treated as a gift and part either was treated as a gift or was furnished by a third party.

(b) *Value of gift when entire consideration is of the type described in paragraph (a) of this section.*—If the entire consideration for the creation of a tenancy by the entirety was treated as a gift or contributed by a third party, the determination of the amount, if any, of a gift made at the termination of the tenancy will be made by the application of the general principles set forth in § 25.2511-1. Under those principles, when a spouse surrenders a property interest in a tenancy, the creation of which was treated as a gift, and in return receives an amount (whether in the form of cash, property, or an interest in property) less than the value of the property interest surrendered, that spouse is deemed to have made a gift in an amount equal to the difference between the value at the time of termination, of the property interest surrendered by such spouse and the amount received in exchange. Thus, if the husband's interest in such a tenancy at the time of termination is worth $44,971 and the wife's interest therein at the time is worth $55,029, the property is sold for $100,000, and each spouse received $50,000 out of the proceeds of the sale, the wife has made a gift to the husband of $5,029. The principles applied in paragraph (c) of § 25.2515-2 for the method of determining the value of the respective interests of the spouses at the time of the creation of a tenancy by the entirety are equally applicable in determining the value of each spouse's interest in the tenancy at termination, except that the actuarial factors to be applied are those for the respective spouses at the ages attained at the date of termination.

(c) *Valuation of gift where both types of consideration are involved.*—If the consideration furnished consists in part of the type described in paragraph (a) of § 25.2515-3 (consideration furnished by the spouses after 1954, and not treated as a gift in the calendar quarter or calendar year in which it was furnished) and in part of the type described in paragraph (a) of this section (consideration furnished by the spouses and treated as a gift or furnished by a third party), the amount of the gift is determined as follows:

(1) By applying the principles set forth in paragraph (b) of § 25.2515-3 to that portion of the total proceeds of termination which the consideration described in paragraph (a) of § 25.2515-3 bears to the total consideration furnished;

(2) By applying the principles set forth in paragraph (b) of this section to the remaining portion of the total proceeds of termination; and

(3) By subtracting the proceeds of termination received by the donor from the total of the amounts which under the principles referred to in subparagraphs (1) and (2) of this paragraph are to be compared with the proceeds of termination received by a spouse in determining whether a gift was made by that spouse. For example, assume that consideration of $30,000 was furnished by the husband in 1954. Assume also that on February 1, 1955, the husband contributed $12,000 and the wife $8,000, the husband's contribution not being treated as a gift (see paragraph (b) of § 25.2515-1). Assume further that between 1957 and 1965 the property appreciated in value by $40,000 and was sold in 1965 for $90,000 (of which the husband received $40,000 and the wife $50,000). The principles set forth in paragraph (b) of § 25.2515-3 are applied to $36,000 (20,000/50,000 × $90,000) in arriving at the amount which is compared with the

proceeds of termination received by a spouse. Applying the principles set forth in paragraph (b) of § 25.2515-3, this amount in the case of the husband is $21,600 (12,000/20,000 × $36,000). Similarly, the principles set forth in paragraph (b) of this section are applied to $54,000 ($90,000 – 36,000), the remaining portion of the proceeds of termination, in arriving at the amount which is compared with the proceeds of termination received by a spouse. If in this case either spouse, without the consent of the other spouse, can bring about a severance of his interest in the tenancy, the amount determined under paragraph (b) of this section in the case of the husband would be $27,000 (1/2 of $54,000). The total of the two amounts which are to be compared with the proceeds of termination received by the husband is $48,600 ($21,600 + 27,000). This sum of $48,600 is then compared with the $40,000 proceeds received by the husband, and the termination of the tenancy has resulted, for gift tax purposes, in a transfer of $8,600 by the husband to his wife in 1965. See paragraph (d) of this section for an additional example illustrating the application of this paragraph.

(d) The application of paragraph (c) of this section may further be illustrated by the following example:

*Example.* X died in 1948 and devised real property to Y and Z (Y's wife) as tenant by the entirety. Under the law of the jurisdiction, both spouses are entitled to share equally in the income from, or the enjoyment of, the property, but neither spouse, acting along, may defeat the right of the survivor of them to the whole of the property. The fair market value of the property at the time of X's death was $100,000 and this amount is the consideration which X furnished toward the creation of the tenancy. In 1955, at which time the fair market value of the property was the same as at the time of X's death, improvements of $50,000 were made to the property, of which Y furnished $40,000 out of his own funds and Z furnished $10,000 out of her own funds. Y did not elect to treat his transfer to the tenancy as resulting in the making of a gift in 1955. In 1956 the property was sold for $300,000 and Y and Z each received $150,000 of the proceeds. At the time the property was sold Y and Z were 45 and 40 years of age, respectively, on their birthdays nearest the date of sale. The value of the gift made by Y to Z is $19,942, computed as follows:

Amount determined under principles set forth in § 25.2515-3:
$50,000 (consideration not treated as gift in year furnished) ÷ $150,000 (total consideration furnished) × $300,000 (proceeds of termination) = $100,000 (proceeds of termination to which principles set forth in § 25.2515-3 apply)
$40,000 (consideration furnished by H and not treated as gift) ÷ $50,000 (total consideration not treated as gift) × $100,000 = $80,000
Amount determined under principles set forth in paragraph (b) of this section:
$300,000 (total proceeds of termination) – $100,000 (proceeds to which principles set forth in § 25.2515-3 apply) = $200,000 (proceeds to which principles set forth in paragraph (b) apply) 0.44971 (factor for Y's latest) × $200,000 = $89,942

Amount of gift:

| | |
|---|---:|
| Amount determined under § 25.2515-3 . . . . . . . . | $80,000 |
| Amount determined under paragraph (b) . . . . . . | 89,942 |
| Total . . . . . . . . . . . . . . . . . . . . . . . . . | 169,942 |
| Less: Proceeds received by Y . . . . . . . . . . . . . . . . | 150,000 |
| Amount of gift made by Y to Z . . . . . . . . . . . . . | 19,942 |

[Reg. § 25.2515-4.]

☐ [*T.D. 6334, 11-15-58. Amended by T.D. 7238, 12-29-72.*]

### [Reg. § 25.2516-1]

**§ 25.2516-1. Certain property settlements.**—(a) Section 2516 provides that transfers of property or interests in property made under the terms of a written agreement between spouses in settlement of their marital or property rights are deemed to be for an adequate and full consideration in money or money's worth and, therefore, exempt from the gift tax (whether or not such agreement is approved by a divorce decree), if the spouses obtain a final decree of divorce from each other within two years after entering into the agreement.

(b) See paragraph (b) of § 25.6019-3 for the circumstances under which information relating to property settlements must be disclosed on the transferor's gift tax return for the "calendar period" (as defined in § 25.2502-1(c)(1)) in which the agreement becomes effective. [Reg. § 25.2516-1.]

☐ [*T.D. 6334, 11-14-58. Amended by T.D. 7238, 12-28-72 and T.D. 7910, 9-6-83.*]

### [Reg. § 25.2516-2]

**§ 25.2516-2. Transfers in settlement of support obligations.**—Transfers to provide a reasonable allowance for the support of children (including legally adopted children) of a marriage during minority are not subject to the gift tax if made pursuant to an agreement which satisfies the requirements of section 2516. [Reg. § 25.2516-2.]

☐ [T.D. 6334, 11-14-58.]

### [Reg. §25.2518-1]

**§25.2518-1. Qualified disclaimers of property; In general.**— (a) *Applicability.*—(1) *In general.*—The rules described in this section, § 25.2518-2, and § 25.2518-3 apply to the qualified disclaimer of an interest in property which is created in the person disclaiming by a transfer made after December 31, 1976. In general, a qualified disclaimer is an irrevocable and unqualified refusal to accept the ownership of an interest in property. For rules relating to the determination of when a transfer creating an interest occurs, see § 25.2518-2(c)(3) and (4).

(2) *Example.*—The provisions of paragraph (a)(1) of this section may be illustrated by the following example:

*Example.* W creates an irrevocable trust on December 10, 1968, and retains the right to receive the income for life. Upon the death of W, which occurs after December 31, 1976, the trust property is distributable to W's surviving issue, *per stirpes.* The transfer creating the remainder interest in the trust occurred in 1968. See § 25.2511-1(c)(2). Therefore, section 2518 does not apply to the disclaimer of the remainder interest because the transfer creating the interest was made prior to January 1, 1977. If, however, W had caused the gift to be incomplete by also retaining the power to designate the person or persons to receive the trust principal at death, and, as a result, no transfer (within the meaning of § 25.2511-1(c)(2)) of the remainder interest was made at the time of the creation of the trust, section 2518 would apply to any disclaimer made after W's death with respect to an interest in the trust property.

(3) Paragraph (a)(1) of this section is applicable for transfers creating the interest to be disclaimed made on or after December 31, 1997.

(b) *Effect of a qualified disclaimer.*—If a person makes a qualified disclaimer as described in section 2518(b) and § 25.2518-2, for purposes of the Federal estate, gift, and generation-skipping transfer tax provisions, the disclaimed interest in property is treated as if it had never been transferred to the person making the qualified disclaimer. Instead, it is considered as passing directly from the transferor of the property to the person entitled to receive the property as a result of the disclaimer. Accordingly, a person making a qualified disclaimer is not treated as making a gift. Similarly, the value of a decedent's gross estate for purposes of the Federal estate tax does not include the value of property with respect to which the decedent, or the decedent's executor or administrator on behalf of the decedent, has made a qualified disclaimer. If the disclaimer is not a qualified disclaimer, for the purposes of the Federal estate, gift, and generation-skipping transfer tax provisions, the disclaimer is disregarded and the disclaimant is treated as having received the interest.

(c) *Effect of local law.*—(1) *In general.*—(i) *Interests created before 1982.*—A disclaimer of an interest created in a taxable transfer before 1982 which otherwise meets the requirements of a qualified disclaimer under section 2518 and the corresponding regulations but which, by itself, is not effective under applicable local law to divest ownership of the disclaimed property from the disclaimant and vest it in another, is nevertheless treated as a qualified disclaimer under section 2518 if, under applicable local law, the disclaimed interest in property is transferred, as a result of attempting the disclaimer, to another person without any direction on the part of the disclaimant. An interest in property will not be considered to be transferred without any direction on the part of the disclaimant if, under applicable local law, the disclaimant has any discretion (whether or not such discretion is exercised) to determine who will receive such interest. Actions by the disclaimant which are required under local law merely to divest ownership of the property from the disclaimant and vest ownership in another person will not disqualify the disclaimer for purposes of section 2518(a). See § 25.2518-2(d)(1) for rules relating to the immediate vesting of title in the disclaimant.

(ii) *Interests created after 1981.*—[Reserved].

(2) *Creditor's claims.*—The fact that a disclaimer is voidable by the disclaimant's creditors has no effect on the determination of whether such disclaimer constitutes a qualified disclaimer. However, a disclaimer that is wholly void or that is voided by the disclaimant's creditors cannot be a qualified disclaimer.

(3) *Examples.*—The provisions of paragraphs (c)(1) and (2) of this section may be illustrated by the following examples:

*Example (1).* F dies testate in State Y on June 17, 1978. G and H are beneficiaries under the will. The will provides that any disclaimed property is to pass to the residuary estate. H has no interest in the residuary estate. Under the applicable laws of State Y, a disclaimer must be made within 6 months of the death of the testator. Seven months after F's death, H disclaimed the real property H received under the will. The disclaimer statute of State Y has a provision stating that an untimely disclaimer will be treated as an assignment of the interest disclaimed to those persons who would have taken had the disclaimer been valid. Pursuant to this provision, the disclaimed property became part of the residuary estate. Assuming the remaining requirements of section 2518 are met, H has made a qualified disclaimer for purposes of section 2518(a).

*Example (2).* Assume the same facts as in example (1) except that the law of State Y does not treat an ineffective disclaimer as a transfer to alternative takers. H assigns the disclaimed interest by deed to those who would have taken had the disclaimer been valid. Under these circumstances, H has not made a qualified disclaimer for purposes of section 2518(a) because the disclaimant directed who would receive the property.

*Example (3).* Assume the same facts as in example (1) except that the law of State Y requires H to pay a transfer tax in order to effectuate the transfer under the ineffective disclaimer provision. H pays the transfer tax. H has made a qualified disclaimer for purposes of section 2518(a).

(d) *Cross-reference.*—For rules relating to the effect of qualified disclaimers on the estate tax charitable and marital deductions, see §§ 20.2055-2(c) and 20.2056(d)-1 respectively. For rules relating to the effect of a qualified disclaimer of a general power of appointment, see § 20.2041-3(d). [Reg. § 25.2518-1.]

☐ [T.D. 8095, 8-6-89. Amended by T.D. 8744, 12-30-97.]

### [Reg § 25.2518-2]

**§25.2518-2. Requirements for a qualified disclaimer.**—(a) *In general.*—For the purposes of section 2518(a), a disclaimer shall be a qualified disclaimer only if it satisfies the requirements of this section. In general, to be a qualified disclaimer—

(1) The disclaimer must be irrevocable and unqualified;

(2) The disclaimer must be in writing;

(3) The writing must be delivered to the person specified in paragraph (b)(2) of this section within the time limitations specified in paragraph (c)(1) of this section;

(4) The disclaimant must not have accepted the interest disclaimed or any of its benefits; and

(5) The interest disclaimed must pass either to the spouse of the decedent or to a person other than the disclaimant without any direction on the part of the person making the disclaimer.

(b) *Writing.*—(1) *Requirements.*—A disclaimer is a qualified disclaimer only if it is in writing. The writing must identify the interest in property disclaimed and be signed either by the disclaimant or by the disclaimant's legal representative.

(2) *Delivery.*—The writing described in paragraph (b)(1) of this section must be delivered to the transferor of the interest, the transferor's legal representative, the holder of the legal title to the property to which the interest relates, or the person in possession of such property.

(c) *Time limit.*—(1) *In general.*—A disclaimer is a qualified disclaimer only if the writing described in paragraph (b)(1) of this section is delivered to the persons described in paragraph (b)(2) of this section no later than the date which is 9 months after the later of—

(i) The date on which the transfer creating the interest in the disclaimant is made, or

(ii) The day on which the disclaimant attains age 21.

(2) *A timely mailing of a disclaimer treated as a timely delivery.*— Although section 7502 and the regulations under that section apply only to documents to be filed with the Service, a timely mailing of a disclaimer to the person described in paragraph (b)(2) of this section is treated as a timely delivery if the mailing requirements under paragraphs (c)(1), (c)(2) and (d) of § 301.7502-1 are met. Further, if the last day of the period specified in paragraph (c)(1) of this section falls on Saturday, Sunday or a legal holiday (as defined in paragraph (b) of § 301.7503-1), then the delivery of the writing described in paragraph (b)(1) of this section shall be considered timely if delivery is made on the first succeeding day which is not Saturday, Sunday or a legal holiday. See paragraph (d)(3) of this section for rules applicable to the exception for individuals under 21 years of age.

(3) *Transfer.*—(i) For purposes of the time limitation described in paragraph (c)(1)(i) of this section, the 9-month period for making a disclaimer generally is to be determined with reference to the transfer creating the interest in the disclaimant. With respect to inter vivos transfers, a transfer creating an interest occurs when there is a completed gift for Federal gift tax purposes regardless of whether a gift tax is imposed on the completed gift. Thus, gifts qualifying for the

gift tax annual exclusion under section 2503(b) are regarded as transfers creating an interest for this purpose. With respect to transfers made by a decedent at death or transfers that become irrevocable at death, the transfer creating the interest occurs on the date of the decedent's death, even if an estate tax is not imposed on the transfer. For example, a bequest of foreign-situs property by a nonresident alien decedent is regarded as a transfer creating an interest in property even if the transfer would not be subject to estate tax. If there is a transfer creating an interest in property during the transferor's lifetime and such interest is later included in the transferor's gross estate for estate tax purposes (or would have been included if such interest were subject to estate tax), the 9-month period for making the qualified disclaimer is determined with reference to the earlier transfer creating the interest. In the case of a general power of appointment, the holder of the power has a 9-month period after the transfer creating the power in which to disclaim. If a person to whom any interest in property passes by reason of the exercise, release, or lapse of a general power desires to make a qualified disclaimer, the disclaimer must be made within a 9-month period after the exercise, release, or lapse regardless of whether the exercise, release, or lapse is subject to estate or gift tax. In the case of a nongeneral power of appointment, the holder of the power, permissible appointees, or takers in default of appointment must disclaim within a 9-month period after the original transfer that created or authorized the creation of the power. If the transfer is for the life of an income beneficiary with succeeding interests to other persons, both the life tenant and the other remaindermen, whether their interests are vested or contingent, must disclaim no later than 9 months after the original transfer creating an interest. In the case of a remainder interest in property which an executor elects to treat as qualified terminable interest property under section 2056(b)(7), the remainderman must disclaim within 9 months of the transfer creating the interest, rather than 9 months from the date such interest is subject to tax under section 2044 or 2519. A person who receives an interest in property as the result of a qualified disclaimer of the interest must disclaim the previously disclaimed interest no later than 9 months after the date of the transfer creating the interest in the preceding disclaimant. Thus, if A were to make a qualified disclaimer of a specific bequest and as a result of the qualified disclaimer the property passed as part of the residue, the beneficiary of the residue could make a qualified disclaimer no later than 9 months after the date of the testator's death. See paragraph (d)(3) of this section for the time limitation rule with reference to recipients who are under 21 years of age.

(ii) Sentences 1 through 10 and 12 of paragraph (c)(3)(i) of this section are applicable for transfers creating the interest to be disclaimed made on or after December 31, 1997.

(4) *Joint property.*—(i) *Interests in joint tenancy with right of survivorship or tenancies by the entirety.*—Except as provided in paragraph (c)(4)(iii) of this section (with respect to joint bank, brokerage, and other investment accounts), in the case of an interest in a joint tenancy with right of survivorship or a tenancy by the entirety, a qualified disclaimer of the interest to which the disclaimant succeeds upon creation of the tenancy must be made no later than 9 months after the creation of the tenancy regardless of whether such interest can be unilaterally severed under local law. A qualified disclaimer of the survivorship interest to which the survivor succeeds by operation of law upon the death of the first joint tenant to die must be made no later than 9 months after the death of the first joint tenant to die regardless of whether such interest can be unilaterally severed under local law and, except as provided in paragraph (c)(4)(ii) of this section (with respect to certain tenancies created on or after July 14, 1988), such interest is deemed to be a one-half interest in the property. (See, however, section 2518(b)(2)(B) for a special rule in the case of disclaimers by persons under age 21.) This is the case regardless of the portion of the property attributable to consideration furnished by the disclaimant and regardless of the portion of the property that is included in the decedent's gross estate under section 2040 and regardless of whether the interest can be unilaterally severed under local law. See paragraph (c)(5), Examples (7) and (8), of this section.

(ii) *Certain tenancies in real property between spouses created on or after July 14, 1988.*—In the case of a joint tenancy between spouses or a tenancy by the entirety in real property created on or after July 14, 1988, to which section 2523(i)(3) applies (relating to the creation of a tenancy where the spouse of the donor is not a United States citizen), the surviving spouse may disclaim any portion of the joint interest that is includible in the decedent's gross estate under section 2040. See paragraph (c)(5), *Example (9)*, of this section.

(iii) *Special rule for joint bank, brokerage, and other investment accounts (e.g., accounts held at mutual funds) established between spouses or between persons other than husband and wife.*—In the case of a transfer to a joint bank, brokerage, or other investment account (e.g., an account held at a mutual fund), if a transferor may unilaterally regain the transferor's own contributions to the account without the consent of the other cotenant, such that the transfer is not a completed gift under § 25.2511-1(h)(4), the transfer creating the survivor's interest in the decedent's share of the account occurs on the death of the deceased cotenant. Accordingly, if a surviving joint tenant desires to make a qualified disclaimer with respect to funds contributed by a deceased cotenant, the disclaimer must be made within 9 months of the cotenant's death. The surviving joint tenant may not disclaim any portion of the joint account attributable to consideration furnished by that surviving joint tenant. See paragraph (c)(5), *Examples(12)*, *(13)*, and *(14)*, of this section, regarding the treatment of disclaimed interests under sections 2518, 2033 and 2040.

(iv) *Effective date.*—This paragraph (c)(4) is applicable for disclaimers made on or after December 31, 1997.

(5) *Examples.*—The provisions of paragraphs (c)(1) through (c)(4) of this section may be illustrated by the following examples. For purposes of the following examples, assume that all beneficiaries are over 21 years of age.

*Example (1).* On May 13, 1978, in a transfer which constitutes a completed gift for Federal gift tax purposes, A creates a trust in which B is given a lifetime interest in the income from the trust. B is also given a nongeneral testamentary power of appointment over the corpus of the trust. The power of appointment may be exercised in favor of any of the issue of A and B. If there are no surviving issue at B's death or if the power is not exercised, the corpus is to pass to E. On May 13, 1978, A and B have two surviving children, C and D. If A, B, C or D wishes to make a qualified disclaimer, the disclaimer must be made no later than 9 months after May 13, 1978.

*Example (2).* Assume the same facts as in example (1) except that B is given a general power of appointment over the corpus of the trust. B exercises the general power of appointment in favor of C upon B's death on June 17, 1989. C may make a qualified disclaimer no later than 9 months after June 17, 1989. If B had died without exercising the general power of appointment, E could have made a qualified disclaimer no later than 9 months after June 17, 1989.

*Example (3).* F creates a trust on April 1, 1978, in which F's child G is to receive the income from the trust for life. Upon G's death, the corpus of the trust is to pass to G's child H. If either G or H wishes to make a qualified disclaimer, it must be made no later than 9 months after April 1, 1978.

*Example (4).* A creates a trust on February 15, 1978, in which B is named the income beneficiary for life. The trust further provides that upon B's death the proceeds of the trust are to pass to C, if then living. If C predeceases D, the proceeds shall pass to D or D's estate. To have timely disclaimers for purposes of section 2518, B, C, and D must disclaim their respective interests no later than 9 months after February 15, 1978.

*Example (5).* A, a resident of State Q, dies on January 10, 1979, devising certain real property to B. The disclaimer laws of State Q require that a disclaimer be made within a reasonable time after a transfer. B disclaims the entire interest in real property on November 10, 1979. Although B's disclaimer may be effective under State Q law, it is not a qualified disclaimer under section 2518 because the disclaimer was made later than 9 months after the taxable transfer to B.

*Example (6).* A creates a revocable trust on June 1, 1980, in which B and C are given the income interest for life. Upon the death of the last income beneficiary, the remainder interest is to pass to D. The creation of the trust is not a completed gift for Federal gift tax purposes, but each distribution of trust income to B and C is a completed gift at the date of distribution. B and C must disclaim each income distribution no later than 9 months after the date of the particular distribution. In order to disclaim an income distribution in the form of a check, the recipient must return the check to the trustee uncashed along with a written disclaimer. A dies on September 1, 1982, causing the trust to become irrevocable, and the trust corpus is includible in A's gross estate for Federal estate tax purposes under section 2038. If B or C wishes to make a qualified disclaimer of his income interest, he must do so no later than 9 months after September 1, 1982. If D wishes to make a qualified disclaimer of his remainder interest, he must do so no later than 9 months after September 1, 1982.

*Example (7).* On February 1, 1990, A purchased real property with A's funds. Title to the property was conveyed to "A and B, as joint tenants with right of survivorship." Under applicable state law, the joint interest is unilaterally severable by either tenant. B dies on May 1, 1998, and is survived by A. On January 1, 1999, A disclaims the one-half survivorship interest in the property to which A succeeds as a result of B's death. Assuming that the other requirements of section 2518(b) are satisfied, A has made a qualified disclaimer of the one-half survivorship interest (but not the interest retained by A upon the creation of the tenancy, which may not be disclaimed by A). The result is the same whether or not A and B are married and regardless of the proportion of consideration furnished by A and B in purchasing the property.

*Example (8).* Assume the same facts as in *Example (7)* except that A and B are married and title to the property was conveyed to "A and B, as tenants by the entirety." Under applicable state law, the tenancy cannot be unilaterally severed by either tenant. Assuming that the other requirements of section 2518(b) are satisfied, A has made a qualified disclaimer of the one-half survivorship interest (but not the interest retained by A upon the creation of the tenancy, which may not be disclaimed by A). The result is the same regardless of the proportion of consideration furnished by A and B in purchasing the property.

*Example (9).* On March 1, 1989, H and W purchase a tract of vacant land which is conveyed to them as tenants by the entirety. The entire consideration is paid by H. W is not a United States citizen. H dies on June 1, 1998. W can disclaim the entire joint interest because this is the interest includible in H's gross estate under section 2040(a). Assuming that W's disclaimer is received by the executor of H's estate no later than 9 months after June 1, 1998, and the other requirements of section 2518(b) are satisfied, W's disclaimer of the property would be a qualified disclaimer. The result would be the same if the property was held in joint tenancy with right of survivorship that was unilaterally severable under local law.

*Example (10).* In 1986, spouses A and B purchased a personal residence taking title as tenants by the entirety. B dies on July 10, 1998. A wishes to disclaim the one-half undivided interest to which A would succeed by right of survivorship. If A makes the disclaimer, the property interest would pass under B's will to their child C. C, an adult, and A resided in the residence at B's death and will continue to reside there in the future. A continues to own a one-half undivided interest in the property. Assuming that the other requirements of section 2518(b) are satisfied, A may make a qualified disclaimer with respect to the one-half undivided survivorship interest in the residence if A delivers the written disclaimer to the personal representative of B's estate by April 10, 1999, since A is not deemed to have accepted the interest or any of its benefits prior to that time and A's occupancy of the residence after B's death is consistent with A's retained undivided ownership interest. The result would be the same if the property was held in joint tenancy with right of survivorship that was unilaterally severable under local law.

*Example (11).* H and W, husband and wife, reside in state X, a community property state. On April 1, 1978, H and W purchase real property with community funds. The property is not held by H and W as jointly owned property with rights of survivorship. H and W hold the property until January 3, 1985, when H dies. H devises his portion of the property to W. On March 15, 1985, W disclaims the portion of the property devised to her by H. Assuming all the other requirements of section 2518(b) have been met, W has made a qualified disclaimer of the interest devised to her by H. However, W could not disclaim the interest in the property that she acquired on April 1, 1978.

*Example (12).* On July 1, 1990, A opens a bank account that is held jointly with B, A's spouse, and transfers $50,000 of A's money to the account. A and B are United States citizens. A can regain the entire account without B's consent, such that the transfer is not a completed gift under §25.2511-1(h)(4). A dies on August 15, 1998, and B disclaims the entire amount in the bank account on October 15, 1998. Assuming that the remaining requirements of section 2518(b) are satisfied, B made a qualified disclaimer under section 2518(a) because the disclaimer was made within 9 months after A's death at which time B had succeeded to full dominion and control over the account. Under state law, B is treated as predeceasing A with respect to the disclaimed interest. The disclaimed account balance passes through A's probate estate and is no longer joint property includible in A's gross estate under section 2040. The entire account is, instead, includible in A's gross estate under section 2033. The result would be the same if A and B were not married.

*Example (13).* The facts are the same as *Example (12)*, except that B, rather than A, dies on August 15, 1998. A may not make a qualified disclaimer with respect to any of the funds in the bank account, because A furnished the funds for the entire account and A did not relinquish dominion and control over the funds.

*Example (14).* The facts are the same as *Example (12)*, except that B disclaims 40 percent of the funds in the account. Since, under state law, B is treated as predeceasing A with respect to the disclaimed interest, the 40 percent portion of the account balance that was disclaimed passes as part of A's probate estate, and is no longer characterized as joint property. This 40 percent portion of the account balance is, therefore, includible in A's gross estate under section 2033. The remaining 60 percent of the account balance that was not disclaimed retains its character as joint property and, therefore, is includible in A's gross estate as provided in section 2040(b). Therefore, 30 percent (1/2 x 60 percent) of the account balance is includible in A's gross estate under section 2040(b), and a total of 70 percent of the aggregate account balance is includible in A's gross estate. If A and B were not married, then the 40 percent portion of the account subject to the disclaimer would be includible in A's gross estate as provided in section 2033 and the 60 percent portion of the account not subject to the disclaimer would be includible in A's gross estate as provided in section 2040(a), because A furnished all of the funds with respect to the account.

(d) *No acceptance of benefits.*—(1) *Acceptance.*—A qualified disclaimer cannot be made with respect to an interest in property if the disclaimant has accepted the interest or any of its benefits, expressly or impliedly, prior to making the disclaimer. Acceptance is manifested by an affirmative act which is consistent with ownership of interest in property. Acts indicative of acceptance include using the property or the interest in property; accepting dividends, interest, or rents from the property; and directing others to act with respect to the property or interest in property. However, merely taking delivery of an instrument of title, without more, does not constitute acceptance. Moreover, a disclaimant is not considered to have accepted property merely because under applicable local law title to the property vests immediately in the disclaimant upon the death of a decedent. The acceptance of one interest in property will not, by itself, constitute an acceptance of any other separate interests created by the transferor and held by the disclaimant in the same property. In the case of residential property, held in joint tenancy by some or all of the residents, a joint tenant will not be considered to have accepted the joint interest merely because the tenant resided on the property prior to disclaiming his interest in the property. The exercise of a power of appointment to any extent by the donee of the power is an acceptance of its benefits. In addition, the acceptance of any consideration in return for making the disclaimer is an acceptance of the benefits of the entire interest disclaimed.

(2) *Fiduciaries.*—If a beneficiary who disclaims an interest in property is also a fiduciary, actions taken by such person in the exercise of fiduciary powers to preserve or maintain the disclaimed property shall not be treated as an acceptance of such property or any of its benefits. Under this rule, for example, an executor who is also a beneficiary may direct the harvesting of a crop or the general maintenance of a home. A fiduciary, however, cannot retain a wholly discretionary power to direct the enjoyment of the disclaimed interest. For example, a fiduciary's disclaimer of a beneficial interest does not meet the requirements of a qualified disclaimer if the fiduciary exercised or retains a discretionary power to allocate enjoyment of that interest among members of a designated class. See paragraph (e) of this section for rules relating to the effect of directing the redistribution of disclaimed property.

(3) *Under 21 years of age.*—A beneficiary who is under 21 years of age has until 9 months after his twenty-first birthday in which to make a qualified disclaimer of his interest in property. Any actions taken with regard to an interest in property by a beneficiary or a custodian prior to the beneficiary's twenty-first birthday will not be an acceptance by the beneficiary of the interest.

(4) *Examples.*—The provisions of paragraphs (d)(1), (2) and (3) of this section may be illustrated by the following examples:

*Example (1).* On April 9, 1977, A established a trust for the benefit of B, then age 22. Under the terms of the trust, the current income of the trust is to be paid quarterly to B. Additionally, one half the principal is to be distributed to B when B attains the age of 30 years. The balance of the principal is to be distributed to B when B attains the age of 40 years. Pursuant to the terms of the trust, B received a distribution of income on June 30, 1977. On August 1, 1977, B disclaimed B's right to receive both the income from the trust and the principal of the trust. B's disclaimer of the income interest is not a qualified disclaimer for purposes of section 2518(a) because B accepted income prior to making the disclaimer. B's disclaimer of the principal, however, does satisfy section 2518(b)(3). See also §25.2518-3 for rules relating to the disclaimer of less than an entire interest in property.

*Example (2).* B is the recipient of certain property devised to B under the will of A. The will stated that any disclaimed property was to pass to C. B and C entered into negotiations in which it was decided that B would disclaim all interest in the real property that was devised to B. In exchange, C promised to let B live in the family home for life. B's disclaimer is not a qualified disclaimer for purposes of section 2518(a) because B accepted consideration for making the disclaimer.

*Example (3).* A received a gift of Blackacre on December 25, 1978. A never resided on Blackacre but when property taxes on Blackacre became due on July 1, 1979, A paid them out of personal funds. On August 15, 1979, A disclaimed the gift of Blackacre. Assuming all the requirements of section 2518(b) have been met, A has made a qualified disclaimer of Blackacre. Merely paying the property taxes does not constitute an acceptance of Blackacre even though A's personal funds were used to pay the taxes.

*Example (4).* A died on February 15, 1978. Pursuant to A's will, B received a farm in State Z. B requested the executor to sell the farm and to give the proceeds to B. The executor then sold the farm pursuant to B's request. B then disclaimed $50,000 of the proceeds from the sale of the farm. B's disclaimer is not a qualified disclaimer. By requesting the executor to sell the farm B accepted the farm even though the executor may not have been legally obligated to comply with B's request. See also § 25.2518-3 for rules relating to the disclaimer of less than an entire interest in property.

*Example (5).* Assume the same facts as in example (4) except that instead of requesting the executor to sell the farm, B pledged the farm as security for a short-term loan which was paid off prior to distribution of the estate. B then disclaimed his interest in the farm. B's disclaimer is not a qualified disclaimer. By pledging the farm as security for the loan, B accepted the farm.

*Example (6).* A delivered 1,000 shares of stock in Corporation X to B as a gift on February 1, 1980. A had the shares registered in B's name on that date. On April 1, 1980, B disclaimed the interest in the 1,000 shares. Prior to making the disclaimer, B did not pledge the shares, accept any dividends or otherwise commit any acts indicative of acceptance. Assuming the remaining requirements of section 2518 are satisfied, B's disclaimer is a qualified disclaimer.

*Example (7).* On January 1, 1980, A created an irrevocable trust in which B was given a testamentary general power of appointment over the trust's corpus. B executed a will on June 1, 1980, in which B provided for the exercise of the power of appointment. On September 1, 1980, B disclaimed the testamentary power of appointment. Assuming the remaining requirements of section 2518(b) are satisfied, B's disclaimer of the testamentary power of appointment is a qualified disclaimer.

*Example (8).* H and W reside in X, a community property state. On January 1, 1981, H and W purchase a residence with community funds. They continue to reside in the house until H dies testate on February 1, 1990. Although H could devise his portion of the residence to any person, H devised his portion of the residence to W. On September 1, 1990, W disclaims the portion of the residence devised to her pursuant to H's will but continues to live in the residence. Assuming the remaining requirements of section 2518(b) are satisfied, W's disclaimer is a qualified disclaimer under section 2518(a). W's continued occupancy of the house prior to making the disclaimer will not by itself be treated as an acceptance of the benefits of the portion of the residence devised to her by H.

*Example (9).* In 1979, D established a trust for the benefit of D's minor children E and F. Under the terms of the trust, the trustee is given the power to make discretionary distributions of current income and corpus to both children. The corpus of the trust is to be distributed equally between E and F when E becomes 35 years of age. Prior to attaining the age of 21 years on April 8, 1982, E receives several distributions of income from the trust. E receives no distributions of income between April 8, 1982 and August 15, 1982, which is the date on which E disclaims all interest in the income from the trust. As a result of the disclaimer the income will be distributed to F. If the remaining requirements of section 2518 are met, E's disclaimer is a qualified disclaimer under section 2518(a). To have a qualified disclaimer of the interest in corpus, E must disclaim the interest no later than 9 months after April 8, 1982, E's 21st birthday.

*Example (10).* Assume the same facts as in example (9) except that E accepted a distribution of income on May 13, 1982. E's disclaimer is not a qualified disclaimer under section 2518 because by accepting an income distribution after attaining the age of 21, E accepted benefits from the income interest.

*Example (11).* F made a gift of 10 shares of stock to G as custodian for H under the State X Uniform Gifts to Minors Act. At the time of the gift, H was 15 years old. At age 18, the local age of majority, the 10 shares were delivered to and registered in the name of H. Between the receipt of the shares and H's 21st birthday, H received dividends from the shares. Within 9 months of attaining age 21, H disclaimed the 10 shares. Assuming H did not accept any dividends from the shares after attaining age 21, the disclaimer by H is a qualified disclaimer under section 2518.

(e) *Passage without direction by the disclaimant of beneficial enjoyment of disclaimed interest.*—(1) *In general.*—A disclaimer is not a qualified disclaimer unless the disclaimed interest passes without any direction on the part of the disclaimant to a person other than the disclaimant (except as provided in paragraph (e)(2) of this section). If there is an express or implied agreement that the disclaimed interest in property is to be given or bequeathed to a person specified by the disclaimant, the disclaimant shall be treated as directing the transfer of the property interest. The requirements of a qualified disclaimer under section 2518 are not satisfied if—

(i) The disclaimant, either alone or in conjunction with another, directs the redistribution or transfer of the property or interest in property to another person (or has the power to direct the redistribution or transfer of the property or interest in property to another person unless such power is limited by an ascertainable standard); or

(ii) The disclaimed property or interest in property passes to or for the benefit of the disclaimant as a result of the disclaimer (except as provided in paragraph (e)(2) of this section).

If a power of appointment is disclaimed, the requirements of this paragraph (e)(1) are satisfied so long as there is no direction on the part of the disclaimant with respect to the transfer of the interest subject to the power or with respect to the transfer of the power to another person. A person may make a qualified disclaimer of a beneficial interest in property even if after such disclaimer the disclaimant has a fiduciary power to distribute to designated beneficiaries, but only if the power is subject to an ascertainable standard. See examples (11) and (12) of paragraph (e)(5) of this section.

(2) *Disclaimer by surviving spouse.*—In the case of a disclaimer made by a decedent's surviving spouse with respect to property transferred by the decedent, the disclaimer satisfies the requirements of this paragraph (e)(2) if the interest passes as a result of the disclaimer without direction on the part of the surviving spouse either to the surviving spouse or to another person. If the surviving spouse, however, retains the right to direct the beneficial enjoyment of the disclaimed property in a transfer that is not subject to Federal estate and gift tax (whether as trustee or otherwise), such spouse will be treated as directing the beneficial enjoyment of the disclaimed property, unless such power is limited by an ascertainable standard. See examples (4), (5), and (6) in paragraph (e)(5) of this section.

(3) *Partial failure of disclaimer.*—If a disclaimer made by a person other than the surviving spouse is not effective to pass completely an interest in property to a person other than the disclaimant because—

(i) The disclaimant also has a right to receive such property as an heir at law, residuary beneficiary, or by any other means; and

(ii) The disclaimant does not effectively disclaim these rights, the disclaimer is not a qualified disclaimer with respect to the portion of the disclaimed property which the disclaimant has a right to receive. If the portion of the disclaimed interest in property which the disclaimant has a right to receive is not severable property or an undivided portion of the property, then the disclaimer is not a qualified disclaimer with respect to any portion of the property. Thus, for example, if a disclaimant who is not a surviving spouse receives a specific bequest of a fee simple interest in property and as a result of the disclaimer of the entire interest, the property passes to a trust in which the disclaimant has a remainder interest, then the disclaimer will not be a qualified disclaimer unless the remainder interest in the property is also disclaimed. See § 25.2518-3(a)(1)(ii) for the definition of severable property.

(4) *Effect of precatory language.*—Precatory language in a disclaimer naming takers of disclaimed property will not be considered as directing the redistribution or transfer of the property or interest in property to such persons if the applicable State law gives the language no legal effect.

(5) *Examples.*—The provisions of this paragraph (e) may be illustrated by the following examples:

*Example (1).* A, a resident of State X, died on July 30, 1978. Pursuant to A's will, B, A's son and heir at law, received the family home. In addition, B and C each received 50 percent of A's residuary estate. B disclaimed the home. A's will made no provision for the distribution of property in the case of a beneficiary's disclaimer. Therefore, pursuant to the disclaimer laws of State X, the disclaimed property became part of the residuary estate. Because B's 50 percent share of the residuary estate will be increased by 50 percent of the value of the family home, the disclaimed property will not pass solely to another person. Consequently, B's disclaimer of the family home is a qualified disclaimer only with respect to the 50 percent portion ($60,000) that passes solely to C. Had B also disclaimed B's 50 percent interest in the residuary estate, the disclaimer would have been a qualified disclaimer under section 2518 of the entire interest in the home (assuming the remaining requirements of a qualified disclaimer were satisfied). Similarly, if under the laws of State X, the disclaimer has the effect of divesting B of all interest in the home, both as devisee and as a beneficiary of the residuary estate, including any property resulting from its sale, the disclaimer would be a qualified disclaimer of B's entire interest in the home.

*Example (2).* D, a resident of State Y, died testate on June 30, 1978. E, an heir at law of D, received specific bequests of certain severable personal property from D. E disclaimed the property transferred by D under the will. The will had no residuary clause and made no provision for the distribution of property in the case of a beneficiary's disclaimer. The disclaimer laws of State Y provide that such property shall pass to the decedent's heirs at law in the same manner as if the disclaiming beneficiary had died immediately before the testator's death. Because State Y's law treats E as predeceasing D, the property disclaimed by E does not pass to E as an heir at law or otherwise. Consequently, if the remaining requirements of section 2518(b) are

Reg. § 25.2518-2(e)(5)

satisfied, E's disclaimer is a qualified disclaimer under section 2518(a).

*Example (3).* Assume the same facts as in example (2) except that State Y has no provision treating the disclaimant as predeceasing the testator. E's disclaimer satisfies section 2518(b)(4) only to the extent that E does not have a right to receive the property as an heir at law. Had E disclaimed both the share E received under D's will and E's intestate share, the requirement of section 2518(b)(4) would have been satisfied.

*Example (4).* B died testate on February 13, 1980. B's will established both a marital trust and a nonmarital trust. The decedent's surviving spouse, A, is an income beneficiary of the marital trust and has a testamentary general power of appointment over its assets. A is also an income beneficiary of the nonmarital trust, but has no power to appoint or invade the corpus. The provisions of the will specify that any portion of the marital trust disclaimed is to be added to the nonmarital trust. A disclaimed 30 percent of the marital trust. (See § 25.2518-3(b) for rules relating to the disclaimer of an undivided portion of an interest in property.) Pursuant to the will, this portion of the marital trust property was transferred to the nonmarital trust without any direction on the part of A. This disclaimer by A satisfies section 2518(b)(4).

*Example (5).* Assume the same facts as in example (4) except that A, the surviving spouse, has both an income interest in the nonmarital trust and a testamentary nongeneral power to appoint among designated beneficiaries. This power is not limited by an ascertainable standard. The requirements of section 2518(b)(4) are not satisfied unless A also disclaims the nongeneral power to appoint the portion of the trust corpus that is attributable to the property that passed to the nonmarital trust as a result of A's disclaimer. Assuming that the fair market value of the disclaimed property on the date of the disclaimer is $250,000 and that the fair market value of the nonmarital trust (including the disclaimed property) immediately after the disclaimer is $750,000, A must disclaim the power to appoint one-third of the nonmarital trust's corpus. The result is the same regardless of whether the nongeneral power is testamentary or inter vivos.

*Example (6).* Assume the same facts as in example (4) except that A has both an income interest in the nonmarital trust and a power to invade corpus if needed for A's health or maintenance. In addition, an independent trustee has power to distribute to A any portion of the corpus which the trustee determines to be desirable for A's happiness. Assuming the other requirements of section 2518 are satisfied, A may make a qualified disclaimer of interests in the marital trust without disclaiming any of A's interests in the nonmarital trust.

*Example (7).* B died testate on June 1, 1980. B's will created both a marital trust and a nonmarital trust. The decedent's surviving spouse, C, is an income beneficiary of the marital trust and has a testamentary general power of appointment over its assets. C is an income beneficiary of the nonmarital trust, and additionally has the noncumulative right to withdraw yearly the greater of $5,000 or 5 percent of the aggregate value of the principal. The provisions of the will specify that any portion of the marital trust disclaimed is to be added to the nonmarital trust. C disclaims 50 percent of the marital trust corpus. Pursuant to the will, this amount is transferred to the nonmarital trust. Assuming the remaining requirements of section 2518(b) are satisfied, C's disclaimer is a qualified disclaimer.

*Example (8).* A, a resident of State X, died on July 19, 1979. A was survived by a spouse B, and three children, C, D, and E. Pursuant to A's will, B received one-half of A's estate and the children received equal shares of the remaining one-half of the estate. B disclaimed the entire interest B had received. The will made no provisions for the distribution of property in the case of a beneficiary's disclaimer. The disclaimer laws of State X provide that under these circumstances disclaimed property passes to the decedent's heirs at law in the same manner as if the disclaiming beneficiary had died immediately before the testator's death. As a result, C, D, and E are A's only remaining heirs at law, and will divide the disclaimed property equally among themselves. B's disclaimer includes language stating that "it is my intention that C, D, and E will share equally in the division of this property as a result of my disclaimer." State X considers these to be precatory words and gives them no legal effect. B's disclaimer meets all other requirements imposed by State X on disclaimers, and is considered an effective disclaimer under which the property will vest solely in C, D, and E in equal shares without any further action required by B. Therefore, B is not treated as directing the redistribution or transfer of the property. If the remaining requirements of section 2518 are met, B's disclaimer is a qualified disclaimer.

*Example (9).* C died testate on January 1, 1979. According to C's will, D was to receive $1/3$ of the residuary estate with any disclaimed property going to E. D was also to receive a second $1/3$ of the residuary estate with any disclaimed property going to F. Finally, D was to receive a final $1/3$ of the residuary estate with any disclaimed

property going to G. D specifically states that he is disclaiming the interest in which the disclaimed property is designated to pass to E. D has effectively directed that the disclaimed property will pass to E and therefore D's disclaimer is not a qualified disclaimer under section 2518(a).

*Example (10).* Assume the same facts as in example (9) except that C's will also states that D was to receive Blackacre and Whiteacre. C's will further provides that if D disclaimed Blackacre then such property was to pass to E and that if D disclaimed Whiteacre then Whiteacre was to pass to F. D specifically disclaims Blackacre with the intention that it pass to E. Assuming the other requirements of section 2518 are met, D has made a qualified disclaimer of Blackacre. Alternatively, D could disclaim an undivided portion of both Blackacre and Whiteacre. Assuming the other requirements of section 2518 are met, this would also be a qualified disclaimer.

*Example (11).* G creates an irrevocable trust on February 16, 1983, naming H, I and J as the income beneficiaries for life and F as the remainderman. F is also named the trustee and as trustee has the discretionary power to invade the corpus and make discretionary distributions to H, I or J during their lives. F disclaims the remainder interest on August 8, 1983, but retains his discretionary power to invade the corpus. F has not made a qualified disclaimer because F retains the power to direct enjoyment of the corpus and the retained fiduciary power is not limited by an ascertainable standard.

*Example (12).* Assume the same facts as in example (11) except that F may only invade the corpus to make distributions for the health, maintenance or support of H, I or J during their lives. If the other requirements of section 2518(b) are met, F has made a qualified disclaimer of the remainder interest because the retained fiduciary power is limited by an ascertainable standard.

[Reg. § 25.2518-2.]

☐ [*T.D. 8095, 8-6-86. Amended by T.D. 8744, 12-30-97.*]

## [Reg. § 25.2518-3]

**§ 25.2518-3. Disclaimer of less than an entire interest.—** (a) *Disclaimer of a partial interest.*—(1) *In general.*—(i) *Interest.*—If the requirements of this section are met, the disclaimer of all or an undivided portion of any separate interest in property may be a qualified disclaimer even if the disclaimant has another interest in the same property. In general, each interest in property that is separately created by the transferor is treated as a separate interest. For example, if an income interest in securities is bequeathed to A for life, then to B for life, with the remainder interest in such securities bequeathed to A's estate, and if the remaining requirements of section 2518(b) are met, A could make a qualified disclaimer of either the income interest or the remainder, or an undivided portion of either interest. A could not, however, make a qualified disclaimer of the income interest for a certain number of years. Further, where local law merges interests separately created by the transferor, a qualified disclaimer will be allowed only if there is a disclaimer of the entire merged interest or an undivided portion of such merged interest. See example (12) in paragraph (d) of this section. See § 25.2518-3(b) for rules relating to the disclaimer of an undivided portion. Where the merger of separate interests would occur but for the creation by the transferor of a nominal interest (as defined in paragraph (a)(1)(iv) of this section), a qualified disclaimer will be allowed only if there is a disclaimer of all the separate interests, or an undivided portion of all such interests, which would have merged but for the nominal interest.

(ii) *Severable property.*—A disclaimant shall be treated as making a qualified disclaimer of a separate interest in property if the disclaimer relates to severable property and the disclaimant makes a disclaimer which would be a qualified disclaimer if such property were the only property in which the disclaimant had an interest. If applicable local law does not recognize a purported disclaimer of severable property, the disclaimant must comply with the requirements of paragraph (c)(1) of § 25.2518-1 in order to make a qualified disclaimer of the severable property. Severable property is property which can be divided into separate parts each of which, after severance, maintains a complete and independent existence. For example, a legatee of shares of corporate stock may accept some shares of the stock and make a qualified disclaimer of the remaining shares.

(iii) *Powers of appointment.*—A power of appointment with respect to property is treated as a separate interest in such property and such power of appointment with respect to all or an undivided portion of such property may be disclaimed independently from any other interests separately created by the transferor in the property if the requirements of section 2518(b) are met. See example (21) of paragraph (d) of this section. Further, a disclaimer of a power of appointment with respect to property is a qualified disclaimer only if any right to direct the beneficial enjoyment of the property which is retained by the disclaimant is limited by an ascertainable standard. See example (9) of paragraph (d) of this section.

(iv) *Nominal interest.*—A nominal interest is an interest in property created by the transferor that—

(A) Has an actuarial value (as determined under §20.2031-7) of less than 5 percent of the total value of the property at the time of the taxable transfer creating the interest,

(B) Prevents the merger under local law of two or more other interests created by the transferor, and

(C) Can be clearly shown from all the facts and circumstances to have been created primarily for the purpose of preventing the merger of such other interests.

Factors to be considered in determining whether an interest is created primarily for the purpose of preventing merger include (but are not limited to) the following: the relationship between the transferor and the interest holder; the age difference between the interest holder and the beneficiary whose interests would have merged; the interest holder's state of health at the time of the taxable transfer; and, in the case of a contingent remainder, any other factors which indicate that the possibility of the interest vesting as a fee simple is so remote as to be negligible.

(2) *In trust.*—A disclaimer is not a qualified disclaimer under section 2518 if the beneficiary disclaims income derived from specific property transferred in trust while continuing to accept income derived from the remaining properties in the same trust unless the disclaimer results in such property being removed from the trust and passing, without any direction on the part of the disclaimant, to persons other than the disclaimant or to the spouse of the decedent. Moreover, a disclaimer of both an income interest and a remainder interest in specific trust assets is not a qualified disclaimer if the beneficiary retains interests in other trust property unless, as a result of the disclaimer, such assets are removed from the trust and pass, without any direction on the part of the disclaimant, to persons other than the disclaimant or to the spouse of the decedent. The disclaimer of an undivided portion of an interest in a trust may be a qualified disclaimer. See also paragraph (b) of this section for rules relating to the disclaimer of an undivided portion of an interest in property.

(b) *Disclaimer of undivided portion.*—A disclaimer of an undivided portion of a separate interest in property which meets the other requirements of a qualified disclaimer under section 2518(b) and the corresponding regulations is a qualified disclaimer. An undivided portion of a disclaimant's separate interest in property must consist of a fraction or percentage of each and every substantial interest or right owned by the disclaimant in such property and must extend over the entire term of the disclaimant's interest in such property and in other property into which such property is converted. A disclaimer of some specific rights while retaining other rights with respect to an interest in the property is not a qualified disclaimer of an undivided portion of the disclaimant's interest in property. Thus, for example, a disclaimer made by the devisee of a fee simple interest in Blackacre is not a qualified disclaimer if the disclaimant disclaims a remainder interest in Blackacre but retains a life estate.

(c) *Disclaimer of a pecuniary amount.*—A disclaimer of a specific pecuniary amount out of a pecuniary or nonpecuniary bequest or gift which satisfies the other requirements of a qualified disclaimer under section 2518(b) and the corresponding regulations is a qualified disclaimer provided that no income or other benefit of the disclaimed amount inures to the benefit of the disclaimant either prior to or subsequent to the disclaimer. Thus, following the disclaimer of a specific pecuniary amount from a bequest or gift, the amount disclaimed and any income attributable to such amount must be segregated from the portion of the gift or bequest that was not disclaimed. Such a segregation of assets making up the disclaimer of a pecuniary amount must be made on the basis of the fair market value of the assets on the date of the disclaimer or on a basis that is fairly representative of value changes that may have occurred between the date of transfer and the date of the disclaimer. A pecuniary amount distributed to the disclaimant from the bequest or gift prior to the disclaimer shall be treated as a distribution of corpus from the bequest or gift. However, the acceptance of a distribution from the gift or bequest shall also be considered to be an acceptance of a proportionate amount of income earned by the bequest or gift. The proportionate share of income considered to be accepted by the disclaimant shall be determined at the time of the disclaimer according to the following formula:

$$\frac{\text{total amount of distributions received by the disclaimant out of the gift or bequest}}{\text{total value of the gift or bequest on the date of transfer}} \times \frac{\text{total amount of income earned by the gift or bequest between date of transfer and date of disclaimer.}}{}$$

See examples (17), (18), and (19) in §25.2518-3 (d) for illustrations of the rules set forth in this paragraph (c).

(d) *Examples.*—The provisions of this section may be illustrated by the following examples:

*Example (1).* A, resident of State Q, died on August 1, 1978. A's will included specific bequests of 100 shares of stock in X corporation; 200 shares of stock in Y corporation; 500 shares of stock in Z corporation; personal effects consisting of paintings, home furnishings, jewelry, and silver; and a 500 acre farm consisting of a residence, various outbuildings, and 500 head of cattle. The laws of State Q provide that a disclaimed interest passes in the same manner as if the disclaiming beneficiary had died immediately before the testator's death. Pursuant to A's will, B was to receive both the personal effects and the farm. C was to receive all the shares of stock in Corporation X and Y and D was to receive all the shares of stock in Corporation Z. B disclaimed 2 of the paintings and all the jewelry, C disclaimed 50 shares of Y corporation stock, and D disclaimed 100 shares of Z corporation stock. If the remaining requirements of section 2518(b) and the corresponding regulations are met, each of these disclaimers is a qualified disclaimer for purposes of section 2518(a).

*Example (2).* Assume the same facts as in example (1) except that D disclaimed the income interest in the shares of Z corporation stock while retaining the remainder interest in such shares. D's disclaimer is not a qualified disclaimer.

*Example (3).* Assume the same facts as in example (1) except that B disclaimed 300 identified acres of the 500 acres. Assuming that B's disclaimer meets the remaining requirements of section 2518(b), it is a qualified disclaimer.

*Example (4).* Assume the same facts as in example (1) except that A devised the income from the farm to B for life and the remainder interest to C. B disclaimed 40 percent of the income from the farm. Assuming that it meets the remaining requirements of section 2518(b), B's disclaimer of an undivided portion of the income is a qualified disclaimer.

*Example (5).* E died on September 13, 1978. Under the provisions of E's will, E's shares of stock in X, Y, and Z corporations were to be transferred to a trust. The trust provides that all income is to be distributed currently to F and G in equal parts until F attains the age of 45 years. At that time the corpus of the trust is to be divided equally between F and G. F disclaimed the income arising from the shares of X stock. G disclaimed 20 percent of G's interest in the trust. F's disclaimer is not a qualified disclaimer because the X stock remains in the trust. If the remaining requirements of section 2518(b) are met, G's disclaimer is a qualified disclaimer.

*Example (6).* Assume the same facts as in example (5) except that F disclaimed both the income interest and the remainder interest in the shares of X stock. F's disclaimer results in the X stock being transferred out of the trust to G without any direction on F's part. F's disclaimer is a qualified disclaimer under section 2518(b).

*Example (7).* Assume the same facts as in example (5) except that F is only an income beneficiary of the trust. The X stock remains in the trust after F's disclaimer of the income arising from the shares of X stock. F's disclaimer is not a qualified disclaimer under section 2518.

*Example (8).* Assume the same facts as in example (5) except that F disclaimed the entire income interest in the trust while retaining the interest F has in corpus. Alternatively, assume that G disclaimed G's entire corpus interest while retaining G's interest in the income from the trust. If the remaining requirements of section 2518(b) are met, either disclaimer will be a qualified disclaimer.

*Example (9).* G creates an irrevocable trust on May 13, 1980, with H, I, and J as the income beneficiaries. In addition, H, who is the trustee, holds the power to invade corpus for H's health, maintenance, support and happiness and a testamentary power of appointment over the corpus. In the absence of the exercise of the power of appointment, the property passes to I and J in equal shares. H disclaimed the power to invade corpus for H's health, maintenance, support and happiness. Because H retained the testamentary power to appoint the property in the corpus, H's disclaimer is not a qualified disclaimer. If H also disclaimed the testamentary power of appointment, H's disclaimer would have been a qualified disclaimer.

*Example (10).* E creates an irrevocable trust on May 1, 1980, in which D is the income beneficiary for life. Subject to the trustee's discretion, E's children, A, B, and C, have the right to receive corpus during D's lifetime. The remainder passes to D if D survives A, B, C, and all their issue. D also holds an inter vivos power to appoint the trust corpus to A, B, and C. On September 1, 1980, D disclaimed the remainder interest. D's disclaimer is not a qualified disclaimer because D retained the power to direct the use and enjoyment of corpus during D's life.

*Example (11).* Under H's will, a trust is created from which W is to receive all of the income for life. The trustee has the power to invade the trust corpus for the support or maintenance of D during the life of W. The trust is to terminate at W's death, at which time the trust property is to be distributed to D. D makes a timely disclaimer of the right to corpus during W's lifetime, but does not disclaim the remainder interest. D's disclaimer is a qualified disclaimer assuming the remaining requirements of section 2518 are met.

*Example (12).* Under the provisions of G's will A received a life estate in a farm, and was the sole beneficiary of property in the residuary estate. The will also provided that the remainder interest in the farm pass to the residuary estate. Under local law A's interests merged to give A a fee simple in the farm. A made a timely disclaimer of the life estate. A's disclaimer of a partial interest is not a qualified disclaimer under section 2518(a). If A makes a disclaimer of the entire merged interest in the farm or an undivided portion of such merged interest then A would be making a qualified disclaimer assuming all the other requirements of section 2518(b) are met.

*Example (13).* A, a resident of State Z, dies on September 3, 1980. Under A's will, Blackacre is devised to C for life, then to D for 1 month, remainder to C. Had A not created D's interest, State Z law would have merged C's life estate and the remainder to C to create a fee simple interest in C. Assume that the actuarial value of D's interest is less than 5 percent of the total value of Blackacre on the date of A's death. Further assume that facts and circumstances (particularly the duration of D's interest) clearly indicate that D's interest was created primarily for the purpose of preventing the merger of C's two interests in Blackacre. D's interest in Blackacre is a nominal interest and C's two interests will, for purposes of making a qualified disclaimer, be considered to have merged. Thus, C cannot make a qualified disclaimer of his remainder while retaining the life estate. C can, however, make a qualified disclaimer of both of these interests entirely or an undivided portion of both.

*Example (14).* A, a resident of State X, dies on October 12, 1978. Under A's will, Blackacre was devised to B for life, then to C for life if C survives B, remainder to B's estate. On the date of A's death, B and C are both 8 year old grandchildren of A. In addition, C is in good health. The actual value of C's interest is less than 5 percent of the total value of Blackacre on the date of A's death. No facts are present which would indicate that the possibility of C's contingent interest vesting is so remote as to be negligible. Had C's contingent life estate not been created, B's life estate and remainder interests would have merged under local law to give B a fee simple interest in Blackacre. Although C's interest prevents the merger of B's two interests and has an actual value of less than 5 percent, C's interest is not a nominal interest within the meaning of § 25.2518-3(a)(1)(iv) because the facts and circumstances do not clearly indicate that the interest was created primarily for the purpose of preventing the merger of other interests in the property. Assuming all the other requirements of section 2518(b) are met, B can make a qualified disclaimer of the remainder while retaining his life estate.

*Example (15).* In 1981, A transfers $60,000 to a trust created for the benefit of B who was given the income interest for life and who also has a testamentary nongeneral power of appointment over the corpus. A transfers an additional $25,000 to the trust on June 1, 1984. At that time the trust corpus (exclusive of the $25,000 transfer) has a fair market value of $75,000. On January 1, 1985, B disclaims the right to receive income attributable to 25 percent of the corpus

| $25,000 | (1984 transfer) | |
|---|---|---|
| $100,000 | (Fair market value of corpus immediately after the 1984 transfer) | = 25%. |

Assuming that no distributions were made to B attributable to the $25,000, B's disclaimer is a qualified disclaimer for purposes of section 2518(a) if all the remaining requirements of section 2518(b) are met.

*Example (16).* Under the provisions of B's will, A is left an outright cash legacy of $50,000 and has no other interest in B's estate. A timely disclaimer by A of any stated dollar amount is a qualified disclaimer under section 2518(a).

*Example (17).* D bequeaths his brokerage account to E. The account consists of stocks and bonds and a cash amount earning interest. The total value of the cash and assets in the account on the date of D's death is $100,000. Four months after D's death, E makes a withdrawal of cash from the account for personal use amounting to $40,000. Eight months after D's death, E disclaims $60,000 of the account without specifying any particular assets or cash. The cumulative fair market value of the stocks and bonds in the account on the date of the disclaimer is equal to the value of such stocks and bonds on the date of D's death. The income earned by the account between the date of D's death and the date of E's disclaimer was $20,000. The amount of income earned by the account that E accepted by withdrawing $40,000 from the account prior to the disclaimer is determined by applying the formula set forth in § 25.2518-3(c) as follows:

$$\frac{\$40,000}{\$100,000} \times \$20,000 = \$8,000$$

E is considered to have accepted $8,000 of the income earned by the account. If (i) the $60,000 disclaimed by E and the $12,000 of income earned prior to the disclaimer which is attributable to that amount are segregated from the $8,000 of income E is considered to have accepted, (ii) E does not accept any benefits of the $72,000 so segregated, and (iii) the other requirements of section 2518(b) are met, then E's disclaimer of $60,000 from the account is a qualified disclaimer.

*Example (18).* A bequeathed his residuary estate to B. The residuary estate had a value of $1 million on the date of A's death. Six months later, B disclaimed $200,000 out of this bequest. B received distributions of all the income from the entire estate during the period of administration. When the estate was distributed, B received the entire residuary estate except for $200,000 in cash. B did not make a qualified disclaimer since he accepted the benefits of the $200,000 during the period of estate administration.

*Example (19).* Assume the same facts as in example (18) except that no income was paid to B and the value of the residuary estate on the date of the disclaimer (including interest earned from date of death) was $1.5 million. In addition, as soon as B's disclaimer was made, the executor of A's estate set aside assets worth $300,000

$$\frac{\$200,000}{\$1,000,000} \times \$1,500,000$$

and the interest earned after the disclaimer on that amount in a separate fund so that none of the income was paid to B. B's disclaimer is a qualified disclaimer under section 2518(a).

*Example (20).* A bequeathed his residuary estate to B. B disclaims a fractional share of the residuary estate. Any disclaimed property will pass to A's surviving spouse, W. The numerator of the fraction disclaimed is the smallest amount which will allow A's estate to pass free of Federal estate tax and the denominator is the value of the residuary estate. B's disclaimer is a qualified disclaimer.

*Example (21).* A created a trust on July 1, 1979. The trust provides that all current income is to be distributed equally between B and C for the life of B. B also is given a testamentary general power of appointment over the corpus. If the power is not exercised, the corpus passes to C or C's heirs. B disclaimed the testamentary power to appoint an undivided one-half of the trust corpus. Assuming the remaining requirements of section 2518(b) are satisfied, B's disclaimer is a qualified disclaimer under section 2518(a). [Reg. § 25.2518-3.]

☐ [*T.D. 8095, 8-6-86. Amended by T.D. 8540, 6-9-94.*]

**[Reg. § 25.2519-1]**

**§ 25.2519-1. Dispositions of certain life estates.**—(a) *In general.*— If a donee spouse makes a disposition of all or part of a qualifying income interest for life in any property for which a deduction was allowed under section 2056(b)(7) or section 2523(f) for the transfer creating the qualifying income interest, the donee spouse is treated for purposes of chapters 11 and 12 of subtitle B of the Internal Revenue Code as transferring all interests in property other than the qualifying income interest. For example, if the donee spouse makes a disposition of part of a qualifying income interest for life in trust corpus, the spouse is treated under section 2519 as making a transfer subject to chapters 11 and 12 of the entire trust other than the qualifying income interest for life. Therefore, the donee spouse is treated as making a gift under section 2519 of the entire trust less the qualifying income interest, and is treated for purposes of section 2036 as having transferred the entire trust corpus, including that portion of the trust corpus from which the retained income interest is payable. A transfer of all or a portion of the income interest of the spouse is a transfer by the spouse under section 2511. See also section 2702 for special rules applicable in valuing the gift made by the spouse under section 2519.

(b) *Presumption.*—Unless the donee spouse establishes to the contrary, section 2519 applies to the entire trust at the time of the disposition. If a deduction is taken on either the estate or gift tax return with respect to the transfer which created the qualifying income interest, it is presumed that the deduction was allowed for purposes of section 2519. To avoid the application of section 2519 upon a transfer of all or part of the donee spouse's income interest, the donee spouse must establish that a deduction was not taken for the transfer of property which created the qualifying income interest. For example, to establish that a deduction was not taken, the donee spouse may produce a copy of the estate or gift tax return filed with respect to the transfer creating the qualifying income interest for life establishing that no deduction was taken under section 2056(b)(7) or section 2523(f). In addition, the donee spouse may establish that no return was filed on the original transfer by the donor spouse because the value of the first spouse's gross estate was below the threshold requirement for filing under section 6018. Similarly, the donee spouse could establish that the transfer creating the qualifying income interest for life was made before the effective date of section 2056(b)(7) or section 2523(f), whichever is applicable.

(c) *Amount treated as a transfer.*—(1) *In general.*—The amount treated as a transfer under this section upon a disposition of all or part of a qualifying income interest for life in qualified terminable interest property is equal to the fair market value of the entire property subject to the qualifying income interest, determined on the date of the disposition (including any accumulated income and not reduced by any amount excluded from total gifts under section 2503(b) with respect to the transfer creating the interest), less the value of the qualifying income interest in the property on the date of the disposition. The gift tax consequences of the disposition of the qualifying income interest are determined separately under § 25.2511-2. See paragraph (c)(4) of this section for the effect of gift tax that the donee spouse is entitled to recover under section 2207A.

(2) *Disposition of interest in property with respect to which a partial election was made.*—If, in connection with the transfer of property that created the spouse's qualifying income interest for life, a deduction was allowed under section 2056(b)(7) or section 2523(f) for less than the entire interest in the property (i.e., for a fractional or percentage share of the entire interest in the transferred property) the amount treated as a transfer by the donee spouse under this section is equal to the fair market value of the entire property subject to the qualifying income interest on the date of the disposition, less the value of the qualifying income interest for life, multiplied by the fractional or percentage share of the interest for which the deduction was taken.

(3) *Reduction for distributions charged to nonelective portion of trust.*—The amount determined under paragraph (c)(2) of this section (if applicable) is appropriately reduced if—

(i) The donee spouse's interest is in a trust and distributions of principal have been made to the donee spouse;

(ii) The trust provides that distributions of principal are made first from the qualified terminable interest share of the trust; and

(iii) The donee spouse establishes the reduction in that share based on the fair market value of the trust assets at the time of each distribution.

(4) *Effect of gift tax entitled to be recovered under section 2207A on the amount of the transfer.*—The amount treated as a transfer under paragraph (c)(1) of this section is further reduced by the amount the donee spouse is entitled to recover under section 2207A(b) (relating to the right to recover gift tax attributable to the remainder interest). If the donee spouse is entitled to recover gift tax under section 2207A(b), the amount of gift tax recoverable and the value of the remainder interest treated as transferred under section 2519 are determined by using the same interrelated computation applicable for other transfers in which the transferee assumes the gift tax liability. The gift tax consequences of failing to exercise the right of recovery are determined separately under § 25.2207A-1(b).

(5) *Interest in previously severed trust.*—If the donee spouse's interest is in a trust consisting of only qualified terminable interest property, and the trust was previously severed (in compliance with § 20.2056(b)-7(b)(2)(ii) of this chapter or § 25.2523(f)-1(b)(3)(ii) from a trust that, after the severance, held only property that was not qualified terminable interest property, only the value of the property in the severed portion of the trust at the time of the disposition is treated as transferred under this section.

(d) *Identification of property transferred.*—If only part of the property in which a donee spouse has a qualifying income interest for life is qualified terminable interest property, the donee spouse is, in the case of a disposition of all or part of the income interest within the meaning of section 2519, deemed to have transferred a pro rata portion of the entire qualified terminable interest property for purposes of this section.

(e) *Exercise of power of appointment.*—The exercise by any person of a power to appoint qualified terminable interest property to the donee spouse is not treated as a disposition under section 2519, even though the donee spouse subsequently disposes of the appointed property.

(f) *Conversion of qualified terminable interest property.*—The conversion of qualified terminable interest property into other property in which the donee spouse has a qualifying income interest for life is not, for purposes of this section, treated as a disposition of the qualifying income interest. Thus, the sale and reinvestment of assets

of a trust holding qualified terminable interest property is not a disposition of the qualifying income interest, provided that the donee spouse continues to have a qualifying income interest for life in the trust after the sale and reinvestment. Similarly, the sale of real property in which the spouse possesses a legal life estate and thus meets the requirements of qualified terminable interest property, followed by the transfer of the proceeds into a trust which also meets the requirements of qualified terminable interest property, or by the reinvestment of the proceeds in income producing property in which the donee spouse has a qualifying income interest for life, is not considered a disposition of the qualifying income interest. On the other hand, the sale of qualified terminable interest property, followed by the payment to the donee spouse of a portion of the proceeds equal to the value of the donee spouse's income interest, is considered a disposition of the qualifying income interest.

(g) *Examples.*—The following examples illustrate the application of paragraphs (a) through (f) of this section. Except as provided otherwise in the examples, assume that the decedent, D, was survived by spouse, S, that in each example the section 2503(b) exclusion has already been fully utilized for each year with respect to the donee in question, that section 2503(e) is not applicable to the amount deemed transferred, and that the gift taxes on the amount treated as transferred under paragraph (c) are offset by S's unified credit. The examples are as follows:

*Example 1. Transfer of the spouse's life estate in residence.* Under D's will, a personal residence valued for estate tax purposes at $250,000 passes to S for life, and after S's death to D's children. D's executor made a valid election to treat the property as qualified terminable interest property. During 1995, when the fair market value of the property is $300,000 and the value of S's life interest in the property is $100,000, S makes a gift of S's entire interest in the property to D's children. Pursuant to section 2519, S makes a gift in the amount of $200,000 (i.e., the fair market value of the qualified terminable interest property of $300,000 less the fair market value of S's qualifying income interest in the property of $100,000). In addition, under section 2511, S makes a gift of $100,000 (i.e., the fair market value of S's income interest in the property). See § 25.2511-2.

*Example 2. Sale of spouse's life estate.* The facts are the same as in *Example 1* except that during 1995, S sells S's interest in the property to D's children for $100,000. Pursuant to section 2519, S makes a gift of $200,000 ($300,000 less $100,000 value of the qualifying income interest in the property). S does not make a gift of the income interest under section 2511, because the consideration received for S's income interest is equal to the value of the income interest.

*Example 3. Transfer of income interest in trust subject to partial election.* D's will established a trust valued for estate tax purposes at $500,000, all of the income of which is payable annually to S for life. After S's death, the principal of the trust is to be distributed to D's children. Assume that only 50 percent of the trust was treated as qualified terminable interest property. During 1995, S makes a gift of all of S's interest in the trust to D's children at which time the fair market value of the trust is $400,000 and the fair market value of S's life income interest in the trust is $100,000. Pursuant to section 2519, S makes a gift of $150,000 (the fair market value of the qualified terminable interest property, 50 percent of $400,000, less the $50,000 income interest in the qualified terminable interest property). S also makes a gift pursuant to section 2511 of $100,000 (i.e., the fair market value of S's life income interest).

*Example 4. Transfer of a portion of income interest in trust subject to a partial election.* The facts are the same as in *Example 3* except that S makes a gift of only 40 percent of S's interest in the trust. Pursuant to section 2519, S makes a gift of $150,000 (i.e., the fair market value of the qualified terminable interest property, 50 percent of $400,000, less the $50,000 value of S's qualified income interest in the qualified terminable interest property). S also makes a gift pursuant to section 2511 of $40,000 (i.e., the fair market value of 40 percent of S's life income interest). See also section 2702 for additional rules that may affect the value of the total amount of S's gift under section 2519 to take into account the fact that S's 30 percent retained income interest attributable to the qualifying income interest is valued at zero under that section, thereby increasing the value of S's section 2519 gift to $180,000. In addition, under § 25.2519-1(d), S's disposition of 40 percent of the income interest is deemed to be a transfer of a pro rata portion of the qualified terminable interest property. Thus, assuming no further lifetime dispositions by S, 30 percent (60 percent of 50 percent) of the trust property is included in S's gross estate under section 2036 and an adjustment is made to S's adjusted taxable gifts under section 2001(b)(1)(B). If S later disposes of all or a portion of the retained income interest, see § 25.2702-6.

*Example 5. Transfer of a portion of spouse's interest in a trust from which corpus was previously distributed to the spouse.* D's will established a trust valued for estate tax purposes at $500,000, all of the income of which is payable annually to S for life. The trustee is granted the discretion to distribute trust principal to S. All appointments of principal must be made from the portion of the trust subject to the section 2056(b)(7) election. After S's death, the principal of the trust is to be distributed to D's children. The executor makes the section 2056(b)(7) election with respect to 50 percent of the trust. In 1994, pursuant to the terms of D's will, the trustee distributed $50,000 of principal to S and charged the entire distribution to the qualified terminable interest portion of the trust. Immediately prior to the distribution, the value of the entire trust was $550,000 and the value of the qualified terminable interest portion was $275,000 (50 percent of $550,000). Provided S can establish the above facts, the qualified terminable interest portion of the trust immediately after the distribution is $225,000 or 45 percent of the value of the trust ($225,000/$500,000). In 1996, when the value of the trust is $400,000 and the value of S's income interest is $100,000, S makes a transfer of 40 percent of S's income interest. S's gift under section 2519 is $135,000; i.e., the fair market value of the qualified terminable interest property, 45 percent of $400,000 ($180,000), less the value of the income interest in the qualified terminable interest property, $45,000 (45 percent of $100,000). S also makes a gift under section 2511 of $40,000; i.e., the fair market value of 40 percent of S's income interest. S's disposition of 40 percent of the income interest is deemed to be a transfer under section 2519 of the entire 45 percent portion of the remainder subject to the section 2056(b)(7) election. Since S retained 60 percent of the income interest, 27 percent (60 percent of 45 percent) of the trust property is includible in S's gross estate under section 2036. See also section 2702 and *Example 4* as to the principles applicable in valuing S's gift under section 2702 and adjusted taxable gifts upon S's subsequent death.

*Example 6. Transfer of Spousal Annuity Payable From Trust.* D died prior to October 24, 1992. D's will established a trust valued for estate tax purposes at $500,000. The trust instrument required the trustee to pay an annuity to S of $20,000 a year for life. All the trust income other than the amounts paid to S as an annuity are to be accumulated in the trust and may not be distributed during S's lifetime to any person other than S. After S's death, the principal of the trust is to be distributed to D's children. Because D died prior to the effective date of section 1941 of the Energy Policy Act of 1992, S's annuity interest qualifies as a qualifying income interest for life. Under § 20.2056(b)-7(e) of this chapter, based on an applicable 10 percent interest rate, 40 percent of the property, or $200,000, is the value of the deductible interest. During 1996, S makes a gift of the annuity interest to D's children at which time the fair market value of the trust is $800,000 and the fair market value of S's annuity interest in the trust is $100,000. Pursuant to section 2519, S is treated as making a gift of $220,000 (the fair market value of the qualified terminable interest property, 40 percent of $800,000 ($320,000), less the $100,000 annuity interest in the qualified terminable interest property). S is also treated pursuant to section 2511 as making a gift of $100,000 (the fair market value of S's annuity interest). [Reg. § 25.2519-1.]

☐ *[T.D. 8522, 2-28-94. Amended by T.D. 9077, 7-17-2003.]*

### [Reg. § 25.2519-2]

**§ 25.2519-2. Effective date.**—Except as specifically provided in § 25.2519-1(g), *Example 6*, the provisions of § 25.2519-1 are effective with respect to gifts made after March 1, 1994. With respect to gifts made on or before such date, the donee spouse of a section 2056(b)(7) or section 2523(f) transfer may rely on any reasonable interpretation of the statutory provisions. For these purposes, the provisions of § 25.2519-1 (as well as project LR-211-76, 1984-1 C.B., page 598, see § 601.601(d)(2)(ii)(*b*) of this chapter), are considered a reasonable interpretation of the statutory provisions. [Reg. § 25.2519-2.]

☐ *[T.D. 8522, 2-28-94.]*

# DEDUCTIONS

### [Reg. § 25.2522(a)-1]

**§ 25.2522(a)-1. Charitable and similar gifts; citizens or residents.**—(a) In determining the amount of taxable gifts for the "calendar period" (as defined in § 25.2502-1(c)(1)) there may be deducted, in the case of a donor who was a citizen or resident of the United States at the time the gifts were made, all gifts included in the "total amount of gifts" made by the donor during the calendar period (see section 2503 and the regulations thereunder) and made to or for the use of:

(1) The United States, any State, Territory, or any political subdivision thereof, or the District of Columbia, for exclusively public purposes.

(2) Any corporation, trust, community chest, fund, or foundation organized and operated exclusively for religious, charitable, scientific, literary, or educational purposes, including the encouragement of art and the prevention of cruelty to children or animals, if no part of the net earnings of the organization inures to the benefit of any private shareholder or individual, if it is not disqualified for tax exemption under section 501(c)(3) by reason of attempting to influence legislation, and if, in the case of gifts made after December 31, 1969, it does not participate in, or intervene in (including the publishing or distributing of statements), any political campaign on behalf of or in opposition to any candidate for public office.

(3) A fraternal society, order, or association, operating under the lodge system, provided the gifts are to be used by the society, order or association exclusively for one or more of the purposes set forth in subparagraph (2) of this paragraph.

(4) Any post or organization of war veterans or auxiliary unit or society thereof, if organized in the United States or any of its possessions, and if no part of its net earnings inures to the benefit of any private shareholder or individual.

The deduction is not limited to gifts for use within the United States or to gifts to or for the use of domestic corporations, trusts, community chests, funds, or foundations, or fraternal societies, orders, or associations operating under the lodge system. An organization will not be considered to meet the requirements of subparagraph (2) of this paragraph, or of paragraph (b)(2) or (3) of this section, if such organization engages in any activity which would cause it to be classified as an "action" organization under paragraph (c)(3) of § 1.501(c)(3)-1 of this chapter (Income Tax Regulations). For the deductions for charitable and similar gifts made by a nonresident who was not a citizen of the United States at the time the gifts were made, see § 25.2522(b)-1. See § 25.2522(c)-1 and § 25.2522(c)-2 for rules relating to the disallowance of deductions to trusts and organizations which engage in certain prohibited transactions or whose governing instruments do not contain certain specified requirements.

(b) The deduction under section 2522 is not allowed for a transfer to a corporation, trust, community chest, fund, or foundation unless the organization or trust meets the following four tests:

(1) It must be organized and operated exclusively for one or more of the specified purposes.

(2) It must not be disqualified for tax exemption under section 501(c)(3) by reason of attempting to influence legislation.

(3) In the case of gifts made after December 31, 1969, it must not participate in, or intervene in (including the publishing or distributing of statements), any political campaign on behalf of any candidate for public office.

(4) Its net earnings must not inure in whole or in part to the benefit of private shareholders or individuals other than as legitimate objects of the exempt purposes.

(c) In order to prove the right to the charitable, etc., deduction provided by section 2522, the donor must submit such data as may be requested by the Internal Revenue Service. As to the extent the deductions provided by this section are allowable, see section 2524. [Reg. § 25.2522(a)-1.]

☐ *[T.D. 6334, 11-14-58. Amended by T.D. 7012, 5-14-69; T.D. 7238, 12-28-72; T.D. 7318, 7-10-74; T.D. 7910, 9-6-83 and T.D. 8308, 8-30-90.]*

### [Reg. § 25.2522(b)-1]

**§ 25.2522(b)-1. Charitable and similar gifts; nonresidents not citizens.**—(a) The deduction for charitable and similar gifts in the case of a nonresident who was not a citizen of the United States at the time he made the gifts is governed by the same rules as those applying to gifts by citizens or residents, subject, however, to the following exceptions:

(1) If the gifts are made to or for the use of a corporation, the corporation must be one created or organized under the laws of the United States or of any State or Territory thereof.

(2) If the gifts are made to or for the use of a trust, community chest, fund or foundation, or a fraternal society, order or association operating under the lodge system, the gifts must be for use within the United States exclusively for religious, charitable, scientific, literary or educational purposes, including encouragement of art and the prevention of cruelty to children or animals. [Reg. § 25.2522(b)-1.]

☐ *[T.D. 6334, 11-14-58.]*

### [Reg. § 25.2522(c)-1]

**§ 25.2522(c)-1. Disallowance of charitable, etc., deductions because of "prohibited transactions" in the case of gifts made before January 1, 1970.**—(a) Sections 503(e) and 681(b)(5) provide that no deduction which would otherwise be allowable under section 2522 for a gift for religious, charitable, scientific, literary or educational purposes, including the encouragement of art and the prevention of cruelty to children or animals, is allowed if—

(1) The gift is made in trust and, for income tax purposes for the taxable year of the trust in which the gift is made, the deduction otherwise allowable to the trust under section 642(c) is limited by section 681(b)(1) by reason of the trust having engaged in a prohibited transaction described in section 681(b)(2); or

(2) The gift is made to any corporation, community chest, fund or foundation which, for its taxable year in which the gift is made, is not exempt from income tax under section 501(a) by reason of having engaged in a prohibited transaction described in section 503(c).

(b) For purposes of section 503(e) and section 681(b)(5), the term "gift" includes any gift, contribution, or transfer without adequate consideration.

(c) Regulations relating to the income tax contain the rules for the determination of the taxable year of the trust for which the deduction under section 642(c) is limited by section 681(b), and for the determination of the taxable year of the organization for which an exemption is denied under section 503(a). Generally, such taxable year is a taxable year subsequent to the taxable year during which the trust or organization has been notified by the Internal Revenue Service that it has engaged in a prohibited transaction. However, if the trust or organization during or prior to the taxable year entered into the prohibited transaction for the purpose of diverting its corpus or income from the charitable or other purposes by reason of which it is entitled to a deduction or exemption, and the transaction involves a substantial part of such income or corpus, then the deduction of the trust under section 642(c) for such taxable year is limited by section 681(b), or the exemption of the organization for such taxable year is denied under section 503(a), whether or not the organization has previously received notification by the Internal Revenue Service that it has engaged in a prohibited transaction. In certain cases, the limitation of section 503 or 681 may be removed or the exemption may be reinstated for certain subsequent taxable years under the rules set forth in the income tax regulations under sections 503 and 681.

(d) In cases in which prior notification by the Internal Revenue Service is not required in order to limit the deduction of the trust under section 681(b), or to deny exemption of the organization under section 503, the deduction otherwise allowable under §25.2522(a)-1 is not disallowed with respect to gifts made during the same taxable year of the trust or organization in which a prohibited transaction occurred, or in a prior taxable year, unless the donor or a member of his family was a party to the prohibited transaction. For purposes of the preceding sentence, the members of the donor's family include only his brothers and sisters (whether by whole or half blood), spouse, ancestors, and lineal descendants.

(e) This section applies only to gifts made before January 1, 1970. In the case of gifts made after December 31, 1969, see §25.2522(c)-2. [Reg. §25.2522(c)-1.]

☐ [*T.D. 6334, 11-14-58. Amended by T.D. 7318, 7-10-74.*]

### [Reg. §25.2522(c)-2]

**§25.2522(c)-2. Disallowance of charitable, etc., deductions in the case of gifts made after December 31, 1969.**—(a) *Organizations subject to section 507(c) tax.*—Section 508(d)(1) provides that, in the case of gifts made after December 31, 1969, a deduction which would otherwise be allowable under section 2522 for a gift to or for the use of an organization upon which the tax provided by section 507(c) has been imposed shall not be allowed if the gift is made by the donor after notification is made under section 507(a) or if the donor is a substantial contributor (as defined in section 507(d)(2)) who makes such gift in his taxable year (as defined in section 441) which includes the first day on which action is taken by such organization that culminates in the imposition of the tax under section 507(c) and any subsequent taxable year. This paragraph does not apply if the entire amount of the unpaid portion of the tax imposed by section 507(c) is abated under section 507(g) by the Commissioner or his delegate.

(b) *Taxable private foundations, section 4947 trusts, etc.*—Section 508(d)(2) provides that, in the case of gifts made after December 31, 1969, a deduction which would otherwise be allowable under section 2522 shall not be allowed if the gift is made to or for the use of—

(1) A private foundation or a trust described in section 4947(a)(2) in a taxable year of such organization for which such organization fails to meet the governing instrument requirements of section 508(e) (determined without regard to section 508(e)(2)(B) and (C)), or

(2) Any organization in a period for which it is not treated as an organization described in section 501(c)(3) by reason of its failure to give notification under section 508(a) of its status to the Commissioner.

For additional rules, see §1.508-2(b)(1) of this chapter (Income Tax Regulations).

(c) *Foreign organizations with substantial support from foreign sources.*—Section 4948(c)(4) provides that, in the case of gifts made after December 31, 1969, a deduction which would otherwise be allowable under section 2522 for a gift to or for the use of a foreign organization which has received substantially all of its support (other than gross investment income) from sources without the United States shall not be allowed if the gift is made (1) after the date on which the Commissioner has published notice that he has notified such organization that it has engaged in a prohibited transaction or (2) in a taxable year of such organization for which it is not exempt from taxation under section 501(a) because it has engaged in a prohibited transaction after December 31, 1969. [Reg. §25.2522(c)-2.]

☐ [*T.D. 7318, 6-10-74.*]

### [Reg. §25.2522(c)-3]

**§25.2522(c)-3. Transfers not exclusively for charitable, etc., purposes in the case of gifts made after July 31, 1969.**—(a) *Remainders and similar interests.*—If a trust is created or property is transferred for both a charitable and a private purpose, deduction may be taken of the value of the charitable beneficial interest only insofar as that interest is presently ascertainable, and hence severable from the noncharitable interest.

(b) *Transfers subject to a condition or a power.*—(1) If, as of the date of the gift, a transfer for charitable purposes is dependent upon the performance of some act or the happening of a precedent event in order that it might become effective, no deduction is allowable unless the possibility that the charitable transfer will not become effective is so remote as to be negligible. If an estate or interest has passed to, or is vested in, charity on the date of the gift and the estate or interest would be defeated by the performance of some act or the happening of some event, the possibility of occurrence of which appeared on such date to be so remote as to be negligible, the deduction is allowable. If the donee or trustee is empowered to divert the property or fund, in whole or in part, to a use or purpose which would have rendered it, to the extent that it is subject to such power, not deductible had it been directly so given by the donor, the deduction will be limited to that portion, if any, of the property or fund which is exempt from an exercise of the power.

(2) The application of this paragraph may be illustrated by the following examples:

*Example (1).* In 1965, A transfers certain property in trust in which charity is to receive the income for his life. The assets placed in trust by the donor consist of stock in a corporation the fiscal policies of which are controlled by the donor and his family. The trustees of the trust and the remainderman are members of the donor's family and the governing instrument contains no adequate guarantee of the requisite income to the charitable organization. Under such circumstances, no deduction will be allowed. Similarly, if the trustees are not members of the donor's family but have no power to sell or otherwise dispose of the closely held stock, or otherwise insure the requisite enjoyment of income to the charitable organization, no deduction will be allowed.

*Example (2).* C transfers a tract of land to a city government for as long as the land is used by the city for a public park. If on the date of gift the city does plan to use the land for a public park and the possibility that the city will not use the land for a public park is so remote as to be negligible, a deduction will be allowed.

(c) *Transfers of partial interests in property.*—(1) *Disallowance of deduction.*—(i) *In general.*—If a donor transfers an interest in property after July 31, 1969, for charitable purposes and an interest in the same property is retained by the donor, or is transferred or has been transferred for private purposes after such date (for less than an adequate and full consideration in money or money's worth), no deduction is allowed under section 2522 for the value of the interest which is transferred or has been transferred for charitable purposes unless the interest in property is a deductible interest described in subparagraph (2) of this paragraph. The principles that are used in applying section 2523 and the regulations thereunder shall apply for purposes of determining under this subparagraph whether an interest in property is retained by the donor, or is transferred or has been transferred by the donor. If, however, as of the date of the gift, a retention of an interest by a donor, or a transfer for a private purpose, is dependent upon the performance of some act or the happening of a precedent event in order that it may become effective, an interest in property will be considered retained by the donor, or transferred for a private purpose, unless the possibility of occurrence of such act or event is so remote as to be negligible. The application of this subparagraph may be illustrated by the following examples, in each of which it is assumed that the property interest which is transferred for private purposes is not transferred for an adequate and full consideration in money or money's worth:

*Example (1).* In 1973, H creates a trust which is to pay the income of the trust to W for her life, the reversionary interest in the trust being retained by H. In 1975, H gives the reversionary interest to charity, while W is still living. For purposes of this paragraph (c)(1)(i), interests in the same property have been transferred by H for charitable purposes and for private purposes.

*Example (2).* In 1973, H creates a trust which is to pay the income of the trust to W for her life and upon termination of the life estate to transfer the remainder to S. In 1975, S gives his remainder interest to charity, while W is still living. For purposes of this paragraph (c)(1)(i), interests in the same property have not been transferred by H or S for charitable purposes and for private purposes.

*Example (3).* H transfers Blackacre to A by gift, reserving the right to the rentals of Blackacre for a term of 20 years. After 4 years H transfers the right to the remaining rentals to charity. For purposes of this paragraph (c)(1)(i) the term "property" refers to Blackacre, and the right to rentals from Blackacre consists of an interest in Blackacre. An interest in Blackacre has been transferred by H for charitable purposes and for private purposes.

*Example (4).* H transfers property in trust for the benefit of A and a charity. An annuity of $5,000 a year is to be paid to charity for 20 years. Upon termination of the 20-year term the corpus is to be distributed to A if living. However, if A should die during the 20-year term, the corpus is to be distributed to charity upon termination of the term. An interest in property has been transferred by H for charitable purposes. In addition, an interest in the same property has been transferred by H for private purposes unless the possibility that A will survive the 20-year term is so remote as to be negligible.

*Example (5).* H transfers property in trust, under the terms of which an annuity of $5,000 a year is to be paid to charity for 20 years. Upon termination of the term, the corpus is to pass to such of A's children and their issue as A may appoint. However, if A should die during the 20-year term without exercising the power of appointment, the corpus is to be distributed to charity upon termination of the term. Since the possible appointees include private persons, an interest in the corpus of the trust is considered to have been transferred by H for private purposes.

(ii) *Works of art and copyright treated as separate properties.*—For purposes of paragraphs (c)(1)(i) and (c)(2) of this section, rules similar to the rules in § 20.2055-2(e)(1)(ii) shall apply in the case of transfers made after December 31, 1981.

(2) *Deductible interests.*—A deductible interest for purposes of subparagraph (i) of this paragraph is a charitable interest in property where—

(i) *Undivided portion of donor's entire interest.*—The charitable interest is an undivided portion, not in trust, of the donor's entire interest in property. An undivided portion of a donor's entire interest in property must consist of a fraction or percentage of each and every substantial interest or right owned by the donor in such property and must extend over the entire term of the donor's interest in such property and in other property into which such property is converted. For example, if the donor gave a life estate in an office building to his wife for her life and retained a reversionary interest in the office building, the gift by the donor of one-half of that reversionary interest to charity while his wife is still alive will not be considered the transfer of a deductible interest; because an interest in the same property has already passed from the donor for private purposes, the reversionary interest will not be considered the donor's entire interest in the property. If, on the other hand, the donor had been given a life estate in Blackacre for the life of his wife and the donor had no other interest in Blackacre on or before the time of gift, the gift by the donor of one-half of that life estate to charity would be considered the transfer of a deductible interest; because the life estate would be considered the donor's entire interest in the property, the gift would be of an undivided portion of such entire interest. An undivided portion of a donor's entire interest in property includes an interest in property whereby the charity is given the right, as a tenant in common with the donor, to possession, dominion, and control of the property for a portion of each year appropriate to its interest in such property. However, except as provided in paragraphs (c)(2)(ii), (iii), and (iv) of this section, for purposes of this subdivision a charitable contribution of an interest in property not in trust where the decedent transfers some specific rights to one party and transfers other substantial rights to another party will not be considered a contribution of an undivided portion of the decedent's entire interest in property. A gift of an open space easement in gross in perpetuity shall be considered a gift of an undivided portion of the donor's entire interest in property. A gift to charity made on or before December 17, 1980, of an open space easement in gross in perpetuity shall be considered the transfer to charity of an undivided portion of the donor's entire interest in property.

(ii) *Remainder interest in a personal residence.*—The charitable interest is an irrevocable remainder interest, not in trust, in a personal residence. Thus, for example, if the donor gives to charity a remainder interest in a personal residence and retains an estate in such property for life or a term of years the value of such remainder interest is deductible under section 2522. For purposes of this subdivision, the term "personal residence" means any property which is used by the donor as his personal residence even though it is not used as his principal residence. For example, a donor's vacation home may be a personal residence for purposes of this subdivision. The term "personal residence" also includes stock owned by the donor on the date of gift as a tenant-stockholder in a cooperative housing corporation (as those terms are defined in section 216(b)(1) and (2)) if the dwelling which the donor is entitled to occupy as such stockholder is used by him as his personal residence.

(iii) *Remainder interest in a farm.*—The charitable interest is an irrevocable remainder interest, not in trust, in a farm. Thus, for example, if the donor gives to charity a remainder interest in a farm and retains an estate in such property for life or a term of years, the value of such remainder interest is deductible under section 2522. For purposes of this subdivision, the term "farm" means any land used by the donor or his tenant for the production of crops, fruits, or other agricultural products or for the sustenance of livestock. The term "livestock" includes cattle, hogs, horses, mules, donkeys, sheep, goats, captive fur-bearing animals, chickens, turkeys, pigeons, and other poultry. A farm includes the improvements thereon.

(iv) *Qualified conservation contribution.*—The charitable interest is a qualified conservation contribution. For the definition of a qualified conservation contribution, see § 1.170A-14.

(v) *Charitable remainder trust and pooled income funds.*—The charitable interest is a remainder interest in a trust which is a charitable remainder annuity trust, as defined in section 664(d)(1) and § 1.664-2 of this chapter; a charitable remainder unitrust, as defined in section 664(d)(2) and (3) and § 1.664-3 of this chapter; or a pooled income fund, as defined in section 642(c)(5) and § 1.642(c)-5 of this chapter. The charitable organization to or for the use of which the remainder interest is transferred must meet the requirements of both section 2522(a) or (b) and section 642(c)(5)(A), section 664(d)(1)(C), or section 664(d)(2)(C), whichever applies. For example, the charitable organization to which the remainder interest in a charitable remainder annuity trust is transferred may not be a foreign corporation.

(vi) *Guaranteed annuity interest.*—(a) The charitable interest is a guaranteed annuity interest, whether or not such interest is in trust. For purposes of this paragraph (c)(2)(vi), the term "guaranteed annuity interest" means an irrevocable right pursuant to the instrument of transfer to receive a guaranteed annuity. A guaranteed annuity is an arrangement under which a determinable amount is paid periodically, but not less often than annually, for a specified term of years or for the life or lives of certain individuals, each of whom must be living at the date of the gift and can be ascertained at such date. Only one or more of the following individuals may be used as measuring lives: the donor, the donor's spouse, and an individual who, with respect to all remainder beneficiaries (other than charitable organizations described in section 170, 2055, or 2522), is either a lineal ancestor or the spouse of a lineal ancestor of those beneficiaries. A trust will satisfy the requirement that all noncharitable remainder beneficiaries are lineal descendants of the individual who is the measuring life, or that individual's spouse, if there is less than a 15% probability that individuals who are not lineal descendants will receive any trust corpus. This probability must be computed, based on the current applicable Life Table contained in § 20.2031-7, at the time property is transferred to the trust taking into account the interests of all primary and contingent remainder beneficiaries who are living at that time. An interest payable for a specified term of years can qualify as a guaranteed annuity interest even if the governing instrument contains a savings clause intended to ensure compliance with a rule against perpetuities. The savings clause must utilize a period for vesting of 21 years after the deaths of measuring lives who are selected to maximize, rather than limit, the term of the trust. The rule in this paragraph that a charitable interest may be payable for the life or lives of only certain specified individuals does not apply in the case of a charitable guaranteed annuity interest payable under a charitable remainder trust described in section 664. An amount is determinable if the exact amount which must be paid under the conditions specified in the instrument of transfer can be ascertained as of the date of gift. For example, the amount to be paid may be a stated sum for a term of years, or for the life of the donor, at the expiration of which it may be changed by a specified amount, but it may not be redetermined by reference to a fluctuating index such as the cost of living index. In further illustration, the amount to be paid may be expressed as a fraction or percentage of the cost of living index on the date of gift.

(b) A charitable interest is a guaranteed annuity interest only if it is a guaranteed annuity interest in every respect. For example, if the charitable interest is the right to receive from a trust each year a payment equal to the lesser of a sum certain or a fixed percentage of the net fair market value of the trust assets, determined annually, such interest is not a guaranteed annuity interest.

(c) Where a charitable interest in the form of a guaranteed annuity interest is not in trust, the interest will be considered a guaranteed annuity interest only if it is to be paid by an insurance company or by an organization regularly engaged in issuing annuity contracts.

(d) Where a charitable interest in the form of a guaranteed annuity interest is in trust, the governing instrument of the trust may provide that income of the trust which is in excess of the amount required to pay the guaranteed annuity interest shall be paid to or for the use of a charity. Nevertheless, the amount of the deduction under section 2522 shall be limited to the fair market value of the guaranteed annuity interest as determined under paragraph (d)(2)(iv) of this section.

(e) Where a charitable interest in the form of a guaranteed annuity interest is in trust and the present value on the date of gift of all income interests for a charitable purpose exceeds 60 percent of the aggregate fair market value of all amounts in such trust (after the payment of liabilities), the charitable interest will not be considered a guaranteed annuity interest unless the governing instrument of the trust prohibits both the acquisition and the retention of assets which would give rise to a tax under section 4944 if the trustee had acquired such assets. The requirement in this (e) for a prohibition in the governing instrument against the retention of assets which would give rise to a tax under section 4944 if the trustee had acquired the assets shall not apply to a gift made on or before May 21, 1972.

(f) Where a charitable interest in the form of a guaranteed annuity interest is in trust, and the gift of such interest is made after May 21, 1972, the charitable interest generally is not a guaranteed annuity interest if any amount may be paid by the trust for a private purpose before the expiration of all the charitable annuity interests. There are two exceptions to this general rule. First, the charitable interest is a guaranteed annuity interest if the amount payable for a private purpose is in the form of a guaranteed annuity interest and the trust's governing instrument does not provide for any preference or priority in the payment of the private annuity as opposed to the charitable annuity. Second, the charitable interest is a guaranteed annuity interest if under the trust's governing instrument the amount that may be paid for a private purpose is payable only from a group of assets that are devoted exclusively to private purposes and to which section 4947(a)(2) is inapplicable by reason of section 4947(a)(2)(B). For purposes of this paragraph (c)(2)(vi)(f), an amount is not paid for a private purpose if it is paid for an adequate and full consideration in money or money's worth. See §53.4947-1(c) of this chapter for rules relating to the inapplicability of section 4947(a)(2) to segregated amounts in a split-interest trust.

(g) For rules relating to certain governing instrument requirements and to the imposition of certain excise taxes where the guaranteed annuity interest is in trust and for rules governing payment of private income interests by a split-interest trust, see section 4947(a)(2) and (b)(3)(A), and the regulations thereunder.

(vii) *Unitrust interest.*—(a) The charitable interest is a unitrust interest, whether or not such interest is in trust. For purposes of this paragraph (c)(2)(vii), the term "unitrust interest" means an irrevocable right pursuant to the instrument of transfer to receive payment, not less often than annually, of a fixed percentage of the net fair market value, determined annually, of the property which funds the unitrust interest. In computing the net fair market value of the property which funds the unitrust interest, all assets and liabilities shall be taken into account without regard to whether particular items are taken into account in determining the income from the property. The net fair market value of the property which funds the unitrust interest may be determined on any one date during the year or by taking the average of valuations made on more than one date during the year, provided that the same valuation date or dates and valuation methods are used each year. Where the charitable interest is a unitrust interest to be paid by a trust and the governing instrument of the trust does not specify the valuation date or dates, the trustee shall select such date or dates and shall indicate his selection on the first return on Form 1041 which the trust is required to file. Payments under a unitrust interest may be paid for a specified term of years or for the life or lives of certain individuals, each of whom must be living at the date of the gift and can be ascertained at such date. Only one or more of the following individuals may be used as measuring lives: the donor, the donor's spouse, and an individual who, with respect to all remainder beneficiaries (other than charitable organizations described in section 170, 2055, or 2522), is either a lineal ancestor or the spouse of a lineal ancestor of those beneficiaries. A trust will satisfy the requirement that all noncharitable remainder beneficiaries are lineal descendants of the individual who is the measuring life, or that individual's spouse, if there is less than a 15%

probability that individuals who are not lineal descendants will receive any trust corpus. This probability must be computed, based on the current applicable Life Table contained in §20.2031-7, at the time property is transferred to the trust taking into account the interests of all primary and contingent remainder beneficiaries who are living at that time. An interest payable for a specified term of years can qualify as a unitrust interest even if the governing instrument contains a savings clause intended to ensure compliance with a rule against perpetuities. The savings clause must utilize a period for vesting of 21 years after the deaths of measuring lives who are selected to maximize, rather than limit, the term of the trust. The rule in this paragraph that a charitable interest may be payable for the life or lives of only certain specified individuals does not apply in the case of a charitable unitrust interest payable under a charitable remainder trust described in section 664.

(b) A charitable interest is a unitrust interest only if it is a unitrust interest in every respect. For example, if the charitable interest is the right to receive from a trust each year a payment equal to the lesser of a sum certain or a fixed percentage of the net fair market value of the trust assets, determined annually, such interest is not a unitrust interest.

(c) Where a charitable interest in the form of a unitrust interest is not in trust, the interest will be considered a unitrust interest only if it is to be paid by an insurance company or by an organization regularly engaged in issuing interests otherwise meeting the requirements of a unitrust interest.

(d) Where a charitable interest in the form of a unitrust interest is in trust, the governing instrument of the trust may provide that income of the trust which is in excess of the amount required to pay the unitrust interest shall be paid to or for the use of a charity. Nevertheless, the amount of the deduction under section 2522 shall be limited to the fair market value of the unitrust interest as determined under paragraph (d)(2)(v) of this section.

(e) Where a charitable interest in the form of a unitrust interest is in trust, the charitable interest generally is not a unitrust interest if any amount may be paid by the trust for a private purpose before the expiration of all the charitable unitrust interests. There are two exceptions to this general rule. First, the charitable interest is a unitrust interest if the amount payable for a private purpose is in the form of a unitrust interest and the trust's governing instrument does not provide for any preference or priority in the payment of the private unitrust interest as opposed to the charitable unitrust interest. Second, the charitable interest is a unitrust interest if under the trust's governing instrument the amount that may be paid for a private purpose is payable only from a group of assets that are devoted exclusively to private purposes and to which section 4947(a)(2) is inapplicable by reason of section 4947(a)(2)(B). For purposes of this paragraph (c)(2)(vii)(e), an amount is not paid for a private purpose if it is paid for an adequate and full consideration in money or money's worth. See §53.4947-1(c) of this chapter for rules relating to the inapplicability of section 4947(a)(2) to segregated amounts in a split-interest trust.

(f) For rules relating to certain governing instrument requirements and to the imposition of certain excise taxes where the unitrust interest is in trust and for rules governing payment of private income interests by a split-interest trust, see sections 4947(a)(2) and (b)(3)(A), and the regulations thereunder.

(d) *Valuation of charitable interest.*—(1) *In general.*—The amount of the deduction in the case of a contribution of a partial interest in property to which this section applies is the fair market value of the partial interest on the date of gift. The fair market value of an annuity, life estate, term for years, remainder, reversion or unitrust interest is its present value.

(2) *Certain transfers after July 31, 1969.*—In the case of a transfer after July 31, 1969, of an interest described in paragraph (c)(2)(v), (vi), or (vii) of this section, the present value of such interest is to be determined under the following rules:

(i) The present value of a remainder interest in a charitable remainder annuity trust is to be determined under §1.664-2(c) of this chapter (Income Tax Regulations).

(ii) The present value of a remainder interest in a charitable remainder unitrust is to be determined under §1.664-4 of this chapter.

(iii) The present value of a remainder interest in a pooled income fund is to be determined under §1.642(c)-6 of this chapter.

(iv) The present value of a guaranteed annuity interest described in paragraph (c)(2)(vi) of this section is to be determined under §25.2512-5 except that, if the annuity is issued by a company regularly engaged in the sale of annuities, the present value is to be determined under §25.2512-6. If by reason of all the conditions and circumstances surrounding a transfer of an income interest in property in trust it appears that the charity may not receive the beneficial enjoyment of the interest, a deduction will be allowed under section

**Reg. §25.2522(c)-3(d)(2)(iv)**

2522 only for the minimum amount it is evident the charity will receive.

*Example (1).* In 1975, B transfers $20,000 in trust with the requirement that a designated charity be paid a guaranteed annuity interest (as defined in paragraph (c)(2)(vi) of this section) of $4,100 a year, payable annually at the end of each year for a period of 6 years and that the remainder be paid to his children. The fair market value of an annuity of $4,100 a year for a period of 6 years is $20,160.93 ($4,100 × 4.9173), as determined under §25.2512-5A(c). The deduction with respect to the guaranteed annuity interest will be limited to $20,000, which is the minimum amount it is evident the charity will receive.

*Example (2).* In 1975, C transfers $40,000 in trust with the requirement that D, an individual, and X Charity be paid simultaneously guaranteed annuity interests (as defined in paragraph (c)(2)(vi) of this section) of $5,000 a year each, payable annually at the end of each year, for a period of 5 years and that the remainder be paid to C's children. The fair market value of two annuities of $5,000 each a year for a period of 5 years is $42,124 ([$5,000 × 4.2124] × 2), as determined under §25.2512-5A(c). The trust instrument provides that in the event the trust fund is insufficient to pay both annuities in a given year, the trust fund will be evenly divided between the charitable and private annuitants. The deduction with respect to the charitable annuity will be limited to $20,000, which is the minimum amount it is evident the charity will receive.

*Example (3).* In 1975, D transfers $65,000 in trust with the requirement that a guaranteed annuity interest (as defined in paragraph (c)(2)(vi) of this section) of $5,000 a year, payable annually at the end of each year, be paid to Y Charity for a period of 10 years and that a guaranteed annuity interest (as defined in paragraph (c)(2)(vi) of this section) of $5,000 a year, payable annually at the end of each year, be paid to W, his wife, aged 62[,]for 10 years or until her prior death. The annuities are to be paid simultaneously, and the remainder is to be paid to D's children. The fair market value of the private annuity is $33,877 ($5,000 × 6.7754), as determined pursuant to §25.2512-5A(c) and by the use of factors involving one life and a term of years as published in Publication 723A (12-70). The fair market value of the charitable annuity is $36,800.50 ($5,000 × 7.3601), as determined under §25.2512-5A(c). It is not evident from the governing instrument of the trust or from local law that the trustee would be required to apportion the trust fund between the wife and charity in the event the fund were insufficient to pay both annuities in a given year. Accordingly, the deduction with respect to the charitable annuity will be limited to $31,123 ($65,000 less $33,877 [the value of the private annuity]), which is the minimum amount it is evident the charity will receive.

(v) The present value of a unitrust interest described in paragraph (c)(2)(vii) of this section is to be determined by subtracting the present value of all interests in the transferred property other than the unitrust interest from the fair market value of the transferred property.

(3) *Other transfers.*—The present value of an interest not described in paragraph (d)(2) of this section is to be determined under §25.2512-5.

(4) *Special computations.*—If the interest transferred is such that its present value is to be determined by a special computation, a request for a special factor, accompanied by a statement of the date of birth and sex of each individual the duration of whose life may affect the value of the interest, and by copies of the relevant instruments, may be submitted by the donor to the Commissioner who may, if conditions permit, supply the factor requested. If the Commissioner furnishes the factor, a copy of the letter supplying the factor must be attached to the tax return in which the deduction is claimed. If the Commissioner does not furnish the factor, the claim for deduction must be supported by a full statement of the computation of the present value made in accordance with the principles set forth in this paragraph.

(e) *Effective/applicability date.*—This section applies only to gifts made after July 31, 1969. In addition, the rule in paragraphs (c)(2)(vi)(a) and (c)(2)(vii)(a) of this section that guaranteed annuity interests or unitrust interests, respectively, may be payable for a specified term of years or for the life or lives of only certain individuals applies to transfers made on or after April 4, 2000. If a transfer is made on or after April 4, 2000, that uses an individual other than one permitted in paragraphs (c)(2)(vi)(a) and (c)(2)(vii)(a) of this section, the interest may be reformed into a lead interest payable for a specified term of years. The term of years is determined by taking the factor for valuing the annuity or unitrust interest for the named individual measuring life and identifying the term of years (rounded up to the next whole year) that corresponds to the equivalent term of years factor for an annuity or unitrust interest. For example, in the case of an annuity interest payable for the life of an individual age 40 at the time of the transfer on or after May 1, 2009 (the effective date of

Table S), assuming an interest rate of 7.4 percent under section 7520, the annuity factor from column 1 of Table S(7.4), contained in IRS Publication 1457, Actuarial Valuations Version 3A, for the life of an individual age 40 is 12.1519 (1 – .10076 / .074). Based on Table B(7.4), contained in Publication 1457, "Actuarial Valuations Version 3A", the factor 12.1519 corresponds to a term of years between 32 and 33 years. Accordingly, the annuity interest must be reformed into an interest payable for a term of 33 years. A judicial reformation must be commenced prior to October 15th of the year following the year in which the transfer is made and must be completed within a reasonable time after it is commenced. A non-judicial reformation is permitted if effective under state law, provided it is completed by the date on which a judicial reformation must be commenced. In the alternative, if a court, in a proceeding that is commenced on or before July 5, 2001, declares any transfer, made on or after April 4, 2000, and on or before March 6, 2001, null and void ab initio, the Internal Revenue Service will treat such transfers in a manner similar to that described in section 2055(e)(3)(J). [Reg. §25.2522(c)-3.]

☐ [T.D. 7318, 7-10-74. *Amended by* T.D. 7340, 1-6-75; T.D. 7955, 5-10-84; T.D. 7957, 5-16-84; T.D. 8069, 1-13-86, T.D. 8540, 6-9-94; T.D. 8630, 12-12-95; T.D. 8923, 1-4-2001; T.D. 9068, 7-3-2003; T.D. 9448, 5-1-2009 *and* T.D. 9540, 8-9-2011.]

### [Reg. §25.2522(c)-4]

**§25.2522(c)-4. Disallowance of double deduction in the case of qualified terminable interest property.**—No deduction is allowed under section 2522 for the transfer of an interest in property if a deduction is taken from the *total amount of gifts* with respect to that property by reason of section 2523(f). See §25.2523(h)-1. [Reg. §25.2522(c)-4.]

☐ [T.D. 8522, 2-28-94.]

### [Reg. §25.2522(d)-1]

**§25.2522(d)-1. Additional cross references.**—(a) See section 14 of the Wild and Scenic Rivers Act (Public Law 90-542, 82 Stat. 918) for provisions relating to the claim and allowance of the value of certain easements as a gift under section 2522.

(b) For treatment of gifts accepted by the Secretary of State or the Secretary of Commerce, for the purpose of organizing and holding an international conference to negotiate a Patent Corporation Treaty, as gifts to or for the use of the United States, see section 3 of Joint Resolution of December 24, 1969 (Public Law 91-160, 83 Stat. 443).

(c) For treatment of gifts accepted by the Secretary of the Department of Housing and Urban Development, for the purpose of aiding or facilitating the work of the Department, as gifts to or for the use of the United States, see section 7(k) of the Department of Housing and Urban Development Act (42 U. S. C. 3535), as added by section 905 of Public Law 91-609 (84 Stat. 1809).

(d) For treatment of certain property accepted by the Chairman of the Administrative Conference of the United States, for the purpose of aiding and facilitating the work of the Conference, as gifts to the United States, see 5 U. S. C. 575(c)(12), as added by section 1(b) of the Act of October 21, 1972 (Public Law 92-526, 86 Stat. 1048).

(e) For treatment of the Board for International Broadcasting as a corporation described in section 2522(a)(2), see section 7 of the Board for International Broadcasting Act of 1973 (Public Law 93-129, 87 Stat. 459). [Reg. §25.2522(d)-1.]

☐ [T.D. 7318, 6-10-74.]

### [Reg. §25.2523(a)-1]

**§25.2523(a)-1. Gift to spouse; in general.**—(a) *In general.*—In determining the amount of taxable gifts for the calendar quarter (with respect to gifts made after December 31, 1970, and before January 1, 1982), or calendar year (with respect to gifts made before January 1, 1971, or after December 31, 1981), a donor may deduct the value of any property interest transferred by gift to a donee who at the time of the gift is the donor's spouse, except as limited by paragraphs (b) and (c) of this section. See §25.2502-1(c)(1) for the definition of calendar quarter. This deduction is referred to as the *marital deduction.* In the case of gifts made prior to July 14, 1988, no marital deduction is allowed with respect to a gift if, at the time of the gift, the donor is a nonresident not a citizen of the United States. Further, in the case of gifts made on or after July 14, 1988, no marital deduction is allowed (regardless of the donor's citizenship or residence) for transfers to a spouse who is not a citizen of the United States at the time of the transfer. However, for certain special rules applicable in the case of estate and gift tax treaties, see section 7815(d)(14) of Pub. L. 101-239. The donor must submit any evidence necessary to establish the donor's right to the marital deduction.

(b) *Deductible interests and nondeductible interests.*—(1) *In general.*—The property interests transferred by a donor to his spouse consist of either transfers with respect to which the marital deduction is authorized (as described in subparagraph (2) of this paragraph) or transfers with respect to which the marital deduction is not authorized (as described in subparagraph (3) of this paragraph). These transfers are referred to in this section and in §§ 25.2523(b)-1 through 25.2523(f)-1 as *deductible interests* and *nondeductible interests,* respectively.

(2) *Deductible interest.*—A property interest transferred by a donor to his spouse is a *deductible interest* if it does not fall within either class of *nondeductible interests* described in subparagraph (3) of this paragraph.

(3) *Nondeductible interests.*—(i) A property interest transferred by a donor to his spouse which is a *terminable interest,* as defined in § 25.2523(b)-1, is a *nondeductible interest* to the extent specified in that section.

(ii) Any property interest transferred by a donor to the donor's spouse is a *nondeductible interest* to the extent it is not required to be included in a gift tax return for a calendar quarter (for gifts made after December 31, 1970, and before January 1, 1982) or calendar year (for gifts made before January 1, 1971, or after December 31, 1981).

(c) *Computation.*—(1) *In general.*—The amount of the marital deduction depends upon when the interspousal gifts are made, whether the gifts are terminable interests, whether the limitations of § 25.2523(f)-1A (relating to gifts of community property before January 1, 1982) are applicable, and whether § 25.2523(f)-1 (relating to the election with respect to life estates) is applicable, and (with respect to gifts made on or after July 14, 1988) whether the donee spouse is a citizen of the United States (see section 2523(i)).

(2) *Gifts prior to January 1, 1977.*—Generally, with respect to gifts made during a calendar quarter prior to January 1, 1977, the marital deduction allowable under section 2523 is 50 percent of the aggregate value of the deductible interests. See section 2524 for an additional limitation on the amount of the allowable deduction.

(3) *Gifts after December 31, 1976, and before January 1, 1982.*—Generally, with respect to gifts made during a calendar quarter beginning after December 31, 1976, and ending prior to January 1, 1982, the marital deduction allowable under section 2523 is computed as a percentage of the deductible interests in those gifts. If the aggregate amount of deductions for such gifts is $100,000 or less, a deduction is allowed for 100 percent of the deductible interests. No deduction is allowed for otherwise deductible interests in an aggregate amount that exceeds $100,000 and is equal to or less than $200,000. For deductible interests in excess of $200,000, the deduction is limited to 50 percent of such deductible interests. If a donor remarries, the computations in this paragraph (c)(3) are made on the basis of aggregate gifts to all persons who at the time of the gifts are the donor's spouse. See section 2524 for an additional limitation on the amount of the allowable deduction.

(4) *Gifts after December 31, 1981.*—Generally, with respect to gifts made during a calendar year beginning after December 31, 1981 (other than gifts made on or after July 14, 1988, to a spouse who is not a United States citizen on the date of the transfer), the marital deduction allowable under section 2523 is 100 percent of the aggregate value of the deductible interests. See section 2524 for an additional limitation on the amount of the allowable deduction, and section 2523(i) regarding disallowance of the marital deduction for gifts to a spouse who is not a United States citizen.

(d) *Examples.*—The following examples (in which it is assumed that the donors have previously utilized any specific exemptions provided by section 2521 for gifts prior to January 1, 1977) illustrate the application of paragraph (c) of this section and the interrelationship of sections 2523 and 2503. Generally, the marital deduction is equal to one-half of the aggregate value of the "deductible interests." The following examples (in each of which it is assumed that the donor has previously utilized his entire $30,000 specific exemption provided by section 2521) illustrate the marital deduction computation and the interrelationship of sections 2503(b) and 2523(a):

*Example 1.* A donor made a transfer by gift of $6,000 cash to his spouse on December 25, 1971. The donor made no other transfers during 1971. The amount of the marital deduction for the fourth calendar quarter of 1971 is $3,000 (one-half of $6,000); the amount of the annual exclusion under § 2503(b) is $3,000; and the amount of taxable gifts is zero ($6,000 – $3,000 (annual exclusion) – $3,000 (marital deduction)).

*Example 2.* A donor made transfers by gift to his spouse of $3,000 cash on January 1, 1971, and $3,000 cash on May 1, 1971. The donor made no other transfers during 1971. For the first calendar quarter of 1971 the marital deduction is zero because the amount excluded under section 2503(b) is $3,000, and the amount of taxable gifts is also zero. For the second calendar quarter of 1971 the marital deduction is $1,500 (one-half of $3,000), and the amount of taxable gifts is $1,500

($3,000 – $1,500 (marital deduction)). Under section 2503(b) no amount of the second $3,000 gift may be excluded because the entire $3,000 annual exclusion was applied against the gift made in the first calendar quarter of 1971.

*Example 3.* A donor made a transfer by gift to his spouse of $10,000 cash on April 1, 1972. The donor made no other transfers during 1972. For the second calendar quarter of 1972 the amount of the marital deduction is $5,000 (one-half of $10,000); the amount excluded under section 2503(b) is $3,000; the amount of taxable gifts is $2,000 ($10,000 – $3,000 (annual exclusion) – $5,000 (marital deduction)).

*Example 4.* A donor made transfers by gift to his spouse of $2,000 cash on January 1, 1971, $2,000 cash on April 5, 1971, and $10,000 cash on December 1, 1971. The donor made no other transfers during 1971. For the first calendar quarter of 1971 the marital deduction is zero because the amount excluded under section 2503(b) is $2,000, and the amount of taxable gifts is also zero. For the second calendar quarter of 1971 the marital deduction is $1,000 (one-half of $2,000) (see section 2524); the amount excluded under section 2503(b) is $1,000 because $2,000 of the $3,000 annual exclusion was applied against the gift made in the first calendar quarter of 1971; and the amount of taxable gifts is zero ($2,000 – $1,000 (annual exclusion) – $1,000 (marital deduction)). For the fourth calendar quarter of 1971, the marital deduction is $5,000 (one-half of $10,000); the amount excluded under section 2503(b) is zero because the entire $3,000 annual exclusion was applied against the gifts made in the first and second calendar quarters of 1971; and the amount of taxable gifts is $5,000 ($10,000 – $5,000 (marital deduction)).

*Example 5.* A donor made transfers by gift to his spouse of $2,000 cash on January 10, 1972, $2,000 cash on May 1, 1972, and a remainder interest valued at $16,000 on June 1, 1972. The donor made no other transfers during 1972. For the first calendar quarter of 1972, the marital deduction is zero because $2,000 is excluded under section 2503(b), and the amount of taxable gifts is also zero. For the second calendar quarter of 1972 the marital deduction is $9,000 (one-half of $16,000 plus one-half of $2,000); the amount excluded under section 2503(b) is $1,000 because $2,000 of the $3,000 annual exclusion was applied against the gift made in the first calendar quarter of 1971 [1972]; and the amount of taxable gifts is $8,000 ($18,000 – $1,000 (annual exclusion) – $9,000 (marital deduction)).

*Example 6.* A donor made transfers by gift to his spouse of $2,000 cash on January 1, 1972, a remainder interest valued at $16,000 on January 5, 1972, and $2,000 cash on April 30, 1972. The donor made no other transfers during 1972. For the first calendar quarter of 1972, the marital deduction is $9,000 (one-half of $16,000 plus one-half of $2,000); the amount excluded under section 2503(b) is $2,000; and the amount of taxable gifts is $7,000 ($18,000 – $2,000 (annual exclusion) – $9,000 (marital deduction)). For the second calendar quarter of 1972 the marital deduction is $1,000 (one-half of $2,000); the amount excluded under section 2503(b) is $1,000 because $2,000 of the $3,000 annual exclusion was applied against the gift of the present interest in the first calendar quarter of 1971 [1972]; and the amount of taxable gifts is zero ($2,000 – $1,000 (annual exclusion) – $1,000 (marital deduction)).

*Example 7.* A donor made a transfer by gift to his spouse of $12,000 cash on July 17, 1955. The donor made no other transfers during 1955. For the calendar year 1955 the amount of the marital deduction is $6,000 (one-half of $12,000); the amount excluded under section 2503(b) is $3,000; and the amount of taxable gifts is $3,000 ($12,000 – $3,000 (annual exclusion) – $6,000 (marital deduction)).

*Example 8.* A donor made a transfer by gift to the donor's spouse, a United States citizen, of $200,000 cash on January 1, 1995. The donor made no other transfers during 1995. For calendar year 1995, the amount excluded under section 2503(b) is $10,000; the marital deduction is $190,000; and the amount of taxable gifts is zero ($200,000 – $10,000 (annual exclusion) – $190,000 (marital deduction)).

(e) *Valuation.*—If the income from property is made payable to the donor or another individual for life or for a term of years, with remainder to the donor's spouse or to the estate of the donor's spouse, the marital deduction is computed (pursuant to § 25.2523(a)-1(c)) with respect to the present value of the remainder, determined under section 7520. The present value of the remainder (that is, its value as of the date of gift) is to be determined in accordance with the rules stated in § 25.2512-5 or, for certain periods, § 25.2512-5A. See the example in paragraph (d) of § 25.2512-5. If the remainder is such that its value is to be determined by a special computation, a request for a specific factor, accompanied by a statement of the dates of birth of each person, the duration of whose life may affect the value of the remainder, and by copies of the relevant instruments may be submitted by the donor to the Commissioner who, if conditions permit, may supply the factor requested. If the Commissioner does not furnish the factor, the claim for deduction must be supported by a full statement of the computation of the present value, made in accordance with the principles set forth in

§ 25.2512-5(d) or, for certain periods, § 25.2512-5A. [Reg. § 25.2523(a)-1.]

☐ [T.D. 6334, 11-14-58. Amended by T.D. 7012, 5-14-69; T.D. 7238, 12-28-72; T.D. 7955, 5-10-84; T.D. 8522, 2-28-94 and T.D. 8540, 6-9-94.]

### [Reg. § 25.2523(b)-1]

**§ 25.2523(b)-1. Life estate or other terminable interest.**—(a) *In general.*—(1) The provisions of section 2523(b) generally disallow a marital deduction with respect to certain property interests (referred to generally as *terminable interests* and defined in paragraph (a)(3) of this section) transferred to the donee spouse under the circumstances described in paragraph (a)(2) of this section, unless the transfer comes within the purview of one of the exceptions set forth in § 25.2523(d)-1 (relating to certain joint interests); § 25.2523(e)-1 (relating to certain life estates with powers of appointment); § 25.2523(f)-1 (relating to certain qualified terminable interest property); or § 25.2523(g)-1 (relating to certain qualified charitable remainder trusts).

(2) If a donor transfers a terminable interest in property to the donee spouse, the marital deduction is disallowed with respect to the transfer if the donor spouse also—

(i) Transferred an interest in the same property to another donee (see paragraph (b) of this section), or

(ii) Retained an interest in the same property in himself (see paragraph (c) of this section), or

(iii) Retained a power to appoint an interest in the same property (see paragraph (d) of this section).

Notwithstanding the preceding sentence, the marital deduction is disallowed under these circumstances only if the other donee, the donor, or the possible appointee, may, by reason of the transfer or retention, possess or enjoy any part of the property after the termination or failure of the interest therein transferred to the donee spouse.

(3) For purposes of this section, a distinction is to be drawn between "property," as such term is used in section 2523, and an "interest in property." The "property" referred to is the underlying property in which various interests exist; each such interest is not, for this purpose, to be considered as "property." A "terminable interest" in property is an interest which will terminate or fail on the lapse of time or on the occurrence or failure to occur of some contingency. Life estates, terms for years, annuities, patents, and copyrights are therefore terminable interests. However, a bond, note, or similar contractual obligation, the discharge of which would not have the effect of an annuity or term for years, is not a terminable interest.

(b) *Interest in property which another donee may possess or enjoy.*—(1) Section 2523(b) provides that no marital deduction shall be allowed with respect to the transfer to the donee spouse of a "terminable interest" in property, in case—

(i) The donor transferred (for less than an adequate and full consideration in money or money's worth) an interest in the same property to any person other than the donee spouse (or the estate of such spouse), and,

(ii) By reason of such transfer, such person (or his heirs or assigns) may possess or enjoy any part of such property after the termination or failure of the interest therein transferred to the donee spouse.

(2) In determining whether the donor transferred an interest in property to any person other than the donee spouse, it is immaterial whether the transfer to the person other than the donee spouse was made at the same time as the transfer to such spouse, or at any earlier time.

(3) Except as provided in § 25.2523(e)-1 or 25.2523(f)-1, if at the time of the transfer it is impossible to ascertain the particular person or persons who may receive a property interest transferred by the donor, such interest is considered as transferred to a person other than the donee spouse for the purpose of section 2523(b). This rule is particularly applicable in the case of the transfer of a property interest by the donor subject to a reserved power. See § 25.2511-2. Under this rule, any property interest over which the donor reserved a power to revest the beneficial title in himself, or over which the donor reserved the power to name new beneficiaries or to change the interests of the beneficiaries as between themselves, is for the purpose of section 2523(b), considered as transferred to a "person other than the donee spouse." The following examples, in which it is assumed that the donor did not make an election under sections 2523(f)(2)(C) and (f)(4), illustrate the application of the provisions of this paragraph (b)(3):

*Example 1.* If a donor transferred property in trust, naming his wife as the irrevocable income beneficiary for 10 years, and providing that, upon the expiration of that term, the corpus should be distributed among his wife and children in such proportions as the trustee should determine, the right to the corpus, for the purpose of the marital deduction, is considered as transferred to a "person other than the donee spouse."

*Example 2.* If, in the above example, the donor had provided that, upon the expiration of the 10-year term, the corpus was to be paid to his wife, but also reserved the power to revest such corpus in himself, the right to corpus, for the purpose of the marital deduction, is considered as transferred to a "person other than the donee spouse."

(4) The term "person other than the donee spouse" includes the possible unascertained takers of a property interest, as, for example, the members of a class to be ascertained in the future. As another example, assume that the donor created a power of appointment over a property interest, which does not come within the purview of § 25.2523(e)-1. In such a case, the term "person other than the donee spouse" refers to the possible appointees and takers in default (other than the spouse) of such property interest.

(5) An exercise or release at any time by the donor (either alone or in conjunction with any person) of a power to appoint an interest in property, even though not otherwise a transfer by him is considered as a transfer by him in determining, for the purpose of section 2523(b), whether he transferred an interest in such property to a person other than the donee spouse.

(6) The following examples illustrate the application of this paragraph. In each example, it is assumed that the donor made no election under sections 2523(f)(2)(C) and (f)(4) and that the property interest that the donor transferred to a person other than the donee spouse is not transferred for adequate and full consideration in money or money's worth:

*Example 1.* H (the donor) transferred real property to W (his wife) for life, with remainder to A and his heirs. No marital deduction may be taken with respect to the interest transferred to W, since it will terminate upon her death and A (or his heirs or assigns) will thereafter possess or enjoy the property.

*Example 2.* H transferred property for the benefit of W and A. The income was payable to W for life and upon her death the principal was to be distributed to A or his issue. However, if A should die without issue, leaving W surviving, the principal was then to be distributed to W. No marital deduction may be taken with respect to the interest transferred to W, since it will terminate in the event of her death if A or his issue survive, and A or his issue will thereafter possess or enjoy the property.

*Example 3.* H purchased for $100,000 a life annuity for W. If the annuity payments made during the life of W should be less than $100,000, further payments were to be made to A. No marital deduction may be taken with respect to the interest transferred to W, since A may possess or enjoy a part of the property following the termination of W's interest. If, however, the contract provided for no continuation of payments, and provided for no refund upon the death of W, or provided that any refund was to go to the estate of W, then a marital deduction may be taken with respect to the gift.

*Example 4.* H transferred property to A for life with remainder to W provided W survives A, but if W predeceases A, the property is to pass to B and his heirs. No marital deduction may be taken with respect to the interest transferred to W.

*Example 5.* H transferred real property to A, reserving the right to the rentals of the property for a term of 20 years. H later transferred the right to the remaining rentals to W. No marital deduction may be taken with respect to the interest since it will terminate upon the expiration of the balance of the 20-year term and A will thereafter possess or enjoy the property.

*Example 6.* H transferred a patent to W and A as tenants in common. In this case, the interest of W will terminate upon the expiration of the term of the patent, but possession and enjoyment of the property by A must necessarily cease at the same time. Therefore, since A's possession or enjoyment cannot outlast the termination of W's interest, the provisions of section 2523(b) do not disallow the marital deduction with respect to the interest.

(c) *Interest in property which the donor may possess or enjoy.*—(1) Section 2523(b) provides that no marital deduction is allowed with respect to the transfer to the donee spouse of a "terminable interest" in property, if—

(i) The donor retained in himself an interest in the same property, and

(ii) By reason of such retention, the donor (or his heirs or assigns) may possess or enjoy any part of the property after the termination or failure of the interest transferred to the donee spouse. However, as to a transfer to the donee spouse as sole joint tenant with the donor or as tenant by the entirety, see § 25.2523(d)-1.

(2) In general, the principles illustrated by the examples under paragraph (b) of this section are applicable in determining whether the marital deduction may be taken with respect to a property interest transferred to the donee spouse subject to the retention by the donor of an interest in the same property. The application of this paragraph may be further illustrated by the following example, in

which it is assumed that the donor made no election under sections 2523(f)(2)(C) and (f)(4):

*Example.* The donor purchased three annuity contracts for the benefit of his wife and himself. The first contract provided for payments to the wife for life, with refund to the donor in case the aggregate payments made to the wife were less than the cost of the contract. The second contract provided for payments to the donor for life, and then to the wife for life if she survived the donor. The third contract provided for payments to the donor and his wife for their joint lives and then to the survivor of them for life. No marital deduction may be taken with respect to the gifts resulting from the purchases of the contracts since, in the case of each contract, the donor may possess or enjoy a part of the property after the termination or failure of the interest transferred to the wife.

(d) *Interest in property over which the donor retained a power to appoint.*—(1) Section 2523(b) provides that no marital deduction is allowed with respect to the transfer to the donee spouse of a "terminable interest" in property if—

(i) The donor had, immediately after the transfer, a power to appoint an interest in the same property, and

(ii) The donor's power was exercisable (either alone or in conjunction with any person) in such manner that the appointee may possess or enjoy any part of the property after the termination or failure of the interest transferred to the donee spouse.

(2) For the purposes of section 2523(b), the donor is to be considered as having, immediately after the transfer to the donee spouse, such a power to appoint even though the power cannot be exercised until after the lapse of time, upon the occurrence of an event or contingency, or upon the failure of an event or contingency to occur. It is immaterial whether the power retained by the donor was a taxable power of appointment under section 2514.

(3) The principles illustrated by the examples under paragraph (b) of this section are generally applicable in determining whether the marital deduction may be taken with respect to a property interest transferred to the donee spouse subject to retention by the donor of a power to appoint an interest in the same property. The application of this paragraph may be further illustrated by the following example:

*Example.* The donor, having a power of appointment over certain property, appointed a life estate to his spouse. No marital deduction may be taken with respect to such transfer, since, if the retained power to appoint the remainder interest is exercised, the appointee thereunder may possess or enjoy the property after the termination or failure of the interest taken by the donee spouse. [Reg. § 25.2523(b)-1.]

☐ [*T.D.* 6334, 11-14-58. *Amended by T.D.* 8522, 2-28-94.]

**[Reg. § 25.2523(c)-1]**

**§ 25.2523(c)-1. Interest in unidentified assets.**—(a) Section 2523(c) provides that if an interest passing to a donee spouse may be satisfied out of a group of assets (or their proceeds) which include a particular asset that would be a nondeductible interest if it passed from the donor to his spouse, the value of the interest passing to the spouse is reduced, for the purpose of the marital deduction, by the value of the particular asset.

(b) In order for this section to apply, two circumstances must coexist, as follows:

(1) The property interest transferred to the donee spouse must be payable out of a group of assets. An example of a property interest payable out of a group of assets is a right to a share of the corpus of a trust upon its termination.

(2) The group of assets out of which the property interest is payable must include one or more particular assets which, if transferred by the donor to the donee spouse, would not qualify for the marital deduction. Therefore, section 2523(c) is not applicable merely because a group of assets includes a terminable interest, but would only be applicable if the terminable interest were nondeductible under the provisions of § 25.2523(b)-1.

(c) If both of the circumstances set forth in paragraph (b) of this section exist, only a portion of the property interest passing to the spouse is a deductible interest. The portion qualifying as a deductible interest is an amount equal to the excess, if any, of the value of the property interest passing to the spouse over the aggregate value of the asset (or assets) that if transferred to the spouse would not qualify for the marital deduction. See paragraph (c) of § 25.2523(a)-1 to determine the percentage of the deductible interest allowable as a marital deduction. The application of this section may be illustrated by the following example:

*Example.* H was absolute owner of a rental property and on July 1, 1950, transferred it to A by gift, reserving the income for a period of 20 years. On July 1, 1955, he created a trust to last for a period of 10 years. H was to receive the income from the trust and at the termination of the trust the trustee is to turn over to H's wife, W, property

having a value of $100,000. The trustee has absolute discretion in deciding which properties in the corpus he shall turn over to W in satisfaction of the gift to her. The trustee received two items of property from H. Item (1) consisted of shares of corporate stock. Item (2) consisted of the right to receive the income from the rental property during the unexpired portion of the 20-year term. Assume that at the termination of the trust on July 1, 1965, the value of the right to the rental income from the then unexpired term of 5 years (item 2) will be $30,000. Since item (2) is a nondeductible interest and the trustee can turn it over to W in partial satisfaction of her gift, only $70,000 of the $100,000 receivable by her on July 1, 1965, will be considered as property with respect to which a marital deduction is allowable. The present value on July 1, 1955, of the right to receive $70,000 at the end of 10 years is $49,624.33 as determined under § 25.2512-5A(c). The value of the property qualifying for the marital deduction, therefore, is $49,624.33 and a marital deduction is allowed for one-half of that amount, or $24,812.17. [Reg. § 25.2523(c)-1.]

☐ [*T.D.* 6334, 11-14-58. *Amended by T.D.* 8522, 2-28-94 *and T.D.* 8540, 6-9-94.]

**[Reg. § 25.2523(d)-1]**

**§ 25.2523(d)-1. Joint interests.**—Section 2523(d) provides that if a property interest is transferred to the donee spouse as sole joint tenant with the donor or as a tenant by the entirety, the interest of the donor in the property which exists solely by reason of the possibility that the donor may survive the donee spouse, or that there may occur a severance of the tenancy, is not for the purposes of section 2523(b), to be considered as an interest retained by the donor in himself. Under this provision, the fact that the donor may, as surviving tenant, possess or enjoy the property after the termination of the interest transferred to the donee spouse does not preclude the allowance of the marital deduction with respect to the latter interest. Thus, if the donor purchased real property in the name of the donor and the donor's spouse as tenants by the entirety or as joint tenants with rights of survivorship, a marital deduction is allowable with respect to the value of the interest of the donee spouse in the property (subject to the limitations set forth in § 25.2523(a)-1). See paragraph (c) of § 25.2523(b)-1 and section 2524. [Reg. § 25.2523(d)-1.]

☐ [*T.D.* 6334, 11-14-58. *Amended by T.D.* 7238, 12-28-72 *and T.D.* 8522, 2-28-94.]

**[Reg. § 25.2523(e)-1]**

**§ 25.2523(e)-1. Marital deduction; life estate with power of appointment in donee spouse.**—(a) *In general.*—Section 2523(e) provides that if an interest in property is transferred by a donor to his spouse (whether or not in trust) and the spouse is entitled for life to all the income from the entire interest or all the income from a specific portion of the entire interest, with a power in her to appoint the entire interest or the specific portion, the interest transferred to her is a deductible interest, to the extent that it satisfies all five of the conditions set forth below (see paragraph (b) of this section if one or more of the conditions is satisfied as to only a portion of the interest):

(1) The donee spouse must be entitled for life to all of the income from the entire interest or a specific portion of the entire interest, or to a specific portion of all the income from the entire interest.

(2) The income payable to the donee spouse must be payable annually or at more frequent intervals.

(3) The donee spouse must have the power to appoint the entire interest or the specific portion to either herself or her estate.

(4) The power in the donee spouse must be exercisable by her alone and (whether exercisable by will or during life) must be exercisable in all events.

(5) The entire interest or the specific portion must not be subject to a power in any other person to appoint any part to any person other than the donee spouse.

(b) *Specific portion; deductible amount.*—If either the right to income or the power of appointment given to the donee spouse pertains only to a specific portion of a property interest, the portion of the interest which qualifies as a deductible interest is limited to the extent that the rights in the donee spouse meet all of the five conditions described in paragraph (a) of this section. While the rights over the income and the power must coexist as to the same interest in property, it is not necessary that the rights over the income or the power as to such interest be in the same proportion. However, if the rights over income meeting the required conditions set forth in paragraph (a)(1) and (2) of this section extend over a small share of the property interest than the share with respect to which the power of appointment requirements set forth in paragraph (a)(3) through (5) of this section are satisfied, the deductible interest is limited to the smaller share. Conversely, if a power of appointment meeting all the requirements extends to a smaller portion of the property interest than the portion over which the income rights pertain, the deductible interest cannot exceed the value of the portion to which such power of appointment applies. Thus, if the donor gives to the donee spouse the right to receive annually all of the income from a particular property interest and a power of appointment meeting the specifications prescribed in paragraph (a)(3) through (5) of this section as to only one-half of the property interest, then only one-half of the property interest is treated as a deductible interest. Correspondingly, if the income interest of the spouse satisfying the requirements extends to only one-fourth of the property interest and a testamentary power of appointment satisfying the requirements extends to all of the property interest, then only one-fourth of the interest in the spouse qualifies as a deductible interest. Further, if the donee spouse has no right to income from a specific portion of a property interest but a testamentary power of appointment which meets the necessary conditions over the entire interest, then none of the interest qualifies for the deduction. In addition, if, from the time of the transfer, the donee spouse has a power of appointment meeting all of the required conditions over three-fourths of the entire property interest and the prescribed income rights over the entire interest, but with a power in another person to appoint one-half of the entire interest, the value of the interest in the donee spouse over only one-half of the property interest will qualify as a deductible interest.

(c) *Meaning of specific portion.*—(1) *In general.*—Except as provided in paragraphs (c)(2) and (c)(3) of this section, a partial interest in property is not treated as a *specific portion* of the entire interest. In addition, any specific portion of an entire interest in property is nondeductible to the extent the specific portion is subject to invasion for the benefit of any person other than the donee spouse, except in the case of a deduction allowable under section 2523(e), relating to the exercise of a general power of appointment by the donee spouse.

(2) *Fraction or percentage share.*—Under section 2523(e), a partial interest in property is treated as a specific portion of the entire interest if the rights of the donee spouse in income, and the required rights as to the power described in § 25.2523(e)-1(a), constitute a fractional or percentage share of the entire property interest, so that the donee spouse's interest reflects its proportionate share of the increase or decrease in the value of the entire property interest to which the income rights and the power relate. Thus, if the spouse's right to income and the spouse's power extend to a specified fraction or percentage of the property, or its equivalent, the interest is in a specific portion of the property. In accordance with paragraph (b) of this section, if the spouse has the right to receive the income from a specific portion of the trust property (after applying paragraph (c)(3) of this section) but has a power of appointment over a different specific portion of the property (after applying paragraph (c)(3) of this section), the marital deduction is limited to the lesser specific portion.

(3) *Special rule in the case of gifts made on or before October 24, 1992.*—In the case of gifts within the purview of the effective date rule contained in paragraph (c)(3)(iii) of this section:

(i) A specific sum payable annually, or at more frequent intervals, out of the property and its income that is not limited by the income of the property is treated as the right to receive the income from a specific portion of the property. The specific portion, for purposes of paragraph (c)(2) of this section, is the portion of the property that, assuming the interest rate generally applicable for the valuation of annuities at the time of the donor's gift, would produce income equal to such payments. However, a pecuniary amount payable annually to a donee spouse is not treated as a right to the income from a specific portion of trust property for purposes of this paragraph (c)(3)(i) if any person other than the donee spouse may receive, during the donee spouse's lifetime, any distribution of the property. To determine the applicable interest rate for valuing annuities, see sections 2512 and 7520 and the regulations under those sections.

(ii) The right to appoint a pecuniary amount out of a larger fund (or trust corpus) is considered the right to appoint a specific portion of such fund or trust in an amount equal to such pecuniary amount.

(iii) The rules contained in paragraphs (c)(3)(i) and (ii) of this section apply with respect to gifts made on or before October 24, 1992.

(4) *Local law.*—A partial interest in property is treated as a specific portion of the entire interest if it is shown that the donee spouse has rights under local law that are identical to those the donee spouse would have acquired had the partial interest been expressed in terms satisfying the requirements of paragraph (c)(2) of this section (or paragraph (c)(3) of this section if applicable).

(5) *Examples.*—The following examples illustrate the application of paragraphs (b) and (c) of this section, where D, the donor, transfers property to D's spouse, S:

*Example 1. Spouse entitled to the lesser of an annuity or a fraction of trust income.* Prior to October 24, 1992, D transferred in trust 500 identical shares of X Company stock, valued for gift tax purposes at $500,000. The trust provided that during the lifetime of D's spouse, S, the trustee is to pay annually to S the lesser of one-half of the trust income or $20,000. Any trust income not paid to S is to be accumulated in the trust and may not be distributed during S's lifetime. S has a testamentary general power of appointment over the entire trust principal. The applicable interest rate for valuing annuities as of the date of D's gift under section 7520 is 10 percent. For purposes of paragraphs (a) through (c) of this section, S is treated as receiving all of the income from the lesser of one-half of the stock ($250,000), or $200,000, the specific portion of the stock which, as determined in accordance with § 25.2523(e)-1(c)(3)(i) of this chapter, would produce annual income of $20,000 (20,000÷.10). Accordingly, the marital deduction is limited to $200,000 (200,000÷500,000 or $^2$/5th of the value of the trust.)

*Example 2. Spouse possesses power and income interest over different specific portions of trust.* The facts are the same as in *Example 1* except that S's testamentary general power of appointment is exercisable over only $^1$/4th of the trust principal. Consequently, under section 2523(e), the marital deduction is allowable only for the value of $^1$/4th of the trust ($125,000); i.e., the lesser of the value of the portion with respect to which S is deemed to be entitled to all of the income ($^2$/5th of the trust or $200,000), or the value of the portion with respect to which S possesses the requisite power of appointment ($^1$/4th of the trust or $125,000).

*Example 3. Power of appointment over shares of stock constitutes a power over a specific portion.* D transferred 250 identical shares of Y company stock to a trust under the terms of which trust income is to be paid annually to S, during S's lifetime. S was given a testamentary general power of appointment over 100 shares of stock. The trust provides that if the trustee sells the Y company stock, S's general power of appointment is exercisable with respect to the sale proceeds or the property in which the proceeds are reinvested. Because the amount of property represented by a single share of stock would be altered if the corporation split its stock, issued stock dividends, made a distribution of capital, etc., a power to appoint 100 shares at the time of S's death is not necessarily a power to appoint the entire interest that the 100 shares represented on the date of D's gift. If it is shown that, under local law, S has a general power to appoint not only the 100 shares designated by D but also $^{100}$/250 of any distributions by the corporation that are included in trust principal, the requirements of paragraph (c)(2) of this section are satisfied and S is treated as having a general power to appoint $^{100}$/250 of the entire interest in the 250 shares. In that case, the marital deduction is limited to 40 percent of the trust principal. If local law does not give S that power, the 100 shares would not constitute a specific portion under § 25.2523(e)-1(c) (including § 25.2523(e)-1(c)(3)(ii)). The nature of the asset is such that a change in the capitalization of the corporation could cause an alteration in the original value represented by the shares at the time of the transfer and is thus not a specific portion of the trust.

(d) *Definition of "entire interest".*—Since a marital deduction is allowed for each qualifying separate interest in property transferred by the donor to the donee spouse, for purposes of paragraphs (a) and (b) of this section, each property interest with respect to which the donee spouse received some rights is considered separately in determining whether her rights extend to the entire interest or to a specific portion of the entire interest. A property interest which consists of several identical units of property (such as a block of 250 shares of stock, whether the ownership is evidenced by one or several certificates) is considered one property interest, unless certain of the units are to be segregated and accorded different treatment, in which case each segregated group of items is considered a separate property interest. The bequest of a specified sum of money constitutes the bequest of a separate property interest if immediately following the transfer and thenceforth it, and the investments made with it, must be so segregated or accounted for as to permit its identification as a separate item of property. The application of this paragraph may be illustrated by the following examples:

*Example (1).* The donor transferred to a trustee three adjoining farms, Blackacre, Whiteacre, and Greenacre. The trust instrument provided that during the lifetime of the donee spouse the trustee should pay her all of the income from the trust. Upon her death, all of Blackacre, a one-half interest in Whiteacre, and a one-third interest in Greenacre were to be distributed to the person or persons appointed by her in her will. The donee spouse is considered as being entitled to all of the income from the entire interest in Blackacre, all of the income from the entire interest in Whiteacre, and all of the income from the entire interest in Greenacre. She also is considered as having a power of appointment over the entire interest in Blackacre, over one-half of the entire interest in Whiteacre, and over one-third of the entire interest in Greenacre.

*Example (2)*. The donor transferred $250,000 to C, as trustee. C is to invest the money and pay all of the income from the investments to W, the donor's spouse, annually. W was given a general power, exercisable by will, to appoint one-half of the corpus of the trust. Here, immediately following establishment of the trust, the $250,000 will be sufficiently segregated to permit its identification as a separate item, and the $250,000 will constitute an entire property interest. Therefore, W has a right to income and a power of appointment such that one-half of the entire interest is a deductible interest.

*Example (3)*. The donor transferred 100 shares of Z Corporation stock to D, as trustee. W, the donor's spouse, is to receive all of the income of the trust annually and is given a general power, exercisable by will, to appoint out of the trust corpus the sum of $25,000. In this case the $25,000 is not, immediately following establishment of the trust, sufficiently segregated to permit its identification as a separate item of property in which the donee spouse has the entire interest. Therefore, the $25,000 does not constitute the entire interest in a property for the purpose of paragraphs (a) and (b) of this section.

(e) *Application of local law.*—In determining whether or not the conditions set forth in paragraph (a)(1) through (5) of this section are satisfied by the instrument of transfer, regard is to be had to the applicable provisions of the law of the jurisdiction under which the interest passes and, if the transfer is in trust, the applicable provisions of the law governing the administration of the trust. For example, silence of a trust instrument as to the frequency of payment will not be regarded as a failure to satisfy the condition set forth in paragraph (a)(2) of this section that income must be payable to the donee spouse annually or more frequently unless the applicable law permits payment to be made less frequently than annually. The principles outlined in this paragraph and paragraphs (f) and (g) of this section which are applied in determining whether transfers in trust meet such conditions are equally applicable in ascertaining whether, in the case of interests not in trust, the donee spouse has the equivalent in rights over income and over the property.

(f) *Right to income.*—(1) If an interest is transferred in trust, the donee spouse is "entitled for life to all of the income from the entire interest or a specific portion of the entire interest," for the purpose of the condition set forth in paragraph (a)(1) of this section, if the effect of the trust is to give her substantially that degree of beneficial enjoyment of the trust property during her life which the principles of the law of trusts accord to a person who is unqualifiedly designated as the life beneficiary of a trust. Such degree of enjoyment is given only if it was the donor's intention, as manifested by the terms of the trust instrument and the surrounding circumstances, that the trust should produce for the donee spouse during her life such an income, or that the spouse should have such use of the trust property as is consistent with the value of the trust corpus and with its preservation. The designation of the spouse as sole income beneficiary for life of the entire interest or a specific portion of the entire interest will be sufficient to qualify the trust unless the terms of the trust and the surrounding circumstances considered as a whole evidence an intention to deprive the spouse of the requisite degree of enjoyment. In determining whether a trust evidences that intention, the treatment required or permitted with respect to individual items must be considered in relation to the entire system provided for the administration of the trust. In addition, the spouse's interest shall meet the condition set forth in paragraph (a)(1) of this section if the spouse is entitled to income as defined or determined by applicable local law that provides for a reasonable apportionment between the income and remainder beneficiaries of the total return of the trust and that meets the requirements of § 1.643(b)-1 of this chapter.

(2) If the over-all effect of a trust is to give to the donee spouse such enforceable rights as will preserve to her the requisite degree of enjoyment, it is immaterial whether that result is effected by rules specifically stated in the trust instrument, or, in their absence, by the rules for the management of the trust property and the allocation of receipts and expenditures supplied by the State law. For example, a provision in the trust instrument for amortization of bond premium by appropriate periodic charges to interest will not disqualify the interest transferred in trust even though there is no State law specifically authorizing amortization or there is a State law denying amortization which is applicable only in the absence of such a provision in the trust instrument.

(3) In the case of a trust, the rules to be applied by the trustee in allocation of receipts and expenses between income and corpus must be considered in relation to the nature and expected productivity of the assets transferred in trust, the nature and frequency of occurrence of the expected receipts, and any provisions as to change in the form of investments. If it is evident from the nature of the trust assets and the rules provided for management of the trust that the allocation to income of such receipts as rents, ordinary cash dividends and interest will give to the spouse the substantial enjoyment during life required by the statute, provisions that such receipts as stock dividends and proceeds from the conversion of trust assets shall be treated as corpus will not disqualify the interest transferred in trust. Similarly, provision for a depletion charge against income in the case of trust assets which are subject to depletion will not disqualify the interest transferred in trust, unless the effect is to deprive the spouse of the requisite beneficial enjoyment. The same principle is applicable in the case of depreciation, trustees' commissions, and other charges.

(4) Provisions granting administrative powers to the trustees will not have the effect of disqualifying an interest transferred in trust unless the grant of powers evidences the intention to deprive the donee spouse of the beneficial enjoyment required by the statute. Such an intention will not be considered to exist if the entire terms of the instrument are such that the local courts will impose reasonable limitations upon the exercise of the powers. Among the powers which if subject to reasonable limitations will not disqualify the interest transferred in trust are the power to determine the allocation or apportionment of receipts and disbursements between income and corpus, the power to apply the income or corpus for the benefit of the spouse, and the power to retain the assets transferred to the trust. For example, a power to retain trust assets which consist substantially of unproductive property will not disqualify the interest if the applicable rules for the administration of the trust require, or permit the spouse to require, that the trustee either make the property productive or convert it within a reasonable time. Nor will such a power disqualify the interest if the applicable rules for administration of the trust require the trustee to use the degree of judgment and care in the exercise of the power which a prudent man would use if he were owner of the trust assets. Further, a power to retain a residence for the spouse or other property for the personal use of the spouse will not disqualify the interest transferred in trust.

(5) An interest transferred in trust will not satisfy the condition set forth in paragraph (a)(1) of this section that the donee spouse be entitled to all the income if the primary purpose of the trust is to safeguard property without providing the spouse with the required beneficial enjoyment. Such trusts include not only trusts which expressly provide for the accumulation of the income but also trusts which indirectly accomplish a similar purpose. For example, assume that the corpus of a trust consists substantially of property which is not likely to be income producing during the life of the donee spouse and that the spouse cannot compel the trustee to convert or otherwise deal with the property as described in subparagraph (4) of this paragraph. An interest transferred to such a trust will not qualify unless the applicable rules for the administration require, or permit the spouse to require, that the trustee provide the required beneficial enjoyment, such as by payments to the spouse out of other assets of the trust.

(6) If a trust may be terminated during the life of the donee spouse, under her exercise of a power of appointment or by distribution of the corpus to her, the interest transferred in trust satisfies the condition set forth in paragraph (a)(1) of this section (that the spouse be entitled to all the income) if she (i) is entitled to the income until the trust terminates, or (ii) has the right, exercisable in all events, to have the corpus distributed to her at any time during her life.

(7) An interest transferred in trust fails to satisfy the condition set forth in paragraph (a)(1) of this section, that the spouse be entitled to all the income, to the extent that the income is required to be accumulated in whole or in part or may be accumulated in the discretion of any person other than the donee spouse; to the extent that the consent of any person other than the donee spouse is required as a condition precedent to distribution of the income; or to the extent that any person other than the donee spouse has the power to alter the terms of the trust so as to deprive her of her right to the income. An interest transferred in trust will not fail to satisfy the condition that the spouse be entitled to all the income merely because its terms provide that the right of the donee spouse to the income shall not be subject to assignment, alienation, pledge, attachment or claims of creditors.

(8) In the case of an interest transferred in trust, the terms "entitled for life" and "payable annually or at more frequent intervals", as used in the conditions set forth in paragraph (a)(1) and (2) of this section, require that under the terms of the trust the income referred to must be currently (at least annually; see paragraph (e) of this section) distributable to the spouse or that she must have such command over the income that it is virtually hers. Thus, the conditions in paragraph (a)(1) and (2) of this section are satisfied in this respect if, under the terms of the trust instrument, the donee spouse has the right exercisable annually (or more frequently) to require distribution to herself of the trust income, and otherwise the trust income is to be accumulated and added to corpus. Similarly, as respects the income for the period between the last distribution date and the date of the spouse's death, it is sufficient if that income is subject to the spouse's power to appoint. Thus, if the trust instrument provides that income accrued or undistributed on the date of the spouse's death is to be disposed of as if it had been received after her

death, and if the spouse has a power of appointment over the trust corpus, the power necessarily extends to the undistributed income.

(g) *Power of appointment in donee spouse.*—(1) The conditions set forth in paragraph (a)(3) and (4) of this section, that is, that the donee spouse must have a power of appointment exercisable in favor of herself or her estate and exercisable alone and in all events, are not met unless the power of the donee spouse to appoint the entire interest or a specific portion of it falls within one of the following categories:

(i) A power so to appoint fully exercisable in her own favor at any time during her life (as, for example, an unlimited power to invade); or

(ii) A power so to appoint exercisable in favor of her estate. Such a power, if exercisable during life, must be fully exercisable at any time during life, or, if exercisable by will, must be fully exercisable irrespective of the time of her death; or

(iii) A combination of the powers described under subdivisions (i) and (ii) of this subparagraph. For example, the donee spouse may, until she attains the age of 50 years, have a power to appoint to herself and thereafter have a power to appoint to her estate. However, the condition that the spouse's power must be exercisable in all events is not satisfied unless irrespective of when the donee spouse may die the entire interest or a specific portion of it will at the time of her death be subject to one power or the other.

(2) The power of the donee spouse must be a power to appoint the entire interest or a specific portion of it as unqualified owner (and free of the trust if a trust is involved, or free of the joint tenancy if a joint tenancy is involved) or to appoint the entire interest or a specific portion of it as a part of her estate (and free of the trust if a trust is involved), that is, in effect, to dispose of it to whomsoever she pleases. Thus, if the donor transferred property to a son and the donee spouse as joint tenants with right of survivorship and under local law the donee spouse has a power of severance exercisable without consent of the other joint tenant, and by exercising this power could acquire a one-half interest in the property as a tenant in common, her power of severance will satisfy the condition set forth in paragraph (a)(3) of this section that she have a power of appointment in favor of herself or her estate. However, if the donee spouse entered into a binding agreement with the donor to exercise the power only in favor of their issue, that condition is not met. An interest transferred in trust will not be regarded as failing to satisfy the condition merely because takers in default of the donee spouse's exercise of the power are designated by the donor. The donor may provide that, in default of exercise of the power, the trust shall continue for an additional period.

(3) A power is not considered to be a power exercisable by a donee spouse alone and in all events as required by paragraph (a)(4) of this section if the exercise of the power in the donee spouse to appoint the entire interest or a specific portion of it to herself or to her estate requires the joinder or consent of any other person. The power is not "exercisable in all events" if it can be terminated during the life of the donee spouse by any event other than her complete exercise or release of it. Further, a power is not "exercisable in all events" if it may be exercised for a limited purpose only. For example, a power which is not exercisable in the event of the spouse's remarriage is not exercisable in all events. Likewise, if there are any restrictions, either by the terms of the instrument or under applicable local law, on the exercise of a power to consume property (whether or not held in trust) for the benefit of the spouse, the power is not exercisable in all events. Thus, if a power of invasion is exercisable only for the spouse's support, or only for her limited use, the power is not exercisable in all events. In order for a power of invasion to be exercisable in all events, the donee spouse must have the unrestricted power exercisable at any time during her life to use all or any part of the property subject to the power, and to dispose of it in any manner, including the power to dispose of it by gift (whether or not she has power to dispose of it by will).

(4) If the power is in existence at all times following the transfer of the interest, limitations of a formal nature will not disqualify the interest. Examples of formal limitations on a power exercisable during life are requirements that an exercise must be in a particular form, that it must be filed with a trustee during the spouse's life, that reasonable notice must be given, or that reasonable intervals must elapse between successive partial exercises. Examples of formal limitations on a power exercisable by will are that it must be exercised by a will executed by the donee spouse after the making of the gift or that exercise must be by specific reference to the power.

(5) If the donee spouse has the requisite power to appoint to herself or her estate, it is immaterial that she also has one or more lesser powers. Thus, if she has a testamentary power to appoint to her estate, she may also have a limited power of withdrawal or of appointment during her life. Similarly, if she has an unlimited power of withdrawal, she may have a limited testamentary power.

(h) *Existence of a power in another.*—Paragraph (a)(5) of this section provides that a transfer described in paragraph (a) is nondeductible to the extent that the donor created a power in the trustee or in any other person to appoint a part of the interest to any person other than the donee spouse. However, only powers in other persons which are in opposition to that of the donee spouse will cause a portion of the interest to fail to satisfy the condition set forth in paragraph (a)(5) of this section. Thus, a power in a trustee to distribute corpus to or for the benefit of the donee spouse will not disqualify the trust. Similarly, a power to distribute corpus to the spouse for the support of minor children will not disqualify the trust if she is legally obligated to support such children. The application of this paragraph may be illustrated by the following examples:

*Example (1).* Assume that a donor created a trust, designating his spouse as income beneficiary for life with an unrestricted power in the spouse to appoint the corpus during her life. The donor further provided that in the event the donee spouse should die without having exercised the power, the trust should continue for the life of his son with a power in the son to appoint the corpus. Since the power in the son could become exercisable only after the death of the donee spouse, the interest is not regarded as failing to satisfy the condition set forth in paragraph (a)(5) of this section.

*Example (2).* Assume that the donor created a trust, designating his spouse as income beneficiary for life and as donee of a power to appoint by will the entire corpus. The donor further provided that the trustee could distribute 30 percent of the corpus to the donor's son when he reached the age of 35 years. Since the trustee has a power to appoint 30 percent of the entire interest for the benefit of a person other than the donee spouse, only 70 percent of the interest placed in trust satisfied the condition set forth in paragraph (a)(5) of this section. If, in this case, the donee spouse had a power, exercisable by her will, to appoint only one-half of the corpus as it was constituted at the time of her death, it should be noted that only 35 percent of the interest placed in the trust would satisfy the condition set forth in paragraph (a)(3) of this section. [Reg. § 25.2523(e)-1.]

☐ [T.D. 6334, 11-14-58. *Amended by* T.D. 6542, 1-19-61; T.D. 8522, 2-28-94 *and* T.D. 9102, 12-30-2003.]

**[Reg. § 25.2523(f)-1A]**

**§ 25.2523(f)-1A. Special rule applicable to community property transferred prior to January 1, 1982.**—(a) *In general.*—With respect to gifts made prior to January 1, 1982, the marital deduction is allowable with respect to any transfer by a donor to the donor's spouse only to the extent that the transfer is shown to represent a gift of property that was not, at the time of the gift, held as *community property*, as defined in paragraph (b) of this section.

(b) *Definition of "community property".*—(1) For the purpose of paragraph (a) of this section, the term "community property" is considered to include—

(i) Any property held by the donor and his spouse as community property under the law of any State, Territory, or possession of the United States, or of any foreign country, except property in which the donee spouse had at the time of the gift merely an expectant interest. The donee spouse is regarded as having, at any particular time, merely an expectant interest in property held at that time by the donor and herself as community property under the law of any State, Territory, or possession of the United States, or of any foreign country, if, in case such property were transferred by gift into the separate property of the donee spouse, the entire value of such property (and not merely one-half of it), would be treated as the amount of the gift.

(ii) Separate property acquired by the donor as a result of a "conversion," after December 31, 1941, of property held by him and the donee spouse as community property under the law of any State, Territory, or possession of the United States, or of any foreign country (except such property in which the donee spouse had at the time of the "conversion" merely an expectant interest), into their separate property, subject to the limitation with respect to value contained in subparagraph (5) of this paragraph.

(iii) Property acquired by the donor in exchange (by one exchange or a series of exchanges) for separate property resulting from such "conversion."

(2) The characteristics of property which acquired a noncommunity instead of a community status by reason of an agreement (whether antenuptial or postnuptial) are such that section 2523(f) classifies the property as community property of the donor and his spouse in the computation of the marital deduction. In distinguishing property which thus acquired a noncommunity status from property which acquired such a status solely by operation of the community property law, section 2523(f) refers to the former category of property as "separate property" acquired as a result of a "conversion" of "property held as such community property." As used in section 2523(f) the phrase "property held as such community property" is used to denote the body of property comprehended

within the community property system; the expression "separate property" includes any noncommunity property, whether held in joint tenancy, tenancy by the entirety, tenancy in common, or otherwise; and the term "conversion" includes any transaction or agreement which transforms property from a community status into a noncommunity status.

(3) The separate property which section 2523(f) classifies as community property is not limited to that which was in existence at the time of the conversion. The following are illustrative of the scope of section 2523(f):

(i) A partition of community property between husband and wife, whereby a portion of the property became the separate property of each, is a conversion of community property.

(ii) A transfer of community property into some other form of coownership, such as a joint tenancy, is a conversion of the property.

(iii) An agreement (whether made before or after marriage) that future earnings and gains which would otherwise be community property shall be shared by the spouses as separate property effects a conversion of such earnings and gains.

(iv) A change in the form of ownership of property which causes future rentals, which would otherwise have been acquired as community property, to be acquired as separate property effects a conversion of the rentals.

(4) The rules of section 2523(f) are applicable, however, only if the conversion took place after December 31, 1941, and only to the extent stated in this section.

(5) If the value of the separate property acquired by the donor as a result of a conversion did not exceed the value of the separate

$$\frac{\$64,000 \text{ (value of property acquired by donee spouse)}}{\$160,000 \text{ (value of property acquired by donor spouse)}}$$

The marital deduction with respect to the gift is, therefore, limited to one-half of $120,000 (the difference between $200,000, the value of the gift, and $80,000, the portion of the gift considered to have been of "community property"). The marital deduction with respect to the gift is, therefore, $60,000. [Reg. § 25.2523(f)-1A.]

☐ [T.D. 6334, 11-14-58. Redesignated and amended by T.D. 8522, 2-28-94.]

## [Reg. § 25.2523(f)-1]

**§ 25.2523(f)-1. Election with respect to life estate transferred to donee spouse.**—(a) In general.—(1) With respect to gifts made after December 31, 1981, subject to section 2523(i), a marital deduction is allowed under section 2523(a) for transfers of qualified terminable interest property. Qualified terminable interest property is terminable interest property described in section 2523(b)(1) that satisfies the requirements of section 2523(f)(2) and this section. Terminable interests that are described in section 2523(b)(2) cannot qualify as qualified terminable interest property. Thus, if the donor retains a power described in section 2523(b)(2) to appoint an interest in qualified terminable interest property, no deduction is allowable under section 2523(a) for the property.

(2) All of the property for which a deduction is allowed under this paragraph (a) is treated as passing to the donee spouse (for purposes of § 25.2523(a)-1), and no part of the property is treated as retained by the donor or as passing to any person other than the donee spouse (for purposes of § 25.2523(b)-1(b)).

(b) Qualified terminable interest property.—(1) Definition.—Section 2523(f)(2) provides the definition of qualified terminable interest property.

(2) Meaning of property.—For purposes of section 2523(f)(2), the term property generally means an entire interest in property (within the meaning of § 25.2523(e)-1(d)) or a specific portion of the entire interest (within the meaning of § 25.2523(e)-1(c)).

(3) Property for which the election may be made.—(i) In general.—The election may relate to all or any part of property that meets the requirements of section 2523(f)(2)(A) and (B), provided that any partial election must be made with respect to a fractional or percentage share of the property so that the elective portion reflects its proportionate share of the increase or decrease in the entire property for purposes of applying sections 2044 or 2519. Thus, if the interest of the donee spouse in a trust (or other property in which the spouse has a qualifying income interest) meets the requirements of this section, the election may be made under section 2523(f)(2)(C) with respect to a part of the trust (or other property) only if the election relates to a defined fraction or percentage of the entire trust (or other property) or specific portion thereof within the meaning of § 25.2523(e)-1(c). The fraction or percentage may be defined by formula.

property thus acquired by the donee spouse, the entire separate property thus acquired by the donor is to be considered, for the purposes of this section, as held by him and the donee spouse as community property. If the value (at the time of conversion) of the separate property so acquired by the donor exceeded the value (at that time) of the separate property so acquired by the donee spouse, only a part of the separate property so acquired by the donor (and only the same fractional part of property acquired by him in exchange for such separate property) is to be considered, for purposes of this section, as held by him and the donee spouse as community property. The part of such separate property (or property acquired in exchange for it) which is considered as so held is the same proportion of it which the value (at the time of the conversion) of the separate property so acquired by the donee spouse is of the value (at the time) of the separate property so acquired by the donor. The following example illustrates the application of the provisions of this paragraph:

Example. During 1942 the donor and his spouse partitioned certain real property held by them under community property laws. The real property then had a value of $224,000. A portion of the property, then having a value of $160,000, was converted into the donor's separate property, and the remaining portion, then having a value of $64,000, was converted into his spouse's separate property. In 1955 the donor made a gift to his spouse of the property acquired by him as a result of the partition, which property then had a value of $200,000. The portion of the property transferred by gift which is considered as community property is

$$\times \$200,000 = \$80,000$$

(ii) Division of trusts.—If the interest of the donee spouse in a trust meets the requirements of this section, the trust may be divided into separate trusts to reflect a partial election that has been made, if authorized under the terms of the governing instrument or otherwise permissible under local law. A trust may be divided only if the fiduciary is required, either by applicable local law or by the express or implied provisions of the governing instrument, to divide the trust according to the fair market value of the assets of the trust at the time of the division. The division of the trusts must be done on a fractional or percentage basis to reflect the partial election. However, the separate trusts do not have to be funded with a pro rata portion of each asset held by the undivided trust.

(4) Manner and time of making election.—(i) An election under section 2523(f)(2)(C) (other than a deemed election with respect to a joint and survivor annuity as described in section 2523(f)(6)), is made on a gift tax return for the calendar year in which the interest is transferred. The return must be filed within the time prescribed by section 6075(b) (determined without regard to section 6019(a)(2)), including any extensions authorized under section 6075(b)(2) (relating to an automatic extension of time for filing a gift tax return where the donor is granted an extension of time to file the income tax return).

(ii) If the election is made on a return for the calendar year that includes the date of death of the donor, the return (as prescribed by section 6075(b)(3)) must be filed no later than the time (including extensions) for filing the estate tax return. The election, once made, is irrevocable.

(c) Qualifying income interest for life.—(1) In general.—For purposes of this section, the term qualifying income interest for life is defined as provided in section 2056(b)(7)(B)(ii) and § 20.2056(b)-7(d)(1).

(i) Entitled for life to all the income.—The principles outlined in § 25.2523(e)-1(f) (relating to whether the spouse is entitled for life to all of the income from the entire interest or a specific portion of the entire interest) apply in determining whether the donee spouse is entitled for life to all the income from the property, regardless of whether the interest passing to the donee spouse is in trust. An income interest granted for a term of years, or a life estate subject to termination upon the occurrence of a specified event (e.g., divorce) is not a qualifying income interest for life.

(ii) Income between last distribution date and date of spouse's death.—An income interest does not fail to constitute a qualifying income interest for life solely because income for the period between the last distribution date and the date of the donee spouse's death is not required to be distributed to the estate of the donee spouse. See § 20.2044-1 of this chapter relating to the inclusion of such undistributed income in the gross estate of the donee spouse.

(iii) Pooled income funds.—An income interest in a pooled income fund described in section 642(c)(5) constitutes a qualifying income interest for life for purposes of this section.

(iv) *Distribution of principal for the benefit of the donee spouse.*— An income interest does not fail to constitute a qualifying income interest for life solely because the trustee has a power to distribute principal to or for the benefit of the donee spouse. The fact that property distributed to a donee spouse may be transferred by the spouse to another person does not result in a failure to satisfy the requirement of section 2056(b)(7)(B)(ii)(II). However, if the governing instrument requires the donee spouse to transfer the distributed property to another person without full and adequate consideration in money or money's worth, the requirement of section 2056(b)(7)(B)(ii)(II) is not satisfied.

(2) *Immediate right to income.*—In order to constitute a qualifying income interest for life, the donee spouse must be granted the immediate right to receive the income from the property. Thus, an income interest does not constitute a qualifying income interest for life if the donee spouse receives the right to trust income commencing at some time in the future, e.g., on the termination of a preceding life income interest of the donor spouse.

(3) *Annuities payable from trusts in the case of gifts made on or before October 24, 1992.*—(i) In the case of gifts made on or before October 24, 1992, a donee spouse's lifetime annuity interest payable from a trust or other group of assets passing from the donor is treated as a qualifying income interest for life for purposes of section 2523(f)(2)(B). The deductible interest, for purposes of § 25.2523(a)-1(b), is the specific portion of the property that, assuming the applicable interest rate for valuing annuities at the time the annuity interest is transferred, would produce income equal to the minimum amount payable annually to the donee spouse. If, based on the applicable interest rate, the entire property from which the annuity may be satisfied is insufficient to produce income equal to the minimum annual payment, the value of the deductible interest is the entire value of the property. The value of the deductible interest may not exceed the value of the property from which the annuity is payable. If the annual payment may increase, the increased amount is not taken into account in valuing the deductible interest.

(ii) An annuity interest is not treated as a qualifying income interest for life for purposes of section 2523(f)(2)(B) if any person other than the donee spouse may receive during the donee spouse's lifetime, any distribution of the property or its income from which the annuity is payable.

(iii) To determine the applicable interest rate for valuing annuities, see sections 2512 and 7520 and the regulations under those sections.

(4) *Joint and survivor annuities.*—[Reserved]

(d) *Treatment of interest retained by the donor spouse.*—(1) *In general.*—Under section 2523(f)(5)(A), if a donor spouse retains an interest in qualified terminable interest property, any subsequent transfer by the donor spouse of the retained interest in the property is not treated as a transfer for gift tax purposes. Further, the retention of the interest until the donor spouse's death does not cause the property subject to the retained interest to be includible in the gross estate of the donor spouse.

(2) *Exception.*—Under section 2523(f)(5)(B), the rule contained in paragraph (d)(1) of this section does not apply to any property after the donee spouse is treated as having transferred the property under section 2519, or after the property is includible in the gross estate of the donee spouse under section 2044.

(e) *Application of local law.*—The provisions of local law are taken into account in determining whether or not the conditions of section 2523(f)(2)(A) and (B), and the conditions of paragraph (c) of this section, are satisfied. For example, silence of a trust instrument on the frequency of payment is not regarded as a failure to satisfy the requirement that the income must be payable to the donee spouse annually or more frequently unless applicable local law permits payments less frequently to the donee spouse.

(f) *Examples.*—The following examples illustrate the application of this section, where D, the donor, transfers property to D's spouse, S. Unless stated otherwise, it is assumed that S is not the trustee of any trust established for S's benefit:

*Example 1. Life estate in residence.* D transfers by gift a personal residence valued at $250,000 on the date of the gift to S and D's children, giving S the exclusive and unrestricted right to use the property (including the right to continue to occupy the property as a personal residence or rent the property and receive the income for her lifetime). After S's death, the property is to pass to D's children. Under applicable local law, S's consent is required for any sale of the property. If D elects to treat all of the transferred property as qualified terminable interest property, the deductible interest is $250,000, the value of the property for gift tax purposes.

*Example 2. Power to make property productive.* D transfers assets having a fair market value of $500,000 to a trust pursuant to which S is given the right exercisable annually to require distribution of all the trust income to S. No trust property may be distributed during S's lifetime to any person other than S. The assets used to fund the trust include both income producing assets and nonproductive assets. Applicable local law permits S to require that the trustee either make the trust property productive or sell the property and reinvest the proceeds in productive property within a reasonable time after the transfer. If D elects to treat the entire trust as qualified terminable interest property, the deductible interest is $500,000. If D elects to treat only 20 percent of the trust as qualified terminable interest property, the deductible interest is $100,000; i.e., 20 percent of $500,000.

*Example 3. Power of distribution over fraction of trust income.* The facts are the same as in *Example 2* except that S is given the power exercisable annually to require distribution to S of only 50 percent of the trust income for life. The remaining trust income may be accumulated or distributed among D's children and S in the trustee's discretion. The maximum amount that D may elect to treat as qualified terminable interest property is $250,000; i.e., the value of the trust for gift tax purposes ($500,000) multiplied by the percentage of the trust in which S has a qualifying income interest for life (50 percent). If D elects to treat only 20 percent of the portion of the trust in which S has a qualifying income interest as qualified terminable interest property, the deductible interest is $50,000; i.e., 20 percent of $250,000.

*Example 4. Power to distribute trust corpus to other beneficiaries.* D transfers $500,000 to a trust providing that all the trust income is to be paid to D's spouse, S, during S's lifetime. The trustee is given the power to use annually $5,000 from the trust for the maintenance and support of S's minor child, C. Any such distribution does not necessarily relieve S of S's obligation to support and maintain C. S does not have a qualifying income interest for life in any portion of the trust because the gift fails to satisfy the condition in sections 2523(f)(3) and 2056(b)(7)(B)(ii)(II) that no person have a power, other than a power the exercise of which takes effect only at or after S's death, to appoint any part of the property to any person other than S. The trust would also be nondeductible under section 2523(f) if S, rather than the trustee, were given the power to appoint a portion of the principal to C. However, in the latter case, if S made a qualified disclaimer (within the meaning of section 2518) of the power to appoint to C, the trust could qualify for the marital deduction pursuant to section 2523(f), assuming that the power was personal to S and S's disclaimer terminates the power. Similarly, if C made a qualified disclaimer of the right to receive distributions from the trust, the trust would qualify under section 2523(f) assuming that C's disclaimer effectively negates the trustee's power under local law.

*Example 5. Spouse's interest terminable on divorce.* The facts are the same as in *Example 3* except that if S and D divorce, S's interest in the trust will pass to C. S's income interest is not a qualifying income interest for life because it is terminable upon S's divorce. Therefore, no portion of the trust is deductible under section 2523(f).

*Example 6. Spouse's interest in trust in the form of an annuity.* Prior to October 24, 1992, D established a trust funded with income producing property valued for gift tax purposes at $800,000. The trustee is required by the trust instrument to pay $40,000 a year to S for life. Any income in excess of the annuity amount is to be accumulated in the trust and may not be distributed during S's lifetime. S's lifetime annuity interest is treated as a qualifying income interest for life. If D elects to treat the entire portion of the trust in which S has a qualifying income interest as qualified terminable interest property, the value of the deductible interest is $400,000, because that amount would yield an income to S of $40,000 a year (assuming a 10 percent interest rate applies in valuing annuities at the time of the transfer).

*Example 7. Value of spouse's annuity exceeds value of trust corpus.* The facts are the same as in *Example 6*, except that the trustee is required to pay S $100,000 a year for S's life. If D elects to treat the entire portion of the trust in which S has a qualifying income interest for life as qualified terminable interest property, the value of the deductible interest is $800,000, which is the lesser of the entire value of the property ($800,000) or the amount of property that (assuming a 10 percent interest rate) would yield an income to S of $100,000 a year ($1,000,000).

*Example 8. Transfer to pooled income fund.* D transfers $200,000 on June 1, 1994, to a pooled income fund (described in section 642(c)(5)) designating S as the only life income beneficiary. If D elects to treat the entire $200,000 as qualified terminable interest property, the deductible interest is $200,000.

*Example 9. Retention by donor spouse of income interest in property.* On October 1, 1994, D transfers property to an irrevocable trust under the terms of which trust income is to be paid to D for life, then to S for life and, on S's death, the trust corpus is to be paid to D's children. Because S does not possess an immediate right to receive trust income, S's interest does not qualify as a qualifying income interest for life under section 2523(f)(2). Further, under section 2702(a)(2) and § 25.2702-2(b), D is treated for gift tax purposes as making a gift with a value equal to the entire value of the property. If D dies in 1996 survived by S, the trust corpus will be includible in D's gross estate under section 2036. However, in computing D's estate tax liability, D's adjusted taxable gifts under section 2001(b)(1)(B) are adjusted to reflect the inclusion of the gifted property in D's gross estate. In addition, if S survives D, the trust property is eligible for treatment as qualified terminable interest property under section 2056(b)(7) in D's estate.

*Example 10. Retention by donor spouse of income interest in property.* On October 1, 1994, D transfers property to an irrevocable trust under the terms of which trust income is to be paid to S for life, then to D for life and, on D's death, the trust corpus is to be paid to D's children. D elects under section 2523(f) to treat the property as qualified terminable interest property. D dies in 1996, survived by S. S subsequently dies in 1998. Under § 2523(f)-1(d)(1), because D elected to treat the transfer as qualified terminable interest property, no part of the trust corpus is includible in D's gross estate because of D's retained interest in the trust corpus. On S's subsequent death in 1998, the trust corpus is includible in S's gross estate under section 2044.

*Example 11. Retention by donor spouse of income interest in property.* The facts are the same as in *Example 10*, except that S dies in 1996 survived by D, who subsequently dies in 1998. Because D made an election under section 2523(f) with respect to the trust, on S's death the trust corpus is includible in S's gross estate under section 2044. Accordingly, under section 2044(c), S is treated as the transferor of the property for estate and gift tax purposes. Upon D's subsequent death in 1998, because the property was subject to inclusion in S's gross estate under section 2044, the exclusion rule in § 25.2523(f)-1(d)(1) does not apply under § 25.2523(f)-1(d)(2). However, because S is treated as the transferor of the property, the property is not subject to inclusion in D's gross estate under section 2036 or section 2038. If the executor of S's estate made a section 2056(b)(7) election with respect to the trust, the trust is includible in D's gross estate under section 2044 upon D's later death. [Reg. § 25.2523(f)-1.]

☐ [*T.D. 8522, 2-28-94.*]

### [Reg. § 25.2523(g)-1]

**§ 25.2523(g)-1. Special rule for charitable remainder trusts.**—(a) *In general.*—(1) With respect to gifts made after December 31, 1981, subject to section 2523(i), if the donor's spouse is the only noncharitable beneficiary (other than the donor) of a charitable remainder annuity trust or charitable remainder unitrust described in section 664 (qualified charitable remainder trust), section 2523(b) does not apply to the interest in the trust transferred to the donee spouse. Thus, the value of the annuity or unitrust interest passing to the spouse qualifies for a marital deduction under section 2523(g) and the value of the remainder interest qualifies for a charitable deduction under section 2522.

(2) A marital deduction for the value of the donee spouse's annuity or unitrust interest in a qualified charitable remainder trust to which section 2523(g) applies is allowable only under section 2523(g). Therefore, if an interest in property qualifies for a marital deduction under section 2523(g), no election may be made with respect to the property under section 2523(f).

(3) The donee spouse's interest need not be an interest for life to qualify for a marital deduction under section 2523(g). However, for purposes of section 664, an annuity or unitrust interest payable to the spouse for a term of years cannot be payable for a term that exceeds 20 years or the trust does not qualify under section 2523(g).

(4) A deduction is allowed under section 2523(g) even if the transfer to the donee spouse is conditioned on the donee spouse's payment of state death taxes, if any, attributable to the qualified charitable remainder trust.

(5) For purposes of this section, the term *noncharitable beneficiary* means any beneficiary of the qualified charitable remainder trust other than an organization described in section 170(c).

(b) *Charitable remainder trusts where the donee spouse and the donor are not the only noncharitable beneficiaries.*—In the case of a charitable remainder trust where the donor and the donor's spouse are not the only noncharitable beneficiaries (for example, where the noncharitable interest is payable to the donor's spouse for life and then to another individual (other than the donor) for life), the qualification of the interest as qualified terminable interest property is determined solely under section 2523(f) and not under section 2523(g). Accordingly, if the transfer to the trust is made prior to October 24, 1992, the spousal annuity or unitrust interest may qualify under § 25.2523(f)-(1)(c)(3) as a qualifying income interest for life. [Reg. § 25.2523(g)-1.]

☐ [*T.D. 8522, 2-28-94.*]

### [Reg. § 25.2523(h)-1]

**§ 25.2523(h)-1. Denial of double deduction.**—The value of an interest in property may not be deducted for Federal gift tax purposes more than once with respect to the same donor. For example, assume that D, a donor, transferred a life estate in a farm to D's spouse, S, with a remainder to charity and that D elects to treat the property as qualified terminable interest property. The entire value of the property is deductible under section 2523(f). No part of the value of the property qualifies for a charitable deduction under section 2522 for gift tax purposes. [Reg. § 25.2523(h)-1.]

☐ [*T.D. 8522, 2-28-94.*]

### [Reg. § 25.2523(h)-2]

**§ 25.2523(h)-2. Effective Dates.**—Except as specifically provided, in § § 25.2523(e)-1(c)(3), 25.2523(f)-1(c)(3), and 25.2523(g)-1(b), the provisions of § § 25.2523(e)-1(c), 25.2523(f)-1, 25.2523(g)-1, and 25.2523(h)-1 are effective with respect to gifts made after March 1, 1994. With respect to gifts made on or before such date, donors may rely on any reasonable interpretation of the statutory provisions. For these purposes, the provisions of § § 25.2523(e)-1(c), 25.2523(f)-1, 25.2523(g)-1, and 25.2523(h)-1, (as well as project LR-211-76, 1984-1 C.B., page 598, see § 601.601(d)(2)(ii)(*b*) of this chapter), are considered a reasonable interpretation of the statutory provisions. In addition, the rule in the last sentence of § 25.2523(e)-1 (f)(1) regarding the determination of income under applicable local law applies to trusts for taxable years ending after January 2, 2004. [Reg. § 25.2523(h)-2.]

☐ [*T.D. 8522, 2-28-94. Amended by T.D. 9102, 12-30-2003.*]

### [Reg. § 25.2523(i)-1]

**§ 25.2523(i)-1. Disallowance of marital deduction when spouse is not a United States citizen.**—(a) *In general.*—Subject to § 20.2056A-1(c) of this chapter, section 2523(i)(1) disallows the marital deduction if the spouse of the donor is not a citizen of the United States at the time of the gift. If the spouse of the donor is a citizen of the United States at the time of the gift, the gift tax marital deduction under section 2523(a) is allowed regardless of whether the donor is a citizen or resident of the United States at the time of the gift, subject to the otherwise applicable rules of section 2523.

(b) *Exception for certain joint and survivor annuities.*—Paragraph (a) does not apply to disallow the marital deduction with respect to any transfer resulting in the acquisition of rights by a noncitizen spouse under a joint and survivor annuity described in section 2523(f)(6).

(c) *Increased annual exclusion.*—(1) *In general.*—In the case of gifts made from a donor to the donor's spouse for which a marital deduction is not allowable under this section, if the gift otherwise qualifies for the gift tax annual exclusion under section 2503(b), the amount of the annual exclusion under section 2503(b) is $100,000 in lieu of $10,000. However, in the case of gifts made after June 29, 1989, in order for the increased annual exclusion to apply, the gift in excess of the otherwise applicable annual exclusion under section 2503(b) must be in a form that qualifies for the marital deduction but for the disallowance provision of section 2523(i)(1). See paragraph (d), *Example 4*, of this section.

(2) *Status of donor.*—The $100,000 annual exclusion for gifts to a noncitizen spouse is available regardless of the status of the donor. Accordingly, it is immaterial whether the donor is a citizen, resident or a nonresident not a citizen of the United States, as long as the spouse of the donor is not a citizen of the United States at the time of the gift and the conditions for allowance of the increased annual exclusion have been satisfied. See § 25.2503-2(f).

(d) *Examples.*—The principles outlined in this section are illustrated in the following examples. Assume in each of the examples that the donee, S, is D's spouse and is not a United States citizen at the time of the gift.

*Example 1. Outright transfer of present interest.* In 1995, D, a United States citizen, transfers to S, outright, 100 shares of X corporation stock valued for federal gift tax purposes at $130,000. The transfer is a gift of a present interest in property under section 2503(b). Additionally, the gift qualifies for the gift tax marital deduction except for the disallowance provision of section 2523(i)(1). Accordingly, $100,000 of the $130,000 gift is excluded from the total amount of gifts made during the calendar year by D for gift tax purposes.

*Example 2. Transfer of survivor benefits.* In 1995, D, a United States citizen, retires from employment in the United States and elects to receive a reduced retirement annuity in order to provide S with a survivor annuity upon D's death. The transfer of rights to S in the joint and survivor annuity is a gift by D for gift tax purposes. However, under paragraph (b) of this section, the gift qualifies for the gift tax marital deduction even though S is not a United States citizen.

*Example 3. Transfer of present interest in trust property.* In 1995, *D*, a resident alien, transfers property valued at $500,000 in trust to *S*, who is also a resident alien. The trust instrument provides that the trust income is payable to *S* at least quarterly and *S* has a testamentary general power to appoint the trust corpus. The transfer to *S* qualifies for the marital deduction under section 2523 but for the provisions of section 2523(i)(1). Because *S* has a life income interest in the trust, *S* has a present interest in a portion of the trust. Accordingly, *D* may exclude the present value of *S*'s income interest (up to $100,000) from *D*'s total 1995 calendar year gifts.

*Example 4. Transfer of present interest in trust property.* The facts are the same as in *Example 3*, except that *S* does not have a testamentary general power to appoint the trust corpus. Instead, *D*'s child, *C*, has a remainder interest in the trust. If *S* were a United States citizen, the transfer would qualify for the gift tax marital deduction if a qualified terminable interest property election was made under section 2523(f)(4). However, because *S* is not a U.S. citizen, *D* may not make a qualified terminable interest property election. Accordingly, the gift does not qualify for the gift tax marital deduction but for the disallowance provision of section 2523(i)(1). The $100,000 annual exclusion under section 2523(i)(2) is not available with respect to *D*'s transfer in trust and *D* may not exclude the present value of *S*'s income interest in excess of $10,000 from *D*'s total 1995 calendar year gifts.

*Example 5. Spouse becomes citizen after transfer.* *D*, a United States citizen, transfers a residence valued at $350,000 on December 20, 1995, to *D*'s spouse, *S*, a resident alien. On January 31, 1996, *S* becomes a naturalized United States citizen. On *D*'s federal gift tax return for 1995, *D* must include $250,000 as a gift ($350,000 transfer less $100,000 exclusion). Although *S* becomes a citizen in January, 1996, *S* is not a citizen of the United States at the time the transfer is made. Therefore, no gift tax marital deduction is allowable. However, the transfer does qualify for the $100,000 annual exclusion. [Reg. § 25.2523(i)-1.]

☐ [T.D. 8612, 8-21-95.]

### [Reg. § 25.2523(i)-2]

**§ 25.2523(i)-2. Treatment of spousal joint tenancy property where one spouse is not a United States citizen.**—(a) *In general.*—In the case of a joint tenancy with right of survivorship between spouses, or a tenancy by the entirety, where the donee spouse is not a United States citizen, the gift tax treatment of the creation and termination of the tenancy (regardless of whether the donor is a citizen, resident or nonresident not a citizen of the United States at such time), is governed by the principles of sections 2515 and 2515A (as such sections were in effect before their repeal by the Economic Recovery Tax Act of 1981). However, in applying these principles, the donor spouse may not elect to treat the creation of a tenancy in real property as a gift, as provided in section 2515(c) (prior to its repeal by the Economic Recovery Tax Act of 1981, Pub. L. 97-34, 95 Stat. 172).

(b) *Tenancies by the entirety and joint tenancies in real property.*—(1) *Creation of the tenancy on or after July 14, 1988.*—Under the principles of section 2515 (without regard to section 2515(c)), the creation of a tenancy by the entirety (or joint tenancy) in real property (either by one spouse alone or by both spouses), and any additions to the value of the tenancy in the form of improvements, reductions in indebtedness thereon, or otherwise, is not deemed to be a transfer of property for purposes of the gift tax, regardless of the proportion of the consideration furnished by each spouse, but only if the creation of the tenancy would otherwise be a gift to the donee spouse who is not a citizen of the United States at the time of the gift.

---

$200,000 (consideration furnished by A)
────────────────────────────────────── ×
$250,000 (total consideration furnished by both spouses)

$300,000 (proceeds of termination) = $240,000 (Proceeds of termination attributable to *A*.)
$240,000 − $225,000 (proceeds received by *A*) = $15,000 gift by *A* to *B*.

*Example 2.* In 1986, *A* purchased real property for $300,000 and took title in the names of *A* and *B*, *A*'s spouse, as joint tenants. Under section 2511 and § 25.2511-1(h)(1) of the regulations, *A* was treated as making a gift of one-half of the value of the property ($150,000) to *B*. In 1995, the real property is sold for $400,000 and *B* receives the entire proceeds of sale. For purposes of determining the amount of the gift

---

$150,000 (consideration furnished by A)
────────────────────────────────────── ×
$300,000 (total consideration deemed furnished by both spouses)

$400,000 (proceeds of termination) = $200,000 (Proceeds of termination attributable to *A*.)
$200,000 − 0 (proceeds received by *A*) = $200,000 gift by *A* to *B*.

(c) *Tenancies by the entirety in personal property where one spouse is not a United States citizen.*—(1) *In general.*—In the case of the creation (either by one spouse alone or by both spouses where at least one of the spouses is not a United States citizen) of a joint interest in

---

(2) *Termination.*—(i) *Tenancies created after December 31, 1954 and before January 1, 1982 not subject to an election under section 2515(c), and tenancies created on or after July 14, 1988.*—When a tenancy to which this paragraph (b) applies is terminated on or after July 14, 1988, other than by reason of the death of a spouse, then, under the principles of section 2515, a spouse is deemed to have made a gift to the extent that the proportion of the total consideration furnished by the spouse, multiplied by the proceeds of the termination (whether in the form of cash, property, or interests in property), exceeds the value of the proceeds of termination received by the spouse. See section 2523(i), and § 25.2523(i)-1 and § 25.2503-2(f) as to certain of the tax consequences that may result upon termination of the tenancy. This paragraph (b)(2)(i) applies to tenancies created after December 31, 1954, and before January 1, 1982, not subject to an election under section 2515(c), and to tenancies created on or after July 14, 1988.

(ii) *Tenancies created after December 31, 1954 and before January 1, 1982 subject to an election under section 2515(c) and tenancies created after December 31, 1981 and before July 14, 1988.*—When a tenancy to which this paragraph (a) is terminated on or after July 14, 1988, other than by reason of the death of a spouse, then, under the principles of section 2515, a spouse is deemed to have made a gift to the extent that the proportion of the total consideration furnished by the spouse, multiplied by the proceeds of the termination (whether in the form of cash, property, or interests in property), exceeds the value of the proceeds of termination received by the spouse. See section 2523(i), and § § 25.2523(i)-1 and 25.2503-2(f) as to certain of the tax consequences that may result upon termination of the tenancy. In the case of tenancies to which this paragraph applies, if the creation of the tenancy was treated as a gift to the noncitizen donee spouse under section 2515(c) (in the case of tenancies created prior to 1982) or section 2511 (in the case of tenancies created after December 31, 1981 and before July 14, 1988), then, upon termination of the tenancy, for purposes of applying the principles of section 2515 and the regulations thereunder, the amount treated as a gift on creation of the tenancy is treated as consideration originally belonging to the noncitizen spouse and never acquired by the noncitizen spouse from the donor spouse. This paragraph (b)(2)(ii) applies to tenancies created after December 31, 1954, and before January 1, 1982, subject to an election under section 2515(c), and to tenancies created after December 31, 1981, and before July 14, 1988.

(3) *Miscellaneous provisions.*—(i) *Tenancy by the entirety.*—For purposes of this section, *tenancy by the entirety* includes a joint tenancy between husband and wife with right of survivorship.

(ii) *No election to treat as gift.*—The regulations under section 2515 that relate to the election to treat the creation of a tenancy by the entirety as constituting a gift and the consequences of such an election upon termination of the tenancy (§ § 25.2515-2 and 25.2515-4) do not apply for purposes of section 2523(i)(3).

(4) *Examples.*—The application of this section may be illustrated by the following examples:

*Example 1.* In 1992, *A*, a United States citizen, furnished $200,000 and *A*'s spouse *B*, a resident alien, furnished $50,000 for the purchase and subsequent improvement of real property held by them as tenants by the entirety. The property is sold in 1998 for $300,000. *A* receives $225,000 and *B* receives $75,000 of the sales proceeds. The termination results in a gift of $15,000 by *A* to *B*, computed as follows:

on termination of the tenancy under the principles of section 2515 and the regulations thereunder, the amount treated as a gift to *B* on creation of the tenancy under section 2511 is treated as *B*'s contribution towards the purchase of the property. Accordingly, the termination of the tenancy results in a gift of $200,000 from *A* to *B* determined as follows:

personal property with right of survivorship, or additions to the value thereof in the form of improvements, reductions in the indebtedness thereof, or otherwise, the retained interest of each spouse, solely for purposes of determining whether there has been a gift by the donor to the spouse who is not a citizen of the United States at the time of the gift, is treated as one-half of the value of the joint interest. See section 2523(i) and §§ 25.2523(i)-1 and 25.2503-2(f) as to certain of the tax consequences that may result upon creation and termination of the tenancy.

(2) *Exception.*—The rule provided in paragraph (c)(1) of this section does not apply with respect to any joint interest in property if the fair market value of the interest in property (determined as if each spouse had a right to sever) cannot reasonably be ascertained except by reference to the life expectancy of one or both spouses. In these cases, actuarial principles may need to be resorted to in determining the gift tax consequences of the transaction. [Reg. § 25.2523(i)-2.]

☐ [*T.D.* 8612, 8-21-95.]

### [Reg. § 25.2523(i)-3]

**§ 25.2523(i)-3. Effective date.**—The provisions of §§ 25.2523(i)-1 and 25.2523(i)-2 are effective in the case of gifts made after August 22, 1995. [Reg. § 25.2523(i)-3.]

☐ [*T.D.* 8612, 8-21-95.]

### [Reg. § 25.2524-1]

**§ 25.2524-1. Extent of deductions.**—Under the provisions of section 2524, the charitable deduction provided for in section 2522 and the marital deduction provided for in section 2523 are allowable only to the extent that the gifts, with respect to which those deductions are authorized, are included in the "total amount of gifts" made during the "calendar period" (as defined in § 25.2502-1(c)(1)), computed as

provided in section 2503 and § 25.2503-1 (i.e., the total gifts less exclusions). The following examples (in both of which it is assumed that the donor has previously utilized his entire $30,000 specific exemption provided by section 2521 which was in effect at the time) illustrate the application of the provisions of this section:

*Example (1).* A donor made transfers by gift to his spouse of $5,000 cash on January 1, 1971, and $1,000 cash on April 5, 1971. The donor made no other transfers during 1971. The first $3,000 of such gifts for the calendar year is excluded under the provisions of section 2503(b) in determining the "total amount of gifts" made during the first calendar quarter of 1971. The marital deduction for the first calendar quarter of $2,500 (one-half of $5,000) otherwise allowable is limited by section 2524 to $2,000. The amount of taxable gifts is zero ($5,000 – $3,000 (annual exclusion) – $2,000 (marital deduction)). For the second calendar quarter of 1971, the marital deduction is $500 (one-half of $1,000); the amount excluded under section 2503(b) is zero because the entire $3,000 annual exclusion was applied against the gift in the first calendar quarter of 1971; and the amount of taxable gifts is $500 ($1,000 – $500 (marital deduction)).

*Example (2).* The only gifts made by a donor to his spouse during calendar year 1969 were a gift of $2,400 in May and a gift of $3,000 in August. The first $3,000 of such gifts is excluded under the provisions of section 2503(b) in determining the "total amount of gifts" made during the calendar year. The marital deduction for 1969 of $2,700 (one-half of $2,400 plus one-half of $3,000) otherwise allowable is limited by section 2524 to $2,400. The amount of taxable gifts is zero ($5,400 – $3,000 (annual exclusion) – $2,400 (marital deduction)). [Reg. § 25.2524-1.]

☐ [*T.D.* 6334, 11-14-58. *Amended by T.D.* 7238, 12-28-72 *and T.D.* 7910, 9-6-83.]

→ *Caution: Reg. §§ 25.6001-1, 25.6011-1, 25.6019-1—25.6019-4, 25.6061-1, 25.6065-1, 25.6075-1—25.6075-2, 25.6081-1, 25.6091-1—25.6091-2, 25.6151-1, 25.6161-1, 25.6165-1, 25.6321-1, 25.6323-1, 25.6324-1, 25.6601-1, 25.6905-1, and 25.7101-1, dealing with administration of the gift tax, are reproduced in Code section numerical order.*

# Tax on Generation-Skipping Transfers

## TAX IMPOSED

See p. 20,601 for regulations not amended to reflect law changes

□ [*T.D. 8644, 12-26-95. Amended by T.D. 8912, 12-19-2000; T.D. 9208, 6-28-2005; T.D. 9214, 7-15-2005; T.D. 9348, 8-1-2007 and T.D. 9421, 7-30-2008.*]

**[Reg. § 26.2601-1]**

**§ 26.2601-1. Effective dates.**—(a) *Transfers subject to the generation-skipping transfer tax.*—(1) *In general.*—Except as otherwise provided in this section, the provisions of chapter 13 of the Internal Revenue Code of 1986 (Code) apply to any generation-skipping transfer (as defined in section 2611) made after October 22, 1986.

(2) *Certain transfers treated as if made after October 22, 1986.*—Solely for purposes of chapter 13, an inter vivos transfer is treated as if it were made on October 23, 1986, if it was—

(i) Subject to chapter 12 (regardless of whether a tax was actually incurred or paid); and

(ii) Made after September 25, 1985, but before October 23, 1986. For purposes of this paragraph, the value of the property transferred shall be the value of the property on the date the property was transferred.

(3) *Certain trust events treated as if occurring after October 22, 1986.*—For purposes of chapter 13, if an inter vivos transfer is made to a trust after September 25, 1985, but before October 23, 1986, any subsequent distribution from the trust or termination of an interest in the trust that occurred before October 23, 1986, is treated as occurring immediately after the deemed transfer on October 23, 1986. If more than one distribution or termination occurs with respect to a trust, the events are treated as if they occurred on October 23, 1986, in the same order as they occurred. See paragraph (b)(1)(iv)(B) of this section for rules determining the portion of distributions and terminations subject to tax under chapter 13. This paragraph (a)(3) does not apply to transfers to trusts not subject to chapter 13 by reason of the transition rules in paragraphs (b)(2) and (3) of this section. The provisions of this paragraph (a)(3) do not apply in determining the value of the property under chapter 13.

(4) *Example.*—The following example illustrates the principle that paragraph (a)(2) of this section is not applicable to transfers under a revocable trust that became irrevocable by reason of the

transferor's death after September 25, 1985, but before October 23, 1986:

*Example.* T created a revocable trust on September 30, 1985, that became irrevocable when T died on October 10, 1986. Although the trust terminated in favor of a grandchild of T, the transfer to the grandchild is not treated as occurring on October 23, 1986, pursuant to paragraph (a)(2) of this section because it is not an inter vivos transfer subject to chapter 12. The transfer is not subject to chapter 13 because it is in the nature of a testamentary transfer that occurred prior to October 23, 1986.

(b) *Exceptions.*—(1) *Irrevocable trusts.*—(i) *In general.*—The provisions of chapter 13 do not apply to any generation-skipping transfer under a trust (as defined in section 2652(b)) that was irrevocable on September 25, 1985. The rule of the preceding sentence does not apply to a pro rata portion of any generation-skipping transfer under an irrevocable trust if additions are made to the trust after September 25, 1985. See paragraph (b)(1)(iv) of this section for rules for determining the portion of the trust that is subject to the provisions of chapter 13. Further, the rule in the first sentence of this paragraph (b)(1)(i) does not apply to a transfer of property pursuant to the exercise, release, or lapse of a general power of appointment that is treated as a taxable transfer under chapter 11 or chapter 12. The transfer is made by the person holding the power at the time the exercise, release, or lapse of the power becomes effective, and is not considered a transfer under a trust that was irrevocable on September 25, 1985. See paragraph (b)(1)(v)(B) of this section regarding the treatment of the release, exercise, or lapse of a power of appointment that will result in a constructive addition to a trust. See § 26.2652-1(a) for the definition of a transferor.

(ii) *Irrevocable trust defined.*—(A) *In general.*—Unless otherwise provided in either paragraph (b)(1)(ii)(B) or (C) of this section, any trust (as defined in section 2652(b)) in existence on September 25, 1985, is considered an irrevocable trust.

(B) *Property includible in the gross estate under section 2038.*—For purposes of this chapter a trust is not an irrevocable trust to the extent that, on September 25, 1985, the settlor held a power with respect to such trust that would have caused the value of the trust to be included in the settlor's gross estate for Federal estate tax purposes by reason of section 2038 (without regard to powers relinquished before September 25, 1985) if the settlor had died on September 25, 1985. A trust is considered subject to a power on September 25, 1985, even though the exercise of the power was subject to the precedent giving of notice, or even though the exercise could take effect only on the expiration of a stated period, whether or not on or before September 25, 1985, notice had been given or the power had been exercised. A trust is not considered subject to a power if the power is, by its terms, exercisable only on the occurrence of an event or contingency not subject to the settlor's control (other than the death of the settlor) and if the event or contingency had not in fact taken place on September 25, 1985.

(C) *Property includible in the gross estate under section 2042.*—A policy of insurance on an individual's life that is treated as a trust under section 2652(b) is not considered an irrevocable trust to the extent that, on September 25, 1985, the insured possessed any incident of ownership (as defined in § 20.2042-1(c) of this chapter, and without regard to any incidents of ownership relinquished before September 25, 1985), that would have caused the value of the trust, (i.e., the insurance proceeds) to be included in the insured's gross estate for Federal estate tax purposes by reason of section 2042, if the insured had died on September 25, 1985.

(D) *Examples.*—The following examples illustrate the application of this paragraph (b)(1):

*Example 1. Section 2038 applicable.* On September 25, 1985, T, the settlor of a trust that was created before September 25, 1985, held a testamentary power to add new beneficiaries to the trust. T held no other powers over any portion of the trust. The testamentary power held by T would have caused the trust to be included in T's gross estate under section 2038 if T had died on September 25, 1985. Therefore, the trust is not an irrevocable trust for purposes of this section.

*Example 2. Section 2038 not applicable when power held by a person other than settlor.* On September 25, 1985, S, the spouse of the settlor of a trust in existence on that date, had an annual right to withdraw a portion of the principal of the trust. The trust was otherwise irrevocable on that date. Because the power was not held by the settlor of the trust, it is not a power described in section 2038. Thus, the trust is considered an irrevocable trust for purposes of this section.

*Example 3. Section 2038 not applicable.* In 1984, T created a trust and retained the right to expand the class of remaindermen to include any of T's afterborn grandchildren. As of September 25, 1985,

all of T's grandchildren were named remaindermen of the trust. Since the exercise of T's power was dependent on there being afterborn grandchildren who were not members of the class of remaindermen, a contingency that did not exist on September 25, 1985, the trust is not considered subject to the power on September 25, 1985, and is an irrevocable trust for purposes of this section. The result is not changed even if grandchildren are born after September 25, 1985, whether or not T exercises the power to expand the class of remaindermen.

*Example 4. Section 2042 applicable.* On September 25, 1985, T purchased an insurance policy on T's own life and designated child, C, and grandchild, GC, as the beneficiaries. T retained the power to obtain from the insurer a loan against the surrender value of the policy. T's insurance policy is a trust (as defined in section 2652(b)) for chapter 13 purposes. The trust is not considered an irrevocable trust because, on September 25, 1985, T possessed an incident of ownership that would have caused the value of the policy to be included in T's gross estate under section 2042 if T had died on that date.

*Example 5. Trust partially irrevocable.* In 1984, T created a trust naming T's grandchildren as the income and remainder beneficiaries. T retained the power to revoke the trust as to one-half of the principal at any time prior to T's death. T retained no other powers over the trust principal. T did not die before September 25, 1985, and did not exercise or release the power before that date. The half of the trust not subject to T's power to revoke is an irrevocable trust for purposes of this section.

(iii) *Trust containing qualified terminable interest property.*—(A) *In general.*—For purposes of chapter 13, a trust described in paragraph (b)(1)(ii) of this section that holds qualified terminable interest property by reason of an election under section 2056(b)(7) or section 2523(f) (made either on, before or after September 25, 1985) is treated in the same manner as if the decedent spouse or the donor spouse (as the case may be) had made an election under section 2652(a)(3). Thus, transfers from such trusts are not subject to chapter 13, and the decedent spouse or the donor spouse (as the case may be) is treated as the transferor of such property. The rule of this paragraph (b)(1)(iii) does not apply to that portion of the trust that is subject to chapter 13 by reason of an addition to the trust occurring after September 25, 1985. See § 26.2652-2(a) for rules where an election under section 2652(a)(3) is made. See § 26.2652-2(c) for rules where a portion of a trust is subject to an election under section 2652(a)(3).

(B) *Examples.*—The following examples illustrate the application of this paragraph (b)(1)(iii):

*Example 1. QTIP election made after September 25, 1985.* On March 28, 1985, T established a trust. The trust instrument provided that the trustee must distribute all income annually to T's spouse, S, during S's life. Upon S's death, the remainder is to be distributed to GC, the grandchild of T and S. On April 15, 1986, T elected under section 2523(f) to treat the property in the trust as qualified terminable interest property. On December 1, 1987, S died and soon thereafter the trust assets were distributed to GC. Because the trust was irrevocable on September 25, 1985, the transfer to GC is not subject to tax under chapter 13. T is treated as the transferor with respect to the transfer of the trust assets to GC in the same manner as if T had made an election under section 2652(a)(3) to reverse the effect of the section 2523(f) election for chapter 13 purposes.

*Example 2. Section 2652(a)(3) election deemed to have been made.* Assume the same facts as in *Example 1*, except the trust instrument provides that after S's death all income is to be paid annually to C, the child of T and S. Upon C's death, the remainder is to be distributed to GC. C died on October 1, 1992, and soon thereafter the trust assets are distributed to GC. Because the trust was irrevocable on September 25, 1985, the termination of C's interest is not subject to chapter 13.

(iv) *Additions to irrevocable trusts.*—(A) *In general.*—If an addition is made after September 25, 1985, to an irrevocable trust which is excluded from chapter 13 by reason of paragraph (b)(1) of this section, a pro rata portion of subsequent distributions from (and terminations of interests in property held in) the trust is subject to the provisions of chapter 13. If an addition is made, the trust is thereafter deemed to consist of two portions, a portion not subject to chapter 13 (the non-chapter 13 portion) and a portion subject to chapter 13 (the chapter 13 portion), each with a separate inclusion ratio (as defined in section 2642(a)). The non-chapter 13 portion represents the value of the assets of the trust as it existed on September 25, 1985. The applicable fraction (as defined in section 2642(a)(2)) for the non-chapter 13 portion is deemed to be 1 and the inclusion ratio for such portion is 0. The chapter 13 portion of the trust represents the value of all additions made to the trust after September 25, 1985. The inclusion ratio for the chapter 13 portion is determined under section 2642. This paragraph (b)(1)(iv)(A) requires separate portions of one trust only for purposes of determining inclusion ratios. For purposes of chapter 13, a constructive addition under paragraph (b)(1)(v) of this section is treated as an addition. See paragraph (b)(4) of this section for exceptions to the additions rule of this paragraph (b)(1)(iv). See § 26.2654-1(a)(2) for rules treating additions to a trust by an individual other than the initial transferor as a separate trust for purposes of chapter 13.

(B) *Terminations of interests in and distributions from trusts.*— Where a termination or distribution described in section 2612 occurs with respect to a trust to which an addition has been made, the portion of such termination or distribution allocable to the chapter 13 portion is determined by reference to the allocation fraction, as defined in paragraph (b)(1)(iv)(C) of this section. In the case of a termination described in section 2612(a) with respect to a trust, the portion of such termination that is subject to chapter 13 is the product of the allocation fraction and the value of the trust (to the extent of the terminated interest therein). In the case of a distribution described in section 2612(b) from a trust, the portion of such distribution that is subject to chapter 13 is the product of the allocation fraction and the value of the property distributed.

(C) *Allocation fraction.*—(1) *In general.*—The allocation fraction allocates appreciation and accumulated income between the chapter 13 and non-chapter 13 portions of a trust. The numerator of the allocation fraction is the amount of the addition (valued as of the date the addition is made), determined without regard to whether any part of the transfer is subject to tax under chapter 11 or chapter 12, but reduced by the amount of any Federal or state estate or gift tax imposed and subsequently paid by the recipient trust with respect to the addition. The denominator of the allocation fraction is the total value of the entire trust immediately after the addition. For purposes of this paragraph (b)(1)(iv)(C), the total value of the entire trust is the fair market value of the property held in trust (deter-

$$\frac{\text{Value of addition}}{\text{Total value of trust}} =$$

(ii) Thus, immediately after the transfer, 20 percent of the value of future generation-skipping transfers under the trust will be subject to chapter 13.

*Example 2. Effect of expenses.* Assume the same facts as in *Example 1,* except immediately prior to the transfer on October 1, 1986, the fair market value of the individual assets in the trust totaled $400,000. Also, assume that the trust had accrued and unpaid debts, expenses, and taxes totaling $300,000. Assume further that the entire $300,000 represented amounts that would be deductible under section 2053 if the trust were includible in the transferor's gross estate. The numerator of the allocation fraction is $100,000 and the denomi-

$$\frac{\text{Total value of additions}}{\text{Total value of trust}} = \frac{\$120,000 + \$40,000}{\$600,000 + \$40,000} = \frac{\$160,000}{\$640,000} = .25$$

(ii) Thus, immediately after the transfer, 25 percent of the value of future generation-skipping transfers under the trust will be subject to chapter 13.

*Example 4. Allocation fraction at time of generation-skipping transfer.* Assume the same facts as in *Example 3,* except on March 1, 1989, when the value of the trust is $800,000, C dies. A generation-skipping transfer occurs at C's death because of the termination of C's life estate. Therefore, $200,000 ($800,000 x .25) is subject to tax under chapter 13.

(v) *Constructive additions.*—(A) *Powers of Appointment.*—Except as provided in paragraph (b)(1)(v)(B) of this section, where any portion of a trust remains in the trust after the post-September 25, 1985, release, exercise, or lapse of a power of appointment over that portion of the trust, and the release, exercise, or lapse is treated to any extent as a taxable transfer under chapter 11 or chapter 12, the value of the entire portion of the trust subject to the power that was released, exercised, or lapsed is treated as if that portion had been withdrawn and immediately retransferred to the trust at the time of the release, exercise, or lapse. The creator of the power will be considered the transferor of the addition except to the extent that the release, exercise, or lapse of the power is treated as a taxable transfer under chapter 11 or chapter 12. See § 26.2652-1 for rules for determining the identity of the transferor of property for purposes of chapter 13.

(B) *Special rule for certain powers of appointment.*—The release, exercise, or lapse of a power of appointment (other than a general power of appointment as defined in § 2041(b)) is not treated as an addition to a trust if—

mined under the rules of section 2031), reduced by any amount attributable to or paid by the trust and attributable to the transfer to the trust that is similar to an amount that would be allowable as a deduction under section 2053 if the addition had occurred at the death of the transferor, and further reduced by the same amount that the numerator was reduced to reflect Federal or state estate or gift tax incurred by and subsequently paid by the recipient trust with respect to the addition. Where there is more than one addition to principal after September 25, 1985, the portion of the trust subject to chapter 13 after each such addition is determined pursuant to a revised fraction. In each case, the numerator of the revised fraction is the sum of the value of the chapter 13 portion of the trust immediately before the latest addition, and the amount of the latest addition. The denominator of the revised fraction is the total value of the entire trust immediately after the addition. If the transfer to the trust is a generation-skipping transfer, the numerator and denominator are reduced by the amount of the generation-skipping transfer tax, if any, that is imposed by chapter 13 on the transfer and actually recovered from the trust. The allocation fraction is rounded off to five decimal places (.00001).

(2) *Examples.*—The following examples illustrate the application of paragraph (b)(1)(iv) of this section. In each of the examples, assume that the recipient trust does not pay any Federal or state transfer tax by reason of the addition.

*Example 1. Post September 25, 1985, addition to trust.* (i) On August 16, 1980, T established an irrevocable trust. Under the trust instrument, the trustee is required to distribute the entire income annually to T's child, C, for life, then to T's grandchild, GC, for life. Upon GC's death, the remainder is to be paid to GC's issue. On October 1, 1986, when the total value of the entire trust is $400,000, T transfers $100,000 to the trust. The allocation fraction is computed as follows:

$$\frac{\$100,000}{\$400,000 + \$100,000} = .2$$

nator of the allocation fraction is $200,000 (($400,000 - $300,000) + $100,000). Thus, the allocation fraction is .5 ($100,000/$200,000) and 50 percent of the value of future generation-skipping transfers will be subject to chapter 13.

*Example 3. Multiple additions.* (i) Assume the same facts as in *Example 1,* except on January 30, 1988, when the total value of the entire trust is $600,000, T transfers an additional $40,000 to the trust. Before the transfer, the value of the portion of the trust that was attributable to the prior addition was $120,000 ($600,000 x .2). The new allocation fraction is computed as follows:

(1) Such power of appointment was created in an irrevocable trust that is not subject to chapter 13 under paragraph (b)(1) of this section; and

(2) In the case of an exercise, the power of appointment is not exercised in a manner that may postpone or suspend the vesting, absolute ownership or power of alienation of an interest in property for a period, measured from the date of creation of the trust, extending beyond any life in being at the date of creation of the trust plus a period of 21 years plus, if necessary, a reasonable period of gestation (the perpetuities period). For purposes of this paragraph (b)(1)(v)(B)(2), the exercise of a power of appointment that validly postpones or suspends the vesting, absolute ownership or power of alienation of an interest in property for a term of years that will not exceed 90 years (measured from the date of creation of the trust) will not be considered an exercise that postpones or suspends vesting, absolute ownership or the power of alienation beyond the perpetuities period. If a power is exercised by creating another power, it is deemed to be exercised to whatever extent the second power may be exercised.

(C) *Constructive addition if liability is not paid out of trust principal.*—Where a trust described in paragraph (b)(1) of this section is relieved of any liability properly payable out of the assets of such trust, the person or entity who actually satisfies the liability is considered to have made a constructive addition to the trust in an amount equal to the liability. The constructive addition occurs when the trust is relieved of liability (e.g., when the right of recovery is no longer enforceable). But see § 26.2652-1(a)(3) for rules involving the application of section 2207A in the case of an election under section 2652(a)(3).

(D) *Examples.*—The following examples illustrate the application of this paragraph (b)(1)(v):

*Example 1. Lapse of a power of appointment.* On June 19, 1980, T established an irrevocable trust with a corpus of $500,000. The trust instrument provides that the trustee shall distribute the entire income from the trust annually to T's spouse, S, during S's life. At S's death, the remainder is to be distributed to T and S's grandchild, GC. T also gave S a general power of appointment over one-half of the trust assets. On December 21, 1989, when the value of the trust corpus is $1,500,000, S died without having exercised the general power of appointment. The value of one-half of the trust corpus, $750,000 ($1,500,000 x .5) is included in S's gross estate under section 2041(a) and is subject to tax under Chapter 11. Because the value of one-half of the trust corpus is subject to tax under Chapter 11 with respect to S's estate, S is treated as the transferor of that property for purposes of Chapter 13 (see section 2652(a)(1)(A)). For purposes of the generation-skipping transfer tax, the lapse of S's power of appointment is treated as if $750,000 ($1,500,000 x .5) had been distributed to S and then transferred back to the trust. Thus, S is considered to have added $750,000 ($1,500,000 x .5) to the trust at the date of S's death. Because this constructive addition occurred after September 25, 1985, 50 percent of the corpus of the trust became subject to Chapter 13 at S's death.

*Example 2. Multiple actual additions.* On June 19, 1980, T established an irrevocable trust with a principal of $500,000. The trust instrument provides that the trustee shall distribute the entire income from the trust annually to T's spouse, S, during S's life. At S's death, the remainder is to be distributed to GC, the grandchild of T and S. On October 1, 1985, when the trust assets were valued at $800,000, T added $200,000 to the trust. After the transfer on October 1, 1985, the allocation fraction was .2 ($200,000/$1,000,000). On December 21, 1989, when the value of the trust principal is $1,000,000, T adds $1,000,000 to the trust. After this addition, the new allocation fraction is 0.6 ($1,200,000/$2,000,000). The numerator of the fraction is the value of that portion of trust assets that were subject to chapter 13 immediately prior to the addition (by reason of the first addition), $200,000 (.2 x $1,000,000), plus the value of the second transfer, $1,000,000, which equals $1,200,000. The denominator of the fraction, $2,000,000, is the total value of the trust assets immediately after the second transfer. Thus, 60 percent of the principal of the trust becomes subject to chapter 13.

*Example 3. Entire portion of trust subject to lapsed power is treated as an addition.* On September 25, 1985, B possessed a general power of appointment over the assets of an irrevocable trust that had been created by T in 1980. Under the terms of the trust, B's power lapsed on July 20, 1987. For Federal gift tax purposes, B is treated as making a gift of ninety-five percent (100% - 5%) of the value of the principal (see section 2514). However, because the entire trust was subject to the power of appointment, 100 percent (that portion of the trust subject to the power) of the assets of the trust are treated as a constructive addition. Thus, the entire amount of all generation-skipping transfers occurring pursuant to the trust instrument after July 20, 1987, are subject to chapter 13.

*Example 4. Exercise of power of appointment in favor of another trust.* On March 1, 1985, T established an irrevocable trust as defined in paragraph (b)(1)(ii) of this section. Under the terms of the trust instrument, the trustee is required to distribute the entire income annually to T's child, C, for life, then to T's grandchild, GC, for life. GC has the power to appoint any or all of the trust assets to Trust 2 which is an irrevocable trust (as defined in paragraph (b)(1)(ii) of this section) that was established on August 1, 1985. The terms of Trust 2's governing instrument provide that the trustee shall pay income to T's great grandchild, GGC, for life. Upon GGC's death, the remainder is to be paid to GGC's issue. GGC was alive on March 1, 1985, when Trust 1 was created. C died on April 1, 1986. On July 1, 1987, GC exercised the power of appointment. The exercise of GC's power does not subject future transfers from Trust 2 to tax under chapter 13 because the exercise of the power in favor of Trust 2 does not suspend the vesting, absolute ownership, or power of alienation of an interest in property for a period, measured from the date of creation of Trust 1, extending beyond the life of GGC (a beneficiary under Trust 2 who was in being at the date of creation of Trust 1) plus a period of 21 years. The result would be the same if Trust 2 had been created after the effective date of chapter 13.

*Example 5. Exercise of power of appointment in favor of another trust.* Assume the same facts as in *Example 4*, except that GGC was born on March 28, 1986. The valid exercise of GC's power in favor of Trust 2 causes the principal of Trust 1 to be subject to chapter 13, because GGC was not born until after the creation of Trust 1. Thus, such exercise may suspend the vesting, absolute ownership, or power of alienation of an interest in the trust principal for a period, measured from the date of creation of Trust 1, extending beyond the life of GGC (a beneficiary under Trust 2 who was not a life in being at the date of creation of Trust 1).

*Example 6. Extension for the longer of two periods.* Prior to the effective date of chapter 13, GP established an irrevocable trust under which the trust income was to be paid to GP's child, C, for life. C was given a testamentary power to appoint the remainder in further trust for the benefit of C's issue. In default of C's exercise of the power, the remainder was to pass to charity. C died on February 3, 1995, survived by a child who was alive when GP established the trust. C exercised the power in a manner that validly extends the trust in favor of C's issue until the later of May 15, 2064 (80 years from the date the trust was created), or the death of C's child plus 21 years. C's exercise of the power is a constructive addition to the trust because the exercise may extend the trust for a period longer than the permissible periods of either the life of C's child (a life in being at the creation of the trust) plus 21 years or a term not more than 90 years measured from the creation of the trust. On the other hand, if C's exercise of the power could extend the trust based only on the life of C's child plus 21 years or only for a term of 80 years from the creation of the trust (but not the later of the two periods) then the exercise of the power would not have been a constructive addition to the trust.

*Example 7. Extension for the longer of two periods.* The facts are the same as in *Example 6* except local law provides that the effect of C's exercise is to extend the term of the trust until May 15, 2064, whether or not C's child predeceases that date by more than 21 years. C's exercise is not a constructive addition to the trust because C exercised the power in a manner that cannot postpone or suspend vesting, absolute ownership, or power of alienation for a term of years that will exceed 90 years. The result would be the same if the effect of C's exercise is either to extend the term of the trust until 21 years after the death of C's child or to extend the term of the trust until the first to occur of May 15, 2064 or 21 years after the death of C's child.

(vi) *Appreciation and income.*—Except to the extent that the provisions of paragraphs (b)(1)(iv) and (v) of this section allocate subsequent appreciation and accumulated income between the original trust and additions thereto, appreciation in the value of the trust and undistributed income added thereto are not considered an addition to the principal of a trust.

(2) *Transition rule for wills or revocable trusts executed before October 22, 1986.*—(i) *In general.*—The provisions of chapter 13 do not apply to any generation-skipping transfer under a will or revocable trust executed before October 22, 1986, provided that—

(A) The document in existence on October 21, 1986, is not amended at any time after October 21, 1986, in any respect which results in the creation of, or an increase in the amount of, a generation-skipping transfer;

(B) In the case of a revocable trust, no addition is made to the revocable trust after October 21, 1986, that results in the creation of, or an increase in the amount of, a generation-skipping transfer; and

(C) The decedent dies before January 1, 1987.

(ii) *Revocable trust defined.*—For purposes of this section, the term *revocable trust* means any trust (as defined in section 2652(b)) except to the extent that, on October 22, 1986, the trust—

(A) Was an irrevocable trust described in paragraph (b)(1) of this section; or

(B) Would have been an irrevocable trust described in paragraph (b)(1) of this section had it not been created or become irrevocable after September 25, 1985, and before October 22, 1986.

(iii) *Will or revocable trust containing qualified terminable interest property.*—The rules contained in paragraph (b)(1)(iii) of this section apply to any will or revocable trust within the scope of the transition rule of this paragraph (b)(2).

(iv) *Amendments to will or revocable trust.*—For purposes of this paragraph (b)(2), an amendment to a will or a revocable trust in existence on October 21, 1986, is not considered to result in the creation of, or an increase in the amount of, a generation-skipping transfer where the amendment is—

(A) Basically administrative or clarifying in nature and only incidentally increases the amount transferred; or

(B) Designed to ensure that an existing bequest or transfer qualifies for the applicable marital or charitable deduction for estate, gift, or generation-skipping transfer tax purposes and only incidentally increases the amount transferred to a skip person or to a generation-skipping trust.

(v) *Creation of, or increase in the amount of, a GST.*—In determining whether a particular amendment to a will or revocable trust creates, or increases the amount of, a generation-skipping transfer for purposes of this paragraph (b)(2), the effect of the instrument(s) in existence on October 21, 1986, is measured against the effect of the instrument(s) in existence on the date of death of the decedent or on the date of any prior generation-skipping transfer. If the effect of an amendment cannot be immediately determined, it is deemed to create, or increase the amount of, a generation-skipping transfer until a determination can be made.

(vi) *Additions to revocable trusts.*—Any addition made after October 21, 1986, but before the death of the settlor, to a revocable trust subjects all subsequent generation-skipping transfers under the trust to the provisions of chapter 13. Any addition made to a revocable trust after the death of the settlor (if the settlor dies before January 1, 1987) is treated as an addition to an irrevocable trust. See paragraph (b)(1)(v) of this section for rules involving constructive additions to trusts. See paragraph (b)(1)(v)(B) of this section for rules providing that certain transfers to trusts are not treated as additions for purposes of this section.

(vii) *Examples.*—The following examples illustrate the application of paragraph (b)(2)(iv) of this section:

(A) *Facts applicable to Examples 1 through 5.*—In each of *Examples 1* through *5* assume that T executed a will prior to October 22, 1986, and that T dies on December 31, 1986.

*Example 1. Administrative change.* On November 1, 1986, T executes a codicil to T's will removing one of the co-executors named in the will. Although the codicil may have the effect of lowering administrative costs and thus increasing the amount transferred, it is considered administrative in nature and thus does not cause generation-skipping transfers under the will to be subject to chapter 13.

*Example 2. Effect of amendment not immediately determinable.* On November 1, 1986, T executes a codicil to T's will revoking a bequest of $100,000 to C, a non-skip person (as defined under section 2613(b)) and causing that amount to be added to a residuary trust held for a skip person. The amendment is deemed to increase the amount of a generation-skipping transfer and prevents any transfers under the will from qualifying under paragraph (b)(2)(i) of this section. If, however, C dies before T and under local law the property would have been added to the residue in any event because the bequest would have lapsed, the codicil is not considered an amendment that increases the amount of a generation-skipping transfer.

*Example 3. Refund of tax paid because of amendment.* T's will provided that an amount equal to the maximum allowable marital deduction would pass to T's spouse with the residue of the estate passing to a trust established for the benefit of skip persons. On October 23, 1986, the will is amended to provide that the marital share passing to T's spouse shall be the lesser of the maximum allowable marital deduction or the minimum amount that will result in no estate tax liability for T's estate. The amendment may increase the amount of a generation-skipping transfer. Therefore, any generation-skipping transfers under the will are subject to tax under chapter 13. If it becomes apparent that the amendment does not increase the amount of a generation-skipping transfer, a claim for refund may be filed with respect to any generation-skipping transfer tax that was paid within the period set forth in section 6511. For example, it would become apparent that the amendment did not result in an increase in the residue if it is subsequently determined that the maximum marital deduction and the minimum amount that will result in no estate tax liability are equal in amount.

*Example 4. An amendment that increases a generation-skipping transfer causes complete loss of exempt status.* T's will provided for the creation of two trusts for the benefit of skip persons. On November 1, 1986, T executed a codicil to the will specifically increasing the amount of a generation-skipping transfer under the will. All transfers made pursuant to the will or either of the trusts created thereunder are precluded from qualifying under the transition rule of paragraph (b)(2)(i) of this section and are subject to tax under chapter 13.

*Example 5. Corrective action effective.* Assume that T in *Example 4* later executes a second codicil deleting the increase to the generation-skipping transfer. Because the provision increasing a generation-skipping transfer does not become effective, it is not considered an amendment to a will in existence on October 22, 1986.

(B) *Facts applicable to Examples 6 through 8.*—T created a trust on September 30, 1985, in which T retained the power to revoke the transfer at any time prior to T's death. The trust provided that, upon the death of T, the income was to be paid to T's spouse, W, for life and then to A, B, and C, the children of T's sibling, S, in equal shares for life, with one-third of the principal to be distributed per stirpes to each child's surviving issue upon the death of the child. The trustee has the power to make discretionary distributions of trust principal to T's sibling, S.

*Example 6. Amendment that affects only a person who is not a skip person.* A became disabled, and T modified the trust on December 1, 1986, to increase A's share of the income. Since the amendment does not result in the creation of, or increase in the amount of, a generation-skipping transfer, transfers pursuant to the trust are not subject to chapter 13.

*Example 7. Amendment that adds a skip person.* Assume that T amends the trust to add T's grandchild, D, as an income beneficiary. The trust will be subject to the provisions of chapter 13 because the amendment creates a generation-skipping transfer.

*Example 8. Refund of tax paid during interim period when effect of amendment is not determinable.* Assume that T amends the trust to provide that the issue of S are to take a one-fourth share of the principal per stirpes upon S's death. Because the distribution to be made upon S's death may involve skip persons, the amendment is considered an amendment that creates or increases the amount of a generation-skipping transfer until a determination can be made. Accordingly, any distributions from (or terminations of interests in) such trust are subject to chapter 13 until it is determined that no skip person has been added to the trust. At that time, a claim for refund may be filed within the period set forth in section 6511 with respect to any generation-skipping transfer tax that was paid.

(3) *Transition rule in the case of mental incompetency.*—(i) *In general.*—If an individual was under a mental disability to change the disposition of his or her property continuously from October 22, 1986, until the date of his or her death, the provisions of chapter 13 do not apply to any generation-skipping transfer—

(A) Under a trust (as defined in section 2652(b)) to the extent such trust consists of property, or the proceeds of property, the value of which was included in the gross estate of the individual (other than property transferred by or on behalf of the individual during the individual's life after October 22, 1986); or

(B) Which is a direct skip (other than a direct skip from a trust) that occurs by reason of the death of the individual.

(ii) *Mental disability defined.*—For purposes of this paragraph (b)(2), the term *mental disability* means mental incompetence to execute an instrument governing the disposition of the individual's property, whether or not there was an adjudication of incompetence and regardless of whether there has been an appointment of a guardian, fiduciary, or other person charged with either the care of the individual or the care of the individual's property.

(iii) *Decedent who has not been adjudged mentally incompetent.*—(A) If there has not been a court adjudication that the decedent was mentally incompetent on or before October 22, 1986, the executor must file, with Form 706, either—

(1) A certification from a qualified physician stating that the decedent was—

(i) mentally incompetent at all times on and after October 22, 1986; and

(ii) did not regain competence to modify or revoke the terms of the trust or will prior to his or her death; or

(2) Sufficient other evidence demonstrating that the decedent was mentally incompetent at all times on and after October 22, 1986, as well as a statement explaining why no certification is available from a physician; and

(3) Any judgement or decree relating to the decedent's incompetency that was made after October 22, 1986.

(B) Such items in paragraphs (b)(3)(iii)(A), (1), (2), and (3) of this section will be considered relevant, but not determinative, in establishing the decedent's state of competency.

(iv) *Decedent who has been adjudged mentally incompetent.*—If the decedent has been adjudged mentally incompetent on or before October 22, 1986, a copy of the judgment or decree, and any modification thereof, must be filed with the Form 706.

(v) *Rule applies even if another person has power to change trust terms.*—In the case of a transfer from a trust, this paragraph (b)(3) applies even though a person charged with the care of the decedent or the decedent's property has the power to revoke or modify the terms of the trust, provided that the power is not exercised after October 22, 1986, in a manner that creates, or increases the amount of, a generation-skipping transfer. See paragraph (b)(2)(iv) of this section for rules concerning amendments that create or increase the amount of a generation-skipping transfer.

(vi) *Example.*—The following example illustrates the application of paragraph (b)(3)(v) of this section:

*Example.* T was mentally incompetent on October 22, 1986, and remained so until death in 1993. Prior to becoming incompetent, T created a revocable generation-skipping trust that was includible in T's gross estate. Prior to October 22, 1986, the appropriate court issued an order under which P, who was thereby charged with the care of T's property, had the power to modify or revoke the revocable trust. Although P exercised the power after October 22, 1986, and while T was incompetent, the power was not exercised in a manner that created, or increased the amount of, a generation-skipping transfer. Thus, the existence and exercise of P's power did not cause the trust to lose its exempt status under paragraph (b)(3) of this section.

The result would be the same if the court order was issued after October 22, 1986.

(4) *Retention of trust's exempt status in the case of modifications, etc.*—(i) *In general.*—This paragraph (b)(4) provides rules for determining when a modification, judicial construction, settlement agreement, or trustee action with respect to a trust that is exempt from the generation-skipping transfer tax under paragraph (b)(1), (2), or (3) of this section (hereinafter referred to as an exempt trust) will not cause the trust to lose its exempt status. In general, unless specifically provided otherwise, the rules contained in this paragraph are applicable only for purposes of determining whether an exempt trust retains its exempt status for generation-skipping transfer tax purposes. Thus (unless specifically noted), the rules do not apply in determining, for example, whether the transaction results in a gift subject to gift tax, or may cause the trust to be included in the gross estate of a beneficiary, or may result in the realization of gain for purposes of section 1001.

(A) *Discretionary powers.*—The distribution of trust principal from an exempt trust to a new trust or retention of trust principal in a continuing trust will not cause the new or continuing trust to be subject to the provisions of chapter 13, if—

(1) Either—

(i) The terms of the governing instrument of the exempt trust authorize distributions to the new trust or the retention of trust principal in a continuing trust, without the consent or approval of any beneficiary or court; or

(ii) at the time the exempt trust became irrevocable, state law authorized distributions to the new trust or retention of principal in the continuing trust, without the consent or approval of any beneficiary or court; and

(2) The terms of the governing instrument of the new or continuing trust do not extend the time for vesting of any beneficial interest in the trust in a manner that may postpone or suspend the vesting, absolute ownership, or power of alienation of an interest in property for a period, measured from the date the original trust became irrevocable, extending beyond any life in being at the date the original trust became irrevocable plus a period of 21 years, plus if necessary, a reasonable period of gestation. For purposes of this paragraph (b)(4)(i)(A), the exercise of a trustee's distributive power that validly postpones or suspends the vesting, absolute ownership, or power of alienation of an interest in property for a term of years that will not exceed 90 years (measured from the date the original trust became irrevocable) will not be considered an exercise that postpones or suspends vesting, absolute ownership, or the power of alienation beyond the perpetuities period. If a distributive power is exercised by creating another power, it is deemed to be exercised to whatever extent the second power may be exercised.

(B) *Settlement.*—A court-approved settlement of a bona fide issue regarding the administration of the trust or the construction of terms of the governing instrument will not cause an exempt trust to be subject to the provisions of chapter 13, if—

(1) The settlement is the product of arm's length negotiations; and

(2) The settlement is within the range of reasonable outcomes under the governing instrument and applicable state law addressing the issues resolved by the settlement. A settlement that results in a compromise between the positions of the litigating parties and reflects the parties' assessments of the relative strengths of their positions is a settlement that is within the range of reasonable outcomes.

(C) *Judicial construction.*—A judicial construction of a governing instrument to resolve an ambiguity in the terms of the instrument or to correct a scrivener's error will not cause an exempt trust to be subject to the provisions of chapter 13, if—

(1) The judicial action involves a bona fide issue; and

(2) The construction is consistent with applicable state law that would be applied by the highest court of the state.

(D) *Other changes.*—(1) A modification of the governing instrument of an exempt trust (including a trustee distribution, settlement, or construction that does not satisfy paragraph (b)(4)(i)(A), (B), or (C) of this section) by judicial reformation, or nonjudicial reformation that is valid under applicable state law, will not cause an exempt trust to be subject to the provisions of chapter 13, if the modification does not shift a beneficial interest in the trust to any beneficiary who occupies a lower generation (as defined in section 2651) than the person or persons who held the beneficial interest prior to the modification, and the modification does not extend the time for vesting of any beneficial interest in the trust beyond the period provided for in the original trust.

(2) For purposes of this section, a modification of an exempt trust will result in a shift in beneficial interest to a lower generation beneficiary if the modification can result in either an increase in the amount of a GST transfer or the creation of a new GST transfer. To determine whether a modification of an irrevocable trust will shift a beneficial interest in a trust to a beneficiary who occupies a lower generation, the effect of the instrument on the date of the modification is measured against the effect of the instrument in existence immediately before the modification. If the effect of the modification cannot be immediately determined, it is deemed to shift a beneficial interest in the trust to a beneficiary who occupies a lower generation (as defined in section 2651) than the person or persons who held the beneficial interest prior to the modification. A modification that is administrative in nature that only indirectly increases the amount transferred (for example, by lowering administrative costs or income taxes) will not be considered to shift a beneficial interest in the trust. In addition, administration of a trust in conformance with applicable local law that defines the term income as a unitrust amount (or permits a right to income to be satisfied by such an amount) or that permits the trustee to adjust between principal and income to fulfill the trustee's duty of impartiality between income and principal beneficiaries will not be considered to shift a beneficial interest in the trust, if applicable local law provides for a reasonable apportionment between the income and remainder beneficiaries of the total return of the trust and meets the requirements of § 1.643(b)-1 of this chapter.

(E) *Examples.*—The following examples illustrate the application of this paragraph (b)(4). In each example, assume that the trust established in 1980 was irrevocable for purposes of paragraph (b)(1)(ii) of this section and that there have been no additions to any trust after September 25, 1985. The examples are as follows:

*Example 1. Trustee's power to distribute principal authorized under trust instrument.* In 1980, Grantor established an irrevocable trust (Trust) for the benefit of Grantor's child, A, A's spouse, and A's issue. At the time Trust was established, A had two children, B and C. A corporate fiduciary was designated as trustee. Under the terms of Trust, the trustee has the discretion to distribute all or part of the trust income to one or more of the group consisting of A, A's spouse or A's issue. The trustee is also authorized to distribute all or part of the trust principal to one or more trusts for the benefit of A, A's spouse, or A's issue under terms specified by the trustee in the trustee's discretion. Any trust established under Trust, however, must terminate 21 years after the death of the last child of A to die who was alive at the time Trust was executed. Trust will terminate on the death of A, at which time the remaining principal will be distributed to A's issue, per stirpes. In 2002, the trustee distributes part of Trust's principal to a new trust for the benefit of B and C and their issue. The new trust will terminate 21 years after the death of the survivor of B and C, at which time the trust principal will be distributed to the issue of B and C, per stirpes. The terms of the governing instrument of Trust authorize the trustee to make the distribution to a new trust without the consent or approval of any beneficiary or court. In addition, the terms of the governing instrument of the new trust do not extend the time for vesting of any beneficial interest in a manner that may postpone or suspend the vesting, absolute ownership or power of alienation of an interest in property for a period, measured from the date of creation of Trust, extending beyond any life in being at the date of creation of Trust plus a period of 21 years, plus if necessary, a reasonable period of gestation. Therefore, neither Trust nor the new trust will be subject to the provisions of chapter 13 of the Internal Revenue Code.

*Example 2. Trustee's power to distribute principal pursuant to state statute.* In 1980, Grantor established an irrevocable trust (Trust) for the benefit of Grantor's child, A, A's spouse, and A's issue. At the time Trust was established, A had two children, B and C. A corporate fiduciary was designated as trustee. Under the terms of Trust, the trustee has the discretion to distribute all or part of the trust income or principal to one or more of the group consisting of A, A's spouse or A's issue. Trust will terminate on the death of A, at which time the trust principal will be distributed to A's issue, per stirpes. Under a state statute enacted after 1980 that is applicable to Trust, a trustee who has the absolute discretion under the terms of a testamentary instrument or irrevocable inter vivos trust agreement to invade the principal of a trust for the benefit of the income beneficiaries of the trust, may exercise the discretion by appointing so much or all of the principal of the trust in favor of a trustee of a trust under an instrument other than that under which the power to invade is created, or under the same instrument. The trustee may take the action either with consent of all the persons interested in the trust but without prior court approval, or with court approval, upon notice to all of the parties. The exercise of the discretion, however, must not reduce any fixed income interest of any income beneficiary of the trust and must be in favor of the beneficiaries of the trust. Under state law prior to the enactment of the state statute, the trustee did not have the authority to make distributions in trust. In 2002, the trustee distributes one-half of Trust's principal to a new trust that provides for the payment of trust income to A for life and further provides that, at A's death, one-half of the trust remainder will pass to B or B's issue and one-half of the trust will pass to C or C's issue. Because the state statute was enacted after Trust was created and requires the consent of all of the parties, the transaction constitutes a modification of Trust. However, the modification does not shift any beneficial interest in Trust to a beneficiary or beneficiaries who occupy a lower generation than the person or persons who held the beneficial interest prior to the modification. In addition, the modification does not extend the time for vesting of any beneficial interest in Trust beyond the period provided for in the original trust. The new trust will terminate at the same date provided under Trust. Therefore, neither Trust nor the new trust will be subject to the provisions of chapter 13 of the Internal Revenue Code.

*Example 3. Construction of an ambiguous term in the instrument.* In 1980, Grantor established an irrevocable trust for the benefit of Grantor's children, A and B, and their issue. The trust is to terminate on the death of the last to die of A and B, at which time the principal is to be distributed to their issue. However, the provision governing the termination of the trust is ambiguous regarding whether the trust principal is to be distributed per stirpes, only to the children of A and B, or per capita among the children, grandchildren, and more remote issue of A and B. In 2002, the trustee files a construction suit with the appropriate local court to resolve the ambiguity. The court issues an order construing the instrument to provide for per capita distributions to the children, grandchildren, and more remote issue of A and B living at the time the trust terminates. The court's construction resolves a bona fide issue regarding the proper interpretation of the instrument and is consistent with applicable state law as it would be interpreted by the highest court of the state. Therefore, the trust will not be subject to the provisions of chapter 13 of the Internal Revenue Code.

*Example 4. Change in trust situs.* In 1980, Grantor, who was domiciled in State X, executed an irrevocable trust for the benefit of Grantor's issue, naming a State X bank as trustee. Under the terms of the trust, the trust is to terminate, in all events, no later than 21 years after the death of the last to die of certain designated individuals living at the time the trust was executed. The provisions of the trust do not specify that any particular state law is to govern the administration and construction of the trust. In State X, the common law rule against perpetuities applies to trusts. In 2002, a State Y bank is named as sole trustee. The effect of changing trustees is that the situs of the trust changes to State Y, and the laws of State Y govern the administration and construction of the trust. State Y law contains no rule against perpetuities. In this case, however, in view of the terms of the trust instrument, the trust will terminate at the same time before and after the change in situs. Accordingly, the change in situs does not shift any beneficial interest in the trust to a beneficiary who occupies a lower generation (as defined in section 2651) than the person or persons who held the beneficial interest prior to the transfer. Furthermore, the change in situs does not extend the time for vesting of any beneficial interest in the trust beyond that provided for in the original trust. Therefore, the trust will not be subject to the provisions of chapter 13 of the Internal Revenue Code. If, in this example, as a result of the change in situs, State Y law governed such that the time for vesting was extended beyond the period prescribed under the terms of the original trust instrument, the trust would not retain exempt status.

*Example 5. Division of a trust.* In 1980, Grantor established an irrevocable trust for the benefit of his two children, A and B, and their issue. Under the terms of the trust, the trustee has the discretion to distribute income and principal to A, B, and their issue in such amounts as the trustee deems appropriate. On the death of the last to die of A and B, the trust principal is to be distributed to the living issue of A and B, per stirpes. In 2002, the appropriate local court approved the division of the trust into two equal trusts, one for the benefit of A and A's issue and one for the benefit of B and B's issue. The trust for A and A's issue provides that the trustee has the discretion to distribute trust income and principal to A and A's issue in such amounts as the trustee deems appropriate. On A's death, the trust principal is to be distributed equally to A's issue, per stirpes. If A dies with no living descendants, the principal will be added to the trust for B and B's issue. The trust for B and B's issue is identical (except for the beneficiaries), and terminates at B's death at which time the trust principal is to be distributed equally to B's issue, per stirpes. If B dies with no living descendants, principal will be added to the trust for A and A's issue. The division of the trust into two trusts does not shift any beneficial interest in the trust to a beneficiary who occupies a lower generation (as defined in section 2651) than the person or persons who held the beneficial interest prior to the division. In addition, the division does not extend the time for vesting of any beneficial interest in the trust beyond the period provided for in the original trust. Therefore, the two partitioned trusts resulting from the division will not be subject to the provisions of chapter 13 of the Internal Revenue Code.

*Example 6. Merger of two trusts.* In 1980, Grantor established an irrevocable trust for Grantor's child and the child's issue. In 1983, Grantor's spouse also established a separate irrevocable trust for the benefit of the same child and issue. The terms of the spouse's trust and Grantor's trust are identical. In 2002, the appropriate local court approved the merger of the two trusts into one trust to save administrative costs and enhance the management of the investments. The merger of the two trusts does not shift any beneficial interest in the trust to a beneficiary who occupies a lower generation (as defined in section 2651) than the person or persons who held the beneficial interest prior to the merger. In addition, the merger does not extend the time for vesting of any beneficial interest in the trust beyond the period provided for in the original trust. Therefore, the trust that resulted from the merger will not be subject to the provisions of chapter 13 of the Internal Revenue Code.

*Example 7. Modification that does not shift an interest to a lower generation.* In 1980, Grantor established an irrevocable trust for the benefit of Grantor's grandchildren, A, B, and C. The trust provides that income is to be paid to A, B, and C, in equal shares for life. The trust further provides that, upon the death of the first grandchild to die, one-third of the principal is to be distributed to that grandchild's issue, per stirpes. Upon the death of the second grandchild to die, one-half of the remaining trust principal is to be distributed to that grandchild's issue, per stirpes, and upon the death of the last grandchild to die, the remaining principal is to be distributed to that grandchild's issue, per stirpes. In 2002, A became disabled. Subsequently, the trustee, with the consent of B and C, petitioned the appropriate local court and the court approved a modification of the trust that increased A's share of trust income. The modification does not shift a beneficial interest to a lower generation beneficiary because the modification does not increase the amount of a GST transfer under the original trust or create the possibility that new GST transfers not contemplated in the original trust may be made. In this case, the modification will increase the amount payable to A who is a member of the same generation as B and C. In addition, the modification does not extend the time for vesting of any beneficial interest in the trust beyond the period provided for in the original trust. Therefore, the trust as modified will not be subject to the provisions of chapter 13 of the Internal Revenue Code. However, the modification increasing A's share of trust income is a transfer by B and C to A for Federal gift tax purposes.

*Example 8. Conversion of income interest into unitrust interest.* In 1980, Grantor established an irrevocable trust under the terms of which trust income is payable to A for life and, upon A's death, the remainder is to pass to A's issue, per stirpes. In 2002, the appropriate local court approves a modification to the trust that converts A's income interest into the right to receive the greater of the entire income of the trust or a fixed percentage of the trust assets valued annually (unitrust interest) to be paid each year to A for life. The modification does not result in a shift in beneficial interest to a beneficiary who occupies a lower generation (as defined in section 2651) than the person or persons who held the beneficial interest prior to the modification. In this case, the modification can only operate to increase the amount distributable to A and decrease the amount distributable to A's issue. In addition, the modification does not extend the time for vesting of any beneficial interest in the trust beyond the period provided for in the original trust. Therefore, the trust will not be subject to the provisions of chapter 13 of the Internal Revenue Code.

*Example 9. Allocation of capital gain to income.* In 1980, Grantor established an irrevocable trust under the terms of which trust income is payable to Grantor's child, A, for life, and upon A's death, the remainder is to pass to A's issue, per stirpes. Under applicable state law, unless the governing instrument provides otherwise, capital gain is allocated to principal. In 2002, the trust is modified to allow the trustee to allocate capital gain to the income. The modification does not shift any beneficial interest in the trust to a beneficiary who occupies a lower generation (as defined in section 2651) than the person or persons who held the beneficial interest prior to the modification. In this case, the modification can only have the effect of increasing the amount distributable to A, and decreasing the amount distributable to A's issue. In addition, the modification does not extend the time for vesting of any beneficial interest in the trust beyond the period provided for in the original trust. Therefore, the trust will not be subject to the provisions of chapter 13 of the Internal Revenue Code.

*Example 10. Administrative change to terms of a trust.* In 1980, Grantor executed an irrevocable trust for the benefit of Grantor's issue, naming a bank and five other individuals as trustees. In 2002, the appropriate local court approves a modification of the trust that decreases the number of trustees which results in lower administrative costs. The modification pertains to the administration of the trust and does not shift a beneficial interest in the trust to any beneficiary who occupies a lower generation (as defined in section 2651) than the person or persons who held the beneficial interest prior to the modification. In addition, the modification does not extend the time for vesting of any beneficial interest in the trust beyond the period provided for in the original trust. Therefore, the trust will not be subject to the provisions of chapter 13 of the Internal Revenue Code.

*Example 11. Conversion of income interest to unitrust interest under state statute.* In 1980, Grantor, a resident of State X, established an irrevocable trust for the benefit of Grantor's child, A, and A's issue. The trust provides that trust income is payable to A for life and upon A's death the remainder is to pass to A's issue, per stirpes. In 2002, State X amends its income and principal statute to define income as a unitrust amount of 4% of the fair market value of the trust assets valued annually. For a trust established prior to 2002, the statute provides that the new definition of income will apply only if all the beneficiaries who have an interest in the trust consent to the change within two years after the effective date of the statute. The statute provides specific procedures to establish the consent of beneficiaries. A and A's issue consent to the change in the definition of income within the time period, and in accordance with the procedures, prescribed by the state statute. The administration of the trust, in accordance with the state statute defining income to be a 4% unitrust amount, will not be considered to shift any beneficial interest in the trust. Therefore, the trust will not be subject to the provisions of chapter 13 of the Internal Revenue Code. Further, under these facts, no trust beneficiary will be treated as having made a gift for federal gift tax purposes, and neither the trust nor any trust beneficiary will be treated as having made a taxable exchange for federal income tax purposes. Similarly, the conclusions in this example would be the same if the beneficiaries' consent was not required, or, if the change in administration of the trust occurred because the situs of the trust was changed to State X from a state whose statute does not define income as a unitrust amount or if the situs was changed to such a state from State X.

*Example 12. Equitable adjustments under state statute.* The facts are the same as in *Example 11*, except that in 2002, State X amends its income and principal statute to permit the trustee to make adjustments between income and principal when the trustee invests and manages the trust assets under the state's prudent investor standard, the trust describes the amount that shall or must be distributed to a beneficiary by referring to the trust's income, and the trustee after applying the state statutory rules regarding allocation of receipts between income and principal is unable to administer the trust impartially. The provision permitting the trustees to make these adjustments is effective in 2002 for trusts created at any time. The trustee invests and manages the trust assets under the state's prudent investor standard, and pursuant to authorization in the state statute, the trustee allocates receipts between the income and principal accounts in a manner to ensure the impartial administration of the trust. The administration of the trust in accordance with the state statute will not be considered to shift any beneficial interest in the trust. Therefore, the trust will not be subject to the provisions of chapter 13 of the Internal Revenue Code. Further, under these facts, no trust beneficiary will be treated as having made a gift for federal gift tax purposes, and neither the trust nor any trust beneficiary will be treated as having made a taxable exchange for federal income tax purposes. Similarly, the conclusions in this example would be the same if the change in administration of the trust occurred because the situs of the trust was changed to State X from a state whose statute does not authorize the trustee to make adjustments between income and principal or if the situs was changed to such a state from State X.

(ii) *Effective dates.*—The rules in this paragraph (b)(4) are generally applicable on and after December 20, 2000. However, the rule in the last sentence of paragraph (b)(4)(i)(D)(2) of this section and *Example 11* and *Example 12* in paragraph (b)(4)(i)(E) of this section regarding the administration of a trust and the determination of income in conformance with applicable state law applies to trusts for taxable years ending after January 2, 2004.

(5) *Exceptions to additions rule.*—(i) *In general.*—Any addition to a trust made pursuant to an instrument or arrangement covered by the transition rules in paragraph (b)(1), (2) or (3) of this section is not treated as an addition for purposes of this section. Moreover, any property transferred inter vivos to a trust is not treated as an addition if the same property would have been added to the trust pursuant to an instrument covered by the transition rules in paragraph (b)(2) or (3) of this section.

(ii) *Examples.*—The following examples illustrate the application of paragraph (b)(4)(i) of this section:

*Example 1. Addition pursuant to terms of exempt instrument.* On December 31, 1980, T created an irrevocable trust having a principal of $100,000. Under the terms of the trust, the principal was to be held for the benefit of T's grandchild, GC. Pursuant to the terms of T's will, a document entitled to relief under the transition rule of paragraph (b)(2) of this section, the residue of the estate was paid to the trust. Because the addition to the trust was paid pursuant to the terms of an instrument (T's will) that is not subject to the provisions of chapter 13 because of paragraph (b)(2) of this section, the payment to the trust is not considered an addition to the principal of the trust. Thus, distributions to or for the benefit of GC, are not subject to the provisions of chapter 13.

*Example 2. Property transferred inter vivos that would have been transferred to the same trust by the transferor's will.* T is the grantor of a trust that was irrevocable on September 25, 1985. T's will, which was executed before October 22, 1986, and not amended thereafter, provides that, upon T's death, the entire estate will pour over into T's trust. On October 1, 1985, T transfers $100,000 to the trust. While T's will otherwise qualifies for relief under the transition rule in paragraph (b)(2) of this section, the transition rule is not applicable unless T dies prior to January 1, 1987. Thus, if T dies after December 31, 1986, the transfer is treated as an addition to the trust for purposes of any distribution made from the trust after the transfer to the trust on October 1, 1985. If T dies before January 1, 1987, the entire trust (as well as any distributions from or terminations of interests in the trust prior to T's death) is exempt, under paragraph (b)(2) of this section, from chapter 13 because the $100,000 would have been added to the trust under a will that would have qualified under paragraph (b)(2) of this section. In either case, for any generation-skipping transfers made after the transfer to the trust on October 1, 1985, but before T's death, the $100,000 is treated as an addition to the trust and a proportionate amount of the trust is subject to chapter 13.

*Example 3. Pour over to a revocable trust.* T and S are the settlors of separate revocable trusts with equal values. Both trusts were established for the benefit of skip persons (as defined in section 2613). S dies on December 1, 1985, and under the provisions of S's trust, the principal pours over into T's trust. If T dies before January 1, 1987, the entire trust is excluded under paragraph (b)(2) of this section from the operation of chapter 13. If T dies after December 31, 1986, the entire trust is subject to the generation-skipping transfer tax provisions because T's trust is not a trust described in paragraph (b)(1) or (2) of this section. In the latter case, the fact that S died before January 1, 1987, is irrelevant because the principal of S's trust was added to a trust that never qualified under the transition rules of paragraph (b)(1) or (2) of this section.

*Example 4. Pour over to exempt trust.* Assume the same facts as in *Example 3*, except upon the death of S on December 1, 1985, S's trust continues as an irrevocable trust and that the principal of T's trust is to be paid over upon T's death to S's trust. Again, if T dies before January 1, 1987, S's entire trust falls within the provisions of paragraph (b)(2) of this section. However, if T dies after December 31, 1986, the pour-over is considered an addition to the trust. Therefore, S's trust is not a trust excluded under paragraph (b)(2) of this section because an addition is made to the trust.

*Example 5. Lapse of a general power of appointment.* S, the spouse of the settlor of an irrevocable trust that was created in 1980, had, on September 25, 1985, a general power of appointment over the trust assets. The trust provides that should S fail to exercise the power of appointment the property is to remain in the trust. On October 21, 1986, S executed a will under which S failed to exercise the power of appointment. If S dies before January 1, 1987, without having exercised the power in a manner which results in the creation of, or increase in the amount of, a generation-skipping transfer (or amended the will in a manner that results in the creation of, or increase in the amount of, a generation-skipping transfer), transfers pursuant to the trust or the will are not subject to chapter 13 because the trust is an irrevocable trust and the will qualifies under paragraph (b)(2) of this section.

*Example 6. Lapse of general power of appointment held by intestate decedent.* Assume the same facts as in *Example 5*, except on October 22, 1986, S did not have a will and that S dies after that date. Upon S's death, or upon the prior exercise or release of the power, the value of the entire trust is treated as having been distributed to S, and S is treated as having made an addition to the trust in the amount of the entire principal. Any distribution or termination pursuant to the trust occurring after S's death is subject to chapter 13. It is immaterial whether S's death occurs before January 1, 1987, since paragraph (b)(2) of this section is only applicable where a will or revocable trust was executed before October 22, 1986.

(c) *Additional effective dates.*—Except as otherwise provided, the regulations under §§ 26.2611-1, 26.2612-1, 26.2613-1, 26.2632-1, 26.2641-1, 26.2642-1, 26.2642-2, 26.2642-3, 26.2642-4, 26.2642-5, 26.2652-1, 26.2652-2, 26.2653-1, 26.2654-1, 26.2663-1, and 26.2663-2 are effective with respect to generation-skipping transfers as defined in § 26.2611-1 made on or after December 27, 1995. However, taxpayers may, at their option, rely on these regulations in the case of generation-skipping transfers made, and trusts that became irrevocable, after December 23, 1992, and before December 27, 1995. The last four sentences in paragraph (b)(1)(i) of this section are applicable on and after November 18, 1999. [Reg. § 26.2601-1.]

☐ [*T.D. 8644, 12-26-95. Amended by T.D. 8912, 12-19-2000 (corrected 2-21-2001) and T.D. 9102, 12-30-2003.*]

### [Reg. §26.2611-1]

**§26.2611-1. Generation-skipping transfer defined.**—A generation-skipping transfer (GST) is an event that is either a direct skip, a taxable distribution, or a taxable termination. See §26.2612-1 for the definition of these terms. The determination as to whether an event is a GST is made by reference to the most recent transfer subject to the estate or gift tax. See §26.2652-1(a)(2) for determining whether a transfer is subject to Federal estate or gift tax. [Reg. §26.2611-1.]

☐ [*T.D. 8644, 12-26-95.*]

### [Reg. §26.2612-1]

**§26.2612-1. Definitions.**—(a) *Direct skip.*—A direct skip is a transfer to a skip person that is subject to Federal estate or gift tax. If property is transferred to a trust, the transfer is a direct skip only if the trust is a skip person. Only one direct skip occurs when a single transfer of property skips two or more generations. See paragraph (d) of this section for the definition of skip person. See §26.2652-1(b) for the definition of trust. See §26.2632-1(c)(4) for the time that a direct skip occurs if the transferred property is subject to an estate tax inclusion period.

(b) *Taxable termination.*—(1) *In general.*—Except as otherwise provided in this paragraph (b), a taxable termination is a termination (occurring for any reason) of an interest in trust unless—

(i) A transfer subject to Federal estate or gift tax occurs with respect to the property held in the trust at the time of the termination;

(ii) Immediately after the termination, a person who is not a skip person has an interest in the trust; or

(iii) At no time after the termination may a distribution, other than a distribution the probability of which occurring is so remote as to be negligible (including a distribution at the termination of the trust) be made from the trust to a skip person. For this purpose, the probability that a distribution will occur is so remote as to be negligible only if it can be ascertained by actuarial standards that there is less than a 5 percent probability that the distribution will occur.

(2) *Partial termination.*—If a distribution of a portion of trust property is made to a skip person by reason of a termination occurring on the death of a lineal descendant of the transferor, the termination is a taxable termination with respect to the distributed property.

(3) *Simultaneous terminations.*—A simultaneous termination of two or more interests creates only one taxable termination.

(c) *Taxable distribution.*—(1) *In general.*—A taxable distribution is a distribution of income or principal from a trust to a skip person unless the distribution is a taxable termination or a direct skip. If any portion of GST tax (including penalties and interest thereon) imposed on a distributee is paid from the distributing trust, the payment is an additional taxable distribution to the distributee. For purposes of chapter 13, the additional distribution is treated as having been made on the last day of the calendar year in which the original taxable distribution is made. If Federal estate or gift tax is imposed on any individual with respect to an interest in property held by a trust, the interest in property is treated as having been distributed to the individual to the extent that the value of the interest is subject to Federal estate or gift tax. See §26.2652-1(a)(6) *Example 5*, regarding the treatment of the lapse of a power of appointment as a transfer to a trust.

(2) *Look-through rule not to apply.*—Solely for purposes of determining whether any transfer from a trust to another trust is a taxable distribution, the rules of section 2651(e)(2) do not apply. If the transferring trust and the recipient trust have the same transferor, see §26.2642-4(a)(1) and (2) for rules for recomputing the applicable fraction of the recipient trust.

(d) *Skip person.*—A skip person is—

(1) An individual assigned to a generation more than one generation below that of the transferor (determined under the rules of section 2651); or

(2) A trust if—

(i) All interests in the trust are held by skip persons; or

(ii) No person holds an interest in the trust and no distributions, other than a distribution the probability of which occurring is so remote as to be negligible (including distributions at the termination of the trust), may be made after the transfer to a person other than a skip person. For this purpose, the probability that a distribution will occur is so remote as to be negligible only if it can be ascertained by actuarial standards that there is less than a 5 percent probability that the distribution will occur.

(e) *Interest in trust.*—(1) *In general.*—An interest in trust is an interest in property held in trust as defined in section 2652(c) and these regulations. An interest in trust exists if a person—

(i) Has a present right to receive trust principal or income;

(ii) Is a permissible current recipient of trust principal or income and is not described in section 2055(a); or

(iii) Is described in section 2055(a) and the trust is a charitable remainder annuity trust or unitrust (as defined in section 664(d)) or a pooled income fund (as defined in section 642(c)(5)).

(2) *Exceptions.*—(i) *Support obligations.*—In general, an individual has a present right to receive trust income or principal if trust income or principal may be used to satisfy the individual's support obligations. However, an individual does not have an interest in a trust merely because a support obligation of that individual may be satisfied by a distribution that is either within the discretion of a fiduciary or pursuant to provisions of local law substantially equivalent to the Uniform Gifts (Transfers) to Minors Act.

(ii) *Certain interests disregarded.*—An interest which is used primarily to postpone or avoid the GST tax is disregarded for purposes of chapter 13. An interest is considered as used primarily to postpone or avoid the GST tax if a significant purpose for the creation of the interest is to postpone or avoid the tax.

(3) *Disclaimers.*—An interest does not exist to the extent it is disclaimed pursuant to a disclaimer that constitutes a qualified disclaimer under section 2518.

(f) *Examples.*—The following examples illustrate the provisions of this section.

*Example 1. Direct skip.* T gratuitously conveys Blackacre to T's grandchild. Because the transfer is a transfer to a skip person of property subject to Federal gift tax, it is a direct skip.

*Example 2. Direct skip of more than one generation.* T gratuitously conveys Blackacre to T's great-grandchild. The transfer is a direct skip. Only one GST tax is imposed on the direct skip although two generations are skipped by the transfer.

*Example 3. Withdrawal power in trust.* T transfers $50,000 to a new trust providing that trust income is to be paid to T's child, C, for life and, on C's death, the trust principal is to be paid to T's descendants. Under the terms of the trust, T grants four grandchildren the right to withdraw $10,000 from the trust for a 60 day period following the transfer. Since C, who is not a skip person, has an interest in the trust, the trust is not a skip person. T's transfer to the trust is not a direct skip.

*Example 4. Taxable termination.* T establishes an irrevocable trust under which the income is to be paid to T's child, C, for life. On the death of C, the trust principal is to be paid to T's grandchild, GC. Since C has an interest in the trust, the trust is not a skip person and the transfer to the trust is not a direct skip. If C dies survived by GC, a taxable termination occurs at C's death because C's interest in the trust terminates and thereafter the trust property is held by a skip person who occupies a lower generation than C.

*Example 5. Direct skip of property held in trust.* T establishes a testamentary trust under which the income is to be paid to T's surviving spouse, S, for life and the remainder is to be paid to a grandchild of T and S. T's executor elects to treat the trust as qualified terminable interest property under section 2056(b)(7). The transfer to the trust is not a direct skip because S, a person who is not a skip person, holds a present right to receive income from the trust. Upon S's death, the trust property is included in S's gross estate under section 2044 and passes directly to a skip person. The GST occurring at that time is a direct skip because it is a transfer subject to chapter 11. The fact that the interest created by T is terminated at S's death is immaterial because S becomes the transferor at the time of the transfer subject to chapter 11.

*Example 6. Taxable termination.* T establishes an irrevocable trust for the benefit of T's child, C, T's grandchild, GC, and T's great-grandchild, GGC. Under the terms of the trust, income and principal may be distributed to any or all of the living beneficiaries at the discretion of the trustee. Upon the death of the second beneficiary to die, the trust principal is to be paid to the survivor. C dies first. A taxable termination occurs at that time because, immediately after C's interest terminates, all interests in the trust are held by skip persons (GC and GGC).

*Example 7. Taxable termination resulting from distribution.* The facts are the same as in *Example 6*, except twenty years after C's death the trustee exercises its discretionary power and distributes the entire principal to GGC. The distribution results in a taxable termination because GGC's interest in the trust terminates as a result of the distribution of the entire trust property to GGC, a skip person. The result would be the same if the trustee retained sufficient funds to pay the GST tax due by reason of the taxable termination, as well as any expenses of winding up the trust.

*Example 8. Simultaneous termination of interests of more than one beneficiary.* T establishes an irrevocable trust for the benefit of T's child, C, T's grandchild, GC, and T's great-grandchild, GGC. Under the terms of the trust, income and principal may be distributed to any or all of the living beneficiaries at the discretion of the trustee. Upon the death of C, the trust property is to be distributed to GGC if then living. If C is survived by both GC and GGC, both C's and GC's interests in the trust will terminate on C's death. However, because both interests will terminate at the same time and as a result of one event, only one taxable termination occurs.

*Example 9. Partial taxable termination.* T creates an irrevocable trust providing that trust income is to be paid to T's children, A and B, in such proportions as the trustee determines for their joint lives. On the death of the first child to die, one-half of the trust principal is to be paid to T's then living grandchildren. The balance of the trust principal is to be paid to T's grandchildren on the death of the survivor of A and B. If A predeceases B, the distribution occurring on the termination of A's interest in the trust is a taxable termination and not a taxable termination. It is a taxable termination because the distribution is a distribution of a portion of the trust that occurs as a result of the death of A, a lineal descendant of T. It is immaterial that a portion of the trust continues and that B, a person other than a skip person, thereafter holds an interest in the trust.

*Example 10. Taxable distribution.* T establishes an irrevocable trust under which the trust income is payable to T's child, C, for life. When T's grandchild, GC, attains 35 years of age, GC is to receive one-half of the principal. The remaining one-half of the principal is to be distributed to GC on C's death. Assume that C survives until GC attains age 35. When the trustee distributes one-half of the principal to GC on GC's 35th birthday, the distribution is a taxable distribution because it is a distribution to a skip person and is neither a taxable termination nor a direct skip.

*Example 11. Exercise of withdrawal right as taxable distribution.* The facts are the same as in *Example 10*, except GC holds a continuing right to withdraw trust principal and after one year GC withdraws $10,000. The withdrawal by GC is not a taxable termination because the withdrawal does not terminate C's interest in the trust. The withdrawal by GC is a taxable distribution to GC.

*Example 12. Interest in trust.* T establishes an irrevocable trust under which the income is to be paid to T's child, C, for life. On the death of C, the trust principal is to be paid to T's grandchild, GC. Because C has a present right to receive income from the trust, C has an interest in the trust. Because GC cannot currently receive distributions from the trust, GC does not have an interest in the trust.

*Example 13. Support obligation.* T establishes an irrevocable trust for the benefit of T's grandchild, GC. The trustee has discretion to distribute property for GC's support without regard to the duty or ability of GC's parent, C, to support GC. Because GC is a permissible current recipient of trust property, GC has an interest in the trust. C does not have an interest in the trust because the potential use of the trust property to satisfy C's support obligation is within the discretion of a fiduciary. C would be treated as having an interest in the trust if the trustee was required to distribute trust property for GC's support. [Reg. § 26.2612-1.]

☐ [*T.D. 8644*, 12-26-95. *Amended by T.D. 9214*, 7-15-2005.]

### [Reg. § 26.2613-1]

**§ 26.2613-1. Skip person.**—For the definition of *skip person* see § 26.2612-1(d). [Reg. § 26.2613-1.]

☐ [*T.D. 8644*, 12-26-95.]

### [Reg. § 26.2632-1]

**§ 26.2632-1. Allocation of GST exemption.**—(a) *General rule.*—Except as otherwise provided in this section, an individual or the individual's executor may allocate the individual's $1 million GST exemption at any time from the date of the transfer through the date for filing the individual's Federal estate tax return (including any extensions for filing that have been actually granted). If no estate tax return is required to be filed, the GST exemption may be allocated at any time through the date a Federal estate tax return would be due if a return were required to be filed (including any extensions actually granted). If property is held in trust, the allocation of GST exemption is made to the entire trust rather than to specific trust assets. If a transfer is a direct skip to a trust, the allocation of GST exemption to the transferred property is also treated as an allocation of GST exemption to the trust for purposes of future GSTs with respect to the trust by the same transferor.

(b) *Lifetime allocations.*—(1) *Automatic allocation to direct skips.*—(i) *In general.*—If a direct skip occurs during the transferor's lifetime, the transferor's GST exemption not previously allocated (unused GST exemption) is automatically allocated to the transferred property (but not in excess of the fair market value of the property on the date

of the transfer). The transferor may prevent the automatic allocation of GST exemption by describing on a timely-filed United States Gift (and Generation-Skipping Transfer) Tax Return (Form 709) the transfer and the extent to which the automatic allocation is not to apply. In addition, a timely-filed Form 709 accompanied by payment of the GST tax (as shown on the return with respect to the direct skip) is sufficient to prevent an automatic allocation of GST exemption with respect to the transferred property. See paragraph (c)(4) of this section for special rules in the case of direct skips treated as occurring at the termination of an estate tax inclusion period.

(ii) *Time for filing Form 709.*—A Form 709 is timely filed if it is filed on or before the date required for reporting the transfer if it were a taxable gift (i.e., the date prescribed by section 6075(b), including any extensions to file actually granted (the due date)). Except as provided in paragraph (b)(1)(iii) of this section, the automatic allocation of GST exemption (or the election to prevent the allocation, if made) is irrevocable after the due date. An automatic allocation of GST exemption is effective as of the date of the transfer to which it relates. Except as provided above, a Form 709 need not be filed to report an automatic allocation.

(iii) *Transitional rule.*—An election to prevent an automatic allocation of GST exemption filed on or before January 26, 1996, becomes irrevocable on July 24, 1996.

(2) *Automatic allocation to indirect skips made after December 31, 2000.*—(i) *In general.*—An indirect skip is a transfer of property to a GST trust as defined in section 2632(c)(3)(B) provided that the transfer is subject to gift tax and does not qualify as a direct skip. In the case of an indirect skip made after December 31, 2000, to which section 2642(f) (relating to transfers subject to an estate tax inclusion period (ETIP)) does not apply, the transferor's unused GST exemption is automatically allocated to the property transferred (but not in excess of the fair market value of the property on the date of the transfer). The automatic allocation pursuant to this paragraph is effective whether or not a Form 709 is filed reporting the transfer, and is effective as of the date of the transfer to which it relates. An automatic allocation is irrevocable after the due date of the Form 709 for the calendar year in which the transfer is made. In the case of an indirect skip to which section 2642(f) does apply, the indirect skip is deemed to be made at the close of the ETIP and the GST exemption is deemed to be allocated at that time. In either case, except as otherwise provided in paragraph (b)(2)(ii) of this section, the automatic allocation of exemption applies even if an allocation of exemption is made to the indirect skip in accordance with section 2632(a).

(ii) *Prevention of automatic allocation.*—Except as otherwise provided in forms or other guidance published by the Service, the transferor may prevent the automatic allocation of GST exemption with regard to an indirect skip (including indirect skips to which section 2642(f) may apply) by making an election, as provided in paragraph (b)(2)(iii) of this section. Notwithstanding paragraph (b)(2)(iii)(B) of this section, the transferor may also prevent the automatic allocation of GST exemption with regard to an indirect skip by making an affirmative allocation of GST exemption on a Form 709 filed at any time on or before the due date for timely filing (within the meaning of paragraph (b)(1)(ii) of this section) of an amount that is less than (but not equal to) the value of the property transferred as reported on that return, in accordance with the provisions of paragraph (b)(4) of this section. See paragraph (b)(4)(iii) *Example 6* of this section. Any election out of the automatic allocation rules under this section has no effect on the application of the automatic allocation rules applicable after the transferor's death under section 2632(e) and paragraph (d) of this section.

(iii) *Election to have automatic allocation rules not apply.*—(A) *In general.*—A transferor may prevent the automatic allocation of GST exemption (elect out) with respect to any transfer or transfers constituting an indirect skip made to a trust or to one or more separate shares that are treated as separate trusts under § 26.2654-1(a)(1) (collectively referred to hereinafter as a trust). In the case of a transfer treated under section 2513 as made one-half by the transferor and one-half by the transferor's spouse, each spouse shall be treated as a separate transferor who must satisfy separately the requirements of paragraph (b)(2)(iii)(B) to elect out with respect to the transfer. A transferor may elect out with respect to—

(1) One or more prior-year transfers subject to section 2642(f) (regarding ETIPs) made by the transferor to a specified trust or trusts;

(2) One or more (or all) current-year transfers made by the transferor to a specified trust or trusts;

(3) One or more (or all) future transfers made by the transferor to a specified trust or trusts;

(4) All future transfers made by the transferor to all trusts (whether or not in existence at the time of the election out); or

(5) Any combination of paragraphs (b)(2)(iii)(A)(1) through (4) of this section.

(B) *Manner of making an election out.*—Except as otherwise provided in forms or other guidance published by the IRS, an election out is made as described in this paragraph (b)(2)(iii)(B). To elect out, the transferor must attach a statement (election out statement) to a Form 709 filed within the time period provided in paragraph (b)(2)(iii)(C) of this section (whether or not any transfer was made in the calendar year for which the Form 709 was filed, and whether or not a Form 709 otherwise would be required to be filed for that year). See paragraph (b)(4)(iv) *Example 7* of this section. The election out statement must identify the trust (except for an election out under paragraph (b)(2)(iii)(A)(4) of this section), and specifically must provide that the transferor is electing out of the automatic allocation of GST exemption with respect to the described transfer or transfers. Prior-year transfers that are subject to section 2642(f), and to which the election out is to apply, must be specifically described or otherwise identified in the election out statement. Further, unless the election out is made for all transfers made to the trust in the current year and/or in all future years, the current-year transfers and/or future transfers to which the election out is to apply must be specifically described or otherwise identified in the election out statement.

(C) *Time for making an election out.*—To elect out, the Form 709 with the attached election out statement must be filed on or before the due date for timely filing (within the meaning of paragraph (b)(1)(ii) of this section) of the Form 709 for the calendar year in which—

(1) For a transfer subject to section 2642(f), the ETIP closes; or

(2) For all other elections out, the first transfer to be covered by the election out was made.

(D) *Effect of election out.*—An election out does not affect the automatic allocation of GST exemption to any transfer not covered by the election out statement. Except for elections out for transfers described in paragraph (b)(2)(iii)(A)(1) of this section that are specifically described in an election out statement, an election out does not apply to any prior-year transfer to a trust, including any transfer subject to an ETIP (even if the ETIP closes after the election is made). An election out does not prevent the transferor from allocating the transferor's available GST exemption to any transfer covered by the election out, either on a timely filed Form 709 reporting the transfer or at a later date in accordance with the provisions of paragraph (b)(4) of this section. An election out with respect to future transfers remains in effect unless and until terminated. Once an election out with respect to future transfers is made, a transferor need not file a Form 709 in future years solely to prevent the automatic allocation of the GST exemption to any future transfer covered by the election out.

(E) *Termination of election out.*—Except as otherwise provided in forms or other guidance published by the IRS, an election out may be terminated as described in this paragraph (b)(2)(iii)(E). Pursuant to this section, a transferor may terminate an election out made on a Form 709 for a prior year, to the extent that election out applied to future transfers or to a transfer subject to section 2642(f). To terminate an election out, the transferor must attach a statement (termination statement) to a Form 709 filed on or before the due date of the Form 709 for the calendar year in which is made the first transfer to which the election out is not to apply (whether or not any transfer was made in the calendar year for which the Form 709 was filed, and whether or not a Form 709 otherwise would be required to be filed for that year). The termination statement must identify the trust (if applicable), describe the prior election out that is being terminated, specifically provide that the prior election out is being terminated, and either describe the extent to which the prior election out is being terminated or describe any current-year transfers to which the election out is not to apply. Consequently, the automatic allocation rules contained in section 2632(c)(1) will apply to any current-year transfer described on the termination statement and, except as otherwise provided in this paragraph, to all future transfers that otherwise would have been covered by the election out. The termination of an election out does not affect any transfer, or any election out, that is not described in the termination statement. The termination of an election out will not revoke the election out for any prior-year transfer, except for a prior-year transfer subject to section 2642(f) for which the election out is revoked on a timely filed Form 709 for the calendar year in which the ETIP closes or for any prior calendar year. The termination of an election out does not preclude the transferor from making another election out in the same or any subsequent year.

(3) *Election to treat trust as a GST trust.*—(i) *In general.*—A transferor may elect to treat any trust as a GST trust (GST trust election),

without regard to whether the trust is subject to section 2642(f), with respect to—

(A) Any current-year transfer (or any or all current-year transfers) by the electing transferor to the trust;

(B) Any selected future transfers by the electing transferor to the trust;

(C) All future transfers by the electing transferor to the trust; or

(D) Any combination of paragraphs (b)(3)(i)(A) through (C) of this section.

(ii) *Time and Manner of making GST trust election.*—Except as otherwise provided in forms or other guidance published by the Internal Revenue Service, a GST trust election is made as described in this paragraph (b)(3)(ii). To make a GST trust election, the transferor must attach a statement (GST trust election statement) to a Form 709 filed on or before the due date for timely filing (within the meaning of paragraph (b)(1)(ii) of this section) of the Form 709 for the calendar year in which the first transfer to be covered by the GST trust election is made (whether or not any transfer was made in the calendar year for which the Form 709 was filed, and whether or not a Form 709 otherwise would be required to be filed for that year). The GST trust election statement must identify the trust, specifically describe or otherwise clearly identify the transfers to be covered by the election, and specifically provide that the transferor is electing to have the trust treated as a GST trust with respect to the covered transfers.

(iii) *Effect of GST trust election.*—Except as otherwise provided in this paragraph, a GST trust election will cause all transfers made by the electing transferor to the trust that are subject to the election to be deemed to be made to a GST trust as defined in section 2632(c)(3)(B). Thus, the electing transferor's unused GST exemption may be allocated automatically to such transfers in accordance with paragraph (b)(2) of this section. A transferor may prevent the automatic allocation of GST exemption to future transfers to the trust either by terminating the GST trust election in accordance with paragraph (b)(3)(iv) of this section (in the case of trusts that would not otherwise be treated as GST trusts) or by electing out of the automatic allocation of GST exemption in accordance with paragraph (b)(2) of this section.

(iv) *Termination of GST trust election.*—Except as otherwise provided in forms or other guidance published by the Service, a GST trust election may be terminated as described in this paragraph (b)(3)(iv). A transferor may terminate a GST trust election made on a Form 709 for a prior year, to the extent that election applied to future transfers or to a transfer subject to section 2642(f). To terminate a GST trust election, the transferor must attach a statement (termination statement) to a Form 709 filed on or before the due date for timely filing (within the meaning of paragraph (b)(1)(ii) of this section) a Form 709 for the calendar year: in which is made the electing transferor's first transfer to which the GST trust election is not to apply; or that is the first calendar year for which the GST trust election is not to apply, even if no transfer is made to the trust during that year. The termination statement must identify the trust, describe the current-year transfer (if any), and provide that the prior GST trust election is terminated. Accordingly, if the trust otherwise does not satisfy the definition of a GST trust, the automatic allocation rules contained in section 2632(c)(1) will not apply to the described current-year transfer or to any future transfers made by the transferor to the trust, unless and until another election under this paragraph (b)(3) is made.

(4) *Allocation to other transfers.*—(i) *In general.*—An allocation of GST exemption to property transferred during the transferor's lifetime, other than in a direct skip, is made on Form 709. The allocation must clearly identify the trust to which the allocation is being made, the amount of GST exemption allocated to it, and if the allocation is late or if an inclusion ratio greater than zero is claimed, the value of the trust assets at the effective date of the allocation. See paragraph (b)(4)(ii) of this section. The allocation should also state the inclusion ratio of the trust after the allocation. Except as otherwise provided in this paragraph, an allocation of GST exemption may be made by a formula; e.g., the allocation may be expressed in terms of the amount necessary to produce an inclusion ratio of zero. However, formula allocations made with respect to charitable lead annuity trusts are not valid except to the extent they are dependent on values as finally determined for Federal estate or gift tax purposes. With respect to a timely allocation, an allocation of GST exemption becomes irrevocable after the due date of the return. Except as provided in § 26.2642-3 (relating to charitable lead annuity trusts), an allocation of GST exemption to a trust is void to the extent the amount allocated exceeds the amount necessary to obtain an inclusion ratio of zero with respect to the trust. See § 26.2642-1 for the definition of inclusion ratio. An allocation is also void if the allocation is made with respect to a trust that has no GST potential with respect to the transferor

making the allocation, at the time of the allocation. For this purpose, a trust has GST potential even if the possibility of a GST is so remote as to be negligible.

(ii) *Effective date of allocation.*—(A) *In general.*—(1) Except as otherwise provided, an allocation of GST exemption is effective as of the date of any transfer as to which the Form 709 on which it is made is a timely filed return (a timely allocation). If more than one timely allocation is made, the earlier allocation is modified only if the later allocation clearly identifies the transfer and the nature and extent of the modification. Except as provided in paragraph (d)(1) of this section, an allocation to a trust made on a Form 709 filed after the due date for reporting a transfer to the trust (a late allocation) is effective on the date the Form 709 is filed and is deemed to precede in point of time any taxable event occurring on such date. For purposes of this paragraph (b)(4)(ii), the Form 709 is deemed filed on the date it is postmarked to the Internal Revenue Service address as directed in forms or other guidance published by the Service. See § 26.2642-2 regarding the effect of a late allocation in determining the inclusion ratio, etc. See paragraph (c)(1) of this section regarding allocation of GST exemption to property subject to an estate tax inclusion period. If it is unclear whether an allocation of GST exemption on a Form 709 is a late or a timely allocation to a trust, the allocation is effective in the following order—

(i) To any transfer to the trust disclosed on the return as to which the return is a timely return;

(ii) As a late allocation; and

(iii) To any transfer to the trust not disclosed on the return as to which the return would be a timely return.

(2) A late allocation to a trust may be made on a Form 709 that is timely filed with respect to another transfer. A late allocation is irrevocable when made.

(B) *Amount of allocation.*—If other transfers exist with respect to which GST exemption could be allocated under paragraphs (b)(4)(ii)(A)(1)(*ii*) and (*iii*), any GST exemption allocated under paragraph (b)(4)(ii)(A)(1)(*i*) of this section is allocated in an amount equal to the value of the transferred property as reported on the Form 709. Thus, if the GST exemption allocated on the Form 709 exceeds the value of the transfers reported on that return that have generation-skipping potential, the initial allocation under paragraph (b)(4)(ii)(A)(1)(*i*) of this section is in the amount of the value of those transfers as reported on that return. Any remaining amount of GST exemption allocated on that return is then allocated pursuant to paragraphs (b)(4)(ii)(A)(1)(*ii*) and (*iii*) of this section, notwithstanding any subsequent upward adjustment in value of the transfers reported on the return.

(iii) *Examples.*—The following examples illustrate the provisions of this paragraph (b):

*Example 1. Modification of allocation of GST exemption.* On December 1, 2003, T transfers $100,000 to an irrevocable GST trust described in section 2632(c)(3)(B). The transfer to the trust is not a direct skip. The date prescribed for filing the gift tax return reporting the taxable gift is April 15, 2004. On February 10, 2004, T files a Form 709 on which T properly elects out of the automatic allocation rules contained in section 2632(c)(1) with respect to the transfer in accordance with paragraph (b)(2)(iii) of this section, and allocates $50,000 of GST exemption to the trust. On April 13th of the same year, T files an additional Form 709 on which T confirms the election out of the automatic allocation rules contained in section 2632(c)(1) and allocates $100,000 of GST exemption to the trust in a manner that clearly indicates the intention to modify and supersede the prior allocation with respect to the 2003 transfer. The allocation made on the April 13 return supersedes the prior allocation because it is made on a timely-filed Form 709 that clearly identifies the trust and the nature and extent of the modification of GST exemption allocation. The allocation of $100,000 of GST exemption to the trust is effective as of December 1, 2003. The result would be the same if the amended Form 709 decreased the amount of the GST exemption allocated to the trust.

*Example 2. Modification of allocation of GST exemption.* The facts are the same as in *Example 1* except, on July 8, 2004, T files a Form 709 attempting to reduce the earlier allocation. The return filed on July 8, 2004, is not a timely filed return. The $100,000 GST exemption allocated to the trust, as amended on April 13, 2004, remains in effect because an allocation, once made, is irrevocable and may not be modified after the last date on which a timely filed Form 709 may be filed.

*Example 3. Effective date of late allocation of GST exemption.* On November 15, 2003, T transfers $100,000 to an irrevocable GST trust described in section 2632(c)(3)(B). The transfer to the trust is not a direct skip. The date prescribed for filing the gift tax return reporting the taxable gift is April 15, 2004. On February 10, 2004, T files a Form 709 on which T properly elects out of the automatic allocation rules

contained in section 2632(c)(1) in accordance with paragraph (b)(2)(iii) of this section with respect to that transfer. On December 1, 2004, T files a Form 709 and allocates $50,000 to the trust. The allocation is effective as of December 1, 2004.

*Example 4. Effective date of late allocation of GST exemption.* T transfers $100,000 to an irrevocable GST trust on December 1, 2003, in a transfer that is not a direct skip. On April 15, 2004, T files a Form 709 on which T properly elects out of the automatic allocation rules contained in section 2632(c)(1) with respect to the entire transfer in accordance with paragraph (b)(2)(iii) of this section and T does not make an allocation of any GST exemption on the Form 709. On September 1, 2004, the trustee makes a taxable distribution from the trust to T's grandchild in the amount of $30,000. Immediately prior to the distribution, the value of the trust assets was $150,000. On the same date, T allocates GST exemption to the trust in the amount of $50,000. The allocation of GST exemption on the date of the transfer is treated as preceding in point of time the taxable distribution. At the time of the GST, the trust has an inclusion ratio of .6667 (1 - (50,000/150,000)).

*Example 5. Automatic allocation to split-gift.* On December 1, 2003, T transfers $50,000 to an irrevocable GST Trust described in section 2632(c)(3)(B). The transfer to the trust is not a direct skip. On April 30, 2004, T and T's spouse, S, each files an initial gift tax return for 2003, on which they consent, pursuant to section 2513, to have the gift treated as if one-half had been made by each. In spite of being made on a late-filed gift tax return for 2003, the election under section 2513 is valid because neither spouse had filed a timely gift tax return for that year. Previously, neither T nor S filed a timely gift tax return electing out of the automatic allocation rules contained in section 2632(c)(1). As a result of the election under section 2513, which is retroactive to the date of T's transfer, T and S are each treated as the transferor of one-half of the property transferred in the indirect skip. Thus, $25,000 of T's unused GST exemption and $25,000 of S's unused GST exemption is automatically allocated to the trust. Both allocations are effective on and after the date that T made the transfer. The result would be the same if T's transfer constituted a direct skip subject to the automatic allocation rules contained in section 2632(b).

*Example 6. Partial allocation of GST exemption.* On December 1, 2003, T transfers $100,000 to an irrevocable GST trust described in section 2632(c)(3)(B). The transfer to the trust is not a direct skip. The date prescribed for filing the gift tax return reporting the taxable gift is April 15, 2004. On February 10, 2004, T files a Form 709 on which T allocates $40,000 of GST exemption to the trust. By filing a timely Form 709 on which a partial allocation is made of $40,000, T effectively elected out of the automatic allocation rules for the remaining value of the transfer for which T did not allocate GST exemption.

(iv) *Example.*—The following example illustrates language that may be used in the statement required under paragraph (b)(2)(iii) of this section to elect out of the automatic allocation rules under various scenarios:

*Example 1.* On March 1, 2006, T transfers $100,000 to Trust B, a GST trust described in section 2632(c)(3)(B). Subsequently, on September 15, 2006, T transfers an additional $75,000 to Trust B. No other transfers are made to Trust B in 2006. T attaches an election out statement to a timely filed Form 709 for calendar year 2006. Except with regard to paragraph (v) of this *Example 1*, the election out statement identifies Trust B as required under paragraph (b)(2)(iii)(B) of this section, and contains the following alternative election statements:

(i) "T hereby elects that the automatic allocation rules will not apply to the $100,000 transferred to Trust B on March 1, 2006." The election out of the automatic allocation rules will be effective only for T's March 1, 2006, transfer and will not apply to T's $75,000 transfer made on September 15, 2006.

(ii) "T hereby elects that the automatic allocation rules will not apply to any transfers to Trust B in 2006." The election out of the automatic allocation rules will be effective for T's transfers to Trust B made on March 1, 2006, and September 15, 2006.

(iii) "T hereby elects that the automatic allocation rules will not apply to any transfers to Trust B made by T in 2006 or to any additional transfers T may make to Trust B in subsequent years." The election out of the automatic allocation rules will be effective for T's transfers to Trust B in 2006 and for all future transfers to be made by T to Trust B, unless and until T terminates the election out of the automatic allocation rules.

(iv) "T hereby elects that the automatic allocation rules will not apply to any transfers T has made or will make to Trust B in the years 2006 through 2008." The election out of the automatic allocation rules will be effective for T's transfers to Trust B in 2006 through 2008. T's transfers to Trust B after 2008 will be subject to the automatic allocation rules, unless T elects out of those rules for one or more years after 2008. T may terminate the election out of the automatic allocation rules for 2007, 2008, or both in accordance with the termination rules of paragraph (b)(2)(iii)(E) of this section. T may terminate the election out for one or more of the transfers made in 2006 only on a later but still timely filed Form 709 for calendar year 2006.

(v) "T hereby elects that the automatic allocation rules will not apply to any current or future transfer that T may make to any trust." The election out of the automatic allocation rules will be effective for all of T's transfers (current-year and future) to Trust B and to any and all other trusts (whether such trusts exist in 2006 or are created in a later year), unless and until T terminates the election out of the automatic allocation rules. T may terminate the election out with regard to one or more (or all) of the transfers covered by the election out in accordance with the termination rules of paragraph (b)(2)(iii)(E) of this section.

(c) *Special rules during an estate tax inclusion period.*—(1) *In general.*—(i) *Automatic allocations with respect to direct skips and indirect skips.*—A direct skip or an indirect skip that is subject to an estate tax inclusion period (ETIP) is deemed to have been made only at the close of the ETIP. The transferor may prevent the automatic allocation of GST exemption to a direct skip or an indirect skip by electing out of the automatic allocation rules at any time prior to the due date of the Form 709 for the calendar year in which the close of the ETIP occurs (whether or not any transfer was made in the calendar year for which the Form 709 was filed, and whether or not a Form 709 otherwise would be required to be filed for that year). See paragraph (b)(2)(i) of this section regarding the automatic allocation of GST exemption to an indirect skip subject to an ETIP.

(ii) *Other allocations.*—An affirmative allocation of GST exemption cannot be revoked, but becomes effective as of (and no earlier than) the date of the close of the ETIP with respect to the trust. If an allocation has not been made prior to the close of the ETIP, an allocation of exemption is effective as of the close of the ETIP during the transferor's lifetime if made by the due date for filing the Form 709 for the calendar year in which the close of the ETIP occurs (timely ETIP return). An allocation of exemption is effective in the case of the close of the ETIP by reason of the death of the transferor as provided in paragraph (d) of this section.

(iii) *Portion of trust subject to ETIP.*—If any part of a trust is subject to an ETIP, the entire trust is subject to the ETIP. See § 26.2642-1(b)(2) for rules determining the inclusion ratio applicable in the case of GSTs during an ETIP.

(2) *Estate tax inclusion period defined.*—(i) *In general.*—An ETIP is the period during which, should death occur, the value of transferred property would be includible (other than by reason of section 2035) in the gross estate of—

(A) The transferor; or

(B) The spouse of the transferor.

(ii) *Exceptions.*—(A) For purposes of paragraph (c)(2) of this section, the value of transferred property is not considered as being subject to inclusion in the gross estate of the transferor or the spouse of the transferor if the possibility that the property will be included is so remote as to be negligible. A possibility is so remote as to be negligible if it can be ascertained by actuarial standards that there is less than a 5 percent probability that the property will be included in the gross estate.

(B) For purposes of paragraph (c)(2) of this section, the value of transferred property is not considered as being subject to inclusion in the gross estate of the spouse of the transferor, if the spouse possesses with respect to any transfer to the trust, a right to withdraw no more than the greater of $5,000 or 5 percent of the trust corpus, and such withdrawal right terminates no later than 60 days after the transfer to the trust.

(C) The rules of this paragraph (c)(2) do not apply to qualified terminable interest property with respect to which the special election under § 26.2652-2 has been made.

(3) *Termination of an ETIP.*—An ETIP terminates on the first to occur of—

(i) The death of the transferor;

(ii) The time at which no portion of the property is includible in the transferor's gross estate (other than by reason of section 2035) or, in the case of an individual who is a transferor solely by reason of an election under section 2513, the time at which no portion would be includible in the gross estate of the individual's spouse (other than by reason of section 2035);

(iii) The time of a GST, but only with respect to the property involved in the GST; or

(iv) In the case of an ETIP arising by reason of an interest or power held by the transferor's spouse under subsection (c)(2)(i)(B) of this section, at the first to occur of—

(A) The death of the spouse; or

(B) The time at which no portion of the property would be includible in the spouse's gross estate (other than by reason of section 2035).

(4) *Treatment of direct skips.*—If property transferred to a skip person is subject to an ETIP, the direct skip is treated as occurring on the termination of the ETIP.

(5) *Examples.*—The following examples illustrate the rules of this section as they apply to the termination of an ETIP during the lifetime of the transferor. In each example assume that T transfers $100,000 to an irrevocable trust:

*Example 1. Allocation of GST exemption during ETIP.* The trust instrument provides that trust income is to be paid to T for 9 years or until T's prior death. The trust principal is to be paid to T's grandchild on the termination of T's income interest. If T dies within the 9-year period, the value of the trust principal is includible in T's gross estate under section 2036(a). Thus, the trust is subject to an ETIP. T files a timely Form 709 reporting the transfer and allocating $100,000 of GST exemption to the trust. The allocation of GST exemption to the trust is not effective until the termination of the ETIP.

*Example 2. Effect of prior allocation on termination of ETIP.* The facts are the same as in *Example 1*, except the trustee has the power to invade trust principal on behalf of T's grandchild, GC, during the term of T's income interest. In year 4, when the value of the trust is $200,000, the trustee distributes $15,000 to GC. The distribution is a taxable distribution. The ETIP with respect to the property distributed to GC terminates at the time of the taxable distribution. See paragraph (c)(3)(iii) of this section. Solely for purposes of determining the trust's inclusion ratio with respect to the taxable distribution, the prior $100,000 allocation of GST exemption (as well as any additional allocation made on a timely ETIP return) is effective immediately prior to the taxable distribution. See § 26.2642-1(b)(2). The trust's inclusion ratio with respect to the taxable distribution is therefore .50 (1-(100,000/200,000)).

*Example 3. Split-gift transfers subject to ETIP.* The trust instrument provides that trust income is to be paid to T for 9 years or until T's prior death. The trust principal is to be paid to T's grandchild on the termination of T's income interest. T files a timely Form 709 reporting the transfer. T's spouse, S, consents to have the gift treated as made one-half by S under section 2513. Because S is treated as transferring one-half of the property to T's grandchild, S becomes the transferor of one-half of the trust for purposes of chapter 13. Because the value of the trust would be includible in T's gross estate if T died immediately after the transfer, S's transfer is subject to an ETIP. If S should die prior to the termination of the trust, S's executor may allocate S's GST exemption to the trust, but only to the portion of the trust for which S is treated as the transferor. However, the allocation does not become effective until the earlier of the expiration of T's income interest or T's death.

*Example 4. Transfer of retained interest as ETIP termination.* The trust instrument provides that trust income is to be paid to T for 9 years or until T's prior death. The trust principal is to be paid to T's grandchild on the termination of T's income interest. Four years after the initial transfer, T transfers the income interest to T's sibling. The ETIP with respect to the trust terminates on T's transfer of the income interest because, after the transfer, the trust property would not be includible in T's gross estate (other than by reason of section 2035) if T died at that time.

*Example 5. Election out of automatic allocation of GST exemption for trust subject to an ETIP.* On December 1, 2003, T transfers $100,000 to Trust A, an irrevocable GST trust described in section 2632(c)(3) that is subject to an estate tax inclusion period (ETIP). T made no other gifts in 2003. The ETIP terminates on December 31, 2008. T timely files a gift tax return (Form 709) reporting the gift on April 15, 2004. On May 15, 2006, T files a Form 709 on which T properly elects out of the automatic allocation rules contained in section 2632(c)(1) with respect to the December 1, 2003, transfer to Trust A in accordance with paragraph (b)(2)(iii) of this section. Because the indirect skip is not deemed to occur until December 31, 2008, T's election out of automatic GST allocation filed on May 15, 2006, is timely, and will be effective as of December 31, 2008 (unless revoked on a Form 709 filed on or before the due date of a Form 709 for calendar year 2008).

(d) *Allocations after the transferor's death.*—(1) *Allocation by executor.*—Except as otherwise provided in this paragraph (d), an allocation of a decedent's unused GST exemption by the executor of the decedent's estate is made on the appropriate United States Estate (and Generation-Skipping Transfer) Tax Return (Form 706 or Form 706NA) filed on or before the date prescribed for filing the return by section 6075(a) (including any extensions actually granted (the due date)). An allocation of GST exemption with respect to property included in the gross estate of a decedent is effective as of the date of death. A timely allocation of GST exemption by an executor with respect to a lifetime transfer of property that is not included in the transferor's gross estate is made on a Form 709. A late allocation of

GST exemption by an executor, other than an allocation that is deemed to be made under section 2632(b)(1) or (c)(1), with respect to a lifetime transfer of property is made on Form 706, Form 706NA, or Form 709 (filed on or before the due date of the transferor's estate tax return) and applies as of the date the allocation is filed. An allocation of GST exemption to a trust (whether or not funded at the time the Form 706 or Form 706NA is filed) is effective if the notice of allocation clearly identifies the trust and the amount of the decedent's GST exemption allocated to the trust. An executor may allocate the decedent's GST exemption by use of a formula. For purposes of this section, an allocation is void if the allocation is made for a trust that has no GST potential with respect to the transferor for whom the allocation is being made, as of the date of the transferor's death. For this purpose, a trust has GST potential even if the possibility of a GST is so remote as to be negligible.

(2) *Automatic allocation after death.*—A decedent's unused GST exemption is automatically allocated on the due date for filing Form 706 or Form 706NA to the extent not otherwise allocated by the decedent's executor on or before that date. The automatic allocation occurs whether or not a return is actually required to be filed. Unused GST exemption is allocated pro rata (subject to the rules of § 26.2642-2(b)), on the basis of the value of the property as finally determined for purposes of chapter 11 (chapter 11 value), first to direct skips treated as occurring at the transferor's death. The balance, if any, of unused GST exemption is allocated pro rata (subject to the rules of § 26.2642-2(b)) on the basis of the chapter 11 value of the nonexempt portion of the trust property (or in the case of trusts that are not included in the gross estate, on the basis of the date of death value of the trust) to trusts with respect to which a taxable termination may occur or from which a taxable distribution may be made. The automatic allocation of GST exemption is irrevocable, and an allocation made by the executor after the automatic allocation is made is ineffective. No automatic allocation of GST exemption is made to a trust that will have a new transferor with respect to the entire trust prior to the occurrence of any GST with respect to the trust. In addition, no automatic allocation of GST exemption is made to a trust if, during the nine month period ending immediately after the death of the transferor—

(i) No GST has occurred with respect to the trust; and

(ii) At the end of such period no future GST can occur with respect to the trust.

(e) *Effective dates.*—This section is applicable as provided in § 26.2601-1(c), with the following exceptions:

(1) Paragraphs (b)(2) and (b)(3), the third sentence of paragraph (b)(4)(i), the fourth sentence of paragraph (b)(4)(ii)(A)(1), paragraphs (b)(4)(iii) and (b)(4)(iv), and the fourth sentence of paragraph (d)(1) of this section, which will apply to elections made on or after July 13, 2004; and

(2) Paragraph (c)(1), and *Example 5* of paragraph (c)(5), which will apply to elections made on or after June 29, 2005. [Reg. § 26.2632-1.]

☐ [*T.D. 8644, 12-26-95. Amended by T.D. 9208, 6-28-2005.*]

### [Reg. § 26.2641-1]

**§ 26.2641-1. Applicable rate of tax.**—The rate of tax applicable to any GST (applicable rate) is determined by multiplying the maximum Federal estate tax rate in effect at the time of the GST by the inclusion ratio (as defined in § 26.2642-1). For this purpose, the maximum Federal estate tax rate is the maximum rate set forth under section 2001(c) (without regard to section 2001(c)(2)). [Reg. § 26.2641-1.]

☐ [*T.D. 8644, 12-26-95.*]

### [Reg. § 26.2642-1]

**§ 26.2642-1. Inclusion ratio.**—(a) *In general.*—Except as otherwise provided in this section, the inclusion ratio is determined by subtracting the applicable fraction (rounded to the nearest one-thousandth (.001)) from 1. In rounding the applicable fraction to the nearest one-thousandth, any amount that is midway between one one-thousandth and another one-thousandth is rounded up to the higher of those two amounts. For generation-skipping transfer tax rules related to an ABLE account established under section 529A, see § 1.529A-4 of this chapter.

(b) *Numerator of applicable fraction.*—(1) *In general.*—Except as otherwise provided in this paragraph (b), and in §§ 26.2642-3 (providing a special rule for charitable lead annuity trusts) and 26.2642-4 (providing rules for the redetermination of the applicable fraction), the numerator of the applicable fraction is the amount of GST exemption allocated to the trust (or to the transferred property in the case of a direct skip not in trust).

(2) *GSTs occurring during an ETIP.*—(i) *In general.*—For purposes of determining the inclusion ratio with respect to a taxable termination or a taxable distribution that occurs during an ETIP, the numerator of the applicable fraction is the sum of—

(A) The GST exemption previously allocated to the trust (including any allocation made to the trust prior to any taxable termination or distribution) reduced (but not below zero) by the nontax amount of any prior GSTs with respect to the trust; and

(B) Any GST exemption allocated to the trust on a timely ETIP return filed after the termination of the ETIP. See § 26.2632-1(c)(5) *Example 2.*

(ii) *Nontax amount of a prior GST.*—(1) The nontax amount of a prior GST with respect to the trust is the amount of the GST multiplied by the applicable fraction attributable to the trust at the time of the prior GST.

(2) For rules regarding the allocation of GST exemption to property during an ETIP, see § 26.2632-1(c).

(c) *Denominator of applicable fraction.*—(1) *In general.*—Except as otherwise provided in this paragraph (c) and in §§ 26.2642-3 and 26.2642-4, the denominator of the applicable fraction is the value of the property transferred to the trust (or transferred in a direct skip not in trust) (as determined under § 26.2642-2) reduced by the sum of—

(i) Any Federal estate tax and any State death tax incurred by reason of the transfer that is chargeable to the trust and is actually recovered from the trust;

(ii) The amount of any charitable deduction allowed under section 2055, 2106, or 2522 with respect to the transfer; and

(iii) In the case of a direct skip, the value of the portion of the transfer that is a nontaxable gift. See paragraph (c)(3) of this section for the definition of nontaxable gift.

(2) *Zero denominator.*—If the denominator of the applicable fraction is zero, the inclusion ratio is zero.

(3) *Nontaxable gifts.*—Generally, for purposes of chapter 13, a transfer is a nontaxable gift to the extent the transfer is excluded from taxable gifts by reason of section 2503(b) (after application of section 2513) or section 2503(e). However, a transfer to a trust for the benefit of an individual is not a nontaxable gift for purposes of this section unless—

(i) Trust principal or income may, during the individual's lifetime, be distributed only to or for the benefit of the individual; and

(ii) The assets of the trust will be includible in the gross estate of the individual if the individual dies before the trust terminates.

(d) *Examples.*—The following examples illustrate the provisions of this section. See § 26.2652-2(d) *Examples 2* and *3* for illustrations of the computation of the inclusion ratio where the special (reverse QTIP) election may be applicable.

*Example 1. Computation of the inclusion ratio.* T transfers $100,000 to a newly-created irrevocable trust providing that income is to be accumulated for 10 years. At the end of 10 years, the accumulated income is to be distributed to T's child, C, and the trust principal is to be paid to T's grandchild. T allocates $40,000 of T's GST exemption to the trust on a timely-filed gift tax return. The applicable fraction with respect to the trust is .40 ($40,000 (the amount of GST exemption allocated to the trust) over $100,000 (the value of the property transferred to the trust)). The inclusion ratio is .60 (1 − .40). If the maximum Federal estate tax rate is 55 percent at the time of a GST, the rate of tax applicable to the transfer (applicable rate) will be .333 (55 percent (the maximum estate tax rate) x .60 (the inclusion ratio)).

*Example 2. Gift entirely nontaxable.* On December 1, 1996, T transfers $10,000 to an irrevocable trust for the benefit of T's grandchild, GC. GC possesses a right to withdraw any contributions to the trust such that the entire transfer qualifies for the annual exclusion under section 2503(b). Under the terms of the trust, the income is to be paid to GC for 10 years or until GC's prior death. Upon the expiration of GC's income interest, the trust principal is payable to GC or GC's estate. The transfer to the trust is a direct skip. T made no prior gifts to or for the benefit of GC during 1996. The entire $10,000 transfer is a nontaxable transfer. For purposes of computing the tax on the direct skip, the denominator of the applicable fraction is zero, and thus, the inclusion ratio is zero.

*Example 3. Gift nontaxable in part.* T transfers $12,000 to an irrevocable trust for the benefit of T's grandchild, GC. Under the terms of the trust, the income is to be paid to GC for 10 years or until GC's prior death. Upon the expiration of GC's income interest, the trust principal is payable to GC or GC's estate. Further, GC has the right to withdraw $10,000 of any contribution to the trust such that $10,000 of the transfer qualifies for the annual exclusion under section 2503(b). The amount of the nontaxable transfer is $10,000. Solely for purposes of computing the tax on the direct skip, T's transfer is divided into two portions. One portion is equal to the amount of the nontaxable transfer ($10,000) and has a zero inclusion ratio; the other portion is $2,000 ($12,000 - $10,000). With respect to the $2,000 portion, the denominator of the applicable fraction is $2,000. Assuming that T has sufficient GST exemption available, the numerator of the applicable fraction is $2,000 (unless T elects to have the automatic allocation provisions not apply). Thus, assuming T does not elect to have the automatic allocation not apply, the applicable fraction is one ($2,000/$2,000 = 1) and the inclusion ratio is zero (1 - 1 = 0).

*Example 4. Gift nontaxable in part.* Assume the same facts as in *Example 3*, except T files a timely Form 709 electing that the automatic allocation of GST exemption not apply to the $12,000 transferred in the direct skip. T's transfer is divided into two portions, a $10,000 portion with a zero inclusion ratio and a $2,000 portion with an applicable fraction of zero (0/$2,000 = 0) and an inclusion ratio of one (1 - 0 = 1). [Reg. § 26.2642-1.]

☐ [*T.D. 8644, 12-26-95. Amended by T.D. 9923, 11-18-2020.*]

**[Reg. § 26.2642-2]**

**§ 26.2642-2. Valuation.**—(a) *Lifetime transfers.*—(1) *In general.*—For purposes of determining the denominator of the applicable fraction, the value of property transferred during life is its fair market value on the effective date of the allocation of GST exemption. In the case of a timely allocation under § 26.2632-1(b)(2)(ii), the denominator of the applicable fraction is the fair market value of the property as finally determined for purposes of chapter 12.

(2) *Special rule for late allocations during life.*—If a transferor makes a late allocation of GST exemption to a trust, the value of the property transferred to the trust is the fair market value of the trust assets determined on the effective date of the allocation of GST exemption. Except as otherwise provided in this paragraph (a)(2), if a transferor makes a late allocation of GST exemption to a trust, the transferor may, solely for purposes of determining the fair market value of the trust assets, elect to treat the allocation as having been made on the first day of the month during which the late allocation is made (valuation date). An election under this paragraph (a)(2) is not effective with respect to a life insurance policy or a trust holding a life insurance policy, if the insured individual has died. An allocation subject to the election contained in this paragraph (a)(2) is not effective until it is actually filed with the Internal Revenue Service. The election is made by stating on the Form 709 on which the allocation is made—

(i) That the election is being made;

(ii) The applicable valuation date; and

(iii) The fair market value of the trust assets on the valuation date.

(b) *Transfers at death.*—(1) *In general.*—Except as provided in paragraphs (b)(2) and (3) of this section, in determining the denominator of the applicable fraction, the value of property included in the decedent's gross estate is its value for purposes of chapter 11. In the case of qualified real property with respect to which the election under section 2032A is made, the value of the property is the value determined under section 2032A provided the recapture agreement described in section 2032A(d)(2) filed with the Internal Revenue Service specifically provides for the signatories' consent to the imposition of, and personal liability for, additional GST tax in the event an additional estate tax is imposed under section 2032A(c). See § 26.2642-4(a)(4). If the recapture agreement does not contain these provisions, the value of qualified real property as to which the election under section 2032A is made is the fair market value of the property determined without regard to the provisions of section 2032A.

(2) *Special rule for pecuniary payments.*—(i) *In general.*—If a pecuniary payment is satisfied with cash, the denominator of the applicable fraction is the pecuniary amount. If property other than cash is used to satisfy a pecuniary payment, the denominator of the applicable fraction is the pecuniary amount only if payment must be made with property on the basis of the value of the property on—

(A) The date of distribution; or

(B) A date other than the date of distribution, but only if the pecuniary payment must be satisfied on a basis that fairly reflects net appreciation and depreciation (occurring between the valuation date and the date of distribution) in all of the assets from which the distribution could have been made.

(ii) *Other pecuniary amounts payable in kind.*—The denominator of the applicable fraction with respect to any property used to satisfy any other pecuniary payment payable in kind is the date of distribution value of the property.

(3) *Special rule for residual transfers after payment of a pecuniary payment.*—(i) *In general.*—Except as otherwise provided in this para-

graph (b)(3), the denominator of the applicable fraction with respect to a residual transfer of property after the satisfaction of a pecuniary payment is the estate tax value of the assets available to satisfy the pecuniary payment reduced, if the pecuniary payment carries appropriate interest (as defined in paragraph (b)(4) of this section), by the pecuniary amount. The denominator of the applicable fraction with respect to a residual transfer of property after the satisfaction of a pecuniary payment that does not carry appropriate interest is the estate tax value of the assets available to satisfy the pecuniary payment reduced by the present value of the pecuniary payment. For purposes of this paragraph (b)(3)(i), the present value of the pecuniary payment is determined by using—

(A) The interest rate applicable under section 7520 at the death of the transferor; and

(B) The period between the date of the transferor's death and the date the pecuniary amount is paid.

(ii) *Special rule for residual transfers after pecuniary payments payable in kind.*—The denominator of the applicable fraction with respect to any residual transfer after satisfaction of a pecuniary payment payable in kind is the date of distribution value of the property distributed in satisfaction of the residual transfer, unless the pecuniary payment must be satisfied on the basis of the value of the property on—

(A) The date of distribution; or

(B) A date other than the date of distribution, but only if the pecuniary payment must be satisfied on a basis that fairly reflects net appreciation and depreciation (occurring between the valuation date and the date of distribution) in all of the assets from which the distribution could have been made.

(4) *Appropriate interest.*—(i) *In general.*—For purposes of this section and § 26.2654-1 (relating to certain trusts treated as separate trusts), appropriate interest means that interest must be payable from the date of death of the transferor (or from the date specified under applicable State law requiring the payment of interest) to the date of payment at a rate—

(A) At least equal to—

(1) The statutory rate of interest, if any, applicable to pecuniary bequests under the law of the State whose law governs the administration of the estate or trust; or

(2) If no such rate is indicated under applicable State law, 80 percent of the rate that is applicable under section 7520 at the death of the transferor; and

(B) Not in excess of the greater of—

(1) The statutory rate of interest, if any, applicable to pecuniary bequests under the law of the State whose law governs the administration of the trust; or

(2) 120 percent of the rate that is applicable under section 7520 at the death of the transferor.

(ii) *Pecuniary payments deemed to carry appropriate interest.*—For purposes of this paragraph (b)(4), if a pecuniary payment does not carry appropriate interest, the pecuniary payment is considered to carry appropriate interest to the extent—

(A) The entire payment is made or property is irrevocably set aside to satisfy the entire pecuniary payment within 15 months of the transferor's death; or

(B) The governing instrument or applicable local law specifically requires the executor or trustee to allocate to the pecuniary payment a pro rata share of the income earned by the fund from which the pecuniary payment is to be made between the date of death of the transferor and the date of payment. For purposes of paragraph (b)(4)(ii)(A) of this section, property is irrevocably set aside if it is segregated and held in a separate account pending distribution.

(c) *Examples.*—The following examples illustrate the provisions of this section:

*Example 1.* T transfers $100,000 to a newly-created irrevocable trust on December 15, 1996. The trust provides that income is to be paid to T's child for 10 years. At the end of the 10-year period, the trust principal is to be paid to T's grandchild. T does not allocate any GST exemption to the trust on the gift tax return reporting the transfer. On November 15, 1997, T files a Form 709 allocating $50,000 of GST exemption to the trust. Because the allocation was made on a late filed return, the value of the property transferred to the trust is determined on the date the allocation is filed (unless an election is made pursuant to paragraph (a)(2) of this section to value the trust property as of the first day of the month in which the allocation document is filed with the Internal Revenue Service). On November 15, 1997, the value of the trust property is $150,000. Effective as of November 15, 1997, the applicable fraction with respect to the trust is .333 ($50,000 (the amount of GST exemption allocated to the trust) over $150,000 (the value of the trust principal on the effective date of the GST exemption allocation)), and the inclusion ratio is .667 (1.0 - .333).

*Example 2.* The facts are the same as in *Example 1*, except the value of the trust property is $80,000 on November 15, 1997. The applicable fraction is .625 ($50,000 over $80,000) and the inclusion ratio is .375 (1.0 - .625).

*Example 3.* T transfers $100,000 to a newly-created irrevocable trust on December 15, 1996. The trust provides that income is to be paid to T's child for 10 years. At the end of the 10-year period, the trust principal is to be paid to T's grandchild. T does not allocate any GST exemption to the trust on the gift tax return reporting the transfer. On November 15, 1997, T files a Form 709 allocating $50,000 of GST exemption to the trust. T elects to value the trust principal on the first day of the month in which the allocation is made pursuant to the election provided in paragraph (a)(2) of this section. Because the late allocation is made in November, the value of the trust is determined as of November 1, 1997. [Reg. §26.2642-2.]

☐ [T.D. 8644, 12-26-95.]

### [Reg. §26.2642-3]

**§26.2642-3. Special rule for charitable lead annuity trusts.—** (a) *In general.*—In determining the applicable fraction with respect to a charitable lead annuity trust—

(1) The numerator is the adjusted generation-skipping transfer tax exemption (adjusted GST exemption); and

(2) The denominator is the value of all property in the trust immediately after the termination of the charitable lead annuity.

(b) *Adjusted GST exemption defined.*—The adjusted GST exemption is the amount of GST exemption allocated to the trust increased by an amount equal to the interest that would accrue if an amount equal to the allocated GST exemption were invested at the rate used to determine the amount of the estate or gift tax charitable deduction, compounded annually, for the actual period of the charitable lead annuity. If a late allocation is made to a charitable lead annuity trust, the adjusted GST exemption is the amount of GST exemption allocated to the trust increased by the interest that would accrue if invested at such rate for the period beginning on the date of the late allocation and extending for the balance of the actual period of the charitable lead annuity. The amount of GST exemption allocated to a charitable lead annuity trust is not reduced even though it is ultimately determined that the allocation of a lesser amount of GST exemption would have resulted in an inclusion ratio of zero. For purposes of chapter 13, a charitable lead annuity trust is any trust providing an interest in the form of a guaranteed annuity described in §25.2522(c)-3(c)(2)(vi) of this chapter for which the transferor is allowed a charitable deduction for Federal estate or gift tax purposes.

(c) *Example.*—The following example illustrates the provisions of this section:

*Example.* T creates a charitable lead annuity trust for a 10-year term with the remainder payable to T's grandchild. T timely allocates an amount of GST exemption to the trust which T expects will ultimately result in a zero inclusion ratio. However, at the end of the charitable lead interest, because the property has not appreciated to the extent T anticipated, the numerator of the applicable fraction is greater than the denominator. The inclusion ratio for the trust is zero. No portion of the GST exemption allocated to the trust is restored to T or to T's estate. [Reg. §26.2642-3.]

☐ [T.D. 8644, 12-26-95.]

### [Reg. §26.2642-4]

**§26.2642-4. Redetermination of applicable fraction.—**(a) *In general.*—The applicable fraction for a trust is redetermined whenever additional exemption is allocated to the trust or when certain changes occur with respect to the principal of the trust. Except as otherwise provided in this paragraph(a), the numerator of the redetermined applicable fraction is the sum of the amount of GST exemption currently being allocated to the trust (if any) plus the value of the nontax portion of the trust, and the denominator of the redetermined applicable fraction is the value of the trust principal immediately after the event occurs. The nontax portion of a trust is determined by multiplying the value of the trust assets, determined immediately prior to the event, by the then applicable fraction.

(1) *Multiple transfers to a single trust.*—If property is added to an existing trust, the denominator of the redetermined applicable fraction is the value of the trust immediately after the addition reduced as provided in §26.2642-1(c).

(2) *Consolidation of separate trusts.*—If separate trusts created by one transferor are consolidated, a single applicable fraction for the consolidated trust is determined. The numerator of the redetermined applicable fraction is the sum of the nontax portions of each trust immediately prior to the consolidation.

(3) *Property included in transferor's gross estate.*—If the value of property held in a trust created by the transferor, with respect to which an allocation was made at a time that the trust was not subject to an ETIP, is included in the transferor's gross estate, the applicable fraction is redetermined if additional GST exemption is allocated to the property. The numerator of the redetermined applicable fraction is an amount equal to the nontax portion of the property immediately after the death of the transferor increased by the amount of GST exemption allocated by the executor of the transferor's estate to the trust. If additional GST exemption is not allocated to the trust, then, except as provided in this paragraph (a)(3), the applicable fraction immediately before death is not changed, if the trust was not subject to an ETIP at the time GST exemption was allocated to the trust. In any event, the denominator of the applicable fraction is reduced to reflect any federal or state, estate or inheritance taxes paid from the trust.

(4) *Imposition of recapture tax under section 2032A.*—(i) If an additional estate tax is imposed under section 2032A and if the section 2032A election was effective (under §26.2642-2(b)) for purposes of the GST tax, the applicable fraction with respect to the property is redetermined as of the date of death of the transferor. In making the redetermination, any available GST exemption not allocated at the death of the transferor (or at a prior recapture event) is automatically allocated to the property. The denominator of the applicable fraction is the fair market value of the property at the date of the transferor's death reduced as provided in §26.2642-1(c) and further reduced by the amount of the additional GST tax actually recovered from the trust.

(ii) The GST tax imposed with respect to any taxable termination, taxable distribution, or direct skip occurring prior to the recapture event is recomputed based on the applicable fraction as redetermined. Any additional GST tax as recomputed is due and payable on the date that is six months after the event that causes the imposition of the additional estate tax under section 2032A. The additional GST tax is remitted with Form 706-A and is reported by attaching a statement to Form 706-A showing the computation of the additional GST tax.

(iii) The applicable fraction, as redetermined under this section, is also used in determining any GST tax imposed with respect to GSTs occurring after the date of the recapture event.

(b) *Examples.*—The following examples illustrate the principles of this section:

*Example 1. Allocation of additional exemption.* T transfers $200,000 to an irrevocable trust under which the income is payable to T's child, C, for life. Upon the termination of the trust, the remainder is payable to T's grandchild, GC. At a time when no ETIP exists with respect to the trust property, T makes a timely allocation of $100,000 of GST exemption, resulting in an inclusion ratio of .50. Subsequently, when the entire trust property is valued at $500,000, T allocates an additional $100,000 of T's unused GST exemption to the trust. The inclusion ratio of the trust is recomputed at that time. The numerator of the applicable fraction is $350,000 ($250,000 (the nontax portion as of the date of the allocation) plus $100,000 (the GST exemption currently being allocated)). The denominator is $500,000 (the date of allocation fair market value of the trust). The inclusion ratio is .30 (1 - .70).

*Example 2. Multiple transfers to a trust, allocation both timely and late.* On December 10, 1993, T transfers $10,000 to an irrevocable trust that does not satisfy the requirements of section 2642(c)(2). T makes identical transfers to the trust on December 10, 1994, 1995, 1996, and on January 15, 1997. Immediately after the transfer on January 15, 1997, the value of the trust principal is $40,000. On January 14, 1998, when the value of the trust principal is $50,000, T allocates $30,000 of GST exemption to the trust. T discloses the 1997 transfer on the Form 709 filed on January 14, 1998. Thus, T's allocation is a timely allocation with respect to the transfer in 1997, $10,000 of the allocation is effective as of the date of that transfer, and, on and after January 15, 1997, the inclusion ratio of the trust is .75 (1 - ($10,000/$40,000)). The balance of the allocation is a late allocation with respect to prior transfers to the trust and is effective as of January 14, 1998. In redetermining the inclusion ratio as of that date, the numerator of the redetermined applicable fraction is $32,500 ($12,500 (.25 x $50,000), the nontax portion of the trust on January 14, 1998 plus $20,000 (the amount of GST exemption allocated late to the trust). The denominator of the new applicable fraction is $50,000 (the value of the trust principal at the time of the late allocation).

*Example 3. Excess allocation.* (i) T creates an irrevocable trust for the benefit of T's child and grandchild in 1996 transferring $50,000 to the trust on the date of creation. T allocates no GST exemption to the trust on the Form 709 reporting the transfer. On July 1, 1997 (when the value of the trust property is $60,000), T transfers an additional $40,000 to the trust.

(ii) On April 15, 1998, when the value of the trust is $150,000, T files a Form 709 reporting the 1997 transfer and allocating $150,000 of GST exemption to the trust. The allocation is a timely allocation of $40,000 with respect to the 1997 transfer and is effective as of that date. Thus, the applicable fraction for the trust as of July 1, 1997 is .40 ($40,000/$100,000 ($40,000 + $60,000)).

(iii) The allocation is also a late allocation of $90,000, the amount necessary to attain a zero inclusion ratio on April 15, 1998, computed as follows: $60,000 (the nontax portion immediately prior to the allocation (.40 X $150,000)) plus $90,000 (the additional allocation necessary to produce a zero inclusion ratio based on a denominator of $150,000)/$150,000 equals one and, thus, an inclusion ratio of zero. The balance of the allocation, $20,000 ($150,000 less the timely allocation of $40,000 less the late allocation of $90,000) is void.

*Example 4. Undisclosed transfer.* (i) The facts are the same as in *Example 3*, except that on February 1, 1998 (when the value of the trust is $150,000), T transfers an additional $50,000 to the trust and the value of the entire trust corpus on April 15, 1998 is $220,000. The Form 709 filed on April 15, 1998 does not disclose the 1998 transfer. Under the rule in § 26.2632-1(b)(2)(ii), the allocation is effective first as a timely allocation to the 1997 transfer; second, as a late allocation to the trust as of April 15, 1998; and, finally as a timely allocation to the February 1, 1998 transfer. As of April 15, 1998, $55,000, a pro rata portion of the trust assets, is considered to be the property transferred to the trust on February 1, 1998 (($50,000/$200,000) X $220,000). The balance of the trust, $165,000, represents prior transfers to the trust.

(ii) As in *Example 3*, the allocation is a timely allocation as to the 1997 transfer (and the applicable fraction as of July 1, 1997 is .40) and a late allocation as of 1998. The amount of the late allocation is $99,000, computed as follows: (.40 X $165,000 plus $99,000)/$165,000 = one.

(iii) The balance of the allocation, $11,000 ($150,000 less the timely allocation of $40,000 less the late allocation of $99,000) is a timely allocation as of February 1, 1998. The applicable fraction with respect to the trust, as of February 1, 1998, is .355, computed as follows: $60,000 (the nontax portion of the trust immediately prior to the February 1, 1998 transfer (.40 X $150,000)) plus $11,000 (the amount of the timely allocation to the 1998 transfer)/$200,000 (the value of the trust on February 1, 1998, after the transfer on that date) = $71,000/$200,000 = .355.

(iv) The applicable fraction with respect to the trust, as of April 15, 1998, is .805 computed as follows: $78,100 (the nontax portion immediately prior to the allocation (.355 X $220,000)) plus $99,000 (the amount of the late allocation)/$220,000 = $177,100/$220,000 = .805.

*Example 5. Redetermination of inclusion ratio on ETIP termination.* (i) T transfers $100,000 to an irrevocable trust. The trust instrument provides that trust income is to be paid to T for 9 years or until T's prior death. The trust principal is to be paid to T's grandchild, GC, on the termination of T's income interest. The trustee has the power to invade trust principal for the benefit of GC during the term of T's income interest. The trust is subject to an ETIP while T holds the retained income interest. T files a timely Form 709 reporting the transfer and allocates $100,000 of GST exemption to the trust. In year 4, when the value of the trust is $200,000, the trustee distributes $15,000 to GC. The distribution is a taxable distribution. Because of the existence of the ETIP, the inclusion ratio with respect to the taxable distribution is determined immediately prior to the occurrence of the GST. Thus, the inclusion ratio applicable to the year 4 GST is .50 (1 - ($100,000/$200,000)).

(ii) In year 5, when the value of the trust is again $200,000, the trustee distributes another $15,000 to GC. Because the trust is still subject to the ETIP in year 5, the inclusion ratio with respect to the year 5 GST is again computed immediately prior to the GST. In computing the new inclusion ratio, the numerator of the applicable fraction is reduced by the nontax portion of prior GSTs occurring during the ETIP. Thus, the numerator of the applicable fraction with respect to the GST in year 5 is $92,500 ($100,000 - (.50 X $15,000)) and the inclusion ratio applicable with respect to the GST in year 5 is .537 (1 - ($92,500/$200,000) = .463). Any additional GST exemption allocated on a timely ETIP return with respect to the GST in year 5 is effective immediately prior to the transfer. [Reg. § 26.2642-4.]

☐ [*T.D.* 8644, 12-26-95.]

### [Reg. § 26.2642-5]

**§ 26.2642-5. Finality of inclusion ratio.**—(a) *Direct skips.*—The inclusion ratio applicable to a direct skip becomes final when no additional GST tax (including additional GST tax payable as a result of a cessation, etc. of qualified use under section 2032A(c)) may be assessed with respect to the direct skip.

(b) *Other GSTs.*—With respect to taxable distributions and taxable terminations, the inclusion ratio for a trust becomes final, on the later of—

(1) The expiration of the period for assessment with respect to the first GST tax return filed using that inclusion ratio (unless the trust is subject to an election under section 2032A in which case the applicable date under this subsection is the expiration of the period of assessment of any additional GST tax due as a result of a cessation, etc. of qualified use under section 2032A); or

(2) The expiration of the period for assessment of Federal estate tax with respect to the estate of the transferor. For purposes of this paragraph (b)(2), if an estate tax return is not required to be filed, the period for assessment is determined as if a return were required to be filed and as if the return were timely filed within the period prescribed by section 6075(a). [Reg. § 26.2642-5.]

☐ [*T.D.* 8644, 12-26-95.]

### [Reg. § 26.2642-6]

**§ 26.2642-6. Qualified severance.**—(a) *In general.*—If a trust is divided in a qualified severance into two or more trusts, the separate trusts resulting from the severance will be treated as separate trusts for generation-skipping transfer (GST) tax purposes and the inclusion ratio of each new resulting trust may differ from the inclusion ratio of the original trust. Because the post-severance resulting trusts are treated as separate trusts for GST tax purposes, certain actions with respect to one resulting trust will generally have no GST tax impact with respect to the other resulting trust(s). For example, GST exemption allocated to one resulting trust will not impact on the inclusion ratio of the other resulting trust(s); a GST tax election made with respect to one resulting trust will not apply to the other resulting trust(s); the occurrence of a taxable distribution or termination with regard to a particular resulting trust will not have any GST tax impact on any other trust resulting from that severance. In general, the rules in this section are applicable only for purposes of the GST tax and are not applicable in determining, for example, whether the resulting trusts may file separate income tax returns or whether the severance may result in a gift subject to gift tax, may cause any trust to be included in the gross estate of a beneficiary, or may result in a realization of gain for purposes of section 1001. See § 1.1001-1(h) of this chapter for rules relating to whether a qualified severance will constitute an exchange of property for other property differing materially either in kind or in extent.

(b) *Qualified severance defined.*—A qualified severance is a division of a trust (other than a division described in § 26.2654-1(b)) into two or more separate trusts that meets each of the requirements in paragraph (d) of this section.

(c) *Effective date of qualified severance.*—A qualified severance is applicable as of the date of the severance, as defined in § 26.2642-6(d)(3), and the resulting trusts are treated as separate trusts for GST tax purposes as of that date.

(d) *Requirements for a qualified severance.*—For purposes of this section, a qualified severance must satisfy each of the following requirements:

(1) The single trust is severed pursuant to the terms of the governing instrument, or pursuant to applicable local law.

(2) The severance is effective under local law.

(3) The date of severance is either the date selected by the trustee as of which the trust assets are to be valued in order to determine the funding of the resulting trusts, or the court-imposed date of funding in the case of an order of the local court with jurisdiction over the trust ordering the trustee to fund the resulting trusts on or as of a specific date. For a date to satisfy the definition in the preceding sentence, however, the funding must be commenced immediately upon, and funding must occur within a reasonable time (but in no event more than 90 days) after, the selected valuation date.

(4) The single trust (original trust) is severed on a fractional basis, such that each new trust (resulting trust) is funded with a fraction or percentage of the original trust, and the sum of those fractions or percentages is one or one hundred percent, respectively. For this purpose, the fraction or percentage may be determined by means of a formula (for example, that fraction of the trust the numerator of which is equal to the transferor's unused GST tax exemption, and the denominator of which is the fair market value of the original trust's assets on the date of severance). The severance of a trust based on a pecuniary amount does not satisfy this requirement. For example, the severance of a trust is not a qualified severance if the trust is divided into two trusts, with one trust to be funded with $1,500,000 and the other trust to be funded with the balance of the original trust's assets. With respect to the particular assets to be distributed to each separate trust resulting from the severance, each such trust may be funded with the appropriate fraction or percentage (pro rata portion) of each asset held by the original trust. Alternatively, the assets may be divided among the resulting trusts on a non-pro rata basis, based on the fair market value of the assets on the date of severance. However, if a resulting

trust is funded on a non-pro rata basis, each asset received by a resulting trust must be valued, solely for funding purposes, by multiplying the fair market value of the asset held in the original trust as of the date of severance by the fraction or percentage of that asset received by that resulting trust. Thus, the assets must be valued without taking into account any discount or premium arising from the severance, for example, any valuation discounts that might arise because the resulting trust receives less than the entire interest held by the original trust. See paragraph (j), *Example 6* of this section.

(5) The terms of the resulting trusts must provide, in the aggregate, for the same succession of interests of beneficiaries as are provided in the original trust. This requirement is satisfied if the beneficiaries of the separate resulting trusts and the interests of the beneficiaries with respect to the separate trusts, when the separate trusts are viewed collectively, are the same as the beneficiaries and their respective beneficial interests with respect to the original trust before severance. With respect to trusts from which discretionary distributions may be made to any one or more beneficiaries on a non-pro rata basis, this requirement is satisfied if—

(i) The terms of each of the resulting trusts are the same as the terms of the original trust (even though each permissible distributee of the original trust is not a beneficiary of all of the resulting trusts);

(ii) Each beneficiary's interest in the resulting trusts (collectively) equals the beneficiary's interest in the original trust, determined by the terms of the trust instrument or, if none, on a per-capita basis. For example, in the case of the severance of a discretionary trust established for the benefit of A, B, and C and their descendants with the remainder to be divided equally among those three families, this requirement is satisfied if the trust is divided into three separate trusts of equal value with one trust established for the benefit of A and A's descendants, one trust for the benefit of B and B's descendants, and one trust for the benefit of C and C's descendants;

(iii) The severance does not shift a beneficial interest in the trust to any beneficiary in a lower generation (as determined under section 2651) than the person or persons who held the beneficial interest in the original trust; and

(iv) The severance does not extend the time for the vesting of any beneficial interest in the trust beyond the period provided for in (or applicable to) the original trust.

(6) In the case of a qualified severance of a trust with an inclusion ratio as defined in §26.2642-1 of either one or zero, each trust resulting from the severance will have an inclusion ratio equal to the inclusion ratio of the original trust.

(7)(i) In the case of a qualified severance occurring after GST tax exemption has been allocated to the trust (whether by an affirmative allocation, a deemed allocation, or an automatic allocation pursuant to the rules contained in section 2632), if the trust has an inclusion ratio as defined in §26.2642-1 that is greater than zero and less than one, then either paragraph (d)(7)(ii) or (iii) of this section must be satisfied.

(ii) The trust is severed initially into only two resulting trusts. One resulting trust must receive that fractional share of the total value of the original trust as of the date of severance that is equal to the applicable fraction, as defined in §26.2642-1(b) and (c), used to determine the inclusion ratio of the original trust immediately before the severance. The other resulting trust must receive that fractional share of the total value of the original trust as of the date of severance that is equal to the excess of one over the fractional share described in the preceding sentence. The trust receiving the fractional share equal to the applicable fraction shall have an inclusion ratio of zero, and the other trust shall have an inclusion ratio of one. If the applicable fraction with respect to the original trust is .50, then, with respect to the two equal trusts resulting from the severance, the trustee may designate which of the resulting trusts will have an inclusion ratio of zero and which will have an inclusion ratio of one. Each separate trust resulting from the severance then may be further divided in accordance with the rules of this section. See paragraph (j), *Example 7*, of this section.

(iii) The trust is severed initially into more than two resulting trusts. One or more of the resulting trusts in the aggregate must receive that fractional share of the total value of the original trust as of the date of severance that is equal to the applicable fraction used to determine the inclusion ratio of the original trust immediately before the severance. The trust or trusts receiving such fractional share shall have an inclusion ratio of zero, and each of the other resulting trust or trusts shall have an inclusion ratio of one. (If, however, two or more of the resulting trusts each receives the fractional share of the total value of the original trust equal to the applicable fraction, the trustee may designate which of those resulting trusts will have an inclusion ratio of zero and which will have an inclusion ratio of one.) The resulting trust or trusts with an inclusion ratio of one must receive in the aggregate that fractional share of the total value of the original trust as of the date of severance that is equal to the excess of one over the fractional share described in the

second sentence of this paragraph. See paragraph (j), *Example 9*, of this section.

(e) *Reporting a qualified severance.*—(1) *In general.*—A qualified severance is reported by filing Form 706-GS(T), "Generation-Skipping Transfer Tax Return for Terminations," (or such other form as may be provided from time to time by the Internal Revenue Service (IRS) for the purpose of reporting a qualified severance). Unless otherwise provided in the applicable form or instructions, the IRS requests that the filer write "Qualified Severance" at the top of the form and attach a Notice of Qualified Severance (Notice). The return and attached Notice should be filed by April 15th of the year immediately following the year during which the severance occurred or by the last day of the period covered by an extension of time, if an extension of time is granted, to file such form.

(2) *Information concerning the original trust.*—The Notice should provide, with respect to the original trust that was severed—
(i) The name of the transferor;
(ii) The name and date of creation of the original trust;
(iii) The tax identification number of the original trust; and
(iv) The inclusion ratio before the severance.

(3) *Information concerning each new trust.*—The Notice should provide, with respect to each of the resulting trusts created by the severance—
(i) The name and tax identification number of the trust;
(ii) The date of severance (within the meaning of paragraph (c) of this section);
(iii) The fraction of the total assets of the original trust received by the resulting trust;
(iv) Other details explaining the basis for the funding of the resulting trust (a fraction of the total fair market value of the assets on the date of severance, or a fraction of each asset); and
(v) The inclusion ratio.

(f) *Time for making a qualified severance.*—(1) A qualified severance of a trust may occur at any time prior to the termination of the trust. Thus, provided that the separate resulting trusts continue in existence after the severance, a qualified severance may occur either before or after—
(i) GST tax exemption has been allocated to the trust;
(ii) A taxable event has occurred with respect to the trust; or
(iii) An addition has been made to the trust.

(2) Because a qualified severance is effective as of the date of severance, a qualified severance has no effect on a taxable termination as defined in section 2612(a) or a taxable distribution as defined in section 2612(b) that occurred prior to the date of severance. A qualified severance shall be deemed to occur before a taxable termination or a taxable distribution that occurs by reason of the qualified severance. See paragraph (j) *Example 8* of this section.

(g) *Trusts that were irrevocable on September 25, 1985.*—(1) *In general.*—See §26.2601-1(b)(4) for rules regarding severances and other actions with respect to trusts that were irrevocable on September 25, 1985.

(2) *Trusts in receipt of a post-September 25, 1985, addition.*—A trust described in §26.2601-1(b)(1)(iv)(A) that is deemed for GST tax purposes to consist of one separate share not subject to GST tax (the non-chapter 13 portion) with an inclusion ratio of zero, and one separate share subject to GST tax (the chapter 13 portion) with an inclusion ratio determined under section 2642, may be severed into two trusts in accordance with §26.2654-1(a)(3). One resulting trust will hold the non-chapter 13 portion of the original trust (the non-chapter 13 trust) and will not be subject to GST tax, and the other resulting trust will hold the chapter 13 portion of the original trust (the chapter 13 trust) and will have the same inclusion ratio as the chapter 13 portion immediately prior to the severance. The chapter 13 trust may be further divided in a qualified severance in accordance with the rules of this section. The non-chapter 13 trust may be further divided in accordance with the rules of §26.2601-1(b)(4).

(h) *Treatment of trusts resulting from a severance that is not a qualified severance.*—Trusts resulting from a severance (other than a severance recognized for GST tax purposes under §26.2654-1) that does not meet the requirements of a qualified severance under paragraph (b) of this section will be treated, after the date of severance, as separate trusts for purposes of the GST tax, provided that the trusts resulting from such severance are recognized as separate trusts under applicable state law. The post-severance treatment of the resulting trusts as separate trusts for GST tax purposes generally permits the allocation of GST tax exemption, the making of various elections permitted for GST tax purposes, and the occurrence of a taxable distribution or termination with regard to a particular resulting trust, with no GST tax impact on any other trust resulting from that severance. Each trust resulting from a severance described in this paragraph (h), however, will have the same inclusion ratio immediately after the severance as that of the original trust immediately before the severance. (See § 26.2654-1 for the inclusion ratio of each trust resulting from a severance described in that section.) Further, any trust resulting from a nonqualified severance may be severed subsequently, pursuant to a qualified severance described in this § 26.2642-6.

(i) [Reserved].

(j) *Examples.*—The rules of this section are illustrated by the following examples:

*Example 1. Succession of interests.* T dies in 2006. T's will establishes a testamentary trust (Trust) providing that income is to be paid to T's sister, S, for her life. On S's death, one-half of the corpus is to be paid to T's child, C (or to C's estate if C fails to survive S), and one-half of the corpus is to be paid to T's grandchild, GC (or to GC's estate if GC fails to survive S). On the Form 706, "United States Estate (and Generation-Skipping Transfer) Tax Return," filed for T's estate, T's executor allocates all of T's available GST tax exemption to other transfers and trusts, such that Trust's inclusion ratio is 1. Subsequent to filing the Form 706 in 2007 and in accordance with applicable state law, the trustee divides Trust into two separate trusts, Trust 1 and Trust 2, with each trust receiving 50 percent of the value of the assets of the original trust as of the date of severance. Trust 1 provides that trust income is to be paid to S for life with remainder to C or C's estate, and Trust 2 provides that trust income is to be paid to S for life with remainder to GC or GC's estate. Because Trust 1 and Trust 2 provide for the same succession of interests in the aggregate as provided in the original trust, the severance constitutes a qualified severance, provided that all other requirements of section 2642(a)(3) and this section are satisfied.

*Example 2. Succession of interests in discretionary trust.* In 2006, T establishes Trust, an irrevocable trust providing that income may be paid from time to time in such amounts as the trustee deems advisable to any one or more members of the group consisting of T's children (A and B) and their respective descendants. In addition, the trustee may distribute corpus to any trust beneficiary in such amounts as the trustee deems advisable. On the death of the last to die of A and B, the trust is to terminate and the corpus is to be distributed in two equal shares, one share to the then-living descendants of each child, per stirpes. T elects, under section 2632(c)(5), to not have the automatic allocation rules contained in section 2632(c) apply with respect to T's transfers to Trust, and T does not otherwise allocate GST tax exemption with respect to Trust. As a result, Trust has an inclusion ratio of one. In 2008, the trustee of Trust, pursuant to applicable state law, divides Trust into two equal but separate trusts, Trust 1 and Trust 2, each of which has terms identical to the terms of Trust except for the identity of the beneficiaries. Trust 1 and Trust 2 each has an inclusion ratio of one. Trust 1 provides that income is to be paid in such amounts as the trustee deems advisable to A and A's descendants. In addition, the trustee may distribute corpus to any trust beneficiary in such amounts as the trustee deems advisable. On the death of A, Trust 1 is to terminate and the corpus is to be distributed to the then-living descendants of A, per stirpes, but, if A dies with no living descendants, the principal will be added to Trust 2. Trust 2 contains identical provisions, except that B and B's descendants are the trust beneficiaries and, if B dies with no living descendants, the principal will be added to Trust 1. Trust 1 and Trust 2 in the aggregate provide for the same beneficiaries and the same succession of interests as provided in Trust, and the severance does not shift any beneficial interest to a beneficiary who occupies a lower generation than the person or persons who held the beneficial interest in Trust. Accordingly, the severance constitutes a qualified severance, provided that all other requirements of section 2642(a)(3) and this section are satisfied.

*Example 3. Severance based on actuarial value of beneficial interests.* In 2004, T establishes Trust, an irrevocable trust providing that income is to be paid to T's child C during C's lifetime. Upon C's death, Trust is to terminate and the assets of Trust are to be paid to GC, C's child, if living, or, if GC is not then living, to GC's estate. T properly elects, under section 2632(c)(5), not to have the automatic allocation rules contained in section 2632(c) apply with respect to T's transfers to Trust, and T does not otherwise allocate GST tax exemption with respect to Trust. Thus, Trust has an inclusion ratio of one. In 2009, the trustee of Trust, pursuant to applicable state law, divides Trust into two separate trusts, Trust 1 for the benefit of C (and on C's death to C's estate), and Trust 2 for the benefit of GC (and on GC's death to GC's estate). The document severing Trust directs that Trust 1 is to be funded with an amount equal to the actuarial value of C's interest in Trust prior to the severance, determined under section 7520 of the Internal Revenue Code. Similarly, Trust 2 is to be funded with an amount equal to the actuarial value of GC's interest in Trust prior to the severance, determined under section 7520. Trust 1 and Trust 2 do not provide for the same succession of interests as provided under the terms of the original trust. Therefore, the severance is not a

qualified severance. Furthermore, because the severance results in no non-skip person having an interest in Trust 2, Trust 2 constitutes a skip person under section 2613 and, therefore, the severance results in a taxable termination subject to GST tax.

*Example 4. Severance of a trust with a 50% inclusion ratio.* On September 1, 2006, T transfers $100,000 to a trust for the benefit of T's grandchild, GC. On a timely filed Form 709, "United States Gift (and Generation-Skipping Transfer) Tax Return," reporting the transfer, T allocates all of T's remaining GST tax exemption ($50,000) to the trust. As a result of the allocation, the applicable fraction with respect to the trust is .50 [$50,000 (the amount of GST tax exemption allocated to the trust) divided by $100,000 (the value of the property transferred to the trust)]. The inclusion ratio with respect to the trust is .50 [1 - .50]. In 2007, pursuant to authority granted under applicable state law, the trustee severs the trust into two trusts, Trust 1 and Trust 2, each of which is identical to the original trust and each of which receives a 50 percent fractional share of the total value of the original trust, valued as of the date of severance. Because the applicable fraction with respect to the original trust is .50 and the trust is severed into two equal trusts, the trustee may designate which resulting trust has an inclusion ratio of one, and which resulting trust has an inclusion ratio of zero. Accordingly, in the Notice of Qualified Severance reporting the severance, the trustee designates Trust 1 as having an inclusion ratio of zero, and Trust 2 as having an inclusion ratio of one. The severance constitutes a qualified severance, provided that all other requirements of section 2642(a)(3) and this section are satisfied.

*Example 5. Funding of severed trusts on a non-pro rata basis.* T's will establishes a testamentary trust (Trust) for the benefit of T's descendants, to be funded with T's stock in Corporation A and Corporation B, both publicly traded stocks. T dies on May 1, 2004, at which time the Corporation A stock included in T's gross estate has a fair market value of $100,000 and the stock of Corporation B included in T's gross estate has a fair market value of $200,000. On a timely filed Form 706, T's executor allocates all of T's remaining GST tax exemption ($270,000) to Trust. As a result of the allocation, the applicable fraction with respect to Trust is .90 [$270,000 (the amount of GST tax exemption allocated to the trust) divided by $300,000 (the value of the property transferred to the trust)]. The inclusion ratio with respect to Trust is .10 [1 - .90]. On August 1, 2008, in accordance with applicable local law, the trustee executes a document severing Trust into two trusts, Trust 1 and Trust 2, each of which is identical to Trust. The instrument designates August 3, 2008, as the date of severance (within the meaning of paragraph (d)(3) of this section). The terms of the instrument severing Trust provide that Trust 1 is to be funded on a non-pro rata basis with assets having a fair market value on the date of severance equal to 90% of the value of Trust's assets on that date, and Trust 2 is to be funded with assets having a fair market value on the date of severance equal to 10% of the value of Trust's assets on that date. On August 3, 2008, the value of the Trust assets totals $500,000, consisting of Corporation A stock worth $450,000 and Corporation B stock worth $50,000. On August 4, 2008, the trustee takes all action necessary to transfer all of the Corporation A stock to Trust 1 and to transfer all of the Corporation B stock to Trust 2. On August 6, 2008, the stock transfers are completed and the stock is received by the appropriate resulting trust. Accordingly, Trust 1 is funded with assets having a value equal to 90% of the value of Trust as of the date of severance, August 3, 2008, and Trust 2 is funded with assets having a value equal to 10% of the value of Trust as of the date of severance. Therefore, the severance constitutes a qualified severance, provided that all other requirements of section 2642(a)(3) and this section are satisfied. Trust 1 will have an inclusion ratio of zero and Trust 2 will have an inclusion ratio of one.

*Example 6. Funding of severed trusts on a non-pro rata basis.* (i) T's will establishes an irrevocable trust (Trust) for the benefit of T's descendants. As a result of the allocation of GST tax exemption, the applicable fraction with respect to Trust is .60 and Trust's inclusion ratio is .40 [1 - .60]. Pursuant to authority granted under applicable state law, on August 1, 2008, the trustee executes a document severing Trust into two trusts, Trust 1 and Trust 2, each of which is identical to Trust. The instrument of severance provides that the severance is intended to qualify as a qualified severance within the meaning of section 2642(a)(3) and designates August 3, 2008, as the date of severance (within the meaning of paragraph (d)(3) of this section). The instrument further provides that Trust 1 and Trust 2 are to be funded on a non-pro rata basis with Trust 1 funded with assets having a fair market value on the date of severance equal to 40% of the value of Trust's assets on that date and Trust 2 funded with assets having a fair market value equal to 60% of the value of Trust's assets on that date. The fair market value of the assets used to fund each trust is to be determined in compliance with the requirements of paragraph (d)(4) of this section.

(ii) On August 3, 2008, the fair market value of the Trust assets totals $4,000,000, consisting of 52% of the outstanding common stock in Company, a closelyheld corporation, valued at $3,000,000 and

$1,000,000 in cash and marketable securities. Trustee proposes to divide the Company stock equally between Trust 1 and Trust 2, and thus transfer 26% of the Company stock to Trust 1 and 26% of the stock to Trust 2. In addition, the appropriate amount of cash and marketable securities will be distributed to each trust. In accordance with paragraph (d)(4) of this section, for funding purposes, the interest in the Company stock distributed to each trust is valued as a pro rata portion of the value of the 52% interest in Company held by Trust before severance, without taking into account, for example, any valuation discount that might otherwise apply in valuing the non-controlling interest distributed to each resulting trust.

(iii) Accordingly, for funding purposes, each 26% interest in Company stock distributed to Trust 1 and Trust 2 is valued at $1,500,000 (.5 × $3,000,000). Therefore, Trust 1, which is to be funded with $1,600,000 (.40 × $4,000,000), receives $100,000 in cash and marketable securities valued as of August 3, 2008, in addition to the Company stock, and Trust 2, which is to be funded with $2,400,000 (.60 × $4,000,000), receives $900,000 in cash and marketable securities in addition to the Company stock. Therefore, the severance is a qualified severance, provided that all other requirements of section 2642(a)(3) and this section are satisfied.

*Example 7. Statutory qualified severance.* T dies on October 1, 2004. T's will establishes a testamentary trust (Trust) to be funded with $1,000,000. Trust income is to be paid to T's child, S, for S's life. The trustee may also distribute trust corpus from time to time, in equal or unequal shares, for the benefit of any one or more members of the group consisting of S and T's three grandchildren (GC1, GC2, and GC3). On S's death, Trust is to terminate and the assets are to be divided equally among GC1, GC2, and GC3 (or their respective then-living descendants, per stirpes). On a timely filed Form 706, T's executor allocates all of T's remaining GST tax exemption ($300,000) to Trust. As a result of the allocation, the applicable fraction with respect to the trust is .30 [$300,000 (the amount of GST tax exemption allocated to the trust) divided by $1,000,000 (the value of the property transferred to the trust)]. The inclusion ratio with respect to the trust is .70 [1 - .30]. On June 1, 2007, the trustee determines that it is in the best interest of the beneficiaries to sever Trust to provide a separate trust for each of T's three grandchildren and their respective families. The trustee severs Trust into two trusts, Trust 1 and Trust 2, each with terms and beneficiaries identical to Trust and thus each providing that trust income is to be paid to S for life, trust principal may be distributed for the benefit of any or all members of the group consisting of S and T's grandchildren, and, on S's death, the trust is to terminate and the assets are to be divided equally among GC1, GC2, and GC3 (or their respective then-living descendants, per stirpes). The instrument severing Trust provides that Trust 1 is to receive 30% of Trust's assets and Trust 2 is to receive 70% of Trust's assets. Further, each such trust is to be funded with a pro rata portion of each asset held in Trust. The trustee then severs Trust 1 into three equal trusts, Trust GC1, Trust GC2, and Trust GC3. Each trust is named for a grandchild of T and provides that trust income is to be paid to S for life, trust principal may be distributed for the benefit of S and T's grandchild for whom the trust is named, and, on S's death, the trust is to terminate and the trust proceeds distributed to the respective grandchild for whom the trust is named. If that grandchild has predeceased the termination date, the trust proceeds are to be distributed to that grandchild's then-living descendants, per stirpes, or, if none, then equally to the other two trusts resulting from the severance of Trust 1. Each such resulting trust is to be funded with a pro rata portion of each Trust 1 asset. The trustee also severs Trust 2 in a similar manner, into Trust GC1(2), Trust GC2(2), and Trust GC3(2). The severance of Trust into Trust 1 and Trust 2, the severance of Trust 1 into Trust GC1, Trust GC2, Trust GC3, and the severance of Trust 2 into Trust GC1(2), Trust GC2(2) and Trust GC3(2), constitute qualified severances, provided that all other requirements of section 2642(a)(3) and this section are satisfied with respect to each severance. Trust GC1, Trust GC2, Trust GC3 will each have an inclusion ratio of zero and Trust GC1(2), Trust GC2(2), and Trust GC3(2) will each have an inclusion ratio of one.

*Example 8. Qualified severance deemed to precede a taxable termination.* In 2004, T establishes an inter vivos irrevocable trust (Trust) for a term of 10 years providing that Trust income is to be paid annually in equal shares to T's child C and T's grandchild GC (the child of another then-living child of T). If either C or GC dies prior to the expiration of the 10-year term, the deceased beneficiary's share of Trust's income is to be paid to that beneficiary's then-living descendants, per stirpes, for the balance of the trust term. At the expiration of the 10-year trust term, the corpus is to be distributed equally to C and GC; if either C or GC is not then living, then such decedent's share is to be distributed instead to such decedent's then-living descendants, per stirpes. T allocates T's GST tax exemption to Trust such that Trust's applicable fraction is .50 and Trust's inclusion ratio is .50 [1-.50]. In 2006, pursuant to applicable state law, the trustee severs the trust into two equal trusts, Trust 1 and Trust 2. The instrument severing Trust provides that Trust 1 is to receive 50% of

the Trust assets, and Trust 2 is to receive 50% of Trust's assets. Both resulting trusts are identical to Trust, except that each has different beneficiaries: C and C's descendants are designated as the beneficiaries of Trust 1, and GC and GC's descendants are designated as the beneficiaries of Trust 2. The severance constitutes a qualified severance, provided all other requirements of section 2642(a)(3) and this section are satisfied. Because the applicable fraction with respect to Trust is .50 and Trust was severed into two equal trusts, the trustee may designate which resulting trust has an inclusion ratio of one, and which has an inclusion ratio of zero. Accordingly, in the Notice of Qualified Severance reporting the severance, the trustee designates Trust 1 as having an inclusion ratio of one, and Trust 2 as having an inclusion ratio of zero. Because Trust 2 is a skip person under section 2613, the severance of Trust resulting in the distribution of 50% of Trust's corpus to Trust 2 would constitute a taxable termination or distribution (as described in section 2612(a)) of that 50% of Trust for GST tax purposes, but for the rule that a qualified severance is deemed to precede a taxable termination that is caused by the qualified severance. Thus, no GST tax will be due with regard to the creation and funding of Trust 2 because the inclusion ratio of Trust 2 is zero.

*Example 9. Regulatory qualified severance.* (i) In 2004, T establishes an inter vivos irrevocable trust (Trust) providing that trust income is to be paid annually in equal shares to T's children, A and B, for 10 years. Trust provides that the trustee has discretion to make additional distributions of principal to A and B during the 10-year term without adjustments to their shares of income or the trust remainder. If either (or both) dies prior to the expiration of the 10-year term, the deceased child's share of trust income is to be paid to the child's then living descendants, per stirpes, for the balance of the trust term. At the expiration of the 10-year term, the corpus is to be distributed equally to A and B; if A and B (or either or them) is not then living, then such decedent's share is to be distributed instead to such decedent's then living descendants, per stirpes. T allocates GST tax exemption to Trust such that Trust's applicable fraction is .25 and its inclusion ratio is .75.

(ii) In 2006, pursuant to applicable state law, the trustee severs the trust into three trusts: Trust 1, Trust 2, and Trust 3. The instrument severing Trust provides that Trust 1 is to receive 50% of Trust's assets, Trust 2 is to receive 25% of Trust's assets, and Trust 3 is to receive 25% of Trust's assets. All three resulting trusts are identical to Trust, except that each has different beneficiaries: A and A's issue are designated as the beneficiaries of Trust 1, and B and B's issue are designated as the beneficiaries of Trust 2 and Trust 3. The severance constitutes a qualified severance, provided that all other requirements of section 2642(a)(3) and this section are satisfied. Trust 1 will have an inclusion ratio of 1. Because both Trust 2 and Trust 3 have each received the fractional share of Trust's assets equal to Trust's applicable fraction of .25, trustee designates that Trust 2 will have an inclusion ratio of one and that Trust 3 will have an inclusion ratio of zero.

*Example 10. Beneficiary's interest dependent on inclusion ratio.* On August 8, 2006, T transfers $1,000,000 to Trust and timely allocates $400,000 of T's remaining GST tax exemption to Trust. As a result of the allocation, the applicable fraction with respect to Trust is .40 [$400,000 divided by $1,000,000] and Trust's inclusion ratio is .60 [1 - .40]. Trust provides that all income of Trust will be paid annually to C, T's child, for life. On C's death, the corpus is to pass in accordance with C's exercise of a testamentary limited power to appoint the corpus of Trust to C's lineal descendants. However, Trust provides that if, at the time of C's death, Trust's inclusion ratio is greater than zero, then C may also appoint that fraction of the trust corpus equal to the inclusion ratio to the creditors of C's estate. On May 3, 2008, pursuant to authority granted under applicable state law, the trustee severs Trust into two trusts. Trust 1 is funded with 40% of Trust's assets, and Trust 2 is funded with 60% of Trust's assets in accordance with the requirements of this section. Both Trust 1 and Trust 2 provide that all income of Trust will be paid annually to C during C's life. On C's death, Trust 1 corpus is to pass in accordance with C's exercise of a testamentary limited power to appoint the corpus to C's lineal descendants. Trust 2 is to pass in accordance with C's exercise of a testamentary power to appoint the corpus of Trust to C's lineal descendants and to the creditors of C's estate. The severance constitutes a qualified severance, provided that all other requirements of section 2642(a)(3) and this section are satisfied. No additional contribution or allocation of GST tax exemption is made to either Trust 1 or Trust 2 prior to C's death. Accordingly, the inclusion ratio with respect to Trust 1 is zero. The inclusion ratio with respect to Trust 2 is one until C's death, at which time C will become the transferor of Trust 2 for GST tax purposes. (Some or all of C's GST tax exemption may be allocated to Trust 2 upon C's death.)

*Example 11. Date of severance.* Trust is an irrevocable trust that has both skip person and non-skip person beneficiaries. Trust holds two parcels of real estate, Property A and Property B, stock in Company X, a publicly traded company, and cash. On June 16, 2008, the local court with jurisdiction over Trust issues an order, pursuant to the trustee's petition authorized under state law, severing Trust into two resulting trusts of equal value, Trust 1 and Trust 2. The court order directs that Property A will be distributed to Trust 1 and Property B will be distributed to Trust 2, and that an appropriate amount of stock and cash will be distributed to each trust such that the total value of property distributed to each trust as of the date of severance will be equal. The court order does not mandate a particular date of funding. Trustee receives notice of the court order on June 24, and selects July 16, 2008, as the date of severance. On June 26, 2008, Trustee commences the process of transferring title to Property A and Property B to the appropriate resulting trust(s), which process is completed on July 8, 2008. Also on June 26, the Trustee hires a professional appraiser to value Property A and Property B as of the date of severance and receives the appraisal report on Friday, October 3, 2008. On Monday, October 6, 2008, Trustee commences the process of transferring to Trust 1 and Trust 2 the appropriate amount of Company X stock valued as of July 16, 2008, and that transfer (as well as the transfer of Trust's cash) is completed by October 9, 2008. Under the facts presented, the funding of Trust 1 and Trust 2 occurred within 90 days of the date of severance selected by the trustee, and within a reasonable time after the date of severance taking into account the nature of the assets involved and the need to obtain an appraisal. Accordingly, the date of severance for purposes of this section is July 16, 2008, the resulting trusts are to be funded based on the value of the original trust assets as of that date, and the severance is a qualified severance assuming that all other requirements of section 2642(a)(3) and this section are met. (However, if Trust had contained only marketable securities and cash, then in order to satisfy the reasonable time requirement, the stock transfer would have to have been commenced, and generally completed, immediately after the date of severance, and the cash distribution would have to have been made at the same time.)

*Example 12. Other severance that does not meet the requirements of a qualified severance.* (i) In 2004, T establishes an irrevocable inter vivos trust (Trust) providing that Trust income is to be paid to T's children, A and B, in equal shares for their joint lives. Upon the death of the first to die of A and B, all Trust income will be paid to the survivor of A and B. At the death of the survivor, the corpus is to be distributed in equal shares to T's grandchildren, W and X (with any then-deceased grandchild's share being paid in accordance with that grandchild's testamentary general power of appointment). W is A's child and X is B's child. T elects under section 2632(c)(5) not to have the automatic allocation rules contained in section 2632(c) apply with respect to T's transfers to Trust, but T allocates GST tax exemption to Trust resulting in Trust having an inclusion ratio of .30.

(ii) In 2009, the trustee of Trust, as permitted by applicable state law, divides Trust into two separate trusts, Trust 1 and Trust 2. Trust 1 provides that trust income is to be paid to A for life and, on A's death, the remainder is to be distributed to W (or pursuant to W's testamentary general power of appointment). Trust 2 provides that trust income is to be paid to B for life and, on B's death, the remainder is to be distributed to X (or pursuant to X's testamentary general power of appointment). Because Trust 1 and Trust 2 do not provide A and B with the contingent survivor income interests that were provided to A and B under the terms of Trust, Trust 1 and Trust 2 do not provide for the same succession of interests in the aggregate as provided by Trust. Therefore, the severance does not satisfy the requirements of this section and is not a qualified severance. Provided that Trust 1 and Trust 2 are recognized as separate trusts under applicable state law, Trust 1 and Trust 2 will be recognized as separate trusts for GST tax purposes pursuant to paragraph (h) of this section, prospectively from the date of the severance. However, Trust 1 and Trust 2 each have an inclusion ratio of .30 immediately after the severance, the same as the inclusion ratio of Trust prior to severance.

*Example 13. Qualified severance following a non-qualified severance.* Assume the same facts as in *Example 12*, except that, as of November 4, 2010, the trustee of Trust 1 severs Trust 1 into two trusts, Trust 3 and Trust 4, in accordance with applicable local law. The instrument severing Trust 1 provides that both resulting trusts have provisions identical to Trust 1. The terms of the instrument severing Trust 1 further provide that Trust 3 is to be funded on a pro rata basis with assets having a fair market value as of the date of severance equal to 70% of the value of Trust 1's assets on that date, and Trust 4 is to be funded with assets having a fair market value as of the date of severance equal to 30% of the value of Trust 1's assets on that date. The severance constitutes a qualified severance, provided that all other requirements of section 2642(a)(3) and this section are satisfied. Trust 3 will have an inclusion ratio of zero and Trust 4 will have an inclusion ratio of one.

(k) *Effective/applicability date.*—(1) *In general.*—Except as otherwise provided in this paragraph (k), this section applies to severances occurring on or after August 2, 2007. Paragraph (d)(7)(iii), paragraph

(h), and *Examples 9, 12* and *13* of paragraph (j) of this section apply to severances occurring on or after September 2, 2008.

(2) *Transition rule.*—In the case of a qualified severance occurring after December 31, 2000, and before August 2, 2007, taxpayers may rely on any reasonable interpretation of section 2642(a)(3) as long as reasonable notice concerning the qualified severance and identification of the trusts involved has been given to the IRS. For this purpose, the proposed regulations (69 FR 51967) are treated as a reasonable interpretation of the statute. For purposes of the reporting provisions of § 26.2642-6(e), notice to the IRS should be mailed by the due date of the gift tax return (including extensions granted) for gifts made during the year in which the severance occurred. If no gift tax return is filed, notice to the IRS should be mailed by April 15th of the year immediately following the year during which the severance occurred. For severances occurring between December 31, 2000, and January 1, 2007, notification should be mailed to the IRS as soon as reasonably practicable after August 2, 2007, if sufficient notice has not already been given. [Reg. § 26.2642-6.]

☐ [*T.D. 9348, 8-1-2007. Amended by T.D. 9421, 7-30-2008.*]

### [Reg. § 26.2651-1]

**§ 26.2651-1. Generation assignment.**—(a) *Special rule for persons with a deceased parent.*—(1) *In general.*—This paragraph (a) applies for purposes of determining whether a transfer to or for the benefit of an individual who is a descendant of a parent of the transferor (or the transferor's spouse or former spouse) is a generation-skipping transfer. If that individual's parent, who is a lineal descendant of the parent of the transferor (or the transferor's spouse or former spouse), is deceased at the time the transfer (from which an interest of such individual is established or derived) is subject to the tax imposed on the transferor by chapter 11 or 12 of the Internal Revenue Code, the individual is treated as if that individual were a member of the generation that is one generation below the lower of—

(i) The transferor's generation; or

(ii) The generation assignment of the individual's youngest living lineal ancestor who is also a descendant of the parent of the transferor (or the transferor's spouse or former spouse).

(2) *Special rules.*—(i) *Corresponding generation adjustment.*—If an individual's generation assignment is adjusted with respect to a transfer in accordance with paragraph (a)(1) of this section, a corresponding adjustment with respect to that transfer is made to the generation assignment of each—

(A) Spouse or former spouse of that individual;

(B) Descendant of that individual; and

(C) Spouse or former spouse of each descendant of that individual.

(ii) *Continued application of generation assignment.*—If a transfer to a trust would be a generation-skipping transfer but for paragraph (a)(1) of this section, any generation assignment determined under this paragraph (a) continues to apply in determining whether any subsequent distribution from (or termination of an interest in) the portion of the trust attributable to that transfer is a generation-skipping transfer.

(iii) *Ninety-day rule.*—For purposes of paragraph (a)(1) of this section, any individual who dies no later than 90 days after a transfer occurring by reason of the death of the transferor is treated as having predeceased the transferor.

(iv) *Local law.*—A living person is not treated as having predeceased the transferor solely by reason of a provision of applicable local law; e.g., an individual who disclaims is not treated as a predeceased parent solely because state law treats a disclaimant as having predeceased the transferor for purposes of determining the disposition of the disclaimed property.

(3) *Established or derived.*—For purposes of section 2651(e) and paragraph (a)(1) of this section, an individual's interest is established or derived at the time the transferor is subject to transfer tax on the property. See § 26.2652-1(a) for the definition of a transferor. If the same transferor, on more than one occasion, is subject to transfer tax imposed by either chapter 11 or 12 of the Internal Revenue Code on the property so transferred (whether the same property, reinvestments thereof, income thereon, or any or all of these), then the relevant time for determining whether paragraph (a)(1) of this section applies is the earliest time at which the transferor is subject to the tax imposed by either chapter 11 or 12 of the Internal Revenue Code. For purposes of section 2651(e) and paragraph (a)(1) of this section, the interest of a remainder beneficiary of a trust for which an election under section 2523(f) or section 2056(b)(7) (QTIP election) has been made will be deemed to have been established or derived, to the extent of the QTIP election, on the date as of which the value of the trust corpus is first subject to tax under section 2519 or section

2044. The preceding sentence does not apply to a trust, however, to the extent that an election under section 2652(a)(3) (reverse QTIP election) has been made for the trust because, to the extent of a reverse QTIP election, the spouse who established the trust will remain the transferor of the trust for generation-skipping transfer tax purposes.

(4) *Special rule in the case of additional contributions to a trust.*—If a transferor referred to in paragraph (a)(1) of this section contributes additional property to a trust that existed before the application of paragraph (a)(1), then the additional property is treated as being held in a separate trust for purposes of chapter 13 of the Internal Revenue Code. The provisions of §26.2654-1(a)(2), regarding treatment as separate trusts, apply as if different transferors had contributed to the separate portions of the single trust. Additional subsequent contributions from that transferor will be added to the new share that is treated as a separate trust.

(b) *Limited application to collateral heirs.*—Paragraph (a) of this section does not apply in the case of a transfer to any individual who is not a lineal descendant of the transferor (or the transferor's spouse or former spouse) if the transferor has any living lineal descendant at the time of the transfer.

(c) *Examples.*—The following examples illustrate the provisions of this section:

*Example 1.* T establishes an irrevocable trust, Trust, providing that trust income is to be paid to T's grandchild, GC, for 5 years. At the end of the 5-year period or on GC's prior death, Trust is to terminate and the principal is to be distributed to GC if GC is living or to GC's children if GC has died. The transfer that occurred on the creation of the trust is subject to the tax imposed by chapter 12 of the Internal Revenue Code and, at the time of the transfer, T's child, C, who is a parent of GC, is deceased. GC is treated as a member of the generation that is one generation below T's generation. As a result, GC is not a skip person and Trust is not a skip person. Therefore, the transfer to Trust is not a direct skip. Similarly, distributions to GC during the term of Trust and at the termination of Trust will not be GSTs.

*Example 2.* On January 1, 2004, T transfers $100,000 to an irrevocable inter vivos trust that provides T with an annuity payable for four years or until T's prior death. The annuity satisfies the definition of a qualified interest under section 2702(b). When the trust terminates, the corpus is to be paid to T's grandchild, GC. The transfer is subject to the tax imposed by chapter 12 of the Internal Revenue Code and, at the time of the transfer, T's child, C, who is a parent of GC, is living. C dies in 2006. In this case, C was alive at the time the transfer by T was subject to the tax imposed by chapter 12 of the Internal Revenue Code. Therefore, section 2651(e) and paragraph (a)(1) of this section do not apply. When the trust subsequently terminates, the distribution to GC is a taxable termination that is subject to the GST tax to the extent the trust has an inclusion ratio greater than zero. See section 2642(a).

*Example 3.* T dies testate in 2002, survived by T's spouse, S, their children, C1 and C2, and C1's child, GC. Under the terms of T's will, a trust is established for the benefit of S and of T and S's descendants. Under the terms of the trust, all income is payable to S during S's lifetime and the trustee may distribute trust corpus for S's health, support and maintenance. At S's death, the corpus is to be distributed, outright, to C1 and C2. If either C1 or C2 has predeceased S, the deceased child's share of the corpus is to be distributed to that child's then-living descendants, per stirpes. The executor of T's estate makes the election under section 2056(b)(7) to treat the trust property as qualified terminable interest property (QTIP) but does not make the election under section 2652(a)(3) (reverse QTIP election). In 2003, C1 dies survived by S and GC. In 2004, S dies, and the trust terminates. The full fair market value of the trust is includible in S's gross estate under section 2044 and S becomes the transferor of the trust under section 2652(a)(1)(A). GC's interest is considered established or derived at S's death, and because C1 is deceased at that time, GC is treated as a member of the generation that is one generation below the generation of the transferor, S. As a result, GC is not a skip person and the transfer to GC is not a direct skip.

*Example 4.* The facts are the same as in *Example 3.* However, the executor of T's estate makes the election under section 2652(a)(3) (reverse QTIP election) for the entire trust. Therefore, T remains the transferor because, for purposes of chapter 13 of the Internal Revenue Code, the election to be treated as qualified terminable interest property is treated as if it had not been made. In this case, GC's interest is established or derived on T's death in 2002. Because C1 was living at the time of T's death, the predeceased parent rule under section 2651(e) does not apply, even though C1 was deceased at the time the transfer from S to GC was subject to the tax under chapter 11 of the Internal Revenue Code. When the trust terminates, the distribution to GC is a taxable termination that is subject to the GST tax to

the extent the trust has an inclusion ratio greater than zero. See section 2642(a).

*Example 5.* T establishes an irrevocable trust providing that trust income is to be paid to T's grandniece, GN, for 5 years or until GN's prior death. At the end of the 5-year period or on GN's prior death, the trust is to terminate and the principal is to be distributed to GN if living, or if GN has died, to GN's then-living descendants, per stirpes. S is a sibling of T and the parent of N. N is the parent of GN. At the time of the transfer, T has no living lineal descendant, S is living, N is deceased, and the transfer is subject to the gift tax imposed by chapter 12 of the Internal Revenue Code. GN is treated as a member of the generation that is one generation below T's generation because S, GN's youngest living lineal ancestor who is also a descendant of T's parent, is in T's generation. As a result, GN is not a skip person and the transfer to the trust is not a direct skip. In addition, distributions to GN during the term of the trust and at the termination of the trust will not be GSTs.

*Example 6.* On January 1, 2004, T transfers $50,000 to a great-grandniece, GGN, who is the great-grandchild of B, a brother of T. At the time of the transfer, T has no living lineal descendants and B's grandchild, GN, who is a parent of GGN and a child of B's living child, N, is deceased. GGN will be treated as a member of the generation that is one generation below the lower of T's generation or the generation assignment of GGN's youngest living lineal ancestor who is also a descendant of the parent of the transferor. In this case, N is GGN's youngest living lineal ancestor who is also a descendant of the parent of T. Because N's generation assignment is lower than T's generation, GGN will be treated as a member of the generation that is one generation below N's generation assignment (i.e., GGN will be treated as a member of her parent's generation). As a result, GGN remains a skip person and the transfer to GGN is a direct skip.

*Example 7.* T has a child, C. C and C's spouse, S, have a 20-year-old child, GC. C dies and S subsequently marries S2. S2 legally adopts GC. T transfers $100,000 to GC. Under section 2651(b)(1), GC is assigned to the generation that is two generations below T. However, since GC's parent, C, is deceased at the time of the transfer, GC will be treated as a member of the generation that is one generation below T. As a result, GC is not a skip person and the transfer to GC is not a direct skip.

[Reg. §26.2651-1.]

☐ [T.D. 9214, 7-15-2005.]

## [Reg. §26.2651-2]

§26.2651-2. **Individual assigned to more than 1 generation.**—(a) *In general.*—Except as provided in paragraph (b) or (c) of this section, an individual who would be assigned to more than 1 generation is assigned to the youngest of the generations to which that individual would be assigned.

(b) *Exception.*—Notwithstanding paragraph (a) of this section, an adopted individual (as defined in this paragraph) will be treated as a member of the generation that is one generation below the adoptive parent for purposes of determining whether a transfer to the adopted individual from the adoptive parent (or the spouse or former spouse of the adoptive parent, or a lineal descendant of a grandparent of the adoptive parent) is subject to chapter 13 of the Internal Revenue Code. For purposes of this paragraph (b), an adopted individual is an individual who is—

(1) Legally adopted by the adoptive parent;

(2) A descendant of a parent of the adoptive parent (or the spouse or former spouse of the adoptive parent);

(3) Under the age of 18 at the time of the adoption; and

(4) Not adopted primarily for the purpose of avoiding GST tax. The determination of whether an adoption is primarily for GST tax-avoidance purposes is made based upon all of the facts and circumstances. The most significant factor is whether there is a bona fide parent/child relationship between the adoptive parent and the adopted individual, in which the adoptive parent has fully assumed all significant responsibilities for the care and raising of the adopted child. Other factors may include (but are not limited to), at the time of the adoption—

(i) The age of the adopted individual (for example, the younger the age of the adopted individual, or the age of the youngest of siblings who are all adopted together, the more likely the adoption will not be considered primarily for GST tax-avoidance purposes); and

(ii) The relationship between the adopted individual and the individual's parents (for example, objective evidence of the absence or incapacity of the parents may indicate that the adoption is not primarily for GST tax-avoidance purposes).

(c) *Special rules.*—(1) *Corresponding generation adjustment.*—If an individual's generation assignment is adjusted with respect to a transfer in accordance with paragraph (b) of this section, a corresponding adjustment with respect to that transfer is made to the generation assignment of each—

(i) Spouse or former spouse of that individual;

(ii) Descendant of that individual; and

(iii) Spouse or former spouse of each descendant of that individual.

(2) *Continued application of generation assignment.*—If a transfer to a trust would be a generation-skipping transfer but for paragraph (b) of this section, any generation assignment determined under paragraph (b) or (c) of this section continues to apply in determining whether any subsequent distribution from (or termination of an interest in) the portion of the trust attributable to that transfer is a generation-skipping transfer.

(d) *Example.*—The following example illustrates the provisions of this section:

*Example.* T has a child, C. C has a 20-year-old child, GC. T legally adopts GC and transfers $100,000 to GC. GC's generation assignment is determined by section 2651(b)(1) and GC is assigned to the generation that is two generations below T. In addition, because T has legally adopted GC, GC is generally treated as a child of T under state law. Under these circumstances, GC is an individual who is assigned to more than one generation and the exception in § 26.2651-2(b) does not apply. Thus, the special rule under section 2651(f)(1) applies and GC is assigned to the generation that is two generations below T. GC remains a skip person with respect to T and the transfer to GC is a direct skip.

[Reg. § 26.2651-2.]

☐ [*T.D.* 9214, 7-15-2005.]

### [Reg. § 26.2651-3]

**§ 26.2651-3. Effective dates.**—(a) *In general.*—The rules of §§ 26.2651-1 and 26.2651-2 are applicable for terminations, distributions, and transfers occurring on or after July 18, 2005.

(b) *Transition rule.*—In the case of transfers occurring after December 31, 1997, and before July 18, 2005, taxpayers may rely on any reasonable interpretation of section 2651(e). For this purpose, these final regulations, as well as the proposed regulations issued on September 3, 2004 (69 FR 53862), are treated as a reasonable interpretation of the statute. [Reg. § 26.2651-3.]

☐ [*T.D.* 9214, 7-15-2005.]

### [Reg. § 26.2652-1]

**§ 26.2652-1. Transferor defined; other definitions.**—(a) *Transferor defined.*—(1) *In general.*—Except as otherwise provided in paragraph (a)(3) of this section, the individual with respect to whom property was most recently subject to Federal estate or gift tax is the transferor of that property for purposes of chapter 13. An individual is treated as transferring any property with respect to which the individual is the transferor. Thus, an individual may be a transferor even though there is no transfer of property under local law at the time the Federal estate or gift tax applies. For purposes of this paragraph, a surviving spouse is the transferor of a qualified domestic trust created by the deceased spouse that is included in the surviving spouse's gross estate, provided the trust is not subject to the election described in § 26.2652-2 (reverse QTIP election). A surviving spouse is also the transferor of a qualified domestic trust created by the surviving spouse pursuant to section 2056(d)(2)(B). For generation-skipping transfer tax rules related to an ABLE account established under section 529A, see § 1.529A-4 of this chapter.

(2) *Transfers subject to Federal estate or gift tax.*—For purposes of this chapter, a transfer is subject to Federal gift tax if a gift tax is imposed under section 2501(a) (without regard to exemptions, exclusions, deductions, and credits). A transfer is subject to Federal estate tax if the value of the property is includible in the decedent's gross estate as determined under section 2031 or section 2103.

(3) *Special rule for certain QTIP trusts.*—Solely for purposes of chapter 13, if a transferor of qualified terminable interest property (QTIP) elects under § 26.2652-2(a) to treat the property as if the QTIP election had not been made (reverse QTIP election), the identity of the transferor of the property is determined without regard to the application of sections 2044, 2207A, and 2519.

(4) *Split-gift transfers.*—In the case of a transfer with respect to which the donor's spouse makes an election under section 2513 to treat the gift as made one-half by the spouse, the electing spouse is treated as the transferor of one-half of the entire value of the property transferred by the donor, regardless of the interest the electing spouse is actually deemed to have transferred under section 2513. The donor is treated as the transferor of one-half of the value of the

entire property. See § 26.2632-1(c)(5) *Example 3*, regarding allocation of GST exemption with respect to split-gift transfers subject to an ETIP.

(5) *Examples.*—The following examples illustrate the principles of this paragraph (a):

*Example 1. Identity of transferor.* T transfers $100,000 to a trust for the sole benefit of T's grandchild. The transfer is subject to Federal gift tax because a gift tax is imposed under section 2501(a) (without regard to exemptions, deductions, and credits). Thus, for purposes of chapter 13, T is the transferor of the $100,000. It is immaterial that a portion of the transfer is excluded from the total amount of T's taxable gift by reason of section 2503(b).

*Example 2. Gift splitting and identity of transferor.* The facts are the same as in *Example 1*, except T's spouse, S, consents under section 2513 to split the gift with T. For purposes of chapter 13, S and T are each treated as a transferor of $50,000 to the trust.

*Example 3. Change of transferor on subsequent transfer tax event.* T transfers $100,000 to a trust providing that all the net trust income is to be paid to T's spouse, S, for S's lifetime. T elects under section 2523(f) to treat the transfer as a transfer of qualified terminable interest property, and T does not make the reverse QTIP election under section 2652(a)(3). On S's death, the trust property is included in S's gross estate under section 2044. Thus, S becomes the transferor at the time of S's death.

*Example 4. Effect of transfer of an interest in trust on identity of the transferor.* T transfers $100,000 to a trust providing that all of the net income is to be paid to T's child, C, for C's lifetime. At C's death, the trust property is to be paid to T's grandchild. C transfers the income interest to X, an unrelated party, in a transfer that is a completed transfer for Federal gift tax purposes. Because C's transfer is a transfer of a term interest in the trust that does not affect the rights of other parties with respect to the trust property, T remains the transferor with respect to the trust.

*Example 5. Effect of lapse of withdrawal right on identity of transferor.* T transfers $10,000 to a new trust providing that the trust income is to be paid to T's child, C, for C's life and, on the death of C, the trust principal is to be paid to T's grandchild, GC. The trustee has discretion to distribute principal for GC's benefit during C's lifetime. C has a right to withdraw $10,000 from the trust for a 60-day period following the transfer. Thereafter, the power lapses. C does not exercise the withdrawal right. The transfer by T is subject to Federal gift tax because a gift tax is imposed under section 2501 (without regard to exemptions, deductions, and credits) and, thus, T is treated as having transferred the entire $10,000 to the trust. On the lapse of the withdrawal right, C becomes a transferor to the extent C is treated as having made a completed transfer for purposes of chapter 12. Therefore, except to the extent that the amount with respect to which the power of withdrawal lapses exceeds the greater of $5,000 or 5% of the value of the trust property, T remains the transferor of the trust property for purposes of chapter 13.

*Example 6. Effect of reverse QTIP election on identity of the transferor.* T establishes a testamentary trust having a principal of $500,000. Under the terms of the trust, all trust income is payable to T's surviving spouse, S, during S's lifetime. T's executor makes an election to treat the trust property as qualified terminable interest property and also makes the reverse QTIP election. For purposes of chapter 13, T is the transferor with respect to the trust. On S's death, the then full fair market value of the trust is includible in S's gross estate under section 2044. However, because of the reverse QTIP election, S does not become the transferor with respect to the trust; T continues to be the transferor.

*Example 7. Effect of reverse QTIP election on constructive additions.* The facts are the same as in *Example 6*, except the inclusion of the QTIP trust in S's gross estate increased the Federal estate tax liability of S's estate by $200,000. The estate does not exercise the right of recovery from the trust granted under section 2207A. Under local law, the beneficiaries of S's residuary estate (which bears all estate taxes under the will) could compel the executor to exercise the right of recovery but do not do so. Solely for purposes of chapter 13, the beneficiaries of the residuary estate are not treated as having made an addition to the trust by reason of their failure to exercise their right of recovery. Because of the reverse QTIP election, for GST purposes, the trust property is not treated as includible in S's gross estate and, under those circumstances, no right of recovery exists.

*Example 8. Effect of reverse QTIP election on constructive additions.* S, the surviving spouse of T, dies testate. At the time of S's death, S was the beneficiary of a trust with respect to which T's executor made a QTIP election under section 2056(b)(7). Thus, the trust is includible in S's gross estate under section 2044. T's executor also made the reverse QTIP election with respect to the trust. S's will provides that all death taxes payable with respect to the trust are payable from S's residuary estate. Since the transferor of the property is determined without regard to section 2044 and section 2207A, S is not treated as making a constructive addition to the trust by reason of the tax apportionment clause in S's will.

*Example 9. Split-gift transfers.* T transfers $100,000 to an inter vivos trust that provides T with an annuity payable for ten years or until T's prior death. The annuity satisfies the definition of a qualified interest under section 2702(b). When the trust terminates, the corpus is to be paid to T's grandchild, GC. T's spouse, S, consents under section 2513 to have the gift treated as made one-half by S. Under section 2513, only the actuarial value of the gift to GC is eligible to be treated as made one-half by S. However, because S is treated as the donor of one-half of the gift to GC, S becomes the transferor of one-half of the entire trust ($50,000) for purposes of Chapter 13.

(b) *Trust defined.*—(1) *In general.*—A trust includes any arrangement (other than an estate) that has substantially the same effect as a trust. Thus, for example, arrangements involving life estates and remainders, estates for years, and insurance and annuity contracts are trusts. Generally, a transfer as to which the identity of the transferee is contingent upon the occurrence of an event is a transfer in trust; however, a transfer of property included in the transferor's gross estate, as to which the identity of the transferee is contingent upon an event that must occur within 6 months of the transferor's death, is not considered a transfer in trust solely by reason of the existence of the contingency.

(2) *Examples.*—The following examples illustrate the provisions of this paragraph (b):

*Example 1. Uniform gifts to minors transfers.* T transfers cash to an account in the name of T's child, C, as custodian for C's child, GC (who is a minor), under a state statute substantially similar to the Uniform Gifts to Minors Act. For purposes of chapter 13, the transfer to the custodial account is treated as a transfer to a trust.

*Example 2. Contingent transfers.* T bequeaths $200,000 to T's child, C, provided that if C does not survive T by more than 6 months, the bequest is payable to T's grandchild, GC. C dies 4 months after T. The bequest is not a transfer in trust because the contingency that determines the recipient of the bequest must occur within 6 months of T's death. The bequest to GC is a direct skip.

*Example 3. Contingent transfers.* The facts are the same as in *Example 2,* except C must survive T by 18 months to take the bequest. The bequest is a transfer in trust for purposes of chapter 13, and the death of C is a taxable termination.

(c) *Trustee defined.*—The trustee of a trust is the person designated as trustee under local law or, if no such person is so designated, the person in actual or constructive possession of property held in trust.

(d) *Executor defined.*—For purposes of chapter 13, the executor is the executor or administrator of the decedent's estate. However, if no executor or administrator is appointed, qualified or acting within the United States, the executor is the fiduciary who is primarily responsible for payment of the decedent's debts and expenses. If there is no such executor, administrator or fiduciary, the executor is the person in actual or constructive possession of the largest portion of the value of the decedent's gross estate.

(e) *Interest in trust.*—See § 26.2612-1(e) for the definition of *interest in trust.* [Reg. § 26.2652-1.]

☐ [*T.D. 8644, 12-26-95. Amended by T.D. 8720, 5-19-97 and T.D. 9923, 11-18-2020.*]

### [Reg. § 26.2652-2]

**§ 26.2652-2. Special election for qualified terminable interest property.**—(a) *In general.*—If an election is made to treat property as qualified terminable interest property (QTIP) under section 2523(f) or section 2056(b)(7), the person making the election may, for purposes of chapter 13, elect to treat the property as if the QTIP election had not been made (reverse QTIP election). An election under this section is irrevocable. An election under this section is not effective unless it is made with respect to all of the property in the trust to which the QTIP election applies. See, however, § 26.2654-1(b)(1). Property that qualifies for a deduction under section 2056(b)(5) is not eligible for the election under this section.

(b) *Time and manner of making election.*—An election under this section is made on the return on which the QTIP election is made. If a protective QTIP election is made, no election under this section is effective unless a protective reverse QTIP election is also made.

(c) *Transitional rule.*—If a reverse QTIP election is made with respect to a trust prior to December 27, 1995, and GST exemption has been allocated to that trust, the transferor (or the transferor's executor) may elect to treat the trust as two separate trusts, one of which has a zero inclusion ratio by reason of the transferor's GST exemption previously allocated to the trust. The separate trust with the zero inclusion ratio consists of that fractional share of the value of the entire trust equal to the value of the nontax portion of the trust under § 26.2642-4(a). The reverse QTIP election is treated as applying only to the trust with the zero inclusion ratio. An election under this paragraph (c) is made by attaching a statement to a copy of the return on which the reverse QTIP election was made under section 2652(a)(3). The statement must indicate that an election is being made to treat the trust as two separate trusts and must identify the values of the two separate trusts. The statement is to be filed in the same place in which the original return was filed and must be filed before June 24, 1996. A trust subject to the election described in this paragraph is treated as a trust that was created by two transferors. See § 26.2654-1(a)(2) for special rules involving trusts with multiple transferors.

(d) *Examples.*—The following examples illustrate the provisions of this section:

*Example 1. Special (reverse QTIP) election under section 2652(a)(3).* T transfers $1,000,000 to a trust providing that all trust income is to be paid to T's spouse, S, for S's lifetime. On S's death, the trust principal is payable to GC, a grandchild of S and T. T elects to treat all of the transfer as a transfer of QTIP and also makes the reverse QTIP election for all of the property. Because of the reverse QTIP election, T continues to be treated as the transferor of the property after S's death for purposes of chapter 13. A taxable termination rather than a direct skip occurs on S's death.

*Example 2. Election under transition rule.* In 1994, T died leaving $4 million in trust for the benefit of T's surviving spouse, S. On January 16, 1995, T's executor filed T's Form 706 on which the executor elects to treat the entire trust as qualified terminable interest property. The executor also makes a reverse QTIP election. The reverse QTIP election is effective with respect to the entire trust even though T's executor could allocate only $1 million of GST exemption to the trust. T's executor may elect to treat the trust as two separate trusts, one having a value of 25% of the value of the single trust and an inclusion ratio of zero, but only if the election is made prior to June 24, 1996. If the executor makes the transitional election, the other separate trust, having a value of 75% of the value of the single trust and an inclusion ratio of one, is not treated as subject to the reverse QTIP election.

*Example 3. Denominator of the applicable fraction of QTIP trust.* T bequeaths $1,500,000 to a trust in which T's surviving spouse, S, receives an income interest for life. Upon the death of S, the property is to remain in trust for the benefit of C, the child of T and S. Upon C's death, the trust is to terminate and the trust property paid to the descendants of C. The bequest qualifies for the estate tax marital deduction under section 2056(b)(7) as QTIP. The executor does not make the reverse QTIP election under section 2652(a)(3). As a result, S becomes the transferor of the trust at S's death when the value of the property in the QTIP trust is included in S's gross estate under section 2044. For purposes of computing the applicable fraction with respect to the QTIP trust upon S's death, the denominator of the fraction is reduced by any Federal estate tax (whether imposed under section 2001, 2101 or 2056A(b)) and State death tax attributable to the trust property that is actually recovered from the trust. [Reg. § 26.2652-2.]

☐ [*T.D. 8644, 12-26-95.*]

### [Reg. § 26.2653-1]

**§ 26.2653-1. Taxation of multiple skips.**—(a) *General rule.*—If property is held in trust immediately after a GST, solely for purposes of determining whether future events involve a skip person, the transferor is thereafter deemed to occupy the generation immediately above the highest generation of any person holding an interest in the trust immediately after the transfer. If no person holds an interest in the trust immediately after the GST, the transferor is treated as occupying the generation above the highest generation of any person in existence at the time of the GST who then occupies the highest generation level of any person who may subsequently hold an interest in the trust. See § 26.2612-1(e) for rules determining when a person has an interest in property held in trust.

(b) *Examples.*—The following examples illustrate the provisions of this section:

*Example 1.* T transfers property to an irrevocable trust for the benefit of T's grandchild, GC, and great-grandchild, GGC. During GC's life, the trust income may be distributed to GC and GGC in the trustee's absolute discretion. At GC's death, the trust property passes to GGC. Both GC and GGC have an interest in the trust for purposes of chapter 13. The transfer by T to the trust is a direct skip, and the property is held in trust immediately after the transfer. After the direct skip, the transferor is treated as being one generation above GC, the highest generation individual having an interest in the trust. Therefore, GC is no longer a skip person and distributions to GC are not taxable distributions. However, because GGC occupies a generation that is two generations below the deemed generation of T, GGC is a skip person and distributions of trust income to GGC are taxable distributions.

*Example 2.* T transfers property to an irrevocable trust providing that the income is to be paid to T's child, C, for life. At C's death, the trust income is to be accumulated for 10 years and added to principal. At the end of the 10-year accumulation period, the trust income is to be paid to T's grandchild, GC, for life. Upon GC's death, the trust property is to be paid to T's great-grandchild, GGC, or to GGC's estate. A GST occurs at C's death. Immediately after C's death and during the 10-year accumulation period, no person has an interest in the trust within the meaning of section 2652(c) and §26.2612-1(e) because no one can receive current distributions of income or principal. Immediately after C's death, T is treated as occupying the generation above the generation of GC (the trust beneficiary in existence at the time of the GST who then occupies the highest generation level of any person who may subsequently hold an interest in the trust). Thus, subsequent income distributions to GC are not taxable distributions. [Reg. §26.2653-1.]

☐ [T.D. 8644, 12-26-95.]

### [Reg. §26.2654-1]

**§26.2654-1. Certain trusts treated as separate trusts.**—(a) *Single trust treated as separate trusts.*—(1) *Substantially separate and independent shares.*—(i) *In general.*—If a single trust consists solely of substantially separate and independent shares for different beneficiaries, the share attributable to each beneficiary (or group of beneficiaries) is treated as a separate trust for purposes of Chapter 13. The phrase "substantially separate and independent shares" generally has the same meaning as provided in §1.663(c)-3. However, except as provided in paragraph (a)(1)(iii) of this section, a portion of a trust is not a separate share unless such share exists from and at all times after the creation of the trust. For purposes of this paragraph (a)(1), a trust is treated as created at the date of death of the grantor if the trust is includible in its entirety in the grantor's gross estate for Federal estate tax purposes. Further, except with respect to shares or trusts that are treated as separate trusts under local law, treatment of a single trust as separate trusts under this paragraph (a)(1) does not permit treatment of those portions as separate trusts for purposes of filing returns and payment of tax or for purposes of computing any other tax imposed under the Internal Revenue Code. Also, additions to, and distributions from, such trusts are allocated pro rata among the separate trusts, unless the governing instrument expressly provides otherwise. See §26.2642-6 and paragraph (b) of this section regarding the treatment, for purposes of Chapter 13, of separate trusts resulting from the discretionary severance of a single trust.

(ii) *Certain pecuniary amounts.*—For purposes of this section, if a person holds the current right to receive a mandatory (i.e., nondiscretionary and noncontingent) payment of a pecuniary amount at the death of the transferor from an inter vivos trust that is includible in the transferor's gross estate, or a testamentary trust, the pecuniary amount is a separate and independent share if—

(A) The trustee is required to pay appropriate interest (as defined in §26.2642-2(b)(4)(i) and (ii)) to the person; and

(B) If the pecuniary amount is payable in kind on the basis of value other than the date of distribution value of the assets, the trustee is required to allocate assets to the pecuniary payment in a manner that fairly reflects net appreciation or depreciation in the value of the assets in the fund available to pay the pecuniary amount measured from the valuation date to the date of payment.

(iii) *Mandatory severances.*—For purposes of this section, if the governing instrument of a trust requires the division or severance of a single trust into separate trusts upon the future occurrence of a particular event not within the discretion of the trustee or any other person, and if the trusts resulting from such a division or severance are recognized as separate trusts under applicable state law, then each resulting trust is treated as a separate trust for purposes of Chapter 13. For this purpose, the rules of paragraph (b)(1)(ii)(C) of this section apply with respect to the severance and funding of the trusts. Similarly, if the governing instrument requires the division of a single trust into separate shares under the circumstances described in this paragraph, each such share is treated as a separate trust for purposes of Chapter 13. The post-severance treatment of the resulting shares or trusts as separate trusts for GST tax purposes generally permits the allocation of GST tax exemption, the making of various elections permitted for GST tax purposes, and the occurrence of a taxable distribution or termination with regard to a particular resulting share or trust, with no GST tax impact on any other trust or share resulting from that severance. The treatment of a single trust as separate trusts under this paragraph (a)(1), however, does not permit treatment of those portions as separate trusts for purposes of filing returns and payment of tax or for purposes of computing any other tax imposed under the Internal Revenue Code, if those portions are not treated as separate trusts under local law. Also, additions to, and

distributions from, such trusts are allocated pro rata among the separate trusts, unless the governing instrument expressly provides otherwise. Each separate share and each trust resulting from a mandatory division or severance described in this paragraph will have the same inclusion ratio immediately after the severance as that of the original trust immediately before the division or severance.

(2) *Multiple transferors with respect to single trust.*—(i) *In general.*—If there is more than one transferor with respect to a trust, the portions of the trust attributable to the different transferors are treated as separate trusts for purposes of chapter 13. Treatment of a single trust as separate trusts under this paragraph (a)(2) does not permit treatment of those portions as separate trusts for purposes of filing returns and payment of tax or for purposes of computing any other tax imposed under the Internal Revenue Code. Also, additions to, and distributions from, such trusts are allocated pro rata among the separate trusts unless otherwise expressly provided in the governing instrument.

(ii) *Addition by a transferor.*—If an individual makes an addition to a trust of which the individual is not the sole transferor, the portion of the single trust attributable to each separate trust is determined by multiplying the fair market value of the single trust immediately after the contribution by a fraction. The numerator of the fraction is the value of the separate trust immediately after the contribution. The denominator of the fraction is the fair market value of all the property in the single trust immediately after the transfer.

(3) *Severance of a single trust.*—A single trust treated as separate trusts under paragraphs (a)(1) or (2) of this section may be divided at any time into separate trusts to reflect that treatment. For this purpose, the rules of paragraph (b)(1)(ii)(C) of this section apply with respect to the severance and funding of the severed trusts.

(4) *Allocation of exemption.*—(i) *In general.*—With respect to a separate share treated as a separate trust under paragraph (a)(1) or (2) of this section, an individual's GST exemption is allocated to the separate trust. See §26.2632-1 for rules concerning the allocation of GST exemption.

(ii) *Automatic allocation to direct skips.*—If the transfer is a direct skip to a trust that occurs during the transferor's lifetime and is treated as a transfer to separate trusts under paragraphs (a)(1) or (a)(2) of this section, the transferor's GST exemption not previously allocated is automatically allocated on a pro rata basis among the separate trusts. The transferor may prevent an automatic allocation of GST exemption to a separate share of a single trust by describing on a timely-filed United States Gift (and Generation-Skipping Transfer) Tax Return (Form 709) the transfer and the extent to which the automatic allocation is not to apply to a particular share. See §26.2632-1(b) for rules for avoiding the automatic allocation of GST exemption.

(5) *Examples.*—The following examples illustrate the principles of this section (a):

*Example 1. Separate shares as separate trusts.* T transfers $100,000 to a trust under which income is to be paid in equal shares for 10 years to T's child, C, and T's grandchild, GC (or their respective estates). The trust does not permit distributions of principal during the term of the trust. At the end of the 10-year term, the trust principal is to be distributed to C and GC in equal shares. The shares of C and GC in the trust are separate and independent and, therefore, are treated as separate trusts. The result would not be the same if the trust permitted distributions of principal unless the distributions could only be made from a one-half separate share of the initial trust principal and the distributee's future rights with respect to the trust are correspondingly reduced. T may allocate part of T's GST exemption under section 2632(a) to the share held for the benefit of GC.

*Example 2. Separate share rule inapplicable.* The facts are the same as in *Example 1*, except the trustee holds the discretionary power to distribute the income in any proportion between C and GC during the last year of the trust. The shares of C and GC in the trust are not separate and independent shares throughout the entire term of the trust and, therefore, are not treated as separate trusts for purposes of chapter 13.

*Example 3. Pecuniary payment as separate share.* T creates a lifetime revocable trust providing that on T's death $500,000 is payable to T's spouse, S, with the balance of the principal to be held for the benefit of T's grandchildren. The value of the trust is includible in T's gross estate upon T's death. Under the terms of the trust, the payment to S is required to be made in cash, and under local law S is entitled to receive interest on the payment at an annual rate of 6 percent, commencing immediately upon T's death. For purposes of chapter 13, the trust is treated as created at T's death, and the $500,000 payable to S from the trust is treated as a separate share. The result would be the same if the payment to S could be satisfied using noncash assets at their value on the date of distribution. Further, the result would be the same if the decedent's probate estate poured over to the revocable trust on the decedent's death and was then distributed in accordance with the terms of the trust.

*Example 4. Pecuniary payment not treated as separate share.* The facts are the same as in *Example 3*, except the bequest to S is to be paid in noncash assets valued at their values as finally determined for Federal estate tax purposes. Neither the trust instrument nor local law requires that the assets distributed in satisfaction of the bequest fairly reflect net appreciation or depreciation in all the assets from which the bequest may be funded. S's $500,000 bequest is not treated as a separate share and the trust is treated as a single trust for purposes of chapter 13.

*Example 5. Multiple transferors to single trust.* A transfers $100,000 to an irrevocable generation-skipping trust; B simultaneously transfers $50,000 to the same trust. As of the time of the transfers, the single trust is treated as two trusts for purposes of chapter 13. Because A contributed 2/3 of the value of the initial corpus, 2/3 of the single trust principal is treated as a separate trust created by A. Similarly, because B contributed 1/3 of the value of the initial corpus, 1/3 of the single trust is treated as a separate trust created by B. A or B may allocate their GST exemption under section 2632(a) to the respective separate trusts.

*Example 6. Additional contributions.* A transfers $100,000 to an irrevocable generation-skipping trust; B simultaneously transfers $50,000 to the same trust. When the value of the single trust has increased to $180,000, A contributes an additional $60,000 to the trust. At the time of the additional contribution, the portion of the single trust attributable to each grantor's separate trust must be redetermined. The portion of the single trust attributable to A's separate trust immediately after the contribution is 3/4 (((2/3 x $180,000) + $60,000)/$240,000). The portion attributable to B's separate trust after A's addition is 1/4.

*Example 7. Distributions from a separate share.* The facts are the same as in *Example 6*, except that, after A's second contribution, $50,000 is distributed to a beneficiary of the trust. Absent a provision in the trust instrument that charges the distribution against the contribution of either A or B, 3/4 of the distribution is treated as made from the separate trust of which A is the transferor and 1/4 from the separate trust of which B is the transferor.

*Example 8. Subsequent mandatory division into separate trusts.* T creates an irrevocable trust that provides the trustee with the discretionary power to distribute income or corpus to T's children and grandchildren. The trust provides that, when T's youngest child reaches age 21, the trust will be divided into separate shares, one share for each child of T. The income from a respective child's share will be paid to the child during the child's life, with the remainder passing on the child's death to such child's children (grandchildren of T). The separate shares that come into existence when the youngest child reaches age 21 will be recognized as of that date as separate trusts for purposes of Chapter 13. The inclusion ratio of the separate trusts will be identical to the inclusion ratio of the trust before the severance. Any allocation of GST tax exemption to the trust after T's youngest child reaches age 21 may be made to any one or more of the separate shares. The result would be the same if the trust instrument provided that the trust was to be divided into separate trusts when T's youngest child reached age 21, provided that the severance and funding of the separate trusts meets the requirements of this section.

(b) *Division of a trust included in the gross estate.*—(1) *In general.*—The severance of a trust that is included in the transferor's gross estate (or created under the transferor's will) into two or more trusts is recognized for purposes of chapter 13 if—

(i) The trust is severed pursuant to a direction in the governing instrument providing that the trust is to be divided upon the death of the transferor; or

(ii) The governing instrument does not require or otherwise direct severance but the trust is severed pursuant to discretionary authority granted either under the governing instrument or under local law; and

(A) The terms of the new trusts provide in the aggregate for the same succession of interests and beneficiaries as are provided in the original trust;

(B) The severance occurs (or a reformation proceeding, if required, is commenced) prior to the date prescribed for filing the Federal estate tax return (including extensions actually granted) for the estate of the transferor; and

(C) Either—

(1) The new trusts are severed on a fractional basis. If severed on a fractional basis, the separate trusts need not be funded with a pro rata portion of each asset held by the undivided trust. The trusts may be funded on a nonpro rata basis provided funding is based on either the fair market value of the assets on the date of funding or in a manner that fairly reflects the net appreciation or

depreciation in the value of the assets measured from the valuation date to the date of funding; or

(2) If the severance is required (by the terms of the governing instrument) to be made on the basis of a pecuniary amount, the pecuniary payment is satisfied in a manner that would meet the requirements of paragraph (a)(1)(ii) of this section if it were paid to an individual.

(2) *Special rule.*—If a court order severing the trust has not been issued at the time the Federal estate tax return is filed, the executor must indicate on a statement attached to the return that a proceeding has been commenced to sever the trust and describe the manner in which the trust is proposed to be severed. A copy of the petition or other instrument used to commence the proceeding must also be attached to the return. If the governing instrument of a trust or local law authorizes the severance of the trust, a severance pursuant to that authorization is treated as meeting the requirement of paragraph (b)(1)(ii)(B) of this section if the executor indicates on the Federal estate tax return that separate trusts will be created (or funded) and clearly sets forth the manner in which the trust is to be severed and the separate trusts funded.

(3) *Allocation of exemption.*—An individual's GST exemption under §2632 may be allocated to the separate trusts created pursuant to this section at the discretion of the executor or trustee.

(4) *Examples.*—The following examples illustrate the provisions of this section (b):

*Example 1. Severance of single trust.* T's will establishes a testamentary trust providing that income is to be paid to T's spouse for life. At the spouse's death, one-half of the corpus is to be paid to T's child, C, or C's estate (if C fails to survive the spouse) and one-half of the corpus is to be paid to T's grandchild, GC, or GC's estate (if GC fails to survive the spouse). If the requirements of paragraph (b) of this section are otherwise satisfied, T's executor may divide the testamentary trust equally into two separate trusts, one trust providing an income interest to spouse for life with remainder to C, and the other trust with an income interest to spouse for life with remainder to GC. Furthermore, if the requirements of paragraph (b) of this section are satisfied, the executor or trustee may further divide the trust for the benefit of GC. GST exemption may be allocated to any of the divided trusts.

*Example 2. Severance of revocable trust.* T creates an inter vivos revocable trust providing that, at T's death and after payment of all taxes and administration expenses, the remaining corpus will be divided into two trusts. One trust, for the benefit of T's spouse, is to be funded with the smallest amount that, if qualifying for the marital deduction, will reduce the estate tax to zero. The other trust, for the benefit of T's descendants, is to be funded with the balance of the revocable trust corpus. The trust corpus is includible in T's gross estate. Each trust is recognized as a separate trust for purposes of chapter 13.

*Example 3. Formula severance.* T's will establishes a testamentary marital trust (Trust) that meets the requirements of qualified terminable interest property (QTIP) if an election under section 2056(b)(7) is made. Trust provides that all trust income is to be paid to T's spouse for life. On the spouse's death, the trust corpus is to be held in further trust for the benefit of T's then-living descendants. On T's date of death in January of 2004, T's unused GST tax exemption is $1,200,000, and T's will includes $200,000 of bequests to T's grandchildren. Prior to the due date for filing the Form 706, "United States Estate (and Generation-Skipping Transfer) Tax Return," for T's estate, T's executor, pursuant to applicable state law, divides Trust into two separate trusts, Trust 1 and Trust 2. Trust 1 is to be funded with that fraction of the Trust assets, the numerator of which is $1,000,000, and the denominator of which is the value of the Trust assets as finally determined for federal estate tax purposes. Trust 2 is to be funded with that fraction of the Trust assets, the numerator of which is the excess of the Trust assets over $1,000,000, and the denominator of which is the value of the Trust assets as finally determined for federal estate tax purposes. On the Form 706 filed for the estate, T's executor makes a QTIP election under section 2056(b)(7) with respect to Trust 1 and Trust 2 and a "reverse" QTIP election under section 2652(a)(3) with respect to Trust 1. Further, T's executor allocates $200,000 of T's available GST tax exemption to the bequests to T's grandchildren, and the balance of T's exemption ($1,000,000) to Trust 1. If the requirements of paragraph (b) of this section are otherwise satisfied, Trust 1 and Trust 2 are recognized as separate trusts for GST tax purposes. Accordingly, the "reverse" QTIP election and allocation of GST tax exemption with respect to Trust 1 are recognized and effective for generation-skipping transfer tax purposes.

(c) *Cross reference.*—For rules applicable to the qualified severance of trusts (whether or not includible in the transferor's gross estate), see §26.2642-6.

(d) *Effective date.*—Paragraph (a)(1)(i), paragraph (a)(1)(iii), and *Example* 8 of paragraph (a)(5) apply to severances occurring on or after September 2, 2008. [Reg. § 26.2654-1.]

☐ [*T.D. 8644*, 12-26-95. *Amended by T.D. 9348*, 8-1-2007 *and T.D. 9421*, 7-30-2008.]

# ADMINISTRATION

**[Reg. § 26.2662-1]**

**§26.2662-1. Generation-skipping transfer tax return requirements.**—(a) *In general.*—Chapter 13 imposes a tax on generation-skipping transfers(as defined in section 2611). The requirements relating to the return of tax depend on the type of generation-skipping transfer involved. This section contains rules for filing the required tax return. Paragraph (c)(2) of this section provides special rules concerning the return requirements for generation-skipping transfers pursuant to certain trust arrangements (as defined in paragraph (c)(2)(ii) of this section), such as life insurance policies and annuities.

(b) *Form of return.*—(1) *Taxable distributions.*—Form 706GS(D) must be filed in accordance with its instructions for any taxable distribution (as defined in section 2612(b)). The trust involved in a transfer described in the preceding sentence must file Form 706GS(D-1) in accordance with its instructions. A copy of Form 706GS(D-1) shall be sent to each distributee.

(2) *Taxable terminations.*—Form 706GS(T) must be filed in accordance with its instructions for any taxable termination (as defined in section 2612(a)).

(3) *Direct skip.*—(i) *Inter vivos direct skips.*—Form 709 must be filed in accordance with its instructions for any direct skip (as defined in section 2612(c)) that is subject to chapter 12 and occurs during the life of the transferor.

(ii) *Direct skips occurring at death.*—(A) *In general.*—Form 706 or Form 706NA must be filed in accordance with its instructions for any direct skips (as defined in section 2612(c)) that are subject to chapter 11 and occur at the death of the decedent.

(B) *Direct skips payable from a trust.*—Schedule R-1 of Form 706 must be filed in accordance with its instructions for any direct skip from a trust if such direct skip is subject to chapter 11. See paragraph (c)(2) of this section for special rules relating to the person liable for tax and required to make the return under certain circumstances.

(c) *Person liable for tax and required to make return.*—(1) *In general.*—Except as otherwise provided in this section, the following person is liable for the tax imposed by section 2601 and must make the required tax return—

(i) The transferee in a taxable distribution (as defined in section 2612(b));

(ii) The trustee in the case of a taxable termination (as defined in section 2612(a));

(iii) The transferor (as defined in section 2652(a)(1)(B)) in the case of an inter vivos direct skip (as defined in section 2612(c));

(iv) The trustee in the case of a direct skip from a trust or with respect to property that continues to be held in trust; or

(v) The executor in the case of a direct skip (other than a direct skip described in paragraph (c)(1)(iv) of this section) if the transfer is subject to chapter 11. See paragraph (c)(2) of this section for special rules relating to direct skips to or from certain trust arrangements (as defined in paragraph (c)(2)(ii) of this section).

(2) *Special rule for direct skips occurring at death with respect to property held in trust arrangements.*—(i) *In general.*—In the case of certain property held in a trust arrangement (as defined in paragraph (c)(2)(ii) of this section) at the date of death of the transferor, the person who is required to make the return and who is liable for the tax imposed by chapter 13 is determined under paragraphs (c)(2)(iii) and (iv) of this section.

(ii) *Trust arrangement defined.*—For purposes of this section, the term *trust arrangement* includes any arrangement (other than an estate) which, although not an explicit trust, has the same effect as an explicit trust. For purposes of this section, the term "explicit trust" means a trust described in § 301.7701-4(a).

(iii) *Executor's liability in the case of transfers with respect to decedents dying on or after June 24, 1996, if the transfer is less than $250,000.*—In the case of a direct skip occurring at death, the executor of the decedent's estate is liable for the tax imposed on that direct skip by chapter 13 and is required to file Form 706 or Form 706NA (and not Schedule R-1 of Form 706) if, at the date of the decedent's death—

(A) The property involved in the direct skip is held in a trust arrangement; and

(B) The total value of the property involved in direct skips with respect to the trustee of that trust arrangement is less than $250,000.

(iv) *Executor's liability in the case of transfers with respect to decedents dying prior to June 24, 1996, if the transfer is less than $100,000.*—In the case of a direct skip occurring at death with respect to a decedent dying prior to June 24, 1996, the rule in paragraph (c)(2)(iii) of this section that imposes liability upon the executor applies only if the property involved in the direct skip with respect to the trustee of the trust arrangement, in the aggregate, is less than $100,000.

(v) *Executor's right of recovery.*—In cases where the rules of paragraphs (c)(2)(iii) and (iv) of this section impose liability for the generation-skipping transfer tax on the executor, the executor is entitled to recover from the trustee (if the property continues to be held in trust) or from the recipient of the property (in the case of a transfer from a trust), the generation-skipping transfer tax attributable to the transfer.

(vi) *Examples.*—The following examples illustrate the application of this paragraph (c)(2) with respect to decedents dying on or after June 24, 1996:

*Example 1. Insurance proceeds less than $250,000.* On August 1, 1997, T, the insured under an insurance policy, died. The proceeds ($200,000) were includible in T's gross estate for Federal estate tax purposes. T's grandchild, GC, was named the sole beneficiary of the policy. The insurance policy is treated as a trust under section 2652(b)(1), and the payment of the proceeds to GC is a transfer from a trust for purposes of chapter 13. Therefore, the payment of the proceeds to GC is a direct skip. Since the proceeds from the policy ($200,000) are less than $250,000, the executor is liable for the tax imposed by chapter 13 and is required to file Form 706.

*Example 2. Aggregate insurance proceeds of $250,000 or more.* Assume the same facts as in *Example 1*, except T is the insured under two insurance policies issued by the same insurance company. The proceeds ($150,000) from each policy are includible in T's gross estate for Federal estate tax purposes. T's grandchild, GC1, was named the sole beneficiary of Policy 1, and T's other grandchild, GC2, was named the sole beneficiary of Policy 2. GC1 and GC2 are skip persons (as defined in section 2613). Therefore, the payments of the proceeds are direct skips. Since the total value of the policies ($300,000) exceeds $250,000, the insurance company is liable for the tax imposed by chapter 13 and is required to file Schedule R-1 of Form 706.

*Example 3. Insurance proceeds of $250,000 or more held by insurance company.* On August 1, 1997, T, the insured under an insurance policy, dies. The policy provides that the insurance company shall make monthly payments of $750 to GC, T's grandchild, for life with the remainder payable to T's great grandchild, GGC. The face value of the policy is $300,000. Since the proceeds continue to be held by the insurance company (the trustee), the proceeds are treated as if they were transferred to a trust for purposes of chapter 13. The trust is a skip person (as defined in section 2613(a)(2)) and the transfer is a direct skip. Since the total value of the policy ($300,000) exceeds $250,000, the insurance company is liable for the tax imposed by chapter 13 and is required to file Schedule R-1 of Form 706.

*Example 4. Insurance proceeds less than $250,000 held by insurance company.* Assume the same facts as in *Example 3*, except the policy provides that the insurance company shall make monthly payments of $500 to GC and that the face value of the policy is $200,000. The transfer is a transfer to a trust for purposes of chapter 13. However, since the total value of the policy ($200,000) is less than $250,000, the executor is liable for the tax imposed by chapter 13 and is required to file Form 706.

*Example 5.* On August 1, 1997, A, the insured under a life insurance policy, dies. The insurance proceeds on A's life that are payable under policies issued by Company X are in the aggregate amount of $200,000 and are includible in A's gross estate. Because the proceeds are includible in A's gross estate, the generation-skipping transfer that occurs upon A's death, if any, will be a direct skip rather than a taxable distribution or a taxable termination. Accordingly, because the aggregate amount of insurance proceeds with respect to Company X is less than $250,000, Company X may pay the proceeds without regard to whether the beneficiary is a skip person in relation to the decedent-transferor.

(3) *Limitation on personal liability of trustee.*—Except as provided in paragraph (c)(3)(iii) of this section, a trustee is not personally liable for any increases in the tax imposed by section 2601 which is attributable to the fact that—

(i) A transfer is made to the trust during the life of the transferor for which a gift tax return is not filed; or

(ii) The inclusion ratio with respect to the trust, determined by reference to the transferor's gift tax return, is erroneous, the actual inclusion ratio being greater than the reported inclusion ratio.

(iii) This paragraph (c)(3) does not apply if the trustee has or is deemed to have knowledge of facts sufficient to reasonably conclude that a gift tax return was required to be filed or that the inclusion ratio is erroneous. A trustee is deemed to have knowledge of such facts if the trustee's agent, employee, partner, or co-trustee has knowledge of such facts.

(4) *Exceptions.*—(i) *Legal or mental incapacity.*—If a distributee is legally or mentally incapable of making a return, the return may be made for the distributee by the distributee's guardian or, if no guardian has been appointed, by a person charged with the care of the distributee's person or property.

(ii) *Returns made by fiduciaries.*—See section 6012(b) for a fiduciary's responsibilities regarding the returns of decedents, returns of persons under a disability, returns of estates and trusts, and returns made by joint fiduciaries.

(d) *Time and manner of filing return.*—(1) *In general.*—Forms 706, 706NA, 706GS(D), 706GS(D-1), 706GS(T), 709, and Schedule R-1 of Form 706 must be filed with the Internal Revenue Service office with which an estate or gift tax return of the transferor must be filed. The return shall be filed—

(i) *Direct skip.*—In the case of a direct skip, on or before the date on which an estate or gift tax return is required to be filed with respect to the transfer (see section 6075(b)(3)); and

(ii) *Other transfers.*—In all other cases, on or before the 15th day of the 4th month after the close of the calendar year in which such transfer occurs. See paragraph (d)(2) of this section for an exception to this rule when an election is made under section 2624(c) to value property included in certain taxable terminations in accordance with section 2032.

(2) *Exception for alternative valuation of taxable termination.*—In the case of a taxable termination with respect to which an election is made under section 2624(c) to value property in accordance with section 2032, a Form 706GS(T) must be filed on or before the 15th day of the 4th month after the close of the calendar year in which the taxable termination occurred, or on or before the 10th month following the month in which the death that resulted in the taxable termination occurred, whichever is later.

(e) *Place for filing returns.*—See section 6091 for the place for filing any return, declaration, statement, or other document, or copies thereof, required by chapter 13.

(f) *Lien on property.*—The liens imposed under sections 6324, 6324A, and 6324B are applicable with respect to the tax imposed under chapter 13. Thus, a lien under section 6324 is imposed in the amount of the tax imposed by section 2601 on all property transferred in a generation-skipping transfer until the tax is fully paid or becomes uncollectible by reason of lapse of time. The lien attaches at the time of the generation-skipping transfer and is in addition to the lien for taxes under section 6321. [Reg. § 26.2662-1.]

☐ [*T.D.* 8644, 12-26-95.]

**[Reg. § 26.2663-1]**

**§ 26.2663-1. Recapture tax under section 2032A.**—See § 26.2642-4(a)(4) for rules relating to the recomputation of the applicable fraction and the imposition of additional GST tax, if additional estate tax is imposed under section 2032A. [Reg. § 26.2663-1.]

☐ [*T.D.* 8644, 12-26-95.]

**[Reg. § 26.2663-2]**

**§ 26.2663-2. Application of chapter 13 to transfers by nonresidents not citizens of the United States.**—(a) *In general.*—This section provides rules for applying chapter 13 of the Internal Revenue Code to transfers by a transferor who is a nonresident not a citizen of the United States (NRA transferor). For purposes of this section, an individual is a resident or citizen of the United States if that individual is a resident or citizen of the United States under the rules of chapter 11 or 12 of the Internal Revenue Code, as the case may be. Every NRA transferor is allowed a GST exemption of $1,000,000. See § 26.2632-1 regarding the allocation of the exemption.

(b) *Transfers subject to chapter 13.*—(1) *Direct skips.*—A transfer by a NRA transferor is a direct skip subject to chapter 13 only to the extent that the transfer is subject to the Federal estate or gift tax within the meaning of § 26.2652-1(a)(2). See § 26.2612-1(a) for the definition of *direct skip.*

(2) *Taxable distributions and taxable terminations.*—Chapter 13 applies to a taxable distribution or a taxable termination to the extent that the initial transfer of property to the trust by a NRA transferor, whether during life or at death, was subject to the Federal estate or gift tax within the meaning of § 26.2652-1(a)(2). See § 26.2612-1(b) for the definition of a *taxable termination* and § 26.2612-1(c) for the definition of a *taxable distribution.*

(c) *Trusts funded in part with property subject to chapter 13 and in part with property not subject to chapter 13.*—(1) *In general.*—If a single trust created by a NRA transferor is in part subject to chapter 13 under the rules of paragraph (b) of this section and in part not subject to chapter 13, the applicable fraction with respect to the trust is determined as of the date of the transfer, except as provided in paragraph (c)(3) of this section.

(i) *Numerator of applicable fraction.*—The numerator of the applicable fraction is the sum of the amount of GST exemption allocated to the trust (if any) plus the value of the nontax portion of the trust.

(ii) *Denominator of applicable fraction.*—The denominator of the applicable fraction is the value of the property transferred to the trust reduced as provided in § 26.2642-1(c).

(2) *Nontax portion of the trust.*—The nontax portion of a trust is a fraction, the numerator of which is the value of property not subject to chapter 13 determined as of the date of the initial completed transfer to the trust, and the denominator of which is the value of the entire trust. For example, T, a NRA transferor, transfers property that has a value of $1,000 to a generation-skipping trust. Of the property transferred to the trust, property having a value of $200 is subject to chapter 13 and property having a value of $800 is not subject to chapter 13. The nontax portion is .8 ($800 (the value of the property not subject to chapter 13) over $1,000 (the total value of the property transferred to the trust)).

(3) *Special rule with respect to the estate tax inclusion period.*—For purposes of this section, the provisions of § 26.2632-1(c), providing rules applicable in the case of an estate tax inclusion period (ETIP), apply only if the property transferred by the NRA transferor is subsequently included in the transferor's gross estate. If the property is not subsequently included in the gross estate, then the nontax portion of the trust and the applicable fraction are determined as of the date of the initial transfer. If the property is subsequently included in the gross estate, then the nontax portion and the applicable fraction are determined as of the date of death.

(d) *Examples.*—The following examples illustrate the provisions of this section. In each example T, a NRA, is the transferor; C is T's child; and GC is C's child and a grandchild of T:

*Example 1. Direct transfer to skip person.* T transfers property to GC in a transfer that is subject to Federal gift tax under chapter 12 within the meaning of § 26.2652-1(a)(2). At the time of the transfer, C and GC are NRAs. T's transfer is subject to chapter 13 because the transfer is subject to gift tax under chapter 12.

*Example 2. Transfers of both U.S. and foreign situs property.* (i) T's will established a testamentary trust for the benefit of C and GC. The trust was funded with stock in a publicly traded U.S. corporation having a value on the date of T's death of $100,000, and property not situated in the United States (and therefore not subject to estate tax) having a value on the date of T's death of $400,000.

(ii) On a timely filed estate tax return (Form 706NA), the executor of T's estate allocates $50,000 of GST exemption under section 2632(a) to the trust. The numerator of the applicable fraction is $450,000, the sum of $50,000 (the amount of exemption allocated to the trust) plus $400,000 (the value of the nontax portion of the trust (4/5 x $500,000)). The denominator is $500,000. Hence, the applicable fraction with respect to the trust is .9 ($450,000/$500,000), and the inclusion ratio is .1 (1 - 9/10).

*Example 3. Inter vivos transfer of U.S. and foreign situs property to a trust and a timely allocation of GST exemption.* T establishes a trust providing that trust income is payable to T's child for life and the remainder is to be paid to T's grandchild. T transfers property to the trust that has a value of $100,000 and is subject to chapter 13. T also transfers property to the trust that has a value of $300,000 but is not subject to chapter 13. T allocates $100,000 of exemption to the trust on a timely filed United States Gift (and Generation-Skipping Transfer) Tax Return (Form 709). The applicable fraction with respect to the trust is 1, determined as follows: $300,000 (the value of the nontax portion of the trust) plus $100,000 (the exemption allocated to the trust)/$400,000 (the total value of the property transferred to the trust).

*Example 4. Inter vivos transfer of U.S. and foreign situs property to a trust and a late allocation of GST exemption.* (i) In 1996, T transfers $500,000 of property to an inter vivos trust the terms of which provide that income is payable to C, for life, with the remainder to GC. The property transferred to the trust consists of property subject to chapter 13 that has a value of $400,000 on the date of the transfer and property not subject to chapter 13 that has a value of $100,000. T does not allocate GST exemption to the trust. On the transfer date, the nontax portion of the trust is .2 ($100,000/$500,000) and the applicable fraction is also .2 determined as follows: $100,000 (the value of the nontax portion of the trust)/$500,000 (the value of the property transferred to the trust).

(ii) In 1999, when the value of the trust is $800,000, T allocates $100,000 of GST exemption to the trust. The applicable fraction of the trust must be recomputed. The numerator of the applicable fraction is $260,000 ($100,000 (the amount of GST exemption allocated to the trust)) plus $160,000 (the value of the nontax portion of the trust as of the date of allocation (.2 x $800,000)). The denominator of the applicable fraction is $800,000. Accordingly, the applicable fraction with respect to the trust after the allocation is .325 ($260,000/$800,000) and the inclusion ratio is .675 (1 - .325).

*Example 5. Taxable termination.* The facts are the same as in *Example 4* except that, in 2006, when the value of the property is $1,200,000, C dies and the trust corpus is distributed to GC. The termination is a taxable termination. If no further GST exemption has been allocated to the trust, the applicable fraction remains .325 and the inclusion ratio remains .675.

*Example 6. Estate Tax Inclusion Period.* (i) T transferred property to an inter vivos trust the terms of which provided T with an annuity payable for 10 years or until T's prior death. The annuity satisfies the definition of a qualified interest under section 2702(b). The trust also provided that, at the end of the trust term, the remainder will pass to GC or GC's estate. The property transferred to the trust consisted of property subject to chapter 13 that has a value of $100,000 and property not subject to chapter 13 that has a value of $400,000. T allocated $100,000 of GST exemption to the trust. If T dies within the 10 year period, the value of the trust principal will be subject to inclusion in T's gross estate to the extent provided in sections 2103 and 2104(b). Accordingly, the ETIP rule under paragraph (c)(3) of this section applies.

(ii) In year 6 of the trust term, T died. At T's death, the trust corpus had a value of $800,000, and $500,000 was includible in T's gross estate as provided in sections 2103 and 2104(b). Thus, $500,000 of the trust corpus is subject to chapter 13 and $300,000 is not subject to chapter 13. The $100,000 GST exemption allocation is effective as of T's date of death. Also, the nontax portion of the trust and the applicable fraction are determined as of T's date of death. In this case, the nontax portion of the trust is .375, determined as follows: $300,000 (the value of the trust not subject to chapter 13)/$800,000 (the value of the trust). The numerator of the applicable fraction is $400,000, determined as follows: $100,000 (GST exemption previously allocated to the trust) plus $300,000 (the value of the nontax portion of the trust). The denominator of the applicable fraction is $800,000. Thus, the applicable fraction with respect to the trust is .50, unless additional exemption is allocated to the trust by T's executor or the automatic allocation rules of §26.2632-1(d)(2) apply.

*Example 7.* The facts are the same as in *Example 6* except that T survives the termination date of T's retained annuity and the trust corpus is distributed to GC. Since the trust was not included in T's gross estate, the ETIP rules do not apply. Accordingly, the nontax portion of the trust and the applicable fraction are determined as of the date of the transfer to the trust. The nontax portion of the trust is .80 ($400,000/$500,000). The numerator of the applicable fraction is $500,000 determined as follows: $100,000 (GST exemption allocated to the trust) plus $400,000 (the value of the nontax portion of the trust). Accordingly, the applicable fraction is 1, and the inclusion ratio is zero.

(e) *Transitional rule for allocations for transfers made before December 27, 1995.*—If a NRA made a GST (inter vivos or testamentary) after December 23, 1992, and before December 27, 1995, that is subject to chapter 13 (within the meaning of §26.2663-2), the NRA will be treated as having made a timely allocation of GST exemption to the transfer in a calendar year in the order prescribed in section 2632(c). Thus, a NRA's unused GST exemption will initially be treated as allocated to any direct skips made during the calendar year and then to any trusts with respect to which the NRA made transfers during the same calendar year and from which a taxable distribution or a taxable termination may occur. Allocations within the above categories are made in the order in which the transfers occur. Allocations among simultaneous transfers within the same category are made pursuant to the principles of section 2632(c)(2). This transitional allocation rule will not apply if the NRA transferor, or the executor of the NRA's estate, as the case may be, elected to have an automatic allocation of GST exemption not apply by describing on a timely-filed Form 709 for the year of the transfer, or a timely filed Form 706NA, the details of the transfer and the extent to which the allocation was not to apply. [Reg. §26.2663-2.]

☐ [T.D. 8644, 12-26-95.]

# Special Valuation Rules

See p. 20,601 for regulations not amended to reflect law changes

(c) Minimum value rule.
  (1) In general.
  (2) Junior equity interest.
  (3) Indebtedness.
(d) Examples.

**§ 25.2701-4. Accumulated qualified payments.**
(a) In general.
(b) Taxable event.
  (1) In general.
  (2) Exception.
  (3) Individual treated as interest holder.
(c) Amount of increase.
  (1) In general.
  (2) Due date of qualified payments.
  (3) Appropriate discount rate.
  (4) Application of payments.
  (5) Payment.
  (6) Limitation.
(d) Taxpayer election.
  (1) In general.
  (2) Limitation not applicable.
  (3) Time and manner of election.
  (4) Example.

**§ 25.2701-5. Adjustments to mitigate double taxation.**
(a) Reduction of transfer tax base.
  (1) In general.
  (2) Federal gift tax modification.
  (3) Federal estate tax modification.
  (4) Section 2701 interest.
(b) Amount of reduction.
(c) Duplicated amount.
  (1) In general.
  (2) Transfer tax value—in general.
  (3) Special transfer tax value rules.
(d) Examples.
(e) Computation of reduction if initial transfer is split under section 2513.
  (1) In general.
  (2) Transfers during joint lives.
  (3) Transfers at or after death of either spouse.
(f) Examples.
(g) Double taxation otherwise avoided.
(h) Effective date.

**§ 25.2701-6. Indirect holding of interests.**
(a) In general.
  (1) Attribution to individuals.
  (2) Corporations.
  (3) Partnerships.
  (4) Estates, trusts, and other entities.
  (5) Multiple attribution.
(b) Examples.

**§ 25.2701-7. Separate interests.**

**§ 25.2701-8. Effective dates.**
[Reg. § 25.2701-0.]

☐ [*T.D. 8395, 1-28-92. Amended by T.D. 8536, 5-4-94.*]

**[Reg. § 25.2701-1]**

**§ 25.2701-1. Special valuation rules in the case of transfers of certain interests in corporations and partnerships.**—(a) *In general.*—(1) *Scope of section 2701.*—Section 2701 provides special valuation rules to determine the amount of the gift when an individual transfers an equity interest in a corporation or partnership to a member of the individual's family. For section 2701 to apply, the transferor or an applicable family member (as defined in paragraph (d)(2) of this section) must, immediately after the transfer, hold an applicable retained interest (a type of equity interest defined in § 25.2701-2(b)(1)). If certain subsequent payments with respect to the applicable retained interest do not conform to the assumptions used in valuing the interest at the time of the initial transfer, § 25.2701-4 provides a special rule to increase the individual's later taxable gifts or taxable estate. Section 25.2701-5 provides an adjustment to mitigate the effects of double taxation when an applicable retained interest is subsequently transferred.

(2) *Effect of section 2701.*—If section 2701 applies to a transfer, the amount of the transferor's gift, if any, is determined using a subtraction method of valuation (described in § 25.2701-3). Under this method, the amount of the gift is determined by subtracting the value of any family-held applicable retained interests and other non-transferred equity interests from the aggregate value of family-held interests in the corporation or partnership (the "entity"). Generally, in determining the value of any applicable retained interest held by the transferor or an applicable family member—

(i) Any put, call, or conversion right, any right to compel liquidation, or any similar right is valued at zero if the right is an "extraordinary payment right" (as defined in § 25.2701-2(b)(2));

(ii) Any distribution right in a controlled entity (*e.g.,* a right to receive dividends) is valued at zero unless the right is a "qualified payment right" (as defined in § 25.2701-2(b)(6)); and

(iii) Any other right (including a qualified payment right) is valued as if any right valued at zero did not exist but otherwise without regard to section 2701.

(3) *Example.*—The following example illustrates rules of this paragraph (a).

*Example.* A, an individual, holds all the outstanding stock of S Corporation. A exchanges A's shares in S for 100 shares of 10-percent cumulative preferred stock and 100 shares of voting common stock. A transfers the common stock to A's child. Section 2701 applies to the transfer because A has transferred an equity interest (the common stock) to a member of A's family, and immediately thereafter holds an applicable retained interest (the preferred stock). A's preferred stock is valued under the rules of section 2701. A's gift is determined under the subtraction method by subtracting the value of A's preferred stock from the value of A's interest in S immediately prior to the transfer.

(b) *Transfers and other triggering events.*—(1) *Completed transfers.*—Section 2701 applies to determine the existence and amount of any gift, whether or not the transfer would otherwise be a taxable gift under chapter 12 of the Internal Revenue Code. For example, section 2701 applies to a transfer that would not otherwise be a gift under chapter 12 because it was a transfer for full and adequate consideration.

(2) *Transactions treated as transfers.*—(i) *In general.*—Except as provided in paragraph (b)(3) of this section, for purposes of section 2701, transfer includes the following transactions:

(A) A contribution to the capital of a new or existing entity;

(B) A redemption, recapitalization, or other change in the capital structure of an entity (a "capital structure transaction"), if—

(*1*) The transferor or an applicable family member receives an applicable retained interest in the capital structure transaction;

(*2*) The transferor or an applicable family member holding an applicable retained interest before the capital structure transaction surrenders an equity interest that is junior to the applicable retained interest (a "subordinate interest") and receives property other than an applicable retained interest; or

(*3*) The transferor or an applicable family member holding an applicable retained interest before the capital structure transaction surrenders an equity interest in the entity (other than a subordinate interest) and the fair market value of the applicable retained interest is increased; or

(C) The termination of an indirect holding in an entity (as defined in § 25.2701-6) (or a contribution to capital by an entity to the extent an individual indirectly holds an interest in the entity), if—

(*1*) The property is held in a trust as to which the indirect holder is treated as the owner under subchapter J of chapter 1 of the Internal Revenue Code; or

(*2*) If the termination (or contribution) is not treated as a transfer under paragraph (b)(2)(i)(C)(*1*) of this section, to the extent the value of the indirectly-held interest would have been included in the value of the indirect holder's gross estate for Federal estate tax purposes if the indirect holder died immediately prior to the termination.

(ii) *Multiple attribution.*—For purposes of paragraph (b)(2)(i)(C) of this section, if the transfer of an indirect holding in property is treated as a transfer with respect to more than one indirect holder, the transfer is attributed in the following order:

(A) First, to the indirect holder(s) who transferred the interest to the entity (without regard to section 2513);

(B) Second, to the indirect holder(s) possessing a presently exercisable power to designate the person who shall possess or enjoy the property;

(C) Third, to the indirect holder(s) presently entitled to receive the income from the interest;

(D) Fourth, to the indirect holder(s) specifically entitled to receive the interest at a future date; and

(E) Last, to any other indirect holder(s) proportionally.

(3) *Excluded transactions.*—For purposes of section 2701, a transfer does not include the following transactions:

(i) A capital structure transaction, if the transferor, each applicable family member, and each member of the transferor's family holds substantially the same interest after the transaction as that individual held before the transaction. For this purpose, common stock with non-lapsing voting rights and nonvoting common stock are interests that are substantially the same;

(ii) A shift of rights occurring upon the execution of a qualified disclaimer described in section 2518; and

(iii) A shift of rights occurring upon the release, exercise, or lapse of a power of appointment other than a general power of appointment described in section 2514, except to the extent the release, exercise, or lapse would otherwise be a transfer under chapter 12.

(c) *Circumstances in which section 2701 does not apply.*—To the extent provided, section 2701 does not apply in the following cases:

(1) *Marketable transferred interests.*—Section 2701 does not apply if there are readily available market quotations on an established securities market for the value of the transferred interests.

(2) *Marketable retained interests.*—Section 25.2701-2 does not apply to any applicable retained interest if there are readily available market quotations on an established securities market for the value of the applicable retained interests.

(3) *Interests of the same class.*—Section 2701 does not apply if the retained interest is of the same class of equity as the transferred interest or if the retained interest is of a class that is proportional to the class of the transferred interest. A class is the same class as is (or is proportional to the class of) the transferred interest if the rights are identical (or proportional) to the rights of the transferred interest, except for non-lapsing differences in voting rights (or, for a partnership, non-lapsing differences with respect to management and limitations on liability). For purposes of this section, non-lapsing provisions necessary to comply with partnership allocation requirements of the Internal Revenue Code (*e.g.*, section 704(b)) are non-lapsing differences with respect to limitations on liability. A right that lapses by reason of Federal or State law is treated as a non-lapsing right unless the Secretary determines, by regulation or by published revenue ruling, that it is necessary to treat such a right as a lapsing right to accomplish the purposes of section 2701. An interest in a partnership is not an interest in the same class as the transferred interest if the transferor or applicable family members have the right to alter the liability of the transferee.

(4) *Proportionate transfers.*—Section 2701 does not apply to a transfer by an individual to a member of the individual's family of equity interests to the extent the transfer by that individual results in a proportionate reduction of each class of equity interest held by the individual and all applicable family members in the aggregate immediately before the transfer. Thus, for example, section 2701 does not apply if P owns 50 percent of each class of equity interest in a corporation and transfers a portion of each class to P's child in a manner that reduces each interest held by P and any applicable family members, in the aggregate, by 10 percent even if the transfer does not proportionately reduce P's interest in each class. See § 25.2701-6 regarding indirect holding of interests.

(d) *Family definitions.*—(1) *Member of the family.*—A member of the family is, with respect to any transferor—

(i) The transferor's spouse;

(ii) Any lineal descendant of the transferor or the transferor's spouse; and

(iii) The spouse of any such lineal descendant.

(2) *Applicable family member.*—An applicable family member is, with respect to any transferor—

(i) The transferor's spouse;

(ii) Any ancestor of the transferor or the transferor's spouse; and

(iii) The spouse of any such ancestor.

(3) *Relationship by adoption.*—For purposes of section 2701, any relationship by legal adoption is the same as a relationship by blood.

(e) *Examples.*—The following examples illustrate provisions of this section:

*Example 1.* P, an individual, holds all the outstanding stock of X Corporation. Assume the fair market value of P's interest in X immediately prior to the transfer is $1.5 million. X is recapitalized so that P holds 1,000 shares of $1,000 par value preferred stock bearing an annual cumulative dividend of $100 per share (the aggregate fair market value of which is assumed to be $1 million) and 1,000 shares of voting common stock. P transfers the common stock to P's child.

Section 2701 applies to the transfer because P has transferred an equity interest (the common stock) to a member of P's family and immediately thereafter holds an applicable retained interest (the preferred stock). P's right to receive annual cumulative dividends is a qualified payment right and is valued for purposes of section 2701 at its fair market value of $1,000,000. The amount of P's gift, determined using the subtraction method of § 25.2701-3, is $500,000 ($1,500,000 minus $1,000,000).

*Example 2.* The facts are the same as in *Example 1*, except that the preferred dividend right is noncumulative. Under § 25.2701-2, P's preferred dividend right is valued at zero because it is a distribution right in a controlled entity, but is not a qualified payment right. All of P's other rights in the preferred stock are valued as if P's dividend right does not exist but otherwise without regard to section 2701. The amount of P's gift, determined using the subtraction method, is $1,500,000 ($1,500,000 minus $0). P may elect, however, to treat the dividend right as a qualified payment right as provided in § 25.2701-2(c)(2). [Reg. § 25.2701-1.]

☐ [*T.D. 8395, 1-28-92. Amended by T.D. 8536, 5-4-94.*]

### [Reg. § 25.2701-2]

**§ 25.2701-2. Special valuation rules for applicable retained interests.**—(a) *In general.*—In determining the amount of a gift under § 25.2701-3, the value of any applicable retained interest (as defined in paragraph (b)(1) of this section) held by the transferor or by an applicable family member is determined using the rules of chapter 12, with the modifications prescribed by this section. See § 25.2701-6 regarding the indirect holding of interests.

(1) *Valuing an extraordinary payment right.*—Any extraordinary payment right (as defined in paragraph (b)(2) of this section) is valued at zero.

(2) *Valuing a distribution right.*—Any distribution right (as defined in paragraph (b)(3) of this section) in a controlled entity is valued at zero, unless it is a qualified payment right (as defined in paragraph (b)(6) of this section). Controlled entity is defined in paragraph (b)(5) of this section.

(3) *Special rule for valuing a qualified payment right held in conjunction with an extraordinary payment right.*—If an applicable retained interest confers a qualified payment right and one or more extraordinary payment rights, the value of all these rights is determined by assuming that each extraordinary payment right is exercised in a manner that results in the lowest total value being determined for all the rights, using a consistent set of assumptions and giving due regard to the entity's net worth, prospective earning power, and other relevant factors (the "lower of" valuation rule). See §§ 20.2031-2(f) and 20.2031-3 for rules relating to the valuation of business interests generally.

(4) *Valuing other rights.*—Any other right (including a qualified payment right not subject to the prior paragraph) is valued as if any right valued at zero does not exist and as if any right valued under the lower of rule is exercised in a manner consistent with the assumptions of that rule but otherwise without regard to section 2701. Thus, if an applicable retained interest carries no rights that are valued at zero or under the lower of rule, the value of the interest for purposes of section 2701 is its fair market value.

(5) *Example.*—The following example illustrates rules of this paragraph (a).

*Example.* P, an individual, holds all 1,000 shares of X Corporation's $1,000 par value preferred stock bearing an annual cumulative dividend of $100 per share and holds all 1,000 shares of X's voting common stock. P has the right to put all the preferred stock to X at any time for $900,000. P transfers the common stock to P's child and immediately thereafter holds the preferred stock. Assume that at the time of the transfer, the fair market value of X is $1,500,000, and the fair market value of P's annual cumulative dividend right is $1,000,000. Because the preferred stock confers both an extraordinary payment right (the put right) and a qualified payment right (*i.e.*, the right to receive cumulative dividends), the lower of rule applies and the value of these rights is determined as if the put right will be exercised in a manner that results in the lowest total value being determined for the rights (in this case, by assuming that the put will be exercised immediately). The value of P's preferred stock is $900,000 (the lower of $1,000,000 or $900,000). The amount of the gift is $600,000 ($1,500,000 minus $900,000).

(b) *Definitions.*—(1) *Applicable retained interest.*—An applicable retained interest is any equity interest in a corporation or partnership with respect to which there is either—

(i) An extraordinary payment right (as defined in paragraph (b)(2) of this section), or

(ii) In the case of a controlled entity (as defined in paragraph (b)(5) of this section), a distribution right (as defined in paragraph (b)(3) of this section).

(2) *Extraordinary payment right.*—Except as provided in paragraph (b)(4) of this section, an extraordinary payment right is any put, call, or conversion right, any right to compel liquidation, or any similar right, the exercise or nonexercise of which affects the value of the transferred interest. A call right includes any warrant, option, or other right to acquire one or more equity interests.

(3) *Distribution right.*—A distribution right is the right to receive distributions with respect to an equity interest. A distribution right does not include—

(i) Any right to receive distributions with respect to an interest that is of the same class as, or a class that is subordinate to, the transferred interest;

(ii) Any extraordinary payment right; or

(iii) Any right described in paragraph (b)(4) of this section.

(4) *Rights that are not extraordinary payment rights or distribution rights.*—Mandatory payment rights, liquidation participation rights, rights to guaranteed payments of a fixed amount under section 707(c), and non-lapsing conversion rights are neither extraordinary payment rights nor distribution rights.

(i) *Mandatory payment right.*—A mandatory payment right is a right to receive a payment required to be made at a specific time for a specific amount. For example, a mandatory redemption right in preferred stock requiring that the stock be redeemed at its fixed par value on a date certain is a mandatory payment right and therefore not an extraordinary payment right or a distribution right. A right to receive a specific amount on the death of the holder is a mandatory payment right.

(ii) *Liquidation participation rights.*—A liquidation participation right is a right to participate in a liquidating distribution. If the transferor, members of the transferor's family, or applicable family members have the ability to compel liquidation, the liquidation participation right is valued as if the ability to compel liquidation—

(A) Did not exist, or

(B) If the lower of rule applies, is exercised in a manner that is consistent with that rule.

(iii) *Right to a guaranteed payment of a fixed amount under section 707(c).*—The right to a guaranteed payment of a fixed amount under section 707(c) is the right to a guaranteed payment (within the meaning of section 707(c)) the amount of which is determined at a fixed rate (including a rate that bears a fixed relationship to a specified market interest rate). A payment that is contingent as to time or amount is not a guaranteed payment of a fixed amount.

(iv) *Non-lapsing conversion right.*—(A) *Corporations.*—A non-lapsing conversion right, in the case of a corporation, is a non-lapsing right to convert an equity interest in a corporation into a fixed number or a fixed percentage of shares of the same class as the transferred interest (or into an interest that would be of the same class but for non-lapsing differences in voting rights), that is subject to proportionate adjustments for changes in the equity ownership of the corporation and to adjustments similar to those provided in section 2701(d) for unpaid payments.

(B) *Partnerships.*—A non-lapsing conversion right, in the case of a partnership, is a non-lapsing right to convert an equity interest in a partnership into a specified interest (other than an interest represented by a fixed dollar amount) of the same class as the transferred interest (or into an interest that would be of the same class but for non-lapsing differences in management rights or limitations on liability) that is subject to proportionate adjustments for changes in the equity ownership of the partnership and to adjustments similar to those provided in section 2701(d) for unpaid payments.

(C) *Proportionate adjustments in equity ownership.*—For purposes of this paragraph (b)(4), an equity interest is subject to proportionate adjustments for changes in equity ownership if, in the case of a corporation, proportionate adjustments are required to be made for splits, combinations, reclassifications, and similar changes in capital stock, or, in the case of a partnership, the equity interest is protected from dilution resulting from changes in the partnership structure.

(D) *Adjustments for unpaid payments.*—For purposes of this paragraph (b)(4), an equity interest is subject to adjustments similar to those provided in section 2701(d) if it provides for—

(1) Cumulative payments;

(2) Compounding of any unpaid payments at the rate specified in § 25.2701-4(c)(2); and

(3) Adjustment of the number or percentage of shares or the size of the interest into which it is convertible to take account of accumulated but unpaid payments.

(5) *Controlled entity.*—(i) *In general.*—For purposes of section 2701, a controlled entity is a corporation or partnership controlled, immediately before a transfer, by the transferor, applicable family members, and any lineal descendants of the parents of the transferor or the transferor's spouse. See § 25.2701-6 regarding indirect holding of interests.

(ii) *Corporations.*—(A) *In general.*—In the case of a corporation, control means the holding of at least 50 percent of the total voting power or total fair market value of the equity interests in the corporation.

(B) *Voting rights.*—Equity interests that carry no right to vote other than on liquidation, merger, or a similar event are not considered to have voting rights for purposes of this paragraph (b)(5)(ii). Generally, a voting right is considered held by an individual to the extent that the individual, either alone or in conjunction with any other person, is entitled to exercise (or direct the exercise of) the right. However, if an equity interest carrying voting rights is held in a fiduciary capacity, the voting rights are not considered held by the fiduciary, but instead are considered held by each beneficial owner of the interest and by each individual who is a permissible recipient of the income from the interest. A voting right does not include a right to vote that is subject to a contingency that has not occurred, other than a contingency that is within the control of the individual holding the right.

(iii) *Partnerships.*—In the case of any partnership, control means the holding of at least 50 percent of either the capital interest or the profits interest in the partnership. Any right to a guaranteed payment under section 707(c) of a fixed amount is disregarded in making this determination. In addition, in the case of a limited partnership, control means the holding of any equity interest as a general partner. See § 25.2701-2(b)(4)(iii) for the definition of a right to a guaranteed payment of a fixed amount under section 707(c).

(6) *Qualified payment right.*—(i) *In general.*—A qualified payment right is a right to receive qualified payments. A qualified payment is a distribution that is—

(A) A dividend payable on a periodic basis (at least annually) under any cumulative preferred stock, to the extent such dividend is determined at a fixed rate;

(B) Any other cumulative distribution payable on a periodic basis (at least annually) with respect to an equity interest, to the extent determined at a fixed rate or as a fixed amount; or

(C) Any distribution right for which an election has been made pursuant to paragraph (c)(2) of this section.

(ii) *Fixed rate.*—For purposes of this section, a payment rate that bears a fixed relationship to a specified market interest rate is a payment determined at a fixed rate.

(c) *Qualified payment elections.*—(1) *Election to treat a qualified payment right as other than a qualified payment right.*—Any transferor holding a qualified payment right may elect to treat all rights held by the transferor of the same class as rights that are not qualified payment rights. An election may be a partial election, in which case the election must be exercised with respect to a consistent portion of each payment right in the class as to which the election has been made.

(2) *Election to treat other distribution rights as qualified payment rights.*—Any individual may elect to treat a distribution right held by that individual in a controlled entity as a qualified payment right. An election may be a partial election, in which case the election must be exercised with respect to a consistent portion of each payment right in the class as to which the election has been made. An election under this paragraph (c)(2) will not cause the value of the applicable retained interest conferring the distribution right to exceed the fair market value of the applicable retained interest (determined without regard to section 2701). The election is effective only to the extent—

(i) Specified in the election, and

(ii) That the payments elected are permissible under the legal instrument giving rise to the right and are consistent with the legal right of the entity to make the payment.

(3) *Elections irrevocable.*—Any election under paragraph (c)(1) or (c)(2) of this section is revocable only with the consent of the Commissioner.

(4) *Treatment of certain payments to applicable family members.*—Any payment right described in paragraph (b)(6) of this section held by an applicable family member is treated as a payment right that is not a qualified payment right unless the applicable family member

**Reg. § 25.2701-2(c)(4)**

elects (pursuant to paragraph (c)(2) of this section) to treat the payment right as a qualified payment right. An election may be a partial election, in which case the election must be exercised with respect to a consistent portion of each payment right in the class as to which the election has been made.

(5) *Time and manner of elections.*—Any election under paragraph (c)(1) or (c)(2) of this section is made by attaching a statement to the Form 709, Federal Gift Tax Return, filed by the transferor on which the transfer is reported. An election filed after the time of the filing of the Form 709 reporting the transfer is not a valid election. An election filed as of March 28, 1992, for transfers made prior to its publication is effective. The statement must—

(i) Set forth the name, address, and taxpayer identification number of the electing individual and of the transferor, if different;

(ii) If the electing individual is not the transferor filing the return, state the relationship between the individual and the transferor;

(iii) Specifically identify the transfer disclosed on the return to which the election applies;

(iv) Describe in detail the distribution right to which the election applies;

(v) State the provision of the regulation under which the election is being made; and

(vi) If the election is being made under paragraph (c)(2) of this section—

(A) State the amounts that the election assumes will be paid, and the times that the election assumes the payments will be made;

(B) Contain a statement, signed by the electing individual, in which the electing individual agrees that—

*(1)* If payments are not made as provided in the election, the individual's subsequent taxable gifts or taxable estate will, upon the occurrence of a taxable event (as defined in § 25.2701-4(b)), be increased by an amount determined under § 25.2701-4(c), and

*(2)* The individual will be personally liable for any increase in tax attributable thereto.

(d) *Examples.*—The following examples illustrate provisions of this section:

*Example 1.* On March 30, 1991, P transfers non-voting common stock of X Corporation to P's child, while retaining $100 par value voting preferred stock bearing a cumulative annual dividend of $10. Immediately before the transfer, P held 100 percent of the stock. Because X is a controlled entity (within the meaning of paragraph (b)(5) of this section), P's dividend right is a distribution right that is subject to section 2701. See § 25.2701-2(b)(3). Because the distribution right is an annual cumulative dividend, it is a qualified payment right. See § 25.2701-2(b)(6).

*Example 2.* The facts are the same as in *Example 1,* except that the dividend right is non-cumulative. P's dividend right is a distribution right in a controlled entity, but is not a qualified payment right because the dividend is non-cumulative. Therefore, the non-cumulative dividend right is valued at zero under § 25.2701-2(a)(2). If the corporation were not a controlled entity, P's dividend right would be valued without regard to section 2701.

*Example 3.* The facts are the same as in *Example 1.* Because P holds sufficient voting power to compel liquidation of X, P's right to participate in liquidation is an extraordinary payment right under paragraph (b)(2) of this section. Because P holds an extraordinary payment right in conjunction with a qualified payment right (the right to receive cumulative dividends), the lower of rule applies.

*Example 4.* The facts are the same as in *Example 1,* except that immediately before the transfer, P, applicable family members of P, and members of P's family, hold 60 percent of the voting rights in X. Assume that 80 percent of the vote is required to compel liquidation of any interest in X. P's right to participate in liquidation is not an extraordinary payment right under paragraph (b)(2) of this section, because P and P's family cannot compel liquidation of X. P's preferred stock is an applicable retained interest that carries no rights that are valued under the special valuation rules of section 2701. Thus, in applying the valuation method of § 25.2701-3, the value of P's preferred stock is its fair market value determined without regard to section 2701.

*Example 5.* L holds 10-percent non-cumulative preferred stock and common stock in a corporation that is a controlled entity. L transfers the common stock to L's child. L holds no extraordinary payment rights with respect to the preferred stock. L elects under paragraph (c)(2) of this section to treat the noncumulative dividend right as a qualified payment right consisting of the right to receive a cumulative annual dividend of 5 percent. Under § 25.2701-2(c)(2), the value of the distribution right pursuant to the election is the lesser of—

(A) The fair market value of the right to receive a cumulative 5-percent dividend from the corporation, giving due regard to the corporation's net worth, prospective earning power, and dividend-paying capacity; or

(B) The value of the distribution right determined without regard to section 2701 and without regard to the terms of the qualified payment election. [Reg. § 25.2701-2.]

☐ [T.D. 8395, 1-28-92.]

**[Reg. § 25.2701-3]**

**§ 25.2701-3. Determination of amount of gift.**—(a) *Overview.*—(1) *In general.*—The amount of the gift resulting from any transfer to which section 2701 applies is determined by a subtraction method of valuation. Under this method, the amount of the transfer is determined by subtracting the values of all family-held senior equity interests from the fair market value of all family-held interests in the entity determined immediately before the transfer. The values of the senior equity interests held by the transferor and applicable family members generally are determined under section 2701. Other family-held senior equity interests are valued at their fair market value. The balance is then appropriately allocated among the transferred interests and other family-held subordinate equity interests. Finally, certain discounts and other appropriate reductions are provided, but only to the extent permitted by this section.

(2) *Definitions.*—The following definitions apply for purposes of this section.

(i) *Family-held.*—Family-held means held (directly or indirectly) by an individual described in § 25.2701-2(b)(5)(i).

(ii) *Senior equity interest.*—Senior equity interest means an equity interest in the entity that carries a right to distributions of income or capital that is preferred as to the rights of the transferred interest.

(iii) *Subordinate equity interest.*—Subordinate equity interest means an equity interest in the entity as to which an applicable retained interest is a senior equity interest.

(b) *Valuation methodology.*—The following methodology is used to determine the amount of the gift when section 2701 applies.

(1) *Step 1—Valuation of family-held interests.*—(i) *In general.*—Except as provided in paragraph (b)(1)(ii) of this section[,] determine the fair market value of all family-held equity interests in the entity immediately after the transfer. The fair market value is determined by assuming that the interests are held by one individual, using a consistent set of assumptions.

(ii) *Special rule for contributions to capital.*—In the case of a contribution to capital, determine the fair market value of the contribution.

(2) *Step 2—Subtract the value of senior equity interests.*—*In general.*—If the amount determined in *Step 1* of paragraph (b)(1) of this section is not determined under the special rule for contributions to capital, from that value subtract the following amounts:

(A) An amount equal to the sum of the fair market value of all family-held senior equity interests, (other than applicable retained interests held by the transferor or applicable family members) and the fair market value of any family-held equity interests of the same class or a subordinate class to the transferred interests held by persons other than the transferor, members of the transferor's family, and applicable family members of the transferor. The fair market value of an interest is its pro rata share of the fair market value of all family-held senior equity interests of the same class (determined, immediately after the transfer, as is [if] all family-held senior equity interests were held by one individual); and

(B) The value of all applicable retained interests held by the transferor or applicable family members (other than an interest received as consideration for the transfer) determined under § 25.2701-2, taking into account the adjustment described in paragraph (b)(5) of this section.

(ii) *Special rule for contributions to capital.*—If the value determined in *Step 1* of paragraph (b)(1) of this section is determined under the special rule for contributions to capital, subtract the value of any applicable retained interest received in exchange for the contribution to capital determined under § 25.2701-2.

(3) *Step 3—Allocate the remaining value among the transferred interests and other family-held subordinate equity interests.*—The value remaining after Step 2 is allocated among the transferred interests and other subordinate equity interests held by the transferor, applicable family members, and members of the transferor's family. If more than one class of family-held subordinate equity interest exists, the value remaining after Step 2 is allocated, beginning with the most senior class of subordinate equity interest, in the manner that would most fairly approximate their value if all rights valued under section

2701 at zero did not exist (or would be exercised in a manner consistent with the assumptions of the rule of §25.2702-2(a)(4), if applicable). If there is no clearly appropriate method of allocating the remaining value pursuant to the preceding sentence, the remaining value (or the portion remaining after any partial allocation pursuant to the preceding sentence) is allocated to the interests in proportion to their fair market values determined without regard to section 2701.

(4) *Step 4—Determine the amount of the gift.*—(i) *In general.*—The amount allocated to the transferred interests in step 3 is reduced by the amounts determined under this paragraph (b)(4).

(ii) *Reduction for minority or similar discounts.*—Except as provided in §25.2701-3(c), if the value of the transferred interest (determined without regard to section 2701) would be determined after application of a minority or similar discount with respect to the transferred interest, the amount of the gift determined under section 2701 is reduced by the excess, if any, of—

(A) A pro rata portion of the fair market value of the family-held interests of the same class (determined as if all voting rights conferred by family-held equity interests were held by one person who had no interest in the entity other than the family-held interests of the same class, but otherwise without regard to section 2701), over

(B) The value of the transferred interest (without regard to section 2701).

(iii) *Adjustment for transfers with a retained interest.*—If the value of the transferor's gift (determined without regard to section 2701) would be reduced under section 2702 to reflect the value of a retained interest, the value determined under section 2701 is reduced by the same amount.

(iv) *Reduction for consideration.*—The amount of the transfer (determined under section 2701) is reduced by the amount of consideration in money or money's worth received by the transferor, but not in excess of the amount of the gift (determined without regard to section 2701). The value of consideration received by the transferor in the form of an applicable retained interest in the entity is determined under section 2701 except that, in the case of a contribution to capital, the Step 4 value of such an interest is zero.

(5) *Adjustment in Step 2.*—(i) *In general.*—For purposes of paragraph (b)(2) of this section, if the percentage of any class of applicable retained interest held by the transferor and by applicable family members (including any interest received as consideration for the transfer) exceeds the family interest percentage, the excess is treated as a family-held interest that is not held by the transferor or an applicable family member.

(ii) *Family interest percentage.*—The family interest percentage is the highest ownership percentage (determined on the basis of relative fair market values) of family-held interests in—

(A) Any class of subordinate equity interest; or

(B) All subordinate equity interests, valued in the aggregate.

(c) *Minimum value rule.*—(1) *In general.*—If section 2701 applies to the transfer of an interest in an entity, the value of a junior equity interest is not less than its pro-rata portion of 10 percent of the sum of—

(i) The total value of all equity interests in the entity, and

(ii) The total amount of any indebtedness of the entity owed to the transferor and applicable family members.

(2) *Junior equity interest.*—For purposes of paragraph (c)(1) of this section, junior equity interest means common stock or, in the case of a partnership, any partnership interest under which the rights to income and capital are junior to the rights of all other classes of partnership interests. Common stock means the class or classes of stock that, under the facts and circumstances, are entitled to share in the reasonably anticipated residual growth in the entity.

(3) *Indebtedness.*—(i) *In general.*—For purposes of paragraph (c)(1) of this section, indebtedness owed to the transferor (or an applicable family member) does not include—

(A) Short-term indebtedness incurred with respect to the current conduct of the entity's trade or business (such as amounts payable for current services);

(B) Indebtedness owed to a third party solely because it is guaranteed by the transferor or an applicable family member; or

(C) Amounts permanently set aside in a qualified deferred compensation arrangement, to the extent the amounts are unavailable for use by the entity.

(ii) *Leases.*—A lease of property is not indebtedness, without regard to the length of the lease term, if the lease payments represent full and adequate consideration for use of the property. Lease pay-

ments are considered full and adequate consideration if a good faith effort is made to determine the fair rental value under the lease and the terms of the lease conform to the value so determined. Arrearages with respect to a lease are indebtedness.

(d) *Examples.*—The application of the subtraction method described in this section is illustrated by the following examples:

*Example 1.* Corporation X has outstanding 1,000 shares of $1,000 par value voting preferred stock, each share of which carries a cumulative annual dividend of 8 percent and a right to put the stock to X for its par value at any time. In addition, there are outstanding 1,000 shares of non-voting common stock. A holds 600 shares of the preferred stock and 750 shares of the common stock. The balance of the preferred and common stock is held by B, a person unrelated to A. Because the preferred stock confers both a qualified payment right and an extraordinary payment right, A's rights are valued under the "lower of" rule of §25.2701-2(a)(3). Assume that A's rights in the preferred stock are valued at $800 per share under the "lower of" rule (taking account of A's voting rights). A transfers all of A's common stock to A's child. The method for determining the amount of A's gift is as follows—

Step 1: Assume the fair market value of all the family-held interests in X, taking account of A's control of the corporation, is determined to be $1 million.

Step 2: From the amount determined under Step 1, subtract $480,000 (600 shares × $800 (the section 2701 value of A's preferred stock, computed under the "lower of" rule of §25.2701-2(a)(3))).

Step 3: The result of Step 2 is a balance of $520,000. This amount is fully allocated to the 750 shares of family-held common stock.

Step 4: Because no consideration was furnished for the transfer, the adjustment under Step 4 is limited to the amount of any appropriate minority or similar discount. Before the application of Step 4 the amount of A's gift is $520,000.

*Example 2.* The facts are the same as in *Example 1*, except that prior to the transfer A holds only 50 percent of the common stock and B holds the remaining 50 percent. Assume that the fair market value of A's 600 shares of preferred stock is $600,000.

Step 1: Assume that the result of this step (determining the value of the family-held interest) is $980,000.

Step 2: From the amount determined under Step 1, subtract $500,000 ($400,000, the value of 500 shares of A's preferred stock determined under section 2701 plus $100,000, the fair market value of A's other 100 shares of preferred stock determined without regard to section 2701 pursuant to the valuation adjustment determined under paragraph (b)(5) of this section). The adjustment in Step 2 applies in this example because A's percentage ownership of the preferred stock (60 percent) exceeds the family interest percentage of the common stock (50 percent). Therefore, 100 shares of A's preferred stock are valued at fair market value, or $100,000 (100 × $1,000). The balance of A's preferred stock is valued under section 2701 at $400,000 (500 shares × $800). The value of A's preferred stock for purposes of section 2701 equals $500,000 ($100,000 plus $400,000).

Step 3: The result of Step 2 is $480,000 ($980,000 minus $500,000) which is allocated to the family-held common stock. Because A transferred all of the family-held subordinate equity interests, all of the value determined under Step 2 is allocated to the transferred shares.

Step 4: The adjustment under Step 4 is the same as in *Example 1*. Thus, the amount of the gift is $480,000.

*Example 3.* Corporation X has outstanding 1,000 shares of $1,000 par value non-voting preferred stock, each share of which carries a cumulative annual dividend of 8 percent and a right to put the stock to X for its par value at any time. In addition, there are outstanding 1,000 shares of voting common stock. A holds 600 shares of the preferred stock and 750 shares of the common stock. The balance of the preferred and common stock is held by B, a person unrelated to A. Assume further that steps one through three, as in *Example 1*, result in $520,000 being allocated to the family-held common stock and that A transfers only 75 shares of A's common stock. The transfer fragments A's voting interest. Under Step 4, an adjustment is appropriate to reflect the fragmentation of A's voting rights. The amount of the adjustment is the difference between 10 percent (75/750) of the fair market value of A's common shares and the fair market value of the transferred shares, each determined as if the holder thereof had no other interest in the corporation.

*Example 4.* On December 31, 1990, the capital structure of Y corporation consists of 1,000 shares of voting common stock held three-fourths by A and one-fourth by A's child, B. On January 15, 1991, A transfers 250 shares of common stock to Y in exchange for 300 shares of nonvoting, noncumulative 8% preferred stock with a section 2701 value of zero. Assume that the fair market value of Y is $1,000,000 at the time of the exchange and that the exchange by A is for full and adequate consideration in moneys' worth. However, for purposes of section 2701, if a subordinate equity interest is transferred in exchange for an applicable retained interest, consideration in the exchange is determined with reference to the section 2701 value of the senior interest. Thus, A is treated as transferring the common stock to the corporation for no consideration. Immediately after the transfer, B is treated as holding one-third (250/750) of the common stock and A is treated as holding two-thirds (500/750). The amount of the gift is determined as follows:

Step 1. Because Y is held exclusively by A and B, the Step 1 value is $1,000,000.

Step 2. The result of Step 2 is $1,000,000 ($1,000,000 − 0).

Step 3. The amount allocated to the transferred common stock is $250,000 (250/1,000 × $1,000,000). That amount is further allocated in proportion to the respective holdings of A and B in the common stock ($166,667 and $83,333, respectively).

Step 4. There is no Step 4 adjustment because the section 2701 value of the consideration received by A was zero and no minority discount would have been involved in the exchange. Thus, the amount of the gift is $83,333. If the section 2701 value of the applicable retained interests were $100,000, the Step 4 adjustment would have been a $33,333 reduction for consideration received ((250/750) × $100,000).

*Example 5.* The facts are the same as in *Example 4,* except that on January 6, 1992, when the fair market value of Y is still $1,000,000, A transfers A's remaining 500 shares of common stock to Y in exchange for 2500 shares of preferred stock. The second transfer is also for full and adequate consideration in money or money's worth. The result of Step 2 is the same—$1,000,000.

Step 3. The amount allocated to the common stock is $666,667 (500/750 × $1,000,000). Since A holds no common stock immediately after the transfer, A is treated as transferring the entire interest to the other shareholder (B). Thus, the amount of the gift is $666,667.

Step 4. There is no Step 4 adjustment because the section 2701 value of the consideration received by A was zero and no minority discount would have been involved in the exchange. Thus, the amount of the gift is the difference between $666,667 and the fair market value of B's shares immediately prior to the transfer to which section 2701 applied. [Reg. § 25.2701-3.]

☐ [T.D. 8395, 1-28-92.]

### [Reg. § 25.2701-4]

**§ 25.2701-4. Accumulated qualified payments.**—(a) *In general.*—If a taxable event occurs with respect to any applicable retained interest conferring a distribution right that was previously valued as a qualified payment right (a "qualified payment interest"), the taxable estate or taxable gifts of the individual holding the interest are increased by the amount determined under paragraph(c) of this section.

(b) *Taxable event.*—(1) *In general.*—Except as otherwise provided in this section, taxable event means the transfer of a qualified payment interest, either during life or at death, by the individual in whose hands the interest was originally valued under section 2701 (the "interest holder") or by any individual treated pursuant to paragraph (b)(3) of this section in the same manner as the interest holder. Except as provided in paragraph (a)(2) of this section, any termination of an individual's rights with respect to a qualified payment interest is a taxable event. Thus, for example, if an individual is treated as indirectly holding a qualified payment interest held by a trust, a taxable event occurs on the earlier of—

(i) The termination of the individual's interest in the trust (whether by death or otherwise), or

(ii) The termination of the trust's interest in the qualified payment interest (whether by disposition or otherwise).

(2) *Exception.*—If, at the time of a termination of an individual's rights with respect to a qualified payment interest, the value of the property would be includible in the individual's gross estate for Federal estate tax purposes if the individual died immediately after the termination, a taxable transfer does not occur until the earlier of—

(i) The time the property would no longer be includible in the individual's gross estate (other than by reason of section 2035), or

(ii) The death of the individual.

(3) *Individual treated as interest holder.*—(i) *In general.*—If a taxable event involves the transfer of a qualified payment interest by the interest holder (or an individual treated as the interest holder) to an applicable family member of the individual who made the transfer to which section 2701 applied (other than the spouse of the individual transferring the qualified payment interest), the transferee applicable family member is treated in the same manner as the interest holder with respect to late or unpaid qualified payments first due after the taxable event. Thus, for example, if an interest holder transfers during life a qualified payment interest to an applicable family member, that transfer is a taxable event with respect to the interest holder

whose taxable gifts are increased for the year of the transfer as provided in paragraph (c) of this section. The transferee is treated thereafter in the same manner as the interest holder with respect to late or unpaid qualified payments first due after the taxable event.

(ii) *Transfers to spouse.*—(A) *In general.*—If an interest holder (or an individual treated as the interest holder) transfers a qualified payment interest, the transfer is not a taxable event to the extent a marital deduction is allowed with respect to the transfer under sections 2056, 2106(a)(3), or 2523 or, in the case of a transfer during the individual's lifetime, to the extent the spouse furnishes consideration for the transfer. If this exception applies, the transferee spouse is treated as if he or she were the holder of the interest from the date the transferor spouse acquired the interest. If the deduction for a transfer to a spouse is allowable under section 2056(b)(8) or 2523(g) (relating to charitable remainder trusts), the transferee spouse is treated as the holder of the entire interest passing to the trust.

(B) *Marital bequests.*—If the selection of property with which a marital bequest is funded is discretionary, a transfer of a qualified payment interest will not be considered a transfer to the surviving spouse unless—

(1) The marital bequest is funded with the qualified payment interest before the due date for filing the decedent's Federal estate tax return (including extensions actually granted) (the "due date"), or

(2) The executor—

(i) Files a statement with the return indicating the extent to which the marital bequest will be funded with the qualified payment interest, and

(ii) Before the date that is one year prior to the expiration of the period of limitations on assessment of the Federal estate tax, notifies the District Director having jurisdiction over the return of the extent to which the bequest was funded with the qualified payment interest (or the extent to which the qualified payment interest has been permanently set aside for that purpose).

(C) *Purchase by the surviving spouse.*—For purposes of this section, the purchase (before the date prescribed for filing the decedent's estate tax return, including extensions actually granted) by the surviving spouse (or a trust described in section 2056(b)(7)) of a qualified payment interest held (directly or indirectly) by the decedent immediately before death is considered a transfer with respect to which a deduction is allowable under section 2056 or section 2106(a)(3), but only to the extent that the deduction is allowed to the estate. For example, assume that A bequeaths $50,000 to A's surviving spouse, B, in a manner that qualifies for deduction under section 2056, and that subsequent to A's death B purchases a qualified payment interest from A's estate for $200,000, its fair market value. The economic effect of the transaction is the equivalent of a bequest by A to B of the qualified payment interest, one-fourth of which qualifies for the marital deduction. Therefore, for purposes of this section, one-fourth of the qualified payment interest purchased by B ($50,000 ÷ $200,000) is considered a transfer of an interest with respect to which a deduction is allowed under [section] 2056. If the purchase by the surviving spouse is not made before the due date of the decedent's return, the purchase of the qualified payment interest will not be considered a bequest for which a marital deduction is allowed unless the executor—

(1) Files a statement with the return indicating the qualified payment interests to be purchased by the surviving spouse (or a trust described in section 2056(b)(7)), and

(2) Before the date that is one year prior to the expiration of the period of limitations on assessment of the Federal estate tax, notifies the District Director having jurisdiction over the return that the purchase of the qualified payment interest has been made (or that the funds necessary to purchase the qualified payment interest have been permanently set aside for that purpose).

(c) *Amount of increase.*—(1) *In general.*—Except as limited by paragraph (c)(6) of this section, the amount of the increase to an individual's taxable estate or taxable gifts is the excess, if any, of—

(i) The sum of—

(A) The amount of qualified payments payable during the period beginning on the date of the transfer to which section 2701 applied (or, in the case of an individual treated as the interest holder, on the date the interest of the prior interest holder terminated) and ending on the date of the taxable event; and

(B) The earnings on those payments, determined hypothetically as if each payment were paid on its due date and reinvested as of that date at a yield equal to the appropriate discount rate (as defined below); over

(ii) The sum of—

(A) The amount of the qualified payments actually paid during the same period;

(B) The earnings on those payments, determined hypothetically as if each payment were reinvested as of the date actually paid at a yield equal to the appropriate discount rate; and

(C) To the extent required to prevent double inclusion, by an amount equal to the sum of—

(1) The portion of the fair market value of the qualified payment interest solely attributable to any right to receive unpaid qualified payments determined as of the date of the taxable event;

(2) The fair market value of any equity interest in the entity received by the individual in lieu of qualified payments and held by the individual at the taxable event; and

(3) The amount by which the individual's aggregate taxable gifts were increased by reason of the failure of the individual to enforce the right to receive qualified payments.

(2) *Due date of qualified payments.*—With respect to any qualified payment, the "due date" is that date specified in the governing instrument as the date on which payment is to be made. If no date is specified in the governing instrument, the due date is the last day of each calendar year.

(3) *Appropriate discount rate.*—The appropriate discount rate is the discount rate that was applied in determining the value of the qualified payment right at the time of the transfer to which section 2701 applied.

(4) *Application of payments.*—For purposes of this section, any payment of an unpaid qualified payment is applied in satisfaction of unpaid qualified payments beginning with the earliest unpaid qualified payment. Any payment in excess of the total of all unpaid qualified payments is treated as a prepayment of future qualified payments.

(5) *Payment.*—For purposes of this paragraph (c), the transfer of a debt obligation bearing compound interest from the due date of the payment at a rate not less than the appropriate discount rate is a qualified payment if the term of the obligation (including extensions) does not exceed four years from the date issued. A payment in the form of an equity interest in the entity is not a qualified payment. Any payment of a qualified payment made (or treated as made) either before or during the four-year period beginning on the due date of the payment but before the date of the taxable event is treated as having been made on the due date.

(6) *Limitation.*—(i) *In general.*—The amount of the increase to an individual's taxable estate or taxable gifts is limited to the applicable percentage of the excess, if any, of—

(A) The sum of—

(1) The fair market value of all outstanding equity interests in the entity that are subordinate to the applicable retained interest, determined as of the date of the taxable event without regard to any accrued liability attributable to unpaid qualified payments; and

(2) Any amounts expended by the entity to redeem or otherwise acquire any such subordinate interest during the period beginning on the date of the transfer to which section 2701 applied (or, in the case of an individual treated as an interest holder, on the date the interest of the prior interest holder terminated) and ending on the date of the taxable event (reduced by any amounts received on the resale or issuance of any such subordinate interest during the same period); over

(B) The fair market value of all outstanding equity interests in the entity that are subordinate to the applicable retained interest, determined as of the date of the transfer to which section 2701 applied (or, in the case of an individual treated as an interest holder, on the date the interest of the prior interest holder terminated).

(ii) *Computation of limitation.*—For purposes of computing the limitation applicable under this paragraph (c)(6), the aggregate fair market value of the subordinate interests in the entity are determined without regard to § 25.2701-3(c).

(iii) *Applicable percentage.*—The applicable percentage is determined by dividing the number of shares or units of the applicable retained interest held by the interest holder (or an individual treated as the interest holder) on the date of the taxable event by the total number of such shares or units outstanding on the same date. If an individual holds applicable retained interests in two or more classes of interests, the applicable percentage is equal to the largest applicable percentage determined with respect to any class. For example, if T retains 40 percent of the class A preferred and 60 percent of the class B preferred in a corporation, the applicable percentage with respect to T's holdings is 60 percent.

(d) *Taxpayer election.*—(1) *In general.*—An interest holder (or individual treated as an interest holder) may elect to treat as a taxable event the payment of an unpaid qualified payment occurring more than four years after its due date. Under this election, the increase under paragraph (c) of this section is determined only with respect to that payment and all previous payments for which an election was available but not made. Payments for which an election applies are treated as having been paid on their due dates for purposes of subsequent taxable events. The election is revocable only with the consent of the Commissioner.

(2) *Limitation not applicable.*—If a taxable event occurs by reason of an election described in paragraph (d)(1) of this section, the limitation described in paragraph (c)(6) of this section does not apply.

(3) *Time and manner of election.*—(i) *Timely-filed returns.*—The election may be made by attaching a statement to a Form 709, Federal Gift Tax Return, filed by the recipient of the qualified payment on a timely basis for the year in which the qualified payment is received. In that case, the taxable event is deemed to occur on the date the qualified payment is received.

(ii) *Election on late returns.*—The election may be made by attaching a statement to a Form 709, Federal Gift Tax Return, filed by the recipient of the qualified payment other than on a timely basis for the year in which the qualified payment is received. In that case, the taxable event is deemed to occur on the first day of the month immediately preceding the month in which the return is filed. If an election, other than an election on a timely return, is made after the death of the interest holder, the taxable event with respect to the decedent is deemed to occur on the later of—

(A) The date of the recipient's death, or

(B) The first day of the month immediately preceding the month in which the return is filed.

(iii) *Requirements of statement.*—The statement must—

(A) Provide the name, address, and taxpayer identification number of the electing individual and the interest holder, if different;

(B) Indicate that a taxable event election is being made under paragraph (d) of this section;

(C) Disclose the nature of the qualified payment right to which the election applies, including the due dates of the payments, the dates the payments were made, and the amounts of the payments;

(D) State the name of the transferor, the date of the transfer to which section 2701 applied, and the discount rate used in valuing the qualified payment right; and

(E) State the resulting amount of increase in taxable gifts.

(4) *Example.*—The following example illustrates the rules of this paragraph (d).

*Example.* A holds cumulative preferred stock that A retained in a transfer to which section 2701 applied. No dividends were paid in years 1 through 5 following the transfer. In year 6, A received a qualified payment that, pursuant to paragraph (c)(3) of this section, is considered to be in satisfaction of the unpaid qualified payment for year 1. No election was made to treat that payment as a taxable event. In year 7, A receives a qualified payment that, pursuant to paragraph (c)(4) of this section, is considered to be in satisfaction of the unpaid qualified payment for year 2. A elects to treat the payment in year 7 as a taxable event. The election increases A's taxable gifts in year 7 by the amount computed under paragraph (c) of this section with respect to the payments due in both year 1 and year 2. For purposes of any future taxable events, the payments with respect to years 1 and 2 are treated as having been made on their due dates. [Reg. § 25.2701-4.]

☐ [*T.D. 8395, 1-28-92.*]

**[Reg. § 25.2701-5]**

**§ 25.2701-5. Adjustments to mitigate double taxation.**— (a) *Reduction of transfer tax base.*—(1) *In general.*—This section provides rules under which an individual (the initial transferor) making a transfer subject to section 2701 (the initial transfer) is entitled to reduce his or her taxable gifts or adjusted taxable gifts (the reduction). The amount of the reduction is determined under paragraph(b) of this section. See paragraph (e) of this section if section 2513 (split gifts) applied to the initial transfer.

(2) *Federal gift tax modification.*—If, during the lifetime of the initial transferor, the holder of a section 2701 interest (as defined in paragraph (a)(4) of this section) transfers the interest to or for the benefit of an individual other than the initial transferor or an applicable family member of the initial transferor in a transfer subject to Federal estate or gift tax, the initial transferor may reduce the amount on which the initial transferor's tentative tax is computed under section 2502(a). The reduction is first applied on any gift tax return required to be filed for the calendar year in which the section 2701 interest is transferred; any excess reduction is carried forward and

applied in each succeeding calendar year until the reduction is exhausted. The amount of the reduction that is used in a calendar year is the amount of the initial transferor's taxable gifts for that year. Any excess reduction remaining at the death of the initial transferor may be applied by the executor of the initial transferor's estate as provided under paragraph (a)(3) of this section. See paragraph (a)(4) of this section for the definition of a section 2701 interest. See § 25.2701-6 for rules relating to indirect ownership of equity interests transferred to trusts and other entities.

(3) *Federal estate tax modification.*—Except as otherwise provided in this paragraph (a)(3), in determining the Federal estate tax with respect to an initial transferor, the executor of the initial transferor's estate may reduce the amount on which the decedent's tentative tax is computed under section 2001(b) (or section 2101(b)) by the amount of the reduction (including any excess reduction carried forward under paragraph (a)(2) of this section). The amount of the reduction under this paragraph (a)(3) is limited to the amount that results in zero Federal estate tax with respect to the estate of the initial transferor.

(4) *Section 2701 interest.*—A section 2701 interest is an applicable retained interest that was valued using the special valuation rules of section 2701 at the time of the initial transfer. However, an interest is a section 2701 interest only to the extent the transfer of that interest effectively reduces the aggregate ownership of such class of interest by the initial transferor and applicable family members of the initial transferor below that held by such persons at the time of the initial transfer (or the remaining portion thereof).

(b) *Amount of reduction.*—Except as otherwise provided in paragraphs (c)(3)(iv) (pertaining to transfers of partial interests) and (e) (pertaining to initial split gifts) of this section, the amount of the reduction is the lesser of—

(1) The amount by which the initial transferor's taxable gifts were increased as a result of the application of section 2701 to the initial transfer; or

(2) The amount (determined under paragraph (c) of this section) duplicated in the transfer tax base at the time of the transfer of the section 2701 interest (the duplicated amount).

(c) *Duplicated amount.*—(1) *In general.*—The duplicated amount is the amount by which the transfer tax value of the section 2701 interest at the time of the subsequent transfer exceeds the value of that interest determined under section 2701 at the time of the initial transfer. If, at the time of the initial transfer, the amount allocated to the transferred interest under § 25.2701-3(b)(3) (*Step 3* of the valuation methodology) is less than the entire amount available for allocation at that time, the duplicated amount is a fraction of the amount described in the preceding sentence. The numerator of the fraction is the amount allocated to the transferred interest at the time of the initial transfer (pursuant to § 25.2701-3(b)(3)) and the denominator of the fraction is the amount available for allocation at the time of the initial transfer (determined after application of § 25.2701-3(b)(2)).

(2) *Transfer tax value—in general.*—Except as provided in paragraph (c)(3) of this section, for purposes of paragraph (c)(1) of this section the transfer tax value of a section 2701 interest is the value of that interest as finally determined for Federal transfer tax purposes under chapter 11 or chapter 12, as the case may be (including the right to receive any distributions thereon (other than qualified payments)), reduced by the amount of any deduction allowed with respect to the section 2701 interest to the extent that the deduction would not have been allowed if the section 2701 interest were not included in the transferor's total amount of gifts for the calendar year or the transferor's gross estate, as the case may be. Rules similar to the rules of section 691(c)(2)(C) are applicable to determine the extent that a deduction would not be allowed if the section 2701 interest were not so included.

(3) *Special transfer tax value rules.*—(i) *Transfers for consideration.*—Except as provided in paragraph (c)(3)(iii) of this section, if, during the life of the initial transferor, a section 2701 interest is transferred to or for the benefit of an individual other than the initial transferor or an applicable family member of the initial transferor for consideration in money or money's worth, or in a transfer that is treated as a transfer for consideration in money or money's worth, the transfer of the section 2701 interest is deemed to occur at the death of the initial transferor. In this case, the estate of the initial transferor is entitled to a reduction in the same manner as if the initial transferor's gross estate included a section 2701 interest having a chapter 11 value equal to the amount of consideration in money or money's worth received in the exchange (determined as of the time of the exchange).

(ii) *Interests held by applicable family members at date of initial transferor's death.*—If a section 2701 interest in existence on the date of

the initial transferor's death is held by an applicable family member and, therefore, is not included in the gross estate of the initial transferor, the section 2701 interest is deemed to be transferred at the death of the initial transferor to or for the benefit of an individual other than the initial transferor or an applicable family member of the initial transferor. In this case, the transfer tax value of that interest is the value that the executor of the initial transferor's estate can demonstrate would be determined under chapter 12 if the interest were transferred immediately prior to the death of the initial transferor.

(iii) *Nonrecognition transactions.*—If an individual exchanges a section 2701 interest in a nonrecognition transaction (within the meaning of section 7701(a)(45)), the exchange is not treated as a transfer of a section 2701 interest and the transfer tax value of that interest is determined as if the interest received in exchange is the section 2701 interest.

(iv) *Transfer of less than the entire section 2701 interest.*—If a transfer is a transfer of less than the entire section 2701 interest, the amount of the reduction under paragraph (a)(2) or (a)(3) of this section is reduced proportionally.

(v) *Multiple classes of section 2701 interest.*—For purposes of paragraph (b) of this section, if more than one class of section 2701 interest exists, the amount of the reduction is determined separately with respect to each such class.

(vi) *Multiple initial transfers.*—If an initial transferor has made more than one initial transfer, the amount of the reduction with respect to any section 2701 interest is the sum of the reductions computed under paragraph (b) of this section with respect to each such initial transfer.

(d) *Examples.*—The following examples illustrate the provisions of paragraphs (a) through (c) of this section.

*Facts.* (1) *In general.* (i) P, an individual, holds 1,500 shares of $1,000 par value preferred stock of X corporation (bearing an annual noncumulative dividend of $100 per share that may be put to X at any time for par value) and 1,000 shares of voting common stock of X. There is no other outstanding common stock of X.

(ii) On January 15, 1991, when the aggregate fair market value of the preferred stock is $1,500,000 and the aggregate fair market value of the common stock is $500,000, P transfers common stock to P's child. The fair market value of P's interest in X (common and preferred) immediately prior to the transfer is $2,000,000, and the section 2701 value of the preferred stock (the section 2701 interest) is zero. Neither P nor P's spouse, S, made gifts prior to 1991.

(2) *Additional facts applicable to Examples 1 through 3.* P's transfer consists of all 1,000 shares of P's common stock. With respect to the initial transfer, the amount remaining after Step 2 of the subtraction method of § 25.2701-3 is $2,000,000 ($2,000,000 minus zero), all of which is allocated to the transferred stock. P's aggregate taxable gifts for 1991 (including the section 2701 transfer) equal $2,000,000.

(3) *Additional facts applicable to Examples 4 and 5.* P's initial transfer consists of one-half of P's common stock. With respect to the initial transfer in this case, only $1,000,000 (one-half of the amount remaining after Step 2 of the subtraction method of § 25.2701-3) is allocated to the transferred stock. P's aggregate taxable gifts for 1991 (the section 2701 transfer and P's other transfers) equal $2,500,000.

*Example 1. Inter vivos transfer of entire section 2701 interest.* (i) On October 1, 1994, at a time when the value of P's preferred stock is $1,400,000, P transfers all of the preferred stock to P's child. In computing P's 1994 gift tax, P, as the initial transferor, is entitled to reduce the amount on which P's tentative tax is computed under section 2502(a) by $1,400,000.

(ii) The amount of the reduction computed under paragraph (b) of this section is the lesser of $1,500,000 (the amount by which the initial transferor's taxable gifts were increased as a result of the application of section 2701 to the initial transfer) or $1,400,000 (the duplicated amount). The duplicated amount is 100 percent (the portion of the section 2701 interest subsequently transferred) times $1,400,000 (the amount by which the gift tax value of the preferred stock ($1,400,000 at the time of the subsequent transfer) exceeds zero (the section 2701 value of the preferred stock at the time of the initial transfer)).

(iii) The result would be the same if the preferred stock had been held by P's parent, GM, and GM had, on October 1, 1994, transferred the preferred stock to or for the benefit of an individual other than P or an applicable family member of P. In that case, in computing the tax on P's 1994 and subsequent transfers, P would be entitled to reduce the amount on which P's tentative tax is computed under section 2502(a) by $1,400,000. If the value of P's 1994 gifts is less than $1,400,000, P is entitled to claim the excess adjustment in computing the tax with respect to P's subsequent transfers.

*Example 2. Transfer of section 2701 interest at death of initial transferor.* (i) P continues to hold the preferred stock until P's death. The chapter

11 value of the preferred stock at the date of P's death is the same as the fair market value of the preferred stock at the time of the initial transfer. In computing the Federal estate tax with respect to P's estate, P's executor is entitled to a reduction of $1,500,000 under paragraph (a)(3) of this section.

(ii) The result would be the same if P had sold the preferred stock to any individual other than an applicable family member at a time when the value of the preferred stock was $1,500,000. In that case, the amount of the reduction is computed as if the preferred stock were included in P's gross estate at a fair market value equal to the sales price. If the value of P's taxable estate is less than $1,500,000, the amount of the adjustment available to P's executor is limited to the actual value of P's taxable estate.

(iii) The result would also be the same if the preferred stock had been held by P's parent, GM, and at the time of P's death, GM had not transferred the preferred stock.

*Example 3. Transfer of after-acquired preferred stock.* On September 1, 1992, P purchases 100 shares of X preferred stock from an unrelated party. On October 1, 1994, P transfers 100 shares of X preferred stock to P's child. In computing P's 1994 gift tax, P is not entitled to reduce the amount on which P's tentative tax is computed under section 2502(a) because the 1994 transfer does not reduce P's preferred stock holding below that held at the time of the initial transfer. See paragraph (a)(4) of this section.

*Example 4. Inter vivos transfer of entire section 2701 interest.* (i) On October 1, 1994, at a time when the value of P's preferred stock is $1,400,000, P transfers all of the preferred stock to P's child. In computing P's 1994 gift tax, P, as the initial transferor, is entitled to reduce the amount on which P's tentative tax is computed under section 2502(a) by $700,000.

(ii) The amount of the reduction computed under paragraph (b) of this section is the lesser of $750,000 (($1,500,000 × .5 ($1,000,000 over $2,000,000)) the amount by which the initial transferor's taxable gifts were increased as a result of the application of section 2701 to the initial transfer) or $700,000 (($1,400,000 × .5) the duplicated amount). The duplicated amount is 100 percent (the portion of the section 2701 interest subsequently transferred) times $700,000; e.g., one-half (the fraction representing the portion of the common stock transferred in the initial transfer ($1,000,000/$2,000,000)) of the amount by which the gift tax value of the preferred stock at the time of the subsequent transfer ($1,400,000) exceeds zero (the section 2701 value of the preferred stock at the time of the initial transfer).

*Example 5. Subsequent transfer of less than the entire section 2701 interest.* On October 1, 1994, at a time when the value of P's preferred stock is $1,400,000, P transfers only 250 of P's 1,000 shares of preferred stock to P's child. In this case, the amount of the reduction computed under paragraph (b) is $175,000 (one-fourth (250/1,000) of the amount of the reduction available if P had transferred all 1,000 shares of preferred stock.

(e) *Computation of reduction if initial transfer is split under section 2513.*—(1) *In general.*—If section 2513 applies to the initial transfer (a split initial transfer), the special rules of this paragraph (e) apply.

(2) *Transfers during joint lives.*—If there is a split initial transfer and the corresponding section 2701 interest is transferred during the joint lives of the donor and the consenting spouse, for purposes of determining the reduction under paragraph (a)(2) of this section each spouse is treated as if the spouse was the initial transferor of one-half of the split initial transfer.

(3) *Transfers at or after death of either spouse.*—(i) *In general.*—If there is a split initial transfer and the corresponding section 2701 interest is transferred at or after the death of the first spouse to die, the reduction under paragraph (a)(2) or (a)(3) of this section is determined as if the donor spouse was the initial transferor of the entire initial transfer.

(ii) *Death of donor spouse.*—Except as provided in paragraph (e)(3)(iv) of this section, the executor of the estate of the donor spouse in a split initial transfer is entitled to compute the reduction as if the donor spouse was the initial transferor of the section 2701 interest otherwise attributable to the consenting spouse. In this case, if the consenting spouse survives the donor spouse—

(A) The consenting spouse's aggregate sum of taxable gifts used in computing each tentative tax under section 2502(a) (and, therefore, adjusted taxable gifts under section 2001(b)(1)(B) (or section 2101(b)(1)(B)) and the tax payable on the consenting spouse's prior taxable gifts under section 2001(b)(2) (or section 2101(b)(2))) is reduced to eliminate the remaining effect of the section 2701 interest; and

(B) Except with respect to any excess reduction carried forward under paragraph (a)(2) of this section, the consenting spouse ceases to be treated as the initial transferor of the section 2701 interest.

(iii) *Death of consenting spouse.*—If the consenting spouse predeceases the donor spouse, except for any excess reduction carried forward under paragraph (a)(2) of this section, the reduction with respect to any section 2701 interest in the split initial transfer is not available to the estate of the consenting spouse (regardless of whether the interest is included in the consenting spouse's gross estate). Similarly, if the consenting spouse predeceases the donor spouse, no reduction is available to the consenting spouse's adjusted taxable gifts under section 2001(b)(1)(B) (or section 2101(b)(1)(B)) or to the consenting spouse's gift tax payable under section 2001(b)(2) (or section 2101(b)(2)). See paragraph (a)(2) of this section for rules involving transfers by an applicable family member during the life of the initial transferor.

(iv) *Additional limitation on reduction.*—If the donor spouse (or the estate of the donor spouse) is treated under this paragraph (e) as the initial transferor of the section 2701 interest otherwise attributable to the consenting spouse, the amount of additional reduction determined under paragraph (b) of this section is the amount determined under that paragraph with respect to the consenting spouse. If a reduction was previously available to the consenting spouse under this paragraph (e), the amount determined under this paragraph (e)(3)(iv) with respect to the consenting spouse is determined as if the consenting spouse's taxable gifts in the split initial transfer had been increased only by that portion of the increase that corresponds to the remaining portion of the section 2701 interest. The amount of the additional reduction (i.e., the amount determined with respect to the consenting spouse) is limited to the amount that results in a reduction in the donor spouse's Federal transfer tax no greater than the amount of the increase in the consenting spouse's gift tax incurred by reason of the section 2701 interest (or the remaining portion thereof).

(f) *Examples.*—The following examples illustrate the provisions of paragraph (e) of this section. The examples assume the facts set out in this paragraph (f).

*Facts.* (1) In each example assume that P, an individual, holds 1,500 shares of $1,000 par value preferred stock of X corporation (bearing an annual noncumulative dividend of $100 per share that may be put to X at any time for par value) and 1,000 shares of voting common stock of X. There is no other outstanding stock of X. The annual exclusion under section 2503 is not allowable with respect to any gift.

(2) On January 15, 1991, when the aggregate fair market value of the preferred stock is $1,500,000 and the aggregate fair market value of the common stock is $500,000, P transfers all 1,000 shares of the common stock to P's child. Section 2701 applies to the initial transfer because P transferred an equity interest (the common stock) to a member of P's family and immediately thereafter held an applicable retained interest (the preferred stock). The fair market value of P's interest in X immediately prior to the transfer is $2,000,000 and the section 2701 value of the preferred stock (the section 2701 interest) is zero. With respect to the initial transfer, the amount remaining after Step 2 of the subtraction method of § 25.2701-3 was $2,000,000 ($2,000,000 minus zero), all of which is allocated to the transferred stock. P had made no gifts prior to 1991. The sum of P's aggregate taxable gifts for the calendar year 1991 (including the section 2701 transfer) is $2,500,000. P's spouse, S, made no gifts prior to 1991.

(3) P and S elected pursuant to section 2513 to treat one-half of their 1991 gifts as having been made by each spouse. Without the application of section 2701, P and S's aggregate gifts would have been $500,000 and each spouse would have paid no gift tax because of the application of the unified credit under section 2505. However, because of the application of section 2701, both P and S are each treated as the initial transferor of aggregate taxable gifts in the amount of $1,250,000 and, after the application of the unified credit under section 2505, each paid $255,500 in gift tax with respect to their 1991 transfers. On October 1, 1994, at a time when the value of the preferred stock is the same as at the time of the initial transfer, P transfers the preferred stock (the section 2701 interest) to P's child.

*Example 1. Inter vivos transfer of entire section 2701 interest.* P transfers all of the preferred stock to P's child. P and S are each entitled to a reduction of $750,000 in computing their 1994 gift tax. P is entitled to the reduction because P subsequently transferred the one-half share of the section 2701 interest as to which P was the initial transferor to an individual who was not an applicable family member of P. S is entitled to the reduction because P, an applicable family member with respect to S, transferred the one-half share of the section 2701 interest as to which S was the initial transferor to an individual other than S or an applicable family member of S. S may claim the reduction against S's 1994 gifts. If S's 1994 taxable gifts are less than $750,000, S may claim the remaining amount of the reduction against S's next succeeding lifetime transfers.

*Example 2. Inter vivos transfer of portion of section 2701 interest.* P transfers one-fourth of the preferred stock to P's child. In this case, P and S are each entitled to a reduction of $187,500, the corresponding portion of the reduction otherwise available to each spouse (one-fourth of $750,000).

*Example 3. Transfer at death of donor spouse.* P, the donor spouse in the section 2513 election, dies on October 1, 1994, while holding all of the preferred stock. The executor of P's estate is entitled to a reduction in the computation of the tentative tax under section 2001(b). Since no reduction had been previously available with respect to the section 2701 interest, P's estate is entitled to a full reduction of $750,000 with respect to the one-half share of the preferred stock as to which P was the initial transferor. In addition, P's estate is entitled to an additional reduction of up to $750,000 for the remaining section 2701 interest as to which S was the initial transferor. The reduction for the consenting spouse's remaining section 2701 interest is limited to that amount that will produce a tax saving in P's Federal estate tax of $255,500, the amount of gift tax incurred by S by reason of the application of section 2701 to the split initial transfer.

*Example 4. Transfer after death of donor spouse.* The facts are the same as in *Example 3*, except that S acquires the preferred stock from P's estate and subsequently transfers the preferred stock to S's child. S is not entitled to a reduction because S ceased to be an initial transferor upon P's death (and S's prior taxable gifts were automatically adjusted at that time to the level that would have existed had the split initial transfer not been subject to section 2701).

*Example 5. Death of donor spouse after inter vivos transfer.* (i) P transfers one-fourth of the preferred stock to P's child. In this case, P and S are each entitled to a reduction of $187,500, the corresponding portion of the reduction otherwise available to each spouse (one-fourth of $750,000). S may claim the reduction against S's 1994 or subsequent transfers. P dies on November 1, 1994.

(ii) P's executor is entitled to include, in computing the reduction available to P's estate, the remaining reduction to which P is entitled and an additional amount of up to $562,500 ($750,000 minus $187,500, the amount of the remaining reduction attributable to the consenting spouse determined immediately prior to P's death). The amount of additional reduction available to P's estate cannot exceed the amount that will reduce P's estate tax by $178,625, the amount that S's 1991 gift tax would have been increased if the application of section 2701 had increased S's taxable gifts by only $562,500 ($750,000 − $187,500).

(g) *Double taxation otherwise avoided.*—No reduction is available under this section if—

(1) Double taxation is otherwise avoided in the computation of the estate tax under section 2001 (or section 2101); or

(2) A reduction was previously taken under the provisions of section 2701(e)(6) with respect to the same section 2701 interest and the same initial transfer.

(h) *Effective date.*—This section is effective for transfers of section 2701 interests after May 4, 1994. If the transfer of a section 2701 interest occurred on or before May 4, 1994, the initial transferor may rely on either this section, project PS-30-91 (1991-2 C.B. 1118, and 1992-1 C.B. 1239 (see §601.601(d)(2)(ii)(b) of this chapter)) or any other reasonable interpretation of the statute. [Reg. §25.2701-5.]

☐ *T.D. 8536, 5-4-94.*]

## [Reg. §25.2701-6]

**§25.2701-6. Indirect holding of interests.**—(a) *In general.*—(1) *Attribution to individuals.*—For purposes of section 2701, an individual is treated as holding an equity interest to the extent the interest is held indirectly through a corporation, partnership, estate, trust, or other entity. If an equity interest is treated as held by a particular individual in more than one capacity, the interest is treated as held by the individual in the manner that attributes the largest total ownership of the equity interest. An equity interest held by a lower-tier entity is attributed to higher-tier entities in accordance with the rules of this section. For example, if an individual is a 50-percent beneficiary of a trust that holds 50 percent of the preferred stock of a corporation, 25 percent of the preferred stock is considered held by the individual under these rules.

(2) *Corporations.*—A person is considered to hold an equity interest held by or for a corporation in the proportion that the fair market value of the stock the person holds bears to the fair market value of all the stock in the corporation (determined as if each class of stock were held separately by one individual). This paragraph applies to any entity classified as a corporation or as an association taxable as a corporation for federal income tax purposes.

(3) *Partnerships.*—A person is considered to hold an equity interest held by or for a partnership in the proportion that the fair market value of the larger of the person's profits interest or capital interest in the partnership bears to the total fair market value of the corresponding profits interests or capital interests in the partnership, as the case may be (determined as if each class were held by one individual).

This paragraph applies to any entity classified as a partnership for federal income tax purposes.

(4) *Estates, trusts and other entities.*—(i) *In general.*—A person is considered to hold an equity interest held by or for an estate or trust to the extent the person's beneficial interest therein may be satisfied by the equity interest held by the estate or trust, or the income or proceeds thereof, assuming the maximum exercise of discretion in favor of the person. A beneficiary of an estate or trust who cannot receive any distribution with respect to an equity interest held by the estate or trust, including the income therefrom or the proceeds from the disposition thereof, is not considered the holder of the equity interest. Thus, if stock held by a decedent's estate has been specifically bequeathed to one beneficiary and the residue of the estate has been bequeathed to other beneficiaries, the stock is considered held only by the beneficiary to whom it was specifically bequeathed. However, any person who may receive distributions from a trust is considered to hold an equity interest held by the trust if the distributions may be made from current or accumulated income from or the proceeds from the disposition of the equity interest, even though under the terms of the trust the interest can never be distributed to that person. This paragraph applies to any entity that is not classified as a corporation, an association taxable as a corporation, or a partnership for federal income tax purposes.

(ii) *Special rules.*—(A) Property is held by a decedent's estate if the property is subject to claims against the estate and expenses of administration.

(B) A person holds a beneficial interest in a trust or an estate so long as the person may receive distributions from the trust or the estate other than payments for full and adequate consideration.

(C) An individual holds an equity interest held by or for a trust if the individual is considered an owner of the trust (a "grantor trust") under subpart E, part 1, subchapter J of the Internal Revenue Code (relating to grantors and others treated as substantial owners). However, if an individual is treated as the owner of only a fractional share of a grantor trust because there are multiple grantors, the individual holds each equity interest held by the trust, except to the extent that the fair market value of the interest exceeds the fair market value of the fractional share.

(5) *Multiple attribution.*—(i) *Applicable retained interests.*—If this section attributes an applicable retained interest to more than one individual in a class consisting of the transferor and one or more applicable family members, the interest is attributed within that class in the following order—

(A) If the interest is held in a grantor trust, to the individual treated as the holder thereof;

(B) To the transferor;

(C) To the transferor's spouse; or

(D) To each applicable family member on a pro rata basis.

(ii) *Subordinate equity interests.*—If this section attributes a subordinate equity interest to more than one individual in a class consisting of the transferor, applicable family members, and members of the transferor's family, the interest is attributed within that class in the following order—

(A) To the transferee;

(B) To each member of the transferor's family on a pro rata basis;

(C) If the interest is held in a grantor trust, to the individual treated as the holder thereof;

(D) To the transferor;

(E) To the transferor's spouse; or

(F) To each applicable family member on a pro rata basis.

(b) *Examples.*—The following examples illustrate the provisions of this section:

*Example 1.* A, an individual, holds 25 percent by value of each class of stock of Y Corporation. Persons unrelated to A hold the remaining stock. Y holds 50 percent of the stock of Corporation X. Under paragraph (a)(2) of this section, Y's interests in X are attributed proportionately to the shareholders of Y. Accordingly, A is considered to hold a 12.5 percent (25 percent × 50 percent) interest in X.

*Example 2.* Z Bank's authorized capital consists of 100 shares of common stock and 100 shares of preferred stock. A holds 60 shares of each (common and preferred) and A's child, B, holds 40 shares of common stock. Z holds the balance of its own preferred stock, 30 shares as part of a common trust fund it maintains and 10 shares permanently set aside to satisfy a deferred obligation. For purposes of section 2701, A holds 60 shares of common stock and 66 shares of preferred stock in Z, 60 shares of each class directly and 6 shares of preferred stock indirectly (60 percent of the 10 shares set aside to fund the deferred obligation).

*Example 3.* An irrevocable trust holds a 10-percent general partnership interest in Partnership Q. One-half of the trust income is required to be distributed to O Charity. The other one-half of the income is to be distributed to D during D's life and thereafter to E for such time as E survives D. D holds one-half of the trust's interest in Q by reason of D's present right to receive one-half of the trust's income, and E holds one-half of the trust's interest in Q by reason of E's future right to receive one-half of the trust's income. Nevertheless, no family member is treated as holding more than one-half of the trust's interest in Q because at no time will either D or E actually hold, in the aggregate, any right with respect to income or corpus greater than one-half.

*Example 4.* An irrevocable trust holds a 10-percent general partnership interest in partnership M. One-half of the trust income is to be paid to D for D's life. The remaining income may, in the trustee's discretion, be accumulated or paid to or for the benefit of a class that includes D's child F, in such amounts as the trustee determines. On the death of the survivor of D and F, the trust corpus is required to be distributed to O Charity. The trust's interest in M is held by the trust's beneficiaries to the extent that present and future income or corpus may be distributed to them. Accordingly, D holds one-half of the trust's interest in M because D is entitled to receive one-half of the trust income currently. F holds the entire value of the interest because F is a member of the class eligible to receive the entire trust income for such time as F survives D. See paragraph (a)(5) of this section for rules applicable in the case of multiple attribution.

*Example 5.* The facts are the same as in *Example 4*, except that all the income is required to be paid to O Charity for the trust's initial year. The result is the same as in *Example 4*. [Reg. § 25.2701-6.]

☐ [*T.D.* 8395, 1-28-92.]

## [Reg. § 25.2701-7]

**§ 25.2701-7. Separate interests.**—The Secretary may, by regulation, revenue ruling, notice, or other document of general application, prescribe rules under which an applicable retained interest is treated as two or more separate interests for purposes of section 2701. In addition, the Commissioner may, by ruling issued to a taxpayer upon request, treat any applicable retained interest as two or more separate interests as may be necessary and appropriate to carry out the purposes of section 2701. [Reg. § 25.2701-7.]

☐ [*T.D.* 8395, 1-28-92.]

## [Reg. § 25.2701-8]

**§ 25.2701-8. Effective dates.**—Sections 25.2701-1 through 25.2701-4 and §§ 25.2701-6 and 25.2701-7 are effective as of January 28, 1992. For transfers made prior to January 28, 1992, taxpayers may rely on any reasonable interpretation of the statutory provisions. For these purposes, the provisions of the proposed regulations and the final regulations are considered a reasonable interpretation of the statutory provisions. [Reg. § 25.2701-8.]

☐ [*T.D.* 8395, 1-28-92.]

## [Reg. § 25.2702-0]

**§ 25.2702-0. Table of contents.**—This section lists the major paragraphs contained in §§ 25.2702-1 through 25.2702-7.

[Reg. § 25.2702-0.]

☐ [*T.D.* 8395, 1-28-92. Amended by *T.D.* 9181, 2-24-2005.]

## [Reg. § 25.2702-1]

**§ 25.2702-1. Special valuation rules in the case of transfers of interests in trust.**—(a) *Scope of section 2702.*—Section 2702 provides special rules to determine the amount of the gift when an individual makes a transfer in trust to (or for the benefit of) a member of the individual's family and the individual or an applicable family member retains an interest in the trust. Section 25.2702-4 treats certain transfers of property as transfers in trust. Certain transfers, including transfers to a personal residence trust, are not subject to section 2702. See paragraph (c) of this section. Member of the family is defined in § 25.2702-2(a)(1). Applicable family member is defined in § 25.2701-1(d)(2).

(b) *Effect of section 2702.*—If section 2702 applies to a transfer, the value of any interest in the trust retained by the transferor or any applicable family member is determined under § 25.2702-2(b). The amount of the gift, if any, is then determined by subtracting the value of the interests retained by the transferor or any applicable family member from the value of the transferred property. If the retained interest is not a qualified interest (as defined in § 25.2702-3), the retained interest is generally valued at zero, and the amount of the gift is the entire value of the property.

(c) *Exceptions to section 2702.*—Section 2702 does not apply to the following transfers.

(1) *Incomplete gift.*—A transfer no portion of which would be treated as a completed gift without regard to any consideration received by the transferor. If a transfer is wholly incomplete as to an undivided fractional share of the property transferred (without regard to any consideration received by the transferor), for purposes of this paragraph the transfer is treated as incomplete as to that share.

(2) *Personal residence trust.*—A transfer in trust that meets the requirements of § 25.2702-5.

(3) *Charitable remainder trust.*—(i) For transfers made on or after May 19, 1997, a transfer to a pooled income fund described in section 642(c)(5); a transfer to a charitable remainder annuity trust described in section 664(d)(1); a transfer to a charitable remainder unitrust described in section 664(d)(2) if under the terms of the governing instrument the unitrust amount can be computed only under section 664(d)(2)(A); and a transfer to a charitable remainder unitrust if under the terms of the governing instrument the unitrust amount can be computed under section 664(d)(2) and (3) and either there are only two consecutive noncharitable beneficial interests and the transferor holds the second of the two interests, or the only permissible recipients of the unitrust amount are the transferor, the transferor's U.S. citizen spouse, or both the transferor and the transferor's U.S. citizen spouse.

(ii) For transfers made before May 19, 1997, a transfer in trust if the remainder interest in the trust qualifies for a deduction under section 2522.

(4) *Pooled income fund.*—A transfer of property to a pooled income fund (as defined in section 642(c)(5)).

(5) *Charitable lead trust.*—A transfer in trust if the only interest in the trust, other than the remainder interest or a qualified annuity or unitrust interest, is an interest that qualifies for deduction under section 2522.

(6) *Certain assignments of remainder interests.*—The assignment of a remainder interest if the only retained interest of the transferor or an applicable family member is as the permissible recipient of distributions of income in the sole discretion of an independent trustee (as defined in section 674(c)).

(7) *Certain property settlements.*—A transfer in trust if the transfer of an interest to a spouse is deemed to be for full and adequate consideration by reason of section 2516 (relating to certain property settlements) and the remaining interests in the trust are retained by the other spouse.

(8) *Transfer or assignment to a Qualified Domestic Trust.*—A transfer or assignment (as described in section 2056(d)(2)(B)) by a noncitizen surviving spouse of property to a Qualified Domestic Trust under the circumstances described in § 20.2056A-4(b) of this chapter, where the surviving spouse retains an interest in the transferred property that is not a qualified interest and the transfer is not described in section 2702(a)(3)(A)(ii) or 2702(c)(4). [Reg. § 25.2702-1.]

☐ [*T.D. 8395, 1-28-92. Amended by T.D. 8612, 8-21-95 and T.D. 8791, 12-9-98.*]

### [Reg. § 25.2702-2]

**§ 25.2702-2. Definitions and valuation rules.**—(a) *Definitions.*—The following definitions apply for purposes of section 2702 and the regulations thereunder.

(1) *Member of the family.*—With respect to any individual, member of the family means the individual's spouse, any ancestor or lineal descendant of the individual or the individual's spouse, any brother or sister of the individual, and any spouse of the foregoing.

(2) *Transfer in trust.*—A transfer in trust includes a transfer to a new or existing trust and an assignment of an interest in an existing trust. Transfer in trust does not include—

(i) The exercise, release or lapse of a power of appointment over trust property that is not a transfer under chapter 12; or

(ii) The execution of a qualified disclaimer (as defined in section 2518).

(3) *Retained.*—Retained means held by the same individual both before and after the transfer in trust. In the case of the creation of a term interest, any interest in the property held by the transferor immediately after the transfer is treated as held both before and after the transfer.

(4) *Interest.*—An interest in trust includes a power with respect to a trust if the existence of the power would cause any portion of a transfer to be treated as an incomplete gift under chapter 12.

(5) *Holder.*—The holder is the person to whom the annuity or unitrust interest is payable during the fixed term of that interest. References to holder shall also include the estate of that person.

(6) *Qualified interest.*—Qualified interest means a qualified annuity interest, a qualified unitrust interest, or a qualified remainder interest. If a transferor retains a power to revoke a qualified annuity interest or qualified unitrust interest of the transferor's spouse, then the revocable qualified annuity or unitrust interest of the transferor's spouse is treated as a retained qualified interest of the transferor. In order for the transferor to be treated as having retained a qualified interest under the preceding sentence, the interest of the transferor's spouse (the successor holder) must be an interest that meets the requirements of a qualified annuity interest in accordance with § 25.2702-3(b) and (d), or a qualified unitrust interest in accordance with § 25.2702-3(c) and (d), but for the transferor's retained power to revoke the interest.

(7) *Qualified annuity interest.*—Qualified annuity interest means an interest that meets all the requirements of § 25.2702-3(b) and (d).

(8) *Qualified unitrust interest.*—Qualified unitrust interest means an interest that meets all the requirements of § 25.2702-3(c) and (d).

(9) *Qualified remainder interest.*—Qualified remainder interest means an interest that meets all the requirements of § 25.2702-3(f).

(10) *Governing instrument.*—Governing instrument means the instrument or instruments creating and governing the operation of the trust arrangement.

(b) *Valuation of retained interests.*—(1) *In general.*—Except as provided in paragraphs (b)(2) and (c) of this section, the value of any interest retained by the transferor or an applicable family member is zero.

(2) *Qualified interest.*—The value[s] of a qualified annuity interest and a qualified remainder interest following a qualified annuity interest are determined under section 7520. The value[s] of a qualified unitrust interest and a qualified remainder interest following a qualified unitrust interest are determined as if they were interests described in section 664.

(c) *Valuation of a term interest in certain tangible property.*—(1) *In general.*—If section 2702 applies to a transfer in trust of tangible property described in paragraph (c)(2) of this section ("tangible property"), the value of a retained term interest (other than a qualified interest) is not determined under section 7520 but is the amount the transferor establishes as the amount a willing buyer would pay a willing seller for the interest, each having reasonable knowledge of the relevant facts and neither being under any compulsion to buy or sell. If the transferor cannot reasonably establish the value of the term interest pursuant to this paragraph (c)(1), the interest is valued at zero.

(2) *Tangible property subject to rule.*—(i) *In general.*—Except as provided in paragraph (c)(2)(ii) of this section, paragraph (c)(1) of this section applies only to tangible property—

(A) For which no deduction for depreciation or depletion would be allowable if the property were used in a trade or business or held for the production of income; and

(B) As to which the failure to exercise any rights under the term interest would not increase the value of the property passing at the end of the term interest.

(ii) *Exception for de minimis amounts of depreciable property.*—In determining whether property meets the requirements of this paragraph (c)(2) at the time of the transfer in trust, improvements that would otherwise cause the property not to qualify are ignored if the fair market value of the improvements, in the aggregate, do [sic] not exceed 5 percent of the fair market value of the entire property.

(3) *Evidence of value of property.*—The best evidence of the value of any term interest to which this paragraph (c) applies is actual sales or rentals that are comparable both as to the nature and character of the property and the duration of the term interest. Little weight is accorded appraisals in the absence of such evidence. Amounts determined under section 7520 are not evidence of what a willing buyer would pay a willing seller for the interest.

(4) *Conversion of property.*—(i) *In general.*—Except as provided in paragraph (c)(4)(iii) of this section, if a term interest in property is valued under paragraph (c)(1) of this section, and during the term the property is converted into property a term interest in which would not qualify for valuation under paragraph (c)(1) of this section, the conversion is treated as a transfer for no consideration for purposes of chapter 12 of the value of the unexpired portion of the term interest.

(ii) *Value of unexpired portion of term interest.*—For purposes of paragraph (c)(4)(i) of this section, the value of the unexpired portion of a term interest is the amount that bears the same relation to the value of the term interest as of the date of conversion (determined under section 7520 using the rate in effect under section 7520 on the date of the original transfer and the fair market value of the property as of the date of the original transfer) as the value of the term interest as of the date of the original transfer (determined under paragraph (c)(1) of this section) bears to the value of the term interest as of the date of the original transfer (determined under section 7520).

(iii) *Conversion to qualified annuity interest.*—The conversion of tangible property previously valued under paragraph (c)(1) of this section into property a term interest in which would not qualify for valuation under paragraph (c)(1) of this section is not a transfer of the value of the unexpired portion of the term interest if the interest thereafter meets the requirements of a qualified annuity interest. The rules of § 25.2702-5(d)(8) (including governing instrument requirements) apply for purposes of determining the amount of the annuity payment required to be made and the determination of whether the interest meets the requirements of a qualified annuity interest.

(5) *Additions or improvements to property.*—(i) *Additions or improvements substantially affecting nature of property.*—If an addition or improvement is made to property a term interest in which was valued under paragraph (c)(1) of this section, and the addition or improvement affects the nature of the property to such an extent that the property would not be treated as property meeting the requirements of paragraph (c)(2) of this section if the property had included the addition or improvement at the time it was transferred, the entire property is deemed, for purposes of paragraph (c)(4) of this section, to convert (effective as of the date the addition or improvement is commenced) into property a term interest in which would not qualify for valuation under paragraph (c)(1) of this section.

(ii) *Other additions or improvements.*—If an addition or improvement is made to property, a term interest in which was valued under paragraph (c)(1) of this section, and the addition or improvement does not affect the nature of the property to such an extent that the property would not be treated as property meeting the requirements of paragraph (c)(2) of this section if the property had included the addition or improvement at the time it was transferred, the addition or improvement is treated as an additional transfer (effective as of the date the addition or improvement is commenced) subject to § 25.2702-2(b)(1).

(d) *Examples.*—(1) The following examples illustrate the rules of § 25.2702-1 and § 25.2702-2. Each example assumes that all applicable requirements of those sections not specifically described in the example are met.

*Example 1.* A transfers property to an irrevocable trust, retaining the right to receive the income of the trust for 10 years. On the expiration of the 10-year term, the trust is to terminate and the trust corpus is to be paid to A's child. However, if A dies during the 10-year term, the entire trust corpus is to be paid to A's estate. Each retained interest is valued at zero because it is not a qualified interest. Thus, the amount of A's gift is the fair market value of the property transferred to the trust.

*Example 2.* A transfers property to an irrevocable trust, retaining a 10-year annuity interest that meets the requirements set forth in § 25.2702-3 for a qualified annuity interest. Upon expiration of the 10-year term, the trust is to terminate and the trust corpus is to be paid to A's child. The amount of A's gift is the fair market value of the property transferred to the trust less the value of the retained qualified annuity interest determined under section 7520.

*Example 3.* D transfers property to an irrevocable trust under which the income is payable to D's spouse for life. Upon the death of D's spouse, the trust is to terminate and the trust corpus is to be paid to D's child. D retains no interest in the trust. Although the spouse is an applicable family member of D under section 2702, the spouse has not retained an interest in the trust because the spouse did not hold the interest both before and after the transfer. Section 2702 does not apply because neither the transferor nor an applicable family member has retained an interest in the trust. The result is the same whether or not D elects to treat the transfer as a transfer of qualified terminable interest property under section 2056(b)(7).

*Example 4.* A transfers property to an irrevocable trust, under which the income is to be paid to A for life. Upon termination of the trust, the trust corpus is to be distributed to A's child. A also retains certain powers over principal that cause the transfer to be wholly incomplete for federal gift tax purposes. Section 2702 does not apply because no portion of the transfer would be treated as a completed gift.

*Example 5.* The facts are the same as in *Example 4,* except that the trust is divided into separate fractional shares and A's retained powers apply to only one of the shares. Section 2702 applies except with respect to the share of the trust as to which A's retained powers cause the transfer to be an incomplete gift.

(2) The following facts apply for *Examples 6* through *8* (examples illustrating § 25.2702-2(c)—tangible property exception):

*Facts.* A transfers a painting having a fair market value of $2,000,000 to A's child, B, retaining the use of the painting for 10 years. The painting does not possess an ascertainable useful life. Assume that the painting would not be depreciable if it were used in a trade or business or held for the production of income. Assume that the value of A's term interest, determined under section 7520, is $1,220,000, and that A establishes that a willing buyer of A's interest would pay $500,000 for the interest.

*Example 6.* A's term interest is not a qualified interest under § 25.2702-3. However, because of the nature of the property, A's failure to exercise A's rights with regard to the painting would not be expected to cause the value of the painting to be higher than it would otherwise be at the time it passes to B. Accordingly, A's interest is valued under § 25.2702-2(c)(1) at $500,000. The amount of A's gift is $1,500,000, the difference between the fair market value of the painting and the amount determined under § 25.2702-2(c)(1).

*Example 7.* Assume that the only evidence produced by A to establish the value of A's 10-year term interest is the amount paid by a museum for the right to use a comparable painting for 1 year. A asserts that the value of the 10-year term is 10 times the value of the 1-year term. A has not established the value of the 10-year term interest because a series of short-term rentals the aggregate duration of which equals the duration of the actual term interest does not establish what a willing buyer would pay a willing seller for the 10-year term interest. However, the value of the 10-year term interest is not less than the value of the 1-year term because it can be assumed that a willing buyer would pay no less for a 10-year term interest than a 1-year term interest.

*Example 8.* Assume that after 24 months A and B sell the painting for $2,000,000 and invest the proceeds in a portfolio of securities. A continues to hold an income interest in the securities for the duration of the 10-year term. Under § 25.2702-2(c)(4) the conversion of the painting into a type of property a term interest in which would not qualify for valuation under § 25.2702-2(c)(1) is treated as a transfer by A of the value of the unexpired portion of A's original term interest, unless the property is thereafter held in a trust meeting the requirements of a qualified annuity interest. Assume that the value of A's remaining term interest in $2,000,000 (determined under section 7520 using the section 7520 rate in effect on the date of the original transfer) is $1,060,000. The value of the unexpired portion of A's interest is $434,426, the amount that bears the same relation to $1,060,000 as $500,000 (the value of A's interest as of the date of the original transfer determined under paragraph (c)(1) of this section) bears to $1,220,000 (the value of A's interest as of the date of the original transfer determined under section 7520). [Reg. § 25.2702-2.]

☐ [*T.D.* 8395, 1-28-92. *Amended by T.D.* 9181, 2-24-2005.]

### [Reg. § 25.2702-3]

**§ 25.2702-3. Qualified interests.**—(a) *In general.*—This section provides rules for determining if an interest is a qualified annuity interest, a qualified unitrust interest, or a qualified remainder interest.

(b) *Special rules for qualified annuity interests.*—An interest is a qualified annuity interest only if it meets the requirements of this paragraph and paragraph (d) of this section.

(1) *Payment of annuity amount.*—(i) *In general.*—A qualified annuity interest is an irrevocable right to receive a fixed amount. The annuity amount must be payable to (or for the benefit of) the holder of the annuity interest at least annually. A right of withdrawal, whether or not cumulative, is not a qualified annuity interest. Issuance of a note, other debt instrument, option, or other similar financial arrangement, directly or indirectly, in satisfaction of the annuity amount does not constitute payment of the annuity amount.

(ii) *Fixed amount.*—A fixed amount means—

(A) A stated dollar amount payable periodically, but not less frequently than annually, but only to the extent the amount does not exceed 120 percent of the stated dollar amount payable in the preceding year; or

(B) A fixed fraction or percentage of the initial fair market value of the property transferred to the trust, as finally determined for federal tax purposes, payable periodically but not less frequently than annually, but only to the extent the fraction or percentage does not exceed 120 percent of the fixed fraction or percentage payable in the preceding year.

(iii) *Income in excess of the annuity amount.*—An annuity interest does not fail to be a qualified annuity interest merely because the trust permits income in excess of the amount required to pay the annuity amount to be paid to or for the benefit of the holder of the qualified annuity interest. Nevertheless, the right to receive the excess income is not a qualified interest and is not taken into account in valuing the qualified annuity interest.

(2) *Incorrect valuations of trust property.*—If the annuity is stated in terms of a fraction or percentage of the initial fair market value of the trust property, the governing instrument must contain provisions meeting the requirements of § § 1.664-2(a)(1)(iii) of this chapter (relating to adjustments for any incorrect determination of the fair market value of the property in the trust).

(3) *Period for payment of annuity amount.*—The annuity amount may be payable based on either the anniversary date of the creation of the trust or the taxable year of the trust. In either situation, the annuity amount may be paid annually or more frequently, such as semi-annually, quarterly, or monthly. If the payment is made based on the anniversary date, proration of the annuity amount is required only if the last period during which the annuity is payable to the grantor is a period of less than 12 months. If the payment is made based on the taxable year, proration of the annuity amount is required for each short taxable year of the trust during the grantor's term. The prorated amount is the annual annuity amount multiplied by a fraction, the numerator of which is the number of days in the short period and the denominator of which is 365 (366 if February 29 is a day included in the numerator).

(4) *Payment of the annuity amount in certain circumstances.*—An annuity amount payable based on the anniversary date of the creation of the trust must be paid no later than 105 days after the anniversary date. An annuity amount payable based on the taxable year of the trust may be paid after the close of the taxable year, provided the payment is made no later than the date by which the trustee is required to file the Federal income tax return of the trust for the taxable year (without regard to extensions). If the trustee reports for the taxable year pursuant to § 1.671-4(b) of this chapter, the annuity payment must be made no later than the date by which the trustee would have been required to file the Federal income tax return of the trust for the taxable year (without regard to extensions) had the trustee reported pursuant to § 1.671-4(a) of this chapter.

(5) *Additional contributions prohibited.*—The governing instrument must prohibit additional contributions to the trust.

(c) *Special rules for qualified unitrust interests.*—An interest is a qualified unitrust interest only if it meets the requirements of this paragraph and paragraph (d) of this section.

(1) *Payment of unitrust amount.*—(i) *In general.*—A qualified unitrust interest is an irrevocable right to receive payment periodically, but not less frequently than annually, of a fixed percentage of the net fair market value of the trust assets, determined annually. For rules relating to computation of the net fair market value of the trust assets see § 25.2522(c)-3(c)(2)(vii). The unitrust amount must be payable to (or for the benefit of) the holder of the unitrust interest at least annually. A right of withdrawal, whether or not cumulative, is not a qualified unitrust interest. Issuance of a note, other debt instrument, option, or other similar financial arrangement, directly or indirectly, in satisfaction of the unitrust amount does not constitute payment of the unitrust amount.

(ii) *Fixed percentage.*—A fixed percentage is a fraction or percentage of the net fair market value of the trust assets, determined annually, payable periodically but not less frequently than annually, but only to the extent the fraction or percentage does not exceed 120 percent of the fixed fraction or percentage payable in the preceding year.

(iii) *Income in excess of unitrust amount.*—A unitrust interest does not fail to be a qualified unitrust interest merely because the trust permits income in excess of the amount required to pay the unitrust amount to be paid to or for the benefit of the holder of the

qualified unitrust interest. Nevertheless, the right to receive the excess income is not a qualified interest and is not taken into account in valuing the qualified unitrust interest.

(2) *Incorrect valuations of trust property.*—The governing instrument must contain provisions meeting the requirements of § 1.664-3(a)(1)(iii) of this chapter (relating to the incorrect determination of the fair market value of the property in the trust).

(3) *Period for payment of unitrust amount.*—The unitrust amount may be payable based on either the anniversary date of the creation of the trust or the taxable year of the trust. In either situation, the unitrust amount may be paid annually or more frequently, such as semi-annually, quarterly, or monthly. If the payment is made based on the anniversary date, proration of the unitrust amount is required only if the last period during which the annuity is payable to the grantor is a period of less than 12 months. If the payment is made based on the taxable year, proration of the unitrust amount is required for each short taxable year of the trust during the grantor's term. The prorated amount is the annual unitrust amount multiplied by a fraction, the numerator of which is the number of days in the short period and the denominator of which is 365 (366 if February 29 is a day included in the numerator).

(4) *Payment of the unitrust amount in certain circumstances.*—A unitrust amount payable based on the anniversary date of the creation of the trust must be paid no later than 105 days after the anniversary date. A unitrust amount payable based on the taxable year of the trust may be paid after the close of the taxable year, provided the payment is made no later than the date by which the trustee is required to file the Federal income tax return of the trust for the taxable year (without regard to extensions). If the trustee reports for the taxable year pursuant to § 1.671-4(b) of this chapter, the unitrust payment must be made no later than the date by which the trustee would have been required to file the Federal income tax return of the trust for the taxable year (without regard to extensions) had the trustee reported pursuant to § 1.671-4(a) of this chapter.

(d) *Requirements applicable to qualified annuity interests and qualified unitrust interests.*—(1) *In general.*—To be a qualified annuity or unitrust interest, an interest must be a qualified annuity interest in every respect or a qualified unitrust interest in every respect. For example, if the interest consists of the right to receive each year a payment equal to the lesser of a fixed amount of the initial trust assets or a fixed percentage of the annual value of the trust assets, the interest is not a qualified interest. If, however, the interest consists of the right to receive each year a payment equal to the greater of a stated dollar amount or a fixed percentage of the initial trust assets or a fixed percentage of the annual value of the trust assets, the interest is a qualified interest that is valued at the greater of the two values. To be a qualified interest, the interest must meet the definition of and function exclusively as a qualified interest from the creation of the trust.

(2) *Contingencies.*—A holder's qualified interest must be payable in any event to or for the benefit of the holder for the fixed term of that interest. Thus, payment of the interest cannot be subject to any contingency other than either the survival of the holder until the commencement, or throughout the term, of that holder's interest, or, in the case of a revocable interest described in § 25.2702-2(a)(6), the transferor's right to revoke the qualified interest of that transferor's spouse.

(3) *Amounts payable to other persons.*—The governing instrument must prohibit distributions from the trust to or for the benefit of any person other than the holder of the qualified annuity or unitrust interest during the term of the qualified interest.

(4) *Term of the annuity or unitrust interest.*—The governing instrument must fix the term of the annuity or unitrust and the term of the interest must be fixed and ascertainable at the creation of the trust. The term must be for the life of the holder, for a specified term of years, or for the shorter (but not the longer) of those periods. Successive term interests for the benefit of the same individual are treated as the same term interest.

(5) *Commutation.*—The governing instrument must prohibit commutation (prepayment) of the interest of the holder.

(6) *Use of debt obligations to satisfy the annuity or unitrust payment obligation.*—(i) *In general.*—In the case of a trust created on or after September 20, 1999, the trust instrument must prohibit the trustee from issuing a note, other debt instrument, option, or other similar financial arrangement in satisfaction of the annuity or unitrust payment obligation.

(ii) *Special rule in the case of a trust created prior to September 20, 1999.*—In the case of a trust created prior to September 20, 1999, the interest will be treated as a qualified interest under section 2702(b) if—

(A) Notes, other debt instruments, options, or similar financial arrangements are not issued after September 20, 1999, to satisfy the annuity or unitrust payment obligation; and

(B) Any notes or any other debt instruments that were issued to satisfy the annual payment obligation on or prior to September 20, 1999, are paid in full by December 31, 1999, and any option or similar financial arrangement issued to satisfy the annual payment obligation is terminated by December 31, 1999, such that the grantor receives cash or other trust assets in satisfaction of the payment obligation. For purposes of the preceding sentence, an option will be considered terminated only if the grantor receives cash or other trust assets equal in value to the greater of the required annuity or unitrust payment plus interest computed under section 7520 of the Internal Revenue Code, or the fair market value of the option.

(e) *Examples.*—The following examples illustrate the rules of paragraphs (b), (c), and (d) of this section. Each example assumes that all applicable requirements for a qualified interest are met unless otherwise specifically stated.

*Example 1.* A transfers property to an irrevocable trust, retaining the right to receive the greater of $10,000 or the trust income in each year for a term of 10 years. Upon expiration of the 10-year term, the trust is to terminate and the entire trust corpus is to be paid to A's child, provided that if A dies within the 10-year term the trust corpus is to be paid to A's estate. A's annual payment right is a qualified annuity interest to the extent of the right to receive $10,000 per year for 10 years or until A's prior death, and is valued under section 7520 without regard to the right to receive any income in excess of $10,000 per year. The contingent reversion is valued at zero. The amount of A's gift is the fair market value of the property transferred to the trust less the value of the qualified annuity interest.

*Example 2.* U transfers property to an irrevocable trust, retaining the right to receive $10,000 in each of years 1 through 3, $12,000 in each of years 4 through 6, and $15,000 in each of years 7 through 10. The interest is a qualified annuity interest to the extent of U's right to receive $10,000 per year in years 1 through 3, $12,000 in years 4 through 6, $14,400 in year 7, and $15,000 in years 8 through 10, because those amounts represent the lower of the amount actually payable each year or an amount that does not exceed 120 percent of the stated dollar amount for the preceding year.

*Example 3.* S transfers property to an irrevocable trust, retaining the right to receive $50,000 in each of years 1 through 3 and $10,000 in each of years 4 through 10. S's entire retained interest is a qualified annuity interest.

*Example 4.* R transfers property to an irrevocable trust retaining the right to receive annually an amount equal to the lesser of 8 percent of the initial fair market value of the trust property or the trust income for the year. R's annual payment right is not a qualified annuity interest to any extent because R does not have the irrevocable right to receive a fixed amount for each year of the term.

*Example 5.* A transfers property to an irrevocable trust, retaining the right to receive 5 percent of the net fair market value of the trust property, valued annually, for 10 years. If A dies within the 10-year term, the unitrust amount is to be paid to A's estate for the balance of the term. The interest of A (and A's estate) to receive the unitrust amount for the specified term of 10 years in all events is a qualified unitrust interest for a term of 10 years.

*Example 6.* The facts are the same as in *Example 5*, except that if A dies within the 10-year term the unitrust amount will be paid to A's estate for an additional 35 years. As in *Example 5*, the interest of A (and A's estate) to receive the unitrust amount for a specified term of 10 years in all events is a qualified unitrust interest for a term of 10 years. However, the right of A's estate to continue to receive the unitrust amount after the expiration of the 10-year term if A dies within that 10-year period is not fixed and ascertainable at the creation of the interest and is not a qualified unitrust interest.

*Example 7.* B transfers property to an irrevocable trust retaining the right to receive annually an amount equal to 8 percent of the initial fair market value of the trust property for 10 years. Upon expiration of the 10-year term, the trust is to terminate and the entire trust corpus is to be paid to B's child. The governing instrument provides that income in excess of the annuity amount may be paid to B's child in the trustee's discretion. B's interest is not a qualified annuity interest to any extent because a person other than the individual holding the term interest may receive distributions from the trust during the term.

*Example 8.* A transfers property to an irrevocable trust, retaining the right to receive an annuity equal to 6 percent of the initial net fair market value of the trust property for 10 years, or until A's prior death. At the expiration of the 10-year term, or on A's death prior to the expiration of the 10-year term, the annuity is to be paid to B, A's spouse, if then living, for 10 years or until B's prior death. A retains

an inter vivos and testamentary power to revoke B's interest during the initial 10-year term. If not exercised by A during the initial 10-year term (whether during A's life or on A's death), A's right to revoke B's interest will lapse upon either A's death during the 10-year term, or the expiration of A's 10-year term (assuming A survives the term). Upon expiration of B's interest (or on the expiration of A's interest if A revokes B's interest or if B predeceases A), the trust terminates and the trust corpus is payable to A's child. Because A has made a completed gift of the remainder interest, the transfer of property to the trust is not incomplete as to all interests in the property and section 2702 applies. A's annuity interest (A's right to receive the annuity for 10 years, or until A's prior death) is a retained interest that is a qualified annuity interest under paragraphs (b) and (d) of this section. In addition, because A has retained the power to revoke B's interest, B's interest is treated as an interest retained by A for purposes of section 2702. B's successive annuity interest otherwise satisfies the requirements for a qualified interest contained in paragraph (d) of this section, but for A's power to revoke. The term of B's interest is specified in the governing instrument and is fixed and ascertainable at the creation of the trust, and B's right to receive the annuity is contingent only on B's survival, and A's power to revoke. Following the expiration of A's interest, the annuity is to be paid for a 10-year term or for B's (the successor holder's) life, whichever is shorter. Accordingly, A is treated as retaining B's revocable qualified annuity interest pursuant to § 25.2702-2(a)(6). Because both A's interest and B's interest are treated as qualified interests retained by A, the value of the gift is the value of the property transferred to the trust less the value of both A's qualified interest and B's qualified interest (subject to A's power to revoke), each valued as a single-life annuity. If A survives the 10-year term without having revoked B's interest, then A's power to revoke lapses and A will make a completed gift to B at that time. Further, if A revokes B's interest prior to the commencement of that interest, A is treated as making an additional completed gift at that time to A's child. In either case, the amount of the gift would be the present value of B's interest determined under section 7520 and the applicable regulations, as of the date the revocation power lapses or the interest is revoked. See § 25.2511-2(f).

*Example 9.* (i) A transfers property to an irrevocable trust, retaining the right to receive 6 percent of the initial net fair market value of the trust property for 10 years, or until A's prior death. If A survives the 10-year term, the trust terminates and the trust corpus is payable to A's child. If A dies prior to the expiration of the 10-year term, the annuity is payable to B, A's spouse, if then living, for the balance of the 10-year term, or until B's prior death. A retains the right to revoke B's interest. Upon expiration of B's interest (or upon A's death if A revokes B's interest or if B predeceases A), the trust terminates and the trust corpus is payable to A's child. As is the case in *Example 8*, A's retained annuity interest (A's right to receive the annuity for 10 years, or until A's prior death) is a qualified annuity interest under paragraphs (b) and (d) of this section. However, B's interest does not meet the requirements of paragraph (d) of this section. The term of B's annuity is not fixed and ascertainable at the creation of the trust, because it is not payable for the life of B, a specified term of years, or for the shorter of those periods. Rather, B's annuity is payable for an unspecified period that will depend upon the number of years left in the original term after A's death. Further, B's annuity is payable only if A dies prior to the expiration of the 10-year term. Thus, payment of B's annuity is not dependent solely on B's survival, but rather is dependent on A's failure to survive.

(ii) Accordingly, the amount of the gift is the fair market value of the property transferred to the trust reduced by the value of A's qualified interest (A's right to receive the stated annuity for 10 years or until A's prior death). B's interest is not a qualified interest and is thus valued at zero under section 2702.

(f) *Qualified remainder interest.*—(1) *Requirements.*—An interest is a qualified remainder interest only if it meets all of the following requirements:

(i) It is a qualified remainder interest in every respect.

(ii) It meets the definition of and functions exclusively as a qualified interest from the creation of the interest.

(iii) It is non-contingent. For this purpose, an interest is non-contingent only if it is payable to the beneficiary or the beneficiary's estate in all events.

(iv) All interests in the trust, other than non-contingent remainder interests, are qualified annuity interests or qualified unitrust interests. Thus, an interest is a qualified remainder interest only if the governing instrument does not permit payment of income in excess of the annuity or unitrust amount to the holder of the qualified annuity or unitrust interest.

(2) *Remainder interest.*—Remainder interest is the right to receive all or a fractional share of the trust property on termination of all or a fractional share of the trust. Remainder interest includes a reversion.

A transferor's right to receive an amount that is a stated or pecuniary amount is not a remainder interest. Thus, the right to receive the original value of the trust corpus (or a fractional share) is not a remainder interest.

(3) *Examples*.—The following examples illustrate rules of this paragraph (f). Each example assumes that all applicable requirements of a qualified interest are met unless otherwise specifically stated.

*Example 1*. A transfers property to an irrevocable trust. The income of the trust is payable to A's child for life. On the death of A's child, the trust is to terminate and the trust corpus is to be paid to A. A's remainder interest is not a qualified remainder interest because the interest of A's child is neither a qualified annuity interest nor a qualified unitrust interest.

*Example 2*. The facts are the same as in *Example 1*, except that A's child has the right to receive the greater of the income of the trust or $10,000 per year. A's remainder interest is not a qualified remainder interest because the right of A's child to receive income in excess of the annuity amount is not a qualified interest.

*Example 3*. A transfers property to an irrevocable trust. The trust provides a qualified annuity interest to A's child for 12 years. An amount equal to the initial value of the trust corpus is to be paid to A at the end of that period and the balance is to be paid to A's grandchild. A's interest is not a qualified remainder interest because the amount A is to receive is not a fractional share of the trust property.

*Example 4*. U transfers property to an irrevocable trust. The trust provides a qualified unitrust interest to U's child for 15 years, at which time the trust terminates and the trust corpus is paid to U or, if U is not then living, to U's child. Because U's remainder interest is contingent, it is not a qualified remainder interest. [Reg. § 25.2702-3.]

☐ [*T.D.* 8395, 1-28-92. *Amended by T.D.* 8536, 5-4-94; *T.D.* 8633, 12-20-95; *T.D.* 8899, 9-1-2000 (*corrected* 11-27-2000) *and T.D.* 9181, 2-24-2005.]

### [Reg. § 25.2702-4]

**§ 25.2702-4. Certain property treated as held in trust.**—(a) *In general*.—For purposes of section 2702, a transfer of an interest in property with respect to which there are one or more term interests is treated as a transfer in trust. A term interest is one of a series of successive (as contrasted with concurrent) interests. Thus, a life interest in property or an interest in property for a term of years is a term interest. However, a term interest does not include a fee interest in property merely because it is held as a tenant in common, a tenant by the entireties, or a joint tenant with right of survivorship.

(b) *Leases*.—A leasehold interest in property is not a term interest to the extent the lease is for full and adequate consideration (without regard to section 2702). A lease will be considered for full and adequate consideration if, under all the facts and circumstances as of the time the lease is entered into or extended, a good faith effort is made to determine the fair rental value of the property and the terms of the lease conform to the value so determined.

(c) *Joint purchases*.—Solely for purposes of section 2702, if an individual acquires a term interest in property and, in the same transaction or series of transactions, one or more members of the individual's family acquire an interest in the same property, the individual acquiring the term interest is treated as acquiring the entire property so acquired, and transferring to each of those family members the interests acquired by that family member in exchange for any consideration paid by that family member. For purposes of this paragraph (c), the amount of the individual's gift will not exceed the amount of consideration furnished by that individual for all interests in the property.

(d) *Examples*.—The following examples illustrate rules of this section:

*Example 1*. A purchases a 20-year term interest in an apartment building and A's child purchases the remainder interest in the property. A and A's child each provide the portion of the purchase price equal to the value of their respective interests in the property determined under section 7520. Solely for purposes of section 2702, A is treated as acquiring the entire property and transferring the remainder interest to A's child in exchange for the portion of the purchase price provided by A's child. In determining the amount of A's gift, A's retained interest is valued at zero because it is not a qualified interest.

*Example 2*. K holds rental real estate valued at $100,000. K sells a remainder interest in the property to K's child, retaining the right to receive the income from the property for 20 years. Assume the purchase price paid by K's child for the remainder interest is equal to the value of the interest determined under section 7520. K's retained interest is not a qualified interest and is therefore valued at zero. K

has made a gift in the amount of $100,000 less the consideration received from K's child.

*Example 3*. G and G's child each acquire a fifty percent undivided interest as tenants in common in an office building. The interests of G and G's child are not term interests to which section 2702 applies.

*Example 4*. B purchases a life estate in property from R, B's grandparent, for $100 and B's child purchases the remainder interest for $50. Assume that the value of the property is $300, the value of the life estate determined under section 7520 is $250 and the value of the remainder interest is $50. B is treated as acquiring the entire property and transferring the remainder interest to B's child. However, the amount of B's gift is $100, the amount of consideration ($100) furnished by B for B's interest.

*Example 5*. H and W enter into a written agreement relative to their marital and property rights that requires W to transfer property to an irrevocable trust, the terms of which provide that the income of the trust will be paid to H for 10 years. On the expiration of the 10-year term, the trust is to terminate and the trust corpus is to be paid to W. H and W divorce within two years after the agreement is entered into. Pursuant to section 2516, the transfer to H would otherwise be deemed to be for full and adequate consideration. Section 2702 does not apply to the acquisition of the term interest by H because no member of H's family acquired an interest in the property in the same transaction or series of transactions. The result would not be the same if, on the termination of H's interest in the trust, the trust corpus were distributable to the children of H and W rather than W. [Reg. § 25.2702-4.]

☐ [*T.D.* 8395, 1-28-92.]

### [Reg. § 25.2702-5]

**§ 25.2702-5. Personal residence trusts.**—(a)(1) *In general*.—Section 2702 does not apply to a transfer in trust meeting the requirements of this section. A transfer in trust meets the requirements of this section only if the trust is a personal residence trust (as defined in paragraph (b) of this section). A trust meeting the requirements of a qualified personal residence trust (as defined in paragraph (c) of this section) is treated as a personal residence trust. A trust of which the term holder is the grantor that otherwise meets the requirements of a personal residence trust (or a qualified personal residence trust) is not a personal residence trust (or a qualified personal residence trust) if, at the time of transfer, the term holder of the trust already holds term interests in two trusts that are personal residence trusts (or qualified personal residence trusts) of which the term holder was the grantor. For this purpose, trusts holding fractional interests in the same residence are treated as one trust.

(2) *Modification of trust*.—A trust that does not comply with one or more of the regulatory requirements under paragraph (b) or (c) of this section will, nonetheless, be treated as satisfying these requirements if the trust is modified, by judicial reformation (or nonjudicial reformation if effective under state law), to comply with the requirements. In the case of a trust created after December 31, 1996, the reformation must be commenced within 90 days after the due date (including extensions) for the filing of the gift tax return reporting the transfer of the residence under section 6075 and must be completed within a reasonable time after commencement. If the reformation is not completed by the due date (including extensions) for filing the gift tax return, the grantor or grantor's spouse must attach a statement to the gift tax return stating that the reformation has been commenced or will be commenced within the 90-day period. In the case of a trust created before January 1, 1997, the reformation must be commenced within 90 days after December 23, 1997, and must be completed within a reasonable time after commencement.

(b) *Personal residence trust*.—(1) *In general*.—A personal residence trust is a trust the governing instrument of which prohibits the trust from holding, for the original duration of the term interest, any asset other than one residence to be used or held for use as a personal residence of the term holder and qualified proceeds (as defined in paragraph (b)(3) of this section). A residence is held for use as a personal residence of the term holder so long as the residence is not occupied by any other person (other than the spouse or a dependent of the term holder) and is available at all times for use by the term holder as a personal residence. A trust does not meet the requirements of this section if, during the original duration of the term interest, the residence may be sold or otherwise transferred by the trust or may be used for a purpose other than as a personal residence of the term holder. In addition, the trust does not meet the requirements of this section unless the governing instrument prohibits the trust from selling or transferring the residence, directly or indirectly, to the grantor, the grantor's spouse, or an entity controlled by the grantor or the grantor's spouse, at any time after the original duration of the term interest during which the trust is a grantor trust. For purposes of the preceding sentence, a sale or transfer to another grantor trust of the grantor or the grantor's spouse is considered a sale or transfer to the grantor or the grantor's spouse; however, a distribution (for no consideration) upon or after the expiration of the original duration of the term interest to another grantor trust of the grantor or the grantor's spouse pursuant to the express terms of the trust will not be considered a sale or transfer to the grantor or the grantor's spouse if such other grantor trust prohibits the sale or transfer of the property to the grantor, the grantor's spouse, or an entity controlled by the grantor or the grantor's spouse. In the event the grantor dies prior to the expiration of the original duration of the term interest, this paragraph (b)(1) does not apply to the distribution (for no consideration) of the residence to any person (including the grantor's estate) pursuant to the express terms of the trust or pursuant to the exercise of a power retained by the grantor under the terms of the trust. Further, this paragraph (b)(1) does not apply to any outright distribution (for no consideration) of the residence to the grantor's spouse after the expiration of the original duration of the term interest pursuant to the express terms of the trust. For purposes of this paragraph (b)(1), a *grantor trust* is a trust treated as owned in whole or in part by the grantor or the grantor's spouse pursuant to sections 671 through 678, and *control* is defined in § 25.2701-2(b)(5)(ii) and (iii). Expenses of the trust whether or not attributable to trust principal may be paid directly by the term holder of the trust.

(2) *Personal residence.*—(i) *In general.*—For purposes of this paragraph (b), a personal residence of a term holder is either—

(A) The principal residence of the term holder (within the meaning of section 1034);

(B) One other residence of the term holder (within the meaning of section 280A(d)(1) but without regard to section 280A(d)(2)); or

(C) An undivided fractional interest in either.

(ii) *Additional property.*—A personal residence may include appurtenant structures used by the term holder for residential purposes and adjacent land not in excess of that which is reasonably appropriate for residential purposes (taking into account the residence's size and location). The fact that a residence is subject to a mortgage does not affect its status as a personal residence. The term personal residence does not include any personal property (*e.g.,* household furnishings).

(iii) *Use of residence.*—A residence is a personal residence only if its primary use is as a residence of the term holder when occupied by the term holder. The principal residence of the term holder will not fail to meet the requirements of the preceding sentence merely because a portion of the residence is used in an activity meeting the requirements of section 280A(c)(1) or (4) (relating to deductibility of expenses related to certain uses), provided that such use is secondary to use of the residence as a residence. A residence is not used primarily as a residence if it is used to provide transient lodging and substantial services are provided in connection with the provision of lodging (*e.g.* a hotel or a bed and breakfast). A residence is not a personal residence if, during any period not occupied by the term holder, its primary use is other than as a residence.

(iv) *Interests of spouses in the same residence.*—If spouses hold interests in the same residence (including community property interests), the spouses may transfer their interests in the residence (or a fractional portion of their interests in the residence) to the same personal residence trust, provided that the governing instrument prohibits any person other than one of the spouses from holding a term interest in the trust concurrently with the other spouse.

(3) *Qualified proceeds.*—Qualified proceeds means the proceeds payable as a result of damage to, or destruction or involuntary conversion (within the meaning of section 1033) of, the residence held by a personal residence trust, provided that the governing instrument requires that the proceeds (including any income thereon) be reinvested in a personal residence within two years from the date on which the proceeds are received.

(c) *Qualified personal residence trust.*—(1) *In general.*—A qualified personal residence trust is a trust meeting all the requirements of this paragraph (c). These requirements must be met by provisions in the governing instrument, and these governing instrument provisions must by their terms continue in effect during the existence of any term interest in the trust.

(2) *Personal residence.*—(i) *In general.*—For purposes of this paragraph (c), a personal residence of a term holder is either—

(A) The principal residence of the term holder (within the meaning of section 1034);

(B) One other residence of the term holder (within the meaning of section 280A(d)(1) but without regard to section 280A(d)(2)); or

(C) An undivided fractional interest in either.

(ii) *Additional property.*—A personal residence may include appurtenant structures used by the term holder for residential purposes and adjacent land not in excess of that which is reasonably appropriate for residential purposes (taking into account the residence's size and location). The fact that a residence is subject to a mortgage does not affect its status as a personal residence. The term personal residence does not include any personal property (*e.g.,* household furnishings).

(iii) *Use of residence.*—A residence is a personal residence only if its primary use is as a residence of the term holder when occupied by the term holder. The principal residence of the term holder will not fail to meet the requirements of the preceding sentence merely because a portion of the residence is used in an activity meeting the requirements of section 280A(c)(1) or (4) (relating to deductibility of expenses related to certain uses), provided that such use is secondary to use of the residence as a residence. A residence is not used primarily as a residence if it is used to provide transient lodging and substantial services are provided in connection with the provision of lodging (*e.g.* a hotel or a bed and breakfast). A residence is not a personal residence if, during any period not occupied by the term holder, its primary use is other than as a residence.

(iv) *Interests of spouses in the same residence.*—If spouses hold interests in the same residence (including community property interests), the spouses may transfer their interests in the residence (or a fractional portion of their interests in the residence) to the same qualified personal residence trust, provided that the governing instrument prohibits any person other than one of the spouses from holding a term interest in the trust concurrently with the other spouse.

(3) *Income of the trust.*—The governing instrument must require that any income of the trust be distributed to the term holder not less frequently than annually.

(4) *Distributions from the trust to other persons.*—The governing instrument must prohibit distributions of corpus to any beneficiary other than the transferor prior to the expiration of the retained term interest.

(5) *Assets of the trust.*—(i) *In general.*—Except as otherwise provided in paragraphs (c)(5)(ii) and (c)(8) of this section, the governing instrument must prohibit the trust from holding, for the entire term of the trust, any asset other than one residence to be used or held for use (within the meaning of paragraph (c)(7)(i) of this section) as a personal residence of the term holder (the "residence").

(ii) *Assets other than personal residence.*—Except as otherwise provided, the governing instrument may permit a qualified personal residence trust to hold the following assets (in addition to the residence) in the amounts and in the manner described in this paragraph (c)(5)(ii):

(A) *Additions of cash for payment of expenses, etc.*—(1) *Additions.*—The governing instrument may permit additions of cash to the trust, and may permit the trust to hold additions of cash in a separate account, in an amount which, when added to the cash already held in the account for such purposes, does not exceed the amount required:

(i) For payment of trust expenses (including mortgage payments) already incurred or reasonably expected to be paid by the trust within six months from the date the addition is made;

(ii) For improvements to the residence to be paid by the trust within six months from the date the addition is made; and

(iii) For purchase by the trust of the initial residence, within three months of the date the trust is created, provided that no addition may be made for this purpose, and the trust may not hold any such addition, unless the trustee has previously entered into a contract to purchase that residence; and

(iv) For purchase by the trust of a residence to replace another residence, within three months of the date the addition is made, provided that no addition may be made for this purpose, and the trust may not hold any such addition, unless the trustee has previously entered into a contract to purchase that residence.

(2) *Distributions of excess cash.*—If the governing instrument permits additions of cash to the trust pursuant to paragraph (c)(5)(ii)(A)(1) of this section, the governing instrument must require that the trustee determine, not less frequently than quarterly, the amounts held by the trust for payment of expenses in excess of the amounts permitted by that paragraph and must require that those amounts be distributed immediately thereafter to the term holder. In addition, the governing instrument must require, upon termination of the term holder's interest in the trust, any amounts held by the trust for the purposes permitted by paragraph (c)(5)(ii)(A)(1) of this section that are not used to pay trust expenses due and payable on

the date of termination (including expenses directly related to termination) be distributed outright to the term holder within 30 days of termination.

(B) *Improvements.*—The governing instrument may permit improvements to the residence to be added to the trust and may permit the trust to hold such improvements, provided that the residence, as improved, meets the requirements of a personal residence.

(C) *Sale proceeds.*—The governing instrument may permit the sale of the residence (except as set forth in paragraph (c)(9) of this section) and may permit the trust to hold proceeds from the sale of the residence, in a separate account.

(D) *Insurance and insurance proceeds.*—The governing instrument may permit the trust to hold one or more policies of insurance on the residence. In addition, the governing instrument may permit the trust to hold, in a separate account, proceeds of insurance payable to the trust as a result of damage to or destruction of the residence. For purposes of this paragraph, amounts (other than insurance proceeds payable to the trust as a result of damage to or destruction of the residence) received as a result of the involuntary conversion (within the meaning of section 1033) of the residence are treated as proceeds of insurance.

(6) *Commutation.*—The governing instrument must prohibit commutation (prepayment) of the term holder's interest.

(7) *Cessation of use as a personal residence.*—(i) *In general.*—The governing instrument must provide that a trust ceases to be a qualified personal residence trust if the residence ceases to be used or held for use as a personal residence of the term holder. A residence is held for use as a personal residence of the term holder so long as the residence is not occupied by any other person (other than the spouse or a dependent of the term holder) and is available at all times for use by the term holder as a personal residence. See § 25.2702-5(c)(8) for rules governing disposition of assets of a trust as to which the trust has ceased to be a qualified personal residence trust.

(ii) *Sale of personal residence.*—The governing instrument must provide that the trust ceases to be a qualified personal residence trust upon sale of the residence if the governing instrument does not permit the trust to hold proceeds of sale of the residence pursuant to paragraph (c)(5)(ii)(C) of this section. If the governing instrument permits the trust to hold proceeds of sale pursuant to that paragraph, the governing instrument must provide that the trust ceases to be a qualified personal residence trust with respect to all proceeds of sale held by the trust not later than the earlier of—

(A) The date that is two years after the date of sale;

(B) The termination of the term holder's interest in the trust; or

(C) The date on which a new residence is acquired by the trust.

(iii) *Damage to or destruction of personal residence.*—(A) *In general.*—The governing instrument must provide that, if damage or destruction renders the residence unusable as a residence, the trust ceases to be a qualified personal residence trust on the date that is two years after the date of damage or destruction (or the date of termination of the term holder's interest in the trust, if earlier) unless, prior to such date—

(1) Replacement of or repairs to the residence are completed; or

(2) A new residence is acquired by the trust.

(B) *Insurance proceeds.*—For purposes of this paragraph (C)(7)(iii), if the governing instrument permits the trust to hold proceeds of insurance received as a result of damage to or destruction of the residence pursuant to paragraph (c)(5)(ii)(D) of this section, the governing instrument must contain provisions similar to those required by paragraph (c)(7)(ii) of this section.

(8) *Disposition of trust assets on cessation as personal residence trust.*—(i) *In general.*—The governing instrument must provide that, within 30 days after the date on which the trust has ceased to be a qualified personal residence trust with respect to certain assets, either—

(A) The assets be distributed outright to the term holder;

(B) The assets be converted to and held for the balance of the term holder's term in a separate share of the trust meeting the requirements of a qualified annuity interest; or

(C) In the trustee's sole discretion, the trustee may elect to comply with either paragraph (C)(8)(i)(A) or (B) of this section pursuant to their terms.

(ii) *Requirements for conversion to a qualified annuity interest.*— (A) *Governing instrument requirements.*—For assets subject to this paragraph (c)(8) to be converted to and held as a qualified annuity interest, the governing instrument must contain all provisions required by § 25.2702-3 with respect to a qualified annuity interest.

(B) *Effective date of annuity.*—The governing instrument must provide that the right of the term holder to receive the annuity amount begins on the date of sale of the residence, the date of damage to or destruction of the residence, or the date on which the residence ceases to be used or held for use as a personal residence, as the case may be ("the cessation date"). Notwithstanding the preceding sentence, the governing instrument may provide that the trustee may defer payment of any annuity amount otherwise payable after the cessation date until the date that is 30 days after the assets are converted to a qualified annuity interest under paragraph (c)(8)(i)(B) of this section ("the conversion date"); provided that any deferred payment must bear interest from the cessation date at a rate not less than the section 7520 rate in effect on the cessation date. The governing instrument may permit the trustee to reduce aggregate deferred annuity payments by the amount of income actually distributed by the trust to the term holder during the deferral period.

(C) *Determination of annuity amount.*—(1) *In general.*—The governing instrument must require that the annuity amount be no less than the amount determined under this paragraph (C).

(2) *Entire trust ceases to be a qualified personal residence trust.*—If, on the conversion date, the assets of the trust do not include a residence used or held for use as a personal residence, the annuity may not be less than an amount determined by dividing the lesser of the value of all interests retained by the term holder (as of the date of the original transfer or transfers) or the value of all the trust assets (as of the conversion date) by an annuity factor determined—

(i) For the original term of the term holder's interest; and

(ii) At the rate used in valuing the retained interest at the time of the original transfer.

(3) *Portion of trust continues as qualified personal residence trust.*—If, on the conversion date, the assets of the trust include a residence used or held for use as a personal residence, the annuity must not be less than the amount determined under paragraph (c)(8)(ii)(C)(2) of this section multiplied by a fraction. The numerator of the fraction is the excess of the fair market value of the trust assets on the conversion date over the fair market value of the assets as to which the trust continues as a qualified personal residence trust, and the denominator of the fraction is the fair market value of the trust assets on the conversion date.

(9) *Sale of residence to grantor, grantor's spouse, or entity controlled by grantor or grantor's spouse.*—The governing instrument must prohibit the trust from selling or transferring the residence, directly or indirectly, to the grantor, the grantor's spouse, or an entity controlled by the grantor or the grantor's spouse during the retained term interest of the trust, or at any time after the retained term interest that the trust is a grantor trust. For purposes of the preceding sentence, a sale or transfer to another grantor trust of the grantor or the grantor's spouse is considered a sale or transfer to the grantor or the grantor's spouse; however, a distribution (for no consideration) upon or after the expiration of the retained term interest to another grantor trust of the grantor or the grantor's spouse pursuant to the express terms of the trust will not be considered a sale or transfer to the grantor or the grantor's spouse if such other grantor trust prohibits the sale or transfer of the property to the grantor, the grantor's spouse, or an entity controlled by the grantor or the grantor's spouse. In the event the grantor dies prior to the expiration of the retained term interest, this paragraph (c)(9) does not apply to the distribution (for no consideration) of the residence to any person (including the grantor's estate) pursuant to the express terms of the trust or pursuant to the exercise of a power retained by the grantor under the terms of the trust. Further, this paragraph (c)(9) does not apply to an outright distribution (for no consideration) of the residence to the grantor's spouse after the expiration of the retained trust term pursuant to the express terms of the trust. For purposes of this paragraph (c)(9), a *grantor trust* is a trust treated as owned in whole or in part by the grantor or the grantor's spouse pursuant to sections 671 through 678, and *control* is defined in § 25.2701-2(b)(5)(ii) and (iii).

(d) *Examples.*—The following examples illustrate rules of this section. Each example assumes that all applicable requirements of a personal residence trust (or qualified personal residence trust) are met unless otherwise stated.

*Example 1.* C maintains C's principal place of business in one room of C's principal residence. The room meets the requirements of section 280A(c)(1) for deductibility of expenses related to such use. The residence is a personal residence.

*Example 2.* L owns a vacation condominium that L rents out for six months of the year, but which is treated as L's residence under section 280A(d)(1) because L occupies it for at least 18 days per year. L provides no substantial services in connection with the rental of the condominium. L transfers the condominium to an irrevocable trust, the terms of which meet the requirements of a qualified personal residence trust. L retains the right to use the condominium during L's lifetime. The trust is a qualified personal residence trust.

*Example 3.* W owns a 200-acre farm. The farm includes a house, barns, equipment buildings, a silo, and enclosures for confinement of farm animals. W transfers the farm to an irrevocable trust, retaining the use of the farm for 20 years, with the remainder to W's child. The trust is not a personal residence trust because the farm includes assets not meeting the requirements of a personal residence.

*Example 4.* A transfers A's principal residence to an irrevocable trust, retaining the right to use the residence for a 20-year term. The governing instrument of the trust does not prohibit the trust from holding personal property. The trust is not a qualified personal residence trust.

*Example 5.* T transfers a personal residence to a trust that meets the requirements of a qualified personal residence trust, retaining a term interest in the trust for 10 years. During the period of T's retained term interest, T is forced for health reasons to move to a nursing home. T's spouse continues to occupy the residence. If the residence is available at all times for T's use as a residence during the term (without regard to T's ability to actually use the residence), the residence continues to be held for T's use and the trust does not cease to be a qualified personal residence trust. The residence would cease to be held for use as a personal residence of T if the trustee rented the residence to an unrelated party, because the residence would no longer be available for T's use at all times.

*Example 6.* T transfers T's personal residence to a trust that meets the requirements of a qualified personal residence trust, retaining the right to use the residence for 12 years. On the date the residence is transferred to the trust, the fair market value of the residence is $100,000. After 6 years, the trustee sells the residence, receiving net proceeds of $250,000, and invests the proceeds of sale in common stock. After an additional eighteen months, the common stock has paid $15,000 in dividends and has a fair market value of $260,000. On that date, the trustee purchases a new residence for $200,000. On the purchase of the new residence, the trust ceases to be a qualified personal residence trust with respect to any amount not reinvested in the new residence. The governing instrument of the trust provides that the trustee, in the trustee's sole discretion, may elect either to distribute the excess proceeds or to convert the proceeds into a qualified annuity interest. The trustee elects the latter option. The amount of the annuity is the amount of the annuity that would be payable if no portion of the sale proceeds had been reinvested in a personal residence multiplied by a fraction. The numerator of the fraction is $60,000 (the amount remaining after reinvestment) and the denominator of the fraction is $260,000 (the fair market value of the trust assets on the conversion date). The obligation to pay the annuity commences on the date of sale, but payment of the annuity that otherwise would have been payable during the period between the date of sale and the date on which the trust ceased to be a qualified personal residence trust with respect to the excess proceeds may be deferred until 30 days after the date on which the new residence is purchased. Any amount deferred must bear compound interest from the date the annuity is payable at the section 7520 rate in effect on the date of sale. The $15,000 of income distributed to the term holder during that period may be used to reduce the annuity amount payable with respect to that period if the governing instrument so provides and thus reduce the amount on which compound interest is computed. [Reg. § 25.2702-5.]

☐ [T.D. 8395, 1-28-92. *Amended by T.D. 8743, 12-22-97.*]

### [Reg. § 25.2702-6]

**§ 25.2702-6. Reduction in taxable gifts.**—(a) *Transfers of retained interests in trust.*—(1) *Inter vivos transfers.*—If an individual subsequently transfers by gift an interest in trust previously valued (when held by that individual) under § 25.2702-2(b)(1) or (c), the individual is entitled to a reduction in aggregate taxable gifts. The amount of the reduction is determined under paragraph(b) of this section. Thus, for example, if an individual transferred property to an irrevocable trust, retaining an interest in the trust that was valued at zero under § 25.2702-2(b)(1), and the individual later transfers the retained interest by gift, the individual is entitled to a reduction in aggregate taxable gifts on the subsequent transfer. For purposes of this section, aggregate taxable gifts means the aggregate sum of the individual's taxable gifts for the calendar year determined under section 2502(a)(1).

(2) *Testamentary transfers.*—If either—

(i) A term interest in trust is included in an individual's gross estate solely by reason of section 2033, or

(ii) A remainder interest in trust is included in an individual's gross estate,

and the interest was previously valued (when held by that individual) under § 25.2702-2(b)(1) or (c), the individual's estate is entitled to a reduction in the individual's adjusted taxable gifts in computing the Federal estate tax payable under section 2001. The amount of the reduction is determined under paragraph (b) of this section.

(3) *Gift splitting on subsequent transfer.*—If an individual who is entitled to a reduction in aggregate taxable gifts (or adjusted taxable gifts) subsequently transfers the interest in a transfer treated as made one-half by the individual's spouse under section 2513, the individual may assign one-half of the amount of the reduction to the consenting spouse. The assignment must be attached to the Form 709 on which the consenting spouse reports the split gift.

(b) *Amount of reduction.*—(1) *In general.*—The amount of the reduction in aggregate taxable gifts (or adjusted taxable gifts) is the lesser of—

(i) The increase in the individual's taxable gifts resulting from the interest being valued at the time of the initial transfer under § 25.2702-2(b)(1) or (c); or

(ii) The increase in the individual's taxable gifts (or gross estate) resulting from the subsequent transfer of the interest.

(2) *Treatment of annual exclusion.*—For purposes of determining the amount under paragraph (b)(1)(ii) of this section, the exclusion under section 2503(b) applies first to transfers in that year other than the transfer of the interest previously valued under § 25.2702-2(b)(1) or (c).

(3) *Overlap with section 2001.*—Notwithstanding paragraph (b)(1) of this section, the amount of the reduction is reduced to the extent section 2001 would apply to reduce the amount of an individual's adjusted taxable gifts with respect to the same interest to which paragraph (b)(1) of this section would otherwise apply.

(c) *Examples.*—The rules of this section are illustrated by the following examples. The following facts apply for *Examples 1-4:*

*Facts.* In 1992, X transferred property to an irrevocable trust retaining the right to receive the trust income for life. On the death of X, the trust is to terminate and the trust corpus is to be paid to X's child, C. X's income interest had a value under section 7520 of $40,000 at the time of the transfer; however, because X's retained interest was not a qualified interest, it was valued at zero under § 25.2702-2(b)(1) for purposes of determining the amount of X's gift. X's taxable gifts in 1992 were therefore increased by $40,000. In 1993, X transfers the income interest to C for no consideration.

*Example 1.* Assume that the value under section 7520 of the income interest on the subsequent transfer to C is $30,000. If X makes no other gifts to C in 1993, X is entitled to a reduction in aggregate taxable gifts of $20,000, the lesser of the amount by which X's taxable gifts were increased as a result of the income interest being valued at zero on the initial transfer ($40,000) or the amount by which X's taxable gifts are increased as a result of the subsequent transfer of the income interest ($30,000 minus $10,000 annual exclusion).

*Example 2.* Assume that in 1993, 4 months after X transferred the income interest to C, X transferred $5,000 cash to C. In determining the increase in taxable gifts occurring on the subsequent transfer, the annual exclusion under section 2503(b) is first applied to the cash gift. X is entitled to a reduction in aggregate taxable gifts of $25,000, the lesser of the amount by which X's taxable gifts were increased as a result of the income interest being valued at zero on the initial transfer ($40,000) or the amount by which X's taxable gifts are increased as a result of the subsequent transfer of the income interest ($25,000 (($30,000 + $5,000) – $10,000 annual exclusion).

*Example 3.* Assume that the value under section 7520 of the income interest on the subsequent transfer to C is $55,000. X is entitled to reduce aggregate taxable gifts by $40,000, the lesser of the amount by which X's taxable gifts were increased as a result of the income interest being valued at zero on the initial transfer ($40,000) or the amount by which X's taxable gifts are increased as a result of the subsequent transfer of the income interest ($55,000 minus $10,000 annual exclusion = $45,000).

*Example 4.* Assume that X and X's spouse, S, split the subsequent gift to C. X is entitled to assign one-half the reduction to S. If the assignment is made, each is entitled to reduce aggregate taxable gifts by $17,500, the lesser of their portion of the increase in taxable gifts on the initial transfer by reason of the application of section 2702 ($20,000) and their portion of the increase in taxable gifts on the subsequent transfer of the retained interest ($27,500 – $10,000 annual exclusion).

*Example 5.* In 1992, A transfers property to an irrevocable trust, retaining the right to receive the trust income for 10 years. On the expiration of the 10-year term, the trust is to terminate and the trust corpus is to be paid to A's child, B. Assume that A's term interest has a value under section 7520 of $20,000 at the time of the transfer; however, because A's retained interest was not a qualified interest, it was valued at zero under §25.2702-2(b)(1) for purposes of determining the amount of A's gift. Assume also that A and A's spouse, S, split the gift of the remainder interest under section 2513. In 1993, A transfers A's term interest to D, A's other child, for no consideration. A is entitled to reduce A's aggregate taxable gifts on the transfer. Assume that A and S also split the subsequent gift to D, and that A dies one month after making the subsequent transfer of the term interest and S dies six months later. The gift of the term interest is included in A's gross estate under section 2035(d)(2). To the extent S's taxable gifts are reduced pursuant to section 2001(e), S is entitled to no reduction in aggregate or adjusted taxable gifts under this section.

*Example 6.* T transfers property to an irrevocable trust retaining the power to direct the distribution of trust income for 10 years among T's descendants in whatever shares T deems appropriate. On the expiration of the 10-year period, the trust corpus is to be paid in equal shares to T's children. T's transfer of the remainder interest is a completed gift. Because T's retained interest is not a qualified interest, it is valued at zero under §25.2702-2(b)(1) and the amount of T's gift is the fair market value of the property transferred to the trust. The distribution of income each year is not a transfer of a retained interest in trust. Therefore, T is not entitled to reduce aggregate taxable gifts as a result of the distributions of income from the trust.

*Example 7.* The facts are the same as in *Example 6,* except that after 3 years T exercises the right to direct the distribution of trust income by assigning the right to the income for the balance of the term to T's child, C. The exercise is a transfer of a retained interest in trust for purposes of this section. T is entitled to reduce aggregate taxable gifts by the lesser of the increase in taxable gifts resulting from the application of section 2702 to the initial transfer or the increase in taxable gifts resulting from the transfer of the retained interest in trust.

*Example 8.* In 1992, V purchases an income interest for 10 years in property in the same transaction or series of transactions in which G, V's child, purchases the remainder interest in the same property. V dies in 1997 still holding the term interest, the value of which is includible in V's gross estate under section 2033. V's estate would be entitled to a reduction in adjusted taxable gifts in the amount determined under paragraph (b) of this section. [Reg. §25.2702-6.]

☐ [T.D. 8395, 1-28-92.]

### [Reg. §25.2702-7]

**§25.2702-7. Effective dates.**—Except as provided in this section, §§25.2702-1 through 25.2702-6 apply as of January 28, 1992. With respect to transfers to which section 2702 applied made prior to January 28, 1992, taxpayers may rely on any reasonable interpretation of the statutory provisions. For these purposes, the provisions of the proposed regulations and the final regulations are considered a reasonable interpretation of the statutory provisions. The fourth through eighth sentences of §25.2702-5(b)(1) and §25.2702-5(c)(9) apply with respect to trusts created after May 16, 1996. Section 25.2702-2(a)(5), the second and third sentences of §25.2702-2(a)(6), §25.2702-3(d)(2), the first two sentences of §25.2702-3(d)(4), the last sentence of §25.2702-3(e), *Example 5,* the last two sentences of §25.2702-3(e), *Example 6,* and §25.2702-3(e), *Examples 8* and *9,* apply for trusts created on or after July 26, 2004. However, the Internal Revenue Service will not challenge any prior application of the changes to *Examples 5* and *6* in §25.2702-3(e). [Reg. §25.2702-7.]

☐ [T.D. 8395, 1-28-92. *Amended by T.D. 8743, 12-22-97 and T.D. 9181, 2-24-2005.*]

### [Reg. §25.2703-1]

**§25.2703-1. Property subject to restrictive arrangements.**— (a) *Disregard of rights or restrictions.*—(1) *In general.*—For purposes of subtitle B (relating to estate, gift, and generation-skipping transfer taxes), the value of any property is determined without regard to any right or restriction relating to the property.

(2) *Right or restriction.*—For purposes of this section, right or restriction means—

(i) Any option, agreement, or other right to acquire or use the property at a price less than fair market value (determined without regard to the option, agreement, or right); or

(ii) Any restriction on the right to sell or use the property.

(3) *Agreements, etc., containing rights or restrictions.*—A right or restriction may be contained in a partnership agreement, articles of incorporation, corporate bylaws, a shareholders' agreement, or any other agreement. A right or restriction may be implicit in the capital structure of an entity.

(4) *Qualified easements.*—A perpetual restriction on the use of real property that qualified for a charitable deduction under either

section 2522(d) or section 2055(f) of the Internal Revenue Code is not treated as a right or restriction.

(b) *Exceptions.*—(1) *In general.*—This section does not apply to any right or restriction satisfying the following three requirements—

(i) The right or restriction is a bona fide business arrangement;

(ii) The right or restriction is not a device to transfer property to the natural objects of the transferor's bounty for less than full and adequate consideration in money or money's worth; and

(iii) At the time the right or restriction is created, the terms of the right or restriction are comparable to similar arrangements entered into by persons in an arm's length transaction.

(2) *Separate requirements.*—Each of the three requirements described in paragraph (b)(1) of this section must be independently satisfied for a right or restriction to meet this exception. Thus, for example, the mere showing that a right or restriction is a bona fide business arrangement is not sufficient to establish that the right or restriction is not a device to transfer property for less than full and adequate consideration.

(3) *Exception for certain rights or restrictions.*—A right or restriction is considered to meet each of the three requirements described in paragraph (b)(1) of this section if more than 50 percent by value of the property subject to the right or restriction is owned directly or indirectly (within the meaning of §25.2701-6) by individuals who are not members of the transferor's family. In order to meet this exception, the property owned by those individuals must be subject to the right or restriction to the same extent as the property owned by the transferor. For purposes of this section, members of the transferor's family include the persons described in §25.2701-2(b)(5) and any other individual who is a natural object of the transferor's bounty. Any property held by a member of the transferor's family under the rules of §25.2701-6 (without regard to §25.2701-6(a)(5)) is treated as held only by a member of the transferor's family.

(4) *Similar arrangement.*—(i) *In general.*—A right or restriction is treated as comparable to similar arrangements entered into by persons in an arm's length transaction if the right or restriction is one that could have been obtained in a fair bargain among unrelated parties in the same business dealing with each other at arm's length. A right or restriction is considered a fair bargain among unrelated parties in the same business if it conforms with the general practice of unrelated parties under negotiated agreements in the same business. This determination generally will entail consideration of such factors as the expected term of the agreement, the current fair market value of the property, anticipated changes in value during the term of the arrangement, and the adequacy of any consideration given in exchange for the rights granted.

(ii) *Evidence of general business practice.*—Evidence of general business practice is not met by showing isolated comparables. If more than one valuation method is commonly used in a business, a right or restriction does not fail to evidence general business practice merely because it uses only one of the recognized methods. It is not necessary that the terms of a right or restriction parallel the terms of any particular agreement. If comparables are difficult to find because the business is unique, comparables from similar businesses may be used.

(5) *Multiple rights or restrictions.*—If property is subject to more than one right or restriction described in paragraph (a)(2) of this section, the failure of a right or restriction to satisfy the requirements of paragraph (b)(1) of this section does not cause any other right or restriction to fail to satisfy those requirements if the right or restriction otherwise meets those requirements. Whether separate provisions are separate rights or restrictions, or are integral parts of a single right or restriction, depends on all the facts and circumstances.

(c) *Substantial modification of a right or restriction.*—(1) *In general.*— A right or restriction that is substantially modified is treated as a right or restriction created on the date of the modification. Any discretionary modification of a right or restriction, whether or not authorized by the terms of the agreement, that results in other than a *de minimis* change to the quality, value, or timing of the rights of any party with respect to property that is subject to the right or restriction is a substantial modification. If the terms of the right or restriction require periodic updating, the failure to update is presumed to substantially modify the right or restriction unless it can be shown that updating would not have resulted in a substantial modification. The addition of any family member as a party to a right or restriction (including by reason of a transfer of property that subjects the transferee family member to a right or restriction with respect to the transferred property) is considered a substantial modification unless the addition is mandatory under the terms of the right or restriction or the added family member is assigned to a generation (determined under the rules of section 2651 of the Internal Revenue Code) no lower than the lowest generation occupied by individuals already party to the right or restriction).

(2) *Exceptions.*—A substantial modification does not include—

(i) A modification required by the terms of a right or restriction;

(ii) A discretionary modification of an agreement conferring a right or restriction if the modification does not change the right or restriction;

(iii) A modification of a capitalization rate used with respect to a right or restriction if the rate is modified in a manner that bears a fixed relationship to a specified market interest rate; and

(iv) A modification that results in an option price that more closely approximates fair market value.

(d) *Examples.*—The following examples illustrate the provisions of this section:

*Example 1.* T dies in 1992 owning title to Blackacre. In 1991, T and T's child entered into a lease with respect to Blackacre. At the time the lease was entered into, the terms of the lease were not comparable to leases of similar property entered into among unrelated parties. The lease is a restriction on the use of the property that is disregarded in valuing the property for Federal estate tax purposes.

*Example 2.* T and T's child, C, each own 50 percent of the outstanding stock of X corporation. T and C enter into an agreement in 1987 providing for the disposition of stock held by the first to die at the time of death. The agreement also provides certain restrictions with respect to lifetime transfers. In 1992, as permitted (but not required) under the agreement, T transfers one-half of T's stock to T's spouse, S. S becomes a party to the agreement between T and C by reason of the transfer. The transfer is the addition of a family member to the right or restriction. However, it is not a substantial modification of the right or restriction because the added family member would be assigned to a generation under section 2651 of the Internal Revenue Code no lower than the generation occupied by C.

*Example 3.* The facts are the same as in *Example 2*. In 1993, the agreement is amended to reflect a change in the company's name and a change of address for the company's registered agent. These changes are not a substantial modification of the agreement conferring the right or restriction because the right or restriction has not changed. [Reg. § 25.2703-1.]

☐ [T.D. 8395, 1-28-92.]

### [Reg. § 25.2703-2]

**§ 25.2703-2. Effective date.**—Section 25.2703-1 applies to any right or restriction created or substantially modified after October 8, 1990, and is effective as of January 28, 1992. With respect to transfers occurring prior to January 28, 1992, and for purposes of determining whether an event occurring prior to January 28, 1992 constitutes a substantial modification, taxpayers may rely on any reasonable interpretation of the statutory provisions. For these purposes, the provisions of the proposed regulations and the final regulations are considered a reasonable interpretation of the statutory provisions. [Reg. § 25.2703-2.]

☐ [T.D. 8395, 1-28-92.]

### [Reg. § 25.2704-1]

**§ 25.2704-1. Lapse of certain rights.**—(a) *Lapse treated as transfer.*—(1) *In general.*—The lapse of a voting right or a liquidation right in a corporation or partnership (an "entity") is a transfer by the individual directly or indirectly holding the right immediately prior to its lapse (the "holder") to the extent provided in paragraphs (b) and (c) of this section. This section applies only if the entity is controlled by the holder and members of the holder's family immediately before and after the lapse. The amount of the transfer is determined under paragraph (d) of this section. If the lapse of a voting right or a liquidation right occurs during the holder's lifetime, the lapse is a transfer by gift. If the lapse occurs at the holder's death, the lapse is a transfer includible in the holder's gross estate.

(2) *Definitions.*—The following definitions apply for purposes of this section:

(i) *Control.*—Control has the meaning given it in § 25.2701-2(b)(5).

(ii) *Member of the family.*—Member of the family has the meaning given it in § 25.2702-2(a)(1).

(iii) *Directly or indirectly held.*—An interest is directly or indirectly held only to the extent the value of the interest would have been includible in the gross estate of the individual if the individual had died immediately prior to the lapse.

(iv) *Voting right.*—Voting right means a right to vote with respect to any matter of the entity. In the case of a partnership, the right of a general partner to participate in partnership management is a voting right. The right to compel the entity to acquire all or a portion of the holder's equity interest in the entity by reason of aggregate voting power is treated as a liquidation right and is not treated as a voting right.

(v) *Liquidation right.*—Liquidation right means a right or ability to compel the entity to acquire all or a portion of the holder's equity interest in the entity, including by reason of aggregate voting power, whether or not its exercise would result in the complete liquidation of the entity.

(vi) *Subordinate.*—Subordinate has the meaning given it in § 25.2701-3(a)(2)(iii).

(3) *Certain temporary lapses.*—If a lapsed right may be restored only upon the occurrence of a future event not within the control of the holder or members of the holder's family, the lapse is deemed to occur at the time the lapse becomes permanent with respect to the holder, *i.e.* either by a transfer of the interest or otherwise.

(4) *Source of right or lapse.*—A voting right or a liquidation right may be conferred by and may lapse by reason of a State law, the corporate charter or bylaws, an agreement, or other means.

(b) *Lapse of voting right.*—A lapse of a voting right occurs at the time a presently exercisable voting right is restricted or eliminated.

(c) *Lapse of liquidation right.*—(1) *In general.*—A lapse of a liquidation right occurs at the time a presently exercisable liquidation right is restricted or eliminated. Except as otherwise provided, a transfer of an interest that results in the lapse of a liquidation right is not subject to this section if the rights with respect to the transferred interest are not restricted or eliminated. However, a transfer that results in the elimination of the transferor's right or ability to compel the entity to acquire an interest retained by the transferor that is subordinate to the transferred interest is a lapse of a liquidation right with respect to the subordinate interest.

(2) *Exceptions.*—Section 2704(a) does not apply to the lapse of a liquidation right under the following circumstances.

(i) *Family cannot obtain liquidation value.*—(A) *In general.*—Section 2704(a) does not apply to the lapse of a liquidation right to the extent the holder (or the holder's estate) and members of the holder's family cannot immediately after the lapse liquidate an interest that the holder held directly or indirectly and could have liquidated prior to the lapse.

(B) *Ability to liquidate.*—Whether an interest can be liquidated immediately after the lapse is determined under the State law generally applicable to the entity, as modified by the governing instruments of the entity, but without regard to any restriction described in section 2704(b). Thus, if, after any restriction described in section 2704(b) is disregarded, the remaining requirements for liquidation under the governing instruments are less restrictive than the State law that would apply in the absence of the governing instruments, the ability to liquidate is determined by reference to the governing instruments.

(ii) *Rights valued under section 2701.*—Section 2704(a) does not apply to the lapse of a liquidation right previously valued under section 2701 to the extent necessary to prevent double taxation (taking into account any adjustment available under § 25.2701-5).

(iii) *Certain changes in State law.*—Section 2704(a) does not apply to the lapse of a liquidation right that occurs solely by reason of a change in State law. For purposes of this paragraph, a change in the governing instrument of an entity is not a change in State law.

(d) *Amount of transfer.*—The amount of the transfer is the excess, if any, of—

(1) The value of all interests in the entity owned by the holder immediately before the lapse (determined immediately after the lapse as if the lapsed right was nonlapsing); over

(2) The value of the interests described in the preceding paragraph immediately after the lapse (determined as if all such interests were held by one individual).

(e) *Application to similar rights.*—[RESERVED]

(f) *Examples.*—The following examples illustrate the provisions of this section:

*Example 1.* Prior to D's death, D owned all the preferred stock of Corporation Y and D's children owned all the common stock. At that time, the preferred stock had 60 percent of the total voting power and the common stock had 40 percent. Under the corporate by-laws, the voting rights of the preferred stock terminated on D's death. The value of D's interest immediately prior to D's death (determined as if the voting rights were non-lapsing) was $100X. The value of that interest immediately after death would have been $90X if the voting rights had been non-lapsing. The decrease in value reflects the loss in value resulting from the death of D (whose involvement in Y was a key factor in Y's profitability). Section 2704(a) applies to the lapse of voting rights on D's death. D's gross estate includes an amount equal to the excess, if any, of $90X over the fair market value of the preferred stock determined after the lapse of the voting rights.

*Example 2.* Prior to D's death, D owned all the preferred stock of Corporation Y. The preferred stock and the common stock each carried 50 percent of the total voting power of Y. D's children owned 40 percent of the common stock and unrelated parties own the remaining 60 percent. Under the corporate by-laws, the voting rights of the preferred stock terminate on D's death. Section 2704(a) does not apply to the lapse of D's voting rights because members of D's family do not control Y after the lapse.

*Example 3.* The by-laws of Corporation Y provide that the voting rights of any transferred shares of the single outstanding class of stock are reduced to $1/2$ vote per share after the transfer but are fully restored to the transferred shares after 5 years. D owned 60 percent of the shares prior to death and members of D's family owned the balance. On D's death, D's shares pass to D's children and the voting rights are reduced pursuant to the by-laws. Section 2704(a) applies to the lapse of D's voting rights. D's gross estate includes an amount equal to the excess, if any, of the fair market value of D's stock (determined immediately after D's death as though the voting rights had not been reduced and would not be reduced) over the stock's fair market value immediately after D's death.

*Example 4.* D owns 84 percent of the single outstanding class of stock of Corporation Y. The by-laws require at least 70 percent of the vote to liquidate Y. D gives one-half of D's stock in equal shares to D's three children (14 percent to each). Section 2704(a) does not apply to the loss of D's ability to liquidate Y, because the voting rights with respect to the corporation are not restricted or eliminated by reason of the transfer.

*Example 5.* D and D's two children, A and B, are partners in Partnership X. Each has a $3^1/3$ percent general partnership interest and a 30 percent limited partnership interest. Under State law, a general partner has the right to participate in partnership management. The partnership agreement provides that when a general partner withdraws or dies, X must redeem the general partnership interest for its liquidation value. Also, under the agreement any general partner can liquidate the partnership. A limited partner cannot liquidate the partnership and a limited partner's capital interest will be returned only when the partnership is liquidated. A deceased limited partner's interest continues as a limited partnership interest. D dies, leaving his limited partnership interest to D's spouse. Because of a general partner's right to dissolve the partnership, a limited partnership interest has a greater fair market value when held in conjunction with a general partnership interest than when held alone. Section 2704(a) applies to the lapse of D's liquidation right because after the lapse, members of D's family could liquidate D's limited partnership interest. D's gross estate includes an amount equal to the excess of the value of all D's interests in X immediately before D's death (determined immediately after D's death but as though the liquidation right had not lapsed and would not lapse) over the fair market value of all D's interests in X immediately after D's death.

*Example 6.* The facts are the same as in *Example 5*, except that under the partnership agreement D is the only general partner who holds a unilateral liquidation right. Assume further that the partnership agreement contains a restriction described in section 2704(b) that prevents D's family members from liquidating D's limited partnership interest immediately after D's death. Under State law, in the absence of the restriction in the partnership agreement, D's family members could liquidate the partnership. The restriction on the family's ability to liquidate is disregarded and the amount of D's gross estate is increased by reason of the lapse of D's liquidation right.

*Example 7.* D owns all the stock of Corporation X, consisting of 100 shares of non-voting preferred stock and 100 shares of voting common stock. Under the by-laws, X can only be liquidated with the consent of at least 80 percent of the voting shares. D transfers 30 shares of common stock to D's child. The transfer is not a lapse of a liquidation right with respect to the common stock because the voting rights that enabled D to liquidate prior to the transfer are not restricted or eliminated. The transfer is not a lapse of a liquidation right with respect to the retained preferred stock because the preferred stock is not subordinate to the transferred common stock.

*Example 8.* D owns all of the single class of stock of Corporation Y. D recapitalizes Y, exchanging D's common stock for voting common stock and non-voting, non-cumulative preferred stock. The preferred

stock carries a right to put the stock for its par value at any time during the next 10 years. D transfers the common stock to D's grandchild in a transfer subject to section 2701. In determining the amount of D's gift under section 2701, D's retained put right is valued at zero. D's child, C, owns the preferred stock when the put right lapses. Section 2704(a) applies to the lapse, without regard to the application of section 2701, because the put right was not valued under section 2701 in the hands of C.

*Example 9.* A and A's two children are equal general and limited partners in Partnership Y. Under the partnership agreement, each general partner has a right to liquidate the partnership at any time. Under State law that would apply in the absence of contrary provisions in the partnership agreement, the death or incompetency of a general partner terminates the partnership. However, the partnership agreement provides that the partnership does not terminate on the incompetence or death of a general partner, but that an incompetent partner cannot exercise rights as a general partner during any period of incompetency. A partner's full rights as general partner are restored if the partner regains competency. A becomes incompetent. The lapse of A's voting right on becoming incompetent is not subject to section 2704(a) because it may be restored to A in the future. However, if A dies while incompetent, a lapse subject to section 2704(a) is deemed to occur at that time because the lapsed right cannot thereafter be restored to A. [Reg. § 25.2704-1.]

☐ [*T.D.* 8395, 1-28-92.]

**[Reg. § 25.2704-2]**

**§ 25.2704-2. Transfers subject to applicable restrictions.**—(a) *In general.*—If an interest in a corporation or partnership (an "entity") is transferred to or for the benefit of a member of the transferor's family, any applicable restriction is disregarded in valuing the transferred interest. This section applies only if the transferor and members of the transferor's family control the entity immediately before the transfer. For the definition of control, see § 25.2701-2(b)(5). For the definition of member of the family, see § 25.2702-2(a)(1).

(b) *Applicable restriction defined.*—An applicable restriction is a limitation on the ability to liquidate the entity (in whole or in part) that is more restrictive than the limitations that would apply under the State law generally applicable to the entity in the absence of the restriction. A restriction is an applicable restriction only to the extent that either the restriction by its terms will lapse at any time after the transfer, or the transferor (or the transferor's estate) and any members of the transferor's family can remove the restriction immediately after the transfer. Ability to remove the restriction is determined by reference to the State law that would apply but for a more restrictive rule in the governing instruments of the entity. See § 25.2704-1(c)(1)(B) for a discussion of the term "State law." An applicable restriction does not include a commercially reasonable restriction on liquidation imposed by an unrelated person providing capital to the entity for the entity's trade or business operations whether in the form of debt or equity. An unrelated person is any person whose relationship to the transferor, the transferee, or any member of the family of either is not described in section 267(b) of the Internal Revenue Code, provided that for purposes of this section the term "fiduciary of a trust" as used in section 267(b) does not include a bank as defined in section 581 of the Internal Revenue Code. A restriction imposed or required to be imposed by Federal or State law is not an applicable restriction. An option, right to use property, or agreement that is subject to section 2703 is not an applicable restriction.

(c) *Effect of disregarding an applicable restriction.*—If an applicable restriction is disregarded under this section, the transferred interest is valued as if the restriction does not exist and as if the rights of the transferor are determined under the State law that would apply but for the restriction. For example, an applicable restriction with respect to preferred stock will be disregarded in determining the amount of a transfer of common stock under section 2701.

(d) *Examples.*—The following examples illustrate the provisions of this section:

*Example 1.* D owns a 76 percent interest and each of D's children, A and B, owns a 12 percent interest in General Partnership X. The partnership agreement requires the consent of all the partners to liquidate the partnership. Under the State law that would apply in the absence of the restriction in the partnership agreement, the consent of partners owning 70 percent of the total partnership interests would be required to liquidate X. On D's death, D's partnership interest passes to D's child, C. The requirement that all the partners consent to liquidation is an applicable restriction. Because A, B and C (all members of D's family), acting together after the transfer, can remove the restriction on liquidation, D's interest is valued without regard to the restriction; *i.e.*, as though D's interest is sufficient to liquidate the partnership.

*Example 2.* D owns all the preferred stock in Corporation X. The preferred stock carries a right to liquidate X that cannot be exercised until 1999. D's children, A and B, own all the common stock of X. The common stock is the only voting stock. In 1994, D transfers the preferred stock to D's child, A. The restriction on D's right to liquidate is an applicable restriction that is disregarded. Therefore, the preferred stock is valued as though the right to liquidate were presently exercisable.

*Example 3.* D owns 60 percent of the stock of Corporation X. The corporate by-laws provide that the corporation cannot be liquidated for 10 years after which time liquidation requires approval by 60 percent of the voting interests. In the absence of the provision in the by-laws, State law would require approval by 80 percent of the voting interests to liquidate X. D transfers the stock to a trust for the benefit of D's child, A, during the 10-year period. The 10-year restriction is an applicable restriction and is disregarded. Therefore, the value of the stock is determined as if the transferred block could currently liquidate X.

*Example 4.* D and D's children, A and B, are partners in Limited Partnership Y. Each has a 3.33 percent general partnership interest and a 30 percent limited partnership interest. Any general partner has the right to liquidate the partnership at any time. As part of a loan agreement with a lender who is related to D, each of the partners agree that the partnership may not be liquidated without the lender's consent while any portion of the loan remains outstanding. During the term of the loan agreement, D transfers one-half of both D's partnership interests to each of A and B. Because the lender is a related party, the requirement that the lender consent to liquidation is an applicable restriction and the transfers of D's interests are valued as if such consent were not required.

*Example 5.* D owns 60 percent of the preferred and 70 percent of the common stock in Corporation X. The remaining stock is owned by individuals unrelated to D. The preferred stock carries a put right that cannot be exercised until 1999. In 1995, D transfers the common stock to D's child in a transfer that is subject to section 2701. The restriction on D's right to liquidate is an applicable restriction that is disregarded in determining the amount of the gift under section 2701. [Reg. § 25.2704-2.]

☐ [*T.D.* 8395, 1-28-92.]

### [Reg. § 25.2704-3]

**§ 25.2704-3. Effective date.**—Section 25.2704-1 applies to lapses occurring after January 28, 1992, of rights created after October 8, 1990. Section 25.2704-2 applies to transfers occurring after January 28, 1992, of property subject to applicable restrictions created after October 8, 1990. In determining whether a voting right or a liquidation right has lapsed prior to that date, and for purposes of determining whether the lapse is subject to section 2704(a), taxpayers may rely on any reasonable interpretation of the statutory provisions. For transfers of interests occurring before January 28, 1992, taxpayers may rely on any reasonable interpretation of the statutory provisions in determining whether a restriction is an applicable restriction that must be disregarded in determining the value of the transferred interest. For these purposes, the provisions of the proposed regulations and the final regulations are considered a reasonable interpretation of the statutory provisions. [Reg. § 25.2704-3.]

☐ [*T.D.* 8395, 1-28-92.]

[The next page is 61,371.]

# EMPLOYMENT TAXES

## Federal Insurance Contributions Act

## INTRODUCTION

See p. 20,601 for regulations not amended to reflect law changes

### [Reg. §31.0-1]

**§31.0-1. Introduction.**—(a) *In general.*—The regulations in this part relate to the employment taxes imposed by subtitle C (chapters 21 to 25, inclusive) of the Internal Revenue Code of 1954, as amended. References in the regulations to the "Internal Revenue Code" or the "Code" are references to the Internal Revenue Code of 1954, as amended, unless otherwise indicated. References to the Federal Insurance Contributions Act, the Railroad Retirement Tax Act, and the Federal Unemployment Tax Act are references to chapters 21, 22, and 23, respectively, of the Code. References to sections of law are references to sections of the Internal Revenue Code unless otherwise indicated. The regulations in this part also provide rules relating to the deposit of other taxes by electronic funds transfer.

(b) *Division of regulations.*—The regulations in this part are divided into 7 subparts. Subpart A contains provisions relating to general definitions and use of terms, the division and scope of the regulations in this part, and the extent to which the regulations in this part supersede prior regulations relating to employment taxes. Subpart B relates to the taxes under the Federal Insurance Contributions Act. Subpart C relates to the taxes under the Railroad Retirement Tax Act. Subpart D relates to the tax under the Federal Unemployment Tax Act. Subpart E relates to the collection of income tax at source on wages under chapter 24 of the Code. Subpart F relates to the provisions of chapter 25 of the Code which are applicable in respect of the taxes imposed by chapters 21 to 24, inclusive, of the Code. Subpart G relates to selected provisions of subtitle F of the Code, relating to procedure and administration, which have special application in respect of the taxes imposed by subtitle C of the Code. Inasmuch as these regulations constitute Part 31 of Title 26 of the Code of Federal Regulations, each section of the regulations is preceded by a section symbol and 31 followed by a decimal point (§31.). Sections of law or references thereto are preceded by "Sec." or the word "section". [Reg. §31.0-1.]

☐ [*T.D. 6516, 12-20-60. Amended by T.D. 8723, 7-11-97.*]

### [Reg. §31.0-2]

**§31.0-2. General definitions and use of terms.**—(a) *In general.*— As used in the regulations in this part, unless otherwise expressly indicated—

(1) The terms defined in the provisions of law contained in the regulations in this part shall have the meanings so assigned to them.

(2) The Internal Revenue Code of 1954 means the Act approved August 16, 1954 (26 U.S.C.), entitled "An act to revise the internal revenue laws of the United States", as amended.

(3) The Internal Revenue Code of 1939 means the Act approved February 10, 1939 (53 Stat., Part 1), as amended.

(4) The Social Security Act means the Act approved August 14, 1935 (42 U.S.C. c.7), as amended.

(5)(i) The Social Security Amendments of 1954 means the act approved September 1, 1954 (68 Stat. 1052), as amended.

(ii) The Social Security Amendments of 1956 means the act approved August 1, 1956 (70 Stat. 807), as amended.

(iii) The Social Security Amendments of 1958 means the act approved August 28, 1958 (72 Stat. 1013), as amended.

(iv) The Social Security Amendments of 1960 means the act approved September 13, 1960 (74 Stat. 924).

(v) The Social Security Amendments of 1961 means the act approved June 30, 1961 (75 Stat. 131).

(vi) The Social Security Amendments of 1965 means the act approved July 30, 1965 (79 Stat. 286).

(vii) The Social Security Amendments of 1967 means the act approved January 2, 1968 (81 Stat. 821).

(viii) The Social Security Amendments of 1972 means the act approved October 30, 1972 (86 Stat. 1329).

(6) The Social Security Administration means the Social Security Administration of the Department of Health, Education, and Welfare. (See the Statement of Organization and Delegations of Authority of the Department of Health, Education, and Welfare (20 F.R. 1996).)

(7) District director means district director of internal revenue. The term also includes the Director of International Operations in all cases where the authority to perform the functions which may be performed by a district director has been delegated to the Director of International Operations.

(8) Person includes an individual, a corporation, a partnership, a trust or estate, a joint-stock company, an association, or a syndicate, group, pool, joint venture or other unincorporated organization or group, through or by means of which any business, financial operation, or venture is carried on. It includes a guardian, committee, trustee, executor, administrator, trustee in bankruptcy, receiver, assignee for the benefit of creditors, conservator, or any person acting in a fiduciary capacity.

(9) Calendar quarter means a period of 3 calendar months ending on March 31, June 30, September 30, or December 31.

(10) Account number means the identifying number of an employee assigned, as the case may be, under the Internal Revenue Code of 1954, under subchapter A of chapter 9 of the Internal Revenue Code of 1939, or under title VIII of the Social Security Act. See also §301.7701-11 of this chapter (Regulations on Procedure and Administration).

(11) Identification number means the identifying number of an employer assigned, as the case may be, under the Internal Revenue Code of 1954, under subchapter A or D of chapter 9 of the Internal Revenue Code of 1939, or under title VIII of the Social Security Act. See also §301.7701-12 of this chapter (Regulations on Procedure and Administration).

(12) Regulations 90 means the regulations approved February 17, 1936 (26 CFR (1939) Part 400), as amended, relating to the excise tax on employers under title IX of the Social Security Act, and such regulations as made applicable to subchapter C of chapter 9 and other provisions of the Internal Revenue Code of 1939 by Treasury Decision 4885, approved February 11, 1939 (26 CFR (1939) 1943 Cum. Supp., p. 5876), together with any amendments to such regulations as so made applicable to the Internal Revenue Code of 1939.

(13) Regulations 91 means the regulations approved November 9, 1936 (26 CFR (1939) Part 401), as amended, relating to the employees' tax and the employers' tax under title VIII of the Social Security Act, and such regulations as made applicable to subchapter A of chapter 9 and other provisions of the Internal Revenue Code of 1939 by Treasury Decision 4885, approved February 11, 1939 (26 CFR (1939) 1943 Cum. Supp., p. 5876), together with any amendments to such regulations as so made applicable to the Internal Revenue Code of 1939.

(14) Regulations 106 means the regulations approved February 24, 1940 (26 CFR (1939) Part 402), as amended, relating to the employees' tax and the employers' tax under the Federal Insurance Contributions Act (subchapter A of chapter 9 of the Internal Revenue Code of 1939) with respect to the period after 1939 and before 1951.

(15) Regulations 107 means the regulations approved September 12, 1940 (26 CFR (1939) Part 403), as amended, relating to the excise tax on employers under the Federal Unemployment Tax Act (subchapter C of chapter 9 of the Internal Revenue Code of 1939) with respect to the period after 1939 and before 1955.

(16) Regulations 114 means the regulations approved December 30, 1948 (26 CFR (1939) Part 411), as amended, relating to the employers' tax, employees' tax, and employee representatives' tax under the Railroad Retirement Tax Act (subchapter B of chapter 9 of the Internal Revenue Code of 1939) with respect to compensation paid after 1948 for services rendered after 1946 and before 1955.

(17) Regulations 120 means the regulations approved December 22, 1953 (26 CFR (1939) Part 406), as amended, relating to collection of income tax at source on wages under subchapter D of chapter 9 of the Internal Revenue Code of 1939 with respect to the period after 1953 and before 1955.

(18) Regulations 128 means the regulations approved December 6, 1951 (26 CFR (1939) Part 408), as amended, relating to the employee tax and the employer tax under the Federal Insurance Contributions Act (subchapter A of chapter 9 of the Internal Revenue Code of 1939) with respect to the period after 1950 and before 1955.

(19) The cross references in the regulations in this part to other portions of the regulations, when the word "see" is used, are made only for convenience and shall be given no legal effect.

(b) *Subpart B.*—As used in subpart B of this part, unless otherwise expressly indicated—

(1) Act means the Federal Insurance Contributions Act.

(2) Taxes means the employee tax and the employer tax, as respectively defined in this paragraph.

(3) Employee tax means the tax (with respect to wages received by an employee after December 31, 1965, the taxes) imposed by section 3101 of the Code.

(4) Employer tax means the tax (with respect to wages paid by an employer after December 31, 1965, the taxes) imposed by section 3111 of the Code.

(c) *Subpart C.*—As used in subpart C of this part, unless otherwise expressly indicated—

(1) Act means the Railroad Retirement Tax Act.

(2) Railway Labor Act means the Act approved May 20, 1926 (45 U.S.C. c.8), as amended.

(3) Railroad Retirement Act of 1937 means the Act approved June 24, 1937 (45 U.S.C. 228a and following), as amended.

(4) Railroad Retirement Board means the board established pursuant to section 10 of the Railroad Retirement Act of 1937 (45 U.S.C. 228j).

(5) Tax means the employee tax, the employee representative tax, or the employer tax, as respectively defined in this paragraph.

(6) Employee tax means the tax imposed by section 3201 of the Code.

(7) Employee representative tax means the tax imposed by section 3211 of the Code.

(8) Employer tax means the tax imposed by section 3221 of the Code.

(d) *Subpart D.*—As used in subpart D of this part, unless otherwise expressly indicated—

(1) Act means the Federal Unemployment Tax Act.

(2) Railroad Unemployment Insurance Act means the Act approved June 25, 1938 (45 U.S.C. c. 11), as amended.

(3) Tax means the tax imposed by section 3301 of the Code.

(e) *Subpart E.*—As used in subpart E of this part, unless otherwise expressly indicated, tax means the tax required to be deducted and withheld from wages under section 3402 of the Code. [Reg. §31.0-2.]

☐ [*T.D.* 6516, 12-20-60. *Amended by* T.D.6606, 8-25-62; *T.D.* 6658, 6-27-63; *T.D.* 6983, 12-4-68 *and T.D.* 7280, 7-10-73.]

**[Reg. §31.0-3.]**

**§31.0-3. Scope of regulations.**—(a) *Subpart B.*—The regulations in his part relate to the imposition of the employee tax and the employer tax under the Federal Insurance Contributions Act with respect to wages paid and received after 1954 for employment performed after 1936. In addition to employment in the case of remuneration therefor paid and received after 1954, the regulations in Subpart B of this part relate also to employment performed after 1954 in the case of remuneration therefor paid and received before 1955. The regulations in Subpart B of this part include provisions relating to the definition of terms applicable in the determination of the taxes under the Federal Insurance Contributions Act, such as "employee", "wages", and "employment". The provisions of Subpart B of this part relating to "employment" are applicable also, to the extent provided in §31.3121(b)-2, to services performed before 1955 the remuneration for which is paid after 1954. (For prior regulations on similar subject matter, see 26 CFR (1939) Part 408 (Regulations 128).)

(b) *Subpart C.*—The regulations in subpart C of this part relate to the imposition of the employee tax, the employee representative tax, and the employer tax under the Railroad Retirement Tax Act with respect to compensation paid after 1954, for services rendered after such date. The regulations in subpart C of this part include provisions relating to the definition of terms applicable in the determination of the taxes under the Railroad Retirement Tax Act, such as "employee", "employee representative", "employer", and "compensation". (For prior regulations on similar subject matter, see 26 CFR (1939) Part 411 (Regulations 114).)

(c) *Subpart D.*—The regulations in subpart D of this part relate to the imposition on employers of the excise tax under the Federal

Unemployment Tax Act for the calendar year 1955 and subsequent calendar years with respect to wages paid after 1954 for employment performed after 1938. In addition to employment in the case of remuneration therefor paid after 1954, the regulations in subpart D of this part relate also to employment performed after 1954 in the case of remuneration therefor paid before 1955. The regulations in subpart D of this part include provisions relating to the definition of terms applicable in the determination of the tax under the Federal Unemployment Tax Act, such as "employee", "employer", "employment", and "wages". The regulations in subpart D of this part also include provisions relating to the credits against the Federal tax for State contributions. (For prior regulations on similar subject matter, see 26 CFR (1939) Part 403 (Regulations 107).)

(d) *Subpart E.*—The regulations in subpart E of this part relate to the withholding under chapter 24 of the Code of income tax at source on wages paid after 1954, regardless of when such wages were earned. The regulations in subpart E of this part include provisions relating to the definition of terms applicable in the determination of the tax under chapter 24 of the Code, such as "employee", "employer", and "wages". (For prior regulations on similar subject matter, see 26 CFR (1939) Part 406 (Regulations 120).)

(e) *Subpart F.*—The regulations in subpart F of this part deal with the general provisions contained in chapter 25 of the Code, which relate to the employment taxes imposed by chapters 21 to 24, inclusive, of the Code. (For prior regulations on the subject matter of section 3503, see 26 CFR (1939) 411.802 and 408.803 (Regulations 114 and 128, respectively). (For prior regulations on the subject matter of section 3504, see 26 CFR (1939) 406.807 and 408.906 (Regulations 120 and 128, respectively).)

(f) *Subpart G.*—The regulations in subpart G of this part, which are prescribed under selected provisions of subtitle F of the Code, relate to the procedural and administrative requirements in respect of records, returns, deposits, payments, and related matters applicable to the employment taxes imposed by subtitle C (chapters 21 to 25, inclusive) of the Code. In addition, the provisions of subpart G of this part relate to adjustments and to claims for refund, credit, or abatement, made after 1954, in connection with the employment taxes imposed by subtitle C of the Internal Revenue Code of 1954, by chapter 9 of the Internal Revenue Code of 1939, or by the corresponding provisions of prior law, but not to any adjustment reported, or credit taken, in whole or in part on any return or supplemental return filed on or before July 31, 1960. The provisions of subpart G of this part also relate to deposits of taxes imposed by subchapter B of chapter 9 of the 1939 Code or by corresponding provisions of prior law with respect to compensation paid after 1954 for services rendered before 1955. For other administrative provisions which have application to the employment taxes imposed by subtitle C of the Code, see Part 301 of this chapter (Regulations on Procedure and Administration). (The administrative and procedural regulations applicable with respect to a particular employment tax for a prior period were combined with the substantive regulations relating to such tax for such period. For the regulations applicable to the respective taxes for prior periods, see paragraphs (a), (b), (c), and (d) of this section.) Subpart G of this part also provides rules relating to the deposit of other taxes by electronic funds transfer. [Reg. §31.0-3.]

☐ [*T.D.* 6516, 12-20-60. *Amended by* T.D. 6744, 7-2-64, T.D. 8723, 7-11-97 *and* T.D. 9849, 3-11-2019.]

**[Reg. §31.0-4]**

**§31.0-4. Extent to which the regulations in this part supersede prior regulations.**—The regulations in this part, with respect to the subject matter within the scope thereof, supersede 25 CFR (1939) Parts 403, 406, 408, and 411 (Regulations 107, 120, 128, and 114, respectively). The Regulations on Monthly Returns and Payment of Employment Taxes (23 F.R. 5006) are also superseded. [Reg. §31.0-4.]

☐ [*T.D.* 6516, 12-20-60.]

# TAX ON EMPLOYEES

**[Reg. §31.3101-1]**

**§31.3101-1. Measure of employee tax.**—The employee tax is measured by the amount of wages received after 1954 with respect to employment after 1936. See §31.3121(a)-1, relating to wages; and

§§31.3121(b)-1 to 31.3121(b)-4, inclusive, relating to employment. For provisions relating to the time of receipt of wages, see §31.3121(a)-2.[Reg. §31.3101-1.]

☐ [*T.D.* 6190, 7-14-56. *Republished in T.D.* 6516, 12-20-60. *Amended by* T.D. 6744, 7-2-64.]

➤➤➤ *Caution: This regulation has not been amended to reflect the changes enacted by P.L. 95-216.*

### [Reg. §31.3101-2]

**§31.3101-2. Rates and computation of employee tax.**—(a) *Old-Age, Survivors, and Disability Insurance.*—The rates of employee tax for Old-Age, Survivors, and Disability Insurance (OASDI) with re-

| | Percent |
|---|---|
| Calendar year | |
| 1984, 1985, 1986, or 1987 | 5.7 |
| 1988 or 1989 | 6.06 |
| 1990 and subsequent years | 6.2 |

(b)(1) *Hospital Insurance.*—The rates of employee tax for Hospital Insurance (HI) with respect to wages received in calendar years after 1973 are as follows:

| | Percent |
|---|---|
| Calendar year | |
| 1974, 1975, 1976, or 1977 | 0.90 |
| 1978 | 1.00 |
| 1979 or 1980 | 1.05 |
| 1981, 1982, 1983, or 1984 | 1.30 |
| 1985 | 1.35 |
| 1986 and subsequent years | 1.45 |

(2) *Additional Medicare Tax.*—(i) The rate of Additional Medicare Tax with respect to wages received in taxable years beginning after December 31, 2012, is as follows:

| | Percent |
|---|---|
| Taxable year | |
| Beginning after December 31, 2012 | 0.9 |

(ii) Individuals are liable for Additional Medicare Tax with respect to wages received in taxable years beginning after December 31, 2012, which are in excess of:

| Filling Status | Threshold |
|---|---|
| Married individual filing a joint return | $250,000 |
| Married individual filing a separate return | $125,000 |
| Any other case | $200,000 |

(c) *Computation of employee tax.*—The employee tax is computed by applying to the wages received by the employee the rates in effect at the time such wages are received.

*Example.* In 1989, A performed services for X which constituted employment (see §31.3121(b)-2). In 1990 A receives from X $1,000 as remuneration for such services. The tax is payable at the 6.2 percent OASDI rate and the 1.45 percent HI rate in effect for the calendar year 1990 (the year in which the wages are received) and not at the 6.06 percent OASDI rate and the 1.45 percent HI rate which were in effect for the calendar year 1989 (the year in which the services were performed).

(d) *Effective/applicability date.*—Paragraphs (a), (b), and (c) of this section apply to quarters beginning on or after November 29, 2013. [Reg. §31.3101-2.]

□ [*T.D.* 6190, 7-14-56. *Republished in T.D.* 6516, 12-20-60. *Amended by T.D.* 6744, 7-2-64; *T.D.* 6983, 12-4-68; *T.D.* 7374, 7-24-75 *and T.D.* 9645, 11-26-2013 (*corrected* 1-28-2014).]

### [Reg. §31.3101-3]

**§31.3101-3. When employee tax attaches.**—The employee tax attaches at the time that the wages are received by the employee. For provisions relating to the time of such receipt see §31.3121(a)-2. [Reg. §31.3101-3.]

□ [*T.D.* 6190, 7-14-56. *Republished in T.D.* 6516, 12-20-60.]

### [Reg. §31.3102-1]

**§31.3102-1. Collection of, and liability for, employee tax; in general.**—(a) The employer shall collect from each of his employees the employee tax with respect to wages for employment performed for the employer by the employee. The employer shall make the collection by deducting or causing to be deducted the amount of the employee tax from such wages as and when paid. (For provisions relating to the time of such payment, see §31.3121(a)-2.) The employer is required to collect the tax, notwithstanding the wages are paid in something other than money, and to pay over the tax in money. (As to the exclusion from wages of remuneration paid in any medium other than cash for certain types of services, see §31.3121(a)(7)-1, relating to such remuneration paid for service not in the course of the employer's trade or business or for domestic service in a private home of the employer; and §31.3121(a)(8)-1, relating to such remuneration paid for agricultural labor.) For provisions relating to the collection of, and liability for, employee tax in respect of tips, see §31.3102-3. For special rules relating to Additional Medicare Tax imposed under section 3101(b)(2), see §31.3102-4.

spect to wages received in calendar years after 1983 are as follows (these regulations do not reflect off-Code revisions to the following rates):

(b) The employer is permitted, but not required, to deduct amounts equivalent to employee tax from payments to an employee of cash remuneration to which the sections referred to in this paragraph (b) are applicable prior to the time that the sum of such payments equals—

(1) $100 in the calendar year, for service not in the course of the employer's trade or business, to which §31.3121(a)(7)-1 is applicable;

(2) The applicable dollar threshold (as defined in section 3121(x)) in the calendar year, for domestic service in a private home of the employer, to which §31.3121(a)(7)-1 is applicable;

(3) $150 in the calendar year, for agricultural labor, to which §31.3121(a)(8)-1(c)(1)(i) is applicable; or

(4) $100 in the calendar year, for service performed as a home worker, to which §31.3121(a)(10)-1 is applicable.

(c) At such time as the sum of the cash payments in the calendar year for a type of service referred to in paragraph (b)(1), (b)(2), (b)(3) or (b)(4) of this section equals or exceeds the amount specified, the employer is required to collect from the employee any amount of employee tax not previously deducted. If an employer pays cash remuneration to an employee for two or more of the types of service referred to in paragraph (b)(1), (b)(2), (b)(3) or (b)(4) of this section, the provisions of paragraph (b) of this section and this paragraph (c) are to be applied separately to the amount of remuneration attributable to each type of service. For provisions relating to the repayment to an employee, or other disposition, of amounts deducted from an employee's remuneration in excess of the correct amount of employee tax, see §31.6413(a)-1.

(d) In collecting employee tax, the employer shall disregard any fractional part of a cent of such tax unless it amounts to one-half cent or more, in which case it shall be increased to 1 cent. The employer is liable for the employee tax with respect to all wages paid by him to each of his employees whether or not it is collected from the employee. If, for example, the employer deducts less than the correct amount of tax, or if he fails to deduct any part of the tax, he is nevertheless liable for the correct amount of the tax. Until collected from him the employee also is liable for the employee tax with respect to all the wages received by him. Any employee tax collected by or on behalf of an employer is a special fund in trust for the United States. See section 7501. The employer is indemnified against the claims and demands of any person for the amount of any payment of such tax made by the employer to the district director.

(e)(1) The provisions of paragraphs (a) and (d) of this section apply to any payment made on or after January 1, 1955.

(2) The provisions of paragraphs (b) and (c) of this section that apply to any payment made for service not in the course of the employer's trade or business or for service performed as a home

worker within the meaning of section 3121(d)(3)(C) apply to any such payment made on or after January 1, 1978. The provisions of paragraphs (b) and (c) of this section that apply to any payment made for domestic service in a private home of the employer apply to any such payment made on or after January 1, 1994. The provisions of paragraphs (b) and (c) of this section that apply to any payment made for agricultural labor apply to any such payment made on or after January 1, 1988. For rules applicable to any payment for these services made prior to the dates set forth in this paragraph (e)(2), see §31.3102-1 in effect at such time (see 26 CFR part 31 contained in the edition of 26 CFR Parts 30 to 39, revised as of April 1, 2006).

(f) *Effective/applicability date.*—Paragraph (a) of this section applies to quarters beginning on or after November 29, 2013. [Reg. §31.3102-1.]

☐ [*T.D.* 6190, 7-14-56. *Republished in T.D.* 6516, 12-20-60. *Amended by T.D.* 6744, 7-2-64; *T.D.* 7001, 1-23-69; *T.D.* 9266, 6-16-2006 *and T.D.* 9645, 11-26-2013.]

**[Reg. §31.3102-2]**

**§31.3102-2. Manner and time of payment of employee tax.**—The employee tax is payable to the district director in the manner and at the time prescribed in Subpart G of the regulations in this part. For provisions relating to the payment by an employee of employee tax in respect of tips, see paragraph (d) of §31.3102-3. [Reg. §31.3102-2.]

☐ [*T.D.* 6190, 7-14-56. *Republished in T.D.* 6516, 12-20-60; *T.D.* 7001, 1-23-69.]

**[Reg. §31.3102-3]**

**§31.3102-3. Collection of, and liability for, employee tax on tips.**—(a) *Collection of tax from employee.*—(1) *In general.*—Subject to the limitations set forth in subparagraph (2) of this paragraph, the employer shall collect from each of his employees the employee tax on those tips received by the employee which constitute wages for purposes of the tax imposed by section 3101. (For provisions relating to the treatment of tips as wages, see §§31.3121(a)(12) and 31.3121(q).) The employer shall make the collection by deducting or causing to be deducted the amount of the employee tax from wages (exclusive of tips) which are under the control of the employer or other funds turned over by the employee to the employer (see subparagraph (3) of this paragraph). For purposes of this section the term "wages (exclusive of tips) which are under the control of the employer" means, with respect to a payment of wages, an amount equal to wages as defined in section 3121(a) except that tips and noncash remuneration which are wages are not included, less the sum of—

(i) The tax under section 3101 required to be collected by the employer in respect of wages as defined in section 3121(a) (exclusive of tips);

(ii) The tax under section 3402 required to be collected by the employer in respect of wages as defined in section 3401(a) (exclusive of tips); and

(iii) The amount of taxes imposed on the remuneration of an employee withheld by the employer pursuant to State and local law (including amounts withheld under an agreement between the employer and the employee pursuant to such law) except that the amount of taxes taken into account in this subdivision shall not include any amount attributable to tips.

(2) *Limitations.*—An employer is required to collect employee tax on tips which constitute wages only in respect of those tips which are reported by the employee to the employer in a written statement furnished to the employer pursuant to section 6053(a). The employer is responsible for the collection of employee tax on tips reported to him only to the extent that the employer can—

(i) During the period beginning at the time the written statement is submitted to him and ending at the close of the 10th day of the month following the month in which the statement was submitted, or

(ii) In the case of an employer who elects to deduct the tax on an estimated basis (see paragraph (c) of this section), during the period beginning at the time the written statement is submitted to him and ending at the close of the 30th day following the quarter in which the statement was submitted,
collect the employee tax by deducting it or causing it to be deducted as provided in subparagraph (1).

(3) *Furnishing of funds to employer.*—If the amount of employee tax in respect of tips reported by the employee to the employer in a written statement (or statements) furnished pursuant to section 6053(a) exceeds the wages (exclusive of tips) which are under the control of the employer, the employee may furnish to the employer, within the period specified in subparagraph (2)(i) or (ii) of this

paragraph (whichever is applicable), an amount of money equal to the amount of such excess.

(b) *Less than $20 of tips.*—Notwithstanding the provisions of paragraph (a) of this section, if an employee furnishes to his employer a written statement—

(1) Covering a period of less than one month, and

(2) The statement is furnished to the employer prior to the close of the 10th day of the month following the month in which the tips were actually received by the employee, and

(3) The aggregate amount of tips reported in the statement and in all other statements previously furnished by the employee covering periods within the same month is less than $20, and the statements, collectively, do not cover the entire month,
the employer may deduct amounts equivalent to employee tax on such tips from wages (exclusive of tips) which are under the control of the employer or other funds turned over by the employee to the employer. For provisions relating to the repayment to an employee, or other disposition, of amounts deducted from an employee's remuneration in excess of the correct amount of employee tax, see §31.6413(a)-1. (As to the exclusions from wages of tips of less than $20, see §31.3121(a)(12)-1.)

(c) *Collection of employee tax on estimated basis.*—(1) *In general.*—Subject to certain limitations and conditions, an employer may, at his discretion, make collection of the employee tax in respect of tips reported by an employee to the employer on an estimated basis. An employer who elects to make collection of the employee tax on an estimated basis shall:

(i) In respect of each employee, make an estimate of the amount of tips that will be reported, pursuant to section 6053(a), by the employee to the employer in a calendar quarter.

(ii) Determine the amount which must be deducted upon each payment of wages (exclusive of tips) which are under the control of the employer to be made during the quarter by the employer to the employee in order to collect from the employee during the quarter an amount equal to the amount obtained by multiplying the estimated quarterly tips by the sum of the rates of tax under subsections (a) and (b) of section 3101.

(iii) Deduct from any payment of such employee's wages (exclusive of tips) which are under the control of the employer, or from funds referred to in paragraph (a)(3) of this section, such amount as may be necessary to adjust the amount of tax withheld on the estimated basis to conform to the amount of employee tax imposed upon, and required to be deducted in respect of, tips reported by the employee to the employer during the calendar quarter in written statements furnished to the employer pursuant to section 6053(a). If an adjustment is required, the additional employee tax required to be collected may be deducted upon any payment of the employee's wages (exclusive of tips) which are under the control of the employer during the quarter and within the first 30 days following the quarter or from funds turned over by the employee to the employer for such purposes within such period. For provisions relating to the repayment to an employee, or other disposition, of amounts deducted from an employee's remuneration in excess of the correct amount of employee tax, see §31.6413(a)-1.

(2) *Estimating tips employee will report.*—(i) *Initial estimate.*—The initial estimate of the amount of tips that will be reported by a particular employee in a calendar quarter shall be made on the basis of the facts and circumstances surrounding the employment of that employee. However, if a number of employees are employed under substantially the same circumstances and working conditions, the initial estimate established for one such employee may be used as the initial estimate for other employees in that group.

(ii) *Adjusting estimate.*—If the quarterly estimate of tips in respect of a particular employee continues to differ substantially from the amount of tips reported by the employee and there are no unusual factors involved (for example, an extended absence from work due to illness) the employer shall make an appropriate adjustment of his estimate of the amount of tips that will be reported by the employee.

(iii) *Reasonableness of estimate.*—The employer must be prepared, upon request of the district director, to disclose the factors upon which he relied in making the estimate, and his reasons for believing that the estimate is reasonable.

(d) *Employee tax not collected by employer.*—If—

(1) The amount of the employee tax imposed by section 3101 in respect of those tips received by an employee which constitute wages exceeds

(2) The amount of employee tax imposed by section 3101 (in respect of tips reported by the employee to the employer) which can be collected by the employer from such employee's wages (exclusive

of tips) which are under the control of the employer or from funds referred to in paragraph (a)(3) of this section,

the employee shall be liable for the payment of tax in an amount equal to such excess. For provisions relating to the manner and time of payment of employee tax by an employee, see paragraph (d) of §31.6011(a)-1 and paragraph (a)(4) of §31.6071(a)-1. For provisions relating to statements required to be furnished by employers to employees in respect of uncollected employee tax on tips reported to the employer, see §31.6053-2. [Reg. §31.3102-3.]

☐ [*T.D. 7001, 1-23-69, as corrected 1-31-69.*]

### [Reg. §31.3102-4]

**§31.3102-4. Special rules regarding Additional Medicare Tax.—**
(a) *Collection of tax from employee.*—An employer is required to collect from each of its employees the tax imposed by section 3101(b)(2) (Additional Medicare Tax) with respect to wages for employment performed for the employer by the employee only to the extent the employer pays wages to the employee in excess of $200,000 in a calendar year. This rule applies regardless of the employee's filing status or other income. Thus, the employer disregards any amount of wages or Railroad Retirement Tax Act (RRTA) compensation paid to the employee's spouse. The employer also disregards any RRTA compensation paid by the employer to the employee or any wages or RRTA compensation paid to the employee by another employer.

*Example.* H, who is married and files a joint return, receives $100,000 in wages from his employer for the calendar year. I, H's spouse, receives $300,000 in wages from her employer for the same calendar year. H's wages are not in excess of $200,000, so H's employer does not withhold Additional Medicare Tax. I's employer is required to collect Additional Medicare Tax only with respect to wages it pays which are in excess of the $200,000 threshold (that is, $100,000) for the calendar year.

(b) *Collection of amounts not withheld.*—To the extent the employer does not collect Additional Medicare Tax imposed on the employee by section 3101(b)(2), the employee is liable to pay the tax.

*Example.* J, who is married and files a joint return, receives $190,000 in wages from his employer for the calendar year. K, J's spouse, receives $150,000 in wages from her employer for the same calendar year. Neither J's nor K's wages are in excess of $200,000, so neither J's nor K's employers are required to withhold Additional Medicare Tax. J and K are liable to pay Additional Medicare Tax on $90,000 ($340,000 minus the $250,000 threshold for a joint return).

(c) *Employer's liability for tax.*—If the employer deducts less than the correct amount of Additional Medicare Tax, or if it fails to deduct any part of Additional Medicare Tax, it is nevertheless liable for the correct amount of tax that it was required to withhold, unless and until the employee pays the tax. If an employee subsequently pays the tax that the employer failed to deduct, the tax will not be collected from the employer. The employer will not be relieved of its liability for payment of the tax required to be withheld unless it can show that the tax under section 3101(b)(2) has been paid. The employer, however, will remain subject to any applicable penalties or additions to tax resulting from the failure to withhold as required.

(d) *Effective/applicability date.*—This section applies to quarters beginning on or after November 29, 2013. [Reg. §31.3102-4.]

☐ [*T.D. 9645, 11-26-2013.*]

# TAX ON EMPLOYERS

### [Reg. §31.3111-1]

**§31.3111-1. Measure of employer tax.**—The employer tax is measured by the amount of wages paid after 1954 with respect to employment after 1936. See §31.3121(a)-1, relating to wages, and §§31.3121(b)-1 to 31.3121(b)-4, inclusive, relating to employment. For provisions relating to time of payment of wages, see §31.3121(a)-2. [Reg. §31.3111-1.]

☐ [*T.D. 6190, 7-14-56. Republished in T.D. 6516, 12-20-60. Amended by T.D. 6744, 7-2-64.*]

⟫⟫→ *Caution: This regulation has not been amended to reflect the changes enacted by P.L. 95-216.*

### [Reg. §31.3111-2]

**§31.3111-2. Rates and computation of employer tax.**—(a) *Old-age, survivors, and disability insurance.*—The rates of employer tax for old-age survivors, and disability insurance with respect to wages paid in calendar years after 1954 are as follows:

| Calendar years | Percent |
| --- | --- |
| 1955 and 1956 | 2 |
| 1957 and 1958 | 2.25 |
| 1959 | 2.5 |
| 1960 and 1961 | 3 |
| 1962 | 3.125 |
| 1963 to 1965, both inclusive | 3.625 |
| 1966 | 3.85 |
| 1967 | 3.9 |
| 1968 | 3.8 |
| 1969 and 1970 | 4.2 |
| 1971 and 1972 | 4.6 |
| 1973 | 4.85 |
| 1974 to 2010, both inclusive | 4.95 |
| 2011 and subsequent calendar years | 5.95 |

(b) *Hospital insurance.*—The rates of employer tax for hospital insurance with respect to wages paid in calendar years after 1965 are as follows:

| Calendar years | Percent |
| --- | --- |
| 1966 | 0.35 |
| 1967 | 0.50 |
| 1968 to 1972, both inclusive | 0.60 |
| 1973 | 1.0 |
| 1974 to 1977, both inclusive | 0.90 |
| 1978 to 1980, both inclusive | 1.10 |
| 1981 to 1985, both inclusive | 1.35 |
| 1986 and subsequent calendar years | 1.50 |

(c) *Computation of employer tax.*—The employer tax is computed by applying to the wages paid by the employer the rate in effect at the time such wages are paid. [Reg. §31.3111-2.]

☐ [*T.D. 6190, 7-14-56. Republished in T.D. 6516, 12-20-60. Amended by T.D. 6744, 7-2-64, T.D. 6983, 12-4-68 and T.D. 7374, 7-24-75.*]

### [Reg. §31.3111-3]

**§31.3111-3. When employer tax attaches.**—The employer tax attaches at the time that the wages are paid by the employer. For provisions relating to the time of such payment, see §31.3121(a)-2. [Reg. §31.3111-3.]

☐ [*T.D. 6190, 7-14-56. Republished in T.D. 6516, 12-20-60.*]

### [Reg. §31.3111-4]

**§31.3111-4. Liability for employer tax.**—The employer is liable for the employer tax with respect to the wages paid to his employees for employment performed for him. [Reg. §31.3111-4.]

☐ [*T.D. 6190, 7-14-56. Republished in T.D. 6516, 12-20-60.*]

### [Reg. §31.3111-5]

**§31.3111-5. Manner and time of payment of employer tax.**—The employer tax is payable to the district director in the manner and at the time prescribed in subpart G of the regulations in this part. [Reg. §31.3111-5.]

☐ [*T.D. 6190, 7-14-56. Republished in T.D. 6516, 12-20-60.*]

### [Reg. §31.3111-6T]

**§31.3111-6T. Recapture of credits under the Families First Coronavirus Response Act and the Coronavirus Aid, Relief, and Economic Security Act.**—(a) *Recapture of erroneously refunded credits under the Families First Coronavirus Response Act.*—Any amount of credits for qualified sick leave wages or qualified family leave wages under sections 7001 and 7003, respectively, of the Families First Coronavirus Response Act (Families First Act), Public Law 116-127, 134 Stat. 178 (2020), as modified by section 3606 of the Coronavirus Aid, Relief, and Economic Security Act (CARES Act), Public Law 116-136, 134 Stat. 281 (2020), plus any amount of credits for qualified health plan expenses under sections 7001 and 7003, and including any increases in those credits under section 7005 of the Families First Act, that are treated as overpayments and refunded or credited to an employer under section 6402(a) or section 6413(b) of the Internal Revenue Code (Code) and to which the employer is not entitled, resulting in an erroneous refund to the employer, shall be treated as an underpayment of the taxes imposed by section 3111(a) of the Code and may be assessed and collected by the Secretary in the same manner as the taxes.

(b) *Recapture of erroneously refunded credits under the Coronavirus Aid, Relief, and Economic Security Act.*—Any amount of credits for qualified wages under section 2301 of the CARES Act that is treated as an overpayment and refunded or credited to an employer under section 6402(a) or section 6413(b) of the Code and to which the employer is not entitled, resulting in an erroneous refund to the employer, shall be treated as an underpayment of the taxes imposed by section 3111(a) of the Code and may be assessed and collected by the Secretary in the same manner as the taxes.

(c) *Advance credit amounts erroneously refunded.*—The determination of any amount of credits erroneously refunded as described in paragraphs (a) and (b) of this section must take into account any amount of credits advanced to an employer under the process established by the Internal Revenue Service in accordance with sections 7001(b)(4)(A)(ii) and 7003(b)(3)(B) of the Families First Act, as modified by section 3606 of the CARES Act, and section 2301(l)(1) of the CARES Act.

(d) *Third party payors.*—For purposes of this section, employers against whom an erroneous refund of the credits under sections 7001 and 7003 of the Families First Act (including any increases in those credits under section 7005 of the Families First Act), as modified by section 3606 of the CARES Act, and the credits under section 2301 of the CARES Act can be assessed as an underpayment of the taxes imposed by section 3111(a) include persons treated as the employer under sections 3401(d), 3504, and 3511 of the Code, consistent with their liability for the section 3111(a) taxes against which the credit applied.

(e) *Applicability date.*—This regulation applies to all credit refunds under sections 7001 and 7003 of the Families First Act (including any increases in those credits under section 7005 of the Families First Act), as modified by section 3606 of the CARES Act, advanced or paid on or after April 1, 2020 and all credit refunds under section 2301 of the CARES Act advanced or paid on or after March 13, 2020. [Reg. § 31.3111-6T.]

☐ [T.D. 9904, 7-24-2020.]

**[Reg. § 31.3112-1]**

**§ 31.3112-1. Instrumentalities of the United States specifically exempted from the employer tax.**—Section 3112 makes ineffectual as to the employer tax imposed by section 3111 those provisions of law which grant to an instrumentality of the United States an exemption from taxation from taxation, unless such provisions grant a specific exemption from the tax imposed by section 3111 by an express reference to such section or the corresponding section of prior law (section 1410 of the Internal Revenue Code 1939). Thus, the general exemptions from Federal taxation granted by various statutes to certain instrumentalities of the United States without specific reference to the tax imposed by section 3111 or by section 1410 of the 1939 Code are rendered inoperative insofar as such exemptions relate to the tax imposed by section 3111. For provisions relating to the exception from employment of services performed in the employ of an instrumentality of the United States specifically exempted from the employer tax, see § 31.3121(b)(5)-1. For provisions relating to services performed for an instrumentality exempt on December 31, 1950, from the employer tax, see paragraph (c) of § 31.3121(b)(6)-1. [Reg. § 31.3112-1.]

☐ [T.D. 6190, 7-14-56. Republished in T.D. 6516, 12-20-60.]

# GENERAL PROVISIONS

**[Reg. § 31.3121(a)-1]**

**§ 31.3121(a)-1. Wages.**—(a) Whether remuneration paid after 1954 for employment performed after 1936 constitutes wages is determined under section 3121 (a). This section and § § 31.3121(a)(1)-1 to 31.3121(a)(15)-1, inclusive (relating to the statutory exclusions from wages), apply with respect only to remuneration paid after 1954 for employment performed after 1936. Whether remuneration paid after 1936 and before 1940 for employment performed after 1936 constitutes wages shall be determined in accordance with the applicable provisions of law and of 26 CFR (1939) Part 401 (Regulations 91). Whether remuneration paid after 1939 and before 1951 for employment performed after 1936 constitutes wages shall be determined in accordance with the applicable provisions of law and of 26 CFR (1939) Part 402 (Regulations 106). Whether remuneration paid after 1950 and before 1955 for employment performed after 1936 constitutes wages shall be determined in accordance with the applicable provisions of law and of 26 CFR (1939) Part 408 (Regulations 128).

(b) The term "wages" means all remuneration for employment unless specifically excepted under section 3121(a) (see § § 31.3121(a)(1)-1 to 31.3121(a)(15)-1, inclusive) or paragraph (j) of this section.

(c) The name by which the remuneration for employment is designated is immaterial. Thus, salaries, fees, bonuses, and commissions on sales or on insurance premiums, are wages if paid as compensation for employment.

(d) Generally the basis upon which the remuneration is paid is immaterial in determining whether the remuneration constitutes wages. Thus, it may be paid on the basis of piecework, or a percentage of profits; and it may be paid hourly, daily, weekly, monthly, or annually. See, however, § 31.3121(a)(8)-1 which relates to the treatment of cash remuneration computed on a time basis for agricultural labor.

(e) Generally the medium in which the remuneration is paid is also immaterial. It may be paid in cash or in something other than cash, as for example, goods, lodging, food, or clothing. Remuneration paid in items other than cash shall be computed on the basis of the fair value of such items at the time of payment. See, however, § § 31.3121(a)(7)-1, 31.3121(a)(8)-1, 31.3121-(a)(10)-1, and 31.3121(a)(12)-1, relating to the treatment of remuneration paid in any medium other than cash for services not in the course of the employer's trade or business and for domestic service in a private home of the employer, for agricultural labor, for services performed by certain home workers, and as tips, respectively.

(f) Ordinarily, facilities or privileges (such as entertainment, medical services, or so-called "courtesy" discounts on purchases), furnished or offered by an employer to his employees generally, are not considered as remuneration for employment if such facilities or privileges are of relatively small value and are offered or furnished by the employer merely as a means of promoting the health, good will, contentment, or efficiency of his employees. The term "facilities or privileges," however, does not ordinarily include the value of meals or lodging furnished, for example, to restaurant or hotel employees, or to seamen or other employees aboard vessels, since generally these items constitute an appreciable part of the total remuneration of such employees.

(g) Amounts of so-called "vacation allowances" paid to an employee constitute wages. Thus, the salary of an employee on vacation, paid notwithstanding his absence from work, constitutes wages.

(h) Amounts paid specifically—either as advances or reimbursements—for traveling or other bona fide ordinary and necessary expenses incurred or reasonably expected to be incurred in the business of the employer are not wages. For amounts that are received by an employee on or after July 1, 1990, with respect to expenses paid or incurred on or after July 1, 1990, see § 31.3121(a)-3.

(i) Remuneration for employment, unless such remuneration is specifically excepted under section 3121(a) or paragraph (j) of this section, constitutes wages even though at the time paid the relationship of employer and employee no longer exists between the person in whose employ the services were performed and the individual who performed them.

*Example.* A is employed by B during the month of January 1955 in employment and is entitled to receive remuneration of $100 for the services performed for B, the employer, during the month. A leaves the employ of B at the close of business on January 31, 1955. On February 15, 1955 (when A is no longer an employee of B), B pays A the remuneration of $100 which was earned for the services performed in January. The $100 is wages and the taxes are payable with respect thereto.

(j) In addition to the exclusions specified in § § 31.3121(a)(1)-1 to 31.3121(a)(15)-1, inclusive, the following types of payments are excluded from wages:

(1) Remuneration for services which do not constitute employment under section 3121(b) and which are not deemed to be employment under section 3121(c) (see § 31.3121(c)-1).

(2) Remuneration for services which are deemed not to be employment under section 3121(c) (see § 31.3121(c)-1).

(3) Tips or gratuities paid, prior to January 1, 1966, directly to an employee by a customer of an employer, and not accounted for by the employee to the employer. For provisions relating to the treatment of tips received by an employee after December 31, 1965, as wages, see § § 31.3121(a)(12) and 31.3121(q).

(k) *Split-dollar life insurance arrangements.*—Except as otherwise provided under section 3121(v), see § § 1.61-22 and 1.7872-15 of this chapter for rules relating to the treatment of split-dollar life insurance arrangements. [Reg. § 31.3121(a)-1.]

☐ [T.D. 6190, 7-14-56. Republished in T.D. 6516, 12-20-60. Amended by T.D. 6744, 7-2-64; T.D. 7374, 7-24-75; T.D. 8324, 12-17-90 and T.D. 9092, 9-11-2003.]

## [Reg. §31.3121(a)-1T]

**§31.3121(a)-1T. Question and answer relating to the definition of wages in section 3121(a) (Temporary).**—The following question and answer relates to the definition of wages in section 3121(a) of the Internal Revenue Code of 1954, as amended by section 531(d)(1)(A) of the Tax Reform Act of 1984 (98 Stat. 885):

*Q-1:* Are fringe benefits included in the definition of "wages" under section 3121(a)?

*A-1:* Yes, unless specifically excluded from the definition of "wages" pursuant to section 3121(a)(1) through (20). For example, a fringe benefit provided to or on behalf of an employee is excluded from the definition of "wages" if at the time such benefit is provided it is reasonable to believe that the employee will be able to exclude such benefit from income under section 117 or 132. [Temporary Reg. §31.3121(a)-1T.]

☐ [*T.D. 8004, 1-2-85.*]

## [Reg. §31.3121(a)-2]

**§31.3121(a)-2. Wages; when paid and received.**—(a) In general, wages are received by an employee at the time that they are paid by the employer to the employee. Wages are paid by an employer at the time that they are actually or constructively paid unless under paragraph (c) of this section they are deemed to be subsequently paid. For provisions relating to the time when tips received by an employee are deemed paid to the employee, see §31.3121(q)-1.

(b) Wages are constructively paid when they are credited to the account of or set apart for an employee so that they may be drawn upon by him at any time although not then actually reduced to possession. To constitute payment in such a case the wages must be credited to or set apart for the employee without any substantial limitation or restriction as to the time or manner of payment or condition upon which payment is to be made, and must be made available to him so that they may be drawn upon at any time, and their payment brought within his own control and disposition. For provisions relating to the treatment of deductions from remuneration as payments of remuneration, see §31.3123-1.

(c)(1) The first $100 of cash remuneration paid, either actually or constructively, by an employer in any calendar year to an employee for—

(i) Service not in the course of the employer's trade or business, to which §31.3121(a)(7)-1 is applicable, shall be deemed to be paid by the employer to the employee at the first moment of time in such calendar year that the sum of such cash payments made within such year is at least $100; or

(ii) Service performed as a home worker within the meaning of section 3121(d)(3)(C), to which §31.3121(a)(10)-1 is applicable, shall be deemed to be paid by the employer to the employee at the first moment of time in such calendar year that the sum of such cash payments made within such year is at least $100.

(2) Cash remuneration paid, either actually or constructively, by an employer in any calendar year to an employee for domestic service in a private home of the employer to which §31.3121(a)(7)-1 is applicable, and before the sum of the payments of such cash remuneration equals or exceeds the applicable dollar threshold (as defined in section 3121(x)) for such year, shall be deemed to be paid by the employer to the employee at the first moment of time in such calendar year that the sum of such cash payments made within such year equals or exceeds the applicable dollar threshold (as defined in section 3121(x)) for such year.

(3) Cash remuneration paid, either actually or constructively, by an employer in any calendar year to an employee for agricultural labor to which §31.3121(a)(8)-1 is applicable, and before either of the events described in paragraphs (c)(3)(i) and (c)(3)(ii) of this section has occurred, shall be deemed to be paid by the employer to the employee at the first moment of time in such calendar year that—

(i) The sum of the payments of such remuneration is $150 or more; or

(ii) The employer's expenditures for agricultural labor in such calendar year equals or exceeds $2,500, except that this paragraph (c)(3)(ii) shall not apply in determining when such remuneration is deemed to be paid under this paragraph if such employee—

(A) Is employed as a hand-harvest laborer and is paid on a piece rate basis in an operation which has been, and is customarily and generally recognized as having been, paid on a piece rate basis in the region of employment;

(B) Commutes daily from his permanent residence to the farm on which he is so employed; and

(C) Has been employed in agriculture less than 13 weeks during the preceding calendar year.

(4) If an employer pays cash remuneration to an employee for two or more of the types of service referred to in this paragraph, the provisions of this paragraph are to be applied separately to the amount of remuneration attributable to each type of service.

(d)(1) The provisions of paragraphs (a) and (b) of this section apply to any payment of wages made on or after January 1, 1955.

(2) The provisions of paragraph (c) of this section that apply to any payment of wages made for service not in the course of the employer's trade or business or for service performed as a home worker within the meaning of section 3121(d)(3)(C) apply to any such payment made on or after January 1, 1978. The provisions of paragraph (c) of this section that apply to any payment of wages made for domestic service in a private home of the employer apply to any such payment made on or after January 1, 1994. The provisions of paragraph (c) of this section that apply to any payment of wages made for agricultural labor apply to any such payment made on or after January 1, 1988. For rules applicable to any payment of wages for these services made prior to the dates set forth in this paragraph (d)(2), see §31.3121(a)-2 in effect at such time (see 26 CFR part 31 contained in the edition of 26 CFR Parts 30 to 39, revised as of April 1, 2006). [Reg. §31.3121(a)-2.]

☐ [*T.D. 6190, 12-14-56. Republished in T.D. 6516, 12-20-60. Amended by T.D. 6744, 7-2-64; T.D. 7001, 1-23-69 and T.D. 9266, 6-16-2006.*]

## [Reg. §31.3121(a)-3]

**§31.3121(a)-3. Reimbursement and other expense allowance amounts.**—(a) *When excluded from wages.*—If a reimbursement or other expense allowance arrangement meets the requirements of section 62(c) of the Code and §1.62-2 and the expenses are substantiated within a reasonable period of time, payments made under the arrangement that do not exceed the substantiated expenses are treated as paid under an accountable plan and are not wages. In addition, if both wages and the reimbursement or other expense allowance are combined in a single payment, the reimbursement or other expense allowance must be identified either by making a separate payment or by specifically identifying the amount of the reimbursement or other expense allowance.

(b) *When included in wages.*—(1) *Accountable plans.*—(i) *General rule.*—Except as provided in paragraph (b)(1)(ii) of this section, if a reimbursement or other expense allowance arrangement satisfies the requirements of section 62(c) and §1.62-2, but the expenses are not substantiated within a reasonable period of time or amounts in excess of the substantiated expenses are not returned within a reasonable period of time, the amount paid under the arrangement in excess of the substantiated expenses is treated as paid under a nonaccountable plan, is included in wages, and is subject to withholding and payment of employment taxes no later than the first payroll period following the end of the reasonable period.

(ii) *Per diem or mileage allowances.*—If a reimbursement or other expense allowance arrangement providing a per diem or mileage allowance satisfies the requirements of section 62(c) and §1.62-2, but the allowance is paid at a rate for each day or mile of travel that exceeds the amount of the employee's expenses deemed substantiated for a day or mile of travel, the excess portion is treated as paid under a nonaccountable plan and is included in wages. In the case of a per diem or mileage allowance paid as a reimbursement, the excess portion is subject to withholding and payment of employment taxes when paid. In the case of a per diem or mileage allowance paid as an advance, the excess portion is subject to withholding and payment of employment taxes no later than the first payroll period following the payroll period in which the expenses with respect to which the advance was paid (i.e., the days or miles of travel) are substantiated. The Commissioner may, in his discretion, prescribe special rules in pronouncements of general applicability regarding the timing of withholding and payment of employment taxes on per diem and mileage allowances.

(2) *Nonaccountable plans.*—If a reimbursement or other expense allowance arrangement does not satisfy the requirements of section 62(c) and §1.62-2 (e.g., the arrangement does not require expenses to be substantiated or require amounts in excess of the substantiated expenses to be returned), all amounts paid under the arrangement are treated as paid under a nonaccountable plan, are included in wages, and are subject to withholding and payment of employment taxes when paid.

(c) *Effective dates.*—This section generally applies to payments made under reimbursement or other expense allowance arrangements received by an employee on or after July 1, 1990, with respect to expenses paid or incurred on or after July 1, 1990. Paragraph (b)(1)(ii) of this section applies to payments made under reimbursement or other expense allowance arrangements received by an employee on or after January 1, 1991, with respect to expenses paid or incurred on or after January 1, 1991. [Reg. §31.3121(a)-3.]

☐ [*T.D. 8324, 12-17-90.*]

⋙→ *Caution:  Reg. §31.3121(a)(1)-1 does not reflect P.L. 95-216 or P.L. 101-508.*

[Reg. §31.3121(a)(1)-1]

**§31.3121(a)(1)-1. Annual wage limitation.**—(a) *In general.*—(1) The term "wages" does not include that part of the remuneration paid by an employer to an employee within any calendar year—

(i) After 1954 and before 1959 which exceeds the first $4,200 of remuneration,

(ii) After 1958 and before 1966 which exceeds the first $4,800 of remuneration,

(iii) After 1965 and before 1968 which exceeds the first $6,600 of remuneration,

(iv) After 1967 and before 1972 which exceeds the first $7,800 of remuneration,

(v) After 1971 and before 1973 which exceeds the first $9,000 of remuneration,

(vi) After 1972 and before 1974 which exceeds the first $10,800 of remuneration,

(vii) After 1973 and before 1975 which exceeds the first $13,200 of remuneration, or

(viii) After 1974 which exceeds the amount equal to the contribution and benefit base (as determined under section 230 of the Social Security Act) which is effective for such calendar year (exclusive of remuneration excepted from wages in accordance with paragraph (j) of §31.3121(a)-1 or §§31.3121(a)(2)-1 to 31.3121(a)(15)-1, inclusive) paid within the calendar year by an employer to the employee for employment performed for him at any time after 1936. For provisions relating to the treatment of tips for purposes of the annual wage limitation see §31.3121(q)-1.

(2) The annual wage limitation applies only if the remuneration received during any one calendar year by an employee from the same employer for employment performed after 1936 exceeds the amount of such limitation. The limitation in such case relates to the amount of remuneration received during any one calendar year for employment after 1936 and not to the amount of remuneration for employment performed in any one calendar year.

*Example.* Employee A, in 1967 receives $7,000 from employer B in part payment of $8,000 due him from employment performed in 1967. In 1968 A receives from employer B the balance of $1,000 due him for employment performed in 1967, and thereafter in 1968 also receives $7,000 for employment performed in 1968 for employer B. The first $6,600 of the $7,000 received during 1967 is subject to the taxes in 1967. The remaining $400 received in 1967 is not included as wages and is not subject to the taxes. The balance of $1,000 received in 1968 for employment during 1967 is subject to the taxes during 1968 as is also the first $6,800 of the $7,000 thereafter received in 1968 ($1,000 plus $6,800 totaling $7,800, which is the annual wage limitation applicable to remuneration received in 1968 by an employee from any one employer). The remaining $200 received in 1968 is not included as wages and is not subject to the taxes.

(3) If during a calendar year the employee receives remuneration from more than one employer, the annual wage limitation does not apply to the aggregate remuneration received from all of such employers, but instead applies to the remuneration received during such calendar year from each employer with respect to employment after 1936. In such case the first remuneration received in any calendar year after 1974 up to the amount equal to the contribution and benefit base (as determined under section 230 of the Social Security Act) (the first $13,200 received in 1974, the first $10,800 received in 1973, the first $9,000 received in 1972, the first $7,800 received in any calendar year after 1967 and before 1972, the first $6,600 received in any calendar year after 1965 and before 1968, the first $4,800 received in any calendar year after 1958 and before 1966, or the first $4,200 received in any calendar year after 1954 and before 1959) from each employer constitutes wages and is subject to the taxes, even though, under section 6413(c), the employee may be entitled to a special credit or refund of a portion of the employee tax deducted from his wages received during the calendar year. In this connection and in connection with the two examples immediately following, see §31.6413(c)-1, relating to special credits or refunds of employee tax. In connection with the annual wage limitation in the case of remuneration paid for services performed in the employ of the United States or a wholly owned instrumentality thereof, see §31.3122. In connection with the annual wage limitation in the case of remuneration paid for services performed in the employ of the Government of Guam, the Government of American Samoa, the District of Columbia, a political subdivision of the Government of Guam, or the Government of American Samoa, or any instrumentality of any of the foregoing which is wholly owned thereby, see §31.3125. In connection with the application of the annual wage limitation, see also paragraph (b) of this section, relating to the circumstances under which wages paid by a predecessor employer are deemed to be paid by his successor. In connection with the annual wage limitation in the case of remuneration paid after December 31, 1978, from two or more related corporations that compensate an employee through a common paymaster, see §31.3121(s)-1.

*Example (1).* During 1968 employee C receives from employer D a salary of $1,300 a month for employment performed for D during the first 7 months of 1968, or total remuneration of $9,100. At the end of the sixth month C has received $7,800 from employer D, and only that part of his total remuneration from D constitutes wages subject to the taxes. The $1,300 received by employee C from employer D in the seventh month is not included as wages and is not subject to the taxes. At the end of the seventh month C leaves the employ of D and enters the employ of E. C receives remuneration of $1,560 a month from employer E in each of the remaining 5 months of 1968, or total remuneration of $7,800 from employer E. The entire $7,800 received by C from employer E constitutes wages and is subject to the taxes. Thus, the first $7,800 received from employer D and the entire $7,800 received from employer E constitute wages.

*Example (2).* During the calendar year 1968 F is simultaneously an officer (an employee) of the X Corporation, the Y Corporation, and the Z Corporation and during such year receives a salary of $7,800 from each corporation. Each $7,800 received by F from each of the Corporations X, Y, and Z (whether or not such corporations are related) constitutes wages and is subject to the taxes.

(b) *Wages paid by predecessor attributed to successor.*—(1) If an employer (hereinafter referred to as a successor) during any calendar year acquires substantially all the property used in a trade or business of another employer (hereinafter referred to as a predecessor), or used in a separate unit of a trade or business of a predecessor, and if immediately after the acquisition the successor employs in his trade or business an individual who immediately prior to the acquisition was employed in the trade or business of such predecessor, then, for purposes of the application of the annual wage limitation set forth in paragraph (a) of this section, any remuneration (exclusive of remuneration excepted from wages in accordance with paragraph (j) of §31.3121(a)-1 or §§31.3121(a)(2)-1 to 31.3121(a)(15)-1, inclusive) with respect to employment paid (or considered under this paragraph as having been paid) to such individual by the predecessor during such calendar year and prior to the acquisition shall be considered as having been paid by the successor.

(2) The wages paid, or considered as having been paid, by a predecessor to an employee shall, for purposes of the annual wage limitation, be treated as having been paid to such employee by a successor, if:

(i) the successor during a calendar year acquired substantially all the property used in a trade or business, or used in a separate unit of a trade or business, of the predecessor;

(ii) such employee was employed in the trade or business of the predecessor immediately prior to the acquisition and is employed by the successor in his trade or business immediately after the acquisition; and

(iii) such wages were paid during the calendar year in which the acquisition occurred and prior to such acquisition.

(3) The method of acquisition by an employer of the property of another employer is immaterial. The acquisition may occur as a consequence of the incorporation of a business by a sole proprietor or a partnership, the continuance without interruption of the business of a previously existing partnership by a new partnership or by a sole proprietor, or a purchase or any other transaction whereby substantially all the property used in a trade or business, or used in a separate unit of a trade or business, of one employer is acquired by another employer.

(4) Substantially all the property used in a separate unit of a trade or business may consist of substantially all the property used in the performance of an essential operation of the trade or business, or it may consist of substantially all the property used in a relatively self-sustaining entity which forms a part of the trade or business.

*Example (1).* The M Corporation which is engaged in the manufacture of automobiles, including the manufacture of automobile engines, discontinues the manufacture of the engines and transfers all the property used in such manufacturing operation to the N Company. The N Company is considered to have acquired a separate unit of the trade or business of the M Corporation, namely, its engine manufacturing unit.

*Example (2).* The R Corporation which is engaged in the operation of a chain of grocery stores transfers one of such stores to the S Company. The S Company is considered to have acquired a separate unit of the trade or business of the R Corporation.

(5) A successor may receive credit for wages paid to an employee by a predecessor only if immediately prior to the acquisition the employee was employed by the predecessor in his trade or business which was acquired by the successor and if immediately after the acquisition such employee is employed by the successor in his trade or business (whether or not in the same trade or business in

which the acquired property is used). If the acquisition involves only a separate unit of a trade or business of the predecessor, the employee need not have been employed by the predecessor in that unit provided he was employed in the trade or business of which the acquired unit was a part.

*Example.* The Y Corporation in 1968 acquires by purchase all the property of the X Company and immediately after the acquisition employs in its trade or business employee A, who, immediately prior to the acquisition, was employed by the X Company. The X Company has in 1968 (the calendar year in which the acquisition occurs) and prior to the acquisition paid $5,000 of wages to A. The Y Corporation in 1968 pays to A remuneration of $5,000 with respect to employment. Only $2,800 of the remuneration paid by the Y Corporation is considered to be wages. For purposes of the $7,800 limitation, the Y Corporation is credited with the $5,000 paid to A by the X Company. If, in the same calendar year, the Z Company acquires the property by purchase from the Y Corporation and A immediately after the acquisition is employed by the Z Company in its trade or business, no part of the remuneration paid to A by the Z Company in the year of the acquisition will be considered to be wages. The Z Company will be credited with the remuneration paid to A by the Y Corporation and also with the wages paid to A by the X Company

**>>>→ Caution: Regulation §31.3121(a)(2)-1 does not reflect changes made by P.L. 100-203.**

### [Reg. §31.3121(a)(2)-1]

**§31.3121(a)(2)-1. Payments on account of sickness or accident disability, medical or hospitalization expenses, or death.**—(a) The term "wages" does not include the amount of any payment (including any amount paid by an employer for insurance or annuities, or into a fund, to provide for any such payment) made to, or on behalf of, an employee or any of his dependents under a plan or system established by an employer which makes provision for his employees generally (or for his employees generally and their dependents) or for a class or classes of his employees (or for a class or classes of his employees and their dependents), on account of—

(1) Sickness or accident disability of an employee or any of his dependents, only if payment is received under a workers' compensation law,

(2) Medical or hospitalization expenses in connection with sickness or accident disability of an employee or any of his dependents, or

(3) Death of an employee or any of his dependents.

(b) The plan or system established by an employer need not provide for payments on account of all of the specified items, but such plan or system may provide for any one or more of such items. Payments for any one or more of such items under a plan or system established by an employer solely for the dependents of his employees are not within this exclusion from wages.

(c) Dependents of an employee include the employee's husband or wife, children, and any other members of the employee's immediate family.

(d) *Workers' compensation law.*—(1) For purposes of paragraph (a)(1) of this section, a payment made under a workers' compensation law includes a payment made pursuant to a statute in the nature of a workers' compensation act.

(2) For purposes of paragraph (a)(1) of this section, a payment made under a workers' compensation law does not include a payment made pursuant to a State temporary disability insurance law.

(3) If an employee receives a payment on account of sickness or accident disability that is not made under a workers' compensation law or a statute in the nature of a workers' compensation act, the payment is not excluded from wages as defined by section 3121(a)(2)(A) even if the payment must be repaid if the employee receives a workers' compensation award or an award under a statute in the nature of a workers' compensation act with respect to the same period of absence from work.

**>>>→ Caution: Temporary Regulation §32.1, below, is applicable to payments made on account of sickness or accident disability on or after January 1, 1982.**

### [Reg. §32.1]

**§32.1. Social security taxes with respect to payments on account of sickness or accident disability.**—(a) *General rule.*—The amount of any payment on or after January 1, 1982, made to, or on behalf of, an employee or any of his dependents on account of sickness or accident disability is not excluded from the term wages as defined in section 3121(a)(2)(A) unless such payment is—

(1) Received under a workmen's compensation law (as defined in 31.3121(a)(2)-1(d)(3) for payments made on or after December 15, 2005, or

(2) Made by a third party pursuant to a contractual agreement between the employer and third party entered into prior to December 14, 1981, but then only if—

(considered for purposes of the application of the $7,800 limitation as having also been paid by the Y Corporation).

(6) Where a corporation described in section 501(c)(3) which is exempt from income tax under section 501(a) has in effect a certificate filed pursuant to section 3121(k), or pursuant to section 1426(l) of the Internal Revenue Code of 1939, waiving its exemption from the taxes imposed by the Act, the activity in which such corporation is engaged is considered to be its trade or business for the purpose of determining whether the transferred property was used in the trade or business of the predecessor and for the purpose of determining whether the employment by the predecessor and the successor of an individual whose services were retained by the successor constitute employment in a trade or business. Thus, if a charitable or religious organization, subject to the taxes by virtue of its certificate, acquires all the property of another such organization likewise subject to the taxes and retains the services of employees of the predecessor, wages paid to such employees by the predecessor in the year of the acquisition (and prior to such acquisition) will be attributed to the successor for purposes of the annual wage limitation. [Reg. §31.3121(a)(1)-1.]

☐ [T.D. 6190, 12-14-56. *Republished in T.D.* 6516, 12-20-60. *Amended by T.D.* 6744, 7-2-64; *T.D.* 6983, 12-4-68; *T.D.* 7374, 7-24-75 *and T.D.* 7660, 12-19-79.]

(4) If an employee receives a payment on account of non-occupational injury sickness or accident disability such payment is not excluded from wages, as defined by section 3121(a)(2)(A).

(e) *Examples.*—The following examples illustrate the principles of paragraph (d) of this section:

*Example 1.* A local government employee is injured while performing work-related activities. The employee is not covered by the State workers' compensation law, but is covered by a local government ordinance that requires the local government to pay the employee's full salary when the employee is out of work as a result of an injury incurred while performing services for the local government. The ordinance does not limit or otherwise affect the local government's liability to the employee for the work-related injury. The local ordinance is not a workers' compensation law, but it is in the nature of a workers' compensation act. Therefore, the salary the employee receives while out of work as a result of the work-related injury is excluded from wages under section 3121(a)(2)(A).

*Example 2.* The facts are the same as in *Example 1* except that the local ordinance requires the employer to continue to pay the employee's full salary while the employee is unable to work due to an injury whether or not the injury is work-related. Thus, the local ordinance does not limit benefits to instances of work-related disability. A benefit paid under an ordinance that does not limit benefits to instances of work-related injuries is not a statute in the nature of a workers' compensation act. Therefore, the salary the injured employee receives from the employer while out of work is wages subject to FICA even though the employee's injury is work-related.

*Example 3.* The facts are the same as in *Example 1* except that the local ordinance includes a rebuttable presumption that certain injuries, including any heart attack incurred by a firefighter or other law enforcement personnel is work-related. The presumption in the ordinance does not eliminate the requirement that the injury be work-related in order to entitle the injured worker to full salary. Therefore, the ordinance is a statute in the nature of a workers' compensation act, and the salary the injured employee receives pursuant to the ordinance is excluded from wages under section 3121(a)(2)(A).

(f) It is immaterial for purposes of this exclusion whether the amount or possibility of such benefit payments is taken into consideration in fixing the amount of an employee's remuneration or whether such payments are required, expressly or impliedly, by the contract of service. [Reg. §31.3121(a)(2)-1.]

☐ [T.D. 6190, 7-14-56. *Republished in T.D.* 6516, 12-20-60. *Amended by T.D.* 9233, 12-14-2005.]

(i) The third party's coverage for that employee's group ceases prior to March 1, 1982,

(ii) No third party payment is made to such employee under that contract after February 28, 1982, and

(iii) The cessation of the third party's coverage for that employee's group indefinitely terminates the contractual relationship between the third party and the employer as to sickness and accident disability benefits for that employee's group.

See section 3121(a)(4) and §31.3121(a)(4)-1 for the exclusion from the term "wages" of any payment on account of sickness or accident disability made after the expiration of 6 calendar months following the last calendar month in which the employee worked.

**Reg. §32.1(a)(2)(iii)**

(b) *Examples.*—The application of the provisions of subparagraph (2) of paragraph (a) may be illustrated by the following examples:

*Example (1).* Company Q enters into a contract on August 31, 1981, with Insurance Company R to provide sickness and accident disability payments to Q's employees. The contract expires on February 28, 1982. On March 1, 1982, Q enters into a new contract with R to provide sickness and accident disability payments to Q's employees. Payments made by R pursuant to the contract expiring February 28, 1982, are included in "wages" as defined in section 3121(a)(2)(B).

*Example (2).* Company S enters into a contract on November 15, 1981, with Insurance Company T to provide sickness and accident disability payments to S's employees. The contract expires on February 15, 1982, and is not renewed. A, one of S's employees, has been receiving sickness payments from T since December 1, 1981. T makes its final payment to A on February 22, 1982. The payments made by T to A pursuant to its contract with S are not included in "wages" as defined in section 3121(a)(2)(B).

(c) *Workmen's compensation laws.*—(1) For purposes of paragraph (a)(1) of this section, a payment made under a workmen's compensation law does not include a payment made pursuant to a State temporary disability insurance law.

(2) If an employee receives a payment on account of sickness or accident disability which is not made under a workmen's compensation law and which must be repaid if the employee receives a workmen's compensation award with respect to the same period of absence from work, such payment is not excluded from the term "wages" as defined in section 3121(a)(2)(B).

(d) *Sickness or accident disability.*—For purposes of paragraph (a) of this section, a payment made on account of sickness or accident disability includes any payment for personal injuries or sickness includible in gross income under section 105(a) and the regulations thereunder and thus does not include—

(1) Any amount which is expended for medical care as described in section 105(b) and § 1.105-2,

(2) Any payment which is unrelated to absence from work as described in section 105(c) and § 1.105-3, or

(3) Any payment or a portion thereof which is attributable to a contribution by the employee as determined in paragraphs (d) and (e) of § 1.105-1.

A payment made on account of sickness or accident disability does not include any payment which is excludable from gross income under section 104(a)(2), (4), or (5). An employee who elects to reduce his compensation or to forgo an increase in his compensation under a salary reduction agreement with an employer will not be deemed to have made employee contributions to the sickness or accident disability plan or system if the employee is not subject to income or social security taxes on the reduction in compensation. A tax which is paid by an employee to fund a State temporary disability insurance program is considered a contribution by the employee for purposes of paragraph (d)(3) of this section.

(e) *Payments by third parties.*—(1) Any third party making a payment on account of sickness or accident disability which payment is not excluded from the term "wages" under paragraph (a) of this section shall be treated as the employer with respect to such wages, except as provided in subparagraphs (2) and (3) of this paragraph. Accordingly, such third party must withhold from such payment the tax imposed on the employee by section 3101, pay the tax imposed on employers by section 3111, deposit such taxes pursuant to section 6302 and § 31.6302(c)-1(a), and provide the receipts required by section 6051 and §§ 31.6051-1 and 31.6051-2.

(2) If any third party who is treated as the employer solely by reason of the applicability of subparagraph (1) of this paragraph promptly—

(i) Withholds the tax imposed on the employee by section 3101,

(ii) Deposits such tax pursuant to section 6302 and § 31.6302(c)-1(a), and

(iii) Notifies the employer for whom services are normally rendered of the amount of wages paid on which tax was withheld and deposited, then the employer (and not the third party) shall be required to pay the tax imposed by section 3111 and to comply with the requirements of section 6051 and §§ 31.6051-1 and 31.6051-2 with respect to the wages. For purposes of subdivision (ii) of this subparagraph, the taxes described in subdivision (i) shall be treated by the third party as if included in the term "taxes" as defined in § 31.6302(c)-1a)(1)(iii). For purposes of subdivision (iii) of this subparagraph, the notice must be provided by the third party within the time required for the deposit of the tax under subdivision (ii) of this subparagraph. For the purpose of providing the notice, the rules of section 7502(a), relating to timely mailing being treated as timely filing, shall apply. The employer, if notified pursuant to subdivision (iii) of this subparagraph by a third party who has complied with the

requirements of subdivisions (i) and (ii) of this subparagraph, must deposit the tax imposed by section 3111 in accordance with § 31.6302(c)-1.a. For purposes of § 31.6302(c)-1(a)(1)(iii)(b), with respect to the employer for whom services are normally rendered the term "taxes" shall not include any tax imposed on employers by section 3111 that is required to be paid by a third party under subparagraph (1) of this paragraph until the employer receives notification from the third party under subdivision (iii) of this subparagraph (2).

(3) A third party making a payment on account of sickness or accident disability to an employee as agent for the employer or making such a payment directly to the employer shall not be treated as the employer under subparagraph (1) with respect to such payment unless the agency agreement so provides. The determining factor as to whether a third party is an agent of the employer is whether the third party bears any insurance risk. If the third party bears no insurance risk and is reimbursed on a cost plus fee basis, the third party is an agent of the employer even if the third party is responsible for making determinations of the eligibility of individual employees of the employer for payments on account of sickness or accident disability. If the third party is paid an insurance premium and not reimbursed on a cost plus fee basis, the third party is not an agent of the employer, but the third party is treated as the employer as provided in subparagraph (1) of this paragraph (e).

(4) In order to avoid overpayment of taxes which would result from paying taxes—

(i) On remuneration which exceeds the annual contribution and benefit base (as described in section 3121(a)(1)),

(ii) With respect to a period of time which exceeds the 6-calendar-month period described in section 3121(a)(4), or

(iii) On a payment or a portion thereof which is attributable to a contribution by the employee,

the third party may request information from the employer as the total wages earned by the employee for the calendar year in which the third party is making payments, as to the last date on which the employee worked for the employer during such year, and as to the amount of any contribution by the employee. Except if the third party has reason not to believe any information supplied by the employer as the result of a request made pursuant to the preceding sentence, the third party may rely on such information in complying with the requirements of subparagraphs (1) and (2) of this paragraph (e). The third party may not rely on representations of the employee as to the information which may be requested of the employer in complying with the requirements of subparagraphs (1) and (2) of this paragraph (e).

(5) The application of the provisions of this paragraph may be illustrated by the following examples:

*Example (1).* Pursuant to an agreement with Company U, Insurance Company V makes payments on account of sickness or accident disability to U's employees. Such payments are not made under a workmen's compensation law. U reimburses V for all such payments and pays V a fee for its expenses of administering the payments. V is not treated as the employer with respect to such payments.

*Example (2).* Pursuant to an agreement with Company W, Insurance Company X indemnifies W for the amount of any payments which W must make to an employee on account of sickness or accident disability. Such payments are not made under a workmen's compensation law. X makes its indemnity payments directly to W. W makes the payments to its employees. X is not treated as the employer with respect to such payments.

*Example (3).* Pursuant to an agreement with company Y (which is not an agency agreement described in subparagraph (3) of this § 32.1(e)). Insurance Company Z makes payments on account of sickness or accident disability to Y's employees. Such payments are not made under a workmen's compensation law. Z does not notify Y of the amount of such payments. Z is treated as the employer with respect to such payments.

(f) *Penalties and interest on payments made from January 1, 1982, to June 30, 1982.*—[Note: An *IRS Release* of 7-2-82 extended the grace period to September 30, 1982—CCH.] No penalty under section 6656(a) or interest under section 6601 will be assessed for the failure to make timely payments of the tax imposed by section 3101 or section 3111 on payments made on account of sickness or accident disability, which payments of tax are made after December 31, 1981, and before July 1, 1982, to the extent that the failure is due to reasonable cause and not willful neglect.

(g) *Special rules.*—(1) For purposes of subdivision (iii) of paragraph (e)(2), the last employer for whom the employee worked prior to becoming sick or disabled or for whom the employee was working at the time he became sick or disabled shall be deemed to be the employer for whom services are normally rendered, provided that such employer made contributions on behalf of such employee to the plan or system under which the employee is being paid.

(2) The application of the provisions of subparagraph (1) of this paragraph (g) may be illustrated by the following examples:

*Example (1).* B is employed by Company M. B becomes sick and is absent from work for 3 months. While B is absent from work, he receives sick pay from Insurance Company N pursuant to a plan established by M and to which M has made contributions on behalf of B. M is the employer for whom services are normally rendered by B.

*Example (2).* C is employed by Company O and is also employed on a part-time basis by Company Q. C becomes sick while at work at Q's place of business. C is absent from work for 3 months. While C is absent from work, he receives sick pay from Insurance Company P pursuant to a plan established by O and to which O has made contributions on behalf of C. O is the employer for whom services are normally rendered by C.

*Example (3).* D is a member of a labor union whose members receive health and welfare benefit payments from a trust fund which is supported by the contributions of the various employers who employ the labor union's members. D has been employed by Company R for 4 days when he becomes sick and is absent from work for 3 months. While D is absent from work he receives sick pay from his union's trust fund to which R has made contributions on D's half. R is the employer for whom services are normally rendered by D.

(3) For purposes of paragraph (e) of this section, in the case of payments on account of sickness or accident disability made to employees by a third party insurer pursuant to a contract of insur-ance with a multiemployer plan which is obligated to make payments on account of sickness or accident disability to such employees pursuant to a collectively bargained agreement, if the third party insurer making the payments complies with the requirements of subdivisions (i) and (ii) of subparagraph (2) of paragraph (e) and notifies the plan of the amount of wages paid on which tax was withheld and deposited within the time required for notification of the employer under subparagraph (2) of paragraph (e), then the plan (and not the third party insurer) shall be required to pay the tax imposed by section 3111 and to comply with the requirements of section 6051 and §§ 31.6051-1 and 31.6051-2 with respect to such payments unless, within 6 business days of the receipt of such notification, the plan notifies the employer for whom services are normally rendered of the amount of the wages on which tax was withheld and deposited. If the plan provides such notice to the employer, the employer (and not the plan) shall be required to pay the tax imposed by section 3111 and to comply with the requirements of section 6051 and §§ 31.6051-1 and 31.6051-2 with respect to the wages. [Reg. § 32.1.]

☐ [*T.D.* 7823, 7-6-82. *Amended by T.D.* 7867, 1-7-83 *and T.D.* 9233, 12-14-2005.]

### [Reg. § 32.2]

**§ 32.2. Railroad retirement taxes with respect to payments on account of sickness or accident disability.**—[Not reproduced—CCH.]

>>>→ *Caution: Reg. § 31.3121(a)(3)-1 does not reflect changes made by P.L. 98-21.*

### [Reg. § 31.3121(a)(3)-1]

**§ 31.3121(a)(3)-1. Retirement payments.**—The term "wages" does not include any payment made by an employer to an employee (including any amount paid by an employer for insurance or annuities, or into a fund, to provide for any such payment) on account of the employee's retirement. Thus, payments made to an employee on account of his retirement are excluded from wages under this exception even though not made under a plan or system. [Reg. § 31.3121(a)(3)-1.]

☐ [*T.D.* 6190, 7-14-56. *Republished in T.D.* 6516, 12-20-60.]

### [Reg. § 31.3121(a)(4)-1]

**§ 31.3121(a)(4)-1. Payments on account of sickness or accident disability, or medical or hospitalization expenses.**—The term "wages" does not include any payment made by an employer to, or on behalf of, an employee on account of the employee's sickness or accident disability or the medical or hospitalization expenses in connection with the employee's sickness or accident disability, if such payment is made after the expiration of six calendar months following the last calendar month in which such employee worked for such employer. Such payments are excluded from wages under this exception even though not made under a plan or system. If the employee does not actually perform services for the employer during the requisite period, the existence of the employer-employee relationship during that period is immaterial. [Reg. § 31.3121(a)(4)-1.]

☐ [*T.D.* 6190, 7-14-56. *Republished in T.D.* 6516, 12-20-60.]

>>>→ *Caution: Reg. § 31.3121(a)(5)-1 has not been amended to reflect the change made by P.L. 96-222 and P.L. 96-499.*

### [Reg. § 31.3121(a)(5)-1]

**§ 31.3121(a)(5)-1. Payments from or to certain tax-exempt trusts, or under or to certain annuity plans or bond purchase plans.**—(a) *Payments from or to certain tax-exempt trusts.*—The term "wages" does not include any payment made—

(1) By an employer, on behalf of an employee or his beneficiary, into a trust, or

(2) To, or on behalf of; an employee or his beneficiary from a trust, if at the time of such payment the trust is exempt from tax under section 501(a) as an organization described in section 401(a). A payment made to an employee of such a trust for services rendered as an employee of the trust and not as a beneficiary thereof is not within this exclusion from wages.

(b) *Payments under or to certain annuity plans.*—(1) The term "wages" does not include any payment made after December 31, 1962—

(i) By an employer, on behalf of an employee or his beneficiary, into an annuity plan, or

(ii) To, or on behalf of, an employee or his beneficiary under an annuity plan,

if at the time of such payment the annuity plan is a plan described in section 403(a).

(2) The term "wages" does not include any payment made before January 1, 1963—

(i) By an employer, on behalf of an employee or his beneficiary, into an annuity plan, or

(ii) To, or on behalf of, an employee or his beneficiary under an annuity plan,

if at the time of such payment the annuity plan meets the requirements of section 401(a)(3), (4), (5) and (6).

(c) *Payments under or to certain bond purchase plans.*—The term "wages" does not include any payment made after December 31, 1962—

(1) By an employer, on behalf of an employee or his beneficiary, into a bond purchase plan, or

(2) To, or on behalf of, an employee or his beneficiary under a bond purchase plan,

if at the time of such payment the plan is a qualified bond purchase plan described in section 405(a). [Reg. § 31.3121(a)(5)-1.]

☐ [*T.D.* 6190, 7-14-56. *Republished in T.D.* 6516, 12-20-60. *Amended by T.D.* 6876, 2-10-66.]

### [Reg. § 31.3121(a)(5)-2]

**§ 31.3121(a)(5)-2. Payments under or to an annuity contract described in section 403(b)..**—(a) *Salary reduction agreement defined.*—For purposes of section 3121(a)(5)(D), the term *salary reduction agreement* means a plan or arrangement (whether evidenced by a written instrument or otherwise) whereby payment will be made by an employer, on behalf of an employee or his or her beneficiary, under or to an annuity contract described in section 403(b)—

(1) If the employee elects to reduce his or her compensation pursuant to a cash or deferred election as defined at § 1.401(k)-1(a)(3) of this chapter;

(2) If the employee elects to reduce his or her compensation pursuant to a one-time irrevocable election made at or before the time of initial eligibility to participate in such plan or arrangement (or pursuant to a similar arrangement involving a one-time irrevocable election); or

(3) If the employee agrees as a condition of employment (whether such condition is set by statute, contract, or otherwise) to make a contribution that reduces his or her compensation.

(b) *Effective/applicability date.*—This section is applicable on November 15, 2007. [Reg. § 31.3121(a)(5)-2.]

☐ [*T.D.* 9367, 11-14-2007.]

⫸➔ *Caution: This regulation has not been amended to reflect the change made by P.L. 96-499.*

**[Reg. §31.3121(a)(6)-1]**

**§31.3121(a)(6)-1. Payment by an employer of employee tax under section 3101 or employee contributions under a State law.**—The term "wages" does not include any payment by an employer (without deduction from the remuneration of, or other reimbursement from, the employee) of either (a) the employee tax imposed by section 3101 or the corresponding section of prior law, or (b) any payment required from an employee under a State unemployment compensation law. [Reg. §31.3121(a)(6)-1.]

☐ [*T.D. 6190, 7-14-56. Republished in T.D. 6516, 12-20-60.*]

**[Reg. §31.3121(a)(7)-1]**

**§31.3121(a)(7)-1. Payments for services not in the course of employer's trade or business or for domestic service.**—(a) *Meaning of terms.*—(1) *Services not in the course of employer's trade or business.*—The term "services not in the course of the employer's trade or business" includes services that do not promote or advance the trade or business of the employer. Such term does not include services performed for a corporation. As used in this section, the term does not include service not in the course of the employer's trade or business performed on a farm operated for profit or domestic service in a private home of the employer. See paragraph (f) of §31.3121(g)-1 for provisions relating to services not in the course of the employer's trade or business performed on a farm operated for profit.

(2) *Domestic service in a private home of the employer.*—Services of a household nature performed by an employee in or about a private home of the person by whom he is employed constitute domestic service in a private home of the employer. A private home is a fixed place of abode of an individual or family. A separate and distinct dwelling unit maintained by an individual in an apartment house, hotel, or other similar establishment may constitute a private home. If a dwelling house is used primarily as a boarding or lodging house for the purpose of supplying board or lodging to the public as a business enterprise, it is not a private home. In general, services of a household nature in or about a private home include services performed by cooks, waiters, butlers, housekeepers, governesses, maids, valets, baby sitters, janitors, laundresses, furnacemen, caretakers, handymen, gardeners, footmen, grooms, and chauffeurs of automobiles for family use. The term "domestic service in a private home of the employer" does not include the services enumerated above unless such services are performed in or about a private home of the employer. Services not of a household nature, such as services performed as a private secretary, tutor, or librarian, even though performed in the employer's home, are not included within the term "domestic service in a private home of the employer." As used in this section, the term does not include domestic service in a private home of the employer performed on a farm operated for profit or service not in the course of the employer's trade or business. See paragraph (f) of §31.3121(g)-1 for provisions relating to domestic service in a private home of the employer performed on a farm operated for profit.

(b) *Payments other than in cash.*—The term "wages" does not include remuneration paid in any medium other than cash (1) for service not in the course of the employer's trade or business, or (2) for domestic service in a private home of the employer. Cash remuneration includes checks and other monetary media of exchange. Remuneration paid in any medium other than cash, such as lodging, food, clothing, car tokens, transportation passes or tickets, or other goods or commodities, for service not in the course of the employer's trade or business or for domestic service in a private home of the employer does not constitute wages.

(c) *Cash payments.*—(1) The term wages does not include cash remuneration paid by an employer in any calendar year to an employee for—

(i) Domestic service in a private home of the employer, unless the cash remuneration paid in such year by the employer to the employee for such service equals or exceeds the applicable dollar threshold (as defined in section 3121(x)) for such year; or

(ii) Service not in the course of the employer's trade or business, unless the cash remuneration paid in such year by the employer to the employee for such service equals or exceeds $100.

(2) The tests relating to cash remuneration are based on the remuneration paid in a calendar year rather than on the remuneration earned during a calendar year. The following example illustrates this provision:

*Example.* On March 31, 2004, employer X pays employee A cash remuneration of $100 for service not in the course of X's trade or business. Such remuneration constitutes wages subject to the taxes even though $10 thereof represents payment for such service performed by A for X in December 2003.

(3) In determining whether wages have been paid either for domestic service in a private home of the employer or for service not in the course of the employer's trade or business, only cash remuneration for such service shall be taken into account. Cash remuneration includes checks and other monetary media of exchange. Remuneration paid in any other medium, such as lodging, food, clothing, car tokens, transportation passes or tickets, or other goods or commodities, is disregarded in determining whether the cash-remuneration test is met. If an employee receives cash remuneration from an employer in a calendar year for both types of services the pertinent cash-remuneration test is to be applied separately to each type of service. If an employee receives cash remuneration from more than one employer in a calendar year for domestic service in a private home of the employer or for service not in the course of the employer's trade or business, the pertinent cash-remuneration test is to be applied separately to the remuneration received from each employer.

(d) *Cross references.*—(1) For provisions relating to deduction of employee tax or amounts equivalent to the tax from cash payments for the services described in this section, see §31.3102-1;

(2) For provisions relating to time of payment of wages for such services, see §31.3121(a)-2;

(3) For provisions relating to computations to the nearest dollar of any payment of cash remuneration for domestic service in a private home of the employer, see §31.3121(i)-1.

(e) *Effective dates.*—(1) The provisions of this section apply to any cash payment for service not in the course of the employer's trade or business made on or after January 1, 1978 and for domestic service in a private home of the employer made on or after January 1, 1994.

(2) For rules applicable to any cash payment made prior to the dates set forth in paragraph (e)(1), see §31.3121(a)(7)-1 in effect at such time (see 26 CFR part 31 contained in the edition of 26 CFR Parts 30 to 39, revised as of April 1, 2006). [Reg. §31.3121(a)(7)-1.]

☐ [*T.D. 6190, 7-14-56. Republished in T.D. 6516, 12-20-60. Amended by T.D. 9266, 6-16-2006.*]

**[Reg. §31.3121(a)(8)-1]**

**§31.3121(a)(8)-1. Payments for agricultural labor.**—(a) *Scope of this section.*—For purposes of the regulations in this section, the term "agricultural labor" means only such agricultural labor (see §31.3121(g)-1) as constitutes employment or is deemed to constitute employment by reason of the rules relating to included and excluded services contained in section 3121(c) (see §31.3121(c)-1) or the corresponding section of prior law.

(b) *Payments other than in cash.*—The term "wages" does not include remuneration paid in any medium other than cash for agricultural labor. For meaning of the term "cash remuneration", see paragraph (f) of the regulations in this section.

(c) *Cash payments.*—(1) The term wages does not include cash remuneration paid by an employer in any calendar year to an employee for agricultural labor unless—

(i) The cash remuneration paid in such year by the employer to the employee for such labor is $150 or more; or

(ii) The employer's expenditures for agricultural labor in such year equal or exceed $2,500, except that this paragraph (c)(1)(ii) shall not apply in determining whether remuneration paid to an employee constitutes wages for agricultural labor if such employee—

(A) Is employed as a hand-harvest laborer and is paid on a piece rate basis in an operation which has been, and is customarily and generally recognized as having been, paid on a piece rate basis in the region of employment;

(B) Commutes daily from his permanent residence to the farm on which he is so employed; and

(C) Has been employed in agriculture less than 13 weeks during the preceding calendar year.

(2) The application of the provisions of paragraph (c)(1) of this section may be illustrated by the following example:

*Example.* Employer X pays A $140 in cash for agricultural labor in calendar year 2004. X makes no other payments to A during the year and makes no other payment for agricultural labor to any other employee. Employee A is not employed as a hand-harvest laborer. Neither the $150-cash-remuneration test nor the $2,500-employer's-expenditures-for-agricultural-labor test is met. Accordingly, the remuneration paid by X to A is not subject to the taxes. If in 2004 X had paid A $140 in cash for agricultural labor and had made expenditures of $2,360 or more to other employees for agricultural labor, the $140 paid by X to A would have been subject to tax because the $2,500-employer's-expenditures-for-agricultural-labor test would have been met. Or, if X had paid A $150 in cash in 2004 and made no other payments to any other employee for agricultural labor, the $150 paid by X to A would have been subject to tax because the $150-cash-remuneration test would have been met.

(d) *Application of cash-remuneration test.*—(1) If an employee receives cash remuneration from an employer both for services which constitute agricultural labor and for services which do not constitute agricultural labor, only the amount of such remuneration which is attributable to agricultural labor shall be included in determining whether cash remuneration of $150 or more has been paid in the calendar year by the employer to the employee for agricultural labor. The following example illustrates this paragraph (d)(1):

*Example.* Employer X operates a store and also is engaged in farming operations. Employee A, who regularly performs services for X in connection with the operation of the store, works on X's farm when additional help is required for the farm activities. In the calendar year 2004, X pays A $140 in cash for services performed in agricultural labor, and $4,000 for services performed in connection with the operation of the store. X has no additional expenditures for agricultural labor in 2004. Since the cash remuneration paid by X to A in the calendar year 2004 for agricultural labor is less than $150, the $150-cash-remuneration test is not met. The $140 paid by X to A in 2004 for agricultural labor does not constitute wages and is not subject to the taxes.

(2) The test relating to cash remuneration of $150 or more is based on the cash remuneration paid in a calendar year rather than on the remuneration earned during a calendar year. It is immaterial if such cash remuneration is paid in a calendar year other than the year in which the agricultural labor is performed. The following example illustrates this paragraph (d)(2):

*Example.* Employer X pays cash remuneration of $150 in the calendar year 2004 to employee A for agricultural labor. Such remuneration constitutes wages even though $10 of such amount represents payment for agricultural labor performed by A for X in December 2003.

(3) In determining whether $150 or more has been paid to an employee for agricultural labor, only cash remuneration for such labor shall be taken into account. If an employee receives cash remuneration in any one calendar year from more than one employer for agricultural labor, the cash-remuneration test is to be applied with respect to the remuneration received by the employee from each employer in such calendar year for such labor.

(e) *Application of employer's-expenditures-for-agricultural-labor test.*—(1) If an employer has expenditures in a calendar year for agricultural labor and for non-agricultural labor, only the amount of such expenditures for agricultural labor shall be included in determining whether the employer's expenditures for agricultural labor in such year equal or exceed $2,500. The following example illustrates this paragraph (e)(1):

*Example.* Employer X operates a store and also is engaged in farming operations. Employee A, who regularly performs services for X in connection with the operation of the store, works on X's farm when additional help is required for the farm activities. In calendar year 2004, X pays A $140 in cash for services performed in agricultural labor, and $4,000 for services performed in connection with the operation of the store. X has no additional expenditures for agricultural labor in 2004. Since X's expenditures for agricultural labor in 2004 are less than $2,500, the employer's-expenditures-for-agricultural-labor test is not met. The $140 paid by X to A in 2004 for agricultural labor does not constitute wages and is not subject to the taxes.

(2) The test relating to an employer's expenditures of $2,500 or more for agricultural labor is based on the expenditures paid by the employer in a calendar year rather than on the expenses incurred by the employer during a calendar year. It is immaterial if the expenditures are paid in a calendar year other than the year in which the agricultural labor is performed. The following example illustrates this paragraph (e)(2):

*Example.* Employer X employs A to construct fences on a farm owned by X. The work constitutes agricultural labor and is performed over the course of November and December 2003. A is not employed by X at any other time, however X does have other employees to whom X pays remuneration of $2,000 for agricultural labor in 2003. X pays A $140 in cash in November 2003 and $140 in cash in January 2004, in full payment for the work. The $140 payment to A made in November is not wages for calendar year 2003 because the $150-cash-remuneration test is not met and X's total expenditures for agricultural labor for such year are not equal to or in excess of $2,500. The $140 payment to A made in January is not wages for 2004 because the $150 cash-remuneration test is not met. However, if X pays additional remuneration to employees for agricultural labor in 2004 that equals or exceeds $2,360, the employer's-expenditures-for-agricultural-labor test will be met and the $140 paid by X to A in 2004 will be considered wages. It is immaterial that the work was performed in 2003.

(f) *Meaning of "cash remuneration."*—Cash remuneration includes checks and other monetary media of exchange. Cash remuneration does not include payments made in any other medium, such as lodging, food, clothing, car tokens, transportation passes or tickets, farm products, or other goods or commodities.

(g) *Cross references.*—(1) For provisions relating to deduction of employee tax or amounts equivalent to the tax from cash payments for agricultural labor, see § 31.3102-1.

(2) For provisions relating to the time of payment of wages for agricultural labor, see § 31.3121(a)-2.

(3) For provisions relating to records to be kept with respect to agricultural labor, see paragraph (b) of § 31.6001-2.

(h) *Effective dates.*—The provisions of this section apply to any payment for agricultural labor made on or after January 1, 1988. For rules applicable to any payment for agricultural labor made prior to January 1, 1988, see § 31.3121(a)(8)-1 in effect at such time (see 26 CFR part 31 contained in the edition of 26 CFR Parts 30 to 39, revised as of April 1, 2006). [Reg. § 31.3121(a)(8)-1.]

☐ [T.D. 6190, 7-14-56. *Republished in T.D.* 6516, 12-20-60. *Amended by* T.D. 6744, 7-2-64 *and T.D.* 9266, 6-16-2006.]

## [Reg. § 31.3121(a)(9)-1]

### § 31.3121(a)(9)-1. [Reserved].

☐ [T.D. 6190, 7-14-56. *Republished in T.D.* 6516, 12-20-60. *Amended by* T.D. 6744, 7-2-64, T.D. 7373, 7-24-75. *Removed and reserved by T.D.* 9849, 3-11-2019.]

## [Reg. § 31.3121(a)(10)-1]

### § 31.3121(a)(10)-1. Payments to certain home workers.—(a) The term wages does not include remuneration paid by an employer in any calendar year to an employee for service performed as a home worker who is an employee by reason of the provisions of section 3121(d)(3)(C) (see § 31.3121(d)-1(d)), unless the cash remuneration paid in such calendar year by the employer to the employee for such services is $100 or more. The test relating to cash remuneration of $100 or more is based on remuneration paid in a calendar year rather than on remuneration earned during a calendar year. If cash remuneration of $100 or more is paid in a particular calendar year, it is immaterial whether such remuneration is in payment for services performed during the year of payment or during any other year.

(b) The application of paragraph (a) of this section may be illustrated by the following example:

*Example.* A, a home worker, performs services for X, a manufacturer, in 2003 and 2004. In the performance of the home work A is an employee by reason of section 3121(d)(3)(C). In March 2004, A returns to X articles made by A at home from materials received by A from X in 2003. X pays A cash remuneration of $100 for such work when the finished articles are delivered. The $100 includes $10 which represents remuneration for home work performed by A in 2003. The entire $100 is subject to the taxes. Any additional cash remuneration paid by X to A in 2004 for such services is also subject to the taxes.

(c) In the event an employee receives remuneration in any one calendar year from more than one employer for services performed as a home worker of the character described in paragraph (a) of this section, the regulations in this section are to be applied with respect to the remuneration received by the employee from each employer in such calendar year for such services. This exclusion from wages has no application to remuneration paid for services performed as a home worker who is an employee under section 3121(d)(2) (see § 31.3121(d)-1(c)) relating to common law employees.

(d) Cash remuneration includes checks and other monetary media of exchange. Remuneration paid in any other medium, such as clothing, car tokens, transportation passes or tickets, or other goods or commodities, is disregarded in determining whether the $100 cash-remuneration test is met. If the cash remuneration paid in any calendar year by an employer to an employee for services performed as a home worker of the character described in paragraph (a) of this section is $100 or more, then no remuneration, whether in cash or in any medium other than cash, paid by the employer to the employee in such calendar year for such services is excluded from wages under this exception.

(e)(1) For provisions relating to deductions of employee tax or amounts equivalent to the tax from cash payments for services performed as a home worker within the meaning of section 3121(d)(3)(C), see § 31.3102-1.

(2) For provisions relating to the time of payment of wages for services performed as a home worker within the meaning of section 3121(d)(3)(C), see § 31.3121(a)-2.

(3) For provisions relating to records to be kept with respect to payment of wages for services performed as a home worker within the meaning of section 3121(d)(3)(C), see § 31.6001-2.

(f) The provisions of this section apply to any payment for services performed as a home worker within the meaning of section 3121(d)(3)(C) made on or after January 1, 1978. For rules applicable to any payment for services performed as a home worker within the meaning of section 3121(d)(3)(C) made prior to January 1, 1978, see §31.3121(a)(10)-1 in effect at such time (see 26 CFR part 31 contained in the edition of 26 CFR Parts 30 to 39, revised as of April 1, 2006). [Reg. §31.3121(a)(10)-1.]

☐ [*T.D.* 6190, 7-14-56. *Republished in T.D.* 6516, 12-20-60. *Amended by T.D.* 9266, 6-16-2006.]

### [Reg. §31.3121(a)(11)-1]

**§31.3121(a)(11)-1. Moving expenses.**—(a) The term "wages" does not include remuneration paid on or after November 1, 1964, to or on behalf of an employee, either as an advance or a reimbursement, specifically for moving expenses incurred or expected to be incurred, if (and to the extent that) at the time of payment it is reasonable to believe that a corresponding deduction is or will be allowable to the employee under section 217. The reasonable belief contemplated by the statute may be based upon any evidence reasonably sufficient to induce such belief, even though such evidence may be insufficient upon closer examination by the district director or the courts finally to establish that a deduction is allowable under section 217. The reasonable belief shall be based upon the application of section 217 and the regulations thereunder in Part 1 of this chapter (Income Tax Regulations). When used in this section, the term "moving expenses" has the same meaning as when used in section 217 and the regulations thereunder.

(b) Except as otherwise provided in paragraph (a) of this section, or in a numbered paragraph of section 3121(a), amounts paid to or on behalf of an employee for moving expenses are wages for purposes of section 3121(a). [Reg. §31.3121(a)(11)-1.]

☐ [*T.D.* 7375, 7-12-75.]

### [Reg. §31.3121(a)(12)-1]

**§31.3121(a)(12)-1. Tips.**—The term "wages" does not include remuneration received by an employee after December 1965 in the form of tips if—

(a) The tips are paid in any medium other than cash, or

(b) The cash tips received by an employee in any calendar month in the course of his employment by an employer are less than $20.

If the cash tips received by an employee in a calendar month after December 1965 in the course of his employment by an employer amount to $20 or more, none of the cash tips received by the employee in such calendar month are excluded from the term "wages" under this section. The cash tips to which this section applies include checks and other monetary media of exchange. Tips received by an employee in any medium other than cash, such as passes, tickets, or other goods or commodities do not constitute wages. If an employee in any calendar month performs services for two or more employers and receives tips in the course of his employment by each employer, the $20 test is to be applied separately with respect to the cash tips received by the employee in respect of his services for each employer and not to the total cash tips received by the employee during the month. As to the time tips are deemed paid, see §31.3121(q)-1. For provisions relating to the treatment of tips received by an employee prior to 1966, see paragraph (j)(3) of §31.3121(a)-1. [Reg. §31.3121(a)(12)-1.]

☐ [*T.D.* 7001, 1-23-69.]

### [Reg. §31.3121(a)(13)-1]

**§31.3121(a)(13)-1. Payments under certain employers' plans after retirement, disability, or death.**—(a) *In general.*—The term "wages" does not include the amount of any payment or series of payments made after January 2, 1968, by an employer to, or on behalf of, an employee or any of his dependents under a plan established by the employer which makes provisions for his employees generally (or for his employees generally and their dependents) or for a class or classes of his employees (or for a class or classes of his employees and their dependents), which is paid or commences to be paid upon or within a reasonable time after the termination of an employee's employment relationship because of the employee's—

(1) Death,

(2) Retirement for disability, or

(3) Retirement after attaining an age specified in the plan established by the employer or in a pension plan of the employer at the age at which a person in the employee's circumstances is eligible for retirement.

A payment or series of payments made under the circumstances described in the preceding sentence is excluded from "wages" even if made pursuant to an incentive compensation plan which also provides for the making of other types of payments. However, any payment or series of payments which would have been paid if the employee's relationship had not been terminated is not excluded

from "wages" under this section and section 3121(a)(13). For example, lump-sum payments for unused vacation time or a final paycheck received after retirement are payments which the employee would have received whether or not he retired and therefore are not excluded from "wages" under this section. Further, if any payment is made upon or after termination of employment for any reason other than those set out in subparagraphs (1), (2), and (3) of this paragraph such payment is not excludable from "wages" by this section. For example, if a pension plan provides for retirement upon disability, completion of 30 years of service, or attainment of age 65, and if an employee who is not disabled retires at age 61 after 30 years of service, none of the retirement payments made to the employee under the pension plan (including any made after he is 65) is excludable from "wages" under this section. However, if the pension plan had conditioned retirement after 30 years of service upon attainment of age 60, all of the retirement payments would have been excludable.

(b) *Plan.*—The plan or system established by an employer need not provide for payments because of termination of employment for all the reasons set out in subparagraphs (1), (2), and (3) of paragraph (a), but such plan or system may provide for payments because of termination for any one or more of such reasons. Payments because of termination of employment for any one or more of such reasons under a plan or system established by an employer solely for the dependents of his employees are not within this exclusion from wages.

(c) *Dependents.*—Dependents of an employee include the employee's husband or wife, children, and any other members of the employee's immediate family.

(d) *Benefit payment.*—It is immaterial for purposes of this exclusion whether the amount or possibility of benefit payments is paid on account of services rendered or taken into consideration in fixing the amount of an employee's remuneration or whether such payments are required, expressly or impliedly, by the contract of service.

(e) *Example.*—The application of this section may be illustrated by the following example:

*Example.* A, an employee, receives a salary of $1,500 a month, payable on the 5th day of the month following the month for which the salary is earned. A's employer has established an incentive compensation plan for a class of his employees, including A, providing for the payment of deferred compensation on termination of employment, including termination upon an employee's death, retirement at age 65 (the retirement age specified in the plan), or retirement for disability. On March 1, 1973, A attains the age of 65 and retires. On March 5, 1973, A receives $5,500 from his employer of which $1,500 represents A's salary for services he performed in February 1973, and $4,000 represents incentive compensation paid under the employer's plan. The amount of $4,000 is excluded from "wages" under this section. The amount of $1,500 is not excluded from "wages" under this section. [Reg. §31.3121(a)(13)-1.]

☐ [*T.D.* 7374, 7-24-75.]

### [Reg. §31.3121(a)(14)-1]

**§31.3121(a)(14)-1. Payments by employer to survivor or estate of former employee.**—The term "wages" does not include any payment by an employer to a survivor or the estate of a former employee made after 1972 and after the calendar year in which such employee died. [Reg. §31.3121(a)(14)-1.]

☐ [*T.D.* 7373, 7-24-75.]

### [Reg. §31.3121(a)(15)-1]

**§31.3121(a)(15)-1. Payments by employer to disabled former employee.**—The term "wages" does not include any payment made after 1972 by an employer to an employee, if at the time such payment is made such employee is entitled to disability insurance benefits under section 223(a) of the Social Security Act and such entitlement commenced prior to the calendar year in which such payment is made, and if such employee did not perform any service for such employer during the period for which such payment is made. [Reg. §31.3121(a)(15)-1.]

☐ [*T.D.* 7373, 7-24-75.]

### [Reg. §31.3121(a)(18)-1]

**§31.3121(a)(18)-1. Payments or benefits under a qualified educational assistance program.**—The term "wages" does not include any payment made, or benefit furnished, to or for the benefit of an employee in a taxable year beginning after December 31, 1978, if at the time of such payment or furnishing it is reasonable to believe that the employee will be able to exclude such payment or benefit from income under section 127. [Reg. §31.3121(a)(18)-1.]

☐ *T.D.* 7898, 7-6-83.

### [Reg. §31.3121(b)-1]

**§31.3121(b)-1. Employment; services to which the regulations in this suppart apply.**—(a) The provisions of the regulations in this subpart relating to the term "employment" apply with respect to services performed after 1954. Certain provisions also apply with respect to services performed before 1955 for which the remuneration is paid after 1954 (see paragraph (b) of §31.3121(b)-2). For provisions relating generally to services performed before 1955, see paragraph (a) of §31.3121(b)-2. For provisions relating to the circumstances under which services which do not constitute employment are nevertheless deemed to be employment, and relating to the circumstances under which services which constitute employment are nevertheless deemed not to be employment, see §31.3121(c)-1. For provisions relating to who are employees and who are employers, see §§31.3121(d)-1 and 31.3121(d)-2, respectively.

(b) The taxes apply with respect to remuneration paid after 1954 for services performed before 1955, as well as for services performed after 1954, to the extent that the remuneration and services constitute wages and employment. See §§31.3121(a)-1 to 31.3121(a)(13)-1 relating to wages. [Reg. §31.3121(b)-1.]

☐ *T.D. 6190, 7-14-56. Republished in T.D. 6516, 12-20-60. Amended by T.D. 6983, 12-4-68.*

### [Reg. §31.3121(b)-2]

**§31.3121(b)-2. Employment; services performed before 1955.**—(a) *General rule.*—(1) Subject to the provisions of paragraph (b) of this section,

(i) Services performed after 1936 and before 1955 which were employment under the applicable law in effect before 1955 constitute employment under section 3121(b).

(ii) Services performed after 1936 and before 1955 which were not employment under the applicable law in effect before 1955 do not constitute employment under section 3121(b).

(2) Except as provided in paragraph (b) of this section, determination of whether services performed before 1955 constitute employment shall be made in accordance with the applicable provisions of law in effect before 1955 and of the regulations thereunder. The regulations applicable in determining whether services performed after 1936 and before 1955 constitute employment are as follows:

(i) Services performed after 1936 and before 1940—26 CFR (1939) Part 401 (Regulations 91).

(ii) Services performed after 1939 and before 1951—26 CFR (1939) Part 402 (Regulations 106).

(iii) Services performed after 1950 and before 1955—26 CFR (1939) Part 408 (Regulations 128).

(b) *Certain services performed before 1955 the remuneration for which is paid after 1954.*—(1) Services of the following character performed before 1955,

for which remuneration is paid after 1954, constitute employment under section 3121(b):

(i) Agricultural labor, as defined in section 3121(g) (see §31.3121(g)-1), other than services of the character described in section 3121(b)(1) (relating to services performed in connection with the production or harvesting of certain oleoresinous products and services performed by certain foreign agricultural workers), which, at the time performed, constituted employment under section 1426(b) of the 1939 Code, or would have constituted employment except for the provisions of section 1426(b)(1) of such Code, as in effect at the time the services were performed.

(ii) Services not in the course of the employer's trade or business (see paragraph (a)(1) of §31.3121(a)(7)-1 which, at the time performed, constituted employment under section 1426(b) of the 1939 Code, or would have constituted employment except for the provisions of section 1426(b)(3) of such Code, as in effect at the time the services were performed.

(2) Services of the character described in paragraphs (a) and (b) of §31.3121(b)(1)-1, which were performed by certain foreign agricultural workers before 1955 and the remuneration for which is paid after 1954, do not constitute employment under section 3121(b), irrespective of whether they constituted employment under section 1426(b) of the 1939 Code, as in effect at the time the services were performed.

(3) This paragraph has no application to services performed before 1955 and the remuneration for which was paid before 1955. [Reg. §31.3121(b)-2.]

☐ *T.D. 6190, 7-14-56. Republished in T.D. 6516, 12-20-60. Amended by T.D. 6744, 7-2-64.*

### [Reg. §31.3121(b)-3]

**§31.3121(b)-3. Employment; services performed after 1954.**—(a) *In general.*—Whether services performed after 1954 constitute

employment is determined in accordance with the provisions of section 3121(b).

(b) *Services performed within the United States.*—Services performed after 1954 within the United States (see §31.3121(e)-1) by an employee for his employer, unless specifically excepted by section 3121(b), constitute employment. With respect to services performed within the United States, the place where the contract of service is entered into is immaterial. The citizenship or residence of the employee or of the employer also is immaterial except to the extent provided in any specific exception from employment. Thus, the employee and the employer may be citizens and residents of a foreign country and the contract of service may be entered into in a foreign country, and yet, if the employee under such contract performs services within the United States, there may be to that extent employment.

(c) *Services performed outside the United States.*—(1) *In general.*—Except as provided in subparagraphs (2) and (3) of this paragraph, services performed outside the United States (see §31.3121(e)-1) do not constitute employment.

(2) *On or in connection with an American vessel or American aircraft.*—(i) Services performed after 1954 by an employee for an employer "on or in connection with" an American vessel or American aircraft outside the United States (see §31.3121(e)-1) constitute employment if:

(a) The employee is also employed "on and in connection with" such vessel or aircraft when outside the United States; and

(b) The services are performed under a contract of service, between the employee and the employer, which is entered into within the United States, or during the performance of the contract under which the services are performed and while the employee is employed on the vessel or aircraft it touches at a port within the United States; and

(c) The services are not excepted under section 3121(b).

(ii) An employee performs services on and in connection with the vessel or aircraft if he performs services on such vessel or aircraft which are also in connection with the vessel or aircraft. Services performed on the vessel by employees as officers or members of the crew, or as employees of concessionaires, of the vessel, for example, are performed under such circumstances, since such services are also connected with the vessel. Similarly, services performed *on* the aircraft by employees as officers or members of the crew of the aircraft are performed on and in connection with such aircraft. Services may be performed on the vessel or aircraft, however, which have no connection with it, as in the case of services performed by an employee while on the vessel or aircraft merely as a passenger in the general sense. For example, the services of a buyer in the employ of a department store while he is a passenger on a vessel are not in connection with the vessel.

(iii) If services are performed by an employee "on and in connection with" an American vessel or American aircraft when outside the United States and conditions listed in subdivision (i)(b) and (c) of this subparagraph are met, then the services of that employee performed on or in connection with the vessel or aircraft constitute employment. The expression "on or in connection with" refers not only to services performed on the vessel or aircraft but also to services connected with the vessel or aircraft which are not actually performed on it (for example, shore services performed as officers or members of the crew, or as employees of concessionaires, of the vessel).

(iv) Services performed by a member of the crew or other employee whose contract of service is not entered into within the United States, and during the performance of which and while the employee is employed on the vessel or aircraft it does not touch at a port within the United States, do not constitute employment under this subparagraph, notwithstanding services performed by other members of the crew or other employees on or in connection with the vessel or aircraft may constitute employment.

(v) A vessel includes every description of watercraft, or other contrivance, used as a means of transportation on water. An aircraft includes every description of craft, or other contrivance, used as a means of transportation through the air. In the case of an aircraft, the term "port" means an airport. An airport means an area on land or water used regularly by aircraft for receiving or discharging passengers or cargo. For definitions of "American vessel" and "American aircraft," see §31.3121(f)-1.

(vi) With respect to services performed outside the United States on or in connection with an American vessel or American aircraft, the citizenship or residence of the employee is immaterial, and the citizenship or residence of the employer is material only in case it has a bearing in determining whether a vessel is an American vessel.

(3) *By a citizen of the United States as an employee for an American employer.*—Services performed after 1954 outside the United States by a citizen of the United States as an employee for an American employer constitute employment provided the services are not specifically excepted under section 3121(b). For definitions of "citizen of the United States" and "American employer", see § § 31.3121(e)-1 and 31.3121(h)-1, respectively.

(4) *By a citizen of the United States as an employee for a foreign subsidiary corporation.*—For provisions relating to the extension of the Federal old-age and survivors insurance system established by title II of the Social Security Act to certain services not constituting employment which are performed outside the United States by citizens of the United States in the employ of a foreign subsidiary of a domestic corporation, see section 3121(l) and Part 36 of this chapter (Regulations Relating to Contract Coverage of Employees of Foreign Subsidiaries). [Reg. § 31.3121(b)-3.]

☐ *T.D.* 6190, 7-14-56. *Republished in T.D.* 6516, 12-20-60. *Amended by T.D.* 6744, 7-2-64.

### [Reg. § 31.3121(b)-4]

**§ 31.3121(b)-4. Employment; excepted services in general.**—(a) Services performed by an employee for an employer do not constitute employment for purposes of the taxes if they are specifically excepted from employment under any of the numbered paragraphs of section 3121(b). Services so excepted do not constitute employment for purposes of the taxes even though they are performed within the United States, or are performed outside the United States on or in connection with an American vessel or American aircraft, or are performed outside the United States by a citizen of the United States for an American employer. If not otherwise provided in the regulations relating to the numbered paragraphs of section 3121(b), such regulations apply to services performed after 1954.

(b) The exception attaches to the services performed by the employee and not to the employee as an individual; that is, the exception applies only to the services in an excepted class rendered by the employee.

*Example.* A is an individual who is employed part time by B to perform services which are specifically excepted from employment under one of the numbered paragraphs of section 3121(b). A is also employed by C part time to perform services which constitute employment. While no tax liability is incurred with respect to A's remuneration for services performed in the employ of B (the services being excepted from employment), the exception does not embrace the services performed by A in the employ of C (which constitute employment) and the taxes attach with respect to the wages (see § 31.3121(a)-1) for such services.

(c) For provisions relating to the circumstances under which services which are excepted are nevertheless deemed to be employment, and relating to the circumstances under which services which are not excepted are nevertheless deemed not to be employment, see § 31.3121(c)-1. [Reg. § 31.3121(b)-4.]

☐ *T.D.* 6190, 7-14-56. *Republished in T.D.* 6516, 12-20-60. *Amended by T.D.* 6744, 7-2-64.

### [Reg. § 31.3121(b)(1)-1]

**§ 31.3121(b)(1)-1. Certain services performed by foreign agricultural workers, or performed before 1959 in connection with oleoresinous products.**—(a) *Services of workers from Mexico.*—Services performed before 1965 by foreign agricultural workers from the Republic of Mexico under contracts entered into in accordance with title V of the Agricultural Act of 1949, as amended, are excepted from employment. Contracts entered into pursuant to the provisions of such title V may provide for the performance only of services which constitute "agricultural employment". The term "agricultural employment" includes certain services which do not constitute "agricultural labor" as that term is defined in section 3121(g) (see § 31.3121(g)-1). For purposes of title V of the Agricultural Act of 1949, as amended, the term "agricultural employment" includes services or activities included within the provisions of section 3(f) of the Fair Labor Standards Act of 1938, as amended, or section 3121(g) of the Internal Revenue Code. Under section 507 of the Agricultural Act of 1949, as amended, and as in effect before October 3, 1961, the term "agricultural employment" included also horticultural employment, cotton ginning, compressing and storing, crushing of oil seeds, and

the packing, canning, freezing, drying, or other processing of perishable or seasonable agricultural products.

(b) *Services of workers from British West Indies.*—Services performed by a foreign agricultural worker lawfully admitted to the United States from the Bahamas, Jamaica, or the other British West Indies, on a temporary basis to perform agricultural labor are excepted from employment.

(c) *Services performed after 1956 by foreign workers.*—Services performed after 1956 by a foreign agricultural worker lawfully admitted to the United States from any foreign country or possession thereof, including the Republic of Mexico, on a temporary basis to perform agricultural labor are excepted from employment.

(d) *Services performed before 1959 in connection with the production or harvesting of certain oleoresinous products.*—Services performed before 1959 in connection with the production or harvesting of crude gum (oleoresin) from a living tree or the processing of such crude gum into gum spirits of turpentine and gum rosin, provided the processing is carried on by the original producer of the crude gum, are excepted from employment. However, the services to which this paragraph relates constitute agricultural labor as defined in section 3121(g) (see paragraph (d) of § 31.3121(g)-1). Thus, any cash remuneration paid for such services, to the extent that the services are deemed to constitute employment by reason of the rules relating to included and excluded services contained in section 3121(c) (see § 31.3121(c)-1), is taken into account in applying the test prescribed in section 3121(a)(8)(B) for determining whether cash remuneration paid for agricultural labor constitutes wages (see paragraph (c) of § 31.3121(a)(8)-1).

(e) *Cross-reference.*—See paragraph (b) of § 31.3121(b)-2 for provisions relating to the status of services of the character to which paragraphs (a) and (b) of this section apply which were performed before 1955 and the remuneration for which is paid after 1954. [Reg. § 31.3121(b)(1)-1.]

☐ *T.D.* 6190, 7-14-56. *Republished in T.D.* 6516, 12-20-60. *Amended by T.D.* 6744, 7-2-64.

### [Reg. § 31.3121(b)(2)-1]

**§ 31.3121(b)(2)-1. Domestic service performed by students for certain college organizations.**—(a) Services of a household nature performed in or about the club rooms or house of a local college club, or in or about the club rooms or house of a local chapter of a college fraternity or sorority, by a student who is enrolled and regularly attending classes at a school, college, or university are excepted from employment. For the purposes of this exemption, the statutory tests are the type of services performed by the employee, the character of the place where the services are performed, and the status of the employee as a student enrolled and regularly attending classes at a school, college, or university.

(b) In general, services of a household nature in or about the club rooms or house of a local college club or local chapter of a college fraternity or sorority include services rendered by cooks, waiters, butlers, maids, janitors, laundresses, furnacemen, handymen, gardeners, housekeepers, and housemothers.

(c) A local college club or local chapter of a college fraternity or sorority does not include an alumni club or chapter. If the club rooms or house of a local college club or local chapter of a college fraternity or sorority is used primarily for the purpose of supplying board or lodging to students or the public as a business enterprise, the services performed therein are not within the exception.

(d) An organization is a *school, college, or university* within the meaning of section 3121(b)(2) if its primary function is the presentation of formal instruction, it normally maintains a regular faculty and curriculum, and it normally has a regularly enrolled body of students in attendance at the place where its educational activities are regularly carried on. See section 170(b)(1)(A)(ii) and the regulations thereunder.

(e) Services of a household nature are not within the exception if performed in or about rooming or lodging houses, boarding houses, clubs (except local college clubs), hotels, hospitals, eleemosynary institutions, or commercial offices or establishments.

(f) For provisions relating to domestic service in a private home of the employer, see § 31.3121(a)(7)-1. [Reg. § 31.3121(b)(2)-1.]

☐ *T.D.* 6190, 7-14-56. *Republished in T.D.* 6516, 12-20-60. *Amended by T.D.* 9167, 12-20-2004.

**≫→ Caution:** *This regulation has not been amended to reflect changes enacted by the Omnibus Budget Reconciliation Act of 1987 (P.L. 100-203).*

### [Reg. §31.3121(b)(3)-1]

**§31.3121(b)(3)-1. Family employment.**—(a) Certain services are excepted from employment because of the existence of a family relationship between the employee and the individual employing him. The exceptions are as follows:

(1) Services performed by an individual in the employ of his or her spouse;

(2)(i) Services performed before 1961 by a father or mother in the employ of his or her son or daughter;

(ii) Services not in the course of the employer's trade or business, or domestic service in a private home of the employer, performed after 1960 but prior to 1968 by a father or mother in the employ of his or her son or daughter;

(iii) Services not in the course of the employer's trade or business, or domestic service in a private home of the employer, performed after 1967 by a father or mother in the employ of his or her son or daughter unless (a) the employer has a child (including an adopted child or stepchild) living in his or her home who is under age 18 or who has a mental or physical condition which requires the personal care and supervision of an adult for at least 4 continuous weeks in the calendar quarter in which the services are rendered; and (b) the employer is during the calendar quarter in which the services are rendered:

*(1)* A widow or widower;

*(2)* A divorced person who has not remarried; or

*(3)* A married person who has a spouse living in the home who has a mental or physical condition which results in such spouse's being incapable of caring for such child for at least 4 continuous weeks in the calendar quarter in which the services are rendered; and

(3) Services performed by a son or daughter under the age of 21 in the employ of his or her father or mother.

(b) Under paragraph (a)(1) and (2)(i) of this section, the exception is conditioned solely upon the family relationship between the employee and the individual employing him. Under paragraph (a)(2)(ii) and (iii) of this section, in addition to the family relationship, there is a further requirement that the services performed after 1960 and before 1968 for purposes of paragraph (a)(2)(ii) and after 1967 for purposes of paragraph (a)(2)(iii) shall be services not in the course of the employer's trade or business or shall be domestic service in a private home of the employer. The terms "services not in the course of the employer's trade or business" and "domestic service in a private home of the employer" have the same meaning as when used in §31.3121(a)(7)-1, except that it is immaterial under paragraphs (a)(2)(ii) and (iii) of this section whether or not such services are performed on a farm operated for profit. The mere fact that a mental or physical disability, whether temporary or permanent, renders a child or spouse incapable of self-support does not necessarily mean that the child requires the personal care and supervision of an adult or that the spouse is incapable of caring for a child within the meaning of paragraph (a)(2)(iii) of this section. A written statement by a doctor of the existence of the mental or physical condition of the child or spouse which states that the child requires the personal care and supervision of an adult or that the spouse is incapable of caring for a child and which sets forth the period of time during which the condition has existed and is likely to exist will usually be sufficient evidence to establish the existence and duration of the condition at the time of the statement. Under paragraph (a)(3) of this section, in addition to the family relationship, there is a further requirement that the son or daughter shall be under the age of 21, and the exception continues only during the time that the son or daughter is under the age of 21.

(c) Services performed in the employ of a partnership are within the exception described in paragraph (a) of this section only if the requisite family relationship exists between the employee and each of the partners comprising the partnership.

(d) Services performed in the employ of a corporation are not within the exception described in paragraph (a) of this section, except that services performed in the employ of an entity that is treated as a corporation under §301.7701-2(c)(2)(iv)(B) of this chapter may qualify for the exception if the requirements of the exception are otherwise met. An entity that is treated as a corporation under §301.7701-2(c)(2)(iv)(B) of this chapter is not treated as the employer for purposes of applying section 3121(b)(3) and this section. For purposes of applying section 3121(b)(3) and this section, the owner of an entity that is treated as a corporation under §301.7701-2(c)(2)(iv)(B) of this chapter is treated as the employer.

(e) Paragraphs (c) and (d) of this section apply to wages paid on or after November 1, 2011. However, taxpayers may apply paragraphs (c) and (d) of this section to wages paid on or after January 1, 2009. [Reg. §31.3121(b)(3)-1.]

□ [*T.D. 6190, 7-14-56. Republished in T.D. 6516, 12-20-60. Amended by T.D. 6744, 7-2-64; T.D. 7374, 7-24-75, T.D. 9554, 10-31-2011 and T.D. 9670, 6-25-2014.*]

### [Reg. §31.3121(b)(4)-1]

**§31.3121(b)(4)-1. Services performed on or in connection with a non-American vessel or aircraft.**—(a) Services performed within the United States by an employee for an employer "on or in connection with" a vessel not an American vessel, or "on or in connection with" an aircraft not an American aircraft, are excepted from employment if—

(1) The employee is employed by such employer "on and in connection with" such vessel or aircraft when outside the United States, and

(2)(i) The employee is not a citizen of the United States, or (ii) the employer is not an American employer.

(b) An employee performs services on and in connection with the vessel or aircraft if he performs services on the vessel or aircraft when outside the United States which are also in connection with the vessel or aircraft. Services performed on the vessel outside the United States by employees as officers or members of the crew, or by employees of concessionaires, of the vessel, for example, are performed under such circumstances, since such services are also connected with the vessel. Similarly, services performed on the aircraft outside the United States by employees as officers or members of the crew of the aircraft are performed on and in connection with such aircraft. Services may be performed on the vessel or aircraft, however, which have no connection with it, as in the case of services performed by an employee while on the vessel or aircraft merely as a passenger in the general sense. For example, the services of a buyer in the employ of a department store while he is a passenger on a vessel are not in connection with the vessel.

(c) The expression "on or in connection with" refers not only to services performed on the vessel or aircraft but also to services connected with the vessel or aircraft which are not actually performed on it (for example, shore services performed as officers or members of the crew, or as employees of concessionaires, of the vessel).

(d) Services performed within the United States on or in connection with a non-American vessel or aircraft for an employer by an employee who is not a citizen of the United States are excepted from employment, irrespective of whether the employer is or is not an American employer, provided the employee also is employed by such employer on and in connection with the vessel or aircraft when outside the United States. Services performed within the United States on or in connection with a non-American vessel or aircraft by an employee for an employer who is not an American employer also are excepted from employment, irrespective of whether the employee is or is not a citizen of the United States, provided the employee also is employed by such employer on and in connection with the vessel or aircraft when outside the United States. Services performed within the United States on or in connection with a non-American vessel or aircraft for an American employer by an employee who is a citizen of the United States are not excepted from employment under section 3121(b)(4), irrespective of whether the employee is employed by such employer on and in connection with the vessel or aircraft when outside the United States. Further, section 3121(b)(4) does not except from employment services performed within the United States for an employer, whether or not an American employer, on or in connection with a non-American vessel or aircraft by an employee, whether or not a citizen of the United States, who is not also employed by such employer on and in connection with the vessel or aircraft when outside the United States.

(e) Services performed outside the United States on or in connection with a vessel not an American vessel, or on or in connection with an aircraft not an American aircraft, by a citizen of the United States as an employee for an American employer are not excepted from employment under section 3121(b)(4), irrespective of whether the employee is employed on and in connection with such vessel or aircraft when outside the United States. Services performed outside the United States on or in connection with a vessel not an American vessel or on or in connection with an aircraft not an American aircraft, either by an employee who is not a citizen of the United States or for an employer who is not an American employer, do not, in any event, constitute employment. See paragraph (c) of §31.3121(b)-3, relating to services performed outside the United States which constitute employment.

(f) See paragraph (c)(2)(v) of §31.3121(b)-3 for definitions of "vessel" and "aircraft," §31.3121(f)-1, for definitions of "American vessel" and "American aircraft," §31.3121(e)-1, for definition of "citizen of the United States," and §31.3121(h)-1, for definition of "American employer." [Reg. §31.3121(b)(4)-1.]

☐ *T.D. 6190, 7-14-56. Republished in T.D. 6516, 12-20-60.*

### [Reg. § 31.3121(b)(5)-1]

**§ 31.3121(b)(5)-1. Services in employ of an instrumentality of the United States specifically exempted from the employer.**—Services performed in the employ of an instrumentality of the United States are excepted from employment if such instrumentality is exempt from the employer tax imposed by section 3111 by virtue of any other provision of law which specifically refers to such section 3111 or the corresponding section of prior law (section 1410 of the Internal Revenue Code of 1939) in granting exemption from the employer tax. This exception does not operate to exclude from employment services performed in the employ of an instrumentality of the United States unless the Congress has granted to such instrumentality a specific exemption from the tax imposed by section 3111 or the corresponding section of prior law. For provisions which make general exemptions from Federal taxation ineffectual as to the employer tax imposed by section 3111, see § 31.3112-1. For other exceptions from employment applicable with respect to services performed in the employ of an instrumentality of the United States, see § 31.3121(b)(6)-1.

The IRS has revoked, effective July 1, 1992, previously issued but unidentified letter rulings under which an exempt organization did not have to pay the employer's portion of the FICA tax imposed by Code Sec. 3111. The IRS applied this revocation prospectively after finding that: (1) there was no misstatement or omission of material facts by the organization; (2) any differences between the facts now and the facts on which the rulings were based were not material; (3) while there has been a change in applicable law, that change did not impact upon the tax at issue here; (4) that ruling was issued in connection with an ongoing transaction; and (5) the organization reasonably relied on the rulings, and retroactive revocation would be to the taxpayer's detriment. [Reg. § 31.3121(b)(5)-1.]

☐ *T.D. 6190, 7-14-56. Republished in T.D. 6516, 12-20-60.*

### [Reg. § 31.3121(b)(6)-1]

**§ 31.3121(b)(6)-1. Services in employ of United States or instrumentality thereof.**—(a) *In general.*—This section relates to services performed in the employ of the United States Government or in the employ of an instrumentality of the United States. Particular services which are not excepted from employment under one rule set forth in this section may nevertheless be excepted under another rule set forth in this section or under § 31.3121(b)(5)-1, relating to services in the employ of an instrumentality of the United States specifically exempted from the employer tax. Moreover, services performed in the employ of the United States or of any instrumentality thereof which are not excepted from employment under paragraph (5) or (6) of section 3121(b) may nevertheless be excepted under some other paragraph of such section. For provisions relating generally to the application of the taxes in the case of services performed in the employ of the United States or a wholly owned instrumentality thereof, see § 31.3122. For provisions relating to the computation of remuneration for service performed by an individual as a member of a uniformed service or for service performed by an individual as a volunteer or volunteer leader within the meaning of the Peace Corps Act, see § 31.3121(i)-2 and § 31.3121(i)-3, respectively.

(b) *Services covered under a retirement system established by a law of the United States.*—Services performed in the employ of the United States or in the employ of any instrumentality thereof are excepted from employment under section 3121(b)(6)(A) if such services are covered under a law enacted by the Congress of the United States which specifically provides for the establishment of a retirement system for employees of the United States or of such instrumentality. Determinations as to whether services are covered by a retirement system of the requisite character are to be made as of the time such services are performed. Services of an employee who has an option to have his services covered under a retirement system are not covered under such retirement system unless and until he exercises such option. The test is whether particular services performed by an employee are covered by a retirement system of the requisite character rather than whether the position in which such services are performed is covered by such retirement system.

(c) *Services performed for an instrumentality not subject to employer tax on December 31, 1950, and covered under a retirement system established by such instrumentality.*—(1) Subject to the provisions of subparagraph (4) of this paragraph, services performed in the employ of an instrumentality of the United States are excepted from employment under section 3121(b)(6)(B) if—

(i) The particular instrumentality was not subject on December 31, 1950, to the employer tax imposed by section 1410 of the Internal Revenue Code of 1939, and

(ii) The services are covered by a retirement system established by such instrumentality.

(2) If the particular instrumentality was not in existence on December 31, 1950, but is created thereafter under a law which was in effect on December 31, 1950, services performed in the employ of such instrumentality are excepted from employment (unless otherwise provided in subparagraph (c)(4) of this paragraph) if—

(i) The instrumentality had it been in existence on December 31, 1950, would not have been subject on that date to the employer tax imposed by section 1410 of the Internal Revenue Code of 1939, and

(ii) The services are covered by a retirement system established by such instrumentality.—It is immaterial, for purposes of this exception, whether the exemption from the employer tax on December 31, 1950, resulted, or would have resulted, from a tax exemption as such in effect on December 31, 1950, or from the provisions of section 1426(b)(6) of the Internal Revenue Code of 1939 in effect on that date, relating to the exception from employment of services performed in the employ of certain instrumentalities of the United States.

(3) Determinations as to whether services performed in the employ of an instrumentality referred to in subparagraph (1) or (2) of this paragraph are covered by a retirement system established by such instrumentality are to be made as of the time such services are performed. Services of an employee who has an option to have his services covered under a retirement system established by the instrumentality are not covered under such retirement system unless and until he exercises such option. The test is whether particular services performed by an employee are covered by a retirement system established by the instrumentality rather than whether the position in which such services are performed is covered by such retirement system.

(4) The exception from employment provided in section 3121(b)(6)(B) has no application with respect to any of the following classes of services:

(i) Services performed in the employ of a corporation which is wholly owned by the United States;

(ii) Services performed in the employ of a production credit association, a Federal Reserve Bank, or a Federal Credit Union; services performed before December 31, 1959, in the employ of a national farm loan association; services performed after December 30, 1959, in the employ of a Federal land bank association; and services performed after December 31, 1959, in the employ of a Federal land bank, a Federal intermediate credit bank, or a bank for cooperatives; services performed after December 31, 1972, in the employ of a Federal home loan bank; and services performed after December 31, 1966, and before January 1, 1973, in the employ of a Federal home loan bank, in the case of individuals who are in such employ on the latter date, provided that an amount equal to the taxes imposed by sections 3101 and 3111 with respect to all such services performed by all such individuals are paid under the provisions of section 3122 by July 1, 1973;

(iii) Services performed in the employ of a State, county, or community committee under the Commodity Stabilization Service;

(iv) Services performed by a civilian employee, not compensated from funds appropriated by the Congress, in the Army and Air Force Exchange Service, Army and Air Force Motion Picture Service, Navy Exchanges, Marine Corps Exchanges, or other activities, conducted by an instrumentality of the United States subject to the jurisdiction of the Secretary of Defense, at installations of the Department of Defense for the comfort, pleasure, contentment, and mental and physical improvement of personnel of such Department, or

(v) Services performed by a civilian employee, not compensated from funds appropriated by the Congress, in the Coast Guard Exchanges or other activities, conducted by an instrumentality of the United States subject to the jurisdiction of the Secretary of the Treasury, at installations of the Coast Guard for the comfort, pleasure, contentment, and mental and physical improvement of personnel of the Coast Guard.

(d) *Special classes of services.*—The following classes of services performed either in the employ of the United States or in the employ of any instrumentality thereof are excepted from employment under section 3121(b)(6)(C):

(1) Services performed as the President or Vice President of the United States or as a Member, Delegate, or Resident Commissioner, of or to the Congress of the United States;

(2) Services performed in the legislative branch of the United States Government;

(3) Services performed in a penal institution of the United States by an inmate thereof;

(4)(i) Except as provided in subdivision (ii) of this subparagraph, services performed by student nurses, medical or dental interns, residents in training, student dietitians, student physical therapists, or student occupational therapists, assigned or attached to a hospital, clinic, or medical or dental laboratory operated by any department, agency, or instrumentality of the United States Government, or by certain other student employees described in section 5351(2) of title 5, United States Code.

(ii) The provisions of subdivision (i) of this subparagraph have no application to services performed after 1965 by medical or dental interns or by medical or dental residents in training.

(5) Services performed by an individual as an employee serving on a temporary basis in case of fire, storm, earthquake, flood, or other similar emergency; and

(6)(i) Except as provided in subdivision (ii) of this subparagraph, services performed by an individual to whom subchapter III of chapter 83 of title 5, United States Code (civil service retirement) does not apply because he is, with respect to such services, subject to another retirement system, established either by a law of the United States or by the agency or instrumentality of the United States for which such services are performed.

(ii) The provisions of subdivision (i) of this subparagraph have no application to service performed by an individual to whom subchapter III of chapter 83 of title 5, United States Code (civil service retirement) does not apply because such individual is subject to the retirement system of the Tennessee Valley Authority, if such service is subject to the plan approved by the Secretary of Health, Education, and Welfare on December 28, 1956, pursuant to section 104(i)(2) of the Social Security Amendments of 1956 (70 Stat. 827). See section 201(m)(4) of such Amendments for provisions relating to the timeliness of payment of tax with respect to remuneration paid before 1957 for such services, and barring the imposition of interest on the amount of any such tax due for any period before December 28, 1956. [Reg. § 31.3121(b)(6)-1.]

☐ *T.D. 6190, 7-14-56. Republished in T.D. 6516, 12-20-60. Amended by T.D. 6744, 7-2-64, T.D. 6983, 12-4-68, and T.D. 7373, 7-24-75.*

### [Reg. § 31.3121(b)(7)-1]

**§ 31.3121(b)(7)-1. Services in employ of States or their political subdivisions or instrumentalities.**—(a) *In general.*—Except as provided in other paragraphs of this section, services performed in the employ of any State, any political subdivision of a State, or any instrumentality of one or more States or political subdivisions thereof which is wholly owned by one or more States or political subdivisions are excepted from employment. For the definition of the term "State," as used in this section, see § 31.3121(e)-1.

(b) *Covered transportation service.*—The exception from employment under section 3121(b)(7) does not apply to covered transportation service as defined in section 3121(j). See §§ 31.3121(j) and 31.3121(j)-1.

(c) *Government of American Samoa.*—The exception from employment under section 3121(b)(7) does not apply to services performed after 1960 in the employ of the Government of American Samoa, any political subdivision thereof, or any instrumentality of such Government or political subdivision, or combination thereof, which is wholly owned thereby, performed by an officer or employee thereof (including a member of the legislature of such Government or political subdivision).

(d) *District of Columbia.*—The exception from employment under section 3121(b)(7) does not apply to services performed after September 30, 1965, in the employ of the District of Columbia or any instrumentality which is wholly owned thereby, if such service is not covered by a retirement system established by a law of the United States. Notwithstanding the preceding sentence the following classes of services performed either in the employ of the District of Columbia or in the employ of any instrumentality which is wholly owned thereby are excepted from employment:

(1) Services performed in a hospital or penal institution by a patient or inmate thereof.

(2) Services performed by student nurses, student dietitians, student physical therapists, or student occupational therapists assigned or attached to a hospital, clinic, or medical or dental laboratory operated by the District of Columbia or by any wholly owned instrumentality thereof, or by certain other student employees described in section 5351(2) of title 5, United States Code. This subparagraph does not apply to services performed by medical or dental interns or by medical or dental residents in training described in such section 5351(2).

(3) Services performed by an individual as an employee serving on a temporary basis in case of fire, storm, snow, earthquake, flood, or other similar emergency.

(4) Services performed by a member of a board, committee, or council of the District of Columbia, paid on a per diem, meeting, or other fee basis.

(e) *Government of Guam.*—The exception from employment under section 3121(b)(7) does not apply to services performed after 1972 in the employ of the Government of Guam or any instrumentality which is wholly owned thereby, by an employee properly classified as a temporary or intermittent employee, if such service is not covered by a retirement system established by a law of Guam. The preceding sentence shall not apply to the services performed by an elected official or a member of the legislature or in a hospital or penal institution by a patient or inmate thereof. For purposes of this paragraph—

(1) Any person whose services as an officer or employee of such Government or instrumentality are not covered by a retirement system established by a law of the United States shall not, with respect to such service, be regarded as an employee of the United States or any agency or instrumentality thereof, and

(2) The remuneration for services described in subparagraph (1) (including fees paid to a public official) shall be deemed to have been paid by such Government or instrumentality. [Reg. § 31.3121(b)(7)-1.]

☐ *T.D. 6190, 7-14-56. Republished in T.D. 6516, 12-20-60. Amended by T.D. 6744, 7-2-64, T.D. 6983, 12-4-68, and T.D. 7373, 7-24-75.*

### [Reg. § 31.3121(b)(7)-2]

**§ 31.3121(b)(7)-2. Service by employees who are not members of a public retirement system.**—(a) *Table of contents.*—This paragraph contains a listing of the major headings of this section 31.3121(b)(7)-2.

*§ 31.3121(b)(7)-2 Service by employees who are not members of a public retirement system.*

  (a) Table of contents.
  (b) Introduction.
  (c) General rule.
    (1) Inclusion in employment of service by employees who are not members of a retirement system.
    (2) Treatment of individuals employed in more than one position.
  (d) Definition of qualified participant.
    (1) General rule.
    (2) Special rule for part-time, seasonal and temporary employees.
    (3) Alternative lookback rule.
    (4) Treatment of former participants.
  (e) Definition of retirement system.
    (1) Requirement that system provide retirement-type benefits.
    (2) Requirement that system provide minimum level of benefits.
  (f) Transition rules.
    (1) Application of qualified participant rules during 1991.
    (2) Additional transition rules for plans in existence on November 5, 1990.

(b) *Introduction.*—Under section 3121(b)(7)(F), wages of an employee of a State or local government are generally subject to tax under FICA after July 1, 1991, unless the employee is a member of a retirement system maintained by the State or local government entity. This section 31.3121(b)(7)-2 provides rules for determining whether an employee is a "member of a retirement system". These rules generally treat an employee as a member of a retirement system if he or she participates in a system that provides retirement benefits, and has an accrued benefit or receives an allocation under the system that is comparable to the benefits he or she would have or receive under Social Security. In the case of part-time, seasonal and temporary employees, this minimum retirement benefit is required to be nonforfeitable.

(c) *General rule.*—(1) *Inclusion in employment of service by employees who are not members of a retirement system.*—Except in the case of service described in section 3121(b)(7)(F)(i) through (v), the exception from employment under section 3121(b)(7) does not apply to service in the employ of a State or any political subdivision thereof, or of any instrumentality of one or more of the foregoing that is wholly owned thereby, after July 1, 1991, unless the employee is a member of a retirement system of such State, political subdivision or instrumentality at the time the service is performed. An employee is not a member of a retirement system at the time service is performed unless at that time he or she is a qualified participant (as defined in paragraph (d) of this section) in a retirement system that meets the requirements of paragraph (e) of this section with respect to that employee.

(2) *Treatment of individuals employed in more than one position.*—Under section 3121(b)(7)(F), whether an employee is a member of a retirement system is determined on an entity-by-entity rather than a position-by-position basis. Thus, if an employee is a member of a retirement system with respect to service he or she performs in one position in the employ of a State, political subdivision or instrumentality thereof, the employee is generally treated as a member of a

retirement system with respect to all service performed for the same State, political subdivision or instrumentality in any other positions. A State is a separate entity from its political subdivisions, and an instrumentality is a separate entity from the State or political subdivision by which it is owned for purposes of this rule. See paragraph (e)(2) of this section, however, for rules relating to service and compensation required to be taken into account in determining whether an employee is a member of a retirement system for purposes of this section. This rule is illustrated by the following examples:

*Example (1).* An individual is employed full-time by a county and is a qualified participant (as defined in paragraph (d) of this section) in its retirement plan with regard to such employment. In addition to this full-time employment, the individual is employed part-time in another position with the same county. The part-time position is not covered by the county retirement plan, however, and neither the service nor the compensation in the part-time position is considered in determining the employee's retirement benefit under the county retirement plan. Nevertheless, if the retirement plan meets the requirements of paragraph (e) of this section with respect to the individual, the exclusion from employment under section 3121(b)(7) applies to both the employee's full-time and part-time service with the county.

*Example (2).* An individual is employed full-time by a State and is a member of its retirement plan. The individual is also employed part-time by a city located in the State, but does not participate in the city's retirement plan. The services of the individual for the city are not excluded from employment under section 3121(b)(7), because the determination of whether services constitute employment for such purposes is made separately with respect to each political subdivision for which services are performed.

(d) *Definition of qualified participant.*—(1) *General rule.*—(i) *Defined benefit retirement systems.*—Whether an employee is a qualified participant in a defined benefit retirement system is determined as services are performed. An employee is a qualified participant in a defined benefit retirement system (within the meaning of paragraph (e)(1) of this section) with respect to services performed on a given day if, on that day, he or she is or ever has been an actual participant in the retirement system and, on that day, he or she actually has a total accrued benefit under the retirement system that meets the minimum retirement benefit requirement of paragraph (e)(2) of this section. An employee may not be treated as an actual participant or as actually having an accrued benefit for this purpose to the extent that such participation or benefit is subject to any conditions (other than vesting), such as a requirement that the employee attain a minimum age, perform a minimum period of service, make an election in order to participate, or be present at the end of the plan year in order to be credited with an accrual, that have not been satisfied. The rules of this paragraph (d)(1)(i) are illustrated by the following examples:

*Example (1).* A State maintains a defined benefit plan that is a retirement system within the meaning of paragraph (e)(1) of this section. Under the terms of the plan, employees in positions covered by the plan must complete 6 months of service before becoming participants. The exception from employment in section 3121(b)(7) does not apply to services of an employee during the employee's 6 months of service prior to his or her initial entry into the plan. The same result occurs even if, upon the satisfaction of this service requirement, the employee is given credit under the plan for all service with the employer (i.e., if service is credited for the 6-month waiting period). This is true even if the employee makes a required contribution in order to gain the retroactive credit. The same result also occurs if the employee can elect to participate in the plan before the end of the 6-month waiting period, but does not elect to do so.

*Example (2).* A political subdivision maintains a defined benefit plan that is a retirement system within the meaning of paragraph (e)(1) of this section. Under the terms of the plan, service during a plan year is not credited for accrual purposes unless a participant has at least 1,000 hours of service during the year. Benefits that accrue only upon satisfaction of this 1,000-hour requirement may not be taken into account in determining whether an employee is a qualified participant in the plan before the 1,000-hour requirement is satisfied.

(ii) *Defined contribution retirement systems.*—Whether an employee is a qualified participant in a defined contribution retirement system is determined as services are performed. An employee is a qualified participant in a defined contribution or other individual account retirement system (within the meaning of paragraph (e)(1) of this section) with respect to services performed on a given day if, on that day, he or she has satisfied all conditions (other than vesting) for receiving an allocation to his or her account (exclusive of earnings) that meets the minimum retirement benefit requirement of paragraph (e)(2) of this section with respect to compensation during any period ending on that day and beginning on or after the beginning of the

plan year of the retirement system. This is the case regardless of whether the allocations were made or accrued before the effective date of section 3121(b)(7)(F). This rule is illustrated by the following examples:

*Example (1).* A State-owned hospital maintains a nonelective defined contribution plan that is a retirement system within the meaning of paragraph (e)(1) of this section. Under the terms of the plan, employees must be employed on the last day of a plan year in order to receive any allocation for the year. Employees may not be treated as qualified participants in the plan before the last day of the year.

*Example (2).* Assume the same facts as in *Example (1)* except that, under the terms of the plan, an employee who terminates service before the end of a plan year receives a pro rata portion of the allocation he or she would have received at the end of the year, e.g., based on compensation earned since the beginning of the plan year. If the pro rata allocation available on a given day would meet the minimum retirement benefit requirement of paragraph (e)(2) of this section with respect to compensation from the beginning of the plan year through that day (or some later day), employees are treated as qualified participants in the plan on that day.

*Example (3).* A political subdivision maintains an elective defined contribution plan that is a retirement system within the meaning of paragraph (e)(1) of this section. The plan has a calendar year plan year and two open seasons—in December and June—when employees can change their contribution elections. In December, an employee elects not to contribute to the plan. In June, the employee elects (beginning July 1) to contribute a uniform percentage of compensation for each pay period to the plan for the remainder of the plan year. The employee is not a qualified participant in the plan during the period January-June, because no allocations are made to the employee's account with respect to compensation during that time, and it is not certain at that time that any allocations will be made. If the level of contributions during the period July-December meets the minimum retirement benefit requirement of paragraph (e)(2) of this section with respect to compensation during that period, however, the employee is treated as a qualified participant during that period.

*Example (4).* Assume the same facts as in *Example (3),* except that the plan allows participants to cancel their elections in cases of economic hardship. In October, the employee suffers an economic hardship and cancels the election (effective November 1). If the contributions during the period July-October are high enough to meet the minimum retirement benefit requirement of paragraph (e)(2) of this section with respect to compensation during that period, the employee is treated as a qualified participant during that period. In addition, if the contributions during the period July-October are high enough to meet the requirements for the entire period July-December, the employee is treated as a qualified participant in the plan throughout the period July-December, even though no allocations are made to the employee's account in the last two months of the year. There is no requirement that the period used to determine whether an employee is a qualified participant on a given day remain the same from day to day, as long as the period begins on or after the beginning of the plan year and ends on the date the determination is being made.

(2) *Special rule for part-time, seasonal and temporary employees.*—(i) *In general.*—A part-time, seasonal or temporary employee is generally not a qualified participant on a given day unless any benefit relied upon to meet the requirements of paragraph (d)(1) of this section is 100-percent nonforfeitable on that day. This requirement may be applied solely to the portion of an employee's benefit under the retirement system attributable to compensation and service while an employee is a part-time, seasonal or temporary employee, provided that such service is taken into account with respect to the remaining portion of the benefit for vesting purposes. Rules similar to the rules in section 411(a)(11) are applicable in determining whether a benefit is nonforfeitable. Thus, a benefit does not fail to be nonforfeitable solely because it can be immediately distributed upon separation of service without the consent of the employee, provided that the present value of the benefit does not exceed the cash-out limit in effect under § 1.411(a)-11(c)(3)(ii) of this chapter.

(ii) *Treatment of employees entitled to certain distributions upon death or separation from service.*—A part-time, seasonal or temporary employee's benefit under a retirement system is considered nonforfeitable within the meaning of paragraph (d)(2)(i) of this section on a given day if on that day the employee is unconditionally entitled under the retirement system to a single-sum distribution on account of death or separation from service of an amount that is at least equal to 7.5 percent of the participant's compensation (within the meaning of paragraph (e)(2)(iii)(B) of this section) for all periods of credited service taken into account in determining whether the employee's benefit under the retirement system meets the minimum retirement benefit requirement of paragraph (e)(2) of this section. An employee will be considered to be unconditionally entitled to a single-sum distribution notwithstanding the fact that the distribution may be forfeitable (in whole or in part) upon a finding of such employee's criminal misconduct. The participant must be entitled to interest on the distributable amount through the date of distribution, at a rate meeting the requirements of paragraph (e)(2)(iii)(C) of this section, as part of the single sum. See paragraph (f)(2)(i)(C) for a transition rule relating to this nonforfeitable benefit safe harbor. The rule of this paragraph (d)(2)(ii) is illustrated by the following example:

*Example.* An employee is required to contribute 7.5 percent of his or her compensation to a State's defined benefit plan each year. The contribution is "picked up" by the employer in accordance with section 414(h). Under the plan, these amounts plus interest accrued since the date each amount was contributed are refundable to the employee in all cases upon the employee's death or separation from service with the employer. If the interest rate meets the requirements of paragraph (e)(2)(iii)(C) of this section, then the employee's benefits under the plan are considered nonforfeitable and thus meet the requirement of paragraph (d)(2)(i) of this section. Of course, the benefit under the plan must still meet the minimum retirement benefit requirement for defined benefit plans of paragraph (e)(2)(ii) of this section.

(iii) *Definitions of part-time, seasonal and temporary employee.*—(A) *Definition of part-time employee.*—For purposes of this section, a part-time employee is any employee who normally works 20 hours or less per week. A teacher employed by a post-secondary educational institution (e.g., a community or junior college, post-secondary vocational school, college, university or graduate school) is not considered a part-time employee for purposes of this section if he or she normally has classroom hours of one-half or more of the number of classroom hours designated by the educational institution as constituting full-time employment, provided that such designation is reasonable under all the facts and circumstances. In addition, elected officials and election workers (otherwise described in section 3121(b)(7)(F)(iv) but paid in excess of $100 annually) are not considered part-time, seasonal or temporary employees for purposes of this section. The rules of this paragraph (d)(2)(iii) are illustrated by the following example:

*Example.* A community college treats a teacher as a full-time employee if the teacher is assigned to work 15 classroom hours per week. A new teacher is assigned to work 8 classroom hours per week. Because the assigned classroom hours of the teacher are at least one-half of the school's definition of full-time teacher, the teacher is not a part-time employee.

(B) *Definition of seasonal employee.*—For purposes of this section, a seasonal employee is any employee who normally works on a full-time basis less than 5 months in a year. Thus, for example, individuals who are hired by a political subdivision during the tax return season in order to process incoming returns and work full-time over a 3-month period are seasonal employees.

(C) *Definition of temporary employee.*—For purposes of this section, a temporary employee is any employee performing services under a contractual arrangement with the employer of 2 years or less duration. Possible contract extensions may be considered in determining the duration of a contractual arrangement, but only if, under the facts and circumstances, there is a significant likelihood that the employee's contract will be extended. Future contract extensions are considered significantly likely to occur for purposes of this rule if on average 80 percent of similarly situated employees (i.e., those in the same or a similar job classification with expiring employment contracts) have had bona fide offers to renew their contracts in the immediately preceding 2 academic or calendar years. In addition, future contract extensions are considered significantly likely to occur if the employee with respect to whom the determination is being made has a history of contract extensions with respect to his or her current position. An employee is not considered a temporary employee for purposes of this rule solely because he or she is included in a unit of employees covered by a collective bargaining agreement of 2 years or less duration.

(D) *Treatment of employees participating in certain systems.*—Whether an employee is a part-time, seasonal or temporary employee with respect to allocations or benefits under a retirement system is generally determined based on service in the position in which the allocations or benefits were earned, and does not take into account service in other positions with the same or different States, political subdivisions or instrumentalities thereof. All of an employee's service in other positions with the same or different States, political subdivisions or instrumentalities thereof may be taken into account for purposes of determining whether an employee is a part-time, seasonal or temporary employee with respect to benefits under the retirement system, however, provided that: the employee's ser-

vice in the other positions is or was covered by the retirement system; all service aggregated for purposes of determining whether an employee is a part-time, seasonal or temporary employee (and related compensation) is aggregated under the system for all purposes in determining benefits (including vesting); and the employee is treated at least as favorably as a full-time employee under the retirement system for benefit accrual purposes. The rule of this paragraph (d)(2)(iii)(D) is illustrated by the following example:

*Example.* Assume that an employee works 15 hours per week for a county and 10 hours per week for a municipality, and that both of these political subdivisions contribute to the same state-wide public employee retirement system. Assume further that the employee's service in both positions is aggregated under the system for all purposes in determining benefits (including vesting). If the employee is covered under the retirement system with respect to both positions and is treated for benefit accrual purposes at least as favorably as full-time employees under the retirement system, then the employee is not considered a part-time employee of either the county or the municipality for purposes of the nonforfeitable benefit requirement of paragraph (d)(2)(i) of this section.

(3) *Alternative lookback rule.*—(i) *In general.*—An employee may be treated as a qualified participant in a retirement system throughout a calendar year if he or she was a qualified participant in such system (within the meaning of paragraphs (d)(1) and (2) of this section) at the end of the plan year of the system ending in the previous calendar year. This rule is illustrated by the following examples:

*Example 1.* A political subdivision maintains a plan that is a retirement system within the meaning of paragraph (e)(1) of this section. An employee is a qualified participant within the meaning of paragraph (d)(1) of this section in the plan on the last day of the plan year ending on May 31, 1995. If the alternative lookback rule is used to determine FICA liability, no such liability exists with respect to the employee or employer for calendar year 1996 by reason of section 3121(b)(7)(F). The same result would apply if the determination is being made with respect to calendar year 1992 and the lookback year was the plan year ending May 31, 1991, even though that plan year ended before the effective date of section 3121(b)(7)(F).

*Example 2.* A political subdivision maintains an elective defined contribution plan described in section 457(b) of the Code. An employee is eligible to participate in the plan but does not elect to contribute for a plan year. Under the general rule of paragraph (d)(1) of this section, the employee is not a qualified participant in the plan during the plan year because contributions sufficient to meet the minimum retirement benefit requirement of paragraph (e)(2) of this section are not being made. However, if an employee's status as a qualified participant is being determined under the alternative lookback rule, then the employee is a qualified participant for the calendar year in which the determination is being made if he or she was a qualified participant as of the end of the plan year that ended in the previous calendar year.

(ii) *Application in first year of participation.*—If the alternative lookback rule is used, an employee who participates in the retirement system may be treated as a qualified participant on any given day during his or her first plan year of participation in a retirement system (within the meaning of paragraph (e)(1) of this section) if and only if it is reasonable on such day to believe that the employee will be a qualified participant (within the meaning of paragraphs (d)(1) and (2) of this section) on the last day of such plan year. In the case of a defined contribution retirement system, the determination of whether the employee is actually (or is expected to be) a qualified participant at the end of the plan year must take into account all compensation since the commencement of participation. See paragraph (d)(3)(iv) of this section. If this reasonable belief is correct, and the employee is a qualified participant on the last day of his or her first plan year of participation, then the exception from employment in section 3121(b)(7) will apply without regard to section 3121(b)(7)(F) to services of the employee for the balance of the calendar year in which the plan year ends. For purposes of this paragraph (d)(3)(ii), it is not reasonable to assume the establishment of a new plan until such establishment actually occurs. In addition, the rule in this paragraph (d)(3)(ii) may not be used to treat an employee as a qualified participant until the employee actually becomes a participant in the retirement system. In the case of a retirement system that does not permit a new employee to participate until the first day of the first month beginning after the employee's commencement of service, or some earlier date, a new employee who is not a part-time, seasonal or temporary employee may be treated as a qualified participant until such date. This 1-month rule of administrative convenience applies without regard to whether the employer has a reasonable belief that the employee will be a qualified participant. The rules of this paragraph (d)(3)(ii) are illustrated by the following examples:

*Example 1.* A political subdivision maintains a plan that is a retirement system within the meaning of paragraph (e)(1) of this section and uses the alternative lookback rule of this paragraph (d)(3). Under the terms of the plan, service during a plan year is not credited for accrual purposes unless a participant has at least 1,000 hours of service during the year. Assume that an employee becomes a participant. If it is reasonable to believe that the employee will be credited with 1,000 hours of service by the last day of his or her first year of participation and thereby become a qualified participant by reason of accruing a benefit that meets the minimum retirement benefit requirement of paragraph (e)(2) of this section, the services of the employee are not subject to FICA tax from the date of initial participation until the end of that plan year. If the employee is a qualified participant on the last day of his or her first plan year of participation, then the exception from employment for purposes of FICA will apply to services of the employee for the balance of the calendar year in which the plan year ended.

*Example 2.* Assume the same facts as *Example 1,* except that the employee is a newly hired employee and the plan provides that an employee may not participate until the first day of his or her first full month of employment. Under the 1-month rule of convenience, the employee may be treated as a qualified participant until the first date on which he or she could participate in the plan.

(iii) *Application in last year of participation.*—If the alternative lookback rule is used, an employee may be treated as a qualified participant on any given day during his or her last year of participation in a retirement system (within the meaning of paragraph (e)(1) of this section) if and only if it is reasonable to believe on such day that the employee will be a qualified participant (within the meaning of paragraphs (d)(1) and (2) of this section) on his or her last day of participation. For purposes of this paragraph (d)(3)(iii), an employee's last year of participation means the plan year that the employer reasonably ascertains is the final year of such employee's participation (e.g., where the employee has a scheduled retirement date or where the employer intends to terminate the plan).

(iv) *Special rule for defined contribution retirement systems.*—An employee may not be treated as a qualified participant in a defined contribution retirement system under this paragraph (d)(3) if compensation for less than a full plan year or other 12-month period is regularly taken into account in determining allocations to the employee's account for the plan year unless, under all of the facts and circumstances, such arrangement is not a device to avoid the imposition of FICA taxes. For example, an arrangement under which compensation taken into account is limited to the contribution base described in section 3121(x)(1) is not considered a device to avoid FICA taxes by reason of such limitation. See paragraph (e)(2)(iii)(B) of this section for a rule permitting the use of such limitation. This rule is illustrated by the following example:

*Example.* A political subdivision maintains a defined contribution plan that covers all of its full-time employees and is a retirement system within the meaning of paragraph (e)(1) of this section. Under the plan, a portion of each participant's compensation in the final month of every plan year is allocated to the participant's account. Employees covered under the plan generally may not be treated as qualified participants under the alternative lookback rule for any portion of the calendar year following the year in which such allocation is made.

(v) *Consistency requirement.*—Beginning with calendar year 1992, if the alternative lookback rule is used to determine whether an employee is a qualified participant, it must be used consistently from year to year and with respect to all employees of the State, political subdivision or instrumentality thereof making the determination. If a retirement system is sponsored by more than one State, political subdivision or instrumentality, this consistency requirement applies separately to each plan sponsor.

(4) *Treatment of former participants.*—(i) *In general.*—In general, the rules of this paragraph (d) apply equally to former participants who continue to perform service for the same State, political subdivision or instrumentality thereof or who return after a break in service. Thus, for example, a former employee of a political subdivision with a deferred benefit under a defined benefit retirement system maintained by the political subdivision who is reemployed by the political subdivision but does not resume participation in the retirement system, may continue to be a qualified participant in the system after becoming reemployed if his or her total accrued benefit under the system meets the minimum retirement benefit requirement of paragraph (e)(2) of this section (taking into account all periods of service (including current service) required to be taken into account under that paragraph). See also paragraph (e)(2)(v) of this section for situations in which benefits under a retirement system may be taken into account even though they relate to service for another employer.

(ii) *Treatment of re-hired annuitants.*—An employee who is a former participant in a retirement system maintained by a State, political subdivision or instrumentality thereof, who has previously retired from service with the State, political subdivision or instrumentality, and who is either in pay status (i.e., is currently receiving retirement benefits) under the retirement system or has reached normal retirement age under the retirement system, is deemed to be a qualified participant in the retirement system without regard to whether he or she continues to accrue a benefit or whether the distribution of benefits under the retirement system has been suspended pending cessation of services. This rule also applies in the case of an employee who has retired from service with another State, political subdivision or instrumentality thereof that maintains the same retirement system as the current employer, provided the employee is a former participant in the system by reason of the employee's former employment. Thus, for example, if a teacher retires from service with a school district that participates in a state-wide teachers' retirement system, begins to receive benefits from the system, and later becomes a substitute teacher in another school district that participates in the same state-wide system, the employee is treated as a re-hired annuitant under this paragraph (d)(4)(ii).

(e) *Definition of retirement system.*—(1) *Requirement that system provide retirement-type benefits.* For purposes of section 3121(b)(7)(F), a retirement system includes any pension, annuity, retirement or similar fund or system within the meaning of section 218 of the Social Security Act that is maintained by a State, political subdivision or instrumentality thereof to provide retirement benefits to its employees who are participants. Whether a plan is maintained to provide retirement benefits with respect to an employee is determined under the facts and circumstances of each case. For example, a plan providing only retiree health insurance or other deferred welfare benefits is not considered a retirement system for this purpose. The legal form of the system is generally not relevant. Thus, for example, a retirement system may include a plan described in section 401(a), an annuity plan or contract under section 403 or a plan described in section 457(b) or (f) of the Internal Revenue Code. In addition, the Social Security system is not a retirement system for purposes of section 3121(b)(7)(F) and this section. These rules are illustrated by the following examples:

*Example 1.* Under an employment arrangement, a portion of an employee's compensation is regularly deferred for 5 years. Because a plan that defers the receipt of compensation for a short span of time rather than until retirement is not a plan that provides retirement benefits, this arrangement is not a retirement system for purposes of section 3121(b)(7)(F).

*Example 2.* An individual holds two positions with the same political subdivision. The wages earned in one position are subject to FICA tax pursuant to an agreement (under section 218 of the Social Security Act) between the Secretary of Health and Human Services and the State in which the political subdivision is located. Because the Social Security system is not a retirement system for purposes of section 3121(b)(7)(F), the exception from employment in section 3121(b)(7) does not apply to service in the other position unless the employee is otherwise a member of a retirement system of such political subdivision.

(2) *Requirement that system provide minimum level of benefits.*—(i) *In general.*—A pension, annuity, retirement or similar fund or system is not a retirement system with respect to an employee unless it provides a retirement benefit to the employee that is comparable to the benefit provided under the Old-Age portion of the Old-Age, Survivor and Disability Insurance program of Social Security. Whether a retirement system meets this requirement is generally determined on an individual-by-individual basis. Thus, for example, a pension plan that is not a retirement system with respect to an employee may nevertheless be a retirement system with respect to other employees covered by the system.

(ii) *Defined benefit retirement systems.*—A defined benefit retirement system maintained by a State, political subdivision or instrumentality thereof meets the requirements of this paragraph (e)(2) with respect to an employee on a given day if and only if, on that day, the employee has an accrued benefit under the system that entitles the employee to an annual benefit commencing on or before his or her Social Security retirement age that is at least equal to the annual Primary Insurance Amount the employee would have under Social Security. For this purpose, the Primary Insurance Amount an individual would have under Social Security is determined as it would be under the Social Security Act if the employee had been covered under Social Security for all periods of service with the State, political subdivision or instrumentality, had never performed service for any other employer, and had been fully insured within the meaning of section 214(a) of the Social Security Act, except that all periods of service with the State, political subdivision or instrumentality must be taken into account (i.e., without reduction for low-earning years).

(iii) *Defined contribution retirement systems.*—(A) *In general.*—A defined contribution retirement system maintained by a state, political subdivision or instrumentality thereof meets the requirements of paragraph (e)(2)(i) of this section with respect to an employee if and only if allocations to the employee's account (not including earnings) for a period are at least 7.5 percent of the employee's compensation for service for the State, political subdivision or instrumentality during the period. Matching contributions by the employer may be taken into account for this purpose.

(B) *Definition of compensation.*—The definition of compensation used in determining whether a defined contribution retirement system meets the minimum retirement benefit requirement must generally be no less inclusive than the definition of the employee's base pay as designated by the employer or the retirement system, provided such designation is reasonable under all the facts and circumstances. Thus, for example, a defined contribution retirement system will not fail to meet this requirement merely because it disregards for all purposes one or more of the following: overtime pay, bonuses, or single-sum amounts received on account of death or separation from service under a bona fide vacation, compensatory time or sick pay plan, or under severance pay plans. Furthermore, any compensation remaining after such amounts are disregarded that is in excess of the contribution base described in section 3121(x)(1) at the beginning of the plan year may also be disregarded. The rules of this paragraph are illustrated by the following example:

*Example.* A political subdivision maintains an elective defined contribution plan that is a retirement system within the meaning of paragraph (e)(1) of this section. The plan has a calendar year plan year. In 1995, an employee contributes to the plan at a rate of 7.5 percent of base pay. Assume that the employee will reach the maximum contribution base described in section 3121(x)(1) in October of 1995. The employee is a qualified participant in the plan for all of the 1995 plan year without regard to whether the employee ceases to participate at any time after reaching the maximum contribution base.

(C) *Reasonable interest rate requirement.*—A defined contribution retirement system does not satisfy this paragraph (e)(2) with respect to an employee unless the employee's account is credited with earnings at a rate that is reasonable under all the facts and circumstances, or employees' accounts are held in a separate trust that is subject to general fiduciary standards and are credited with actual earnings on the trust fund. Whether the interest rate with which an employee's account is credited is reasonable is determined after reducing the rate to adjust for the payment of any administrative expenses. The rule of this paragraph (e)(2)(iii)(C) is illustrated by the following example:

*Example.* A political subdivision maintains a defined contribution plan described in section 457(b). Under the plan, the accounts of participants are credited annually on the basis of a variable interest rate formula determined as of the beginning of the plan year. The formula requires an interest rate (after adjustment for administrative expense payments) equal to 100 percent of the Applicable Federal Rate for long-term debt instruments. This interest rate constitutes a reasonable rate of interest.

(iv) *Treatment of employees employed in more than one position with the same entity.*—All service and compensation of an employee with respect to his or her employment with a State, political subdivision or instrumentality thereof must generally be considered in determining whether a benefit meets the requirement of this paragraph (e)(2). However, for individuals employed simultaneously in multiple positions with the same entity, this determination may (but is not required to) be made solely by reference to the service and compensation related to a single position of the employee with the State, political subdivision or instrumentality thereof making the determination, provided that the position is not a part-time, seasonal or temporary position.

(v) *Treatment of employees participating in certain systems.*—In general, only compensation from and service for the State, political subdivision or instrumentality thereof that employs the employee (and the allocations or benefits related to such compensation or service) on a given day are considered in determining whether the employee's benefit under the retirement system on that day meets the requirements of this paragraph (e)(2), even if the employee has other allocations or benefits under the same retirement system from service with another State, political subdivision or instrumentality thereof. However, an employee's total allocations or benefits under a retirement system maintained by multiple States, political subdivisions or instrumentalities thereof (including the current employer) may be taken into account if:

(A) The compensation and service on which the additional allocations or benefits are based are also taken into account in determining whether the employee's allocations or benefits satisfy the minimum retirement benefit requirement;

(B) The retirement system takes all service and compensation of the employee in all positions covered by the system into account for all benefit determination purposes; and

(C) If the employee is a part-time, seasonal or temporary employee, he or she is treated under the plan for benefit accrual purposes in as favorable a manner as a full-time employee participating in the system.

(vi) *Additional testing methods.*—Additional testing methods may be designated by the Commissioner in revenue procedures, revenue rulings, notices or other documents of general applicability.

(f) *Transition rules.*—(1) *Application of qualified participant rules during 1991.*—(i) *In general.*—An employee may be treated as a qualified participant in a retirement system (within the meaning of paragraph (e)(1) of this section) on a given day during the period July 1 through December 31, 1991, if it is reasonable on that day to believe that he or she will be a qualified participant under the general rule in paragraphs (d)(1) and (2) of this section by January 1, 1992 (taking into account only service and compensation on or after such date). For purposes of this paragraph (f)(1)(i), given the facts and circumstances of a particular case, it may be reasonable to assume that the terms of a plan will be changed or that a new retirement system will be established by the end of calendar year 1991, as long as affirmative steps have been taken to accomplish this result.

(ii) *Extension of reliance period if legislative action required.*—If a plan amendment or other action is necessary in order to treat an employee as a member of a retirement system for purposes of this section, such amendment or other action may only be taken by a legislative body that does not convene during the period July 1, 1991, through December 31, 1991, and the other requirements of paragraph (f)(1)(i) of this section are met, the end of the reasonable reliance period (including the rule that service and compensation prior to that date may be disregarded) provided under paragraph (f)(1)(i) of this section is extended from December 31, 1991, to the date that is the last day of the first legislative session commencing after December 31, 1991. These rules are illustrated by the following examples:

*Example 1.* A State maintains a defined benefit plan that meets the requirements of paragraph (e) of this section. The plan does not cover a particular class of full-time employees as of July 1, 1991. However, in light of the enactment of section 3121(b)(7)(F), state officials administering the plan for the State intend to request that the legislature amend the State statute to include that class of employees in the existing plan and otherwise to modify the terms of the plan to meet the requirements of section 3121(b)(7)(F) and this section. The State legislature meets from January through March each year, and legislative action is required to expand coverage under the plan. State officials administering the plan have publicized the proposed amendment providing for the addition of these employees to the plan. Under the transition rule for 1991, if it is reasonable to believe that the legislature will pass this bill in the 1992 session, service by the employees who will be covered under the plan by reason of the amendment is not treated as employment by reason of section 3121(b)(7)(F) during the period prior to April 1, 1992. This is true regardless of whether the plan provides retroactive coverage for the period July 1, 1991 through March 31, 1992.

*Example 2.* Assume the same facts as in *Example 1*, except that legislative action is not required in order to expand coverage under the plan, and that publication of the proposed change to the plan occurs in 1991. Assume further that coverage is expanded under the plan to include the new class of full-time employees as of April 1, 1992. Despite this action, in this situation the service by those employees during the period January 1, 1992 through March 31, 1992 is not excluded from "employment" under section 3121(b)(7)(F), and wages for that period are generally subject to FICA taxes even if the plan provides retroactive coverage for any portion of the period July 1, 1991 to March 31, 1992.

(2) *Additional transition rules for plans in existence on November 5, 1990.*—(i) *Application of minimum retirement benefit requirement to defined benefit retirement systems in plan years beginning before 1993.*—(A) *In general.*—A defined benefit retirement system maintained by a State, political subdivision or instrumentality thereof on November 5, 1990, is not subject to the minimum retirement benefit requirement of paragraph (e)(2) of this section for any plan year beginning before January 1, 1993, with respect to individuals who were actually covered under the system on November 5, 1990. Such a retirement system is also not subject to the minimum retirement benefit requirement of paragraph (e)(2) of this section with respect to an employee who becomes a participant after November 5, 1990, if he or she is employed in a position that was covered under the retirement system

on November 5, 1990, without regard to whether such coverage was mandatory or elective. A retirement system is not described in this paragraph (f)(2)(i)(A) if there has been a material decrease in the level of retirement benefits under the retirement system pursuant to an amendment adopted subsequent to November 5, 1990. Whether such a material decrease in benefits has occurred is determined under the facts and circumstances of each case. A decrease in benefits is not material to the extent that it does not decrease the benefit payable at normal retirement age. These rules are illustrated by the following examples:

*Example 1.* The retirement formula under a retirement plan that was in existence on November 5, 1990, is amended to use career average compensation instead of a high 3-year average, without any increase in the benefit formula. This amendment constitutes a material decrease in the level of benefit under the retirement plan. Therefore, the retirement plan is subject to the minimum retirement benefit requirement for the plan year for which the amendment is effective and for all succeeding plan years.

*Example 2.* A defined benefit retirement plan that was in existence on November 5, 1990, is subsequently amended to include part-time employees. Previously, this class of employees was not covered under the plan either on a mandatory or on an elective basis. The plan is subject to the minimum retirement benefit requirement with respect to the part-time employees because this class of employees was previously excluded from coverage under the retirement plan. Of course, the nonforfeitable benefit rule applies to the benefit relied upon to meet the minimum retirement benefit requirement with respect to any part-time, seasonal or temporary employee covered during this period.

(B) *Treatment in plan years beginning after 1992 of benefits accrued during previous plan years.*—The general rule that a defined benefit retirement system meets the minimum retirement benefit requirement on the basis of total benefits and service accrued to date is modified for plans in existence on November 5, 1990. If a defined benefit retirement system in existence on November 5, 1990, does not meet the minimum retirement benefit requirement solely because the benefits accrued for an employee (with respect to whom the system is entitled to relief under paragraph (f)(2)(i)(A) of this section) as of the last day of the last plan year beginning before January 1, 1993, do not meet the minimum retirement benefit requirement of paragraph (e)(2) of this section with respect to service and compensation before that time, then the retirement system will be deemed to comply with the requirements of paragraph (e)(2) of this section if the future service accruals would comply with the requirement of paragraph (e)(2) of this section. If retirement benefits under a retirement system in existence on November 5, 1990, are materially decreased within the meaning of paragraph (f)(2)(i)(A) of this section, then the date the decrease is effective is substituted for January 1, 1993, for purposes of this paragraph. The rule of this paragraph (f)(2)(i)(B) is illustrated by the following example:

*Example.* A defined benefit plan maintained by a State was in existence on November 5, 1990. It provides a retirement benefit on the last day of the 1992 plan year that is insufficient to meet the requirements of paragraph (e)(2) of this section based on employees' total service and compensation with the State at that time. The plan will nevertheless meet the requirements of paragraph (e)(2) of this section if it is amended to provide benefits sufficient to meet the requirements of paragraph (e)(2) of this section based on employees' service and compensation in plan years beginning after December 31, 1992.

(C) *Treatment of part-time, seasonal or temporary employees.*—A defined benefit retirement system is not exempt from the minimum retirement benefit requirement with respect to a part-time, seasonal or temporary employee during the transition period provided in paragraph (f)(2)(i)(A) of this section unless any retirement benefit provided to the employee is 100-percent nonforfeitable within the

meaning of paragraph (d)(2) of this section. In determining whether the benefit is nonforfeitable, the special rule in paragraph (d)(2)(ii) of this section is modified in two respects during the transition period: first, the percentage of compensation required to be available for distribution is reduced from 7.5 percent to 6 percent; and second, the period of service with respect to which compensation must be determined is modified to include all periods of participation by the employee in the system since July 1, 1991.

(ii) *Application of minimum retirement benefit requirement to defined contribution retirement systems in plan years beginning before 1993.*—A defined contribution retirement system maintained by a State, political subdivision or instrumentality thereof on November 5, 1990, meets the minimum retirement benefit requirement of paragraph (e)(2) of this section with respect to an employee for any plan year beginning before January 1, 1993, if mandatory allocations to the employee's account (not including earnings) for a period are at least 6 percent (rather than 7.5 percent) of the employee's compensation for service to the State, political subdivision or instrumentality during the period, and the plan otherwise meets the requirements of paragraph (e)(2)(iii) of this section. This transition rule is only available with respect to an employee who is actually covered under the system on November 5, 1990, and to an employee who becomes a participant after November 5, 1990, if he or she is employed in a position that was covered under the retirement system on November 5, 1990, without regard to whether such coverage was mandatory or elective. In addition, this transition rule is not available with respect to a part-time, seasonal or temporary employee unless the mandatory allocation required under this paragraph (f)(2)(ii) is 100-percent nonforfeitable within the meaning of paragraph (d)(2) of this section. A retirement system is not described in this paragraph (f)(2)(ii) if there has been a material decrease in the level of retirement benefits under the retirement system pursuant to an amendment adopted subsequent to November 5, 1990. Whether such a material decrease in benefits has occurred is determined under all the facts and circumstances.

(iii) *Application of qualified participant rules.*—A participant with respect to whom relief is granted under paragraph (f)(2)(i)(A) of this section may be treated as a qualified participant in the defined benefit retirement system on a given day if, on that day, he or she is actually a participant in the retirement system, and, on that day, it is reasonable to believe that the participant will actually accrue a benefit before the end of the plan year of such retirement system in which the determination is made. A participant is not treated as accruing a benefit for purposes of this rule if his or her accrued benefits increase solely as a result of an increase in compensation. However, an employee is treated as a qualified participant for a plan year if the employee meets all of the applicable conditions for accruing the maximum current benefit for such year but fails to accrue a benefit solely because of a uniformly applicable benefit limit under the plan. In addition, an employee may be treated as a qualified participant in the system on a given day if the employee is a re-hired annuitant within the meaning of paragraph (d)(4)(ii) of this section. This rule is illustrated by the following example:

*Example.* A political subdivision maintains a defined benefit plan that is a retirement system within the meaning of paragraph (e)(1) of this section but does not meet the requirements of paragraph (e)(2) of this section. If the plan is not subject to the minimum retirement benefit requirement, an employee who is a participant in the retirement plan as of the end of a plan year beginning before January 1, 1993, and may reasonably be expected to accrue a benefit under the plan by the end of such plan year may be treated as a qualified participant in the plan throughout the plan year regardless of the actual amount of the accrual. [Reg. §31.3121(b)(7)-2.]

☐ [*T.D. 8354, 6-28-91. Amended by T.D. 8794, 12-18-98 and T.D. 8891, 7-18-2000.*]

⟩⟩⟩→ *Caution: The following regulation has not been revised to reflect the automatic extension of self-employment coverage to ministers, Christian Science practitioners, and members of religious orders who have not applied for an exemption from coverage.*

### [Reg. §31.3121(b)(8)-1]

**§31.3121(b)(8)-1. Services performed by a minister of a church or a member of a religious order.**—(a) *In general.*—Services performed by a duly ordained, commissioned, or licensed minister of a church in the exercise of his ministry, or by a member of a religious order in the exercise of duties required by such order, are excluded from employment, except that services performed by a member of such an order in the exercise of such duties (whether performed for the order or for another employer) are included in employment if an election of coverage under section 3121(r) and §31.3121(r)-1 is in effect with respect to such order or with respect to the autonomous subdivision thereof to which such member belongs. For provisions relating to the election available to certain ministers and members of religious orders with respect to the extension of the Federal old-age, survivors,

and disability insurance system established by Title II of the Social Security Act to certain services performed by them, see Part 1 of this chapter (Income Tax Regulations).

(b) *Service by a minister in the exercise of his ministry.*—Except as provided in paragraph (c)(3) of this section, service performed by a minister in the exercise of his ministry includes the ministration of sacerdotal functions and the conduct of religious worship, and the control, conduct, and maintenance of religious organizations (including the religious boards, societies, and other integral agencies of such organizations), under the authority of a religious body constituting a church or church denomination. The following rules are applicable in determining whether services performed by a minister are performed in the exercise of his ministry:

(1) Whether service performed by a minister constitutes the conduct of religious worship or the ministration of sacerdotal functions depends on the tenets and practices of the particular religious body constituting his church or church denomination.

(2) Service performed by a minister in the control, conduct, and maintenance of a religious organization relates to directing, managing, or promoting the activities of such organization. Any religious organization is deemed to be under the authority of a religious body constituting a church or church denomination if it is organized and dedicated to carrying out the tenets and principles of a faith in accordance with either the requirements or sanctions governing the creation of institutions of the faith. The term "religious organization" has the same meaning and application as is given to the term for income tax purposes.

(3)(i) If a minister is performing service in the conduct of religious worship or the ministration of sacerdotal functions, such service is in the exercise of his ministry whether or not it is performed for a religious organization.

(ii) The rule in subdivision (i) of this subparagraph may be illustrated by the following example:

*Example.* M, a duly ordained minister, is engaged to perform service as chaplain at N university. M devotes his entire time to performing his duties as chaplain which include the conduct of religious worship, offering spiritual counsel to the university students, and teaching class in religion. M is performing service in the exercise of his ministry.

(4)(i) If a minister is performing service for an organization which is operated as an integral agency of a religious organization under the authority of a religious body constituting a church or church denomination, all service performed by the minister in the conduct of religious worship, in the ministration of sacerdotal functions, or in the control, conduct, and maintenance of such organization (see subparagraph (2) of this paragraph) is in the exercise of his ministry.

(ii) The rule in subdivision (i) of this subparagraph may be illustrated by the following example:

*Example.* M, a duly ordained minister, is engaged by the N Religious Board to serve as director of one of its departments. He performs no other service. The N Religious Board is an integral agency of O, a religious organization operating under the authority of a religious body constituting a church denomination. M is performing service in the exercise of his ministry.

(5)(i) If a minister, pursuant to an assignment or designation by a religious body constituting his church, performs service for an organization which is neither a religious organization nor operated as an integral agency of a religious organization, all service performed by him, even though such service may not involve the conduct of religious worship or the ministration of sacerdotal functions, is in the exercise of his ministry.

(ii) The rule in subdivision (i) of this subparagraph may be illustrated by the following example:

*Example.* M, a duly ordained minister, is assigned by X, the religious body constituting his church, to perform advisory service to Y Company in connection with the publication of a book dealing with the history of M's church denomination. Y is neither a religious organization nor operated as an integral agency of a religious organization. M performs no other service for X or Y. M is performing service in the exercise of his ministry.

(c) *Service by a minister not in the exercise of his ministry.*—(1) Section 3121(b)(8)(A) does not except from employment service performed by a duly ordained, commissioned, or licensed minister of a church which is not in the exercise of his ministry.

(2)(i) If a minister is performing service for an organization which is neither a religious organization nor operated as an integral agency of a religious organization and the service is not performed pursuant to an assignment or designation by his ecclesiastical superiors, then only the service performed by him in the conduct of religious worship or the ministration of sacerdotal functions is in the exercise of his ministry. See, however, subparagraph (3) of this paragraph.

(ii) The rule in subdivision (i) of this subparagraph may be illustrated by the following example:

*Example.* M, a duly ordained minister, is engaged by N University to teach history and mathematics. He performs no other service for N although from time to time he performs marriages and conducts funerals for relatives and friends. N University is neither a religious organization nor operated as an integral agency of a religious organization. M is not performing the service for N pursuant to an assignment or designation by his ecclesiastical superiors. The service performed by M for N University is not in the exercise of his ministry. However, service performed by M in performing marriages and conducting funerals is in the exercise of his ministry.

(3) Service performed by a duly ordained, commissioned, or licensed minister of a church as an employee of the United States, or a State, Territory, or possession of the United States, or the District of Columbia, or a foreign government, or a political subdivision of any of the foregoing, is not considered to be in the exercise of his ministry for purposes of the taxes, even though such service may involve the ministration of sacerdotal functions or the conduct of religious worship. Thus, for example, service performed by an individual as a chaplain in the Armed Forces of the United States is considered to be performed by a commissioned officer in his capacity as such, and not by a minister in the exercise of his ministry. Similarly, service performed by an employee of a State as a chaplain in a State prison is considered to be performed by a civil servant of the State and not by a minister in the exercise of his ministry.

(d) *Service in the exercise of duties required by a religious order.*— Service performed by a member of a religious order in the exercise of duties required by such order includes all duties required of the member by the order. The nature or extent of such service is immaterial so long as it is a service which he is directed or required to perform by his ecclesiastical superiors. [Reg. § 31.3121(b)(8)-1.]

☐ [*T.D.* 6190, 7-14-56. *Republished in T.D.* 6516, 12-20-60. *Amended by T.D.* 7280, 7-10-73.]

## [Reg. § 31.3121(b)(9)-1]

**§ 31.3121(b)(9)-1. Railroad industry; services performed by an employee or an employee representative as defined in section 3231.**—Services performed by an individual as an "employee" or as an "employee representative," as those terms are defined in section 3231, are excepted from employment. For definitions of employee and employee representative, see § § 31.3231(b)-1 and 31.3231(c)-1. [Reg. § 31.312(b)(9)-1.]

☐ [*T.D.* 6190, 7-14-56.]

**»»→ *Caution: This regulation has not been amended to reflect the new test for low-paid employees of exempt organizations.***

## [Reg. § 31.3121(b)(10)-1]

**§ 31.3121(b)(10)-1. Services for remuneration of less than $50 for calendar quarter in the employ of certain organizations exempt from income tax.**—(a) Services performed by an employee in a calendar quarter in the employ of an organization exempt from income tax under section 501(a) (other than an organization described in section 401(a)) or under section 521 are excepted from employment, if the remuneration for the services is less than $50. The test relating to remuneration of $50 is based on the remuneration earned during a calendar quarter rather than on the remuneration paid in a calendar quarter. The exception applies separately with respect to each organization for which the employee renders services in a calendar quarter. The type of services performed by the employee and the place where the services are performed are immaterial; the statutory tests are the character of the organization in the employ of which the services are performed and the amount of the remuneration for services performed by the employee in the calendar quarter. For provisions relating to exemption from income tax under section 501(a) or 521, see Part 1 of this chapter (Income Tax Regulations).

*Example (1).* X is a local lodge of a fraternal organization and is exempt from income tax under section 501(a) as an organization of the character described in section 501(c)(8). X has two paid employees, A, who serves exclusively as recording secretary for the lodge, and B, who performs services for the lodge as janitor of its clubhouse. For services performed during the first calendar quarter of 1955 (that is, January 1, 1955, through March 31, 1955, both dates inclusive) A earns a total of $30. For services performed during the same calendar quarter B earns $180. Since the remuneration for the services performed by A during such quarter is less than $50, all of such services are excepted, and the taxes do not attach with respect to any of the remuneration for such services. Since the remuneration for the services performed by B during such quarter, however, is not less than $50, none of such services are excepted, and the taxes attach with respect to all of the remuneration for such services (that is, $180) as and when paid.

*Example (2).* The facts are the same as in example (1), above, except that on April 1, 1955, A's salary is increased and, for services performed during the calendar quarter beginning on that date (that is, April 1, 1955, through June 30, 1955, both dates inclusive), A earns a total of $60. Although all of the services performed by A during the first quarter were excepted, none of A's services performed during the second quarter are excepted since the remuneration for such services is not less than $50. The taxes attach with respect to all of the remuneration for services performed during the second quarter (that is, $60) as and when paid.

*Example (3).* The facts are the same as in example (1), above, except that A earns $120 for services performed during the year 1955, and such amount is paid to him in a lump sum at the end of the year. The services performed by A in any calendar quarter during the year are excepted if the portion of the $120 attributable to services performed in that quarter is less than $50. If, however, the portion of the $120 attributable to services performed in any calendar quarter during the year is not less than $50, the services during that quarter are not excepted, and the taxes attach with respect to that portion of the remuneration attributable to his services in that quarter.

(b) See §31.3121(b)(8)-1, relating to services performed by a minister of a church in the exercise of his ministry or by a member of a religious order in the exercise of duties required by such order; §31.3121(b)(10)-2, relating to services performed by certain students in the employ of a school, college, or university or of a nonprofit organization auxiliary to a school, college, or university; and §31.3121(b)(13)-1, relating to services performed by certain student nurses and hospital interns. [Reg. §31.3121(b)(10)-1.]

☐ [*T.D.* 6190, 7-14-56. *Republished in T.D.* 6516, 12-20-60. *Amended by T.D.* 7373, 7-24-75 *and T.D.* 9849, 3-11-2019.]

### [Reg. §31.3121(b)(10)-2]

**§31.3121(b)(10)-2. Services performed by certain students in the employ of a school, college, or university, or of a nonprofit organization auxiliary to a school, college, or university.**—(a) *General rule.*—(1) Services performed in the employ of a school, college, or university within the meaning of paragraph (c) of this section (whether or not the organization is exempt from income tax) are excepted from employment, if the services are performed by a student within the meaning of paragraph (d) of this section who is enrolled and is regularly attending classes at the school, college, or university.

(2) Services performed in the employ of an organization which is—

(i) Described in section 509(a)(3) and §1.509(a)-4;

(ii) Organized, and at all times thereafter operated, exclusively for the benefit of, to perform the functions of, or to carry out the purposes of a school, college, or university within the meaning of paragraph (c) of this section; and

(iii) Operated, supervised, or controlled by or in connection with the school, college, or university; are excepted from employment, if the services are performed by a student who is enrolled and regularly attending classes within the meaning of paragraph (d) of this section at the school, college, or university. The preceding sentence shall not apply to services performed in the employ of a school, college, or university of a State or a political subdivision thereof by a student referred to in section 218(c)(5) of the Social Security Act (42 U.S.C. 418(c)(5)) if such services are covered under the agreement between the Commissioner of Social Security and such State entered into pursuant to section 218 of such Act. For the definitions of "operated, supervised, or controlled by", "supervised or controlled in connection with", and "operated in connection with", see paragraphs (g), (h), and (i), respectively, of §1.509(a)-4.

(b) *Statutory tests.*—For purposes of this section, if an employee has the status of a student within the meaning of paragraph (d) of this section, the amount of remuneration for services performed by the employee, the type of services performed by the employee, and the place where the services are performed are not material. The statutory tests are:

(1) The character of the organization in the employ of which the services are performed as a school, college, or university within the meaning of paragraph (c) of this section, or as an organization described in paragraph (a)(2) of this section, and

(2) The status of the employee as a student enrolled and regularly attending classes within the meaning of paragraph (d) of this section at the school, college, or university within the meaning of paragraph (c) of this section by which the employee is employed or with which the employee's employer is affiliated within the meaning of paragraph (a)(2) of this section.

(c) *School, college, or university.*—An organization is a *school, college, or university* within the meaning of section 3121(b)(10) if its primary function is the presentation of formal instruction, it normally maintains a regular faculty and curriculum, and it normally has a regularly enrolled body of students in attendance at the place where its educational activities are regularly carried on. See section 170(b)(1)(A)(ii) and the regulations thereunder.

(d) *Student status—general rule.*—Whether an employee has the status of a student performing the services shall be determined based on the relationship of the employee with the organization employing the employee. In order to have the status of a student, the employee must perform services in the employ of a school, college, or university within the meaning of paragraph (c) of this section at which the employee is enrolled and regularly attending classes in pursuit of a course of study within the meaning of paragraphs (d)(1) and (2) of

this section. In addition, the employee's services must be incident to and for the purpose of pursuing a course of study within the meaning of paragraph (d)(3) of this section at such school, college, or university. An employee who performs services in the employ of an affiliated organization within the meaning of paragraph (a)(2) of this section must be enrolled and regularly attending classes at the affiliated school, college, or university within the meaning of paragraph (c) of this section in pursuit of a course of study within the meaning of paragraphs (d)(1) and (2) of this section. In addition, the employee's services must be incident to and for the purpose of pursuing a course of study within the meaning of paragraph (d)(3) of this section at such school, college, or university.

(1) *Enrolled and regularly attending classes.*—An employee must be enrolled and regularly attending classes at a school, college, or university within the meaning of paragraph (c) of this section at which the employee is employed to have the status of a student within the meaning of section 3121(b)(10). An employee is enrolled within the meaning of section 3121(b)(10) if the employee is registered for a course or courses creditable toward an educational credential described in paragraph (d)(2) of this section. In addition, the employee must be regularly attending classes to have the status of a student. For purposes of this paragraph (d)(1), a class is an instructional activity led by a faculty member or other qualified individual hired by the school, college, or university within the meaning of paragraph (c) of this section for identified students following an established curriculum. Traditional classroom activities are not the sole means of satisfying this requirement. For example, research activities under the supervision of a faculty advisor necessary to complete the requirements for a Ph.D. degree may constitute classes within the meaning of section 3121(b)(10). The frequency of these and similar activities determines whether an employee may be considered to be regularly attending classes.

(2) *Course of study.*—An employee must be pursuing a course of study in order to have the status of a student. A course of study is one or more courses the completion of which fulfills the requirements necessary to receive an educational credential granted by a school, college, or university within the meaning of paragraph (c) of this section. For purposes of this paragraph, an educational credential is a degree, certificate, or other recognized educational credential granted by an organization described in paragraph (c) of this section. A course of study also includes one or more courses at a school, college or university within the meaning of paragraph (c) of this section the completion of which fulfills the requirements necessary for the employee to sit for an examination required to receive certification by a recognized organization in a field.

(3) *Incident to and for the purpose of pursuing a course of study.*—(i) *General rule.*—An employee's services must be incident to and for the purpose of pursuing a course of study in order for the employee to have the status of a student. Whether an employee's services are incident to and for the purpose of pursuing a course of study shall be determined on the basis of the relationship of the employee with the organization for which such services are performed as an employee. The educational aspect of the relationship between the employer and the employee, as compared to the service aspect of the relationship, must be predominant in order for the employee's services to be incident to and for the purpose of pursuing a course of study. The educational aspect of the relationship is evaluated based on all the relevant facts and circumstances related to the educational aspect of the relationship. The service aspect of the relationship is evaluated based on all the relevant facts and circumstances related to the employee's employment. The evaluation of the service aspect of the relationship is not affected by the fact that the services performed by the employee may have an educational, instructional, or training aspect. Except as provided in paragraph (d)(3)(iii) of this section, whether the educational aspect or the service aspect of an employee's relationship with the employer is predominant is determined by considering all the relevant facts and circumstances. Relevant factors in evaluating the educational and service aspects of an employee's relationship with the employer are described in paragraphs (d)(3)(iv) and (v) of this section respectively. There may be facts and circumstances that are relevant in evaluating the educational and service aspects of the relationship in addition to those described in paragraphs (d)(3)(iv) and (v) of this section.

(ii) *Student status determined with respect to each academic term.*—Whether an employee's services are incident to and for the purpose of pursuing a course of study is determined separately with respect to each academic term. If the relevant facts and circumstances with respect to an employee's relationship with the employer change significantly during an academic term, whether the employee's services are incident to and for the purpose of pursuing a course of study is reevaluated with respect to services performed during the remainder of the academic term.

(iii) *Full-time employee.*—The services of a full-time employee are not incident to and for the purpose of pursuing a course of study. The determination of whether an employee is a full-time employee is based on the employer's standards and practices, except regardless of the employer's classification of the employee, an employee whose normal work schedule is 40 hours or more per week is considered a full-time employee. An employee's normal work schedule is not affected by increases in hours worked caused by work demands unforeseen at the start of an academic term. However, whether an employee is a full-time employee is reevaluated for the remainder of the academic term if the employee changes employment positions with the employer. An employee's work schedule during academic breaks is not considered in determining whether the employee's normal work schedule is 40 hours or more per week. The determination of an employee's normal work schedule is not affected by the fact that the services performed by the employee may have an educational, instructional, or training aspect.

(iv) *Evaluating educational aspect.*—The educational aspect of an employee's relationship with the employer is evaluated based on all the relevant facts and circumstances related to the educational aspect of the relationship. The educational aspect of an employee's relationship with the employer is generally evaluated based on the employee's course workload. Whether an employee's course workload is sufficient in order for the employee's employment to be incident to and for the purpose of pursuing a course of study depends on the particular facts and circumstances. A relevant factor in evaluating an employee's course workload is the employee's course workload relative to a full-time course workload at the school, college or university within the meaning of paragraph (c) of this section at which the employee is enrolled and regularly attending classes.

(v) *Evaluating service aspect.*—The service aspect of an employee's relationship with the employer is evaluated based on the facts and circumstances related to the employee's employment. Services of an employee with the status of a full-time employee within the meaning of paragraph (d)(3)(iii) of this section are not incident to and for the purpose of pursuing a course of study. Relevant factors in evaluating the service aspect of an employee's relationship with the employer are described in paragraphs (d)(3)(v)(A), (B), and (C) of this section.

(A) *Normal work schedule and hours worked.*—If an employee is not a full-time employee within the meaning of paragraph (d)(3)(iii) of this section, then the employee's normal work schedule and number of hours worked per week are relevant factors in evaluating the service aspect of the employee's relationship with the employer. As an employee's normal work schedule or actual number of hours worked approaches 40 hours per week, it is more likely that the service aspect of the employee's relationship with the employer is predominant. The determination of an employee's normal work schedule and actual number of hours worked is not affected by the fact that some of the services performed by the employee may have an educational, instructional, or training aspect.

(B) *Professional employee.*—(1) If an employee has the status of a professional employee, then that suggests. the service aspect of the employee's relationship with the employer is predominant. A professional employee is an employee—

(i) Whose primary duty consists of the performance of work requiring knowledge of an advanced type in a field of science or learning customarily acquired by a prolonged course of specialized intellectual instruction and study, as distinguished from a general academic education, from an apprenticeship, and from training in the performance of routine mental, manual, or physical processes;

(ii) Whose work requires the consistent exercise of discretion and judgment in its performance; and

(iii) Whose work is predominantly intellectual and varied in character (as opposed to routine mental, manual, mechanical, or physical work) and is of such character that the output produced or the result accomplished cannot be standardized in relation to a given period of time.

(2) *Licensed, professional employee.*—If an employee is a licensed, professional employee, then that further suggests the service aspect of the employee's relationship with the employer is predominant. An employee is a licensed, professional employee if the employee is required to be licensed under state or local law to work in the field in which the employee performs services and the employee is a professional employee within the meaning of paragraph (d)(3)(v)(B)(1) of this section.

(C) *Employment benefits.*—Whether an employee is eligible to receive one or more employment benefits is a relevant factor in evaluating the service aspect of an employee's relationship with the employer. For example, eligibility to receive vacation, paid holiday,

and paid sick leave benefits; eligibility to participate in a retirement plan or arrangement described in sections 401(a), 403(b), or 457(a); or eligibility to receive employment benefits such as reduced tuition (other than qualified tuition reduction under section 117(d)(5) provided to a teaching or research assistant who is a graduate student), or benefits under sections 79 (life insurance), 127 (qualified educational assistance), 129 (dependent care assistance programs), or 137 (adoption assistance) suggest that the service aspect of an employee's relationship with the employer is predominant. Eligibility to receive health insurance employment benefits is not considered in determining whether the service aspect of an employee's relationship with the employer is predominant. The weight to be given the fact that an employee is eligible for a particular employment benefit may vary depending on the type of benefit. For example, eligibility to participate in a retirement plan is generally more significant than eligibility to receive a dependent care employment benefit. Additional weight is given to the fact that an employee is eligible to receive an employment benefit if the benefit is generally provided by the employer to employees in positions generally held by non-students. Less weight is given to the fact that an employee is eligible to receive an employment benefit if eligibility for the benefit is mandated by state or local law.

(e) *Examples.*—The following examples illustrate the principles of paragraphs (a) through (d) of this section:

*Example 1.* (i) Employee C is employed by State University T to provide services as a clerk in T's administrative offices, and is enrolled and regularly attending classes at T in pursuit of a B.S. degree in biology. C has a course workload during the academic term which constitutes a full-time course workload at T. C is considered a part-time employee by T during the academic term, and C's normal work schedule is 20 hours per week, but occasionally due to work demands unforeseen at the start of the academic term C works 40 hours or more during a week. C is compensated by hourly wages, and receives no other compensation or employment benefits.

(ii) In this *example*, C is employed by T, a school, college, or university within the meaning of paragraph (c) of this section. C is enrolled and regularly attending classes at T in pursuit of a course of study. C is not a full-time employee based on T's standards, and C's normal work schedule does not cause C to have the status of a full-time employee, even though C may occasionally work 40 hours or more during a week due to unforeseen work demands. C's part-time employment relative to C's full-time course workload indicates that the educational aspect of C's relationship with T is predominant. Additional facts supporting this conclusion are that C is not a professional employee, and C does not receive any employment benefits. Thus, C's services are incident to and for the purpose of pursuing a course of study. Accordingly, C's services are excepted from employment under section 3121(b)(10).

*Example 2.* (i) Employee D is employed in the accounting department of University U, and is enrolled and regularly attending classes at U in pursuit of an M.B.A. degree. D has a course workload which constitutes a half-time course workload at U. D is considered a full-time employee by U under U's standards and practices.

(ii) In this *example*, D is employed by U, a school, college, or university within the meaning of paragraph (c) of this section. In addition, D is enrolled and regularly attending classes at U in pursuit of a course of study. However, because D is considered a full-time employee by U under its standards and practices, D's services are not incident to and for the purpose of pursuing a course of study. Accordingly, D's services are not excepted from employment under section 3121(b)(10).

*Example 3.* (i) The facts are the same as in Example 2, except that D is not considered a full-time employee by U, and D's normal work schedule is 32 hours per week. In addition, D's work is repetitive in nature and does not require the consistent exercise of discretion and judgment, and is not predominantly intellectual and varied in character. However, D receives vacation, sick leave, and paid holiday employment benefits, and D is eligible to participate in a retirement plan maintained by U described in section 401(a).

(ii) In this *example*, D's half-time course workload relative to D's hours worked and eligibility for employment benefits indicates that the service aspect of D's relationship with U is predominant, and thus D's services are not incident to and for the purpose of pursuing a course of study. Accordingly, D's services are not excepted from employment under section 3121(b)(10).

*Example 4.* (i) Employee E is employed by University V to provide patient care services at a teaching hospital that is an unincorporated division of V. These services are performed as part of a medical residency program in a medical specialty sponsored by V. The residency program in which E participates is accredited by the Accreditation Counsel for Graduate Medical Education. Upon completion of the program, E will receive a certificate of completion, and be eligible to sit for an examination required to be certified by a recognized organization in the medical specialty. E's normal work schedule, which includes services having an educational, instructional, or training aspect, is 40 hours or more per week.

(ii) In this *example*, E is employed by V, a school, college, or university within the meaning of paragraph (c) of this section. However, E's normal work schedule calls for E to perform services 40 or more hours per week. E is therefore a full-time employee, and the fact that some of E's services have an educational, instructional, or training aspect does not affect that conclusion. Thus, E's services are not incident to and for the purpose of pursuing a course of study. Accordingly, E's services are not excepted from employment under section 3121(b)(10) and there is no need to consider other relevant factors, such as whether E is a professional employee or whether E is eligible for employment benefits.

*Example 5.* (i) Employee F is employed in the facilities management department of University W. F has a B.S. degree in engineering, and is completing the work experience required to sit for an examination to become a professional engineer eligible for licensure under state or local law. F is not attending classes at W.

(ii) In this *example*, F is employed by W, a school, college, or university within the meaning of paragraph (c) of this section. However, F is not enrolled and regularly attending classes at W in pursuit of a course of study. F's work experience required to sit for the examination is not a course of study for purposes of paragraph (d)(2) of this section. Accordingly, F's services are not excepted from employment under section 3121(b)(10).

*Example 6.* (i) Employee G is employed by Employer X as an apprentice in a skilled trade. X is a subcontractor providing services in the field in which G wishes to specialize. G is pursuing a certificate in the skilled trade from Community College C. G is performing services for X pursuant to an internship program sponsored by C under which its students gain experience, and receive credit toward a certificate in the trade.

(ii) In this *example*, G is employed by X. X is not a school, college or university within the meaning of paragraph (c) of this section. Thus, the exception from employment under section 3121(b)(10) is not available with respect to G's services for X.

*Example 7.* (i) Employee H is employed by a cosmetology school Y at which H is enrolled and regularly attending classes in pursuit of a certificate of completion. Y's primary function is to carry on educational activities to prepare its students to work in the field of cosmetology. Prior to issuing a certificate, Y requires that its students gain experience in cosmetology services by performing services for the general public on Y's premises. H is scheduled to work and in fact works significantly less than 30 hours per week. H's work does not require knowledge of an advanced type in a field of science or learning, nor is it predominantly intellectual and varied in character. H receives remuneration in the form of hourly compensation from Y for providing cosmetology services to clients of Y, and does not receive any other compensation and is not eligible for employment benefits provided by Y.

(ii) In this *example*, H is employed by Y, a school, college or university within the meaning of paragraph (c) of this section, and is enrolled and regularly attending classes at Y in pursuit of a course of study. Factors indicating the educational aspect of H's relationship with Y is predominant are that H's hours worked are significantly less than 30 per week, H is not a professional employee, and H is not eligible for employment benefits. Based on the relevant facts and circumstances, the educational aspect of H's relationship with Y is predominant. Thus, H's services are incident to and for the purpose of pursuing a course of study. Accordingly, H's services are excepted from employment under section 3121(b)(10).

*Example 8.* (i) Employee J is a graduate teaching assistant at University Z. J is enrolled and regularly attending classes at Z in pursuit of a graduate degree. J has a course workload which constitutes a full-time course workload at Z. J's normal work schedule is 20 hours per week, but occasionally due to work demands unforeseen at the start of the academic term J works more than 40 hours during a week. J's duties include grading quizzes and exams pursuant to guidelines set forth by the professor, providing class and laboratory instruction pursuant to a lesson plan developed by the professor, and preparing laboratory equipment for demonstrations. J receives a cash stipend and employment benefits in the form of eligibility to make elective employee contributions to an arrangement described in section 403(b). In addition, J receives qualified tuition reduction benefits within the meaning of section 117(d)(5) with respect to the tuition charged for the credits earned for being a graduate teaching assistant.

(ii) In this *example*, J is employed by Z, a school, college or university within the meaning of paragraph (c) of this section, and is enrolled and regularly attending classes at Z in pursuit of a course of study. J's full-time course workload relative to J's normal work schedule of 20 hours per week indicates that the educational aspect of J's relationship with Z is predominant. In addition, J is not a professional employee because J's work does not require the consistent exercise of discretion and judgment in its performance. On the

other hand, the fact that J receives employment benefits in the form of eligibility to make elective employee contributions to an arrangement described in section 403(b) indicates that the employment aspect of J's relationship with Z is predominant. Balancing the relevant facts and circumstances, the educational aspect of J's relationship with Z is predominant. Thus, J's services are incident to and for the purpose of pursuing a course of study. Accordingly, J services are excepted from employment under section 3121(b)(10).

(f) *Effective date.*—Paragraphs (a), (b), (c), (d) and (e) of this section apply to services performed on or after April 1, 2005.

(g) For provisions relating to domestic service performed by a student in a local college club, or local chapter of a college fraternity or sorority, see § 31.3121(b)(2)-1. [Reg. § 31.3121(b)(10)-2.]

☐ [*T.D. 6190,* 7-14-56. *Republished in T.D. 6516,* 12-20-60. *Amended by T.D. 7373,* 7-24-75 *and T.D. 9167,* 12-20-2004.]

## [Reg. § 31.3121(b)(11)-1]

**§ 31.3121(b)(11)-1. Services in the employ of foreign government.**—(a) Services performed by an employee in the employ of a foreign government are excepted from employment. The exception includes not only services performed by ambassadors, ministers, and other diplomatic officers and employees but also services performed as a consular or other officer or employee of a foreign government, or as a nondiplomatic representative thereof.

(b) For purposes of this exception, the citizenship or residence of the employee is immaterial. It is also immaterial whether the foreign government grants an equivalent exemption with respect to similar services performed in the foreign country by citizens of the United States. [Reg. § 31.2121(b)(11)-1.]

☐ [*T.D. 6190,* 7-14-56. *Republished in T.D. 6516,* 12-20-60.]

## [Reg. § 31.3121(b)(12)-1]

**§ 31.3121(b)(12)-1. Services in employ of wholly owned instrumentality of foreign government.**—(a) Services performed by an employee in the employ of certain instrumentalities of a foreign government are excepted from employment. The exception includes all services performed in the employ of an instrumentality of the government of a foreign country, if—

(1) The instrumentality is wholly owned by the foreign government;

(2) The services are of a character similar to those performed in foreign countries by employees of the United States Government or of an instrumentality thereof; and

(3) The Secretary of State certifies to the Secretary of the Treasury that the foreign government, with respect to whose instrumentality and employees thereof exemption is claimed, grants an equivalent exemption with respect to services performed in the foreign country by employees of the United States Government and of instrumentalities thereof.

(b) For purposes of this exception, the citizenship or residence of the employee is immaterial. [Reg. § 31.31212(b)(12)-1.]

☐ [*T.D. 6190,* 7-14-56. *Republished in T.D. 6516,* 12-20-60.]

## [Reg. § 31.3121(b)(13)-1]

**§ 31.3121(b)(13)-1. Services of student nurse or hospital intern.**—(a) Services performed as a student nurse in the employ of a hospital or a nurses' training school are excepted from employment, if the student nurse is enrolled and regularly attending classes in a nurses' training school and such nurses' training school is chartered or approved pursuant to State law.

(b) Services performed before 1966 as an intern (as distinguished from a resident doctor), in the employ of a hospital are excepted from employment, if the intern has completed a 4 years' course in a medical school chartered or approved pursuant to State law. [Reg. § 31.3121(b)(13)-1.]

☐ [*T.D. 6190,* 7-14-56. *Republished in T.D. 6516,* 12-20-60. *Amended by T.D. 6983,* 12-4-68.]

## [Reg. § 31.3121(b)(14)-1]

**§ 31.3121(b)(14)-1. Services in delivery or distribution of newspapers, shopping news, or magazines.**—(a) *Services of individuals under age 18.*—Services performed by an employee under the age of 18 in the delivery or distribution of newspapers or shopping news, not including delivery or distribution (as, for example, by a regional distributor) to any point for subsequent delivery or distribution, are excepted from employment. Thus, the services performed by an employee under the age of 18 in making house-to-house delivery or sale of newspapers or shopping news, including handbills and other similar types of advertising material, are excepted from employment. The services are excepted irrespective of the form or method of compensation. Incidental services by the employee who makes the house-to-house delivery, such as services in assembling newspapers, are considered to be within the exception. The exception continues only during the time that the employee is under the age of 18.

(b) *Services of individuals of any age.*—Services performed by an employee in, and at the time of, the sale of newspapers or magazines to ultimate consumers under an arrangement under which the newspapers or magazines are to be sold by him at a fixed price, his compensation being based on the retention of the excess of such price over the amount at which the newspapers or magazines are charged to him, are excepted from employment. The services are excepted whether or not the employee is guaranteed a minimum amount of compensation for such services, or is entitled to be credited with the unsold newspapers or magazines turned back. Moreover, the services are excepted without regard to the age of the employee. Services performed other than at the time of sale to the ultimate consumer are not within the exception. Thus, the services of a regional distributor which are antecedent to but not immediately part of the sale to the ultimate consumer are not within the exception. However, incidental services by the employee who makes the sale to the ultimate consumer, such as services in assembling newspapers or in taking newspapers or magazines to the place of sale, are considered to be within the exception. [Reg. § 31.3121(b)(14)-1.]

☐ [*T.D.* 6190, 7-14-56. *Republished in T.D.* 6516, 12-20-60.]

### [Reg. § 31.3121(b)(15)-1]

§ 31.3121(b)(15)-1. **Services in employ of international organization.**—(a) Subject to the provisions of section 1 of the International Organizations Immunities Act (22 U.S.C. 288), services performed in the employ of an international organization as defined in section 7701(a)(18) are excepted from employment.

(b)(1) Section 7701(a)(18) provides as follows:

Sec. 7701. *Definitions.* (a) When used in this title, where not otherwise distinctly expressed or manifestly incompatible with the intent thereof—

\* \* \*

(18) *International organization.* The term "international organization" means a public international organization entitled to enjoy privileges, exemptions, and immunities as an international organization under the International Organizations Immunities Act (22 U.S.C. 288-288f).

(2) Section 1 of the International Organizations Immunities Act provides as follows:

Sec. 1. [*International Organizations Immunities Act.*]For the purposes of this title [International Organizations Immunities Act], the term "international organization" means a public international organization in which the United States participates pursuant to any treaty or under the authority of any Act of Congress authorizing such participation or making an appropriation for such participation, and which shall have been designated by the President through appropriate Executive order as being entitled to enjoy the privileges, exemptions, and immunities herein provided. The President shall be authorized, in the light of the functions performed by any such international organization, by appropriate Executive order to withhold or withdraw from any such organization or its officers or employees any of the privileges, exemptions, and immunities provided for in this title (including the amendments made by this title) or to condition or limit the enjoyment by any such organization or its officers or employees of any such privilege, exemption, or immunity. The President shall be authorized, if in his judgment such action should be justified by reason of the abuse by an international organization or its officers and employees of the privileges, exemptions, and immunities herein provided or for any other reason, at any time to revoke the designation of any international organization under this section, whereupon the international organization in question shall cease to be classed as an international organization for the purposes of this title. [Reg. § 31.3121(b)(15)-1.]

☐ [*T.D.* 6190, 7-14-56. *Republished in T.D.* 6516, 12-20-60.]

### [Reg. § 31.3121(b)(16)-1]

§ 31.3121(b)(16)-1. **Services performed under share-farming arrangement.**—(a) The term "employment" does not include services performed by an individual under an arrangement with the owner or tenant of land pursuant to which—

(1) Such individual undertakes to produce agricultural or horticultural commodities (including livestock, bees, poultry, and fur-bearing animals and wildlife) on such land,

(2) The agricultural or horticultural commodities produced by such individual, or the proceeds therefrom, are to be divided between such individual and such owner or tenant, and

(3) The amount of such individual's share depends on the amount of the agricultural or horticultural commodities produced.

For purposes of this exception, the arrangement pursuant to which the individual's services are performed must meet the specified statutory conditions.

(b) If the arrangement between the parties provides that the individual who undertakes to produce a crop or livestock is to be compensated at a specified rate of pay or is to receive a fixed sum of money or a stipulated quantity of the commodities to be produced, without regard to the amount actually produced, as distinguished from a proportionate share of the crop or livestock, or the proceeds therefrom, the services performed by such individual in the production of such crop or livestock is not within the exception.

(c) For provisions relating to the status, under the Self-Employment Contributions Act of 1954, of the services which are excepted from "employment" under this section, see the regulations under section 1402(a) in Part 1 of this chapter (Income Tax Regulations). [Reg. § 31.3121(16)-1.]

☐ [*T.D.* 6744, 7-2-64.]

### [Reg. § 31.3121(b)(17)-1]

§ 31.3121(b)(17)-1. **Services in employ of Communist organization.**—The term "employment" does not include services performed in the employ of any organization in any calendar quarter beginning after June 30, 1956, and during any part of which such organization is registered, or there is in effect a final order of the Subversive Activities Control Board requiring such organization to register, under the Internal Security Act of 1950 (50 U.S.C. 781 *et seq.*), as amended, as a Communist-action organization, a Communist-front organization, or a Communist-infiltrated organization. [Reg. § 31.3121(b)(17)-1.]

☐ [*T.D.* 6744, 7-2-64.]

### [Reg. § 31.3121(b)(18)-1]

§ 31.3121(b)(18)-1. **Services performed by a resident of the Republic of the Philippines while temporarily in Guam.**—(a) Services performed after 1960 by a resident of the Republic of the Philippines while in Guam on a temporary basis as a nonimmigrant alien admitted to Guam pursuant to section 101(a)(15)(H)(ii) of the Immigration and Nationality Act (8 U.S.C. 1101) are excepted from employment.

(b) Section 101(a)(15)(H) of the Immigration and Nationality Act provides as follows:

\* \* \*

Sec. 101. *Definitions.* [Immigration and Nationality Act (66 Stat. 166)]

(a) As used in this chapter—

\* \* \*

(15) The term "immigrant" means every alien except an alien who is within one of the following classes of nonimmigrant aliens—

\* \* \*

(H) An alien having a residence in a foreign country which he has no intention of abandoning (i) who is of distinguished merit and ability and who is coming temporarily to the United States to perform temporary services of an exceptional nature requiring merit and ability; or (ii) who is coming temporarily to the United States to perform other temporary services or labor, if unemployed persons capable of performing such service or labor cannot be found in this country; or (iii) who is coming temporarily to the United States as an industrial trainee;

\* \* \*

[Reg. § 31.3121(b)(18)-1.]

☐ [*T.D.* 6744, 7-2-64.]

**⋙→ *Caution: This regulation has not been amended to reflect changes enacted by the Social Security Independence and Program Improvements Act of 1994 (P.L. 103-296).***

### [Reg. § 31.3121(b)(19)-1]

§ 31.3121(b)(19)-1. **Services of certain nonresident aliens.**—(a)(1) Services performed after 1961 by a nonresident alien individual who is temporarily present in the United States as a nonimmigrant under subparagraph (F) or (J) of section 101(a)(15) of the Immigration and Nationality Act (8 U.S.C. 1101), as amended, are excepted from employment if the services are performed to carry out a purpose for which the individual was admitted. For purposes of this section an alien individual who is temporarily present in the United States as a nonimmigrant under such subparagraph (F) or (J) is deemed to be a nonresident alien individual. The preceding sentence does not apply to the extent it is inconsistent with section 7701(b) and the regulations under that section. A nonresident alien individual who is temporarily present in the United States as a nonimmigrant under subparagraph (J) includes an alien individual admitted to the United States as an "exchange visitor" under section 201 of the United States Information and Educational Exchange Act of 1948 (22 U.S.C. 1446).

(2) If services are performed by a nonresident alien individual's alien spouse or minor child, who is temporarily present in the United States as a nonimmigrant under subparagraph (F) or (J) of section 101(a)(15) of the Immigration and Nationality Act, as amended, the services are not deemed for purposes of this section to be performed to carry out a purpose for which such individual was admitted. The services of such spouse or child are excepted from employment under this section only if the spouse or child was admitted for a purpose specified in such subparagraph (F) or (J) and if the services are performed to carry out such purpose.

(b) Section 101 of the Immigration and Nationality Act (8 U.S.C. 1101), as amended, provides in part as follows:

Sec. 101. *Definitions.* [Immigration and Nationality Act (66 Stat. 166)]

(a) As used in this chapter—

\* \* \*

(15) The term "immigrant" means every alien except an alien who is within one of the following classes of nonimmigrant aliens—

\* \* \*

(F)(i) An alien having a residence in a foreign country which he has no intention of abandoning, who is a bona fide student qualified to pursue a full course of study and who seeks to enter the United States temporarily and solely for the purpose of pursuing such a course of study at an established institution of learning or other recognized place of study in the United States, particularly designated by him and approved by the Attorney General after consultation with the Office of Education of the United States, which institution or place of study shall have agreed to report to the Attorney General the termination of attendance of each nonimmigrant student, and if any such institution of learning or place of study fails to make reports promptly the approval shall be withdrawn, and (ii) the alien spouse and minor children of any such alien if accompanying him or following to join him;

\* \* \*

(J) An alien having a residence in a foreign country which he has no intention of abandoning who is a bona fide student, scholar, trainee, teacher, professor, research assistant, specialist, or leader in a field of specialized knowledge or skill, or other person of similar description who is coming temporarily to the United States as a participant in a program designated by the Secretary of State, for the purpose of teaching, instructing or lecturing, studying, observing, conducting research, consulting, demonstrating special skills, or receiving training and who, if he is coming to the United States to participate in a program under which he will receive graduate medical education or training, also meets the requirements of section 1182(j) of this title, and of the alien spouse and minor children of any such alien if accompanying him or following to join him.

\* \* \*

[Sec. 101, Immigration and Nationality Act, as amended by sec. 101, Act of June 27, 1952, 66 Stat. 166; sec.109, Act of Sept. 21,1961. 75 Stat. 534.]

[Reg. §31.3121(b)(19)-1.]

☐ [*T.D. 6744, 7-2-64. As amended by T.D. 8411, 4-27-92.* Note that Sec. 101(a)(15) of the Immigration and Nationality Act as reproduced above does not reflect current law.—CCH.]

### [Reg. §31.3121(b)(20)-1]

**§31.3121(b)(20)-1. Service performed on a boat engaged in catching fish.**—(a) *In general.*—(1) *Service performed on or after December 31, 1954, by an individual on a boat engaged in catching fish or other forms of aquatic animal life (hereinafter "fish") are excepted from employment if—*

(i) The individual receives a share of the boat's (or boats' for a fishing operation involving more than one boat) catch of fish or a share of the proceeds from the sale of the catch.

(ii) The amount of the individual's share depends solely on the amount of the boat's (or boats' for a fishing operation involving more than one boat) catch of fish.

(iii) The individual does not receive and is not entitled to receive, any cash remuneration, other than remuneration that is described in subdivision (1) of this subparagraph, and

(iv) The crew of the boat (or of each boat from which the individual receives a share of the catch) normally is made up of fewer than 10 individuals.

(2) The requirement of subdivision (ii) of subparagraph (1) is not satisfied if there exists an agreement with the boat's (or boats') owner or operator by which the individual's remuneration is determined partially or fully by a factor not dependent on the size of the catch. For example, if a boat is operated under a remuneration arrangement, *e.g.*, a collective agreement which specifies that crew members, in addition to receiving a share of the catch, are entitled to an hourly wage for repairing nets, regardless of whether this wage is actually paid, then all the crew members covered by the arrangement are entitled to receive cash remuneration other than a share of the

catch and their services are not excepted from employment by section 3121(b)(20).

(3) The operating crew of a boat includes all persons on the boat (including the captain) who receive any form of remuneration in exchange for services rendered while on a boat engaged in catching fish. See §1.6050A-1 for reporting requirements for the operator of a boat engaged in catching fish with respect to individuals performing services described in this section.

(4) During the same return period, service performed by a crew member may be excepted from employment by section 3121(b)(20) and this section for one voyage and not so excepted on a subsequent voyage on the same or on a different boat.

(5) During the same voyage, service performed by one crew member may be excepted from employment by section 3121(b)(20) and this section but service performed by another crew member may not be so excepted.

(b) *Special rule.*—Services performed after December 31, 1954, and before October 4, 1976, on a boat by an individual engaged in catching fish are not excepted from employment for any voyage (for purposes of section 3121(b) and the corresponding regulations), even though the individual satisfies the requirements of subdivision (i) through (iv) of paragraph (a)(1) of this section, if the owner or operator of the boat engaged in catching fish treated the individual as an employee. For purposes of this subparagraph, the individual was treated as an employee if—

(1) Form 941 was voluntarily filed by the boat operator or owner, regardless of whether the tax imposed by chapter 21 was withheld. For purposes of this subdivision, the filing of Form 941 is not voluntary if the filing was the result of action taken by the Service pursuant to section 6651(a) (relating to addition to the tax for failure to file tax return or to pay tax);

(2) The boat owner or operator withheld from the individual's share the tax imposed by chapter 21, regardless of whether the tax was paid over to the Service; or

(3) The boat owner or operator made full or partial payment of the tax imposed by chapter 21, unless the payment was made pursuant to section 7422(a) (relating to no civil actions for refund prior to filing claim for refund). However, for purposes of this paragraph crew members whose services, but for subdivisions (i) through (iii), would have been excepted from employment by section 3121(b)(20) are not required to pay self-employment tax on income earned in performing those services. See §1.1402(c)-3(g). Moreover, in such cases the employer is not entitled to a refund of the employer's share of any tax imposed by chapter 21 that was paid. [Reg. §31.3121(b)(20)-1.]

☐ [T.D. 7716, 8-27-80.]

### [Reg. §31.3121(c)-1]

**§31.3121(c)-1. Included and excluded services.**—(a) If a portion of the services performed by an employee for an employer during a pay period constitutes employment, and the remainder does not constitute employment, all the services performed by the employee for the employer during the period shall for purposes of the taxes be treated alike, that is, either all as included or all as excluded. The time during which the employee performs services which under section 3121(b) constitute employment, and the time during which he performs services which under such section do not constitute employment, within the pay period, determine whether all the services during the pay period shall be deemed to be included or excluded.

(b) If one-half or more of the employee's time in the employ of a particular person in a pay period is spent in performing services which constitute employment, then all the services of that employee for that person in that pay period shall be deemed to be employment.

(c) If less than one-half of the employee's time in the employ of a particular person in a pay period is spent in performing services which constitute employment, then none of the services of that employee for that person in that pay period shall be deemed to be employment.

(d) The application of the provisions of paragraphs (a), (b), and (c) of this section may be illustrated by the following example:

*Example.* The AB Club, which is a local college club within the meaning of section 3121(b)(2), employs D, a student who is enrolled and is regularly attending classes at a university, to perform domestic service for the club and to keep the club's books. The domestic services performed by D for the AB Club do not constitute employment, and his services as the club's bookkeeper constitute employment. D receives a payment at the end of each month for all services which he performs for the club. During a particular month D spends 60 hours in performing domestic service for the club and 40 hours as the club's bookkeeper. None of D's services during the month are deemed to be employment, since less than one-half of his services during the month constitutes employment. During another month D spends 35 hours in the performance of domestic services and 60 hours in keeping the club's books. All of D's services during the month are deemed to be employment, since one-half or more of his services during the month constitutes employment.

(e) For purposes of this section, a "pay period" is the period (of not more than 31 consecutive calendar days) for which a payment of remuneration is ordinarily made to the employee by the employer. Thus, if the periods for which payments of remuneration are made to the employee by the employer are of uniform duration, each such period constitutes a "pay period." If, however, the periods occasionally vary in duration, the "pay period" is the period for which a payment of remuneration is ordinarily made to the employee by the employer, even though that period does not coincide with the actual period for which a particular payment of remuneration is made. For example, if an employer ordinarily pays a particular employee for each calendar week at the end of the week, but the employee receives a payment in the middle of the week for the portion of the week already elapsed and receives the remainder at the end of the week, the "pay period" is still the calendar week; or if, instead, that employee is sent on a trip by such employer and receives at the end of the third week a single remuneration payment for three weeks' services, the "pay period" is still the calendar week.

(f) If there is only one period (and such period does not exceed 31 consecutive calendar days) for which a payment of remuneration is made to the employee by the employer, such period is deemed to be a "pay period" for purposes of this section.

(g) The rules set forth in this section do not apply (1) with respect to any services performed by the employee for the employer if the periods for which such employer makes payments of remuneration to the employee vary to the extent that there is no period "for which a payment or remuneration is ordinarily made to the employee," or (2) with respect to any services performed by the employee for the employer if the period for which a payment of remuneration is ordinarily made to the employee by such employer exceeds 31 consecutive calendar days, or (3) with respect to any service performed by the employee for the employer during a pay period if any of such service is excepted by section 3121(b)(9) (see § 31.3121(b)(9)-1).

(h) If during any period for which a person makes a payment of remuneration to an employee only a portion of the employee's services constitutes employment, but the rules prescribed in this section are not applicable, the taxes attach with respect to such services as constitute employment as defined in section 3121(b). [Reg. § 31.3121(c)-1.]

□ [T.D. 6190, 7-14-56. *Republished in T.D. 6516, 12-20-60, Amended by* T.D. 7-2-64.]

**⋙→ Caution: Reg. §31.3121(d)-1 has not been amended to reflect §530 of P.L. 95-600 or P.L. 104-188.**

**[Reg. §31.3121(d)-1]**

**§31.3121(d)-1. Who are employees.**—(a) *In general.*—(1) Whether an individual is an employee with respect to services performed after 1954 is determined in accordance with section 3121(d) and (o) and section 3506. This section of the regulations applies with respect only to services performed after 1954. Whether an individual is an employee with respect to services performed after 1936 and before 1940 shall be determined in accordance with the applicable provisions of law and of 26 CFR (1939) Part 401 (Regulations 91). Whether an individual is an employee with respect to services performed after 1939 and before 1951 shall be determined in accordance with the applicable provisions of law and of 26 CFR (1939) Part 402 (Regulations 106). Whether an individual is an employee with respect to services performed after 1950 and before 1955 shall be determined in accordance with the applicable provisions of law and of 26 CFR (1939) Part 408. (Regulations 128).

(2) Section 3121(d) contains three separate and independent tests for determining who are employees. Paragraphs (b), (c), and (d) of this section relate to the respective tests. Paragraph (b) relates to the test for determining whether an officer of a corporation is an employee of the corporation. Paragraph (c) relates to the test for determining whether an individual is an employee under the usual common law rules. Paragraph (d) relates to the test for determining which individuals in certain occupational groups who are not employees under the usual common law rules are included as employees. If an individual is an employee under any one of the tests, he is to be considered an employee for purposes of the regulations in this subpart whether or not he is an employee under any of the other tests.

(3) If the relationship of employer and employee exists, the designation or description of the relationship by the parties as anything other than that of employer and employee is immaterial. Thus, if such relationship exists, it is of no consequence that the employee is designated as a partner, co-adventurer, agent, independent contractor, or the like.

(4) All classes or grades of employees are included within the relationship of employer and employee. Thus, superintendents, managers, and other supervisory personnel are employees.

(5) Although an individual may be an employee under this section, his services may be of such a nature, or performed under such circumstances, as not to constitute employment (see § 31.3121(b)-3).

(b) *Corporate officers.*—Generally, an officer of a corporation is an employee of the corporation. However, an officer of a corporation who as such does not perform any services or performs only minor services and who neither receives nor is entitled to receive, directly or indirectly, any remuneration is considered not to be an employee of the corporation. A director of a corporation in his capacity as such is not an employee of the corporation.

(c) *Common law employees.*—(1) Every individual is an employee if under the usual common law rules the relationship between him and the person for whom he performs services is the legal relationship of employer and employee.

(2) Generally such relationship exists when the person for whom services are performed has the right to control and direct the individual who performs the services, not only as to the result to be accomplished by the work but also as to the details and means by which that result is accomplished. That is, an employee is subject to the will and control of the employer not only as to what shall be done but how it shall be done. In this connection, it is not necessary that the employer actually direct or control the manner in which the services are performed; it is sufficient if he has the right to do so. The right to discharge is also an important factor indicating that the person possessing that right is an employer. Other factors characteristic of an employer, but not necessarily present in every case, are the furnishing of tools and the furnishing of a place to work, to the individual who performs the services. In general, if an individual is subject to the control or direction of another merely as to the result to be accomplished by the work and not as to the means and methods for accomplishing the result, he is an independent contractor. An individual performing services as an independent contractor is not as to such services an employee under the usual common law rules. Individuals such as physicians, lawyers, dentists, veterinarians, construction contractors, public stenographers, and auctioneers, engaged in the pursuit of an independent trade, business, or profession, in which they offer their services to the public, are independent contractors and not employees.

(3) Whether the relationship of employer and employee exists under the usual common law rules will in doubtful cases be determined upon an examination of the particular facts of each case.

(d) *Special classes of employees.*—(1) In addition to individuals who are employees under paragraph (b) or (c) of this section, other individuals are employees if they perform services for remuneration under certain prescribed circumstances in the following occupational groups:

(i) as an agent-driver or commission-driver engaged in distributing meat products, vegetable products, fruit products, bakery products, beverages (other than milk), or laundry or dry-cleaning services for his principal;

(ii) as a full-time life insurance salesman;

(iii) as a homeworker performing work, according to specifications furnished by the person for whom the services are performed, on materials or goods furnished by such person which are required to be returned to such person or a person designated by him; or

(iv) as a traveling or city salesman, other than as an agent-driver or commission-driver, engaged upon a full-time basis in the solicitation on behalf of, and the transmission to, his principal (except for side-line sales activities on behalf of some other person) of orders from wholesalers, retailers, contractors, or operators of hotels, restaurants, or other similar establishments for merchandise for resale or supplies for use in their business operations.

(2) In order for an individual to be an employee under this paragraph, the individual must perform services in an occupation falling within one of the enumerated groups. If the individual does not perform services in one of the designated occupational groups, he is not an employee under this paragraph. An individual who is not an employee under this paragraph may nevertheless be an employee under paragraph (b) or (c) of this section. The language used to designate the respective occupational groups relates to fields of endeavor in which particular designations are not necessarily in universal use with respect to the same service. The designations are addressed to the actual services without regard to any technical or colloquial labels which may be attached to such services. Thus, a determination whether services fall within one of the designated occupational groups depends upon the facts of the particular situation.

(3) The factual situations set forth below are illustrative of some of the individuals falling within each of the above enumerated occupational groups. The illustrative factual situations are as follows:

(i) *Agent-driver or commission-driver.*—This occupational group includes agent-drivers or commission-drivers who are engaged in distributing meat or meat products, vegetables or vegetable products, fruit or fruit products, bakery products, beverages (other than milk), or laundry or dry-cleaning services for their principals. An agent-driver or commission-driver includes an individual who operates his own truck or the truck of the person for whom he performs services, serves customers designated by such person as well as those solicited on his own, and whose compensation is a commission on his sales or the difference between the price he charges his customers and the price he pays to such person for the product or service.

(ii) *Full-time life insurance salesman.*—An individual whose entire or principal business activity is devoted to the solicitation of life insurance or annuity contracts, or both, primarily for one life insurance company is a full-time life insurance salesman. Such a salesman ordinarily uses the office space provided by the company or its general agent, and stenographic assistance, telephone facilities, forms, rate books, and advertising materials are usually made available to him without cost. An individual who is engaged in the general insurance business under a contract or contracts of service which do not contemplate that the individual's principal business activity will be the solicitation of life insurance or annuity contracts, or both, for one company, or any individual who devotes only part time to the solicitation of life insurance contracts, including annuity contracts, and is principally engaged in other endeavors, is not a full-time life insurance salesman.

(iii) *Home workers.*—This occupational group includes a worker who performs services off the premises of the person for whom the services are performed, according to specifications furnished by such person, on materials or goods furnished by such person which are required to be returned to such person or a person designated by him. For provisions relating to the determination of wages in the case of a home worker to whom this subdivision is applicable, see § 31.3121(a)(10)-1.

(iv) *Traveling or city salesman.*—(a) This occupational group includes a city or traveling salesman who is engaged upon a full-time basis in the solicitation on behalf of, and the transmission to, his principal (except for side-line sales activities on behalf of some other person or persons) of orders from wholesalers, retailers, contractors, or operators of hotels, restaurants, or other similar establishments for merchandise for resale or supplies for use in their business operations. An agent-driver or commission-driver is not within this occupational group. City or traveling salesmen who sell to retailers or to the others specified, operate off the premises of their principals, and are generally compensated on a commission basis, are within this occupational group. Such salesmen are generally not controlled as to the details of their services or the means by which they cover their territories, but in the ordinary case they are expected to call on regular customers with a fair degree of regularity.

(b) In order for a city or traveling salesman to be included within this occupational group, his entire or principal business activity must be devoted to the solicitation of orders for one principal. Thus, the multiple-line salesman generally is not within this occupational group. However, if the salesman solicits orders primarily for one principal, he is not excluded from this occupational group solely because of side-line sales activities on behalf of one or more other persons. In such a case, the salesman is within this occupational group only with respect to the services performed for the person for whom he primarily solicits orders and not with respect to the services performed for such other persons. The following examples illustrate the application of the foregoing provisions:

*Example (1).* Salesman A's principal business activity is the solicitation of orders from retail pharmacies on behalf of the X Wholesale Drug Company. A also occasionally solicits orders for drugs on behalf of the Y and Z companies. A is within this occupational group with respect to his services for the X Company but not with respect to his services for either the Y Company or the Z Company.

*Example (2).* Salesman B's principal business activity is the solicitation of orders from retail hardware stores on behalf of the R Tool Company and the S Cooking Utensil Company. B regularly solicits orders on behalf of both companies. B is not within this occupational group with respect to the services performed for either the R Company or the S Company.

*Example (3).* Salesman C's principal business activity is the house-to-house solicitation of orders on behalf of the T brush company. C occasionally solicits such orders from retail stores and restaurants. C is not within this occupational group.

(4)(i) The fact that an individual falls within one of the enumerated occupational groups, however, does not make such individual an employee under this paragraph unless (*a*) the contract of service contemplates that substantially all the services to which the contract relates in the particular designated occupation are to be performed personally by such individual; (*b*) such individual has no substantial investment in the facilities used in connection with the performance of such services (other than in facilities for transportation), and (*c*) such services are part of a continuing relationship with the person for whom the services are performed and are not in the nature of a single transaction.

(ii) The term "contract of service," as used in this paragraph, means an arrangement, formal or informal, under which the particular services are performed. The requirement that the contract of service shall contemplate that substantially all the services to which the contract relates in the particular designated occupation are to be performed personally by the individual means that it is not contemplated that any material part of the services to which the contract relates in such occupation will be delegated to any other person by the individual who undertakes under the contract to perform such services.

(iii) The facilities to which reference is made in this paragraph include equipment and premises available for the work or enterprise as distinguished from education, training, and experience, but do not include such tools, instruments, equipment, or clothing, as are commonly or frequently provided by employees. An investment in an automobile by an individual which is used primarily for his own transportation in connection with the performance of services for another person has no significance under this paragraph, since such investment is comparable to outlays for transportation by an individual performing similar services who does not own an automobile. Moreover, the investment in facilities for the transportation of the goods or commodities to which the services relate is to be excluded in determining the investment in a particular case. If an individual has a substantial investment in facilities of the requisite character, he is not an employee within the meaning of this paragraph, since a substantial investment of the requisite character standing alone is sufficient to exclude the individual from the employee concept under this paragraph.

(iv) If the services are not performed as part of a continuing relationship with the person for whom the services are performed, but are in the nature of a single transaction, the individual performing such services is not an employee of such person within the meaning of this paragraph. The fact that the services are not performed on consecutive workdays does not indicate that the services are not performed as part of a continuing relationship. [Reg. § 31.3121(d)-1.]

☐ [*T.D.* 6190, 7-14-56. *Republished in T.D.* 6516, 12-20-60. *Amended by T.D.* 6744, 7-2-64 *and T.D.* 7691, 4-9-80.]

**[Reg. § 31.3121(d)-2]**

**§ 31.3121(d)-2. Who are employers.**—(a) Every person is an employer if he employs one or more employees. Neither the number of employees employed nor the period during which any such employee is employed is material for the purpose of determining whether the person for whom the services are performed is an employer.

(b) An employer may be an individual, a corporation, a partnership, a trust, an estate, a joint-stock company, an association, or a syndicate, group, pool, joint venture, or other unincorporated organization, group, or entity. A trust or estate, rather than the fiduciary acting for or on behalf of the trust or estate, is generally the employer.

(c) Although a person may be an employer under this section, services performed in his employ may be of such a nature, or performed under such circumstances, as not to constitute employment (see § 31.3121(b)-3). [Reg. § 31.3121(d)-2.]

☐ [*T.D.* 6190, 7-14-56. *Republished in T.D.* 6516, 12-20-60.]

**[Reg. § 31.3121(e)-1]**

**§ 31.3121(e)-1. State, United States, and citizen.**—(a) When used in the regulations in this subpart, the term "State" includes the District of Columbia, the Commonwealth of Puerto Rico, the Virgin Islands, the Territories of Alaska and Hawaii before their admission as States, and (when used with respect to services performed after 1960) Guam and American Samoa.

(b) When used in the regulations in this subpart, the term "United States", when used in a geographical sense, means the several states (including the Territories of Alaska and Hawaii before their admission as States), the District of Columbia, the Commonwealth of Puerto Rico, and the Virgin Islands. When used in the regulations in this subpart with respect to services performed after 1960, the term "United States" also includes Guam and American Samoa when the term is used in a geographical sense. The term "citizen of the United States" includes a citizen of the Commonwealth of Puerto Rico or the Virgin Islands, and, effective January 1, 1961, a citizen of Guam or American Samoa. [Reg. § 31.3121(e)-1.]

☐ [*T.D. 6190, 7-14-56. Republished in T.D. 6516, 12-20-60. Amended by T.D. 6744, 7-2-64.*]

### [Reg. § 31.3121(f)-1]

**§ 31.3121(f)-1. American vessel and aircraft.**—(a) The term "American vessel" means any vessel which is documented (that is, registered, enrolled, or licensed) or numbered in conformity with the laws of the United States. It also includes any vessel which is neither documented nor numbered under the laws of the United States, nor documented under the laws of any foreign country, if the crew of such vessel is employed solely by one or more citizens or residents of the United States or corporations organized under the laws of the United States or of any State. (For provisions relating to the terms "State" and "citizens", see § 31.3121(e)-1.)

(b) The term "American aircraft" means any aircraft registered under the laws of the United States.

(c) For provisions relating to services performed outside the United States on or in connection with an American vessel or American aircraft, see paragraph (c)(2) of § 31.3121(b)-3. [Reg. § 31.3121(f)-1.]

☐ [*T.D. 6190, 7-14-56. Republished in T.D. 6516, 12-20-60. Amended by T.D. 6744, 7-2-64.*]

### [Reg. § 31.3121(g)-1]

**§ 31.3121(g)-1. Agricultural labor.**—(a) *In general.*—(1) The term "agricultural labor" as defined in section 3121(g) includes services of the character described in paragraphs (b), (c), (d), (e) and (f) of this section. In general, however, the term does not include services performed in connection with forestry, lumbering, or landscaping.

(2) The term "farm" as used in the regulations in this subpart includes stock, dairy, poultry, fruit, fur-bearing animal, and truck farms, plantations, ranches, nurseries, ranges, orchards, and such greenhouses and other similar structures as are used primarily for the raising of agricultural or horticultural commodities. Greenhouses and other similar structures used primarily for other purposes (for example, display, storage, and fabrication of wreaths, corsages, and bouquets) do not constitute "farms".

(3) For provisions relating to the exception from employment provided with respect to services performed by certain foreign agricultural workers and to services performed before 1959 in connection with the production or harvesting of certain oleo-resinous products, see § 31.3121(b)(1)-1. For provisions relating to the exclusion from wages of remuneration paid in any medium other than cash for agricultural labor and to the test for determining whether cash remuneration paid for agricultural labor constitutes wages, see § 31.3121(a)(8)-1.

(b) *Services described in section 3121(g)(1).*—(1) Services performed on a farm by an employee of any person in connection with any of the following activities constitute agricultural labor:

(i) The cultivation of the soil;

(ii) The raising, shearing, feeding, caring for, training, or management of livestock, bees, poultry, fur-bearing animals, or wildlife; or

(iii) The raising or harvesting of any other agricultural or horticultural commodity.

(2) Services performed in connection with the production or harvesting of maple sap, or in connection with the raising or harvesting of mushrooms, or in connection with the hatching of poultry constitute agricultural labor only if such services are performed on a farm. Thus, services performed in connection with the operation of a hatchery, if not operated as part of a poultry or other farm, do not constitute agricultural labor.

(c) *Services described in section 3121(g)(2).*—(1) The following services performed by an employee in the employ of the owner or tenant or other operator of one or more farms constitute agricultural labor, provided the major part of such services is performed on a farm:

(i) Services performed in connection with the operation, management, conservation, improvement, or maintenance of any of such farms or its tools or equipment; or

(ii) Services performed in salvaging timber, or clearing land of brush and other debris, left by a hurricane.

(2) The services described in subparagraph (1)(i) of this paragraph may include, for example, services performed by carpenters, painters, mechanics, farm supervisors, irrigation engineers, bookkeepers, and other skilled or semi-skilled workers, which contribute in any way to the conduct of the farm or farms, as such, operated by

the person employing them, as distinguished from any other enterprise in which such person may be engaged.

(3) Since the services described in this paragraph must be performed in the employ of the owner or tenant or other operator of the farm, the term "agricultural labor" does not include services performed by employees of a commercial painting concern, for example, which contracts with a farmer to renovate his farm properties.

(d) *Services described in section 3121(g)(3).*—Services performed by an employee in the employ of any person in connection with any of the following operations constitute agricultural labor without regard to the place where such services are performed:

(1) The ginning of cotton;

(2) The operation or maintenance of ditches, canals, reservoirs, or waterways, not owned or operated for profit, used exclusively for supplying or storing water for farming purposes; or

(3) The production or harvesting of crude gum (oleoresin) from a living tree or the processing of such crude gum into gum spirits of turpentine and gum rosin, provided such processing is carried on by the original producer of such crude gum.

(e) *Services described in section 3121(g)(4).*—(1) Services performed by an employee in the handling, planting, drying, packing, packaging, processing, freezing, grading, storing, or delivering to storage or to market or to a carrier for transportation to market, of any agricultural or horticultural commodity constitute agricultural labor if:

(i) Such services are performed by the employee in the employ of an operator of a farm or in the employ of a group of operators of farms (other than a cooperative organization);

(ii) Such services are performed with respect to the commodity in its unmanufactured state; and

(iii) Such operator produced more than one-half of the commodity with respect to which such services are performed during the pay period, or such group of operators produced all of the commodity with respect to which such services are performed during the pay period.

(2) The term "operator of a farm" as used in this paragraph means an owner, tenant, or other person, in possession of a farm and engaged in the operation of such farm.

(3) The services described in this paragraph do not constitute agricultural labor if performed in the employ of a cooperative organization. The term "organization" includes corporations, joint-stock companies, and associations which are treated as corporations pursuant to section 7701(a)(3) of the Internal Revenue Code. For purposes of this paragraph, any unincorporated group of operators shall be deemed a cooperative organization if the number of operators comprising such group is more than 20 at any time during the calendar quarter in which the services involved are performed.

(4) Processing services which change the commodity from its raw or natural state do not constitute agricultural labor. For example, the extraction of juices from fruits or vegetables is a processing operation which changes the character of the fruits or vegetables from their raw or natural state and, therefore, does not constitute agricultural labor. Likewise, services performed in the processing of maple sap into maple sirup or maple sugar do not constitute agricultural labor. On the other hand, services rendered in the cutting and drying of fruits or vegetables are processing operations which do not change the character of the fruits or vegetables and, therefore, constitute agricultural labor, if the other requisite conditions are met. Services performed with respect to a commodity after its character has been changed from its raw or natural state by a processing operation do not constitute agricultural labor.

(5) The term "commodity" refers to a single agricultural or horticultural product, for example, all apples are to be treated as a single commodity, while apples and peaches are to be treated as two separate commodities. The services with respect to each such commodity are to be considered separately in determining whether the condition set forth in subparagraph (1)(iii) of this paragraph has been satisfied. The portion of the commodity produced by an operator or group of operators with respect to which the services described in this paragraph are performed by a particular employee shall be determined on the basis of the pay period in which such services were performed by such employee.

(6) The services described in this paragraph do not include services performed in connection with commercial canning or commercial freezing or in connection with any commodity after its delivery to a terminal market for distribution for consumption. Moreover, since the services described in this paragraph must be rendered in the actual handling, planting, drying, packing, packaging, processing, freezing, grading, storing, or delivering to storage or to market or to a carrier for transportation to market, of the commodity, such services do not, for example, include services performed as stenographers, bookkeepers, clerks, and other office employees, even though such services may be in connection with such activities. However, to the extent that the services of such individuals are performed in the

employ of the owner or tenant or other operator of a farm and are rendered in major part on a farm, they may be within the provisions of paragraph (c) of this section.

(f) *Services described in section 3121(g)(5).*—(1) Service not in the course of the employer's trade or business (see paragraph (a)(1) of §31.3121(a)(7)-1) or domestic service in a private home of the employer (see paragraph (a)(2) of §31.3121(a)(7)-1) constitutes agricultural labor if such service is performed on a farm operated for profit. The determination whether remuneration for any such service performed on a farm operated for profit constitutes wages is to be made under §31.3121(a)(8)-1 rather than under §31.3121(a)(7)-1. For provisions relating to the exception from employment provided with respect to any such service performed after 1960 by a father or mother in the employ of his or her son or daughter, see §31.3121(b)(3)-1.

(2) Generally, a farm is not operated for profit if it is occupied by the employer primarily for residential purposes, or is used primarily for the pleasure of the employer or his family such as for the entertainment of guests or as a hobby of the employer or his family. [Reg. §31.3121(g)-1.]

☐ [T.D. 6190, 7-14-56. *Republished in T.D. 6516, 12-20-60. Amended by* T.D. 6744, 7-2-64.]

### [Reg. §31.3121(h)-1]

**§31.3121(h)-1. American employer.**—(a) The term "American employer" means an employer which is (1) the United States or any instrumentality thereof, (2) an individual who is a resident of the United States, (3) a partnership, if two-thirds or more of the partners are residents of the United States, (4) a trust, if all of the trustees are residents of the United States, or (5) a corporation organized under the laws of the United States or of any State. For provisions relating to the terms "State" and "United States," see §31.3121(e)-1.

(b) For provisions relating to services performed outside the United States by a citizen of the United States as an employee for an American employer, see paragraph (c)(3) of §31.3121(b)-3 and paragraph (e) of §31.3121(b)(4)-1. [Reg. §31.3121(h)-1.]

☐ [T.D. 6190, 7-14-56. *Republished in T.D. 6516, 12-20-60. Amended by* T.D. 6744, 7-2-64.]

⫸→ *Caution: This regulation has not been amended to reflect changes enacted by the Omnibus Budget Reconciliation Act of 1987 (P.L. 100-203).*

### [Reg. §31.3121(i)-2]

**§31.3121(i)-2. Computation of remuneration for service performed by an individual as a member of a uniformed service.**—In the case of an individual performing service after December 31, 1956, as a member of a uniformed service (see §31.3121(n)), to which the provisions of section 3121(m)(1) (see §31.3121(m)) are applicable, the

⫸→ *Caution: This regulation has not been amended to reflect changes enacted by the Omnibus Budget Reconciliation Act of 1987 (P.L. 100-203).*

### [Reg. §31.3121(i)-3]

**§31.3121(i)-3. Computation of remuneration for service performed by an individual as a volunteer or volunteer leader within the meaning of the Peace Corps Act.**—In the case of an individual performing service in his capacity as a volunteer or volunteer leader within the meaning of the Peace Corps Act (see §31.3121(p)), the term "wages" shall, subject to the provisions of section 3121(a)(1) (see §31.3121(a)-1), include as such individual's remuneration for such service only amounts paid pursuant to section 5(c) or section 6(1) of the Peace Corps Act (22 U.S.C. 2501; 75 Stat. 612). [Reg. §31.3121(i)-3.]

☐ [T.D. 6744, 7-2-64.]

### [Reg. §31.3121(i)-4]

**§31.3121(i)-4. Computation of remuneration for service performed by certain members or religious orders.**—In any case where an individual is a member of a religious order (as defined in section 3121(r)(2) and paragraph (b) of §31.3121(r)-1) performing service in the exercise of duties required by such order, and an election of coverage under section 3121(r) and §31.3121(r)-1 is in effect with respect to such order or its autonomous subdivision to which such member belongs, the term "wages" shall, subject to the provisions of section 3121(a)(1) (relating to definition of wages), include as such individual's remuneration for such service the fair market value of any board, lodging, clothing, and other perquisites furnished to such member by such order or subdivision or by any other person or organization pursuant to an agreement (whether written or oral) with such order or subdivision. Such other perquisites shall include any cash either paid by such order or subdivision or paid by another employer and not required by such order or subdivision to be remitted to it. For purposes of this section, perquisites shall be considered to be furnished over the period during which the member receives the benefit of them. (See example (4) of this section.) In no case shall the amount included as such individual's remuneration under this

### [Reg. §31.3121(i)-1]

**§31.3121(i)-1. Computation to nearest dollar of cash remuneration for domestic service.**—(a) An employer may, for purposes of the Act, elect to compute to the nearest dollar any payment of cash remuneration for domestic service described in section 3121(a)(7)(B) (see §31.3121(a)(7)-1) which is more or less than a whole-dollar amount. For the purpose of the computation to the nearest dollar, the payment of a fractional part of a dollar shall be disregarded unless it amounts to one-half dollar or more, in which case it shall be increased to one dollar. For example, any amount actually paid between $4.50 and $5.49, inclusive, may be treated as $5 for purposes of the taxes imposed by the Act. If an employer elects this method of computation with respect to any payment of cash remuneration made in a calendar year for domestic service in his private home, he must use the same method in computing each payment of cash remuneration of more or less than a whole-dollar amount made to each of his employees in such calendar year for domestic service in his private home. Moreover, if an employer elects this method of computation with respect to payments of the prescribed character made in any calendar year, the amount of each payment of cash remuneration so computed to the nearest dollar shall, in lieu of the amount actually paid, be deemed to constitute the amount of cash remuneration for purposes of the Act. Thus, the amount of cash payments so computed to the nearest dollar shall be used for purposes of determining whether such payments constitute wages, for purposes of applying the employee and employer tax rates to the wage payments, for purposes of any required record keeping, and for purposes of reporting and paying the employee tax and employer tax with respect to such wage payments.

(b) The provisions of this section apply to any cash payment for domestic service in a private home of the employer made on or after January 1, 1994. For rules applicable to any cash payment for domestic service in a private home of the employer made prior to January 1, 1994, see §31.3121(i)-1 in effect at such time (see 26 CFR part 31 contained in the edition of 26 CFR Parts 30 to 39, revised as of April 1, 2006). [Reg. §31.3121(i)-1.]

☐ [T.D. 6190, 7-14-56. *Republished in T.D. 6516, 12-20-60. Amended by* T.D. 9266, 6-16-2006.]

term "wages" shall, subject to the provisions of section 3121(a)(1) (see §31.3121(a)-1), include as the individual's remuneration for such service only his basic pay as described in section 102(10) of the Servicemen's and Veterans' Survivor Benefits Act (38 U.S.C., 401(1), 403; 72 Stat. 1126). [Reg. §31.3121(i)-2.]

☐ [T.D. 6744, 7-2-64.]

paragraph be less than $100 a month. All relevant facts and elements of value shall be considered in every case. Where the fair market value of any board, lodging, clothing, and other perquisites furnished to all members of an electing religious order or autonomous subdivision (or to all in a group of members) does not vary significantly, such order or subdivision may treat all of its members (or all in such group of members) as having a uniform wage. The provisions of this section may be illustrated by the following examples of the treatment of particular perquisites:

*Example (1).* M is a religious order which requires its members to take a vow of poverty and which has made an election under section 3121(r). Under section 3121(i)(4), M must include in the wages of its members the fair market value of the clothing it provides for its members. M and several other religious orders using essentially the same type of religious habit purchase clothing for their members from either of two suppliers in arms-length transactions. The fair market value of such clothing (*i.e.,* the price at which such items would change hands between a willing buyer and a willing seller, neither being under any compulsion to buy or to sell) is determined by reference to the actual sales price of these suppliers to the religious orders.

*Example (2).* N is a religious order which requires its members to take a vow of poverty and which has made an election under section 3121(r). N operates a seminary adjacent to a university. Students at the university obtain lodging and board on campus from the university for its fair market value of $2,000 for the school year. Such lodging and board is essentially the same as that provided by N at its seminary to N's members subject to a vow of poverty. Accordingly, the amount to be included in the "wages" of such members with respect to lodging and board for the same period of time is $2,000.

*Example (3).* O is a religious order which requires its members to take a vow of poverty and to observe silence, and which has made an election under section 3121(r). O operates a monastery in a remote rural area. Under section 3121(i)(4), O must include in the wages of its members assigned to this monastery the fair market value of the board and lodging furnished to them. In making a determination of the fair market value of such board and lodging, the remoteness of the monastery, as well as the smallness of the rooms and the simplicity of their furnishings, affect this determination. However, the facts that the facility is used by a religious order as a monastery and that the order's members maintain silence do not affect the fair market value of such items.

*Example (4).* P is a religious order which requires its members to take a vow of poverty and which has made an election under section 3121(r). Several of P's members are attending a university on a full-time basis. The fair market value of the board and lodging of each of such members at the university is $1,000 per semester. P pays the university $1,000 at the beginning of each semester for the board and lodging of each of such members. In addition, P gives each such member a $400 cash advance to cover his miscellaneous expenses during the semester. Under section 3121(i)(4), P must prorate the fair market value of such members' board and lodging, as well as the miscellaneous items, over the semester and include such value in the determination of "wages."

*Example (5).* Q is a religious order which is a corporation organized under the laws of Wisconsin, which requires its members to take a vow of poverty, and which has made an election under section 3121(r). Q has convents in rural South America and in suburbs and central city areas of the United States. Characteristically, in the United States its suburban convents provide somewhat larger and newer rooms for its members than do its convents in city areas. Moreover, its suburban convents have more extensive grounds and somewhat more elaborate facilities than do its older convents in city areas. However, both types of convents limit resident members to a single, plainly furnished room and provide them meals which are comparable. Q's members in South America live in extremely primitive dwellings and otherwise have extremely modest perquisites. Under section 3121(i)(4), Q may report a uniform wage for its members who live in suburban convents and city convents in the United States, as the board, lodging, and perquisites furnished these members do not vary significantly from one convent to the other. Q may report another uniform wage (but not less than $100 per month apiece) for its members who are citizens of the United States and who reside in South America based on the fair market value of the perquisites furnished these individuals, as the fair market value of the perquisites furnished these individuals varies significantly from that of those furnished its members who live in its domestic convents but does not vary significantly among members in South America whose wages are subject to tax. [Reg. § 31.3121(i)-4.]

☐ [*T.D. 7280, 7-10-73.*]

**[Reg. § 31.3121(j)-1]**

**§ 31.3121(j)-1. Covered transportation service.**—(a) *Transportation systems acquired in whole or in part after 1936 and before 1951.*—(1) *In general.*—Except as provided in subparagraph (2) of this paragraph, all service performed in the employ of a State or political subdivision thereof in connection with its operation of a public transportation system constitutes covered transportation service if any part of the transportation system was acquired from private ownership after 1936 and before 1951. For purposes of this subparagraph, it is immaterial whether any part of the transportation system was acquired before 1937 or after 1950, whether the employee was hired before, during, or after 1950, or whether the employee had been employed by the employer from whom the State or political subdivision acquired its transportation system or any part thereof.

(2) *General retirement system protected by State constitution.*—Except as provided in subparagraph (3) of this paragraph, service performed in the employ of a State or political subdivision in connection with its operation of a public transportation system acquired in whole or in part from private ownership after 1936 and before 1951 does not constitute covered transportation service, if substantially all service in connection with the operation of the transportation system was, on December 31, 1950, covered under a general retirement system providing benefits which are protected from diminution or impairment under the State constitution by reason of an express provision, dealing specifically with retirement systems established by the State or political subdivisions of the State, which forbids such diminution or impairment.

(3) *Additions to certain transportation systems by acquisition after 1950.*—This subparagraph is applicable only in case of an acquisition after 1950 from private ownership of an addition to an existing public transportation system which was acquired in whole or in part by a State or political subdivision thereof from private ownership after 1936 and before 1951 and then only in case service for such existing transportation system did not constitute covered transportation service by reason of the provisions of subparagraph (2) of this paragraph. Service in connection with the operation of such

transportation system (including any additions acquired after 1950) constitutes covered transportation service commencing with the first day of the third calendar quarter following the calendar quarter in which the addition to the existing transportation system was acquired, if such service is performed by an employee who became an employee of the State or political subdivision in connection with and at the time of its acquisition from private ownership of such addition and who before the acquisition of such addition rendered service in employment in connection with the operation of the addition so acquired by such State or political subdivision. However, service performed by such employee in connection with the operation of the transportation system does not constitute covered transportation service if, on the first day of the third calendar quarter following the calendar quarter in which the addition was acquired, such service is covered by a general retirement system which does not, with respect to such employee, contain special provisions applicable only to employees who became employees of the State or political subdivision in connection with and at the time of its acquisition of such addition.

(b) *Transportation systems in operation on December 31, 1950, no part of which was acquired after 1936 and before 1951.*—(1) *In general.*—Except as provided in subparagraph (2) of this paragraph, no service performed in the employ of a State or a political subdivision thereof in connection with its operation of a public transportation system constitutes covered transportation service if no part of such transportation system operated by the State or political subdivision on December 31, 1950, was acquired from private ownership after 1936 and before 1951.

(2) *Additions acquired after 1950.*—This subparagraph is applicable only in case of an acquisition after 1950 from private ownership of an addition to an existing public transportation system which was operated by a State or political subdivision on December 31, 1950, but no part of which was acquired from private ownership after 1936 and before 1951. Service in connection with the operation of such transportation system (including any additions acquired after 1950) constitutes covered transportation service commencing with the first day of the third calendar quarter following the calendar quarter in which the addition to the existing transportation system was acquired, if such service is performed by an employee who became an employee of the State or political subdivision in connection with and at the time of its acquisition from private ownership of such addition and who before the acquisition of such addition rendered service in employment in connection with the operation of the addition so acquired by such State or political subdivision. However, service performed by such employee in connection with the operation of the transportation system does not constitute covered transportation service if, on the first day of the third calendar quarter following the calendar quarter in which the addition was acquired, such service is covered by a general retirement system which does not, with respect to such employee, contain special provisions applicable only to employees who became employees of the State or political subdivision in connection with and at the time of its acquisition of such addition.

(c) *Transportation systems acquired after 1950.*—All service performed in the employ of a State or political subdivision thereof in connection with its operation of a public transportation system constitutes covered transportation service if the transportation system was not operated by the State or political subdivision before 1951 and, at the time of its first acquisition after 1950 from private ownership of any part of its transportation system, the State or political subdivision did not have a general retirement system covering substantially all service performed in connection with the operation of the transportation system.

(d) *Definitions.*—For purposes of this section:

(1) The term "general retirement system" means any pension, annuity, retirement, or similar fund or system established by a State or by a political subdivision thereof for employees of the State, political subdivision, or both; but such term does not include such a fund or system which covers only service performed in positions connected with the operation of its public transportation system.

(2) A transportation system or a part thereof is considered to have been acquired by a State or political subdivision from private ownership if prior to the acquisition service performed by employees in connection with the operation of the system or an acquired part thereof constituted employment under the Act or under subchapter A of chapter 9 of the Internal Revenue Code of 1939 or was covered by an agreement entered into pursuant to section 218 of the Social Security Act, and some of such employees became employees of the State or political subdivision in connection with and at the time of such acquisition.

(3) The term "political subdivision" includes an instrumentality of a State, of one or more political subdivisions of a State, or of a State and one or more of its political subdivisions.

(4) The term "employment" includes service covered by an agreement entered into pursuant to section 218 of the Social Security Act. [Reg. §31.3121(j)-1.]

□ [*T.D.* 6190, 7-14-56. *Republished in T.D.* 6516, 12-20-60.]

### [Reg. §31.3121(l)-1]

**§31.3121(l)-1. Agreements entered into by domestic corporations with respect to foreign subsidiaries.**—For provisions relating to the extension of the Federal old-age, survivors, and disability insurance system established by title II of the Social Security Act to certain services performed outside the United States by citizens of the United States in the employ of a foreign subsidiary of a domestic corporation, see the Regulations Relating to Contract Coverage of Employees of Foreign Subsidiaries (Part 36 of this chapter). [Reg. §31.3121(l)-1.]

□ [*T.D.* 6190, 7-14-56. *Republished in T.D.* 6516, 12-20-60.]

### [Reg. §36.3121(l)-0]

**§36.3121(l)-0. Introduction.**—(a) The regulations in this part deal with the circumstances under which a domestic corporation may enter into an agreement with the Internal Revenue Service for the purpose of extending the insurance system established by title II of the Social Security Act to certain services performed outside the United States by citizens of the United States as employees of a foreign subsidiary of the domestic corporation, and with the obligations of a domestic corporation which enters into such an agreement. The provisions of the Internal Revenue Code of 1954, as amended, to which the regulations in this part pertain are contained in section 3121(l). The liabilities assumed under an agreement entered into pursuant to such section are based on the remuneration for services covered by the agreement. Such agreement may not be effective prior to January 1, 1955.

(b) Although the obligations incurred under an agreement entered into pursuant to section 3121(l) of the Internal Revenue Code of 1954, as amended, must be distinguished from the obligations imposed on employers with respect to the taxes under the Federal Insurance Contributions Act, the two are similar in many respects. Accordingly, the regulations in this part are prescribed as a supplement to the regulations (26 CFR (1954), Part 31, Subpart B) relating to the employee tax and the employer tax imposed by the Federal Insurance Contributions Act. The terms used in the regulations in this part have the same meaning, unless otherwise provided, as when used in the regulations relating to the taxes imposed by such act.

(c) The regulations in this part constitute Part 36 of title 26 of the Code of Federal Regulations. As used in the regulations in this part, the word "Code" means the Internal Revenue Code of 1954, as amended, and the term "Federal Insurance Contributions Act" means chapter 21 of such Code. All references to sections of law are references to the Code unless otherwise indicated. The number of each section of the regulations begins with 36 followed by a decimal point (36.). Numbers which do not begin with 36 followed by a decimal point are numbers of sections of law unless otherwise indicated. In identifying sections of regulations, the symbol "§" is used. [Reg. §36.3121(l)-0.]

□ [*T.D.* 6145, 12-31-60. *Amended by T.D.* 7012, 5-15-69 *and T.D.* 7665, 1-25-80.]

### [Reg. §36.3121(l)(1)-1]

**§36.3121(l)(1)-1. Agreements entered into by domestic corporations with respect to foreign subsidiaries.**—(a) *In general.*—(1) Any domestic corporation having one or more foreign subsidiaries may request the Internal Revenue Service to enter into an agreement for the purpose of extending the Federal old-age, survivors, and disability insurance system established by title II of the Social Security Act to certain services performed outside the United States by all citizens of the United States who are employees of any such foreign subsidiary. See §36.3121(l)(8)-1, relating to the definition of foreign subsidiary. Except as provided in §36.3121(l)(5)-1, relating to the effect of the termination of an agreement entered into pursuant to the provisions of section 3121(l), the Internal Revenue Service shall, at the request of a domestic corporation enter into such agreement on Form 2032 in any case where a Form 2032 is executed, and submitted by the domestic corporation in the manner prescribed in this section. A domestic corporation may not have in effect at the same moment of time more than one agreement on Form 2032.

(2) An agreement authorized in section 3121(l)(1) may not be made applicable to any services performed outside the United States which would not constitute employment, for purposes of the taxes imposed under the Federal Insurance Contributions Act, if the services were performed within the United States. Thus, such an agreement shall have no application with respect to any services performed outside the United States which, if performed within the United States, would be specifically excepted from employment

under any of the numbered paragraphs of section 3121(b), or which, although not so excepted, would be deemed not to be employment by application of section 3121(c), relating to included and excluded services. Further, an agreement may not be made applicable with respect to any services performed outside the United States which constitute employment, as defined in section 3121(b). Thus, an agreement may not be made applicable to services for any employer performed by any employee on or in connection with an American vessel or American aircraft when outside the United States, if (i) performed under a contract of service which is entered into within the United States or (ii) during the performance of which and while the employee is employed on the vessel or aircraft it touches at a port in the United States, because such services constitute employment as defined in section 3121(b). An agreement may not be made applicable to remuneration which would not constitute wages, as defined in section 3121(a), even if the services to which such remuneration is attributable had constituted employment.

(3) The terms "corporation", "domestic", and "foreign", as used in the regulations in this part, have the meaning assigned by paragraphs (3), (4), and (5), respectively, of section 7701(a). Section 701(a) (3), (4), and (5) provides as follows:

SEC. 7701. *Definitions.* (a) When used in this title [Internal Revenue Code of 1954], where not otherwise distinctly expressed or manifestly incompatible with the intent thereof—

\* \* \*

(3) *Corporation.* The term "corporation" includes associations, joint-stock companies, and insurance companies.

(4) *Domestic.* The term "domestic" when applied to a corporation \* \* \* means created or organized in the United States or under the law of the United States or of any State or Territory.

(5) *Foreign.* The term "foreign" when applied to a corporation \* \* \* means a corporation \* \* \* which is not domestic.

(b) *Form and contents of agreement.*—Form 2032 is the form prescribed for the agreement authorized in section 3121(l)(1). The agreement shall include provisions substantially as follows:

(1) That the agreement shall apply to all services performed outside the United States by all citizens of the United States who are in the employ of the foreign subsidiary or subsidiaries to which the agreement is made applicable, but only to the extent that the remuneration paid each employee for such services would constitute wages if paid by one employer for services performed in the United States;

(2) That the agreement shall not apply to any services which constitute employment within the meaning of section 3121;

(3) That the agreement shall become effective on the first day of the calendar quarter in which the Form 2032 is signed by the district director or director of the service center or on the first day of the next succeeding calendar quarter, whichever is specified in the agreement;

(4) That the domestic corporation will pay, as required by the regulations in this part, amounts equivalent to the sum of the taxes which would be imposed by sections 3101 and 3111, respectively, if the remuneration for the services covered by the agreement constituted wages;

(5) That the domestic corporation will pay, in accordance with written notification and demand therefor to the domestic corporation, amounts equivalent to the interest, additions to the taxes, additional amounts, and penalties which would be applicable if the remuneration for services covered by the agreement constituted wages; and

(6) That the domestic corporation will comply with all provisions of the regulations in this part.

(c) *Execution and filing of Form 2032.*—The request of any domestic corporation that the Internal Revenue Service enter into an agreement with the corporation on Form 2032 shall be signified by the corporation by executing and filing Form 2032 in triplicate. Such form shall be executed and filed in accordance with the regulations in this part and the instructions relating to the form. Each copy of the form shall be signed and dated by the officer of the corporation authorized to enter into the agreement, shall show the title of such officer, and shall have the corporate seal affixed thereto. A certified copy of the minutes of the meeting of the board of directors of the domestic corporation, or other evidence, showing the authority of such officer so to act shall accompany the form. Form 2032 executed and filed as provided in this paragraph shall be signed and dated by the district director or director of the service center and, upon such signing, the Form 2032 so executed and filed will constitute the agreement authorized in section 3121(l)(1). The Internal Revenue Service will return one copy of the agreement to the domestic corporation, will transmit one copy of the Department of Health, Education, and Welfare, and will retain one copy (together with all related papers). [Reg. §36.3121(l)(1)-1.]

☐ [*T.D. 6145, 9-8-55. Amended by T.D. 7012, 5-15-69.*]

### [Reg. §36.3121(l)(1)-2]

**§36.3121(l)(1)-2. Amendment of agreement.**—(a) An agreement entered into by a domestic corporation as provided in §36.3121(l)(1)-1 may be amended so as to be made applicable, in the same manner and under the same conditions, with respect to any one or more of the foreign subsidiaries of the domestic corporation not previously named in the agreement. See §36.3121(l)(2)-1(b), relating to the effective period of an amendment of an agreement.

(b) Form 2032 Supplement is the form prescribed for use in amending an agreement entered into by a domestic Corporation as provided in §36.3121(l)(1)-1.

(c) A domestic corporation shall signify its desire to amend an agreement entered into by the corporation as provided in §36.3121(l)(1)-1 by executing and filing Form 2032 Supplement in triplicate.

(d) Form 2032 Supplement shall be executed and filed in the manner and in conformity with the requirements prescribed in the instructions relating to such form and in §36.3121(l)(1)-1(c) in respect of an agreement on Form 2032. Form 2032 Supplement executed and filed as provided in this paragraph shall be signed and dated by the district director or director of the service center, and, upon such signing, the Form 2032 Supplement so executed and filed will constitute an amendment of the agreement entered into on Form 2032. The Internal Revenue Service will return one copy of the amendment to the domestic corporation, will transmit one copy to the Department of Health, Education, and Welfare, and will retain one copy (together with all related papers). [Reg. §36.3121(l)(1)-2.]

☐ [*T.D. 6145, 12-31-60. Amended by T.D. 7012, 5-15-69.*]

### [Reg. §36.3121(l)(1)-3]

**§36.3121(l)(1)-3. Effect of agreement.**—(a) *Liability for amounts equivalent to tax.*—(1) *In general.*—A domestic corporation which has entered into an agreement (as provided in §36.3121(l)(1)-1, or any amendment thereof (as provided in §36.3121(l)(1)-2, incurs liability under the agreement in respect of certain remuneration paid by each foreign subsidiary named in the agreement, or any amendment thereof. Liability is incurred in respect of the remuneration paid to all those employees of the foreign subsidiaries who are citizens of the United States and who perform services outside the United States (other than services which constitute employment) for the foreign subsidiaries. However, liability is incurred only with respect to that portion of such remuneration paid by the foreign subsidiary which is attributable to services performed during the period for which the agreement is in effect with respect to such subsidiary, and then only to the extent that the remuneration would constitute wages if the services to which the remuneration is attributable were performed in the United States. Liability with respect to such remuneration is incurred in an amount equivalent to the sum of the employee and employer taxes which would be imposed by sections 3101 and 3111, respectively, if such remuneration constituted wages. If an individual performs services for more than one of the foreign subsidiaries named in an agreement, including any amendment thereof, such services are regarded as being performed in the employ of a single employer for purposes of determining the amount of the remuneration for such services which would constitute wages if the services were performed in the United States. See §36.3121(l)(9)-1, relating to the treatment of a domestic corporation as a separate entity in its capacity as a party to an agreement.

(2) *Examples.*—The application of paragraph (a)(1) of this section may be illustrated by the following examples:

*Example 1.* P. a domestic corporation, has entered into an agreement as provided in §36.3121(l)(1)-1, effective with respect to services performed on and after January 1, 1955. Three foreign subsidiaries, S-1, S-2, and S-3 are named in the agreement. A, a citizen of the United States, is employed during 1955 by S-1, S-2, and S-3, for the performance outside the United States of services covered by the agreement. In 1955 A is paid remuneration of $2,500 for such services by each of the foreign subsidiaries. The circumstances are such that the entire $7,500 would constitute wages if the services has been performed in the United States. However, only $4,200 of such remuneration would constitute wages if the services had been performed in the United States for a single employer, and it is with respect to this amount only that P incurs liability under its agreement.

*Example 2.* On August 1, 1955, P, the domestic corporation in the preceding example, amends its agreement to include therein its foreign subsidiary S-4. The amendment is in effect with respect to S-4 for the period beginning with October 1, 1955. B, a citizen of the United States, is employed by S-4 throughout 1955 for the performance of services outside the United States. B is paid remuneration of $500 in each month of 1955 for these services. The circumstances are

such that the first $4,200 of such remuneration would constitute wages if the services had been performed in the United States, and, except for the $4,200 limitation, the remainder of such remuneration would constitute wages if the services had been so performed. P incurs no liability with respect to remuneration paid B for services performed for S-4 prior to October 1, 1955. However, P incurs liability under its agreement with respect to the $1,500 paid B in October, November, and December 1955, for services performed in these months. Since the remuneration paid to B for services performed during the first nine months of 1955 is not covered by the agreement, such remuneration is not taken into account in computing the $4,200 limitation or the liability under the agreement.

*Example 3.* Assume the same facts as in example 2 except that B's services for S-4 during December 1955 are of a character which if performed within the United States would be excepted from employment. Accordingly, P incurs no liability under the agreement with respect to the $500.00 paid in December 1955 for such services.

(3) *Determination of liability.*—The amount of the liability referred to in paragraph (a)(1) of this section incurred by a domestic corporation for any period shall be determined in the same manner as liability for the employee tax and for the employer tax imposed by the Federal Insurance Contributions Act is determined, pursuant to regulations relating to the taxes under such act as in effect for the same period, with respect to wages paid by an employer to an employee.

(b) *Liability for amounts equivalent to interest or penalties.*—A domestic corporation which has entered into an agreement as provided in §36.3121(l)(1)-1 also incurs liability under the agreement for amounts equivalent to the amount of interest, additions to the taxes, additional amounts, and penalties which would be applicable if the remuneration for services covered by the agreement constituted wages.

(c) *Deductions from employees' remuneration.*—There is no obligation to deduct, or cause to be deducted, from the remuneration of any employee of a foreign subsidiary any part of the amount due from a domestic corporation under its agreement. Whether such deduction shall be made is a matter for settlement between the employee and the domestic corporation or such other person as may be concerned.

(d) *Cross reference.*—For other obligations of a domestic corporation under an agreement, see §36.3121(l)(1)-1. [Reg. §36.3121(l)(1)-3.]

☐ [*T.D. 6145, 9-8-55. Amended by T.D. 6390, 6-13-59.*]

### [Reg. §36.3121(l)(2)-1]

**§36.3121(l)(2)-1. Effective period of agreement.**—(a) *In general.*—An agreement entered into as provided in §36.3121(l) (1)-1 shall be in effect for the period beginning with the first day of the calendar quarter in which the agreement is signed by the district director or director of the service center, or the first day of the calendar quarter following the calendar quarter in which the agreement is signed by the district director or director of the service center, whichever is specified in the agreement. In no case, however, shall the agreement be effective for any calendar quarter which begins prior to January 1, 1955.

(b) *Amendment of agreement.*—If an amendment on Form 2032 Supplement (filed by a domestic corporation to include in its agreement services performed for a foreign subsidiary not previously named therein) is signed by the district director or director of the service center, within the quarter for which the agreement is first effective or within the first calendar month following such quarter, the agreement shall be effective with respect to the subsidiary named in the amendment as of the date such agreement first became effective. However, if the amendment is signed by the district director or director of the service center after the last day of the fourth month for which the agreement is in effect, such agreement shall be in effect with respect to the subsidiary named in the amendment for the period beginning with the first day of the calendar quarter following the calendar quarter in which the amendment is signed by the district director or director of the service center. [Reg. §36.3121(l)(2)-1.]

☐ [*T.D. 7012, 5-15-69.*]

### [Reg. §36.3121(l)(3)-1]

**§36.3121(l)(3)-1. Termination of agreement by domestic corporation or by reason of change in stock ownership.**—(a) *Termination by domestic corporation.*—(1) A domestic corporation which has entered into an agreement under section 3121(l)(1) with respect to one or more of its foreign subsidiaries may terminate such agreement in part or in its entirety by giving (for calendar quarters beginning before 1969, to the district director for the internal revenue district in which is located the principal place of business in the United States of the domestic corporation; and for calendar quarters beginning after 1968, except as provided in paragraph (b) of §301.6091-1 (relating to hand-carried documents) to the director of the service center serving such internal revenue district 2 years' advance notice in writing of its desire so to terminate the agreement at the end of a specified calendar quarter: *Provided*, That, at the time of the receipt of such notice by such internal revenue officer, the agreement has been in effect with respect to the subsidiary or subsidiaries covered by the notice for at least 8 years. The notice of termination shall be signed and dated and shall show (i) the title of the officer authorized to sign the notice, (ii) the name, address, and identification number of the domestic corporation, (iii) the internal revenue officer with whom the agreement was entered into, (iv) the name and address of each foreign subsidiary with respect to which the agreement is to be terminated, (v) the date on which the agreement became effective with respect to each such foreign subsidiary, and (vi) the date on which the agreement is to be terminated with respect to each such foreign subsidiary. The notice shall be submitted in duplicate and shall be accompanied by a certified copy of the minutes of the meeting of the board of directors of the domestic corporation, or other evidence, showing authorization for the notice of termination. No particular form is prescribed for the notice of termination. The Internal Revenue Service will transmit one copy of the notice of termination to the Department of Health, Education, and Welfare.

(2) A notice of termination given by a domestic corporation in respect of any one or more of its foreign subsidiaries may be revoked by the corporation with respect to any such subsidiary or subsidiaries by giving, prior to the close of the calendar quarter specified in the notice of termination, written notice of revocation. The notice of revocation shall be filed with the internal revenue officer with whom the notice of termination was filed. Such notice of revocation shall be signed and dated and shall show (i) the title of the officer authorized to sign the notice of revocation, (ii) the name, address, and identification number of the domestic corporation, (iii) the name and address of each foreign subsidiary with respect to which the notice of termination is revoked, and (iv) the date of the notice of termination to be revoked. The notice shall be submitted in duplicate and shall be accompanied by a certified copy of the minutes of the meeting of the board of directors of the domestic corporation, or other evidence, showing authorization for the notice of revocation. No particular form is prescribed for the notice of revocation. The Internal Revenue Service will transmit one copy of the notice of revocation to the Department of Health, Education, and Welfare.

(b) *Termination by reason of change in stock ownership.*—(1) The period for which an agreement entered into by a domestic corporation as provided in §36.3121(l)(1)-1 is in effect with respect to a foreign corporation is automatically terminated at the end of the calendar quarter in which the foreign corporation ceases, at any time in such quarter, to be a foreign subsidiary of the domestic corporation. See §36.3121(l)(8)-1, relating to definition of foreign subsidiary.

(2) A domestic corporation which has entered into an agreement as provided in §36.3121(l)(1)-1 shall furnish (for calendar quarters beginning before 1969, to the district director for the internal revenue district in which is located its principal place of business in the United States; and for calendar quarters beginning after 1968, except as provided in paragraph (b) of §301.6091-1 (relating to hand-carried documents) to the director of the service center serving such internal revenue district) written notification in the event that a foreign corporation named in the agreement, including any amendment thereof, as a foreign subsidiary of the domestic corporation ceases to be its foreign subsidiary. The written notification shall be furnished in duplicate on or before the last day of the first month following the close of the calendar quarter in which the foreign corporation ceases, at any time in such quarter, to be a foreign subsidiary of the domestic corporation. Such notification shall be signed and dated by the president or other principal officer of the domestic corporation. The written notification shall show (i) the title of the officer signing the notice, (ii) the name, address, and identification number of the domestic corporation, (iii) the internal revenue officer with whom the agreement was entered into, (iv) the date on which the agreement was entered into, (v) the name and address of the foreign corporation with respect to which the notification is furnished, and (vi) the date on which the foreign corporation ceased to be a foreign subsidiary of the domestic corporation. No particular form is prescribed for the written notification. The Internal Revenue Service will transmit one copy of the written notification to the Department of Health, Education, and Welfare. [Reg. §36.3121(l)(3)-1.]

☐ [*T.D.* 6145, 12-31-60. *Amended by T.D.* 7012, 5-15-69.]

### [Reg. §36.3121(l)(4)-1]

**§36.3121(l)(4)-1. Termination of agreement by Commissioner.**— (a) *Notice of termination.*—The period for which an agreement entered into with a domestic corporation as provided in §36.3121(l)(1)-1 is in effect may be terminated by the Commissioner, with the prior con-

currence of the Secretary of Health, Education, and Welfare, upon a finding by the Commissioner that the domestic corporation has failed to comply substantially with the terms of the agreement. The Commissioner shall give the corporation not less than 60 days' advance notice in writing that the period for which the agreement is in effect will terminate at the end of the calendar quarter specified in the notice of termination.

(b) *Revocation of notice of termination.*—A notice of termination given to a domestic corporation by the Commissioner may be revoked by the Commissioner, with the prior concurrence of the Secretary of Health, Education, and Welfare by giving written notice of revocation to the corporation prior to the close of the calendar quarter specified in the notice of termination. [Reg. §36.3121(l)(4)-1.]

☐ [*T.D.* 6145, 9-8-55, 12-31-60.]

### [Reg. §36.3121(l)(5)-1]

**§36.3121(l)(5)-1. Effect of termination.**—(a) *Termination of entire agreement.*—(1) If the effective period of an agreement entered into by a domestic corporation as provided in §36.3121(l)(1)-1 is terminated by the domestic corporation, pursuant to §36.3121(l)(3)-1(a), with respect to all foreign subsidiaries named in the agreement, including any amendment thereof, an agreement may not again be entered into by the domestic corporation under the provisions of section 3121(l)(1).

(2) If the effective period of an agreement entered into by a domestic corporation as provided in §36.3121(l)(1)-1 is terminated by the Commissioner, pursuant to §36.3121(l)(4)-1 (a), an agreement may not again be entered into by the domestic corporation under the provisions of section 3121(l)(1).

(3) If the effective period of an agreement entered into by a domestic corporation as provided in §36.3121(l)(1)-1 is terminated automatically by reason of a change in stock ownership (see §36.3121(l)(3)-1(b)) with respect to all foreign corporations named in the agreement, including any amendment thereof, a new agreement may be entered into by the domestic corporation, as provided in §36.3121(l)(1)-1, with respect to any foreign corporation which is a foreign subsidiary of the domestic corporation.

(b) *Partial termination of agreement.*—(1) If the effective period of an agreement entered into by a domestic corporation as provided in §36.3121(l)(1)-1 is terminated by the domestic corporation, pursuant to §36.3121(l)(3)-1(a), with respect to one or more foreign subsidiaries named in the agreement, including any amendment thereof, the period for which the agreement is in effect will continue with respect to any other foreign subsidiary or subsidiaries named in the agreement (or amendment). However, the agreement may not thereafter be amended to include any foreign subsidiary with respect to which the effective period of the agreement has been terminated.

(2) If the effective period of an agreement entered into by a domestic corporation as provided in §36.3121(l)(1)-1 is terminated automatically by reason of a change in stock ownership (see §36.3121(l)(3)-1(b)) with respect to a foreign corporation which has ceased to be a foreign subsidiary of the domestic corporation, but the period for which the agreement is in effect continues with respect to one or more other foreign subsidiaries, the agreement may not thereafter be amended to include such foreign corporation even though the foreign corporation may again become a foreign subsidiary of the domestic corporation. [Reg. §36.3121(l)(5)-1.]

☐ [*T.D.* 6145, 9-8-55, 12-31-60.]

### [Reg. §36.3121(l)(7)-1]

**§36.3121(l)(7)-1. Overpayments and underpayments.**— (a) *Adjustments.*—(1) *In general.*—Errors in the payment of amounts for which liability equivalent to the employee and employer taxes with respect to any payment of remuneration is incurred by a domestic corporation pursuant to its agreement are adjustable by the domestic corporation in certain cases without interest. However, not all corrections made under this section constitute adjustments within the meaning of the regulations in this part. The various situations in which such corrections constitute adjustments are set forth in paragraphs (a)(2) and (3) of this section. All corrections in respect of underpayments and all adjustments or credits in respect of overpayments made under this section must be reported on a return filed by the domestic corporation under the regulations in this part and not on a return filed with respect to the employee and employer taxes imposed by sections 3101 and 3111, respectively. Every return on which such a correction (by adjustment, credit, or otherwise) is reported pursuant to this section must have securely attached as a part thereof a statement explaining the error in respect of which the correction is made, designating the calendar quarter in which the error was ascertained, and setting forth such other information as would be required if the correction were in respect of an overpayment or underpayment of taxes under the Federal Insurance Contributions Act. An error is ascertained when the domestic corporation has sufficient knowledge of the error to be able to correct it. An underpayment may not be corrected under this section after receipt from the district director or director of the service center of written notification of the amount due and demand for payment thereof, but the amount shall be paid in accordance with such notification.

(2) *Underpayments.*—If a domestic corporation fails to report, on a return filed under the regulations in this part, all or any part of the amount for which liability equivalent to the employee and employer taxes is incurred under its agreement with respect to any payment of remuneration, the domestic corporation shall adjust the underpayment by reporting the additional amount due as an adjustment on a return or supplemental return filed on or before the last day on which the return for the return period in which the error is ascertained is required to be filed. The amount of each underpayment adjusted in accordance with this subparagraph shall be paid, without interest, at the time fixed for reporting the adjustment. If an adjustment is reported pursuant to this subparagraph but the amount thereof is not paid when due, interest thereafter accrues.

(3) *Overpayments.*—If a domestic corporation pays more than the amount for which liability equivalent to the employee and employer taxes is incurred under its agreement with respect to any payment of remuneration, the domestic corporation may correct the error, subject to the requirements and under the conditions stated in this paragraph, by deducting the amount of the overpayment from the amount of liability reported on a return filed by the domestic corporation, except that—

(i) A correction may not be made in respect of any part of an overpayment which was collected from an individual by reason of the agreement unless the domestic corporation (a) has repaid the amount so collected to the individual, has secured the written receipt of the individual showing the date and amount of the repayment, and retains such receipt as a part of its records, or (b) has reimbursed the individual by reducing the amounts which otherwise should have been deducted from his remuneration by reason of the agreement; and

(ii) A correction may not be made in one calendar year in respect of any part of an overpayment which was collected from an individual in a prior calendar year unless the domestic corporation has secured the written statement of the individual showing that he has not claimed and will not claim refund or credit of the amount so collected, and retains such receipt as a part of its records. See §31.6413(c)-1 of this chapter, relating to claims for special credit or refund.

The correction constitutes an adjustment under this subparagraph only if it is reported on the return for the period in which the error is ascertained or on the return for the next following period, and then only if the correction is reported within the statutory period of limitation upon refund or credit of overpayments of amounts due under the agreement. See paragraph (b)(2)(iii) of this section relating to such statutory period. A claim for credit or refund may be filed in accordance with the provisions of paragraph (b)(2) of this section for any overpayment of an amount due under the agreement which is not adjusted under this subparagraph.

(b) *Errors not adjustable.*—(1) *Underpayments.*—If a domestic corporation fails to report all or any part of the amount for which liability equivalent to the employee and employer taxes is incurred under its agreement with respect to any payment of remuneration, and such underpayment is not reported as an adjustment within the time prescribed by paragraph (a)(2) of this section, the amount of such underpayment shall be reported on the domestic corporation's next return, or shall be reported immediately on a supplemental return for the return period in which such payment of remuneration was made. The reporting of an underpayment under this subparagraph does not constitute an adjustment without interest.

(2) *Overpayments.*—(i) If more than the correct amount due from a domestic corporation pursuant to its agreement (including the amount of any interest or addition) is paid and the amount of the overpayment is not adjusted under paragraph (a)(3) of this section, the domestic corporation may file a claim for refund or credit. Except as otherwise provided in this subparagraph, such claim shall be made in the same manner and subject to the same conditions as to allowance of the claim as would be the case if the claim were in respect of an overpayment of taxes under the Federal Insurance Contributions Act. Refund or credit of an amount erroneously paid by a domestic corporation under its agreement may be allowed only to the domestic corporation.

(ii) Any claim filed under this subparagraph shall be plainly marked "Claim under section 3121(1)."

(iii) No refund or credit of an overpayment of the amount due from a domestic corporation under its agreement will be allowed after the expiration of 2 years after the date of payment of such overpayment, except upon one or more of the grounds set forth in a claim filed prior to the expiration of such 2-year period.

(c) *Deductions from employees' remuneration.*—If a domestic corporation deducts, or causes to be deducted, from the remuneration of an individual for services covered by the agreement amounts which are more or less than the employee tax which would be deductible therefrom if such remuneration constituted wages, any repayment to the individual (except to the extent otherwise provided in this section), or further collection from the individual, in respect of such deduction is a matter for settlement between the individual and the domestic corporation or such other person as may be concerned. [Reg. §36.3121(1)(7)-1.]

☐ [T.D. 6145, 12-31-60. *Amended by T.D. 7012, 5-15-69.*]

### [Reg. §36.3121(l)(8)-1]

§36.3121(l)(8)-1. **Definition of foreign subsidiary.**—(a) *Prior to August 1, 1956.*—(1) For the period January 1, 1955 to July 31, 1956, inclusive, a foreign corporation is a foreign subsidiary of a domestic corporation, within the meaning of the regulations in this part, if—

(i) More than 50 percent of the voting stock of the foreign corporation is owned by the domestic corporation; or

(ii) More than 50 percent of the voting stock of the foreign corporation is owned by a second foreign corporation and more than 50 percent of the voting stock of the second foreign corporation is owned by the domestic corporation.

(2) The application of subparagraph (1) of this paragraph may be illustrated by the following examples:

*Example 1.* P, a domestic corporation, owns 51 percent of the voting stock of S-1, a foreign corporation. S-1 owns 51 percent of the voting stock of S-2, a foreign corporation. S-2 owns 51 percent of the voting stock of S-3, a foreign corporation. S-1 and S-2 are foreign subsidiaries of P for purposes of the regulations in this part. Since neither P nor S-1 owns more than 50 percent of the voting stock of S-3, S-3 is not a foreign subsidiary of P within the meaning of the regulations in this part.

*Example 2.* Assume the same facts as those stated in example 1 except that 25 percent of the voting stock of S-2 is transferred by S-1 to P. P owns no other voting stock of S-2. Accordingly, after the transfer, P and S-1 together own more than 50 percent of the voting stock of S-2, but neither P nor S-1 alone owns more than 50 percent of such stock. S-2 ceases to be a foreign subsidiary of P when such transfer is effected.

(b) *On or after August 1, 1956.*—(1) Beginning August 1, 1956, a foreign corporation is a foreign subsidiary of a domestic corporation, within the meaning of the regulations in this part, if—

(i) Not less than 20 percent of the voting stock of the foreign corporation is owned by the domestic corporation; or

(ii) More than 50 percent of the voting stock of the foreign corporation is owned by a second foreign corporation and not less than 20 percent of the voting stock of the second foreign corporation is owned by the domestic corporation.

(2) The application of subparagraph (1) of this paragraph may be illustrated by the following examples:

*Example 1.* P, a domestic corporation owns 20 percent of the voting stock of S-1, a foreign corporation. S-1 is, therefore, a foreign subsidiary of P. S-1 owns 51 percent and P owns 15 percent of the voting stock of S-2, a foreign corporation. S-2 is also a foreign subsidiary of P, and this would be so even if P owned none of the voting stock of S-2. S-2 owns 51 percent, S-1 owns 39 percent, and P owns 10 percent of the voting stock of S-3, a foreign corporation. Since P owns less than 20 percent of the voting stock of S-2 and less than 20 percent of the voting stock of S-3, and since S-1 owns not more than 50 percent of the voting stock of S-3, S-3 is not a foreign subsidiary of P within the meaning of the regulations in this part.

*Example 2.* Assume the same facts as those stated in example 1 except that 4 percent of the voting stock of S-2 is transferred by S-1 to P. After, as well as before, the transfer of 66 percent of the voting stock of S-2 is owned by P and S-1 together. After the transfer, however, P owns less than 20 percent and S-1 owns not more than 50 percent of the voting stock of S-2. When such transfer is effected S-2 ceases to be a foreign subsidiary of P for purposes of the regulations in this part.

(c) *Transfer of stock ownership.*—The transfer of the voting stock of a foreign corporation which is a foreign subsidiary of a domestic corporation within the meaning of section 3121(l)(8) will not affect the status of the foreign corporation as such a foreign subsidiary if at all times either of the percentage tests stated in section 3121(l)(8), relating to ownership of the voting stock of such foreign corporation, is met.

(d) *Meaning of "stock".*—The term "stock", as used in the regulations in this part, has the meaning assigned by paragraph (7) of section 7701(a). Section 7701(a)(7) provides as follows:

SEC. 7701. *Definitions.* (a) When used in this title [Internal Revenue Code of 1954], where not otherwise distinctly expressed or manifestly incompatible with the intent thereof—

\* \* \*

(7) *Stock.* The term "stock" includes shares in an association, joint-stock company, or insurance company.
[Reg. § 36.3121(l)(8)-1.]

☐ [*T.D.* 6390, 6-13-59.]

### [Reg. § 36.3121(l)(9)-1]

**§ 36.3121(l)(9)-1. Domestic corporation as separate entity.**—A domestic corporation which enters into an agreement as provided in § 36.3121(l)(1)-1 shall, for purposes of the regulations in this part and for purposes of section 6413(c)(2)(C), relating to special credits or refunds, be considered an employer in its capacity as a party to such agreement separate and apart from its identity as an employer incurring liability for the employee tax and employer tax on the wages of its own employees. Thus, if a citizen of the United States performs services in employment for the domestic corporation and at any time within the same calendar year performs services covered by the agreement as an employee of one or more foreign subsidiaries named therein, the limitation on wages provided in section 3121(a) (1) has application separately as to the wages for employment performed in the employ of the domestic corporation and as to the remuneration for services covered by the agreement performed in the employ of such foreign subsidiary or subsidiaries. All services covered by the agreement whether performed in the employ of one or more than one such foreign subsidiary are regarded for purposes of the wage limitation as having been performed in the employ of the domestic corporation in its separate capacity as a party to the agreement. Similarly, any remuneration for such services which, if the services were performed in the United States, would be excluded from wages unless a certain amount of such remuneration is paid by a single employer within a specified period (for example, remuneration for agricultural labor) is regarded, for purposes of determining whether the domestic corporation incurs liability under its agreement with respect to such remuneration, as having been paid by the domestic corporation in its separate capacity as a party to the agreement. All remuneration received by an employee for services covered by the agreement is deemed, for purposes of the special credit or refund provisions contained in section 6413(c), to have been received from the domestic corporation as an employer in its separate capacity as a party to the agreement. [Reg. § 36.3121(l)(9)-1.]

☐ [*T.D.* 6145, 9-8-55, 12-31-60.]

### [Reg. § 36.3121(l)(10)-1]

**§ 36.3121(l)(10)-1. Requirements in respect of liability under agreement.**—To the extent not inconsistent with, or otherwise provided in, the regulations in this part, the requirements and duties (relating to identification number, account numbers, wage information statements to employees, record keeping, etc.) imposed on an employer for any period with respect to the taxes imposed by the Federal Insurance Contributions Act are hereby made applicable to a domestic corporation with respect to its obligations and liabilities, for the same period, under an agreement entered into as provided in § 36.3121(l)(1)-1. [Reg. § 36.3121(l)(10)-1.]

☐ [*T.D.* 6145, 9-8-55, 12-31-60.]

### [Reg. § 36.3121(l)(10)-2]

**§ 36.3121(l)(10)-2. Identification.**—(a) *Domestic corporation.*—A domestic corporation which has secured, or is required to secure, an identification number as an employer having in its employ one or more individuals in employment for wages is not required to secure an identification number under the regulations in this part.

(b) *Employees.*—Every employee performing services covered by an agreement shall have the same duties in respect of an account number as would be the case if the employee were performing services in employment for the domestic corporation. [Reg. § 36.3121(l)(10)-2.]

☐ [*T.D.* 6145, 9-8-55, 12-31-60.]

### [Reg. § 36.3121(l)(10)-3]

**§ 36.3121(l)(10)-3. Returns.**—(a) The forms prescribed for use in making returns of the taxes imposed by the Federal Insurance Contributions Act (except any forms particularly prescribed for use by household employers or by employers filing returns in Puerto Rico) shall be used by a domestic corporation in making returns of its liability under an agreement entered into as provided in § 36.3121(l)(1)-1. Returns of such liability shall be made separate and apart from any returns required of the domestic corporation in respect of the taxes imposed by the Federal Insurance Contributions Act. The domestic corporation shall plainly mark "3121(l) Agreement" at the top of each return, each detachable schedule thereof, and each paper or document constituting a part of the return, filed by the domestic corporation pursuant to the regulations in this part. Returns required under the regulations in this part shall be made by the domestic corporation as if all services covered by the agreement, whether performed in the employ of one or more than one foreign subsidiary, were performed in the employ of the domestic corporation as an employer in its separate capacity as a party to the agreement.

(b) Each return required under the regulations in this part must be filed on or before the last day of the month following the period for which the return is made. [Reg. § 36.3121(l)(10)-3.]

☐ [*T.D.* 6145, 9-8-55. *Amended by T.D.* 6390, 6-13-59.]

### [Reg. § 36.3121(l)(10)-4]

**§ 36.3121(l)(10)-4. Payment of amounts equivalent to tax.**—A domestic corporation which has entered into an agreement as provided in § 36.3121(l)(1)-1 is not required to make deposits with an authorized financial institution of any amount for which liability is incurred under its agreement. [Reg. § 36.3121(l)(10)-4.]

☐ [*T.D.* 6145, 9-8-55, 12-31-60. *Amended by T.D.* 7953, 5-9-84 *and T.D.* 8952, 6-26-2001.]

### [Reg. § 31.3121(o)-1]

**§ 31.3121(o)-1. Crew leader.**—The term "crew leader" means an individual who furnishes individuals to perform agricultural labor for another person, if such individual pays (either on his own behalf or on behalf of such person) the individuals so furnished by him for the agricultural labor performed by them and if such individual has not entered into a written agreement with such person whereby such individual has been designated as an employee of such person. For purposes of this chapter a crew leader is deemed to be the employer of the individuals furnished by him to perform agricultural labor, after 1956, for another person, and the crew leader is deemed not to be an employee of such other person with respect to the performance of services by him after 1956 in furnishing such individuals or as a member of the crew. An individual is not a crew leader within the meaning of section 3121(o) and of this section if he does not pay the agricultural workers furnished by him to perform agricultural labor for another person, or if there is an agreement between such individual and the person for whom the agricultural labor is performed whereby such individual is designated as an employee of such person. Whether or not such individual is an employee will be determined under the usual common-law rules (see paragraph (c) of § 31.3121(d)-1). [Reg. § 31.3121(o)-1.]

☐ [*T.D.* 6744, 7-2-64.]

⟫⟫→ *Caution: This regulation has not been amended to reflect changes enacted by the Omnibus Budget Reconciliation Act of 1987 (P.L. 100-203).*

### [Reg. § 31.3121(q)-1]

**§ 31.3121(q)-1. Tips included for employee taxes.**—(a) *In general.*—Except as otherwise provided in paragraph (b) of this section, tips received after 1965 by an employee in the course of his employment shall be considered remuneration for employment. (For definition of the term "employee" see §§ 31.3121(d) and 31.3121(d)-1.) Tips reported by an employee to his employer in a written statement furnished to the employer pursuant to section 6053(a) (see § 31.6053-1) shall be deemed to be paid to the employee at the time the written statement is furnished to the employer. Tips received by an employee which are not reported to his employer in a written statement furnished pursuant to section 6053(a) shall be deemed to be paid to the employee at the time the tips are actually received by

the employee. For provisions relating to the collection of employee tax in respect of tips from the employee, see § 31.3102-3.

(b) *Tips not included for employer taxes.*—Tips received after 1965 by an employee in the course of his employment do not constitute remuneration for employment for purposes of computing wages subject to the taxes imposed by subsections (a) and (b) of section 3111.

(c) *Tips received by an employee in course of his employment.*—Tips are considered to be received by an employee in the course of his employment for an employer regardless of whether the tips are received by the employee from a person other than his employer or are paid to the employee by the employer. However, only those tips which are received by an employee on his own behalf (as distinguished from tips received on behalf of another employee) shall be considered as remuneration paid to the employee. Thus, where employees practice tip splitting (for example, where waiters pay a portion of the tips received by them to the busboys), each employee who receives a portion of a tip left by a customer of the employer is considered to have received tips in the course of his employment.

(d) *Computation of annual wage limitation.*—In connection with the application of the annual wage limitation (see § 31.3121(a)(1)-1), tips reported by an employee to his employer in a written statement furnished to the employer pursuant to section 6053(a) shall be taken into account for purposes of the tax imposed by section 3101. However, since tips received by an employee in the course of his employment do not constitute remuneration for employment for purposes of the tax imposed by section 3111, they are disregarded for purposes of the annual wage limitation in respect of such tax. Accordingly, separate computations for purposes of the annual wage limitation may be required in respect of an employee who receives tips. The provisions of this paragraph may be illustrated by the following example:

*Example.* During 1966, A is employed as a waiter by X restaurant and is paid wages by X restaurant at the rate of $100 a week. At the end of October 1966, A has been paid weekly wages in the amount of $4,300 and has reported tips in the amount of $2,200. On November 6, 1966, A is paid an additional week's wages in the amount of $100 and on November 9, 1966, A furnishes X restaurant a report of tips actually received by him during October. The annual wage limitation of $6,600 (weekly wages of $4,400 ($4,300 plus $100) and tips of $2,200) had been reached for purposes of the tax imposed by section 3101 prior to November 9 and, accordingly, no portion of the tips included in the report furnished on that date constitutes wages. However, since tips do not constitute remuneration for employment for purposes of the tax imposed by section 3111, the weekly wages paid to A during the remainder of 1966 will be subject to the tax imposed by section 3111. [Reg. § 31.3121(q)-1.]

☐ [*T.D. 7001*, 1-23-69.]

### [Reg. § 31.3121(r)-1]

**§ 31.3121(r)-1. Election of coverage by religious orders.**—(a) *In general.*—A religious order whose members are required to take a vow of poverty, or any autonomous subdivision of such an order, may elect to have the Federal old-age, survivors, and disability insurance system established by title II of the Social Security Act extended to services performed by its members in the exercise of duties required by such order or subdivision. See section 3121(i)(4) and § 31.3121(i)-4 for provisions relating to the computation of the amount of remuneration of such members. For purposes of this section, a subdivision of a religious order is autonomous if it directs and governs its members, if it is responsible for its members' care and maintenance, if it is responsible for the members' support and maintenance in retirement, and if the members live under the authority of a religious superior who is elected by them or appointed by higher authority.

(b) *Definition of member.*—(1) *In general.*—For purposes of section 3121(r) and this section, a member of a religious order means any individual who is subject to a vow of poverty as a member of such order, who performs tasks usually required (and to the extent usually required) of an active member of such order, and who is not considered retired because of old age or total disability.

(2) *Retirement because of old age.*—(i) *In general.*—For purposes of section 3121(r)(2) and this paragraph, an individual is considered retired because of old age if (A) in view of all the services performed by the individual and the surrounding circumstances it is reasonable to consider him to be retired, and (B) his retirement occurred by reason of old age. Even though an individual performs some services in the exercise of duties required by the religious order, the first test (the retirement test) is met where it is reasonable to consider the individual to be retired.

(ii) *Factors to be considered.*—In determining whether it is reasonable to consider an individual to be retired, consideration is first to be given to all of the following factors:

(A) *Nature of services.*—Consideration is given to the nature of the services performed by the individual in the exercise of duties required by his religious order. The more highly skilled and valuable such services are, the more likely the individual rendering such services is not reasonably considered retired. Also, whether such services are of a type performed principally by retired members of the individual's religious order may be significant.

(B) *Amount of time.*—Consideration is also given to the amount of time the individual devotes to the performance of services in the exercise of duties required by his religious order. This time includes all the time spent by him in any activity in connection with services which might appropriately be performed in the exercise of duties required of active members by the order. Normally, an individual who, solely by reason of his advanced age, performs services of less than 45 hours per month shall be considered retired. In no event shall an individual who, solely by reason of his advanced age, performs services of less than 15 hours per month not be considered retired.

(C) *Comparison of services rendered before and after retirement.*—In addition, consideration is given to the nature and extent of the services rendered by the individual before he "retired," as compared with the services performed thereafter. A large reduction in the importance or amount of services performed by the individual in the exercise of duties required by his religious order tends to show that the individual is retired; absence of such reduction tends to show that the individual is not retired. Normally, an individual who reduces by at least 75 percent the amount of services performed shall be considered retired.

Where consideration of the factors described in paragraph (b)(2)(ii) of this section does not establish whether an individual is or is not reasonably considered retired, all other factors are considered.

(iii) *Examples.*—The rules of this subparagraph may be illustrated by the following examples:

*Example (1).* A is a member of a religious order who is subject to a vow of poverty. A's religious order is principally engaged in providing nursing services, and A has been fully trained in the nursing profession. In accordance with the practices of her order, upon attaining the age of 65, A is relieved of her nursing duties by reason of her age, and is assigned to a mother house where she is required to perform only such duties as light housekeeping and ordinary gardening. A is reasonably considered retired since the services she is performing are simple in nature, are markedly less skilled than those professional services which she previously performed, are of a type performed principally by retired members of her order, and are performed at a location to which members frequently retire.

*Example (2).* Assume the same facts as in example (1) except that A is not reassigned to a mother house. Instead, she is reassigned to full-time duties in a hospital not utilizing her nursing skills. Whether A has met the retirement test requires consideration of the nature of her work. If A's new duties are almost entirely of a make-work nature primarily to occupy her body and mind, she is reasonably considered retired. However, if they are essential to the operation of the hospital, she is not reasonably considered retired.

*Example (3).* B is a member of a religious order who is subject to a vow of poverty. As such, he provides supportive services to his order, such as housekeeping, cooking, and gardening. By reason of having attained the age of 62, he reduces the number of hours spent per day in these services from 8 hours to 2 hours. B is reasonably considered retired in view of the large reduction in the amount of time he devotes to his duties.

*Example (4).* C is a member of a religious order who is subject to a vow of poverty. In his capacity as a member of the order, he performs duties as president of a university. Upon attaining the age of 65, C is relieved of his duties as president of the university and instead becomes a member of its faculty, teaching two courses whereas full time members of the faculty normally teach four comparable courses. Although C's duties are no longer as demanding as those he previously performed, and although the amount of his time required for them is less than full time, he is nonetheless performing duties requiring a high degree of skill for a substantial amount of time. Accordingly, C is not reasonably considered retired.

*Example (5).* Assume the same facts as in example (4), except that C teaches only one course upon being relieved of his position as president by reason of age. C is reasonably considered retired.

*Example (6).* D is a member of a contemplative order who is subject to a vow of poverty. In accordance with the practices of his order, upon attaining the age of 70, D reduces by 50 percent the amount of time spent performing the normal duties of active members of his order. D is not reasonably considered retired.

*Example (7).* Assume the same facts as in example (6), except that because of his age D no longer participates in the more rigorous liturgical services of the order and that the amount of time which he spends in all duties which might appropriately be performed by active members of his order is reduced by 75 percent. D is reasonably considered retired in view of the large reduction in his participation in the usual devotional routine of his order.

(3) *Retirement because of total disability.*—For purposes of section 3121(r)(2) and this paragraph, an individual is considered retired because of total disability (i) if he is unable, by reason of a medically determinable physical or mental impairment, to perform the tasks usually required of an active member of his order to the extent

necessary to maintain his status as an active member, and (ii) if such impairment is reasonably expected to prevent his resumption of the performance of such tasks to such extent. A physical or mental impairment is an impairment that results from anatomical, physiological, or psychological abnormalities which are demonstrable by medically acceptable clinical and laboratory diagnostic techniques. Statements of the individual, including his own description of his impairment (symptoms), are, alone, insufficient to establish the presence of a physical or mental impairment.

(4) *Evidentiary requirements with respect to retirement.*—There shall be attached to the return of taxes paid pursuant to an election under section 3121(r) a summary of the facts upon which any determination has been made by the religious order or autonomous subdivision that one or more of its members retired during the period covered by such return. Each summary shall contain the name and social security number of each such retired member as well as the date of retirement. Such order or subdivision shall maintain records of the details relating to each such "retirement" sufficient to show whether or not such member or members has in fact retired.

(c) *Certificates of election.*—(1) *In general.*—A religious order or an autonomous subdivision of such an order desiring to make an election of coverage pursuant to section 3121(r) and this section shall file a certificate of election on Form SS-16 in accordance with the instructions thereto. However, in the case of an election made before [30th day after the date of publication of this section in final regulations] a document other than Form SS-16 shall constitute a certificate of election if it purports to be a binding election of coverage and if it is filed with an appropriate official of the Internal Revenue Service. Such a document shall be given the effect it would have if it were a certificate of election containing the provisions required by subparagraph (2) of this paragraph. However, it should subsequently be supplemented by a Form SS-16.

(2) *Provisions of certificates.*—Each certificate of election shall provide that—

(i) Such election of coverage by such order or subdivision shall be irrevocable,

(ii) Such election shall apply to all current and future members of such order, or in the case of a subdivision thereof to all current and future members of such order who belong to such subdivision,

(iii) All services performed by a member of such order or subdivision in the exercise of duties required by such order or subdivision shall be deemed to have been performed by such member as an employee of such order or subdivision, and

(iv) The wages of each member, upon which such order or subdivision shall pay the taxes imposed on employees and employers by sections 3101 and 3111, will be determined as provided in section 3121(i)(4).

(d) *Effective date of election.*—(1) *In general.*—Except as provided in paragraph (e) of this section, a certificate of election of coverage filed by a religious order or its subdivision pursuant to section 3121(r) and this section shall be in effect, for purposes of section 3121(b)(8)(A) and for purposes of section 210(a)(8)(A) of the Social Security Act, for the period beginning with whichever of the following may be designated by the electing religious order or subdivision:

(i) The first day of the calendar quarter in which the certificate is filed,

(ii) The first day of the calendar quarter immediately following the quarter in which the certificate is filed, or

(iii) The first day of any calendar quarter preceding the calendar quarter in which the certificate is filed, except that such date may not be earlier than the first day of the 20th calendar quarter preceding the quarter in which such certificate is filed.

(2) *Retroactive elections.*—Whenever a date is designated as provided in paragraph (d)(1)(iii) of this section, the election shall apply to services performed before the quarter in which the certificate is filed only if the member performing such services was a member at the time such services were performed and is living on the first day of the quarter in which such certificate is filed. Thus, the election applies to an individual who is no longer a member of a religious order on the first day of such quarter if he performed services as a member at any time on or after the date so designated and is living on the first day of the quarter in which such certificate is filed. For purposes of computing interest and for purposes of section 6651 (relating to additions to tax for failure to file tax return or to pay tax), in any case in which such a date is designated the due date for the return and payment of the tax, for calendar quarters prior to the quarter in which the certificate is filed, resulting from the filing of such certificate shall be the last day of the calendar month following the calendar quarter in which the certificate is filed. The statutory period for the assessment of the tax for such prior calendar quarters

shall not expire before the expiration of 3 years from such due date. [Reg. §31.3121(r)-1.]

☐ [*T.D. 7280, 7-10-73. Amended by T.D. 9849, 3-11-2019.*]

**[Reg. §31.3121(s)-1]**

**§31.3121(s)-1. Concurrent employment by related corporations with common paymaster.**—(a) *In general.*—For purposes of section 3102, 3111, and 3121(a)(1), except as otherwise provided in paragraph (c) of this section, when two or more related corporations concurrently employ the same individual and compensate that individual through a common paymaster which is one of the related corporations that employs the individual, each of the corporations is considered to have paid only the remuneration it actually disburses to that individual. This rule applies whether the remuneration was paid with respect to the employment relationship of the individual with the disbursing corporation or was paid on behalf of another related corporation. Accordingly, if all of the remuneration to the individual from the related corporations is disbursed through the common paymaster, the total amount of taxes imposed with respect to the remuneration under sections 3102 and 3111 is determined as though the individual has only one employer (the common paymaster). The common paymaster is responsible for filing information and tax returns and issuing Forms W-2 with respect to wages it is considered to have paid under this section. Section 3121(s) and this section apply only to remuneration disbursed in the form of money, check, or similar instrument by one of the related corporations or its agent.

(b) *Definitions.*—The definitions contained in this paragraph are applicable only for purposes of this section and §31.3306(p)-1.

(1) *Related corporations.*—Corporations shall be considered related corporations for an entire calendar quarter (as defined in §31.0-2(a)(9)) if they satisfy any one of the following four tests at any time during that calendar quarter:

(i) The corporations are members of a "controlled group of corporations", as defined in section 1563 of the Code, or would be members if section 1563(a)(4) and (b) did not apply and if the phrase "more than 50 percent" were substituted for the phrase "at least 80 percent" wherever it appears in section 1563(a).

(ii) In the case of a corporation that does not issue stock, either fifty percent or more of the members of one corporation's board of directors (or other governing body) are members of the other corporation's board of directors (or other governing body), or the holders of fifty percent or more of the voting power to select such members are concurrently the holders of fifty percent or more of that power with respect to the other corporation.

(iii) Fifty percent or more of one corporation's officers are concurrently officers of the other corporation.

(iv) Thirty percent or more of one corporation's employees are concurrently employees of the other corporation.

The following examples illustrate the application of this paragraph:

*Example (1).* (a) X Corporation employs individuals A, B, D, E, F, G, and H. Y Corporation employs individuals A, B, and C. Z Corporation employs individuals A, C, I, J, K, L, and M. X Corporation is the paymaster for all thirteen individuals. The corporations have no officers or stockholders in common.

(b) X and Y are related corporations because at least 30 percent of Y's employees are also employees of X. Y and Z are related corporations because at least 30 percent of Y's employees are also employees of Z. X and Z are not related corporations because neither corporation has 30 percent of its employees concurrently employed by the other corporation.

(c) For purposes of determining the amount of the tax liability under sections 3102 and 3111, individual B is treated as having one employer. Individual C has two employers for these purposes, although Y and Z are related corporations, because C is not employed by X Corporation, the common paymaster. Individual A also is treated as having two employers for the purposes of these sections because X and Y Corporations are treated as one employer, and Z Corporation is treated as a second employer (since it is not related to the paymaster, X Corporation). Of course, individuals D, E, F, G, H, I, J, K, L, and M are not concurrently employed by two or more corporations, and, accordingly, section 3121(s) is inapplicable to them.

*Example (2).* M and N Corporations are both related to Corporation O but are not related to each other. Individual A is concurrently employed by all three corporations and paid by O, their common paymaster. Although M and N are not related, O is treated as the employer for A's employment with M, N, and O.

*Example (3).* Corporations X, Y, and Z meet the definition of related corporations for the first time on April 12, 1979, and cease to meet it on July 5, 1979. A is concurrently employed by X, Y, and Z throughout 1979. In each of the four calendar quarters of 1979, A's remuneration from X, Y, and Z is $2,000, $10,000, and $30,000, respectively. All of the remuneration to A from X, Y, and Z for the year is disbursed by X, the common paymaster. Under these circumstances, the amount of wages subject to sections 3102 and 3111 is as follows:

| For the first calendar quarter | | |
|---|---|---|
| X | Y | Z |
| $2,000 | $10,000 | $22,900 |
| For the second calendar quarter | | |
| X | Y | Z |
| $20,900 | 0 | 0 |
| ($22,900 – $2,000) | | |
| For the third calendar quarter | | |
| X | Y | Z |
| 0 | 0 | 0 |
| For the fourth calendar quarter | | |
| X | Y | Z |
| 0 | $10,000 | 0 |

Of course, if the corporations had been related throughout all of 1979, only $22,900 of X's first quarter disbursement would have constituted wages subject to sections 3102 and 3111.

(2) *Common paymaster.*—(i) *In general.*—A common paymaster of a group of related corporations is any member thereof that disburses remuneration to employees of two or more of those corporations on their behalf and that is responsible for keeping books and records for the payroll with respect to those employees. The common paymaster is not required to disburse remuneration to all the employees of those two or more related corporations, but the provisions of this section do not apply to any remuneration to an employee that is not disbursed through a common paymaster. The common paymaster may pay concurrently employed individuals under this section by one combined paycheck, drawn on a single bank account, or by separate paychecks, drawn by the common paymaster on the accounts of one or more employing corporations.

(ii) *Multiple common paymasters.*—A group of related corporations may have more than one common paymaster. Some of the related corporations may use one common paymaster and others of the related corporations use another common paymaster with respect to a certain class of employees. A corporation that uses a common paymaster to disburse remuneration to certain of its employees may use a different common paymaster to disburse remuneration to other employees.

(iii) *Examples.*—The rules of this subparagraph are illustrated by the following examples:

*Example (1).* S, T, U, and V are related corporations with 2,000 employees collectively. Forty of these employees are concurrently employed by two or more of the corporations, during a calendar quarter. The four corporations arrange for S to disburse remuneration to thirty of these forty employees for their services. Under these facts, S is the common paymaster of S, T, U, and V with respect to the thirty employees. S is not a common paymaster with respect to the remaining employees.

*Example (2).* (a) W, X, Y, and Z are related corporations. The corporations collectively have 20,000 employees. Two hundred of the employees are top-level executives and managers, sixty of whom are concurrently employed by two or more of the corporations during a calendar quarter. Six thousand of the employees are skilled artisans, all of whom are concurrently employed by two or more of the corporations during the calendar year. The four corporations arrange for Z to disburse remuneration to the sixty executives who are concurrently employed by two or more of the corporations. W and X arrange for X to disburse remuneration to the artisans who are concurrently employed by W and X.

(b) A is an executive who is concurrently employed only by W, Y, and Z during the calendar year. Under these facts, Z is a common paymaster for W, Y, and Z with respect to A. Assuming that the other requirements of this section are met, the amount of the tax liability under sections 3102 and 3111 is determined as if Z were A's only employer for the calendar quarter.

(c) B is a skilled artisan who is concurrently employed only by W and X during the calendar year. Under these facts, X is a common paymaster for S and X with respect to B. Assuming that the other requirements of this section are met, the amount of the tax liability under sections 3102 and 3111 is determined as if X were B's only employer for the calendar quarter.

(3) *Concurrent employment.*—For purposes of this section, the term "concurrent employment" means the contemporaneous existence of an employment relationship (within the meaning of section 3121 (b)) between an individual and two or more corporations. Such a relationship contemplates the performance of services by the employee for the benefit of the employing corporation (not merely for the benefit of the group of corporations), in exchange for remuneration which, if deductible for the purposes of Federal income tax, would be deductible by the employing corporation. The contemporaneous existence of an employment relationship with each corporation is the decisive factor; if it exists, the fact that a particular employee is on leave or otherwise temporarily inactive is immaterial. However, employment is not concurrent with respect to one of the related corporations if the employee's employment relationship with that corporation is completely nonexistent during periods when the employee is not performing services for that corporation. An employment relationship is completely nonexistent if all rights and obligations of the employer and employee with respect to employment have terminated, other than those that customarily exist after employment relationships terminate. Examples of rights and obligations that customarily exist after employment relationships terminate include those with respect to remuneration not yet paid, employer's property used by the employee not yet returned to the employer, severance pay, and lump-sum termination payments from a deferred compensation plan. Circumstances that suggest that an employment relationship has become completely nonexistent include unconditional termination of participation in deferred compensation plans of the employer, forfeiture of seniority claims, and forfeiture of unused fringe benefits such as vacation or sick pay. Of course, the continued existence of an employment relationship between an individual and a corporation is not necessarily established by the individual's continued participation in a deferred compensation plan, retention of seniority rights, etc., since continuation of those benefits may be attributable to employment with a second corporation related to the first corporation if the corporations have common benefit plans or if the benefits are continued as a matter of corporate reciprocity. An individual who does not perform substantial services in exchange for remuneration from a corporation is presumed not employed by that corporation. Concurrent employment need not exist for any particular length of time to meet the requirements of this section, but this section only applies to remuneration disbursed by a common paymaster to an individual who is concurrently employed by the common paymaster and at least one other related corporation at the time the individual performs the services for which the remuneration is paid. If the employment relationship is nonexistent during a quarter, that employee may not be counted towards the 30-percent test set forth in paragraph (b)(1)(iv) of this section; however, even if the employment relationship is nonexistent, section 3121(s) of the Code applies to remuneration paid to the former employee for services rendered while the employee was a common employee. The principles of this subparagraph are illustrated by the following examples:

*Example (1).* M, N, and O are related corporations which use N as a common paymaster with respect to officers. Their respective headquarters are located in three separate cities several hundred miles apart. A is an officer of M, N, and O who performs substantial services for each corporation. A does not work a set length of time at each corporate headquarters, and when A leaves one corporate headquarters, it is not known when A will return, although it is expected that A will return. Under these facts, A is concurrently employed by the three corporations.

*Example (2).* P, Q, and R are related corporations whose geographical zones of business activity do not overlap. P, Q, and R have a common pension plan and arrange for Q to be a common paymaster for managers and executives. All three corporations maintain cafeterias for the use of their employees. B is a cafeteria manager who has worked at P's headquarters for 3 years. On June 1, 1980, B is transferred from P to the position of cafeteria manager of R. There are no plans for B's return to P. B's accrued pension benefits, vacation and sick pay, do not change as a result of the transfer. The decision to transfer B was made by Q, the parent corporation. Under these facts, B is not concurrently employed by P and R, because B's employment relationship with P was completely nonexistent during B's employment with R. Furthermore, section 3121(s) is inapplicable since B also was not employed by Q, the common paymaster, because B never contracted to perform services for remuneration from Q, and Q did not have the right to control the day-to-day duties of B's work.

*Example (3).* C is employed by two related corporations, S and T. C was concurrently employed by these corporations between April 1, 1979, and June 30, 1979. The corporations used T as the common paymaster with respect to C's wages between May 1, 1979, and September 30, 1979. T pays C on May 15 for services performed between April 1 and April 30, on July 15 for services performed between June 1 and June 30, and on August 15 for services performed between July 1 and July 31. Section 3121(s) applies to the first two payments but does not apply to the third payment (there was no concurrent employment). However, if the third payment was made by T for services performed for T, T counts the amounts previously disbursed to C in 1979 while C was concurrently employed by S and T towards the wage base (see section 3121(a)(1)).

(c) *Allocation of employment taxes.*—(1) *Responsibility to pay tax.*—If the requirements of this section are met, the common paymaster has the primary responsibility for remitting taxes pursuant to sections 3102 and 3111 with respect to the remuneration it disburses as the common paymaster. The common paymaster computes these taxes as though it were the sole employer of the concurrently employed individuals. If the common paymaster fails to remit these taxes (in whole or in part), it remains liable for the full amount of the unpaid portion of these taxes. In addition, each of the other related corporations using the common paymaster is jointly and severally liable for its appropriate share of these taxes. That share is an amount equal to the lesser of:

(i) The amount of the liability of the common paymaster under section 3121(s), after taking account of any tax payments made, or

(ii) The amount of the liability under sections 3102 and 3111 which, but for section 3121(s), would have existed with respect to the remuneration from such other related corporation, reduced by an allocable portion of any taxes previously paid by the common paymaster with respect to that remuneration.

The portion of taxes previously paid by the common paymaster that is allocable to each related corporation is determined by

$$\frac{\begin{array}{l}\text{Portion of wage payment constituting} \\ \text{remuneration to the employee for} \\ \text{services performed for the corporation} \end{array}}{\begin{array}{l}\text{Total wage payment constituting} \\ \text{remuneration to the employee for all} \\ \text{services performed for the related} \\ \text{corporations using the common} \\ \text{paymaster}\end{array}}$$

If the remuneration disbursed to an employee for services performed for a corporation is inappropriate, the district director may adjust the remuneration records of the related corporations to reflect appropriate remuneration. The district director may use the principles of § 1.482-2(b) in making the adjustments.

multiplying the amount of taxes paid by a fraction, the numerator of which is the portion of the amount of employment tax liability of the common paymaster under section 3121(s) that is allocable to such related corporation under paragraph (c)(2) of this section, and the denominator of which is the total amount of the common paymaster's liability under section 3121(s), both determined without regard to any prior tax payments. These rules apply whether or not the tax on employees was withheld from the employees' wages.

(2) *Allocation of tax.*—(i) *In general.*—If the related corporations maintain a record of the remuneration disbursed to the employee for services performed for each corporation, the remuneration-based allocation rules of paragraph (c)(2)(ii) of this section apply. If the related corporations do not maintain this record of remuneration, the group-wide allocation rules of paragraph (c)(2)(iii) of this section apply. In all cases, allocations must be made with respect to each payment of wages. The allocation of employment tax liabilities pursuant to this subparagraph also determines which related corporation may be entitled to income tax deductions with respect to the payments of those taxes.

(ii) *Remuneration-based allocation rules.*—Under the remuneration-based method of allocation, each related corporation that remunerates an employee through a common paymaster has allocated to it for each pay period an amount of tax determined according to the following formula:

$$\times \quad \begin{array}{l}\text{Tax on employees under section 3102} \\ \text{and tax on employers under section} \\ \text{3111 that the common paymaster is} \\ \text{required to remit with respect to the} \\ \text{wage payment.}\end{array}$$

*Example.* (i) X and Y are related corporations which use Y as common paymaster for their executives. A is a concurrently employed executive who performs services during the first quarter of 1979 for X and Y. Y remunerates $4,000 gross pay every week to A, calculated as follows:

| Wage payments | Remuneration | | | Tax on employers under section 3111 | Tax on employees withheld under section 3102 | Total |
|---|---|---|---|---|---|---|
| | X | Y | Total | | | |
| 1 | $3,000 | $1,000 | $4,000 | $245.20 | $245.20 | $490.40 |
| 2—3 | ....... | 8,000 | 8,000 | 490.40 | 490.40 | 980.80 |
| 4 | 1,000 | 3,000 | 4,000 | 245.20 | 245.20 | 490.40 |
| 5 | 4,000 | ....... | 4,000 | 245.20 | 245.20 | 490.40 |
| 6 | 2,000 | 2,000 | 4,000 | 177.77 | 177.77 | 355.54 |
| 7—13 | 10,000 | 18,000 | 28,000 | 0 | 0 | 0 |
| | $20,000 | $32,000 | $52,000 | $1,403.77 | $1,403.77 | $2,807.54 |

The amounts of remuneration to A are determined by the district director to be appropriate. Under these facts, the tax is allocated to X and Y in the following amounts:

| Wage Payments | X | Y |
|---|---|---|
| 1 | $\frac{\$3,000}{\$4,000} \times \$490.40 = \$367.80$ | $\frac{\$1,000}{\$4,000} \times \$490.40 = \$122.60$ |
| 2—3 | .................... | $\frac{\$8,000}{\$8,000} \times \$980.80 = \$980.80$ |
| 4 | $\frac{\$1,000}{\$4,000} \times \$490.40 = \$122.60$ | $\frac{\$3,000}{\$4,000} \times \$490.40 = \$367.80$ |
| 5 | $\frac{\$4,000}{\$4,000} \times \$490.40 = \$490.40$ | .................... |
| 6 | $\frac{\$2,000}{\$4,000} \times \$355.54 = \$177.77$ | $\frac{\$2,000}{\$4,000} \times \$355.54 = \$177.77$ |
| 7—13 | $\frac{\$10,000}{\$28,000} \times -0- = -0-$ | $\frac{\$28,000}{\$28,000} \times -0- = -0-$ |
| | $1,158.57 | $1,648.97 |

Reg. §31.3121(s)-1(c)(1)

*Example* (ii) If Y remits none of the taxes to the Internal Revenue Service, X is liable for $2,452.00 (the entire amount due pursuant to sections 3102 and 3111 with respect to the remuneration to A from X) (12.26% × $20,000). Any amount remitted by X to the Internal Revenue Service under these circumstances is also credited against the liability of the common paymaster, Y. However, only the portion of the employment taxes allocated to X under (i) above may be deducted by X as employment taxes paid by it in respect of wages paid by it to its employees.

*Example* (iii) If Y remits $1,000.00 of the total $2,807.54 due, Y as common paymaster remains liable for $1,807.54 ($2,807.54 minus $1,000). X's liability is the lesser of $1,807.54 (the liability of the common paymaster), or X's total liability, in the absence of section 3121(s), on wages paid through the common paymaster $2,452.00) minus a credit for an allocable part of the amount remitted by Y. The part is $412.66

$$\frac{\$1,158.57 \text{ (X's allocable share of tax)}}{\$2,807.54 \text{ (total tax)}} \times \$1,000$$

(tax remitted). Since $1,807.54 is less than $2,039.34 ($2,452.00 minus $412.66), X and Y are jointly and severally liable for $1,807.54.

(iii) *Group-wide allocation rules.*—Under the group-wide method of allocation, the Commissioner may allocate the taxes imposed by sections 3102 and 3111 in an appropriate manner to a related corporation that remunerates an employee through a common paymaster if the common paymaster fails to remit the taxes to the Internal Revenue Service. Allocation in an appropriate manner varies according to the circumstances. It may be based on sales, property, corporate payroll, or any other basis that reflects the distribution of the services performed by the employee, or a combination of the foregoing bases. To the extent practicable, the Commissioner may use the principles of § 1.482-2(b) of this chapter in making the allocations with respect to wages paid after December 31, 1978, and on or before July 31, 2009. To the extent practicable, the Commissioner may use the principles of § 1.482-9 of this chapter in making the allocations with respect to wages paid after July 31, 2009.

(d) *Effective/applicability date.*—(1) *In general.*—This section is applicable with respect to wages paid after December 31, 1978. The fourth sentence of paragraph (c)(2)(iii) of this section is applicable with respect to wages paid after December 31, 1978, and on or before July 31, 2009. The fifth sentence of paragraph (c)(2)(iii) of this section is applicable with respect to wages paid after July 31, 2009.

(2) *Election to apply regulation to earlier taxable years.*—A person may elect to apply the fifth sentence of paragraph (c)(2)(iii) of this section to earlier taxable years in accordance with the rules set forth in § 1.482-9(n)(2) of this chapter. [Reg. § 31.3121(s)-1.]

☐ [*T.D. 7660, 12-19-79, as corrected*, 3-20-80. *Amended by T.D.* 9278, 7-31-2006 *and T.D.* 9456, 7-31-2009.]

### [Reg. § 31.3121(v)(2)-1]

**§ 31.3121(v)(2)-1. Treatment of amounts deferred under certain nonqualified deferred compensation plans.**—(a) *Timing of wage inclusion.*—(1) *General timing rule for wages.*—Remuneration for employment that constitutes wages within the meaning of section 3121(a) generally is taken into account for purposes of the Federal Insurance Contributions Act (FICA) taxes imposed under sections 3101 and 3111 at the time the remuneration is actually or constructively paid. See § 31.3121(a)-2(a).

(2) *Special timing rule for an amount deferred under a nonqualified deferred compensation plan.*—(i) *In general.*—To the extent that remuneration deferred under a nonqualified deferred compensation plan constitutes wages within the meaning of section 3121(a), the remuneration is subject to the special timing rule described in this paragraph (a)(2). Remuneration is considered deferred under a nonqualified deferred compensation plan within the meaning of section 3121(v)(2) and this section only if it is provided pursuant to a plan described in paragraph (b) of this section. The amount deferred under a nonqualified deferred compensation plan is determined under paragraph (c) of this section.

(ii) *Special timing rule.*—Except as otherwise provided in this section, an amount deferred under a nonqualified deferred compensation plan is required to be taken into account as wages for FICA tax purposes as of the later of—

(A) The date on which the services creating the right to that amount are performed (within the meaning of paragraph (e)(2) of this section); or

(B) The date on which the right to that amount is no longer subject to a substantial risk of forfeiture (within the meaning of paragraph (e)(3) of this section).

(iii) *Inclusion in wages only once (nonduplication rule).*—Once an amount deferred under a nonqualified deferred compensation plan is taken into account (within the meaning of paragraph (d)(1) of this section), then neither the amount taken into account nor the income attributable to the amount taken into account (within the meaning of paragraph (d)(2) of this section) is treated as wages for FICA tax purposes at any time thereafter.

(iv) *Benefits that do not result from a deferral of compensation.*—If a nonqualified deferred compensation plan (within the meaning of paragraph (b)(1) of this section) provides both a benefit that results from the deferral of compensation (within the meaning of paragraph (b)(3) of this section) and a benefit that does not result from the deferral of compensation, the benefit that does not result from the deferral of compensation is not subject to the special timing rule described in this paragraph (a)(2). For example, if a nonqualified deferred compensation plan provides retirement benefits which result from the deferral of compensation and disability pay (within the meaning of paragraph (b)(4)(iv)(C) of this section) which does not result from the deferral of compensation, the retirement benefits provided under the plan are subject to the special timing rule in this paragraph (a)(2) and the disability pay is not.

(v) *Remuneration that does not constitute wages.*—If remuneration under a nonqualified deferred compensation plan does not constitute wages within the meaning of section 3121(a), then that remuneration is not taken into account as wages for FICA tax purposes under either the general timing rule described in paragraph (a)(1) of this section or the special timing rule described in this paragraph (a)(2). For example, benefits under a death benefit plan described in section 3121(a)(13) do not constitute wages for FICA tax purposes. Therefore, these benefits are not included as wages under the general timing rule described in paragraph (a)(1) of this section or the special timing rule described in this paragraph (a)(2), even if the death benefit plan would otherwise be considered a nonqualified deferred compensation plan within the meaning of paragraph (b)(1) of this section.

(b) *Nonqualified deferred compensation plan.*—(1) *In general.*—For purposes of this section, the term *nonqualified deferred compensation plan* means any plan or other arrangement, other than a plan described in section 3121(a)(5), that is established (within the meaning of paragraph (b)(2) of this section) by an employer for one or more of its employees, and that provides for the deferral of compensation (within the meaning of paragraph (b)(3) of this section). A nonqualified deferred compensation plan may be adopted unilaterally by the employer or may be negotiated among or agreed to by the employer and one or more employees or employee representatives. A plan may constitute a nonqualified deferred compensation plan under this section without regard to whether the deferrals under the plan are made pursuant to an election by the employee or whether the amounts deferred are treated as deferred compensation for income tax purposes (e.g., whether the amounts are subject to the deduction rules of section 404). In addition, a plan may constitute a nonqualified deferred compensation plan under this section whether or not it is an employee benefit plan under section 3(3) of the Employee Retirement Income Security Act of 1974 (ERISA), as amended (29 U.S.C. 1002(3)). For purposes of this section, except where the context indicates otherwise, the term *plan* includes a plan or other arrangement.

(2) *Plan establishment.*—(i) *Date plan is established.*—For purposes of this section, a plan is established on the latest of the date on which it is adopted, the date on which it is effective, and the date on which the material terms of the plan are set forth in writing. For purposes of this section, a plan will be deemed to be set forth in writing if it is set forth in any other form that is approved by the Commissioner. The material terms of the plan include the amount (or the method or formula for determining the amount) of deferred compensation to be provided under the plan and the time when it may or will be provided.

(ii) *Plan amendments.*—In the case of an amendment that increases the amount deferred under a nonqualified deferred compensation plan, the plan is not considered established with respect to the additional amount deferred until the plan, as amended, is established in accordance with paragraph (b)(2)(i) of this section.

(iii) *Transition rule for written plan requirement.*—For purposes of this section, an unwritten plan that was adopted and effective before March 25, 1996, is treated as established under this section as of the later of the date on which it was adopted or became effective, provided that the material terms of the plan are set forth in writing before January 1, 2000.

(3) *Plan must provide for the deferral of compensation.*—(i) *Deferral of compensation defined.*—A plan provides for the *deferral of compensation* with respect to an employee only if, under the terms of the plan and the relevant facts and circumstances, the employee has a legally binding right during a calendar year to compensation that has not been actually or constructively received and that, pursuant to the terms of the plan, is payable to (or on behalf of) the employee in a later year. An employee does not have a legally binding right to compensation if that compensation may be unilaterally reduced or eliminated by the employer after the services creating the right to the compensation have been performed. For this purpose, compensation is not considered subject to unilateral reduction or elimination merely because it may be reduced or eliminated by operation of the objective terms of the plan, such as the application of an objective provision creating a substantial risk of forfeiture (within the meaning of section 83). Similarly, an employee does not fail to have a legally binding right to compensation merely because the amount of compensation is determined under a formula that provides for benefits to be offset by benefits provided under a plan that is qualified under section 401(a), or because benefits are reduced due to investment losses or, in a final average pay plan, subsequent decreases in compensation.

(ii) *Compensation payable pursuant to the employer's customary payment timing arrangement.*—There is no deferral of compensation (within the meaning of this paragraph (b)(3)) merely because compensation is paid after the last day of a calendar year pursuant to the timing arrangement under which the employer ordinarily compensates employees for services performed during a payroll period described in section 3401(b).

(iii) *Short-term deferrals.*—If, under a nonqualified deferred compensation plan, there is a deferral of compensation (within the meaning of this paragraph (b)(3)) that causes an amount to be deferred from a calendar year to a date that is not more than a brief period of time after the end of that calendar year, then, at the employer's option, that amount may be treated as if it were not subject to the special timing rule described in paragraph (a)(2) of this section. An employer may apply this option only if the employer does so for all employees covered by the plan and all substantially similar nonqualified deferred compensation plans. For purposes of this paragraph (b)(3)(iii), whether compensation is deferred to a date that is not more than a brief period of time after the end of a calendar year is determined in accordance with § 1.404(b)-1T, Q&A-2, of this chapter.

(4) *Plans, arrangements, and benefits that do not provide for the deferral of compensation.*—(i) *In general.*—Notwithstanding paragraph (b)(3)(i) of this section, an amount or benefit described in any of paragraphs (b)(4)(ii) through (viii) of this section is not treated as resulting from the deferral of compensation for purposes of section 3121(v)(2) and this section and, thus, is not subject to the special timing rule of paragraph (a)(2) of this section.

(ii) *Stock options, stock appreciation rights, and other stock value rights.*—The grant of a stock option, stock appreciation right, or other stock value right does not constitute the deferral of compensation for purposes of section 3121(v)(2). In addition, amounts received as a result of the exercise of a stock option, stock appreciation right, or other stock value right do not result from the deferral of compensation for purposes of section 3121(v)(2) if such amounts are actually or constructively received in the calendar year of the exercise. For purposes of this paragraph (b)(4)(ii), a *stock value right* is a right granted to an employee with respect to one or more shares of employer stock that, to the extent exercised, entitles the employee to a payment for each share of stock equal to the excess, or a percentage of the excess, of the value of a share of the employer's stock on the date of exercise over a specified price (greater than zero). Thus, for example, the term stock value right does not include a phantom stock or other arrangement under which an employee is awarded the right to receive a fixed payment equal to the value of a specified number of shares of employer stock.

(iii) *Restricted property.*—If an employee receives property from, or pursuant to, a plan maintained by an employer, there is no deferral of compensation (within the meaning of section 3121(v)(2)) merely because the value of the property is not includible in income (under section 83) in the year of receipt by reason of the property being nontransferable and subject to a substantial risk of forfeiture. However, a plan under which an employee obtains a legally binding right to receive property (whether or not the property is restricted property) in a future year may provide for the deferral of compensation within the meaning of paragraph (b)(3) of this section and, accordingly, may constitute a nonqualified deferred compensation plan, even though benefits under the plan are or may be paid in the form of property.

(iv) *Certain welfare benefits.*—(A) *In general.*—Vacation benefits, sick leave, compensatory time, disability pay, severance pay, and death benefits do not result from the deferral of compensation for purposes of section 3121(v)(2), even if those benefits constitute wages within the meaning of section 3121(a).

(B) *Severance pay.*—Benefits that are provided under a severance pay arrangement (within the meaning of section 3(2)(B)(i) of ERISA) that satisfies the conditions in 29 CFR 2510.3-2(b)(1)(i) through (iii) are considered severance pay for purposes of this paragraph (b)(4)(iv). If benefits are provided under a severance pay arrangement (within the meaning of section 3(2)(B)(i) of ERISA), but do not satisfy one or more of the conditions in 29 CFR 2510.3-2(b)(1)(i) through (iii), then whether those benefits are severance pay within the meaning of this paragraph (b)(4)(iv) depends upon the relevant facts and circumstances. For this purpose, relevant facts and circumstances include whether the benefits are provided over a short period of time commencing immediately after (or shortly after) termination of employment or for a substantial period of time following termination of employment and whether the benefits are provided after any termination or only after retirement (or another specified type of termination). Benefits provided under a severance pay arrangement (within the meaning of section 3(2)(B)(i) of ERISA) are in all cases severance pay within the meaning of this paragraph (b)(4)(iv) if the benefits payable under the plan upon an employee's termination of employment are payable only if that termination is involuntary.

(C) *Death benefits and disability pay.*—(1) *General definition.*—Payments made under a nonqualified deferred compensation plan in the event of death are death benefits within the meaning of this paragraph (b)(4)(iv), but only to the extent the total benefits payable under the plan exceed the lifetime benefits payable under the plan. Similarly, payments made under a nonqualified deferred compensation plan in the event of disability are disability pay within the meaning of this paragraph (b)(4)(iv), but only to the extent the disability benefits payable under the plan exceed the lifetime benefits payable under the plan. Accordingly, any benefits that a nonqualified deferred compensation plan provides in the event of death or disability that are associated with an amount deferred under this section are disregarded in applying this section to the extent the benefits payable under the plan in the event of death or in the event of disability have a value in excess of the lifetime benefits payable under the plan.

(2) *Total benefits payable defined.*—For purposes of paragraph (b)(4)(iv)(C)(1) of this section, the term *total benefits payable* under a plan means the present value of the total benefits payable to or on behalf of the employee (including benefits payable in the event of the employee's death) under the plan, disregarding any benefits that are payable only in the event of disability and determined separately with respect to each form of distribution or other election that may apply with respect to the employee.

(3) *Disability benefits payable defined.*—For purposes of paragraph (b)(4)(iv)(C)(1) of this section, the term *disability benefits payable* under a plan means the present value of the benefits payable to or on behalf of the employee under the plan, including benefits payable in the event of the employee's disability but excluding death benefits within the meaning of this paragraph (b)(4)(iv).

(4) *Lifetime benefits payable defined.*—For purposes of paragraph (b)(4)(iv)(C)(1) of this section, the term *lifetime benefits payable* under a plan means the present value of the benefits that could be payable to the employee under the plan during the employee's lifetime, determined under the plan's optional form of distribution or other election that is or was available to the employee at any time with respect to the amount deferred and that provides the largest present value to the employee during the employee's lifetime of any such form or election so available.

(5) *Rules of application.*—For purposes of determining present value under this paragraph (b)(4)(iv)(C), present value is determined as of the time immediately preceding the time the amount deferred under a nonqualified deferred compensation plan is required to be taken into account under paragraph (e) of this section, using actuarial assumptions that are reasonable as of that date but taking into consideration only benefits that result from the deferral of compensation, as determined under this paragraph (b), and benefits payable in the event of death or disability. In addition, for purposes of paragraph (b)(4)(iv)(C)(4) of this section, present value must be determined without any discount for the probability that the em-

ployee may die before benefit payments commence and without regard to any benefits payable solely in the event of disability.

(v) *Certain benefits provided in connection with impending termination.*—(A) *In general.*—Benefits provided in connection with impending termination of employment under paragraph (b)(4)(v)(B) or (C) of this section do not result from the deferral of compensation within the meaning of section 3121(v)(2).

(B) *Window benefits.*—(1) *In general.*—For purposes of this paragraph (b)(4)(v), except as provided in paragraph (b)(4)(v)(B)(3) of this section, a window benefit is provided in connection with impending termination of employment. For this purpose, a *window benefit* is an early retirement benefit, retirement-type subsidy, social security supplement, or other form of benefit made available by an employer for a limited period of time (no greater than one year) to employees who terminate employment during that period or to employees who terminate employment during that period under specified circumstances.

(2) *Special rule for recurring window benefits.*—A benefit will not be considered a window benefit if an employer establishes a pattern of repeatedly providing for similar benefits in similar situations for substantially consecutive, limited periods of time. Whether the recurrence of these benefits constitutes a pattern of amendments is determined based on the facts and circumstances. Although no one factor is determinative, relevant factors include whether the benefits are on account of a specific business event or condition, the degree to which the benefits relate to the event or condition, and whether the event or condition is temporary or discrete or is a permanent aspect of the employer's business.

(3) *Transition rule for window benefits.*—In the case of a window benefit that is made available for a period of time that begins before January 1, 2000, an employer may choose to treat the window benefit as a benefit that results from the deferral of compensation if the sole reason the window benefit would otherwise fail to be provided pursuant to a nonqualified deferred compensation plan is the application of paragraph (b)(4)(v)(B)(1) of this section.

(C) *Termination within 12 months of establishment of a benefit or plan.*—For purposes of this paragraph (b)(4)(v), a benefit is provided in connection with impending termination of employment, without regard to whether it constitutes a window benefit, if—

(1) An employee's termination of employment occurs within 12 months of the establishment of the plan (or amendment) providing the benefit; and

(2) The facts and circumstances indicate that the plan (or amendment) is established in contemplation of the employee's impending termination of employment.

(vi) *Benefits established after termination.*—Benefits established with respect to an employee after the employee's termination of employment do not result from a deferral of compensation within the meaning of section 3121(v)(2). However, cost-of-living adjustments on benefit payments under a nonqualified deferred compensation plan (within the meaning of paragraph (b) of this section) shall not be considered benefits established after the employee's termination of employment for purposes of this paragraph (b)(4)(vi) merely because the employee does not obtain the right to the adjustment until after the employee's termination of employment. For purposes of the preceding sentence, *cost-of-living adjustments* are payments that satisfy conditions similar to those of 29 CFR 2510.3-2(g)(1)(ii) and (iii).

(vii) *Excess parachute payments.*—An excess parachute payment (as defined in section 280G(b)) under an agreement entered into or renewed after June 14, 1984, in taxable years ending after such date, does not result from the deferral of compensation within the meaning of section 3121(v)(2). For this purpose, any contract entered into before June 15, 1984, that is amended after June 14, 1984, in any relevant significant aspect, is treated as a contract entered into after June 14, 1984.

(viii) *Compensation for current services.*—A plan does not provide for the deferral of compensation within the meaning of section 3121(v)(2) if, based on the relevant facts and circumstances, the compensation is paid for current services.

(5) *Examples.*—This paragraph (b) is illustrated by the following examples:

*Example 1.* (i) In December of 2001, Employer L tells Employee A that, if specified goals are satisfied for 2002, Employee A will receive a bonus on July 1, 2003, equal to a specified percentage of 2002 compensation. Because Employee A meets the specified goals, Employer L pays the bonus to Employee A on July 1, 2003, consistent with its oral commitment.

(ii) This arrangement is not a nonqualified deferred compensation plan under this section because its terms were not set forth in

writing and, therefore, it was not established in accordance with paragraph (b)(2) of this section.

*Example 2.* (i) In 2004, Employer M establishes a compensation arrangement for Employee B under which Employer M agrees to pay Employee B a specified amount based on a percentage of his salary for 2004. The amount due is to be paid out of the general assets of Employer M and is payable in 2008.

(ii) Employee B has a legally binding right during 2004 to an amount of compensation that has not been actually or constructively received and that, pursuant to the terms of the arrangement, is payable in a later year. Therefore, the arrangement provides for the deferral of compensation.

*Example 3.* (i) Employer N establishes a nonqualified deferred compensation plan (within the meaning of paragraph (b)(1) of this section) for Employee C in 1984. The plan is amended on January 1, 2001, to increase benefits, and the amendment provides that the increase in benefits is on account of Employee C's performance of services for Employer N from 1985 through 2000.

(ii) The additional benefits that resulted from the plan amendment cannot be taken into account as amounts deferred for 1985 through 2000, even though the plan was established before then. Pursuant to paragraphs (b)(2)(ii) and (e)(1) of this section, the additional benefits cannot be taken into account before the latest of the date on which the amendment is adopted, the date on which the amendment is effective, or the date on which the material terms of the plan, as amended, are set forth in writing.

*Example 4.* (i) In 2002, Employer O, a state or local government, establishes a plan for certain employees that provides for the deferral of compensation and that is subject to section 457(a).

(ii) Paragraph (b)(1) of this section provides that nonqualified deferred compensation plan means any plan that is established by an employer and that provides for the deferral of compensation, other than a plan described in section 3121(a)(5). Section 3121(a)(5) lists, among other plans, an exempt governmental deferred compensation plan as defined in section 3121(v)(3). Under section 3121(v)(3)(A), this definition does not include any plan to which section 457(a) applies. Thus, the plan established by Employer O is not an exempt governmental deferred compensation plan described in section 3121(v)(3) and, consequently, is not a plan described in section 3121(a)(5). Accordingly, the plan is a nonqualified deferred compensation plan within the meaning of section 3121(v)(2) and paragraph (b)(1) of this section.

(iii) However, the general timing rule of paragraph (a)(1) of this section and the special timing rule of paragraph (a)(2) of this section apply only to remuneration for employment that constitutes wages. Under section 3121(b)(7), certain service performed in the employ of a state, or any political subdivision of a state, is not employment. Thus, even though the plan is a nonqualified deferred compensation plan, the extent to which section 3121(v)(2) applies to a participating employee will depend on whether or not the service performed for Employer O is excluded from the definition of employment under section 3121(b)(7).

*Example 5.* (i) In 2000, Employer P establishes a plan that provides for bonuses to be paid to employees based on an objective formula that takes into account the employees' performance for the year. Employer P does not have the discretion to reduce the amount of any employee's bonus after the end of the year. The bonus is not actually calculated until March 1 of the following year, and is paid on March 15 of that following year.

(ii) The plan provides for the deferral of compensation because the employees have a legally binding right, as of the last day of a calendar year, to an amount of compensation that has not been actually or constructively received and, pursuant to the terms of the plan, that compensation is payable in a later year. However, because the bonuses under the plan are paid within a brief period of time after the end of the calendar year from which they are deferred, Employer P may choose, pursuant to paragraph (b)(3)(iii) of this section, to treat all the bonuses as if they are not subject to the special timing rule of paragraph (a)(2) of this section.

(iii) If the employer uses the special timing rule, the amount deferred would be taken into account as wages on December 31, 2000. If the employer chooses not to use the special timing rule, the amount of the bonus is wages on the date it is actually or constructively paid, March 15, 2000.

*Example 6.* (i) Employer Q establishes a plan under which bonuses based on performance in one year may be paid on February 1 of the following year at the discretion of the board of directors. The board of directors meets in January of each year to determine the amount, if any, of the bonuses to be paid based on performance in the prior year.

(ii) Because an employee does not have a legally binding right to any bonus until January of the year in which the bonus is paid, any bonus paid under the plan in that year is not deferred from the preceding calendar year, and the plan does not provide for the deferral of compensation within the meaning of paragraph (b)(3)(i) of this section.

*Example 7.* (i) Employer R maintains a plan for employees that provides nonqualified stock options described in § 1.83-7(a) of this chapter. Under the plan, employees are granted in 2001 the option to acquire shares of employer stock at the fair market value of the shares on the date of grant ($50 per share). The options can be exercised at any time from the date of grant through 2010. The options do not have a readily ascertainable fair market value for purposes of section 83 at the date of grant, and shares are issued upon the exercise of the options without being subject to a substantial risk of forfeiture within the meaning of section 83. In 2005, when the fair market value of a share of employer stock is $80, Employee D exercises an option to acquire 1,000 shares.

(ii) Under paragraph (b)(4)(ii) of this section, neither the grant of a stock option nor amounts received currently as a result of the exercise of a stock option result from the deferral of compensation for purposes of section 3121(v)(2). Thus, under the general timing rule of paragraph (a)(1) of this section, the $30,000 spread between the amount paid for the shares ($50,000) and the fair market value of the shares on the date of exercise ($80,000) is taken into account as wages for FICA tax purposes in the year of exercise.

(iii) If the options had been granted at $45 per share, $5 per share below the fair market value on date of grant, the $35,000 spread between the amount paid for the shares ($45,000) and the fair market value of the shares on the date of exercise ($80,000) would similarly be taken into account as wages for FICA tax purposes in the year of exercise.

*Example 8.* (i) Employer T establishes a phantom stock plan for certain employees. Under the plan, an employee is credited on the last day of each calendar year with a dollar amount equal to the fair market value of 1,000 shares of employer stock. Upon termination of employment for any reason, each employee is entitled to receive the value on the date of termination, in cash or employer stock, of the shares with which he or she has been credited.

(ii) Because compensation to which the employee has a legally binding right as of the last day of one year is paid in a subsequent year, the phantom stock plan provides for the deferral of compensation. The phantom stock plan does not provide stock value rights within the meaning of paragraph (b)(4)(ii) of this section because it provides for awards equal in value to the full fair market value of a specified number of shares of Employer T stock, rather than the excess of that fair market value over a specified price.

*Example 9.* (i) Employer U establishes a severance pay arrangement (within the meaning of section 3(2)(b)(i) of ERISA) which provides for payments solely upon an employee's death, disability, or dismissal from employment. The amount of the payments to an employee is based on the length of continuous active service with Employer U at the time of dismissal, and is paid in monthly installments over a period of three years.

(ii) Because benefits payable under the plan upon termination of employment are payable only upon an employee's involuntary termination, the plan is a severance pay plan within the meaning of paragraph (b)(4)(iv)(B) of this section. Thus, the benefits are not treated as resulting from the deferral of compensation for purposes of section 3121(v)(2).

*Example 10.* (i) Employer V establishes a nonqualified deferred compensation plan under which employees will receive benefit payments commencing at age 65 as a life annuity or in one of several actuarially equivalent annuity forms. If an employee dies before benefit payments commence under the plan, a benefit is payable to the employee's designated beneficiary in a single lump sum payment equal to the present value of the employee's annuity benefit. This benefit (sometimes called a full reserve death benefit) is calculated using the applicable interest rate specified in section 417(e) and, for the period after age 65, the applicable mortality table specified in section 417(e), both of which are reasonable actuarial assumptions. During 2002, Employee E obtains a legally binding right to an annuity benefit under the plan, payable at age 65. This annuity benefit has a present value of $10,000 at the end of 2002, determined using the same assumptions as are used under the plan to calculate the full reserve death benefit.

(ii) The present value, at the end of 2002, of the total benefits payable to or on behalf of Employee E (i.e., the sum of the present value of the annuity benefit commencing at age 65, and the present value of the full reserve death benefit, with both determined using the actuarial assumptions described in paragraph (i) of this *Example 10*, except also taking into account the probability of death prior to age 65) is $10,000. This present value does not exceed the present value of the annuity benefits that could be payable to Employee E under the plan during Employee E's lifetime determined without a discount for the possibility that Employee E might die before age 65 (also $10,000). Thus, the benefit payable in the event of Employee E's

death is not a death benefit for purposes of paragraph (b)(4)(iv) of this section.

(iii) The same result would apply in the case of a plan that bases benefits on an interest bearing account balance and pays the account balance at termination of employment or death (because the sum of the deferred benefits payable in the future if the employee terminates employment before death with a discount for the probability of death before that date plus the present value of the benefit payable in the event of death necessarily equals the present value of the deferred benefits payable with no discount for the probability of death).

*Example 11.* (i) The facts are the same as in *Example 10*, except that, in lieu of the full reserve death benefit, the plan provides a monthly life annuity benefit to an employee's spouse in the event of the employee's death before benefit payments commence equal to 100 percent of the monthly annuity that would be payable to the employee at age 65 under the life annuity form. Employee E is age 63 and has a spouse who is age 51. The sum of the present value of Employee E's annuity benefit commencing at age 65 determined with a discount for the possibility that Employee E might die before age 65 and the present value of the 100 percent annuity death benefit for Employee E's spouse exceeds $10,000.

(ii) The amount deferred for 2002 is $10,000 (because the 100 percent annuity death benefit for Employee E's spouse is disregarded to the extent that the total benefits payable to or on behalf of Employee E exceeds the present value of the annuity benefits that could be payable to Employee E under the plan during Employee E's lifetime without a discount for the probability of Employee E's death before benefit payments commence).

*Example 12.* (i) On January 1, 2001, Employer W establishes a plan that covers only Employee F, who owns a significant portion of the business and who has 30 years of service as of that date. The plan provides that, upon Employee F's termination of employment at any time, he will receive $200,000 per year for each of the immediately succeeding five years. Employee F terminates employment on March 1, 2001.

(ii) Because Employee F terminates employment within 12 months of the establishment of the plan and the facts and circumstances set forth above indicate that the plan was established in contemplation of impending termination of employment, the plan is considered to be established in connection with impending termination within the meaning of paragraph (b)(4)(v) of this section. Therefore, the benefits provided under the plan are not treated as resulting from the deferral of compensation for purposes of section 3121(v)(2).

*Example 13.* (i) Employer X establishes a plan on January 1, 2004, to supplement the qualified retirement benefits of recently hired 55-year old Employee G, who forfeited retirement benefits with her former employer in order to accept employment with Employer X. The plan provides that Employee G will receive $50,000 per year for life beginning at age 65, regardless of when she terminates employment. On April 15, 2004, Employee G unexpectedly terminates employment.

(ii) The facts and circumstances indicate that the plan was not established in contemplation of impending termination. Thus, even though Employee G terminated employment within 12 months of the establishment of the plan, the plan is not considered to be established in connection with impending termination within the meaning of paragraph (b)(4)(v) of this section. Benefits provided under the plan are treated as resulting from the deferral of compensation for purposes of section 3121(v)(2).

*Example 14.* (i) Employer Y establishes a plan to provide supplemental retirement benefits to a group of management employees who are at various stages of their careers. All employees covered by the plan are subject to the same benefit formula. Employee H is planning to (and actually does) retire within six months of the date on which the plan is established.

(ii) Even though Employee H terminated employment within 12 months of the establishment of the plan, the plan is not considered to have been established in connection with Employee H's impending termination within the meaning of paragraph (b)(4)(v) of this section because the facts and circumstances indicate otherwise.

*Example 15.* (i) Employee J owns 100 percent of Employer Z, a corporation that provides consulting services. Substantially all of Employer Z's revenue is derived as a result of the services performed by Employee J. In each of 2001, 2002, and 2003, Employer Z has gross receipts of $180,000 and expenses (other than salary) of $80,000. In each of 2001 and 2002, Employer Z pays Employee J a salary of $100,000 for services performed in each of those years. On December 31, 2002, Employer Z establishes a plan to pay Employee J $80,000 in 2003. The plan recites that the payment is in recognition of prior services. In 2003, Employer Z pays Employee J a salary of $20,000 and the $80,000 due under the plan.

(ii) The facts and circumstances described above indicate that the $80,000 paid pursuant to the plan is based on services performed by Employee J in 2003 and, thus, is paid for current services within the meaning of paragraph (b)(4)(viii) of this section. Accordingly, the plan does not provide for the deferral of compensation within the meaning of section 3121(v)(2), and the $80,000 payment is included as wages in 2003 under the general timing rule of paragraph (a)(1) of this section.

(c) *Determination of the amount deferred.*—(1) *Account balance plans.*—(i) *General rule.*—For purposes of this section, if benefits for an employee are provided under a nonqualified deferred compensation plan that is an account balance plan, the amount deferred for a period equals the principal amount credited to the employee's account for the period, increased or decreased by any income attributable to the principal amount through the date the principal amount is required to be taken into account as wages under paragraph (e) of this section.

(ii) *Definitions.*—(A) *Account balance plan.*—For purposes of this section, an *account balance plan* is a nonqualified deferred compensation plan under the terms of which a principal amount (or amounts) is credited to an individual account for an employee, the income attributable to each principal amount is credited (or debited) to the individual account, and the benefits payable to the employee are based solely on the balance credited to the individual account.

(B) *Income.*—For purposes of this section, *income* means any increase or decrease in the amount credited to an employee's account that is attributable to amounts previously credited to the employee's account, regardless of whether the plan denominates that increase or decrease as income.

(iii) *Additional rules.*—(A) *Commingled accounts.*—A plan does not fail to be an account balance plan merely because, under the terms of the plan, benefits payable to an employee are based solely on a specified percentage of an account maintained for all (or a portion of) plan participants under which principal amounts and income are credited (or debited) to such account.

(B) *Bifurcation permitted.*—An employer may treat a portion of a nonqualified deferred compensation plan as a separate account balance plan if that portion satisfies the requirements of this paragraph (c)(1) and the amount payable to employees under that portion is determined independently of the amount payable under the other portion of the plan.

(C) *Actuarial equivalents.*—A plan does not fail to be an account balance plan merely because the plan permits employees to elect to receive their benefits under the plan in a form of benefit other than payment of the account balance, provided the amount of benefit payable in that other form is actuarially equivalent to payment of the account balance using actuarial assumptions that are reasonable. Conversely, a plan is not an account balance plan if it provides an optional form of benefit that is not actuarially equivalent to the account balance using actuarial assumptions that are reasonable. For this purpose, the determination of whether forms are actuarially equivalent using actuarial assumptions that are reasonable is determined under the rules applicable to nonaccount balance plans under paragraph (c)(2)(iii) of this section.

(2) *Nonaccount balance plans.*—(i) *General rule.*—For purposes of this section, if benefits for an employee are provided under a nonqualified deferred compensation plan that is not an account balance plan (a nonaccount balance plan), the amount deferred for a period equals the present value of the additional future payment or payments to which the employee has obtained a legally binding right (as described in paragraph (b)(3)(i) of this section) under the plan during that period.

(ii) *Present value defined.*—For purposes of this section, *present value* means the value as of a specified date of an amount or series of amounts due thereafter, where each amount is multiplied by the probability that the condition or conditions on which payment of the amount is contingent will be satisfied, and is discounted according to an assumed rate of interest to reflect the time value of money. For purposes of this section, the present value must be determined as of the date the amount deferred is required to be taken into account as wages under paragraph (e) of this section using actuarial assumptions and methods that are reasonable as of that date. For this purpose, a discount for the probability that an employee will die before commencement of benefit payments is permitted, but only to the extent that benefits will be forfeited upon death. In addition, the present value cannot be discounted for the probability that payments will not be made (or will be reduced) because of the unfunded status of the plan, the risk associated with any deemed or actual investment of amounts credited under the plan, the risk that the employer, the trustee, or another party will be unwilling or unable to pay, the possibility of future plan amendments, the possibility of a future change in the law, or similar risks or contingencies. Nor is the present value affected by the possibility that some of the payments due

under the plan will be eligible for one of the exclusions from wages in section 3121(a).

(iii) *Treatment of actuarially equivalent benefits.*—(A) *In general.*—In the case of a nonaccount balance plan that permits employees to receive their benefits in more than one form or commencing at more than one date, the amount deferred is determined by assuming that payments are made in the normal form of benefit commencing at normal commencement date if the requirements of paragraph (c)(2)(iii)(B) of this section are satisfied. Accordingly, in the case of a nonaccount balance plan that permits employees to receive their benefits in more than one form or commencing at more than one date, unless the requirements of paragraph (c)(2)(iii)(B) of this section are satisfied, the amount deferred is treated as not reasonably ascertainable under the rules of paragraph (e)(4)(i)(B) of this section until a form of benefit and a time of commencement are selected.

(B) *Use of normal form commencing at normal commencement date.*—The requirements of this paragraph (c)(2)(iii)(B) are satisfied by a nonaccount balance plan if the plan has a single normal form of benefit commencing at normal commencement date for the amount deferred and each other optional form is actuarially equivalent to the normal form of benefit commencing at normal commencement date using actuarial assumptions that are reasonable. For this purpose, each form of benefit for payment of the amount deferred commencing at a date is a separate optional form. For purposes of this paragraph (c)(2)(iii)(B), each optional form is actuarially equivalent to the normal form of benefit commencing at normal commencement date only if the terms of the plan in effect when the amount is deferred provide for every optional form to be actuarially equivalent and further provide for actuarial assumptions to determine actuarial equivalency that will be reasonable at the time the optional form is selected, without regard to whether market interest rates are higher or lower at the time the optional form is selected than at the time the amount is deferred. Thus, a plan that provides for every optional form to be actuarially equivalent satisfies this paragraph (c)(2)(iii)(B) if it provides for actuarial equivalence to be determined—

(1) When an optional form is selected or when benefit payments under the optional form commence, based on assumptions that are reasonable then;

(2) Based on an index that reflects market rates of interest from time to time (for example, the plan specifies that all benefits will be actuarially equivalent using the applicable interest rate and applicable mortality table specified in section 417(e)); or

(3) Based on actuarial assumptions specified in the plan and provides for those assumptions to be revised to be reasonable assumptions if they cease to be reasonable assumptions.

(C) *Fixed mortality assumptions permitted.*—A plan does not fail to satisfy paragraph (c)(2)(iii)(B) of this section merely because the plan specifies a fixed mortality assumption that is reasonable at the time the amount is deferred, even if that assumption is not reasonable at the time the optional form is selected. (But see paragraph (c)(2)(iii)(E) of this section for additional rules that apply if the mortality assumption is not reasonable at the time the optional form is selected.)

(D) *Normal form of benefit commencing at normal commencement date defined.*—For purposes of this paragraph (c)(2)(iii), the normal form of benefit commencing at normal commencement date under the plan is the form, and date of commencement, under which the payments due to the employee under the plan are expressed, prior to adjustments for form or timing of commencement of payments.

(E) *Rule applicable if actuarial assumptions cease to be reasonable.*—If the terms of the plan in effect when an amount is deferred provide for actuarial assumptions to determine actuarial equivalency that will be reasonable at the time the optional form is selected or payments commence as provided in paragraph (c)(2)(iii)(B) of this section, but, at that time, the actuarial assumptions used under the plan are not reasonable, the employee will be treated as obtaining a legally binding right at that time (or, if earlier, at the date on which the plan is amended to provide actuarial assumptions that are not reasonable) to any additional benefits that result from the use of an unreasonable actuarial assumption. This might occur, for example, if the plan specifies that the actuarial assumptions will be reasonable assumptions to be set at the time the optional form is selected and the assumptions used are in fact not reasonable at that time.

(3) *Separate determination for each period.*—The amount deferred under this paragraph (c) is determined separately for each period for which there is an amount deferred under the plan. In addition, paragraphs (d) and (e) of this section are applied separately with respect to the amount deferred for each such period. Thus, for example, the fraction described in paragraph (d)(1)(ii)(B) of this section and the amount of the true-up at the resolution date de-

scribed in paragraph (e)(4)(ii)(B) of this section are determined separately with respect to each amount deferred. See paragraph (e)(4)(ii)(D) of this section for special rules for allocating amounts deferred over more than one year.

(4) *Examples.*—This paragraph (c) is illustrated by the following examples. (The examples illustrate the rules in this paragraph (c) and include various interest rate and mortality table assumptions, including the applicable section 417(e) mortality table, the GAM 83 (male) mortality table, and UP-84 mortality table. These tables can be obtained from the Society of Actuaries at its internet site at *http://www.soa.org.*) The examples are as follows:

*Example 1.* (i) Employer M establishes a nonqualified deferred compensation plan for Employee A. Under the plan, 10 percent of annual compensation is credited on behalf of Employee A on December 31 of each year. In addition, a reasonable rate of interest is credited quarterly on the balance credited to Employee A as of the last day of the preceding quarter. All amounts credited under the plan are 100 percent vested and the benefits payable to Employee A are based solely on the balance credited to Employee A's account.

(ii) The plan is an account balance plan. Thus, pursuant to paragraph (c)(1) of this section, the amount deferred for a calendar year is equal to 10 percent of annual compensation.

*Example 2.* (i) Employer N establishes a nonqualified deferred compensation plan for Employee B. Under the plan, 2.5 percent of annual compensation is credited quarterly on behalf of Employee B. In addition, a reasonable rate of interest is credited quarterly on the balance credited to Employee B's account as of the last day of the preceding quarter. All amounts credited under the plan are 100 percent vested, and the benefits payable to Employee B are based solely on the balance credited to Employee B's account. As permitted by paragraph (e)(5) of this section, any amount deferred under the plan for the calendar year is taken into account as wages on the last day of the year.

(ii) The plan is an account balance plan. Thus, pursuant to paragraph (c)(1) of this section, the amount deferred for a calendar year equals 10 percent of annual compensation (i.e., the sum of the principal amounts credited to Employee B's account for the year) plus the interest credited with respect to that 10 percent principal amount through the last day of the calendar year. If Employer N had not chosen to apply paragraph (e)(5) of this section and, thus, had taken into account 2.5 percent of compensation quarterly, the interest credited with respect to those quarterly amounts would not have been treated as part of the amount deferred for the year.

*Example 3.* (i) Employer O establishes a nonqualified deferred compensation plan for a group of five employees. Under the plan, a specified sum is credited to an account for the benefit of the group of employees on July 31 of each year. Income on the balance of the account is credited annually at a rate that is reasonable for each year. The benefit payable to an employee is equal to one-fifth of the account balance and is payable, at the employee's option, in a lump sum or in 10 annual installments that reflect income on the balance.

(ii) The plan is an account balance plan notwithstanding the fact that the employee's benefit is equal to a specified percentage of an account maintained for a group of employees.

*Example 4.* (i) The facts are the same as in *Example 3*, except that the plan also permits an employee to elect a life annuity that is actuarially equivalent to the account balance based on the applicable interest rate and applicable mortality table specified in section 417(e) at the time the benefit is elected by the employee.

(ii) Under paragraphs (c)(1)(iii)(C) and (c)(2)(iii) of this section, the plan does not fail to be an account balance plan merely because the plan permits employees to elect to receive their benefits under the plan in a form that is actuarially equivalent to payment of the account balance using actuarial assumptions that are reasonable at the time the form is selected.

*Example 5.* (i) Employer P establishes a nonqualified deferred compensation plan for a group of employees. Under the plan, each participating employee has a fully vested right to receive a life annuity, payable monthly beginning at age 65, equal to the product of 2 percent for each year of service and the employee's highest average annual compensation for any 3-year period. The plan also provides that, if an employee dies before age 65, the present value of the future payments will be paid to his or her beneficiary. As permitted under paragraph (e)(5) of this section, any amount deferred under the plan for a calendar year is taken into account as FICA wages as of the last day of the year. As of December 31, 2002, Employee C is age 60, has 25 years of service, and high 3-year average compensation of $100,000 (the average for the years 2000 through 2002). As of December 31, 2003, Employee C is age 61, has 26 years of service, and has high 3-year average compensation of $104,000. As of December 31, 2004, Employee C is age 62, has 27 years of service, and has high 3-year average compensation of $105,000. The assumptions that Employer P uses to determine the amount deferred for 2003 (a 7 percent interest rate and, for the period after commencement of benefit payments, the GAM 83 (male) mortality table) and for 2004 (a 7.5 percent interest rate and, for the period after commencement of benefit payments, the GAM 83 (male) mortality table) are assumed, solely for purposes of this example, to be reasonable actuarial assumptions.

(ii) As of December 31, 2002, Employee C has a legally binding right to receive lifetime payments of $50,000 (2 percent × 25 years × $100,000) per year. As of December 31, 2003, Employee C has a legally binding right to receive lifetime payments of $54,080 (2 percent × 26 years × $104,000) per year. Thus, during 2003, Employee C has earned a legally binding right to additional lifetime payments of $4,080 ($54,080 − $50,000) per year beginning at age 65. The amount deferred for 2003 is the present value, as of December 31, 2003, of these additional payments, which is $28,767 ($4,080 × the present value factor for a deferred annuity payable at age 65, using the specified actuarial assumptions for 2003). Similarly, during 2004, Employee C has earned a legally binding right to additional lifetime payments of $2,620 (2 percent × 27 years × $105,000, minus $54,080) per year beginning at age 65. The amount deferred for 2004 is the present value, as of December 31, 2004, of these additional payments, which is $18,845 ($2,620 × the present value factor for a deferred annuity payable at age 65, using the specified actuarial assumptions for 2004).

*Example 6.* (i) Employer Q establishes a nonqualified deferred compensation plan for Employee D on January 1, 2001, when Employee D is age 63. During 2001, Employee D obtains a fully vested right to receive a life annuity under the nonqualified deferred compensation plan equal to the excess of $200,000 over the life annuity benefits payable to Employee D under a qualified defined benefit pension plan sponsored by Employer Q. The life annuity benefit payable annually under the qualified plan is the lesser of $200,000 and the section 415(b)(1)(A) limitation in effect for the year, where the section 415(b)(1)(A) limitation is automatically adjusted to reflect changes in the cost of living. Benefits under both the qualified and nonqualified plan are payable monthly beginning at age 65. For purposes of this example, the section 415(b)(1)(A) limit for 2001 is assumed to be $140,000. The nonqualified plan provides no benefits in the event Employee D dies prior to commencement of benefit payments. As permitted under paragraph (e)(5) of this section, any amount deferred under the plan for a calendar year is taken into account as FICA wages as of the last day of the year. The assumptions that Employer Q uses to determine the amount deferred for 2001 (a 7 percent interest rate, a 3 percent increase in the cost of living and the GAM 83 (male) mortality table) are assumed, solely for purposes of this example, to be reasonable actuarial assumptions. As of December 31, 2001, Employee D has a legally binding right to receive lifetime payments as set forth in the following table:

| Year | Annual Gross Amount | Assumed Qualified Plan Annual Payment (based on cost of living) | Net Annual Payment under Nonqualified Plan |
|---|---|---|---|
| 2003 | $200,000 | $145,000 | $55,000 |
| 2004 | $200,000 | $150,000 | $50,000 |
| 2005 | $200,000 | $155,000 | $45,000 |
| 2006 | $200,000 | $160,000 | $40,000 |
| 2007 | $200,000 | $165,000 | $35,000 |
| 2008 | $200,000 | $170,000 | $30,000 |
| 2009 | $200,000 | $175,000 | $25,000 |
| 2010 | $200,000 | $180,000 | $20,000 |
| 2011 | $200,000 | $185,000 | $15,000 |
| 2012 | $200,000 | $190,000 | $10,000 |
| 2013 | $200,000 | $195,000 | $5,000 |
| 2014 and thereafter | $200,000 | $205,000 or greater | $0 |

(ii) The amount deferred for 2001 is the present value, as of December 31, 2001, of the net lifetime payments under the nonqualified plan, or $223,753.

(d) *Amounts taken into account and income attributable thereto.*—(1) *Amounts taken into account.*—(i) *In general.*—For purposes of this section, an amount deferred under a nonqualified deferred compensation plan is taken into account as of the date it is included in computing the amount of *wages* as defined in section 3121(a), but only to the extent that any additional FICA tax that results from such inclusion (including any interest and penalties for late payment) is actually paid before the expiration of the applicable period of limitations for the period in which the amount deferred was required to be taken into account under paragraph (e) of this section. Because an amount deferred for a calendar year is combined with the employee's other wages for the year for purposes of computing FICA taxes with respect to the employee for the year, if the employee has other wages that equal or exceed the wage base limitations for the Old-Age, Survivors, and Disability Insurance (OASDI) portion (or, in the case of years before 1994, the Hospital Insurance (HI) portion) of FICA for the year, no portion of the amount deferred will actually result in additional OASDI (or HI) tax. However, because there is no wage base limitation for the HI portion of FICA for years after 1993, the entire amount deferred (in addition to all other wages) is subject to the HI tax for the year and, thus, will not be considered taken into account for purposes of this section unless the HI tax relating to the amount deferred is actually paid. In determining whether any additional FICA tax relating to the amount deferred is actually paid, any FICA tax paid in a year is treated as paid with respect to an amount deferred only after FICA tax is paid on all other wages for the year.

(ii) *Amounts not taken into account.*—(A) *Failure to take an amount deferred into account under the special timing rule.*—If an amount deferred for a period (as determined under paragraph (c) of this section) is not taken into account, then the nonduplication rule of paragraph (a)(2)(iii) of this section does not apply, and benefit payments attributable to that amount deferred are included as wages in accordance with the general timing rule of paragraph (a)(1) of this section. For example, if an amount deferred is required to be taken into account in a particular year under paragraph (e) of this section, but the employer fails to pay the additional FICA tax resulting from that amount, then the amount deferred and the income attributable to that amount must be included as wages when actually or constructively paid.

(B) *Failure to take a portion of an amount deferred into account under the special timing rule.*—If, as of the date an amount deferred is required to be taken into account, only a portion of the amount deferred (as determined under paragraph (c) of this section) has been taken into account, then a portion of each subsequent benefit payment that is attributable to that amount is excluded from wages pursuant to the nonduplication rule of paragraph (a)(2)(iii) of this section and the balance is subject to the general timing rule of paragraph (a)(1) of this section. The portion that is excluded from wages is fixed immediately before the attributable benefit payments commence (or, if later, the date the amount deferred is required to be taken into account) and is determined by multiplying each such payment by a fraction, the numerator of which is the amount that was taken into account (plus income attributable to that amount determined under paragraph (d)(2) of this section through the date the portion is fixed) and the denominator of which is the present value of the future benefit payments attributable to the amount deferred, determined as of the date the portion is fixed. For this purpose, if the requirements of paragraph (c)(2)(iii)(B) of this section are satisfied, the present value is determined by assuming that payments are made in the normal form of benefit commencing at normal commencement date. In addition, if the employer demonstrates that the amount deferred was determined using reasonable actuarial assumptions as determined by the Commissioner, the present value of the future benefit payments attributable to the amount deferred is determined using those assumptions. In any other case, see paragraph (d)(2)(iii) of this section.

(2) *Income attributable to the amount taken into account.*— (i) *Account balance plans.*—(A) *In general.*—For purposes of the nonduplication rule of paragraph (a)(2)(iii) of this section, in the case of an account balance plan, the *income attributable to the amount taken into account* means any amount credited on behalf of an employee under the terms of the plan that is income (within the meaning of paragraph (c)(1)(ii)(B) of this section) attributable to an amount previously taken into account (within the meaning of paragraph (d)(1) of this section), but only if the income reflects a rate of return that does not exceed either the rate of return on a predetermined actual investment (as determined in accordance with paragraph (d)(2)(i)(B) of this section) or, if the income does not reflect the rate of return on a predetermined actual investment (as so determined), a reasonable rate of interest (as determined in accordance with paragraph (d)(2)(i)(C) of this section).

(B) *Rules relating to actual investment.*—(1) *In general.*—For purposes of this paragraph (d)(2)(i), the rate of return on a predetermined actual investment for any period means the rate of total return (including increases or decreases in fair market value) that would

apply if the account balance were, during the applicable period, actually invested in one or more investments that are identified in accordance with the plan before the beginning of the period. For this purpose, an account balance plan can determine income based on the rate of return of a predetermined actual investment regardless of whether assets associated with the plan or the employer are actually invested therein and regardless of whether that investment is generally available to the public. For example, an account balance plan could provide that income on the account balance is determined based on an employee's prospective election among various investment alternatives that are available under the employer's section 401(k) plan, even if one of those investment alternatives is not generally available to the public. In addition, an actual investment includes an investment identified by reference to any stock index with respect to which there are positions traded on a national securities exchange described in section 1256(g)(7)(A).

(2) *Certain rates of return not based on predetermined actual investment.*—A rate of return will not be treated as the rate of return on a predetermined actual investment within the meaning of this paragraph (d)(2)(i)(B) if the rate of return (to any extent or under any conditions) is based on the greater of the rate of return of two or more actual investments, is based on the greater of the rate of return on an actual investment and a rate of interest (whether or not the rate of interest would otherwise be reasonable under paragraph (d)(2)(i)(C) of this section), or is based on the rate of return on an actual investment that is not predetermined. For example, if a plan bases the rate of return on the greater of the rate of return on a predetermined actual investment (such as the value of the employer's stock), and a 0 percent interest rate (i.e., without regard to decreases in the value of that investment), the plan is using a rate of return that is not a rate of return on a predetermined actual investment within the meaning of this paragraph (d)(2)(i)(B).

(C) *Rules relating to reasonable interest rates.*—(1) *In general.*— If income for a period is credited to an account balance plan on a basis other than the rate of return on a predetermined actual investment (as determined in accordance with paragraph (d)(2)(i)(B) of this section), then, except as otherwise provided in this paragraph (d)(2)(i)(C), the determination of whether the income for the period is based on a reasonable rate of interest will be made at the time the amount deferred is required to be taken into account and annually thereafter.

(2) *Fixed rates permitted.*—If, with respect to an amount deferred for a period, an account balance plan provides for a fixed rate of interest to be credited, and the rate is to be reset under the plan at a specified future date that is not later than the end of the fifth calendar year that begins after the beginning of the period, the rate is reasonable at the beginning of the period, and the rate is not changed before the reset date, then the rate will be treated as reasonable in all future periods before the reset date.

(ii) *Nonaccount balance plans.*—For purposes of the nonduplication rule of paragraph (a)(2)(iii) of this section, in the case of a nonaccount balance plan, the *income attributable to the amount taken into account* means the increase, due solely to the passage of time, in the present value of the future payments to which the employee has obtained a legally binding right, the present value of which constituted the amount taken into account (determined as of the date such amount was taken into account), but only if the amount taken into account was determined using reasonable actuarial assumptions and methods. Thus, for each year, there will be an increase (determined using the same interest rate used to determine the amount taken into account) resulting from the shortening of the discount period before the future payments are made, plus, if applicable, an increase in the present value resulting from the employee's survivorship during the year. As a result, if the amount deferred for a period is determined using a reasonable interest rate and other reasonable actuarial assumptions and methods, and the amount is taken into account when required under paragraph (e) of this section, then, under the nonduplication rule of paragraph (a)(2)(iii) of this section, none of the future payments attributable to that amount will be subject to FICA tax when paid.

(iii) *Unreasonable rates of return.*—(A) *Account balance plans.*— This paragraph (d)(2)(iii)(A) applies to an account balance plan under which the income credited is based on neither a predetermined actual investment, within the meaning of paragraph (d)(2)(i)(B) of this section, nor a rate of interest that is reasonable, within the meaning of paragraph (d)(2)(i)(C) of this section, as determined by the Commissioner. In that event, the employer must calculate the amount that would be credited as income under a reasonable rate of interest, determine the excess (if any) of the amount credited under the plan over the income that would be credited using the reasonable rate of interest, and take that excess into account as an additional amount deferred in the year the income is credited. If the employer fails to calculate the amount that would be credited as income under a reasonable rate of interest and to take the excess into account as an additional amount deferred in the year the income is credited, or the employer otherwise fails to take the full amount deferred into account, then the excess of the income credited under the plan over the income that would be credited using AFR will be treated as an amount deferred in the year the income is credited. For purposes of this section, *AFR* means the mid-term applicable federal rate (as defined pursuant to section 1274(d)) for January 1 of the calendar year, compounded annually. In addition, pursuant to paragraph (d)(1)(ii) of this section, the excess over the income that would result from the application of AFR and any income attributable to that excess are subject to the general timing rule of paragraph (a)(1) of this section.

(B) *Nonaccount balance plans.*—If any actuarial assumption or method used to determine the amount taken into account under a nonaccount balance plan is not reasonable, as determined by the Commissioner, then the income attributable to the amount taken into account is limited to the income that would result from the application of the AFR and, if applicable, the applicable mortality table under section 417(e)(3)(A)(ii)(I) (the 417(e) mortality table), both determined as of the January 1 of the calendar year in which the amount was taken into account. In addition, paragraph (d)(1)(ii)(B) of this section applies and, in calculating the fraction described in paragraph (d)(1)(ii)(B) of this section (at the date specified in paragraph (d)(1)(ii)(B) of this section), the numerator is the amount taken into account plus income (as limited under this paragraph (d)(2)(iii)(B)), and the present value in the denominator is determined using the AFR, the 417(e) mortality table, and reasonable assumptions as to cost of living, each determined as of the time the amount deferred was required to be taken into account.

(3) *Examples.*—This paragraph (d) is illustrated by the following examples:

*Example 1.* (i) In 2001, Employer M establishes a nonqualified deferred compensation plan for Employee A under which all benefits are 100 percent vested. In 2002, Employee A has $200,000 of current annual compensation from Employer M that is subject to FICA tax. The amount deferred under the plan on behalf of Employee A for 2002 is $20,000. Thus, Employee A has total wages for FICA tax purposes of $220,000. Because Employee A has other wages that exceed the OASDI wage base for 2002, no additional OASDI tax is due as a result of the $20,000 amount deferred. Because there is no wage base limitation for the HI portion of FICA, additional HI tax liability results from the $20,000 amount deferred. However, Employer M fails to pay the additional HI tax.

(ii) Under paragraph (d)(1)(i) of this section, an amount deferred is considered taken into account as wages for FICA tax purposes as of the date it is included in computing FICA wages, but only if any additional FICA tax liability that results from inclusion of the amount deferred is actually paid. Because the HI tax resulting from the $20,000 amount deferred was not paid, that amount deferred was not taken into account within the meaning of paragraph (d)(1) of this section. Thus, pursuant to paragraph (d)(1)(ii) of this section, benefit payments attributable to the $20,000 amount deferred will be included as wages in accordance with the general timing rule of paragraph (a)(1) of this section and will be subject to the HI portion of FICA tax when actually or constructively paid (and the OASDI portion of FICA tax to the extent Employee A's wages do not exceed the OASDI wage base limitation).

*Example 2.* (i) The facts are the same as in *Example 1*, except that Employer M takes all actions necessary to correct its failure to pay the additional tax before the applicable period of limitations expires for 2002 (including payment of any applicable interest and penalties).

(ii) Because the HI tax resulting from the $20,000 amount deferred is paid, that amount deferred is considered taken into account for 2002. Thus, in accordance with paragraph (a)(2)(iii) of this section, neither the amount deferred nor the income attributable to the amount taken into account will be treated as wages for FICA tax purposes at any time thereafter.

*Example 3.* (i) Employer N establishes a nonqualified deferred compensation plan under which all benefits are 100 percent vested. Under the plan, an employee's account is credited with a contribution equal to 10 percent of salary on December 31 of each year. The employee's account balance also is increased each December 31 by *interest* on the total amounts credited to the employee's account as of the preceding December 31. The interest rate specified in the plan results in income credits that are not based on the rate of return on a predetermined actual investment within the meaning of paragraph (d)(2)(i)(B) of this section, and that are greater than the income that would result from application of a reasonable rate of interest within the meaning of paragraph (d)(2)(i)(C) of this section. Employer N fails to take into account an additional amount for the excess of the income credited under the plan over a reasonable rate of interest.

(ii) Pursuant to paragraph (d)(2)(iii)(A) of this section, the income credits in excess of the income that would be credited using the AFR are considered additional amounts deferred in the year credited.

*Example 4.* (i) The facts are the same as in *Example 3*, except that the annual increase is based on Moody's Average Corporate Bond Yield.

(ii) Because this index reflects a reasonable rate of interest, the income credited under the plan is considered income attributable to the amount taken into account within the meaning of paragraph (d)(2)(i) of this section.

*Example 5.* (i) The facts are the same as in *Example 3*, except that the annual increase (or decrease) is based on the rate of total return on Employer N's publicly traded common stock.

(ii) Because the income credited under the plan does not exceed the actual rate of return on a predetermined actual investment, the income credited is considered income attributable to the amount taken into account within the meaning of paragraph (d)(2)(i) of this section.

*Example 6.* (i) The facts are the same as in *Example 3*, except that the annual rate of increase or decrease is equal to the greater of the rate of total return on a specified aggressive growth mutual fund or the rate of return on a specified income-oriented mutual fund. Employer N fails to take into account an additional amount for the excess of the income credited under the plan over a reasonable rate of interest.

(ii) Because the rate of increase or decrease is based on the greater of two rates of returns, the increase is not based on the return on a predetermined actual investment within the meaning of paragraph (d)(2)(i)(B) of this section. Thus, if the rate of return credited under the plan (i.e., the greater of the rates of return of the two mutual funds) exceeds the income that would be credited using the AFR, the excess is not considered income attributable to the amount taken into account within the meaning of paragraph (d)(2)(i) of this section and, pursuant to paragraph (d)(2)(iii)(A) of this section, is considered an additional amount deferred.

*Example 7.* (i) The facts are the same as in *Example 6*, except that the annual increase or decrease with respect to 50 percent of the employee's account is equal to the rate of total return on the specified aggressive growth mutual fund and the annual increase or decrease with respect to the other 50 percent of the employee's account is equal to the increase or decrease in the Standard & Poor's 500 Index.

(ii) Because the increase or decrease attributable to any portion of the employee's account is based on the return on a predetermined actual investment, the entire increase or decrease is considered income attributable to the amount taken into account within the meaning of paragraph (d)(2)(i) of this section.

*Example 8.* (i) The facts are the same as in *Example 3*, except that, pursuant to the terms of the plan, before the beginning of each year, the board of directors of Employer N designates a specific investment on which the following year's annual increase or decrease will be based. The board is authorized to switch investments more frequently on a prospective basis. Before the beginning of 2004, the board designates Company A stock as the investment for 2004. Before the beginning of 2005, the board designates Company B stock as the investment for 2005. At the end of 2005, the board determines that the return on Company B stock was lower than expected and changes its designation for 2005 to the rate of return on Company C stock, which had a higher return during 2005. Employer N fails to take into account an additional amount for the excess of the income credited under the plan over a reasonable rate of interest.

(ii) The annual increase or decrease for 2004 is based on the return of a predetermined actual investment. Although the annual increase or decrease for 2005 is based on an actual investment, the actual investment is not predetermined since it was not designated before the beginning of 2005. Pursuant to paragraph (d)(2)(iii)(A) of this section, the excess of the income credited under the plan over the income determined using AFR is an additional amount deferred for 2005.

*Example 9.* (i) Employer O establishes a nonqualified deferred compensation plan for Employee B. Under the plan, if Employee B survives until age 65, he has a fully vested right to receive a lump sum payment at that age, equal to the product of 10 percent per year of service and Employee B's highest average annual compensation for any 3-year period, but no benefits are payable in the event Employee B dies prior to age 65. As permitted under paragraph (e)(5) of this section, any amount deferred under the plan for the calendar year is taken into account as wages as of the last day of the year. As of December 31, 2002, Employee B has 25 years of service and Employee B's high 3-year average compensation is $100,000 (the average for the years 2000 through 2002). As of December 31, 2002, Employee B has a legally binding right to receive a payment at age 65 of $250,000 (10 percent × 25 years × $100,000). As of December 31, 2003, Employee B is age 63, has 26 years of service, and has high 3-year average compensation of $104,000. As of December 31, 2003,

Employee B has a legally binding right to receive a payment at age 65 of $270,400 (10 percent × 26 years × $104,000). Thus, during 2003, Employee B has earned a legally binding right to an additional payment at age 65 of $20,400 ($270,400 – $250,000). The assumptions that Employer O uses to determine the amount deferred for 2003 are a 7 percent interest rate and the GAM 83 (male) mortality table, which, solely for purposes of this example, are assumed to be reasonable actuarial assumptions. The amount deferred for 2003 is the present value, as of December 31, 2003, of the $20,400 payment, which is $17,353. Employer O takes this amount into account by including it in Employee B's FICA wages for 2003 and paying the additional FICA tax.

(ii) Under paragraph (d)(2)(ii) of this section, the income attributable to the amount that was taken into account is the increase in the present value of the future payment due solely to the passage of time, because the amount deferred was determined using reasonable actuarial assumptions and methods. As of the payment date at age 65, the present value of the future payment earned during 2003 is $20,400. The entire difference between the $20,400 and the $17,353 amount deferred ($3,047) is the increase in the present value of the future payment due solely to the passage of time, and thus constitutes income attributable to the amount taken into account. Because the amount deferred was taken into account, the entire payment of $20,400 represents either an amount deferred that was previously taken into account ($17,353) or income attributable to that amount ($3,047). Accordingly, pursuant to the nonduplication rule of paragraph (a)(2)(iii) of this section, none of the payment is included in wages.

*Example 10*. (i) The facts are the same as in *Example 9*, except that, instead of providing a lump sum equal to 10 percent of average compensation per year of service, the plan provides Employee B with a fully vested right to receive a life annuity, payable monthly beginning at age 65, equal to the product of 2 percent for each year of service and Employee B's highest average annual compensation for any 3-year period. The plan also provides that, if Employee B dies before age 65, the present value of the future payments will be paid to his or her beneficiary. As of December 31, 2002, Employee B has a legally binding right to receive lifetime payments of $50,000 (2 percent × 25 years × $100,000) per year. As of December 31, 2003, Employee B has a legally binding right to receive lifetime payments of $54,080 (2 percent × 26 years × $104,000) per year. Thus, during 2003, Employee B has earned a legally binding right to additional lifetime payments of $4,080 ($54,080 $50,000) per year beginning at age 65. The amount deferred for 2003 is $32,935, which is the present value, as of December 31, 2003, of these additional payments, determined using the same actuarial assumptions and methods used in *Example 9*, except that there is no discount for the probability of death prior to age 65. Employer O takes this amount into account by including it in Employee B's FICA wages for 2003 and paying the additional FICA tax.

(ii) Under paragraph (d)(2)(ii) of this section, the income attributable to the amount that was taken into account is the increase in the present value of the future payments due solely to the passage of time, because the amount deferred was determined using reasonable actuarial assumptions and methods. Because the amount deferred was taken into account, each annual payment of $4,080 attributable to the amount deferred in 2003 represents either an amount deferred that was previously taken into account or income attributable to that amount. Accordingly, pursuant to the nonduplication rule of paragraph (a)(2)(iii) of this section, none of the payments are included in wages.

*Example 11*. (i) The facts are the same as in *Example 10*, except that no amount is taken into account for 2003 because Employer O fails to pay the additional FICA tax.

(ii) Under paragraph (d)(1)(ii)(A) of this section, if an amount deferred for a period is not taken into account, then the benefit payments attributable to that amount deferred are included as wages in accordance with the general timing rule of paragraph (a)(1) of this section. In this case, assuming that the amounts deferred in other periods were taken into account, $4,080 of each year's total benefit payments will be included in wages when actually or constructively paid, in accordance with the general timing rule.

*Example 12*. (i) Employer P establishes an account balance plan on January 1, 2002, under which all benefits are 100 percent vested. The plan provides that amounts deferred will be credited annually with interest beginning in 2002 at a rate that is greater than a reasonable rate of interest. Employer P treats the excess over the applicable interest rate in section 417(e) as an additional amount deferred for 2002 and in each year thereafter, and takes the additional amount into account by including it in FICA wages and paying the additional FICA tax for the year.

(ii) Under the nonduplication rule in paragraph (a)(2)(iii) of this section, the benefits paid under the plan will be excluded from wages for FICA tax purposes.

*Example 13*. (i) The facts are the same as in *Example 9*, except that, in determining the amount deferred, Employer O uses a 15 percent interest rate, which, solely for purposes of this example, is assumed not to be a reasonable interest rate. Employer O determines that the amount deferred for 2003 is the present value, as of December 31, 2003, of the $20,400 payment, which is $15,023. Employer O includes $15,023 in wages and pays any resulting FICA tax. Solely for purposes of this example, it is assumed that the AFR as of January 1, 2003, is 7 percent.

(ii) Under paragraph (d)(2)(iii)(B) of this section, if any actuarial assumption or method is not reasonable, then the income attributable to the amount taken into account is limited to the income that would result from application of the AFR and, if applicable, the 417(e) mortality table. Because the 15 percent interest rate is unreasonable, the income attributable to the amount taken into account is limited to the income that would result from using a 7 percent interest rate and, in this case, an increase for survivorship using the 417(e) mortality table. Under these assumptions, the income attributable to the $15,023 amount taken into account for 2003 is $1,199 in 2004 and $1,313 in 2005. Under paragraph (d)(1)(ii) of this section, the sum of these amounts ($17,535) is excluded from Employee B's wages pursuant to the nonduplication rule of paragraph (a)(2)(iii) of this section, and the balance of the payment ($2,865) is subject to the general timing rule of paragraph (a)(1) of this section and, thus, is included in Employee B's wages when actually or constructively paid.

(iii) The same result can be reached by multiplying the attributable benefit payments by a fraction, the numerator of which is the amount taken into account, and the denominator of which is the amount deferred that would have been taken into account at the same time had the amount deferred been calculated using the AFR and the 417(e) mortality table. These assumptions are determined as of January 1 of the calendar year in which the amount was taken into account. In this *Example 13*, the fraction would be $15,023 divided by $17,478, which equals .85954. The $20,400 payment is multiplied by this fraction to determine the amount of the payment that is excluded from wages pursuant to the nonduplication rule of paragraph (a)(2)(iii) of this section. Thus, $17,535 ($20,400 × .85954) is excluded from wages and the balance ($2,865) is subject to FICA tax when actually or constructively paid.

*Example 14*. (i) The facts are the same as *Example 10*, except that Employer O calculates the amount deferred for 2003 as $18,252 and takes that amount into account by including that amount in wages and paying any resulting FICA tax. The assumptions that Employer O uses to determine the amount deferred are a 15 percent interest rate and, for the period after commencement of benefit payments, the GAM 83 (male) mortality table. The 15 percent interest rate is assumed, solely for purposes of this example, not to be a reasonable actuarial assumption. Solely for purposes of this example, it is assumed that the AFR as of January 1, 2003, is 7 percent.

(ii) Under paragraph (d)(2)(iii)(B) of this section, if any actuarial assumption or method used is not reasonable, then the income attributable to the amount taken into account is limited to the income that would result from application of the AFR and, if applicable, the 417(e) mortality table. Because the 15 percent interest rate is not reasonable, the income attributable to the amount taken into account is equal to the income that would result from using a 7 percent interest rate and the amount taken into account is treated as if it represented a portion of the amount deferred for purposes of applying paragraph (d)(1)(ii)(B) of this section. Under these assumptions, the income attributable to the $18,252 amount taken into account for 2003 is $1,278 in 2004 and $1,367 in 2005. Under paragraph (d)(1)(ii)(B) of this section, the portion of each benefit payment attributable to the amount deferred that is excluded from wages pursuant to the nonduplication rule of paragraph (a)(2)(iii) of this section is determined at benefit commencement by multiplying each benefit payment by a fraction, the numerator of which is the amount taken into account (plus income attributable to that amount) and the denominator of which is the present value of future benefit payments attributable to the amount deferred. Because the interest rate assumption is not reasonable, not only is the income limited to the application of the AFR, but the present value in the denominator must be determined using the AFR and (if applicable) the 417(e) mortality table. In this case, the present value is $40,283 and thus the fraction is $20,897 divided by $40,283, or .51875. Thus, $2,116 (.51875 × $4,080) of each year's benefit payment is excluded from wages and the balance of each year's payment ($1,964) is subject to the general timing rule of paragraph (a)(1) of this section and is included in wages when actually or constructively paid.

(iii) The same result can be reached by multiplying the attributable benefit payments by a fraction the numerator of which is the amount taken into account, and the denominator of which is the amount deferred that would have been taken into account at the same time had the amount deferred been calculated using the AFR and the 417(e) mortality table. These assumptions are determined as of January 1 of the calendar year in which the amount was taken into account. In this *Example 14*, the fraction would be $18,252 divided by $35,185, which equals .51875. The $4,080 annual payment is multiplied by this fraction to determine the amount of the payment that is excluded from wages pursuant to the nonduplication rule of paragraph (a)(2)(iii) of this section. Thus, $2,116 ($4,080 × .51875) is excluded from wages and the balance ($1,964) is subject to FICA tax when actually or constructively paid.

(e) *Time amounts deferred are required to be taken into account.*—(1) *In general.*—Except as otherwise provided in this paragraph (e), an amount deferred under a nonqualified deferred compensation plan must be taken into account as wages for FICA tax purposes as of the later of the date on which services creating the right to the amount deferred are performed (within the meaning of paragraph (e)(2) of this section) or the date on which the right to the amount deferred is no longer subject to a substantial risk of forfeiture (within the meaning of paragraph (e)(3) of this section). However, in no event may any amount deferred under a nonqualified deferred compensation plan be taken into account as wages for FICA tax purposes prior to the establishment of the plan providing for the amount deferred (or, if later, the plan amendment providing for the amount deferred). Therefore, if an amount is deferred pursuant to the terms of a legally binding agreement that is not put in writing until after the amount would otherwise be taken into account under this paragraph (e)(1), the amount deferred (including any attributable income) must be taken into account as wages for FICA tax purposes as of the date the material terms of the plan are put in writing.

(2) *Services creating the right to an amount deferred.*—For purposes of this section, services creating the right to an amount deferred under a nonqualified deferred compensation plan are considered to be performed as of the date on which, under the terms of the plan and all the facts and circumstances, the employee has performed all of the services necessary to obtain a legally binding right (as described in paragraph (b)(3)(i) of this section) to the amount deferred.

(3) *Substantial risk of forfeiture.*—For purposes of this section, the determination of whether a substantial risk of forfeiture exists must be made in accordance with the principles of section 83 and the regulations thereunder.

(4) *Amount deferred that is not reasonably ascertainable under a nonaccount balance plan.*—(i) *In general.*—(A) *Date required to be taken into account.*—Notwithstanding any other provision of this paragraph (e), an amount deferred under a nonaccount balance plan is not required to be taken into account as wages under the special timing rule of paragraph (a)(2) of this section until the first date on which all of the amount deferred is reasonably ascertainable (the resolution date). In this case, the amount required to be taken into account as of the resolution date is determined in accordance with paragraph (c)(2) of this section.

(B) *Definition of reasonably ascertainable.*—For purposes of this paragraph (e)(4), an amount deferred is considered reasonably ascertainable on the first date on which the amount, form, and commencement date of the benefit payments attributable to the amount deferred are known, and the only actuarial or other assumptions regarding future events or circumstances needed to determine the amount deferred are interest and mortality. For this purpose, the form and commencement date of the benefit payments attributable to the amount deferred are treated as known if the requirements of paragraph (c)(2)(iii)(B) of this section (under which payments are treated as being made in the normal form of benefit commencing at normal commencement date) are satisfied. In addition, an amount deferred does not fail to be reasonably ascertainable on a date merely because the exact amount of the benefit payable cannot readily be calculated on that date or merely because the exact amount of the benefit payable depends on future changes in the cost of living. If the exact amount of the benefit payable depends on future changes in the cost of living, the amount deferred must be determined using a reasonable assumption as to the future changes in the cost of living. For example, the amount of a benefit is treated as known even if the exact amount of the benefit payable cannot be determined until future changes in the cost of living are reflected in the section 415 limitation on benefits payable under a qualified retirement plan.

(ii) *Earlier inclusion permitted.*—(A) *In general.*—With respect to an amount deferred that is not reasonably ascertainable, an employer may choose to take an amount into account at any date or dates (an early inclusion date or dates) before the resolution date (but not before the date described in paragraph (e)(1) of this section with respect to the amount deferred). Thus, for example, with respect to an amount deferred under a nonaccount balance plan that is not reasonably ascertainable because the plan permits employees to receive their benefits in more than one form or commencing at more than one date (and the requirements of paragraph (c)(2)(iii) of this section are not satisfied), an employer may choose to take an amount

into account on the date otherwise described in paragraph (e)(1) of this section before the form and commencement date are selected (based on assumptions as to the form and commencement date for the benefit payments) or may choose to wait until the form and commencement date of the benefit payments are selected. An employer that chooses to take an amount into account at an early inclusion date under this paragraph (e)(4)(ii) for an employee under a plan is not required until the resolution date to identify the period to which the amount taken into account relates.

(B) *True-up at resolution date.*—If, with respect to an amount deferred for a period, an employer chooses to take an amount into account as of an early inclusion date in accordance with this paragraph (e)(4)(ii) and the benefit payments attributable to the amount deferred exceed the benefit payments that are actuarially equivalent to the amount taken into account at the early inclusion date (payable in the same form and using the same commencement date as the benefit payments attributable to the amount deferred), then the present value of the difference in the benefits, determined in accordance with paragraph (c)(2) of this section, must be taken into account as of the resolution date.

(C) *Actuarial assumptions.*—For purposes of determining the benefits that are actuarially equivalent to the amount taken into account as of an early inclusion date, the amount taken into account is converted to an actuarially equivalent benefit payable in the same form and commencing on the same date as the actual benefit payments attributable to the amount deferred using an interest rate, and, if applicable, mortality and cost-of-living assumptions, that were reasonable as of the early inclusion date. Thus, with respect to an amount deferred for a period, the amount required to be taken into account as of the resolution date is the present value (determined using an interest rate, and, if applicable, mortality and cost-of-living assumptions, that are reasonable as of the resolution date) of the excess, if any, of the future benefit payments attributable to the amount deferred over the future benefits payable in the same form and commencing on the same date that are actuarially equivalent to the portion of the amount deferred that was taken into account as of the early inclusion date (where actuarial equivalence is determined using an interest rate, and, if applicable, mortality and cost-of-living assumptions, that were reasonable as of the early inclusion date).

(D) *Allocation rules for amounts deferred over more than one period.*—(1) *General rule.*—The rules of this paragraph (e)(4)(ii)(D) apply for purposes of determining whether an amount has been included under this paragraph (e)(4) before the earliest date permitted under paragraph (e)(1) of this section.

(2) *Future compensation increases.*—Increases in an employee's compensation after the early inclusion date must be disregarded.

(3) *Early retirement subsidies.*—An early retirement subsidy that the employee ultimately receives may be taken into account at an early inclusion date if the employee would have a legally binding right to the subsidy at the early inclusion date but for any condition that the employee continue to render services. Accordingly, an employer may take into account at an early inclusion date any early retirement subsidy that the employee ultimately receives to the extent that elimination or reduction of that subsidy would violate section 411(d)(6)(B)(i) if that section applied to the plan.

(4) *Allocation with respect to offsets.*—In any case in which a series of amounts are deferred over more than one period, the amounts deferred are not reasonably ascertainable until a single resolution date and the benefit payments attributable to the entire series are determined under a formula that provides a gross benefit that in the aggregate is subject to an objective reduction for future events under the terms of the plan, such as an offset for the aggregate benefits payable under a plan qualified under section 401(a), the attribution of benefit payments to the amount deferred in each period is determined under the rules of this paragraph (e)(4)(ii)(D)(4). In a case described in the preceding sentence, the benefit payments made as a result of the series of amounts deferred may be treated as attributable to the amount deferred as of the earliest period in which the employee obtained a legally binding right to a benefit under the plan equal to the excess, if any, of the amount of the gross benefit attributable to that period (determined at the resolution date), over the amount of the reduction determined as of the end of that period. Thus, for example, if an employee obtains a legally binding right in each of several years to benefit payments from a nonqualified deferred compensation plan that provides for a specified gross benefit for the years to be offset by the benefits payable under a qualified plan, the amount deferred in the first year may be treated as equal to the gross benefit for the year, reduced by the offset applicable at the end of the year (even if the offset increases after the end of the year).

(E) *Treatment of benefits paid before the resolution date.*—If a benefit payment is attributable to an amount deferred that is not reasonably ascertainable at the time of payment (or is paid before the date selected under paragraph (e)(5) of this section), and the employer has previously taken an amount into account with respect to the amount deferred under the early inclusion rule of this paragraph (e)(4), then, in lieu of the pro rata rule provided in paragraph (d)(1)(ii)(B) of this section, a first-in-first-out rule applies in determining the portion of the benefit payment attributable to the amount taken into account. Under this first-in-first-out rule, the benefit payment is compared to the sum of the amount taken into account at the early inclusion date and the income attributable to that amount. If the benefit payment equals or exceeds the amount taken into account at the early inclusion date and the income attributable to that amount as of the date of the benefit payment, the benefit payment is included as wages under the general timing rule of paragraph (a)(1) of this section to the extent of any excess, and the amount taken into account at the early inclusion date (and income attributable to that amount) is disregarded thereafter with respect to the amount deferred. If the amount taken into account at the early inclusion date and the income attributable to that amount as of the date of the benefit payment exceeds the benefit payment, the benefit payment is not included as wages under the general timing rule of paragraph (a)(1) of this section and, in determining the amount that must be taken into account thereafter with respect to the amount deferred, the amount taken into account at the early inclusion date, plus attributable income as of the date of the benefit payment, is reduced by the amount of the benefit payment, and only the excess plus future income attributable to the excess (credited using assumptions that were reasonable on the early inclusion date) is taken into consideration. If amounts have been taken into account at more than one early inclusion date, this paragraph (e)(4)(ii)(E) applies on a first-in-first-out basis, beginning with the amount taken into account at the earliest early inclusion date (including income attributable thereto).

(5) *Rule of administrative convenience.*—For purposes of this section, an employer may treat an amount deferred as required to be taken into account under this paragraph (e) on any date that is later than, but within the same calendar year as, the actual date on which the amount deferred is otherwise required to be taken into account under this paragraph (e). For example, if services creating the right to an amount deferred are considered performed under paragraph (e)(2) of this section periodically throughout a year, the employer may nevertheless treat the services creating the right to that amount deferred as performed on December 31 of that year. If an employer uses the rule of administrative convenience described in this paragraph (e)(5), any determination of whether the income attributable to an amount deferred under an account balance plan is based on a reasonable rate of interest or whether the actuarial assumptions used to determine the present value of an amount deferred in a nonaccount balance plan are reasonable will be made as of the date the employer selects to take the amount into account.

(6) *Portions of an amount deferred required to be taken into account on more than one date.*—If different portions of an amount deferred are required to be taken into account under paragraph (e)(1) of this section on more than one date (e.g., on account of a graded vesting schedule), then each such portion is considered a separate amount deferred for purposes of this section.

(7) *Examples.*—This paragraph (e) is illustrated by the following examples:

*Example 1.* (i) Employer M establishes a nonqualified deferred compensation plan for Employee A on November 1, 2005. Under the plan, which is an account balance plan, Employee A obtains a legally binding right on the last day of each calendar year (if Employee A is employed on that date) to be credited with a principal amount equal to 5 percent of compensation for the year. In addition, a reasonable rate of interest is credited quarterly. Employee A's account balance is nonforfeitable and is payable upon Employee A's termination of employment. For 2006, the principal amount credited to Employee A under the plan (which, in this case, is also the amount deferred within the meaning of paragraph (c) of this section) is $25,000.

(ii) Under paragraph (e)(2) of this section, the services creating the right to the $25,000 amount deferred are considered performed as of December 31, 2006, the date on which Employee A has performed all of the services necessary to obtain a legally binding right to the amount deferred. Thus, in accordance with paragraph (e)(1) of this section, the $25,000 amount deferred must be taken into account as of December 31, 2006, which is the later of the date on which services creating the right to the amount deferred are performed or the date on which the right to the amount deferred is no longer subject to a substantial risk of forfeiture.

*Example 2.* (i) The facts are the same as in *Example 1*, except that the principal amount credited under the plan on the last day of each

year (and attributable interest) is forfeited if the employee terminates employment within five years of that date.

(ii) Under paragraph (e)(3) of this section, the determination of whether the right to an amount deferred is subject to a substantial risk of forfeiture is made in accordance with the principles of section 83. Under §1.83-3(c) of this chapter, a substantial risk of forfeiture generally exists where rights in property that are transferred are conditioned, directly or indirectly, upon the future performance of substantial services. Because Employee A's right to receive the $25,000 principal amount (and attributable interest) is conditioned on the performance of services for five years, a substantial risk of forfeiture exists with respect to that amount deferred until December 31, 2011.

(iii) December 31, 2011, is the later of the date on which services creating the right to the amount deferred are performed or the date on which the right to the amount deferred is no longer subject to a substantial risk of forfeiture. Thus, in accordance with paragraph (e)(1) of this section, the amount deferred (which, pursuant to paragraph (c)(1) of this section, is equal to the $25,000 principal amount credited to Employee A's account on December 31, 2006, plus the interest credited with respect to that principal amount through December 31, 2011) must be taken into account as of December 31, 2011.

*Example 3.* (i) The facts are the same as in *Example 2*, except that the principal amount credited under the plan on the last day of each year (and attributable interest) becomes nonforfeitable according to a graded vesting schedule under which 20 percent is vested as of December 31, 2007; 40 percent is vested as of December 31, 2008; 60 percent is vested as of December 31, 2009; 80 percent is vested as of December 31, 2010; and 100 percent is vested as of December 31, 2011. Because these dates are later than the date on which the services creating the right to the amount deferred are considered performed (December 31, 2006), the amount deferred is required to be taken into account as of these dates that fall in five different years.

(ii) Paragraph (e)(6) of this section provides that, if different portions of an amount deferred are required to be taken into account under paragraph (e)(1) of this section on more than one date, then each such portion is considered a separate amount deferred for purposes of this section. Thus, $5,000 of the principal amount, plus interest credited through December 31, 2007, is taken into account as an amount deferred on December 31, 2007; $5,000 of the principal amount, plus interest credited through December 31, 2008, is taken into account as a separate amount deferred on December 31, 2008; etc.

*Example 4.* (i) On November 21, 2001, Employer N establishes a nonqualified deferred compensation plan under which all benefits are 100 percent vested. The plan provides for Employee B (who is age 45) to receive a lump sum benefit of $500,000 at age 65. This benefit will be forfeited if Employee B dies before age 65.

(ii) Because the amount, form, and commencement date of the benefit are known, and the only assumptions needed to determine the amount deferred are interest and mortality, the amount deferred is reasonably ascertainable within the meaning of paragraph (e)(4)(i) of this section on November 21, 2001.

*Example 5* (i) The facts are the same as in *Example 4*, except that plan provides that the lump sum will be paid at the later of age 65 or termination of employment and provides that the $500,000 payable to Employee B is increased by 5 percent per year for each year that payment is deferred beyond age 65.

(ii) Because the commencement date of the benefit payment is contingent on when Employee B terminates employment, the commencement date of the benefit payment is not known. Thus, the amount deferred is not reasonably ascertainable within the meaning of paragraph (e)(4)(i) of this section, unless the plan satisfies the requirements of paragraph (c)(2)(iii)(B) of this section. Because the fixed 5 percent factor may not be reasonable at the time benefit payments commence (i.e., 5 percent might be higher or lower than a reasonable interest rate when payments commence), the plan fails to satisfy paragraph (c)(2)(iii)(B) of this section and accordingly the amount deferred is not reasonably ascertainable until termination of employment,

*Example 6.* (i) The facts are the same as in *Example 4*, except that the $500,000 is payable to Employee B at the later of age 55 or termination of employment.

(ii) Because the commencement date of the benefit payment is contingent on when Employee B terminates employment, the commencement date of the benefit payment is not known. Thus, the amount deferred is not reasonably ascertainable until termination of employment.

*Example 7.* (i) The facts are the same as in *Example 4*, except that Employee B may elect to take the benefit in the form of a life annuity of $50,000 per year (commencing at age 65).

(ii) Because the plan permits employees to elect to receive benefits in more than one form and the alternative forms may not have the same value when Employee B makes his election, the plan fails to satisfy the requirements of paragraph (c)(2)(iii)(B) of this section until a form of benefit is selected. Thus, the amount deferred is not reasonably ascertainable until then.

*Example 8.* (i) Employer O establishes a nonqualified deferred compensation plan. The plan is a supplemental executive retirement plan (SERP) that provides Employee C with a fully vested right to receive a pension, in the form of a life annuity payable monthly, beginning at age 65, equal to the excess of 3 percent of Employee C's final 3-year average pay for each year of participation up to 15 years, over the amount payable to Employee C from Employer O's qualified pension plan. The amount payable under the qualified pension plan is a life annuity payable monthly, beginning at age 65, equal to 1.5 percent of final 3-year average pay for each year of employment, excluding pay in excess of the section 401(a)(17) compensation limit. No benefits are payable under the SERP if Employee C dies before age 65. Employee C becomes a participant in the SERP on January 1, 2001, at age 44. The amount deferred under the SERP for any year is not reasonably ascertainable prior to termination of employment because the amount of the benefit is not known and the determination of the amount deferred requires assumptions other than interest and mortality (e.g., an assumption as to Employee C's average pay for the final three years of employment). As permitted by paragraph (e)(4)(i) of this section, Employer O chooses not to take any amount into account for any year before the resolution date. Employee C terminates employment on December 31, 2018 when he is age 62.

(ii) As of the date Employee C terminates employment, the amount of the benefit is known and the only actuarial or other assumptions needed to determine the amount deferred are an interest rate assumption and a mortality assumption. At that time, the amount deferred in each past year becomes reasonably ascertainable, and Employer O is able to determine that during 2001 Employee C earned a legally binding right to a life annuity of $4,000 per year beginning in 2021 when Employee C is age 65. Employer O determines the present value of Employee C's future benefit payments under the SERP as of this resolution date (December 31, 2018), using a 7 percent interest rate and the UP-84 mortality table, which, solely for purposes of this example, are assumed to be reasonable actuarial assumptions for December 31, 2018. The special timing rule will be satisfied if the resulting present value, $26,950, is taken into account on that date in accordance with paragraph (d)(1) of this section.

*Example 9.* (i) The facts are the same as in *Example 8*, except that the plan provides that Employee C may choose to receive early retirement benefits on an unreduced basis at any time after age 60 if Employee C has completed 15 years of service by that date.

(ii) As of the date Employee C terminates employment, the amount of the benefit is known and the only actuarial or other assumptions needed to determine the amount deferred are an interest rate assumption and a mortality assumption. At that time, the amount deferred in each past year becomes reasonably ascertainable, and Employer O is able to determine that during 2001 Employee C earned a legally binding right to a life annuity of $4,000 per year beginning on December 31, 2018 when Employee C is age 62. Employer O determines the present value of Employee C's future benefit payments under the SERP as of this resolution date (December 31, 2018), using a 7 percent interest rate and the UP-84 mortality table, which, solely for purposes of this example, are assumed to be reasonable actuarial assumptions for December 31, 2018. The special timing rule will be satisfied if the resulting present value, $37,576, is taken into account on that date in accordance with paragraph (d)(1) of this section.

*Example 10.* (i) The facts are the same as in *Example 9*, except that, as permitted under paragraph (e)(4)(ii) of this section, Employer O chooses to take an amount into account before the amount deferred for 2001 is reasonably ascertainable. The amount that Employer O takes into account on December 31, 2001, is $13,043 (the present value of a life annuity of $4,000 per year, payable at age 62, using a 6 percent interest rate and the UP-84 mortality table). Employer O does not take any other amount into account before the resolution date.

(ii) In accordance with paragraph (e)(4)(ii)(B) of this section, Employer O must determine any additional amount required to be taken into account in 2018. If the $4,000 payable in the form of a life annuity beginning at age 62 exceeds the life annuity which is actuarially equivalent to the $13,043 previously taken into account, the present value of the excess must be taken into account. In this *Example 10*, the $13,043 previously taken into account is actuarially equivalent to a $4,000 annuity commencing at age 62 using a 6 percent interest rate and the UP-84 mortality table ( which, solely for purposes of this example, are assumed to be reasonable actuarial assumptions for December 31, 2001). Accordingly, no additional amount need be taken into account in 2018, regardless of any changes in market rates of interest between 2001 and 2018.

*Example 11.* (i) The facts are the same as in *Example 9*, except that, as permitted under paragraph (e)(4)(ii) of this section, Employer O chooses to take an amount into account before the amount deferred

for 2001 is reasonably ascertainable. The amount that Employer O takes into account on December 31, 2001, is $9,569 (the present value of a life annuity of $4,000 per year, payable at age 65, using a 6 percent interest rate and the UP-84 mortality table). Employer O does not take any other amount into account before the resolution date.

(ii) In accordance with paragraph (e)(4)(ii)(B) of this section, Employer O must determine any additional amount required to be taken into account in 2018. If the $4,000 payable in the form of a life annuity beginning in 2018 at age 62 exceeds the life annuity which is actuarially equivalent to the $9,569 previously taken into account, the present value of the excess must be taken into account. In this case, the $9,569 previously taken into account is actuarially equivalent to a $2,935 annuity commencing at age 62 using a 6 percent interest rate and the UP-84 mortality table (which, solely for purposes of this example, are assumed to be reasonable actuarial assumptions for December 31, 2001). Accordingly, an additional amount needs to be taken into account in 2018 equal to the present value of the excess of the $4,000 annual stream of benefit payments to which Employee C obtained a legally binding right during 2001 over the $2,935 annual stream of benefit payments which is actuarially equivalent to the amount previously taken into account. This present value (i.e., the present value of a life annuity equal to $4,000 minus $2,935, or $1,065 annually) is determined by Employer O to be $10,005 as of the resolution date using a 7 percent interest rate and the UP-84 mortality table (which, solely for purposes of this example, are assumed to be reasonable actuarial assumptions for December 31, 2018).

*Example 12.* (i) The facts are the same as in *Example 9*, except that the amount that Employer O takes into account on December 31, 2001, is $15,834 (the present value of $4,000, payable at age 60, using a 6 percent interest rate and the UP-84 mortality table). Employer O does not take any other amount into account before the resolution date.

(ii) In accordance with paragraph (e)(4)(ii)(B) of this section, Employer O must determine any additional amount required to be taken into account in 2018. If the $4,000 payable in the form of a life annuity beginning at age 62 exceeds the life annuity which is actuarially equivalent to the $15,834 previously taken into account, the present value of the excess must be taken into account. In this case, the $15,834 previously taken into account is actuarially equivalent to a $4,856 annuity commencing at age 62 using a 6 percent interest rate and the UP-84 mortality table (which, solely for purposes of this example, are assumed to be reasonable actuarial assumptions for December 31, 2001). Because the life annuity of $4,856 per year (which is equivalent to the amount taken into account at the early inclusion date) exceeds the $4,000 annuity attributable to the amount deferred in 2001, no additional amount is required to be taken into account for that amount deferred as of the resolution date. Employer O may claim a refund or credit for the overpayment of FICA tax with respect to amounts taken into account prior to the resolution date to the extent permitted by sections 6402, 6413, and 6511.

*Example 13.* (i) The facts are the same as in *Example 12*, except that Employee C became a participant in the SERP on January 1, 2000. In addition, Employer O determines in 2018 that during 2000 Employee C earned a legally binding right to a life annuity of $1,500 per year beginning on December 31, 2018.

(ii) Employer O may allocate the $15,834 previously taken into account among any amounts deferred on or before the early inclusion date. At the resolution date, Employer O will have to take into account the present value of an annuity equal to the excess of the life annuity attributable to the amounts deferred for 2000 and 2001 over a life annuity of $4,856 per year.

*Example 14.* (i) In 2003, Employer P establishes a nonqualified deferred compensation plan for Employee D. The plan provides that, in consideration of Employee D's services to be performed on Project X in 2004, Employee D will have a nonforfeitable right to receive 1 percent per year of Employer P's net profits associated with Project X for each of the immediately succeeding three years. No services beyond 2004 are required. The 1 percent of net profits payable each year will be paid on March 31 of the immediately succeeding year. One percent of net profits associated with Project X is $750,000 in 2005, $400,000 in 2006, and $90,000 in 2007. Employee D receives $750,000 on March 31, 2006, $400,000 on March 31, 2007, and $90,000 on March 31, 2008.

(ii) Because the services creating the right to all of the amount deferred are performed in 2004, the benefit payments based on the 2005, 2006, and 2007 net profits are all attributable to the amount deferred in 2004. However, because the present value of Employee D's future benefit is contingent on future profits, the determination of the amount deferred requires the use of assumptions other than interest, mortality, and cost of living. Thus, all of the amount deferred in 2004 will not be reasonably ascertainable within the meaning of paragraph (e)(4)(i) of this section until December 31, 2007 (which is the resolution date). Employer P does not choose to take any amount into account prior to the amount deferred becoming reasonably ascertainable.

(iii) However, paragraph (d)(1)(ii)(A) of this section provides that a benefit payment attributable to an amount deferred under a nonqualified deferred compensation plan must be included as wages when actually or constructively paid if the amount deferred has not been taken into account as wages under the special timing rule of paragraph (a)(2) of this section. Thus, the benefit payments in 2006 and 2007 must be included as wages when paid.

(iv) As of December 31, 2007, all of the amount deferred under the plan becomes reasonably ascertainable because the amount of the benefit payable attributable to the amount deferred is treated as known under paragraph (e)(4)(i)(B) of this section, and the only assumption needed to determine the present value of the future benefits is interest. However, since Employer P was required to treat the payments in 2006 and 2007 as wages when paid under the general timing rule of paragraph (a)(1) of this section, only the present value of the payment to be made in 2008 is required to be taken into account as of the resolution date (December 31, 2007) under the special timing rule of paragraph (a)(2) of this section. Using an interest rate of 10 percent per year (which, solely for purposes of this *Example 14*, is assumed to be reasonable), Employer P determines that on December 31, 2007, the present value of the future benefits is $87,881, and Employer P includes that additional amount in wages for 2007. (Note that Employer P can choose to use the lag method of withholding described in paragraph (f)(3) of this section, which allows the resolution date amount to be taken into account no later than March 31, 2008, provided that the amount deferred is increased by interest using the AFR for January of 2008.)

*Example 15.* (i) The facts are the same as in *Example 14*, except that Employer P chooses the early inclusion option permitted by paragraph (e)(4)(ii) of this section to take $1,000,000 into account on December 31, 2004, before the amount deferred for 2004 is reasonably ascertainable.

(ii) Pursuant to paragraph (e)(4)(ii)(E) of this section, in applying the nonduplication rule of paragraph (a)(2)(iii) of this section, a first-in-first-out rule applies in determining the benefit payments that are attributable to amounts previously taken into account. Using the 10 percent interest rate, Employer P determines that the $750,000 benefit payment on March 31, 2006, and the March 31, 2007, benefit payment of $400,000 are less than the $1,000,000 taken into account at the early inclusion date, plus attributable income, and, therefore, are not included in wages when paid.

(iii) Under paragraph (e)(4)(ii)(E) of this section, if an employer chooses to take an amount into account before the resolution date, the amount taken into account (plus income attributable to that amount) is disregarded to the extent the amount is attributed to benefit payments made before the resolution date. Thus, Employer P must reduce the $1,000,000 taken into account in 2004 (plus income attributable to that amount) based upon the two benefit payments ($750,000 and $400,000) that were excluded from wages. Using an interest rate of 10 percent, Employer P determines that the amount taken into account in 2004 plus interest to the resolution date and reduced based upon the two benefit payments is $15,228 and the additional amount that is required to be taken into account as of December 31, 2007, is $72,653 ($87,881 − $15,228).

*Example 16.* (i) Employee E obtains a fully vested, legally binding right during 2002, 2003, and 2004 to payments from a nonqualified deferred compensation plan of Employer Q under which the benefits are based on a formula that includes an actuarial offset by the account balance under a qualified defined contribution plan of Employer Q as of December 31, 2004. The payments from the nonqualified deferred compensation plan are to commence on December 31, 2005. At the resolution date for the amounts earned during 2002, 2003, and 2004, which is December 31, 2004, Employee E has a legally binding right to a net annual benefit of $100,000 payable for life to commence on December 31, 2005. On the resolution date, Employer Q determines that on December 31, 2002, Employee E had a legally binding right to receive $100,000 annually for life beginning on December 31, 2005 (as a result of the gross benefit under the nonqualified plan being $120,000 annually for life, and the offset being $20,000 annually for life, as of December 31, 2002). On December 31, 2003, Employee E had a legally binding right to receive $95,000 annually for life beginning on December 31, 2005 (as a result of the gross benefit under the nonqualified plan being $135,000 annually for life, and the offset being $40,000 annually for life, as of December 31, 2003). On December 31, 2004, Employee E had a legally binding right to receive $100,000 annually for life beginning on December 31, 2005 (as a result of the gross benefit under the nonqualified plan being $145,000 annually for life, and the offset being $45,000 annually for life, as of December 31, 2004).

(ii) In this case, pursuant to paragraph (e)(4)(ii)(D)(4) of this section, Employer Q can attribute the entire $100,000 life annuity to the amount deferred for 2002, even though Employee E's benefit

under the nonqualified deferred compensation plan is reduced to $95,000 in 2003.

*Example 17.* (i) In 2010, Employee F performs services for which she earns a right to 10 percent of the proceeds from the sale of a motion picture. In 2011, Employee F performs services for which she earns a right to 10 percent of the proceeds from the sale of another motion picture. These proceeds are calculated by subtracting the total advertising expenses for both movies. Payment is to be made in the year following the date on which both pictures have been sold, but not later than 2018. At the end of 2010, the advertising expenses for both pictures totaled $300,000. The first motion picture is sold for $10,000,000 in 2014. The second motion picture is sold for $17,000,000 in 2017. At the end of 2017, the advertising expenses totaled $1,700,000. In 2018, Employee F is paid $2,530,000 (10 percent of the sum of $10,000,000 and $17,000,000 minus $1,700,000).

(ii) Pursuant to paragraph (e)(4)(ii)(D)(4) of this section, $970,000 (10 percent of the excess of the gross proceeds from the sale of the first motion picture at the resolution date in 2017 over the advertising expenses incurred at the end of 2010) of the payment made in 2018 can be attributed to the amount deferred in 2010 (and with the remaining payment of $1,560,000 to be attributed to the amount deferred in 2011).

(f) *Withholding.*—(1) *In general.*—Unless an employer applies an alternative method described in paragraph (f)(2) or (3) of this section, an amount deferred under a nonqualified deferred compensation plan for any employee is treated, for purposes of withholding and depositing FICA tax, as wages paid by the employer and received by the employee at the time it is taken into account in accordance with paragraph (e) of this section. However, paragraphs (f)(2) and (3) of this section provide alternative methods which may be used with respect to an amount deferred for an employee. An employer is not required to be consistent in applying the alternatives described in this paragraph (f) with respect to different employees or amounts deferred.

(2) *Estimated method.*—(i) *In general.*—Under the alternative method provided in this paragraph (f)(2), the employer may make a reasonable estimate of the amount deferred on the date on which the amount is taken into account in accordance with paragraph (e) of this section and take that estimated amount into account as wages paid by the employer and received by the employee on that date (the estimate date), for purposes of withholding and depositing FICA tax.

(ii) *Underestimate of the amount deferred.*—(A) *General rule.*—If the employer underestimates the amount deferred (as determined after calculating the actual amount deferred that should have been taken into account as of the date on which the amount was taken into account in accordance with paragraph (e) of this section, using an interest rate and other actuarial assumptions that are reasonable as of that date), the employer may treat the shortfall as wages paid as of the estimate date or as of any date that is no later than three months after the estimate date. In either case, the shortfall does not include the income credited to the amount deferred after the amount is taken into account in accordance with paragraph (e) of this section.

(B) *Shortfall is treated as wages paid on a date after the estimate date.*—If the employer chooses to treat the shortfall as wages paid on a date that is no later than three months after the estimate date, the employer must take that shortfall into account as wages paid by the employer and received by the employee on that date, for purposes of withholding and depositing FICA tax.

(C) *Shortfall is treated as wages paid on the estimate date.*—If the employer chooses to treat the shortfall as wages paid as of the estimate date, the shortfall is treated as an error for purposes of withholding and depositing FICA tax. Appropriate adjustments may be made in accordance with section 6205(a) and the regulations thereunder; however, for purposes of § 31.6205-1(b), the error need not be treated as ascertained before the date that is three months after the estimate date.

(D) *Reporting.*—The employer must report the shortfall as wages on Form 941, Employer's Quarterly Federal Tax Return (and, if applicable, Form 941c, Supporting Statement to Correct Information) and Form W-2, Wage and Tax Statement (or, if applicable, Form W-2c, Corrected Wage and Tax Statement) in accordance with its treatment of the shortfall under paragraph (f)(2)(ii)(B) or (C) of this section.

(iii) *Overestimate of the amount deferred.*—If the employer overestimates the amount deferred (as determined after calculating the actual amount deferred that should have been taken into account as of the date on which the amount was taken into account in accordance with paragraph (e) of this section, using an interest rate and actuarial assumptions that are reasonable as of that date) and deposits more than the amount required, the employer may claim a refund or credit in accordance with sections 6402, 6413, and 6511. A Form 941c, or an equivalent statement, must accompany each claim for refund. In addition, Form W-2 or, if applicable, Form W-2c must also reflect the actual amount deferred that should have been taken into account.

(3) *Lag method.*—Under the alternative method provided in this paragraph (f)(3), an amount deferred, plus interest, may be treated as wages paid by the employer and received by the employee, for purposes of withholding and depositing FICA tax, on any date that is no later than three months after the date the amount is required to be taken into account in accordance with paragraph (e) of this section. For purposes of this paragraph (f)(3), the amount deferred must be increased by interest through the date on which the wages are treated as paid, at a rate that is not less than AFR. If the employer withholds and deposits FICA tax in accordance with this paragraph (f)(3), the employer will be treated as having taken into account the amount deferred plus income to the date on which the wages are treated as paid.

(4) *Examples.*—This paragraph (f) is illustrated by the following examples:

*Example 1.* (i) Employer M maintains a nonqualified deferred compensation plan that is an account balance plan. The plan provides for annual bonuses based on current year profits to be deferred until termination of employment. Employer M's profits for 2003, and thus the amount deferred, is reasonably ascertainable, but Employer M calculates the amount deferred on March 3, 2004, when the relevant data is available.

(ii) In accordance with the alternative method described in paragraph (f)(2) of this section, Employer M makes a reasonable estimate that the amount deferred that must be taken into account as of December 31, 2003, for Employee A is $20,000, and withholds and deposits FICA tax on that amount as if it were wages paid by Employer M and received by Employee A on that date. In January of 2004, Employer M files and furnishes Form W-2 for Employee A including the $20,000 in FICA wages. On March 3, 2004, Employer M determines that the actual amount deferred that should have been taken into account on December 31, 2003, was $22,000.

(iii) In accordance with the alternative method described in paragraph (f)(2)(ii) of this section, Employer M may treat the additional $2,000 as wages paid to and received by Employee A on December 31, 2003, the estimate date. Employer M may treat the $2,000 shortfall as an error ascertained on March 3, 2004, and withhold and deposit FICA tax on that amount. Form W-2c for Employee A for 2003 must include the $2,000 shortfall in FICA wages. Employer M must also correct the information on Form 941 for the last quarter of 2003, reporting the adjustment on Form 941 for the first quarter of 2004, accompanied by Form 941c for the last quarter of 2003.

(iv) Instead, Employer M may treat the $2,000 shortfall as wages paid on March 31, 2004, and withhold and deposit FICA tax on that amount as if it were wages paid by Employer M and received by Employee A on that date. Form W-2 for Employee A for 2004 and Form 941 for the first quarter of 2004 must include the $2,000 shortfall in FICA wages.

*Example 2.* (i) The facts are the same as in *Example 1*, except that on March 3, 2004, Employer M determines that the actual amount deferred that should have been taken into account on December 31, 2003, was $19,000.

(ii) Under paragraph (f)(2)(iii) of this section, Employer M may, in accordance with sections 6402, 6413, and 6511, claim a refund or credit for the overpayment of tax resulting from the overestimate. In addition, Employer M must file and furnish Form W-2c for Employee A and must correct the information on Form 941 for the last quarter of 2003.

*Example 3.* (i) The facts are the same as in *Example 1*, except that Employer M does not make a reasonable estimate of the amount deferred that must be taken into account as of December 31, 2003. Instead, Employer M withholds and deposits FICA tax on the amount deferred plus interest on that amount using AFR (for January 2004) as if it were wages paid by Employer M and received by Employee A on March 15, 2004.

(ii) Under the alternative method described in paragraph (f)(3) of this section, the amount taken into account on March 15, 2004 (including the interest), will be treated as FICA wages paid to and received by Employee A on March 15, 2004.

*Example 4.* (i) The facts are the same as in *Example 1*, except that an amount is also deferred for Employee B which is required to be taken into account on October 15, 2003, and Employer M chooses to use the lag method in paragraph (f)(3) of this section in order to provide time to calculate the amount deferred.

(ii) Employer M may use any date not later than January 15, 2004, to take the amount deferred into account (provided that the amount deferred includes interest, at AFR for January 1, 2003,

through December 31, 2003, and at AFR for January 1, 2004, through January 15, 2004).

(g) *Effective date and transition rules.*—(1) *General effective date.*— Except for paragraphs (g)(2) through (4) of this section, this section is applicable on and after January 1, 2000. Thus, paragraphs (a) through (f) of this section apply to amounts deferred on or after January 1, 2000; to amounts deferred before January 1, 2000, which cease to be subject to a substantial risk of forfeiture on or after January 1, 2000, or for which a resolution date occurs on or after January 1, 2000; and to benefits actually or constructively paid on or after January 1, 2000.

(2) *Reasonable, good faith interpretation for amounts deferred and benefits paid before January 1, 2000.*—(i) *In general.*—For periods before January 1, 2000 (including amounts deferred before January 1, 2000, and any benefits actually or constructively paid before January 1, 2000, that are attributable to those amounts deferred), an employer may rely on a reasonable, good faith interpretation of section 3121(v)(2), taking into account pre-existing guidance. An employer will be deemed to have determined FICA tax liability and satisfied FICA withholding requirements in accordance with a reasonable, good faith interpretation of section 3121(v)(2) if the employer has complied with paragraphs (a) through (f) of this section. For purposes of paragraphs (g)(2) through (4) of this section, and subject to paragraphs (g)(2)(ii) and (iii) of this section, whether an employer that has not complied with paragraphs (a) through (f) of this section has determined FICA tax liability and satisfied FICA withholding requirements in accordance with a reasonable, good faith interpretation of section 3121(v)(2) will be determined based on the relevant facts and circumstances, including consistency of treatment by the employer and the extent to which the employer has resolved unclear issues in its favor.

(ii) *Plan must be established or adopted.*—If an amount is deferred under a plan before January 1, 2000, and benefit payments attributable to that amount are actually or constructively paid on or after January 1, 2000, then in no event will an employer's treatment of the amount deferred be considered to be in accordance with a reasonable, good faith interpretation of section 3121(v)(2) if the employer treats that amount as taken into account as wages for FICA tax purposes prior to the establishment of the plan (within the meaning of paragraph (b)(2) of this section) providing for the deferred compensation (or, if later, the establishment of the plan as amended to provide for the deferred compensation, as provided in paragraph (b)(2)(ii) of this section). If an amount is deferred under a plan before January 1, 2000, and benefit payments attributable to that amount are actually or constructively paid before January 1, 2000, then in no event will the employer's treatment of that amount deferred be considered to be in accordance with a reasonable, good faith interpretation of section 3121(v)(2) if the employer treats that amount as taken into account as wages for FICA tax purposes prior to the adoption of the plan providing for the deferred compensation (or, if later, the adoption of the plan amendment providing the deferred compensation). For example, awards, bonuses, raises, incentive payments, and other similar amounts granted under a plan as compensation for past services may not be taken into account under section 3121(v)(2) prior to the establishment (or, if applicable, the adoption) of the plan.

(iii) *Certain changes in position for stock options, stock appreciation rights, and other stock value rights not reasonable, good faith interpretation.*—In the case of a stock option, stock appreciation right, or other stock value right (as defined in paragraph (b)(4)(ii) of this section) that is exercised before January 1, 2000, an employer that treats the exercise as not subject to FICA tax as a result of the nonduplication rule of section 3121(v)(2)(B) is not acting in accordance with a reasonable, good faith interpretation of section 3121(v)(2) if the employer has not treated that grant and all earlier grants as subject to section 3121(v)(2) by reporting the current value of such options and rights as FICA wages on Form 941 filed for the quarter during which each grant was made (or, if later, for the quarter during which each grant ceased to be subject to a substantial risk of forfeiture).

(3) *Optional adjustments to conform with this section for pre-effective-date open periods.*—(i) *General rule.*—If an employer determined FICA tax liability with respect to section 3121(v)(2) in any period ending before January 1, 2000, for which the applicable period of limitations has not expired on January 1, 2000 (pre-effective-date open periods), in a manner that was not in accordance with this section, the employer may adjust its FICA tax determination for that period to conform to this section. Thus, if an amount deferred was taken into account in a pre-effective-date open period when it was not required to be taken into account (e.g., an amount taken into account before it became reasonably ascertainable), the employer may claim a refund or credit for any FICA tax paid on that amount to the extent permitted by sections 6402, 6413, and 6511.

(ii) *Consistency required.*—In the case of a plan that is not a nonqualified deferred compensation plan (within the meaning of paragraph (b)(1) of this section), if any payment was actually or constructively paid to an employee under the plan in a pre-effective-date open period and that payment was not included in FICA wages by reason of the employer's treatment of the plan as a nonqualified deferred compensation plan, then the employer may claim a refund or credit for FICA tax paid on amounts treated as amounts deferred under the plan (in accordance with the employer's treatment of the plan as a nonqualified deferred compensation plan) for that employee for pre-effective-date open periods only to the extent that the FICA tax paid on all amounts treated as amounts deferred for the employee in all pre-effective-date open periods under the plan exceeds the FICA tax that would have been due on the benefits actually or constructively paid to the employee in those periods under the plan if those benefits were included in FICA wages when paid. If any benefit payments attributable to amounts deferred after December 31, 1993, were actually or constructively paid to an employee under a nonqualified deferred compensation plan (within the meaning of paragraph (b)(1) of this section) in a pre-effective-date open period, but these payments were treated as subject to FICA tax because the employer treated the plan as not being a nonqualified deferred compensation plan, then the employer may claim a refund or credit for the FICA tax paid on those benefit payments only to the extent that the FICA tax paid on those benefit payments exceeds the FICA tax that would have been due on the amounts deferred to which those benefit payments are attributable if those amounts deferred had been taken into account when they would have been required to have been taken into account under this section (if this section had been in effect then).

(iii) *Reporting.*—Any employer that adjusts its FICA tax determination in accordance with paragraphs (g)(3)(i) and (ii) of this section must make appropriate adjustments on Form 941 and Form 941c for the affected periods, and, in addition, must file and furnish Form W-2, or, if applicable, Form W-2c, for any affected employee so that the Social Security Administration may correctly post the amount deferred to the employee's earnings record. The adjustments may be made in accordance with section 6205(a) and the regulations thereunder; however, for purposes of §31.6205-1(b), the error is not required to be treated as ascertained before March 31, 2000.

(4) *Application of reasonable, good faith standard.*—(i) *Plans that are not subject to section 3121(v)(2).*—If a plan is not a nonqualified deferred compensation plan within the meaning of paragraph (b)(1) of this section, but, for a period ending prior to January 1, 2000, and, pursuant to a reasonable, good faith interpretation of section 3121(v)(2), an amount under the plan was taken into account (within the meaning of paragraph (d)(1) of this section) as an amount deferred under a nonqualified deferred compensation plan, then, pursuant to paragraph (g)(2) of this section, the following rules shall apply—

(A) With respect to benefit payments actually or constructively paid before January 1, 2000, that are attributable to amounts previously taken into account under the plan, no additional FICA tax will be due;

(B) On or after January 1, 2000, benefit payments under the plan must be taken into account as wages when actually or constructively paid in accordance with paragraph (a)(1) of this section; and

(C) To the extent permitted by paragraph (g)(3) of this section, the emp6oyer may claim a refund or credit for FICA tax actually paid on amounts taken into account prior to January 1, 2000.

(ii) *Plans that are subject to section 3121(v)(2) for which the amount deferred has not been fully taken into account.*—(A) *In general.*— The rules of paragraphs (g)(4)(ii)(B) through (E) of this section apply if a plan is a nonqualified deferred compensation plan (within the meaning of paragraph (b)(1) of this section) and, with respect to an amount deferred under the plan for an employee prior to January 1, 2000, the employer, in accordance with a reasonable, good faith interpretation of section 3121(v)(2), either took into account an amount that is less than the amount that would have been required to be taken into account if paragraphs (a) through (f) of this section had been in effect for that period or took no amount into account. Thus, paragraphs (g)(4)(ii)(B) through (E) of this section apply both to an employer that treated the plan as if it were not a nonqualified deferred compensation plan within the meaning of section 3121(v)(2) (by withholding and paying FICA tax due on benefits actually or constructively paid under the plan during that period, if any) and to an employer that treated the plan as a nonqualified deferred compensation plan within the meaning of section 3121(v)(2).

(B) *No additional tax required.*—Pursuant to paragraph (g)(2) of this section, no additional FICA tax will be due for any period ending prior to January 1, 2000.

(C) *General timing rule applicable.*—In accordance with paragraph (d)(1)(ii) of this section, except as provided in paragraphs (g)(4)(ii)(D) and (E), the general timing rule described in paragraph (a)(1) of this section applies to benefits actually or constructively paid on or after January 1, 2000, attributable to an amount deferred in a period before January 1, 2000, to the extent the amount taken into account was less than the amount that would have been required to be taken into account if paragraphs (a) through (f) of this section had been in effect before January 1, 2000.

(D) *Special rule for amounts deferred before 1994.*—The difference between the amount that was taken into account in any period ending prior to January 1, 1994, and the amount that would have been required or permitted to be taken into account in that period if paragraphs (a) through (f) of this section had been in effect is treated as if it had been taken into account within the meaning of paragraph (d)(1) of this section. For example, in the case of an amount deferred before 1994 that was not reasonably ascertainable (and which was not subject to a substantial risk of forfeiture), the employer is treated as if it had anticipated the actual amount, form, and commencement date for the benefit payments attributable to the amount deferred and had taken the amount deferred into account at an early inclusion date before 1994 using a method permitted under this section. Thus, with respect to such an amount deferred, the employer is not required to take any additional amount into account when the amount deferred becomes reasonably ascertainable, and no additional FICA tax will be due when the benefit payments attributable to the amount deferred are actually or constructively paid.

(E) *Special rule for amounts required to be taken into account in 1994 or 1995.*—In the case of an amount deferred that would have been required to be taken into account in 1994 or 1995 if paragraphs (a) through (f) of this section had been in effect, an employer will be treated as taking the amount deferred into account under paragraph (d)(1) of this section to the extent the employer takes the amount into account by treating it as wages paid by the employer and received by the employee as of any date prior to April 1, 2000.

(iii) *Plans that are subject to section 3121(v)(2) for which more than the amount deferred has been taken into account.*—If a plan is a nonqualified deferred compensation plan (within the meaning of paragraph (b)(1) of this section) and an amount was taken into account under the plan for an employee before January 1, 2000, in accordance with a reasonable, good faith interpretation of section 3121(v)(2), but that amount could not have been taken into account before January 1, 2000, if paragraphs (a) through (f) of this section had been in effect then, the following rules apply—

(A) The determination of the amount deferred for any period beginning on or after January 1, 2000, must be made in accordance with paragraph (c) of this section, and the time when amounts deferred under the plan are required to be taken into account must be determined in accordance with paragraph (e) of this section, without regard to any such amount that was taken into account for any period ending before January 1, 2000; and

(B) To the extent permitted by sections 6402, 6413, and 6511, the employer may claim a refund or credit for an overpayment of tax caused by the overinclusion of wages that occurred before January 1, 2000.

(5) *Examples.*—This paragraph (g) is illustrated by the following examples:

*Example 1.* (i) In 1996, Employer M establishes a nonqualified deferred compensation plan that is a nonaccount balance plan for Employee A. All benefits under the plan are 100 percent vested. In order to determine the amount deferred on behalf of Employee A under the plan for 1996 and 1997, Employer M must make assumptions as to the date on which Employee A will retire and the form of benefit Employee A will elect, in addition to interest, mortality, and cost-of-living assumptions. Based on assumptions made with respect to all of these contingencies, Employer M determines that the amount deferred for 1996 is $50,000 and the amount deferred for 1997 is $55,000. In 1996 and 1997, Employee A's total wages (without regard to the amounts deferred) exceed the OASDI wage bases. Employer M withholds and deposits HI tax on the $50,000 and $55,000 amounts. Employee A does not retire before January 1, 2000. Employer M chooses under paragraph (g)(3) of this section to apply this section to 1996 and 1997 before the January 1, 2000, general effective date.

(ii) Under this section, the amounts deferred in 1996 and 1997 are not reasonably ascertainable (within the meaning of paragraph (e)(4)(i) of this section) before January 1, 2000. Thus, as long as the applicable period of limitations has not expired for the periods in 1996 and 1997, Employer M may, to the extent permitted under paragraph (g)(3) of this section, apply for a refund or credit for the HI tax paid on the amounts deferred for 1996 and 1997 and, in accordance with paragraph (e)(4) of this section, take into account the amounts deferred when they become reasonably ascertainable.

*Example 2.* (i) Employer N adopts a plan on January 1, 1994, that covers Employee B, who has 10 years of service as of that date. The plan provides that, in consideration of Employee B's outstanding services over the past 10 years, Employee B will be paid a $500,000 lump sum distribution upon termination of employment at any time. On January 15, 1996, Employee B terminates employment with Employer N. Employer N determines, based on a reasonable, good faith interpretation of section 3121(v)(2), that the plan is a nonqualified deferred compensation plan under that section. Employer N treats the $500,000 as having been taken into account as an amount deferred in 1993 and earlier years.

(ii) Under paragraph (g)(2)(ii) of this section, if all amounts are deferred and all benefits are paid under a plan before January 1, 2000, then in no event will an employer's treatment of amounts deferred under the plan be considered to be in accordance with a reasonable, good faith interpretation of section 3121(v)(2) if the employer treats these amounts as taken into account as wages for FICA tax purposes prior to the adoption of the plan. Accordingly, Employer N's treatment is not in accordance with a reasonable, good faith interpretation of section 3121(v)(2) because Employer N treated amounts as taken into account in years before the adoption of the plan. As a result, the payment made to Employee B in 1996 was subject to both the OASDI and HI portions of FICA tax when paid.

*Example 3.* (i) Employer O adopts a bonus plan on December 1, 1993, that becomes effective and legally binding on January 1, 1994. Under the plan, which is not set forth in writing, a specified bonus amount (which is 100 percent vested) is credited to Employee C's account each December 31. A reasonable rate of interest on Employee C's account balance is credited quarterly. Employee C's account balance will begin to be paid in equal annual installments over 10 years beginning on January 1, 2000. Employer O determines, based on a reasonable, good faith interpretation of section 3121(v)(2), that the bonus plan is a nonqualified deferred compensation plan under that section and, therefore, treats the amounts credited from January 1, 1994, through December 31, 1999, as amounts deferred and, in accordance with a reasonable, good faith interpretation of section 3121(v)(2), takes those amounts deferred into account as wages for FICA tax purposes as of those dates. The bonus plan is set forth in writing on May 1, 1999, and, thus, is treated as established as of January 1, 1994.

(ii) Under paragraph (g)(2)(ii) of this section, if an amount is deferred before January 1, 2000, and the attributable benefit is paid on or after January 1, 2000, then in no event will an employer's treatment of the amount deferred under a plan be considered to be in accordance with a reasonable, good faith interpretation of section 3121(v)(2) if the employer treats the amount deferred as taken into account as wages for FICA tax purposes prior to the establishment of the plan (within the meaning of paragraph (b)(2) of this section). Because the bonus plan is treated as established on January 1, 1994 (pursuant to the transition rule for unwritten plans in paragraph (b)(2)(iii) of this section), and because Employer O, in accordance with a reasonable, good faith interpretation of section 3121(v)(2), took amounts deferred into account in 1994 through 1999, the amounts paid to Employee C attributable to those amounts deferred will not be subject to FICA tax when paid.

*Example 4.* (i) In 1985, Employer P establishes a compensation arrangement for Employee D that provides for a lump sum payment to be made after termination of employment but the arrangement is not a nonqualified deferred compensation plan (within the meaning of paragraph (b)(1) of this section). However, prior to January 1, 2000, and in accordance with a reasonable, good faith interpretation of section 3121(v)(2), Employer P treats the arrangement as a nonqualified deferred compensation plan under section 3121(v)(2). Employer P determines that Employee D's total wages (without regard to the amount deferred) for each year from 1985 through 1993 exceed the applicable OASDI and HI wage bases for each of those years and, consequently, there is no FICA tax liability with respect to the amounts deferred for those years. In 1994, Employee D's total wages (without regard to the amount deferred) exceed the OASDI wage base. However, because there is no limit on the HI wage base, the amount deferred for 1994 results in additional HI tax liability of $290, which is timely paid by Employer P.

(ii) Employee D terminates employment with Employer P in 1995 and receives a plan payment of $50,000. In that year, Employee D also receives wages of $60,000 from Employer P. In accordance with its treatment of the plan as a nonqualified deferred compensation plan under section 3121(v)(2), Employer P does not treat the $50,000 payment in 1995 as wages for FICA tax purposes in that year.

(iii) Because amounts under a plan were taken into account (within the meaning of paragraph (d)(1) of this section) as amounts deferred under a nonqualified deferred compensation plan pursuant to a reasonable, good faith interpretation of section 3121(v)(2)(A), but that plan is not a nonqualified deferred compensation plan within the meaning of paragraph (b)(1) of this section, the transition rules

provided in paragraph (g)(4)(i) of this section apply. Thus, no additional FICA tax will be due on the benefits paid in 1995.

(iv) Because $290 of HI tax was paid on the amount deferred in 1994, Employer P is entitled to a refund or credit for that amount to the extent permitted under sections 6402, 6413, and 6511— but only to the extent that $290 exceeds the FICA tax that would have been due on the $50,000 payment in 1995 if that payment had been subject to FICA tax when paid (i.e., if paragraphs (a) through (f) of this section had been effective for those years). In 1995, Employee D had other wages of $60,000. Thus, only $1,200 (the $61,200 OASDI wage base, less the $60,000 of other wages) of the $50,000 payment would have been subject to OASDI; the full $50,000 would have been subject to HI. This would have resulted in $148.80 of OASDI tax ($1,200 × 12.4 percent) and $1,450 of HI tax ($50,000 × 2.9 percent). Employer P is not entitled to a refund or credit under the consistency rule of paragraph (g)(3)(ii) because the $290 of HI tax paid in 1994 is less than the total $1,598.80 of FICA tax liability that would have resulted if this section had applied for 1995.

(v) However, if the benefit payment is instead actually or constructively paid on or after January 1, 2000, the benefit payment must be taken into account as wages when actually or constructively paid in accordance with the general timing rule of paragraph (a)(1) of this section (and paragraph (g)(4)(i)(B) of this section).

*Example 5.* (i) In 1985, Employer Q establishes a compensation arrangement for Employee E that is a nonqualified deferred compensation plan within the meaning of paragraph (b)(1) of this section. However, prior to January 1, 2000, Employer Q determines, based on a reasonable, good faith interpretation of section 3121(v)(2), that the arrangement is not a nonqualified deferred compensation plan within the meaning of that section. Thus, when Employee E retires at the end of 1996 and benefit payments under the arrangement begin in 1997, Employer Q withholds and deposits FICA tax on the amounts paid to Employee E. Payments under the arrangement continue on or after January 1, 2000. Employer Q does not choose (under paragraph (g)(3) of this section) to adjust its FICA tax determination for a pre-effective-date open period by treating this section as in effect for all amounts deferred and benefits actually or constructively paid for any such period. The periods in 1994 and 1995 are not pre-effective-date open periods for Employer Q.

(ii) Under paragraph (g)(4)(ii) of this section, for purposes of determining whether benefits actually or constructively paid on or after January 1, 2000, were previously taken into account for purposes of applying the nonduplication rule of section 3121(v)(2)(B), any amount that would have been required to have been taken into account before 1994 will be treated as if it had been taken into account within the meaning of paragraph (d)(1) of this section. Under the nonduplication rule, benefit payments attributable to an amount that has been so treated as taken into account is not treated as wages for FICA tax purposes at any later time (such as upon payment).

(iii) Because Employer Q does not adjust its FICA tax determination by treating this section as in effect for all amounts deferred for periods ending after December 31, 1993, any benefit payments attributable to amounts deferred in periods ending after December 31, 1993, will be included in wages when actually or constructively paid in accordance with the general timing rule of paragraph (a)(1) of this section.

*Example 6.* (i) The facts are the same as in *Example 5*, except that Employer Q chooses (in accordance with paragraph (g)(3) of this section) to adjust its FICA tax determination for all pre-effective-date open periods by treating this section as in effect for all amounts deferred for those periods. In addition, Employer Q chooses (in accordance with paragraph (g)(4)(ii)(E) of this section) to take the amounts deferred for 1994 and 1995 into account by treating these amounts as FICA wages paid and received by Employee E on January 15, 2000.

(ii) In accordance with the nonduplication rule of paragraph (a)(2)(iii) of this section, because all amounts deferred for Employee E under the plan were taken into account (or treated as taken into account), any benefit payments made to Employee E under the plan will not be included as FICA wages when actually or constructively paid.

*Example 7.* (i) The facts are the same as in *Example 5*, except that Employer Q does not withhold and deposit the FICA tax due on benefits actually or constructively paid before January 1, 2000.

(ii) Because Employer Q did not withhold and deposit the FICA tax due on benefits actually or constructively paid before January 1, 2000, Employer Q did not determine FICA tax liability and satisfy FICA tax withholding requirements in accordance with a reasonable, good faith interpretation of section 3121(v)(2). Thus, the transition rules provided in paragraphs (g)(3) and (4) of this section do not apply. As a result, any amount that would have been required to have been taken into account under this section before 1994 is not treated as if it had been so taken into account under paragraph (g)(4)(ii)(D) of this section, and benefit payments attributable to amounts deferred before January 1, 2000, are treated as FICA wages when actually or constructively paid in accordance with the general timing rule of paragraph (a)(1) of this section.

*Example 8.* (i) In 1993, Employer R establishes a nonqualified deferred compensation plan for Employee F under which Employee F will have a fully vested right to receive a lump sum payment in 2000 equal to 50 percent of Employee F's highest rate of salary. On December 31, 1993, Employee F's highest salary is $1 million. In accordance with a reasonable, good faith interpretation of section 3121(v)(2), Employer R determines that, for 1993, there is an amount deferred that must be taken into account as wages for FICA tax purposes. Based on Employer R's estimate that Employee F's highest salary will be $3 million in 2000, Employer R determines that the amount deferred is equal to the present value in 1993 of $1.5 million payable in 2000. However, because Employee F has other wages in 1993 that exceed the applicable OASDI and HI wage bases for that year, no additional FICA tax is paid as a result of that amount deferred being taken into account for 1993. In addition, Employer R takes no amounts into account under the plan after 1993 for Employee F. Under paragraphs (e)(1) and (4)(ii)(D)(2) of this section, the largest amount that could have been taken into account in 1993 is the present value of a lump sum payment of $500,000, payable in 2000, because that is the maximum amount to which Employee F has a legally binding right as of December 31, 1993. Employee F's highest salary is, in fact, $3 million in 2000 and Employee F receives $1.5 million under the plan on December 31, 2000.

(ii) In accordance with paragraphs (g)(1) and (4)(iii)(A) of this section, the determination of the amount deferred under the plan for any period beginning on or after January 1, 2000, and the time when that amount deferred is required to be taken into account must be determined in accordance with this section. In addition, these determinations must be made without regard to any amount deferred that was taken into account for any period ending before January 1, 2000, that could not be taken into account before January 1, 2000, if paragraphs (a) through (f) of this section had been in effect. Because no FICA tax was actually paid on that $1 million in 1993, no overpayment of tax was caused by the overinclusion of wages in 1993 and, thus, Employer R is not entitled to a refund or credit (even assuming that the period of limitations has been kept open for periods in 1993). In addition, because the difference between the present value of the $1.5 million payment and the present value of a $500,000 payment was not taken into account for periods beginning on or after January 1, 1994, $1 million must be included in FICA wages under the general timing rule when paid.

[Reg. § 31.3121(v)(2)-1.]

☐ [T.D. 8814, 1-28-99 (corrected 3-31-99).]

### [Reg. § 31.3121(v)(2)-2]

**§ 31.3121(v)(2)-2. Effective dates and transition rules.**—
(a) *General statutory effective date.*—Except as otherwise provided in paragraphs (b) through (e) of this section, section 3121(v)(2) and the amendments made to section 3121(a)(2), (a)(3), and (a)(13) by the Social Security Amendments of 1983 (Public Law 98-21, 97 Stat. 65), as amended by section 2662(f)(2) of the Deficit Reduction Act of 1984 (Public Law 98-369, 98 Stat. 494), apply to amounts deferred and benefits paid after December 31, 1983.

(b) *Definitions.*—For purposes of § 31.3121(v)(2)-1 and this section, the following definitions apply:

(1) *FICA.*—FICA means the Federal Insurance Contributions Act (26 U.S.C. 3101 et seq.).

(2) *457(a) plan.*—A *457(a) plan* means an eligible deferred compensation plan of a State or local government or of a tax-exempt organization to which section 457(a) applies.

(3) *Gap agreement.*—*Gap agreement* means an agreement adopted after March 24, 1983, and on or before December 31, 1983, between an individual and a nonqualified deferred compensation plan within the meaning of § 31.3121(v)(2)-1(b). Such an agreement does not fail to be a gap agreement merely because the terms of the plan are changed after December 31, 1983.

(4) *Individual party to a gap agreement.*—*Individual party to a gap agreement* means an individual who was eligible to participate in a gap agreement on December 31, 1983, under the terms of the agreement on that date. An individual will be treated as an individual party to a gap agreement even if the individual has not accrued any benefits under the plan by December 31, 1983, and regardless of whether the individual has taken any specific action to become a party to the agreement. However, an individual who becomes eligible to participate in a gap agreement after December 31, 1983, is not an individual party to a gap agreement.

(5) *Individual party to a March 24, 1983 agreement.*—*Individual party to a March 24, 1983 agreement* means an individual who was eligible to participate in a March 24, 1983 agreement under the terms of the agreement on March 24, 1983. An individual will be treated as an individual party to a March 24, 1983 agreement even if the individual has not accrued any benefits under the plan by March 24, 1983, and regardless of whether the individual has taken any specific action to become a party to the agreement. However, an individual who becomes eligible to participate in a March 24, 1983 agreement after March 24, 1983, is not an individual party to a March 24, 1983 agreement.

(6) *March 24, 1983 agreement.*—*March 24, 1983 agreement* means an agreement in existence on March 24, 1983, between an individual and a nonqualified deferred compensation plan within the meaning of § 31.3121(v)(2)-1(b). Such an agreement does not fail to be a March 24, 1983 agreement merely because the terms of the plan are changed after March 24, 1983. In addition, for purposes of this paragraph (b)(6) only, any plan (or agreement) that provides for payments that qualify for one of the retirement payment exclusions is treated as a nonqualified deferred compensation plan. For example, § 31.3121(v)(2)-1(b)(4)(v) provides that certain benefits established in connection with impending termination do not result from the deferral of compensation and thus are not considered deferred under a nonqualified deferred compensation plan. However, a plan that provides such benefits and that was in existence on March 24, 1983, is treated as a nonqualified deferred compensation plan for purposes of this paragraph (b) to the extent it provides benefits that would have satisfied one of the retirement payment exclusions.

(7) *Retirement payment exclusions.*—*Retirement payment exclusions* are the exclusions from wages (for FICA tax purposes) for retirement payments under section 3121(a)(2)(A), (a)(3), and (a)(13)(A)(iii), as in effect on April 19, 1983 (the day before enactment of the Social Security Amendments of 1983).

(8) *Transition benefits.*—*Transition benefits* are payments made after December 31, 1983, attributable to services rendered before January 1, 1984. For this purpose, transition benefits are determined without regard to any changes made in the terms of the plan after March 24, 1983, in the case of a March 24, 1983 agreement or after December 31, 1983, in the case of a gap agreement.

(c) *Transition rules.*—(1) *In general.*—Except as provided in paragraph (c)(2) or (3) of this section, the general statutory effective date described in paragraph (a) of this section applies to benefit payments after December 31, 1983. Thus, except as provided in paragraph (c)(2) or (3) of this section, section 3121(v)(2) applies, and the retirement payment exclusions do not apply, to benefit payments made after December 31, 1983, even if the benefit payments are made under a March 24, 1983 agreement or a gap agreement.

(2) *Transition benefits under a March 24, 1983 agreement.*—With respect to an individual party to a March 24, 1983 agreement, transition benefits paid under that March 24, 1983 agreement (except for those paid under a 457(a) plan) are not subject to the special timing rule of section 3121(v)(2) and are subject to section 3121(a) as in effect on April 19, 1983. Thus, transition benefits under a March 24, 1983 agreement (except for those under a 457(a) plan) to an individual party to a March 24, 1983 agreement are excluded from wages (for FICA tax purposes) only if they qualify for any of the retirement payment exclusions (or any other exclusion provided under section 3121(a) as in effect on April 19, 1983).

(3) *Transition benefits under a gap agreement.*—With respect to an individual party to a gap agreement, the payor of transition benefits under the gap agreement must choose to either—

(i) Take the transition benefits into account as wages when paid; or

(ii) Take the amount deferred (within the meaning of § 31.3121(v)(2)-1(c)) with respect to the transition benefits into account as wages under section 3121(v)(2) (as if section 3121(v)(2) had applied before its general statutory effective date).

(d) *Determining transition benefit portion.*—For purposes of determining the portion of total benefits under a nonqualified deferred compensation plan that represents transition benefits, if, under the terms of the plan, benefit payments are not attributed to specific years of service, the employer may use any reasonable method. For example, if a plan provides that the employee will receive benefits equal to 2 percent of high 3-year average compensation multiplied by years of service, and the employee retires after 25 years of service, 9 of which are before 1984, the employer may determine that 9/25 of the total benefit payments to be received beginning in 2000 are transition benefits attributable to services performed before 1984.

(e) *Order of payment.*—If an employer determines, in accordance with paragraph (d) of this section, that a portion of the total benefits under a nonqualified deferred compensation plan constitutes transition benefits, then, for purposes of determining the portion of each benefit payment that constitutes transition benefits, the employer must treat each benefit payment as consisting of transition benefits in the same proportion as the transition benefits that have not been paid (as of January 1, 2000) bear to total benefits that have not been paid (as of January 1, 2000), unless such allocation is inconsistent with the terms of the plan. However, for a benefit payment made before January 1, 2000, the employer may use any reasonable allocation method to determine the portion of a payment that consists of transition benefits, provided that the allocation method is consistent with the terms of the plan. [Reg. § 31.3121(v)(2)-2.]

☐ [*T.D.* 8814, 1-28-99.]

#### [Reg. § 31.3123-1]

**§ 31.3123-1. Deductions by an employer from remuneration of an employee.**—Any amount deducted by an employer from the remuneration of an employee is considered to be part of the employee's remuneration and is considered to be paid to the employee as remuneration at the time that the deduction is made. It is immaterial that any act of Congress or the law of any State requires or permits such deductions and the payment of the amount thereof to the United States, a State, or any political subdivision thereof. [Reg. § 31.3123-1.]

☐ [*T.D.* 6190, 7-14-56. *Republished in T.D.* 6516, 12-20-60.]

#### [Reg. § 31.3127-1]

**§ 31.3127-1. Exemption for employers and their employees if both are members of religious faiths opposed to participation in Social Security Act programs.**—(a) *Exemption.*—(1) *Employer.*—Except as provided in paragraph (b) of this section, an employer is exempt from the taxes imposed by section 3111 on wages paid to an employee if—

(i) The employer (or if the employer is a partnership, each partner therein) and its employee are members of a recognized religious sect or division described in section 1402(g)(1);

(ii) Both the employer (or if the employer is a partnership, each partner therein) and the employee adhere to the tenets and teachings of that sect; and

(iii) Both the employer and the employee have filed and had approved applications under section 3127(b) for exemption from the taxes imposed by sections 3111 and 3101.

(2) *Employee.*—If an employer is exempt from the taxes imposed by section 3111 under paragraph (a)(1) of this section, then each employee described in paragraph (a)(1) of this section is exempt from the taxes imposed by section 3101 on the wages received with respect to employment with that employer.

(b) *Corporation.*—Services performed in the employ of a corporation are not within the exemption described in paragraph (a) of this section, except that services performed in the employ of an entity that is treated as a corporation under § 301.7701-2(c)(2)(iv)(B) of this chapter may qualify for the exemption if the requirements of the exemption are otherwise met. An entity that is treated as a corporation under § 301.7701-2(c)(2)(iv)(B) of this chapter is not treated as the employer for purposes of applying section 3127 and this section. For purposes of applying section 3127 and paragraph (a) of this section, the owner of an entity that is treated as a corporation under § 301.7701-2(c)(2)(iv)(B) of this chapter is treated as the employer.

(c) *Effective/applicability date.*—This section applies to wages paid on or after November 1, 2011. However, taxpayers may apply this section to wages paid on or after January 1, 2009. [Reg. § 31.3127-1.]

☐ [*T.D.* 9670, 6-25-2014.]

# Railroad Retirement Tax Act

## TAX ON EMPLOYEES

See p. 20,601 for regulations not amended to reflect law changes

#### [Reg. § 31.3201-1]

**§ 31.3201-1. Measure of employee tax.**—The employee tax is measured by the amount of compensation received for services rendered as an employee. For provisions relating to compensation, see § 31.3231(e)-1. For provisions relating to the circumstances under which certain compensation is to be disregarded for the purpose of determining the employee tax, see paragraphs (b)(1) and (2) of § 31.3231(e)-1. [Reg. § 31.3201-1.]

☐ [*T.D.* 8582, 12-23-94.]

#### [Reg. § 31.3201-2]

**§ 31.3201-2. Rates and computation of employee tax.**—(a) *Rates.*—(1)(i) *Tier 1 tax.*—The Tier 1 employee tax rate equals the sum of the tax rates in effect under section 3101(a) relating to old-age, survivors, and disability insurance, and section 3101(b), relating to hospital insurance. The Tier 1 employee tax rate is applied to compensation up to the contribution base described in section 3231(e)(2)(B)(i). The contribution base is determined under section 230 of the Social Security Act and is identical to the old-age, survivors, and disability insurance wage base and the hospital insurance wage base, respectively, under the Federal Insurance Contributions Act.

(ii) *Example.*—The rule in paragraph (a)(1)(i) of this section is illustrated by the following example.

*Example.* A received compensation of $60,000 in 1992. The section 3101(a) rate of 6.2 percent would be applied to A's compensation up to $55,500, the applicable contribution base for 1992. The section 3101(b) rate of 1.45 percent would be applied to the entire $60,000 of A's compensation because the applicable contribution base for 1992 is $130,200.

(2)(i) *Tier 2 tax.*—The Tier 2 employee tax rate equals the percentage set forth in section 3201(b) of the Code. This rate is applied to compensation up to the contribution base described in section 3231(e)(2)(B)(ii).

(ii) *Example.*—The rule in paragraph (a)(2)(i) of this section is illustrated by the following example.

*Example.* A received compensation of $60,000 in 1992. The section 3201(b) rate of 4.90 percent would be applied to A's compensation up to $41,400, the applicable contribution base for 1992.

(b)(1) *Computation.*—The employee tax is computed by multiplying the amount of the employee's compensation with respect to which the employee tax is imposed by the rate applicable to such compensation, as determined under paragraph (a) of this section. The applicable rate is the rate in effect when the compensation is received by the employee. For rules relating to the time of receipt, see § 31.3121(a)-2 (a) and (b).

(2) *Example.*—The rule in paragraph (b)(1) of this section is illustrated by the following example.

*Example.* In 1990, employee A received compensation of $1,000 as remuneration for services performed for employer R in 1989. The employee tax is payable at the rate of 12.55 percent (7.65 percent plus 4.90 percent) in effect for 1990 (the year the compensation was received), and not the 12.41 percent rate (7.51 percent plus 4.90 percent) in effect for 1989 (the year the services were performed). [Reg. § 31.3201-2.]

☐ [*T.D.* 8582, 12-23-94.]

#### [Reg. § 31.3202-1]

**§ 31.3202-1. Collection of, and liability for, employee tax.**—(a) *Collection; general rule.*—The employer shall collect from each of his employees the employee tax imposed with respect to the compensation of the employee by deducting or causing to be deducted the amount of such tax from the compensation subject to the tax as and when such compensation is paid. As to the measure of the employee tax, see § 31.3201-1.

(b) *Collection; payments by two or more employers in excess of annual compensation limitation.*—For rules relating to payments by two or more employers in excess of the annual compensation limitation see § 31.3121(a)(1)-1.

(c) *Undercollections or overcollections.*—Any undercollection or overcollection of employee tax resulting from the employer's inability to determine, at the time compensation is paid, the correct amount of compensation with respect to which the deduction should be made shall be corrected in accordance with the provisions of Subpart G of the regulations in this part relating to adjustments, credits, refunds, and abatements.

(d) *When fractional part of cent may be disregarded.*—In collecting the employee tax, the employer shall disregard any fractional part of a cent of such tax unless it amounts to one-half cent or more, in which case it shall be increased to one cent.

(e) *Employer's liability.*—The employer is liable for the employee tax with respect to compensation paid by him, whether or not collected from the employee. If the employer deducts less than the correct amount of employee tax or fails to deduct any part of the tax, he is nevertheless liable for the correct amount of the tax. Until collected from him, the employee is also liable for the employee tax. Any employee tax collected by or on behalf of an employer is a special fund in trust for the United States. See section 7501. An employer is not liable to any person for the amount of the employee tax deducted by him and paid to the district director.

(f) *Concurrent employment.*—If two or more related corporations who are rail employers concurrently employ the same individual and compensate that individual through a common paymaster, which is one of the related corporations employing the individual, see § 31.3121(s)-1.

(g) *Special rules regarding Additional Medicare Tax.*—(1) An employer is required to collect from each of its employees the portion of the tax imposed by section 3201(a) (as calculated under section 3101(b)(2)) (Additional Medicare Tax) with respect to compensation for employment performed for the employer by the employee only to the extent the employer pays compensation to the employee in excess of $200,000 in a calendar year. This rule applies regardless of the employee's filing status or other income. Thus, the employer disregards any amount of compensation or Federal Insurance Contributions Act (FICA) wages paid to the employee's spouse. The employer also disregards any FICA wages paid by the employer to the employee or any compensation or FICA wages paid to the employee by another employer.

*Example.* A, who is married and files a joint return, receives $100,000 in compensation from her employer for the calendar year. B, A's spouse, receives $300,000 in compensation from his employer for the same calendar year. A's compensation is not in excess of $200,000, so A's employer does not withhold Additional Medicare Tax. B's employer is required to collect Additional Medicare Tax only with respect to compensation it pays to B that is in excess of the $200,000 threshold (that is, $100,000) for the calendar year.

(2) To the extent the employer does not collect Additional Medicare Tax imposed on the employee by section 3201(a) (as calculated under section 3101(b)(2)), the employee is liable to pay the tax.

*Example.* C, who is married and files a joint return, receives $190,000 in compensation from her employer for the calendar year. D, C's spouse, receives $150,000 in compensation from his employer for the same calendar year. Neither C's nor D's compensation is in excess of $200,000, so neither C's nor D's employers are required to withhold Additional Medicare Tax. C and D are liable to pay Additional Medicare Tax on $90,000 ($340,000 minus the $250,000 threshold for a joint return).

(3) If the employer deducts less than the correct amount of Additional Medicare Tax, or if it fails to deduct any part of Additional Medicare Tax, it is nevertheless liable for the correct amount of tax that it was required to withhold, unless and until the employee pays the tax. If an employee subsequently pays the tax that the employer failed to deduct, the tax will not be collected from the employer. The employer will not be relieved of its liability for payment of the tax required to be withheld unless it can show that the tax under section 3201(a) (as calculated under section 3101(b)(2)) has been paid. The employer, however, will remain subject to any applicable penalties or additions to tax resulting from the failure to withhold as required.

(h) *Effective/applicability date.*—Paragraph (g) of this section applies to quarters beginning on or after November 29, 2013. [Reg. § 31.3202-1.]

□ [*T.D.* 6516, 12-20-60. *Amended by T.D.* 6541, 1-20-61; *T.D.* 6727, 5-5-64; *T.D.* 8582, 12-23-94 *and T.D.* 9645, 11-26-2013.]

# TAX ON EMPLOYEE REPRESENTATIVES

**[Reg. § 31.3211-1]**

**§ 31.3211-1. Measure of employee representative tax.**—The employee representative tax is measured by the amount of compensation received for services rendered as an employee representative. For provisions relating to compensation, see § 31.3231(e)-1. [Reg. § 31.3211-1.]

□ [*T.D.* 8582, 12-23-94.]

**[Reg. § 31.3211-2]**

**§ 31.3211-2. Rates and computation of employee representative tax.**—(a) *Rates.*—(1)(i) *Tier 1 tax.*—The Tier 1 employee representative tax rate equals the sum of the tax rates in effect under sections 3101(a) and 3111(a), relating to the employee and the employer tax for old-age, survivors, and disability insurance, and sections 3101(b) and 3111(b), relating to the employee and the employer tax for hospital insurance. The Tier 1 employee representative tax rate is applied to compensation up to the contribution base described in section 3231(e)(2)(B)(i). The contribution base is determined under section 230 of the Social Security Act, and is identical to the old-age, survivors, and disability insurance wage base and the hospital insurance wage base, respectively, under the Federal Insurance Contributions Act.

(ii) *Example.*—The rule in paragraph (a)(1)(i) of this section is illustrated by the following example.

*Example.* B, an employee representative received compensation of $60,000 in 1992. The sections 3101(a) and 3111(a) rates of 12.4 percent (6.2 percent plus 6.2 percent) would be applied to B's compensation up to $55,500, the applicable contribution base for 1992. The sections 3101(b) and 3111(b) rates of 2.9 percent (1.45 percent plus 1.45 percent) would be applied to the entire $60,000 of B's compensation because the applicable contribution base for 1992 is $130,200.

(2)(i) *Tier 2 tax.*—The Tier 2 employee representative tax rate equals the percentage set forth in section 3211(a)(2) of the Code. This rate is applied up to the contribution base described in section 3231(e)(2)(B)(ii).

(ii) *Example.*—The rule in paragraph (a)(2)(i) of this section is illustrated by the following example.

*Example.* B received compensation of $60,000 in 1992. The section 3211(a)(2) rate of 14.75 percent would be applied to B's compensation up to $41,400, the applicable contribution base for 1992.

(3) *Supplemental annuity tax.*—The supplemental annuity tax for each work-hour for which compensation is paid to an employee representative for services rendered as an employee representative is imposed at the same rate as the excise tax imposed on every employer under section 3221(c). See also § 31.3211-3.

(b)(1) *Computation.*—The employee representative tax is computed by multiplying the amount of the employee representative's compensation with respect to which the employee representative tax is imposed by the rate applicable to such compensation, as determined under paragraph (a) of this section. The applicable rate is the rate in effect when the compensation is received by the employee representative. For rules relating to the time of receipt, see § 31.3121(a)-2 (a) and (b).

(2) *Example.*—The rule in paragraph (b)(1) of this section is illustrated by the following example.

*Example.* In 1990, employee representative B received $1,000 as remuneration for services performed for employer R in 1989. The employee representative tax is payable at the rate of 30.05 percent (15.30 percent plus 14.75 percent) in effect for 1990 (the year the compensation was received), and not the 29.77 percent rate (15.02 percent plus 14.75 percent) in effect for 1989 (the year the services were performed).

(c)(1) *Rule where compensation is received both as an employee representative and employee.*—The following rule applies to an individual who renders service both as an employee representative and as an employee. The employee representative tax is imposed on compensation received as an employee representative under the rules described in § 31.3211-2. The employee tax is imposed on compensation received as an employee under the rules described in § 31.3201-2. However, if the total compensation received is greater than the applicable contribution base, the employee representative tax is imposed on the amount equal to the contribution base less the amount received for services rendered as an employee.

(2) *Example.*—The rule in paragraph (c)(1) of this section is illustrated by the following example.

*Example.* C performed services both as an employee and an employee representative in 1992. C received compensation of $40,000 as an employee and $20,000 as an employee representative. C's entire compensation of $40,000 is subject to tax under the rules described in § 31.3201-2. The amount of employee representative compensation subject to the section 3101(a) and the section 3111(a) rate is $15,500 ($55,500 − $40,000). The entire $20,000 is subject to the sections 3101(b) and 3111(b) rates since the combined compensation is less

than $130,200, the applicable contribution base for 1992. The amount of the employee representative compensation subject to the section 3211(a)(2) rate is $1,400 ($41,400 – $40,000).
[Reg. § 31.3211-2.]

☐ [*T.D.* 8582, 12-23-94.]

### [Reg. § 31.3211-3]

**§ 31.3211-3. Employee representative supplemental tax.**—See paragraphs (a), (b), and (c) of § 31.3221-3 for rules applicable to the supplemental tax for each work-hour for which compensation is paid to an employee representative for services rendered as an employee representative. [Reg. § 31.3211-3.]

☐ [*T.D.* 8525, 3-1-94.]

### [Reg. § 31.3212-1]

**§ 31.3212-1. Determination of compensation.**—See § 31.3231(e)-1 for regulations applicable to compensation. [Reg. § 31.3212-1.]

# TAX ON EMPLOYERS

### [Reg. § 31.3221-1]

**§ 31.3221-1. Measure of employer tax.**—(a) *General rule.*—The employer tax is measured by the amount of compensation paid by an employer to its employees. For provisions relating to compensation, see § 31.3231(e)-1. For provisions relating to the circumstances under which certain compensation is to be disregarded for purposes of determining the employer tax, see paragraphs (b) (1) and (2) of § 31.3231(e)-1.

(b) *Payments by two or more employers in excess of annual compensation limitation.*—For rules relating to payments by two or more employers in excess of the annual compensation limitation, see § 31.3121(a)(1)-1.

(c) *Underpayments or overpayments.*—Any underpayment or overpayment of employer tax resulting from the employer's inability to determine, at the time such tax is paid, the correct amount of compensation with respect to which the tax should be paid shall be corrected in accordance with the provisions of Subpart G of the regulations in this part relating to adjustments, credits, refunds, and abatements. [Reg. § 31.3221-1.]

☐ [*T.D.* 6516, 12-20-60. *Amended by T.D.* 6541, 1-20-61 *and T.D.* 8582, 12-23-94.]

### [Reg. § 31.3221-2]

**§ 31.3221-2. Rates and computation of employer tax.**—(a) *Rates.*—(1)(i) *Tier 1 tax.*—The Tier 1 employer tax rate equals the sum of the tax rates in effect under section 3111(a), relating to old-age, survivors, and disability insurance, and section 3111(b) relating to hospital insurance. The Tier 1 employer tax rate is applied to compensation up to the contribution base described in section 3231(e)(2)(B)(i). The contribution base is determined under section 230 of the Social Security Act and is identical to the old-age, survivors, and disability insurance wage base and the hospital insurance wage base, respectively, under the Federal Insurance Contributions Act.

(ii) *Example.*—The rule in paragraph (a)(1)(i) of this section is illustrated by the following example.

*Example.* R's employee, A, received compensation of $60,000 in 1992. The section 3111(a) rate of 6.2 percent would be applied to A's compensation up to $55,500, the applicable contribution base for 1992. The section 3111(b) rate of 1.45 percent would be applied to the entire $60,000 of A's compensation because the applicable contribution base for 1992 is $130,200.

(2)(i) *Tier 2 tax.*—The Tier 2 employer tax rate equals the percentage set forth in section 3221(b) of the Internal Revenue Code. This rate is applied up to the contribution base described in section 3231(e)(2)(B)(ii).

(ii) *Example.*—The rule in paragraph (a)(2)(i) of this section is illustrated by the following example.

*Example.* R's employee, A, received compensation of $60,000 in 1992. The section 3221(b) rate of 16.10 percent would be applied to A's compensation up to $41,400, the applicable contribution base for 1992.

(3) *Supplemental annuity tax.*—The supplemental annuity tax for each work-hour for which compensation is paid by an employer for services rendered during any calendar quarter by employees is imposed at the tax rate determined each calendar quarter by the Railroad Retirement Board. See also § 31.3221-3.

(b)(1) *Computation.*—The employer tax is computed by multiplying the amount of the compensation with respect to which the employer tax is imposed by the rate applicable to such compensation, as determined under paragraph (a) of this section. The applicable rate is the rate in effect at the time the compensation is paid. For rules relating to the time of payment, see § 31.3121(a)-2(a) and (b).

(2) *Example.*—The rule in paragraph (b)(1) of this section is illustrated by the following example.

*Example.* In 1990, R's employee A received $1,000 as remuneration for services performed for R in 1989. The employer tax is payable at the rate of 23.75 percent (7.65 percent plus 16.10 percent) in effect for 1990 (the year the compensation was received) and not the 23.61 percent rate (7.51 percent plus 16.10 percent) in effect for 1989 (the year the services were performed).
[Reg. § 31.3221-2.]

☐ [*T.D.* 8582, 12-23-94.]

### [Reg. § 31.3221-3]

**§ 31.3221-3. Supplemental tax.**—(a) *Introduction.*—(1) *In general.*—Section 3221(c) imposes an excise tax on every employer, as defined in section 3231(a) and § 31.3231(a)-1, with respect to individuals employed by the employer. The tax is imposed for each work-hour for which the employer pays compensation, as defined in section 3231(e) and § 31.3231(e)-1, for services rendered to the employer during a calendar quarter. This § 31.3221-3 provides rules for determining the number of taxable work-hours.

(2) *Overview.*—Paragraph (b) of this section defines *work-hours.* Paragraph (c) of this section demonstrates the calculation of work-hours. Paragraph (d) of this section offers a safe harbor calculation of work-hours for use by any employer in lieu of calculating the number of work-hours for each employee.

(b) *Definition of work-hours.*—(1) *In general.*—For purposes of section 3221(c) and this section, *work-hours* are hours for which the employee is compensated, whether or not the employee performs services.

(i) *Payments included in work-hours.*—Work-hours include regular time worked; overtime; time paid for vacations and holidays; time allowed for meals; away-from-home terminal time; called and not used, runaround, and deadheading time; time for attending court, participating in investigations, and attending claim and safety meetings; and guaranteed time not worked. Work-hours also include conversion hours, that is, compensation converted into work-hours. Conversion hours may be derived from payment by the mile or by the piece. Work-hours also include time for which the employee is paid for periods of absence not due to sickness or accident disability, such as for routine medical and dental examinations or for time lost.

(ii) *Payments excluded from work-hours.*—Certain kinds of payments are not subject to conversion into work-hours. These include those payments that are specifically excluded from compensation within the meaning of section 3231(e), such as certain sick pay payments (section 3231(e)(1)(i)); tips (section 3231(e)(1)(ii)); and amounts paid specifically (either as an advance, as reimbursement, or allowance) for traveling expenses (section 3231(e)(1)(iii)). Traveling expenses paid under a nonaccountable plan are excluded from work-hours even though they are includible in compensation. See § 31.3231(e)-1(a)(5). Also excluded from work-hours are amounts representing bonuses, amounts received pursuant to the exercise of an employee stock option, and all separation payments or severance allowances.

(2) *Hourly compensation.*—Because the tax under section 3221(c) is calculated on the basis of work-hours, the number of hours for which an employee receives compensation is the figure used to determine work-hours. In the case of an hourly-rated employee, each hour for which the employee receives compensation is one work-hour.

(3) *Daily, weekly, monthly compensation.*—(i) If an employee is paid by the day, week, month, or other period of time, the tax is imposed on the number of hours comprehended in the rate and, if any, the number of overtime hours for which additional compensation is paid. Thus, in the case of an office worker who receives an annual salary based on an 8-hour, 5-day-a-week work schedule that

includes paid holidays, vacations, and sick time, the number of work-hours for one month is 174 (2088 hours/year ÷ 12 months).

(ii) The rule in paragraph (b)(3)(i) of this section is illustrated by the following examples.

*Example 1.* A, an office worker, receives an annual salary that is paid monthly. The salary is based on an 8-hour, Monday through Friday work schedule. A is not paid for overtime hours. A is not expected to work on holidays, during A's annual vacation, or during periods that A is ill. The number of work-hours for one month is 174 (2088 hours/year ÷ 12 months). This figure remains constant, even though some months have more workdays than others.

*Example 2.* B is paid a stated amount for each day B works, regardless of the number of hours worked. However, if B works more than 8 hours during any day, B is paid overtime for each additional hour worked that day. B is not paid for holidays, vacations, or sick time. During May, B worked 6 hours on 4 days, 7 hours on 6 days, 8 hours on 6 days, and 9 hours on 5 days. Because B is paid a daily rate for up to 8 hours, 8 hours are comprehended in the daily rate. Therefore, the number of work-hours for May is 173 (21 days × 8 hours/day + 5 overtime hours), even though B actually worked 159 hours.

(4) *Conversion hours.*—(i) Compensation not based on time (hour, day, month, etc.), such as compensation paid by the mile or by the piece, must be converted into the number of hours represented by the compensation paid. Thus, if an employee is paid by the mile, 1 work-hour equals the number of miles constituting a workday, divided by 8 hours. However, in the case of a collective bargaining agreement that specifies a number of hours as constituting a workday, the number of hours specified under the agreement may be used instead of 8.

(ii) The rule in paragraph (b)(4)(i) of this section is illustrated by the following example.

*Example.* C's normal workday consists of 2 150-mile round trips that together take 6 hours. C is paid by the mile. The collective bargaining agreement does not specify the number of hours in a workday. Thus, the number of work-hours for each day C works is 8, or 1 work-hour for each 37.5 miles (300 miles/day ÷ 8 hours/day)). If the applicable collective bargaining agreement specifies that 6 hours constitute a workday, the number of work-hours for each day C works would be 6.

(c) *Calculation of work-hours.*—(1) An employer may calculate the work-hours separately for each employee, as described in the examples in this paragraph. If the employer chooses to calculate work-hours separately for each employee, the employer must calculate the number of regular hours, overtime hours, and conversion hours for each employee for each month. In lieu of separate calculations, the employer may calculate the work-hours for all the employer's employees using the safe harbor formula described in paragraph (d) of this section.

(2) The rules in paragraph (c) of this section are illustrated by the following examples.

*Example 1.* D worked 8 hours a day, Monday through Friday, during the months of February and March 1992. D did not work on President's Day, but was paid for the holiday. D's work-hours for February were 160 (19 days × 8 hours a day + 8 holiday hours). D's work-hours for March were 176 (22 days × 8 hours a day).

*Example 2.* E worked 7-hour shifts every Tuesday through Saturday during the months of February and March 1992. E also worked 7 overtime hours during February and 21 overtime hours during March. Also, E was paid for 7 hours on President's Day, even though E did not work on that day. The number of work-hours for February was 161 (21 days × 7 hours a day + 7 overtime hours + 7 holiday hours). The number of work-hours for March was 168 (21 days × 7 hours a day + 21 overtime hours). Because E receives an hourly wage and was paid for the President's Day holiday, the number of hours (7) for which E was paid are added to the hours E actually worked. If E had worked on President's Day and had received extra pay for working on a holiday and holiday pay for 7 hours, the employer would include 14 hours in E's work-hours for that day, the 7 hours E actually worked and the 7 holiday hours for which E was paid.

*Example 3.* Employment beginning during month. F began employment on March 16, a Monday, and worked 8 hours a day, Monday through Friday. The employer calculates that F's hours for the month were 96, because F worked 12 8-hour days during the month. If March 16 were on a Friday, the employer would calculate 11 days, or 88 hours.

*Example 4.* Employment ending during month. G's last day of employment was Friday, March 13. G worked 8 hours a day, Monday through Friday, except for March 3, when G was ill. G was paid for 8 hours for March 3. The employer calculates that G's work-hours for March were 80, because G worked 9 8-hour days and was paid for an additional 8 hours.

(d) *Safe harbor.*—(1) *In general.*—In lieu of calculating work-hours separately for each employee, an employer may use the safe harbor for all employees. If the employer elects to use the safe harbor for a calendar year, the employer must use the safe harbor for all employees for the entire calendar year. If an employer uses the safe harbor for a calendar year, the employer need not elect the safe harbor for the following calendar year. An employer that elects the safe harbor for a calendar year may not subsequently elect to separately calculate employee work-hours for that calendar year.

(2) *Method of calculation.*—The safe harbor treats each employee of the employer as receiving monthly compensation for a number of hours equal to the safe harbor number. To determine the number of work-hours for a month, the employer multiplies the safe harbor number by the number that equals the total number of employees to whom the employer paid compensation during the month.

(i) *Safe harbor number defined.*—The safe harbor number is the number established in guidance of general applicability promulgated by the Commissioner.

(ii) *Employee defined.*—Solely for purposes of this paragraph, an employee is any individual who is paid compensation, within the meaning of §31.3231(e)-1, regardless of the amount, during the month. Thus, for example, a part-time, temporary, or seasonal employee is counted as an employee. A terminated employee is counted in the month of termination (provided the terminated employee received compensation in the month of termination), but not in any subsequent month in which the employee does not perform service for the employer as an employee, even if the terminated employee is paid compensation in a subsequent month. Thus, for example, an employee who terminates employment during the month, receives compensation during the month of termination, and receives a final paycheck the following month is counted as an employee of the employer for the month of termination but not for the following month.

(3) *Method of election.*—An employer makes the safe harbor election for a calendar year on the employment tax return filed for the previous calendar year.

(4) *Additional rules.*—The Commissioner may, in revenue procedures, revenue rulings, notices, or other guidance of general applicability, revise the safe harbor number or provide additional safe harbors that satisfy section 3221(c).

(e) *Effective dates.*—This §31.3221-3 is effective for calendar years beginning after December 31, 1992, except that paragraph (d) is effective for calendar years beginning after December 31, 1993. Taxpayers may apply the rules in paragraphs (a), (b), and (c) of this section before January 1, 1993. [Reg. §31.3221-3.]

☐ [T.D. 8525, 3-1-94.]

**[Reg. §31.3221-4]**

**§31.3221-4. Exception from supplemental tax.**—(a) *General rule.*—Section 3221(d) provides an exception from the excise tax imposed by section 3221(c). Under this exception, the excise tax imposed by section 3221(c) does not apply to an employer with respect to employees who are covered by a supplemental pension plan, as defined in paragraph (b) of this section, that is established pursuant to an agreement reached through collective bargaining between the employer and employees, within the meaning of paragraph (c) of this section.

(b) *Definition of supplemental pension plan.*—(1) *In general.*—A plan is a supplemental pension plan covered by the section 3221(d) exception described in paragraph (a) of this section only if it meets the requirements of paragraphs (b)(2) through (b)(4) of this section.

(2) *Pension benefit requirement.*—A plan is a supplemental pension plan within the meaning of this section only if the plan is a pension plan within the meaning of §1.401-1(b)(1)(i) of this chapter. Thus, a plan is a supplemental pension plan only if the plan provides for the payment of definitely determinable benefits to employees over a period of years, usually for life, after retirement. A plan need not be funded through a qualified trust that meets the requirements of section 401(a) or an annuity contract that meets the requirements of section 403(a) in order to meet the requirements of this paragraph (b)(2). A plan that is a profit-sharing plan within the meaning of §1.401-1(b)(1)(ii) of this chapter or a stock bonus plan within the meaning of §1.401-1(b)(1)(iii) of this chapter is not a supplemental pension plan within the meaning of this paragraph (b).

(3) *Railroad Retirement Board determination with respect to the plan.*—A plan is a supplemental pension plan within the meaning of this paragraph (b) with respect to an employee only during any period for which the Railroad Retirement Board has made a determi-

nation under 20 CFR 216.42(d) that the plan is a private pension, the payments from which will result in a reduction in the employee's supplemental annuity payable under 45 U.S.C. 231a(b). A plan is not a supplemental pension plan for any time period before the Railroad Retirement Board has made such a determination, or after that determination is no longer in force.

(4) *Other requirements.*—[Reserved]

(c) *Collective bargaining agreement.*—A plan is established pursuant to a collective bargaining agreement with respect to an employee only if, in accordance with the rules of §1.410(b)-6(d)(2) of this chapter, the employee is included in a unit of employees covered by an agreement that the Secretary of Labor finds to be a collective bargaining agreement between employee representatives and one or more employers, provided that there is evidence that retirement benefits were the subject of good faith bargaining between employee representatives and the employer or employers.

(d) *Substitute section 3221(d) excise tax.*—Section 3221(d) imposes an excise tax on any employer who has been excepted from the excise tax imposed under section 3221(c) by the application of section 3221(d) and paragraph (a) of this section with respect to an employee. The excise tax is equal to the amount of the supplemental annuity paid to that employee under 45 U.S.C. 231a(b), plus a percentage thereof determined by the Railroad Retirement Board to be sufficient to cover the administrative costs attributable to such payments under 45 U.S.C. 231a(b).

(e) *Effective date.*—(1) *In general.*—Except as provided in paragraph (e)(2) of this section, this section applies beginning on October 1, 1998.

(2) *Delayed effective date for collective bargaining agreement provisions.*—Paragraph (c) of this section applies beginning on January 1, 2000. [Reg. §31.3221-4.]

☐ [*T.D.* 8832, 8-5-99.]

### [Reg. §31.3221-5T]

**§31.3221-5T. Recapture of credits under the Families First Coronavirus Response Act and the Coronavirus Aid, Relief, and Economic Security Act.**—(a) *Recapture of erroneously refunded credits under the Families First Coronavirus Response Act.*—Any amount of credits for qualified sick leave wages or qualified family leave wages under sections 7001 and 7003, respectively, of the Families First Coronavirus Response Act (Families First Act), Public Law 116-127,

134 Stat. 178 (2020), as modified by section 3606 of the Coronavirus Aid, Relief, and Economic Security Act (CARES Act), Public Law 116-136, 134 Stat. 281 (2020), plus any amount of credits for qualified health plan expenses under sections 7001 and 7003, that are treated as overpayments and refunded or credited to an employer under section 6402(a) or section 6413(b) of the Internal Revenue Code (Code) and to which the employer is not entitled, resulting in an erroneous refund to the employer, shall be treated as an underpayment of the taxes imposed by section 3221(a) of the Code and may be assessed and collected by the Secretary in the same manner as the taxes.

(b) *Recapture of erroneously refunded credits under the Coronavirus Aid, Relief, and Economic Security Act.*—Any amount of credits for qualified wages under section 2301 of the CARES Act that is treated as an overpayment and refunded or credited to an employer under section 6402(a) or section 6413(b) of the Code and to which the employer is not entitled, resulting in an erroneous refund to the employer, shall be treated as an underpayment of the taxes imposed by section 3221(a) of the Code and may be assessed and collected by the Secretary in the same manner as the taxes.

(c) *Advance credit amounts erroneously refunded.*—The determination of any amount of credits erroneously refunded as described in paragraphs (a) and (b) of this section must take into account any amount of credits advanced to an employer under the process established by the Internal Revenue Service in accordance with sections 7001(b)(4)(A)(ii) and 7003(b)(3)(B) of the Families First Act, as modified by section 3606 of the CARES Act, and section 2301(l)(1) of the CARES Act.

(d) *Third party payors.*—For purposes of this section, employers against whom an erroneous refund of the credits under sections 7001 and 7003 of the Families First Act, as modified by section 3606 of the CARES Act, and the credits under section 2301 of the CARES Act can be assessed as an underpayment of the taxes imposed by section 3221(a) include persons treated as the employer under sections 3401(d), 3504, and 3511 of the Code, consistent with their liability for the section 3221(a) taxes against which the credit applied.

(e) *Applicability date.*—This regulation applies to all credit refunds under sections 7001 and 7003 of the Families First Act, as modified by section 3606 of the CARES Act, advanced or paid on or after April 1, 2020, and all credit refunds under section 2301 of the CARES Act advanced or paid on or after March 13, 2020. [Reg. §31.3221-5T.]

☐ [*T.D.* 9904, 7-24-2020.]

# GENERAL PROVISIONS

### [Reg. §31.3231(a)-1]

**§31.3231(a)-1. Who are employers.**—(a) Each of the following persons is an employer within the meaning of the act:

(1) Any carrier, that is, any express carrier, sleeping car carrier, or rail carrier providing transportation subject to subchapter I of chapter 105 of title 49;

(2) Any company—

(i) Which is directly or indirectly owned or controlled by one or more employers as defined in paragraph (a)(1) of this section, or under common control therewith, and

(ii) Which operates any equipment or facility or performs any service (except trucking service, casual service, and the casual operation of equipment or facilities) in connection with—

*(a)* The transportation of passengers or property by railroad, or

*(b)* The receipt, delivery, elevation, transfer in transit, refrigeration or icing, storage, or handling of property transported by railroad;

(3) Any receiver, trustee, or other individual or body, judicial or otherwise, when in the possession of the property or operating all or any part of the business of any employer as defined in paragraph (a)(1) or (2) of this section;

(4) Any railroad association, traffic association, tariff bureau, demurrage bureau, weighing and inspection bureau, collection agency, and any other association, bureau, agency, or organization controlled and maintained wholly or principally by two or more employers as defined in paragraph (a)(1), (2) or (3) of this section and engaged in the performance of services in connection with or incidental to railroad transportation;

(5) Any railway labor organization, national in scope, which has been or may be organized in accordance with the provisions of the Railway Labor Act; and

(6) Any subordinate unit of a national railway-labor-organization employer, that is, any State or National legislative committee, general committee, insurance department, or local lodge or division,

of an employer as defined in paragraph (a)(5) of this section, established pursuant to the constitution and bylaws of such employer.

(b) As used in paragraph (a)(2) of this section, the term "controlled" includes direct or indirect control, whether legally enforceable and however exercisable or exercised. The control may be by means of stock ownership, or by agreements, licenses, or any other devices which insure that the operation of the company is in the interest of one or more carriers. It is the reality of the control, however, which is decisive, not its form nor the mode of its exercise.

(c) As used in paragraph (a)(2) of this section, the term *casual* applies when the service rendered or the operation of equipment or facilities by a controlled company or person in connection with the transportation of passengers or property by railroad is so irregular or infrequent as to afford no substantial basis for an inference that such service or operation will be repeated, or whenever such service or operation is insubstantial.

(d) The term "employer" does not include any street, interurban, or suburban electric railway, unless such railway is operating as a part of a general steam-railroad system of transportation, but shall not exclude any part of the general steam-railroad system of transportation which is operated by any other motive power.

(e) The term "employer" does not include any company by reason of its being engaged in the mining of coal, the supplying of coal to an employer where delivery is not beyond the mine tipple and the operation of equipment or facilities for such mining or supplying of coal, or in any of such activities.

(f) Any company that is described in paragraph (a)(2) of this section is an employer under section 3231. In certain cases, based on all the facts and circumstances, it may be appropriate to segregate those businesses engaged in rail services and therefore subject to the Railroad Retirement Tax Act from those businesses engaged exclusively in nonrail services and therefore not subject to the Railroad Retirement Tax Act. The factors considered are set forth in guidance published by the Internal Revenue Service. [Reg. §31.3231(a)-1.]

☐ [*T.D.* 6516, 12-20-60. *Amended by T.D.* 8582, 12-23-94.]

**[Reg. §31.3231(b)-1]**

**§31.3231(b)-1. Who are employees.**—(a) *In general.*—(1) An individual who is in the service of one or more employers for compensation is an employee within the meaning of the act. (For definitions of the terms "employer", "service", and "compensation", see subsections (a), (d), and (e), respectively, of section 3231.) An individual is in the service of an employer, with respect to services rendered for compensation, if—

(i) He is subject to the continuing authority of the employer to supervise and direct the manner in which he renders such services; or

(ii) He is rendering professional or technical services and is integrated into the staff of the employer; or

(iii) He is rendering, on the property used in the employer's operations, other personal services the rendition of which is integrated into the employer's operations.

(2) In order that an individual may be in the service of an employer within the meaning of paragraph (a)(1)(i) of this section, it is not necessary that the employer actually direct or control the manner in which the services are rendered; it is sufficient if the employer has the right to do so. The right of an employer to discharge an individual is also an important factor indicating that the individual is subject to the continuing authority of the employer to supervise and direct the manner of rendition of the services. Other factors indicating that an individual is subject to the continuing authority of the employer to supervise and direct the manner of rendition of the services are the furnishing of tools and the furnishing of a place to work by the employer to the individual who renders the services.

(3) In general, if an individual is subject to the control or direction of an employer merely as to the result to be accomplished by the work and not as to the means and methods for accomplishing the result, he is an independent contractor. On individual performing services as an independent contractor is not, as to such services, in the service of an employer within the meaning of paragraph (a)(1)(i) of this section. However, an individual performing services as an independent contractor may be, as to such services, in the service of an employer within the meaning of paragraph (a)(1) (ii) or (iii) of this section.

(4) Whether or not an individual is an employee will be determined upon an examination of the particular facts of the case.

(5) If an individual is an employee, it is of no consequence that he is designated as a partner, coadventurer, agent, independent contractor, or otherwise, or that he performs services on a part-time basis.

(6) No distinction is made between classes or grades of employees. Thus, superintendents, managers, and other supervisory personnel are employees within the meaning of the act. An officer of an employer is an employee, but a director as such is not.

(7) In determining whether an individual is an employee with respect to services rendered within the United States, the citizenship or residence of the individual, or the place where the contract of service was entered into is immaterial.

(8) If an individual performs services for an employer (other than a local lodge or division or a general committee of a railway-labor-organization employer) which does not conduct the principal part of its business within the United States, such individual shall be deemed to be in the service of such employer only to the extent that he performs services for it in the United States. Thus, with respect to services rendered for such employer outside the United States, such individual is not in the service of an employer.

(9) If an individual performs services for an employer (other than a local lodge or division or a general committee of a railway-labor-organization employer) which conducts the principal part of its business within the United States, he is in the service of such employer whether his services are rendered within or without the United States. In the case of an individual, not a citizen or resident of the United States, rendering services in a place outside the United States to an employer which is required under the laws applicable in such place to employ, in whole or in part, citizens or residents thereof, such individual shall not be deemed to be in the service of an employer with respect to services so rendered.

(10) The term "employee" does not include any individual while he is engaged in the physical operations consisting of the mining of coal, the preparation of coal, the handling (other than movement by rail with standard railroad locomotives) of coal not beyond the mine tipple, or the loading of coal at the tipple.

(b) *Employees of local lodges or divisions of railway-labor-organization employers.*—(1) An individual is in the service of a local lodge or division of a railway-labor-organization employer (see paragraph (a)(6) of §31.3231(a)-1) only if—

(i) All, or substantially all, the individuals constituting the membership of such local lodge or division are employees of an employer conducting the principal part of its business in the United States; or

(ii) The headquarters of such local lodge or division is located in the United States.

(2)(i) An individual in the service of a local lodge or division is not an employee within the meaning of the act unless he was, on or after August 29, 1935, in the service of a carrier (see §31.3231(g) for definition of carrier) or he was, on August 29, 1935, in the "employment relation" to a carrier.

(ii) An individual shall be deemed to have been in the employment relation to a carrier on August 29, 1935, if (a) he was on that date on leave of absence from his employment expressly granted to him by the carrier by whom he was employed, or by a duly authorized representative or such carrier, and the grant of such leave of absence was established to the satisfaction of the Railroad Retirement Board before July 1947; or (b) he was in the service of a carrier after August 29, 1935, and before January 1946 in each of six calendar months whether or not consecutive; or (c) before August 29, 1935, he did not retire and was not retired or discharged from the service of the last carrier by whom he was employed or its corporate or operating successor, but (1) solely by reason of his physical or mental disability he ceased before August 29, 1935, to be in the service of such carrier and thereafter remained continuously disabled until he attained age sixty-five or until August 1945, or (2) solely for such last stated reason a carrier by whom he was employed before August 29, 1935, or a carrier who is its successor did not on or after August 29, 1935, and before August 1945 call him to return to service, or (3) if he was so called he was solely for such reason unable to render service in six calendar months as provided in (b) of this subdivision; or (d) he was on August 29, 1935, absent from the service of a carrier by reason of a discharge which, within one year after the effective date thereof, was protested, to an appropriate labor representative or to the carrier, as wrongful, and which was followed within 10 years of the effective date thereof by his reinstatement in good faith to his former service with all his seniority rights. However, an individual shall not be deemed to have been in the employment relation to a carrier on August 29, 1935, if before that date he was granted a pension or gratuity on the basis of which a pension was awarded to him pursuant to section 6 of the Railroad Retirement Act of 1937 (45 U.S.C. 228f), or if during the last payroll period before August 29, 1935, in which he rendered service to a carrier he was not, with respect to any service in such payroll period, in the service of an employer (see paragraph (a) of this section).

(c) *Employees of general committees of railway-labor-organization employers.*—An individual is in the service of a general committee of a railway-labor-organization employer (see paragraph (a)(6) of §31.3231(a)-1) only if—

(1) He is representing a local lodge or division described in paragraph (b)(1) of this section; or

(2) All, or substantially all, the individuals represented by such general committee are employees of an employer conducting the principal part of its business in the United States; or

(3) He acts in the capacity of a general chairman or an assistant general chairman of a general committee which represents individuals rendering service in the United States to an employer. In such case, if his office or headquarters is not located in the United States and the individuals represented by such general committee are employees of an employer not conducting the principal part of its business in the United States, only a part of his remuneration for such service shall be regarded as compensation. The part of his remuneration regarded as compensation shall be in the same proportion to his total remuneration as the mileage in the United States under the jurisdiction of such general committee bears to the total mileage under its jurisdiction, unless such mileage formula is inapplicable, in which case such other formula as the Railroad Retirement Board may have prescribed pursuant to section 1(c) of the Railroad Retirement Act of 1937 (45 U.S.C. 228a) shall be applicable. However, no part of his remuneration for such service shall be regarded as compensation if the application of such mileage formula, or such other formula as the Railroad Retirement Board may have prescribed, would result in his compensation for the service being less than 10 percent of his remuneration for such service. [Reg. §31.3231(b)-1.]

**[Reg. §31.3231(c)-1]**

**§31.3231(c)-1. Who are employee representatives.**—(a) An employee representative within the meaning of the act is—

(1) Any officer or official representative of a railway labor organization which is not included as an employer under section 3231(a) who—

(i) Was in the service of an employer either before or after June 29, 1937, and

(ii) Is duly authorized and designated to represent employees in accordance with the Railway Labor Act.

For railway labor organizations which are employers under section 3231(a), see paragraph (a) (5) and (6) of §31.3231(a)-1.

(2) Any individual who is regularly assigned to or regularly employed by an employee representative, as defined in paragraph (a)(1) of this section, in connection with the duties of such employee representative's office.

(b) In determining whether an individual is an employee representative, his citizenship or residence is material only insofar as those factors may affect the determination of whether he was "in the service of an employer" (see paragraph (a) of §31.3231(b)-1). [Reg. §31.3231(c)-1.]

### [Reg. §31.3231(d)-1]

**§31.3231(d)-1. Service.**—See §31.3231(b)-1 for regulations relating to the term "in the service of an employer." [Reg. §31.3231(d)-1.]

### [Reg. §31.3231(e)-1]

**§31.3231(e)-1. Compensation.**—(a) *Definition.*—(1) The term *compensation* has the same meaning as the term *wages* in section 3121(a), determined without regard to section 3121(b)(9), except as specifically limited by the Railroad Retirement Tax Act (chapter 22 of the Internal Revenue Code) or regulation. The Commissioner may provide any additional guidance that may be necessary or appropriate in applying the definitions of sections 3121(a) and 3231(e).

(2) A payment made by an employer to an individual through the employer's payroll is presumed, in the absence of evidence to the contrary, to be compensation for services rendered as an employee of the employer. Likewise, a payment made by an employee organization to an employee representative through the organization's payroll is presumed, in the absence of evidence to the contrary, to be compensation for services rendered by the employee representative as such. For rules regarding the treatment of deductions by an employer from remuneration of an employee, see §31.3123-1.

(3) The term *compensation* is not confined to amounts paid for active service, but includes amounts paid for an identifiable period during which the employee is absent from the active service of the employer and, in the case of an employee representative, amounts paid for an identifiable period during which the employee representative is absent from the active service of the employee organization.

(4) Compensation includes amounts paid to an employee for loss of earnings during an identifiable period as the result of the displacement of the employee to a less remunerative position or occupation as well as pay for time lost.

(5) For rules regarding the treatment of reimbursement and other expense allowance amounts, see §31.3121(a)-3. For rules regarding the inclusion of fringe benefits in compensation, see §31.3121(a)-1T.

(6) *Split-dollar life insurance arrangements.*—See §§1.61-22 and 1.7872-15 of this chapter for rules relating to the treatment of split-dollar life insurance arrangements.

(b) *Special rules.*—(1) If the amount of compensation earned in any calendar month by an individual as an employee in the service of a local lodge or division of a railway-labor-organization employer is less than $25, the amount is disregarded for purposes of determining the employee tax under section 3201 and the employer tax under section 3221.

(2) Compensation for service as a delegate to a national or international convention of a railway-labor-organization employer is disregarded for purposes of determining the employee tax under section 3201 and the employer tax under section 3221 if the individual rendering the service has not previously rendered service, other than as a delegate, which may be included in the individual's years of service for purposes of the Railroad Retirement Act.

(3) For special provisions relating to the compensation of certain general chairs or assistant general chairs of a general committee of a railway-labor-organization employer, see paragraph (c)(3) of §31.3231(b)-1. [Reg. §31.3231(e)-1.]

☐ [*T.D. 8582, 12-23-94. Amended by T.D. 9092, 9-11-2003.*]

### [Reg. §31.3231(e)-2]

**§31.3231(e)-2. Contribution base.**—The term *compensation* does not include any remuneration paid during any calendar year by an employer to an employee for services rendered in excess of the applicable contribution base. For rules applying this provision, see §31.3121(a)(1)-1. [Reg. §31.3231(e)-2.]

☐ [*T.D. 8582, 12-23-94.*]

# Federal Unemployment Tax Act

**See p. 20,601 for regulations not amended to reflect law changes**

### [Reg. §31.3301-1]

**§31.3301-1. Persons liable for tax.**—Every person who is an employer as defined in section 3306(a) (see §31.3306(a)-1) is liable for the tax. Even if an employer is not subject to any State unemployment compensation law, he or she is nevertheless liable for the tax. However, if the employer is subject to such a State law, he or she may be entitled to certain credits against the tax (see §§31.3302(a)-1 to 31.3302(c)-1, inclusive). For provisions relating to payment of the tax, see Subpart G of the regulations in this part. [Reg. §31.3301-1.]

>>>→ *Caution: Reg. §31.3301-3 does not reflect P.L. 91-373, P.L. 92-329, P.L. 94-566, P.L. 100-203 or P.L. 105-33.*

### [Reg. §31.3301-3]

**§31.3301-3. Rate and computation of tax.**—(a) The rates of tax with respect to wages paid in calendar years after 1954 are as follows:

|  | Percent |
|---|---|
| In the calendar years 1955 to 1960, both inclusive | 3 |
| In the calendar year 1961 | 3.1 |
| In the calendar year 1962 | 3.5 |
| In the calendar year 1963 | 3.35 |
| In the calendar year 1964 and subsequent calendar years | 3.1 |

(b) The tax is computed by applying to the wages paid in calendar year, with respect to employment after December 31, 1938, the rate in effect at the time the wages are paid. [Reg. §31.3301-3.]

>>>→ *Caution: Reg. §31.3302(a)-1 does not reflect P.L. 91-373, P.L. 92-329 and P.L. 94-566.*

### [Reg. §31.3302(a)-1]

**§31.3302(a)-1. Credit against tax for contributions paid.**—(a) *In general.*—Subject to the provisions of paragraphs (b) and (c) of this section and to the provisions of §31.3302(c)-1, the taxpayer may credit against the tax for any taxable year the total amount of contributions paid by him into an unemployment fund maintained during such year under a State law which has been found by the Secretary of

☐ [*T.D. 6199, 9-5-56. Republished in T.D. 6516, 12-20-60.*]

### [Reg. §31.3301-2]

**§31.3301-2. Measure of tax.**—The tax for any calendar year is measured by the amount of wages paid by the employer during such year with respect to employment after December 31, 1938. (See §31.3306(b)-1, relating to wages, and §§31.3306(c)-1 to 31.3306(c)-3, inclusive, relating to employment.) [Reg. §31.3301-2.]

☐ [*T.D. 6199, 9-5-56. Republished in T.D. 6516, 12-20-60; T.D. 6658, 6-27-63.*]

☐ [*T.D. 6199, 9-5-56. Republished in T.D. 6516, 12-20-60; T.D. 6658, 6-27-63.*]

### [Reg. §31.3301-4]

**§31.3301-4. When wages are paid.**—Wages are paid when actually or constructively paid. Wages are constructively paid when they are credited to the account of or set apart for an employee so that they may be drawn upon by him at any time although not then actually reduced to possession. To constitute payment in such a case the wages must be credited to or set apart for the employee without any substantial limitation or restriction as to the time or manner of payment or condition upon which payment is to be made, and must be made available to him so that they may be drawn upon at any time, and their payment brought within his own control and disposition. See §31.6011(a)-3, relating to the return on which wages are to be reported. [Reg. §31.3301-4.]

☐ [*T.D. 6199, 9-5-56. Republished in T.D. 6516, 12-20-60.*]

Labor to contain the provisions specified in section 3304(a); *Provided, however,* That no credit may be taken for contributions under a State law if such State has not been duly certified for the calendar year to the Secretary of the Treasury by the Secretary of Labor. The contributions may be credited against the tax whether or not they are paid with respect to employment as defined in section 3306(c). For provisions relating to additional credit against the tax, see §31.3302(b)-1.

(b) *Limitation on the taxable year with respect to which contributions are allowable.*—In order to be allowable as credit against the tax for any taxable year, the contributions must have been paid with respect to such year.

*Example (1).* Under the unemployment compensation law of State X, employer M is required to report in his contribution return for the quarter ending December 31, 1955, all remuneration payable for services rendered in such quarter. A portion of such remuneration is not paid to his employees until February 1, 1956. On January 20, 1056, M pays to the State the total amount of contributions due with respect to all remuneration so required to be reported. Such contributions, including those with respect to the remuneration paid on February 1, 1956, may be included in computing the credit against the tax for the calendar year 1955. This is true even though the remuneration paid on February 1, 1956 (if it constitutes "wages") is required to be reported in the Federal return for 1956 and not in the Federal return for 1955.

*Example (2).* Under the unemployment compensation law of State Y, employer N is required to include in his contribution return for the quarter ending December 31, 1955, certain remuneration paid on December 30, 1955, to an employee for services to be rendered after December 31. On January 20, 1956, N pays to the State the total amount of contributions due with respect to all remuneration required to be reported on the contribution return. Such contributions, including those with respect to the remuneration paid on December 30, 1955, may be included in computing the credit against the tax for the calendar year 1955.

(c) *Limitation on amount of credit allowable based on time when contributions are paid.*—(1) *In general.*—The amount of credit allowable for contributions paid into a State unemployment fund depends in part on the time of payment of such contributions. Although contributions paid at any time may be credited against the tax (subject to the limitations referred to in subparagraphs (2) and (3) of this paragraph), no refund or credit of the tax based on credit for contributions paid will be allowed unless the contributions are paid prior to the expiration of the period of limitations applicable to refund or credit of the tax. For general provisions relating to the limitation period and to refunds, credits and abatements of the tax, see respectively §§ 301.6511(a)-1, 301.6402-2 and 301.6404-1 of this chapter (Regulations on Procedure and Administration).

(2) *Amount of credit allowable when contributions are paid on or before last day for filing return.*—Contributions paid into a State unemployment fund on or before the last day upon which the Federal return for the taxable year is required to be filed may be credited against the tax in an amount equal to such contributions, but not, however, to exceed the total credits determined pursuant to § 31.3302(c)-1. For provisions relating to the time for filing the return, see § 31.6071(a)-1 in Subpart G of this part.

(3) *Amount of credit allowable when contributions are paid after last day for filing return.*—Contributions paid into a State unemployment fund after the last day upon which the Federal return for the taxable year is required to be filed may be credited against the tax in an amount not to exceed 90 percent of the amount which would have been allowable as credit on account of such contributions had they been paid into a State unemployment fund on or before such last day. However, see subparagraph (4) of this paragraph relating to the payment of contributions to the wrong State. For general provisions relating to refunds, credits, or abatements of the tax, see §§ 301.6402-2 and 301.6404-1 of this chapter (Regulations on Procedure and Administration).

*Example (1).* The Federal return of the M Company for the calendar year 1961 discloses total wages of $400,000. The Federal tax, imposed at the rate of 3.1 percent, is $12,400. The company is liable for total State contributions of $8,000 for 1961. The due date of the Federal return is January 31, 1962, no extension of time for filing the return having been granted. The contributions are not paid until February 1, 1962. If the contributions had been paid on or before January 31, 1962, the entire amount of $8,000 could have been credited against the tax. (Credits could not exceed 2.7 percent of the wages, or $10,800. See § 31.3302(c)-1.) Since the contributions were paid after January 31, 1962, the M Company is entitled to a credit of 90 percent of the amount which would have been allowable as credit had the contributions been paid on time (90 percent of $8,000, or $7,200), the net liability for Federal tax being $5,200 ($12,400 minus $7,200).

*Example (2).* The facts are the same as in example (1), except that the M Company is liable for and pays total State contributions of $12,000, instead of $8,000. If the contributions had been paid on or before January 31, 1962, the amount allowable as credit would have been $10,800 (2.7 percent of wages of $400,000). Since the contributions were paid after January 31, 1962, the M Company is entitled to a credit of 90 percent of $10,800, or $9,720, the net liability for Federal tax being $2,680 ($12,400 minus $9,720).

*Example (3).* The Federal return of the R Company for the calendar year 1961 discloses a total tax of $3,100. The company is liable for total State contributions of $2,700 for such year. The due date of the Federal return is January 31, 1962, no extension of time for filing the return having been granted. The R Company pays $1,700 of the total State contributions on or before such date, and the remaining $1,000 on February 1, 1962. If the $1,000 had been paid on or before January 31, 1962, that amount could have been credited against the tax (such amount plus the $1,700 paid on or before January 31, 1962, not exceeding the aggregate credit allowable). Since the $1,000 was paid after January 31, 1962, the R Company is entitled to a credit of 90 percent of this amount or $900, plus the credit of $1,700 allowable for the contributions paid on or before January 31, 1962. The net liability for Federal tax is thus $500 ($3,100 minus $2,600).

(4) *Amount of credit allowable when contributions are paid to wrong State.*—Contributions for the taxable year paid into a State unemployment fund which are required under the unemployment compensation law of that State, but which are paid with respect to remuneration on the basis of which the taxpayer had, prior to such payment, erroneously paid an amount as contributions under another unemployment compensation law, shall be deemed for purposes of the credit to have been paid at the time of the erroneous payment. If, by reason of such other law, the taxpayer was entitled to cease paying contributions for such taxable year with respect to services subject to such other law, the payment into the proper fund shall be deemed for purposes of credit to have been made on the date the Federal return for such year was actually filed by the taxpayer under § 31.6011(a)-(3).

*Example.* Employer N, whose Federal return for the calendar year 1961 discloses a total tax of $3,100, employs individuals in State X and State Y during the calendar year 1961. N assumes in good faith that the services of his employees are covered by the unemployment compensation law of State Y, and pays as contributions to State Y the amount of $2,700 based upon the remuneration of the employees. All of the services were in fact covered by the unemployment compensation law of State X, and none by the law of State Y. The payment to State Y was made on January 31, 1962. When the error was discovered thereafter, N paid to State X contributions in the amount of $2,700 based upon such remuneration. Since the contributions were paid to State Y on January 31, 1962, the contributions to State X are, for purposes of the credit, deemed to have been paid on such date. N is entitled to a credit of $2,700 against the Federal tax of $3,100, the net liability for Federal tax being $400 ($3,100 minus $2,700). [Reg. § 31.3302(a)-1.]

☐ [*T.D. 6199, 9-5-56. Republished in T.D. 6516, 12-20-60; T.D. 6658, 6-27-63.*]

### [Reg. § 31.3302(a)-2]

**§ 31.3302(a)-2. Refund of State contributions.**—If, subsequent to the filing of the return, a refund is made by a State to the taxpayer of any part of his contribution credited against the tax, the taxpayer is required to advise the district director of the date and amount of such refund and the reason therefor, and to pay the tax, if any, due as a result of such refund, together with interest from the date when the tax was due. [Reg. § 31.3302(a)-2.]

☐ [*T.D. 6199, 9-5-56. Republished in T.D. 6516, 12-20-60.*]

### [Reg. § 31.3302(a)-3]

**§ 31.3302(a)-3. Proof of credit under section 3302(a).**—Credit against the tax for any calendar year for contributions paid into State unemployment funds shall not be allowed unless there is submitted to the district director:

(a) A certificate of the proper officer of each State (the laws of which required the contributions to be paid) showing, for the taxpayer:

(1) The total amount of contributions required to be paid under the State law with respect to such calendar year (exclusive of penalties and interest) which was actually paid on or before the date the Federal return is required to be filed; and

(2) The amounts and dates of such required payments (exclusive of penalties and interest) actually paid after the date the Federal return is required to be filed.

(b) A statement by the taxpayer that no part of any payment made by him into a State unemployment fund for such calendar year, which is claimed as a credit against the tax, was deducted or is to be deducted from the remuneration of individuals in his employ. Such statement shall contain or be verified by a written declaration that it is made under the penalties of perjury.

(c) Such other or additional proof as the Commissioner or the district director may deem necessary to establish the right to the credit provided for under section 3302(a). [Reg. § 31.3302(a)-3.]

☐ [*T.D. 6199, 9-5-56. Republished in T.D. 6516, 12-20-60.*]

### [Reg. § 31.3302(b)-1]

**§ 31.3302(b)-1. Additional credit against tax.**—(a) In general.—In addition to the credit against the tax allowable for contributions actually paid to State unemployment funds (see § 31.3302(a)-1), the taxpayer may be entitled to a credit under section 3302(b). This additional credit is allowable to the taxpayer with respect to the amount of contributions which he is relieved from paying to an unemployment fund under the provisions of a State law which have been certified for the taxable year as provided in section 3303. Generally, an additional credit is available to an employer, if under the provisions of a State law which have been so certified he is permitted to pay contributions to such State for the taxable year, or portion thereof, at a rate which is both lower than the highest rate applied under such law in such year and lower than 2.7 percent. No additional credit is allowable except with respect to a State law certified by the Secretary of Labor for the taxable year as provided in section 3303 (or with respect to any provisions thereof so certified).

(b) *Method of computing amount of additional credit allowable with respect to a State law.*—(1) *Certification of a State law as a whole.*—In ascertaining the additional credit for any taxable year with respect to a particular State law which the Secretary of Labor certifies as a whole to the Secretary of the Treasury in accordance with the provisions of section 3303, the taxpayer must first compute the following amounts:

(i) The amount of contributions (whether or not with respect to employment as defined in section 3306(c)) which the taxpayer would have been required to pay under the State law for such year if throughout the year he had been subject to the highest rate applied under such law in such year, or to a rate of 2.7 percent, whichever rate is lower.

(ii) The amount of contributions (whether or not with respect to employment as defined in section 3306(c)) he was required to pay under the State law with respect to such year, whether or not paid.

The amount computed under subdivision (ii) of this subparagraph should then be subtracted from the amount computed under subdivision (i) of this subparagraph and the result will be the additional credit for the taxable year with respect to the law of that State.

*Example.* A employs individuals only in State X during the calendar year 1955. The unemployment compensation law of State X has been certified in its entirety to the Secretary of the Treasury by the Secretary of Labor for such year. The highest rate applied in such year under such State law to any taxpayer is 3 percent. However, A has obtained a rate of 1 percent under the law of such State and is required to pay his entire year's contribution at that rate. The amount of remuneration of A's employees subject to contributions under such State law is $25,000. A's additional credit under section 3302(b) is $425, computed as follows:

| | |
|---|---:|
| Remuneration subject to contributions . . . . . . . . . . | $25,000 |
| Contributions at 2.7 percent rate . . . . . . . . . . . . . . | 675 |
| Less: | |
|     Contributions required to be paid at 1 | |
|     percent rate . . . . . . . . . . . . . . . . . . . | 250 |
| Additional credit to A . . . . . . . . . . . . . . . . . . . | $425 |

Since the 2.7 percent rate is less than the highest rate applied (3 percent), the 2.7 percent rate is used in computing the amount ($675)

from which the amount of contributions required to be paid at the 1 percent rate ($250) is deducted in order to ascertain the additional credit ($425).

(2) *Certification with respect to particular provisions of a State law.*—If the Secretary of Labor makes a certification to the Secretary of the Treasury with respect to particular provisions of a State law for any taxable year pursuant to section 3303, the additional credit of the taxpayer for such year with respect to such law shall be computed in such manner as the Commissioner shall determine.

(c) *Amount of additional credit allowable to taxpayer with respect to more than one State law.*—If the taxpayer is entitled to additional credit with respect to more than one State law in any taxable year, the additional credit allowable with respect to each State law shall be computed separately (in accordance with paragraph (b) of this section) and the total additional credit allowable against the tax for such year shall be the aggregate of the additional credits allowable with respect to such State laws. For limitation on total credits, see §31.3302(c)-1. [Reg. §31.3302(b)-1.]

☐ [T.D. 6199, 9-5-56. *Republished in* T.D. 6516, 12-20-60; T.D. 6658, 6-27-63.]

---

**[Reg. §31.3302(b)-2]**

**§31.3302(b)-2. Proof of additional credit under section 3302(b).**—Additional credit under section 3302(b) shall not be allowed against the tax for any calendar year unless there is submitted—

(a) To the Commissioner a certificate of the proper officer of each State (with respect to the law of which the additional credit is claimed) showing the highest rate of contributions applied under the State law in such calendar year to any person having individuals in his employ; and

(b) To the district director a certificate of the proper officer of each State (with respect to the law of which the additional credit is claimed) showing for the taxpayer—

(1) The total remuneration with respect to which contributions were required to be paid by the taxpayer under the State law with respect to such calendar year; and

(2) The rate of contributions applied to the taxpayer under the State law with respect to such calendar year.

If under the law of such State different rates of contributions were applied to the taxpayer during particular periods of such calendar year, the certificate shall set forth the information called for in subparagraphs (1) and (2) of this paragraph with respect to each such period.

(c) Such other or additional proof as the Commissioner or the district director may deem necessary to establish the right to the additional credit provided for under section 3302(b). [Reg. §31.3302(b)-2.]

☐ [T.D. 6199, 9-5-56. *Republished in* T.D. 6516, 12-20-60.]

---

⧁⧁→ *Caution: The following regulation has not been revised to reflect provisions of P.L. 94-45 regarding repayment of advances, or to reflect certain technical amendments in P.L. 94-455, or to reflect the cap on federal credit reductions in the Omnibus Budget Reconciliation Act of 1981 (P.L. 97-35).*

---

**[Reg. §31.3302(c)-1]**

**§31.3302(c)-1. Limit on total credits.**—(a) *In general.*—Paragraph (b) of this section relates to the limitation on the aggregate of the credits allowable under section 3302(a) and (b). Paragraph (c) of this section relates to reductions, under certain circumstances, of the total credits allowable after applying section 3302(a), (b), and (c)(1). In paragraph (c) of this section, subparagraphs (1), (2), and (3) relate, respectively, to reductions of credits in respect of advances under title XII of the Social Security Act before September 13, 1960, advances under title XII of the Social Security Act after September 12, 1960, and payments under the Temporary Unemployment Compensation Act of 1958. A reduction of credit under subparagraph (1), (2), or (3) of paragraph (c) of this section applies separately from, and in addition to, a reduction under any other such subparagraph. See section 3302(d) and §31.3302(d)-1 for definitions and special rules relating to section 3302(c), and for a provision that, in applying section 3302(c), the Federal tax shall be computed at the rate of 3 percent.

(b) *Limitation on aggregate credit.*—The aggregate of the credit under section 3302(a) and the additional credit under section 3302(b) shall not exceed 90 percent of the tax against which credit is taken, computed as if the tax were imposed at the rate of 3 percent. Thus, the aggregate of the credit which is allowable to an employer for any taxable year shall not exceed 2.7 percent of the wages paid by the employer during the year.

(c) *Reductions of amount of credit otherwise allowable.*—(1) *Advances before September 13, 1960, under title XII of Social Security Act.*—(i) *Credit reductions for 1961 and 1962.*—Pursuant to section 3302(c)(2), as applicable to credit allowable for any year ended before 1963, the total credits otherwise allowable under section 3302 to a taxpayer subject to the unemployment compensation law of the State of—

(a) Alaska shall be reduced for the taxable year 1961 by an amount equal to 0.15 percent of the wages paid by the taxpayer during 1961 which are attributable to Alaska, and shall be reduced for the taxable year 1962 by an amount equal to 0.3 percent of the wages paid by the taxpayer during 1962 which are attributable to Alaska; or

(b) Michigan shall be reduced for the taxable year 1962 by an amount equal to 0.15 percent of the wages paid by the taxpayer during 1962 which are attributable to Michigan.

(ii) *Credit reductions for 1963 and subsequent years.*—If any balance of an advance or advances under title XII of the Social Security Act, made before September 13, 1960, to the unemployment account of a State, remains unpaid on January 1, 1963, or on January 1 of any succeeding taxable year, the total credits otherwise allowable under section 3302 to a taxpayer subject to the unemployment compensation law of the State shall be reduced for the taxable year unless—

(a) No balance of such advance or advances exists as of the beginning of November 10 of the taxable year, or

(b) The State pays into the Federal unemployment account, before November 10 of the taxable year, the amount certified by the

Secretary of Labor pursuant to section 3302(c)(2), and designates such payment as being made for purposes of the last sentence of section 3302(c)(2).

The credit reduction for a taxable year shall be a percentage of the wages paid by the taxpayer during that taxable year which are attributable to the State. The percentage for the taxable year 1963, or for any succeeding taxable year beginning before January 1, 1968, is 0.15 percent (that is, 5 percent of the Federal tax, computed as if imposed at the rate of 3 percent of the wages.) The percentage for any taxable year beginning on or after January 1, 1968, is the percentage reduction for the immediately preceding taxable year plus 0.15 percent. Thus, for 1968 the percentage is 0.3 percent, for 1969 the percentage is 0.45 percent, and for 1970 the percentage is 0.6 percent.

(2) *Advances after September 12, 1960 under the title XII of Social Security Act.*—(i) *In general.*—If any balance of an advance or advances under title XII of the Social Security Act, made after September 12, 1960, to the unemployment account of a State, remains unpaid on January 1 of two consecutive taxable years, the total credits otherwise allowable under section 3302 to a taxpayer subject to the unemployment compensation law of the State shall be reduced for the taxable year beginning with the second consecutive January 1, unless prior to November 10 of that taxable year the total amount of any such advance or advances made to the account of the State has been fully repaid. The reduction made pursuant to this subdivision in the total credits otherwise allowable for the taxable year beginning with the second consecutive January 1 shall be .3 percent of the wages paid by the taxpayer during the taxable year which are attributable to the State (that is, 10 percent of the Federal tax, computed as if imposed at the rate of 3 percent of the wages). In the case of any succeeding taxable year beginning with a consecutive January 1 on which there exists such a balance of an unreturned advance or advances made after September 12, 1960, the total credits otherwise allowable shall be further reduced unless prior to November 10 of that succeeding taxable year the total amount of any such advance or advances made to the account of the State has been fully repaid. The reduction for each such succeeding taxable year beginning with a consecutive January 1 on which such a balance exists shall be a percentage of the wages paid by the taxpayer during that succeeding taxable year which are attributable to the State. The percentage reduction for any such succeeding taxable year shall be the aggregate of (*a*) the percentage reduction (without regard to subdivision (ii) or (iii) of this subparagraph) for the immediately preceding taxable year, (*b*) .3 percent of the wages paid by the taxpayer during the taxable year which are attributable to the State, and (*c*) the percentage, if any, described in subdivision (ii) or (iii) of this subparagraph.

(ii) *Additional reduction if a balance of advances exists after third or fourth consecutive January 1.*—If the credit reduction described in subdivision (i) of this subparagraph is made for the third or fourth consecutive taxable year, the total credits otherwise allowable under section 3302 to a taxpayer subject to the unemployment compensation law of the State shall be further reduced for the taxable year unless the average employer contribution rate (see section 3302(d)(4)) for such State for the calendar year preceding such taxable year is at least 2.7 percent. The percentage of reduction, if any, under this subdivision shall be the percentage referred to in section 3302(c)(3)(B) which is certified by the Secretary of Labor pursuant to section 3302(d)(7).

(iii) *Additional reduction if a balance of advances exists after fifth or any succeeding consecutive January 1.*—If the credit reduction described in subdivision (i) of this subparagraph is made for the fifth or any succeeding taxable year, the total credits otherwise allowable under section 3302 to a taxpayer subject to the unemployment compensation law of the State shall be further reduced for the taxable year unless the average employer contribution rate (see section 3302(d)(4)) for the State for the calendar year preceding such taxable year equals or exceeds the 5-year benefit cost rate (see section 3302(d)(5)) applicable to the State for the taxable year or 2.7 percent, whichever is higher. The percentage of reduction, if any, under this subdivision for a taxable year shall be the percentage referred to in section 3302(c)(3)(C) which is certified by the Secretary of Labor pursuant to section 3302(d)(7).

**⟫⟶ Caution: The following regulation has not been revised to reflect technical changes in IRC §3302(c) enacted by P.L. 94-455.**

**[Reg. §31.3302(d)-1]**

**§31.3302(d)-1. Definitions and special rules relating to limit on total credits.**—(a) *Rate of tax deemed to be 3 percent.*—In applying the provisions of section 3302(c) relating to the limitation on total credits, and to reductions of credits otherwise allowable, the tax imposed by section 3301 shall be computed at the rate of 3 percent in lieu of any other rate prescribed in section 3301 (see §31.3301-3).

(3) *Payments under the Temporary Unemployment Compensation Act of 1958.*—If any amount of temporary unemployment compensation was paid in a State under the Temporary Unemployment Compensation Act of 1958, the total credits otherwise allowable under section 3302 to a taxpayer with respect to wages attributable to the State for the taxable year beginning January 1, 1963, and for each taxable year thereafter, shall be reduced unless prior to November 10 of the taxable year—

(i) There have been restored to the Treasury the amounts of temporary unemployment compensation paid in the State (except amounts paid to individuals who exhausted their unemployment compensation under title XV of the Social Security Act and title IV of the Veterans' Readjustment Assistance Act of 1952 prior to their making their first claims under the Temporary Unemployment Compensation Act of 1958), the amount of costs incurred in the administration of the Temporary Unemployment Compensation Act of 1958 with respect to the State, and the amount estimated by the Secretary of Labor as the State's proportionate share of other costs incurred in the administration of such Act, or

(ii) The State restores to the general fund of the Treasury the amount certified by the Secretary of Labor pursuant to section 104 of the Temporary Unemployment Compensation Act of 1958, and designates such restoration as being made for purposes of the last sentence of such section.

The credit reduction for a taxable year shall be a percentage of the wages paid by the taxpayer during that year which are attributable to the State. The percentage for the taxable year 1963 is 0.15 percent (that is, 5 percent of the Federal tax, computed as if imposed at the rate of 3 percent). The percentage for any succeeding year is 0.3 percent (that is, 10 percent of the Federal tax, computed as if imposed at the rate of 3 percent).

(4) *Example.*—The cumulative effect of the credit reductions described in this paragraph may be illustrated by the following example:

*Example.* Advances to the unemployment account of State X were made in 1957 and in 1961 under title XII of the Social Security Act. Payments under the Temporary Unemployment Compensation Act of 1958 were made in State X in 1958. No portion of the advances or payments is returned before November 10, 1964. As a consequence:

(a) The credit reduction applicable under subparagraph (1) of this paragraph is made for 1964 at the rate of 0.15 percent;

(b) The credit reduction described in subparagraph (2) of this paragraph has been made for 1963 (the second successive year after 1961) at the rate of 0.3 percent. The rate of credit reduction under subparagraph (2) for 1964 is 1 percent (the aggregate of 0.6 percent under section 3302(c)(3)(A) and 0.4 percent (assumed for purposes of this example to be the percentage referred to in section 3302(c)(3)(B) which is certified by the Secretary of Labor); and

(c) The credit reduction described in subparagraph (3) of this paragraph has been made for 1963 at the rate of 0.15 percent. The rate of credit reduction for 1964 is 0.3 percent.

The cumulative rate of credit reduction applicable for 1964 to wages attributable to State X is 1.45 percent, representing the aggregate of the percentage reductions applicable under subparagraphs (1), (2), and (3) of this paragraph (.0.15 percent, 1 percent, and 0.3 percent, respectively). In 1964 Employer A paid wages of $100,000, all of which are subject to the unemployment compensation law of State X. The credit which would be allowable (under section 3302(a), (b), and (c)(1)) if there were no credit reduction is $2,700. Employer A's tax is computed as follows for 1964:

| | | |
|---|---:|---:|
| Total taxable wages (attributable to State X) . . . . . . . | | $100,000 |
| Gross Federal tax (3.1 percent of wages) . . . . . . . . . . | | 3,100 |
| Less credit: | | |
|   Gross credit . . . . . . . . . . . . . . . . . | $2,700 | |
|   Credit reduction (1.45 percent of | | |
|   wages) . . . . . . . . . . . . . . . . . . . | 1,450 | |
|   Net credit . . . . . . . . . . . . . . . . . . | | 1,250 |
| Amount of Federal tax due . . . . . . . . . . . . . . . . . | | $1,850 |

[Reg. §31.3302(c)-1.]

☐ [*T.D.* 6199, 9-5-56. *Republished in T.D.* 6516, 12-20-60; *T.D.* 6658, 6-27-63; *T.D.* 6708, 3-10-64.]

(b) *Wages attributable to a particular State.*—For purposes of section 3302(c)(2) or (3), wages are attributable to a particular State if they are subject to the unemployment compensation law of the State. If wages are not subject to the unemployment compensation law of any State, the determination as to whether such wages, or any portion thereof, are attributable to the particular State with respect to which the reduction in total credits is imposed shall be made in accordance with rules prescribed by the Commissioner.

(c) *Employment Security Act of 1960.*—The Employment Security Act of 1960, referred to in section 3302(c)(2), means title V of the Social Security Amendments of 1960. [Reg. § 31.3302(d)-1.]

☐ [*T.D.* 6658, 6-27-63.]

### [Reg. § 31.3302(e)-1]

**§ 31.3302(e)-1. Successor employer.**—(a) *In general.*—In addition to the credits against the tax allowable under section 3302(a) and (b) for any taxable year after 1960, the taxpayer may be entitled to an amount of credit under section 3302(e). Credit under section 3302(e) is provided in the case of a taxpayer who (1) acquires substantially all of the property used in a trade or business, or in a separate unit of a trade or business, of another person (referred to in this section as a predecessor) who is not an employer (see § 31.3306(a)-1) for the calendar year in which the acquisition takes place, and (2) immediately after the acquisition employs in his trade or business one or more individuals who immediately prior to the acquisition were employed in the trade or business of the predecessor.

(b) *Method of computing credit under section 3302(e).*—(1) Except as provided in subparagraph (2) of this paragraph, the amount of credit to which the taxpayer may be entitled under section 3302(e) is the amount of credit to which the predecessor would be entitled under section 3302(a), (b), and (e), without regard to the limits in section 3302(c), if the predecessor were an employer.

(2) If, during the calendar year in which the acquisition takes place, the predecessor pays remuneration, subject to contributions under the unemployment compensation law of a State, to any employee other than the individuals referred to in paragraph (a) of this section, the taxpayer will be entitled only to a portion of the amount of credit described in subparagraph (1) of this paragraph. The portion is determined by multiplying such amount by a fraction. The numerator of the fraction is the total amount of remuneration, subject to such contributions, paid by the predecessor during such year to the individuals referred to in paragraph (a) of this section. The denominator of the fraction is the total amount of remuneration, subject to such contributions, paid by the predecessor during such

year to all employees for services performed by them in the trade or business, or unit thereof, acquired by the taxpayer.

*Example.* In April 1961 the X Partnership terminated after selling all of its property to the Y Corporation. During 1961, the X Partnership paid its employees and former employees a total of $1,000,000 as remuneration subject to contributions under the employment compensation law of a State. (Note that the X Partnership did not qualify as an employer for 1961 for purposes of the Federal unemployment tax, because it had employees during less than 20 weeks in 1961. When the Y Corporation acquired the property it concurrently employed all individuals who were then in the employ of the X Partnership. Assume that the X Partnership, if it had qualified as an employer for 1961, would have been entitled to a total credit against the Federal tax of $30,000 under section 3302(a) and (b), without regard to the limits in section 3302(c). Of the $1,000,000 remuneration paid by the X Partnership in 1961, one-fifth (or $200,000) was paid to individuals who were employed by the Y Corporation at the time it acquired the property of the X Partnership. Under section 3302(e), therefore, the Y Corporation is entitled to credit of $6,000, which is one-fifth of the credit ($30,000) which would have been available to the X Partnership.

(3) The aggregate amount of credit allowable to the taxpayer under section 3302(a), (b), and (e) is subject to the limits in section 3302(c).

(c) *Proof of credit under section 3302(e).*—Credit under section 3302(e) shall not be allowed against the tax for any taxable year unless there is submitted to the district director (1) such information or proof as may be called for in the return on which the credit is reported, or in the instructions relating to the return, and (2) such other or additional proof as the Commissioner or the district director may deem necessary to establish the right to the credit provided for under section 3302(e).

(d) *Cross-references.*—See paragraph (b) of § 31.3306(b)(1)-1 for examples of the acquisition of property used in a trade or business, or in a separate unit thereof. [Reg. § 31.3302(e)-1.]

☐ [*T.D.* 6658, 6-27-63.]

**⋙→** *Caution: The following regulation has not been revised to reflect the amendments affecting "employer" status made by P.L. 91-373 and P.L. 94-566.*

### [Reg. § 31.3306(a)-1]

**§ 31.3306(a)-1. Who are employers.**—(a) *Definition.*—(1) *For calendar years 1956 through 1969, inclusive.*—Every person who employs 4 or more employees in employment (within the meaning of section 3306 (c) and (d)) on a total of 20 or more calendar days during any calendar year after 1955 and before 1970, each such day being in a different calendar week, is with respect to such year an employer subject to the tax.

(1a) *For 1970 and subsequent calendar years.*—Every person who employs 4 or more employees in employment (within the meaning of section 3306 (c) and (d)) on a total of 20 or more calendar days during a calendar year after 1969, or during the calendar year immediately preceding such a calendar year, each such day being in a different calendar week, is with respect to such year an employer subject to the tax.

(2) *For calendar year 1955.*—Every person who employs 8 or more employees in employment (within the meaning of section 3306(c) and (d)) on a total of 20 or more calendar days during the calendar year 1955, each such day being in a different calendar week, is with respect to such year an employer subject to the tax.

(3) *General agents of the Secretary of Commerce.*—For provisions relating to the circumstances under which an employee who performs services as an officer or member of the crew of an American vessel (i) which is owned by or bareboat chartered to the United States and (ii) whose business is conducted by a general agent of the Secretary of Commerce shall be deemed to be performing services for such general agent rather than for the United States, see § 31.3306(n)-1.

(b) The several weeks in each of which occurs a day on which the prescribed number of employees are employed need not be consecutive weeks. It is not necessary that the employees so employed be the same individuals; they may be different individuals on each day. Neither is it necessary that the prescribed number of employees be employed at the same moment of time or for any particular length of time or on any particular basis of compensation. It is sufficient if the total number of employees employed during the 24 hours of a calendar day is 4 or more (8 or more for the calendar year 1955).

(c) In determining whether a person employs a sufficient number of employees to be an employer subject to the tax, each employee is counted with respect to services which constitute employment as defined in section 3306(c) (see § 31.3306(c)-2). No employee is

counted with respect to services which do not constitute employment as so defined. See, however, paragraph (d) of this section.

(d) The provisions of paragraph (c) of this section are subject to the provisions of section 3306(d), relating to services which do not constitute employment but which are deemed to be employment, and relating to services which constitute employment but which are deemed not to be employment (see § 31.3306(d)-1). For example, if the services of an employee during a pay period are deemed to be employment under section 3306(d), even though a portion thereof does not constitute employment under section 3306(c), the employee is counted with respect to all services during the pay period. On the other hand, if the services of an employee during a pay period are deemed not to be employment, even though a portion thereof constitutes employment, the employee is not counted with respect to any services during the pay period. [Reg. § 31.3306(a)-1.]

☐ [*T.D.* 6199, 9-5-56. *Republished in T.D.* 6516, 12-20-60. *Amended by* T.D. 7037, 4-28-70.]

### [Reg. § 31.3306(b)-1]

**§ 31.3306(b)-1. Wages.**—(a) *Applicable law and regulations.*—(1) *Remuneration paid after 1954.*—Whether remuneration paid after 1954 for employment performed after 1938 constitutes wages is determined under section 3306(b). Accordingly, only remuneration paid after 1954 for employment performed after 1938 is covered by this section of the regulations and by the sections relating to the statutory exclusions from wages (§ § 31.3306(b)(1)-1 to 31.3306(b)(10)-1).

(2) *Remuneration paid after 1939 and before 1955.*—Whether remuneration paid after 1939 and before 1955 for employment performed after 1938 constitutes wages shall be determined in accordance with the applicable provisions of law and of 26 CFR (1939) Part 403 (Regulations 107).

(3) *Remuneration paid in 1939.*—Whether remuneration paid in 1939 for employment performed after 1938 constitutes wages shall be determined in accordance with the applicable provisions of law and of 26 CFR (1939) Part 400 (Regulations 90).

(b) The term "wages" means all remuneration for employment unless specifically excepted under section 3306(b) (see § § 31.3306(b)(1)-1 to 31.3306(b)(10)-1, inclusive) or paragraph (j) of this section.

(c) The name by which the remuneration for employment is designated is immaterial. Thus, salaries, fees, bonuses, and commissions are wages if paid as compensation for employment.

(d) The basis upon which the remuneration is paid is immaterial in determining whether the remuneration constitutes wages. Thus, it may be paid on the basis of piecework or a percentage of profits; and it may be paid hourly, daily, weekly, monthly, or annually.

(e) Except in the case of remuneration paid for services not in the course of the employer's trade or business (see § 31.3306(b)(7)-1), the medium in which the remuneration is paid is also immaterial. It may be paid in cash or in something other than cash, as for example, goods, lodging, food, or clothing. Remuneration paid in items other than cash shall be computed on the basis of the fair value of such items at the time of payment.

(f) Ordinarily, facilities or privileges (such as entertainment, medical services, or so-called "courtesy" discounts on purchases), furnished or offered by an employer to his employees generally, are not considered as remuneration for employment if such facilities or privileges are of relatively small value and are offered or furnished by the employer merely as a means of promoting the health, good will, contentment, or efficiency of his employees. The term "facilities or privileges," however, does not ordinarily include the value of meals or lodging furnished, for example, to restaurant or hotel employees, or to seamen or other employees aboard vessels, since generally these items constitute an appreciable part of the total remuneration of such employees.

(g) Amounts of so-called "vacation allowances" paid to an employee constitute wages. Thus, the salary of an employee on vacation, paid notwithstanding his absence from work, constitutes wages.

(h) Amounts paid specifically—either as advances or reimbursements—for traveling or other bona fide ordinary and necessary expenses incurred or reasonably expected to be incurred in the business of the employer are not wages. For amounts that are received by an employee on or after July 1, 1990, with respect to expenses paid or incurred on or after July 1, 1990, see § 31.3306(b)-2.

(i) Remuneration paid by an employer to an individual for employment, unless such remuneration is specifically excepted under section 3306(b), constitutes wages even though at the time paid the individual is no longer an employee.

*Example.* A is employed by B, an employer, during the month of June 1955 in employment and is entitled to receive remuneration of $100 for the services performed for B during the month. A leaves the employ of B at the close of business on June 30, 1955. On July 15, 1955 (when A is no longer an employee of B), B pays A the remuneration of $100 which was earned for the services performed in June. The $100 is wages, and the tax is payable with respect thereto.

(j) In addition to the exclusions specified in §§ 31.3306(b)(1)-1 to 31.3306(b)(10)-1, inclusive, the following types of payments are excluded from wages:

(1) Remuneration for services which do not constitute employment under section 3306(c).

(2) Remuneration for services which are deemed not to be employment under section 3306(d) (§ 31.3306(d)-1).

(3) Tips or gratuities paid directly to an employee by a customer of an employer, and not accounted for by the employee to the employer.

(k) For provisions relating to the treatment of deductions from remuneration as payments of remuneration, see § 31.3307-1.

(l) *Split-dollar life insurance arrangements.*—Except as otherwise provided under section 3306(r), see §§ 1.61-22 and 1.7872-15 of this chapter for rules relating to the treatment of split-dollar life insurance arrangements. [Reg. § 31.3306(b)-1.]

□ [*T.D.* 6199, 9-5-56. *Republished in T.D.* 6516, 12-20-60; *T.D.* 6658, 6-27-63. *Amended by T.D.* 7375, 9-12-75; *T.D.* 8324, 12-17-90 *and T.D.* 9092, 9-11-2003.]

**[Reg. § 31.3306(b)-2]**

**§ 31.3306(b)-2. Reimbursement and other expense allowance amounts.**—(a) *When excluded from wages.*—If a reimbursement or other expense allowance arrangement meets the requirements of section 62(c) of the Code and § 1.62-2 and the expenses are substantiated within a reasonable period of time, payments made under the arrangement that do not exceed the substantiated expenses are treated as paid under an accountable plan and are not wages. In addition, if both wages and the reimbursement or other expense allowance are combined in a single payment, the reimbursement or other expense allowance must be identified either by making a separate payment or by specifically identifying the amount of the reimbursement or other expense allowance.

(b) *When included in wages.*—(1) *Accountable plans.*—(i) *General rule.*—Except as provided in paragraph (b)(1)(ii) of this section, if a reimbursement or other expense allowance arrangement satisfied the requirements of section 62(c) and § 1.62-2, but the expenses are not substantiated within a reasonable period of time or amounts in excess of the substantiated expenses are not returned within a reasonable period of time, the amount paid under the arrangement in excess of the substantiated expenses is treated as paid under a nonaccountable plan, is included in wages, and is subject to withholding and payment of employment taxes no later than the first payroll period following the end of the reasonable period.

(ii) *Per diem or mileage allowances.*—If a reimbursement or other expense allowance arrangement providing a per diem or mileage allowance satisfies the requirements of section 62(c) and § 1.62-2, but the allowance is paid at a rate for each day or mile of travel that exceeds the amount of the employee's expenses deemed substantiated for a day or mile of travel, the excess portion is treated as paid under a nonaccountable plan and is included in wages. In the case of a per diem or mileage allowance paid as a reimbursement, the excess portion is subject to withholding and payment of employment taxes when paid. In the case of a per diem or mileage allowance paid as an advance, the excess portion is subject to withholding and payment of employment taxes no later than the first payroll period following the payroll period in which the expenses with respect to which the advance was paid (i.e., the days or miles of travel) are substantiated. The Commissioner may, in his discretion, prescribe special rules in pronouncements of general applicability regarding the timing of withholding and payment of employment taxes on per diem and mileage allowances.

(2) *Nonaccountable plans.*—If a reimbursement or other expense allowance arrangement does not satisfy the requirements of section 62(c) and § 1.62-2 (e.g., the arrangement does not require expenses to be substantiated or require amounts in excess of the substantiated expenses to be returned), all amounts paid under the arrangement are treated as paid under a nonaccountable plan, are included in wages, and are subject to withholding and payment of employment taxes when paid.

(c) *Effective dates.*—This section generally applies to payments made under reimbursement or other expense allowance arrangements received by an employee on or after July 1, 1990, with respect to expenses paid or incurred on or after July 1, 1990. Paragraph (b)(1)(ii) of this section applies to payments made under reimbursement or other expense allowance arrangements received by an employee on or after January 1, 1991, with respect to expenses paid or incurred on or after January 1, 1991. [Reg. § 31.3306(b)-2.]

□ [*T.D.* 8324, 12-17-90.]

**»»→** *Caution: The following regulation has not been revised to reflect the increases in the taxable wage base to $4,200 after 1971 as enacted by P.L. 91-373, to $6,000 after 1977 as enacted by P.L. 94-566, and to $7,000 after 1982 as enacted by P.L. 97-248.*

**[Reg. § 31.3306(b)(1)-1]**

**§ 31.3306(b)(1)-1. $3,000 limitation.**—(a) *In general.*—(1) The term "wages" does not include that part of the remuneration paid within any calendar year by an employer to an employee which exceeds the first $3,000 of remuneration (exclusive of remuneration excepted from wages in accordance with paragraph (j) of § 31.3306(b)-1 or §§ 31.3306(b)(2)-1 to 31.3306(b)(8)-1, inclusive), paid within such calendar year by such employer to such employee for employment performed for him at any time after 1938.

(2) The $3,000 limitation applies only if the remuneration paid during any one calendar year by an employer to the same employee for employment performed after 1938 exceeds $3,000. The limitation in such case relates to the amount of remuneration paid during any one calendar year for employment performed after 1938 and not to the amount of remuneration for employment performed in any one calendar year.

*Example.* Employer B, in 1955, pays employee A $2,500 on account of $3,000 due him for employment performed in 1955. In 1956 employer B pays employee A the balance of $500 due him for employment performed in the prior year (1955), and thereafter in 1956 also pays A $3,000 for employment performed in 1956. The $2,500 paid in 1955 is subject to tax in 1955. The balance of $500 paid in 1956 for employment during 1955 is subject to tax in 1956, as is also the first $2,500 paid of the $3,000 for employment during 1956 (this $500 for 1955 employment added to the first $2,500 paid for 1956 employment constitutes the maximum wages subject to the tax which could be paid in 1956 by B to A). The final $500 paid by B to A in 1956 is not included as wages and is not subject to the tax.

(3) If during a calendar year an employee is paid remuneration by more than one employer, the limitation of wages to the first $3,000 of remuneration paid applies, not to the aggregate remuneration paid by all employers with respect to employment performed after 1938, but instead to the remuneration paid during such calendar year by each employer with respect to employment performed after 1938. In such case the first $3,000 paid during the calendar year by each employer constitutes wages and is subject to the tax. In connection

with the application of the $3,000 limitation, see also paragraph (b) of this section relating to the circumstances under which wages paid by a predecessor employer are deemed to be paid by his successor. In connection with the annual wage limitation in the case of remuneration after December 31, 1978 from two or more related corporations that compensate an employee through a common paymaster, see § 31.3306(p)-1.

*Example (1).* During 1955 employer D pays to employee C a salary of $600 a month for employment performed for D during the first seven months of 1955, or total remuneration of $4,200. At the end of the fifth month C has been paid $3,000 by employer D, and only that part of his total remuneration from D constitutes wages subject to the tax. The $600 paid to employee C by employer D in the sixth month, and the like amount paid in the seventh month, are not included as wages and are not subject to the tax. At the end of the seventh month C leaves the employ of D and enters the employ of E. Employer E pays to C remuneration of $600 a month in each of the remaining five months of 1955, or total remuneration of $3,000. The entire $3,000 paid by E to employee C constitutes wages and is subject to the tax. Thus, the first $3,000 paid by employer D and the entire $3,000 paid by employer E constitute wages.

*Example (2).* During the calendar year 1955 F is simultaneously an officer (an employee) of the X Corporation, the Y Corporation, and the Z Corporation, each such corporation being an employer for such year. During such year F is paid a salary of $3,000 by each corporation. Each $3,000 paid to F by each of the corporations, X, Y, and Z (whether or not such corporations are related), constitutes wages and is subject to the tax.

(b) *Wages paid by predecessor attributed to successor.*—(1) If an employer (hereinafter referred to as a successor) during any calendar year acquires substantially all the property used in a trade or business of another employer (hereinafter referred to as a predecessor), or used in a separate unit of a trade or business of a predecessor, and if immediately after the acquisition the successor employs in his trade or business an individual who immediately prior to the acquisition was employed in the trade or business of such predecessor, then, for purposes of the application of the $3,000 limitation set forth in paragraph (a) of this section, any remuneration (exclusive of remuneration excepted from wages in accordance with paragraph (j) of § 31.3306(b)-1 or §§ 31.3306(b)(2)-1 to 31.3306(b)(8)-1, inclusive), with respect to employment paid (or considered under this provision as having been paid) to such individual by such predecessor during such calendar year and prior to such acquisition shall be considered as having been paid by such successor. Wages paid by a predecessor shall not be considered as having been paid by the successor unless both the predecessor and the successor are employers as defined in section 3306(a) for the calendar year in which the acquisition occurs (see § 31.3306(a)-1, relating to who are employers).

(2) The wages paid, or considered as having been paid, by a predecessor to an employee shall, for purposes of the $3,000 limitation, be treated as having been paid to such employee by a successor, if:

(i) The successor during a calendar year acquired substantially all the property used in a trade or business, or used in a separate unit of a trade or business, of the predecessor;

(ii) Such employee was employed in the trade or business of the predecessor immediately prior to the acquisition and is employed by the successor in his trade or business immediately after the acquisition; and

(iii) Such wages were paid during the calendar year in which the acquisition occurred and prior to such acquisition.

(3) The method of acquisition by an employer of the property of another employer is immaterial. The acquisition may occur as a consequence of the incorporation of a business by a sole proprietor or a partnership, the continuance without interruption of the business of a previously existing partnership by a new partnership or by a sole proprietor, or a purchase or any other transaction whereby substantially all the property used in a trade or business, or used in a separate unit of a trade or business, of one employer is acquired by another employer.

(4) Substantially all the property used in a separate unit of a trade or business may consist of substantially all the property used in the performance of an essential operation of the trade or business, or it may consist of substantially all the property used in a relatively self-sustaining entity which forms a part of the trade or business.

*Example (1).* The M Corporation which is engaged in the manufacture of automobiles, including the manufacture of automobile engines, discontinues the manufacture of the engines and transfers all the property used in such manufacturing operations to the N Company. The N Company is considered to have acquired a separate unit of the trade or business of the M Corporation, namely, its engine manufacturing unit.

*Example (2).* The R Corporation which is engaged in the operation of a chain of grocery stores transfers one of such stores to the S Company. The S Company is considered to have acquired a separate unit of the trade or business of the R Corporation.

(5) A successor may receive credit for wages paid to an employee by a predecessor only if immediately prior to the acquisition the employee was employed by the predecessor in his trade or business which was acquired by the successor and if immediately after the acquisition such employee is employed by the successor in his trade or business (whether or not in the same trade or business in which the acquired property is used). If the acquisition involves only a separate unit of a trade or business of the predecessor, the employee need not have been employed by the predecessor in that unit provided he was employed in the trade or business of which the acquired unit was a part.

*Example.* The Y Corporation in 1955 acquires all the property of the X Manufacturing Company and immediately after the acquisition employs in its trade or business employee A, who, immediately prior to the acquisition, was employed by the X Company. Both the Y Corporation and the X Company are employers, as defined in the Act, for the calendar year 1955. The X Company has in 1955 (the calendar year in which the acquisition occurs) and prior to the acquisition paid $2,000 of wages to A. The Y Corporation in 1955 pays to A remuneration with respect to employment of $2,000. Only $1,000 of such remuneration is considered to be wages. For purposes of the $3,000 limitation, the Y Corporation is credited with the $2,000 paid to A by the X Company. If, in the same calendar year, the property is acquired from the Y Corporation by the Z Company, an employer for such year, and A immediately after the acquisition is employed by the Z Company in its trade or business, no part of the remuneration paid to A by the Z Company in the year of the acquisition will be considered to be wages. The Z Company will be credited with the remuneration paid to A by the Y Corporation and also with the wages paid to A by the X Company (considered for purposes of the application of the $3,000 limitation as having also been paid by the Y Corporation). [Reg. § 31.3306(b)(1)-1.]

☐ [*T.D.* 6199, 9-5-56. *Republished in T.D.* 6516, 12-20-60; *T.D.* 6658, 6-27-63; *T.D.* 7660, 12-19-79.]

**»»→ Caution: This regulation has not been amended to reflect the fact that, effective in 1985, most sick pay is includible in taxable wages.**

**[Reg. § 31.3306(b)(2)-1]**

**§ 31.3306(b)(2)-1. Payments under employers' plans on account of retirement, sickness or accident disability, medical or hospitalization expenses, or death.**—(a) The term "wages" does not include the amount of any payment (including any amount paid by an employer for insurance or annuities, or into a fund, to provide for any such payment) made to, or on behalf of, an employee or any of his dependents under a plan or system established by an employer which makes provision for his employees generally (or for his employees generally and their dependents) or for a class or classes of his employees (or for a class or classes of his employees and their dependents), on account of:

(1) An employee's retirement,

(2) Sickness or accident disability of an employee or any of his dependents,

(3) Medical or hospitalization expenses in connection with sickness or accident disability of an employee or any of his dependents, or

(4) Death of an employee or any of his dependents.

(b) The plan or system established by an employer need not provide for payments on account of all of the specified items, but such plan or system may provide for any one or more of such items. Payments for any one or more of such items under a plan or system established by an employer solely for the dependents of his employees are not within this exclusion from wages.

(c) Dependents of an employee include the employee's husband or wife, children, and any other members of the employee's immediate family.

(d) It is immaterial for purposes of this exclusion whether the amount or possibility of such benefit payments is taken into consideration in fixing the amount of an employee's remuneration or whether such payments are required, expressly or impliedly, by the contract of service. [Reg. § 31.3306(b)(2)-1.]

☐ [*T.D.* 6199, 9-5-56. *Republished in T.D.* 6516, 12-20-60.]

>>>→ *Caution: This regulation has not been amended to reflect the repeal of IRC §3306(b)(3), as made by P.L. 98-21, §324(b)(3)(B).*

**[Reg. §31.3306(b)(3)-1]**

**§31.3306(b)(3)-1. Retirement payments.**—The term "wages" does not include any payment made by an employer to an employee (including any amount paid by an employer for insurance or annuities, or into a fund, to provide for any such payment) on account of the employee's retirement. Thus, payments made to an employee on account of his retirement are excluded from wages under this exception even though not made under a plan or system. [Reg. §31.3306(b)(3)-1.]

☐ [T.D. 6199, 9-5-56. *Republished in T.D. 6516, 12-20-60.*]

**[Reg. §31.3306(b)(4)-1]**

**§31.3306(b)(4)-1. Payments on account of sickness or accident disability, or medical or hospitalization expenses.**—The term

>>>→ *Caution: This regulation has not been amended to reflect the change made by P.L. 96-222.*

**[Reg. §31.3306(b)(5)-1]**

**§31.3306(b)(5)-1. Payments from or to certain tax-exempt trusts, or under or to certain annuity plans or bond purchase plans.**—(a) *Payments from or to certain tax-exempt trusts.*—The term "wages" does not include any payment made—

(1) By an employer, on behalf of an employee or his beneficiary, into a trust, or

(2) To, or on behalf of, an employee or his beneficiary from a trust,

if at the time of such payment the trust is exempt from tax under section 501(a) as an organization described in section 401(a). A payment made to an employee of such a trust for services rendered as an employee of the trust and not as a beneficiary thereof is not within this exclusion from wages.

(b) *Payments under or to certain annuity plans.*—(1) The term "wages" does not include any payment made after December 31, 1962,—

(i) By an employer, on behalf of an employee or his beneficiary, into an annuity plan, or

(ii) To, or on behalf of, an employee or his beneficiary under an annuity plan,

>>>→ *Caution: This regulation has not been amended to reflect the change made by P.L. 96-499.*

**[Reg. §31.3306(b)(6)-1]**

**§31.3306(b)(6)-1. Payment by an employer of employee tax under sectin 3101 or employee contributions under a State law.**—The term "wages" does not include any payment by an employer (without deduction from the remuneration of, or other reimbursement from, the employee) of either (a) the employee tax imposed by section 3101 [FICA employee tax] or the corresponding section of prior law, or (b) any payment required from an employee under a State unemployment compensation law. [Reg. §31.3306(b)(6)-1.]

☐ [T.D. 6199, 9-5-56. *Republished in T.D. 6516, 12-20-60.*]

**[Reg. §31.3306(b)(7)-1]**

**§31.3306(b)(7)-1. Payments other than in cash for service not in the course of employer's trade or business.**—The term "wages" does not include remuneration paid in any medium other than cash for service not in the course of the employer's trade or business. Cash remuneration includes checks and other monetary media of exchange. Remuneration paid in any medium other than cash, such as lodging, food, or other goods or commodities, for service not in the course of the employer's trade or business does not constitute wages. Remuneration paid in any medium other than cash for other types of services does not come within this exclusion from wages. For provisions relating to the circumstances under which service not in the course of the employer's trade or business does not constitute employment, see §31.3306(c)(3)-1. [Reg. §31.3306(b)(7)-1.]

☐ [T.D. 6199, 9-5-56. *Republished in T.D. 6516, 12-20-60.*]

**[Reg. §31.3306(b)(8)-1]**

**§31.3306(b)(8)-1. Payments to employees for non-work periods.**—The term "wages" does not include any payment (other than vacation or sick pay) made by an employer to an employee after the calendar month in which the employee attains age 65, if—

(a) Such employee does no work (other than being subject to call for the performance of work) for such employer in the period for which such payment is made; and

(b) The employer-employee relationship exists between the employer and employee throughout the period for which such payment is made.

Vacation or sick pay is not within this exclusion from wages. If the employee does any work for the employer in the period for which

"wages" does not include any payment made by an employer to, or on behalf of, an employee on account of the employee's sickness or accident disability or the medical or hospitalization expenses in connection with the employee's sickness or accident disability, if such payment is made after the expiration of 6 calendar months following the last calendar month in which such employee worked for such employer. Such payments are excluded from wages under this exception even though not made under a plan or system. If the employee does not actually perform services for the employer during the requisite period, the existence of the employer-employee relationship during that period is immaterial.[Reg. §31.3306(b)(4)-1.]

☐ [T.D. 6199, 9-5-56. *Republished in T.D. 6516, 12-20-60.*]

if at the time of such payment the annuity plan is a plan described in section 403(a).

(2) The term "wages" does not include any payment made before January 1, 1963,—

(i) By an employer, on behalf of an employee or his beneficiary, into an annuity plan, or

(ii) To, or on behalf of, an employee or his beneficiary under an annuity plan,

if at the time of such payment the annuity plan meets the requirements of section 401(a)(3), (4), (5), and (6).

(c) *Payments under or to certain bond purchase plans.*—The term "wages" does not include any payment made after December 31, 1962,—

(1) By an employer, on behalf of an employee or his beneficiary, into a bond purchase plan, or

(2) To, or on behalf of, an employee or his beneficiary under a bond purchase plan,

if at the time of such payment the plan is a qualified bond purchase plan described in section 405(a). [Reg. §31.3306(b)(5)-1.]

☐ [T.D. 6199, 9-5-56. *Republished in T.D. 6516, 12-20-60; T.D. 6658, 6-27-63.*]

the payment is made, no remuneration paid by such employer to such employee with respect to such period is within this exclusion from wages. For example, if employee A, who attained the age of 65 in January 1955, is employed by the X Company on a stand-by basis and is paid $200 by the X Company for being subject to call during the month of February 1955 and an additional $25 for work performed for the X Company on one day in February 1955, then none of the $225 is excluded from wages under this exception. [Reg. §31.3306(b)(8)-1.]

☐ [T.D. 6199, 9-5-56. *Republished in T.D. 6516, 12-20-60; T.D. 6708, 3-10-64.*]

**[Reg. §31.3306(b)(9)-1]**

**§31.3306(b)(9)-1. Moving expenses.**—(a) The term "wages" does not include remuneration paid on or after November 1, 1964, to or on behalf of an employee, either as an advance or a reimbursement, specifically for moving expenses incurred or expected to be incurred, if (and to the extent that) at the time of payment it is reasonable to believe that a corresponding deduction is or will be allowable to the employee under section 217. The reasonable belief contemplated by the statute may be based upon any evidence reasonably sufficient to induce such belief, even though such evidence may be insufficient upon closer examination by the district director or the courts finally to establish that a deduction is allowable under section 217. The reasonable belief shall be based upon the application of section 217 and the regulations thereunder in Part 1 of this chapter (Income Tax Regulations). When used in this section, the term "moving expenses" has the same meaning as when used in section 217 and the regulations thereunder.

(b) Except as otherwise provided in paragraph (a) of this section, or in a numbered paragraph of section 3306(b), amounts paid to or on behalf of an employee for moving expenses are wages for purposes of section 3306(b). [Reg. §31.3306(b)(9)-1.]

☐ [T.D. 7375, 9-12-75.]

**[Reg. §31.3306(b)(10)-1]**

**§31.3306(b)(10)-1. Payments under certain employers' after retirement, disability, or death.**—(a) *In general.*—The term "wages" does not include the amount of any payment or series of payments made after January 2, 1968, by an employer to, or on behalf of, an employee or any of his dependents under a plan established by the employer which makes provisions for his employees generally (or for his employees generally and their dependents) or for a class or classes of his employees (or for a class or classes of his employees and their dependents), which is paid or commences to be paid under or within a reasonable time after the termination of an employee's employment relationship because of the employee's—

(1) Death,

(2) Retirement for disability, or

(3) Retirement after attaining an age specified in the plan established by the employer or in a pension plan of the employer at the age at which a person in the employee's circumstances is eligible for retirement.

A payment or series of payments made under the circumstances described in the preceding sentence is excluded from "wages" even if made pursuant to an incentive compensation plan which also provides for the making of other types of payments. However, any payment or series of payments which would have been paid if the employee's relationship had not been terminated is not excluded from "wages" under this section and section 3306(b)(10). For example, lump-sum payments for unused vacation time or a final paycheck received after retirement are payments which the employee would have received whether or not he retired and therefore are not excluded from "wages." Further, if any payment is made upon or after termination of employment for any reason other than those set out in subparagraphs (1), (2), and (3) of this paragraph such payment is not excludable from "wages" by this section. For example, if a pension plan provides for retirement upon disability, completion of 30 years of service, or attainment of age 65, and if an employee who is not disabled retires at age 61 after 30 years of service, none of the retirement payments made to the employee under the pension plan (including any made after he is 65) is excludable from "wages" under this section. However, if the pension plan had conditioned retirement after 30 years of service upon attainment of age 60, all of the retirement payments would have been excludable.

(b) *Plan.*—The plan or system established by an employer need not provide for payments because of termination of employment for all the reasons set out in subparagraphs (1), (2), and (3) of paragraph (a), but such plan or system may provide for payments because of termination for any one or more of such reasons. Payments because of termination of employment for any one or more of such reasons under a plan or system established by an employer solely for the dependents of his employes are not within this exclusion from wages.

(c) *Dependents.*—Dependents of an employee include the employee's husband or wife, children, and any other members of the employee's immediate family.

(d) *Benefit payments.*—It is immaterial for purposes of this exclusion whether the amount or possibility of such benefit payments is paid on account of services rendered or taken into consideration in fixing the amount of an employee's remuneration or whether such payments are required expressly or impliedly, by the contract of service.

(e) *Example.*—The application of this section may be illustrated by the following example:

*Example.* A, an employee, receives a salary of $1,500 a month, payable on the 5th day of the month following the month for which the salary is earned. A's employer has established an incentive compensation plan for a class of his employees, including A, providing for the payment of deferred compensation on termination of employment, including termination upon an employee's death, retirement at age 65 (the retirement age specified in the plan), or retirement for disability. On March 1, 1973, A attains the age of 65 and retires. On March 5, 1973, A receives $5,500 from his employer of which $1,500 represents A's salary for services he performed in February 1973, and $4,000 represents incentive compensation paid under the employer's plan. The amount of $4,000 is excluded from "wages" under this section. The amount of $1,500 is not excluded from "wages" under this section. [Reg. §31.3306(b)(10)-1.]

☐ [*T.D. 7374, 7-24-75.*]

⟫⟫➤ *Caution: The following provisions of the regulation have not been revised to reflect the amendments made by P.L. 91-373 and 94-566.*

(c) *Services performed outside the United States.*—(1) *In general.*— Except as provided in subparagraph (2) of this paragraph, services performed outside the United States (see §31.3306(j)-1) do not constitute employment.

(2) *On or in connection with an American vessel or American aircraft.*—(i) This subparagraph relates to services performed after 1954 "on or in connection with" an American vessel, and to services performed after 1961 "on or in connection with" an American aircraft to the extent that the remuneration for the latter services is paid after

**§31.3306(b)(13)-1. Payments or benefits under a qualified educational assistance program.**—The term "wages" does not include any payment made, or benefit furnished, to or for the benefit of an employee in a taxable year beginning after December 31, 1978, if at the time of such payment or furnishing it is reasonable to believe that the employee will be able to exclude such payment or benefit from income under section 127. [Reg. §31.3306(b)(13)-1.]

☐ [*T.D. 7898, 7-6-83.*]

**§31.3306(b)-1T. Question and answer relating to the definition of wages in section 3306(b) (Temporary).**—

The following question and answer relate to the definition of wages in section 3306(b) of the Internal Revenue Code of 1954, as amended by section 531(d)(3) of the Tax Reform Act of 1984 (98 Stat. 885):

*Q-1:* Are fringe benefits included in the definition of wages under section 3306(b)?

*A-1:* Yes, unless specifically excluded from the definition of "wages" pursuant to section 3306(b)(1) through (16). For example, a fringe benefit provided to or on behalf of an employee is excluded from the definition of "wages" if at the time such benefit is provided it is reasonable to believe that the employee will be able to exclude such benefit from income under section 117 or 132. [Temporary Reg. §31.3306(b)-1T.]

☐ [*T.D. 8004, 1-7-85. Amended by T.D. 8009, 2-20-85.*]

**§31.3306(c)-1. Employment; services performed after 1955.**— (a) Services performed after 1938 and before 1955 constitute employment under section 3306(c) if such services were employment under the law applicable to the period in which they were performed.

(b) The tax applies with respect to remuneration paid by an employer after 1954 for services performed after 1938 and before 1955, as well as for services performed after 1954, to the extent that the remuneration and services constitute wages and employment. See §§31.3306(b)-1 to 31.3306(b)(8)-1, inclusive, relating to wages.

(c) Determination of whether services performed after 1938 and before 1955 constitute employment shall be made in accordance with the provisions of law applicable to the period in which they were performed and of the regulations thereunder. The regulations applicable in determining whether services performed after 1938 and before 1955 constitute employment are as follows:

(1) Services performed in 1939-26 CFR (1939) Part 400 (Regulations 90).

(2) Services performed after 1939 and before 1955-26 CFR (1939) Part 403 (Regulations 107). [Reg. §31.3306(c)-1.]

☐ [*T.D. 6199, 9-5-56. Republished in T.D. 6516, 12-20-60.*]

**§31.3306(c)-2. Employment; services performed after 1954.**— (a) *In general.*—Whether services performed after 1954 constitute employment is determined under subsection (c) and (n) of section 3306.

(b) *Services performed within the United States.*—Services performed after 1954 within the United States (see §31.3306(j)-1) by an employee for the person employing him, unless specifically excepted under section 3306(c), constitute employment. With respect to services performed within the United States, the place where the contract of service is entered into is immaterial. The citizenship or residence of the employee or of the person employing him also is immaterial except to the extent provided in any specific exception from employment. Thus, the employee and the person employing him may be citizens and residents of a foreign country and the contract of service may be entered into in a foreign country, and yet, if the employee under such contract performs services within the United States, there may be to that extent employment.

1961. Such services performed outside the United States by an employee for the person employing him constitute employment if:

*(a)* The employee is also employed "on and in connection with" such vessel or aircraft when outside the United States; and

*(b)* The services are performed under a contract of service, between the employee and the person employing him, which is entered into within the United States, or during the performance of the contract under which the services are performed and while the employee is employed on the vessel or aircraft it touches at a port within the United States; and

*(c)* The services are not excepted under section 3306(c). (See particularly § 31.3306(c)(17)-1, relating to fishing.)

(ii) An employee performs services on and in connection with the vessel or aircraft if he performs services on the vessel or aircraft which are also in connection with the vessel or aircraft. Services performed on the vessel by employees as officers or members of the crew, or as employees of concessionaires, of the vessel, for example, are performed under such circumstances, since the services are also connected with the vessel. Similarly, services performed on the aircraft by employees as officers or members of the crew of the aircraft are performed on and in connection with such aircraft. Services may be performed on the vessel or aircraft, however, which have no connection with it, as in the case of services performed by an employee while on the vessel or aircraft merely as a passenger in the general sense. For example, the services of a buyer in the employ of a department store while he is a passenger on a vessel are not in connection with the vessel.

(iii) If services are performed by an employee "on and in connection with" an American vessel or American aircraft when outside the United States and the conditions in (b) and (c) of subdivision (i) of this subparagraph are met, then the services of that employee performed on or in connection with the vessel or aircraft constitute employment. The expression "on or in connection with" refers not only to services performed on the vessel or aircraft but also to services connected with the vessel or aircraft which are not actually performed on it (for example, shore services performed as officers or members of the crew, or as employees of concessionaires, of the vessel).

(iv) Services performed by a member of the crew or other employee whose contract of service is not entered into within the United States, and during the performance of which and while the employee is employed on the vessel or aircraft it does not touch at a port within the United States, do not constitute employment, notwithstanding that services performed by other members of the crew or other employees on or in connection with the vessel or aircraft may constitute employment.

(v) A vessel includes every description of watercraft, or other contrivance, used as a means of transportation on water. An aircraft includes every description of craft, or other contrivance, used as a means of transportation through the air. In the case of an aircraft, the term "port" means an airport. An airport means an area on land or water used regularly by aircraft for receiving or discharging passengers or cargo. For definitions of "American vessel" and "American aircraft", see § 31.3306(m)-1.

(vi) With respect to services performed outside the United States on or in connection with an American vessel or American aircraft, the citizenship or residence of the employee is immaterial, and the citizenship or residence of the employer is material only in case it has a bearing in determining whether a vessel is an American vessel. [Reg. § 31.3306(c)-2.]

☐ [*T.D. 6199, 9-5-56. Republished in T.D. 6516, 12-20-60; T.D. 6658, 6-27-63.*]

### [Reg. § 31.3306(c)-3]

**§ 31.3306(c)-3. Employment; excepted services in general.—** (a) Services performed by an employee for the person employing him do not constitute employment for purposes of the tax if they are specifically excepted from employment under any of the numbered paragraphs of section 3306(c). Services so excepted do not constitute employment for purposes of the tax even though they are performed within the United States, or are performed outside the United States on or in connection with an American vessel or American aircraft. If not otherwise provided in the regulations relating to the numbered paragraphs of section 3306(c), such regulations apply with respect to services performed after 1954.

(b) The exception attaches to the services performed by the employee and not to the employee as an individual; that is, the exception applies only to the services rendered by the employee in an excepted class.

*Example.* A is an individual who is employed part time by B to perform services which constitute "agricultural labor" (see § 31.3306(k)-1). A is also employed by C part time to perform services as a grocery clerk in a store owned by him. While A's services which constitute "agricultural labor" are excepted, the exception does not embrace the services performed by A as a grocery clerk in the employ of C and the latter services are not excepted from employment.

(c) For provisions relating to the circumstances under which services which are excepted are nevertheless deemed to be employment, and relating to the circumstances under which services which are not excepted are nevertheless deemed not to be employment, see § 31.3306(d)-1. [Reg. § 31.3306(c)-3.]

☐ [*T.D. 6199, 9-5-56. Republished in T.D. 6516, 12-20-60; T.D. 6658, 6-27-63.*]

### [Reg. § 31.3306(c)(1)-1]

**§ 31.3306(c)(1)-1. Agricultural labor.—**Services performed by an employee for the person employing him which constitute "agricultural labor" as defined in section 3306(k) are excepted from employment. For provisions relating to the definition of the term "agricultural labor," see § 31.3306(k)-1. [Reg. § 31.3306(c)(1)-1.]

☐ [*T.D. 6199, 9-5-56. Republished in T.D. 6516, 12-20-60.*]

### [Reg. § 31.3306(c)(2)-1]

**§ 31.3306(c)(2)-1. Domestic service.—**(a) *In a private home.—* (1) Services of a household nature performed by an employee in or about a private home of the person by whom he is employed are excepted from the employment. A private home is a fixed place of abode of an individual or family. A separate and distinct dwelling unit maintained by an individual in an apartment house, hotel, or other similar establishment may constitute a private home. If a dwelling house is used primarily as a boarding or lodging house for the purpose of supplying board or lodging to the public as a business enterprise, it is not a private home and the services performed therein are not excepted.

(2) In general, services of a household nature in or about a private home include services performed by cooks, waiters, butlers, housekeepers, governesses, maids, valets, baby sitters, janitors, laundresses, furnacemen, caretakers, handymen, gardeners, footmen, grooms, and chauffeurs of automobiles for family use.

(b) *In a local college club or local chapter of a college fraternity or sorority.—*(1) Services of a household nature performed by an employee in or about the club rooms or house of a local college club or of a local chapter of a college fraternity or sorority by which he is employed are excepted from employment. A local college club or local chapter of a college fraternity or sorority does not include an alumni club or chapter. If the club room or house of a local college club or local chapter of a college fraternity or sorority is used primarily for the purpose of supplying board or lodging to students or the public as a business enterprise the services performed therein are not within the exception.

(2) In general, services of a household nature in or about the club rooms or house of a local college club or local chapter of a college fraternity or sorority include services rendered by cooks, waiters, butlers, maids, janitors, laundresses, furnacemen, handymen, gardeners, housekeepers, and housemothers.

(c) *Services not excepted.—*Services not of a household nature, such as services performed as a private secretary, tutor, or librarian, even though performed in the employer's private home or in a local college club or local chapter of a college fraternity or sorority, are not within the exception. Services of a household nature are not within the exception if performed in or about rooming or lodging houses, boarding houses, clubs (except local college clubs), hotels, hospitals, eleemosynary institutions, or commercial offices or establishments. [Reg. § 31.3306(c)(2)-1.]

☐ [*T.D. 6199, 9-5-56. Republished in T.D. 6516, 12-20-60.*]

### [Reg. § 31.3306(c)(3)-1]

**§ 31.3306(c)(3)-1. Services not in the course of employer's trade or business.—**(a) Services not in the course of the employer's trade or business performed by an employee for an employer in a calendar quarter are excepted from employment unless—

(1) The cash remuneration paid for such services performed by the employee for the employer in the calendar quarter is $50 or more; and

(2) Such employee is regularly employed in the calendar quarter by such employer to perform such services.

Unless the tests set forth in both subparagraphs (1) and (2) of this paragraph are met, the services are excepted from employment.

(b) The term "services not in the course of the employer's trade or business" includes services that do not promote or advance the trade or business of the employer. Services performed for a corporation do not come within the exception.

(c) The test relating to cash remuneration of $50 or more is based on the remuneration earned during a calendar quarter rather than on the remuneration paid in a calendar quarter. However, for purposes of determining whether the test is met, it is also required that the remuneration be paid, although it is immaterial when the remuneration is paid. Furthermore, in determining whether $50 or more has been paid for services not in the course of the employer's trade or business, only cash remuneration for such services shall be taken into account. The term "cash remuneration" includes checks and other monetary media of exchange. Remuneration paid in any other medium, such as lodging, food, or other goods or commodities, is disregarded in determining whether the cash-remuneration test is met.

(d) For purposes of this exception, an individual is deemed to be regularly employed by an employer during a calendar quarter only if—

(1) Such individual performs services not in the course of the employer's trade or business for such employer for some portion of the day on at least 24 days (whether or not consecutive) during such calendar quarter; or

(2) Such individual was regularly employed (as determined under subparagraph (1) of this paragraph) by such employer in the performance of services not in the course of the employer's trade or busines during the preceding calendar quarter (including the last calendar quarter of 1954).

(e) In detemining whether an employee has performed services not in the course of the employer's trade or business on at least 24 days during a calendar quarter, there shall be counted as one day—

(1) Any day or portion thereof on which the employee actually performs such services; and

(2) Any day or portion thereof on which the employee does not perform services of the prescribed character but with respect to which cash remuneration is paid or payable to the employee for such services, such as a day on which the employee is sick or on vacation. An employee who on a particualr day reports for work and, at the direction of his employer, holds himself in readiness to perform services not in the course of the employer's trade or business shall be considered to be engaged in the actual performance of such services on that day. For purposes of this exception, a day is a period of 24 hours commencing at midnight and ending at midnight.

(f) For provisions relating to the exclusion from wages of remuneration paid in any medium oher than cash for services not in the course of the employer's trade or business, see §31.3306(b)(7)-1. [Reg. §31.3306(c)(3)-1.]

☐ [*T.D.* 6199, 9-5-56. *Republished in T.D.* 6516, 12-20-60.]

### [Reg. §31.3306(c)(4)-1]

**§31.3306(c)(4)-1. Services on or in connection with a non-American vessel or aircraft.**—(a) Services performed within the United States by an employee for an employer "on or in connection with" a vessel not an American vessel, or "on or in connection with" an aircraft not an American aircraft, are excepted from employment if the employee is employed by the employer "on and in connection with" the vessel or aircraft when outside the United States.

(b) An employee performs services on and in connection with the vessel or aircraft if he performs services on the vessel or aircraft when outside the United States which are also in connection with the vessel or aircraft. Services performed on the vessel outside the United States by employees as officers or members of the crew, or by employees of concessionaires, of the vessel, for example, are performed under such circumstances, since such services are also connected with the vessel. Similarly, services performed on the aircraft outside the United States by employees as officers or members of the crew of the aircraft are performed on and in connection with such aircraft. Services may be performed on the vessel or aircraft, however, which have no connection with it, as in the case of services performed by an employee while on the vessel or aircraft merely as a passenger in the general sense. For example, the services of a buyer in the employ of a department store while he is a passenger on a vessel are not in connection with the vessel.

(c) The expression "on or in connection with" refers not only to services performed on the vessel or aircraft but also to services connected with the vessel or aircraft which are not actually performed on it (for example, shore services performed as officers or members of the crew, or as employees of concessionaires, of the vessel).

(d) The citizenship or residence of the employee and the place where the contract of service is entered into are immaterial for purposes of this exception, and the citizenship or residence of the person employing him is material only in case it has a bearing in determining whether the vessel is an American vessel. For definitions of the terms "vessel" and "aircraft", see paragraph (c)(2)(v) of §31.3306(c)-2. For definitions of the terms "American vessel" and "American aircraft", see §31.3306(m)-1.

(e) Since the only services performed outside the United States which constitute employment are those described in section 3306(c) and paragraph (c) of §31.3306(c)-2 (relating to services performed outside the United States on or in connection with an American vessel or American aircraft), services performed outside the United States on or in connection with a vessel not an American vessel, or an aircraft not an American aircraft, do not constitute employment in any event.

(f) The provisions of section 3306(c)(4) and of this section, insofar as they relate to services performed on or in connection with an aircraft not an American aircraft, apply only to services performed after 1961 for which remuneration is paid after 1961. [Reg. §31.3306(c)(4)-1.]

☐ [*T.D.* 6199, 9-5-56. *Republished in T.D.* 6516, 12-20-60; *T.D.* 6658, 6-27-63.]

### [Reg. §31.3306(c)(5)-1]

**§31.3306(c)(5)-1. Family employment.**—(a) Certain services are excepted from employment because of the existence of a family relationship between the employee and the individual employing him. The exceptions are as follows:

(1) Services performed by an individual in the employ of his or her spouse;

(2) Services performed by a father or mother in the employ of his or her son or daughter; and

(3) Services performed by a son or daughter under the age of 21 in the employ of his or her father or mother.

(b) Under paragraph (a)(1) and (2) of this section, the exception is conditioned solely upon the family relationship between the employee and the individual employing him. Under paragraph (a)(3) of this section, in addition to the family relationship, there is a further requirement that the son or daughter shall be under the age of 1, and the exception continues only during the time that such son or daughter is under the age of 21.

(c) Services performed in the employ of a partnership are within the exception described in paragraph (a) of this section only if the requisite family relationship exists between the employee and each of the partners comprising the partnership.

(d) Services performed in the employ of a corporation are not within the exception described in paragraph (a) of this section, except that services performed in the employ of an entity that is treated as a corporation under §301.7701-2(c)(2)(iv)(B) of this chapter may qualify for the exception if the requirements of the exception are otherwise met. An entity that is treated as a corporation under §301.7701-2(c)(2)(iv)(B) of this chapter is not treated as the employer for purposes of applying section 3306(c)(5) and this section. For purposes of applying section 3306(c)(5) and this section, the owner of an entity that is treated as a corporation under §301.7701-2(c)(2)(iv)(B) of this chapter is treated as the employer.

(e) Paragraphs (c) and (d) of this section apply to wages paid on or after November 1, 2011. However, taxpayers may apply paragraphs (c) and (d) of this section to wages paid on or after January 1, 2009. [Reg. §31.3306(c)(5)-1.]

☐ [*T.D.* 6199, 9-5-56. *Republished in T.D.* 6516, 12-20-60. *Amended by T.D.* 9554, 10-31-2011 *and T.D.* 9670, 6-25-2014.]

### [Reg. §31.3306(c)(6)-1]

**§31.3306(c)(6)-1. Services in employ of United States or instrumentality thereof.**—(a) *Services in employ of United States or wholly-owned instrumentality thereof.*—Services performed in the employ of the United States Government, except as provided in section 3306(n) (see §31.3306(n)-1), are excepted from employment. Services performed in the employ of an instrumentality of the United States which is wholly owned by the United States also are excepted from employment.

(b) *Services in employ of instrumentality not wholly owned by United States.*—(1) *Services performed after 1961.*—Services performed after 1961 in the employ of an instrumentality of the United States which is partially owned by the United States are excepted from employment, if the remuneration for such service is paid after 1961. Services performed after 1961 in the employ of an instrumentality of the United States which is neither wholly owned or partially owned by the United States are excepted from employment if (i) the instrumentality is exempt from the tax imposed by section 3301 by virtue of any provision of law which specifically refers to section 3301 or the corresponding section of prior law in granting exemption from such tax, and (ii) the remuneration for such service is paid after 1961. For provisions which make general exemptions from Federal taxation ineffectual as to the tax imposed by section 3301, see §31.3308-1.

(2) *Services performed before 1962.*—Services performed in the employ of an instrumentality of the United States which is not wholly owned by the United States are excepted from employment if the instrumentality is exempt from the tax imposed by section 3301 by virtue of any other provision of law, and (i) the services are performed before 1962 or (ii) remuneration for the services is paid before 1962. [Reg. §31.3306(c)(6)-1.]

☐ [*T.D.* 6199, 9-5-56. *Republished in T.D.* 6516, 12-20-60; *T.D.* 6658, 6-27-63.]

>>>→ *Caution: P.L. 91-373 has made state coverage of certain services performed for state, county, and municipal hospitals and institutions of higher learning a condition for approval of state laws after 1971.*

### [Reg. §31.3306(c)(7)-1]

**§31.3306(c)(7)-1. Services in employ of States or their political subdivisions or instrumentalities.**—(a) Services performed in the employ of any State, or of any political subdivision thereof, are excepted from employment. Services performed in the employ of an instrumentality of one or more States or political subdivisions thereof are excepted if the instrumentality is wholly owned by one or more of the foregoing. Services performed in the employ of an instrumen-tality of one or more of the several States or political subdivisions thereof which is not wholly owned by one or more of the foregoing are excepted only to the extent that the instrumentality is with respect to such services immune under the Constitution of the United States from the tax imposed by section 3301.

(b) For provisions relating to the term "State" see §31.3306(j)-1. [Reg. §31.3306(c)(7)-1.]

☐ [*T.D.* 6199, 9-5-56. *Republished in T.D.* 6516, 12-20-60; *T.D.* 6658, 6-27-63.]

>>>→ *Caution: P.L. 91-373 has made state coverage of certain services performed for nonprofit organizations a condition for approval of state laws after 1971.*

### [Reg. §31.3306(c)(8)-1]

**§31.3306(c)(8)-1. Services in employ of religious, charitable, educational, or certain other organizations exempt from income tax.**—(a) *Services performed after 1961.*—Services performed by an employee after 1961 in the employ of a religious, charitable, educational, or other organization described in section 501(c)(3) which is exempt from income tax under section 501(a) are excepted from employment, if the remuneration for such service is paid after 1961. For provisions relating to exemption from income tax of an organization described in section 501(c)(3), see Part 1 of this chapter (Income Tax Regulations).

(b) *Services performed before 1962.*—(1) Services performed by an employee in the employ of an organization described in section 3306(c)(8) as in effect before 1962, that is, a corporation, community chest, fund, or foundation, organized and operated exclusively for religious, charitable, scientific, testing for public safety, literary, or educational purposes, or for the prevention of cruelty to children or animals, no part of the net earnings of which inures to the benefit of any private shareholder or individual, and no substantial part of the activities of which is carrying on propaganda, or otherwise attempt-ing, to influence legislation, are excepted from employment if (i) the services are performed before 1962, or (ii) remuneration for the services is paid before 1962.

(2) Any organization which is an organization of a type de-scribed in section 501(c)(3) and which—

(i) Is exempt from income tax under section 501(a), or

(ii) Has been denied exemption from income tax under sec-tion 501(a) by reason of the provisions of section 503 or 504, relating to prohibited transactions and to accumulations out of income, respectively,

is an organization of a type described in section 3306(c)(8) as in effect before 1962. An organization which would be an organization of a type described in section 501(c)(3) except for those provisions of section 501(c)(3) which are contained in section 3306(c)(8) as in effect before 1962 (provisions relating to participation or intervention in a political campaign on behalf of a candidate for public office) is also an organization of a type described in section 3306(c)(8) as in effect before 1962. [Reg. §31.3306(c)(8)-1.]

☐ [*T.D.* 6199, 9-5-56. *Republished in T.D.* 6516, 12-20-60; *T.D.* 6658, 6-27-63.]

### [Reg. §31.3306(c)(9)-1]

**§31.3306(c)(9)-1. Railroad industry; services performed by an employee or an employee representative under the Railroad Unem-ployment Insurance Act.**—(a) Services performed by an individual as an "employee" or as an "employee representative", as those terms are defined in section 1 of the Railroad Unemployment Insurance Act, as amended, are excepted from employment.

(b) Section 1 of the Railroad Unemployment Insurance Act (45 U.S.C. 351), as amended, provides, in part, as follows:

For the purposes of this Act, except when used in amending the provisions of other Acts—

(a) The term "employer" means any carrier (as defined in subsec-tion (b) of this section), and any company which is directly or indirectly owned or controlled by one or more such carriers or under common control therewith, and which operates any equipment or facility or performs any service (except trucking service, casual ser-vice, and the casual operation of equipment or facilities) in connec-tion with the transportation of passengers or property by railroad, or the receipt, delivery, elevation, transfer in transit, refrigeration or icing, storage, or handling of property transported by railroad, and any receiver, trustee, or other individual or body, judicial or other-wise, when in the possession of the property or operating all or any part of the business of any such employer: *Provided, however*, That the term "employer" shall not include any street, interurban, or subur-ban electric railway, unless such railway is operating as a part of a general steam-railroad system of transportation, but shall not exclude any part of the general steam-railroad system of transportation now or hereafter operated by any other motive power. The Interstate Commerce Commission is hereby authorized and directed upon request of the Board, or upon complaint of any party interested, to determine after hearing whether any line operated by electric power falls within the terms of this proviso. The term "employer" shall also include railroad associations, traffic associations, tariff bureaus, de-murrage bureaus, weighing and inspection bureaus, collection agen-cies, and other associations, bureaus, agencies, or organizations controlled and maintained wholly or principally by two or more employers as hereinbefore defined and engaged in the performance of services in connection with or incidental to railroad transportation; and railway labor organizations, national in scope, which have been or may be organized in accordance with the provisions of the Rail-way Labor Act, and their State and National legislative committees and their general committees pursuant to the constitution and by-laws of such organizations. The term "employer" shall not include any company by reason of its being engaged in the mining of coal, the supplying of coal to an employer where delivery is not beyond the mine tipple, and the operation of equipment or facilities therefor, or in any of such activities.

(b) The term "carrier" means an express company, sleeping-car company, or carrier by railroad, subject to part I of the interstate Commerce Act.

(c) The term "company" includes corporations, associations, and joint-stock companies.

(d) The term "employee" (except when used in phrases establish-ing a different meaning) means any individual who is or has been (i) in the service of one or more employers for compensation, or (ii) an employee representative. The term "employee" shall include an em-ployee of a local lodge or division defined as an employer in section 1(a) only if he was in the service of a carrier on or after August 29, 1935. The term "employee" includes an officer of an employer.

The term "employee" shall not include any individual while such individual is engaged in the physical operations consisting of the mining of coal, the preparation of coal, the handling (other than movement by rail with standard railroad locomotives) of coal not beyond the mine tipple, or the loading of coal at the tipple.

(e) An individual is in the service of an employer whether his service is rendered within or without the United States if (i) he is subject to the continuing authority of the employer to supervise and direct the manner of rendition of his service, or he is rendering professional or technical services and is integrated into the staff of the employer, or he is rendering, on the property used in the em-ployer's operations, other personal services the rendition of which is integrated into the employer's operations, and (ii) he renders such service for compensation: *Provided, however*, That an individual shall be deemed to be in the service of an employer, other than a local lodge or division or a general committee of a railway-labor-organiza-tion employer, not conducting the principal part of its business in the United States only when he is rendering service to it in the United States; and an individual shall be deemed to be in the service of such a local lodge or division only if (1) all, or substantially all, the individuals constituting its membership are employees of an em-ployer conducting the principal part of its business in the United States; or (2) the headquarters of such local lodge or division is located in the United States; and an individual shall be deemed to be in the service of such a general committee only if (1) he is represent-ing a local lodge or division described in clauses (1) or (2) immedi-ately above; or (2) all, or substantially all, the individuals represented by it are employees of an employer conducting the principal part of its business in the United States; or (3) he acts in the capacity of a general chairman or an assistant general chairman of a general committee which represents individuals rendering service in the United States to an employer, but in such case if his office or headquarters is not located in the United States and the individuals represented by such general committee are employees of an em-ployer not conducting the principal part of its business in the United States, only such proportion of the remuneration for such service shall be regarded as compensation as the proportion which the mileage in the United States under the jurisdiction of such general committee bears to the total mileage under its jurisdiction, unless such mileage formula is inapplicable, in which case the Board may prescribe such other formula as it finds to be equitable, and if the application of such mileage formula, or such other formula as the Board may prescribe, would result in the compensation of the individual being less than 10 per centum of his remuneration for such service no part of such remuneration shall be regarded as compensation: *Provided further,* That an individual not a citizen or resident of the United States shall not be deemed to be in the service of an employer when rendering service outside the United States to an employer who is required under the laws applicable in the place where the service is rendered to employ therein, in whole or in part, citizens or residents thereof.

(f) The term "employee representative" means any officer or official representative of a railroad labor organization other than a labor organization included in the term employer as defined in section 1(a) who before or after August 29, 1935, was in the service of an employer as defined in section 1(a) and who is duly authorized and designated to represent employees in accordance with the Railway Labor Act, and any individual who is regularly assigned to or regularly employed by such officer or official representative in connection with the duties of his office.

* * *

(i) The term "compensation" means any form of money remuneration, including pay for time lost but excluding tips, paid for services rendered as an employee to one or more employers, or as an employee representative: *Provided, however,* That in computing the compensation paid to an employee, no part of any month's compensation in excess of $300 for any month before July 1, 1954, or in excess of $350 for any month after June 30, 1954, and before the calendar month next following the month [May] in which this Act was amended in 1959, or in excess of $400 for any month after the month [May] in which this Act was so amended, shall be recognized. A payment made by an employer to an individual through the employer's pay roll shall be presumed, in the absence of evidence to the contrary, to be compensation for service rendered by such individual as an employee of the employer in the period with respect to which the payment is made. An employee shall be deemed to be paid, "for time lost" the amount he is paid by an employer with respect to an identifiable period of absence from the active service of the employer, including absence on account of personal injury, and the amount he is paid by the employer for loss of earnings resulting from his displacement to a less remunerative position or occupation. If a payment is made by an employer with respect to a personal injury and includes pay for time lost, the total payment shall be deemed to be paid for time lost unless, at the time of payment, a part of such payment is specifically apportioned to factors other than time lost, in which event only such part of the payment as is not so apportioned shall be deemed to be paid for time lost. Compensation earned in any calendar month before 1947 shall be deemed paid in such month regardless of whether or when payment will have been in fact made, and compensation earned in any calendar year after 1946 but paid after the end of such calendar year shall be deemed to be compensation paid in the calendar year in which it will have been earned if it is so reported by the employer before February 1 of the next succeeding calendar year or, if the employee establishes, subject to the provisions of section 8, the period during which such compensation will have been earned.

* * *

(r) The term "Board" means the Railroad Retirement Board.

(s) The term "United States", when used in a geographical sense, means the States, Alaska, Hawaii, and the District of Columbia.

* * *

[Sec. 1, Railroad Unemployment Insurance Act, as amended by secs. 1 and 2, Act of June 20, 1939, 53 Stat. 845; secs. 1 and 3, Act of Aug. 13, 1940, 54 Stat. 785, 786; sec. 15, Act of Apr. 8, 1942, 56 Stat. 210; secs. 1 and 2, Act of July 31, 1946, 60 Stat. 722; sec. 302, Act of Aug. 31, 1954, 68 Stat. 1040; sec. 301, Act of May 19, 1959, Pub. Law 86-28, 7 Stat. 30.] [Reg. § 31.3306(c)(9)-1.]

☐ [*T.D. 6199,* 9-5-56. *Republished in T.D. 6516,* 12-20-60; *T.D. 6658,* 6-27-63.]

**[Reg. § 31.3306(c)(10)-1]**

**§ 31.3306(c)(10)-1. Services in the employ of certain organizations exempt from income tax.**—(a) *In general.*—(1) This section deals with the exception from employment of certain services performed in the employ of any organization exempt from income tax under section 501(a) (other than an organization described in section 401(a)) or under section 521. (See the provisions of §§ 1.401-1, 1.501(a)-1, and 1.521-1 of this chapter (Income Tax Regulations).) If the services meet the tests set forth in paragraphs (b), (c), (d), or (e) of this section, the services are excepted.

(2) See also § 31.3306(c)(8)-1 for provisions relating to the exception of services performed in the employ of religious, charitable, educational, or certain other organizations exempt from income tax; § 31.3306(c)(10)-2 for provisions relating to the exception of services performed by certain students in the employ of a school, college, or university; and § 31.3306(c)(10)-3 for provisions relating to the exception of services performed before 1962 in the employ of certain employees' beneficiary associations.

(b) *Remuneration less than $50 for calendar quarter.*—Services performed by an employee in a calendar quarter in the employ of an organization exempt from income tax under section 501(a) (other than an organization described in section 401(a)) or under section 521 are excepted from employment, if the remuneration for the services is less than $50. The test relating to remuneration of $50 is based on the remuneration earned during a calendar quarter rather than on the remuneration paid in a calendar quarter. The exception applies separately with respect to each organization for which the employee renders services in a calendar quarter. The type of services performed by the employee and the place where the services are performed are immaterial; the statutory tests are the character of the organization in the employ of which the services are performed and the amount of the remuneration for services performed by the employee in the calendar quarter.

*Example (1).* X is a local lodge of a fraternal organization and is exempt from income tax under section 501(a) as an organization of the character described in section 501(c)(8). X has a number of paid employees, among them being A who serves exclusively as recording secretary for the lodge, and B who performs services for the lodge as janitor of its clubhouse. For services performed during the first calendar quarter of 1955 (that is, January 1, 1955, through March 31, 1955, both dates inclusive) A earns a total of $30. For services performed during the same calendar quarter of 1955 (that is, January 1, 1955, through March 31, 1955, both dates inclusive) A earns a total of $30. For services performed during the same calendar quarter B earns $180. Since the remuneration for the services performed by A during such quarter is less than $50, all of such services are excepted. Thus, A is not counted as an employee in employment on any of the days during such quarter for purposes of determining whether the X organization is an employer (see § 31.3306(a)-1). Even though it is subsequently determined that X is an employer, A's remuneration of $30 for services performed during the first calendar quarter of such year is not subject to tax. B's services, however, are not excepted during such quarter since the remuneration therefor is not less than $50. Thus, B is counted as an employee in employment during all of such quarter for purposes of determining whether the X organization is an employer. If it is determined that the X organization is an employer, B's remuneration of $180 for services performed during the first calendar quarter is included in computing the tax.

*Example (2).* The facts are the same as in example (1), above, except that on April 1, 1955, A's salary is increased and, for services performed during the calendar quarter beginning on that date (that is, April 1, 1955, through June 30, 1955, both dates inclusive), A earns $60. Although all of the services performed by A during the first quarter were excepted, none of A's services performed during the second quarter are excepted since the remuneration for such services is not less than $50. A, therefore, is counted as an employee in employment during all of the second quarter for the purpose of determining whether the X organization is an employer. If it is determined that the X organization is an employer, A's remuneration of $60 for services performed during the second calendar quarter is included in computing the tax.

*Example (3).* The facts are the same as in example (1), above, except that A earns $120 for services performed during the year 1955, and such amount is paid to him in a lump sum at the end of the year. The services performed by A in any calendar quarter during the year are excepted if the portion of the $120 attributable to services performed in that quarter is less than $50. In such case, A is not counted as an employee in employment on any of the days during such quarter for purposes of determining whether the X organization is an employer. If, however, the portion of the $120 attributable to services performed in any calendar quarter during the year is not less than $50, the services during that quarter are not excepted. In the latter case, A is counted as an employee in employment during all of such quarter and, if it is determined that the X organization is an employer, that portion of the $120 attribuable to services performed in such quarter is included in computing the tax.

(c) *Collection of dues or premiums for fraternal beneficiary societies, and ritualistic services in connection with such societies, before 1962.*—The following services performed by an employee in the employ of a fraternal beneficiary society, order, or association exempt from income tax under section 501(a) are excepted from employment if the services are performed before 1962 or if remuneration for the services is paid before 1962:

(1) Services performed away from the home office of such a society, order, or association in connection with the collection of dues or premiums for such society, order, or association; and

(2) Ritualistic services (wherever performed) in connection with such a society, order, or association.

For purposes of this paragraph the amount of the remuneration for services performed by the employee in the calendar quarter is immaterial; the tests are the character of the organization in whose employ the services are performed, the type of services, and, in the case of collection of dues or premiums, the place where the services are performed.

(d) *Students employed before 1962.*—(1) Services performed in the employ of an organization exempt from income tax under section 501(a) (other than an organization described in section 401(a)) or under section 521 by a student who is enrolled and is regularly attending classes at a school, college, or university, are excepted from employment if the services are performed before 1962 or if remuneration for the services is paid before 1962. For purposes of this paragraph, the amount of remuneration for services performed by the employee in the calendar quarter, the type of services, and the place where the services are performed are immaterial; the tests are the character of the organization in whose employ the services are performed and the status of the employee as a student enrolled and regularly attending classes at a school, college, or university.

(2) The term "school, college, or university" as used in this paragraph is to be taken in its commonly or generally accepted sense. For provisions relating to services performed before 1962 by a student enrolled and regularly attending classes at a school, college, or university not exempt from income tax in the employ of such school, college, or university, see paragraph (b) of § 31.3306(c)(10)-2. For provisions relating to services performed after 1961 by a student enrolled and regularly attending classes at a school, college, or uni-

versity in the employ of such school, college, or university, see paragraph (a) of § 31.3306(c)(10)-2.

(e) *Services performed before 1962 in employ of agricultural or horticultural organization exempt from income tax.*—(1) Services performed by an employee in the employ of an agricultural or horticultural organization which is described in section 501(c)(5) and the regulations thereunder and which is exempt from income tax under section 501(a) are excepted from employment if the services are performed before 1962 or if remuneration of the services is paid before 1962.

(2) For purposes of this paragraph, the type of services performed by the employee, the amount of remuneration for the services, and the place where the services are performed are immaterial; the test is the character of the organization in whose employ the services are performed. [Reg. § 31.3306(c)(10)-1.]

☐ [*T.D. 6199*, 9-5-56. Republished in *T.D.* 6516, 12-20-60; *T.D.* 6658, 6-27-63.]

### [Reg. §31.3306(c)(10)-2]

**§ 31.3306(c)(10)-2. Services of student in employ of school, college, or university.**—(a) *Services performed after 1961.*—Services performed after 1961 in the employ of a school, college, or university, by a student who is enrolled and is regularly attending classes at the school, college, or university, are excepted from employment (whether or not the school, college, or university is exempt from income tax), if remuneration for the services is paid after 1961.

(b) *Services performed before 1962.*—Services performed in the employ of a school, college, or university not exempt from income tax under section 501(a), by a student who is enrolled and is regularly attending classes at the school, college, or university, are excepted from employment if the services are performed before 1962 or if remuneration for the services is paid before 1962.

⟫⟫→ *Caution: Reg. §31.3306(c)(10)-2(c), below, prior to amendment by T.D. 9167, is applicable for services performed before April 1, 2005.*

(c) *Application of section.*—(1) For purposes of this section, the type of services performed by the employee, the place where the services are performed, and the amount of remuneration for services performed by the employee are immaterial; the tests are the character of the organization in the employ of which the services are performed and the status of the employee as a student enrolled and regularly attending classes at the school, college, or university in the employ of which he performs the services.

(2) The status of the employee as a student performing the services shall be determined on the basis of the relationship of such

employee with the organization for which the services are performed. An employee who performs services in the employ of a school, college, or university as an incident to and for the purpose of pursuing a course of study at such school, college, or university has the status of a student in the performance of such services.

(3) The term "school, college, or university" as used in this section is to be taken in its commonly or generally accepted sense.

(4) For provisions relating to services performed before 1962 by a student in the employ of an organization exempt from income tax, see paragraph (d) of § 31.3306(c)(10)-1.

⟫⟫→ *Caution: Reg. §31.3306(c)(10)-2(c), below, as amended by T.D. 9167, is applicable for services performed on or after April 1, 2005.*

(c) *General rule.*—(1) For purposes of this section, the tests are the character of the organization in the employ of which the services are performed and the status of the employee as a student enrolled and regularly attending classes at the school, college, or university described in paragraph (c)(2) of this section, in the employ of which the employee performs the services. If an employee has the status of a student within the meaning of paragraph (d) of this section, the type of services performed by the employee, the place where the services are performed, and the amount of remuneration for services performed by the employee are not material.

(2) *School, college, or university.*—An organization is a *school, college, or university* within the meaning of section 3306(c)(10)(B) if its primary function is the presentation of formal instruction, it normally maintains a regular faculty and curriculum, and it normally has a regularly enrolled body of students in attendance at the place where its educational activities are regularly carried on. See section 170(b)(1)(A)(ii) and the regulations thereunder.

(d) *Student status—general rule.*—Whether an employee has the status of a student within the meaning of section 3306(c)(10)(B) performing the services shall be determined based on the relationship of the employee with the organization for which the services are performed. In order to have the status of a student within the meaning of section 3306(c)(10)(B), the employee must perform services in the employ of a school, college, or university described in paragraph (c)(2) of this section at which the employee is enrolled and regularly attending classes in pursuit of a course of study within the meaning of paragraphs (d)(1) and (2) of this section. In addition, the employee's services must be incident to and for the purpose of pursuing a course of study at such school, college, or university within the meaning of paragraph (d)(3) of this section.

(1) *Enrolled and regularly attending classes.*—An employee must be enrolled and regularly attending classes at a school, college, or university within the meaning of paragraph (c)(2) of this section at which the employee is employed to have the status of a student within the meaning of section 3306(c)(10)(B). An employee is enrolled within the meaning of section 3306(c)(10)(B) if the employee is regis-

tered for a course or courses creditable toward an educational credential described in paragraph (d)(2) of this section. In addition, the employee must be regularly attending classes to have the status of a student. For purposes of this paragraph (d)(1), a class is an instructional activity led by a faculty member or other qualified individual hired by the school, college, or university within the meaning of paragraph (c)(2) of this section for identified students following an established curriculum. The frequency of these and similar activities determines whether an employee may be considered to be regularly attending classes.

(2) *Course of study.*—An employee must be pursuing a course of study in order to have the status of a student within the meaning of section 3306(c)(10)(B). A course of study is one or more courses the completion of which fulfills the requirements necessary to receive an educational credential granted by a school, college, or university within the meaning of paragraph (c)(2) of this section. For purposes of this paragraph, an educational credential is a degree, certificate, or other recognized educational credential granted by an organization described in paragraph (c)(2) of this section. In addition, a course of study is one or more courses at a school, college or university within the meaning of paragraph (c)(2) of this section the completion of which fulfills the requirements necessary for the employee to sit for an examination required to receive certification by a recognized organization in a field.

(3) *Incident to and for the purpose of pursuing a course of study.*— (i) *General rule.*—An employee's services must be incident to and for the purpose of pursuing a course of study in order for the employee to have the status of a student. Whether an employee's services are incident to and for the purpose of pursuing a course of study shall be determined on the basis of the relationship of the employee with the organization for which such services are performed as an employee. The educational aspect of the relationship between the employer and the employee, as compared to the service aspect of the relationship, must be predominant in order for the employee's services to be incident to and for the purpose of pursuing a course of study. The educational aspect of the relationship is evaluated based on all the relevant facts and circumstances related to the educational aspect of

the relationship. The service aspect of the relationship is evaluated based on all the relevant facts and circumstances related to the employee's employment. The evaluation of the service aspect of the relationship is not affected by the fact that the services performed by the employee may have an educational, instructional, or training aspect. Except as provided in paragraph (d)(3)(iii) of this section, whether the educational aspect or the service aspect of an employee's relationship with the employer is predominant is determined by considering all the relevant facts and circumstances. Relevant factors in evaluating the educational and service aspects of an employee's relationship with the employer are described in paragraphs (d)(3)(iv) and (v) of this section respectively. There may be facts and circumstances that are relevant in evaluating the educational and service aspects of the relationship in addition to those described in paragraphs (d)(3)(iv) and (v) of this section.

(ii) *Student status determined with respect to each academic term.*—Whether an employee's services are incident to and for the purpose of pursuing a course of study is determined separately with respect to each academic term. If the relevant facts and circumstances with respect to an employee's relationship with the employer change significantly during an academic term, whether the employee's services are incident to and for the purpose of pursuing a course of study is reevaluated with respect to services performed during the remainder of the academic term.

(iii) *Full-time employee.*—The services of a full-time employee are not incident to and for the purpose of pursuing a course of study. The determination of whether an employee is a full-time employee is based on the employer's standards and practices, except regardless of the employer's classification of the employee, an employee whose normal work schedule is 40 hours or more per week is considered a full-time employee. An employee's normal work schedule is not affected by increases in hours worked caused by work demands unforeseen at the start of an academic term. However, whether an employee is a full-time employee is reevaluated for the remainder of the academic term if the employee changes employment positions with the employer. An employee's work schedule during academic breaks is not considered in determining whether the employee's normal work schedule is 40 hours or more per week. The determination of the employee's normal work schedule is not affected by the fact that the services performed by the individual may have an educational, instructional, or training aspect.

(iv) *Evaluating educational aspect.*—The educational aspect of an employee's relationship with the employer is evaluated based on all the relevant facts and circumstances related to the educational aspect of the relationship. The educational aspect of an employee's relationship with the employer is generally evaluated based on the employee's course workload. Whether an employee's course workload is sufficient in order for the employee's employment to be incident to and for the purpose of pursuing a course of study depends on the particular facts and circumstances. A relevant factor in evaluating an employee's course workload is the employee's course workload relative to a full-time course workload at the school, college or university within the meaning of paragraph (c)(2) of this section at which the employee is enrolled and regularly attending classes.

(v) *Evaluating service aspect.*—The service aspect of an employee's relationship with the employer is evaluated based on the facts and circumstances related to the employee's employment. Services of an employee with the status of a full-time employee within the meaning of paragraph (d)(3)(iii) of this section are not incident to and for the purpose of pursuing a course of study. Relevant factors in evaluating the service aspect of an employee's relationship with the employer are described in paragraphs (d)(3)(v)(A), (B), and (C) of this section.

(A) *Normal work schedule and hours worked.*—If an employee is not a full-time employee within the meaning of paragraph (d)(3)(iii) of this section, then the employee's normal work schedule and number of hours worked per week are relevant factors in evaluating the service aspect of the employee's relationship with the employer. As an employee's normal work schedule or actual number of hours worked approaches 40 hours per week, it is more likely that the service aspect of the employee's relationship with the employer is predominant. The determination of the employee's normal work schedule and actual number of hours worked is not affected by the fact that some of the services performed by the individual may have an educational, instructional, or training aspect.

(B) *Professional employee.*—(1) If an employee has the status of a professional employee, then that suggests that the service aspect of the employee's relationship with the employer is predominant. A professional employee is an employee—

(i) Whose primary duty consists of the performance of work requiring knowledge of an advanced type in a field of science or learning customarily acquired by a prolonged course of specialized intellectual instruction and study, as distinguished from a general academic education, from an apprenticeship, and from training in the performance of routine mental, manual, or physical processes;

(ii) Whose work requires the consistent exercise of discretion and judgment in its performance; and

(iii) Whose work is predominantly intellectual and varied in character (as opposed to routine mental, manual, mechanical, or physical work) and is of such character that the output produced or the result accomplished cannot be standardized in relation to a given period of time.

(2) *Licensed, professional employee.*—If an employee is a licensed, professional employee, then that further suggests the service aspect of the employee's relationship with the employer is predominant. An employee is a licensed, professional employee if the employee is required to be licensed under state or local law to work in the field in which the employee performs services and the employee is a professional employee within the meaning of paragraph (d)(3)(v)(B)(1) of this section.

(C) *Employment benefits.*—Whether an employee is eligible to receive employment benefits is a relevant factor in evaluating the service aspect of an employee's relationship with the employer. For example, eligibility to receive vacation, paid holiday, and paid sick leave benefits; eligibility to participate in a retirement plan described in section 401(a); or eligibility to receive employment benefits such as reduced tuition, or benefits under section 79 (life insurance), 127 (qualified educational assistance), 129 (dependent care assistance programs), or 137 (adoption assistance) suggest that the service aspect of an employee's relationship with the employer is predominant. Eligibility to receive health insurance employment benefits is not considered in determining whether the service aspect of an employee's relationship with the employer is predominant. The weight to be given the fact that an employee is eligible for a particular benefit may vary depending on the type of employment benefit. For example, eligibility to participate in a retirement plan is generally more significant than eligibility to receive a dependent care employment benefit. Additional weight is given to the fact that an employee is eligible to receive an employment benefit if the benefit is generally provided by the employer to employees in positions generally held by non-students.

(e) *Effective date.*—Paragraphs (c) and (d) of this section apply to services performed on or after April 1, 2005. [Reg. § 31.3306(c)(10)-2.]

☐ [*T.D.* 6199, 9-5-56. *Republished in T.D.* 6516, 12-20-60; *T.D.* 6658, 6-27-63 *and T.D.* 9167, 12-20-2004.]

**[Reg. § 31.3306(c)(10)-3]**

**§ 31.3306(c)(10)-3. Services before 1962 in employ of certain employees' beneficiary associations.**—(a) *Voluntary employees' beneficiary associations.*—Services performed by an employee in the employ of a voluntary employees' beneficiary association providing for the payment of life, sick, accident, or other benefits to the members of such association or their dependents are excepted from employment if—

(1) No part of its net earnings inures (other than through such payments) to the benefit of any private shareholder or individual,

(2) 85 percent or more of the income consists of amounts collected from members for the sole purpose of making such payments and meeting expenses, and

(3) The services are performed before 1962, or remuneration for the services is paid before 1962.

(b) *Federal employees' beneficiary associations.*—Services performed by an employee in the employ of a voluntary employees' beneficiary association providing for the payment of life, sick, accident, or other benefits to the members of such association or their dependents or their designated beneficiaries are excepted from employment if—

(1) Admission to membership in the association is limited to individuals who are officers or employees of the United States Government,

(2) No part of the net earnings of the association inures (other than through such payments) to the benefit of any private shareholder or individual, and

(3) The services are performed before 1962, or remuneration for the services is paid before 1962.

(c) *Application of tests.*—For purposes of this section, the type of services performed by the employee, the amount of remuneration for the services, and the place where the services are performed are immaterial; the test is the character of the organization in whose employ the services are performed. [Reg. § 31.3306(c)(10)-3.]

☐ [*T.D.* 6199, 9-5-56. *Republished in T.D.* 6516, 12-20-60; *T.D.* 6658, 6-27-63.]

### [Reg. §31.3306(c)(11)-1]

§31.3306(c)(11)-1. **Services in employ of foreign government.**—(a) Services performed by an employee in the employ of a foreign government are excepted from employment. The exception includes not only services performed by ambassadors, ministers, and other diplomatic officers and employees but also services performed as a consular or other officer or employee of a foreign government, or as a nondiplomatic representative thereof.

(b) For purposes of this exception, the citizenship or residence of the employee is immaterial. It is also immaterial whether the foreign government grants an equivalent exemption with respect to similar services performed in the foreign country by citizens of the United States.[Reg. §31.3306(c)(11)-1.]

☐ [*T.D.* 6199, 9-5-56. *Republished in T.D.* 6516, 12-20-60.]

### [Reg. §31.3306(c)(12)-1]

§31.3306(c)(12)-1. **Services in employ of wholly owned instrumentality of foreign government.**—(a) Services performed by an employee in the employ of certain instrumentalities of a foreign government are excepted from employment. The exception includes all services performed in the employ of an instrumentality of the government of a foreign country, if—

(1) The instrumentality is wholly owned by the foreign government;

(2) The services are of a character similar to those performed in foreign countries by employees of the United States Government or of an instrumentality thereof; and

(3) The Secretary of States certifies to the Secretary of the Treasury that the foreign government, with respect to whose instrumentality exemption is claimed, grants an equivalent exemption with respect to services performed in the foreign country by employees of the United States Government and of instrumentalities thereof.

(b) For purposes of this exception, the citizenship or residence of the employee is immaterial. [Reg. §31.3306(c)(12)-1.]

☐ [*T.D.* 6199, 9-5-56. *Republishd in T.D.* 6516, 12-20-60.]

### [Reg. §31.3306(c)(13)-1]

§31.3306(c)(13)-1. **Services of student nurse or hospital intern.**—(a) Services performed as a student nurse in the employ of a hospital or a nurses' training school are excepted from employment, if the student nurse is enrolled and regularly attending classes in a nurses' training school and such nurses' training school is chartered or approved pursuant to State law.

(b) Services performed as an intern (as distinguished from a resident doctor) in the employ of a hospital are excepted from employment, if the intern has completed a 4 years' course in a medical school chartered or approved pursuant to State law. [Reg. §31.3306(c)(13)-1.]

☐ [*T.D.* 6199, 9-5-56. *Republished in T.D.* 6516, 12-20-60.]

### [Reg. §31.3306(c)(14)-1]

§31.3306(c)(14)-1. **Services of insurance agent or solicitor.**—(a) Services performed for a person by an employee as an insurance agent or insurance solicitor are excepted from employment, if all such services performed for such person by such individual are performed for remuneration solely by way of commission.

(b) If all or any part of the remuneration of an employee for services performed as an insurance agent or insurance solicitor for a person is a salary, none of his services performed as an insurance agent or insurance solicitor for such person are excepted from employment, and his total remuneration (for example, salary, or salary and commissions) for such services is included for purposes of computing the tax. [Reg. §31.3306(c)(14)-1.]

☐ [*T.D.* 6199, 9-5-56. *Republished in T.D.* 6516, 12-20-60.]

### [Reg. §31.3306(c)(15)-1]

§31.3306(c)(15)-1. **Services in delivery or distribution of newspapers, shopping news or magazines.**—(a) *Services of individuals under age 18.*—Services performed by an employee under the age of 18 in the delivery or distribution of newspapers or shopping news, not including delivery or distribution (as, for example, by a regional distributor) to any point for subsequent delivery or distribution, are excepted from employment. Thus, the services performed by an employee under the age of 18 in making house-to-house delivery or sale of newspapers or shopping news, including handbills and other similar types of advertising material, are excepted. The services are excepted irrespective of the form or method of compensation. Incidental services by the employee who makes the house-to-house delivery, such as services in assembling newspapers, are considered

to be within the exception. The exception continues only during the time that the employee is under the age of 18.

(b) *Services of individuals of any age.*—Services performed by an employee in, and at the time of, the sale of newspapers or magazines to ultimate consumers under an arrangement under which the newspapers or magazines are to be sold by him at a fixed price, his compensation being based on the retention of the excess of such price over the amount at which the newspapers or magazines are charged to him, are excepted from employment. The services are excepted whether or not the employee is guaranteed a minimum amount of compensation for such services, or is entitled to be credited with the unsold newspapers or magazines turned back. Moreover, the services are excepted without regard to the age of the employee. Services performed other than at the time of sale to the ultimate consumer are not within the exception. Thus, the services of a regional distributor which are antecedent to but not immediately part of the sale to the ultimate consumer are not within the exception. However, incidental services by the employee who makes the sale to the ultimate consumer, such as services in assembling newspapers or in taking newspapers or magazines to the place of sale, are considered to be within the exception. [Reg. §31.3306(c)(15)-1.]

☐ [*T.D.* 6199, 9-5-56. *Republished in T.D.* 6516, 12-20-60.]

### [Reg. §31.3306(c)(16)-1]

§31.3306(c)(16)-1. **Services in employ of international organization.**—(a) Subject to the provisions of section 1 of the International Organizations Immunities Act (22 U.S.C. 288), services performed in the employ of an international organization as defined in section 7701 (a)(18) are excepted from employment.

(b)(1) Section 7701(a)(18) provides as follows:

Sec. 7701. *Definitions.* (a) When used in this title, where not otherwise distinctly expressed or manifestly incompatible with the intent thereof—

\* \* \*

(18)*International organization.* The term "international organization" means a public international organization entitled to enjoy privileges, exemptions, and immunities as an international organization under the International Organizations Immunities Act (22 U.S.C. 288-288f).

(2) Section 1 of the International Organizations Immunities Act provides as follows:

Sec. 1. [*International Organizations Immunities Act.*]For the purposes of this title [International Organizations Immunities Act], the term "international organization" means a public international organization in which the United States participates pursuant to any treaty or under the authority of any Act of Congress authorizing such participation or making an appropriation for such participation, and which shall have been designated by the President through appropriate Executive order as being entitled to enjoy the privileges, exemptions, and immunities herein provided. The President shall be authorized, in the light of the functions performed by any such international organization, by appropriate Executive order to withhold or withdraw from any such organization or its officers or employees any of the privileges, exemptions, and immunities provided for in this title (including the amendments made by this title) or to condition or limit the enjoyment by any such organization or its officers or employees of any such privilege, exemption, or immunity. The President shall be authorized, if in his judgment such action should be justified by reason of the abuse by an international organization or its officers and employees of the privileges, exemptions, and immunities herein provided or for any other reason, at any time to revoke the designation of any international organization under this section, whereupon the international organization in question shall cease to be classed as an international organization for the purposes of this title. [Reg. §31.3306(c)(16)-1.]

☐ [*T.D.* 6199, 9-5-56. *Republished in T.D.* 6516, 12-20-60.]

### [Reg. §31.3306(c)(17)-1]

§31.3306(c)(17)-1. **Fishing services.**—(a) *In general.*—Subject to the limitations prescribed in paragraphs (b) and (c) of this section, services described in this paragraph are excepted from employment. Services performed by an individual in the catching, taking, harvesting, cultivating, or farming of any kind of fish, shellfish (for example, oysters, clams, and mussels), crustacea (for example, lobsters, crabs, and shrimps), sponges, seaweeds, or other aquatic forms of animal and vegetable life are excepted. The exception extends to services performed as an officer or member of the crew of a vessel while the vessel is engaged in any such activity whether or not the officer or member of the crew is himself so engaged. In the case of an individual who is engaged in any such activity in the employ of any person, the services performed, by such individual in the employ of such person, as an ordinary incident to any such activity are excepted. Similarly, for example, the shore services of an officer or member of the crew of a vessel engaged in any such activity are excepted if such services are an ordinary incident to any such activity. Services performed as an ordinary incident to any such activity may include, for example, services performed in such cleaning, icing, and packing of fish as are necessary for the immediate preservation of the catch.

(b) *Salmon and halibut fishing.*—Services performed in connection with the catching or taking of salmon or halibut, for commercial purposes, are not within the exception. Thus, neither the services of an officer or member of the crew of a vessel (irrespective of its tonnage) which is engaged in the catching or taking of salmon or halibut, for commercial purposes, nor the services of any other individual in connection with such activity, are within the exception.

(c) *Vessels of more than 10 net tons.*—Services described in paragraph (a) of this section performed on or in connection with a vessel of more than 10 net tons are not within the exception. For purposes of the exception, the tonnage of the vessel shall be determined in the manner provided for determining the register tonnage of merchant vessels under the laws of the United States. [Reg. § 31.3306(c)(17)-1.]

☐ [*T.D.* 6199, 9-5-56. *Republished in T.D.* 6516, 12-20-60.]

≫→ *Caution: This regulation has not been amended to reflect the changes made by P.L. 100-647.*

### [Reg. § 31.3306(c)(18)-1]

**§ 31.3306(c)(18)-1. Services of certain nonresident aliens.**—(a)(1) Services performed after 1961 by a nonresident alien individual who is temporarily present in the United States as a nonimmigrant under subparagraph (F) or (J) of section 101(a)(15) of the Immigration and Nationality Act (8 U.S.C. 1101), as amended, are excepted from employment if the services are performed to carry out a purpose for which the individual was admitted. For purposes of this section an alien individual who is temporarily present in the United States as a nonimmigrant under such subparagraph (F) or (J) is deemed to be a nonresident alien individual. The preceding sentence does not apply to the extent it is inconsistent with section 7701(b) and the regulations under that section. A nonresident alien individual who is temporarily present in the United States as a nonimmigrant under such subparagraph (J) includes an alien individual admitted to the United States as an "exchange visitor" under section 201 of the United States Information and Educational Exchange Act of 1948 (22 U.S.C. 1446).

(2) If services are performed by a nonresident alien individual's alien spouse or minor child, who is temporarily present in the United States as a nonimmigrant under subparagraph (F) or (J) of section 101(a)(15) of the Immigration and Nationality Act, as amended, the services are not deemed for purposes of this section to be performed to carry out a purpose for which such individual was admitted. The services of such spouse or child are excepted from employment under this section only if the spouse or child was admitted for a purpose specified in such subparagraph (F) or (J) and if the services are performed to carry out such purpose.

(b) Section 101 of the Immigration and Nationality Act (8 U.S.C. 1101), as amended, provides, in part, as follows:

Sec. 101. *Definitions.* [Immigration and Nationality Act (66 Stat. 166)]

(a) As used in this chapter—* * *

(15) The term *immigrant* means every alien except an alien who is within one of the following classes of nonimmigrant aliens—

* * *

(F)(i) An alien having a residence in a foreign country which he has no intention of abandoning, who is a bona fide student qualified to pursue a full course of study and who seeks to enter the United States temporarily and solely for the purpose of pursuing such a course of study at an established institution of learning or other recognized place of study in the United States, particularly designated by him and approved by the Attorney General after consultation with the Office of Education of the United States, which institution or place of study shall have agreed to report to the Attorney General the termination of attendance of each nonimmigrant student, and if any such institution of learning or place of study fails to make reports promptly the approval shall be withdrawn, and (ii) the alien spouse and minor children of any such alien if accompanying him or following to join him:

* * *

(J) An alien having a residence in a foreign country which he has no intention of abandoning who is a bona fide student, scholar, trainee, teacher, professor, research assistant, specialist, or leader in a field of specialized knowledge or skill, or other person of similar description, who is coming temporarily to the United States as a participant in a program designated by the Secretary of State, for the purpose of teaching, instructing or lecturing, studying, observing, conducting research, consulting, demonstrating special skills, or receiving training, and the alien spouse and minor children of any such alien if accompanying him or following to join him.

* * *

[Sec. 101, Immigration and Nationality Act, as amended by sec. 101, Act of June 27, 1952, 66 Stat. 166; sec. 109, Act of Sept. 21, 1961, 75 Stat. 534] [Reg. § 31.3306(c)(18)-1.]

☐ [*T.D.* 6658, 6-27-63. *Amended by T.D.* 8411, 4-27-92.]

### [Reg. § 31.3306(d)-1]

**§ 31.3306(d)-1. Included and excluded service.**—(a) If a portion of the services performed by an employee for the person employing him during a pay period constitutes employment, and the remainder does not constitute employment, all the services of the employee during the period shall for purposes of the tax be treated alike, that is, either all as included or all as excluded. The time during which the employee performs services which under section 3306(c) constitute employment, and the time during which he performs services which under such section do not constitute employment, within the pay period, determine whether all the services during the pay period shall be deemed to be included or excluded.

(b) If one-half or more of the employee's time in the employ of a particular person in a pay period is spent in performing services which constitute employment, then all the services of that employee for that person in that pay period shall be deemed to be employment.

(c) If less than one-half of the employee's time in the employ of a particular person in a pay period is spent in performing services which constitute employment, then none of the services of that employee for that person in that pay period shall be deemed to be employment.

(d) The application of the provisions of paragraphs (a), (b), and (c) of this section may be illustrated by the following examples:

*Example (1).* Employer B, who operates a farm and a store, employs A to perform services in connection with both operations. A's services on the farm are such that they are excepted as agricultural labor and do not constitute employment, and his services in the store constitute employment. He is paid at the end of each month. During a particular month A works 120 hours on the farm and 80 hours in the store. None of A's services during the month are deemed to be employment, since less than one-half of his services during the month constitutes employment. During another month A works 75 hours on the farm and 120 hours in the store. All of A's services during the month are deemed to be employment, since one-half or more of his services during the month constitutes employment.

*Example (2).* Employee C is employed as a maid by D, a medical doctor, whose home and office are located in the same building. C's services in the home are excepted as domestic service and do not constitute employment, and her services in the office constitute employment. She is paid each week. During a particular week C works 20 hours in the home and 20 hours in the office. All of C's services during that week are deemed to be employment, since one-half or more of her services during the week constitutes employment. During another week C works 22 hours in the home and 15 hours in the office. None of C's services during that week are deemed to be employment, since less than one-half of her services during the week constitutes employment.

(e) For purposes of this section, a "pay period" is the period (of not more than 31 consecutive calendar days) for which a payment of remuneration is ordinarily made to the employee by the person employing him. Thus, if the periods for which payments of remuneration are made to the employee by such person are of uniform duration, each such period constitutes a "pay period." If, however, the periods occasionally vary in duration, the "pay period" is the period for which a payment of remuneration is ordinarily made to the employee by such person, even though that period does not coincide with the actual period for which a particular payment of remuneration is made. For example, if a person ordinarily pays a particular employee for each calendar week at the end of the week, but the employee receives a payment in the middle of the week for the portion of the week already elapsed and receives the remainder at the end of the week, the "pay period" is still the calendar week; or if, instead, that employee is sent on a trip by such person and receives at the end of the third week a single remuneration payment for 3 weeks' services, the "pay period" is still the calendar week.

(f) If there is only one period (and such period does not exceed 31 consecutive calendar days) for which a payment of remuneration is made to the employee by the person employing him, such period is deemed to be a "pay period" for purposes of this section.

(g) The rules set forth in this section do not apply (1) with respect to any services performed by the employee for the person employing him if the periods for which such person makes payments of remuneration to the employee vary to the extent that there is no period "for which a payment of remuneration is ordinarily made to the employee," or (2) with respect to any services performed by the employee for the person employing him if the period for which a payment of remuneration is ordinarily made to the employee by such person exceeds 31 consecutive calendar days, or (3) with respect to any service performed by the employee for the person employing him during a pay period if any of such service is excepted by section 3306(c)(9) (see §31.3306(c)(9)-1).

(h) If during any period for which a person makes a payment of remuneration to an employee only a portion of the employee's

services constitutes employment, but the rules prescribed in this section are not applicable, the tax attaches with respect to such services as constitute employment as defined in section 3306(c) (provided such person is an employer as defined in section 3306(a) and §31.3306(a)-1). [Reg. §31.3306(d)-1.]

☐ [*T.D.* 6199, 9-5-56. *Republished in T.D. 6516, 12-20-60.*]

*»»→ Caution: The following regulation has not been revised to reflect the amendments made by P.L. 91-373.*

### [Reg. §31.3306(i)-1]

**§31.3306(i)-1. Who are employees.**—(a) Every individual is an employee if the relationship between him and the person for whom he performs services is the legal relationship of employer and employee. (The word "employer" as used in this section only, notwithstanding the provisions of §31.3306(a)-1, includes a person who employs one or more employees.)

(b) Generally such relationship exists when the person for whom services are performed has the right to control and direct the individual who performs the services, not only as to the result to be accomplished by the work but also as to the details and means by which that result is accomplished. That is, an employee is subject to the will and control of the employer not only as to what shall be done but how it shall be done. In this connection, it is not necessary that the employer actually direct or control the manner in which the services are performed; it is sufficient if he has the right to do so. The right to discharge is also an important factor indicating that the person possessing that right is an employer. Other factors characteristic of an employer, but not necessarily present in every case, are the furnishing of tools and the furnishing of a place to work, to the individual who performs the services. In general, if an individual is subject to the control or direction of another merely as to the result to be accomplished by the work and not as to the means and methods for accomplishing the result, he is an independent contractor. An individual performing services as an independent contractor is not as to such services an employee. Individuals such as physicians, lawyers, dentists, veterinarians, construction contractors, public stenog-

raphers, and auctioneers, engaged in the pursuit of an independent trade, business, or profession, in which they offer their services to the public, are independent contractors and not employees.

(c) Whether the relationship of employer and employee exists will in doubtful cases be determined upon an examination of the particular facts of each case.

(d) If the relationship of employer and employee exists, the designation or description of the relationship by the parties as anything other than that of employer and employee is immaterial. Thus, if such relationship exists, it is of no consequence that the employee is designated as a partner, coadventurer, agent, independent contractor, or the like.

(e) All classes or grades of employees are included within the relationship of employer and employee. Thus, superintendents, managers, and other supervisory personnel are employees. Generally, an officer of a corporation is an employee of the corporation. However, an officer of a corporation who as such does not perform any services or performs only minor services and who neither receives nor is entitled to receive, directly or indirectly, any remuneration is considered not to be an employee of the corporation. A director of a corporation in his capacity as such is not an employee of the corporation.

(f) Although an individual may be an employee under this section, his services may be of such a nature, or performed under such circumstances, as not to constitute employment (see §31.3306(c)-2). [Reg. §31.3306(i)-1.]

☐ [*T.D.* 6199, 9-5-56. *Republished in T.D. 6516, 12-20-60.*]

*»»→ Caution: The following regulation has not been revised to reflect the amendments made by P.L. 94-566.*

### [Reg. §31.3306(j)-1]

**§31.3306(j)-1. State, United States, and citizen.**—(a) When used in the regulations in this subpart, the term "State" includes the District of Columbia, the Territories of Alaska and Hawaii before their admission as States, and (when used with respect to remuneration paid after 1960 for services performed after 1960) the Commonwealth of Puerto Rico.

(b) When used in the regulations in this subpart, the Term "United States", when used in a geographical sense, means the several States

(including the Territories of Alaska and Hawaii before their admission as States), and the District of Columbia. When used in the regulations in this subpart with respect to remuneration paid after 1960 for services performed after 1960, the term "United States" also includes the Commonwealth of Puerto Rico when the term is used in a geographical sense, and the term "citizen of the United States" includes a citizen of the Commonwealth of Puerto Rico. [Reg. §31.3306(j)-1.]

☐ [*T. D.* 6658, 6-27-63.]

*»»→ Caution: The following regulation has not been revised to reflect the amendments made by P.L. 91-373.*

### [Reg. §31.3306(k)-1]

**§31.3306(k)-1. Agricultural labor.**—(a) *In general.*—(1) Services performed by an employee for the person employing him which constitute "agricultural labor" as defined in section 3306(k) are excepted from employment by reason of section 3306(c)(1). See §31.3306(c)(1)-1. The term "agricultural labor" as defined in section 3306(k) includes services of the character described in paragraphs (b), (c), (d), and (e) of this section. In general, however, the term does not include services performed in connection with forestry, lumbering, or landscaping.

(2) The term "farm" as used in this subpart includes stock, dairy, poultry, fruit, fur-bearing animal, and truck farms, plantations, ranches, nurseries, ranges, orchards, and such greenhouses and other similar structures as are used primarily for the raising of agricultural or horticultural commodities. Greenhouses and other similar structures used primarily for other purposes (for example, display, storage, and fabrication of wreaths, corsages, and bouquets) do not constitute "farms."

(b) *Services described in section 3306(k)(1).*—Services performed on a farm by an employee of any person in connection with any of the following activities constitute agricultural labor:

(1) The cultivation of the soil;

(2) The raising, shearing, feeding, caring for, training, or management of livestock, bees, poultry, fur-bearing animals, or wildlife; or

(3) The raising or harvesting of any other agricultural or horticultural commodity.

(c) *Services described in section 3306(k)(2).*—(1) The following services performed by an employee in the employ of the owner or tenant or other operator of one or more farms constitute agricultural labor, if the major part of such services is performed on a farm:

(i) Services performed in connection with the operation, management, conservation, improvement, or maintenance of any such farms or its tools or equipment; or

(ii) Services performed in salvaging timber, or clearing land of brush and other debris, left by a hurricane.

(2) The services described in subparagraph (1)(i) of this paragraph may include, for example, services performed by carpenters, painters, mechanics, farm supervisors, irrigation engineers, bookkeepers, and other skilled or semi-skilled workers, which contribute in any way to the conduct of the farm or farms, as such, operated by the person employing them, as distinguished from any other enterprise in which such person may be engaged.

(3) Since the services described in this paragraph must be performed in the employ of the owner or tenant or other operator of the farm, services performed by employees of a commercial painting concern, for example, which contracts with a farmer to renovate his farm properties, do not constitute agricultural labor.

(d) *Services described in section 3306(k)(3).*—Services performed by an employee in the employ of any person in connection with any of the following operations constitute agricultural labor without regard to the place where such services are performed:

(1) The ginning of cotton;

(2) The hatching of poultry;

(3) The raising or harvesting of mushrooms;

(4) The operation or maintenance of ditches, canals, reservoirs, or waterways used exclusively for supplying or storing water for farming purposes;

(5) The production or harvesting of maple sap or the processing of maple sap into maple sirup or maple sugar (but not the subsequent blending or other processing of such sirup or sugar with other products); or

(6) The production or harvesting of crude gum (oleoresin) from a living tree or the processing of such crude gum into gum spirits of

turpentine and gum rosin, provided such processing is carried on by the original producer of such crude gum.

(e) *Services described in section 3306(k)(4).*—(1)(i) Services performed by an employee in the employ of a farmer or a farmers' cooperative organization or group in the handling, planting, drying, packing, packaging, processing, freezing, grading, storing, or delivering to storage or to market or to a carrier for transportation to market, of any agricultural or horticultural commodity, other than fruits and vegetables (see subparagraph (2) of this paragraph), produced by such farmer or farmer-members of such organization or group of farmers constitute agricultural labor, if such services are performed as an incident to ordinary farming operations.

(ii) Generally services are performed "as an incident to ordinary farming operations" within the meaning of this paragraph if they are services of the character ordinarily performed by the employees of a farmer or of a farmers' cooperative organization or group as a prerequisite to the marketing, in its unmanufactured state, of any agricultural or horticultural commodity produced by such farmer or by the members of such farmers' organization or group. Services performed by employees of such farmer or farmers' organization or group in the handling, planting, drying, packing, packaging, processing, freezing, grading, storing, or delivering to storage or to market or to a carrier for transportation to market, of commodities produced by persons other than such farmer or members of such farmers' organization or group are not performed "as an incident to ordinary farming operations".

(2) Services performed by an employee in the employ of any person in the handling, planting, drying, packing, packaging, processing, freezing, grading, storing, or delivering to storage or to market or to a carrier for transportation to market, of fruits and vegetables, whether or not of a perishable nature, constitute agricultural labor, if such services are performed as an incident to the preparation of such fruits and vegetables for market. For example, if services in the sorting, grading, or storing of fruits, or in the cleaning of beans, are performed as an incident to their preparation for market, such services may constitute agricultural labor, whether performed in the employ of a farmer, a farmers' cooperative, or a commercial handler of such commodities.

(3) The services described in subparagraphs (1) and (2) of this paragraph do not include services performed in connection with commercial canning or commercial freezing or in connection with any commodity after its delivery to a terminal market for distribution for consumption. Moreover, since the services described in such subparagraphs must be rendered in the actual handling, planting, drying, packing, packaging, processing, freezing, grading, storing, or delivering to storage or to market or to carrier for transportation to market, of the commodity, such services do not, for example, include services performed as stenographers, bookkeepers, clerks, and other office employees, even though such services may be in connection with such activities. However, to the extent that the services of such individuals are performed in the employ of the owner or tenant or other operator of a farm and are rendered in major part on a farm, they may be within the provisions of paragraph (c) of this section. [Reg. §31.3306(k)-1.]

☐ [*T. D.* 6199, 9-5-56. *Republished in T. D.* 6516, 12-20-60.]

### [Reg. §31.3306(m)-1]

**§31.3306(m)-1. American vessel and aircraft.**—(a) The term "American vessel" means any vessel which is documented (that is, registered, enrolled, or licensed) or numbered in conformity with the laws of the United States. It also includes any vessel which is neither documented nor numbered under the laws of the United States, nor documented under the laws of any foreign country, if the crew of such vessel is employed solely by one or more citizens or residents of the United States or corporations organized under the laws of the United States or of any State. (For provisions relating to the terms "State" and citizen", see §31.3306(j)-1.)

(b) The term "American aircraft" means any aircraft registered under the laws of the United States.

(c) For provisions relating to services performed outside the United States on or in connection with an American vessel or American aircraft, see paragraph (c) of §31.3306(c)-2. [Reg. §31.3306(m)-1.]

☐ [*T.D.* 6199, 9-5-56. *Republished in T.D.* 6516, 12-20-60; *T.D.* 6658, 6-27-63.]

### [Reg. §31.3306(n)-1]

**§31.3306(n)-1. Services on American vessel whose business is conducted by general agent of Secretary of Commerce.**—(a) Section 3306(n) and this section of the regulations apply with respect only to services performed by an officer or member of the crew of an American vessel (1) which is owned by or bareboat chartered to the United States, and (2) whose business is conducted by a general agent of the Secretary of Commerce. Whether services performed by

such an officer or member of a crew under the above conditions constitute employment is determined under section 3306(c) and (n), but without regard to section 3306(c)(6). See §31.3306(c)(6)-1, relating to services performed in the employ of the United States and instrumentalities thereof. If, without regard to section 3306(c)(6), such services constitute employment, they are not excepted from employment by reason of the fact that they are performed on or in connection with an American vessel which is owned by or bareboat chartered to the United States and whose business is conducted by a general agent of the Secretary of Commerce, that is, such services are not excepted from employment by section 3306(c)(6). For provisions relating to services performed within the United States and services performed outside the United States which constitute employment, see §31.3306(c)-2.

(b) The expression "officer or member of the crew" includes the master or officer in charge of the vessel, however, designated, and every individual, subject to his authority, serving on board and contributing in any way to the operation and welfare of the vessel. Thus, the expression includes, for example, the master, mates, pilots, pursers, surgeons, stewards, engineers, firemen, cooks, clerks, carpenters, and deck hands.

(c) An employee of the United States who performs services as an officer or member of the crew of an American vessel which is owned by or bareboat chartered to the United States and whose business is conducted by a general agent of the Secretary of Commerce shall be deemed, under section 3306(n), to be performing services for such general agent rather than for the United States. Any such general agent of the Secretary of Commerce is considered a legal entity in his capacity as such general agent, separate and distinct from his identity as a person employing individuals on his own account. Each such general agent who in his capacity as such qualifies as an employer under section 3306(a) is with respect to each calendar year for which he so qualifies subject to the tax imposed by section 3301, and to all the requirements imposed upon an employer as defined in section 3306(a) by the regulations in this part, with respect to services which constitute employment by reason of section 3306(n) and this section of the regulations. [Reg. §31.3306(n)-1.]

☐ [*T.D.* 6199, 9-5-56. *Republished in T.D.* 6516, 12-20-60.]

### [Reg. §31.3306(p)-1]

**§31.3306(p)-1. Employees or related corporations.**—(a) *In general.*—For purposes of sections 3301, 3302, and 3306(b)(1), when two or more related corporations concurrently employ the same individual and compensate that individual through a common paymaster which is one of the related corporations for which the individual performs services, each of the corporations is considered to have paid only the remuneration it actually disburses to that individual (unless the disbursing corporation fails to remit the taxes due). Paragraphs (b) and (c) of §31.3121(s)-1 contains rules defining related corporations, common paymasters, and concurrent employment, and rules for determining the liability of the other related corporations for employment taxes if the common paymaster fails to remit the taxes pursuant to sections 3102 and 3111, and for allocating these taxes among the related corporations. Those rules also apply to the tax under section 3301. For purposes of applying those rules to this section, references in those rules to section 3111 are considered references to sections 3301 and 3302, and references to section 3121 are considered references to section 3306.

(b) *Allocation of credit for contributions to State unemployment funds.*—A special rule for applying the rules of §31.3121(s)-1 to this section applies if it is necessary to determine the ultimate liability of each related corporation for which services are performed in the event the common paymaster fails to remit the tax to the Internal Revenue Service. In determining the ultimate liability of a corporation, the credit for contributions to State unemployment funds that the corporation may claim under section 3302 is calculated as if each corporation were a separate employer.

(c) *Effective date.*—This section is effective with respect to wages paid after December 31, 1978. [Reg. §31.3306(p)-1.]

☐ [*T.D.* 7660, 12-19-79.]

### [Reg. §31.3306(r)(2)-1]

**§31.3306(r)(2)-1. Treatment of amounts deferred under certain nonqualified deferred compensation plans.**—(a) *In general.*—Section 3306(r)(2) provides a special timing rule for the tax imposed by section 3301 with respect to any amount deferred under a nonqualified deferred compensation plan. Section 31.3121(v)(2)-1 contains rules relating to when amounts deferred under certain nonqualified deferred compensation plans are wages for purposes of sections 3121(v)(2), 3101, and 3111. The rules in §31.3121(v)(2)-1 also apply to the special timing rule of section 3306(r)(2). For purposes of applying the rules in §31.3121(v)(2)-1 to section 3306(r)(2) and this paragraph (a), references to the Federal Insurance Contributions Act are considered references to the Federal Unemployment Tax Act (26 U.S.C. 3301 et seq.), references to FICA are considered references to FUTA, references to section 3101 or 3111 are considered references to section 3301, references to section 3121(v)(2) are considered references to section 3306(r)(2), references to section 3121(a), (a)(5), and (a)(13) are considered references to section 3306(b), (b)(5), and (b)(10), respectively, and references to §31.3121(a)-2(a) are considered references to §31.3301-4.

(b) *Effective dates and transition rules.*—Except as otherwise provided, section 3306(r)(2) applies to remuneration paid after December 31, 1984. Section 31.3121(v)(2)-2 contains effective date rules for certain remuneration paid after December 31, 1983, for purposes of section 3121(v)(2). The rules in §31.3121(v)(2)-2 also apply to section 3306(r)(2). For purposes of applying the rules in §31.3121(v)(2)-2 to section 3306(r)(2) and this paragraph (b), references to section 3121(v)(2) are considered references to section 3306(r)(2), and references to section 3121(a)(2), (a)(3), or (a)(13) are considered references to section 3306(b)(2), (b)(3), or (b)(10), respectively. In addition, references to §31.3121(v)(2)-1 are considered references to paragraph (a) of this section. For purposes of applying the rules of §31.3121(v)(2)-2 to this paragraph (b)—

(1) References to "December 31, 1983" are considered references to "December 31, 1984";

(2) References to "before 1984" are considered references to "before 1985";

(3) References to "Federal Insurance Contributions Act" are considered references to "Federal Unemployment Tax Act"; and

(4) References to "FICA" are considered references to "FUTA". [Reg. §31.3306(r)(2)-1.]

☐ [*T.D.* 8815, 1-28-99.]

**[Reg. §31.3307-1]**

**§31.3307-1. Deductions by an employer from remuneration of an employee.**—Any amount deducted by an employer from the remuneration of an employee is considered to be a part of the employee's remuneration and is considered to be paid to the employee as remuneration at the time that the deduction is made. It is immaterial that any act of Congress or the law of any State requires or permits such deductions and the payment of the amount thereof to the United States, a State, or any political subdivision thereof. [Reg. §31.3307-1.]

☐ [*T.D.* 6199, 9-5-56. *Republished in T.D.* 6516, 12-20-60.]

**[Reg. §31.3308-1]**

**§31.3308-1. Instrumentalities of the United States specifically exempted from tax imposed by section 3301.**—Section 3308 makes ineffectual as to the tax imposed by section 3301 (with respect to remuneration paid after 1961 for services performed after 1961) those provisions of law which grant to an instrumentality of the United States an exemption from taxation, unless such provisions grant a specific exemption from the tax imposed by section 3301 by an express reference to such section or the corresponding section of prior law. Thus, the general exemptions from Federal taxation granted by various statutes to certain instrumentalities of the United States without specific reference to the tax imposed by section 3301 or the corresponding section of prior law are rendered inoperative insofar as such exemptions relate to the tax imposed by section 3301. For provisions relating to the exception from employment of services performed in the employ of an instrumentality of the United States specificially exempted from the tax imposed by section 3301, see §31.3306(c)(6)-1. [Reg. §31.3308-1.]

☐ [*T.D.* 6658, 6-27-63.]

# Collection of Income Tax at Source on Wages

## WITHHOLDING FROM WAGES

See p. 20,601 for regulations not amended to reflect law changes

**[Reg. §31.3401(a)-1]**

**§31.3401(a)-1. Wages.**—(a) *In general.*—(1) The term "wages" means all remuneration for services performed by an employee for his employer unless specifically excepted under section 3401(a) or excepted under section 3402(e).

(2) The name by which the remuneration for services is designated is immaterial. Thus, salaries, fees, bonuses, commission on sales or on insurance premiums, pensions, and retired pay are wages within the meaning of the statute if paid as compensation for services performed by the employee for his employer.

(3) The basis upon which the remuneration is paid is immaterial in determining whether the remuneration constitutes wages. Thus, it may be paid on the basis of piecework, or a percentage of profits; and may be paid hourly, daily, weekly, monthly, or annually.

(4) Generally the medium in which remuneration is paid is also immaterial. It may be paid in cash or in something other than cash, as for example, stocks, bonds, or other forms of property. (See, however, §31.3401(a)(11)-1, relating to the exclusion from wages of remuneration paid in any medium other than cash for services not in the course of the employer's trade or business, and §31.3401(a)(16)-1, relating to the exclusion from wages of tips paid in any medium other than cash.) If services are paid for in a medium other than cash, the fair market value of the thing taken in payment is the amount to be included as wages. If the services were rendered at a stipulated price, in the absence of evidence to the contrary, such price will be presumed to be the fair value of the remuneration received. If a corporation transfers to its employees its own stock as remuneration for services rendered by the employee, the amount of such remuneration is the fair market value of the stock at the time of the transfer.

(5) Remuneration for services, unless such remuneration is specifically excepted by the statute, constitutes wages even though at the time paid the relationship of employer and employee no longer exists between the person in whose employ the services were performed and the individual who performed them.

*Example.* A is employed by R during the month of January 1955 and is entitled to receive remuneration of $100 for the services performed for R, the employer, during the month. A leaves the employ of R at the close of business on January 31, 1955. On February 15, 1955 (when A is no longer an employee of R), R pays A the remuneration of $100 which was earned for the services performed in January. The $100 is wages within the meaning of the statute.

(b) *Certain specific items.*—(1) *Pensions and retirement pay.*—(i) In general, pensions and retired pay are wages subject to withholding.

However, no withholding is required with respect to amounts paid to an employee upon retirement which are taxable as annuities under the provisions of section 72 or 403. So-called pensions awarded by one to whom no services have been rendered are mere gifts or gratuities and do not constitute wages. Those payments of pensions or other benefits by the Federal Government under Title 38 of the United States Code which are excluded from gross income are not wages subject to withholding.

(ii) Amounts received as retirement pay for service in the Armed Forces of the United States, the Coast and Geodetic Survey, or the Public Health Service or as a disability annuity paid under the provisions of section 831 of the Foreign Service Act of 1946, as amended (22 U.S.C. 1081; 60 Stat. 1021), are subject to withholding unless such pay or disability annuity is excluded from gross income under section 104(a)(4), or is taxable as an annuity under the provisions of section 72. Where such retirement pay or disability annuity (not excluded from gross income under section 104(a)(4) and not taxable as an annuity under the provisions of section 72) is paid to a nonresident alien individual, withholding is required only in the case of such amounts paid to a nonresident alien individual who is a resident of Puerto Rico.

(2) *Traveling and other expenses.*—Amounts paid specifically—either as advances or reimbursements—for traveling or other bona fide ordinary and necessary expenses incurred or reasonably expected to be incurred in the business of the employer are not wages and are not subject to withholding. Traveling and other reimbursed expenses must be identified either by making a separate payment or by specifically indicating the separate amounts where both wages and expense allowances are combined in a single payment. For amounts that are received by an employee on or after July 1, 1990, with respect to expenses paid or incurred on or after July 1, 1990, see §31.3401(a)-4.

(3) *Vacation allowances.*—Amounts of so-called "vacation allowances" paid to an employee constitute wages. Thus, the salary of an employee on vacation, paid notwithstanding his absence from work, constitutes wages.

(4) *Dismissal payments.*—Any payments made by an employer to an employee on account of dismissal, that is, involuntary separation from the service of the employer, constitute wages regardless of whether the employer is legally bound by contract, statute, or otherwise to make such payments.

(5) *Deductions by employer from remuneration of an employee.*—Any amount deducted by an employer from the remuneration of an employee is considered to be a part of the employee's remuneration and is considered to be paid to the employee as remuneration at the time that the deduction is made. It is immaterial that any act of Congress, or the law of any State or of Puerto Rico, requires or permits such deductions and the payment of the amounts thereof to the United States, a State, a Territory, Puerto Rico, or the District of Columbia, or any political subdivision of any one or more of the foregoing.

(6) *Payment by an employer of employee's tax, or employee's contributions under a State law.*—The term "wages" includes the amount paid by an employer on behalf of an employee (without deduction from the remuneration of, or other reimbursement from, the employee) an account of any payment required from an employee under a State unemployment compensation law, or on account of any tax imposed upon the employee by any taxing authority, including the taxes imposed by sections 3101 and 3201.

(7) *Remuneration for services as employee of nonresident alien individual or foreign entity.*—The term "wages" includes remuneration for services performed by a citizen or resident (including, in regard to wages paid after February 28, 1979, an individual treated as a resident under section 6013(g) or (h)) of the United States as an employee of a nonresident alien individual, foreign partnership, or foreign corporation whether or not such alien individual or foreign entity is engaged in trade or business within the United States. Any person paying wages on behalf of a nonresident alien individual, foreign partnership, or foreign corporation, not engaged in trade or business within the United States (including Puerto Rico as if a part of the United States), is subject to all the provisions of law and regulations applicable with respect to an employer. See §31.3401(d)-1, relating to the term "employer", and §31.3401(a)(8)(C)-1, relating to remuneration paid for services performed by a citizen of the United States in Puerto Rico.

(8) *Amounts paid under accident or health plans.*—(i) *Amounts paid in taxable years beginning on or after January 1, 1977.*—(a) *In general.*—Withholding is required on all payments of amounts includible in gross income under section 105(a) and §1.105-1 (relating to amounts attributable to employer contributions), made in taxable years beginning on or after January 1, 1977, to an employee under an accident or health plan for a period of absence from work on account of personal injuries or sickness. Payments on which withholding is required by this subdivision are wages as defined in section 3401(a), and the employer shall deduct and withhold in accordance with the requirements of chapter 24 of subtitle C of the Code. Third party payments of sick pay, as defined in section 3402(o) and the regulations thereunder, are not wages for purposes of this section.

(b) *Payments made by an agent of the employer.*—(1) Payments are considered made by the employer if a third party makes the payments as an agent of the employer. The determining factor as to whether a third party is an agent of the employer is whether the third party bears any insurance risk. If the third party bears no insurance risk and is reimbursed on a cost plus fee basis, the third party is an agent of the employer even if the third party is responsible for making determinations of the eligibility of individual employees of the employer for sick pay payments. If the third party is paid an insurance premium and not reimbursed on a cost plus fee basis, the third party is not an agent of the employer, but the third party is a payor of third party sick pay for purposes of voluntary withholding from sick pay under sections 3402(o) and 6051(f) and the regulations thereunder. If a third party and an employer enter into an agency agreement as provided in paragraph (c) of §31.6051-3 (relating to statements required in case of sick pay paid by third parties), that agency agreement does not make the third party an agent of the employer for purposes of this paragraph.

(2) Payments made by agents subject to this paragraph are supplemental wages as defined in §31.3402(g)-1, and are therefore subject to the rules regarding withholding tax on supplemental wages provided in §31.3402(g)-1. For purposes of those rules, unless the agent is also an agent for purposes of withholding tax from the employee's regular wages, the agent may deem tax to have been withheld from regular wages paid to the employee during the calendar year.

(3) This paragraph is only applicable to amounts paid on or after May 25, 1983, unless the agent actually withheld taxes before that date.

(c) *Exceptions to withholding.*—(1) Withholding is not required on payments that are specifically excepted under the numbered paragraphs of section 3401(a) (relating to the definition of wages), under section 3402(e) (relating to included and excluded wages), or under section 3402(n) (relating to employees incurring no income tax liability).

(2) Withholding is not required on disability payments to the extent that the payments are excludable from gross income under section 105(d). In determining the excludable portion of the disability payments, the employer may assume that payments that the employer makes to the employee are the employee's sole source of income. This exception applies only if the employee furnishes the employer with adequate verification of disability. A certificate from a qualified physician attesting that the employee is permanently and totally disabled (within the meaning of section 105(d)) shall be deemed to constitute adequate verification. This exception does not affect the requirement that a statement (which includes any amount paid under section 105(d)) be furnished under either section 6041 (relating to information at source) or section 6051 (relating to receipts for employees) and the regulations thereunder.

(ii) *Amounts paid after December 31, 1955 and before January 1, 1977.*—(a) *In general.*—The term "wage continuation payment", as used in this subdivision, means any payment to an employee which is made after December 31, 1955, and before January 1, 1977, under a wage continuation plan (as defined in paragraph (a)(2)(i) of §1.105-4 and §1.105-5 of Part 1 of this chapter (Income Tax Regulations)) for a period of absence from work on account of personal injuries or sickness, to the extent such payment is attributable to contributions made by the employer which were not includible in the employee's gross income or is paid by the employer. Any such payment, whether or not excluded from the gross income of the employee under section 105(d), constitutes "wages" (unless specifically excepted under any of the numbered paragraphs of section 3401(a) or under section 3402(e)) and withholding thereon is required except as provided in paragraphs (b)(8)(ii)(b), (c), and (d) of this section.

(b) *Amounts paid before January 1, 1977, by employer for whom services are performed for period of absence beginning after December 31, 1963.*—(1) Withholding is not required upon the amount of any wage continuation payment for a period of absence beginning after December 31, 1963, paid before January 1, 1977, to an employee directly by the employer for whom he performs services to the extent that such payment is excludable from the gross income of the employee under the provisions of section 105(d) in effect with respect to such payments, provided the records maintained by the employer—

(i) Separately show the amount of each such payment and the excludable portion thereof, and

(ii) Contain data substantiating the employee's entitlement to the exclusion provided in section 105(d) with respect to such amount, either by a written statement from the employee specifying whether his absence from work during the period for which the payment was made was due to a personal injury or to sickness and whether he was hospitalized for at least one day during this period; or by any other information which the employer reasonably believes establishes the employee's entitlement to the exclusion under section 105(d). Employers shall not be required to ascertain the accuracy of any written statement submitted by an employee in accordance with this subdivision (b)(1)(ii).

For purposes of this subdivision (b)(1), wage continuation payments reasonably expected by the employer to be made on behalf of the employer by another person shall be taken into account in determining whether the 75 percent test contained in section 105(d) is met and in computing the amount of any wage continuation payment made directly by the employer for whom services are performed by the employee which is within the $75 or $100 weekly rate of exclusion from the gross income of the employee provided in section 105(d). In making this latter computation, the amount excludable under section 105(d) shall be applied first against payments reasonably expected to be made on behalf of the employer by the other person and then, to the extent any part of the exclusion remains, against the payments made directly by the employer. In a case in which wage continuation payments are not paid at a constant rate for the first 30 calendar days of the period of absence, the determination of whether the 75 percent test contained in section 105(d) is met shall be based upon the length of the employee's absence as of the end of the period for which the payment by the employer is made, without regard to the effect which any further extension of such absence may have upon the excludability of the payment.

(2) The computation of the amount of any wage continuation payment with respect to which the employer may refrain from withholding may be illustrated by the following examples:

*Example (1).* A, an employee of B, normally works Monday through Friday and has a regular weekly rate of wages of $100. On Monday, November 5, 1974, A becomes ill, and as a result is absent from work for two weeks, returning to work on Monday, November 19, 1974. A is not hospitalized. Under B's noncontributory wage continuation plan, A receives no benefits for the first three working days of absence and is paid benefits directly by B at the rate of $85 a week thereafter ($34 for the last two days of the first week of absence and $85 for the second week of absence). No wage continuation payment is made by any other person. Since the benefits are entirely attributable to contributions to the plan by B, such benefits are wage continuation payments in their entirety. The wage continuation payments for the first seven calendar days of absence are not excludable from A's gross income because A was not hospitalized for at least one day during his period of absence, and therefore B must withhold with respect to such payments. Under section 105(d), the wage continuation payments attributable to absence after the first seven calendar days of absence are excludable to the extent that they do not exceed a rate of $75 a week. Under the principles stated in paragraph (e)(6)(iv) of §1.105-4 of this chapter (Income Tax Regulations), the wage continuation payments in the case are at a rate not in excess of 75 percent (119/200 or 59.5 percent) of A's regular weekly rate of wages. Accordingly, B may refrain from withholding with respect to $75 of the wage continuation payment attributable to the second week of absence.

*Example (2).* Assume the facts in example (1) except that A is unable to return to work until Monday, February 11, 1975, and that, of the $85 a week of wage continuation payments $35 is paid directly by B and $50 is reasonably expected by B to be paid by C, an insurance company, on behalf of B. In such a case, both the $50 and the $35 payments constitute wage continuation payments and the amount of such payments which is attributable to the first 30 calendar days of absence is at a rate not in excess of 75 percent (323/440 or 73.4 percent) of A's regular weekly rate of wages. Therefore, under section 105(d), the portion of such payments which is attributable to absence after the first seven calendar days of absence is excludable to the extent that it does not exceed a rate of $75 a week for the eighth through the thirtieth calendar day of absence and does not exceed a rate of $100 a week thereafter. B may refrain from withholding with respect to $25 a week (the amount by which the $75 maximum excludable amount exceeds the $50 reasonably expected by B to be paid by C) of his direct payments for the eighth through the thirtieth calendar days of absence. Thereafter, B may refrain from withholding with respect to the entire $35 paid directly by him, since the maximum excludable amount ($100 a week) exceeds the total of payments made by B and payments which B reasonably expects will be made by C.

*(c) Amounts paid by employer for whom services are performed for period of absence beginning before January 1, 1964.*—Withholding is not required upon the amount of any wage continuation payment for a period of absence beginning before January 1, 1964, made to an employee directly by the employer for whom he performs services to the extent that such payment is excludable from the gross income of the employee under the provisions of section 105(d) in effect with respect to such payments, provided the records maintained by the employer—

*(1)* Separately show the amount of each such payment and the excludable portion thereof, and

*(2)* Contain data substantiating the employee's entitlement to the exclusion provided in section 105(d) with respect to such amount, either by a written statement from the employee specifying whether his absence from work during the period for which the payment was made was due to a personal injury or whether such absence was due to sickness, and, if the latter, whether he was hospitalized for at least one day during this period; or by any other information which the employer reasonably believes establishes the employee's entitlement to the exclusion under section 105(d). Employers shall not be required to ascertain the accuracy of the information contained in any written statement submitted by an employee in accordance with this paragraph (b)(8)(ii)*(c)(2)*.

For purposes of this paragraph (b)(8)(ii)*(c)*, the computation of the amount excludable from the gross income of the employee under section 105(d) may be made either on the basis of the wage continuation payments which are made directly by the employer for whom the employee performs services, or on the basis of such payments in conjunction with any wage continuation payments made on behalf of the employer by a person who is regarded as an employer under section 3401(d)(1).

*(d) Amounts paid before January 1, 1977 by person other than the employer for whom services are performed.*—No tax shall be withheld upon any wage continuation payment made to an employee by or on behalf of a person who is not the employer for whom the employee performs services but who is regarded as an employer under section 3401(d)(1). For example, no tax shall be withheld with respect to wage continuation payments made on behalf of an employer by an insurance company under an accident or health policy, by a separate trust under an accident or health plan, or by a State agency from a sickness and disability fund maintained under State law.

*(e) Cross references.*—See sections 6001 and 6051 and the provisions thereunder in subpart G of the regulations in this part for

rules with respect to the records which must be maintained in connection with wage continuation payments and for rules with respect to the statements which must be furnished an employee in connection with wage continuation payments, respectively. See also section 105 and the provisions thereunder in the Income Tax Regulations (26 CFR Part 1).

(9) *Value of meals and lodging.*—The value of any meals or lodging furnished to an employee by his employer is not subject to withholding if the value of the meals or lodging is excludable from the gross income of the employee. See the Income Tax Regulations (Part 1 of this chapter) under section 119.

(10) *Facilities or privileges.*—Ordinarily, facilities or privileges (such as entertainment, medical services, or so-called "courtesy" discounts on purchases), furnished or offered by an employer to his employees generally, are not considered as wages subject to withholding if such facilities or privileges are of relatively small value and are offered or furnished by the employer merely as a means of promoting the health, good will, contentment, or efficiency of his employees.

(11) *Tips or gratuities.*—Tips or gratuities paid, prior to January 1, 1966, directly to an employee by a customer of an employer, and not accounted for by the employee to the employer are not subject to withholding. For provisions relating to the treatment of tips received by an employee after December 31, 1965, as wages, see §§31.3401(f)-1 and 31.3402(k)-1.

(12) *Remuneration for services performed by permanent resident of Virgin Islands.*—(i) *Exemption from withholding.*—No tax shall be withheld for the United States under chapter 24 from a payment of wages by an employer, including the United States or any agency thereof, to an employee if at the time of payment it is reasonable to believe that the employee will be required to satisfy his income tax obligations with respect to such wages under section 28(a) of the Revised Organic Act of the Virgin Islands. That section provides that all persons whose permanent residence is in the Virgin Islands "shall satisfy their income tax obligations under applicable taxing statutes of the United States by paying their tax on income derived from all sources both within and outside the Virgin Islands into the treasury of the Virgin Islands".

(ii) *Claiming exemption.*—If the employee furnishes to the employer a statement in duplicate that he expects to satisfy his income tax obligations under section 28(a) of the Revised Organic Act of the Virgin Islands with respect to all wages subsequently to be paid to him by the employer during the taxable year to which the statement relates, the employer may, in the absence of information to the contrary, rely on such statement as establishing reasonable belief that the employee will so satisfy his income tax obligations. The employee's statement shall identify the taxable year to which it relates, and both the original and the duplicate copy thereof shall be signed and dated by the employee.

(iii) *Disposition of statement.*—The original of the statement shall be retained by the employer. The duplicate copy of the statement shall be sent by the employer to the Director of International Operations, Washington 25, D.C., on or before the last day of the calendar year in which the employer receives the statement from the employee.

(iv) *Applicability of subparagraph.*—This subparagraph has no application with respect to any payment of remuneration which is not subject to withholding by reason of any other provision of the regulations in this subpart.

(13) *Federal employees resident in Puerto Rico.*—Except as provided in paragraph (d) of §31.3401(a)(6)-1, the term "wages" includes remuneration for services performed by a nonresident alien individual who is a resident of Puerto Rico if such services are performed as an employee of the United States or any agency thereof. The place where the services are performed is immaterial for purposes of this subparagraph.

(14) *Supplemental unemployment compensation benefits.*—(i) Supplemental unemployment compensation benefits paid to an individual after December 31, 1970, shall be treated (for purposes of the provisions of Subparts E, F, and G of this part which relate to withholding of income tax) as if they were wages, to the extent such benefits are includible in the gross income of such individual.

(ii) For purposes of this subparagraph, the term "supplemental unemployment compensation benefits" means amounts which are paid to an employee, pursuant to a plan to which the employer is a party, because of the employee's involuntary separation from the employment of the employer, whether or not such separation is temporary, but only when such separation is one resulting directly from a reduction in force, the discontinuance of a plant or operation, or other similar conditions.

(iii) For the meanings of the terms "involuntary separation from the employment of the employer" and "other similar conditions", see subparagraphs (3) and (4) of § 1.501(c)(17)-1(b) of this chapter (Income Tax Regulations).

(iv) As used in this subparagraph, the term "employee" means an employee within the meaning of paragraph (a) of § 31.3401(c)-1, the term "employer" means an employer within the meaning of paragraph (a) of § 31.3401(d)-1, and the term "employment" means employment as defined under the common law rules.

(v) References in this chapter to wages as defined in section 3401(a) shall be deemed to refer also to supplemental unemployment compensation benefits which are treated under this subparagraph as if they were wages.

(15) *Split-dollar life insurance arrangements.*—See § 1.61-22 of this chapter for rules relating to the treatment of split-dollar life insurance arrangements.

(c) *Geographical definitions.*—For definition of the term "United States" and for other geographical definitions relating to the continental shelf, see section 638 and § 1.638-1 of this chapter. [Reg. § 31.3401(a)-1.]

□ [*T.D.* 6155, 12-29-55 *and T.D.* 6259, 10-25-57. *Amended by T.D.* 6654, 5-27-63; *T.D.* 6908, 12-30-66; *T.D.* 7001, 1-17-69; *T.D.* 7068, 11-10-70; *T.D.* 7277, 5-14-73; *T.D.* 7493, 6-29-77; *T.D.* 7670, 1-30-80; *T.D.* 7888, 4-22-83; *T.D.* 8276, 12-7-89; *T.D.* 8324, 12-14-90; *T.D.* 9092, 9-11-2003 *and T.D.* 9276, 7-24-2006.]

### [Reg. § 31.3401(a)-1T]

**§ 31.3401(a)-1T. Question and answer relating to the definition of wages in section 3401(a).**—The following question and answer relates to the definition of wages in section 3401(a) of the Internal Revenue Code of 1954, as amended by section 531(d)(4) of the Tax Reform Act of 1984 (98 Stat. 886):

Q-1: Are fringe benefits included in the definition of "wages" under section 3401(a)?

A-1: Yes, unless specifically excluded from the definition of "wages" pursuant to section 3401(a)(1) through (20). For example, a fringe benefit provided to or on behalf of an employee is excluded from the definition of "wages" if at the time such benefit is provided it is reasonable to believe that the employee will be able to exclude such benefit from income under section 117 or 132. [Reg. § 31.3401(a)-1T.]

□ [*T.D.* 8004, 1-2-85.]

### [Reg. § 31.3401(a)-2]

**§ 31.3401(a)-2. Exclusions from wages.**—(a) *In general.*—(1) The term "wages" does not include any remuneration for services performed by an employee for his employer which is specifically excepted from wages under section 3401(a).

(2) The exception attaches to the remuneration for services performed by an employee and not to the employee as an individual; that is, the exception applies only to the remuneration in an excepted category.

*Example.* A is an individual who is employed part time by B to perform domestic service in his home (see § 31.3401(a)(3)-1). A is also employed by C part time to perform services as a clerk in a department store owned by him. While no withholding is required with respect to A's remuneration for services performed in the employ of B (the remuneration being excluded from wages), the exception does not embrace the remuneration for services performed by A in the employ of C and withholding is required with respect to the wages for such services.

(3) For provisions relating to the circumstances under which remuneration which is excepted is nevertheless deemed to be wages, and relating to the circumstances under which remuneration which is not excepted is nevertheless deemed not to be wages, see § 31.3402(e)-1.

(4) For provisions relating to payments with respect to which a voluntary withholding agreement is in effect, which are not defined as wages in section 3401(a) but which are nevertheless deemed to be wages, see § § 31.3401(a)-3 and 31.3402 (p)-1.

(b) *Fees paid a public official.*—(1) Authorized fees paid to public officials such as notaries public, clerks of courts, sheriffs, etc., for services rendered in the performance of their official duties are excepted from wages and hence are not subject to withholding. However, salaries paid such officials by the Government, or by a Government agency or instrumentality, are subject to withholding.

(2) Amounts paid to precinct workers for services performed at election booths in State, county, and municipal elections and fees paid to jurors and witnesses are in the nature of fees paid to public

officials and therefore are not subject to withholding. [Reg. § 31.3401(a)-2.]

□ [*T.D.* 6259, 10-25-59. *Amended by T.D.* 6654, 5-27-63 *and T.D.* 7096, 3-17-71.]

### [Reg. § 31.3401(a)-3]

**§ 31.3401(a)-3. Amounts deemed wages under voluntary withholding agreements.**—(a) *In general.*—Notwithstanding the exceptions to the definition of wages specified in section 3401(a) and the regulations thereunder, the term "wages" includes the amounts described in paragraph (b)(1) of this section with respect to which there is a voluntary withholding agreement in effect under section 3402(p). References in this chapter to the definition of wages contained in section 3401(a) shall be deemed to refer also to this section (§ 31.3401(a)-3).

(b) *Remuneration for services.*—(1) Except as provided in subparagraph (2) of this paragraph, the amounts referred to in paragraph (a) of this section include any remuneration for services performed by an employee for an employer which, without regard to this section, does not constitute wages under section 3401(a). For example, remuneration for services performed by an agricultural worker or a domestic worker in a private home (amounts which are specifically excluded from the definition of wages by section 3401(a)(2) and (3), respectively) are amounts with respect to which a voluntary withholding agreement may be entered into under section 3402(p). See § § 31.3401(c)-1 and 31.3401(d)-1 for the definitions of "employee" and "employer."

(2) For purposes of this paragraph, remuneration for services shall not include amounts not subject to withholding under § 31.3401(a)-1(b)(12) (relating to remuneration for services performed by a permanent resident of the Virgin Islands), § 31.3401(a)-2(b) (relating to fees paid to a public official), section 3401(a)(5) (relating to remuneration for services for foreign government or international organization), section 3401(a)(8)(B) (relating to remuneration for services performed in a possession of the United States (other than Puerto Rico) by citizens of the United States), section 3401(a)(8)(C) (relating to remuneration for services performed in Puerto Rico by citizens of the United States), section 3401(a)(11) (relating to remuneration other than in cash for service not in the course of employer's trade or business), section 3401(a)(12) (relating to payments from or to certain tax-exempt trusts, or under or to certain annuity plans or bond purchase plans), section 3401(a)(14) (relating to group-term life insurance), section 3401(a)(15) (relating to moving expenses), or section 3401(a)(16)(A) (relating to tips paid in any medium other than cash). [Reg. § 31.3401(a)-3.]

□ [*T.D.* 7096, 3-17-71.]

### [Reg. § 31.3401(a)-4]

**§ 31.3401(a)-4. Reimbursements and other expense allowance amounts.**—(a) *When excluded from wages.*—If a reimbursement or other expense allowance arrangement meets the requirements of section 62(c) of the Code and § 1.62-2 and the expenses are substantiated within a reasonable period of time, payments made under the arrangement that do not exceed the substantiated expenses are treated as paid under an accountable plan and are not wages. In addition, if both wages and the reimbursement or other expense allowance are combined in a single payment, the reimbursement or other expense allowance must be identified either by making a separate payment or by specifically identifying the amount of the reimbursement or other expense allowance.

(b) *When included in wages.*—(1) *Accountable plans.*—(i) *General rule.*—Except as provided in paragraph (b)(1)(ii) of this section, if a reimbursement or other expense allowance arrangement satisfies the requirements of section 62(c) and § 1.62-2, but the expenses are not substantiated within a reasonable period of time or amounts in excess of the substantiated expenses are not returned within a reasonable period of time, the amount paid under the arrangement in excess of the substantiated expenses is treated as paid under a nonaccountable plan, is included in wages, and is subject to withholding and payment of employment taxes no later than the first payroll period following the end of the reasonable period.

(ii) *Per diem or mileage allowances.*—If a reimbursement or other expense allowance arrangement providing a per diem or mileage allowance satisfies the requirements of section 62(c) and § 1.62-2, but the allowance is paid at a rate for each day or mile of travel that exceeds the amount of the employee's expenses deemed substantiated for a day or mile of travel, the excess portion is treated as paid under a nonaccountable plan and is included in wages. In the case of a per diem or mileage allowance paid as a reimbursement, the excess portion is subject to withholding and payment of employment taxes when paid. In the case of a per diem or mileage allowance paid as an advance, the excess portion is subject to withholding and payment of employment taxes no later than the first payroll period in which the expenses with respect to which the advance was paid (i.e., the days or miles of travel) are substantiated. The Commissioner may, in his discretion, prescribe special rules in pronouncements of general applicability regarding the timing of withholding and payment of employment taxes on per diem and mileage allowances.

(2) *Nonaccountable plans.*—If a reimbursement or other expense allowance arrangement does not satisfy the requirements of section 62(c) and §1.62-2 (e.g., the arrangement does not require expenses to be substantiated or require amounts in excess of the substantiated expenses to be returned), all amounts paid under the arrangement are treated as paid under a nonaccountable plan, are included in wages, and are subject to withholding and payment of employment taxes when paid.

(c) *Withholding rate.*—Payments made under reimbursement or other expense allowance arrangements that are subject to income tax withholding are supplemental wages as defined in §31.3402(g)-1. Accordingly, withholding on such supplemental wages is calculated under the rules provided with respect to supplemental wages in §31.3402(g)-1.

(d) *Effective date.*—This section applies to payments made under reimbursement or other expense allowance arrangements received by an employee on or after July 1, 1990, with respect to expenses paid or incurred on or after July 1, 1990. Paragraph (b)(1)(ii) of this section applies to payments made under reimbursement or other expense allowance arrangements received by an employee on or after January 1, 1991, with respect to expenses paid or incurred on or after January 1, 1991. [Reg. §31.3401(a)-4.]

☐ [*T.D. 8324,*12-14-90. *Amended by T.D. 9276, 7-24-2006.*]

### [Reg. §31.3401(a)(1)-1]

**§31.3401(a)(1)-1. Remuneration of members of the Armed Forces of the United States for active service in combat zone or while hospitalized as a result of such service.**—Remuneration paid for active service as a member of the Armed Forces of the United States performed in a month during any part of which such member served in a combat zone (as determined under section 112) or is hospitalized at any place as a result of wounds, disease, or injury incurred while serving in such a combat zone is excepted from wages and is, therefore, not subject to withholding. The exception with respect to hospitalization is applicable, however, only if during all of such month there are combatant activities in some combat zone (as determined under section 112). See the Income Tax Regulations (Part 1 of this chapter) under section 112. [Reg. §31.3401(a)(1)-1.]

☐ [*T.D. 6259, 10-25-57.*]

### [Reg. §31.3401(a)(2)-1]

**§31.3401(a)(2)-1. Agricultural labor.**—The term "wages" does not include remuneration for services which constitute agricultural labor as defined in section 3121(g). For regulations relating to the definition of the term "agricultural labor", see §31.3121(g)-1 in subpart B of this part. [Reg. §31.3401(a)(2)-1.]

☐ [*T.D. 6259, 10-25-57.*]

### [Reg. §31.3401(a)(3)-1]

**§31.3401(a)(3)-1. Remuneration for domestic service.**—(a) *In a private home.*—(1) Remuneration paid for services of a household nature performed by an employee in or about a private home of the person by whom he is employed is excepted from wages and hence is not subject to withholding. A private home is a fixed place of abode of an individual or family. A separate and distinct dwelling unit maintained by an individual in an apartment house, hotel, or other similar establishment may constitute a private home. If a dwelling house is used primarily as a boarding or lodging house for the purpose of supplying board or lodging to the public as a business enterprise, it is not a private home, and the remuneration paid for services performed therein is not within the exception.

(2) In general, services of a household nature in or about a private home include services performed by cooks, waiters, butlers, housekeepers, governesses, maids, valets, baby sitters, janitors, laundresses, furnacemen, caretakers, handymen, gardeners, footmen, grooms, and chauffeurs of automobiles for family use.

(b) *In a local college club or local chapter of a college fraternity or sorority.*—(1) Remuneration paid for services of a household nature performed by an employee in or about the club rooms or house of a local college club or of a local chapter of a college fraternity or sorority by which he is employed is excepted from wages and hence is not subject to withholding. A local college club or local chapter of a college fraternity or sorority does not include an alumni club or chapter. If the club rooms or house of a local college club or local

chapter of a college fraternity or sorority is used primarily for the purpose of supplying board or lodging to students or the public as a business enterprise, the remuneration paid for services performed therein is not within the exception.

(2) In general, services of a household nature in or about the club rooms or house of a local college club or local chapter of a college fraternity or sorority include services rendered by cooks, waiters, butlers, maids, janitors, laundresses, furnacemen, handymen, gardeners, housekeepers and housemothers.

(c) *Remuneration not excepted.*—Remuneration paid for services not of a household nature, such as services performed as a private secretary, tutor, or librarian, even though performed in the employer's private home or in a local college club or local chapter of a college fraternity or sorority, is not within the exception. Remuneration paid for services of a household nature is not within the exception if performed in or about rooming or lodging houses, boarding houses, clubs (except local college clubs), hotels, hospitals, eleemosynary institutions, or commercial offices or establishments. [Reg. §31.3401(a)(3)-1.]

☐ [*T.D. 6259, 10-25-57.*]

### [Reg. §31.3401(a)(4)-1]

**§31.3401(a)(4)-1. Cash remuneration for service not in the course of employer's trade or business.**—(a) Cash remuneration paid for services not in the course of the employer's trade or business performed by an employee for an employer in a calendar quarter is excepted from wages and hence is not subject to withholding unless—

(1) The cash remuneration paid for such services performed by the employee for the employer in the calendar quarter is $50 or more; and

(2) Such employee is regularly employed in the calendar quarter by such employer to perform such services.

Unless the tests set forth in both subparagraphs (1) and (2) of this paragraph are met, cash remuneration for service not in the course of the employer's trade or business is excluded from wages. (For provisions relating to the exclusion from wages of remuneration paid in any medium other than cash for services not in the course of the employer's trade or business, see §31.3401(a)(11)-1.)

(b) The term "services not in the course of the employer's trade or business" includes services that do not promote or advance the trade or business of the employer. As used in this section, the term does not include service not in the course of the employer's trade or business performed on a farm operated for profit or domestic service in a private home, local college club, or local chapter of a college fraternity or sorority. Accordingly, this exception does not apply with respect to remuneration which is excepted from wages, under section 3401(a)(2) or section 3401(a)(3) (see §§31.3401(a)(2)-1 and 31.3401(a)(3)-1, respectively). Remuneration paid for service performed for a corporation does not come within the exception.

(c) The test relating to cash remuneration of $50 or more is based on the remuneration earned during a calendar quarter rather than on the remuneration paid in a calendar quarter. However, for purposes of determining whether the test is met, it is also required that the remuneration be paid, although it is immaterial when the remuneration is paid. Furthermore, in determining whether $50 or more has been paid for service not in the course of the employer's trade or business, only cash remuneration for such service shall be taken into account. The term "cash remuneration" includes checks and other monetary media of exchange. Remuneration paid in any other medium, such as lodging, food, or other goods or commodities, is disregarded in determining whether the cash-remuneration test is met.

(d) For purposes of this exception, an individual is deemed to be regularly employed by an employer during a calendar quarter only if—

(1) Such individual performs service not in the course of the employer's trade or business for such employer for some portion of the day on at least 24 days (whether or not consecutive) during such calendar quarter; or

(2) Such individual was regularly employed (as determined under subparagraph (1) of this paragraph) by such employer in the performance of service not in the course of the employer's trade or business during the preceding calendar quarter.

(e) In determining whether an employee has performed service not in the course of the employer's trade or business on at least 24 days during a calendar quarter, there shall be counted as one day—

(1) Any day or portion thereof on which the employee actually performs such service; and

(2) Any day or portion thereof on which the employee does not perform service of the prescribed character but with respect to which cash remuneration is paid or payable to the employee for such service, such as a day on which the employee is sick or on vacation.

An employee who on a particular day reports for work and, at the direction of his employer, holds himself in readiness to perform service not in the course of the employer's trade or business shall be considered to be engaged in the actual performance of such service on that day. For purposes of this exception, a day is a continuous period of 24 hours commencing at midnight and ending at midnight. [Reg. § 31.3401(a)(4)-1.]

☐ [*T.D.* 6259, 10-25-57.]

### [Reg. § 31.3401(a)(5)-1]

**§ 31.3401(a)(5)-1. Remuneration for services for foreign government or international organization.**—(a) *Services for foreign government.*—(1) Remuneration paid for services performed as an employee of a foreign government is excepted from wages and hence is not subject to withholding. The exception includes not only remuneration paid for services performed by ambassadors, ministers, and other diplomatic officers and employees but also remuneration paid for services performed as a consular or other officer or employee of a foreign government or as a nondiplomatic representative of such a government. However, the exception does not include remuneration for services performed for a corporation created or organized in the United States or under the laws of the United States or any State (including the District of Columbia or the Territory of Alaska or Hawaii) or of Puerto Rico even though such corporation is wholly owned by such a government.

(2) The citizenship or residence of the employee and the place where the services are performed are immaterial for purposes of the exception.

(b) *Services for international organization.*—(1) Subject to the provisions of section 1 of the International Organizations Immunities Act, remuneration aid for services performed within or without the United States by an employee for an international organization as defined in section 7701(a)(18) is excepted from wages and hence is not subject to withholding. The term "employee" as used in the preceding sentence includes not only an employee who is a citizen or resident of the United States but also an employee who is a nonresident alien individual. The term "employee" also includes an officer. An organization designated by the President through appropriate Executive order as entitled to enjoy the privileges, exemptions, and immunities provided in the International Organizations Immunities Act may enjoy the benefits of the exclusion from wages with respect to remuneration paid for services performed for such organization prior to the date of the issuance of such Executive order, if (i) the Executive order does not provide otherwise and (ii) the organization is a public international organization in which the United States participates, pursuant to a treaty or under the authority of an Act of Congress authorizing such participation or making an appropriation for such participation, at the time such services are performed.

(2) Section 7701(a)(18) provides as follows:

"Sec. 7701. *Definitions.* (a) When used in this title, where not otherwise distinctly expressed or manifestly incompatible with the intent thereof—

\* \* \*

"(18) *International organization.* The term 'international organization' means a public international organization entitled to enjoy privileges, exemptions, and immunities as an international organization under the International Organizations Immunities Act (22 U.S.C. 288-288f)."

(3) Section 1 of the International Organizations Immunities Act provides as follows:

"SECTION 1. [INTERNATIONAL ORGANIZATIONS IMMUNITIES ACT.] For the purposes of this title [International Organizations Immunities Act], the term 'international organization' means a public international organization in which the United States participates pursuant to any treaty or under the authority of any Act of Congress authorizing such participation or making an appropriation for such participation, and which shall have been designated by the President through appropriate Executive order as being entitled to enjoy the privileges, exemptions, and immunities herein provided. The President shall be authorized, in the light of the functions performed by any such international organization, by appropriate Executive order to withhold or withdraw from any such organization or its officers or employees any of the privileges, exemptions, and immunities provided for in this title (including the amendments made by this title) or to condition or limit the enjoyment by any such organization or its officers or employees of any such privilege, exemption, or immunity. The President shall be authorized, if in his judgment such action should be justified by reason of the abuse by an international organization or its officers and employees of the privileges, exemptions, and immunities herein provided or for any other reason, at any time to revoke the designation of any international organization under this section, whereupon the international organization in question

shall cease to be classed as an international organization for the purposes of this title." [Reg. § 31.3401(a)(5)-1.]

☐ [*T.D.* 6259, 10-25-57.]

### [Reg. § 31.3401(a)(6)-1]

**§ 31.3401(a)(6)-1. Remuneration for services of nonresident alien individuals.**—(a) *In general.*—All remuneration paid after December 31, 1966, for services performed by a nonresident alien individual, if such remuneration otherwise constitutes wages within the meaning of § 31.3401(a)-1 and if such remuneration is effectively connected with the conduct of a trade or business within the United States, is subject to withholding under section 3402 unless excepted from wages under this section. In regard to wages paid under this section after February 28, 1979, the term "nonresident alien individual" does not include a nonresident alien individual treated as a resident under section 6013(g) or (h).

(b) *Remuneration for services performed outside the United States.*—Remuneration paid to a nonresident alien individual (other than a resident of Puerto Rico) for services performed outside the United States is excepted from wages and hence is not subject to withholding.

(c) *Remuneration for services of residents of Canada or Mexico who enter and leave the United States at frequent intervals.*—(1) *Transportation service.*—Remuneration paid to a nonresident alien individual who is a resident of Canada or Mexico and who, in the performance of his duties in transportation service between points in the United States and points in such foreign country, enters and leaves the United States at frequent intervals, is excepted from wages and hence is not subject to withholding. This exception applies to personnel engaged in railroad, bus, truck, ferry, steamboat, aircraft, or other transportation services and applies whether the employer is a domestic or foreign entity. Thus, the remuneration of a nonresident alien individual who is a resident of Canada and an employee of a domestic railroad, for services as a member of the crew of a train operating between points in Canada and points in the United States, is not subject to withholding under section 3402.

(2) *Service on international projects.*—Remuneration paid to a nonresident alien individual who is a resident of Canada or Mexico and who, in the performance of his duties in connection with the construction, maintenance, or operation of a waterway, viaduct, dam, or bridge traversed by, or traversing, the boundary between the United States and Canada or the boundary between the United States and Mexico, as the case may be, enters and leaves the United States at frequent intervals, is excepted from wages and hence is not subject to withholding. Thus, the remuneration of a nonresident alien individual who is a resident of Canada, for services as an employee in connection with the construction, maintenance, or operation of the Saint Lawrence Seaway and who, in the performance of such services, enters and leaves the United States at frequent intervals, is not subject to withholding under section 3402.

(3) *Limitation.*—The exceptions provided by this paragraph do not apply to the remuneration of a resident of Canada or of Mexico who is employed wholly within the United States as, for example, where such a resident is employed to perform service at a fixed point or points in the United States, such as a factory, store, office, or designated area or areas within the United States, and who commutes from his home in Canada or Mexico, in the pursuit of his employment within the United States.

(4) *Certificate required.*—In order for an exception provided by this paragraph to apply for any taxable year, the nonresident alien employee must furnish his employer a statement in duplicate for the taxable year setting forth the employee's name, address, and taxpayer identifying number, and certifying (i) that he is not a citizen or resident of the United States, (ii) that he is a resident of Canada or Mexico, as the case may be, and (iii) that he expects to meet the requirements of subparagraph (1) or (2) of this paragraph with respect to remuneraion to be paid during the taxable year in respect of which the statement is filed. The statement shall be dated, shall identify the taxable year to which it relates, shall be signed by the employee, and shall contain, or be verified by, a written declaration that is made under the penalties of perjury. No particular form is prescribed for this statement. The duplicate copy of each statement filed during any calendar year pursuant to this paragraph shall be forwarded by the employer with, and attached to, the Form 1042S required by paragraph (c) of § 1.1461-2 with respect to such remuneration for such calendar year.

(d) *Remuneration for services performed by residents of Puerto Rico.*—(1) Remuneration paid for services performed in Puerto Rico by a nonresident alien individual who is a resident of Puerto Rico for an employer (other than the United States or any agency thereof) is excepted from wages and hence is not subject to withholding.

(2) Remuneration paid for services performed outside the United States but not in Puerto Rico by a nonresident alien individual who is a resident of Puerto Rico for an employer (other than the United States or any agency thereof) is excepted from wages and hence is not subject to withholding if such individual does not expect to be a resident of Puerto Rico during the entire taxable year. In order for the exception provided by this subparagraph to apply for any taxable year, the nonresident alien employee must furnish his employer a statement for the taxable year setting forth the employee's name and address and certifying (i) that he is not a citizen or resident of the United States and (ii) that he is a resident of Puerto Rico but does not expect to be a resident of Puerto Rico during the entire taxable year. The statement shall be dated, shall identify the taxable year to which it relates, shall be signed by the employee, and shall contain, or be verified by, a written declaration that it is made under the penalties of perjury. No particular form is prescribed for this statement.

(3) Remuneration paid for services performed outside the United States by a nonresident alien individual who is a resident of Puerto Rico as an employee of the United States or any agency thereof is excepted from wages and hence is not subject to withholding if such individual does not expect to be a resident of Puerto Rico during the entire taxable year. In order for the exception provided by this subparagraph to apply for any taxable year, the nonresident alien employee must furnish his employer a statement for the taxable year setting forth the employee's name and address and certifying (i) that he is not a citizen or resident of the United States and (ii) that he is a resident of Puerto Rico but does not expect to be a resident of Puerto Rico during the entire taxable year. This statement shall be dated, shall identify the taxable year to which it relates, shall be signed by the employee, and shall contain, or be verified by, a written declaration that it is made under the penalties of perjury. No particular form is prescribed for this statement.

(e) *Exemption from income tax for remuneration paid for services performed before January 1, 2001.*—Remuneration paid for services performed within the United States by a nonresident alien individual before January 1, 2001, is excepted from wages and hence is not subject to withholding if such remuneration is, or will be, exempt from income tax imposed by chapter 1 of the Internal Revenue Code by reason of a provision of the Internal Revenue Code or an income tax convention to which the United States is a party. In order for the exception provided by this paragraph to apply for any taxable year, the nonresident alien employee must furnish his employer a statement in duplicate for the taxable year setting forth the employee's name, address, and taxpayer identifying number, and certifying (1) that he is not a citizen or resident of the United States, (2) that the remuneration to be paid to him during the taxable year is, or will be, exempt from the tax imposed by chapter 1 of the Code, and (3) the reason why such remuneration is so exempt from tax. If the remuneration is claimed to be exempt from tax by reason of a provision of an income tax convention to which the United States is a party, the statement shall also indicate the provision and tax convention under which the exemption is claimed, the country of which the employee is a resident, and sufficient facts to justify the claim to exemption. The statement shall be dated, shall identify the taxable year for which it is to apply and the remuneration to which it relates, shall be signed by the employee, and shall contain, or be verified by, a written declaration that is made under the penalties of perjury. No particular form is prescribed for this statement. The duplicate copy of each statement filed during any calendar year pursuant to this paragraph shall be forwarded by the employer with, and attached to, the Form 1042S required by paragraph (c) of §1.1461-2 with respect to such remuneration for such calendar year.

(f) *Exemption from income tax for remuneration paid for services performed after December 31, 2000.*—Remuneration paid for services performed within the United States by a nonresident alien individual after December 31, 2000, is excepted from wages and hence is not subject to withholding if such remuneration is, or will be, exempt from the income tax imposed by chapter 1 of the Internal Revenue Code by reason of a provision of the Internal Revenue Code or an income tax convention to which the United States is a party. An employer may rely on a claim that the employee is entitled to an exemption from tax if it complies with the requirements of §1.1441-1(e)(1)(ii) of this chapter (for a claim based on a provision of the Internal Revenue Code) or §1.1441-4(b)(2) of this chapter (for a claim based on an income tax convention). [Reg. §31.3401(a)(6)-1.]

☐ [T.D. 6908, 12-30-66. *Amended by T.D. 7670,* 1-30-80; *T.D. 7977,* 9-19-84; *T.D. 8734,* 10-6-97; *T.D. 8804,* 12-30-98 *and T.D. 8856,* 12-29-99.]

[Reg. §31.3401(a)(7)-1]

**§31.3401(a)(7)-1. Remuneration paid before January 1, 1967, for services performed by nonresident alien individuals who are residents of a contiguous country and who enter and leave the United States at frequent intervals.**—(a) *Transportation service.*—Remuneration paid to nonresident aliens who are residents of a contiguous country (Canada or Mexico) and who, in the performance of their duties in transportation service between points in the United States and points in a contiguous country, enter and leave the United States at frequent intervals, is excepted from wages and hence is not subject to withholding. This exception applies to personnel engaged in railroad, bus, ferry, steamboat, and aircraft services and applies whether the employer is a domestic or foreign entity. This, the remuneration of a nonresident alien individual who is a resident of Canada and an employee of a domestic railroad, for services as a member of the crew of a train operating between points in Canada and points in the United States, is not subject to withholding under section 3402.

(b) *Service on international projects.*—Remuneration paid to nonresident aliens who are residents of a contiguous country (Canada or Mexico) and who, in the performance of their duties in connection with the construction, maintenance or operation of a waterway, viaduct, dam, or bridge traversed by or traversing the boundary between the United States and Canada or the boundary between the United States and Mexico, as the case may be, enter and leave the United States at frequent intervals, is excepted from wages and hence is not subject to withholding. Thus, the remuneration of a nonresident alien individual who is a resident of Canada, for services as an employee in connection with the construction, maintenance, or operation of the Saint Lawrence Seaway and who, in the performance of such services, enters and leaves the United States at frequent intervals, is not subject to withholding under section 3402.

(c) *Limitation on application of section.*—The exception provided by this section has no application to the remuneration of a resident of Canada or of Mexico who is employed wholly within the United States as, for example, where such a resident is employed to performed service at a fixed point or points in the United States, such as a factory, store, office, or designated area or areas within the United States, and who commutes from his home in Canada or Mexico in the pursuit of his employment within the United States.

(d) *Certificate required.*—In order for the exception to apply, the nonresident alien employee must furnish his employer a statement setting forth the employee's name and address and certifying (1) that his is not a citizen of the United States, (2) that he is a resident of Canada or Mexico, as the case may be, and (3) the approximate period of time during which he has had such status. Such statement shall be dated, shall be signed by the employee, and shall contain, or be verified by, a written declaration that it is made under the penalties of perjury. No particular form is prescribed for this statement.

(e) *Effective date.*—This section shall not apply with respect to remuneration paid after December 31, 1966. For rules with respect to such remuneration see §31.3401(a)(6)-1. [Reg. §31.3401(a)(7)-1.]

☐ [T.D. 6259, 10-25-57. *Republished in T.D. 6516,* 12-19-60. *Amended by T.D. 6908,* 12-30-66.]

[Reg. §31.3401(a)(8)(A)-1]

**§31.3401(a)(8)(A)-1. Remuneration for services performed outside the United States by citizens of the United States.**—(a) *Remuneration excluded from gross income under section 911.*—(1)(i) Remuneration paid for services performed outside the United States for an employer (other than the United States or any agency thereof) by a citizen of the United States does not constitute wages and hence is not subject to withholding, if at the time of payment it is reasonable to believe that such remuneration will be excluded from gross income under the provisions of section 911. The reasonable belief contemplated by the statute may be based upon any evidence reasonably sufficient to induce such belief, even though such evidence may be insufficient upon closer examination by the district director or the courts finally to establish that the remuneration is excludable from gross income under the provisions of section 911. The reasonable belief shall be based upon the application of section 911 and the regulations thereunder in Part 1 of this chapter (Income Tax Regulations).

(ii) Remuneration paid by an employer to an employee constitutes wages, and hence is subject to withholding, only to the extent that the remuneration is expected to exceed the aggregate amount which is excludable from the employee's gross income under section 911(a). For amounts paid after December 31, 1984, the determination of the amount subject to withholding shall be made by applying the excludable amount, on a pro rata basis, to each payment of remuneration to the employee. For this purpose, an employer is not required to ascertain information with respect to amounts received by his employee from any other source; but, if the employer has such information, he shall take it into account in determining whether the earned income of the employee is in excess of the applicable limitation. For purposes of section 911(d)(5) and § 1.911-2(c), relating to an employee who states to the authorities of a foreign country that he is not a resident of that country, the employer is not required to ascertain whether such a statement has been made; but if an employer knows that such a statement has been made, he shall presume that the employee is not a bona fide resident of that country, unless the employer also knows that the authorities of the foreign country have determined, notwithstanding the statement, that the employee is a resident of that country. For purposes of section 911(d)(1) or § 1.911-2(a) relating to the definition of a qualified individual, the reasonable belief contemplated by the statute may be based on a presumption as set forth in subparagraph (2) or (3) of this paragraph. For purposes of sections 911(a)(2) and 911(c)(2) and § 1.911-4(b) and (d)(1), relating to the housing cost amount exclusion and the definition of housing expenses, the reasonable belief contemplated by the statute may be based on the presumption set forth in subparagraph (4) of this paragraph.

(2)(i) The employer may, in the absence of cause for a reasonable belief to the contrary, presume that an employee will maintain a tax home in a foreign country or countries and be a bona fide resident of a foreign country or countries, within the meaning of section 911(d)(1), for an uninterrupted period which includes each taxable year of the employee, or applicable portion thereof, in respect of which the employee properly executes and delivers to the employer a statement that the employee meets or will meet the requirement of § 1.911-2(a) relating to maintaining a tax home and a bona fide residence in a foreign country for the taxable year. This statement must set forth the facts alleged as the basis for this determination and contain a declaration by the employee that the statement is made under the penalties of perjury. Sample forms of acceptable statements may be obtained by writing to the Foreign Operations District, Internal Revenue Service, Washington, D.C. 20225 (Form IO-673).

(ii) If the employer was entitled to presume for the two consecutive taxable years immediately preceding an employee's current taxable year that such employee was a bona fide resident of a foreign country or countries for an uninterrupted period which includes such preceding taxable years, he may, if such employee is residing in a foreign country on the first day of such current taxable year, presume, in the absence of cause for a reasonable belief to the contrary, and without obtaining from the employee the statement prescribed in subdivision (i) of this subparagraph, that the employee will be a bona fide resident of a foreign country or countries in such current taxable year.

(3) The employer may, in the absence of cause for a reasonable belief to the contrary, presume that an employee will maintain a tax home in a foreign country or countries and be present in a foreign country or countries during at least 330 full days during any period of twelve consecutive months, within the meaning of section 911(d)(1), and that such period includes each taxable year of the employee, or applicable portion thereof, in respect of which the employee properly executes and delivers to the employer a statement that the employee meets or will meet the requirements of § 1.911-2(a) relating to maintaining a tax home and being physically present in a foreign country for the taxable year. This statement must set forth the facts alleged as the basis for this determination and contain a declaration by the employee that the statement is made under the penalties of perjury. Sample forms of acceptable statements may be obtained by writing to the Foreign Operations District, Internal Revenue Service, Washington, D.C. 20225 (Form IO-673).

(4) The employer may, in the absence of cause for a reasonable belief to the contrary, presume that an employee's housing cost amount will be the amount shown on a statement properly executed and delivered to the employer. This statement must set forth the employee's estimation of the following items: housing expenses (as defined in § 1.911-4(b)), the housing cost amount exclusion (as defined in § 1.911-4(d)(1)), and the qualifying period (as defined in § 1.911-2(a)). The statement must contain a declaration by the employee that it is made under the penalties of perjury. Sample forms of acceptable statements may be obtained by writing to the Foreign Operations District, Internal Revenue Service, Washington, D.C. 20225 (IO-673). The employer may not rely on a statement from an employee if the employer, based on his or her knowledge of housing costs in the vicinity of the employee's tax home (as defined in § 1.911-2(b)), believes the employee's housing expenses are lavish or extravagant under the circumstances.

(b) *Remuneration subject to withholding of income tax under law of a foreign country or a possession of the United States.*—(1) Remuneration paid for services in a foreign country or in a possession of the United States for an employer (other than the United States or any agency

thereof) by a citizen of the United States does not constitute wages and hence is not subject to withholding, if at the time of the payment of such remuneration the employer is required by the law of any foreign country or of any possession of the United States to withhold income tax upon such remuneration. This paragraph, insofar as it relates to remuneration paid for services performed in a possession of the United States, applies only with respect to remuneration paid on or after August 9, 1955.

(2) Remuneration is not exempt from withholding under this paragraph if the employer is not required by the law of a foreign country or of a possession of the United States to withhold income tax upon such remuneration. Mere agreements between the employer and the employee whereby the estimated income tax of a foreign country or of a possession of the United States is withheld from the remuneration in anticipation of actual liability under the law of such country or possession will not suffice.

(3) The exemption from withholding provided by this paragraph does not apply by reason of withholding of income tax pursuant to the law of a territory of the United States, of a political subdivision of a possession of the United States, or of a political subdivision of a foreign state.

(4) For provisions relating to remuneration for services performed by a permanent resident of the Virgin Islands, see paragraph (b)(12) of § 31.3401(a)-1.

(c) *Limitation on application of section.*—This section has no application to the remuneration paid to a citizen of the United States for services performed outside the United States as an employee of the United States or any agency thereof. [Reg. § 31.3401(a)(8)(A)-1.]

☐ [*T.D. 6259, 10-25-57. Amended by T.D. 6697, 12-16-63, and T.D. 8006, 1-17-85.*]

### [Reg. § 31.3401(a)(8)(B)-1]

**§ 31.3401(a)(8)(B)-1. Remuneration for services performed in possession of the United States (other than Puerto Rico) by citizen of the United States.**—(a) Remuneration paid for services for an employer (other than the United States or any agency thereof) performed by a citizen of the United States within a possession of the United States (other than Puerto Rico) does not constitute wages and hence is not subject to withholding, if it is reasonable to believe that at least 80 percent of the remuneration to be paid to the employee by such employer during the calendar year will be for such services. The reasonable belief contemplated by section 3401(a)(8)(B) may be based upon any evidence reasonably sufficient to induce such belief, even though such evidence may be insufficient upon closer examination by the district director or the courts finally to establish that at least 80 percent of the remuneration paid by the employer to the employee during the calendar year was for services performed within such a possession of the United States.

(b) This section has no application to remuneration paid to a citizen of the United States for services performed in any possession of the United States as an employee of the United States or any agency thereof.

(c) For provisions relating to remuneration for services performed by a permanent resident of the Virgin Islands, see § 31.3401(a)-1(b)(12). [Reg. § 31.3401(a)(8)(B)-1.]

☐ [*T.D. 6259, 10-25-57.*]

### [Reg. § 31.3401(a)(8)(C)-1]

**§ 31.3401(a)(8)(C)-1. Remuneration for services performed in Puerto Rico by citizen of the United States.**—(a) Remuneration paid for services performed within Puerto Rico for an employer (other than the United States or any agency thereof) by a citizen of the United States does not constitute wages and hence is not subject to withholding, if it is reasonable to believe that during the entire calendar year the employee will be a bona fide resident of Puerto Rico. The reasonable belief contemplated by section 3401 (a)(8)(C) may be based upon any evidence reasonably sufficient to induce such belief, even though such evidence may be insufficient upon closer examination by the district director or the courts finally to establish that the employee was a bona fide resident of Puerto Rico for the entire calendar year.

(b) The employer may, in the absence of cause for a reasonable belief to the contrary, presume that an employee will be a bona fide resident of Puerto Rico during the entire calendar year—

(1) Unless the employee is known by the employer to have maintained his abode at a place outside Puerto Rico at some time during the current or the preceding calendar year; or

(2) In any case where the employee files with the employer a statement (containing a declaration under the penalties of perjury that such statement is true to the best of the employees's knowledge and belief) that such employee has at all times during the current calendar year been a bona fide resident of Puerto Rico and that he

intends to remain a bona fide resident of Puerto Rico during the entire remaining portion of such current calendar year.

(c) This section has no application to remuneration paid to a citizen of the United States for services performed in Puerto Rico as an employee of the United States or any agency thereof. [Reg. §31.3401(a)(8)(C)-1.]

☐ [T.D. 6259, 10-25-57.]

### [Reg. §31.3401(a)(9)-1]

**§31.3401(a)(9)-1. Remuneration for services performed by a minister of a church or a member of a religious order.**—(a) *In general.*— Remuneration paid for services performed by a duly ordained, commissioned, or licensed minister of a church in the exercise of his ministry, or by a member of a religious order in the exercise of duties required by such order, is excepted from wages and hence is not subject to withholding.

(b) *Service by a minister in the exercise of his ministry.*—Except as provided in paragraph (c)(3) of this section, service performed by a minister in the exercise of his ministry includes the ministration of sacerdotal functions and the conduct of religious worship, and the control, conduct, and maintenance of religious organizations (including the religious boards, societies, and other integral agencies of such organizations), under the authority of a religious body, constituting a church or church denomination. The following rules are applicable in determining whether services performed by a minister are performed in the exercise of his ministry:

(1) Whether service performed by a minister constitutes the conduct of religious worship or the ministration of sacerdotal functions depends on the tenets and practices of the particular religious body constituting his church or church denomination.

(2) Service performed by a minister in the control, conduct, and maintenance of a religious organization relates to directing, managing, or promoting the activities of such organization. Any religious organization is deemed to be under the authority of a religious body constituting a church or church denomination if it is organized and dedicated to carrying out the tenets and principles of a faith in accordance with either the requirements or sanctions governing the creation of institutions of the faith. The term "religious organization" has the same meaning and application as is given to the term for income tax purposes.

(3)(i) If a minister is performing service in the conduct of religious worship or the ministration of sacerdotal functions, such service is in the exercise of his ministry whether or not it is performed for a religious organization.

(ii) The rule in subdivision (i) of this subparagraph may be illustrated by the following example:

*Example.* M, a duly ordained minister, is engaged to perform service as chaplain at N University. M devotes his entire time to performing his duties as chaplain which include the conduct of religious worship, offering spiritual counsel to the university students, and teaching a class in religion. M is performing service in the exercise of his ministry.

(4)(i) If a minister is performing service for an organization which is operated as an integral agency of a religious organization under the authority of a religious body constituting a church or church denomination, all service performed by the minister in the conduct of religious worship, in the ministration of sacerdotal functions, or in the control, conduct, and maintenance of such organization (see subparagraph (2) of this paragraph) is in the exercise of his ministry.

(ii) The rule in subdivision (i) of this subparagraph may be illustrated by the following example:

*Example.* M, a duly ordained minister, is engaged by the N Religious Board to serve as director of one of its departments. He performs no other service. The N Religious Board is an integral agency of O, a religious organization operating under the authority of a religious body constituting a church denomination. M is performing service in the exercise of his ministry.

(5)(i) If a minister, pursuant to an assignment or designation by a religious body constituting his church, performs service for an organization which is neither a religious organization nor operated as an integral agency of a religious organization, all service performed by him, even though such service may not involve the conduct of religious worship or the ministration of sacerdotal functions, is in the exercise of his ministry.

(ii) The rule in subdivision (i) of this subparagraph may be illustrated by the following example:

*Example.* M, a duly ordained minister, is assigned by X, the religious body constituting his church, to perform advisory service to Y Company in connection with the publication of a book dealing with the history of M's church denomination. Y is neither a religious organization nor operated as an integral agency of a religious organi-

zation. M performs no other service for X or Y. M is performing service in the exercise of his ministry.

(c) *Service by a minister not in the exercise of his ministry.*—(1) Section 3401(a)(9) does not except from wages remuneration for service performed by a duly ordained, commissioned, or licensed minister of a church which is not in the exercise of his ministry.

(2)(i) If a minister is performing service for an organization which is neither a religious organization nor operated as an integral agency of a religious organization and the service is not performed pursuant to an assignment or designation by his ecclesiastical superiors, then only the service performed by him in the conduct of religious worship or the ministration of sacerdotal functions is in the exercise of his ministry. See, however, subparagraph (3) of this paragraph.

(ii) The rule in subdivision (i) of this subparagraph may be illustrated by the following example:

*Example.* M, a duly ordained minister, is engaged by N University to teach history and mathematics. He performs no other service for N although from time to time he performs marriages and conducts funerals for relatives and friends. N University is neither a religious organization nor operated as an integral agency of a religious organization. M is not performing the service for N pursuant to an assignment or designation by his ecclesiastical superiors. However, service performed by M in performing marriages and conducting funerals is in the exercise of his ministry.

(3) Service performed by a duly ordained, commissioned, or licensed minister of a church as an employee of the United States, or a State, Territory, or possession of the United States, or the District of Columbia, or a foreign government, or a political subdivision of any of the foregoing, is not considered to be in the exercise of his ministry for purposes of the collection of income tax at source on wages, even though such service may involve the ministration of sacerdotal functions or the conduct of religious worship. Thus, for example, service performed by an individual as a chaplain in the Armed Forces of the United States is considered to be performed by a commissioned officer in his capacity as such, and not by a minister in the exercise of his ministry. Similarly, service performed by an employee of a State as a chaplain in a State prison is considered to be performed by a civil servant of the State and not by a minister in the exercise of his ministry.

(d) *Service in the exercise of duties required by a religious order.*— Service performed by a member of a religious order in the exercise of duties required by such order includes all duties required of the member by the order. The nature or extent of such service is immaterial so long as it is a service which he is directed or required to perform by his ecclesiastical superiors. [Reg. §31.3401(a)(9)-1.]

☐ [T.D. 6259, 10-25-57.]

### [Reg. §31.3401(a)(10)-1]

**§31.3401(a)(10)-1. Remuneration for services in delivery or distribution of newspapers, shopping news, or magazines.**— (a) *Services of individuals under age 18.*—Remuneration for services performed by an employee under the age of 18 in the delivery or distribution of newspapers, or shopping news, not including delivery or distribution (as, for example, by a regional distributor) to any point for subsequent delivery or distribution, is excepted from wages and hence is not subject to withholding. Thus, remuneration for services performed by an employee under the age of 18 in making house-to-house delivery or sale of newspapers or shopping news, including handbills and other similar types of advertising material, is excepted from wages. The remuneration is excepted irrespective of the form or method thereof. Remuneration for incidental services by the employee who makes the house-to-house delivery, such as services in assembling newspapers, is considered to be within the exception. The exception continues only during the time that the employee is under the age of 18.

(b) *Services of individuals of any age.*—Remuneration for services performed by an employee in, and at the time of, the sale of newspapers or magazines to ultimate consumers under an arrangement under which the newspapers or magazines are to be sold by him at at fixed price, his remuneration being based on the retention of the excess of such price over the amount at which the newspapers or magazines are charged to him, is excepted from wages and hence is not subject to withholding. The remuneration is excepted whether or not the employee is guaranteed a minimum amount of remuneration, or is entitled to be credited with the unsold newspapers or magazines turned back. Moreover, the remuneration is excepted without regard to the age of the employee. Remuneration for services performed other than at the time of sale to the ultimate consumer is not within the exception. Thus, remuneration for services of a regional distributor which are antecedent to but not immediately part of the sale to the ultimate consumer is not within the exception.

However, remuneration for incidental services by the employee who makes the sale to the ultimate consumer, such as services in assembling newspapers or in taking newspapers or magazines to the place of sale, is considered to be within the exception. [Reg. §31.3401(a)(10)-1.]

☐ [*T.D. 6259, 10-25-57.*]

### [Reg. §31.3401(a)(11)-1]

**§31.3401(a)(11)-1. Remuneration other than in cash for service not in the course of employer's trade or business.—** (a) Remuneration paid in any medium other than cash for services not in the course of the employer's trade or business is excepted from wages and hence is not subject to withholding. Cash remuneration includes checks and other monetary media of exchange. Remuneration paid in any medium other than cash, such as lodging, food, or other goods or commodities, for services not in the course of the employer's trade or business does not constitute wages. Remuneration paid in any medium other than cash for other types of services does not come within this exception from wages. For provisions relating to cash remuneration for service not in the course of employer's trade or business, see §31.3401(a)(4)-1.

(b) As used in this section, the term "services not in the course of the employer's trade or business" has the same meaning as when used in §31.3401(a)(4)-1. [Reg. §31.3401(a)(11)-1.]

☐ [*T.D. 6259, 10-25-57.*]

### [Reg. §31.3401(a)(12)-1]

**§31.3401(a)(12)-1. Payments from or to certain tax-exempt trusts, or under or to certain annuity plans or bond purchase plans.—** (a) *Payments from or to certain tax-exempt trusts.*—The term "wages" does not include any payment made—

(1) By an employer, on behalf of an employee or his beneficiary, into a trust, or

(2) To, or on behalf of, an employee or his beneficiary from a trust, if at the time of such payment the trust is exempt from tax under section 501(a) as an organization described in section 401(a). A payment made to an employee of such a trust for services rendered as an employee of the trust and not as a beneficiary thereof is not within this exclusion from wages. Also, since supplemental unemployment compensation benefits are treated under paragraph (b)(14) of §31.3401(a)-1 as if they were wages for purposes of this chapter, this section does not apply to such benefits.

(b) *Payments under or to certain annuity plans.*—(1) The term "wages" does not include any payment made after December 31, 1962,—

(i) By an employer, on behalf of an employee or his beneficiary, into an annuity plan, or

(ii) To, or on behalf of, an employee or his beneficiary under an annuity plan,

if at the time of such payment the annuity plan is a plan described in section 403(a).

(2) The term "wages" does not include any payment made before January 1, 1963,—

(i) By an employer, on behalf of an employee or his beneficiary, into an annuity plan, or

(ii) To, or on behalf of, an employee or his beneficiary under an annuity plan,

if at the time of such payment the annuity plan meets the requirements of section 401(a)(3), (4), (5), and (6).

(c) *Payments under or to certain bond purchase plans.*—The term "wages" does not include any payment made after December 31, 1962,—

(1) By an employer, on behalf of an employee or his beneficiary, into a bond purchase plan, or

(2) To, or on behalf of, an employee or his beneficiary under a bond purchase plan,

if at the time of such payment the plan is qualified bond purchase plan described in section 405(a).

(d) *Payment to individual retirement plans.*—(1) The term "wages" does not include any payment to an individual retirement plan described in section 7701(a)(37) by an employer after December 31, 1974, on behalf of an employee, if, at the time of such payment, it is reasonable for the employer to believe that the employee will be entitled to a deduction for such payment under section 219(a).

(2) The term "wages" does not include any payment to an individual retirement plan described in section 7701(a)(37) by an employer after December 31, 1976, on behalf of an employee, if, at the time of such payment, it is reasonable for the employer to believe that the employee on whose behalf the payment is made will be entitled to a deduction for such payment under section 220(a).

(3) The term "wages" does not include any payment to a simplified employee pension arrangement described in section 408(k) by an employer after December 31, 1978, on behalf of an employee, if, at the time of such payment, it is reasonable for the employer to believe that the employee on whose behalf the payment is made will be entitled to a deduction for such payment under section 219(a). [Reg. §31.3401(a)(12)-1.]

☐ [*T.D. 6259, 10-25-57. Amended by T.D. 6654, 5-27-63, T.D. 7068, 11-10-70 and T.D. 7730, 10-31-80.*]

### [Reg. §31.3401(a)(13)-1]

**§31.3401(a)(13)-1. Remuneration for services performed by Peace Corps volunteers.—**(a) Remuneration paid after September 22, 1961, for services performed as a volunteer or volunteer leader within the meaning of the Peace Corps Act (22 U.S.C. 2501) is excepted from wages, and hence is not subject to withholding, unless the remuneration is paid pursuant to section 5(c) or section 6(1) of the Peace Corps Act.

(b) Sections 5 and 6 of the Peace Corps Act (22 U.S.C. 2504, 2505) provide, in part, as follows:

Sec. 5. *Peace Corps Volunteers* [Peace Corps Act (75 Stat. 613); as amended by sec. 2(b), Act of December 13, 1963 (P.L. 88-200, 77 Stat. 359); sec 2(a), Act of August 24, 1965, (P.L. 89-134, 79 Stat. 549); sec. 3(a), Act of July 24, 1970 (P.L. 91-352, 84 Stat. 464)]

* * *

(c) *Readjustment allowances.* Volunteers shall be entitled to receive a readjustment allowance at a rate not to exceed $75 for each month of satisfactory service as determined by the President; except that, in the cases of volunteers who have one or more minor children at the time of their entering a period of pre-enrollment training, one parent shall be entitled to receive a readjustment allowance at a rate not to exceed $125 for each month of satisfactory service as determined by the President. The readjustment allowance of each volunteer shall be payable on his return to the United States: *Provided, however,* That, under such circumstances as the President may determine, the accrued readjustment allowance, or any part thereof, may be paid to the volunteer, members of his family or others, during the period of his service, or prior to his return to the United States. In the event of the volunteer's death during the period of his service, the amount of any unpaid readjustment allowance shall be paid in accordance with the provisions of section 5582(b) of Title 5. For purposes of the Internal Revenue Code of 1954, a volunteer shall be deemed to be paid and to receive each amount of a readjustment allowance to which he is entitled after December 31, 1964, when such amount is transferred from funds made available under this chapter to the fund from which such readjustment allowance is payable.

* * *

Sec. 6. *Peace Corps Volunteer Leaders; number; applicability of chapter; benefits* [Peace Corps Act (75 Stat. 615), as amended by sec. 3, Act of December 13, 1963 (P.L. 88-200, 77 Stat. 360)] The President may enroll in the Peace Corps qualified citizens or nationals of the United States whose services are required for supervisory or other special duties or responsibilities in connection with programs under this chapter (referred to in this Act as "volunteer leaders"). The ratio of the total number of volunteer leaders to the total number of volunteers in service at any one time shall not exceed one to twenty-five. Except as otherwise provided in this Act, all of the provisions of this Act applicable to volunteers shall be applicable to volunteer leaders, and the term "volunteers" shall include "volunteer leaders": *Provided, however,* That—

(1) Volunteer leaders shall be entitled to receive a readjustment allowance at a rate not to exceed $125 for each month of satisfactory service as determined by the President;

* * *

[Reg. §31.3401(a)(13)-1.]

☐ [*T.D. 62654, 5-27-63 Amended by T.D. 7943, 6-29-77.*]

### [Reg. §31.3401(a)(14)-1]

**§31.3401(a)(14)-1. Group-term life insurance.—**(a) The cost of group-term life insurance on the life of an employee is excepted from wages, and hence is not subject to withholding. For provisions relating generally to such remuneration, and for reporting requirements with respect to such remuneration, see sections 79 and 6052, respectively, and the regulations thereunder in Part 1 of this chapter (Income Tax Regulations).

(b) The cost of group-term life insurance on the life of an employee's spouse or children is not subject to withholding if it is excludable from the employee's gross income because it is merely incidental. See paragraph (d)(2)(ii)(*b*) of §1.161-2 in Part 1 of this chapter (Income Tax Regulations). [Reg. §31.3401(a)(14)-1.]

☐ [*T.D. 7493, 6-29-77.*]

## [Reg. §31.3401(a)(15)-1]

§31.3401(a)(15)-1. Moving expenses.—(a) An amount paid to or on behalf of an employee after March 4, 1964, either as an advance or a reimbursement, specifically for moving expenses incurred or expected to be incurred is excepted from wages, and hence is not subject to withholding, if (and to the extent that) at the time of payment it is reasonable to believe that a corresponding deduction is or will be allowable to the employee under section 217. The reasonable belief contemplated by the statute may be based upon any evidence reasonably sufficient to induce such belief, even though such evidence may be insufficient upon closer examination by the district director or the courts finally to establish that a deduction is allowable under section 217. The reasonable belief shall be based upon the application of section 217 and the regulations thereunder in Part 1 of this chapter (Income Tax Regulations). When used in this section, the term "moving expenses" has the same meaning as when used in section 217. See §1.6041-2(a) in Part 1 of this chapter (Income Tax Regulations), relating to return of information as to payments to employees, and §31.6051-1(e), relating to the reporting of reimbursements of or payments of certain moving expenses.

(b) Except as otherwise provided in paragraph (a) of this section, or in a numbered paragraph of section 3401(a), amounts paid to or on behalf of an employee for moving expenses constitute wages subject to withholding. [Reg. §31.3401(a)(15)-1.]

☐ [T.D. 7493, 6-29-77.]

## [Reg. §31.3401(a)(16)-1]

§31.3401(a)(16)-1. Tips.—Tips paid to an employee are excepted from wages and hence not subject to withholding if—

(a) The tips are paid in any medium other than cash, or

(b) The cash tips received by an employee in any calendar month in the course of his employment by an employer are less than $20.

However, if the cash tips received by an employee in a calendar month in the course of his employment by an employer amount to $20 or more, none of the cash tips received by the employee in such calendar month are excepted from wages under this section. The cash tips to which this section applies include checks and other monetary media of exchange. Tips received by an employee in any medium other than cash, such as passes, tickets, or other goods or commodities do not constitute wages. If an employee in any calendar month performs services for two or more employers and receives tips in the course of his employment by each employer, the $20 test is to be applied separately with respect to the cash tips received by the employee in respect of his services for each employer and not to the total cash tips received by the employee during the month. As to the time tips are deemed paid, see §31.3401(f)-1. For provisions relating to the treatment of tips received by an employee prior to 1966, see paragraph (b)(11) of §31.3401(a)-1. [Reg. §31.3401(a)(16)-1.]

☐ [T.D. 7001, 1-17-69.]

## [Reg. §31.3401(a)(17)-1]

§31.3401(a)(17)-1. Remuneration for services performed on a boat engaged in catching fish.—(a) Remuneration for services performed on or after December 31, 1954, by an individual on a boat engaged in catching fish or other forms of aquatic animal life (hereinafter "fish") is excepted from wages and hence is not subject to withholding if—

(1) The individual receives a share of the boat's (or boats' for a fishing operation involving more than one boat) catch of fish or a share of the proceeds from the sale of the catch,

(2) The amount of the individual's share depends solely on the amount of the boat's (or boats' for a fishing operation involving more than one boat) catch of fish,

(3) The individual does not receive, and is not entitled to receive, any cash remuneration, other than remuneration that is described in subparagraph (1) of this paragraph, and

(4) The crew of the boat (or of each boat from which the individual receives a share of the catch) normally is made up of fewer than 10 individuals.

(b) The requirement of subparagraph (2) of paragraph (a) is not satisfied if there exists an agreement with the boat's (or boats') owner or operator by which the individual's remuneration is determined partially or fully by a factor not dependent on the size of the catch. For example, if a boat is operated under a remuneration arrangement, e.g., a union contract, which specifies that crew members, in addition to receiving a share of the catch, are entitled to an hourly wage for repairing nets, regardless of whether this wage is actually paid, then all the crew members covered by the arrangement are entitled to receive cash remuneration other than as a share of the catch and are not excepted from employment by section 3121(b)(20).

(c) The operating crew of a boat includes all persons on the boat (including the captain) who receive any form of remuneration in exchange for services rendered while on a boat engaged in catching fish. See §1.6050A-1 for reporting requirements for the operator of a boat engaged in catching fish with respect to individuals performing services described in this section.

(d) During the same return period, service performed by a crew member may be excepted from employment by section 3121(b)(20) and this section for one voyage and not so excepted on a subsequent voyage on the same or on a different boat. [Reg. §31.3401(a)(17)-1.]

☐ [T.D. 7716, 8-26-80.]

## [Reg. §31.3401(a)(18)-1]

§31.3401(a)(18)-1. Payments or benefits under a qualified educational assistance program.—A payment made, or benefit furnished, to or for the benefit of an employee in a taxable year beginning after December 31, 1978, does not constitute wages and hence is not subject to withholding if, at the time of such payment or furnishing, it is reasonable to believe that the employee will be able to exclude such payment or benefit from income under section 127. [Reg. §31.3401(a)(18)-1.]

☐ [T.D. 7898, 7-5-83.]

## [Reg. §31.3401(a)(19)-1]

§31.3401(a)(19)-1. Reimbursements under a self-insured medical reimbursement plan.—Amounts reimbursed to or on behalf of an employee after December 31, 1979, as a medical care reimbursement under a self-insured medical reimbursement plan (within the meaning of section 105(h)(6)) do not constitute wages and hence are not subject to withholding even though such reimbursement is includible in the gross income of an employee. For rules with respect to self-insured medical reimbursement plans, see section 105(h) and §1.105-11 of this Chapter (Income Tax Regulations). [Reg. §31.3401(a)(19)-1.]

☐ [T.D. 7754, 1-13-81.]

## [Reg. §31.3401(b)-1]

§31.3401(b)-1. Payroll period.—(a) The term "payroll period" means the period of service for which a payment of wages is ordinarily made to an employee by his employer. It is immaterial that the wages are not always paid at regular intervals. For example, if an employer ordinarily pays a particular employee for each calendar week at the end of the week, but if for some reason the employee in a given week receives a payment in the middle of the week for the portion of the week already elapsed and receives the remainder at the end of the week, the payroll period is still the calendar week; or if, instead, that employee is sent on a 3-week trip by his employer and receives at the end of the trip a single wage payment for three weeks' services, the payroll period is still the calendar week, and the wage payment shall be treated as though it were three separate weekly wage payments.

(b) For the purpose of section 3402, an employee can have but one payroll period with respect to wages paid by any one employer. Thus, if an employee is paid a regular wage for a weekly payroll period and in addition thereto is paid supplemental wages (for example, bonuses) determined with respect to a different period, the payroll period is the weekly payroll period. For computation of tax on supplemental wage payments, see §31.3402(g)-1.

(c) The term "payroll period" also means the period of accrual of supplemental unemployment compensation benefits for which a payment of such benefits is ordinarily made. Thus if benefits are ordinarily accrued and paid on a monthly basis, the payroll period is deemed to be monthly.

(d) The term "miscellaneous payroll period" means a payroll period other than a daily, weekly, biweekly, semimonthly, monthly, quarterly, semiannual, or annual payroll period. [Reg. §31.3401(b)-1.]

☐ [T.D. 6259, 10-25-57. Amended by T.D. 7068, 11-10-70.]

## [Reg. §31.3401(c)-1]

§31.3401(c)-1. Employee.—(a) The term "employee" includes every individual performing services if the relationship between him and the person for whom he performs such services is the legal relationship of employer and employee. The term includes officers and employees, whether elected or appointed, of the United States, a State, Territory, Puerto Rico, or any political subdivision thereof, or the District of Columbia, or any agency or instrumentality of any one or more of the foregoing.

(b) Generally the relationship of employer and employee exists when the person for whom services are performed has the right to control and direct the individual who performs the services, not only as to the result to be accomplished by the work but also as to the details and means by which that result is accomplished. That is, an employee is subject to the will and control of the employer not only as to what shall be done but how it shall be done. In this connection,

Reg. §31.3401(c)-1(b)

it is not necessary that the employer actually direct or control the manner in which the services are performed; it is sufficient if he has the right to do so. The right to discharge is also an important factor indicating that the person possessing that right is an employer. Other factors characteristic of an employer, but not necessarily present in every case, are the furnishing of tools and the furnishing of a place to work to the individual who performs the services. In general, if an individual is subject to the control or direction of another merely as to the result to be accomplished by the work and not as to the means and methods for accomplishing the result, he is not an employee.

(c) Generally, physicians, lawyers, dentists, veterinarians, contractors, subcontractors, public stenographers, auctioneers, and others who follow an independent trade, business, or profession, in which they offer their services to the public, are not employees.

(d) Whether the relationship of employer and employee exists will in doubtful cases be determined upon an examination of the particular facts of each case.

(e) If the relationship of employer and employee exists, the designation or description of the relationship by the parties as anything other than that of employer and employee is immaterial. Thus, if such relationship exists, it is of no consequence that the employee is designated as a partner, coadventurer, independent contractor, or the like.

(f) All classes or grades of employees are included within the relationship of employer and employee. Thus, superintendents, managers, and other supervisory personnel are employees. Generally, an officer of a corporation is an employee of the corporation. However, an officer of a corporation who as such does not perform any services or performs only minor services and who neither receives nor is entitled to receive, directly or indirectly, any remuneration is not considered to be an employee of the corporation. A director of a corporation in his capacity as such is not an employee of the corporation.

(g) The term "employee" includes every individual who receives a supplemental unemployment compensation benefit which is treated under paragraph (b)(14) of §31.3401(a)-1 as if it were wages.

(h) Although an individual may be an employee under this section, his services may be of such a nature, or performed under such circumstances, that the remuneration paid for such services does not constitute wages within the meaning of section 3401(a). [Reg. §31.3401(c)-1.]

☐ [*T.D. 6259*, 10-25-57. *Amended by T.D. 7068*, 11-10-70.]

### [Reg. §31.3401(d)-1]

**§31.3401(d)-1. Employer.**—(a) The term "employer" means any person for whom an individual performs or performed any service, of whatever nature, as the employee of such person.

(b) It is not necessary that the services be continuing at the time the wages are paid in order that the status of employer exist. Thus, for purposes of withholding, a person for whom an individual has performed past services for which he is still receiving wages from such person is an "employer."

(c) An employer may be an individual, a corporation, a partnership, a trust, an estate, a joint-stock company, an association, or a syndicate, group, pool, joint venture, or other unincorporated organization, group, or entity. A trust or estate, rather than the fiduciary acting for or on behalf of the trust or estate, is generally the employer.

(d) The term "employer" embraces not only the individuals and organizations engaged in trade or business, but organizations exempt from income tax, such as religious and charitable organizations, educational institutions, clubs, social organizations and societies, as well as the governments of the United States, the States, Territories, Puerto Rico, and the District of Columbia, including their agencies, instrumentalities, and political subdivisions.

(e) The term "employer" also means (except for the purpose of the definition of "wages") any person paying wages on behalf of a nonresident alien individual, foreign partnership, or foreign corporation, not engaged in trade or business within the United States (including Puerto Rico as if a part of the United States).

(f) If the person for whom the services are or were performed does not have legal control of the payment of the wages for such services, the term "employer" means (except for the purpose of the definition of "wages") the person having such control. For example, where wages, such as certain types of pensions or retired pay, are paid by a trust and the person for whom the services were performed has no legal control over the payment of such wages, the trust is the "employer."

(g) The term "employer" also means a person making a payment of a supplemental unemployment compensation benefit which is treated under paragraph (b)(14) of §31.3401(a)-1 as if it were wages. For example, if supplemental unemployment compensation benefits are paid from a trust which was created under the terms of a collective bargaining agreement, the trust shall generally be deemed

to be the employer. However, if the person making such payment is acting solely as an agent for another person, the term "employer" shall mean such other person and not the person actually making the payment.

(h) It is a basic purpose to centralize in the employer the responsibility for withholding, returning, and paying the tax, and for furnishing the statements required under section 6051 and §31.6051-1. The special definitions of the term "employer" in paragraphs (e), (f), and (g) of this section are designed solely to meet special or unusual situations. They are not intended as a departure from the basic purpose. [Reg. §31.3401(d)-1.]

☐ [*T.D. 6259*, 10-25-57. *Amended by T.D. 7068*, 11-10-70.]

### [Reg. §31.3401(f)-1]

**§31.3401(f)-1. Tips.**—(a) *Tips considered wages.*—Tips received after 1965 by an employee in the course of his employment are considered to be wages, and thus subject to withholding of income tax at source. For an exception to the rule that tips constitute wages, see §§31.3401(a)(16) and 31.3401(a)(16)-1, relating to tips paid in a medium other than cash and cash tips of less than $20. For definition of the term "employee", see §§31.3401(c) and 31.3401(c)-1.

(b) *When tips deemed paid.*—Tips reported by an employee to his employer in a written statement furnished to the employer pursuant to section 6053(a) (see §31.6053-1) shall be deemed to be paid to the employee at the time the written statement is furnished to the employer. Tips received by an employee which are not reported to his employer in a written statement furnished pursuant to section 6053(a) shall be deemed to be paid to the employee at the time the tips are actually received by the employee. [Reg. §31.3401(f)-1.]

☐ [*T.D. 7001*, 1-17-69.]

### [Reg. §31.3402(a)-1]

**§31.3402(a)-1. Requirement of withholding.**—(a) Section 3402 provides alternative methods, at the election of the employer, for use in computing the amount of income tax to be collected at source on wages. Under the percentage method of withholding (see §31.3402(b)-1), the employer is required to deduct and withhold a tax computed in accordance with the provisions of section 3402(a). Under the wage bracket method of withholding (see §31.3402(c)-1), the employer is required to deduct and withhold a tax determined in accordance with the provisions of section 3402(c). The employer may elect to use the percentage method, the wage bracket method, or certain other methods (see §31.3402(h)(4)-1). Different methods may be used by the employer with respect to different groups of employees.

(b) The employer is required to collect the tax by deducting and withholding the amount thereof from the employee's wages as and when paid, either actually or constructively. Wages are constructively paid when they are credited to the account of or set apart for an employee so that they may be drawn upon by him at any time although not then actually reduced to possession. To constitute payment in such a case, the wages must be credited to or set apart for the employee without any substantial limitation or restriction as to the time or manner of payment or condition upon which payment is to be made, and must be made available to him so that they may be drawn upon at any time, and their payment brought within his own control and disposition.

(c) Except as provided in sections 3402(j) and (k) (see §§31.3402(j)-1 and 31.3402(k)-1, relating to noncash remuneration paid to retail commission salesman and to tips received by an employee in the course of his employment, respectively), an employer is required to deduct and withhold the tax notwithstanding the wages are paid in something other than money (for example, wages paid in stocks or bonds; see §31.3401(a)-1) and to pay over the tax in money. If wages are paid in property other than money, the employer should make necessary arrangements to insure that the amount of the tax required to be withheld is available for payment in money.

(d) For provisions relating to the circumstances under which tax is required to be deducted and withheld from certain amounts received under accident and health plans, see paragraph (b)(8) of §31.3401(a)-1.

(e) As a matter of business administration, certain of the mechanical details of the withholding process may be handled by representatives of the employer. Thus, in the case of an employer having branch offices, the branch manager or other representative may actually, as a matter of internal administration, withhold the tax or prepare the statements required under section 6051. Nevertheless, the legal responsibility for withholding, paying, and returning the tax and furnishing such statements rests with the employer. For provisions relating to statements under section 6051, see the regulations under such section in Subpart G of this part.

(f) The amount of any tax withheld and collected by the employer is a special fund in trust for the United States. See section 7501.

(g) For purposes of Chapter 24 of the Code and this Subpart:

(1) References to "withholding exemption certificate" include "withholding allowance certificate" unless otherwise stated in this subpart.

(2) [Reserved]

(h) The provisions of paragraph (g) of this section apply on and after October 6, 2020. Taxpayers may choose to apply paragraph (g) of this section on or after January 1, 2020 and before October 6, 2020. [Reg. § 31.3402(a)-1.]

□ *T.D. 6259, 10-25-57. Amended by T.D. 7001, 1-17-69, T.D. 7115, 5-20-71, T.D. 7888, 4-22-83 and T.D. 9924, 10-5-2020.]*

### [Reg. § 31.3402(b)-1]

**§ 31.3402(b)-1. Percentage method of withholding.—** (a) *Percentage method of withholding.*—The amount of tax to be deducted and withheld from an employee's wages under the percentage method of withholding is determined based on the entry for the employee's anticipated filing status or marital status and other entries on the employee's withholding allowance certificate using the applicable percentage method tables and computational procedures set forth in the applicable forms, instructions, publications, and other guidance prescribed by the Commissioner issued with respect to the period in which wages are paid.

(b) *Applicability date.*—The provisions of this section apply on and after October 6, 2020. Taxpayers may choose to apply this section on or after January 1, 2020 and before October 6, 2020. For rules that apply before October 6, 2020, see 26 CFR part 31, revised as of April 1, 2020. [Reg. § 31.3402(b)-1.]

□ *[T.D. 7915, 9-26-83. Amended by T.D. 9924 10-5-2020.]*

### [Reg. § 31.3402(c)-1]

**§ 31.3402(c)-1. Wage bracket withholding.—**(a) *In general.*— (1) The employer may elect to use the wage bracket method provided in section 3402(c) instead of the percentage method with respect to any employee. The tax computed under the wage bracket method shall be in lieu of the tax required to be deducted and withheld under section 3402(a).

(2) The amount of tax to be deducted and withheld from an employee's wages under the wage bracket method of withholding is determined based on the entry for the employee's anticipated filing status or marital status and other entries on the employee's withholding allowance certificate using the applicable wage bracket method tables and computational procedures set forth in the applicable forms, instructions, publications, and other guidance prescribed by the Commissioner issued with respect to the period in which wages are paid.

(3) For provisions relating to the treatment of wages paid under accident and health plans and wages paid other than in cash to retail commission salesmen, see §§ 31.3401(a)-1(b)(8) and 31.3402(j)-1, respectively.

(b) *Established payroll periods, other than daily or miscellaneous, covered by wage bracket withholding tables.*—The wage bracket withholding tables applicable to the employee's filing status set forth in forms, instructions, publications, and other guidance prescribed by the Commissioner for established periods other than daily or miscellaneous should be used in determining the tax to be deducted and withheld for any such period without reference to the time the employee is actually engaged in the performance of services during such payroll period.

(c) *Periods to which the tables for a daily or miscellaneous payroll period are applicable.*—(1) *In general.*—The tables applicable to a daily or miscellaneous payroll period show the tentative amount of tax to be deducted and withheld from an employee's wages for the employee's filing status for one day. Where the withholding is computed under the rules applicable to a miscellaneous payroll period, the wages and the amounts shown in the applicable table must be placed on a comparable basis. This may be accomplished by reducing the wages paid for the period to a daily basis by dividing the total wages by the number of days (including Sundays and holidays) in the period. The amount of the tax shown in the applicable table as the tax required to be withheld from the wages, as so reduced to a daily basis, should then be multiplied by the number of days (including Sundays and holidays) in the period.

(2) *Period not a payroll period.*—If wages are paid for a period which is not a payroll period, the amount to be deducted and withheld under the wage bracket method shall be the amount applicable in the case of a miscellaneous payroll period containing a number of days (including Sundays and holidays) equal to the number of days (including Sundays and holidays) in the period with respect to which such wages are paid.

*Example.* An individual performs services for a contractor in connection with a construction project. He has in effect a withholding exemption certificate indicating that he claims two withholding exemptions and that he is married. Wages have been fixed at the rate of $36 per day, to be paid upon completion of the project. The project is completed before July 1, 1971, in 12 consecutive days, at the end of which period the individual is paid wages of $360 for 10 days' services performed during the period. Under the wage bracket method the amount to be deducted and withheld from such wages is determined by dividing the amount of the wages ($360) by the number of days in the period (12), the result being $30. The amount of tax required to be withheld is determined under the appropriate table applicable to a miscellaneous payroll period for an employee who is married. Under this table the tax required to be withheld is $47.40 (12 × $3.95).

(3) *Wages paid without regard to any period.*—If wages are paid to an employee without regard to any particular period, as, for example, commissions paid to a salesman upon consummation of a sale, the amount of tax to be deducted and withheld shall be determined in the same manner as in the case of a miscellaneous payroll period containing a number of days (including Sundays and holidays) equal to the number of days (including Sundays and holidays) which have elapsed, beginning with the latest of the following days:

(i) The first day after the last payment of wages to such employee by such employer in the calendar year, or

(ii) The date on which such individual's employment with such employer began in the calendar year, or

(iii) January 1 of such calendar year, and ending with (and including) the date on which such wages are paid.

*Example.* On April 2, 1971, C is employed by the X Real Estate Company to sell real estate on a commission basis, commissions to be paid only upon consummation of sales. C has in effect a withholding exemption certificate indicating that he claims one withholding exemption and that he is not married. On May 22, 1971, C receives a commission of $300, his first commission since April 2, 1971. Again, on June 19, 1971, C receives a commission of $420. Under the wage bracket method, the amount of tax to be deducted and withheld in respect of the commission paid on May 22, is $10.00, which amount is obtained by multiplying $0.20 (tax per day under the appropriate wage bracket table applicable to a daily or miscellaneous payroll period for an employee who is not married where wages are at least $6 but less than $6.25 a day) by 50 (number of days elapsed); and the amount of tax to be withheld with respect to the commission paid on June 19 is $54.60, which amount is obtained by multiplying $1.95 (tax under the appropriate wage bracket table for a daily or miscellaneous payroll period where wages are at least $15 but less than $15.50 a day) by 28 (number of days elapsed).

(d) *Period or elapsed time less than one week.*—(1) It is the general rule that if wages are paid for a payroll period or other period of less than one week, the tax to be deducted and withheld under the wage bracket method shall be the amount computed for a daily payroll period, or for a miscellaneous payroll period containing the same number of days (including Sundays and holidays) as the payroll period, or other period, for which such wages are paid. In the case of wages paid without regard to any period, if the elapsed time computed as provided in paragraph (c) of this section is less than 1 week, the same rule is applicable.

*Example (1).* On May 14, 1971, an employee who has a daily payroll period is paid wages of $15 per day. The employee has in effect a withholding exemption certificate indicating that he claims one withholding exemption and that he is not married. Under the applicable table for a daily payroll period for an employee who is not married, the amount of tax to be deducted and withheld from each such payment of wages is $1.95.

*Example (2).* An employee works for a certain employer on four consecutive days for which he is paid wages totalling $60 on July 25, 1971 The employee has in effect a withholding exemption certificate claiming two withholding exemptions and indicating that he is married. The amount of tax to be deducted and withheld under the wage bracket method is $5.60 (4 × $1.40).

(2) If the payroll period, other period, or elapsed time where wages are paid without regard to any period, is less than one week, the employer may, under certain conditions, elect to deduct and withhold the tax determined by the application of the wage table for a weekly payroll period to the aggregate of the wages paid to the employee during the calendar week. The election to use the weekly wage table in such cases is subject to the limitations and conditions prescribed in Circular E with respect to employers using the percentage method in similar cases.

(3) As used in this paragraph the term "calendar week" means a period of seven consecutive days beginning with Sunday and ending with Saturday.

(e) *Rounding off of wage payment.*—In determining the amount to be deducted and withheld under the wage bracket method the employer may, at the election of the employer, be computed to the nearest dollar, provided such wages are in excess of the highest wage bracket of the applicable table. For the purpose of the computation to the nearest dollar, the payment of a fractional part of a dollar shall be disregarded unless it amounts to one-half dollar or more, in which case it shall be increased to $1.00. Thus, if the payroll period of an employee is weekly and the wage payment of such employee is $255.49, the employer may compute the tax on the excess over $200 as if the excess were $55 instead of $55.49. If the weekly wage payment is $255.50, the employer may, in computing the tax, consider the excess over $200 to be $56 instead of $55.50.

(f) *Applicability date.*—The provisions of this section apply on and after October 6, 2020. Taxpayers may choose to apply this section on or after January 1, 2020 and before October 6, 2020. For rules that apply before October 6, 2020, see 26 CFR part 31, revised as of April 1, 2020. [Reg. § 31.3402(c)-1.]

☐ [*T.D. 6259,* 10-25-57. *Amended by T.D. 6860,* 11-3-65, *T.D. 7115,* 5-20-71, *T.D. 7888,* 4-22-83, *T.D. 7915,* 9-26-83 *and T.D. 9924,* 10-5-2020.]

### [Reg. § 31.3402(d)-1]

**§ 31.3402(d)-1. Failure to withhold.**—If the employer in violation of the provisions of section 3402 fails to deduct and withhold the tax, and thereafter the income tax against which the tax under section 3402 may be credited is paid, the tax under section 3402 shall not be collected from the employer. Such payment does not, however, operate to relieve the employer from liability for penalties or additions to the tax applicable in respect of such failure to deduct and withhold. The employer will not be relieved of his liability for payment of the tax required to be withheld unless he can show that the tax against which the tax under section 3402 may be credited has been paid. See § 31.3403-1, relating to liability for tax. [Reg. § 31.3402(d)-1.]

☐ [*T.D. 6259,* 10-25-57.]

### [Reg. § 31.3402(e)-1]

**§ 31.3402(e)-1. Included and excluded wages.**—(a) If a portion of the remuneration paid by an employer to his employee for services performed during a payroll period of not more than 31 consecutive days constitutes wages, and the remainder does not constitute wages, all the remuneration paid the employee for services performed during such period shall for purposes of withholding be treated alike, that is, either all included as wages or all excluded. The time during which the employee performs services, the remuneration for which under section 3401(a) constitutes wages, and the time during which he performs services, the remuneration for which under such section does not constitute wages, determine whether all the remuneration for services performed during the payroll period shall be deemed to be included or excluded.

(b) If one-half or more of the employee's time in the employ of a particular employer in a payroll period is spent in performing services the remuneration for which constitutes wages, then all the remuneration paid the employee for services performed in that payroll period shall be deemed to be wages.

(c) If less than one-half of the employee's time in the employ of a particular employer in a payroll period is spent in performing services the remuneration for which constitutes wages, then none of the remuneration paid the employee for services performed in that payroll period shall be deemed to be wages.

(d) The application of the provisions of paragraphs (a), (b), and (c) of this section may be illustrated by the following examples:

*Example (1).* Employer B, who operates a store and a farm, employs A to perform services in connection with both operations. The remuneration paid A for services on the farm is excepted as remuneration for agricultural labor, and the remuneration for services performed in the store constitutes wages. Employee A is paid on a monthly basis. During the particular month, A works 120 hours on the farm and 80 hours in the store. None of the remuneration paid by B to A for services performed during the month is deemed to be wages, since the remuneration paid for less than one-half of the services performed during the month constitutes wages. During another month A works 75 hours on the farm and 120 hours in the store. All of the remuneration paid by B to A for services performed during the month is deemed to be wages since the remuneration paid for one-half or more of the services performed during the month constitutes wages.

*Example (2).* Employee C is employed as a maid by D, a physician, whose home and office are located in the same building. The remuneration paid C for services in the home is excepted as remuneration for domestic service, and the remuneration paid for her services in the office constitutes wages. C is paid on a weekly basis. During a particular week C works 20 hours in the home and 20 hours in the office. All of the remuneration paid [by] D to C for services performed during that week is deemed to be wages, since the remuneration paid for one-half or more of the services performed during the week constitutes wages. During another week C works 22 hours in the home and 15 hours in the office. None of the remuneration paid by D to C for services performed during that week is deemed to be wages, since the remuneration paid for less than one-half of the services performed during the week constitutes wages.

(e) The rules set forth in this section do not apply (1) with respect to any remuneration paid for services performed by an employee for his employer if the periods for which remuneration is paid by the employer vary to the extent that there is no period which constitutes a payroll period within the meaning of section 3401(b) (see § 31.3401(b)-1), or (2) with respect to any remuneration paid for services performed by an employee for his employer if the payroll period for which remuneration is paid exceeds 31 consecutive days. In any such case withholding is required with respect to that portion of such remuneration which constitutes wages. [Reg. § 31.3402(e)-1.]

☐ [*T.D. 6259,* 10-25-57.]

### [Reg. § 31.3402(f)(1)-1]

**§ 31.3402(f)(1)-1. Withholding allowance.**—(a) *In general.*—(1) Except as otherwise provided in section 3402(f)(6) (see § 31.3402(f)(6)-1), an employee receiving wages will, on any day, be entitled to a withholding allowance as provided in section 3402(f)(1) and paragraph (b) of this section. In order to receive the benefit of the withholding allowance, the employee must furnish to the employer a valid withholding allowance certificate in effect for the calendar year as provided in section 3402(f)(2) and § 31.3402(f)(2)-1.

(2) The employer is not required to ascertain whether the withholding allowance claimed is greater than the withholding allowance to which the employee is entitled. For rules relating to invalid withholding allowance certificates, see § 31.3402(f)(2)-1(f)(3), for rules relating to required submission of copies of certain withholding allowance certificates to the Internal Revenue Service, see § 31.3402(f)(2)-1(g)(1), and for rules relating to the notice of the maximum withholding allowance permitted, see § 31.3402(f)(2)-1(g)(2).

(b) *Withholding allowance defined.*—(1) Generally, the withholding allowance to which an employee is entitled is determined under the computational procedures prescribed by the Commissioner in forms, instructions, publications, and other guidance for the calendar year for which the withholding allowance certificate is in effect.

(2) The withholding allowance is determined based on the following—

(i) Whether the employee is an individual for whom a deduction is allowable with respect to another taxpayer under section 151;

(ii) If the employee is married, whether the employee's spouse is an individual for whom a deduction is allowable with respect to another taxpayer under section 151 but only if such spouse does not have in effect a withholding allowance certificate claiming such deduction;

(iii) If the employee is married, whether the employee's spouse is entitled to additional deductions, credits, or other items the employee elects to take into account under § 31.3402(m)-1 or would be so entitled if the employee's spouse were an employee receiving wages, but only if such spouse does not have in effect a withholding allowance certificate claiming such allowance;

(iv) Any credit under section 24(a) that the employee reasonably expects to be able to claim on the employee's income tax return for the calendar year for which the withholding allowance certificate is in effect, except that the employee may not take into account any credit under section 24(a) if this credit is claimed on another valid withholding allowance certificate in effect with respect to another employer of the employee or the employee's spouse. In addition, an employee whose employer must withhold for that employee pursuant to a notice under § 31.3402(f)(2)-1(g)(2) must offset any tax benefit resulting from a credit under section 24(a) with any anticipated income tax attributable to items other than wages includible in the employee's gross income in the manner prescribed by the Commissioner;

(v) Any additional deductions, credits, or other items the employee elects to take into account under § 31.3402(m)-1 for the calendar year for which the withholding allowance certificate is in effect;

(vi) The basic standard deduction (as defined in section 63(c)(2)) relating to the filing status the employee reasonably expects to claim on the employee's income tax return for the calendar year for which the withholding allowance certificate is in effect; and

(vii) Any adjustment resulting from multiple withholding allowance certificates the employee, the employee's spouse, or both have or reasonably expect to have in effect with respect to one or more employers, determined based on the instructions to the withholding allowance certificate and other guidance for the calendar year for which the withholding allowance certificate is in effect.

(c) *Applicability date.*—The provisions of this section apply on and after October 6, 2020. Taxpayers may choose to apply this section on or after January 1, 2020 and before October 6, 2020. For rules that apply before October 6, 2020, see 26 CFR part 31, revised as of April 1, 2020. [Reg. §31.3402(f)(1)-1.]

☐ [*T.D. 6259, 10-25-57. Amended by T.D. 6654, 5-27-63, T.D. 7065, 10-22-70, T.D. 7114, 5-17-71, T.D. 7115, 5-20-71, T.D. 7670, 1-30-80, T.D. 7915, 9-26-83, T.D. 8164, 11-30-87 and T.D. 9924, 10-5-2020.]*

### [Reg. §31.3402(f)(2)-1]

**§31.3402(f)(2)-1. Furnishing of withholding allowance certificates.**—(a) *On commencement of employment.*—(1) On or before the date on which an individual commences employment with an employer, the individual must furnish the employer with a signed withholding allowance certificate (see §31.3402(f)(5)-1) relating to the filing status the employee reasonably expects to claim under §31.3402(l)-1(b) for the calendar year for which the withholding allowance certificate is in effect and the withholding allowance under §31.3402(f)(1)-1(b) that the employee claims.

(2) In no event may the withholding allowance exceed the withholding allowance that the employee is entitled to as determined based on the employee's reasonable expectations and the instructions set forth in forms, instructions, publications, and other guidance prescribed by the Commissioner.

(3) The employee may claim exemption from withholding if the certifications described in section 3402(n) and §31.3402(n)-1(a)(1) and (2) are true with respect to the employee.

(4) If an employee has no valid withholding allowance certificate in effect with the employer at the time of the payment of the wages, and fails to furnish a valid withholding allowance certificate to the employer, the employee will be treated as single but having the withholding allowance provided in forms, instructions, publications, and other guidance prescribed by the Commissioner.

(b) *Change of status that affects calendar year.*—(1) *General rule.*—If, on any day during the calendar year, the employee experiences a change of status that reduces the employee's withholding allowance or withholding allowances, in the manner described in paragraph (b)(2) of this section, the employee must, within 10 days after the change occurs, furnish the employer with a new withholding allowance certificate claiming the withholding allowance to which the employee is entitled under §31.3402(f)(1)-1(b), unless paragraph (b)(3) of this section applies to the employee.

(2) *Changes of status.*—A change of status occurs if any of the following changes occur on any day during the calendar year:

(i) The employee's filing status changes in the manner described in §31.3402(l)-1(c).

(ii) The employee no longer has only one withholding allowance certificate in effect for the employee, the employee's spouse, or both, and the employee or the employee's spouse selects higher withholding rate tables on the additional withholding allowance certificate, but higher withholding rate tables are not selected on any previously furnished withholding allowance certificate.

(iii) The employee has multiple withholding allowance certificates in effect on which higher withholding rate tables are not selected, and the employee or the employee's spouse reasonably expects an increase in regular wages for the calendar year (as defined in §31.3402(g)-1(a)(1)(ii)) in excess of $10,000.

(iv) The employee has included on a valid withholding allowance certificate the child tax credit allowed under section 24(a) but reasonably expects the number of individuals who satisfy the definition of "qualifying child" as defined in section 24(c) who will be reported on the employee's income tax return for the year for which tax is being withheld to be less than the number taken into account in completing the withholding allowance certificate.

(v) The employee has included on a valid withholding allowance certificate a tax credit allowed under section 24(a) or other tax credits allowed under §31.3402(m)-1 but reasonably expects the employee's tax credits that will be reported on the employee's income tax return for the year for which tax is being withheld to decrease by more than $500 from the amount taken into account in completing the withholding allowance certificate.

(vi) The employee has included on a valid withholding allowance certificate deductions allowed under §31.3402(m)-1 but reasonably expects the employee's included income tax deductions that will be reported on the employee's income tax return for the year for which tax is being withheld to decrease by more than $2,300 from the amount taken into account in completing the withholding allowance certificate.

(vii) It is no longer reasonable for an employee who has furnished the employer with a withholding allowance certificate

which relies upon the certifications described in §31.3402(n)-1(a) to anticipate that the employee will incur no liability for income tax imposed under subtitle A of the Code for the current or previous taxable year.

(3) *Exception.*—If one or more of the changes described in paragraph (b)(2) of this section occurs, but the total effect of the changes together with any other changes affecting the employee's anticipated tax liability under subtitle A is not anticipated to result in an amount of tax to be deducted and withheld from the employee's wages under section 3402 for the year that is less than the employee's anticipated tax liability under subtitle A, the employee is not required to furnish a new withholding allowance certificate.

(c) *Increase in withholding allowance.*—If, on any day during the calendar year, the employee experiences a change of status that increases the employee's withholding allowance, the employee may furnish the employer with a new withholding allowance certificate claiming the withholding allowance the employee is entitled to under §31.3402(f)(1)-1(b).

(d) *Exemption from withholding.*—If, on any day during the calendar year, the certifications described in section 3402(n) and §31.3402(n)-1(a)(1) and (2) are true with respect to an employee, the employee may furnish the employer with a withholding allowance certificate claiming exemption from withholding in the manner described in forms, instructions, publications, and other guidance prescribed by the Commissioner.

(e) *Change of status which affects next calendar year.*—(1) *General rule.*—If, on any day during the calendar year, the withholding allowance to which the employee will be, or may reasonably be expected to be, entitled under §31.3402(f)(1)-1(b) for the next calendar year, but not for the current calendar year, decreases in the manner prescribed in paragraph (b)(2) of this section, the employee must furnish a new withholding allowance certificate claiming the withholding allowance the employee is entitled to under §31.3402(f)(1)-1(b) to take effect in the next calendar year by the later of December 1 of the calendar year of the year in which the change occurs or within 10 days after the change occurs, unless paragraph (e)(2) of this section applies to the employee.

(2) *Exception.*—If one or more of the changes in paragraph (b)(2) of this section occurs, but the total effect of the changes together with any other changes affecting the employee's anticipated tax liability under subtitle A is not anticipated to result in an amount of tax to be deducted and withheld from the employee's wages under section 3402 for the employee's next year that is less than the employee's anticipated tax liability under subtitle A, the employee is not required to furnish a new withholding allowance certificate.

(f) *Special rules.*—(1) *Employer requests.*—Before December 1 of each year, every employer should request each employee to furnish a new withholding allowance certificate for the next calendar year, in the event of a change to the employee's withholding allowance.

(2) *Social security account numbers.*—Every individual to whom a social security number has been assigned must include such number on any withholding allowance certificate furnished to an employer. An employee may not use a truncated social security number (see §301.6109-4 of this chapter) in completing the withholding allowance certificate. For provisions relating to the obtaining of an account number from the Social Security Administration, see §31.6011(b)-2.

(3) *Invalid withholding allowance certificates.*—(i) *General rule.*—Any alteration of or unauthorized addition to a withholding allowance certificate causes such certificate to be invalid; see §31.3402(f)(5)-1(b) for the definitions of alteration and unauthorized addition. Any withholding allowance certificate which the employee clearly indicates to be false by an oral statement or by a written statement (other than one made on the withholding allowance certificate itself) made by the employee to the employer on or before the date on which the employee furnishes such certificate is also invalid. For purposes of the preceding sentence, the term "employer" includes any individual authorized by the employer either to receive withholding allowance certificates, to make withholding computations, or to make payroll distributions.

(ii) *Employer disregard of invalid withholding allowance certificate.*—If an employer receives an invalid withholding allowance certificate, the employer must disregard it for purposes of computing withholding. The employer must inform the employee who furnished the certificate that it is invalid and must request another withholding allowance certificate from the employee. If the employee who furnished the invalid certificate fails to comply with the employer's request, the employer must treat the employee as single but having the withholding allowance provided by the forms, instructions, publications, and other guidance prescribed by the Commissioner. If, however, a prior certificate is in effect with respect to the employee, the employer must continue to withhold in accordance with the prior certificate.

(g) *Submission of certain withholding allowance certificates and notice of maximum withholding allowance permitted.*—(1) *Submission of certain withholding allowance certificates.*—(i) *In general.*—An employer must submit to the Internal Revenue Service (IRS) a copy of any currently effective withholding allowance certificate as directed in a written notice to the employer from the IRS or as directed in published guidance.

(A) *Notice to submit withholding allowance certificates.*—A notice to the employer to submit withholding allowance certificates may relate either to one or more named employees, to one or more reasonably segregable units of the employer, or to withholding allowance certificates under certain specified criteria. The notice will designate the IRS office to which the copies of the withholding allowance certificates must be submitted. Alternatively, upon notice from the IRS, the employer must make available for inspection by an IRS employee withholding allowance certificates received from one or more named employees, from one or more reasonably segregable units of the employer, or from employees who have furnished withholding allowance certificates under certain specified criteria.

(B) *Published guidance.*—Employers may also be required to submit copies of withholding allowance certificates under certain specified criteria when directed to do so by the IRS in published guidance in the Internal Revenue Bulletin (see §601.601(d)(2) of this chapter).

(ii) *Withholding after submission of withholding allowance certificate.*—After a copy of a withholding allowance certificate has been submitted to the IRS under this paragraph (g)(1), the employer must withhold tax on the basis of the withholding allowance certificate, if the withholding allowance certificate meets the requirements of §31.3402(f)(5)-1. However, the employer may not withhold on the basis of the withholding allowance certificate if the certificate must be disregarded based on a notice of the maximum withholding allowance permitted under the provisions of paragraph (g)(2) of this section.

(2) *Notice of the maximum withholding allowance permitted.*—(i) *Notice to employer.*—The IRS may notify the employer in writing that the employee is not entitled to claim a complete exemption from withholding or more than the maximum withholding allowance specified by the IRS in the written notice. The notice will also specify the applicable filing status for purposes of calculating the required amount of withholding. The notice will specify the IRS office to be contacted for further information. The notice of maximum withholding allowance permitted may be issued if—

(A) The IRS determines that a copy of a withholding allowance certificate submitted under paragraph (g)(1) of this section or otherwise provided to the IRS includes a materially incorrect statement or determines, after a request to the employee for verification of the statements on the certificate, that the IRS lacks sufficient information to determine if the certificate is correct; or

(B) The IRS otherwise determines that the employee is not entitled to claim a complete exemption from withholding and is not entitled to claim more than a specified number of withholding exemptions, withholding allowances, or a specified withholding allowance.

(ii) *Notice to employee.*—If the IRS provides a notice to the employer under this paragraph (g)(2), the IRS will also provide the employer with a similar notice for the employee (employee notice) that identifies the maximum withholding allowance permitted and specifies the filing status to be used for calculating the required amount of withholding for the employee. The employee notice will indicate the process by which the employee can provide additional information to the IRS for purposes of determining the appropriate withholding allowance and/or modifying the specified filing status. The IRS will also mail a similar notice to the employee's last known address. For further guidance regarding the definition of last known address, see §301.6212-2 of this chapter. If the IRS is unable to determine a last known address for the employee, the IRS will use other available information as appropriate to mail the notice to the employee.

(iii) *Requirement to furnish.*—If the employee is employed by the employer as of the date of the notice, the employer must furnish the employee notice to the employee within 10 business days of receipt. The employer may follow any reasonable business practice to furnish the copy of the notice to the employee. For purposes of this paragraph (g)(2)(iii), the determination of whether an employee is employed as of the date of the notice is based on all the facts and circumstances, including whether the employer has treated the employment relationship as terminated for other purposes. An employee who is not performing services for the employer as of the date of the notice is employed by the employer as of the date of the notice for purposes of this paragraph (g)(2)(iii) if—

(A) The employer pays wages with respect to prior employment to the employee subject to income tax withholding on or after the date specified in the notice;

(B) The employer reasonably expects the employee to resume the performance of services for the employer within twelve months of the date of the notice; or

(C) The employee is on a bona fide leave of absence and either the period of such leave does not exceed twelve months or the employee retains a right to reemployment with the employer under an applicable statute or by contract.

(iv) *Requirement to withhold based on the notice.*—If the employer is required to furnish the employee notice to the employee under paragraph (g)(2)(iii) of this section, then the employer must withhold tax on the basis of the maximum withholding allowance and the filing status specified in the notice for any wages paid after the date specified in the notice, except as provided in paragraphs (g)(2)(v) through (ix) of this section. The employer must withhold tax in accordance with the notice as of the date specified in the notice, which shall be no earlier than 45 calendar days after the date of the notice. If the notice was provided to the employer based on computational procedures applicable to a withholding allowance certificate that was in effect on December 31, 2019 or earlier, the employer may comply with the requirement in this paragraph (g)(2)(iv) to withhold on the basis of the notice by implementing the maximum withholding allowance and filing status permitted by using the computational bridge entries as set forth in forms, instructions, publications, and other guidance prescribed by the Commissioner to calculate withholding for a withholding allowance certificate that was in effect on December 31, 2019 or earlier.

(v) *Employment resumes after twelve months.*—If the employer is required to furnish the employee notice to the employee only pursuant to paragraph (g)(2)(iii)(B) of this section and the employee resumes the performance of services for the employer more than 12 months after the date of the notice, then the employer is not required to withhold based on the notice.

(vi) *Requirement to withhold based on an existing Form W-4.*—If a withholding allowance certificate is in effect with respect to the employee before the employer receives a notice of the maximum withholding allowance permitted under this paragraph (g)(2), the employer must continue to withhold tax in accordance with the existing withholding allowance certificate, rather than on the basis of the notice, if the existing withholding allowance certificate does not claim complete exemption from withholding and claims a filing status, a withholding allowance, and any additional amount under §31.3402(i)-1(a)(1) and (2) that results in more withholding than would result from applying the filing status and withholding allowance specified in the notice.

(vii) *Modification notice.*—After issuing the notice specifying the maximum withholding allowance permitted and the filing status, the IRS may issue a subsequent notice to the employer and the employee that modifies the original notice (modification notice). The modification notice may change the filing status and/or the withholding allowance permitted. The employer must withhold based on the modification notice as of the date specified in the modification notice. If the modification notice was provided to the employer based on computational procedures applicable to a withholding allowance certificate that was in effect on December 31, 2019 or earlier, the employer may comply with the requirement in this paragraph (g)(2)(vii) to withhold on the basis of the modification notice by implementing the maximum withholding allowance and filing status permitted by using the optional computational bridge entries as set forth in forms, instructions, publications, and other guidance prescribed by the Commissioner to calculate withholding for a withholding allowance certificate that was in effect on December 31, 2019 or earlier.

(viii) *Requirement to withhold after termination of employment.*—If the employee is employed as of the date of the notice under paragraph (g)(2)(iii) of this section but the employer or employee terminates the employment relationship after the date of the notice, the employer must continue to withhold based on the maximum withholding allowance and the filing status specified in the notice or a modification notice if any wages subject to income tax withholding are paid with respect to the prior employment after such date. Furthermore, the employer must withhold based on the notice or modification notice if the employee resumes an employment relationship with the employer within 12 months after the termination of the employment relationship. Whether the employment relationship is terminated is based on all the facts and circumstances.

(ix) *Requirement to withhold based on new Form W-4.*—The employee may furnish a new withholding allowance certificate after the employer receives a notice or modification notice from the IRS of the maximum withholding allowance permitted under this paragraph (g)(2).

(A) *Employee requests more withholding.*—If the employee furnishes a new withholding allowance certificate after the employer receives the notice or modification notice, the employer must withhold tax on the basis of that new certificate only if the new certificate does not claim complete exemption from withholding and claims a filing status, a withholding allowance, and any additional amount under § 31.3402(i)-1(a)(1) and (2) that results in more withholding than would result under the notice or modification notice.

(B) *Employee requests less withholding.*—If the employee furnishes a new withholding allowance certificate after the employer receives the notice or modification notice, the employer must disregard the new certificate and withhold on the basis of the notice or modification notice if the employee claims complete exemption from withholding or claims a filing status, a withholding allowance, and any additional amount under § 31.3402(i)-1(a)(1) and (2) that results in less withholding than would result under the notice or modification notice. If the employee wants to put a new certificate into effect that results in less withholding than that required under the notice or modification notice, the employee must contact the IRS. The employer must withhold on the basis of the notice or modification notice unless the IRS subsequently notifies the employer to withhold based on the new certificate.

(3) *Definition of employer.*—For purposes of this paragraph (g), the term "employer" includes any person authorized by the employer to receive withholding allowance certificates, to make withholding computations, or to make payroll distributions.

(4) *Examples.*—The following examples illustrate the rules of this section.

(i) *Example 1.*—Employer U receives a notice from the IRS that identifies the maximum withholding allowance permitted and specifies the filing status for Employee A. Employee A is not currently performing any services for Employer U. However, Employer U is continuing to make certain wage payments to Employee A. Employer U must furnish the employee notice to Employee A within 10 business days of receipt and must withhold based on the notice on any wages paid to Employee A on or after the date specified in the notice.

(ii) *Example 2.*—Employer V receives a notice in October of Year 1 from the IRS that identifies the maximum withholding allowance permitted and specifies the filing status for Employee B. Employee B has not performed services for Employer V since August of Year 1. However, since Employee B has performed services for Employer V for several years on a seasonal basis, Employer V reasonably expects Employee B to resume the performance of services for Employer V in June of Year 2, a date that is within 12 months of the date of the notice. Employer V is required to furnish the notice to Employee B within 10 business days of receipt. Employee B does not resume the performance of services with Employer V until June of Year 3. Employer V is not required to withhold based on the notice.

(iii) *Example 3.*—Employer W receives a notice from the IRS that identifies the maximum withholding allowance permitted and specifies the filing status for Employee C. Employee C began a 4-month unpaid maternity leave of absence three weeks before Employer W received the notice. Employer W must furnish the employee notice to Employee C within 10 business days of receipt. When her maternity leave ends and Employee C resumes performing services for Employer W, Employer W must withhold based on the notice.

(iv) *Example 4.*—Employer X receives a notice from the IRS in Year 1 that identifies the maximum withholding allowance permitted and specifies the filing status for Employee D. Employer X must furnish the employee notice to Employee D within 10 business days of receipt and withhold based on the notice. In Year 2, Employee D terminates the employment relationship. Employee D applies for a different position with Employer X and resumes employment 10 months after having left her previous position with Employer X. Since Employer X rehired Employee D within 12 months after the termination of employment, Employer X must withhold based on the notice.

(v) *Example 5.*—Employer Y receives a notice from the IRS that identifies the maximum withholding allowance permitted and speci-

fies the filing status for Employee E. Employer Y must furnish the employee notice to Employee E within 10 business days of receipt. After receipt of this notice, Employee E contacts the IRS and establishes that the employee is entitled to claim a modified filing status and withholding allowance. Employer Y receives a modification notice from the IRS that changes the maximum withholding allowance permitted for Employee E. Employer Y must withhold tax based on the modification notice as of the date specified in such notice.

(vi) *Example 6.*—Employer Z pays remuneration to Employee F, a United States citizen, for services performed in Country M. Employer Z receives a notice from the IRS in Year 1 that identifies the maximum withholding allowance permitted and specifies the filing status for Employee F. Employer Z must furnish the employee notice to Employee F within 10 business days of receipt. Employer Z reasonably believes all the remuneration paid to Employee F in Year 1 is excluded from Employee F's gross income under section 911. Since section 3401(a)(8)(B) excludes such remuneration from wages for income tax withholding purposes, Employer X does not have to withhold on such remuneration, notwithstanding the maximum withholding allowance permitted and filing status specified in the notice. In Year 2, Employee F returns to the United States to perform services. Employer Z does not reasonably believe any part of Employee F's remuneration paid in Year 2 is excluded from Employee F's gross income under section 911. Rather, Employer Z reasonably believes that remuneration paid to Employee F in Year 2 is subject to income tax withholding. Employer Z must withhold on the remuneration paid to Employee F in Year 2 based on the notice.

(h) *Applicability date.*—The provisions of paragraph (g) of this section apply on February 13, 2020. Taxpayers may choose to apply paragraph (g) of this section on or after January 1, 2020 and before February 13, 2020. For rules that apply under paragraph (g) of this section before February 13, 2020, see 26 CFR part 31, revised as of April 1, 2020. The provisions of paragraphs (a) through (f) of this section apply on and after October 6, 2020. Taxpayers may choose to apply the provisions of paragraph (a) through (f) of this section on or after January 1, 2020 and before October 6, 2020. For rules that apply before October 6, 2020, see 26 CFR part 31, revised as of April 1, 2020. [Reg. § 31.3402(f)(2)-1.]

☐ *[T.D. 6259, 10-25-57. Amended by T.D. 6606, 8-24-62, T.D. 6654, 5-27-63, T.D. 7048, 6-23-70, T.D. 7065, 10-22-70, T.D. 7423, 6-24-76, T.D. 7577, 12-19-78, T.D. 7598, 3-12-79, T.D. 7682, 3-10-80, T.D. 7772, 3-17-81, T.D. 7083, 1-21-82, T.D. 7915, 9-26-82, T.D. 8164, 11-30-87 T.D. 9196, 4-13-2005, T.D. 9337, 7-12-2007 and T.D. 9924, 10-5-2020.]*

### [Reg. § 31.3402(f)(3)-1]

**§ 31.3402(f)(3)-1. When withholding allowance certificate takes effect.**—(a) *No withholding allowance certificate on file.*—A withholding allowance certificate furnished to the employer in any case in which no previous withholding allowance certificate is in effect with such employer, takes effect as of the beginning of the first payroll period ending, or the first payment of wages made without regard to a payroll period, on or after the date on which such certificate is so furnished.

(b) *Withholding allowance certificate on file.*—Except as provided in paragraph (c) of this section, a withholding allowance certificate furnished to the employer in any case in which a previous withholding allowance certificate is in effect with such employer takes effect as of the beginning of the first payroll period ending (or the first payment of wages made without regard to a payroll period) on or after the 30th day after the day on which such certificate is so furnished. However, the employer may elect to put a withholding allowance certificate into effect earlier, beginning with any payment of wages on or after the day on which the certificate is so furnished.

(c) *Withholding allowance certificate furnished to take effect in next calendar year.*—A withholding allowance certificate furnished to the employer pursuant to section 3402(f)(2)(C) (see § 31.3402(f)(2)-1(e) or § 31.3402(l)-1(c)) which effects a change for the next calendar year, does not take effect, and may not be made effective, with respect to the calendar year in which the certificate is furnished.

(d) *Applicability date.*—The provisions of this section apply on and after October 6, 2020. Taxpayers may choose to apply this section on or after January 1, 2020 and before October 6, 2020. For rules that apply before October 6, 2020, see 26 CFR part 31, revised as of April 1, 2020. [Reg. § 31.3402(f)(3)-1.]

☐ *[T.D. 6259, 10-25-57. Amended by T.D. 7048, 6-23-70, T.D. 7065, 10-22-70, T.D. 7115, 5-20-71, T.D. 7915, 9-26-83 and T.D. 9924, 10-5-2020.]*

### [Reg. § 31.3402(f)(4)-1]

**§ 31.3402(f)(4)-1. Effective period of a withholding allowance certificate.**—(a) *In general.*—Except as provided in paragraph (b) of this section and § 31.3402(f)(2)-1(g)(2), a withholding allowance certificate that takes effect under section 3402(f) of the Internal Revenue Code of 1986 continues in effect with respect to the employee until another withholding allowance certificate takes effect under section 3402(f). An employer's use of computational bridge entries as set forth in forms, instructions, publications, and other guidance prescribed by the Commissioner to calculate withholding for a withholding allowance certificate that was in effect on December 31, 2019 or earlier continues in effect an employee's withholding allowance certificate under this paragraph (a).

(b) *Certifications under section 3402(n) eliminating requirement of withholding.*—The certifications described in § 31.3402(n)-1(a) made by an employee with respect to the employee's preceding taxable year and current taxable year are effective until either a new withholding allowance certificate furnished by the employee takes effect or the existing certificate that relies upon such certifications expires. If an employee's certificate expires and the employee fails to furnish a valid withholding allowance certificate, the employee will be treated as single but having the withholding allowance provided in forms, instructions, publications, and other guidance prescribed by the Commissioner. In no case shall a withholding allowance certificate that relies upon such certifications be effective with respect to any payment of wages made to an employee:

(1) In the case of an employee whose liability for tax under subtitle A of the Code is determined on a calendar year basis, after February 15 of the calendar year following the estimation year, or

(2) In the case of an employee to whom paragraph (b)(1) of this section does not apply, after the 15th day of the 2nd calendar month following the last day of the estimation year.

(c) *Estimation year.*—The estimation year is the taxable year including the day on which the employee furnishes the withholding allowance certificate to the employer, except that if the employee furnishes the withholding allowance certificate to the employer and specifies on the certificate that the certificate is not to take effect until a specified future date, the estimation year will be the taxable year including that specified future date.

(d) *Applicability to notice of maximum withholding allowance.*—If a withholding allowance certificate is no longer in effect because of the application of § 31.3402(f)(2)-1(g)(2), the employer is no longer required to withhold pursuant to any notice under § 31.3402(f)(2)-1(g)(2), and the employee fails to furnish the employer a valid withholding allowance certificate, then the employee will be treated as single but having the withholding allowance provided in forms, instructions, publications, and other guidance prescribed by the Commissioner, in accordance with § 31.3402(f)(2)-1(a)(4).

(e) *Applicability date.*—The provisions of this section apply on and after October 6, 2020. Taxpayers may choose to apply this section on or after January 1, 2020 and before October 6, 2020. For rules that apply before October 6, 2020, see 26 CFR part 31, revised as of April 1, 2020. [Reg. § 31.3402(f)(4)-1.]

☐ [*T.D.* 7915, 9-26-83. *Redesignated and amended by T.D.* 9924, 10-5-2020.]

### [Reg. § 31.3402(f)(5)-1]

**§ 31.3402(f)(5)-1. Form and contents of withholding allowance certificates.**—(a) *In general.*—(1) *Form W-4.*—Form W-4, "Employee's Withholding Certificate," previously called "Employee's Withholding Allowance Certificate," is the form prescribed for the withholding allowance certificate required to be furnished under section 3402(f)(2). A withholding allowance certificate must be prepared in accordance with the instructions applicable thereto and must set forth fully and clearly the information that is called for therein. In lieu of the prescribed form, an employer may prepare and provide to employees a form the provisions of which are identical to those of the prescribed form, but only if the employer also provides employees with all the tables, instructions, and worksheets set forth in the Form W-4 in effect at that time, and only if the employer complies with all revenue procedures and other guidance prescribed by the Commissioner relating to substitute forms in effect at that time.

(2) *Employee substitute forms.*—Employers are prohibited from accepting a substitute form developed by an employee, and an employee furnishing such form will be treated as failing to furnish a withholding allowance certificate. For further guidance regarding the employer's obligations when an employee is treated as failing to furnish a withholding allowance certificate, see § 31.3402(f)(2)-1.

(3) *Current year revision.*—Only the Form W-4 revision in effect for a calendar year may be furnished by an employee in that calendar year and given legal effect by the employer, unless provided other-

wise in forms, instructions, publications, or other guidance, except that an employee may furnish the Form W-4 revision for the following calendar year in the current calendar year to take effect for the following calendar year.

(4) *Examples.*—The following examples illustrate the rule in paragraph (a)(3) of this section.

(i) *Example 1.*—Employee A furnishes a 2019 Form W-4 to Employer X in calendar year 2020. The 2019 Form W-4 furnished by Employee A in 2020 has no legal effect. Employer X must disregard this 2019 Form W-4 furnished in 2020 and continue to withhold based on a previously furnished Form W-4 that has been in effect for Employee A, if any. If Employee A has no Form W-4 in effect, she is treated as having no valid withholding allowance certificate in effect.

(ii) *Example 2.*—Employee A furnishes a 2021 Form W-4 to Employer X in calendar year 2020 to take effect in calendar year 2021. The 2021 Form W-4 is valid, and the employer must put this form into effect in 2021 in accordance with the timing rules in § 31.3402(f)(3)-1.

(b) *Invalid Form W-4.*—A Form W-4 does not meet the requirements of section 3402(f)(5) or this section and is invalid if it includes an alteration or unauthorized addition. For purposes of § 31.3402(f)(2)-1(f)(3) and this paragraph (b)—

(1) An alteration of a withholding allowance certificate is any deletion of the language of the jurat or other similar provision of such certificate by which the employee certifies or affirms the correctness of the completed certificate, or any material defacing of such certificate; and

(2) An unauthorized addition to a withholding allowance certificate is any writing on such certificate other than the entries requested on the Form W-4 (*e.g.*, name, address, and filing status) or permitted by instructions or other guidance. For purposes of this paragraph (b)(2), an entry claiming exemption from withholding that is accompanied by other entries on the Form W-4 (other than the employee's filing status) that could potentially affect the amount of income tax deducted and withheld from the employee's pay is an unauthorized addition; consequently, the employer must treat the Form W-4 as an invalid Form W-4.

(c) *Electronic Form W-4.*—(1) *In general.*—An employer may establish a system for its employees to furnish withholding allowance certificates electronically.

(2) *Requirements.*—(i) *In general.*—The electronic system must ensure that the information received is the information sent and must document all occasions of employee access that result in the furnishing of a Form W-4. In addition, the design and operation of the electronic system, including access procedures, must make it reasonably certain that the person accessing the system and furnishing the Form W-4 is the employee identified in the form.

(ii) *Information to employer.*—The electronic furnishing must provide the employer with exactly the same information as the current version of the official Internal Revenue Service (IRS) Form W-4 available on irs.gov.

(iii) *Information to employee.*—The electronic Form W-4 system must provide the employee with the same information as the current version of the official IRS Form W-4 available on irs.gov and must satisfy any requirements specified by the IRS in forms, publications, and other guidance. The electronic Form W-4 system must provide employees the ability to claim exemption from withholding under section 3402(n) and must include the two certifications described in § 31.3402(n)-1(a).

(iv) *Jurat and signature requirements.*—The electronic furnishing must be signed by the employee under penalties of perjury.

(A) *Jurat.*—The jurat (perjury statement) must contain the language that appears on the paper Form W-4. The electronic program must inform the employee that he or she must make the declaration set forth in the jurat and that the declaration is made by signing the Form W-4. The instructions and the language of the jurat must immediately follow the employee's income tax withholding selections and immediately precede the employee's electronic signature.

(B) *Electronic signature.*—The electronic signature must identify the employee furnishing the electronic Form W-4 and authenticate and verify the furnishing. For purposes of this paragraph (c)(2)(iv)(B), the terms "authenticate" and "verify" have the same meanings as they do when applied to a written signature on a paper Form W-4. An electronic signature can be in any form that satisfies the foregoing requirements. The electronic signature must be the final entry in the employee's Form W-4 furnished electronically.

**Collection of Income Tax at Source on Wages**
See p. 20,601 for regulations not amended to reflect law changes
**61,475**

(v) *Copies of electronic Forms W-4.*—Upon request by the Internal Revenue Service, the employer must supply a hard copy of the electronic Form W-4 and a statement that, to the best of the employer's knowledge, the electronic Form W-4 was furnished by the named employee. The hardcopy of the electronic Form W-4 must provide exactly the same information as, but need not be a facsimile of, the paper Form W-4.

(d) *Applicability date.*—The provisions of paragraphs (a)(3) and (4) of this section apply on and after March 16, 2020. Taxpayers may choose to apply the provisions of paragraphs (a)(3) and (4) of this section on or after January 1, 2020 and before March 16, 2020. For the provision of paragraph (a)(3) of this section that applies before March 16, 2020, see 26 CFR part 31, revised as of April 1, 2020. The provisions of paragraphs (a)(1) and (2), (b), and (c) of this section apply on and after October 6, 2020. Taxpayers may choose to apply paragraphs (a)(1) and (2), (b), and (c) of this section on or after January 1, 2020 and before October 6, 2020. For rules that apply before October 6, 2020, see 26 CFR part 31, revised as of April 1, 2020. [Reg. §31.3402(f)(5)-1.]

☐ [*T.D. 6259, 10-25-57. Amended by T.D. 7048, 6-23-70; T.D. 7423, 6-24-76; T.D. 7915, 9-26-83; T.D. 8706, 12-31-96; T.D. 9196, 4-13-2005, T.D. 9337, 7-12-2007 and T.D. 9924, 10-5-2020.*]

### [Reg. §31.3402(f)(6)-1]

**§31.3402(f)(6)-1. Withholding exemptions for nonresident alien individuals.**—(a) *In general.*—(1) A nonresident alien individual (other than a nonresident alien individual treated as a resident under section 6013(g) or (h)) subject to withholding under section 3402 is on any one day entitled to the number of withholding exemptions corresponding to the number of personal exemptions to which the nonresident alien is entitled on such day by reason of the application of section 873(b)(3) or section 876, whichever applies. Thus, a nonresident alien individual who is not a resident of Canada or Mexico and who is not a resident of Puerto Rico during the entire taxable year, is allowed only one withholding exemption.

(2) The withholding exemption in paragraph (a) of this section and section 3402(f)(6) is the deduction allowed to the nonresident alien individual under section 151.

(b) *Additional guidance.*—A nonresident alien individual (other than a nonresident alien individual treated as a resident under section 6013(g) or (h)) subject to withholding must follow administrative guidance such as forms, instructions, publications, or other guidance prescribed by the Commissioner to determine the nonresident alien's withholding allowance.

(c) *Applicability date.*—The provisions of this section apply on and after October 6, 2020. Taxpayers may choose to apply this section on or after January 1, 2020 and before October 6, 2020. For rules that apply before October 6, 2020, see 26 CFR part 31, revised as of April 1, 2020. [Reg. §31.3402(f)(6)-1.]

☐ [*T.D. 6654, 5-27-63. Amended by T.D. 6908, 12-30-66, T.D. 7670, 1-30-80 and T.D. 9924, 10-5-2020.*]

### [Reg. §31.3402(g)-1]

**§31.3402(g)-1. Supplemental wage payments.**—(a) *In general and withholding on supplemental wages in excess of $1,000,000.*—(1) *Determination of supplemental wages and regular wages.*—(i) *Supplemental wages.*—An employee's remuneration may consist of regular wages and supplemental wages. Supplemental wages are all wages paid by an employer that are not regular wages. Supplemental wages include wage payments made without regard to an employee's payroll period, but also may include payments made for a payroll period. Examples of wage payments that are included in supplemental wages include reported tips (except as provided in paragraph (a)(1)(v) of this section), overtime pay (except as provided in paragraph (a)(1)(iv) of this section), bonuses, back pay, commissions, wages paid under reimbursement or other expense allowance arrangements, nonqualified deferred compensation includible in wages, wages paid as noncash fringe benefits, sick pay paid by a third party as an agent of the employer, amounts that are includible in gross income under section 409A, income recognized on the exercise of a nonstatutory stock option, wages from imputed income for health coverage for a non-dependent, and wage income recognized on the lapse of a restriction on restricted property transferred from an employer to an employee. Amounts that are described as supplemental wages in this definition are supplemental wages regardless of whether the employer has paid the employee any regular wages during either the calendar year of the payment or any prior calendar year. Thus, for example, if the only wages that an employer has ever paid an employee are payments of noncash fringe benefits and income recognized on the exercise of a nonstatutory stock option, such payments are classified as supplemental wages.

(ii) *Regular wages.*—As distinguished from supplemental wages, regular wages are amounts that are paid at a regular hourly, daily, or similar periodic rate (and not an overtime rate) for the current payroll period or at a predetermined fixed determinable amount for the current payroll period. Thus, among other things, wages that vary from payroll period to payroll period (such as commissions, reported tips, bonuses, or overtime pay) are not regular wages, except that an employer may treat tips as regular wages under paragraph (a)(1)(v) of this section and an employer may treat overtime pay as regular wages under paragraph (a)(1)(iv) of this section.

(iii) *Amounts that are not wages subject to income tax withholding.*—If an amount of remuneration is not wages subject to income tax withholding, it is neither regular wages nor supplemental wages. Thus, for example, income from the disqualifying dispositions of shares of stock acquired pursuant to the exercise of statutory stock options, as described in section 421(b), is not included in regular wages or supplemental wages.

(iv) *Optional treatment of overtime pay as regular wages.*—Employers may treat overtime pay as regular wages rather than supplemental wages. For this purpose, overtime pay is defined as any pay required to be paid pursuant to federal (Fair Labor Standards Act), state, or local governmental laws at a rate higher than the normal wage rate of the employee because the employee has worked hours in excess of the number of hours deemed to constitute a normal work week or work day.

(v) *Optional treatment of tips as regular wages.*—Employers may treat tips as regular wages rather than supplemental wages. For this purpose, tips are defined as including all tips which are reported to the employer pursuant to section 6053.

(vi) *Amount to be withheld.*—The calculation of the amount of the income tax withholding with respect to supplemental wage payments is provided for under paragraph (a)(2) through (a)(7) of this section.

(2) *Mandatory flat rate withholding.*—If a supplemental wage payment, when added to all supplemental wage payments previously made by one employer (as defined in paragraph (a)(3) of this section) to an employee during the calendar year, exceeds $1,000,000, the rate used in determining the amount of withholding on the excess (including any excess which is a portion of a supplemental wage payment) shall be equal to the highest rate of tax applicable under section 1 for such taxable years beginning in such calendar year. This flat rate shall be applied without regard to whether income tax has been withheld from the employee's regular wages, and without regard to any entries on Form W-4, including whether the employee has claimed exempt status on Form W-4 or whether the employee has requested additional withholding on Form W-4, and without regard to the withholding method used by the employer. Withholding under this paragraph (a)(2) is mandatory flat rate withholding.

(3) *Certain persons treated as one employer.*—(i) *Persons under common control.*—For purposes of paragraph (a)(2) of this section, all persons treated as a single employer under subsection (a) or (b) of section 52 shall be treated as one employer.

(ii) *Agents.*—For purposes of paragraph (a)(2) of this section, any payment made to an employee by a third party acting as an agent for the employer (regardless of whether such person shall have been designated as an agent pursuant to section 3504) shall be considered as made by the employer except as provided in paragraph (a)(4)(iii) of this section.

(4) *Treatment of certain items in determining applicability of mandatory flat rate withholding.*—(i) *Optional treatment of compensation not subject to income tax withholding.*—For purposes of paragraph (a)(2) of this section, employers may determine whether an employee has received $1,000,000 of supplemental wages during a calendar year by including in supplemental wages amounts includible in income but not subject to withholding that are reported as wages, tips, other compensation on Form W-2.

(ii) *Allocation of salary reduction deferrals.*—In allocating salary reduction deferral amounts excludable from wages for purposes of determining whether the employer has paid $1,000,000 of supplemental wages under paragraph (a)(2) of this section, employers must allocate such salary reduction deferral amounts to the type of compensation (i.e., gross amounts of regular wage payments or gross amounts of supplemental wage payments) actually being deferred.

(iii) *Optional de minimis exception for certain payments by agents.*—For purposes of paragraph (a)(2) of this section, if an agent makes total wage payments (including regular wages and supplemental wages) of less than $100,000 to an individual during any calendar year, an employer or other agent may disregard such payments in determining whether the individual has received $1,000,000 of supplemental wages during the calendar year, and such agent need not consider whether the individual has received other supplemental wages in determining the amount of income tax to be withheld from the payments. An employer may not avail itself of this exception if the employer is making payments to the employee using five or more agents and a principal effect of such use of agents is to reduce the applicability of mandatory flat rate withholding to the employee. For purposes of paragraph (a)(2) of this section, if an agent makes total wage payments of $100,000 or more to an individual during any calendar year, the entire amount of supplemental wages paid by the agent during the calendar year to the employee must be taken into account (by other agents of the employer that make total wage payments to the employee of $100,000 or more, by the agent, and by the employer for which the agent is acting) in determining whether the employee has received $1,000,000 of supplemental wages.

(iv) *Treatment of supplemental wage payment exceeding $1,000,000 cumulative threshold.*—In the case of a supplemental wage payment that, when added to all supplemental wage payments previously made by the employer to the employee in the calendar year, results in the employee having received in excess of $1,000,000 supplemental wages for the calendar year, the employer is required to impose withholding under paragraph (a)(2) of this section only on the portion of the payment that is in excess of $1,000,000 (taking into account all prior supplemental wage payments during the year). However, an employer may subject the entire amount of such supplemental wage payment to the withholding imposed by paragraph (a)(2) of this section.

(5) *Withholding on supplemental wages that are not subject to mandatory flat rate withholding.*—To the extent that paragraph (a)(2) of this section does not apply to a supplemental wage payment (or a portion of a payment), the amount of the tax required to be withheld on the supplemental wages when paid shall be determined under the rules provided in paragraphs (a)(6) and (7) of this section.

(6) *Aggregate procedure for withholding on supplemental wages.*—(i) *Applicability.*—The employer is required to determine withholding upon supplemental wages under this paragraph (a)(6) if paragraph (a)(2) of this section does not apply to the payment or portion of the payment and if paragraph (a)(7) of this section may not be used with respect to the payment. In addition, employers have the option of using this paragraph (a)(6) to calculate withholding with respect to a supplemental wage payment, if paragraph (a)(2) of this section does not apply to the payment, but if paragraph (a)(7) of this section could be used with respect to the payment.

(ii) *Procedure.*—Provided this procedure applies under paragraph (a)(6)(i) of this section, the supplemental wages, if paid concurrently with wages for a payroll period, are aggregated with the wages paid for such payroll period. If not paid concurrently, the supplemental wages are aggregated with the wages paid or to be paid within the same calendar year for the last preceding payroll period or for the current payroll period, if any. The amount of tax to be withheld is determined as if the aggregate of the supplemental wages and the regular wages constituted a single wage payment for the regular payroll period. The withholding method used by the employer with respect to regular wages would then be used to calculate the withholding on this single wage payment and the employer would take into consideration the Form W-4 submitted by the employee. This procedure is the aggregate procedure for withholding on supplemental wages.

(7) *Optional flat rate withholding on supplemental wages.*—(i) *Applicability.*—The employer may determine withholding upon supplemental wages under this paragraph (a)(7) if three conditions are met—

(A) Paragraph (a)(2) of this section does not apply to the payment or the portion of the payment;

(B) The supplemental wages are either not paid concurrently with regular wages or are separately stated on the payroll records of the employer; and

(C) Income tax has been withheld from regular wages of the employee during the calendar year of the payment or the preceding calendar year.

(ii) *Procedure.*—The determination of the tax to be withheld under paragraph (a)(7)(iii) of this section is made without reference to any payment of regular wages and without regard to any entries on the Form W-4 other than the entry claiming exempt status on Form W-4 (see §31.3402(n)-1(b)). Withholding under this procedure is optional flat rate withholding.

(iii) *Rate applicable for purposes of optional flat rate withholding.*—Provided the conditions of paragraph (a)(7)(i) of this section have been met, the employer may determine the tax to be withheld—

(A) From supplemental wages paid after April 30, 1966, and prior to January 1, 1994, by using a flat percentage rate of 20 percent;

(B) From supplemental wages paid after December 31, 1993, and on or before August 6, 2001, by using a flat percentage rate of 28 percent;

(C) From supplemental wages paid after August 6, 2001, and on or before December 31, 2001, by using a flat percentage rate of 27.5 percent;

(D) From supplemental wages paid after December 31, 2001, and on or before May 27, 2003, by using a flat percentage rate of 27 percent;

(E) From supplemental wages paid after May 27, 2003, and on or before December 31, 2004, by using a flat percentage rate of 25 percent; and

(F) From supplemental wages paid after December 31, 2004, by using a flat percentage rate of 28 percent (or the corresponding rate in effect under section 1(i)(2) for taxable years beginning in the calendar year in which the payment is made).

(8) *Examples.*—For purposes of these examples, it is assumed that the rate for purposes of mandatory flat rate withholding for 2007 is 35 percent, and the rate for purposes of optional flat rate withholding for 2007 is 25 percent. The following examples illustrate this paragraph (a):

*Example 1.* (i) Employee A is an employee of three entities (X, Y, and Z) that are treated as a single employer under section 52(a) or (b). In 2007, X pays regular wages to A on a monthly payroll period for services performed for X, Y, and Z. The regular wages are paid on the third business day of each month. Income tax is withheld from the regular wages of A during the year. A receives only the following supplemental wage payments during 2007 in addition to the regular wages paid by X—

(A) A bonus of $600,000 from X on March 15, 2007;

(B) A bonus of $2,300,000 from Y on November 15, 2007; and

(C) A bonus of $10,000 from Z on December 31, 2007.

(ii) In this *Example 1*, the $600,000 bonus from X is a supplemental wage payment. The withholding on the $600,000 payment from X could be determined under either paragraph (a)(6) or (7) of this section because income tax has been withheld from the regular wages of A. If X elects to use the aggregate procedure under paragraph (a)(6) of this section, the amount of withholding on the supplemental wages would be based on aggregating the supplemental wages and the regular wages paid by X either for the current or last payroll period and treating the total of the regular wages paid by X and the $600,000 supplemental wages as a single wage payment for a regular payroll period. The withholding method used by the employer with respect to regular wages would then be used to calculate the withholding on this single wage payment, and the employer would take into consideration the Form W-4 furnished by the employee.

(iii) In this *Example 1*, the $2,300,000 bonus from Y is a supplemental wage payment. To calculate the withholding on the $2,300,000 supplemental wage payment from Y, the $600,000 of supplemental wages X has already paid to A in 2007 must be taken into account because X and Y are treated as the same employer under section 52(a) or (b). Thus, the withholding on the first $400,000 of the payment (i.e., the cumulative supplemental wages not in excess of $1,000,000) is computed separately from the withholding on the remaining $1,900,000 of the payment (i.e., the amount of the cumulative supplemental wages in excess of $1,000,000). With respect to the first $400,000, the withholding could be computed under either paragraph (a)(6) or (a)(7) of this section, because income tax has been withheld from the regular wages of the employee. If Y elected to withhold income tax using paragraph (a)(7) of this section, Y would withhold on the $400,000 component at 25 percent (pursuant to paragraph (a)(7)(iii)(F) of this section), which would result in $100,000 tax withheld. The remaining $1,900,000 of the bonus would be subject to mandatory flat rate withholding at the maximum rate of tax in effect under section 1 for 2007 (35%) without regard to the Form W-4 submitted by A. The amount withheld from the $1,900,000 would be $665,000. The withholding on the first component and the withholding on the second component then would be added together to determine the total income tax withholding on the supplemental wage payment from Y. Alternatively, under paragraph (a)(4)(iv) of this section, Y could treat the entire $2,300,000 bonus payment as subject to mandatory flat rate withholding at the maximum rate of tax (35%), in which case the amount to be withheld would be 35 percent of $2,300,000, or $805,000.

(iv) The $10,000 bonus paid from Z is also a supplemental wage payment. To calculate the withholding on the $10,000 bonus, the $2,900,000 in cumulative supplemental wages already paid to A in 2007 by X and Y must be taken into account because X, Y, and Z are treated as a single employer. The entire $10,000 bonus would be subject to mandatory flat rate withholding at the maximum rate of tax in effect under section 1 for 2007. The income tax required to be withheld on this payment would be 35 percent of $10,000 or $3,500.

*Example 2.* Employees B and C work for employer M. Each employee receives a monthly salary of $3,000 in 2007. As a result of the withholding allowances claimed by B, there has been no income tax withholding on the regular wages M pays to B during either 2007 or 2006. In contrast, M has withheld income tax from regular wages M pays to C during 2007. Together with the monthly salary check paid in December 2007 to each employee, M includes a bonus of $2,000, which is the only supplemental wage payment each employee receives from M in 2007. The bonuses are separately stated on the payroll records of M. Because M has withheld no income tax from B's regular wages during either the calendar year of the $2,000 bonus or the preceding calendar year, M cannot use optional flat rate withholding provided under paragraph (a)(7) of this section to calculate the income tax withholding on B's $2,000 bonus. Consequently, M must use the aggregate procedure set forth in paragraph (a)(6) of this section to calculate the income tax withholding due on the $2,000 bonus to B. With respect to the bonus paid to C, M has the option of using either the aggregate procedure provided under paragraph (a)(6) of this section or the optional flat rate withholding provided under paragraph (a)(7) of this section to calculate the income tax withholding due.

*Example 3.* (i) Employee D works as an employee of Corporation R. Corporations R and T are treated as a single employer under section 52(a) or (b). R makes regular wage payments to Employee D of $200,000 on a monthly basis in 2007, and income tax is withheld from those wages. R pays D a bonus for his services as an employee equal to $3,000,000 on June 30, 2007. Unrelated company U pays D sick pay as an agent of the employer R and such sick pay is supplemental wages pursuant to § 31.3401(a)-1(b)(8)(i)(*b*)(*2*). U pays D $50,000 of sick pay on October 31, 2007. Corporation T decides to award bonuses to all employees of R and T, and pays a bonus of $100,000 to D on December 31, 2007. D received no other payments from R, T, or U.

(ii) In chronological summary, D is paid the following wages other than the regular monthly wages paid by R:

(A) June 30, 2007 — $3,000,000 (bonus from R);

(B) October 31, 2007 — $50,000 (sick pay from U); and

(C) December 31, 2007 — $100,000 (bonus from T).

(iii) In this *Example 3*, each payment of wages other than the regular monthly wage payments from R is considered to be supplemental wages for purposes of withholding under § 31.3402(g)-1(a)(2). The amount of regular wages from R is irrelevant in determining when mandatory flat rate withholding on supplemental wages must be applied.

(iv) Because income tax has been withheld on D's regular wages, income tax may be withheld on $1,000,000 of the $3,000,000 bonus paid on June 30, 2007, under either paragraph (a)(6) or (7) of this section. If R elects to use optional flat rate withholding provided under paragraph (a)(7)(iii)(f) of this section, withholding would be calculated at 25 percent of the $1,000,000 portion of the payment and would be $250,000.

(v) Income tax withheld on the following supplemental wage payments (or portion of a payment) as follows is required to be calculated at the maximum rate in effect under section 1, or 35 percent in 2007—

(A) $2,000,000 of the $3,000,000 bonus paid by R on June 30, 2007; and

(B) all of the $100,000 bonus paid by T on December 31, 2007.

(vi) Pursuant to paragraph (a)(4)(iii) of this section, because the total wage payments made by U, an agent of the employer, to D are less than $100,000, U is permitted to determine the amount of income tax to be withheld without regard to other supplemental wage payments made to the employee. Income tax withholding on the $50,000 in sick pay may be determined under either paragraph (a)(6) or (7) of this section. If U elects to withhold income tax at the flat rate provided under paragraph (a)(7)(iii)(F) of this section, withholding on the $50,000 of sick pay would be calculated at 25 percent of the $50,000 payment and would be $12,500. Alternatively, U may choose to take account of the $3,000,000 in supplemental wages paid by the

employer during 2007 prior to payment of the $50,000 sick pay, and withholding on the $50,000 of sick pay could be calculated applying the mandatory flat rate of 35 percent, resulting in withholding of $17,500 on the $50,000 payment.

*Example 4.* (i) Employer J has decided it wants to grant its employee B a $1,000,000 net bonus (after withholding) to be paid in 2007. Employer J has withheld income tax from the regular wages of the employee. Employer J has made no other supplemental wage payments to B during the year.

(ii) This *Example 4* requires grossing up the supplemental wage payment to determine the gross wages necessary to result in a net payment of $1,000,000. If the employer elected to use optional flat rate withholding, the first $1,000,000 of the wages would be subject to 25 percent withholding. However, any wages above that, including amounts representing gross-up payments, would be subject to mandatory 35 percent withholding. The withholding applicable to the first $1,000,000 (i.e., $250,000) would thus be required to be grossed-up at a 35 percent rate to determine the gross wage amount in excess of $1,000,000. Thus, the wages in excess of $1,000,000 would be equal to $250,000 divided by .65 (computed by subtracting .35 from 1) or $384,615.38. Thus the total supplemental wage payment, taking into account income tax withholding only (and not Federal Insurance Contributions Act taxes), to B would be $1,384,615.38, and the total withholding with respect to the payment if Employer J elected optional flat rate withholding with respect to the first $1,000,000, would be $384,615.38.

(9) *Certain noncash payments to retail commission salesmen.*—For provisions relating to the treatment of wages that are not subject to paragraph (a)(2) of this section and that are paid other than in cash to retail commission salesmen, see § 31.3402(j)-1.

(10) *Alternative methods.*—The Secretary may provide by publication in the Internal Revenue Bulletin (see § 601.601(d)(2)(ii)(b) of this chapter) for alternative withholding methods that will allow an employer to meet its responsibility for the mandatory flat rate withholding required by paragraph (a)(2) of this section.

(b) *Special rule where aggregate withholding exemption exceeds wages paid.*—(1) *Procedure.*—This rule does not apply to the extent that paragraph (a)(2) of this section applies to the supplemental wage payment. If supplemental wages are paid to an employee during a calendar year for a period which involves two or more consecutive payroll periods, for which other wages also are paid during such calendar year, and the aggregate of such other wages is less than the aggregate of the amounts determined under the table provided in section 3402(b)(1) as the withholding exemptions applicable for such payroll periods, the amount of the tax required to be withheld on the supplemental wages shall be computed as follows:

*Step 1.* Determine an average wage for each of such payroll periods by dividing the sum of the supplemental wages and the wages paid for such payroll periods by the number of such payroll periods.

*Step 2.* Determine a tax for each payroll period as if the amount of the average wage constituted the wages paid for such payroll period.

*Step 3.* From the sum of the amounts of tax determined in Step 2 subtract the total amount of tax withheld, or to be withheld, from the wages, other than the supplemental wages, for such payroll periods. The remainder, if any, shall constitute the amount of the tax to be withheld upon the supplemental wages.

*Example.* An employee has a weekly payroll period ending on Saturday of each week, the wages for which are paid on Friday of the succeeding week. On the 10th day of each month he is paid a bonus based upon production during the payroll periods for which wages were paid in the preceding month. The employee is paid a weekly wage of $64 on each of the five Fridays occurring in July 1966. On August 10, 1966, the employee is paid a bonus of $125 based upon production during the five payroll periods covered by the wages paid in July. On the date of payment of the bonus, the employee, who is married and has three children, has a withholding exemption certificate in effect indicating that he is married and claiming five withholding exemptions. The amount of the tax to be withheld from the bonus paid on August 10, 1966, is computed as follows:

| | |
|---|---:|
| Wages paid in July 1966 for 5 payroll periods (5 × $64) | $320.00 |
| Bonus paid August 10, 1966 | 125.00 |
| Aggregate of wages and bonus | $445.00 |
| Average wage per payroll period ($445 ÷ 5) | $89.00 |
| Computation of tax under percentage method: Withholding exemptions (5 × $13.50) | $67.50 |
| Remainder subject to tax | $21.50 |
| Tax on average wage for 1 week under percentage method of withholding (married person with weekly payroll period) (14 percent of $17.50 (excess over $4)) | $2.45 |
| Tax on average wage for 5 weeks | $12.25 |

Reg. § 31.3402(g)-1(b)(1)

Less: Tax previously withheld on weekly wage payments of $64 . . . . . . . . . . . . . . . . . . . . . . . . . . . . . . . . . . . . . . None

Tax to be withheld on supplemental wages . . . . . . . . . . . . . . . . . . . . . . . . . . . . . . . . . . . . . . . . . . . . . . . . $12.25

Computation of tax under wage bracket method: Tax on $89 wage under weekly wage table for married person ($2.50 per
week for 5 weeks) . . . . . . . . . . . . . . . . . . . . . . . . . . . . . . . . . . . . . . . . . . . . . . . . . . . . . . . . . . . . . . . . . $12.50

Less: Tax previously withheld on weekly wage payments of $64 . . . . . . . . . . . . . . . . . . . . . . . . . . . . . . . . . . . . . . None

Tax to be withheld on supplemental wages . . . . . . . . . . . . . . . . . . . . . . . . . . . . . . . . . . . . . . . . . . . . . . . . $12.50

(2) *Applicability.*—The rules prescribed in this paragraph (b) shall, at the election of the employer, be applied in lieu of the rules prescribed in paragraph (a) of this section except that this paragraph shall not be applicable in any case in which the payroll period of the employee is less than one week or to the extent that paragraph (a)(2) of this section applies to the supplemental wage payment.

(c) *Vacation allowances.*—Amounts of so-called "vacation allowances" shall be subject to withholding as though they were regular wage payments made for the period covered by the vacation. If the vacation allowance is paid in addition to the regular wage payment for such period, the rules applicable with respect to supplemental wage payments shall apply to such vacation allowance.

(d) *Applicability date.*—The provisions of paragraphs (a)(2) and (a)(7)(ii) of this section apply on and after October 6, 2020. Taxpayers may choose to apply paragraphs (a)(2) and (a)(7)(ii) of this section on or after January 1, 2020 and before October 6, 2020. For the provisions of paragraphs (a)(2) and (a)(7)(ii) of this section that apply before October 6, 2020, see 26 CFR part 31, revised as of April 1, 2020. [Reg. §31.3402(g)-1.]

□ [*T.D.* 6259, 10-25-57. *Amended by T.D.* 6860, 11-3-65; *T.D.* 6882, 4-11-66 *and T.D.* 9276, 7-24-2006 (*corrected* 10-2-2006 *and* 12-26-2006) *and T.D.* 9924, 10-5-2020.]

### [Reg. §31.3402(g)-2]

**§31.3402(g)-2. Wages paid for payroll period of more than one year.**—If wages are paid to an employee for a payroll period of more than one year, for the purpose of determining the amount of tax required to be deducted and withheld in respect of such wages—

(a) Under the percentage method, the amount of the tax shall be determined as if such payroll period constituted an annual payroll period, and

(b) Under the wage bracket method, the amount of the tax shall be determined as if such payroll period constituted a miscellaneous payroll period of 365 days. [Reg. §31.3402(g)-2.]

□ [*T.D.* 6259, 10-25-57.]

### [Reg. §31.3402(g)-3]

**§31.3402(g)-3. Wages paid through an agent, fiduciary, or other person on behalf of two or more employers.**—(a) If a payment of wages is made to an employee by an employer through an agent, fiduciary, or other person who also has the control, receipt, custody, or disposal of, or pays the wages payable by another employer to such employee, the amount of the tax required to be withheld on each wage payment made through such agent, fiduciary, or person shall, whether the wages are paid separately on behalf of each employer or paid in a lump sum of all such employers, be determined upon the aggregate amount of such wage payment or payments in the same manner as if such aggregate amount had been paid by one employer. Hence, under either the percentage method or the wage bracket method the tax shall be determined upon the aggregate amount of the wage payment.

(b) In any such case, each employer shall be liable for the return and payment of a pro rata portion of the tax so determined, such portion to be determined in the ratio which the amount contributed by the particular employer bears to the aggregate of such wages.

(c) For example, three companies maintain a central management agency which carries on the administrative work of the several companies. The central agency organization consists of a staff of clerks, bookkeepers, stenographers, etc., who are the common employees of the three companies. The expenses of the central agency, including wages paid to the foregoing employees, are borne by the several companies in certain agreed proportions. Company X pays 45 percent, Company Y pays 35 percent and Company Z pays 20 percent of such expenses. The amount of the tax required to be withheld on the wages paid to persons employed in the central agency should be determined in accordance with the provisions of this section. In such event, Company X is liable as an employer for the return and payment of 45 percent of the tax required to be withheld, Company Y is liable for the return and payment of 35 percent of the tax and Company Z is liable for the return and payment of 20 percent of the tax. (See §31.3504-1, relating to acts to be performed by agents.) [Reg. §31.3402(g)-3.]

□ [*T.D.* 6259, 10-25-57.]

### [Reg. §31.3402(h)(1)-1]

**§31.3402(h)(1)-1. Withholding on basis of average wages.**—(a) *In general.*—An employer may determine the amount of tax to be deducted and withheld upon a payment of wages to an employee on the basis of the employee's average estimated wages, with necessary adjustments, for any quarter. This paragraph applies only where the method desired to be used includes wages other than tips (whether or not tips are also included).

(b) *Withholding on the basis of average estimated tips.*—(1) *In general.*—Subject to certain limitations and conditions, an employer may, at his discretion, withhold the tax under section 3402 in respect of tips reported by an employee to the employer on an estimated basis. An employer who elects to make withholding of the tax on an estimated basis shall:

(i) In respect of each employee, make an estimate of the amount of tips that will be reported, pursuant to section 6053, by the employee to the employer in a calendar quarter.

(ii) Determine the amount which must be deducted and withheld upon each payment of wages (exclusive of tips) which are under the control of the employer to be made during the quarter by the employer to the employee. The total amount which must be deducted and withheld shall be determined by assuming that the estimated tips for the quarter represent the amount of wages to be paid to the employee in the form of tips in the quarter and that such tips will be ratably (in terms of pay periods) paid during the quarter.

(iii) Deduct and withhold from any payment of wages (exclusive of tips) which are under the control of the employer, or from funds referred to in section 3402(k) (see §§31.3402(k) and 31.3402(k)-1), such amount as may be necessary to adjust the amount of tax withheld on the estimated basis to conform to the amount required to be withheld in respect of tips reported by the employee to the employer during the calendar quarter in written statements furnished to the employer pursuant to section 6053(a). If an adjustment is required, the additional tax required to be withheld may be deducted upon any payment of wages (exclusive of tips) which are under the control of the employer during the quarter and within the first 30 days following the quarter or from funds turned over by the employee to the employer for such purpose within such period. For provisions relating to the repayment to an employee, or other disposition, of amounts deducted from an employee's remuneration in excess of the correct amount of tax, see §31.6413(a)-1.

(2) *Estimating tips employee will report.*—(i) *Initial estimate.*—The initial estimate of the amount of tips that will reported by a particular employee in a calendar quarter shall be made on the basis of the facts and circumstances surrounding the employment of that employee. However, if a number of employees are employed under substantially the same circumstances and working conditions, the initial estimate established for one such employee may be used as the initial estimate for other employees in that group.

(ii) *Adjusting estimate.*—If the quarterly estimate of tips in respect of a particular employee continues to differ substantially from the amount of tips reported by the employee and there are no unusual factors involved (for example, an extended absence from work due to illness) the employer shall make an appropriate adjustment of his estimate of the amount of tips that will be reported by the employee.

(iii) *Reasonableness of estimate.*—The employer must be prepared, upon request of the district director, to disclose the factors upon which he relied in making the estimate, and his reasons for believing that the estimate is reasonable. [Reg. §31.3402(h)(1)-1.]

□ [*T.D.* 6259, 10-27-57. *Amended by T.D.* 7001, 1-17-69 *and T.D.* 7053, 7-20-70.]

### [Reg. §31.3402(h)(2)-1]

**§31.3402(h)(2)-1. Withholding on basis of annualized wages.**—An employer may determine the amount of tax to be deducted and withheld upon a payment of wages to an employee by taking the following steps:

*Step 1.* Multiply the amount of the employee's wages for the payroll period by the number of such periods in the calendar year.

*Step 2.* Determine the amount of tax which would be required to be deducted and withheld upon the amount determined in Step 1 if that amount constituted the actual wages for the calendar year and the payroll period of the employee were an annual payroll period.

*Step 3.* Divide the amount of tax determined in Step 2 by the number of periods by which the employee's wages were multiplied in Step 1.

*Example.* On July 1, 1970, A, a single person who is on a weekly payroll period and claims one exemption, receives wages of $100 from X Co., his employer. X Co. multiplies the weekly wage of $100 by 52 weeks to determine an annual wage of $5,200. It then subtracts $650 for A's withholding exemption and arrives at a balance of $4,550. The applicable table in section 3402(a) for annual payroll periods indicates that the amount of tax to be withheld thereon is $376 plus $314.50 (17 percent of excess over $2,700), or a total of $690.50. The annual tax of $690.50, when divided by 52 to arrive at the portion thereof attributable to the weekly payroll period, equals $13.28. X Co. may, if it chooses, withhold $13.28 rather than the amount specified in section 3402(a) or (c) for a weekly payroll period. [Reg. § 31.3402(h)(2)-1.]

☐ [*T.D. 7053, 7-20-70.*]

### [Reg. § 31.3402(h)(3)-1]

**§ 31.3402(h)(3)-1. Withholding on basis of cumulative wages.—**
(a) *In general.*—In the case of an employee who has in effect a request that the amount of tax to be withheld from his wages be computed

| | |
|---|---|
| July 20 | |
| August 3 | |
| August 17 | |
| August 31 | |
| September 14 | |
| September 28 | |

On October 5, B requests that Y Co. withhold on the basis of his cumulative wages with respect to his wages to be paid on October 12 and thereafter. Y Co. adds the $300 in wages to be paid to B on October 12 to the payments of wages already made to B during the calendar year, and determines that the aggregate amount of wages is $2,800. The average amount of wages for the 7 biweekly payroll periods is $400. The total amount of tax required to be deducted and withheld for payments of $400 for each of 7 biweekly payroll periods is $485.87 under section 3402(a). Since the total amount of tax which has been deducted and withheld by Y Co. through September 28 is $484.86, Y Co. may, if it chooses, deduct and withhold $1.01 (the amount by which $485.87 exceeds the total amount already withheld by Y Co.) from the payment of wages to B on October 12 rather than the amount specified in section 3402(a) or (c).

(b) *Employee's request and revocation of request.*—An employee's request that his employer withhold on the basis of his cumulative wages and a notice of revocation of such request shall be in writing and in such form as the employer may prescribe. An employee's request furnished to his employer pursuant to this section shall be effective, and may be acted upon by his employer, after the furnishing of such request and before a revocation thereof is effective. A revocation of such request may be made at any time by the employee furnishing his employer with a notice of revocation. The employer may give immediate effect to a revocation, but, in any event, a revocation shall be effective with respect to payments of wages made on or after the first "status determination date" (see section

on the basis of his cumulative wages, and whose wages since the beginning of the current calendar year have been paid with respect to the same category of payroll period (e.g., weekly or semimonthly) the employer may determine the amount of tax to be deducted and withheld upon a payment of wages made to the employee after December 31, 1969, by taking the following steps:

*Step 1.* Add the amount of the wages to be paid the employee for the payroll period to the total amount of wages paid by the employer to the employee during the calendar year.

*Step 2.* Divide the aggregate amount of wages computed in Step 1 by the number of payroll periods to which that amount relates.

*Step 3.* Compute the total amount of tax that would have been required to be deducted and withheld under section 3402(a) if the average amount of wages (as computed in Step 2) had been paid to the employee for the number of payroll periods to which the aggregate amount of wages (computed in Step 1) relates.

*Step 4.* Determine the excess, if any, of the amount of tax computed in Step 3 over the total amount of tax already deducted and withheld by the employer from wages paid to the employee during the calendar year.

*Example.* On July 1, 1970, Y Co. employs B, a single person claiming one exemption. Y Co. pays B the following amounts of wages on the basis of a biweekly payroll period on the following pay days:

| | |
|---|---:|
| July 20 | $1,000 |
| August 3 | 300 |
| August 17 | 300 |
| August 31 | 300 |
| September 14 | 300 |
| September 28 | 300 |

3402(f)(3)(B)) which occurs at least 30 days after the date on which such notice is furnished.

(c) *Requests due to increases or decreases in allowances.*—An employee may request pursuant to this section that his employer withhold on the basis of the employee's cumulative wages when the employee is entitled to claim an increased or decreased number of withholding allowances under § 31.3402(m)-1 during the estimation year (as defined in § 31.3402(m)-1(c)(1)). [Reg. § 31.3402(h)(3)-1.]

☐ [*T.D. 7053, 7-20-70. Amended by T.D. 7915, 9-26-83.*]

### [Reg. § 31.3402(h)(4)-1]

**§ 31.3402(h)(4)-1. Other methods.**—(a) *Maximum permissible deviations.*—An employer may use any other method of withholding under which the employer will deduct and withhold upon wages paid to an employee after December 31, 1969, for a payroll period substantially the same amount as would be required to be deducted and withheld by applying section 3402(a) with respect to the payroll period. For purposes of section 3402(h)(4) and this section, an amount is substantially the same as the amount required to be deducted and withheld under section 3402(a) if its deviation from the latter amount is not greater than the maximum permissible deviation prescribed in this paragraph. The maximum permissible deviation under this paragraph is determined by annualizing wages as provided in Step 1 of § 31.3402(h)(2)-1 and applying the following table to the amount of tax required to be deducted and withheld under section 3402(a) with respect to such annualized wages, as determined under Step 2 of § 31.3402(h)(2)-1:

| If the tax required to be withheld under the annual percentage rate schedule is— | The maximum permissible annual deviation is— |
|---|---|
| $10 to $100 | $10, plus 10% of excess over $10 |
| $100 to $1,000 | $19, plus 3% of excess over $100 |
| $1,000 or over | $46, plus 1% of excess over $1,000 |

In any case, an amount which is less than $10 more or less per year than the amount required to be deducted and withheld under section 3402(a) is substantially the same as the latter amount. If any method produces results which are not greater than the prescribed maximum deviations only with respect to some of his employees, the employer may use such method only with respect to such employees. An employer should thoroughly test any method which he contemplates using to ascertain whether it meets the tolerances prescribed by this paragraph. An employer may not use any method one of the principal purposes of which is to consistently produce amounts to be deducted and withheld which are less (though substantially the same) than the amount required to be deducted and withheld by applying section 3402(a).

(b) *Part-year employment method of withholding.*—(1) *In general.*—In addition to the methods authorized by other paragraphs of this section, in the case of part-year employment (as defined in subpara-

graph (4) of this paragraph) of an employee who determines his liability for tax under subtitle A of the Code on a calendar-year basis and who has in effect a request that the amount of tax to be withheld from his wages be computed according to the part-year employment method described in this paragraph, the employer may determine the amount of tax to be deducted and withheld upon a payment of wages made to the employee on or after January 5, 1973, by taking the following steps:

*Step 1.* Add the amount of wages to be paid to the employee for the current payroll period to the total amount of wages paid by the employer to the employee for all preceding payroll periods included in the current term of continuous employment (as defined in subparagraph (3) of this paragraph) of the employee by the employer;

*Step 2.* Divide the aggregate amount of wages computed in Step 1 by the total of the number of payroll periods to which that amount relates plus the equivalent number of payroll periods (as defined in subparagraph (2) of this paragraph) in the employee's term of continuous unemployment immediately preceding the current term of continuous employment, such term of continuous unemployment to be exclusive of any days prior to the beginning of the current calendar year;

*Step 3.* Determine the total amount of tax that would have been required to be deducted and withheld under section 3402 if the average amount of wages (as computed in Step 2) had been paid to the employee for the number of payroll periods determined in Step 2 (including the equivalent number of payroll periods); and

*Step 4.* Determine the excess, if any, of the amount of tax computed in Step 3 over the total amount of tax already deducted and withheld by the employer from wages paid to the employee for all payroll periods during the current term of continuous employment. The use of the method described in this paragraph does not preclude the employee from claiming additional withholding allowances pursuant to section 3402(m) or the standard deduction allowance pursuant to section 3402(f)(1)(G).

(2) *Equivalent number of payroll periods.*—For purposes of this paragraph, the equivalent number of payroll periods shall be determined by dividing the number of calendar days contained in the current payroll period into the number of calendar days between the later of (i) the day certified by the employee as his last day of employment prior to his current term of continuous employment during the calendar year in which such term commenced, or (ii) the last day of the calendar year immediately preceding the current calendar year, and the first day of the current term of continuous employment. For purposes of the preceding sentence, the term "calendar days" includes holidays, Saturdays, and Sundays. In determining the equivalent number of payroll periods, any fraction obtained in the division described in the first sentence of this subparagraph shall be disregarded. An employee paid for a miscellaneous payroll period shall be considered to have a daily payroll period for purposes of this subparagraph. In a case in which an employee is paid for a daily or miscellaneous payroll period and the employer elects under Circular E to compute the tax to be withheld as if the aggregate of the wages paid to the employee during the calendar week were paid for a weekly period, the employer shall determine the equivalent number of payroll periods for purposes of the computation of the tax to be withheld for the calendar week on the basis of a weekly payroll period (notwithstanding the fact that a determination of the equivalent number of payroll periods for purposes of the computation of the tax to be withheld upon wages paid for daily or miscellaneous payroll periods within such calendar week has been made on the basis of a daily or miscellaneous payroll period).

(3) *Term of continuous employment.*—For purposes of this paragraph, a term of employment is continuous if it is either a single term of employment or two or more consecutive terms of employment with the same employer. A term of continuous employment begins on the first day on which any services are performed by the employee for the employer for which compensation is paid or payable. Such term ends on the earlier of (i) the last day during the current term of continuous employment on which any services are performed by the employee for the employer, or (ii) if the employee performs no services for the employer for a period of more than 30 calendar days, the last day preceding such period on which any services are performed by the employee for the employer. For example, a professional athlete who signs a contract on December 31, 1973, to perform services from July 1 through December 31 for the calendar years 1974, 1975, and 1976 has a new term of employment beginning each July 1 and accordingly may qualify for use of the part-year withholding method in each of such years. Likewise, a term of continuous employment is not broken by a temporary layoff of no more than 30 days. On the other hand, when an employment relationship is actually terminated the term of continuous employment is ended even though a new employment relationship is established with the same employer within 30 days. A "term of continuous employment" includes all days on which an employee performs any services for an employer and includes days on which services are not performed because of illness or vacation, or because such days are holidays or are regular days off (such as Saturdays and Sundays, or days off in lieu of Saturdays and Sundays), or other days for which the employee is not scheduled to work. For example, an employee who is employed two days a week for the same employer from March 1 through December 31 has a term of continuous employment of 306 days.

(4) *Part-year employment.*—For purposes of this paragraph, "part-year employment" means one or more terms of continuous employment with all employers which term or terms will not aggregate more than 245 days within a calendar year. For example, A graduates from college in May and was not employed from January through May. A accepts a permanent position with X Co., beginning June 1. Since the total duration of A's term of continuous employ-

ment will, during the current calendar year, not exceed 245 days it does qualify as part-year employment for purposes of this section. If, however, A had also worked for Y Co. from December 15 of the previous year through February 5 of the current calendar year, the total duration of A's terms of continuous employment will, during the current calendar year, exceed 245 days (36 days (January 1 through February 5) plus 214 days (June 1 through December 31) equals 250 days). This year's employment does not therefore qualify as part-year employment for purposes of this section.

(5) *Employee's request.*—(i) An employee's request that his employer withhold according to the part-year employment method shall be in writing and in such form as the employer may prescribe. Such request shall be made under the penalties of perjury and shall contain the following information—

(*a*) The last day of employment (if any) by any employer prior to the current term of continuous employment during the calendar year in which such term commenced,

(*b*) A statement that the employee reasonably anticipates that he will be employed for an aggregate of no more than 245 days in all terms of continuous employment during the current calendar year, and

(*c*) The employee uses a calendar-year accounting period. An employee's request furnished to his employer pursuant to this section shall be effective, and may be acted upon by his employer, with respect to wages paid after the furnishing of such request, and shall cease to be effective with respect to any wages paid on or after the beginning of the payroll period during which the current calendar year will end.

(ii) If, on any day during the calendar year, any of the anticipations stated by the employee in his statement provided pursuant to subdivision (i)(*b*) of this subparagraph becomes unreasonable, the employee shall revoke the request described in this subparagraph before the end of the payroll period during which it becomes unreasonable. The revocation shall be effective as of the beginning of the payroll period during which it is made.

(c) *Applicability date.*—The removal of paragraph (b) from this section as of October 6, 2020, provided for combined FICA and income tax withholding tables, applies on and after January 1, 2020. For rules that apply before January 1, 2020, see 26 CFR part 31, revised as of April 1, 2020. [Reg. § 31.3402(h)(4)-1.]

☐ [*T.D. 7053, 7-20-70. Amended by T.D. 7251, 12-29-72, T.D. 7915, 9-26-83 and T.D. 9924, 10-5-2020.*]

### [Reg. § 31.3402(i)-1]

**§ 31.3402(i)-1. Increases in withholding.**—(a) *Increases in withholding.*—(1) *In general.*—In addition to the tax required to be deducted and withheld in accordance with the provisions of section 3402, the employee may request, after September 30, 1981, that the employer deduct and withhold an additional amount from the employee's wages. The employer must comply with the employee's request, except that the employer shall comply with the employee's request only to the extent that the amount that the employee requests to be deducted and withheld under this section does not exceed the amount that remains after the employer has deducted and withheld all amounts otherwise required to be deducted and withheld by Federal law (other than by section 3402 (i) and this section), State law, and local law (other than by State or local law that provides for voluntary withholding). The employer must comply with the employee's request in accordance with the time limitations of § 31.3402(f)(3)-1 (relating to when withholding exemption certificate takes effect). The employee must make his request on Form W-4 as provided in § 31.3402(f)(5)-1 (relating to form and contents of withholding exemption certificates), and this Form W-4 shall take effect and remain effective in accordance with section 3402(f) and the regulations thereunder.

(2) *Increases in withholding based on additional income.*—(i) The employee may request that the employer add an additional amount to the employee's wages and that the employer deduct and withhold an additional amount of income tax resulting from this addition under the computational procedures prescribed by the Commissioner in forms, instructions, publications, and other guidance for the calendar year for which the withholding allowance certificate claiming an additional amount to add to the employee's wages is furnished;

(ii) The employee may request that the employer deduct and withhold additional amounts of income tax resulting from the employee selecting higher withholding rate tables on the withholding allowance certificate;

(iii) The employer must comply with the employee's request under paragraph (a)(1)(i) or (ii) of this section, except that the employer shall comply with the employee's request only to the extent that the amount that the employee requests to be deducted and withheld under this section does not exceed the amount that remains after the employer has deducted and withheld all amounts otherwise required to be deducted and withheld by Federal law (other than by section 3402(i) and this section), State law, and local law (other than by State or local law that provides for voluntary withholding); and

(iv) The employer must comply with the employee's request in accordance with the time limitations in §31.3402(f)(3)-1. The employee must make the request on Form W-4 as provided in §31.3402(f)(5)-1 (relating to form and contents of withholding allowance certificates), and this Form W-4 shall take effect and remain effective in accordance with section 3402(f) and §31.3402(f)(4)-1.

(3) *Amount deducted treated as tax.*—The amount deducted and withheld pursuant to paragraphs (a)(1) and (2) of this section shall be treated as tax required to be deducted and withheld under section 3402.

(b) *Applicability date.*—The provisions of paragraphs (a)(2) and (3) of this section apply on and after October 6, 2020. Taxpayers may choose to apply paragraphs (a)(2) and (3) this section on or after January 1, 2020 and before October 6, 2020. [Reg. §31.3402(i)-1.]

☐ [*T.D.* 7915, 9-26-83. *Redesignated and amended by T.D.* 9924, 10-5-2020.]

### [Reg. §31.3402(j)-1]

**§31.3402(j)-1. Remuneration other than in cash for service performed by retail commission salesman.**—(a) *In general.*—(1) An employer, in computing the amount to be deducted and withheld as tax in accordance with section 3402, may, at his election, disregard any wages paid, after August 9, 1955, in a medium other than cash for services performed for him by an employee if (i) the noncash remuneration is paid for services performed by the employee as a retail commission salesman and (ii) the employer ordinarily pays the employee remuneration solely by way of cash commissions for services performed by him as a retail commission salesman.

(2) Section 3402(j) and this section are not applicable with respect to wages paid to the employee that are subject to withholding under §31.3402(g)-1(a)(2). Section 3402(j) and this section are not applicable with respect to noncash wages paid to a retail commission salesman for services performed by him in a capacity other than as such a salesman. Such sections are not applicable with respect to noncash wages paid by an employer to an employee for services performed as a retail commission salesman if the employer ordinarily pays the employee remuneration other than by way of cash commissions for such services. Thus, noncash remuneration may not be disregarded in computing the amount to be deducted and withheld in a case where the employee, for services performed as a retail commission salesman, is paid both a salary and cash commissions on sales, or is ordinarily paid in something other than cash (stocks, bonds or other forms of property) notwithstanding that the amount of remuneration paid to the employee is measured by sales.

(b) *Retail commission salesman.*—For purposes of section 3402(j) and this section, the term "retail commission salesman" includes an employee who is engaged in the solicitation of orders at retail, that is, from the ultimate consumer, for merchandise or other products offered for sale by his employer. The term does not include an employee salesman engaged in the solicitation on behalf of his employer of orders from wholesalers, retailers, or others, for merchandise for resale. However, if the salesman solicits orders for more than one principal, he is not excluded from the term solely because he solicits orders from wholesalers or retailers on behalf of one or more principals. In such case the salesman may be a retail commission salesman with respect to services performed for one or more principals and not with respect to services performed for his other principals.

(c) *Noncash remuneration.*—The term "noncash remuneration" includes remuneration paid in any medium other than cash, such as goods or commodities, stocks, bonds, or other forms of property. The term does not include checks or other monetary media of exchange.

(d) *Cross reference.*—For provisions relating to records required to be kept and statements which must be furnished an employee with respect to wage payments, see sections 6001 and 6051 and the regulations thereunder in Subpart G of this part. [Reg. §31.3402(j)-1.]

☐ [*T.D.* 6259, 10-25-57. *Amended by T.D.* 9276, 7-24-2006.]

### [Reg. §31.3402(k)-1]

**§31.3402(k)-1. Special rule for tips.**—(a) *Withholding of income tax in respect of tips.*—(1) *In general.*—Subject to the limitations set forth in subparagraph (2) of this paragraph, an employer is required to deduct and withhold from each of his employees tax in respect of those tips received by the employee which constitute wages. (For provisions relating to the treatment of tips as wages, see

§§31.3401(a)(16) and 31.3401(f).) The employer shall make the withholding by deducting or causing to be deducted the amount of the tax from wages (exclusive of tips) which are under control of the employer or other funds turned over by the employee to the employer (see subparagraph (3) of this paragraph). For purposes of this section the term "wages (exclusive of tips) which are under the control of the employer" means, with respect to a payment of wages, an amount equal to wages as defined in section 3401(a) except that tips and noncash remuneration which are wages are not included, less the sum of—

(i) The tax under section 3101 required to be collected by the employer in respect of wages as defined in section 3121(a) (exclusive of tips);

(ii) The tax under section 3402 required to be collected by the employer in respect of wages as defined in section 3401(a) (exclusive of tips); and

(iii) The amount of taxes imposed on the remuneration of an employee withheld by the employer pursuant to State and local law (including amounts withheld under an agreement between the employer and the employee pursuant to such law) except that the amount of taxes taken into account in this subdivision shall not include any amount attributable to tips.

(2) *Limitations.*—An employer is required to deduct and withhold the tax on tips which constitute wages only in respect of those tips which are reported by the employee to the employer in a written statement furnished to the employer pursuant to section 6053(a). The employer is responsible for the collection of the tax on tips reported to him only to the extent that the employer can, during the period beginning at the time the written statement is submitted to him and ending at the close of the calendar year in which the statement was submitted, collect the tax by deducting it or causing it to be deducted as provided in subparagraph (1) of this paragraph.

(3) *Furnishing of funds to employer.*—If the amount of the tax in respect of tips reported by the employee to the employer in a written statement furnished pursuant to section 6053(a) exceeds the wages (exclusive of tips) which are under the control of the employer from which the employer is required to withhold the tax in respect of such tips, the employee may furnish to the employer, within the period specified in subparagraph (2) of this paragraph, an amount of money equal to the amount of such excess.

(b) *Less than $20 of tips.*—Notwithstanding the provisions of paragraph (a) of this section, if an employee furnishes to his employer a written statement—

(1) Covering a period of less than one month, and

(2) The statement is furnished to the employer prior to the close of the 10th day of the month following the month in which the tips were actually received by the employee, and

(3) The aggregate amount of tips reported in the statement and in all other statements previously furnished by the employee covering periods within the same month is less than $20, and such statements, collectively, do not cover the entire month,

the employer may deduct amounts equivalent to the tax on such tips from wages (exclusive of tips) which are under the control of the employer or other funds turned over by the employee to the employer. For provisions relating to the repayment to an employee, or other disposition, of amounts deducted from an employee's remuneration in excess of the correct amount of tax, see §31.6413(a)-1. (As to the exclusion from wages of tips of less than $20, see §31.3401(a)(16)-1.)

(c) *Priority of tax collection.*—(1) *In general.*—In the case of a payment of wages (exclusive of tips), the employer shall deduct or cause to be deducted in the following order:

(i) The tax under section 3101 and the tax under section 3402 with respect to such payment of wages.

(ii) Any tax under section 3101 which, at the time of the payment of the wages, the employer is required to collect—

(*a*) In respect of tips reported by the employee to the employer in a written statement furnished to the employer pursuant to section 6053(a), or

(*b*) By reason of the employer's election to make collection of the tax under section 3101 in respect of tips on an estimated basis, but which has not been collected by the employer and which cannot be deducted from funds turned over by the employee to the employer for such purpose. (See §31.3102-3, relating to collection of, and liability for, employee tax on tips.)

(iii) Any tax under section 3402 which, at the time of the payment of the wages, the employer is required to collect—

(*a*) In respect of tips reported by the employee to the employer in a written statement furnished to the employer pursuant to section 6053(a), or

(b) By reason of the employer's election to make collection of the tax under section 3402 in respect of tips on an estimated basis, but which has not been collected by the employer and which cannot be deducted from funds turned over by the employee to the employer for such purpose. For provisions relating to the withholding of tax on the basis of average estimated tips, see paragraph (b) of §31.3402(h)(1)-1.

(2) *Examples.*—The application of subparagraph (1) of this paragraph may be illustrated by the following examples (The amounts used in the following examples are intended for illustrative purposes and do not necessarily reflect currently effective rates or amounts.):

*Example (1).* W is a waiter employed by R restaurant. W's principal remuneration for his services is in the form of tips received from patrons of R; however, he also receives a salary from R of $40 per week, which is paid to him every Friday. W is a member of a labor union which has a contract with R pursuant to which R is to collect dues for the union by withholding from the wages of its employees at the rate of $1 per week. In addition to the taxes required to be withheld under the Internal Revenue Code, W's wages are subject to withholding of a state income tax imposed upon both his regular wage and his tips received and reported to R.

On Monday of a given week W furnishes a written statement to R pursuant to section 6053(a) in which he reports the receipt of $160 in tips. The $40 wage to be paid to W on Friday of the same week is subject to the following items of withholding:

| | Taxes with Respect to Regular Wage | Taxes with Respect to Tips | Total |
|---|---|---|---|
| Section 3101 (F.I.C.A.) | $1.76 | $7.04 | $8.80 |
| Section 3402 (Income Tax at Source) | 5.65 | 28.30 | 33.95 |
| State Income Tax | 1.20 | 4.80 | 6.00 |
| Union Dues | | | 1.00 |
| Total | | | $49.75 |

W does not turn over any funds to R. R should satisfy the taxes imposed by sections 3101 and 3402 out of W's $40 wage as follows: The taxes imposed with respect to the regular wage (a total of $7.41) should be satisfied first. The taxes imposed with respect to tips are to be withheld only out of "wages (exclusive of tips) which are under the control of the employer" as that phrase is defined in §§31.3102-3(a)(1) and 31.3402(k)-1(a)(1). The amount of such wages under the control of employer in this example is $31.39, or $40, less the amounts applied in satisfaction of the Federal and state withholding taxes imposed with respect to the regular $40 wage ($8.61). This $31.39 is applied first in satisfaction of the tax under section 3101 with respect to tips ($7.04) and the balance of $24.35 is applied in partial satisfaction of the withholding of income tax at source under section 3402 with respect to tips. The amount of the tax with respect to tips under section 3402 which remains unsatisfied ($3.95) should be withheld from wages under the control of the employer the following week.

*Example (2).* During the week following the week dealt with in example (1), W furnishes a written statement to R pursuant to section 6053(a) in which he reports the receipt of $130 in tips. In addition, R receives a notice of garnishment of W's wages issued by the state court, pursuant to which R is required to withhold $10 per week from W's wages for a period of ten weeks. The $40 wage to be paid to W at the end of the week is subject to the following items of withholding:

| | Taxes with Respect to Regular Wage | Taxes with Respect to Tips | Total |
|---|---|---|---|
| Section 3101 (F.I.C.A.) | $1.76 | $5.72 | $7.48 |
| Section 3402 (Income Tax at Source): | | | |
| Current week | 5.65 | 22.30 | 27.95 |
| Carryover from prior week | .. | 3.95 | 3.95 |
| State Income Tax | 1.20 | 3.90 | 5.10 |
| Union Dues | | | 1.00 |
| Garnishment | | | 10.00 |
| Total | | | $55.48 |

As in example (1), the amount of "wages (exclusive of tips) which are under the control of the employer" is $31.39. This amount is applied first in satisfaction of the tax under section 3101 with respect to tips ($5.72) and the balance is applied in partial satisfaction of the withholding of income tax at source under section 3402 with respect to tips (a total of $26.25), including that portion of the amount required to be withheld from the prior week's wages which remained unsatisfied. The amount of the tax with respect to tips under section 3402 which remains unsatisfied ($0.58) should be withheld from wages under the control of the employer the following week. [Reg. §31.3402(k)-1.]

☐ [T.D. 7001, 1-17-69. Amended by T.D. 7053, 7-20-70.]

### [Reg. §31.3402(l)-1]

**§31.3402(l)-1. Determination and disclosure of marital or filing status.**—(a) *In general.*—An employer shall apply the applicable percentage method or wage bracket method withholding tables corresponding to the marital status or filing status that the employee selects on a valid withholding allowance certificate as set forth in forms, instructions, publications, and other guidance prescribed by the Commissioner.

(b) *Employee's filing status.*—An employee will be treated as single unless the employee selects head of household or married filing jointly filing status on a valid withholding allowance certificate. Employees may select a filing status other than single, subject to the following conditions:

(1) The employee may select head of household filing status on the employee's withholding allowance certificate only if the employee reasonably expects to be eligible to claim head of household filing status under section 2(b) and §1.2-2(b) of this chapter on the employee's income tax return.

(2) The employee may select married filing jointly filing status on the employee's withholding allowance certificate only if paragraph (d) of this section applies to the employee and the employee reasonably expects to file jointly a single return of income under subtitle A of the code with the employee's spouse. If an employee is married and expects to file a separate return from the employee's spouse, the employee must select single or married filing separately filing status on the employee's withholding allowance certificate.

(c) *Change in filing status.*—(1) *In general.*—Unless paragraph (c)(2) of this section applies, the employee must within 10 days furnish the employer with a new withholding allowance certificate if the employee's filing status changes—

(i) From married filing jointly (or qualifying widow(er)) to head of household, married filing separately, or single; or

(ii) From head of household to married filing separately or single

(2) *Exception.*—If the employee's filing status changes in the manner described in paragraph (c)(1)(i) or (ii) of this section, but the total effect of the changes together with other changes affecting the employee's anticipated tax liability under subtitle A does not result in an amount of tax to be deducted and withheld from the employee's wages for the taxable year that is less than the employee's anticipated tax liability under subtitle A, the employee is not required to furnish a new withholding allowance certificate within 10 days. However, the employee must furnish a new withholding allowance certificate to take effect the following calendar year by the later of December 1 of the calendar year in which the employee's filing status changes, or within 10 days of such change.

(d) *Determination of marital status.*—For the purposes of section 3402(l)(2) and paragraph (b) of this section, paragraphs (d)(1) and (2) of this section shall be applied in determining whether an employee is a single person or a married person:

(1) An employee shall on any day be considered as a single person and not married if—

(i) The employee is legally separated from the employee's spouse under a decree of divorce or separate maintenance; or

(ii) Either the employee or the employee's spouse is, or on any preceding day within the same calendar year was, a nonresident alien unless the employee has made or reasonably expects to make an election under section 6013(g) in the time and manner prescribed in §1.6013-6(a)(4) of this chapter.

(2) An employee shall on any day be considered as a married person if paragraph (d)(1) of this section does not apply and—

(i) The employee is married within the meaning of §301.7701-18(b) of this chapter on the day the withholding allowance certificate is furnished;

(ii) The employee's spouse died during the employee's taxable year; or

(iii) The employee's spouse died during one of the two taxable years immediately preceding the current taxable year and, on the basis of facts existing at the beginning of such day, the employee reasonably expects, at the close of the taxable year, to be a surviving spouse as defined in section 2 and §1.2-2(a) of this chapter. The employee must reasonably expect to file an income tax return claiming qualifying widow(er) status.

(e) *Applicability date.*—The provisions of this section apply on and after October 6, 2020. Taxpayers may choose to apply paragraphs (a)(2) and (3) this section on or after January 1, 2020 and before October 6, 2020. For rules that apply before October 6, 2020, see 26 CFR part 31, revised as of April 1, 2020. [Reg. §31.3402(l)-1.]

☐ [*T.D. 7115, 5-20-71. Amended by T.D. 9924, 10-5-2020.*]

### [Reg. §31.3402(m)-1]

**§31.3402(m)-1. Additional withholding allowance.**—(a) *In general.*—In determining the withholding allowance or additional reductions in withholding under section 3402(m) on employee withholding allowance certificates furnished to the employer to be effective on or after January 1, 2020, employees may take into account the estimated tax deductions described in paragraph (b) of this section, the estimated tax credits described in paragraph (c) of this section, and estimated tax payments described in paragraph (d) of this section. Employees may only claim items in paragraphs (b), (c), and (d) of this section to the extent provided in paragraph (e) of this section.

(b) *Estimated tax deductions.*—Employees may take into account the following income tax deductions in chapter 1 of the Code:

(1) Estimated itemized deductions (as defined in section 63(d)) allowable under chapter 1;

(2) Estimated deductions described in section 62(a), except for—

(i) Any deduction described in section 62(a)(1);

(ii) Any deduction described in section 62(a)(2) if the reimbursement or payment for the amount allowable as such deduction is excludable from wages subject to income tax withholding;

(iii) Any deduction described in section 62(a)(3); (iv) Any deduction described in section 62(a)(4); and

(v) Any deduction described in section 62(a)(5);

(3) Estimated deductions for net operating loss carryovers under section 172;

(4) The estimated aggregate net losses from schedules C (Profit or Loss from Business), D (Capital Gains and Losses), E (Supplemental Income and Loss), and F (Profit or Loss from Farming) of Form 1040 and from the last line of Part II of Form 4797 (Sale of Business Property);

(5) Estimated additional standard deduction for the aged and blind provided under section 63(c)(3) and section 63(f);

(6) Estimated deduction allowed under section 199A; and

(7) Estimated deduction or deductions allowed under section 151.

(c) *Estimated tax credits.*—Employees may take into account the estimated income tax credits allowable under chapter 1, except for—

(1) The credit under section 31(a) for taxes withheld under chapter 24 of the code (which includes taxes withheld on wages and amounts treated as wages for chapter 24 purposes, such as pension withholding under section 3405 and backup withholding under section 3406) unless, on the day the employee estimates this amount, the amount has been actually withheld from the employee's wages (or another payment treated as wages for this purpose), the employee enters this amount of tax withheld pursuant to the instructions in the Tax Withholding Estimator (or successor) or Publication 505 (or successor), and the employee is not an employee whose employer must withhold for that employee pursuant to a notice under §31.3402(f)(2)-1(g)(2);

(2) The credit for tax withheld at source for nonresident aliens and foreign corporations under section 33; and

(3) Any credit to the extent that the employee has filed or expects to file any IRS form claiming such credit other than the employee's United States Individual Income Tax Return (Form 1040).

(d) *Estimated tax payments.*—Employees may take into account estimated tax payments only if—

(1) The employee's employer is not obligated to withhold on the employee's wages pursuant to a notice under §31.3402(f)(2)-1(g)(2);

(2) The amount claimed has been paid with the payment voucher from Form 1040-ES (or was otherwise designated by the taxpayer as a payment of estimated tax) or is planned to be made with respect to nonwage items but only if the planned amount does not decrease withholding below the pro-rata share of chapter 1 tax attributable to wages as determined under forms, instructions, publications, and other guidance prescribed by the Commissioner;

(3) The employee uses the Tax Withholding Estimator (or successor) or Publication 505 (or successor) and enters the amount claimed pursuant to the instructions in the Tax Withholding Estimator (or successor) or Publication 505 (or successor); and

(4) In using the Tax Withholding Estimator (or successor) or Publication 505 (or successor), the employee includes all items of nonwage income the Tax Withholding Estimator (or successor) or Publication 505 (or successor) prompts or instructs the employee to enter or include.

(e) *Definitions and special rules.*—(1) *Estimated.*—The term "estimated" as used in this section to modify the terms "deduction," "deductions," "credits," "losses," and "amount of decrease" means with respect to an employee the aggregate dollar amount of a particular item that the employee reasonably expects will be allowable to the employee on the employee's income tax return for the estimation year under the section of the Code specified for each item. In no event shall that amount exceed the sum of:

(i) The amount shown for that particular item on the income tax return that the employee has filed for the taxable year preceding the estimation year (or, if such return has not yet been filed, then the income tax return that the employee filed for the taxable year preceding such year), which amount the employee also reasonably expects to show on the income tax return for the estimation year; plus

(ii) The determinable additional amounts (as defined in paragraph (e)(1)(iii) of this section) for each item for the estimation year.

(iii) The determinable additional amounts are amounts that are not included in paragraph (e)(1)(i) of this section and that are demonstrably attributable to identifiable events during the estimation year or the preceding year. Amounts are demonstrably attributable to identifiable events if they relate to payments already made during the estimation year, to binding obligations to make payments (including the payment of taxes) during the year, and to other transactions or occurrences, the implementation of which has begun and is verifiable at the time the employee furnishes a withholding allowance certificate. The estimation year is the taxable year including the day on which the employee furnishes the withholding allowance certificate to the employer, except that if the employee furnishes the withholding allowance certificate to the employer and specifies on the certificate that the certificate is not to take effect until a specified future date, the estimation year shall be the taxable year including that specified future date. It is not reasonable for an employee to include in his or her withholding computation for the estimation year any amount that is shown for a particular item on the income tax return that the employee has filed for the taxable year preceding the estimation year (or, if such return has not yet been filed, then the income tax return that the employee filed for the taxable year preceding such year) and that has been disallowed by the Service as part of an adjustment described in §601.103(b) of this chapter (relating to examination and determination of tax liability) and §601.105(b) through (d) of this chapter (relating to examination of returns), without regard to any pending request for reconsideration, protest, request for consideration by an Appeals office, or civil action in which such proposed adjustment is at issue.

(2) *Restriction for employees with nonwage income.*—The employee must offset any deduction described in paragraph (b) of this section with items includible in the employee's gross income for which no Federal income tax is withheld in accordance with forms, instructions, publications, and other guidance prescribed by the Commissioner. In addition, an employee whose employer must withhold for that employee pursuant to a notice under §31.3402(f)(2)-1(g)(2) must offset any tax benefit resulting from any deduction or credit described in paragraph (b) or (c) of this section with the anticipated income tax attributable to items other than wages includible in the employee's gross income in the manner determined by the Commissioner.

(3) *Multiple withholding allowance certificates.*—(i) *In general.*—The employee may not take into account deductions, credits, or estimated tax payments described in paragraph (b), (c), or (d) of this section if these deductions, credits, or estimated tax payments are claimed on another valid withholding allowance certificate in effect with respect to another employer of the employee or any employer of the employee's spouse.

(ii) *Married taxpayers filing jointly.*—Married taxpayers who reasonably expect to file as married filing jointly on their Federal income tax return for the estimation year determine the withholding allowance to which they are entitled under section 3402(m) on the basis of their combined wages, allowable credits or deductions, and estimated tax payments permitted to be taken into account. The deductions, credits, or estimated tax payments described in paragraphs (b), (c), and (d) of this section to which either spouse is entitled may be claimed by either spouse or may be allocated between both spouses. However, one spouse may not claim deductions, credits, or estimated tax payments described in paragraphs (b), (c), and (d) of this section claimed on the other spouse's withholding allowance certificate.

(iii) *Married taxpayers filing separately.*—A married taxpayer who reasonably expects to file a separate income tax return from the employee's spouse for the estimation year determines the withholding allowance deductions, credits, or estimated tax payments described in paragraphs (b), (c), and (d) of this section on the basis of the employee's individual wages, deductions, credits, and estimated tax payments.

(4) *IRS instructions.*—An employee must follow the instructions to the Form W-4, and other IRS forms, instructions, publications, and related guidance in determining the employee's withholding allowance or other reductions in withholding permitted under section 3402(m) for deductions, credits, or estimated tax payments described in paragraphs (b), (c), and (d) of this section.

(f) *Applicability date.*—The provisions of this section apply on or after October 6, 2020. Taxpayers may choose to apply paragraphs (a)(2) and (3) this section on or after January 1, 2020 and before October 6, 2020. For rules that apply before October 6, 2020, see 26 CFR part 31, revised as of April 1, 2020. [Reg. §31.3402(m)-1.]

☐ [*T.D. 7065, 10-22-70. Amended by T.D. 7915, 9-26-83 and T.D. 9924, 10-5-2020.*]

### [Reg. §31.3402(n)-1]

**§31.3402(n)-1. Employees incurring no income tax liability.**—(a) *In general.*—Notwithstanding any other provision of this subpart (except to the extent a payment of wages is subject to withholding under §31.3402(g)-1(a)(2)), an employer shall not deduct and withhold any tax under chapter 24 of the code upon a payment of wages made to an employee, if there is in effect with respect to the payment a withholding allowance certificate furnished to the employer by the employee which certifies that—

(1) The employee incurred no liability for income tax imposed under subtitle A of the Internal Revenue Code for the employee's preceding taxable year; and

(2) The employee anticipates that the employee will incur no liability for income tax imposed under subtitle A for the employee's current taxable year.

(b) *Mandatory flat rate withholding.*—To the extent wages are subject to income tax withholding under §31.3402(g)-1(a)(2), such wages are subject to such income tax withholding regardless of whether a withholding allowance certificate under section 3402(n) and this section has been furnished to the employer.

(c) *Liability for income tax.*—For purposes of section 3402(n) and this section, an employee is not considered to incur liability for income tax imposed under subtitle A if the amount of such tax imposed is equal to or less than the total amount of credits against such tax which are allowable under chapter 1 of the Internal Revenue Code, other than those credits allowable under section 31 or section 34. For purposes of this section, an employee who files a joint return under section 6013 is considered to incur liability for any tax shown on such return. An employee who is entitled to file a joint return under section 6013 shall not certify that the employee anticipates that he or she will incur no liability for income tax imposed by subtitle A for the employee's current taxable year if such statement would not be true in the event that the employee files a joint return for such year, unless the employee filed a separate return for the preceding taxable year and anticipates that the employee will file a separate return for the current taxable year.

(d) *Rules about withholding allowance certificates.*—For rules relating to invalid withholding allowance certificates, see §31.3402(f)(2)-1(h), and for rules relating to disregarding certain withholding allowance certificates on which an employee claims a complete exemption from withholding, see §31.3402(f)(2)-1(i).

(e) *Examples.*—The following examples illustrate this section:

(1) *Example 1.*—A, an unmarried, calendar-year basis taxpayer, files an income tax return for 2020 on April 10, 2021, showing that A had adjusted gross income of $5,000 and is not liable for any income

tax for 2020. A had $180 of income tax withheld during 2020. A anticipates that A's gross income for 2021 will be approximately the same amount, and that A will not incur income tax liability for that year. On April 20, 2021, A commences employment and furnishes the employer a withholding allowance certificate certifying that A incurred no liability for income tax imposed under subtitle A for 2020, and that A anticipates that A will incur no liability for income tax imposed under subtitle A for 2021. A's employer shall not deduct and withhold on payments of wages made to A on or after April 20, 2021. Under §31.3402(f)(4)-1(b), unless A furnishes a new withholding allowance certificate including the certifications described in paragraph (a) of this section to the employer, the employer is required to deduct and withhold upon payments of wages to A made after February 15, 2022.

(2) *Example 2.*—Assume the facts are the same as in paragraph (e)(1) of this section (Example 1) except that A had been employed by the employer prior to April 20, 2021, and had furnished the employer a withholding allowance certificate prior to furnishing the withholding allowance certificate including the certifications described in paragraph (a) of this section on April 20, 2021. Under §31.3402(f)(3)-1(b), the employer would be required to give effect to the new withholding allowance certificate no later than the beginning of the first payroll period ending (or the first payment of wages made without regard to a payroll period) on or after May 20, 2021. However, under §31.3402(f)(3)-1(b), the employer could, if it chose, make the new withholding allowance certificate effective with respect to any payment of wages made on or after April 20, 2021, and before the effective date mandated by section 3402(f)(3)(B)(i) and §31.3402(f)(3)-1(b). Under §31.3402(f)(4)-1(b), unless A furnishes a new withholding allowance certificate including the certifications described in §31.3402(n)-1(a) to A's employer, the employer is required to deduct and withhold upon payments of wages to A made after February 15, 2022.

(3) *Example 3.*—Assume the facts are the same as in paragraph (e)(1) of this section (Example 1) except that for 2020 A has taxable income of $8,000, income tax liability of $839, and income tax withheld of $1,195. Although A received a refund of $356 due to income tax withholding of $1,195, A may not certify on A's withholding allowance certificate that A incurred no liability for income tax imposed by subtitle A for 2020.

(f) *Applicability date.*—The provisions of this section apply on and after October 6, 2020. Taxpayers may choose to apply paragraphs (a)(2) and (3) this section on or after January 1, 2020 and before October 6, 2020. For rules that apply before October 6, 2020, see 26 CFR part 31, revised as of April 1, 2020. [Reg. §31.3402(n)-1.]

☐ [*T.D. 7048, 6-23-70. Amended by T.D. 7423, 6-24-76, T.D. 7577, 12-19-78, T.D. 7598, 3-12-79, T.D. 7682, 3-10-80, T.D. 7772, 3-17-81; T.D. 7803, 1-21-82, and T.D. 9276, 7-24-2006 and T.D. 9924, 10-5-2020.*]

### [Reg. §31.3402(o)-1]

**§31.3402(o)-1. Extension of withholding to supplemental unemployment compensation benefits.**—(a) *In general.*—Withholding of income tax is required under section 3402(o) with respect to payments of supplemental unemployment compensation benefits made after December 31, 1970, which are treated under paragraph (b)(14) of §31.3401(a)-1 as if they were wages.

(b) *Withholding exemption certificates.*—For purposes of section 3402(f)(2) and (3) and the regulations thereunder (relating to withholding exemption certificates), in the case of supplemental unemployment compensation benefits an employment relationship shall be considered to commence with either the date on which such benefits begin to accrue or January 1, 1971, whichever is later, and the withholding exemption certificate furnished the employer with respect to such commencement of employment shall be considered the first certificate furnished the employer. The withholding exemption certificate furnished by the employee to his former employer (with whom his employment has been involuntarily terminated, within the meaning of paragraph (b)(14)(ii) of §31.3401(a)-1) shall be treated as meeting the requirements of section 3402(f)(2)(A) and the regulations thereunder if such former employer furnishes such certificate to the employee's current employer, as defined in paragraph (g) of §31.3401(d)-1, or if such former employer is the agent of such current employer with respect to the employee's withholding exemption certificate. However, the preceding sentence shall not be applicable if such employee furnishes a new withholding exemption certificate to such current employer (or his agent), provided that such withholding exemption certificate meets the requirements of section 3402(f)(2)(A) and the regulations thereunder. See the definitions of payroll period in paragraph (c) of §31.3401(b)-1 and of employee in paragraph (g) of §31.3401(c)-1. [Reg. §31.3402(o)-1.]

☐ [*T.D. 7068, 11-10-70.*]

[Reg. §31.3402(o)-2]

**§31.3402(o)-2. Extension of withholding to annuity payments if requested by payee.**—(a) *In general.*—Under section 3402(o) of the Internal Revenue Code of 1954 and this section, the payee (as defined in paragraph (g)(2) of this section) of an annuity (as defined in paragraph (g)(1) of this section) may request the payor (as defined in paragraph (g)(3) of this section) of the annuity to withhold income tax with respect to payments of the annuity made after December 31, 1970. If such a request is made, the payor shall deduct and withhold as requested.

(b) *Manner of making request.*—A payee who wishes a payor to deduct and withhold income tax from annuity payments shall file a request with the payor to deduct and withhold a specific whole dollar amount from each annuity payment. Such specific dollar amount requested shall be at least $5 per month and shall not reduce the net amount of any annuity payment received by the payee below $10. The request shall be made on Form W-4P (annuitant's withholding exemption certificate and request) in accordance with the instructions applicable thereto, and shall set forth fully and clearly the data therein called for. In lieu of Form W-4P, payers may prepare and use a form the provisions of which are identical with those of Form W-4P. For the requirements relating to Form W-4P with respect to qualified State individual income taxes, see paragraph (d)(3)(i) of §301.6361-1 of this chapter (Regulations on Procedure and Administration).

(c) *When request takes effect.*—Upon receipt of a request under this section the payor of the annuity with respect to which such request was made shall deduct and withhold the amount specified in such request from each annuity payment commencing with the first annuity payment made on or after the date which occurs—

(1) In a case in which no previous request is in effect, three calendar months after the date on which such request is furnished to such payor, and

(2) In a case in which a previous request is in effect, the first status determination date (see section 3402(f)(3)(B) and paragraph (d) of §31.3402(f)(3)-1 of this chapter) which occurs at least 30 days after the date on which such request is so furnished.

However, the payor may, at his election, commence to deduct and withhold such specified amount with respect to an annuity payment which is made prior to the annuity payment described in the preceding sentence with respect to which the payor must commence to deduct and withhold.

(d) *Duration and termination of request.*—A request under this section shall continue in effect until terminated. The payee may terminate the request by furnishing the payor a signed written notice of termination. Such notice of termination shall, except as hereinafter provided, take effect with respect to the first payment of an amount in respect of which the request is in effect which is made on or after the first status determination date (see section 3402(f)(3)(B) and paragraph (d) of §31.3402(f)(3)-1 of this chapter) which occurs at least 30 days after the date on which such notice is so furnished. However, at the election of such payor, such notice may be made effective with respect to any payment of an amount in respect of which the request is in effect which is made on or after the date on which such notice is so furnished and before such status determination date.

(e) *Special rules.*—For purposes of chapter 24 of subtitle C of the Internal Revenue Code of 1954 (relating to collection of income tax at source on wages) and of subtitle F of such Code (relating to procedure and administration), and the regulations thereunder—

(1) An amount which is requested to be withheld pursuant to this section shall be deemed a tax required to be deducted and withheld under section 3402.

(2) An amount deducted and withheld pursuant to this section shall be deemed an amount deducted and withheld under section 3402.

(3) The term "wages" includes the gross amount of an annuity payment with respect to which there is in effect a request for withholding under this section. However, references to the definition of wages in section 3401(a) which are made in section 6014 (relating to election by the taxpayer not to compute the tax on his annual return) and section 6015(a) (relating to declaration of estimated tax by individuals) shall not be deemed to include any portion of such an annuity payment.

(4) The term "employer" includes a payor with respect to whom a request for withholding is in effect under this section.

(5) The term "employee" includes a payee with respect to whom a request for withholding is in effect under this section.

(6) The term "payroll period" includes the period of accrual with respect to which payments of an annuity which is subject to withholding under this section are ordinarily made.

(f) *Returns of income tax withheld and statements for payees.*—(1) Form W-2P is to be used in lieu of Form W-2, which is required to be furnished by an employer to an employee under §31.6051-1 of this chapter and to the Social Security Administration under paragraph (a) of §31.6051-2 of this chapter, with respect to an annuity subject to withholding under this section. If an amount is required to be deducted and withheld under this section from any or all of the payments made to a payee under an annuity contract during a calendar year, all payments with respect to that annuity contract are required to be reported on Form W-2P, in lieu of Form 1099, as prescribed in §§1.6041-1, 1.6041-2, and 1.6047-1 of this chapter; any other annuity payments made by the same payor to the same payee may, at the option of the payor, be reported on Form W-2P.

(2) Each statement on Form W-2P shall show the following:

(i) The gross amount of annuity payments made during the calendar year, whether or not income tax withholding under this section was in effect with respect to all such payments,

(ii) The total amount deducted and withheld as tax under section 3402 of this section, and

(iii) The information required to be shown by Form W-2P and the instructions applicable thereto.

For the requirements relating to Form W-2P with respect to qualified State individual income taxes, see paragraph (d)(3)(ii) of §301.6361-1 of this chapter (Regulations on Procedure and Administration).

(3) The provisions of §1.9101-1 of this chapter (relating to permission to submit information required by certain returns and statements on magnetic tape) shall be applicable to the information required to be furnished on Form W-2P.

(4) The provisions of §31.6109-1 of this chapter (relating to supplying of identifying numbers) shall be applicable to Form W-2P and to any payee of an annuity to whom a statement on Form W-2P is required to be furnished.

(g) *Definitions.*—For purposes of this section—

(1) The term "annuity" means periodic payments which are payable over a period greater than one year and which are treated under section 72 as amounts received as an annuity, whether or not such periodic payments are variable in amount. Also, periodic payments to an individual who is retired before the normal retirement age for reasons of disability, to which the provisions of section 105(d) apply, shall be deemed to be an annuity for purposes of this section. A lump-sum payment (including a total distribution under section 72(n)) is not an annuity.

(2) The term "payee" means an individual who is a citizen or resident of the United States and who receives an annuity payment.

(3) The term "payor" means a person making an annuity payment except that, if the person making the payment is acting solely as an agent for another person, the term "payor" shall mean such other person and not the person actually making the payment. For example, if a bank makes an annuity payment only as agent for an employees' trust, the trust shall be deemed to be the "payor." Notwithstanding the preceding two sentences, any person who, under section 3401(a)(5) or (8), would not be required to deduct and withhold the tax under section 3402 if the annuity payment were remuneration for services shall not be considered a "payor." [Reg. §31.3402(o)-2.]

☐ [T.D. 7804, 1-21-82.]

[Reg. §31.3402(o)-3]

**§31.3402(o)-3. Extension of withholding to sick pay.**—(a) *In general.*—Under section 3402(o) of the Internal Revenue Code of 1954 and this section, the payee (as defined in subparagraph (h)(2) of this section) of sick pay (as defined in subparagraph (h)(1) of this section) may request the payor (as defined in subparagraph (h)(3) of this section) of the sick pay to withhold income tax with respect to payments of sick pay made on or after May 1, 1981. If such a request is made, the payor must deduct and withhold as requested.

(b) *Manner of making request.*—A payee who wishes a payor to deduct and withhold income tax from sick pay shall file a written request with the payor to deduct and withhold a specific whole dollar amount (subject to the limitations of paragraph (c) of this section) from each sick pay payment. The request shall be made on Form W-4S in accordance with the instructions applicable thereto, and shall set forth fully and clearly the data therein called for. In lieu of Form W-4S, payors may prepare and use a form the provisions of which are identical to those of Form W-4S. The payee must include his social security account number in the request.

(c) *Amount requested to be withheld.*—The payee shall request that the payor withhold a specific whole dollar amount. The specific whole dollar amount shall be at least $20 per weekly payment of sick pay. If the payee is paid sick pay computed on a daily basis, the specific whole dollar amount shall be at least $4 per daily payment of sick pay. If the payee is paid sick pay on a biweekly basis, the specific whole dollar amount shall be at least $40 per 2 week payment of sick pay. If the payee is paid sick pay on a semimonthly basis, the specific whole dollar amount shall be at least $44 per semimonthly payment of sick pay. If the payee is paid sick pay on a monthly basis, the specific whole dollar amount shall be at least $88 per monthly payment of sick pay. If the payee is paid sick pay on a basis other than weekly, daily, biweekly, semimonthly, or monthly, the specific whole dollar amount shall be the equivalent of at least $4 per day, assuming a 5 day work week of 8 hours per day (40 hours total) in each 7 day calendar week. In the case of a payment which is greater or less than a full payment, the amount withheld is to bear the same relation to the specific whole dollar amount requested to be withheld as such payment bears to a full payment. For example, assume an individual receives sick pay of $100 per week and requests that $25 per week be withheld for taxes. After 4 full weeks of absence, the individual returns to work on a Wednesday (having been absent on sick leave Monday and Tuesday). For the week the individual returns to work, the individual would be entitled to $40 of sick pay, $10 of which would be withheld for taxes. The payor may, at his option, permit the payee to request that the payor withhold a specific percentage from each payment. The specific percentage shall be at least 10 percent. If the payor so opts, the payor must also accept requests under the whole dollar method. If the amount requested to be withheld under either the whole dollar method or the optional percentage method reduces the net amount of a sick pay payment received by the payee to below $10, no income tax shall be withheld from that payment by the payor.

(d) *When request takes effect.*—The payor must deduct and withhold the amount specified in the request with respect to payments made more than 7 days after the date on which the request is received by the payor. At the election of the payor, the request may take effect before this deadline.

(e) *Duration and termination of request.*—A request under this section shall continue in effect until changed or terminated. The payee may change the request by filing a new written request that meets all of the requirements of paragraphs (b) and (c) of this section. The new request shall take effect as specified in paragraph (d) of this section and the old request shall be deemed terminated when the new request takes effect. The payee may terminate the request by furnishing the payor a signed written notice of termination containing both a request to terminate withholding and all the information contained in the request to withhold. This written notice of termination shall take effect with respect to payments made more than 7 days after the date on which the notice of termination is received by the payor. At the election of the payor, the request may take effect before this deadline.

(f) *Special rules.*—For purposes of chapter 24 of subtitle C of the Internal Revenue Code of 1954 (relating to collection of income tax at source on wages) and of subtitle F of the Code (relating to procedure and administration), and the regulations thereunder—

(1) An amount which is requested to be withheld pursuant to this section shall be deemed a tax required to be deducted and withheld under section 3402.

(2) An amount deducted and withheld pursuant to this section shall be deemed an amount deducted and withheld under section 3402.

(3) The term "wages" includes the gross amount of a sick pay payment with respect to which there is in effect a request for withholding under this section. However, references to the definition of wages in section 3401(a) which are made in section 6014 (relating to election by the taxpayer not to compute the tax on his annual return) and section 6015(a) (relating to declaration of estimated tax by individuals) shall not be deemed to include any portion of such a sick pay payment.

(4) The term "employer" includes a payor with respect to whom a request for withholding is in effect under this section.

(5) The term "employee" includes a payee with respect to whom a request for withholding is in effect under this section.

(6) The term "payroll period" includes the period of accrual with respect to which payments of sick pay which are subject to withholding under this section are ordinarily made.

(g) *Statements required to be furnished to payees.*—See section 6051(f) and the regulations thereunder for requirements relating to statements required to be furnished to payees.

(h) *Definitions.*—(1)(i) The term "sick pay" means any **payment** made to an individual which does not constitute wages (**determined** without regard to section 3402(o) and this section), which is **paid** to an employee pursuant to a plan to which the employer is a party, and which constitutes remuneration or a payment in lieu of remuneration for any period during which the employee is temporarily absent from work on account of personal injuries or sickness. The

term "personal injuries or sickness" shall have the same meaning as ascribed thereto by section 105(a) and the regulations thereunder. The term "sick pay" does not include any amounts either excludable from gross income under section 104(a)(1), (2), (4), or (5) or section 105(b) or (c) or paid under section 3402(o)(1)(B). The term "sick pay" does not include amounts paid under a plan if all amounts paid under the plan are paid to individuals who are described in the first sentence of section 105(d)(4) (relating to the definition of permanent and total disability) and the regulations thereunder. Amounts paid under any other plan shall be deemed to be paid for a period during which the employee is temporarily absent from work. For sick pay paid in 1981 only, however, the payor may opt not to follow the rules of the two preceding sentences but to follow instead the rule that an employee is temporarily absent if his absence is not described in section 105(d)(4) (relating to the definition of permanent and total disability) and the regulations thereunder. An employer is not a party to the plan if the plan is a contract between only employees and a third party payor or the employer makes no contributions to provide sick pay benefits under the plan, even if the employer withholds amounts from the employees' salaries and pays the amounts over to the third party payor.

(ii) This subparagraph (1) may be illustrated by the following examples:

*Example (1).* Employee A works for P Company and Employee B works for Q Company. P Company has contracted with R Insurance Company for R to pay P's employees the equivalent of their normal wages when they are temporarily absent from work because of sickness or personal injury. Q Company has neither entered into such a contract nor will it make such payments directly from its own funds. B consequently goes to S Insurance Company and purchases directly an insurance policy which will pay him the equivalent of his normal wages when he is unable to work because of sickness or personal injury. Both A and B are subsequently temporarily absent from work on account of sickness or personal injuries. A receives payments from R and B receives payments from S. Neither the payments made by R to A nor the payments made by S to B constitute wages (determined without regard to section 3402(o) and this section). A may request that R withhold income taxes under section 3402(o) and this section from the payments he receives because the payments are sick pay as defined in section 3402(o) and this section. B may not request that S withhold income taxes under section 3402(o) and this section from the payments he receives because the payments are not paid pursuant to a plan to which Q Company is a party and thus are not sick pay as defined in section 3402(o) and this section.

*Example (2).* Employees C and D both work for T Company, which has contracted with U Insurance Company for U to pay T's employees for all sickness or injury claims. Employee C is sick and out from work for a month. U pays C the equivalent of C's regular pay. Employee D loses his arm in an accident and U pays D $10,000. C may request that U withhold income taxes under section 3402(o) and this section from the payments he receives because the payments constitute remuneration or a payment in lieu of remuneration for any period during which the employee is temporarily absent from work on account of sickness or personal injuries. D may not request that U withhold income taxes from the payments he receives because the payments do not constitute remuneration or a payment in lieu of remuneration for any period during which the employee is temporarily absent from work on account of sickness or personal injuries.

(2) The term "payee" means an individual who is a citizen or resident of the United States and who receives a sick pay payment.

(3)(i) The term "payor" means any person making a sick pay payment who is not the employer (as defined in section 3401 and in §31.3401(d)-1 (except paragraph (f) thereof)) of the payee. If however the person making the payment is acting solely as an agent for another person, the term "payor" shall mean the other person and not the person actually making the payment.

(ii) This subparagraph (3) may be illustrated by the following examples:

*Example (1).* X Company contracts with Y Insurance Company for Y to pay X's employees the equivalent of their normal wages when they are temporarily absent from work because of sickness or personal injury. Y computes the amount to be paid and determines the date payment is to be made for each of X's employees. Y then instructs Z Bank to issue a check for that amount on that date. Y reimburses Z for the amount of the check plus Z's administrative costs. Under these circumstances, Z is the agent of Y and Y is the payor under section 3402(o) and this section.

*Example (2).* V Company contracts with W Company for W to pay V's employees the equivalent of their normal wages when they are temporarily absent from work on account of sickness or personal injury. Under the contractual arrangement, V advises W of the wages normally paid to each of V's employees. V tells W when an employee of V is temporarily absent from work on account of sickness or personal injury, and W computes the amount to be paid the employee and makes payments of sick pay to the employee during the period of the employee's absence. V subsequently reimburses W for the amount of those payments and pays W a fee for W's services. Under these circumstances, W is acting solely as the agent of V, and a payee may not request under section 3402(o) and these regulations that W withhold income taxes from his payments. However, see section 3401 and the regulations thereunder for the obligation of V to withhold income taxes from the payments that W makes as the agent of V, which are not excluded from income under section 105 and the regulations thereunder and which are wages under section 3401 and the regulations thereunder. See also §31.3402(g)-1 (relating to supplemental wage payments) for the conditions under which a flat percentage rate of withholding may be used.

 *Example (3).* Assume the same facts as in Example (2), except that the consideratin for W's services is a set insurance premium rather than reimbursement for costs plus a fee. Under these circumstances W is the payor and is not acting solely as the agent of V. An employee of V to whom W makes payments under the agreement may request under section 3402(o) and the regulations thereunder that W withhold income taxes from those payments.

 (i) *Special rules for sick pay paid pursuant to certain collective-bargaining agreements.*—(1) Special rules (enumerated in subparagraph (2)) apply to sick pay where all of the following tests are met.

 (i) The sick pay must be paid pursuant to a collective-bargaining agreement between employee representatives and one or more employers.

 (ii) The agreement must contain a provision that section 3402(o)(5) is to apply to sick pay paid pursuant to the agreement.

 (iii) The agreement must contain a provision for determining the amount to be deducted and withheld from each payment of sick pay.

 (iv) The social security number of the payee must be furnished to the payor. The agreement may provide that the employer will furnish this or the payee may furnish his social security number directly to the payor.

 (v) The payor must be furnished with information that is necessary for the payor to determine whether the payment is pursuant to the agreement and to determine the amount to be deducted and withheld. The agreement may provide that the employer will furnish this information directly to the payor.

 (2) The following special rules apply to sick pay where all of the tests of subparagraph (1) are met.

 (i) The requirement of section 3402(o)(1)(c) and this section that a request for withholding be in effect does not apply.

 (ii) The amount to be deducted and withheld from the sick pay shall be determined according to the provisions of the agreement and not according to this section. This rule shall not however apply—

 (A) To payments enumerated in section 3402(n) (relating to employees incurring no income tax liability) and the regulations thereunder, or

 (B) To payments made to a payee more than 7 days after the date that the payor receives a statement from the payee that the payee expects to claim an exclusion from gross income under section 105(d). Such statement must include adequate verification of disability. A certificate from a qualified physician attesting that the employee is permanently and totally disabled (within the meaning of section 105(d)) shall be deemed to constitute adequate verification. If the payor receives such a statement, the payor shall not withhold any income tax from the payments made to the payee, regardless of the provisions of the collective bargaining agreement. This exception from withholding does not affect the requirements of §31.6051-3. [Reg. §31.3402(o)-3.]

 ☐ [*T.D. 7813, 3-15-82. Amended by T.D. 7915, 9-26-83.*]

### [Reg. §31.3402(p)-1]

**§31.3402(p)-1. Voluntary withholding agreements.**—(a) *Employer-employee agreement.*—An employee and his employer may enter into an agreement under section 3402(p)(3)(A) to provide for the withholding of income tax upon payments of amounts described in paragraph (b)(1) of §31.3401(a)-3, made after December 31, 1970. An agreement may be entered into under this section only with respect to amounts which are includible in the gross income of the employee under section 61, and must be applicable to all such amounts paid by the employer to the employee. The amount to be withheld pursuant to an agreement under section 3402(p)(3)(A) shall be determined under the rules contained in section 3402 and the regulations thereunder. See §31.3405(c)-1, Q&A-3 concerning agreements to have more than 20-percent Federal income tax withheld from eligible rollover distributions within the meaning of section 402.

 (b) *Form and duration of employer-employee agreement.*—(1)(i) Except as provided in subdivision (ii) of this subparagraph, an employee who desires to enter into an agreement under section 3402(p)(3)(A) shall furnish his employer with Form W-4 (withholding exemption certificate) executed in accordance with the provisions of section 3402(f) and the regulations thereunder. The furnishing of such Form W-4 shall constitute a request for withholding.

 (ii) In the case of an employee who desires to enter into an agreement under section 3402(p)(3)(A) with his employer, if the employee performs services (in addition to those to be the subject of the agreement) the remuneration for which is subject to mandatory income tax withholding by such employer, or if the employee wishes to specify that the agreement terminate on a specific date, the employee shall furnish the employer with a request for withholding which shall be signed by the employee, and shall contain—

 (a) The name, address, and social security number of the employee making the request,

 (b) The name and address of the employer,

 (c) A statement that the employee desires withholding of Federal income tax, and, if applicable, of qualified State individual income tax (see paragraph (d)(3)(i) of §301.6361-1 of this chapter (Regulations on Procedure and Administration)), and

 (d) If the employee desires that the agreement terminate on a specific date, the date of termination of the agreement.

If accepted by the employer as provided in subdivision (iii) of this subparagraph, the request shall be attached to, and constitute part of, the employee's Form W-4. An employee who furnishes his employer a request for withholding under this subdivision shall also furnish such employer with Form W-4 if such employee does not already have a Form W-4 in effect with such employer.

 (iii) No request for withholding under section 3402(p)(3)(A) shall be effective as an agreement between an employer and an employee until the employer accepts the request by commencing to withhold from the amounts with respect to which the request was made.

 (2) An agreement under section 3402(p)(3)(A) shall be effective for such period as the employer and employee mutually agree upon. However, either the employer or the employee may terminate the agreement prior to the end of such period by furnishing a signed written notice to the other. Unless the employer and employee agree on an earlier termination date, the notice shall be effective with respect to the first payment of an amount in respect of which the agreement is in effect which is made on or after the first "status determination date" (January 1, May 1, July 1, and October 1 of each year) that occurs at least 30 days after the date on which the notice is furnished. If the employee executes a new Form W-4, the request upon which an agreement under section 3402(p)(3)(A) is based shall be attached to, and constitute a part of, such new Form W-4.

 (c) *Other payments.*—The Secretary may issue guidance by publication in the Internal Revenue Bulletin (IRB) (which will be available at www.IRS.gov) describing other payments for which withholding under a voluntary withholding agreement would be appropriate and authorizing payors to agree to withhold income tax on such payments if requested by the payee. Requirements regarding the form and duration of voluntary withholding agreements authorized by this paragraph (c) will be provided in the IRB guidance issued regarding specific types of payments.

 (d) *Effective/applicability date.*—(1) This section applies on and after September 16, 2014. [Reg. §31.3402(p)-1.]

 ☐ [*T.D. 7096, 3-17-71. Amended by T.D. 7577, 12-19-78; T.D. 8619, 9-15-95 and T.D. 9692, 9-15-2014.*]

### [Reg. §31.3402(q)-1]

**§31.3402(q)-1. Extension of withholding to certain gambling winnings.**—(a) *Withholding obligation.*—(1) *General rule.*—Every person, including the Government of the United States, a State, or a political subdivision thereof, or any instrumentality of any of the foregoing making any payment of "winnings subject to withholding" (defined in paragraph (b) of the section) must deduct and withhold a tax in an amount equal to the product of the third lowest rate of tax applicable under section 1(c) and the payment. The tax must be deducted and withheld upon payment of the winnings by the person making the payment ("payer"). See paragraph (c)(5)(ii) of this section for a special rule relating to the time for making deposits of withheld amounts and filing the return with respect to those amounts. Any person receiving a payment of winnings subject to withholding must furnish the payer a statement as required in paragraph (d) of this section. Payers of winnings subject to withholding must file a return with the Internal Revenue Service and furnish a statement to the payee as required in paragraph (e) of this section. With respect to reporting requirements for certain payments of gambling winnings not subject to withholding, see section 6041 and the regulations thereunder.

(2) *Exceptions.*—The tax imposed under section 3402(q)(1) and this section shall not apply (i) with respect to a payment of winnings which is made to a nonresident alien individual or foreign corporation under the circumstances described in paragraph (c)(4) of this section or (ii) with respect to a payment of winnings from a slot machine play, or a keno or bingo game.

(b) *Winnings subject to withholding.*—(1) *In general.*—Winnings subject to withholding means any payment from—

(i) A wager placed in a State-conducted lottery (defined in paragraph (c)(2) of this section) but only if the proceeds from the wager exceed $5,000;

(ii) A wager placed in a sweepstakes, wagering pool, or lottery other than a State-conducted lottery but only if the proceeds from the wager exceed $5,000; or

(iii) Any other wagering transaction (as defined in paragraph (c)(3) of this section) but only if the proceeds from the wager:

(A) Exceed $5,000; and

(B) Are at least 300 times as large as the amount of the wager.

(2) *Total proceeds subject to withholding.*—If proceeds from the wager qualify as winnings subject to withholding, then the total proceeds from the wager, and not merely amounts in excess of $5,000, are subject to withholding.

(c) *Definitions; special rules.*—(1) *Rules for determining amount of proceeds from a wager.*—(i) *In general.*—The amount of proceeds from a wager is the amount paid with respect to the wager, less the amount of the wager.

(ii) *Amount of the wager in the case of horse races, dog races, and jai alai.*—In the case of a wagering transaction with respect to horse races, dog races, or jai alai, all wagers placed in a single parimutuel pool and represented on a single ticket are aggregated and treated as a single wager for purposes of determining the amount of the wager. A ticket in the case of horse races, dog races, or jai alai is a written or electronic record that the payee must present to collect proceeds from a wager or wagers.

(iii) *Amount paid with respect to a wager.*—(A) *Identical wagers.*—Amounts paid with respect to identical wagers are treated as paid with respect to a single wager for purposes of calculating the amount of proceeds from a wager. Two or more wagers are identical wagers if winning depends on the occurrence (or non-occurrence) of the same event or events; the wagers are placed with the same payer; and, in the case of horse races, dog races, or jai alai, the wagers are placed in the same parimutuel pool. Wagers may be identical wagers even if the amounts wagered differ as long as the wagers are otherwise treated as identical wagers under this paragraph (c)(1)(iii)(A). Tickets purchased in a lottery generally are not identical wagers, because the designation of each ticket as a winner generally would not be based on the occurrence of the same event, for example, the drawing of a particular number.

(B) *Non-monetary proceeds.*—In determining the amount paid with respect to a wager, proceeds which are not money are taken into account at the fair market value.

(C) *Periodic payments.*—Periodic payments, including installment payments or payments which are to be made periodically for the life of a person, are aggregated for purposes of determining the amount paid with respect to the wager. The aggregate amount of periodic payments to be made for a person's life is based on that person's life expectancy. See §§ 1.72–5 and 1.72–9 of this chapter for rules used in computing the expected return on annuities. For purposes of determining the amount subject to withholding, the first periodic payment must be reduced by the amount of the wager.

(2) *Wager placed in a State-conducted lottery.*—The term "wager placed in a State-conducted lottery" means a wager placed in a lottery conducted by an agency of the State acting under authority of State law provided that the wager is placed with the State agency conducting such lottery or with its authorized employees or agents. This term includes wagers placed in State- conducted lotteries in which the amount of winnings is determined by a parimutuel system.

(3) *Other wagering transaction.*—The term "other wagering transaction" means any wagering transaction other than one in a lottery, sweepstakes, or wagering pool. This term includes a wagering transaction in a parimutuel pool with respect to horse races, dog races, or jai alai.

(4) *Certain payments to nonresident aliens or foreign corporations.*—A payment of winnings that is subject to withholding tax under section 1441(a) (relating to withholding on nonresident aliens) or 1442(a) (relating to withholding on foreign corporations) is not sub-

ject to the tax imposed by section 3402(q) and this section when the payee is a foreign person, as determined under the rules of section 1441(a) and the regulations thereunder. A payment is treated as being subject to withholding tax under section 1441(a) or 1442(a) notwithstanding that the rate of such tax is reduced (even to zero) as may be provided by an applicable treaty with another country. However, a reduced or zero rate of withholding of tax must not be applied by the payer in lieu of the rate imposed by sections 1441 and 1442 unless the person receiving the winnings has provided to the payer the documentation required by §1.1441–6 of this chapter to establish entitlement to treaty benefits.

(5) *Gambling winnings treated as payments by employer to employee.*—(i) Except as provided in subdivision (ii), for purposes of sections 3403 and 3404 and the regulations thereunder and for purposes of so much of subtitle F (except section 7205) and the regulations thereunder as relate to chapter 24, payments to any person of winnings subject to withholding under this section shall be treated as if they are wages paid by an employer to an employee.

(ii) Solely for purposes of applying the deposit rules under 6302(c) and the return requirement of section 6011, the withholding from winnings shall be deemed to have been made no earlier than at the time the winner's identity is known to the payer. Thus, for example, winnings from a State-conducted lottery are subject to withholding when actually or constructively paid, whichever is earlier; however, the time for depositing the withheld taxes and filing a return with respect thereto shall be determined by reference to the date on which the winner's identity is known to the State, if such date is later than the date on which the winnings are actively or constructively paid. If a payer's obligation to pay winnings terminates other than by payment, all liabilities and requirements resulting from the requirement that the payer deduct and withhold with respect to such winnings shall also terminate.

(d) *Statement furnished by payee.*—(1) *In general.*—Each person who is making a payment subject to withholding under this section must obtain from the payee a statement described in paragraph (d)(2) of this section.

(2) *Contents of statement.*—Each person who is to receive a payment of winnings subject to withholding under this section must furnish the payer a statement on Form W–2G or 5754 (whichever is applicable) made under the penalties of perjury containing—

(i) The name, address, and taxpayer identification number of the winner accompanied by a declaration that no other person is entitled to any portion of such payment, or

(ii) The name, address, and taxpayer identification number of the payee and of every person entitled to any portion of the payment.

(3) *Multiple payments.*—If more than one payment of winnings subject to withholding is to be made with respect to a single wager, for example in the case of an annuity, the payee is required to furnish the payer a statement with respect to the first payment only, provided that the other payments are taken into account in a return required by paragraph (e) of this section.

(4) *Reliance on statement for identical wagers.*—If the payee furnishes the statement which may be required pursuant to § 1.6011–3 of this chapter (regarding the requirement of a statement from payees of certain gambling winnings), indicating that the payee (and any other persons entitled to a portion of the winnings) is entitled to winnings from identical wagers, as defined in paragraph (c)(1)(iii)(A) of this section, and indicating the amount of the winnings, if any, then the payer may rely upon the statement in determining the total amount of proceeds from the wager under paragraph (c)(1) of this section.

(e) *Return of payer.*—(1) *In general.*—Every person making payment of winnings for which a statement is required under paragraph (d) of this section must file a return on Form W–2G at the Internal Revenue Service location designated in the instructions to the form on or before February 28 (March 31 if filed electronically) of the calendar year following the calendar year in which the payment of winnings is made. The return required by this paragraph (e) need not include the statement by the payee required by paragraph (d) of this section and, therefore, need not be signed by the payee, provided the statement is retained by the payer as long as its contents may become material in the administration of any internal revenue law. In addition, the return required by this paragraph (e) need not contain the information required by paragraph (e)(1)(v) of this section provided the information is obtained with respect to the payee and retained by the payer as long as its contents may become material in the administration of any internal revenue law. For payments to more than one winner, a separate Form W–2G, which in no event need be signed by the winner, must be filed with respect to each such winner. Each Form W–2G must contain the following:

(i) The name, address, and taxpayer identification number of the payer;

(ii) The name, address, and taxpayer identification number of the winner;

(iii) The date, amount of the payment, and amount withheld;

(iv) The type of wagering transaction;

(v) Except with respect to winnings from a wager placed in a State-conducted lottery, a general description of the two types of identification (as described in paragraph (e)(2) of this section), one of which must have the payee's photograph on it (except in the case of tribal member identification cards in certain circumstances as described in paragraph (e)(3) of this section), that the payer relied on to verify the payee's name, address, and taxpayer identification number;

(vi) The amount of winnings from identical wagers; and

(vii) Any other information required by the form, instructions, or other applicable guidance published in the Internal Revenue Bulletin.

(2) *Identification.*—The following items are treated as identification for purposes of paragraph (e)(1)(v) of this section—

(i) Government-issued identification (for example, a driver's license, passport, social security card, military identification card, tribal member identification card issued by a federally-recognized Indian tribe, or voter registration card) in the name of the payee; and

(ii) A Form W-9, "Request for Taxpayer Identification Number and Certification," signed by the payee that includes the payee's name, address, taxpayer identification number, and other information required by the form. A Form W-9 is not acceptable for this purpose if the payee has modified the form (other than pursuant to instructions to the form) or if the payee has deleted the jurat or other similar provisions by which the payee certifies or affirms the correctness of the statements contained on the form.

(3) *Special rule for tribal member identification cards.*—A tribal member identification card need not contain the payee's photograph to meet the identification requirement described in paragraph (e)(1)(v) of this section if—

(i) The payee is a member of a federally-recognized Indian tribe;

(ii) The payee presents the payer with a tribal member identification card issued by a federally-recognized Indian tribe stating that the payee is a member of such tribe; and

(iii) The payer is a gaming establishment (as described in § 1.6041-10(b)(2)(iv) of this chapter) owned or licensed (in accordance with 25 U.S.C. 2710) by the tribal government that issued the tribal member identification card referred to in paragraph (e)(3)(ii) of this section.

(4) *Transmittal form.*—Persons making payments of winnings subject to withholding must use Form 1096 to transmit Forms W–2G to the Internal Revenue Service.

(5) *Furnishing a statement to the payee.*—Every payer required to make a return under paragraph (e)(1) of this section must also make and furnish to each payee, with respect to each payment of winnings subject to withholding, a written statement that contains the information that is required to be included on the return under paragraph (e)(1) of this section. The payer must furnish the statement to the payee on or before January 31st of the year following the calendar year in which payment of the winnings subject to withholding is made. The statement will be considered furnished to the payee if it is provided to the payee at the time of payment or if it is mailed to the payee on or before January 31st of the year following the calendar year in which payment was made.

(f) *Examples.*—The provisions of this section may be illustrated by the following examples:

*Example (1).* A purchases a lottery ticket for $1 in the State W lottery from an authorized agent of State W. On February 1, 1977, the drawing is held and A wins $5,001. Since the proceeds of the wager ($5,001 – $1) are not greater than $5,000, State W is not required to withhold or deduct any amount from A's winnings.

*Example (2).* Assume the same facts as in example (1) except that A purchases two $1 tickets and that A wins $5,002 when one of the tickets is drawn. State W must deduct and withhold tax at a rate of 20% from $5,001 ($5,002 less the $1 wager), or $1,000.20.

*Example (3).* C purchases a lottery ticket for $1. On June 1, 1979, the lottery drawing is held and C wins the grand prize of $50,000, payable $500 monthly. The payer must deduct and withhold tax at the rate of 20% from each payment of winnings. Therefore, $99.80 must be withheld from the first monthly payment to B (($500 – $1) × 20% = $99.80) and $100 ($500 × 20%) must be withheld from each monthly payment thereafter.

*Example (4).* Assume the same facts as in example (3), except that C wins an automobile rather than the grand prize. The fair market value of the automobile on the date on which it is made available to C is $10,001. The payer must deduct and withhold a tax of $2,000

(($10,001 – $1) × 20%). This may be accomplished, for example, if C pays $2,000 to the payer. Alternatively, if the payer, as part of the prize, pays all taxes required to be deducted and withheld, the payer must deduct and withhold tax not only on the fair market value of the automobile less the wager, but also on the taxes it pays that are required to be deducted and withheld. This results in a pyramiding of taxes requiring the use of an algebraic formula. Under this formula, the payer must deduct and withhold a tax of 25 percent of the fair market value of the automobile less the wager ($2,500) and, in addition, the payer must indicate on Form W-2G the amount of such winnings as $12,501 ($10,001 + 25% ($10,001 – $1)).

*Example (5).* D purchases a ticket for $1 in the State Y lottery from an authorized agent of State Y. On January 1, 1976, a drawing is held and D wins $100 a month for the rest of D's life. It is actuarially determined that, on January 3, 1977, D's life expectancy is 5 years. Based on that determination, the proceeds from the wager paid to D on or after January 3, 1977, will exceed $5,000. Therefore, State Y must deduct and withhold $20 from each monthly payment made on or after January 3, 1977. (None of such payments is reduced by the amount of the wager because the amount of the wager was offset by the first payment of winnings which was made before January 3, 1977).

*Example (6).* Assume the same facts as in example (5) except that State Y purchases in its own name, as owner, an annuity of $100 a month for D's life from E Corporation, in order to fund its own obligation to make the payments. Although State Y remains liable for the withholding of tax, E Corporation as paying agent for State Y, making payments directly to D, should deduct and withhold from each monthly payment in the manner described in example (5).

*Example (7).* E purchases a sweepstakes ticket for $1 in a sweepstakes conducted by W. E purchases the ticket on behalf of himself and on behalf of F and G, who have contributed equal amounts toward the purchase of the ticket and who have agreed to share equally in any prizes won. The ticket which E purchases wins $1,002. Since the proceeds of the wager ($1,002 – $1) are greater than $1,000 W is required to withhold and deduct 20 percent of such proceeds.

*Example (8).* On February 1, 1977, a drawing is held in the State X lottery in which a winning ticket is selected. The person holding the winning ticket is entitled to proceeds of $100,000 payable either as a lump sum upon demand or $10,000 a year for 10 years. Under State law, the winning ticket must be presented to an authorized agent of State X before February 1, 1978. Until the ticket is presented, State X does not know the identity of the winner. On December 1, 1977, H, the winner, presents the winning ticket to an authorized agent of the State X lottery. The winnings are constructively paid to H on February 1, 1977. Since H has the option of receiving the entire proceeds upon demand, State X is required to deduct and withhold $20,000 ($100,000 × 20%) from the proceeds of H's winnings on February 1, 1977; but for purposes of determining the time at which the deposit and inclusion on Form 941 of these taxes is to be made, the withholding shall be deemed to have been made on December 1, 1977.

*Example (9).* J purchases a subscription to N magazine, at the regular subscription price. All new subscribers are automatically eligible for a special drawing. The drawing is held and J wins $50,000. Since J has not paid any more than the regular subscription price, J has not placed a wager or entered a wagering transaction. Therefore, N is not required to deduct and withhold from J's winnings.

*Example 10.* (i) B places a $15 bet at the cashier window at the racetrack for horse A to win the fifth race at the racetrack that day. After placing the first bet, B gains confidence in horse A's prospects to win and places an additional $40 bet at the cashier window at the racetrack for horse A to win the fifth race, receiving a second ticket for this second bet. Horse A wins the fifth race, and B wins a total of $5,500 (100 to 1 odds) on those bets. The $15 bet and the $40 bet are identical wagers under paragraph (c)(1)(iii)(A) of this section because winning on both bets depended on the occurrence of the same event and the bets are placed in the same parimutuel pool with the same payer. This is true regardless of the fact that the amount of the wager differs in each case.

(ii) B cashes the tickets at different cashier windows. Pursuant to paragraph (d) of this section and § 1.6011-3, B completes a Form W-2G indicating that the amount of winnings is from identical wagers and provides the form to each cashier. The payments by each cashier of $1,500 and $4,000 are less than the $5,000 threshold for withholding, but under paragraph (c)(1)(iii)(A) of this section, identical wagers are treated as paid with respect to a single wager for purposes of determining the proceeds from a wager. The payment is not subject to withholding or reporting because although the proceeds from the wager are $5,445 ($1,500 + $4,000 - $55), the proceeds from the wager are not at least 300 times as great as the amount wagered ($55 x 300 = $16,500).

*Example 11.* B makes two $1,000 bets in a single "show" pool for the same jai alai game, one bet on Player X to show and one bet on

Player Y to show. A show bet is a winning bet if the player comes in first, second, or third in a single game. The bets are placed at the same time at the same cashier window, and B receives a single ticket showing both bets. Player X places second in the game, and Player Y does not place first, second, or third in the game. B wins $8,000 from his bet on Player X. Because winning on both bets does not depend on the occurrence of the same event, the bets are not identical bets under paragraph (c)(1)(iii)(A) of this section. However, pursuant to the rule in paragraph (c)(1)(ii) of this section, the amount of the wager is the aggregate amount of both wagers ($2,000) because the bets were placed in a single parimutuel pool and reflected on a single ticket. The payment is not subject to withholding or reporting because although the proceeds from the wager are $6,000 ($8,000 - $2,000), the proceeds from the wager are not at least 300 times as great as the amount wagered ($2,000 x 300 = $600,000).

*Example 12.* B bets a total of $120 on a three-dog exacta box bet ($20 for each one of the six combinations played) at the dog racetrack and receives a single ticket reflecting the bet from the cashier. B wins $5,040 from one of the selected combinations. Pursuant to the rule in paragraph (c)(1)(ii) of this section, the amount of the wager is $120, not $20 for the single winning combination of the six combinations played. The payment is not subject to withholding under section 3402(q) because the proceeds from the wager are $4,920 ($5,040-$120), which is below the section 3402(q) withholding threshold.

*Example 13.* B makes two $12 Pick 6 bets at the horse racetrack at two different cashier windows and receives two different tickets each representing a single $12 Pick 6 bet. In his two Pick 6 bets, B selects the same horses to win races 1-5 but selects different horses to win race 6. All Pick 6 bets on those races at that racetrack are part of a single parimutuel pool from which Pick 6 winning bets are paid. B wins $5,020 from one of his Pick 6 bets. Pursuant to the rule in paragraph (c)(1)(ii) of this section, the bets are not aggregated for purposes of determining the amount of the wager because the bets are reflected on separate tickets. Assuming that the applicable rate is 25%, the racetrack must deduct and withhold $1,252 (($5,020-$12) x 25%) because the amount of the proceeds of $5,008 ($5,020 - $12) is greater than $5,000 and is at least 300 times as great as the amount wagered ($12 x 300 = $3,600). The racetrack also must report B's winnings on Form W-2G pursuant to paragraph (e) of this section and furnish a copy of the Form W-2G to B.

*Example 14.* C makes two $50 bets in two different parimutuel pools for the same jai alai game. One bet is an "exacta" in which C bets on player M to win and player N to "place." The other bet is a "trifecta" in which C bets on player M to win, player N to "place," and player O to "show." C wins both bets and is paid $2,000 with respect to the bet in the "exacta" pool and $3,100 with respect to the bet in the "trifecta" pool. Under paragraph (c)(1)(iii)(A) of this section, the bets are not identical bets. Under paragraph (c)(1)(ii) of this section, the bets are not aggregated for purposes of determining the amount of the wager for either payment because they are not wagers in the same parimutuel pool. No section 3402(q) withholding is required on either payment because neither payment separately exceeds the $5,000 withholding threshold.

*Example 15.* C makes two $100 bets for the same dog to win a particular race. C places one bet at the racetrack and one bet at an off-track betting establishment, but the two pools constitute a single pool. C receives separate tickets for each bet. C wins both bets and is paid $4,000 from the racetrack and $4,000 from the off-track betting establishment. Under paragraph (c)(1)(ii) of this section, the bets are not aggregated for purposes of determining the amount of the wager because the wager placed at the racetrack and the wager placed at the off-track betting establishment are reflected on separate tickets, despite being placed in the same parimutuel pool. No section 3402(q) withholding is required because neither payment separately exceeds the $5,000 withholding threshold.

*Example 16.* C places a $200 Pick 6 bet for a series of races at the racetrack on a particular day and receives a single ticket for the bet. No wager correctly picks all six races that day, so that portion of the pool carries over to the following day. On the following day, C places an additional $200 Pick 6 bet for that day's series of races and receives a new ticket for that bet. C wins $100,000 on the second day. Pursuant to the rule in paragraph (c)(1)(ii) of this section, the bets are on two separate tickets, so C's two Pick 6 bets are not aggregated for purposes of determining the amount of the wager. Assuming that the applicable rate is 25%, the racetrack must deduct and withhold $24,950 (($100,000 - $200) x 25%) because the amount of the proceeds of $99,800 ($100,000 - $200) is greater than $5,000, and is at least 300 times as great as the amount wagered ($200 x 300 = $60,000). The racetrack also must report C's winnings on Form W-2G pursuant to paragraph (e) of this section and furnish a copy of the Form W-2G to C.

(g) *Applicability date.*—The rules in this section apply to payments made with respect to a winning event that occurs after November 13, 2017. For rules that apply to payments made with respect to a

winning event on or before that date, see §31.3402(q)-1 as contained in 26 CFR part 31, revised April 1, 2017. [Reg. §31.3402(q)-1.]

☐ [*T.D.* 7787, 9-22-81. *Amended by T.D.* 7919, 10-11-83; *T.D.* 7943, 2-10-84; *T.D.* 8895, 8-17-2000 *and T.D.* 9824, 9-25-2017.]

## [Reg. §31.3402(r)-1]

**§31.3402(r)-1. Withholding on distributions of Indian gaming profits to tribal members.**—(a)(1) *General rule.*—Section 3402(r)(1) requires every person, including an Indian tribe, making a payment to a member of an Indian tribe from the net revenues of any class II or class III gaming activity, as defined in 25 U.S.C. 2703, conducted or licensed by such tribe to deduct and withhold from such payment a tax in an amount equal to such payment's proportionate share of the annualized tax, as that term is defined in section 3402(r)(3).

(2) *Withholding tables.*—Except as provided in paragraph (a)(4) of this section, the amount of a payment's proportionate share of the annualized tax shall be determined under the applicable table provided by the Commissioner.

(3) *Annualized amount of payment.*—Section 3402(r)(5) provides that payments shall be placed on an annualized basis under regulations prescribed by the Secretary. A payment may be placed on an annualized basis by multiplying the amount of the payment by the total number of payments to be made in a calendar year. For example, a monthly payment may be annualized by multiplying the amount of the payment by 12. Similarly, a quarterly payment may be annualized by multiplying the amount of the payment by 4.

(4) *Alternate withholding procedures.*—(i) *In general.*—Any procedure for determining the amount to be deducted and withheld under section 3402(r) may be used, provided that the amount of tax deducted and withheld is substantially the same as it would be using the tables provided by the Commissioner under paragraph (a)(2) of this section. At the election of an Indian tribe, the amount to be deducted and withheld under section 3402(r) shall be determined in accordance with this alternate procedure.

(ii) *Method of election.*—It is sufficient for purposes of making an election under this paragraph (a)(4) that an Indian tribe evidence the election in any reasonable way, including use of a particular method. Thus, no written election is required.

(5) *Additional withholding permitted.*—Consistent with the provisions of section 3402(p), a tribal member and a tribe may enter into an agreement to provide for the deduction and withholding of additional amounts from payments in order to satisfy the anticipated tax liability of the tribal member. The agreement may be made in a manner similar to that described in §31.3402(p)-1 (with respect to voluntary withholding agreements between employees and employers).

(b) *Effective date.*—This section applies to payments made after December 31, 1994. [Reg. §31.3402(r)-1.]

☐ [*T.D.* 8634, 12-18-95.]

## [Reg. §31.3403-1]

**§31.3403-1. Liability for tax.**—Every employer required to deduct and withhold the tax under section 3402 from the wages of an employee is liable for the payment of such tax whether or not it is collected from the employee by the employer. If, for example, the employer deducts less than the correct amount of tax, or if he fails to deduct any part of the tax, he is nevertheless liable for the correct amount of the tax. See, however, §31.3402(d)-1. The employer is relieved of liability to any other person for the amount of any such tax withheld and paid to the district director or deposited with a duly designated depositary of the United States. [Reg. §31.3403-1.]

☐ [*T.D.* 6259, 10-25-57.]

## [Reg. §31.3404-1]

**§31.3404-1. Return and payment by governmental employer.**—If the United States, or a State, Territory, Puerto Rico, or a political subdivision thereof, or the District of Columbia, or any agency or instrumentality of any one or more of the foregoing, is an employer required to deduct and withhold tax under chapter 24, the return of the amount deducted and withheld as such tax may be made by the officer or employee having control of the payment of the wages or other officer or employee appropriately designated for that purpose. (For provisions relating to the execution and filing of returns, see Subpart G of the regulations in this part.) [Reg. §31.3404-1.]

☐ [*T.D.* 6259, 10-25-57.]

## [Reg. §31.3405(a)-1]

**§31.3405(a)-1. Questions and answers relating to Federal income tax withholding on periodic retirement and annuity payments.**—

(a) The following questions and answers relate to Federal income tax withholding on periodic payments under section 3405(a), as amended by section 11041(c)(2)(G) of the Tax Cuts and Jobs Act (Public Law 115-97, 131 Stat. 2054 (2017)). The withholding rules of section 3405(a) do not apply to periodic payments that are eligible rollover distributions (as defined in section 402(f)(2)(A)). See generally section 3405(c) and §31.3405(c)-1 for Federal income tax withholding rules applicable to eligible rollover distributions. See section 3405(e)(13) for additional rules applicable to certain periodic payments under section 3405(a) and nonperiodic distributions under section 3405(b) that are to be delivered outside the United States and its possessions. For additional guidance regarding periodic payments, see §§ 35.3405-1 and 35.3405-1T of this chapter.

(b)(1) Q-1: How will Federal income tax be withheld from a periodic payment?

(2) A-1: In the case of a periodic payment that is subject to withholding under section 3405(a), amounts are withheld as if the payment were a payment of wages by an employer to the employee for the appropriate payroll period. If the payee has not furnished a withholding certificate, the amount to be withheld is determined in the manner described in the applicable forms, instructions, publications, and other guidance prescribed by the Commissioner. The rules for withholding when the payee has not furnished a withholding certificate apply regardless of whether the payor is aware of the payee's actual marital status or actual Federal income tax filing status.

(c)(1) Q-2: Do rules similar to those for wage withholding apply to the furnishing of a withholding certificate for periodic payments?

(2) A-2: Yes. Unless the rules of section 3405 specifically conflict with the rules of section 3402, the rules for withholding on periodic payments that are not eligible rollover distributions will parallel the rules for wage withholding. Thus, if a withholding certificate is furnished by a payee, it will generally take effect in accordance with section 3402(f)(3) and as provided in applicable forms, instructions, publications, and other guidance prescribed by the Commissioner. If no withholding certificate is furnished, the amount withheld must be determined in the manner described in the applicable forms, instructions, publications, and other guidance prescribed by the Commissioner for withholding on periodic payments when no withholding certificate is furnished.

(d)(1) Q-3: What is the applicability date of this section?

(2) A-3: This section applies with respect to periodic payments made after December 31, 2020. [Reg. § 31.3405(a)-1.]

☐ [*T.D. 9920, 9-30-2020.*]

### [Reg. § 31.3405(c)-1]

**§ 31.3405(c)-1. Withholding on eligible rollover distributions; questions and answers.**—The following questions and answers relate to withholding on eligible rollover distributions under section 3405(c) of the Internal Revenue Code of 1986, as added by section 522(b) of the Unemployment Compensation Amendments of 1992 (Public Law 102-318, 106 Stat. 290) (UCA). For additional UCA guidance under sections 401(a)(31), 402(c), 402(f), and 403(b)(8) and (10), see §§ 1.401(a)(31)-1, 1.402(c)-2, 1.402(f)-1, and 1.403(b)-2 of this chapter, respectively.

### LIST OF QUESTIONS

Q-1: What are the withholding requirements under section 3405 for distributions from qualified plans and section 403(b) annuities?

Q-2: May a distributee elect under section 3405(c) not to have Federal income tax withheld from an eligible rollover distribution?

Q-3: May a distributee be permitted to elect to have more than 20-percent Federal income tax withheld from an eligible rollover distribution?

Q-4: Who has responsibility for complying with section 3405(c) relating to the 20-percent income tax withholding on eligible rollover distributions?

Q-5: May the plan administrator shift the withholding responsibility to the payor and, if so, how?

Q-6: How does the 20-percent withholding requirement under section 3405(c) apply if a distributee elects to have a portion of an eligible rollover distribution paid to an eligible retirement plan in a direct rollover and to have the remainder of that distribution paid to the distributee?

Q-7: Will the plan administrator be subject to liability for tax, interest, or penalties for failure to withhold 20 percent from an eligible rollover distribution that, because of erroneous information provided by a distributee, is not paid to an eligible retirement plan even though the distributee elected a direct rollover?

Q-8: Is an eligible rollover distribution that is paid to a qualified defined benefit plan subject to 20-percent withholding?

Q-9: If property other than cash, employer securities, or plan loans is distributed, how is the 20-percent income tax withholding required under section 3405(c) accomplished?

Q-10: What assumptions may a plan administrator make regarding whether a benefit is an eligible rollover distribution for purposes of determining the amount of a distribution that is subject to 20-percent mandatory withholding?

Q-11: Are there special rules for applying the 20-percent withholding requirement to employer securities and a plan loan offset amount distributed in an eligible rollover distribution?

Q-12: How does the mandatory withholding rule apply to net unrealized appreciation from employer securities?

Q-13: Does the 20-percent withholding requirement apply to eligible rollover distributions from a qualified plan distributed annuity contract?

Q-14: Must a payor or plan administrator withhold tax from an eligible rollover distribution for which a direct rollover election was not made if the amount of the distribution is less than $200?

Q-15: If eligible rollover distributions are made from a qualified plan, who has responsibility for making the returns and reports required under these regulations?

Q-16: What eligible rollover distributions must be reported on Form 1099-R?

Q-17: Must the plan administrator, trustee or custodian of the eligible retirement plan report amounts received in a direct rollover?

### QUESTIONS AND ANSWERS

Q-1: What are the withholding requirements under section 3405 for distributions from qualified plans and section 403(b) annuities?

A-1: (a) *General rule.* Section 3405(c), added by UCA, provides that any designated distribution that is an eligible rollover distribution (as defined in section 402(f)(2)(A)) from a qualified plan or a section 403(b) annuity is subject to income tax withholding at the rate of 20 percent unless the distributee of the eligible rollover distribution elects to have the distribution paid directly to an eligible retirement plan in a direct rollover. See § 1.402(c)-2, Q&A-2 of this chapter for the definition of a qualified plan and § 1.403(b)-7(b) of this chapter for the definition of a section 403(b) annuity. For purposes of section 3405 and this section, with respect to a distribution from a qualified plan, an eligible retirement plan is a trust qualified under section 401(a), an annuity plan described in section 403(a), or an individual retirement plan (as described in § 1.402(c)-2, Q&A-2 of this chapter). For purposes of section 3405 and this section, with respect to a distribution from a section 403(b) annuity, an eligible retirement plan is an annuity contract, a custodial account, a retirement income account described in section 403(b), or an individual retirement plan. If a designated distribution is not an eligible rollover distribution, it is subject to the elective withholding provisions of section 3405(a) and (b) and § 35.3405-1 of this chapter and is not subject to the mandatory withholding provisions of section 3405(c) and this section.

(b) *Application of other statutory provisions.* See § 1.401(a)(31)-1 of this chapter concerning the requirements and the procedures for electing a direct rollover under section 401(a)(31). See section 402(c)(2) and (4), and § 1.402(c)-2, Q&A-3 through Q&A-10 and Q&A-14 of this chapter for rules to determine what constitutes an eligible rollover distribution. See § 1.402(f)-1, Q&A-1 through Q&A-3 and § 1.403(b)-7(b) of this chapter concerning the notice that must be provided to a distributee, within a reasonable period of time before making an eligible rollover distribution. See § 1.403(b)-7(b) of this chapter for guidance concerning the rollover provisions and direct rollover requirements for distributions from annuities described in section 403(b).

(c) *Effective date*—(1) *Statutory effective date*—(i) *General rule.* Section 3405(c), as added by UCA, applies to eligible rollover distributions made on or after January 1, 1993, even if the employee's employment with the employer maintaining the plan terminated before January 1, 1993 and even if the eligible rollover distribution is part of a series of payments that began before January 1, 1993.

(ii) *Special rule for governmental section 403(b) annuities.* Section 522 of UCA provides a special effective date for governmental section 403(b) annuities. This special effective date appears in § 1.403(b)-2T of this chapter (as it appeared in the April 1, 1995 edition of 26 CFR part 1).

(2) *Regulatory effective date.* This section applies to eligible rollover distributions made on or after October 19, 1995. For eligible rollover distributions made on or after January 1, 1993 and before October 19, 1995, § 31.3405(c)-1T (as it appeared in the April 1, 1995 edition of 26 CFR part 1), applies. However, for any distribution made on or after January 1, 1993 but before October 19, 1995, a plan administrator or payor may comply with the withholding requirements of section 3405(c) by substituting any or all provisions of this section for the corresponding provisions of § 31.3405(c)-1T, if any.

Q-2: May a distributee elect under section 3405(c) not to have Federal income tax withheld from an eligible rollover distribution?

A-2: No. The 20-percent income tax withholding imposed under section 3405(c)(1) applies to an eligible rollover distribution unless the distributee elects under section 401(a)(31) to have the eligible rollover distribution paid directly to an eligible retirement plan in a direct rollover. See § 1.401(a)(31)-1 and § 1.403(b)-7(b) of this chapter for provisions concerning the requirement that a distributee of an eligible rollover distribution be permitted to elect a distribution in the form of a direct rollover.

Q-3: May a distributee be permitted to elect to have more than 20-percent Federal income tax withheld from an eligible rollover distribution?

A-3: Yes. Under section 3402(p), a distributee of an eligible rollover distribution and the plan administrator or payor are permitted to enter into an agreement to provide for withholding in excess of 20 percent from an eligible rollover distribution. Any agreement must be made in accordance with applicable forms and instructions. However, no request for withholding will be effective between the plan administrator or payor and the distributee until the plan administrator or payor accepts the request by commencing to withhold from the amounts with respect to which the request was made. An agreement under section 3402(p) shall be effective for such period as the plan administrator or payor and the distributee mutually agree upon. However, either party to the agreement may terminate the agreement prior to the end of such period by furnishing a signed written notice to the other.

Q-4: Who has responsibility for complying with section 3405(c) relating to the 20-percent income tax withholding on eligible rollover distributions?

A-4: Section 3405(d) generally requires the plan administrator of a qualified plan and the payor of a section 403(b) annuity to withhold under section 3405(c)(1) an amount equal to 20 percent of the portion of an eligible rollover distribution that the distributee does not elect to have paid in a direct rollover. When an amount is paid under a qualified plan distributed annuity contract as defined in § 1.402(c)-2, Q&A-10 of this chapter, the payor is treated as the plan administrator. See Q&A-13 of this section concerning eligible rollover distributions from a qualified plan distributed annuity contract.

Q-5: May the plan administrator shift the withholding responsibility to the payor and, if so, how?

A-5: Yes. The plan administrator may shift the withholding responsibility to the payor by following the procedures set forth in § 35.3405-1, Q&A E-2 through E-5 of this chapter (relating to elective withholding on pensions, annuities and certain other deferred income) with appropriate adjustments, including the plan administrator's identification of amounts that constitute required minimum distributions.

Q-6: How does the 20-percent withholding requirement under section 3405(c) apply if a distributee elects to have a portion of an eligible rollover distribution paid to an eligible retirement plan in a direct rollover and to have the remainder of that distribution paid to the distributee?

A-6: If a distributee elects to have a portion of an eligible rollover distribution paid to an eligible retirement plan in a direct rollover and to receive the remainder of the distribution, the 20-percent withholding requirement under section 3405(c) applies only to the portion of the eligible rollover distribution that the distributee receives and not to the portion that is paid in a direct rollover.

Q-7: Will the plan administrator be subject to liability for tax, interest, or penalties for failure to withhold 20 percent from an eligible rollover distribution that, because of erroneous information provided by a distributee, is not paid to an eligible retirement plan even though the distributee elected a direct rollover?

A-7: (a) *General rule.* If the plan administrator reasonably relied on adequate information provided by the distributee (as described in paragraph (b) of this Q&A), the plan administrator will not be subject to liability for taxes, interest, or penalties for failure to withhold income tax from an eligible rollover distribution solely because the distribution is paid to an account or plan that is not an eligible retirement plan (as defined, with respect to distributions from qualified plans, in section 402(c)(8)(B) and § 1.402(c)-2, Q&A-2 of this chapter and, with respect to a distributions from section 403(b) annuities, in § 1.403(b)-7(b) of this chapter. Although the plan administrator is not required to verify independently the accuracy of information provided by the distributee, the plan administrator's reliance on the information furnished must be reasonable. For example, it is not reasonable for the plan administrator to rely on information that is clearly erroneous on its face.

(b) *Adequate information.* The plan administrator has obtained from the distributee adequate information on which to rely in making a direct rollover if the distributee furnishes to the plan administrator: the name of the eligible retirement plan; a representation that the recipient plan is an individual retirement plan, a qualified plan, or a section 403(b) annuity, as appropriate; and any other information that is necessary in order to permit the plan administrator to accomplish the direct rollover by the means it has selected. This information must include any information needed to comply with the specific requirements of § 1.401(a)(31)-1, Q&A-3 and Q&A-4 of this

chapter. For example, if the direct rollover is to be made by mailing a check to the trustee of an individual retirement account, the plan administrator must obtain, in addition to the name of the individual retirement account and the representation described above, the name and address of the trustee of the individual retirement account.

Q-8: Is an eligible rollover distribution that is paid to a qualified defined benefit plan subject to 20-percent withholding?

A-8: No. If an eligible rollover distribution is paid in a direct rollover to an eligible retirement plan within the meaning of section 402(c)(8), including a qualified defined benefit plan, it is reasonable to believe that the distribution is not includible in gross income pursuant to section 402(c)(1). Accordingly, pursuant to section 3405(e)(1)(B), the distribution is not a designated distribution and is not subject to 20-percent withholding.

Q-9: If property other than cash, employer securities, or plan loans is distributed, how is the 20-percent income tax withholding required under section 3405(c) accomplished?

A-9: When all or a portion of an eligible rollover distribution subject to 20-percent income tax withholding under section 3405(c) consists of property other than cash, employer securities, or plan loan offset amounts, the plan administrator or payor must apply § 35.3405-1, Q&A F-2 of this chapter and may apply § 35.3405-1, Q&A F-3 of this chapter in determining how to satisfy the withholding requirements.

Q-10: What assumptions may a plan administrator make regarding whether a benefit is an eligible rollover distribution for purposes of determining the amount of a distribution that is subject to 20-percent mandatory withholding?

A-10: (a) *In general.* For purposes of determining the amount of a distribution that is subject to 20-percent mandatory withholding, a plan administrator may make the assumptions described in paragraphs (b), (c), and (d) of this Q&A in determining the amount of a distribution that is an eligible rollover distribution and a designated distribution. Section 1.401(a)(31)-1, Q&A-18 of this chapter provides assumptions for purposes of complying with section 401(a)(31). See § 1.402(c)-2, Q&A-15 of this chapter concerning the effect of these assumptions for purposes of section 402(c).

(b) *$5,000 death benefit.* A plan administrator may assume that a distribution that qualifies for the $5,000 death benefit exclusion under section 101(b) is the only death benefit being paid with respect to a deceased employee that qualifies for that exclusion. Thus, in such a case, the plan administrator may assume that the distribution is not an eligible rollover distribution to the extent that it would be excludible from gross income based on this assumption.

(c) *Required minimum distributions.* The plan administrator is permitted to determine the amount of the minimum distribution required to satisfy section 401(a)(9)(A) for any calendar year by assuming that there is no designated beneficiary.

(d) *Valuation of property.* In the case of a distribution that includes property, in calculating the amount of the distribution for purposes of applying section 3405(c), the value of the property may be determined in accordance with § 35.3405-1, Q&A F-1 of this chapter.

Q-11: Are there special rules for applying the 20-percent withholding requirement to employer securities and a plan loan offset amount distributed in an eligible rollover distribution?

A-11: Yes. The maximum amount to be withheld on any designated distribution (including any eligible rollover distribution) under section 3405(c) must not exceed the sum of the cash and the fair market value of property (excluding employer securities) received in the distribution. The amount of the sum is determined without regard to whether any portion of the cash or property is a designated distribution or an eligible rollover distribution. For purposes of this rule, any plan loan offset amount, as defined in § 1.402(c)-2, Q&A-9 of this chapter, is treated in the same manner as employer securities. Thus, although employer securities and plan loan offset amounts must be included in the amount that is multiplied by 20-percent, the total amount required to be withheld for an eligible rollover distribution is limited to the sum of the cash and the fair market value of property received by the distributee, excluding any amount of the distribution that is a plan loan offset amount or that is distributed in the form of employer securities. For example, if the only portion of an eligible rollover distribution that is not paid in a direct rollover consists of employer securities or a plan loan offset amount, withholding is not required. In addition, if a distribution consists solely of employer securities and cash (not in excess of $200) in lieu of fractional shares, no amount is required to be withheld as income tax from the distribution under section 3405 (including section 3405(c) and this section). For purposes of section 3405 and this section, employer securities means securities of the employer corporation within the meaning of section 402(e)(4)(E)(ii).

Q-12: How does the mandatory withholding rule apply to net unrealized appreciation from employer securities?

A-12: An eligible rollover distribution can include net unrealized appreciation from employer securities, within the meaning of section

402(e)(4), even if the net unrealized appreciation is excluded from gross income under section 402(e)(4). However, to the extent that it is excludible from gross income pursuant to section 402(e)(4), net unrealized appreciation is not a designated distribution pursuant to section 3405(e)(1)(B) because it is reasonable to believe that it is not includible in gross income. Thus, to the extent that net unrealized appreciation is excludible from gross income pursuant to section 402(e)(4), net unrealized appreciation is not included in the amount of an eligible rollover distribution that is subject to 20-percent withholding.

Q-13: Does the 20-percent withholding requirement apply to eligible rollover distributions from a qualified plan distributed annuity contract?

A-13: The 20-percent withholding requirement applies to eligible rollover distributions from a qualified plan distributed annuity contract as defined in Q&A-10 of § 1.402(c)-2 of this chapter. In the case of an eligible rollover distribution from such an annuity contract, the payor is treated as the plan administrator for purposes of section 3405. See § 1.401(a)(31)-1, Q&A-17 of this chapter concerning the direct rollover requirements that apply to distributions from such an annuity contract and see § 1.402(c)-2, Q&A-10 of this chapter concerning the treatment of distributions from such annuity contracts as eligible rollover distributions.

Q-14: Must a payor or plan administrator withhold tax from an eligible rollover distribution for which a direct rollover election was not made if the amount of the distribution is less than $200?

A-14: No. However, all eligible rollover distributions received within one taxable year of the distributee under the same plan must be aggregated for purposes of determining whether the $200 floor is reached. If the plan administrator or payor does not know at the time of the first distribution (that is less than $200) whether there will be additional eligible rollover distributions during the year for which aggregation is required, the plan administrator need not withhold from the first distribution. If distributions are made within one taxable year under more than one plan of an employer, the plan administrator or payor may, but need not, aggregate distributions for purposes of determining whether the $200 floor is reached. However, once the $200 threshold has been reached, the sum of all payments during the year must be used to determine the applicable amount to be withheld from subsequent payments during the year.

Q-15: If eligible rollover distributions are made from a qualified plan, who has responsibility for making the returns and reports required under these regulations?

A-15: Generally, the plan administrator, as defined in section 414(g), is responsible for maintaining the records and making the required reports with respect to eligible rollover distributions from qualified plans. However, if the plan administrator fails to keep the required records and make the required reports, the employer maintaining the plan is responsible for the reports and returns.

Q-16: What eligible rollover distributions must be reported on Form 1099-R?

A-16: Each eligible rollover distribution, including each eligible rollover distribution that is paid directly to an eligible retirement plan in a direct rollover, must be reported on Form 1099-R in accordance with the instructions for Form 1099-R. For purposes of the reporting required under section 6047(e), a direct rollover is treated as a distribution that is immediately rolled over to an eligible retirement plan. Distributions that are not eligible rollover distributions are subject to the reporting requirements set forth in § 35.3405-1 of this chapter and applicable forms and instructions.

Q-17: Must the plan administrator, trustee or custodian of the eligible retirement plan report amounts received in a direct rollover?

A-17: (a) *Individual retirement plan.* If a distributee elects to have an eligible rollover distribution paid to an individual retirement plan in a direct rollover, the eligible rollover distribution is reported on Form 5498 as a rollover contribution to the individual retirement plan, in accordance with the instructions for Form 5498.

(b) *Qualified plan or section 403(b) annuity.* If a distributee elects to have an eligible rollover distribution paid to a qualified plan or section 403(b) annuity, the recipient plan or annuity is not required to report the receipt of the rollover contribution.

[Reg. § 31.3405(c)-1.]

☐ [*T.D. 8619, 9-15-95. Amended by T.D. 8880, 4-20-2000 and T.D. 9340, 7-23-2007.*]

### [Reg. § 35.3405-1]

**§ 35.3405-1. Questions and answers relating to withholding on pensions, annuities, and certain other deferred income.**—The following questions and answers relate to withholding on pensions, annuities, and other deferred income under section 3405 of the Internal Revenue Code of 1986, as added by section 334 of the Tax Equity and Fiscal Responsibility Tax Act of 1982 (Public Law 97-248) (TEFRA).

a-1 through d-34 [Reserved]. For further guidance, see § 35.3405-1T.

d-35. Q. *Through what medium may a payor provide the notice required under section 3405 to a payee?*

A. A payor may provide the notice required under section 3405 (including the abbreviated notice described in d-27 of § 35.3405-1T and the annual notice described in d-31 of § 35.3405-1T) to a payee on a written paper document. However, see § 1.401(a)-21 of this chapter for rules permitting the use of electronic media to provide applicable notices to recipients with respect to retirement plans and individual retirement plans.

[Reg. § 35.3405-1.]

☐ [*T.D. 8873, 2-7-2000 (corrected 3-30-2000) and T.D. 9294, 10-19-2006.*]

### [Reg. § 35.3405-1T]

**§ 35.3405-1T. Questions and answers relating to withholding on pensions, annuities, and certain other deferred income (temporary).**—The following questions and answers relate to withholding on pensions, annuities, and other deferred income under section 3405 of the Internal Revenue Code of 1954, as added by section 334 of the Tax Equity and Fiscal Responsibility Act of 1982 (P.L. 97-248) (TEFRA):

*TABLE OF CONTENTS*

A. In general.
B. Periodic payments.
C. Nonperiodic distributions.
D. Notice and election procedures.
E. Reporting and recordkeeping.

*A. In general.*

A-1. Q. How did TEFRA change the law on withholding requirements for pensions, annuities, and other deferred income?

A. TEFRA amended the Internal Revenue Code to impose withholding requirements on designated distributions paid after December 31, 1982. Further, although under prior law individuals could elect to have Federal income tax withheld from certain pension and annuity payments, TEFRA requires withholding on all designated distributions unless the payee elects not to have withholding apply.

A-2. Q. What type of payment is a designated distribution that is subject to the new withholding rules?

A. A designated distribution is any distribution or payment from or under an employer deferred compensation plan, an individual retirement plan (as defined in section 7701(a)(37)), or a commercial annuity. However, a designated distribution does not include any portion of a distribution which it is reasonable to believe is not includible in the gross income of the payee. For rules concerning when it is reasonable to believe that all or part of a distribution is not includible in the gross income of the recipient, see questions A-24 through A-33. In addition, a payment or distribution that is treated as wages under section 3401(a) is not a designated distribution subject to the new withholding rules. For examples of these payments, see questions A-18 through A-23.

A-3. Q. What is an employer deferred compensation plan for purposes of the new withholding rules?

A. An employer deferred compensation plan is any pension, annuity, profit-sharing, stock bonus, or other plan that defers the receipt of compensation.

A-4. Q. What is a commercial annuity for purposes of the new withholding rules?

A. A commercial annuity is an annuity, endowment, or life insurance contract issued by an insurance company licensed to do business under the laws of any State. See, also, question F-21.

A-5. Q. When does the new law take effect?

A. In general, withholding is required on any designated distribution made after December 31, 1982. In the case of periodic payments beginning before January 1, 1983, the first payment after December 31, 1982 is treated as the first periodic payment for purposes of the withholding requirements. The Secretary has authority to delay (but not beyond June 30, 1983) the application of these withholding provisions to any payor if the payor can establish that it is impossible to comply with these provisions without undue hardship. Additionally, no penalty will be imposed for failure to withhold on periodic payments if the failure occurs before July 1, 1983, and if a good faith attempt is made to comply.

Procedures for requesting a delay in implementation of the withholding provisions are under consideration.

A-6. Q. What effect does the new law have on the old law provisions relating to withholding of tax from annuity payments by request?

A. If payment is part of a designated distribution, the rules of section 3402(o) (relating to voluntary withholding on certain payments) do not apply. Therefore, a payee receiving amounts that are subject to withholding under the new provisions described in this regulation may not choose to use the voluntary withholding system of section 3402(o) with respect to those amounts. Also, if a payee had a fixed amount withheld by request, a different amount will probably be withheld when the new provisions take effect unless the rule provided in question A-7 applies. However, section 3402(o) will continue to apply to annuity payments that are not designated distributions, to sick pay, and to supplemental unemployment benefits.

A-7. Q. If a recipient of a pension or annuity has previously elected voluntary withholding under section 3402(o), is the Form W-4P effective for withholding on payments after December 31, 1982?

A. Yes, if the plan administrator or payor wishes to honor it; the Form W-4P can be treated by the plan administrator or payor as an election to withhold the flat dollar amount specified on the form if the payee is notified of his right to elect out of withholding and if he is notified that his previously filed W-4P will remain effective unless he elects out of withholding or files a new withholding certificate. If these requirements are met the plan administrator or payor may treat the Form W-4P as a voluntary withholding agreement under section 3402(p). See, also, section 3402(i). These amounts withheld should be reported in the same manner as amounts withheld under section 3405.

A-8. Q. What amount of Federal income tax will be withheld from designated distributions?

A. The amount to be withheld by any payor (or, in certain cases, a plan administrator) depends upon whether the payment is a periodic payment, a nonperiodic distribution other than a qualified total distribution, or a qualified total distribution. However, the maximum amount to be withheld cannot exceed the sum of the amount of money and the fair market value of property (other than employer securities as defined in section 402(a)(3)) received in the distribution.

A-9. Q. What is a periodic payment?

A. A periodic payment is an annuity or similar periodic payment whether paid by a licensed life insurance company, a financial institution, or a plan. The term "annuity" means a series of payments payable over a period greater than one year and taxable under section 72 as amounts received as an annuity, whether or not the payments are variable in amount.

A-10. Q. [Reserved]

A. [Reserved]

A-11. Q. How will Federal income tax be withheld from a "qualified total distribution?"

A. A "qualified total distribution" means any designated distribution which it is reasonable to believe is made within one taxable year of the payee, is made from or under a qualified plan described in section 401(a) or section 403(a), and consists of the balance to the credit of the employee under the plans. For additional questions and answers concerning qualified total distributions, see part C. The amount to be withheld on qualified total distributions will be determined under tables prescribed by the Secretary that approximate the tax that would be imposed under section 402(e) if the payee elected to treat the distribution as a lump sum distribution within the meaning of section 402(e)(4)(A). See, in this respect, question C-8.

A-12. Q. What amount of Federal income tax will be withheld from a designated distribution that is not a periodic payment or a qualified total distribution?

A. If a designated distribution is not a periodic payment or a qualified total distribution, the amount to be withheld is computed by multiplying the amount of the designated distribution by 10 percent.

A-13. Q. Who must withhold?

A. Generally, the payor of a designated distribution must withhold, and is liable for payment of, the tax required to be withheld. However, in the case of a distribution from a plan described in section 401(a) (relating to pension, profit-sharing, and stock bonus plans), section 403(a) (relating to certain annuity plans), or section 301(d) of the Tax Reduction Act of 1975 (relating to certain employee stock ownership plans, sometimes called "TRASOP's"), the plan administrator must withhold, and is liable for payment of, the withheld tax unless he directs the payor to withhold the tax and furnishes the payor with any information that may be required by the Secretary in forms or regulations. This provision applies to qualified plans as well as once qualified plans that are no longer qualified. For a description of the material that the plan administrator must furnish to the payor, see question E-3.

A-14. Q. Who is a plan administrator?

A. Under section 414(g), the plan administrator is the person specifically designated as the plan administrator by the terms of the plan or trust. If the plan or trust does not specifically designate the plan administrator (as provided in section 1.414(g)-1(a) of the Income Tax Regulations), then the plan administrator is generally determined as follows:

(1) In the case of a plan maintained by a single employer, the employer is the plan administrator.

(2) In the case of a plan maintained by two or more employers or jointly by one or more employers and one or more employee organizations, the association, committee, joint board of trustees, or other similar group of representatives who maintain the plan is the plan administrator.

(3) In the case in which (1) or (2) does not apply, the person actually responsible for the control, disposition, or management of the assets is the plan administrator.

A-15. Q. If a bank trustee, regulated investment company, or insurance company makes a periodic payment to a payee solely at the direction of an employer sponsored individual retirement account (IRA), is the bank trustee, regulated investment company or insurance company a payor subject to the pension withholding provisions?

A. Yes. The term "payor" generally means the person actually paying the annuity or other payment (even if the person is acting as an agent). Because this is not a payment from a plan described in section 401(a) or 403(a), responsibility for withholding is on the bank trustee, regulated investment company, or insurance company and not on the employer who sponsors the account.

A-16. Q. If a bank trustee transfers plan funds to the employer who sponsors a plan described in section 410(a) and the employer makes the designated distributions, is the employer a payor?

A. Yes. The employer is a payor because it acts as an agent for the bank trustee. Even though the plan administrator has transferred liability to the bank trustee under section 3405(c)(2), the transfer of funds to the employer does not relieve the bank trustee of its liability for withholding because the rule on transfer of liability only applies to plan administrators. Therefore, if the employer fails to withhold on designated distributions, either the employer or the bank trustee may be liable for failure to withhold. Note, however, that the plan administrator could transfer liability for withholding to the employer as payor under section 3405(c)(2). See, in this respect, questions E-2 and E-3.

A-17. Q. Do the withholding provisions apply to annuities paid from an employer deferred compensation plan, an individual retirement plan, or a commercial annuity to the surviving spouse or other beneficiary or a deceased payee?

A. Yes.

A-18. Q. Do these withholding provisions apply to designated distributions under all nonqualified employer deferred compensation plans?

A. No. The withholding provisions relating to pensions and annuities do not apply to any amounts that are wages without regard to these provisions. Wages to which the general wage withholding rules apply mean any remuneration paid by an employer for services performed by an employee unless the amount paid falls within one of the exceptions of section 3401(a). For example, wages do not include remuneration paid to, or on behalf of, an employee or beneficiary from or to a trust qualified under section 401(a) and tax-exempt under section 501(a). There is no exception for contributions to, or benefits paid from, some nonqualified plans. In general, any contributions to, or benefits from, a nonqualified plan that are taxable under section 83 are subject to wage withholding at the time that they are includible in the recipient's gross income.

A-19. Q. Do these withholding provisions apply to designated distributions from a bond purchase plan described in section 405(a)?

A. Yes. Although a bond purchase plan is not a qualified plan, section 3402(a) does not apply to contributions to, or distributions from, such a plan. Therefore, designated distributions from a bond purchase plan are subject to the new withholding rules of section 3405. Similarly, the new withholding rules apply to designated distributions of an individual retirement bond described in section 409 or from an annuity plan described in section 403(a). For purposes of the withholding provisions of section 3405, a designated distribution from a bond purchase plan described in section 405(a) or an individual retirement bond described in section 409 occurs when an individual redeems a bond.

A-20. Q. Do these withholding provisions apply to designated distributions from a tax-sheltered annuity described in section 403(b)?

A. Yes. Section 31.3401(a)-1(b)(1)(i) of the Employment Tax Regulations provides that there is no withholding required under the wage withholding provisions to the extent that any amounts are taxable under the rules of section 72 or 403. Because designated distributions are not subject to the general wage withholding provisions, the new provisions of section 3405 apply to these designated distributions.

A-21. Q. An employer maintains a nonqualified deferred compensation plan such as a supplemental executive retirement ("top hat") plan. Payments under the plan are made in the form of a single sum payment at retirement. Amounts paid at retirement are includible in income as compensation in the year received. Must the payor withhold on these amounts according to the rules in section 3405?

A. No. Section 3405(d)(1)(B)(i) provides that a designated distribution on which withholding is required does not include amounts that are wages without regard to the rules of section 3405. Therefore, withholding on payments that are includible in income as compensation are based on the rules for withholding on wages contained in section 3402.

A-22. Q. Do the withholding provisions of section 3405 apply to a retirement plan maintained by a State or local government on behalf of its employees?

A. Yes. A retirement plan maintained by a State or local government on behalf of its employees is a plan that defers the receipt of compensation. The fact that a plan deferring the receipt of compensation is maintained by a governmental unit does not make the withholding provisions inapplicable. Thus, annuity payments and other distributions under the Federal Civil Service Retirement System or under the plan of any State or municipality are subject to withholding.

A-23. Q. Are payments from a state or local plan of deferred compensation described in section 457 subject to the withholding requirements of section 3405?

A. No. Amounts paid from a plan described in section 457 are paid from a plan that defers the receipt of compensation. However, amounts paid from a deferred compensation plan described in section 457 are wages under section 3401(a). Therefore, the general wage withholding rules, not the special rules of section 3405, apply to these payments.

A-24. Q. An individual retires and begins receiving periodic payments under a commercial annuity contract that was distributed to him from a contributory qualified plan. The insurance company is the payor and is liable for withholding because the plan administrator has transferred liability under the rules of section 3405(c)(2). Must the payor determine whether the employee's investment in the contract is recoverable within three years?

A. Yes. Under section 72(d), if the annuity payments during the first three years equal or exceed the amount contributed by the employee to the plan, no amounts are includible in income until the employee's contributions are recovered. Because the application of section 72(d) may affect the extent to which it is reasonable to believe that amounts are not includible in income and, therefore, not subject to withholding, the payor must determine whether section 72(d) applies to the annuity payments. As a general rule, the information necessary to determine the employee's investment in the contract must be provided to the payor by the plan administrator. See, however, questions A-27 and A-33.

A-25. Q. If the payor in question A-24 determines that the employee's investment in the contract is not recoverable within 3 years, must the payor compute the exclusion ratio under section 72(b) to calculate the amount of each payment that is not includible in gross income?

A. Yes. The operation of section 72(b) affects the extent to which it is reasonable to believe that amounts are not includible in gross income. Therefore, the payor must compute the exclusion ratio to determine what portion of each payment is subject to withholding under section 3405. As a general rule, the information necessary to determine the employee's exclusion ratio must be provided to the payor by the plan administrator. See, however, questions A-27 and A-33.

A-26. Q. In questions A-24 and A-25, may the payor (*i.e.*, the insurance company) rely on the information furnished by the plan administrator to determine the amounts that are includible in gross income?

A. In the absence of information to the contrary supplied by the payee, the payor may rely on the information furnished by the plan administrator. See, with respect to the plan administrator's duty to report to the payor, questions E-2 and E-3.

A-27. Q. What is the result in questions A-24 and A-25 if the plan administrator fails to provide the payor with any information concerning the amount of employee contributions?

A. Until the earlier of December 31, 1983, or the date on which the plan administrator provides the payor with information concerning the amount of employee contributions, it is reasonable for the payor to assume that the employee's investment in the annuity contract is zero unless the payor has independent specific knowledge of the amount of employee contributions. Additionally, if the payee notifies the payor of the amount of employee contributions, the payor must compute the taxable portion of the payment based on the information supplied by the payee. If the plan administrator fails to provide the payor with this information on or before December 31, 1983, the plan administrator will be liable for failure to withhold and pay the tax due. See questions E-2 through E-5 for rules on the plan administrator's ability to transfer liability for withholding to the payor. See

also question A-33 with respect to the plan administrator's failure to provide the necessary information prior to December 31, 1983.

A-28. Q. If a beneficiary receives the balance to the credit of an employee from an annuity described in section 403(b) on account of the employee's death, is it reasonable to believe that the $5,000 death benefit exclusion of section 101(b) is not includible in gross income?

A. Yes. Although the amount of the death benefit exclusion allowable may be limited by section 101(b)(2)(B)(iii), the payor, for withholding purposes, may use the maximum death benefit exclusion ($5,000) in computing the amount of the distribution that is subject to withholding. See also, in this respect, question C-3.

A-29. Q. What is the appropriate treatment of a distribution (whether periodic or nonperiodic) that includes employer securities?

A. Employer securities are significant in the calculation of amounts subject to withholding in two respects. First, the maximum amount to be withheld cannot exceed the sum of the amount of money plus the fair market value of property received, *except* employer securities. In other words, a payor will not be forced to dispose of employer securities in order to meet withholding tax liability. Thus, for example, if an individual receives a distribution from a stock bonus plan that includes $1,000 worth of employer stock and $5 in cash for payment of fractional shares of stock, all of the cash, but none of the stock, may be retained by the payor to satisfy the withholding obligation. Second, under certain circumstances, the net unrealized appreciation in employer securities is not includible in gross income. See, in this respect, the rules of sections 402(a)(1) and 402(e)(4)(J).

A-30. Q. Is it reasonable to believe that all net unrealized appreciation from employer securities is not includible in gross income in the case of a qualified total distribution?

A. Yes. Although a qualified total distribution may include a distribution that is not a lump sum distribution, it is reasonable to believe that all net unrealized appreciation from employer securities is not includible in gross income.

A-31. Q. Is it reasonable to believe that a distribution is not includible in gross income if the distribution consists of employee contributions from a plan described in section 401(a) and the amount distributed is not specifically designated as accumulated deductible employee contributions?

A. Yes. Employee contributions to a plan described in section 401(a) are not deductible from gross income when contributed unless they are deductible employee contributions under section 72(o)(5). Unless the payor has specific knowledge that employee contributions distributed from a plan described in section 401(a) are accumulated deductible employee contributions, it is reasonable to assume that the amounts are excludible from gross income in the year when received.

A-32. Q. In the case of disability payments paid under a noncontributory plan to a disability retiree who has not attained age 65, is it reasonable to believe that all amounts paid to the payee are includible in gross income?

A. Yes. Whether or not all or part of the disability payments paid under a noncontributory plan to a permanently disabled retiree who has not attained age 65 are includible in gross income depends on the adjusted gross income of the taxpayer and on whether the taxpayer is permanently and totally disabled. In this situation, it is reasonable for the payor to assume that all amounts paid to the payee are includible in gross income unless the payor has specific independent knowledge that all or part of the periodic payments are not includible in gross income. Additionally, if the payee notifies the payor of the amount excludible from gross income, the payor must compute the taxable portion of the payment based on information provided by the payee.

A-33. Q. In the case of a periodic payment, is it reasonable to believe that all amounts paid to the payee are includible in gross income?

A. Yes. As an alternative to the general rule that a designated distribution does not include amounts which it is reasonable to believe are not includible in gross income, the payor of any periodic payment may assume that the entire amount of the payment is includible in gross income. The wage withholding tables must be used without adjustment for the fact that Federal income tax is being withheld on the gross amount. If the payor uses this alternative method of calculating the amount of the designated distribution, he must include with the notice of the election not to have withholding apply to the following additional statements:

(1) tax will be withheld on the gross amount of the payment even though the payee may be receiving amounts that are not subject to withholding because they are excludible from gross income;

(2) this withholding procedure may result in excess withholding on the payment; and

(3) the payee may adjust the allowances claimed on the withholding certificate if he wants a lesser amount withheld from each payment or he may provide the payor with the information necessary to calculate the taxable portion of each payment.

This alternative will not apply to periodic payments made after the earlier of December 31, 1983, or the date on which the plan administrator supplies the payor with the information necessary to calculate the taxable portion of the distribution.

See, also, questions E-3, E-4, and E-5.

A-34. Q. May the payor rely on a plan administrator's computation of the amount to be withheld?

A. Yes. Although the plan administrator is not required to compute the amount to be withheld in order to transfer liability for withholding to the payor, the plan administrator may provide such information to the payor, and the payor may rely on such computations unless the payor knows or has reason to know that the computations are incorrect.

A-35. Q. Under the plans of certain States, individuals may receive payments from more than one retirement system, such as payments from the state's teacher's retirement plan and from the state's regular retirement plan. Must these payments be aggregated for purposes of providing a single notice and election to a payee or for purposes of determining whether the floor on withholding tax (i.e., $5,400 for a married individual claiming three allowances) has been reached?

A. No. However, if it is feasible to aggregate payments under more than one retirement system, the payor is permitted to do so for these purposes.

A-36. Q. If a payment is made by one check to more than one beneficiary, such as a surviving spouse and a minor child, how is the amount to be withheld computed?

A. The payor may compute the withholding on a payment made by one check to more than one beneficiary as if the payment were made to only one beneficiary. In this case, the payor must base withholding for the total amount of the designated distribution on the withholding certificate of the payee to whom the election was sent.

Alternatively, if each payee files a withholding certificate and the payor knows the amount of the payment to which each payee is entitled, the payor may determine the amount to be withheld with respect to each payee. If the payor does not know the amount of the payment to which each payee is entitled, he may treat the payment as being made pro-rata to each payee. If only one withholding certificate is received, the payor must base withholding for the total amount of the designated distribution on the withholding certificate of one of the payees, such as the surviving spouse's certificate. Thus, if notice of the election not to have withholding apply is supplied to each payee at the times required in section 3405(c)(10) and only one payee makes the election or files a certificate, the payor must assume that the election or filing was made by the payee on behalf of the other payees.

A-37. Q. If a payor makes an error in computing the amount of a designated distribution that is subject to withholding, must the payor make a retroactive correction of the error?

A. No, provided the error was a reasonable one. Thus, if a payor either underwithholds or overwithholds because the amount of the designated distribution (i.e., the taxable portion of the payment) was incorrectly calculated, no retroactive make-up is required if one of the following applies: (1) the payor reasonably relied on information furnished by the plan administrator (including the computation of the amount to be withheld), (2) the payor relied on a payee's representations on the withholding certificate, (3) the payor reasonably relied on the rules of this regulation, or (4) the payor made a mathematical error in computations. However, if the amount of the designated distribution is correctly computed, but the payor makes an error in applying the withholding tables, the normal rules concerning failure to withhold and pay the tax will apply.

*B. Withholding on Periodic Payments.*

B-1. Q. Is the payor of periodic payments required to aggregate such payments with a payee's compensation to determine the amount of tax to be withheld under section 3405(a)(1)?

A. No. Although the payor must withhold from any periodic payment the amount that has to be withheld if the payment were a payment of wages by an employer to an employee for a payroll period, the amount to be withheld under section 3405(a)(1) is calculated separately of any amounts that actually are wages to the payee for the same period.

B-2. Q. Can either the percentage method (section 3402(b)) or the wage bracket method (section 3402(c)) be used to determine the withholding liability on a periodic payment?

A. Yes. Withholding on a periodic payment is accomplished by treating the payment as if it were wages. Therefore, unless the employee has elected not to have withholding apply, any method of withholding that is an appropriate method for withholding on wages is also an appropriate method for withholding on periodic payments. Refer to the Employer's Tax Guide (Circular E) and Publication 493, Alternative Tax Withholding Methods and Tables for the general procedures on withholding, deposit, payment, and reporting of Fed-

eral income tax withheld. Note, however, that any specific procedures contained in this regulation take precedence over any contrary rules in Circular E and Publication 493.

B-3. Q. [Reserved]

A. [Reserved]

B-4. Q. [Reserved]

A. [Reserved]

B-5. Q. May a payor determine whether payments to an individual are subject to withholding based on the amount of the first periodic payment for the year?

A. No. Periodic payments can vary during a calendar year because of make-up or past due payments, variable rates of payments, or cost-of-living adjustments, so that withholding based on the first payment within a year may be an inaccurate measure of withholding on total payments for the year. Therefore, the amount to be withheld is determined each payment period in the same manner as applies to withholding on wages. See, in this respect, Circular E and the regulations under section 3402.

B-6. Q. If a payment period is specified as by the terms of a commercial annuity contract, must this period be used as the appropriate period for determining the amount to be withheld?

A. Yes. Similarly, if the payment period is designated in a plan administrator's report or on an individual retirement account payout schedule agreed to by payor and payee, this period must be used as the appropriate payment period.

B-7. Q. If the payor received no report from the plan administrator or beneficiary concerning the payment period, but knows the frequency of payments, can the known frequency be used as the appropriate payment period?

A. Yes. However, if no report is received and the payor has no knowledge of the frequency of payments, then he must treat the distribution as a nonperiodic distribution. Therefore, a distribution cannot be a periodic payment unless the frequency of payments is known. See, in this respect, questions B-8 and C-2. For rules concerning the plan administrator's failure to provide this information, see questions E-2 and E-3.

B-8. Q. If a payee receives a one-time payment that is a make-up payment resulting from an insurance company's incorrect calculation of a monthly annuity amount, is the one-time payment part of a series of periodic payments?

A. Yes. Because the one-time payment is a catch-up of prior amounts due as periodic payments, it is treated as part of a series of periodic payments. These payments are treated for withholding purposes in a manner similar to the treatment of supplemental wage payments in section 31.3402(g)-1 of the Employment Tax Regulations.

*C. Withholding on Nonperiodic Distributions.*

C-1. Q. Must an individual receive a lump-sum distribution within the meaning of section 402(e)(4) to have a qualified total distribution?

A. No. A "qualified total distribution" is any distribution that (i) is a designated distribution, (ii) is reasonable to believe is made within one taxable year of the recipient, (iii) is made under a plan described in section 401(a) or 403(a), and (iv) consists of the balance to the credit of the employee under such plan. Thus, a distribution from a plan described in section 401(a) that does not meet the requirements (such as the minimum 5-year period of participation in section 402(e)(4)(H)) for a lump sum distribution within the meaning of section 402(e)(4) may still be a qualified total distribution for purposes of withholding.

C-2. Q. If a class year plan permits annual withdrawal of participants' vested amounts, are these withdrawals considered periodic payments?

A. No. A class year plan is a plan under which amounts contributed by an employer for a year become vested a number of years (e.g., five years) after the year in which the amounts are contributed. Generally, class year plans permit withdrawals each year of amounts that have vested during the year. However, these distributions are not made with respect to an established frequency of payments, so the withdrawals must be treated as nonperiodic distributions, subject to withholding at the 10 percent rate.

C-3. Q. If a beneficiary receives the balance to the credit of a payee from an annuity contract on account of the payee's death, is this final payment a nonperiodic distribution?

A. Yes. The lump sum death benefit in this situation is a one-time payment that cannot be characterized as a periodic payment. The payment may be a qualified total distribution if the requirements of section 3405(c)(4) are satisfied, but otherwise it will be treated as a nonperiodic distribution other than a qualified total distribution.

C-4. Q. Is it permissible to assume that an individual is a calendar year taxpayer for purposes of determining whether a distribution is a "qualified total distribution?"

A. Yes, unless the payor or plan administrator has reason to believe that the payee is not a calendar year taxpayer. The payor or plan administrator has reason to believe that the payee is not a calendar year taxpayer if the payee tells the payor or plan administrator that he is not a calendar year taxpayer.

C-5. Q. Is a distribution of accumulated deductible employee contributions with earnings that is paid on account of an employee's separation from service treated as a qualified total distribution?

A. Yes. As long as the other requirements for a qualified total distribution are met, a distribution of accumulated deductible employee contributions with earnings is eligible for withholding at the rate applicable to qualified total distributions even though the distribution could never be a lump sum distribution. Because accumulated deductible employee contributions are treated separately in determining whether a distribution is a qualified total distribution, the answer would be the same even if the recipient received none (or a portion) of the vested employer contributions in his account.

C-6. Q. What is meant by the "balance to the credit" of an employee under a plan described in section 401(a) or 403(a)?

A. In general, the balance to the credit of an employee includes any amount credited to the employee under the plan on the date the distribution commences. The balance to the credit of an employee includes an amount credited after the date the distribution commences if it is attributable to services performed before that date or is attributable to earnings on an amount credited to the employee before that date. Additionally, the balance to the credit of an employee includes any amount payable as an annuity with respect to the employee under the plan. Amounts that have been placed in a separate account for the funding of medical benefits under section 401(h) or amounts that are forfeitable under the plan are not included in the balance to the credit of an employee. Finally, accumulated deductible employee contributions (within the meaning of section 72(o)(5)(B)) are not included in the balance to the credit of an employee for the purposes of determining whether a distribution is a "qualified total distribution."

C-7. Q. Can a payor rely on a plan administrator's report in determining whether a distribution consists of the balance to the credit of an employee under a plan?

A. Yes. If the plan administrator does not inform the payor that the distribution consists of the balance to the credit of the employee, the payor may not assume that the distribution is a qualified total distribution and must treat the distribution as a nonperiodic distribution that is not a qualified total distribution. However, the payor may rely on the payee's representations that a distribution does consist of the balance to the credit of the employee under the plan.

C-8. Q. What table must be used to calculate the amount to be withheld from a "qualified total distribution?"

A. The table to be used for withholding on "qualified total distributions" will be published by the Secretary in the near future.

### D. Notice and Election Procedures.

D-1. Q. May a payee elect not to have Federal income tax withheld from a designated distribution?

A. Yes. Withholding is not required on any periodic payment or nonperiodic distribution if the payee elects not to have withholding apply. If the payee makes this election, it is effective until revoked. The payor is required to provide each payee with notice of the right to elect not to have withholding apply and of the right to revoke the election.

D-2. Q. In the case of a designated distribution made on account of the death of an employee, who makes the election not to have withholding apply?

A. The election may be made by the beneficiary of plan benefits specified by the decedent in accordance with plan procedures or, if there is no designated beneficiary, by the beneficiary specified under the terms of the plan. If there is not a designated beneficiary and the terms of the plan do not specify a beneficiary, then the election may be made by the executor or the personal representative of the decedent.

D-3. Q. Who is required to provide notice to the payee of the payee's right not to have withholding apply?

A. Section 3405(d)(10)(B) requires the payor to provide notice to the payee of the payee's right to elect not to have withholding apply. Thus, even if the plan administrator has failed to transfer liability for withholding to the payor, the payor must provide notice to the payees.

D-4. Q. When must notice of the right to elect not to have withholding apply be given for periodic payments?

A. In the case of periodic payments, notice of the election must be provided not earlier than six months before the first payment and not later than when making the first payment. However, even if notice is provided at a date before the first payment, notice must also be given when making the first payment. Thereafter, notice must be provided at least once each calendar year of the right to make the election and to revoke the election.

D-5. Q. Must notice of the right to elect not to have withholding apply be provided to those payees whose annual payments are less than $5,400?

A. Yes. However, under the statute, notice is only required to be provided when making the first payment. Therefore, a payor may provide notice to a payee with annual payments less than $5,400 by indicating to the payee when making the first payment that no Federal income tax will be withheld unless the payee chooses to have withholding apply by filing a withholding certificate, if the payor also provides information concerning where a withholding certificate may be obtained.

D-6. Q. Must notice of the right to elect not to have withholding apply be provided in the same manner to all payees?

A. No. If the payor provides notice to all payees when making the first payment, the payor may, in addition, provide earlier notice as provided in section 3405(d)(10)(B)(i)(I) to selected groups of payees, such as those payees whose annual payments are over $5,400.

D-7. Q. Must notice be attached to the first payment to satisfy the requirement that notice be provided "when making" the first payment?

A. No. Because many payees utilize electronic funds transfer to deposit their pension or annuity checks, notice does not have to be attached physically to the check.

D-8. Q. If a payee utilizes electronic funds transfer and notice is mailed directly to the payee at the same time the check is issued, is the notice requirement satisfied even though the payee receives the notice fifteen days after the check is deposited?

A. Yes. Although it is desirable that the notice reach the payee immediately prior to or concurrent with receipt of the check, the notice requirement is deemed to be satisfied if the payee receives the notice within 15 days before or after receipt of the first payment.

D-9. Q. When is the payor required to notify the payee of his right to elect not to have withholding apply to a nonperiodic distribution?

A. Section 3405(d)(10)(B)(ii) requires that notice must be provided to the payee at the time of a nonperiodic distribution. Since notice provided at the time of the distribution could result in delay of receipt of the benefit check if the payee elects out of withholding, notice for nonperiodic distributions should be given not earlier than six months prior to the distribution and not later than the time that will give the payee reasonable time to elect not to have withholding apply and to reply to the payor with the election information. What is reasonable time depends upon the facts and circumstances of each case.

D-10. Q. What is a "reasonable time" for notice with respect to a nonperiodic distribution from a qualified plan?

A. The "reasonable time" requirement is satisfied with respect to a nonperiodic distribution if the notice is included in the basic claim for benefits application that is provided to the participant by the plan administrator.

D-11. Q. If the payor of a periodic payment provides notice of the election not to have withholding apply within the time specified by section 3405(d)(10)(B)(i)(I), may the payor specify a time prior to distribution by which the election must be made?

A. Yes. The election not to have withholding apply is generally given effect as provided in section 3402(f)(3) for a certificate filed to replace an existing certificate. However, the payor may require that the election is made up to 30 days before the first payment to be effective for the first payment. See question B-3.

D-12. Q. If the payor of a nonperiodic distribution provides notice of the election not to have withholding apply within a reasonable time prior to the distribution, may the payor specify a time prior to distribution by which the election must be made?

A. No. The payee has the right to make or revoke an election at any time prior to the distribution. Therefore, the payor may place a deadline on the time to elect without delaying payment of the distribution, but must accept any election or revocation made up to the time of distribution.

D-13. Q. What is a "reasonable time" for notice with respect to a distribution from an individual retirement account?

A. A payor may provide notice of the election not to have withholding apply at the time the beneficiary requests a withdrawal from his individual retirement account. This rule also applies to distributions from bank sponsored prototype plans and other plans that permit withdrawals on request.

D-14. Q. If notice is provided to a payee prior to the first payment of a periodic payment, why must it also be provided at the time of the first payment or distribution?

A. Section 3405(d)(10)(B)(i)(II) of the Internal Revenue Code requires such notice. In addition, because the payee has the right to make an election or to revoke a prior election at any time prior to the beginning of the payment period, notice must be provided when making the first payment in order to offer the payee ample opportunity to make or revoke an election not to have withholding apply even if the election will not be effective until later payments.

D-15. Q. If a payee who has been receiving periodic payments is rehired by the same employer, has his benefits suspended, and then recommences receiving periodic payments, must notice again be provided to the payee?

A. Yes. Upon recommencement of benefits, the first payment thereafter is treated as the first payment for purposes of the notice requirements.

D-16. Q. Must a payor provide notice if it is reasonable to believe that the entire amount payable is excludible from the payee's gross income?

A. No. Amounts which it is reasonable to believe are not includible in gross income are not designated distributions. Therefore, no notice is required of the ability to elect not to have withholding apply.

D-17. Q. If the payor of a periodic payment under a qualified plan knows that an employee's investment in an annuity contract will be recovered within three years, must he provide notice of the right to elect out of withholding at the time the first payment is made?

A. No. The first payment is not a designated distribution, and, therefore, is not a periodic payment subject to the notice requirements of section 3405(d)(10)(B)(i). There is no withholding obligation until the employee's investment in the contract is recovered because those amounts that equal the investment in the contract are not includible in gross income and, therefore, are not designated distributions. Therefore, the first payment after the employee's investment in the contract is recouped is the first payment for purposes of the notice requirements.

D-18. Q. What information concerning the election not to have withholding apply must be provided by the payor to the payee?

A. Notice to a payee must contain the following information:

(1) notice of the payee's right to elect not to have withholding apply to any payment or distribution and how to make that election,

(2) notice of the payee's right to revoke such an election at any time and a statement that the election remains effective until revoked,

(3) a statement to advise payees that penalties may be incurred under the estimated tax payment rules if the payments of estimated tax are not adequate and sufficient tax is not withheld from the payment or distribution.

In the event that the payor does not know what part of a distribution is includible in gross income and treats these payments as provided in question A-33, the following additional statements must be included with the notice:

(1) tax will be withheld on the gross amount of the payment even though the payee may be receiving amounts that are not subject to withholding because they are excludible from gross income,

(2) this withholding procedure may result in excess withholding on the payment, and

(3) the payee may adjust his allowances claimed on the withholding certificate if he wants a lesser amount withheld from each payment or he may provide the payor with the information necessary to calculate the taxable portion of each payment.

D-19. Q. Is there any information that, although not required, it is desirable to include in the notice to payees?

A. It is desirable to include a statement in the notice to payees that the election not to have withholding apply is prospective only and that any election made after a payment or distribution to the payee is not an election with respect to that payment or distribution.

D-20. Q. May the plan administrator provide the notice to payees on behalf of the payor?

A. The plan administrator may provide notice on behalf of the payor. However, the payor has sole responsibility for providing this notice whether or not the plan administrator has shifted liability for withholding to the payor, and if the plan administrator fails to provide adequate notice, the payor is responsible.

D-21. Q. Is there a sample notice that can be used to satisfy the notice requirement for periodic payments?

A. Yes. Any payor who uses the following sample notice is deemed to satisfy the notice requirement if notice is timely provided:

*NOTICE OF WITHHOLDING ON PERIODIC PAYMENTS*

Beginning on January 1, 1983, the [pension] OR [annuity] payments you receive from the [insert name of plan or company] will be subject to Federal income tax withholding unless you elect not to have withholding apply. Withholding will only apply to the portion of your [pension]OR [annuity] payment that is already included in your income subject to Federal income tax and will be like wage withholding. Thus, there will be no withholding on the return of your own nondeductible contributions to the [plan] OR [contract].

You may elect not to have withholding apply to your [pension]OR [annuity] payments by returning the signed and dated election [manner may be specified] to [insert name and address]. Your election will remain in effect until you revoke it. You may revoke your election at any time by returning the signed and dated revocation to [insert

appropriate name or address]. Any election or revocation will be effective no later than the January 1, May 1, July 1, or October 1 after it is received, so long as it is received at least 30 days before that date. You may make and revoke elections not to have withholding apply as often as you wish. Additional elections may be obtained from [insert name and address].

If you do not return the election by [insert date], Federal income tax will be withheld from the taxable portion of your [pension]OR [annuity] payments as if you were a married individual claiming three withholding allowances. As a result, no Federal income tax will be withheld if the taxable portion of your annual [pension] OR [annuity]payments are less than $5,400.

If you elect not to have withholding apply to your [pension]OR [annuity] payments, or if you do not have enough Federal income tax withheld from your [pension] OR [annuity] payments, you may be responsible for payment of estimated tax. You may incur penalties under the estimated tax rules if your withholding and estimated tax payments are not sufficient.

D-22. Q. Is there sample language that may be used to elect not to have withholding apply or to revoke a prior election not to have withholding apply?

A. Yes. A payee may elect not to have withholding apply or revoke a prior election in any manner that clearly shows the payee's intent. The following language would suffice:

*ELECTION FOR RECIPIENTS OF PERIODIC PAYMENTS*

*Instructions:* Check Box A if you do not want any Federal income tax withheld from your [pension] OR [annuity]. Check Box B to revoke an election not to have withholding apply. Return the signed and dated election to [insert name and address].

Even if you elect not to have Federal income tax withheld, you are liable for payment of Federal income tax on the taxable portion of your [pension] OR [annuity]. You also may be subject to tax penalties under the estimated tax payment rules if your payments of estimated tax and withholding, if any, are not adequate.

A ☐ I do not want to have Federal income tax withheld from my [pension] OR [annuity].

B ☐ I want to have Federal income tax withheld from my [pension] OR [annuity].

Signed: . . . . . . . . . . . . . . . . . . . . . . . . . . . . . . . . . . . .
                     Name             Date

Return your completed election to: [insert name and address]

D-23. Q. May the payee's election be combined with a withholding certificate?

A. Yes. The payor may provide a single statement for the payee to fill out and return that would enable the payee to elect not to have withholding apply or to revoke a previous election and, at the same time, would enable the payee to claim the number of withholding allowances and, also, the dollar amount the payee wants withheld.

D-24. Q. Will a notice mailed to the last known address of the payee fulfill notice requirement of section 3405(d)(10)(B)?

A. Yes.

D-25. Q. Is there a sample notice that can be used to satisfy the notice requirement for nonperiodic distributions?

A. Yes. Any payor who uses the following sample notice is deemed to satisfy the notice requirement if notice is timely provided:

*NOTICE OF WITHHOLDING ON DISTRIBUTIONS OR WITHDRAWALS FROM ANNUITIES, IRAS, PENSION, PROFIT SHARING, STOCK BONUS, AND OTHER DEFERRED COMPENSATION PLANS*

The [distributions] or [withdrawals] you receive from the [insert name of plan or company] are subject to Federal income tax withholding unless you elect not to have withholding apply. Withholding will only apply to the portion of your [distribution] OR [withdrawal] that is included in your income subject to Federal income tax. Thus, for example, there will be no withholding on the return of your own nondeductible contributions to the [plan] OR [contract].

You may elect not to have withholding apply to your [distribution]OR [withdrawal] payments by signing and dating the attached election and returning it [manner may be specified] to [insert name and address].

If you do not return the election by [insert date]receipt of your payments may be delayed. If you do not respond by the date your [distribution] OR [withdrawal] is scheduled to begin, Federal income tax will be withheld from the taxable portion of your [distribution]OR [withdrawal]. [Insert information on rates if desired].

If you elect not to have withholding apply to your [distribution]OR [withdrawal] payments, or if you do not have enough Federal income tax withheld from your [distribution] OR [withdrawal], you may be responsible for payment of estimated tax. You may incur penalties under the estimated tax rules if your withholding and estimated tax payments are not sufficient.

D-26. Q. Is there sample language that may be used for payees of nonperiodic distributions to elect not to have withholding apply?

A. Yes. A payee of a nonperiodic distribution may elect not to have withholding apply in any manner that clearly shows the payee's intent. The following language would suffice:

*ELECTION FOR PAYEES OF NONPERIODIC PAYMENTS*

*Instructions:* If you do not want any Federal income tax withheld from your [distribution] OR [withdrawal], sign and date this election and return it to [insert name and address].

Even if you elect not to have Federal income tax withheld, you are liable for payment of Federal income tax on the taxable portion of your [distribution] OR [withdrawal]. You also may be subject to tax penalties under the estimated tax payment rules if your payments of estimated tax and withholding, if any, are not adequate.

I do not want to have Federal income tax withheld from my [distribution]OR [withdrawal].

Signed: . . . . . . . . . . . . . . . . . . . . . . . . . . . . . . . . . .
                 Name                  Date

Return your completed election to: [insert name and address]

D-27. Q. If the payor provides notice prior to making the first payment, can an abbreviated notice be used to satisfy the notice requirement of section 3405(d)(10)(B)(i)(II)?

A. Yes. It is permissible to provide with the payment a statement that the payee has the right to elect out of withholding. For example, the following sample notice could be used to satisfy the notice requirement if the payor has provided notice previously:

If Federal income taxes have been withheld from the [pension]OR [annuity] payments you are receiving and if you do not wish to have taxes withheld, you should notify [insert name and address]. However, if you elect not to have withholding apply to your [pension]OR [annuity] payments, or if you do not have enough Federal income tax withheld from your [pension] OR [annuity] payment, you may be responsible for payment of estimated tax. You may incur penalties under the estimated tax rules if your withholding and estimated tax payments are not sufficient.

If Federal income taxes are not being withheld from your [pension]OR [annuity] payment because you have elected not to have withholding apply and if you wish to revoke that election and have Federal income taxes withheld from your [pension] OR [annuity] payments, you should notify [insert name and address].

D-28. Q. Must an employee who receives a distribution from a plan described in section 401(a) that includes amounts attributable to employer contributions and to accumulated deductible employee contributions make two elections not to have withholding apply?

A. No. Although accumulated deductible employee contributions are treated separately in determining whether a distribution is a qualified total distribution, an employee needs to make only one election not to have withholding apply to any distributions occurring at the same time from or under the same plan. However, the plan administrator could require the employee to make separate elections with respect to the distributions.

D-29. Q. If the administrator of a plan described in section 401(a) makes a qualified total distribution to an employee out of funds contained in two or more trusts, must the employee make a separate election not to have withholding apply with respect to the distribution from each trust?

A. No. The fact that a plan may use several trusts does not eliminate treatment of the distribution as a single qualified total distribution for which only one election is necessary.

D-30. Q. Is it permissible to provide notice to persons already in pay status on January 1, 1983, in a newsletter of the plan administrator?

A. Yes, provided that this notice is received by the payee within 15 days of the payee's receipt of the first periodic payment after December 31, 1982, and such notice provides the means to make an election and instructions for electing not to have withholding apply. It is desirable that payees be afforded the maximum opportunity to make the election provided by section 3405(a)(2). Payors are encouraged to give payees notice of their election opportunities at least 30 days before the first periodic payment after December 31, 1982.

D-31. Q. Is it permissible to provide the annual notice required by section 3405(d)(10)(B)(i)(III) on January 1, 1984, December 31, 1985, and January 1, 1986?

A. No. The annual notice required by section 3405(d)(10)(B)(i)(III) should be provided at approximately the same time each calendar year.

D-32. Q. Under what circumstances may an election made with respect to a nonperiodic distribution apply to subsequent distributions?

A. Generally, any election not to have withholding apply to a nonperiodic distribution may apply to any subsequent payment or distribution from or under the same plan or arrangement. However, the payor must still provide notice of the election and revocation

procedures upon each subsequent distribution and must include the statement concerning liability for payment of estimated tax if the payee does not have withholding applied.

D-33. Q. How may a payee who intends to make a qualifying rollover (as defined in section 402(a)(5) or section 408(d)(3)) of a distribution elect not to have Federal income tax withheld from the distribution?

A. The payee may elect not to have withholding apply by making the election on the form provided by the payor. Alternatively, if the payee directs the payor to pay over the distribution to a qualified plan or an individual retirement account, the payor may treat this direction as an election not to have withholding apply.

D-34. Q. If a payee claims more than 14 withholding allowances on a withholding certificate, must the payor remit a copy of the withholding certificate to the Internal Revenue Service?

A. No. Because a payee may, at any time, elect out of withholding, the rules of section 31.3402(f)(2)-1(g) of the Employment Tax Regulations do not apply. Therefore, a payee may claim more than 14 allowances and the payor need not remit the withholding certificate to the Internal Revenue Service.

*E. Reporting and Recordkeeping.*

E-1. Q. If designated distributions are made from or under a plan described in section 401(a), who has responsibility for making the returns and reports required by section 6047(e)?

A. Generally, the plan administrator, as defined in section 414(g), is responsible for maintaining the records and making the reports required by section 6047(e). However, if the plan administrator fails to keep the required records and make the required reports, the employer maintaining the plan is responsible for the reports and returns.

E-2. Q. How may a plan administrator of a plan described in section 401(a) or 403(a) transfer his duty to withhold to a payor?

A. A plan administrator of a plan described in section 401(a) or 403(a) may transfer the liability for withholding by (1) directing the payor in writing to withhold the tax and (2) providing the payor with any required information. This direction is presumed to remain in effect until the plan administrator revokes it in writing.

E-3. Q. What information must the plan administrator provide to the payor in order to transfer his liability for withholding?

A. The general rule is that the plan administrator must provide the payor with all information necessary to compute correctly the withholding tax liability. To satisfy this requirement, the plan administrator must explicitly inform the payor of the information that would be reportable on the Form W-2P or 1099R or that such information is not applicable to a particular payee or to any payments under the plan. For example, if the plan administrator is silent with respect to any employee contributions, he has not satisfied his reporting obligation even if there are no employee contributions to the plan. Thus, the plan administrator is expected to provide the payor with the following minimum information:

(1) the name, address, and social security number of the payee and the payee's spouse or other beneficiary if applicable,

(2) the existence and amount of any employee contributions,

(3) the amount of accumulated deductible employee contributions, if any,

(4) the payee's cost basis in any employer securities and the current fair market value of the securities,

(5) the existence and amount of any premiums paid for the current cost of life insurance that were previously includible in income,

(6) a statement of the reason (*e.g.*, death, disability, retirement) for the payment or distribution,

(7) the date on which payments commence and the amount and frequency of payments,

(8) the age of the payee and of the payee's spouse or designated beneficiary if applicable, and

(9) any other information required by Form W-2P or 1099R.

If, prior to December 31, 1983, the plan administrator fails to provide the payor with the information required in items (2) through (5) the payor is liable for withholding. However, the payor may withhold on the payment as if all amounts are includible in gross income. See question A-33.

E-4. Q. If, after December 31, 1983, the plan administrator does not notify the payor of the amount of employee contributions with respect to one payee, has withholding liability shifted to the payor?

A. Yes. The plan administrator satisfies the requirements of question E-3 as to the information that must be supplied to the payor so long as the failure to provide the required information occurs on an infrequent basis or the plan administrator informs the payor in writing that he has made a good faith effort to supply all the required information but the amount of employee contributions as to a particular payee is unavailable.

E-5. Q. If, after December 31, 1983, the plan administrator fails to supply the payor with any information concerning the existence or amount of any employee contributions, has withholding liability shifted to the payor?

A. No. The plan administrator has not satisfied his reporting obligation as required in question E-3 as to employee contributions even if there are no employee contributions unless he affirmatively states that there are no employee contributions or states that the reporting of this item is not applicable in determining the payee's tax liability.

E-6. Q. Is it permissible to satisfy the requirements of section 6047(e) by maintaining records necessary to provide the information contained on Forms W-2P and 1099R?

A. Section 6047(e) will be satisfied if, in addition to the information necessary to complete Forms W-2P and 1099R, the following information is maintained:

(1) payee's date of birth (if known), and date of spouse's or designated beneficiary's birth (if applicable and known);

(2) plan administrator's name, address, and employer identification number (EIN);

(3) plan's name and identification number and sponsor's name, address, and EIN; and

(4) date on which payments commence and amount and frequency of payments.

E-7. Q. If the interim method of withholding on periodic payments (*i.e.*, withholding on the gross amount) is used, must the employer, plan administrator, or issuer of any contract still maintain the information required by Form W-2P?

A. Yes. Even if this interim method is used, the recipient must be provided with the information that will enable him to determine his tax liability and adjust his claimed exemptions or claim a credit or refund.

E-8. Q. What events trigger the reporting requirements of section 6047(e)?

A. Reporting is required any time there is a designated distribution to which section 3405 applies. Therefore, the old law rule that distributions of less than $600 per year do not require reporting no longer applies. Additionally, an exchange of insurance contracts under which any designated distribution (including a tax-free exchange under section 1035) may be made is a reportable event even though a designated distribution does not occur. To insure proper reporting when a designated distribution is made under the new contract, it is anticipated that the issuer of the contract to be exchanged will provide the information necessary to compute the amount to be withheld to the policyholder and to the issuer of the new contract.

E-9. Q. Will the reporting requirement be satisfied if Form W-2P or Form 1099R is filed?

A. Yes. In the absence of other forms or regulations, the reporting requirement is satisfied if Form W-2P or Form 1099R is filed with respect to each payee.

E-10. Q. How should the payor or plan administrator remit payments of amounts withheld under section 3405?

A. The payor or plan administrator must deposit the amount withheld under section 3405 with an authorized financial institution in accordance with the provisions of § 31.6302(c)-1(a)(1)(i) of the Procedure and Administration Regulations, which provides the procedures for depositing employment taxes. For purposes of applying these procedures to amounts withheld under section 3405, the term "taxes" as defined in § 31.6302(c)-1(a)(1)(iii) includes the income tax withheld under section 3405 with respect to designated distributions. A payor or plan administrator who remits these amounts in accordance with those rules must report the amounts deposited on the same Form 941 or 941E, whichever is appropriate, that he uses to report the employment taxes he had deposited under § 31.6302(c)-1(a)(1)(i).

### F. Other.

F-1. Q. If a plan administrator or other payor distributes property other than cash to payees, is it permissible to use the value of the property as of the last preceding valuation date to determine the amount of Federal income tax that must be withheld from each distribution?

A. Yes. In many situations, the plan administrator or payor will not be able to determine the value of property to be distributed as of the date of distribution without delaying payment to the payee. In these cases, the plan administrator or payor may determine the value of the property to be distributed as of the last preceding valuation date prior to the date of distribution, as long as the valuation is made at least once each year. If the most recent valuation date occurred within the 90 days immediately preceding the date of distribution, the next most recent valuation date may be used.

F-2. Q. How is withholding accomplished if a payee receives only property other than employer securities?

A. A payor or plan administrator must satisfy the obligation to withhold on distributions of property other than employer securities

even if this requires selling all or part of the property and distributing the cash remaining after Federal income tax is withheld. However, the payor or plan administrator may instead permit the payee to remit to the payor or plan administrator sufficient cash to satisfy the withholding obligation. Additionally, if a distribution of property other than cash includes property that is not includible in a designated distribution, such as the distribution of U.S. Savings Bonds or an annuity contract, such property need not be sold or redeemed to meet any withholding obligation.

F-3. Q. If a designated distribution includes cash and property other than employer securities, is it permissible to satisfy the withholding obligation with respect to the entire distribution by using the cash distributed, provided the cash distributed is sufficient to satisfy the withholding obligation?

A. Yes, as long as there is sufficient cash to satisfy the withholding obligation for the entire distribution. There is no requirement that tax be withheld from each type of property in proportion to its value.

F-4. Q. If a loan from a qualified plan is treated as a distribution under section 72(p), is the amount of the loan subject to withholding under section 3405?

A. Yes. If, and to the extent that, the loan is treated as a distribution when made, withholding is accomplished by withholding tax from the amount of the loan that is treated as a distribution. Thus, for example, if a loan of $12,000 that must be repaid within 5 years is made to a common law employee with a vested account balance of $5,000, $2,000 is treated as a distribution under section 72(p), and the payor or plan administrator must withhold tax from the $2,000.

F-5. Q. Is a loan that is treated as a distribution under section 72(p) a nonperiodic distribution other than a qualified total distribution?

A. Yes.

F-6. Q. Must a payor or plan administrator withhold tax on a nonperiodic distribution (including a qualified total distribution) if the amount of the distribution is less than $200?

A. No. However, all amounts received within one taxable year of the payee from the payor or plan administrator under the same plan or arrangement must be aggregated for purposes of determining whether the $200 floor is reached. If the payor or plan administrator does not know at the time a first payment of $200 or less is made whether there will be additional payments during the year for which aggregation is required, the payor or plan administrator need not withhold from the first payment. If distributions are made within one taxable year under more than one plan of an employer, the plan administrator or payor may, but need not, aggregate the distributions for purposes of determining whether the $200 floor is reached.

F-7. Q. If a nonperiodic distribution (including a qualified total distribution) to a payee will be less than $200, must the payor provide notice to the payee of the right to elect not to have withholding apply?

A. No.

F-8. Q. How is withholding accomplished if a qualified total distribution is paid in installments during one taxable year of the payee?

A. Withholding can be accomplished on a qualified total distribution that is paid in installments within one taxable year by either one of the following methods:

Under Option 1, the tax on the first installment is calculated under the qualified total distribution table. The tax on each subsequent installment is calculated by finding the tax under the table on the cumulative amount of the installments for the year and subtracting the amount of tax already withheld from the tax due with respect to the cumulative amount of the installments.

Under Option 2, the payor or plan administrator can withhold the tax on all installments except the final installment at a 10 percent rate. The tax on the final installment may be calculated by finding the tax under the qualified total distribution table on the cumulative amount of the installments for the year and subtracting the amount of tax already withheld from the installments. Option 2 may be used even if the amount of the tax that should be withheld from the final installment under the qualified total distribution tables exceeds the amount of the final installment. The plan administrator or payor will not be subject to penalties under section 6651 with respect to the difference between the tax that should have been withheld from the final installment under the qualified total distribution tables and the amount of the final installment.

The effect of these alternatives is illustrated by the following example:

An individual receives within one taxable year the balance to his credit under a plan described in section 401(a) or 403(a). The balance to his credit is paid in three installments of $1,000, $10,000, and $60,000. The amount of tax to be withheld from the installments may be calculated under Option 1 or Option 2.

Option 1—Withholding on each installment computed by finding tax under qualified total distribution tables on the cumulative amount of the distribution and subtracting the tax already withheld.

A.  1. Amount of installment 1 . . . . . . . . . . . . . . .    $1,000
    2. Withholding obligation on installment 1 . . . .    50
B.  1. Amount of installments 1 and 2 . . . . . . . . .    $11,000
    2. Withholding obligation on installments 1 and 2

    . . . . . . . . . . . . . . . . . . . . . . . . . . . . . .    550
    3. Withholding paid on installment 1 . . . . . . . .    50
    4. Withholding obligation on installment 2 . . . .    500
    (2 minus 3)
C.  1. Amount of installments 1, 2, and 3 . . . . . . . .    $71,000
    2. Withholding obligation on installments 1, 2, and
    3 . . . . . . . . . . . . . . . . . . . . . . . . . . . . . .    9,580
    3. Withholding paid on installments 1 and 2 . . .    550
    4. Withholding obligation on installment 3 . . . .    $9,030
    (2 minus 3)
          Total withholding obligation . . . . . .    $9,580

Option 2—Withholding computed by withholding at 10 percent rate for all but the final installment. Withholding on the final installment computed by finding tax under qualified total distribution table for the cumulative amount of the distribution and subtracting the amount of tax already withheld:

A.  1. Amount of installment 1 . . . . . . . . . . . . . . .    $1,000
    2. Withholding obligation on installment 1 . . . .    100
B.  1. Amount of installment 2 . . . . . . . . . . . . . . .    $10,000
    2. Withholding obligation on installment 2 . . . .    1,000
C.  1. Amount of installments 1, 2, and 3 . . . . . . . .    $71,000
    2. Withholding obligation on installments 1, 2, and
    3 . . . . . . . . . . . . . . . . . . . . . . . . . . . . . .    9,580
    3. Withholding paid on installments 1 and 2 . . .    1,100
    4. Withholding obligation on installment 3 . . . .    8,480
    (2 minus 3)
          Total withholding obligation . . . . . .    $9,580

F-9. Q. A plan described in section 401(a) invests in life insurance contracts for its participants. Each year the current cost of the life insurance element (PS 58 cost) is taxable to the participants under section 72. Is withholding required on this amount even though there is no amount actually distributed to the participant?

A. No. Because the PS 58 costs are not distributed or deemed to be distributed, they are not designated distributions for which withholding is required.

F-10. Q. The plan administrator or payor of a plan described in section 401(a) has been properly reporting distributions on a multiple contract basis for purposes of section 72. How should the plan administrator or payor determine the amount of each payment that is includible in gross income for withholding purposes?

A. In the absence of revenue rulings or regulations to the contrary, the plan administrator or payor of a plan that properly reports distributions on a multiple contract basis should use that method to determine the taxable portion of a payment for withholding purposes.

F-11. Q. The plan administrator or payor of a plan described in section 401(a) has been reporting distributions on a multiple contract basis for purposes of section 72 and has properly switched to the single contract method for reporting distributions. How should the plan administrator or payor determine the amount of each payment that is includible in gross income for withholding purposes?

A. If a plan has properly switched from the multiple contract basis to the single contract basis for reporting distributions, the plan administrator or payor may assume that all amounts prior to the year of switch were reported by the payees on a multiple contract basis. Therefore, for example, in the case of an individual whose annuity payments have not commenced prior to the date of the switch to a single contract basis, the payee's investment in the contract can be assumed to have been recovered on a multiple contract basis prior to the year of the switch and on a single contract basis thereafter for purposes of determining the amount of each payment that is includible in gross income for withholding purposes. This rule applies even though payees may have amended their income tax returns for prior years to report all payments on a single contract basis.

F-12. Q. If a plan that makes payments subject to the withholding and notice requirements of section 3405 makes separate payments to the same individual as a retired participant and as a surviving spouse of a retired participant, must the two payments be aggregated for withholding purposes?

A. No, unless the payor wishes to aggregate them.

F-13. Q. An insurance company makes payments under certain variable annuity contracts. The Investment Company Act of 1940 (§22(e)) applies to these variable annuity contracts and requires that the insurance company make a pay-out within 7 days after a payee requests a withdrawal from his contract. Under these circumstances,

how may notice be provided to a payee of his right to elect out of withholding for a nonperiodic distribution?

A. In this situation, the insurance company has only seven days in which to notify a payee of his right to elect out of withholding. It is not feasible for the insurance company to secure an election in writing unless the payee supplies the written election at the time he requests a withdrawal. Therefore, the notice and election can be provided in the following manner: 1) the insurance company may mail a notice to a payee on the day the request for withdrawal is received and 2) the notice may specify that unless the payee calls the company at a toll-free telephone number supplied on the notice within seven days of the date the request was received, the company will withhold from the distribution. Notice provided in this manner is deemed to satisfy the "reasonable time" requirement of question d-9. Insurance companies that encounter this problem are encouraged to supply an election form to a payee at the time an annuity contract is purchased. If a payee supplies an election with the request for withdrawal, notice still must be given but the insurance company may honor the election received if no other communication is received after notice is provided to the payee.

F-14. Q. If an individual receives periodic payments from two or more plans of one member of a controlled group of corporations, separate periodic payments from two members of a controlled group of corporations out of one plan, or periodic payments from separate plans of two members of a controlled group, must the periodic payments be aggregated for withholding purposes?

A. No, unless the plan administrator or payor wishes to aggregate the payments. Section 414(b) does not require that plans of a controlled group of corporations be aggregated for withholding purposes. The same rule applies to a group of trades or businesses under common control or an affiliated service group described in section 414(c) or (m).

F-15. Q. How is withholding applied to a designated distribution from an individual retirement account (IRA) described in section 408(a) that is payable upon demand even though payments are scheduled to be made over a period certain greater than one year?

A. Distributions from IRAs that are payable upon demand are not periodic payments taxable under section 72 because they do not constitute annuity contracts within the meaning of section 408(d)(2). Therefore, designated distributions from an IRA that are payable upon demand are treated as nonperiodic distributions subject to withholding at the 10% rate even if the distributions are paid over a period certain.

F-16. Q. Under the rules of section 72, a portion of certain payments that may vary because of investment experience, cost of living indices, or similar criteria is treated as not received as an annuity. For withholding purposes, must these amounts be treated as nonperiodic distributions even though part of each payment is a periodic payment?

A. No. For withholding purposes, amounts will be considered periodic payments even though a portion of each payment is treated as an amount not received as an annuity under §1.72-2(b)(3) of the Income Tax Regulations.

F-17. Q. Is the payor of distributions under a funded nonqualified deferred compensation plan that are payable as an annuity and taxable under section 72 required to withhold under section 3405?

A. Yes. Section 31.3401(a)-1(b)(1)(i) of the Employment Tax Regulations provides that any amounts received as an annuity and taxable under section 72 are excepted from the general definition of wages. Therefore, to the extent that section 402(b) requires that distributions from nonqualified plans which are received as an annuity are taxable under the rules of section 72, section 3405 will apply. See, however, question a-18 for the rules relating to distributions from a nonqualified deferred compensation plan that are taxable under section 83. Therefore, whether the payor or plan administrator of a nonqualified plan is required to withhold under section 3402 or section 3405 depends upon what section of the Code governs the taxation of amounts contributed or distributed.

F-18. Q. Are amounts paid in connection with a partial or complete surrender or upon the maturity or endowment of a commercial annuity subject to the new withholding rules?

A. Yes. Amounts paid in connection with a partial or complete surrender or upon the maturity or endowment of a commercial annuity are subject to the new withholding rules to the extent that they are designated distributions. Thus, withholding is required on the complete or partial surrender of an annuity, life insurance or endowment contract to the extent they are designated distributions.

F-19. Q. Are amounts paid in connection with a partial surrender of a commercial annuity periodic payments?

A. Generally, no. Unless the amount paid in connection with the partial surrender is one of a series of payments payable over a period of greater than one year and taxable under section 72 as an amount received as an annuity, the amount paid is not a periodic payment.

Reg. §35.3405-1T

F-20. Q. Are amounts paid in connection with a complete surrender of a commercial annuity a qualified total distribution?

A. A qualified total distribution must be made under a plan described in section 401(a) or 403(a). Unless the commercial annuity is surrendered under such a plan and meets the other requirements for a qualified total distribution, the total surrender will be treated as a nonperiodic payment that is not a qualified total distribution.

F-21. Q. Is it reasonable to believe that amounts distributed in connection with a commercial annuity that was acquired on or before August 13, 1982, or are otherwise described in section 72(e)(5), which are not treated as amounts received as an annuity under section 72, will not be includible in the gross income of the recipient?

A. Generally, yes. Under the rules of section 72(e) prior to the passage of TEFRA, amounts not received as an annuity were not taxable until the investment in the contract was recovered. Thus, for distributions that are not received as an annuity under a commercial annuity contract acquired on or before August 13, 1982, it is reasonable to believe that amounts distributed are not includible in the payee's gross income to the extent they represent unrecovered investment in the contract. The special transitional rule of question a-33, available for plan administrators, may be used until December 31, 1983, by payors of commercial annuities who lack records with regard to the payee's unrecovered investment in the contract.

F-22. Q. For commercial annuity contracts entered into after August 13, 1982, which are not described in section 72(e)(5), is it reasonable to believe that amounts distributed, which are not amounts received as an annuity under section 72, are not includible in gross income?

A. Generally, no. TEFRA amended section 72(e) to provide that amounts not received as an annuity will be includible in gross income until all earnings or other amounts that are not part of the investment in the contract have been distributed. Thus, it is not reasonable to believe that amounts distributed in connection with a comercial annuity contract entered into after August 13, 1982, are excludible from gross income until all earnings or other amounts that are not part of the investment in the contract have been distributed. This new rule does not apply to distributions from commercial annuities described in section 72(e)(5). Question f-21 provides the proper rule with respect to distributions from commercial annuities described in section 72(e)(5).

F-23. Q. Is it reasonable to believe that amounts involved solely in connection with an exchange of commercial annuities under section 1035 of the Code will not be includible in the gross income of the recipient?

A. Yes. Designated distributions include only amounts that it is reasonable to believe are includible in the gross income of the recipient. In the case of a commercial annuity exchange under section 1035 in which no cash or other property is exchanged, it is reasonable to believe that no portion is includible in the gross income of a recipient. An annuity exchange includes an exchange of annuity, endowment, or life insurance contracts issued by a life insurance company licensed to do business under the laws of any State. Thus, such exchanges are not subject to the withholding rules of section 3405. However, see question e-8 concerning recordkeeping requirements with respect to the nontaxable exchange of commercial annuity contracts under section 1035.

F-24. Q. Is it reasonable to believe that amounts distributed in connection with a surrender of a life insurance or endowment contract, or in connection with an exchange of life insurance or endowment contracts in which cash or other property is distributed, will not be includible in gross income?

A. Generally, no. Amounts distributed in connection with the surrender of a life insurance or endowment contract, or in connection with an exchange of life insurance or endowment contracts in which cash or other property is distributed are includible in income to the extent that the amount received exceeds the policyholder's investment in the contract. However, if a life insurance or endowment contract issued before August 13, 1982, is surrendered within ten years of the date of its issuance, or is exchanged within ten years of the date of its issuance, the payor may assume that no amounts are includible in the gross income of the policyholder if the cash or other property received by the policyholder in connection with the surrender or exchange of the life insurance or endowment contract does not exceed $10,000. If a life insurance or endowment contract issued before August 13, 1982, is surrendered or exchanged ten years or more after the date of its issuance, the payor may assume that no amounts are includible in the gross income of the policyholder if the cash or other property received by the policyholder in connection with the surrender or exchange of the life insurance or endowment contract does not exceed $5,000. If the payor utilizes the special rule in the two preceding sentences, the payor must notify the policyholder, at the time described in question d-4, that all or part of the amount distributed may be includible in the policyholder's gross

income. See question f-23 for additional rules concerning certain exchanges of annuity contracts.

F-25. Q. Do the requirements of section 3405(d)(10), relating to the time at which notice must be provided, also apply to the time at which an election out of withholding may be made?

A. Generally, yes. For example, an individual may not at commencement of employment execute an election out of withholding to be honored by a plan administrator or payor when the individual terminates employment and receives a distribution from a deferred compensation plan. See, however, question f-13 for a special rule applicable to certain annuity contracts.

F-26. Q. If a payor provided notice prior to January 1, 1983, but failed to include all of the information required by question d-18, may the abbreviated notice of question d-27 be supplied when making the first payment?

A. Yes, as long as the abbreviated notice contains all of the information required by question d-18 that was not supplied with the earlier notice.

F-27. Q. When must notice of the right to elect not to have withholding apply be given as to designated distributions from an individual retirement account (IRA) described in section 408(a) that is payable on demand even though payments are scheduled to be made over a period greater than one year?

A. Under question f-15, designated distributions from an IRA that are payable upon demand are treated as nonperiodic distributions subject to withholding at the 10 percent rate even if the distributions are paid over a period certain. Section 3405(d)(10)(B)(i) requires the payor of a nonperiodic distribution to transmit to the payee notice, at the time of the distribution or at such earlier time as may be provided in regulations, of the right to elect not to have withholding apply. If distributions from an IRA have begun and are scheduled to be made at quarterly or more frequent intervals, then, in lieu of providing a notice at the time of each distribution, the payor may furnish a blanket notice applicable to all such distributions that are expected to be made to the payee from the account during a calendar year. Such a blanket notice must be furnished at a reasonable time before the first payment made in the calendar year to which the notice relates, except that a blanket notice relating to distributions from the IRA during 1983 may be made by the later of October 1, 1983, or the date of the first designated distribution from the IRA.

### G. Delay Procedures.

G-1. Q. When does the new law take effect?

A. In general, withholding is required on any designated distributions made after December 31, 1982.

G-2. Q. Is there a penalty for failure to withhold under section 3405 on designated distributions made after December 31, 1982?

A. Yes. In general, section 6651 governs the failure to file a return and to withhold tax under section 3405.

G-3. Q. Are there any circumstances under which the withholding and notice requirements of section 3405 may be delayed to a date later than January 1, 1983?

A. Yes. The Secretary has authority to delay, but not beyond June 30, 1983, the application of these withholding provisions to any payor or plan administrator if the payor or plan administrator can establish that he is unable to comply with these provisions without undue hardship.

G-4. Q. Under what circumstances may a payor or plan administrator who is experiencing undue hardship in complying with section 3405 delay implementation of the notice and withholding requirements?

A. For those payors and plan administrators who experience undue hardship in complying with the provisions of section 3405, the withholding and notice requirements of section 3405 may be delayed so long as undue hardship exists up to July 1, 1983.

G-5. Q. Must approval be obtained from the Internal Revenue Service to be entitled to the delay referred to in question g-4 if the delay will be no later than April 1, 1983?

A. No. If a payor or plan administrator can establish that undue hardship would result if required to comply with the provisions of this section before April 1, 1983, prior approval from the Internal Revenue Service is not required and should not be requested. For purposes of this delay up to April 1, 1983, undue hardship will be presumed to exist, in the absence of bad faith, as long as the payor or plan administrator can establish that at least one of the conditions listed in question g-6 is present.

The payor or plan administrator should prepare and retain a statement of undue hardship as described in question g-9 and should maintain any documents necessary to support the representations made in that statement.

G-6. Q. What constitutes undue hardship?

A. For purposes of these delay procedures, the term "undue hardship" generally means more than an inconvenience or increased costs to the payor or plan administrator. In the case of a payor or plan

**Collection of Income Tax at Source on Wages**
See p. 20,601 for regulations not amended to reflect law changes
**61,503**

administrator who complies with the notice and withholding requirements of section 3405 on or before April 1, 1983, undue hardship will be presumed to exist if one or more of the following conditions is present:

(1) The payor or plan administrator encounters significant delay or other substantial difficulty in obtaining authorization for funds to develop forms, to mail notices, to process responses, to develop new computer programs, or to obtain and train personnel to implement withholding.

(2) The payor or plan administrator incurs substantial increases in unbudgeted costs to develop forms, to mail notices, to process responses, to develop new computer programs, or to obtain and train personnel.

(3) There is difficulty in obtaining trained personnel, including professional or semi-professional individuals, whose skills are necessary to implement withholding.

(4) Training new or present employees or hiring new employees to implement withholding would cause substantially increased costs or would disrupt the payor's or plan administrator's operations, and such disruption or increased costs would not occur if withholding were implemented at a later date.

(5) Plan benefits change due to a collective bargaining agreement concluded between October 1, 1982, and April 1, 1983.

(6) A payor who provided notice prior to January 1, 1983, receives a substantial number of inquiries from payees. These inquiries indicate the payees' lack of understanding of the new withholding provisions and the payor cannot answer all questions and receive responses by January 1, 1983.

(7) The payor or plan administrator is unable to implement withholding on account of the occurrence of an event, such as fire, flood, earthquake, explosion, or strike, beyond the control of the payor or plan administrator.

(8) The payor or plan administrator is scheduled to install a new data processing hardware package or system between December 1, 1982, and July 1, 1983, that will be used for the process of pension withholding.

An example of a circumstance not considered as resulting in undue hardship would be changes in the withholding tables effective July 1, 1983.

The following examples illustrate situations in which an undue hardship that will permit delay in implementation of the notice and withholding provisions exists:

*Example (1).* A is the payor and plan administrator of a deferred compensation plan that is the subject of a collective bargaining agreement. The collectively bargained plan has fewer than 100 participants receiving annuity payments. All of A's available budget is scheduled to be used to pay plan benefits and administrative costs, and no funds are available to implement the new withholding requirements. A must obtain authorization to expend funds to implement withholding. Meetings at which A can obtain such authorization are held August 1 and February 1 of each year. After obtaining authorization on February 1, 1983, A will need to develop and mail withholding notices and elections, process responses and determine the amount to be withheld from each payee's annuity payment. A can implement withholding on April 1, 1983, without substantially disrupting its operations, but earlier implementation would disrupt its normal operations. Under these facts, A experiences undue hardship until at least April 1, 1983, as a result of the circumstances described in items (1) and (4) of question g-6.

*Example (2).* B, a bank, is a payor of pensions and annuities under plans described in section 401(a). The plan administrators of all these plans have transferred liability to B for withholding under section 3405. After T.D. 7839, relating to withholding from pensions, annuities and other deferred income, was published in the Federal Register on October 14, 1982, B determines that the withholding provisions can be implemented before April 1, 1983, on a reasonable schedule, without substantial increases in costs or disruption of daily bank operations, according to the following schedule:

| | | |
|---|---|---|
| (a) B's counsel analyzes regulations and reports requirements to operations personnel; operations personnel develop new forms, which are reviewed and revised by management and legal personnel; new forms are printed; personnel begin reprogramming computers | 8 weeks | (Dec. 9, 1982) |
| (b) Forms distributed to branch offices | 1 week | (Dec. 16, 1982) |
| (c) Forms mailed to payees | 1 week | (Dec. 23, 1982) |
| (d) Time allowed for response to mailing of notices, answering questions, mailing follow-up notices to payees | 6 weeks | (Feb. 3, 1983) |
| (e) Withholding calculated and entered into payment system | 6 weeks | (Mar. 17, 1983) |
| Total: | 22 weeks | |

Implementation is scheduled to begin March 17, 1983. Implementation prior to March 17, 1983, would substantially increase costs and would disrupt B's operations.

Under these facts, B experiences undue hardship under item (4) of question g-6 up to March 17, 1983, the scheduled date of implementation.

G-7. Q. If a payor or plan administrator qualifies for the delay described in question g-5, is there a procedure for requesting an additional delay up to July 1, 1983?

A. Yes. However, any request made for this additional delay will be considered on a case-by-case basis. It is anticipated these requests will be carefully scrutinized and generally will be granted only in circumstances where the payor or plan administrator can reasonably expect that more than one of the conditions described in question g-6 will exist on or after April 1, 1983, and up to July 1, 1983.

G-8. Q. How may a payor or plan administrator request this additional delay of up to 3 months for undue hardship?

A. The payor or plan administrator may request an additional delay of up to 3 months by filing in duplicate a written statement of undue hardship signed under penalties of perjury with the director of the service center where the payor or plan administrator files Form 941 or Form 941E. This written request must state on the envelope and at the top of the letter "PENSION WITHHOLDING: Undue Hardship" and must include all the information required in a statement of undue hardship as described in question g-9.

G-9. Q. What information must the statement of undue hardship include?

A. The statement of undue hardship must include the following information:

(1) The name, address, and taxpayer identification number of the payor or plan administrator.

(2) A complete statement of the facts upon which the payor is relying to show a delay beyond April 1, 1983, is warranted. This statement must include as many of the conditions of undue hardship listed in question g-6 as pertain to the payor or plan administrator.

(3) A schedule or plan of implementation showing dates on which the payor will implement the provisions of this section, with no date later than July 1, 1983. This schedule should provide a complete timetable that includes such items as development of forms, mailing of notices, time for responses, programming computers, and calculation of withholding.

(4) An explanation of the steps taken which demonstrate the payor's or plan administrator's good faith attempt to comply with these notice and withholding requirements.

G-10. Q. When must the plan administrator or payor file this request for delay and statement of undue hardship?

A. Payors or plan administrators must file the statement of undue hardship on or before March 1, 1983. However, no request for delay may be filed with the Internal Revenue Service before January 1, 1983.

G-11. Q. Who must request the delay?

A. The delay should be requested by the payor or plan administrator who is actually liable for withholding. Therefore, generally the payor should request the delay. However, in the case of a distribution from a plan described in section 401(a), section 403(a), or section 301(d) of the Tax Reduction Act of 1975, the plan administrator is liable for withholding and should request the delay unless the plan administrator has transferred liability for withholding to the payor under section 3405(c).

G-12. Q. If a plan administrator has not yet transferred liability for withholding under section 3405(c) or has inadequately transferred liability, and the payor requests a delay, will the request for delay be treated as if the plan administrator had requested it?

A. Yes.

G-13. Q. If a plan administrator and a payor both file requests for delay and statements of undue hardship with respect to the same plan, will there be two separate three-month extensions?

A. No. A request for delay will delay the effective date only up to three months and in no case will it extend it past July 1, 1983.

G-14. Q. What are the consequences for failure to file the request for delay and statement of undue hardship in a timely manner?

A. If the request for delay and statement of undue hardship are not filed in a timely manner, the payor or plan administrator will not be entitled to any delay beyond the delay to which he may be entitled under question g-5. This rule will not apply in the case of an event such as strike, fire, flood, earthquake, or explosion that occurs after March 1, 1983, if compliance with the withholding provisions would have been possible absent the occurrence of the event.

G-15. Q. Will a payor or plan administrator receive a response from the Internal Revenue Service as to whether a delay after April 1, 1983, has been granted?

A. Yes. Since these requests for delay will be reviewed on a case-by-case basis, the payor or plan administrator will receive a response by April 1, 1983, as to whether or not a requested delay has been granted. If the request for delay is denied by the director of the service center, the payor or plan administrator is required to begin withholding by the later of April 1, 1983, or 10 days from the date of the response. No penalties will be imposed under section 6651 for failure to withhold between April 1, 1983, and the day 10 days from the date on the response.

G-16. Q. If the director of the service center grants a delay up to July 1, 1983, must the payor or plan administrator retain a copy of the response from the Internal Revenue Service?

A. Yes. In addition, the payor or plan administrator must attach a copy of the response to the first Form 941 or 941E filed after the response is received.

G-17. Q. If a plan administrator or payor begins withholding before April 1, 1983, or July 1, 1983, can the payee request a refund from the plan administrator or payor of the amounts withheld?

A. No. Because plan administrators and payors are required to comply with the withholding and notice requirements as soon as they no longer experience undue hardship, they cannot refund any amounts withheld to a payee, except as provided in the regulations under section 6413 (in the case of a mistake by the payor or plan administrator).

G-18. Q. If a payor or plan administrator properly files the statement of undue hardship and receives a delay as provided in question g-7, will withholding from payments made after the delay period be required to make up for amounts that would have been withheld if there had been no delay granted?

A. No. No catch-up withholding is required for plan administrators or payors who are entitled to a delay up to April 1, 1983, as provided in question g-5 or granted a delay up to July 1, 1983, as provided in question g-7. However, if a payor or plan administrator who is entitled to a delay up to April 1, 1983, as provided in question g-5, is not granted a delay up to July 1, 1983, but is unable to implement withholding until July 1, 1983, despite a good faith effort to comply, no penalties will be imposed under section 6651 if the payor or plan administrator withholds between July 1, 1983, and December 31, 1983, both the amounts required to be withheld during that period and the amounts that should have been withheld between April 1, 1983, and June 30, 1983.

G-19. Q. If a payor or plan administrator does not receive and is not otherwise entitled to a delay under these regulations, will withholding from future payments be required to make up for amounts that would have been withheld if there had been no delay?

A. Yes, to the extent possible. An example of a situation in which a payor or plan administrator would not be able to withhold enough from subsequent payments to satisfy pre-July 1, 1983, withholding obligations is one where the recipient of a single life annuity died on July 1, 1983, before the payor or plan administrator began to withhold income tax from the annuity. In addition, a payor or plan administrator would not be able to satisfy the pre-July 1, 1983, withholding requirements if the payee elects out of withholding before all of the make-up withholding has been accomplished.

G-20. Q. What are the consequences if the payor or plan administrator cannot establish undue hardship and does not comply on January 1, 1983?

A. In general, if the payor or plan administrator cannot establish undue hardship and fails to withhold beginning January 1, 1983, the payor or plan administrator will be liable for the tax that should have been withheld and, in addition, the penalties provided in section 6651 will apply. However, the payor or plan administrator will not be liable for penalties for failure to file a return and for failure to pay the tax if a good faith effort is made to comply, and if, to the extent possible, withholding from post-implementation payments is sufficient to satisfy the pre-implementation withholding obligation. Whether the payor or plan administrator has made a good faith effort to comply depends on the facts and circumstances of each case. The facts and circumstances that will be considered include, but are not limited to, those conditions listed in question g-6.

G-21. Q. If a payor or plan administrator is required to make up amounts that should have been withheld, must he withhold from the first subsequent payment the entire amount that should have been previously withheld?

A. No. A payor or plan administrator may withhold a proportional amount out of each subsequent payment made before January 1, 1984.

G-22. Q. Will the notice requirements of section 3405 apply before July 1, 1983, with respect to recipients of periodic payments that total less than $5,400 per year?

A. No.

G-23. Q. Will the notice and withholding requirements of section 3405 apply before July 1, 1983, with respect to payments to nonresident alien individuals?

A. No.

G-24. Q. Does a payor or plan administrator who requested a delay prior to the publication of these procedures in the Federal Register need to resubmit the request in light of these procedures?

A. Yes. In order to be entitled to a delay, payors and plan administrators must follow the procedures required by these temporary regulations.

G-25. Q. Will the notice and withholding requirements of section 3405 apply before January 1, 1984, with respect to the exchange or complete or partial surrender of a commercial annuity under which the recipient had not irrevocably chosen, prior to January 1, 1984, to receive payments in the form of an annuity?

A. In the case of the exchange or complete or partial surrender of a commercial annuity under which the recipient had not irrevocably chosen, prior to January 1, 1984, to receive payments in the form of an annuity, the application of the notice and withholding provisions of this section may be delayed, so long as undue hardship exists, up to January 1, 1984. Prior approval from the Internal Revenue Service is not required for such delay, and should not be requested. For purposes of this delay, undue hardship will be presumed to exist, in the absence of bad faith, so long as the payor can establish that at least one of the conditions in question g-6 is present. The payor should prepare and retain a statement of undue hardship as described in question g-9 and should maintain any documents necessary to support the representations made in that statement.
[Temporary Reg. § 35.3405-1T.]

☐ [*T.D. 7839*, 10-8-82. *Amended by T.D. 7858*, 11-26-82 *and T.D. 7904*, 8-2-83. *Redesignated by T.D. 8873*, 2-7-2000. *Amended by T.D. 8952*, 6-25-2001 *and T.D. 9920*, 9-30-2020.]

### [Reg. § 31.3406-0]

**§ 31.3406-0. Outline of the backup withholding regulations.—** This section lists paragraphs contained in § § 31.3406(a)-1 through 31.3406(i)-1.

*§ 31.3406(a)-1 Backup withholding requirement on reportable payments.*
  (a) Overview.
  (b) Conditions that invoke the backup withholding requirement.
    (1) Conditions applicable to all reportable payments.
    (2) Conditions applicable only to reportable interest or dividend payments.
  (c) Exceptions.
  (d) Cross references.

*§ 31.3406(a)-2 Definition of payors obligated to backup withhold.*
  (a) In general.
  (b) Persons treated as payors.
  (c) Persons not treated as payors.
  (d) Effective date.

*§ 31.3406(a)-3 Scope and extent of accounts subject to backup withholding.*

*§ 31.3406(a)-4 Time when payments are considered to be paid and subject to backup withholding.*
  (a) Timing.
    (1) In general.
    (2) Special rules for dividends.
  (b) Amounts reportable under section 6045.
    (1) In general.
    (2) Special rule for interest accrued on bonds.
  (c) Middlemen.
    (1) In general.
    (2) Special rule for common trust funds.
    (3) Special rule for certain grantor trusts.

*§ 31.3406(b)(2)-1 Reportable interest payment.*
  (a) Interest subject to backup withholding.
    (1) In general.
    (2) Special rule for tax-exempt interest.
  (b) Amount subject to backup withholding.

(1) In general.
(2) Special rule to adjust for premature withdrawal penalty.

*§ 31.3406(b)(2)-2 Original issue discount.*
(a) Original issue discount subject to backup withholding.
(b) Amount subject to backup withholding and time when backup withholding is imposed with respect to short-term obligations.
(c) Transferred short-term obligations.
(1) Subsequent holder may establish purchase price.
(2) Subsequent holder unable (or not permitted) to establish purchase price.
(3) Transferred obligation.
(d) Amount subject to backup withholding and time when backup withholding is imposed with respect to long-term obligations.
(1) No cash payments prior to maturity.
(2) Registered long-term obligations with cash payments prior to maturity.
(3) Transferred registered long-term obligations with payments prior to maturity.
(e) Bearer long-term obligations.
(1) Payments prior to maturity.
(2) Payments at maturity.

*§ 31.3406(b)(2)-3 Window transactions.*
(a) Requirement to backup withhold.
(b) Window transaction defined.
(c) Manner of furnishing taxpayer identification number in the case of a window transaction.

*§ 31.3426(b)(2)-4 Reportable dividend payment.*
(a) Dividends subject to backup withholding.
(b) Dividends not subject to backup withholding.
(c) Amount subject to backup withholding.
(1) In general.
(2) Reasonable estimate of amount of dividend subject to backup withholding.
(3) Reinvested dividends.

*§ 31.3406(b)(2)-5 Reportable patronage dividend payment.*
(a) Patronage dividends subject to backup withholding.
(b) Amount subject to backup withholding.
(1) Failure to provide taxpayer identification number or notification of incorrect taxpayer identification number.
(2) Notified payee underreporting or payee certification failure.

*§ 31.3406(b)(3)-1 Reportable payments of rents, commissions, nonemployee compensation, etc.*
(a) Section 6041 and 6041A(a) payments subject to backup withholding.
(b) Amount subject to backup withholding.
(1) In general.
(2) Net commissions.
(3) Payments aggregating $600 or more for the calendar year.

*§ 31.3406(b)(3)-2 Reportable barter exchanges and gross proceeds of sales of securities or commodities by brokers.*
(a) Transactions subject to backup withholding.
(b) Amount subject to backup withholding.
(1) In general.
(2) Forward contracts, including foreign currency contracts, and regulated futures contracts.
(3) Security sales made through a margin account.
(4) Security short sales.
(5) Fractional shares.

*§ 31.3406(b)(3)-3 Reportable payments by certain fishing boat operators.*
(a) Payments subject to backup withholding.
(b) Amount subject to backup withholding.

*§ 31.3406(b)(3)-4 Reportable payments of royalties.*
(a) Royalty payments subject to backup withholding.
(b) Amount subject to backup withholding.

*§ 31.3406(b)(3)-5 Reportable payments of payment card and third party network transactions.*
(a) Payment card and third party network transactions subject to backup withholding.
(b) Amount subject to backup withholding.
(c) Time when payments are considered to be subject to backup withholding.
(d) Backup withholding from an alternate source.

(e) Effective/applicability date.

*§ 31.3406(b)(4)-1 Exemption for certain minimal payments.*
(a) In general.
(b) Manner of making the election.
(c) How to annualize.
(1) In general.
(2) Special aggregation rule for reportable interest and dividends.
(d) Exception for window transactions and original issue discount.

*§ 31.3406(c)-1 Notified payee underreporting of reportable interest or dividend payments.*
(a) Overview.
(b) Definitions.
(1) Notified payee underreporting.
(2) Payee underreporting.
(c) Notice to payors regarding backup withholding due to notified payee underreporting.
(1) In general.
(2) Additional requirements for payors that are also brokers.
(3) Payor identification of accounts of the payee subject to backup withholding due to notified payee underreporting.
(d) Notice from payors of backup withholding due to notified payee underreporting.
(1) In general.
(2) Procedures.
(e) Period during which backup withholding is required.
(1) In general.
(2) Stop withholding.
(3) Dormant accounts.
(f) Notice to payees from the Internal Revenue Service.
(1) Notice period.
(2) Payee subject to backup withholding.
(3) Disclosure of names of payors and brokers.
(4) Backup withholding certification.
(g) Determination by the Internal Revenue Service that backup withholding should not start or should be stopped.
(1) In general.
(2) Date notice to stop backup withholding will be provided.
(3) Grounds for determination.
(4) No underreporting.
(5) Correcting any payee underreporting.
(6) Undue hardship.
(7) Bona fide dispute.
(h) Payees filing a joint return.
(1) In general.
(2) Exceptions.
(i) [Reserved.]
(j) Penalties.

*§ 31.3406(d)-1 Manner required for furnishing a taxpayer identification number.*
(a) Requirement to backup withhold.
(b) Reportable interest or dividend account.
(1) Manner required for furnishing a taxpayer identification number with respect to a pre-1984 account or instrument.
(2) Determination of pre-1984 account or instrument.
(3) Manner required for furnishing a taxpayer identification number with respect to an account or instrument that is not a pre-1984 account.
(4) Special rule with respect to the acquisition of a readily tradable instrument in a transaction between certain parties acting without the assistance of a broker.
(c) Brokerage account.
(1) Manner required for furnishing a taxpayer identification number with respect to a brokerage relationship that is not a post-1983 brokerage account.
(2) Manner required for furnishing a taxpayer identification number with respect to a post-1983 brokerage account.
(d) Rents, commissions, nonemployee compensation, and certain fishing boat operators, etc.—Manner required for furnishing a taxpayer identification number.

*§ 31.3406(d)-2 Payee certification failure.*
(a) Requirement to backup withhold.
(b) Exceptions.

*§ 31.3406(d)-3 Special 30-day rules for certain reportable payments.*
(a) Accounts or readily tradable instruments acquired directly from the payor (including a broker who holds an instrument in street name) by electronic transmission or by mail.

**Reg. § 31.3406-0**

(b) Sale of an instrument for a customer by electronic transmission or by mail.

(c) Application to foreign payees.

*§ 31.3406(d)-4 Special rules for readily tradable instruments acquired through a broker.*

(a) Readily tradable instruments acquired through post-1983 brokerage accounts with a broker who is not a payor.

(1) In general.

(2) Additional requirements.

(3) Transactions entered into through a brokerage account that is not a post-1983 brokerage account.

(4) Payor must notify payee.

(b) Notices.

(1) Form of notice by broker to payor.

(2) Form of notice by payor to payee.

(c) Payor's reliance on information from broker.

(1) In general.

(2) Amount subject to backup withholding.

*§ 31.3406(d)-5 Backup withholding when the Service or a broker notifies the payor to withhold because the payee's taxpayer identification number is incorrect.*

(a) Overview.

(b) Definitions and special rules.

(1) Definition of an incorrect name/TIN combination.

(2) Definition of account.

(3) Definition of business day.

(4) Certain exceptions.

(c) Notice regarding an incorrect name/TIN combination.

(1) In general.

(2) Additional requirements for payors that are also brokers.

(3) Payor identification of the account or accounts of the payee that have the incorrect taxpayer identification number.

(4) Special rule for joint accounts.

(5) Date of receipt.

(d) Notice from payors of backup withholding due to an incorrect name/TIN combination.

(1) In general.

(2) Procedures.

(e) Period during which backup withholding is required due to notification of an incorrect name/TIN combination.

(1) In general.

(2) Grace periods.

(3) Dormant accounts.

(f) Manner required for payee to furnish certified taxpayer identification number.

(g) Receipt of two notices within a 3-year period.

(1) In general.

(2) Notice to payee who has provided two incorrect name/TIN combinations within 3 calendar years.

(3) Period during which backup withholding is required due to a second notice of an incorrect name/TIN combination within 3 calendar years.

(4) Receipt of two notices in one calendar year.

(5) Notification from the Social Security Administration (or the Internal Revenue Service) validating a name/TIN combination.

(h) Payors must use newly provided certified number.

(i) Effective date.

(j) Examples.

*§ 31.3406(e)-1 Period during which backup withholding is required.*

(a) In general.

(b) Failure to furnish a taxpayer identification number in the manner required.

(1) Start withholding.

(2) Stop withholding.

(c) Notification of an incorrect taxpayer identification number.

(d) Notified payee underreporting.

(e) Payee certification failure.

(1) Start withholding.

(2) Stop withholding.

(f) Rule for determining when the payor receives a taxpayer identification number or certificate from a payee.

*§ 31.3406(f)-1 Confidentiality of information.*

(a) Confidentiality and liability for violation.

(b) Permissible use of information.

(1) In general.

(2) Window transactions.

(c) Specific restrictions on the use of information.

*§ 31.3406(g)-1 Exception for payments to certain payees and certain other payments.*

(a) Exempt recipients.

(1) In general.

(2) Nonexclusive list.

(b) Determination of whether a person is described in paragraph (a)(1) of this section.

(c) Prepaid or advance premium life-insurance contracts.

(d) Reportable payments made to Canadian nonresident alien individuals.

(e) Certain reportable payments made outside the United States by foreign persons, foreign offices of United States banks and brokers, and others.

(f) Special rule for certain payment card transactions.

*§ 31.3406(g)-2 Exception for reportable payments for which backup withholding is otherwise required.*

(a) In general.

(b) Payment of wages.

(c) Distribution from a pension, annuity, or other plan of deferred compensation.

(d) Gambling winnings.

(1) In general.

(2) Definition of a reportable gambling winning and determination of amount subject to backup withholding.

(3) Special rules.

(e) Certain real estate transactions.

(f) Certain payments after an acquisition of accounts or instruments.

(g) Certain gross proceeds.

(h) Applicability date.

*§ 31.3406(g)-3 Exemption while payee is waiting for a taxpayer identification number.*

(a) In general.

(1) Backup withholding not required for 60 days.

(2) Reserve method.

(3) Alternative rule; 7-day grace period.

(b) Special rule for readily tradable instruments.

(c) Exceptions.

(1) In general.

(2) Special rule for amounts subject to reporting under section 6045 other than proceeds of redemptions of bearer obligations.

(d) Awaiting-TIN certificate.

(e) Form for awaiting-TIN certificate.

*§ 31.3406(h)-1 Definitions.*

(a) In general.

(b) Taxpayer identification number.

(1) In general.

(2) Obviously incorrect number.

(c) Broker.

(d) Readily tradable instrument.

(e) Day.

(f) Business day.

*§ 31.3406(h)-2 Special rules.*

(a) Joint accounts.

(1) Relevant name and taxpayer identification number combination.

(2) Optional rule for accounts subject to backup withholding under section 3406(a)(1)(B) or (C) where the names are switched.

(3) Joint foreign payees.

(b) Backup withholding from an alternative source.

(1) In general.

(2) Exceptions for payments made in property.

(c) Trusts.

(d) Adjustment of prior withholding by middleman.

(e) Conversion of amounts paid in foreign currency into United States dollars.

(f) Coordination with other sections.

(g) Tax liabilities and penalties.

(h) To whom payor is liable for amount withheld.

*§ 31.3406(h)-3 Certificates.*

(a) Prescribed form to furnish information under penalties of perjury.

(1) In general.

(2) Use of a single or multiple Forms W-9 for accounts of the same payee.

(b) Prescribed form to furnish a noncertified taxpayer identification number.

(c) Forms prepared by payors or brokers.

(1) Substitute forms; in general.

(2) Form for exempt recipient.

(d) Special rule for brokers.

(e) Reasonable reliance on certificate.

(1) In general.

(2) Circumstances establishing reasonable reliance.

(f) Who may sign certificate.

(1) In general.

(2) Notified payee underreporting.

(g) Retention of certificates.

(1) Accounts or instruments that are not pre-1984 accounts and brokerage relationships that are post-1983 brokerage accounts.

(2) Accounts or instruments that are pre-1984 accounts and brokerage relationships that are not post-1983 brokerage accounts.

(h) Cross references.

[Reg. § 31.3406-0.]

□ [T.D. 8409, 4-10-92. *Amended by T.D. 8637, 12-20-95; T.D. 8734,* 10-6-97 (T.D. 8804 delayed the effective date of T.D. 8734 from January 1, 1999, to January 1, 2000; T.D. 8856 further delayed the effective date of T.D. 8734 until January 1, 2001); *T.D. 9010, 7-25-2002; T.D. 9496, 8-13-2010 and T.D. 9824, 9-25-2017.*]

### [Reg. § 31.3406(a)-1]

**§ 31.3406(a)-1. Backup withholding requirement on reportable payments.**—(a) *Overview.*—Under section 3406, a payor must deduct and withhold 31 percent of a reportable payment if a condition for withholding exists. *Reportable payments* mean interest and dividend payments (as defined in section 3406(b)(2)) and other reportable payments (as defined in section 3406(b)(3)). The conditions described in paragraph (b)(1) of this section apply to all reportable payments, including reportable interest and dividend payments. The conditions described in paragraph (b)(2) of this section apply only to reportable interest and dividend payments.

(b) *Conditions that invoke the backup withholding requirement.*—(1) *Conditions applicable to all reportable payments.*—A payor of a reportable payment must deduct and withhold under section 3406 if—

(i) The payee of the reportable payment does not furnish the payee's taxpayer identification number to the payor, as required in section 3406(a)(1)(A) and § 31.3406(d)-1; or

(ii) The Internal Revenue Service or a broker notifies the payor that the taxpayer identification number furnished by its payee for a reportable payment is incorrect, as described in section 3406(a)(1)(B) and § 31.3406(d)-5.

(2) *Conditions applicable only to reportable interest or dividend payments.*—A payor of a reportable interest or dividend payment must deduct and withhold under section 3406 if—

(i) The Internal Revenue Service or a broker notifies the payor that its payee has underreported interest or dividend income, as described in section 3406(a)(1)(C) and § 31.3406(c)-1; or

(ii) The payee fails to certify to the payor or broker that the payee is not subject to withholding due to notified payee underreporting, as described in section 3406(a)(1)(D) and § 31.3406(d)-2.

(c) *Exceptions.*—The requirement to withhold does not apply to certain minimal payments as described in § 31.3406(b)(4)-1 or to payments exempt from withholding under §§ 31.3406(g)-1 through 31.3406(g)-3.

(d) *Cross references.*—For the definition of *payor,* see § 31.3406(a)-2. For the definition of *taxpayer identification number,* see § 31.3406(h)-1(b). [Reg. § 31.3406(a)-1.]

□ [T.D. 8637, 12-20-95.]

### [Reg. § 31.3406(a)-2]

**§ 31.3406(a)-2. Definition of payors obligated to backup withhold.**—(a) *In general.*—*Payor* means the person that is required to make an information return under section 6041, 6041A(a), 6042, 6044, 6045, 6049, 6050A, 6050N, or 6050W with respect to any reportable payment (as described in section 3406(b)), or that is described in paragraph (b) of this section.

(b) *Persons treated as payors.*—The following persons are treated as payors for purposes of section 3406—

(1) A grantor trust established after December 31, 1995, all of which is owned by two or more grantors (treating for this purpose spouses filing a joint return as one grantor);

(2) A grantor trust with ten or more grantors established on or after January 1, 1984 but before January 1, 1996;

(3) A common trust fund; and

(4) A partnership or an S corporation that makes a reportable payment.

(c) *Persons not treated as payors.*—A person on the following list is not treated as a payor for purposes of section 3406 if the person does not have a reporting obligation under the section on information reporting to which the payment relates—

(1) A trust (other than a grantor trust as described in paragraph (b)(1) or (2) of this section) that files a Form 1041 containing information required to be shown on an information return, including amounts withheld under section 3406; or

(2) A partnership making a payment of a distributive share or an S corporation making a similar distribution.

(d) *Effective date.*—The provisions of this section apply to payments made after December 31, 2002. [Reg. § 31.3406(a)-2.]

[T.D. 8637, 12-20-95. *Amended by T.D. 9010, 7-25-2002 and T.D. 9496,* 8-13-2010.]

### [Reg. § 31.3406(a)-3]

**§ 31.3406(a)-3. Scope and extent of accounts subject to backup withholding.**—A payor who is required to withhold under § 31.3406(a)-1 must withhold—

(a) On the accounts subject to withholding under § 31.3406(a)-1(b)(1)(i) or (b)(2)(ii); and

(b) On the accounts subject to withholding under § 31.3406(a)-1(b)(1)(ii) or (b)(2)(i), as described under § 31.3406(d)-5 (relating to notification of incorrect TIN) or § 31.3406(c)-1 (relating to notified payee underreporting), respectively. [Reg. § 31.3406(a)-3.]

□ [T.D. 8637, 12-20-95.]

### [Reg. § 31.3406(a)-4]

**§ 31.3406(a)-4. Time when payments are considered to be paid and subject to backup withholding.**—(a) *Timing.*—(1) *In general.*—If backup withholding is required under section 3406 on a reportable payment (as defined in section 3406(b)), the payor must withhold at the time it makes the payment to the payee or to the payee's account that is subject to withholding. Amounts are considered paid when they are credited to the account of, or made available to, the payee. Amounts are not considered paid solely because they are posted (e.g., an informational notation on the payee's passbook) if they are not actually credited to the payee's account or made available to the payee. See paragraph (c) of this section for the timing of withholding by a middleman.

(2) *Special rules for dividends.*—For purposes of section 3406 and this section—

(i) *Record date earlier than payment date.*—In the case of stock for which the record date is earlier than the payment date, the dividends are considered paid on the payment date.

(ii) *Dividends paid in corporate reorganizations.*—In the case of a corporate reorganization, if a payee is required to exchange stock held in the former corporation for stock in the new corporation before the dividends that have been paid with respect to the stock in the new corporation will be provided to the payee, the dividend is considered paid on the date the payee actually exchanges the stock and receives the dividend.

(b) *Amounts reportable under section 6045.*—(1) *In general.*—Notwithstanding paragraph (a) of this section, in the case of a transaction reportable under section 6045 (except in the case of forward contracts (including foreign currency contracts), regulated futures contracts, and security short sales), the obligation to withhold under section 3406 arises on the date the sale is entered on the books of the broker or the date the exchange occurs as provided in § 1.6045-1(f)(3) of this chapter. A broker (in its capacity as payor) is not required, however, to satisfy its withholding liability until payment is made. See § 31.3406(b)(3)-2(b)(2) for special rules applicable to forward contracts (including foreign currency contracts), regulated futures contracts, and security short sales.

(2) *Special rule for interest accrued on bonds.*—For purposes of determining the time that interest is considered paid and subject to withholding under section 3406 when bonds are sold between interest payment dates, the portion of the sales price representing interest accrued to the date of sale is considered a portion of a reportable payment of gross proceeds under section 6045 (provided that the accrued interest is not tax-exempt as described in section 103(a), relating to certain governmental obligations), and is not considered to be a payment of interest for purposes of section 6049.

(c) *Middlemen.*—(1) *In general.*—A person that is a middleman and is a person defined in § 31.3406(a)-2(b) or in the section on information reporting to which the payment relates must withhold under section 3406 at the time the reportable payment is received by or credited to the middleman. If the middleman makes or credits the reportable payment to the payee prior to the middleman's receipt of the corresponding payment, the middleman may withhold at the time the reportable payment is made or credited to the payee.

(2) *Special rule for common trust funds.*—A common trust fund (as defined in section 584) must withhold either—

(i) At the time the reportable payment is received by or credited to the common trust fund as provided in paragraph (c)(1) of this section;

(ii) On the date on which the assets of the common trust fund are valued; or

(iii) At the time the common trust fund pays or credits the reportable payment to a participant of the common trust fund.

(3) *Special rule for certain grantor trusts.*—For grantor trusts described in §31.3406(a)-2(b)(1) or (2), reportable payments made to the trust are treated as paid by the trust to each grantor, in an amount equal to the distribution made by the trust to each grantor, on the date that the reportable payment is paid to the trust (except for gross proceeds reportable under section 6045). Paragraph (b)(2) of this section applies to a grantor trust making a payment of gross proceeds under section 6045 subject to withholding under section 3406. For purposes of this paragraph (c)(3) a husband and wife filing a joint return are considered to be one grantor. [Reg. §31.3406(a)-4.]

☐ [T.D. 8637, 12-20-95. Amended by T.D. 9010, 7-25-2002.]

**[Reg. §31.3406(b)(2)-1]**

**§31.3406(b)(2)-1. Reportable interest payment.**—(a) *Interest subject to backup withholding.*—(1) *In general.*—A payment of a kind, and to a payee, that is required to be reported under section 6049 (relating to returns regarding interest and original issue discount) is a reportable payment for purposes of section 3406, subject to the special rules of §31.3406(b)(2)-2 (relating to original issue discount) and §31.3406(b)(2)-3 (relating to window transactions). See §31.6051-4 for the requirement to furnish a statement to the payee if tax is withheld under section 3406.

(2) *Special rule for tax-exempt interest.*—When an issuer is required to make an information return under §1.6049-4(d)(8) of this chapter because a payee provided a signed written statement on the envelope or shell incorrectly claiming that the interest was exempt from taxation under section 103(a)(as described in §1.6049-5(b)(1)(ii) of this chapter), the issuer is not required to impose withholding under section 3406.

(b) *Amount subject to backup withholding.*—(1) *In general.*—The amount of interest subject to withholding under section 3406 is the amount subject to reporting under section 6049.

(2) *Special rule to adjust for premature withdrawal penalty.*—Solely for purposes of computing the amount subject to withholding under section 3406, the payor may elect not to withhold from the portion of any interest payment that is not received by the payee because a penalty is in fact imposed for premature withdrawal of funds deposited in a time savings account, certificate of deposit, or similar class of deposit. [Reg. §31.3406(b)(2)-1.]

☐ [T.D. 8637, 12-20-95.]

**[Reg. §31.3406(b)(2)-2]**

**§31.3406(b)(2)-2. Original issue discount.**—(a) *Original issue discount subject to backup withholding.*—The amount of original issue discount, treated as interest, subject to withholding under section 3406 is the amount subject to reporting under section 6049, but is limited to the amount of cash paid. In addition, if an original issue discount obligation, subject to reporting under section 6045, is sold prior to maturity and with respect to the seller a condition exists for imposing withholding under section 3406 on the gross proceeds, then withholding under §31.3406(b)(3)-2 applies to the gross proceeds of the sale reportable under section 6045, and not to the amount of any original issue discount includible in the gross income of the seller for the calendar year of the sale. See §31.6051-4 for the requirement to furnish a statement to the payee if tax is withheld under section 3406.

(b) *Amount subject to backup withholding and time when backup withholding is imposed with respect to short-term obligations.*—In the case of an obligation with a fixed maturity date not exceeding one year from the date of issue (a short-term obligation), withholding under section 3406 applies to any payment of original issue discount on the obligation includible in the gross income of the holder to the extent of the cash amount of the payment. See §1.1273-1 of this chapter to determine the amount of original issue discount on a short-term obligation. See §1.446-2(e)(1) of this chapter to determine the amount of a payment treated as original issue discount.

(c) *Transferred short-term obligations.*—(1) *Subsequent holder may establish purchase price.*—(i) *In general.*—At maturity of a short-term obligation, a subsequent holder (i.e., any person who purchased or

otherwise obtained the obligation after the obligation was issued to the original holder) may establish the price of the obligation. The price established by the subsequent holder must then be treated as the original issue price for purposes of computing the amount of the original issue discount subject to withholding under section 3406. The price of a short-term obligation may be established by confirmation receipt or other record of a similar type or, if the obligation is redeemed by or through the person from whom the obligation was purchased or otherwise obtained, by the records of the person from whom or through whom the obligation was purchased or otherwise obtained. The subsequent holder is not required to certify under penalties of perjury that the price determined under this paragraph (c)(1)(i) is correct.

(ii) *Exception.*—A payor may elect to disregard the price at which the subsequent holder purchased or otherwise obtained the obligation if the payor's computer or recordkeeping system on which the details of the obligation are stored is not able to accept that price without significant manual intervention.

(2) *Subsequent holder unable (or not permitted) to establish purchase price.*—If a subsequent holder fails (or is unable, pursuant to paragraph (c)(1)(ii) of this section) to establish the purchase price of the obligation, then the person redeeming the obligation must determine the amount subject to withholding under section 3406 as though the obligation had been purchased by the holder on the date of issue. If the person redeeming the obligation is the issuer of the obligation, then the issuer must determine the amount subject to withholding from its records. If a person other than the issuer of the obligation redeems the obligation and the obligation is listed in Internal Revenue Service Publication 1212, List of Original Issue Discount Obligations, that person must determine the amount subject to withholding by using the issue price indicated in Publication 1212.

(3) *Transferred obligation.*—If a short-term obligation is transferred, no part of the purchase price is considered a reportable interest payment under section 6049. Withholding under section 3406 applies, however, to the gross proceeds of the sale of the obligation if the transfer is subject to reporting under section 6045 and a condition exists for imposing withholding. For the rules regarding withholding for amounts subject to reporting under section 6045, see §31.3406(b)(3)-2.

(d) *Amount subject to backup withholding and time when backup withholding is imposed with respect to long-term obligations.*—(1) *No cash payments prior to maturity.*—In the case of an obligation with a fixed maturity date that is more than one year from the date of issue (a long-term obligation) and with no cash payments prior to maturity, withholding under section 3406 applies at the maturity of the obligation to the amount of original issue discount includible in the gross income of the holder for the calendar year in which the obligation matures. The amount required to be withheld must not exceed the amount of the cash payment.

(2) *Registered long-term obligations with cash payments prior to maturity.*—In the case of a long-term obligation in registered form that provides for cash payments prior to maturity, withholding under section 3406 applies at the time cash payments are made to the sum of the amounts of qualified stated interest and original issue discount includible in the gross income of the holder for the calendar year in which the cash payments are made. The amount required to be withheld at the time of any cash payment, however, must not exceed the amount of the cash payment. If more than one cash payment is made during a calendar year, the tax that is required to be withheld with respect to original issue discount must be allocated among all the expected cash payments in the ratio that each cash payment bears to the total of the expected cash payments.

(3) *Transferred registered long-term obligations with payments prior to maturity.*—In the case of a long-term obligation that is transferred after its issuance from the original holder, the amount subject to withholding under section 3406 with respect to a subsequent holder is the amount of original issue discount includible in the gross income of all holders during the calendar year (without regard to any amount paid by a subsequent holder at the time of transfer). If the person redeeming the obligation at maturity is the issuer of the obligation, the issuer must determine the amount subject to withholding through its records by treating the holder as if he were the original holder. If a person redeeming the obligation at maturity is a person other than the issuer of the obligation, and the obligation is listed in Internal Revenue Service Publication 1212, List of Original Issue Discount Obligations, the person must determine the amount subject to withholding by using the issue price indicated in Publication 1212.

(e) *Bearer long-term obligations.*—In the case of a bearer long-term obligation with cash payments prior to maturity—

(1) *Payments prior to maturity.*—Withholding under section 3406 applies prior to maturity only to the payment of qualified stated interest (and not to any amount of original issue discount) includible in the gross income of the holder for the calendar year.

(2) *Payments at maturity.*—At maturity of the obligation, withholding applies to the sum of any qualified stated interest payment made at maturity and the total amount of original issue discount includible in the gross income of the holder during the calendar year of maturity. The amount required to be withheld at the time of the cash payment, however, must not exceed the amount of the cash payment. [Reg. § 31.3406(b)(2)-2.]

☐ [*T.D.* 8637, 12-20-95.]

### [Reg. § 31.3406(b)(2)-3]

**§ 31.3406(b)(2)-3. Window transactions.**—(a) *Requirement to backup withhold.*—Withholding under section 3406 applies to a window transaction (as defined in paragraph (b) of this section) only if the payee does not furnish a taxpayer identification number to the payor in the manner required in paragraph (c) of this section or furnishes an obviously incorrect number as described in § 31.3406(h)-1(b)(2). Withholding does not apply to a window transaction even though the Internal Revenue Service notifies the payor of the payee's incorrect taxpayer identification number under section 3406(a)(1)(B) or of notified payee underreporting under section 3406(a)(1)(C). The payee in a window transaction is not required to certify under penalties of perjury that the payee is not subject to withholding due to notified payee underreporting (as described in § 31.3406(d)-2(b)(2)).

(b) *Window transaction defined. Window transaction.*—means payment of interest with respect to any of the following obligations:

(1) An interest coupon in bearer form that is subject to taxation (i.e., other than exempt interest described in § 1.6049-5(b)(1)(ii) of this chapter);

(2) A United States savings bond; or

(3) A discount obligation having a maturity at issue of one year or less, including commercial paper and bankers' acceptances that are in definitive form (i.e., evidenced by a paper document other than a confirmation receipt) but not including short-term government obligations (as defined in section 1271(a)(3)(B)).

(c) *Manner of furnishing taxpayer identification number in the case of a window transaction.*—A payee must furnish the payee's taxpayer identification number to the payor with respect to a window transaction either orally or in writing at the time that the window transaction occurs. See § 31.3406(g)-3(c)(1)(i), which provides that a payee may not claim the payee is awaiting receipt of a taxpayer identification number with respect to a window transaction. The payee is not required to certify, under penalties of perjury, that the taxpayer identification number provided is correct. [Reg. § 31.3406(b)(2)-3.]

☐ [*T.D.* 8637, 12-20-95.]

### [Reg. § 31.3406(b)(2)-4]

**§ 31.3406(b)(2)-4. Reportable dividend payment.**—(a) *Dividends subject to backup withholding.*—A payment of a kind, and to a payee, that is required to be reported under section 6042 (relating to returns regarding payments of dividends and corporate earnings and profits) is a reportable payment for purposes of section 3406. See paragraph (b) of this section for certain dividends not subject to withholding under section 3406. See § 31.6051-4 for the requirement to furnish a statement to the payee if tax is withheld under section 3406.

(b) *Dividends not subject to backup withholding.*—Except as provided in § 31.3406(b)(3)-2 (relating to transactions reportable under section 6045), withholding under section 3406 does not apply to—

(1) Any amount treated as a taxable dividend by reason of section 302 (relating to redemptions of stock), section 304 (relating to redemptions through the use of related corporations), section 306 (relating to disposition of certain stock), section 356 (relating to receipt of additional consideration in connection with certain reorganizations), or section 1081(e)(2)(relating to certain distributions pursuant to an order of the Securities and Exchange Commission);

(2) Any exempt-interest dividend, as defined in section 852(b)(5)(A), paid by a regulated investment company; or

(3) Any amount paid or treated as paid during a year by a regulated investment company, provided that the payor reasonably estimates, as provided in paragraph (c)(2) of this section, that 95 percent or more of all dividends paid or treated as paid during the year are exempt-interest dividends.

(c) *Amount subject to backup withholding.*—(1) *In general.*—The amount of a dividend subject to withholding under section 3406 is the amount subject to reporting under section 6042, including any dividend that is reinvested pursuant to a plan under which a share-holder may elect to receive stock as a dividend instead of property. Except as otherwise provided in this paragraph (c), withholding applies to the entire amount of the distribution.

(2) *Reasonable estimate of amount of dividend subject to backup withholding.*—Pursuant to section 6042(b)(3) and § 1.6042-3(c) of this chapter, if the payor is unable to determine the portion of a distribution that is a dividend, the entire amount of the distribution must be treated as a dividend for information reporting under section 6042. Hence, withholding applies to the entire amount of the distribution. If a payor is able reasonably to estimate under section 6042 and § 1.6042-3(c) of this chapter the portion of a distribution that is not a dividend, however, the payor must not withhold on that portion (which is not considered a dividend). A payor making a payment, all or a portion of which may not be a dividend, may use previous experience to estimate the portion of a distribution that is not a dividend. The payor's estimate is considered reasonable if—

(i) The estimate does not exceed the proportion of the distributions made by the payor during the most recent calendar year for which a Form 1099 was required to be filed that was not reported by the payor as a dividend; and

(ii) The payor has no reasonable basis to expect that the proportion of the distribution that is not a dividend will be substantially different for the current year.

(3) *Reinvested dividends.*—In the case of a dividend paid pursuant to a dividend reinvestment plan, withholding under section 3406 applies, pursuant to § 31.3406(a)-4(a), at the time and to the amount made available to the shareholder or credited to the shareholder's account. At the discretion of the payor, withholding under section 3406 need not be applied to any excess of the fair market value of the shares of stock received by the shareholder or credited to the shareholder's account over the purchase price of the shares (including shares acquired by the shareholder at a discount in connection with the dividend distribution) or to any fee that is paid by the payor in the nature of a broker's fee for purchase of the stock or service charge for maintenance of the shareholder's account. The payor must, however, treat any excess amounts and fees on a consistent basis for each calendar year. [Reg. § 31.3406(b)(2)-4.]

☐ [*T.D.* 8637, 12-20-95.]

### [Reg. § 31.3406(b)(2)-5]

**§ 31.3406(b)(2)-5. Reportable patronage dividend payment.**—(a) *Patronage dividends subject to backup withholding.*—A payment of a kind, and to a payee, that is required to be reported under section 6044 (relating to returns regarding patronage dividends) is a reportable payment for purposes of section 3406. See § 31.6051-4 for the requirement to furnish a statement to the payee if tax is withheld under section 3406.

(b) *Amount subject to backup withholding.*—(1) *Failure to provide taxpayer identification number or notification of incorrect taxpayer identification number.*—For purposes of sections 3406(a)(1)(A) and (B), the amount of a payment described in paragraph (a) of this section that is subject to withholding under section 3406 is the amount subject to reporting under section 6044, but only to the extent the payment is made in money. For purposes of this paragraph (b), *money* includes cash or a qualified check (as defined in section 1388(c)(4)).

(2) *Notified payee underreporting or payee certification failure.*—For purposes of sections 3406(a)(1)(C) and (D), the amount of a payment described in paragraph (a) of this section that is subject to withholding under section 3406 is the amount subject to withholding under paragraph (b)(1) of this section, but only if 50 percent or more of that reportable amount is paid in money. Thus, a payor is required to withhold according to this paragraph (b)(2) on a payment if—

(i) There has been a notified payee underreporting described in section 3406(a)(1)(C) and § 31.3406(c)-1 or there has been a payee certification failure described in section 3406(a)(1)(D) and § 31.3406(d)-2;

(ii) The payor makes a reportable payment subject to reporting under section 6044 to the payee; and

(iii) Fifty percent or more of the payment is in cash or by qualified check. [Reg. § 31.3406(b)(2)-5.]

☐ [*T.D.* 8637, 12-20-95.]

### [Reg. § 31.3406(b)(3)-1]

**§ 31.3406(b)(3)-1. Reportable payments of rents, commissions, nonemployee compensation, etc.**—(a) *Section 6041 and 6041A(a) payments subject to backup withholding.*—A payment of a kind, and to a payee, that is required to be reported under section 6041 (relating to information reporting of rents, commissions, nonemployee compensation, etc.) or a payment that is required to be reported under section 6041A(a)(relating to information reporting of payments to nonemployees for services) is a reportable payment for purposes of section 3406. See paragraph (b) of this section for an exception concerning payments aggregating less than $600. See §31.6051-4 for the requirement to furnish a statement to the payee if tax is withheld under section 3406.

(b) *Amount subject to backup withholding.*—(1) *In general.*—The amount of a payment described in paragraph (a) of this section subject to withholding under section 3406 is the amount subject to reporting under section 6041 or section 6041A(a).

(2) *Net commissions.*—Withholding under section 3406 does not apply to net commissions paid to unincorporated special agents with respect to insurance policies that are subject to reporting under section 6041, provided that no cash is actually paid by the payor to the special agent.

(3) *Payments aggregating $600 or more for the calendar year.*—(i) *In general.*—A payment is a reportable payment under paragraph (a) of this section only if the aggregate amount of the current payment and all previous payments to the payee during the calendar year aggregate $600 or more. The amount subject to withholding is the entire amount of the payment that causes the total amount paid to the payee to equal $600 or more and the amount of any subsequent payments made to the payee during the calendar year. This paragraph (b)(3)(i) does not apply to gambling winnings (as provided in §31.3406(g)-2(e)(1)).

(ii) *Exceptions.*—(A) *The $600 aggregation rule.*—The $600 aggregation rule of paragraph (b)(3)(i) of this section does not apply if the payor was required to make an information return under section 6041 or 6041A(a) for the preceding calendar year with respect to payments to the payee, or the payor was required to withhold under section 3406 during the preceding calendar year with respect to payments to the payee that were reportable under section 6041 or 6041A(a).

(B) *Determination of whether payments aggregate $600 or more.*—In determining whether payments to a payee aggregate $600 or more during a calendar year for purposes of withholding under section 3406, the payor must aggregate only payments of the same kind made to the same payee. For this purpose, payments are of the same kind if they are of the same type, regardless of whether they are reportable under the same section. However, a payor with different paying departments making reportable payments of the same kind is not required to aggregate payments made by all those departments unless it is the payor's customary method to aggregate those payments. A payor may, in its discretion, aggregate—

(1) Payments not of the same kind to the same payee, reportable under either section 6041 or 6041A(a); and

(2) Payments reportable under section 6041 with payments reportable under section 6041A(a). [Reg. §31.3406(b)(3)-1.]

☐ [T.D. 8637, 12-20-95.]

#### [Reg. §31.3406(b)(3)-2]

**§31.3406(b)(3)-2. Reportable barter exchanges and gross proceeds of sales of securities or commodities by brokers.**—(a) *Transactions subject to backup withholding.*—A payment of a kind, and to a payee, that any broker (as defined in section 6045(c) and §1.6045-1(a)(1) of this chapter) or any barter exchange (as defined in section 6045(c) and §1.6045-1(a)(4) of this chapter) is required to report under section 6045 is a reportable payment for purposes of section 3406. See §31.6051-4 for the requirement to furnish a statement to the payee if tax is withheld under section 3406.

(b) *Amount subject to backup withholding.*—(1) *In general.*—The amount subject to withholding under section 3406 is the amount subject to reporting under section 6045. The amount subject to withholding with respect to broker reporting is the amount of gross proceeds (as determined under §1.6045-1(d)(5) of this chapter). The amount subject to withholding with respect to barter exchanges is the amount received by any member or client (as determined under §1.6045-1(f)(4) of this chapter).

(2) *Forward contracts, including foreign currency contracts, and regulated futures contracts.*—(i) *In general.*—If a customer is subject to withholding under section 3406 with respect to a forward contract (subject to information reporting under §1.6045-1(c)(5) of this chapter), including a foreign currency contract (as defined in section 1256(g)(2)), or a regulated futures contract (as defined in section 1256(g)(1)), or with respect to an account through which those contracts are disposed of or acquired, the broker must withhold on both of the following amounts:

(A) All cash or property withdrawn from the account by the customer during the relevant year; and

(B) The amount of cash in the account available for withdrawal by the customer at the relevant year-end (including both gross proceeds and variation margin).

(ii) *Rules concerning withdrawals.*—A withdrawal includes the use of money (including both gross proceeds and variation margin) or property in the account to purchase any property other than property acquired in connection with the closing of a contract. For this purpose, the acceptance of a warehouse receipt or other taking of delivery to close a contract is in connection with the closing of a contract only if the property acquired is disposed of by the close of the seventh trading day following the trading day that the customer takes delivery under the contract. In addition, making delivery to close a contract is in connection with the closing of a contract only if the broker is able to determine that the property used to close the contract was acquired no earlier than the seventh trading day prior to the trading day on which delivery is made. Withdrawals do not include repayments of debt incurred in connection with making or taking delivery that meets the requirements of this paragraph (b)(2). Withdrawals also do not include payments of commissions, fees, transfers of cash from the account to another futures account that is subject to this paragraph (b)(2) or cash withdrawals traceable to dispositions of property other than futures (not including profit on the contract separately reportable under §1.6045-1(c)(5)(i)(*b*) of this chapter).

(iii) *Special rule for forward contracts, including foreign currency contracts, and regulated futures contracts.*—The determination of whether the customer is subject to withholding under section 3406 with respect to an account containing forward contracts, including foreign currency contracts, or regulated futures contracts must be made at the time of the cash or property withdrawals or the relevant year-end, whichever is applicable.

(3) *Security sales made through a margin account.*—The amount described in paragraph (a) of this section that is subject to withholding under section 3406 in the case of a security sale made through a margin account (as defined in 12 CFR part 220 (Regulation T)) is the gross proceeds (as defined in §1.6045-1(d)(5) of this chapter) of the sale. The amount required to be withheld with respect to the sale, however, is limited to the amount of cash available for withdrawal by the customer immediately after the settlement of the sale. For this purpose, the amount available for withdrawal by the customer does not include amounts required to satisfy margin maintenance under Regulation T, rules and regulations of the National Association of Securities Dealers and national securities exchanges, and generally applicable self-imposed rules of the margin account carrier.

(4) *Security short sales.*—(i) *Amount subject to backup withholding.*—The amount subject to withholding under section 3406 with respect to a short sale of securities is the gross proceeds (as defined in §1.6045-1(d)(5) of this chapter) of the short sale. At the option of the broker, however, the amount subject to withholding may be the gain upon the closing of the short sale (if any); consequently, the obligation to withhold under section 3406 would be deferred until the closing transaction. A broker may use this alternative method of determining the amount subject to withholding under section 3406 with respect to a short sale only if at the time the short sale is initiated, the broker expects that the amount of gain realized upon the closing of the short sale will be determinable from the broker's records. If, due to events unforeseen at the time the short sale was initiated, the broker is unable to determine the basis of the property used to close the short sale, the property must be assumed for this purpose to have a basis of zero.

(ii) *Time of backup withholding.*—The determination of whether a short seller is subject to withholding under section 3406 must be made on the date of the initiation or closing, as the case may be, or on the date that the initiation or closing, as the case may be, is entered on the broker's books and records.

(5) *Fractional shares.*—A broker is not required to withhold under section 3406 with respect to a sale of a fractional share of stock resulting in less than $20 of gross proceeds (as described in §1.6045-1(c)(3)(x) of this chapter). [Reg. §31.3406(b)(3)-2.]

☐ [T.D. 8637, 12-20-95. *Amended by T.D. 9010, 7-25-2002.*]

#### [Reg. §31.3406(b)(3)-3]

**§31.3406(b)(3)-3. Reportable payments by certain fishing boat operators.**—(a) *Payments subject to backup withholding.*—A payment of a kind, and to a payee, that is required to be reported under section 6050A (relating to information reporting by certain fishing boat operators) is a reportable payment for purposes of section 3406. See §31.6051-4 for the requirement to furnish a statement to the payee if tax is withheld under section 3406.

**Collection of Income Tax at Source on Wages**
See p. 20,601 for regulations not amended to reflect law changes
**61,511**

(b) *Amount subject to backup withholding.*—The amount described in paragraph (a) of this section subject to withholding under section 3406 is the amount subject to reporting under section 6050A, but only to the extent the amount is paid in money and represents a share of the proceeds of the catch. [Reg. § 31.3406(b)(3)-3.]

☐ [*T.D. 8637, 12-20-95.*]

### [Reg. § 31.3406(b)(3)-4]

**§ 31.3406(b)(3)-4. Reportable payments of royalties.**—(a) *Royalty payments subject to backup withholding.*—A payment of a kind, and to a payee, that is required to be reported under section 6050N (relating to information reporting of payments of royalties) is a reportable pay-

**⋙→ Caution: Reg. § 31.3406(b)(3)-5, below, applies to amounts paid after December 31, 2011.**

### [Reg. § 31.3406(b)(3)-5]

**§ 31.3406(b)(3)-5. Reportable payments of payment card and third party network transactions.**—(a) *Payment card and third party network transactions subject to backup withholding.*—The gross amount of a reportable transaction that is required to be reported under section 6050W (relating to information reporting for payment card and third party network transactions) is a reportable payment for purposes of section 3406. See § 31.6051-4 for the requirement to furnish a statement to the payee if tax is withheld under section 3406.

(b) *Amount subject to backup withholding.*—In general, the amount described in paragraph (a) of this section that is subject to withholding under section 3406 is the amount subject to reporting under section 6050W. In the case of payments made in settlement of third party network transactions, the amount subject to withholding under section 3406 is determined without regard to the exception for de minimis payments by third party settlement organizations in section 6050W(e) and the associated regulations.

(c) *Time when payments are considered to be subject to backup withholding.*—(1) *In general.*—In the case of a payment card or third party network transaction reportable under section 6050W, the obligation to withhold arises on the date of the transaction. A payor is not required, however, to satisfy its withholding liability until the time that payment is made.

(2) *Example.*—The provisions of paragraph (c)(1) are illustrated by the following example:

*Example.* On Day 1, Customer A uses a payment card to purchase $100 worth of goods from Merchant B. Bank X, the merchant acquiring entity for B, is the party with the contractual obligation to make payment to B in settlement of the transaction. On Day 2, X, after deducting fees of $2, makes payment of $98 to settle the transaction for the sale of goods from B to A. Under paragraph (a)(6) of § 1.6050W-1, X must report the amount of $100, the amount of the transaction on Day 1, without any reduction for fees or any other amount, as the gross amount of this reportable payment transaction on the annual information return filed under paragraph (a)(1) of § 1.6050W-1. Under paragraph (c)(1) of this section, X's obligation, if any, to backup withhold arises on Day 1, the backup withholding obligation must be satisfied on Day 2, and the amount subject to backup withholding is $100 (the gross amount of the reportable payment transaction (as defined in paragraph (a)(6) of § 1.6050W-1)).

(d) *Backup withholding from an alternate source.*—(1) *In general.*—A payor may not withhold under section 3406 from a source maintained by the payor other than the source with respect to which there exists a liability to withhold under section 3406 with respect to the payee. See section 3403 and § 31.3403-1, which provide that the payor is liable for the amount required to be withheld regardless of whether the payor withholds.

(2) *Exceptions for backup withholding when there are no funds available.*—(i) *Backup withholding from an alternative source.*—In the event there are no funds available in the source with respect to which there exists a liability to withhold under section 3406 with respect to the payee, the payor may withhold under section 3406 from another source maintained by the payee with the payor. The source from which the tax is withheld under section 3406 must be payable to at least one of the persons listed on the account subject to withholding. If the account or source is not payable exclusively to the same person or persons listed on the account subject to withholding under section 3406, then the payor must obtain a written statement from all other persons to whom the account or source is payable authorizing the payor to withhold under section 3406 from the alternative account or source. A payor that elects to withhold under section 3406 from an alternative source may determine the account or source from which the tax is to be withheld, or may allow the payee to designate the alternative source.

(ii) *Deferral of withholding.*—If the payor cannot locate, with reasonable care (following procedures substantially similar to those

ment for purposes of section 3406. See § 31.6051-4 for the requirement to furnish a statement to the payee if tax is withheld under section 3406.

(b) *Amount subject to backup withholding.*—In general, the amount described in paragraph (a) of this section that is subject to withholding under section 3406 is the amount *subject* to reporting under section 6050N. However, if the reportable payment is for an oil or gas interest, the amount subject to withholding is the net amount the payee receives (i.e., the gross proceeds less production-related taxes such as state severance taxes). [Reg. § 31.3406(b)(3)-4.]

☐ [*T.D. 8637, 12-20-95.*]

set forth in § 31.3406(d)-5(c)(3)(ii)(A) and (B)), an alternative source of cash from which the payor may satisfy its withholding obligation pursuant to paragraph (d)(2)(i) of this section, the payor may defer its obligation to withhold under section 3406 until the earlier of—

(A) The date on which cash, in a sufficient amount to satisfy the obligation in full, is deposited in the account subject to withholding under section 3406; or

(B) The close of the fourth calendar year after the obligation arose.

(iii) *Termination of obligation to backup withhold.*—If, at the close of the fourth calendar year after the backup withholding arose, the payor has not located an alternate source of cash from which the payor may satisfy its withholding obligation, and sufficient cash to satisfy the obligation in full has not been deposited in the account subject to withholding under section 3406, then the obligation to backup withhold terminates at the close of the fourth calendar year.

(e) *Effective/applicability date.*—The provisions of this section apply to amounts paid after December 31, 2011. [Reg. § 31.3406(b)(3)-5.]

☐ [*T.D. 9496, 8-13-2010.*]

### [Reg. § 31.3406(b)(4)-1]

**§ 31.3406(b)(4)-1. Exemption for certain minimal payments.**—(a) *In general.*—A payor of reportable interest or dividends (as described in section 3406(b)(2)) or of royalties (as described in section 3406(b)(3)(E)) may elect not to withhold from a payment that does not exceed $10 and that on an annualized basis does not exceed $10 (see paragraph (c) of this section). A broker or barter exchange may elect not to withhold on gross proceeds of $10 or less without regard to the annualization requirement. See § 31.6051-4 for the requirement to furnish a statement to the payee if tax is withheld under section 3406.

(b) *Manner of making the election.*—The election not to withhold from payments that do not exceed $10 can be made only for payments described in paragraph (a) of this section. The election may be made on a payment-by-payment basis.

(c) *How to annualize.*—(1) *In general.*—To annualize a reportable interest payment, dividend payment, or royalty payment, a payor must calculate what the amount of the payment would be if it were paid for a 1-year period (instead of the period for which it actually is paid). The annualized amount is determined by dividing the amount of the payment by the number of days in the period for which it is being paid and then multiplying that result by the number of days in the year. If the annualized amount is $10 or less, the payor may elect not to withhold on that payment regardless of whether more than $10 may be or has been paid to the payee in other reportable payments during the calendar year. Conversely, if the annualized amount is more than $10, withholding applies even if $10 or less is actually paid to the payee during the calendar year. For purposes of computing the annualized amount, the payor may assume that February always consists of 28 days and that the year always consists of 360 days. For amounts that are deposited with a payor in a new account or certificate between the dates on which the payor customarily pays or credits interest, the payor may assume that the period for which the interest is paid is the payor's customary period for paying or crediting interest.

(2) *Special aggregation rule for reportable interest and dividends.*—If a payor maintains records that reflect multiple holdings of one payee and the payor makes an aggregate payment of reportable interest or dividends (as defined in section 3406(b)(2)) with respect to those multiple holdings (such as a dividend check that reflects payment on all stock owned by the payee), the payor must annualize the aggregate payment.

(d) *Exception for window transactions and original issue discount.*—A payor is not required to annualize payments made in window transactions (as defined in § 31.3406(b)(2)-3(b)) or payments of original issue discount. With respect to a window transaction, however, the payor is required to aggregate all payments made in the same transaction (e.g., payments made with respect to coupons or obligations presented for payment at the same time as described in § 1.6049-4(e)(4) of this chapter). [Reg. § 31.3406(b)(4)-1.]

☐ *[T.D. 8637, 12-20-95.]*

### [Reg. § 31.3406(c)-1]

**§ 31.3406(c)-1. Notified payee underreporting of reportable interest or dividend payments.**—(a) *Overview.*—Withholding under section 3406(a)(1)(C) applies to any reportable interest or dividend payment (as defined in section 3406(b)(2)) made with respect to an account of a payee if the Internal Revenue Service or a broker notifies a payor under paragraph (c)(1) or (2) of this section that the payee is subject to withholding due to notified payee underreporting (as defined in paragraph (b)(1) of this section), and the payor is required under paragraph (c)(3) of this section to identify that account. After receiving the notice and identifying accounts, the payor must notify the payee, in accordance with paragraph (d) of this section, that withholding due to notified payee underreporting has started. Paragraph (e) of this section describes the period for which withholding due to notified payee underreporting is required. Paragraph (f) of this section provides rules concerning notices that the Internal Revenue Service will send to a payee before notifying a payor that the payee is subject to withholding due to notified payee underreporting. Paragraph (g) of this section provides rules that a payee can use to prevent withholding due to notified payee underreporting from starting or to stop it once it has started. Paragraph (h) of this section provides special rules for joint accounts of payees who have filed a joint return. See section 6682 for the penalties that may apply to a payee subject to withholding under section 3406(a)(1)(C).

(b) *Definitions.*—(1) *Notified payee underreporting.*—*Notified payee underreporting* means that the Internal Revenue Service has—

(i) Determined that there was a payee underreporting (as defined in paragraph (b)(2) of this section);

(ii) Mailed at least four notices under paragraph (f)(1) of this section to the payee (over a period of at least 120 days) with respect to the underreporting; and

(iii) Assessed any deficiency attributable to the underreporting in the case of any payee who has filed a return.

(2) *Payee underreporting.*—(i) *In general.*—*Payee underreporting* means that the Internal Revenue Service has determined, for a taxable year, that—

(A) A payee failed to include in the payee's return of tax under chapter 1 of the Internal Revenue Code for that year any portion of a reportable interest or dividend payment required to be shown on that tax return; or

(B) A payee may be required to file a return for that year and to include a reportable interest or dividend payment in the return, but failed to file the return.

(ii) *Payments included in making payee underreporting determination.*—The determination of whether there is payee underreporting is made by treating as reportable interest or dividend payments, all payments of dividends reported under section 6042, all patronage dividends reported under section 6044, and all interest and original issue discount reported under section 6049, regardless of whether withholding due to notified payee underreporting applies to those payments.

(c) *Notice to payors regarding backup withholding due to notified payee underreporting.*—(1) *In general.*—If the Internal Revenue Service or a broker notifies a payor that a payee is subject to withholding due to notified payee underreporting, the payor must—

(i) Identify any accounts of the payee under the rules of paragraph (c)(3) of this section; and

(ii) Notify the payee and withhold under section 3406 on reportable interest or dividend payments made with respect to any identified account under the rules of paragraphs (d) and (e) of this section.

(2) *Additional requirements for payors that are also brokers.*—(i) *In general.*—A broker must notify the payor of a readily tradable instrument that the payee of the instrument is subject to withholding due to notified payee underreporting if—

(A) The broker (in its capacity as a payor) receives a notice from the Internal Revenue Service under paragraph (c)(1) of this section that a payee is subject to withholding due to notified payee underreporting and the broker is required to identify an account of the payee under paragraph (c)(3) of this section;

(B) The payee subsequently acquires the instrument from the broker through the same account; and

(C) The acquisition of the instrument occurs after the close of the 30th business day after the date that the broker receives the

notice (or on any earlier date that the broker may begin applying this paragraph (c)(2) after receipt of the notice described in paragraph (c)(1) of this section).

(ii) *Transfer out of street name.*—For purposes of this paragraph (c)(2), an acquisition includes a transfer of an instrument out of street name into the name of the registered owner (i.e., the payee).

(iii) *Method of providing notice.*—A broker must provide the notice required under this paragraph (c)(2) to the payor of the instrument with the transfer instructions for the acquisition. See § 31.3406(d)-4a(a)(2).

(iv) *Termination of obligation to provide information.*—The obligation of a broker to provide notice to payors under this paragraph (c)(2) terminates simultaneously with the termination of the broker's obligation to withhold (in its capacity as payor) due to notified payee underreporting on reportable interest or dividends made with respect to the account.

(3) *Payor identification of accounts of the payee subject to backup withholding due to notified payee underreporting.*—(i) *In general.*—(A) *Notice from the Internal Revenue Service.*—If a payor receives a notice from the Internal Revenue Service under paragraph (c)(1) of this section, the payor must identify, exercising reasonable care, all accounts using the same taxpayer identification number for information reporting purposes as the one provided in the notice. The notice may provide, however, that the payor need only identify the account or accounts corresponding to any account number or designation and related taxpayer identification number used for information reporting purposes as that listed on the notice.

(B) *Notice from a broker.*—If a payor receives a notice from a broker under paragraphs (c)(1) and (2) of this section, the payor is not required to identify any account other than the account identified in the notice.

(ii) *Exercise of reasonable care.*—If an account identified pursuant to paragraph (c)(3)(i)(A) of this section contains a customer identifier that can be used to retrieve systemically any other accounts that use the same taxpayer identification number for information reporting purposes, the payor must identify all accounts that can be so retrieved. Otherwise, a payor is considered to exercise reasonable care in identifying accounts subject to withholding under section 3406(a)(1)(C) if the payor searches any computer or other recordkeeping system for the region, division, or branch that serves the geographic area in which the payee's mailing address is located and that was established (or is maintained) to reflect reportable interest or dividend payments.

(iii) *Newly opened accounts.*—(A) In general, a new account is not subject to withholding under section 3406(a)(1)(C) if the payee provides to the payor a Form W-9 (or other acceptable substitute) on which the payor may reasonably rely (within the meaning of § 31.3406(h)-3(e)(2) without regard to § 31.3406(h)-3(e)(2)(v)), unless the payor has actual knowledge (within the meaning of paragraph (c)(3)(iii)(B) of this section) that the statements made on the form are not true.

(B) For purposes of paragraph (c)(3)(iii)(A) of this section, a payor is considered to have actual knowledge that a payee's statement that the payee is not subject to withholding under section 3406(a)(1)(C) is not true if—

(1) The employee or individual agent of the payor who receives the payee's certification knows that the statement is not true;

(2) In conducting the investigation, if any, required by paragraph (c)(3)(iii)(C) of this section, the payor identifies any other accounts of the payee that are already subject to withholding under section 3406(a)(1)(C); or

(3) In the course of processing the certification or in administering an account to which a certification relates, the payor discovers that the payor was previously notified by the Internal Revenue Service that the payee is subject to withholding under section 3406(a)(1)(C) and no notice was received to stop withholding pursuant to section 3406(c)(3) prior to the time of the discovery.

(C) Except as provided in this paragraph (c)(3)(iii)(C), a payor is not required to investigate whether the statements made on the Form W-9 described in paragraph (c)(3)(iii)(A) of this section are true. If, however, in opening a new account, the payor relies on the same Form W-9 (or appropriate substitute) that it relied on previously in opening another account, the payor must investigate whether any such existing account is subject to withholding under section 3406(a)(1)(C). Similarly, if the payor utilizes a universal account system described in the first sentence of paragraph (c)(3)(ii) of this section, and in opening a new account the payor searches its records to determine whether the new account should be identified under an existing identifier (because the payee has existing accounts with the payor), the payor must investigate whether any existing

**Collection of Income Tax at Source on Wages**
See p. 20,601 for regulations not amended to reflect law changes
**61,513**

accounts identified with the same identifier are subject to withholding under section 3406(a)(1)(C).

(d) *Notice from payors of backup withholding due to notified payee underreporting.*—(1) *In general.*—If a payor receives notice from the Internal Revenue Service or a broker under paragraph (c)(1) of this section and is required to identify an account under paragraph (c)(3) of this section as an account of the payee, the payor must notify the payee in accordance with paragraph (d)(2) of this section that withholding due to notified payee underreporting has started.

(2) *Procedures.*—The payor must send the notice required by paragraph (d)(1) of this section to the payee no later than 15 days after the date that the payor makes the first payment subject to withholding due to notified payee underreporting. The payor must send the notice by first-class mail to the payee at the payee's last known address. The notice to the payee required by paragraph (d)(1) of this section must state—

(i) That the Internal Revenue Service has given notice that the payee has underreported reportable interest or dividends;

(ii) That, as a result of the underreporting, the payor is required under section 3406(a)(1)(C) of the Internal Revenue Code to withhold 31 percent of reportable interest or dividend payments made to the payee;

(iii) The date that the payor started (or plans to start) withholding due to notified payee underreporting under section 3406(a)(1)(C);

(iv) The account number or numbers that are subject to withholding due to notified payee underreporting;

(v) That the payee must obtain a determination from the Internal Revenue Service in order to stop the withholding due to notified payee underreporting; and

(vi) That while the payee is subject to withholding due to notified payee underreporting, the payee may not certify to a payor making reportable interest or dividend payments (or to a broker acquiring a readily tradable instrument for the payee) that the payee is not subject to withholding due to notified underreporting.

(e) *Period during which backup withholding is required.*—(1) *In general.*—If a payor receives notice from the Internal Revenue Service or a broker under paragraph (c)(1) of this section, the payor must impose withholding under section 3406(a)(1)(C) on all reportable interest or dividend payments with respect to any account of the payee required to be identified under paragraph (c)(3) of this section made after the close of the 30th business day after the day on which the payor receives that notice and before the stop date (as described in paragraph (e)(2) of this section). A payor may choose to start withholding under this paragraph (e)(1) at any time during the 30-business-day period described in the preceding sentence.

(2) *Stop withholding.*—(i) *When no underreporting exists or undue hardship exists.*—(A) *Stop date.*—In the case of a determination under paragraph (g)(3)(i) or (iii) of this section that no underreporting exists or that an undue hardship exists, the stop date is the day that is 30 days after the earlier of—

(*1*) The date on which the payor receives written notification from the Internal Revenue Service under paragraph (g) of this section that withholding is to stop; or

(*2*) The date on which the payor receives a copy of the written certification provided to the payee by the Internal Revenue Service under paragraph (g) of this section that withholding is to stop.

(B) *Acceleration of stop date.*—A payor may choose to stop withholding at any time during the 30-day period described in paragraph (e)(2)(i)(A) of this section.

(ii) *When underreporting is corrected or bona fide dispute exists.*— In the case of a determination under paragraph (g)(3)(ii) or (iv) of this section that the underreporting has been corrected or that a bona fide dispute exists, the stop date occurs on the first day of January (immediately following a period of at least twelve months ending on October 15 of any calendar year in which the determination has been made) or if later, the stop date determined under paragraph (e)(2)(i) of this section.

(3) *Dormant accounts.*—The requirement that a payor withhold under this paragraph (e) on reportable interest or dividend payments made with respect to an account terminates no later than the close of the third calendar year ending after the later of—

(i) The date that the most recent reportable interest or dividend payment was made with respect to that account; or

(ii) The date that the payor received notice under paragraph (c)(1) of this section.

(f) *Notice to payees from the Internal Revenue Service.*—(1) *Notice period.*—After the Internal Revenue Service determines under para-

graph (b)(2) of this section that payee underreporting exists, the Internal Revenue Service will mail to the payee at least four notices over a period of at least 120 days (the notice period) before payors will be notified under paragraph (c)(1) of this section that the payee is subject to withholding due to notified payee underreporting. The notices may be accompanied by, or incorporated in, other notices provided to the payee by the Internal Revenue Service.

(2) *Payee subject to backup withholding.*—After the Internal Revenue Service provides the notices described in paragraph (f)(1) of this section, the Internal Revenue Service will send notices to payors under paragraph (c)(1) of this section unless—

(i) A payee obtains a determination under paragraph (g) of this section; or

(ii) In the case of a payee who has filed a tax return, the Internal Revenue Service has not assessed the deficiency attributable to the underreporting.

(3) *Disclosure of names of payors and brokers.*—Pursuant to section 3406(c)(5) the Internal Revenue Service may require a payee subject to withholding due to notified payee underreporting to disclose the names of all the payee's payors of reportable interest or dividend payments and the names of all of the brokers with whom the payee has accounts which may involve reportable interest or dividend payments. To the extent required in the request from the Internal Revenue Service, the payee must also provide the payee's account numbers and other information necessary to identify the payee's accounts.

(4) *Backup withholding certification.*—After a payee receives a final notice from the Internal Revenue Service under paragraph (f)(1) of this section, the payee is not permitted to certify to any payor or broker, under penalties of perjury, that the payee is not subject to withholding under section 3406(a)(1)(C), until the payee receives the certification from the Internal Revenue Service under paragraph (g) of this section advising the payee that the payee is no longer subject to withholding under section 3406(a)(1)(C). A final notice will contain the information described in this paragraph (f)(4). See sections 6682 and 7205(b) for civil and criminal penalties for making a false certification.

(g) *Determination by the Internal Revenue Service that backup withholding should not start or should be stopped.*—(1) *In general.*—A payee may prevent withholding due to notified payee underreporting from starting, or stop the withholding once it has started, by requesting and receiving a determination from the Internal Revenue Service under one or more of the provisions of paragraph (g)(3) of this section. Following its review of a request for a determination under paragraph (g)(3) of this section, the Internal Revenue Service will either make the determination or provide the payee with a written report informing the payee that the request for determination is being denied and the reasons for the denial. If a determination is made during the notice period (as defined in paragraph (f)(1) of this section), the payee is not subject to withholding due to notified payee underreporting with respect to any taxable year for which a determination was made. If a determination is made after the notice period, the Internal Revenue Service will, at the time prescribed in paragraph (g)(2) of this section, provide written certification to a payee that withholding is to stop, and will notify payors who were contacted pursuant to paragraph (c)(1) of this section to stop withholding. A broker who (in its capacity as payor) under this paragraph (g)(1) receives a notice from the Internal Revenue Service or a copy of the certification provided to a payee by the Internal Revenue Service is not required to provide a corresponding notice to any payors whom the broker has previously notified under paragraph (c)(2) of this section.

(2) *Date notice to stop backup withholding will be provided.*— (i) *Underreporting corrected or bona fide dispute.*—If the Internal Revenue Service makes a determination under paragraph (g)(3)(ii) or (iv) of this section during the 12-month period ending on October 15 of any calendar year (as described in paragraph (e)(2)(ii) of this section), the Internal Revenue Service will provide the certification and the notices described in paragraph (g)(1) of this section no later than December 1 of that calendar year.

(ii) *No underreporting or undue hardship.*—If the Internal Revenue Service makes a determination under paragraph (g)(3)(i) or (iii) of this section, the Internal Revenue Service will provide the notices described in paragraph (g)(1) of this section no later than the 45th day after the day on which the Internal Revenue Service makes its determination.

(3) *Grounds for determination.*—The Internal Revenue Service will make a determination that withholding due to notified payee underreporting should not start or should stop once it has started if the payee—

(i) Shows that there was no payee underreporting (as provided in paragraph (g)(4) of this section) for each taxable year with respect to which the Internal Revenue Service determined under paragraph (b)(2) of this section that there was payee underreporting;

(ii) Corrects any payee underreporting (as provided in paragraph (g)(5) of this section) for each taxable year with respect to which the Internal Revenue Service determined under paragraph (b)(2) of this section that there was payee underreporting;

(iii) Shows that withholding will cause or is causing an undue hardship (as defined in paragraph (g)(6) of this section) and that it is unlikely that the payee will underreport interest or dividend payments again; or

(iv) Shows that a bona fide dispute exists regarding whether any underreporting has occurred (as provided in paragraph (g)(7) of this section) for each taxable year with respect to which the Internal Revenue Service determined under paragraph (b)(2) of this section that there was payee underreporting.

(4) *No underreporting.*—A payee may show that no underreporting of reportable interest or dividends payments exists by presenting—

(i) Receipts or other satisfactory documentation to the Internal Revenue Service showing that all taxes relating to the payments were reported; or

(ii) Evidence showing that the payee did not have to file a return for the taxable year in question (e.g., because the payee did not make enough income) or that the underreporting determination was based upon a factual, clerical, or other error.

(5) *Correcting any payee underreporting.*—(i) *Before issuance of a statutory notice of deficiency.*—Before a statutory notice of deficiency is issued to a payee pursuant to section 6212, the payee may correct underreporting—

(A) By filing a return if one was not previously filed and including the unreported interest and dividends thereon;

(B) By filing an amended return in the event a return was filed and including the unreported interest and dividends thereon; or

(C) By consenting to the additional assessment according to applicable notices and forms sent to the payee by the Internal Revenue Service with respect to the underreporting, and paying taxes, penalties, and interest due with respect to any underreported interest or dividend payments.

(ii) *After issuance of a statutory notice of deficiency.*—After a statutory notice of deficiency is issued to a payee—

(A) The payee may correct underreporting at any time, by filing a return if one was not previously filed and paying the entire deficiency and any other taxes including penalties and interest attributable to any payee underreporting of interest or dividend payments; or

(B) The payee may correct underreporting after the mailing of the statutory notice of deficiency but before the expiration of the 90-day or 150-day period described in section 6213(a) or, if a petition is filed with the United States Tax Court, before the decision of the Tax Court is final, by making a remittance to the Internal Revenue Service of the amounts described in paragraph (g)(5)(ii)(A) of this section. The payee must specifically designate in writing that the remittance is a deposit in the nature of a cash bond.

(iii) *Special rules.*—For purposes of paragraph (g)(5)(ii) of this section, the payee will not be deemed to have corrected the payee underreporting under paragraph (g)(5)(ii)(B) of this section after the remittance is returned to the payee in the manner described in any applicable administrative procedure. For further guidance on a deposit in the nature of a cash bond, see subparagraph 2 of section 4.01 of Rev. Proc. 84-58 (1984-2 C.B. 501). (See § 601.601(d)(2) of this chapter.) Once the remittance is returned to the payee, the rules of this section will apply. If the Internal Revenue Service previously contacted payors of the payee to start withholding with respect to the notified payee underreporting, however, the Internal Revenue Service will recontact those payors to start withholding under paragraph (c)(1) of this section with respect to the payee underreporting without regard to paragraph (f) of this section.

(6) *Undue hardship.*—(i) *In general.*—A determination of undue hardship will be based on the overall impact to the payee of having reportable interest or dividend payments withheld at a 31 percent rate under section 3406. In addition, a determination of undue hardship will be made only if the Internal Revenue Service concludes that it is unlikely that any payee underreporting will occur again.

(ii) *Factors.*—Factors that will be considered in determining whether withholding causes undue hardship include, but are not limited to, the following—

(A) Whether estimated tax payments, and other credits for current tax liabilities, or amounts withheld on employee wages or pensions, in addition to withholding under section 3406, would cause significant overwithholding;

(B) The payee's health, including the payee's ability to pay foreseeable medical expenses;

(C) The extent of the payee's reliance on interest and dividend payments to meet necessary living expenses and the existence, if any, of other sources of income;

(D) Whether other income of the payee is limited or fixed (e.g., social security, pension, and unearned income);

(E) The payee's ability to sell or liquidate stocks, bonds, bank accounts, trust accounts, or other assets, and the consequences of doing so;

(F) Whether the payee reported and timely paid the most recent year's tax liability, including interest and dividend income; and

(G) Whether the payee has filed a bankruptcy petition with the United States Bankruptcy Court.

(7) *Bona fide dispute.*—The Internal Revenue Service may make a determination under this paragraph (g)(7) if there is a dispute between the payee and the Internal Revenue Service on a question of fact or law that is material to a determination under paragraph (g)(3)(i) of this section, and, based upon all the facts and circumstances, the Internal Revenue Service finds that the dispute is asserted in good faith by the payee and there is a reasonable basis for the payee's position.

(h) *Payees filing a joint return.*—(1) *In general.*—For purposes of this section, if payee underreporting is found to exist with respect to a joint return, then the provisions of this section apply to both payees (i.e., the husband and wife). As a result, both payees are subject to withholding on accounts in their individual names as well as accounts in their joint names. Either or both payees may satisfy the criteria for a determination that no payee underreporting exists, that the underreporting has been corrected, or that a bona fide dispute exists (as provided in paragraph (g)(3)(i), (ii), or (iv) of this section). Both payees, however, must satisfy the criteria for a determination that withholding will cause or is causing undue hardship (as provided in paragraph (g)(3)(iii) of this section).

(2) *Exceptions.*—(i) *Innocent spouse.*—A spouse who files a joint return may obtain a determination that withholding should stop or not start with respect to payments made to his or her individual accounts, if the spouse shows that—

(A) He or she did not underreport income because he or she is a spouse described in section 6013(e), i.e, innocent spouse; or

(B) There is a bona fide dispute regarding whether he or she is an innocent spouse and hence did not underreport income.

(ii) *Divorced or legally separated payee.*—A payee who, at the time of the request for a determination under paragraph (g) of this section, is divorced or separated under state law may obtain a determination that undue hardship exists (or would exist) under paragraph (g)(3)(iii) of this section with respect to reportable interest or dividend payments made to his or her individual accounts if the divorced or legally separated payee satisfies the criteria for a determination under paragraph (g)(6) of this section.

(i) *Reserved.*

(j) *Penalties.*—For the application of penalties related to this section, see sections 6682 and 7205(b). [Reg. § 31.3406(c)-1.]

☐ [T.D. 8637, 12-20-95.]

### [Reg. § 31.3406(d)-1]

**§ 31.3406(d)-1. Manner required for furnishing a taxpayer identification number.**—(a) *Requirement to backup withhold.*—Withholding under section 3406(a)(1)(A) applies to a reportable payment (as defined in section 3406(b)) if the payee does not furnish the payee's taxpayer identification number to the payor in the manner required by this section. The period for which withholding is required is described in § 31.3406(e)-1(b). See § 31.3406(d)-3(a) and (b) for special rules when an account is established directly with, or an instrument is acquired directly from, the payor by electronic transmission or by mail, or an instrument is sold through a broker by electronic transmission or by mail. See § 31.3406(d)-4 for special rules applicable to readily tradable instruments acquired through a broker. See § 31.3406(h)-3(e) for the rules on when a payor may rely on a Form W-9. See also § 31.3406(g)-3 for rules regarding a payee awaiting receipt of a taxpayer identification number. See the applicable information reporting sections and section 6109 and the regulations thereunder to determine whose taxpayer identification number should be provided.

(b) *Reportable interest or dividend account.*—(1) *Manner required for furnishing a taxpayer identification number with respect to a pre-1984*

**Collection of Income Tax at Source on Wages**
See p. 20,601 for regulations not amended to reflect law changes
**61,515**

*account or instrument.*—A payee must furnish the payee's taxpayer identification number to the payor with respect to any obligation, deposit, certificate, share, membership, contract, investment, account, or other relationship or instrument established or acquired on or before December 31, 1983 (a pre-1984 account) and with respect to which the payor makes a reportable interest or dividend payment (as defined in section 3406(b)(2)). The manner of determining whether an account or an instrument is a pre-1984 account is described in paragraph (b)(2) of this section. The payee of a pre-1984 account may furnish the payee's taxpayer identification number to the payor orally or in writing. The payee is not required to certify under penalties of perjury that the taxpayer identification number is correct.

(2) *Determination of pre-1984 account or instrument.*—(i) *In general.*—An account that is in existence before January 1, 1984, will be considered a pre-1984 account, regardless of whether additional deposits are made to the account on or after January 1, 1984. An account established as an expansion of a credit union prime account in existence prior to January 1, 1984, constitutes a pre-1984 account. If funds taken from one account in existence prior to January 1, 1984, are used to create a new account on or after that date, however, the new account does not constitute a pre-1984 account except as provided in the preceding sentence. An instrument acquired prior to January 1, 1984, is a pre-1984 account. Regardless of when an instrument was acquired, if it is negotiated in a window transaction as defined in §31.3406(b)(2)-3(b), it is treated as an instrument acquired after December 31, 1983. An obligation in bearer form and subject to reporting under section 6045, whenever acquired, is not a pre-1984 account. Any instrument, whenever acquired, that is held in a brokerage account is considered a pre-1984 account if the brokerage account is not a post-1983 brokerage account (as described in paragraph (c)(1)(ii) of this section). If shares of a corporation are held before January 1, 1984 (or considered held before that date by operation of this paragraph (b)(2)), and additional shares are acquired by the holder, irrespective of whether the shares are received by reason of a stock dividend, investing new cash, or otherwise, the new shares, in the discretion of the payor, may be considered a pre-1984 account. In the case of a qualified employee trust that distributes instruments in kind, any instrument distributed from the trust is considered a pre-1984 account with respect to employees who were participants in the trust before 1984. Similarly, when a payor offers participants in a plan the opportunity to purchase stock of the payor after a specified time, using the money that the payee invested during that period of time, the stock so purchased after December 31, 1983, is considered a pre-1984 account with respect to participants in the plan who either owned shares or invested money in the plan before January 1, 1984.

(ii) *Account or instrument automatically acquired on the maturity or termination of an account.*—When an account is opened, or an instrument is acquired, automatically on the maturity or termination of an account that was in existence or an instrument that was held before January 1, 1984 (or considered to have been in existence or held before that date by operation of this paragraph (b)(2)(ii)), without the participation of the payee, the new account or instrument, in the discretion of the payor, may be considered a pre-1984 account. For purposes of the preceding sentence, a payee is not considered to have participated in the acquisition of the new account or instrument solely because the payee failed to exercise a right to withdraw funds at the maturity or termination of the old account or instrument.

(iii) *Insurance policies.*—In the case of insurance policies in effect on December 31, 1983, the election of a dividend accumulation option pursuant to which interest is paid (as defined in §1.6049-5(a)(4) of this chapter), or the creation of an account in which proceeds of a policy are held for the policy beneficiary, may, in the payor's discretion, be treated as a pre-1984 account.

(iv) *Acquisitions of accounts and instruments.*—(A) *Pre-1984 or post-1983 status known.*—If a payor acquires accounts or instruments of another payor (including through a tax-free reorganization under section 368), the acquiring payor must treat the persons specified in this paragraph (b)(2)(iv)(A) as having the same requirement to furnish a taxpayer identification number in the manner required under this paragraph (b) to the acquiring payor for information reporting, withholding, and related tax provisions as existed with respect to the payor whose accounts or instruments were acquired. Persons specified in this paragraph (b)(2)(iv)(A) are persons who held accounts or instruments in the other payor immediately before the acquisition and who receive an account or instrument in the acquiring payor immediately after the acquisition.

(B) *Pre-1984 or post-1983 status unknown.*—If the acquiring payor, as described in paragraph (b)(2)(iv)(A) of this section, is unable to identify from the business records of the other payor whether any or all of the accounts or instruments of the persons specified in paragraph (b)(2)(iv)(A) of this section are pre-1984 (or

post-1983) accounts or instruments, then the acquiring payor may treat these unidentified accounts or instruments as pre-1984 accounts or instruments.

(C) *Cross reference.*—See §31.3406(g)-2(g) for the limited exception from withholding under section 3406(a)(1)(A) on accounts or instruments described in paragraphs (b)(2)(iv)(A) and (B) of this section for which the payor does not have a taxpayer identification number.

(3) *Manner required for furnishing a taxpayer identification number with respect to an account or instrument that is not a pre-1984 account.*—A payee who receives reportable interest or dividend payments (as defined in section 3406(b)(2)) from a payor must certify under penalties of perjury that the taxpayer identification number the payee furnishes to the payor is the payee's correct taxpayer identification number. The payee must make the certification only with respect to an account or instrument that is not a pre-1984 account (as described in paragraph (b)(2) of this section). See §31.3406(h)-3 for a description of the certificate on which the certification must be made. See §31.3406(d)-2 for the requirement that the payee must certify under penalties of perjury that the payee is not subject to withholding due to notified payee underreporting. See §31.3406(d)-3(a) with respect to an account established directly with, or an instrument acquired directly from, the payor by electronic transmission or by mail. See §31.3406(d)-4 for the rules applicable to readily tradable instruments acquired through a broker.

(4) *Special rule with respect to the acquisition of a readily tradable instrument in a transaction between certain parties acting without the assistance of a broker.*—If a payee, at any time, acquires a readily tradable instrument without the assistance of a broker, and no party to the acquisition is a broker or an agent of the payor, the payee must furnish the payee's taxpayer identification number to the payor prior to the time reportable payments are made on the instrument. The payee is not required to certify under penalties of perjury that the number is correct. See §31.3406(d)-2 for the rule that a payee is not subject to withholding due to notified payee underreporting with respect to a readily tradable instrument acquired in the manner described in this paragraph (b)(4). A broker is considered to provide assistance in the acquisition of an instrument if the person effecting the acquisition would be required to make an information return under section 6045 if such person were to sell the instrument. See §31.3406(d)-4 for rules relating to an acquisition of a readily tradable instrument when a broker is involved.

(c) *Brokerage account.*—(1) *Manner required for furnishing a taxpayer identification number with respect to a brokerage relationship that is not a post-1983 brokerage account.*—(i) *In general.*—With respect to any instrument, investment, or deposit made through a brokerage account that is not a post-1983 brokerage account, a payee must furnish the payee's taxpayer identification number to the broker either orally or in writing. The payee is not required to certify under penalties of perjury that the taxpayer identification number is correct. See paragraph (b)(2)(i) of this section for the rule that any instrument, whenever acquired, that is held in a brokerage account that is not a post-1983 brokerage account, is considered held in an account that is not a post-1983 brokerage account. For example, in 1983 a payee established and acquired a readily tradable instrument from a brokerage account; no activity took place through that account until the payee purchased a readily tradable instrument in 1995. That readily tradable instrument is not held in a post-1983 brokerage account; therefore, the payee need not certify under penalties of perjury that the payee's taxpayer identification number is correct.

(ii) *Definition of a brokerage account that is not a post-1983 brokerage account.*—A brokerage account that was established by a payee before January 1, 1984, through which during 1983 the broker either bought or sold securities for the payee or held securities on behalf of the payee as a nominee (i.e., in street name), is an account that is not a post-1983 brokerage account.

(2) *Manner required for furnishing a taxpayer identification number with respect to a post-1983 brokerage account.*—(i) *In general.*—With respect to a post-1983 brokerage account, the payee must furnish the payee's taxpayer identification number to the broker and certify under penalties of perjury that the taxpayer identification number furnished is correct, except as provided in §31.3406(d)-3(b).

(ii) *Definition of a post-1983 brokerage account.*—A brokerage account established after December 31, 1983 (or before January 1, 1984, through which during 1983 the broker neither bought nor sold securities nor held securities on behalf of the payee as a nominee (i.e., in street name)), is a post-1983 brokerage account.

(d) *Rents, commissions, nonemployee compensation, certain fishing boat operators, and payment card and third party network transactions, etc.*— *Manner required for furnishing a taxpayer identification number.*—For accounts, contracts, or relationships subject to information reporting under section 6041 (relating to information reporting at source on rents, royalties, salaries, etc.), section 6041A(a) (relating to information reporting of payments for nonemployee services), section 6050A (relating to information reporting by certain fishing boat operators), section 6050N (relating to information reporting of payments of royalties), or section 6050W (relating to information reporting for payment card and third party network transactions), the payee must furnish the payee's taxpayer identification number to the payor either orally or in writing. Except as provided in §31.3406(d)-5, the payee is not required to certify under penalties of perjury that the taxpayer identification number is correct regardless of when the account, contract, or relationship is established. [Reg. §31.3406(d)-1.]

□ [T.D. 8637, 12-20-95. Amended by T.D. 9496, 8-13-2010.]

### [Reg. §31.3406(d)-2]

**§31.3406(d)-2. Payee certification failure.**—(a) *Requirement to backup withhold.*—Withholding under section 3406(a)(1)(D) applies to a reportable interest or dividend payment (as defined in section 3406(b)(2)) if, and only if, the payee fails to certify to the payor, under penalties of perjury, that the payee is not subject to withholding due to notified payee underreporting under section 3406(a)(1)(C). The period for which withholding applies is described in §31.3406(e)1(e). See §31.3406(d)-3(a) for special rules when an account is established directly with, or an instrument is acquired directly from, the payor by electronic transmission or by mail. See §31.3406(c)-1(c)(3)(iv) for rules with respect to a payor's reliance on a payee certification for a new account following notified payee underreporting. See §31.3406(d)-4 for special rules relating to the acquisition of a readily tradable instrument through a broker. The certificate on which the certification should be made is described in §31.3406(h)-3.

(b) *Exceptions.*—Withholding under section 3406(a)(1)(D) and paragraph (a) of this section does not apply to reportable interest or dividend payments (as defined in section 3406(b)(2)) made—

(1) With respect to a pre-1984 account (as defined in §31.3406(d)-1(b)(1);

(2) In a window transaction (as defined in §31.3406(b)(2)-3(b));

(3) With respect to a readily tradable instrument described in §31.3406(d)-1(b)(2)(iv) or §31.3406(d)-4(a)(3); or

(4) During the period and with respect to an account or readily tradable instrument described in §31.3406(d)-3. [Reg. §31.3406(d)-2.]

□ [T.D. 8637, 12-20-95.]

### [Reg. §31.3406(d)-3]

**§31.3406(d)-3. Special 30-day rules for certain reportable payments.**—(a) *Accounts or readily tradable instruments acquired directly from the payor (including a broker who holds an instrument in street name) by electronic transmission or by mail.*—In the case of an account established directly with, or a readily tradable instrument acquired directly from, the payor by means of electronic transmission (i.e., telephone or wire instruction) or by mail, the payor may permit the payee to furnish the certifications required in §31.3406(d)-1(b)(3)(relating to certification that the payee's taxpayer identification number is correct) and §31.3406(d)-2 (relating to certification of notified payee underreporting) within 30 days after the establishment or acquisition without subjecting the account to withholding during the 30 days. The preceding sentence applies only if the payee furnishes a taxpayer identification number to the payor at the time of the establishment or acquisition, and the payee does not withdraw more than 69 percent of a reportable interest or dividend payment before the certifications are received within the 30 days. If the payee does not provide the required certifications within 30 days of the establishment or acquisition, the payor must withhold 31 percent of any reportable interest or dividend payments made to the account after its acquisition. For purposes of this section, an account or instrument is considered acquired directly from the payor if the instrument was acquired by the payee without the assistance of a broker or the instrument was acquired directly from a broker who holds the instrument as nominee for the payee (i.e., in street name) and who is considered a payor under §31.3406(a)-2. For payments made after December 31, 1998, see §1.6049-5(d)(2)(ii) of this chapter for the application of a 90-day grace period in lieu of the 30-day grace period described in this paragraph (a) if, at the beginning of the 90-day grace period, certain conditions are satisfied. If the grace period provisions of §1.6049-5(d)(2)(ii) or §1.1441-1(b)(3)(iv) of this chapter are applied with respect to a new account, the grace period provisions of this paragraph (a) shall not apply to that account.

(b) *Sale of an instrument for a customer by electronic transmission or by mail.*—The special rules set forth in paragraph (a) of this section apply comparably with respect to certification of the taxpayer identification number for the sale of an instrument under section 6045 (as described in §31.3406(b)(3)-2) through a post-1983 brokerage account

(as described in §31.3406(d)-1(c)(2)) for a customer by electronic transmission or by mail. However, the 30-day rules may apply only if the payee furnishes the payee's taxpayer identification number before the sale occurs. For purposes of applying the 30-day rules under this paragraph (b), a payee's reinvestment of the gross proceeds of the sale into other instruments constitutes a withdrawal.

(c) *Application to foreign payees.*—The rules of paragraphs (a) and (b) of this section also apply to a payee from whom the payor is required to obtain a Form W-8 (or an acceptable substitute) or other evidence of foreign status (pursuant to relevant regulations under an applicable Internal Revenue Code section without regard to the requirement to furnish a taxpayer identifying number, and the certifications described in §§31.3406(d)-1(b)(3) and 31.3406(d)-2), provided the payee represents orally or otherwise, before or at the time of the acquisition or sale of the instrument or the establishment of the account, that the payee is not a United States citizen or resident. The 30-day rules described in paragraph (a) or (b) of this section may apply only if the payee does not qualify for, or the payor does not apply, the 90-day grace period described in §1.6049-5(d)(2)(ii) or §1.1441-1(b)(3)(iv) of this chapter. [Reg. §31.3406(d)-3.]

□ [T.D. 8637, 12-20-95. Amended by T.D. 8734, 10-6-97 (T.D. 8804 delayed the effective date of T.D. 8734 from January 1, 1999, to January 1, 2000; T.D. 8856 further delayed the effective date of T.D. 8734 until January 1, 2001).]

### [Reg. §31.3406(d)-4]

**§31.3406(d)-4. Special rules for readily tradable instruments acquired through a broker.**—(a) *Readily tradable instruments acquired through post-1983 brokerage accounts with a broker who is not a payor.*— (1) *In general.*—If a readily tradable instrument is acquired through a post-1983 brokerage account (as defined in §31.3406(d)-1(c)(2)) and the broker is not a broker holding a security (including stock) for a customer in street name, the broker must—

(i) Obtain once with respect to each account the certifications described in §31.3406(d)-2(a) and §31.3406(d)-1(b) and (c)(2) from the payee (relating to certification regarding payee underreporting and taxpayer identification number, respectively);

(ii) Furnish the payee's taxpayer identification number to the payor; and

(iii) Notify the payor to impose withholding if the payee fails to make either of the required certifications to the broker or if the broker has been notified by the Internal Revenue Service before the acquisition of the instrument that the payee is subject to withholding due to notified payee underreporting under section 3406(a)(1)(C) or that the payee is subject to withholding because the payee's taxpayer identification number is incorrect under section 3406(a)(1)(B)(as described in §31.3406(d)-5).

(2) *Additional requirements.*—The broker must give the information required by paragraphs (a)(1)(ii) and (iii) of this section to the payor with the transfer instructions for the acquisition (including account registration instructions transmitted by a broker in the case of acquisitions of shares in a mutual fund). A notice including the information described in paragraph (b)(1) of this section fulfills the broker's requirement to give notice to the payor. Once the broker transmits the transfer instructions containing the information required by this section, the broker has no further responsibility to obtain a missing taxpayer identification number or missing certification or to provide additional notices to the payee or payor with respect to the acquisition of the instrument. Upon receiving the notice from a broker, the payor must impose withholding on the account pursuant to §31.3406(a)-1.

(3) *Transactions entered into through a brokerage account that is not a post-1983 brokerage account.*—If a broker acquires readily tradable instruments for a payee through an account (with the broker) that is not a post-1983 brokerage account (as defined in §31.3406(d)-1(c)(1)), and the broker is not the payor of the instruments, the broker must furnish the payee's taxpayer identification number to the payor. In addition, if the broker has been notified by the Internal Revenue Service that the payee is subject to withholding under section 3406 either because of an incorrect taxpayer identification number or due to notified payee underreporting as described in section 3406(a)(1)(B) or (C), respectively, the broker must notify the payor of the instrument to impose withholding with respect to that payee and transmit the information in the manner described in this paragraph (a). After a payor receives a notice from a broker pursuant to section 3406(d)(2)(B) and this paragraph (a), the payor must impose withholding on any accounts of the payee paying reportable interest or dividends as defined in section 3406(b)(2) in accordance with §31.3406(a)-1.

(4) *Payor must notify payee.*—(i) *Failure to provide certifications.*—If a payor is notified by a broker, as required in paragraph (a)(1) of this section, that a payee is subject to withholding because the payee

failed to provide the certifications, as described in §31.3406(d)-2(a) and §31.3406(d)-1(b)(3) and (c)(2), and the payor has not received the certifications from the payee, then the payor must notify the payee that withholding has started (or will start) no later than 15 days after the payor makes the first payment to the payee that is subject to withholding under section 3406. A notice that contains the information described in paragraph (b)(2) of this section satisfies the payor's requirement to give notice to the payee. If the broker notifies the payor that the payee failed to make a required certification and the payor has received the certification from the payee, the payor may disregard the notice from the broker.

(ii) *Notified payee underreporting and incorrect taxpayer identification number.*—The payor must notify the payee under this section if the Internal Revenue Service or a broker notifies the payor to withhold either because of an incorrect taxpayer identification number under section 3406(a)(1)(B)(as described in §31.3406(d)-5) or due to notified payee underreporting under section 3406(a)(1)(C)(as described in §31.3406(c)-1). If a payor is notified by the Internal Revenue Service or a broker with respect to a readily tradable instrument, the payor may not ignore the notice even if the payee previously provided the payee's taxpayer identification number under penalties of perjury to the payor and even if the payee certified to the payor that the payee is not subject to backup withholding due to a notified payee underreporting. See §31.3406(d)-5(c)(1) and (2) and (f)(2) for notice requirements under section 3406(a)(1)(B) due to an incorrect taxpayer identification number. See §31.3406(c)-1(c)(2) for notice requirements under section 3406(a)(1)(C) due to notified payee underreporting.

(b) *Notices.*—(1) *Form of notice by broker to payor.*—A broker who is required under paragraphs (a)(1)(iii) and (2) of this section to notify the payor with respect to a readily tradable instrument may notify the payor in connection with the transfer instructions by means of magnetic media, machine readable document, or any other medium, provided that the notice includes the following information—

(i) The payee's name, address, and taxpayer identification number (if provided to the broker); and

(ii) A statement that the payee is subject to withholding under section 3406(a)(1)(A), (B), (C), or (D) of the Internal Revenue Code, whichever section applies; and

(iii) When applicable, a statement that the broker was notified by the Internal Revenue Service that the payee is subject to withholding under section 3406(a)(1)(B) or (C).

(2) *Form of notice by payor to payee.*—A payor who is required to notify a payee that the payee is subject to withholding must provide notice that is substantially similar to the following—

(i) For a notification concerning a failure to provide a taxpayer identification number in the required manner under section 3406(a)(1)(A) or a failure to make the following certification described in section 3406(a)(1)(D):

Recently, you purchased (identify security acquired). Because of the existence of one or more of the following conditions, payments of interest, dividends, and other reportable amounts that are made to you will be subject to withholding of tax at a 31 percent rate: (specify the condition or conditions, described below, that are applicable)

(1) You failed to provide a taxpayer identification number, or failed to provide this number under penalties of perjury, in connection with the purchase of the acquired security. (An individual's taxpayer identification number is his or her social security number.)

(2) You failed to certify, under penalties of perjury, that you are not subject to withholding due to notified payee underreporting as required under section 3406(a)(1)(D) of the Internal Revenue Code.

If condition (1) applies, you may stop withholding by providing your taxpayer identification number on the enclosed Form W-9, signing the form, and returning it to us. If you do not have a taxpayer identification number, but have applied (or will soon apply) for one, you may so indicate on the Form W-9. Withholding may apply during the 60-day period you are waiting for your taxpayer identification number. You must provide us with your taxpayer identification number promptly after you receive it in order to avoid withholding after the end of the 60-day period or to stop withholding if it has already begun. Certain persons, described on the enclosed Form W-9, are exempt from withholding. Follow the instructions on that form if applicable to you.

If condition (2) applies, you may stop withholding by certifying on the enclosed Form W-9 that you are not subject to withholding due to notified payee underreporting, signing the form, and returning it to us.

If more than one condition applies, you must remove all applicable conditions to stop withholding.

Please address any questions concerning this notice to: [Insert payor identifying information].

(Do not address questions to the broker who purchased the securities for you.)

(ii) For the form of the notice concerning imposition of withholding due to an incorrect taxpayer identification number, see §31.3406(d)-5(d)(2) and (g)(2).

(iii) For the form of the notice concerning the imposition of withholding due to notified payee underreporting, see §31.3406(c)-1(d)(2).

(c) *Payor's reliance on information from broker.*—(1) *In general.*—A payor of an instrument acquired by a payee through a broker may rely on the information that the payor receives from the broker pursuant to paragraphs (a) and (b) of this section.

(2) *Amount subject to backup withholding.*—The payor is required to withhold under section 3406 depending on the payor's customary method of making payment on an instrument or instruments owned by a payee. If it is the practice of a payor to combine in one account all readily tradable instruments of the same issue owned by a payee and if only certain of those instruments are subject to withholding, the payor must withhold on the aggregate payment made with respect to all the instruments in the account. Otherwise, the payor must withhold on the payment made on the instrument or instruments with respect to which the payee is subject to withholding. [Reg. §31.3406(d)-4.]

☐ [*T.D. 8637, 12-20-95. Amended by T.D. 9010, 7-25-2002.*]

### [Reg. §31.3406(d)-5]

**§31.3406(d)-5. Backup withholding when the Service or a broker notifies the payor to withhold because the payee's taxpayer identification number is incorrect.**—(a) *Overview.*—Backup withholding under section 3406(a)(1)(B) applies to any reportable payment made with respect to an account of a payee if the Internal Revenue Service or a broker notifies a payor under paragraph (c)(1) or (2) of this section that the payee's name and taxpayer identification number combination ("name/TIN combination") is incorrect and the payor is required under paragraph (c)(3) of this section to identify that account as having the same name/TIN combination. After receiving a notice from the Internal Revenue Service or a broker under paragraph (c)(1) or (2) of this section and identifying an account as having the incorrect name/TIN combination under paragraph (c)(3) of this section, the payor must notify the payee in accordance with paragraph (d) of this section. In addition, under paragraph (e) of this section, the payor must backup withhold on all reportable payments made to such account after the close of the 30th business day after the date that the payor receives the notice and on or before the close of the 30th calendar day after the date that the payor receives from the payee the certification required under paragraph (f) of this section. Under paragraph (g) of this section, if a payor receives 2 notices from the Internal Revenue Service or broker within 3 calendar years with respect to a payee's account, the payor must notify the payee in accordance with paragraph (g)(2) (rather than paragraph (d) of this section. In addition, the payor must backup withhold on all reportable payments made with respect to the account after the close of the 30th business day after the date that the payor receives the second notice and on or before the 30th calendar day after the date that the payor receives notification from the Social Security Administration (or the Internal Revenue Service) validating a name/TIN combination for the account. Paragraph (h) of this section requires a payor to use a corrected name/TIN combination on subsequent information returns.

(b) *Definitions and special rules.*—(1) *Definition of incorrect name/TIN combination.*—An incorrect name/TIN combination is a combination of a name and taxpayer identification number provided on an information return with respect to which the Internal Revenue Service determines that the taxpayer identification number provided is not assigned under section 6109 to the name provided.

(2) *Definition of account.*—The term "account" means any account, instrument, or other relationship with the payor.

(3) *Definition of business day.*—The term "business day" means any day other than a Saturday, Sunday, or legal holiday (within the meaning of section 7503).

(4) *Certain exceptions.*—(i) *In general.*—This section does not apply with respect to any notice received under paragraph (c)(1) or (2) of this section with respect to payments that—

(A) Were made to a fiduciary or nominee account; or

(B) Were not reportable payments (for example, because the payments were made to an exempt recipient).

See §301.6724-1(f)(3) of this chapter for certain solicitation rules applicable after receipt of a notice under paragraph (c)(1) or (2) of this section with respect to a fiduciary or nominee account.

(ii) *Definition of fiduciary or nominee account.*—A fiduciary or nominee account is an account with respect to which at least one person named in the registration is identified as acting in the capacity as nominee or as administrator, conservator, custodian, receiver, tutor, curator, committee, executor, guardian, trustee, or other fiduciary capacity recognized under governing law.

(c) *Notice regarding an incorrect name/TIN combination.*—(1) *In general.*—If the Internal Revenue Service notifies a payor that a payee's name/TIN combination is incorrect and that the payor must commence backup withholding as required on reportable payments made with respect to accounts of the payee with the same name/TIN combination, the payor must—

(i) Identify under paragraph (c)(3) of this section any account or accounts of the payee having the same name/TIN combination;

(ii) Except as provided in paragraph (g) of this section, notify the payee and backup withhold on reportable payments made to the account or accounts under the rules of paragraphs (d), (e), and (f) of this section.

This paragraph (c)(1) also applies if the payor receives notice from a broker under paragraph (c)(2) of this section.

(2) *Additional requirements for payors that are also brokers.*—(i) *In general.*—A broker must notify the payor of an instrument of the information required under paragraph (c)(2)(ii) of this section, if—

(A) The broker (in its capacity as a payor) receives a notice from the Internal Revenue Service under paragraph (c)(1) of this section that a payee's name/TIN combination is incorrect and is required to identify an account of the payee pursuant to paragraph (c)(3) of this section as having the name/TIN combination;

(B) The payee acquires through the same account with the broker a readily tradable instrument with respect to which the broker is not the payor; and

(C) The acquisition of such instrument occurs after the close of the 30th business day after the date that the broker receives that notice (or on any earlier date that the broker chooses to begin applying this paragraph (c)(2)).

For purposes of this paragraph (c)(2)(i), with respect to notices under paragraph (c)(1) of this section received on or after September 1, 1992, an acquisition includes a transfer of an instrument out of street name into the name of the registered owner, *i.e.,* the payee.

(ii) *Required information.*—The information required to be provided under this paragraph (c)(2)(ii) is:

(A) The fact that the broker was notified by the Internal Revenue Service that the payee furnished an incorrect name/TIN combination;

(B) The incorrect name/TIN combination; and

(C) The fact that the named payee is subject to backup withholding under section 3406(a)(1)(B).

The broker is required to provide this information to the payor of the instrument in connection with the transfer instructions for the acquisition.

(iii) *Termination of obligation to provide information.*—The obligation of a broker to provide information to payors under this paragraph (c)(2) terminates simultaneously with the termination of the broker's obligation to backup withhold (in its capacity as payor) on reportable payments to the account.

(3) *Payor identification of the account or accounts of the payee that have the incorrect taxpayer identification number.*—(i) *In general.*—If an account number or designation is provided in the notice received under paragraph (c)(1) of this section, the payor need only identify any account or accounts corresponding to that number or designation that has the same name/TIN combination provided in the notice. If no account number or designation is provided in the notice received under paragraph (c)(1) of this section, the payor must identify, using reasonable care, all accounts of the payee having the same name/TIN combination provided in the notice. If a payor receives notice from a broker under paragraph (c)(2) of this section with respect to the acquisition of a readily tradable instrument, the payor is not required to identify any other account of the payee.

(ii) *Reasonable care where no account number or designation is provided.*—A payor who satisfies the following two-part facts-and-circumstances test will be considered to have exercised reasonable care for purposes of this paragraph (c)(3).

(A) Part one of the test is satisfied if a payor searches for accounts of the payee on the computer or other recordkeeping system that the payor can reasonably associate with the information return that generated the notice under paragraph (c)(1) of this section. For example, a payor who maintains separate computer or recordkeeping systems for different product lines will have identified and used the appropriate system if the payor searches for accounts of

the payee on the computer or recordkeeping system that contains the product line for the type of payments reported on the information return. A payor with the same product line on several nonintegrated computer or record systems will have identified and used the appropriate system if the payor searches for accounts of the payee on any computer or record system that the payor otherwise can reasonably associate with the information return.

(B) Part two of the test is satisfied if the payor inputs the name/TIN combination provided on the notice from the Internal Revenue Service under paragraph (c)(1) of this section into the system that is described in paragraph (c)(3)(ii)(A) of this section. If the system of a payor cannot utilize the name/TIN combination, the payor must input appropriate data or criteria, as determined by the capability of the payor's computer or recordkeeping system.

(iii) *No identification if error is caused by payor.*—A payor may treat an account as not having the incorrect name/TIN combination if the error resulted because the name or taxpayer identification number on such account is not the name or taxpayer identification number that was provided to the payor. This may occur, for example, where a payor transposes numbers in the taxpayer identification number when incorporating it into the payor's business records.

(4) *Special rules for joint accounts.*—(i) *In general.*—In the case of a joint account, the relevant name/TIN combination for purposes of this section is the name/TIN combination used for information reporting purposes.

(ii) *Transitional rule.*—With respect to notices received under paragraph (c)(1) or (2) of this section prior to September 1, 1993, a payor may treat the name/TIN combination of the first person on a joint account as the relevant name/TIN combination, unless that person is an exempt foreign person and the account registration includes names of persons who are not foreign persons.

(iii) *Optional rule where names are switched.*—A payor may backup withhold under this section on reportable payments made to a joint account if the order of the names (or taxpayer identification numbers) on the account is merely changed subsequent to receipt of a notice under paragraph (c)(1) or (2) of this section, provided that the name of the person to which the incorrect name/TIN combination originally applies remains on the account.

(5) *Date of receipt.*—For purposes of this section, the date set forth on the notice from the Internal Revenue Service or broker under paragraph (c)(1) or (2) of this section is considered to be the date of receipt of the notice by the payor. However, if the payor demonstrates to the satisfaction of the Internal Revenue Service that the date of actual receipt of the notice is later than the date on the notice, the actual date of receipt is controlling.

(d) *Notice from payors of backup withholding due to an incorrect name/TIN combination.*—(1) *In general.*—Except as provided in paragraph (g) of this section, if a payor receives notice under paragraph (c)(1) or (2) of this section and is required to identify an account as having the incorrect name/TIN combination under paragraph (c)(3) of this section, the payor must send a copy of the notice (or an acceptable substitute notice) to the payee of the account in accordance with the procedures of paragraph (d)(2) of this section.

(2) *Procedures.*—(i) *In general.*—The notice that a payor must send to a payee under paragraph (d)(1) of this section must comply with such procedural requirements as the Internal Revenue Service provides in the Internal Revenue Bulletin such as to form and manner of delivery. A payor must send the notice to the payee within 15 business days after the date that the payor receives the notice from the Internal Revenue Service or a broker under paragraph (c)(1) or (2) of this section.

(ii) *Two or more notices for an account for the same year or received in the same year.*—A payor who receives, under the same payor taxpayer identification number, two or more notices under paragraph (c)(1) or (2) of this section with respect to the same payee's account for the same year, or in the same calendar year, need only send one notice to the payee under this section.

(e) *Period during which backup withholding is required due to notification of an incorrect name/TIN combination.*—(1) *In general.*—Except as provided in paragraph (g) of this section, if a payor receives a notice under paragraph (c)(1) or (2) of this section and is required to identify an account as having the same name/TIN combination under paragraph (c)(3) of this section, the payor must impose backup withholding on all reportable payments made with respect to the account after the close of the 30th business day after the date the payor receives that notice and on or before the close of the 30th calendar day after the day the payor receives from the payee the certification required under paragraph (f) of this section.

(2) *Grace periods.*—(i) *Starting backup withholding.*—A payor may, on an account-by-account basis or in general, choose to begin backup withholding under this paragraph (e) at any time during the 30-business-day period described in paragraph (e)(1) of this section.

(ii) *Stopping backup withholding.*—A payor may, on an account-by-account basis or in general, choose to stop backup withholding under this paragraph (e) at any time within 30 calendar days after the payor receives from the payee the certification required under paragraph (f) of this section.

(3) *Dormant accounts.*—The requirement that a payor backup withhold under this paragraph (e) on reportable payments made with respect to an account terminates no later than the close of the third calendar year ending after the later of—

(i) The date that the last reportable payment was made to that account; or

(ii) The date that the payor received the notice under paragraph (c)(1) or (2) of this section.

(f) *Manner required for payee to furnish certified taxpayer identification number.*—(1) Except as provided in paragraph (g) of this section, in order to prevent backup withholding under paragraph (e) of this section from starting, or to stop it once it has begun, a payee with respect to whom the payor has been notified under paragraph (c)(1) or (2) that the payee's name/TIN combination is incorrect is required on Form W-9 (or an acceptable substitute form) to—

(i) Provide the payee's name and taxpayer identification number; and

(ii) Certify, under penalties of perjury, that the taxpayer identification number being provided is correct.

(2) The certification must be made even if the account is a pre-1984 account and even if the payment to the account is reportable payment other than interest, dividends, patronage dividends, original issue discount, or proceeds of a sale of a security or commodity. In order to prevent backup withholding under paragraph (e) of this section from starting or to stop it once it has begun, a payee is not required to certify, under penalties of perjury, that the payee is not subject to backup withholding due to notified payee underreporting under section 3406(a)(1)(C). With respect to notices received under paragraph (c)(1) or (2) of this section on or after September 1, 1993, the requirements of this paragraph (f) are not satisfied if a payee provides only an awaiting TIN certification. As a result, a payor must not fail to begin backup withholding under paragraph (e) of this section solely because the payee provided an awaiting TIN certification, or stop once it has begun solely because the payee provided an awaiting TIN certification.

(g) *Receipt of two notices within a three-year period.*—(1) *In general.*— If a payor receives notification under paragraph (c)(1) or (2) of this section twice within three calendar years, and in each case the payor is required to identify the same account as having the incorrect name/TIN combination, the payor must—

(i) Disregard any future certifications (described in paragraph (f) of this section) furnished by the payee with respect to the account until the payor receives notice from the Social Security Administration (or the Internal Revenue Service) validating a name/TIN combination under paragraph (g)(5) of this section;

(ii) Send the notice described in paragraph (g)(2) of this section to the payee (and not the notice required under paragraph (d) of this section) within 15 business days after the date that the payor receives the second notice; and

(iii) Impose backup withholding on the account for the period described in paragraph (g)(3) of this section.
The payor must maintain sufficient records to determine whether the payor has received notices under paragraph (c)(1) or (2) of this section twice within three calendar years with respect to the same account.

(2) *Notice to payee who has provided two incorrect name/TIN combinations within three calendar years.*—The notice to the payee required by paragraph (g)(1) of this section must comply with such procedural requirements as the Internal Revenue Service provides in the Internal Revenue Bulletin such as to form and manner of delivery.

(3) *Period during which backup withholding is required due to a second notice of an incorrect name/taxpayer identification combination within three calendar years.*—(i) *In general.*—If paragraph (g)(1) of this section applies, the payor must backup withhold on all reportable payments made with respect to the account of the payee after the close of the 30th business day after the date that the payor receives the second notice under paragraph (c)(1) or (2) of this section and on or before the close of the 30th calendar day after the date that the payor receives notice from the Social Security Administration (or the Internal Revenue Service) validating a name/TIN combination under paragraph (g)(5) of this section for the account. However, a payor

may choose not to commence backup withholding under this paragraph (g) until January 1, 1992.

(ii) *Grace periods.*—(A) *Starting backup withholding.*—A payor may, on an account-by-account basis or in general, choose to begin backup withholding under this paragraph (g) at any time during the 30-business-day period described in paragraph (g)(3)(i) of this section.

(B) *Stopping backup withholding.*—A payor may, on an account-by-account basis or in general, choose to stop backup withholding under this paragraph (g) at any time within 30 calendar days after the date the payor receives notice from the Social Security Administration (or the Internal Revenue Service) validating a name/TIN combination under paragraph (g)(5) of this section for the account.

(iii) *Dormant accounts.*—The requirement that a payor backup withhold under this paragraph (g) on reportable payments made with respect to an account terminates no later than the close of the third calendar year ending after the later of—

(A) The date that the last reportable payment was made to that account; or

(B) The date that the payor received the second notice under paragraph (c)(1) or (2) of this section.

(4) *Receipt of two notices for the same year or in the same calendar year.*—A payor who receives, under the same payor taxpayer identification number, two or more notices under paragraph (c)(1) or (2) of this section with respect to the same payee's account for the same year, or in the same calendar year, must treat such notices as one notice for purposes of this paragraph (g).

(5) *Notification from the Social Security Administration (or the Internal Revenue Service) validating a name/TIN combination.*—The Social Security Administration (or the Internal Revenue Service) will notify a payor after it validates a name/TIN combination that the payee provides for an account to which paragraph (g)(1) of this section applies. Notification from the Social Security Administration (or the Internal Revenue Service) validating a name/TIN combination satisfies the requirements of this paragraph (g)(5) only if it complies with such procedural requirements as the Internal Revenue Service provides in the Internal Revenue Bulletin such as to form and manner of delivery. In order to obtain notification from the Social Security Administration (or the Internal Revenue Service) validating a name/TIN combination for an account, a payee who receives notice from a payor under paragraph (g)(2) of this section should follow such procedures as the Internal Revenue Service provides in the Internal Revenue Bulletin.

(h) *Payors must use newly provided certified number.*—If a payor receives a certification under paragraph (f) of this section or a notification under paragraph (g)(5) of this section for an account, the payor must use the name/TIN combination provided on such certification or notification on information returns for the account for which the due date (without regard to extensions) is more than 30 calendar days after the date that the payor receives the certification or notification. A payor who uses that name/TIN combination on the first such information return satisfies the requirement of section 3406(h)(9) to provide this information to the Internal Revenue Service. If the payor is not required to file any information returns with respect to the account after the date that the payor receives the certification or notification, a payor is deemed to satisfy the requirements of section 3406(h)(9).

(i) *Effective date.*—Except as otherwise provided in this section, the provisions of this section are effective with respect to notices received on or after September 1, 1990, under paragraph (c)(1) or (2) of this section.

(j) *Examples.*—The application of the provisions of this section may be illustrated by the following examples:

*Example 1.* D opened an account with Bank O prior to 1984 and furnished a taxpayer identification number to O at the time he opened the account. O pays interest on the account at the end of each calendar month, and the account is a pre-1984 account. On October 1, 1990, the Internal Revenue Service notifies Bank O that the name/TIN combination provided by D is incorrect. O timely notifies D as required in paragraph (d)(1) of this section. O does not receive the certification required under paragraph (f) of this section from D. O is required to backup withhold 20 percent of all reportable payments made after November 14, 1990 (which is 30 business days after the date the Internal Revenue Service notified O). Therefore, O is not required to backup withhold on the reportable payment made on October 31, 1990, but is required to backup withhold on the reportable payment made on November 30, 1990. O is required to continue to backup withhold under section 3406(a)(1)(B) until O receives the certification required under paragraph (f) of this section from D (or, if earlier, until backup withholding terminates under paragraph (e)(3) of this section).

*Example 2.* Assume that same facts as in *Example 1* except that D furnishes a new taxpayer identification number to O on November 1, 1990, but does not certify, under penalties of perjury, that it is his correct taxpayer identification number as required under paragraph (f) of this section. Even though the account is a pre-1984 account, O is required to withhold 20 percent of all reportable payments made after November 14, 1990 (which is 30 business days after the date the Internal Revenue Service notified O), and before the date O receives the certification required under paragraph (f) of this section from D.

*Example 3.* Assume the same facts as in *Example 2* except that D provides O with the certification required under paragraph (f) of this section on November 20, 1990. D elects pursuant to paragraph (e)(2)(ii) of this section to treat the certification as received on November 20, 1990. Even though D did not provide the certification to O within 30 business days after the Internal Revenue Service notified O that D provided an incorrect taxpayer identification number, O is not required to backup withhold under section 3406(a)(1)(B) because O did not make any reportable payment to D after 30 business days after notification of an incorrect name/TIN combination and before O received D's certification under paragraph (f) of this section (or, if earlier, until backup withholding terminates under paragraph (e)(3) of this section).

*Example 4.* Individual F has two post-1983 accounts with Bank R that pay reportable interest: a savings account and a money market account. The money market account was opened in 1986, and the savings account was opened on February 1, 1991. R treats each of these accounts as a separate account on its books and records for business purposes. On October 1, 1990, the Internal Revenue Service notified R pursuant to paragraph (c)(1) of this section that F furnished an incorrect name/TIN combination with respect to the money market account. R timely sends F the notice required under paragraph (d) of this section and receives the certification required under paragraph (f) of this section from F on November 1, 1990. On October 1, 1991, the Internal Revenue Service again notifies R that F furnished an incorrect name/TIN combination with respect to the money market account. Further, R determines from its business records that two notifications of an incorrect name/TIN combination have been received with respect to the money market account within 3 calendar years. R must send F the notice required under paragraph (g)(2) of this section and must commence backup withholding on reportable interest paid on the money market account pursuant to paragraph (g)(3) of this section after November 14, 1991, which is 30 business days after R received the second notice. R must continue to backup withhold under paragraph (g) of this section on the money market account until R receives notification from the Social Security Administration as described in paragraph (g)(5) of this section (or, if earlier, until backup withholding terminates under paragraph (g)(3)(iii) of this section). R is not required to backup withhold on the savings account unless and until it receives notice under paragraph (c)(1) or (2) of this section with respect to the savings account. [Reg. §31.3406(d)-5.]

☐ [*T.D. 8409, 4-10-92. Amended by T.D. 9055, 4-28-2003.*]

### [Reg. §31.3406(e)-1]

**§31.3406(e)-1. Period during which backup withholding is required.**—(a) *In general.*—A payor must withhold under section 3406 at a rate of 31 percent on any reportable payment (as defined in section 3406(b)) made to a payee during the period described in this section (irrespective of the number of conditions for imposing withholding under section 3406 that exist with respect to the payee). A payor must continue to withhold under section 3406 until no condition for imposing backup withholding exists with respect to the payee.

(b) *Failure to furnish a taxpayer identification number in the manner required.*—(1) *Start withholding.*—A payor is required to withhold under section 3406(a)(1)(A) at a rate of 31 percent on any reportable payment (as defined in section 3406(b)) at the time the payor pays the reportable payment (as described in §31.3406(a)-4) to a payee if—

(i) The payor has not received the payee's taxpayer identification number in the manner required in §31.3406(d)-1; or

(ii) The payor has received notice from a broker (as required in §31.3406(d)-4(a)(1)(iii)) with respect to a readily tradable instrument that the payee did not furnish a taxpayer identification number to the broker in the manner required in §31.3406(d)-1 and the payor has not received the taxpayer identification number from the payee in this manner.

(2) *Stop withholding.*—The payor must stop withholding under section 3406(a)(1)(A) within 30 days after the payor receives—

(i) The payee's taxpayer identification number in the manner required under §31.3406(d)-1; or

(ii) A statement, in such form and containing such information as is required under applicable regulations, that the payee is not a United States person.

(c) *Notification of an incorrect taxpayer identification number.*—See §31.3406(d)-5(e) and (g)(3) for the period for which withholding is required in the case of notification of an incorrect taxpayer identification number.

(d) *Notified payee underreporting.*—See §31.3406(c)-1(e) for the period for which withholding is required in the case of notified payee underreporting.

(e) *Payee certification failure.*—(1) *Start withholding.*—A payor is required to withhold under section 3406(a)(1)(D) at a rate of 31 percent on any reportable interest or dividend payment (as defined in section 3406(b)(2)) at the time the payor pays such reportable interest or dividend payment (as described in §31.3406(a)-4) to a payee if—

(i) The payor has not received from the payee the certification required in §31.3406(d)-2; or

(ii) The payor has received notice from a broker (as required in §31.3406(d)-4(a)(1)(iii)) with respect to a readily tradable instrument that the payee did not make the required certification and the payor has not received the required certification from the payee.

(2) *Stop withholding.*—The payor must stop withholding under section 3406(a)(1)(D) on any reportable interest or dividend payment within 30 days after the payor receives the certification from the payee in the manner required by §31.3406(d)-2.

(f) *Rule for determining when the payor receives a taxpayer identification number or certificate from a payee.*—In determining whether a payee has failed to provide a taxpayer identification number or any certification to a payor (including a Form W-8 or substitute form), a payor is required to process the taxpayer identification number or certification within 30 days after the payor receives the taxpayer identification number or certification from the payee or in certain cases, from a broker. Thus, the payor may take up to 30 days to treat the taxpayer identification number or a certificate as having been received. [Reg. §31.3406(e)-1.]

☐ [*T.D. 8637, 12-20-95.*]

### [Reg. §31.3406(f)-1]

**§31.3406(f)-1. Confidentiality of information.**—(a) *Confidentiality and liability for violation.*—Pursuant to section 3406(f) no person may use any information obtained under section 3406 for any purpose except for the purpose of complying with the requirements of section 3406 or for purposes permitted under section 6103 (subject to the safeguards of section 6103). See section 7431 for civil damages for violating the confidential use of the information (subject to an exception for good faith).

(b) *Permissible use of information.*—(1) *In general.*—A payor or broker may transmit information on a Form W-9, Form W-8, or other acceptable form relating to withholding to the department, institution, or firm (or to any employee therein) responsible for withholding or processing of taxpayer identification numbers, certifications described in §31.3406(h)-3, or other substitute forms. In addition, a broker may notify the payor with respect to a readily tradable instrument of the requirement to withhold and the condition or conditions for imposing withholding (as described in §31.3406(d)-4) that exist with respect to the payee. A payor or broker may, without violating the Internal Revenue Code, close an account of, refuse to open an account for, issue an instrument to, or redeem an instrument for, a person solely because the person fails to furnish the person's taxpayer identification number or documentation of foreign status in the manner required in §31.3406(d)-1 and §31.3406(g)-1, respectively. A payor who closes an account of a payee in the calendar year in which the account was opened and during which no taxpayer identification number or evidence of foreign status was provided for that account will be presumed in the absence of evidence to the contrary to have closed the account without violating section 3406(f) even though the payee is subject to backup withholding under section 3406(a)(1)(A). A payor, except as provided in §§31.3406(d)-3 and 31.3406(g)-3, may not prohibit a payee who fails to furnish the payee's taxpayer identification number in the manner required in §31.3406(d)-1 from withdrawing any funds in the account.

(2) *Window transactions.*—In the case of a window transaction (as defined in §31.3406(b)(2)-3(b)), a payor may, without violating the Internal Revenue Code, refuse to redeem or may refuse to make payment if the payee fails to provide a taxpayer identification number regardless of when the obligation was issued or acquired.

(c) *Specific restrictions on the use of information.*—Except as provided in paragraph (b) of this section, a payor or broker is not permitted to—

(1) Close an account (or instrument) of a payee solely because that payee (or the account of a payee) is subject to withholding under section 3406(a)(1)(A), (B), (C), or (D);

(2) Refuse to open an account or to issue an instrument if the person fails to certify, under penalties of perjury, that the person is not subject to withholding under section 3406(a)(1)(C)(relating to notified payee underreporting);

(3) Use information obtained under section 3406 (including a payee's failure or inability to certify that the payee is not subject to withholding due to notified payee underreporting or the fact that the account is subject to withholding), surcharge an account (i.e., charge an account more than the fee charged a similar account that was not subject to withholding under section 3406), or use that information to determine whether to open or close an account, whether to issue or redeem an instrument, or whether to extend credit to the payee. [Reg. § 31.3406(f)-1.]

☐ [*T.D. 8637*, 12-20-95.]

### [Reg. §31.3406(g)-1]

**§31.3406(g)-1. Exception for payments to certain payees and certain other payments.**—(a) *Exempt recipients.*—(1) *In general.*—A payor of any reportable payment (as defined in section 3406(b)) must not withhold under section 3406 if the payee is—

(i) An organization exempt from taxation under section 501(a) or an individual retirement account;

(ii) The United States or any wholly owned agency or instrumentality thereof;

(iii) A state, the District of Columbia, a possession of the United States, any political subdivision of any of the foregoing, or any wholly owned agency or instrumentality of any one or more of the foregoing;

(iv) A foreign government, a political subdivision of a foreign government, or any wholly owned agency or instrumentality of any one or more of the foregoing (as defined in regulations under section 892); or

(v) An international organization or any wholly owned agency or instrumentality thereof (as defined in section 7701(a)(18)).

(2) *Nonexclusive list.*—Paragraph (a)(1) of this section does not prescribe an exclusive list of payees that are exempt from information reporting and also are exempt from withholding under section 3406.

(b) *Determination of whether a person is described in paragraph (a)(1) of this section.*—The determination of whether a person is a payee described in paragraph (a)(1) of this section must be made as provided in the applicable provisions of section 6049 and the regulations issued thereunder. A payor, even if permitted to treat a person as an exempt recipient without requiring a certificate under the provisions of section 6049, may require a payee, otherwise not required to file a certificate regarding its exempt status, to file a certificate and may treat a payee who fails to file the certificate as a person who is not an exempt recipient. See §31.3406(h)-3 for a description of the Form W-9 or a substitute form prescribed under section 3406 for claiming exempt status.

(c) *Prepaid or advance premium life-insurance contracts.*—A payor of a reportable payment (as defined in section 3406(b)(1)) may, but is not required to, withhold under section 3406 on reportable payments made from January 1, 1984, to December 31, 1996, on prepaid or advance premium life-insurance contracts to a payee who is the owner for tax purposes of the prepaid or advance premium life-insurance contract. For purposes of this exception from backup withholding, a prepaid or advance premium life-insurance contract is one entered into on or before June 30, 1984, by the payee and under which the increment in value of the prepaid or advance premium is used for the payment of premiums during the period in which the exception from backup withholding applies.

(d) *Reportable payments made to nonresident alien individuals.*—A payment of interest to a nonresident alien individual that is described in §1.6049-(8)(a) of this chapter is not subject to withholding under section 3406 if the payor may treat the payee as a foreign beneficial owner or foreign payee under the rules of §1.6049-5(b)(12). (For interest paid to a Canadian nonresident alien individual on or before December 31, 2012, see paragraph (d) of this section as in effect and contained in 26 CFR part 1 revised April 1, 2000.)

(e) *Certain reportable payments made outside the United States by foreign persons, foreign offices of United States banks and brokers, and others.*—For reportable payments made after June 30, 2014, a payor is not required to backup withhold under section 3406 on a reportable payment that is paid and received outside the United States (as defined in §1.6049-4(f)(16)) with respect to an offshore obligation (as defined in §1.6049-5(c)(1)) or on gross proceeds from a sale effected outside the United States (as defined in §1.6045-1(g)(3)(iii)), unless

the payor has actual knowledge that the payee is a United States person. Further, no backup withholding is required on a reportable payment of an amount already withheld upon by a participating FFI (as defined in §1.1471-1(b)(91)) or another payor in accordance with the withholding provisions under chapter 3 or 4 of the Code and the regulations under those chapters even if the payee is a known U.S. person. For example, a participating FFI is not required to backup withhold on a reportable payment allocable to its chapter 4 withholding rate pool (as defined in §1.6049-4(f)(5)) of recalcitrant account holders (as described in §1.6049-4(f)(11)), if withholding was applied to the payment (either by the participating FFI or another payor) pursuant to §1.1471-4(b) or §1.1471-2(a). For rules applicable to notional principal contracts, see §1.6041-1(d)(5) of this chapter. For rules applicable to reportable payments made before July 1, 2014, see this paragraph (e) as in effect and contained in 26 CFR part 1 revised April 1, 2013.)

(f) *Effective/applicability date.*—This section applies on or after January 6, 2017. (For payments made after June 30, 2014, and before January 6, 2017, see this section as in effect and contained in 26 CFR part 1, revised April 1, 2016). [Reg. §31.3406(g)-1.]

☐ [*T.D. 8637*, 12-20-95. *Amended by T.D. 8664*, 4-15-96; *T.D. 8734*, 10-6-97; *T.D. 8804*, 12-30-98; *T.D. 8856*, 12-29-99 *T.D. 9136*, 7-12-2004; *T.D. 9584*, 4-17-2012; *T.D. 9658*, 2-28-2014; *T.D. 9699*, 10-24-2014 *and T.D. 9808*, 12-30-2016.]

### [Reg. §31.3406(g)-2]

**§31.3406(g)-2. Exception for reportable payments for which withholding is otherwise required.**—(a) *In general.*—A payor of a reportable payment (as defined in section 3406(b)) must not withhold under section 3406 if the payment is subject to withholding under any other provision of the Internal Revenue Code.

(b) *Payment of wages.*—A payor who is required to make an information return under section 6041 with respect to a payment of wages (as defined in section 3401) because, e.g., the employee makes a certification under section 3402(n)(relating to employees incurring no income tax liability), must not withhold under section 3406 on those wages.

(c) *Distribution from a pension, annuity, or other plan of deferred compensation.*—An amount reportable under section 6047, such as a designated distribution under section 3405, is not a reportable payment subject to withholding under section 3406. See section 3406(b). Designated distributions not subject to withholding under section 3406 include—

(1) Distributions from a pension, annuity, profit-sharing, stock bonus plan, or other plan deferring the receipt of compensation;

(2) Distributions from an individual retirement account or annuity;

(3) Distributions from an owner-employee plan; and

(4) Certain surrenders of life insurance contracts.

(d) *Gambling winnings.*—(1) *In general.*—A payor of a reportable gambling winning must not withhold under section 3406 if tax is required to be withheld from the gambling winning under section 3402(q)(relating to the extension of withholding to certain gambling winnings). If the reportable gambling winning is not required to be withheld upon under section 3402(q), withholding under section 3406 applies to the gambling winning if, and only if, the payee does not furnish a taxpayer identification number to the payor. Section 31.3406(b)(3)-1(b)(3) does not apply to a reportable gambling winning. The payor of a reportable gambling winning is not required to aggregate all such winnings made to a payee during a calendar year, nor is the payor required to determine whether an information return was required to be made with respect to the payee for the preceding year.

(2) *Definition of a reportable gambling winning and determination of amount subject to backup withholding.*—For purposes of withholding under section 3406, a reportable gambling winning is any gambling winning subject to information reporting under section 6041. A gambling winning (other than a winning from bingo, keno, or slot machines) is a reportable gambling winning only if the amount paid with respect to the wager is $600 or more and if the proceeds are at least 300 times as large as the amount wagered. See §1.6041-10 of this chapter to determine whether a winning from bingo, keno, or slot machines is a reportable gambling winning and thus subject to withholding under section 3406. The amount of a reportable gambling winning is—

(i) The amount paid with respect to the amount of the wager reduced, at the option of the payer; by

(ii) The amount of the wager.

(3) *Special rules.*—For special rules for determining the amount of the wager in a wagering transaction with respect to horse racing,

dog racing, and jai alai, or amounts paid with respect to identical wagers, see § 31.3402(q)–1(c).

(e) *Certain real estate transactions.*—A real estate reporting person (the so-called broker) as defined in section 6045(e)(2) must not withhold under section 3406 on a payment made with respect to a real estate transaction that is subject to reporting under sections 6045(a) and (e) and § 1.6045-4 of this chapter.

(f) *Certain payments after an acquisition of accounts or instruments.*— A payor who acquires pre-1984 accounts or instruments described in § 31.3406(d)-1(b)(2)(iv) for which the payor does not have a taxpayer identification number or has an obviously incorrect taxpayer identification number as defined in § 31.3406(h)-1(b)(2) must start withholding under section 3406(a)(1)(A) and § 31.3406(d)-1 on those accounts or instruments no later than sixty days following the date of the payor's acquisition of those accounts or instruments.

(g) *Certain gross proceeds.*—No withholding under section 3406 is required with respect to any portion of the original issue discount on an instrument or security that is subject to withholding under section 3406 as reportable gross proceeds of such instrument or security under section 6045.

(h) *Applicability date.*—The rules apply to reportable gambling winnings paid with respect to a winning event that occurs after November 13, 2017. For rules that apply to payments made with respect to a winning event on or before that date, see § 31.3406(g)-2 as contained in 26 CFR part 31, revised April 1, 2017. [Reg. § 31.3406(g)-2.]

☐ [T.D. 8637, 12-20-95. *Amended by T.D. 9524, 5-6-2011, T.D. 9586, 4-24-2012; T.D. 9807, 12-29-2016 and T.D. 9824, 9-25-2017.*]

**[Reg. § 31.3406(g)-3]**

**§ 31.3406(g)-3. Exemption while payee is waiting for a taxpayer identification number.**—(a) *In general.*—(1) *Backup withholding not required for 60 days.*—If a payor has received an awaiting-TIN certificate from a payee with respect to an account or instrument receiving reportable interest or dividends as described in section 3406(b)(2), the payor must exempt the payee from withholding under section 3406(a)(1)(A) during the 60-day exemption period to the extent and in the manner described in either paragraph (a)(2) or (3) of this section. The 60-day exemption period means the 60-consecutive-day period beginning with the day the payor receives the awaiting-TIN certificate. The payor must withhold under section 3406 beginning after the 60-day exemption period if the payor has not received a taxpayer identification number from the payee in the manner required in § 31.3406(d)-1. Regardless of whether the payee provides an awaiting-TIN certificate to a payor, the payor is required to withhold under section 3406(a)(1)(D) and § 31.3406(d)-2 on reportable interest or dividend payments as described in § 31.3406(d)-2 if the payee fails to certify, under penalties of perjury, that the payee is not subject to withholding due to notified payee underreporting as required in section 3406(a)(1)(D) and § 31.3406(d)-2.

(2) *Reserve method.*—A payor must not withhold under section 3406 during the 60-day exemption period unless the payee (or a joint payee in the case of a joint account) desires to make a withdrawal of more than $500 of either principal or interest from the account in any single transaction during the period. If a payee (or a joint payee) desires to make a withdrawal of more than $500 during the 60-day exemption period, the payor is required under section 3406 to withhold 31 percent of all reportable payments made during the period and at the time of withdrawal unless the payee reserves 31 percent of all reportable payments made to the account during the period.

(3) *Alternative rule; 7-day grace period.*—(i) *In general.*—A payor who receives an awaiting-TIN certificate may elect, on a payee-by-payee basis or in general, to exempt reportable interest or dividend payments to a payee from withholding under section 3406 applying the rules in paragraph (a)(3)(ii) or (iii) of this section.

(ii) *Withholding on withdrawals.*—Under this paragraph (a)(3)(ii), a payor must obtain a certified taxpayer identification number from the payee within 60 days after the date that the payor receives the awaiting-TIN certification. In addition, the payor must withhold under section 3406 on any withdrawals made after the close of 7 business days after the date the awaiting-TIN certification is received and before the earlier of the date that the payor receives a certified taxpayer identification number from the payee, the date the account is closed (in which case the payor must withhold on any reportable payment made at the time the account or relationship is closed), or the date withholding under section 3406 starts on all reportable payments made to the account, instrument, or relationship. All cash withdrawals in an amount up to the reportable payments made from the day after the date of receipt of the awaiting-

TIN certification to the date of withdrawal are treated as reportable payments.

(iii) *Withholding regardless of withdrawals.*—Under this paragraph (a)(3)(iii), a payor must start withholding under section 3406 on the account not later than 7 business days after the date the payor receives the awaiting-TIN certification on reportable payments thereafter made to the account (whether or not the payee makes a cash withdrawal). The payor must withhold under section 3406 until the earlier of the date the payor receives a certified taxpayer identification number from the payee, the date the account is closed, or the date withholding under section 3406 starts on all reportable payments made to the account, instrument, or relationship. The payor must obtain a certified taxpayer identification number from the payee within 60 days after the date that the payor receives the awaiting-TIN certificate or undertake a mailing each year soliciting the certified taxpayer identification number from the payee until the earlier of the calendar year that the certified taxpayer identification number is received, or the calendar year in which the account is closed. However, if the account is closed in December of a calendar year, the mailing must be made after the account is closed and before January 31 of the subsequent calendar year.

(b) *Special rule for readily tradable instruments.*—The 60-day awaiting-TIN exemption described in paragraph (a)(1) of this section applies to payments made with respect to readily tradable instruments only if the payee provides an awaiting-TIN certificate directly to the payor. If a broker acquires a readily tradable instrument through a post-1983 brokerage account (as described in § 31.3406(d)-1(c)(2)) for a payee who has no taxpayer identification number, the broker must advise the payor as required in § 31.3406(d)-4(a)(1) that the payee failed to provide a taxpayer identification number under penalties of perjury, regardless of whether the payee provides an awaiting-TIN certificate to the broker. Once a payor is notified by a broker that a payee failed to provide a taxpayer identification number in the required manner, or that the payee is subject to withholding under section 3406(a)(1)(B) or (C), the payor must impose withholding under section 3406 for the appropriate period described in § 31.3406(e)-1.

(c) *Exceptions.*—(1) *In general.*—The 60-day awaiting-TIN exemption described in paragraph (a) of this section does not apply to—

(i) Window transactions (as defined in § 31.3406(b)(2)-3(b));

(ii) Redemptions of bearer obligations that are subject to reporting under section 6045; or

(iii) Other amounts that are subject to reporting under section 6045 (except as described in paragraph (c)(2) of this section).

(2) *Special rule for amounts subject to reporting under section 6045 other than proceeds of redemptions of bearer obligations.*—If a broker's customer does not provide a taxpayer identification number to the broker, and the broker effects a sale that is subject to reporting under section 6045 (other than a redemption of a bearer obligation), § 31.3406(d)-3(b) applies, whether or not the sale is pursuant to an instruction by electronic transmission, provided the customer furnishes an awaiting-TIN certificate to the broker before the sale. For purposes of this paragraph (c)(2), the 30-day period provided in § 31.3406(d)-3(b) is a 60-day period.

(d) *Awaiting-TIN certificate.*—A payee qualifies for the 60-day awaiting-TIN exemption provided in paragraph (a) of this section if the payee furnishes a written statement to the payor, signed under penalties of perjury, that the payee has not been issued a taxpayer identification number, that the payee has applied for a taxpayer identification number or intends to apply for a number in the near future, and that the payee understands that if the payee does not provide a number to the payor within 60 days, the payor is required under section 3406 to withhold 31 percent of any reportable payment thereafter made to the payee until the payor receives a number, and 31 percent of a withdrawal to the extent of reportable payments made to the payee during the 60-day period, as described in paragraph (a) of this section. Language that is substantially similar to the awaiting-TIN certification on Form W-9 will satisfy the requirements of this paragraph (d).

(e) *Form for awaiting-TIN certificate.*—A payor may use Form W-9 for the awaiting-TIN certificate, or a payor may include language that is substantially similar to the awaiting-TIN certification on Form W-9 in any other document of the payor. See § 31.3406(h)-3, which provides that Form W-9 is the prescribed form but permits use of substitute forms, and specifies the length of time the payor is required to retain the form. If Form W-9 is used, the payee should write "Applied For" in the space reserved for the taxpayer identification number. [Reg. § 31.3406(g)-3.]

☐ [*T.D. 8637, 12-20-95.*]

**Collection of Income Tax at Source on Wages**
See p. 20,601 for regulations not amended to reflect law changes
**61,523**

[Reg. §31.3406(h)-1]

**§31.3406(h)-1. Definitions.**—(a) *In general.*—For purposes of section 3406 and the regulations thereunder, the definitions of this section apply.

(b) *Taxpayer identification number.*—(1) *In general.*—*Taxpayer identification number* means the identifying number assigned to a person under section 6109 (relating to identifying numbers, generally a nine-digit social security number for an individual and a nine-digit employer identification number for a nonindividual, e.g., a corporation, partnership, trust, or estate). An obviously incorrect number is not considered a taxpayer identification number. See §31.6011(b)-2 and §301.6109-1 of this chapter for provisions relating to obtaining a taxpayer identification number.

(2) *Obviously incorrect number.*—*Obviously incorrect number* means a number that does not contain nine digits or a number that includes an alpha character as one of the nine digits.

(c) *Broker.*—*Broker* is defined in section 6045(c)(1) and §1.6045-1(a)(1) of this chapter. If there could be more than one broker with respect to any acquisition, only the broker having the closest contact (as determined under §1.6045-1(c)(3)(iii) and (iv) of this chapter) with the payee is treated as a broker. In the case of any instrument, the term *broker* does not include any person who is the payor with respect to the instrument as described in §31.3406(a)-2.

(d) *Readily tradable instrument. Readily tradable instrument.*—means—

(1) Any instrument that is part of an issue any portion of which is traded on an established securities market (within the meaning of section 453(f)(5)); or

(2) Any instrument that is regularly quoted by brokers or dealers making a market.

(e) *Day.*—*Day* means a calendar day unless specified otherwise under any section of the regulations under section 3406. For example, see §§31.3406(d)-5(a) and 31.3406(g)-3(a)(2).

(f) *Business day.*—*Business day* means any day other than a Saturday, Sunday, or legal holiday (within the meaning of section 7503). [Reg. §31.3406(h)-1.]

☐ [T.D. 8637, 12-20-95. Amended by T.D. 9010, 7-25-2002.]

[Reg. §31.3406(h)-2]

**§31.3406(h)-2. Special rules.**—(a) *Joint accounts.*—(1) *Relevant name and taxpayer identification number combination.*—For purposes of identifying the account subject to withholding under sections 3406(a)(1)(B) and (C), the relevant name and taxpayer identification number combination is that which is used for information reporting purposes.

(2) *Optional rule for accounts subject to backup withholding under section 3406(a)(1)(B) or (C) where the names are switched.*—See §31.3406(d)-5(c)(4)(iii) under which a payor may withhold under section 3406(a)(1)(B) as required even though the names or taxpayer identification numbers on the account have been switched. The rules under §31.3406(d)-5(c)(4)(iii) may be applied comparably by a payor who is required to withhold under section 3406(a)(1)(C).

(3) *Joint foreign payees.*—(i) *In general.*—If the relevant payee listed on a jointly owned account or instrument provides a Form W-8 or documentary evidence described in §1.1441-1(e)(1)(ii) regarding its foreign status, withholding under section 3406 applies unless every joint payee provides the statement regarding foreign status (under the provisions of chapters 3 or 61 of the Internal Revenue Code and the regulations under those provisions); any one of the joint owners who has not established foreign status provides a taxpayer identification number to the payor in the manner required in §§31.3406(d)-1 through 31.3406(d)-5; or, in the case of a withholdable payment (as defined in §1.6049-4(f)(15)), any joint payee does not appear to be an individual as described in §1.1471-3(f)(7). See §1.6049-5(d)(2)(iii) of this chapter for corresponding joint payees provisions.

(ii) *Information reporting on an account including foreign payees.*—If any one of the joint payees who has not established foreign status provides a taxpayer identification number under paragraph (a)(3)(i)(B) of this section, that number is the taxpayer identification number that is required to be furnished for purposes of information reporting and withholding under section 3406.

(b) *Backup withholding from an alternative source.*—(1) *In general.*—A payor may not withhold under section 3406 from a source maintained by the payor other than the source with respect to which there exists a liability to withhold under section 3406 with respect to the payee. See section 3403 and §31.3403-1, which provide that the payor

is liable for the amount required to be withheld regardless of whether the payor withholds.

(2) *Exceptions for payments made in property.*—(i) *Backup withholding from alternative source.*—In the case of a payment that is made in property (other than money), the payor must withhold under section 3406, 31 percent of the fair market value of the property determined immediately before or on the date of payment. The payor may withhold under section 3406 from the principal amount being deposited with the payor or from another source maintained by the payee with the payor. The source from which the tax is withheld under section 3406 must be payable to at least one of the persons listed on the account subject to withholding. If the account or source is not payable exclusively to the same person or persons listed on the account subject to withholding under section 3406, then the payor must obtain a written statement from all other persons to whom the account or source is payable authorizing the payor to withhold under section 3406 from the alternative account or source. A payor that elects to withhold under section 3406 from an alternative source may determine the account or source from which the tax is to be withheld, or may allow the payee to designate the alternative source. A payee may not, however, require a payor to withhold under section 3406 from a specific alternative source. See §31.3402(q)-1(d), *Example 5*, for methods of withholding on prizes, awards, and gambling winnings paid in property other than cash.

(ii) *Deferral of withholding.*—If the payor cannot locate, using reasonable care (following procedures substantially similar to those set forth in §31.3406(d)-5(c)(3)(ii)(A) and (B)), an alternative source of cash from which the payor may satisfy its withholding obligation pursuant to paragraph (b)(2)(i) of this section, the payor may defer its obligation to withhold under section 3406, except for reportable payments of property made in connection with prizes, awards, or gambling winnings, until the earlier of—

(A) The date the payor makes a cash payment to the account subject to withholding under section 3406 or cash is otherwise deposited in the account in a sufficient amount to satisfy the obligation in full; or

(B) The close of the fourth calendar year after the obligation arose.

(iii) *Barter exchanges.*—In the case of a barter exchange that issues scrip to, or credits the account of, a member or client of the exchange in payment for property or services, the barter exchange may withhold under section 3406 from—

(A) The scrip or credit, if converted to cash in order to satisfy the deposit requirements of section 6302 and §31.6302-4; or

(B) Any other source maintained by the exchange for the member or client in the manner described in paragraph (b)(2) of this section.

(c) *Trusts.*—Withholding under section 3406 applies to reportable payments made to a trust if any of the conditions for imposing withholding under section 3406 apply to the trust. Generally, a trust is not a payor and will not be required to withhold under section 3406 on reportable payments that it makes to its beneficiary who is subject to withholding under section 3406. The preceding sentence does not apply, however, to a grantor trust described in §31.3406(a)-2(b)(1) or (2), which is treated as a payor. The trustee of a trust described in this paragraph (c) may certify that the trust's taxpayer identification number is correct and that the trust is not subject to withholding due to notified payee underreporting, without regard to the status of the beneficiaries of the trust.

(d) *Adjustment of prior withholding by middlemen.*—A middleman payor (as defined in §31.3406(a)-2(b) or in the section on information reporting to which the payment relates) who receives a payment from which tax has been erroneously withheld under section 3406 may seek a refund of the tax withheld by the payor from whom the middleman payor received the payment (referred to as the "upstream payor"). Alternatively, the middleman payor may obtain a refund of the tax by claiming a credit for the amount of tax withheld by the upstream payor against the deposit of any tax imposed by this chapter which the middleman payor is required to withhold and deposit (as described in section 6413 and §31.6413(a)-2). In either case, the middleman payor must pay or credit the gross amount of the payment (including the tax withheld) to its payee as though it had received the gross amount of the payment from the upstream payor and must withhold under section 3406 only if one of the conditions for imposing backup withholding exists with respect to its payee. If its payee is not subject to withholding under section 3406, the payor must pay or credit the full amount of the payment to the payee, unless, with respect to payments made after December 31, 2000, the payor chooses to apply prior withholding under section 3406 to an amount required to be withheld under another section of the Internal Revenue Code (such as under section 1441) to the extent permitted under procedures prescribed by the Internal Revenue Service (see § 601.601(d)(2) of this chapter). See § 31.6413(a)-3 regarding repayment by a payor of tax erroneously collected from a payee.

(e) *Conversion of amounts paid in foreign currency into United States dollars.*—If a payment is made in a currency other than the United States dollar, the amount subject to withholding under section 3406 is determined by applying the statutory rate of backup withholding to the foreign currency payment and converting the amount withheld into United States dollars on the date of payment at the spot rate (as defined in § 1.988-1(d)(1) of this chapter) or pursuant to a reasonable spot rate convention. For example, a withholding agent may use a month-end spot rate or a monthly average spot rate. A spot rate convention must be used consistently with respect to all non-dollar amounts withheld and from year to year. Such convention cannot be changed without the consent of the Commissioner.

(f) *Coordination with other sections.*—For purposes of section 31, chapter 24 (other than section 3402(n)) of subtitle C of the Internal Revenue Code (relating to employment taxes and collection of income tax at source) and so much of subtitle F (other than section 7205) of the Internal Revenue Code (relating to procedure and administration) as relates to this chapter, and the regulations thereunder—

(1) An amount required to be withheld under section 3406 must be treated as a tax required to be withheld under section 3402;

(2) An amount withheld under section 3406 must be treated as an amount withheld under section 3402;

(3) An amount withheld under section 3406 must be deposited as required under § 31.6302-4;

(4) *Wages* includes the gross amount of any reportable payment (as defined in section 3406(b)) except for purposes of section 6014 (relating to an election by the taxpayer not to compute the tax on his annual return);

(5) *Employee* includes a payee of any reportable payment; and

(6) *Employer* includes a payor who is required to withhold the tax under section 3406 (as defined in § 31.3406(a)-2) with respect to any reportable payment (as defined in section 34069(b)).

(g) *Tax liabilities and penalties.*—A payor is subject to the same civil and criminal penalties for failing to impose withholding under section 3406 as an employer who fails to withhold on a payment of wages. In addition, a broker may be subject to the penalty under section 6705 (failure of a broker to provide notice to a payor).

(h) *To whom payor is liable for amount withheld.*—A payor is not liable to any person for any amount withheld under section 3406. A payor is liable only to the United States for an amount that is required to be withheld as provided in § 31.3403-1.

(i) *Effective/applicability date.*—This section applies to payments made on or after January 6, 2017. (For payments made after June 30, 2014, and before January 6, 2017, see this section as in effect and contained in 26 CFR part 1, revised April 1, 2016.) [Reg. § 31.3406(h)-2.]

☐ [T.D. 8637, 12-20-95. Amended by T.D. 8734, 10-6-97; T.D. 8804, 12-30-98; T.D. 8856, 12-29-99; T.D. 9010, 7-25-2002, T.D. 9658, 2-28-2014 and T.D. 9808, 12-30-2016.]

### [Reg. § 31.3406(h)-3]

**§ 31.3406(h)-3. Certificates.**—(a) *Prescribed form to furnish information under penalties of perjury.*—(1) *In general.*—Except as provided in paragraph (c) of this section, the Form W-9 is the form prescribed under section 3406 on which a payee that is a U.S. person certifies, under penalties of perjury, that—

(i) The taxpayer identification number furnished to the payor is correct (as required in § 31.3406(d)-1 and § 31.3406(d)-5);

(ii) The payee is not subject to withholding due to notified payee underreporting (as required in § 31.3406(d)-2);

(iii) The payee is an exempt recipient (as described in § 31.3406(g)-1); or

(iv) The payee is awaiting receipt of a taxpayer identification number (as described in § 31.3406(g)-3).

(2) *Use of a single or multiple Forms W-9 for accounts of the same Payee.*—A valid Form W-9 must include the name and taxpayer identification number of the payee. Except as provided in paragraph (b) of this section, the payee must sign under penalties of perjury and date the Form W-9 in order to satisfy the requirements of this section. A payor or broker may require a payee to furnish a separate Form W-9 for each obligation, deposit, certificate, share, membership, contract, or other instrument, or one Form W-9 for all the payee's obligations or relationships with the payor or broker. In addition, a payee of a mutual fund that has a common investment advisor or common principal underwriter with other mutual funds (within the same family of funds) may be permitted, in the discretion of the mutual fund, to provide one Form W-9 with respect to shares acquired or owned in any of the funds.

(b) *Prescribed form to furnish a noncertified taxpayer identification number.*—With respect to accounts or other relationships where the payee is not required to certify, under penalties of perjury, that the taxpayer identification number being furnished is correct, the payor or broker may obtain the taxpayer identification number orally or may use Form W-9, a substitute form, or any other document, but the payee is not required to sign the form.

(c) *Forms prepared by payors or brokers.*—(1) *Substitute forms; in general.*—A payor or broker may prepare and use a form that contains provisions that are substantially similar to those of the official Form W-9. A payor or broker may use any document relating to the transaction, such as the signature card for an account, so long as the certifications are clearly set forth. A payor or broker who uses a substitute form may furnish orally or in writing the instructions for the Form W-9 that relate to the account. A payor or broker may refuse to accept certifications (including the official Form W-9) that are not made on the form or forms provided by the payor or broker. A payor or broker may refuse to accept a certification provided by a payee only if the payor or broker furnishes the payee with an acceptable form immediately upon receipt of an unacceptable form or within 5 business days of receipt of an unacceptable form. An acceptable form for this purpose must contain a notice that the payor or broker has refused to accept the form submitted by the payee and that the payee must submit the acceptable form provided by the payor in order for the payee not to be subject to withholding under section 3406. If the payor or broker requires the payee to furnish a form for each account of the payee, the payor or broker is not required to furnish an acceptable form until the payee furnishes the payor or broker with the payee's account numbers. A payor or broker may use separate substitute forms to have a payee certify under penalties of perjury that—

(i) The payee's taxpayer identification number is correct; and

(ii) The payee is not subject to withholding under section 3406 due to notified payee underreporting.

(2) *Form for exempt recipient.*—A payor or broker may use a substitute form for the payee to certify, under penalties of perjury, that the payee is an exempt recipient (described in § 31.3406(g)-1 or described in the respective reporting section), provided the form contains provisions that are substantially similar to those of the official Form W-9 relating to exempt recipients. A certificate must be prepared in accordance with the instructions applicable to exempt recipients on Form W-9, and must set forth fully and clearly the data called for therein. If a payor will treat the payee as an exempt recipient only if the payee files a certificate as to its exempt status, the certificate is valid only if it contains the payee's taxpayer identification number. Thus, a payee must include the payee's taxpayer identification number on a certificate that a payor requires to be made in order to treat the payee as an exempt recipient.

(d) *Special rule for brokers.*—A broker may act as the payee's agent for purposes of furnishing a taxpayer identification number or certification to a payor with respect to any readily tradable instrument (as defined in § 31.3406(h)-1(d)) provided the payee provides a taxpayer identification number on Form W-9 or other acceptable substitute form to the broker. The payor may rely on a taxpayer identification number provided by the broker unless certification is required (as described in § 31.3406(d)-4) and the broker notifies the payor that the number was not certified.

(e) *Reasonable reliance on certificate.*—(1) *In general.*—A payor is not liable for the tax imposed under section 3406 if the payor's failure to deduct and withhold the tax is due to reasonable reliance, as defined in paragraph (e)(2) of this section, on a Form W-9 (or other acceptable substitute) required by this section.

(2) *Circumstances establishing reasonable reliance.*—For purposes of paragraph (e)(1) of this section, a payor can reasonably rely on a Form W-9 (or other acceptable substitute) unless—

(i) The form does not contain the name and taxpayer identification number of the payee (or does not state, in lieu of a taxpayer identification number, that the payee is awaiting receipt of a taxpayer identification number (i.e., an awaiting-TIN certificate));

(ii) The form is not signed and dated by the payee;

(iii) The form does not contain the statement, when required, that the payee is not subject to withholding due to notified payee underreporting;

(iv) The payee has deleted the jurat or other similar provisions by which the payee certifies or affirms the correctness of the statements contained on the form; or

(v) For purposes of section 3406(a)(1)(C), the payor is required to subject the account to which the form relates to withholding under section 3406(a)(1)(C) under the circumstances described in §31.3406(c)-1(c)(3)(iii).

(f) *Who may sign certificate.*—(1) *In general.*—A Form W-9 or other acceptable substitute form may be signed by any person who is authorized to sign a declaration under penalties of perjury on behalf of the payee as provided in section 6061 and the regulations thereunder (relating to who may sign generally for an individual, which includes certain agents who may sign returns and other documents), section 6062 and the regulations thereunder (relating to who may sign corporate returns), and section 6063 and the regulations thereunder (relating to who may sign partnership returns).

(2) *Notified payee underreporting.*—A payee who has not been notified that he is subject to withholding under section 3406(a)(1)(C) as a result of notified payee underreporting may make the certification related to notified payee underreporting. In addition, a payee who was subject to withholding under section 3406(a)(1)(C) due to notified payee underreporting may certify that he is not subject to withholding under section 3406(a)(1)(C) due to notified payee underreporting if the Internal Revenue Service has provided the payee with written certification that withholding under section 3406(a)(1)(C) due to notified payee underreporting has terminated.

(g) *Retention of certificates.*—(1) *Accounts or instruments that are not pre-1984 accounts and brokerage relationships that are post-1983 brokerage accounts.*—With respect to an account or instrument that is not a pre-1984 account (as described in §31.3406(d)-1(b)(3)), or with respect to a brokerage relationship that is a post-1983 brokerage account (as described in §31.3406(d)-1(c)(2)), a payor or broker who receives a Form W-9 or other acceptable substitute form related to withholding under section 3406 must retain the form in its records for 3 years from the date the account is opened or the instrument is purchased. The form may be retained on microfilm or microfiche.

(2) *Accounts or instruments that are pre-1984 accounts and brokerage relationships that are not post-1983 brokerage accounts.*—With respect to a pre-1984 account (as described in §31.3406(d)-1(b)(1)) or or with respect to a brokerage relationship that is not a post-1983 brokerage account (as described in §31.3406(d)-1(c)(1)), a payor or broker is not required to retain any Form W-9 or other acceptable substitute form. If, however, the payor or broker requires the payee to file only one Form W-9 or substitute form for all accounts or instruments of the payee, the payor or broker must retain the single form in the manner and for the period of time described in paragraph (g)(1) of this section if that form relates to any account or instrument that is not a pre-1984 account or relates to a post-1983 brokerage account. If a payee has certified that the payee is an exempt recipient described in §31.3406(g)-1, the payor or broker must retain the form unless the payor or broker can establish the existence of procedures that are reasonably calculated to ensure that a payee who has so certified is accurately identified in the payor's or broker's records.

(h) *Cross references.*—For the requirement to file an information return (and furnish the related statement) with respect to a reportable payment, particularly if that payment has been subject to withholding under section 3406, see subtitle F, chapter 61, subparts B and C of the Internal Revenue Code. See §31.6302-4 for the requirement to deposit amounts withheld under section 3406 on either a monthly or semi-weekly basis. See §31.6011(a)-4(b) for the requirement to file Form 945, Annual Return of Withheld Federal Income Tax, to reflect amounts withheld under section 3406. See §31.6071(a)-1 for the time for filing the Form 945. [Reg. §31.3406(h)-3.]

☐ [*T.D. 8637, 12-20-95. Amended by T.D. 8881, 5-15-2000.*]

**⟫⟫ Caution: Caution: Reg. §35a.3406-2, below, is effective until December 31, 1996.**

**[Reg. §35a.3406-2]**

**§35a.3406-2. Imposition of backup withholding for notified payee underreporting of reportable interest or dividend payments (Temporary).**—(a) *Requirement that a payor backup withhold due to a notified payee underre porting.*—(1) *In general.*—Except as otherwise provided in paragraph (a)(5) of this section, backup withholding under section 3406(a)(1)(C) applies to any reportable interest or dividend payment (as defined in section 3406(b)(2) and paragraph (a)(4) of this section) made to a payee, if the Internal Revenue Service or a broker (as defined in section 3406(h)(5) and paragraph (a)(7) of this section and pursuant to section 3406(d)(2)(B)(ii)(III)) notifies a payor (as defined in section 3406(h)(4) and in paragraph (a)(6) of this section) that the payee is subject to backup withholding due to a notified payee underreporting (as defined in paragraph (a)(2) of this section). The payor is required under section 3406(c)(4) and paragraph (c)(1) of this section to inform the payee that backup withholding under section 3406(a)(1)(C) has begun. The requirements for the

**[Reg. §31.3406(i)-1]**

**§31.3406(i)-1. Effective date.**—Sections 31.3406-0 through 31.3406(i)-1 (except §§31.3406(d)-5 and 31.3406(g)-1(c) and except for international transactions) are effective after December 31, 1996, and, optionally, for reportable payments made and transactions occurring on or after December 21, 1995. For the effective date of §31.3406(d)-5, see §31.3406(d)-5(i). Section 31.3406(g)-1(c) is effective before January 1, 1997. See §§35a.9999-0T through 35a.9999-5 of this chapter for rules that apply to international transactions after December 31, 1996. [Reg. §31.3406(i)-1.]

☐ [*T.D. 8637, 12-20-95.*]

**[Reg. §31.3406(j)-1]**

**§31.3406(j)-1. Taxpayer Identification Number (TIN) matching program.**—(a) *The matching program.*—Under section 3406(i), the Commissioner has the authority to establish Taxpayer Identification Number (TIN) matching programs. The Commissioner may prescribe in a revenue procedure (see §601.601(d)(2) of this chapter) or other appropriate guidance the scope and the terms and conditions of participating in any TIN matching program. In general, under a matching program, prior to filing information returns with respect to reportable payments as defined in section 3406(b)(1), a payor of those reportable payments who is entitled to participate in the matching program may contact the Internal Revenue Service (IRS) with respect to the TIN furnished by a payee who has received or is likely to receive a reportable payment. The IRS will inform the payor whether or not a name/TIN combination furnished by the payee matches a name/TIN combination maintained in the data base utilized for the particular matching program. For purposes of this section, the term payor includes an agent designated by the payor to participate in TIN matching on the payor's behalf.

(b) *Notice of incorrect TIN.*—No matching details received by a payor through a matching program will constitute a notice regarding an incorrect name/TIN combination under §31.3406(d)-5(c) for purposes of imposing backup withholding under section 3406(a)(1)(B).

(c) *Application of section 3406(f).*—The provisions of section 3406(f), relating to confidentiality of information, apply to any matching details received by a payor through the matching program. A payor may not take into account any such matching details in determining whether to open or close an account with a payee.

(d) *Reasonable cause.*—The IRS will not use either a payor's decision not to participate in an available TIN matching program or the results received by a payor from participation in a TIN matching program implemented under the authority of this section as a basis to assert that the payor lacks reasonable cause under section 6724(a) for the failure to file an information return under section 6721 or to furnish a correct payee statement under section 6722. If the establishment of reasonable cause may be relevant to a substantial number of the participants in a TIN matching program implemented under the authority of this section, the extent to which, if any, a payor may establish reasonable cause by participating in the TIN matching program will be set forth in the guidance establishing the program.

(e) *Definition of account.*—Account means any account, instrument, or other relationship with a payor and with respect to which a payor has made or is likely to make a reportable payment as defined in section 3406(b)(1).

(f) *Effective date.*—The last sentence in paragraph (a) of this section is applicable on January 31, 2003. All other provisions of this section are applicable on and after June 18, 1997. [Reg. §31.3406(j)-1.]

☐ [*T.D. 8721, 6-17-97. Amended by T.D. 9041, 1-30-2003 and T.D. 9136, 7-12-2004.*]

notice that a payor must send to a payee are set forth in paragraph (c)(2) and (3) of this section. The period for which backup withholding is required due to a notified payee underreporting is described in section 3406(e)(3)(A) and in paragraph (e) of this section. See section 3406(c)(3) and paragraph (g) of this section for the rules regarding how a payee may obtain a determination from the Internal Revenue Service that withholding under section 3406(a)(1)(C) be stopped or not started.

(2) *Definition of notified payee underreporting.*—The term "notified payee underreporting" means that the Internal Revenue Service has—

(i) Determined that there was a payee underreporting as defined in paragraph (a)(3) of this section,

(ii) Mailed at least four notices to the payee (over a period of at least 120 days) with respect to the underreporting as prescribed in paragraph (f)(1) of this section, and

⋙➤ *Caution: Caution: Reg. §35a.3406-2, below, is effective until December 31, 1996.*

(iii) Assessed any deficiency attributable to the underreporting in the case of any payee who has filed a return.

(3) *Definition of a payee underreporting.*—The term "payee underreporting" means that the Internal Revenue Service has determined, for a taxable year, that—

(i) A payee failed to include in his return of tax under chapter 1 of the Internal Revenue Code for such year any portion of a reportable interest or dividend payment required to be shown on such tax return, or

(ii) A payee may be required to file a return for such year and to include a reportable interest or dividend payment in such return, but failed to file such return.

See paragraph (a)(5) of this section for certain payments to be taken into account in determining whether there is payee underreporting even though those payments may not be defined as reportable interest or dividend payments in paragraph (a)(4) of this section or even though backup withholding under section 3406(a)(1)(C) may not apply to such payments.

(4) *Definition of a reportable interest or dividend payment.*—(i) *In general.*—See section 3406(b)(2), A-2 of §35a.9999-1, A-5 of §35a.9999-3, and A-15 of §35a.9999-2 for the definition of reportable interest or dividend payment.

(ii) *Exceptions.*—(A) *Patronage dividends.*—Patronage dividends are treated as reportable interest or dividend payments for purposes of backup withholding under section 3406(a)(1)(C) only if 50 percent or more of the reportable amount is paid in money or by qualified check (as defined in section 1388(c)(4)), and then only to the extent that the payment is in money or by qualified check. See the second paragraph in A-10 of §35a.9999-3 for an example of how this rule applies.

(B) *Window payments.*—Pursuant to section 3406(b)(7), window payments as defined in A-42 of §35a.9999-1 and A-9 of §35a.9999-2 are not treated as reportable interest or dividend payments for purposes of backup withholding under section 3406(a)(1)(C).

(5) *Reportable interest or dividend payments excluded from backup withholding.*—The following reportable interest or dividend payments are not subject to backup withholding:

(i) *Certain dividends.*—Certain dividend payments as defined in A-9 of §35a.9999-3.

(ii) *Minimal payments.*—Minimal payments as defined in A-19 of §35a.9999-2 if the payor elects not to impose backup withholding on such amounts.

(iii) *Original issue discount.*—Original issue discount as defined in section 1273, unless there is a payment in cash. See A-15 of §35a.9999-2.

(iv) *Payments subject to other withholding.*—Payments already subject to withholding under another provision of the Internal Revenue Code. Reportable minimal payments (to the extent reported on an information return), patronage dividends, original issue discount, and window payments shall be taken into account in determining whether underreporting (as defined in paragraph (a)(3) of this section) has occurred, even though those payments may not be defined as reportable interest or dividend payments under paragraph (a)(4) of this section or even though backup withholding under section 3406(a)(1)(C) may not apply to such payments.

(6) *Definition of payor.*—See section 3406(h)(4), A-41 of §35a.9999-1, and A-1 of §35a.9999-3 for the definition of payor. The term payor includes a broker who holds an instrument in street name.

(7) *Definition of broker.*—See section 3406(h)(5) for the definition of broker.

(b) *Notice to payors and brokers regarding backup withholding.*—(1) *Notice from the Internal Revenue Service.*—The Internal Revenue Service will notify—

(i) Payors to begin backup withholding on reportable interest or dividend payments due to a notified payee underreporting pursuant to section 3406(a)(1)(C); and

(ii) Brokers pursuant to section 3406(c)(5) that a payee is subject to backup withholding under section 3406(a)(1)(C).

(2) *Notice from a broker.*—A broker who receives a notice from the Internal Revenue Service that a payee is subject to backup withholding due to a notified payee underreporting and through whom the payee subsequently acquires a readily tradable instrument (as de-

fined in section 3406(h)(6)) with respect to which the broker is not the payor is required to notify the payor of that instrument that the payee is subject to backup withholding under section 3406(a)(1)(C) in the time and manner provided in A-41 of §35a.9999-1.

(3) *Accounts subject to backup withholding.*—(i) *In general.*—After receiving notice from the Internal Revenue Service or from a broker, as provided in section 3406(d)(2)(B) and paragraphs (b)(1)(i) and (2) of this section, that a payee is subject to backup withholding under section 3406(a)(1)(C), payors are required to withhold 20 percent of all reportable interest or dividend payments subject to backup withholding made with respect to all accounts of the payee.

(ii) *Joint accounts.*—Payors are required to withhold on joint accounts if the payee subject to backup withholding under section 3406(a)(1)(C) is the first person listed on the account at the time the payor receives the notice to begin backup withholding. Backup withholding shall continue to apply to reportable interest and dividend payments made to that account even if the order of the names on the account is subsequently changed, provided that the name of the payee subject to backup withholding remains on the account.

(iii) *Exception.*—Payors are not required to withhold on reportable interest or dividend payments made with respect to an account of the payee that could not be located with reasonable care. The payor will be considered to have exercised reasonable care if the payor uses the name and taxpayer identification number (or names and taxpayer identification numbers if a joint return was filed by the payees) provided on the notice from the Internal Revenue Service or from a broker as prescribed in paragraphs (b)(1)(i) and (2) of this section and in certain circumstances identified in this paragraph (b)(3)(iii) any account numbers provided by the Internal Revenue Service in locating all accounts of a payee or payees. If a payee uses a different name on an account than the name stated on the notice from the Internal Revenue Service or from a broker (for instance, due to marriage or adoption) and the payor can associate both names with the payee using records kept in the ordinary course of business, the payor will be treated as exercising reasonable care if the payor uses both names to locate accounts of the payee. If the taxpayer identification number is not provided to the payor or broker by the Internal Revenue Service, or if the taxpayer identification number provided by the Internal Revenue Service does not match the taxpayer identification number of the payee on the records that the payor or broker maintains in the ordinary course of business, the payor or broker is required to use any account numbers provided by the Internal Revenue Service to identify the payee and that payee's taxpayer identification number. This information must be used by the payor to locate other accounts of the payee and by the broker to locate the payors with respect to whom the payee subsequently acquires a readily tradable instrument through that broker.

(c) *Notice from payors of backup withholding due to a payee underreporting.*—(1) *In general.*—A payor is required under section 3406(c)(4) to notify the payee in accordance with paragraph (c)(2) of this section that backup withholding has begun because of a notified payee underreporting. Payors who are notified by a broker that a payee is subject to backup withholding under section 3406(a)(1)(C) are also required to send the notice in accordance with paragraph (c)(2) of this section. As a result, the notice requirements provided in A-39 of §35a.9999-1 and in the appendix to §35a.9999-2 shall not apply to those payors notified by a broker that a payee is subject to backup withholding under section 3406(a)(1)(C). The payor must send the notice required by paragraph (c)(2) of this section to the payee no later than 15 days after the date that the payor makes the first payment subject to backup withholding under section 3406(a)(1)(C). The payor must send the notice of backup withholding by first-class mail to the payee at his last known address. Rules similar to the rules in A-17, A-18, A-19, and A-20 of §35a.9999-1 shall apply to the requirement to provide notice by first-class mail.

(2) *Form of the notice to the payee with respect to notified payee underreporting.*—The notice to the payee required by paragraph (c)(1) of this section must state—

(i) That the Internal Revenue Service has given notice that the payee has underreported reportable interest or dividends;

(ii) That, as a result of such underreporting, the payor is required under section 3406(a)(1)(C) of the Internal Revenue Code to withhold 20 percent of reportable interest and dividend payments made to the payee no later than the close of the day 30 days after the date that the payor received the notice;

(iii) The date that the payor received the notice to begin backup withholding under 3406(a)(1)(C);

(iv) That the payee must obtain a determination from the Internal Revenue Service in order to stop the backup withholding under section 3406(a)(1)(C); and

⫸→ *Caution: Caution: Reg. §35a.3406-2, below, is effective until December 31, 1996.*

(v) That while he is subject to backup withholding due to payee underreporting, the payee may not certify to a payor making reportable interest or dividend payments (or to a broker acquiring a readily tradable instrument for the payee) that he is not subject to backup withholding under section 3406(a)(1)(C). See section 3406(a)(1)(D) for the backup withholding rules with respect to a payee's failure to make the certification under section 3406(a)(1)(D).

(3) *Exceptions.*—A notice provided to a payee on or before April 23, 1987, will be deemed to satisfy the provisions of paragraph (c)(2) of this section if it informs the payee that the payor has been instructed by the Internal Revenue Service to start backup withholding on reportable interest or dividend payments to the payee. If a payor who has started backup withholding due to notified payee underreporting on or before April 23, 1987, has not provided adequate notice to the payee on or before April 23, 1987, then the payor must provide notice to the payee in the manner prescribed in paragraph (c)(2) of this section by the date that is 45 days after April 23, 1987.

(d) *Notice to stop backup withholding.*—(1) *In general.*—The Internal Revenue Service will provide written certification to the payee that backup withholding is to stop and will notify the payors who were contacted pursuant to paragraph (b) of this section to stop withholding after the Internal Revenue Service makes a determination under paragraph (g) of this section that backup withholding with respect to a payee should stop. The Internal Revenue Service will also notify the brokers who were contacted pursuant to paragraph (b) of this section that the payee is no longer subject to backup withholding under section 3406(a)(1)(C) and that the brokers are no longer obligated to provide notices to payors under paragraph (b)(2) of this section. A broker who receives a certification under this section from the Internal Revenue Service is not required to provide the certification to any payors to which the broker has previously provided the notice required under paragraph (b)(2).

(2) *Date notice to stop withholding will be provided.*—(i) *Underreporting corrected or bona fide dispute.*—If the Internal Revenue Service makes a determination as set forth in paragraph (g)(1)(ii) or (iv) of this section during the 12-month period ending on October 15 of any calendar year, the Internal Revenue Service will provide the certification or notice required by paragraph (d)(1) of this section no later than December 1 of such calendar year.

(ii) *No underreporting or undue hardship.*—If the Internal Revenue Service makes a determination as set forth in paragraph (g)(1)(i) or (iii), the Internal Revenue Service will provide the notices required by paragraph (d)(1) of this section no later than the 45th day after the day on which the Internal Revenue Service makes its determination.

(e) *Period during which withholding is required.*—(1) *In general.*—Upon receiving notice from the Internal Revenue Service after April 23, 1987, to begin backup withholding under section 3406(a)(1)(C) or notification from a broker stating that the payee is subject to backup withholding under section 3406(a)(1)(C), the payor must impose backup withholding on all reportable interest and dividend payments made to the payee during the period beginning after the close of the 30th day after the day on which the payor receives the notice provided in paragraph (b)(1)(i) or (2) of this section and ending as of the close of the day before the stop date (as described in paragraph (e)(2) of this section). Pursuant to section 3406(e)(5)(C), the payor may elect to begin backup withholding at any time during the 30-day period described in this paragraph.

(2) *Stop date.*—(i) *Underreporting corrected or bona fide dispute.*—In the case of a determination that the underreporting has been corrected or that a bona fide dispute exists (as defined in paragraphs (g)(1)(ii) or (iv) of this section), the stop date is—

(A) January 1 following the 12-month period ending on October 15th of any calendar year in which the determination has been made or, if later,

(B) The day that is 30 days after the earlier of—

(1) The date on which the payor receives written notification from the Internal Revenue Service (under paragraph (d)(2) of this section) that withholding is to stop, or

(2) The date on which the payor receives a copy of the written certification provided to the payee by the Internal Revenue Service that withholding is to stop.

(ii) *No underreporting or undue hardship.*—In the case of a determination that no payee underreporting occurred or that an undue hardship exists or could exist (as defined in paragraph (g)(1)(i) or (iii) of this section), the stop date is the date specified in paragraph (e)(2)(i)(B) of this section.

(iii) *Payor election to shorten or eliminate grace period.*—The payor with respect to any payee may elect to determine the stop date without regard to the grace period provided in section 3406(e)(5)(B) (*i.e.,* without regard to the words "the day that is 30 days after" in paragraph (e)(2)(i)(B) of this section) or by substituting a shorter grace period.

(iv) *Examples.*—The provisions of paragraph (e)(2)(i) may be illustrated by the following examples:

*Example (1).* The Internal Revenue Service makes a determination by October 15, 1987, that any underreporting with respect to A has been corrected. X, a payor who has been notified to backup withhold on payments of interest to A due to notified payee underreporting, receives written notice from the Internal Revenue Service on December 1, 1987, informing X that A is no longer subject to backup withholding under section 3406(a)(1)(C) and that X must stop backup withholding as of the close of December 31, 1987, or if later, the earlier of the close of the day 30 days after receipt of the notice from the Internal Revenue Service or receipt of the copy of the written certification provided to the payee by the Internal Revenue Service. The stop date, as provided in paragraph (e)(2)(i)(A) of this section, is January 1, 1988, and the payor must stop backup withholding as of the close of December 31, 1987.

*Example (2).* Assume the same facts as in *Example (1)* except that X, due to a change of address or for other reasons, does not receive the notice from the Internal Revenue Service to stop backup withholding until December 15, 1987. In addition, A does not provide X with a copy of the certification that was provided to A by the Internal Revenue Service until December 15, 1987. The stop date, as provided in paragraph (e)(2)(i)(B) of this section, is January 14, 1988 (30 days after December 15, 1987), because that date is later than January 1, 1988. However, if a payor elects pursuant to section 3406(e)(5)(C) and paragraph (e)(2)(iii) of this section to determine the stop date without regard to that 30-day grace period, the stop date is January 1, 1987.

*Example (3).* Assume the same facts as in *Example (2)* except that on December 10, 1987 (rather than on December 15, 1987), A provides X with a copy of the certification from the Internal Revenue Service. The stop date, as provided in paragraph (e)(2)(i)(B) of this section, is January 9, 1988 (30 days after December 10, 1987), because that date is earlier than January 14, 1988 (30 days after the day X received notice from the Internal Revenue Service), but later than January 1, 1988.

(f) *Notice to payees from the Internal Revenue Service.*—(1) *Notice period.*—After the Internal Revenue Service determines that a payee underreporting exists as defined in paragraph (a)(3) of this section, the Internal Revenue Service, pursuant to section 3406(c)(1)(B), will mail to the payee at least four notices over a period of at least 120 days (hereafter referred to as the "notice period") before payors and brokers will be notified that the payee is subject to backup withholding due to a notified payee underreporting as provided in paragraph (b)(1) of this section. The notices may be incorporated with other notices provided to the payee by the Internal Revenue Service.

(2) *Payee subject to withholding.*—After the Internal Revenue Service provides the notices described in paragraph (f)(1) of this section, the Internal Revenue Service will send the notices required by paragraph (b) of this section unless—

(i) A payee obtains a determination under paragraph (g) of this section, or

(ii) In the case of a payee who has filed a tax return, the Internal Revenue Service has not assessed the deficiency attributable to the underreporting.

(3) *Disclosure of names of payors and brokers.*—The Internal Revenue Service pursuant to section 3406(c)(5) may require a payee subject to backup withholding due to a notified payee underreporting to disclose the names of all of his payors of reportable interest or dividend payments and the names of all of the brokers with whom the payee has accounts which may involve reportable interest or dividend payments. To the extent required in the request from the Internal Revenue Service, the payee shall also provide his account numbers and other information necessary to identify the payee's accounts.

(4) *Backup withholding certification.*—Once a payee receives a final notice from the Internal Revenue Service notifying him that his reportable interest or dividend payments are subject to backup withholding due to notified payee underreporting under section 3406(a)(1)(C), the payee shall not certify to any payor or broker, under penalties of perjury, that he is not subject to backup withholding under section 3406(a)(1)(C). See paragraph (k)(2) of this section for the penalties that will apply to a payee who makes a false certification. The payee may not make the certification until the

**Reg. §35a.3406-2(f)(4)**

**⋙→** *Caution: Caution: Reg. §35a.3406-2, below, is effective until December 31, 1996.*

payee receives the certification provided in paragraph (d)(1) of this section from the Internal Revenue Service advising the payee that he is no longer subject to backup withholding under section 3406(a)(1)(C) (as provided in A-33 of §35a.9999-1). See A-37 of §35a.9999-1 for the rule applicable to a payor who makes reportable interest or dividend payments to a payee who fails to certify that he is not subject to backup withholding due to notified payee underreporting.

(g) *Determination by the Internal Revenue Service that backup withholding should not start or should be stopped.*—(1) *In general.*—A payee may prevent backup withholding from starting or stop it once it has started if, for the taxable year with respect to which there is a notified payee underreporting and any other taxable years for which there is any payee underreporting, the payee—

(i) Shows that there was no payee underreporting (as provided in paragraph (g)(2) of this section);

(ii) Corrects any payee underreporting (as provided in paragraph (g)(3) of this section);

(iii) Shows that backup withholding will cause or is causing an undue hardship (as defined in paragraph (g)(4) of this section) and that it is unlikely that the payee will underreport interest or dividend payments again; or

(iv) Shows that a bona fide dispute exists as to whether any underreporting has occurred (as provided in paragraph (g)(5) of this section).

(2) *No underreporting.*—A payee may show that no underreporting of interest or dividends exists by presenting receipts or other satisfactory documentation to the Internal Revenue Service showing that all taxes relating to such payments were reported and paid timely or evidence showing that the payee did not have to file a return for the taxable year in question or that the underreporting determination is based upon a factual, clerical, or other mistake.

(3) *Correcting any payee underreporting.*—(i) *Before issuance of a statutory notice of deficiency.*—Before a statutory notice of deficiency is issued to a payee pursuant to section 6212, the payee may correct underreporting by filing a return if one was not previously filed and paying taxes, penalties, and interest due with respect to any underreported interest or dividend payments.

(ii) *After issuance of a statutory notice of deficiency.*—After a statutory notice of deficiency is issued to a payee, the payee may correct underreporting at any time by filing a return if one was not previously filed and paying the entire deficiency and any other taxes including penalties and interest attributable to any payee underreporting of interest or dividend payments. Thus, for example, a payee may correct underreporting after assessment of a deficiency by paying the entire assessment with respect to that deficiency and any other taxes including penalties and interest attributable to any payee underreporting of interest or dividend payments for other taxable years.

(4) *Undue hardship.*—A determination of undue hardship will be based on the overall impact to the payee of having 20 percent of reportable interest and dividend payments withheld. Factors that will be considered in determining whether backup withholding causes undue hardship include, but are not limited to, the following:

(i) Whether estimated tax payments, and other credits for current tax liabilities, or amounts withheld on employee wages or pensions, in addition to backup withholding, would cause significant over-withholding;

(ii) The payee's health, including the payee's ability to pay foreseeable medical expenses;

(iii) The extent of the payee's reliance on interest and dividend payments to meet necessary living expenses and the existence, if any, of other sources of income;

(iv) Whether other income of the payee is limited or fixed (*e.g.,* social security, pension, and unearned income);

(v) The payee's ability to sell or liquidate stocks, bonds, bank accounts, trust accounts, or other assets, and the consequences of doing so;

(vi) Whether the payee reported and timely paid the most recent year's tax liability, including interest and dividend income; and

(vii) Whether the payee has filed a bankruptcy petition with the United States Bankruptcy Court.

In addition to the above factors, the Internal Revenue Service must conclude that it is unlikely that any payee underreporting will occur again.

(5) *Bona fide dispute.*—The Internal Revenue Service may make a determination under this paragraph if there is a dispute between the payee and the Internal Revenue Service on a question of fact or law that is material to a determination under paragraph (g)(1)(i) and, based upon all the facts and circumstances, the Internal Revenue Service finds that the dispute is asserted in good faith by the payee and there is a reasonable basis for the payee's position. See the example provided in paragraph (j)(2)(ii) of this section for an illustration of this provision.

(h) *Requests for determinations.*—(1) *In general.*—A payee may request a determination under one or more of the provisions of paragraph (g) of this section. Following its review of a request for a determination under paragraph (g) of this section, the Internal Revenue Service will either provide the payee with a written certification as prescribed in paragraph (d) of this section if the evidence presented warrants the requested determination or will provide the payee with a written notice informing him that a determination was not made.

(2) *Determinations made during the notice period.*—In general, if a determination is made during the notice period as defined in paragraph (f)(1) of this section, then the payee will not be subject to backup withholding due to a notified payee underreporting with respect to any taxable year for which a determination was made.

(3) *Determinations made after the notice period.*—If a determination is made after the notice period, as defined in paragraph (f)(1) of this section, the Internal Revenue Service will provide a notice to payors and brokers, and a certification to the payee as provided in paragraph (d)(1) of this section.

(i) [Reserved].

(j) *Payees filing a joint return.*—(1) *In general.*—For purposes of section 3406(a)(1)(C), if payee underreporting is found to exist with respect to a joint return filed by a husband and wife, then the provisions of this section shall apply to the payees collectively. As a result, both payees will be subject to backup withholding on accounts in their individual names as well as accounts in their joint names. Either or both payees may satisfy the criteria for a determination that no payee underreporting exists, that the underreporting has been corrected, or that a bona fide dispute exists (as provided in paragraphs (g)(1)(i), (ii), or (iv) of this section). Both payees, however, must satisfy the criteria for a determination that backup withholding will cause or is causing undue hardship (as provided in paragraph (g)(1)(iii) of this section).

(2) *Exceptions.*—(i) *Innocent spouse.*—A spouse who files a joint return may obtain a determination that withholding should stop or not start with respect to payments made to his or her individual accounts, if the spouse—

(A) Shows that he or she did not underreport income because he or she is an innocent spouse as described in section 6013(e), or

(B) Shows that there is a bona fide dispute as to whether he or she is an innocent spouse and hence did not underreport income.

(ii) *Example.*—The provisions of paragraph (j)(2)(i) may be illustrated by the following example:

*Example.*—H and W filed a joint return in 1986 on which H failed to include $2,000 of interest income. In 1987, the Internal Revenue Service determined that a payee underreporting exists with respect to H and W for the 1986 tax year. After properly notifying H and W of the underreporting and assessing the tax, the Internal Revenue Service sent notices to payors to begin backup withholding on the joint and individual accounts of H and W and to brokers informing them that H and W are subject to backup withholding under section 3406(a)(1)(C) on their joint and individual accounts. W claims that she is an innocent spouse and requests a determination that she did not underreport interest or dividend income so that her individual accounts will not be subject to backup withholding.

The Internal Revenue Service questions her status as an innocent spouse. If the Internal Revenue Service determines, based upon all the facts and circumstances, that there is a reasonable basis for W's claim to be an innocent spouse and that the claim is made in good faith, W will have a bona fide dispute with the Internal Revenue Service. Consequently, the individual accounts of W will not be subject to further backup withholding due to a notified payee underreporting as provided in paragraph (g)(5) of this section.

The Internal Revenue Service will notify payors to stop backup withholding under section 3406(a)(1)(C) and brokers that W is no longer subject to backup withholding under section 3406(a)(1)(C) on W's individual accounts. Backup withholding will not restart on those accounts unless the Internal Revenue Service ultimately determines that W is not an innocent spouse. In that event the Internal Revenue Service will notify the payors to start backup withholding under section 3406(a)(1)(C) and the brokers that W is

>>> → *Caution: Caution: Reg. §35a.3406-2, below, is effective until December 31, 1996.*

subject to backup withholding under section 3406(a)(1)(C) with respect to the individual accounts of W.

(iii) *Divorced or legally separated payee.*—A payee who, at the time of the request for a determination under paragraph (g) of this section, is divorced or legally separated under state law may obtain a determination that undue hardship exists (or would exist) under paragraph (g)(1)(iii) of this section with respect to reportable interest and dividend payments made to his or her individual accounts if the divorced or legally separated payee satisfies the criteria for a determination under paragraph (g)(4) of this section.

(k) *Penalties.*—(1) *Failure to withhold.*—See A-2 of § 35a.9999-3 for rules relating to penalties applicable to a payor who fails to withhold on reportable interest and dividend payments made to a payee subject to backup withholding.

(2) *False certification.*—*(i) *Criminal penalty under section 7205 (b).*—If any individual willfully makes a false certification under section 3406 (d)(1) or (2), then that individual shall, in addition to any other penalty provided by law, upon conviction thereof, be fined not more than $1,000, or imprisoned not more than 1 year, or both.

(ii) *Civil penalty under section 6682.*—(A) *In general.*—In addition to any criminal penalty provided by law, if any individual makes a statement under section 3406 which results in a decrease in the amounts deducted and withheld under chapter 24 of the Internal Revenue Code and, as of the time the statement was made, there was no reasonable basis for the statement, the individual shall pay a penalty of $500 for the statement. The penalty is due upon notice and demand and pursuant to section 6682 collection is not subject to the deficiency procedures of subchapter B of chapter 63 of the Internal Revenue Code. See section 6682.

(B) *Waiver of penalty.*—The payee may obtain a waiver (in whole or part) of the penalty imposed under section 6682(a) and paragraph (k)(2)(ii)(A) of this section if it is established to the satisfaction of the Internal Revenue Service that the taxes imposed under subtitle A of the Internal Revenue Code with respect to the payee for the taxable year in which the false certification was made are equal to or less than the sum of—

(1) The credits against taxes allowed by part IV of subchapter A of chapter 1 of the Internal Revenue Code, and

(2) The payments of estimated tax which are considered payments on account of such taxes.

(C) *Procedure for seeking a waiver.*—To request a waiver under section 6682(b) and paragraph (k)(2)(ii)(B) of this section, the payee must submit to the Internal Revenue Service a written statement with supporting documents to establish all the facts necessary in order to obtain the waiver. The statement must be signed by the person that otherwise would be subject to the penalty imposed by section 6682(a) and paragraph (k)(2)(ii)(A) of this section and must contain a declaration that it is made under penalties of perjury.

(3) *Delay of assessment.*—If a payee institutes or maintains a suit with the United States Tax Court primarily to delay assessment and the payee's position is frivolous or groundless, or the payee unreasonable failed to pursue available administrative remedies, the court may award up to $5,000 in damages under section 6673. The damages will be assessed against and collected from the payee in the same manner as the underlying tax.

(l) Effective date. This section is effective until December 31, 1996. [Temporary Reg. § 35a.3406-2.]

☐ [*T.D. 8137, 4-20-87. Amended by T.D. 8637, 12-20-95. Corrected on 3-20-96.*]

# General Provisions Relating to Employment Taxes

See p. 20,601 for regulations not amended to reflect law changes

[Reg. § 31.3501(a)-1T]

**§ 31.3501(a)-1T. Question and answer relating to the time employers must collect and pay the taxes on noncash fringe benefits (Temporary).**—The following questions and answers relate to the time employers must collect and pay the taxes imposed by subtitle C on noncash fringe benefits:

Q-1: If a noncash fringe benefit constitutes "wages" under section 3121(a), 3306(b), or 3401(a), or constitutes "compensation" under section 3231(e), when must an employer collect and pay the taxes imposed by subtitle C?

A-1: For purposes of an employer's liability to collect and pay the taxes imposed by subtitle C, an employer may deem such fringe benefit to be paid at any time on or after the date on which it is provided, as long as such date is on or before the last day of the calendar quarter in which such benefit is provided. An employer may consider the benefit to be provided in two or more parts for purposes of the preceding sentence. For example, if a fringe benefit with a fair market value of $1,000 is provided on January 1, 1985, the employer could deem $500 paid on February 28, 1985 and $500 paid on March 31, 1985.

With respect to noncash fringe benefits provided during the first calendar quarter of 1985, a special rule applies. Such benefits may be deemed paid at any time on or after the date on which they are provided as long as the date they are deemed paid is on or before the last day of the second calendar quarter of 1985.

In addition, for purposes of § 31.6302(c)-1(a)(1)(i), the term "tax" does not include the employer tax under section 3111 with respect to noncash fringe benefits which are deemed by the employer to be paid on the last day of any calendar quarter. For purposes of the first sentence of § 31.6302(c)-2(a)(1), the phrase "employer tax imposed after December 31, 1983, under section 3221(a) and (b)" will not include any such employer tax with respect to noncash fringe benefits which are deemed by the employer to be paid on the last day of the quarter; provided that for purposes of deposits required under § 31.6302(c)-1(a)(1)(v), such first sentence applies to such noncash fringe benefits.

Notwithstanding anything in this section to the contrary, if an employer in fact withholds, the amount withheld is subject to the general deposit rules.

The manner in which and the time at which the employer withholds amounts from the wages of an employee to pay the taxes imposed under section 3101, 3201, and/or 3402 will generally be left to be determined by the employer and the employee. Any delay in withholding, however, does not affect the employer's obligation, upon the filing of an employment tax return, to pay amounts which would be due under this subtitle if the employer had withheld, with respect to noncash fringe benefits, the amount which would have been required to be withheld if such noncash fringe benefits had been paid in cash on the date the benefits were deemed paid. However, if such amounts are not withheld from the wages of an employee within a reasonable period after payment of the taxes by the employer, payment by the employer may be deemed additional compensation of the employee.

Q-2: Are any fringe benefits excepted from the rules contained in Q/A-1 of this section?

A-2: Yes. The rules contained in Q/A-1 of this section do not apply to the transfer of personal property (both tangible and intangible) of a kind held for investment or to the transfer of real property. Accordingly, an employer is liable for the collection and payment of taxes imposed by this subtitle when such property is transferred. For example, stock transferred in connection with the performance of services is paid, for purposes of this subtitle C, on the date the stock is transferred, i.e., on the date the stock vests pursuant to section 83 (absent a section 83(b) election).

Q-3: What is an example of the application of the rules contained in Q/A-1 of this section with respect to obligations under Chapters 21 and 24 of subtitle C?

A-3: All of employer A's employees received $100 in cash as wages each week from A. In addition, during a calendar quarter, each such employee receives noncash fringe benefits, the fair market value of which is $500. A deems all such noncash fringe benefits to be paid on the last day of the quarter. As of the end of the quarter, no amount has been withheld from the employees' wages with respect to such noncash fringe benefits, and A has "undeposited taxes" (within the meaning of § 31.6302(c)-1(a)(1)(i)) of more than $3,000 attributable to amounts actually withheld under section 3102 or section 3402 or due under section 3111 with respect to cash wages of A's employees. The amount which A must deposit within 3 banking days after the end of the quarter will be determined without regard to the noncash fringe benefits deemed paid on the last day of the quarter.

During the month following the quarter, A withholds from its employees with respect to the noncash fringe benefits deemed paid on the last day of the quarter. As A withholds amounts, such amounts become "taxes" subject to § 31.6302(c)-1(a)(1)(i). If, as of the date of filing of the return for the period which includes the last day of the quarter, A has not deposited all amounts with respect to the quarter which are due under section 3111 or which would have been due had A withheld, under sections 3102 and 3402, with respect to noncash fringe benefits, the amount which would have been required to be withheld had such benefits been paid in cash, A shall pay the balance with its return. A must make such payment regardless of whether, at the time the return is filed, he has actually withheld all amounts which he would have been required to withhold had such benefits been paid in cash.

Q-4: If an employee is provided with a noncash fringe benefit and separates from service before the benefit is deemed paid by the employer, is the employer liable for the taxes imposed by subtitle C?

A-4: Yes. The employer's liability is unaffected by his ability to collect the tax from the former employee.

Q-5: If an entity other than the employer provides a noncash fringe benefit to an employee, is that entity considered the employer of such employee with respect to such noncash fringe benefit for any purposes of subtitle C?

A-5: The provision of noncash fringe benefits by an entity to an employee of another employer does not make such entity the employer of such employee with respect to such noncash fringe benefit for any purpose of subtitle C, so long as such noncash fringe benefits are incidental to the provision of wages by the employer to such employee. For example, if two unrelated airlines, A and B, enter into a reciprocal agreement whereby the parents of employees of both airlines are entitled to free flights on both airlines, the fact that A is providing a noncash fringe benefit to the employees of B generally will not make A the employer of such employees for purposes of subtitle C.

Q-6: Do special rules apply to the provision of taxable noncash fringe benefits by a nonemployer under a reciprocal agreement with the employee's employer?

A-6: If the provision of taxable noncash fringe benefits meets the requirements of Q/A-5 of this section, the nonemployer provider of the benefits is not required to withhold. The employer must take the steps necessary to obtain the relevant information from the provider of the benefits in order to enable the employer to satisfy, in a timely manner, its obligations under subtitle C to collect and pay taxes with respect to the noncash fringe benefits provided by the nonemployer.

Q-7: For purposes of subtitle C, how is the fair market value of an employer-provided automobile or other road vehicle during any time period to be determined?

A-7: The value of the availability of an employer-provided automobile or other road vehicle must be determined under the rules provided in §§ 1.61-21 and 1.132-1. (For purposes of this section, the terms "automobile" and "road vehicle" have the meaning given those terms in § 1.61-21). For example, assume that an employee adopts the special rule provided in § 1.61-21 and that the Annual Lease Value, as defined in § 1.61-21, of an automobile is $2,100. The automobile is provided to employee A on January 1, 1985. As of March 31, A had driven the automobile 1,000 personal miles and 3,000 miles in the course of his employer's business. For the quarter, A would have had wages of $131.25 attributable to his personal use of the automobile computed by subtracting a $393.75 working condition fringe from $525 ($2,100 divided by 4). See section 132(d) and § 1.132-1T. During the second quarter of 1985, A drives the automobile only 1,000 miles, all of which are personal. In order to calculate the value of the wages provided to A in the second quarter in the form of the availability of an employer-provided automobile, first A's employer calculates the Annual Lease Value attributable to the first six months of 1985 which is $1,050 ($2,100 divided by 2). Second, A's employer calculates the working condition fringe exclusion which is $630 ($1,050 multiplied by a fraction the numerator of which is A's business mileage (3,000 miles) and the denominator of which is A's total mileage (5,000 miles)). These calculations result in a total inclusion of $420 ($1,050–$630). From the total inclusion of $420, the wages provided in the first quarter, $131.25, are subtracted, leaving $288.75 as the wages includible in the second quarter attributable to the availability to A of the employer-provided automobile.

Q-8: May an employer treat any part of the Annual Lease Value or Daily Lease Value (as defined in § 1.61-21), or the fair market value if the special rule of § 1.61-21 is not or cannot be used, of an automobile or other road vehicle made available to an employee as includible in the employee's gross income without regard to whether the employee has used the automobile or other road vehicle in the employer's business?

A-8: No, except as otherwise provided in this Q/A-8, an employer may not include any amount in an employee's income with respect to an employer-provided automobile or other road vehicle unless such inclusion is based on:

(a) Records or a statement submitted by an employee that contain the business and total mileage for the period beginning on January 1, 1985, and ending on the last day of the employer's taxable year that began in 1984, or

(b) Records that satisfy the employer's "adequate contemporaneous record" requirement under section 274(d)(4) and the regulations thereunder for the employer's taxable years beginning after December 31, 1984.

For example, an employer who is subject to (b) of this Q/A-8 may rely on a statement submitted by the employee indicating for the period the number of miles driven by the employee in the employer's business and the total number of miles driven by the employee unless the employer knows or has reason to know the statement submitted is not based on "adequate contemporaneous records". (For purposes of this section, if a road vehicle is available to any person and such availability would be taxable to an employee, miles driven by that person will be considered miles driven by the employee).

Notwithstanding the preceding paragraph of this Q/A-8, an employer may include in an employee's income the value of the availability of an employer-provided road vehicle, calculated without regard to a working condition fringe exclusion based on business mileage if one of the conditions listed in § 1.274-6T(f)(1) is satisfied with respect to the relevant period.

In addition, the employer must, before including any amount in an employee's income with respect to an employer-provided road vehicle, take into account other working condition fringe exclusions, such as the security exclusion discussed in § 1.132-1T. If proper calculation of an exclusion requires information from the employee and the employee does not respond within a reasonable period of time to a request for that information or produces information which the employer knows or has reason to know is not accurate, the employer may disregard such exclusion in reporting the employee's gross income.

Q-8a. May an employer withhold amounts attributable to noncash fringe benefits on the basis of average wages as permitted under section 3402(h)(1)?

A-8a. In general, yes. In estimating wages under section 3402(h)(1)(A), however, the employer must take into account estimated business use of the benefit (such as an employer-provided road vehicle). In no event, however, may the amount reported by the employer as "wages" for any employee for any quarter be based on an estimation. However, the rules in Q/A-1 of this section regarding permissible delays in actual withholding apply.

Q-9: If an employee purchases any property or service from an employer at a discount and the discount is not excludable under section 132 and any applicable regulations thereunder, when is the noncash fringe benefit provided?

A-9: Such property or service is provided at the time that ownership is transferred, in the case of property, or the time service is rendered, in the case of services. This will be true regardless of when the employee pays for such property or service or the date payment is due or the rate of interest charged prior to payment. The time at which ownership of the property is transferred must be determined under general tax principles.

Q-10: What rules apply with respect to the treatment of the payment of any noncash fringe benefit as the payment of supplemental wages under section 3402?

A-10: An employer may treat the payment of any noncash fringe benefit as the payment of supplemental wages. Thus, if noncash fringe benefits are provided and tax has been withheld from the employee's regular wages, the employer may determine the tax to be withheld with respect to such noncash fringe benefits by using a flat percentage rate of 20 percent, without allowance for exemptions and without reference to any regular payment of wages. For example, assume that during a calendar quarter A receives from his employer a taxable noncash fringe benefit with a fair market value of $1,000. If the requirements specified above are satisfied, A's employer may determine the tax to be withheld with respect to such benefit by using a flat percentage rate of 20 percent. The employer may also determine the tax to be withheld with respect to such benefit by use of the method described in § 31.3402(g)-1(a)(2).

[Reg. § 31.3501(a)-1T.]

☐ [*T.D.* 8004, 1-2-85. *Amended by T.D.* 8009, 2-15-85 *and T.D.* 9849, 3-11-2019.]

### [Reg. § 31.3502-1]

**§ 31.3502-1. Nondeductibility of taxes in computing taxable income.**—For provisions relating to the nondeductibility, in computing taxable income under subtitle A, of the taxes imposed by sections 3101, 3201, and 3211, and of the tax deducted and withheld under chapter 24, see §§ 1.164-2 and 1.275-1 of this chapter (Income Tax Regulations). For provisions relating to the credit allowable to the recipient of the income in respect of the tax deducted and withheld under chapter 24, see § 1.31-1 of this chapter (Income Tax Regulations). [Reg. § 31.3502-1.]

☐ [*T.D.* 6354, 1-13-59. *Amended by T.D.* 6780, 12-21-64.]

### [Reg. § 31.3503-1]

**§ 31.3503-1. Tax under chapter 21 or 22 paid under wrong chapter.**—If, for any period, an amount is paid as tax—

(a) Under chapter 21 or corresponding provisions of prior law by a person who is not liable for tax for such period under such chapter or prior law, but who is liable for tax for such period under chapter 22 or corresponding provisions of prior law, or

(b) Under chapter 22 or corresponding provisions of prior law by a person who is not liable for tax for such period under such chapter or prior law, but who is liable for tax for such period under chapter 21 or corresponding provisions of prior law,

the amount so paid shall be credited against the tax for which such person is liable and the balance, if any, shall be refunded. Each claim for refund or credit under this section shall be made on Form 843 and in accordance with § 31.6402(a)-2 and the applicable provisions of section 6402(a) and the regulations thereunder in Part 301 of this chapter (Regulations on Procedure and Administration). [Reg. § 31.3503-1.]

☐ [*T.D. 6354*, 1-13-59.]

**[Reg. § 31.3504-1]**

**§ 31.3504-1. Designation of agent by application.**—(a) *In general.*—In the event wages as defined in chapter 21 or 24 of the Internal Revenue Code (Code), or compensation as defined in chapter 22 of the Code, of an employee or group of employees, employed by one or more employers, is paid by a fiduciary, agent, or other person ("agent"), or if that agent has the control, receipt, custody, or disposal of (collectively "pays") wages or compensation, the Internal Revenue Service may, subject to the terms and conditions as it deems proper, authorize that agent to perform the acts required of the employer or employers under those provisions of the Code and the regulations that apply, for purposes of the taxes imposed by the chapter or chapters, with respect to wages or compensation paid by the agent. If the agent is authorized by the Internal Revenue Service to perform such acts, all provisions of law (including penalties) and of the regulations applicable to an employer with respect to such acts shall be applicable to the agent. However, each employer for whom the agent acts shall remain subject to all provisions of law (including penalties) and of the regulations applicable to an employer with respect to such acts. Any application to authorize an agent to perform such acts, signed by the agent and the employer, shall be made on the form prescribed by the Internal Revenue Service and shall be filed with the Internal Revenue Service as prescribed in the instructions to the form and other applicable guidance.

(b) *Special rule for home care service recipients.*—(1) *In general.*—In the event an agent is authorized pursuant to paragraph (a) of this section to perform the acts required of an employer under chapters 21 or 24 on behalf of one or more home care service recipients, as defined in paragraph (b)(3) of this section, the Internal Revenue Service may authorize that agent to perform the acts as are required of employers for purposes of the tax imposed by chapter 23 of the Code with respect to wages paid by the agent for home care services, as defined in paragraph (b)(2) of this section, rendered to the home care service recipient. If the agent is authorized by the Internal Revenue Service to perform such acts, all provisions of law (including penalties) and of the regulations applicable to an employer in respect of such acts shall be applicable to the agent. However, each employer for whom the agent acts shall remain subject to all provisions of law (including penalties) and of the regulations applicable to an employer with respect to such acts.

(2) *Home care services.*—For purposes of this section, the term *home care services* includes health care and personal attendant care services rendered to the home care service recipient.

(3) *Home care service recipient.*—For purposes of this section, the term *home care service recipient* means any individual who receives home care services, as defined in paragraph (b)(2) of this section, while enrolled, and for the remainder of the calendar year after ceasing to be enrolled, in a program administered by a Federal, state, or local government agency that provides Federal, state, or local government funds, to pay, in whole or in part, for home care services for that individual.

(c) *Effective/applicability dates.*—An authorization under paragraph (a) in effect prior to December 12, 2013 continues to be in effect after that date. Paragraph (b) of this section applies to wages paid on or after January 1, 2014. However, pursuant to section 7805(b), taxpayers may rely on paragraph (b) of this section for all taxable years for which a valid designation is in effect under paragraph (a) of this section. [Reg. § 31.3504-1.]

☐ [*T.D. 6354*, 1-13-59. *Amended by T.D. 7012*, 5-14-69 *and T.D. 9649*, 12-11-2013.]

**[Reg. § 31.3504-2]**

**§ 31.3504-2. Designation of payor to perform acts of an employer.**—(a) *In general.*—A person (as defined in section 7701(a)(1)) that pays wages or compensation ("payor") to the individual(s) performing services for any client pursuant to a service agreement, except as provided in paragraph (d) of this section, is designated to perform the acts required of an employer with respect to the wages or compensation paid. For purposes of this section the term *wages* has the same meaning as the term wages has for purposes of chapters 21, 23, and 24, and the term *compensation* has the same meaning as the term compensation has for purposes of chapter 22. This section is not applicable if the payor has been authorized as an agent of the employer under § 31.3504-1.

(b) *Definitions.*—(1) *Client.*—The term *client* means an individual or entity that enters into a service agreement with the payor.

(2) *Service agreement.*—(i) The term *service agreement* means an agreement pursuant to which the payor —

(A) Asserts it is the employer (or "co-employer") of the individual(s) performing services for the client;

(B) Pays wages or compensation to the individual(s) for services the individual(s) perform for the client; and

(C) Assumes responsibility to collect, report, and pay, or assumes liability for, any taxes applicable under subtitle C of the Code with respect to the wages or compensation paid by the payor to the individual(s) performing services for the client.

(ii) For purposes of paragraph (b)(2)(i)(A) of this section, the payor may implicitly or explicitly assert it is the employer (or "co-employer") of the individual(s) performing services for the client, including by agreeing to—

(A) Recruit and hire employees for the client or assign employees as permanent or temporary members of the client's work force, or participate with the client in these actions;

(B) Hire the client's employees as its own and then provide them back to the client to perform services for the client; or

(C) File employment tax returns using its own employer identification number that include wages or compensation paid to the individual(s) performing services for the client.

(c) *Effects of designation.*—If a payor is designated to perform the acts required of an employer under this section then the following rules apply—

(1) A payor must perform the acts required of an employer under each applicable chapter of the Code and the relevant regulations with respect to the wages or compensation paid by such payor. All provisions of law (including penalties) and the regulations applicable to the employer are applicable to the payor so designated with respect to the wages or compensation paid by the payor; and

(2) Each employer for whom the payor is designated remains subject to all provisions of law (including penalties) and of the regulations applicable to an employer.

(d) *Exceptions.*—A payor is not designated to perform the acts required of an employer under this section for any wages or compensation paid by the payor to the individual(s) performing services for a client if—

(1) The wages or compensation are reported on a return filed under the client's employer identification number (as defined in section 6109 and the applicable regulations);

(2) The payor is a common paymaster under sections 3121(s) or 3231(i);

(3) The payor is the employer of the individual(s) (including an employer within the meaning of section 3401(d)(1)); or

(4) The payor is treated as an employer under section 3121(a)(2)(A).

(e) *Examples.*—The following examples illustrate the application of this section:

(1) *Example 1.* Corporation P enters into an agreement with Employer, effective January 1, 2015. Under the agreement, Corporation P hires the Employer's employees as its own employees and provides them back to Employer to perform services for Employer. Corporation P also assumes responsibility to make payment of the individuals' wages and for the collection, reporting, and payment of applicable taxes. For all pay periods in 2015, Employer provides Corporation P with an amount equal to the gross payroll (that is, wage and tax amounts) of the individuals, and Corporation P pays wages (less the applicable withholding) to the individuals performing services for Employer. Corporation P also reports the wage and tax amounts on Form 941, *Employer's QUARTERLY Federal Tax Return*, filed for each quarter of 2015 under Corporation P's employer identification number. Corporation P is not a common paymaster, the employer of the individuals (including an employer within the meaning of section 3401(d)(1)), or treated as the employer of the individual under section 3121(a)(2)(A). Corporation P is designated to perform the acts of an employer with respect to all of the wages Corporation P paid to the individuals performing services for Employer for all quarters of 2015. Employer and Corporation P are each

subject to all provisions of law (including penalties) applicable in respect of employers for all quarters of 2015 with respect to such wages.

(2) *Example 2.* Same facts as *Example 1*, except that Corporation P only reports the wage and tax amounts on Form 941, *Employer's QUARTERLY Federal Tax Return,* filed for the 1st and 2nd quarters of 2015. Neither Corporation P nor Employer files returns for the 3rd and 4th quarters of 2015. Corporation P is designated to perform the acts of an employer with respect to all of the wages Corporation P paid to the individuals performing services for Employer for all quarters of 2015. Employer and Corporation P are each subject to all provisions of law (including penalties) applicable in respect of employers for all quarters of 2015 with respect to such wages.

(3) *Example 3.* Same facts as *Example 1*, except that neither Corporation P nor Employer reports the wage and tax amounts on Form 941, *Employer's QUARTERLY Federal Tax Return,* for any quarter of 2015. Corporation P is designated to perform the acts of an employer with respect to all of the wages Corporation P paid to the individuals performing services for Employer for all quarters of 2015. Employer and Corporation P are each subject to all provisions of law (including penalties) applicable in respect of employers for all quarters of 2015 with respect to such wages.

(4) *Example 4.* Same facts as *Example 1*, except that Employer provides only net payroll (that is, wages less tax amounts) to Corporation P for each pay period. Corporation P is designated to perform the acts of an employer with respect to all of the wages Corporation P paid to the individuals performing services for Employer for all quarters of 2015. Employer and Corporation P are each subject to all provisions of law (including penalties) applicable in respect of employers for all quarters of 2015 with respect to such wages.

(5) *Example 5.* Same facts as *Example 1*, except that after Corporation P reports the wage and tax amounts on Form 941, *Employer's QUARTERLY Federal Tax Return,* filed for each quarter of 2015 under Corporation P's employer identification number, Corporation P files a claim for refund of the employment taxes it paid for each quarter of 2015 that are related to wages Corporation P paid to the individuals performing services for Employer. The basis for Corporation P's refund claim is that Corporation P is not the employer of the individuals that performed services for Employer. Corporation P is designated to perform the acts of an employer with respect to all of the wages Corporation P paid to the individuals performing services for Employer for all quarters of 2015. Accordingly, Corporation P is not entitled to a refund. Employer and Corporation P are each subject to all provisions of law (including penalties) applicable in respect of employers for all quarters of 2015 with respect to such wages.

(6) *Example 6.* Corporation S enters into an agreement with Employer, effective January 1, 2015. Under the agreement, Corporation S provides payroll services, including payment of wages to individuals performing services for Employer, and assumes responsibility for the collection, reporting, and payment of applicable taxes. For all pay periods in 2015, Employer provides Corporation S with an amount equal to the gross payroll (that is, wage and tax amounts) of the individuals, and Corporation S pays wages (less the applicable withholding) to the individuals performing services for Employer. Corporation S also reports the wage and tax amounts on Form 941, *Employer's QUARTERLY Federal Tax Return,* filed for each quarter of 2015 under Employer's employer identification number. Corporation S is not designated to perform the acts of an employer with respect to all of the wages Corporation S paid to the individuals performing services for Employer for all quarters of 2015. Corporation S did not assert it was the employer and filed Forms 941 using Employer's employer identification number. Accordingly, Corporation S is not liable for the applicable employment taxes under this section. Employer remains subject to all provisions of law (including penalties) applicable in respect of employers for all quarters of 2015 with respect to such wages.

(7) *Example 7.* Corporation T enters into a consulting agreement with Manufacturer effective January 1, 2015, to provide consulting services to Manufacturer. Corporation T is responsible to pay wages to the individuals providing the consulting services to Manufacturer and to collect, report, and pay the applicable taxes. Corporation T has the right to direct and control the individuals as to when and how to perform the consulting services and, thus, is the common law employer of the individuals providing the consulting services. Corporation T is not designated to perform the acts of an employer with respect to all of the wages Corporation T pays to individuals providing consulting services to Manufacturer. However, as the common law employer of the individuals, Corporation T is subject to all provisions of law (including penalties) applicable in respect of employers with respect to such wages.

(8) *Example 8.* On January 1, 2015, Corporation U enters into an agreement with Employer for Employer to farm Corporation U's property. Under the agreement, Corporation U and Employer agree to split the proceeds of the sale of the products grown on the property. Employer hires workers to assist it with the farming. Employer has the right to direct and control the workers as to when and how to perform the services and, thus, is the common law employer of the workers. However, Employer is unable to pay the workers until after the products are sold. Therefore, Corporation U pays wages to the workers and deducts this amount from Employer's share of the profits. Corporation U controls the payment of wages within the meaning of section 3401(d)(1). Corporation U is not designated to perform the acts of an employer with respect to all of the wages Corporation U paid to workers providing services for Employer. However, as the section 3401(d)(1) employer of the workers performing services for Employer, Corporation U is subject to all provisions of law (including penalties) applicable in respect of employers with respect to such wages.

(9) *Example 9.* Corporation V and Employer execute and submit a Form 2678, *Employer/Payer Appointment of Agent,* to the Service, requesting approval to authorize Corporation V to report, deposit, and pay taxes with respect to wages it pays, as agent of Employer for purposes of Form 941, *Employer's QUARTERLY Federal Tax Return.* The Form 2678 is approved by the Service and effective for all quarters of 2015. Accordingly, Corporation V reports the wages it pays to individuals performing services for Employer and related tax amounts on Form 941 and Schedule R (Form 941), *Allocation Schedule for Aggregate Form 941 Filers,* filed for each quarter of 2015 under Corporation V's employer identification number. Corporation V is not designated under this section to perform the acts of an employer with respect to all of the wages Corporation V paid to the individuals performing services for Employer for all quarters of 2015. However, as an agent authorized under §31.3504-1(a), Corporation V is subject to all provisions of law (including penalties) applicable in respect of employers for all quarters of 2015 with respect to such wages. Employer also remains subject to all provisions of law (including penalties) applicable in respect of employers for all quarters of 2015 with respect to such wages.

(f) *Effective/applicability date.*—These final regulations are effective for wages or compensation paid by a payor in quarters beginning on or after March 31, 2014. [Reg. §31.3504-2.]

☐ [*T.D.* 9662, 3-28-2014 (*corrected* 5-30-2014).]

### [Reg. §31.3505-1]

**§31.3505-1. Liability of third parties paying or providing for wages.**—(a) *Personal liability in case of direct payment of wages.*—(1) *In general.*—A lender, surety, or other person—

(i) Who is not an employer for purposes of section 3102 (relating to deduction of tax from wages under the Federal Insurance Contributions Act), section 3202 (relating to deduction of tax from compensation under the Railroad Retirement Tax Act), or section 3402 (relating to deduction of income tax from wages) with respect to an employee or group of employees, and

(ii) Who pays wages on or after January 1, 1967, directly to such employee or group of employees, employed by one or more employers, or to an agent on behalf of such employee or employees, shall be liable in his own person and estate for payment to the United States of an amount equal to the sum of the taxes required to be deducted and withheld from those wages by the employer under subtitle C of the Code and interest from the due date of the employer's return relating to such taxes for the period in which the wages are paid.

(2) *Example.*—The provisions of this paragraph may be illustrated by the following example:

*Example.* Pursuant to a wage claim of $200, A, a surety company, paid a net amount of $158 to B, an employee of the X Construction Company. This was done in accordance with A's payment bond covering a private construction job on which B was an employee. If X Construction Company fails to make timely payment or deposit of $42.00, the amount of tax required by subtitle C of the Code to be deducted and withheld from a $200 wage payment to B, A becomes personally liable for $42.00 (*i.e.,* an amount equal to the unpaid taxes), plus interest upon this amount from the due date of X's return.

(b) *Personal liability where funds are supplied.*—(1) *In general.*—A lender, surety, or other person who—

(i) Advances funds to or for the account of an employer for the specific purpose of paying wages of the employees of that employer, and

(ii) At the time the funds are advanced, has actual notice or knowledge (within the meaning of section 6323(i)(1)) that the employer does not intend to, or will not be able to, make timely payment or deposit of the amounts of tax required by subtitle C of the Code to be deducted and withheld by the employer from those wages, shall be liable in his own person and estate for payment to the United States of an amount equal to the sum of the taxes which are required by subtitle C of the Code to be deducted and withheld from wages paid on or after January 1, 1967, and which are not paid over to the United States by the employer, and interest from the due date of the employer's return relating to such taxes. However, the liability of the lender, surety, or other person shall not exceed 25 percent of the amount supplied by him for the payment of wages. The preceding sentence and the second sentence of section 3505(b) limit the liability of a lender, surety, or other person arising solely by reason of section 3505, and they do not limit the liability which the lender, surety or other person may incur to the United States as a third-party beneficiary of an agreement between the lender, surety, or other person and the employer. The liability of a lender, surety, or other person does not include penalties imposed on the taxpayer.

(2) *Examples.*—The provisions of this paragraph may be illustrated by the following examples:

*Example (1).* D, a savings and loan association, advances $10,000 to Y for the specific purpose of paying the net wages of Y's employees. D advances those funds with knowledge that Y will not be able to make timely payment of the taxes required to be deducted and withheld from these wages by subtitle C of the Code. Y uses the $10,000 to pay the net wages of his employees but fails to remit withholding taxes under subtitle C in the amount of $2,600. D's liability, under this section, is limited to $2,500, 25 percent of the amount supplied for the payment of wages to Y's employees.

*Example (2).* E, a loan company, advances $15,000 to F, a contractor, for the specific purpose of paying $20,000 of net wages due to F's employees. E advances those funds with knowledge that F will not be able to make timely payment of the taxes required to be deducted and withheld from these wages by subtitle C of the Code. F applies $5,000 of its own funds toward payment of these wages. The amount of tax required to be deducted and withheld from the gross wages is $4,500. The limitation applicable to E's liability is $3,750 (25% of $15,000). However, because E furnished only a portion of the total net wages, E is liable for $3,375 of the taxes required to be deducted and withheld (4,500 × $15,000/$20,000).

(3) *Ordinary working capital loan.*—The provisions of section 3505(b) do not apply in the case of an ordinary working capital loan made to an employer, even though the person supplying the funds knows that part of the funds advanced may be used to make wage payments in the ordinary course of business. Generally, an ordinary working capital loan is a loan which is made to enable the borrower to meet current obligations as they arise. The person supplying the funds is not obligated to determine the specific use of an ordinary working capital loan or the ability of the employer to pay the amounts of tax required by subtitle C of the Code to be deducted and withheld. However, section 3505(b) is applicable where the person supplying the funds has actual notice or knowledge (within the meaning of section 6323(i)(1)) at the time of the advance that the funds, or a portion thereof, are to be used specifically to pay net wages, whether or not the written agreement under which the funds are advanced states a different purpose. Whether or not a lender has actual notice or knowledge that the funds are to be used to pay net wages, or merely that the funds may be so used, depends upon the facts and circumstances of each case. For example, a lender, who has actual notice or knowledge that the withheld taxes will not be paid, will be deemed to have actual notice or knowledge that the funds are to be used specifically to pay net wages where substantially all of the employer's ordinary operating expenses consist of salaries and wages even though funds for other incidental operating expenses may be supplied pursuant to an agreement described as a working capital loan agreement.

(c) *Definition of other person.*—(1) *In general.*—As used in this section, the term "other person" means any person who directly pays the wages or supplies funds for the specific purpose of paying the wages of an employee or group of employees of another employer. It does not include a person acting only as agent of the employer or as agent of the employees.

(2) *Examples.*—The provisions of this paragraph may be illustrated by the following examples:

*Example (1).* Pursuant to an agreement between L, a labor union, and M, an employer, M makes monthly vacation payments (of a sum equal to a certain percentage of the remuneration paid to each union member employed by M during the previous month) to a union administered pool plan under which each employee's rights are fully vested and nonforfeitable from the time the money is paid by M. Vacation allowances are accumulated by the plan and distributed to eligible employees during their vacations. L, acting merely as a conduit with respect to these payments, would incur no liability under section 3505.

*Example (2).* N, a construction company, maintains a payroll account with the O Bank in which N deposits its own funds. Pursuant to an automated payroll service agreement between N and O, O prepares payroll checks and earnings statements for each of N's employees reflecting the net pay due each such employee. These checks are delivered to N for signature. After the checks are signed, O distributes them directly to N's employees on the regularly scheduled pay day. O, acting only in the capacity of a disbursing agent of N's funds, would incur no liability under section 3505 with respect to these payroll distributions. However, O may incur liability under section 3505 in the capacity of a lender if it supplies the funds for the payment of wages.

(d) *Payment of taxes and interest.*—(1) *Procedure for payment.*—A lender, surety, or other person may satisfy the personal liability imposed upon him by section 3505 by executing Form 4219 and filing it, accompanied by payment of the amount of tax and interest due the United States, in accordance with the instructions for the form. In the event the lender, surety, or other person does not satisfy the liability imposed by section 3505, the United States may collect the liability by appropriate civil proceeding commenced within 10 years after assessment of the tax against the employer.

(2) *Effect of payment.*—(i) *In general.*—A person paying the amounts of tax required to be deducted and withheld by subtitle C of the Code as a result of section 3505 and this section is not required to pay the employer's portion of the payroll taxes upon those wages, or file an employer's tax return with respect to those wages, or furnish annual wage and tax statements to the employees.

(ii) *Amounts paid by a lender, surety, or other person.*—Any amounts paid by the lender, surety, or other person to the United States pursuant to this section shall be credited against the liability of the employer on whose behalf those payments are made and shall also reduce the total liability imposed upon the lender, surety, or other person under section 3505 and this section.

(iii) *Amounts paid by the employer.*—Any amounts paid to the United States by an employer and applied to his liability under subtitle C of the Code shall reduce the total liability imposed upon that employer by subtitle C. Such payments will also reduce the liability imposed upon a lender, surety, or other person under section 3505 except that such liability shall not be reduced by any portion of an employer's payment applied against the employer's liability under subtitle C which is in excess of the total liability imposed upon the lender, surety, or other person under section 3505. For example, if a lender supplies $1,000 to an employer for the payment of net wages, upon which $300 withholding tax liability is imposed, a part-payment of $25 by the employer which is applied to this liability would reduce the employer's total liability under subtitle C of the Code by that amount, but the liability imposed upon the lender by section 3505(b) in an amount equal to the withholding tax liability of the employer, which is limited to 25 percent of the amount supplied by him, would remain $250. However, if the employer makes another payment of $200 which is applied to his liability for the withholding taxes, the lender's liability under section 3505 attributable to the withholding taxes is reduced by $175 ($225 less $50 (the amount by which the employer's liability exceeds the lender's liability after application of the limitation)). Thus, after the second payment by the employer, the lender's liability under section 3505(b) is $75 ($250 less $175) plus interest due on the underpayment for the period of underpayment to a maximum of $250, 25 percent of the funds supplied.

(3) *Extensions of the period for collection.*—Prior to the expiration of the 10-year period for collection after assessment against the employer, the lender, surety, or other third party may agree in writing with the district director, service center director, or compliance center director to extend the 10-year period for collection. The period so agreed upon may be extended by subsequent agreements in writing made before the expiration of the period previously agreed upon. If any timely proceeding in court for the collection of the tax and any applicable interest is commenced, the period during which such tax and interest may be collected shall be extended and shall not expire until the liability for the tax (or a judgment against the lender, surety, or other third party arising from such liability) is satisfied or becomes unenforceable.

(e) *Returns required by employers and statements for employees.*—This section does not relieve the employer of the responsibilities imposed upon him to file the returns and supply the receipts and statements required under subchapter A, Chapter 61 of the Code (relating to returns and records).

(f) *Time when liability arises.*—The liability under section 3505 and this section of a lender, surety, or other person paying or supplying funds for the payment of wages is incurred on the last day prescribed for the filing of the employer's Federal employment tax return (determined without regard to any extension of time) in respect of such wages.

(g) *Effective date.*—These regulations are effective on August 1, 1995. [Reg. § 31.3505-1.]

□ [*T.D. 7430, 8-19-76. Amended by T.D. 8604, 7-31-95.*]

## [Reg. § 31.3506-1]

**§ 31.3506-1. Companion sitting placement services.—**
(a) *Definitions.*—(1) *Companion sitting placement service.*—For purposes of this section, the term "companion sitting placement service" means a person (whether or not an individual) engaged in the trade or business of placing sitters with individuals who wish to avail themselves of the sitters' services.

(2) *Sitters.*—For purposes of this section, the term "sitters" means individuals who furnish personal attendance, companionship, or household care services to children or to individuals who are elderly or disabled.

(b) *General rule.*—For purposes of subtitle C of the Internal Revenue Code of 1954 (relating to employment taxes), a companion sitting placement service shall not be treated as the employer of its sitters, and the sitters shall not be treated as the employees of the placement service. However, the rule of the preceding sentence shall apply only if the companion sitting placement service neither pays nor receives (directly or through an agent) the salary or wages of the sitters, but is compensated, if at all, on a fee basis by the sitters or the individuals for whom the sitting is performed.

(c) *Individuals deemed self-employed.*—Any individual who, by reason of this section, is deemed not to be the employee of a companion sitting placement service shall be deemed to be self-employed for purposes of the tax on self-employment income (see sections 1401-1403 and the regulations thereunder in part 1 of this chapter (Income Tax Regulations)).

(d) *Scope of rules.*—The rules of this section operate only to remove sitters and companion sitting placement services from the employee-employer relationship when, under § § 31.3121(d)-1 and 31.3121(d)-2, that relationship would otherwise exist. Thus, if, under § § 31.3121(d)-1 and 31.3121(d)-2, a sitter is considered to be the employee of the individual for whom the sitting is performed rather than the employee of the companion sitting placement service, this section has no effect upon that employee-employer relationship.

(e) *Examples.*—The provisions of this section may be illustrated by the following examples:

*Example (1).* X is an agency that places babysitters with individuals who desire babysitting services. X furnishes all the sitters with an instruction manual regarding their conduct and appearance, requires them to file semimonthly reports, and determines the total fee to be charged the individual for whom the sitting is performed. Individuals who need a babysitter contact the agency, are informed of the charges, and, if agreement is reached, a sitter is sent to perform the services. The sitter collects the entire amount of the charges and remits a percentage to X as a fee for the placement. X is a companion sitting placement service within the meaning of paragraph (a)(1) of this section. Therefore, since the agency does not actually pay or receive the wages of the sitters, X is not treated as the employer of the sitters for purposes of this subtitle. The sitters are deemed to be self-employed for the purpose of the tax imposed by section 1401.

*Example (2).* Assume the same facts as in example (1), except that the individual for whom the sitting is performed pays to X the entire amount of the charges. X retains a percentage and pays the difference to the sitter. Since X actually receives and pays the wages of the sitters, X is the employer of the sitters.

*Example (3).* As a service to the community a neighborhood association maintains a list of individuals who are available to babysit. Parents in need of a sitter contact the association and are provided with a list of names and telephone numbers. The association charges no fee for the service and takes no action other than compiling the list of sitters and making it available to members of the community. Issues such as hours of work, amount of payment, and the method by which the services are performed are all resolved between the sitter and parent. A, a parent, used the list to hire B to sit for A's child. B performs the services four days a week in A's home and follows specific instructions given by A. Under § 31.3121(d)-1, B is the employee of A rather than the employee of the neighborhood association. Consequently, this section does not apply and B remains the employee of A.

(f) *Effective date.*—This section shall apply to remuneration received after December 31, 1974. [Reg. § 31.3506-1.]

□ [*T.D. 7691, 4-8-80.*]

## [Reg. § 31.3507-1]

**§ 31.3507-1. Advance payments of earned income credit.—**
(a) *General rule.*—(1) *In general.*—Every employer paying wages after June 30, 1979, to an employee with respect to whom an earned income credit advance payment certificate is in effect must, at the time of paying the wages, also pay the employee the advance earned income credit amount of that employee. For the purposes of applying this section and § 31.3507-2—

(i) In the case of an individual who receives wages which are subject to income tax withholding, the term "employee" has the same meaning as set forth in section 3401(c) and the regulations thereunder, and the term "wages" has the same meaning as set forth in sections 3401(a) and 3402(e) and the regulations under those sections; and

(ii) In the case of an individual who does not receive wages which are subject to income tax withholding, but who receives wages which are subject to employee FICA taxes, the term "employee" has the same meaning as set forth in section 3121(d) and the regulations thereunder and the term "wages" has the same meaning as set forth in section 3121(a) and the regulations thereunder.

An individual not having wages subject to either income tax withholding or employee FICA taxes is not entitled to advance payments of the earned income credit. Moreover, notwithstanding subdivisions (i) and (ii) of this paragraph (a)(1), employers are not required to pay advance earned income credit amounts to agricultural workers paid on a daily basis. For this purpose an "agricultural worker" is an employee who performs "agricultural labor", as that term is defined in section 3121(g) and the regulations thereunder.

(2) *Cross references.*—For determination of the advance earned income credit amount of an employee, see paragraph (b) of this section. For rules relating to the treatment of the payment of an employee's advance earned income credit amount as equivalent to payment by the employer of withholding and FICA taxes, see paragraph (c) of this section. For rules describing the earned income credit advance payment certificate, see § 31.3507-2(a) and (b). For rules relating to the employee's furnishing of the earned income credit advance payment certificate and the payroll periods for which the certificate is effective, see § 31.3507-2(c) and (d).

(b) *Advance earned income credit amount.*—The advance earned income credit amount of an employee is determined, with respect to any payroll period, on the basis of the employee's wages from the employer for the period and in accordance with the advance amount tables prescribed by the Commissioner of Internal Revenue and then in effect for the payroll period. See, however, paragraph (c)(2) of this section. The advance amount paid is reflected on the employee's W-2 form as a separate item (and neither as a reduction of withholding nor an increase in compensation). For purposes of applying this section and § 31.3507-2, the term "payroll period" has the meaning set forth in section 3401(b) and the regulations thereunder. As required by section 3507(c)(2)(A), these advance amount tables must be similar in form to, and coordinated with, the tables prescribed under section 3402 (relating to income tax collected at the source). Sections 3507(c)(2)(B) and 3507(c)(2)(C) provide, respectively, separate rules for the treatment in the advance amount tables of the advance earned income credit of the following two separate classes of employees:

(1) Employees who are not married (within the meaning of section 143), or employees whose spouses do not have an earned income credit advance payment certificate in effect; and

(2) Employees whose spouses have an earned income credit advance payment certificate in effect.

If during the calendar year an employer has paid an employee amounts of earned income, within the meaning of section 43(c)(2)(A)(i), which in the aggregate equal or exceed $10,000, the employer need not make further payments of advance earned income credit to the employee during that calendar year.

(c) *Payment of advance earned income credit amount as payment of withholding and FICA taxes.*—(1) *In general.*—(i) The provisions of this paragraph (c) apply for all purposes of the Internal Revenue Code of 1954. Payments of advance earned income credit amounts pursuant to paragraph (a)(1) of this section do not constitute the payment of compensation. These payments by the employer are treated as made—

(A) First, from the aggregate amount, with respect to all employees, required to be deducted and withheld for the payroll period under section 3401 (relatinig to income tax withholding);

(B) Second, from the aggregate amount, with respect to all employees, required to be deducted for the payroll period under section 3102 (relating to employee FICA taxes); and

(C) Third, from the aggregate amount of the taxes imposed for the payroll period under section 3111 (relating to employer FICA taxes). For purposes of the requirements of sections 3401, 3102, and 3111, as the case may be, and 6302, amounts equal to the advance earned income credit amounts paid to employees are treated as if paid to the Treasury Department on the day on which the wages (and advance amounts) are paid to the employees. The employer must report the payment and treatment of the advance amounts on the employer's Form 941, 941E, 942, or 943, as the case may be, in accordance with the applicable instructions.

(ii) The provisions of paragraph (c)(1)(i) of this section may be illustrated by the following example:

*Example.* Employer X has ten employees, each of whom is entitled to advance earned income credit payment of $10. The total of advance amounts paid by the employer to the ten employees for the payroll period is $100. The total of income tax withholding for the payroll period is $90. The total of employee FICA taxes for the payroll period is $61.30, and the total of employer FICA taxes for the payroll period is also $61.30. Under the rules of paragraph (c)(1)(i) of this section, the total of advance amounts paid to employees is treated as if X had paid the Treasury Department on the day X paid the employees' wages: first, the $90 aggregate amount of income tax withholding; and second, $10 of the aggregate amount of employee FICA tax. X remains liable only for $112.60 of the aggregate FICA tax [$51.30 + $61.30 = $112.60].

(2) *Advance payments exceeding taxes due.*—(i) If, for any payroll period, the aggregate amount of advance earned income credit amounts required to be paid by an employer under paragraph (a)(1) of this section exceeds the sum of the amounts for the payroll period referred to in paragraphs (c)(1)(i)(A) through (C) of this section, the employer reduces each advance amount paid for the payroll period by an amount which bears the same ratio to the excess of the advance amounts as the subject advance amount bears to the aggregate of advance amounts for the payroll period. However, this paragraph (c)(2) does not apply if the employer makes the election provided by paragraph (c)(3) of this section.

(ii) The provisions of paragraph (c)(2) of this section may be illustrated by the following example.

*Example.* Assume the same facts as the example in paragraph (c)(1)(ii) of this section, except that the employer is a state government which does not pay FICA taxes. Under these facts, the advance amounts would be $10 greater than the $90 total of income tax withholding for the payroll period. Assume 10 employees each receiving $10 in advance payments. Under the rule of this paragraph (c)(2), the employer X reduces the amount of the advance amount paid to each employee by 1/10, computed as follows:

$$\frac{\$10}{\$100} = 1/10$$

This is the same result as would be obtained by reducing the advance payment of $10 for each of the ten employees by one-tenth $^{10}/_{100}$ of the $10 excess or $1.00.

(3) *Election to treat excess amounts as advance tax payment.*—In lieu of reducing advance payments under paragraph (c)(2) of this section, an employer may elect under this paragraph (c)(3) to pay in full all advance earned income credit amounts. However, if no election is made, the employer is required to reduce advance amounts paid in accordance with paragraph (c)(2) of this section. The election, if made, applies to all advance earned income credit amounts required to be paid for the payroll period. The employer reflects the election on the employer's Form 941, 941E, 942, or 943, as the case may be, and must specify (with supporting computations) the amount of the excess of the advance amounts paid and the payroll period to which the excess relates. Separate elections may be made for separate payroll periods. The excess of advance amounts paid is treated as an advance payment by the employer of employment taxes described in subdivisions (i) through (iii) of this paragraph (c)(3) and due for the period reported on the Form 941, 941E, 942, or 943 which includes the payroll period during which the excess amounts were paid. The amount of the excess advance payment is applied to the amounts of the employer's liability—

(i) First, for income tax withholding due under section 3401 for the reporting period in which the payment is made;

(ii) Second, for employee FICA taxes due under section 3102 for the reporting period in which the payment is made; and

(iii) Third, for employer FICA taxes due under section 3111 for the reporting period in which the payment is made.

If the amount of the employment taxes (as described) for which the employer remains liable for the reporting period in which the excess payment is made is less than the excess payment, the employer may claim a refund of that portion of the excess amount paid which exceeds the employer's remaining liability for these taxes for the reporting period. This refund may be claimed, in the same manner as a refund of wage withholding taxes paid by the employer under section 3401, on the employer's Form 941, 941E, 942, or 943, as the

case may be, for the reporting period. In the absence of a claim for refund, that portion of the excess amount will be applied by the Internal Revenue Service against the employer's liability for employment taxes reported on the employer's Form 941, 941E, 942, or 943, as the case may be, filed for the next reporting period.

(4) *Failure to make advance payments.*—The failure to pay an employee, at the time required by paragraph (a)(1) of this section, all or any part of an advance earned income credit amount as required by this section is treated, for all purposes including penalties, as a failure by the employer as of that time to deduct and withhold under chapter 24 of the Internal Revenue Code of 1954 an amount equal to the advance amount (or part thereof) not paid. This treatment applies to the failure to pay an advance amount to an eligible employee without regard to whether the employee is ultimately not entitled to claim the earned income credit (in full or in part) on a return for the year, so long as the employee has a valid earned income credit advance payment certificate in effect with the employer at the time when the wages were paid. If an employer fails to pay an advance earned income credit amount as required under this section, the advance amount will not be collected by the Internal Revenue Service from the employer if the employer has properly withheld and deposited all income taxes and FICA taxes applicable with respect to the employee. However, such amount may be collected if the employer has not properly withheld and deposited these taxes. [Reg. §31.3507-1.]

☐ [*T.D.* 7766, 1-28-81 (previously issued as Temporary Reg. §38.3507-1 by *T.D.* 7619).]

### [Reg. §31.3507-2]

**§31.3507-2. Earned income credit advance payment certificates.**—(a) *Definition.*—For the purposes of this section and §31.3507-1, an earned income credit advance payment certificate is a statement furnished by an employee to the employer which—

(1) Certifies that the employee reasonably expects to be eligible to receive the earned income credit provided by section 43 for the employee's last taxable year under subtitle A of the Internal Revenue Code of 1954 which begins in the calendar year in which the wages are paid;

(2) Certifies that the employee does not have an earned income credit advance payment certificate in effect for the calendar year (in which the wages are paid) with respect to the payment of wages by another employer; and

(3) States if the employee's spouse has an earned income credit advance payment certificate in effect with any employer. For the rule for determining if an employee's spouse has a certificate in effect, see paragraph (c)(3) of this section.

(b) *Form and content of earned income credit advance payment certificate.*—(1) *In general.*—Form W-5 (Earned Income Credit Advance Payment Certificate) is the prescribed form for the earned income credit advance payment certificate. The Form W-5 must be prepared in accordance with the instructions applicable thereto and must set forth fully and clearly the data therein called for. In lieu of the prescribed form, a form the provisions of which are identical with those of the prescribed form may be used.

(2) *Invalid certificates.*—A Form W-5 does not meet the requirements of section 3507 or this section and is invalid if it is not completed or signed or contains an alteration or unauthorized addition (as defined in §31.3402(f)(5)-1(b)(1) and (2)). Any earned income credit advance payment certificate which the employee clearly indicates to be false by oral statement or written statement to the employer must be treated by the employer as a certificate which is invalid as of the date of the employee's statement. For purposes of the preceding sentence, the term "employer" includes any individual authorized by the employer to receive earned income credit advance payment certificates or to make payroll distributions. If an employer receives from an employee an invalid certificate, the employer must consider it a nullity with respect to all payments of wages thereafter to the employee and must inform the employee of the certificate's invalidity. The employer is not required to ascertain whether any completed and signed earned income credit advance payment certificate is correct. However, the employer should inform the district director if the employer has reason to believe that the certificate contains any incorrect statement.

(c) *When earned income credit advance payment certificate takes effect.*—(1) *No previous certificate.*—An earned income credit advance payment certificate furnished the employer where no previous certificate is or has been in effect with the employer for that employee for the calendar year takes effect with—

(i) The date of the beginning of the first payroll period ending on or after the date on which the certificate is received by the employer;

(ii) The date of the first payment of wages made without regard to a payroll period on or after the date on which the certificate is received by the employer; or

(iii) The first day of the calendar year for which the certificate is furnished, if that day is later than the otherwise applicable effective date specified in subdivision (i) or (ii) of this paragraph (c)(1).

(2) *Previous certificate.*—Except as otherwise provided in this paragraph (c)(2), an earned income credit advance payment certificate furnished the employer where a previous certificate is or has been in effect with the employer for that employee for the calendar year takes effect on the date of the first payment of wages made on or after the first status determination date (as defined in paragraph (c)(4) of this section) occurring at least thirty days after the date on which the certificate is received by the employer. However, if the employer so chooses, the employer may treat the certificate as effective on the date of any payment of wages made on or after the date on which the certificate is received by the employer (without regard to any status determination date).

(3) *Certificate of spouse.*—For the sole purpose of applying paragraph (a)(3) of this section, in determining if a certificate is in effect with respect to an employee's spouse, the spouse's certificate is treated as then in effect if the spouse's certificate will be or is reasonably expected to be in effect on the first status determination date following the date on which the employer receives the employee's certificate.

(4) *Status determination date.*—For the purposes of this section, the term "status determination date" means January 1, May 1, July 1, and October 1 of each year.

(d) *Period during which certificate remains in effect; change of status.*—(1) *Period certificate remains in effect.*—An earned income credit advance payment certificate which takes effect during a calendar year continues in effect with respect to the employee only during that calendar year and until revoked by the employee or until another certificate takes effect. See paragraphs (d)(2) and (c)(2) of this section.

(2) *Change of status.*—(i) *Revocation of certificate.*—If, after an employee has furnished an earned income credit advance payment certificate—

(A) The employee no longer wishes to receive advance earned income credit payments; or

(B) There has been a change of circumstances which has the effect of either making the employee ineligible for the earned income credit for the taxable year or causing a certificate to be in effect for the employee's spouse,

then the employee must revoke the certificate previously furnished by furnishing the employer a new certificate (Form W-5 or identical form) in revocation of the earlier certificate. Depending upon the nature of the change of circumstances, the employer may be required, pursuant to the new certificate, to pay further advance earned income credit amounts to the employee (but in different amounts than previously paid to the employer). The Form W-5 (or identical form) must be prepared in accordance with the instructions applicable thereto and must set forth fully and clearly the data therein called for. In the case of revocation due to change of circumstances, the new certificate in revocation must be delivered to the employer within ten days after the employee first learns of the change of circumstances. The new certificate is effective under the rules provided in paragraph (c)(2) of this section for later certificates. A new certificate furnished by an employee which is invalid within the meaning of paragraph (b)(2) of this section is considered a nullity with respect to all payments of wages thereafter to the employee. The prior certificate of the employee remains in effect, unless the employee clearly indicates by an oral or written statement to the employer that the prior certificate is invalid. See paragraph (b)(2) of this section. The employer is not required to ascertain whether any employee has experienced a change of circumstances described in subdivision (i)(B) of this paragraph which necessitates the employee's furnishing a new certificate. However, the employer should inform the district director if the employer has reason to believe that an employee has experienced a change of circumstances as described if the employee does not deliver a new certificate to the employer within the ten day period.

(ii) *Change in spouse's certificate.*—If, after an employee has furnished an earned income credit advance payment certificate stating that a certificate is in effect for the spouse of the employee, the certificate of the spouse is no longer in effect, the employee may furnish the employer with a new certificate which reflects this change of circumstances. [Reg. § 31.3507-2.]

☐ [*T.D.* 7766, 1-28-81 (previously issued as Temporary Reg. § 38.3507-2 by *T.D.* 7619).]

**[Reg. § 31.3511-1]**

**§ 31.3511-1. Certified professional employer organization.**—(a) *Treatment as employer.*—(1) *In general.*—For purposes of the federal employment taxes and other obligations imposed under chapters 21 through 25 of subtitle C of the Internal Revenue Code (federal employment taxes), a certified professional employer organization (CPEO) (as defined in § 301.7705-1(b)(1) of this chapter) is treated as the employer of any covered employee (as defined in § 301.7705-1(b)(5) of this chapter), but only with respect to remuneration remitted by the CPEO to the covered employee.

(2) *Work site employee.*—In the case of a covered employee who is a work site employee (as defined in § 301.7705-1(b)(17) of this chapter) of the customer, no person other than the CPEO is treated as the employer of the work site employee with respect to the customer for purposes of federal employment taxes imposed on remuneration remitted by the CPEO to the work site employee.

(3) *Non-work site covered employee.*—In the case of a covered employee who is not a work site employee, a person other than the CPEO is also treated as an employer of the employee for purposes of federal employment taxes imposed on remuneration remitted by the CPEO to the employee if such person is determined to be an employer of the employee without regard to the application of this paragraph (a) and section 3511.

(b) *Exemptions, exclusions, definitions, and other rules.*—(1) *In general.*—Solely for purposes of federal employment taxes imposed on remuneration remitted by a CPEO to a covered employee, the application of exemptions, exclusions, definitions, and other rules that are based on the type of employer is presumed to be based on the type of employer of the customer of the CPEO for whom the covered employee performs services. If a covered employee performs services for more than one customer of the CPEO during the calendar year, the presumption described in the previous sentence applies separately to remuneration remitted by the CPEO to the covered employee for services performed with respect to each such customer.

(2) *Presumption rebutted.*—The presumption set forth in paragraph (b)(1) of this section may be rebutted if either the Commissioner determines, or the CPEO demonstrates by clear and convincing evidence, that the relationship between the customer and the covered employee is not the legal relationship of employer and employee as set forth in § 31.3401(c)-1. If such a determination or demonstration is made, then, with respect to remuneration remitted by a CPEO to a covered employee, the application of exemptions, exclusions, definitions, and other rules that are based on the type of employer will be based on the type of employer of the person determined by the Commissioner or demonstrated by the CPEO to be the common law employer of the covered employee in accordance with § 31.3401(c)-1.

(3) *No inference from presumption.*—The presumption set forth in paragraph (b)(1) of this section does not create any inference with respect to the determination of who is an employer or employee or whether the legal relationship of employer and employee exists for federal tax purposes or for purposes of any other provision of law (other than for paragraph (b)(1) of this section).

(c) *Annual wage limitation, contribution base, and withholding threshold.*—(1) *CPEO has separate taxable wage base, contribution base, and withholding threshold.*—For purposes of applying the annual wage limitations under sections 3121(a)(1) and 3306(b)(1) (relating to the Federal Insurance Contributions Act and the Federal Unemployment Tax Act, respectively), the contribution base under section 3231(e)(2) (relating to the Railroad Retirement Tax Act), and the withholding threshold under section 3102(f)(1) (relating to the Additional Medicare Tax), remuneration received by a covered employee from a CPEO for performing services for a customer of the CPEO within any calendar year is subject to a separate annual wage limitation, contribution base, and withholding threshold that are each computed without regard to any remuneration received by the covered employee during the calendar year from any other employer (including, if applicable, remuneration received directly from the customer receiving services from the employee). Notwithstanding the preceding sentence, a CPEO is treated as a successor or predecessor employer for purposes of the annual wage limitations and contribution base upon entering into or terminating a CPEO contract (as defined in § 301.7705-1(b)(3) of this chapter) with respect to a work site employee, as described in paragraph (d) of this section.

(2) *Performance of services for more than one customer.*—If, during a calendar year, a covered employee receives remuneration from a CPEO for services performed by the covered employee for more than one customer of the CPEO, the annual wage limitation, contribution base, and withholding threshold do not apply to the aggregate remuneration received by the covered employee from the CPEO for

services performed for all such customers. Rather, the annual wage limitation, contribution base, and withholding threshold apply separately to the remuneration received by the covered employee from the CPEO with respect to services performed for each customer.

(d) *Successor employer status.*—(1) *In general.*—For purposes of sections 3121(a)(1), 3231(e)(2)(C), and 3306(b)(1), a CPEO and its customer are treated as—

(i) A successor and predecessor employer, respectively, upon entering into a CPEO contract with respect to a work site employee who is performing services for the customer; and

(ii) A predecessor and successor employer, respectively, upon termination of the CPEO contract between the CPEO and the customer with respect to the work site employee who is performing services for the customer.

(2) *Non-work site covered employee.*—A CPEO entering into a CPEO contract with a customer during a calendar quarter with respect to a covered employee who is not a work site employee at any time during that calendar quarter will not be treated as a successor employer (and the customer will not be treated as a predecessor employer) for purposes of paragraph (d)(1)(i) of this section regardless of whether, during the term of the CPEO contract, the covered employee subsequently becomes a work site employee. Similarly, a CPEO terminating a CPEO contract with a customer during a calendar quarter with respect to a covered employee who is not a work site employee at any time during that calendar quarter will not be treated as a predecessor employer (and the customer will not be treated as a successor employer) for purposes of paragraph (d)(1)(ii) of this section regardless of whether, during the term of the CPEO contract, the covered employee had previously been a work site employee.

(e) *Treatment of credits.*—(1) *In general.*—For purposes of the credits specified in paragraph (e)(2) of this section—

(i) The credit with respect to a work site employee performing services for a customer applies to the customer, not to the CPEO; and

(ii) In computing the credit, the customer, and not the CPEO, is to take into account wages and federal employment taxes paid by the CPEO with respect to the work site employee and for which the CPEO receives payment from the customer.

(2) *Credits specified.*—A credit is specified in this paragraph (e) if such credit is allowed under—

(i) Section 41 (credit for increasing research activity);

(ii) Section 45A (Indian employment credit);

(iii) Section 45B (credit for portion of employer social security taxes paid with respect to employee cash tips);

(iv) Section 45C (clinical testing expenses for certain drugs for rare diseases or conditions);

(v) Section 45R (employee health insurance expenses for small employers);

(vi) Section 45S (employer credit for paid family and medical leave);

(vii) Section 51 (work opportunity credit);

(viii) Section 1396 (empowerment zone employment credit);

(ix) Statutory employee retention credits that are similar to the employee retention credit in section 1400R and that provide disaster relief to employers in designated disaster areas; and

(x) Any other section specified by the Commissioner in further guidance (as defined in § 301.7705-1(b)(8) of this chapter).

(f) *Section not applicable to related customers, self-employed individuals, and other circumstances.*—This section does not apply—

(1) In the case of any customer that—

(i) Has a relationship to a CPEO described in section 267(b) (including, by cross-reference, section 267(f)) or section 707(b), except that "10 percent" shall be substituted for "50 percent" wherever it appears in such sections; or

(ii) Has commenced a CPEO contract with the CPEO but such commencement has not been reported to the IRS as described in paragraph (g)(3)(i) of this section; or

(2) To remuneration paid by a CPEO to any self-employed individual (as defined in § 301.7705-1(b)(14) of this chapter) in that capacity;

(3) To any CPEO contract that a CPEO enters into while its certification has been suspended by the IRS; or

(4) To any CPEO whose certification has been revoked or voluntarily terminated for periods after the effective date of revocation or voluntary termination.

(g) *Reporting and recordkeeping.*—(1) *Reporting and recordkeeping for employers.*—A CPEO that is treated as an employer of a covered employee pursuant to paragraph (a) of this section must meet all reporting and recordkeeping requirements described in subtitle F of the Code that are applicable to employers in a manner consistent with such treatment.

(2) *Reporting on magnetic media.*—(i) *In general.*—A CPEO must file on magnetic media any Form 940, "Employer's Annual Federal Unemployment (FUTA) Tax Return," Form 941, "Employer's QUARTERLY Federal Tax Return," and Form 943, "Employer's Annual Federal Tax Return for Agricultural Employees," and all required accompanying schedules, as well as such other returns, schedules, and other required forms and documents as is required by further guidance.

(ii) *Waiver.*—The Commissioner may waive the requirements of this paragraph (g)(2) in case of undue economic hardship (including economic hardship resulting from temporary software and technological issues). The principal factor in determining hardship will be the amount, if any, by which the cost of filing the return, schedule, or other required form or document on magnetic media in accordance with this paragraph (g)(2) exceeds the cost of filing on or by other media. A request for a waiver must be made in accordance with applicable guidance. The waiver must specify the type of filing (that is, the name of the form or schedule) and the period to which it applies. In addition, the waiver will be subject to such terms and conditions regarding the method of filing as may be prescribed by the Commissioner in further guidance.

(iii) *Magnetic media.*—The term magnetic media means any magnetic media permitted under applicable guidance. These generally include electronic filing, as well as other media specifically permitted under the applicable guidance.

(3) *Reporting to the IRS by CPEOs.*—A CPEO must report the following to the IRS in such time and manner, and including such information, as the Commissioner may prescribe in further guidance:

(i) The commencement or termination of any CPEO contract (as defined in § 301.7705-1(b)(3) of this chapter) with a customer, or any service agreement as described in § 31.3504-2(b)(2) with a client, and the name and employer identification number (EIN) of such customer or client.

(ii) With any Form 940, Form 941, and Form 943 that it files, all required schedules, including, but not limited to, the applicable Schedule R (or any successor form), containing such information as the Commissioner may require about each of its customers under a CPEO contract (as defined in § 301.7705-1(b)(3) of this chapter) and each of its clients under a service agreement (as described in § 31.3504-2(b)(2)). A CPEO must file Form 940, Form 941, and Form 943, along with all required schedules, on magnetic media, unless the CPEO is granted a waiver by the Commissioner in accordance with paragraph (g)(2)(ii) of this section.

(iii) A periodic verification that it continues to meet the requirements of § 301.7705-2 of this chapter, as described in § 301.7705-2(j).

(iv) Any change that materially affects the continuing accuracy of any agreement or information that was previously made or provided by the CPEO to the IRS, as described in § 301.7705-2(k) of this chapter.

(v) A copy of its audited financial statements and an opinion of a certified public accountant regarding such financial statements, as described in § 301.7705-2(e)(1) of this chapter.

(vi) The quarterly statements, assertions, and attestations regarding those assertions described in § 301.7705-2(f)(1) of this chapter.

(vii) Any information the IRS determines is necessary to promote compliance with respect to the credits described in paragraph (e)(2) of this section and provided in section 3302.

(viii) Any other information the Commissioner may prescribe in further guidance.

(4) *Reporting to customers by CPEOs.*—A CPEO must meet the following reporting requirements with respect to its customers in such time and manner, and including such information, as the Commissioner may prescribe in further guidance:

(i) Provide each of its customers with the information necessary for the customer to claim the credits described in paragraph (e)(2) of this section.

(ii) Notify any customer if its CPEO contract has been transferred to another person (or if another person will report, withhold, or pay, under such other person's EIN, any applicable federal employment taxes with respect to the wages of any individuals covered by its CPEO contract) and provide the customer with the name and EIN of such other person.

(iii) If the CPEO's certification is suspended or revoked as described in § 301.7705-2(n) of this chapter, notify each of its current customers of such suspension or revocation.

(iv) If any covered employees are not, or cease to be, work site employees because they perform services at a location at which the

85 percent threshold described in § 301.7705-1(b)(17) of this chapter is not met, notify the customer that it may also be liable for federal employment taxes imposed on remuneration remitted by the CPEO to such covered employees, as described in paragraph (a)(3) of this section.

(5) *Information and agreements in any contract or agreement between a CPEO and a customer or client.*—Any CPEO contract (as defined in § 301.7705-1(b)(3) of this chapter) between a CPEO and a customer or service agreement described in § 31.3504-2(b)(2) between a CPEO and a client must—

(i) In the case of a contract that is a CPEO contract—

(A) Contain the name and EIN of the CPEO reporting, withholding, and paying any applicable federal employment taxes with respect to any remuneration paid to individuals covered by the contract or agreement;

(B) Require the CPEO to provide to the customer the notices and information required by paragraph (g)(4) of this section;

(C) Describe the information that the CPEO will provide that is necessary for the customer to claim the credits specified in paragraph (e)(2) of this section; and

(D) Require the CPEO to notify the customer that the customer may also be liable for federal employment taxes on remuneration remitted by the CPEO to covered employees if the work sites at which they perform services do not (or ever cease to) meet the 85 percent threshold described in § 301.7705-1(b)(17) of this chapter; and

(ii) In the case of a service agreement described in § 31.3504-2(b)(2) that is not a CPEO contract (and thus the individuals covered by that contract are not covered employees), or if this section does not apply to the contract under paragraph (f) of this section, notify, or be accompanied by a notification to, the client that the service agreement or contract is not covered by section 3511 and does not alter the client's liability for federal employment taxes on remuneration remitted by the CPEO to the employees covered by the service agreement or contract.

(h) *Penalties and additions to tax.*—(1) *In general.*—A CPEO that is treated as an employer of a covered employee under this section and that is required to meet the reporting requirements of an employer is subject to the same penalties and additions to tax as an employer with respect to such reporting requirements, including, but not limited to, penalties and additions to tax under sections 6651, 6656, 6672, 6721, 6722, and 6723.

(2) *Failures to timely make reports required under section 3511.*—CPEOs are subject to penalty under section 6652(n) with respect to reports required to be made to the IRS in paragraphs (g)(1) and (3) of this section and reports required to be made to customers in paragraph (g)(4) of this section.

(3) *Failures to attach Schedule R.*—A CPEO is subject to penalty under section 6652(n) for failure to attach Schedule R (or successor form) to Forms 941, 940, or 943 as required by paragraph (g)(3)(ii) of this section. A CPEO is also subject to penalty under section 6723 for failure to include the EIN of each customer on Schedule R of Form 941, 940, or 943. See § 301.6723-1 of this chapter for the application of the section 6723 penalty in the case of multiple failures on a single document.

(4) *Failures to file on magnetic media.*—With respect to the requirement in paragraph (g)(3)(ii) of this section that a CPEO must file Forms 940, 941, and 943, along with all required schedules, on magnetic media, a failure to file on magnetic media does not constitute a failure to file for purposes of section 6651(a)(1) nor does it constitute a failure to make a report for purposes of section 6652(n). Rather, the requirement to file Forms 940, 941, and 943 on magnetic media is a condition of maintaining certification as a CPEO.

(i) *Applicability date.*—The rules in this section apply on and after May 3, 2019. [Reg. § 31.3511-1.]

☐ [*T.D.* 9860, 5-23-2019.]

[The next page is 62,351.]

# MISCELLANEOUS EXCISE TAXES
## Retail Excise Taxes
### See p. 20,601 for regulations not amended to reflect law changes

[Reg. §48.0-1]

§48.0-1. Introduction.—The regulations in this part 48 are designated "Manufacturers and Retailers Excise Tax Regulations." The regulations relate to the excise taxes imposed by chapter[s] 31 and 32 of the Internal Revenue Code. Chapter 31 (relating to retail taxes) imposes tax on certain luxury items, special fuels, fuel used in commercial transportation on inland waterways, and heavy trucks and trailers. Chapter 32 (relating to manufacturers taxes) imposes tax on gas guzzler automobiles, highway-type tires, taxable fuel, aviation fuel, coal, certain vaccines, sporting goods, and taxable medical devices. Although chapter 32 also imposes a tax on firearms, this tax is under the jurisdiction of the Bureau of Alcohol, Tobacco, and Firearms. See part 40 of this chapter for regulations relating to returns, payments, and deposits of taxes imposed by chapters 31 and 32 (other than the tax on firearms imposed by section 4181). [Reg. §48.0-1.]

☐ [T.D. 8442, 10-21-92. Amended by T.D. 8659, 3-13-96 and T.D. 9604, 12-5-2012.]

[Reg. §48.0-2]

§48.0-2. General definitions and attachment of tax.—(a) Meaning of terms.—As used in the regulations in this part, unless otherwise expressly indicated—

(1) The terms defined in the provisions of law contained in the regulations in this part shall have the meanings so assigned to them.

(2) [Reserved]

(3) The term "calendar quarter" means a period of 3 calendar months ending on March 31, June 30, September 30, or December 31.

(4)(i) The term "manufacturer" includes any person who produces a taxable article from scrap, salvage, or junk material, or from new or raw material, by processing, manipulating, or changing the form of an article or by combining or assembling two or more articles. The term also includes a "producer" and an "importer." An "importer" of a taxable article is any person who brings such an article into the United States from a source outside the United States, or who withdraws such an article from a customs bonded warehouse for sale or use in the United States. If the nominal importer of a taxable article is not its beneficial owner (for example, the nominal importer is a customs broker engaged by the beneficial owner), the beneficial owner is the "importer" of the article for purposes of chapter 32 and is liable for tax on his sale or use of the article in the United States. See section 4219 and the regulations thereunder for the circumstances under which sales by persons other than the manufacturer or importer are subject to the manufacturers excise tax.

(ii) Under certain circumstances, as where a person manufactures or produces a taxable article for another person who furnishes materials under an agreement whereby the person who furnished the materials retains title thereto and to the finished article, the person for whom the taxable article is manufactured or produced, and not the person who actually manufactures or produces it, will be considered the manufacturer.

(iii) A manufacturer who sells a taxable article in a knockdown condition is liable for the tax as a manufacturer. Whether the person who buys such component parts and assembles a taxable article from them will also be liable for tax as a further manufacturer of a taxable article will depend on the relative amount of labor, material, and overhead required to assemble the completed article and on whether the article is assembled for a business or personal use. See section 4218 and the regulations thereunder.

(5) The term "sale" means an agreement whereby the seller transfers the property (that is, the title or the substantial incidents of ownership) in goods to the buyer for a consideration called the price, which may consist of money, services, or other things.

(6) The term "taxable article" means any article taxable under section 4041 or chapter 32, Subtitle D, of the Code.

(7) The term "vendor" includes a lessor except that, with respect to the manufacturers excise taxes, this rule applies only where the lessor is also the manufacturer of the article.

(8) The term "purchaser" includes a lessee except that, with respect to the manufacturers excise taxes, this rule applies only where the lessor is also the manufacturer of the article.

(9) The term "exporter" means the person named as shipper or consignor in the export bill of lading.

(10) The term "exportation" means the severance of an article from the mass of things belonging with the United States with the intention of uniting it with the mass of things belonging within some foreign country or within a possession of the United States.

(11) The term "possession of the United States" includes Guam, the Midway Islands, Palmyra, the Panama Canal Zone, the Commonwealth of Puerto Rico, American Samoa, the Virgin Islands, and Wake Island.

(b) Attachment of tax.—(1) For purposes of this part, the manufacturers excise tax generally attaches when the title to the article sold passes from the manufacturer to a purchaser, and the retailers excise tax generally attaches when the title to the article sold passes from the retailer to a purchaser.

(2) When title passes is dependent upon the intention of the parties as gathered from the contract of sale and the attendant circumstances. In the absence of expressed intention, the legal rules of presumption followed in the jurisdiction where the sale is made govern in determining when title passes.

(3) In the case of a sale on credit, the tax attaches whether or not the purchase price is actually collected.

(4) Where a consignor (such as a manufacturer) consigns articles to a consignee (such as a dealer), retaining ownership in them until they are disposed of by the consignee, title does not pass, and the tax does not attach, until sale by the consignee. Where the relationship between a manufacturer and a dealer is that of principal and agent, title does not pass, and the tax does not attach, until sale by the dealer.

(5) In the case of a lease, an installment sale, a conditional sale, or a chattel mortgage arrangement or similar arrangement creating a security interest, a proportionate part of the tax attaches to each payment. See section 4217 and the regulations thereunder for a limitation on the amount of tax payable on lease payments.

(6) In the case of use by the manufacturer, the tax attaches at the time the use begins. [Reg. §48.0-2.]

☐ [T.D. 6408. Amended by T.D. 7536, 3-27-78 and T.D. 8879, 3-30-2000.]

[Reg. §48.0-3]

§48.0-3. Exemption certificates.—Several sections of the regulations in this part, relating to sales exempt from retailers or manufacturers excise tax, require the retailer or manufacturer (as the case may be) to obtain an exemption certificate from the purchaser to substantiate the exempt character of the sale. Many of these sections also contain specimen forms of acceptable exemption certificates. However, any form of exemption certificate will be acceptable if it includes all the information required to be contained in such a certificate by the pertinent sections of the regulations in this part. If it contains all the required information, a form of exemption certificate that is processed by data processing equipment is acceptable. [Reg. §48.0-3.]

☐ [T.D. 7536, 3-27-78. Amended by T.D. 8043, 8-8-85.]

[Reg. §48.4041-0]

§48.4041-0. Applicability of regulations relating to diesel fuel after December 31, 1993.—Sections 48.4041-3 through 48.4041-17 do not apply to sales or uses of diesel fuel after December 31, 1993. For rules relating to the diesel fuel tax imposed by section 4041 after that date, see §48.4082-4. [Reg. §48.4041-0.]

☐ [T.D. 8659, 3-13-96.]

[Reg. §48.4041-3]

§48.4041-3. Application of tax on sales of special motor fuel for use in motor vehicles and motorboats.—(a) In general.—The tax imposed by paragraph (2)(A) of section 4041(a), (or before April 1, 1983, paragraph (1) of section 4041 (b)), applies to the taxable sale of special motor fuel by any person to an owner, lessee, or other operator of a motor vehicle or motorboat, for use as a fuel in the motor vehicle or motorboat. The tax does not apply to special motor fuel sold for use on or after April 1, 1983, and before October 1, 1988, in an off-highway business use.

(b) Liability for tax.—The tax on the taxable sale of special motor fuel is payable by the person who sells the special motor fuel to the owner, lessee, or other operator of a motor vehicle or motorboat.

(c) Rate of tax.—(1) In general.—Tax is imposed on the sale of special motor fuel at the rate applicable on the date on which the special motor fuel is sold. See §48.4041-1(b)(2) for rates. The test of taxability at the rates specified in §48.4041-1(b)(2)(i)(A) and (ii)(A) is whether the fuel is to be used in a motor vehicle or motorboat. For purposes of paragraphs (c)(2) and (3) of this section, the term "qualified business use" has the same meaning as that given to the term "off-highway business use" by section 6421(d)(2).

(2) *Special motor fuel sold for use as a fuel in a motor vehicle.*—Tax at the rates specified in paragraphs (b)(2)(i)(A) and (ii)(A) of § 48.4041-1 applies in the case of the sale of special motor fuel for use as a fuel in a motor vehicle. Tax at the rates specified in that section applies regardless of whether the motor vehicle is a highway vehicle. However, a reduced rate of tax from that imposed by paragraphs (b)(2)(i)(A) of § 48.4041-1 is allowed by paragraph (b)(2)(i)(C) of § 48.4041-1 if special motor fuel is sold for use in a qualified business use. An exemption from the tax imposed by paragraph (b)(2)(ii)(A) of § 48.4041-1 is allowed by paragraph (b)(2)(ii)(C) of § 48.4041-1 if the special motor fuel is sold for use in an off-highway business use.

(3) *Special motor fuel sold for use as fuel in a motorboat.*—Tax at the rates specified in paragraphs (b)(2)(i)(A) and (ii)(A) of § 48.4041-1 applies in the case of the sale of special motor fuel for use as fuel in a motorboat. The qualified business use reduced rate of tax set forth in paragraph (b)(2)(i)(C) of § 48.4041-1 and the off-highway business use exemption set forth in paragraph (b)(2)(ii)(C) of § 48.4041-1 are not applicable to motorboats unless the motorboat is a vessel employed in the fisheries or whaling business. See section 6421(d)(2)(B).

(d) *Example.*—Application of the tax to the sale of special motor fuels may be illustrated by the following example.

*Example.* The N Company is engaged in the manufacture of ceramic products. It has a vehicle which is used to haul clay from a clay pit to its factory. This vehicle has not been registered for highway use and under the applicable State law is not required to be registered for highway use since none of the hauling of clay is done on public highways. The N Company also uses a ditch digging machine in the vicinity of the clay pit for the construction of drains. A fork lift truck is used to move cartons of merchandise from place to place inside the company's warehouse and to assist in the loading of merchandise onto the company's highway trucks for delivery to purchasers. The highway trucks are registered by the State for use on highways. Special motor fuel is used for the operation of all of these items of equipment. Before April 1, 1983, the special motor fuel sold for use as a fuel in the registered highway trucks is subject to tax at the rate specified in § 48.4041-1(b)(2)(i)(A). On or after January 1, 1979, and before April 1, 1983, the special motor fuel sold for use as a fuel in the unregistered truck used to haul clay from the pit to the factory and in the fork lift truck, assuming both of these are used in qualified business uses, is subject to tax at the rate specified in § 48.4041-1(b)(2)(i)(C). If the unregistered truck and forklift are not used in qualified business uses, then the special motor fuel sold for use in these vehicles is taxable at the rate specified in § 48.4041-1(b)(2)(i)(A) since both are motor vehicles. No tax is payable with respect to the special motor fuel sold for use in the ditch digging machine since that machine is not a motor vehicle. On and after April 1, 1983, and before October 1, 1988, special motor fuel sold for use in the registered trucks is taxable at the rate specified in § 48.4041-1(b)(2)(ii)(A) because the trucks are motor vehicles. On and after April 1, 1983, and before October 1, 1988, special motor fuel sold for use in the unregistered truck and the fork lift, assuming that both vehicles are used in off-highway business uses, is exempt from tax as specified in § 48.4041-1(b)(2)(ii)(C). If the unregistered truck and fork lift are not used in off-highway business uses, then the special motor fuel sold for use in these vehicles is taxable at the rate specified in § 48.4041-1(b)(2)(ii)(A) since both are motor vehicles. No tax is payable with respect to the special motor fuel sold for use in the ditch digging machine since that machine is not a motor vehicle.

(e) *Cross reference.*—(1) For the tax applicable in certain cases based on the use of special motor fuel as a fuel in a motor vehicle or motorboat, see § 48.4041-6.

(2) For the definition of the terms "highway", "motor vehicle", "special motor fuel", and "registered", see paragraphs (a), (c), (f), and (i) of § 48.4041-8. For the definition of the term "off-highway business use", see section 6421(d)(2).

(3) For the exemption from tax with respect to special motor fuel sold for use on a farm for farming purposes or as supplies for vessels, see §§ 48.4041-9 and 48.4041-10, respectively.

(4) For credit or refund of tax paid on special motor fuel resold or used otherwise than for the purpose for which purchased, see section 6427(a). [Reg. § 48.4041-3.]

☐ [T.D. 8066, 1-2-86.]

#### [Reg. § 48.4041-4]

**§ 48.4041-4. Application of tax on sales of liquid for use as fuel in aircraft in noncommercial aviation.**—(a) *In general.*—The taxes imposed by subparagraphs (1)(A) and (2)(A) of section 4041(c) apply to the taxable sale of any liquid by any person to an owner, lessee, or other operator of an aircraft, for use as a fuel in the aircraft in noncommercial aviation.

(b) *Liability of tax.*—The tax on the taxable sale of any liquid used as fuel in aircraft in noncommercial aviation is payable by the person who sells the liquid to the owner, lessee, or operator of an aircraft in noncommercial aviation.

(c) *Rate of tax.*—Tax is imposed on the sale of liquids used as fuel in aircraft in noncommercial aviation at the rate applicable on the date on which the liquid is sold. See § 48.4041-1(b)(3) for rates.

(d) *Cross references.*—(1) For the tax applicable on the basis of the use of fuel in an aircraft in noncommercial aviation, see § 48.4041-6.

(2) For the definition of the term "noncommercial aviation", see paragraph (j) of § 48.4041-8.

(3) For the exemption of tax with respect to liquids used as fuel in aircraft in noncommercial aviation sold for use on a farm for farming purposes or as supplies for vessels or aircraft, see §§ 48.4041-9 and 48.4041-10, respectively. For tax-free sales if sellers and purchasers are registered, see § 48.4041-11.

(4) For credit or refund of tax paid on fuel used in noncommercial aviation that is resold or used otherwise than for the purpose for which purchased, see section 6427(a).

(e) *Effective date.*—The provisions of this section shall apply to sales or uses occurring before October 1, 1980, and to sales or uses occurring on or after September 1, 1982, and ending before January 1, 1988. [Reg. § 48.4041-4.]

☐ [T.D. 8066, 1-2-86.]

#### [Reg. § 48.4041-5]

**§ 48.4041-5. Sales of diesel and special motor fuels and fuel for use in aircraft; rules of general application.**—(a) *Taxability of liquid fuel delivered into purchaser's tanks.*—(1) *Fuel supply tanks.*—(i) The sale of diesel fuel to an owner, lessee, or other operator of a diesel-powered highway vehicle, or of special motor fuel to an owner, lessee, or other operator of a motor vehicle or motorboat, or of fuel to an owner, lessee, or other operator of an aircraft used in noncommercial aviation is considered a taxable sale of the liquid fuel if the liquid fuel is delivered by the seller into the fuel supply tank of the vehicle, motorboat, or aircraft. For purposes of this paragraph (a), liquid fuel sold at a location unattended by the seller (such as under a cardlock or meter system) on or after January 2, 1986, is considered to be delivered into the fuel supply tank by the seller except as provided in paragraph (a)(1)(ii) of this section. In this regard, see section 6427(a) for credit or refund of tax if liquid fuel acquired in a transaction subject to tax is used in a nontaxable use.

(ii) If the seller maintains special devices at the unattended location to account accurately for sales of liquid fuel for nontaxable uses (such as assigning a separate "nontaxable" meter or, in a cardlock system, issuing a special "nontaxable" card to a customer who regularly purchases fuel for nontaxable uses), then such sales of liquid fuel shall be considered nontaxable. The seller must maintain sufficient records of such nontaxable sales and include in these records the name of the purchaser, the date of the purchase, and the quantity of fuel purchased in each sale.

(2) *Bulk tanks.*—The sale of diesel fuel to an owner, lessee, or other operator of a diesel-powered highway vehicle, or of special motor fuel to an owner, lessee, or other operator of a motor vehicle or motorboat, or of fuel to an owner, lessee, or other operator of an aircraft used in noncommercial aviation is considered a taxable sale of the liquid fuel if—

(i) The liquid fuel is delivered by the seller into a bulk supply tank (or other container) that is not the fuel supply tank of a vehicle, motorboat, or aircraft; and

(ii) The purchaser furnishes a written statement to the seller before or at the time of the sale stating that the entire quantity of the liquid fuel covered by the sale is for a taxable purpose as a fuel in such a vehicle, motorboat, or aircraft. If the purchaser fails to provide the written statement required by paragraph (a)(2)(ii) of this section, the purchaser is liable for the tax on the later taxable sale or use. If a purchaser acquires both fuel that is to be used for taxable purposes and fuel that is to be used for nontaxable purposes, and the fuel that is to be used for taxable purposes is stored in a different storage tank (or container) from the tank used to store the fuel to be used for nontaxable purposes, the written statement described in paragraph (a)(2)(ii) of this section will relate to the fuel to be used for taxable purposes if proper records are kept by the purchaser that sufficiently identify the tanks (or containers) into which tax-paid fuel is delivered and the quantities of fuel delivered into those tanks (or containers). If only occasional sales for delivery into a bulk storage tank (or other container) are made to a purchaser, a separate statement must be furnished for each order. However, if sales are regularly or frequently made to a purchaser, a written statement covering all orders for a specified period not to exceed 12 calendar quarters is acceptable.

(b) *Sales for resale and to consignees.*—(1) A sale to a dealer for resale is not subject to tax even if it is known at the time of the sale that the liquid fuel will be resold by the dealer for use as a fuel in a diesel-powered highway vehicle, motor vehicle, motorboat, or aircraft.

(2) The tax is payable by the person who makes the taxable sale. If a taxable liquid fuel is consigned to a person for sale and the consignor retains ownership in the liquid fuel until it is disposed of by the consignee, the consignor is the person liable for the tax when a taxable sale of the liquid fuel is made by the consignee. If the consignor transfers ownership in the taxable liquid fuel to the consignee before sale of the liquid fuel by the consignee, the consignee is the person liable for the tax upon a subsequent taxable sale of the liquid. However, if ownership of the liquid fuel is transferred back to the consignor or to another person before a taxable sale is made, as described in paragraph (a) of this section, and thereafter a taxable sale of the liquid fuel is made by such person or by another person acting as the person's agent, such person is liable for the tax. See paragraph (d) of §48.4041-8 for definition of the term "taxable liquid fuel." [Reg. §48.4041-5.]

□ [*T.D. 8066, 1-2-86. Amended by T.D. 8154, 8-24-87.*]

### [Reg. §48.4041-6]

**§48.4041-6. Application of tax on use of taxable liquid fuel.**— (a) *In general.*—(1) *Diesel fuel.*—(i) If, before April 1, 1983, a person acquires any diesel fuel by any means other than through a transaction subject to tax under section 4041(a)(1) and uses it as a fuel in a diesel powered highway vehicle, the person is liable for a tax under section 4041(a)(2) on the quantity of diesel fuel so used at the appropriate rate set forth in §48.4041-1(b)(1)(i). If a person acquired any diesel fuel through a transaction which is subject to tax at the rate set forth in paragraph (b)(1)(i)(C) or (D) of §48.4041-1, and uses it for a use described in paragraph (b)(1)(i)(A) or (B) of §48.4041-1 the person is liable for an additional tax under section 4041(a)(2) on the quantity of diesel fuel so used. See §48.4041-1(b)(1)(i)(E), (F), or (G) for the applicable rate of tax. See section 6427(a) for credit or refund of tax where diesel fuel acquired in a transaction subject to tax at the rate set forth in paragraph (b)(1)(i)(A) or (B) of §48.4041-1 is used as described in paragraph(b)(1)(i)(C) or (D) of §48.4041-1 or in a nontaxable use.

(ii) On or after April 1, 1983, and before August 1, 1984, if a person acquires any diesel fuel by any means other than through a transaction subject to tax under section 4041(a)(1)(A) and uses it as a fuel in a diesel-powered highway vehicle, the person is liable for a tax under section 4041(a)(1)(B) on the quantity of diesel fuel so used at the appropriate rate set forth in paragraph (b)(1)(ii) of §48.4041-1. If a person acquired any diesel fuel through a transaction for which no tax is imposed by reason of paragraph (b)(1)(ii)(C) of §48.4041-1 and uses it in other than a nontaxable use, the person is liable for a tax under section 4041(a)(1)(B) on the quantity of fuel so used. See paragraph (b)(1)(ii)(D) or (E) of §48.4041-1 for the applicable rate of tax. See section 6427(a) for credit or refund of tax where diesel fuel acquired in a transaction subject to tax at the rate set forth in paragraph (b)(1)(ii)(A) of §48.4041-1 is used as described in paragraph (b)(1)(ii)(C) of §48.4041-1 or in another nontaxable use.

(iii) On or after August 1, 1984, and before October 1, 1988, if a person acquires any diesel fuel by any means other than through a transaction subject to tax under section 4041(a)(1)(A) and uses it as a fuel in a diesel-powered highway vehicle, the person is liable for a tax under section 4041(a)(1)(B) on the quantity of diesel fuel so used at the appropriate rate set forth in paragraph (b)(1)(iii) of §48.4041-1. If a person acquired any diesel fuel through a transaction for which no tax is imposed by reason of paragraph (b)(1)(iii)(C) of §48.4041-1 and uses it in other than a nontaxable use, the person is liable for a tax under section 4041(a)(1)(B) on the quantity of fuel so used. See paragraph (b)(1)(iii)(D) of §48.4041-1 for the applicable rate of tax. See section 6427(a) for credit or refund of tax where diesel fuel acquired in a transaction subject to tax at the rate set forth in paragraph (b)(1)(iii)(A) of §48.4041-1 is used as described in paragraph (b)(1)(iii)(C) of §48.4041-1 or in another nontaxable use.

(2) *Special motor fuel.*—(i) On or after January 1, 1979, and before April 1, 1983, if a person acquired any special motor fuel by any means other than through a transaction subject to tax under section 4041(b)(1) and uses it as a fuel in a motor vehicle or motorboat, the person is liable for a tax under section 4041(b)(2) on the quantity of special motor fuel so used at the appropriate rate set forth in §48.4041-1(b)(2)(i). If a person acquired any special motor fuel through a transaction which is subject to a tax at the rate set forth in paragraph (b)(2)(i)(C) of §48.4041-1 and uses it in a use other than one for which the reduced rate applies, the person is liable for an

additional tax under section 4041(b)(2) on the quantity of special motor fuel so used. See §48.4041-1(b)(2)(i)(D) or (E) for the applicable rate of tax. See section 6427(a) for credit or refund of tax where special motor fuel acquired in a transaction subject to tax at the rate set forth in paragraph (b)(2)(i)(A) of §48.4041-1 is used for a purpose described in paragraph (b)(2)(i)(C) of §48.4041-1 or in a nontaxable use.

(ii) On or after April 1, 1983, and before October 1, 1988, if a person acquired any special motor fuel by any means other than through a transaction subject to tax under section 4041(a)(2)(A) and uses it as a fuel in a motor vehicle or motorboat, the person is liable for a tax under section 4041(a)(2)(B) on the quantity of special motor fuel so used at the appropriate rate set forth in paragraph (b)(2)(ii) of §48.4041-1. If a person acquired any special motor fuel through a transaction for which no tax is imposed by reason of paragraph (b)(2)(ii)(C) of §48.4041-1 and uses it in other than a nontaxable use, the person is liable for a tax under section 4041(a)(2)(B) on the quantity of fuel so used. See paragraph (b)(2)(ii)(D) of §48.4041-1 for the applicable rate of tax. See section 6427(a) for credit or refund of tax where special motor fuel acquired in a transaction subject to tax at the rate set forth in paragraph (b)(2)(ii)(A) of §48.4041-1 is used for a purpose described in paragraph (b)(2)(ii)(C) of §48.4041-1 or in another nontaxable use.

(3) *Noncommercial aviation.*—If a person acquires any liquid fuel by any means other than through a transaction subject to tax under section 4041(c)(1)(A) or section 4041(c)(2)(A) and uses it as fuel in an aircraft in noncommercial aviation, the person is liable for a tax under section 4041(c)(1)(B) or section 4041(c)(2)(B) on the quantity of the liquid fuel so used at the appropriate rate set forth in §48.4041-1(b)(3).

(b) *Bulk purchases by users.*—Taxpayers who purchase taxable liquid fuel in bulk delivered into storage tanks or other containers and use it for taxable or nontaxable purposes or in registered and nonregistered vehicles must maintain adequate records of all fuel used for each purpose to permit verification of the tax paid and of any credits, refunds, or exemptions claimed. [Reg. §48.4041-6.]

□ [*T.D. 8066, 1-2-86.*]

### [Reg. §48.4041-7]

**§48.4041-7. Dual use of taxable liquid fuel.**—Tax applies to all taxable liquid fuel sold for use or used as a fuel in the motor which is used to propel a diesel-powered vehicle or in the motor used to propel a motor vehicle, motorboat, or aircraft, even though the motor is also used for a purpose other than the propulsion of the vehicle, motorboat, or aircraft. Thus, if the motor of a diesel-powered highway vehicle or a motorboat operates special equipment by means of a power take-off or power transfer, tax applies to all taxable liquid fuel sold for this use or so used, whether or not the special equipment is mounted on the vehicle or boat. For example, tax applies to diesel fuel sold to operate the mixing unit on a concrete mixer truck of the mixing unit is operated by means of a power take-off from the motor of the vehicle. Similarly, tax applies to all taxable liquid fuel sold for use or used in a motor propelling a fuel oil truck even though the same motor is used to operate the pump (whether or not mounted on the truck) for discharging the fuel into customers' storage tanks. However, tax does not apply to liquid fuel sold for use or used in a separate motor to operate special equipment (whether or not the equipment is mounted on the vehicle). If the taxable liquid fuel used in a separate motor is drawn from the same tank as the one which supplies fuel for the propulsion of the vehicle, a reasonable determination of the quantity of taxable liquid fuel used in such separate motor or during such period is acceptable for purposes of application of the tax. This determination must be based, however, on the operating experience of the person using the taxable liquid fuel, and the taxpayer must maintain records which support the allocation used. Devices to measure the number of miles the vehicle has traveled, such as hubometers, may be used in making a preliminary determination of the number of gallons of fuel used to propel the vehicle. In order to make a final determination of the number of gallons of fuel used to propel the vehicle, there must be added to this preliminary determination the amount of fuel consumed while idling or warming up the motor preparatory to propelling the vehicle. [Reg. §48.4041-7.]

□ [*T.D. 8066, 1-2-86.*]

### [Reg. §48.4041-8]

**§48.4041-8. Definitions.**—For purposes of the regulations in this subpart, unless otherwise expressly indicated:

(a) *Highway.*—The term "highway" includes any road (whether a Federal highway, State highway, city street, rural road, or otherwise) in the United States which is not a private roadway.

(b) *Highway vehicle.*—(1) *In general.*—The term "highway vehicle" means any self-propelled vehicle, or any trailer or semi-trailer, designed to perform a function of transporting a load over highways, whether or not also designed to perform other functions, but does not include a vehicle described in paragraph (b)(2) of this section. For purposes of this definition, a vehicle consists of a chassis, or a chassis and a body if the vehicle has a body, but does not include the vehicle's load. Therefore, in determining whether a vehicle is a "highway vehicle", it is immaterial that the vehicle is designed to perform a highway transportation function for only a particular kind of load, such as passengers, furnishings and personal effects (as in a house, office, or utility trailer), a special type of cargo, goods, supplies, or materials, or, except to the extent otherwise provided in paragraph (b)(2)(i) of this section, machinery or equipment specially designed to perform some off-highway task unrelated to highway transportation. In the case of specially designed machinery or equipment, it is also immaterial, except as provided in paragraph (b)(2)(i) of this section, that such machinery or equipment is permanently mounted on the vehicle. For purposes of paragraph (b) of this section, the term "transport" includes the term "tow". A vehicle which is not a highway vehicle within the meaning of this paragraph shall be treated as a non-highway vehicle for purposes of section 4041. Examples of vehicles that are designed to perform a function of transporting a load over the public highways are passenger automobiles, motorcycles, buses, and highway-type trucks, truck tractors, trailers, and semi-trailers.

(2) *Exceptions.*—(i) *Certain specially designed mobile machinery for nontransportation functions.*—A self-propelled vehicle, or trailer or semi-trailer, is not a highway vehicle if it (A) consists of a chassis to which there has been permanently mounted (by welding, bolting, riveting, or other means) machinery or equipment to perform a construction, manufacturing, processing, farming, mining, drilling, timbering, or other operation similar to any one of the foregoing enumerated operations if the operation of the machinery or equipment is unrelated to transportation on or off the public highways, (B) the chassis has been specially designed to serve only as a mobile carriage and mount (and a power source, where applicable) for the particular machinery or equipment involved, whether or not such machinery or equipment is in operation, and (C) by reason of such special design, such chassis could not, without substantial structural modification, be used as a component of a vehicle designed to perform a function of transporting any load other than that particular machinery or equipment or similar machinery or equipment requiring such a specially designed chassis.

(ii) *Certain vehicles specially designed for off-highway transportation.*—A self-propelled vehicle, or a trailer or semi-trailer, is not a highway vehicle if it is (A) specially designed for the primary function of transporting a particular type of load other than over the public highway in connection with a construction, manufacturing, processing, farming, mining, drilling, timbering, or other operation similar to any one of the foregoing enumerated operations, and (B) if by reason of such special design, the use of such vehicle to transport such load over the public highways is substantially limited or substantially impaired. For purposes of applying the rule of clause (b) of this paragraph (b)(2)(ii), account may be taken of whether the vehicle may travel at regular highway speeds, requires a special permit for highway use, is overweight, overheight or overwidth for regular use, and any other relevant considerations. Solely for purposes of determinations under this paragraph (b)(2)(ii), where there is affixed to the vehicle equipment used for loading, unloading, storing, vending, handling, processing, preserving, or otherwise caring for a load transported by the vehicle over the public highways, the functions are related to the transportation of a load over the public highways even though the functions may be performed off the public highways.

(iii) *Certain trailers and semi-trailers specially designed to perform nontransportation functions off the public highways.*—A trailer or semi-trailer is not a highway vehicle if it is specially designed to serve no purpose other than providing an enclosed stationary shelter for the carrying on of a function which is directly connected with and necessary to, and at the off-highway site of, a construction, manufacturing, processing, mining, drilling, farming, timbering, or other operation similar to any one of the foregoing enumerated operations, such as a trailer specially designed to serve as an office for such an operation.

(3) *Optional application.*—For purposes of section 4041, if any rules existing immediately prior to January 13, 1977, would, if applicable, unequivocally resolve an issue involving the definition of a highway vehicle with respect to a period prior to such date, at the option of the taxpayer, such rules existing prior to such date shall be applied to resolve the issue for all periods prior to such date, and the rules of paragraph (b)(1) and (2) of this section, which define the

term "highway vehicle", shall not apply with respect to such issue for all periods prior to such date.

(4) *Diesel-powered highway vehicle.*—The term "diesel-powered highway vehicle" means any highway vehicle (within the meaning of paragraph (b)(1) of this section) which is also a motor vehicle (as defined in paragraph (c) of this section) and which uses diesel fuel (as defined in paragraph (e) of this section) for propulsion purposes,

(c) *Motor vehicles.*—The term "motor vehicle" includes all types of vehicles propelled by motor that are designed for carrying or towing loads from one place to another, regardless of the type of load or material carried or towed and whether or not the vehicle is registered or required to be registered for highway use. Included are fork lift trucks used to carry loads at railroad stations, industrial plants, warehouses, etc. The term does not include farm tractors, trench diggers, power shovels, bulldozers, road graders or rollers, and similar equipment which does not carry or tow a load; nor does it include any vehicle which moves exclusively on rails. For periods prior to January 6, 1977, a vehicle which is designed for towing, but not carrying, loads shall not be considered to be a motor vehicle.

(d) *Taxable liquid fuel.*—The term "taxable liquid fuel" (or "taxable liquid") means any liquid which is either—

(1) Diesel fuel as defined in paragraph (e) of this section,

(2) Special motor fuel as defined in paragraph (f) of this section, or

(3) Any liquid fuel used in an aircraft in "noncommercial aviation", as defined in paragraph (h) of this section.

(e) *Diesel fuel.*—The term "diesel fuel" means any liquid (other than a product taxable as gasoline under the provisions of section 4081) which is sold for use or used as a fuel in a diesel-powered highway vehicle.

(f) *Special motor fuel.*—(1) Except as provided in paragraph (f)(2) of this section, *special motor fuel* means any liquid fuel, including—

(i) Any liquefied petroleum gas (such as propane, butane, pentane, or mixtures of the same);

(ii) Liquefied natural gas; or

(iii) Benzol, benezene, naptha, or any other liquid, whether a refined, partly refined, or unrefined product, 10 percent of which has been recovered when the thermometer reads 347° F. (175° C.) or 95 percent of which has been recovered when the thermometer reads 464°F. (240° C.) when subjected to distillation in accordance with the "Standard Method of Test for Distillation of Gasoline, Naptha, Kerosene, and Similar Petroleum Products" (A.S.T.M. designation: D86) of the American Society for Testing Materials, regardless of the trade name under which sold.

(2) The term "special motor fuel" does not include any product taxable under the provisions of section 4081, nor does it include "kerosene, gas oil, or fuel oil", as defined in paragraph (g) of this section.

(g) *Kerosene, gas oil, or fuel oil.*—(1) The term "kerosene, gas oil, or fuel oil" means any product (i) 10 percent of which has not been recovered when the thermometer reads 347° F. (175° C.), and (ii) 95 percent of which has not been recovered when the thermometer reads 464° F. (240° C.), when subjected to distillation in accordance with the "Standard Method of Test for Distillation of Gasoline, Naptha, Kerosene, and Similar Petroleum Products" (A.S.T.M. designation: D86) of the American Society for Testing Materials.

(2) Products designated as kerosene, gas oil, or fuel oil which do not fall within the specifications of both paragraphs (g)(1)(i) and (ii) of this section are taxable as special motor fuel if sold or used as a fuel in a motor vehicle or motorboat.

(h) *Fuel used in the aircraft in noncommercial aviation.*—The term "fuel used in an aircraft in noncommercial aviation" means any liquid (including any product taxable under section 4081) that is sold for use or used as a fuel in an aircraft in noncommercial aviation (as defined in paragraph (j) of this section).

(i) *Registered.*—The term "registered", when used with reference to a highway vehicle, means—

(1) Registered for highway use under the laws of any State, District of Columbia, or foreign country, or

(2) Required to be registered for highway use under the law of the State, District of Columbia, or foreign country in which it is operated or situated. Any highway vehicle which is operated under a dealer's tag, license, or permit is considered to be registered. A highway vehicle is not considered to be "registered" solely because there has been issued a special permit for operation of the vehicle at particular times and under specified conditions. However, a highway vehicle which is required to be registered and which also has been issued a special permit for operation of the vehicle under specified

conditions, such as carrying an oversized load, is still considered to be "registered".

(j) *Noncommercial aviation.*—The term "noncommercial aviation" means any use of an aircraft, other than in a business of transporting persons or property for compensation or hire by air. The term also includes any use of an aircraft, in a business described in the preceding sentence, which is properly allocable to any transportation exempt from taxes imposed by sections 4261 (transportation of persons) and 4271 (transportation of property) by reason of section 4281 (use of small aircraft on nonestablished lines) or 4282 (transportation of members of affiliated group). [Reg. § 48.4041-8.]

☐ [*T.D. 8066, 1-2-86. Amended by T.D. 8609, 8-4-95.*]

### [Reg. § 48.4041-9]

**§ 48.4041-9. Exemption for farm use.**—(a) *In general.*—The tax imposed by section 4041 does not apply to diesel fuel or special motor fuel, or fuel used in noncommercial aviation, sold for use or used on a farm in the United States for farming purposes. The tax applies in the case of diesel fuel delivered into the fuel supply tank of a highway vehicle, or special motor fuel delivered into the fuel supply tank of a motor vehicle or motorboat, even if it is known that the liquid fuel is to be used on a farm for farming purposes. Credit or refund of the tax paid in such case may be claimed as provided by section 6427(c) upon proof that the taxable liquid was used on a farm for farming purposes. A tax-free sale of fuel delivered into the fuel supply tank of an aircraft in noncommercial aviation where such fuel is to be used on the farm for farming purposes may be made only if the requirements of § 48.4041-11 are met. The terms "used on a farm for farming purposes", and related terms, have the same meaning for purposes of the exemption in section 4041(f) and the regulations in this section as these terms are defined in paragraphs (1), (2), and (3) of section 6420(c) and the regulations contained in § 48.6420-4.

(b) *Application of exemption.*—The exemption referred to in paragraph (a) of this section does not apply with respect to diesel fuel or special motor fuel or fuel used in noncommercial aviation sold for use or used for nonfarming purposes, or diesel fuel or special motor fuel or fuel used in noncommercial aviation sold for use or used off a farm, regardless of the nature of the use. Thus, if a vehicle, motorboat, or aircraft is used both on a farm and off the farm, or if it is used on a farm both for farming and nonfarming purposes, the exemption applies only with respect to that portion of the diesel fuel or special motor fuel or fuel used in noncommercial aviation which is sold for use or used "on a farm for farming purposes". For purposes of this exemption, it is immaterial whether or not a vehicle is registered for highway use. However, the actual use of the vehicle and the place where it is used are material. For example, if a truck used on a farm for farming purposes is also used on the highways (even though in connection with operating the farm), tax applies to that diesel fuel or special motor fuel which is sold for use or used in operating the truck on the highways, since the fuel was used off the farm.

(c) *Termination of exemption.*—The exemption referred to in paragraph (a) of this section shall not apply on and after October 1, 1988. [Reg. § 48.4041-9.]

☐ [*T.D. 8066, 1-2-86.*]

### [Reg. § 48.4041-10]

**§ 48.4041-10. Exemption for use as supplies for vessels or aircraft.**—(a) *Application of exemption.*—The tax imposed by section 4041 does not apply to any fuels which are sold for use or used as supplies for vessels or aircraft within the meaning of section 4221(a)(3) and (d)(3), and § 48.4221-4. In the case of a liquid sold for use as fuel in an aircraft, a tax-free sale may be made only if the requirements of § 48.4041-11 are met. For credit or refund of tax paid on fuels which have been sold or used as supplies for vessels or aircraft, see section 6416(b)(2)(B), section 6427, and paragraph (f) of this section.

(b) *Evidence required to establish exemption.*—(1) In order to establish exemption from tax in the case of a sale of fuels for use as supplies for vessels or aircraft, it is necessary that the seller obtain from the owner, charterer, or authorized agent of the vessel or aircraft and retain in its possession a properly executed exemption certificate in the form prescribed by paragraph (c) of this section. If fuel is sold tax free for use as supplies for civil aircraft employed in foreign trade or in trade between the United States and any of its possessions, the exemption certificate must show the name of the country in which the aircraft is registered.

(2) If only occasional sales of fuels are made to a purchaser for use which is exempt from tax as provided in this section, a separate exemption certificate must be furnished for each order. However, if sales are regularly or frequently made to a purchaser for such exempt use, a certificate covering all orders for a specified period not to exceed 12 calendar quarters is acceptable. Such certificates and proper records of invoices, orders, etc., relative to tax-free sales must be kept for inspection by the district director as provided in section 6001. If a seller's records with respect to any sale claimed to be tax free do not include a proper certificate, with supporting invoices and such other evidence as may be necessary to establish the exempt character of the sale, tax is payable by the seller on the sale.

(c) *Acceptable form of exemption certificate.*—The following form of exemption certificate, which must be adhered to in substance, is acceptable for the purposes of this section.

EXEMPTION CERTIFICATE

(For use by purchasers of fuels for use as supplies for certain vessels or aircraft (section 4041(g) of the Internal Revenue Code of 1954).)

(Date) . . . . . ., 19 . . . .

The undersigned purchaser hereby certifies that he/she is the . . . . . . (owner, charterer, or authorized agent of owner or charterer) of . . . . . . . (Name of company and vessel) and that the fuel specified in the accompanying order, or as specified below or on the reverse side hereof, will be used only as fuel supplies for a vessel belonging to one of the following classes of vessels (including aircraft) to which section 4041(g) of the Internal Revenue Code applies:

(Check class to which vessel belongs):

(1) Vessels (including aircraft) engaged in foreign trade.

(2) Vessels engaged in trade between the Atlantic and Pacific ports of the United States.

(3) Vessels (including aircraft) engaged in trade between the United States and any of its possessions.

(4) Vessels employed in the fisheries or whaling business.

(5) Vessels (including aircraft) of war of the United States or a foreign nation.

The undersigned understands that if the fuels are sold or used otherwise than as stated above and for a taxable purpose specified in section 4041 of the Internal Revenue Code, the undersigned will be liable for the tax upon such sale or use. It is also understood that this certificate may not be used in purchasing fuels, if such fuels are for use as fuels in pleasure vessels, or of any type of aircraft except (1) civil aircraft employed in foreign trade or trade between the United States and any of its possessions, and otherwise entitled to exemption, and (2) aircraft owned by the United States or any foreign country and constituting a part of the armed forces thereof.

The undersigned understands that the fraudulent use of this certificate to secure exemption will subject the undersigned and all others making fraudulent use to a penalty equivalent to the amount of tax due on the sale of the fuel and, upon conviction, to a fine of not more than $10,000, or to imprisonment for not more than 5 years, or both, together with the costs of prosecution. The purchaser also understands that it must be prepared to establish by satisfactory evidence the purpose for which the fuel purchased under this certificate was used.

(Signature) . . . . . . . . . . . . . . . . . . . . .

(Address) . . . . . . . . . . . . . . . . . . . . .

. . . . . . . . . . . . . . . . . . . . . . . . . . . .

Registration Number if fuel used as supplies for civil aircraft engaged in foreign trade or in trade between the United States and any of its possessions.

(d) *Exemption certificate not obtained prior to filing of seller's excise tax return.*—If the exemption certificate is not obtained prior to the time the seller files a return covering taxes due for the period during which the sale was made, the seller must include the tax on the sale in its return for that period. However, if the certificate is later obtained, a claim for refund of the tax paid on the sale may be filed on Form 843, or a credit for the tax paid may be taken upon a subsequent return as provided by section 6416(b)(2)(B) and § 48.6416(b)-2(c).

(e) *Liability of purchaser.*—The person who purchases fuels tax free as provided in this section is liable for the tax imposed by section 4041 if the person sells or uses such fuel in a sale or use that is not exempt under any provision of law applicable to the taxes imposed by section 4041.

(f) *Credit or refund.*—(1) If diesel fuel or special motor fuel upon which the tax imposed by section 4041(a)(1) or (2), has been paid, is sold or used as supplies for vessels, a credit or refund of the tax is available under section 6416(b)(2)(B) to the retail dealer who paid the tax. As an alternative, a credit or refund of tax is available under section 6427 to the operator of the vessel who used the fuel. Where the retail dealer claims refund of the tax, the dealer, in accordance with section 6416(a), must reimburse the operator of the vessel for the amount of tax or obtain the written consent of the operator to the filing of such claim.

(2) If aviation fuel upon which the tax imposed by section 4041(c) has been paid is sold or used as supplies for aircraft, credit or refund of the tax is available only as a payment under section 6427 to the operator of the aircraft who uses the fuel or to the person who resells the fuel for such use. [Reg. § 48.4041-10.]

☐ [T.D. 8066, 1-2-86.]

### [Reg. § 48.4041-11]

**§ 48.4041-11. Tax-free sales of fuel for use in noncommercial aviation only if sellers and certain purchasers are registered.—** (a) *In general.*—Any sale of liquid fuel for delivery into a fuel supply tank of an aircraft is presumed to be subject to tax under section 4041(c), unless both the seller and purchaser of the liquid fuel are registered as provided in paragraph (b) of this section or are within one of the exceptions provided in paragraph (c) of this section.

(b) *Form of registration.*—Except as provided in paragraph (c) of this section (relating to exceptions for State and local governments, for fuel purchased from customs bonded warehouses or continuous customs custody, and for fuel purchased for use in certain aircraft of the United States or of any foreign nation), tax-free sales under section 4041(c) may be made only if both the seller and the purchaser have registered as required by section 4041(i) and this paragraph (b). If fuel is purchased tax paid for use in noncommercial aviation but is used for a nontaxable purpose, see section 6427(a) for provisions relating to refunds or credits of tax for tax-paid fuels not used for the purpose for which sold. Any person desiring to be registered in order to sell or purchase fuel free of the tax imposed by section 4041(c) must, before making any tax-free sale or purchase, file Form 637A, in duplicate. Form 637A must be filed with the District Director of Internal Revenue for the district in which the principal place of business of the applicant is located (or if the applicant has no principal place of business in the United States, with the Director of International Operations, Internal Revenue Service, Washington, DC 20224). The person who receives a validated Certificate of Registry (Validated Form 637A) is considered to be registered for purposes of selling or purchasing fuel tax free as provided in this section.

(c) *Transactions excepted from registration.*—(1) A State or local government purchasing fuel delivered into a fuel supply tank of an aircraft it operates for its exclusive use may, but is not required to, register as provided in this section.

(2) Any purchaser of aircraft fuel who purchases fuel from any customs bonded warehouse or from continuous customs custody elsewhere than in a bonded warehouse is not required to register to purchase aircraft fuel from these sources tax free.

(3) Any purchaser of fuel for use in an aircraft which is owned by the United States or any foreign country and constitutes a part of the armed forces thereof is not required to register to purchase aircraft fuel tax free.

(4) The exceptions from registration in paragraphs (c)(1), (2), and (3) of this section do not relieve purchasers from the requirement of furnishing an exemption certificate as required by paragraph (d) of this section.

(d) *Evidence of tax-free sale.*—(1) To establish the right of a purchaser to purchase fuel delivered into the fuel supply tank of an aircraft tax free, the seller must obtain from the purchaser and retain in its possession a certificate, properly executed and signed by or on behalf of the purchaser, containing the following information:

(1) Date of purchase,

(ii) The purchaser's registration number (or the exception from registration which is relied upon), and

(iii) A brief statement of the intended tax-free use of fuel (for example, by an airline in the business of transporting persons or property for hire).

(2) The following form of certificate which must be adhered to in substance, is acceptable for the purposes of this paragraph.

(Date) . . . . . . , 19 . . . .

The undersigned signifies that he/she, or the . . . . . . (Name of purchaser if other than undersigned) if the undersigned is . . . . . . (Title) holds Certificate of Registry No. . . . . . . or has not registered because . . . . . . (Brief statement of exception from registration relied upon) delivered into a supply tank of the subject aircraft may be purchased free of tax because the fuel will be used . . . . . . (Brief statement of tax-free use)

The undersigned understands that if the fuel is used otherwise than as stated above and for a purpose taxable under section 4041 of the Internal Revenue Code, the undersigned will be liable for the tax upon such use, and that the undersigned must be prepared to establish by satisfactory evidence the purpose for which the fuel purchased under this certificate was used.

The undersigned also understands that the fraudulent use of this certificate to secure exemption will subject the undersigned and all others making fraudulent use to a penalty equivalent to the amount of tax due on the sale of the fuel and, upon conviction, to a fine of not more than $10,000, or to imprisonment for not more than 5 years, or both, together with the costs of prosecution.

(Signature) . . . . . . . . . . . . . . . . . .

(Address) . . . . . . . . . . . . . . . . . .

(3) Except as provided in paragraph (d)(4) of this section, a separate exemption certificate must be furnished for each sale of fuel delivered into a fuel supply tank of an aircraft. If a portion of the fuel is intended to be used for a nontaxable purpose, the entire amount of the fuel may be sold tax free. Exemption certificates and proper supporting records such as invoices, orders, etc., relative to tax-free sales must be readily accessible for inspection by internal revenue officers and retained as provided in section 6001 of the Code and the regulations thereunder.

(4) If the purchaser of fuel to be used in an aircraft has reasonable grounds to believe that 90 percent or more of the total of the fuel to be purchased by it during a specified period not to exceed 12 calendar quarters will be used in a tax-free use, it may furnish each of its suppliers an exemption certificate covering all purchases for the specified period. The certificate shall be substantially in the same form as the certificate in paragraph (d)(2) of this section, except that in place of the date the purchaser shall specify the period covered by the certificate, and the purchaser shall give a brief explanation of its grounds for belief that 90 percent or more of its total fuel will be used in a tax-free use.

(5) The presumption under section 4041(i) that any liquid delivered into a fuel supply tank of an aircraft is taxable places the duty on the seller of the liquid fuel to use reasonable diligence to satisfy itself that a tax-free sale of fuel to the purchaser is allowed by law. In the absence of circumstances surrounding a sale that would raise a question as to whether a tax-free sale is allowable, the requirement of reasonable diligence is satisfied if the seller receives and retains the required certificate evidencing the right of the purchaser to buy the fuel tax free. However, if the circumstances are such as to indicate the seller has failed to use reasonable diligence, it is not relieved of liability for the tax imposed by section 4041(c). In addition, if the seller fails to obtain and retain the evidence of tax-free sales as required by this paragraph (d), it is not relieved of liability for the tax imposed by section 4041(c). [Reg. § 48.4041-11.]

☐ [T.D. 8066, 1-2-86.]

### [Reg. § 48.4041-12]

**§ 48.4041-12. Sales by United States, etc.—**The taxes imposed by section 4041 apply to the sale at retail of taxable liquid fuels by the United States or by any agency or instrumentality of the United States, unless by statute specifically exempted from these taxes. However, the exemptions from these taxes provided by section 4041(f), (g), and (h) and the regulations thereunder contained in this subpart F are available to the extent therein provided. [Reg. § 48.4041-12.]

☐ [T.D. 8066, 1-2-86.]

### [Reg. § 48.4041-13]

**§ 48.4041-13. Other credits or refunds.—**(a) *In general.*—For provisions relating to credit or refund of tax paid on taxable liquid fuel resold by the purchaser, or used otherwise than for the purpose for which purchased, see section 6427 and the regulations thereunder contained in Subpart O of this part.

(b) *Tax-paid liquid fuel used by local transit systems.*—For provisions relating to credit or refund in the case of taxable liquid fuel used in vehicles while engaged in furnishing scheduled common carrier public passenger land transportation service along regular routes, see section 6427(b) and the regulations thereunder contained in Subpart O of this part.

(c) *Credit or refund of diesel fuel differential amount.*—For provisions relating to an income tax credit or refund of the increased diesel fuel tax for original purchasers of diesel-powered automobiles and light trucks, see section 6427(g) and the regulations thereunder contained in Subpart O of this part. [Reg. § 48.4041-13.]

☐ [T.D. 8066, 1-2-86.]

### [Reg. § 48.4041-14]

**§ 48.4041-14. Exemption for sale to or use by certain aircraft museums.—**(a) *In general.*—(1) The tax imposed by section 4041 does not apply to liquids which are sold for use or used by an aircraft museum in an aircraft or vehicle owned by such museum and used exclusively for the procurement, care, and exhibition of aircraft of the type used for combat or transport in World War II.

(2) In the case of liquid sold for use in a aircraft owned by an aircraft museum and to be used for the purposes described in paragraph (a)(1) of this section, a tax-free sale may be made only if the requirements of § 48.4041-11 are met.

(b) *Cross reference.*—For the definition of aircraft museum, see section 4041(h)(2). [Reg. § 48.4041-14.]

☐ [*T.D.* 8066, 1-2-86.]

### [Reg. § 48.4041-15]

**§ 48.4041-15. Sales to States or political subdivisions thereof.**—(a) *Application of exemption.*—The taxes imposed by section 4041 do not apply in the case of a sale of any liquid by any person for the exclusive use of any State or any political subdivision thereof, the District of Columbia, or in the case of the use of any liquid by any State or any political subdivision thereof, or the District of Columbia, as a fuel in a motor vehicle, motorboat, or aircraft.

EXEMPTION CERTIFICATE
(For use by States and local governments. (section 4041(g)(2) of the Internal Revenue Code).)
(Date) _____, 19_____

I hereby certify that I am _____ of __ (State or local government); that I am authorized to execute this certificate; and that

(Check applicable type of certificate)

__ the liquid or liquids specified in the accompanying order, or on the reverse side hereof, (or)

__ all orders placed by the purchaser for the period commencing _____ (Date) and ending _____ (Date) (period not to exceed 12 calendar quarters) are, or will be, purchased from _____ (Name of vendor) for the exclusive use of _____ (Government unit) of _____ (State or local government).

I understand that the exemption from tax in the case of sales of liquids under this exemption certificate is limited to the sale of articles purchased for the exclusive use of a State, etc. I understand that the fraudulent use of this certificate for the purpose of securing this exemption will subject me and all parties making such fraudulent use of this certificate to a fine of not more than $10,000, or to imprisonment for not more than five years, or both, together with costs of prosecution.

_____
(Signature)

_____
(Address)

[Reg. § 48.4041-15.]

☐ [*T.D.* 7536, 3-27-78. *Redesignated by T.D.* 8066, 1-2-86.]

### [Reg. § 48.4041-16]

**§ 48.4041-16. Sales for export.**—(a) *General rule.*—In order for a sale to be exempt from tax under section 4041 as a sale for export, it is necessary that the liquid be (1) identified as having been sold by the retailer for export and (2) exported in due course. To establish exemption from tax in the case of a taxable article for export, it is necessary that the retailer maintain adequate records and have in his possession documentary evidence showing that the article was so sold.

(b) *Proof of exportation.*—Exportation may be evidenced by any one of (1) a copy of the export bill of lading issued by the delivering carrier, (2) a certificate by the agent or representative of the export carrier showing actual exportation of the liquid, (3) a certificate of lading signed by a customs officer of the foreign country to which the liquid is exported, or (4) a statement of the foreign consignee showing receipt of the liquid.

(c) *Shipment to possessions of the United States.*—The same provisions as relate to sales for export and proof of exportation will apply to sales for shipment to a possession of the United States, within the meaning of § 48.0-2. [Reg. § 48.4041-16.]

☐ [*T.D.* 7536, 3-27-78. *Redesignated by T.D.* 8066, 1-2-86.]

### [Reg. § 48.4041-17]

**§ 48.4041-17. Tax-free retail sales to certain nonprofit educational organizations.**—(a) *In general.*—The taxes imposed by section 4041 do not apply in the case of a sale of any liquid by any person to a nonprofit educational organization (as defined in paragraph (b) of this section) for its exclusive use, or in the case of the use of any

(b) *Evidence required to establish exemption.*—Any vendor claiming exemption under this section shall be prepared to produce evidence that will establish the right to exemption from the tax imposed by section 4041. Generally, orders or contracts of a State or a political subdivision thereof, or the District of Columbia, when signed by an authorized officer thereof will be accepted in support of the exemption. However, in the absence of such orders or contracts, a certificate signed by such an authorized officer that the liquid sold was purchased for the exclusive use of a State or political subdivision thereof, or the District of Columbia, will be acceptable. The certificate shall be in substantially the following form:

liquid by such an organization. In the case of a school operated as an activity of an organization described in section 501(c)(3), as referred to in paragraph (b) of this section, the liquid must be sold for the exclusive use of the school, or the liquid must be used exclusively by the school.

(b) *Definition of nonprofit educational organization.*—For purposes of section 4041(g)(4) and this section, the term "nonprofit educational organization" means an organization described in section 170(b)(1)(A)(ii), that is exempt from income tax under section 501(a), whose primary function is the presentation of formal instruction and which normally maintains a regular faculty and curriculum and normally has a regularly enrolled body of pupils or students in attendance at the place where its educational activities are regularly carried on. The term also includes a school operated as an activity of an organization described in section 501(c)(3) which is exempt from income tax under section 501(a), provided such school normally maintains a regular faculty and curriculum and normally has a regularly enrolled body of pupils or students in attendance at the place where its educational activities are regularly carried on.

(c) *Evidence required to establish tax-free sales to a nonprofit educational organization; general rule.*—To establish the right to exemption, the retailer must obtain from the purchaser and retain in its possession a properly executed certificate as set forth in paragraph (d) of this section.

(d) *Forms of exemption certificates.*—The following forms of exemption certificates will be acceptable for the purpose of this section and must be adhered to in substance.

(1) Form of certificate for exemption from retailers excise taxes for use by a nonprofit educational organization, other than a school operated as an activity of a church or other exempt organization that in itself is not a nonprofit educational organization:

EXEMPTION CERTIFICATE

(For use by a nonprofit educational organization (other than a school operated as an activity of a church or other exempt organization that in itself is not a nonprofit educational organization) purchasing articles subject to retailers excise tax for its exclusive use)

(Date) . . . . . . . . . . ., 19_____

I hereby certify that I am . . . . . . . . . . (Title) of . . . . . . . . . . (Exempt organization); that I am authorized to execute this certificate; and that the articles specified in the accompanying order or on the reverse side hereof are purchased by such organization exclusively for use in its educational activities.

I understand that this exemption certificate is for use only by a nonprofit educational organization in the tax-free purchase for its exclusive use of articles subject to the retailers excise tax; and it is agreed that if any article purchased tax free under this exemption certificate is used otherwise, such fact will be reported to the retailer from whom the tax-free purchase was made.

**Reg. § 48.4041-17(d)(1)**

The organization claiming exemption under this certificate has received a determination letter (or a ruling) from the Internal Revenue Service holding the organization to be exempt from income tax as an organization described in section 170(b)(1)(A)(ii) that is exempt from income tax under section 501(a) of the Internal Revenue Code (or has received a determination letter (or ruling) under the corresponding provisions of prior revenue laws). The date of such determination letter (or ruling) is . . . . . . . . . . . . . . . . . . . . and such determination letter (or ruling) has not been withdrawn or revoked.

I understand that the fraudulent use of this certificate for the purpose of securing this exemption will subject me and all parties making such fraudulent use of this certificate to a fine of not more than $10,000, or to imprisonment for not more than five years, or both, together with costs of prosecution.

. . . . . . . . . . . . . . . . . . . . . . . . . . . . . . . . . . . . . . . . . . . . . . . .
(Signature of authorized individual)

. . . . . . . . . . . . . . . . . . . . . . . . . . . . . . . . . . . . . . . . . . . . . . . .
(Address)

(2) Form of certificate for exemption from retailers excise taxes for use by a school operated as an activity of a church or other organization described in section 501(c)(3) that in itself is not an educational organization described in section 170(b)(1)(A)(ii) of the Code:

## EXEMPTION CERTIFICATE

(For use by or for a school operated as an activity of a church or other organization described in section 501(c)(3) of the Internal Revenue Code of 1954, that is not, in itself, an educational organization described in section 170(b)(1)(A)(ii), purchasing articles subject to retailers excise tax for the exclusive use of the school)

(Date) . . . . . . . . . . . , 19____

I hereby certify that I am . . . . . . . . . . (Title) of . . . . . . . . . . (School, church, parish, etc.); that I am authorized to execute this certificate; and that the articles specified in the accompanying order or on the reverse side hereof are purchased by such institution exclusively for use in its educational activities.

I understand that this exemption certificate is for use only by a school operated as an activity of a church or other organization described in section 501(c)(3) of the Internal Revenue Code of 1954, in the tax-free purchase for its exclusive use of articles subject to the retailers excise tax; or by a church, or other organization in the tax-free purchase of any such article for the exclusive use of its school which qualifies for the exemption; and it is agreed that if any article purchased tax free under this exemption certificate is used otherwise, such fact will be reported to the retailer from whom the tax-free purchase was made.

The school operated as an activity of the church or other organization described in section 501(c)(3) of the Internal Revenue Code of 1954, normally maintains a regular faculty and curriculum and normally has a regularly enrolled body of pupils or students in attendance at the place where its educational activities are regularly carried on.

I understand that the fraudulent use of this certificate for the purpose of securing this exemption will subject me and all parties making such fraudulent use of this certificate to a fine of not more than $10,000, or to imprisonment for not more than five years, or both, together with costs of prosecution.

_____
(Signature of authorized individual)

_____
(Address)

(e) *Frequency of certificates.*—Where only occasional sales are made by a retailer to a nonprofit educational organization, as defined in paragraph (b) of this section, a separate exemption certificate should be furnished for each order. However, where sales by the retailer to the educational organization are regularly or frequently made, a certificate covering all orders for a specified period not to exceed 12 calendar quarters will be acceptable. Such certificate and proper records of invoices, orders, etc., relative to tax-free sales must be readily accessible for inspection by internal revenue officers and retained as provided in section 6001 of the Code and the regulations thereunder.

(f) *Prima facie evidence of exempt use.*—The exemption certificate procured by the retailer from the purchasing nonprofit educational organization will be acceptable as prima facie evidence that the article is purchased for the exclusive use of such organization.

(g) *Exemption certificate not obtained prior to filing of retailer's excise tax return.*—If the sale is otherwise exempt but the exemption certificate is not obtained prior to the time the retailer files a return covering taxes due for the period in which the sale was made, the retailer must include the tax on such sale in its return for that period. However, if the certificate is later obtained, a credit may be taken on a subsequent return or a claim for refund of the tax paid on such sale may be filed, within the period of limitation prescribed by section 6511(b) of the Code and §301.6511(b)-1 of this chapter. [Reg. §48.4041-17.]

☐ [T.D. 7536, 3-27-78. Redesignated by T.D. 8066, 1-2-86.]

### [Reg. §48.4041-18]

**§48.4041-18. [Reserved].**

☐ [T.D. 7658, 12-4-79. Redesignated by T.D. 8066, 1-2-86. Amended by T.D. 8152, 8-20-87. Removed and reserved by T.D. 9849, 3-11-2019.]

### [Reg. §48.4041-19]

**§48.4041-19. Exemption for qualified methanol and ethanol fuel.**—(a) *In general.*—Under section 4041(b)(2), the tax imposed upon the sale or use of motor fuels under section 4041(a) does not apply to the sale or use of qualified methanol or ethanol fuel.

(b) *Qualified methanol or ethanol fuel defined.*—For purposes of section 4041(b)(2) and this section, qualified methanol or ethanol fuel is liquid motor fuel, 85% of the volume of which consists of alcohol, as defined in section 4081(c) and §48.4081-2(a)(4) of the regulations as modified by the following sentence. For purposes of section 4041(b)(2) and this section, the alcohol contained in a qualified methanol or ethanol fuel may be produced from coal. The actual gallonage of each component of the mixture (without adjustment for temperature) shall be used in determining whether the 85 percent alcohol has been met. Further, in determining whether a particular mixture containing less than 85 percent alcohol satisfies this percentage requirement, the District Director shall take into account the existence of any facts and circumstances, that establish that but for the commercial and operational realities of the blending process, it may reasonably be concluded that the mixture would have contained at least 85 percent alcohol. The necessary facts and circumstances will not be found to exist if over a period of time the mixtures blended by a blender show a consistent pattern of failing to contain 85 percent alcohol.

(c) *Mixtures which do not qualify as qualified methanol or ethanol fuel.*—If a methanol or ethanol fuel does not qualify as qualified methanol or ethanol fuel under this section, the entire mixture is taxed at the rate of tax applicable to sales of special motor fuels under section 4041(a)(2) of the Code.

(d) *Refunds relating to fuels used to produce qualified fuels.*—See section 6427 for rules which relate to the allowance of a refund or credit to a person who uses tax-paid diesel, special motor or noncommercial aviation fuels to produce a qualified methanol or ethanol fuel and section 6416 for rules which relate to the allowance of a refund or credit to a person who uses tax-paid gasoline to produce a qualified methanol or ethanol fuel.

(e) *Later blending.*—If a qualified methanol or ethanol fuel is blended with other motor fuel in a mixture less than 85 percent of which consists of alcohol, the subsequent sale or use of such alcohol mixture fuel is taxable under the provisions of section 4041 or section 4081 subject to the requirements, limitations and exemptions of those sections. Thus, if the alcohol mixture fuel is at least 10% alcohol by volume, sale or use of the fuel is taxed at the rates provided in section 4041(k) or section 4081(c), but if the fuel is less than 10% alcohol, sale or use of the fuel is taxed at the rates provided in section 4041(a) or section 4081(a).

(f) *Effective date.*—Section 4041(b)(2) applies to sales or uses after March 31, 1983, and before October 1, 1988. [Reg. § 48.4041-19.]

☐ [*T.D. 8152, 8-20-87.*]

### [Reg. §48.4041-20]

**§48.4041-20. Partially exempt methanol and ethanol fuel.**—(a) *In general.*—Under section 4041(m), the sale or use of partially exempt methanol or ethanol fuel is taxed at the rate of $4^{1}/_{2}$ cents per gallon of fuel sold or used. The amount of tax is based upon the total volume of fuel and not merely upon the nonalcohol portion of the fuel.

(b) *Partially exempt methanol or ethanol fuel defined.*—For purposes of section 4041(m) and this section, partially exempt methanol or ethanol fuel is liquid motor fuel, 85% of which by volume consists of alcohol, as defined in section 4081 and § 48.4081-2(a)(4) of the regulations, as modified by the following sentence. For purposes of section 4041(m) and this section, the alcohol contained in partially exempt methanol or ethanol fuel must be produced from natural gas. The actual gallonage of each component of the mixture (without adjustment for temperature) shall be used in determining whether the 85 percent alcohol requirement has been met. Further, in determining whether a particular mixture containing less than 85 percent alcohol satisfies this percentage requirement, the District Director shall take into account the existence of any facts and circumstances that establish that but for the commercial and operational realities of the blending process, it may reasonably be concluded that the mixture would have contained at least 85 percent alcohol. The necessary facts and circumstances will not be found to exist if over a period of time the mixtures blended by a blender show a consistent pattern of failing to contain 85 percent alcohol. See paragraph (f) of this section for rules relating to information required to be attached to the taxpayer's return of the tax imposed by chapter 31 relating to the alcohol content of the partially exempt methanol or ethanol fuel for which tax is paid.

(c) *Mixtures which do not qualify as partially exempt methanol or ethanol fuel.*—If methanol or ethanol fuel does not qualify as partially exempt methanol or ethanol fuel under this section, the entire mixture is taxed at the rate of tax applicable under section 4041(a)(2) of the Code.

(d) *Refunds relating to fuels.*—See section 6427 for rules which relate to the allowance of a refund or credit to a person who uses tax-paid diesel, special motor or noncommercial aviation fuel to produce a partially exempt methanol or ethanol fuel and section 6416 for rules which relate to the allowance of a refund or credit to a person who uses tax-paid gasoline to produce a partially exempt methanol or ethanol fuel.

(e) *Later blending.*—If a partially exempt methanol or ethanol fuel is blended with other motor fuel in a mixture less than 85 percent of which consists of alcohol, the subsequent sale or use of such blended motor fuel is taxable under the provisions of section 4041(a) or section 4081(a), subject to the requirements, limitations and exemptions of those sections.

(f) *Records required to be furnished by the taxpayer.*—A taxpayer making a return of the tax imposed by chapter 31 indicating payment of the tax under section 4041(m) and § 48.4041-20 at the reduced rate must attach a statement to the return indicating the total number of gallons of partially exempt methanol or ethanol fuel containing at least 85 percent alcohol and the total number of gallons of partially exempt methanol or ethanol fuel containing less than 85 percent alcohol, but qualifying for taxation at the reduced rate under the rules of paragraph (b) of this section. However, the taxpayer does not have to specify the precise mixture ratio of every mixture blended for which tax is being paid.

(g) *Effective date.*—Section 4041(m) applies to sales and uses after July 31, 1984. If methanol or ethanol fuel meeting the requirements of paragraph (b) of this section was put into the tank of a vehicle prior to August 1, 1984, the fuel is considered used prior to that date and is subject to the tax described in paragraph (a) of section 4041. [Reg. § 48.4041-20.]

☐ [*T.D. 8152, 8-20-87.*]

### [Reg. §48.4041-21]

**§48.4041-21. Compressed natural gas (CNG).**—(a) *Delivery of CNG into the fuel supply tank of a motor vehicle or motorboat.*—(1) *Imposition of tax.*—Tax is imposed on the delivery of compressed natural gas (CNG) into the fuel supply tank of the propulsion engine of a motor vehicle or motorboat unless tax was previously imposed on the CNG under paragraph (b) of this section.

(2) *Liability for tax.*—If the delivery of the CNG is in connection with a sale, the seller of the CNG is liable for the tax imposed under paragraph (a)(1) of this section. If the delivery of the CNG is not in connection with a sale, the operator of the motor vehicle or motorboat, as the case may be, is liable for the tax imposed under paragraph (a)(1) of this section.

(b) *Bulk sales of CNG.*—(1) *In general.*—Tax is imposed on the sale of CNG that is not in connection with the delivery of the CNG into the fuel supply tank of the propulsion engine of a motor vehicle or motorboat if, by the time of the sale—

(i) The buyer has given the seller a written statement stating that the entire quantity of the CNG covered by the statement is for use by the buyer for a taxable use as a fuel in a motor vehicle or motorboat; and

(ii) The seller has given the buyer a written acknowledgement of receipt of the statement described in paragraph (b)(1)(i) of this section.

(2) *Liability for tax.*—The seller of the CNG is liable for the tax imposed under this paragraph (b).

(c) *Exemptions.*—(1) *In general.*—The taxes imposed under this section do not apply to a delivery or sale of CNG for a use described in section 4041(a)(3)(B), (b)(1), (f), (g), or (h). However, if the person otherwise liable for tax under this section is the seller of the CNG, the exemption under this section applies only if, by the time of sale, the seller receives an unexpired certificate (as described in this paragraph (c)) from the buyer and has no reason to believe any information in the certificate is false.

(2) *Certificate; in general.*—The certificate to be provided by a buyer of CNG is to consist of a statement that is signed under penalties of perjury by a person with authority to bind the buyer, should be in substantially the same form as the model certificate provided in paragraph (c)(4) of this section, and should contain all information necessary to complete the model certificate. A new certificate must be given if any information in the current certificate changes. The certificate may be included as part of any business records normally used to document a sale. The certificate expires on the earliest of the following dates:

(i) The date one year after the effective date of the certificate (which may be no earlier than the date it is signed).

(ii) The date a new certificate is provided to the seller.

(iii) The date the seller is notified by the Internal Revenue Service or the buyer that the buyer's right to provide a certificate has been withdrawn.

(3) *Withdrawal of the right to provide a certificate.*—The Internal Revenue Service may withdraw the right of a buyer of CNG to provide a certificate under this paragraph (c) if the buyer uses CNG to which a certificate applies in a taxable use. The Internal Revenue Service may notify any seller to whom the buyer has provided a certificate that the buyer's right to provide a certificate has been withdrawn.

(4) *Model certificate.*

CERTIFICATE OF PERSON BUYING COMPRESSED NATURAL GAS (CNG)
FOR A NONTAXABLE USE
(To support tax-free sales of CNG under section 4041 of the Internal Revenue Code.)

_____

Name, address, and employer identification number of seller
_____ ("Buyer") certifies the following under penalties of perjury:
    Name of buyer
    The CNG to which this certificate relates will be used in a nontaxable use.
    This certificate applies to the following (complete as applicable):
    If this is a single purchase certificate, check here ___ and enter:
1. Invoice or delivery ticket number _____
2. ___ (number of MCFs)

If this is a certificate covering all purchases under a specified account or order number, check here ___ and enter:

1. Effective date _____

2. Expiration date _____

(period not to exceed 1 year after the effective date)

3. Buyer account or order number _____

Buyer will not claim a credit or refund under section 6427 of the Internal Revenue Code for any CNG to which this certificate relates.

Buyer will provide a new certificate to the seller if any information in this certificate changes.

Buyer understands that if Buyer violates the terms of this certificate, the Internal Revenue Service may withdraw Buyer's right to provide a certificate.

Buyer has not been notified by the Internal Revenue Service that its right to provide a certificate has been withdrawn. In addition, the Internal Revenue Service has not notified Buyer that the right to provide a certificate has been withdrawn from a purchaser to which Buyer sells CNG tax free.

Buyer understands that the fraudulent use of this certificate may subject Buyer and all parties making any fraudulent use of this certificate to a fine or imprisonment, or both, together with the costs of prosecution.

Printed or typed name of person signing _____

Title of person signing _____

Employer identification number _____

Address of Buyer _____

Signature and date signed

(d) *Rate of tax.*—The rate of the tax imposed under this section is the rate prescribed by section 4041(a)(3).

(e) *Effective date.*—This section is effective October 1, 1995. [Reg. §48.4041-21.]

☐ [*T.D.* 8303, 6-5-90. *Amended by T.D.* 8609, 8-4-95; *T.D.* 8659, 3-13-96; *T.D.* 8879, 3-30-2000 *and T.D.* 9051, 4-1-2003.]

**[Reg. §48.4042-1]**

**§48.4042-1. Tax on fuel used in commercial waterway transportation.**—(a) *In general.*—Section 4042(a) imposes an excise tax on the use of liquid fuel in the propulsion system of commercial transportation vessels while traveling on certain inland and intracoastal waterways (*see*§48.4042-1(f)). The tax applies generally to all types of vessels, including ships, bargers, and tugboats. It is in addition to all other taxes imposed on the sale or use of fuel.

(b) *Amount of tax.*—For the amount of tax, see section 4042(b).

(c) *Person liable for tax.*—The person operating the vessel in which the propulsion fuel is consumed is the user of liquid fuel for purposes of section 4042(a). Thus, a person who operates (or whose employees operate) a vessel is responsible for filing returns and paying the tax. If a vessel owner (or lessee) contracts with an independent contractor to operate the vessel, the independent contractor is the user of liquid fuel for purposes of section 4042(a), regardless of who purchases the fuel.

(d) *Time of use.*—Fuel is not taxed by section 4042(a) when put into a vessel's tanks. For purposes of section 4042(a), fuel is used when it is actually consumed by a vessel's engine.

(e) *Liquid fuels.*—For purposes of the tax imposed under this section, *liquid fuel* means any liquid fuel including gasoline, diesel fuel, special motor fuel, or Bunker C residual fuel oil.

(f) *Commercial waterway transportation.*—(1) *In general.*—For purposes of section 4042(a) and §48.4042-2(c)(1), the term "commercial waterway transportation" means the use of a vessel on the waterways specified in paragraphs (g)(1) through (27) of this section if—

(i) Use of the vessel is in the business of transporting property for compensation or hire, or

(ii) Use of the vessel is in transporting property in the business of the owner, lessee, or operator of the vessel (whether or not a fee is charged).

Except for the operation of certain fishing vessels, the operation of all vessels satisfying the requirements of paragraphs (f) (1)(i) or (1)(ii) of this section will be deemed "commercial waterway transportation," regardless of whether the vessel is actually engaged in the transportation of property on a particular voyage. Thus, "commercial waterway transportation" includes the operation of vessels while moving empty of cargo, while awaiting passage through locks, while dislodging vessels grounded on a sandbar, while moving to or from a repair facility, while maneuvering around loading and unloading docks, and while fleeting barges into a single tow.

(2) *Fishing vessels exception.*—A vessel does not transport property in the business of the owner, lessee, or operator, for purposes of paragraph (f)(1)(ii) of this section, by merely transporting fish or other aquatic animal life caught on the voyage. The tax imposed by section 4042(a) does not apply to fuel used by a fishing vessel while traveling to a fishing site, while engaged in fishing, or while returning from the fishing site with its catch. However, the tax applies

to fuel used by a commercial vessel along the taxable waterways while traveling to pick up aquatic animal life caught by another vessel and while transporting the catch of such other vessel.

(g) *Specified waterways.*—Only fuel used on those waterways specified in section 206 of the Inland Waterways Revenue Act of 1978 (specified waterways) is taxable. The specified waterways are as follows:

(1) Alabama-Coosa Rivers: From junction with the Tombigbee River at river mile (hereinafter referred to as RM) 0 to junction with the Coosa River at RM 314.

(2) Allegheny River: From confluence with the Monongahela River to form the Ohio River at RM 0 to the head of the existing project at East Brady, Pennsylvania, RM 72.

(3) Apalachicola-Chattahoochee and Flint Rivers: Apalachicola River from mouth at Apalachicola Bay (intersection with the Gulf Intracoastal Waterway) RM 0 to junction with Chattachoochee and Flint Rivers at RM 107.8. Chattachoochee River from junction with Apalachicola and Flint Rivers at RM 0 to Columbus, Georgia, at RM 155 and Flint River, from junction with Apalachicola and Chattachoochee Rivers at RM 0 to Bainbridge, Georgia, at RM 28.

(4) Arkansas River (McClellan-Kerr Arkansas River Navigation System): From junction with Mississippi River at RM 0 to port of Catoosa, Oklahoma, at RM 448.2.

(5) Atchafalaya River: From RM 0 at its intersection with the Gulf Intracoastal Waterway at Morgan City, Louisiana, upstream to junction with Red River at RM 116.8

(6) Atlantic Intracoastal Waterway (A.I.W.W.): Two inland water routes approximately paralleling the Atlantic coast between Norfolk, Virginia, and Miami, Florida, for 1,192 miles via both the Albermarle and Chesapeake Canal and Great Dismal Swamp Canal routes. For vessels traveling along the A.I.W.W. no matter how short the distance, the A.I.W.W. includes the main channel, all alternate channels, and all adjoining bays and sounds, regardless of depth. However, vessels merely crossing the A.I.W.W. on route either to a coastal port or to a nonspecified waterway will not be treated as traveling on the A.I.W.W.

(7) Black Warrior-Tombigbee-Mobile Rivers: Black Warrior River System from RM 2.9, Mobile River (at Chickasaw Creek) to confluence with Tombigbee River at RM 45. Tombigbee River (to Demopolis at RM 215.4) to port of Birmingham, RM's 374—411 and upstream to head of navigation on Mulberry Fork (RM 429.6), Locust Fork (RM 407.8), and Sipsey Fork (RM 430.4).

(8) Columbia River (Columbia-Snake Rivers Inland Waterways). From The Dalles at RM 191.5 to Pasco, Washington (McNary Pool), at RM 330, Snake River from RM 0 at the mouth to RM 231.5 at Johnson Bar Landing, Idaho.

(9) Cumberland River: Junction with Ohio River at RM 0 to head of navigation, upstream to Carthage, Tennessee, at RM 313.5

(10) Green and Barren Rivers: Green River from junction with the Ohio River at RM 0 to head of navigation at RM 149.1.

(11) Gulf Intracoastal Waterway (G.I.W.W.): From the mouth of St. Mark's River, Florida, to Brownsville, Texas, 1,134.5 miles. For vessels traveling along the G.I.W.W. no matter how short the distance, the G.I.W.W. includes the main channel, all alternate channels, and all adjoining bays and sounds, regardless of depth. However, vessels merely crossing the G.I.W.W. on route either to a coastal port or to a nonspecified waterway will not be treated as traveling on the G.I.W.W.

(12) Illinois Waterway: Illinois River from junction with the Mississippi River at RM 0 to the Des Plaines River and along the Des

Plaines River to Lockport Lock and Dam at RM 291. Chicago Sanitary and Ship Canal from Lockport Lock and Dam at RM 291 to the South Branch Chicago River and along the South Branch Chicago River to Lake Street, Chicago at RM 325.5 near Chicago Harbor. Calumet-Sag Channel from junction with the Chicago Sanitary and Ship Canal to the Little Calumet River and along the Little Calumet and Calumet Rivers to turning basin 5, near the entrance to Lake Calumet, an additional 23.8 RMs. Total waterway distance approximately 350 RMs.

(13) Kanawha River: From junction with Ohio River at RM 0 to RM 90.6 at Deepwater, West Virginia.

(14) Kaskaskia River: From junction with the Mississippi River at RM 0 to RM 36.2 at Fayetteville, Illinois.

(15) Kentucky River: From junction with Ohio River at RM 0 to confluence of Middle and North Forks at RM 258.6.

(16) Lower Mississippi River: From Baton Rouge, Louisiana, RM 233.9 to Cairo, Illinois, RM 953.8.

(17) Upper Mississippi River: From Cairo, Illinois, RM 953.8 to Minneapolis, Minnesota, RM 1,811.4.

(18) Missouri River: From junction with Mississippi River at RM 0 to Sioux City, Iowa, at RM 734.8.

(19) Monongahela River: From junction with Allegheny River to form the Ohio River at RM 0 to junction of the Tygart and West Fork Rivers, Fairmont, West Virginia, at RM 128.7.

(20) Ohio River: From junction with the Mississippi River at RM 0 to junction of the Allegheny and Monongahela Rivers at Pittsburgh, Pennsylvania, at RM 981.

(21) Ouachita-Black Rivers: From the mouth of the Black River at its junction with the Red River at RM 0 to RM 351 at Camden, Arkansas.

(22) Pearl River: From junction of West Pearl River with the Rigolets at RM 0 to Bogalusa, Louisiana, RM 58.

(23) Red River: From RM 0 to the mouth of Cypress Bayou at RM 236.

(24) Tennessee River: From junction with Ohio River at RM 0 to confluence with Holstein and French Rivers at RM 652.

(25) Tennessee-Tombigbee Waterway: From its confluence with the Tennessee River to the Warrior River at Demopolis, Alabama.

(26) White River: From RM 9.8 to RM 255 at Newport, Arkansas.

(27) Willamette River: From RM 21 upstream of Portland, Oregon, to Harrisburg, Oregon, at RM 194. [Reg. §48.4042-1.]

☐ [T.D. 7727, 10-27-80. Amended by T.D. 8659, 3-13-96.]

**[Reg. §48.4042-2]**

§48.4042-2. Special rules.—(a) *Dual use of liquid fuels.*—(1) *Dual use by the propulsion engine.*—The tax imposed by section 4042(a) applies to all taxable liquid used as a fuel in the propulsion system of the vessel, regardless of whether the engine (or other propulsion system) is used for a purpose other than propulsion of the vessel. For purposes of this section, any engines generating movement of a vessel (including bow thrusters used for steering) are part of the propulsion system. The tax does not apply to fuel consumed in engines which are not used to generate movement of a vessel. When the propulsion engine operates special equipment by means of a power take-off or power transfer, the tax applies to all liquid fuel consumed by that engine. For example, the tax applies to all fuel used in the engine operating an alternator, a generator, or pumps, if that engine is used to generate movement of a vessel.

(2) *Common tank.*—If the liquid fuel consumed by a nonpropulsion engine is drawn from the same tank as fuel consumed by a propulsion engine, a reasonable determination of the quantity of fuel used in such a separate engine will be acceptable for purposes of excluding from taxation a portion of the fuel consumed by the vessel. The determination of the amount of fuel consumed by the nonpropulsion engine may be based primarily on the operating experience of the person using the fuel; however, in order to exclude fuel from taxation under the rules set out in this paragraph (a)(2), the taxpayer must maintain records which will support the allocation used.

(b) *Voyages crossing boundaries of the specified waterways.*—Fuel consumed by a vessel traveling along the specified waterways is taxable only to the extent of fuel consumed for propulsion while on the specified waterways. Generally, the operator may calculate the amount of fuel consumed while on the specified waterways during a particular voyage by multiplying total fuel consumed in the propulsion engine by a fraction. The numerator of the fraction is the time spent operating on the specified waterways; the denominator is the total time spent operating on the specified and nonspecified waterways during the voyage. This calculation may not be used when it is unreasonable. It may be determined to be unreasonable by:

(1) Better evidence of fuel consumed (*e.g.*, readings from an accurate fuel gauge or records from similar voyages); or

(2) The existence of factors causing a substantial discrepancy between the rate of fuel consumption on the specified and nonspecified waterways.

(c) *Records required.*—(1) All operators of vessels used in commercial waterway transportation must maintain records sufficient to establish to the satisfaction of the district director the amount of fuel used for taxable purposes. Those records may include, when relevant to establish liability:

(i) Quantity of fuel and date of acquisition of all liquid fuels acquired for both taxable and nontaxable purposes, whether delivered to storage tanks or tanks on a vessel;

(ii) Date and quantity of fuel pumped into tanks on each vessel;

(iii) Identification number or name of each vessel using fuel; and

(iv) Departure time, departure point, route traveled, destination, and arrival time for each vessel.

(2) Vessel operators seeking a tax exemption provided by section 4042(c) must maintain records which will support any exemption claimed. Where applicable, the records shall contain:

(i) The draft of the vessel on each voyage (for exemption under section 4042(c)(1));

(ii) The type of vessel in which fuel is consumed and the type of vessel in which cargo is transported (for exemption under section 4042(c)(1), (2) or (4); and

(iii) The ultimate use of cargo transported (for exemption under section 4042(c)(3)). [Reg. §48.4042-2.]

☐ [T.D. 7727, 10-27-80. Amended by T.D. 8442, 10-21-92.]

**[Reg. §48.4042-3]**

§48.4042-3. Certain types of commercial waterway transportation excluded.—(a) *Deep draft ocean-going vessels.*—(1) *In general.*—Under section 4042(c)(1), there is no tax imposed by section 4042(a) if:

(i) the vessel was designed primarily for use on the high seas; and

(ii) the vessel has a draft of more than 12 feet on the voyage for which the fuel tax exclusion is sought (*e.g.* 12 feet 1 inch).

(2) *Meaning of "designed primarily for use on the high seas.".*—Section 4042(c)(1) requires a determination of the primacy of the design features rendering the vessel useful for service on the high seas, as opposed to the features which render the vessel useful for service on all less turbulent waters. Thus, whether a ship is "designed primarily for use on the high seas" must be determined from all the facts, including structural features and equipment. If the predominant use of a vessel is on the high seas, it shall be presumed to be "designed primarily for use on the high seas." If the predominant use of a vessel is on waters other than the high seas, it shall be presumed not to be "designed primarily for use on the high seas."

(3) *Meaning of "high seas.".*—For purposes of this section, "high seas" shall mean waters other than the territorial waters of the United States or any other country. Thus, the high seas shall not include the internal waters of any country, the Great Lakes, harbors, or narrow coastal indentations.

(4) *Twelve foot draft.*—(i) Definition. For purposes of section 4042(c)(1), "draft" shall mean the maximum vertical distance between the mean water line and the bottom of the keel. In cases where a vessel has a skeg or other appendage extending locally below the line of the keel, the draft shall be measured from the deepest appendage. A separate determination of draft must be made for each voyage when the vessel has its greatest load of cargo and fuel. For purposes of this determination, the term "voyage" means a round trip voyage. Therefore, if a vessel travels into the specified waterway system to pick up cargo and has a draft sufficient to qualify for the exclusion when loaded, then for purposes of section 4042(c)(1) the vessel satisfies the 12 foot draft requirement for the entire voyage. Similarly, if a vessel loaded with cargo travels into the specified waterway system with a draft sufficient to qualify for the exclusion provided by section 4042(c)(1), then the fuel consumed on the entire voyage may be excluded, regardless of the vessel's draft after the cargo is unloaded.

(ii) *Example.*—The following example illustrates the application of paragraph (a)(4)(i) of this section:

*Example.* A ship with a design draft of 20 feet (maximum certified draft when fully loaded) travels into a taxable waterway with only a partial load, such that the draft is 12 feet. The ship unloads and departs the waterway empty. The portion of the fuel consumed for propulsion of the vessel on the specified waterway is taxable because only vessels with a draft greater than 12 feet are eligible for the section 4042(c)(1) exemption from tax.

(b) *Commercial passenger vessels.*—Under section 4042(c)(2), the tax imposed by section 4042(a) does not apply to fuel consumed by vessels used primarily for the transportation of persons. Thus, commercial passenger vessels while being operated as passenger vessels are not subject to tax, even if such vessels in fact transport property in addition to transporting passengers. Similarly, ferry boats carrying passengers are not subject to tax, even if such vessels carry the passengers' automobiles.

(c) *Exemption for State or local governments.*—(1) *In general.*—Under section 4042(c)(3), there is no tax imposed by section 4042(a) if:

(i) The vessel is being used by a State or local government; and

(ii) The vessel is being used in transporting property in the State or local government's business.

(2) *State or local government.*—For purposes of paragraph (c)(1)(i) of this section a "vessel is being used by a State or local government" if it is operated by any State, the District of Columbia, or any political subdivision of a State. If a private party is contracted to haul for a State or local government, the vessel is not "being used by a State or local government." Similarly, if a person other than a State or local government is contracted to supply vessel operators, the fuel consumed by the vessel is not used "by a State or local government," regardless of ownership of the vessel. However, when a local government leases barges and employees of the local government operate the barges, the vessel is being used by the local government.

(3) *Government business.*—The test for whether a vessel is being used "in transporting in a State or local government's business," within the meaning of paragraph (c)(1)(ii) of this section, is whether the ultimate use of the cargo is for a function which is ordinarily carried out by governmental units. For example, when the cargo transported is salt to be spread on icy roads, the vessel is being used "in transporting in a State or local business" because the use to which the cargo will be put (road maintenance) is a function ordinarily performed by governmental units. Fuel consumed in a vessel transporting property for compensation or in furtherance of a business not ordinarily carried out by a governmental unit is not exempt from taxation by section 4042(c)(3).

(d) *Ocean-going barges.*—Under section 4042(c)(4), the tax imposed by section 4042(a) does not apply to fuel consumed by tugs moving exclusively barges released by ocean-going carriers soley to pick up or deliver international cargos. The tax exemption provided by section 4042(c)(4) applies to LASH barges, SEABEE barges, and all other ocean-going barges carried aboard ocean-going vessels. There is no exemption under section 4042(c)(4) while:

(1) One or more of the barges in the tow is not a LASH barge, SEABEE barge, or other ocean-going barge carried aboard an ocean-going vessel; or

(2) One or more of the barges in the tow is not on an international voyage; or

(3) Part of the cargo in the tow is not being transported internationally. [Reg. § 48.4042-3.]

☐ [*T.D. 7727,* 10-27-80.]

## [Reg. § 145.4051-1]

**§ 145.4051-1. Imposition of tax on heavy trucks and trailers sold at retail.**—(a) *Imposition of tax.*—(1) *In general.*—Section 4051(a)(1) imposes a tax on the first retail sale (as defined in § 145.4052-1(a)) of the following articles (including in each case parts or accessories therefor sold on or in connection therewith or with the sale thereof):

(i) Automobile truck chassis and bodies;

(ii) Truck trailer and semitrailer chassis and bodies; and

(iii) Tractors of the kind chiefly used for highway transportation in combination with a trailer or semitrailer.

A sale of an automobile truck, truck trailer or semitrailer, shall be considered to be a sale of a chassis and of a body enumerated in this paragraph (a)(1).

(2) *Special rule applicable to chassis and bodies.*—A chassis or body enumerated in paragraph (a)(1) of this section is taxable under section 4051(a)(1) only if such chassis or body is sold for use as a component part of a highway vehicle (as defined in paragraph (d) of § 48.4061(a)-1 (Regulations on Manufacturers and Retailers Excise Taxes)), which is an automobile truck, truck trailer or semitrailer, or a tractor of the kind chiefly used for highway transportation in combination with a trailer or semitrailer. Furthermore, a chassis or body which is not enumerated in paragraph (a)(1) of this section is not taxable under section 4051(a)(1) even though such chassis or body is

used as a component part of a highway vehicle (e.g., a chassis or body of a passenger automobile). See paragraphs (e)(1) and (e)(2) of this section for the definitions of a tractor and truck. See paragraphs (e)(1) through (5) of § 145.4052-1 for other provisions applicable to this section. See paragraph (f) of this section, relating to tax-free sales of non-highway vehicles.

(3) *Parts or accessories sold on or in connection with chassis, bodies, etc.*—The tax applies in respect of parts or accessories sold on or in connection with or with the sale of the vehicles specified in section 4051(a)(1). Thus, for example, if at the time the article is sold by the retailer, the part or accessory has been ordered from the retailer, the part or accessory will be considered as sold in connection with and with the sale of the vehicle. The tax applies in such a case whether or not the parts or accessories are billed separately by the retailer. If a taxable chassis, body, or tractor is sold by the retailer, without parts or accessories which are considered equipment essential for the operation or appearance of the taxable article, the sale of such parts or accessories by the retailer to the purchaser of the taxable article will be considered, in the absence of evidence to the contrary, to have been made in connection with the sale of the taxable article even though they are shipped separately, at the same time or on a different date. For example, if a retailer sells to any person a chassis and the bumpers for such chassis, or sells a taxable tractor and the fifth wheel and attachments, the tax applies to such parts or accessories regardless of the method of billing or the time at which the shipments were made. Parts and accessories that are spares or replacements are not subject to tax.

(4) *Exclusions.*—No tax is imposed by section 4051(a)(1) on the sale of automobile truck chassis and bodies, suitable for use with a vehicle which has a gross vehicle weight of 33,000 pounds or less, or truck trailer and semitrailer chassis and bodies, suitable for use with a trailer or semitrailer which has a gross vehicle weight of 26,000 pounds or less. For purposes of this paragraph (a)(4) the term "suitable for use" means practical and commercial fitness for such use. A chassis or body possesses practical fitness for use with a vehicle if it performs its intended function up to a generally acceptable standard of efficiency with the vehicle, and a chassis or body possesses commercial fitness for use with a vehicle if it is generally available for use with the vehicle at a price that is reasonably competitive with other articles that may be used for the same purpose. Thus, a truck chassis which is suitable for use with a vehicle having a gross vehicle weight of 33,000 pounds or less, is not subject to the tax imposed by section 4051(a)(1) regardless of the body actually mounted thereon. A truck trailer or semitrailer chassis suitable for use with a vehicle having a gross vehicle weight of 26,000 pounds or less, is not subject to tax regardless of the body actually mounted thereon. Where an exempt body is mounted on a taxable chassis, or a taxable body is mounted on an exempt chassis, the taxable chassis or body, as the case may be, nevertheless remains subject to such tax, if the resulting vehicle is a highway vehicle as defined in § 48.4061(a)-1.

(b) *Rate of tax.*—With respect to the articles enumerated in paragraph (a)(1) of this section, the rate of tax imposed by section 4051(a)(1) is 12 percent of the price for which the article is sold on or after April 1, 1983. See paragraph (d) of this section relating to vehicles on which a 10 percent tax was imposed under section 4061(a)(1).

(c) *Separate purchase of truck or trailer and parts and accessories therefor.*—(1) *In general.*—If the owner, lessee, or operator of any vehicle, which contains an article taxable under paragraph (a)(1) of this section, installs (or causes to be installed) any part or accessory on such vehicle, and such installation is not later than 6 months after the date such vehicle (as it contains such article) was first placed in service, section 4051(b)(1) imposes a tax on such installation equal to 12 percent of the price of such part or accessory and its installation. For purposes of the tax imposed by section 4051(b)(1) and this paragraph (c)(1) the term "parts and accessories" does not include those parts and accessories which were previously exempt from tax under sections 4061(b)(1) and (2) as in effect prior to January 7, 1983. Thus, for example, articles of general use are exempt from tax. See § 48.4061(b)-2(b). See paragraphs (d)(1) through (4) of § 145.4052-1 for determination of price.

(2) *Placed in service.*—For purposes of paragraph (c)(1) of this section, a vehicle shall be considered placed in service on the date on which the owner of the vehicle took actual possession of the vehicle. This date can be established by the delivery ticket signed by the owner or other comparable document indicating delivery to and acceptance by the owner.

(3) *Exceptions.*—The tax imposed by section 4051(b)(1) and paragraph (c)(1) of this section shall not apply if—

(i) The part or accessory installed is a replacement part or accessory, or

(ii) The aggregate price of the parts and accessories (and their installation) described in paragraph (c)(1) of this section with respect to any vehicle does not exceed $200.

For purposes of paragraph (c)(3)(i) of this section, a part is a replacement part, regardless of when it is ordered, if its use with a vehicle is as a replacement for a part on such vehicle. For purposes of paragraph (c)(3)(ii) of this section, the term "aggregate price of parts and accessories (and their installation)" refers to all purchases and installation charges, not including replacement parts and accessories, made with respect to a vehicle within the 6 month period provided for in paragraph (c)(1) of this section. If the aggregate price of parts and accessories (and their installation) during the 6 month period exceeds $200, the tax imposed under section 4051(b)(1) and paragraph (c)(1) of this section shall apply to the cost of all parts and accessories (and their installation) during such period. For example, a vehicle is purchased and placed in service on July 1, 1983. On August 1, 1983, the owner purchases and has installed parts and accessories at a cost of $150. On September 1, 1983, the owner purchases and has installed parts and accessories at a cost of $300. On September 1, 1983 a tax of $54 will be imposed (12 percent × $450). Any costs of additional parts and accessories installed with respect to the vehicle before January 1, 1984 (and the cost of installation) will also be subject to the 12 percent tax.

(d) *Transitional rule.*—In the case of an article taxable under paragraph (a)(1) of this section, on which a tax was imposed under section 4061(a)(1), the rate of tax set forth in paragraph (b) shall be applied by substituting "2 percent" for "12 percent." For example, if a manufacturer sells a tractor to a dealer on February 1, 1983, for $20,000 (which includes the Federal excise tax), for which a 10 percent tax was paid, and the dealer sells the tractor on April 10, 1983 for $25,000, a tax of 2 percent will be imposed on the $25,000 sales price. See paragraphs (d)(1) through (4) of §145.4052-1 relating to determination of price.

(e) *Definitions.*—For purposes of this section—

(1) *Tractor.*—(i) The term "tractor" means a highway vehicle primarily designed to tow a vehicle, such as a trailer or semitrailer, but does not carry cargo on the same chassis as the engine. A vehicle equipped with air brakes and/or towing package will be presumed to be primarily designed as a tractor.

(ii) An incomplete chassis cab shall be treated as a tractor if it is equipped with one or more of the following:

(A) A device for supplying pressure from the chassis cab to the brake system (air or hydraulic) of the towed vehicle;

(B) A mechanism for protecting the chassis cab brake system from the effects of a loss of pressure in the brake system of the towed vehicle;

(C) A control linking the brake system of the chassis to the brake system of the towed vehicle;

(D) A control in the cab for operating the towed vehicle's brakes independently of the chassis cab's brakes; or

(E) Any other equipment designed to make it suitable for use as a tractor.

An incomplete chassis cab which is not equipped with any of the devices set forth in paragraphs (e)(1)(ii)(A) through (E) of this section shall be treated as a truck if the purchaser certifies in writing that the vehicle will not be equipped for use as a tractor.

(2) *Truck.*—The term "truck" refers to a highway vehicle that is primarily designed to transport its load on the same chassis as the engine even if it is also equipped to tow a vehicle, such as a trailer or semitrailer.

(3) *Gross vehicle weight.*—(i) For purposes of this section the term "gross vehicle weight" means the maximum total weight of a loaded vehicle. Except as otherwise provided in paragraphs (e)(3)(ii) through (v) of this section, such maximum total weight shall be the gross vehicle weight rating of the article as specified by the manufacturer or established by the seller of the completed article, unless the Commissioner finds that such rating is unreasonable in light of the facts and circumstances in a particular case.

(ii) A seller must specify or establish a weight rating for each chassis, body, or vehicle sold on or after April 1, 1983 if such article requires no additional manufacture other than (A) the addition of readily attachable articles, such as tire or rim assemblies or minor accessories, (B) the performance of minor finishing operations, such as painting, or (C) in the case of a chassis, the addition of a body. If an article is specially equipped to the purchaser's specifications, such specifications may be used to establish the gross vehicle weight of the article.

(iii) A seller shall maintain a record of the gross vehicle weight rating of each truck, trailer and semitrailer sold and excluded from the tax imposed by section 4051(a)(1) by reason of sections

4051(a)(2), (3) and paragraphs (e)(3)(i) through (v) of this section. For this purpose, a record of the serial number of each such article shall be treated as a record of the gross vehicle weight rating of the article if such rating is indicated by the serial number.

(iv) If (A) the seller's rating indicated in a label or identifying device affixed to an article, (B) the rating set forth in the sales invoice or warranty agreement, and (C) the advertised rating for that article (or two or more identical articles) are inconsistent, the highest of such ratings will be considered to be the seller's gross vehicle weight rating specified or established for purposes of the tax imposed by section 4051(a)(1).

(v) The seller's gross vehicle weight rating must take into account, among other things, the strength of the chassis frame and the axle capacity and placement. The Commissioner may exclude from the gross vehicle weight rating any readily attachable parts to the extent the Commissioner finds that the use of such parts in computing the gross vehicle weight rating is unreasonable.

(f) *Tax-free sales.*—With respect to tax-free sales of a chassis or body for use as a component of a vehicle other than a highway vehicle, similar provisions to paragrahs (e)(2)(ii), (iii), and (iv) of §48.4061(a)-1 shall apply.

(g) *Effective date.*—The provisions of this section shall be effective for articles sold on or after April 1, 1983. [Temporary Reg. §145.4051-1.]

☐ [T.D. 7882, 3-30-83. *Amended by T.D. 8879, 3-30-2000.*]

### [Reg. §48.4052-1]

**§48.4052-1. Heavy trucks and trailers; certification requirement.**—(a) *In general.*—Tax is not imposed by section 4051 on the sale of an article for resale or leasing in a long-term lease if, by the time of sale, the seller has in good faith accepted from the buyer a statement that the buyer executed in good faith and that is in substantially the same form, and subject to the same conditions, as the certificate described in §145.4052-1(a)(6) of this chapter, except that the certificate must be signed under penalties of perjury and need not refer to Form 637 or include a registration number.

(b) *References to §145.4052-1(a)(2) of this chapter.*—References to §145.4052-1(a)(2) of this chapter appearing in §145.4052-1 of this chapter apply also to paragraph (a) of this section.

(c) *Effective date.*—This section is applicable after June 30, 1998. In addition, tax is not imposed on a sale occurring after December 31, 1997, and before July 1, 1998, if the conditions of paragraph (a) of this section are satisfied. [Reg. §48.4052-1.]

☐ [T.D. 8879, 3-30-2000.]

### [Reg. §145.4052-1]

**§145.4052-1. Special rules and definitions.**—(a) *First retail sale.*—(1) *General rule.*—For purposes of section 4051(a)(1) and §145.4051-1, the term "first retail sale" means a taxable sale described in paragraph (a)(2) of this section.

(2) *Taxable sale.*—The sale of an article is a taxable sale unless—

(i) The sale is a tax-free sale under section 4221,

(ii) [Reserved]. For sales after June 30, 1998, see §48.4052-1 of this chapter,

(iii) There has been a prior taxable sale of the article. Notwithstanding the preceding clause, the sale of a chassis or body of a trailer or semitrailer ("trailer or semitrailer") less than six months after a taxable sale of the article shall be treated as a taxable sale.

(3) *Computation of tax.*—(i) *In general.*—If the sale of an article is a taxable sale under paragraph (a)(2) of this section, the tax shall be computed on the price as determined under paragraph (d) of this section.

(ii) *Exception.*—If the taxable sale of an article is a taxable use of such article under paragraph (c) of this section, the tax shall be computed on the price as determined under paragraph (c) of this section.

(4) *Special rule for tax-paid trailer and semitrailer.*—In the case of a taxable sale of a trailer or semitrailer less than six months after a taxable sale of the article, the seller in the subsequent sale ("the subsequent seller") may claim a credit equal to the amount of tax previously paid by another person ("the previous taxpayer") under section 4051(a)(1) with respect to the prior taxable sale of the article. The credit for such tax will be allowed to the subsequent seller only if the form on which the credit is claimed is accompanied by a statement, signed by the subsequent seller, indicating the amount of the credit being claimed under this paragraph (a)(4) and stating that—

(i) The subsequent seller has not been repaid any portion of such tax by the previous taxpayer,

(ii) The subsequent seller has not provided the previous taxpayer with written consent to allow the previous taxpayer to claim a credit or refund of such tax under section 6416(a), and

(iii) The subsequent seller has records (*e.g.* invoices) substantiating the amount of tax paid by the previous taxpayer with respect to the prior taxable sale of such article.

In no case shall the amount of the credit allowable under this paragraph (a)(4) with respect to an article exceed the tax liability of the subsequent seller with respect to the sale of such article.

(5) *No installment payments of tax.*—If a lease or an installment sale (or another form of sale under which the sales price is paid in installments) is, or is deemed to be, a taxable sale under this section, then the liability for the entire tax arises at the time of the lease or

installment sale. No portion of the tax is deferred by reason of the fact that the sales price is paid in installments.

(6) *Certificate.*—A certificate signed by the purchaser, or an officer or employee authorized by the purchaser to sign the certificate, may be accepted by a seller in support of a nontaxable sale to the purchaser. If it is impracticable to furnish a separate certificate for each sale because of the frequency of sales to such purchaser, a certificate covering all orders between given dates (such period not to exceed 12 calendar quarters) will be acceptable. The purchaser may revoke the certificate by sending a written revocation to the seller. The certificate and proper records of invoices, orders, etc., relating to sales made pursuant to such certificate, must be retained by the seller as provided in section 6001 and the regulations thereunder. The certificate shall be substantially in the following form:

## EXEMPTION CERTIFICATE

I hereby certify that I am _____

(Title)

of _____, that I am authorized to execute

(Name of purchaser)

this certificate, and that:

(Check appropriate line)

\_\_\_ the article or articles specified in the accompanying order, or on the reverse side hereof, (or)

\_\_\_all orders placed by the purchaser for the period commencing _____(Date) (period not to exceed 12 calendar

quarters), are purchased either for resale or for lease on a long-term basis.

I have filed Form 637 and have received registration number_____.

I understand that the fraudulent use of this certificate to secure exemption will subject me and all parties making such fraudulent use to a fine of not more than $10,000, or to imprisonment for not more than 5 years, or both, together with costs of prosecution.

_____

(Signature)

_____

(Address)

(b) *Tax treatment of leases.*—(1) *Long-term lease.*—For purposes of this section and §145.4051-1, the leasing of an article on a long-term basis (as defined in paragraph (d)(6) of this section) will be deemed to be a sale of the article and will be deemed to be a taxable sale unless one of the exceptions contained in paragraph (a)(2) of this section applies. Thus, if a dealer purchases an article tax-free under an exception contained in paragraph (a)(2) of this section and then leases the article on a long-term basis, the leasing of the article will be treated as a taxable sale.

(2) *Short-term lease.*—For purposes of this section and §145.4051-1, the leasing of an article on a short-term basis (as defined in paragraph (d)(6) of this section) will be deemed to be a taxable use of such article under paragraph (c) of this section and will be deemed to be a taxable sale unless one of the exceptions contained in paragraph (a)(2) of this section applies.

(3) *Computation of tax.*—(i) *Long-term lease by manufacturer, producer, or importer.*—When a manufacturer, producer, or importer is the lessor of an article on a long-term basis (as defined in paragraph (d)(6) of this section) and such lease is deemed to be a taxable sale under paragraph (b)(1) of this section, the tax shall be computed on a presumptive retail sales price as determined under paragraph (d)(4)(i) of this section. The manufacturer, producer, or importer shall be liable for the tax as if the article were sold at retail by such manufacturer, importer, or retailer.

(ii) *Long-term lease by persons other than manufacturer, producer, or importer.*—When a person other than a manufacturer, producer, or importer is the lessor of an article on a long-term basis (as defined in paragraph (d)(6) of this section) and such lease is deemed to be a taxable sale under paragraph (b)(1) of this section, the tax shall be computed on a presumptive retail sales price as determined under paragraph (d)(5)(i) of this section. Such person shall be liable for the tax as if the article were sold at retail by such person.

(c) *Use treated as sale.*—(1) *In general.*—For purposes of this section and §145.4051-1, the use of an article will be deemed to be a sale of the article. Furthermore, if a person purchases a vehicle for which no tax was imposed under section 4051(a)(1) and thereafter converts such vehicle into an article which would have been taxable under section 4051(a)(1) and uses it, such person shall be liable for the tax as if such article were sold at retail by such person. For example, a truck having a gross vehicle weight rating of 24,000 pounds is sold at retail. The purchaser adds a lift axle, thereby increasing the gross vehicle weight rating to 34,000 pounds. If the purchaser thereafter uses the vehicle the purchaser shall be liable for the tax as if such article were sold at retail.

(2) *Exemption for use in further manufacture.*—The tax on the use of an article to which paragraph (c)(1) of this section applies shall not apply to use of the article by such person as material in the manufacture or production of, or as a component part of, another article to be manufactured or produced by the same user.

(3) *Time of application of tax.*—In the case of taxable use of an article by the seller, the tax attaches at the time such use begins. If tax applies by reason of the sale of an article on or in connection with, or with the sale of another article, the tax attaches at the time of the sale of such other article.

(4) *Events subsequent to taxable use of article.*—Liability for tax incurred on the use of an article is not extinguished or reduced because of any subsequent sale or lease of the article even if such sale or lease would have been exempt if the article had been sold or leased prior to use. If a seller of an article incurs liability for tax on his or her use of an article, and thereafter sells or leases the article in a transaction which otherwise would be subject to tax, liability for tax is not incurred on such sale or lease.

(5) *Computation of tax.*—(i) Except as provided in paragraph (c)(5)(ii) and (c)(5)(iii) of this section, the tax liability incurred on the use of an article shall be computed on the price at which such or similar articles are generally sold in the ordinary course of trade by retailers.

(ii) If the seller of an article regularly sells such articles at retail in arm's length transactions, tax liability on its use of any such article shall be computed on its lowest established retail price for such articles in effect at the time of the taxable use. In establishing such price, there shall be included and excluded, as applicable, the charges and readjustments specified in sections 4216(a), 4216(f), and 6416(b)(1) as in effect at the time the tax liability on the use of the article is incurred. If the seller of an article does not regularly sell such articles at retail in arm's length transactions, a constructive price on which the tax shall be computed will be determined by the Commissioner. This price will be established after considering the selling practices and price structures of sellers of similar articles.

(iii) In the case of any short-term lease (as defined in paragraph (d)(6) of this section) by any person other than a manufacturer, producer, or importer (or related person as defined in paragraph (d)(2)(ii) of this section) of an article that is deemed to be a taxable use of such article under paragraph (b)(2) of this section, the tax imposed by section 4051(a)(1) shall be computed on a price equal to the sum of—

(A) The price (as determined under paragraph (d) of this section) at which such article was sold to the lessor plus the cost of any parts and accessories installed by the lessor (or an agent of the lessor) on such article before the first use of lease by the lessor, plus

(B) The product of the sum described in paragraph (c)(5)(iii)(A) of this section and the presumed markup percentge (as defined in paragraph (d)(7) of this section).

(d) *Determination of price.*—(1) *In general.*—The price for which an article is sold includes the total consideration paid for the article whether that consideration is paid in money, services, or other forms. In addition, there shall be included any charge incident to placing the article in condition ready for use. Similar rules to section 4216(a) and the regulations thereunder, relating to charges to be included in the price and excluded from the price, shall apply. For example, charges for transportation, delivery, insurance, and installation (other than installation charges to which section 4051(b) applies), and other expenses actually incurred in connection with the delivery of an article to a purchaser pursuant to a bona fide sale shall be excluded from the price in computing the tax.

(2) *Presumptive retail sales price where tax paid by manufacturer, producer, or importer.*—(i) *In general.*—In the case of a taxable sale (other than a taxable sale described in paragraph (b)(1) of this section) where a manufacturer, producer, importer, or related person is liable for the tax imposed by section 4051, such tax shall be computed on a price equal of the sum of—

(A) The price that would (but for this paragraph (d)(2)) be determined under this paragraph (d), and

(B) The product of the price determined under paragraph (d)(2)(i)(A) of this section and the presumed markup percentage (as defined in paragraph (d)(7) of this section).

(ii) *Related person defined.*—(A) *In general.*—Except as provided in paragraph (d)(2)(ii)(B) of this section, the term "related person" means any person that is a member of the same controlled group (within the meaning of section 5061(e)(3)) as the manufacturer, producer, or importer.

(B) *Exception for permanent retail establishment.*—A person shall not be treated as a related person with respect to the sale of any article if—

(1) Such person sells the article through a permanent retail establishment in the normal course of business of being a retailer, and

(2) Such person has records (*e.g.*, invoices) that substantiate that the article was sold for a price that included a markup equal to or greater than the presumed markup percentage (as defined in paragraph (d)(7) of this section).

(3) *Retail sales price where tax paid by person other than a manufacturer, producer, importer, or related person.*—(i) *In general.*—In the case of a taxable sale (other than a taxable sale defined in paragraph (b)(1) of this section) where a person other than a manufacturer, producer, importer, or related person is liable for the tax imposed by section 4051, such tax shall be computed on a price determined under paragraph (d)(1) of this section.

(ii) *Exception.*—When a person other than a manufacturer, producer, importer, or related person is liable for the tax imposed by section 4051, such tax shall be computed on a price determined under paragraph (d)(2)(i) of this section if—

(A) Such person does not perform any significant activities relating to the processing of the sale of an article,

(B) The principal purpose for processing the sale through such person is to avoid or evade the presumed markup under paragraph (d)(2)(i)(B) of this section, and

(C) Such person does not have records (*e.g.*, invoices) substantiating that the article was sold for a price that included a markup equal to or greater than the presumed markup percentage as defined in paragraph (d)(7) of this section.

(4) *Presumptive retail sales price in the case of a lease by a manufacturer, producer, or importer.*—In the case of any long-term lease (as defined in paragraph (d)(6) of this section) by a manufacturer, producer, importer, or a related person (as defined in paragraph (d)(2)(ii) of this section) of an article that is deemed to be a taxable sale of such article under paragraph (b)(1) of this section, the tax imposed by section 4051(a)(1) shall be computed on a price equal to the sum of—

(i) A constructive sales price established by the Commissioner based on the price at which such article would be sold by a manufacturer, producer, or importer in a sale other than a taxable sale (*e.g.*, a sale to which the exceptions contained in paragraph (a)(2)(ii) of this section apply) on the date the lease is made, and

(ii) The product of the constructive sales price referred to in paragraph (d)(4)(i) of this section and the presumed markup percentage as defined in paragraph (d)(7) of this section.

(5) *Presumptive retail sales price in the case of a long-term lease by any other person.*—In the case of any long-term lease (as defined in paragraph (d)(6) of this section) of an article in which any person other than a manufacturer, producer, or importer (or related person as defined in paragraph (d)(2)(ii) of this section) is the lessor and the long-term lease is deemed to be a taxable sale of such article under paragraph (b)(1) of this section, the tax imposed by section 4051 (a)(1) shall be computed on a price equal to the sum of—

(i) The price (as determined under this paragraph (d)) at which such article was sold to the lessor plus the cost of any parts and accessories installed by the lessor (or an agent of the lessor) on such article before the first use by the lessee or leased in connection with such long-term lease, and

(ii) The product of the sum described in paragraph (d)(5)(i) of this section and the presumed markup percentage as defined in paragraph (d)(7) of this section.

(6) *Long-term and short-term lease defined.*—For purposes of this section, the term "long-term lease" means any lease with a term of one year or more. The term "short-term lease" means any lease with a term of less than one year. In determining a lease term, options to renew shall be taken into account. In addition, two or more successive leases that are part of the same transaction (or a series of related transactions) with respect to the same or substantially similar article, shall be treated as one lease.

(7) *Presumed markup percentage.*—(i) *In general.*—Except as provided in paragraph (d)(7)(ii) of this section, for purposes of this section the term "presumed markup percentage" shall be four percent.

(ii) *Exceptions.*—For purposes of this section the "presumed markup percentage" for trailers, semitrailers, and remanufactured automobile truck chassis and bodies and tractors shall be zero percent. For purposes of this section an article is a remanufactured article if—

(A) The refurbishing, renovation, or repair of the article causes it to be subject to the tax imposed by section 4051, and

(B) Before remanufacture, such article was previously subject to the tax imposed by section 4051 (or section 4061 prior to its repeal).

(8) *Items excluded from price.*—There shall be excluded from the price—

(i) The amount of tax imposed under sections 4051(a)(1) and (b)(1);

(ii) If stated as a separate charge, the amount of any retail sales tax imposed by any state or political subdivision thereof or the District of Columbia, whether the liability for such tax is imposed on the vendor or vendee; and

(iii) The fair market value (including any tax imposed by section 4071) at retail of any tires (not including any metal rim or rim base). For purposes of this paragraph (d)(8)(iii), fair market value at retail shall be determined by the lowest established price for which the vehicle retailer would sell such tires at retail in the ordinary course of trade. The lowest established price is the lowest price for which the vehicle retailer sells, or offers to sell, a single tire to an independent purchaser who would not ordinarily be expected to buy more than one. If the vehicle retailer has no lowest established price the Commissioner will accept any price provided, under the facts and circumstances, such price is not unreasonable. For vehicles sold on or after April 1, 1983, and before October 15, 1985, a price will not be considered unreasonable if it is no more than an amount equal to 50 percent of the manufacturer's suggested retail price.

(9) *Trade-ins.*—If, in connection with the sale of an article subject to the tax imposed under section 4051(a)(1) or (b)(1) on the price for which sold, a vendor receives from its vendee another article in exchange, the tax on the vendor's sale shall be computed on the basis of the full price of the article sold, unreduced by any amount allowed for the article received from the vendee. For example, where a vehicle costing $20,000 is purchased for $16,000 cash plus a used vehicle valued at $4,000, tax is $2,400 (12 percent × $20,000).

(10) *Sales not at arm's length.*—For purposes of § 145.4051-1 and this section, a sale is considered to be made under circumstances otherwise than at "arm's length" if—

(i) One of the parties is controlled (in law or in fact) by the other, or there is common control, whether or not such control is actually exercised to influence the sale price, or

(ii) The sale is made pursuant to special arrangements between a seller and a purchaser.

In the case of an article sold otherwise than at arm's length, and sold at less than the fair market price, the tax imposed under section 4051(a)(1) or (b)(1) shall be computed on the price for which similar articles are sold at retail in the ordinary course of trade, as determined by the Commissioner. Once such a price has been determined, no further adjustment of such price shall be made.

(e) *Examples.*—The provisions of this section may be illustrated by the following examples:

*Example (1).* M manufactures trucks that are taxable under section 4051. On July 11, 1988, D, a corporation that is a dealer, purchases one truck from M for $50,000. M does not own any stock in D. Prior to this transaction, D gave M a certificate that meets the specifications detailed in paragraph (a)(6) of this section. The certificate states that the truck will be resold or leased on a long-term basis. M's sale to D is not a taxable sale of the truck (within the meaning of paragraph (a)(2) of this section). On July 20, 1988, D resells the truck to a purchaser, P, for $52,000. The additional $2,000 includes the dealer's mark-up, costs of transporting the truck from M to D, and overhead. No parts or accessories were added to the truck. P did not give D a certificate and did not have an agreement with D under which all vehicles purchased were to be resold. The sale of the truck by D to P is a taxable sale within the meaning of paragraph (a)(3) of this section. Therefore, D has a tax liability of $6,240 (12% × $52,000).

*Example (2).* Assume the same facts as in example (1) except that M owns 80 percent of D's stock. D and M are members of the same controlled group (within the meaning of section 5061(e)(3)). Therefore, D is a related person under paragraph (d)(2)(ii)(A) of this section. On July 20, 1988, D sells the truck to P for $51,000. D does not have records substantiating that the truck was sold for a price that included a markup equal to or greater than the presumed markup percentage. The tax on the sale of the truck to P is determined under paragraph (d)(2)(i) of this section. Therefore, D has a tax liability of $6,240 (12% × ($50,000 + ($50,000 × 4%))).

*Example (3).* Assume the same facts as in example (1) except that D does not perform any significant activities relating to the sale. Assume further that the principal purpose for processing the sale through D is to avoid the presumed markup and that D did not sell the truck for a price that included a markup equal to or greater then the presumed markup percentage. D, however, is designated the seller of the truck on the invoice. Pursuant to paragraph (d)(3)(ii) of this section, the price of the truck shall be computed on a price determined under paragraph (d)(2)(i). Therefore, D, the taxpayer, has a liability of $6,240 [12% × ($50,000 + ($50,000 × 4%))].

*Example (4).* Assume the same facts as in example (1) except that on July 20, 1988, D leases the truck for a two-year period (*i.e.*, on a long-term basis) to L, a lessee. D's leasing of the truck to L is treated as a taxable sale under paragraph (b)(1) of this section and the tax is computed on the price as determined under paragraph (d)(5)(i) of this section. D has a tax liability of $6,240 [12% × ($50,000 + ($50,000 × 4%))].

*Example (5).* Assume the same facts as in example (1) except that on July 20, 1988, D leases the truck to L for a six-month period (*i.e.*, a short-term lease). The lease is treated as a use under paragraph (b)(2) of this section. The tax is computed on the price as determined under paragraph (c)(5) of this section. D has a tax liability of $6,240 [12% × ($50,000 + ($50,000 × 4%))].

*Example (6).* Assume the same facts as in example (1) except that D does not give M a certificate. The sale by M to D is a taxable sale of the truck under paragraph (a)(2) of this section. M's tax liability is $6,240 [12% × ($50,000 + ($50,000 × 4%))]. On July 20, 1988 D leases the truck to L, a lessee. The lease has a two-year term. Since the lease to L occurred after a taxable sale of the truck, paragraph (b)(1) of this section does not apply, and the lease is not treated as a taxable sale under this section.

*Example (7).* M manufactures trucks that are taxable under section 4051. On July 11, 1988, M leases a truck to a lessee, L. The lease has a two-year term. The lease is treated as a taxable sale under paragraph (b)(1) of this section and the tax is computed on the price as determined under paragraph (d)(4)(i) of this section. The constructive sales price established by the Commissioner, pursuant to paragraph (d)(4)(i) of this section, is $50,000. M has a tax liability of $6,240 [12% × ($50,000 + ($50,000 × 4%))].

*Example (8).* Assume the same facts as in example (7) except that the lease has a six-month term. The lease is treated as a taxable use under paragraph (b)(2) of this section and the tax is computed under paragraph (c)(5) of this section. The constructive sales price estab-

lished by the Commissioner, pursuant to paragraph (c)(5)(i) of this section, is $52,000. M has a tax liability of $6,240 (12% × $52,000).

*Example (9).* M manufactures truck trailers and semitrailers that are taxable under section 4051. On July 5, 1988, D, a dealer, purchases a trailer from M for $10,000. Prior to this transaction, D did not give M a certificate and D did not have an agreement with M to resell all articles purchased. The sale by M to D is a taxable sale of the trailer under paragraph (a)(2) of this section. M has a tax liability of $1,200 (12% × $10,000 + ($10,000 × 0%)).

*Example (10).* Assume the same facts as in example (9) except that on July 12, 1988, D resells the trailer to P, a purchaser, for $10,500 (the additional $500 includes the dealer's markup, costs of transporting the trailer from M to D, and overhead). P did not give D a certificate and P did not have an agreement with D that stipulates that all articles purchased were to be leased on a long-term basis or resold. The sale of the trailer by D to P is a taxable sale within the meaning of paragraph (a)(3) of this section. Therefore, D has a tax liability of $1,260 (12% × $10,500). D, however, may file for a credit or $1,200 under section 6402 provided that the requirements of paragraph (a)(4) of this section are met.

(f) *Other rules made applicable.*—For purposes of § 145.4051-1 and this section, rules similar to the following provisions shall apply:

(1) Section 48.0-2, relating to general definitions and attachment of tax;

(2) Paragraphs (a)(2) and (3) of § 48.4061(a)-1;

(3) The exemptions provided by sections 4063(a) and (d) and the regulations thereunder;

(4) Section 4216(f) and the regulations thereunder, relating to the incorporation of used components; and

(5) Section 4221 and the regulations thereunder, relating to certain tax-free sales.

(g) *Effective date.*—(1) *In general.*—Except as provided below, the provisions of this section shall be effective for articles sold or leased on or after April 1, 1983.

(2) *Certain sales made prior to November 12, 1985.*—If a sale to a lessor before November 12, 1985, was not taxable under § 145.4052-1 of the temporary regulations contained in 26 CFR part 145 revised as of April 1, 1983, (the "prior regulations") and it was so treated by the parties, a subsequent sale or lease that was or would have been treated as the first retail sale of the article under the prior regulations will be treated as a taxable sale for purposes of this section. The tax on such subsequent sale will be based on a price determined under paragraph (d) of this section. For example, if an article was sold to a purchaser who intended to lease such article long-term, the sale would not have been taxable under the prior regulations even though the seller did not receive a certificate of the purchaser's intent to lease the vehicle. If such a sale was treated as nontaxable by the parties, and the purchaser leases it long-term on or after October 1, 1987, the lease will be treated as a taxable sale of the article. The tax is to be computed under paragraph (b) (3) (ii) of this section and the price will be computed under paragraph (d) (5).

(3) *Certain sales made after November 11, 1985, and before October 1, 1987.*—(i) *Sales not treated as taxable by purchaser and seller.*—If a sale to a purchaser after November 11, 1985, and before October 1, 1987, was not treated as taxable by the parties, a subsequent sale or lease that was or would have been treated as the first retail sale of the article under the temporary regulations published in the September 13, 1985, issue of the FEDERAL REGISTER (50 FR 37350) ("the interim regulations") will be treated as a taxable sale for the purposes of this section. The tax on a sale or lease after September 30, 1987, will be based on a price determined under paragraph (d) of this section. For example, if a vehicle was sold on January 3, 1987, to a purchaser who intended to resell the article and who was not in the business of leasing to any extent, the sale would not have been taxable under the interim regulations even though the seller did not receive a certificate indicating the purchaser's intent to resell the article. If such a sale was not treated as a taxable sale by the parties, and the purchaser resells the article, the resale will be treated as a taxable sale of the article under paragraph (a)(2) of this section.

(ii) *Sales treated as first retail sale by purchaser and seller.*—If the sale of an article after November 11, 1985, and before October 1, 1987, was treated as a taxable sale by the parties and tax was paid with respect to the article under the interim regulations, the subsequent sale of the article by the purchaser will not be treated as a taxable sale under paragraph (a)(2) of this section. [Temporary Reg. § 145.4052-1.]

☐ [T.D. 7882, 3-30-83. *Amended by* T.D. 8050, 9-13-85; T.D. 8200, 5-11-88; T.D. 8774, 6-26-98 *and* T.D. 8879, 3-30-2000.]

# Manufacturers Excise Taxes

See p. 20,601 for regulations not amended to reflect law changes

[Reg. § 48.4061(a)-1]

§ 48.4061(a)-1. Imposition of tax; exclusion for light-duty trucks, etc.—(a) *Imposition of tax.*—(1) *In general.*—Section 4061(a)(1) imposes a tax on the sale by the manufacturer, producer, or importer of the following articles (including in each case parts and accessories therefor sold on or in connection therewith or with the sale thereof):

    (i) Automobile truck and bus chassis and bodies;

    (ii) Truck and bus trailer and semitrailer chassis and bodies; and

    (iii) Tractors of the kind chiefly used for highway transportation in combination with a trailer or semitrailer.

For purposes of this section, a sale of an automobile truck or bus, or a truck or bus trailer or semitrailer, shall be considered to be a sale of a chassis and of a body enumerated in this paragraph (a)(1).

(2) *Special rule applicable to chassis and bodies.*—A chassis or body enumerated in paragraph (a)(1) of this section is taxable under section 4061(a)(1) only if such chassis or body is, within the meaning of paragraph (e) of this section, sold for use as a component part of a highway vehicle (as defined in paragraph (d) of this section), which is an automobile truck or bus, a truck or bus trailer or semitrailer, or a tractor of the kind chiefly used for highway transportation in combination with a trailer or semitrailer. Furthermore, a chassis or body which is not enumerated in paragraph (a)(1) of this section is not taxable under section 4061(a)(1) even though such chassis or body is used as a component part of a higway vehicle (*e.g.*, a chassis or body of a passenger automobile).

(3) *Equipment installed on chassis or bodies.*—(i) For purposes of the tax imposed by section 4061(a)(1), equipment or machinery installed on a taxable chassis or body is considered to be an integral part of the taxable chassis or body if the machinery or equipment contributes toward the highway transportation function of the chassis or body, regardless of whether separate sales of the machinery or equipment would be subject to the tax on automotive parts or accessories imposed by section 4061(b). Therefore, the amount of the sale price of a taxable chassis or body that is attributable to such machinery or equipment must be included in the tax base when computing the tax due on a manufacturer's or importer's sale or use of a taxable chassis or body.

Examples of the type of machinery or equipment that contribute to the highway transportation function of a chassis or body are the following: loading and unloading equipment; towing winches; and all other machinery or equipment contributing to either the maintenance or safety of the vehicle, the preservation of cargo (other than refrigeration units), or the comfort or convenience of the driver or passengers.

    (ii) Amounts charged for machinery or equipment that is installed on a taxable chassis or body are not part of the taxable sale price of the chassis or body if (A) such machinery or equipment does not contribute toward the highway transportation function of the chassis or body and (B) the reasonableness of the charge for the machinery or equipment is supportable by adequate records. Examples of such machinery or equipment are the following: equipment designed to spread materials on the highway; machinery or equipment used solely in the operation of mobile amusement rides; television equipment mounted in a mobile television studio; machine shop equipment mounted in a mobile machine shop; and car crushing equipment mounted on the chassis of a mobile car crusher.

(4) *Passenger automobile chassis and bodies, motorcycles, etc.*—No tax is imposed under section 4061(a) on the sale of a motorcycle or, in the case of a sale made after December 10, 1971, on the sale of automobile chassis and bodies not enumerated in paragraph (a)(1) of this section, or of trailer and semitrailer chassis and bodies suitable for use in combination with passenger automobiles. For tax on certain sales made after December 31, 1958, and before December 11, 1971, see paragraph (b)(4) of this section.

(5) *Cross references.*—For additional rules relating to the sale of a chassis or body enumerated in this paragraph for use as a component part of a highway vehicle, see paragraph (e) of this section. For exclusion of certain light-duty highway vehicles, see paragraph (f) of this section. For provisions relating to the tax-free sale of bodies to certain manufacturers, see section 4063(b) and the regulations thereunder. For other exemptions from the tax imposed under section 4061(a), see sections 4063 and 4221 and the regulations thereunder. For special rules relating to the sale by a manufacturer of a vehicle consisting of a tax-paid chassis and a body manufactured by him, see § 48.4061(a)-5.

(b) *Rate and computation of tax.*—(1) *In general.*—With respect to the articles enumerated in paragraph (a)(1) of this section, the rate of tax imposed by section 4061(a)(1) is:

| | | *Percent* |
|---|---|---|
| (i) | For articles sold during the period beginning on January 1, 1959, and ending on September 30, 1979 . . . . . . . . . . . . . . | 10 |
| (ii) | For articles sold on or after October 1, 1979 . . . . . . . . . . . . . . . . . . . . . . . . . | 5 |

(2) *Determination of price subject to tax.*—The tax is computed by applying to the price for which the article is sold the rate in effect at the time of the sale. For definition of the term "price" and for application of the tax to leases of articles, see sections 4216 and 4217, respectively, and the regulations thereunder. If an article subject to tax under section 4061(a) has equipment mounted thereon to perform functions other than in connection with the transportation of persons or property, no tax under section 4061(a) attaches to that part of the selling price on the invoice to the customer or can otherwise be established by adequate records. For other rules relating to the sale of parts or accessories in connection with the sale of a chassis, body, or completed unit, see § 48.4061(a)-4. For special rules relating to the determination of selling price when equipment or machinery is permanently installed on a taxable chassis or body, see paragraph (a)(3) of this section.

(3) *Tax on trailers sold before December 11, 1971.*—With respect to sales made after December 31, 1958, and before December 11, 1971, the rate of tax imposed under section 4061(a) on a trailer or semitrailer chassis or body that is a highway vehicle within the meaning of paragraph (d) of this section depends upon a classification of the article. The sale during this period of a trailer or semitrailer chassis or body (other than a house trailer) suitable for use in combination with passenger automobiles is subject to tax as set forth in paragraph (b)(4) of this section. A trailer suitable for use in combination with a passenger automobile which is designed for purposes other than living or sleeping, commonly referred to as a "utility trailer", is an example of a trailer taxable at the 7 percent rate set forth in paragraph (b)(4) of this section. The sale of a trailer or semitrailer chassis or body that is not suitable for use in combination with passenger automobiles is subject to tax as set forth in paragraph (b)(1) of this section.

(4) *Passenger automobile chassis and bodies and related articles sold before December 11, 1971.*—With respect to the sale after December 31, 1958, and before December 11, 1971, of (i) automobile chassis and bodies not enumerated in paragraph (a)(1) of this section or (ii) trailer and semitrailer chassis and bodies suitable for use in combination with passenger automobiles, the tax imposed by section 4061(a) is computed in accordance with paragraph (b)(2) of this section at the rate of 10 percent for sales prior to June 22, 1965, and at the rate of 7 percent thereafter.

(c) *Liability for tax.*—The tax imposed by section 4061(a) is payable by the manufacturer, producer, or importer making the sale.

(d) *Highway vehicle.*—(1) *Definition.*—For purposes of this subchapter, the term "highway vehicle" means any self-propelled vehicle, or any trailer or semitrailer, designed to perform a function of transporting a load over public highways, whether or not also designed to perform other functions, but does not include a vehicle described in paragraph (d)(2) of this section. For purposes of this definition, a vehicle consists of a chassis, or a chassis and a body if the vehicle has a body, but does not include the vehicle's load. Therefore, in determining whether a vehicle is a "highway vehicle", it is immaterial that the vehicle is designed to perform a highway transportation function for only a particular kind of load, such as passengers, furnishings and personal effects (as in a house, office, or utility trailer), a special type of cargo, goods, supplies, or materials, or, except to the extent otherwise provided in paragraph (d)(2)(i) of this section, machinery or equipment specially designed to perform some off-highway task unrelated to highway transportation. In the case of specially designed machinery or equipment, it is also immaterial, except as provided in paragraph (d)(2)(i) of this section, that such machinery or equipment is permanently mounted on the vehicle. For purposes of paragraph (d) of this section, the term "transport" includes the term "tow", and the term "public highway" includes any road (whether a Federal highway, State highway, city street, or otherwise) in the United States which is not a private roadway. A vehicle which is not a highway vehicle within the meaning of this paragraph shall be treated as a nonhighway vehicle for purposes of this subchapter. Examples of vehicles that are designed to perform a function of transporting a load over the public highways are passenger automobiles, motorcycles, buses, and highway-type trucks, truck tractors, trailers, and semi-trailers.

(2) *Exceptions.*—(i) *Certain specially designed mobile machinery for nontransportation functions.*—A self-propelled vehicle, or trailer or semi-trailer, is not a highway vehicle if it (A) consists of a chassis to which there has been permanently mounted (by welding, bolting, riveting, or other means) machinery or equipment to perform a construction, manufacturing, processing, farming, mining, drilling, timbering, or operation similar to any one of the foregoing enumerated operations if the operation of the machinery or equipment is unrelated to transportation on or off the public highways, (B) the chassis has been specially designed to serve only as a mobile carriage and mount (and a power source, where applicable) for the particular machinery or equipment involved, whether or not such machinery or equipment is in operation, and (C) by reason of such special design, such chassis could not, without substantial structural modification, be used as a component of a vehicle designed to perform a function of transporting any load other than that particular machinery or equipment or similar machinery or equipment requiring such a specially designed chassis.

(ii) *Certain vehicles specially designed for off-highway transportation.*—A self-propelled vehicle, or a trailer or semi-trailer, is not a highway vehicle if it is (A) specially designed for the primary function of transporting a particular type of load other than over the public highway in connection with a construction, manufacturing, processing, farming, mining, drilling, timbering, or operation similar to any one of the foregoing enumerated operations, and (B) if by reason of such special design, the use of such vehicle to transport such load over the public highways is substantially limited or substantially impaired. For purposes of applying the rule of (B) of this subdivision, account may be taken of whether the vehicle may travel at regular highway speeds, requires a special permit for highway use, is overweight, overheight or overwidth for regular highway use, and any other relevant considerations. Solely for purposes of determinations under this paragraph (d)(2)(ii), where there is affixed to the vehicle equipment used for loading, unloading, storing, vending, handling, processing, preserving, or otherwise caring for a load transported by the vehicle over the public highways, the functions are related to the transportation of a load over the public highways even though such functions may be performed off the public highways.

(iii) *Certain trailers and semi-trailers specially designed to perform non-transportation functions off the public highways.*—A trailer or semi-trailer is not a highway vehicle if it is specially designed to serve no purpose other than providing an enclosed stationary shelter for the carrying on of a function which is directly connected with and necessary [to, and at the off-highway site of, a con-] struction, manufacturing, processing, mining, drilling, farming, timbering, or operation similar to any one of the foregoing enumerated operations such as a trailer specially designed to serve as an office for such an operation.

(3) *Optional application.*—For purposes of this subchapter, if any rules existing immediately prior to January 13, 1977, would, if applicable, unequivocally resolve an issue involving the definition of a highway vehicle with respect to a period prior to such date, at the option of the taxpayer, such rules existing prior to such date shall be applied to resolve the issue for all periods prior to such date, and the rules of paragraph (d)(1) and (2) of this section, which define the term "highway vehicle", shall not apply with respect to such issue for all periods prior to such date.

(4) *Highway vehicles not subject to section 4061 tax.*—Although for purposes of this paragraph (d) passenger automobiles, automobile trailers and semi-trailers, motor homes, motorcycles, light-duty trucks, etc., will be considered to be highway vehicles because they are designed to perform a function of transporting a load over public highways, the tax imposed under section 4061(a) does not apply to the sale of such vehicles because they either are not articles subject to tax under such section or are excluded from tax under section 4061(a)(2). See also paragraphs (a)(4) and (f) of this section. Despite the fact that passenger automobiles, passenger automobile trailers and semi-trailers, motor homes, motorcycles, light-duty trucks, etc., are not subject to the manufacturers excise tax on highway vehicles imposed by section 4061(a), the fact that they are nevertheless considered highway vehicles for purposes of this subchapter can be of material significance in determining the applicability of such excise taxes as the tax imposed by section 4041 (relating to diesel and special motor fuels), the tax imposed by section 4071(a)(1) (relating to tires of the type used on highway vehicles), or the tax imposed by section 4481 (relating to highway use tax on highway motor vehicles). In addition, the definition of the term "highway vehicle" is material in determining the credits or refunds provided by section 6416(b)(2)(I) (relating to diesel fuel used in certain highway vehicles), section 6421(a) (relating to gasoline used for a nonhighway purpose), section 6424 (relating to lubricating oil used otherwise than in a

highway motor vehicle), and section 6427(a) (relating to diesel or special motor fuel not used for a taxable purpose).

(e) *Sale of a chassis or body for use as a component of a vehicle other than a highway vehicle.*—(1) *In general.*—Except as otherwise provided in paragraphs (a)(4), (e)(2), or (f) of this section, the sale of a chassis or body shall be deemed to be a sale of a chassis or body enumerated in paragraph (a)(1) of this section if such chassis or body is, in any sense, reasonably suitable for use as a component part of a highway vehicle that is either an automobile truck or bus, a truck or bus trailer or semitrailer, or a tractor of the kind chiefly used for highway transportation in combination with a trailer or semitrailer.

(2) *Exceptions based on unitary concept.*—(i) *Completed vehicles not qualifying as highway vehicles.*—With respect to the sale of a vehicle after January 13, 1977, which would otherwise be treated under paragraph (e)(1) of this section as a sale of a chassis or body enumerated in paragraph (a)(1) of this section, the tax imposed under section 4061(a) shall not apply to such sale if the vehicle (considered as a completed unit) is not considered to be a highway vehicle within the meaning of paragraph (d) of this section.

(ii) *Tax-free sales of chassis and bodies.*—With respect to the sale after January 13, 1977 of a chassis or body (not including the sale of a completed vehicle described in paragraph (e)(2)(i) of this section) which would otherwise be treated under paragraph (e)(1) of this section as a sale of a chassis or body enumerated in paragraph (a)(1) of this section, the tax imposed under section 4061(a) shall not apply to such sale if the chassis or body is actually sold for use, or for resale for use, as a component part of a vehicle that is not a highway vehicle within the meaning of paragraph (d) of this section. For purposes of determining the liability of the manufacturer or reseller for the tax imposed under section 4061(a), the test of the preceding sentence will be considered to be met if (A) the purchaser furnishes the statement set forth in paragraph (e)(2)(iv) of this section to the seller before the manufacturer files a return covering excise taxes for the period in which the sale was made, and (B) the manufacturer or reseller complies with the requirements set forth in paragraph (e)(2)(iii) of this section. However, even though the purchaser and manufacturer (or reseller) have complied with the foregoing, the tax imposed under section 4061(a), shall apply to such sale if the manufacturer or reseller has received a written notification (applicable with respect to such sale) from the Internal Revenue Service that sales of a specified type or types of chassis or bodies may not be made tax free pursuant to this paragraph (e)(2)(ii) until further notification. Any such notification issued by the Internal Revenue Service shall be effective only with respect to sales after the manufacturer has received such notification.

(iii) *Requirements to be met.*—In order for a manufacturer or reseller to sell free of tax under paragraph (e)(2)(ii) of this section an otherwise taxable chassis or body, the manufacturer or reseller must—

(A) Retain in his possession the statement required to be furnished by the purchaser and such other evidence as may be furnished by the purchaser to support the tax-free sale. Such evidence shall be retained for at least 3 years from the due date of the tax that would be due if the transaction in question had been a taxable sale; and

(B) Indicate on the invoice with respect to the sale of the chassis or body that the sale of such article is made free of tax under paragraph (e)(2)(ii) of this section.

(iv) *Form of statement.*—In order for an otherwise taxable chassis or body to be sold free of tax under paragraph (e)(2)(ii) of this section, the purchaser must execute and furnish to the manufacturer or reseller a statement that substantially complies with the following form: . . . . . . . . . . . . . . . . . . . . . . . . . . , 19 . . . . . .

Under the penalty of perjury, the undersigned certifies that he, or the . . . . (Name of purchaser if other than the undersigned), of which he is . . . . (Title), is in the business of . . . . (State nature of business), and that the chassis and/or bodies covered by the accompanying order or contract for purchase from . . . . . . . . . . . . . . . . . . . . . . . . . . . . . . . . . . . . . . . . (Name and address of seller) are purchased for (check one) □ use, or for □ resale for use, as components of the following type or types of nonhighway vehicles:

1. . . . . . . . . . . . . . . . . . . .
2. . . . . . . . . . . . . . . . . . . .
3. . . . . . . . . . . . . . . . . . . .

The undersigned understands that he must be prepared to establish by satisfactory evidence the actual use or disposition of such chassis or bodies and that, upon their use or disposition other than use as components of a nonhighway vehicle, he consents to be treated as the manufacturer of any such chassis or body purchased by him free of the tax imposed by section 4061(a).

The undersigned also understands that he and all guilty parties will, for use of this statement to willfully attempt to evade or defeat the tax imposed under section 4061, be subject, under section 7201, to a fine of not more than $10,000, or imprisonment for not more than 5 years, or both, together with the costs of prosecution.

The undersigned agrees to retain in his possession a copy of this statement for at least 3 years from its date.

. . . . . . . . . . . . . . . . . . . . . . . . . . . . . . . .
(Signature)

. . . . . . . . . . . . . . . . . . . . . . . . . . . . . . . .
(Address)

(v) *Refund or credit of overpayment.*—If a purchaser furnishes the manufacturer with the statement described in paragraph (e)(2)(iv) of this section after the time the manufacturer has filed a return covering excise taxes for the period in which the sale was made, the manufacturer must include the tax on the sale in his return for the period. However, in such case, if the conditions prescribed in paragraph (e)(2)(iii) of this section are met, a claim for refund of the tax paid on such sale may be filed by the manufacturer on Form 843, or a credit taken on a subsequent return, in accordance with the provisions of sections 6402(a) and 6416(a) and § 48.6416(a)-1.

(vi) *Cross reference.*—For special rules relating to the sale by a manufacturer of a vehicle consisting of a tax-paid chassis and a body manufactured by him, see § 48.4061(a)-5.

(f) *Exclusion of light-duty trucks, buses, and related articles from tax.*—(1) *In general.*—(i) No tax is imposed by section 4061(a)(1) on the sale after December 10, 1971, of the following articles, if suitable for use with a vehicle having a gross vehicle weight of 10,000 pounds or less (as determined under paragraph (f)(3) of this section):

(A) Automobile truck and bus chassis and bodies, and

(B) Truck trailer and semitrailer chassis and bodies, suitable for use with a trailer or semitrailer having a gross vehicle weight of 10,000 pounds or less (as so determined).

(ii) For purposes of this part, a chassis or body is suitable for use with a vehicle having a gross vehicle weight of 10,000 pounds or less (hereafter referred to in this paragraph (f) as a "light-duty vehicle") if such chassis or body is commonly used with such a vehicle or possesses actual, practical, and commercial fitness for such use. A truck or bus chassis, sold after December 10, 1971, which is suitable for use with a light-duty vehicle, is not subject to the tax imposed by section 4061(a)(1) regardless of the body actually mounted thereon. Similarly, a truck trailer or semitrailer chassis sold after such date, suitable for use with a trailer or semitrailer having a gross vehicle weight of 10,000 pounds or less, which trailer or semitrailer is suitable for use in connection with a light-duty towing vehicle, is not subject to such tax regardless of the body actually mounted thereon. A truck or bus body, sold after such date, which is suitable for use with a light-duty vehicle, is not subject to such tax even though it may also be suitable for use with (and is actually a component of) a vehicle having a gross vehicle weight in excess of 10,000 pounds. Similarly, a truck trailer or semitrailer body sold after such date, suitable for use with a trailer or semitrailer having a gross vehicle weight of 10,000 pounds or less, which trailer or semitrailer is suitable for use with a light-duty towing vehicle, is not subject to such tax even though it may also be suitable for use with (and is actually a component of) a trailer or semitrailer having a gross vehicle weight of more than 10,000 pounds, or is used in connection with a vehicle having a gross vehicle weight of more than 10,000 pounds.

(iii) Where an exempt body is mounted on a taxable chassis, or a taxable body is mounted on an exempt chassis, the taxable chassis or taxable body, as the case may be, nevertheless remains subject to such tax, if the resulting vehicle is a highway vehicle as defined in paragraph (d) of this section.

(iv) Where the modification of an article, exempt from tax when sold by the original manufacturer, constitutes further manufacture after the original manufacturer's sale, a tax may be imposed on the subsequent manufacturer's sale or use of the modified article.

(2) *Parts and accessories.*—(i) The sale of a part or accessory which, if sold on December 10, 1971, would be subject to the tax imposed by section 4061(a)(1) as in effect at such time, is not subject to the tax imposed by section 4061(a)(1) as in effect after such date if—

(A) It is sold by the manufacturer on or in connection therewith, or with the sale of, a vehicle enumerated in paragraph (f)(1)(i) of this section which is not subject to such tax, and

(B) It is not a replacement part (as defined in paragraph (f)(2)(ii) of this section).

(ii) For purposes of this paragraph (f)(2), a part or accessory is considered sold with a vehicle if, as of the time the article is sold by the manufacturer, the part or accessory has been ordered from such manufacturer for use with the vehicle. Thus, for example, original equipment sold after December 10, 1971, with a light-duty vehicle, consisting of parts and accessories which are ordered from the manufacturer of the vehicle not later than the time at which such vehicle is

sold by him (whether or not installed as of such time) are not subject to such tax. For purposes of this paragraph (f)(2), a part is a replacement part, regardless of when ordered, if its use with a vehicle is as a replacement for a part of such vehicle. Therefore, spare parts or accessories sold separately or ordered with a light-duty truck are subject to the tax imposed on sales of parts or accessories by section 4061(b)(1), unless they are excluded from tax as articles used interchangeably between truck and passenger vehicles under the provisions of section 4061(b)(2).

(3) *Gross vehicle weight.*—(i) For purposes of paragraph (f)(1) of this section, gross vehicle weight means the maximum total weight of a loaded vehicle. Except as otherwise provided in this paragraph (f)(3), such maximum total weight shall be the gross vehicle weight rating of the article (as manufactured) as specified or established by the manufacturer of the completed article, unless such rating is unreasonable in light of the facts and circumstances in a particular case.

(ii) A manufacturer must specify or establish a weight rating for each chassis, body, or vehicle sold by him after September 22, 1971, if such article requires no additional manufacture other than (A) the addition of readily attachable articles, such as tire or rim assemblies or minor accessories, (B) the performance of minor finishing operations, such as painting, or (C) in the case of a chassis, the addition of a body. If an article is specially manufactured to the purchaser's specifications, such specifications may be used to establish the gross vehicle weight of the article.

(iii) A manufacturer shall maintain a record of the gross vehicle weight rating of each truck, bus, trailer, and semitrailer sold by him and excluded from the tax imposed by section 4061(a)(1) by reason of section 4061(a)(2) and this paragraph (f). For this purpose, a record of the serial number of each such article shall be treated as a record of the gross vehicle weight rating of the article if such rating is indicated by the serial number.

(iv) If (A) the manufacturer's rating indicated in a label or identifying device affixed to an article, (B) the rating set forth in his sales invoice or warranty agreement, and (C) his advertised rating for that article (or two or more identical articles) are inconsistent, the highest of such ratings will be considered to be the manufacturer's gross vehicle weight rating specified or established for purposes of the tax imposed by section 4061(a)(1).

(v) With respect to articles sold after January 31, 1972, the manufacturer's gross vehicle weight rating must take into account the strength of the chassis frame, the axle capacity and placement, and the spring, brake, rim, and tire capacities. The component with the lowest weight rating ordinarily shall be considered determinative of the gross vehicle weight. If the capacity of any of the readily attachable components (springs, brakes, rims, or tires) would otherwise be determinative of a gross vehicle weight rating of 10,000 pounds or less, no readily attachable component will be taken into account in determining such rating unless the rating determined solely on the basis of the chassis frame or the total of the axle ratings is 12,000 pounds or less.

(vi) For purposes of paragraph (f)(3)(v) of this section, the term "total of the axle ratings" means the sum of the maximum load carrying capability (capacity and placement) of the axles (without regard to springs, brakes, rims, and tires) and, in the case of a trailer or semitrailer, the weight, if any, that is to be borne by a vehicle used in combination with the trailer or semitrailer for which gross vehicle weight is determined. [Reg. § 48.4061(a)-1.]

☐ [*T.D. 6648*, 4-12-63. *Amended by T.D. 6694*, 12-4-63; *T.D. 6753*, 9-8-64; *T.D. 7461*, 1-12-77 *and T.D. 7566*, 9-15-78.]

### [Reg. § 48.4061(a)-2]

**§ 48.4061(a)-2. Bonding of importers.**—(a) *Authority for requiring bond.*—Section 623 of the Tariff Act of 1930, as amended (19 U.S.C. 1623), provides as follows:

"SEC. 623. *Bonds and other security.* (a) In any case in which bond or other security is not specifically required by law, the Secretary of the Treasury may by regulation or specific instruction require, or authorize collectors of customs to require, such bonds or other security as he, or they, may deem necessary for the protection of the revenue or to assure compliance with any provision of law, regulation, or instruction which the Secretary of the Treasury or the Customs Service may be authorized to enforce.

"(b) Whenever a bond is required or authorized by a law, regulation, or instruction which the Secretary of the Treasury or the Customs Service is authorized to enforce, the Secretary of the Treasury may—

"(1) Except as otherwise specifically provided by law, prescribe the conditions and form of such bond, and fix the amount of penalty thereof, whether for the payment of liquidated damages or of a penal sum: *Provided,* That when a consolidated bond authorized by paragraph 4 of this subsection is taken, the Secretary of the Treasury may fix the penalty of such bond without regard to any other provision of law, regulation, or instruction.

"(2) Provide for the approval of the sureties on such bond, without regard to any general provision of law.

"(3) Authorize the execution of a term bond the conditions of which shall extend to and cover similar cases of importations over such period of time, not to exceed one year, or such longer period as he may fix when in his opinion special circumstances existing in a particular instance require such longer period.

"(4) Authorize, to the extent that he may deem necessary, the taking of a consolidated bond (single entry of term), in lieu of separate bonds to assure compliance with two or more provisions of law, regulations, or instructions which the Secretary of the Treasury or the Customs Service is authorized to enforce. A consolidated bond taken pursuant to the authority contained in this subsection shall have the same force and effect in respect of every provision of law, regulation, or instruction for the purposes for which it is required as though separate bonds had been taken to assure compliance with each such provision.

"(c) The Secretary of the Treasury may authorize the cancellation of any bond provided for in this section, or of any charge that may have been made against such bond, in the event of a breach of any condition of the bond, upon the payment of such lesser amount or penalty or upon such other terms and conditions as he may deem sufficient.

"(d) No condition in any bond taken to assure compliance with any law, regulation, or instruction which the Secretary of the Treasury or the Customs Service is authorized to enforce shall be held invalid on the ground that such condition is not specified in the law, regulation, or instruction authorizing or requiring the taking of such bond.

"(e) The Secretary of the Treasury is authorized to permit the deposit of money or obligations of the United States, in such amount and upon such conditions as he may by regulation prescribe, in lieu of sureties on any bond required or authorized by a law, regulation, or instruction which the Secretary of the Treasury or the Customs Service is authorized to enforce."

(b) *Application for determination whether bond required.*—(1) *Requirement of application.*—(i) *In general.*—Except as otherwise provided in subparagraph (2) of this paragraph, every importer of articles taxable under section 4061(a) shall make application for a determination whether the importer is required to give bond in accordance with the provisions of paragraph (c) of this section. Such application shall be submitted in writing to the district director for the district in which the importer will file returns of any tax under section 4061(a) for which he may incur liability.

(ii) *Form of application.*—No form is prescribed for making the application required under subdivision (i) of this subparagraph, but such application shall include the following information:

(a) The name of the person making the application and the address of his principal place of business, and, if the principal place of business of such person is outside the United States, the address of his principal place of business, office, or agency in the United States.

(b) Information establishing that the person making the application is an importer of articles taxable under section 4061(a).

(c) The kind and approximate number of automobiles, trucks, buses, etc., which the importer may be expected to import during an average calendar quarter and the approximate amount of tax under section 4061(a) for which the importer may be expected to incur liability in respect of such articles.

(d) Whether the importer has filed returns of tax under chapter 31 or chapter 32 within the 2-year period immediately preceding the date on which the application is filed, and, if so, the internal revenue district in which such returns were filed.

(e) Facts pertaining to the importer's assets and liabilities which will aid the district director in determining whether a bond shall be required.

(2) *Exceptions.*—The provisions of subparagraph (1) of this paragraph shall have no application in any case where an article taxable under section 4061(a) is—

(i) Incidentally imported by an individual for his personal use.

(ii) Brought into the United States for export to a foreign country or possession of the United States.

(iii) Admitted to the United States free of duty as an instrument of international traffic.

(iv) Admitted to the United States free of duty as a temporary importation under bond.

(v) Returned to the United States after having been sold in the United States and exported.

(c) *Requirement of bond.*—(1) *In general.*—If the district director determines that a bond is necessary in order to insure payment of the tax under section 4061(a), and to assure compliance with all provisions of the Code and regulations thereunder, with respect to articles imported by any importer required to make application for a determination under paragraph (b) of this section, such bond shall be given by such importer. Such bond shall be submitted, in duplicate, to the district director for the district in which the importer will file returns of any tax under section 4061(a) for which he may incur liability.

(2) *Execution of bond.*—(i) *In general.*—The bond required under this paragraph shall be executed with satisfactory surety. (For provisions as to what will be considered "satisfactory surety", see subparagraph (3) of this paragraph.) Such bond shall be conditioned that the principal shall not engage in any attempt, by himself or by collusion with others, to defraud the United States of any tax under section 4061(a); that he shall render truly and completely all returns, statements, and other documents required of him by law or regulations in respect of such tax; that he shall timely pay all such tax for which he is liable; and in the case of any such tax in respect of an article released from customs custody by reason of such bond, that he shall pay such tax, whether the liability therefor is incurred by him or by some other person as the importer of the articles covered by the bond, unless such other person makes payment of such tax on or before the due date. The bond shall be in an amount which the district director believes to be sufficient to protect the interests of the United States with respect to all articles taxable under section 4061(a) which are released from customs custody by reason of such bond, but in no event shall the bond be in an amount less than the approximate amount of tax under section 4061(a) for which the principal may be expected to incur liability during an average calendar quarter. Such bond shall be signed by the individual, if the principal is an individual; the president, vice president, or other principal officer, if the principal is a corporation; a responsible and duly authorized member or officer having knowledge of its affairs, if the principal is a partnership or other unincorporated organization; or the fiduciary, if the principal is a trust or estate.

(ii) *Cancellation clause.*—The bond required under this paragraph may be accepted with a cancellation clause incorporated therein. Such cancellation clause shall provide that:

(a) Any surety on the bond may at any time give notice to the principal and the district director that he desires to be relieved of liability under said bond after a date named, which shall be at least 60 days after the receipt of notice by the district director.

(b) If the notice is not withdrawn in writing prior to the date named in the notice, the rights of the principal as supported by said bond shall be terminated on such date (unless supported by another bond or bonds). The surety shall, however, remain liable with respect to any tax under section 4061(a) (plus penalties and interest) the liability for which is incurred in respect of articles released from customs custody by reason of the bond.

(c) Said notice may not be given by an agent of the surety, unless it is accompanied by power of attorney duly executed by the surety authorizing the agent to give such notice or by a verified statement that such power of attorney is on file with the Treasury Department.

(iii) *Changes in bond.*—After filing of the bond required under this paragraph, no change may be made in the terms thereof except with the consent of the surety or sureties and subject to the approval of the district director.

(3) *Satisfactory surety.*—(i) *Approved surety company or bonds or notes of the United States.*—For purposes of subparagraph (2) of this paragraph, a bond shall be considered executed with satisfactory surety if:

(a) It is executed by a surety company holding a certificate of authority from the Secretary as an acceptable surety on Federal bonds; or

(b) It is secured by bonds or notes of the United States as provided in 6 U.S.C. 15 (see 31 CFR Part 225).

(ii) *Other surety acceptable in discretion of district director.*—For purposes of subparagraph (2) of this paragraph, a bond may, in the discretion of the district director, be considered executed with satisfactory surety if, in lieu of being executed or secured as provided in subdivision (i) of this subparagraph, it is—

(a) Executed by a corporate surety (other than a surety company), provided such corporate surety establishes that it is within its corporate powers to act as surety for another corporation or an individual;

(b) Executed by two or more individual sureties, provided such individual sureties meet the conditions contained in subdivision (iii) of this subparagraph;

**Reg. § 48.4061(a)-2(b)(1)**

(c) Secured by a mortgage on real or personal property;

(d) Secured by a certified, cashier's, or treasurer's check drawn on any bank or trust company incorporated under the laws of the United States or any State, Territory, or possession of the United States, or by a United States postal, bank, express, or telegraph money order;

(e) Secured by corporate bonds or stocks, or by bonds issued by a State or political subdivision thereof, of recognized stability; or

(f) Secured by any other acceptable collateral. Collateral shall be deposited with the district director or, in his discretion, with a responsible financial institution acting as escrow agent.

(iii) *Conditions to be met by individual sureties.*—If a bond is executed by two or more individual sureties, the following conditions must be met by each such individual surety:

(a) He must reside within the State in which the principal place of business or legal residence of the primary obligor is located;

(b) He must have property subject to execution of a current market value, above all encumbrances, equal to at least the penalty of the bond;

(c) All real property which he offers as security must be located in the State in which the principal place of business or legal residence of the primary obligor is located;

(d) He must agree not to mortgage, or otherwise encumber, any property offered as security while the bond continues in effect without first securing the permission of the district director; and

(e) He must file with the bond, and annually thereafter so long as the bond continues in effect, an affidavit as to the adequacy of his security, executed on the appropriate form furnished by the district director.

Partners may not act as sureties upon bonds of their partnership. Stockholders of a corporate principal may be accepted as sureties provided their qualifications as such are independent of their holdings of the stock of the corporation.

(iv) *Adequacy of surety.*—No surety or security shall be accepted if it does not adequately protect the interest of the United States.

(4) *New or additional bond.*—The district director may require a new or additional bond under this section in any case where he deems it necessary or desirable in order to protect the interests of the United States.

(d) *Termination of requirement.*—(1) *Application for relief from requirement.*—Any importer who has given bond as required under paragraph (c) of this section may make application for relief from such requirement at any time after the last day of the first month following the close of the calendar quarter in which the bond was given. Any such application shall be submitted to the district director to whom the bond was furnished and shall set forth such facts as will be of assistance to the district director in determining whether the relief shall be granted.

(2) *Relief from requirement.*—In any case where the district director determines that the bond required under paragraph (c) of this section to be given by an importer is no longer necessary to insure payment of any tax under section 4061(a) for which liability may be incurred by such importer, such importer shall no longer be required to give such bond.

(e) *Evidence required for release of imported articles from customs custody.*—(1) *In general.*—Each article taxable under section 4061(a) which arrives in the United States from any foreign country or possession of the United States on or after the first day of the first calendar quarter beginning more than 60 days after the date of publication of this Treasury decision in the Federal Register, and which is imported by any person required under paragraph (b) of this section to make application for a determination whether bond shall be given, shall not, if subject to customs examination and release, be released from customs custody until the evidence prescribed in subparagraph (2)(i) or (ii) of this paragraph has been furnished by such person to the collector of customs.

(2) *Form of evidence.*—The evidence required under subparagraph (1) of this paragraph shall be in the form of a statement, executed, signed, and dated by the district director. Such statement shall show the following:

(i) *Bond required.*—If the importer is required to give bond under this section, the statement shall show—

(a) The total number of articles in respect of which the statement is given.

(b) The model number of each such article.

(c) The name and address of the importer of such articles.

(d) If the articles are to be released from customs custody to a person other than the importer, the name and address of such other person.

(e) That the importer has given a bond which the district director finds sufficient to protect the interests of the United States with respect to any tax under section 4061(a) for which liability may be incurred in respect of such articles.

A statement under this subdivision shall be furnished to the importer by the district director, upon request of the importer, in every case where such importer furnishes the district director with information which establishes to the satisfaction of the district director that the importer has given bond in an amount sufficient to protect the interests of the United States with respect to any tax under section 4061(a) which may become due in respect of the articles to which the request relates, and with such other information as is required under this subdivision to be shown in the statement. Such request, together with such information, shall be submitted by the importer immediately upon receipt by him of notice that articles taxable under section 4061(a) have been exported to his order. A separate request shall be made in respect of each shipment. Each statement given under this subdivision shall be executed in duplicate. The original of such statement shall be furnished by the district director to the importer and the copy shall be retained by the district director.

(ii) *No bond required.*—If the importer is not required to give bond under this section, the statement shall show—

(a) The name and address of the importer.

(b) That bond under this section is not required of such importer.

A statement under this subdivision shall be furnished to the importer by the district director on the date on which the district director determines that the importer is not required to give a bond under this section. Such statement shall be executed in triplicate. The original of such statement and one signed copy shall be furnished by the district director to the importer, and one copy shall be retained by the district director. Additional signed copies of such statement will be furnished by the district director to the importer upon request of the importer. However, once such statement, or a signed copy thereof, has been furnished by the importer to a collector of customs, the requirements imposed by subparagraph (1) of this paragraph are deemed to be satisfied in respect of all articles taxable under section 4061(a) which thereafter arrive in the United States for release to or for the importer in a port under the jurisdiction of such collector of customs, until such time, if any, as such collector of customs receives written notification from the district director or the Commissioner of Customs that such statement has been withdrawn. [Reg. § 48.4061(a)-2.]

☐ [T.D. 6499. *Amended by T.D. 7517, 11-11-77.*]

### [Reg. § 48.4061(a)-3]

**§ 48.4061(a)-3. Definitions.**—For purposes of the tax imposed by section 4061, unless otherwise expressly indicated:

(a) *Automobile truck.*—The term "automobile truck" includes automobile buses, and truck and bus trailers and semitrailers.

(b) *Other automobile.*—The term "other automobile" means all automobiles other than automobile trucks, and includes trailers and semitrailers suitable for use in connection with passenger automobiles, but does not include house trailers.

(c) *Tractor.*—The term "tractor" means any tractor chiefly used for highway transportation in combination with a trailer or semitrailer. [Reg. § 48.4061(a)-3.]

☐ [T.D. 6648, 4-12-63.]

### [Reg. § 48.4061(a)-4]

**§ 48.4061(a)-4. Parts or accessories sold on or in connection with chassis, bodies, etc.**—(a) *In general.*—The tax attaches in respect of parts or accessories for articles specified in section 4061(a) sold on or in connection therewith or with the sale thereof at the rate applicable to the sale of the basic article. The tax attaches in such case whether or not the parts or accessories are billed separately. For the tax applicable to parts or accessories which are not sold on or in connection with the sale of a taxable chassis, body, or tractor, see § 48.4061(b)-1.

(b) *Essential equipment.*—If taxable chassis, bodies, or tractors are sold by the manufacturer, producer, or importer without parts or accessories which are considered equipment essential for the operation or appearance of such articles, the sale of such parts or accessories will be considered, in the absence of evidence to the contrary, to have been made in connection with the sale of the basic article even though they are shipped separately at the same time or on a different date. For example, if a manufacturer sells to any person a chassis and the bumpers for such chassis, or sells a taxable tractor and the fifth wheel and attachments, the tax applies to such parts or accessories at the same rate as on the chassis or tractor regardless of the method of billing or the time at which the shipments were made. [Reg. §48.4061(a)-4.]

☐ [*T.D. 6648, 4-12-63.*]

### [Reg. §48.4061(a)-5]

**§48.4061(a)-5. Sale of automobile truck bodies and chassis.—**
(a) *Sale of completed vehicle.*—An automobile truck (as defined by §48.4061(a)-3(a)) for purposes of the tax imposed by section 4061(a) consists of two parts, namely, a body and a chassis. Generally, the tax applies to the sale by the manufacturer of each. Thus, if the purchaser of a tax-paid chassis attaches to it a taxable body manufactured by him and sells the completed vehicle, he is liable for tax based on the sale price of the body only. However, in such a case, the tax attaches to the selling price of the entire vehicle unless adequate records are available to show the portion of the total selling price attributable to the body.

(1)    Parts or accessories sold during the period January 1, 1959, to June 30, 1965, inclusive . . . . . . . . . . . .    8
(2)    Parts or accessories sold on or after July 1, 1965 . . . . . . . . . . . . . . . . . . . . . . . . . . . . . .    5

The tax is computed by applying to the price for which the part or accessory is sold the rate in effect at the time of the sale. For definition of the term "price" see section 4216 and the regulations thereunder contained in Subpart M of this part.

(c) *Liability for tax.*—The tax imposed by section 4061(b) is payable by the manufacturer, producer, or importer making the sale. [Reg. §48.4061(b)-1.]

☐ [*T.D. 6648, 4-12-63. Amended by T.D. 6694, 12-4-63, and T.D. 6753, 9-8-64.*]

### [Reg. §48.4061(b)-2]

**§48.4061(b)-2. Definition of parts or accessories.—**(a) *In general.*—The term "parts or accessories" includes (1) any article the primary use of which is to improve, repair, replace, or serve as a component part of an automobile truck or bus chassis or body, or other automobile chassis or body, or taxable tractor, (2) any article designed to be attached to or used in connection with such chassis, body, or tractor to add to its utility or ornamentation, and (3) any article the primary use of which is in connection with such chassis, body, or tractor, whether or not essential to its operation or use. The term "parts or accessories" includes all articles which have reached such a stage of manufacture as to be commonly known as parts or accessories whether or not fitting operations are required in connection with their installation. An article shall not be deemed to be a taxable part or accessory even though it is designed to be attached to the vehicle or to be primarily used in connection therewith if the article is in effect the load being transported and the primary function of the article is to serve a purpose unrelated to the vehicle as such. For example, a construction derrick attached to a truck is not a taxable part or accessory inasmuch as the derrick is the load of the truck and its use is in connection with construction work at a construction site rather than in connection with the transportation or loading or unloading function of the truck. On the other hand, an article such as a towing cradle or loading or unloading equipment designed to be attached to or to be primarily used in connection with a truck is a taxable part or accessory inasmuch as the article contributes to the load-carrying function of the truck. The term "parts or accessories" does not include tires, inner tubes, or automobile radio or television receiving sets, since these articles are expressly exempted by section 4061(b) from the tax. However, the term "parts or accessories" includes tire valves designed for use on tires or tubes for articles taxable under section 4061(a).

(b) *Articles of a general use.*—The term "parts or accessories" does not include articles which are not used primarily in the manufacture, repair, etc., of automobile trucks, other automobiles, or tractors, but have a general use in the manufacture, repair, etc., of various articles. For example, commodities such as ball and roller bearings, bolts, nuts, washers, screws, nails, tacks, rivets, pins, studs, cotters, pipe fittings such as plugs, tees, ells, and elbows, drain cocks, grease cups, oilers, and similar articles are not of themselves parts or accessories unless so constructed as to be used primarily in the manufacture, repair, etc., of automobile trucks, other automobiles, or tractors. On the other hand, parts for automobile parts or accessories are in themselves taxable unless they are articles of a type not specifically designed for use primarily in the automobile field. For example, the tax applies to the sale of gears, flexible shafts, and flexible housings designed as replacement parts for automotive speedometers; as well as replacement parts for automobile engines, transmissions, differentials, steering mechanisms, timers, windshield-wiper motors, and other automobile parts or accessories.

(b) *Cross references.*—For special rules relating to the sale of a chassis or body to a purchaser who will use it in the manufacture or assembly of an nonhighway vehicle, see §48.4061(a)-1(e). With respect to bodies sold to a chassis manufacturer, see also section 4063(b) and the regulations thereunder. [Reg. §48.4061(a)-5.]

☐ [*T.D. 6648, 4-12-63.*]

### [Reg. §48.4061(b)-1]

**§48.4061(b)-1. Imposition of tax.—**(a) *In general.*—Section 4061(b) imposes a tax on the sale by the manufacturer, producer, or importer of parts or accessories (other than tires and inner tubes and other than automobile radio and television receiving sets) for any of the articles enumerated in section 4061(a) (see paragraph (a) of §48.4061(a)-1).

(b) *Rates of tax.*—Tax is imposed on the sale of parts or accessories for any of the articles enumerated in section 4061(a) at the rates specified below:

(c) *Materials of a general use.*—(1) *General rule.*—The term "parts or accessories" also does not include material such as glass, cloth, leather, matting linoleum, and other materials sold in rolls or by the foot, such as brake lining, tape, binding, wire, cable, metal and rubber tubing, packing, conduit, and similar material. However, except as provided in subparagraph (2) of this paragraph, when any such material is cut or otherwise transformed by any person into an automobile part or accessory, tax attaches at the time such part or accessory is sold by such person.

(2) *Articles made for immediate installation or repair.*—If in connection with an immediate installation in an automobile truck, other automobile, or tractor an article is produced through the use of special machinery or as a result of specialized skills from lengths or rolls of material, the person producing such article is considered to have manufactured an automobile part or accessory and the tax applies to his sale of such part or accessory. For example, tax applies to the sale of automobile glass cut to size to replace broken glass, or automobile seat covers, automobile floor mats, or fitted truck top covers produced to replace worn seat covers, floor mats, or truck top covers. However, if an article of a minor nature is produced by simple operation from lengths or rolls of material for immediate use by a repairman in the repair of an automobile truck, other automobile, or tractor on which he is then working, the person producing such article is not considered to have manufactured an automobile part or accessory and tax does not apply on his sale of such article. For example, tax does not apply where a wire, hose, or board is cut to size in order to replace a damaged wire, hose, or board of an automobile truck, other automobile, or tractor.

(d) *Examples of articles taxable as parts or accessories.*—Examples of articles which are taxable as parts or accessories are: Automobile air conditioners; baby seats for automobiles; automobile beds; automobile hammocks; automobile clutches; bottle warmers and heating pads designed to operate from an automobile cigarette lighter; automobile radio antennae; automobile license plate frames; automobile clocks; automobile mirrors and mirror brackets; purses for carrying parking meter coins or cases for carrying registration cards when designed for attachment to an automobile; safes primarily designed for use in taxable motor vehicles; electric bulbs primarily designed and adapted for use on automobiles; automobile floor mats; jacks of the mechanical or hydraulic bumper, screw, ratchet, scissors, or other type primarily designed to be carried as accessories in automobiles as distinguised from jacks designed especially for use in garages and repair shops; dollies of the type commonly known as converter dollies which are used as connectors to convert semitrailers to full trailers; tool kits recommended for use with automobiles; automobile seat covers of any construction whether they are ready-made or custom fitted; fitted truck top covers; glass cut to size for installation in automobiles; and automobile bearings, such as automobile crankshaft or connecting rod bearings.

(e) *Effective date.*—This section shall be effective with respect to sales made on or after January 1, 1964. For the definition of parts or accessories applicable to sales thereof prior to such date, see §48.4061(b)-2 of this chapter (Manufacturers and Retailers Excise Tax Regulations).

(f) *Cross references.*—For provisions relating to the tax imposed upon:

(1) Tires and inner tubes, see section 4071 and the regulations thereunder contained in Subpart H of this part:

(2) Automobile radio and television receiving sets, see section 4141 and the regulations thereunder contained in Subpart J of this part; and

(3) Fare registers and fare boxes for use on buses and automobiles, see section 4191 and the regulations thereunder contained in Subpart L of this part. [Reg. § 48.4061(b)-2.]

☐ [*T.D.* 6648, 4-21-63. *Amended by T.D.* 6655, 5-23-63.]

### [Reg. § 48.4062(a)-1]

**§ 48.4062(a)-1. Specific parts or accessories.**—Spark plugs, storage batteries, leaf springs, coils, timers, and tire chains, which are suitable for use on or in connection with, or as component parts of, automobile trucks, other automobiles, tractors, or other vehicles enumerated in section 4061(a), are considered parts of, or accessories for, such articles whether or not primarily designed or adapted for such use. [Reg. § 48.4062(a)-1.]

☐ [*T.D.* 6648, 4-12-63.]

### [Reg. § 48.4062(b)-1]

**§ 48.4062(b)-1. Rebuilt parts or accessories sold on an exchange basis.**—The sale price of a rebuilt part or accessory on which the tax is to be computed shall not include the value of a like part or accessory accepted in exchange. The total amount charged in excess of the amount allowed for a like article accepted in an exchange will be the basis for tax. For example, if a rebuilt automobile engine is sold for $100, plus another automobile engine, the tax on the rebuilt engine will be computed on the basis of $100. [Reg. § 48.4062(b)-1.]

☐ [*T.D.* 6648, 4-12-63.]

### [Reg. § 48.4063-1]

**§ 48.4063-1. Tax-free sales of bodies to chassis manufacturers.**—Under the provisions of section 4063(b), the tax imposed by section 4061 (a) shall not apply to bodies sold by the manufacturer thereof to a manufacturer (but not an importer) of automobile trucks (as defined by § 48.4061(a)-3(a)) to be sold by the purchaser. Thus, a manufacturer of automobile truck bodies is permitted to sell such bodies tax free to manufacturers of automobile truck chassis. This section does not apply with respect to the sale of an automobile truck chassis to manufacturers of automobile truck bodies. However, see § 48.4061(a)-1(e) with respect to the sale of an automobile truck chassis for use in the manufacture or assembly of a nonhighway vehicle (within the meaning of § 48.4061(a)-1(d)). In order to effect a tax-free sale of a body as provided in this section both the seller and purchaser must comply with the registration and other requirements of section 4222 and the regulations thereunder. A chassis manufacturer who purchases a body tax free as provided in this section shall, for purposes of application of the tax imposed by section 4061(a), be considered the manufacturer of such body. [Reg. § 48.4063-1.]

☐ [*T.D.* 6648, 4-12-63. *Amended by T.D.* 7461, 1-12-77.]

### [Reg. § 48.4063-2]

**§ 48.4063-2. Tax-free sales of parts or accessories sold for resale on or in connection with the first retail sale of a light-duty truck.**—

(a) *In general.*—Under section 4063(e), the 8-percent manufacturers excise tax imposed by section 4061(b) on the sale of truck parts or accessories does not apply to the sale by the manufacturer, producer, or importer of any parts which are to be resold by the purchaser on or in connection with the first retail sale of a light-duty truck as defined in section 4061(a)(2), or which are to be resold by the purchaser to a second purchaser for resale by the second purchaser on or in connection with the first retail sale of a light-duty truck. A tax-free sale is also allowed under section 4063(e) if an ultimate purchaser makes a direct purchase from a manufacturer of a part or accessory for use on or in connection with a substantially contemporaneous purchase of a new light-duty truck.

(b) *Evidence required for tax-free sales of light-duty truck parts and accessories.*—(1) *In general.*—The provisions of section 4063(e) do not apply with respect to any sale unless the manufacturer, the first purchaser, and the second purchaser, if any, are all registered as required under section 4222, and unless they comply with all the requirements under that section relating to tax-free sales. To effectuate a tax-free sale directly from the manufacturer, first or second purchaser to an ultimate purchaser, the ultimate purchaser must, in every case, satisfy the provisions of paragraphs (b)(3)(i), (ii) and (iii) of this section. Persons not required to be registered under section 4222(b) may purchase articles tax free by following the same procedures that apply to them in the case of other tax-free sales. See § 48.4222(b)-1.

(2) *Revocation or suspension of registration or right to use exemption certificate.*—A person's registration and right to sell or purchase articles tax free through the use of an exemption certificate may be revoked or suspended. See § 48.4222(c)-1. Such a revocation or suspension shall be in addition to any other penalties that may apply. Any person who purchases articles tax free and who sells or uses them for a non-exempt purpose shall notify its vendor of the taxable sale or use.

(3) *Exemption certificate.*—(i) To establish exemption from tax under section 4061(b) in those instances where a sale is made directly to an ultimate purchaser, the manufacturer, first, or second purchaser must obtain (prior to or at the time of sale) from the ultimate purchaser and retain in its possession a properly executed exemption certificate in the form prescribed in paragraph (b)(3)(iii) of this section.

(ii) Where only occasional sales are made, a separate exemption certificate shall be furnished for each order. However, where sales are regularly or frequently made to a purchaser for such exempt use, a certificate covering all sales for a specified period not to exceed 12 calendar quarters will be acceptable. Such certificates and proper records of invoices, orders, etc. relative to tax-free sales must be kept for inspection by the district director as provided in section 6001 and the regulations thereunder.

(iii) The following form of exemption certificate will be acceptable for purposes of this section and must be adhered to in substance.

**Exemption Certificate**

(For use by ultimate purchaser who purchase[s] parts or accessories from a manufacturer, producer, importer, first or second purchaser for use on or in connection with the first retail sale of a light-duty truck. (Section 4063 of the Internal Revenue Code.))

(Date) . . . . . . . . , 19 . . . .

1. I, the undersigned, certify that I am, or the . . . . . . . . . . . . . . . . . (Name of company) of which I am . . . . . . . . . . . . (Position held), is purchasing from the manufacturer, producer, importer, first or second purchaser the parts or accessories specified in section 2 below (or in the purchase order or invoice attached hereto) for use on or in connection with a substantially contemporaneous purchase of a new light-duty truck specified in section 3 below. I also certify that (check applicable type of certificate) . . . . the article or articles specified in the accompanying order, as described below, or . . . . all orders placed by the purchaser for the period commencing . . . . . . . . . . . (Date) and ending . . . . . . . . . . . (Date) (period not to exceed 12 calendar quarters), will be used only for the above stated tax-exempt purposes and will not be used as a replacement part.

I understand that the willful use of this exemption certificate to evade or defeat the manufacturers excise tax otherwise applicable to these parts or accessories will subject me to a fine of not more than $10,000 or imprisonment for not more than 5 years, or both, together with cost of prosecution.

. . . . . . . . . . . . . . . . . . . . . . . . . . . . . . . . . . . . . . . .

(Signature)

. . . . . . . . . . . . . . . . . . . . . . . . . . . . . . . . . . . . . . . .

(Address)

**2. Description of parts and accessories**

| *Type* | *Quantity* | *Price* | *Total* |
|---|---|---|---|
| . . . . . . . . . . . . | . . . . . . . . . . . . | . . . . . . . . . . . . | . . . . . . . . . . . . |
| . . . . . . . . . . . . | . . . . . . . . . . . . | . . . . . . . . . . . . | . . . . . . . . . . . . |
| . . . . . . . . . . . . | . . . . . . . . . . . . | . . . . . . . . . . . . | . . . . . . . . . . . . |

**3. Description of new light-duty truck**
(a) Type:
(b) Quantity,
(c) Serial Number.
(d) GVWR:
(e) Date of Sale,
(f) Invoice Number.
(g) Name and Address of Vendor of Vehicle.

(c) *Information; records.*—(1) *Information to be furnished to vendee.*—A vendor (including the manufacturer) selling light-duty truck parts and accessories tax free under section 4063(e) shall indicate to its vendee that the vendee is obtaining the parts or accessories tax free for the purpose of resale (or used) on or in connection with the first retail sale of a light-duty truck. This information may be transmitted by any convenient means, such as coding of sales invoices, provided that the information is presented with sufficient particularity so that the purchaser is informed that the purchaser has obtained the light duty truck parts or accessories tax free.

(2) *Records of vendor.*—A manufacturer or vendor selling light-duty truck parts or accessories tax free under section 4063(e) shall maintain in its records the identity of the purchaser, a signed statement of the exempt purpose for purchasing the light-duty truck parts or accessories, and the quantity of light-duty truck parts or accessories sold tax free to each purchaser.

(3) *Records of vendee.*—A person purchasing light-duty truck parts or accessories tax free under section 4063(e) must maintain sufficient records to establish that the parts or accessories purchased tax free have actually been resold (or used) on or in connection with the first retail sale of a light-duty truck or have been resold to a second purchaser for such a resale by the second purchaser.

(d) *Duty of selling manufacturer to ascertain validity of tax-free sale.*—The selling manufacturer of light-duty truck parts is not relieved of liability under the provisions of section 4063(e) by reason of section 4221(c) for the tax imposed by section 4061(b) if at the time of sale the selling manufacturer has knowledge or reason to believe that the light-duty truck parts or accessories sold by it to the purchaser are not intended for resale (or use) on or in connection with the first retail sale of a light-duty truck. The selling manufacturer is also not relieved of liability if it has knowledge or reason to believe that the purchaser has failed to register, refused to execute an exemption certificate, or that its registration or its right to purchase tax free through the use of an exemption certificate has been revoked or suspended.

Miles per gallon:
| | |
|---|---|
| At least 15 . . . . . . . . . . . . . . . . . . . . . . . . . . . . . . . . . | 0 |
| At least 14 but less than 15 . . . . . . . . . . . . . . . . . . . . . . . . | $200 |
| At least 13 but less than 14 . . . . . . . . . . . . . . . . . . . . . . . . | 300 |
| Less than 13 . . . . . . . . . . . . . . . . . . . . . . . . . . . . . . . . | 550 |

(ii) In the case of a 1981 model year automobile:

Miles per gallon:
| | |
|---|---|
| At least 17 . . . . . . . . . . . . . . . . . . . . . . . . . . . . . . . . . | 0 |
| At least 16 but less than 17 . . . . . . . . . . . . . . . . . . . . . . . . | $200 |
| At least 15 but less than 16 . . . . . . . . . . . . . . . . . . . . . . . . | 350 |
| At least 14 but less than 15 . . . . . . . . . . . . . . . . . . . . . . . . | 450 |
| At least 13 but less than 14 . . . . . . . . . . . . . . . . . . . . . . . . | 550 |
| Less than 13 . . . . . . . . . . . . . . . . . . . . . . . . . . . . . . . . | 650 |

(iii) In the case of a 1982 model year automobile:

Miles per gallon:
| | |
|---|---|
| At least 18.5 . . . . . . . . . . . . . . . . . . . . . . . . . . . . . . . . | 0 |
| At least 17.5 but less than 18.5 . . . . . . . . . . . . . . . . . . . . . . | $200 |
| At least 16.5 but less than 17.5 . . . . . . . . . . . . . . . . . . . . . . | 350 |
| At least 15.5 but less than 16.5 . . . . . . . . . . . . . . . . . . . . . . | 450 |
| At least 14.5 but less than 15.5 . . . . . . . . . . . . . . . . . . . . . . | 600 |
| At least 13.5 but less than 14.5 . . . . . . . . . . . . . . . . . . . . . . | 750 |
| At least 12.5 but less than 13.5 . . . . . . . . . . . . . . . . . . . . . . | 950 |
| Less than 12.5 . . . . . . . . . . . . . . . . . . . . . . . . . . . . . . . | 1,200 |

(iv) In the case of a 1983 model year automobile:

Miles per gallon:
| | |
|---|---|
| At least 19 . . . . . . . . . . . . . . . . . . . . . . . . . . . . . . . . . | 0 |
| At least 18 but less than 19 . . . . . . . . . . . . . . . . . . . . . . . . | $350 |
| At least 17 but less than 18 . . . . . . . . . . . . . . . . . . . . . . . . | 500 |

(e) *Cross reference.*—For credit or refund, see section 6416(b)(2).

(f) *Effective date.*—Section 4063(e) (relating to light-duty truck parts and accessories) applies to sales on or after December 1, 1978. Light-duty truck parts or accessories sold prior to that date are not exempt from tax under section 4061(b) by reason of section 4063(e). [Reg. § 48.4063-2.]

☐ [*T.D.* 7834.]

**[Reg. § 48.4063-3]**

**§ 48.4063-3. Other tax-free sales.**—For provisions relating to tax-free sales of articles referred to in section 4061, see—
(a) Section 4221, relating to certain tax-free sales;
(b) Section 4222, relating to registration; and
(c) Section 4223, relating to special rules pertaining to further manufacture; and the regulations thereunder contained in Subpart N of this part. [Reg. § 48.4063-3.]

☐ [*T.D.* 6648, 4-12-63.]

**[Reg. § 48.4064-1]**

**§ 48.4064-1. Gas guzzler tax.**—(a) *General rule.*—(1) *In general.*—Section 4064 imposes on the sale by the manufacturer of an automobile a tax determined in accordance with the tables in section 4064(a)(1) through (7), and in paragraph (a)(2) of this section. The tax is applicable to model types of 1980 and later model year automobiles that have a fuel economy level below the applicable tax-free fuel economy level. Paragraph (b) of this section defines the following terms: sale, manufacturer, automobile, model year, model type, fuel economy, and fuel. Paragraph (c) of this section contains rules relating to the determination of fuel economy. Paragraph (d) of this section contains a special rule for certain small manufacturers. Paragraph (e) of this section contains rules relating to the tax-free sales of emergency vehicles.

(2) *Tables.*—(i) In the case of a 1980 model year automobile: If the fuel economy of the model type in which the automobile falls is:
The tax is—

(ii) If the fuel economy of the model type in which the automobile falls is:
The tax is—

(iii) If the fuel economy of the model type in which the automobile falls is:
The tax is—

(iv) If the fuel economy of the model type in which the automobile falls is:
The tax is—

| | The tax is— |
|---|---|
| At least 16 but less than 17 | 650 |
| At least 15 but less than 16 | 800 |
| At least 14 but less than 15 | 1,000 |
| At least 13 but less than 14 | 1,250 |
| Less than 13 | 1,550 |

(v) In the case of a 1984 model year automobile:   If the fuel economy of the model type in which the automobile falls is:

| Miles per gallon: | The tax is— |
|---|---|
| At least 19.5 | 0 |
| At least 18.5 but less than 19.5 | $450 |
| At least 17.5 but less than 18.5 | 600 |
| At least 16.5 but less than 17.5 | 750 |
| At least 15.5 but less than 16.5 | 950 |
| At least 14.5 but less than 15.5 | 1,150 |
| At least 13.5 but less than 14.5 | 1,450 |
| At least 12.5 but less than 13.5 | 1,750 |
| Less than 12.5 | 2,150 |

(vi) In the case of a 1985 model year automobile:   If the fuel economy of the model type in which the automobile falls is:

| Miles per gallon: | The tax is— |
|---|---|
| At least 21 | 0 |
| At least 20 but less than 21 | $500 |
| At least 19 but less than 20 | 600 |
| At least 18 but less than 19 | 800 |
| At least 17 but less than 18 | 1,000 |
| At least 16 but less than 17 | 1,200 |
| At least 15 but less than 16 | 1,500 |
| At least 14 but less than 15 | 1,800 |
| At least 13 but less than 14 | 2,200 |
| Less than 13 | 2,650 |

(vii) In the case of a 1986 or later model year automobile:   If the fuel economy of the model type in which the automobile falls is:

| Miles per gallon: | The tax is— |
|---|---|
| At least 22.5 | 0 |
| At least 21.5 but less than 22.5 | $500 |
| At least 20.5 but less than 21.5 | 650 |
| At least 19.5 but less than 20.5 | 850 |
| At least 18.5 but less than 19.5 | 1,050 |
| At least 17.5 but less than 18.5 | 1,300 |
| At least 16.5 but less than 17.5 | 1,500 |
| At least 15.5 but less than 16.5 | 1,850 |
| At least 14.5 but less than 15.5 | 2,250 |
| At least 13.5 but less than 14.5 | 2,700 |
| At least 12.5 but less than 13.5 | 3,200 |
| Less than 12.5 | 3,850 |

(3) *Liability for tax.*—The tax imposed by section 4064 is payable by the manufacturer making the sale. An automobile sold before the time a determination of fuel economy is made for the model type (as defined in paragraph (b)(6) of this section) is subject to tax if it is subsequently determined that the fuel economy level of that model type of automobile is within the taxable range (see paragraph (a)(1) of this section).

(b) *Definitions.*—(1) *Sale.*—Sale includes the use (within the meaning of section 4218) or the first lease (within the meaning of section 4217(e)) of an automobile by the manufacturer.

(2) *Manufacturer.*—The term "manufacturer" has the same meaning assigned to such term under §48.0-2(a)(4). The term "manufacturer" includes a producer or importer. An importer is a person who imports an automobile whether or not in connection with a trade or business.

(3) *Automobile.*—The term "automobile" means any four-wheeled vehicle—

(i) Propelled by an engine powered by fuel;

(ii) Manufactured primarily for use on public streets, roads, and highways (except any vehicle operated exclusively on a rail or rails);

(iii) Rated at 6,000 pounds gross vehicle weight or less; and

(iv) Requiring no further manufacturing operations to perform its intended function, other than the addition of readily attacha-

ble components, such as mirrors or tire and rim assemblies, or minor finishing operations, such as painting. For this purpose, gross vehicle weight means the value specified by the manufacturer as the maximum design loaded weight of a single vehicle. An automobile does not include a nonpassenger automobile as defined in regulations in effect on November 9, 1978 (49 CFR 523.5 (1978)), which were prescribed by the Secretary of Transportation for section 501 of the Motor Vehicle Information and Cost Savings Act (15 U.S.C. 2001). In addition, an automobile does not include the following: any vehicle sold for use and used primarily as an ambulance or combination ambulance-hearse; any vehicle sold for use and used by the United States or by a State or local government primarily for police or other law enforcement purposes; or any vehicle sold for use and used primarily for fire-fighting purposes.

(4) *Model year.*—The term "model year" means the manufacturer's annual production period (as determined by the Administrator of the Environmental Protection Agency) which includes January 1 of any particular calendar year. If the manufacturer has no annual production year, the model year is the calendar year.

(5) *Model type.*—The term "model type" means a particular class of automobile, as determined by regulations in effect on November 9, 1978 (40 CFR 600.002.79(a)(19) (1978)), which were prescribed by the Administrator of the Environmental Protection Agency.

(6) *Fuel economy.*—The term "fuel economy" means the average number of miles traveled by an automobile per gallon of fuel con-

Reg. §48.4064-1(b)(6)

sumed, rounded to the nearest .1 mile per gallon. The fuel economy for any model type is determined by the Environmental Protection Agency (as determined in accordance with the procedures provided in paragraph (c) of this section). For this purpose, the fuel economy is a combined (urban-highway weighted average) mileage figure estimated in connection with the determination (or redetermination) of general label value (fuel economy information displayed on a sticker that is affixed to new automobiles) mandated under section 506 of the Motor Vehicle Information and Cost Savings Act (15 U.S.C. 2006) and regulations thereunder (40 CFR 600).

(7) *Fuel.*—The term "fuel" means gasoline and diesel fuel.

(c) *Determination of fuel economy.*—For purposes of this section, the fuel economy for any model type is determined (or redetermined) in accordance with the testing and calculation procedures utilized by the Environmental Protection Agency Administrator for model year 1975 (weighted 55 percent urban cycle and 45 percent highway cycle), or any other procedures (yielding comparable results) established by the Administrator. The Environmental Protection Agency's determination (or redetermination) of a model type's fuel economy is made at the time the general label fuel economy value is calculated (or recalculated). This determination (or redetermination) is conclusive for purposes of this section. A redetermination of a model type's fuel economy value shall be effective only with respect to those automobiles for which the manufacturer is required (or is permitted and chooses) under Environmental Protection Agency regulations to affix labels with the recalculated general label fuel economy value.

(d) *Special rule for small manufacturers.*—(1) *In general.*—A small manufacturer (as defined in subparagraph (2)(i) of this paragraph) may apply for a determination that it is not feasible for that manufacturer to meet the statutory tax-free fuel economy level for the model year, with respect to all automobiles produced by that manufacturer, or with respect to a particular model type. For this purpose, the Commissioner (or his delegate) will make a determination of maximum feasible fuel economy level with respect to the automobiles that are the subject of the determination, but only after consultation with the Secretary of Energy, the Secretary of Transportation, and the Administrator of the Environmental Protection Agency (or their delegates) to obtain their views. A finding that it is not feasible for the manufacturer to meet the statutory tax-free fuel economy level will be made by the Internal Revenue Service if the maximum feasible fuel economy level (as defined in subparagraph (3)(i) of this paragraph) of the automobiles that are the subject of the determination is lower than the statutory tax-free fuel economy level for those automobiles. If it is determined that it is not feasible for a small manufacturer to meet the statutory tax-free fuel economy level, the Secretary (or his delegate) has the discretion to grant to the manufacturer the alternate rate schedule prescribed in paragraph (d)(3)(iii) of this section in lieu of the applicable statutory tax table prescribed in section 4064(a). The decision whether to grant the alternate rate schedule shall be based on the consideration set forth in paragraph (d)(3)(ii) of this section. If a small manufacturer for which an alternate rate schedule under this paragraph (d) is applicable sells an automobile to an importer, the alternate rate schedule applies to the sale by the importer of such automobile if such automobile is of the model year and type to which such alternate schedule applies.

(2) *Definitions.*—(i) *Small manufacturer.*—A small manufacturer is any manufacturer who produced (whether or not in the United States) fewer than 10,000 automobiles in the second model year

preceding the affected model year (the model year for which the determination under this paragraph is being made), and who can reasonably be expected to produce (whether or not in the United States) fewer than 10,000 automobiles in the affected model year.

(ii) *Manufacturer.*—For purposes of this paragraph, the term "manufacturer" does not include a person who is only an importer, but does include a producer of automobiles outside the United States who is also an importer.

(iii) *Members of a controlled group.*—For purposes of this paragraph, persons who are members of a controlled group of corporations (as defined in section 1563(a) of the Internal Revenue Code, except that "more than 50 percent" is substituted for "at least 80 percent" each place it appears in section 1563(a)) are treated as one manufacturer.

(3) *Basis for determination.*—(i) *Maximum feasible fuel economy level.*—For purposes of this paragraph, the maximum feasible fuel economy level is determined by taking into account the same factors used in determining the maximum feasible fuel economy level under section 502(e) of the Motor Vehicle Information and Cost Savings Act (as amended) and the regulations thereunder in effect on November 9, 1978. (Those regulations for small manufacturers are prescribed in 49 CFR 525 (1978).) In making this determination, the Commissioner (or his delegate) will consult with the National Highway Traffic Safety Administration of the Department of Transportation.

(ii) *Decision to grant alternate rate schedule.*—In deciding whether to grant an alternate rate schedule, the Secretary (or his delegate) will consider whether the use (in the United States) of the automobile serves an important public policy (*e.g.*, providing public transportation or transportation for the handicapped) that overrides the United States' need to conserve energy. The manufacturer has the burden of demonstrating that the public policy consideration involved overrides the United States' need to conserve energy. The Commissioner (or his delegate), after consultation with the Secretary of Energy, the Secretary of Transportation, and the Administrator of the Environmental Protection Agency (or their delegates), will review the information submitted by the manufacturer and report findings and recommendations to the Secretary (or his delegate).

(iii) *Alternate rate schedule and tax.*—If an alternate rate schedule is granted, the maximum feasible fuel economy level shall be deemed to be the statutory tax-free fuel economy level. Accordingly, a tax is imposed only on automobiles sold that fail to meet the deemed tax-free fuel economy level. The alternate rate schedule shall be determined by substituting the maximum feasible fuel economy level for the tax-free fuel economy level in the applicable statutory tax table set forth in section 4064(a), and by substituting for the miles per gallon amount prescribed in that applicable table an amount that is the tax-free fuel economy decreased by one mile per gallon increments, while keeping the same corresponding tax amount prescribed in that applicable table. The rule for determining an alternate rate schedule may be illustrated by the following example:

*Example.* Manufacturer X, a small manufacturer of automobiles specifically designed to accommodate disabled passengers, applied for a determination that it is not feasible for X to meet the statutory tax-free fuel economy level for a particular model type of X's 1982 model year automobiles. It was determined that the maximum feasible fuel economy level for that model type was 15 miles per gallon. The Secretary decided to grant X an alternate rate schedule. The alternate rate schedule for the model type would be as follows:

| If the fuel economy of the automobile is: Miles per gallon: | The tax is— |
|---|---|
| At least 15 | 0 |
| At least 14 but less than 15 | $200 |
| At least 13 but less than 14 | 350 |
| At least 12 but less than 13 | 450 |
| At least 11 but less than 12 | 600 |
| At least 10 but less than 11 | 750 |
| At least 9 but less than 10 | 950 |
| Less than 9 | 1,200 |

Thus, if X's 1982 automobiles of that model year and type attain only 12 miles per gallon (because X fails to modify them to reach the maximum feasible fuel economy level before they are sold), the tax imposed upon the sale of each automobile is $450 (instead of the $1,200 tax (see the applicable statutory tax table set forth in section 4064(a)(3)), which would have been imposed had no alternate rate schedule been prescribed).

(4) *Duration of determination.*—A determination under this paragraph does not apply to more than three model years.

(5) *Requirements for application.*—Each application for a determination under this section must—

(i) Identify the model year or years, and particular model type or types for which a determination is requested;

(ii)(A) In the case of an application for model year 1980, be submitted not later than May 8, 1980;

(B) In the case of an application for model year 1981, be submitted not later than 9 months before the beginning of that model year of March 10, 1980, whichever is later;

(C) In the case of an application for model year 1982 or any subsequent model year, be submitted not later than 9 months before that model year;

(iii) Be submitted in three copies to: Commissioner of Internal Revenue, Attention: Associate Chief Counsel (Technical), 1111 Constitution Avenue, N.W., Washington, D.C. 20224;

(iv) Be written in the English language;

(v) Set forth the full name, address, and title of the official responsible for preparing the application;

(vi) State whether the applicant is a member of a controlled group of corporations (as defined in paragraph (d)(2)(iii) of this section);

(vii) State the total number of automobiles manufactured (whether or not in the United States) by the applicant (or the controlled group of corporations in the case where the applicant is a member of the group) in the second model year immediately preceding each affected model year and the total number of automobiles likely to be manufactured in the affected model year;

(viii) Set forth the same information required by an application pursuant to section 502(c) of the Motor Vehicle Information and Cost Savings Act (as amended) and the regulations thereunder (see 49 CFR 525 (1978)) and state whether or not the applicant under this paragraph has also made an application pursuant to such Act; and

(ix) Set forth the reasons why an alternate rate schedule should be granted under paragraph (d)(3)(ii) of this section.

(6) *Update of application.*—A manufacturer making an application under this section must update the application when a material change of circumstances occurs or material information not available at the time of applying becomes available. The manufacturer must also furnish any further information that may be required by the Internal Revenue Service.

(7) *Processing of applications.*—If a manufacturer's application is found not to contain the information required by this paragraph, the applicant will be informed of the areas of insufficiency. The application will not receive further consideration until the required information is submitted. Each applicant will be informed in writing whether an application has been granted or denied.

(e) *Tax-free sales of emergency vehicles.*—(1) *In general.*—The tax imposed by section 4064(a) shall not apply to vehicles sold by a manufacturer for use and used (i) primarily as an ambulance or combination ambulance-hearse, (ii) by the United States or by a State or local government primarily for police or other law enforcement purposes, or (iii) primarily for fire-fighting purposes. A vehicle may be sold tax-free by the manufacturer under this paragraph only in those cases where the sale is made directly to a purchaser for an emergency use prescribed in this subparagraph. In order to effect a tax-free sale, the requirements of section 4222 and the regulations thereunder must be met.

(2) *Credit or refund.*—Where tax is paid on the sale of a vehicle, but the vehicle is used or resold for an emergency use prescribed in subparagraph (1) of this paragraph, a claim for refund of the tax paid on such sale may be filed by the manufacturer on Form 8849 (or on such other form as the Commissioner may designate), or a credit may be taken on a subsequent return, in accordance with the provisions of sections 6402(a) and 6416(a) and § 48.6416(a)-1. [Reg. § 48.4064-1.]

☐ [T.D. 8036, 4-23-85. Amended by T.D. 8659, 3-13-96.]

### [Reg. § 48.4071-1]

**§ 48.4071-1. Imposition and rate of tax.**—(a) *Imposition of tax.*—(1) *Imposition of tax before January 1, 1984.*—Section 4071 imposes a tax at the rates set forth in paragraph (b)(1) of this section on tires made wholly or in part of rubber, inner tubes (for tires) made wholly or in part of rubber and tread rubber which are sold by the manufacturer thereof before January 1, 1984.

(2) *Imposition of tax after December 31, 1983.*—Section 4071 imposes a tax at the rates set forth in paragraph (b)(2) of this section on tires of the type used on highway vehicles and made wholly or in part of rubber which are sold by the manufacturer thereof after December 31, 1983.

(3) *Definitions.*—For definitions of the terms "tires," "inner tubes," "tread rubber," "rubber" and "manufacturer," see § 48.4072-1 of the regulations.

(b) *Rates and computation of tax.*—(1) *Rates of tax before January 1, 1984.*

(i) *Tires:*

(A) Of the type used on highway vehicles:

(1) For the period July 1, 1965 to December 31, 1980, inclusive—10 cents per pound.

(2) For the period January 1, 1981 to December 31, 1983, inclusive—9.75 cents per pound.

(B) Of the type used on other than highway vehicles:

(1) For the period July 1, 1965 to December 31, 1980, inclusive—5 cents per pound.

(2) For the period January 1, 1981 to December 31, 1983, inclusive—4.875 cents per pound.

(C) Laminated tires for the period July 1, 1965 to December 31, 1983, inclusive—1 cent per pound.

(ii) *Inner tubes:*

For the period July 1, 1965 to December 31, 1983, inclusive—10 cents per pound.

(iii) *Tread Rubber:*

For the period July 1, 1965 to December 31, 1983, inclusive—5 cents per pound.

(2) *Rates of tax on or after January 1, 1984.*—Tires of the type used on highway vehicles:

(i) Tires weighing not more than 40 pounds—0 cents.

(ii) Tires weighing more than 40 pounds but not more than 70 pounds—15 cents for each pound in excess of 40 pounds.

(iii) *Tread Rubber:*

For the period July 1, 1965 to December 31, 1983, inclusive—5 cents per pound.

(2) *Rates of tax on or after January 1, 1984.*—Tires of the type used on highway vehicles:

(i) Tires weighing not more than 40 pounds—0 cents.

(ii) Tires weighing more than 40 pounds but not more than 70 pounds—15 cents for each pound in excess of 40 pounds.

(iii) Tires weighing more than 70 pounds but not more than 90 pounds—$4.50 plus 30 cents for each pound in excess of 70 pounds.

(iv) Tires weighing more than 90 pounds—$10.50 plus 50 cents for each pound in excess of 90 pounds.

(3) *Computation of tax.*—The tax on tires, inner tubes, and tread rubber is computed by applying to the total weight (including a fractional part of a pound) of the article the rate in effect at the time the article is sold. See § 48.4071-2, relating to determination of weight.

(c) *Liability for tax.*—The tax imposed by section 4071 is payable by the manufacturer when the manufacturer makes a sale of a taxable article, or as provided in section 4071(b) and § 48.4071-3 for a manufacturer who sells at retail, when the manufacturer delivers a taxable article to a retail store, or to a retail outlet, of the manufacturer.

(d) *Recapped or retreaded tires.*—The recapping or retreading of a tire, whether from shoulder-to-shoulder or bead-to-bead, does not constitute manufacture of a taxable tire. The tax on tires imposed by section 4071 does not apply to the sale of a recapped or retreaded tire, except that a used tire or tire carcass not previously sold in the United States that is recapped or retreaded from shoulder-to-shoulder or bead-to-bead in a foreign country and imported into the United States is subject to the tax imposed by section 4071 when such tire is sold or used by the importer. This paragraph (d) is effective for recapped and retreaded tires sold on or after January 1, 1984. [Reg. § 48.4071-1.]

☐ [T.D. 7809. Amended by T.D. 8057, and T.D. 8152, 8-20-87.]

### [Reg. § 48.4071-2]

**§ 48.4071-2. Determination of weight.**—(a) *In general.*—(1) *Tires.*—(i) Metal rims or rim bases are not to be included in determining the total weight of a tire. However, the wire, staples, darts, clips, and other material or fastening devices which form a part of the tire or are required for its use must be included in determining the total weight of the tire. Studs are considered to be part of a tire and are to be included when determining the weight of a tire. In the case of a tubeless tire, the total weight includes the weight of the air valve and stem or any other mechanism that functions as a part of the tire and is used in connection with inflating the tire or maintaining its air pressure.

(ii) When tires are sold with metal rims or rim bases attached, the manufacturer must maintain records that will establish what portion of the total weight of the finished product represents the tire exclusive of the metal rim or rim base.

(2) *Inner tubes.*—The total weight of an inner tube includes the weight of the air valve and stem or any other mechanism attached to the inner tube that is used in connection with inflating the tube or maintaining its air pressure.

(b) *Alternative method of determining the weight of tires after December 1983.*—A manufacturer who has received permission from the Commissioner may, subject to such conditions as the Commissioner may prescribe, determine total weight of tires manufactured and sold by the manufacturer on the basis of the average weight for each type, size, grade, and classification. The average weights must be established in accordance with the method approved by the Commissioner and apply for such periods as the Commissioner may prescribe. The Commissioner may terminate the approval granted any manufacturer. In the case of the termination of the approval granted any manufacturer, the termination becomes effective 10 days from the date of the receipt by the manufacturer of the notice of termination. A manufacturer may effect termination, as of a specified date, of the privilege to determine total weight in accordance with provisions of this paragraph by giving no less than 10 days' written notice of such intention to the Commissioner. The termination of the approval given a manufacturer does not affect a manufacturer's tax liability for tires sold prior to the effective date of the notice of termination. [Reg. § 48.4071-2.]

☐ [*T.D. 7809. Amended by T.D. 8152, 8-20-87.*]

**[Reg. § 48.4071-3]**

**§ 48.4071-3. Imposition of tax on tires and tubes delivered to manufacturer's retail outlet.**—(a) *General rule.*—If, on or after October 1, 1966, a tire or inner tube is delivered by the manufacturer thereof to a retail outlet of the manufacturer, the manufacturer is liable for tax in respect of the tire or tube at the rate set forth in section 4071 in the same manner as if the tire or tube had been sold at the time it was delivered to the retail outlet. The amount of tax payable shall be computed in accordance with the provisions of paragraph (b)(2) of § 48.4071-1, and of § 48.4071-2.

(b) *Definition of retail outlet.*—For purposes of this section, the term "retail outlet" includes the term "retail store." A retail outlet is a facility maintained by a manufacturer for selling tires or tubes at retail. A facility may be a retail outlet even though some sales are made at wholesale at such facility; see paragraph (d)(1) of this section. A facility may also be considered to be a retail outlet for the purposes of this section notwithstanding that its main activity is in another area than selling tires or inner tubes. For example, if a manufacturer operates a facility for both automotive repair and the selling of tires at retail, the facility is considered a retail outlet for the purposes of this section even if the primary activity of the facility is automotive repair. No facility is considered a retail outlet for the purposes of this section if it is determined that less than 15 percent of the taxable tires and inner tubes removed from such facility are sold at retail by such facility. The determination described in the preceding sentence is made on the basis of the experience of a representative period, of at least 12 consecutive calendar months during the 2-year period immediately preceding the first day included in the return period for which tax under section 4071(b) is reported. If a facility has not been in existence during such a 12-month period, the determination is made on the basis of the available experience of the manufacturer. See also paragraph (c)(3) of this section, relating to imposition of tax where a retail outlet is maintained as an adjunct to a production facility or distribution center.

(c) *Delivery.*—(1) *In general.*—A manufacturer of tires or inner tubes may, at its option, treat either of the following events as constituting delivery to a retail outlet:

(i) Delivery of tires or inner tubes to a common carrier (or, where the tires or tubes are transported by the manufacturer, the placing of the tires or tubes into the manufacturer's over-the-road vehicle) for shipment from the plant in which the tires or tubes are manufactured, or from a regional distribution center of tires and inner tubes, to a retail outlet or to a location in the immediate vicinity of a retail outlet primarily for future delivery to the retail outlet.

(ii) Arrival of the tires or tubes at the retail outlet, or, where shipment is to a location in the immediate vicinity of a retail outlet primarily for future delivery to the retail outlet, the arrival of the tires or tubes at such location.

In its excise tax return for the first return period beginning after September 30, 1966, a manufacturer of tires or inner tubes must elect to determine the date of delivery to retail outlets in accordance with one of the two subdivisions of this paragraph (c)(1) and must determine the dates of all deliveries made to all retail outlets in accordance with the subdivision which the manufacturer has elected to apply. The election may be made in a statement attached to the return for such period. Having elected to treat one of the events listed in subdivision (i) or (ii) of this paragraph (c)(1) as constituting delivery to a retail outlet for purposes of its return for the first return period after September 30, 1966, the manufacturer may not use a different criterion for a subsequent return period unless permission of the district director is obtained in advance.

(2) *Deliveries made in the immediate vicinity of a retail outlet primarily for future delivery to the retail outlet.*—(i) For purposes of this section, any delivery which is made in the immediate vicinity of a

retail outlet primarily for future delivery to the retail outlet is deemed to be a delivery to the retail outlet. For the purpose of the preceding sentence, a location is considered to be in the immediate vicinity of a retail outlet if the distance between the location and the retail outlet is sufficiently small so that it is feasible to transport tires and inner tubes between the location and the retail outlet by means of dollies, fork lift trucks, pushcarts, and similar vehicles of the type normally used around the premises of factories and similar establishments, as opposed to highway motor vehicles. For the purpose of the preceding sentence, it is immaterial that a public thoroughfare must be used in order to transport tires or inner tubes to a retail outlet from another location. Tires and inner tubes delivered to a location in the immediate vicinity of a retail outlet are considered to be delivered to the location "primarily for future delivery" to the retail outlet if it is determined that a majority (by number) of the tires and tubes removed from the location are delivered to the retail outlet. The determination described in the preceding sentence is made on the basis of the experience of a representative period of at least 12 consecutive calendar months during the 2-year period immediately preceding the first day included in the return period for which tax under section 4071(b) is reported. If a facility has not been in existence during such a 12-month period, the determination is made on the basis of the available experience of the manufacturer. If it is determined that the majority of all tires and inner tubes removed from a given location are delivered to a retail outlet of the manufacturer in the immediate vicinity of the location, tax is imposed upon all tires and tubes delivered by the manufacturer to the location, even though all or part of the tires or tubes comprising a particular shipment to the location may be intended for further transportation to a location other than the retail outlet. If it is determined that a majority of all tires and inner tubes removed from a given location are not delivered to a retail outlet of the manufacturer in the immediate vicinity of the location, tax is imposed upon the removal of a tire or inner tube from the location to the premises of the retail outlet. See also paragraph (d)(2) of this section, relating to sales by the manufacturer at facilities other than retail outlets.

(ii) The provisions of this paragraph (c)(2) may be illustrated by the following example:

*Example.* A manufacturer of tires and tubes whose plant is located in City X operates two facilities in City Y, Warehouse A and Store Q. Store Q is a retail outlet within the meaning of paragraph (b) of this section, and Warehouse A is in the immediate vicinity of Store Q. During the 12-month period ending September 30, 1966, 60 percent of the tires and inner tubes removed from Warehouse A were delivered to Store Q. All tires or inner tubes delivered by the manufacturer to Warehouse A are subject to tax under section 4071(b) and this section (unless, before such delivery, tax was imposed on the same tires and tubes).

(3) *Retail outlet maintained as adjunct of production or distribution facility.*—If a retail outlet is maintained as an adjunct to and in the immediate vicinity of a facility which is not a retail outlet (as, for example, a production plant or a regional distribution center), delivery to the retail outlet is deemed to occur at the earlier of—

(i) The date when a tire or inner tube is removed from the general storage facilities in the facility which is not a retail outlet for transfer to the premises of the retail outlet, or

(ii) The date when a tire or inner tube is designated to be sold by or at the retail outlet.

(d) *Special rules.*—(1) *Retail outlets which also sell at wholesale.*—Tax applies to all shipments of tires and inner tubes delivered to a retail outlet, as defined in paragraph (b)(2) of this section. Thus, for the purposes of section 4071(b) and this section, it is immaterial that all or part of the tires or inner tubes of a particular delivery to a retail outlet are intended for sale at wholesale. See also paragraph (d)(3) of this section.

(2) *Sales by manufacturer at facilities other than retail outlets.*—Sales by the manufacturer of tires and inner tubes at facilities other than retail outlets are subject to tax under section 4071(a).

(3) *Deliveries of tires or tubes on which tax has been previously imposed.*

(i) Tax is not imposed under section 4071(b) and this section on any tire or inner tube in respect of which there was previously imposed a tax under section 4071(a). Similarly, a tire or inner tube is taxed only once under section 4071(b) and this section.

(ii) The provisions of this paragraph (d)(3) may be illustrated by the following example:

*Example.* A manufacturer has two selling facilities, Store No. 1 and Store No. 2. Only retail sales are made at Store No. 2, which obtains its merchandise from Store No. 1. Assume that, although wholesaling and distribution activities are conducted at Store No. 1, the sale of tires and tubes at retail is conducted at Store No. 1 to the extent that Store No. 1 is a retail outlet within the meaning of paragraph (b) of this section, with the result that tax is imposed on deliveries by the manufacturer of tires and tubes to Store No. 1. Tax is not imposed on a delivery of tires or inner tubes from Store No. 1 to Store No. 2. [Reg. § 48.4071-3.]

☐ [T.D. 7809.]

## [Reg. § 48.4071-4]

**§ 48.4071-4. Original equipment tires on imported articles.**—The tax imposed by section 4071(a) applies with respect to tires and inner tubes (other than bicycle tires and inner tubes) that are original equipment for an imported article upon which no tax is imposed under section 4061 if the article is sold on or after December 11, 1971. In such a case, the importer of the article is treated as the manufacturer and vendor of the tires and inner tubes with which the article is equipped. However, the tax imposed by section 4071(a) is not imposed with respect to tires and inner tubes if the imported article is an automobile bus chassis or an automobile bus body. Solely for purposes of this section, the provisions of section 4218 (relating to use by a manufacturer or importer considered a sale) do not apply in cases where an individual imports an article having original equipment tires and tubes and on which article no tax is imposed under section 4061 if the article is imported solely for the individual's personal use and is so used. [Reg. § 48.4071-4.]

☐ [T.D. 7809.]

## [Reg. § 48.4072-1]

**§ 48.4072-1. Definitions.**—For purposes of the regulations in this part, unless otherwise expressly indicated:

(a) *Rubber.*—The term "rubber" includes synthetic and substitute rubber.

(b) *Tread rubber.*—The term "tread rubber" means any material (1) which is commonly or commercially known as tread rubber or camelback, or (2) which is a substitute for any material commonly or commercially known as tread rubber or camelback and is of a type used in recapping or retreading tires. The term includes, for example, strips of material, wholly or partially of rubber, natural or synthetic, intended to be vulcanized or otherwise affixed to a tire casing to form the outside perimeter of the tire, smooth or treaded. It also includes treading material produced by reprocessing scrap, salvage, or junk rubber and a continuous rubber ribbon produced through an extrusion process for direct application in recapping or retreading a tire casing. The term does not include rubber in various forms such as strip, slab, pellet, etc. which is used as raw material for the extrusion process. Tread rubber loses its identity as such when it has been used in the recapping or retreading of a tire of a type used on a highway vehicle (without regard to the actual use ultimately made of the tire) or has deteriorated in quality to the point where it is no longer suitable for use in recapping or retreading of a tire. (In the case of such deterioration, see section 6416(b)(2) and § 48.6416(b)-2 to secure a refund or credit of the tax paid.)

(c) *Tires of the type used on highway vehicles.*—(1) The term "tires of the type used on highway vehicles", for purposes of §§ 48.4071-1 through 48.4073-3 means tires of the type used on—

(i) Motor vehicles that are highway vehicles (within the meaning of § 48.4061(a)-1(d)), or

(ii) Vehicles of the type used in connection with motor vehicles that are highway vehicles (within the meaning of § 48.4061(a)-1(d)). The term "tires of the type used on highway vehicles" does not include bicycle tires. Bicycle tires, however, are included in the term "other tires" as used in section 4071(a)(2).

(2) For purposes of paragraph (c)(1)(i) of this section, tires of the type used on motor vehicles that are highway vehicles include tires used on motor trucks, buses, passenger automobiles, motor homes, highway tractors, trolley buses or coaches, and motorcycles.

(3) For purposes of paragraph (c)(1)(ii) of this section, tires of the types used on vehicles of the type used in connection with motor vehicles that are highway vehicles include tires used on truck or bus trailers, truck semi-trailers, mobile homes, housetrailers, or utility trailers.

(d) *Inner tubes.*—The term "inner tubes" includes air containers of all types made wholly or in part of rubber and designed and manufactured for use in pneumatic tires.

(e) *Tires.*—The term "tires" includes rubber casings, hoops, and strips or bands of all kinds designed and shaped or built to form the tread of or to fit a vehicle wheel. Tires of either the pneumatic or solid type which fit or form the tread for wheels of any article which is capable of use as a means of transporting a person or burden are taxable as tires. Examples of articles which may be equipped with

taxable tires are motor scooters, minibikes, industrial trucks, farm tractors, wheelbarrows, and similar articles. See section 4073(a) and § 48.4073-1 with respect to the exemption of tires of certain sizes, and section 4073(b) and § 48.4073-2 with respect to the exemption for tires with internal wire fastening.

(f) *Laminated tires.*—For purposes of the tax imposed by section 4071, the term "laminated tires" means tires (1) which are not "tires of the type used on highway vehicles" within the meaning of paragraph (c) of this section, and (2) which consist wholly of scrap rubber from used tire casings with an internal metal fastening agent.

(g) *Manufacturer.*—The term "manufacturer" means manufacturer, producer or importer. A person who converts, by any process, a new tire taxable under section 4071 at one rate of tax into a tire taxable under section 4071 at a different rate (as for example, an off highway-type tire converted into a highway-type tire) is considered to be a manufacturer of the converted tire. If a conversion results in a reduced rate of tax for the converted tire, see section 6416(b)(2) and § 48.6416(b)-2 to secure a credit or refund of part of the tax paid. The term "manufactured" includes "produced" and "imported".

(h) *Cross references.*—For other definitions, see § 48.0-2. [Reg. § 48.4072-1.]

☐ [T.D. 7809.]

## [Reg. § 48.4073-1]

**§ 48.4073-1. Exemption of tires of certain sizes.**—The tax does not apply to sales of tires of all-rubber construction (whether hollow center or solid) if they have no fabric or metal reinforcement and do not exceed either of these measurements:(a) 20 inches in diameter measured to the outside circumferences, and (b) 1³/₄ inches in cross-section. The exemption provided by section 4073(a) is to be determined solely on the measurements of the tire and not on the purpose for which it is designed or used. [Reg. § 48.4073-1.]

☐ [T.D. 7809.]

## [Reg. § 48.4073-2]

**§ 48.4073-2. Exemption of tires with internal wire fastening.**—The tax does not apply to sales of tires of any size or dimension manufactured from extruded tiring that is fastened or held together by means of internal wire or other metallic material. [Reg. § 48.4073-2.]

## [Reg. § 48.4073-3]

**§ 48.4073-3. Exemption of tread rubber used for recapping non-highway tires.**—(a) *Sold direct by manufacturer for nontaxable use.*—The tax does not apply to the sale of tread rubber by the manufacturer to any person for use by that person otherwise than in the recapping or retreading of tires of the type used on highway vehicles. In determining whether tread rubber is sold for a taxable or nontaxable use, the type of vehicle on which the recapped or retreaded tire is to be used, or the actual or intended use of the recapped or retreaded tire, is immaterial. The controlling factor is whether the tire resulting from the recapping or retreading is of a type that is used otherwise than on a highway vehicle. For definition of "tires of the type used on highway vehicles", see paragraph (c) of § 48.4072-1.

(b) *Sales for resale for nontaxable use.*—No sale of tread rubber may be made tax free for resale even though it is known at the time of the sale that the tread rubber will be resold for use otherwise than in the recapping or retreading of tires of the type used on highway vehicles. However, where the tread rubber is resold for such use, the manufacturer who paid the tax on a sale of the tread rubber may secure a refund or credit in accordance with the provisions of section 6416(b)(2) and § 48.6416(b)-2.

(c) *Evidence required to establish exemption.*—(1) To establish the right to sell tread rubber tax free under section 4073(c), the manufacturer must obtain from the purchaser and retain in its possession a properly executed exemption certificate.

(2) Where only occasional sales of tread rubber for exempt use are made to a purchaser, a separate exemption certificate should be furnished for each order. However, where sales are regularly and frequently made to a purchaser for exempt use, a certificate covering all purchases during the period not to exceed 12 calendar quarters is acceptable. The certificates and proper records of invoices, order, etc., relative to tax-free sales must be kept for inspection by the district director as provided in section 6001 and the regulations in Subpart O.

(d) *Acceptable form of exemption certificate.*—The following form of exemption certificate is acceptable for the purposes of this section and must be adhered to in substance:

EXEMPTION CERTIFICATE

(For use by persons who purchase tread rubber from the manufacturer, producer, or importer thereof for use otherwise than in recapping or retreading tires of the type used on highway vehicles (section 4073(c) of the Internal Revenue Code).)

(Date)_____ 19____
I, the undersigned, certify that I am the purchaser, or the (Title) _____ of (Name of purchaser of other than the undersigned) _____ who is the purchaser of: _____ The tread rubber specified in the accompanying order or contract, or _____ All tread rubber specified in contracts or orders entered into or placed with (Name of seller) _____ for the period commencing _____ and ending _____ (period not to exceed 12 calendar quarters) and that such tread rubber will not be used in the recapping or retreading of tires of the type used on highway vehicles, but will be used for the following purposes:

_____

_____

_____

_____

The undersigned understands that if the tread rubber is used for the recapping or retreading of tires of the type used on highway vehicles, or is sold or otherwise disposed of, such fact must be promptly reported to the manufacturer. The undersigned also understands that the fraudulent use of this certificate for the purpose of securing this exemption will subject the undersigned or any other party making such fraudulent use to a fine of not more than $10,000, or to imprisonment for not more than 5 years, or both, together with costs of prosecution. The purchaser also understands that the purchaser must be prepared to establish by satisfactory evidence the purpose for which the tread rubber was used.
(Signature) _____

(Address) _____

(e) *Exemption certificate not obtained prior to filing of manufacturer's excise tax return.*—If the sale is otherwise exempt but the exemption certificate is not obtained prior to the time the manufacturer files a return covering taxes due for the period during which the sale was made, the manufacturer must include the tax on the sale in its return for that period. However, if the certificate is later obtained, a claim for refund of the tax paid on the sale may be filed, or a credit for the amount may be taken upon a subsequent return, as provided by section 6416(b)(2) and § 48.6416(b)-2. [Reg. § 48.4073-3.]

☐ [T.D. 7809, 2-9-82.]

**[Reg. § 48.4073-4]**

**§ 48.4073-4. Other tax-free sales.**—(a) *Cross references.*—For provisions relating to tax-free sales of articles referred to in section 4071, see:

(1) Section 4221, relating to certain tax-free sales, and the regulations thereunder in Subpart H;

(2) Section 4222, relating to registration, and the regulations thereunder in Subpart H;

(3) Section 4223, relating to special rules pertaining to further manufacture, and the regulations thereunder in Subpart H; and

(4) 28 FR 348, January 12, 1963, relating to the authorization of an exemption from the tax imposed by section 4071 by the Secretary of the Treasury under section 4293 for sales of certain tires and inner tubes sold to the American Red Cross on or after March 1, 1963. [Reg. § 48.4073-4.]

☐ [T.D. 7809, 2-9-82.]

**[Reg. § 48.4081-1]**

**§ 48.4081-1. Taxable fuel; definitions.**—(a) *Overview.*—This section provides definitions for purposes of the tax on taxable fuel imposed by section 4081.

(b) *Definitions.*

*Approved terminal or refinery* means a terminal or refinery that is operated, respectively, by a taxable fuel registrant that is a terminal operator, or by a taxable fuel registrant that is a refiner.

*Aviation gasoline* means all special grades of gasoline that are suitable for use in aviation reciprocating engines and covered by ASTM specification D 910 or military specification MIL-G-5572. For availability of ASTM and military specifications, see paragraph (d) of this section.

*Blender* means any person that produces blended taxable fuel.

*Bulk transfer* means any transfer of taxable fuel by pipeline or vessel.

*Bulk transfer/terminal system* means the taxable fuel distribution system consisting of refineries, pipelines, vessels, and terminals. Thus, taxable fuel in a refinery, pipeline, vessel, or terminal is in the bulk transfer/terminal system. Taxable fuel in the fuel supply tank of any engine, or in any tank car, rail car, trailer, truck, or other equipment suitable for ground transportation is not in the bulk transfer/terminal system.

*Bus* means automobile bus.

*Diesel-powered bus* means any bus that is propelled by a diesel-powered engine.

*Diesel-powered highway vehicle* means a highway vehicle, as defined in § 48.4061(a)-1(d), that is propelled by a diesel-powered engine.

*Diesel-powered train* means any diesel-powered equipment or machinery that rides on rails. Thus, for example, the term includes a locomotive, work train, switching engine, and track maintenance machine.

*Enterer* generally means the importer of record (under customs law) with respect to the taxable fuel, except that—

(1) If the importer of record is a customs broker engaged by the owner of the taxable fuel, the person for whom the broker is acting is the enterer; and

(2) If there is no importer of record for taxable fuel entered into the United States, the owner of the taxable fuel at the time it is brought into the United States is the enterer.

*Entry* of taxable fuel into the United States occurs when—

(1) The taxable fuel is brought into the United States and applicable customs law requires that the taxable fuel be entered into the United States for consumption, use, or warehousing; or

(2) The taxable fuel is brought into the United States from Puerto Rico and applicable customs law would require that the taxable fuel be entered into the United States for consumption, use, or warehousing if the taxable fuel were brought into the United States from somewhere other than Puerto Rico.

*Excluded liquid* means any liquid that—

(1) Contains less than four percent normal paraffins; or

(2) Has a—

(i) Distillation range of 125[degree] F. or less;

(ii) Sulfur content of 10 ppm or less; and

(iii) Minimum color of +27 Saybolt.

*Finished gasoline* means all products (including gasohol (as defined in § 48.4081-6(b)(2))) that are commonly or commercially known or sold as gasoline and are suitable for use as a motor fuel, other than products that have an ASTM octane number of less than 75 as determined by the motor method.

*Gasoline* means finished gasoline and gasoline blendstocks.

*Industrial user* means any person that receives gasoline blendstocks by bulk transfer for its own use in the manufacture of any product other than finished gasoline.

*Kerosene* means any liquid that meets the specifications for kerosene or would meet those specifications but for the presence in the liquid of a dye of the type described in § 48.4082-1(b). A liquid meets the specifications for kerosene if it is one of the two grades of kerosene (No. 1-K and No. 2-K) covered by ASTM specification D 3699, or kerosene-type jet fuel covered by ASTM specification D 1655 or military specification MIL-DTL-5624T (Grade JP-5) or MIL-DTL-83133E (Grade JP-8). For availability of ASTM and military specifications, see paragraph (d) of this section. However, the term does not include *excluded liquid.*

*Position holder* means, with respect to taxable fuel in a terminal, the person that holds the inventory position in the taxable fuel, as reflected on the records of the terminal operator. A person holds the inventory position in taxable fuel when that person has a contractual agreement with the terminal operator for the use of storage facilities and terminaling services at a terminal with respect to the taxable fuel. The term also includes a terminal operator that owns taxable fuel in its terminal.

*Rack* means a mechanism capable of delivering taxable fuel into a means of transport other than a pipeline or vessel.

*Refiner* means any person that owns, operates, or otherwise controls a refinery.

*Refinery* means a facility used to produce taxable fuel and from which taxable fuel may be removed by pipeline, by vessel, or at a rack. However, the term does not include a facility where only blended fuel or gasohol (as defined in § 48.4081-6(b)(2)), and no other type of taxable fuel, is produced. For this purpose blended fuel is any mixture that, if produced outside the bulk transfer/terminal system, would be blended taxable fuel.

*Removal* means any physical transfer of taxable fuel, and any use of taxable fuel other than as a material in the production of taxable fuel or special fuels. However, taxable fuel is not removed when it evaporates or is otherwise lost or destroyed.

*Sale* means—

(1) The transfer of title to, or substantial incidents of ownership in, taxable fuel (other than taxable fuel in a terminal) to the buyer for a consideration, which may consist of money, services, or other property; or

(2) The transfer of the inventory position in the taxable fuel in a terminal if the transferee becomes the position holder with respect to the taxable fuel.

*State* includes any State, any political subdivision of a State, the District of Columbia, the American Red Cross, and, to the extent provided by section 7871, any Indian tribal government.

*Taxable fuel* means gasoline, diesel fuel, and kerosene.

*Taxable fuel registrant* means an enterer, industrial user, refiner, terminal operator, or throughputter that is registered as such under section 4101.

*Terminal* means a taxable fuel storage and distribution facility that is supplied by pipeline or vessel and from which taxable fuel may be removed at a rack. However, the term does not include any facility at which gasoline blendstocks are used in the manufacture of products other than finished gasoline and from which no gasoline is removed. Also, effective January 2, 1998, the term does not include any facility where finished gasoline, undyed diesel fuel, or undyed kerosene is stored if the facility is operated by a taxable fuel registrant and all such taxable fuel stored at the facility has been previously taxed under section 4081 upon removal from a refinery or terminal.

*Terminal operator* means any person that owns, operates, or otherwise controls a terminal.

*Throughputter* means any person that—

(1) Owns taxable fuel within the bulk transfer/terminal system (other than in a terminal); or

(2) Is a position holder.

*Vessel* means a waterborne taxable fuel transporting vessel.

(c) *Blended taxable fuel, diesel fuel, and gasoline blendstocks; definitions.*—(1) *Blended taxable fuel.*—(i) *In general.*—Except as provided in paragraphs (c)(1)(ii) and (c)(1)(iii) of this section, *blended taxable fuel* means any taxable fuel that is produced outside the bulk transfer/terminal system by mixing—

(A) Taxable fuel with respect to which tax has been imposed under section 4041(a)(1) or 4081(a) (other than taxable fuel for which a credit or payment has been allowed); and

(B) Any other liquid on which tax has not been imposed under section 4081.

(ii) *Exclusion; minor blending.*—A mixture described in paragraph (c)(1)(i) of this section is not blended taxable fuel if, during the calendar quarter in which the blender removes or sells the mixture, all such mixtures removed or sold by the blender contain, in the aggregate, less than 400 gallons of liquid described in paragraph (c)(1)(i)(B) of this section.

(iii) *Exclusion; gasohol.*—Blended taxable fuel does not include any gasohol (as defined in § 48.4081-6(b)(2)) if, disregarding the alcohol, the gasohol is not blended taxable fuel and contains, in addition to permitted amounts of liquids described in paragraph (c)(1)(i)(B) of this section, only gasoline with respect to which—

(A) Tax was imposed under section 4081(a) at a rate described in § 48.4081-6(e) (relating to the gasohol production tax rate and the gasohol tax rate); or

(B) A valid claim is made under section 6427(f).

(2) *Diesel fuel.*—(i) *In general.*—Except as provided in paragraph (c)(2)(ii) of this section, *diesel fuel* means any liquid that, without further processing or blending, is suitable for use as a fuel in a diesel-powered highway vehicle or diesel-powered train. A liquid is suitable for this use if the liquid has practical and commercial fitness for use in the propulsion engine of a diesel-powered highway vehicle or diesel-powered train. A liquid may possess this practical and commercial fitness even though the specified use is not the liquid's predominant use. However, a liquid does not possess this practical and commercial fitness solely by reason of its possible or rare use as a fuel in the propulsion engine of a diesel-powered highway vehicle or diesel-powered train.

(ii) *Exclusion.*—Diesel fuel does not include gasoline, kerosene, excluded liquid, No. 5 and No. 6 fuel oils covered by ASTM specification D 396, or F-76 (Fuel Naval Distillate) covered by military specification MIL-F-16884. For availability of ASTM and military specifications, see paragraph (d) of this section.

(3) *Gasoline blendstocks.*—(i) *In general.*—Except as provided in paragraph (c)(3)(ii) of this section, *gasoline blendstocks* means—

(A) Alkylate;

(B) Butane;

(C) Butene;

(D) Catalytically cracked gasoline;

(E) Coker gasoline;

(F) Ethyl tertiary butyl ether (ETBE);

(G) Hexane;

(H) Hydrocrackate;

(I) Isomerate;

(J) Methyl tertiary butyl ether (MTBE);

(K) Mixed xylene (not including any separated isomer of xylene);

(L) Natural gasoline;

(M) Pentane;

(N) Pentane mixture;

(O) Polymer gasoline;

(P) Raffinate;

(Q) Reformate;

(R) Straight-run gasoline;

(S) Straight-run naphtha;

(T) Tertiary amyl methyl ether (TAME);

(U) Tertiary butyl alcohol (gasoline grade) (TBA);

(V) Thermally cracked gasoline;

(W) Toluene; and

(X) Transmix containing gasoline.

(ii) *Exclusion.*—Gasoline blendstocks does not include any product that cannot, without further processing, be used in the production of finished gasoline. For example, a mixed hydrocarbon stream that is produced in a natural gas processing plant is not a gasoline blendstock if the stream cannot be used to produce finished gasoline without further processing.

(d) *ASTM and military specifications.*—ASTM specifications may be obtained from the American Society for Testing and Materials, 100 Barr Harbor Drive, West Conshohocken, PA 19428. Military specifications may be obtained from the Standardization Document Order Desk, Building 4, Section D, 700 Robbins Avenue, Philadelphia, PA 19111.

(e) *Other definitions.*—For other definitions relating to taxable fuel, see § § 48.4081-6(b), 48.4082-5(b), 48.4082-6(b), 48.4082-7(b), 48.4101-1(b), 48.6427-9(b), 48.6427-10(b), and 48.6427-11(b).

(f) *Effective date.*—(1) Except as provided in paragraph (f)(2) of this section, this section is applicable after December 31, 1993.

(2) In paragraph (b) of this section the definition of aviation gasoline and the third sentence in the definition of terminal are applicable after January 1, 1998, the definition of kerosene, excluded liquid, and taxable fuel are applicable after June 30, 1998, and the definition of enterer is applicable to entries of taxable fuel after September 27, 2004. Paragraph (c)(2) of this section is applicable after December 31, 1997. [Reg. § 48.4081-1.]

☐ [*T.D.* 6433, 12-21-59. *Amended by T.D.* 6574, 10-10-61; *T.D.* 7908, 9-2-83; *T.D.* 8421, 7-21-92; *T.D.* 8659, 3-13-96; *T.D.* 8748, 12-31-97; *T.D.* 8879, 3-30-2000; *T.D.* 9051, 4-1-2003; *T.D.* 9145, 7-29-2004 *and T.D.* 9346, 7-26-2007.]

**[Reg. § 48.4081-2]**

**§ 48.4081-2. Taxable fuel; tax on removal at a terminal rack.—** (a) *Overview.*—This section provides the general rule that all removals of taxable fuel at a terminal rack are subject to tax and the position holder with respect to the fuel is liable for the tax.

(b) *Imposition of tax.*—Tax is imposed on the removal of taxable fuel from a terminal if the taxable fuel is removed at the rack.

(c) *Liability for tax.*—(1) *In general.*—The position holder with respect to the taxable fuel is liable for the tax imposed under paragraph (b) of this section.

(2) *Joint and several liability of terminal operator; unregistered position holder.*—(i) *In general.*—The terminal operator is jointly and severally liable for the tax imposed under paragraph (b) of this section if—

(A) The position holder with respect to the taxable fuel is a person other than the terminal operator and is not a taxable fuel registrant; and

(B) The terminal operator has not met the conditions of paragraph (c)(2)(ii) of this section.

(ii) *Conditions for avoidance of liability.*—A terminal operator is not liable for tax under this paragraph (c)(2) if, at the time of the removal, the terminal operator—

(A) Is a taxable fuel registrant;

(B) Has an unexpired notification certificate (as described in § 48.4081-5) from the position holder; and

(C) Has no reason to believe that any information in the notification certificate is false.

(3) *Joint and several liability of terminal operator; incorrect information provided.*—The terminal operator is jointly and severally liable for the tax imposed under paragraph (b) of this section if, in connection with the removal of diesel fuel or kerosene that is not dyed and marked in accordance with § 48.4082-1, the terminal operator provides any person (including the position holder with respect to the fuel) with any bill of lading, shipping paper, record, or similar document indicating that the diesel fuel or kerosene is dyed and marked in accordance with § 48.4082-1.

(4) *Example.*—The following example illustrates this paragraph (c) and § 48.4082-1:

*Example.* (i) TO is a terminal operator and PH is the position holder with respect to, and owner of, 8,000 gallons of diesel fuel stored in TO's terminal. TO and PH are taxable fuel registrants. When the fuel is removed from the terminal at the rack, the fuel is not dyed and marked in accordance with § 48.4082-1, and TO does not provide any person with any paperwork indicating that the fuel is dyed and marked. After the removal from the terminal, PH sells the fuel to individuals for use as heating oil, a nontaxable use.

(ii) Because PH is the position holder of the fuel at the time of the removal from the terminal, PH is liable for the tax imposed by section 4081. The removal is subject to tax because the fuel is not dyed and marked in accordance with § 48.4082-1, and later use of the fuel in a nontaxable use does not make the removal from the terminal exempt from tax.

(iii) Because PH is a taxable fuel registrant and TO did not provide any person with any paperwork indicating that the fuel is dyed and marked, TO is not jointly and severally liable for tax under paragraph (c)(2) or (3) of this section.

(d) *Rate of tax.*—For the rate of tax generally, see section 4081(a). For the rate of tax on gasohol and on gasoline removed for gasohol production, see § 48.4081-6.

(e) *Exemptions.*—For exemptions from the tax imposed under this section, see §§ 48.4081-4 (relating to gasoline blendstocks), 48.4082-1 (relating to dyed diesel fuel and dyed kerosene), 48.4082-5 (relating to diesel fuel and kerosene used in Alaska), 48.4082-6 (relating to aviation-grade kerosene), and 48.4082-7 (relating to kerosene used for a feedstock purpose).

(f) *Effective date.*—This section is applicable after December 31, 1993. [Reg. § 48.4081-2.]

☐ [*T.D. 7658,* 12-4-79. *Amended by T.D. 8152,* 8-30-87; *T.D. 8399,* 3-3-92; *T.D. 8421,* 7-21-92; *T.D. 8659,* 3-13-96 *and T.D. 8879,* 3-30-2000.]

**[Reg. § 48.4081-3]**

**§ 48.4081-3. Taxable fuel; taxable events other than removal at the terminal rack.**—(a) *Overview.*—Although tax is imposed when taxable fuel is removed from the terminal at the rack, tax also is imposed in certain other situations described in this section.

(b) *Tax on removal from a refinery.*—(1) *Imposition of tax.*—Tax is imposed on the following removals from a refinery:

(i) A removal of taxable fuel by bulk transfer if the refiner or the owner of the taxable fuel immediately before the removal is not a taxable fuel registrant.

(ii) A removal of taxable fuel at the rack.

(iii) After September 30, 1995, a removal of a batch of gasohol from an approved refinery by bulk transfer if the refiner treats itself with respect to the removal as a person that is not registered under section 4101. See § 48.4101-1(a). For the rule providing that no deposit is required in the case of the tax imposed under this paragraph (b)(1)(iii), see § 40.6302(c)-1(f)(4) of this chapter. For the rule allowing inspections of facilities where gasohol is produced, see section 4083.

(2) *Exception for certain refineries.*—The tax imposed under paragraph (b)(1)(ii) of this section does not apply to a removal of taxable fuel if—

(i) The taxable fuel is removed from an approved refinery that is not served by pipeline (other than a pipeline for the receipt of crude oil) or vessel;

(ii) The taxable fuel is received at a facility that is operated by a taxable fuel registrant and is located within the bulk transfer/terminal system;

(iii) The removal from the refinery is by—

(A) Rail car; or

(B) In the case of diesel fuel, a trailer or semi-trailer that is used exclusively for the transport service described in paragraphs (b)(2)(i) and (b)(2)(ii) of this section;

(iv) In the case of taxable fuel removed by rail car, the facility at which the fuel is received is operated by the same person that operates the refinery from which the fuel was removed; and

(v) In the case of diesel fuel removed by a trailer or semi-trailer, the facility at which the fuel is received is less than 20 miles from the refinery from which the diesel fuel was removed.

(3) *Liability for tax.*—The refiner is liable for the tax imposed under paragraph (b)(1) of this section.

(c) *Tax on entry into the United States.*—(1) *Imposition of tax.*—Tax is imposed on the entry of taxable fuel into the United States if—

(i) The entry is by bulk transfer and the enterer is not a taxable fuel registrant; or

(ii) The entry is not by bulk transfer.

(2) *Liability for tax.*—(i) *In general.*—The enterer is liable for the tax imposed under paragraph (c)(1) of this section.

(ii) *Joint and several liability of the importer of record.* The importer of record with respect to the taxable fuel is jointly and severally liable with the enterer for the tax imposed under paragraph (c)(1) of this section if—

(A) The importer of record is not the enterer of the taxable fuel; and

(B) The enterer is not a taxable fuel registrant.

(iii) *Conditions for avoidance of liability.* The importer of record is not liable for the tax under paragraph (c)(2)(ii) of this section if, at the time of the entry, the importer of record—

(A) Has an unexpired notification certificate (as described in § 48.4081-5) from the enterer; and

(B) Has no reason to believe that any information in the notification certificate is false.

(iv) *Customs bond.*—The Customs bond posted with respect to the importation of the fuel will not be charged for the tax imposed on the entry of the fuel if the enterer is a taxable fuel registrant. A Customs bond will not be charged for the tax imposed on the entry of the fuel covered by the bond, if at the time of entry, the surety—

(A) Has an unexpired notification certificate (as described in § 48.4081-5) from the enterer; and

(B) Has no reason to believe that any information in the notification certificate is false.

(d) *Tax on bulk transfers from a terminal by an unregistered position holder.*—(1) *Imposition of tax.*—Tax is imposed on the removal by bulk transfer of taxable fuel from a terminal if the position holder with respect to the taxable fuel is not a taxable fuel registrant.

(2) *Liability for tax.*—(i) *In general.*—The position holder with respect to the taxable fuel is liable for the tax imposed under paragraph (d)(1) of this section.

(ii) *Joint and several liability of terminal operator.*—The terminal operator is jointly and severally liable for the tax imposed under paragraph (d)(1) of this section if—

(A) The position holder with respect to the taxable fuel is a person other than the terminal operator; and

(B) The terminal operator has not met the conditions of paragraph (d)(2)(iii) of this section.

(iii) *Conditions for avoidance of liability.*—A terminal operator is not liable for tax under this paragraph (d)(2) if, at the time of the bulk transfer, the terminal operator—

(A) Is a taxable fuel registrant;

(B) Has an unexpired notification certificate (described in § 48.4081-5) from the position holder; and

(C) Has no reason to believe that any information in the notification certificate is false.

(e) *Tax on bulk transfers not received at an approved terminal or refinery.*—(1) *Imposition of tax.*—Tax on taxable fuel is imposed if—

(i) Taxable fuel is removed by bulk transfer from a refinery or terminal, or entered by bulk transfer into the United States;

(ii) No tax was imposed on such removal or entry under paragraph (b), (c), or (d) of this section; and

(iii) Upon removal from the pipeline or vessel, the taxable fuel is not received at an approved terminal or refinery (or at another pipeline or vessel).

(2) *Liability for tax.*—(i) *In general.*—The owner of the taxable fuel when it is removed from the pipeline or vessel is liable for the tax imposed under paragraph (e)(1) of this section if the owner has not met the conditions of paragraph (e)(2)(ii) of this section.

(ii) *Conditions for avoidance of liability.*—An owner of taxable fuel is not liable for tax under paragraph (e)(2)(i) of this section if, at the time the taxable fuel is removed from the pipeline or vessel, the owner of the taxable fuel—

(A) Is a taxable fuel registrant;

(B) Has an unexpired notification certificate (described in § 48.4081-5) from the operator of the terminal or refinery where the taxable fuel is received; and

(C) Has no reason to believe that any information in the notification certificate is false.

(iii) *Liability of the operator of the facility where the taxable fuel is received.*—The operator of the facility where the taxable fuel is received is liable for the tax imposed under paragraph (e)(1) of this section if the owner of the taxable fuel has met the conditions of paragraph (e)(2)(ii) of this section and is jointly and severally liable for the tax if the owner has not met such conditions.

(f) *Tax on sales within the bulk transfer/terminal system.*—(1) *Imposition of tax.*—Tax is imposed on the sale of taxable fuel located within the bulk transfer/terminal system if the sale is to a person that is not a taxable fuel registrant and tax has not been imposed on such taxable fuel under § 48.4081-2, or paragraph (b), (c), (d), or (e) of this section.

(2) *Exception for certain sales of taxable fuel for export.*—The tax imposed under paragraph (f)(1) of this section does not apply to a sale of taxable fuel if—

(i) The buyer's principal place of business is not within the United States;

(ii) The sale of the fuel occurs as the fuel is delivered into a transport vessel;

(iii) The vessel has a capacity of at least 20,000 barrels of fuel;

(iv) The seller is a taxable fuel registrant and the exporter of record of the fuel; and

(v) The fuel was exported in due course.

(3) *Liability for tax.*—(i) *In general.*—The seller of the taxable fuel is liable for the tax imposed under paragraph (f)(1) of this section if the seller has not met the conditions of paragraph (f)(3)(ii) of this section.

(ii) *Conditions for avoidance of liability.*—A seller is not liable for tax under paragraph (f)(3)(i) of this section if, at the time of the sale, the seller—

(A) Is a taxable fuel registrant;

(B) Has an unexpired notification certificate (described in § 48.4081-5) from the buyer; and

(C) Has no reason to believe that any information in the certificate is false.

(iii) *Liability of the buyer.*—The buyer of the taxable fuel is liable for the tax imposed under paragraph (f)(1) of this section if the seller of the taxable fuel has met the conditions of paragraph (f)(3)(ii) of this section and is jointly and severally liable for the tax if the seller has not met such conditions.

(4) *Example.*—The following example illustrates this paragraph (f) and the definition of the term *sale* in § 48.4081-1:

*Example.* PH owns one million gallons of untaxed gasoline that is stored in TO's terminal. PH also is the position holder with respect to the gasoline. While the gasoline remains stored in the terminal, PH transfers title to 200,000 gallons of the gasoline to A, a person that is not a taxable fuel registrant. PH continues to hold the inventory position on TO's records with respect to the one million gallons. Because PH continues as the position holder with respect to the gasoline, the transfer of title to the gasoline from PH to A is not a sale of gasoline. Because this transfer of title from PH to A is not a sale of

gasoline, the tax imposed under paragraph (f) of this section does not apply to the transfer.

(g) *Tax on removal or sale of blended taxable fuel by the blender.*—(1) *Imposition of tax.*—A tax is imposed on the removal or sale of blended taxable fuel by the blender thereof. Tax is computed on the difference between the total number of gallons of blended taxable fuel removed or sold and the number of gallons of previously taxed taxable fuel used to produce the blended taxable fuel. For this purpose, the alcohol in gasohol is treated as previously taxed taxable fuel.

(2) *Liability for tax.*—(i) *Liability of the blender.*—The blender is liable for the tax imposed under paragraph (g)(1) of this section.

(ii) *Liability of seller of untaxed liquid.*—On and after April 2, 2003, a person that sells any liquid that is used to produce blended taxable fuel is jointly and severally liable for the tax imposed under paragraph (g)(1) of this section on the removal or sale of that blended taxable fuel if the liquid—

(A) Is described in § 48.4081-1(c)(1)(i)(B) (relating to liquids on which tax has not been imposed under section 4081); and

(B) Is sold by that person as gasoline, diesel fuel, or kerosene that has been taxed under section 4081.

(3) *Examples.*—The following examples illustrate the provisions of this paragraph (g) and the definitions of *blended taxable fuel* and *diesel fuel* in § 48.4081-1(c):

*Example 1.* (i) *Facts.* W is a wholesale distributor of petroleum products and R is a retailer of petroleum products. W sells to R 1,000 gallons of an untaxed liquid (a liquid described in § 48.4081-1(c)(1)(i)(B)) and delivers the liquid into a storage tank (tank) at R's retail facility. However, W's invoice to R states that the liquid is undyed diesel fuel. At the time of the delivery, the tank contains 4,000 gallons of undyed diesel fuel, a taxable fuel that has been taxed under section 4081. The resulting 5,000 gallon mixture is suitable for use as a fuel in a diesel-powered highway vehicle because it has practical and commercial fitness for use in the propulsion engine of a diesel-powered highway vehicle. The mixture does not satisfy the dyeing requirements of § 48.4082-1. R sells the mixture from the tank to a construction company for off-highway business use.

(ii) *Analysis*—(A) *Production of blended taxable fuel.* R is a blender within the meaning of § 48.4081-1 because R has produced blended taxable fuel, as defined in § 48.4081-1, by mixing 1,000 gallons of a liquid that has not been taxed under section 4081 with 4,000 gallons of diesel fuel that has been taxed under section 4081. The mixing occurs outside of the bulk transfer/terminal system and the resulting product is diesel fuel because it is suitable for use as a fuel in a diesel-powered highway vehicle.

(B) *Imposition of tax.* Under paragraph (g)(1) of this section, tax is imposed on R's sale of the 5,000 gallons of blended taxable fuel to the construction company. Even though the blended taxable fuel is sold for off-highway business use, which is a nontaxable use as defined in section 4082(b), the sale is not exempt from tax because the blended taxable fuel does not satisfy the dyeing requirements of § 48.4082-1. Tax is computed on 1,000 gallons, which is the difference between the number of gallons of blended taxable fuel R sells (5,000) and the number of gallons of previously taxed taxable fuel used to produce the blended taxable fuel (4,000).

(C) *Liability for tax.* R, as the blender, is liable for this tax under paragraph (g)(2)(i) of this section. W is jointly and severally liable for this tax under paragraph (g)(2)(ii) of this section because the blended taxable fuel is produced using an untaxed liquid that W sold as undyed diesel fuel (that is, as diesel fuel that was taxed under section 4081).

*Example 2.* (i) *Facts.* W, a wholesale distributor of petroleum products, buys 7,000 gallons of diesel fuel at a terminal rack. The diesel fuel is delivered into a tank trailer. Tax is imposed on the diesel fuel under § 48.4081-2 when the diesel fuel is removed at the rack. W then goes to another location where X, the operator of a chemical plant, sells W 1,000 gallons of an untaxed liquid (a liquid described in § 48.4081-1(c)(1)(i)(B)). However, X's invoice to W states that the liquid is undyed diesel fuel. This liquid is delivered into the tank trailer already containing the 7,000 gallons of diesel fuel. The resulting 8,000 gallon mixture is suitable for use as a fuel in a diesel-powered highway vehicle because it has practical and commercial fitness for use in the propulsion engine of a diesel-powered highway vehicle. The mixture does not satisfy the dyeing requirements of § 48.4082-1. W sells the mixture to R, a retailer of petroleum products, and delivers the mixture into a storage tank at R's retail facility. R sells the mixture to its customers.

(ii) *Analysis*—(A) *Production of blended taxable fuel.* W is a blender within the meaning of § 48.4081-1 because W has produced blended taxable fuel, as defined in § 48.4081-1, by mixing 1,000 gallons of a liquid that has not been taxed under section 4081 with 7,000 gallons

**Reg. § 48.4081-3(g)(3)**

of diesel fuel that has been taxed under section 4081. The mixing occurs outside of the bulk transfer/terminal system and the resulting product is diesel fuel because it is suitable for use as a fuel in a diesel-powered highway vehicle. Thus, R has bought blended taxable fuel.

(B) *Imposition of tax.* Under paragraph (g)(1) of this section, tax is imposed on W's sale of the 8,000 gallons of blended taxable fuel to R. Tax is computed on 1,000 gallons, which is the difference between the number of gallons of blended taxable fuel W sells (8,000) and the number of gallons of previously taxed taxable fuel used to produce the blended taxable fuel (7,000). No tax is imposed on R's subsequent sale of the blended taxable fuel because tax is imposed only with respect to a removal or sale by the blender.

(C) *Liability for tax.* W, as the blender, is liable for this tax under paragraph (g)(2)(i) of this section. X is jointly and severally liable for this tax under paragraph (g)(2)(ii) of this section because the blended taxable fuel is produced using an untaxed liquid that X sold as undyed diesel fuel (that is, as diesel fuel that was taxed under section 4081). R has no liability for tax because R is not a blender and did not sell any untaxed liquid as a taxed taxable fuel. R only sold taxed taxable fuel, the blended taxable fuel bought from W.

(h) *Rate of tax.*—For the rate of tax generally imposed under this section, see section 4081(a). For the rate of tax on gasohol and on gasoline removed or entered for gasohol production, see § 48.4081-6.

(i) *Exemptions.*—For exemptions from the taxes imposed under this section, see §§ 48.4081-4 (relating to gasoline blendstocks), 48.4082-1 (relating to dyed diesel fuel and dyed kerosene), 48.4082-5 (relating to diesel fuel and kerosene used in Alaska), 48.4082-6 (relating to aviation-grade kerosene), and 48.4082-7 (relating to kerosene used for a feedstock purpose).

(j) Effective/applicability date: This section is applicable January 1, 1994, except that paragraphs (c)(2)(ii) through (iv) of this section are applicable to entries of taxable fuel after September 27, 2004. [Reg. § 48.4081-3.]

☐ [*T.D.* 8421, 7-21-92. *Amended by T.D.* 8609, 8-4-95; *T.D.* 8659, 3-13-96; *T.D.* 8879, 3-30-2000; *T.D.* 9051, 4-1-2003; *T.D.* 9145, 7-29-2004 *and T.D.* 9346, 7-26-2007.]

**[Reg. § 48.4081-4]**

**§ 48.4081-4. Gasoline; special rules for gasoline blendstocks.—**
(a) *Overview.*—This section provides rules exempting from tax certain removals, entries, and sales of gasoline blendstocks. Generally, under prescribed conditions, tax is not imposed on gasoline blendstocks that are not used to produce finished gasoline or that are received at an approved terminal or refinery.

(b) *Nonbulk removals and entries of gasoline blendstocks not used to produce gasoline.*—(1) *Removals and entries not in connection with sales.*—Tax is not imposed under § 48.4081-2(b), 48.4081-3(b)(1)(ii), or 48.4081-3(c)(1)(ii) on the removal or entry of gasoline blendstocks not in connection with a sale if—

(i) The person otherwise liable for tax under § 48.4081-2(c)(1) (the position holder), 48.4081-3(b)(3) (the refiner), or 48.4081-3(c)(2) (the enterer) is a taxable fuel registrant; and

(ii) Such person does not use the gasoline blendstocks to produce finished gasoline.

(2) *Removals and entries in connection with sales.*—Tax is not imposed under § 48.4081-2(b), 48.4081-3(b)(1)(ii), or 48.4081-3(c)(1)(ii) on the removal or entry of gasoline blendstocks in connection with a sale if—

(i) The person otherwise liable for tax under § 48.4081-2(c)(1) (the position holder), 48.4081-3(b)(3) (the refiner), or 48.4081-3(c)(2) (the enterer) is a taxable fuel registrant; and

(ii) At the time of the sale, such person has an unexpired certificate (described in paragraph (e) of this section) from the buyer and has no reason to believe any information in the certificate is false.

(3) *Tax on sales after certain nonbulk removals or entries.*—(i) *In general.*—If paragraph (b)(1) or (2) of this section applies to the removal or entry of gasoline blendstocks, tax is imposed on any sale of such blendstocks unless, at the time of the sale, the seller—

(A) Has an unexpired certificate (described in paragraph (e) of this section) from its buyer; and

(B) Has no reason to believe any information in the certificate is false.

(ii) *Liability for tax.*—The seller is liable for the tax imposed under this paragraph (b)(3).

(iii) *Rate of tax.*—For the rate of tax, see section 4081.

(c) *Nonbulk removals and entries of gasoline blendstocks received at an approved terminal or refinery.*—Tax is not imposed under § 48.4081-2(b), 48.4081-3(b)(1)(ii), or 48.4081-3(c)(1)(ii) on the removal or entry of gasoline blendstocks that are received at a terminal or refinery if the person otherwise liable for tax under § 48.4081-2(c)(1) (the position holder), 48.4081-3(b)(3) (the refiner), or 48.4081-3(c)(2) (the enterer)—

(1) Is a taxable fuel registrant;

(2) Has an unexpired notification certificate (described in § 48.4081-5) from the operator of the terminal or refinery where the gasoline blendstocks are received; and

(3) Has no reason to believe that any information in the certificate is false.

(d) *Bulk transfers to a registered industrial user.*—Tax is not imposed under § 48.4081-3(e)(1) if, upon the removal of gasoline blendstocks from a pipeline or vessel, the gasoline blendstocks are received by a taxable fuel registrant that is an industrial user.

(e) *Certificate.*—(1) *In general.*—The certificate to be provided by a buyer of gasoline blendstocks consists of a statement that is signed under penalties of perjury by a person with authority to bind the buyer, is in substantially the same form as the model certificate provided in paragraph (e)(3) of this section, and contains all information necessary to complete such model certificate. A new certificate must be given if any information in the current certificate changes. The certificate may be included as part of any business records normally used to document a sale. The certificate expires on the earliest of the following dates:

(i) The date one year after the effective date of the certificate (which may be no earlier than the date it is signed).

(ii) The date a new certificate is provided to the seller.

(iii) The date the seller is notified by the Internal Revenue Service or the buyer that the buyer's right to provide a certificate has been withdrawn.

(2) *Withdrawal of right to provide certificate.*—The Internal Revenue Service may withdraw the right of a buyer of gasoline blendstocks to provide a certificate under this paragraph (e) if such buyer uses gasoline blendstocks to which a certificate applies in the production of finished gasoline or resells the gasoline blendstocks without obtaining a certificate from its buyer. The Internal Revenue Service may notify any seller to whom the buyer has provided a certificate that the buyer's right to provide a certificate has been withdrawn.

(3) *Model certificate.*

---

CERTIFICATE OF PERSON BUYING GASOLINE BLENDSTOCKS FOR USE
OTHER THAN IN THE PRODUCTION OF FINISHED GASOLINE
(To support tax-free sales under section 4081 of the Internal Revenue Code.)

_____

_____
Name, address, and employer identification number of seller

The undersigned buyer ("Buyer") hereby certifies the following under penalties of perjury:
The gasoline blendstocks to which this certificate relates will not be used to produce finished gasoline.
This certificate applies to the following (complete as applicable):
If this is a single purchase certificate, check here _____ and enter:
1. Invoice or delivery ticket number _____
2. _____ (number of gallons) of _____ (type of gasoline blendstocks)
If this is a certificate covering all purchases under a specified account or order number, check here _____ and enter:
1. Effective date _____
2. Expiration date _____
(period not to exceed 1 year after the effective date)
3. Type (or types) of gasoline blendstocks _____
4. Buyer account or order number _____
Buyer will not claim a credit or refund under section 6427(h) of the Internal Revenue Code for any gasoline blendstocks covered by this certificate.

Buyer will provide a new certificate to the seller if any information in this certificate changes.

If Buyer resells the gasoline blendstocks to which this certificate relates, Buyer will be liable for tax unless Buyer obtains a certificate from the purchaser stating that the gasoline blendstocks will not be used to produce finished gasoline and otherwise complies with the conditions of § 48.4081-4(b)(3) of the Manufacturers and Retailers Excise Tax Regulations.

Buyer understands that if Buyer violates the terms of this certificate, the Internal Revenue Service may withdraw Buyer's right to provide a certificate.

Buyer has not been notified by the Internal Revenue Service that its right to provide a certificate has been withdrawn. In addition, the Internal Revenue Service has not notified Buyer that the right to provide a certificate has been withdrawn from a purchaser to which Buyer sells gasoline blendstocks tax free.

Buyer understands that the fraudulent use of this certificate may subject Buyer and all parties making such fraudulent use of this certificate to a fine or imprisonment, or both, together with the costs of prosecution.

_____
Signature and date signed

_____
Printed or typed name of person signing

_____
Title of person signing

_____
Name of Buyer

_____
Employer identification number

_____
Address of Buyer

(f) *Effective date.*—This section is effective January 1, 1994. [Reg. § 48.4081-4.]

☐ [*T.D. 8421, 7-21-92. Amended by T.D. 8659, 3-13-96.*]

### [Reg. § 48.4081-5]

**§ 48.4081-5. Taxable fuel; notification certificate of taxable fuel registrant.**—(a) *Overview.*—This section sets forth requirements for the notification certificate under § § 48.4081-2(c)(2)(ii), 48.4081-3(c)(2)(iii) and (iv), 48.4081-3(d)(2)(iii), 48.4081-3(e)(2)(iii), 48.4081-3(f)(2)(ii), and 48.4081-4(c) to notify another person of the taxable fuel registrant's registration status.

(b) *Certificate.*—(1) *In general.*—The certificate to be provided by a taxable fuel registrant consists of a statement that is signed under penalties of perjury by a person with authority to bind the registrant, is in substantially the same form as the model provided in paragraph (b)(2) of this section, and contains all information necessary to complete such model. A new certificate must be given if any information in the most recently provided certificate changes. The certificate may be included as part of any business records normally used to document a sale. The certificate expires on the earlier of the following dates:

(i) The date the registrant provides a new certificate.

(ii) The date the recipient of the certificate is notified by either the Internal Revenue Service or the registrant that the registrant's registration has been revoked or suspended.

(2) *Model certificate.*

NOTIFICATION CERTIFICATE OF TAXABLE FUEL REGISTRANT

_____
Name, address, and employer identification number of person receiving certificate

The undersigned taxable fuel registrant ("Registrant") hereby certifies under penalties of perjury that Registrant is registered by the Internal Revenue Service with registration number_____ and that Registrant's registration has not been revoked or suspended by the Internal Revenue Service.

Registrant understands that the fraudulent use of this certificate may subject Registrant and all parties making such fraudulent use of this certificate to a fine or imprisonment, or both, together with the costs of prosecution.

_____
Signature and date signed

_____
Printed or typed name of person signing

_____
Title of person signing

_____
Name of registrant

_____
Employer identification number

_____
Address of registrant

(3) *Use of Form 637 as a notification certificate prohibited.*—A copy of the certificate of registry (Form 637) or letter of registration issued to a registrant by the Internal Revenue Service is not a notification certificate described in paragraph (b)(2) of this section.

(c) *Effective date.*—This section is effective January 1, 1994. [Reg. § 48.4081-5.]

☐ [*T.D. 8421, 7-21-92. Amended by T.D. 8659, 3-13-96; T.D. 9145, 7-29-2004 and T.D. 9346, 7-26-2007.*]

### [Reg. § 48.4081-6]

**§ 48.4081-6. Gasoline; gasohol.**—(a) *Overview.*—This section provides rules for determining the applicability of reduced rates of tax on a removal or entry of gasohol or of gasoline used to produce gasohol. Rules are also provided for the imposition of tax on the separation of gasoline from gasohol and the failure to use gasoline that has been taxed at a reduced rate to produce gasohol.

(b) *Explanation of terms.*—(1) *Alcohol.*—(i) *In general; source of the alcohol.*—Except as provided in paragraph (b)(1)(ii) of this section, alcohol means any alcohol that is not a derivative product of petroleum, natural gas, or coal (including peat). Thus, the term includes methanol and ethanol that are not derived from petroleum, natural gas, or coal (including peat). The term also includes alcohol produced either within or outside the United States.

(ii) *Proof and denaturants.*—Alcohol does not include alcohol with a proof of less than 190 degrees (determined without regard to added denaturants). If the alcohol added to a fuel/alcohol mixture (the added alcohol) includes impurities or denaturants, the volume of alcohol in the mixture is determined under the following rules:

(A) The volume of alcohol in the mixture includes the volume of any impurities (other than added denaturants and any fuel with which the alcohol is mixed) that reduce the purity of the added alcohol to not less than 190 proof (determined without regard to added denaturants).

(B) The volume of alcohol in the mixture includes the volume of any approved denaturants that reduce the purity of the added alcohol, but only to the extent that the volume of the approved denaturants does not exceed five percent of the volume of the added alcohol (including the approved denaturants). If the volume of the approved denaturants exceeds five percent of the volume of the added alcohol, the excess over five percent is considered part of the nonalcohol content of the mixture.

(C) For purposes of this paragraph (b)(1)(ii), approved denaturants are any denaturants (including gasoline and nonalcohol fuel denaturants) that reduce the purity of the added alcohol and are added to such alcohol under a formula approved by the Secretary.

(iii) *Products derived from alcohol.*—If alcohol described in paragraphs (b)(1)(i) and (ii) of this section has been chemically trans-

**Reg. § 48.4081-6(b)(1)(iii)**

formed in producing another product (that is, the alcohol is no longer present as a separate chemical in the other product) and there is no significant loss in the energy content of the alcohol, any mixture containing the product includes the volume of alcohol used to produce the product. Thus, for example, a mixture of gasoline and ethyl tertiary butyl ether (ETBE), or of gasoline and methyl tertiary butyl ether (MTBE), includes any alcohol described in paragraphs (b)(1)(i) and (ii) of this section that is used to produce the ETBE or MTBE, respectively, in a chemical reaction in which there is no significant loss in the energy content of the alcohol.

(2) *Gasohol.*—(i) *In general.*—(A) Gasohol is a mixture of gasoline and alcohol that is 10 percent gasohol, 7.7 percent gasohol, or 5.7 percent gasohol. The determination of whether a particular mixture is 10 percent gasohol, 7.7 percent gasohol, or 5.7 percent gasohol is made on a batch-by-batch basis. A batch of gasohol is a discrete mixture of gasoline and alcohol.

(B) If a particular mixture is produced within the bulk transfer/terminal system (for example, at a refinery), the determination of whether the mixture is gasohol is made at the time of the taxable removal or entry of the mixture.

(C) If a particular mixture is produced outside of the bulk transfer/terminal system (for example, by splash blending after the gasoline has been removed from the terminal at the rack), the determination of whether the mixture is gasohol is made immediately after the mixture is produced. In such a case, the contents of the batch typically correspond to a gasoline meter delivery ticket and an alcohol meter delivery ticket, each of which shows the number of gallons of liquid delivered into the mixture. The volume of each component in a batch (without adjustment for temperature) ordinarily is determined by the number of metered gallons shown on the delivery tickets for the gasoline and alcohol delivered. However, if metered gallons of gasoline and alcohol are added to a tank already containing more than a minor amount of liquid, the determination of whether a batch satisfies the alcohol-content requirement will be made by taking into account the amount of alcohol and non-alcohol fuel contained in the liquid already in the tank. Ordinarily, any amount in excess of 0.5 percent of the capacity of the tank will not be considered minor.

(ii) *10 percent gasohol.*—(A) *In general.*—A batch of gasoline/alcohol mixture is 10 percent gasohol if it contains at least 9.8 percent alcohol by volume, without rounding.

(B) *Batches containing less than 10 percent but at least 9.8 percent alcohol.*—If a batch of mixture contains less than 10 percent alcohol but at least 9.8 percent alcohol, without rounding, only a portion of the batch is considered to be 10 percent gasohol. That portion equals the number of gallons of alcohol in the batch multiplied by 10. Any remaining liquid in the mixture is excess liquid.

(iii) *7.7 percent gasohol.*—(A) *In general.*—A batch of gasoline/alcohol mixture is 7.7 percent gasohol if it contains less than 9.8 percent alcohol but at least 7.55 percent alcohol by volume, without rounding.

(B) *Batches containing less than 7.7 percent but at least 7.55 percent alcohol.*—If a batch of mixture contains less than 7.7 percent alcohol but at least 7.55 percent alcohol, without rounding, only a portion of the batch is considered to be 7.7 percent gasohol. That portion equals the number of gallons of alcohol in the batch multiplied by 12.987. Any remaining liquid in the mixture is excess liquid.

(iv) *5.7 percent gasohol.*—(A) *In general.*—A batch of gasoline/alcohol mixture is 5.7 percent gasohol if it contains less than 7.55 percent alcohol but at least 5.59 percent alcohol by volume, without rounding.

(B) *Batches containing less than 5.7 percent but at least 5.59 percent alcohol.*—If a batch of mixture contains less than 5.7 percent alcohol but at least 5.59 percent alcohol, without rounding, only a portion of the batch is considered to be 5.7 percent gasohol. That portion equals the number of gallons of alcohol in the batch multiplied by 17.544. Any remaining liquid in the mixture is excess liquid.

(v) *Tax on excess liquid.*—If tax was imposed on the excess liquid in any gasohol at the gasohol production tax rate (as defined in paragraph (e)(1) of this section), the excess liquid in the batch is considered to be gasoline with respect to which there is a failure to blend into gasohol for purposes of paragraph (f) of this section. If tax was imposed on the excess liquid at the rate of tax described in

section 4081(a), a credit or refund under section 6427(f) is not allowed with respect to the excess liquid.

(vi) *Examples.*—The following examples illustrate this paragraph (b)(2). In these examples, a gasohol blender creates a gasoline/alcohol mixture by pumping a specified amount of gasoline into an empty tank and then adding a specified amount of alcohol.

*Example 1. Mixtures containing exactly 10 percent alcohol.* The applicable delivery tickets show that the mixture is made with 7200 metered gallons of gasoline and 800 metered gallons of alcohol. Accordingly, the mixture contains 10 percent alcohol (as determined based on the delivery tickets provided to the blender) and qualifies as 10 percent gasohol.

*Example 2. Mixtures containing less than 10 percent alcohol but at least 9.8 percent alcohol.* The applicable delivery tickets show that the mixture is made with 7205 metered gallons of gasoline and 795 metered gallons of alcohol. Because the mixture contains less than 10 percent alcohol, but more than 9.8 percent alcohol (as determined based on the delivery tickets provided to the blender), 7950 gallons of the mixture qualify as 10 percent gasohol. If tax was imposed on the gasoline in the mixture at the gasohol production rate applicable to 10 percent gasohol, the remaining 50 gallons of the mixture (the excess liquid) are treated as gasoline with respect to which there was a failure to blend into gasohol for purposes of paragraph (f) of this section. If tax was imposed on the gasoline in the mixture at the rate of tax described in section 4081(a), a credit or refund under section 6427(f) is allowed only with respect to 7155 gallons of gasoline.

*Example 3. Mixtures containing less than 5.59 percent alcohol.* The applicable delivery tickets show that the mixture is made with 7568 metered gallons of gasoline and 436 metered gallons of alcohol. Because the mixture contains only 5.45 percent alcohol (as determined based on the delivery tickets provided to the blender), the mixture does not qualify as gasohol.

(3) *Gasohol blender.*—Gasohol blender means any person that regularly produces gasohol outside of the bulk transfer/terminal system for sale or use in its trade or business.

(4) *Registered gasohol blender.*—*Registered gasohol blender* means a person that is registered under section 4101 as a gasohol blender.

(c) *Rate of tax on gasoline removed or entered for gasohol production.*—(1) *In general.*—The rate of tax imposed on gasoline under §48.4081-2(b) (relating to tax imposed at the terminal rack), §48.4081-3(b)(1) (relating to tax imposed at the refinery), or §48.4081-3(c)(1) (relating to tax imposed on entries) is the gasohol production tax rate if—

(i) The person liable for tax under §48.4081-2(c)(1) (the position holder), §48.4081-3(b)(3) (the refiner), or §48.4081-3(c)(2) (the enterer) is a taxable fuel registrant and a registered gasohol blender, and such person produces gasohol with the gasoline within 24 hours after removing or entering the gasoline; or

(ii) The gasoline is sold in connection with the removal or entry, the person liable for tax under §48.4081-2(c)(1) (the position holder), §48.4081-3(b)(3) (the refiner), or §48.4081-3(c)(2) (the enterer) is a taxable fuel registrant and the person, at the time of the sale,—

(A) Has an unexpired certificate (as described in paragraph (c)(2) of this section) from the buyer; and

(B) Has no reason to believe that any information in the certificate is false.

(2) *Certificate.*—(i) *In general.*—The certificate referred to in paragraph (c)(1)(ii)(A) of this section is a statement that is to be provided by a registered gasohol blender that is signed under penalties of perjury by a person with authority to bind the registered gasohol blender, is in substantially the same form as the model certificate provided in paragraph (c)(2)(ii) of this section, and contains all information necessary to complete such model certificate. A new certificate must be given if any information in the current certificate changes. The certificate may be included as part of any business records normally used to document a sale. The certificate expires on the earliest of the following dates:

(A) The date one year after the effective date of the certificate (which may be no earlier than the date it is signed).

(B) The date the registered gasohol blender provides a new certificate to the seller.

(C) The date the seller is notified by the Internal Revenue Service or the gasohol blender that the gasohol blender's registration has been revoked or suspended.

(ii) *Model certificate.*

CERTIFICATE OF REGISTERED GASOHOL BLENDER
(To support sales of gasoline at the gasohol production tax rate under section 4081(c) of the Internal Revenue Code)

_____

Name, address, and employer identification number of seller
_____("Buyer") certifies the following under penalties of perjury:
     Name of buyer
Buyer is registered as a gasohol blender with registration number _____. Buyer's registration has not been suspended or revoked by the Internal
Revenue Service.
The gasoline bought under this certificate will be used by Buyer to produce gasohol (as defined in §48.4081-6(b) of the Manufacturers and Retailers Excise Tax
Regulations) within 24 hours after buying the gasoline.
Type of gasohol Buyer will produce (check one only):
_____10% gasohol
_____7.7% gasohol
_____5.7% gasohol
If the gasohol the Buyer will produce will contain ethanol, check here: _____
This certificate applies to the following (complete as applicable):
If this is a single purchase certificate, check here_____ and enter:
1. Account number _____
2. Number of gallons _____
If this is a certificate covering all purchases under a specified account or order number, check here _____ and enter:
1. Effective date _____
2. Expiration date _____
(period not to exceed 1 year after the effective date)
3. Buyer account or order number _____
Buyer will not claim a credit or refund under section 6427(f) of the Internal Revenue Code for any gasoline covered by this certificate.
Buyer agrees to provide seller with a new certificate if any information on this certificate changes.
Buyer understands that Buyer's registration may be revoked if the gasoline covered by this certificate is resold or is used other than in Buyer's production of the type of
gasohol identified above.
Buyer will reduce any alcohol mixture credit under section 40(b) by an amount equal to the benefit of the gasohol production tax rate under section 4081(c) for the
gasohol to which this certificate relates.
Buyer understands that the fraudulent use of this certificate may subject Buyer and all parties making any fraudulent use of this certificate to a fine or imprisonment, or
both, together with the costs of prosecution.

_____

Printed or typed name of person signing

_____

Title of person signing

_____

Employer identification number

_____

Address of Buyer

_____

Signature and date signed

(iii) _Use of Form 637 or letter of registration as a gasohol blender's certificate prohibited._—A copy of the certificate of registry (Form 637) or letter of registration issued to a gasohol blender by the Internal Revenue Service is not a gasohol blender's certificate described in paragraph (c)(2)(ii) of this section.

(d) _Rate of tax on gasohol removed or entered._—The rate of tax imposed on removals or entries of any gasohol under §§ 48.4081-2(b), 48.4081-3(b)(1), and 48.4081-3(c)(1) is the gasohol tax rate. The rate of tax imposed on removals and entries of excess liquid described in paragraph (b)(2) of this section is the rate of tax applicable to gasoline under section 4081(a).

(e) _Tax rates._—(1) _Gasohol production tax rate._—The gasohol production tax rate is the applicable rate of tax determined under section 4081(c)(2)(A).

(2) _Gasohol tax rate._—The gasohol tax rate is the applicable alcohol mixture rate determined under section 4081(c)(4)(A).

(f) _Later separation and failure to blend._—(1) _Later separation._—(i) _Imposition of tax._—A tax is imposed on the removal or sale of gasoline separated from gasohol with respect to which tax was imposed at a rate described in paragraph (e) of this section or with respect to which a credit or payment was allowed or made by reason of section 6427(f)(1).

(ii) _Liability for tax._—The person that owns the gasohol at the time gasoline is separated from the gasohol is liable for the tax imposed under paragraph (f)(1)(i) of this section.

(iii) _Rate of tax._—The rate of tax imposed under paragraph (f)(1)(i) of this section is the difference between the rate of tax applicable to gasoline not described in this section and the applicable gasohol production tax rate.

(2) _Failure to blend._—(i) _Imposition of tax._—Tax is imposed on the entry, removal, or sale of gasoline (including excess liquid described in paragraph (b)(2) of this section) with respect to which tax was imposed at a gasohol production tax rate if—

(A) The gasoline was not blended into gasohol; or

(B) The gasoline was blended into gasohol but the gasohol production tax rate applicable to the type of gasohol produced is greater than the rate of tax originally imposed on the gasoline.

(ii) _Liability for tax._—(A) In the case of gasoline with respect to which tax was imposed at the gasohol production tax rate under paragraph (c)(1)(i) of this section, the person liable for the tax imposed by paragraph (f)(2)(i) of this section is the person that was liable for tax on the entry or removal.

(B) In the case of gasoline with respect to which tax was imposed at the gasohol production tax rate under paragraph (c)(1)(ii) of this section, the person that bought the gasoline in connection with the entry or removal is liable for the tax imposed under paragraph (f)(2)(i) of this section.

(iii) _Rate of tax._—The rate of tax imposed on gasoline described in paragraph (f)(2)(i)(A) of this section is the difference between the rate of tax applicable to gasoline not described in this section and the rate of tax previously imposed on the gasoline. The rate of tax imposed on gasoline described in paragraph (f)(2)(i)(B) of this section is the difference between the gasohol production tax rate applicable to the type of gasohol produced and the rate of tax previously imposed on the gasoline.

(iv) _Example._—The following example illustrates this paragraph (f)(2):
_Example._ (i) A registered gasohol blender bought gasoline in connection with a removal described in paragraph (c)(1)(ii) of this section. Based on the blender's certification (described in paragraph (c)(2) of this section) that the blender would produce 10 percent gasohol with the gasoline, tax at the gasohol production tax rate applicable to 10 percent gasohol was imposed on the removal.

(ii) The blender then produced a mixture by splash blending in a tank holding approximately 8000 gallons of mixture. The applicable delivery tickets show that the mixture was blended by first pumping 7220 metered gallons of gasoline into the empty tank, and then pumping 780 metered gallons of alcohol into the tank. Because

**Reg. §48.4081-6(f)(2)(iv)**

the mixture contains 9.75 percent alcohol (as determined based on the delivery tickets provided to the blender) the entire mixture qualifies as 7.7 percent gasohol, rather than 10 percent gasohol.

(iii) Because the 7220 gallons of gasoline were taxed at the gasohol production tax rate applicable to 10 percent gasohol but the gasoline was blended into 7.7 percent gasohol, a failure to blend has occurred with respect to the gasoline. As the person that bought the gasoline in connection with the taxable removal, the blender is liable for the tax imposed under paragraph (f)(2)(i) of this section. The amount of tax imposed is the difference between—

(A) 7220 gallons times the gasohol production tax rate applicable to 7.7 percent gasohol; and

(B) 7220 gallons times the gasohol production tax rate applicable to 10 percent gasohol.

(iv) Because the gasohol does not contain exactly 7.7 percent alcohol, the benefit of the gasohol production tax rate with respect to the alcohol is less than the amount of the alcohol mixture credit under section 40(b) (determined before the application of section 40(c)). Accordingly, the blender may be entitled to claim an alcohol mixture credit for the alcohol used in the gasohol. Under section 40(c), however, the amount of the alcohol mixture credit must be reduced to take into account the benefit provided with respect to the alcohol by the gasohol production tax rate.

(g) *Effective date.*—This section is effective August 7, 1995. [Reg. §48.4081-6.]

☐ [*T.D. 8421, 7-21-92. Amended by T.D. 8609, 8-4-95; T.D. 8659, 3-13-96 and T.D. 8879, 3-30-2000.*]

## [Reg. §48.4081-7]

**§48.4081-7. Taxable fuel; conditions for refunds of taxable fuel tax under section 4081(e).**—(a) *Overview.*—This section provides re-

porting requirements and other conditions that a person paying tax to the government under section 4081 must satisfy to receive a refund (but not a credit) under section 4081(e) with respect to taxable fuel on which a prior tax was paid to the government under section 4081. No credit against any tax imposed under the Internal Revenue Code is allowed under this section.

(b) *Conditions to allowance of refund.*—A claim for refund of tax imposed by section 4081 with respect to taxable fuel is allowed under section 4081(e) and this section only if—

(1) A tax imposed by section 4081 with respect to the taxable fuel was paid to the government and not credited or refunded (the "first tax");

(2) After imposition of the first tax, another tax was imposed by section 4081 with respect to the same taxable fuel and was also paid to the government (the "second tax");

(3) The person that paid the second tax to the government has filed a timely claim for refund that contains the information required under paragraph (d) of this section; and

(4) The person that paid the first tax to the government has met the reporting requirements of paragraph (c) of this section.

(c) *Reporting requirements.*—(1) *Reporting by persons paying the first tax.*—Except as provided in paragraph (c)(3) of this section, the person that paid the first tax under §48.4081-3 (the first taxpayer) must file a report that is in substantially the same form as the model report provided in paragraph (c)(2) of this section (or such other model report as the Commissioner may prescribe) and contains all information necessary to complete such model report (the first taxpayer's report). A first taxpayer's report must be filed with the return to which the report relates (or at such other time, or in such other manner, as prescribed by the Commissioner).

(2) *Model first taxpayer's report.*

FIRST TAXPAYER'S REPORT

1. _____

First Taxpayer's name, address, and employer identification number

2. _____

Name, address, and employer identification number of the buyer of the taxable fuel subject to tax

3. _____

Date and location of removal, entry, or sale

4. _____

Volume and type of taxable fuel removed, entered, or sold

5. Check type of taxable event:

_____Removal from refinery

_____Entry into United States

_____Bulk transfer from terminal by unregistered position holder

_____Bulk transfer not received at an approved terminal

_____Sale within the bulk transfer/terminal system

_____Removal at the terminal rack

_____Removal or sale by the blender

6. _____

Amount of Federal excise tax paid on account of the removal, entry, or sale

The undersigned taxpayer (the "Taxpayer") has not received, and will not claim, a credit with respect to, or a refund of, the tax on the taxable fuel to which this form relates.

Under penalties of perjury, the Taxpayer declares that Taxpayer has examined this statement, including any accompanying schedules and statements, and, to the best of Taxpayer's knowledge and belief, they are true, correct and complete.

_____

Signature and date signed

_____

Printed or typed name of person signing this report

_____

Title

(3) *Optional reporting for certain taxable events.*—Paragraph (c)(1) of this section does not apply with respect to a tax imposed under §48.4081-2 (removal at a terminal rack), §48.4081-3(c)(1)(ii) (nonbulk entries into the United States), or §48.4081-3(g) (removals or sales by blenders). However, if the person liable for the tax expects that another tax will be imposed under section 4081 with respect to the taxable fuel, that person should (but is not required to) file a first taxpayer's report.

(4) *Information provided to subsequent owners, etc.*—(i) *By person required to file first taxpayer's report.*—A first taxpayer required to file a first taxpayer's report under paragraph (c)(1) of this section must give a copy of the report to—

(A) The person to whom the first taxpayer sells (within the meaning of §48.4081-1) the taxable fuel within the bulk transfer/terminal system; or

(B) The owner of the taxable fuel immediately before the imposition of the first tax, if the first taxpayer is not the owner at that time.

(ii) *By person filing optional first taxpayer's report.*—A first taxpayer filing a first taxpayer's report under paragraph (c)(3) of this section should (but is not required to) give a copy of the report to—

(A) The person to whom the first taxpayer sells the taxable fuel; or

(B) The owner of the taxable fuel immediately before the imposition of the first tax, if the first taxpayer is not the owner at that time.

(iii) *By person receiving first taxpayer's report.*—A person that receives a copy of the first taxpayer's report and subsequently sells (within the meaning of §48.4081-1) the taxable fuel within the bulk transfer/terminal system must give the copy and a statement that satisfies the requirements of paragraph (c)(4)(iv) of this section to the buyer. A person that receives a copy of the first taxpayer's report and subsequently sells the taxable fuel outside the bulk transfer/terminal system should (but is not required to) give the copy and a statement that satisfies the requirements of paragraph (c)(4)(iv) of this section to the buyer, if that person expects that another tax will be imposed under section 4081 with respect to the taxable fuel.

(iv) *Form of statement.*—(A) *In general.*—A statement satisfies the requirements of this paragraph (c)(4)(iv) if it is provided at the bottom or on the back of the copy of the first taxpayer's report (or in an attached document). This statement must contain all information

STATEMENT OF SUBSEQUENT SELLER

1. _____

Name, address, and employer identification number of seller in subsequent sale

2. _____

Name, address, and employer identification number of buyer in subsequent sale

3. _____

Date and location of subsequent sale

4. _____

Volume and type of taxable fuel sold

The undersigned seller (the "Seller") has received the copy of the first taxpayer's report provided with this statement in connection with Seller's purchase of the taxable fuel described in this statement.

Under penalties of perjury, Seller declares that Seller has examined this statement, including any accompanying schedules and statements, and, to the best of Seller's knowledge and belief, they are true, correct and complete.

_____

Signature and date signed

_____

Printed or typed name of person signing this statement

_____

Title

(v) *Sale to multiple buyers.*—If the first taxpayer's report relates to taxable fuel divided among more than one buyer, multiple copies of the first taxpayer's report must be made at the stage that the taxable fuel is divided and each buyer must be given a copy of the report.

(d) *Form and content of claim.*—(1) *In general.*—The following rules apply to claims for refund under section 4081(e):

(i) The claim must be made by the person that paid the second tax to the government and must include all the information described in paragraph (d)(2) of this section.

(ii) The claim must be made on Form 8849 (or such other form as the Commissioner may designate) in accordance with the instructions on the form. The form should be marked *Section 4081(e) Claim* at the top. Section 4081(e) claims must not be included with a claim for a refund under any other provision of the Internal Revenue Code.

(2) *Information to be included in the claim.*—Each claim for a refund under section 4081(e) must contain the following information with respect to the taxable fuel covered by the claim:

(i) Volume and type of taxable fuel.

(ii) Date on which the claimant incurred the tax liability to which this claim relates (the second tax).

(iii) Amount of second tax that claimant paid to the government and a statement that claimant has not included the amount of this tax in the sales price of the taxable fuel to which this claim relates and has not collected that amount from the person that bought the taxable fuel from claimant.

(iv) Name, address, and employer identification number of the person that paid the first tax to the government.

(v) A copy of the first taxpayer's report that relates to the taxable fuel covered by the claim.

(vi) If the taxable fuel covered by the claim was bought other than from the first taxpayer, a copy of the statement of subsequent seller that the claimant received with respect to that taxable fuel.

(e) *Time for filing claim.*—A claim for refund under section 4081(e) may be filed any time after the claimant has filed the return of the second tax and before the end of the period prescribed by section 6511 for the filing of a claim for a refund.

(f) *Examples.*—The following examples illustrate the provisions of this section.

*Example 1.* (i) A is a taxable fuel registrant that owns 10,000 gallons of gasoline, and on April 5, 1996, is transporting the gasoline by barge on a waterway in the United States. That day, A sells the gasoline to B, a person that is not a taxable fuel registrant. A is liable for tax on the sale under §48.4081-3(f). A pays this tax to the government and attaches to its return of the gasoline tax for the 2nd quarter of 1996 the first taxpayer's report described in paragraph (c) of this section. A also gives a copy of this report to B.

(ii) On April 9, 1996, B sells the gasoline to C, a taxable fuel registrant. B also gives C a copy of the first taxpayer's report and the statement of subsequent seller (required under paragraph (c)(4) of this section). On April 14, 1996, the gasoline is removed from a terminal at the rack. C is the position holder of the gasoline at the time of the removal and thus is liable for tax on the removal under §48.4081-2(c)(1). C pays this tax to the government.

(iii) After C has filed a return of the second tax and before the end of the period prescribed by section 6511 for filing a claim for a refund, C files a claim for a refund of the second tax. The claim is in the form prescribed in paragraph (d)(2) of this section. C includes

with its claim a copy of the first taxpayer's report and statement of subsequent seller. Because the conditions to allowance of a refund under paragraph (b) of this section have been met, C is allowed a refund of the second tax.

*Example 2.* The facts are the same as in *Example 1* except that A does not pay the tax to the government. Because the first tax was not paid to the government as required by paragraph (b)(1) of this section, the conditions to allowance of a refund under paragraph (b) of this section have not been met. Therefore, C is not allowed a refund of the second tax.

(g) *Effective date.*—This section is effective in the case of taxable fuel with respect to which the first tax is imposed after September 30, 1995. [Reg. §48.4081-7.]

☐ [*T.D. 8421, 7-21-92. Amended by T.D. 8609, 8-4-95; T.D. 8659, 3-13-96 and T.D. 8879, 3-30-2000.*]

### [Reg. §48.4081-8]

**§48.4081-8. Taxable fuel; measurement.**—(a) *In general.*—Volumes of taxable fuel may be measured on the basis of actual volumetric gallons or gallons adjusted to 60 degrees Fahrenheit.

(b) *Effective date.*—This section is applicable January 1, 1994. [Reg. §48.4081-8.]

☐ [*T.D. 8421, 7-21-92. Amended by T.D. 8659, 3-13-96; T.D. 8879, 3-30-2000 and T.D. 8945, 5-17-2001.*]

### [Reg. §48.4082-1]

**§48.4082-1. Diesel fuel and kerosene; exemption for dyed fuel.**—(a) *Exemption.*—Tax is not imposed by section 4081 on the removal, entry, or sale of any diesel fuel or kerosene if—

(1) The person otherwise liable for tax is a taxable fuel registrant;

(2) In the case of a removal from a terminal, the terminal is an approved terminal; and

(3) The diesel fuel or kerosene satisfies the dyeing and marking requirements of paragraphs (b), (c), and (d) of this section.

(b) *Dyeing requirements.*—Diesel fuel or kerosene satisfies the dyeing requirement of this paragraph (b) only if the diesel fuel or kerosene contains—

(1) The dye Solvent Red 164 (and no other dye) at a concentration spectrally equivalent to at least 3.9 pounds of the solid dye standard Solvent Red 26 per thousand barrels of diesel fuel or kerosene; or

(2) Any dye of a type and in a concentration that has been approved by the Commissioner.

(c) *Marking requirements.*—[Reserved]

(d) [Reserved]. For further guidance, see §48.4082-1T(d).

(e) *Effective date.*—(1) Except as provided in paragraph (e)(2) of this section, this section is applicable March 14, 1996.

(2) [Reserved]For further guidance, see §48.4082-1T(e)(2). [Reg. §48.4082-1.]

☐ [*T.D. 8550, 6-28-94. Amended by T.D. 8659, 3-13-96; T.D. 8879, 3-30-2000 and T.D. 9199, 4-25-2005.*]

### [Reg. §48.4082-1T]

**§48.4082-1T. Diesel fuel and kerosene; exemption for dyed fuel (temporary).**—(a) through (c) [Reserved]. For further guidance, see §48.4082-1(a) through (c).

(d) *Time and method for adding dye.*—(1) *In general.*—Except as provided by paragraph (d)(6) of this section, diesel fuel or kerosene satisfies the dyeing requirements of this paragraph (d) only if the dye required by § 48.4082-1(b) is combined with the diesel fuel or kerosene by means of a mechanical injection system that is approved by the Commissioner for use at the facility where the dyeing occurs. Application for approval must be made in the form and manner required by the Commissioner. Rules similar to the rules of § 48.4101-1(g) apply to the Commissioner's action on the applications.

(2) *Mechanical injection system; requirements.*—The Commissioner will approve a mechanical injection system only if—

(i) The system has features that automatically inject an amount of dye that satisfies the concentration requirements of § 48.4082-1(b) into diesel fuel or kerosene as the diesel fuel or kerosene is delivered from the bulk transfer/terminal system into the transport compartment of a truck, trailer, railroad car, or other means of nonbulk transfer;

(ii) The system has calibrated devices that accurately measure and record the amount of dye and the amount of diesel fuel and kerosene that is dispensed for each removal;

(iii) The system has automatic shut-off devices that prevent the removal of more than 100 gallons of undyed diesel fuel or kerosene in the case of a system malfunction;

(iv) The system is secured by either—

(A) Unbroken seals that are issued, installed, and maintained by the terminal operator and secure the measurement devices, shut-off devices, and other access points to the injection system; or

(B) A secured container that controls access to the measurement devices, shut-off devices, and other access points and is secured by an unbroken seal issued, installed, and maintained by the terminal operator;

(v) Each seal securing the system bears a unique identifying number or code and is produced in a manner that provides adequate assurance against duplication; and

(vi) The operator of the facility has written procedures in place for complying with its duty, described in paragraph (d)(4) of this section, to maintain the system's security standards.

(3) *Mechanical injection system; basis for approval.*—In determining whether to approve a mechanical injection system, the Commissioner will take into account the individual circumstances of each facility, including local fire and safety codes, to ensure that the cost of acquiring and maintaining the appropriate levels of security are reasonable for that facility.

(4) *Mechanical injection system; duty of the operator of a mechanical injection system to maintain the system's security standards.*—Each operator of a mechanical injection system must—

(i) Maintain a record for each seal, including its identifying number or code, the location of the seal, the date(s) on which the seal was issued and installed, and the reason for the installation;

(ii) Visually inspect each installed seal not less than once during every 24 hour period to ascertain that each seal and lock mechanism, if applicable, has not been physically altered;

(iii) Check the identifying number or code for each seal against the records maintained by the terminal operator no less frequently than once during each seven day period and record each inspection and verification;

(iv) Promptly notify the Commissioner if inspection of a seal reveals any inconsistency in the records pertaining to that seal, or if the seal has been damaged or removed (other than a removal authorized by the operator for testing or maintenance);

(v) Maintain a record of each seal that has been replaced to include the seal number or code, the date the seal was issued, the location of the seal, the date the seal was replaced, and the reason the seal was replaced;

(vi) Promptly destroy and replace seals that have been removed from the system;

(vii) Restrict access to unused seal inventory to individuals specifically designated by the operator and maintain a record of such individuals;

(viii) Maintain a record of each installation, inspection, and destruction described in this paragraph (d)(4), including the name of the individual who conducts the installation, inspection, or destruction;

(ix) Make available for the Commissioner's immediate inspection the seals and records described in this paragraph (d)(4); and

(x) Promptly notify the Commissioner if, and when, the dye injection system is placed out of service.

(5) *Mechanical injection system; revocation or suspension of approval.*—The Commissioner may revoke or suspend its approval of a dye injection system if the Commissioner determines that the system

does not meet the standards of paragraph (d)(2) of this section or if the operator of the system has not complied with the requirements of paragraph (d)(4) of this section.

(6) *Sales and entries.*—For purposes of determining whether tax is imposed by section 4081 on a sale or entry of diesel fuel or kerosene, such fuel satisfies the dyeing requirements of this paragraph (d) only if the dye required by § 48.4082-1(b) is combined with the fuel before the sale or entry and the seller or enterer has in its records evidence (such as a certificate from the terminal operator providing the fuel) establishing that the dye was combined with the fuel by means of a mechanical injection system. Thus, for example, diesel fuel or kerosene that is entered into the United States by means of nonbulk transfer (such as a railroad car) does not satisfy the requirements of this paragraph (d) if the required dye and marker are combined with diesel fuel or kerosene after the diesel fuel or kerosene has been entered into the United States.

(7) *Cross reference.*—For the penalty relating to mechanical dye injection systems, see section 6715A.

(e) and (e)(1) [Reserved]. For further guidance, see § 48.4082-1(e) and (e)(1).

(2) This section is applicable on October 24, 2005. [Temporary Reg. § 48.4082-1T.]

☐ [*T.D.* 9199, 4-25-2005.]

### [Reg. § 48.4082-2]

**§ 48.4082-2. Diesel fuel and kerosene; notice required for dyed fuel.**—(a) *In general.*—A legible and conspicuous notice stating "*DYED DIESEL FUEL, NONTAXABLE USE ONLY, PENALTY FOR TAXABLE USE*" must be posted by a seller on any retail pump or other delivery facility where it sells dyed diesel fuel for use by its buyer. A legible and conspicuous notice stating "*DYED KEROSENE, NONTAXABLE USE ONLY, PENALTY FOR TAXABLE USE*" must be posted by a seller on any retail pump or other delivery facility where it sells dyed kerosene for use by its buyer. Any seller that fails to post the required notice on any retail pump or other delivery facility where it sells dyed fuel is, for purposes of the penalty imposed by section 6715, presumed to know that the fuel will not be used for a nontaxable use.

(b) *Cross reference; terminal operators.*—For the requirement that terminal operators provide a notice with respect to dyed fuel, see § 48.4101-1(h)(3) (relating to terms and conditions of registration for terminal operators).

(c) *Effective date.*—This section is applicable with respect to diesel fuel after December 31, 1993, and with respect to kerosene after June 30, 1998. [Reg. § 48.4082-2.]

☐ [*T.D.* 8659, 3-13-96. *Amended by T.D.* 8685, 11-8-96 *and T.D.* 8879, 3-30-2000.]

### [Reg. § 48.4082-3]

**§ 48.4082-3. Diesel fuel and kerosene; visual inspection devices.**—[Reserved]

☐ [*T.D.* 8659, 3-13-96. *Amended by T.D.* 8879, 3-30-2000.]

### [Reg. § 48.4082-4]

**§ 48.4082-4. Diesel fuel and kerosene; back-up tax.**—(a) *Imposition of tax.*—(1) *In general.*—Tax is imposed by section 4041 on the delivery into the fuel supply tank of the propulsion engine of a diesel-powered highway vehicle (other than a diesel-powered bus) of—

(i) Any diesel fuel or kerosene on which tax has not been imposed by section 4081;

(ii) Any diesel fuel or kerosene for which a credit or payment has been allowed under section 6427; or

(iii) Any liquid (other than taxable fuel) for use as fuel.

(2) *Liability for tax.*—(i) *In general.*—The operator of the highway vehicle into which the fuel is delivered is liable for the tax imposed under paragraph (a)(1) of this section.

(ii) *Joint and several liability of the seller.*—The seller of the fuel is jointly and severally liable for the tax imposed under paragraph (a)(1) of this section if the seller knows or has reason to know that the fuel will not be used in a nontaxable use.

(3) *Rate of tax.*—The rate of tax is the rate imposed on diesel fuel by section 4081(a).

(b) *Tax on diesel fuel and kerosene; buses and trains.*—(1) *In general.*—Tax is imposed by section 4041 on the delivery into the fuel supply tank of the propulsion engine of a diesel-powered bus or a diesel-powered train of—

(i) Any diesel fuel or kerosene on which tax has not been imposed by section 4081;

(ii) Any diesel fuel or kerosene for which a credit or payment has been allowed under section 6427; or

(iii) Any liquid (other than taxable fuel) for use as fuel.

(2) *Liability for tax.*—(i) *In general.*—Except as provided in paragraph (b)(2)(ii) of this section, the operator of the bus or train into which the fuel is delivered is liable for the tax imposed under paragraph (b)(1) of this section.

(ii) *Special rule for certain train operators.*—The person that delivers the fuel into the fuel supply tank of a train, rather than the train operator, is liable for the tax imposed under paragraph (b)(1) of this section if, at the time of the delivery—

(A) The deliverer of the fuel and the operator of the train are both registered as train operators under § 48.4101-1; and

(B) A written agreement between the deliverer of the fuel and the operator requires the deliverer to pay the tax imposed under paragraph (b)(1) of this section.

(3) *Rate of tax.*—(i) *Buses.*—(A) *In general.*—The rate of tax under paragraph (b)(1) of this section is the sum of the rates described in sections 4041(a)(1)(C)(iii)(I) and 4041(d)(1) (the bus rate) if the bus is used to furnish (for compensation) passenger land transportation available to the general public and either such transportation is scheduled and along regular routes or the seating capacity of the bus is at least 20 adults (not including the driver). A bus is available to the general public if the bus is available for hire to more than a limited number of persons, groups, or organizations.

(B) *Other uses.*—The rate of tax under paragraph (b)(1) of this section is the rate of tax imposed on diesel fuel by section 4081(a) if the bus is used for a purpose other than that described in paragraph (b)(3)(i)(A) of this section.

(ii) *Trains.*—The rate of tax under paragraph (b)(1) of this section is the rate prescribed in section 4041 for diesel fuel sold for use in a train (the train rate).

(4) *Cross reference.*—For the registration requirement relating to certain bus and train operators, see § 48.4101-1(c)(2).

(c) *Exemptions.*—The taxes imposed under paragraphs (a) and (b) of this section do not apply to a delivery of any liquid for—

(1) Use on a farm for farming purposes as that term and related terms are defined in § 48.6420-4(a) through (g);

(2) The exclusive use of a State;

(3) Use described in section 4041(h) (relating to use in a vehicle owned by an aircraft museum);

(4) Use in a bus while the bus is engaged in the transportation of students and employees of schools (as defined in the last sentence of section 4221(d)(7)(C));

(5) Use in a qualified local bus (as defined in section 6427(b)(2)(D)) while the bus is engaged in furnishing (for compensation) intracity passenger land transportation that is available to the general public and is scheduled and along regular routes;

(6) Use in a highway vehicle that—

(i) Is not registered (and is not required to be registered) for highway use under the laws of any State or foreign country; and

(ii) Is used in the operator's trade or business or in an activity of the operator described in section 212 (relating to the production of income);

(7) The exclusive use of a nonprofit educational organization, as defined in § 48.4221-6(b); or

(8) Use in a highway vehicle that is owned by the United States and is not used on the highway.

(d) *Effective date.*—This section is applicable after December 31, 1993, except that references to kerosene are applicable after June 30, 1998. [Reg. § 48.4082-4.]

☐ [*T.D.* 8659, 3-13-96. *Amended by T.D.* 8879, 3-30-2000.]

### [Reg. § 48.4082-5]

**§ 48.4082-5. Diesel fuel and kerosene; Alaska.**—(a) *Application.*—This section applies to diesel fuel or kerosene removed, entered, or sold in Alaska for ultimate sale or use in an exempt area of Alaska.

(b) *Definitions.*

*Exempt area of Alaska* means the area of Alaska in which the sulfur content requirements for diesel fuel (see section 211(i) of the Clean Air Act (42 U.S.C. 7545(i))) do not apply because the Administrator of the Environmental Protection Agency has granted an exemption under section 211(i)(4) of that Act.

*Nontaxable use* means a use described in section 4082(b).

*Qualified dealer* means any person that holds a qualified dealer license from the state of Alaska or has been registered by the district director as a qualified retailer. The district director will register a person as a qualified retailer only if the district director—

(1) Determines that the person, in the course of its trade or business, regularly sells diesel fuel or kerosene for use by its buyer in a nontaxable use; and

(2) Is satisfied with the filing, deposit, payment, and claim history for all federal taxes of the person and any related person.

(c) *Tax-free removals and entries.*—Notwithstanding § 48.4082-1, tax is not imposed by section 4081 on the removal or entry of any diesel fuel or kerosene in an exempt area of Alaska if—

(1) The person that would be liable for tax under § 48.4081-2 or 48.4081-3 is a taxable fuel registrant and satisfies the requirements of paragraph (e) of this section;

(2) In the case of a removal from a terminal, the terminal is an approved terminal; and

(3) The owner of the diesel fuel or kerosene immediately after the removal or entry holds the fuel for its own use in a nontaxable use or is a qualified dealer.

(d) *Sales after removals and entries.*—(1) *In general.*—Paragraph (c) of this section does not apply with respect to diesel fuel or kerosene that is subsequently sold by a qualified dealer unless—

(i) The fuel is sold in an exempt area of Alaska;

(ii) The buyer purchases the fuel for its own use in a nontaxable use or is a qualified dealer; and

(iii) The seller satisfies the requirements of paragraph (e) of this section.

(2) *Tax imposed at time of sale: liability for tax.*—Notwithstanding §§ 48.4081-2 and 48.4081-3, in any case in which paragraph (c) of this section does not apply with respect to diesel fuel or kerosene because of a subsequent sale by a qualified dealer, the tax with respect to that fuel is imposed at the time of the subsequent sale and the qualified dealer is liable for the tax.

(3) *Rate of tax.*—For the rate of tax, see section 4081.

(e) *Evidence of tax-free transactions.*—The requirements of section 4082(c)(2) (relating to certification) and this paragraph (e) are satisfied if the person otherwise liable for tax is able to show the district director satisfactory evidence of the exempt nature of the transaction and has no reason to believe that the evidence is false. Satisfactory evidence may include copies of qualified dealer licenses or exemption certificates obtained for state tax purposes.

(f) *Registration.*—With respect to each person that has been registered as a qualified retailer by the district director, the rules of § 48.4101-1(g), (h), and (i) apply.

(g) *Cross reference.*—For the tax on previously untaxed diesel fuel or kerosene that is used for a taxable purpose, see § 48.4082-4.

(h) *Effective date.*—This section is applicable with respect to diesel fuel removed or entered after December 31, 1996, and with respect to kerosene removed or entered after June 30, 1998. A person registered by the district director as a qualified retailer before April 2, 1998, may be treated, to the extent the district director determines appropriate, as a qualified dealer for the period before that date. [Reg. § 48.4082-5.]

☐ [*T.D.* 8693, 12-16-96. *Redesignated and amended by T.D.* 8748, 12-31-97. *Amended by T.D.* 8879, 3-30-2000.]

### [Reg. § 48.4082-6]

**§ 48.4082-6. Kerosene; exemption for aviation-grade kerosene.**—(a) *Overview.*—This section prescribes the conditions under which tax does not apply to the removal or entry of aviation-grade kerosene that is destined for use as a fuel in an aircraft.

(b) *Definition.*—For purposes of this section, *aviation-grade kerosene* means kerosene-type jet fuel covered by ASTM specification D 1655 or military specification MIL-DTL-5624T (Grade JP-5) or MIL-DTL-83133E (Grade JP-8). For availability of ASTM and military specifications, see § 48.4081-1(d).

(c) *Exemption for certain removals and entries.*—Tax is not imposed under § 48.4081-2(b), 48.4081-3(b)(1)(ii), or 48.4081-3(c)(1)(ii) on the removal or entry of aviation-grade kerosene if—

(1) The person otherwise liable for tax is a taxable fuel registrant;

(2) In the case of a removal from a terminal, the terminal is an approved terminal; and

(3)(i) The person otherwise liable for tax delivers the kerosene into the fuel supply tank of an aircraft and this delivery is not in connection with a sale; or

(ii) The kerosene is sold for use as a fuel in an aircraft and, at the time of the sale, the person otherwise liable for tax has an unexpired certificate (described in paragraph (e) of this section) from the buyer and has no reason to believe any information in the certificate is false.

(d) *Certain later sales.*—(1) *In general.*—Paragraph (c) of this section does not apply with respect to kerosene that is sold as described in paragraph (c)(3)(ii) of this section if there is a later disqualifying sale of the kerosene. A later disqualifying sale is any later sale other than a later sale—

(i) By a person that, at the time of the sale, has an unexpired certificate (described in paragraph (e) of this section) from the buyer and has no reason to believe that any information in the certificate is false; or

(ii) In connection with the delivery of the kerosene into the fuel supply tank of an aircraft.

(2) *Imposition of tax; liability for tax.*—Notwithstanding §§ 48.4081-2 and 48.4081-3, in any case in which paragraph (d)(1) of this section applies, tax is imposed with respect to that kerosene at the time of the first later disqualifying sale and the seller in that sale is liable for the tax.

(3) *Rate of tax.*—For the rate of tax, see section 4081.

(e) *Certificate.*—(1) *In general.*—The certificate described in this paragraph (e) is a statement by a buyer that is signed under penalties of perjury by a person with authority to bind the buyer, is in substantially the same form as the model certificate provided in paragraph (e)(3) of this section, and contains all information necessary to complete the model certificate. A new certificate or notice that the current certificate is invalid must be given if any information in the current certificate changes. The certificate may be included as part of any business records normally used to document a sale. The certificate expires on the earliest of the following dates:

(i) The date one year after the effective date of the certificate (which may be no earlier than the date it is signed).

(ii) The date the buyer provides the seller a new certificate or notice that the current certificate is invalid.

(iii) The date the Internal Revenue Service or the buyer notifies the seller that the buyer's right to provide a certificate has been withdrawn.

(2) *Withdrawal of the right to provide a certificate.*—The Internal Revenue Service may withdraw the right of a buyer of aviation-grade kerosene to provide a certificate under this section if the buyer uses the aviation-grade kerosene to which a certificate relates other than as a fuel in an aircraft or sells the kerosene without first obtaining a certificate from its buyer. The Internal Revenue Service may notify any seller to whom the buyer has provided a certificate that the buyers right to provide a certificate has been withdrawn.

(3) *Model certificate.*

### CERTIFICATE OF PERSON BUYING AVIATION-GRADE KEROSENE FOR USE AS A FUEL IN AN AIRCRAFT
(To support tax-free removals and entries of aviation-grade kerosene under section 4082 of the Internal Revenue Code.)

_____ (Buyer) certifies the following under penalties of perjury:

Name of Buyer

The aviation-grade kerosene to which this certificate applies will be used by Buyer as a fuel in an aircraft or resold by Buyer for that use.

This certificate applies to_____ percent of Buyer's purchases from_____ (name, address, and employer identification number of seller) as follows (complete as applicable):

1. A single purchase on invoice or delivery ticket number _____.

2. All purchases between _____ (effective date) and _____ (expiration date) (period not to exceed one year after the effective date) under account or order number(s) _____. If this certificate applies only to Buyer's purchases for certain locations, check here _____ and list the locations.

_____

_____

Buyer is buying the kerosene for (check either or both as applicable):

_____ Buyer's use as a fuel in an aircraft.

_____ Resale for use as a fuel in an aircraft.

Buyer will provide a new certificate to the seller if any information in this certificate changes.

If Buyer sells the aviation-grade kerosene to which this certificate relates and does not deliver it into the fuel supply tank of an aircraft, Buyer will be liable for tax unless Buyer obtains a certificate from its buyer stating that the aviation-grade kerosene will be used as a fuel in an aircraft.

If Buyer violates the terms of this certificate, the Internal Revenue Service may withdraw Buyer's right to provide a certificate.

Buyer has not been notified by the Internal Revenue Service that its right to provide a certificate has been withdrawn.

The fraudulent use of this certificate may subject Buyer and all parties making any fraudulent use of this certificate to a fine or imprisonment, or both, together with the costs of prosecution.

_____

Printed or typed name of person signing

_____

Title of person signing

_____

Employer identification number

_____

Address of Buyer

_____

Signature and date signed

(f) *Effective date.*—This section is applicable after March 30, 2000, except that paragraph (d) of this section is applicable after June 30, 2000. [Reg. § 48.4082-6.]

☐ [T.D. 8879, 3-30-2000.]

### [Reg. § 48.4082-7]

**§ 48.4082-7. Kerosene; exemption for feedstock purposes.**—(a) *Overview.*—This section prescribes the conditions under which tax does not apply to the removal or entry of kerosene for use for a feedstock purpose.

(b) *Definitions.*—The following definitions apply to this section:

*Feedstock purpose* means the use of kerosene for nonfuel purposes in the manufacture or production of any substance other than gasoline, diesel fuel, or special fuels referred to in section 4041. Thus, for example, kerosene is used for a feedstock purpose when it is used as an ingredient in the production of paint and is not used for a feedstock purpose when it is used to power machinery at a factory where paint is produced.

*Feedstock user* means a person that uses kerosene for a feedstock purpose.

*Registered feedstock user* means a feedstock user that is—

(1) Registered under section 4101 as a feedstock user; or

(2) With respect to removals and entries before October 1, 2000, a taxable fuel registrant.

(c) *Exemption for removals and entries.*—Tax is not imposed on the removal or entry of kerosene if—

(1) The person otherwise liable for tax is a taxable fuel registrant;

(2) In the case of a removal from a terminal, the terminal is an approved terminal; and

(3)(i) The person otherwise liable for tax uses the kerosene for a feedstock purpose; or

(ii) The kerosene is sold for use by the buyer for a feedstock purpose and, at the time of the sale, the person otherwise liable for tax has an unexpired certificate (described in paragraph (e) of this section) from the buyer and has no reason to believe any information in the certificate is false.

(d) *Later sale.*—(1) *In general.*—Paragraph (c) of this section does not apply with respect to kerosene that is sold as described in paragraph (c)(3)(ii) of this section if the buyer in that sale (the certifying buyer) sells the kerosene.

(2) *Imposition of tax; liability for tax.*—Notwithstanding §§ 48.4081-2 and 48.4081-3, in any case in which paragraph (d)(1) of this section applies, tax with respect to that kerosene is imposed at

the time of the sale by the certifying buyer and the certifying buyer is liable for the tax.

(3) *Rate of tax.*—For the rate of tax, see section 4081.

(e) *Certificate.*—(1) *In general.*—The certificate described in this paragraph (e) is a statement by a buyer that is signed under penalties of perjury by a person with authority to bind the buyer, is in substantially the same form as the model certificate provided in paragraph (e)(2) of this section, and contains all information necessary to complete the model certificate. A new certificate or notice that the current certificate is invalid must be given if any information in

the current certificate changes. The certificate may be included as part of any business records normally used to document a sale. The certificate expires on the earliest of the following dates:

(i) The date one year after the effective date of the certificate (which may be no earlier than the date it is signed).

(ii) The date the buyer provides the seller a new certificate or notice that the current certificate is invalid.

(iii) The date the seller is notified by the Internal Revenue Service or the buyer that the buyer's registration has been revoked or suspended.

(2) *Model certificate.*

**CERTIFICATE OF REGISTERED FEEDSTOCK USER**
(To support tax-free removals and entries of kerosene under section 4082 of the Internal Revenue Code.)

_____ (Buyer) certifies the following under penalties of perjury:

Name of Buyer

Buyer is a registered feedstock user with registration number _____. Buyer's registration has not been revoked or suspended.

The kerosene to which this certificate applies will be used by Buyer for a feedstock purpose.

This certificate applies to _____ percent of Buyer's purchases from _____ (name, address, and employer identification number of seller as follows (complete as applicable):

1. A single purchase on invoice or delivery ticket number _____

2. All purchases between _____ (effective date) and _____ (expiration date) (period not to exceed one year after the effective date) under account or order number(s) _____. If this certificate applies only to Buyer's purchases for certain locations, check here _____ and list the locations.

_____

_____

_____

If Buyer sells the kerosene to which this certificate relates, Buyer will be liable for tax on that sale.

Buyer will provide a new certificate to the seller if any information in this certificate changes.

If Buyer violates the terms of this certificate, the Internal Revenue Service may revoke Buyer's registration.

Buyer understands that the fraudulent use of this certificate may subject Buyer and all parties making any fraudulent use of this certificate to a fine or imprisonment, or both, together with the costs of prosecution.

Printed or typed name of person signing

Title of person signing

Employer identification number

Address of Buyer

Signature and date signed

(f) *Effective date.*—This section is applicable after March 30, 2000, except that paragraph (d) of this section is applicable after June 30, 2000. [Reg. § 48.4082-7.]

☐ [*T.D. 8879, 3-30-2000.*]

## [Reg. § 48.4083-1]

**§ 48.4083-1. Taxable fuel; administrative authority.**—(a) *In general.*—(1) *Authority to inspect.*—Officers or employees of the IRS designated by the Commissioner, upon presenting appropriate credentials and a written notice to the owner, operator, or agent in charge, are authorized to enter any place and to conduct inspections in accordance with paragraphs (a) through (c) of this section.

(2) *Reasonableness.*—Inspections will be performed in a reasonable manner and at times that are reasonable under the circumstances, taking into consideration the normal business hours of the place to be entered.

(b) *Place of inspection.*—(1) *In general.*—Inspections may be at any place at which taxable fuel is (or may be) produced or stored or at any inspection site where evidence of activities described in section 6715(a) may be discovered. These places may include, but are not limited to—

(i) Any terminal;

(ii) Any fuel storage facility that is not a terminal;

(iii) Any retail fuel facility; or

(iv) Any designated inspection site.

(2) *Designated inspection sites.*—A designated inspection site is any State highway inspection station, weigh station, agricultural inspection station, mobile station, or other location designated by the Commissioner to be used as a fuel inspection site. A designated inspection site will be identified as a fuel inspection site.

(c) *Scope of inspection.*—(1) *Inspection.*—Officers or employees may physically inspect, examine or otherwise search any tank, reservoir, or other container that can or may be used for the production, storage, or transportation of fuel, fuel dyes, or fuel markers. Inspection may also be made of any equipment used for, or in connection with, production, storage, or transportation of fuel, fuel dyes, or fuel markers. This includes any equipment used for the dyeing or marking of fuel. This also includes books and records, if any, that are

maintained at the place of inspection and are kept to determine excise tax liability under section 4081.

(2) *Detainment.*—Officers or employees may detain any vehicle or train for the purpose of inspecting its fuel tanks and storage tanks. Detainment will be either on the premises under inspection or at a designated inspection site. Detainment may continue for such reasonable period of time as is necessary to determine the amount and composition of the fuel.

(3) *Removal of samples.*—Officers or employees may take and remove samples of fuel in such quantities as are reasonably necessary to determine the composition of the fuel.

(d) *Refusal to submit to inspection.*—For the penalty for any refusal to permit an entry or inspection authorized by this section, see section 4083(c)(3). This penalty is in addition to any tax that may be imposed by section 4041 or 4081 and any penalty that may be imposed by section 6715.

(e) *Effective date.*—This section is effective January 1, 1994. [Reg. § 48.4083-1.]

☐ [*T.D. 8659, 3-13-96. Amended by T.D. 8685, 11-8-96 and T.D. 8879, 3-30-2000.*]

## [Reg. § 48.4091-3]

**§ 48.4091-3. [Reserved].**

☐ [*T.D. 8774, 6-26-98. Redesignated by T.D. 8879, 3-30-2000. Removed and reserved by T.D. 9849, 3-11-2019.*]

## [Reg. § 48.4101-1]

**§ 48.4101-1. Taxable fuel; registration.**—(a) *In general.*—(1) This section provides rules relating to registration under section 4101 for purposes of the federal excise tax on taxable fuel imposed by sections 4041(a)(1) and 4081 and the credit or payment allowed to certain ultimate vendors of diesel fuel and kerosene under section 6427.

(2) A person is registered under section 4101 only if the district director has issued a registration letter to the person and the registration has not been revoked or suspended. However, the United States is treated as registered under section 4101.

(3) A refiner that is registered under section 4101 may, with respect to the bulk removal of any batch of gasohol from its refinery, treat itself as a person that is not registered. See § 48.4081-3(b)(1)(iii).

(4) Each business unit that has, or is required to have, a separate employer identification number is treated as a separate person. Thus, two business units (for example, a parent corporation and a subsidiary corporation, or a proprietorship and a related partnership), each of which has a different employer identification number, are two persons.

(5) A registration in effect on December 31, 1993, with respect to the tax on gasoline or diesel fuel is subject to the district director's review, and to revocation or suspension, under the standards set forth in this section, but remains in effect until the earlier of—

(i) The effective date of a registration issued under paragraph (g)(3) of this section; or

(ii) The effective date of the revocation or suspension of the registration under paragraph (i) of this section.

(6)(i) A person is treated as a taxable fuel registrant if on June 30, 1998, the person—

(A) Is an enterer, refiner, terminal operator, or throughputter with respect to kerosene and is registered under section 4101 as a producer or importer of aviation fuel;

(B) Operates one or more terminals that store kerosene (and no other type of taxable fuel); or

(C) Is a commercial airline, an operator of aircraft in noncommercial aviation, or a fixed base operator and is also a position holder with respect to kerosene.

(ii) A person treated as registered under paragraph (a)(6)(i) of this section is treated as registered from July 1, 1998, until the earlier of—

(A) The date of a subsequent denial of an application for registration under paragraph (g)(2) of this section;

(B) The effective date of a subsequent registration issued under paragraph (g)(3) of this section;

(C) The effective date of a subsequent revocation or suspension of registration under paragraph (i) of this section; or

(D) July 1, 1999.

(b) *Definitions.*—(1) *Applicant.*—An *applicant* is a person that has applied for registration under paragraph (e) of this section.

(2) *Bonded registrant.*—A *bonded registrant* is a person that has given a bond to the district director under paragraph (j) of this section as a condition of registration.

(3) *Gasohol bonding amount.*—The *gasohol bonding amount* is the product of—

(i) The rate of tax applicable to later separation, as described in § 48.4081-6(f)(1)(iii); and

(ii) The total number of gallons of gasoline expected to be bought at the gasohol production tax rate by the gasohol blender during a representative 6-month period (as determined by the district director).

(4) *Penalized for a wrongful act.*—A person has been *penalized for a wrongful act* if the person has—

(i) Been assessed any penalty under chapter 68 of the Internal Revenue Code (or similar provision of the law of any State) for fraudulently failing to file any return or pay any tax, and the penalty has not been wholly abated, refunded, or credited;

(ii) Been assessed any penalty under chapter 68 of the Internal Revenue Code, such penalty has not been wholly abated, refunded, or credited, and the district director determines that the conduct resulting in the penalty is part of a consistent pattern of failing to deposit, pay, or pay over a substantial amount of tax;

(iii) Been convicted of a crime under chapter 75 of the Internal Revenue Code (or similar provision of the law of any State), or of conspiracy to commit such a crime, and the conviction has not been wholly reversed by a court of competent jurisdiction;

(iv) Been convicted, under the laws of the United States or any State, of a felony for which an element of the offense is theft, fraud, or the making of false statements, and the conviction has not been wholly reversed by a court of competent jurisdiction;

(v) Been assessed any tax under section 4103 and the tax has not been wholly abated, refunded, or credited; or

(vi) Had its registration under section 4101 or 4222 revoked.

(5) *Related person.*—A *related person* is a person that—

(i) Directly or indirectly exercises control over an activity of the applicant if the activity is described in paragraph (c)(1) or (d) of this section;

(ii) Owns, directly or indirectly, five percent or more of the applicant;

(iii) Is under a duty to assure the payment of a tax for which the applicant is responsible;

(iv) Is a member, with the applicant, of a group of organizations (as defined in §1.52-1(b) of this chapter) that would be treated as a group of trades or businesses under common control for purposes of §1.52-1 of this chapter; or

(v) Distributed or transferred assets to the applicant in a transaction in which the applicant's basis in the assets is determined by reference to the basis of the assets in the hands of the distributor or transferor.

(6) *Registrant.*—A *registrant* is a person that the district director has, in accordance with paragraph (g)(3) of this section, registered under section 4101 and whose registration has not been revoked or suspended.

(7) *Pipeline operator.*—A *pipeline operator* is any person that operates a pipeline within the bulk transfer/terminal system.

(8) *Vessel operator.*—A *vessel operator* is any person that operates a vessel within the bulk transfer/terminal system. However, for purposes of this definition, *vessel* does not include a deep draft ocean-going vessel (as defined in §48.4042-3(a)).

(9) *Other definitions.*—For other definitions relating to taxable fuel, see §§48.4081-1, 48.4081-6(b), 48.4082-5(b), 48.4082-6(b), 48.4082-7(b), 48.6427-9(b), 48.6427-10(b), and 48.6427-11(b).

(c) *Persons required to be registered.*—(1) *In general.*—A person is required to be registered under section 4101 if the person is—

(i) A blender;

(ii) An enterer;

(iii) A pipeline operator;

(iv) A position holder;

(v) A refiner;

(vi) A terminal operator; or

(vii) A vessel operator.

(2) *Bus and train operators.*—Every operator of a bus or train is required to be registered under section 4101 at any time it incurs any liability for tax under section 4041 at the bus rate (as described in §48.4082-4(b)(3)(i)) or the train rate (as described in §48.4082-4(b)(3)(ii)).

(3) *Consequences of failing to register.*—For the criminal penalty imposed for failure to register, see section 7232. For the civil penalty imposed for failure to register, see section 7272.

(d) *Persons that may, but are not required to, be registered.*—A person may, but is not required to, be registered under section 4101 if the person is—

(1) A feedstock user;

(2) A gasohol blender;

(3) An industrial user;

(4) A throughputter that is not a position holder;

(5) An ultimate vendor; or

(6) An ultimate vendor (blocked pump).

(e) *Application instructions.*—Application for registration under section 4101 must be made in accordance with the instructions for Form 637 (or such other form as the Commissioner may designate).

(f) *Registration tests.*—(1) *In general.*—(i) *Persons other than ultimate vendors, pipeline operators, and vessel operators.*—Except as provided in paragraph (f)(1)(ii) of this section, the district director will register an applicant only if the district director determines that the applicant meets the following three tests (collectively, the registration tests):

(A) The activity test of paragraph (f)(2) of this section.

(B) The acceptable risk test of paragraph (f)(3) of this section.

(C) The adequate security test of paragraph (f)(4) of this section.

(ii) *Ultimate vendors, pipeline operators, and vessel operators.*—The district director will register an applicant as an ultimate vendor, ultimate vendor (blocked pump), pipeline operator, or vessel operator only if the district director—

(A) Determines that the applicant meets the activity test of paragraph (f)(2) of this section; and

(B) Is satisfied with the filing, deposit, payment, and claim history for all federal taxes of the applicant and any related person.

(2) *The activity test.*—An applicant meets the activity test of this paragraph (f)(2) only if the district director determines that the applicant—

(i) Is, in the course of its trade or business, regularly engaged as an operator of a bus or train or in the characteristic activity of a person described in paragraph (c)(1) or (d) of this section; or

(ii) Is likely to be (because of such factors as the applicant's business experience, financial standing, or trade connections), in the course of its trade or business, regularly engaged as an operator of a bus or train or in the characteristic activity of a person described in paragraph (c)(1) or (d) of this section within a reasonable time after becoming registered under section 4101.

(3) *Acceptable risk test.*—(i) *In general.*—An applicant meets the acceptable risk test of this paragraph (f)(3) only if—

(A) Neither the applicant nor a related person has been penalized for a wrongful act; or

(B) Even though the applicant or a related person has been penalized for a wrongful act, the district director determines, after review of evidence offered by the applicant, that the registration of the applicant does not create a significant risk of nonpayment or late payment of the tax imposed by sections 4041(a)(1) and 4081.

(ii) *Significant risk of nonpayment or late payment of tax.*—In making the determination described in paragraph (f)(3)(i)(B) of this section, the district director may consider factors such as the following:

(A) The time elapsed since the applicant or related person was penalized for a wrongful act.

(B) The present relationship between the applicant and any related person that was penalized for any wrongful act.

(C) The degree of rehabilitation of the person penalized for any wrongful act.

(D) The amount of bond given by the applicant. In this regard, the district director may accept a bond under paragraph (j) of this section, without regard to the limits on the amount of the bond set by paragraph (j)(2) of this section.

(4) *Adequate security test.*—(i) *In general.*—An applicant meets the adequate security test of this paragraph (f)(4) only if the district director determines that the applicant has both adequate financial resources and a satisfactory tax history, or the applicant gives the district director a bond (under the provisions of paragraph (j) of this section).

(ii) *Adequate financial resources.*—(A) *In general.*—An applicant has adequate financial resources only if the district director determines that the applicant is financially capable of paying—

(1) Its expected tax liability under sections 4041(a)(1) and 4081 for a representative 6-month period (as determined by the district director);

(2) In the case of a terminal operator, the expected tax liability under section 4081 of persons other than the terminal operator with respect to taxable fuel removed at the racks of its terminals during a representative 1-month period (as determined by the district director); and

(3) In the case of a gasohol blender, the gasohol bonding amount.

(B) *Basis for determination.*—The determination under § 48.4101-1(f)(4)(ii) must be based on all information relevant to the applicant's financial status.

(iii) *Satisfactory tax history.*—An applicant has a satisfactory tax history only if the district director is satisfied with the filing, deposit, and payment history for all federal taxes of the applicant and any related person.

(g) *Action on the application by the district director.*—(1) *Review of application.*—The district director may investigate the accuracy and completeness of any representations made by an applicant, request any additional relevant information from the applicant, and inspect the applicant's premises during normal business hours without advance notice.

(2) *Denial.*—If the district director determines that an applicant does not meet all of the applicable registration tests described in paragraph (f) of this section, the district director must notify the applicant, in writing, that its application for registration is denied and state the basis for the denial.

(3) *Approval.*—If the district director determines that an applicant meets all of the applicable registration tests described in paragraph (f) of this section, the district director must register the applicant under section 4101 and issue the applicant a letter of registration containing the effective date of the registration. The effective date of the registration must be no earlier than the date on which the district director signs the letter of registration. A copy of an application for registration (Form 637) is not a letter of registration.

(h) *Terms and conditions of registration.*—(1) *Affirmative duties.*—Each registrant must—

(i) Make deposits, file returns, and pay taxes required by the Internal Revenue Code and the regulations;

(ii) Keep records sufficient to show the registrant's tax liability under sections 4041(a)(1) and 4081 and payments or deposits of such liability;

(iii) Make all information reports required under section 4101(d);

(iv) Make available for inspection on demand by the Internal Revenue Service during normal business hours records relevant to a determination of tax liability under sections 4041(a)(1) and 4081; and

(v) Notify the district director of any change (such as a change in ownership) in the information the registrant submitted in connection with its application for registration, or previously submitted under this paragraph (h)(1)(v), within 10 days after the change occurs.

(2) *Prohibited actions.*—A registrant may not—

(i) Sell, lease or otherwise allow another person to use its registration;

(ii) Make any false statement to the district director in connection with a submission under paragraph (h)(1) or (h)(3) of this section;

(iii) Make any false statement on, or violate the terms of, any certificate given to another person to support an exemption from, or a reduced rate of, the tax imposed by section 4081; or

(iv) In the case of an ultimate vendor (blocked pump), deliver kerosene (or allow kerosene to be delivered) into the fuel supply tank of a diesel-powered highway vehicle or diesel-powered train from a blocked pump.

(3) *Additional terms and conditions for terminal operators.*—(i) *Notice required with respect to dyed diesel fuel and dyed kerosene.*—A legible and conspicuous notice stating "DYED DIESEL FUEL, NONTAXABLE USE ONLY, PENALTY FOR TAXABLE USE" must be provided by each terminal operator to any person that receives dyed diesel fuel at a terminal rack of that operator. A legible and conspicuous notice stating "DYED KEROSENE, NONTAXABLE USE ONLY, PENALTY FOR TAXABLE USE" must be provided by each terminal operator to any person that receives dyed kerosene at a terminal rack of that operator. These notices must be provided by the time of the removal and must appear on all shipping papers, bills of lading, and similar documents that are provided by the terminal operator to accompany the removal of the fuel.

(ii) *Records to be maintained relating to removals of diesel fuel or kerosene.*—Each terminal operator must keep the following information with respect to each rack removal of diesel fuel or kerosene at each terminal it operates:

(A) The bill of lading or other shipping document.

(B) The record of whether the fuel was dyed and marked in accordance with § 48.4082-1.

(C) The volume and date of the removal.

(D) The identity of the person, such as a common carrier, that physically received the fuel.

(E) Any other information required by the Commissioner.

(iii) *Records to be maintained relating to dye.*—With respect to each of its terminals, a terminal operator must keep records relating to dye inventories and usage.

(iv) [Reserved]. For further guidance, see § 48.4101-1T(h)(3)(iv).

(v) *Prohibition on providing incorrect information.*—In connection with the removal of diesel fuel or kerosene that is not dyed and marked in accordance with § 48.4082-1, a terminal operator may not provide any person (including the position holder with respect to the fuel) with any bill of lading, shipping paper, or similar document indicating that the diesel fuel or kerosene is dyed and marked in accordance with § 48.4082-1.

(i) *Adverse actions by the district director against a registrant.*—(1) *Mandatory revocation or suspension.*—The district director must revoke or suspend the registration of any registrant if the district director determines that the registrant, at any time—

(i) Does not meet one or more of the applicable registration tests under paragraph (f) of this section and has not corrected the deficiency within a reasonable period of time after notification by the district director;

(ii) Has used its registration to evade, or attempt to evade, the payment of any tax imposed by section 4041(a)(1) or 4081, or to postpone or in any manner to interfere with the collection of any such tax, or to make a fraudulent claim for a credit or payment;

(iii) Has aided or abetted another person in evading, or attempting to evade, payment of any tax imposed by section 4041(a)(1) or 4081, or in making a fraudulent claim for a credit or payment; or

(iv) Has sold, leased, or otherwise allowed another person to use its registration.

(2) *Remedial action permitted in other cases.*—If the district director determines that a registrant has, at any time, failed to comply with the terms and conditions of registration under paragraph (h) of this section, made a false statement to the district director in connection with its application for registration or retention of registration, or otherwise used its registration in a manner that creates a significant risk of nonpayment or late payment of tax, then the district director may—

(i) Revoke or suspend the registrant's registration;

(ii) In the case of a registrant other than an ultimate vendor or an ultimate vendor (blocked pump), require the registrant to give a bond under the provisions of paragraph (j) of this section as a condition of retaining its registration; and

(iii) In the case of a registrant other than an ultimate vendor or an ultimate vendor (blocked pump), require the registrant to file monthly or semimonthly returns under § 40.6011(a)-1(b) of this chapter as a condition of retaining its registration.

(3) *Action by the district director to revoke or suspend a registration.*—If the district director revokes or suspends a registration, the district director must so notify the registrant in writing and state the basis for the revocation or suspension. The effective date of the revocation or suspension may not be earlier than the date on which the district director notifies the registrant.

(j) *Bonds.*—(1) *Form.*—Each bond given to the district director as a condition of registration under paragraph (f)(4)(i) or (i)(2)(ii) of this section must be executed in the form prescribed by the district director. Each bond must be—

(i) A public debt obligation of the United States Government;

(ii) An obligation the principal and interest of which are unconditionally guaranteed by the United States Government;

(iii) A bond executed by a surety company listed in Department of the Treasury Circular 570 as an acceptable surety or reinsurer of federal bonds (a surety bond); or

(iv) Any other bond with security (including liens under section 4101(b)(1)(B)) considered acceptable by the district director.

(2) *Amount of bond.*—A bond given under this paragraph (j) must be in an amount that the district director determines will ensure timely collection of the taxes imposed by sections 4041(a)(1) and 4081, taking into account the applicant's financial capabilities, tax history, and expected liability under sections 4041(a)(1) and 4081. The district director may increase or decrease the amount of the required bond to take into account changes in the applicant's financial capabilities, tax history, and expected liability under sections 4041(a)(1) and 4081. However, in no case may the amount of the bond be greater than the amount that the district director determines is equal to—

(i) The applicant's expected tax liability under sections 4041(a)(1) and 4081 for a representative 6-month period (as determined by the district director);

(ii) In the case of a terminal operator, the expected tax liability of persons other than the terminal operator under section 4081 with respect to taxable fuel removed at the racks of its terminals (determined as if all removals of taxable fuel were taxable) during a representative 1-month period (as determined by the district director); and

(iii) In the case of a gasohol blender, the gasohol bonding amount.

(3) *Collection of taxes from a bond.*—If a bonded registrant does not pay the amount of tax it incurs under section 4041(a)(1) or 4081 by the time prescribed in section 6151 for paying that tax, the district director may collect the amount of the unpaid tax (including penalties and interest with respect to that tax) from the bonded registrant's bond.

(4) *Termination of bonds.*—(i) *Surety bonds.*—A surety on a bond may give written notice to the district director and the bonded registrant that the surety desires to be relieved of liability under the bond after a certain date, which date must be at least 60 days after the receipt of the notice by the district director. The surety will be relieved of any liability that the bonded registrant incurs after the date named in the notice. However, the surety remains liable for the amount of tax that the bonded registrant incurred under sections 4041(a)(1) and 4081 during the term of the bond and for penalties and interest with respect to that tax.

(ii) *Other bonds.*—A bond (other than a surety bond) given to the district director may be returned to the bonded registrant only after the earlier of—

(A) The district director's determination that the bonded registrant has paid all taxes that the bonded registrant incurred under sections 4041(a)(1) and 4081 during the period covered by the bond and any penalties and interest with respect to the taxes;

(B) The expiration of the period for assessment of the taxes that the bonded registrant incurred under sections 4041(a)(1) and 4081 taxes during the period covered by the bond, as determined under the provisions of subchapter A of chapter 66 of the Internal Revenue Code; or

(C) The date that the district director receives from the registrant a substitute bond given under this paragraph (j).

(5) *Determination that bond is no longer required.*—If the district director determines that the bonded registrant meets the adequate security test of paragraph (f)(4) of this section without a bond, the registrant is to be released from the obligation to give a bond as a condition of registration under section 4101.

(k) *Cross references.*—For a rule relating to the filing of monthly and semimonthly returns by certain persons that are registered under section 4101, see § 40.6011(a)-1(b)(2) of this chapter. For rules relating to the tax on taxable fuel, see § § 48.4081-1 through 48.4083-1. For rules relating to claims by registered ultimate vendors, see § 48.6427-9. For rules relating to claims by registered ultimate vendors (blocked pump), see § 48.6427-10.

(l) *Effective dates.*—(1) Except as otherwise provided in this paragraph (l), this section is applicable as of January 1, 1994.

(2) Paragraph (c)(1) of this section (relating to persons required to be registered) is applicable as of January 1, 1995, except that paragraphs (c)(1)(iii) and (c)(1)(vii) of this section are applicable after March 31, 2001.

(3) Paragraph (h)(3)(iii) of this section (relating to certain record-keeping requirements) is applicable as of July 1, 1996.

(4) References in this section to kerosene are applicable after June 30, 1998.

(5) *Applicability date.*—Paragraph (f)(4)(ii)(B) of this section applies on and after July 6, 2011. [Reg. § 48.4101-1.]

☐ [*T.D.* 6434, 12-21-59. *Amended by T.D.* 7908, 9-2-83; *T.D.* 8659, 3-13-96; *T.D.* 8879, 3-30-2000 (*corrected* 5-5-2000); 9199, 4-25-2005; *T.D.* 9533, 7-1-2011 *and T.D.* 9637, 9-5-2013.]

**[Reg. § 48.4101-2]**

**§ 48.4101-2. Information reporting.**—(a) *In general.*—Each information report under section 4101(d) must be—

(1) Made in the form required by the Commissioner;

(2) Made for a period of one calendar month; and

(3) Filed by the last day of the first month following the month for which the report is made, except that a report relating to any month during 2000 must be filed by February 28, 2001.

(b) *Effective date.*—This section is applicable after March 30, 2000. [Reg. § 48.4101-2.]

☐ [*T.D.* 8659, 3-13-96. *Amended by T.D.* 8879, 3-30-2000.]

**[Reg. § 48.4102-1]**

**§ 48.4102-1. Inspection of records by State or local tax officers.**—(a) *Inspection of records maintained by taxpayer.*—The records that a taxpayer is required to keep with respect to the taxes imposed by section 4081 or 4091 must be open to inspection by any officer of any State or political subdivision thereof, or of the District of Columbia, who is charged with the enforcement or collection of any tax on taxable fuel or aviation fuel.

(b) *Inspection of records maintained by Internal Revenue Service.*—(1) *In general.*—The records maintained by the Internal Revenue Service with respect to the taxes imposed by sections 4081 and 4091 shall, upon the request of an officer (described in paragraph (b)(2) of this section) of a State or political subdivision thereof, or of the District of Columbia, be open to inspection by the officer for purposes of collection or enforcement.

(2) *Requests for inspection.*—Requests for inspection under this paragraph shall be made in writing, signed by any officer of a State, political subdivision, or the District of Columbia, who is charged with the enforcement or collection of any tax on taxable fuel or aviation fuel imposed by the State, political subdivision, or the District of Columbia, and shall be addressed to the director of the Internal Revenue Service Center having custody of the records which it is desired to inspect. Each such request shall state (i) the kind of records (whether pertaining to taxable fuel or aviation fuel) it is desired to inspect, (ii) the period or periods covered by the records involved, (iii) the name of the officer by whom the inspection is to be made, (iv) the name of the representative of the officer who has been designated to make the inspection, (v) by specific reference, the law of the State, political subdivision, or the District of Columbia imposing the tax which the officer is charged with collecting or enforcing, and the law under which the officer is so charged, and (vi) the purpose for which the inspection is to be made. The service center

director will notify the person making the request upon approval or disapproval of the request.

(3) *Time and place for inspection.*—In any case where a request for inspection under this paragraph (b) is approved, the inspection shall be made in the office of the service center director having custody of the records which it is desired to inspect, but only in the presence of an internal revenue officer or employee and during the regular hours of business of the office. [Reg. §48.4102-1.]

☐ [T.D. 6434, 12-21-59. *Amended by T.D. 7908, 9-2-83 and T.D. 8659, 3-13-96.*]

### [Reg. §48.4121-1]

**§48.4121-1. Imposition and rate of tax on coal.**—(a) *Imposition of tax.*—(1) *In general.*—Section 4121(a) imposes a tax on coal mined at any time in this country if the coal is sold or used by the producer after March 31, 1978 (see section 4218 and the regulations under that section for rules relating to the use of coal being treated as a sale of coal). For purposes of this section, the term "producer" means the person in whom is vested ownership of the coal under state law immediately after the coal is severed from the ground, without regard to the existence of any contractual arrangement for the sale or other disposition of the coal or the payment of any royalties between the producer and third parties. The term includes any person who extracts coal from coal waste refuse piles or from the silt waste product which results from the wet washing (or similarly processing) of coal. However, the excise tax does not apply to a producer who sells the silt waste product without extracting the coal from it, or to the producer who uses the silt waste product without extracting the coal from it. Furthermore, the excise tax does not apply to the sale or use of the silt waste product after any coal has been extracted from it.

(2) *Examples.*—Paragraph (a)(1) of this section may be illustrated by the following examples:

*Example (1).* A, a limited partnership, is the owner of land on which a coal mine is located. A contracts with XYZ Company to extract the coal for a set price per ton. XYZ Company is an independent contractor and has no ownership interest in the coal mined. Under state law, A is the owner of the coal immediately after severance. After XYZ extracts the coal from the mine, A sells the coal. A is the producer of the coal and is responsible for the payment of the excise tax.

*Example (2).* A, a limited partnership, is the owner of land on which a coal mine is located. A leases the land to XYZ Company, and XYZ Company extracts coal from the mine and sells it. Under state law, XYZ is the owner of the coal immediately after the coal is severed from the ground. XYZ Company is the producer and must pay the excise tax. This is true even though the lease agreement requires XYZ to pay a royalty to A.

*Example (3).* XYZ Company purchases a coal waste refuse pile from B and extracts the coal from the waste refuse pile and sells the coal. XYZ is the producer and must pay the excise tax.

*Example (4).* XYZ Company is a producer of coal and operates its own cleaning plant. After wet washing the coal, it sells the coal and the silt waste product. The sale of the coal is subject to the excise tax whereas the sale of the silt is not.

*Example (5).* Assume the same facts as in example (4) except that before selling the silt waste product XYZ Company extracts a small quantity of finely sized coal from the silt waste product and then sells both the finely sized coal and the silt waste product. The sale of the finely sized coal is subject to the excise tax whereas the sale of the silt is not.

(b) *Rate of tax.*—(1) *Underground mines: surface mines.*—The rate of tax imposed on coal from underground mines located in the United States is the lower of 50 cents per ton (2,000 pounds), or 2 percent of the sale price. The rate of tax imposed on coal from surface mines located in the United States is the lower of 25 cents per ton (2,000 pounds) or 2 percent of the sale price. If a sale or use includes a portion of a ton, the tax is applied proportionately. Thus, if 1200 pounds of coal from an underground mine are sold for $35.00, the tax is 30 cents.

(2) *Combination.*—If a single mine yields coal from both surface and underground mining, the producer must determine the rate (50 cents or 25 cents per ton) for each ton of coal mined: It is presumed that coal is mined from underground mines (50 cents per ton) unless the producer keeps sufficient records to establish to the satisfaction of the Secretary that the coal was mined from a surface mine.

(c) *Exemptions.*—(1) *Lignite or imported coal.*—The excise tax on coal does not apply to lignite or imported coal. Lignite is defined in accordance with the standard specification for classification of coals by rank of the American Society for Testing and Materials (Annual Book of ASTM Standards Part 26, D 388). The procedures specified in D 388 must be followed. If a producer extracts both taxable coal and

lignite, then the producer must maintain adequate records to establish the portion of the mineral mined that is exempt from the tax. In determining whether all or a portion of the mineral extracted is lignite, the Service will consider all the facts and circumstances. For example, if a producer sells lignite and coal, the Service will examine all the facts and circumstances, including the contract price, contract specifications, and the amount of lignite extracted as it compares to the amount of lignite sold.

(2) *Other exemptions not applicable.*—There are not exemptions for sales for further manufacture, for export, for use as supplies for vessels or aircraft, for the use of a State or local government, or for the use of a nonprofit educational organization. Furthermore, the Secretary does not have discretion to exempt sales of coal for use of the United States from the tax. There is also no exemption from the coal excise tax when the coal is used in further manufacture of another article that is subject to manufacturers excise tax. For example, if a producer of coal converts coal into gasoline which the producer then sells, the producer is liable for the coal excise tax when the coal is converted into gasoline and also liable for the manufacturers excise tax on gasoline when the gasoline is sold.

(d) *Definitions and special rules.*—(1) *Coal produced from surface mine.*—Coal is treated as produced from a surface mine if all of the geological matter (e.g., trees, earth, rock) above the coal is removed before the coal is mined.In addition, both coal mined by auger and coal that is reclaimed from coal waste refuse piles are treated as produced from a surface mine.

(2) *Coal produced from underground mine.*—Coal is treated as produced from an underground mine if it is not produced from a surface mine.

(3) *Coal used by the producer.*—For purposes of this section, the term "coal used by the producer" means use by the producer in other than a mining process. A mining process is determined the same way it is determined for percentage depletion purposes. For example, a producer who mines coal does not "use" the coal and thereby becomes liable for the tax merely because, before selling the coal, the producer breaks it, cleans it, sizes it, or applies one of the other processes listed in section 613(c)(4)(A) of the Code. In such a case, the producer will be liable for the tax only when he sells the coal. On the other hand, a producer who mines coal does become liable for the tax when he uses the coal as fuel, as an ingredient in making coke, or in another process not treated as "mining" under section 613(c).

(4) *Tonnage sold and sales price.*—For purposes of determining both the amount of coal sold by a producer and the sales price of the coal, the point of sale is f.o.b. mine, or f.o.b. cleaning point if the producer cleans the coal before selling it. This is true even if the producer sells the coal on the basis of a delivered price. Accordingly, f.o.b. mine or cleaning point is the point at which the number of tops sold is to be determined for purposes of applying the applicable tonnage rate, and the point at which the sales price is to be determined for purposes of the tax under the 2 percent rate.

(5) *Constructive sale price.*—If a producer uses coal mined by the producer in other than a mining process, a constructive sale price must be used in determining the tax under the 2 percent rate. This constructive price is determined under section 613(c) and 4218(e) of the Code, and is based on sales of like kind and grade of coal by the producer or other producers made f.o.b. mine (if the coal is used without first being cleaned) or f.o.b. cleaning plant (if the coal is cleaned before it is used). Normally, this constructive price will be the same as the constructive price used in determining the producer's percentage depletion deduction. [Reg. §48.4121-1.]

☐ [T.D. 7726, 10-6-80, *as amended on 10-20-80. Amended by T.D. 8442, 10-21-92.*]

### [Reg. §48.4161(a)-1]

**§48.4161(a)-1. Imposition and rate of tax; fishing equipment.**—(a) *Imposition of tax.*—Section 4161(a) imposes a tax on the sale of the following articles of fishing equipment (including in each case parts or accessories of such articles sold on or in connection therewith or with the sale thereof) by the manufacturer, producer, or importer thereof:

(1) Fishing rods;

(2) Fishing creels;

(3) Fishing reels; and

(4) Artificial lures, baits, and flies.

The tax applies only to those items of fishing equipment specified in section 4161(a) and this paragraph. Therefore, other items of fishing equipment, such as fishing nets, lines, hooks, sinkers, gaffs, etc., are not subject to the tax. Furthermore, the tax applies only to those specified articles of fishing equipment that are designed or constructed for use in the sport of fishing. Accordingly, the tax does not apply to those articles which, although nominally articles that are specified in section 4161(a), are in the nature of toys or novelties that merely simulate articles of a type referred to in section 4161(a), and are not designed or constructed for practical use in the sport of fishing.

(b) *Rate of tax.*—Tax is imposed on the sale of the articles enumerated in section 4161(a) and paragraph (a) of this section at the rate of 10 percent of the price for which such articles are sold. For the definition of the term "price" see section 4216 and the regulations thereunder.

(c) *Liability for tax.*—The tax imposed by section 4161(a) is payable by the manufacturer, producer, or importer making the sale. For determining who is the manufacturer, producer, or importer, see §48.0-2(a)(4). [Reg. §48.4161(a)-1.]

☐ [*T.D. 7328, 10-10-74. Amended by T.D. 8043, 8-8-85.*]

**[Reg. §48.4161(a)-2]**

**§48.4161(a)-2. Meaning of terms.**—(a) *Fishing rods.*—The term "fishing rods" includes all articles, however designated, that are designed or constructed for use in conjunction with a fishing reel for casting a line and hook in the sport of fishing. The term does not include any article that is neither designed for use in casting, nor suitable for such use. A so-called fishing rod "blank" is not considered to be a "fishing rod" unless the blank contains an affixed handle and reel seat, or is sold in the form of a kit that contains a rod blank, a handle, and a reel seat.

(b) *Fishing creels.*—The term "fishing creels" includes all portable containers, of whatever material made, that are designed for storing and carrying fish from the time they are caught until such time as they are removed form the container for consumption or preservation. The terms does not include any article primarily designed for use in the commercial fishing industry, or an article such as a collapsible wire basket designed to be hung over the side of a boat to keep fish captive and alive in the water.

(c) *Fishing reels.*—The term "fishing reels" includes all mechanical and electrical devices that contain a spool for dispensing and recovering fishing line, and are designed to use with fishing rods in casting and in reeling in hooked fish in the sport of fishing. The term also includes reels designed for use with bows, in the sport of bow-fishing.

(d) *Artificial lures, baits, and flies.*—The term "artificial lures, baits, and flies" includes all artifacts, of whatever materials made, that simulate an article considered edible by fish and are designed to be attached to a line or hook to attract fish so that they may be captured. Thus, the term includes such artifacts as imitation flies, blades, spoons, and spinners, and edible materials that have been processed so as to resemble a different edible article considered more attractive to fish, such as bread crumbs treated so as to simulate salmon eggs, and pork rind cut and dyed to resemble frogs, eels, or tadpoles. [Reg. §48.4161(a)-2.]

☐ [*T.D. 7328, 10-10-74. Amended by T.D. 8043, 8-8-85.*]

**[Reg. §48.4161(a)-3]**

**§48.4161(a)-3. Parts and accessories.**—(a) *In general.*—The tax attaches with respect to parts and accessories for articles specified in section 4161(a) and §48.4161(a)-1 that are sold on or in connection with such articles, or with the sale thereof, at the same rate applicable to the sale of the basic articles. The tax attaches in such cases whether or not charges for the parts or accessories are billed separately. To be considered a part or accessory for an article specified in section 4161(a), an item must be either essential to the operation of the specified article, or be designed to directly improve the performance of the specified article, or to improve its appearance. For example, a carrying case for a fishing rod is not considered to be a part or accessory for a fishing rod, despite the fact that it is designed for use with the rod, because it is neither essential to the use of the rod, nor does it in any way improve its performance or appearance. A sale of a part or accessory, which would otherwise be considered a sale "on or in connection with" the sale of an article taxable under section 4161(a), is not subject to tax if the part or accessory is sold as a replacement for an identical part or accessory being sold with the taxable article.

(b) *Essential equipment.*—If taxable articles are sold by the manufacturer, producer, or importer thereof, without parts or accessories that are essential for their operation, or are designed directly to improve the performance or appearance of the articles, the separate sale of the parts or accessories to the same vendee will be considered, in the absence of evidence to the contrary, to have been made in connection with the sale of the basic article, even though the parts or

accessories are shipped separately at the same time or on a different date. [Reg. §48.4161(a)-3.]

☐ [*T.D. 7328, 10-10-74. Amended by T.D. 8043, 8-8-85.*]

**[Reg. §48.4161(a)-4]**

**§48.4161(a)-4. Use considered sale.**—For provisions relating to the tax on use of taxable articles by the manufacturer, producer, or importer thereof, see section 4218 relating to use by a manufacturer being considered a sale, and the regulations thereunder. [Reg. §48.4161(a)-4.]

☐ [*T.D. 7328, 10-10-74.*]

**[Reg. §48.4161(a)-5]**

**§48.4161(a)-5. Tax-free sales.**—For provisions relating to the tax-free sales of articles referred to in section 4161(a) see—

(a) Section 4221, relating to certain tax-free sales;

(b) Section 4222, relating to registration;

(c) Section 4223, pertaining to special rules relating to further manufacture; and

(d) Section 4225, relating to exemption of articles manufactured or produced by Indians; and the regulations thereunder. [Reg. §48.4161(a)-5.]

☐ [*T.D. 7328, 10-10-74.*]

**[Reg. §48.4161(b)-1]**

**§48.4161(b)-1. Imposition and rates of tax; bows and arrows.**—(a) *Imposition of tax.*—Section 4161(b) imposes a tax on the sale of the following articles by the manufacturer, producer, or importer thereof:

(1) Any bow that has a draw weight of 10 pounds or more;

(2) Any arrow that measures 18 inches overall or more in length;

(3) Any part or accessory (other than a fishing reel) suitable for inclusion in or attachment to a bow or arrow described in subparagraph (1) or (2) of this paragraph; and

(4) Any quiver suitable for use with arrows described in subparagraph (2) of this paragraph.

(b) *Rate of tax.*—The tax is imposed on the sale of articles enumerated in section 4161(b) and paragraph (a) of this section at the rate of 11 percent of the price for which such articles are sold. For definition of the term "price", see section 4216 and the regulations thereunder.

(c) *Liability for tax.*—The tax imposed by section 4161(b) is payable by the manufacturer, producer, or importer making the sale. For determining who is the manufacturer, producer, or importer, see §48.0-2(a)(4). [Reg. §48.4161(b)-1.]

☐ [*T.D. 7328, 10-10-74. Amended by T.D. 8043, 8-8-85.*]

**[Reg. §48.4161(b)-2]**

**§48.4161(b)-2. Meaning of terms.**—(a) For purposes of the tax imposed by section 4161(b), and unless otherwise expressly indicated:

(1) *Bows.*—The term "bows" includes all articles made of flexible materials, that are designed to be equipped with a string and used for the propelling of arrows in the sport of archery (target shooting), or in hunting or fishing.

(2) *Arrows.*—The term "arrows" includes all articles designed or constructed to be propelled by a bow in the sport of archery (target shooting), or in hunting or fishing. The overall length of an arrow is to be measured from the point of the tip or arrowhead to the end of the arrow nock. In the case of arrows sold by the manufacturer without heads, tips, or nocks, the overall length is to include the length of the shaft plus the length of the nock and head or tip that is normally used with the particular type of arrow shaft.

(b) *Parts and accessories.*—(1) *In general.*—"Parts and accessories" for bows and arrows include all articles (other than fishing reels) suitable for inclusion in, or attachment to, a bow or arrow of the type described in section 4161(b)(1) and paragraph (a) of this section. Examples of parts and accessories for bows are bow handles, bow limbs, bow strings, bow-string silencers, bow stabilizers, arrow rests, bow slings, bow sights, bow levels, bow tip protectors, brush buttons, camouflaged bow covers, and all articles designed to be attached to or included in a bow to assist in aiming or propelling an arrow, or to protect the bow while in use. Examples of parts and accessories for arrows are arrow shafts, nocks, tips, heads, head adapters, and feathers.

(2) *General purpose materials and articles.*—General purpose materials, and articles that are not specifically designed to directly improve the performance or appearance of bows or arrows, or to protect them while in use, are not considered to be "parts and accessories" for bows or arrows, even though such materials may be

intended, after further processing, to be included in or attached to bows or arrows. An example of a nontaxable article that is designed for use with a bow, but is neither attached to a bow, nor serves a purpose directly related to the efficient use of a bow, is a carrying case for a bow. Examples of nontaxable general purpose materials or articles are glues and cements, feathers before they are prepared for use with arrows, and bowstring thread before it is processed into bowstrings. Arrow-shaft material is considered to be taxable part for an arrow, unless the manufacturer, producer, or importer can establish that the particular material is unsuitable for use in the manufacture of arrows that are subject to the tax imposed by section 4161(b)(1)(B). In addition, the term "parts and accessories" does not include articles in the nature of expendable supplies, even though such articles are designed to be applied to, or used with, bows or arrows. Examples of such supply materials are bowstring wax, and archery powder.

(c) *Quivers.*—The term "quivers" includes all articles, of whatever material made, that are designed to contain, and to provide ready access to, taxable arrows during the time an archer is engaged in target shooting, hunting, or fishing. The term does not include any article designed solely for storing or transporting arrows during times when the arrows are not in use. [Reg. § 48.4161(b)-2.]

☐ [*T.D. 7328, 10-10-74.*]

### [Reg. § 48.4161(b)-3]

**§ 48.4161(b)-3. Use considered sale.**—For provisions relating to the tax on use of taxable articles by the manufacturer, producer, or importer thereof, see section 4218 relating to use by a manufacturer considered a sale, and the regulations thereunder. [Reg. § 48.4161(b)-3.]

☐ [*T.D. 7328, 10-10-74.*]

### [Reg. § 48.4161(b)-4]

**§ 48.4161(b)-4. Tax-free sales.**—For provisions relating to tax-free sales of articles referred to in section 4161(b) see—

Section 4221, relating to certain tax-free sales;

(b) Section 4222, relating to registration;

(c) Section 4223, pertaining to special rules relating to further manufacture; and

(d) Section 4225, relating to exemption of articles manufactured or produced by Indians; and the regulations thereunder. [Reg. § 48.4161(b)-4.]

☐ [*T.D. 7328, 10-10-74.*]

### [Reg. § 48.4161(b)-5]

**§ 48.4161(b)-5. Effective date.**—The taxes imposed by section 4161(b) are effective with respect to sales made on and after January 1, 1975. [Reg. § 48.4161(b)-5.]

☐ [*T.D. 7328, 10-10-74.*]

### [Reg. § 48.4191-1]

**§ 48.4191-1. Imposition and rate of tax.**—(a) *Imposition of tax.*—Under section 4191(a), tax is imposed on the sale of any taxable medical device by the manufacturer, producer, or importer of the device. For the definition of the term *taxable medical device*, see § 48.4191-2.

(b) *Rate of tax.*—Tax is imposed on the sale of a taxable medical device at the rate of 2.3 percent of the price for which the device is sold. For the definition of the term *price*, see section 4216 and §§ 48.4216(a)-1 through 48.4216(e)-3.

(c) *Liability for tax.*—The manufacturer, producer, or importer making the sale of a taxable medical device is liable for the tax imposed by section 4191(a). For rules relating to the determination of who the manufacturer, producer, or importer is for purposes of section 4191, see § 48.0-2(a)(4). For the definition of the term *sale*, see § 48.0-2(a)(5). For rules relating to the lease of an article by the manufacturer, producer, or importer, see section 4217 and § 48.4217-1 through § 48.4217-2. For rules relating to the use of an article by the manufacturer, producer, or importer, see section 4218 and § 48.4218-1 through § 48.4218-5.

(d) *Procedural rules.*—For the procedural rules relating to section 4191, see part 40 of this chapter.

(e) *Tax-free sales for further manufacture or export.*—For rules relating to tax-free sales of taxable medical devices for further manufacture or export, see section 4221 and § 48.4221-1 through § 48.4221-3.

(f) *Payments made on or after January 1, 2013, pursuant to lease, installment sale, or sale on credit contracts.*—For rules relating to the taxability of payments made on or after January 1, 2013, pursuant to

a lease, installment sale, or sale on credit contract entered into on or after March 30, 2010, see § 48.4216(c)-1(e)(1). For rules relating to the taxability of payments made on or after January 1, 2013, pursuant to a lease, installment sale, or sale on credit contract entered into before March 30, 2010, see § 48.4216(c)-1(e)(2).

(g) *Effective/applicability date.*—This section applies to sales of taxable medical devices on and after January 1, 2013. [Reg. § 48.4191-1.]

☐ [*T.D. 9604, 12-5-2012.*]

### [Reg. § 48.4191-2]

**§ 48.4191-2. Taxable medical device.**—(a) *Taxable medical device.*—(1) *In general.*—A taxable medical device is any device, as defined in section 201(h) of the Federal Food, Drug, and Cosmetic Act (FFDCA), that is intended for humans. For purposes of this section, a device defined in section 201(h) of the FFDCA that is intended for humans means a device that is listed as a device with the Food and Drug Administration (FDA) under section 510(j) of the FFDCA and 21 CFR part 807, pursuant to FDA requirements.

(2) *Devices that should have been listed with the FDA.*—If a device is not listed as a device with the FDA but the FDA determines that the device should have been listed as a device, the device will be deemed to be listed as a device with the FDA as of the date FDA notifies the manufacturer or importer in writing that corrective action with respect to listing is required.

(b) *Exemptions.*—(1) *Specific exemptions.*—The term *taxable medical device* does not include eyeglasses, contact lenses, and hearing aids.

(2) *Retail exemption.*—The term *taxable medical device* does not include any device of a type that is generally purchased by the general public at retail for individual use (the retail exemption). A device will be considered to be of a type that is generally purchased by the general public at retail for individual use if it is regularly available for purchase and use by individual consumers who are not medical professionals, and if the design of the device demonstrates that it is not primarily intended for use in a medical institution or office or by a medical professional. Whether a device is of a type described in the preceding sentence is evaluated based on all the relevant facts and circumstances. Factors relevant to this evaluation are enumerated in paragraphs (b)(2)(i) and (ii) of this section. Further, there may be facts and circumstances that are relevant in evaluating whether a device is of a type generally purchased by the general public at retail for individual use in addition to those described in paragraphs (b)(2)(i) and (ii) of this section. The determination of whether a device is of a type that qualifies for the retail exemption is made based on the overall balance of factors relevant to the particular type of device. The fact that a device is of a type that requires a prescription is not a factor in the determination of whether or not the device falls under the retail exemption.

(i) *Regularly available for purchase and use by individual consumers.*—The following factors are relevant in determining whether a device is of a type that is regularly available for purchase and use by individual consumers who are not medical professionals:

(A) Whether consumers who are not medical professionals can purchase the device in person, over the telephone, or over the internet, through retail businesses such as drug stores, supermarkets, or medical supply stores and retailers that primarily sell devices (for example, specialty medical stores, durable medical equipment, prosthetics, orthotics, and supplies (DMEPOS) suppliers and similar vendors);

(B) Whether consumers who are not medical professionals can use the device safely and effectively for its intended medical purpose with minimal or no training from a medical professional; and

(C) Whether the device is classified by the FDA under Subpart D of 21 CFR part 890 (Physical Medicine Devices).

(ii) *Primarily for use in a medical institution or office or by a medical professional.*—The following factors are relevant in determining whether a device is designed primarily for use in a medical institution or office or by a medical professional:

(A) Whether the device generally must be implanted, inserted, operated, or otherwise administered by a medical professional;

(B) Whether the cost to acquire, maintain, and/or use the device requires a large initial investment and/or ongoing expenditure that is not affordable for the average individual consumer;

(C) Whether the device is a Class III device under the FDA system of classification;

(D) Whether the device is classified by the FDA under—

(*1*) 21 CFR part 862 (Clinical Chemistry and Clinical Toxicology Devices), 21 CFR part 864 (Hematology and Pathology Devices), 21 CFR part 866 (Immunology and Microbiology Devices), 21

CFR part 868 (Anesthesiology Devices), 21 CFR part 870 (Cardiovascular Devices), 21 CFR part 874 (Ear, Nose, and Throat Devices), 21 CFR part 876 (Gastroenterology - Urology Devices), 21 CFR part 878 (General and Plastic Surgery Devices), 21 CFR part 882 (Neurological Devices), 21 CFR part 886 (Ophthalmic Devices), 21 CFR part 888 (Orthopedic Devices), or 21 CFR part 892 (Radiology Devices);

(2) Subpart B, Subpart D, or Subpart E of 21 CFR part 872 (Dental Devices);

(3) Subpart B, Subpart C, Subpart D, Subpart E, or Subpart G of 21 CFR part 884 (Obstetrical and Gynecological Devices); or

(4) Subpart B of 21 CFR part 890 (Physical Medicine Devices); and

(E) Whether the device qualifies as durable medical equipment, prosthetics, orthotics, and supplies for which payment is available exclusively on a rental basis under the Medicare Part B payment rules, and is an "item requiring frequent and substantial servicing" as defined in 42 CFR 414.222.

(iii) *Safe Harbor.*—The following devices will be considered to be of a type generally purchased by the general public at retail for individual use:

(A) Devices that are included in the FDA's online IVD Home Use Lab Tests (Over-the-Counter Tests) database, available at http://www.accessdata.fda.gov/scripts/cdrh/cfdocs/cfIVD/Search.cfm.

(B) Devices that are described as "OTC" or "over the counter" devices in the relevant FDA classification regulation heading.

(C) Devices that are described as "OTC" or "over the counter" devices in the FDA's product code name, the FDA's device classification name, or the "classification name" field in the FDA's device registration and listing database, available at http://www.accessdata.fda.gov/scripts/cdrh/cfdocs/cfrl/rl.cfm.

(D) Devices that qualify as durable medical equipment, prosthetics, orthotics, and supplies, as described in Subpart C of 42 CFR part 414 (Parenteral and Enteral Nutrition) and Subpart D of 42 CFR part 414 (Durable Medical Equipment and Prosthetic and Orthotic Devices), for which payment is available on a purchase basis under Medicare Part B payment rules, and are—

(1) "Prosthetic and orthotic devices," as defined in 42 CFR 414.202, that do not require implantation or insertion by a medical professional;

(2) "Parenteral and enteral nutrients, equipment, and supplies" as defined in 42 CFR 411.351 and described in 42 CFR 414.102(b);

(3) "Customized items," as described in 42 CFR 414.224;

(4) "Therapeutic shoes," as described in 42 CFR 414.228(c); or

(5) Supplies necessary for the effective use of durable medical equipment (DME), as described in section 110.3 of chapter 15 of the Medicare Benefit Policy Manual (Centers for Medicare and Medicaid Studies Publication 100-02).

(iv) *Examples.*—The following examples illustrate the rules of this paragraph (b)(2).

*Example 1.* X manufactures non-sterile absorbent tipped applicators. X sells the applicators to distributors Y and Z, which, in turn, sell the applicators to medical institutions and offices, medical professionals, and retail businesses. The FDA requires manufacturers of non-sterile absorbent tipped applicators to list the applicators as a device with the FDA. The applicators are classified by the FDA under 21 CFR part 880 (General Hospital and Personal Use Devices) and product code KXF.

Absorbent tipped applicators do not fall within a retail exemption safe harbor set forth in paragraph (b)(2)(iii) of this section. Therefore, the determination of whether the absorbent tipped applicators are devices of a type generally purchased by the general public at retail for individual use must be made on a facts and circumstances basis.

Individual consumers who are not medical professionals can regularly purchase the absorbent tipped applicators at drug stores, supermarkets, cosmetic supply stores or other similar businesses, and can use the applicators safely and effectively for their intended medical purpose without training from a medical professional. Further, the absorbent tipped applicators do not need to be implanted, inserted, operated, or otherwise administered by a medical professional, do not require a large investment and/or ongoing expenditure, are not a Class III device, are not classified by the FDA under a category described in paragraph (b)(2)(ii)(D) of this section, and are not "items requiring frequent and substantial servicing" as defined in 42 CFR 414.222.

Thus, the applicators have multiple factors under paragraph (b)(2)(i) of this section that tend to show they are regularly available for purchase and use by individual consumers and none of the

factors under paragraph (b)(2)(ii) of this section tend to show they are designed primarily for use in a medical institution or office or by medical professionals. Based on the totality of the facts and circumstances, the applicators are devices that are of a type that are generally purchased by the general public at retail for individual use.

*Example 2.* X manufactures adhesive bandages. X sells the adhesive bandages to distributors Y and Z, which, in turn, sell the bandages to medical institutions and offices, medical professionals, and retail businesses. The FDA requires manufacturers of adhesive bandages to list the bandages as a device with the FDA. The adhesive bandages are classified by the FDA under 21 CFR part 880 (General Hospital and Personal Use Devices) and product code KGX.

Adhesive bandages do not fall within a retail exemption safe harbor set forth in paragraph (b)(2)(iii) of this section. Therefore, the determination of whether the adhesive bandages are devices of a type generally purchased by the general public at retail for individual use must be made on a facts and circumstances basis.

Individual consumers who are not medical professionals can regularly purchase the adhesive bandages at drug stores, supermarkets, or other similar businesses, and can use the adhesive bandages safely and effectively for their intended medical purpose without training from a medical professional. Further, the adhesive bandages do not need to be implanted, inserted, operated, or otherwise administered by a medical professional, do not require a large investment and/or ongoing expenditure, are not Class III devices, are not classified by the FDA under a category described in paragraph (b)(2)(ii)(D) of this section, and are not "items requiring frequent and substantial servicing" as defined in 42 CFR 414.222.

Thus, the adhesive bandages have multiple factors under paragraph (b)(2)(i) of this section that tend to show they are regularly available for purchase and use by individual consumers and none of the factors under paragraph (b)(2)(ii) of this section tend to show they are designed primarily for use in a medical institution or office or by medical professionals. Based on the totality of the facts and circumstances, the adhesive bandages are devices that are of a type that are generally purchased by the general public at retail for individual use.

*Example 3.* X manufactures snake bite suction kits. X sells the snake bite suction kits to distributors Y and Z, which, in turn, sell the kits to medical institutions and offices, medical professionals, and retail businesses. The FDA requires manufacturers of snake bite suction kits to list the kits as a device with the FDA. The FDA classifies the snake bit suction kits under 21 CFR part 880 (General Hospital and Personal Use Devices) and product code KYP.

Snake bite suction kits do not fall within a retail exemption safe harbor set forth in paragraph (b)(2)(iii) of this section. Therefore, the determination of whether the snake bite suction kits are devices of a type generally purchased by the general public at retail for individual use must be made on a facts and circumstances basis.

Individual consumers who are not medical professionals can regularly purchase the snake bite suction kits at sporting goods stores, camping stores, or other similar retail businesses, and can use the kits safely and effectively for their intended medical purpose without training from a medical professional. Further, the snake bite suction kits do not need to be implanted, inserted, operated, or otherwise administered by a medical professional, do not require a large investment and/or ongoing expenditure, are not Class III devices, are not classified by the FDA under a category described in paragraph (b)(2)(ii)(D) of this section, and are not "items requiring frequent and substantial servicing" as defined in 42 CFR 414.222.

Thus, the snake bite suction kits have multiple factors under paragraph (b)(2)(i) of this section that tend to show they are regularly available for purchase and use by individual consumers and none of the factors under paragraph (b)(2)(ii) of this section tend to show they are designed primarily for use in a medical institution or office or by medical professionals. Based on the totality of the facts and circumstances, the snake bite suction kits are devices that are of a type that are generally purchased by the general public at retail for individual use.

*Example 4.* X manufactures denture adhesives. X sells the denture adhesives to distributors Y and Z, which, in turn, sell the adhesives to dental offices and retail businesses. The FDA requires manufacturers of denture adhesives to list the adhesive as a device with the FDA. The FDA classifies the denture adhesives under 21 CFR part 872 (Dental Devices) and product code KXX.

The denture adhesives do not fall within a retail exemption safe harbor set forth in paragraph (b)(2)(iii) of this section. Therefore, the determination of whether the denture adhesives are devices of a type generally purchased by the general public at retail for individual use must be made on a facts and circumstances basis.

Individual consumers who are not medical professionals can regularly purchase the denture adhesives at drug stores, supermarkets, or other similar businesses, and can use the adhesives safely and effectively for their intended medical purpose with minimal or no training from a medical professional. Further, the denture adhesives do not need to be implanted, inserted, operated, or otherwise administered by a medical professional, do not require a large investment and/or ongoing expenditure, are not Class III devices, are not classified by the FDA under a category described in paragraph (b)(2)(ii)(D) of this section, and are not "items requiring frequent and substantial servicing" as defined in 42 CFR 414.222.

Thus, the denture adhesives have multiple factors under paragraph (b)(2)(i) of this section that tend to show they are regularly available for purchase and use by individual consumers and none of the factors under paragraph (b)(2)(ii) of this section tend to show they are designed primarily for use in a medical institution or office or by medical professionals. Based on the totality of the facts and circumstances, the denture adhesives are devices that are of a type that are generally purchased by the general public at retail for individual use.

*Example 5.* X manufactures mobile x-ray systems. X sells the x-ray systems to distributors Y and Z, which, in turn, sell the systems generally to medical institutions and offices, as well as medical professionals. The FDA requires manufacturers of mobile xray systems to list the systems as a device with the FDA. The FDA classifies the mobile x-ray systems under 21 CFR part 892 (Radiology Devices) and product code IZL.

Mobile x-ray systems do not fall within a retail exemption safe harbor set forth in paragraph (b)(2)(iii) of this section. Therefore, the determination of whether the mobile x-ray systems are devices of a type generally purchased by the general public at retail for individual use must be made on a facts and circumstances basis.

Individual consumers who are not medical professionals can regularly purchase the mobile x-ray systems over the internet. However, individual consumers cannot use the x-ray systems safely and effectively for their intended medical purpose without training from a medical professional. Although the mobile x-ray systems are not Class III devices and are not "items requiring frequent and substantial servicing" as defined in 42 CFR 414.222, they need to be operated by a medical professional, may require a large investment and/or ongoing expenditure, and are classified by the FDA under a category described in paragraph (b)(2)(ii)(D) of this section (21 CFR part 892 (Radiology Devices).

Thus, with regard to the factors under paragraph (b)(2)(i) of this section, the mobile x-ray systems have one factor that tends to show they are regularly available for purchase and use by individual consumers and one factor that tends to show that they are not regularly available for purchase and use by individual consumers. With regard to the factors under paragraph (b)(2)(ii) of this section, the mobile x-ray systems have multiple factors that tend to show they are designed primarily for use in a medical institution or office or by medical professionals. Based on the totality of the facts and circumstances, the mobile x-ray systems are not devices that are of a type that are generally purchased by the general public at retail for individual use.

*Example 6.* X manufactures pregnancy test kits. X sells the kits to distributors Y and Z, which, in turn, sell the pregnancy test kits to medical institutions and offices, medical professionals, and retail businesses. The FDA requires manufacturers of pregnancy test kits to list the kits as a device with the FDA. The FDA classifies the kits under 21 CFR part 862 (Clinical Chemistry and Clinical Toxicology Devices) and product code LCX.

The pregnancy test kits are included in the FDA's online IVD Home Use Lab Tests (Over-the-Counter Tests) database. Therefore, the over the counter pregnancy test kits fall within the safe harbor set forth in paragraph (b)(2)(iii)(A) of this section. Further, the FDA product code name for LCX is "Kit, Test, Pregnancy, HCG, Over The Counter." Therefore, the pregnancy test kits also fall within the safe harbor set forth in paragraph (b)(2)(iii)(C) of this section. Accordingly, the pregnancy test kits are devices that are of a type that are generally purchased by the general public at retail for individual use.

*Example 7.* X manufactures blood glucose monitors, blood glucose test strips, and lancets. X sells the blood glucose monitors, test strips, and lancets to distributors Y and Z, which, in turn, sell the monitors, test strips, and lancets to medical institutions and offices, medical professionals, and retail businesses. The FDA requires manufacturers of blood glucose monitors, test strips, and lancets to list the items as devices with the FDA. The FDA classifies the blood glucose monitors under 21 CFR part 862 (Clinical Chemistry and Clinical Toxicology Devices) and product code NBW. The FDA classifies the test strips under 21 CFR part 862 (Clinical Chemistry and Clinical Toxicology Devices) and product code NBW. The FDA classifies the lancets under 21 CFR part 878 (General and Plastic Surgery Devices) and product code FMK.

The blood glucose monitors and test strips are included in the FDA's online IVD Home Use Lab Tests (Over-the-Counter Tests) database. Therefore, the blood glucose monitors and test strips fall within the safe harbor set forth in paragraph (b)(2)(iii)(A) of this

section. Further, the FDA product code name for NBW is "System, Test, Blood Glucose, Over the Counter." Therefore, the blood glucose monitors and test strips also fall within the safe harbor set forth in paragraph (b)(2)(iii)(C) of this section.

In addition, the lancets are supplies necessary for the effective use of DME as described in section 110.3 of chapter 15 of the Medicare Policy Benefit Manual. Therefore, the lancets fall within the safe harbor set forth in paragraph (b)(2)(iii)(D)(5) of this section.

Accordingly, the blood glucose monitors, test strips, and lancets are devices that are of a type that are generally purchased by the general public at retail for individual use.

*Example 8.* X manufactures single axis endoskeletal knee shin systems, which are used in the manufacture of prosthetic legs. X sells the knee shin systems to Y, a business that makes prosthetic legs. The FDA requires manufacturers of knee shin systems and prosthetic legs to list the items as devices with the FDA. The FDA classifies prosthetic leg components, including knee shin systems, as external limb prosthetic components under Subpart D of 21 CFR part 890.3420 and product code ISH. The FDA classifies prosthetic legs as an external assembled lower limb prosthesis under 21 CFR part 890.3500 and product code ISW / KFX. In addition, the Centers for Medicare and Medicaid Services have assigned the knee shin systems Healthcare Procedure Coding System code L5810.

Prosthetic legs and certain prosthetic leg components, including single axis endoskeletal knee shin systems, fall within the safe harbor for prosthetic and orthotic devices that do not require implantation or insertion by a medical profession that is set forth in paragraph (b)(2)(iii)(D)(1) of this section. Accordingly, both the single axis endoskeletal knee shin systems manufactured by X and the prosthetic legs made by Y are devices that are of a type that are generally purchased by the general public at retail for individual use.

*Example 9.* X manufactures mechanical and powered wheelchairs. X sells the wheelchairs to distributors Y and Z, which, in turn, sell the wheelchairs to medical institutions and offices, medical professionals, nursing homes, and retail businesses. The FDA requires manufacturers of manual and powered wheelchairs to list the items as devices with the FDA. The FDA classifies the manual and powered wheelchairs under Subpart D of 21 CFR part 890 (Physical Medicine Devices). The FDA classifies mechanical wheelchairs under product code IOR. The FDA classifies powered wheelchairs under product code product code ITI.

Mechanical and powered wheelchairs do not fall within a retail exemption safe harbor set forth in paragraph (b)(2)(iii) of this section. Therefore, the determination of whether the mechanical and powered wheelchairs are devices of a type generally purchased by the general public at retail for individual use must be made on a facts and circumstances basis.

Individual consumers who are not medical professionals can regularly purchase the wheelchairs in drug stores, medical specialty stores, or DME suppliers, as well as over the internet. In addition, individual consumers can use the wheelchairs safely and effectively for their intended medical purpose with minimal or no training from a medical professional, and the wheelchairs are classified by the FDA under Subpart D of 21 CFR part 890 (Physical Medicine Devices). Further, although the wheelchairs may require a large initial investment and/or ongoing expenditure, they do not need to be implanted, inserted, operated, or otherwise administered by a medical professional, are not Class III devices, are not classified by the FDA under a category described in paragraph (b)(2)(ii)(D) of this section, and are not "items requiring frequent and substantial servicing" as defined in 42 CFR 414.222.

Thus, the wheelchairs have multiple factors under paragraph (b)(2)(i) of this section that tend to show they are regularly available for purchase and use by individual consumers and, at most, only one factor under paragraph (b)(2)(ii) of this section tends to show they are designed primarily for use in a medical institution or office or by medical professionals. Based on the totality of the facts and circumstances, the mechanical and powered wheelchairs are devices that are of a type that are generally purchased by the general public at retail for individual use.

*Example 10.* X manufactures portable oxygen concentrators. X sells the portable oxygen concentrators to distributors Y and Z, which, in turn, sell the portable oxygen concentrators to medical institutions and offices, medical professionals, and retail businesses. The FDA requires manufacturers of portable oxygen concentrators to list the items as devices with the FDA. The FDA classifies the oxygen regulators under 21 CFR part 868 (Anesthesiology Devices) and product code CAW.

Portable oxygen concentrators do not fall within a retail exemption safe harbor set forth in paragraph (b)(2)(iii) of this section. Therefore, the determination of whether the oxygen concentrators are devices of a type generally purchased by the general public at retail for individual use must be made on a facts and circumstances basis.

Individual consumers who are not medical professionals can regularly purchase the portable oxygen concentrators in retail pharmacies, medical specialty stores, or DME suppliers, as well as over the internet. In addition, individual consumers can use the portable oxygen concentrators safely and effectively for their intended medical purpose with minimal or no training from a medical professional. Further, although the portable oxygen concentrators are classified by the FDA under a category described in paragraph (b)(2)(ii)(D) of this section, they do not need to be implanted, inserted, operated, or otherwise administered by a medical professional, do not require a large investment and/or ongoing expenditure, are not Class III devices, and are not "items requiring frequent and substantial servicing" as defined in 42 CFR 414.222.

Thus, the portable oxygen concentrators have multiple factors under paragraph (b)(2)(i) of this section that tend to show they are regularly available for purchase and use by individual consumers and only one factor under paragraph (b)(2)(ii) of this section that tends to show they are designed primarily for use in a medical institution or office or by medical professionals. Based on the totality of the facts and circumstances, the portable oxygen concentrators are devices that are of a type that are generally purchased by the general public at retail for individual use.

*Example 11.* X manufactures urinary ileostomy bags. X sells the urinary ileostomy bags to distributors Y and Z, which, in turn, sell the urinary ileostomy bags to medical institutions and offices, medical professionals, and retail businesses. The FDA requires manufacturers of urinary ileostomy bags to list the items as devices with the FDA. The FDA classifies the urinary ileostomy bags under 21 CFR part 876 (Gastroenterology - Urology Devices) and product code EXH.

The urinary ileostomy bags are "Prosthetic and orthotic devices," as defined in 42 CFR 414.202, that do not require implantation or insertion by a medical professional. Therefore, the urinary ileostomy bags fall within the safe harbor set forth in paragraph (b)(2)(iii)(D)(1) of this section. Accordingly, the urinary ileostomy bags are devices that are of a type that are generally purchased by the general public at retail for individual use.

*Example 12.* X manufactures nonabsorbable silk sutures. X sells the nonabsorbable silk sutures to distributors Y and Z, which, in turn, sell the nonabsorbable silk sutures to medical institutions and offices, medical professionals, and retail businesses. The FDA requires manufacturers of nonabsorbable silk sutures to list the items as devices with the FDA. The FDA classifies the nonabsorbable silk sutures under 21 CFR part 878 (General and Plastic Surgery Devices) and product code GAP.

Nonabsorbable silk sutures do not fall within a retail exemption safe harbor set forth in paragraph (b)(2)(iii) of this section. Therefore, the determination of whether the nonabsorbable silk sutures are devices of a type generally purchased by the general public at retail for individual use must be made on a facts and circumstances basis.

Individual consumers who are not medical professionals can regularly purchase the nonabsorbable silk sutures over the internet. However, individual consumers cannot use nonabsorbable silk sutures safely and effectively for their intended medical purpose with minimal or no training from a medical professional. Further, although the nonabsorbable silk sutures do not require a large investment and/or ongoing expenditure, are not Class III devices, and are not "items requiring frequent and substantial servicing" as defined in 42 CFR 414.222, the nonabsorbable silk sutures are classified by the FDA under a category described in paragraph (b)(2)(ii)(D) of this section, and they need to be administered by a medical professional.

Thus, with regard to the factors under paragraph (b)(2)(i) of this section, the nonabsorbable silk sutures have one factor that tends to show they are regularly available for purchase and use by individual consumers and one factor that tends to show that they are not regularly available for purchase and use by individual consumers. With regard to the factors under paragraph (b)(2)(ii) of this section, the nonabsorbable silk sutures have multiple factors that tend to show they are designed primarily for use in a medical institution or office or by medical professionals. Based on the totality of the facts and circumstances, the nonabsorbable silk sutures are not devices that are of a type that are generally purchased by the general public at retail for individual use.

*Example 13.* X manufactures nuclear magnetic resonance imaging (NMRI) systems (also known as magnetic resonance imaging (MRI) systems). X sells the NMRI systems to distributor Y, which, in turn, sells the systems to medical institutions. The FDA requires manufacturers of NMRI systems to list the systems as a device with the FDA. The FDA classifies the magnetic resonance diagnostic device under 21 CFR part 892 (Radiology Devices) and product code LNH.

NMRI systems do not fall within a retail exemption safe harbor set forth in paragraph (b)(2)(iii) of this section. Therefore, the determination of whether the NMRI systems are devices of a type generally purchased by the general public at retail for individual use must be made on a facts and circumstances basis.

Individual consumers who are not medical professionals may be able to regularly purchase the NMRI systems over the internet. However, individual consumers cannot use the NMRI systems safely and effectively for their intended medical purpose without training from a medical professional. Although the NMRI systems are not Class III devices and are not "items requiring frequent and substantial servicing" as defined in 42 CFR 414.222, they need to be operated by a medical professional, and are of a type classified by the FDA under 21 CFR part 892 (Radiology Devices). Further, the cost to acquire, maintain, and/or use the NMRI systems requires a large initial investment and/or ongoing expenditure that is not affordable for the average consumer.

Thus, with regard to the factors under paragraph (b)(2)(i), the NMRI systems have, at most, one factor that tends to show that they are regularly available for purchase and use by individual consumers and at least one factor that tends to show that they are not regularly available for purchase and use by individual consumers. With regard to the factors under paragraph (b)(2)(ii), the NMRI systems have multiple factors that tend to show they are designed primarily for use in a medical institution or office or by medical professionals. Based on the totality of the facts and circumstances, the NMRI systems are not devices that are of a type that are generally purchased by the general public at retail for individual use.

*Example 14.* X manufactures therapeutic AC powered adjustable home use beds. X sells the beds to distributors Y and Z, which, in turn, sell the beds to retail businesses. The FDA requires manufacturers of therapeutic AC powered adjustable home use beds to list the items as devices with the FDA. The FDA classifies the therapeutic AC powered adjustable home use beds under 21 CFR part 880 (General Hospital Devices) and product code LLI.

Therapeutic AC powered adjustable home use beds do not fall within a retail exemption safe harbor set forth in paragraph (b)(2)(iii) of this section. Therefore, the determination of whether the beds are devices of a type generally purchased by the general public at retail for individual use must be made on a facts and circumstances basis.

Although the beds may require a large initial investment and/or ongoing expenditure, individual consumers who are not medical professionals can regularly purchase the beds in medical specialty stores or from DME suppliers, as well as over the internet. In addition, individual consumers can use the beds safely and effectively for their intended medical purpose with minimal or no training from a medical professional. Further, the beds are not classified by the FDA under a category described in paragraph (b)(2)(ii)(D) of this section, do not need to be implanted, inserted, operated, or otherwise administered by a medical professional, are not Class III devices, and are not "items requiring frequent and substantial servicing" as defined in 42 CFR 414.222.

Thus, the therapeutic AC powered adjustable home use beds have multiple factors under paragraph (b)(2)(i) of this section that tend to show they are regularly available for purchase and use by individual consumers and, at most, only one factor under paragraph (b)(2)(ii) of this section that tends to show they are designed primarily for use in a medical institution or office or by medical professionals. Based on the totality of the facts and circumstances, the therapeutic AC powered adjustable home use beds are devices that are of a type that are generally purchased by the general public at retail for individual use.

*Example 15.* X manufactures powered flotation therapy beds. X sells the beds to distributors Y and Z, which, in turn, sell the beds to medical institutions and offices, and medical professionals. The FDA requires manufacturers of powered flotation therapy beds to list the items as devices with the FDA. The FDA classifies the powered flotation therapy beds under 21 CFR part 890 (Physical Medicine Devices) and product code IOQ.

Powered flotation therapy beds do not fall within a retail exemption safe harbor set forth in paragraph (b)(2)(iii) of this section. Therefore, the determination of whether the beds are devices of a type generally purchased by the general public at retail for individual use must be made on a facts and circumstances basis.

Individual consumers who are not medical professionals may be able to regularly purchase the beds over the internet. However, individual consumers cannot use the beds safely and effectively for their intended medical purpose with minimal or no training from a medical professional. Although the powered flotation therapy beds are not Class III devices and are not "items requiring frequent and substantial servicing" as defined in 42 CFR 414.222, they need to be operated or otherwise administered by a medical professional. Further, the cost to acquire, maintain, and/or use the powered flotation therapy beds requires a large initial investment and/or ongoing expenditure that is not affordable for the average consumer.

Thus, with regard to the factors under paragraph (b)(2)(i) of this section, the powered flotation therapy beds have, at most, one factor that tends to show they are regularly available for purchase and use by individual consumers and at least one factor that tends to show they are not regularly available for purchase and use by individual consumers. With regard to the factors under paragraph (b)(2)(ii) of this section, the powered flotation therapy beds have multiple factors that tend to show they are designed primarily for use in a medical institution or office or by medical professionals. Based on the totality of the facts and circumstances, the powered flotation therapy beds are not devices that are of a type that are generally purchased by the general public at retail for individual use.

(c) *Effective/applicability date.*—This section applies to sales of taxable medical devices on and after January 1, 2013. [Reg. §48.4191-2.]

☐ [T.D. 9604, 12-5-2012 (corrected 3-12-2013).]

### [Reg. §48.4216(a)-1]

**§48.4216(a)-1. Charges to be included in sale price.**—(a) *In general.*—The "price" for which an article is sold includes the total consideration paid for the article, whether that consideration is in the form of money, services, or other things. See §48.0-2(a)(5). However, for purposes of the taxes imposed under chapter 32 certain collateral charges made in connection with the sale of a taxable article must be included in the taxable sale price, whereas others may be excluded. Any charge which is required by a manufacturer, producer, or importer to be paid as a condition of its sale of a taxable article and which is not attributable to an expense falling within one of the exclusions provided in section 4216 or the regulations thereunder is includible in the taxable sale price. It is immaterial for this purpose that the charge may be paid to a person other than the manufacturer, producer, or importer, or that it may be separately billed to the purchaser as a charge earmarked for expenses incurred or to be incurred in his behalf, such as charges for demonstration or display of the article, for sales promotion programs, or otherwise. With respect to the rules relating to exclusion (in the case of sales after December 31, 1960) of charges for local advertising of a manufacturer's products, see section 4216(e) and §48.4216(e)-1. In the case of sales on credit, a carrying, finance, or service charge is excludable from the sale price if it is reasonably related to the costs of carrying the deferred portion of the sale price (such as interest on the deferred portion of the sale price, expenses of bookkeeping necessary to keep the records of such sales, and expenses of correspondence and other communication in connection with collection).

(b) *Tools and dies.*—Separate charges for tools and dies used in the manufacture or production of a taxable article are to be included, in whole or in part, in the sale price on which the tax is based. It is immaterial whether the charges for such items are billed in a lump sum or are amortized or allocated to each of the taxable articles. If, at the termination of a contract to manufacture taxable articles, the tools and dies used in production pass to the purchaser, only the amount of depreciation of the tools and dies incurred in production, computed on a "production output" basis, should be included in the sale price. If the purchaser furnishes the tools and dies, the amount of the cost thereof, to the extent that such cost has been depreciated in the production of the taxable articles (computed on a "production output" basis), shall be included in determining the sale price of the articles for purposes of computing the tax. This paragraph applies to sales by manufacturers after May 5, 1974.

(c) *Charges for warranty.*—A charge for a warranty of an article which the manufacturer, producer, or importer requires the purchaser to pay in order to obtain the article shall be included in the sale price of the article on which the tax is computed. On the other hand, a charge for a warranty of a taxable article paid at the purchaser's option shall not be included in the sale price for purposes of computing tax thereon.

(d) *Charges for coverings, containers, and packing.*—Any charge by the manufacturer, producer, or importer for coverings and containers of whatever nature used to pack an article for shipment shall be included as part of the sale price for the purpose of computing the tax, whether or not the charges are identified as such on the invoice or are billed separately. Even though there is an agreement that the manufacturer, producer, or importer will repay all or a portion of the charge for the coverings or containers upon the return thereof, the full charge nevertheless shall be included in the sale price. It is immaterial whether the charge made at the time of sale is more or less than the actual value of the covering or container. See paragraph (b)(4) of §48.6416(b)-1 for provisions relating to the claiming of a credit or refund in the case of a price readjustment due to the return or repossession of a covering or container. Packing charges are to be included in the sale price whether the charges cover normal packing or special packing services, such as for extra protection of the article or for odd-lot quantities. This rule shall apply whether the packing services are initiated by the manufacturer, producer, or importer or are furnished at the request of the purchaser and whether the packing is performed by the manufacturer, producer, or importer or by another person at his request. If the purchaser supplies packing materials, the fair market value of such materials must be included in the tax base when computing tax liability on the sale of the article.

(e) *Taxable and nontaxable articles sold as a unit.*—Where a taxable article and a nontaxable article are sold by the manufacturer as a unit, the tax attaches to that portion of the manufacturer's sale price of the unit which is properly allocable to the taxing article. For example, where a fishing reel (an article subject to tax under section 4161(a)) is equipped with a fishing line (a nontaxable article) and the reel and line are sold as a unit, the tax imposed by section 4161(a) applies only to that portion of the manufacturer's sale price of the unit which is properly allocable to the fishing reel. Normally, the taxable portion of such a unit may be determined by applying to the manufacturer's sale price of the unit the ratio which the manufacturer's separate sale price of the taxable article bears to the sum of the sale prices of both the taxable and nontaxable articles, if such articles are sold separately by the manufacturer. Where the articles (or either one of them) are not sold separately by the manufacturer and do not have established sale prices, the taxable portion is to be determined from a comparison of the actual costs of the articles to the manufacturer. Thus, if the cost of the taxable article represents four-fifths of the total cost of the complete unit, the tax applies to four-fifths of the price charged by the manufacturer for the unit. [Reg. §48.4216(a)-1.]

☐ [T.D. 7536, 3-27-78.]

### [Reg. §48.4216(a)-2]

**§48.4216(a)-2. Exclusions from sale price.**—(a) *Tax.*—(1) *Tax not part of taxable sale price.*—The tax imposed by chapter 32 of the Code on the sale of an article is not part of the taxable sale price of the article. Thus, if a manufacturer computes the tax on a sale price which is determined without regard to the tax, and it charges the proper tax as a separate item, the amount of tax so charged does not become a part of the taxable sale price and no tax is due on the tax so charged. Where no separate charge is made as tax, it will be presumed that the price charged to the purchaser for the article includes the proper tax, and the proper percentage of such price will be allocated to the tax.

(2) *Computation of tax.*—If an article subject to tax at the rate of 10 percent is sold for $100 and an additional item of $10 is billed as tax, $100 is the taxable selling price and $10 is the amount of tax due thereon. However, if the article is sold for $100 with no separate billing or indication of the amount of the tax, it will be presumed that the tax is included in the $100, and a computation will be necessary to determine what portion of the total amount represents the sale price of the article and what portion represents the tax. The computation is as follows:

$$\text{taxable sale price} = \frac{\text{sale price including tax}}{100 + \text{rate of tax}}$$

Thus, if the tax rate is 10 percent and the sale price including tax is $100, the taxable sale price is $90.91 (that is, $100 divided by (100 + 10)), and the tax is 10 percent of $90.91, or $9.09.

(b) *Transportation, delivery, insurance, or installation charges.*—(1) *Charges incurred pursuant to sale.*—Charges for transportation, delivery, insurance, installation, and other expenses actually incurred in connection with the delivery of an article to a purchaser pursuant to a bona fide sale shall be excluded from the sale price in computing the tax. Such charges include all items of transportation, delivery, insurance, installation, and similar expense incurred after shipment to a customer begins, in response to the customer's order, pursuant to a bona fide sale. However, costs of such nature incurred by a manufacturer, producer, or importer in transporting, in the normal course of business and for its benefit and convenience, articles from a factory or port of entry to a warehouse or other facility (regardless of the location of such warehouse or facility) are not considered as being incurred in connection with the delivery of an article to a purchaser pursuant to a bona fide sale, and charges therefor cannot be excluded from the sale price in computing tax liability. Similarly, an allowance granted by a manufacturer as reimbursement for expenses incurred by the purchaser in shipping used articles to the manufacturer for credit against the purchase price of taxable articles shall not be excluded from the sale price when computing tax due on the sale of the taxable articles. In any event, no charge may be excluded from the sale price unless the conditions set forth in subparagraph (2) of this paragraph are complied with. Said conditions are prescribed under the authority granted the Secretary or his delegate in section 4216(a).

(2) *Only actual expenses to be excluded.*—Where a separate charge is made for transportation or other expenses incurred in connection

with the delivery of an article to the purchaser pursuant to a bona fide sale, there shall be excluded in arriving at the sale price subject to tax only that portion of the charge which represents the actual expenses incurred for the transportation or other excludible expenses. Where a separate charge is less than the actual expense, the difference is presumed to be included in the billed price. Such difference, together with the separate charge, shall be excluded in arriving at the sale price on which the tax is computed. Similarly, where no separate charge is made but the manufacturer, producer, or importer incurs an expense of the type to which this paragraph has application, the amount of such expense actually incurred shall be excluded from the sale price on which the tax is computed. Where transportation expense is incurred in conjunction with a shipment composed of both taxable and nontaxable articles, only the portion of the expense allocable to the taxable articles shall be excludible. In general, unless the taxpayer establishes to the satisfaction of the district director that another method reasonably apportions such freight expense between taxable and nontaxable articles, such expense should be apportioned on the basis of the relative weights (or, if available, the relative published tariff rates applicable to) the taxable and nontaxable articles. Where it is not feasible to apportion such expense on the basis of relative weights or tariff rates, the expense shall be apportioned on another reasonable basis; for example, in the case of a shipment including both taxable and nontaxable automotive parts which are subject to the same tariff rate, it may be appropriate to apportion the transportation expense on the basis of the relative sale prices. A charge for insurance in connection with the delivery of an article to a purchaser is considered to represent an expense actually incurred only to the extent that an amount equivalent to such charge is paid or payable by the manufacturer to a person authorized to assume such insurance risk.

(3) *Transportation, delivery, or installation services performed by manufacturer.*—For purposes of computing the taxable sale price of articles, it is immaterial whether the transportation, delivery, or other services of the type to which this paragraph has application are performed by a common carrier or independent agency for or on behalf of the manufacturer, producer, or importer, or are performed by the manufacturer, producer, or importer with the use of its own vehicles or other facilities. Thus, where a manufacturer, producer, or importer performs the transportation, delivery, or other services with its equipment, tools, employees, etc., the cost of such services allocable to the sale of the taxable article shall be excluded. In determining whether an expense is an excludible transportation or delivery expense, only those expenses incurred by reason of the fact that the purchaser accepts delivery at some point other than the manufacturer's place of business shall be considered excludible transportation or delivery expenses. All expenses incurred in placing an article packed, ready for shipment on the loading dock at the manufacturer's factory are not excludible transportation or delivery expenses. An allowance granted by the manufacturer, producer, or importer to the purchaser for transportation, delivery, or other expenses incurred or to be incurred by the purchaser in connection with the sale shall be excluded in computing the taxable sale price, if charges for similar expenses would be excludible if incurred by the manufacturer.

(4) *Records in support of exclusion.*—Every manufacturer, producer, or importer making sales of taxable articles shall keep records which will disclose the amount of transportation, delivery, insurance, installation or other expense actually incurred by it in connection with the delivery of a taxable article to a purchaser pursuant to a bona fide sale.

(c) *Other charges.*—A charge or expense not within the scope of paragraph (a) or (b) of this section, whether or not separately stated, may not be excluded in computing the taxable sale price unless it can be shown by adequate records that the charge or expense properly is not to be included as a manufacturing or selling expense or is in no way incidental to placing the article in condition packed ready for shipment. Commissions to manufacturers' agents, or allowances, payments, or adjustments made to, and for the benefit of, persons other than the purchaser may not be excluded or deducted, under any condition, in computing the sale price upon which the tax is computed. [Reg. § 48.4216(a)-2.]

☐ [*T.D. 7536, 3-27-78.*]

**[Reg. § 48.4216(a)-3]**

**§ 48.4216(a)-3. Other items relating to tax on sale price.**—(a) *Exchanges.*—If, in connection with the sale of an article subject to a tax imposed under chapter 32 on the price for which sold, a manufacturer receives from its vendee another article in exchange, the tax on the manufacturer's sale shall be computed on the basis of the amount allowed for the article received from the vendee, plus any additional amount charged the vendee.

(b) *Replacements under warranty.*—If an article, subject to a tax imposed under chapter 32 on the price for which sold, is returned to the manufacturer by reason of the failure of the article under a warranty as to its quality or service, and a new article is given by the manufacturer, free, or at a reduced price, the tax on the new article shall be computed on the actual amount, if any, to be paid to the manufacturer for the new article. See paragraph (b)(2) of § 48.6416(b)-1 for the circumstances under which the allowance made by the manufacturer, producer, or importer upon the return of the first article constitutes a price readjustment of the sale price of the first article and the extent, if any, to which a credit may be allowed, or refund made, of the tax paid by the manufacturer, producer, or importer on the sale of the first article.

(c) *Readjustments in sale price.*—Readjustments in sale price (such as allowable discounts, rebates, bonuses, etc.) cannot be anticipated. The tax must be based upon the original price unless the readjustments have actually been made prior to the close of the period for which the tax upon the sale is returned. However, if the price upon which the tax was computed is subsequently readjusted, credit may be taken against the tax due on a subsequent return or a claim for refund filed as provided by section 6416(b)(1) and the regulations thereunder. [Reg. § 48.4216(a)-3.]

☐ [*T.D. 7536, 3-27-78.*]

**[Reg. § 48.4216(b)-1]**

**§ 48.4216(b)-1. Constructive sale price; scope and application.**—(a) *In general.*—Section 4216(b) pertains to those taxes imposed under chapter 32 that are based on the price for which an article is sold, and contains the provisions for constructing a tax base other than the actual sale price of the article, under certain defined conditions.

(b) *Specific applications.*—(1) Section 4216(b)(1) applies to:

(i) Arm's-length sales at retail or on consignment, other than those sales at retail and to retailers to which section 4216(b)(2) and § 48.4216(b)-3 apply; and,

(ii) Sales otherwise than at arm's-length, and at less than fair market price.

(2) Section 4216(b)(2) applies generally to arm's-length sales of an article at retail or to retailers, or both, where the manufacturer also sells the same article to wholesale distributors.

(3) Section 4216(b)(3) provides a formula for determining a constructive sale price for sales of taxable articles between members of an affiliated group of corporations (as "affiliated group" is defined in section 1504(a)) in those instances where the purchasing corporation regularly resells to retailers but does not regularly resell to wholesale distributors, and except for situations where section 4216(b)(4) or (5) applies.

(4) Section 4216(b)(4) provides a special method for computing a constructive sale price for sales of taxable articles between affiliated corporations where the purchasing corporation sells only to retailers, and the normal method of selling within the industry is for manufacturers to sell to wholesale distributors.

(5) Section 4216(b)(5) provides a special method for computing a constructive sale price for sales of articles subject to a tax imposed by section 4061(a) (trucks, buses, tractors, etc.) between affiliated corporations, where the purchasing corporation regularly sells such articles in arm's-length transactions to independent retailers.

(c) *Definitions.*—For purposes of section 4216(b) and the regulations thereunder and unless otherwise indicated:

(1) *Sale at retail.*—A "sale at retail," or a "retail sale," is a sale of an article to a purchaser who intends to use or lease the article rather than resell it. The fact that articles are sold in wholesale lots, or at wholesale prices, will not change the character of such sales as "sales at retail" if the purchaser is not engaged in the business of reselling such articles, and acquires them for the purpose of using them rather than reselling them.

(2) *Retail dealers.*—A "retail dealer," or "retailer," is a person engaged in the business of selling articles at retail.

(3) *Wholesale distributor.*—The term "wholesale distributor" means a person engaged in the business of selling articles to persons engaged in the business of reselling such articles. [Reg. § 48.4216(b)-1.]

☐ [*T.D. 7613, 4-23-79.*]

**[Reg. § 48.4216(b)-2]**

**§ 48.4216(b)-2. Constructive sale price; basic rules.**—(a) *In general.*—Section 4216(b)(1) sets forth the conditions that require the Secretary to construct a sale price on which to compute a tax imposed under chapter 32 on the price for which an article is sold. The section requires a constructive sale price to be established where a taxable article is (1) sold at retail, (2) sold while on consignment, or (3) sold otherwise than through an arm's-length transaction at less than fair market price. See § 48.4216(b)-2(c) for the treatment of articles taxable under section 4061(a).

(b) *Sales at retail.*—Section 4216(b)(1)(A) relates to the determination of a constructive sale price for sales of taxable articles sold at arm's length and at retail. In the case of such sales, the constructive sale price is the highest price for which such articles are sold to wholesale distributors, in the ordinary course of trade, by manufacturers or producers thereof, as determined by the Secretary. If the constructive sale price is less than the actual sale price the constructive sale price shall be used as the tax base. If the constructive sale price is not less than the actual sale price, the actual sale price shall be considered as not less than fair market and shall be used as the tax base. In determining the highest price for which articles are sold by manufacturers to wholesale distributors there must be taken into consideration the normal industry practices with respect to section 4216(a) and (f) inclusions and exclusions. However, once a constructive sale price has been determined by the Secretary, no further adjustment of such price shall be made. The provisions of section 4216(b)(1)(A) and this paragraph shall not apply in those instances where the provisions of section 4216(b)(2) and § 48.4216(b)-3 apply.

(c) *Sales of articles taxable under section 4061(a).*—With respect to sales made after December 31, 1978, in the case of an article the sale of which is taxable under section 4061(a) and which is sold at retail, the tax under this chapter shall be computed on a percentage (as determined by the Secretary but not greater than 100 percent) of the actual selling price based on the highest price for which such articles are sold by manufacturers and producers in the ordinary course of trade. The constructive sale price under this section shall be determined without regard to any individual manufacturer's or producer's cost.

(d) *Sales on consignment.*—As in the case of sales at retail, the constructive sale price for sales on consignment shall be the price for which such articles are sold, in the ordinary course of trade, by manufacturers or producers thereof, as determined by the Secretary. For purposes of section 4216(b)(1)(B) and this paragraph, an article is considered to be sold on consignment if it is sold while it is on consignment to a person which has the right to sell, and does sell, such article in its own name, but never receives title to the article from the manufacturer. Ordinarily, the constructive sale price of an article sold on consignment is the net price received by the manufacturer from the consignee. The provisions of section 4216(b)(1)(B) and this paragraph shall not apply if the provisions of section 4216(b)(2) and § 48.4216(b)-3 apply.

(e) *Sales not at arm's length.*—For purposes of section 4216(b)(1)(C) and this paragraph, a sale is considered to be made under circumstances otherwise than at "arm's length" if:

(1) One of the parties is controlled (in law or in fact) by the other, or there is common control, whether or not such control is actually exercised to influence the sale price, or

(2) The sale is made pursuant to special arrangements between a manufacturer and a purchaser.

In the case of an article sold otherwise than at arm's length, and at less than fair market price, the constructive sale price shall be the price for which such articles are sold, in the ordinary course of trade, by manufacturers or producers thereof, as determined by the Secretary. Once such a constructive sale price has been determined, no further adjustment of such price shall be made. See section 4216(b)(3), (4), and (5), and § 48.4216(b)-4, for specific methods for determining constructive sale prices for inter-company sales under certain defined conditions. [Reg. § 48.4216(b)-2.]

☐ [*T.D. 7613, 4-23-79.*]

### [Reg. § 48.4216(b)-3]

**§ 48.4216(b)-3. Constructive sale price; special rule for arm's-length sales.**—(a) *In general.*—Section 4216(b)(2) provides a special rule under which a manufacturer shall determine a constructive sale price for his sales of taxable articles at retail, and to retail dealers, under certain conditions.

The rule is applicable where:

(1) The manufacturer regularly sells such articles at retail, or to retailers, or both, as the case may be,

(2) The manufacturer also regularly sells such articles to one or more wholesale distributors in arm's-length transactions, and the manufacturer establishes that its prices in such cases are determined without regard to any benefit to be derived under section 4216(b)(2),

(3) The transactions are arm's-length transactions, and

(4) With respect to articles to which the tax imposed by section 4061(a) applies (relating to trucks, buses, tractors, etc.), the normal method of sales for such articles within the industry is not to sell such articles at retail or to retailers, or combinations thereof.

A manufacturer meeting the foregoing requirements shall base its tax liability for sales at retail and sales to retailers on the lower of its actual sale price or the highest price for which it sells the same articles under the same conditions to wholesale distributors.

(b) *Definitions.*—For purposes of section 4216(b)(2) and this section—

(1) *Actual sale price.*—"Actual sale price" means the actual selling price of an article determined in the same manner as sale price is determined for a taxable sale. Accordingly, such price must reflect the inclusions and exclusions set forth in sections 4216(a) and (f), and any price adjustments described in section 6416(b)(1).

(2) *Highest price to wholesale distributors.*—The "highest price" charged wholesale distributors for an article by a manufacturer, producer, or importer thereof, is the highest price at which the manufacturer, producer, or importer sells the article to wholesale distributors, determined without regard to quantity. Such price shall be determined in the same manner as sale price is determined for a taxable sale with respect to sections 4216(a) and (f) inclusions and exclusions; however, since the price is to be a "highest" price, no further adjustment may be made for price readjustments under section 6416(b)(1).

(3) *Regular sales.*—An article is considered to be sold "regularly" at retail or to retailers if sales are made at retail or to retailers periodically and recurringly as a regular part of the seller's business. If a seller makes only isolated or casual sales of an article at retail or to retailers, it is not considered to be selling "regularly" at retail or to retailers. Similarly, a manufacturer is considered to be making regular sales for an article to one or more distributors if it sells the article to at least one distributor periodically and recurringly as a regular part of its business.

(4) *Normal method of sales in industry.*—In the absence of a showing to the Commissioner of Internal Revenue of a more appropriate manner of determining the normal method of sales within an industry which is practical in application, the normal method of sales within an industry shall be regarded as not being at retail or to retailers, or both, if the industry dollar volume of sales which are at retail or to retailers, or both, is less than half the total industry dollar volume of sales at all levels of distribution by manufacturers, producers, or importers, including sales to other manufacturers, producers, or importers.

(5) *Industry.*—Each of the following categories of articles upon which tax is imposed by section 4061(a) constitutes a separate "industry":

(i) Taxable automobile trucks (consisting of automobile truck bodies and chassis);

(ii) Taxable automobile buses (consisting of automobiles bus bodies and chassis);

(iii) Taxable truck and bus trailers and semitrailers (consisting of chassis and bodies of such trailers and semitrailers); and

(iv) Taxable tractors of the kind chiefly used for highway transportation in combination with a trailer or semitrailer.

(6) *Application of section 4216(b)(2) to certain sales before June 22, 1965.*—In the case of sales before June 22, 1965, of articles then taxable under section 4121 (relating to electric, gas, and oil appliances), section 4216(b)(2) also applied in the case of a sale of such an article to a special dealer. The applicability of section 4216(b)(2) to such a sale may be determined by inserting "or to a special dealer" following "or to a retailer" in so much of section 4216(b)(2) as precedes subparagraph (A); by inserting "or to special dealers" following "retailers" in section 4216(b)(2)(A); and by inserting "(other than special dealers)" after "wholesale distributors" in section 4216(b)(2)(B) and so much of section 4216(b)(2) as follows section 4216(b)(2)(D). A "special dealer" was a distributor of articles taxable under section 4121 who did not maintain a sales force to resell the article whose constructive sale price was established under section 4216(b)(2) but relied on salesmen of the manufacturer, producer, or importer of the article. In the case of sales before June 22, 1965, of articles taxable under section 4191 (relating to business machines) or section 4211 (relating to matches), section 4216(b)(2) was applicable is [in] the same manner as in the case of articles taxable under section 4061(a). With respect to sales after September 30, 1962, section 4216(b)(2)(C) applied only to articles taxable under section 4061(a), 4191, or 4211. Section 4216(b)(2)(C) was applicable to sales before October 1, 1962, of all articles subject to tax under Chapter 32. [Reg. § 48.4216(b)-3.]

☐ [*T.D. 7613, 4-23-79.*]

**[Reg. § 48.4216(b)-4]**

**§ 48.4216(b)-4. Constructive sale price; affiliated corporations.—** (a) *In general.*—Sections 4216(b)(3), (4) and (5) establish procedures for determining a constructive sale price under section 4216(b)(1)(C) for sales between corporations that are members of the same "affiliated group," as that term is defined in section 1504.

(b) *Sales to which section 4216(b)(3) applies.*—Section 4216(b)(3), which applies to articles sold after December 31, 1969, provides a procedure for determining a constructive sale price under section 4216(b)(1)(C) in those instances where—

(1) A manufacturer, producer or importer regularly sells a taxable article (other than an article subject to a tax imposed by section 4061(a) (trucks, buses, etc.)) to a wholesale distributor which is a member of the same affiliated group as the manufacturer, producer or importer, and

(2) The wholesale distributor regularly sells such article to one or more independent retailers, but does not regularly sell to wholesale distributors.

Under such circumstances the constructive sale price for the article shall be an amount equal to 90 percent of the lowest price for which the distributor regularly sells the article in arm's-length transactions to such independent retailers. Once the constructive sale price has been determined, no adjustment shall be made for sections 4216(a) and (f) inclusions or exclusions or section 6416(b)(1) price readjustments. If both section 4216(b)(3) and section 4216(b)(4) apply with respect to the sale of an article, the constructive sale price for such article shall be the lower of the prices computed under section 4216(b)(3) and section 4216(b)(4).

(c) *Sales to which section 4216(b)(4) applies.*—Section 4216(b)(4), which applies to articles sold after December 31, 1969, provides a procedure for determining a constructive sale price under section 4216(b)(1)(C) in those instances where—

(1) A manufacturer, producer, or importer regularly sells (except for tax-free sales) a taxable article only to a wholesale distributor which is a member of the same affiliated group as the manufacturer, producer, or importer,

(2) The distributor regularly sells (except for tax-free sales) such article only to retail dealers, and

(3) The normal method of sales for such articles within the industry is to sell such articles in arm's-length transactions to wholesale distributors.

$$\text{Constructive sale price} = [\$15.00 \text{ minus } [\$15.00 \times \frac{(\$16.00 - \$12.00)}{\$16.00}] = \$11.25.$$

(e) *Sales to which section 4216(b)(5) applies.*—Section 4216(b)(5), which applies to articles sold after December 31, 1970, provides a procedure for determining a constructive sale price under section 4216(b)(1)(C) in those circumstances where—

(1) A manufacturer, producer, or importer of an article subject to a tax imposed by section 4061(a) (trucks, buses, etc.) regularly sells such article to a wholesale distributor that is a member of the same affiliated group of corporations as the manufacturer, producer, or importer, and

(2) Such distributor regularly sells such articles to independent retail dealers.

Under such circumstances the constructive sale price of such article shall be 98 1/2 percent of the lowest price for which such distributor regularly sells the article in arm's-length transactions to the independent retail dealers. Once the constructive sale price has been determined, no adjustment shall be made for section 4216(a) and (f) inclusions or exclusions or section 6416(b)(1) price readjustments.

(f) *Determination of "lowest price".*—(1) In addition to other considerations, in determining a "lowest price" for purposes of section 4216(b)(1), (3), and (5), and §§ 48.4216(b)-4(b) and 48.4216(b)-4(e), such price shall be determined—

(i) Without requiring that a given percentage of sales be made at that price (provided that the volume of sales made at that price is great enough to indicate that those sales have not been engaged in primarily to establish a lower tax base), and

(ii) Without including any charge for a fixed amount that the purchaser has an unconditional right to recover on the basis of a contractual arrangement existing at the time of sale.

(2) For purposes of applying section 4216(b)(1) and § 48.4216(b)-2, section 4216(b)(6) and this paragraph apply to articles sold after June 30, 1962. For purposes of applying section 4216(b)(3) and paragraph (b) of this section, section 4216(b)(6) and this paragraph apply to articles sold after December 31, 1969. For purposes of applying section 4216(b)(5) and paragraph (e) of this section, section 4216(b)(6) and this paragraph apply to articles sold after December 31, 1970.

Section 4216(b)(4) applies with respect to articles taxable under section 4061(a) (relating to trucks, buses, etc.) only as to sales after December 31, 1969, and before January 1, 1971. Under section 4216(b)(4), the constructive sale price of such article shall be the median price at which the distributor, at the time of the sale by the manufacturer, resells the article to retail dealers, reduced by a percentage of such price equal to the percentage which—

(i) The difference between the median price for which comparable articles are sold to wholesale distributors, in the ordinary course of trade, by manufacturers or producers thereof, and the median price at which such wholesale distributors in arm's-length transactions sell such comparable articles to retailers, is of

(ii) The median price at which such wholesale distributors in arm's-length transactions sell such comparable articles to retailers.

For purposes of this paragraph, the "median price" for which an article is sold at a particular level of distribution is the price midway between the highest and lowest prices charged vendees at the particular level of distribution. Where only one price is charged at a level of distribution, "median price" is equivalent to "actual price." All sale prices referred to in paragraphs (c) and (d) of this section are prices that must reflect the inclusions and exclusions set forth in sections 4216(a) and (f). However, once a constructive sale price has been determined under these paragraphs, no further adjustment of such price is allowed.

(d) *Application of section 4261(b)(4).*—The application of section 4216(b)(4) and paragraph (c) of this section may be illustrated by the following example:

*Example.* M, a corporation engaged in the manufacture of article X, sold 100 of such articles at $10.00 per article to a wholesale distributor N, a corporation engaged in the business of selling X articles to independent retail dealers. N is a member of the same affiliated group of corporations as M. M sells X articles only to N. The normal method of manufacturers' sales of X articles in the industry is to sell to independent wholesale distributors. N corporation sells X articles to retailers for $15.00 each. The price for which comparable X articles are sold to wholesale distributors in the ordinary course of trade by manufacturers thereof is $12.00 per article. Wholesale distributors sell X articles to retailers in the ordinary course of trade for $16.00 per article. Under the foregoing facts the constructive sale price determined under section 4216(b)(4) and this paragraph is $11.25, computed as follows:

(g) *Definitions.*—For purposes of this section and paragraphs (3), (4), and (5) of section 4216(b), the term "regularly sells" has the same meaning as that accorded the term "regular sales" in subparagraph (3) of § 48.4216(b)-3(b), and the term "normal method of sales in the industry" has the same meaning as accorded that term in subparagraph (4) of § 48.4216(b)-3(b). [Reg. § 48.4216(b)-4.]

☐ [*T.D.* 7613, 4-23-79.]

**[Reg. § 48.4216(c)-1]**

**§ 48.4216(c)-1. Computation of tax on leases and installment sales.—** (a) *Leases.*—When a taxable article is leased by a manufacturer, producer, or importer, liability for tax is incurred, except as provided by section 4217(b) and § 48.4217-2, on each payment made with respect to such lease. Tax is payable on each lease payment as long as the article is leased by the manufacturer, producer, or importer. The tax payable with respect to each lease payment is a percentage of each payment based on the rate of tax, if any, in effect on the date the lease payment is due. If the article is subsequently sold by the manufacturer, producer, or importer, the tax applies also to such sale, without regard to the tax paid when the article was leased. For definition of the term "lease", see paragraph (a) of § 48.4217-1(a).

(b) *Installment sales.*—When a taxable article is sold under an installment payment contract with title reserved in the seller, or under a conditional sale contract, chattel mortgage arrangement or other arrangement creating a security interest with payments to be made in installments, tax shall be computed and paid on each payment made by the purchaser. The tax payable with each payment is a percentage of each payment based on the rate of tax, if any, in effect on the date the payment is due. The part of each payment that is subject to tax is that portion of the payment equal to the percentage of the total charge for the article that is subject to tax. For example, if the total charge for the article is $1,000, and of the total amount charged only 90 percent thereof, or $900, is subject to tax by reason of exclusions, then only 90 percent of the installment payment is subject to tax. If the tax base is a constructive sale price computed under section 4216(b) that is less than the actual sale price of the article, the portion of each payment subject to tax is the percentage of such payment equal to the percentage that the constructive sale price bears to the actual sale price. For example, if an article is sold at retail for $100, and the constructive sale price for such an article computed under the provisions of section 4216(b)(1)(A) is $75, the percentage which the constructive sale price bears to the actual sale price is 75 percent. Accordingly, only 75 percent of each installment payment is subject to tax.

(c) *Sales on credit.*—Where articles are sold on credit under conditions other than those specified in paragraph (b) of this section, the entire tax shall be reported and paid with the return covering the period in which the sale is made, even though the price may not be paid to the manufacturer, producer, or importer until a later date, or not paid at all.

(d) *Effective dates of paragraphs (a) and (b) of this section.*—The rules set forth in paragraphs (a) and (b) of this section are effective as of June 22, 1965. As in effect before June 22, 1965, section 4216(c) required, in the case of a transaction described in section 4216(c)(1), (2), (3), or (4), that there be paid upon each payment with respect to an article that portion of the total tax which was proportionate to the portion of the total amount to be paid represented by such payment.

(e) *Contracts for the lease, installment sale, or sale on credit, of a taxable medical device.*—(1) *General rule.*—Payments made on or after January 1, 2013, pursuant to a contract for the lease, installment sale, or sale on credit of a taxable medical device that was entered into on or after March 30, 2010, are subject to tax under section 4191. The provisions of sections 4216(c) and 4217, paragraphs (a), (b), and (c) of this section, and § 48.4217-2 apply.

(2) *Exception for payments made on or after January 1, 2013, pursuant to written binding contracts entered into prior to March 30, 2010.*—Payments made on or after January 1, 2013, pursuant to a written binding contract for the lease, installment sale, or sale on credit of a taxable medical device that was in effect prior to March 30, 2010, are not subject to tax under section 4191. This exception includes payments made on or after January 1, 2013, if they are made pursuant to a written binding contract that was entered into prior to March 30, 2010. This exception does not apply to payments made under any contract that is materially modified on or after March 30, 2010. For this purpose, a material modification includes only a modification that materially affects the property to be provided under the contract, the terms of payment under the contract, or the amount payable under the contract. Notwithstanding the foregoing, a material modification does not include a modification to the contract required by applicable Federal, State, or local law.

(3) *Effective/applicability date.*—This section applies on and after January 1, 2013. [Reg. § 48.4216(c)-1.]

☐ [*T.D. 7536, 3-27-78. Amended by T.D. 9604, 12-5-2012 (corrected 3-12-2013).*]

### [Reg. § 48.4216(d)-1]

**§ 48.4216(d)-1. Sales of installment accounts.**—(a) *In general.*—Except as provided in paragraph (d) of this section, in case of a sale or other disposition by a manufacturer, producer, or importer of an installment account of the type specified in section 4216(c), the tax shall not apply to subsequent installment payments on such account. Instead, there shall be paid an amount equal to the difference between the tax previously paid on such installment account and the total tax computed by applying—

(1) To each installment due before the sale of the installment account, the rate of tax applicable at the time payment thereof was due, and

(2) To each installment, the time for payment of which has not arrived, the rate of tax which, under the provisions of chapter 32 as in effect on the date of the sale of the installment account, is (or is to be) in effect on the date such installment is due.

However, see paragraph (b) of this section if the sale is made in a bankruptcy or insolvency proceeding. The tax due under this paragraph shall be included in the return for the period in which the account is sold.

(b) *Sale in bankruptcy or insolvency proceeding.*—In the case of a sale of an installment account of a manufacturer, producer, or importer pursuant to the order of, or subject to the approval of, a court of competent jurisdiction in a bankruptcy or insolvency proceeding, the amount of tax due shall be computed and paid as provided in paragraph (a) of this section but shall not exceed the amount of tax computed by multiplying (1) the proportionate share of the amount for which such accounts are sold which is allocable to each unpaid installment payment, by (2) the rate of tax which, under the provisions of chapter 32 as in effect on the date of the sale of the install-

ment account, is (or is to be) in effect on the date such payment is due.

(c) *Collection of installment accounts on behalf of the manufacturer.*—Where a manufacturer, producer, or importer retains title to an installment account but turns it over to another person for collection on a fee basis, no sale of such account (or other disposition as contemplated in section 4216(d)) has been made. The tax shall continue to be paid as provided by section 4216(c).

(d) *Returned installment accounts.*—Where an installment account which has been sold or otherwise disposed of is returned to the manufacturer, producer, or importer who sold it under an agreement under which the account was sold, and credit or refund has been allowed under section 6416(b)(5) and the regulations thereunder, the manufacturer, producer, or importer shall pay tax as provided by section 4216(c) and § 48.4216(c)-1 on any subsequent payments made on such returned installment account until such time as there shall have been paid the total tax liability with respect to the account as computed under paragraph (a) of this section.

(e) *Limitation.*—The sum of the amounts payable under this section and § 48.4216(c)-1 on an installment account shall not exceed the total amount of tax which would be payable if such installment account had not been sold or otherwise disposed of (computed as provided in subsection (c)).

(f) *Applicability of paragraphs (a) and (b) of this section.*—The rules set forth in paragraphs (a) and (b) of this section apply in the case of installment accounts sold after June 21, 1965. In the case of installment accounts sold before June 22, 1965, paragraph (b) of this section shall be applied by substituting, in lieu of subparagraph (2) thereof, "the rate of tax, as set forth in chapter 32 of the Code, which applied on the day on which the transaction giving rise to such installment accounts took place." [Reg. § 48.4216(d)-1.]

☐ [*T.D. 7536, 3-27-78.*]

### [Reg. § 48.4216(e)-1]

**§ 48.4216(e)-1. Exclusion of local advertising charges from sale price.**—(a) *In general.*—Section 4216(e) deals with the treatment to be accorded charges made by a manufacturer for, and reimbursements by a manufacturer of expenditures in connection with, the advertising of certain articles subject to excise tax under chapter 32 of the Code. Section 4216(e) provides an exclusion (which is in addition to the exclusions provided by section 4216(a) and the regulations thereunder) in respect of charges for local advertising, as defined in paragraph (b) of this section, for purposes of determining the price for which an article is sold. See paragraph (c) of this section. The exclusion provided by section 4216(e) and paragraph (c) of this section has application only if—

(1) In the case of articles sold during the period January 1, 1961, through December 31, 1962, the advertising is broadcast over a radio or television station, or appears in a newspaper; and

(2) In the case of articles sold on or after January 1, 1963, the advertising is broadcast over a radio or television station, appears in a newspaper or magazine, or is displayed by means of an outdoor advertising sign or poster.

Section 4216(e) also provides an over-all limitation in respect of the sum of the amount of the exclusions from price as charges for local advertising and the amount of the readjustments authorized under section 6416(b)(1) (relating to credits or refunds for price readjustments) in respect of reimbursements by a manufacturer of expenditures for local advertising. See § 48.4216(e)-2. For provisions prohibiting exclusion from price or readjustment of price in respect of charges for, and reimbursements of expenditures for, advertising other than local advertising, see § 48.4216(e)-3.

(b) *Definition of local advertising.*—(1) *In general.*—For purposes of the regulations under sections 4216(e) and 6416(b)(1), the term "local advertising" means advertising which relates to an article with respect to which tax is imposed under chapter 32 of the Code on the price for which sold and which—

(i) Is initiated or obtained by the purchaser or any subsequent vendee,

(ii) Names the article for which the price is determinable under section 4216 and states the location at which such article may be purchased at retail, and

(iii)*(a)* In the case of articles sold on or after January 1, 1961, and before January 1, 1963, is broadcast over a radio station or television station or appears in a newspaper, or

*(b)* In the case of articles sold on or after January 1, 1963, is broadcast over a radio station or television station, appears in a newspaper or magazine, or is displayed by means of an outdoor advertising sign or poster.

(2) *Initiating or obtaining advertising.*—For purposes of subparagraph (1) of this paragraph, the advertising must be initiated or obtained by one or more of the persons in the chain of distribution of the article (wholesale distributor, jobber, dealer, etc.) who purchased the article for resale. For purposes of this subparagraph, the manufacturer is not considered to be one of the persons in the chain of distribution of the article. In general, advertising of an article is considered to be initiated or obtained by one or more persons in the chain of distribution of the article if any such person—

(i) Takes an active part in the actual planning and development, or in the arrangements or negotiations leading to the development, of the form and content of the advertising, or

(ii) Contracts for the placement of the advertising.

The participation by the manufacturer of the article in the planning, development, or placement of the advertising is immaterial provided the advertising is in fact initiated or obtained by one or more persons in the chain of distribution of the article. Furthermore, it is immaterial whether or not the advertising is subject to the approval of the manufacturer of the article. However, if no person in the chain of distribution of the article takes an active part in the actual planning and development, or in the arrangements or negotiations leading to the development, of the form and content of the advertising, but, rather, all such planning, development, arrangements, and negotiations are accomplished by the manufacturer of the article, then such manufacturer is considered to have initiated the advertising, and if he also contracts for the placement of the advertising, such advertising does not qualify as "local advertising".

(3) *Identification of article and sales location.*—To meet the requirements of subparagraph (1) of this paragraph, the advertising must identify the article for which the price is determinable under section 4216 and give the location or locations at which the article may be purchased at retail. All products taxable at the same rate under the same section of chapter 32 of the Code shall be considered to be an "article" for purposes of the preceding sentence. No specific method or means of identification is prescribed. The identification of the article may be made through the use of the name of the manufacturer or the use of an established trade-mark, such as a seal, picture, letter or letters, etc., or a combination thereof. The advertising must identify the particular retail establishment or establishments at which the article may be purchased at retail but need not specify the location of any such establishment in terms of the number by which the premises are designated or the name of the street on which the retail premises are situated. However, the location of the retail premises must be described sufficiently, as, for example, by reference to a particular named shopping area or shopping center, to enable consumers to find the retail establishment.

(4) *Determination of costs of local advertising.*—Where an advertisement identifies more than one article, and all such articles are not taxable, or are not taxable at the same rate under the same section of chapter 32 of the Code, a reasonable allocation of the cost of the advertisement must be made among (i) articles taxable at the same rate under the same section of the Code and (ii) articles which are not taxable under chapter 32 of the Code. For example, in the case of a single page newspaper or magazine advertisement, an allocation of costs reflecting the lineage or space devoted to the specified categories will be considered to reflect a reasonable allocation of the cost of advertising the different articles. As a general rule, only the cost of the "spot" portion identifying the retail establishment is considered "local advertising" in the case of national television or radio programs.

(5) *Meaning of "newspaper".*—The term "newspaper", as used in subparagraph (1) of this paragraph, is limited to those publications which are commonly understood to be newspapers and which are printed and distributed periodically at daily, weekly, or other short intervals for the dissemination of news of a general character and of a general interest. The term does not include handbills, circulars, flyers, or the like, unless printed and distributed as a part of a publication which constitutes a newspaper within the meaning of this subparagraph. Neither does the term include any publication which is issued to supply information on certain subjects of interest to particular groups, unless such publication otherwise qualifies as a newspaper within the meaning of this subparagraph. For purposes of this subparagraph, advertising is not considered to be news of a general character and of a general interest.

(6) *Meaning of "magazine".*—The term "magazine", as used in subparagraph (1) of this paragraph, is limited to those publications which are (i) commonly understood to be magazines, (ii) printed and distributed periodically at least twice a year, and (iii) published for the dissemination of information of a general nature or of special

interest to particular groups. The term does not include handbills, circulars, flyers or the like, unless printed and distributed as a part of a publication which constitutes a magazine within the meaning of this subparagraph. For purposes of this subparagraph, advertising is not considered to be information of a general nature or information of special interest to particular groups within the contemplation of subdivision (iii) of this subparagraph.

(7) *Meaning of "outdoor advertising sign or poster".*—The term "outdoor advertising sign or poster", as used in subparagraph (1) of this paragraph, means a sign or poster displaying advertising matter, which is located outside of a roofed enclosure. This term includes both signs or posters on billboards, whether placed on or affixed to land, buildings, or other structures, and those which are displayed on or attached to moving objects, provided the signs or posters are located outside of a roofed enclosure. The term "roofed enclosure" means a roofed structure which is enclosed on more than one-half of its sides by walls, fences, or other barriers.

(c) *Exclusion.*—(1) *Conditions and limitations.*—A charge for local advertising which is required by a manufacturer to be paid as a condition to his sale of an article is not a part of the taxable price of the article, to the extent that such charge meets each of the following conditions and limitations:

(i) Such charge does not exceed 5 percent of the difference between (*a*) an amount which would constitute the taxable price of the article (computed at the time of the sale of the article) if no part of any charge for local advertising were excludable in computing taxable price and (*b*) the amount of any separate charge for the local advertising, whatever the amount of such charge may be.

(ii) Such charge is specifically shown as a separate charge for local advertising of the invoice or statement covering the sale of the article.

(iii) Such charge is billed by the manufacturer with the intention on his part of repaying the amount of the charge to the person purchasing the article from him, or to any person who subsequently purchases the article for resale, in reimbursement of costs incurred for local advertising of such article or some other article or articles taxable at the same rate under the same section of the Code. In the absence of evidence to the contrary, the fact of such intention will be assumed in all cases where the manufacturer and his vendees are parties to an advertising plan which calls for such repayments, or the manufacturer can otherwise establish that the vendees to whom he bills such charges understand and expect that such repayments will be made.

(2) *When exclusion ceases to apply.*—To the extent that a charge for local advertising meets the conditions and limitations stated in subparagraph (1) of this paragraph, such charge is excludable in computing the taxable price of the article in respect of which the charge was made. However, the exclusion will cease to apply in respect of any part of such charge which the manufacturer fails to repay, before May 1 of the calendar year following the calendar year in which the article was sold, to the person who purchased the article from him, or to some other person who subsequently purchases the article for resale, in reimbursement of costs incurred for local advertising of such article or some other article or articles taxable at the same rate under the same section of the Code. If, before May 1, such any part of the charge so excluded has not been so repaid, the manufacturer becomes liable for tax on such May 1 in the same manner as if an article taxable under such section of the Code had been sold by him on such May 1 at a taxable price equivalent to that part of the charge not so repaid. However, see paragraph (c)(2) of § 48.6416(b)-1, relating to price readjustments in cases where local advertising charges are not repaid before such May 1 but are subsequently paid over by the manufacturer to his vendees in reimbursement of costs for local advertising. For provisions relating to the method of determining whether a payment by a manufacturer is or is not attributable to an excluded local advertising charge, see paragraph (b)(3) of § 48.4216(e)-2. In any case where the payment is determined to be attributable to such a charge, the date of the sale in connection with which the charge was made shall be determined on a first-in-first-out basis in respect of the vendee to whom the charge was billed by the manufacturer.

(d) *Examples.*—The application of this section may be illustrated by the following examples:

*Example (1).* During the first calendar quarter of 1961, a manufacturer sold refrigerators to one of his distributors at a total charge of $10,500, exclusive of tax, transportation charges, delivery charges, or other charges which are excludable in computing taxable price pursuant to section 4216(a). This total charge of $10,500 was billed as follows:

| | |
|---|---:|
| Refrigerators | $10,000 |
| Local advertising charge | 500 |
| Total charge | $10,500 |

Reg. § 48.4216(e)-1(b)(2)

At the time of the manufacturer's sale of the refrigerators, it was his intention, in accordance with the agreement between him and the distributor, to make repayment to the distributor of the local advertising charge, to the extent of expenditures by the distributor for radio, television, or newspaper advertising specifically naming refrigerators or other articles taxable at the same rate under section 4111 which were manufactured by the manufacturer, and giving the location of various retail stores within the distributor's territory where such articles may be purchased. Pursuant to such agreement, the selection of the advertising medium to be employed is to be made by the distributor, who is to plan the advertising subject to approval by the manufacturer, and contract for its placement. In this example, the advertising for which the charge is made qualifies as local advertising, the charge is billed to the manufacturer's vendee as a separate charge, the manufacturer intends to repay the charge to his vendee in reimbursement of costs incurred by the vendee for local advertising, and the charge does not exceed 5 percent of $10,000. Accordingly, the manufacturer's charge of $500 for local advertising is not includible in the taxable price of the refrigerators for purposes of computing and paying the tax imposed by section 4111.

| | |
|---|---|
| Refrigerators | $10,000 |
| Local advertising charge | 1,000 |
| Total charge | $11,000 |

At the time of the manufacturer's sale of the refrigerators, it was his intention, in accordance with the terms of a cooperative advertising plan to which the manufacturer and the distributor were parties, to make repayment to the distributor of the local advertising charge. Pursuant to the plan, the repayment would be made to the extent of expenditures by the distributor for radio, television, or newspaper advertising, initiated or obtained by him, specifically naming refrigerators or other articles taxable at the same rate under section 4111 which were manufactured by the manufacturer, and giving the location of various retail stores within the distributor's territory where such articles may be purchased. In this example, only $500 of the manufacturer's charge of $1,000 for local advertising may be excluded in determining the taxable price of the refrigerators for purposes of reporting and paying the tax imposed by section 4111. The remaining $500 may not be excluded in computing the taxable price of the refrigerators since this is the amount by which the $1,000 local advertising charge exceeds 5 percent of $10,000. Thus, the taxable price of the refrigerators in this example is $10,500.

*Example (4).* Assume the same facts as those stated in Example (1), except that, pursuant to the agreement between the manufacturer and the distributor, the manufacturer is to contract for the placement of the local advertising. Payment of the $500 local advertising charge is to be made by the manufacturer to the person with whom the advertising is placed in satisfaction of the manufacturer's contractual liability to such person. Under these circumstances, the manufacturer's payment of the $500 charge to the person with whom the advertising is placed does not constitute a refund to the purchaser in reimbursement of costs incurred for local advertising. [Reg. §48.4216(e)-1.]

☐ [T.D. 6635. *Amended by T.D. 6686 and T.D. 7536, 3-27-78.*]

### [Reg. §48.4216(e)-2]

**§48.4216(e)-2. Limitation on aggregate of exclusions and price readjustments.**—(a) *In general.*—The sum of the amount excluded from taxable price in respect of charges for local advertising, as provided in section 4216(e)(1) and §48.4216(e)-1, plus the amount of the readjustments for which credits or refunds may be claimed in respect of local advertising, as provided in section 6416(b)(1) and paragraph (c) of §48.6416(b)-1, is subject to an over-all 5 percent limitation. This limitation applies to each manufacturer, as of the close of each calendar quarter, in respect of all articles taxable under the same section of chapter 32 which were sold by such manufacturer in such quarter (and the preceding quarter or quarters, if any, in the calendar year). For example, a manufacturer selling articles taxable under section 4061 (relating to automobiles, trucks, buses, etc.), and also selling articles taxable under section 4111 (relating to refrigerators, quick-freeze units, etc.), who makes separate charges for local advertising in connection with his sales, or who makes reimbursement of local advertising expenses to his vendees out of moneys previously included in taxable price, in respect of any one or more articles in each of the two groups must apply the limitation separately in relation to the articles taxable under section 4061 and in relation to the articles taxable under section 4111. However, in such case, no breakdown of the separate articles taxable under section 4061, or of the separate articles taxable under section 4111, is required.

(b) *Computation of over-all 5 percent limitation.*—(1) *In general.*—The limitation prescribed by section 4216(e)(2) (the "over-all 5 percent limitation" referred to in paragraph (a) of this section) as to the total of the exclusions from price and readjustments of price which may be

*Example (2).* Assume the same facts as those stated in Example (1), and assume further that prior to May 1, 1962, the manufacturer has repaid to the distributor, in reimbursement of local advertising expenses incurred by the distributor in connection with refrigerators or other articles taxable at the same rate under section 4111 sold to him by the manufacturer, $400 of the $500 billed as a local advertising charge by the manufacturer in connection with his sale of refrigerators to the distributor in the first quarter of 1961. The manufacturer is liable, as of May 1, 1962, for tax in respect of the $100 which has not been repaid to the distributor. The amount of the tax is determinable at the rate in effect under section 4111 on May 1, 1962, in respect of refrigerators and is includible in the manufacturer's return of tax under such section for the second quarter of 1962.

*Example (3).* During the first calendar quarter of 1961, a manufacturer sold refrigerators to one of his distributors at a total charge of $11,000, exclusive of tax, transportation charges, delivery charges, or other charges which are excludable in computing taxable price under section 4216(a). This total charge of $11,000 was billed as follows:

claimed for local advertising in respect of all articles taxable under the same section of chapter 32 of the Code shall be computed as of the close of each calendar quarter of the calendar year. The over-all 5 percent limitation is 5 percent of the difference between (i) the amount which would constitute the total taxable price (computed at the time of sale) of all articles taxable under the same section of chapter 32 of the Code sold by the manufacturer during the elapsed calendar quarters of the calendar year, if no part of any charge for local advertising were excludable in computing taxable price, and (ii) the total of all amounts billed as separate charges for local advertising of such articles (whatever the amount of any single charge or the total of all charges). In making the computations under subdivisions (i) and (ii) of this subparagraph, credits or refunds under section 6416(b) of tax paid on the sale of any such articles are to be disregarded and articles sold tax-free by the manufacturer are to be excluded. The amount by which the over-all 5 percent limitation computed as of the close of a particular calendar quarter in respect of articles taxable under the same section of the Code exceeds the sum of the charges for local advertising excluded in computing the taxable price and the amount of reimbursements for local advertising of such articles made during the elapsed calendar quarters of the calendar year, in respect of which credit or refund has been claimed, represents the unused portion of the over-all 5 percent limitation. Such unused portion is the maximum amount of the reimbursements for local advertising in respect of which credit or refund may be claimed at the close of the particular calendar quarter, subject to the applicable conditions and limitations governing the right to claim a credit or refund in respect of local advertising (see §48.6416(b)-1). The unused portion of the over-all 5 percent limitation as of the close of the fourth calendar quarter of a calendar year in respect of which credit or refund may not be claimed as of the close of such quarter must be disregarded in computing the over-all 5 percent limitation for any subsequent calendar quarter. Moreover, the amount of any reimbursements for local advertising made by a manufacturer in a calendar year which is in excess of the amount of such reimbursements in respect of which credit or refund may be claimed, within the over-all limitation, as of the close of the calendar year, may not subsequently serve as the basis for a credit or refund.

(2) *Alternative method of computation in certain cases.*—If during the portion of the calendar year ending with the date as of which the over-all 5 percent limitation is being computed the amount of the local advertising charge separately billed by the manufacturer has not, in respect of any sale of any articles taxable under the same section of chapter 32 of the Code, exceeded the amount excludable pursuant to paragraph (c) of §48.4216(e)-1 in computing taxable price, the over-all 5 percent limitation as of the close of a particular calendar quarter in respect of articles taxable under such section is 5 percent of the total taxable price (computed at the time of the sale) of all such articles sold tax-paid during the calendar year.

(3) *Allocation of amounts paid in reimbursement of expenditures for local advertising.*—If a manufacturer makes contributions to a local advertising program in connection with which he makes excludable local advertising charges, it is necessary that reimbursements by the manufacturer for local advertising be attributed to the charges for local advertising, to the manufacturer's contributions, or allocated between them. Whether an amount paid by a manufacturer in reimbursement of expenses for local advertising is or is not a repayment of a local advertising charge which was excluded from taxable price under section 4216(e)(1) and §48.4216(e)-1, shall be determined on

the basis of an allocation made under the agreement between the manufacturer and his vendee (or any subsequent vendee).

(c) *Examples.*—The application of paragraphs (a) and (b) of this section may be illustrated by the following examples:

*First Quarter*

| | |
|---|---:|
| Articles taxable under section 4111 | $100,000 |
| Local advertising charges | 3,000 |
| Total charge | $103,000 |

*Second Quarter*

| | |
|---|---:|
| Articles taxable under section 4111 | $150,000 |
| Local advertising charges | 4,000 |
| Total charge | $154,000 |

Assume further that the manufacturer contributes to the advertising plan and that the manufacturer pays $5,500 and $1,000 during the first and second calendar quarters of 1961, respectively, to his distrib-

*Computation as of close of first calendar quarter*

| | | |
|---|---:|---:|
| 1. Amount which would constitute total taxable price (computed at time of sale) if no part of any charge for local advertising were excludable in computing taxable price | | $103,000 |
| 2. Amounts billed as separate charges for local advertising | | 3,000 |
| 3. Difference | | $100,000 |
| 4. Over-all 5 percent limitation (5 percent of item 3) | | 5,000 |
| 5. Amount excluded in computing taxable price | | 3,000 |
| 6. Unused portion of limitation | | $2,000 |
| 7. Allocation, pursuant to agreement, of $5,500 paid to distributors: | | |
| Charges for local advertising | $3,000 | |
| Contributions by manufacturer | 2,500 | |

Readjustment may be claimed in respect of that portion of the total amount repaid to the distributors which is allocated to the manufacturer's contribution ($2,500) to the extent that such portion does not exceed the unused portion of the over-all 5 percent limitation

*Computation as of close of second calendar quarter*

| | | |
|---|---:|---:|
| 1. Amount which would constitute total taxable price (computed at time of sale) if no part of any charge for local advertising were excludable in computing taxable price ($103,000 + $154,000) | | $257,000 |
| 2. Amounts billed as separate charges for local advertising ($3,000 + $4,000) | | 7,000 |
| 3. Difference | | $250,000 |
| 4. Over-all 5 percent limitation (5 percent of item 3) | | $12,500 |
| 5. Amount excluded in computing taxable price ($3,000 + $4,000) plus readjustment claimed at end of first calendar quarter ($2,000) | | 9,000 |
| 6. Unused portion of limitation | | $ 3,500 |
| 7. Allocation, pursuant to agreement, of $6,500 ($5,500 + $1,000) paid to distributors: | | |
| Charges for local advertising | $3,500 | |
| Contributions by manufacturer | 3,000 | |

Although the total reimbursements for local advertising expenses attributable to contributions by the manufacturer ($3,000) does not exceed the unused portion of the over-all 5 percent limitation ($3,500), the manufacturer having taken, at the close of the first calendar quarter, a price readjustment in the amount of $2,000 in respect of his contributions is entitled at the close of the second quarter to claim credit or refund in respect of a price readjustment in the amount of $1,000 ($3,000 – $2,000).

| | |
|---|---:|
| Articles taxable under section 4111 | $100,000 |
| Local advertising charges | 6,000 |
| Total charge | $106,000 |

Assume further that the manufacturer contributes to the advertising plan and that the manufacturer pays $3,000 during the first calendar quarter of 1961 to his distributors in reimbursement of expenses

*Computation as of close of first calendar quarter*

| | | |
|---|---:|---:|
| 1. Amount which would constitute total taxable price (computed at time of sale) if no part of any charge for local advertising were excludable in computing taxable price | | $106,000 |
| 2. Amounts billed as separate charges for local advertising | | 6,000 |
| 3. Difference | | $100,000 |
| 4. Over-all 5 percent limitation (5 percent of item 3) | | $ 5,000 |
| 5. Amount excluded in computing taxable price (see paragraph (c) of § 48.4216(e)-1) | | 5,000 |
| 6. Unused portion of limitation | | 0 |
| 7. Allocation, pursuant to agreement, of $3,000 paid to distributors: | | |
| Charges for local advertising | $2,000 | |
| Contributions by manufacturer | 1,000 | |

Credit or refund may not be claimed in respect of that portion of the total amount repaid to the distributors ($3,000) which is allocated to the manufacturer's contribution ($1,000) since the amount excluded in computing taxable price is equal to the over-all 5 percent limitation. [Reg. § 48.4216(e)-2.]

☐ [*T.D. 6635. Amended by T.D. 7536, 3-27-78.*]

**[Reg. § 48.4216(e)-3]**

**§ 48.4216(e)-3. No exclusion or readjustment for other advertising charges or reimbursements.**—(a) *Exclusions from price.*—No exclusion in computing the taxable price of any article sold by the

*Example (1).* During the first and second calendar quarters of 1961, a manufacturer makes sales of articles taxable under section 4111 to his distributors. The total charges for such sales, exclusive of the tax, transportation charges, delivery charges, or other charges which are excludable, pursuant to section 4216(a), in computing taxable price, are as follows:

utors in reimbursement of expenses incurred by them for local advertising of the articles purchased from the manufacturer.

($2,000). Accordingly, as of the close of the first calendar quarter the manufacturer may claim credit or refund in respect of a readjustment or price in the amount of $2,000.

*Example (2).* During the first calendar quarter of 1961, a manufacturer sold articles taxable under section 4111 to his distributors at a total charge of $106,000, exclusive of the tax, transportation charges, delivery charges, or other charges which are excludable, pursuant to section 4216(a), in computing taxable price. This total charge of $106,000 was billed as follows:

incurred by them for local advertising of the articles purchased from the manufacturer.

manufacturer may be allowed in respect of any charge for advertising if, and to the extent that, such charge—

(1) Is for advertising which does not qualify as local advertising within the meaning of section 4216(e)(4) and paragraphs (a) and (b) of § 48.4216(e)-1, or

(2) Does not satisfy all of the conditions and limitations stated in section 4216(e)(1) and paragraph (c) of § 48.4216(e)-1.

(b) *Readjustments of price.*—No credit or refund under section 6416(b)(1) may be allowed in respect of any amount which was included in the taxable price of an article sold by the manufacturer and which was later paid by him to his vendee in reimbursement of costs incurred for advertising, if, and to the extent that, the amount so paid—

(1) Is for advertising which does not qualify as local advertising within the meaning of section 4216(e)(4) and paragraph (b) of §48.4216(e)-1, or

(2) Is not within the limitation provided in section or 4216(e)(2), as computed in accordance with §48.4216(e)-2, as of the close of the calendar quarter in which the amount is so paid over or as of the close of any subsequent calendar quarter in the same calendar year. See, however, paragraph (c)(2)(ii) of §48.6416(b)-1, relating to redetermination of price readjustments in cases where local advertising charges excluded from taxable price in one calendar year become taxable as of May 1 of the following calendar year. [Reg. §48.4216(e)-3.]

☐ [*T.D. 6635. Amended by T.D. 6686 and T.D. 7536, 3-27-78.*]

### [Reg. §48.4216(f)-1]

**§48.4216(f)-1. Value of used components excluded from price of certain trucks.**—For purposes of the tax imposed by section 4061(a)(1) (relating to trucks, buses, etc.), in determining the price for which an article is sold, the value of any previously used component of such article shall be excluded from the price if the person furnishing the component is the first user of the finished article. For example, where a manufacturer builds a truck for a customer who intends to use, rather than resell the truck, incorporating used parts furnished by the customer, the value of the previously used parts shall not be included in the price for which the truck is considered sold by the manufacturer. [Reg. §48.4216(f)-1.]

☐ [*T.D. 7536, 3-27-78.*]

### [Reg. §48.4217-1]

**§48.4217-1. Lease considered as sale.**—For purposes of chapter 32 of the Code, the lease of an article by a manufacturer, producer, or importer shall be considered a sale of the article. The term "lease" means a contract or agreement, written or verbal, which gives the lessee an exclusive, continuous right to the possession or use of a particular article for a period of time. The term includes any renewal or extension of a lease or any subsequent lease of the article. However, in the case of the lease of an automobile the sale of which by the manufacturer would be taxable under section 4064, the term includes only the first lease (excluding any renewal or extension of the lease) of such automobile by the manufacturer. [Reg. §48.4217-1.]

☐ [*T.D. 7536, 3-27-78. Amended by T.D. 8036, 7-23-85.*]

### [Reg. §48.4217-2]

**§48.4217-2. Limitation on amount of tax applicable to certain leases.**—(a) *Conditions for eligibility.*—Section 4217(b) provides for a limitation on the amount of tax that shall apply to the lease, any renewal, or further lease, of an article which, if sold, would be subject to tax on the basis of sale price. Such limitation on the amount of the tax applies with respect to the lease of an article only if, at the time of making the lease, the lessor is engaged in the business of selling in arm's length transactions the same type and model of article. In case of a lease to which section 4217(b) does not apply, tax shall be computed and paid as provided in section 4216(c) and paragraph (a) of §48.4216(c)-1.

(b) *Lessor engaged in business of selling.*—The lessor will be regarded as being engaged in the business of selling in arm's length transactions the same type and model of an article as the one being leased if it periodically and recurringly makes bona fide offers for sale of such articles in the regular course of operation of its business, which offers if accepted would constitute sales at arm's length. Whether the offers are bona fide shall be determined on the basis of the facts in each case, such as sales actually made, the nature of the advertising, sales literature, and other means used to effectuate sales. It is not necessary that the offers for sale be made to the same class of purchasers as those to whom the article is being leased.

(c) *Same type and model of article.*—To qualify as the "same type and model of article", the article offered for sale must be an unused article essentially the same in size, design, and function as the article being leased. For example, a van-type truck trailer would not be the same type and model as a stake-body of flat-bed truck trailer. Neither would a 25-foot van-type trailer be the same type and model as a 35-foot van-type trailer. Slight differences in appearance or accessories will not render articles dissimilar which are identical in all other respects.

(d) *Basis for tax.*—(1) *Tax payable until total tax is paid.*—In case of a lease of an article to which section 4217(b) applies, tax shall be paid on each lease payment in an amount computed by applying to such lease payment a percentage equal to the rate of tax in effect on the

date of the lease payment. Such tax payments shall continue to be made under such lease, or any subsequent lease of the article, until the cumulative total of the tax payments equals the total tax. Lease payments made thereafter with respect to that article shall not be subject to tax. For definition of the term "total tax", see paragraph (e) of this section.

(2) *Changes in tax rates.*—Except as provided in—

(i) Section 701(a)(3) of the Excise Tax Reduction Act of 1965 (79 Stat. 155) in the case of certain reductions in tax rates effective June 22, 1965, or January 1, 1966, and

(ii) Section 401(h)(3) of the Revenue Act of 1971 (85 Stat. 534) in the case of certain reductions in tax rates effective December 11, 1971,

if the rate of tax is increased or decreased during a lease period, the new rate shall apply to the lease payments made on and after the date of the change, but the amount of the total tax shall remain the same.

(e) *Total tax.*—For purposes of this section, the term "total tax" means the amount of tax, computed at the rate in effect on the date of the first lease of the article to which section 4217(b) applies, which would be due on the constructive sale price of the article as determined under section 4216(b) and §48.4216(b)-2, as if the article had been sold by a manufacturer at retail on such date.

(f) *Sale of article before total tax becomes payable.*—If the lessor sells the article before the total tax has become payable, the tax payable on the sale shall be the lesser of the following amounts—

(1) The difference between (i) the total tax, and (ii) the aggregate tax applicable to lease payments already received; or

(2) A tax computed, at the rate in effect on the date of the sale, on the price for which the article is sold.

For purposes of subparagraph (2) of this paragraph, the provisions of section 4216(b) for determining a constructive sale price shall not apply if the sale is at arm's length. If the sale is not at arm's length, the tax referred to in subparagraph (2) of this paragraph shall be computed on a constructive sale price as provided in §48.4216(b)-2.

(g) *Sale of article after total tax has become payable.*—If the lessor sells an article after the total tax has become payable, the tax imposed under chapter 32 of the Code shall not apply to such sale.

(h) *Special rules applicable to certain leases entered into before January 1, 1959.*—For purposes of this section, in the case of any lease entered into before, and existing on, January 1, 1959—

(1) Such lease shall be considered to have been entered into on January 1, 1959.

(2) The total tax shall be computed on the fair market value of the article on January 1, 1959.

(3) The lease payments under such lease shall include only payments attributable to periods beginning after December 31, 1958.

(i) *Cross-reference.*—In the case of the lease of an automobile the sale of which by the manufacturer would be taxable under section 4064, the foregoing provisions of this section shall not apply. See section 4217(e) for the rules relating to the payment of the gas guzzler tax. [Reg. §48.4217-2.]

☐ [*T.D. 7536, 3-27-78. Amended by T.D. 8036, 7-23-85.*]

### [Reg. §48.4218-1]

**§48.4218-1. Tax on use by manufacturer, producer, or importer.**—(a) *In general.*—Section 4218 imposes tax in respect of certain uses of articles by the actual manufacturer, producer, or importer thereof. This section also applies in respect of the use of articles by any other person who, pursuant to a provision of chapter 32 of the Code, is considered to be, or is treated as, the manufacturer or producer of the articles. See, for example, section 4223 relating to articles purchased tax free for use in further manufacture.

(b) *Taxable articles in general.*—(1) *Application of tax.*—If the manufacturer, producer, or importer of an article taxable under chapter 32 of the Code (other than an article referred to in paragraph (c), (d), or (e) of this section) uses the article for any purpose other than that indicated in subparagraph (3) or (4) of this paragraph, he shall be liable for tax with respect to the use of such article in the same manner as if the article were sold by him.

(2) *Taxable use in manufacture of nontaxable articles.*—(i) *In general.*—In the case of an article to which subparagraph (1) of this paragraph applies, tax attaches when the manufacturer, producer, or importer of the article uses it as material in the manufacture or production of, or as a component part of, another article which is not taxable under chapter 32 of the Code, regardless of the disposition made of such other article. (See paragraph (c) of §48.4218-5 for computation of tax on such use.)

(ii) *Types of use in manufacture of nontaxable articles.*—Taxable use may consist of the incorporation of a taxable article, such as an electric light bulb, into a nontaxable article, such as a flashlight. Taxable use may also result from the combining of a taxable article (or the components thereof) with a nontaxable article (or the components of a nontaxable article) resulting in a combination end article which itself is not taxable. Although the taxable article may not be a completely separable unit, within the contemplation of the law a taxable article has been produced and incorporated in the combination end article. The following are examples of taxable articles so used:

(a) Household type electric or gas clothes drier incorporated in a combination washer-drier.

(b) Household type electric, gas, or oil cooking range combined either with a range using other means of heating or with a nontaxable space heater.

(c) Taxable radio receiving set incorporated in a combination radio receiver-transmitter or in a combination radio receiver-intercommunication system.

If an automobile part or accessory, radio or television component, or camera lens is used as material in the manufacture or production of, or as a component part of, a taxable article to which subparagraph (1) of this paragraph has application and such article in turn is used in the manufacture or production of, or as a component part of, a nontaxable article, the part or accessory, component, or lens is considered to have been used in the manufacture of the taxable article, and not in the manufacture of the nontaxable article. For example, the use of taxable radio components in the production of a taxable radio receiving set is exempt from tax (see paragraph (d) of this section), but the use of the radio receiving set in the production of a nontaxable combination radio receiver-transmitter is subject to tax. See section 6416(b)(2) or 6416(b)(3) and the regulations thereunder contained in Subpart O for credit or refund of tax paid in respect of such radio receiver if the combination radio receiver-transmitter is by any person exported, sold to a State or local government for its exclusive use, sold to a nonprofit educational organization for its exclusive use, or used or sold for use as supplies for vessels or aircraft.

(3) *Nontaxable use in manufacture of taxable articles.*—The tax on the use of an article to which subparagraph (1) of this paragraph has application shall not apply if the article is used by the manufacturer, producer, or importer thereof as material in the manufacture or production of, or as a component part of, another article taxable under chapter 32 to be manufactured or produced by him. It is immaterial what disposition is made of such other article.

(4) *Gasoline.*—The tax on the use of an article shall not apply in the case of gasoline used on or after October 1, 1961, by any person, for nonfuel purposes, as a material in the manufacture or production of another article to be manufactured or produced by him. See section 4221 and the regulations thereunder contained in Subpart N. For provisions applicable to use of gasoline by a producer or importer otherwise than in the production of other gasoline, or special motor fuel taxable under section 4041(b), see section 4082(c) and paragraph (c) of § 48.4082-1 contained in Subpart H.

(c) *Tires, inner tubes, and automobile radio or television receiving sets.*—If the manufacturer, producer, or importer of a tire or inner tube taxable under section 4071 (other than a bicycle or inner tube referred to in paragraph (e) of this section), or an automobile radio or television receiving set taxable under section 4141, sells such article on or in connection with the sale of any other article or uses it for any purpose, he shall be liable for tax with respect to such tire, inner tube, or radio or television receiving set in the same manner as if it were sold by him as a separate article. However, tax does not apply where the manufacturer, producer, or importer of the tire, inner tube, or automobile radio or television receiving set sells such article on or in connection with the sale of another article manufactured by him for any of the exempt purposes specified in paragraphs (2) to (5), inclusive, of section 4221(a) and the regulations thereunder contained in Subpart N.

(d) *Automobile parts or accessories, radio or television components, and camera lenses.*—(1) *Application of tax.*—If the manufacturer, producer, or importer of an automobile part or accessory taxable under section 4061(b), a radio or television component taxable under section 4141, or a camera lens taxable under section 4171, uses the article for any purpose other than that indicated in subparagraph (2) of this paragraph, he shall be liable for tax with respect to the use of the article in the same manner as if the article were sold by him. For example, tax applies if the manufacturer, producer, or importer uses the article referred to in this subparagraph for repair or replacement purposes in connection with equipment used by him in the operation of his business.

(2) *Nontaxable use in manufacture of other articles.*—The tax on the use of an article referred to in subparagraph (1) of this paragraph shall not apply if the article is used by the manufacturer, producer, or importer thereof as material in the manufacture or production of, or as a component part of, any other article (whether or not taxable under chapter 32) to be manufactured or produced by him. It is immaterial what disposition is made of such other article.

(e) *Bicycle tires and inner tubes.*—(1) *Application of tax.*—If the manufacturer, producer, or importer of a bicycle tire as defined in section 4221(e)(4)(B) or an inner tube for such tire uses the tire or inner tube for any purpose other than as indicated in subparagraph (2) of this paragraph, he shall be liable for tax with respect to the use of the tire or inner tube in the same manner as if the article were sold by him.

(2) *Nontaxable use in manufacture of other articles.*—The tax on the use of a bicycle tire or inner tube referred to in subparagraph (1) of this paragraph shall not apply if the tire or inner tube is used by the manufacturer, producer, or importer thereof as material in the manufacture or production of, or as a component part of, a new bicycle to be manufactured or produced by him. It is immaterial what disposition is made of the new bicycle. Tax, however, applies in the case of the use of a bicycle tire or inner tube by the manufacturer, producer, or importer thereof in the rebuilding or reconditioning of a used bicycle.

(3) *Effective date.*—The provisions of this paragraph shall apply to the use on or after May 1, 1960, of a bicycle tire or inner tube by the manufacturer, producer, or importer thereof. Liability for tax on the use prior to that date of a bicycle tire or inner tube by the manufacturer, producer, or importer thereof shall be based on the provisions of paragraph (c) of this section which apply to tires and inner tubes in general.

(f) *Use after lease.*—If the manufacturer, producer, or importer of a taxable article leases such article and thereafter uses the article, he incurs liability for tax on such use as provided in these regulations to the same extent as if the article were sold after being leased. See section 4217 and the regulations thereunder in this subpart for application and computation of tax in case of leased articles.

(g) *Time of application of tax.*—In the case of a taxable use of an article by the manufacturer, producer, or importer thereof, the tax attaches at the time such use begins. If tax applies by reason of the sale of an article by the manufacturer, producer, or importer thereof on or in connection with his sale of another article, the tax attaches at the time of the sale of such other article.

(h) *Exemption because of other statutory provisions.*—Tax does not apply on the use of an article by the manufacturer, producer, or importer thereof if under the applicable provisions of the Code the sale of the article for a similar use would not be subject to tax. For example, the use of gasoline by the producer thereof to propel tankers engaged in foreign trade which are owned or leased by the producer would not be subject to tax under section 4218 since a sale for such use would be exempt from tax as provided in section 4221(a)(3). Also, tax need not be paid with respect to the use of an article by the manufacturer, producer, or importer thereof if such use would qualify, under the provisions of section 6416(b), for credit or refund of the tax paid. [Reg. § 48.4218-1.]

☐ [T.D. 6687.]

**[Reg. § 48.4218-2]**

**§ 48.4218-2. Business or personal use of articles.**—(a) *Business use.*—Section 4218 applies to the use by a person, in the operation of any business in which he is engaged of a taxable article which has been manufactured, produced, or imported by him or his agent. For example, a person engaged in the operation of a dairy business incurs liability for tax with respect to a truck body manufactured by him and used in the operation of his dairy business.

(b) *Personal use.*—The tax on use of a taxable article does not attach in cases where an individual incidentally manufactures, produces, or imports a taxable article for his personal use or causes a taxable article to be manufactured, produced, or imported for his personal use. [Reg. § 48.4218-2.]

☐ [T.D. 6687.]

**[Reg. § 48.4218-3]**

**§ 48.4218-3. Events subsequent to taxable use of article.**—Liability for tax incurred on the use of an article is not extinguished or reduced because of any subsequent sale or lease of the article even if such sale or lease would have been exempt if the article had been so sold or leased prior to use. If a manufacturer, producer, or importer of an article incurs liability for tax on his use thereof, and thereafter sells or leases the article in a transaction which otherwise would be subject to tax, liability for tax is not incurred on such sale or lease. [Reg. § 48.4218-3.]

☐ [T.D. 6687.]

### [Reg. § 48.4218-4]

**§ 48.4218-4. Use in further manufacture.**—For purposes of section 4218 and § 48.4218-1, an article is used as material in the manufacture or production of, or as a component part of, another article, if it is incorporated in, or is a part or accessory of, the other article. Lubricating oil in the crankcase of a new truck is an example of a taxable article used as material in the manufacture or production of, or as a component part of, another article. In addition, an article (other than gasoline used as a fuel) is considered to be used as material in the manufacture of another article if it is partly or entirely consumed in testing such other article; for example, shells or cartridges used in testing new firearms. Similarly, if an article is partly or wholly consumed in quality testing a production run of like articles (as, for example, an automotive part destroyed in stress testing) such article is also considered to have been used as material in the manufacture of another article. However, if a taxable article that has been used tax free and only partly consumed in testing is later sold, or put to a taxable use, by the manufacturer, tax attaches to such sale or use. An article that is consumed in the manufacturing process other than in testing, so that it is not a physical part of the manufactured article, is not used as material in the manufacture or production of, or as a component part of, such other article. Thus, lubricating oil consumed in operating plant machinery in the course of the manufacture of automobile trucks chasis is not used as material in the manufacture or production of, or as a component part of, the truck chassis. [Reg. § 48.4218-4.]

☐ [T.D. 6687. *Amended by T.D. 7536, 3-27-78.*]

### [Reg. § 48.4218-5]

**§ 48.4218-5. Computation of tax.**—(a) *Tax based on price.*—Except as provided in paragraph (d) of this section, tax liability incurred on the use of an article shall be computed on the price at which such or similar articles are sold in the ordinary course of trade by manufacturers, producers, or importers thereof and in the absence of special arrangements. For additional provisions applicable in computing the tax in the case of the use of an article by a manufacturer or producer who purchased the article free of tax under section 4221(a)(1) for use by him in further manufacture, see section 4223(b) and the regulations thereunder.

(b) *Articles regularly sold by manufacturer.*—If the manufacturer, producer, or importer of an article regularly sells such articles at wholesale in arm's length transactions, tax liability on his use of any such article shall be computed on his lowest established wholesale price for such articles in effect at the time of the taxable use. In establishing such price, there shall be included and excluded, as applicable, the charges and readjustments specified in sections 4216(a), 4216(f), and 6416(b)(1), as in effect at the time tax liability on the use of the article is incurred, and the regulations thereunder contained in this subpart and subpart O. If the manufacturer, producer, or importer of an article does not regularly sell such articles at wholesale in arm's length transactions, a constructive price on which the use tax shall be computed will be determined by the Commissioner. This price will be established after considering the selling practices and price structures of manufacturers, producers, and importers of similar articles.

(c) *Articles governed by section 4218(a) used in manufacture of nontaxable combination articles.*—If the manufacturer, producer, or importer of an article to which section 4218(a) applies does not regularly sell such article separately but uses it as material in the manufacture or production of, or as a component part of, a nontaxable combination article consisting of a taxable and nontaxable article, liability for tax on his use shall be computed on the constructive price of the taxable article at the time of use. To determine the constructive price of the taxable article in such case, the combination article is considered to be composed of (1) parts used exclusively in the functioning of the taxable article in the combination, (2) parts used exclusively in the functioning of the nontaxable article in the combination, and (3) parts, called common parts, which serve a dual function in connection with the parts in both subparagraphs (1) and (2) of this paragraph. The ratio which the cost of the parts in subparagraph (1) of this paragraph bears to the sum of the cost of such parts and the parts in subparagraph (2) of this paragraph is applied to the lowest established wholesale price for which like combination articles are at the time of the taxable use being sold by the manufacturer or producer in the ordinary course of trade. The resulting amount is the constructive sale price for the taxable article on which tax is to be computed. The cost of the common parts is allocable to the parts in subparagraphs (1) and (2) of this paragraph in the same ratio, and, therefore, need not be taken into account in the computation since

the inclusion and allocation of the cost of such parts in the determination would not result in a different ratio. In determining the lowest established wholesale price for the combination article, there shall be included and excluded, as applicable, the charges and readjustments specified in sections 4216(a), 4216(f), and 6416(b)(1), as in effect at the time tax liability on the use of the taxable article is incurred, and the regulations thereunder contained in this subpart and subpart O of this part. The tax applicable to the use of the article for which a constructive sale price has been computed is not affected by any charges or readjustments of the price for which the nontaxable combination article is sold, whether by reason of the return or repossession of the nontaxable article or its covering or container, or by a bona fide discount, rebate, allowance, or other factor. The application of this subparagraph may be illustrated by the following example:

*Example.* A manufacturer of a nontaxable washer-drier combination produces and uses an electric clothes drier taxable under section 4121 in the manufacture of the combination article. The lowest established wholesale price of the manufacturer for the washer-drier combination at the time of the taxable use is $150 with respect to identical combinations after including and excluding applicable charges and readjustments. The manufacturer does not regularly sell such drier separately. In the manufacture of the washer-drier the two units are integrated to the extent that certain component parts function both in the operation of the washer and of the drier. The parts used exclusively in the operation of the washer cost $30 and those used exclusively in the operation of the drier cost $20. The taxable cost ratio in this instance is 20/50, or 40 percent. Applying 40 percent to the manufacturer's lowest established wholesale price of $150 for the washer-drier results in $60 as the constructive price for the taxable article in the combination at the time tax liability is incurred. No additional charges or readjustments in connection with, or subsequent to, the sale of the washer-drier combination may affect the tax liability incurred at the time of use.

(d) *Tax based on weight or volume.*—Where liability for tax is incurred on the use of an article subject, if sold, to a tax based on—

(1) the weight of the article (such as a tire), or

(2) the volume of the article (such as gasoline or lubricating oil), the tax due shall be computed on the basis which would be applicable if such article were sold. [Reg. § 48.4218-5.]

☐ [T.D. 6687, 11-4-63.]

### [Reg. § 48.4219-1]

**§ 48.4219-1. Sale of taxable articles by a person other than the manufacturer, producer, or importer.**—(a) *General rule.*—If the title to, or ownership of, an article taxable under chapter 32 of the Code is transferred from the manufacturer, producer, or importer thereof, and, under the law, no tax attaches to such transfer, the subsequent sale, lease, or use of such article by the transferee is subject to tax to the same extent and in the same manner as if such transferee were the manufacturer, producer, or importer of the article. The following examples illustrate this rule:

(1) The surviving spouse, child or children, executors or administrators, or other legal representatives, as the case may be, of a deceased manufacturer, producer, or importer of taxable articles, incur liability for tax on all such articles sold by them.

(2) A receiver or trustee in a bankruptcy who under a court order conducts or liquidates the business of a manufacturer, producer, or importer of taxable articles, incurs liability for tax on all taxable articles sold by him, regardless of whether the articles were manufactured, produced, or imported before or after he took charge of the business.

(3) An assignee for the benefit of creditors of a manufacturer, producer, or importer incurs liability for tax with respect to all taxable articles sold by him as such assignee.

(4) If one or more members of a partnership withdraw, or if new partners are admitted, the new partnership so constituted incurs liability for tax on all taxable articles sold by it regardless of when such articles were manufactured, produced, or imported.

(5) A person who acquires title to taxable articles as a result of default of the manufacturer, producer, or importer pursuant to an agreement under the terms of which the articles were pledged as collateral incurs liability of tax with respect to his sale of the articles so acquired.

(6) A person who succeeds to the business of a manufacturer, producer, or importer of taxable articles, such as—

(i) a corporation which results from a consolidation, merger, or reorganization;

(ii) a corporation which acquires the business of an individual or partnership; or

(iii) a stockholder in a corporation who, after its dissolution, continues the business;

incurs liability for tax on all taxable articles sold by such person. However, where a manufacturer, producer, or importer sells only his assets, rather than ownership of his business, he incurs liability for tax on the sale of any taxable articles included in such assets.

(b) *Transfer of title to damaged articles.*—If title to a damaged taxable article is transferred by the manufacturer, producer, or importer thereof to a carrier or insurance company in adjustment of a damage claim, such transfer is not considered a taxable sale of the article. If the article is usable, even though damaged, the carrier or insurance company incurs liability for tax on its sale, lease, or use of the article. Where the article has been damaged to the extent that its only value is as scrap, and it is not restored to usable condition, sale thereof by the carrier or insurance company is not subject to tax. [Reg. §48.4219-1.]

☐ [*T.D.* 6687, 11-4-63.]

### [Reg. §48.4221-1]

**§48.4221-1. Tax-free sales; general rule.**—(a) *Application of regulations under section 4221.*—(1) *In general.*—The regulations under section 4221 provide rules under which the manufacturer, producer, or importer of an article subject to tax under chapter 32 (or the retailer of an article subject to tax under subchapter A or C of chapter 31) may sell the article tax free under section 4221.

(2) *Limitations.*—The following restrictions must be taken into account in applying the regulations under section 4221:

(i) The exemptions under section 4221(a)(4) and (a)(5) do not apply to the tax imposed by section 4064 (gas guzzler tax).

(ii) The exemptions under section 4221 do not apply to the tax imposed by section 4081 (taxable fuel tax).

(iii) The exemptions under section 4221 do not apply to the tax imposed by section 4091 (aviation fuel tax). For rules relating to tax-free sales of aviation fuel, see section 4092 and the regulations thereunder.

(iv) The exemptions under section 4221 do not apply to the tax imposed by section 4121 (coal tax).

(v) The exemptions under section 4221(a)(3) through (a)(5) do not apply to the tax imposed by section 4131 (vaccine tax). In addition, the exemption under section 4221(a)(2) applies to the vaccine tax only to the extent provided in §48.4221-3(e) (relating to tax-free sales of vaccine for export).

(vi) The exemptions under section 4221(a) apply only in those cases where the exportation or use referred to is to occur before any other use.

(vii) The exemptions under section 4221(a)(3) through (a)(6) do not apply to the tax imposed by section 4191 (medical device tax).

(b) *Manufacturer relieved of liability in certain cases.*—(1) *General rule.*—Under the provisions of section 4221(c), if an article subject to tax under chapter 32 of the Code is sold free of tax by the manufacturer of the article for an exempt purpose referred to in section 4221(c) and paragraph (b)(2) of this section, the manufacturer shall be relieved of any tax liability under chapter 32 with respect to such sale if the manufacturer in good faith accepts a proper certification by the purchaser that the article or articles will be used by the purchaser in the stated exempt manner. See paragraph (b)(2) of this section for a list of the exempt purposes referred to in section 4221(c).

(2) The following are situations wherein section 4221(c) is applicable with respect to sales made tax free on the assumption that one of the following sections of the Code provides exemption for such sales:

(i) Section 4221(a)(1), to the extent that it relates to sales for further manufacture by a first purchaser (see §48.4221-2),

(ii) Section 4221(a)(3), relating to supplies for vessels and aircraft (see §48.4221-4),

(iii) Section 4221(a)(4), relating to sales to State or local governments (see §48.4221-5),

(iv) Section 4221(a)(5), relating to sales to nonprofit educational organizations (see §48.4221-6), and

(v) Section 4221(e)(3), relating to the sale of tires used on intercity, local, or school buses (see §48.4221-8).

(3) *Duty of seller to ascertain validity of tax-free sale.*—If the manufacturer at the time of its sale has reason to believe that the article sold by it is not intended for the exempt purpose indicated by the purchaser, or that the purchaser has failed to register as required, the manufacturer is not considered to have accepted certification from the purchaser in good faith, and is not relieved from liability under the provisions of section 4221(c).

(4) *Information to be furnished to purchaser.*—A manufacturer selling articles free of tax under this section after December 31, 1978, shall indicate to the purchaser that (i) certain articles normally subject to tax are being sold tax free and (ii) the purchaser is obtaining those articles tax free for an exempt purpose under an exemption certificate or its equivalent. The manufacturer may transmit this information by

any convenient means, such as coding of sales invoices, provided that the information is presented with sufficient particularity so that the purchaser is informed that he has obtained the articles tax free and—

(i) The purchaser can compute and remit the tax due if an article sold tax free for further manufacture is diverted to a taxable use,

(ii) The manufacturer can remit the tax due with respect to an article purchased tax free for resale for use in further manufacture or for export if, within the 6-month period described in §48.4221-2(c) or §48.4221-3(c), the manufacturer does not receive proof that the article has been exported or resold for use in further manufacture, or

(iii) The purchaser can notify the manufacturer if an article otherwise purchased tax free is diverted to a taxable use.

(c) *Evidence required in support of tax-free sales.*—(1) *Purchasers required to be registered.*—Every purchaser who is required to be registered (see §48.4222(a)-1) shall furnish to the seller, as evidence in support of each tax-free sale made by the seller to such purchaser, the exempt purpose for which the article or articles are being purchased and the registration number of the purchaser. Such information must be in writing and may be noted on the purchase order or other document furnished by the purchaser to the seller in connection with each sale.

(2) *Purchasers not required to be registered.*—For the evidence which purchasers not required to register must furnish to the seller in support of each tax-free sale made by the seller to such purchasers, see paragraph (b) of §48.4221-3 for sales or resales to a foreign purchaser for export, paragraph (d) of §48.4221-4 for sales of supplies to vessels or aircraft, paragraph (c) of §48.4221-5 for sales to State and local governments, and paragraph (c) of §48.4222(b)-1 for sales and purchases by the United States. [Reg. §48.4221-1.]

☐ [*T.D.* 7536, 3-27-78. *Amended by T.D.* 8036, 7-23-85; *T.D.* 8659, 3-13-96; *T.D.* 8879, 3-30-2000 *and T.D.* 9604, 12-5-2012.]

### [Reg. §48.4221-2]

**§48.4221-2. Tax-free sale of articles to be used for, or resold for, further manufacture.**—(a) *Further manufacture.*—(1) *In general.*—Under prescribed conditions, an article subject to tax under chapter 32 (other than a tire taxable under section 4071, which is given special treatment under section 4221(e)(2) and §48.4221-7) may be sold tax free by the manufacturer, pursuant to section 4221(a)(1), for use by the purchaser in further manufacture, or for resale by the purchaser to a second purchaser for use by the second purchaser in further manufacture. See section 4221(d)(6) and paragraph (b) of this section for the circumstances under which an article is considered to have been sold for use in further manufacture. See section 6416(b)(3) and §48.6416(b)-3 for the circumstances under which credit or refund is available when tax-paid articles are used in further manufacture.

(2) *Proof of resale for use in further manufacture.*—See section 4221(b)(1) and paragraph (c) of this section for provisions under which the exemption provided in section 4221(a)(1) shall cease to apply in the case of an article sold by the manufacturer to a purchaser for resale to a second purchaser for use in further manufacture unless the manufacturer receives timely proof of resale for further manufacture.

(b) *Circumstances under which an article is considered to have been sold for use in further manufacture.*—(1) An article shall be treated as sold for use in further manufacture if the article is sold for use by the buyer as material in the manufacture or production of, or as a component part of, another article taxable under chapter 32 of the Internal Revenue Code.

(2) An article is used as material in the manufacture or production of, or as a component of, another article if it is incorporated in, or is a part or accessory of, the other article when the other article is sold by the manufacturer. In addition, an article is considered to be used as material in the manufacture of another article if it is consumed in whole or in part in testing such other article. However, an article that is consumed in the manufacturing process other than in testing, so that it is not a physical part of the manufactured article, is not considered to have been used as material in the manufacture of, or as a component part of, another article.

(c) *Proof of resale for further manufacture.*—(1) *Cessation of exemption.*—The exemption provided in section 4221(a)(1) and described in paragraph (a) of this section in respect of an article sold by the manufacturer to a purchaser for resale to a second purchaser for use by the second purchaser in further manufacture shall cease to apply on the first day following the close of the 6-month period which begins on the date of the sale of such article by the manufacturer, or the date of shipment of the article by the manufacturer, whichever is earlier, unless, within such 6-month period, the manufacturer receives proof, in the form prescribed by paragraph (c)(2) of this section, that the article was actually resold by the purchaser to a second purchaser for such use. If, on the first day following the close of the 6-month period, such proof has not been received, the manufacturer shall become liable for tax at that time at the rate in effect when the sale was made but otherwise in the same manner as if the article had been sold by it on such first day at a taxable price equivalent to that at which the article was actually sold. If the manufacturer later obtains such proof, it may file a claim for refund or credit of this tax. The payment of this tax by the manufacturer is not considered an overpayment by the subsequent manufacturer or producer for which the subsequent manufacturer or producer is entitled to a credit or refund under section 6416(b)(3). See section 4221(d)(6) and paragraph (b) of this section for the circumstances

under which an article is considered to have been sold for use in further manufacture.

(2) *Proof of resale.*—(i) *Certificate of purchaser.*—The proof of resale to be received by the manufacturer, as required under section 4221(b)(1), may consist of either a copy of the invoice of the manufacturer's vendee directed to his purchaser which discloses the certificate of registry number held by each party or a statement described below. In the case of an invoice of manufacturer's vendee, it must appear from such invoice (or by statement attached thereto) that the article was in fact resold for use in further manufacture. In lieu of such an invoice, proof of resale may consist of a statement, executed and signed by the manufacturer's vendee. Such statement shall be in substantially the following form:

### STATEMENT OF MANUFACTURER'S VENDEE

(To support tax-free sales of taxable articles to a purchaser for resale to a second purchaser for use in further manufacture (section 4221(a)(1) of the Internal Revenue Code).)

. . . . . . . . . . Date, 19 .

The undersigned, or the (Name of manufacturer's vendee if other than undersigned) . . . . . . . . . . . . . . . . . . . . of which I am (Title) . . . . . . . . holds certificate of registry No. . . . . , issued by the District Director of Internal Revenue

at . . . . . . . . .

The article or articles specified below or on the reverse side thereof were purchased tax free by me, or by (Name of manufacturer's vendee if other than undersigned) . . . . . . . . . . . . . . . . . , on (Date) . . . . . . . . and were thereafter resold to a purchaser who holds certificate of registry No. . . . . . . . , issued by the District Director of Internal Revenue at . . . . . . . . . . . , for use by it as material in the manufacture or production of, or as a component part or parts of, an article or articles taxable under chapter 32 of the Internal Revenue Code, or, if the article or articles are automobile parts or accessories (to which section 4061(b) applies) or gasoline, for use by it as material (for nonfuel uses in the case of gasoline) in the manufacture or production of, or as a component part or parts of, any article or articles.

The undersigned, or (Name of manufacturer's vendee if other than undersigned) . . . . . . . . . . . . . . . . . . . . . . , has in my/its possession proof of tax-free resale of such article or articles in the form of related purchase orders and sales invoices, and proof of tax-free resale will be retained by me or (Name of manufacturer's vendee if other than undersigned) . . . . . . . . . . . . . . . . . . . . . . , for at least 3 years from the date of this statement, and will be made readily available for inspection by Government officers during such 3-year period.

I have not previously executed a statement in respect of such certificate of resale, and I understand that the fraudulent use of this statement may subject me and all parties making such fraudulent use of this statement to a fine of not more than $10,000, or imprisonment for not more than five years, or both, together with the costs of prosecution.

(Signature) . . . . . . . . . . . . . . . . . .

(Address) . . . . . . . . . . . . . . . . .

(ii) *Period covered.*—Any statement executed and signed by the manufacturer's vendee, as provided in subdivision (i) of this paragraph (c)(2), may be executed with respect to any one or more articles purchased tax free from a manufacturer and resold for use in further manufacture within the 6-month period prescribed in section 4221(a)(1) and paragraph (c)(1) of this section. Such statement (or other prescribed proof of resale) must be retained for inspection by the district director as provided in section 6001. [Reg. § 48.4221-2.]

☐ [T.D. 7536, 3-27-78. *Amended by T.D. 7681, 2-29-80; T.D. 7753, 1-13-81; T.D. 7882, 3-30-83 and T.D. 8659, 3-13-96.]*

### [Reg. § 48.4221-3]

**§ 48.4221-3. Tax-free sale of articles for export, or for resale by the purchaser to a second purchaser for export.**—(a) *In general.*—(1) An article subject to tax under chapter 32 of the Code may be sold tax free by the manufacturer, pursuant to section 4221(a)(2) and this section, for export, or for resale by the purchaser to a second purchaser for export. See paragraph (a)(10) of § 48.0-2 for the meaning of the term "export". An article may be sold tax free by the manufacturer under the provisions of this section only if the person to whom the manufacturer sells the article intends either to export the article or to resell it to a person who intends to export it. An article may not be sold tax free under the provisions of this section by a manufacturer to a purchaser for resale to a second purchaser which does not intend to export the article itself but plans to resell it to a third purchaser for export. See section 6416(b)(2)(A) and paragraph (b)(1) of § 48.6416(b)-2 for the circumstances under which credit or refund of tax is available where tax-paid articles are exported from the United States.

(2) If an article, otherwise taxable under chapter 32 of the Code—

(i) Is sold tax free by the manufacturer pursuant to section 4221(a)(2) and this section, and

(ii) Is returned subsequently to the United States in an unused and undamaged condition,

then the importer is liable for the tax imposed by chapter 32 on the subsequent sale or use of the article in the United States. The provisions of this paragraph (a)(2) may be illustrated by the following examples:

*Example (1).* Q, a U.S. motor vehicle manufacturer, previously sold a truck chassis to R, a company in Canada. The sale was tax free under section 4221(a)(2). R mounted a truck body on the truck chassis and sold the completed vehicle to S. Thereafter S sold the

completed new vehicle to T who imported the vehicle into the United States and sold it. The sale of the completed truck subjects T to an excise tax liability under section 4061(a)(1) with respect to both the body and the chassis.

*Example (2).* X, a U.S. manufacturer of trucks, sold a trash collection truck to Y, a company in France. The sale was tax free under section 4221(a)(2). The truck was sold by Y to the City of Nice, France. After initial use, the city determined that the truck was not suited for its needs and resold the truck to X. X returned the truck to the United States where it was resold. The resale of the truck by X does not subject X to an excise tax liability under section 4061(a)(1).

(b) *Sales or resales to a foreign purchaser for export.*—In the case of sales or resales to a foreign purchaser for export, where the first purchaser or the second purchaser is located in a foreign country or possession of the United States, such purchaser is not required to register as provided in section 4222(a) and § 48.4222(a)-1. To establish the right to sell articles tax free for export to a purchaser who is not registered and who is located in a foreign country or a possession of the United States, the manufacturer must obtain from such purchaser at the time title to the article passes or at the time of shipment, whichever is earlier, either:

(1) A written order or contract of sale showing that the manufacturer is to ship the article to a foreign destination; or

(2) Where delivery by the manufacturer is to be made within the United States, a statement from the purchaser showing:

(i) That the article is purchased either to fill existing or future orders for delivery to a foreign destination or for resale to another person engaged in the business of exporting who will export the article, and

(ii) That such article will be transported to its foreign destination in due course prior to use or further manufacture and prior to any resale except for export.

See section 4221(b) and paragraphs (c) and (d) of this section for requirements as to timely proof of exportation and cessation of the exemption for export unless the evidence to show actual exportation has been received by the manufacturer.

(c) *Cessation of exemption.*—The exemption provided in section 4221(a)(2) and paragraph (a) of this section for an article sold by the manufacturer for export or for resale by the purchaser to a second purchaser for export shall cease to apply on the first day following the close of the 6-month period which begins on the date of the sale of the article by the manufacturer, or the date of shipment of the article by the manufacturer, whichever is earlier, unless within the 6-month period the manufacturer receives proof, in the form prescribed by paragraph (d) of this section, that the article was actually exported. If, on the first day following the close of the 6-month period, the proof has not been received, the manufacturer shall become liable for tax at that time at the rate in effect when the sale was made but otherwise in the same manner as if the article had been sold by it on such first day at a taxable price equivalent to that at which the article was actually sold.

(d) *Proof of exportation.*—(1) Exportation may be evidenced by:

(i) A copy of the export bill of lading issued by the delivering carrier,

(ii) A certificate by the agent or representative of the export carrier showing actual exportation of the article,

(iii) A certificate of lading signed by a customs officer of the foreign country to which the article is exported,

(iv) Where the foreign country has no customs administration, a statement of the foreign consignee showing receipt of the article, or

(v) Where a department or agency of the United States Government is unable to furnish any one of the foregoing four types of proof of exportation, a statement or certification on the department or agency stationery, executed by an authorized officer, that the listed or identified articles have, in fact, been exported.

(2) In any case where the manufacturer is not the exporter, the manufacturer must have in its possession a statement from the vendee to whom the manufacturer sold the article stating that the article was in fact exported in due course by the vendee or was sold to another person who in due course exported the article. The statement must state what evidence is available to establish that the article was in fact exported in due course prior to use or further manufacture and prior to resale in the United States other than for export. Such evidence must be that described in paragraph (d)(1) of this section, and the statement must show where such evidence is readily available for inspection by Government officers, and should be in substantially the following form:

### STATEMENT OF MANUFACTURER'S VENDEE

(To support tax-free sales of taxable articles to a purchaser for export or for resale to a second purchaser for export (section 4221(a)(2) of the Internal Revenue Code).)

The undersigned, or the (Name of manufacturer's vendee if other than undersigned) . . . . . . . . . . . . . . . . of which I am (Title) . . . . . . . . . . . ., holds certificate of registry No. . . ., issued by the District Director of Internal Revenue at . . . . . . . . . . . . . . .

The article or articles specified below or on the reverse side hereof were purchased tax free by me or by (Name of manufacturer's vendee if other than undersigned) . . . . . . . . . . . . . . . . . on (Date) . . . ., and were thereafter exported.

The undersigned or (Name of manufacturer's vendee if other than undersigned) . . . . . . . . . . . . . . . . has in my/its possession proof of exportation in respect of such article or articles. The evidence of export available is . . . . . and is located at (If other than address below) . . . . . . . . . . . . . .

Such proof of exportation will be retained by (Name of manufacturer's vendee) for at least three years from the date of this statement and will be made readily available for inspection by Government officers.

I have not previously executed a statement in respect of the article or articles covered by this statement, and I understand that the fraudulent use of this statement will subject me and all parties making such fraudulent use of this statement to a fine of not more than $10,000, or imprisonment for not more than five years, or both, together with the costs of prosecution.

. . . . . . . . . . . . . . . . . . (Signature)

. . . . . . . . . . . . . . . . (Address)

. . . . . . . . . . . . . . . . . (Date)

(3) The statement executed and signed by the manufacturer's vendee, as provided in paragraph (d)(2) of this section, may be executed with respect to any one or more articles purchased tax free from a manufacturer and exported within the 6-month period prescribed in section 4221(b)(2) and paragraph (c) of this section. Such statement shall be kept for inspection by the district director as provided in section 6001 and the regulations thereunder.

(e) *Vaccines.*—The exemption provided by section 4221(a)(2) applies after August 10, 1993, to the tax imposed on vaccines by section 4131, but only if—

(1) The vaccine is sold by the manufacturer after August 10, 1993; and

(2) In the case of vaccine sold to, or sold for resale to, the United States or any of its agencies or instrumentalities, the United States or such agency or instrumentality notifies the manufacturer that the vaccine is intended for uses other than the vaccination of persons described in 42 U.S.C. 300aa-11(c)(1)(B)(i)(II) (relating to certain U.S. citizens who are vaccinated outside the United States). [Reg. § 48.4221-3.]

☐ [*T.D. 7536, 3-27-78. Amended by T.D. 7729 and T.D. 8561, 8-19-94.*]

### [Reg. § 48.4221-4]

**§ 48.4221-4. Tax-free sale of articles by the purchaser as supplies for vessels or aircraft.**—(a) *Supplies for vessels or aircraft.*—(1) *In general.*—An article subject to tax under chapter 32 may be sold tax free by the manufacturer, pursuant to section 4221(a)(3) and this section, for use by the purchaser as supplies for vessels or aircraft. See paragraph (b) of this section for the meaning of the term "supplies for vessels or aircraft." An article may be sold tax free under the provisions of this section only in those cases where the sale of an article by the manufacturer is made directly to the owner, officer, charterer, or authorized agent of a vessel or aircraft for use as supplies for the vessel or aircraft. No sale may be made tax free to a dealer for resale for use as supplies for vessels or aircraft, even though it is known at the time of sale by the manufacturer that the article will be so resold. See section 6416(b)(2)(B) and paragraph (b)(2) of § 48.6416(b)-2 for circumstances under which credit or refund of tax is available where tax-paid articles are used, or sold for use, as supplies for vessels or aircraft. An article may not be sold tax free under the provisions of this section by the manufacturer to passengers or members of the crew of a vessel or aircraft.

(2) *Civil aircraft of foreign registry.*—In the case of any article sold by the manufacturer for use by the purchaser as supplies for civil aircraft of foreign registry employed in foreign trade or in trade between the United States and any of its possessions, the provisions of this paragraph apply only if the reciprocity requirements of section 4221(e)(1) are met. See paragraph (c) of this section.

(b) *Meaning of terms.*—(1) *Supplies for vessels or aircraft.*—The term "supplies for vessels or aircraft" means fuel supplies, ships' stores, sea stores, or legitimate equipment on vessels of war of the United States or of any foreign nation, vessels employed in the fisheries or in the whaling business, or vessels actually engaged in foreign trade between the Atlantic and Pacific ports of the United States or between the United States and any of its possessions.

(2) *Fuel supplies, ships' stores, and legitimate equipment.*—The terms "fuel supplies", "ships' stores", and "legitimate equipment" include all articles, materials, supplies, and equipment necessary for the navigation, propulsion, and upkeep of vessels of war of the United States or of any foreign nation, vessels employed in the fisheries or in the whaling business, or vessels actually engaged in foreign trade or in trade between the Atlantic and Pacific ports of the United States or between the United States and any of its possessions, even though such vessels may make intermediate stops in the United States. The term does not include supplies for vessels engaged in trade (i) between domestic ports in the Atlantic Ocean and the Gulf of Mexico, (ii) between domestic ports on the Pacific Ocean, (iii) between domestic ports on the Great Lakes, or (iv) on the inland waterways of the United States.

(3) *Sea stores.*—The term "sea stores" includes any article purchased for use or consumption by the passengers or crew, or both, of a vessel during its voyage.

(4) *Vessels.*—The term "vessels" includes (i) every description of watercraft or other contrivance used, or capable of being used, as a means of transportation on water, (ii) civil aircraft registered in the United States and employed in foreign trade or in trade between the United States and any of its possessions, and (iii) civil aircraft registered in a foreign country and employed in foreign trade or in trade between the United States and any of its possessions.

(5) *Vessels of war of the United States or of any foreign nation.*—The term "vessels of war of the United States or of any foreign nation" includes (i) every description of watercraft or other contrivance used, or capable of being used, as a means of transportation on water and

constituting equipment of the armed forces (including the U.S. Coast Guard and U.S. National Guard) of the United States or of a foreign nation, and (ii) aircraft owned by the United States or by any foreign nation and constituting equipment of the armed forces thereof. For purposes of this section, vessels or aircraft owned by armed forces are not considered to be equipment of such armed forces while on lease or loan to an organization that is not part of the armed forces.

(6) *Vessels used in fisheries or whaling business.*—The exemption provided by section 4221(a)(3) and paragraph (a) of this section in the case of articles sold for the prescribed use on vessels employed in the fisheries or whaling business is limited to articles sold by the manufacturer for such use on vessels while employed, and to the extent employed, exclusively in the fisheries or in the whaling business. For purposes of this section, vessels engaged in sport fishing are not considered to be employed in the fisheries.

(7) *Civil aircraft.*—The exemption provided by section 4221(a)(3) and paragraph (a) of this section relating to supplies for vessels or aircraft, with respect to civil aircraft, extends only to civil aircraft when employed in foreign trade, or in trade between the United States and any of its possessions. Sales of supplies to civil aircraft when engaged in trade between the Atlantic and the Pacific ports of the United States are not exempt from the tax imposed under chapter 32. See section 4221(e)(1) and paragraph (c) of this section for requirement of reciprocal exemption in the case of a civil aircraft registered in a foreign country.

(8) *Trade.*—The term "trade" includes the transportation of persons or property for hire and the making of the necessary preparations for such transportation. The term "trade" also includes the transportation of property on a vessel or aircraft owned or chartered by the owner of the property in connection with the purchase, sale, or exchange of the property in a commercial business operation. However, a vessel owned or chartered by a company and used in the transportation of personnel or property of such company to or from its business properties located in a foreign country, or in a possession of the United States, is not engaged in "trade".

(c) *Reciprocity required in the case of civil aircraft.*—The exemption provided by section 4221(a)(3) and paragraph (a) of this section with respect to the sales of supplies for civil aircraft registered in a foreign country is further limited in that the privilege of exemption may be granted only if the Secretary of Commerce advises the Secretary of

the Treasury that the foreign country allows, or will allow, substantially the same reciprocal privileges. If a foreign country discontinues the allowance of such substantially reciprocal exemption, the exemption allowed by the United States will not apply after the Secretary of the Treasury is notified by the Secretary of Commerce of the discontinuance of the exemption allowed by the foreign country.

(d) *Evidence required to establish exemption.*—(1) *In general.*—The exemption provided in section 4221(a)(3) and paragraph (a) of this section for articles sold for use by the purchaser as supplies for vessels or aircraft applies only (i) if both the manufacturer and purchaser are registered under the provisions of section 4222 or (ii) the purchaser or both the manufacturer and the purchaser are not registered but have satisfied the provisions of paragraph (d)(2) of this section. See paragraph (c) of § 48.4221-1 for the evidence required to establish exemption where the purchaser is registered pursuant to section 4222 and § 48.4222(a)-1.

(2) *Exemption certificates for use in support of tax-free sales of supplies for vessels and aircraft.*—(i) In order to establish exemption from tax under section 4221(a)(3) in those instances where the purchaser or both the manufacturer and purchaser are not registered under section 4222, the manufacturer must obtain (prior to or at the time of the sale) from the owner, chartered, or authorized agent of the vessel or aircraft and retain in the manufacturer's possession a properly executed exemption certificate in the form prescribed by subdivision (iii) of this paragraph (d)(2). If articles are sold tax-free for use as supplies for civil aircraft employed in foreign trade or in trade between the United States and any of its possessions, the exemption certificate must show the name of the country in which the aircraft is registered.

(ii) Where only occasional sales of articles are made to a purchaser for use as supplies for vessels or aircraft, a separate exemption certificate shall be furnished for each order. However, where sales are regularly or frequently made to a purchaser for such exempt use, a certificate covering all orders for a specified period not to exceed 12 calendar quarters will be acceptable. Such certificates and proper records of invoices, orders, etc., relative to tax-free sales must be kept for inspection by the district director as provided in section 6001, and the regulations thereunder.

(iii) *Acceptable form of exemption certificate.*—The following form of exemption certificate will be acceptable for the purposes of this section and must be adhered to in substance:

### EXEMPTION CERTIFICATE

(For use by purchasers of articles for use as fuel supplies, ships' stores, sea stores, or legitimate equipment on certain vessels or aircraft (sections 4221 and 4222 of the Internal Revenue Code of 1954).)

(Date) . . . . , 19 .

I, the undersigned purchaser, hereby certify that I am the (Owner, charterer, or authorized agent) . . . . . . . . . . . . . . . of (Name of company and vessel) . . . . . . . . . . . . . . . and that:

(Check applicable type of certificate)

. . The article or articles specified in the accompanying order, or on the reverse side hereof, (or)

. . . All orders placed by the purchaser for the period commencing (Date) . . . . and ending (Date) . . . . (period not to exceed 12 calendar quarters),will be used only for fuel supplies, ships' stores, sea stores, or legitimate equipment on a vessel belonging to one of the following classes of vessels to which section 4221 of the Internal Revenue Code applies:

(Check class to which vessel belongs)

. . . . . . (1) Vessels engaged in foreign trade.

. . . . . . (2) Vessels engaged in trade between the Atlantic and Pacific ports of the United States.

. . . . . . (3) Vessels engaged in trade between the United States and any of its possessions.

. . . . . . (4) Vessels employed in the fisheries or whaling business.

. . . . . . (5) Vessels of war of the United States or a foreign nation.

If the articles are purchased for use on civil aircraft engaged in trade as specified in (1) or (3) above, state the name of the country in which the aircraft is registered: . . . . . . . . . . . . . . . . . . . . . . . . .

I understand that if the articles are used for any purpose other than as stated in this certificate, or are resold or otherwise disposed of, I must report such fact to the manufacturer. I understand that this certificate may not be used in purchasing articles tax free for use as fuel supplies, etc., on pleasure vessels, or on any type of aircraft except (i) civil aircraft employed in foreign trade or trade between the United States and any of its possessions, and (ii) aircraft owned by the United States or any foreign country and constituting a part of the armed forces thereof.

I understand that the fraudulent use of this certificate to secure exemption will subject me and all parties making such fraudulent use of this certificate to a fine of not more than $10,000, or to imprisonment for not more than 5 years, or both, together with costs of prosecution. I also understand that I must be prepared to establish by satisfactory evidence the purpose for which the article was used.

(Signature) . . . . . . . . . . . . . . . . . . . . . . . . . . . . . . . . . . . . .

(Address) . . . . . . . . . . . . . . . . . . . . . . . . . . . . . . . . . . . . . . .

[Reg. § 48.4221-4.]

☐ [*T.D. 7536, 3-27-78.*]

### [Reg. § 48.4221-5]

**§ 48.4221-5. Tax-free sale of articles to States and local governments for their exclusive use.**—(a) *In general.*—An article (excluding an automobile subject to tax under section 4064) subject to tax under chapter 32 of the Code may be sold tax free by the manufacturer, pursuant to section 4221(a)(4) and this section, to a State or local

government for the exclusive use of such State or local government. See paragraph (b) of this section for the meaning of the term "State or local government." An article may be sold tax free by the manufacturer under this paragraph only in those cases where the sale is made directly to a State or local government for its exclusive use. Accordingly, no sale may be made tax free to a dealer for resale to a State or local government for its exclusive use, even though it is known at the time of sale by the manufacturer that the article will be so resold. A sale of an article to a State or local government for resale is not considered to be a sale for the "exclusive use" of the State or local government, within the meaning of section 4221(a)(4), and, therefore, such sales may not be made tax free. Such sales are not exempt regardless of whether the resales are made to government employees, or the fact that the article is an item of equipment the employee is required to possess in carrying out his duties. For example, pistols or revolvers may not be sold tax-free to a State or local government for resale to its police officers. See section 6416(b)(2)(C), and paragraph (b)(3) of §48.6416(b)-2, for the circumstances under which credit or refund of tax is available where tax-paid articles are sold for the exclusive use of a State or local government.

(b) *State or local government.*—The term "State or local government" includes any State, the District of Columbia, and any political subdivision of any of the foregoing.

(c) *Evidence required in support of tax-free sales to States or local governments.*—(1) The evidence required in support of a tax-free sale to the State or local government shall, except as provided in paragraph (c)(2) of this section, consist of a certificate, executed and signed by an officer or employee authorized by the State or local government to execute and sign the certificate. If it is impracticable to furnish a separate certificate for each order or contract because of a frequency of purchases, a certificate covering all orders between given dates (such period not to exceed 12 calendar quarters) will be acceptable. The certificates and proper records of invoices, orders, etc., relative to tax-free sales must be retained by the manufacturer as provided in section 6001 and the regulations thereunder. The certificates shall be in substantially the following form:

EXEMPTION CERTIFICATE

(For use by States and local governments (section 4221(a)(4) of the Internal Revenue Code.))

(Date) . . . . , 19 .

I hereby certify that I am . . . . (Title of Officer) of . . . . (State or local government) that I am authorized to execute this certificate; and that:

(Check applicable type of certificate)

. . the article or articles specified in the accompanying order, or on the reverse side hereof, (or) . . . . all orders placed by the purchaser for the period commencing (Date) . . . . . and ending (Date) . . . . (period not to exceed 12 calendar quarters), are, or will be, purchased from (Name of manufacturer) . . . . . . . . . . . . . . . . for the exclusive use of (Governmental unit) . . . . . . . . . . . . . . . of (State or local government) . . . . . . . . . . . . . . . . .

I understand that the exemption from tax in the case of sales of articles under this exemption certificate to a State, etc., is limited to the sale of articles purchased for its exclusive use. I understand that the fraudulent use of this certificate for the purpose of securing this exemption will subject me and all parties making such fraudulent use of this certificate to a fine of not more than $10,000, or to imprisonment for not more than 5 years, or both, together with costs of prosecution.

(Signature) . . . . . . . . . . . . . . . . . . . . . . . . . . . . . . . . .

(Address) . . . . . . . . . . . . . . . . . . . . . . . . . . . . . . . . .

(2) A purchase order, provided that all of the information required by paragraph (c)(1) of this section is included therein, is acceptable in lieu of a separate exemption certificate.

(d) *Resale of articles purchased tax free by a State or local government.*— If articles purchased tax free for the exclusive use of a State or local government are prior to use by the State or local government resold under circumstances that do not amount to an exclusive use by the State or local government (such as tires that are resold by a volunteer fire department to volunteer firemen), the parties responsible in the State or local government are required to inform the manufacturer, producer, or importer from whom the articles were purchased that they were disposed of in a manner that did not amount to an exclusive use by the State or local government. A willful failure to supply the manufacturer, producer, or importer with the information required by this subparagraph will subject responsible parties to the penalties provided by section 7203. [Reg. §48.4221-5.]

☐ [T.D. 7536, 3-27-78. *Amended by T.D. 8036, 7-23-85 and T.D. 8659, 3-13-96.*]

## [Reg. §48.4221-6]

**§48.4221-6. Tax-free sales of articles to nonprofit educational organizations.**—(a) *In general.*—An article (excluding an automobile subject to tax under section 4064) subject to tax under chapter 32 of the Code may be sold tax free by the manufacturer, pursuant to section 4221(a)(5) and this section, to a nonprofit educational organization for its exclusive use. See paragraph (b) of this section for the meaning of the term "nonprofit educational organization". An article may be sold tax free by the manufacturer under this paragraph only in those cases where the sale of an article by the manufacturer is made directly to a nonprofit educational organization for its exclusive use. Accordingly, no sale may be made tax free to a dealer for resale to a nonprofit educational organization for its exclusive use even though it is known at the time of sale by the manufacturer that the article will be so resold. See section 6416(b)(2)(D), and paragraph (b)(4) of §48.6416(b)-2, for the circumstances under which credit or refund of tax is available where tax-paid articles are sold for the exclusive use of a nonprofit educational organization.

(b) *Nonprofit educational organization.*—The term "nonprofit educational organization" means an organization described in section 170(b)(1)(A)(ii) that is exempt from income tax under section 501(a). Section 170(b)(1)(A)(ii) describes an "educational organization" as one that normally maintains a regular faculty and curriculum and normally has a regularly enrolled body of pupils or students in attendance at the place where its educational activities are regularly carried on. The term also includes a school operated as an activity of an organization described in section 501(c)(3) which is exempt from income tax under section 501(a), provided the primary function of such school is the presentation of formal instruction and provided such school normally maintains a regular faculty and curriculum and normally has a regularly enrolled body of pupils or students in

attendance at the place where its educational activities are regularly carried on.

(c) *Evidence required in support of tax-free sales to nonprofit educational organizations.*—Every nonprofit educational organization purchasing tax free under section 4221(a)(5) must furnish the following information to the seller:

(1) The exempt purpose for which the article or articles are being purchased, and

(2) Its registration number, and the district director's office that issued the registration number.

Such information must be in writing and may be noted on the purchase order or other document furnished by the purchaser to the seller in connection with each sale except that a single notification containing the information described in this paragraph may cover all sales by the seller to the purchaser made during a designated period not to exceed 12 successive calendar quarters. See paragraph (c) of §48.4221-1 for the evidence required to establish exemption. [Reg. §48.4221-6.]

☐ [T.D. 7536, 3-27-78. *Amended by T.D. 7686, 3-18-80 and T.D. 8036, 7-23-85.*]

## [Reg. §48.4221-7]

**§48.4221-7. Tax-free sales of tires and tubes.**—(a) *In general.*—A manufacturer of tires or inner tubes that are taxable under section 4071 may sell such articles tax free if the sale meets the conditions prescribed in section 4221(e)(2) and paragraph (a)(1) and (2) of this section. The following are conditions under which articles taxable under section 4071 may be sold tax free:

(1) The tire or tube is sold for use by the purchaser for sale on or in connection with the sale of another article manufactured or produced by the purchaser; and

(2) The other article is to be sold in a tax-free sale by the purchaser for export, for use as supplies for vessels or aircraft, to a State or local government for its exclusive use, or to a nonprofit educational organization for its exclusive use, or the other article is to be sold by the purchaser for any of such purposes in a sale which would be tax-free but for the fact that the other article is not subject to tax under chapter 32 of the Code.

See section 6416(b)(2)(F) and paragraph (b)(6) of §48.6416(b)-2 for the circumstances under which credit or refund of tax is available for tax-paid tires or tubes that are resold for the purposes described in this paragraph (a).

(b) *Registration requirements.*—In order to effect a tax-free sale under section 4221(e)(2)(A), both the manufacturer and purchaser (except for purchasers who are exempt from the registration requirement under §48.4222(b)-1) must be registered with the District Director of Internal Revenue as required in §48.4222(a)-1. At the time of sale, the registration number assigned to the purchaser by the district director together with the purpose for which the article was purchased must be shown on (or attached to) the invoice, purchase order, or other document used for the sale.

(c) *Proof required in support of tax-free sales of tires and tubes.*—(1) *Cessation of exemption.*—The exemption allowed under section 4221(e)(2)(A) and this section on the sale of a tire or inner tube shall cease to apply unless, within the 6-month period which begins on the date of the tax-free sale by the manufacturer of such article (or, if earlier, on the date of shipment by such manufacturer), the manufacturer receives proof from the purchaser that such article has been used on or in connection with the sale of another article which has been sold for one of the tax-exempt purposes referred to in paragraph (a)(2) of this section. If the manufacturer has not received the required information within such 6-month period, the temporary suspension of the liability for the payment of the tax ceases, and the manufacturer shall include the tax on the sale of the tire or inner tube in his return for the period in which the 6-month period expires. If the required information is received after the expiration of the 6-month period, the manufacturer may file a claim for credit or refund of tax so paid on his sale of the tire or inner tube.

(2) *Required information.*—The information which the manufacturer must receive within the 6-month period, referred to in paragraph (c)(1) of this section, shall be in substantially the following form:

STATEMENT OF MANUFACTURER'S VENDEE

(To support tax-free sales of tires or inner tubes by the manufacturer thereof for use on or in connection with the sale of another article (section 4221(e)(2) of the Internal Revenue Code))

(Date) . . . . . . . , 19

I certify that I, or the . . . . (Name of purchaser if other than undersigned), of which I am . . . . (Title) am/is in the business of selling . . . . (Products handled) and hold(s) certificate of registry No. . . . . issued by the District Director of Internal Revenue at . . . . . . . . ; and that the tires or inner tubes which were purchased or shipped on . . . . . . . , 19 , as specified on the back hereof, have been used on or in connection with the sale of . . . . (Products sold) by such undersigned

*Check one*

. . . . for export by . . . . (Name of carrier) to . . . . (Name of foreign country or U.S. possession) and was so exported on (Date) . . . . , 19 (A copy of the bill of lading or other proof of exportation is attached)

. . . . for use as supplies on . . . . (Name of vessel or aircraft) which is registered in . . . . (Name of country in which vessel or aircraft is registered)

. . . . . to . . . . (Name of State or local government)

. . . . . to . . . . (Name and address of the nonprofit educational organization).

I understand that the fraudulent use of this certificate for the purpose of substantiating the tax-free sale will subject me and all parties making such fraudulent use of this certificate to revocation of the privilege of purchasing articles tax free and to a fine of not more than $10,000 or to imprisonment for not more than 5 years, or both, together with costs of prosecution.

(Signature) . . . . . . . . . . . . . . . . . . . . . . . . . . . . . . . . .

(Address) . . . . . . . . . . . . . . . . . . . . . . . . . . . . . . .

[Reg. § 48.4221-7.]

☐ [T.D. 7536, 3-27-78.]

**[Reg. § 48.4221-8]**

**§ 48.4221-8. Tax-free sales of tires, tubes, and tread rubber used on intercity, local, and school buses.**—(a) *In general.*—Under section 4221(e)(5), the taxes imposed by section 4071(a)(1), (3) and (4) shall not apply to sales by a manufacturer, producer, or importer of tires of the type used on highway vehicles or inner tubes for tires sold for use by the purchaser on or in connection with a qualified bus, or to the sales by a manufacturer, producer, or importer of tread rubber sold for use by the purchaser in the recapping or retreading of any tire to be used by the purchaser on or in connection with a qualified bus if the requirements of this section are met.

(b) *Meaning of terms.*—(1) *Qualified bus.*—"Qualified bus" means an intercity, local or school bus.

(2) *Intercity or local bus.*—"Intercity or local bus" means any automobile bus which is used predominantly (more than 50 percent) in furnishing (for compensation) passenger land transportation available to the general public if such transportation is scheduled and along regular routes, or if the seating capacity of the bus is at least 20 adults (not including the driver). In determining predominant use, mileage travelled with passengers as well as mileage travelled incidental to such passenger transportation, such as "dead-heading", is counted. Under the first alternative, the size of the bus is not relevant for purposes of determining whether or not the use of the bus qualifies for the exemption. Under the second alternative, for non-scheduled bus operations, such as that provided by charter buses, the exemption is available only if the bus has a passenger seating capacity of at least 20 adults and the transportation is available to the general public. For purposes of determining whether the bus has a seating capacity of at least 20 adults, the bus driver is not included. Service is available to the general public if bus service is used in a passenger transportation business in which service is offered to more than a limited number of persons, groups, or organizations.

(3) *School bus.*—"School bus" means any automobile bus in which "substantially all" (85 percent or more) of the use involves transporting students and employees of a school. Incidental use (deadheading) of the school bus without passengers to or from a point to which students or employees of school are transported is considered to be a use which involves transporting students or employees of schools. A school is any educational organization which normally maintains a regular faculty and curriculum and normally has a regularly enrolled body of pupils or students in attendance at the place where its educational activities are carried on. Tax-exempt schools, taxable schools, and a private contractor who operates a bus for tax-exempt or a taxable school may qualify for the tax exemption if all the requirements of this section are met.

(b) *Registration requirements for tires, tubes, and tread rubber; vendees purchasing tax free.*—The provisions of section 4221(e)(5) do not apply with respect to any sale unless the manufacturer and the vendee are registered as required under section 4222, and unless they comply with all the requirements under that section relating to tax-free sales. See § 48.4222(a)-1. Persons not required to be registered under section 4222(b) may purchase articles tax free by following the same procedures that apply to them in the case of other tax-free sales. See § 48.4222(b)-1. A person's registration and right to sell or purchase articles tax free may be revoked or suspended as provided in § 48.4222(c).1. Such a revocation or suspension shall be in addition to any other penalties that may apply.

(c) *Cross reference.*—For credit or refund, see section 6416(b)(2).

(d) *Information; records.*—(1) *Information to be furnished to purchaser.*—A manufacturer selling tires, tubes, or tread rubber tax free under section 4221(e)(5) shall indicate to the purchaser that the purchaser is obtaining the tires or tubes tax free for the purpose of use on or in connection with a qualified bus, and that the purchaser is obtaining the tread rubber tax free for use in the recapping or retreading of tires to be used by the purchaser on or in connection with a qualified bus. The manufacturer may transmit this information by any convenient means, such as coding of sales invoices, provided that the information is presented with sufficient particularity so that the purchaser is informed that the purchaser has obtained the tires, tubes, and tread rubber tax free.

(2) *Records of manufacturer.*—A manufacturer selling tires, tubes, or tread rubber tax free under section 4221(e)(5) shall maintain in its records the identity of the purchaser, a signed statement of the exempt purpose for purchasing the tires, tubes, or tread rubber, and the quantity of tires, tubes, or tread rubber sold tax free to each purchaser.

(3) *Records of purchaser.*—A person purchasing tires, tubes, or tread rubber tax free under section 4221(e)(5) must maintain sufficient records to establish that the tires, tubes, or tread rubber purchased tax free has actually been used for that purpose.

(e) *Duty of selling manufacturer to ascertain validity of tax-free sale.*—The selling manufacturer is not relieved of liability under the provisions of section 4221(e)(5) by reason of section 4221(c) for the tax imposed by section 4061(b) if at the time of sale the selling manufacturer has knowledge or reason to believe that the tires, tubes, or tread rubber sold by it to the purchaser are not intended for use on an intercity, local, or school bus, or that the purchaser has failed to register, or that its registration has been revoked or suspended.

(f) *Effective date.*—Section 4221(e)(5) (relating to tires, tubes, and tread rubber) applies to sales on or after December 1, 1978. The sale of tires, tubes, or tread rubber sold prior to that date is not exempt from tax under section 4221(e)(5). [Reg. § 48.4221-8.]

□ [*T.D. 7834, 9-27-82. Redesignated as Reg. §48.4221-8 by T.D. 8659, 3-13-96.*]

**[Reg. §48.4222(a)-1]**

**§48.4222(a)-1. Registration.**—(a) *General rule.*—Except as provided in §48.4222(b)-1, tax-free sales under section 4221 may be made only if the manufacturer, first purchaser, and second purchaser, as the case may be, have been registered by the Internal Revenue Service.

(b) *Application instructions.*—Application for registration under section 4222 must be made in accordance with instructions for Form 637 (or such other form as the Commissioner may designate).

(c) *Evidence required in support of tax-free sales.*—See subparagraph (1) of §48.4221-1(c) for evidence required in support of tax-free sales to purchasers who are required to be registered.

(d) *Failure to register.*—If either the seller or purchaser is not registered as required by this section of the regulations, tax-free sales may not be made, except as indicated in §48.4222(b)-1.

(e) *Cross references.*—(1) For exceptions to the requirement for registration, see section 4222(b) and §48.4222(b)-1.

(2) For revocation or suspension of registration, see §48.4222(c)-1.

(3) For applicability of section 4222 and these regulations to exemptions provided by sections 4063(b), 4182(b), and 4293, see §48.4222(d)-1. [Reg. §48.4222(a)-1.]

□ [*T.D. 7536, 3-27-78. Amended by T.D. 8659, 3-13-96.*]

**[Reg. §48.4222(b)-1]**

**§48.4222(b)-1. Exceptions to the requirement for registration.**—(a) *State and local governments.*—The Internal Revenue Service will not register State or local governments under section 4222. To establish the right to sell articles tax free to a State or local government, the manufacturer must obtain the information described in §48.4221-5(c).

(b) *Sales or resales to foreign purchasers for export.*—Persons whose principal place of business is not within the United States may, but are not required to, register in order to purchase articles tax free for export. To establish the right to sell articles tax free for export to a purchaser who is not registered and who is located in a foreign country or a possession of the United States, the manufacturer must obtain the evidence required by paragraph (b) of §48.4221-3.

(c) *United States.*—Except as provided in paragraph (b) of §48.4222(d)-1 (relating to sales to the American Red Cross) the registration requirements of the regulations in this part do not apply to purchases and sales by the United States or any of its agencies or instrumentalities. The evidence required in support of such tax-free purchases and sales is a notation on the purchase order or other document furnished to the seller clearly indicating that the article or articles are being purchased tax free as authorized by Chapter 32 of the Code.

(d) *Supplies for vessels and aircraft.*—An article subject to an excise tax imposed by chapter 32 of the Code may be sold tax free by the manufacturer under the provisions of §48.4221-4 for use by the purchaser as supplies for a vessel or aircraft if both the manufacturer and the purchaser are registered under the provisions of §48.4222(a)-1. The article also may, on or after July 1, 1965, be sold tax free for such use even though neither the manufacturer nor the purchaser is so registered if the provisions of paragraph (d) of §48.4221-4 are satisfied. [Reg. §48.4222(b)-1.]

□ [*T.D. 7536, 3-27-78. Amended by T.D. 8659, 3-13-96 and T.D. 8879, 3-30-2000.*]

**[Reg. §48.4222(c)-1]**

**§48.4222(c)-1. Revocation or suspension of registration.**—The district director or the Director of International Operations, as the case may be, is authorized to revoke or temporarily suspend, upon written notice, the registration of any person and the right of such person to sell or purchase articles tax free under section 4221 of the Code in any case in which he finds that (1) the registrant is not a bona fide manufacturer, or a purchaser reselling direct to manufacturers or exporters;(2) the registrant is for some other reason not eligible under these regulations to retain a Certificate of Registry; (3) the registrant has used his registration to avoid the payment of any tax imposed by chapter 32 of the Code, or to postpone or interfere in any manner with the collection of such tax; (4) such revocation or suspension is necessary to protect the revenue; or (5) the registrant failed to comply with the requirements of paragraph (c) of §48.4222(a)-1, relating to

the evidence required to support a tax-free sale. The revocation or suspension of registration is in addition to any other penalty that may apply under the law for any act or failure to act. [Reg. §48.4222(c)-1.]

□ [*T.D. 7536, 3-27-78. Amended by T.D. 7753, 1-13-81 and T.D. 7882, 3-30-83.*]

**[Reg. §48.4222(d)-1]**

**§48.4222(d)-1. Registration in the case of certain other exemptions.**—The registration procedure set forth in §48.4222(a)-1 also applies in the following cases:

(a) Tax-free sales on or after March 10, 1980, under section 4064(b)(1) (C) (relating to emergency vehicles). Both the vendor and vendee (other than a State or local government) must be registered.

(b) Tax-free sales under section 4293 to any corporation created by Act of Congress to act in matters of relief under the treaty of Geneva of August 22, 1864 (American Red Cross) for its exclusive use. Both the vendor and the vendee must be registered. [Reg. §48.4222(d)-1.]

□ [*T.D. 7536, 3-27-78. Amended by T.D. 7834, 9-27-82; T.D. 8036, 7-23-85 and T.D. 8659, 3-13-96.*]

**[Reg. §48.4223-1]**

**§48.4223-1. Special rules relating to further manufacture.**—(a) *Purchasing manufacturer to be treated as the manufacturer.*—For purposes of chapter 32, a manufacturer or producer to whom an article is sold or resold tax free under section 4221(a)(1) of the Code for use by it in further manufacture shall be treated as the manufacturer or producer of such article. If a manufacturer who purchases an article tax free for further manufacture does not use the article for further manufacture, the sale of the article by it, or its use of the article other than in further manufacture, shall, for purposes of the taxes imposed by chapter 32 of the Code, be treated as a sale or use of the article by the manufacturer thereof. See paragraphs (b) and (c) of this section for determination of taxable sale price where an article purchased tax free for further manufacture is resold, or used other than in further manufacture.

(b) *Computation of tax.*—Except as provided in paragraph (c) of this section, the tax liability referred to in paragraph (a) of this section shall be based on the price for which the article was sold by the purchasing manufacturer, or, where the manufacturer uses the article for a purpose other than which it was purchased, the tax shall be based on the price at which such or similar articles are sold, in the ordinary course of trade by manufacturers, producers, or importers thereof. See section 4218(e) and §48.4218-5.

(c) *Election.*—(1) Instead of computing the tax as described under paragraph (b) of this section, the purchasing manufacturer who has incurred liability for tax on its sale or use of an article as provided by paragraph (a) of this section may compute the tax incurred under chapter 32 by using as the tax base either the price for which the article was sold to it by the first purchaser, if any, or the price for which such article was sold by the actual manufacturer, producer, or importer of such article. The purchasing manufacturer must have in its possession information upon which to substantiate such basis for tax. For purposes of this paragraph, the price for which the article was sold by the actual manufacturer or by the first purchaser shall be determined as provided in section 4216 and the regulations thereunder. However, such price shall not be adjusted for any discount, rebate, allowance, return, or repossession of a container or covering, or otherwise.

(2) The election under this paragraph shall be in the form of a statement attached to the return reporting the tax applicable to the sale or use of the article which gave rise to such tax liability. Such election, once made, may not be revoked. [Reg. §48.4223-1.]

□ [*T.D. 7536, 3-27-78.*]

**[Reg. §48.4225-1]**

**§48.4225-1. Exemption of articles manufactured or produced by Indians.**—The exemption provided under section 4225 applies to articles taxable under chapter 32 of the Code that are of native Indian handicraft and are manufactured or produced by Indians on Indian reservations or in Indian schools, or manufactured or produced by Indians who are under the jurisdiction of the United States Government in Alaska. For purposes of this section, Indians who reside on allotments of land adjacent to an Indian reservation and are subject to the supervision, control, and jurisdiction of the Bureau of Indian Affairs are considered to be "Indians on Indian reservations." [Reg. §48.4225-1.]

□ [*T.D. 7536, 3-27-78.*]

# Facilities and Services

See p. 20,601 for regulations not amended to reflect law changes

## [Reg. §49.0-1]

**§49.0-1. Introduction.**—The regulations in this part 49 are designated "Facilities and Services Excise Tax Regulations." The regulations relate to the taxes on communications and transportation by air imposed by chapter 33 of the Internal Revenue Code and the taxes on indoor tanning services imposed by section 5000B. See part 40 of this chapter for regulations relating to returns, payments, and deposits of these taxes. [Reg. §49.0-1.]

☐ [T.D. 8442, 10-21-92. Amended by T.D. 9621, 6-10-2013.]

## [Reg. §49.0-2]

**§49.0-2. General definitions and use of terms.**—As used in the regulations in this part, unless otherwise expressly indicated—

(a) The terms defined in the provisions of law contained in the regulations in this part shall have the meanings so assigned to them.

(b) The Internal Revenue Code of 1954 means the Act approved August 16, 1954 (68A Stat.), entitled "An Act to revise the internal revenue laws of the United States", as amended.

(c) District director means district director of internal revenue. The term also includes the Director of International Operations in all cases where the authority to perform the functions which may be performed by a district director has been delegated to the Director of International Operations.

(d) Calendar quarter means a period of 3 calendar months ending on March 31, June 30, September 30, or December 31. [Reg. §49.0-2.]

☐ [T.D. 6430, 12-3-59.]

| Taxable Service | Rate of tax Percent |
| --- | --- |
| General telephone service | 10 |
| Toll telephone service | 10 |
| Telegraph service | 10 |
| Teletypewriter exchange service | 10 |
| Wire mileage service | 10 |
| Wire and equipment service | 8 |

(b) *Amounts paid.*—The term "amounts paid" means the amounts collected for the communication services specified in paragraph (a) of this section, without regard to whether the charge therefor is paid or satisfied in money, service, or other valuable consideration. For additional provisions relating to the term "amounts paid" see the section of the regulations relating to the particular taxable service listed in paragraph (a) of this section.

(c) *Liability for, and return of, tax.*—The taxes imposed by section 4251 are payable by the person paying for the services rendered, and must be paid to the person rendering the services who is required to collect the tax and return and pay over the tax. [Reg. §49.4251-2.]

☐ [T.D. 6664, 7-15-63. Amended by T.D. 8442, 10-21-92.]

## [Reg. §49.4251-3]

**§49.4251-3. [Reserved].**

☐ [T.D. 6664, 7-15-63. Removed and reserved by T.D. 9849, 3-11-2019.]

## [Reg. §49.4251-4]

**§49.4251-4. Prepaid telephone cards.**—(a) *In general.*—In the case of communications services acquired by means of a prepaid telephone card (PTC), the face amount of the PTC is treated as an amount paid for communications services and that amount is treated as paid when the PTC is transferred by any carrier to any person that is not a carrier. This section provides rules for the application of the section 4251 tax to PTCs.

(b) *Definitions.*—The following definitions apply to this section:

*Carrier* means a telecommunications carrier as defined in 47 U.S.C. 153.

*Comparable PTC* means a currently available dollar card or tariffed unit card (other than a PTC transferred in bulk or under special circumstances, such as for promotional purposes) that provides the same type and amount of communications services as the PTC to which it is being compared.

*Dollar card* means a PTC the value of which is designated by the carrier in dollars (even if also designated in units of service), provided that the designated value is not less than the amount for which the PTC is expected to be sold to a holder.

*Holder* means a person that purchases other than for resale.

## [Reg. §49.4251-1]

**§49.4251-1. Imposition of tax.**—(a) *In general.*—Section 4251 imposes a tax on amounts paid for general telephone service; toll telephone service; telegraph service; teletypewriter exchange service; wire mileage service; and wire and equipment service. See §49.4251-2 for rate and application of tax.

(b) *Termination of tax on general telephone service.*—(1) Except as otherwise provided in subparagraph (2) of this paragraph, no tax is imposed on amounts paid on or after July 1, 1965, for general telephone service rendered on or after such date.

(2) In the case of amounts paid pursuant to bills rendered on or after July 1, 1965, for general telephone service for which no previous bill was rendered, no tax is imposed on that portion of the amount paid pursuant to such bill or bills as is attributable to general telephone service rendered subsequent to April 30, 1965. However, the tax applies to that portion of the amount paid pursuant to any such bill or bills as is attributable to general telephone service rendered prior to May 1, 1965. The tax also applies to amounts paid for general telephone service pursuant to bills rendered before July 1, 1965, without regard to when the payment is made or the service is rendered. [Reg. §49.4251-1.]

☐ [T.D. 6664, 7-15-63. Amended by T.D. 6694, 12-4-63 and T.D. 6753, 9-8-64.]

## [Reg. §49.4251-2]

**§49.4251-2. Rate and application of tax.**—(a) *Rate of tax.*—Tax is imposed on amounts paid for each of the following services rendered at the rate specified below:

*Prepaid telephone card (PTC)* means a card or similar arrangement that permits its holder to obtain a fixed amount of communications services by means of a code (such as a personal identification number (PIN)) or other access device provided by the carrier and to pay for those services in advance.

*Tariff* means a schedule of rates and regulations filed by a carrier with the Federal Communications Commission.

*Tariffed unit card* means a unit card that is transferred by a carrier—

(1) To a holder at a price that does not exceed the designated number of units on the PTC multiplied by the carrier's tariffed price per unit; or

(2) To a transferee reseller subject to a contractual or other arrangement under which the price at which the PTC is sold to a holder will not exceed the designated number of units on the PTC multiplied by the carrier's tariffed price per unit.

*Transferee* means the first person that is not a carrier to whom a PTC is transferred by a carrier.

*Transferee reseller* means a transferee that purchases a PTC for resale.

*Unit card* means a PTC other than a dollar card.

*Untariffed unit card* means a unit card other than a tariffed unit card.

(c) *Determination of face amount.*—(1) *Dollar card.*—The face amount of a dollar card is the designated dollar value.

(2) *Tariffed unit card.*—The face amount of a tariffed unit card is the designated number of units on the PTC multiplied by the tariffed price per unit.

(3) *Untariffed unit card.*—(i) *Transfer to holder.*—The face amount of an untariffed unit card transferred by a carrier to a holder is the amount for which the carrier sells the PTC to the holder.

(ii) *Transfer to transferee reseller.*—(A) *In general.*—The face amount of an untariffed unit card transferred by a carrier to a transferee reseller is at the option of the carrier—

(1) The highest amount for which the carrier sells a PTC that provides the same type and amount of communications services to a holder that ordinarily would not be expected to buy more than one such PTC at a time (if the carrier makes such sales on a regular and arm's-length basis) or the face amount of a comparable PTC (if

the carrier does not make such sales on a regular and arm's-length basis);

(2) 135 percent of the amount for which the carrier sells the PTC to the transferee reseller (including in that amount, in addition to any sum certain fixed at the time of the sale, any contingent amount per unit multiplied by the designated number of units on the PTC); or

(3) If the PTC is of a type that ordinarily is used entirely for domestic communications service, the maximum number of minutes of domestic communications service on the PTC multiplied by the applicable rate.

(B) *Applicable rate.*—The applicable rate under paragraph (c)(3)(ii)(A)(3) of this section with respect to a PTC is $0.30 reduced (but not below $0.20) by $0.01 for each full 20 minutes by which the maximum number of minutes of domestic communications service on the PTC exceeds 40 minutes.

(C) *Sales not at arm's length.*—In the case of a transfer of an untariffed unit card by a carrier to a transferee reseller otherwise than through an arm's-length transaction, the fair market retail value of the PTC shall be substituted for the amount determined in paragraph (c)(3)(ii)(A)(2) of this section.

(4) *Exclusion.*—The amount of any state or local tax imposed on the furnishing or sale of communications services that is separately stated in the bill or on the face of the PTC and the amount of any section 4251 tax separately stated in the bill or on the face of the PTC are disregarded in determining, for purposes of this paragraph (c), the amount for which a PTC is sold.

(d) *Liability for tax.*—(1) *In general.*—Under section 4251(d), the section 4251(a) tax is imposed on the transfer of a PTC by a carrier to a transferee. The person liable for the tax is the transferee. Except as provided in paragraph (d)(2) of this section, the person responsible for collecting the tax is the carrier transferring the PTC to the transferee. If a holder purchases a PTC from a transferee reseller, the amount the holder pays for the PTC is not treated as an amount paid for communications services and thus tax is not imposed on that payment.

(2) *Effect of statement that purchaser is a carrier.*—(i) *On transferor.*—A carrier that transfers a PTC to a purchaser is not responsible for collecting the tax if, at the time of transfer, the transferor carrier has received written notification from the purchaser that the purchaser is a carrier, and the transferor has no reason to believe otherwise. The notification to be provided by the purchaser is a statement, signed under penalties of perjury by a person with authority to bind the purchaser, that the purchaser is a carrier (as defined in paragraph (b) of this section). The statement is not required to take any particular form.

(ii) *On purchaser.*—If a purchaser that is not a carrier provides the notification described in paragraph (d)(2)(i) of this section to the carrier that transfers a PTC, the purchaser remains liable for the tax imposed on the transfer of the PTC.

(3) *Exemptions.*—Any exemptions available under section 4253 apply to the transfer of a PTC from a carrier to a holder. Section 4253 does not apply to the transfer of a PTC from a carrier to a transferee reseller.

(e) *Examples.*—The following examples illustrate the provisions of this section:

*Example 1. Unit card; sold to individual.* (i) On May 1, 2000, A, a carrier, sells a card it calls a prepaid telephone card at A's retail store to P, an individual, for P's use in making telephone calls. A provides P with a PIN. The value of the card is not denominated in dollars, but the face of the card is marked 30 minutes. The sales price is $9. A tariff has not been filed for the minutes on the card. The toll telephone service acquired by purchasing the card will be obtained by entering the PIN and the telephone number to be called.

(ii) Because P purchased from a carrier other than for resale, P is a holder. The card provides its holder, P, with a fixed amount of communications services (30 minutes of toll telephone service) to be obtained by means of a PIN, for which P pays in advance of obtaining service; therefore, the card is a PTC. Because the value of the PTC is not designated in dollars and a tariff has not been filed for the minutes on the PTC, the PTC is an untariffed unit card. Because it is transferred by the carrier to the holder, the face amount is the sales price ($9).

(iii) The card is a PTC; thus, under section 4251(d), the face amount is treated as an amount paid for communications services and that amount is treated as paid when the PTC is transferred from A to P. Accordingly, at the time of transfer, P is liable for the 3 percent tax imposed by section 4251(a). The amount of the tax is $0.27 (3% × the

$9 face amount). Thus, the total paid by P is $9.27, the $9 sales price plus $0.27 tax. A is responsible for collecting the tax from P.

*Example 2. Unit card; given to individual.* (i) The facts are the same as in Example 1, except that instead of selling a card, A gives a 30 minute card to P.

(ii) Although the card provides P with a fixed amount of communications services (30 minutes of toll telephone service) to be obtained by means of a PIN, P does not pay for the service. Therefore, the card is not a PTC, even though it is called a prepaid telephone card by A.

(iii) Because the card is not a PTC, section 4251(d) does not apply. Furthermore, no tax is imposed by section 4251(a) because no amount is paid for the communications services.

*Example 3. Unit card; adding value.* (i) After using the card described in Example 2, P arranges with A by telephone to have 30 minutes of toll telephone service added to the card. The sales price is $9. P is told to continue using the PIN provided with the card.

(ii) Because P purchased from a carrier other than for resale, P is a holder. The arrangement provides its holder, P, with a fixed amount of communications services (30 minutes of toll telephone service) to be obtained by means of a PIN, for which P pays in advance of obtaining service; therefore, the arrangement is a PTC. Because the value of the PTC is not designated in dollars and a tariff has not been filed for the minutes on the PTC, the PTC is an untariffed unit card. Because it is transferred by the carrier to the holder, the face amount is the sales price ($9).

(iii) The arrangement is a PTC; thus, under section 4251(d), the face amount is treated as an amount paid for communications services and that amount is treated as paid when the PTC is transferred from A to P. Accordingly, at the time of transfer, P is liable for the 3 percent tax imposed by section 4251(a). The amount of the tax is $0.27 (3% × the $9 face amount). Thus, the total paid by P is $9.27, the $9 sales price plus $0.27 tax. A is responsible for collecting the tax from P.

*Example 4. Dollar card; sold other than for resale.* (i) On May 1, 2000, B, a carrier, sells 100,000 cards it calls prepaid telephone cards to Q, an auto dealer, for $50,000. Q will give away a card to each person that visits Q's dealership. B provides Q with a PIN for each card. The face of each card is marked $3. The toll telephone service acquired by purchasing the card will be obtained by entering the PIN and the telephone number to be called.

(ii) Because Q purchased from a carrier other than for resale, Q is a holder. Each card provides its holder, Q, with a fixed amount of communications services ($3 of toll telephone service) to be obtained by means of a PIN, for which Q pays in advance of obtaining service; therefore, each card is a PTC even though Q's visitors do not pay for the cards. The value of each PTC is designated in dollars; therefore, each PTC is a dollar card. Because the PTC is a dollar card, the face amount is the designated dollar value ($3).

(iii) The cards are PTCs; thus, under section 4251(d), the face amount is treated as an amount paid for communications services and that amount is treated as paid when the PTCs are transferred from B to Q. Accordingly, at the time of transfer, Q is liable for the 3 percent tax imposed by section 4251(a). The amount of the tax is $9,000 (3% × the $3 face amount × 100,000 PTCs). Thus, the total paid by Q is $59,000, the $50,000 sales price plus $9,000 tax. B is responsible for collecting the tax from Q.

*Example 5. Tariffed unit card; sold to transferee reseller.* (i) On May 1, 2000, C, a carrier, sells 1,000 cards it calls prepaid telephone cards to R, a convenience store owner, for $7,000. C provides R with a PIN for each card. The value of the cards is not denominated in dollars, but the face of each card is marked 30 minutes and a tariff of $0.33 per minute has been filed for the minutes on each card. R agrees that it will sell the cards to individuals for their own use and at a price that does not exceed $0.33 per minute. R actually sells the cards for $9 each (that is, at a price equivalent to $0.30 per minute). The toll telephone service acquired by purchasing the card will be obtained by entering the PIN and the telephone number to be called.

(ii) Because R purchased from a carrier for resale, R is a transferee reseller. Because R's customers will purchase other than for resale, they will be holders. Each card sold by R provides its holder, R's customer, with a fixed amount of communications services (30 minutes of toll telephone service) to be obtained by means of a PIN provided by the carrier, for which R's customer pays in advance of obtaining service; therefore, each card is a PTC. Because the value of each PTC is not designated in dollars and C sells the PTCs to R subject to an arrangement under which the price at which the PTCs are sold to holders will not exceed the designated number of minutes on the PTC multiplied by C's tariffed price per minute, each PTC is a tariffed unit card. Because the PTCs are tariffed unit cards, the face amount of each PTC is $9.90, the designated number of minutes on the PTC multiplied by the tariffed price per minute (30 × $0.33), even though the retail sale price of each card is $9.

(iii) The cards are PTCs; thus, under section 4251(d), the face amount is treated as an amount paid for communications services and that amount is treated as paid when the PTC is transferred from C to R. Accordingly, at the time of transfer, R is liable for the 3 percent tax imposed by section 4251(a). The amount of the tax is $297 (3% × the $9.90 face amount × 1,000 PTCs). Thus, the total paid by R is $7,297, the $7,000 sales price plus $297 tax. C is responsible for collecting the tax from R.

*Example 6. Unit card; sold to transferee reseller.* (i) On May 1, 2000, D, a carrier, sells 10,000 cards it calls prepaid telephone cards to S, a convenience store owner, for $60,000. D provides S with a PIN for each card. The value of the cards is not denominated in dollars, but the face of each card is marked 30 minutes. A tariff has not been filed for the minutes on each card. S will sell the cards to individuals for their own use for $9 each. D also sells a card that provides 30 minutes of the same type of communications service at its retail store for $9. The toll telephone service acquired by purchasing the card will be obtained by entering the PIN and the telephone number to be called.

(ii) Because S purchased from a carrier for resale, S is a transferee reseller. Because S's customers will purchase other than for resale, they will be holders. Each card sold by S provides its holder, S's customer, with a fixed amount of communications services (30 minutes of toll telephone service) to be obtained by means of a PIN provided by the carrier, for which S's customer pays in advance of obtaining service; therefore, each card is a PTC. Because the value of each PTC is not designated in dollars and a tariff has not been filed for the minutes on the PTC, each PTC is an untariffed unit card.

(iii) The PTCs are untariffed unit cards transferred by the carrier to a transferee reseller. Thus, the face amount is determined under paragraph (c)(3)(ii) of this section, which permits D to choose from three alternative methods. Under paragraph (c)(3)(ii)(A)(1) of this section, the face amount of each PTC would be $9, the highest amount for which D sells to holders purchasing a single PTC. Alternatively, under paragraph (c)(3)(ii)(A)(2) of this section, the face amount of each PTC would be $8.10, computed as follows: 135% × the $60,000 sales price ÷ 10,000 PTCs. Finally, under paragraph (c)(3)(ii)(A)(3) of this section (assuming the PTCs are of a type that ordinarily is used entirely for domestic communications services), the face amount of each PTC would be $9 ($0.30 × 30 minutes).

(iv) The cards are PTCs; thus, under section 4251(d), the face amount is treated as an amount paid for communications services and that amount is treated as paid when the PTCs are transferred from D to S. Accordingly, at the time of transfer, S is liable for the 3 percent tax imposed by section 4251(a). Assuming that D chooses to determine the face amount as provided in paragraph (c)(3)(ii)(A)(2) of this section, the amount of the tax is $62,430 (3% × the $8.10 face amount × 10,000 PTCs). Thus, the total paid by S is $62,430, the $60,000 sales price plus $2,430 tax. D is responsible for collecting the tax from S.

*Example 7. Transfer of card that is not a PTC.* (i) On May 1, 2000, E, a carrier, provides a telephone card to T, an individual, for T's use in making telephone calls. E provides T with a PIN. The card provides access to an unlimited amount of communications services. E charges T $0.25 per minute of service, and bills T monthly for services used. The communications services acquired by using the card will be obtained by entering the PIN and the telephone number to be called.

(ii) Although the communications services will be obtained by means of a PIN, T does not receive a fixed amount of communications services. Also, T cannot pay in advance since the amount of T's payment obligation depends upon the number of minutes used. Therefore, the card is not a PTC.

(iii) Because the card is not a PTC, section 4251(d) does not apply. However, the 3 percent tax imposed by section 4251(a) applies to the amounts paid by T to E for the communications services. Accordingly, at the time an amount is paid for communications services, T is liable for tax. E is responsible for collecting the tax from T.

(f) *Effective date.*—This section is applicable with respect to PTCs transferred by a carrier on or after the first day of the first calendar quarter beginning after January 7, 2000. [Reg. § 49.4251-4.]

☐ [*T.D. 8855, 1-6-2000.*]

### [Reg. § 49.4252-1]

**§ 49.4252-1. [Reserved].**

☐ [*T.D. 6664, 7-15-63. Removed and reserved by T.D. 9849, 3-11-2019.*]

### [Reg. § 49.4252-2]

**§ 49.4252-2. Toll telephone service.**—(a) *In general.*—The term "toll telephone service" means any telephone or radio telephone message or conversation for which there is a toll charge, and the charge is paid within the United States. A toll charge is a charge made for such a message or conversation to a place beyond the local service area. For the meaning of the term "United States", see paragraph (d) of § 49.4252-4.

(b) *Amounts paid.*—(1) The tax in respect of toll telephone service is imposed on the total amount paid for the service, including any charge, in addition to the basic toll charge, made for "overtime" in connection with a telephone or radio telephone message or conversation.

(2) The tax attaches to the total charge made to a hotel or similar subscriber for toll telephone service furnished to the hotel or its guests, but no tax attaches to any charge made by the hotel for service rendered in placing the calls for its guests.

(c) *Cross reference.*—For provisions relating to toll telephone messages communicated through the use of coin-operated telephones, see section 4253 (a) and § 49.4253-1. For other provisions relating to toll telephone service. see § 49.4252-4. [Reg. § 49.4252-2.]

☐ [*T.D. 6664, 7-15-63.*]

### [Reg. § 49.4252-3]

**§ 49.4252-3. [Reserved].**

☐ [*T.D. 6664, 7-15-63. Removed and reserved by T.D. 9849, 3-11-2019.*]

### [Reg. § 49.4252-4]

**§ 49.4252-4. Provisions common to telephone and telegraph services.**—(a) *In general.*—The tax applies to all amounts paid for services rendered which are incidental to the transmission of a message or conversation. Where dispatches, messages, or conversations are transmitted by telephone, radiotelephone, telegraph, cable, or radio free of any charge whatsoever, no tax attaches, but where the carrier in fact makes some charge for the transmission, either in money, service, or other valuable consideration, such charge is subject to the tax upon the basis of the amount of the charge computed in money or money's worth. The tax is payable by the person paying the transmission charge and is to be collected by the person receiving the payment. If a message, dispatch, or conversation is transmitted "collect", the person who pays the charge therefor is liable for the tax. All telephone and telegraph transmission services when rendered for hire are subject to tax whether or not the agency furnishing such services is a common carrier. For provisions relating to the computation of tax with respect to charges for telephone and telegraph services, see section 4254 and § § 49.4254-1 and 49.4254-2.

(b) *When transmission begins and ends.*—Transmission begins when the message is delivered by the sender to the carrier, or its agent, and continues until receipt by the addressee or his agent. Thus, an amount paid to a telephone, telegraph, radio, or cable company for messenger service in bringing the recipient of a message to the telephone, or in delivering a dispatch or message, must be included in determining the total amount subject to tax. However, an amount paid for messenger service rendered by a hotel or similar establishment is not to be included in the total charge on which the tax is computed.

(c) *Services rendered under contract.*—(1) Except as an exemption may otherwise be specifically provided for in this part, where, under the provisions of a contract, dispatches, messages, or conversations are transmitted by telephone, radiotelephone, telegraph, cable, or radio in consideration of the payment of a lump sum of money or the performance of services, the amounts paid for such transmissions are subject to tax regardless of whether such dispatches, messages, or conversations relate to the operation of the business of a common carrier and whether they are "on line" or "off line".

(2) Where a telegraph company agrees to transmit over its wires dispatches or messages relating to the business of a carrier free or at reduced rates in consideration of services to be performed by the carrier in transporting men or materials of the telegraph company, all such dispatches or messages are subject to tax.

(d) *Meaning of the term "United States".*—For purposes of section 4252(b) and (c), the term "United States" includes the States and the District of Columbia. Such term also includes inland waters (such as rivers, lakes, bays, etc.) lying wholly within the United States, and, where an international boundary line divides inland waters, such parts of such inland waters as lie within the boundary of the United States, and also the waters known as a marine league from low tide on the coast line. Ships within these limits whether of foreign or domestic registry are considered to be within the United States.

(e) *Exemptions.*—For exemptions from the taxes imposed on amounts paid for telephone and telegraph services, see sections 4253, 4292, 4293, and 4294, and the regulations thereunder contained in this part. [Reg. § 49.4252-4.]

☐ [*T.D. 6664, 7-15-63.*]

### [Reg. § 49.4252-5]

**§ 49.4252-5. Teletypewriter exchange service.**—(a) *In general.*—The term "teletypewriter exchange service" means any service where a teletypewriter (or similar device) may be connected, directly or indirectly, to an exchange operated by a person engaged in the business of furnishing communication service, if by means of such connection communication may be established with any other teletypewriter (or similar device). If the teletypewriter or similar device used in conjunction with such service may be connected to such an exchange, the service constitutes teletypewriter exchange service whether or not it is the practice of the subscriber to the service to make such connection, and whether or not the person engaged in the business of furnishing communication service permits the subscriber to make such connection.

(b) *Amounts paid.*—In determining the amount of tax due, the amount paid for the service shall include all charges made in connection with the furnishing of any teletypewriter exchange service, such as salaries of operators, if in the employ of the person furnishing such service, charges for equipment, instruments, and other apparatus. In cases where a person leases lines or channels, equipment, and other facilities used in conjunction with teletypewriter exchange service, the amounts paid by such person for such lines or channels, equipment, and other facilities constitute amounts paid for teletypewriter exchange service, notwithstanding the fact that the lines or channels, equipment, and other facilities used in conjunction with such service are supplied by different persons or in part by the user of such service.

(c) *Exemptions.*—For exemptions from the tax imposed on amounts paid for teletypewriter exchange service, see sections 4253, 4292, 4293, and 4294, and the regulations thereunder contained in this part. [Reg. § 49.4252-5.]

☐ *[T.D. 6664, 7-15-63.]*

### [Reg. § 49.4253-1]

**§ 49.4253-1. Exemption for certain coin-operated service.**—(a) *In general.*—Except as provided in paragraph (b) of this section, the tax imposed on amounts paid for general telephone service is not applicable to a single telephone conversation paid for by inserting coins in a public coin-operated telephone. The tax imposed on amounts paid for toll telephone service or telegraph service is not applicable to a single telephone conversation for which a toll charge is made (see paragraph (a) of § 49.4252-2), or to a telegraph message, if the charge for such toll telephone service (including any additional charge for overtime) or telegraph service is less than 25 cents and is paid for by inserting coins in a public coin-operated telephone.

(b) *Exception where service furnished for a guaranteed amount.*— Where a coin-operated telephone service is furnished for a guaranteed amount, the amount paid under such guarantee plus any fixed monthly or other periodic charge is subject to the tax imposed on amounts paid for general telephone service. The tax applies to the full amount of the guarantee whether such amount is paid out of receipts from the coin-box of the telephone or from funds of the subscriber. [Reg. § 49.4253-1.]

☐ *[T.D. 6664, 7-15-63.]*

### [Reg. § 49.4253-2]

**§ 49.4253-2. Exemption for news services.**—(a) *In general.*—The exemption for news services provided by section 4253(b) is applicable to payments for services of the kind listed in section 4251, except general telephone service. The exemption will apply only with respect to payments for services which are utilized exclusively:

(1) In the collection of news for the public press or radio or television broadcasting or in the dissemination of news through the public press or by means of radio or television broadcasting; or

(2) In the collection or dissemination of news by a news ticker service furnishing a general news service similar to that of the public press.

For the exemption to apply, the charge for the services must be billed in writing to the person paying for the services and such person must certify in writing that the services are so utilized.

(b) *Scope of the exemption.*—(1) The exemption applies to amounts charged for messages from any newspaper, press association, radio or television news broadcasting agency, or news ticker service, to any other newspaper, press association, radio or television news broadcasting agency, or news ticker service, or to or from their bona fide correspondents, which messages deal exclusively with the collection of news items for, or the dissemination of news items through, the public press, radio or television broadcasting, or a news ticker service furnishing a general news service similar to that of the public press.

The exemption does not extend to messages of an administrative nature such as messages transmitting funds to correspondents, messages to correspondents relating to assignments or hotel accommodations, etc.

(2) The exemption does not extend to the collection and dissemination of information or matters for publication in magazines, periodicals, and trade and scientific publications issued to supply information on certain subjects of interest to particular groups; or to amounts paid by newspapers, press associations, radio or television news broadcasting agencies or networks, or news ticker services, for general telephone service taxable under section 4251. [Reg. § 49.4253-2.]

☐ *[T.D. 6664, 7-15-63.]*

### [Reg. § 49.4253-3]

**§ 49.4253-3. Exemption for certain organizations.**—(a) *The American National Red Cross.*—The taxes imposed by section 4251 do not apply to amounts paid for services furnished to the American National Red Cross.

(b) *International organizations.*—The taxes imposed by section 4251 do not apply to amounts paid for services furnished to an international organization. See section 7701(a)(18) for the definition of "international organization". An international organization is designated as such by the President of the United States through an Executive order or orders. When an organization has been designated by the President as entitled to enjoy the privileges, exemptions, and immunities conferred by the International Organizations Immunities Act, or part thereof, including exemption from tax, the exemption applies to the taxes imposed by section 4251 on amounts paid for services unless the President otherwise provides. The exemption is subject to withdrawal or revocation by the President. In case of withdrawal or revocation, unless otherwise provided by the President, the exemption is inapplicable to payments made on or after the date of issuance of the order of withdrawal or the date of revocation.

(c) *Exemption certificate.*—(1) No exemption certificate is required under this section where the payment for the services furnished is made by the American National Red Cross direct to the person furnishing the services. In all other cases the right to exemption under section 4253(c) shall be evidenced by properly executed exemption certificates in substantially the following form:

EXEMPTION CERTIFICATE

. . . . (Date) 19 .

I certify that . . . . . . . . . . (Name of service) have been furnished by . . . . . . . . . . . (Telephone, telegraph company, etc.) to . . . . . . . . . . . (International Organization, etc.); that the charges of $ . . . . . will be paid from . . . . . . . . . . . (International Organization, etc.) funds; and that the charges are exempt from tax under section 4253(c) of the Internal Revenue Code.

. . . . . . . . . .

(Signature of Officer or Employee)

. . . . . . . . . .

(Address) (Title)

NOTE: Penalty for fraudulent use, $10,000 or imprisonment, or both.

(2) See § 49.4253-11 for further provisions relating to exemption certificates. [Reg. § 49.4253-3.]

☐ *[T.D. 6664, 7-15-63.]*

### [Reg. § 49.4253-4]

**§ 49.4253-4. Exemption for servicemen in combat zone.**—(a) *In general.*—The exemption provided by section 4253(d) is applicable to any payment received for any telephone or radio telephone message or call which originates within a combat zone, as defined in section 112, from a member of the Armed Forces of the United States performing service in such combat zone, if a properly executed certificate of exemption substantially in the form shown in paragraph (c) of this section is furnished to the person receiving such payment.

(b) *Service in combat zone.*—Service is performed in a combat zone only if it is performed in an area which the President of the United States has designated by Executive order, for the purpose of section 112, as an area in which Armed Forces of the United States are or have engaged in combat, and only if it is performed on or after the date designated by the President by Executive order as the date of the commencing of combatant activities in such zone and on or before the date designated by the President by Executive order as the date of the termination of combatant activities in such zone.

(c) *Exemption certificate.*—(1) The exemption certificate shall be in substantially the following form:

## EXEMPTION CERTIFICATE
### (Overseas Telephone Calls)

. . . . . . . . . . . . . . . . . . . . . . . . . . . . . . . . . . . . . . . . (Date) 19 . . . .

I certify that the toll charges of $ . . . . . are for telephone or radio telephone messages originating at . . . . . . . . . . (Point of origin) within a combat zone from . . . . . . . . . . (Name) a member of the Armed Forces of the United States performing service in such combat zone; that the transmission facilities were furnished by . . . . . . . . . . (Name of carrier); and that the charges are exempt from tax under section 4253(d) of the Internal Revenue Code.

. . . . . . . . . . . . . . . . . . . . . . . . . . . . . . . . . . . . .

(Signature of Subscriber)

. . . . . . . . . . . . . . . . . . . . . . . . . . . . . . . . . . . . .

(Address)

NOTE: Penalty for fraudulent use, $10,000 or imprisonment or both.

(2) See §49.4253-11 for further provisions relating to exemption certificates. [Reg. §49.4253-4.]

☐ [*T.D.* 6664, 7-15-63.]

### [Reg. §49.4253-5]

**§49.4253-5. Exemption for items otherwise taxed.**—A dispatch, message, or conversation transmitted by toll telephone, telegraph, or teletypewriter exchange over the combined facilities of several lines or stations of one or more persons is considered to be one dispatch, message, or conversation, and is subject to only one payment of tax under section 4251. [Reg. §49.4253-5.]

☐ [*T.D.* 6664, 7-15-63.]

### [Reg. §49.4253-6]

**§49.4253-6. Exemption for common carriers and communications companies.**—(a) *In general.*—(1) The taxes imposed by section 4251 on amounts paid for wire mileage service and wire and equipment service do not apply to amounts paid for any such services to the extent that the amounts paid are for services utilized by a common carrier, telephone or telegraph company, or television or radio broadcasting station or network in the conduct of its business as such.

(2) The tax imposed by section 4251 on amounts paid for general telephone service does not apply to amounts paid for the use of a continuous telephone or radio telephone line or channel to the extent that the amounts paid are for use by a common carrier, telephone or telegraph company, or television or radio broadcasting station or network in the conduct of its business as such, if such line or channel connects stations between any two of which there would otherwise be a toll charge. A line or channel connects stations between which there would otherwise be a toll charge if the telephone company makes a toll charge for a single message transmitted between the two stations in the case of the ordinary residential and business or commercial telephone service. A line or channel connecting two stations is considered a continuous line or channel if such line or channel does not connect with any switchboard interposed between the two stations, which makes it possible to carry on two or more independent conversations simultaneously. Where a line or channel connects with such a switchboard, the exemption is inapplicable to so much of the amount paid as is attributable to the portion of the line or channel which extends from a station to a switchboard located in the same local service area.

(b) *Exemption inapplicable.*—This particular exemption is not applicable in the case of the taxes imposed on amounts paid for other services by section 4251, even though such services are utilized by the companies described in the conduct of their business as such. [Reg. §49.4253-6.]

☐ [*T.D.* 6664, 7-15-63.]

### [Reg. §49.4253-7]

**§49.4253-7. Exemption for installation charges.**—(a) *In general.*— The taxes imposed by section 4251 do not apply to any amount paid as is properly attributable to the installation of any instrument, wire, pole, switchboard, apparatus, or equipment.

(b) *Maintenance charges subject to tax.*—The exemption provided by section 4253(g) and paragraph (a) of this section is applicable only to amounts paid for installation. Amounts paid for the repair or replacement of instruments, wires, poles, switchboards, apparatus, or equipment, incidental to ordinary maintenance, are subject to tax. [Reg. §49.4253-7.]

☐ [*T.D.* 6664, 7-15-63.]

### [Reg. §49.4253-8]

**§49.4253-8. [Reserved].**

☐ [*T.D.* 6664, 7-15-63. *Removed and reserved by T.D. 9849, 3-11-2019.*]

### [Reg. §49.4253-9]

**§49.4253-9. [Reserved].**

☐ [*T.D.* 6664, 7-15-63. *Removed and reserved by T.D. 9849, 3-11-2019.*]

### [Reg. §49.4253-10]

**§49.4253-10. Exemption for certain private communications services.**—(a) *In general.*—The tax imposed by section 4251 on amounts paid for general telephone service does not apply to amounts paid for any such service furnished on or after January 1, 1963, to the extent that the amounts paid are for use of any telephone or radio telephone line or channel (including equipment, instruments, and other apparatus furnished exclusively for use in connection with the line or channel) in the conduct of a trade or business when such line or channel is furnished between specified locations in different States or between specified locations in different counties, municipalities, or similar political subdivisions of a State. The term "trade or business" as used in this section includes activities of organizations which are conducted with no purpose of gain or profit. A line or channel is considered to be furnished between specified locations only when the line or channel connects preselected points without the use of switching functions performed by a communications company exchange. Where an amount is paid which includes a charge for such a line or channel and also a charge for the service provided by means of switching functions performed by a communications company exchange, the exemption is applicable only to that portion of the amount so paid as is attributable to such a line or channel. The preselected points must be located in different States or in different counties or municipalities of the same State. If the preselected points are located in a State in which the political subdivisions are not denominated as counties or municipalities, then the preselected points must be in different political subdivisions of such State which correspond to counties or municipalities. For purposes of this paragraph the term "municipality" means the largest political subdivision of a State below the level of county or similar subdivision. For the exemption to apply, the charge for the service must be billed in writing to the person paying for the service and such person must certify in writing that the service is for use in the conduct of a trade or business.

(b) *Exemption inapplicable.*—This particular exemption is not applicable in the case of taxes imposed on amounts paid for other services by section 4251, even though such services are utilized in the conduct of a trade or business. [Reg. §49.4253-10.]

☐ [*T.D.* 6664, 7-15-63.]

### [Reg. §49.4253-11]

**§49.4253-11. Use and retention of exemption certificates.**—A separate exemption certificate(as required by §§49.4253-3 and 49.4253-4) shall be furnished for each message paid for as a separate item, but where periodic payments are made, a blanket certificate (for a period not to exceed four calendar quarters) may be accepted as evidence of the right to exemption. An agent of a telegraph, telephone, radio, or cable company should not accept an exemption certificate unless satisfied, on the basis of proper credentials or otherwise, that the person who signed it is the person whom he represents himself to be and that the exemption claimed is allowable under the law. Exemption certificates should be retained with the record of the services rendered for inspection by internal revenue officers as provided in section 6001 and the regulations in Subpart G of this part. [Reg. §49.4253-11.]

☐ [*T.D.* 6664, 7-15-63.]

### [Reg. §49.4253-12]

**§49.4253-12. Cross reference.**—For exemptions applicable to amounts received as payment for services furnished to the government of any State or political subdivision of a State, to the District of Columbia, to the government of the United States, or to certain nonprofit educational organizations, see sections 4292, 4293, and 4294, and the regulations thereunder contained in Subpart F of this part. [Reg. §49.4253-12.]

☐ [*T.D.* 6664, 7-15-63.]

**[Reg. §49.4254-1]**

**§49.4254-1. Computation of tax.**—(a) *General rule.*—Except as provided in paragraph (b) of this section, when a bill is rendered to the taxpayer covering charges for general telephone service, toll telephone service, or telegraph service, with respect to which a tax is imposed by section 4251, the amount upon which the tax with respect to such services shall be based shall be the sum of all such charges for such services included in the bill.

(b) *Special rule in certain cases.*—When a bill is rendered to the taxpayer covering charges for general telephone service, toll telephone service, or telegraph service, with respect to which a tax is imposed by section 4251, by a person who groups individual items for purposes of rendering the bill and computing the tax, then the amount on which the tax with respect to each such group shall be based shall be the sum of all items within that group, and the tax on remaining items not included in any such group shall be based on the charge for each item separately. [Reg. §49.4254-1.]

☐ [*T.D. 6664, 7-15-63.*]

**[Reg. §49.4254-2]**

**§49.4254-2. Payment for toll telephone service or telegraph service in coin-operated telephones.**—Where the tax on a toll telephone or radio telephone message or conversation, or a telegraph, cable, or radio dispatch or message is paid by inserting coins in a coin-operated telephone, the tax shall be computed to the nearest multiple of 5 cents, and where the tax is midway between multiples of 5 cents, the next highest multiple shall apply. In other words, one-half or a greater fraction of 5 cents shall be treated as 5 cents and a smaller fraction shall be ignored. [Reg. §49.4254-2.]

☐ [*T.D. 6664, 7-15-63.*]

**[Reg. §49.4261-1]**

**§49.4261-1. Imposition of tax; in general.**—(a) *In general.*—Section 4261 of the Internal Revenue Code (Code) imposes three separate taxes on amounts paid for certain transportation of persons by air. Tax attaches at the time of payment for any transportation taxable under section 4261. The applicability of each section 4261 tax is generally determined on a flight-by-flight basis.

(1) *Percentage tax.*—Section 4261(a) imposes a 7.5 percent tax on the amount paid for the taxable transportation of any person. *See* section 4262(a) of the Code and §49.4262-1(a) for the definition of the term *taxable transportation*.

(2) *Domestic segment tax.*—Section 4261(b)(1) imposes a $3 tax (indexed annually for inflation pursuant to section 4261(e)(4)) on the amount paid for each domestic segment of taxable transportation. *See* section 4261(b)(2) for the definition of the term *domestic segment*. The domestic segment tax does not apply to a domestic segment beginning or ending at an airport that is a rural airport for the calendar year in which the segment begins or ends (as the case may be). *See* section 4261(e)(1)(B) for the definition of the term *rural airport*.

(3) *International travel facilities tax.*—Section 4261(c) imposes a $12 tax (indexed annually for inflation pursuant to section 4261(e)(4)) on any amount paid (whether within or without the United States) for any transportation by air that begins or ends in the United States. The international travel facilities tax does not apply to any transportation that is entirely taxable under section 4261(a) (determined without regard to sections 4281 and 4282). *See* section 4261(c)(2). A special rule applies to Alaska and Hawaii flights. *See* section 4261(c)(3).

(b) *Payment and collection obligations.*—(1) *In general.*—The taxes imposed by section 4261 are collected taxes. In general, the person making the payment subject to tax is the *taxpayer*. *See* section 4261(d). The person receiving the payment is the *collector* (also commonly referred to as the collecting agent). *See* section 4291 of the Code. The collector must collect the applicable tax from the taxpayer, report the tax on Form 720, *Quarterly Federal Excise Tax Return*, and remit the tax to the Internal Revenue Service. *See* sections 4291, 6011, and 7501 of the Code. *See* §40.6011(a)-1 of this chapter and §49.4291-1. The collector must also make semimonthly deposits of the taxes imposed by section 4261. *See* section 6302(e) of the Code. *See* §§40.0-1(c), 40.6302(c)-1, and 40.6302(c)-3 of this chapter. *See* section 4263(a) and (c) of the Code for special rules relating to the payment and collection of tax.

(2) *Failure to collect tax.*—If any tax imposed by section 4261 is not paid at the time payment for transportation is made, then, to the extent the tax is not collected under any other provision of subchapter C of chapter 33 of the Code, the tax must be paid by the carrier providing the initial segment of transportation that begins or ends in the United States. *See* section 4263(c). *See* section 6672 of the Code for rules relating to the application of the trust fund recovery penalty.

(c) *Type of aircraft.*—The taxes imposed by section 4261 generally apply regardless of the type of aircraft on which the transportation is provided, provided all of the other conditions for liability are present and no specific statutory exemption applies. *See* paragraph (f) of this section for a list of statutory exemptions from tax. Amounts paid for the transportation of persons by air cushion vehicles, also known as hovercraft, are not subject to the taxes imposed by section 4261.

(d) *Purpose of transportation.*—The purpose of the transportation (for example, business or pleasure) is not a factor in determining taxability under section 4261.

(e) *Routes.*—Amounts paid for transportation may be taxable even if the transportation is not between two definite points. Unless otherwise exempt, a payment for continuous transportation that begins and ends at the same point is subject to tax. *See* section 4281 of the Code and §49.4281-1 for the exemption for small aircraft on nonestablished lines.

(f) *Exemptions from tax; cross-references.*—(1) *Aircraft management services.*—For the exemption for certain aircraft management services, see section 4261(e)(5) of the Code and §49.4261-10.

(2) *Hard minerals, oil, and gas.*—For the exemption for certain uses related to the exploration, development, or removal of hard minerals, oil, or gas, see section 4261(f)(1).

(3) *Trees and logging operations.*—For the exemption for certain uses related to trees and logging operations, see section 4261(f)(2).

(4) *Air ambulances.*—For the exemption for air ambulances providing certain emergency medical transportation, see section 4261(g).

(5) *Skydiving.*—For the exemption for certain skydiving uses, see section 4261(h).

(6) *Seaplanes.*—For the exemption for certain seaplane segments, see section 4261(i).

(7) *Fractionally-owned aircraft.*—For the exemption for certain aircraft in fractional ownership aircraft programs, see section 4261(j).

(8) *Small aircraft on nonestablished lines.*—For the exemption for certain small aircraft on nonestablished lines, see section 4281 of the Code and §49.4281-1.

(9) *Affiliated groups.*—For the exemption for certain transportation of members of an affiliated group, see section 4282.

(10) *United States and territories.*—For exemptions authorized by the Secretary of the Treasury or his delegate for the exclusive use of the United States, see section 4293.

(g) *Applicability date.*—This section applies to amounts paid on and after January 19, 2021. For rules that apply before that date, see 26 CFR part 49, revised as of April 1, 2020. [Reg. §49.4261-1.]

☐ [*T.D. 6618, 11-13-62. Amended by T.D. 6694, 12-4-63, T.D. 6753, 9-8-64 and T.D. 9948, 1-14-2021.*]

**[Reg. §49.4261-2]**

**§49.4261-2. Application of tax.**—(a) *Tax on total amount paid.*—The tax imposed by section 4261(a) of the Internal Revenue Code (Code) is measured by the total amount paid for taxable transportation, whether paid in cash or in kind.

(b) *Tax on transportation of each person.*—The taxes imposed by section 4261(b) and (c) of the Code are head taxes and, therefore, apply on a per-passenger basis. The taxes apply to each passenger for whom an amount is paid, regardless of whether the payment is made as a single lump sum or is made individually for each passenger. In the case of charter flights for which a fixed amount is paid, the section 4261(b) and

(c) *Charges for nontransportation services.*—Where a payment covers charges for nontransportation services as well as for transportation of a person, such as charges for meals, hotel accommodations, etc., the charges for the nontransportation services may be excluded in computing the tax payable with respect to such payment, provided such charges are separable and are shown in the exact amounts thereof in the records pertaining to the transportation charge. If the charges for nontransportation services are not separable from the charge for transportation of the person, the tax must be computed upon the full amount of the payment.

(d) *Applicability date.*—Paragraphs (a) and (b) of this section apply to amounts paid on and after January 19, 2021. For rules that apply before that date, *see* 26 CFR part 49, revised as of April 1, 2020. [Reg. §49.4261-2.]

☐ [*T.D. 6430, 12-3-59. Amended by T.D. 6518, 12-21-60, T.D. 6618, 11-14-62 and T.D. 9948, 1-14-2021.*]

**[Reg. §49.4261-3]**

**§49.4261-3. Payments made within the United States.—**
(a) *Transportation beginning and ending in the United States or the 225-mile zone.*—The taxes imposed by section 4261(a) and (b) of the Internal Revenue Code (Code) applies to payments made within the United States for transportation which begins in the United States or in the 225-mile zone and ends in the United States or in the 225-mile zone. For example, an amount paid within the United States for transportation between New York and Montreal, Canada; between Vancouver, Canada, and Windsor, Canada; or between Nogales, Mexico, and Hermosillo, Mexico, would be fully taxable under section 4261(a) and (b). See section 4262(c)(2) and paragraph (b) of §49.4262-3 for the definition of the term "225-mile zone."

(b) *Other transportation.*—In the case of transportation, other than that described in paragraph (a) of this section, for which payment is made in the United States, the taxes imposed by section 4261(a) and (b) apply with respect to the amount paid for that portion of such transportation by air which is directly or indirectly from one port or station in the United States to another port or station in the United States, but only if such portion is not a part of uninterrupted international air transportation within the meaning of section 4262(c)(3) of the Code and §49.4262-3(c). Transportation that:

(1) Begins in the United States or the 225-mile zone and ends outside such area,

(2) Begins outside the United States or the 225-mile zone and ends inside such area, or

(3) Begins outside the United States and ends outside such area, is taxable only with respect to the portion of the transportation by air which is directly or indirectly from one port or station in the United States to another port or station in the United States, but only if such portion is not a part of "uninterrupted international air transportation" within the meaning of section 4262(c)(3) and §49.4262-3(c). Thus, on a trip by air from Chicago to London, England, with a stopover at New York, for which payment is made in the United States, if the portion from Chicago to New York is not a part of "uninterrupted international air transportation" within the meaning of section 4262(c)(3) and §49.4262-3(c), the taxes would apply to the part of the payment which is applicable to the transportation from Chicago to New York. However, if the portion from Chicago to New York is a part of "uninterrupted international air transportation" within the meaning of section 4262(c)(3) and §49.4262-3(c), the taxes would not apply.

(c) *Method of computing tax on taxable portion.*—Where a payment is made for transportation which is partially taxable under paragraph (b) of this section, the tax imposed by section 4261(a) may be computed on that proportion of the total amount paid which the mileage of the taxable portion of the transportation bears to the mileage of the entire trip.

(d) *Cross reference.*—See section 4262(b) of the Code and §49.4262-2 for a partial exclusion with respect to amounts paid for certain transportation.

(e) *Applicability date.*—This section applies to amounts paid on and after January 19, 2021. For rules that apply before that date, *see* 26 CFR part 49, revised as of April 1, 2020. [Reg. §49.4261-3.]

☐ [T.D. 6430, 12-3-59. *Amended by T.D.* 6618, 11-14-62 *and T.D.* 9948, 1-14-2021.]

**[Reg. §49.4261-4]**

**§49.4261-4. Payments made within the United States; evidence of nontaxability.**—(a) *Presumption of taxability.*—The tax imposed by section 4261 of the Internal Revenue Code (Code) shall apply to any amount paid within the United States for the transportation of any person, unless the taxpayer establishes in accordance with the provisions of this section that at the time of payment the transportation is not transportation in respect of which tax is imposed by section 4261 (see section 4263(d) of the Code).

(b) *Through tickets.*—In the case of transportation which is wholly or in part not taxable transportation, the issuance of one ticket (commonly known as a "through ticket") covering such transportation will be sufficient to establish that the amount paid for such transportation is wholly or in part not subject to tax. Thus, if A purchases a through ticket in the United States for transportation by air which begins before November 16, 1962, from Chicago to Edmonton, Canada, with a stopover at Minneapolis, no further evidence will be required to establish that no tax applies with respect to the amount paid for the portion of transportation between Minneapolis and Edmonton. A similar result will be reached if a through ticket is purchased for the same air transportation which begins after November 15, 1962, and the trip is not "uninterrupted international air transportation" within the meaning of section 4262(c)(3) and

paragraph (c) of §49.4262-3. See paragraph (d) of this section for the information to be inscribed on all tickets issued for uninterrupted international air transportation.

(c) *Separate tickets.*—Where a separate ticket or order is issued for taxable transportation as defined in section 4262(a)(1) (referred to in this subpart as the "domestic ticket or order"), but the domestic ticket or order is to be used in conjunction with a ticket or order for additional transportation (referred to in this subpart as the "international ticket or order") which changes the tax consequences, unless the domestic ticket or order and the international ticket or order are purchased from a single agency or carrier at the same time, the person making payment for the domestic ticket or order shall at the time of payment exhibit the international ticket or order to the agency or carrier receiving such payment. The agency or carrier which receives the payment for the domestic ticket or order shall inscribe the tickets or orders for the entire journey in the following manner:

(1) The international ticket or order shall be inscribed or stamped with an appropriate legend (for example, "Cannot be reused to obtain any tax exemption on a domestic ticket or order") to show that a domestic ticket or order has been purchased wholly or partially tax free for use in conjunction therewith.

(2) The domestic ticket or order shall be inscribed to show (i) the identity of the agency or carrier which received payment therefor (unless otherwise shown on the ticket or order), (ii) the origin and destination of the additional transportation, (iii) the identity of the carrier furnishing the additional transportation, and (iv) the serial number of the ticket or order covering such additional transportation. If the domestic ticket or order is not large enough to accommodate the prescribed inscription, a statement setting forth the required information shall be attached to such ticket or order.

(d) *Tickets issued for uninterrupted international air transportation.*—All tickets issued for "uninterrupted international air transportation" within the meaning of section 4262(c)(3) and paragraph (c) of §49.4262-3, whether through tickets or separate tickets, must have inscribed thereon, in addition to the other information required in the regulations in this subpart, sufficient information from which may be ascertained the scheduled arrival and departure time at each stopover to which the 12-hour scheduled interval requirement of section 4262(c)(3) applies. It will be sufficient, for example, if the airline ticket or tickets show the trip number and the date and time of departure of the aircraft from each such stopover point, provided the published airline schedules show the scheduled time of arrival at each such stopover point. [Reg. §49.4261-4.]

☐ [T.D. 6430, 12-3-59. *Amended by T.D.* 6618, 11-14-62 *and T.D.* 9948, 1-14-2021.]

**[Reg. §49.4261-5]**

**§49.4261-5. Payments made outside the United States.**—(a) *In general.*—The tax imposed by section 4261(a) and 4261(b) applies to amounts paid outside the United States for the taxable transportation of persons, but only if such transportation begins and ends in the United States. Thus, in addition to the exclusion provided for certain travel under section 4261(a) and 4261(b), the tax imposed by section 4261(a) and 4261(b) shall not apply unless the transportation both begins and ends within the United States. Accordingly, the tax does not apply to a payment made outside the United States for one-way or round-trip transportation between a point within the United States and a point outside the United States.

(b) *Transportation between two or more points in the United States.*—(1) For purposes of this section, a payment made outside the United States for transportation between two or more points in the United States is a payment for transportation which begins and ends in the United States, even though additional transportation to or from a point outside the United States is involved in the entire journey, if at the time of making payment for the transportation between two or more points in the United States it is not definitely established, under the rules set forth in §49.4261-6, that such transportation is purchased for use in making the journey from or to a point outside the United States. The fact that the entire journey includes transportation from or to a point outside the United States is not in itself determinative of the liability for tax.

(2) The following examples illustrate the application of this paragraph:

*Example (1).* W travels from Havana, Cuba, to New York by way of Miami. He purchases in Havana a steamship ticket for his transportation from Havana to Miami and an exchange order for air transportation from Miami to New York. The ticket for the connecting transportation from Havana to Miami, and the order for the transportation from Miami to New York were not appropriately inscribed by the agency or carrier which received the payment for the air transportation involved at the time such payment was received so as to clearly show that the ticket and order were purchased for use in conjunction with each other. Therefore, the agency or carrier which accepts the exchange order and issues the ticket for the transportation from Miami to New York is required to collect the tax which applied to the amount paid outside the United States for such transportation.

*Example (2).* X travels on a round trip from Montreal, Canada, to Los Angeles by way of New York. He purchases in Montreal air transportation for the round trip between New York and Los Angeles, and uses a private automobile for transportation from Montreal to New York and return to Montreal. The amount paid in Montreal for the round-trip transportation between New York and Los Angeles is a payment for transportation which begins and ends in the United States, and is therefore subject to tax.

(c) *Cross reference.*—See section 4262(b)and §49.4262-2 for a partial exclusion with respect to amounts paid for certain transportation. [Reg. §49.4261-5.]

☐ [*T.D.* 6430, 12-3-59. *Amended by T.D.* 9948, 1-14-2021.]

### [Reg. §49.4261-6]

**§49.4261-6. Payments made outside the United States; evidence of nontaxability.**—(a) *In general.*—The tax does not apply to a payment made outside the United States for transportation which begins or ends outside the United States. For purposes of the preceding sentence, a payment made outside the United States for transportation between two or more points within the United States (such transportation being referred to hereinafter in this section as "the United States portion"), which is part of transportation from or to a point outside the United States is a payment for transportation which begins or ends outside the United States, where it is definitely established at the time of making payment for the United States portion that such portion is purchased for use in making the journey from or to a point outside the United States. The nontaxable character of the payment made outside the United States for the United States portion shall be established under the rules set forth in paragraphs (b) through (e) of this section.

(b) *Through tickets.*—Where one ticket (commonly known as a "through ticket") is issued to cover all of the United States portion of a journey which begins or ends outside the United States and to cover also the connecting transportation from or to a point outside the United States, no further evidence of the nontaxable character of the transportation covered by such ticket will be required.

(c) *Separate tickets.*—Where separate tickets or orders are issued for the United States portion of a journey which begins or ends outside the United States, the agency or carrier which receives payment for such tickets or orders shall definitely determine at the time of receiving the payment that the United States portion is being purchased for use in conjunction with connecting transportation from or to a point outside the United States, and shall appropriately inscribe the tickets or orders issued outside the United States for the United States portion and for the connecting transportation from or to a point outside the United States to show clearly that such tickets or orders are purchased for use in conjunction with each other. Such tickets or orders shall be inscribed in the following manner:

(1) The ticket or order for the connecting transportation from or to a point outside the United States shall be inscribed or stamped with an appropriate legend (for example, "Not to be used again for purchase of tax-free United States transportation") to show that the United States portion has been purchased tax free for use in conjunction therewith.

(2) Where the ticket for the United States portion is issued outside the United States, it shall be inscribed to show (i) the identity of the agency or carrier which received payment therefor (unless otherwise shown on the ticket), (ii) the origin and destination of the connecting transportation, (iii) the identity of the carrier furnishing the connecting transportation, and (iv) the serial number of the ticket or order covering such connecting transportation. If the ticket is not large enough to accommodate the prescribed inscription, a statement setting forth the required information shall be attached to such ticket.

(3) Where an order for the United States portion is issued outside the United States, it shall be inscribed to show (i) the origin and destination of the connecting transportation, (ii) the identity of the carrier furnishing the connecting transportation, and (iii) the serial number of the ticket or order covering such connecting transportation.

(d) *Ticket issued pursuant to inscribed order.*—Where the ticket for the United States portion is issued in the United States pursuant to an order which was purchased and properly inscribed outside the United States under the rules set forth in paragraph (c)(3) of this section, liability for payment or collection of tax will not be incurred upon the issuance of the ticket provided the agency or carrier issuing

such ticket stamps or inscribes thereon an appropriate legend, for example, "Tax not paid—furnished on order", or "Exempt—order".

(e) *Maintenance of records.*—In any case where a payment for the United States portion is not subject to tax under the rules set forth in this section, the carrier furnishing transportation for the United States portion shall procure and maintain appropriate evidence which will clearly show that the tickets or orders for such transportation were purchased for use in conjunction with connecting transportation from or to a point outside the United States.

(f) *Examples.*—The following are examples of nontaxable transportation:

*Example (1).* Y travels from London, England, to San Francisco by way of New York. He purchases from an agency or carrier in England all of the transportation involved in such journey, which includes air transportation from London to New York and from New York to San Francisco, for which separate tickets are issued. The agency or carrier which receives the payment for Y's transportation from New York to San Francisco will not be required to collect tax with respect to the payment, provided it determines at the time such payment is received that the transportation in question is being purchased for use in conjunction with the connecting transportation from London to New York and it appropriately inscribes both of the tickets for the journey.

*Example (2).* Z travels from Havana, Cuba, to New York by way of Miami. He purchases in Havana a ticket for his transportation by water from Havana to Miami, and later purchases from a travel agency in Havana air transportation from Miami to New York for which the travel agency issues an exchange order. To establish the nontaxable character of the payment for Z's transportation from Miami to New York the travel agency shall determine at the time payment is received by it that the transportation is being purchased for use in conjunction with the connecting transportation from Havana to Miami, and shall make the appropriate inscription on the ticket and the order. The carrier which accepts the exchange order and issues the ticket for the transportation from Miami to New York will not be required to collect tax with respect to the ticket so issued if it appropriately inscribes the ticket as provided in paragraph (d) of this section. [Reg. §49.4261-6.]

☐ [*T.D.* 6430, 12-3-59.]

### [Reg. §49.4261-7]

**§49.4261-7. Examples of payments subject to tax.**—The following are examples of payments for transportation which, unless otherwise exempt under section 4261, 4281, 4282, or 4293 of the Internal Revenue Code, are subject to tax:

(a) *Cash fares.*—The tax applies to payments of so-called "cash fares" where no ticket or other evidence of the right to transportation is issued to the passenger.

(b) [Reserved]

(c) *Additional charges.*—Amounts paid as additional charges for changing the class of accommodations, changing the destination or route, extending the time limit of a ticket, as "extra fare", or for exclusive occupancy of a section, etc., are subject to the tax.

(d) [Reserved]

(e) [Reserved]

(f) *Prepaid orders, exchange orders, or similar orders.*—The tax applies to the amounts paid for prepaid orders, exchange orders, or similar orders for transportation. Additional amounts paid in procuring transportation in connection with the use of prepaid orders, exchange orders, or similar orders, are likewise subject to tax.

(g) [Reserved]

(h) *Aircraft charters.*—(1) When no charge is made by the charterer of an aircraft to the persons transported, the amount paid by the charterer for the charter of the aircraft is subject to tax.

(2) The charterer of an aircraft who sells transportation to other persons must collect and account for the tax with respect to all amounts paid to the charterer by such other persons. In such case, no tax will be due on the amount paid by the charterer for the charter of the aircraft but it shall be the duty of the owner of the aircraft to advise the charterer of the charterer's obligation for collecting, accounting for, and paying over the tax to the Internal Revenue Service.

(i) *All-expense tours.*—Amounts paid for all-expense tours are subject to tax with respect to that portion representing transportation which is subject to tax. See §§49.4261-2(c) and 49.4261-8(f)(4).

(j) *Payments remitted to foreign countries by persons in the United States.*—Payments for transportation tickets, prepaid orders, exchange orders, or similar orders are subject to the tax where the payment for such tickets or orders is accomplished by the purchaser either (1) by transmission from within the United States via telegraph or mail of cash, checks, postal or telegraphic money orders, and similar drafts to ticket offices or travel agencies, etc., located in any place without the United States, or (2) by the delivery of the funds to an agency located in the United States for transmission to ticket offices, or travel agencies, etc., without the United States. Such payments are considered to be payments made within the United States.

(k) *Applicability date.*—Paragraph (h) of this section applies to amounts paid on and after January 19, 2021. For rules that apply before that date, *see* 26 CFR part 49, revised as of April 1, 2020. [Reg. §49.4261-7.]

☐ [*T.D. 6430, 12-3-59. Amended by T.D. 6618, 11-14-62 and T.D. 9948, 1-14-2021.*]

### [Reg. §49.4261-8]

**§49.4261-8. Examples of payments not subject to tax.**—In addition to a payment specifically exempt under section 4261, 4281, 4282, or 4293 of the Internal Revenue Code, the following are examples of payments not subject to tax:

(a) *Exchange of prepaid order, scrip, etc., for tickets.*—A ticket issued pursuant to an exchange order, prepaid order, airline pilot order, or scrip is not subject to tax where the tax is paid at the time of payment for the order or scrip.

(b) *Caretakers and messengers accompanying freight shipments.*—The tax on the transportation of persons does not apply to amounts paid for transportation of freight that includes also the transportation of caretakers or messengers for which no specific charge as such is made.

(c) *Special baggage transportation equipment.*—An amount paid for special baggage transportation equipment is not subject to the tax on the transportation of persons if separable from the payment for transportation of persons and if shown in the exact amount of the charge on the records covering the taxable transportation payment.

(d) *Circus or show conveyances.*—The amount paid pursuant to a contract for the movement of a circus or show conveyance where the amount covers only the transportation of the performers, laborers, animals, equipment, etc., by such conveyances is not subject to the tax on the transportation of persons imposed by section 4261. However, if the contract payment also covers the issuance to advance agents, bill posters, etc., of circus or show scrip books, or other evidence of the right to transportation, for use on regular passenger conveyances, that portion of the contract payment properly allocable to such scrip books or other evidence is subject to the tax on the transportation of persons.

(e) *Corpses.*—The tax on the transportation of persons does not apply to the amount paid for the transportation of a corpse, but does apply to the amount paid for the transportation of any person accompanying the corpse.

(f) *Miscellaneous charges.*—Where the charge is separable from the payment for the transportation of a person and is shown in the exact amount thereof on the records pertaining to the transportation payment, the tax on the transportation of persons does not apply to the following and similar charges:

(1) Charges for transportation of baggage, including incidental charges such as excess value, storage, transfer, parcel checking, special delivery, etc.

(2) [Reserved]

(3) [Reserved]

(4) Charges for admissions, guides, meals, hotel accommodations, and other nontransportation services, for example, where such items are included in a lump sum payment for an all-expense tour.

(5) [Reserved]
[Reg. §49.4261-8.]

☐ [*T.D. 6430, 12-3-59. Amended by T.D. 6618, 11-14-62 and T.D. 9948, 1-14-2021.*]

### [Reg. §49.4261-9]

**§49.4261-9. Mileage awards.**—(a) *Tax imposed.*—Any amount paid (and the value of any other benefit provided) to an air carrier (or any related person) for the right to provide mileage awards for or other reductions in the cost of any transportation of persons by air is an amount paid for taxable transportation and is therefore subject to the tax imposed by section 4261(a) of the Internal Revenue Code. *See* section 4261(e)(3)(A).

(b) [Reserved]

(c) *Applicability date.*—This section applies to amounts paid on and after January 19, 2021. [Reg. §49.4261-9.]

☐ [*T.D. 6430, 12-3-59. Amended by T.D. 6618, 11-14-62 and T.D. 9948, 1-14-2021.*]

### [Reg. §49.4261-10]

**§49.4261-10. Aircraft management services.**—(a) *In general.*—(1) *Overview.*—This section prescribes rules relating to the exemption under section 4261(e)(5) of the Internal Revenue Code (Code) for amounts paid (in cash or in kind) by an aircraft owner to an aircraft management services provider for certain aircraft management services (aircraft management services exemption). Pursuant to section 4261(e)(5), the tax imposed by section 4261 of the Code does not apply to amounts paid by an aircraft owner to an aircraft management services provider for aircraft management services related to maintenance and support of the aircraft owner's aircraft; or related to flights on the aircraft owner's aircraft (flight services). The aircraft management services exemption applies to amounts paid by an aircraft owner to an aircraft management services provider for flight services on the aircraft owner's aircraft, even if the aircraft owner is not on the flight. The aircraft management services exemption does not apply to amounts paid to an aircraft management services provider by another person on behalf of an aircraft owner (other than in a principal-agent scenario in which the aircraft owner is the principal). In addition, amounts paid for aircraft management services by a party related to the aircraft owner are not amounts paid by the aircraft owner solely by virtue of the relationship between the aircraft owner and the related party. However, if an aircraft owner leases an aircraft to another person, including a related party, amounts paid by the lessee to an aircraft management services provider for aircraft management services related to the leased aircraft qualify for the aircraft management services exemption, provided the lease is not a disqualified lease and all other requirements of section 4261(e)(5) are satisfied. For example, amounts paid for aircraft management services by one member of an affiliated group (as that term is defined in section 4282 of the Code) for flights on an aircraft owned by another member of the affiliated group are not amounts paid by the aircraft owner unless the member owning the aircraft leases the aircraft to the member of the affiliated group that pays for the aircraft management services. *See* paragraph (b) of this section for definitions of terms used in this section.

(2) *Private aviation.*—The aircraft management services exemption is limited to aircraft management services related to aircraft used in private aviation.

(3) *Adequate records required.*—In order to qualify for the aircraft management services exemption, an aircraft owner and aircraft management services provider must maintain adequate records to show that the amounts paid by the aircraft owner to the aircraft management services provider relate to aircraft management services specifically for the aircraft owner's aircraft or for flights on the aircraft owner's aircraft and to support any allocations required under paragraph (c) under of this section. Such records may include the agreement, if any, between the aircraft owner and the aircraft management services provider, evidence of aircraft ownership, evidence that amounts paid for aircraft management services came from the aircraft owner, and the aircraft management services provider's fee schedule.

(b) *Definitions.*—This paragraph provides definitions applicable to this section.

(1) *Aircraft management services.*—The term *aircraft management services* means—

(i) *Statutory services.*—The services listed in section 4261(e)(5)(B)(i)-(v); and

(ii) *Other services.*—Any service (including, but not limited to, purchasing fuel, purchasing aircraft parts, and arranging for the fueling of an aircraft owner's aircraft) provided directly or indirectly to an aircraft owner in order to provide air transportation to the aircraft owner on the aircraft owner's aircraft at a level and quality of service required under the agreement between the aircraft owner and the aircraft management services provider.

(2) *Aircraft management services provider.*—The term *aircraft management services provider* means a person that provides aircraft management services to an aircraft owner.

(3) *Aircraft owner.*—(i) *In general.*—Except as otherwise provided in this section, the term *aircraft owner* means a person that owns an aircraft managed by an aircraft management services provider (commonly referred to as a managed aircraft), or a person that

leases a managed aircraft (lessee) pursuant to a lease that is not a disqualified lease. A person owns a managed aircraft if the person holds legal title to the aircraft, or if the person holds substantial incidents of ownership in the aircraft for a period of more than 31 days. A lessee includes the beneficiary of an owner trust that holds legal title to the managed aircraft.

(ii) *Persons not included in the definition of aircraft owner.*—A lessee of an aircraft under a disqualified lease cannot be an aircraft owner with respect to the aircraft leased pursuant to the disqualified lease. A person that owns stock in a commercial airline does not qualify as an aircraft owner of that commercial airline's aircraft. A participant in a fractional aircraft ownership program, as defined in section 4043(c)(2) of the Code, does not qualify as an aircraft owner of the program's managed aircraft if the amount paid for such person's participation is exempt from the tax imposed by section 4261 reason of section 4261(j).

(4) *Disqualified lease.*—The term *disqualified lease* has the meaning given to it by section 4261(e)(5)(C)(ii).

(5) *Fair market value.*—The term *fair market value* means the value of comparable flights or services provided with respect to a comparable aircraft as of the date such flights or services are provided. The aircraft management services provider's published fee schedule in effect on the date(s) the flights or services are provided may be used as evidence of fair market value.

(6) *For-hire flight.*—The term *for-hire flight* means the use of an aircraft to transport passengers for compensation that is paid in cash or in kind. The term includes, but is not limited to, charter flights, air taxi flights, and sightseeing flights (commonly referred to as flightseeing flights).

(7) *Owner trust.*—The term *owner trust* means an arrangement in which legal title of an aircraft is held in the name of the trustee of the trust for the limited purpose of registering the aircraft in the United States with the Federal Aviation Administration pursuant to the registration requirements in 49 U.S.C. sections 40102(a) and 44102(a), and 14 CFR part 47.

(8) *Private aviation.*—The term *private aviation* means the use of an aircraft for civilian flights, except scheduled passenger service for which tickets (or substitutes equivalent to tickets) are sold on a seat-by-seat basis to the general public. The term includes, but is not limited to, civilian flights operated under Part 135 (14 CFR Part 135) of the Federal Aviation Regulations prescribed by the Federal Aviation Administration (FARs).

(9) *Substitute aircraft.*—The term *substitute aircraft* means an aircraft, other than the aircraft owner's aircraft, that is provided by an aircraft management services provider to the aircraft owner when the aircraft owner's aircraft is not available, regardless of the reason for the unavailability.

(c) *Pro rata allocation.*—(1) *In general.*—Except as provided in paragraph (c)(2)(iii) of this section, when an amount paid to an aircraft management services provider includes a portion that is subject to the tax imposed by section 4261 and a portion that consists of amounts described in section 4261(e)(5)(A), the exception in section 4261(e)(5) applies on a pro rata basis only to the portion that consists of amounts described in section 4261(e)(5)(A). *See* section 4261(e)(5)(D). In such case, the tax base for the portion that is subject to the tax imposed by section 4261(a) is the amount paid for the flights or services, provided the amount paid is separable and shown in exact amounts in the records pertaining to the charge. If the portion of the amount paid that is subject to the tax imposed by section 4261(a) is not separable, the tax base is the fair market value of the flights or services. However, the tax base determined in the previous sentence may not exceed the total amount paid (that is, the sum of the portion that is subject to the tax imposed by section 4261(a) and the portion that consists of amounts described in section 4261(e)(5)(A)).

(2) *Substitute aircraft.*—(i) *Flight treated as a charter.*—If an aircraft management services provider provides a flight to an aircraft owner on a substitute aircraft, the flight is treated as a charter flight provided by the aircraft management services provider to the aircraft owner, regardless of whether the aircraft owner is on the flight, and the aircraft owner is treated as the charterer of such flight. If the flight constitutes taxable transportation, as defined in section 4262 of the Code, the tax imposed by section 4261(a) applies, unless the flight is exempt from such tax by reason of an exemption other than the aircraft management services exemption. See section 4261(b) and (c) for other taxes that may apply to flights provided by an aircraft management services provider to an aircraft owner on substitute aircraft.

(ii) *General rule for flights provided on substitute aircraft.*—In cases where an aircraft management services provider provides a flight to an aircraft owner on a substitute aircraft and an allocation is required, the rule in paragraph (c)(1) of this section applies in determining the tax base. In all other cases, the tax base and the tax imposed by section 4261(a) thereon must be determined in accordance with the rules of §49.4261-7(h)(1), unless the flight is otherwise exempt from such tax by reason of an exemption other than the aircraft management services exemption.

(iii) *Special rule for for-hire flights provided on substitute aircraft.*—In cases where a substitute aircraft is used to provide a for-hire flight and an amount is paid for the flight by someone other than the aircraft owner, the tax base and the tax imposed by section 4261(a) thereon must be determined in accordance with the rules in §49.4261-7(h)(2), unless the flight is otherwise exempt from such tax by reason of an exemption other than the aircraft management services exemption.

(d) *Choice of flight rules.*—Whether a flight on an aircraft owner's aircraft operates pursuant to the rules under FARs Part 91 (14 CFR part 91) or pursuant to the rules under FARs Part 135 does not affect the application of section 4261(e)(5).

(e) *Aircraft available for hire.*—Whether an aircraft owner permits an aircraft management services provider or other person to use its aircraft to provide for-hire flights (for example, when the aircraft is not being used by the aircraft owner or when the aircraft is being moved in deadhead service) does not affect the application of section 4261(e)(5). However, an amount paid for for-hire flights on the aircraft owner's aircraft, except payments made by the aircraft owner, does not qualify for the aircraft management services exemption under section 4261(e)(5). Therefore, an amount paid by someone other than the aircraft owner for a for-hire flight on the aircraft owner's aircraft is subject to the tax imposed by section 4261 unless the flight is otherwise exempt from such tax by reason of an exemption other than the aircraft management services exemption. *See* §49.4261-7(h) for rules relating to the application of the tax imposed by section 4261 on amounts paid for certain charter flights.

(f) *Billing methods.*—Except as otherwise provided in this section, the method an aircraft management services provider bills, invoices, or otherwise charges an aircraft owner for aircraft management services, whether by specific itemization of costs, flat monthly or hourly fee, or otherwise, does not affect the application of section 4261(e)(5).

(g) *Multiple aircraft management services providers not disqualifying.*—Whether an aircraft owner pays amounts to more than one aircraft management services provider for aircraft management services does not affect the application of section 4261(e)(5).

(h) *Examples.*—The following examples illustrate the provisions of this section.

(1) *Example 1.*—(i) *Facts.* During the first quarter of 2021, an aircraft owner pays a $3,000 monthly management fee to an aircraft management services provider for services related to operating the aircraft owner's aircraft. The aircraft owner used its own aircraft for all but one of the flights the owner took during the period. On the one occasion that the aircraft owner's aircraft was unavailable when the aircraft owner wanted to fly, the aircraft management services provider used a substitute aircraft to transport the aircraft owner. The flight was within the continental United States and the aircraft owner received no compensation for the transportation of other passengers on the flight. The aircraft owner paid $1,000 for the flight on the substitute aircraft. The aircraft management services provider included the $1,000 charge for the substitute aircraft as a separate line item on the monthly management fee invoice.

(ii) *Analysis.* The tax imposed by section 4261(a) applies to services that do not qualify for the section 4261(e)(5) exemption; in this case, the flight provided on the substitute aircraft. The flight provided on the substitute aircraft is treated as a charter flight for purposes of the tax imposed by section 4261(a), and the owner is treated as the charterer of the flight. The amount paid by the aircraft owner for the flight on the substitute aircraft is the section 4261(a) tax base. The monthly invoice from the aircraft management services provider to the aircraft owner included a line item in the amount of $1,000 for the charter flight. Because $1,000 is the actual amount paid for the flight, this amount is the section 4261(a) tax base. The tax imposed by section 4261(b) also applies to the flight on a per-passenger basis. *See* §49.4261-2(b) for rules regarding the application of the tax imposed by section 4261(b).

(2) *Example 2.*—(i) *Facts.* Same facts as in paragraph (h)(1) of this section (Example 1), except the invoice does not show the amount paid for the flight on the substitute aircraft and that amount is not otherwise separable from the monthly management fee. The fair market value of the flight on the substitute aircraft is $1,000.

(ii) *Analysis.* The tax imposed by section 4261(a) applies to the flight provided on the substitute aircraft. The amount paid for the flight on the substitute aircraft is not otherwise separable from the monthly management fee. Because $1,000 is the fair market value of the flight, and such amount does not exceed the $3,000 monthly management fee paid by the aircraft owner, this amount is the section 4261(a) tax base. The tax imposed by section 4261(b) also applies to the flight on a per-passenger basis. *See* § 49.4261-2(b) for rules regarding the application of the tax imposed by section 4261(b).

(3) *Example 3.*—(i) *Facts.* An aircraft owner pays a monthly management fee to an aircraft management services provider for aircraft management services related to the aircraft owner's aircraft. When the aircraft is not being used by the owner, the owner sometimes permits a charter company to use the aircraft to provide charter flights. At other times when the aircraft is not being used by the owner, the owner permits a tour operator to use the aircraft for flightseeing tours. All charter and flightseeing flights on the aircraft constitute taxable transportation, as that term is defined in section 4262, and no exemptions (other than section 4261(e)(5)) apply. No charter or flightseeing flights are provided on a substitute aircraft. The aircraft's maximum certificated takeoff weight is 7,000 pounds.

(ii) *Analysis.* Amounts paid by the aircraft owner to the aircraft management services provider for aircraft management services related to the aircraft owner's aircraft are exempt under section 4261(e)(5). Amounts paid by the charterer or passengers for the charter flights are subject to tax under section 4261(a) and (b). *See* § 49.4261-7(h) for rules relating to the application of the tax imposed by section 4261 on amounts paid for charter flights. *See* § 49.4261-2(b) for rules regarding the application of the tax imposed by section 4261(b). Amounts paid by flightseeing customers for flightseeing tours are also subject to tax under section 4261(a) and (b). If a payment for a flightseeing tour includes charges for nontransportation services, the charges for the nontransportation services may be excluded in computing the tax payable provided the payments are separable and provided in exact amounts. *See* § 49.4261-2(c).

(i) *Applicability date.*—This section applies to amounts paid on and after January 19, 2021. [Reg. § 49.4261-10.]

☐ [*T.D. 6430, 12-3-59. Amended by T.D. 9948, 1-14-2021.*]

### [Reg. § 49.4262-1]

**§ 49.4262-1. Taxable transportation.**—(a) *In general.*—Unless excluded under section 4262(b) of the Internal Revenue Code (Code) (see § 49.4262-2), taxable transportation means—

(1) Transportation by air which begins in the United States or in that portion of Canada or Mexico which is not more than 225 miles from the nearest point in the continental United States (225-mile zone) and ends in the United States or in the 225-mile zone; and

(2) In the case of any other transportation by air, that portion of such transportation that is directly or indirectly from one port or station in the United States to another port or station in the United States, but only if such transportation is not part of *uninterrupted international air transportation* within the meaning of section 4262(c)(3) of the Code and § 49.4262-3(c). Transportation from one port or station in the United States occurs whenever a carrier, after leaving any port or station in the United States, makes a regularly scheduled stop at another port or station in the United States irrespective of whether stopovers are permitted or whether passengers disembark.

(b) *Illustrations of taxable transportation under section 4262(a)(1).*—In each of the following examples the transportation is taxable transportation and the amount paid within the United States for such transportation is subject to the tax:

(1) New York to Seattle;

(2) New York to Vancouver, Canada, with a stop at Toronto, Canada;

(3) Chicago to Monterrey, Mexico;

(4) Montreal, Canada, to Toronto, Canada; and

(5) Miami to Los Angeles via Panama.

If in the examples in paragraph (b)(1) and (5) of this section, payment for the transportation had been made outside the United States, such payment would nevertheless have been subject to the taxes imposed by section 4261(a) and (b) since in each case the transportation begins and ends in the United States.

(c) [Reserved]

(d) *Examples.*—The following examples illustrate the application of section 4262(a)(2) and the taxes imposed by section 4261(a) and (b) of the Code:

(1) *Example (1).*—A purchases in New York a ticket for air transportation from New York to Nassau, Bahamas, with a scheduled stopover of 14 hours in Miami. The part of the transportation from New York to Miami is taxable transportation as defined in section

4262(a) because such transportation is from one station in the United States to another station in the United States and the trip is not uninterrupted international air transportation (because the scheduled stopover interval in Miami is greater than 12 hours). Therefore, the amount paid for the transportation from New York to Miami is subject to the taxes imposed by section 4261(a) and (b).

(2) [Reserved]

(3) *Example (3).*—A purchases a through ticket for air transportation from San Francisco to London with stopovers at Denver, Chicago, Philadelphia, and New York. At each stopover the air carrier has scheduled his arrival and departure within 12 hours. After arriving in Philadelphia, A, for his own convenience, decides to stopover for more than 12 hours. The total amount paid by A for his transportation from San Francisco to New York is subject to the taxes imposed by section 4261(a) and (b) since the scheduled interval between the beginning or end and the end or beginning of any two segments of the domestic portion of international air transportation exceeded 12 hours. If the stopover interval in Philadelphia is extended for more than 12 hours by the carrier solely for its own convenience such as making repairs to the aircraft, the domestic portion of A's trip will not become taxable, provided A continues his international air transportation no later than on the first available flight offered by the carrier.

(4) *Example (4).*—A purchases a through ticket for transportation by air from Los Angeles to Barbados with stopovers at Houston, Mexico City, Mexico, and Miami. At each stopover, except Mexico City, A's scheduled time of arrival and departure is within 12 hours. At Mexico City, A's scheduled time of arrival and departure exceeds 12 hours. The total amount paid by A for his transportation from Los Angeles to Miami, including that part of the transportation to and from Mexico City, is subject to the taxes imposed by section 4261(a) and (b) since the transportation includes a portion which is indirectly from one port or station in the United States to another port or station in the United States (Houston to Miami via Mexico City) and the scheduled interval in Mexico City between two segments of such portion exceeds 12 hours. If A's scheduled arrival and departure at each stopover of his transportation which is directly or indirectly between ports or stations in the United States, including that at Mexico City, had been within a six hour interval and A had arrived and departed at each such stopover within that period, the transportation would have qualified as uninterrupted international air transportation and no part of the amount paid for the transportation by air from Los Angeles to Barbados would be subject to the taxes imposed by section 4261(a) and (b).

(e) *Examples of transportation that is not taxable transportation.*—The following examples illustrate transportation that is not taxable transportation:

(1) New York to Trinidad with no intervening stops;

(2) Minneapolis to Edmonton, Canada, with a stop at Winnipeg, Canada;

(3) Los Angeles to Mexico City, Mexico, with stops at Tijuana and Guadalajara, Mexico;

(4) New York to Whitehorse, Yukon Territory, Canada, by air with a scheduled stopover in Chicago of five hours. Amounts paid for the transportation referred to in examples set forth in paragraphs (e)(1), (2), and (3) of this section are not subject to the tax regardless of where payment is made, since none of the trips:

(i) Begin in the United States or in the 225–mile zone and end in the United States or in the 225–mile zone, nor

(ii) Contain a portion of transportation which is directly or indirectly from one port or station in the United States to another port or station in the United States. The amount paid within the United States for the transportation referred to in the example set forth in paragraph (4) of this section is not subject to tax since the entire trip (including the domestic portion thereof) is *uninterrupted international air transportation* within the meaning of section 4262(c)(3) and § 49.4262-3(c). In the event the transportation is paid for outside the United States, no tax is due since the transportation does not begin and end in the United States.

(f) *Applicability date.*—This section applies to amounts paid on and after January 19, 2021. For rules that apply before that date, *see* 26 CFR part 49, revised as of April 1, 2020. [Reg. § 49.4262-1.]

☐ [*T.D. 6430, 12-3-59. Amended by T.D. 6618, 11-14-62. Redesignated and amended by T.D. 9948, 1-14-2021.*]

### [Reg. § 49.4262-2]

**§ 49.4262-2. Exclusion of certain travel.**—(a) *In general.*—Under section 4262(b) of the Internal Revenue Code taxable transportation does not include that portion of any transportation which meets all four of the following requirements:

(1) Such portion is outside the United States;

(2) Neither such portion nor any segment thereof is directly or indirectly—

(i) Between (a) a point where the route of the transportation leaves or enters the Continental United States, or (b) a port or station in the 225-mile zone, and

(ii) A port or station in the 225-mile zone;

(3) Such portion—

(i) Begins at either (a) at the point where the route of the transportation leaves the United States, or (b) a port or station in the 225-mile zone, and

(ii) Ends at either (a) the point where the route of the transportation enters the United States, or (b) a port or station in the 225-mile zone; and

(4) A direct line from the point (or the port or station) specified in subparagraph (3)(i) of this paragraph, to the point (or the port or station) specified in subparagraph (3)(ii) of this paragraph, passes through or over a point which is not within 225 miles of the United States.

For purposes of this section, the route of the transportation shall be deemed to leave or enter the United States when it passes over (i) the international boundary line between any part of the United States and a contiguous foreign country, or (ii) a point three nautical miles (3.45 statute miles) from low tide on the coast line.

(b) *Transportation to or from Alaska or Hawaii.*—(1) Under the provisions of section 4262(b) transportation between the continental United States or the 225-mile zone and Alaska or Hawaii will be partially exempt from the tax. The portion of such transportation which (i) is outside the United States, (ii) is not transportation between ports or stations within the continental United States or the 225-mile zone, and (iii) is not transportation between ports or stations within Alaska or Hawaii, meets all the requirements set forth in section 4262(b) and is excluded from taxable transportation.

(2) The provisions of subparagraph (1) of this paragraph may be illustrated by the following examples:

*Example (1).* A buys a ticket for transportation by air from Seattle to Fairbanks, Alaska, via Ketchikan and Juneau, Alaska, and Whitehorse, Yukon Territory, Canada. The portion of the transportation between the point where the route of the transportation leaves the continental United States and the point where it first enters Alaska (the three-mile limit or the international boundary) is not subject to tax.

*Example (2).* [Reserved]

*Example (3).* C purchases a ticket in the United States for transportation by air from Vancouver, Canada, to Honolulu, Hawaii. No part of the route followed by the carrier passes through or over any part of the continental United States. The only part of the payment made by C for this transportation which is subject to the tax is that applicable to the portion of the transportation between the three-mile limit off the coast of Hawaii and the airport in Honolulu.

(c) *Method of computing tax on travel not excluded.*—(1) Where a payment is made for transportation which includes transportation excluded under the provisions of section 4262(b)—

(i) The tax may be computed on that proportion of the total amount paid which the mileage of the taxable portion of the transportation bears to the mileage of the entire trip, or

(ii) If the taxable portion of the transportation includes transportation from one port or station to another port or station for which an applicable local fare of a like class is available, the tax may be computed on the amount of such local fare, plus an amount equivalent to that proportion of the remainder of the total amount paid which the mileage of the remainder of the taxable portion of the transportation bears to the remainder of the mileage of the entire trip. If the taxable transportation includes a leg from a station to a coastal gateway point of embarkation for which a uniform fare is charged regardless of the gateway point actually used, the tax on such a leg may be computed on the basis of such uniform fare. In the absence of a fare described in this subparagraph, the tax must be determined in accordance with subdivision (i) of this subparagraph. If the taxable portion of the transportation includes a leg between coastal gateway points of embarkation for which no additional fair is charged, no tax shall be applicable to such leg of the transportation.

(2) The basis for determining the proportions described in subdivisions (i) and (ii) of subparagraph (1) of this paragraph shall be the average mileage of the established route traveled by the carrier between given points under normal circumstances.

(d) *Example.*—The application of paragraph (c) of this section may be illustrated by the following example: A purchases in San Francisco a ticket for transportation by air to Honolulu, Hawaii. The portion of the transportation which is outside the continental United States and is outside Hawaii is excluded from taxable transportation. The tax applies to that part of the payment made by A which is applicable to the portion of the transportation between the airport in San Francisco and the three-mile limit off the coast of California (a distance of 15 miles) and between the three-mile limit off the coast of Hawaii and the airport in Honolulu (a distance of 5 miles). The part of the payment made by A which is applicable to the taxable portion of his transportation and the tax due thereon are computed in accordance with paragraph (c)(1) as follows:

Table 1 to paragraph (d)

| | |
|---|---:|
| Mileage of entire trip (San Francisco airport to Honolulu airport) (miles) | 2,400 |
| Mileage in continental United States (miles) | 15 |
| Mileage in Hawaii (miles) | 5 |
| | 20 |
| Fare from San Francisco to Honolulu | $168.00 |
| Payment for taxable portion (20/2400 x $168) | $1.40 |
| Tax due (7.5% (rate in effect on date of payment) x $1.40) | $0.11 |

(All distances and fares assumed for purposes of this example. This example addresses only the computation of the tax imposed by section 4261(a). It does not address the computation of any other tax imposed by section 4261 that may apply to these facts.)

(e) *Applicability date.*—This section applies to amounts paid on and after January 19, 2021. For rules that apply before that date, *see* 26 CFR part 49, revised as of April 1, 2020. [Reg. § 49.4262-2.]

☐ [T.D. 6430, 12-3-59. *Amended by T.D.* 6618, 11-14-62. *Redesignated and amended by T.D.* 9948, 1-14-2021.]

**[Reg. § 49.4262-3]**

**§ 49.4262-3. Definitions.**—(a) *The continental United States.*—For the purposes of the regulations in this subpart, the term "continental United States" means the District of Columbia and the States other than Alaska and Hawaii, including inland waters (such as rivers, lakes, bays, etc.) lying wholly therein, and, where an international boundary line divides inland waters, such parts of such inland waters as lie within the boundary of the United States, and also the waters 3 nautical miles (3.45 statute miles) from low tide on the coast line.

(b) *The 225-mile zone.*—For purposes of the regulations in this subpart, the term "225-mile zone" means that portion of Canada and Mexico which is not more than 225 miles from the nearest point in the continental United States. Whether any point in Canada or Mexico is more than 225 miles from the continental United States is to be determined by measuring the distance from such point to the nearest point on the boundary of the continental United States.

(c) *Uninterrupted international air transportation.*—(1) For the purpose of the regulations in this subpart, the term "uninterrupted international air transportation" means transportation entirely by air which does not begin in the United States or in the 225-mile zone and end in the United States or in the 225-mile zone provided that

(i) Where the transportation within the United States involves one stop, the scheduled interval between the beginning or end of the United States portion of such air transportation and the end or beginning of the remainder of the air transportation, and

(ii) Where the United States portion of such transportation involves two or more stops, the scheduled interval between the beginning or end of one segment and the end or beginning of the continuing segment of such portion

does not exceed 12 hours. The transportation is considered to be entirely by air even though the passenger may use other means of transportation between two airports provided the scheduled 12-hour limitation for his continuing air transportation is complied with. Transportation which otherwise is uninterrupted international air transportation does not cease to be such because of the use of non-air transportation between ports or stations which are outside the United States, provided the non-air transportation is not a part of transportation which is indirectly from one port or station in the United States to another port or station in the United States.

(2) Where the interval between the arrival and departure time at any stopover point in the United States exceeds 12 hours, such transportation is not uninterrupted international air transportation even though the schedules of the air lines do not make possible a scheduling within the 12-hour limit. Where any interval scheduled for 12 hours or less is increased to exceed 12 hours, the transportation

will continue to be uninterrupted international air transportation if the increase in time is attributable to delays in the arrival or departure of the scheduled air transportation. In such case the transportation shall continue to be uninterrupted international air transportation if the passenger continues his transportation no later than on the first available flight offered by the continuing carrier which affords the passenger substantially the same accommodations as originally purchased. However, if for any other reason such interval at any stopover is increased to more than 12 hours, the transportation will lose its classification of uninterrupted international air transportation. The tax applicable in such case shall be paid as provided in §49.4263-3(a)(2). The transportation from the point of origin in the United States to a port or station outside the United States and the 225-mile zone, with a stopover in the United States, must be scheduled before the time the initial transportation commences in order for the United States portion of such transportation to qualify as uninterrupted international air transportation. For example, where transportation by air from Chicago to New York only is scheduled in Chicago and transportation by air from New York to London, England, is scheduled by the passenger after his arrival in New York, the Chicago to New York trip does not qualify as uninterrupted international air transportation even though the passenger may depart on the London flight within 12 hours after arrival in New York.

(d) *Transportation.*—For purposes of the regulations in this subpart, the term *transportation* includes layover or waiting time and movement of the aircraft in deadhead service.

(e) *Applicability date.*—This section applies to amounts paid on and after January 19, 2021. For rules that apply before that date, *see* 26 CFR part 49, revised as of April 1, 2020. [Reg. §49.4262-3.]

☐ [*T.D.* 6430, 12-3-59. *Amended by T.D.* 6618, 11-14-62. *Redesignated and amended by T.D.* 9948, 1-14-2021.]

### [Reg. §49.4263-1]

**§49.4263-1. Duty to collect the tax; payments made outside the United States.**—(a) *Duty to collect tax.*—Where payment upon which tax is imposed by section 4261 of the Internal Revenue Code is made outside the United States for a prepaid order, exchange order, or similar order, the person furnishing the initial transportation pursuant to such order must collect the applicable tax. *See* section 4291 and the regulations under section 4291 for cases where persons receiving payment must collect the tax. *See* section 6672 for rules relating to the application of the trust fund recovery penalty.

(b) *Applicability date.*—This section applies to amounts paid on and after January 19, 2021. For rules that apply before that date, *see* 26 CFR part 49, revised as of April 1, 2020. [Reg. §49.4263-1.]

☐ [*T.D.* 6430, 12-3-59. *Redesignated and amended by T.D.* 9948, 1-14-2021.]

### [Reg. §49.4263-2]

**§49.4263-2. Duty to collect the tax in the case of certain refunds.**—(a) *Special rule for collection of tax.*—Section 4263(b) of the Internal Revenue Code (Code) provides a special rule for the collection of the tax where an unused ticket or order (or portion thereof) purchased without payment of tax is presented for refund and, as a result of the use of only a portion of the transportation purchased in connection with such ticket or order, liability for payment of tax has been incurred. In such a case, the person making the refund shall deduct the amount of the tax due, to the extent available, from the amount which would otherwise be refundable. If the redemption value of the unused ticket or order (or portion thereof) is less than the amount of the tax due on the amount paid for the travel actually performed, the person redeeming the unused ticket or order (or portion thereof) shall make no refund but shall apply the entire amount against the tax due and shall collect any additional tax due or, within 90 days, shall make a report of the amount of the tax remaining uncollected, together with the name and address of the person who sought the refund. The report shall be made to the Commissioner, and a copy of the report shall be furnished to the person presenting the unused ticket or order for redemption.

(b) *Return of tax.*—Any person who has made a collection of tax in accordance with the preceding paragraph shall include such amount in his regular return of taxes required to be collected under section 4291 of the Code.

(c) *Example.*—A carrier receives for redemption a ticket purchased in the United States for transportation from Calgary, Canada, to Edmonton, Canada, which the purchaser bought for use in conjunction with a ticket for non-stop transportation from Seattle to Calgary. The person applying for the refund does not establish to the satisfaction of the carrier that the tax on the Seattle-Calgary ticket has been paid or that the Seattle-Calgary ticket has been redeemed. The car-

rier, before making any refund for the unused ticket, is required to deduct from the amount otherwise refundable the tax applicable to the amount paid by the purchaser for the transportation from Seattle to Calgary and to report the tax so collected in its quarterly return on Form 720. In the event that the redemption value of the unused Calgary to Edmonton ticket is less than the amount of the tax due on the amount paid for the transportation from Seattle to Calgary, the carrier should not make any refund but should apply against the outstanding tax the entire amount refundable and should either collect the balance of the tax due or make a report, within 90 days, to the Commissioner, setting forth the name and address of the person seeking the refund and the amount of the tax remaining uncollected. [Reg. §49.4263-2.]

☐ [*T.D.* 6430, 12-3-59. *Redesignated and amended by T.D.* 9948, 1-14-2021.]

### [Reg. §49.4263-3]

**§49.4263-3. Special rule for the payment of tax.**—(a) *In general.*—For the rules applicable under section 4263(c) of the Internal Revenue Code, see §49.4261-1(b)(2).

(b) *Relationship to other sections.*—Section 4263(c) and this section are not intended in any way to relieve the person receiving the payment for taxable transportation of persons from his duty under section 4291 of the Code of collecting the tax at the time such payment is received by him.

(c) [Reserved]

(d) *Applicability date.*—This section applies to amounts paid on and after January 19, 2021. For rules that apply before that date, *see* 26 CFR part 49, revised as of April 1, 2020. [Reg. §49.4263-3.]

☐ [*T.D.* 6430, 12-3-59. *Amended by T.D.* 6618, 11-14-62. *Redesignated and amended by T.D.* 9948, 1-14-2021.]

### [Reg. §49.4263-4]

**§49.4263-4. Cross reference.**—For the rules applicable under section 4263(d) see §49.4261-4 relating to payments made within the United States. [Reg. §49.4263-4.]

☐ [*T.D.* 6430, 12-3-59. *Redesignated and amended by T.D.* 9948, 1-14-2021.]

### [Reg. §49.4263-5]

**§49.4263-5. Round trips.**—(a) *In general.*—For purposes of the regulations in this subpart, a round trip shall be considered to consist of two separate trips, i.e., one trip from the point of departure to the destination and a second trip in returning from the destination. A round trip includes certain journeys in which the same routing is not followed on the return trip from the destination to the point of departure as was taken on the going trip (sometimes referred to as "circle trips"). In the case of a cruise or tour (i.e., transportation to no set destination but with one or more intermediate stops en route) the point farthest from the point of departure will be regarded as the destination for purposes of applying the term "round trip". If a cruise or tour ends at a point other than the one at which it began, the rules of "open jaw" transportation set forth in paragraph (b) of this section apply.

(b) *Open jaw transportation.*—Transportation which qualifies under this paragraph as "open jaw" transportation will be treated in the same manner as a round trip. For purposes of the regulations in this subpart, "open jaw" transportation means (1) transportation from the point of departure to a specified destination and return from the specified destination to a point other than the original point of departure, or (2) transportation from the point of departure to a specified destination and return from a point other than the specified destination to the original point of departure, provided that where the points of the open jaw are within the continental United States or the 225-mile zone, the distance between the points of the open jaw does not exceed the distance of the shorter segment traveled. For example, a trip from New York to New Orleans via Panama would be considered as one trip from New York to Panama and separate trip from Panama to New Orleans, since the distance between the points of the open jaw (i.e., New York and New Orleans) is shorter than the distance between Panama and New Orleans (the shorter of the two segments traveled). Both trips would be nontaxable. On the other hand, transportation from New York to Miami via Bermuda does not qualify as "open jaw" transportation (since the points of the open jaw are in the United States and the distance between them is greater than the shorter segment traveled) and therefore would be considered a single trip from New York to Miami and would be taxable. [Reg. §49.4263-5.]

☐ [*T.D.* 6430, 12-3-59. *Redesignated and amended by T.D.* 9948, 1-14-2021.]

[Reg. §49.4263-6]

### §49.4263-6. Transportation outside the northern portion of the Western Hemisphere.—(a) *Transportation which leaves and re-enters the northern portion of the Western Hemisphere.*—For purposes of the regulations in this subpart, transportation, any part of which is outside the northern portion of the Western Hemisphere(as defined in paragraph (c) of this section) shall, if the route of the transportation leaves and re-enters the northern portion of the Western Hemisphere, be considered to consist of transportation to the point outside such northern portion and of separate transportation thereafter. The amount paid for such transportation will be considered to be a payment made for two trips and the taxability of the payment will be determined accordingly. Thus, an amount paid for transportation from New York to San Francisco with a stop at Caracas, Venezuela, will be considered an amount paid for a trip from New York to Caracas and for a separate trip from Caracas to San Francisco, neither of which is taxable transportation.

(b) [Reserved]

(c) *Northern portion of the Western Hemisphere.*—For purposes of the regulations in this subpart, the term "northern portion of the Western Hemisphere" means the area lying west of the 30th meridian west of Greenwich, east of the International Date Line, and north of the equator, but not including any country of South America. [Reg. §49.4263-6.]

☐ [*T.D.* 6430, 12-3-59. *Amended by T.D.* 6618, 11-14-62. *Redesignated and amended by T.D.* 9948, 1-14-2021.]

[Reg. §49.4271-1]

### §49.4271-1. Tax on transportation of property by air.—(a) *Purpose of this section.*—Section 4271 of the Internal Revenue Code (Code) imposes a 6.25 percent tax on amounts paid within or without the United States for the taxable transportation of property (as defined in section 4272 of the Code). This section sets forth rules as to the general applicability of the tax. This section also sets forth rules authorized by section 4272(b)(2) which exempt from tax payments for the transportation of property by air in the course of exportation (including shipment to a possession of the United States) by continuous movement, and in due course so exported.

(b) *Imposition of tax.*—(1) The tax imposed by section 4271 applies only to amounts paid to persons engaged in the business of transporting property by air for hire.

(2) The tax imposed by section 4271 does not apply to amounts paid for the transportation of property by air if such transportation is furnished on an aircraft having a maximum certificated takeoff weight (as defined in section 4281(b) of the Code) of 6,000 pounds or less, unless such aircraft is operated on an established line or when such aircraft is a jet aircraft. The tax imposed by section 4271 also does not apply to any payment made by one member of an affiliated group (as defined in section 4282(b) of the Code) to another member of such group for services furnished in connection with the use of an aircraft if such aircraft is owned or leased by a member of the affiliated group and is not available for hire by persons who are not members of such group.

(c) *Property exported or imported entirely by air.*—(1) The tax does not apply to amounts paid for transportation entirely by air which begins in the United States and ends outside the United States, or which begins outside the United States and ends in the United States. Transportation of property by air will be considered to begin and end at the points of origin and destination shown on a through airwaybill covering shipment of the property, even though there may be stop-overs in the United States (such as, for example, to consolidate cargo at a "gateway" city). If a through airwaybill is issued by a person other than a person engaged in the business of transporting property by air for hire (for example, by a freight forwarder), the air carrier may accept an air freight manifest listing the article to be shipped by weight and destination as evidence of the existence of a through airwaybill.

(2) If a through airwaybill covering air transportation from its beginning in the United States to a foreign destination, or from its beginning abroad to a United States destination, has not been issued, then the export or import character of the shipment must be evidenced by a contract or other written evidence clearly showing the beginning point and ending point of the air transportation.

(3) If a through airwaybill has been issued covering air transportation to a foreign destination, but the transportation nevertheless ends in the United States (for example, because the foreign consignee cancels the order before the shipment leaves a gateway city), then the amount paid for air transportation is taxable. In such a case the air carrier must collect the tax from the shipper or other person who paid for the air transportation.

(4) Any transportation of property by air shipped by the Department of Defense through an aerial port of embarkation and debarkation on a U.S. Government bill of lading shall be considered to—

(i) Begin in the United States and end outside the United States if the bill of lading states that the shipment is "For Export", or

(ii) Begin outside the United States and end in the United States if the bill of lading states that the shipment is "Imported by Air".

If a U.S. Government bill of lading stating that a shipment is "For Export" has been issued but the shipment nevertheless ends in the United States, then the amount paid for air transportation is taxable. In such a case the Department of Defense shall notify the air carrier that the shipment is taxable and shall pay the tax to such carrier.

(d) *Exportation involving two or more modes of transportation.*—(1) Even though transportation of property by air begins and ends in the United States, the tax does not apply if the property is being transported in the course of exportation by continuous movement and in due course is so exported, provided the requirements of this paragraph are satisfied. For example, the tax does not apply to air transportation from Chicago to New York if the property is in the course of exportation, by continuous movement, by boat from New York to Europe and in due course is so exported. Delays caused by circumstances beyond the control of the shipper (such as labor disputes or natural disasters) will not interrupt continuous movement. Property arriving at a gateway city by air may be repacked or consolidated with other property without interrupting continuous movement.

(2)(i) Continuous movement in the course of exportation shall be evidenced by (*a*) the execution of the Export Exemption Certificate, Form 1363, and (*b*) proof that exportation has actually occurred.

(ii) Form 1363 may be used in connection with a separate payment otherwise subject to tax or it may be used, with the permission of the district director, as a blanket exemption certificate by a person who expects to make payments for numerous export shipments over an indefinite period of time. If used in connection with a separate payment, the certificate shall be executed, in duplicate, by the shipper or other person making the payment subject to tax. Such person shall retain the duplicate with the shipping papers for at least 3 years from the last day of the month during which the shipment was made from the point of origin, and shall file the original with the carrier at the time of payment of the transportation charge. The carrier receiving the original certificate shall retain it along with the document showing payment of the transportation charge, for a period of at least 3 years from the last day of the month during which the shipment was made from the point of origin.

(iii) Form 1363 may be used as a blanket exemption certificate by a person who demonstrates to the satisfaction of the district director that it is impracticable to execute a separate Form 1363 for each payment. Permission to execute a blanket exemption certificate shall be requested, in writing, from the district director for the district in which is located the principal place of business or principal office or agency of the shipper or other person seeking permission. If permission is granted a separate certificate shall be executed in duplicate, by the shipper or other person making the payments, for each air carrier to be used in making export shipments. Such person shall retain the duplicate together with all shipping papers, and shall file the original with the air carrier with or before payment of the first transportation charge to be covered by the certificate. The air carrier shall retain the original certificate together with all documents showing payment of the transportation charges. Permission to execute a blanket exemption certificate, if granted, shall remain in force until withdrawn by the person who requested such permission or until withdrawn by the district director who granted such permission. Each person shall retain the certificate for at least 3 years after the last day of the month during which the final shipment covered by the certificate was made from the point of origin. Each person shall retain the shipping and payment documents for at least 3 years after the last day of the month during which the shipment was made from the point of origin.

(3) The filing of a properly executed Form 1363 with the carrier suspends liability for the payment of the tax for a period of six months from the date of shipment from the point of origin. If the person who is liable for the tax has not provided evidence to the carrier of the actual exportation of a shipment within such period, then the temporary suspension of the liability for the payment of the tax ceases and the carrier shall collect the tax from the person who paid the carrier for the transportation charge. If, after collection of the tax by the carrier, proof of exportation is subsequently received by the carrier, credit or refund of the tax may be obtained under the terms set forth in section 6415 of the Internal Revenue Code of 1954.

(4) Documentary evidence of the exportation of the property may consist of a copy of export bill of lading, memorandum from the captain of the vessel, customs official, or a foreign consignee, shipper's export declaration, or other evidence sufficient to establish that

the property has actually been exported. The person making the payment subject to tax shall furnish the appropriate documentary evidence to the carrier, or a statement that he holds such documentary evidence. In the latter case, the statement must: (i) certify that the property covered by the Export Exemption Certificate, Form 1363 was exported; (ii) identify the evidence of exportation; (iii) specify the foreign destination or the possession of the United States to which the property was shipped; and (iv) show the place where such evidence will be available for inspection by internal revenue officers. Any documentary evidence or statement, as the case may be, shall be retained by the carrier and the person making the payment subject to tax for a period of three years from the last day of the month during which the shipment was made from the point of origin. If the person making the payment subject to tax is not the actual exporter and is unable to obtain documentary evidence of exportation, such person shall obtain from the person having custody of the documentary evidence a statement containing the same facts as listed above for a statement furnished to the carrier by the person liable for the tax. The person making the payment subject to tax shall furnish the original of such statement to the carrier and shall retain a copy in his records. The statement shall be retained for the same three year period as the evidence of exportation is to be retained.

(e) *Definitions.*—(1) *Property.*—The term "property" does not include excess baggage accompanying a passenger travelling on an aircraft operated on an established line.

(2) *Transportation.*—The term "transportation" includes layover or waiting time and movement of the aircraft in deadhead service.

(3) *Taxable transportation.*—The term "taxable transportation" is defined in section 4272.

(f) *Collection of tax.*—The tax imposed by section 4271 shall be paid by the person making the payment subject to tax and shall be collected by the person engaged in the business of transporting property by air for hire who receives such payment, except that in the case of amounts subject to tax which are paid by the U.S. Postal Service, the tax shall not be collected by the person engaged in the business of transporting property by air for hire who receives such payment, but instead shall be paid directly by such Service as if it were a collecting agent.

(g) *Applicability date.*—This section applies to amounts paid on and after January 19, 2021. For rules that apply before that date, *see* 26 CFR part 49, revised as of April 1, 2020. [Reg. § 49.4271-1.]

☐ [*T.D. 7054, 7-28-70. Amended by T.D. 7190, 6-28-72; T.D. 7316, 6-18-74; T.D. 7517, 11-11-77; T.D. 7953, 5-9-84. Redesignated and amended by T.D. 8328, 12-28-90. Amended by T.D. 8442, 10-21-92 and T.D. 9948, 1-14-2021.*]

### [Reg. § 49.4271-2]

**§ 49.4271-2. Aircraft management services.**—For rules regarding the exemption for certain amounts paid by aircraft owners for aircraft management services, see § 49.4261-10. This section applies to amounts paid on and after January 19, 2021. For rules that apply before that date, *see* 26 CFR part 49, revised as of April 1, 2020. [Reg. § 49.4271-2.]

☐ [*T.D. 9948, 1-14-2021.*]

### [Reg. § 49.4281-1]

**§ 49.4281-1. Small aircraft on nonestablished lines.**—(a) *In general.*—Amounts paid for the transportation of persons on a small aircraft of the type sometimes referred to as air taxis shall be exempt from the tax imposed under section 4261 of the Internal Revenue Code provided the aircraft has a maximum certificated takeoff weight of 6,000 pounds or less determined as provided in paragraph (b) of this section. The exemption does not apply, however, when the

aircraft is operated on an established line or when the aircraft is a jet aircraft.

(b) *Maximum certificated takeoff weight.*—The term *maximum certificated takeoff weight* means the maximum certificated takeoff weight shown in the type certificate or airworthiness certificate issued by the Federal Aviation Administration.

(c) *Established line.*—The term "operated on an established line" means operated with some degree of regularity between definite points. It does not necessarily mean that strict regularity of schedule is maintained; that the full run is always made; that a particular route is followed; or that intermediate stops are restricted. The term implies that the person rendering the service maintains and exercises control over the direction, route, time, number of passengers carried, etc.

(d) *Jet aircraft.*—For purposes of this section, the term *jet aircraft* does not include any aircraft which is a rotorcraft (such as a helicopter) or propeller aircraft.

(e) *Applicability date.*—This section applies to amounts paid on and after January 19, 2021. For rules that apply before that date, *see* 26 CFR part 49, revised as of April 1, 2020. [Reg. § 49.4281-1.]

☐ [*T.D. 6430, 12-3-59. Redesignated by T.D. 6618, 11-14-62. Redesignated and amended by T.D. 9948, 1-14-2021.*]

### [Reg. § 49.4282-1]

**§ 49.4282-1. [Reserved]**
☐ [*T.D. 9948, 1-14-2021.*]

### [Reg. § 49.4291-1]

**§ 49.4291-1. Persons receiving payment must collect tax.**—Except as otherwise provided in section 4263(a), every person receiving any payment for facilities or services on which a tax is imposed upon the payor thereof under chapter 33 shall collect the amount of the tax from the person making that payment. Under section 7501, all taxes collected in this manner are held by the collecting agent in trust for the United States. If the person from whom the tax is required to be collected refuses to pay it or if for any reason it is impossible for the collecting agent to collect the tax from that person, the collecting agent is required to report to the Commissioner the name and address of that person, the nature of the facility provided or service rendered, the amount paid therefor, and the date on which paid. Applicable October 1, 2004, this report must be made on or before the report due date. Upon receipt of this report the Commissioner will proceed against the person to whom the facilities were provided or the services rendered to assert the amount of tax due, affording that person the same conference, protest, and appellate rights as are available to other excise taxpayers. In addition, when a field or office audit of a collecting agent's records, or of a taxpayer's records, discloses that the collecting agent failed during prior reporting periods to collect taxes due, the Commissioner may assert those taxes directly against the person to whom the facilities were provided or the services rendered, whether or not the collecting agent had attempted collection or the person liable for the tax had refused payment thereof. For purposes of this section, the report due date is—

(a) In the case of a person using the alternative method of making deposits described in § 40.6302(c)-3 of this chapter, the due date of the return on which the item of adjustment relating to the uncollected tax would be reflected if items of adjustment were determined without regard to the limitation in § 40.6302(c)-3 of this chapter; and

(b) In any other case, the due date of the return on which the tax would have been reported but for the refusal to pay or inability to collect. [Reg. § 49.4291-1.]

☐ [*T.D. 8685, 11-8-96. Amended by T.D. 9051, 4-1-2003; T.D. 9149, 8-9-2004 and T.D. 9221, 8-24-2005.*]

## Policies Issued by Foreign Insurers

See p. 20,601 for regulations not amended to reflect law changes

### [Reg. § 46.0-1]

**§ 46.0-1. Amended.**—The regulations in this part 46 relate to the taxes on certain insurance policies and self-insured health plans imposed by chapter 34 of the Internal Revenue Code and the tax on the issuer of registration-required obligations not issued in registered form imposed by chapter 39 of the Internal Revenue Code. See part 40 of this chapter for regulations relating to returns, payments, and deposits of taxes imposed by chapters 34 and 39. [Reg. § 46.0-1.]

☐ [*T.D. 8442, 10-21-92. Amended by T.D. 9602, 12-5-2012.*]

### [Reg. § 46.4371-1]

**§ 46.4371-1. Applicability of subpart.**—The provisions of this subpart apply only to premiums paid on or after January 1, 1966. See Subpart H, Part 47 of this chapter for provisions relating to premiums paid or charged before January 1, 1966. If any portion of the tax imposed by section 4371 was paid on the basis of the premium charged before January 1, 1966, in accordance with the provisions of § 47.4371-2 of this chapter (documentary stamp tax), then, to the extent that such portion was paid by stamp, no further tax is due under the provisions of this subpart. [Reg. § 46.4371-1.]

☐ [*T.D. 7023, 1-21-70.*]

**[Reg. §46.4371-2]**

**§46.4371-2. Imposition of tax on policies issued by foreign insurers; scope of tax.**—(a) *Certain insurance policies, and indemnity, fidelity, or surety bonds.*—Section 4371(1) imposes a tax upon each policy of insurance (other than those referred to in paragraph (b) of this section), upon each indemnity, fidelity, or surety bond, or upon each certificate, binder, covering note, receipt, memorandum, cablegram, letter, or other instrument by whatever name called, whereby a contract of insurance or an obligation in the nature of an indemnity, fidelity, or surety bond is made, continued, or renewed, if issued—

(1) By a nonresident alien individual, a foreign partnership, or a foreign corporation, as insurer (unless the policy or other instrument is signed or countersigned by an officer or agent of the insurer in a State, Territory, or the District of Columbia in which the insurer is authorized to do business); and either

(2) To or for, or in the name of, a domestic corporation, domestic partnership, or an individual resident of the United States, against or with respect to hazards, risks, losses, or liabilities wholly or partly within the United States; or

(3) To or for, or in the name of, a foreign corporation, foreign partnership, or nonresident individual, engaged in a trade or business within the United States with respect to hazards, risks, or liabilities wholly within the United States.

For definition of the term "indemnity bond," see section 4372(c).

(b) *Life insurance, sickness, and accident policies, and annuity contracts.*—Unless the insurer is subject to tax under section 819, section 4371(2) imposes a tax upon each policy of insurance or annuity contract, or upon each certificate, binder, covering note, receipt, memorandum, cablegram, letter, or other instrument by whatever name called, whereby a contract of insurance or an annuity contract is made, continued, or renewed, if issued—

(1) By a nonresident alien individual, a foreign partnership, or a foreign corporation, as insurer (unless the policy or other instrument is signed or countersigned by an officer or agent of the insurer in a State, Territory, or the District of Columbia in which such insurer is authorized to do business); and

(2) To any person with respect to the life or hazards to the person of a citizen or resident of the United States.

(c) *Reinsurance.*—Section 4371(3) imposes a tax upon each policy of reinsurance, certificate, binder, covering note, receipt, memorandum, cablegram, letter, or other instrument by whatever name called, whereby a contract of reinsurance is made, continued, or renewed, if issued—

(1) By a nonresident alien individual, a foreign partnership, or a foreign corporation, as reinsurer (unless the policy or other instrument is signed or countersigned by an officer or agent of the reinsurer in a State, Territory, or the District of Columbia in which such reinsurer is authorized to do business); and

(2) To any person against, or with respect to, any of the hazards, risks, losses, or liabilities covered by contracts described in section 4371(1) or (2).

(d) *Exempt indemnity bonds.*—The tax imposed by section 4371 does not apply to any indemnity bond described in section 4373(2). [Reg. §46.4371-2.]

☐ [*T.D.* 7023, 1-21-70.]

**[Reg. §46.4371-3]**

**§46.4371-3. Rate and computation of tax.**—(a) *Rate of tax.*—(1) The tax under section 4371(1) is imposed at the rate of 4 cents on each dollar, or fractional part thereof, of the premium payment.

(2) The tax under section 4371(2) and (3) is imposed at the rate of 1 cent on each dollar, or fractional part thereof, of the premium payment.

(b) *Meaning of premium payment.*—For purposes of this subpart, the term "premium payment" means the consideration paid for assuming and carrying the risk or obligation, and includes any additional assessment or charge paid under the contract, whether payable in one sum or installments. [Reg. §46.4371-3.]

☐ [*T.D.* 7023, 1-21-70.]

**[Reg. §46.4371-4]**

**§46.4371-4. Records required with respect to foreign insurance policies.**—(a) Each person required under the provisions of §46.4374-1 to remit the tax imposed by section 4371 shall keep or cause to be kept accurate records of all policies or other instruments subject to such tax upon which premiums have been paid. Such records must identify each such policy or other instrument in such a manner as to clearly establish the following:(1) The gross premium paid; (2) whether such policy or other instrument is (i) a policy of casualty insurance or an indemnity bond subject to tax under section

4371(1), (ii) a policy of life, sickness, or accident insurance or an annuity contract subject to tax under section 4371(2), or (iii) a policy of reinsurance subject to tax under section 4371(3); (3) the identity of the insured (as defined in section 4372(d)); (4) the identity of the foreign insurer or reinsurer (as defined in section 4372(a)); and (5) the total premium charged and, if the premium is to be paid in installments, the amount and anniversary date of each such installment.

(b) The records required under the provisions of this section must be kept on file at the place of business or at some other convenient location, for a period of at least 3 years from the date any part of the tax became due or the date any part of the tax is paid, whichever is later, in such manner as to be readily accessible to authorized internal revenue officers or employees. The person having control or possession of a policy or other instrument subject to tax under section 4371 shall retain such policy or other instrument for at least 3 years from the date any part of the tax with respect to such policy was paid. [Reg. §46.4371-4.]

☐ [*T.D.* 7023, 1-21-70. *Redesignated by T.D.* 8328, 12-28-90.]

**[Reg. §46.4374-1]**

**§46.4374-1. Liability for tax.**—(a) *In general.*—Any person who makes, signs, issues, or sells any of the documents and instruments subject to the tax, or for whose use or benefit the same are made, signed, issued, or sold, shall be liable for the tax imposed by section 4371. For purposes of this section, in the case of a reinsurance policy that is subject to the tax imposed by section 4371(3), other than assumption reinsurance, the insured person on the underlying insurance policy, the risk of which is covered in whole or in part by such reinsurance policy, shall not constitute a person for whose use or benefit the reinsurance policy is made, signed, issued, or sold.

(b) *When liability for tax attaches.*—The liability for the tax imposed by section 4371 shall attach at the time the premium payment is transferred to the foreign insurer or reinsurer (including transfers to any bank, trust fund, or similar recipient, designated by the foreign insurer or reinsurer), or to any nonresident agent, solicitor, or broker. A person required to pay tax under this section may remit such tax before the time the tax attaches if he keeps records consistent with such practice.

(c) *Payment of tax.*—The tax imposed by section 4371 shall be paid on the basis of a return by the person who makes payment of the premium to a foreign insurer or reinsurer or to any nonresident agent, solicitor, or broker. If the tax is not paid by the person who paid the premium, the tax imposed by section 4371 shall be paid on the basis of a return by any person who makes, signs, issues, or sells any of the documents or instruments subject to the tax imposed by section 4371, or for whose use or benefit such document or instrument is made, signed, issued, or sold.

(d) *Penalty for failure to pay tax.*—Any person who fails to comply with the requirements of this section with intent to evade the tax shall, in addition to other penalties provided therefor, pay a fine of double the amount of tax. (See section 7270.)

(e) *Effective date.*—This section is applicable for premiums paid on or after November 27, 2002. [Reg. §46.4374-1.]

☐ [*T.D.* 7023, 1-21-70. *Amended by T.D.* 9024, 11-26-2002.]

**[Reg. §46.4375-1]**

**§46.4375-1. Fee on issuers of specified health insurance policies.**—(a) *In general.*—An issuer of a specified health insurance policy is liable for a fee imposed by section 4375 for policy years ending on or after October 1, 2012, and before October 1, 2019. Paragraph (b) of this section provides definitions that apply for purposes of section 4375 and this section. Paragraph (c) of this section provides rules for calculating the fee under section 4375. Paragraph (d) of this section provides the applicability date. For rules relating to filing the required return and paying the fee, see §§ 40.6011(a)-1 and 40.6071(a)-1 of this chapter.

(b) *Definitions.*—The following definitions apply for purposes of section 4375 and this section. See also §46.4377-1 for additional definitions.

(1) *Specified health insurance policy.*—(i) *In general.*—Except as provided in paragraph (b)(1)(ii) of this section and §46.4377-1, *specified health insurance policy* means any accident and health insurance policy (including a policy under a group health plan) issued with respect to individuals residing in the United States (as defined in §46.4377-1(a)(2)), including prepaid health coverage arrangements described in paragraph (b)(2) of this section. *Specified health insurance policy* also includes any policy that provides accident and health coverage to an active employee, former employee, or qualifying beneficiary, as continuation coverage required under the Consoli-

dated Omnibus Budget Reconciliation Act of 1985 (COBRA) or similar continuation coverage under other Federal law or state law.

(ii) *Exceptions.*—The term *specified health insurance policy* does not include—

(A) Any insurance policy if substantially all of its coverage is of excepted benefits described in section 9832(c);

(B) Any group policy issued to an employer where the facts and circumstances show that the group policy was designed and issued specifically to cover primarily employees who are working and residing outside of the United States (as defined in §46.4377-1(a)(3));

(C) Any stop loss or indemnity reinsurance policy; or

(D) Any insurance policy to the extent it provides an employee assistance program, disease management program, or wellness program if the program does not provide significant benefits in the nature of medical care or treatment.

(iii) *Stop loss policy.*—For purposes of paragraph (b)(1)(ii) of this section, *stop loss policy* means an insurance policy in which—

(A) The insurer that issues the policy to a person establishing or maintaining a self-insured health plan becomes liable for all, or an agreed upon portion, of losses that person incurs in covering the applicable lives in excess of a specified amount; and

(B) The person establishing or maintaining the self-insured health plan retains its liability to, and its contractual relationship with, the applicable lives covered.

(iv) *Indemnity reinsurance policy.*—For purposes of paragraph (b)(1)(ii) of this section, *indemnity reinsurance policy* means an agreement between two or more insurance companies under which—

(A) The reinsuring company agrees to accept and to indemnify the issuing company for all or part of the risk of loss under policies specified in the agreement; and

(B) The issuing company retains its liability to, and its contractual relationship with, the applicable lives covered.

(2) *Prepaid health coverage arrangement.*—The term *prepaid health coverage arrangement* means an arrangement under which fixed payments or premiums are received as consideration for a person's agreement to provide or arrange for the provision of accident and health coverage to individuals residing in the United States, regardless of how such coverage is provided or arranged to be provided. For example, any hospital or medical service policy or certificate, hospital or medical service plan contract, or health maintenance organization contract is a specified health insurance policy.

(c) *Calculation of fee.*—(1) *In general.*—The amount of the fee for a policy for a policy year is equal to the product of the average number of lives covered under the policy for the policy year (determined in accordance with paragraphs (c)(2) and (c)(3) of this section) and the applicable dollar amount (determined in accordance with paragraph (c)(4) of this section). For purposes of computing the fee under this paragraph (c), in the case of an issuer that determines the average number of lives covered for all policies in effect during a calendar year using the member months method under paragraph (c)(2)(v) of this section or the state form method under paragraph (c)(2)(vi) of this section, the applicable dollar amount with respect to such issuer's policies for such calendar year is the applicable dollar amount for policy years ending on December 31 of such calendar year (determined in accordance with paragraph (c)(4) of this section), except that the applicable dollar amount with respect to such an issuer's policies for calendar year 2019 is the applicable dollar amount for policy years ending on September 30, 2019. For more information, see the examples in paragraphs (c)(2)(iii)(B), (c)(2)(iv)(B), (c)(2)(v)(B), and (c)(2)(vi)(B) of this section.

(2) *Determination of the average number of lives covered under a policy.*—(i) *In general.*—To determine the average number of lives covered under a specified health insurance policy during a policy year, an issuer must use one of the following methods—

(A) The actual count method (described in paragraph (c)(2)(iii) of this section);

(B) The snapshot method (described in paragraph (c)(2)(iv) of this section);

(C) The member months method (described in paragraph (c)(2)(v) of this section); or

(D) The state form method (described in paragraph (c)(2)(vi) of this section).

(ii) *Consistency requirements.*—An issuer must use the same method of calculating the average number of lives covered under a policy consistently for the duration of the year. In addition, for all policies for which a liability is reported on a Form 720, "Quarterly Federal Excise Tax Return," for a particular year, an issuer must use the same method of computing lives covered. An issuer that deter-

mines the average number of lives covered by using the actual count method described in paragraph (c)(2)(iii) of this section or the snapshot method described in paragraph (c)(2)(iv) of this section may change its method of computing the average lives covered to the snapshot method or actual count method, respectively, provided that the issuer uses the same method for computing the average lives covered for all policies for which a liability is reported on the Form 720 for that year. For example, an issuer with a policy having a policy year that ends on June 30, Policy A, may determine the average number of lives covered under Policy A for July 1, 2013, to June 30, 2014, using the actual count method if the issuer uses the actual count method for all policies for which a liability will be reported on the Form 720 due by July 31, 2015 (the due date for return that will include the liability for the July 2013 to June 2014 policy year for Policy A). The issuer may change its method for determining the average number of lives covered under Policy A to the snapshot method for the July 1, 2014, to June 30, 2015, policy year, provided that the snapshot method is used for all policies for which a liability will be reported on the Form 720 due by July 31, 2016 (the due date for return that will 36 include the liability for the July 2014 to June 2015 policy year for Policy A). An issuer that determines the average number of lives covered by using the member months method under paragraph (c)(2)(v) of this section or the state form method under paragraph (c)(2)(vi) of this section must use the same method for calculating lives covered for all policy years for which the fee applies.

(iii) *Actual count method.*—(A) *Calculation method.*—An issuer may determine the average number of lives covered under a policy for a policy year by adding the total number of lives covered for each day of the policy year and dividing that total by the number of days in the policy year.

(B) *Example.*—The following example illustrates the principles of paragraphs (c)(1) and (c)(2)(iii)(A) of this section:

*Example.* Insurance Company A issues three policies that are in effect during 2014, Group Health Insurance Policy A, which has a policy year from December 1 to November 30, Group Health Insurance Policy B, which has a policy year from March 1 to February 28, and Group Health Insurance Policy C, which has a policy year from January 1 to December 31. To calculate the average number of lives covered for 2014, Insurance Company A must calculate the average number of lives covered for each of its three policies for the policy year that ends in 2014. Insurance Company A chooses to use the actual count method under paragraph (c)(2)(iii)(A) of this section to determine average lives covered for policies having a policy year that ends in 2014. Insurance Company A calculates the sum of lives covered under Policy A for each day of the policy year ending November 30, 2014, as 3,285,000. The average number of lives covered under Policy A for the policy year ending November 30, 2014, is 3,285,000 divided by 365, or 9,000. Insurance Company A calculates the sum of lives covered under Policy B for each day of the policy year ending February 28, 2014, as 547,500. The average number of lives covered under Policy B for the policy year ending on February 28, 2014, is 547,500 divided by 365, or 1,500. Insurance Company A calculates the sum of lives covered under Policy C for each day of the policy year ending December 31, 2014, as 4,380,000. The average number of lives covered under Policy C for the policy year ending December 31, 2014, is 4,380,000 divided by 365, or 12,000. To calculate the section 4375 fee under paragraph (c)(1) of this section for calendar year 2014, Insurance Company A must first determine the applicable dollar amount for each policy under paragraph (c)(4) of this section and multiply that amount by the average number of lives covered for that policy. Insurance Company A then adds the total fees for all three policies to determine the total fee under section 4375 that it must pay for calendar year 2014.

(iv) *Snapshot method.*—(A) *Calculation method.*—An issuer may determine the average number of lives covered under a policy for a policy year by adding the totals of lives covered on a date during the first, second, or third month of each quarter (or more dates in each quarter if an equal number of dates is used for each quarter), and dividing that total by the number of dates on which a count is made. For purposes of this paragraph (c)(2)(iv)(A), each date used for the second, third and fourth quarters must be within three days of the date in that quarter that corresponds to the date used for the first quarter, and all dates used must be within the same policy year. If an issuer uses multiple dates for the first quarter, the issuer must use dates in the second, third, and fourth quarters that correspond to each of the dates used for the first quarter or are within three days of such corresponding dates, and all dates used must be within the same policy year. The 30th and 31st day of a month are treated as the last day of the month for purposes of determining the corresponding date for any month that has fewer than 31 days (for example, if either March 30 or March 31 is used as a counting date for a calendar year policy, June 30 is the corresponding date for the second quarter).

**Reg. §46.4375-1(c)(2)(iv)(A)**

(B) *Example.*—The following example illustrates the principles of paragraphs (c)(1) and (c)(2)(iv)(A) of this section:

*Example.* (i) Insurance Company B issues three policies with 12-month policy years that end in 2014, Group Health Insurance Policy A, which has a policy year from December 1 to November 30, Group Health Insurance Policy B, which has a policy year from March 1 to February 28, and Group Health Insurance Policy C, which has a policy year from January 1 to December 31. To calculate the average number of lives covered for 2014, Insurance Company B must calculate the average number of lives covered for each of its three policies for the policy year that ends in 2014. Insurance Company B chooses to determine the average lives covered using the snapshot method for all policies that have a policy year that ends in 2014 and chooses to count lives covered on a single date of the first month of each quarter of the policy years. Thus, for Policy A, Insurance Company B must count lives covered on a single date falling in each of December 2013, March 2014, June 2014 and September 2014; for Policy B, Insurance Company B must count lives covered on a single date falling in each of March 2014, June 2014, September 2014 and December 2014; and for Policy C, Insurance Company B must count lives covered on a single date falling in each of January 2014, April 2014, July 2014 and October 2014. In addition, the date for each of the second, third, and fourth quarters must fall within three days of the date in such quarter that corresponds to the date used for the first quarter, and must fall within the same policy year.

(ii) On December 6, 2013, Policy A covers 8,900 lives, on March 7, 2014, 9,100 lives, on June 6, 2014, 9,050 lives, and on September 5, 2014, 9,050 lives. Insurance Company B treats the average number of lives covered under Policy A for the policy year ending November 30, 2014, as 36,100 (8,900 + 9,100 + 9,050 + 9,050) divided by 4, or 9,025.

(iii) On March 4, 2013, Policy B covers 1,500 lives, on June 7, 2013, 1,350 lives, on September 6, 2013, 1,400 lives, and on December 6, 2013, 1,550 lives. Insurance Company B treats the average number of lives covered under Policy B for the policy year ending February 28, 2014, as 5,800 (1,500 + 1,350 + 1,400 + 1,550) divided by 4, or 1,450.

(iv) On January 6, 2014, Policy C covers 12,500 lives, on April 4, 2014, 12,250 lives, on July 7, 2014, 12,000 lives, and on October 3, 2014, 11,250 lives. Insurance Company B treats the average number of lives covered under Policy C for the policy year ending December 31, 2014, as 47,750 (12,500 + 12,250 + 12,000 + 11,250) divided by 4, or 12,000.

(v) To calculate the section 4375 fee under paragraph (c)(1) of this section for calendar year 2014, Insurance Company B must first determine the applicable dollar amount for each policy under paragraph (c)(4) of this section and multiply that amount by the number of average lives covered for that policy. Insurance Company B then adds the total fees for all three policies to determine the total fee under section 4375 that it must pay for calendar year 2014.

(v) *Member months method.*—(A) *Calculation method.*—An issuer may determine the average number of lives covered under all policies in effect for a calendar year based on the member months (an amount that equals the sum of the totals of lives covered on pre-specified days in each month of the reporting period) reported on the National Association of Insurance Commissioners (NAIC) Supplemental Health Care Exhibit filed for that calendar year. Under this method, the average number of lives covered under the policies in effect for the calendar year equals the member months divided by 12.

(B) *Example.*—The following example illustrates the principles of paragraphs (c)(1) and (c)(2)(v)(A) of this section:

*Example.* Insurance Company C chooses to determine the average number of lives covered for all years to which the section 4375 fee applies using the member months method of paragraph (c)(2)(v)(A) of this section. Insurance Company C reports 12,000,000 as its member months on the NAIC Supplemental Health Care Exhibit filed for calendar year 2013. Under the member months method, Insurance Company C calculates the average number of lives covered for all its specified health insurance policies in force during calendar year 2013 by dividing 12,000,000 (member months) by 12 (number of months in the reporting period), which equals 1,000,000. To determine the section 4375 fee it must pay for calendar year 2013, Insurance Company C multiplies 1,000,000 by the applicable dollar amount that is in effect at the end of the calendar year under paragraph (c)(4) of this section.

(vi) *State form method.*—(A) *Calculation method.*—An issuer that is not required to file NAIC annual financial statements may determine the number of lives covered under all policies in effect for the calendar year using a form that is filed with the issuer's state of domicile and a method similar to that described in paragraph (c)(2)(v) of this section, if the form reports the number of lives covered in the same manner as member months are reported on the NAIC Supplemental Health Care Exhibit.

(B) *Example.*—The following example illustrates the principles of paragraphs (c)(1) and (c)(2)(vi)(A) of this section:

*Example.* Insurance Company D is not required to file the NAIC Supplemental Health Care Exhibit, but files a form with its state of domicile. Insurance Company D chooses to determine the average number of lives covered for all years to which the section 4375 fee applies using the state form method of paragraph (c)(2)(vi)(A) of this section. The state form reports the number of lives covered in the same manner as member months is reported on the NAIC Supplemental Health Care Exhibit. For calendar year 2013, Insurance Company D reports 12,000,000 as its equivalent member months on the state form. Under the state form method, Insurance Company D calculates the average number of lives covered for all of its specified health insurance policies in force during calendar year 2013 by dividing 12,000,000 (equivalent member months) by 12 (number of months in the reporting period), which equals 1,000,000. To determine the section 4375 fee it must pay for calendar year 2013, Insurance Company D multiplies 1,000,000 by the applicable dollar amount that is in effect at the end of the calendar year under paragraph (c)(4) of this section.

(3) *Special rules for the first year and the last year the fee is in effect.*— (i) *Calculation of the average number of lives covered under the policy for the first year the fee is in effect.*—For issuers that determine the average number of lives covered using data reported on the 2012 NAIC Supplemental Health Care Exhibit or a permitted state form that covers the 2012 calendar year, the average number of lives covered under all policies in effect for the 2012 calendar year equals the average number of lives covered for that year (as determined under paragraph (c)(2)(v) or (vi) of this section) multiplied by 1/4. The resulting number is deemed to be the average number of lives covered for policies with policy years ending on or after October 1, 2012, and before January 1, 2013. For policy years beginning before May 14, 2012, and ending on or after October 1, 2012, issuers that determine the average number of lives covered using the actual count method under paragraph (c)(2)(iii) of this section may calculate the average number of lives covered using data from the period beginning May 14, 2012, through the end of the policy year. For policy years beginning before May 14, 2012, and ending on or after October 1, 2012, issuers that determine the average number of lives covered using the snapshot method under paragraph (c)(2)(iv) of this section may calculate the average number of lives covered using dates from the quarters remaining in the policy year starting on or after May 14, 2012. If an abbreviated year is used, the issuer will divide the number of lives covered by the number of days from May 14, 2012, through the end of the policy year (for the actual count method) or the number of days on which a count was made (for the snapshot method).

(ii) *Calculation of the average number of lives covered under the policy for the last year the fee is in effect.*—For issuers that determine the average number of lives covered using data reported on the 2019 NAIC Supplemental Health Care Exhibit or a permitted state form that covers the 2019 calendar year, the average number of lives covered for all policies in effect during the 2019 calendar year equals the average number of lives covered for that year (as determined under paragraph (c)(2)(v) or (vi) of this section) multiplied by 3/4. The resulting number is deemed to be the average number of lives covered for policies with policy years ending on or after January 1, 2019, and before October 1, 2019.

(iii) *Examples.*—The following examples illustrate the principles of paragraph (c)(3) of this section:

*Example 1.* Insurance Company E issues Group Health Insurance Policy C, which has a policy year that ends on November 30, 2012. Insurance Company E determines the average number of lives covered under a policy by using the actual count method. Under that method, for that policy year, Insurance Company E calculates the sum of lives covered under Policy C for each day between May 14, 2012, and November 30, 2012, as 10,000. The average number of lives covered under Policy C for that policy year is 10,000 divided by the number of days from May 14, 2012, through November 30, 2012. Alternatively, Insurance Company E could have counted the number of lives covered for the entire policy year and divided the sum by 365.

*Example 2.* Insurance Company F reports 12,000,000 as its member months on its NAIC Supplemental Health Care Exhibit filed for calendar year 2012. Under the member months method, Insurance Company F calculates the average number of lives covered for 2012 by dividing 12,000,000 (member months) by 12 (number of months in the reporting period), and then multiplying the result (1,000,000) by 1/4, which equals 250,000. Accordingly, the average number of lives covered for policies with policy years ending on or after October 1, 2012, and before January 1, 2013, is 250,000.

(4) *Applicable dollar amount.*—For policy years ending on or after October 1, 2012, and before October 1, 2013, the applicable dollar amount is $1. For policy years ending on or after October 1, 2013, and before October 1, 2014, the applicable dollar amount is $2. For any policy year ending in any Federal fiscal year beginning on or after October 1, 2014, the applicable dollar amount is the sum of—

(i) The applicable dollar amount for the policy year ending in the previous Federal fiscal year; plus

(ii) The amount equal to the product of—

(A) The applicable dollar amount for the policy year ending in the previous Federal fiscal year; and

(B) The percentage increase in the projected per capita amount of the National Health Expenditures most recently released by the Department of Health and Human Services before the beginning of the Federal fiscal year.

(d) *Effective/Applicability date.*—This section applies for policies with policy years ending on or after October 1, 2012, and before October 1, 2019. [Reg. § 46.4375-1.]

☐ [*T.D. 9602, 12-5-2012.*]

### [Reg. § 46.4376-1]

**§ 46.4376-1. Fee on sponsors of self-insured health plans.**—(a) *In general.*—(1) *General rule.*—A plan sponsor of an applicable self-insured health plan is liable for a fee imposed by section 4376 for plans with plan years ending on or after October 1, 2012, and before October 1, 2019. Paragraph (b) of this section provides the definitions that apply for purposes of section 4376 and this section. Paragraph (c) of this section provides the requirements for calculating the fee imposed by section 4376. Paragraph (d) of this section provides the applicability date. For rules relating to filing the required return and paying the fee, see § § 40.6011(a)-1 and 40.6071(a)-1.

(2) [Reserved]

(b) *Definitions.*—The following definitions apply for purposes of section 4376 and this section. See § 46.4377-1 for additional definitions.

(1) *Applicable self-insured health plan.*—(i) *In general.*—Except as provided in paragraph (b)(1)(ii) of this section and § 46.4377-1, *applicable self-insured health plan* means a plan that provides for accident and health coverage (within the meaning of § 46.4377-1(a)) if any portion of the coverage is provided other than through an insurance policy and the plan is established or maintained—

(A) By one or more employers for the benefit of their employees or former employees;

(B) By one or more employee organizations for the benefit of their members or former members;

(C) Jointly by one or more employers and one or more employee organizations for the benefit of employees or former employees;

(D) By a voluntary employees' beneficiary association, as described in section 501(c)(9);

(E) By an organization described in section 501(c)(6); or

(F) By a multiple employer welfare arrangement (as defined in section 3(40) of the Employee Retirement Income Security Act of 1974 (ERISA)), a rural electric cooperative (as defined in section 3(40)(B)(iv) of ERISA), or a rural cooperative association (as defined in section 3(40)(B)(v) of ERISA).

(ii) *Exceptions.*—The term *applicable self-insured health plan* does not include any of the following:

(A) A plan that provides benefits substantially all of which are excepted benefits, as defined in section 9832(c). For example, a health flexible spending arrangement (health FSA) (as described in section 106(c)(2)) that satisfies the requirements to be treated as an excepted benefit under section 9832(c) and § 54.9831-1(c)(3)(v) of this chapter is not an applicable self-insured health plan. A health FSA that is not treated as an excepted benefit under section 9832(c) and § 54.9831-1(c)(3)(v) is an applicable self-insured health plan.

(B) An employee assistance program, disease management program, or wellness program if the program does not provide significant benefits in the nature of medical care or treatment.

(C) A plan that, as demonstrated by the facts and circumstances surrounding the adoption and operation of the plan, was designed specifically to cover primarily employees who are working and residing outside the United States (as defined in § 46.4377-1(a)(3)).

(iii) *Multiple self-insured arrangements established or maintained by the same plan sponsor.*—For purposes of section 4376, two or more arrangements established or maintained by the same plan sponsor that provide for accident and health coverage (within the meaning of § 46.4377-1(a)) other than through an insurance policy and that have the same plan year may be treated as a single applicable self-insured

health plan for purposes of calculating the fee imposed by section 4376. For example, if a plan sponsor establishes or maintains a self-insured arrangement providing major medical benefits, and a separate self-insured arrangement with the same plan year providing prescription drug benefits, the two arrangements may be treated as one applicable self- insured health plan so that the same life covered under each arrangement would count as only one covered life under the plan for purposes of calculating the fee. Similarly, if a plan sponsor provides a Health Reimbursement Arrangement (HRA) and another applicable self-insured health plan that provides major medical coverage, the HRA and the major medical plan may be treated as one applicable self-insured health plan if the HRA and the self-insured plan have the same plan year.

(iv) *Examples.*—The following examples illustrate the principle of this paragraph (b)(1):

*Example 1.* (i) Plan Sponsor D sponsors and maintains three separate plans to provide certain benefits to its employees - Plan 501, Plan 502, and Plan 503.

(ii) Plan 501 is a calendar year plan that provides accident and health benefits, other than through insurance (that is, on a self-insured basis), to employees of Plan Sponsor D. Plan 502 is a calendar year HRA that can be used to pay for qualified accident and medical expenses for employees of Plan Sponsor D and their eligible dependents. Plan 503 provides dental and vision benefits for employees of Plan Sponsor D and eligible dependents, other than through insurance (that is, on a self-insured basis).

(iii) Because Plan 501 and Plan 502 provide accident and health coverage (within the meaning of § 46.4377-1(a)) and are maintained by Plan Sponsor D for the benefit of its employees, Plans 501 and 502 are applicable self-insured health plans that are subject to the fee imposed by section 4376. Because dental and vision benefits are excepted benefits, as defined in section 9832(c), Plan 503 is not an applicable self-insured health plan subject to the section 4376 fee. Under the special rule set forth in § 46.4376-2(b)(1)(iii), Plan Sponsor D may treat Plans 501 and 502 (both self-insured plans with a calendar year plan year) as a single plan for purposes of calculating the fee imposed by section 4376.

*Example 2.* Same facts as *Example 1*, except Plan 503 is not a Plan that provides dental and vision benefits, but rather a plan that provides accident and health coverage solely to employees who are working and residing outside the United States and does not provide any benefits to employees who are not working and residing outside the United States. Plan 503 is designed specifically to provide coverage to employees working and residing outside the United States because it limits coverage to these employees. Therefore, in accordance with the exception described in § 46.4376-1(b)(1)(ii)(C), Plan 503 is not an applicable self-insured health plan.

(2) *Plan sponsor.*—(i) *In general.*—The term *plan sponsor* means—

(A) The employer, in the case of an applicable self-insured health plan established or maintained by a single employer;

(B) The employee organization, in the case of an applicable self-insured health plan established or maintained by an employee organization;

(C) The joint board of trustees, in the case of a multiemployer plan (as defined in section 414(f));

(D) The committee, in the case of a multiple employer welfare arrangement (as defined in section 3(40) of ERISA);

(E) The cooperative or association that establishes or maintains an applicable self-insured health plan established or maintained by a rural electric cooperative (as defined in section 3(40)(B)(iv) of ERISA) or rural cooperative association (as defined in section 3(40)(B)(v) of ERISA);

(F) The trustee, in the case of an applicable self-insured health plan established or maintained by a voluntary employees' beneficiary association (meaning that the voluntary employees' beneficiary association is not merely serving as a funding vehicle for a plan that is established or maintained by an employer or other person); or

(G) In the case of an applicable self-insured health plan the plan sponsor of which is not described in paragraphs (b)(2)(i)(A) through (F) of this section, the person identified by the terms of the document under which the plan is operated as the plan sponsor, or the person designated by the terms of the document under which the plan is operated as the plan sponsor for section 4376 purposes, provided that designation is made in writing, and that person has consented to the designation in writing, by no later than the date by which the return paying the fee under section 4376 for that plan year is required to be filed, after which date that designation for that plan year may not be changed or revoked, and provided further that a person may be designated as the plan sponsor only if the person is one of the persons establishing or maintaining the plan (for example, one of the employers that establishes or maintains the plan with one or more other employers or employee organizations).

(H) In the case of an applicable self-insured health plan the sponsor of which is not described in paragraphs (b)(2)(i)(A) through (F) of this section, and for which no identification or designation of a plan sponsor has been made pursuant to paragraph (b)(2)(i)(G) of this section, each employer that establishes or maintains the plan (with respect to employees of that employer), each employee organization that establishes or maintains the plan (with respect to members of that employee organization), and each board of trustees, cooperative, or association that establishes or maintains the plan, meaning that each plan sponsor must file a separate Form 720, "Quarterly Federal Excise Tax Return," reflecting its separate liability under section 4376.

(ii) *Examples.*—The following examples illustrate the principles of paragraph (b)(2) of this section:

*Example 1.* (i) Corporation XYZ is a holding company with no employees that owns all the issued and outstanding shares of Employer X, Employer Y, and Employer Z. Employer X, Employer Y, and Employer Z have established the XYZ Group Health Plan to provide accident and health coverage, provided other than through an insurance policy, for the benefit of their employees. The XYZ Group Health Plan has a calendar year plan year. In addition, there is no plan sponsor identified or designated in the plan document.

(ii) Because the XYZ Group Health Plan provides accident and health coverage other than through an insurance policy, and is established by one or more employers for the benefit of their employees, the XYZ Group Health Plan is an applicable self-insured health plan under section 4376(c)(2)(A) and paragraph (b)(1)(i)(A) of this section. Because a plan sponsor is not identified or designated in the governing plan document, the plan sponsor, for purposes of section 4376, is determined under paragraph (b)(2)(i)(H) of this section as each employer that establishes or maintains the plan (Employer X, Employer Y, and Employer Z), each with respect to its employees covered under the plan. Accordingly, Employer X, Employer Y, and Employer Z each must file a Form 720 reflecting their separate liabilities under section 4376, calculated based on lives covered that are employees of that employer (or spouses, dependents, or other beneficiaries of employees of that employer) and the applicable dollar amount in effect for the plan year.

*Example 2.* The same facts as *Example 1,* except that the governing plan document designates Employer X as the plan sponsor of the XYZ Group Health Plan for purposes of the fee under section 4376 and Employer X consents to this designation no later than the due date for paying the fee under section 4376. Accordingly, the plan sponsor for purposes of section 4376 is determined under paragraph (b)(2)(i)(G) of this section as Employer X. Employer X must file a Form 720 reflecting liabilities under section 4376, calculated based upon lives covered that are employees of Employer X, Employer Y, or Employer Z, or spouses, dependents, or other beneficiaries of employees of those employers and the applicable dollar amount in effect for the plan year.

(c) *Calculation of fee.*—(1) *In general.*—The amount of the fee for a plan year is equal to the product of the average number of lives covered under the plan for the plan year (determined in accordance with paragraph (c)(2) of this section) and the applicable dollar amount (determined in accordance with paragraph (c)(3) of this section).

(2) *Determination of the average number of lives covered under the plan.*—(i) *In general.*—To determine the average number of lives covered under an applicable self-insured health plan during a plan year, a plan sponsor must use one of the following methods—

(A) The actual count method (described in paragraph (c)(2)(iii) of this section);

(B) The snapshot method (described in paragraph (c)(2)(iv) of this section); or

(C) The Form 5500 method (described in paragraph (c)(2)(v) of this section).

(ii) *Consistency within plan year.*—A plan sponsor must use the same method of calculating the average number of lives covered under the plan consistently for the duration of the plan year. However, a plan sponsor may use a different method from one plan year to the next.

(iii) *Actual count method.*—(A) *In general.*—A plan sponsor may determine the average number of lives covered under a plan for a plan year by adding the totals of lives covered for each day of the plan year and dividing that total by the number of days in the plan year.

(B) *Example.*—The following example illustrates the principles of paragraphs (c)(1) and (c)(2)(iii)(A) of this section:

*Example.* Employer A is the plan sponsor of the Employer A Self-Insured Health Plan, which has a calendar year plan year. Em-

ployer A calculates the sum of lives covered under the plan for each day of the plan year ending December 31, 2013 as 3,285,000. The average number of lives covered under the plan for the plan year ending December 31, 2013, is 3,285,000 divided by 365, or 9,000. To calculate the section 4376 fee for the plan under paragraph (c)(1) of this section for the plan year ending December 31, 2013, Employer A must determine the applicable dollar amount under paragraph (c)(3) of this section and multiply that amount by 9,000.

(iv) *Snapshot method.*—(A) *In general.*—A plan sponsor may determine the average number of lives covered under an applicable self-insured health plan for a plan year by adding the totals of lives covered on a date during the first, second, or third month of each quarter of the plan year (or more dates in each quarter if an equal number of dates is used in each quarter), and dividing that total by the number of dates on which a count was made. For purposes of this paragraph (c)(2)(iv), each date used for the second, third and fourth quarter must be within three days of the date in that quarter that corresponds to the date used for the first quarter, and all dates used must fall within the same plan year. If a plan sponsor uses multiple dates for the first quarter, the plan sponsor must use dates in the second, third, and fourth quarters that correspond to each of the dates used for the first quarter or are within three days of such corresponding dates, and all dates used must fall within the same plan year. The 30th and 31st day of a month are treated as the last day of the month for purposes of determining the corresponding date for any month that has fewer than 31 days (for example, if either March 30 or March 31 is used for a calendar year plan, June 30 is the corresponding date for the second quarter). For purposes of this paragraph (c)(2)(iv), the number of lives covered on a designated date may be determined using either the snapshot factor method described in paragraph (c)(2)(iv)(B) of this section or the snapshot count method described in paragraph (c)(2)(iv)(C) of this section.

(B) *Snapshot factor method.*—Under the snapshot factor method, the number of lives covered on a date is equal to the sum of—

(i) The number of participants with self-only coverage on that date; plus

(ii) The number of participants with coverage other than self-only coverage on the date multiplied by 2.35.

(C) *Snapshot count method.*—Under the snapshot count method, the number of lives covered on a date equals the actual number of lives covered on the designated date.

(D) *Examples.*—The following examples illustrate the principles of paragraphs (c)(1) and (c)(2)(iv) of this section:

*Example 1.* (i) Employer B is the plan sponsor of the Employer B Self-Insured Health Plan, which has a calendar year plan year. Employer B uses the snapshot method to determine the average number of lives covered under the plan and uses the snapshot count method to determine the number of lives covered on a day in the first month of each calendar quarter of the plan year.

(ii) On January 4, 2013, the Employer B Self-Insured Health Plan covers 2,000 lives, on April 5, 2013, 2,100 lives, on July 5, 2013, 2,050 lives, and on October 4, 2013, 2,050 lives. Under the snapshot method, Employer B must determine the average number of lives covered under the Employer B Self-Insured Health Plan for the plan year ending December 31, 2013, as 8,200 (2,000 + 2,100 + 2,050 + 2,050) divided by 4, or 2,050. To calculate the section 4376 fee under paragraph (c)(1) of this section for the plan year ending December 31, 2013, Employer B must determine the applicable dollar amount under paragraph (c)(3) of this section and multiply that amount by 2,050.

*Example 2.* (i) Same facts as *Example 1,* except that for the 2014 plan year Employer B determines the number of lives covered that are not covered by self-only coverage using the snapshot factor method (that is, based on the number of participants with coverage other than self-only coverage multiplied by 2.35 (the factor set forth in (c)(2)(iv) of this section)).

(ii) On January 10, 2014, Employer B Self-Insured Health Plan provides self-only coverage to 600 employees and other than self-only coverage to 800 employees. On April 11, 2014, Employer B Self-Insured Health Plan provides self-only coverage to 608 employees and other than self-only coverage to 800 employees. On July 11, 2014 and October 10, 2014, Employer B Self-Insured Health Plan provides self-only coverage to 610 employees and other than self-only coverage to 809 employees.

(iii) Under the snapshot factor method, Employer B must determine the average number of lives covered under the Employer B Self-Insured Health Plan for the plan year ending December 31, 2014 as 9,988 [(600+(800 × 2.35)) + (608 + (800 × 2.35)) + (610 + (809 × 2.35)) + (610 + (809 × 2.35))] divided by 4, or 2,497. To calculate the section 4376 fee under paragraph (c)(1) of this section for the plan year ending December 31, 2014, Employer B must determine the applicable dollar amount under paragraph (c)(3) of this section and multiply that amount by 2,497.

(v) *Form 5500 method.*—(A) *Calculation method.*—A plan sponsor may determine the average number of lives covered under a plan for a plan year based on the number of participants reported on the Form 5500, "Annual Return/Report of Employee Benefit Plan," or the Form 5500-SF, "Short Form Annual Return/Report of Small Employee Benefit Plan," that is filed for the applicable self-insured health plan for that plan year, provided that the Form 5500 or Form 5500-SF is filed no later than the due date for the fee imposed by section 4376 for that plan year. For purposes of this paragraph (c)(2)(v), the average number of lives covered under the plan for the plan year for a plan offering only self-only coverage equals the sum of the total participants covered at the beginning and the end of the plan year, as reported on the Form 5500 or Form 5500-SF for the applicable self-insured health plan, divided by 2. For purposes of this paragraph (c)(2)(v), the average number of lives covered under the plan for the plan year for a plan offering self-only coverage and coverage other than self-only coverage equals the sum of total participants covered at the beginning and the end of the plan year, as reported on the Form 5500 or Form 5500-SF filed for the applicable self-insured health plan.

(B) *Examples.*—The following examples illustrate the principles of paragraphs (c)(1) and (c)(2)(v)(A) of this section:

*Example 1.* Employer C is the plan sponsor of the Employer C Self-Insured Health Plan, which has a calendar year plan year ending on December 31, 2013. Employer C is required to file a Form 5500 for the plan for the 2013 plan year by July 31, 2014. However, on July 30, 2014, Employer C obtains an automatic 2-1/2 month extension for filing the 2013 Form 5500. Employer C files the 2013 Form 5500 on September 30, 2014 (that is, before the October 15 extended due date). Employer C is not eligible to use the Form 5500 method to determine the average number of lives covered under Plan C for the plan year ending on December 31, 2013, because the 2013 Form 5500 was not filed by the original due date (that is, by July 31, 2014) for the return that reports liability for the fee imposed by section 4376 for the 2013 plan year.

*Example 2.* Same facts as *Example 1*, except that the Employer C Self-Insured Health Plan has a fiscal year plan year ending on July 31, 2013, and offers only self-only coverage. Employer C files a Form 5500 for the Employer C Self-Insured Health Plan for the plan year ending July 31, 2013 (the 2012 Form 5500), on the extended due date for filing the 2012 Form 5500 (May 15, 2014). Employer C is eligible to use the Form 5500 method to determine the average number of lives covered under Plan C for the plan year ending on July 31, 2013, because the 2012 Form 5500 had been filed by the due date for the return that reports liability for the fee imposed by section 4376 for that plan year (July 31, 2014).

*Example 3.* Same facts as *Example 2*, provided further that the Employer C Self-Insured Health Plan 2012 Form 5500 reports 4,000 plan participants on the first day of the plan year and 4,200 plan participants on the last day of the 2012 plan year. For purposes of calculating the fee under section 4376 using the Form 5500 method, Employer C must treat the number of lives covered for the plan year ending July 31, 2013, as equal to the sum of 4,000 and 4,200 or 8,200, divided by 2, or 4,100. To calculate the section 4376 fee under paragraph (c)(1) of this section for the plan year ending July 31, 2013, Employer C must determine the applicable dollar amount under paragraph (c)(3) of this section and multiply that amount by 4,100.

*Example 4.* Same facts as *Example 3*, except that the Employer C Self-Insured Health plan offers self-only coverage and family coverage. For purposes of calculating the fee under section 4376 using the Form 5500 method, Employer C must treat the number of lives covered for the plan year ending July 31, 2013, as equal to the sum of 4,000 and 4,200, or 8,200. To calculate the section 4376 fee under paragraph (c)(1) of this section for the plan year ending July 31, 2013, Employer C must determine the applicable dollar amount under paragraph (c)(3) of this section and multiply that amount by 8,200.

(vi) *Special rule for health FSAs and HRAs.*—For purposes of this section, if a plan sponsor does not establish or maintain an applicable self-insured health plan other than a health flexible spending arrangement (health FSA) (as described in section 106(c)(2)) or a health reimbursement arrangement (as described in Notice 2002-45 (2002-2 CB 93)) (HRA), the plan sponsor may treat each participant's health FSA or HRA as covering a single life (and therefore the plan sponsor is not required to include as lives covered any spouse, dependent, or other beneficiary of the individual participant in the health FSA or HRA, as applicable). If a health FSA or HRA that is an applicable self-insured health plan has the same plan sponsor and plan year as another applicable self-insured health plan other than a health FSA or HRA, the two arrangements may be treated as a single plan under paragraph (b)(1)(iii) of this section. However, the special counting rule in this paragraph applies only for purposes of the health FSA or HRA and, therefore, applies only for purposes of the participants in the health FSA or HRA that do not participate in the other applicable self-insured health plan. The participants in the health FSA or HRA that participate in the other applicable self-insured health plan will be counted in accordance with the method applied for counting lives covered under that other plan as described in paragraph (b)(2)(i) of this section. See § 601.601(d)(2) of this chapter.

(vii) *Special rule for lives covered solely by the fully-insured options under an applicable self-insured health plan.*—(A) *In general.*—If an applicable self-insured health plan provides accident and health coverage through fully-insured options and self-insured options, the plan sponsor is permitted to disregard the lives that are covered solely under the fully-insured options in determining the lives covered taken into account for the actual count method (described in paragraph (c)(2)(iii) of this section), the snapshot method (described in paragraph (c)(2)(iv) of this section), and the Form 5500 method (described in paragraph (c)(2)(v) of this section).

(B) *Example.*—The following example illustrates the principles of paragraph (c)(2)(vii) of this section:

*Example.* (i) Employer C is the plan sponsor of the Employer C Health Plan (Plan P). The Plan offers self-only or family health and accident coverage under fully-insured or self-insured options. On June 28, 2015, Employer C files a Form 5500 for Plan P for the plan year ending December 31, 2014 indicating: (1) a total of 4,000 plan participants on the first day of the 2014 plan year; and (2) a total of 4,200 plan participants on the last day of the plan year. Employer C determines that there were 3,000 plan participants (and their families, as applicable) covered under the fully-insured option offered under the plan on the first day of the 2014 plan year, and 2,900 plan participants (and their families, as applicable) covered under the fully-insured option on the last day of the 2014 plan year. Employer C uses the Form 5500 method to calculate the number of lives covered for the 2014 plan year.

(ii) Pursuant to paragraph (c)(2)(vii) of this section, Employer C determines the number of lives covered for the 2014 plan year as: the sum of 1,000 (4,000 total participants on the first day of the plan year - 3,000 participants covered by the specified health insurance policy on the first day of the plan year) and 1,300 (4,200 total participants - 2,900 participants covered by the specified health insurance policy on the first day of the plan year), or 2,300. To calculate the section 4376 fee under paragraph (c)(1) of this section for the 2014 plan year, Employer C must determine the applicable dollar amount under paragraph (c)(3) of this section and multiply that amount by 2,300.

(viii) *Special rule for the first year the fee is in effect.*—Notwithstanding paragraph (c)(2)(i) of this section, for a plan year beginning before July 11, 2012, and ending on or after October 1, 2012, a plan sponsor may determine the average number of lives covered under the plan for the plan year using any reasonable method.

(3) *Applicable dollar amount.*—For a plan year ending on or after October 1, 2012, and before October 1, 2013, the applicable dollar amount is $1. For a plan year ending on or after October 1, 2013, and before October 1, 2014, the applicable dollar amount is $2. For any plan year ending in any Federal fiscal year beginning on or after October 1, 2014, the applicable dollar amount is equal to the sum of—

(i) The applicable dollar amount for the plan year ending in the previous Federal fiscal year; plus

(ii) The amount equal to the product of—

(A) The applicable dollar amount for the plan year ending in the previous Federal fiscal year; and

(B) The percentage increase in the projected per capita amount of the National Health Expenditures most recently released by the Department of Health and Human Services before the beginning of the Federal fiscal year.

(4) *Examples.*—The following examples illustrate the principle of paragraph (c)(3) of this section.

*Example 1.* (Calendar year plan). (i) Plan Sponsor C maintains Plan X which has a calendar year plan year; the plan continues in operation for the entire calendar years 2012 through 2019. Plan X is an applicable self-insured health plan, within the meaning of § 46.4376-1(b)(1), and Plan Sponsor C is liable for the fee imposed by section 4376, determined in accordance with these regulations, beginning with the 2012 plan year - the plan year beginning January 1, 2012, and ending December 31, 2012 - and ending with the 2018 plan year - the plan year beginning January 1, 2018, and ending December 31, 2018. In accordance with § 40.6071(a)-1(c) of this chapter:

(ii) The first Form 720 that must be filed to report and pay the fee imposed by section 4376 for Plan X covers the 2012 plan year (January 1, 2012, through December 31, 2012) and must be filed no later than July 31, 2013, and the fee reported on this form must be calculated by multiplying the average number lives by $1 (the applicable dollar amount in effect for plans with plan years beginning on or after October 1, 2012, and before October 1, 2013); and

(iii) The last Form 720 that must be filed to report and pay the fee imposed by section 4376 for Plan X covers the 2018 plan year (January 1, 2018, through December 31, 2018) and must be filed no later than July 31, 2019, and the fee reported on this form must be calculated using the applicable dollar amount in effect for plan years ending on or after October 1, 2018, and before October 1, 2019.

*Example 2.* (Fiscal year plan). (i) Plan Sponsor B maintains Plan W, which has a fiscal year plan year ending on July 31; the plan continues in operation for the entire fiscal year plan years from August 1, 2012, through July 31, 2019. Plan W is an applicable self-insured health plan, within the meaning of §46.4376-1(b)(1), and Plan Sponsor B is liable for the fee imposed by section 4376, determined in accordance with these regulations, beginning with the 2012 plan year - the plan year beginning on August 1, 2012, and ending on July 31, 2013 - and ending with the 2018 plan year - plan year beginning on August 1, 2018, and ending July 31, 2019. In accordance with §40.6071(a)-1(c) of this chapter:

(ii) The first Form 720 that must be filed to report and pay the fee imposed by section 4376 for Plan X covers the 2012 plan year (August 1, 2012, through July 31, 2013) and must be filed no later than July 31, 2014, and the fee reported on this form must be calculated by multiplying the average number lives by $1 (the applicable dollar amount in effect for plans with plans years beginning on or after October 1, 2012, and before October 1, 2013); and

(iii) The last Form 720 that must be filed to report and pay the fee imposed by section 4376 for Plan X covers the 2018 plan year (August 1, 2018, through July 31, 2019) and must be filed no later than July 31, 2020, and the fee must be calculated using the applicable dollar amount in effect for plan years ending on or after October 1, 2018, and before October 1, 2019.

(d) *Effective/Applicability date.*—This section applies for plan years that end on or after October 1, 2012, and before October 1, 2019. [Reg. §46.4376-1.]

☐ *[T.D. 9602, 12-5-2012.]*

### [Reg. §46.4377-1]

**§46.4377-1. Definitions and special rules.**—(a) *Definitions.*—The following definitions apply for purposes of sections 4375 and 4376 and §§46.4375-1 and 46.4376-1.

(1) *Accident and health coverage.*—The term *accident and health coverage* means any coverage that, if provided by an insurance policy, would cause such policy to be a specified health insurance policy (as defined in section 4375(c) and §46.4375-1(b)(1)). Accident and health coverage also includes coverage for an active employee, a former

employee, or a qualifying beneficiary that is continuation coverage required under the Consolidated Omnibus Budget Reconciliation Act of 1985 (COBRA) or similar continuation coverage under other federal law or under state law.

(2) *Individual residing in the United States.*—(i) The term *individual residing in the United States* means an individual with a place of abode in the United States.

(ii) *Determination of place of abode.*—For purposes of paragraph (a)(2) of this section, an issuer or a plan sponsor may rely on the most recent address on file with the issuer or plan sponsor and may treat the primary insured and the primary insured's spouse, dependents, or other beneficiaries covered by the policy as having the same place of abode. For this purpose, the primary insured is the individual covered by the policy whose eligibility for coverage was not due to that individual's status as the spouse, dependent, or other beneficiary of another covered individual.

(3) *United States.*—The term *United States* includes American Samoa, Guam, the Northern Mariana Islands, Puerto Rico, the Virgin Islands, and any other possession of the United States.

(4) *Federal fiscal year.*—The term *Federal fiscal year* means the year beginning on October 1 and ending on the following September 30.

(b) *Treatment of exempt governmental programs.*—(1) *In general.*—The fees imposed by sections 4375 and 4376 do not apply to any covered life under an exempt governmental program as defined in paragraph (b)(2) of this section.

(2) *Exempt governmental program.*—For purposes of this section, *exempt governmental program* means any—

(i) Insurance program established under title XVIII of the Social Security Act;

(ii) Medical assistance program established by title XIX or XXI of the Social Security Act;

(iii) Program established by Federal law for providing medical care (other than through insurance policies) to individuals (or their spouses and dependents) by reason of such individuals being (or having been) members of the Armed Forces of the United States; and

(iv) Program established by Federal law for providing medical care (other than through insurance policies) to members of Indian tribes (as defined in section 4(d) of the Indian Health Care Improvement Act).

(c) *Effective/Applicability date.*—This section applies to all policy and plan years that end on or after October 1, 2012, and before October 1, 2019. [Reg. §46.4377-1.]

☐ *[T.D. 9602, 12-5-2012.]*

# Taxes on Wagering

### [Reg. §44.0-1]

**§44.0-1. Introduction.**—(a) *In general.*—The regulations in this part (Part 44, Subchapter D, Chapter I, Title 26 (1954) Code of Federal Regulations) are designated "Wagering Tax Regulations." The regulations relate to the taxes imposed by chapter 35 of the Internal Revenue Code of 1954, as amended, to certain general provisions of chapter 40 of such Code, and to certain related administrative provisions of subtitle F of such Code. Chapter 35 imposes an excise tax on wagers and a special tax to be paid by each person liable for the tax imposed on wagers and by each person engaged in receiving wagers for or on behalf of any person liable for the tax imposed on wagers. References in these regulations to the "Internal Revenue Code" or the "Code" are references to the Internal Revenue Code of 1954, as amended, unless otherwise indicated. References to a section or other provision of law are references to a section or other provision of the Internal Revenue Code, as amended, unless otherwise indicated.

(b) *Division of regulations.*—The regulations in this part (26 CFR Part 44) are divided into five subparts. Subpart A contains provisions relating to the arrangement and numbering of the sections of the regulations in this part, general definitions and use of terms, scope of the regulations, and the extent to which the regulations in this part supersede prior regulations relating to the taxes imposed by chapter 35 of the Internal Revenue Code. Subpart B relates to the tax on wagers. Subpart C relates to the special tax. Subpart D relates to certain miscellaneous and general provisions having application to taxes imposed by chapter 35. Subpart E relates to selected provisions

of subtitle F of the Code (Procedure and Administration) which have special application to the taxes imposed by chapter 35 of the Code.

(c) *Arrangement and numbering.*—Each section of the regulations in this part (other than subpart A) is designated by a number composed of the part number followed by a decimal point (44.); the section of the Internal Revenue Code which it interprets; a hyphen (-); and a number identifying the section. By use of these designations one can ascertain the sections of the regulations relating to a provision of the Code. For example, the regulations pertaining to section 4401 of the Code are designated §44.4401-1, §44.4401-2, and §44.4401-3. [Reg. §44.0-1.]

☐ *[T.D. 6370. Amended by T.D. 7665.]*

### [Reg. §44.0-2]

**§44.0-2. General definitions and use of terms.**—As used in the regulations in this part, unless otherwise expressly indicated—

(a) The terms defined in the provisions of law contained in the regulations in this part shall have the meanings so assigned to them.

(b) The Internal Revenue Code of 1954 means the Act approved August 16, 1954 (68A Stat.), entitled "An Act To revise the internal revenue laws of the United States", as amended.

(c) District director means district director of internal revenue.

(d) The cross references in the regulations in this part to other portions of the regulations, when the word "see" is used, are made only for convenience and shall be given no legal effect. [Reg. §44.0-2.]

☐ *[T.D. 6370.]*

**[Reg. §44.0-3]**

**§44.0-3. Scope of regulations.**—The regulations in this part apply to wagering activity on and after January 1, 1955. [Reg. §44.0-3.]

☐ [*T.D.* 6370.]

**[Reg. §44.0-4]**

**§44.0-4. Extent to which the regulations in this part supersede prior regulations.**—The regulations in this part, with respect to the subject matter within the scope thereof, supersede Regulations 132, 26 CFR (1939) Part 325. [Reg. §44.0-4.]

☐ [*T.D.* 6370.]

**[Reg. §44.4401-1]**

**§44.4401-1. Imposition of tax.**—(a) *In general.*—Section 4401 imposes a tax on all wagers, as defined in section 4421. See §§44.4421 and 44.4421-1 for definition of the term "wager."

(b) *Rate of tax; amount of wager.*—(1) *Rate of tax.*—The tax is imposed at the rate of 10 percent of the amount of any taxable wager.

(2) *Amount of wager.*—(i) The amount of the wager is the amount risked by the bettor, including any charge or fee incident to the placing of the wager as provided in subdivision (iv) of this subparagraph, rather than the amount which he stands to win. Thus, if a bettor bets $5 against a bookmaker's $7 with respect to the outcome of a prize fight, the amount of the wager subject to tax is $5.

(ii) In the case of a "parlay" wager (i.e., a single wager made by a bettor on the outcome of a series of events, usually horse races), the amount of the taxable wager is the amount initially wagered by the bettor irrespective of whether the parlay is successful. In the case of an "if" wager, the amount of the taxable wager is the total of all amounts wagered on each selection of the bettor. For example, A makes a $10 wager on horse R with the understanding that if horse R wins, $5 is to be wagered on horse S and $5 on horse T. If horse R wins, the taxable wager is $20. If horse R loses, the taxable wager is $10. In determining the amount of a taxable wager involving the features of, or a combination of, "parlay" and "if" bets, such as wagers sometimes referred to as a "whipsaw" or an "if and reverse" bet, the rules set forth above relating to "parlay" and "if" bets are to be followed. For example, assume B wagers $10 on horse R with the understanding that if horse R wins, $5 is to be placed as a parlay wager on horses S and T. In such a case, if horse R loses, the taxable wager is $10; if horse R wins, there are two taxable wagers amounting in the aggregate to $15.

(iii) In the case of punchboards with prizes of merchandise, cash, or free plays listed thereon, the amount of the taxable wager is the amount risked by the bettor for all chances taken by him, including the chances taken by the bettor in lieu of the acceptance of an equivalent amount in cash or merchandise.

(iv) In determining the amount of any wager subject to tax there shall be included any charge or fee incident to the placing of the wager. For example, in the case of a wager with respect to a horse race, any amount paid to a bookmaker for the purpose of guaranteeing the bettor a payoff based on actual track odds is to be included as a part of the wager. Similarly, in the case of a lottery, any amount paid to the operator thereof by the bettor for the privilege of making a contribution to the pool or bank is also to be included in the amount of the wager. However, the amount of the wager subject to tax shall not include the amount of the tax where it is established by actual records of the taxpayer that such amount of tax was collected from the bettor as a separate charge. [Reg. §44.4401-1.]

☐ [*T.D.* 6370.]

**[Reg. §44.4401-2]**

**§44.4401-2. Person liable for tax.**—(a) *In general.*—(1) Every person engaged in the business of accepting wagers with respect to a sports event or a contest is liable for the tax on any such wager accepted by him. Every person who operates a wagering pool or lottery conducted for profit is liable for the tax with respect to any wager or contribution placed in such pool or lottery. To be liable for the tax, it is not necessary that the person engaged in the business of accepting wagers or operating a wagering pool or lottery physically receive the wager or contribution. Any wager or contribution received by an agent or employee on behalf of such person shall be considered to have been accepted by and placed with such person.

(2) Any person required to register under section 4412 by reason of having received wagers for or on behalf of another person, but who fails to register the name and place of residence of such other person (hereinafter in this subparagraph referred to as principal), shall be liable for the tax on all wagers received by him during the period in which he has failed to so register the name and place of residence of such principal. Subsequent compliance with section 4412 by the person receiving wagers for another does not relieve him of

his liability and duty to pay such tax, nor will the fact that such person incurs liability with respect to the tax on such wagers, relieve his principal of liability for the tax imposed under section 4401 with respect to such wagers. Accordingly, both the person receiving the wagers and his principal shall be liable for the tax on such wagers until the tax is paid. Payment of the tax on such wagers shall not relieve the person receiving wagers of any penalty for failure to register as required by section 4412. This subparagraph has application only to wagers received after September 2, 1958.

(b) *In business of accepting wagers.*—A person is engaged in the business of accepting wagers if he makes it a practice to accept wagers with respect to which he assumes the risk of profit or loss depending upon the outcome of the event or the contest with respect to which the wager is accepted. It is not intended that to be engaged in the business of accepting wagers a person must be either so engaged to the exclusion of all other activities or even primarily so engaged. Thus, for example, an individual may be primarily engaged in business as a salesman, and also for the purpose of the tax be engaged in the business of accepting wagers.

(c) *Lay-offs.*—If a person engaged in the business of accepting wagers or conducting a lottery or betting pool for profit lays off all or part of the wagers placed with him with another person engaged in the business of accepting wagers or conducting a betting pool or lottery for profit, he shall, notwithstanding such lay-off, be liable for the tax on the wagers or contributions initially accepted by him. See §44.6419-2 for credit and refund provisions applicable with respect to laid-off wagers. [Reg. §44.4401-2.]

☐ [*T.D.* 6370.]

**[Reg. §44.4401-3]**

**§44.4401-3. When tax attaches.**—The tax attaches when (a) a person engaged in the business of accepting wagers with respect to a sports event or a contest, or (b) a person who operates a wagering pool or lottery for profit, accepts a wager or contribution from a bettor. In the case of a wager on credit, the tax attaches whether or not the amount of the wager is actually collected from the bettor. However, if an amount equivalent to the amount of the wager is paid to the bettor prior to the close of the calendar month in which such wager was accepted, either because of the cancellation of the event upon which the wager was placed, or because the wager was cancelled or rescinded by mutual agreement, the wager need not be reported on the taxpayer's return for such month. Where such cancellation or rescission takes place in a month subsequent to the month in which the wager was accepted, credit or refund of the tax paid with respect to such wager may be made subject to the provisions of §44.6419-1. [Reg. §44.4401-3.]

☐ [*T.D.* 6370.]

**[Reg. §44.4402-1]**

**§44.4402-1. Exemptions.**—(a) *Parimutuel wagering enterprise.*—Section 4402 provides that no tax shall be imposed by section 4401 on any wager placed with, or on any wager placed in a wagering pool conducted by, a parimutuel wagering enterprise licensed under State law.

(b) *Wagering machines.*—(1) *In general.*—Section 4402 provides that no tax shall be imposed by section 4401 on any wager placed in a coin-operated device (as defined in section 4462 as in effect for years beginning before July 1, 1980), or on any amount paid, in lieu of inserting a coin, token, or similar object, to operate a device described in section 4462(a)(2) (as so in effect). These devices include:

(i) So-called "slot" machines that operate by means of the insertion of a coin, token, or similar object and that, by application of the element of chance, may deliver, or entitle the person playing or operating the machine to receive cash, premiums, merchandise, or tokens; and

(ii) Machines that are similar to machines described in paragraph (b)(1)(i) of this section and are operated without the insertion of a coin, token, or similar object.

(2) *Examples.*—The following devices and machines are examples of the devices referred to in paragraph (b)(1) of this section:

(i) A machine that is operated by means of the insertion of a coin, token, or similar object and that, even though it does not dispense cash or tokens, has the features and characteristics of a gaming device whether or not evidence exists as to actual payoffs.

(ii) A so-called crane machine, claw, digger, or rotary merchandising type device that is operated by the insertion of a coin and adjustment of a control lever for the purpose of removing from the machine, by gripping, pushing, or other manipulation articles such as figurines, lighters, etc., in the machine.

(iii) A pinball machine equipped with a pushbutton for releasing free plays and a meter for recording the plays so released, or equipped with provisions for multiple coin insertion for increasing the odds.

(iv) Pinball machines in connection with which free plays are redeemed in cash, tokens, or merchandise, or prizes are offered to any person for the attainment of designated scores.

(v) A coin-operated machine that displays a poker hand or delivers a ticket with a poker hand symbolized on it that entitles the player to a prize if the poker hand displayed by the machine or symbolized on the ticket constitutes a winning hand. [Reg. §44.4402-1.]

☐ [T.D. 8328, 12-28-90. *Redesignated and amended by T.D. 8442,* 10-21-92.]

### [Reg. §44.4403-1]

**§44.4403-1. Daily record.**—Every person liable for tax under section 4401 shall keep such records as will clearly show as to each day's operations:

(a) The gross amount of all wagers accepted;

(b) The gross amount of each class or type of wager accepted on each separate event, contest, or other wagering medium. For example, in the case of wagers accepted on a horse race, the daily record shall show separately the gross amount of each class or type of wagers (straight bets, parlays, "if" bets, etc.) accepted on each horse in the race. Similarly, in the case of the numbers game, the daily record shall show the gross amount of each class or type of wager accepted on each number.

For additional provisions relating to records, see §§44.6001 and 44.6001-1. [Reg. §44.4403-1.]

☐ [T.D. 6370.]

### [Reg. §44.4404-1]

**§44.4404-1. Territorial extent.**—(a) *In general.*—The tax imposed by section 4401 applies to wagers (1) accepted in the United States, or (2) placed by a person who is in the United States (i) with a person who is a citizen or resident of the United States, or (ii) in a wagering pool or lottery conducted by a person who is a citizen or resident of the United States. All wagers made within the United States are taxable irrespective of the citizenship or place of residence of the parties to the wager. Thus, the tax applies to wagers placed within the United States, even though the person for whom or on whose behalf the wagers are received is located in a foreign country and is not a citizen or resident of the United States. Likewise, a wager accepted outside the United States by a citizen or resident of the United States is taxable if the person making such wager is within the United States at the time the wager is made.

(b) *Examples.*—The following examples illustrate the application of paragraph (a) of this section:

*Example (1).* A syndicate which maintains its headquarters in a foreign country has representatives in the United States who receive wagers in the United States for or on behalf of such syndicate. For the purposes of section 4404, such wagers are considered as accepted within the United States, the syndicate is considered to be in the business of accepting wagers within the United States, and such wagers are subject to the tax. This is true regardless of the nationality or residence of the members of the syndicate.

*Example (2).* A Canadian citizen employed in Detroit, Michigan, telephones a horse race bet to a bookmaker who is a United States citizen with his place of business located in Windsor, Canada. The wager is taxable since it is made by a person within the United States with a person who is a United States citizen.

*Example (3).* A United States citizen while visiting Tijuana, Mexico, makes a wager on the outcome of a horse race with a bookmaker who is also a United States citizen located and doing business in Tijuana. The wager is not taxable since both parties to the wager, though United States citizens, were outside the United States at the time the wager was made. [Reg. §44.4404-1.]

☐ [T.D. 6370.]

### [Reg. §44.4411-1]

**§44.4411-1. Imposition of tax.**—(a) *In general.*—A special tax of $50 per year is required to be paid by each person:

(1) Who is liable for the tax imposed by section 4401, or

(2) Who is engaged in receiving wagers for or on behalf of any person who is liable for the tax imposed by section 4401.

(b) *Examples.*—The application of paragraph (a) of this section may be illustrated by the following examples:

*Example (1).* A, who is engaged in the business of accepting horse race bets, employs ten persons to receive on his behalf wagers which are transmitted by telephone. A also employs a secretary and a bookkeeper. A and each of the ten persons who receive wagers by telephone on behalf of A are liable for the special tax. The secretary

and bookkeeper are not liable for the special tax unless they also receive wagers for A.

*Example (2).* B operates a numbers game and has an arrangement with ten persons, who are employed in various capacities, such as bootblacks, elevator operators, news dealers, etc., to receive wagers from the public on his behalf. B also employs C to collect from the ten persons referred to the wagers received by them on B's behalf and to deliver such wagers to B. C performs no other services for B. B and the ten persons who receive wagers on his behalf are liable for the special tax. C is not liable for the special tax since he is not engaged in receiving wagers for B.

(c) *Cross references.*—For provisions relating to the payment of the special tax (computation, manner of payment, etc.), see subpart D of this part. [Reg. §44.4411-1.]

☐ [T.D. 6370.]

### [Reg. §44.4412-1]

**§44.4412-1. Registration.**—(a) *In general.*—Every person required to pay the special tax imposed by section 4411 shall register and file a return on Form 11-C. For provisions relating to the general requirement for filing a return, see §44.6011(a)-1.

(b) *Information to be reported on Form 11-C.*—(1) Every person required to make a return on Form 11-C shall report thereon his full name and place of residence. A person doing business under an alias, style, or trade name shall give his true name, followed by his alias, style, or trade name. In the case of a partnership, association, firm, or company, other than a corporation, the style or trade name shall be given, also the true name of each member and his place of residence. In the case of a corporation, the true name and title of each officer and his place of residence shall be shown.

(2) Each person engaged in the business of accepting wagers on his own account shall report on Form 11-C the name and address of each place where such business will be conducted and the name, address, and number appearing on the special (occupational) stamp of each agent or employee who may receive wagers on his behalf. Thereafter, a return shall be filed on Form 11-C, marked "Supplemental", each time an additional employee or agent is engaged to receive wagers. Such supplemental return shall be filed not later than 10 days after the date such additional employee or agent is engaged to receive wagers and shall show the name, address, and number appearing on the special (occupational) stamp of each such agent or employee. As to a change of address, see §44.4905-2.

(3) Each agent or employee who receives wagers for or on behalf of a person engaged in the business of accepting wagers on his own account shall report on Form 11-C the name and residence address of each person (i.e., individual, partnership, corporation, etc.) on whose behalf wagers are to be received. Thereafter, the agent or employee shall file a return on Form 11-C, marked "Supplemental", each time he is engaged or employed to receive wagers for a person or persons other than the person or persons previously reported on Form 11-C. Such supplemental return shall be filed not later than 10 days after the date he is engaged to receive wagers and shall show the name, business address, or, if none, the residence address of the person or persons by whom he is engaged to receive wagers. As to a change of address, see §44.4905-2.

(c) *Time and place for filing Form 11-C.*—For provisions relating to the time for filing Form 11-C (other than Form 11-C marked "Supplemental"), see §§44.6071 and 44.6071-1. For provisions relating to the place for filing Form 11-C, see §§44.6091 and 44.6091-1. [Reg. §44.4412-1.]

☐ [T.D. 6370.]

### [Reg. §44.4413-1]

**§44.4413-1. Certain provisions made applicable.**—For regulations under sections 4901, 4902, 4904, 4905, and 4906, as extended and made applicable to the special tax imposed by section 4411 and to the persons upon whom such tax is imposed, see subpart D of this part. [Reg. §44.4413-1.]

☐ [T.D. 6370.]

### [Reg. §44.4421-1]

**§44.4421-1. Definitions.**—(a) *Wager.*—The term "wager" means—

(1) Any wager placed with a person engaged in the business of accepting wagers upon the outcome of a sports event or a contest;

(2) Any wager placed in a wagering pool with respect to a sports event or a contest, if such pool is conducted for profit; and

(3) Any wager placed in a lottery conducted for profit.

(b) *Lottery.*—(1) *In general.*—The term "lottery" includes the numbers game, policy, and similar types of wagering. In general, a lottery conducted for profit includes any scheme or method for the distribution of prizes among persons who have paid or promised a consideration for a chance to win such prizes, usually as determined by the numbers or symbols on tickets as drawn from a lottery wheel or other receptacle, or by the outcome of an event, provided such lottery is conducted for profit. The term also includes enterprises commonly known as "policy" or "numbers" and similar types of wagering where the player selects a number, or a combination of numbers, and pays or agrees to pay a certain amount in consideration of which the operator of the lottery, policy, or numbers game agrees to pay a prize or fixed sum of money if the selected number or combination of numbers appear or are published in a manner understood by the parties. For example, the winning number or combination of numbers may appear or be published as a series of numbers in the payoff prices of a series of horse races at a certain race track, or in the United States Treasury balance reports, or the reports of a stock or commodity exchange. This description is not intended to be restrictive; hence, the substitution of letters or other symbols for numbers, or a different arrangement for determining the winning number or combination of numbers, does not alter the fundamental nature of a game which otherwise would be considered a lottery. The operation of a punch board or a similar gaming device for profit is also considered to be the operation of a lottery.

(2) *Certain games excluded.*—(i) *Cards, dice, etc.*—Section 4421 specifically excludes from the term "lottery" any game of a type in which usually (*a*) the wagers are placed, (*b*) the winners are determined, and (*c*) the distribution of prizes or other property is made, in the presence of all persons placing wagers in such game. Thus, for example, no tax would be payable with respect to wagers made in a bingo or keno game since such a game is usually conducted under circumstances in which the wagers are placed, the winners are determined, and the distribution of prizes is made in the presence of all persons participating in the game. For the same reason, no tax would apply in the case of card games, dice games, or games involving wheels of chance, such as roulette wheels and gambling wheels of a type used at carnivals and public fairs.

(ii) *Drawings conducted by an organization exempt from tax under section 501 or 521.*—Section 4421 specifically excludes from the term "lottery" any drawing conducted by an organization exempt from tax under section 501 or 521 if no part of the net proceeds derived from such drawing inures to the benefit of any private shareholder or individual. For provisions relating to exemption from income tax under section 501 or 521, see the Income Tax Regulations (Part 1 of this chapter).

(c) *Other terms used.*—(1) *Wagering pool.*—A wagering pool conducted for profit includes any scheme or method for the distribution of prizes to one or more winning bettors based upon the outcome of a sports event or a contest, or a combination or series of such events or contests, provided such wagering pool is managed and conducted for the purpose of making a profit.

(2) *Sports event.*—A sports event includes every type of sports event, whether amateur, scholastic, or professional, such as horse racing, auto racing, dog racing, boxing and wrestling matches and exhibitions, baseball, football, and basketball games, tennis and golf matches, track meets, etc.

(3) *Contest.*—A contest includes any type of contest involving speed, skill, endurance, popularity, politics, strength, appearances, etc., such as a general or primary election, the outcome of a nominating convention, a dance marathon, a log-rolling, wood-chopping, weight-lifting, corn-husking, beauty contest, etc.

(4) *Conducted for profit.*—A wagering pool or lottery may be conducted for profit even though a direct profit will not inure from the operation thereof. A wagering pool or lottery operated with the section expectancy of a profit in the form of increased sales, increased attendance, or other indirect benefits is conducted for profit for purposes of the wagering tax. [Reg. § 44.4421-1.]

☐ [*T.D.* 6370.]

**[Reg. § 44.4422-1]**

**§ 44.4422-1. Doing business in violation of Federal or State law.**—Payment of any special tax within the scope of the regulations in this part in nowise authorizes the carrying on of any business in violation of a law of the United States or the law of any State. The special tax stamp is not a license or permit and affords no protection from prosecution for violation of any Federal or State law. See also § 44.4906. [Reg. § 44.4422-1.]

☐ [*T.D.* 6370.]

# Certain Other Excise Taxes

**[Reg. § 43.0-1]**

**§ 43.0-1. Introduction.**—The regulations in this part 43 are designated "Excise Tax on Transportation by Water." The regulations relate to the taxes on transportation by water imposed by section 4471 of the Internal Revenue Code. See part 40 of this chapter for regulations relating to returns, payments, and deposits of taxes imposed by section 4471. [Reg. § 43.0-1]

☐ [*T.D.* 8328, 12-28-90. *Redesignated and amended by T.D.* 8422, 7-29-92; *Amended by T.D.* 8442, 10-21-92.]

**[Reg. § 43.4471-1]**

**§ 43.4471-1. Imposition of tax.**—(a) *In general.*—Section 4471 imposes a tax of $3 per passenger on a covered voyage as is defined in section 4472.

(b) *By whom paid.*—The tax is imposed on the person providing the covered voyage (the operator of the vessel). [Reg. § 43.4471-1.]

☐ [*T.D.* 8314, 10-5-90. *Redesignated and amended by T.D.* 8422, 7-29-92.]

**[Reg. § 43.4472-1]**

**§ 43.4472-1. Definitions.**—(a) *In general.*—For definitions of the terms "covered voyage" and "passenger vessel," see sections 4472(1) and (2).

(b) *Voyage.*—For purposes of this section, "voyage" means a journey of a vessel that includes the outward and homeward trips or passages. The voyage commences when the vessel begins to load passengers and continues during the entire ensuing period until the vessel has made one outward and one homeward passage (including intermediate passages, if made). A voyage may be a covered voyage with respect to a passenger even if the passenger does not make both an outward and homeward passage or if the point of first embarkation or disembarkation by the passenger in the United States is an intermediate stop of the vessel.

(c) *Over 1 or more nights.*—A voyage is considered to extend over 1 or more nights if it extends for more than 24 hours.

(d) *Engaged in gambling.*—A passenger is engaged in gambling aboard a vessel if that person is participating as a player in any policy game or other lottery, or any other game of chance, for money or other thing of value, provided that the policy game, other lottery, or game of chance is conducted, sponsored, or operated by the owner or operator of the vessel, as either principal or agent, or by an employee, agent, or franchisee of the owner or operator of the vessel. A passenger is not engaged in gambling aboard a vessel if the passenger participates with other passengers in a casual, "friendly" game of chance that is not conducted, sponsored, or operated by the owner or operator of the vessel or, by an employee, agent, or franchisee of the owner or operator.

(e) *Territorial waters.*—For purposes of sections 4471 and 4472, the territorial waters of the United States are those waters within the international boundary line between the United States and any contiguous foreign country or within 3 nautical miles (3.45 statute miles) from low tide on the coastline. No inference is intended as to the extent of the territorial limits for other tax purposes.

(f) *Passenger.*—For purposes of section 4471 and 4472, "passenger" means an individual carried on the vessel except—

(1) The Master; or

(2) A crew member or other individual engaged in the business of the vessel or its owners. A person is engaged in the business of the vessel or its owners if the person is an employee of the vessel or its owners or has a duty, contractual or otherwise, to perform on the vessel on behalf of the vessel or its owners. For example, a person engaged as an entertainer, instructor, or lecturer for the benefit of the passengers is not a passenger, but a person on a promotional trip such as a travel agent or contest winner is a passenger even though the vessel or its owners may derive some future benefit from the promotion. [Reg. § 43.4472-1.]

☐ [*T.D.* 8422, 7-29-92.]

[Reg. §41.0-1]

**§41.0-1. Introduction.**—The regulations in this part are designated "Highway Use Tax Regulations." The regulations in this part relate to the tax on the use of certain highway vehicles imposed by section 4481 and to certain associated administrative provisions. [Reg. §41.0-1.]

☐ [*T.D.* 6216, 12-6-56. *Amended by T.D. 7665, 1-25-80 and T.D. 8879, 3-30-2000.*]

**⫸→ *Caution: Reg. §41.4481-1, below, prior to amendment by T.D. 9698, applies before July 1, 2015.***

[Reg. §41.4481-1]

**§41.4481-1. Imposition of tax.**—(a) *In general.*—Tax is imposed on the use during a taxable period of any registered highway motor vehicle that (together with the semitrailers and trailers customarily used in connection with highway motor vehicles of the same type as such highway motor vehicle) has a taxable gross weight of at least 55,000 pounds.

(b) *Rate of tax.*—For the rate of tax generally, see section 4481(a). For the rate of tax for certain vehicles used in logging, see section 4483(e). For the rate of tax for certain vehicles base-plated in Canada or Mexico, see section 4483(f). For a special rule for the taxable period in which the tax terminates, see section 4482(d).

(c) *Computation of tax.*—(1) Except as provided in paragraph (c)(2) of this section, the tax on the use of a particular highway motor vehicle a taxable period is computed as follows:

(i) For vehicles with a taxable gross weight of at least 55,000 pounds, but not over 75,000 pounds, add to $100 an amount equal to $22 for each 1,000 pounds (or fraction thereof) in excess of 55,000 pounds; and

(ii) For vehicles with a taxable gross weight over 75,000 pounds, the tax is $550.

(2) If the first taxable use of a particular highway motor vehicle is made after the first month of the taxable period, the tax on the use of such vehicle for such taxable period is computed by multiplying the amount of tax that would be due for a full taxable period as computed under paragraph (c)(1) of this section, by a fraction. Such fraction shall have as its numerator the number of months in the taxable period beginning with the month of first taxable use and as its denominator the number of months in the entire taxable period. For purposes of determining the fraction, any part of a month is counted as a full month. (See example (2) of paragraph (e) of this section.)

(3) If the taxable gross weight of a vehicle increases during the month in which the vehicle is first used in a taxable period, the tax for the vehicle for the taxable period is computed on the basis of the increased weight. If the taxable gross weight of a vehicle increases after the month in which the vehicle was first used in a taxable period, the additional tax liability, if any, that results from the increased weight is calculated according to the following formula:

$$\left[ \left( T_1 \times \frac{P}{12} \right) + \left( T_2 \times \frac{R}{12} \right) \right] - T_1.$$

where:

$T_1$ = Tax imposed for a full taxable period (or partial taxable period as determined under paragraph (c)(2) of this section) at the vehicle's previously reported taxable gross weight.

$T_2$ = Tax imposed for the same taxable period as used in $T_1$ at the vehicle's increased taxable gross weight.

P = The number of months in the taxable period during which the vehicle's taxable gross weight was as previously reported for such taxable period. This number does not include the month in which the vehicle's taxable gross weight increased.

R = The number of months remaining in the taxable period including the month in which the vehicle's taxable gross weight was increased.

If tax was imposed for a partial taxable period as determined under paragraph (c)(2) of this section, the additional tax is determined by substituting the number of months in such partial taxable period for "12" in the above formula.

(4) If in any taxable period the taxable gross weight of a highway motor vehicle is decreased, the computation of tax is not affected and no right to credit or refund of any tax paid under section 4481 arises.

(5) If in any taxable period a highway motor vehicle is destroyed or stolen before the first day of the last month in the taxable period, and is not subsequently used during such taxable period, the tax shall be calculated proportionately from the first day of the month in the period in which the first taxable use of the highway motor vehicle occurs to and including the last day of the month in which the highway motor vehicle was destroyed or stolen. Any tax paid under section 4481(a) on such a highway motor vehicle in excess of the tax calculated in the preceding sentence, shall be an overpayment for which a credit or refund of tax may be claimed. For purposes of this paragraph (c)(5), a highway motor vehicle is destroyed if the vehicle is damaged due to an accident or other casualty to such an extent that it is not economical to rebuild.

(6) If the use of a highway motor vehicle during the taxable period is discontinued (for reasons other than destruction or theft as described in paragraph (c)(5) of this section) or is converted to a use which is exempt from the tax imposed by section 4481(a), the computation of the tax is not affected and no right to a credit or refund of any tax paid under section 4481 arises.

(d) *Credit or refund of tax under section 4481(a).*—(1) Any claim for refund of an overpayment of tax under section 4481(a) due to destruction or theft of the vehicle shall be made in accordance with the applicable provisions of this section and §301.6402-2 (Regulations on Procedure and Administration) and shall be filed by the person in whose name the vehicle is registered or required to be registered when the vehicle is destroyed or stolen. A claim for refund of the tax imposed by section 4481(a) is to be filed on Form 8849 (or such other form as the Commissioner may designate).

(2) Any person entitled to claim a refund of tax under paragraph (d)(1) of this section may, in lieu of claiming a refund of such tax, claim a credit for such tax on the next Form 2290 required to be filed.

(e) *Examples.*—The application of section 4481 and this section may be illustrated by the following examples:

*Example (1).* In the taxable period beginning July 1, 1984, the first taxable use of a particular highway motor vehicle, a bus, having a taxable gross weight of 56,000 pounds, occurs on July 10, 1984, at which time the vehicle is registered in the name of X. A tax of $122 ($100 + $22) is imposed on X for the use of such vehicle for such taxable period.

*Example (2).* On July 1, 1984, X has registered in his name a highway motor vehicle having a taxable gross weight of 60,000 pounds. The vehicle is in "dead storage" until August 10, 1984, at which time X starts using the vehicle on the public highways in carrying on his trucking business. On August 10, 1984, the vehicle is still registered in X's name. Since the first taxable use of this highway motor vehicle during the taxable period occurred on August 10, 1984, X is required to pay a tax of $192.50 ([$100 + (5 × $22)] × $^{11}/_{12}$) for such taxable period.

*Example (3).* On April 15, 1985, a vehicle with a taxable gross weight of 70,000 pounds and registered in the name of Y is completely destroyed. Y had purchased the vehicle from X who had paid the tax for the taxable period beginning July 1, 1984. Y is entitled to a refund of tax for those full months after destruction in the taxable period ending June 30, 1985. Thus, Y may file a claim for a refund of $71.67—$^{2}/_{12}$ of the total tax of $430 ($100 + (15 × $22)). [Reg. §41.4481-1.]

☐ [*T.D.* 6216. *Amended by T.D. 6743, 6-22-64; T.D. 7409, 3-8-76; T.D. 7505, 8-24-77; T.D. 8027, 5-23-85; T.D. 8159, 9-3-87; T.D. 8177, 3-3-88 and T.D. 8879, 3-30-2000.*]

**⫸→ *Caution: Reg. §41.4481-1, below, as amended by T.D. 9698, applies on or after July 1, 2015.***

[Reg. §41.4481-1]

**§41.4481-1. Imposition and computation of tax.**—(a) *In general.*—Tax is imposed on the use during a taxable period of any registered highway motor vehicle that (together with the semitrailers and trailers customarily used in connection with highway motor vehicles of the same type as such highway motor vehicle) has a taxable gross weight of at least 55,000 pounds.

(b) *Rate of tax.*—For the rate of tax generally, see section 4481(a). For the rate of tax for certain vehicles used in logging, see section 4483(e). For the rate of tax for certain vehicles base-plated in Canada or Mexico, see section 4483(f).

(c) *Computation of tax.*—(1) *In general.*—Except as otherwise provided in this paragraph (c), the tax on the use of a particular highway motor vehicle a taxable period is computed as follows:

(i) For vehicles with a taxable gross weight of at least 55,000 pounds, but not over 75,000 pounds, add to $100 an amount equal to $22 for each 1,000 pounds (or fraction thereof) in excess of 55,000 pounds; and

(ii) For vehicles with a taxable gross weight over 75,000 pounds, the tax is $550.

(2) *Certain prorated taxable periods.*—If the first taxable use of a particular highway motor vehicle is made after the first month of the

**>>>→ Caution: Reg. §41.4481-1, below, as amended by T.D. 9698, applies on or after July 1, 2015.**

taxable period, the tax on the use of such vehicle for such taxable period is computed by multiplying the amount of tax that would be due for a full taxable period as computed under paragraph (c)(1) of this section, by a fraction. Such fraction shall have as its numerator the number of months in the taxable period beginning with the month of first taxable use and as its denominator the number of months in the entire taxable period. For purposes of determining the fraction, any part of a month is counted as a full month. (See example (2) of paragraph (e) of this section.)

(3) *Increase in taxable gross weight during the taxable period.*—If the taxable gross weight of a vehicle increases during the month in which the vehicle is first used in a taxable period, the tax for the vehicle for the taxable period is computed on the basis of the increased weight. If the taxable gross weight of a vehicle increases after the month in which the vehicle was first used in a taxable period, the additional tax liability, if any, that results from the increased weight is calculated according to the following formula:

$$\left[ \left( T_1 \times \frac{P}{12} \right) + \left( T_2 \times \frac{R}{12} \right) \right] - T_1.$$

where:

$T_1$ = Tax imposed for a full taxable period (or partial taxable period as determined under paragraph (c)(2) of this section) at the vehicle's previously reported taxable gross weight.

$T_2$ = Tax imposed for the same taxable period as used in $T_1$ at the vehicle's increased taxable gross weight.

P = The number of months in the taxable period during which the vehicle's taxable gross weight was as previously reported for such taxable period. This number does not include the month in which the vehicle's taxable gross weight increased.

R = The number of months remaining in the taxable period including the month in which the vehicle's taxable gross weight was increased.

If tax was imposed for a partial taxable period as determined under paragraph (c)(2) of this section, the additional tax is determined by substituting the number of months in such partial taxable period for "12" in the above formula.

(4) *Prorated taxable period for sold, destroyed, or stolen vehicles.*—(i) *In general.*—The tax on a taxpayer's use of a highway vehicle for a taxable period is determined under paragraph (c)(4)(ii) of this section if—

(A) The vehicle is destroyed or stolen before the first day of the last month in the taxable period and is not later used by the taxpayer during the period; or

(B) The taxpayer sells the vehicle before the first day of the last month in the taxable period and does not later use the vehicle during the period.

(ii) *Computation of tax.*—If the tax on a taxpayer's use of a highway vehicle for a taxable period is determined under this paragraph (c)(4)(ii), the tax is computed by multiplying the amount of tax that would be due for a full taxable period, as computed under paragraph (c)(1) of this section, by a fraction. The fraction has as its numerator the number of months in the period from the first day of the month in the period in which the first taxable use of the highway motor vehicle occurs to and including the last day of the month in which the highway motor vehicle was sold, destroyed, or stolen, and as its denominator the number of months in the entire taxable period. (See paragraph (d) *Example* (3)(i) of this section.)

(iii) *Overpayment.*—If a taxpayer's liability for the tax on the use of a highway vehicle for a taxable period is determined under paragraph (c)(4)(ii) of this section, any tax the taxpayer paid under section 4481(a) on the use of the vehicle for such period in excess of the tax calculated under paragraph (c)(4)(ii) of this section is an overpayment of tax.

(iv) *Definition of destroyed vehicle.*—For purposes of this paragraph (c)(4), a highway motor vehicle is destroyed if the vehicle is damaged due to an accident or other casualty to such an extent that it is not economical to rebuild.

(v) *Form and content of claim.*—A claim for refund of an overpayment described in paragraph (c)(4)(iii) of this section must be made on Form 8849, "Claim for Refund of Excise Taxes" (or such other form as the Commissioner may designate) in accordance with the instructions for that form. A claim for a credit must be made on Form 2290, "Heavy Highway Vehicle Use Tax Return" (or such other form as the Commissioner may designate) in accordance with the instructions for that form. A claim for refund or credit for any vehicle must include—

(A) The vehicle identification number and taxable gross weight of the vehicle;

(B) The date of the sale, destruction, or theft of the vehicle; and

(C) If the vehicle was sold, the name and address of the purchaser of the vehicle.

(vi) *Tax on buyer's use of second-hand vehicles.*—If a vehicle is sold during the taxable period and a credit or refund of the tax imposed by section 4481 is allowable upon the sale under paragraph (c)(4)(iii) of this section, tax is imposed on the use of the vehicle after the sale and before the end of the taxable period. (See paragraph (c)(4)(vii) of this section for the rules regarding the computation of tax after the sale and before the end of the taxable period.)

(vii) *Computation of tax on second-hand vehicles.*—The tax under paragraph (c)(4)(vi) of this section on the use of a vehicle after a sale upon which a credit or refund is allowable is computed by multiplying the amount of tax that would be due for a full taxable period as computed under paragraph (c)(1) of this section by a fraction. The fraction has as its numerator the number of months in the period from the first day of the month in which the first taxable use of the vehicle after the sale occurs (the first day of the month after such month if the first taxable use after the sale occurs in the month of the sale) through the end of the taxable period, and as its denominator the number of months in the entire taxable period. (See paragraph (d) *Example* (3)(ii) of this section.)

(5) *Decrease in taxable gross weight, discontinued use, or converted use.*—The computation of the tax is not affected, and no right to a credit or refund of any tax paid under section 4481 arises, if in any taxable period—

(i) The taxable gross weight of a highway motor vehicle is decreased;

(ii) The use of a highway motor vehicle is discontinued (for reasons other than sale, destruction, or theft as described in paragraph (c)(4) of this section); or

(iii) The highway motor vehicle is converted to a use that is exempt from the tax imposed by section 4481(a).

(d) *Examples.*—The application of §§ 41.4481-1, 41.4481-2, and 41.4482(c)-1(c) may be illustrated by the following examples:

*Example (1).* In the taxable period beginning July 1, 1984, the first taxable use of a particular highway motor vehicle, a bus, having a taxable gross weight of 56,000 pounds, occurs on July 10, 1984, at which time the vehicle is registered in the name of X. A tax of $122 ($100 + $22) is imposed on X for the use of such vehicle for such taxable period.

*Example (2).* On July 1, 1984, X has registered in his name a highway motor vehicle having a taxable gross weight of 60,000 pounds. The vehicle is in "dead storage" until August 10, 1984, at which time X starts using the vehicle on the public highways in carrying on his trucking business. On August 10, 1984, the vehicle is still registered in X's name. Since the first taxable use of this highway motor vehicle during the taxable period occurred on August 10, 1984, X is required to pay a tax of $192.50 ([$100 + (5 × $22)] × $^{11}/_{12}$) for such taxable period.

*Example (3).* (i) In July, X uses a vehicle that is registered in X's name and has a taxable gross weight of 70,000 pounds. The vehicle is not a logging vehicle. X pays the $430 of tax imposed by section 4481 for the taxable period. On September 2 of the same calendar year, X sells the vehicle to Y. X's tax is calculated under paragraph (c)(4)(ii) by multiplying the amount of tax that would be due for a full taxable period by a fraction that has as its numerator the number of months in the period from the first day of the month in which X's first taxable use of the highway motor vehicle occurs to and including the last day of the month in which the vehicle was sold, and as its denominator the number of months in the entire taxable period. Thus, X's tax for the period is $107.50 (3/12 of $430), and X may claim a credit or refund of $322.50 ($430.00 - $107.50) in accordance with § 41.4481-1(c)(4)(v) after X sells the vehicle.

(ii) On September 23, Y uses the vehicle. Y is liable for tax on the use of the vehicle during the taxable period ending June 30 of the following calendar year. Y's tax is calculated under paragraph (c)(4)(vii) by multiplying the amount of tax that would be due for a full taxable period by a fraction that has as its numerator the number of months in the period from the first day of the month in which Y's first taxable use of the vehicle after the sale occurs (the first day of the month after such month if the first taxable use after the sale occurs in the month of the sale) through the end of the taxable period, and as its denominator the number of months in the entire taxable period. Y's first use of the vehicle occurs in the month of the sale. Accordingly, Y's tax is based on the number of months in the period from the first day of October (the month following the month of the first

»»→ *Caution: Reg. §41.4481-1, below, as amended by T.D. 9698, applies on or after July 1, 2015.*

taxable use) through the end of June, and Y owes a section 4481 tax of $322.50 (9/12 of $430) for the taxable period.

*Example* (4). Assume the same facts as in *Example* (3)(i), except that on September 2, X sells the vehicle to Dealer, a dealer in highway motor vehicles. X may claim a credit or refund of $322.50. Dealer operates the vehicle exclusively for the purpose of demonstration, which is not a "use" of the vehicle under §41.4482(c)-1(c). On May 2 of the following calendar year, Dealer sells the vehicle to Y. Dealer does not owe a section 4481 tax and may not claim a refund. Y's first taxable use of the vehicle occurs on May 3. Y's first taxable use of the vehicle does not occur in the month of a sale upon which a credit or refund is allowable. Accordingly, Y's tax is calculated under paragraph (c)(2) by multiplying the amount of tax that would be due for a

full taxable period by a fraction which has as its numerator the number of months in the taxable period beginning with the month of first taxable use and as its denominator the number of months in the entire taxable period. The numerator is the number of months in the period from the first day of May (the month of Y's first taxable use after the sale) through the end of June, and Y owes a section 4481 tax of $71.67 (2/12 of $430) for the taxable period.

(e) *Effective/applicability date.*—This section applies on and after July 1, 2015. For rules applicable before that date, see 26 CFR 41.4481-1 (revised as of April 1, 2014). [Reg. §41.4481-1.]

☐ [*T.D. 6216. Amended by T.D. 6743, 6-22-64; T.D. 7409, 3-8-76; T.D. 7505, 8-24-77; T.D. 8027, 5-23-85; T.D. 8159, 9-3-87; T.D. 8177, 3-3-88; T.D. 8879, 3-30-2000 and T.D. 9698, 10-28-2014.*]

»»→ *Caution: Reg. §41.4481-2, below, prior to amendment by T.D. 9698, applies before July 1, 2015.*

**[Reg. §41.4481-2]**

**§41.4481-2. Persons liable for tax.**—(a) *In general.*—(1)(i) A person is liable for the tax imposed by section 4481 with respect to the use of a highway motor vehicle in a taxable period if the vehicle is registered in the person's name—

(A) At the time of the first use of the vehicle in the taxable period;

(B) In the case of a vehicle under a suspension of tax described in §41.4483-3(a), at the time the use on the public highways during the taxable period exceeds 5,000 miles (7,500 miles for agricultural vehicles);

(C) At the time that an increase in the taxable gross weight of the vehicle results in an additional tax liability (as computed under §41.4481-1(c)(3)) if the increase occurs after the month in which the vehicle was first used in the taxable period; or

(D) At the time of any use during the taxable period that is after the first use during the period, but only to the extent that the tax or any installment payment of the tax has not previously been paid.

(ii) In any case in which more than one person is liable for the tax for a taxable period, the liability of all persons is satisfied to the extent that the tax is paid by any person liable for the tax.

(2) The application of paragraph (a)(1) of this section may be illustrated by the following example:

*Example.* In the taxable period beginning July 1, 1985, the first taxable use of a particular highway motor vehicle having a taxable gross weight of 60,000 pounds occurs on July 10, 1985, at which time the vehicle is registered in the name of Y. On September 1, 1985, Y sells the vehicle to X who registers and uses the vehicle before the end of such taxable period. Since the vehicle was registered in the name of Y at the time of its first taxable use, Y is liable for the total tax of $210 ($100 + (5 × $22)) imposed on the use of the vehicle for the taxable period. X is also liable for $210 tax or any part thereof, but

only to the extent that Y does not pay it. To the extent that either X or Y pays the tax the other party is relieved of such liability.

(b) *Evidence of prior use of secondhand vehicle.*—Every person who, at any time in the taxable period, acquires and has registered in his name a secondhand highway motor vehicle shall obtain and keep as a part of his records evidence, which he believes to be true, showing whether there was or was not a taxable use of such vehicle at any time in such taxable period prior to the time when the vehicle was registered in his name. Such person shall also obtain and keep as evidence a statement from the transferor as to whether there was in effect, at the time the vehicle was acquired, a suspension under §41.4483-3(a) of the tax imposed by section 4481(a). The evidence may take the form of a written statement, signed and dated by the person from whom the vehicle was acquired, showing whether there was or was not a prior taxable use of the vehicle and whether there was a suspension of tax in the taxable period. If the vehicle is acquired from a dealer in highway motor vehicles, the statement may be obtained from such dealer or from the person from whom the dealer acquired such vehicle. If evidence is not obtained showing whether there was or was not a prior taxable use of such vehicle and whether there was a suspension of tax in the taxable period, such person shall keep as a part of his records a written statement of the reason why he was unable to obtain such evidence.

(c) *Cross references.*—(1) For provisions relating to interest on underpayments of tax, see §301.6601-1 of this chapter (Regulations on Procedure and Administration).

(2) For records required to be kept, see §41.6001-1.

(3) For rules applicable to installment payment of tax for highway use tax liability, see §41.6156-1.

(4) For rules applicable to time of filing returns, see §41.6071(a)-1. [Reg. §41.4481-2.]

☐ [*T.D. 6216. Amended by T.D. 6743, 6-22-64; T.D. 8027, 5-23-85 and T.D. 8879, 3-30-2000.*]

»»→ *Caution: Reg. §41.4481-2, below, as amended by T.D. 9698, applies on or after July 1, 2015.*

**[Reg. §41.4481-2]**

**§41.4481-2. Persons liable for tax.**—(a) *In general.*—(1)(i) A person is liable for the tax imposed by section 4481 with respect to the use of a highway motor vehicle in a taxable period if the vehicle is registered in the person's name—

(A) At the time of the first use of the vehicle in the taxable period;

(B) In the case of a vehicle under a suspension of tax described in §41.4483-3(a), at the time the use on the public highways during the taxable period exceeds 5,000 miles (7,500 miles for agricultural vehicles);

(C) At the time that an increase in the taxable gross weight of the vehicle results in an additional tax liability (as computed under §41.4481-1(c)(3)) if the increase occurs after the month in which the vehicle was first used in the taxable period; or

(D) At the time of any use during the taxable period that is after the first use during the period, but only to the extent that the tax has not previously been paid.

(ii) In any case in which more than one person is liable for the tax for a taxable period, the liability of all persons is satisfied to the extent that the tax is paid by any person liable for the tax.

(2) If a vehicle is sold during the taxable period and a credit or refund is allowable upon the sale under §41.4481-1(c)(4)(iii), paragraph (a)(1) of this section is applied with the following modifications:

(i) For purposes of determining the person liable for the tax determined under §41.4481-1(c)(4)(ii), each reference to a taxable period in paragraph (a)(1) of this section is treated as a reference to the period that begins on the first day of the taxable period in which the vehicle is sold and ends on the date of sale.

(ii) For purposes of determining the person liable for the tax determined under §41.4481-1(c)(4)(vi), each reference to a taxable period in paragraph (a)(1) of this section is treated as a reference to the period that begins on the date of the sale and ends on the last day of the taxable period in which the vehicle is sold.

(3) The application of paragraph (a) of this section may be illustrated by *Examples* (3) and (4) in §41.4481-1(d).

(b) *Evidence of prior use of secondhand vehicle.*—Every person who, at any time in the taxable period, acquires and has registered in his name a secondhand highway motor vehicle shall obtain and keep as a part of his records evidence, which he believes to be true, showing whether there was or was not a taxable use of such vehicle at any time in such taxable period prior to the time when the vehicle was registered in his name. Such person shall also obtain and keep as evidence a statement from the transferor as to whether there was in effect, at the time the vehicle was acquired, a suspension under §41.4483-3(a) of the tax imposed by section 4481(a). The evidence may take the form of a written statement, signed and dated by the person from whom the vehicle was acquired, showing whether there was or was not a prior taxable use of the vehicle and whether there was a suspension of tax in the taxable period. If the vehicle is acquired from a dealer in highway motor vehicles, the statement may be obtained from such dealer or from the person from whom the dealer acquired such vehicle. If evidence is not obtained showing whether there was or was not a prior taxable use of such vehicle and whether there was a suspension of tax in the taxable period, such person shall keep as a part of his records a written statement of the reason why he was unable to obtain such evidence. For provisions relating to penalties for aiding and abetting an understatement of tax liability, see section 6701 of the Internal Revenue Code.

⟫→ *Caution: Reg. §41.4481-2, below, as amended by T.D. 9698, applies on or after July 1, 2015.*

(c) *Effective/applicability date.*—This section applies on and after July 1, 2015. For rules applicable before that date, see 26 CFR 41.4481-2 (revised as of April 1, 2014). [Reg. § 41.4481-2.]

☐ [*T.D. 6216. Amended by T.D. 6743, 6-22-64; T.D. 8027, 5-23-85; T.D. 8879, 3-30-2000 and T.D. 9698, 10-28-2014.*]

### [Reg. §41.4481-3]

**§41.4481-3. Registration.**—(a) For purposes of the regulations in this part, the term "registered" when used in reference to a highway motor vehicle means—

(1) Registered under the law of any State or Territory of the United States, the District of Columbia, or contiguous foreign country, or

(2) Required to be registered under the law of any State or Territory of the United States or contiguous foreign country in which such highway motor vehicle is operated or situated or, in case the vehicle is operated or situated in the District of Columbia, under the law of the District of Columbia.

Any highway motor vehicle which is operated under a dealer's tag, license, or permit is considered to be registered in the name of such dealer. A highway motor vehicle is not considered to be registered solely by reason of the fact that there has been issued a special permit for operation of the vehicle at particular times and under specified conditions.

(b) Any highway motor vehicle which, at any time in the taxable period, is registered both in the name of the owner of the vehicle and in the name of any other person, is considered, for purposes of the regulations in this part, to be registered, at such time, solely in the name of the owner of the vehicle. [Reg. § 41.4481-3.]

☐ [*T.D. 6216. Amended by T.D. 6743, 6-22-64 and T.D. 8159, 9-3-87.*]

### [Reg. §41.4482(a)-1]

**§41.4482(a)-1. Definition of highway motor vehicle.**—(a) *Highway motor vehicle.*—The term "highway motor vehicle" means any vehicle that is both—

(1) A vehicle propelled by means of its own motor, whether such motor is powered by gasoline, diesel fuel, special motor fuels, electricity, or otherwise, and

(2) A "highway vehicle" as defined in §48.4061(a)-1(d) of this chapter.

(b) *Treatment of certain excluded vehicles.*—Although trailers and semi-trailers used in combination with highway trucks or truck-tractors are not vehicles the use of which is subject to the tax imposed by section 4481(a), trailers and semitrailers customarily used in combination with highway trucks or truck-tractors are taken into account in determining the taxable gross weight of the highway motor vehicle under §41.4482(b)-1, which is the base of the tax. [Reg. §41.4482(a)-1.]

☐ [*T.D. 6216. Amended by T.D. 7461, 1-12-77 and T.D. 8879, 3-30-2000.*]

### [Reg. §41.4482(b)-1]

**§41.4482(b)-1. Definition of taxable gross weight.**—(a) *Actual unloaded weight.*—(1) *In general.*—Actual unloaded weight means the empty (or tare) weight of the truck, truck-tractor, or bus, fully equipped for service.

(2) *Trucks and truck-tractors.*—A truck or truck-tractor fully equipped for service includes the body (whether or not designed and adapted primarily for transporting cargo, as for example, concrete mixers); all accessories; all equipment attached to or carried on such truck or truck-tractor for use in connection with the movement of the vehicle by means of its own motor or for use in the maintenance of the vehicle; and a full complement of lubricants, fuel, and water. It does not include the driver, any equipment (not including the body) attached to or carried on the vehicle for use in handling, protecting, or preserving cargo, or any special equipment (such as an air compressor, crane, specialized oilfield machinery, etc.) mounted on the vehicle for use on construction jobs, in oilfield operations, etc.

(3) *Buses.*—A bus fully equipped for service includes the body; all accessories; all equipment attached to or carried on such bus for use in connection with the movement of the vehicle by means of its own motor, for use in the maintenance of the vehicle, or for the accommodation of passengers or others (such as air conditioning equipment and sanitation facilities, etc.); and a full complement of lubricants, fuel, and water. It does not include the driver.

(b) *Determination of taxable gross weight.*—(1) *In general.*—The taxable gross weight of a highway motor vehicle is the sum of the actual unloaded weight of the vehicle fully equipped for service, the actual unloaded weight of any semitrailers or trailers fully equipped for service customarily used in combination with the vehicle, and the weight of the maximum load customarily carried on the vehicle and on any semitrailers or trailers customarily used in combination with the vehicle. In the case of a highway motor vehicle that is registered in at least one State that requires a declaration of gross weight to be stated as a specific amount for any purpose (including proportional or prorate registration or the payment of any other fees or taxes), the taxable gross weight of such vehicle must be no less than the highest gross weight declaration (or combined gross weight declaration in the case of a tractor-trailer or truck-trailer combination) made by the registrant in any State with respect to such vehicle. If a highway motor vehicle is registered in at least one State that requires vehicles to register on the basis of gross weight and such vehicle is not registered in any State that requires a declaration of gross weight to be stated as a specific amount by the registrant, the taxable gross weight of such vehicle must fall within the highest gross weight category of such State for which such vehicle is registered during the taxable period. Declarations of weight made in order to obtain special temporary travel permits which allow a vehicle to, (i) operate in a State in which the vehicle is not registered or prorated, (ii) operate at more than a State's maximum statutory weight limit, or (iii) operate at more than the weight that the vehicle is registered in a State, shall not be considered in determining the taxable gross weight of a vehicle.

(2) *Buses.*—For purposes of the tax imposed by section 4481(a), the taxable gross weight of a bus shall be the sum of the weights referred to in paragraph (b)(1) of this section except that "the weight of the maximum load customarily carried" on a bus shall be equal to 150 pounds times the number of units of seating capacity provided for passengers and driver.

(c) *Examples.*—The provisions of this section may be illustrated by the following examples:

*Example (1).* A is the owner of a truck-tractor. On January 1, 1985, A registers the truck-tractor in three states—X, Y, and Z. For purposes of registering the vehicle in State X, A declares the gross operating weight of his truck-tractor to be 60,000 pounds. The declaration of the gross weight of the vehicle at 50,000 pounds places A's truck-tractor in the State X registration category of 55,000 to 62,000 pounds gross weight. Thus, the registered weight of A's vehicle in State X is 62,000 pounds. At the same time as A registers the vehicle in State X, A also proportionally registers the vehicle under the IRP in State Y. A uses the same declared gross weight of 60,000 pounds for purposes of the State Y proportional registration. Registration in State Y at this declared gross weight places A's truck-tractor in the State Y gross weight registration category of 58,000 to 68,000 pounds. Finally, A registers the truck-tractor in State Z. Registration of vehicles in State Z is based on the unladen weight of the vehicle. During the taxable period beginning on July 1, 1985, A's truck-tractor is not registered in any other state. For the taxable period beginning on July 1, 1985, A must declare a taxable gross weight of no less than 60,000 pounds for purposes of the tax imposed by section 4481(a) because that is the highest declared gross weight for state registration or other purposes. Should A declare to any State agency a higher gross operating weight with respect to the truck-tractor during the same taxable period (except for a special temporary permit), A would then be liable for additional tax as determined under paragraph (c)(3) of § 41.4481-1.

*Example (2).* Assume the same facts as in example (1), except that on one occasion during the taxable period, A was issued a special 2-day permit to use his truck-tractor in State Y to haul a load which would give A's unit a total gross weight of 80,000 pounds. A may still declare the taxable gross weight of his unit to be no less than 60,000 pounds because special permits to haul heavier loads on a temporary basis are not considered in determining the taxable gross weight of a vehicle.

*Example (3).* C owns and has registered in his name 2 trucks which are identical in all respects and which are used to carry the same type of load. The first vehicle is registered only in State X at a registered weight of 73,000 pounds based on a declared gross weight of 70,000 pounds. The second vehicle is registered only in State Y at a registered weight of 68,000 pounds based on a declared gross weight of 65,000 pounds. No other declarations of gross weight are made with respect to either vehicle. For purposes of the Federal heavy vehicle use tax, the taxable gross weight of the vehicle registered in State X may be declared at no less than 70,000 pounds and the taxable gross weight of the vehicle registered in State Y may be declared at no less than 65,000 pounds even though the vehicles are identical. [Reg. §41.4482(b)-1.]

☐ [*T.D. 6216, 12-5-56. Amended by T.D. 6743, 6-22-64; T.D. 7011, 5-7-69; T.D. 8027, 5-22-85 and T.D. 8879, 3-30-2000.*]

**[Reg. §41.4482(c)-1]**

**§41.4482(c)-1. Definition of State, taxable period, use, and customarily used.**—(a) *State.*—*State* includes any State, any political subdivision of a State, the District of Columbia, and, to the extent provided by section 7871, any Indian tribal government.

(b) *Taxable period.*—For the definition of *taxable period*, see section 4482(c).

(c) *Use.*—The term "use," as used in the regulations in this part with reference to a highway motor vehicle, means the use of the highway motor vehicle on the public highways in the United States, that is, operation of the vehicle, by means of its own motor, on any roadway (whether a Federal highway, State highway, city street, or otherwise) in the United States which is not a private roadway. Thus, for purposes of the tax, there is no use of a highway motor vehicle while the vehicle is in "dead storage." The term "use" does not include operation of a new highway motor vehicle on a public highway in the United States if such operation is merely for the purpose of transporting the vehicle from the point of manufacture or assembly to the consumer, whether direct or with intermediate deliveries to such points as are involved in the distribution process. For example, operation of a new vehicle for the purpose of delivering it from the factory to a branch establishment of the manufacturer, or from the factory or branch establishment to a dealer, distributor, or consumer, does not constitute use of the vehicle within the meaning of the regulations in this part; likewise, the further operation of the vehicle by a dealer or distributor for the purpose of delivering the vehicle to a consumer does not constitute use of the vehicle. Similarly, the operation of a secondhand highway motor vehicle by a dealer or distributor for the purpose of delivering the vehicle to a purchaser does not constitute use of the vehicle within the meaning of the regulations in this part. Furthermore, the term "use" does not include operation of a new or secondhand highway motor vehicle, if such operation is exclusively for the purpose of demonstration of the vehicle by a dealer in, or distributor of, new or secondhand highway motor vehicles. Operation of a highway motor vehicle on a private roadway, or other private property, does not constitute use of the vehicle within the meaning of the regulations in this part.

(d) *Customarily used.*—A semitrailer or trailer is treated as *customarily used* in connection with a highway motor vehicle if the vehicle is equipped to tow the semitrailer or trailer. [Reg. §41.4482(c)-1.]

☐ [T.D. 6216, 12-6-56. *Amended by T.D. 6518, 12-20-60; T.D. 6743, 6-22-64; T.D. 7409, 3-5-76; T.D. 7505, 8-24-77; T.D. 8027, 5-22-85; T.D. 8159, 9-3-87 and T.D. 8879, 3-30-2000.]*

**[Reg. §41.4483-1]**

**§41.4483-1. State exemption.**—Use of a highway motor vehicle by a State is exempt from the tax imposed by section 4481. For this purpose, the term *use by a State* means the operation by a State on the public highways in the United States of any highway motor vehicle, whether or not such highway motor vehicle is owned by the State. [Reg. §41.4483-1.]

☐ [T.D. 6216, 12-6-56. *Amended by T.D. 8879, 3-30-2000.]*

**[Reg. §41.4483-2]**

**§41.4483-2. Exemption for certain transit-type buses.**—(a) *In general.*—Use in any taxable period, or part thereof, of any bus of the transit type by any person who is engaged in the operation of a transit system is exempt from the tax, if such person meets the 60-percent passenger fare revenue test provided for in paragraph (e) of this section, for the applicable period prescribed in paragraph (c) of this section as the test period for such person for such system for such taxable period, or part thereof.

(b) *Buses of the transit type.*—The term "transit type," when used in the regulations in this part with reference to a bus, means the type of bus which is designed for the mass transportation of persons within an urban area, as distinguished from the intercity-type bus. A transit-type bus is ordinarily distinguishable from an intercity-type bus by comparison of seats, doors, and baggage facilities. The transit-type bus usually has straight-back seats of the bench type, while the intercity-type bus generally has seats which either can be reclined or are in fact permanently fixed in a reclining position. The transit-type bus is more likely to have an accordion or folding-type door at the front of the bus, and often has a second door in the middle or at the rear for passengers to leave the bus, as opposed to the emergency-type rear door which may or may not be included in the intercity-type bus. The typical transit-type bus does not have facilities for storing baggage whereas the typical intercity-type bus has facilities for storing baggage in a compartment underneath the floor of the bus or in overhead racks, or both. Other characteristics which may be taken into account in distinguishing a transit-type bus from an intercity-type bus include gear ratios, acceleration and maximum speed, and aisle space for standees. The transit-type bus ordinarily has a lower gear ratio to provide for quick starts and because, in general, buses of this type are operated at low speeds. The intercity-type bus ordinarily has a higher gear ratio and can be operated at much higher speeds. The transit-type bus usually has wider aisles, with overhead straps or bars to accommodate standees.

(c) *Test period.*—(1) In the case of any person who is engaged in the operation of a transit system at any time in the calendar quarter immediately preceding July 1 of any taxable period, the test period for such system for such taxable period shall be such calendar quarter. However, if passenger fare revenue from scheduled service described in paragraph (e) of this section was derived on less than 30 days during such calendar quarter from operation of such system, the test period for such system for such taxable period shall be the last preceding test period for such system. If such system has no preceding test period, then the test period for such system for such taxable period shall be the calendar quarter beginning with July 1 of such taxable period.

(2) Except as otherwise provided in subparagraph (3) of this paragraph, in the case of any person who commences operation of a transit system at any time on or after July 1 of any taxable period, the test period for such system for that part of such taxable period beginning with the first day on which such operation was commenced shall be the calendar quarter in which falls such first day. However, if passenger fare revenue from scheduled service described in paragraph (e) of this section was derived on less than 30 days during such calendar quarter from operation of such system, the test period for such system for such taxable period shall be the following calendar quarter.

(3) In the case of any person who commences operation of a transit system at any time in the last calendar quarter to which the tax imposed by section 4481 applies, such last calendar quarter shall be the test period for such transit system regardless of the number of days in which passenger fare revenue is derived in such calendar quarter.

(d) The term "transit system," as used in the regulations in this part, means any system for furnishing scheduled common carrier public passenger land transportation service along regular routes.

(e) *60-percent passenger fare revenue test.*—For purposes of this section, a person engaged in the operation of a transit system meets the 60-percent passenger fare revenue test, for the applicable test period prescribed in this section, if—

(1) During such test period such person derived passenger fare revenue from the operation of such system, and

(2) At least 60 percent of the total of such passenger fare revenue derived by such person during such test period was attributable to (i) amounts paid for transportation which do not exceed 60 cents, (ii) amounts paid for commutation or season tickets for single trips of less than 30 miles, or (iii) amounts paid for commutation tickets for one month or less. In determining the total of such passenger fare revenue, revenue from sources such as charter fees, rentals of property, advertising receipts, etc., is not taken into account.

(f) *Examples.*—Application of this section may be illustrated by the following examples:

*Example (1).* The X Transit Company is engaged in the operation of a transit system in the city of A and surrounding area throughout April, May, and June of 1984 and the taxable period beginning July 1, 1984. It derives passenger fare revenue from the operation of such system for 15 days in April and for the entire months of May and June of 1984. On July 1, 1984, the Company is using 60 buses of the transit type and 40 buses of the intercity type. Each of 20 of the transit-type buses and each of 10 of the intercity-type buses has a taxable gross weight of at least 55,000 pounds. (No tax is imposed on the use of either a transit-type bus or an intercity-type bus having a taxable gross weight of less than 55,000 pounds. See §41.4481-1.) Use of the 10 intercity-type buses is subject to the tax for the taxable period beginning with July 1, 1984, since the exemption, if any, applies only to transit-type buses. Use of the 20 transit-type buses is not subject to the tax for such taxable period if at least 60 percent of the total passenger fare revenue derived by the X Transit Company during April, May, and June of 1984 (the test period prescribed in paragraph (c)(1) of this section) from operation of such system was from fares attributable to (i) amounts paid for transportation which do not exceed 60 cents, (ii) amounts paid for commutation or season tickets for single trips of less than 30 miles, or (iii) amounts paid for commutation tickets for one month or less. If the X Transit Company does not meet the 60-percent passenger fare revenue test for April, May, and June of 1984, the tax attaches for the taxable period beginning with July 1, 1984, with respect to the use of each of the 20 transit-type buses having a taxable gross weight of at least 55,000 pounds.

*Example (2).* Assume the same facts as those stated in Example (1), except that the X Transit Company commences operation of the transit system on July 15, 1984, and derives passenger fare revenue from operation of the system throughout the following August and September. In such case, the test period is July, August, and September of 1984, and if the test is met for this period, no tax is imposed on the use by the Company of any bus of the transit type in the period July 15, 1984, through June 30, 1985.

*Example (3).* Assume the same facts as those stated in Example (1), except that the X Transit Company commences operation of the transit system on April 15, 1985, and derives passenger fare revenue from operation of the system throughout the following May and June. In such case the test period is April, May, and June of 1985, and if the test is met for this period, no tax is imposed on the use by the Company of any bus of the transit type in the period April 15 through June 30, 1985 or in the taxable period beginning on July 1, 1985. [Reg. §41.4483-2.]

☐ [*T.D. 6216. Amended by T.D. 6743, 6-22-64; T.D. 8027, 5-23-85 and T.D. 8879, 3-30-2000.*]

### [Reg. §41.4483-3]

**§41.4483-3. Exemption for trucks used for 5,000 or fewer miles and agricultural vehicles used for 7,500 or fewer miles on public highways.**—(a) *Suspension of tax.*—(1) *In general.*—Liability for the tax imposed by section 4481(a) is suspended during a taxable period if it is reasonable to expect that the vehicle will be used for 5,000 or fewer miles on public highways during such taxable period and the owner furnishes in the time and manner required the information required under paragraph (a)(2) of this section. See paragraph (g) of this section regarding special rules for agricultural vehicles. See §41.4482(c)-1(c) for the meaning of "use" on the public highways.

(2) *Information to be supplied in support of suspension of tax.*—The owner of a highway motor vehicle who reasonably expects that the vehicle will be used for 5,000 or fewer miles on public highways during a taxable period shall furnish on the first Form 2290 filed during the taxable period for such motor vehicle, such information as is required by the Form in order to support the suspension of tax under paragraph (a) of this section.

(b) *Cessation of suspension from tax.*—If a highway motor vehicle on which the tax under section 4481(a) is suspended for a particular taxable period under paragraph (a)(1) of this section is used for more than 5,000 miles on public highways during such taxable period, the owner of the vehicle is liable for the tax for the entire taxable period in accordance with section 4481(a).

(c) *Exemption.*—If at the end of any taxable period during which the tax under section 4481(a) on a highway motor vehicle was suspended under paragraph (a)(1) of this section the vehicle has not been used for more than 5,000 miles on public highways, the vehicle shall be exempt from the tax for that taxable period. The owner of the vehicle shall verify that the vehicle was used for less than 5,000 miles in such ended taxable period on the first Form 2290 filed for the next taxable period.

(d) *Examples.*—The provisions of this section may be illustrated by the following examples:

*Example (1).* A is the owner of 6 highway motor vehicles, each of which has a taxable gross weight in excess of 55,000 pounds. None of these 6 vehicles are agricultural vehicles. The vehicles are placed in use during July 1984. Because of the nature of his business, A reports on the first Form 2290 filed after June 30, 1984, that he reasonably expects that none of the vehicles will be used for more than 5,000 miles on public highways. Accordingly, the tax imposed by section 4481(a) is suspended for A's 6 vehicles for the taxable period July 1, 1984, through June 30, 1985.

*Example (2).* Assume the same facts as in example (1) except that during the month of February 1985, the use of one of A's vehicles exceeds 5,000 miles on public highways. A is liable for the full tax for the taxable period July 1, 1984, through June 30, 1985, for that vehicle at the rate set forth in §41.4481-1(b), and must so report on a Form 2290 filed on or before March 31, 1985, the last day of the month following the month in which the use exceeds 5,000 miles.

(e) *Credit or refund of tax for highway motor vehicle used 5,000 or fewer miles.*—(1) If a highway motor vehicle on which the tax imposed by section 4481(a) has been paid for a given taxable period is used for 5,000 or fewer miles on public highways during such taxable period, the person who paid the tax may file a claim for refund of an overpayment of the tax at the end of the taxable period. Claims for refunds of tax made under this paragraph (e) shall be filed in the same manner as claims for refunds filed under §41.4481-1(d). Refunds of tax made under this paragraph (e) shall be without interest.

(2) Any person entitled to claim a refund of tax under paragraph (e)(1) of this section may, in lieu of claiming a refund of such tax, claim credit for such tax on the first Form 2290 filed for the next taxable period.

**⟫→ Caution:** *Reg. §41.4483-3(f), below, prior to amendment by T.D. 9698, applies before July 1, 2015.*

(f) *Relief from liability for tax under certain circumstances.*—If the tax imposed by section 4481(a) on a highway motor vehicle is suspended for any taxable period under paragraph (a) of this section and the vehicle is transferred while the suspension is in effect, the transferor will not be liable for any tax on such vehicle for such taxable period if such transferor furnishes a statement to the transferee on which is included the transferor's name, address and taxpayer identification number, the vehicle identification number, the date of transfer of the vehicle, the number of miles the vehicle has been used on the public highways during the taxable period, the odometer reading at the time of the transfer, and the name, address and taxpayer identification number of the transferee. The suspension from tax under paragraph (a) continues until the vehicle is used on the public highways

for more than 5,000 miles during the taxable period (including use by the transferor for the portion of the taxable period prior to the transfer). If the transferor has furnished the statement required in this paragraph (f), the transferee and not the transferor is liable for the entire tax under section 4481(a) for the taxable period in which the transfer was made. If the transferor has not furnished such statement to the transferee, then the transferor is also liable for the tax on the use of such vehicle for such taxable period to the extent that the tax or an installment payment of the tax has not been previously paid. See paragraph (b) of this section relating to cessation of suspension from tax and §41.6011(a)-1(a)(3) for a requirement that certain transferees described in this paragraph (f) must file a return.

**⟫→ Caution:** *Reg. §41.4483-3(f), below, as amended by T.D. 9698, applies on or after July 1, 2015.*

(f) *Relief from liability for tax under certain circumstances.*—If the tax imposed by section 4481(a) on a highway motor vehicle is suspended for any taxable period under paragraph (a) of this section and the vehicle is transferred while the suspension is in effect, the transferor will not be liable for any tax on such vehicle for such taxable period if such transferor furnishes a statement to the transferee on which is included the transferor's name, address and taxpayer identification number, the vehicle identification number, the date of transfer of the vehicle, the number of miles the vehicle has been used on the public highways during the taxable period, the odometer reading at the time of the transfer, and the name, address and taxpayer identification number of the transferee. The suspension from tax under paragraph (a) continues until the vehicle is used on the public highways for more than 5,000 miles during the taxable period (including use by the transferor for the portion of the taxable period prior to the transfer). If the transferor has furnished the statement required in this paragraph (f), the transferee and not the transferor is liable for the entire tax under section 4481(a) for the taxable period in which the transfer was made. If the transferor has not furnished such statement to the transferee, then the transferor is also liable for the tax on the use of such vehicle for such taxable period (determined in the case of a transfer described in §41.4481-1(c)(4)(i) under §41.4481-1(c)(4)(ii)) to the extent that the tax has not been previously paid. See paragraph (b) of this section relating to cessation of suspension from tax and

§41.6011(a)-1(a)(3) for a requirement that certain transferees described in this paragraph (f) must file a return.

(g) *Special rule for agricultural vehicles.*—(1) *In General.*—In applying the provisions of this section to an agricultural vehicle, "7,500" shall be substituted for "5,000" each place it appears in paragraphs (a) through (f) of this section.

(2) *Meaning of terms.*—(i) *Agriculture vehicle.*—An agricultural vehicle is any highway motor vehicle—

(A) Used (or expected to be used) primarily for farming purposes, and

(B) Registered (under the laws of the State or States in which such vehicle is required to be registered) as a highway motor vehicle used for farming purposes.

A highway motor vehicle is used primarily for farming purposes if more than one-half of such vehicle's use (determined on the basis of mileage) during the taxable period is for farming purposes. Further, the highway motor vehicle must be registered (under the laws of the State or States where such vehicle is required to be registered) as a highway motor vehicle used for farming purposes for the entire taxable period in order to qualify as an agricultural vehicle. See §41.4482(a)-(1) for the definition of "highway motor vehicle". A vehicle will be considered to be registered under the laws of the State as a highway motor vehicle used for farming purposes if such vehicle is so registered under a State statute or legally valid regulations. In addition, no special tag or license plate identifying a vehicle as being used for farming purposes is required.

(ii) *Farming purposes.*—For purposes of this section "farming purposes" means the transporting of any farm commodity to or from a farm, or the use directly in agricultural production.

(iii) *Farm commodity.*—A "farm commodity" is any agricultural or horticultural commodity, feed, seed, fertilizer, livestock, bees, poultry, fur-bearing animals, or wildlife. A farm commodity does not include a commodity which has been changed by a processing operation from its raw or natural state. For example, juice which has been extracted from fruits or vegetables is not a farm commodity for purposes of this paragraph (g).

(iv) *Farm.*—The term "farm" includes stock (including feed yards for fattening cattle), dairy, poultry, fruit, fur-bearing animal, and truck farms, plantations, ranches, nurseries, ranges, orchards, and such greenhouses and other similar structures as are used primarily for the raising of any agricultural or horticultural commodity. Greenhouses and other similar structures used primarily for purposes other than the raising of agricultural or horticultural commodities (for example, display, storage, or fabrication of wreaths, corsages, and bouquets) do not constitute "farms".

(v) *Agricultural production.*—(A) *In general.*—A highway motor vehicle is considered to be used directly in agricultural production only if it is used as indicated in the following paragraphs.

(B) *Use of a highway motor vehicle in connection with cultivating, raising and harvesting.*—A highway motor vehicle is considered to be used directly in agricultural production if such vehicle is used in connection with cultivating the soil, or raising or harvesting any agricultural or horticultural commodity, including the raising, shearing, feeding, caring for, training and management of livestock, bees, poultry, and fur-bearing animals and wildlife. A highway motor vehicle which is used in connection with operations such as canning, freezing, packaging, or other processing operations will not be considered to be used directly in agricultural production.

(C) *Use of a highway motor vehicle in connection with planting, cultivation, caring for, cutting, etc., of trees.*—A highway motor vehicle is used directly for agricultural production if it is used in connection with planting, cultivating, caring for, or cutting of trees, or in connection with the preparation (other than milling) of trees for market; but only if such operations are incidental to farming operations. These farming operations include felling trees and cutting them into logs or firewood, but do not include sawing logs into lumber, chipping, or other milling operations. The operations specified in this paragraph (g)(2)(v)(C) will be considered "incidental to farming operations" only if they are a minor nature in comparison with the total farming operations involved. Therefore, a treefarmer or timbergrower may not claim that a highway motor vehicle used in that trade or business is used directly in agricultural production.

(D) *Use of a highway motor vehicle in connection with the operation, management, conservation, improvement, or maintenance of a farm.*—A highway motor vehicle is used directly for agricultural production if it is used in connection with the operation, management, conservation, improvement, or maintenance of a farm and its tools and equipment. Examples of these operations include clearing land, repairing fences and farm buildings, building terraces or irrigation ditches, cleaning tools or farm machinery, painting, and other activities which contribute in any way to the conduct of a farm as such, as distinguished from any other enterprise in which the owner of the highway motor vehicle may be engaged.

(3) *Mileage on farm not counted toward 7,500 mile limit.*—For purposes of this section, the number of miles which a highway motor vehicle is driven on a farm and not on the public highways shall not

be taken into account when determining whether the vehicle's mileage is in excess of 7,500 miles. Accurate records should be kept by taxpayers of the number of miles that a highway motor vehicle is operated on a farm.

(h) *Owner.*—For purposes of this section the term "owner" means, with respect to any highway motor vehicle, the person described in section 4481(b).

(i) *Effective/applicability date.*—This section applies on and after July 1, 2015. For rules applicable before that date, see 26 CFR 41.4483-3 (revised as of April 1, 2014). [Reg. § 41.4483-3.]

☐ [*T.D. 8027, 5-23-85. Amended by T.D. 8879, 3-30-2000 and T.D. 9698, 10-28-2014.*]

### [Reg. § 41.4483-4]

**§ 41.4483-4. Application of exemptions.**—Any exemption from the tax on the use of a highway motor vehicle has application only with respect to the use of such highway motor vehicle and not with respect to the highway motor vehicle as such. Furthermore, such exemption is subject to those provisions of paragraph (c) of § 41.4481-1 relating to proration of the tax and to the effect of an exempt use of a highway motor vehicle after a taxable use has been made. Thus, if a taxable use is made of a highway motor vehicle at any time in a taxable period, the tax is imposed on the use of such vehicle for such taxable period, computed from the first day of the month in which such taxable use occurred, even though at some time in the same taxable period, before or after such taxable use occurred, the use of the vehicle may have been, or may be, exempt. For example, if a highway motor vehicle is operated exclusively by a State in the period July 1 through September 10 of a taxable period use of such vehicle in such period is exempt from the tax. However, if a taxable use of the vehicle is made on September 11 of such taxable period, the tax imposed on the use of such vehicle for such taxable period is computed from September 1. On the other hand, if a taxable use of the vehicle is made at any time in July of the taxable period, the tax imposed on the use of such vehicle for such taxable period is computed from July 1, even though the vehicle may be operated exclusively by a State in every other month of such period. [Reg. § 41.4483-3.]

☐ [*T.D. 6216. Amended by T.D. 6743, 6-22-64. Redesignated T.D. 8027, 5-23-85.*]

### [Reg. § 41.4483-6]

**§ 41.4483-6. Reduction in tax for trucks used in logging.**—(a) *In general.*—The tax imposed by section 4481 shall be reduced by 25 percent in the case of a truck used in logging.

(b) *Truck used in logging.*—The term "truck used in logging" means any highway motor vehicle which—

(1) Is used exclusively during the taxable period for the transportation, to and from a point located on a forested site, of products harvested from such forested site, and

(2) Is registered (under the laws of the State or States in which such vehicle is required to be registered) as a highway motor vehicle used exclusively in the transportation of harvested forest products.

Products harvested from the forested site may include timber which has been processed for commercial use by sawing into lumber, chipping or other milling operations if such processing occurs prior to transportation from the forested site. A vehicle will be considered to be registered under the laws of a state as a highway motor vehicle used exclusively in the transportation of harvested forest products if such vehicle is so registered under a state statute or legally valid regulations. In addition, no special tag or license plate identifying a vehicle as being used in the transportation of harvested forest products is required. [Reg. § 41.4483-6.]

☐ [*T.D. 8027, 5-23-85.*]

## Environmental Taxes

See p. 20,601 for regulations not amended to reflect law changes

### [Reg. § 52.0-1]

**§ 52.0-1. Introduction.**—The regulations in this part 52 are designated "Environmental Tax Regulations." The regulations relate to the environmental taxes imposed by chapter 38 of the Internal Revenue Code. See part 40 of this chapter for regulations relating to returns, payments, and deposits of taxes imposed by chapter 38. [Reg. § 52.0-1.]

☐ [*T.D. 8442, 10-21-92.*]

### [Reg. § 52.4681-1]

**§ 52.4681-1. Taxes imposed with respect to ozone-depleting chemicals.**—(a) *Taxes imposed.*—Sections 4681 and 4682 impose the following taxes with respect to ozone-depleting chemicals (ODCs):

(1) *Tax on ODCs.*—Section 4681(a)(1) imposes a tax on ODCs that are sold or used by the manufacturer or importer thereof. Except as otherwise provided in § 52.4682-1 (relating to the tax on ODCs), the amount of the tax is equal to the product of—

(i) The weight (in pounds) of the ODC;

(ii) The base tax amount (determined under section 4681(b)(1)(B) or (C)) for the calendar year in which the sale or use occurs; and

(iii) The ozone-depletion factor (determined under section 4682(b)) for the ODC.

(2) *Tax on imported taxable products.*—Section 4681(a)(2) imposes a tax on imported taxable products that are sold or used by the importer thereof. Except as otherwise provided in §52.4682-3 (relating to the tax on imported taxable products), the tax is computed by reference to the weight of the ODCs used as materials in the manufacture of the product. The amount of tax is equal to the tax that would have been imposed on the ODCs under section 4681(a)(1) if the ODCs had been sold in the United States on the date of the sale or use of the imported product. The weight of such ODCs is determined under §52.4682-3.

(3) *Floor stocks tax.*—(i) *Imposition of tax.*—Section 4682(h) imposes a floor stocks tax on ODCs that—

(A) Are held by any person other than the manufacturer or importer of the ODC on a date specified in paragraph (a)(3)(ii) of this section; and

(B) Are held on such date for sale or for use in further manufacture.

(ii) *Dates on which tax imposed.*—The floor stocks tax is imposed on January 1 of each calendar year after 1989.

(iii) *Amount of tax.*—Except as otherwise provided in §52.4682-4 (relating to the floor stocks tax), the amount of the floor stocks tax is equal to the excess of—

(A) The tax that would be imposed on the ODC under section 4681(a)(1) if a sale or use of the ODC by its manufacturer or importer occurred on the date the floor stocks tax is imposed (the tentative tax amount), over

(B) The sum of the taxes previously imposed (if any) on the ODC under sections 4681 and 4682.

(b) *Cross-references.*—(1) *Tax on ODCs.*—Additional rules relating to the tax on ODCs are contained in §§52.4682-1 and 52.4682-2.

(2) *Tax on imported taxable products.*—Additional rules relating to the tax on imported taxable products are contained in §52.4682-3.

(3) *Floor stocks tax.*—Additional rules relating to the floor stocks tax are contained in §52.4682-4.

(4) *Returns, payments, and deposits of tax.*—Rules requiring returns reporting the taxes imposed by sections 4681 and 4682 are contained in part 40 of this chapter. Part 40 of this chapter also provides rules relating to the use of Government depositaries and to the time for filing returns and making payments of tax.

(c) *Definitions of general application.*—The following definitions set forth the meaning of certain terms for purposes of the regulations under sections 4681 and 4682:

(1) *Ozone-depleting chemical.*—The term "ozone-depleting chemical" (ODC) means any chemical listed in section 4682(a)(2).

(2) *United States.*—The term "United States" has the meaning given such term by section 4612(a)(4). Under section 4612(a)(4)—

(i) The term "United States" means the 50 States, the District of Columbia, the Commonwealth of Puerto Rico, any possession of the United States, the Commonwealth of the Northern Mariana Islands, and the Trust Territory of the Pacific Islands; and

(ii) The term includes—

(A) Submarine seabed and subsoil that would be treated as part of the United States (as defined in paragraph (c)(2)(i) of this section) under the principles of section 638 relating to continental shelf areas; and

(B) Foreign trade zones of the United States.

(3) *Manufacture; manufacturer.*—The term "manufacture" when used with respect to any ODC or imported product includes its production, and the term "manufacturer" includes a producer.

(4) *Entry into United States for consumption, use, or warehousing.*—(i) *In general.*—Except as otherwise provided in this paragraph (c)(4), the term "entered into the United States for consumption, use, or warehousing" when used with respect to any goods means—

(A) Brought into the customs territory of the United States (the customs territory) if applicable customs law requires that the goods be entered into the customs territory for consumption, use, or warehousing;

(B) Admitted into a foreign trade zone for any purpose if like goods brought into the customs territory for such purpose would

be entered into the customs territory for consumption, use, or warehousing; or

(C) Imported into any other part of the United States (as defined in paragraph (c)(2) of this section) for any purpose if like goods brought into the customs territory for such purpose would be entered into the customs territory for consumption, use, or warehousing.

(ii) *Entry for transportation and exportation.*—Goods entered into the customs territory for transportation and exportation are not goods entered for consumption, use, or warehousing.

(iii) *Entries described in two or more provisions.*—In the case of any goods with respect to which entries are described in two or more provisions of paragraph (c)(4)(i) of this section, only the first such entry is taken into account. Thus, if the admission of goods into a foreign trade zone is an entry into the United States for consumption, use, or warehousing, the subsequent entry of such goods into the customs territory will not be treated as an entry into the United States for consumption, use or warehousing.

(iv) *Certain imported products not entered for consumption, use, or warehousing.*—Imported products that are entered into the United States for consumption, use, or warehousing do not include any imported products that—

(A) Are entered into the customs territory under Harmonized Tariff Schedule (HTS) heading 9801, 9802, 9803, or 9813;

(B) Would, if entered into the customs territory, be entered under any such heading; or

(C) Are brought into the United States by an individual if the product is brought in for use by the individual and is not expected to be used in a trade or business other than a trade or business of performing services as an employee.

(5) *Importer.*—The term "importer" means the person that first sells or uses goods after their entry into the United States for consumption, use, or warehousing (within the meaning of paragraph (c)(4) of this section).

(6) *Sale.*—The term "sale" means the transfer of title or of substantial incidents of ownership (whether or not delivery to, or payment by, the buyer has been made) for consideration which may include money, services, or property. The determination as to the time a sale occurs shall be made under applicable local law.

(7) *Use.*—(i) *In general.*—Except as otherwise provided in regulations under sections 4681 and 4682, ODCs and imported taxable products are used when they are—

(A) Used as a material in the manufacture of an article, whether by incorporation into such article, chemical transformation, release into the atmosphere, or otherwise; or

(B) Put into service in a trade or business or for production of income.

(ii) *Loss, destruction, packaging, warehousing, and repair.*—The loss, destruction, packaging (including repackaging), warehousing, or repair of ODCs and imported taxable products is not a use of the ODC or product lost, destroyed, packaged, warehoused, or repaired.

(iii) *Cross-references to exceptions.*—For exceptions to the rule contained in paragraph (c)(7)(i) of this section, see—

(A) Section 52.4682-1(b)(2)(iii) (relating to mixture elections), §52.4682-1(b)(2)(iv) (relating to mixtures for export), and §52.4682-1(b)(2)(v) (relating to mixtures for use as a feedstock);

(B) §52.4682-3(c)(2) (relating to the election to treat entry of an imported taxable product as use); and

(C) §52.4682-3(c)(3) (relating to treating sale of an article incorporating an imported taxable product as the first sale or use of the product).

(8) *Pound.*—The term "pound" means a unit of weight that is equal to 16 avoirdupois ounces.

(9) *Post-1990 ODC; post-1989 ODC.*—The term "post-1990 ODC" means any ODC that is listed below Halon-2402 in the table contained in section 4682(a)(2). The term "post-1989 ODC" means any ODC other than a post-1990 ODC.

(d) *Effective date.*—Sections 52.4681-0, 52.4681-1, 52.4682-1, 52.4682-2, 52.4682-3, and 52.4682-4 are effective as of January 1, 1990, and apply to—

(1) Post-1989 ODCs that the manufacturer or importer thereof first sells or uses after December 31, 1989, and post-1990 ODCs that the manufacturer or importer thereof first sells or uses after December 31, 1990;

(2) Imported taxable products that the importer thereof first sells or uses after December 31, 1989 (but, in the case of products first

sold or used before January 1, 1991, by taking into account only the post-1989 ODCs used as materials in their manufacture); and

(3) Post-1989 ODCs held for sale or for use in further manufacture by any person other than the manufacturer or importer thereof on January 1, 1990, and post-1989 and post-1990 ODCs that are so held on January 1 of each calendar year after 1990. [Reg. §52.4681-1.]

☐ [*T.D. 8370*, 11-1-91. *Amended by T.D. 8442*, 10-21-92 *and T.D. 8622*, 10-10-95.]

**[Reg. §52.4682-1]**

**§52.4682-1. Ozone-depleting chemicals.**—(a) *Overview.*—This section provides rules relating to the tax imposed on ozone-depleting chemicals (ODCs) under section 4681, including rules for identifying taxable ODCs and determining when the tax is imposed, and rules prescribing special treatment for certain ODCs. See §52.4681-1(a)(1) and (c) for general rules and definitions relating to the tax on ODCs.

(b) *Taxable ODCs; taxable event.*—(1) *Taxable ODCs.*—(i) *In general.*—Except as provided in paragraphs (c) through (g) of this section, an ODC is taxable if—

(A) It is listed in section 4682(a)(2) on the date it is sold or used by its manufacturer or importer; and

(B) It is manufactured in the United States or entered into the United States for consumption, use, or warehousing.

(ii) *Storage containers.*—An ODC described in paragraph (b)(1)(i) of this section is taxable without regard to the type or size of storage container in which the ODC is held.

(iii) *Example.*—The application of this paragraph (b)(1) may be illustrated by the following example:

*Example.* A brings CFC-12, an ODC listed in section 4682(a)(2), into the customs territory and enters the CFC-12 for transportation and exportation. The ODC is not taxable because it is not entered for consumption, use, or warehousing. The ODC also would not be taxable if it were admitted to a foreign trade zone (rather than brought into the customs territory) for transportation and exportation.

(2) *Taxable event.*—(i) *In general.*—(A) *General rule.*—The tax on an ODC is imposed when the ODC is first sold or used (as defined in §52.4681-1(c)(6) and (7)) by its manufacturer or importer.

(B) *Example.*—The application of this paragraph (b)(2)(i) may be illustrated by the following example:

*Example.* A enters CFC-113, an ODC listed in section 4682(a)(2), into the United States for consumption, use, or warehousing. A warehouses the CFC-113 and then decides to ship the ODC to its factory outside the United States (as defined in §52.4681-1(c)(2)). The CFC-113 is a taxable ODC because the requirements of paragraph (b)(1)(i) of this section have been met. However, tax is not imposed on the ODC because there is no taxable event. A did not sell the ODC and, under §52.4681-1(c)(7), warehousing is not a use.

(ii) *Mixtures.*—Except as provided in paragraphs (b)(2)(iii), (iv), and (v) of this section, the creation of a mixture containing two or more ingredients is treated as a taxable use of the ODCs contained in the mixture. For this purpose, a mixture cannot be represented by a chemical formula, and an ODC is contained in a mixture only if the chemical identity of the ODC is not changed. Thus, except as provided in paragraphs (b)(2)(iii), (iv), and (v) of this section—

(A) The tax on the post-1989 ODCs (as defined in §52.4681-1(c)(9)) contained in mixtures created after December 31, 1989, or on the post-1990 ODCs (as defined in §52.4681-1(c)(9)) contained in mixtures created after December 31, 1990, is imposed when the mixture is created and not on any subsequent sale or use of the mixture; and

(B) No tax is imposed under section 4681 on the post-1989 ODCs contained in mixtures created before January 1, 1990, or on the post-1990 ODCs contained in mixtures created before January 1, 1991.

(iii) *Mixture elections.*—(A) *Permitted elections.*—The only elections permitted under this paragraph (b)(2)(iii) are—

(1) An election for the first calendar quarter beginning after December 31, 1989, and all subsequent periods (the 1990 election); and

(2) An election for the first calendar quarter beginning after December 31, 1990, and all subsequent periods (the 1991 election).

(B) *In general.*—A manufacturer or importer may elect to treat the sale or use of mixtures containing ODCs as the first sale or use of the ODCs contained in the mixtures. If a 1990 election is made under this paragraph (b)(2)(iii), the tax on post-1989 ODCs contained in a mixture sold or used after December 31, 1989 (including any

such mixture created before January 1, 1990) is imposed on the date of such sale or use. Similarly, if a 1991 election is made under this paragraph (b)(2)(iii), the tax on post-1990 ODCs contained in a mixture sold or used after December 31, 1990 (including any such mixture created before January 1, 1991) is imposed on the date of such sale or use.

(C) *Applicability of elections.*—An election under this paragraph (b)(2)(iii) applies—

(1) In the case of a 1990 election, to all post-1989 ODCs contained in mixtures sold or used by the manufacturer or importer after December 31, 1989 (including any such mixture created before January 1, 1990); and

(2) In the case of a 1991 election, to all post-1990 ODCs contained in mixtures sold or used by the manufacturer or importer after December 31, 1990 (including any such mixture created before January 1, 1991).

(D) *Making the election; revocation.*—An election under this paragraph (b)(2)(iii) shall be made in accordance with the instructions for the return on which the manufacturer or importer reports liability for tax under section 4681. After October 9, 1990, the election may be revoked only with the consent of the Commissioner.

(iv) *Special rule for exports.*—The creation of a mixture for export is not a taxable use of the ODCs contained in the mixture. If a manufacturer or importer sells a mixture for export, §52.4682-5 applies to the ODCs contained in the mixture. See §52.4682-5(e) for rules relating to liability of a purchaser for tax if the mixture is not exported.

(v) *Special rule for use as a feedstock.*—The creation of a mixture for use as a feedstock (within the meaning of paragraph (c) of this section) is not a taxable use of the ODCs contained in the mixture.

(c) *ODCs used as a feedstock.*—(1) *Exemption from tax.*—No tax is imposed on an ODC if the manufacturer or importer of the ODC—

(i) Uses the ODC as a feedstock in the manufacture of another chemical; or

(ii) Sells the ODC in a qualifying sale (within the meaning of paragraph (c)(4) of this section) for use as a feedstock.

(2) *Excess payments.*—(i) *In general.*—Under section 4682(d)(2)(B), a credit or refund is allowed to a person if—

(A) The person uses an ODC as a feedstock; and

(B) The amount of any tax paid with respect to the ODC under section 4681 or 4682 was not determined under section 4682(d)(2)(A).

(ii) *Procedural rules.*—See section 6402 and the regulations thereunder for rules relating to claiming a credit or refund of tax paid with respect to ODCs that are used as a feedstock. A credit against the income tax is not allowed for the amount determined under section 4682(d)(2)(B).

(3) *Definition.*—An ODC is used as a feedstock only if the ODC is entirely consumed (except for trace amounts) in the manufacture of another chemical. Thus, the transformation of an ODC into one or more new compounds (such as the transformation of CFC-113 into chlorotrifluoroethylene (CTFE or 1113), of CFC-113 into CFC-115 and CFC-116, or of carbon tetrachloride into hydrochloric acid during petroleum refining or incineration) is treated as use as a feedstock. On the other hand, the ODCs used in a mixture (including an azeotrope such as R-500 or R-502) are not used as a feedstock.

(4) *Qualifying sale.*—A sale of ODCs for use as a feedstock is a qualifying sale if the requirements of §52.4682-2(b)(1) are satisfied with respect to such sale.

(d) *ODCs used in the manufacture of rigid foam insulation.*—(1) *Phase-in of tax.*—(i) *In general.*—The amount of tax imposed on an ODC is determined under section 4682(g) if the manufacturer or importer of the ODC—

(A) Uses the ODC during 1990, 1991, 1992, or 1993 in the manufacture of rigid foam insulation; or

(B) Sells the ODC in a qualifying sale (within the meaning of paragraph (d)(5) of this section) during 1990, 1991, 1992, or 1993.

(ii) *Amount of tax.*—Under section 4682(g), ODCs described in paragraph (d)(1)(i) of this section are not taxed if sold or used during 1990 and are taxed at a reduced rate if sold or used during 1991, 1992, or 1993.

(2) *Excess payments.*—(i) *In general.*—Under section 4682(g)(3), a credit against income tax or a refund is allowed to a person if—

(A) The person uses an ODC during 1990, 1991, 1992, or 1993 in the manufacture of rigid foam insulation; and

(B) The amount of any tax paid with respect to the ODC under section 4681 or 4682 was not determined under section 4682(g).

(ii) *Procedural rules.*—(A) The amount determined under section 4682(g)(3) shall be treated as a credit described in section 34(a) (relating to credits for gasoline and special fuels) unless a claim for refund has been filed.

(B) See section 6402 and the regulations thereunder for rules relating to claiming a credit or refund of the tax paid with respect to ODCs that are used in the manufacture of rigid foam insulation.

(3) *Definition.*—(i) *Rigid foam insulation.*—The term "rigid foam insulation" means any rigid foam that is designed for use as thermal insulation in buildings, equipment, appliances, tanks, railcars, trucks, or vessels, or on pipes, including any such rigid foam actually used for purposes other than insulation. Information such as test reports on R-values and advertising material reflecting R-value claims for a particular rigid foam may be used to show that such rigid foam is designed for use as thermal insulation.

(ii) *Rigid foam.*—(A) *In general.*—The term "rigid foam" means any closed cell polymeric foam (whether or not rigid) in which chlorofluorocarbons are used to fill voids within the polymer.

(B) *Examples of rigid foam products.*—Rigid foam includes extruded polystyrene foam, polyisocyanurate foam, spray and pour-in-place polyurethane foam, polyethylene foam, phenolic foam, and any other product that the Commissioner identifies as rigid foam in a pronouncement of general applicability. The form of a product identified under this paragraph (d)(3)(ii)(B) does not affect its character as rigid foam. Thus, such products are rigid foam whether in the form of a board, sheet, backer rod, or wrapping, or in a form applied by spraying, pouring, or frothing.

(4) *Use in manufacture.*—An ODC is used in the manufacture of rigid foam insulation if it is incorporated into such product or is expended as a propellant or otherwise in the manufacture or application of such product.

(5) *Qualifying sale.*—A sale of an ODC for use in the manufacture of rigid foam insulation is a qualifying sale if the requirements of §52.4682-2(b)(2) are satisfied with respect to such sale.

(e) *Halons; phase-in of tax.*—The amount of tax imposed on Halon-1211, Halon-1301, or Halon-2402 (Halons) is determined under section 4682(g) if the manufacturer or importer of Halons sells or uses Halons during 1990, 1991, 1992, or 1993. Under section 4682(g), Halons are not taxed if sold or used during 1990 and are taxed at a reduced rate if sold or used during 1991, 1992, or 1993.

(f) *Methyl chloroform; reduced rate of tax in 1993.*—The amount of tax imposed on methyl chloroform is determined under section 4682(g)(5) if the manufacturer or importer of the methyl chloroform sells or uses it during 1993.

(g) *ODCs used as medical sterilants.*—(1) *Phase-in of tax.*—The amount of tax imposed on an ODC is determined under section 4682(g)(4) if the manufacturer or importer of the ODC—

(i) Uses the ODC during 1993 as a medical sterilant; or

(ii) Sells the ODC in a qualifying sale (within the meaning of paragraph (g)(4) of this section) during 1993.

(2) *Excess payments.*—(i) *In general.*—Under section 4682(g)(4)(B), a credit against income tax (without interest) or a refund of tax (without interest) is allowed to a person if—

(A) The person uses an ODC during 1993 as a medical sterilant; and

(B) The amount of any tax paid with respect to the ODC under section 4681 or 4682 exceeds the amount that would have been determined under section 4682(g)(4).

(ii) *Amount of credit or refund.*—The amount of credit or refund of tax is equal to the excess of—

(A) The tax that was paid with respect to the ODCs under sections 4681 and 4682; over

(B) The tax that would have been imposed under section 4682(g)(4).

(iii) *Procedural rules.*—(A) The amount determined under section 4682(g)(4)(B) and paragraph (g)(2)(ii) of this section is treated as a credit described in section 34(a) (relating to credits for gasoline and special fuels) unless a claim for refund has been filed.

(B) See section 6402 and the regulations under that section for procedural rules relating to claiming a credit or refund of tax.

(3) *Definition of use as a medical sterilant.*—An ODC is used as a medical sterilant if it is used in the manufacture of sterilant gas.

(4) *Qualifying sale.*—A sale of an ODC for use as a medical sterilant is a qualifying sale if the requirements of §52.4682-2(b)(3) are satisfied with respect to the sale.

(h) *ODCs used as propellants in metered-dose inhalers.*—(1) *Reduced rate of tax.*—The amount of tax imposed on an ODC is determined under section 4682(g)(4) if the manufacturer or importer of the ODC—

(i) Uses the ODC after 1992 as a propellant in a metered-dose inhaler; or

(ii) Sells the ODC in a qualifying sale (within the meaning of paragraph (h)(4) of this section) after 1992.

(2) *Excess payments.*—(i) *In general.*—Under section 4682(g)(4)(B), a credit against income tax (without interest) or a refund of tax (without interest) is allowed to a person if—

(A) The person uses an ODC after 1992 as a propellant in a metered-dose inhaler; and

(B) The amount of any tax paid with respect to the ODC under section 4681 or 4682 exceeds the amount that would have been determined under section 4682(g)(4).

(ii) *Amount of credit or refund.*—The amount of credit or refund of tax is equal to the excess of—

(A) The tax that was paid with respect to the ODCs under sections 4681 and 4682; over

(B) The tax that would have been imposed under section 4682(g)(4).

(iii) *Procedural rules.*—(A) The amount determined under section 4682(g)(4)(B) and paragraph (h)(2)(ii) of this section is treated as a credit described in section 34(a) (relating to credits for gasoline and special fuels) unless a claim for refund has been filed.

(B) See section 6402 and the regulations under that section for procedural rules relating to claiming a credit or refund of tax.

(3) *Definition of metered-dose inhaler.*—A metered-dose inhaler is an aerosol device that delivers a precisely-measured dose of a therapeutic drug.

(4) *Qualifying sale.*—A sale of an ODC for use as a propellant for a metered-dose inhaler is a qualifying sale if the requirements of §52.4682-2(b)(4) are satisfied with respect to the sale.

(i) [Reserved]

(j) *Exports; cross-reference.*—For the treatment of exports of ODCs, see §52.4682-5.

(k) *Recycling.*—[Reserved][Reg. §52.4682-1.]

☐ [*T.D.* 8370, 11-1-91. *Amended by T.D.* 8622, 10-10-95.]

### [Reg. §52.4682-2]

**§52.4682-2. Qualifying sales.**—(a) *In general.*—(1) *Special rules applicable to certain sales.*—Special rules apply to sales of ODCs in the following cases:

(i) Under section 4682(d)(2), §52.4682-1(c), and §52.4682-4(b)(2)(v) (relating to ODCs used as a feedstock), ODCs sold in qualifying sales are not taxed.

(ii) Under section 4682(g), §52.4682-1(d), and §52.4682-4(d)(2) (relating to ODCs used in the manufacture of rigid foam insulation), ODCs sold in qualifying sales are not taxed in 1990 and are taxed at a reduced rate in 1991, 1992, and 1993.

(iii) Under section 4682(g)(4) and §52.4682-1(g) (relating to ODCs used as medical sterilants), ODCs sold in qualifying sales are taxed at a reduced rate in 1993.

(iv) Under section 4682(g)(4) and §52.4682-1(h) (relating to ODCs used as propellants in metered-dose inhalers), ODCs sold in qualifying sales are taxed at a reduced rate in years after 1992.

(2) *Qualifying sales.*—A sale of ODCs is not a qualifying sale unless the requirements of this section are satisfied. Although registration with the Internal Revenue Service is not required to establish that a sale of ODCs is a qualifying sale, the certificates required by this section shall be made available for inspection by internal revenue agents and officers.

(b) *Requirements for qualification.*—(1) *Use as a feedstock.*—A sale of ODCs is a qualifying sale for purposes of §§52.4682-1(c) and 52.4682-4(b)(2)(v) if the manufacturer or importer of the ODCs—

(i) Obtains a certificate in substantially the form set forth in paragraph (d)(2) of this section from the purchaser of the ODCs; and

(ii) Relies on the certificate in good faith.

(2) *Use in the manufacture of rigid foam insulation.*—A sale of ODCs is a qualifying sale for purposes of §§52.4682-1(d) and 52.4682-4(d)(2) if the manufacturer or importer of the ODCs—

(i) Obtains a certificate in substantially the form set forth in paragraph (d)(3) of this section from the purchaser of the OCDs; and

(ii) Relies on the certificate in good faith.

(3) *Use as medical sterilants.*—A sale of ODCs is a qualifying sale for purposes of § 52.4682-1(g) if the manufacturer or importer of the ODCs—

(i) Obtains a certificate in substantially the form set forth in paragraph (d)(4) of this section from the purchaser of the ODCs; and

(ii) Relies on the certificate in good faith.

(4) *Use as propellants in metered-dose inhalers.*—A sale of ODCs is a qualifying sale for purposes of §§ 52.4682-1(h) and 52.4682-4(b)(2)(vii) if the manufacturer or importer of the ODCs—

(i) Obtains a certificate in substantially the form set forth in paragraph (d)(5) of this section from the purchaser of the ODCs; and

(ii) Relies on the certificate in good faith.

(c) *Good faith reliance.*—(1) *In general.*—The requirements of paragraph (b) of this section are not satisfied with respect to a sale of ODCs and the sale is not a qualifying sale if at the time of the sale—

(i) The manufacturer or importer has reason to believe that the purchaser will use the ODCs other than for the purpose set forth in the certificate; or

(ii) The Internal Revenue Service has notified the manufacturer or importer that the purchaser's right to provide a certificate has been withdrawn.

(2) *Withdrawal of right to provide a certificate.*—The Internal Revenue Service may withdraw the right of a purchaser to provide a certificate to its supplier if such purchaser uses the ODCs to which its certificate applies other than for the purpose set forth in such certificate, or otherwise fails to comply with the terms of the certificate. The Internal Revenue Service may notify the supplier to whom the purchaser provided the certificate that the purchaser's right to provide a certificate has been withdrawn.

(d) *Certificate.*—(1) *In general.*—(i) *Rules relating to all certificates.*—This paragraph (d) sets forth certificates that satisfy the requirements of paragraphs (b)(1) through (4) of this section. The certificate shall consist of a statement executed and signed under penalties of perjury by a person with authority to bind the purchaser. A certificate provided under paragraph (d)(2) or (5) of this section may apply to a single purchase or to multiple purchases and need not specify an expiration date. A certificate provided under paragraph (d)(3) or (4) of this section may apply to a single purchase or multiple purchases, and will expire as of December 31, 1993, unless an earlier expiration date is specified in the certificate. A new certificate must be given to the supplier if any information on the current certificate changes. The certificate may be included as part of any business records normally used to document a sale.

(ii) *Special rule relating to certificates executed before January 1, 1992.*—Certificates provided under this paragraph (d)(2) and executed before January 1, 1992, satisfy the requirements of paragraph (b) of this section if they are in substantially the same form as certificates set forth in § 52.4682-2T.

(2) *Certificate relating to ODCs used as a feedstock.*—(i) *ODCs that will be resold for use by the second purchaser as a feedstock.*—If the purchaser will resell the ODCs to a second purchaser for use by such second purchaser as a feedstock, the certificate provided by the purchaser must be in substantially the following form:

CERTIFICATE OF PURCHASER OF CHEMICALS THAT WILL BE RESOLD FOR USE BY THE SECOND PURCHASER AS A FEEDSTOCK
(To support tax-free sales under section 4682(d)(2) of the Internal Revenue Code.)

Date_____

The undersigned purchaser ("Purchaser") hereby certifies the following under penalties of perjury:
The following percentage of ozone-depleting chemicals purchased from

_____
(name and address of seller)

will be resold by Purchaser to persons (Second Purchasers) that certify to Purchaser that they are purchasing the ozone-depleting chemicals for use as a feedstock (as defined in § 52.4682-1(c)(3) of the Environmental Tax Regulations).

| PRODUCT | PERCENTAGE |
|---|---|
| CFC-11 | _____ |
| CFC-12 | _____ |
| CFC-113 | _____ |
| CFC-114 | _____ |
| CFC-115 | _____ |
| Carbon tetrachloride | _____ |
| Methyl chloroform | _____ |
| Other (specify) | _____ |

This certificate applies to (check and complete as applicable):

_____ All shipments to Purchaser at the following location(s):

_____
_____

_____ All shipments to Purchaser under the following Purchaser account number(s):

_____
_____

_____ All shipments to Purchaser under the following purchase order(s):

_____
_____

_____ One or more shipments to Purchaser identified as follows:

_____
_____

Purchaser will not claim a credit or refund under section 4682(d)(2)(B) of the Internal Revenue Code for any ozone-depleting chemicals covered by this certificate.
Purchaser understands that any use by Purchaser of the ozone-depleting chemicals to which this certificate applies other than for the purpose set forth in this certificate may result in the withdrawal by the Internal Revenue Service of Purchaser's right to provide a certificate.
Purchaser will retain the business records needed to document the sales covered by this certificate and will make such records available for inspection by Government officers. Purchaser also will retain and make available for inspection by Government officers the certificates of its Second Purchasers.
Purchaser has not been notified by the Internal Revenue Service that its right to provide a certificate has been withdrawn. In addition, the Internal Revenue Service has not notified Purchaser that the right to provide a certificate has been withdrawn from any Second Purchaser who will purchase ozone-depleting chemicals to which this certificate applies.
Purchaser understands that the fraudulent use of this certificate may subject Purchaser and all parties making such fraudulent use of this certificate to a fine or imprisonment, or both, together with the costs of prosecution.

_____
Signature

_____

Printed or typed name of person signing
_____

Title of person signing
_____

Name of Purchaser
_____

Address
_____
_____

Taxpayer Identifying Number
_____

(ii) *ODCs that will be used by the purchaser as a feedstock.*—If the purchaser will use the ODCs as a feedstock, the certificate provided by the purchaser must be in substantially the following form:

**CERTIFICATE OF PURCHASER OF CHEMICALS THAT WILL BE USED BY THE PURCHASER AS A FEEDSTOCK**
(To support tax-free sales under section 4682(d)(2) of the Internal Revenue Code.)

Date_____

The undersigned purchaser ("Purchaser") hereby certifies the following under penalties of perjury:
The following percentage of ozone-depleting chemicals purchased from
_____
(name and address of seller)
will be used by Purchaser as a feedstock (as defined in §52.4682-1(c)(3) of the Environmental Tax Regulations).

| PRODUCT | PERCENTAGE | KILOGRAMS TO BE TRANSFORMED |
|---|---|---|
| CFC-11 | _____ | _____ |
| CFC-12 | _____ | _____ |
| CFC-113 | _____ | _____ |
| CFC-114 | _____ | _____ |
| CFC-115 | _____ | _____ |
| Carbon tetrachloride | _____ | _____ |
| Methyl chloroform | _____ | _____ |
| Other (specify) | _____ | _____ |

This certificate applies to (check and complete as applicable):
_____ All shipments to Purchaser at the following location(s):
_____

_____ All shipments to Purchaser under the following Purchaser account number(s):
_____

_____ All shipments to Purchaser under the following purchase order(s):
_____

_____ One or more shipments to Purchaser identified as follows:
_____

Purchaser will not claim a credit or refund under section 4682(d)(2)(B) of the Internal Revenue Code for any ozone-depleting chemicals covered by this certificate.
Purchaser understands that any use of the ozone-depleting chemicals to which this certificate applies other than as a feedstock may result in the withdrawal by the Internal Revenue Service of Purchaser's right to provide a certificate.
Purchaser will retain the business records needed to document the use as a feedstock of the ozone-depleting chemicals to which this certificate applies and will make such records available for inspection by Government officers.
Purchaser has not been notified by the Internal Revenue Service that its right to provide a certificate has been withdrawn.
Purchaser understands that the fraudulent use of this certificate may subject Purchaser and all parties making such fraudulent use of this certificate to a fine or imprisonment, or both, together with the costs of prosecution.

Signature
_____

Printed or typed name of person signing
_____

Title of person signing
_____

Name of Purchaser
_____

Address
_____
_____

Taxpayer Identifying Number
_____

(3) *Certificate relating to ODCs used in the manufacture of rigid foam insulation.*—(i) *ODCs that will be resold to a second purchaser for use by the second purchaser in the manufacture of rigid foam insulation.*—If the purchaser will resell the ODCs to a second purchaser for use by such second purchaser in the manufacture of rigid foam insulation, the certificate provided by the purchaser must be in substantially the following form:

**CERTIFICATE OF PURCHASER OF CHEMICALS THAT WILL BE RESOLD FOR USE BY THE SECOND PURCHASER IN THE MANUFACTURE OF RIGID FOAM INSULATION**
(To support tax-free or tax-reduced sales under section 4682(g) of the Internal Revenue Code.)

**Reg. §52.4682-2(d)(3)(i)**

Effective Date_____

Expiration Date_____

(not after 12/31/93)

The undersigned purchaser ("Purchaser") hereby certifies the following under penalties of perjury:
The following percentage of ozone-depleting chemicals purchased from

_____

(name and address of seller)

will be resold by Purchaser to persons (Second Purchasers) that certify to Purchaser that they are purchasing the ozone-depleting chemicals for use in the manufacture of rigid foam insulation (as defined in §52.4682-1(d)(3) and (4) of the Environmental Tax Regulations).

| PRODUCT | PERCENTAGE |
|---|---|
| CFC-11 | _____ |
| CFC-12 | _____ |
| CFC-113 | _____ |
| CFC-114 | _____ |
| CFC-115 | _____ |
| Carbon tetrachloride | _____ |
| Methyl chloroform | _____ |
| Other (specify) | _____ |

This certificate applies to (check and complete as applicable):
____All shipments to Purchaser at the following locations(s):

_____

_____

____All shipments to Purchaser under the following Purchaser account number(s):

_____

_____

____All shipments to Purchaser under the following purchase order(s):

_____

_____

____One or more shipments to Purchaser identified as follows:

_____

_____

Purchaser will not claim a credit or refund under section 4682(g)(3) of the Internal Revenue Code for any ozone-depleting chemicals covered by this certificate.
Purchaser understands that any use by purchaser of the ozone-depleting chemicals to which this certificate applies other than for the purpose set forth in this certificate may result in the withdrawal by the Internal Revenue Service of Purchaser's right to provide a certificate.
Purchaser will retain the business records needed to document the sales covered by this certificate and will make such records available for inspection by Government officers. Purchaser also will retain and make available for inspection by Government officers the certificates of its Second Purchasers.
Purchaser has not been notified by the Internal Revenue Service that its right to provide a certificate has been withdrawn. In addition, the Internal Revenue Service has not notified Purchaser that the right to provide a certificate has been withdrawn from any Second Purchaser who will purchase ozone-depleting chemicals to which this certificate applies.
Purchaser understands that the fraudulent use of this certificate may subject Purchaser and all parties making such fraudulent use of this certificate to a fine or imprisonment, or both, together with the costs of prosecution.

Signature _____

Printed or typed name of person signing _____

Title of person signing _____

Name of Purchaser _____

Address _____

Taxpayer Identifying Number _____

(ii) *ODCs that will be used by the purchaser in the manufacture of rigid foam insulation.*—If the purchaser will use the ODCs in the manufacture of rigid foam insulation, the certificate provided by the purchaser must be in substantially the following form:

CERTIFICATE OF PURCHASER OF CHEMICALS THAT WILL BE USED BY THE PURCHASER IN THE MANUFACTURE OF RIGID FOAM INSULATION
(To support tax-free or tax-reduced sales under section 4682(g) of the Internal Revenue Code.)

Effective Date_____

Expiration Date_____

(not after 12/31/93)

The undersigned purchaser ("Purchaser") hereby certifies the following under penalties of perjury:
The following percentage of ozone-depleting chemicals purchased from

_____

(name and address of seller)

will be used by Purchaser in the manufacture of rigid foam insulation (as defined in §52.4682-1(d)(3) and (4) of the Environmental Tax Regulations).

| PRODUCT | PERCENTAGE |
|---|---|
| CFC-11 | _____ |
| CFC-12 | _____ |
| CFC-113 | _____ |
| CFC-114 | _____ |
| CFC-115 | _____ |
| Carbon tetrachloride | _____ |
| Methyl chloroform | _____ |

**Reg. §52.4682-2(d)(3)(ii)**

Other (specify) _____ _____

This certificate applies to (check and complete as applicable):
___All shipments to Purchaser at the following location(s): _____
_____
_____

___All shipments to Purchaser under the following Purchaser account number(s): _____
_____
_____

___All shipments to Purchaser under the following purchase order(s): _____
_____
_____

___One or more shipments to Purchaser identified as follows: _____
_____
_____

Purchaser will not claim a credit or refund under section 4682(g)(3) of the Internal Revenue Code for any ozone-depleting chemicals covered by this certificate.
Purchaser understands that any use by Purchaser of the ozone-depleting chemicals to which this certificate applies other than in the manufacture of rigid foam insulation may result in the withdrawal by the Internal Revenue Service of Purchaser's right to provide a certificate.
Purchaser will retain the business records needed to document the use in the manufacture of rigid foam insulation of the ozone-depleting chemicals to which this certificate applies and will make such records available for inspection by Government officers.
Purchaser has not been notified by the Internal Revenue Service that its right to provide a certificate has been withdrawn.
Purchaser understands that the fraudulent use of this certificate may subject Purchaser and all parties making such fraudulent use of this certificate to a fine or imprisonment, or both, together with the costs of prosecution.
_____

Signature
_____

Printed or typed name of person signing
_____

Title of person signing
_____

Name of Purchaser
_____

Address
_____

Taxpayer Identifying Number

(4) *Certificate relating to ODCs used as medical sterilants.*— (i) *ODCs that will be resold for use by the second purchaser as medical sterilants.*—If the purchaser will resell the ODCs to a second purchaser for use by such second purchaser as medical sterilants, the certificate provided by the purchaser must be in substantially the following form:

CERTIFICATE OF PURCHASER OF CHEMICALS THAT WILL BE RESOLD
FOR USE BY THE SECOND PURCHASER AS MEDICAL STERILANTS
(To support tax-reduced sales under
section 4682(g)(4) of the Internal Revenue Code.)

Effective Date _____
Effective Date _____

(not after 12/31/93)

The undersigned purchaser (Purchaser) certifies the following under penalties of perjury:
The following percentage of ozone-depleting chemicals purchased from: _____

(Name of seller)
_____

(Address of seller)
will be resold by Purchaser to persons (Second Purchasers) that certify to Purchaser that they are purchasing the ozone-depleting chemicals for use as medical sterilants (as defined in §52.4682-1(g)(3) of the Environmental Tax Regulations).

| Product | Percentage |
|---------|-----------|
| CFC-12  |           |

This certificate applies to (check and complete as applicable):
_____ All shipments to Purchaser at the following location(s): _____
_____
_____

_____ All shipments to Purchaser under the following Purchaser account number(s): _____
_____
_____

_____ All shipments to Purchaser under the following purchase order(s): _____
_____
_____

_____ One or more shipments to Purchaser identified as follows: _____
_____
_____

Purchaser will not claim a credit or refund under section 4682(g)(4) of the Internal Revenue Code for any ozone-depleting chemicals covered by this certificate.
Purchaser understands that any use by Purchaser of the ozone-depleting chemicals to which this certificate applies other than for the purpose set forth in this certificate may result in the withdrawal by the Internal Revenue Service of Purchaser's right to provide a certificate.

Reg. §52.4682-2(d)(4)(i)

Purchaser will retain the business records needed to document the sales covered by this certificate and will make such records available for inspection by Government officers. Purchaser also will retain and make available for inspection by Government officers the certificates of its Second Purchasers.

Purchaser has not been notified by the Internal Revenue Service that its right to provide a certificate has been withdrawn. In addition, the Internal Revenue Service has not notified Purchaser that the right to provide a certificate has been withdrawn from any Second Purchaser who will purchase ozone-depleting chemicals to which this certificate applies.

Purchaser understands that the fraudulent use of this certificate may subject Purchaser and all parties making such fraudulent use of this certificate to a fine or imprisonment, or both, together with the costs of prosecution.

_____

Name of Purchaser
_____
_____

Address of Purchaser
_____

Taxpayer Identifying Number of Purchaser
_____

Title of person signing
_____

Printed or typed name of person signing
_____

Signature

(ii) *ODCs that will be used by the purchaser as medical sterilants.*—If the purchaser will use the ODCs as medical sterilants, the certificate provided by the purchaser must be in substantially the following form:

**CERTIFICATE OF PURCHASER OF CHEMICALS**
**THAT WILL BE USED BY THE PURCHASER AS MEDICAL STERILANTS**
(To support tax-reduced sales under
section 4682(g)(4) of the Internal Revenue Code.)

Effective Date _____
Effective Date _____

(not after 12/31/93)

The undersigned purchaser (Purchaser) certifies the following under penalties of perjury:

The following percentage of ozone-depleting chemicals purchased from:

_____

(Name of seller)
_____

(Address of seller)

will be used by Purchaser as medical sterilants (as defined in §52.4682-1(g)(3) of the Environmental Tax Regulations).

| Product | Percentage |
|---------|-----------|
| CFC-12 | _____ |

This certificate applies to (check and complete as applicable):

_____ All shipments to Purchaser at the following location(s):
_____
_____
_____

_____ All shipments to Purchaser under the following Purchaser account number(s):
_____
_____
_____

_____ All shipments to Purchaser under the following purchase order(s):
_____
_____
_____

_____ One or more shipments to Purchaser identified as follows:
_____
_____
_____

Purchaser will not claim a credit or refund under section 4682(g)(4) of the Internal Revenue Code for any ozone-depleting chemicals covered by this certificate.

Purchaser understands that any use by Purchaser of the ozone-depleting chemicals to which this certificate applies other than as medical sterilants may result in the withdrawal by the Internal Revenue Service of Purchaser's right to provide a certificate.

Purchaser will retain the business records needed to document the use as medical sterilants of the ozone- depleting chemicals to which this certificate applies and will make such records available for inspection by Government officers.

Purchaser has not been notified by the Internal Revenue Service that its right to provide a certificate has been withdrawn.

Purchaser understands that the fraudulent use of this certificate may subject Purchaser and all parties making such fraudulent use of this certificate to a fine or imprisonment, or both, together with the costs of prosecution.

_____

Name of Purchaser
_____

Address of Purchaser
_____

Taxpayer Identifying Number of Purchaser
_____

Title of person signing
_____

Printed or typed name of person signing
_____

Signature

(5) *Certificate relating to ODCs used as propellants in metered-dose inhalers.*—(i) *ODCs that will be resold for use by the second purchaser as propellants in metered-dose inhalers.*—If the purchaser will resell the ODCs to a second purchaser for use by such second purchaser as propellants in metered-dose inhalers, the certificate provided by the purchaser must be in substantially the following form:

CERTIFICATE OF PURCHASER OF CHEMICALS THAT WILL BE RESOLD
FOR USE BY THE SECOND PURCHASER AS PROPELLANTS IN METERED-DOSE INHALERS

(To support tax-reduced sales under
section 4682(g)(4) of the Internal Revenue Code.)

Date _____

The undersigned purchaser (Purchaser) certifies the following under penalties of perjury:
The following percentage of ozone-depleting chemicals purchased from:

_____
(Name of seller)

_____
(Address of seller)

will be resold by Purchaser to persons (Second Purchasers) that certify to Purchaser that they are purchasing the ozone-depleting chemicals for use as propellants in metered-dose inhalers (as defined in §52.4682-1(h)(3) of the Environmental Tax Regulations).

| Product | Percentage |
|---|---|
| CFC-11 | _____ |
| CFC-12 | _____ |
| CFC-114 | _____ |

This certificate applies to (check and complete as applicable):

_____ All shipments to Purchaser at the following location(s):

_____
_____
_____

_____ All shipments to Purchaser under the following Purchaser account number(s):

_____
_____

_____ All shipments to Purchaser under the following purchase order(s):

_____
_____

_____ One or more shipments to Purchaser identified as follows:

_____
_____
_____

Purchaser will not claim a credit or refund under section 4682(g)(4) of the Internal Revenue Code for any ozone-depleting chemicals covered by this certificate.

Purchaser understands that any use by Purchaser of the ozone-depleting chemicals to which this certificate applies other than for the purpose set forth in this certificate may result in the withdrawal by the Internal Revenue Service of Purchaser's right to provide a certificate.

Purchaser will retain the business records needed to document the sales covered by this certificate and will make such records available for inspection by Government officers. Purchaser also will retain and make available for inspection by Government officers the certificates of its Second Purchasers.

Purchaser has not been notified by the Internal Revenue Service that its right to provide a certificate has been withdrawn. In addition, the Internal Revenue Service has not notified Purchaser that the right to provide a certificate has been withdrawn from any Second Purchaser who will purchase ozone-depleting chemicals to which this certificate applies.

Purchaser understands that the fraudulent use of this certificate may subject Purchaser and all parties making such fraudulent use of this certificate to a fine or imprisonment, or both, together with the costs of prosecution.

_____
Name of Purchaser

_____
Address of Purchaser

_____
Taxpayer Identifying Number of Purchaser

_____
Title of person signing

_____
Printed or typed name of person signing

_____
Signature

(ii) *ODCs that will be used by the purchaser as propellants in metered-dose inhalers.*—If the purchaser will use the ODCs as propellants in metered-dose inhalers, the certificate provided by the purchaser must be in substantially the following form:

CERTIFICATE OF PURCHASER OF CHEMICALS THAT WILL BE
USED BY THE PURCHASER AS PROPELLANTS IN METERED-DOSE INHALERS
(To support tax-reduced sales under
section 4682(g)(4) of the Internal Revenue Code.)

Date _____

The undersigned purchaser (Purchaser) certifies the following under penalties of perjury:
The following percentage of ozone-depleting chemicals purchased from:

_____
(Name of seller)

_____
(Address of seller)

will be used by Purchaser as propellants in metered-dose inhalers (as defined in §52.4682-1(h)(3) of the Environmental Tax Regulations).

| Product | Percentage |
|---|---|
| CFC-11 | _____ |
| CFC-12 | _____ |
| CFC-114 | _____ |

This certificate applies to (check and complete as applicable):
_____ All shipments to Purchaser at the following location(s):

**Reg. §52.4682-2(d)(5)(ii)**

_____ All shipments to Purchaser under the following Purchaser account number(s):

_____ All shipments to Purchaser under the following purchase order(s):

_____ One or more shipments to Purchaser identified as follows:

Purchaser will not claim a credit or refund under section 4682(g)(4) of the Internal Revenue Code for any ozone-depleting chemicals covered by this certificate.

Purchaser understands that any use by Purchaser of the ozone-depleting chemicals to which this certificate applies other than as propellants in metered-dose inhalers may result in the withdrawal by the Internal Revenue Service of Purchaser's right to provide a certificate.

Purchaser will retain the business records needed to document the use as propellants in metered-dose inhalers of the ozone-depleting chemicals to which this certificate applies and will make such records available for inspection by Government officers.

Purchaser has not been notified by the Internal Revenue Service that its right to provide a certificate has been withdrawn.

Purchaser understands that the fraudulent use of this certificate may subject Purchaser and all parties making such fraudulent use of this certificate to a fine or imprisonment, or both, together with the costs of prosecution.

_____
Name of Purchaser

_____
Address of Purchaser

_____
Taxpayer Identifying Number of Purchaser

_____
Title of person signing

_____
Printed or typed name of person signing

_____
Signature

[Reg. § 52.4682-2.]

☐ [*T.D.* 8370, 11-1-91. *Amended by T.D.* 8622, 10-10-95.]

### [Reg. § 52.4682-3]

**§ 52.4682-3. Imported taxable products.**—(a) *Overview; references to Tables; special rule for 1990.*—(1) *Overview.*—This section provides rules relating to the tax imposed on imported taxable products under section 4681, including rules for identifying imported taxable products, determining the weight of the ozone-depleting chemicals (ODCs) used as materials in the manufacture of such products, and computing the amount of tax on such products. See § 52.4681-1(a)(2) and (c) for general rules and definitions relating to the tax on imported taxable products.

(2) *References to Tables.*—When used in this section—

(i) The term "Imported Products Table" (Table) refers to the Table set forth in paragraph (f)(6) of this section; and

(ii) The term "current Imported Products Table" (current Table) used with respect to a product refers to the Table in effect on the date such product is first sold or used by the importer thereof.

(3) *Special rule for 1990.*—In the case of products first sold or used before January 1, 1991, post-1990 ODCs (as defined in § 52.4681-1(c)(9)) shall not be taken into account in applying the rules of this section.

(b) *Imported taxable products.*—(1) *In general.*—(i) *Rule.*—Except as provided in paragraph (b)(2) of this section, the term "imported taxable product" means any product that—

(A) Is entered into the United States for consumption, use, or warehousing; and

(B) Is listed in the current Table.

(ii) *Example.*—The application of this paragraph (b)(1) may be illustrated by the following example:

*Example.* A brings a light truck with a Harmonized Tariff Schedule classification of 8704 into the customs territory and enters the truck for transportation and exportation. Although the truck is listed in the current Table, it is not an imported taxable product because it is not entered for consumption, use, or warehousing. The truck also would not be an imported taxable product if it were admitted to a foreign trade zone (rather than brought into the customs territory) for transportation and exportation.

(2) *Exceptions.*—(i) *In general.*—A product is not treated as an imported taxable product if—

(A) The product is listed in Part I of the current Table and the adjusted tax with respect to the product is *de minimis* (within the meaning of paragraph (b)(2)(ii) of this section); or

(B) The product is listed in Part II of the current Table, the adjusted tax with respect to the product is *de minimis* (within the meaning of paragraph (b)(2)(ii) of this section), and the ODCs (other than methyl chloroform) used as materials in the manufacture of the product were not used for purposes of refrigeration or air conditioning, creating an aerosol or foam, or manufacturing electronic components.

(ii) *De minimis adjusted tax.*—The adjusted tax with respect to a product is *de minimis* if such tax is less than one/tenth of one percent of the importer's cost of acquiring such product. The term "adjusted tax" means the tax that would be imposed under section 4681 on the ODCs used as materials in the manufacture of such product if such ODCs were sold in the United States and the base tax amount were $1.00.

(c) *Taxable event.*—(1) *In general.*—Except as otherwise provided in paragraphs (c)(2) and (3) of this section, the tax on an imported taxable product is imposed when the product is first sold or used (as defined in § 52.4681-1(c)(6) and (7)) by its importer. Thus, for example, imported taxable products that are warehoused or repackaged after entry and then exported without being sold or used in the United States are not subject to tax.

(2) *Election to treat importation as use.*—(i) *In general.*—An importer may elect to treat the entry of products into the United States as the use of such products. In the case of imported taxable products to which an election under this paragraph (c)(2) applies—

(A) Tax is imposed on the products on the date of entry (as determined under paragraph (c)(2)(ii) of this section) if the products are entered into the United States after the election becomes effective;

(B) Tax is imposed on the products on the date the election becomes effective if the products were entered into the United States after December 31, 1989, and before the election becomes effective; and

(C) No tax is imposed if the products were entered into the United States before January 1, 1990.

(ii) *Date of entry.*—The date of entry is determined by reference to customs law. If the actual date is unknown, the importer may use any reasonable and consistent method to determine the date of entry, provided that such date is within 10 business days of arrival of products in the United States.

(iii) *Applicability of election.*—An election under this paragraph (c)(2) applies to all imported taxable products that are owned (and

**Reg. § 52.4682-3**

have not been used) by the importer at the time the election becomes effective and all imported taxable products that are entered into the United States by the importer after the election becomes effective. An election under this paragraph (c)(2) becomes effective at the beginning of the first calendar quarter to which the election applies. After October 9, 1990, the election may be revoked only with the consent of the Commissioner.

(iv) *Making the election.*—An election under this paragraph (c)(2) shall be made in accordance with the instructions for the return on which the importer is required to report liability for tax under section 4681.

(3) *Treating the sale of an article incorporating an imported taxable product as the first sale or use of such product.*—(i) *In general.*—In the case of articles to be sold, an importer may treat the sale of an article manufactured or assembled in the United States as the first sale or use of an imported taxable product incorporated in such article, but only if the importer—

(A) Has consistently treated the sale of similar articles as the first sale or use of similar imported taxable products; and

(B) Has not made an election under paragraph (c)(2) of this section.

(ii) *Similar articles and imported taxable products.*—An importer may establish any reasonable criteria for determining whether articles or imported taxable products are similar for purposes of this paragraph (c)(3).

(iii) *Establishment of consistent treatment.*—An importer has consistently treated the sale of similar articles as the first sale or use of similar imported taxable products only if such treatment is reflected in the computation of tax on the importer's returns for all prior calendar quarters in which such treatment would affect tax liability.

(iv) *Example.*—The application of this paragraph (c)(3) may be illustrated by the following example:

*Example.* (a) An importer of printed circuits and other electronic components uses those products in assembling television receivers in the United States and also uses the printed circuits in assembling VCRs in the United States. Under the importer's criteria for determining similarity, printed circuits are similar to other printed circuits, but not to the other electronic components. In addition, television receivers are similar to other television receivers, but not to VCRs. The importer has not made an election under paragraph (c)(2) of this section.

(b) Under this paragraph (c)(3), the importer may treat the sale of the television receivers as the first sale or use of the imported printed circuits incorporated into the television receivers. In that case, the tax on the printed circuits would be imposed when the television receivers are sold rather than when the printed circuits are used in assembling the television receivers.

(c) The importer may treat the sale of the television receivers as the first sale or use of the printed circuits incorporated into the television receivers even if the sale of the television receivers is not treated as the first sale or use of the other electronic components incorporated into the television receivers and even if the sale of VCRs is not treated as the first sale or use of the printed circuits incorporated into the VCRs. Under paragraph (c)(3)(i)(A) of this section, however, the importer must have consistently treated the sale of television receivers as the first sale or use of printed circuits incorporated into the receivers. Thus, in the case of television receivers that were assembled before January 1, 1990, and sold after December 31, 1989, the importer must have treated the sale of the television receivers as the first sale or use of the printed circuits incorporated into the television receivers when reporting tax under section 4681 with respect to such printed circuits.

(d) *ODCs used as materials in the manufacture of imported taxable products.*—(1) *ODC weight.*—The tax imposed on an imported taxable product under section 4681 is computed by reference to the weight of the ODCs used as materials in the manufacture of the product (ODC weight). The ODC weight of a product includes the weight of ODCs used as materials in the manufacture of any components of the product.

(2) *ODCs used as materials in the manufacture of a product.*—Except as provided in paragraph (d)(3) of this section, an ODC is used as a material in the manufacture of a product if the ODC is—

(i) Incorporated into the product;

(ii) Released into the atmosphere in the process of manufacturing the product; or

(iii) Otherwise used in the manufacture of the product (but only to the extent the cost of the ODC is properly allocable to the product).

(3) *Protective packaging.*—ODCs used in the manufacture of protective material in which a product is packaged are not treated as ODCs used as materials in the manufacture of such product.

(4) *Examples.*—The provisions of this paragraph (d) may be illustrated by the following examples:

*Example 1.* A, a manufacturer located outside the United States, uses ODCs as a solvent to clean the printed circuits it manufactures and as a coolant in the air-conditioning system of the factory in which the printed circuits are manufactured. The ODCs used as a solvent are released into the atmosphere, and, under paragraph (d)(2)(ii) of this section, are used as materials in the manufacture of the printed circuits. The ODCs used as a coolant in the air-conditioning system are also used in the manufacture of the printed circuits. Under paragraph (d)(2)(iii) of this section, these ODCs are used as materials in the manufacture of the printed circuits only to the extent the cost of the ODCs is properly allocable to the printed circuits.

*Example 2.* B manufactures television receivers outside the United States and wraps them for shipping in a protective packing material manufactured with ODCs. Under paragraph (d)(3) of this section, the ODCs used in the manufacture of the protective packing material are not treated as ODCs used as a material in the manufacture of the television receivers.

(e) *Methods of determining ODC weight; computation of tax.*—(1) *In general.*—This paragraph (e) sets forth the methods to be used for determining the ODC weight of an imported taxable product and a method to be used in computing the tax when the ODC weight cannot be determined. The amount of tax is computed separately for each imported taxable product and the method to be used in determining the ODC weight or otherwise computing the tax is separately determined for each such product. Thus, an importer may use one method in computing the tax on some imported taxable products and different methods in computing the tax on other products. For example, an importer of telephone sets may compute the tax using the exact method described in paragraph (e)(2) of this section for determining the ODC weight of telephone sets supplied by one manufacturer and using the Table method described in paragraph (e)(3) of this section for telephone sets supplied by other manufacturers that have not provided sufficient information to allow the importer to use the exact method.

(2) *Exact method.*—If the importer determines the weight of each ODC used as a material in the manufacture of an imported taxable product and supports that determination with sufficient and reliable information, the ODC weight of the product is the weight so determined. Under this method, the ODC weight of a mixture is equal to the weight of the ODCs contained in the mixture. Representations by the manufacturer of the product to the importer as to the weight of the ODCs used as materials in the manufacture of the product may be sufficient and reliable information for this purpose. Thus, a letter to the importer signed by the manufacturer may constitute sufficient and reliable information if the letter adequately identifies the product and states the weight of each ODC used as a material in the product's manufacture.

(3) *Table method.*—(i) *In general.*—If the ODC weight of an imported taxable product is not determined using the exact method described in paragraph (e)(2) of this section and the current Table specifies an ODC weight for the product, the ODC weight of the product is the Table ODC weight, regardless of what ODCs were used in the manufacture of the product. In computing the amount of tax, the Table ODC weight shall not be rounded.

(ii) *Special rules.*—(A) *Articles assembled in the United States.*— An importer that assembles finished articles in the United States may compute the amount of tax imposed on the imported taxable products incorporated into the finished article by using the Table ODC weight specified for the article instead of the Table ODC weights specified for the components. In order to compute the tax under this special rule, the importer must determine the actual number of articles manufactured. For example, if an importer manufactures 100 camcorders using imported subassemblies, the importer may compute the amount of tax on the subassemblies by using the Table ODC weight specified for camcorders. Thus, the tax imposed on the subassemblies is equal to the tax that would be imposed on 100 camcorders.

(B) *Combination method.*—This paragraph (e)(3)(ii)(B) applies to an imported taxable product if the current Table specifies weights for two or more ODCs with respect to the product and the importer of the product can determine the weight of any such ODC (and of any ODC used as a substitute for such ODC) and can support such determination with sufficient and reliable information. In determining the ODC weight of any such product, the importer may replace the weight specified in the Table for such ODC with the weight (as determined by the importer) of such ODC and its substitutes. For example, if an importer has sufficient and reliable information to determine the amount of CFC-12 included in a product as a coolant (and to determine that no ODCs have been used as substitutes for CFC-12) but cannot determine the amount of CFC-113 used in manufacturing the product's electronic components, the importer may use the weight specified in the Table for CFC-113 and the actual weight determined by the importer for CFC-12 in determining the ODC weight of the product.

(C) *ODCs used in the manufacture of rigid foam insulation.*—In computing the tax using the method described in this paragraph (e)(3), any ODC for which the Table specifies a weight followed by an asterisk (*) shall be treated as an ODC used in the manufacture of rigid foam insulation (as defined in §52.4682-1(d)(3) and (4)).

(4) *Value method.*—(i) *General rule.*—If the importer cannot determine the ODC weight of an imported taxable product under the exact method described in paragraph (e)(2) of this section and the Table ODC weight of the product is not specified, the tax imposed on the product under section 4681 is one percent of the entry value of the product.

(ii) *Special rule for mixtures.*—If, in the case of an imported taxable product that is a mixture, the tax was determined under the method described in this paragraph (e)(4), the Commissioner may redetermine the tax based on the ODC weight of the mixture.

(5) *Adjustment for prior taxes.*—(i) *In general.*—If any manufacture with respect to an imported taxable product occurred in the United States or the product incorporates a taxed component or a taxed chemical was used in its manufacture, the product's ODC weight (or value) attributable to manufacture within the United States or to taxed components or taxed chemicals shall be disregarded in computing the tax on such product using a method described in paragraph (e)(2), (3), or (4) of this section.

(ii) *Taxed component.*—The term "taxed component" means any component that previously was subject to tax as an imported taxable product or that would have been so taxed if section 4681 had been in effect for periods before January 1, 1990.

(iii) *Taxed chemical.*—The term "taxed chemical" means any ODC that previously was subject to tax.

(6) *Examples.*—The application of this paragraph (e) may be illustrated by the following examples:
*Example 1.* A is an importer (as defined in §52.4681-1(c)(5)) of VCRs. The HTS classification for the VCRs is 8528.10.40. VCRs classified under HTS under HTS heading 8528.10.40 are imported taxable products because they are listed in the Table (contained in paragraph (f)(6) of this section) by name and HTS heading (as described in paragraph (f)(3)(i) of this section). Each VCR is wrapped in protective packing material manufactured with ODCs. A imports and sells 100 VCRs during the first calendar quarter of 1991. A may determine the ODC weight for the VCRs by reference to the Table. The Table ODC weight specified for VCRs classified under HTS heading 8528.10.40 is 0.0586 pound of CFC-113. This weight does not take protective packaging into account. The amount of tax for the first quarter of 1991 is $6.42 (0.0586 (the ODC weight) × 100 (the number of VCRs sold in the quarter) × $1.37 (the base tax amount for CFC-113 in 1991) × 0.8 (the ozone-depletion factor for CFC-113)). If A uses the exact method (as described in paragraph (e)(2) of this section) to determine the ODC weight for the VCRs, A does not take into account the ODCs used in the manufacture of the protective packaging. (Imported protective packaging containing foams made with ODCs other than foams defined in §52.4682-1(d)(3) is subject to tax, however, if the packaging is sold as packaging or first used as packaging in the United States.)
*Example 2.* The facts are the same as in *Example 1,* except that A's VCRs are manufactured using methyl chloroform as the solvent instead of CFC-113. If A does not use the exact method to determine the weight of the methyl chloroform used in the manufacture of the VCRs, A must, under paragraphs (e)(3)(i) and (e)(4)(i) of this section, determine the ODC weight by reference to the Table. If A used the Table ODC weight, the computation of tax is the same as in *Example 1,* using the base tax amount and ozone-depletion factor for CFC-113. A does not substitute the base tax amount and ozone-depletion factor of methyl chloroform for those of CFC-113.
*Example 3.* B imports and sells mixtures of ethylene oxide and CFC-12. The mixture is 88 percent CFC-12 by weight. B also imports and sells R-502. The R-502 is 51 percent CFC-115 by weight. In the first calendar quarter of 1991 B sells 100 pounds of imported ethylene oxide/CFC-12 mixture and 10,000 pounds of imported R-502. The ethylene/CFC-12 mixture and the R-502 are imported taxable products because they are listed in Part I of the Table (contained in paragraph (f)(6) of this section). Under the exact method described in paragraph (e)(2) of this section, B computes the tax based on 88

pounds of CFC-12, the amount of ODCs contained in the imported ethylene oxide mixture, and based on 5100 pounds of CFC-115, the amount of ODCs in the imported R-502.

(f) *Imported Products Table.*—(1) *In general.*—This paragraph (f) contains rules relating to the Imported Products Table (Table) and sets forth the Table. The Table lists all the products that are subject to the tax on imported taxable products and specifies the Table ODC weight of each product for which such a weight has been determined.

(2) *Applicability of Table.*—(i) *In general.*—Except as provided in paragraph (f)(2)(ii) of this section, the Table contained in paragraph (f)(6) of this section is effective on January 1, 1990.

(ii) *Treatment of certain products.*—(A) Products included in a listing that is preceded by a double asterisk (**) in the Table shall not be treated as imported taxable products until October 1, 1990.

(B) Products included in a listing that is preceded by a triple asterisk (***) in the Table shall not be treated as imported taxable products until January 1, 1992.

(3) *Identification of products.*—(i) *In general.*—Each listing in the Table identifies a product by name and includes only products that are described by that name. Most listings (other than listings for mixtures) identify a product by both name and HTS heading. In such cases, a product is included in that listing only if the product is described by that name and the rate of duty on the product is determined by reference to that HTS heading. However, the product is included in that listing even if it is manufactured with or contains a different ODC than the ODC specified in the Table.

(ii) *Electronic items not listed by specific name.*—(A) *In general.*—Part II of the Table contains listings for electronic items that are not included within any other listing in the Table. An imported product is included in these listings only if such imported product—
(1) Is an electronic component listed in chapters 84, 85, or 90 of the Harmonized Tariff Schedule; or
(2) Contains components described in paragraph (f)(3)(ii)(A)(1) of this section and more than 15 percent of the cost of the imported product is attributable to such components.

(B) *Electronic component.*—For purposes of this paragraph (f)(3)(ii), an electronic component is a component whose operation involves the use of nonmechanical amplification or switching devices such as tubes, transistors, and integrated circuits. Such components do not include passive electrical devices such as resistors and capacitors.

(C) *Certain items not included.*—Items such as screws, nuts, bolts, plastic parts, and similar specially fabricated parts that may be used to construct an electronic item are not themselves included in the listing for electronic items not otherwise listed in the Table.

(iii) *Examples.*—The application of this paragraph (f)(3) may be illustrated by the following examples:
*Example 1.* The Table lists "electronic integrated circuits and microassemblies; HTS heading 8542." A bipolar transistor under HTS heading 8542.11.00.05 is included in this listing because a bipolar transistor is a type of electronic integrated circuit and HTS heading 8542.11.00.05 is included within HTS heading 8542.
*Example 2.* The Table lists "radios; HTS heading 8527.19," "radio combinations; HTS heading 8527.11" and "radio combinations; HTS heading 8527.31." A radio classified under HTS heading 8527.19 is not included within either listing for radio combinations. However, a radio classified under HTS heading 8527.19.00.20 is included within the listing for radios; HTS heading 8527.19. A radio combination classified under HTS heading 8527.11.20 is included within the listing for radio combinations; HTS heading 8527.11 but not the listing for radio combinations; HTS heading 8527.31. Any radio or radio combination not classified under the HTS heading for any other listing is included in the listing for electronic items not otherwise listed.

(4) *Rules for listing products.*—Products are listed in the Table in accordance with the following rules:

(i) *Listing in Part I.*—A product is listed in Part I of the Table if it is a mixture containing ODCs. In addition, a product other than a mixture containing ODCs will be listed in Part I of a revised Table if the Commissioner has determined that—
(A) The ODC weight of the product is not *de minimis* when the product is produced using the predominant method of manufacturing the product; and
(B) None of the ODCs used as materials in the manufacture of the product under the predominant method are used for purposes of refrigeration or air conditioning, creating an aerosol or foam, or manufacturing electronic components.

(ii) *Listing in Part II.*—A product is listed in Part II of the Table if the Commissioner has determined that the ODCs used as materials in the manufacture of the product under the predominant method are used for purposes of refrigeration or air conditioning, creating an aerosol or foam, or manufacturing electronic components.

(iii) *Listing in Part III.*—A product is listed in Part III of the Table if the Commissioner has determined that the product is not an imported taxable product and the product would otherwise be included within a listing in Part II of the Table. For example, floppy disk drive units are listed in Part III because they are not imported taxable products and they would, but for their listing in Part III, be included within the Part II listing for electronic items not specifically identified.

(5) *Table ODC weight.*—The Table ODC weight of a product is the weight, determined by the Commissioner, of the ODCs that are used as materials in the manufacture of the product under the predominant method of manufacturing. The Table ODC weight is given in pounds per single unit of product unless otherwise specified.

(6) *Table.*—The Table is set forth below:

## IMPORTED PRODUCTS TABLE

PART I—Products that are mixtures containing ODCs

Mixtures containing ODCs, including but not limited to:
—anti-static sprays
—automotive products such as "carburetor cleaner," "stop leak," and "oil charge"
—cleaning solvents
—contact cleaners
—degreasers
—dusting sprays
—electronic circuit board coolants
—electronic solvents
—ethylene oxide/CFC-12
—fire extinguisher preparations and charges
—flux removers for electronics
—insect and wasp sprays
—mixtures of ODCs
—propellants
—refrigerants

PART II—Products in which ODCs are used for purposes of refrigeration or air conditioning, creating an aerosol or foam, or manufacturing electronic components

| Product Name | Harmonized Tariff Schedule Heading | ODC | ODC Weight |
|---|---|---|---|
| Rigid foam insulation defined in §52.4682-1(d)(3) | | | |
| Foams made with ODCs, other than foams defined in §52.4682-1(d)(3) | | | |
| Scrap flexible foams made with ODCs | | | |
| Medical products containing ODCs: | | | |
|     surgical staplers | | | |
|     cryogenic medical instruments | | | |
|     drug delivery systems | | | |
|     inhalants | | | |
| Dehumidifiers, household | 8415.82.00.50 | CFC-12 | 0.344 |
| Chillers: | 8415.82.00.65 | | |
|   charged with CFC-12 | | CFC-12 | 1600. |
|   charged with CFC-114 | | CFC-114 | 1250. |
|   charged with R-500 | | CFC-12 | 1920. |
| Refrigerator-freezers, household: | | | |
|   not > 184 liters | 8418.10.00.10 | CFC-11 | 1.08* |
| | | CFC-12 | 0.13 |
|   > 184 liters but | 8418.10.00.20 | CFC-11 | 1.32* |
|   not > 269 liters | | CFC-12 | 0.26 |
|   > 269 liters but | 8418.10.00.30 | CFC-11 | 1.54* |
|   not > 382 liters | | CFC-12 | 0.35 |
|   > 382 liters | 8418.10.00.40 | CFC-11 | 1.87* |
| | | CFC-12 | 0.35 |
| Refrigerators, household | | | |
|   not > 184 liters | 8418.21.00.10 | CFC-11 | 1.08* |
| | | CFC-12 | 0.13 |
|   > 184 liters but | 8418.21.00.20 | CFC-11 | 1.32* |
|   not > 269 liters | | CFC-12 | 0.26 |
|   > 269 liters but | 8418.21.00.30 | CFC-11 | 1.54* |
|   not > 382 liters | | CFC-12 | 0.35 |
|   > 382 liters | 8418.21.00.90 | CFC-11 | 1.87* |
| | | CFC-12 | 0.35 |
| Freezers, household | 8418.30 | CFC-11 | 2.* |
| | | CFC-12 | 0.4 |
| Freezers, household | 8418.40 | CFC-11 | 2.* |
| | | CFC-12 | 0.4 |
| Refrigerating | 8418.50 | CFC-11 | 50.* |
|   display counters | | CFC-12 | 260. |
|   not > 227 kg | | | |
| Icemaking machines: | 8418.69 | | |
|   charged with CFC-12 | | CFC-12 | 1.4 |
|   charged with R-502 | | CFC-115 | 3.39 |
| Drinking water coolers: | 8418.69 | | |
|   charged with CFC-12 | | CFC-12 | 0.21 |
|   charged with R-500 | | CFC-12 | 0.22 |
| Centrifugal chillers, hermetic: | 8418.69 | | |
|   charged with CFC-12 | | CFC-12 | 1600. |
|   charged with CFC-114 | | CFC-114 | 1250. |
|   charged with R-500 | | CFC-12 | 1920. |
| Reciprocating chillers: | 8418.69 | | |

| Product Name | Harmonized Tariff Schedule Heading | ODC | ODC Weight |
|---|---|---|---|
| charged with CFC-12 | | CFC-12 | 200. |
| Mobile refrigeration systems: | 8418.99 | | |
| containers | | CFC-12 | 15. |
| trucks | | CFC-12 | 11. |
| trailers | | CFC-12 | 20. |
| Refrigeration condensing units: | | | |
| not > 746W | 8418.99.00.05 | CFC-12 | 0.3 |
| > 746W but not > 2.2KW | 8418.99.00.10 | CFC-12 | 1. |
| > 2.2KW but not > 7.5KW | 8418.99.00.15 | CFC-12 | 3. |
| > 7.5KW but not > 22.3KW | 8418.99.00.20 | CFC-12 | 8.5 |
| > 22.3 KW | 8418.99.00.25 | CFC-12 | 17. |
| Fire extinguishers, charged w/ODCs | 8424 | | |
| Electronic typewriters and word processors | 8469 | CFC-113 | 0.2049 |
| Electronic calculators | 8470.10 | CFC-113 | 0.0035 |
| Electronic calculators w/printing device | 8470.21 | CFC-113 | 0.0057 |
| Electronic calculators | 8470.29 | CFC-113 | 0.0035 |
| Account machines | 8470.40 | CFC-113 | 0.1913 |
| Cash registers | 8470.50 | CFC-113 | 0.1913 |
| Digital automatic data processing machines w/cathode ray tube, not included in subheading 8471.20.00.90 | 8471.20 | CFC-113 | 0.3663 |
| Laptops, notebooks, and pocket computers | 8471.20.00.90 | CFC-113 | 0.03567 |
| Digital processing units w/entry value: | | | |
| not > $100K | 8471.91 | CFC-113 | 0.498 |
| > $100K | 8471.91 | CFC-113 | 27.6667 |
| Combined input/output units (terminals) | 8471.92 | CFC-113 | 0.36 |
| Keyboards | 8471.92 | CFC-113 | 0.0742 |
| Display units | 8471.92 | CFC-113 | 0.0386 |
| Printer units | 8471.92 | CFC-113 | 0.1558 |
| Input or output units | 8471.92 | CFC-113 | 0.1370 |
| Hard magnetic disk drive units not included in subheading 8471.93.10 for a disk of a diameter: | | | |
| not > 9 cm (3$^1$/$_2$ inches) | 8471.93 | CFC-113 | 0.2829 |
| > 9 cm (3$^1$/$_2$ inches) but not > 21 cm (8$^1$/$_4$ inches) | 8471.93 | CFC-113 | 1.1671 |
| Nonmagnetic storage units w/entry value > $1,000 | 8471.93 | CFC-113 | 2.7758 |
| Magnetic disk drive units for a disk of a diameter over 21 cm (8$^1$/$_4$ inches) | 8471.93.10 | CFC-113 | 4.0067 |
| Power supplies | 8471.99.30 | CFC-113 | 0.0655 |
| Electronic office machines | 8472 | CFC-113 | 0.0010 |
| Populated cards for digital processing units in subheading 8471.91 w/ value: | | | |
| not > $100K | 8473.30 | CFC-113 | 0.1408 |
| > $100K | 8473.30 | CFC-113 | 4.82 |
| Automatic goods-vending machines with refrigerating device | 8476.11 | CFC-12 | 0.45 |
| Microwave ovens with electronic controls, with capacity of: | 8516.5 | | |
| 0.99 cu. ft. or less | | CFC-113 | 0.03 |
| 1.0 through 1.3 cu. ft. | | CFC-113 | 0.0441 |
| 1.31 cu. ft. or greater | | CFC-113 | 0.0485 |
| Microwave oven combinations with electronic controls | 8516.60.40.60 | CFC-113 | 0.0595 |
| Telephone sets w/entry value: | | | |
| not > $11.00 | 8517.10 | CFC-113 | 0.0225 |
| > $11.00 | 8517.10 | CFC-113 | 0.1 |
| Teleprinters and teletypewriters | 8517.20 | CFC-113 | 0.1 |
| Switching equipment not included in subheading 8517.30.20 | 8517.30 | CFC-113 | 0.1267 |
| Private branch exchange switching equipment | 8517.30.20 | CFC-113 | 0.0753 |
| Modems | 8517.40 | CFC-113 | 0.0225 |
| Intercoms | 8517.81 | CFC-113 | 0.0225 |
| Facsimile machines | 8517.82 | CFC-113 | 0.0225 |
| Loudspeakers, microphones, headphones, and electric sound amplifier sets, not included in subheading 8518.30.10 | 8518 | CFC-113 | 0.0022 |
| Telephone handsets | 8518.30.10 | CFC-113 | 0.0420 |
| Turntables, record players, cassette players, and other sound reproducing apparatus | 8519 | CFC-113 | 0.0022 |
| Magnetic tape recorders and other sound recording apparatus, not included in subheading 8520.20 | 8520 | CFC-113 | 0.0022 |
| Telephone answering machines | 8520.20 | CFC-113 | 0.1 |
| Color video recording/reproducing apparatus | 8521.10.00.20 | CFC-113 | 0.0586 |
| Videodisc players | 8521.90 | CFC-113 | 0.0106 |
| Cordless handset telephones | 8525.20.50 | CFC-113 | 0.1 |
| Cellular communication equipment | 8525.20.60 | CFC-113 | 0.4446 |
| TV cameras | 8525.30 | CFC-113 | 1.4230 |
| Camcorders | 8525.30 | CFC-113 | 0.0586 |
| Radio combinations | 8527.11 | CFC-113 | 0.0022 |
| Radios | 8527.19 | CFC-113 | 0.0014 |
| Motor vehicle radios with or w/o tape player | 8527.21 | CFC-113 | 0.0021 |
| Radio combinations | 8527.31 | CFC-113 | 0.0022 |
| Radios | 8527.32 | CFC-113 | 0.0014 |
| Tuners w/o speaker | 8527.39.00.20 | CFC-113 | 0.0022 |
| Television receivers | 8528 | CFC-113 | 0.0386 |
| VCRs | 8528.10.40 | CFC-113 | 0.0586 |
| Home satellite earth stations | 8528.10.80.55 | CFC-113 | 0.0106 |
| Electronic assemblies for HTS headings 8525, 8527, & 8528 | 8529.90 | CFC-113 | 0.0816 |
| Indicator panels incorporating liquid crystal devices or light emitting diodes | 8531.20 | CFC-113 | 0.0146 |
| Printed circuits | 8534 | CFC-113 | 0.001 |
| Computerized numerical controls | 8537.10.00.30 | CFC-113 | 0.1306 |

| Product Name | Harmonized Tariff Schedule Heading | ODC | ODC Weight |
|---|---|---|---|
| Diodes, crystals, transistors and other similar discrete semiconductor devices | 8541 | CFC-113 | 0.0001 |
| Electronic integrated circuits and microassemblies | 8542 | CFC-113 | 0.0002 |
| Signal generators | 8543.20 | CFC-113 | 0.6518 |
| Avionics | 8543.90.40 | CFC-113 | 0.9150 |
| Signal generators subassemblies | 8543.90.80 | CFC-113 | 0.1265 |
| Insulated or refrigerated railway freight cars | 8606 | CFC-11 | 100.* |
| Passenger automobiles: | 8703 | | |
|     foams (interior) | | CFC-11 | 0.8 |
|     foams (exterior) | | CFC-11 | 0.7 |
|     with charged a/c | | CFC-12 | 2. |
|     without charged a/c | | CFC-12 | 0.2 |
|     electronics | | CFC-113 | 0.5 |
| Light trucks: | 8704 | | |
|     foams (interior) | | CFC-11 | 0.6 |
|     foams (exterior) | | CFC-11 | 0.1 |
|     with charged a/c | | CFC-12 | 2. |
|     without charged a/c | | CFC-12 | 0.2 |
|     electronics | | CFC-113 | 0.4 |
| ** Heavy trucks and tractors; GVW 33,001 lbs or more: | 8704 | | |
|     foams (interior) | | CFC-11 | 0.6 |
|     foams (exterior) | | CFC-11 | 0.1 |
|     with charged a/c | | CFC-12 | 3. |
|     without charged a/c | | CFC-12 | 0.2 |
|     electronics | | CFC-113 | 0.4 |
| Motorcycles with seat foamed with ODCs | 8711 | CFC-11 | 0.04 |
| Bicycles with seat foamed with ODCs | 8712 | CFC-11 | 0.04 |
| Seats foamed with ODCs | 8714.95 | CFC-11 | 0.04 |
| Aircraft | 8802 | CFC-12 | 0.25 lb/1000 lbs Operating Empty Weight (OEW) |
| | | CFC-13 | 30.0 lbs/1000 lbs OEW |
| Optical fibers | 9001 | CFC-12 | 0.005 lb/thousand feet |
| Electronics cameras | 9006 | CFC-113 | 0.01 |
| Photocopiers | 9009 | CFC-113 | 0.0426 |
| Avionics | 9014.20 | CFC-113 | 0.915 |
| Electronic drafting machines | 9017 | CFC-113 | 0.12 |
| Complete patient | 9018.19.80 | CFC-12 | 0.94 |
|     monitoring systems | | CFC-113 | 3.4163 |
| Complete patient monitoring systems; subassemblies thereof | 9018.19.80.60 | CFC-113 | 1.932 |
| Physical or chemical analysis instruments | 9027 | CFC-12 | 0.0003 |
| | | CFC-113 | 0.0271 |
| Oscilloscopes | 9030 | CFC-11 | 0.49 |
| | | CFC-12 | 0.5943 |
| | | CFC-113 | 0.2613 |
| Foam chairs | 9401 | CFC-11 | 0.3 |
| Foam sofas | 9401 | CFC-11 | 0.75 |
| Foam mattresses | 9404.21 | CFC-11 | 1.6 |
| Electronic games and electronic components thereof | 9504 | CFC-113 | |
| Electronic items not otherwise listed in the Table: | | | |
|     included in HTS chapters 84, 85, 90 | | CFC-113 | 0.0004 pound/ $1.00 of entry value |
|     *** not included in HTS chapters 84, 85, 90 | | CFC-113 | 0.0004 pound/ $1.00 of entry value |

PART III—Products that are not Imported Taxable Products

| Product Name | Harmonized Tariff Schedule Heading |
|---|---|
| Room air conditioners | 8415.10.00.6 |
| Dishwashers | 8422.11 |
| Clothes washers | 8450.11 |
| Clothes dryers | 8451.21 |
| Floppy disk drive units | 8471.93 |
| Transformers and inductors | 8504 |
| Toasters | 8516.72 |
| Unrecorded media | 8523 |
| Recorded media | 8524 |
| Capacitors | 8532 |
| Resistors | 8533 |
| Switching apparatus | 8536 |
| Cathode tubes | 8540 |

* See paragraph (e)(3)(ii)(C) of this section. Denotes an ODC used in the manufacture of rigid foam insulation.

** See paragraph (f)(2)(ii)(A) of this section. Denotes products for which the effective date is October 1, 1990.

*** See paragraph (f)(2)(ii)(B) of this section. Denotes products for which the effective date is January 1, 1992.

(g) *Requests for modification of Table.*—(1) *In general.*—Any manufacturer or importer of a product may request that the Secretary modify the Table in any of the following respects:

(i) Adding a product to the Table and specifying its Table ODC weight.

(ii) Removing a product from the Table.

(iii) Changing or specifying the Table ODC weight of a product.

(2) *Form of request.*—The Secretary will consider a request for modification that includes the following:

(i) The name, address, taxpayer identifying number, and principal place of business of the requester.

(ii) For each product with respect to which a modification is requested:

(A) The name of the product;

(B) The HTS heading or subheading;

(C) The type of modification requested;

(D) The Table ODC weight that should be specified for the product if the request related to adding a product or changing or specifying its Table ODC weight; and

(E) The data supporting the request.

(3) *Address.*—The address for submission of requests under this paragraph (g) is: Internal Revenue Service, P.O. Box 7604, Ben Franklin Station, Attn: CC:CORP:T:R (Imported Products Table), room 5228, Washington, D.C. 20044.

(4) *Public inspection and copying.*—Requests submitted under this paragraph (g) will be available in the Internal Revenue Service Freedom of Information Reading Room for public inspection and copying. [Reg. § 52.4682-3.]

☐ [*T.D.* 8370, 11-1-91.]

### [Reg. § 52.4682-4]

**§ 52.4682-4. Floor stocks tax.**—(a) *Overview.*—This section provides rules for identifying ozone-depleting chemical (ODCs) that are subject to the floor stocks tax imposed by section 4682(h)(1), determining the person that is liable for the tax, and computing the amount of the tax. See § 52.4681-1(a)(3) and (c) for general rules and definitions relating to the floor stocks tax.

(b) *Identifying rules.*—(1) *ODCs subject to floor stocks tax; ODCs held for sale or for use in further manufacture.*—(i) *In general.*—The floor stocks tax is imposed only on an ODC that is held for sale or for use in further manufacture on the date the tax is imposed. This paragraph (b)(1) provides rules for identifying ODCs held for sale or for use in further manufacture.

(ii) *Held for sale.*—(A) *In general.*—For purposes of determining whether an ODC is held for sale, the term "sale" shall have the meaning set forth in § 52.4681-1(c)(6). ODCs held for sale include ODCs that will be sold in connection with the provision of services or in connection with the sale of a manufactured article and, in such cases, include ODCs that will be sold without the statement of a separate charge for those ODCs.

(B) *ODCs held by a government.*—An ODC that is held by a government for its own use is not held for sale even if the ODC will be transferred between agencies or other subdivisions that have or are required to have different employer identification numbers.

(iii) *Held for use in further manufacture.*—Except as otherwise provided in paragraph (b)(2)(v) of this section, an ODC is held for use in further manufacture if—

(A) The ODC will be used as a material (within the meaning of paragraph (b)(1)(iv) of this section) in the manufacture of an article; and

(B) Such article will be held for sale.

(iv) *Use as material.*—(A) *In general.*—Except as provided in paragraph (b)(1)(iv)(B) of this section, an ODC will be used as a material in the manufacture of an article if the ODC will be—

(1) Incorporated into the article; or

(2) Released into the atmosphere in the process of manufacturing the article.

(B) *ODCs used in equipment.*—For purposes of the floor stocks tax, an ODC is not used as a material in the manufacture of an article if the ODC is (or will be) contained in equipment used in such manufacture and the ODC will be used for its intended purpose without being released from such equipment. Thus, ODCs that are (or will be) used as coolants in a factory's air-conditioning system are not used as materials in the manufacture of articles produced in the factory.

(v) *Storage containers.*—The floor stocks tax is imposed on an ODC without regard to the type or size of the storage container in which the ODC is held. Thus, the tax may apply to an ODC whether it is in a 14-ounce can or a 30-pound tank.

(vi) *Examples.*—The provisions of this paragraph (b)(1) may be illustrated by the following examples:

*Example 1.* A, a manufacturer of air conditioners, holds an ODC for use in air conditioners that it will manufacture and sell. A holds the ODC for use in further manufacture.

*Example 2.* B, a manufacturer of electronic components, holds an ODC for use as a solvent to clean printed circuits that it will sell to computer manufacturers. B holds the ODC for use in further manufacture.

*Example 3.* C, an automobile dealer, holds an ODC for use in charging air conditioners installed in automobiles that it sells to retail customers. C does not hold the ODC for use in further manufacture. C does, however, hold the ODC for sale, even if the customers are not separately charged for ODCs used in the automobile air conditioners.

*Example 4.* D operates an air-conditioning repair service and holds an ODC for use in repairing air conditioners for its customers. D holds the ODC for sale even if the customers are not separately charged for ODCs used in the repairs.

*Example 5.* E, a grocery-store chain, holds an ODC for use in its refrigeration units. E does not hold the ODC for sale or for use in further manufacture.

*Example 6.* F, a bank, holds an ODC for use in its fire extinguishers to protect the computer system. F does not hold the ODC for sale or for use in further manufacture.

*Example 7.* G, a government agency, holds an ODC for use in the refrigeration equipment of its various units. The units have separate employer identification numbers. The ODC is stored in a central warehouse until needed by a unit and then transferred to the unit upon request. G does not hold the ODC for sale or for use in further manufacture.

(2) Except as otherwise provided in paragraphs (d)(2) and (d)(3) of this section, the floor stocks tax is not imposed on any ODC in any year in which the base tax amount does not increase.

(i) *Mixtures.*—(A) *Tax imposed on January 1, 1990.*—In the case of the floor stocks tax imposed on January 1, 1990, the tax is not imposed on an ODC that has been mixed with any other ingredients.

(B) *Taxes imposed after 1990.*—(1) *In general.*—In the case of the floor stocks tax imposed on January 1 of a calendar year after 1990, the tax is not imposed on an ODC that has been mixed with any other ingredients, but only if it is established that such ingredients contribute to the accomplishment of the purpose for which the mixture will be used. A mixture is not exempt from tax under this paragraph (b)(2)(i)(B), however, if it contains only an ODC and an inert ingredient that doe snot contribute to the accomplishment of the purpose for which the mixture will be used.

(2) *Exception.*—In the case of a floor stocks tax imposed on or after January 1, 1992, a mixture is not exempt from floor stocks tax under this paragraph (b)(2)(i)(B) if it contains only ODCs and one or more stabilizers. For this purpose, the term "stabilizer" means an ingredient needed to maintain the chemical integrity of the ODC.

(C) *Examples.*—The provisions of this paragraph (b)(2)(i) may be illustrated by the following examples:

*Example 1.* The floor stocks tax is not imposed on the ODCs contained in refrigerants such as R-500 and R-502 because such products are mixtures of ODCs and other chemicals that contribute to the accomplishment of the purpose for which the mixture will be used.

*Example 2.* The floor stocks tax is not imposed on the ODCs contained in automotive products used for checking for leaks because such products are a mixture of ODCs and small amounts of dyes and oils that contribute to the accomplishment of the purpose for which the mixture will be used.

*Example 3.* The floor stocks tax is not imposed on Halon 1301 pressurized with nitrogen. Although nitrogen is an inert ingredient, it contributes to the accomplishment of the purpose for which the mixture will be used.

*Example 4.* On January 1, 1993, the floor stocks tax is imposed on methyl chloroform that is stabilized to prevent hydrolization or chemical reaction during transportation or use, unless the stabilized methyl chloroform has also been mixed with other ingredients that contribute to the accomplishment of the purpose for which the mixture will be used.

(ii) *Manufactured articles.*—The floor stocks tax is not imposed on an ODC that is contained in a manufactured article in which the ODC will be used for its intended purpose without being released from such article. For example, the tax is not imposed on the ODCs contained in the cooling coils of a refrigerator even if the refrigerator is held for sale. However, the tax is imposed on a can of ODC used to recharge an air conditioning unit because the ODC must be expelled from the can in order to be used. Similarly, beginning in 1991, the tax is imposed on Halons contained in a fire extinguisher held for sale because such ODCs must be expelled from the fire extinguisher in order to be used.

(iii) *Recycled ODCs.*—The floor stocks tax is not imposed on ODCs that have been reclaimed or recycled. For example, the tax is not imposed on an ODC that is held for use in further manufacture after being used as a solvent and recycled.

(iv) *ODCs held by the manufacturer or importer.*—The floor stocks tax is not imposed on ODCs held by their manufacturer or importer.

(v) *ODCs used as a feedstock.*—(A) *In general.*—The floor stocks tax is not imposed on any ODC that was sold in a qualifying sale for use as a feedstock (as defined in § 52.4682-1(c)).

(B) *Post-1989 ODCs sold before January 1, 1990; post-1990 ODCs sold before January 1, 1991.*—A post-1989 ODC that was sold by its manufacturer or importer before January 1, 1990, or a post-1990 ODC that was sold by its manufacturer or importer before January 1, 1991, shall be treated, for purposes of this paragraph (b)(2)(v), as an ODC that was sold in a qualifying sale for purposes of § 52.4682-1(c) if the ODC will be used as a feedstock (within the meaning of § 52.4682-1(c)(3)).

(vi) *ODCs to be exported.*—(A) *In general.*—The floor stocks tax is not imposed on any ODC that was sold in a qualifying sale for export (as defined in § 52.4682-5(d)(1)).

(B) *ODCs sold before January 1, 1993.*—An ODC that was sold by its manufacturer or importer before January 1, 1993, is treated, for purposes of this paragraph (b)(2)(vi), as an ODC that was sold in a qualifying sale for export for purposes of § 52.4682-5(d)(1) if the ODC will be exported.

(vii) *ODCs used as propellants in metered-dose inhalers; years after 1992.*—(A) *In general.*—The floor stocks tax is not imposed on January 1 of calendar years after 1992 on any ODC that was sold in a qualifying sale for use as a propellant in a metered-dose inhaler (as defined in § 52.4682-1(h)).

(B) *ODCs sold before January 1, 1993.*—An ODC that was sold by its manufacturer or importer before January 1, 1993, is treated, for purposes of this paragraph (b)(2)(vii), as an ODC that was sold in a qualifying sale for purposes of § 52.4682-1(h) if the ODC will be used as a propellant in a metered-dose inhaler (within the meaning of § 52.4682-1(h)).

(viii) *ODCs used as medical sterilants; 1993.*—The floor stocks tax is not imposed in 1993 on any ODC held for use as a medical sterilant (as defined in § 52.4682-1(g)).

(c) *Person liable for tax.*—(1) *In general.*—The person liable for the floor stocks tax on an ODC is the person that holds the ODC on a date on which the tax is imposed. The person who holds the ODC is the person who has title to the ODC (whether or not delivery to such person has been made) as of the first moment of such date. The person who has title at such time is determined under applicable local law.

(2) *Special rule.*—Each business unit that has, or is required to have, its own employer identification number is treated as a separate person for purposes of the floor stocks tax. For example, a chain of automotive parts stores that has one employer identification number is one person for purposes of the floor stocks tax, and a parent corporation and subsidiary corporation that each have a different employer identification number are two persons for purposes of the floor stocks tax.

(d) *Computation of tax; tentative tax amount.*—(1) *In general.*—(i) *Generally applicable rules.*—This paragraph (d) provides rules for determining the tentative tax amount and the amount of the floor stocks tax. Section 52.4681-1(a)(3) provides that the amount of the floor stocks tax on an ODC is determined by reference to a tentative tax amount. The tentative tax amount is the amount of tax that would be imposed on the ODC under section 4681(a)(1) if a sale of the ODC by the manufacturer or importer had occurred on the date the floor stocks tax is imposed. The amount of the floor stocks tax imposed on the ODCs contained in a nonexempt mixture is computed on the basis of the weight of the ODCs in that mixture.

(ii) *Floor stocks tax imposed on post-1989 ODCs on January 1, 1990.*—The floor stocks tax imposed on post-1989 ODCs (as defined in § 52.4681-1(c)(9)) on January 1, 1990, is equal to the tentative tax amount. See paragraph (d)(2) of this section for rules relating to the floor stocks tax imposed on ODCs used in the manufacture of rigid foam insulation. See paragraph (d)(3) of this section for rules relating to the floor stocks tax imposed on Halons.

(iii) *Floor stocks tax imposed on post-1990 ODCs on January 1, 1991.*—The floor stocks tax imposed on post-1990 ODCs (as defined in § 52.4681-1(c)(9)) on January 1, 1991, is equal to the tentative tax amount.

(iv) *Other floor stocks taxes.*—(A) *In general.*—The following rules apply for floor stocks taxes imposed on post-1989 ODCs after January 1, 1990, and on post-1990 ODCs after January 1, 1991:

(1) The tentative tax amount is determined, except as provided in paragraph (d)(2), (3), or (4) of this section, by reference to the rate of tax prescribed in section 4681(b)(1)(B) and the ozone-depletion factors prescribed in section 4682(b).

(2) The amount of the floor stocks tax on an ODC is equal to the amount by which the tentative tax amount exceeds the amount of taxes previously imposed on the ODC.

(B) *Example.*—The application of this paragraph (d)(1)(iv) may be illustrated by the following example:

*Example.* The floor stocks tax imposed on one pound of CFC-12 held for sale on January 1, 1992, is $0.30 (the amount by which $1.67, the tentative tax, exceeds $1.37, the tax previously imposed on CFC-12).

(2) *ODCs used in the manufacture of rigid foam insulation; 1990, 1991, 1992, and 1993.*—(i) *In general.*—In the case of an ODC that was sold in a qualifying sale for purposes of § 52.4682-1(d) (relating to use in the manufacture of rigid foam insulation) the tentative tax amount is determined under section 4682(g) for purposes of computing the floor stocks tax imposed on the ODC on January 1 of 1990, 1991, 1992 or 1993. For purposes of computing the floor stocks tax imposed on the ODC on January 1, 1990, the tentative tax amount is zero. The floor stocks tax is not imposed on ODCs for use in the manufacture of rigid foam insulation in 1992 and 1993.

(ii) *Post-1989 ODCs sold before January 1, 1990; post-1990 ODCs sold before January 1, 1991.*—A post-1989 ODC that was sold by its manufacturer or importer before January 1, 1990, or a post-1990 ODC that was sold by its manufacturer or importer before January 1, 1991, shall be treated, for purposes of paragraphs (d)(2) and (e) of this section, as an ODC that was sold in a qualifying sale for purposes of § 52.4682-1(d) if the ODC will be used in the manufacture of rigid foam insulation (within the meaning of § 52.4682-1(d)(3) and (4)).

(3) *Halons; 1990, 1991, 1992, and 1993.*—In the case of Halon-1211, Halon-1301, or Halon-2402 (Halons), the tentative tax amount is determined under section 4682(g) for purposes of computing the floor stocks tax imposed on Halons on January 1 of 1990, 1991, 1992, or 1993. For purposes of computing the floor stocks tax imposed on Halons on January 1, 1990, the tentative tax amount is zero. The floor stocks tax is not imposed on Halons in 1992 and 1993.

(4) *Methyl chloroform; 1993.*—In the case of methyl chloroform, the tentative tax amount is determined under section 4682(g)(5) for purposes of computing the floor stocks tax imposed on January 1, 1993.

(e) *De minimis exception.*—(1) *1990 and 1992.*—In the case of the floor stocks tax imposed on January 1 of 1990 or 1992, a person is liable for the tax only if, on the date the tax is imposed, the person holds at least 400 pounds of post-1989 ODCs that are not described in paragraph (d)(2) or (3) of this section and are otherwise subject to tax.

(2) *1991.*—In the case of the floor stocks tax imposed on January 1, 1991, a person is liable for the tax only if, on such date, the person holds at least 400 pounds of ODCs subject to the 1991 floor stocks tax. For this purpose, ODCs subject to the 1991 floor stocks tax are—

(i) Post-1990 ODCs that are subject to tax; and

(ii) Post-1989 ODCs that are described in paragraph (d)(2) or (3) of this section and are otherwise subject to tax.

(3) *1993.*—In the case of the floor stocks tax imposed on January 1, 1993, a person is liable for the tax only if, on such date, the person holds at least 400 pounds of ODCs that are not described in paragraph (d)(2) or (3) of this section and are otherwise subject to tax.

(4) *1994.*—In the case of the floor stocks tax imposed on January 1, 1994, a person is liable for the tax only if, on such date, the person holds—

(i) At least 400 pounds ODCs that are not described in paragraph (d)(2) or (d)(3) of this section and are otherwise subject to tax;

(ii) At least 200 pounds of ODCs that are described in paragraph (d)(2) of this section and are otherwise subject to tax; or

(iii) At least 20 pounds of ODCs that are described in paragraph (d)(3) of this section and are otherwise subject to tax.

(5) *Calendar years after 1994.*—In the case of the floor stocks tax imposed on January 1 of 1995 and each following calendar year, a person is liable for the tax only if, on such date, the person holds—

(i) At least 400 pounds of ODCs that are not described in paragraph (d)(3) or (d)(4) of this section and are otherwise subject to tax;

(ii) At least 50 pounds of ODCs that are described in paragraph (d)(3) of this section and are otherwise subject to tax; or

(iii) At least 1000 pounds of ODCS that are described in paragraph (d)(4) of this section and are otherwise subject to tax.

(6) *Examples.*—The rules of this paragraph (e) may be illustrated by the following examples:

*Example 1.* On January 1, 1990, A holds for sale 300 pounds of CFC-12 (a post-1989 ODC not described in paragraph (d)(2) or (d)(3) of this section) and 500 pounds of R-500 (a mixture). A does not hold at least 400 pounds of ODCs that are taken into account under paragraph (e)(1) of this section and, under paragraph (b)(2)(i) of this section, mixtures are not subject to the floor stocks tax. Thus, A is not liable for the floor stocks tax imposed on January 1, 1990.

*Example 2.* On January 1, 1990, B holds for sale 250 pounds of CFC-12 and 250 pounds of CFC-113 (post-1989 ODCs not described in paragraph (d)(2) or (3) of this section). B holds 500 pounds of ODCs that are taken into account under paragraph (e)(1) of this section. Thus, B is liable for the floor stocks tax imposed on January 1, 1990, because B holds at least 400 pounds of ODCs for sale.

*Example 3.* On January 1, 1990, C holds 200 pounds of post-1990 ODCs and 500 pounds of post-1989 ODCs for use in further manufacture. C will use 300 pounds of the post-1989 ODCs in the manufacture of rigid foam insulation (as defined in §52.4682-1(d)(3) and (4)). The remainder of the ODCs are not described in paragraph (d)(2) or (3) of this section. Under paragraph (e)(1) of this section, post-1990 ODCs and ODCs that will be used in the manufacture of rigid foam insulation are disregarded in determining whether the *de minimis* exception is applicable in 1990. Thus, C holds only 200 pounds of ODCs that are taken into account under paragraph (e)(1) of this section and is not liable for the floor stocks tax imposed on January 1, 1990.

*Example 4.* (a) The facts are the same as in *Example 3*, except that the ODCs are held on January 1, 1991. Under paragraph (e)(2) of this section, the 200 pounds of post-1990 ODCs and the 300 pounds of post-1989 ODCs that will be used in the manufacture of rigid foam insulation are taken into account in determining whether the *de minimis* exception is applicable in 1991. Under paragraph (b)(2) of this section, the remaining 200 pounds of post-1989 ODCs are [is] not taken into account because the base tax amount applicable to post-1989 ODCs does not increase in 1991. Thus, C holds 500 pounds of ODCs that are taken into account under paragraph (e)(2) of this section and is liable for the floor stocks tax imposed on January 1, 1991.

(b) The amount of the floor stocks tax imposed on the 200 pounds of post-1990 ODCs and the 300 pounds of post-1989 ODCs that will be used in the manufacture of rigid foam insulation is equal to the tentative tax amount because those ODCs were not previously subject to tax.

*Example 5.* (a) On January 1, 1994, D holds for sale 300 pounds of CFC-113 (an ODC not described in paragraph (d)(2) or (d)(3) of this section) and 25 pounds of Halon-1301 (an ODC described in paragraph (d)(3) of this section). D is liable for the floor stocks tax imposed on January 1, 1994, because 25 pounds of Halon-1301 exceeds the de minimis amount specified in paragraph (e)(4)(iii) of this section. The 300 pounds of CFC-113 is less than the amount specified in paragraph (e)(4)(i) of this section. Nevertheless, tax is imposed on both the 25 pounds of Halon-1301 and the 300 pounds of CFC-113.

(b) The amount of the floor stocks tax is determined separately for the 300 pounds of CFC-113 and the 25 pounds of Halon-1301 and is equal to the difference between the tentative tax amount and the amount of tax previously imposed on those ODCS. For Halon-1301, for example, the tax is determined as follows. The tentative tax amount is $1,087.50 ($4.35 (the base tax amount in 1994) x 10 (the ozone-depletion factor for Halon-1301) x 25 (the number of pounds held)). The tax previously imposed on the Halon-1301 is $6.28 ($3.35 (the base tax amount in 1993) x 10 (the ozone-depletion factor for Halon-1301) x 0.75 percent (the applicable percentage determined under section 4682(g)(2)(A)) x 25 (the number of pounds held)). Thus, the floor stocks tax imposed on the 25 pounds of Halon-1301 in 1994 is $1,081.22, the difference between $1,087.50 (the tentative tax amount) and $6.28 (the tax previously imposed).

(f) *Inventory.*—(1) *In general.*—If, on the date on which the floor stocks tax is imposed, a person holds ODCs for sale or for use in further manufacture and the ODCs were not manufactured or imported by such person, the following rules apply:

(i) The person shall prepare an inventory of all such ODCs that the person holds on the date on which the tax is imposed.

(ii) The inventory shall be taken as of the first moment of the date on which the tax is imposed, but work-back or work-forward inventories will be acceptable if supported by adequate commercial records of receipt, use, and disposition of ODCs held for sale or for use in further manufacture.

(iii) The person must maintain records of the inventory and make such records available for inspection and copying by internal revenue agents and officers. Records of the inventory are not to be filed with the Internal Revenue Service.

(2) *Circumstances in which an inventory is not required.*—The inventory requirement of paragraph (f)(1) of this section does not apply to any person holding, on a date on which floor stocks tax is imposed, only ODCs that are not subject to tax by reason of a statutory exemption (*e.g.,* use as a feedstock) or regulatory exclusion other than the *de minimis* exception provided by paragraph (e) of this section (*e.g.,* mixtures). In addition, any person that holds ODCs subject to the floor stocks tax and also holds ODCs that are nontaxable under

the provisions of paragraph (b)(2) of this section, is not required to inventory the nontaxable ODCs. However, any person that holds any ODCs that either are subject to the floor stocks tax or would be subject to the floor stocks tax but for the *de minimis* exception must inventory those ODCs.

(3) *Examples.*—The rules of this paragraph (f) may be illustrated by the following examples:

*Example 1.* On January 1, 1990, A holds for sale 300 pounds of CFC-12 (a post-1989 ODC not described in paragraph (d)(2) and (d)(3) of this section) and 500 pounds of R-500 (a mixture). As required by paragraph (f)(1) of this section, A must prepare an inventory of the CFC-12 A holds for sale on that date even though, under paragraph (e)(1) of this section, the 300 pounds of CFC-12 is not taken into account because it is *de minimis*. However, as provided in paragraph (f)(2) of this section, A is not required to inventory the R-500 because, under paragraph (b)(2) of this section, mixtures are not subject to the floor stocks tax.

*Example 2.* On January 1, 1991, B holds for sale 1,000 pounds of CFC-12 (a post-1989 ODC not described in paragraph (d)(2) or (d)(3) of this section). As provided under paragraph (f)(2) of this section, B is not required to prepare an inventory because CFC-12 is not subject to the floor stocks tax in 1991.

(g) *Time for paying tax.*—The floor stocks tax imposed under section 4682(h) shall be paid without assessment or notice. In the case of the floor stocks tax imposed on January 1, 1990, the tax shall be paid by April 1, 1990. In the case of floor stocks taxes imposed after January 1, 1990, the tax shall be paid by June 30 of the year in which the tax is imposed. [Reg. §52.4682-4.]

☐ [T.D. 8370, 11-1-91. Amended by T.D. 8622, 10-10-95.]

**[Reg. §52.4682-5]**

**§52.4682-5. Exports.**—(a) *Overview.*—This section provides rules relating to the tax imposed under section 4681 on ozone-depleting chemicals (ODCs) that are exported. In general, tax is not imposed on ODCs that a manufacturer or importer sells for export, or for resale by the purchaser to a second purchaser for export, if the procedural requirements set forth in paragraph (d) of this section are met. The tax benefit of this exemption is limited, however, to the manufacturer's or importer's exemption amount. Thus, if the tax that would otherwise be imposed under section 4681 on ODCs that a manufacturer or importer sells for export exceeds this exemption amount, a tax equal to the excess is imposed on the ODCS. The exemption amount, which is determined separately for post-1989 ODCs and post-1990 ODCs, is calculated for each calendar year in accordance with the rules of paragraph (c) of this section. This section also provides rules under which a tax imposed under section 4681 on exported ODCs may be credited or refunded, subject to the same limit on tax benefits, if the procedural requirements set forth in paragraph (f) of this section are met. See §52.4681-1(c) for definitions relating to the tax on ODCs.

(b) *Exemption or partial exemption from tax.*—(1) *In general.*—Except as provided in paragraph (b)(2) of this section, no tax is imposed on an ODC if the manufacturer or importer of the ODC sells the ODC in a qualifying sale for export (within the meaning of paragraph (d)(1) of this section).

(2) *Tax imposed if exemption amount exceeded.*—(i) *Post-1989 ODCs.*—The tax imposed on post-1989 ODCs that a manufacturer or importer sells in qualifying sales for export during a calendar year is equal to the excess (if any) of—

(A) The tax that would be imposed on the ODCs but for section 4682(d)(3) and this section; over

(B) The post-1989 ODC exemption amount for the calendar year determined under paragraph (c)(1) of this section.

(ii) *Post-1990 ODCs.*—The tax imposed on post-1990 ODCs that a manufacturer or importer sells in qualifying sales for export during a calendar year is equal to the excess (if any) of—

(A) The tax that would be imposed on the ODCs but for section 4682(d)(3) and this section; over

(B) The post-1990 ODC exemption amount for the calendar year determined under paragraph (c)(2) of this section.

(iii) *Allocation of tax.*—(A) *Post-1989 ODCs.*—The tax (if any) determined under paragraph (b)(2)(i) of this section may be allocated among the post-1989 ODCs on which it is imposed in any manner, provided that the amount allocated to any post-1989 ODC does not exceed the tax that would be imposed on such ODC but for section 4682(d)(3) and this section.

(B) *Post-1990 ODCs.*—The tax (if any) determined under paragraph (b)(2)(ii) of this section may be allocated among the post-1990 ODCs on which it is imposed in any manner, provided that, the amount allocated to any post-1990 ODC does not exceed the tax that would be imposed on such ODC but for section 4682(d)(3) and this section.

(c) *Exemption amount.*—(1) *Post-1989 ODC exemption amount.*—A manufacturer's or importer's post-1989 ODC exemption amount for a calendar year is the sum of the following amounts:

(i) The 1986 export percentage of the aggregate tax that would (but for section 4682(d), section 4682(g), and this section) be imposed under section 4681 on the maximum quantity, determined without regard to additional production allowances, of post-1989 ODCs that the person is permitted to manufacture during the calendar year under rules prescribed by the Environmental Protection Agency (40 CFR part 82).

(ii) The aggregate tax that would (but for section 4682(d), section 4682(g), and this section) be imposed under section 4681 on post-1989 ODCs that the person manufactures during the calendar year under any additional production allowance granted by the Environmental Protection Agency.

(iii) The aggregate tax that would (but for section 4682(d), section 4682(g), and this section) be imposed under section 4681 on post-1989 ODCs imported by the person during the calendar year.

(2) *Post-1990 ODC exemption amount.*—A manufacturer's or importer's post-1990 ODC exemption amount for a calendar year is the sum of the following amounts:

(i) The 1989 export percentage of the aggregate tax that would (but for section 4682(d), section 4682(g), and this section) be imposed under section 4681 on the maximum quantity, determined without regard to additional production allowances, of post-1990 ODCs the person is permitted to manufacture during the calendar year under rules prescribed by the Environmental Protection Agency.

(ii) The aggregate tax that would (but for section 4682(d), section 4682(g), and this section) be imposed under section 4681 on post-1990 ODCs that the person manufactures during the calendar year under any additional production allowance granted by the Environmental Protection Agency.

(iii) The aggregate tax that would (but for section 4682(d), section 4682(g), and this section) be imposed under section 4681 on post-1990 ODCs imported by the person during the calendar year.

(3) *Definitions.*—(i) *1986 export percentage.*—See section 4682(d)(3)(B)(ii) for the meaning of the term *1986 export percentage*.

(ii) *1989 export percentage.*—See section 4682(d)(3)(C) for the meaning of the term *1989 export percentage*.

(d) *Procedural requirements relating to tax-free sales for export.*—(1) *Qualifying sales.*—(i) *In general.*—A sale of ODCs is a qualifying sale for export if—

(A) The seller is the manufacturer or importer of the ODCs and the purchaser is a purchaser for export or for resale to a second purchaser for export;

(B) At the time of the sale, the seller and the purchaser are registered with the Internal Revenue Service; and

(C) At the time of the sale, the seller—

(1) Has an unexpired certificate in substantially the form set forth in paragraph (d)(3)(ii) of this section from the purchaser; and

(2) Relies on the certificate in good faith.

(ii) *Qualifying resale.*—A sale of ODCs is a qualifying resale for export if—

(A) The seller acquired the ODCs in a qualifying sale for export and the purchaser is a second purchaser for export;

(B) At the time of the sale, the seller and the purchaser are registered with the Internal Revenue Service; and

(C) At the time of the sale, the seller—

(1) Has an unexpired certificate in substantially the form set forth in paragraph (d)(3)(ii)(A) of this section from the purchaser of the ODCs; and

(2) Relies on the certificate in good faith.

(iii) *Special rule relating to sales made before July 1, 1993.*—If a sale for export made before July 1, 1993, satisfies all the requirements of paragraph (d)(1)(i) or (ii) of this section other than those relating to registration, the sale will be treated as a qualifying sale (or resale) for export. Thus, a sale made before July 1, 1993, may be a qualifying sale (or resale) even if the parties to the sale are not registered and the required certificate does not contain statements regarding registration.

(iv) *Registration.*—Application for registration is made on Form 637 (or any other form designated for the same use by the Commissioner) according to the instructions applicable to the form. A person is registered only if the district director has issued that person a letter of registration and it has not been revoked or suspended. The effective date of the registration must be no earlier than the date on which the district director signs the letter of registration. Each business unit that has, or is required to have, a separate employer identification number is treated as a separate person.

(2) *Good faith reliance.*—The requirements of paragraph (d)(1) of this section are not satisfied with respect to a sale of ODCs and the sale is not a qualifying sale (or resale) if, at the time of the sale—

(i) The seller has reason to believe that the ODCs are not purchased for export; or

(ii) The Internal Revenue Service has notified the seller that the purchaser's registration has been revoked or suspended.

(3) *Certificate.*—(i) *In general.*—The certificate required under paragraph (d)(1) of this section consists of a statement executed and signed under penalties of perjury by a person with authority to bind the purchaser, in substantially the same form as model certificates provided in paragraph (d)(1)(3)(ii) of this section, and containing all information necessary to complete such model certificate. A new certificate must be given if any information in the current certificate changes. The certificate may be included as part of any business records normally used to document a sale. The certificate expires on the earliest of the following dates—

(A) The date one year after the effective date of the certificate;

(B) The date the purchaser provides a new certificate to the seller; or

(C) The date the seller is notified by the Internal Revenue Service or the purchaser that the purchaser's registration has been revoked or suspended.

(ii) *Model certificates.*—(A) *ODCs sold for export by the purchaser.*—If the purchaser will export the ODCS, the certificate must be in substantially the following form:

CERTIFICATE OF PURCHASER OF CHEMICALS
FOR EXPORT BY THE PURCHASER

(To support tax-free sales under
section 4682(d)(3) of the Internal Revenue Code.)

Effective Date _____

Expiration Date _____

(not more than one year after effective date)

The undersigned purchaser (Purchaser) certifies the following under penalties of perjury:

Purchaser is registered with the Internal Revenue Service as a purchaser of ozone-depleting chemicals for export under registration number _____

Purchaser's registration has not been suspended or revoked by the Internal Revenue Service.

The following percentage of ozone-depleting chemicals purchased from:

_____

(Name of seller)

_____

(Address of seller)

_____

(Taxpayer identifying number of seller)

are purchased for export by Purchaser.

| Product | Percentage |
|---------|-----------|
| CFC-11 | _____ |
| CFC-12 | _____ |
| CFC-113 | _____ |
| CFC-114 | _____ |

Reg. §52.4682-5(d)(3)(ii)(A)

CFC-115 _____
Halon-1211 _____
Halon-1301 _____
Halon-2402 _____
Carbon tetrachloride _____
Methyl chloroform _____

Other (specify) _____ _____

This certificate applies to (check and complete as applicable):
_____ All shipments to Purchaser at the following location(s):

_____
_____

_____ All shipments to Purchaser under the following Purchaser account number(s):

_____
_____

_____ All shipments to Purchaser under the following purchase order(s):

_____
_____

_____ One or more shipments to Purchaser identified as follows:

_____
_____
_____

Purchaser understands that Purchaser will be liable for tax imposed under section 4681 if Purchaser does not export the ODCs to which this certificate applies.

Purchaser understands that any use of the ODCs to which this certificate applies other than for export may result in the revocation of Purchaser's registration.

Purchaser will retain the business records needed to document the export of the ozone-depleting chemicals to which this certificate applies and will make such records available for inspection by Government officers.

Purchaser has not been notified by the Internal Revenue Service that its registration has been revoked or suspended.

Purchaser understands that the fraudulent use of this certificate may subject Purchaser and all parties making such fraudulent use of this certificate to a fine or imprisonment, or both, together with the costs of prosecution.

_____
Name of Purchaser

_____
Address of Purchaser

_____
Taxpayer Identifying Number of Purchaser

_____
Title of person signing

_____
Printed or typed name of person signing

_____
Signature

(B) *ODCs sold by the purchaser for resale for export by the second purchaser.*—If the purchaser will resell the ODCs to a second purchaser for export by the second purchaser, the certificate must be in substantially the following form:

CERTIFICATE OF PURCHASER OF CHEMICALS FOR RESALE
FOR EXPORT BY THE SECOND PURCHASER

(To support tax-free sales under
section 4682(d)(3) of the Internal Revenue Code.)

Effective Date _____
Expiration Date _____
(not more than one year after effective date)

The undersigned purchaser (Purchaser) certifies the following under penalties of perjury:
Purchaser is registered with the Internal Revenue Service as a purchaser of ozone-depleting chemicals for export under registration number _____. Purchaser's registration has not been suspended or revoked by the Internal Revenue Service.

The following percentage of ozone-depleting chemicals purchased from:

_____
(Name of seller)

_____
(Address of seller)

_____
(Taxpayer identifying number of seller)
will be resold by Purchaser to persons (Second Purchasers) that certify to Purchaser that they are (1) registered with the Internal Revenue Service as purchasers of ozone-depleting chemicals for export and (2) purchasing the ozone-depleting chemicals for export.

| Product | Percentage |
|---|---|
| CFC-11 | _____ |
| CFC-12 | _____ |
| CFC-113 | _____ |
| CFC-114 | _____ |
| CFC-115 | _____ |
| Halon-1211 | _____ |
| Halon-1301 | _____ |
| Halon-2402 | _____ |
| Carbon tetrachloride | _____ |
| Methyl chloroform | _____ |
| Other (specify) _____ | _____ |

**Reg. §52.4682-5(d)(3)(ii)(B)**

This certificate applies to (check and complete as applicable):

_____ All shipments to Purchaser at the following location(s):

_____
_____
_____

_____ All shipments to Purchaser under the following Purchaser account number(s):

_____
_____
_____

_____ All shipments to Purchaser under the following purchase order(s):

_____
_____
_____

_____ One or more shipments to Purchaser identified as follows:

_____
_____
_____

Purchaser understands that Purchaser will be liable for tax imposed under section 4681 if Purchaser does not resell the ODCs to which this certificate applies to a Second Purchaser for export or export those ODCs.

Purchaser understands that any use of the ODCs to which this certificate applies other than for resale to Second Purchasers for export may result in the revocation of Purchaser's registration.

Purchaser will retain the business records needed to document the sales to Second Purchasers for export covered by this certificate and will make such records available for inspection by Government officers. Purchaser also will retain and make available for inspection by Government officers the certificates of its Second Purchasers.

Purchaser has not been notified by the Internal Revenue Service that its registration has been revoked or suspended. In addition, the Internal Revenue Service has not notified Purchaser of the revocation or suspension of the registration of any Second Purchaser who will purchase ozone-depleting chemicals to which this certificate applies.

Purchaser understands that the fraudulent use of this certificate may subject Purchaser and all parties making such fraudulent use of this certificate to a fine or imprisonment, or both, together with the costs of prosecution.

_____
Name of Purchaser

_____
Address of Purchaser

_____
Taxpayer Identifying Number of Purchaser

_____
Title of person signing

_____
Printed or typed name of person signing

_____
Signature

(4) *Documentation of export.*—(i) *After December 31, 1992.*—After December 31, 1992, to document the exportation of any ODCs, a person must have the evidence required by the Environmental Protection Agency as proof that the ODCs were exported.

(ii) *Before January 1, 1993.*—Before January 1, 1993, to document the exportation of any ODCs, a person must have evidence substantially similar to that required by the Environmental Protection Agency as proof that the ODCs were exported.

(e) *Purchaser liable for tax.*—(1) *Purchaser in qualifying sale.*—The purchaser of ODCs in a qualifying sale for export is treated as the manufacturer of the ODC and is liable for any tax imposed under section 4681 (determined without regard to exemptions for qualifying sales under this section or §52.4682-1) when it sells or uses the ODCs if that purchaser does not—

(i) Export the ODCs and document the exportation of the ODCs in accordance with paragraph (d)(4) of this section; or

(ii) Sell the ODCs in a qualifying resale for export.

(2) *Purchaser in qualifying resale.*—The purchaser of ODCs in a qualifying resale for export is treated as the manufacturer of the ODC and is liable for any tax imposed under section 4681 (determined without regard to exemptions for qualifying sales under this section or §52.4682-1) when it sells or uses the ODCs if that purchaser does not export the ODCs and document the exportation of the ODCs in accordance with paragraph (d)(4) of this section.

(f) *Credit or refund.*—(1) *In general.*—Except as provided in paragraph (f)(2) of this section, a manufacturer or importer that meets the conditions of paragraph (f)(3) of this section is allowed a credit or refund (without interest) of the tax it paid to the government under section 4681 on ODCs that are exported. Persons other than manufacturers and importers of ODCs cannot file claims for credit or refund of tax imposed under section 4681 on ODCs that are exported.

(2) *Limitation.*—The amount of credits or refunds of tax under this paragraph (f) is limited—

(i) In the case of tax paid on post-1989 ODCs sold during a calendar year, to the amount (if any) by which the post-1989 exemption amount for the year exceeds the tax benefit provided to such post-1989 ODCs under paragraph (b) of this section; and

(ii) In the case of tax paid on post-1990 ODCs sold during a calendar year, to the amount (if any) by which the post-1990 exemption amount for the year exceeds the tax benefit provided to such post-1990 ODCs under paragraph (b) of this section.

(3) *Conditions to allowance of credit or refund.*—The conditions of this paragraph (f)(3) are met if the manufacturer or importer—

(i) Documents the exportation of the ODCs in accordance with paragraph (d)(4) of this section; and

(ii) Establishes that it has—

(A) Repaid or agreed to repay the amount of the tax to the person that exported the ODC; or

(B) Obtained the written consent of the exporter to the allowance of the credit or the making of the refund.

(4) *Procedural rules.*—See section 6402 and the regulations under that section for procedural rules relating to filing a claim for credit or refund of tax.

(g) *Examples.*—The following examples illustrate the provisions of this section. In each example, the sales are qualifying sales for export (within the meaning of paragraph (d)(1) of this section), all registration, certification, and documentation requirements of this section are met, and the ODCs sold for export are exported:

*Example 1.* (i) *Facts.* D, a corporation, manufactures CFC-11, a post-1989 ODC, and does not manufacture or import any other ODCs. In 1993, D manufactures 100,000 pounds of CFC-11, the maximum quantity D is allowed to manufacture in 1993 under EPA regulations. D has no additional production allowance from EPA for 1993. In 1993, the tax on CFC-11 is $3.35 per pound. D's 1986 export percentage for post-1989 ODCs is 50%. In 1993, D sells 80,000 pounds of CFC-11 in qualifying sales for export. The remainder of D's production is not exported.

(ii) *Components of limit on tax benefit.* Under paragraph (c)(1) of this section, D's exemption amount for 1993 is equal to the sum of—

(A) D's 1986 export percentage multiplied by the aggregate tax that would (but for section 4682(d), section 4682(g), and §52.4682-5) be imposed under section 4681 on the maximum quantity of post-1989 ODCs D is permitted to manufacture during 1993;

(B) The aggregate tax that would (but for section 4682(d), section 4682(g), and §52.4682-5) be imposed under section 4681 on post-1989

Reg. §52.4682-5(g)

ODCs that D manufactures during 1993 under an additional production allowance; and

(C) The aggregate tax that would (but for section 4682(d), section 4682(g), and §52.4682-5) be imposed under section 4681 on post-1989 ODCs imported by D during 1993.

(iii) *Limit on tax benefit*. The amounts described in paragraphs (ii)(B) and (C) of this *Example 1* are equal to zero. Thus, D's 1993 exemption amount is $167,500 (50% of $335,000 (the tax that would otherwise be imposed on 100,000 pounds of CFC-11 in 1993)).

(iv) *Application of limit on tax benefit*. Under paragraph (b)(2) of this section, the tax imposed on the CFC-11 D sells for export is equal to the excess of the tax that would have been imposed on those ODCs but for section 4682(d) and §52.4682-5, over D's 1993 exemption amount. But for §52.4682-5, $268,000 ($3.35 × 80,000) of tax would have been imposed on the CFC-11 sold for export. Thus, $100,500 ($268,000 – $167,500) of tax is imposed on the CFC-11 sold for export.

*Example 2*. (i) *Facts*. E, a corporation, manufactures CFC-11, a post-1989 ODC, and does not manufacture or import any other ODCs. In 1993, E manufactures 100,000 pounds of CFC-11, the maximum quantity E is allowed to manufacture in 1993 under EPA regulations. E has no additional production allowance from EPA for 1993. In 1993, the tax on CFC-11 is $3.35 per pound. E's 1986 export percentage for post-1989 ODCs *is* 50%. In 1993, E sells 45,000 pounds of CFC-11 tax free in qualifying sales for export and pays tax under section 4681 on an additional 35,000 pounds of exported CFC-11. The remainder of E's production is not exported.

(ii) *Limit on tax benefit*. E's 1993 exemption amount is $167,500, (50% of $335,000 (the tax that would otherwise be imposed on 100,000 pounds of CFC-11 in 1993)). The credit or refund allowed to E under paragraph (f) of this section is limited under paragraph (f)(2) of this section to the amount by which E's 1993 exemption amount exceeds E's 1993 tax benefit under paragraph (b) of this section.

(iii) *Application of limit on tax benefit*. Because E sold 45,000 pounds of CFC-11 tax free in qualifying sales for export in 1993, E's 1993 tax

benefit under paragraph (b) of this section is $150,750 ($3.35 × 45,000). Thus, the credit or refund allowed to E under paragraph (f) of this section is limited to $16,750 ($167,500 – $150,750).

*Example 3*. (i) *Facts*. F, a corporation, manufactures CFC-11, a post-1989 ODC, and does not manufacture any other ODCs. F also imports CFC-11. In 1993, F manufactures 60,000 pounds of CFC-11 (100,000 pounds is the maximum quantity F is allowed to manufacture in 1993 under EPA regulations) and imports 40,000 pounds. F has no additional production allowance from EPA for 1993. In 1993, the tax on CFC-11 is $3.35 per pound. F's 1986 export percentage for post-1989 ODCs is 50%. In 1993, F sells 45,000 pounds of CFC-11 tax free in qualifying sales for export and pays tax under section 4681 on an additional 35,000 pounds of exported CFC-11. The remainder of F's production is not exported.

(ii) *Limit on tax benefit*. F's 1993 exemption amount is $301,500, ($167,500 (50% of $335,000 (the tax that would otherwise be imposed on 100,000 pounds of CFC-11 in 1993) plus $134,000 (the tax that would otherwise be imposed on the 40,000 pounds imported)). The credit or refund allowed to F under paragraph (f) of this section is limited under paragraph (f)(2) of this section to the amount by which F's 1993 exemption amount exceeds F's 1993 tax benefit under paragraph (b) of this section.

(iii) *Application of limit on tax benefit*. Because F sold 45,000 pounds of CFC-11 tax free in qualifying sales for export in 1993, F's 1993 tax benefit under paragraph (b) of this section is $150,750 ($3.35 × 45,000). Thus, the credit or refund allowed to F under paragraph (f) of this section is limited to $150,750 ($301,500 – $150,750). The limitation does not affect F's credit or refund because the tax F paid on exported ODCs is only $117,250 ($3.35 × 35,000).

(h) *Effective date*.—This section is effective January 1, 1993. [Reg. §52.4682-5.]

☐ [*T.D.* 8622, 10-10-95.]

---

# Registration-Required Obligations

See p. 20,601 for regulations not amended to reflect law changes

### [Reg. §46.4701-1]

**§46.4701-1. Tax on issuer of registration-required obligation not in registered form.**—(a) *In general*.—Section 4701 imposes a tax (determined under paragraph (c) of this section) on any person (referred to as the issuer) who issues an obligation that—

(1) is a registration-required obligation, and

(2) is not issued in registered form.

(b) *Definitions*.—(1) *Person*.—The term "person" includes all governmental entities.

(2) *Obligations*.—The term "obligation" includes bonds, debentures, notes, certificates and other evidences of indebtedness regardless of how denominated.

(3) *Registration-required obligation*.—The term "registration-required obligation" has the same meaning as when used in section 163(f) (and the regulations thereunder) which relates to the denial of a deduction for interest on certain obligations not in registered form. However, the term "registration-required obligation" does not include any obligation which would otherwise be exempt from Federal income tax under section 103(a) or any other provision of law.

(4) *Registered form*.—The term "registered form" has the same meaning as when used in section 103(j) (and the regulations thereunder) which relates to obligations which must be in registered form to be tax-exempt.

(5) *Issuer*.—Except as provided in §1.163-5T(d) (relating to pass-through certificates) and §1.163-5T(e) (relating to REMICs), the "issuer" is the person whose interest deduction would be disallowed solely by reason of section 163(f)(1).

(6) *Date of issuance*.—(i) For obligations intended to be offered to the public, the term "date of issuance" means the date the obligation is first sold to the public at the issue price.

(ii) For an obligation which is privately placed, the term "date of issuance" is the date the obligation is first sold by the issuer.

(7) *Issue price*.—See section 1273(b) and the regulations thereunder for the definition of "issue price".

(c) *Rate and computation of tax*.—The tax under section 4701(a) is imposed in an amount equal to the product of—

(1) 1 percent of the principal amount of the obligation, multiplied by

(2) the number of calendar years (or portions thereof) during the period beginning on the date of issuance of the obligation and ending on the date of maturity.

For purposes of this paragraph, the term "principal amount" for a discounted obligation is the issue price, and for all other obligations, including obligations sold at a premium, the term "principal amount" is the stated redemption price at maturity.

(d) *Payment of tax*.—Every person who incurs liability for the tax imposed by section 4701 is required to file a return in accordance with section 6011 and §46.6011(a)-1 relating to the general requirement of a return, statement or list.

(e) *Effective date*.—The provisions of this section shall apply to obligations issued after December 31, 1982, unless issued on the exercise of a warrant or the conversion of a convertible obligation if the warrant or obligation was offered or sold outside the United States without registration under the Securities Act of 1933 and was issued before August 10, 1982. See section 310(d)(3) of the Tax Equity and Fiscal Responsibility Act of 1982. [Reg. §46.4701-1.]

☐ [*T.D.* 8102, 9-19-86. *Amended by T.D.* 8300, 5-9-90.]

---

# General Provisions Relating to Occupational Taxes

See p. 20,601 for regulations not amended to reflect law changes

### [Reg. §44.4901-1]

**§44.4901-1. Payment of special tax.**—(a) *Condition precedent to carrying on business*.—No persons shall engage in the business of accepting wagers subject to the tax imposed by section 4401 until he has filed a return on Form 11-C and paid the special tax imposed by

section 4411. Likewise, no person shall engage in receiving wagers for or on behalf of any person engaged in the business of accepting wagers until he has filed a return on Form 11-C and paid the special tax imposed by section 4411. For provisions relating to the tax imposed by section 4401 and the special tax imposed by section 4411, see Subparts B and C of this part, respectively.

(b) *Computation of special tax.*—(1) Section 4411 imposes a special tax of $50 per year which is required to be paid by each person who is liable for the tax imposed by section 4401 (tax on wagers) or who is engaged in receiving wagers for or on behalf of any person who is liable for the tax imposed by section 4401. A person engaged both in accepting wagers on his own account and in receiving wagers or or on behalf of some other person is required to purchase but one special tax stamp.

(2) The tax year begins July 1 and ends June 30 of the following calendar year. Persons commencing business between August 1 and June 30 (both dates inclusive) shall pay a proportionate part of the annual tax. "Commencing business" means the initial acceptance by a person of a wager subject to the tax imposed by section 4401 or the initial receiving of a taxable wager by an agent or employee for or on behalf of some other person. Persons in business for only a portion of a month are liable for tax for the full month, i.e., a person first becoming subject to the special tax on, for example, the 20th day of a month, is liable for tax for the entire month.

(c) *Tax payment evidenced by special tax stamp.*—(1) Upon receipt of a return on Form 11-C, together with remittance of the full amount of tax due, the district director will issue a special tax stamp as evidence of payment of the special tax.

(2) District directors will distinctly write or print on the stamp before it is delivered or mailed to the taxpayer the following information: (i) The taxpayer's registered name, and (ii) the business or office address of the taxpayer if he has one; if not, the residence address. Special tax stamps will be transmitted by ordinary mail, unless it is requested that they be transmitted by registered mail in which case additional cost to cover registry fee shall be remitted with the return.

(3) District directors and their collection officers are forbidden to issue receipts in lieu of stamps representing the payment of special taxes.

(d) *Cross references.*—For provisions relating to registration and information required to be reported on Form 11-C, see §44.4412-1. For other provisions relating to Form 11-C, see §§44.6011(a)-1 (relating to returns), 44.6071-1 (time for filing returns and other documents), and 44.6091-1 (place for filing returns or other documents). [Reg. §44.4901-1.]

☐ [*T.D.* 6530, 1-19-61. *Amended by T.D.* 6774, 12-1-64 *and T.D.* 7279, 6-21-73.]

### [Reg. §44.4902-1]

**§44.4902-1. Partnership liability.**—Any number of persons doing business in copartnership shall be required to pay but one special tax. The district director may issue a special tax stamp to a copartnership in a firm or trade name, provided the names and addresses of all members of the partnership are disclosed on Form 11-C. [Reg. §44.4902-1.]

☐ [*T.D.* 6530, 1-19-61.]

### [Reg. §44.4905-1]

**§44.4905-1. Change of ownership.**—(a) *Changes through death.*—Whenever any person who has paid the special tax imposed by section 4411 dies, the surviving spouse or child, or executor or administrator, or other legal representative, may carry on such business for the remainder of the term for which such special tax has been paid without any additional payment, subject to the conditions hereinafter stated. If the surviving spouse or child, or executor or administrator, or other legal representative of the deceased taxpayer continues the business, such person shall within 30 days after the date of the death of the taxpayer execute a return on Form 11-C. Such return shall show the name of the deceased taxpayer, together with all other data required to be reported on Form 11-C (see §44.4412-1), and the stamp issued to such taxpayer shall be submitted with the return for proper notation by the district director.

(b) *Changes from other causes.*—A receiver or trustee in bankruptcy may continue the business under the stamp issued to the taxpayer at the place and for the period for which the special tax was paid. An assignee for the benefit of creditors may continue business under his assignor's special tax stamp without incurring additional special tax liability. In such cases the change shall be registered with the district director in a manner similar to that required by paragraph (a) of this section.

(c) *Changes in firm.*—When one or more members of a firm partnership withdraw, the business may be continued by the remaining partner or partners under the same special tax stamp for the remainder of the period for which the stamp was issued to the old firm. The change shall, however, be registered in the same manner as required in paragraph (a) of this section. If new partners are taken into a firm

the new firm so constituted may not carry on business under the special tax stamp of the old firm. The new firm shall make a return on Form 11-C and pay the special tax imposed by section 4411 reckoned from the first day of the month in which it began business, even though the name of such firm be the same as that of the old. If the members of a partnership, which has paid the special tax, form a corporation to continue the business a new special tax stamp must be obtained in the name of the corporation.

(d) *Change in corporation.*—If a corporation changes its name, no additional tax is due, provided the change in name is registered with the district director in the manner required by paragraph (a) of this section. An increase in the capital stock of a corporation does not create a new special tax liability if the laws of the State under which it is incorporated permit such increase without the formation of a new corporation. A stockholder in a corporation, who after its dissolution continues the business, incurs liability for the special tax imposed by section 4411 unless he already has a special tax stamp obtained in respect of activities conducted as a sole proprietor. [Reg. §44.4905-1.]

☐ [*T.D.* 6530, 1-19-61. *Amended by T.D.* 7279, 6-21-73.]

### [Reg. §44.4905-2]

**§44.4905-2. Change of address.**—(a) *Procedure by taxpayer.*—(1) *After June 30, 1963.*—Whenever, after June 30, 1963, a taxpayer changes his business or residence address to a location other than that specified in his last return on Form 11-C, he shall register the change with the district director from whom the special tax stamp was purchased by filing a new return, Form 11-C, designated "Supplemental Return", setting forth the new address and the date of change. He shall so register the change of address before:

(i) He engages in any wagering activity at the new address, or

(ii) The termination of a 30-day period which begins on the day after the date of such change,

whichever occurs first. The taxpayer's special tax stamp shall accompany the supplemental return for proper notation by the district director. As to liability in case of failure to register a change of address, see §44.4905-3.

(2) *Before July 1, 1963.*—Whenever, before July 1, 1963, a taxpayer changes his business or residence address to a location other than that specified in his last return of Form 11-C, he shall, within 30 days after the date of such change, register the change with the district director from whom the special tax stamp was purchased by filing a new return, Form 11-C, designated "Supplemental Return", setting forth the new address and the date of change. The taxpayer's special tax stamp shall accompany the supplemental return for proper notation by the district director. As to liability in case of failure to register a change of address, see §44.4905-3.

(b) *Procedure by district director; removal within district.*—When registration of a change of address within the same district is made by a taxpayer in the manner specified in paragraph (a) of this section, the district director, if necessary, will enter on his records the new address and the date of change. If the information disclosed on the supplemental return is such as to require a change on the face of the special tax stamp, the district director will make the proper change and return the stamp to the taxpayer.

(c) *Procedure by district director; removal to another district.*—In case of removal of the taxpayer's office or principal place of business (or residence address, if he has no office or principal place of business) to another district, the district director, after noting the transfer on his records, shall transmit the special tax stamp to the district director for the district to which such office or business was removed. The latter will make an entry on his records, as in the case of an original registration in his district, correct the address on the stamp, if necessary, and note also thereon his name, title, date, and district, and then forward the stamp to the taxpayer. [Reg. §44.4905-2.]

☐ [*T.D.* 6530, 1-19-61. *Amended by T.D.* 7279, 6-21-73.]

### [Reg. §44.4905-3]

**§44.4905-3. Liability for failure to register change or removal.**—Any person succeeding to and carrying on a business for which the special tax imposed by section 4411 has been paid, and any taxpayer changing his residence address or his place of business, without registering such change as provided in §§44.4905-1 and 44.4905-2 shall be liable to an additional tax, and to the penalty prescribed in section 6651 for failure to make a return. (For regulations under section 6651, see the Regulations on Procedure and Administration (Part 301 of this chapter).) [Reg. §44.4905-3.]

☐ [*T.D.* 6530, 1-19-61.]

**[Reg. §44.4906-1]**

**§44.4906-1. Cross reference.**—For provisions relating to the applicability of Federal and State laws, see section 4422 and §44.4422-1. [Reg. §44.4906-1.]

☐ [T.D. 6530, 1-19-61.]

# Public Charities

See p. 20,601 for regulations not amended to reflect law changes

**[Reg. §56.4911-0]**

**§56.4911-0. Outline of regulations under section 4911.**—Immediately following is an outline of the regulations under section 4911 of the Internal Revenue Code relating to an excise tax on electing public charities' excess lobbying expenditures.

*§56.4911-0. Outline of regulations under section 4911.*

*§56.4911-1. Tax on excess lobbying expenditures.*
  (a) In general.
  (b) Excess lobbying expenditures.
  (c) Nontaxable amounts.
    (1) Lobbying nontaxable amount.
    (2) Grass roots nontaxable amount.
  (d) Examples.

*§56.4911-2. Lobbying expenditures, direct lobbying communications, and grass roots lobbying communications.*
  (a) Lobbying expenditures.
    (1) In general.
    (2) Overview of §56.4911 and the definitions of "direct lobbying communication" and "grass roots lobbying communication".
  (b) Influencing legislation: direct and grass roots lobbying communications defined.
    (1) Direct lobbying communication.
    (2) Grass roots lobbying communication.
    (3) Exceptions to the definition of influencing legislation.
    (4) Examples.
    (5) Special rule for certain mass media advertisements.
  (c) Exceptions to the definitions of direct lobbying communication and grass roots lobbying communication.
    (1) Nonpartisan analysis, study, or research exception.
    (2) Examinations and discussions of broad social, economic, and similar problems.
    (3) Requests for technical advice.
    (4) Communications pertaining to "self-defense" by the organization.
  (d) Definitions.
    (1) Legislation.
    (2) Action.
    (3) Legislative body.
    (4) Administrative bodies.

*§56.4911-3. Expenditures for direct and/or grass roots lobbying communications.*
  (a) Definition of term "expenditures for".
    (1) In general.
    (2) Allocation of mixed purpose expenditures.
    (3) Allocation of mixed lobbying.
  (b) Examples.
  (c) Certain transfers treated as lobbying expenditures.
    (1) Transfer earmarked for grass roots purposes.
    (2) Transfer earmarked for direct and grass roots lobbying.
    (3) Certain transfers to noncharities that lobby.

*§56.4911-4. Exempt purpose expenditures.*
  (a) Application.
  (b) Included expenditures.
  (c) Excluded expenditures.
  (d) Certain transfers treated as exempt purpose expenditures.
  (e) Transfers not exempt purpose expenditures.
  (f) Definitions.
  (g) Example.

*§56.4911-5. Communications with members.*
  (a) In general.
  (b) Communications (directed only to members) that are not lobbying communications.
  (c) Communications (directed only to members) that are direct lobbying communications.
  (d) Communications (directed only to members) that are grass roots lobbying communications.

  (e) Written communications directed to members and nonmembers.
    (1) In general.
    (2) Direct lobbying directly encouraged.
    (3) Grass roots expenditure if grass roots lobbying directly encouraged.
    (4) No direct encouragement of direct lobbying or of grass roots lobbying.
  (f) Definitions and special rules.
    (1) Member; general rule.
    (2) Member; special rule.
    (3) Member; affiliated group of organizations.
    (4) Member; limited affiliated group of organizations.
    (5) Subscriber.
    (6) Directly encourages.
    (7) Percentages of total distribution.
    (8) Reasonable allocation rule.

*§56.4911-6. Records of lobbying and grass roots expenditures.*
  (a) Records of lobbying expenditures.
  (b) Records of grass roots expenditures.

*§56.4911-7. Affiliated group of organizations.*
  (a) Affiliation between two organizations.
    (1) In general.
    (2) Organizations not described in section 501(c)(3).
    (3) Action on legislative issues.
  (b) Interlocking governing boards.
    (1) In general.
    (2) Majority or quorum.
    (3) Votes required under governing instrument or local law.
    (4) Representatives constituting less than 15% of governing board.
    (5) Representatives.
  (c) Governing instrument.
  (d) Three or more organizations affiliated.
    (1) Two controlled organizations affiliated.
    (2) Chain rule.
  (e) Affiliated group of organizations.
    (1) Defined.
    (2) Multiple membership.
    (3) Taxable year of affiliated group.
    (4) Electing member organization.
    (5) Election of member's year as group's taxable year.
  (f) Examples.

*§56.4911-8. Excess lobbying expenditures of affiliated group.*
  (a) Application.
  (b) Affiliated group treated as one organization.
  (c) Tax imposed on excess lobbying expenditures of affiliated group.
  (d) Liability for tax.
    (1) Electing organizations.
    (2) Tax based on excess lobbying expenditures.
    (3) Tax based on excess grass roots expenditures.
    (4) Tax based on exempt purpose expenditures.
    (5) Taxable year for which liable.
    (6) Organization a member of more than one affiliated group.
  (e) Former member organization.

*§56.4911-9. Application of section 501(h) to affiliated groups of organizations.*
  (a) Scope.
  (b) Determination required.
  (c) Member organizations that are not electing organizations.
  (d) Filing of information relating to affiliated group of organizations.
    (1) Scope.
    (2) In general.
    (3) Additional information required.
    (4) Information required of electing member organization.
  (e) Example.

(f) Cross reference.

*§ 56.4911-10. Members of a limited affiliated group of organizations.*

(a) Scope.

(b) Members of limited affiliated group.

(c) Controlling and controlled organizations.

(d) Expenditures of controlling organization.

(1) Scope.

(2) Expenditures for direct lobbying.

(3) Grass roots expenditures.

(4) Exempt purpose expenditures.

(e) Expenditures of controlled member.

(f) Reports of members of limited affiliated groups.

(1) Controlling member organization's additional information on annual return.

(2) Reports of controlling members to other members.

(3) Reports of controlled member organizations.

(g) National legislative issues.

(h) Examples.

*§ 56.6001-1. Notice or regulations requiring records, statements, and special returns.*

(a) In general.

(b) Cross references.

*§ 56.6011-1. General requirement of return, statement, or list.* [Reg. § 56.4911-0.]

☐ [*T.D. 8308, 8-30-90.*]

### [Reg. § 56.4911-1]

**§ 56.4911-1. Tax on excess lobbying expenditures.**—(a) *In general.*—Section 4911(a) imposes an excise tax of 25 percent on the excess lobbying expenditures (as defined in paragraph (b) of this section) for a taxable year of an organization for which the expenditure test election under section 501(h) is in effect (an "electing public charity"). An electing public charity's annual limit on expenditures for influencing legislation (i.e., the amount of lobbying expenditures on which no tax is due) is the lobbying nontaxable amount or, on expenditures for influencing legislation through grass roots lobbying, the grass roots nontaxable amount (see paragraph (c) of this section). For rules concerning the application of the excise tax imposed by section 4911(a) to the members of an affiliated group of organizations (as defined in § 56.4911-7(e)), see § 56.4911-8.

(b) *Excess lobbying expenditures.*—For any taxable year for which the expenditure test election under section 501(h) is in effect, the amount of an electing public charity's excess lobbying expenditures is the greater of—

(1) The amount by which the organization's lobbying expenditures (within the meaning of § 56.4911-2(a)) exceed the organization's lobbying nontaxable amount, or

(2) The amount by which the organization's grass roots expenditures (within the meaning of § 56.4911-2(a)) exceed the organization's grass roots nontaxable amount.

(c) *Nontaxable amounts.*—(1) *Lobbying nontaxable amount.*—Under section 4911(c)(2), the lobbying nontaxable amount for any taxable year for which the expenditure test election is in effect is the lesser of—

(i) $1,000,000, or

(ii) To the extent of the electing public charity's exempt purpose expenditures (within the meaning of § 56.4911-4) for that year, the sum of 20 percent of the first $500,000 of such expenditures, plus 15 percent of the second $500,000 of such expenditures, plus 10 percent of the third $500,000 of such expenditures, plus 5 percent of the remainder of such expenditures.

(2) *Grass roots nontaxable amount.*—Under section 4911(c)(4), an electing public charity's grass roots nontaxable amount for any taxable year is 25 percent of its lobbying nontaxable amount for that year.

(d) *Examples.*—The provisions of this section are illustrated by the examples in § 1.501(h)-3. [Reg. § 56.4911-1.]

☐ [*T.D. 8308, 8-30-90.*]

### [Reg. § 56.4911-2]

**§ 56.4911-2. Lobbying expenditures, direct lobbying communications, and grass roots lobbying communications.**—(a) *Lobbying expenditures.*—(1) *In general.*—An electing public charity's lobbying expenditures for a year are the sum of its expenditures during that year for direct lobbying communications ("direct lobbying expenditures") plus its expenditures during that year for grass roots lobbying communications ("grass roots expenditures").

(2) *Overview of § 56.4911-2 and the definitions of "direct lobbying communication" and "grass roots lobbying communication".*—Paragraph (b)(1) of this section defines the term "direct lobbying communication." Paragraph (b)(2) of this section provides the general definition of the term "grass roots lobbying communication." (But also see paragraph (b)(5) of this section (special rebuttable presumption regarding certain paid mass media communications) and § 56.4911-5 (special, more lenient definitions for certain communications from an electing public charity to its bona fide members)). Paragraph (b)(3) of this section lists and cross-references various exceptions to the definitions set forth in paragraphs (b)(1) and (2) (the text of the exceptions, along with relevant definitions and examples, is generally set forth in paragraph (c)). Paragraph (b)(4) of this section contains numerous examples illustrating the application of paragraphs (b)(1), (2) and (3). As mentioned above, paragraph (b)(5) of this section sets forth the special rebuttable presumption regarding a limited number of paid mass media communications about highly publicized legislation. Paragraph (d) of this section contains definitions of (and examples illustrating) various terms used in this section.

(b) *Influencing legislation: direct and grass roots lobbying communications defined.*—(1) *Direct lobbying communication.*—(i) *Definition.*—A direct lobbying communication is any attempt to influence any legislation through communication with:

(A) Any member or employee of a legislative body; or

(B) Any government official or employee (other than a member or employee of a legislative body) who may participate in the formulation of the legislation, but only if the principal purpose of the communication is to influence legislation.

(ii) *Required elements.*—A communication with a legislator or government official will be treated as a direct lobbying communication under this § 56.4911-2(b)(1) if, but only if, the communication:

(A) Refers to specific legislation (see paragraph (d)(1) of this section for a definition of the term "specific legislation"); and

(B) Reflects a view on such legislation.

(iii) *Special rule for referenda, ballot initiatives or similar procedures.*—Solely for purposes of this section 4911, where a communication refers to and reflects a view on a measure that is the subject of a referendum, ballot initiative or similar procedure, the general public in the state or locality where the vote will take place constitutes the legislative body, and individual members of the general public are, for purposes of this paragraph (b)(1), legislators. Accordingly, if such a communication is made to one or more members of the general public in that state or locality, the communication is a direct lobbying communication (unless it is nonpartisan analysis, study or research (see paragraph (c)(1) of this section).

(2) *Grass roots lobbying communication.*—(i) *Definition.*—A grass roots lobbying communication is any attempt to influence any legislation through an attempt to affect the opinions of the general public or any segment thereof.

(ii) *Required elements.*—A communication will be treated as a grass roots lobbying communication under this § 56.4911-2(b)(2)(ii) if, but only if, the communication:

(A) Refers to specific legislation (see paragraph (d)(1) of this section for a definition of the term "specific legislation");

(B) Reflects a view on such legislation; and

(C) Encourages the recipient of the communication to take action with respect to such legislation (see paragraph (b)(2)(iii) of this section for the definition of encouraging the recipient to take action).

For special, more lenient rules regarding an organization's communications directed only or primarily to bona fide members of the organization, see § 56.4911-5. For special rules regarding certain paid mass media advertisements about highly publicized legislation, see paragraph (b)(5) of this section. For special rules regarding lobbying on referenda, ballot initiatives and similar procedures, see paragraph (b)(1)(iii) of this section)).

(iii) *Definition of encouraging recipient to take action.*—For purposes of this section, encouraging a recipient to take action with respect to legislation means that the communication:

(A) States that the recipient should contact a legislator or an employee of a legislative body, or should contact any other government official or employee who may participate in the formulation of legislation (but only if the principal purpose of urging contact with the government official or employee is to influence legislation);

(B) States the address, telephone number, or similar information of a legislator or an employee of a legislative body;

(C) Provides a petition, tear-off postcard or similar material for the recipient to communicate with a legislator or an employee of a legislative body, or with any other government official or employee who may participate in the formulation of legislation (but only if the principal purpose of so facilitating contact with the government official or employee is to influence legislation); or

(D) Specifically identifies one or more legislators who will vote on the legislation as: opposing the communication's view with respect to the legislation; being undecided with respect to the legislation; being the recipient's representative in the legislature; or being a member of the legislative committee or subcommittee that will consider the legislation. Encouraging the recipient to take action under this paragraph (b)(2)(iii)(D) does not include naming the main sponsor(s) of the legislation for purposes of identifying the legislation.

(iv) *Definition of directly encouraging recipient to take action.*—Communications described in one or more of paragraphs (b)(2)(iii)(A) through (C) of this section not only "encourage," but also "directly encourage" the recipient to take action with respect to legislation. Communications described in paragraph (b)(2)(iii)(D) of this section, however, do not directly encourage the recipient to take action with respect to legislation. Thus, a communication would encourage the recipient to take action with respect to legislation, but not *directly* encourage such action, if the communication does no more than identify one or more legislators who will vote on the legislation as: opposing the communication's view with respect to the legislation; being undecided with respect to the legislation; being the recipient's representative in the legislature; or being a member of the legislative committee or subcommittee that will consider the legislation. Communications that encourage the recipient to take action with respect to legislation but that do not *directly* encourage the recipient to take action with respect to legislation may be within the exception for nonpartisan analysis, study or research (see paragraph (c)(1) of this section) and thus not be grass roots lobbying communications.

(v) *Subsequent lobbying use of nonlobbying communications or research materials.*—(A) *Limited effect of application.*—Even though certain communications or research materials are initially not grass roots lobbying communications under the general definition set forth in paragraph (b)(2)(ii) of this section, subsequent use of the communications or research materials for grass roots lobbying may cause them to be treated as grass roots lobbying communications. This paragraph (b)(2)(v) does not cause any communications or research materials to be considered direct lobbying communications.

(B) *Limited scope of application.*—Under this paragraph (b)(2)(v), only "*advocacy* communications or research materials" are potentially treated as grass roots lobbying communications. Communications or research materials that are not "*advocacy* communications or research materials" are not treated as grass roots lobbying communications under this paragraph (b)(2)(v). "Advocacy communications or research materials" are any communications or materials that both refer to and reflect a view on specific legislation but that do not, in their initial format, contain a direct encouragement for recipients to take action with respect to legislation.

(C) *Subsequent use in lobbying.*—Where advocacy communications or research materials are subsequently accompanied by a direct encouragement for recipients to take action with respect to legislation, the advocacy communications or research materials themselves are treated as grass roots lobbying communications unless the organization's primary purpose in undertaking or preparing the advocacy communications or research materials was not for use in lobbying. In such a case, all expenses of preparing and distributing the advocacy communications or research materials will be treated as grass roots expenditures.

(D) *Time limit on application of subsequent use rule.*—The characterization of expenditures as grass roots lobbying expenditures under paragraph (b)(2)(v)(C) shall apply only to expenditures paid less than six months before the first use of the advocacy communications or research materials with a direct encouragement to action.

(E) *Safe harbor in determining "Primary Purpose".*—The primary purpose of the organization in undertaking or preparing advocacy communications or research materials will not be considered to be for use in lobbying if, prior to or contemporaneously with the use of the advocacy communications or research materials with the direct encouragement to action, the organization makes a substantial nonlobbying distribution of the advocacy communications or research materials (without the direct encouragement to action). Whether a distribution is substantial will be determined by reference to all of the facts and circumstances, including the normal distribution pattern of similar nonpartisan analyses, studies or research by that and similar organizations.

(F) *Special rule for partisan analysis, study or research.*—In the case of advocacy communications or research materials that are not nonpartisan analysis, study or research, the nonlobbying distribution thereof will not be considered "substantial" unless that distribution is at least as extensive as the lobbying distribution thereof.

(G) *Factors considered in determining primary purpose.*—Where the nonlobbying distribution of advocacy communications or research materials is not substantial, all of the facts and circumstances must be weighed to determine whether the organization's primary purpose in preparing the advocacy communications or research materials was for use in lobbying. While not the only factor, the extent of the organization's nonlobbying distribution of the advocacy communications or research materials is particularly relevant, especially when compared to the extent of their distribution with the direct encouragement to action. Another particularly relevant factor is whether the lobbying use of the advocacy communications or research materials is by the organization that prepared the document, a related organization, or an unrelated organization. Where the subsequent lobbying distribution is made by an unrelated organization, clear and convincing evidence (which must include evidence demonstrating cooperation or collusion between the two organizations) will be required to establish that the primary purpose for preparing the communication was for use in lobbying.

(H) *Examples.*—The provisions of this paragraph (b)(2)(v) are illustrated by the following examples:

*Example (1).* Assume a nonlobbying "report" (that is not nonpartisan analysis, study or research) is prepared by an organization, but distributed to only 50 people. The report, in that format, refers to and reflects a view on specific legislation but does not contain a direct encouragement for the recipients to take action with respect to legislation. Two months later, the organization sends the report to 10,000 people along with a letter urging recipients to write their Senators about the legislation discussed in the report. Because the report's nonlobbying distribution is not as extensive as its lobbying distribution, the report's nonlobbying distribution is not substantial for purposes of this paragraph (b)(2)(v). Accordingly, the organization's primary purpose in preparing the report must be determined by weighing all of the facts and circumstances. In light of the relatively minimal nonlobbying distribution and the fact that the lobbying distribution is by the preparing organization rather than by an unrelated organization, and in the absence of evidence to the contrary, both the report and the letter are grass roots lobbying communications. Assume that all costs of preparing the report were paid within the six months preceding the mailing of the letter. Accordingly, all of the organization's expenditures for preparing and mailing the two documents are grass roots lobbying expenditures.

*Example (2).* Assume the same facts as in Example (1), except that the costs of the report are paid over the two month period of January and February. Between January 1 and 31, the organization pays $1,000 for the report. In February, the organization pays $500 for the report. Further assume that the report is first used with a direct encouragement to action on August 1. Six months prior to August 1 is February 1. Accordingly, no costs paid for the report before February 1 are treated as grass roots lobbying expenditures under the subsequent use rule. Under these facts, the subsequent use rule treats only the $500 paid for the report in February as grass roots lobbying expenditures.

(3) *Exceptions to the definition of influencing legislation.*—In many cases, a communication is not a direct or grass roots lobbying communication under paragraph (b)(1) or (b)(2) of this section if it falls within one of the exceptions listed in paragraph (c) of this section. See paragraph (c)(1), *Nonpartisan analysis, study or research*; paragraph (c)(2), *Examinations and discussions of broad social, economic and similar problems*; paragraph (c)(3), *Requests for technical advice*; and paragraph (c)(4), *Communications pertaining to self-defense by the organization.* In addition, see §56.4911-5, which provides special rules regarding the treatment of certain lobbying communications directed in whole or in part to members of an electing public charity.

(4) *Examples.*—This paragraph (b)(4) provides examples to illustrate the rules set forth in this section regarding direct and grass roots lobbying. The expenditure test election under section 501(h) is assumed to be in effect for all organizations discussed in the examples in this paragraph (b)(4). In addition, it is assumed that the special rules of §56.4911-5, regarding certain of a public charity's communications with its members, do not apply to any of the examples in this paragraph (b)(4).

(i) *Direct lobbying.*—The provisions of this section regarding direct lobbying communications are illustrated by the following examples:

*Example (1).* Organization P's employee, X, is assigned to approach members of Congress to gain their support for a pending bill. X drafts and P prints a position letter on the bill. P distributes the letter to members of Congress. Additionally, X personally contacts several members of Congress or their staffs to seek support for P's position on the bill. The letter and the personal contacts are direct lobbying communications.

*Example (2).* Organization M's president writes a letter to the Congresswoman representing the district in which M is headquartered, requesting that the Congresswoman write an administrative agency regarding proposed regulations recently published by that agency. M's president also requests that the Congresswoman's letter to the agency state the Congresswoman's support of M's application for a particular type of permit granted by the agency. The letter written by M's president is not a direct lobbying communication.

*Example (3).* Organization Z prepares a paper on a particular state's environmental problems. The paper does not reflect a view on any specific pending legislation or on any specific legislative proposal that Z either supports or opposes. Z's representatives give the paper to a state legislator. Z's paper is not a direct lobbying communication.

*Example (4).* State X enacts a statute that requires the licensing of all day care providers. Agency B in State X is charged with preparing rules to implement the bill enacted by State X. One week after enactment of the bill, organization C sends a letter to Agency B providing detailed proposed rules that organization C suggests to Agency B as the appropriate standards to follow in implementing the statute on licensing of day care providers. Organization C's letter to Agency B is not a lobbying communication.

*Example (5).* Organization B researches, prepares and prints a code of standards of minimum safety requirements in an area of common electrical wiring. Organization B sells the code of standards booklet to the public and it is widely used by professionals in the installation of electrical wiring. A number of states have codified all, or part, of the code of standards as mandatory safety standards. On occasion, B lobbies state legislators for passage of the code of standards for safety reasons. Because the primary purpose of preparing the code of standards was the promotion of public safety and the standards were specifically used in a profession for that purpose, separate from any legislative requirement, the research, preparation, printing and public distribution of the code of standards is not an expenditure for a direct (or grass roots) lobbying communication. Costs, such as transportation, photocopying, and other similar expenses, incurred in lobbying state legislators for passage of the code of standards into law are expenditures for direct lobbying communications.

*Example (6).* On the organization's own initiative, representatives of Organization F present written testimony to a Congressional committee. The news media report on the testimony of Organization F, detailing F's opposition to a pending bill. The testimony is a direct lobbying communication but is not a grass roots lobbying communication.

*Example (7).* Organization R's monthly newsletter contains an editorial column that refers to and reflects a view on specific pending bills. R sends the newsletter to 10,000 nonmember subscribers. Senator Doe is among the subscribers. The editorial column in the newsletter copy sent to Senator Doe is not a direct lobbying communication because the newsletter is sent to Senator Doe in her capacity as a subscriber rather than her capacity as a legislator. (Note, though, that the editorial column may be a grass roots lobbying communication if it encourages recipients to take action with respect to the pending bills it refers to and on which it reflects a view).

*Example (8).* Assume the same facts as in Example (7), except that one of Senator Doe's staff members sees Senator Doe's copy of the editorial and writes to R requesting additional information. R responds with a letter that refers to and reflects a view on specific legislation. R's letter is a direct lobbying communication unless it is within one of the exceptions set forth in paragraph (c) of this section (such as the exception for nonpartisan analysis, study or research). (R's letter is not within the scope of the exception for responses to written requests from a legislative body or committee for technical advice (see paragraph (c)(3) of this section) because the letter is not in response to a written request from a legislative body or committee).

(ii) *Grass roots lobbying.*—The provisions of this section regarding grass roots lobbying communications are illustrated in paragraph (b)(4)(ii) (A) of this section by examples of communications that are not grass roots lobbying communications and in paragraph (b)(4)(ii)(B) by examples of communications that are grass roots lobbying communications. The provisions of this section are further illustrated in paragraph (b)(4)(ii)(C), with particular regard to the exception for nonpartisan analysis, study, or research:

(A) *Communications that are not grass roots lobbying communications.*

*Example (1).* Organization L places in its newsletter an article that asserts that lack of new capital is hurting State W's economy. The article recommends that State W residents either invest more in local businesses or increase their savings so that funds will be available to others interested in making investments. The article is an attempt to influence opinions with respect to a general problem that might receive legislative attention and is distributed in a manner so as to reach and influence many individuals. However, the article does not refer to specific legislation that is pending in a legislative body, nor does the article refer to a specific legislative proposal the organization either supports or opposes. The article is not a grass roots lobbying communication.

*Example (2).* Assume the same facts as Example (1), except that the article refers to a bill pending in State W's legislature that is intended to provide tax incentives for private savings. The article praises the pending bill and recommends that it be enacted. However, the article does not encourage readers to take action with respect to the legislation. The article is not a grass roots lobbying communication.

*Example (3).* Organization B sends a letter to all persons on its mailing list. The letter includes an update on numerous environmental issues with a discussion of general concerns regarding pollution, proposed federal regulations affecting the area, and several pending legislative proposals. The letter endorses two pending bills and opposes another pending bill, but does not name any legislator involved (other than the sponsor of one bill, for purposes of identifying the bill), nor does it otherwise encourage the reader to take action with respect to the legislation. The letter is not a grass roots lobbying communication.

*Example (4).* A pamphlet distributed by organization Z discusses the dangers of drugs and encourages the public to send their legislators a coupon, printed with the statement "I support a drug-free America." The term "drug-free America" is not widely identified with any of the many specific pending legislative proposals regarding drug issues. The pamphlet does not refer to any of the numerous pending legislative proposals, nor does the organization support or oppose a specific legislative proposal. The pamphlet is not a grass roots lobbying communication.

*Example (5).* A pamphlet distributed by organization B encourages readers to join an organization and "get involved in the fight against drugs." The text states, in the course of a discussion of several current drug issues, that organization B supports a specific bill before Congress that would establish an expanded drug control program. The pamphlet does not encourage readers to communicate with legislators about the bill (such as by including the names of undecided or opposed legislators). The pamphlet is not a grass roots lobbying communication.

*Example (6).* Organization E, an environmental organization, routinely summarizes in each edition of its newsletter the new environment-related bills that have been introduced in Congress since the last edition of the newsletter. The newsletter identifies each bill by a bill number and the name of the legislation's sponsor. The newsletter also reports on the status of previously introduced environment-related bills. The summaries and status reports do not encourage recipients of the newsletter to take action with respect to legislation, as described in paragraphs (b)(2)(iii) (A) through (D) of this section. Although the summaries and status reports refer to specific legislation and often reflect a view on such legislation, they do not encourage the newsletter recipients to take action with respect to such legislation. The summaries and status reports are not grass roots lobbying communications.

*Example (7).* Organization B prints in its newsletter a report on pending legislation that B supports, the Family Equity bill. The report refers to and reflects a view on the Family Equity bill, but does not directly encourage recipients to take action. Nor does the report specifically identify any legislator as opposing the communication's view on the legislation, as being undecided, or as being a member of the legislative committee or subcommittee that will consider the legislation. However, the report does state the following:

Rep. Doe (D-Ky.) and Rep. Roe (R-Ma.), both ardent supporters of the Family Equity bill, spoke at B's annual convention last week. Both encouraged B's efforts to get the Family Equity bill enacted and stated that they thought the bill could be enacted even over a presidential veto. B's legislative affairs liaison questioned others, who seemed to agree with that assessment. For example, Sen. Roe (I-Ca.) said that he thinks the bill will pass with such a large majority, "the President won't even consider vetoing it".

Assume the newsletter, and thus the report, is sent to individuals throughout the U.S., including some recipients in Kentucky, Massachusetts and California. Because the report is distributed nationally, the mere fact that the report identifies several legislators by party and state as part of its discussion does not mean the report specifically identifies the named legislators as the Kentucky, Massachusetts and California recipients' representatives in the legislature for purposes of paragraph (b)(2)(iii) of this section. The report is not a grass roots lobbying communication.

(B) *Communications that are grass roots lobbying communications.*

*Example (1).* A pamphlet distributed by organization Y states that the "President's plan for a drug-free America," which will establish a drug control program, should be passed. The pamphlet encourages readers to "write or call your senators and representatives and tell them to vote for the President's plan." No legislative proposal formally bears the name "President's plan for a drug-free America," but that and similar terms have been widely used in connection with specific legislation pending in Congress that was initially proposed by the President. Thus, the pamphlet refers to specific legislation, reflects a view on the legislation, and encourages readers to take action with respect to the legislation. The pamphlet is a grass roots lobbying communication.

*Example (2).* Assume the same facts as in Example (1), except that the pamphlet does not encourage the public to write or call representatives, but does list the members of the committee that will consider the bill. The pamphlet is a grass roots lobbying communication.

*Example (3).* Assume the same facts as in Example (1), except that the pamphlet encourages readers to "write the President to urge him to make the bill a top legislative priority" rather than encouraging readers to communicate with members of Congress. The pamphlet is a grass roots lobbying communication.

*Example (4).* Organization B, a nonmembership organization, includes in one of three sections of its newsletter an endorsement of two pending bills and opposition to another pending bill and also identifies several legislators as undecided on the three bills. The section of the newsletter devoted to the three pending bills is a grass roots lobbying communication.

*Example (5).* Organization D, a nonmembership organization, sends a letter to all persons on its mailing list. The letter includes an extensive discussion concluding that a significant increase in spending for the Air Force is essential in order to provide an adequate defense of the nation. Prior to a concluding fund raising request, the letter encourages readers to write their Congressional representatives urging increased appropriations to build the B-1 bomber. The letter is a grass roots lobbying communication.

*Example (6).* The President nominates X for a position in the President's cabinet. Organization Y disagrees with the views of X and does not believe X has the necessary administrative capabilities to effectively run a cabinet-level department. Accordingly, Y sends a general mailing requesting recipients to write to four Senators on the Senate Committee that will consider the nomination. The mailing is a grass roots lobbying communication.

*Example (7).* Organization F mails letters requesting that each recipient contribute money to or join F. In addition, the letters express F's opposition to a pending bill that is to be voted upon by the U.S. House of Representatives. Although the letters are form letters sent as a mass mailing, each letter is individualized to report to the recipient the name of the recipient's congressional representative. The letters are grass roots lobbying communications.

*Example (8).* Organization C sends a mailing that opposes a specific legislative proposal and includes a postcard addressed to the President for the recipient to sign stating opposition to the proposal. The letter requests that the recipient send to C a contribution as well as the postcard opposing the proposal. C states in the letter that it will deliver all the postcards to the White House. The letter is a grass roots lobbying communication.

(C) *Additional examples.*

*Example (1).* The newsletter of an organization concerned with drug issues is circulated primarily to individuals who are not members of the organization. A story in the newsletter reports on the prospects for passage of a specifically identified bill, stating that the organization supports the bill. The newsletter story identifies certain legislators as undecided, but does not state that readers should contact the undecided legislators. The story does not provide a full and fair exposition sufficient to qualify as nonpartisan analysis, study or research. The newsletter story is a grass roots lobbying communication.

*Example (2).* Assume the same facts as in Example (1), except that the newsletter story provides a full and fair exposition sufficient to qualify as nonpartisan analysis, study or research. The newsletter story is *not* a grass roots lobbying communication because it is within the exception for nonpartisan analysis, study or research (since it does not *directly* encourage recipients to take action).

*Example (3).* Assume the same facts as in Example (2), except that the newsletter story explicitly asks readers to contact the undecided legislators. Because the newsletter story directly encourages readers to take action with respect to the legislation, the newsletter story is not within the exception for nonpartisan analysis, study or research. Accordingly, the newsletter story is a grass roots lobbying communication.

*Example (4).* Assume the same facts as in Example (1), except that the story does not identify any undecided legislators. The story is not a grass roots lobbying communication.

*Example (5).* X organization places an advertisement that specifically identifies and opposes a bill that X asserts would harm the farm economy. The advertisement is not a mass media communication described in paragraph (b)(5)(ii) of this section and does not directly encourage readers to take action with respect to the bill. However, the advertisement does state that Senator Y favors the legislation. Because the advertisement refers to and reflects a view on specific legislation, and also encourages the readers to take action with respect to the legislation by specifically identifying a legislator who opposes X's views on the legislation, the advertisement is a grass roots lobbying communication.

*Example (6).* Assume the same facts as in Example (5), except that instead of identifying Senator Y as favoring the legislation, the advertisement identifies the "junior Senator from State Z" as favoring the legislation. The advertisement is a grass roots lobbying communication.

*Example (7).* Assume the same facts as in Example (5), except that instead of identifying Senator Y as favoring the legislation, the advertisement states: "Even though this bill will have a devastating effect upon the farm economy, most of the Senators from the Farm Belt states are inexplicably in favor of the bill." The advertisement does not specifically identify one or more legislators as opposing the advertisement's view on the bill in question. Accordingly, the advertisement is not a grass roots lobbying communication because it does not encourage readers to take action with respect to the legislation.

*Example (8).* Organization V trains volunteers to go door-to-door to seek signatures for petitions to be sent to legislators in favor of a specific bill. The volunteers are wholly unreimbursed for their time and expenses. The volunteers' costs (to the extent any are incurred) are not lobbying or exempt purpose expenditures made by V (but the volunteers may not deduct their out-of-pocket expenditures (see section 170(f)(6)). When V asks the volunteers to contact others and urge them to sign the petitions, V encourages those volunteers to take action in favor of the specific bill. Accordingly, V's costs of soliciting the volunteers' help and its costs of training the volunteers are grass roots expenditures. In addition, the costs of preparing, copying, distributing, etc. the petitions (and any other materials on the same specific subject used in the door-to-door signature gathering effort), are grass roots expenditures.

(5) *Special rule for certain mass media advertisements.*—(i) *In general.*—A mass media advertisement that is not a grass roots lobbying communication under the three-part grass roots lobbying definition contained in paragraph (b)(2) of this section may be a grass roots lobbying communication by virtue of paragraph (b)(5)(ii) of this section. The special rule in paragraph (b)(5)(ii) generally applies only to a limited type of paid advertisements that appear in the mass media.

(ii) *Presumption regarding certain paid mass media advertisements about highly publicized legislation.*—If within two weeks before a vote by a legislative body, or a committee (but not a subcommittee) thereof, on a highly publicized piece of legislation, an organization's paid advertisement appears in the mass media, the paid advertisement will be presumed to be a grass roots lobbying communication, but only if the paid advertisement both reflects a view on the general subject of such legislation and either: refers to the highly publicized legislation; or encourages the public to communicate with legislators on the general subject of such legislation. An organization can rebut this presumption by demonstrating that the paid advertisement is a type of communication regularly made by the organization in the mass media without regard to the timing of legislation (that is, a customary course of business exception) or that the timing of the paid advertisement was unrelated to the upcoming legislative action. Notwithstanding the fact that an organization successfully rebuts the presumption, a mass media communication described in this paragraph (b)(5)(ii) is a grass roots lobbying communication if the communication would be a grass roots lobbying communication under the rules contained in paragraph (b)(2) of this section.

(iii) *Definitions.*—(A) *Mass media.*—For purposes of this paragraph (b)(5), the term "mass media" means television, radio, billboards and general circulation newspapers and magazines. General circulation newspapers and magazines do not include newspapers or magazines published by an organization for which the expenditure test election under section 501(h) is in effect, except where both: the total circulation of the newspaper or magazine is greater than 100,000; and fewer than one-half of the recipients are members of the organization (as defined in §56.4911-5(f)).

(B) *Paid advertisement.*—For purposes of this paragraph (b)(5), where an electing public charity is itself a mass media publisher or broadcaster, all portions of that organization's mass media publications or broadcasts are treated as paid advertisements in the mass media, except those specific portions that are advertisements paid for by another person. The term "mass media" is defined in paragraph (b)(5)(iii)(A).

(C) *Highly publicized.*—For purposes of this paragraph (b)(5), "highly publicized" means frequent coverage on television and radio, and in general circulation newspapers, during the two weeks preceding the vote by the legislative body or committee. In the case of state or local legislation, "highly publicized" means frequent coverage in the mass media that serve the state or local jurisdiction in question. Even where legislation receives frequent coverage, it is "highly publicized" only if the pendency of the legislation or the legislation's general terms, purpose, or effect are known to a significant segment of the general public (as opposed to the particular interest groups directly affected) in the area in which the paid mass media advertisement appears.

(iv) *Examples.*—The special rule of this paragraph (b)(5) is illustrated by the following examples. The expenditure test election under section 501(h) is assumed to be in effect for all organizations discussed in the examples in this paragraph (b)(5)(iv):

*Example (1).* Organization X places a television advertisement advocating one of the President's major foreign policy initiatives, as outlined by the President in a series of speeches and as drafted into proposed legislation. The initiative is popularly known as "the President's World Peace Plan," and is voted upon by the Senate four days after X's advertisement. The advertisement concludes: "SUPPORT THE PRESIDENT'S WORLD PEACE PLAN!" The President's plan and position are highly publicized during the two weeks before the Senate vote, as evidenced by: coverage of the plan on several nightly television network news programs; more than one article about the plan on the front page of a majority of the country's ten largest daily general circulation newspapers; and an editorial about the plan in four of the country's ten largest daily general circulation newspapers. Although the advertisement does not encourage readers to contact legislators or other government officials, the advertisement does refer to specific legislation and reflect a view on the general subject of the legislation. The communication is presumed to be a grass roots lobbying communication.

*Example (2).* Assume the same facts as in Example (1), except that the advertisement appears three weeks before the Senate's vote on the plan. Because the advertisement appears more than two weeks before the legislative vote, the advertisement is *not* within the scope of the special rule for mass media communications on highly publicized legislation. Accordingly, the advertisement is a grass roots lobbying communication only if it is described in the general definition contained in paragraph (b)(2) of this section. Because the advertisement does not encourage recipients to take action with respect to the legislation in question, the advertisement is not a grass roots lobbying communication.

*Example (3).* Organization Y places a newspaper advertisement advocating increased government funding for certain public works projects the President has proposed and that are being considered by a legislative committee. The advertisement explains the President's proposals and concludes: "SUPPORT FUNDING FOR THESE VITAL PROJECTS!" The advertisement does not encourage readers to contact legislators or other government officials nor does it name any undecided legislators, but it does name the legislation being considered by the committee. The President's proposed funding of public works, however, is not highly publicized during the two weeks before the vote: there has been little coverage of the issue on nightly television network news programs, only one front-page article on the issue in the country's ten largest daily general circulation newspapers, and only one editorial about the issue in the country's ten largest daily general circulation newspapers. Two days after the advertisement appears, the committee votes to approve funding of the projects. Although the advertisement appears less than two weeks before the legislative vote, the advertisement is *not* within the scope of the special rule for mass media communications on highly publicized legislation because the issue of funding for public works projects is not highly publicized. Thus, the advertisement is a grass roots lobbying communication only if it is described in the general definition contained in paragraph (b)(2) of this section. Because the advertisement does not encourage recipients to take action with respect to the legislation in question, the advertisement is not a grass roots lobbying communication.

*Example (4).* Organization P places numerous advertisements in the mass media about a bill being considered by the State Assembly. The bill is highly publicized, as evidenced by numerous front-page articles, editorials and letters to the editor published in the state's general circulation daily newspapers, as well as frequent coverage of the bill by the television and radio stations serving the state. The advertisements run over a three week period and, in addition to showing pictures of a family being robbed at gunpoint,

say: "The State Assembly is considering a bill to make gun ownership illegal. This outrageous legislation would violate your constitutional rights and the rights of other law-abiding citizens. If this legislation is passed, you and your family will be criminals if you want to exercise your right to protect yourselves." The advertisements refer to and reflect a view on a specific bill but do not encourage recipients to take action. Sixteen days after the last advertisement runs, a State Assembly committee votes to defeat the legislation. None of the advertisements is a grass roots lobbying communication.

*Example (5).* Assume the same facts as in Example (4), except that it is publicly announced prior to the advertising campaign that the committee vote is scheduled for five days after the last advertisement runs. Because of public pressure resulting from the advertising campaign, the bill is withdrawn and no vote is ever taken. None of the advertisements is a grass roots lobbying communication.

(c) *Exceptions to the definitions of direct lobbying communication and grass roots lobbying communication.*—(1) *Nonpartisan analysis, study, or research exception.*—(i) *In general.*—Engaging in nonpartisan analysis, study, or research and making available to the general public or a segment or members thereof or to governmental bodies, officials, or employees the results of such work constitute neither a direct lobbying communication under §56.4911-2(b)(1) nor a grass roots lobbying communication under §56.4911-2(b)(2).

(ii) *Nonpartisan analysis, study, or research.*—For purposes of this section, "nonpartisan analysis, study, or research" means an independent and objective exposition of a particular subject matter, including any activity that is "educational" within the meaning of §1.501(c)(3)-1(d)(3). Thus, "nonpartisan analysis, study, or research" may advocate a particular position or viewpoint so long as there is a sufficiently full and fair exposition of the pertinent facts to enable the public or an individual to form an independent opinion or conclusion. The mere presentation of unsupported opinion, however, does not qualify as "nonpartisan analysis, study, or research".

(iii) *Presentation as part of a series.*—Normally, whether a publication or broadcast qualifies as "nonpartisan analysis, study, or research" will be determined on a presentation-by-presentation basis. However, if a publication or broadcast is one of a series prepared or supported by an electing organization and the series as a whole meets the standards of paragraph (c)(1)(ii) of this section, then any individual publication or broadcast within the series is not a direct or grass roots lobbying communication even though such individual broadcast or publication does not, by itself, meet the standards of paragraph (c)(1)(ii) of this section. Whether a broadcast or publication is considered part of a series will ordinarily depend upon all the facts and circumstances of each particular situation. However, with respect to broadcast activities, all broadcasts within any period of six consecutive months will ordinarily be eligible to be considered as part of a series. If an electing organization times or channels a part of a series which is described in this paragraph (c)(1)(iii) in a manner designed to influence the general public or the action of a legislative body with respect to a specific legislative proposal, the expenses of preparing and distributing such part of the analysis, study, or research will be expenditures for a direct or grass roots lobbying communication, as the case may be.

(iv) *Making available results of nonpartisan analysis, study, or research.*—An organization may choose any suitable means, including oral or written presentations, to distribute the results of its nonpartisan analysis, study, or research, with or without charge. Such means include distribution of reprints of speeches, articles and reports; presentation of information through conferences, meetings and discussions; and dissemination to the news media, including radio, television and newspapers, and to other public forums. For purposes of this paragraph (c)(1)(iv), such communications may not be limited to, or be directed toward, persons who are interested solely in one side of a particular issue.

(v) *Subsequent lobbying use of certain analysis, study or research.*—Even though certain analysis, study or research is initially within the exception for nonpartisan analysis, study or research, subsequent use of that analysis, study or research for grass roots lobbying may cause that analysis, study or research to be treated as a grass roots lobbying communication that is not within the exception for nonpartisan analysis, study or research. This paragraph (c)(1)(v) does not cause any analysis, study or research to be considered a direct lobbying communication. For rules regarding when analysis, study or research is treated as a grass roots lobbying communication that is not within the scope of the exception for nonpartisan analysis, study or research, see paragraph (b)(2)(v) of this section.

(vi) *Directly encouraging action by recipients of a communication.*—A communication that reflects a view on specific legislation is not within the nonpartisan analysis, study, or research exception of this paragraph (c)(1) if the communication directly encourages the recipient to take action with respect to such legislation. For purposes of this section, a communication directly encourages the recipient to take action with respect to legislation if the communication is described in one or more of paragraphs (b)(2)(iii)(A) through (C) of this section. As described in paragraph (b)(2)(iv) of this section, a communication would encourage the recipient to take action with respect to legislation, but not *directly* encourage such action, if the communication does no more than specifically identify one or more legislators who will vote on the legislation as: opposing the communication's view with respect to the legislation; being undecided with respect to the legislation; being the recipient's representative in the legislature; or being a member of the legislative committee or subcommittee that will consider the legislation.

(vii) *Examples.*—The provisions of this paragraph (c)(1) may be illustrated by the following examples:

*Example (1).* Organization M establishes a research project to collect information for the purpose of showing the dangers of the use of pesticides in raising crops. The information collected includes data with respect to proposed legislation, pending before several State legislatures, which would ban the use of pesticides. The project takes favorable positions on such legislation without producing a sufficiently full and fair exposition of the pertinent facts to enable the public or an individual to form an independent opinion or conclusion on the pros and cons of the use of pesticides. This project is not within the exception for nonpartisan analysis, study, or research because it is designed to present information merely on one side of the legislative controversy.

*Example (2).* Organization N establishes a research project to collect information concerning the dangers of the use of pesticides in raising crops for the ostensible purpose of examining and reporting information as to the pros and cons of the use of pesticides in raising crops. The information is collected and distributed in the form of a published report which analyzes the effects and costs of the use and nonuse of various pesticides under various conditions on humans, animals and crops. The report also presents the advantages, disadvantages, and economic cost of allowing the continued use of pesticides unabated, of controlling the use of pesticides, and of developing alternatives to pesticides. Even if the report sets forth conclusions that the disadvantages as a result of using pesticides are greater than the advantages of using pesticides and that prompt legislative regulation of the use of pesticides is needed, the project is within the exception for nonpartisan analysis, study, or research since it is designed to present information on both sides of the legislative controversy and presents a sufficiently full and fair exposition of the pertinent facts to enable the public or an individual to form an independent opinion or conclusion.

*Example (3).* Organization O establishes a research project to collect information on the presence or absence of disease in humans from eating food grown with pesticides and the presence or absence of disease in humans from eating food not grown with pesticides. As part of the research project, O hires a consultant who prepares a "fact sheet" which calls for the curtailment of the use of pesticides and which addresses itself to the merits of several specific legislative proposals to curtail the use of pesticides in raising crops which are currently pending before State Legislatures. The "fact sheet" presents reports of experimental evidence tending to support its conclusions but omits any reference to reports of experimental evidence tending to dispute its conclusions. O distributes ten thousand copies to citizens' groups. Expenditures by O in connection with this work of the consultant are not within the exception for nonpartisan analysis, study, or research.

*Example (4).* P publishes a bimonthly newsletter to collect and report all published materials, ongoing research, and new developments with regard to the use of pesticides in raising crops. The newsletter also includes notices of proposed pesticide legislation with impartial summaries of the provisions and debates on such legislation. The newsletter does not encourage recipients to take action with respect to such legislation, but is designed to present information on both sides of the legislative controversy and does present such information fully and fairly. It is within the exception for nonpartisan analysis, study, or research.

*Example (5).* X is satisfied that A, a member of the faculty of Y University, is exceptionally well qualified to undertake a project involving a comprehensive study of the effects of pesticides on crop yields. Consequently, X makes a grant to A to underwrite the cost of the study and of the preparation of a book on the effect of pesticides on crop yields. X does not take any position on the issues or control the content of A's output. A produces a book which concludes that the use of pesticides often has a favorable effect on crop yields, and on that basis argues against pending bills which would ban the use of pesticides. A's book contains a sufficiently full and fair exposition of the pertinent facts, including known or potential disadvantages of the use of pesticides, to enable the public or an individual to form an

independent opinion or conclusion as to whether pesticides should be banned as provided in the pending bills. The book does not directly encourage readers to take action with respect to the pending bills. Consequently, the book is within the exception for nonpartisan analysis, study, or research.

*Example (6).* Assume the same facts as Example (2), except that, instead of issuing a report, X presents within a period of 6 consecutive months a two-program television series relating to the pesticide issue. The first program contains information, arguments, and conclusions favoring legislation to restrict the use of pesticides. The second program contains information, arguments, and conclusions opposing legislation to restrict the use of pesticides. The programs are broadcast within 6 months of each other during commensurate periods of prime time. X's programs are within the exception for nonpartisan analysis, study, or research. Although neither program individually could be regarded as nonpartisan, the series of two programs constitutes a balanced presentation.

*Example (7).* Assume the same facts as in Example (6), except that X arranged for televising the program favoring legislation to restrict the use of pesticides at 8:00 on a Thursday evening and for televising the program opposing such legislation at 7:00 on a Sunday morning. X's presentation is not within the exception for nonpartisan analysis, study, or research, since X disseminated its information in a manner prejudicial to one side of the legislative controversy.

*Example (8).* Organization Z researches, writes, prints and distributes a study on the use and effects of pesticide X. A bill is pending in the U.S. Senate to ban the use of pesticide X. Z's study leads to the conclusion that pesticide X is extremely harmful and that the bill pending in the U.S. Senate is an appropriate and much needed remedy to solve the problems caused by pesticide X. The study contains a sufficiently full and fair exposition of the pertinent facts, including known or potential advantages of the use of pesticide X, to enable the public or an individual to form an independent opinion or conclusion as to whether pesticides should be banned as provided in the pending bills. In its analysis of the pending bill, the study names certain undecided senators on the Senate committee considering the bill. Although the study meets the three-part test for determining whether a communication is a grass roots lobbying communication, the study is within the exception for nonpartisan analysis, study or research, because it does not directly encourage recipients of the communication to urge a legislator to oppose the bill.

*Example (9).* Assume the same facts as in Example (8), except that, after stating support for the pending bill, the study concludes: "You should write to the undecided committee members to support this crucial bill." The study is not within the exception for nonpartisan analysis, study or research because it directly encourages the recipients to urge a legislator to support a specific piece of legislation.

*Example (10).* Organization X plans to conduct a lobbying campaign with respect to illegal drug use in the United States. It incurs $5,000 in expenses to conduct research and prepare an extensive report primarily for use in the lobbying campaign. Although the detailed report discusses specific pending legislation and reaches the conclusion that the legislation would reduce illegal drug use, the report contains a sufficiently full and fair exposition of the pertinent facts to enable the public or an individual to form an independent conclusion regarding the effect of the legislation. The report does not encourage readers to contact legislators regarding the legislation. Accordingly, the report does not, in and of itself, constitute a lobbying communication.

Copies of the report are available to the public at X's office, but X does not actively distribute the report or otherwise seek to make the contents of the report available to the general public. Whether or not X's distribution is sufficient to meet the requirement in § 56.4911-2(c)(1)(iv) that a nonpartisan communication be made available, X's distribution is not substantial (for purposes of § 56.4911-2(b)(2)(v)(E)) in light of all of the facts and circumstances, including the normal distribution pattern of similar nonpartisan reports. X then mails copies of the report, along with a letter, to 10,000 individuals on X's mailing list. In the letter, X requests that individuals contact legislators urging passage of the legislation discussed in the report. Because X's research and report were primarily undertaken by X for lobbying purposes and X did not make a substantial distribution of the report (without an accompanying lobbying message) prior to or contemporaneously with the use of the report in lobbying, the report is a grass roots lobbying communication that is not within the exception for nonpartisan analysis, study or research.

*Example (11).* Assume the same facts as in Example (10), except that before using the report in the lobbying campaign, X sends the research and report (without an accompanying lobbying message) to universities and newspapers. At the same time, X also advertises the availability of the report in its newsletter. This distribution is similar in scope to the normal distribution pattern of similar nonpartisan reports. In light of all of the facts and circumstances, X's distribution of the report is substantial. Because of X's substantial distribution of the report, X's primary purpose will be considered to be other than for use in lobbying and the report will not be considered a grass roots lobbying communication. Accordingly, only the expenditures for copying and mailing the report to the 10,000 individuals on X's mailing list, as well as for preparing and mailing the letter, are expenditures for grass roots lobbying communications.

*Example (12).* Organization M pays for a bumper sticker that reads: "STOP ABORTION: Vote *NO* on Prop. X!" M also pays for a 30-second television advertisement and a billboard that similarly advocate opposition to Prop. X. In light of the limited scope of the communications, none of the communications is within the exception for nonpartisan analysis, study or research. First, none of the communications rises to the level of analysis, study or research. Second, none of the communications is nonpartisan because none contains a sufficiently full and fair exposition of the pertinent facts to enable the public or an individual to form an independent opinion or conclusion. Thus, each communication is a direct lobbying communication.

(2) *Examinations and discussions of broad social, economic, and similar problems.*—Examinations and discussions of broad social, economic, and similar problems are neither direct lobbying communications under §56.4911-2(b)(1) nor grass roots lobbying communications under §56.4911-2(b)(2) even if the problems are of the type with which government would be expected to deal ultimately. Thus, under §56.4911-2(b)(1) and (2), lobbying communications do not include public discussion, or communications with members of legislative bodies or governmental employees, the general subject of which is also the subject of legislation before a legislative body, so long as such discussion does not address itself to the merits of a specific legislative proposal and so long as such discussion does not directly encourage recipients to take action with respect to legislation. For example, this paragraph (c)(2) excludes from grass roots lobbying under §56.4911-2(b)(2) an organization's discussions of problems such as environmental pollution or population growth that are being considered by Congress and various State legislatures, but only where the discussions are not directly addressed to specific legislation being considered, and only where the discussions do not directly encourage recipients of the communication to contact a legislator, an employee of a legislative body, or a government official or employee who may participate in the formulation of legislation.

(3) *Requests for technical advice.*—A communication is not a direct lobbying communication under §56.4911-2(b)(1) if the communication is the providing of technical advice or assistance to a governmental body, a governmental committee, or a subdivision of either in response to a written request by the body, committee, or subdivision, as set forth in §53.4945-2(d)(2).

(4) *Communications pertaining to "self-defense" by the organization.*—A communication is not a direct lobbying communication under §56.4911-2(b)(1) if either:

(i) The communication is an appearance before, or communication with, any legislative body with respect to a possible action by the body that might affect the existence of the electing public charity, its powers and duties, its tax-exempt status, or the deductibility of contributions to the organization, as set forth in §53.4945-2(d)(3);

(ii) The communication is by a member of an affiliated group of organizations (within the meaning of §56.4911-7(e)), and is an appearance before, or communication with, a legislative body with respect to a possible action by the body that might affect the existence of any other member of the group, its powers and duties, its tax-exempt status, or the deductibility of contributions to it;

(iii) The communication is by an electing public charity more than 75 percent of the members of which are other organizations that are described in section 501(c)(3), and is an appearance before, or communication with, any legislative body with respect to a possible action by the body which might affect the existence of one or more of the section 501(c)(3) member organizations, their powers, duties, or tax-exempt status, or the deductibility (under section 170) of contributions to one or more of the section 501(c)(3) member organizations, but only if the principal purpose of the appearance or communication is to defend the section 501(c)(3) member organizations (rather than the nonsection 501(c)(3) member organizations); or

(iv) The communication is by an electing public charity that is a member of a limited affiliated group of organizations under §56.4911-10, and is an appearance before, or communication with, the Congress of the United States with respect to a possible action by the Congress that might affect the existence of any member of the limited affiliated group, its powers and duties, tax-exempt status, or the deductibility of contributions to it.

(v) Under the self-defense exception of paragraphs (c)(4)(i) through (iv) of this section, a charity may communicate with an entire legislative body, with committees or subcommittees of a legis-

lative body, with individual legislators, with legislative staff members, or with representatives of the executive branch who are involved with the legislative process, so long as such communication is limited to the prescribed subjects. Similarly, under the self-defense exception, a charity may make expenditures in order to initiate legislation if such legislation concerns only matters which might affect the existence of the charity, its powers and duties, its tax-exempt status, or the deductibility of contributions to such charity. For examples illustrating the application and scope of the self-defense exception of this paragraph (c)(4), see §53.4945-2(d)(3)(ii).

(d) *Definitions.*—For purposes of section 4911 and the regulations thereunder—

(1) *Legislation.*—(i) *In general.*—"Legislation" includes action by the Congress, any state legislature, any local council, or similar legislative body, or by the public in a referendum, ballot initiative, constitutional amendment, or similar procedure. "Legislation" includes a proposed treaty required to be submitted by the President to the Senate for its advice and consent from the time the President's representative begins to negotiate its position with the prospective parties to the proposed treaty.

(ii) *Definition of specific legislation.*—For purposes of paragraphs (b)(1) and (b)(2) of this section, "specific legislation" includes both legislation that has already been introduced in a legislative body and a specific legislative proposal that the organization either supports or opposes. In the case of a referendum, ballot initiative, constitutional amendment, or other measure that is placed on the ballot by petitions signed by a required number or percentage of voters, an item becomes "specific legislation" when the petition is first circulated among voters for signature.

(iii) *Examples.*—The terms "legislation" and "specific legislation" are illustrated using the following examples:

*Example (1).* A nonmembership organization includes in its newsletter an article about problems with the use of pesticide X that states in part: "Legislation that is pending in Congress would prohibit the use of this very dangerous pesticide. Fortunately, the legislation will probably be passed. Write your congressional representatives about this important issue." This is a grass roots lobbying communication that refers to and reflects a view on specific legislation and that encourages recipients to take action with respect to that legislation.

*Example (2).* An organization based in State A notes in its newsletter that State Z has passed a bill to accomplish a stated purpose and then says that State A should pass such a bill. The organization urges readers to write their legislators in favor of such a bill. No such bill has been introduced into the State A legislature. The organization has referred to and reflected a view on a specific legislative proposal and has also encouraged readers to take action thereon.

(2) *Action.*—The term "action" in paragraph (d)(1)(i) of this section is limited to the introduction, amendment, enactment, defeat or repeal of acts, bills, resolutions, or similar items.

(3) *Legislative body.*—"Legislative body" does not include executive, judicial, or administrative bodies.

(4) *Administrative bodies.*—"Administrative bodies" includes school boards, housing authorities, sewer and water districts, zoning boards, and other similar Federal, State, or local special purpose bodies, whether elective or appointive. Thus, for example, for purposes of section 4911, the term "any attempt to influence any legislation" does not include attempts to persuade an executive body or department to form, support the formation of, or to acquire property to be used for the formation or expansion of, a public park or equivalent preserves (such as public recreation areas, game, or forest preserves, and soil demonstration areas) established or to be established by act of Congress, by executive action in accordance with an act of Congress, or by a State, municipality or other governmental unit described in section 170(c)(1), as compared with attempts to persuade a legislative body, a member thereof, or other governmental official or employee, to promote the appropriation of funds for such an acquisition or other legislative authorization of such an acquisition. Therefore, for example, an organization would not be influencing legislation for purposes of section 4911, if it proposed to a Park Authority that it purchase a particular tract of land for a new park, even though such an attempt would necessarily require the Park Authority eventually to seek appropriations to support a new park. However, in such a case, the organization would be influencing legislation, for purposes of section 4911, if it provided the Park Authority with a proposed budget to be submitted to a legislative body, unless such submission is described by one of the exceptions set forth in paragraph (c) of this section. [Reg. §56.4911-2.]

☐ [*T.D.* 8308, 8-30-90.]

[Reg. §56.4911-3]

**§56.4911-3. Expenditures for direct and/or grass roots lobbying communications.**—(a) *Definition of term "expenditures for".*—(1) *In general.*—This §56.4911-3 contains allocation rules regarding what portion of a lobbying communication's costs is a direct lobbying expenditure, what portion is a grass roots expenditure and what portion is, in certain cases, a nonlobbying expenditure. Except as otherwise indicated in this paragraph(a), all costs of preparing a direct or grass roots lobbying communication are included as expenditures for direct or grass roots lobbying. Expenditures for a direct or grass roots lobbying communication ("lobbying expenditures") include amounts paid or incurred as current or deferred compensation for an employee's services attributable to the direct or grass roots lobbying communication, and the allocable portion of administrative, overhead, and other general expenditures attributable to the direct or grass roots lobbying communication. For example, except as otherwise provided in this paragraph (a), all expenditures for researching, drafting, reviewing, copying, publishing and mailing a direct or grass roots lobbying communication, as well as an allocable share of overhead expenses, are included as expenditures for direct or grass roots lobbying.

(2) *Allocation of mixed purpose expenditures.*—(i) *Nonmembership communications.*—Except as provided in paragraph (a)(2)(ii) of this section, lobbying expenditures for a communication that also has a bona fide nonlobbying purpose must include all costs attributable to those parts of the communication that are on the same specific subject as the lobbying message. All costs attributable to those parts of the communication that are not on the same specific subject as the lobbying message are not included as lobbying expenditures for allocation purposes. Whether or not a portion of a communication is on the same specific subject as the lobbying message will depend on the surrounding facts and circumstances. In general, a portion of a communication will be on the same specific subject as the lobbying message if that portion discusses an activity or specific issue that would be directly affected by the specific legislation that is the subject of the lobbying message. Moreover, discussion of the background or consequences of the specific legislation, or discussion of the background or consequences of an activity or specific issue affected by the specific legislation, is also considered to be on the same specific subject as the lobbying communication.

(ii) *Membership communications.*—In the case of lobbying expenditures for a communication that also has a bona fide nonlobbying purpose and that is sent only or primarily to members, an electing public charity must make a reasonable allocation between the amount expended for the lobbying purpose and the amount expended for the nonlobbying purpose. An electing public charity that includes as a lobbying expenditure only the amount expended for the specific sentence or sentences that encourage the recipient to take action with respect to legislation has not made a reasonable allocation. For purposes of this paragraph, a communication is sent only or primarily to members if more than half of the recipients of the communication are members of the electing public charity making the communication within the meaning of §56.4911-5. See §56.4911-5 for separate rules on communications sent only or primarily to members. Nothing in this paragraph (a) shall change any allocation required by §56.4911-5.

(3) *Allocation of mixed lobbying.*—If a communication (to which §56.4911-5 does not apply) is both a direct lobbying communication and a grass roots lobbying communication, the communication will be treated as a grass roots lobbying communication except to the extent that the electing public charity demonstrates that the communication was made primarily for direct lobbying purposes, in which case a reasonable allocation shall be made between the direct and the grass roots lobbying purposes served by the communication.

(b) *Examples.*—The provisions of paragraph (a) of this section are illustrated by the following examples. Except where otherwise explicitly stated, the expenditure test election under section 501(h) is assumed to be in effect for all organizations discussed in the examples in this paragraph (b). See §56.4911-5 for special rules applying to the member communications described in some of the following examples.

*Example (1).* Organization R makes the services of E, one of its paid executives, available to S, an organization described in section 501(c)(4) of the Code. E works for several weeks to assist S in developing materials that urge voters to contact their congressional representatives to indicate their support for specific legislation. In performing this work, E uses office space and clerical assistance provided by R. R pays full salary and benefits to E during this period and receives no reimbursement from S for these payments or for the other facilities and assistance provided. All expenditures of R, including allocable office and overhead expenses, that are attributable to

this assignment are grass roots expenditures because E was engaged in an attempt to influence legislation.

*Example (2).* An organization distributes primarily to nonmembers a pamphlet with two articles on unrelated subjects. The total cost of preparing, printing and mailing the pamphlet is $11,000, $1,000 for preparation and $10,000 for printing and mailing. The cost of preparing one article, a nonlobbying communication, is $600. The article is printed on three of the four pages in the pamphlet. The cost of preparing the second article, a grassroots lobbying communication that addresses only one specific subject, is $400. This article is printed on one page of the four page pamphlet. In this situation, $400 of preparation costs and $2,500 (25% of $10,000) of printing and mailing costs are expenditures for a grass roots lobbying communication.

*Example (3).* Assume the same facts as in Example (2), except that the pamphlet is distributed only to members. In addition, assume the second article states that the recipient members should contact their congressional representatives. The organization allocates $400 of preparation costs and $2,500 of printing and mailing costs as expenditures for direct lobbying (see §56.4911-5(c)). The allocation is reasonable for purposes of §56.4911-3(a)(2)(ii).

*Example (4).* Organization J places a full-page advertisement in a newspaper. The advertisement urges passage of pending legislation to build three additional nuclear powered submarines, and states that readers should write their Congressional representatives in favor of the legislation. The advertisement also provides a general description of J's purposes and activities, invites readers to become members of J and asks readers to contribute money to J. Except for the cost of the portion of the advertisement describing J's purposes and activities and the portion specifically seeking members and contributions, the entire cost of the advertisement is an expenditure for a grass roots lobbying communication, because the entire advertisement, except for the lines specifically describing J and specifically seeking members and contributions, is on the same specific subject as the grass roots lobbying message.

*Example (5).* Assume the same facts as in Example (4), except that J places in the newspaper two separate half-page advertisements instead of one full-page advertisement. One of the two advertisements discusses the need for three additional nuclear powered submarines and urges readers to write their Congressional representatives in favor of the pending legislation to build the three submarines. The other advertisement contains only the membership and fundraising appeals, along with a general description of J's purposes and activities. The half-page advertisement urging readers to write to Congress is a grass roots lobbying communication and all of J's expenditures for producing and placing that advertisement are expenditures for a grass roots lobbying communication. J's expenditures for the other half-page advertisement are not expenditures for a grass roots or direct lobbying communication.

*Example (6).* Assume the same facts as in Example (4), except that the communication by J is in a letter mailed only to members of J, rather than in a newspaper advertisement, and the invitation to become a member of J is an invitation to join a new membership category. In addition, assume that the communication states that the member recipients should ask nonmembers to write their Congressional representatives. J allocates one-half of the cost of the mailing as an expenditure for a grass roots lobbying communication (see §56.4911-5(d)). Because the communication had both bona fide nonlobbying (e.g., membership solicitation and fundraising) purposes as well as lobbying purposes, J's allocation of one-half of the cost of the communication to grass roots lobbying and one-half to nonlobbying is reasonable for purposes of §56.4911-3(a)(2)(ii).

*Example (7).* A particular monthly issue of organizations X's newsletter, which is distributed mainly to nonmembers of X, has three articles of equal length. The first article is a grass roots lobbying communication, the sole specific subject of which is pending legislation to help protect seals from being slaughtered in certain foreign countries. The second article discusses the rapid decline in the world's whale population, particularly because of the illegal hunting of whales by foreign countries. The third article deals with air pollution and the acid rain problem in North America. Because the first article is a grass roots lobbying communication, all of the costs allocable to that article (e.g., one-third of the newsletter's printing and mailing costs) are lobbying expenditures. The second article is not a lobbying communication and the pending legislation relating to seals addressed in the first article does not affect the illegal whale hunting activities. Because the second and third articles are not lobbying communications and are also not on the same specific subject as the first article, no portion of the costs attributable to those articles is a grass roots lobbying expenditure.

*Example (8).* Organization T, a nonmembership organization, prepares a three page document that is mailed to 3,000 persons on T's mailing list. The first two pages of the three page document, titled "The Need for Child Care," support the need for additional child care programs, and include statistics on the number of children living in homes where both parents work or in homes with a single parent. The two pages also make note of the inadequacy of the number of day care providers to meet the needs of these parents. The third page of the document, titled "H.R. 1," indicates T's support of H.R. 1, a bill pending in the U.S. House of Representatives. The document states that H.R. 1 will provide for $10,000,000 in additional subsidies to child care providers, primarily for those providers caring for lower income children. The third page of the document also notes that H.R. 1 includes new federal standards regulating the quality of child care providers. The document ends with T's request that recipients contact their congressional representative in support of H.R. 1. The entire three page document is on the same specific subject, and, therefore, all expenditures of preparing and distributing the three page document are grass roots lobbying expenditures.

*Example (9)*. Assume the same facts as in Example (8), except that the document has a fourth page. The fourth page does not refer to the general need for child care or the specific need for additional child care providers. Instead, the fourth page advocates that a particular federal agency commence, under its existing statutory authority, licensing of day care providers in order to promote safe and effective child care. The cost of the fourth page is not a lobbying expenditure.

*Example (10)*. Assume the same facts as in Example (8), except that T is a membership organization, 75 percent of the recipients of the three page document are members of T, and 25 percent of the recipients are nonmembers and are not subscribers within the meaning of § 56.4911-5(f)(5). Assume also that the document states that readers should write to Congress, but does not state that the readers should urge nonmembers to write to Congress. T treats the document as having a bona fide nonlobbying purpose, the purpose of educating its members about the need for child care. Accordingly, T allocates one-half of the cost of preparing and distributing the document as a lobbying expenditure (see § 56.4911-5(e)(2)(i)), of which 75 percent is a direct lobbying expenditure (see § 56.4911-5(e)(2)(iii)) and 25 percent is a grass roots lobbying expenditure (see § 56.4911-5(e)(2)(ii)). The remaining one-half is allocated as a nonlobbying expenditure. T's allocation is reasonable for purposes of § 56.4911-3(a)(2)(ii) and is correct for purposes of § 56.4911-5(e).

*Example (11)*. Assume the same facts as in Example (10), except that T allocates one percent of the cost of preparing and distributing the document as a lobbying expenditure (for purposes of § 56.4911-5(e)(2)) and 99 percent as a nonlobbying expenditure. T's allocation is based upon the fact that out of 200 lines in the document, only two lines state that the recipient should contact legislators about the pending legislation. T's allocation is unreasonable for purposes of § 56.4911-3(a)(2)(ii).

*Example (12)*. Organization F, a nonmembership organization, sends a one page letter to all persons on its mailing list. The only subject of the letter is the organization's opposition to a pending bill allowing private uses of certain national parks. The letter requests recipients to send letters opposing the bill to their congressional representatives. A second one page letter is sent in the same envelope. The second letter discusses the broad educational activities and publications of the organization in all areas of environmental protection and ends by requesting the recipient to make a financial contribution to organization F. Since the separate second letter is on a different subject from the lobbying letter, and the letters are of equal length, 50 percent of the mailing costs must be allocated as an expenditure for a grass roots lobbying communication.

*Example (13)*. Assume the same facts as in Example (12), except that F is a membership organization and the letters in question are sent primarily (90 percent) to members. The other 10 percent of the recipients are nonmembers and are not subscribers within the meaning of § 56.4911-5(f)(5). Assume also that the first letter does not state that readers should urge nonmembers to write to legislators. F allocates one-half of the mailing costs as a lobbying expenditure, of which 90 percent is a direct lobbying expenditure and 10 percent is a grass roots lobbying expenditure (see § 56.4911-5(e)(2)). F's allocation is reasonable for purposes of § 56.4911-3(a)(2)(ii) and is correct for purposes of § 56.4911-5.

(c) *Certain transfers treated as lobbying expenditures.*—(1) *Transfer earmarked for grass roots purposes.*—A transfer is a grass roots expenditure to the extent that it is earmarked (as defined in § 56.4911-4(f)(4)) for grass roots lobbying purposes and is not described in § 56.4911-4(e).

(2) *Transfer earmarked for direct and grass roots lobbying.*—A transfer that is earmarked for direct lobbying purposes or for direct lobbying and grass roots lobbying purposes is treated as a grass roots expenditure in full except to the extent the transferor demonstrates that all or part of the amounts transferred were expended for direct lobbying purposes, in which case that part of the amounts transferred is a direct lobbying expenditure by the transferor. This paragraph (c)(2) shall not apply to any expenditure described in § 56.4911-4(e).

(3) *Certain transfers to noncharities that lobby.*—(i) *Limited application of paragraph (c)(3).*—(A) *In general.*—This paragraph (c)(3) applies only to transfers for less than fair market value from an electing public charity to any noncharity that makes lobbying expenditures. A noncharity is any entity that is not described in section 501(c)(3). In order for this paragraph to apply, the electing public charity must transfer to a noncharity more in value than it receives in return. For example, this paragraph does not apply to an electing public charity's fair market value payment of rent to a landlord. However, this paragraph does apply where an electing public charity and a noncharity share office space and the electing public charity pays more than fair market value rent to the noncharity. Similarly, this paragraph applies where an electing public charity sells goods or services to a noncharity for less than fair market value. See paragraphs (c)(3)(i)(B), (C) and (D) of this section for exceptions where non-fair market value transfers are not covered by this paragraph (c)(3). See paragraph (c)(3)(i)(E) of this section to determine the amount of any non-fair market value transfer covered by this paragraph (c)(3). See paragraph (c)(3)(ii) of this section for the rules that apply to transfers governed by this paragraph (c)(3).

(B) *Exception for controlled grants.*—Notwithstanding paragraph (c)(3)(i)(A) of this section, this paragraph (c)(3) does not apply where an electing public charity makes a grant to a noncharity that is a controlled grant (as defined in § 56.4911-4(f)(3)).

(C) *Exception for transfers that artificially inflate exempt purpose expenditures.*—Notwithstanding paragraph (c)(3)(i)(A) of this section, this paragraph (c)(3) does not apply where an electing public charity makes a grant to a noncharity that is an expenditure described in § 56.4911-4(e) (relating to grants that artificially inflate exempt purpose expenditures).

(D) *Exception for substantially related activity.*—Notwithstanding paragraph (c)(3)(i)(A) of this section, this paragraph (c)(3) does not apply where an electing public charity, in the course of an activity that is substantially related to the accomplishment of the electing public charity's exempt purposes, makes goods or services widely available for less than fair market value to individual members of the general public and those goods or services are actually purchased (or consumed for no charge) by a substantial number of wholly unrelated individual members of the general public for less than fair market value. For purposes of the preceding sentence, the term "individual member of the general public" does not include any person or entity directly or indirectly affiliated with the electing public charity in question. The following example illustrates this paragraph (c)(3)(i)(D):

*Example*. Organization P is an educational organization dedicated to preserving the environment. One of P's activities is educating the public about the benefits of installing cost-effective passive solar energy systems, thereby helping to preserve the environment. P charges for its extensive literature and advice, but the charges are less than the fair market value of the literature and advice. P makes its literature and advice widely available to individual members of the general public by advertising in various media and by pamphlets distributed in various areas. P annually provides its literature and advice for less than fair market value to 500 wholly unrelated families, businesses, and tax-exempt organizations. Several of the businesses and tax-exempt organizations make lobbying expenditures within the meaning of section 4911. P's provision of its goods and services to these entities is not covered by this paragraph (c)(3) (and thus does not give rise to a lobbying expenditure by P under paragraph (c)(3)(ii)).

(E) *Determination of amount of transfer governed by paragraph (c)(3).*—Where an electing public charity receives nothing of value in return for its transfer, the amount of the transfer governed by this paragraph (c)(3) is the greater of the fair market value or the cost of the goods or services transferred to the noncharity. Where the noncharity transfers something of value to the electing public charity in return for the charity's transfer, but that payment is less than the fair market value of the charity's transfer to the noncharity, the amount of the transfer governed by this paragraph (c)(3) is the excess of: first, the greater of the fair market value or cost of the goods or services transferred to the noncharity over, second, the value of the amount transferred to the charity. For example, if an electing public charity transfers $10,000 of goods and services to a noncharity that makes lobbying expenditures in return for payment by the noncharity of $2,000, the amount of the transfer governed by this paragraph (c)(3) is $8,000.

(ii) *Rules governing transfers to which paragraph (c)(3) applies.*—A transfer to which this paragraph (c)(3) applies is treated in whole or in part as a grass roots and/or direct lobbying expenditure by the transferor in accordance with paragraphs (c)(3)(ii)(A), (B) and (C) of this section. In applying those paragraphs, the expenditures of the transferee will be determined as if the regulations under section 4911 applied to the transferee. This paragraph (c)(3) discusses only when certain transfers are lobbying expenditures by the transferor. This paragraph does not address other issues that may arise when an electing public charity makes a noncontrolled grant to a noncharity. Nothing in this paragraph (c)(3) shall be used to interpret issues relating to noncontrolled grants by charities to noncharities, such as whether the noncontrolled grant is consistent with the continued tax-exempt status of the electing public charity.

(A) *Transfers treated as grass roots expenditures.*—The transfer is treated as a grass roots expenditure to the extent of the lesser of two amounts: the amount of the transfer and the amount of the transferee's grass roots expenditures.

(B) *Transfers treated as direct lobbying expenditures.*—If the transfer is greater than the transferee's grass roots expenditures, the excess is treated as a direct lobbying expenditure, but only to the extent of the transferee's direct lobbying expenditures. (If, however, the transfer is less than the transferee's grass roots expenditures, none of the transfer is a direct lobbying expenditure).

(C) *Transfers treated as non-lobbying.*—If the transfer is greater than the sum of the transferee's grass roots and direct lobbying expenditures, the excess of the transfer over those lobbying expenses is not a lobbying expenditure.

(iii) *Example.*—The following example illustrates the application of this paragraph (c)(3):

*Example.* Organization C, an electing public charity, shares employee E with N, a noncharity that makes lobbying expenditures. N's grass roots expenditures are $5,000 and its direct lobbying expenditures are $25,000. Each organization pays one-half of the $100,000 in direct and overhead costs associated with E. E devotes one-quarter of his time to C and three-quarters of his time to N. In substance, this arrangement is a transfer (for less than fair market value) from C to N in the amount of $25,000 (one-quarter of the $100,000 of direct and overhead costs associated with E's work). Accordingly, C is treated as having made a $5,000 grass roots expenditure (the lesser of N's grass roots expenditures ($5,000) or the amount of the transfer ($25,000)). C is also treated as having made a $20,000 direct lobbying expenditure (the lesser of N's direct lobbying expenditures ($25,000) or the remaining amount of the transfer ($20,000)). [Reg. § 56.4911-3.]

☐ [T.D. 8308, 8-30-90.]

**[Reg. § 56.4911-4]**

**§ 56.4911-4. Exempt purpose expenditures.**—(a) *Application.*—This section provides rules under section 4911(e) for determining an electing public charity's "exempt purpose expenditures" for a taxable year for purposes of section 4911(c)(2) and § 56.4911-1(c)(2). Those two sections generally define an electing public charity's lobbying limit (lobbying nontaxable amount) as a sliding scale percentage of the organization's exempt purpose expenditures. In determining an electing public charity's exempt purpose expenditures, no expenditure shall be counted twice by an organization.

(b) *Included expenditures.*—Amounts paid or incurred by an organization that are exempt purpose expenditures include—

(1) Amounts paid or incurred to accomplish a purpose enumerated in section 170(c)(2)(B), including (but not limited to) the amount of any transfer made by the organization (other than a transfer described in paragraph (e) of this section) to another organization to accomplish the transferor's exempt purposes, and including amounts expended by an organization out of transfers (other than a transfer described in paragraph (e) of this section) for which the organization is the transferee,

(2) Amounts paid or incurred as current or deferred compensation for an employee's services for a purpose enumerated in section 170(c)(2)(B),

(3) The allocable portion of administrative overhead, and other general expenditures attributable to the accomplishment of a purpose enumerated in section 170(c)(2)(B),

(4) Lobbying expenditures (as defined in § 56.4911-2(a)) whether or not for a purpose enumerated in section 170(c)(2)(B),

(5) Amounts paid or incurred for activities described in § 56.4911-2(c),

(6) Amounts paid or incurred for activities described in § 56.4911-5 that are not lobbying expenditures,

(7) A reasonable allowance for exhaustion, wear and tear, obsolescence or amortization, of assets to the extent used for one or more of the purposes described in paragraphs (b)(1) through (6) of this section, computed on a straight-line basis (for this purpose, an allowance for depreciation will be treated as reasonable if based on a useful life that would satisfy section 312(k)(3)(A) as in effect on January 1, 1985), and

(8) Fundraising expenditures (but see section 4911(e)(1)(C) and paragraphs (c)(3) and (4) of this section).

(c) *Excluded expenditures.*—Notwithstanding paragraph (b) of this section, exempt purpose expenditures do not include—

(1) Amounts paid or incurred that are neither expenditures to accomplish a purpose enumerated in section 170(c)(2)(B), lobbying expenditures (as defined in § 56.4911-2(a)), nor expenditures described in paragraph (b)(5), (6) or (8) of this section,

(2) The amount of any transfer described in paragraph (e) of this section,

(3) Amounts paid to or incurred for a separate fundraising unit (as defined in paragraph (f)(2) of this section) of an organization or of an affiliated organization (see § 56.4911-7(a)),

(4) Amounts paid to or incurred for any person not an employee, or any organization not an affiliated organization, if paid or incurred primarily for fundraising, but only if such person or organization engages in fundraising, fundraising counselling or the provision of similar advice or services,

(5) Amounts paid or incurred that are properly chargeable to a capital account, determined in accordance with the principles that apply under section 263 or, as applicable, section 263A, with respect to an unrelated trade or business,

(6) Amounts paid or incurred for a tax that is not imposed in connection with the organization's efforts to accomplish a purpose described in section 170(c)(2)(B), such as taxes imposed under sections 511(a)(1) and 4911(a), and

(7) Amounts paid or incurred for the production of income. For purposes of this section, amounts are paid or incurred for the production of income if they are paid or incurred for a purpose or activity that is not substantially related (aside from the need of the organization for income or funds or the use it makes of the profits derived) to the exercise or performance by the organization of its charitable, educational or other purpose or function constituting the basis for its exemption under section 501. For example, the costs of managing an endowment are amounts that are paid or incurred for the production of income and are thus not exempt purpose expenditures. Fundraising expenditures are not, for purposes of this section, amounts that are paid or incurred for the production of income. Instead, the determination of whether fundraising costs are exempt purpose expenditures must be made with reference to section 4911(e)(1)(C) and paragraphs (b)(8), (c)(3) and (c)(4) of this section.

(d) *Certain transfers treated as exempt purpose expenditures.*—(1) An organization's transfer will be treated as an exempt purpose expenditure under paragraph (b)(1) of this section if it is—

(i) Described in either paragraph (d)(2) or (d)(3) of this section, and

(ii) Not described in paragraph (e) of this section.

(2) A transfer is described in this paragraph (d)(2) if it is made to an organization described in section 501(c)(3) in furtherance of the transferor's exempt purposes and is not earmarked for any purpose other than a purpose described in section 170(c)(2)(B). Thus, a payment of dues by a local or state organization to, respectively, a state or national organization that is described in section 501(c)(3) is considered an exempt purpose expenditure of the transferor to the extent it is not otherwise earmarked.

(3) A transfer is described in this paragraph (d)(3) if it is a controlled grant (as defined in paragraph (f)(3) of this section), but only to the extent of the amounts that are paid or incurred by the transferee that would be exempt purpose expenditures if paid or incurred by the transferor.

(e) *Transfers not exempt purpose expenditures.*—(1) An organization's transfer is described in this paragraph (e) if it is described in one of paragraphs (e)(2) through (e)(4).

(2) A transfer is described in this paragraph (e)(2) if it is made to a member of any affiliated group (as defined in § 56.4911-7(e)) of which the transferor is a member.

(3) A transfer is described in this paragraph (e)(3) if the Commissioner determines that the transfer artificially inflates the amount of the transferor's or transferee's exempt purpose expenditures. In general, the Commissioner will make that determination if a substantial purpose of a transfer is to inflate those exempt purpose expenditures. A transfer described in this paragraph will not be considered an exempt purpose expenditure of the transferor, but will be an exempt purpose expenditure of the transferee to the extent that the transferee expends the transfer in the active conduct of its charitable activities or attempts to influence legislation. Standards similar to those found in § 53.4942(b)-1(b) may be applied in determining whether the transferee has expended amounts in the "active conduct" of its charitable activities or attempts to influence legislation.

(4) A transfer is described in this paragraph (e)(4) if it is not a controlled grant and is made to an organization not described in section 501(c)(3) that does not attempt to influence legislation.

(f) *Definitions.*—(1) For purposes of paragraph (c) of this section, "fundraising" includes—

(i) Soliciting dues or contributions from members of the organization, from persons whose dues are in arrears, or from the general public,

(ii) Soliciting grants from businesses or other organizations, including organizations described in section 501(c)(3), or

(iii) Soliciting grants from a governmental unit referred to in section 170(c)(1), or any agency or instrumentality thereof.

(2) For purposes of paragraph (c) of this section, a separate fundraising unit of any organization must consist of either two or more individuals a majority of whose time is spent on fundraising for the organization, or any separate accounting unit of the organization that is devoted to fundraising. For purposes of paragraph (c) of this section, amounts paid to or incurred for a separate fundraising unit include all amounts incurred for the creation, production, copying, and distribution of the fundraising portion of a separate fundraising unit's communication. (For example, an electing public charity that has a separate fundraising unit may not count the cost of postage for a separate fundraising unit's fundraising communication as an exempt purpose expenditure even though, under the electing public charity's accounting system, that cost is attributable to the mailroom rather than to the separate fundraising unit).

(3) For purposes of this section, a "controlled grant" is a grant made by an eligible organization described in §1.501(h)-2(b) to an organization not described in section 501(c)(3) that meets the following requirements:

(i) The donor limits the grant to a specific project of the recipient that is in furtherance of the donor's (nonlobbying) exempt purposes; and

(ii) The donor maintains records to establish that the grant is used in furtherance of the donor's (nonlobbying) exempt purposes.

(4) A transfer, including a grant or payment of dues, is "earmarked" for a specific purpose—

(i) To the extent that the transferor directs the transferee to add the amount transferred to a fund established to accomplish the purpose, or

(ii) To the extent of the amount transferred or, if less, the amount agreed upon to be expended to accomplish the purpose, if there exists an agreement, oral or written, whereby the transferor may cause the transferee to expend amounts to accomplish the purpose or whereby the transferee agrees to expend an amount to accomplish the purpose.

(g) *Example.*—The provisions of this section are illustrated by the following example:

*Example.* Organization X is an exempt organization described in section 501(c)(3) that is organized for the purpose of rehabilitating alcoholics. X elected to be subject to the provisions of section 501(h) in 1981. For 1981, X had the following expenditures that are included in its exempt purpose expenditures to the extent indicated.

| Description | Total | Includible |
|---|---|---|
| Cost of real estate purchased for use as half-way house for alcoholics, attributable to the following: | | |
|     Land | $30,000 | $–0– |
|     Building | 200,000 | –0– |
|     Depreciation 40-year useful life | –0– | 5,000 |
| Expenses of operating its half-way house | 170,000 | 170,000 |
| Administrative expenses of the organization allocated to the operation of its half-way house | 95,000 | 95,000 |
| Depreciation and allowances for equipment | 10,000 | 10,000 |
| Expenses related to attempts to influence legislation (lobbying expenditures) | 40,000 | 40,000 |
| Amounts paid to Z by the Organization for fundraising | 35,000 | –0– |
|     Total | $580,000 | $320,000 |

Note.—For 1981, X's exempt purpose expenditures total $320,000. The $35,000 paid by X to Z for fundraising is not included in the exempt purpose expenditures total. All lobbying expenses are included in full. Only depreciation computed on a straight-line basis is included in exempt purpose expenditures.

[Reg. §56.4911-4.]

☐ [*T.D.* 8308, 8-30-90.]

## [Reg. §56.4911-5]

**§56.4911-5. Communications with members.**—(a) *In general.*— For purposes of section 4911, expenditures for certain communications between an organization and its members ("membership communications") are treated more leniently than are communications to nonmembers. This §56.4911-5 contains rules about the more lenient treatment. In certain cases, this section provides that expenditures for a membership communication are not lobbying expenditures even though those expenditures would be lobbying expenditures if the communication were to nonmembers. In other cases, this section provides that expenditures for a membership communication are direct lobbying expenditures even though those expenditures would be grass roots expenditures if the communication were to nonmembers. Paragraphs (b), (c) and (d) of this section set forth the more lenient rules that apply for communications that are directed only to members. Paragraph(e) of this section sets forth the more lenient rules that apply for communications that are directed primarily, but not solely, to members. Paragraph (f) of this section sets forth certain definitions and special rules.

(b) *Communications (directed only to members) that are not lobbying communications.*—Expenditures for a communication that refers to, and reflects a view on, specific legislation are not lobbying expenditures if the communication satisfies the following requirements:

(1) The communication is directed only to members of the organization;

(2) The specific legislation the communication refers to, and reflects a view on, is of direct interest to the organization and its members;

(3) The communication does not directly encourage the member to engage in direct lobbying (whether individually or through the organization); and

(4) The communication does not directly encourage the member to engage in grass roots lobbying (whether individually or through the organization).

(c) *Communications (directed only to members) that are direct lobbying communications.*—Expenditures for a communication that refers to, and reflects a view on, specific legislation and that satisfies the requirements of paragraphs (b)(1), (b)(2), and (b)(4) of this section, but does not satisfy the requirements of paragraph (b)(3) of this section, are treated as expenditures for direct lobbying.

(d) *Communications (directed only to members) that are grass roots lobbying communications.*—Expenditures for a communication that refers to, and reflects a view on, specific legislation and that satisfies the requirements of paragraphs (b)(1) and (b)(2) of this section, but does not satisfy the requirements of paragraph (b)(4) of this section, are treated as grass roots expenditures (whether or not the communication satisfies the requirements of paragraph (b)(3) of this section).

(e) *Written communications directed to members and nonmembers.*— (1) *In general.*—Expenditures for any written communication that is designed primarily for members of an organization (but not directed only to members) and that refers to, and reflects a view on, specific legislation of direct interest to the organization and its members, are treated as expenditures for direct or grass roots lobbying in accordance with paragraph (e)(2), (e)(3) or (e)(4) of this section. For purposes of this section, a communication is designed primarily for members of an organization if more than half of the recipients of the communication are members of the organization.

(2) *Direct lobbying directly encouraged.*—(i) *Lobbying expenditure amount.*—If a written communication described in paragraph (e)(1) of this section directly encourages readers to engage individually or through the organization in direct lobbying but does not directly encourage them to engage in grass roots lobbying, the cost of the communication is allocated between expenditures for direct lobbying and grass roots expenditures in accordance with paragraphs (e)(2)(ii) and (iii) of this section. The portion of the cost to be allocated includes all costs of preparing all the material with respect to which readers are urged to engage in direct lobbying plus the mechanical and distribution costs attributable to the lineage devoted to this material (see §1.512(a)-1(f)(6)).

(ii) *Grass roots amount.*—The amount allocable as a grass roots expenditure for a communication described in paragraph (e)(1) of this section is the amount calculated in paragraph (e)(2)(i) of this section multiplied by the sum of the nonmember subscribers percentage and the all other distribution percentage, both as defined in paragraph (f)(7) of this section. Solely for purposes of the allocation described in this paragraph (e)(2)(ii), the nonmember subscribers percentage is treated as zero unless it is greater than 15% of total distribution.

(iii) *Direct lobbying amount.*—The amount allocable as an expenditure for direct lobbying for a communication described in paragraph (e)(1) of this section is the excess of the amount described in paragraph (e)(2)(i) of this section over the amount described in paragraph (e)(2)(ii) of this section.

(3) *Grass roots expenditure if grass roots lobbying directly encouraged.*—If a written communication described in paragraph (e)(1) of this section directly encourages readers to engage individually or collectively (whether through the organization or otherwise) in grass roots lobbying (whether or not it also encourages readers to engage in direct lobbying), the grass roots expenditure includes all the costs of preparing all the material with respect to which readers are urged to engage in grass roots lobbying plus the mechanical and distribution costs attributable to the lineage devoted to this material (see §1.512(a)-1(f)(6)).

(4) *No direct encouragement of direct lobbying or of grass roots lobbying.*—If a written communication described in paragraph (e)(1) of this section does not directly encourage readers to engage in either direct lobbying or grass roots lobbying, expenditures for the communication are not lobbying expenditures.

(f) *Definitions and special rules.*—For purposes of the regulations under section 4911—

(1) *Member; general rule.*—A person is a member of an electing public charity if the person—

(i) Pays dues or makes a contribution of more than a nominal amount,

(ii) Makes a contribution of more than a nominal amount of time, or

(iii) Is one of a limited number of "honorary" or "life" members who have more than a nominal connection with the electing public charity and who have been chosen for a valid reason (such as length of service to the organization or involvement in activities forming the basis of the electing public charity's exemption) unrelated to the electing public charity's dissemination of information to its members.

(2) *Member; special rule.*—A person not a member of an electing public charity within the meaning of paragraph (f)(1) of this section may be treated as a member if the electing public charity demonstrates to the satisfaction of the Internal Revenue Service that there is a good reason for its membership requirements not meeting the requirements of such paragraph (f)(1), and that its membership requirements do not operate to permit an abuse of the rules described in this section.

(3) *Member; affiliated group of organizations.*—For purposes of this section, a person who is a member of an organization that is a member of an affiliated group of organizations (within the meaning of §56.4911-7(e)) is treated as a member of each organization in the affiliated group.

(4) *Member; limited affiliated group of organizations.*—For purposes of this section, a person who is a member of an organization that is a member of a limited affiliated group of organizations (within the meaning of §56.4911-10(b)) is treated as a member of each organization in the limited affiliated group, but only to the extent that the communication relates to a national legislative issue (within the meaning of §56.4911-10(g)).

(5) *Subscriber.*—A person is a subscriber to a written communication if—

(i) The person is a member of the publishing organization and the membership dues expressly include the right to receive the written communication, or

(ii) The person has affirmatively expressed a desire to receive the written communication and has paid more than a nominal amount for the communication.

(6) *Directly encourages.*—(i) *Direct lobbying.*—(A) *In general.*—For purposes of this section, a communication directly encourages a recipient to engage in direct lobbying, whether individually or through the organization, if the communication:

(*1*) States that the recipient should contact a legislator or an employee of a legislative body, or should contact any other government official or employee who may participate in the formulation of legislation (but only if the principal purpose of urging contact with the government official or employee is to influence legislation);

(*2*) States the address, telephone number, or similar information of a legislator or an employee of a legislative body; or

(*3*) Provides a petition, tear-off postcard or similar material for the recipient to communicate his or her views to a legislator or an employee of a legislative body, or to any other government official or employee who may participate in the formulation of legislation (but only if the principal purpose of so facilitating contact with the government official or employee is to influence legislation).

(B) *"Self-defense" exception for communications with members.*—Notwithstanding the provisions of paragraph (f)(6)(i)(A) of this section, for purposes of paragraphs (b)(3), (e)(2)(i), (e)(3) and (e)(4) of this section, a communication that directly encourages a member to engage in direct lobbying activities that are described in section 4911(d)(2)(C) and that would not be attempts to influence legislation if engaged in directly by the organization is treated as a communication that does not directly encourage a member to engage in direct lobbying.

(ii) *Grass roots lobbying.*—For purposes of paragraphs (b)(4), (e)(3) and (e)(4) of this section, a communication directly encourages recipients to engage individually or collectively (whether through the organization or otherwise) in grass roots lobbying if the communication:

(A) States that the recipient should encourage any nonmember to contact a legislator or an employee of a legislative body, or to contact any other government official or employee who may participate in the formulation of legislation (but only if the principal purpose of urging contact with the government official or employee is to influence legislation);

(B) States that the recipient should provide to any nonmember the address, telephone number, or similar information of a legislator or an employee of a legislative body; or

(C) Provides (or requests that the recipient provide to nonmembers) a petition, tear-off postcard or similar material for the recipient (or nonmember) to use to ask any nonmember to communicate views to a legislator or an employee of a legislative body, or to any other government official or employee who may participate in the formulation of legislation, but only if the principal purpose of so facilitating contact with the government official or employee is to influence legislation. For purposes of this paragraph (f)(6)(ii)(C), a petition is provided for the recipient to use to ask any nonmember to communicate views if, for example, the petition has an entire page of preprinted signature blocks. Similarly, for purposes of this paragraph (f)(6)(ii)(C), where a communication is distributed to a single member and provides several tear-off postcards addressed to a legislator, the postcards are presumed to be provided for the member to use to ask a nonmember to communicate with the legislator.

(7) *Percentages of total distribution.*—With respect to a communication described in paragraph (e)(1) of this section—

(i) "Member percentage" means the percentage of total distribution that represents distribution of a single copy to any member;

(ii) "Nonmember subscribers percentage" means the percentage of total distribution that represents distribution to nonmember subscribers (including libraries); and

(iii) "All other distribution percentage" means 100% reduced by the sum of the member percentage and the nonmember subscribers percentage.

(8) *Reasonable allocation rule.*—In the case of lobbying expenditures for a communication that also has a bona fide nonlobbying purpose and that is sent only or primarily to members, an electing public charity must make a reasonable allocation between the amount expended for the lobbying purpose and the amount expended for the nonlobbying purpose. See §56.4911-3(a)(2)(ii). [Reg. §56.4911-5.]

☐ [*T.D.* 8308, 8-30-90.]

**[Reg. §56.4911-6]**

**§56.4911-6. Records of lobbying and grass roots expenditures.**—(a) *Records of lobbying expenditures.*—An electing public charity must keep a record of its lobbying expenditures for the taxable year. Lobbying expenditures of which an organization must keep a record include the following:

(1) Expenditures for grass roots lobbying, as described in paragraph (b) of this section;

(2) Amounts directly paid or incurred for direct lobbying, including payments to another organization earmarked for direct lobbying, fees and expenses paid to individuals or organizations for direct lobbying, and printing, mailing, and other direct costs of reproducing and distributing materials used in direct lobbying;

(3) The portion of amounts paid or incurred as current or deferred compensation for an employee's services for direct lobbying;

(4) Amounts paid for out-of-pocket expenditures incurred on behalf of the organization and for direct lobbying, whether or not incurred by an employee;

(5) The allocable portion of administrative, overhead, and other general expenditures attributable to direct lobbying;

(6) Expenditures for publications or for communications with members to the extent the expenditures are treated as expenditures for direct lobbying under §56.4911-5; and

(7) Expenditures for direct lobbying of a controlled organization (within the meaning of §56.4911-10(c)) to the extent included by a controlling organization (within the meaning of §56.4911-10(c)) in its lobbying expenditures.

(b) *Records of grass roots expenditures.*—An electing public charity must keep a record of its grass roots expenditures for the taxable year. Grass roots expenditures of which an organization must keep a record include the following:

(1) Amounts directly paid or incurred for grass roots lobbying, including payments to other organizations earmarked for grass roots lobbying, fees and expenses paid to individuals or organizations for grass roots lobbying, and the printing, mailing, and other direct costs of reproducing and distributing materials used in grass roots lobbying;

(2) The portion of amounts paid or incurred as current or deferred compensation for an employee's services for grass roots lobbying;

(3) Amounts paid for out-of-pocket expenditures incurred on behalf of the organization and for grass roots lobbying, whether or not incurred by an employee;

(4) The allocable portion of administrative, overhead and other general expenditures attributable to grass roots lobbying;

(5) Expenditures for publications or communications that are treated as expenditures for grass roots lobbying under §56.4911-5; and

(6) Expenditures for grass roots lobbying of a controlled organization (within the meaning of §56.4911-10(c)) to the extent included by a controlling organization (within the meaning of §56.4911-10(c)) in its grass roots expenditures. [Reg. §56.4911-6.]

☐ [T.D. 8308, 8-30-90.]

## [Reg. §56.4911-7]

§56.4911-7. **Affiliated group of organizations.**—(a) *Affiliation between two organizations.*—Sections 4911(f)(1) through (3) contain a limited anti-abuse rule for groups of affiliated organizations. In general, the rule operates to prevent numerous organizations from being created for the purpose of avoiding the sliding-scale percentage limitation on an electing public charity's lobbying expenditures (as well as avoiding the $1,000,000 cap on a single electing public charity's lobbying expenditures). This is generally accomplished by treating the members of an affiliated group as a single organization for purposes of measuring both lobbying expenditures and permitted lobbying expenditures. The anti-abuse rule is implemented by this §56.4911-7 and §§56.4911-8 and -9. This §56.4911-7 defines the term "affiliated group of organizations" and defines the taxable year of an affiliated group of organizations. Section 56.4911-8 provides rules concerning the exempt purpose expenditures, lobbying expenditures and grass roots expenditures of an affiliated group of organizations, as well as rules concerning the application of the excise tax imposed by section 4911(a) on excess lobbying expenditures by the group. Section 56.4911-9 provides rules concerning the application of the section 501(h) lobbying expenditure limits to members of an affiliated group of organizations. (For additional rules for members of a limited affiliated group of organizations (generally, organizations that are affiliated solely by reason of governing instrument provisions that extend control solely with respect to national legislation), see section 4911(f)(4) and §56.4911-10.)

(1) *In general.*—For purposes of the regulations under section 4911, two organizations are affiliated, subject to the limitation described in paragraph (a)(2) of this section, if one organization is able to control action on legislative issues by the other by reason of interlocking governing boards (see paragraph (b) of this section) or by reason of provisions of the governing instruments of the controlled organization (see paragraph (c) of this section). The ability of the controlling organization to control action on legislative issues by the controlled organization is sufficient to establish that the organizations are affiliated; it is not necessary that the control be exercised.

(2) *Organizations not described in section 501(c)(3).*—Two organizations, neither of which is described in section 501(c)(3), are affiliated only if there exists at least one organization described in section 501(c)(3) that is affiliated with both organizations.

(3) *Action on legislative issues.*—For purposes of this section, the term "action on legislative issues" includes taking a position in the organization's name on legislation, authorizing any person to take a position in the organization's name on legislation, or authorizing any lobbying expenditures. The phrase does not include actions taken merely to correct unauthorized actions taken in the organization's name.

(b) *Interlocking governing boards.*—(1) *In general.*—Two organizations have interlocking governing boards if one organization (the controlling organization) has a sufficient number of representatives (within the meaning of paragraph (b)(5) of this section) on the governing board of the second organization (the controlled organization) so that by aggregating their votes, the representatives of the controlling organization can cause or prevent action on legislative issues by the controlled organization. If two organizations have interlocking governing boards, the organizations are affiliated without regard to how or whether the representatives of the controlling organization vote on any particular matter.

(2) *Majority or quorum.*—Except as provided in paragraph (b)(3) or (4) of this section, the number of representatives of an organization (the controlling organization) who are members of the governing board of a second organization (the controlled organization) will be presumed sufficient to cause or prevent action on legislative issues by the controlled organization if that number either—

(i) Constitutes a majority of incumbents on the governing board, or

(ii) Constitutes a quorum, or is sufficient to prevent a quorum, for acting on legislative issues.

(3) *Votes required under governing instrument or local law.*—Except as provided in paragraph (b)(4) of this section, if under the governing documents of an organization (the controlled organization), it can be determined that a lesser number of votes than the number described in paragraph (b)(2) of this section is necessary or sufficient to cause or to prevent action on legislative issues, the number of representatives of the controlling organization who are members of the governing board of the controlled organization will be considered sufficient to cause or prevent action on legislative issues if it equals or exceeds that number.

(4) *Representatives constituting less than 15% of governing board.*—Notwithstanding paragraph (b)(2) or (3) of this section, if the number of representatives of one organization is less than 15 percent of the incumbents on the governing board of a second organization, the two organizations are not affiliated by reason of interlocking governing boards.

(5) *Representatives.*—(i) This paragraph (b)(5) describes members of the governing board of one organization (the controlled organization) who are considered representatives of a second organization (the controlling organization). Under this paragraph (b)(5), a member of the governing board of a controlled organization may be a representative of more than one controlling organization. A person with no authority to vote on any issue being considered by the governing board is not a representative of any organization.

(ii) A board member of one organization (the controlled organization) is a representative of a second organization (the controlling organization) if the controlling organization has specifically designated that person to be a board member of the controlled organization. For purposes of this paragraph (b)(5)(ii) and paragraph (b)(5)(iii) of this section, a board member of the controlled organization is specifically designated by the controlling organization if the board member is selected by virtue of the right of the controlling organization, under the governing instruments of the controlled organization, either to designate a person to be a member of the controlled organization's governing board, or to select a person for a position that entitles the holder of that position to be a member of the controlled organization's governing board.

(iii) A board member of one organization who is specifically designated by a second organization, a majority of the governing board of which is made up of representatives of a third organization, is a representative of the third organization as well as being a representative of the second organization pursuant to paragraph (b)(5)(ii) of this section.

(iv) A board member of one organization who is also a member of the governing board of a second organization is a representative of the second organization.

(v) A board member of one organization who is an officer or paid executive staff member of a second organization is a representative of the second organization. Although titles are significant in determining whether a person is a member of the executive staff of an organization, any employee of an organization who possesses authority commonly exercised by an executive is considered an executive staff member for purposes of this paragraph (b)(5)(v).

(c) *Governing instrument.*—One organization (the "controlling" organization) is affiliated with a second organization (the "controlled" organization) by reason of the governing instruments of the controlled organization if the governing instruments of the controlled organization limit the independent action of the controlled organization on legislative issues by requiring it to be bound by decisions of the other organization on legislative issues.

(d) *Three or more organizations affiliated.*—(1) *Two controlled organizations affiliated.*—If a controlling organization described in this section is affiliated with each of two or more controlled organizations described in this section, then the controlled organizations are affiliated with each other.

(2) *Chain rule.*—If one organization is a controlling organization described in this section with respect to a second organization and that second organization is a controlling organization with respect to a third organization, then the first organization is affiliated with the third.

(e) *Affiliated group of organizations.*—(1) *Defined.*—For purposes of the regulations under section 4911, an affiliated group of organizations is a group of organizations—

(i) Each of which is affiliated with every other member for at least thirty days of the taxable year of the affiliated group (determined without regard to the election provided for in paragraph (e)(5) of this section),

(ii) Each of which is an eligible organization (within the meaning of § 1.501(h)-2(b)(1)), and

(iii) At least one of which is an electing member organization (within the meaning of paragraph (e)(4) of this section).
Each organization in a group of organizations that satisfies the requirements of the preceding sentence is a member of the affiliated group of organizations for the taxable year of the affiliated group.

(2) *Multiple membership.*—For any taxable year of an organization, it may be a member of two or more affiliated groups of organizations.

(3) *Taxable year of affiliated group.*—If all members of an affiliated group have the same taxable year, that taxable year is the taxable year of the affiliated group. If the members of an affiliated group do not all have the same taxable year, the taxable year of the affiliated group is the calendar year, unless the election under paragraph (e)(5) of this section is made.

(4) *Electing member organization.*—For purposes of the regulations under section 4911, an "electing member organization" is an organization to which the expenditure test election under section 501(h) applies on at least one day of the taxable year of the affiliated group of which it is a member. For purposes of the preceding sentence (and notwithstanding § 1.501(h)-2(a)), the expenditure test is not considered to apply to the organization on any day before the date on which it files the Form 5768 making the expenditure test election.

(5) *Election of member's year as group's taxable year.*—The taxable year of an affiliated group may be determined according to the provisions of this paragraph (e)(5) if all of the members of the affiliated group so elect. Under this paragraph (e)(5), each member organization shall apply the provisions of section 501(h) and 4911, and the regulations thereunder (unless the regulations provide otherwise), by treating its own taxable year as the taxable year of the affiliated group. The election may be made by an electing member organization by attaching to its annual return a statement from itself and every other member of the affiliated group that contains: the organization's name, address, and employer identification number; and its signed consent to the election provided for in this paragraph (e)(5). The election must be made no later than the due date of the first annual return of any electing member for its taxable year for which the member is liable for tax under section 4911(a), determined under § 56.4911-8(d). The election may not be made or revoked after the due date of the return referred to in the preceding sentence except upon such terms and conditions as the Commissioner may prescribe.

(f) *Examples.*—The provisions of this section are illustrated by the following examples.

*Example (1).* M, N, and O are eligible organizations within the meaning of § 1.501(h)-2(b)(1). Each has a governing board made up of nine members. Five members on the board of N are also members of the board of M. N designates five individuals from among its board, officers, and executive staff members to serve on the board of O. M is affiliated with N, N is affiliated with O, and M is affiliated with O.

*Example (2).* X, an eligible organization, has a board consisting of 10 members. Five unaffiliated tax-exempt organizations each designate two individuals to serve on the governing board of X. A **simple** majority of the board of X is a quorum and may establish X's **position** on legislative issues. X is not affiliated with any of the five autonomous organizations by reason of interlocking governing boards.

*Example (3).* P and Q are eligible organizations. The governing instruments of Q state that it will not take a position on legislation if P disapproves of the position. In addition, there is regular correspon-

dence between P and Q with regard to positions on legislation. P is affiliated with Q regardless of whether P has ever vetoed a position taken by Q.

*Example (4).* The governing board of organization R resolves to adopt the position taken on legislative issues by organization S. R and S are eligible organizations and do not have interlocking governing boards. The governing instruments of R do not mention organization S and do not indicate that R is to be bound by the decisions of legislation of any organization. R and S are not affiliated.

*Example (5).* Organization Z is bound, under the terms of its governing instruments, by the legislative positions of organization Y. Organization Y, however, is bound, under the terms of its governing instruments, by the legislative positions of organization X. Organization X is affiliated with Y and Z; Y is affiliated with X and Z; and Z is affiliated with X and Y.

*Example (6).* Organizations T and U have interlocking boards of directors. T is the controlling organization. Organization V is bound, under the terms of its governing instruments, by the legislative positions of U. T and V are affiliated because T may cause or prevent action on legislative issues by U, and V is bound by U's action. If U were the controlling organization, T and V would be affiliated as two organizations controlled by the same organization.

*Example (7).* Organization A is described in section 501(c)(4). It is affiliated, as the controlling organization, with organizations K and L, both of which are described in section 501(c)(3) and are eligible to elect under section 501(h). If K elects under section 501(h), K and L are an affiliated group of organizations. Even though A is affiliated with K and L, A is not a member of that affiliated group of organizations because A is not an eligible organization within the meaning of § 1.501(h)-2(b)(1) (see § 56.4911-7(e)(1) for the definition of which affiliated organizations may be members of an affiliated group of organizations).

*Example (8).* G, H, I, and J are eligible organizations. G, H, and I have elected the expenditure test under section 501(h). The governing board of J has nine members. Under the governing instruments of J, organizations G, H, and I each designate three members of the governing board of J. Also under the governing instruments of J, action on legislative issues requires the approval of any seven board members. Because the three representatives of G may prevent action on legislative issues, J is affiliated with G. Similarly, J is affiliated with each of H and I. However, under none of the rules of affiliation is G affiliated with H, or H with I, or I with G. Therefore J is a member of one affiliated group comprising G and J, of another group comprising H and J, and of a third group comprising I and J.

*Example (9).* Organizations C, D, and E have been affiliated for many years and have all elected the expenditure test. Each has a taxable year ending July 31. For every day of the year ending July 31, 1992, they were eligible organizations, electing member organizations, and affiliated with each other. On no day of that year were they affiliated with any other eligible organization having a different taxable year. Therefore, the year ending July 31, 1992, is the taxable year of the affiliated group comprising C, D, and E. [Reg. § 56.4911-7.]

☐ [T.D. 8308, 8-30-90.]

**[Reg. § 56.4911-8]**

**§ 56.4911-8. Excess lobbying expenditures of affiliated group.**—(a) *Application.*—This section provides rules concerning the exempt purpose expenditures, lobbying expenditures, and grass roots expenditures of an affiliated group of organizations, and the application of the excise tax imposed by section 4911(a) on the excess lobbying expenditures of the group.

(b) *Affiliated group treated as one organization.*—Under section 4911(f), an affiliated group of organizations is treated as a single organization for purposes of the tax imposed by section 4911(a). For any taxable year of the affiliated group, the group's lobbying expenditures, grass roots expenditures, and exempt purpose expenditures are equal to the sum of the lobbying expenditures, grass roots expenditures, and exempt purpose expenditures, respectively, paid or incurred by each member during the taxable year of the affiliated group. The lobbying and grass roots nontaxable amounts for the affiliated group for a taxable year are determined under section 4911(c)(2) and (4) and § 56.4911-1(c) and are based on the sum of the exempt purpose expenditures described in the preceding sentence. The lobbying and grass roots ceiling amounts for the affiliated group for a taxable year are calculated under § 1.501(h)-3(c)(3) and (6) based upon the nontaxable amounts determined pursuant to the preceding sentence.

(c) *Tax imposed on excess lobbying expenditures of affiliated group.*—The excise tax under section 4911(a) is imposed for a taxable year of an affiliated group if the group has excess lobbying expenditures. For any taxable year of an affiliated group, the group's excess lobbying expenditures are the greater of—

(1) The amount by which the group's lobbying expenditures exceed the group's lobbying nontaxable amount, or

(2) The amount by which the group's grass roots expenditures exceed the group's grass roots nontaxable amount.

(d) *Liability for tax.*—(1) *Electing organizations.*—As provided in this paragraph (d), an electing member organization is liable for all or a portion of the excise tax imposed by section 4911(a) on the excess lobbying expenditures of an affiliated group of organizations. An organization that is liable under this paragraph (d) is not liable for any excise tax under section 4911 based on its own excess lobbying expenditures. A member of the affiliated group that is not an electing member organization is not liable for any portion of the excise tax that is imposed with respect to the affiliated group.

(2) *Tax based on excess lobbying expenditures.*—If the excise tax imposed by section 4911(a) on the excess lobbying expenditures of an affiliated group of organizations is based upon the amount described in paragraph (c)(1) of this section, and at least one electing member has made lobbying expenditures, each electing member organization is liable for a portion of the tax equal to the amount of the tax multiplied by a fraction, the numerator of which is the electing member organization's lobbying expenditures paid or incurred during the taxable year of the affiliated group, and the denominator of which is the sum of the lobbying expenditures of all electing member organizations in the group paid or incurred during the taxable year of the affiliated group.

(3) *Tax based on excess grass roots expenditures.*—If the excise tax imposed by section 4911(a) on the excess lobbying expenditures of an affiliated group of organizations is based upon the amount described in paragraph (c)(2) of this section, and at least one electing member has made grass roots expenditures, each electing member organization is liable for a portion of the tax equal to the amount of the tax multiplied by the fraction described in paragraph (d)(2) of this section, except that "grass roots expenditures" is substituted for "lobbying expenditures."

(4) *Tax based on exempt purpose expenditures.*—If the excise tax imposed by section 4911(a) on the excess lobbying expenditures of an affiliated group of organizations is based upon the amount described in paragraph (c)(2) of this section, and if paragraphs (d)(2) and (d)(3) of this section do not apply because no electing organization has made lobbying or grass roots expenditures, respectively, each electing member organization is liable for a portion of the tax equal to the amount of tax multiplied by a fraction the numerator of which is the electing member organization's exempt purpose expenditures and the denominator of which is the exempt purpose expenditures of all the electing member organizations in the affiliated group.

(5) *Taxable year for which liable.*—An electing member organization that is liable for all or a portion of the excise tax imposed by section 4911(a) on the excess lobbying expenditures of an affiliated group of organizations is liable for the tax as if the tax were imposed for its taxable year with which or within which ends the taxable year of the affiliated group.

(6) *Organization a member of more than one affiliated group.*—If, under this paragraph (d), an organization is liable for its taxable year for two or more excise taxes imposed by section 4911(a) on the excess lobbying expenditures of two or more affiliated groups, then the organization is liable only for the greater of the two or more taxes.

(e) *Former member organization.*—An electing member organization that ceases to be a member of an affiliated group of organizations, the taxable year of which is different from its own, must thereafter determine its liability under §56.4911-1 for the excise tax imposed by section 4911(a) as if its taxable year were the taxable year of the affiliated group of which it was formerly a member. An organization to which this paragraph (e) applies that is liable for the excise tax imposed by section 4911(a) is liable for the tax as if the tax were imposed for its taxable year within which ends the taxable year of the affiliated group of which it was formerly a member. The Commissioner may, at the Commissioner's discretion, permit an organization to disregard the rules of this paragraph (e) and to determine any liability under section 4911(a) based upon its own taxable year. [Reg. §56.4911-8.]

☐ [*T.D.* 8308, 8-30-90.]

## [Reg. §56.4911-9]

**§56.4911-9. Application of section 501(h) to affiliated groups of organizations.**—(a) *Scope.*—This section provides rules concerning the application of the limitations of section 501(h) to members of an affiliated group of organizations (as defined in § 56.4911-7(e)(1)).

(b) *Determination required.*—For each taxable year of an affiliated group of organizations, the calculations described in

§1.501(h)-3(b)(1)(i) and (ii) must be made, based on the expenditures of the group. If, for a taxable year of an affiliated group, it is determined that the sum of the affiliated group's lobbying or grass roots expenditures for the group's base years exceeds 150 percent of the sum of the group's corresponding nontaxable amounts for the base years, then under section 501(h), each member organization that is an electing member organization (as defined in §56.4911-7(e)(4)) at any time in the taxable year of the affiliated group shall be denied tax exemption beginning with its first taxable year beginning after the end of such taxable year of the affiliated group. Thereafter, exemption shall be denied unless (pursuant to §1.501(h)-3(d)) the organization reapplies and is recognized as exempt as an organization described in section 501(c)(3). For purposes of this section, the term "base years" generally means the taxable year of the affiliated group for which a determination is made and the group's three preceding taxable years. Base years, however, do not include any year preceding the first year in which at least one member of the group was treated as described in section 501(c)(3).

(c) *Member organizations that are not electing organizations.*—An organization that is a member of an affiliated group of organizations but that is not an electing member organization remains subject to the "substantial part test" described in section 501(c)(3) with respect to its activities involving attempts to influence legislation.

(d) *Filing of information relating to affiliated group of organizations.*—(1) *Scope.*—The filing requirements described in this paragraph (d) apply to each member of an affiliated group of organizations for the taxable year of the member with which, or within which, ends the taxable year of the affiliated group.

(2) *In general.*—Each member of an affiliated group of organizations shall provide to every other member of the group, before the first day of the second month following the close of the affiliated group's taxable year, its name, identification number, and the information required under §1.6033-2(a)(2)(ii)(M) for its expenditures during the group's taxable year and for prior taxable years of the group that are base years under paragraph (b). For groups electing under §56.4911-7(e)(5) to have each member file information with respect to the group based on its taxable year, each member shall provide the information required by the preceding sentence by treating each taxable year of any member of the group as a taxable year for the group.

(3) *Additional information required.*—In addition to the information required by §1.6033-2(a)(2)(ii)(M), each member of an affiliated group of organizations must provide on its annual return the group's taxable year and, if the election under §56.4911-7(e)(5) is made, the name, identification number, and taxable year identifying the return with which its consent to the election was filed.

(4) *Information required of electing member organization.*—In addition to the information required by §1.6033-2(a)(2)(ii)(M) and paragraph (d)(3) of this section, each electing member organization (as defined in §56.4911-7(e)(4)) must provide on its annual return—

(i) The name and identification number of each member of the group, and

(ii) The appropriate calculation described in §56.4911-8(d), if the organization is an electing member organization liable for all or any portion of the excise tax imposed by section 4911(a).

(e) *Example.*—The provisions of this section may be illustrated by the following example:

*Example.* (1) M, N, and O are affiliated organizations under §56.4911-7(a). M's taxable year ends November 30, N's, January 31, and O's, June 30. On June 20, 1979, O files Form 5768 to elect to be governed by the expenditure test. M files Form 5768 in December of 1979. Neither M nor O revokes the election, and no organization makes the election provided for in §56.4911-7(e)(5). M, N, and O constitute an affiliated group of organizations, the first taxable year of which is the calendar year 1979.

(2) Because the organizations did not elect under §56.4911-7(e)(5) to use their own taxable years as the group's taxable years, the expenditures of the affiliated group for its first taxable year are the expenditures made by M, N, and O during calendar year 1979, and are reported by M, N, and O on their returns for their taxable years within which falls December 31, 1979. M reports the expenditures of the affiliated group for 1979 on its return for its taxable year ending November 30, 1980; and O, on its return for its taxable year ending June 30, 1980. N is not an electing member (as defined in §56.4911-7(e)(4)). Accordingly, under paragraph (d)(3)(i) of this section, it reports the name and identification number of each member of the group.

(3) The following tables summarize the expenditures by the affiliated group for the calendar years indicated. None of the group's lobbying expenditures for its taxable years 1979 through 1982 were grass roots expenditures.

### Table I. Group's Expenditures

| Year | Exempt Purpose Expenditures (EPE) | Calculation | Lobbying Nontaxable Amount (LNTA) | Lobbying Expenditures (LE) |
|---|---|---|---|---|
| 1979 | $400,000 | (20% × $400,000 =) | $80,000 | $100,000 |
| 1980 | $300,000 | (20% × $300,000 =) | $60,000 | $100,000 |
| 1981 | $600,000 | (20% × $500,000 + 15% × $100,000 =) | $115,000 | $120,000 |
| 1982 | $500,000 | (20% × $500,000 =) | $100,000 | $220,000 |
| Totals: | $1,800,000 | | $355,000 | $540,000 |

### Table II. Expenditures of M and O

| Year | Exempt Purpose Expenditures M | O | Lobbying Nontaxable Amount M | O | Lobbying Expenditures M | O | M plus O |
|---|---|---|---|---|---|---|---|
| 1979 | 125,000 | 100,000 | 25,000 | 20,000 | 60,000 | 20,000 | 80,000 |
| 1980 | 100,000 | 50,000 | 20,000 | 10,000 | 40,000 | 40,000 | 80,000 |
| 1981 | 250,000 | 100,000 | 50,000 | 20,000 | 60,000 | 40,000 | 100,000 |
| 1982 | 200,000 | 100,000 | 40,000 | 20,000 | 160,000 | 40,000 | 200,000 |

(4) For the affiliated group's taxable years 1979, 1980, 1981, and 1982, the group has excess lobbying expenditures. Under section 4911(f)(1)(B) and § 56.4911-8(d), M and O, as electing member organizations, are liable for a portion of the 25 percent excise tax imposed on the group's excess lobbying expenditures, based on their respective shares of the lobbying expenditures of all electing member organizations. For 1979, the excess lobbying expenditures are $20,000 ($100,000 − $80,000). The tax is 25% of $20,000 or $5,000; M must pay $3,750 { ($60,000/$80,000) × $5,000 = $3,750)}, and O must pay $1,250 {($20,000/$80,000)× $5,000 = $1,250}. For 1980, the tax is $10,000 and each must pay $5,000. For 1981, the tax is $1,250, of which M must pay $750 and O must pay $500. For 1982, the tax is $30,000. M must pay $24,000 and O must pay $6,000. M and O are not liable for any separate 4911 excise tax that otherwise would have been imposed on their separate excess lobbying expenditures.

(5) Under § 56.4911-9(b), the group must make the calculation described in § 1.501(h)-3(b)(1) for each of the group's taxable years 1979 through 1982. The following illustrates only the required calculation for the group's taxable year 1982. For its taxable year 1982, the group must determine whether it normally has made lobbying expenditures in excess of its lobbying ceiling amount. The determination takes into account the group's expenditures in base years 1979 through 1982. The sum of the group's lobbying expenditures for the base years ($540,000) exceeds 150% of the sum of the group's lobbying nontaxable amounts for the base years (150%× $355,000 = $532,500). Therefore, for its taxable year 1982, the group normally has made lobbying expenditures in excess of its lobbying ceiling amount. Under section 501(h) and § 56.4911-9(b), M is not exempt from tax under section 501(a) as an organization described in section 501(c)(3) for its taxable year beginning December 1, 1983, and O is not exempt for its year beginning July 1, 1983. Whether N's lobbying expenditures disqualify it for tax exemption at any time after January 1, 1979, is determined under the substantial part test of section 501(c)(3).

(f) *Cross reference.*—For other provisions relating to members of an affiliated group of organizations, see § § 56.4911-2(c)(4)(ii), 56.4911-4(c)(2), 56.4911-4(e), and 56.4911-5(f)(3). [Reg. § 56.4911-9.]

☐ [*T.D.* 8308, 8-30-90. Amended by *T.D.* 9898, 5-26-2020.]

### [Reg. § 56.4911-10]

**§ 56.4911-10. Members of a limited affiliated group of organizations.**—(a) *Scope.*—This section provides additional rules for members of a limited affiliated group of organizations, as defined in paragraph (b) of this section (relating generally to organizations that are affiliated solely by reason of provisions of their governing instruments that extend control solely with respect to national legislation). Except as otherwise provided in this section, § § 56.4911-8 and 56.4911-9 do not apply to members of a limited affiliated group. Thus, as modified by this section, the regulations under sections 501(h) and 4911 apply to electing members of a limited affiliated group individually. For example, § § 56.4911-2 through -4, which, by their terms, include amounts described in paragraph (d) of this section, are used in applying sections 501(h) and 4911 to controlling member organizations(within the meaning of paragraph (c) of this section). Except as otherwise provided in this section, members of a limited affiliated group that are not electing organizations are subject to the substantial part test.

(b) *Members of limited affiliated group.*—For purposes of section 4911, a limited affiliated group consists of two or more organizations that meet the following requirements:

(1) Each organization is a member of an affiliated group of organizations as defined in § 56.4911-7(e);

(2) No two members of the affiliated group described in paragraph (b)(1) of this section are affiliated by reason of interlocking governing boards under § 56.4911-7(b); and

(3) No member of the affiliated group described in paragraph (b)(1) of this section is, under its governing instrument, bound by decisions of one or more of the other such members on legislative issues other than national legislative issues.

Each organization in a group of organizations that satisfies the requirements of the preceding sentence is a member of the limited affiliated group.

(c) *Controlling and controlled organizations.*—For purposes of this section, a member of a limited affiliated group is a controlling member organization if it controls one or more of the other members of the limited affiliated group, and a member of a limited affiliated group is a controlled member organization if it is controlled by one or more of the other members of the limited affiliated group. For purposes of the preceding sentence, whether an organization controls a second organization shall be determined by whether the second organization is bound, under its governing instruments, by actions taken by the first organization on national legislative issues.

(d) *Expenditures of controlling organization.*—(1) *Scope.*—This paragraph (d) applies to a controlling member organization that has the expenditure test election in effect for its taxable year. This paragraph (d) applies whether or not the organization is also a controlled member organization. In determining a controlling member organization's expenditures, no expenditure shall be counted twice.

(2) *Expenditures for direct lobbying.*—A controlling member organization for which the expenditure test election is in effect shall include in its direct lobbying expenditures for its taxable year the direct lobbying expenditures (as defined in § § 56.4911-2 and -3) paid or incurred with respect to national legislative issues during such year by each organization that is a member of the limited affiliated group and is controlled (within the meaning of paragraph (c) of this section) by such controlling member organization.

(3) *Grass roots expenditures.*—A controlling member organization for which the expenditure test election is in effect shall include in its grass roots expenditures for its taxable year the grass roots expenditures (as defined in § § 56.4911-2 and -3) paid or incurred with respect to national legislative issues during such year by each organization that is a member of the limited affiliated group and is controlled (within the meaning of paragraph (c) of this section) by such controlling member organization.

(4) *Exempt purpose expenditures.*—The exempt purpose expenditures of a controlling member organization do not include the exempt purpose expenditures (other than lobbying expenditures described in paragraphs (d)(2) and (d)(3) of this section) of any organization that is a controlled member organization with respect to it.

(e) *Expenditures of controlled member.*—A controlled member organization that is an electing organization but that does not control (within the meaning of paragraph (c) of this section) any organization in the limited affiliated group shall apply sections 501(h) and 4911 and the regulations thereunder without regard to the expenditures of any other member of the limited affiliated group.

(f) *Reports of members of limited affiliated groups.*—(1) *Controlling member organization's additional information on annual return.*—In addition to the information required by § 1.6033-2(a)(2)(ii)(M)), each controlling member organization for which the expenditure test election is in effect must provide on its annual return the name and identification number of each member of the limited affiliated group.

(2) *Reports of controlling members to other members.*—Each controlling member organization for which an expenditure test election is in effect must notify each member that it controls of its taxable year in order for the controlled organization to prepare the report required by paragraph (f)(3) of this section. Such notification must be made before the beginning of the second month after the close of each taxable year of the controlling member for which the election is in effect.

(3) *Reports of controlled member organization.*—Every controlled member organization (whether or not the expenditure test election is in effect with respect to it) shall provide to each member of the limited affiliated group that controls it, before the first day of the second month following the close of the taxable year of each such controlling organization, its name, identification number, and the lobbying expenditures and grass roots expenditures on national legislative issues incurred by the controlled member organization.

(g) *National legislative issues.*—The term "national legislative issue" means legislation, limited to action by the Congress of the United States or by the public in any national procedure. If an issue is both national and local, it is characterized as a national legislative issue if the contemplated legislation is Congressional legislation.

(h) *Examples.*—The provisions of this section are illustrated by the following examples:

*Example (1).* State X has an income tax law that uses definitions contained in the Internal Revenue Code as it may be amended from time to time. Legislation to change a definition in the Internal Revenue Code is pending in Congress. This is a national legislative issue even though Congressional action may affect state law.

*Example (2).* Organization M takes a position favoring approval by Congress of a proposed amendment to the United States Constitution. This is a national legislative issue. After approval by Congress and submission to the states for ratification, the proposed amendment ceases to be a national legislative issue.

*Example (3).* N, O, and P are organizations described in section 501(c)(3) that do not have interlocking governing boards, within the meaning of § 56.4911-7(b). N has elected the expenditure test under section 501(h). By virtue of the governing instruments of O and P, any decision made by N on national legislative issues (such as issues concerning action on acts, bills, resolutions, or similar items by Congress) binds both O and P. Under their governing instruments, O and P are not bound on any other issues. Therefore, N, O, and P

constitute a limited affiliated group. If P sends a series of letters and pamphlets to members of Congress in support of bill V, their cost will be included in N's and P's expenditures for direct lobbying and in N's and P's exempt purposes expenditures, but will not be included in O's lobbying expenditures. If N hires a lobbyist to solicit support for bill V, the cost of hiring the lobbyist will be includable only in N's lobbying expenditures. Any lobbying expenditures incurred by either O or P on any issue that is not a national legislative issue will not be included in N's lobbying expenditures.

*Example (4).* Y is an electing organization and a member of a limited affiliated group of organizations. Y controls organizations A, B, and C with respect to national legislative issues but is not controlled by any other organization. Y's taxable year is the calendar year. During 1982, A dissolves on March 15th and D, also controlled by Y with respect to national legislative issues, is established on May 1st. For 1982 the limited affiliated group comprises Y, A, B, C, and D.

*Example (5).* P, Q, R, and S are electing organizations. The governing instruments of Q require it to adopt the positions on national legislative issues adopted by P. R is similarly bound by Q's positions. R and S have interlocking governing boards, within the meaning of § 56.4911-7(b), but S's governing instruments do not require it to adopt the position of any other organization on any legislative issues. Under § 56.4911-7(e)(1), P, Q, R, and S are members of an affiliated group. Applying paragraph (b) of this section, it is determined that (1) P, Q, R and S are members of an affiliated group; and (2) R and S are affiliated by reason of interlocking governing boards. Accordingly, P, Q, R, and S are not a limited affiliated group. Similarly, P, Q, and R do not constitute a limited affiliated group because they are members of an affiliated group comprising P, Q, R, and S, two of whose members, R and S, are affiliated by reason of interlocking governing boards.

*Example (6).* T, U, V, and W are electing organizations. The governing instruments of U and V require them to adopt the positions on national legislative issues adopted by T, but do not require them to adopt the positions of any organization on any other legislative issues. The governing documents of W require it to adopt the positions of V on all legislative issues. Applying paragraph (b) of this section, it is determined that (1) T, U, V, and W are all members of an affiliated group; (2) no two of T, U, V, and W are affiliated by reason of interlocking governing boards; but (3) W is bound, under its governing instrument, by decisions of V on legislative issues that are not national legislative issues. Accordingly, T, U, V, and W do not constitute a limited affiliated group. Similarly, T, U, and V do not constitute a limited affiliated group. T, U, V, and W are an affiliated group under § 56.4911-7. [Reg. § 56.4911-10.]

☐ [*T.D. 8308, 8-30-90. Amended by T.D. 9898, 5-26-2020.*]

# Private Foundations and Certain Other Tax-Exempt Organizations

## PRIVATE FOUNDATIONS

See p. 20,601 for regulations not amended to reflect law changes

**[Reg. § 53.4940-1]**

**§ 53.4940-1. Excise tax on net investment income.**—(a) *In general.*—For taxable years beginning after September 30, 1977, section 4940 imposes an excise tax of 2 percent of the net investment income (as defined in section 4940(c) and paragraph (c) of this section) of a tax-exempt private foundation (as defined in section 509). For taxable years beginning after December 31, 1969, and before October 1, 1977, the tax imposed by section 4940 is 4 percent of the net investment income. This tax will be reported on the form the foundation is required to file under section 6033 for the taxable year and will be paid annually at the time prescribed for filing such annual return (determined without regard to any extension of time for filing). In addition, an excise tax is imposed in the manner prescribed in paragraph (b) of this section on certain non-exempt private foundations (including certain non-exempt charitable trusts). Except as provided in the succeeding sentence, this tax is to be reported by means of a schedule attached to the organization's income tax return.

For taxable years ending on or after December 31, 1975, the tax imposed by section 4940(b) and paragraph (b) of this section on a trust described in section 4947(a)(1) which is a private foundation shall be reported on Form 5227. The tax imposed by section 4940(b) and this section is to be paid annually at the time the organization is required to pay its income taxes imposed under Subtitle A. Except as otherwise provided herein, no exclusions or deductions from gross investment income or credits against tax are allowable under this section.

(b) *Taxable foundations.*—(1) The excise tax imposed under section 4940 on private foundations which are not exempt from taxation under section 501(a) is equal to:

(i) The amount (if any) by which the sum of

(A) The tax on net investment income imposed under section 4940(a), computed as if such private foundation were exempt from taxation under section 501(a) and described in section 501(c)(3) for the taxable year, plus

(B) The amount of the tax which would have been imposed under section 511 for such taxable year if such private foundation had been exempt from taxation under section 501(a), exceeds

(ii) The tax imposed under subtitle A on such private foundation for the taxable year.

(2) The provisions of this paragraph may be illustrated by the following examples:

*Example (1).* Assume that the tax liability under subtitle A for private foundation X, which is not exempt from taxation under section 501(a) for 1970, is $10,000. Had X been exempt under section 501(a) for 1970, the tax imposed under section 4940(a) would have been $4,000 and the tax imposed under section 511 would have been $7,000. The excess of the sum of the taxes which would have been imposed under sections 4940(a) and 511 ($11,000) over the tax that was imposed under subtitle A ($10,000) is $1,000, the amount of the tax imposed on such organization under section 4940(b).

*Example (2).* Assume the facts stated in Example (1), except that the tax liability under subtitle A is $15,000 rather than $10,000. Because the sum of the taxes which would have been imposed under sections 4940(a) and 511 ($11,000) does not exceed the tax that was imposed under subtitle A ($15,000), there is no tax imposed under section 4940(b) with respect to such foundation.

(c) *Net investment income defined.*—(1) *In general.*—For purposes of section 4940(a), "net investment income" of a private foundation is the amount by which:

(i) The sum of the gross investment income (as defined in section 4940(c)(2) and paragraph (d) of this section) and the capital gain net income (net capital gain for taxable years beginning before January 1, 1977) (within the meaning of section 4940(c)(4) and paragraph (f) of this section) exceeds

(ii) The deductions allowed by section 4940(c)(3) and paragraph (e) of this section.

Except to the extent inconsistent with the provisions of this section, net investment income shall be determined under the principles of subtitle A.

(2) *Tax-exempt income.*—For purposes of computing net investment income under section 4940, the provisions of section 103 (relating to interest on certain governmental obligations) and section 265 (relating to expenses and interest relating to tax-exempt income) and the regulations thereunder shall apply.

(d) *Gross investment income.*—(1) *In general.*—For purposes of paragraph (c) of this section, "gross investment income" means the gross amounts of income from interest, dividends, rents, and royalties (including overriding royalties) received by a private foundation from all sources, but does not include such income to the extent included in computing the tax imposed by section 511. Under this definition, interest, dividends, rents, and royalties derived from assets devoted to charitable activities are includible in gross investment income. Therefore, for example, interest received on a student loan would be includible in the gross investment income of a private foundation making such loan. For purposes of paragraph (c) of this section, gross investment income also includes the items of investment income described in § 1.512(b)-1(a).

(2) *Certain estate and trust disbursements.*—In the case of a distribution from an estate or a trust described in section 4947(a)(1) or (2), such distribution shall not retain its character in the hands of the distributee for purposes of computing the tax under section 4940; except that, in the case of a distribution from a trust described in section 4947(a)(2), the income of such trust attributable to transfers in trust after May 26, 1969, shall retain its character in the hands of a distributee private foundation for purposes of section 4940 (unless such income is taken into account because of the application of section 671).

(3) *Treatment of certain distributions in redemption of stock.*—For purposes of applying section 302(b)(1), any distribution made to a private foundation by a disqualified person (as defined in section 4946(a)), in redemption of stock held by such private foundation in a business enterprise shall be treated as not essentially equivalent to a dividend if all of the following conditions are satisfied: (i) such redemption is of stock which was owned by a private foundation on May 26, 1969 (or which is acquired by a private foundation under the terms of a trust which was irrevocable on May 26, 1969, or under the terms of a will executed on or before such date, which is in effect on such date and at all times thereafter, or would have passed under such a will but before that time actually passes under a trust which would have met the test of this subdivision but for the fact that the trust was revocable (but was not in fact revoked)); (ii) such foundation is required to dispose of such property in order not to be liable for tax under section 4943 (relating to taxes on excess business holdings); and (iii) such foundation receives in return an amount which equals or exceeds the fair market value of such property at the time of such disposition or at the time a contract for such disposition was previously executed in a transaction which would not constitute a prohibited transaction (within the meaning of section 503(b) or the corresponding provisions of prior law). In the case of a disposition before January 1, 1975, section 4943 shall be applied without taking section 4943(c)(4) into account. A distribution which otherwise qualifies under section 302 as a distribution in part or full payment in exchange for stock shall not be treated as essentially equivalent to a dividend because it does not meet the requirements of this subparagraph.

(e) *Deductions.*—(1) *In general.*—(i) For purposes of computing net investment income, there shall be allowed as a deduction from gross investment income all the ordinary and necessary expenses paid or incurred for the production or collection of gross investment income or for the management, conservation, or maintenance of property held for the production of such income, determined with the modifications set forth in subparagraph (2) of this paragraph. Such expenses include that portion of a private foundation's operating expenses which is paid or incurred for the production or collection of gross investment income. Taxes paid or incurred under this section are not paid or incurred for the production or collection of gross investment income. A private foundation's operating expenses in-

clude compensation of officers, other salaries and wages of employees, outside professional fees, interest, and rent and taxes upon property used in the foundation's operations. Where a private foundation's officers or employees engage in activities on behalf of the foundation for both investment purposes and for exempt purposes, compensation and salaries paid to such officers or employees must be allocated between the investment activities and the exempt activities. To the extent a private foundation's expenses are taken into account in computing the tax imposed by section 511, they shall not be deductible for purposes of computing the tax imposed by section 4940.

(ii) Where only a portion of property produces, or is held for the production of, income subject to the section 4940 excise tax, and the remainder of the property is used for exempt purposes, the deductions allowed by section 4940(c)(3) shall be apportioned between the exempt and nonexempt uses.

(iii) No amount is allowable as a deduction under this section to the extent it is paid or incurred for purposes other than those described in subdivision (i) of this subparagraph. Thus, for example, the deductions prescribed by the following sections are not allowable: (1) the charitable deduction prescribed under sections 170 and 642(c); (2) the net operating loss deduction prescribed under section 172; and (3) the special deductions prescribed under Part VIII, subchapter B, chapter 1.

(2) *Deduction modifications.*—The following modifications shall be made in determining deductions otherwise allowable under this paragraph:

(i) The depreciation deduction shall be allowed, but only on the basis of the straight line method provided in section 167(b)(1).

(ii) The depletion deduction shall be allowed, but such deduction shall be determined without regard to section 613, relating to percentage depletion.

(iii) The basis to be used for purposes of the deduction allowed for depreciation or depletion shall be the basis determined under the rules of Part II of subchapter O of chapter 1, subject to the provisions of section 4940(c)(3)(B), and without regard to section 4940(c)(4)(B), relating to the basis for determining gain, or section 362(c). Thus, a private foundation must reduce the cost or other substituted or transferred basis by an amount equal to the straight line depreciation or cost depletion, without regard to whether the foundation deducted such depreciation or depletion during the period prior to its first taxable year beginning after December 31, 1969. However, where a private foundation has previously taken depreciation or depletion deductions in excess of the amount which would have been taken had the straight line or cost method been employed, such excess depreciation or depletion also shall be taken into account to reduce basis. If the facts necessary to determine the basis of property in the hands of the donor or the last preceding owner by whom it was not acquired by gift are unknown to a donee private foundation, then the original basis to such foundation of such property shall be determined under the rules of § 1.1015-1(a)(3).

(iv) The deduction for expenses paid or incurred in any taxable year for the production of gross investment income earned as an incident to a charitable function shall be no greater than the income earned from such function which is includible as gross investment income for such year. For example, where rental income is incidentally realized in 1971 from historic buildings held open to the public, deductions for amounts paid or incurred in 1971 for the production of such income shall be limited to the amount of rental income includible as gross investment income for 1971.

(f) *Capital gain and losses.*—(1) *General rule.*—In determining capital gain net income (net capital gain for taxable years beginning before January 1, 1977) for purposes of the tax imposed by section 4940, there shall be taken into account only capital gains and losses from the sale or other disposition of property held by a private foundation for investment purposes (other than program-related investments, as defined in section 4944(c)), and property used for the production of income included in computing the tax imposed by section 511 except to the extent gain or loss from the sale or other disposition of such property is taken into account for purposes of such tax. For taxable years beginning after December 31, 1972, property shall be treated as held for investment purposes even though such property is disposed of by the foundation immediately upon its receipt, if it is property of a type which generally produces interest, dividends, rents, royalties, or capital gains through appreciation (for example, rental real estate, stock, bonds, mineral interests, mortgages, and securities). Under this subparagraph, gains and losses from the sale or other disposition of property used for the exempt purposes of the private foundation are excluded. For example, gain or loss on the sale of the buildings used for the exempt activities of a private foundation would not be subject to the section 4940 tax. Where the foundation uses property for its exempt purposes, but also incidentally derives income from such property which is subject to the tax imposed by section 4940(a), any gain or loss resulting from the sale or other disposition of such property is not subject to the tax imposed by section 4940(a). For example, if a tax-exempt private foundation maintains buildings of a historical nature and keeps them open for public inspection, but requires a number of its employees to live in these buildings and charges the employees rent, the rent would be subject to the tax imposed by section 4940(a), but any gain or loss resulting from the sale of such property would not be subject to such tax. However, where the foundation uses property for both exempt purposes and (other than incidentally) for investment purposes (for example, a building in which the foundation's charitable and investment activities are carried on), that portion of any gain or loss from the sale or other disposition of such property which is allocable to the investment use of such property must be taken into account in computing net capital gain for such taxable year. For purposes of this paragraph, a distribution of property for purposes described in section 170(c)(1) or (2)(B) which is a qualifying distribution under section 4942 shall not be treated as a sale or other disposition of property.

(2) *Basis.*—(i) The basis for purposes of determining gain from the sale or other disposition of property shall be the greater of:

(A) Fair market value on December 31, 1969, plus or minus all adjustments after December 31, 1969, and before the date of disposition under the rules of part II of subchapter O of chapter 1, provided that the property was held by the private foundation on December 31, 1969, and continuously thereafter to the date of disposition, or

(B) Basis as determined under the rules of part II of subchapter O of chapter 1,

subject to the provisions of section 4940(c)(3)(B) (and without regard to section 362(c)).

(ii) For purposes of determining loss from the sale or other disposition of property, basis as determined in subdivision (i) (B) of this subparagraph shall apply.

(3) *Losses.*—Where the sale or other disposition of property referred to in section 4940(c)(4)(A) results in a capital loss, such loss may be subtracted from capital gains from the sale or other disposition of other such property during the same taxable year, such excess may not be deducted from gross investment income under section 4940(c)(3) in any taxable year, nor may such excess be used to reduce gains in either prior or future taxable years, regardless of whether the foundation is a corporation or a trust.

(4) *Examples.*—The provisions of this paragraph may be illustrated by the following examples:

*Example (1).* A private foundation holds certain depreciable real property on December 31, 1969, having a basis of $102,000. The fair market value of such property on that date was $100,000. For its taxable year 1970 the foundation was allowed depreciation for such property of $5,100 on the straight-line method, the allowable amount computed on the $102,000 basis. The property was sold on January 1, 1971, for $100,000. Because fair market value on December 31, 1969, less straight-line depreciation of $5,100 ($94,900) is less than basis as determined by part II of subchapter O of chapter 1, $96,900 ($102,000 less $5,100), a gain of $3,100 is recognized (*i.e.*, sales price of $100,000 less the greater of the two possible bases).

*Example (2).* Assume the same facts in Example (1), except that the sale price was $95,000. Because the sale price was $1,900 less than the basis for loss ($96,900 as determined by the application of subparagraph (2)(ii) of this paragraph), there is a capital loss of $1,900 which may be deducted against capital gains for 1971 (if any) in determining capital gain net income (for taxable years beginning after December 31, 1976).

*Example (3).* A private foundation holds certain depreciable real property on December 31, 1969, having a basis of $102,000. The fair market value of such property on that date was $110,000. For its taxable year 1970 the foundation was allowed depreciation for such property of $5,100 on the straight line method, the allowable amount computed on the $102,000 basis. The property was sold on January 1, 1971, for $100,000. Fair market value on December 31, 1969, less straight line depreciation of $5,100 ($104,900) exceeds basis as determined by part II of subchapter O of chapter 1, $96,900 ($102,000 less $5,100), and will be used for purposes of determining gain. Because basis for purposes of determining gain exceeds sale price, there is no gain. There is no loss because basis for purposes of determining loss ($96,900) is less than sale price. [Reg. § 53.4940-1.]

☐ [T.D. 7250, 12-29-72. Amended by T.D. 7407, 3-3-76; T.D. 7606, 3-29-79; T.D. 7728, 10-31-80 and T.D. 8423, 7-28-92.]

**[Reg. § 53.4941(a)-1]**

**§ 53.4941(a)-1. Imposition of initial taxes.**—(a) *Tax on self-dealer.*—(1) *In general.*—Section 4941(a)(1) of the Code imposes an excise tax on each act of self-dealing between a disqualified person (as defined

in section 4946(a)) and a private foundation. Except as provided in subparagraph(2) of this paragraph, this tax shall be imposed on a disqualified person even though he had no knowledge at the time of the act that such act constituted self-dealing. Notwithstanding the preceding two sentences, however, a transaction between a disqualified person and a private foundation will not constitute an act of self-dealing if—

(i) The transaction is a purchase or sale of securities by a private foundation through a stockbroker where normal trading procedures on a stock exchange or recognized over-the-counter market are followed;

(ii) Neither the buyer nor the seller of the securities nor the agent of either knows the identity of the other party involved; and

(iii) The sale is made in the ordinary course of business, and does not involve a block of securities larger than the average daily trading volume of that stock over the previous four weeks.

However, the preceding sentence shall not apply to a transaction involving a dealer who is a disqualified person acting as a principal or to a transaction which is an act of self-dealing pursuant to section 4941(d)(1)(B) and §53.4941 (d)-2(c)(1). Tax imposed by section 4941(a)(1) is at the rate of 5 percent of the amount involved (as defined in section 4941(e)(2) and §53.4941(e)-1(b)) with respect to the act of self-dealing for each year or partial year in the taxable period (as defined in section 4941(e)(1)) and shall be paid by any disqualified person (other than a foundation manager acting only in the capacity of a foundation manager) who participates in the act of self-dealing. However, if a foundation manager is also acting as a self-dealer, he may be liable for both the tax imposed by section 4941(a)(1) and the tax imposed by section 4941(a)(2).

(2) *Government officials.*—In the case of a government official (as defined in section 4946(c)), the tax shall be imposed upon such government offical who participates in an act of self-dealing, only if he knows that such act is an act of self-dealing. See paragraph (b)(3) of this section for a definition of "knowing".

(3) *Participation.*—For purposes of this paragraph, a disqualified person shall be treated as participating in an act of self-dealing in any case in which he engages or takes part in the transaction by himself or with others, or directs any person to do so.

(b) *Tax on foundation manager.*—(1) *In general.*—Section 4941(a)(2) of the Code imposes an excise tax on the participation of any foundation manager in the act of self-dealing between a disqualified person and a private foundation. This tax is imposed only in cases in which the following circumstances are present:

(i) A tax is imposed by section 4941(a)(1),

(ii) Such participating foundation manager knows that the act is an act of self-dealing, and

(iii) The participation by the foundation manager is willful and is not due to reasonable cause.

The tax imposed by section 4941(a)(2) is at the rate of $2^1/2$ percent of the amount involved with respect to the act of self-dealing for each year or partial year in the taxable period and shall be paid by any foundation manager described in subdivisions (ii) and (iii) of this subparagraph.

(2) *Participation.*—The term "participation" shall include silence or inaction on the part of a foundation manager where he is under a duty to speak or act, as well as any affirmative action by such manager. However, a foundation manager will not be considered to have participated in an act of self-dealing where he has opposed such act in a manner consistent with the fulfillment of his responsibilities to the private foundation.

(3) *Knowing.*—For purposes of section 4941, a person shall be considered to have participated in a transaction "knowing" that it is an act of self-dealing only if—

(i) He has actual knowledge of sufficient facts so that, based solely upon such facts, such transaction would be an act of self-dealing,

(ii) He is aware that such an act under these circumstances may violate the provisions of federal tax law governing self-dealing, and

(iii) He negligently fails to make reasonable attempts to ascertain whether the transaction is an act of self-dealing, or he is in fact aware that it is such an act.

For purposes of this part, and chapter 42, the term "knowing" does not mean "having reason to know". However, evidence tending to show that a person has reason to know of a particular fact or particular rule is relevant in determining whether he had actual knowledge of such fact or rule. Thus, for example, evidence tending to show that a person has reason to know of sufficient facts so that, based solely upon such facts, a transaction would be an act of self-dealing is relevant in determining whether he has actual knowledge of such facts.

(4) *Willful.*—Participation by a foundation manager shall be deemed willful if it is voluntary, conscious, and intentional. No motive to avoid the restrictions of the law or the incurrence of any tax is necessary to make the participation willful. However, participation by a foundation manager is not willful if he does not know that the transaction in which he is participating is an act of self-dealing.

(5) *Due to reasonable cause.*—A foundation manager's participation is due to reasonable cause if he has exercised his responsibility on behalf of the foundation with ordinary business care and prudence.

(6) *Advice of counsel.*—If a person, after full disclosure of the factual situation to legal counsel (including house counsel), relies on the advice of such counsel expressed in a reasoned written legal opinion that an act is not an act of self-dealing under section 4941, although such act is subsequently held to be an act of self-dealing, the person's participation in such act will ordinarily not be considered "knowing" or "willful" and will ordinarily be considered "due to reasonable cause" within the meaning of section 4941(a)(2). For purposes of this subparagraph, a written legal opinion will be considered "reasoned" even if it reaches a conclusion which is subsequently determined to be incorrect so long as such opinion addresses itself to the facts and applicable law. However, a written legal opinion will not be considered "reasoned" it it does nothing more than recite the facts and express a conclusion. However, the absence of advice of counsel with respect to an act shall not, by itself, give rise to any inference that a person participated in such act knowingly, willfully, or without reasonable cause.

(c) *Burden of proof.*—For provisions relating to the burden of proof in cases involving the issue whether a foundation manager or a government official has knowingly participated in an act of self-dealing, see section 7454(b). [Reg. § 53.4941(a)-1.]

☐ [*T.D. 7270, 4-16-73. Amended by T.D. 7299, 12-21-73.*]

### [Reg. § 53.4941(b)-1]

**§ 53.4941(b)-1. Imposition of additional taxes.**—(a) *Tax on self-dealer.*—Section 4941(b)(1) of the Code imposes an excise tax in any case in which an initial tax is imposed by section 4941(a)(1) on an act of self-dealing by a disqualified person with a private foundation and the act is not corrected within the taxable period (as defined in § 53.4941(e)-1(a)). The tax imposed by section 4941(b)(1) is at the rate of 200 percent of the amount involved and shall be paid by any disqualified person (other than a foundation manager acting only in the capacity of a foundation manager) who participated in the act of self-dealing.

(b) *Tax on foundation manager.*—Section 4941(b)(2) of the Code imposes an excise tax to be paid by a foundation manager in any case in which a tax is imposed by section 4941(b)(1) and the foundation manager refused to agree to part or all of the correction of the self-dealing act. The tax imposed by section 4941(b)(2) is at the rate of 50 percent of the amount involved and shall be paid by any foundation manager who refused to agree to part or all of the correction of the self-dealing act. For the limitations on liability of a foundation manager, see § 53.4941(c)-1(b). [Reg. § 53.4941(b)-1.]

☐ [*T.D. 7270, 4-16-73. Amended by T.D. 8084, 5-1-86.*]

### [Reg. § 53.4941(c)-1]

**§ 53.4941(c)-1. Special rules.**—(a) *Joint and several liability.*—(1) In any case where more than one person is liable for the tax imposed by any paragraph of section 4941(a) or (b), all such persons shall be jointly and severally liable for the taxes imposed under such paragraph with respect to such act of self-dealing.

(2) The provisions of this paragraph may be illustrated by the following example:

*Example.* A and B, who are managers of private foundation X, lend one of the foundation's paintings to G, a disqualified person, for display in G's office, in a transaction which gives rise to liability for tax under section 4941(a)(2) (relating to tax on foundation managers). An initial tax is imposed on both A and B with respect to the act of lending the foundation's painting to G. A and B are jointly and severally liable for the tax.

(b) *Limits on liability for management.*—(1) The maximum aggregate amount of tax collectible under section 4941(a)(2) from all foundation managers with respect to any one act of self-dealing shall be $10,000, and the maximum aggregate amount of tax collectible under section 4941(b)(2) from all foundation managers with respect to any one act of self-dealing shall be $10,000.

(2) The provisions of this paragraph may be illustrated by the following example:

*Example.* A, a disqualified person with respect to private foundation Y, sells certain real estate having a fair market value of $500,000 to Y for $500,000 in cash. B, C, and D, all the managers of foundation Y, authorized the purchase on Y's behalf knowing that such purchase was an act of self-dealing. The actions of B, C, and D in approving the purchase were willful and not due to reasonable cause. Initial taxes are imposed upon the foundation managers under subsections (a)(2) and (c)(2) of section 4941. The tax to be paid by the foundation managers is $10,000 (the lesser of $10,000 or 2¹/₂% of the amount involved). The managers are jointly and severally liable for this $10,000, and the sum may be collected by the Internal Revenue Service from any one of them. [Reg. § 53.4941(c)-1.]

☐ [*T.D. 7270, 4-16-73.*]

### [Reg. § 53.4941(d)-1]

**§ 53.4941(d)-1. Definition of self-dealing.**—(a) *In general.*—For purposes of section 4941, the term "self-dealing" means any direct or indirect transaction described in § 53.4941(d)-2. For purposes of this section it is immaterial whether the transaction results in a benefit or a detriment to the private foundation. The term "self-dealing" does not, however, include a transaction between a private foundation and a disqualified person where the disqualified person status arises only as a result of such transaction. For example, the bargain sale of property to a private foundation is not a direct act of self-dealing if the seller becomes a disqualified person only by reason of his becoming a substantial contributor as a result of the bargain element of the sale. For the effect of section 4942, 4943, 4944, and 4945 upon an act of self-dealing which also results in the imposition of tax under one or more of such sections, see the regulations under those sections.

(b) *Indirect self-dealing.*—(1) *Certain business transactions.*—The term "indirect self-dealing" shall not include any transaction described in § 53.4941(d)-2 between a disqualified person and an organization controlled by a private foundation (within the meaning of subparagraph (5) of this paragraph) if—

(i) The transaction results from a business relationship which was established before such transaction constituted an act of self-dealing (without regard to this paragraph),

(ii) The transaction was at least as favorable to the organization controlled by the foundation as an arm's-length transaction with an unrelated person, and

(iii) Either—

(a) The organization controlled by the foundation could have engaged in the transaction with someone other than a disqualified person only at a severe economic hardship to such organization, or

(b) Because of the unique nature of the product or services provided by the organization controlled by the foundation, the disqualified person could not have engaged in the transaction with anyone else, or could have done so only by incurring severe economic hardship. See example (2) of subparagraph (8) of this paragraph.

(2) *Grants to intermediaries.*—The term "indirect self-dealing" shall not include a transaction engaged in with a government official by an intermediary organization which is a recipient of a grant from a private foundation and which is not controlled by such foundation (within the meaning of subparagraph (5) of this paragraph) if the private foundation does not earmark the use of the grant for any named government official and there does not exist an agreement, oral or written, whereby the grantor foundation may cause the selection of the government official by the intermediary organization. A grant by a private foundation is earmarked if such grant is made pursuant to an agreement, either oral or written, that the grant will be used by any named individual. Thus, a grant by a private foundation shall not constitute an indirect act of self-dealing even though such foundation had reason to believe that certain government officials would derive benefits from such grant so long as the intermediary organization exercises control, in fact, over the selection process and actually makes the selection completely independently of the private foundation. See example (3) of subparagraph (8) of this paragraph.

(3) *Transactions during the administration of an estate or revocable trust.*—The term "indirect self-dealing" shall not include a transaction with respect to a private foundation's interest or expectancy in property (whether or not encumbered) held by an estate (or revocable trust, including a trust which has become irrevocable on a grantor's death), regardless of when title to the property vests under local law, if—

(i) The administrator or executor of an estate or trustee of a revocable trust either—

(a) Possesses a power of sale with respect to the property,

(b) Has the power to reallocate the property to another beneficiary, or

(c) Is required to sell the property under the terms of any option subject to which the property was acquired by the estate (or revocable trust);

(ii) Such transaction is approved by the probate court having jurisdiction over the state (or by another court having jurisdiction over the estate (or trust) or over the private foundation);

(iii) Such transaction occurs before the estate is considered terminated for Federal income tax purposes pursuant to paragraph (a) of §1.641(b)-3 of this chapter (or in the case of a revocable trust, before it is considered subject to section 4947);

(iv) The estate (or trust) receives an amount which equals or exceeds the fair market value of the foundation's interest or expectancy in such property at the time of the transaction, taking into account the terms of any option subject to which the property was acquired by the estate (or trust); and

(v) With respect to transactions occurring after April 16, 1973, the transaction either—

(a) Results in the foundation receiving an interest or expectancy at least as liquid as the one it gave up,

(b) Results in the foundation receiving an asset related to the active carrying out of its exempt purposes, or

(c) Is required under the terms of any option which is binding on the estate (or trust).

(4) *Transactions with certain organizations.*—A transaction between a private foundation and an organization which is not controlled by the foundation (within the meaning of subparagraph (5) of this paragraph), and which is not described in section 4946(a)(1)(E), (F), or (G) because persons described in section 4946(a)(1)(A), (B), (C), or (D) own no more than 35 percent of the total combined voting power or profits or beneficial interest of such organization, shall not be treated as an indirect act of self-dealing between the foundation and such disqualified persons solely because of the ownership interest of such persons in such organization.

(5) *Control.*—For purposes of this paragraph, an organization is controlled by a private foundation if the foundation or one or more of its foundation managers (acting only in such capacity) may, only by aggregating their votes or positions of authority, require the organization to engage in a transaction which if engaged in with the private foundation would constitute self-dealing. Similarly, for purposes of this paragraph, an organization is controlled by a private foundation in the case of such a transaction between the organization and a disqualified person, if such disqualified person, together with one or more persons who are disqualified persons by reason of such person's relationship (within the meaning of section 4946(a)(1)(C) through (G)) to such disqualified person, may, only by aggregating their votes or positions of authority with that of the foundation, require the organization to engage in such a transaction. The "controlled" organization need not be a private foundation; for example, it may be any type of exempt or nonexempt organization including a school, hospital, operating foundation, or social welfare organization. For purposes of this paragraph, an organization will be considered to be controlled by a private foundation or by a private foundation and disqualified persons referred to in the second sentence of this subparagraph if such persons are able, in fact, to control the organization (even if their aggregate voting power is less then 50 percent of the total voting power of the organization's governing body) or if one or more of such persons has the right to exercise veto power over the actions of such organization relevant to any potential acts of self-dealing. A private foundation shall not be regarded as having control over an organization merely because it exercises expenditure responsibility (as defined in section 4945(d)(4) and (h)) with respect to contributions to such organization. See example (6) of subparagraph (8) of this paragraph.

(6) *Certain transactions involving limited amounts.*—The term "indirect self-dealing" shall not include any transaction between a disqualified person and an organization controlled by a private foundation (within the meaning of subparagraph (5) of this paragraph) or between two disqualified persons where the foundation's assets may be affected by the transaction if—

(i) The transaction arises in the normal and customary course of a retail business engaged in with the general public,

(ii) In the case of a transaction between a disqualified person and an organization controlled by a private foundation, the transaction is at least as favorable to the organization controlled by the foundation as an arm's-length transaction with an unrelated person, and

(iii) The total of the amounts involved in such transactions with respect to any one such disqualified person in any one taxable year does not exceed $5,000.

See example (7) of subparagraph (8) of this paragraph.

(7) *Applicability of statutory exceptions to indirect self-dealing.*—The term "indirect self-dealing" shall not include a transaction involving one or more disqualified persons to which a private foundation is not a party, in any case in which the private foundation, by reason of section 4941(d)(2), could itself engage in such a transaction. Thus, for example, even if a private foundation has control (within the meaning of subparagraph (5) of this paragraph) of a corporation, the corporation may pay to a disqualified person except a government official, reasonable compensation for personal services.

(8) *Examples.*—The provisions of this paragraph may be illustrated by the following examples:

*Example (1).* Private foundation P owns the controlling interest of the voting stock of corporation X and, as a result of such interest, elects a majority of the board of directors of X. Two of the foundation managers, A and B, who are also directors of corporation X, form corporation Y for the purpose of building and managing a country club. A and B receive a total of 40 percent of Y's stock, making Y a disqualified person with respect to P under section 4946(a)(1)(E). In order to finance the construction and operation of the country club, Y requested and received a loan in the amount of $4,000,000 from X. The making of the loan by X to Y shall constitute an indirect act of self-dealing between P and Y.

*Example (2).* Private foundation W owns the controlling interest of the voting stock of corporation X, a manufacturer of certain electronic computers. Corporation Y, a disqualified person with respect to W, owns the patent for, and manufactures, one of the essential component parts used in the computers. X has been making regular purchases of the patented component from Y since 1965, subject to the same terms as all other purchasers of such component parts. X could not buy similar components from another source. Consequently, X would suffer severe economic hardship if it could not continue to purchase these components from Y, since it would then be forced to develop a computer which could be constructed with other components. Under these circumstances, the continued purchase by X from Y of these components shall not be an indirect act of self-dealing between W and Y.

*Example (3).* Private foundation Y made a grant to M University, an organization described in section 170(b)(1)(A)(ii), for the purpose of conducting a seminar to study methods for improving the administration of the judicial system. M is not controlled by Y within the meaning of subparagraph (5) of this paragraph. In conducting the seminar, M made payments to certain government officials. By the nature of the grant, Y had reason to believe that government officials would be compensated for participation in the seminar. M, however, had completely independent control over the selection of such participants. Thus, such grant by Y shall not constitute an indirect act of self-dealing with respect to the government officials.

*Example (4).* A, a substantial contributor to P, a private foundation, bequeathed one-half of his estate to his spouse and one-half of his estate to P. Included in A's estate is a one-third interest in AB, a partnership. The other two-thirds interest in AB is owned by B, a disqualified person with respect to P. The one-third interest in AB was subject to an option agreement when it was acquired by the estate. The executor of A's estate sells the one-third interest in AB to B pursuant to such option agreement at the price fixed in such option agreement in the sale which meets the requirements of subparagraph (3) of this paragraph. Under these circumstances, the sale does not constitute an indirect act of self-dealing between B and P.

*Example (5).* A bequeathed $100,000 to his wife and a piece of unimproved real estate of equivalent value to private foundation Z, of which A was the creator and a foundation manager. Under the laws of State Y, to which the estate is subject, title to the real estate vests in the foundation upon A's death. However, the executor has the power under State law to reallocate the property to another beneficiary. During a reasonable period for administration of the estate, the executor exercises this power and distributes the $100,000 cash to the foundation and the real estate to A's wife. The probate court having jurisdiction over the estate approves the executor's action. Under these circumstances, the executor's action does not constitute an indirect act of self-dealing between the foundation and A's wife.

*Example (6).* Private foundation P owns 20 percent of the voting stock of corporation W. A, a substantial contributor with respect to P, owns 16 percent of the voting stock of corporation W. B, A's son, owns 15 percent of the voting stock of the corporation W. The terms of the voting stock are such that P, A, and B could vote their stock in a block to elect a majority of the board of directors of W. W is treated as controlled by P (within the meaning of subparagraph (5) of this paragraph) for purposes of this example. A and B also own 50 percent of the stock of corporation Y, making Y a disqualified person with respect to P under section 4946(a)(1)(E). W makes a loan to Y of $1,000,000. The making of this loan by W to Y shall constitute an indirect act of self-dealing between P and Y.

*Example* (7). A, a disqualified person with respect to private foundation P, enters into a contract with corporation M, which is also a disqualified person with respect to P. P owns 20 percent of M's stock, and controls M within the meaning of subparagraph (5) of this paragraph. M is in the retail department store business. Purchases by A of goods sold by M in the normal and customary course of business at retail or higher prices are not indirect acts of self-dealing so long as the total of the amounts involved in all of such purchases by A in any one year does not exceed $5,000. [Reg. § 53.4941(d)-1.]

☐ [*T.D.* 7270, 4-16-73.]

### [Reg. § 53.4941(d)-2]

**§ 53.4941(d)-2. Specific acts of self-dealing.**—Except as provided in § 53.4941(d)-3 or § 53.4941(d)-4—

(a) *Sale or exchange of property.*—(1) *In general.*—The sale or exchange of property between a private foundation and a disqualified person shall constitute an act of self-dealing. For example, the sale of incidental supplies by a disqualified person to a private foundation shall be an act of self-dealing regardless of the amount paid to the disqualified person for the incidental supplies. Similarly, the sale of stock or other securities by a disqualified person to a private foundation in a "bargain sale" shall be an act of self-dealing regardless of the amount paid for such stock or other securities. An installment sale may be subject to the provisions of both section 4941(d)(1)(A) and section 4941(d)(1)(B).

(2) *Mortgaged property.*—For purposes of subparagraph (1) of this paragraph, the transfer of real or personal property by a disqualified person to a private foundation shall be treated as a sale or exchange if the foundation assumes a mortgage or similar lien which was placed on the property prior to the transfer, or takes subject to a mortgage or similar lien which a disqualified person placed on the property with the 10-year period ending on the date of transfer. For purposes of this subparagraph, the term "similar lien" shall include, but is not limited to, deeds of trust and vendors' liens, but shall not include any other lien if such lien is insignificant in relation to the fair market value of the property transferred.

(b) *Leases.*—(1) *In general.*—Except as provided in subparagraphs (2) and (3) of this paragraph, the leasing of property between a disqualified person and a private foundation shall constitute an act of self-dealing.

(2) *Certain leases without charge.*—The leasing of property by a disqualified person to a private foundation shall not be an act of self-dealing if the lease is without charge.
For purposes of this subparagraph, a lease shall be considered to be without charge even though the private foundation pays for janitorial services, utilities, or other maintenance costs it incurs for the use of the property, so long as the payment is not made directly or indirectly to a disqualified person.

(3) *Certain leases of office space.*—For taxable years beginning after December 31, 1979, the leasing of office space by a disqualified person to a private foundation shall not be an act of self-dealing if—

(i) The leased space is in a building in which there are other tenants who are not disqualified persons,

(ii) The lease is pursuant to a binding lease which was in effect on October 9, 1969, or pursuant to renewals of such a lease,

(iii) The execution of the lease was not a prohibited transaction (within the meaning of section 503(b) or the corresponding provisions of prior law) at the time of such execution, and

(iv) The terms of the lease (or any renewal) reflect an arm's length transaction.
A lease or renewal of such lease is described in this subparagraph (3) only if it satisfies the requirements of § 53.4941(d)-4(c)(1) and (2), applied without regard to the December 31, 1979 deadline described therein.

(c) *Loans.*—(1) *In general.*—Except as provided in subparagraphs (2), (3), and (4) of this paragraph, the lending of money or other extension of credit between a private foundation and a disqualified person shall constitute an act of self-dealing. Thus, for example, an act of self-dealing occurs where a third party purchases property and assumes a mortgage, the mortgagee of which is a private foundation, and subsequently the third party transfers the property to a disqualified person who either assumes liability under the mortgage or takes the property subject to the mortgage. Similarly, except in the case of the receipt and holding of a note pursuant to a transaction described in § 53.4941(d)-1(b)(3), an act of self-dealing occurs where a note, the obligor of which is a disqualified person, is transferred by a third party to a private foundation which becomes the creditor under the note.

(2) *Loans without interest.*—Subparagraph (1) of this paragraph shall not apply to the lending of money or other extension of credit by a disqualified person to a private foundation if the loan or other extension of credit is without interest or other charge.

(3) *Certain evidences of future gifts.*—The making of a promise, pledge, or similar arrangement to a private foundation by a disqualified person, whether evidenced by an oral or written agreement, a promissory note, or other instrument of indebtedness, to the extent motivated by charitable intent and unsupported by consideration, is not an extension of credit (within the meaning of this paragraph) before the date of maturity.

(4) *General banking functions.*—Under section 4941(d)(2)(E) the performance by a bank or trust company which is a disqualified person of trust functions and certain general banking services for a private foundation is not an act of self-dealing, where the banking services are reasonable and necessary to carrying out the exempt purposes of the private foundation, if the compensation paid to the bank or trust company, taking into account the fair interest rate for the use of the funds by the bank or trust company, for such services is not excessive. The general banking services allowed by this subparagraph are:

(i) Checking accounts, as long as the bank does not charge interest on any overwithdrawals,

(ii) Savings accounts, as long as the foundation may withdraw its funds on no more than 30 days' notice without subjecting itself to a loss of interest on its money for the time during which the money was on deposit, and

(iii) Safekeeping activities.
See example (3) of § 53.4941(d)-3(c)(2).

(d) *Furnishing goods, services, or facilities.*—(1) *In general.*—Except as provided in subparagraph (2) or (3) of this paragraph (or § 53.4941(d)-3(b)), the furnishing of goods, services, or facilities between a private foundation and a disqualified person shall constitute an act of self-dealing. This subparagraph shall apply, for example, to the furnishing of goods, services, or facilities such as office space, automobiles, auditoriums, secretarial help, meals, libraries, publications, laboratories, or parking lots. Thus, for example, if a foundation furnishes personal living quarters to a disqualified person (other than a foundation manager or employee) without charge, such furnishing shall be an act of self-dealing.

(2) *Furnishing of goods, services, or facilities to foundation managers and employees.*—The furnishing of goods, services, or facilities such as those described in subparagraph (1) of this paragraph to a foundation manager in recognition of his services as a foundation manager, or to another employee (including an individual who would be an employee but for the fact that he receives no compensation for his services) in recognition of his services in such capacity, is not an act of self-furnishing if the value of such furnishing (whether or not includible as compensation in his gross income) is reasonable and necessary to the performance of his tasks in carrying out the exempt purposes of the foundation and, taken in conjunction with any other payment of compensation or payment or reimbursement of expenses to him by the foundation, is not excessive. For example, if a foundation furnishes meals and lodging which are reasonable and necessary (but not excessive) to a foundation manager by reason of his being a foundation manager, then, without regard to whether such meals and lodging are excludable from gross income under section 119 as furnished for the convenience of the employer, such furnishing is not an act of self-dealing. For the effect of section 4945(d)(5) upon an expenditure for unreasonable administrative expenses, see § 53.4945-6(b)(2).

(3) *Furnishing of goods, services, or facilities by a disqualified person without charge.*—The furnishing of goods, services, or facilities by a disqualified person to a private foundation shall not be an act of self-dealing if they are furnished without charge. Thus, for example, the furnishing of goods such as pencils, stationery, or other incidental supplies, or the furnishing of facilities such as a building, by a disqualified person to a foundation shall be allowed if such supplies or facilities are furnished without charge. Similarly, the furnishing of services (even though such services are not personal in nature) shall be permitted if such furnishing is without charge. For purposes of this subparagraph, a furnishing of goods shall be considered without charge even though the private foundation pays for transportation, insurance, or maintenance costs it incurs in obtaining or using the property, so long as the payment is not made directly or indirectly to the disqualified person.

(e) *Payment of compensation.*—The payment of compensation (or payment or reimbursement of expenses) by a private foundation to a disqualified person shall constitute an act of self-dealing. See, however, § 53.4941(d)-3(c) for the exception for the payment of compensation by a foundation to a disqualified person for personal services which are reasonable and necessary to carry out the exempt purposes of the foundation.

(f) *Transfer or use of the income or assets of a private foundation.*— (1) *In general.*—The transfer to, or use by or for the benefit of, a disqualified person of the income or assets of a private foundation shall constitute an act of self-dealing. For purposes of the preceding sentence, the purchase or sale of stock or other securities by a private foundation shall be an act of self-dealing if such purchase or sale is made in an attempt to manipulate the price of the stock or other securities to the advantage of a disqualified person. Similarly, the indemnification (of a lender) or guarantee (of repayment) by a private foundation with respect to a loan to a disqualified person shall be treated as a use for the benefit of a disqualified person of the income or assets of the foundation (within the meaning of this subparagraph). In addition, if a private foundation makes a grant or other payment which satisfies the legal obligation of a disqualified person, such grant or payment shall ordinarily constitute an act of self-dealing to which this subparagraph applies. However, if a private foundation makes a grant or payment which satisfies a pledge, enforceable under local law, to an organization described in section 501(c)(3), which pledge is made on or before April 16, 1973, such grant or payment shall not constitute an act of self-dealing to which this subparagraph applies so long as the disqualified person obtains no substantial benefit, other than the satisfaction of his obligation, from such grant or payment.

(2) *Certain incidental benefits.*—The fact that a disqualified person receives an incidental or tenuous benefit from the use by a foundation of its income or assets will not, by itself, make such use an act of self-dealing. Thus, the public recognition a person may receive, arising from the charitable activities of a private foundation to which such person is a substantial contributor, does not in itself result in an act of self-dealing since generally the benefit is incidental and tenuous. For example, a grant by a private foundation to a section 509(a)(1), (2), or (3) organization will not be an act of self-dealing merely because such organization is located in the same area as a corporation which is a substantial contributor to the foundation, or merely because one of the section 509(a)(1), (2), or (3) organization's officers, directors, or trustees is also a manager of or a substantial contributor to the foundation. Similarly, a scholarship or a fellowship grant to a person other than a disqualified person, which is paid or incurred by a private foundation in accordance with a program which is consistent with—

(i) The requirements of the foundation's exempt status under section 501(c)(3),

(ii) The requirements for the allowance of deductions under section 170 for contributions made to the foundation, and

(iii) The requirements of section 4945(g)(1),

will not be an act of self-dealing under section 4941(d)(1) merely because a disqualified person indirectly receives an incidental benefit from such grant. Thus, a scholarship or a fellowship grant made by a private foundation in accordance with a program to award scholarships or fellowship grants to the children of employees of a substantial contributor shall not constitute an act of self-dealing if the requirements of the preceding sentence are satisfied. For an example of the kind of scholarship program with an employment nexus that meets the above requirements, see § 53.4945-4(b)(5) (Example 1).

(3) *Non-compensatory indemnification of foundation managers against liability for defense in civil proceedings.*—(i) Except as provided in § 53.4941(d)-3(c), section 4941(d)(1) shall not apply to the indemnification by a private foundation of a foundation manager, with respect to the manager's defense in any civil judicial or civil administrative proceeding arising out of the manager's performance of services (or failure to perform services) on behalf of the foundation, against all expenses (other than taxes, including taxes imposed by chapter 42, penalties, or expenses of correction) including attorneys' fees, judgments and settlement expenditures if—

(A) Such expenses are reasonably incurred by the manager in connection with such proceeding; and

(B) The manager has not acted willfully and without reasonable cause with respect to the act or failure to act which led to such proceeding or to liability for tax under chapter 42.

(ii) Similarly, except as provided in § 53.4941(d)-3(c), section 4941(d)(1) shall not apply to premiums for insurance to make or to reimburse a foundation for an indemnification payment allowed pursuant to this paragraph (f)(3). Neither shall an indemnification or payment of insurance allowed pursuant to this paragraph (f)(3) be treated as part of the compensation paid to such manager for purposes of determining whether the compensation is reasonable under chapter 42.

(4) *Compensatory indemnification of foundation managers against liability for defense in civil proceedings.*—(i) The indemnification by a private foundation of a foundation manager for compensatory ex-

penses shall be an act of self-dealing under this paragraph unless when such payment is added to other compensation paid to such manager the total compensation is reasonable under chapter 42. A compensatory expense for purposes of this paragraph (f) is—

(A) Any penalty, tax (including a tax imposed by chapter 42), or expense of correction that is owed by the foundation manager;

(B) Any expense not reasonably incurred by the manager in connection with a civil judicial or civil administrative proceeding arising out of the manager's performance of services on behalf of the foundation; or

(C) Any expense resulting from an act or failure to act with respect to which the manager has acted willfully and without reasonable cause.

(ii) Similarly, the payment by a private foundation of the premiums for an insurance policy providing liability insurance to a foundation manager for expenses described in this paragraph (f)(4) shall be an act of self-dealing under this paragraph (f) unless when such premiums are added to other compensation paid to such manager the total compensation is reasonable under chapter 42.

(5) *Insurance Allocation.*—A private foundation shall not be engaged in an act of self-dealing if the foundation purchases a single insurance policy to provide its managers both the noncompensatory and the compensatory coverage discussed in this paragraph (f), provided that the total insurance premium is allocated and that each manager's portion of the premium attributable to the compensatory coverage is included in that manager's compensation for purposes of determining reasonable compensation under chapter 42.

(6) *Indemnification.*—For purposes of this paragraph (f), the term *indemnification* shall include not only reimbursement by the foundation for expenses that the foundation manager has already incurred or anticipates incurring but also direct payment by the foundation of such expenses as the expenses arise.

(7) *Taxable Income.*—The determination of whether any amount of indemnification or insurance premium discussed in this paragraph (f) is included in the manager's gross income for individual income tax purposes is made on the basis of the provisions of chapter 1 and without regard to the treatment of such amount for purposes of determining whether the manager's compensation is reasonable under chapter 42.

(8) *De minimis items.*—Any property or service that is excluded from income under section 132(a)(4) may be disregarded for purposes of determining whether the recipient's compensation is reasonable under chapter 42.

(9) *Examples.*—The provisions of this paragraph may be illustrated by the following examples:

*Example (1).* M, a private foundation, makes a grant of $50,000 to the governing body of N City for the purpose of alleviating the slum conditions which exist in a particular neighborhood of N. Corporation P, a substantial contributor to M, is located in the same area in which the grant is to be used. Although the general improvement of the area may constitute an incidental and tenuous benefit to P, such benefit by itself will not constitute an act of self-dealing.

*Example (2).* Private foundation X established a program to award scholarship grants to the children of employees of corporation M, a substantial contributor to X. After disclosure of the method of carrying out such program, X received a determination letter from the Internal Revenue Service stating that X is exempt from taxation under section 501(c)(3), that contributions to X are deductible under section 170, and that X's scholarship program qualifies under section 4945(g)(1). A scholarship grant to a person not a disqualified person with respect to X paid or incurred by X in accordance with such program shall not be an indirect act of self-dealing between X and M.

*Example (3).* Private foundation Y owns voting stock in corporation Z, the management of which includes certain disqualified persons with respect to Y. Prior to Z's annual stockholder meeting, the management solicits and receives the foundation's proxies. The transfer of such proxies in and of itself shall not be an act of self-dealing.

*Example (4).* A, a disqualified person with respect to private foundation S, contributes certain real estate to S for the purpose of building a neighborhood recreation center in a particular underprivileged area. As a condition of the gift, S agrees to name the recreation center after A. Since the benefit to A is only incidental and tenuous, the naming of the recreation center, by itself, will not be an act of self-dealing.

(g) *Payment to a government official.*—Except as provided in section 4941(d)(2)(G) or § 53.4941(d)-3(e), the agreement by a private foundation to make any payment of money or other property to a government official, as defined in section 4946(c), shall constitute an act of self-dealing. For purposes of this paragraph, an individual who is otherwise described in section 4946(c) shall be treated as a government official while on leave of absence from the government without pay. [Reg. § 53.4941(d)-2.]

☐ [T.D. 7270, 4-16-73. Amended by T.D. 7938, 1-30-84 and T.D. 8639, 12-19-95.]

**[Reg. § 53.4941(d)-3]**

**§ 53.4941(d)-3. Exceptions to self-dealing.**—(a) *General rule.*—In general, a transaction described in section 4941(d)(2)(B), (C), (D), (E), (F), (G), or (H) is not an act of self-dealing. Section 4941(d)(2)(B), (C), and (H) provide limited exceptions to certain specific transactions, as described in paragraphs (b)(2), (b)(3), (c)(2), and (d)(3) of § 53.4941(d)-2.

(b) *Furnishing of goods, services, or facilities to a disqualified person.*—(1) *In general.*—Under section 4941(d)(2)(D), the furnishing of goods, services, or facilities by a private foundation to a disqualified person shall not be an act of self-dealing if such goods, services, or facilities are made available to the general public on at least as favorable a basis as they are made available to the disqualified person. This subparagraph shall not apply, however, in the case of goods, services or facilities furnished later than May 16, 1973, unless such goods, services or facilities are functionally related, within the meaning of section 4942(j)(5), to the exercise or performance by a private foundation of its charitable, educational, or other purpose or function constituting the basis for its exemption under section 501(c)(3).

(2) *General public.*—For purposes of this paragraph, the term "general public" shall include those persons who, because of the particular nature of the activities of the private foundation, would be reasonably expected to utilize such goods, services, or facilities. This paragraph shall not apply, however, unless there are a substantial number of persons other than disqualified persons who are actually utilizing such goods, services or facilities. Thus, a private foundation which furnishes recreational or park facilities to the general public may furnish such facilities to a disqualified person provided they are furnished to him on a basis which is not more favorable than that on which they are furnished to the general public. Similarly, the sale of a book or magazine by a private foundation to disqualified persons shall not be an act of self-dealing if the publication of the book or magazine is functionally related to a charitable or educational activity of the foundation and the book or magazine is made available to the disqualified persons and the general public at the same price. In addition, if the terms of the sale require, for example, payment within 60 days from the date of delivery of the book or magazine, such terms are consistent with normal commercial practices, and payment is made within the 60-day period, the transaction shall not be treated as a loan or other extension of credit under § 53.4941(d)-2(c)(1).

(c) *Payment of compensation for certain personal services.*—(1) *In general.*—Under section 4941(d)(2)(E), except in the case of a government official (as defined in section 4946(c)), the payment of compensation (and the payment or reimbursement of expenses, including reasonable advances for expenses anticipated in the immediate future) by a private foundation to a disqualified person for the performance of personal services which are reasonable and necessary to carry out the exempt purpose of the private foundation shall not be an act of self-dealing if such compensation (or payment or reimbursement) is not excessive. For purposes of this subparagraph the term "personal services" includes the services of a broker serving as agent for the private foundation, but not the services of a dealer who buys from the private foundation as principal and resells to third parties. For the determination whether compensation is excessive, see § 1.162-7 of this chapter (Income Tax Regulations). This paragraph applies without regard to whether the person who receives the compensation (or payment or reimbursement) is an individual. The portion of any payment which represents payment for property shall not be treated as payment of compensation (or payment or reimbursement of expenses) for the performance of personal services for purposes of this paragraph. For rules with respect to the performance of general banking services, see § 53.4941(d)-2(c)(4). Further, the making of a cash advance to a foundation manager or employee for expenses on behalf of the foundation is not an act of self-dealing, so long as the amount of the advance is reasonable in relation to the duties and expense requirements of the foundation manager. Except where reasonably allowable pursuant to subdivision (iii) of this subparagraph, such advances shall not ordinarily exceed $500. For example, if a foundation makes an advance to a foundation manager to cover anticipated out-of-pocket current expenses for a reasonable period (such as a month) and the manager accounts to the foundation under a periodic reimbursement program for actual expenses incurred, the foundation will not be regarded as having engaged in an act of self-dealing—

(i) When it makes the advance,

(ii) When it replenishes the funds upon receipt of supporting vouchers from the foundation manager, or

(iii) If it temporarily adds to the advance to cover extraordinary expenses anticipated to be incurred in fulfillment of a special assignment (such as long distance travel).

(2) *Examples.*—The provisions of this paragraph may be illustrated by the following examples:

*Example (1).* M, a partnership, is a firm of ten lawyers engaged in the practice of law. A and B, partners in M, serve as trustees to private foundation W and, therefore, are disqualified persons. In addition, A and B own more than 35 percent of the profits interest in M, thereby making M a disqualified person. M performs various legal services for W from time to time as such services are requested. The payment of compensation by W to M shall not constitute an act of self-dealing if the services performed are reasonable and necessary for the carrying out of W's exempt purposes and the amount paid by W for such services is not excessive.

*Example (2).* C, a manager of private foundation X, owns an investment counseling business. Acting in his capacity as an investment counselor, C manages X's investment portfolio for which he receives an amount which is determined to be not excessive. The payment of such compensation to C shall not constitute an act of self-dealing.

*Example (3).* M, a commercial bank, serves as a trustee for private foundation Y. In addition to M's duties as trustee, M maintains Y's checking and savings accounts and rents a safety deposit box to Y. The use of the funds by M and the payment of compensation by Y to M for such general banking services shall be treated as the payment of compensation for the performance of personal services which are reasonable and necessary to carry out the exempt purposes of Y if such compensation is not excessive.

*Example (4).* D, a substantial contributor to private foundation Z, owns a factory which manufactures microscopes. D contracts with Z to manufacture 100 microscopes for Z. Any payment to D under the contract shall constitute an act of self-dealing, since such payment does not constitute the payment of compensation for the performance of personal services.

(d) *Certain transactions between a foundation and a corporation.*—(1) *In general.*—Under section 4941(d)(2)(F), any transaction between a private foundation and a corporation which is a disqualified person will not be an act of self-dealing if such transaction is engaged in pursuant to a liquidation, merger, redemption, recapitalization, or other corporate adjustment, organization, or reorganization, so long as all the securities of the same class as that held (prior to such transaction) by the foundation are subject to the same terms and such terms provide for receipt by the foundation of no less than fair market value. For purposes of this paragraph, all of the securities are not "subject to the same terms" unless, pursuant to such transaction, the corporation makes a bona fide offer on a uniform basis to the foundation and every other person who holds such securities. The fact that a private foundation receives property, such as debentures, while all other persons holding securities of the same class receive cash for their interests, will be evidence that such offer was not made on a uniform basis. This paragraph may apply even if no other person holds any securities of the class held by the foundation. In such event, however, the consideration received by holders of other classes of securities, or the interests retained by holders of such other classes, when considered in relation to the consideration received by the foundation, must indicate that the foundation received at least as favorable treatment in relation to its interests as the holders of any other class of securities. In addition, the foundation must receive no less than the fair market value of its interests.

(2) *Examples.*—The provisions of this paragraph may be illustrated by the following examples:

*Example (1).* Private foundation X owns 50 percent of the Class A preferred stock of corporation M, which is a disqualified person with respect to X. The terms of such securities provide that the stock may be called for redemption at any time by M at 105 percent of the face amount of the stock. M exercises this right and calls all the Class A preferred stock by paying 105 percent of the face amount in cash. At the time of the redemption of the Class A preferred stock, it is determined that the fair market value of the preferred stock is equal to its face amount. In such case, the redemption by M of the preferred stock of X is not an act of self-dealing.

*Example (2).* Private foundation Y, which is on a calendar year basis, acquires 60 percent of the Class A preferred stock of corporation N by will on January 10, 1970. N, which is also on a calendar year basis, is a disqualified person with respect to Y. In 1971, N offers to redeem all of the Class A preferred stock for a consideration equal to 100 percent of the face amount of such stock by the issuance of debentures. The offer expires January 2, 1972. Both Y and all other holders of the Class A preferred stock accept the offer and enter into the transaction on January 2, 1972, at which time it is determined that the fair market value of the debentures is no less than the fair market value of the preferred stock. The transaction on January 2, 1972, shall not be treated as an act of self-dealing for 1972. However, because under §53.4941(e)-1(e)(1)(i) an act of self-dealing occurs on the first day of each taxable year or portion of a taxable year that an extension of credit from a foundation to a disqualified person goes uncorrected, if such debentures are held by Y after December 31, 1972, except as provided in §53.4941(d)-4(c)(4), such extension of credit shall not be excepted from the definition of an act of self-dealing by reason of the January 2, 1972, transaction. See §53.4941(d)-4(c)(4) for rules indicating that under certain circumstances such debentures could be held by Y until December 31, 1979.

(e) *Certain payments to government officials.*—Under section 4941(d)(2)(G), in the case of a government official, in addition to the exceptions provided in section 4941(d)(2)(B), (C), and (D), section 4941(d)(1) shall not apply to—

(1) A prize or award which is not includible in gross income under section 74(b), if the government official receiving such prize or award is selected from the general public;

(2) A scholarship or a fellowship grant which is excludable from gross income under section 117(a) and which is to be utilized for study at an educational institution described in section 151(e)(4);

(3) Any annuity or other payment (forming part of a stock-bonus, pension, or profit sharing plan) by a trust which constitutes a qualified trust under section 401;

(4) Any annuity or other payment under a plan which meets the requirements of section 404(a)(2);

(5) Any contribution or gift (other than a contribution or gift of money) to, or services or facilities made available to, any government official, if the aggregate value of such contributions, gifts, services, and facilities does not exceed $25 during any calendar year;

(6) Any payment made under 5 U.S.C. chapter 41 (relating to government employees' training programs);

(7) Any payment or reimbursement of traveling expenses (including amounts expended for meals and lodging, regardless of whether the government official is "away from home" within the meaning of section 162(a)(2), and including reasonable advances for such expenses anticipated in the immediate future) for travel solely from one point in the United States to another in connection with one or more purposes described in section 170(c)(1) or (2)(B), but only if such payment or reimbursement does not exceed the actual cost of the transportation involved plus an amount for all other traveling expenses not in excess of 125 percent of the maximum amount payable under 5 U.S.C. 5702(a) for like travel by employees of the United States;

(8) Any agreement to employ or make a grant to a government official for any period after the termination of his government service if such agreement is entered into within 90 days prior to such termination;

(9) If a government official attends or participates in a conference sponsored by a private foundation, the allocable portion of the cost of such conference and other non-monetary benefits (for example, benefits of a professional, intellectual, or psychological nature, or benefits resulting from the publication or the distribution to participants of a record of the conference), as well as the payment or reimbursement of expenses (including reasonable advances for expenses anticipated in connection with such a conference in the near future), received by such government official as a result of such attendance or participation shall not be subject to section 4941(d)(1), so long as the conference is in furtherance of the exempt purposes of the foundation; or

(10) In the case of any government official who was on leave of absence without pay on December 31, 1969, pursuant to a commitment entered into on or before such date for the purpose of engaging in certain activities for which such individual was to be paid by one or more private foundations, any payment of compensation (or payment or reimbursement of expenses, including reasonable advances for expenses anticipated in the immediate future) by such private foundations to such individual for any continuous period after December 31, 1969, and prior to January 1, 1971, during which such individual remains on leave of absence to engage in such activities. A commitment is considered entered into on or before December 31, 1969, if on or before such date, the amount and nature of the payments to be made and the name of the individual receiving such payments were entered on the records of the payor, or were otherwise adequately evidenced, or the notice of the payment to be received was communicated to the payee orally or in writing. [Reg. §53.4941(d)-3.]

☐ [T.D. 7270, 4-16-73. Amended by T.D. 7938, 1-30-84.]

[Reg. §53.4941(d)-4]

§53.4941(d)-4. Transitional rules.—(a) *Certain transactions involving securities acquired by a foundation before May 27, 1969.*—(1) *In general.*—Under section 101(l)(2)(A) of the Tax Reform Act of 1969 (83 Stat. 533), any transaction between a private foundation and a corporation which is a disqualified person shall not be an act of self-dealing if such transaction is pursuant to the terms of securities of such corporation, if such terms were in existence at the time such securities were acquired by the foundation, and if such securities were acquired by the foundation before May 27, 1969.

(2) *Example.*—The provisions of this paragraph may be illustrated by the following example:

*Example.* Private foundation X purchased preferred stock of corporation M, a disqualified person with respect to X, on March 15, 1969. The terms of such securities on such date provided that the stock could be called by M at any time if M paid the outstanding shareholders cash equal to 105 percent of the face amount of the stock. If M exercises this right and calls the stock owned by X on February 15, 1970, such call shall not constitute an act of self-dealing even if such price is not equivalent to fair market value on such date and even if not all of the securities of that class are called.

(b) *Disposition of certain business holdings.*—(1) *In general.*—Under section 101(l)(2)(B) of the Tax Reform Act of 1969 (83 Stat. 533), the sale, exchange, or other disposition of property which is owned by a private foundation on May 26, 1969, to a disqualified person shall not be an act of self-dealing if the foundation is required to dispose of such property in order not to be liable for tax under section 4943 (determined without regard to section 4943(c)(2)(C) and as if every disposition by the foundation were made to disqualified persons) and if such disposition satisfies the requirements of subparagraph (2) of this paragraph. For purposes of applying this paragraph in the case of a disposition completed before January 1, 1975, or after October 4, 1976, and before January 1, 1977, the amount of excess business holdings is determined under section 4943(c) without taking subsection (c)(4) into account.

(2) *Terms of the disposition.*—Subparagraph (1) of this paragraph shall not apply unless—

(i) The private foundation receives an amount which equals or exceeds the fair market value of the business holdings at the time of disposition or at the time a contract for such disposition was previously executed; and

(ii) At the time with respect to which subdivision (i) of this subparagraph is applied, the transaction would not have constituted a prohibited transaction within the meaning of section 503(b) or the corresponding provisions of prior law if such provisions had been applied at such time.

(3) *Property received under a trust or will.*—For purposes of this paragraph, property shall be considered as owned by a private foundation on May 26, 1969, if such property is acquired by such foundation under the terms of a will executed on or before such date, under the terms of a trust which was irrevocable on such date, or under the terms of a revocable trust executed on or before such date if the property would have passed under a will which would have met the requirements of this subparagraph but for the fact that a grantor dies without having revoked the trust. An amendment or republication of a will which was executed on or before May 26, 1969, does not prevent any interest in a business enterprise which was to pass under the terms of such will (which terms were in effect on May 26, 1969, and at all times thereafter) from being treated as owned by a private foundation on or before May 26, 1969, solely because—

(i) There is a reduction in the interest in the business enterprise which the foundation was to receive under the terms of the will (for example, if the foundation is to receive the residuary estate and one class of stock is disposed of by the decedent during his lifetime or by a subsequent codicil),

(ii) Such amendment or republication is necessary in order to comply with section 508(e) and the regulations thereunder,

(iii) There is a change in the executor of the will, or

(iv) There is any other change which does not otherwise change the rights of the foundation with respect to such interest in the business enterprise.

However, if under such amendment or republication there is an increase of the interest in the business enterprise which the foundation was to receive under the terms of the will in effect on May 26, 1969, such increase shall not be treated as owned by the private foundation on or before May 26, 1969, but under such circumstances the interest which would have been acquired before such increase shall be treated as owned by the private foundation on or before May 26, 1969.

**Reg. §53.4941(d)-4(b)(3)(iv)**

(4) *Examples.*—The provisions of this paragraph may be illustrated by the following examples:

*Example (1).* On May 26, 1969, private foundation X owns 10 percent of corporation Y's voting stock, which is traded on the New York Stock Exchange. Disqualified persons with respect to X own an additional 40 percent of such voting stock. X is on a calendar year basis. Prior to January 1, 1975, X privately sold its entire 10 percent for cash to B, a disqualified person, at the price quoted on the stock exchange at the close of the day less commissions. Since the 10 percent owned by X would constitute excess business holdings without the application of section 4943(c)(2)(C) or (4), the disposition will not constitute an act of self-dealing.

*Example (2).* Assume the facts as stated in Example (1), except that the only stock of corporation Y which X owns is 1.5 percent of Y's voting stock. Since the 1.5 percent owned by X would constitute excess business holdings without the application of section 4943(c)(2)(C) or (4), the disposition of the stock to B for cash will not constitute an act of self-dealing.

*Example (3).* Assume the facts as stated in Example (1), except that B, instead of paying cash as consideration for the stock, issued a 10-year secured promissory note as consideration for the stock. The issuance of such promissory note will not be treated as an act of self-dealing until taxable years beginning after December 31, 1979, unless such issuance would have been a prohibited transaction under section 503(b), or unless the transaction does not remain throughout its life at least as favorable as an arm's-length contract negotiated currently. See paragraph (c) of this section.

(c) *Existing leases and loans.*—(1) *In general.*—Under section 101(l)(2)(C) of the Tax Reform Act of 1969 (83 Stat. 533), the leasing of property or the lending of money (or other extension of credit) between a disqualified person and a private foundation pursuant to a binding contract which was in effect on October 9, 1969 (or pursuant to a renewal or modification of such a contract, as described in subparagraph (2) of this paragraph), shall not be an act of self-dealing until taxable years beginning after December 31, 1979, if—

(i) At the time the contract was executed, such contract was not a prohibited transaction (within the meaning of section 503(b) or the corresponding provisions of prior law), and

(ii) The leasing or lending of money (or other extension of credit) remains throughout the term of the lease or extension of credit at least as favorable as a current arm's-length transaction with an unrelated person.

(2) *Renewal or modification of existing contracts.*—A renewal or a modification of an existing contract is referred to in subparagraph (1) of this paragraph only if any modifications of the terms of such contract are not substantial and the relative advantages of the modified contract compared with contracts entered into at arm's-length with an unrelated person at the time of the renewal or modification are at least as favorable to the private foundation as the relative advantages of the original contract compared with contracts entered into at arm's-length with an unrelated person at the time of execution of the original contract. Such renewal or modification need not be provided for in the original contract; it may take place before or after the expiration of the original contract and at any time before the first day of the first taxable year of the private foundation beginning after December 31, 1979. Where, in a normal commercial setting, an unrelated party in the position of a private foundation could be expected to insist upon a renegotiation or termination of a binding contract, the private foundation must so act. Thus, for example, if a disqualified person leases office space from a private foundation on a month-to-month basis, and a party in the position of the private foundation could be expected to renegotiate the rent required in such contract because of a rise in the fair market value of such office space, the private foundation must so act in order to avoid participation in an act of self-dealing. Where the private foundation has no right to insist upon renegotiation, an act of self-dealing shall occur if the terms of the contract become less favorable to the foundation than an arm's-length contract negotiated currently, unless—

(i) The variation from current fair market value is *de minimis*, or

(ii) The contract is renegotiated by the foundation and the disqualified person so that the foundation will receive no less than fair market value.

For purposes of subdivision (i) of this subparagraph *de minimis* ordinarily shall be no more than one-half of 1 percent in the rate of return in the case of a loan, or 10 percent of the rent in the case of a lease.

(3) *Example.*—The provisions of subparagraphs (1) and (2) of this paragraph may be illustrated by the following example.

*Example.* Under a binding contract entered into on January 1, 1964, X, a private foundation, leases a building for 10 years from Z, a disqualified person. At the time the contract was executed, the lease

was not a "prohibited transaction" within the meaning of section 503(b), since the rent charged X was only 50 percent of the rent which would have been charged in an arm's-length transaction with an unrelated person. On January 1, 1974, X renewed the lease for 5 additional years. The terms of the renewal agreement provided for a 20 percent increase in the amount of rent charged X. However, at the time of such renewal, the rent which would have been charged in an arm's-length transaction had also increased by 20 percent from that of 1964. The renewal agreement shall not be treated as an act of self-dealing.

(4) *Certain exchanges of stock or securities for bonds, debentures or other indebtedness.*—(i) In the case of a transaction described in paragraph (a) or (b) of this section or paragraph (d) of § 53.4941(d)-3, where a bond, debenture, or other indebtedness of a disqualified person is acquired by a private foundation in exchange for stock or securities which it held on October 9, 1969, and at all times thereafter, such indebtedness shall be treated as an extension of credit pursuant to a binding contract in effect on October 9, 1969, to which this paragraph applies. Thus, so long as the extension of credit remains at least as favorable as an arm's-length transaction with an unrelated person and neither the acquisition of the securities which were exchanged for the indebtedness nor the exchange of such securities for the indebtedness was a prohibited transaction within the meaning of section 503(b) (or the corresponding provisions of prior law) at the time of such acquisition, such extension of credit shall not be an act of self-dealing until taxable years beginning after December 31, 1979.

(ii) The provisions of this subparagraph may be illustrated by the following examples:

*Example (1).* Assume the facts as stated in Example (2) of § 53.4941(d)-3(d)(2), except that the preferred stock was held by Y on October 9, 1969, and at all times thereafter until the redemption occurred on January 2, 1972. In addition, assume that the acquisition of the preferred stock was not a prohibited transaction within the meaning of section 503(b) at the time of such acquisition and the exchange of the preferred stock for the debentures would not have been a prohibited transaction within the meaning of section 503(b). For 1973 through 1979, the extension of credit arising from the holding of the debentures is not an act of self-dealing so long as the extension of credit remains at least as favorable as an arm's-length transaction with an unrelated person. See, however, Example (3) of § 53.4941(e)-1(e)(1)(ii).

*Example (2).* Assume the same facts as stated in Example (1) of § 53.4941(d)-4(b)(4), except that private foundation X sold its entire 10 percent of corporation Y's voting stock in exchange for Y's secured notes which mature on December 31, 1985. For taxable years beginning before January 1, 1980, the extension of credit arising from the holding of such notes by X is not an act of self-dealing so long as the extension of credit remains at least as favorable as an arm's-length transaction with an unrelated person and neither the acquisition of the securities which were exchanged for the indebtedness nor the exchange of such securities for the indebtedness was a prohibited transaction within the meaning of section 503(b) (or the corresponding provisions of prior law). Under § 53.4941(e)-1, a new extension of credit occurs on the first day of each taxable year in which an indebtedness is outstanding; therefore, if the secured notes are held by X after December 31, 1979, a new extension of credit not excepted from the definition of an act of self-dealing will occur on the first day of the first taxable year beginning after December 31, 1979, and on the first day of each succeeding taxable year in which X holds such secured notes.

(d) *Sharing of goods, services, or facilities before January 1, 1980.*—(1) Under section 101(l)(2)(D) of the Tax Reform Act of 1969 (83 Stat. 533), the use (other than leasing) of goods, services, or facilities which are shared by a private foundation and a disqualified person shall not be an act of self-dealing until taxable years beginning after December 31, 1979, if—

(i) The use is pursuant to an arrangement in effect before October 9, 1969, and at all times thereafter;

(ii) The arrangement was not a prohibited transaction (within the meaning of section 503(b) or the corresponding provisions of prior law) at the time it was made; and

(iii) The arrangement would not be a prohibited transaction if section 503(b) continued to apply.

For purposes of this paragraph, such arrangement need not be a binding contract.

(2) The provisions of this paragraph may be illustrated by the following example:

*Example.* In 1964 X, a private foundation, and B, a disqualified person, arranged for the sharing of computer time in B's son's company for a 10-year period commencing January 1, 1965. B's son has the unilateral right to terminate the arrangement at any time. X uses the computer facilities in connection with an analysis of its grant-making activities, while B's use is related to his business affairs. Both X and B make reasonable fixed payments to the computer company based on the number of hours of computer use and comparable to fees charged in arm's length transactions with unrelated parties. The company imposes a maximum limit per month on the sum of the number of hours for which X and B use the computer facilities. Under these circumstances, the sharing of computer time is not an act of self-dealing.

(e) *Use of certain property acquired before October 9, 1969.*—(1) Under section 101(l)(2)(E) of the Tax Reform Act of 1969 (83 Stat. 533), the use of property in which a private foundation and a disqualified person have a joint or common interest will not be an act of self-dealing if the interests of both in such property were acquired before October 9, 1969.

(2) The provisions of this paragraph may be illustrated by the following example:

*Example.* Prior to October 9, 1969, C, a disqualified person, gave beachfront property to private foundation X for use as a recreational facility for underprivileged, inner-city children during the summer months. However, C retained the right to use such property for his life. The use of such property by C or X is not an act of self-dealing.

(f) *Disposition of leased property.*—(1) *In general.*—Under section 101(l)(2)(F) of the Tax Reform Act of 1969, as amended by the Tax Reform Act of 1976 (90 Stat. 1713), the sale, exchange or other disposition (other than by lease) to a disqualified person of property being leased to the disqualified person by a private foundation is not an act of self-dealing if—

(i) The private foundation is leasing substantially all of the property to the disqualified person under a lease to which paragraph (c) of this section applies;

(ii) The disposition occurs after October 4, 1976, and before January 1, 1978; and

(iii) The disposition satisfies the requirements of paragraph (f)(2) of this section.

(2) *Terms of disposition.*—Paragraph (f)(1) of this section applies only if—

(i) The private foundation receives an amount that equals or exceeds the fair market value of the property either at the time of the disposition or at the time (after June 30, 1976) the contract for such disposition was executed;

(ii) In computing the fair market value of the property, no diminution of that value results from the fact that the property is subject to any lease to disqualified persons; and

(iii) At the time with respect to which subdivision (f)(2)(i) of this section is applied, the transaction would not have constituted a prohibited transaction within the meaning of section 503(b) or the corresponding provisions of prior law if those provisions had been applied at the time of the transaction. [Reg. § 53.4941(d)-4.]

☐ [*T.D. 7270, 4-16-73. Amended by T.D. 7678, 2-25-80.*]

## [Reg. § 53.4941(e)-1]

**§ 53.4941(e)-1. Definitions.**—(a) *Taxable period.*—(1) *In general.*—For purposes of any act of self-dealing, the term "taxable period" means the period beginning with the date on which the act of self-dealing occurs and ending on the earliest of:

(i) The date of mailing of a notice of deficiency under section 6212 with respect to the tax imposed by section 4941(a)(1),

(ii) The date on which the correction of the act of self-dealing is completed, or

(iii) The date on which the tax imposed by section 4941(a)(1) is assessed.

(2) *Date of occurrence.*—An act of self-dealing occurs on the date on which all the terms and conditions of the transaction and the liabilities of the parties have been fixed. Thus, for example, if a private foundation gives a disqualified person a binding option on June 15, 1971, to purchase property owned by the foundation at any time before June 15, 1972, the act of self-dealing has occurred on June 15, 1971. Similarly, in the case of a conditional sales contract, the act of self-dealing shall be considered as occurring on the date the property is transferred subject only to the condition that the buyer make payment for receipt of such property.

(3) *Special rule.*—Where a notice of deficiency referred to in subparagraph (1)(i) of this paragraph is not mailed because a waiver of the restrictions on assessment and collection of a deficiency has been accepted, or because the deficiency is paid, the date of filing of the waiver or the date of such payment, respectively, shall be treated as the end of the taxable period.

(4) *Examples.*—The provisions of this paragraph may be illustrated by the following examples:

*Example (1).* On July 16, 1970, F, a manager of private foundation X acting on behalf of the foundation, knowing his act to be one of

self-dealing, willfully and without reasonable cause engaged in an act of self-dealing by selling certain real estate to A, a disqualified person. On March 25, 1973, the Internal Revenue Service mailed a notice of deficiency to A with respect to the tax imposed on the sale under section 4941(a)(1). The taxable period with respect to the act of self-dealing for both A and F is July 16, 1970, through March 25, 1973.

*Example (2).* Assume the facts as stated in Example (1), except that the act of self-dealing is corrected by A on March 17, 1971. The taxable period with respect to the act of self-dealing for both A and F is July 16, 1970, through March 17, 1971.

*Example (3).* Assume the facts as stated in Example (1), except that on August 20, 1972, A files a waiver of the restrictions on assessment and collection of the tax imposed on the sale under section 4941(a)(1) which is accepted. The taxable period with respect to the act of self-dealing for both A and F is July 16, 1970, through August 20, 1972.

(b) *Amount involved.*—(1) *In general.*—Except as provided in subparagraph (2) of this paragraph, for purposes of any act of self-dealing, the term "amount involved" means the greater of the amount of money and the fair market value of the other property given or the amount of money and the fair market value of the other property received.

(2) *Exceptions.*—(i) In the case of the payment of compensation for personal services to persons other than government officials, the amount involved shall be only the excess compensation paid by the private foundation.

(ii) Where the use of money or other property is involved, the amount involved shall be the greater of the amount paid for such use or the fair market value of such use for the period for which the money or other property is used. Thus, for example, in the case of a lease of a building by a private foundation to a disqualified person, the amount involved is the greater of the amount of rent received by the private foundation from the disqualified person or the fair rental value of the building for the period such building is used by the disqualified person.

(iii) In cases in which a transaction would not have been an act of self-dealing had the private foundation received fair market value, the amount involved is the excess of the fair market value of the property transferred by the private foundation over the amount which the private foundation receives, but only if the parties have made a good faith effort to determine fair market value. For purposes of this subdivision a good faith effort to determine fair market value shall ordinarily have been made where—

(*a*) The person making the valuation is not a disqualified person with respect to the foundation and is both competent to make the valuation and not in a position, whether by stock ownership or otherwise, to derive an economic benefit from the value utilized, and

(*b*) The method utilized in making the valuation is a generally accepted method for valuing comparable property, stock, or securities for purposes of arm's-length business transactions where valuation is a significant factor.

See section 4941(d)(2)(F) and §§ 53.4941(d)-1(b)(3), 53.4941(d)-3(d)(1) and 53.4941(d)-4(b). Thus, for example, if a corporation which is a disqualified person with respect to a private foundation recapitalizes in a transaction which would be described in section 4941(d)(2)(F) but for the fact that the private foundation receives new stock worth only $95,000 in exchange for the stock which it previously held in the corporation and which has a fair market value of $100,000 at the time of the recapitalization, the amount involved would be $5,000 ($100,000 − $95,000) if there had been a good faith attempt to value the stock. Similarly, if an estate enters into a transaction with a disqualified person with respect to a foundation and such transaction would be described in § 53.4941(d)-1(b)(3) but for the fact that the estate receives less than fair market value for the property exchanged, the amount involved is the excess of the fair market value of the property the estate transfers to the disqualified person over the money and the fair market value of the property received by the estate.

(3) *Time for determining fair market value.*—The fair market value of the property or the use thereof, as the case may be, shall be determined as of the date on which the act of self-dealing occurred in the case of the initial taxes imposed by section 4941(a) and shall be the highest fair market value during the taxable period in the case of the additional taxes imposed by section 4941(b).

(4) *Examples.*—The provisions of this paragraph may be illustrated by the following examples:

*Example (1).* A, a disqualified person with respect to private foundation M, uses an airplane owned by M on June 15 and June 16, 1970, for a two-day trip to New York City on personal business and pays M $500 for the use of such airplane. The fair rental value for the use of the airplane for those two days is $3,000. For purposes of section 4941(a), the amount involved with respect to the act of self-dealing is $3,000.

*Example (2).* On April 10, 1970, B, a manager of private foundation P, borrows $100,000 from P at 6 percent interest per annum. Both principal and interest are to be paid one year from the date of the loan. The fair market value of the use of the money on April 10, 1970, is 10 percent per annum. Six months later, B and P terminate the loan, and B repays the $100,000 principal plus $3,000 ($100,000 × 6 percent for one-half year) interest. For purposes of section 4941(a), the amount involved with respect to the act of self-dealing is $5,000 ($100,000 × 10 percent for one-half year) for each year or partial year in the taxable period.

*Example (3).* C, a substantial contributor to private foundation S, leases office space in a building owned by S for $3,600 for 1 year beginning on January 1, 1971. The fair rental value of the building for a one-year lease on January 1, 1971, is $5,600. On December 31, 1971, the lease is terminated. For purposes of section 4941(a), the amount involved with respect to the act of self-dealing is $5,600 for each year or partial year in the taxable period.

*Example (4).* D, a disqualified person with respect to private foundation T, purchases 100 shares of stock from T for $5,000 on June 15, 1982. The fair market value of the 100 shares of stock on that date is $4,800. D sells the 100 shares of stock on December 20, 1983, for $6,000. On December 27, 1983, a notice of deficiency with respect to the taxes imposed under subsections (a) and (b) of section 4941 is mailed to D and the taxable period ends. D fails to correct during the taxable period. Between June 15, 1982, and the end of the taxable period, the stock was quoted on the New York Stock Exchange at a high of $67 per share. The amount involved with respect to the tax imposed under subsection (a) is $5,000, and the amount involved with respect to the tax imposed under subsection (b) for failure to correct is $6,700 (100 shares at $67 per share), the highest fair market value during the taxable period.

*Example (5).* Corporation M, a disqualified person with respect to private foundation V, redeems all of its Class B common stock, some of which is held by V. The redemption of V's stock would be described in section 4941(d)(2)(F) but for the fact that V receives only $95,000 in exchange for stock which has a fair market value of $100,000 at the time of the transaction. The $95,000 value of V's stock, which is not publicly traded, was determined by investment bankers in accordance with accepted methods of valuation that would be utilized if the M stock held by V were to be offered for sale to the public. Therefore, the amount involved with respect to the transaction will ordinarily be limited to $5,000 ($100,000 − $95,000).

(c) *Correction.*—(1) *In general.*—Correction shall be accomplished by undoing the transaction which constituted the act of self-dealing to the extent possible, but in no case shall the resulting financial position of the private foundation be worse than that which it would be if the disqualified person were dealing under the highest fiduciary standards. For example, where a disqualified person sells property to a private foundation for cash, correction may be accomplished by recasting the transaction in the form of a gift by returning the cash to the foundation. Subparagraphs (2) through (6) of this paragraph illustrate the minimum standards of correction in the case of certain specific acts of self-dealing. Principles similar to the principles contained in such subparagraphs shall be applied with respect to other acts of self-dealing. Any correction pursuant to this paragraph and section 4941 shall not be an act of self-dealing.

(2) *Sales by foundation.*—(i) In the case of a sale of property by a private foundation to a disqualified person for cash, undoing the transaction includes, but is not limited to, requiring rescission of the sale where possible. However, in order to avoid placing the foundation in a position worse than that in which it would be if rescission were not required, the amount returned to the disqualified person pursuant to the rescission shall not exceed the lesser of the cash received by the private foundation or the fair market value of property received by the disqualified person. For purposes of the preceding sentence, fair market value shall be the lesser of the fair market value at the time of the act of self-dealing or the fair market value at the time of rescission. In addition to rescission, the disqualified person is required to pay over to the private foundation any net profits he realized after the original sale with respect to the property he received from the sale. Thus, for example, the disqualified person must pay over to the foundation any income derived by him from the property he received from the original sale to the extent such income during the correction period exceeds the income derived by the foundation during the correction period from the cash which the disqualified person originally paid to the foundation.

(ii) If, prior to the end of the correction period, the disqualified person resells the property in an arm's-length transaction to a bona fide purchaser who is not the foundation or another disqualified person, no rescission is required. In such case, the disqualified person must pay over to the foundation the excess (if any) of the

greater of the fair market value of such property on the date on which correction of the act of self-dealing occurs or the amount realized by the disqualified person from such arm's length resale over the amount which would have been returned to the disqualified person pursuant to subdivision (i) of this subparagraph if rescission had been required. In addition, the disqualified person is required to pay over to the foundation any net profits he realized, as described in subdivision (i) of this subparagraph.

(iii) *Examples.*—The provisions of this subparagraph may be illustrated by the following examples:

*Example (1).* On July 1, 1970, private foundation M sold a painting to A, a disqualified person, for $5,000, in a transaction not within any of the exceptions to self-dealing. The fair market value of the painting on such date was $6,000. On March 25, 1971, the painting is still owned by A and has a fair market value of $7,200. A did not derive any income as a result of purchasing the painting. In order to correct the act of self-dealing under this subparagraph on March 25, 1971, the sale must be rescinded by the return of the painting to M. However, pursuant to such rescission, M must not pay A more than $5,000, the original consideration received by M.

*Example (2).* Assume the facts as stated in Example (1), except that A sold the painting on December 15, 1970, in an arm's-length transaction to C, a bona fide purchaser who is not a disqualified person, for $6,100. In addition, assume that the fair market value of the painting on March 25, 1971, is $7,600. In order to correct the act of self-dealing under this subparagraph on March 25, 1971, A must pay M $2,600 ($7,600, the fair market value at the time of correction, less $5,000, the amount which would have been returned to A if rescission had been required). Since the painting was sold to C in an arm's-length transaction prior to correction, no rescission is required.

(3) *Sales to foundation.*—(i) In the case of a sale of property to a private foundation by a disqualified person for cash, undoing the transaction includes, but is not limited to, requiring rescission of the sale where possible. However, in order to avoid placing the foundation in a position worse than that in which it would be if rescission were not required, the amount received from the disqualified person pursuant to the rescission shall be the greatest of the cash paid to the disqualified person, the fair market value of the property at the time of the original sale, or the fair market value of the property at the time of rescission. In addition to rescission, the disqualified person is required to pay over to the private foundation any net profits he realized after the original sale with respect to the consideration he received from the sale. Thus, for example, the disqualified person must pay over to the foundation any income derived by him from the cash he received from the original sale to the extent such income during the correction period exceeds the income derived by the foundation during the correction period from the property which the disqualified person originally transferred to the foundation.

(ii) If, prior to the end of the correction period, the foundation resells the property in an arm's-length transaction to a bona fide purchaser who is not a disqualified person, no rescission is required. In such case, the disqualified person must pay over to the foundation the excess (if any) of the amount which would have been received from the disqualified person pursuant to subdivision (i) of this subparagraph, if rescission had been required over the amount realized by the foundation upon resale of the property. In addition, the disqualified person is required to pay over to the foundation any net profits he realized, as described in subdivision (i) of this subparagraph.

(iii) *Examples.*—The provisions of this subparagraph may be illustrated by the following examples:

*Example (1).* On February 10, 1972, D, a disqualified person with respect to private foundation P, sells 100 shares of X stock to P for $2,500 in a transaction which does not fall within any of the exceptions to self-dealing. The fair market value of the 100 shares of X stock on February 10, 1972, is $3,200. On June 1, 1973, the 100 shares of X stock have a fair market value of $2,900. From February 10, 1972, through June 1, 1973, P has received dividends of $90 from the stock, and D has received interest of $300 from the $2,500 which D received as consideration for the stock. In order to correct the act of self-dealing under this subparagraph on June 1, 1973, the sale must be rescinded by the return of the stock to D. However, pursuant to such rescission, D must pay $3,200, the fair market value of the stock on the date of sale. In addition, D must pay P $210, the amount of income derived by D during the correction period from the $2,500 received from P ($300) minus the income derived by P during the correction period from the stock sold to P ($90).

*Example (2).* Assume the facts as stated in Example (1), except that on September 1, 1972, P sells the 100 shares of X stock to E, a bona fide purchaser who is not a disqualified person, in an arm's length transaction for $2,750. Assume further that P has not received any dividends from the stock prior to the sale to E, but that P receives interest of $260 from the $2,750 received as consideration for the stock for the period from September 1, 1972, to June 1, 1973. In order to correct the act of self-dealing under this subparagraph on June 1, 1973, D must pay P $450 ($3,200, the amount which would have been received from D if rescission had been required, less $2,750, the amount realized by P from the sale to E). In addition, D must pay P $40, the amount of income derived by D during the correction period from the $2,500 received from P ($300) minus the income derived by P during the correction period from the stock sold to P ($260 from the $2,750 received as consideration for the stock). Since the stock was sold to E in an arm's length transaction prior to correction, no rescission is required.

(4) *Use of property by a disqualified person.*—(i) In the case of the use by a disqualified person of property owned by a private foundation, undoing the transaction includes, but is not limited to, terminating the use of such property. In addition to termination, the disqualified person must pay the foundation—

(a) The excess (if any) of the fair market value of the use of the property over the amount paid by the disqualified person for such use until such termination, and

(b) The excess (if any) of the amount which would have been paid by the disqualified person for the use of the property on or after the date of such termination, for the period such disqualified person would have used the property (without regard to any further extensions or renewals of such period) if such termination had not occurred, over the fair market value of such use for such period.

In applying (a) of this subdivision the fair market value of the use of property shall be the higher of the rate (that is, fair rental value per period in the case of use of property other than money or fair interest rate in the case of use of money) at the time of the act of self-dealing (within the meaning of paragraph (e)(1) of this section) or such rate at the time of correction of such act of self-dealing. In applying (b) of this subdivision the fair market value of the use of property shall be the rate at the time of correction.

(ii) The provisions of this subparagraph may be illustrated by the following examples:

*Example (1).* On January 1, 1972, private foundation S rented the third story of its office building to A, a disqualified person, for one year at an annual rent of $10,000, in a transaction not within any of the exceptions to self-dealing. Both S and A are on the calendar year basis. The fair rental value of such office space for a one-year period on January 1, 1972, is $12,000. On June 30, 1972, the fair rental value of such office space for a one-year period is $13,000. In order to correct the act of self-dealing under this subparagraph on June 30, 1972, A must terminate his use of the property. In addition, A must pay S $1,500, the excess of $6,500 (the fair rental value for six months as of June 30, 1972) over $5,000 (the amount paid to S from January 1, 1972, to June 30, 1972).

*Example (2).* On January 1, 1972, private foundation R rented the fourth story of its office building to B, a disqualified person, for one year at an annual rent of $10,000, in a transaction not included in any of the exceptions to self-dealing. Both R and B are on the calendar year basis. On January 1, 1973, B continues to rent the office space as a periodic tenant paying his rent monthly at an annual rate of $10,000. The fair rental value of such office space for a one-year period on January 1, 1972, is $12,000, and as of January 1, 1973, is $1,250 per month. As of December 31, 1973, the fair rental value of such office space is $14,000 for a one-year period and $1,200 on a monthly basis. In order to correct his acts of self-dealing (within the meaning of paragraph (e)(1) of this section) under this subparagraph on December 31, 1973, B must terminate his use of the property. In addition, B must pay R $9,000, $4,000 for his use of the property for 1972 (the excess of $14,000, the fair rental value for one year as of December 31, 1973, over $10,000, the amount B paid R for his use of the property for 1972) and $5,000 for his use of the property for 1973 (the excess of $15,000, the fair rental value for 12 months as of January 1, 1973, over $10,000, the amount B paid R for his use of the property for 1973).

*Example (3).* B, a substantial contributor to private foundation T, leases office space in a building owned by T for $5,000 for one year beginning on November 10, 1972, in a transaction not included in any of the exceptions to self-dealing. The fair rental value of the building for a one-year period on November 10, 1972, is $4,000. On May 10, 1973, the fair rental value of the building for the remaining period of the lease is $2,200. In order to correct the acts of self-dealing under this subparagraph on May 10, 1973, B and T must terminate the lease. In addition, B must pay T $300 (the excess of $2,500, the amount which would have been paid by B for the remaining period of the lease if it had not been terminated, over $2,200, the fair rental value at the time of correction for the remaining period of the lease).

(5) *Use of property by a private foundation.*—(i) In the case of the use by a private foundation of property owned by a disqualified person, undoing the transaction includes, but is not limited to, termi-

nating the use of such property. In addition to termination, the disqualified person must pay the foundation—

(a) The excess (if any) of the amount paid to the disqualified person for such use until such termination over the fair market value of the use of the property, and

(b) The excess (if any) of the fair market value of the use of the property, for the period the foundation would have used the property (without regard to any further extensions or renewals of such period) if such termination had not occurred, over the amount which would have been paid to the disqualified person on or after the date of such termination for such use for such period.

In applying (a) of this subdivision the fair market value of the use of property shall be the lesser of the rate (that is, fair rental value per period in the case of use of property other than money or fair interest rate in the case of use of money) at the time of the act of self-dealing (within the meaning of paragraph (e)(1) of this section) or such rate at the time of correction of such act of self-dealing. In applying (b) of this subdivision the fair market value of the use of property shall be the rate at the time of correction.

(ii) The provisions of this subparagraph may be illustrated by the following examples:

*Example (1).* On July 1, 1972, private foundation X leases office space in a building owned by C, a disqualified person, for one year at an annual rent of $6,000. Both X and C are on the calendar year basis. The fair rental value of such office space for a one-year period as of July 1, 1972, is $4,200. As of January 1, 1973, the fair rental value of such office space for a one-year period is $5,400, and as of June 30, 1973, the fair rental value of such office space for a one-year period is $4,800. In order to correct its acts of self-dealing (within the meaning of paragraph (e)(1) of this section) under this subparagraph on June 30, 1973, C must terminate X's use of the property. In addition, C must pay X $1,500, $900 (the excess of $3,000, the amount paid to C from July 1, 1972, through December 31, 1972, over $2,100, the fair rental value for six months as of July 1, 1972) plus $600 (the excess of $3,000, the amount paid to C from January 1, 1973, through June 30, 1973, over $2,400, the fair rental value for six months as of June 30, 1973).

*Example (2).* On April 1, 1973, D, a disqualified person with respect to private foundation Y, loans $100,000 to Y at 6 percent interest per annum. Both principal and interest are to be paid on April 1, 1978. The fair market value of the use of the money on April 1, 1973, is 9 percent per annum. On April 1, 1974, D and Y terminate the loan. On such date, the fair market value of the use of $100,000 is 10 percent per annum. In order to correct the act of self-dealing on April 1, 1974, in addition to the termination of the loan from D to Y, D must pay Y $16,000, the excess of $40,000 ($100,000 × 10 percent, the fair market value of the use determined at the time of correction, from April 1, 1974, to April 1, 1978) over $24,000 (the amount of interest Y would have paid to D from April 1, 1974, to April 1, 1978, if the loan from D to Y had not been terminated).

(6) *Payment of compensation to a disqualified person.*—In the case of the payment of compensation by a private foundation to a disqualified person for the performance of personal services which are reasonable and necessary to carry out the exempt purpose of such foundation, undoing the transaction requires that the disqualified person pay to the foundation any amount which is excessive. However, termination of the employment or independent contractor relationship is not required.

(7) *Special rule for correction of valuation errors.*—(i) In the case of a transaction described in paragraph (b)(2)(iii) of this section, a "correction" of the act of self-dealing shall ordinarily be deemed to occur if the foundation is paid an amount of money equal to the amount involved (as defined in paragraph (b)(2)(iii) of this section) plus such additional amounts as are necessary to compensate it for the loss of the use of the money or other property during the period commencing on the date of the act of self-dealing and ending on the date the transaction is corrected pursuant to this subparagraph.

(ii) The provisions of this subparagraph may be illustrated by the following example:

*Example.* Assume the same facts as in Example (5) of paragraph (b)(4) of this section. Such transaction shall be considered as corrected by a payment of $5,000 by M to V, together with an additional payment to V of an amount equal to the interest which V could have obtained on $5,000 for the period commencing on the date of the redemption and ending on the date the act is corrected.

(d) *Cross reference.*—For rules relating to taxable events that are corrected within the correction period, defined in section 4963(e), see section 4961(a), and the regulations thereunder.

(e) *Act of self-dealing.*—(1) *Number of acts; use of money or property.*—(i) *In general.*—If a transaction between a private foundation and a disqualified person is determined to be self-dealing (as defined in section 4941(d)), for purposes of section 4941 there is generally one act of self-dealing. For the date on which such act is treated as occurring, see paragraph (a)(2) of this section. If, however, such transaction relates to the leasing of property, the lending of money or other extension of credit, other use of money or property, or payment of compensation, the transaction will generally be treated (for purposes of section 4941 but not section 507 or 6684) as giving rise to an act of self-dealing on the day the transaction occurs plus an act of self-dealing on the first day of each taxable year or portion of a taxable year which is within the taxable period and which begins after the taxable year in which the transaction occurs.

(ii) *Examples.*—The provisions of this subparagraph may be illustrated by the following examples:

*Example (1).* On August 31, 1970, X, a private foundation, sells a building to A, a disqualified person with respect to X. A is on the calendar year basis. Under these circumstances, the transaction between A and X is one act of self- dealing which is treated for purposes of section 4941 as occurring on August 31, 1970.

*Example (2).* Assume the facts as stated in Example (1), except that, instead of selling the building to A, X leases the building to A for a term of four years beginning July 31, 1970, at an annual rental of $12,000. The fair rental value of the building is also $12,000 per annum as of July 31, 1970, and throughout the next four years. This transaction is corrected on September 30, 1973, in accordance with paragraph (c)(4) of this section. Under these circumstances, the transaction between A and X constitutes four separate acts of self-dealing, which are treated for purposes of section 4941 as occurring on July 31, 1970, January 1, 1971, January 1, 1972, and January 1, 1973. Consequently, there are four taxable periods. The first taxable period is from July 31, 1970, to September 30, 1973; the second is from January 1, 1971, to September 30, 1973; the third is from January 1, 1972, to September 30, 1973; and the fourth is from January 1, 1973, to September 30, 1973. For purposes of the initial taxes in section 4941(a), the amount involved is $5,000 for the first taxable period, $12,000 for the second, $12,000 for the third, and $9,000 for the fourth. The initial taxes to be paid by A are thus $1,000 ($5,000 × 5% × 4 taxable years or partial taxable years in the taxable period) for the first act; $1,800 ($12,000 × 5% × 3) for the second act; $1,200 ($12,000 × 5% × 2) for the third act; and $450 ($9,000 × 5% × 1) for the fourth act.

*Example (3).* Assume the facts as stated in Example (1) of § 53.4941(d)-4(c)(4)(ii). If the debentures are held by Y after December 31, 1979, the extension of credit will not be excepted from the definition of an act of self-dealing, because a new act of self-dealing will be treated (for purposes of section 4941) as occurring on January 1, 1980.

(2) *Number of acts; joint participation by disqualified persons.*—(i) *In general.*—If joint participation in a transaction by two or more disqualified persons constitutes self-dealing (such as a joint sale of property to a private foundation or joint use of its money or property), such transaction shall generally be treated as a separate act of self-dealing with respect to each disqualified person for purposes of section 4941. For purposes of section 507 and, in the case of a foundation manager, section 6684, however, such transaction shall be treated as only one act of self-dealing. For purposes of this subparagraph, an individual and one or more members of his family (within the meaning of section 4946(d)) shall be treated as one person, regardless of whether a member of the family is a disqualified person not only by reason of section 4946(a)(1)(D) but also by reason of another subparagraph of section 4946(a)(1). However, the liability imposed on a disqualified person and one or more members of his family for joint participation in an act of self-dealing shall be joint and several in accordance with section 4941(c)(1) and § 53.4941(c)-1(a).

(ii) *Examples.*—The provisions of this subparagraph may be illustrated by the following examples:

*Example (1).* Private foundation X permits A, a substantial contributor to X, and her spouse, H, to use an automobile owned by X and normally used in its foundation activities to travel from State Z to State Y for a vacation on December 1, 1971. The automobile is then returned to X until December 21, 1971, when X again permits them to use the automobile to return to their home in State Z. Under these circumstances, there is one act of self-dealing on December 1, 1971, and a second act of self-dealing on December 21, 1971.

*Example (2).* Assume the facts as stated in Example (1), except that B joined A and H on their vacation and travelled with them both to and from State Y. B is a disqualified person with respect to X, but he is not related by blood or marriage to A or H. Assume also that X is not paid for the use of its automobile, but that the fair rental value during the taxable period is $300 (or $100 per person) for a one-way trip between State Y and State Z. Under these circumstances, there are four acts of self-dealing, two with respect to A and H and two with respect to B. The amount involved with respect to A and H is

$200 for each act, and the amount involved with respect to B is $100 for each act.

(f) *Fair market value.*—For purposes of §§53.4941(a)-1 through 53.4941(f)-1, fair market value shall be determined pursuant to the provisions of §53.4942(a)-2(c)(4). [Reg. §53.4941(e)-1.]

☐ [*T.D. 7270,* 4-16-73. *Amended by T.D. 8084,* 5-1-86.]

### [Reg. §53.4941(f)-1]

**§53.4941(f)-1. Effective dates.**—(a) *In general.*—Except as provided in paragraph (b) of this section, §§53.4941(a)-1 through 53.4941(e)-1 shall apply to all acts of self-dealing engaged in after December 31, 1969.

(b) *Transitional rules.*—(1) *Commitments made prior to January 1, 1970, between private foundations and government officials.*—Section 4941 shall not apply to a payment for one or more purposes described in section 170(c)(1) or (2)(B) made on or after January 1, 1970, by a private foundation to a government official, if such payment is made pursuant to a commitment entered into prior to such date, but only if such commitment was made in accordance with the foundation's usual practices and is reasonable in amount in light of the purposes of the payment. For purposes of this subparagraph, a commitment will be considered entered into prior to January 1, 1970, if prior to such date, the amount and nature of the payments to be made and the name of the payee were entered on the records of the payor, or were otherwise adequately evidenced, or the notice of the payment to be received was communicated to the payee in writing.

(2) *Special transitional rule.*—In the case of an act of self-dealing engaged in prior to July 5, 1971, section 4941(a)(1) shall not apply if—

(i) The participation (as defined in §53.4941(a)-1(a)(3)) by the disqualified person in such act is not willful and is due to reasonable cause (as defined in §53.4941(a)-1(b)(4) and (5)),

(ii) The transaction would not be a prohibited transaction if section 503(b) applied, and

(iii) The act is corrected (within the meaning of §53.4941(e)-1(c)) within a period ending [insert 90 days after date on which final regulations under section 4941 are filed by the Federal Register], extended (prior to the expiration of the original period) by any period which the Commissioner determines is reasonable and necessary (within the meaning of §53.4941(e)-1(d)) to bring about correction of the act of self-dealing. [Reg. §53.4941(f)-1.]

☐ [*T.D. 7270,* 4-16-73.]

### [Reg. §53.4942(a)-1]

**§53.4942(a)-1. Taxes for failure to distribute income.**—(a) *Imposition of tax.*—(1) *Initial tax.*—Except as provided in paragraph (b) of this section, section 4942(a) imposes an excise tax of 15 percent on the undistributed income (as defined in paragraph (a) of §53.4942(a)-2) of a private foundation for any taxable year which has not been distributed before the first day of the second (or any succeeding) taxable year following such taxable year (if such first day falls within the taxable period as defined in paragraph (c)(1) of this section). For purposes of section 4942 and this section, the term "distributed" means distributed as qualifying distributions under section 4942(g). See paragraph (d)(2) of §53.4942(a)-3 with respect to correction of deficient distributions for prior taxable years.

(2) *Additional tax.*—In any case in which an initial excise tax is imposed by section 4942(a) on the undistributed income of a private foundation for any taxable year, section 4942(b) imposes an additional excise tax on any portion of such income remaining undistributed at the close of the correction period (as defined in paragraph (c)(1) of this section). The tax imposed by section 4942(b) is equal to 100 percent of the amount remaining undistributed at the close of the taxable period.

(3) *Payment of tax.*—Payment of the excise taxes imposed by section 4942(a) or (b) is in addition to, and not in lieu of, making the distribution of such undistributed income as required by section 4942. See section 507(a)(2) and the regulations thereunder.

(4) *Examples.*—The provisions of this paragraph may be illustrated by the following examples:

*Example (1).* M, a private foundation which uses the calendar year as its taxable year, has at the end of 1981, $50,000 of undistributed income (as defined in paragraph (a) of §53.4942(a)-2) for 1981. As of January 1, 1983, $40,000 is still undistributed. On August 15, 1983, a notice of deficiency with respect to the excise taxes imposed by section 4942(a) and (b) is mailed to M under section 6212(a) and the taxable period ends. Thus, under these facts, an initial excise tax of $6,000 (15 percent of $40,000) is imposed upon M. An additional excise tax of $40,000 (100 percent of $40,000) is imposed by section 4942(b). Under section 4961(a), however, if the undistributed income is reduced to zero during the correction period, this latter tax will not be assessed, and if assessed, it will be abated, and if collected, it will be credited or refunded as an overpayment.

*Example (2).* Assume the facts as stated in example (1), except that the notice of deficiency is mailed to *M* on September 7, 1984, and as of January 1, 1984, only $10,000 of the $50,000 of undistributed income with respect to 1981 is undistributed. Therefore, initial excise taxes of $6,000 (15 percent of $40,000, *M*'s undistributed income from 1981, as of January 1, 1983) and $1,500 (15 percent of $10,000, *M*'s undistributed income from 1981 as of January 1, 1984) are imposed by section 4942(a). If the $10,000 remains undistributed as of September 7, 1984, the end of the taxable period, an additional excise tax of $10,000 (100 percent of $10,000, *M*'s undistributed income from 1981, as of September 7, 1984) is imposed by section 4942(b).

(b) *Exceptions.*—(1) *In general.*—The initial excise tax imposed by section 4942(a) shall not apply to the undistributed income of a private foundation—

(i) For any taxable year for which it is an operating foundation (as defined in section 4942(j)(3) and the regulations thereunder), or

(ii) To the extent that the foundation failed to distribute any amount solely because of incorrect valuation of assets under paragraph (c)(4) of § 53.4942(a)-2, if—

(*a*) The failure to value the assets properly was not willful and was due to reasonable cause.

(*b*) Such amount is distributed as qualifying distributions (within the meaning of paragraph (a) of § 53.4942(a)-3) by the foundation during the allowable distribution period (as defined in paragraph (c)(2) of this section),

(*c*) The foundation notifies the Commissioner that such amount has been distributed (within the meaning of subdivision (ii) (*b*) of this subparagraph) to correct such failure, and

(*d*) Such distribution is treated under paragraph (d)(2) of § 53.4942(a)-3 as made out of the undistributed income for the taxable year for which a tax would (except for this subdivision) have been imposed by section 4942.

(2) *Improper valuation.*—For purposes of subparagraph (1)(ii) of this paragraph, failure to value an asset properly shall be regarded as "not willful" and "due to reasonable cause" whenever, under all the facts and circumstances, the foundation can show that it has made all reasonable efforts in good faith to value such an asset in accordance with the provisions of paragraph (c)(4) of § 53.4942(a)-2. If a foundation, after full disclosure of the factual situation, obtains a bona fide appraisal of the fair market value of an asset by a person qualified to make such an appraisal (whether or not such a person is a disqualified person with respect to the foundation), and such foundation relies upon such appraisal, then failure to value the asset properly shall ordinarily be regarded as "not willful" and "due to reasonable cause". Notwithstanding the preceding sentence, the failure to obtain such a bona fide appraisal shall not, by itself, give rise to any inference that a foundation's failure to value an asset properly was willful or not due to reasonable cause.

(3) *Example.*—The provisions of this paragraph may be illustrated by the following example:

*Example.* In 1976 M, a private foundation which was established in 1975 and which uses the calendar year as the taxable year, incorrectly values its assets under paragraph (c)(4) of § 53.4942(a) in a manner which is not willful and is due to reasonable cause. As a result of the incorrect valuation of assets, $20,000 which should be distributed with respect to 1976 is not distributed, and as of January 1, 1978, such amount is still undistributed. On March 29, 1978, a notice of deficiency with respect to the excise taxes imposed by section 4942(a) and (b) is mailed to M under section 6212(a). On May 5, 1978 (within the allowable distribution period), M makes a qualifying distribution of $20,000 which is treated under paragraph (d)(2) of § 53.4942(a)-3 as made out of M's undistributed income for 1976. M notifies the Commissioner of its action. Under the stated facts, an initial excess tax of $3,000 (15 percent of $20,000) would (except for the exception contained in subparagraph (1)(ii) of this paragraph) have been imposed by section 4942(a), but since all of the requirements of this subparagraph are satisfied no tax is imposed by section 4942(a).

(c) *Certain periods.*—For purposes of this section—

(1) *Taxable period.*—(i) The term "taxable period" means, with respect to the undistributed income of a private foundation for any taxable year, the period beginning with the first day of the taxable year and ending on the earlier of:

(A) The date of mailing of a notice of deficiency under section 6212(a) with respect to the initial excise tax imposed under section 4942(a), or

(B) The date on which the initial excise tax imposed under section 4942(a) is assessed.

For example, assume M, a private foundation which uses the calendar year as the taxable year, has $15,000 of undistributed income for 1981. A notice of deficiency is mailed to M under section 6212(a) on June 1, 1983. With respect to the undistributed income of M for 1981, the taxable period began on January 1, 1981, and ended on June 1, 1983.

(ii) Where a notice of deficiency referred to in subdivision (i) of this subparagraph is not mailed because there is a waiver of the restrictions on assessment and collection of a deficiency, or because the deficiency is paid, the date of filing of the waiver or the date of such payment, respectively, shall be treated as the end of the taxable period.

(2) *Allowable distribution period.*—(i) The term "allowable distribution period" means the period beginning with the first day of the first taxable year following the taxable year in which the incorrect valuation of foundation assets (described in paragraph (b)(1)(ii) of this section) occurred and ending 90 days after the date of mailing of a notice of deficiency under section 6212(a) with respect to the initial excise tax imposed by section 4942(a). This period shall be extended by any period in which a deficiency cannot be assessed under section 6213(a), and any other period which the Commissioner determines is reasonable and necessary to permit a distribution of undistributed income under section 4942.

(ii) Where a notice of deficiency referred to in subdivision (i) of this subparagraph is not mailed because there is a waiver of the restrictions on assessment and collection of a deficiency, or because the deficiency is paid, the date of filing of the waiver or the date of such payment, respectively, shall be treated as the end of the allowable distribution period.

(3) *Cross reference.*—For rules relating to taxable events that are corrected within the correction period, defined in section 4963(e), see section 4961(a) and the regulations thereunder.

(4) *Examples.*—The provisions of this paragraph may be illustrated by the following examples:

*Example (1).* In 1975 M, a private foundation which uses the calendar year as the taxable year, made an error in valuing its assets which was not willful and was due to reasonable cause. The error caused M not to distribute $25,000 that should have been distributed with respect to 1975. On March 1, 1978, a notice of deficiency with respect to the excise taxes imposed by section 4942(a) and (b) was mailed to M under section 6212(a). With respect to the undistributed income for 1975, the "taxable period" is the period from January 1, 1975, through March 1, 1978, and the "allowable distribution period" is the period from January 1, 1976, through May 30, 1978 (90 days after the mailing of the notice of deficiency).

*Example (2).* Assume the facts as stated in example (1), except that the Commissioner determines that it is reasonable and necessary to extend the period for distribution through June 15, 1978. Thus, the "allowable distribution period" is from January 1, 1976, through June 15, 1978.

(d) *Effective date.*—Except as otherwise specifically provided, section 4942 and the regulations thereunder shall only apply with respect to taxable years beginning after December 31, 1969. [Reg. § 53.4942(a)-1.]

☐ [*T.D. 7256, 2-2-73. Amended by T.D. 8084, 5-1-86.*]

## [Reg. § 53.4942(a)-2]

§ 53.4942(a)-2. **Computation of undistributed income.**—(a) *Undistributed income.*—For purposes of section 4942, the term "undistributed income" means, with respect to any private foundation for any taxable year as of any time, the amount by which—

(1) The distributable amount (as defined in paragraph (b) of this section) for such taxable year, exceeds

(2) The qualifying distributions (as defined in § 53.4942(a)-3) made before such time out of such distributable amount.

(b) *Distributable amount.*—(1) *In general.*—For purposes of paragraph (a) of this section, the term "distributable amount" means—

(i) For taxable years beginning before January 1, 1982, an amount equal to the greater of the minimum investment return (as defined in paragraph (c) of this section) or the adjusted net income (as defined in paragraph (d) of this section); and

(ii) For taxable years beginning after December 31, 1981, an amount equal to the minimum investment return (as defined in paragraph (c) of this section),
reduced by the sum of the taxes imposed on such private foundation for such taxable year under subtitle A of the Code and section 4940, and increased by the amounts received from trusts described in subparagraph (2) of this paragraph.

(2) *Certain trust amounts.*—(i) *In general.*—The distributable amount shall be increased by the income portion (as defined in

subdivision (ii) of this subparagraph) of distributions from trusts described in section 4947(a)(2) with respect to amounts placed in trust after May 26, 1969. If such distributions are made with respect to amounts placed in trust both on or before and after May 26, 1969, such distributions shall be allocated between such amounts to determine the extent to which such distributions shall be included in the foundation's distributable amount. For rules relating to the segregation of amounts placed in trust on or before May 26, 1969, from amounts placed in trust after such date and to the allocation of income derived from such amounts, see paragraph (c)(5) of § 53.4947-1.

(ii) *Income portion of distributions to private foundations.*—For purposes of subdivision (i) of this subparagraph, the income portion of a distribution from a section 4947(a)(2) trust to a private foundation in a particular taxable year of such foundation shall be the greater of:

(a) The amount of such distribution which is treated as income (within the meaning of section 643(b)) of the trust, or

(b) The guaranteed annuity, or fixed percentage of the fair market value of the trust property (determined annually), which the private foundation is entitled to receive for such year, regardless of whether such amount is actually received in such year or in any prior or subsequent year.

(iii) *Limitation.*—Notwithstanding subdivisions (i) and (ii) of this subparagraph, a private foundation shall not be required to distribute a greater amount for any taxable year than would have been required (without regard to this subparagraph) for such year had the corpus of the section 4947(a)(2) trust to which the distribution described in subdivision (ii) of this subparagraph is attributable been taken into account by such foundation as an asset described in paragraph (c)(1)(i) of this section.

(c) *Minimum investment return.*—(1) *In general.*—For purposes of paragraph (b) of this section, the "minimum investment return" for any private foundation for any taxable year is the amount determined by multiplying—

(i) The excess of the aggregate fair market value of all assets of the foundation, other than those described in subparagraph (2) or (3) of this paragraph, over the amount of the acquisition indebtedness with respect to such assets (determined under section 514(c)(1), but without regard to the taxable year in which the indebtedness was incurred), by

(ii) The applicable percentage (as defined in subparagraph (5) of this paragraph) for such year.

For purposes of subdivision (i) of this subparagraph, the aggregate fair market value of all assets of the foundation shall include the average of the fair market values on a monthly basis of securities for which market quotations are readily available (within the meaning of subparagraph (4)(i)(a) of this paragraph), the average of the foundation's cash balances on a monthly basis (less the cash balances excluded from the computation of the minimum investment return by operation of subparagraph (3)(iv) of this paragraph), and the fair market value of all other assets (except those assets described in subparagraph (2) or (3) of this paragraph) for the period of time during the year for which such assets are held by the foundation. Any determination of the fair market value of an asset required pursuant to the provisions of this subparagraph shall be made in accordance with the rules of subparagraph (4) of this paragraph.

(2) *Certain assets excluded.*—For purposes of this paragraph, the assets taken into account in determining minimum investment return shall not include the following:

(i) Any future interest (such as a vested or contingent remainder, whether legal or equitable) of a foundation in the income or corpus of any real or personal property, other than a future interest created by the private foundation, after December 31, 1969, until all intervening interests in, and rights to the actual possession or enjoyment of, such property have expired, or, although not actually reduced to the foundation's possession, until such future interest has been constructively received by the foundation, as where it has been credited to the foundation's account, set apart for the foundation, or otherwise made available so that the foundation may acquire it at any time or could have acquired it if notice of intention to acquire had been given;

(ii) The assets of an estate until such time as such assets are distributed to the foundation or, due to a prolonged period of administration, such estate is considered terminated for Federal income tax purposes by operation of paragraph (a) of § 1.641(b)-3 of this chapter (Income Tax Regulations);

(iii) Any present interest of a foundation in any trust created and funded by another person (see, however, paragraph (b)(2) of this section with respect to amounts received from certain trusts described in section 4947(a)(2));

(iv) Any pledge to the foundation of money or property (whether or not the pledge may be legally enforced); and

(v) Any assets used (or held for use) directly in carrying out the foundation's exempt purpose.

(3) *Assets used (or held for use) in carrying out the exempt purpose.*—(i) *In general.*—For purposes of subparagraph (2)(v) of this paragraph, an asset is "used (or held for use) directly in carrying out the foundation's exempt purpose" only if the asset is actually used by the foundation in the carrying out of the charitable, educational, or other similar purpose which gives rise to the exempt status of the foundation, or if the foundation owns the asset and establishes to the satisfaction of the Commissioner that its immediate use for such exempt purpose is not practical (based on the facts and circumstances of the particular case) and that definite plans exist to commence such use within a reasonable period of time. Consequently, assets which are held for the production of income or for investment (for example, stocks, bonds, interest-bearing notes, endowment funds, or, generally, leased real estate) are not being used (or held for use) directly in carrying out the foundation's exempt purpose, even though the income from such assets is used to carry out such exempt purpose. Whether an asset is held for the production of income or for investment rather than used (or held for use) directly by the foundation to carry out its exempt purpose is a question of fact. For example, an office building used for the purpose of providing offices for employees engaged in the management of endowment funds of the foundation is not being used (or held for use) directly by the foundation to carry out its charitable, educational, or other similar exempt purpose. However, where property is used both for charitable, educational, or other similar exempt purposes and for other purposes, if such exempt use represents 95 percent or more of the total use, such property shall be considered to be used exclusively for a charitable, educational, or other similar exempt purpose. If such exempt use of such property represents less than 95 percent of the total use, reasonable allocation between such exempt and nonexempt use must be made for purposes of this paragraph. Property acquired by the foundation to be used in carrying out its charitable, educational, or other similar exempt purpose may be considered as used (or held for use) directly to carry out such exempt purpose even though the property, in whole or in part, is leased for a limited period of time during which arrangements are made for its conversion to the use for which it was acquired, provided such income-producing use of the property does not exceed a reasonable period of time. Generally, one year shall be deemed to be a reasonable period of time for purposes of the immediately preceding sentence. For treatment of the income derived from such income-producing use, see paragraph (d)(2)(viii) of this section. Where the income-producing use continues beyond a reasonable period of time, the property shall not be deemed to be used by the foundation to carry out its charitable, educational, or other similar exempt purpose, but, instead, as of the time the income-producing use becomes unreasonable, such property shall be treated as disposed of within the meaning of paragraph (d)(2)(iii)(b) of this section to the extent that the acquisition of the property was taken into account as a qualifying distribution (within the meaning of paragraph (a)(2) of § 53.4942(a)-3) for any taxable year. If, subsequently, the property is used by the foundation directly in carrying out its charitable, educational, or other similar exempt purpose, a qualifying distribution in the amount of its then fair market value, determined in accordance with the rules contained in subparagraph (4) of this paragraph, shall be deemed to have been made as of the time such exempt use begins.

(ii) *Illustrations.*—Examples of assets which are "used (or held for use) directly in carrying out the foundation's exempt purpose" include, but are not limited to, the following:

(a) Administrative assets, such as office equipment and supplies which are used by employees or consultants of the foundation, to the extent such assets are devoted to and used directly in the administration of the foundation's charitable, educational, or other similar exempt activities;

(b) Real estate or the portion of a building used by the foundation directly in its charitable, educational, or other similar exempt activities;

(c) Physical facilities used in such activities, such as paintings or other works of art owned by the foundation which are on public display, fixtures and equipment in classrooms, and research facilities and related equipment, which under the facts and circumstances serve a useful purpose in the conduct of such activities;

(d) Any interest in a functionally related business (as defined in subdivision (iii) of this subparagraph) or in a program-related investment (as defined in section 4944(c));

(e) The reasonable cash balances (as described in subdivision (iv) of this subparagraph) necessary to cover current administrative expenses and other normal and current disbursements directly connected with the foundation's charitable, educational, or other similar exempt activities; and

(f) Any property leased by a foundation in carrying out its charitable, educational, or other similar exempt purpose at no cost (or at a nominal rent) to the lessee or for a program-related purpose (within the meaning of section 4944(c)), such as the leasing of renovated apartments to low-income tenants at a low rental as part of the lessor-foundation's program for rehabilitating a blighted portion of a community. For treatment of the income derived from such use, see paragraph (d)(2)(viii) of this section.

(iii) *Functionally related business.—(a) In general.*—The term "functionally related business" means—

(1) A trade or business which is not an unrelated trade or business (as defined in section 513), or

(2) An activity which is carried on within a larger aggregate of similar activities or within a larger complex of other endeavors which is related (aside from the need of the organization for income or funds or the use it makes of the profits derived) to the charitable, educational, or other similar exempt purpose of the organization.

(b) *Examples.*—The provisions of this subdivision may be illustrated by the following examples:

*Example (1).* X, a private foundation, maintains a community of historic value which is open to the general public. For the convenience of the public, X, through a wholly owned, separately incorporated, taxable entity, maintains a restaurant and hotel in such community. Such facilities are within the larger aggregate of activities which makes available for public enjoyment the various buildings of historic interest and which is related to X's exempt purpose. Thus, the operation of the restaurant and hotel under such circumstances constitutes a functionally related business.

*Example (2).* Y, a private foundation, as part of its medical research program under section 501(c)(3), publishes a medical journal in carrying out its exempt purpose. Space in the journal is sold for commercial advertising. Notwithstanding the fact that the advertising activity may be subject to the tax imposed by section 511, such activity is within a larger complex of endeavors which makes available to the scientific community and the general public developments with respect to medical research and is therefore a functionally related business.

(iv) *Cash held for charitable, etc. activities.*—For purposes of subdivision (ii) (e) of this subparagraph, the reasonable cash balance which a private foundation needs to have on hand to cover expenses and disbursements described in such subdivision will generally be deemed to be an amount, computed on an annual basis, equal to one and one-half percent of the fair market value of all assets described in subparagraph (1)(i) of this paragraph, without regard to subdivision (ii)(e) of this subparagraph. However, if the Commissioner is satisfied that under the facts and circumstances an amount in addition to such one and one-half percent is necessary for payment of such expenses and disbursements, then such additional amount may also be excluded from the amount of assets described in subparagraph (1)(i) of this paragraph. All remaining cash balances, including amounts necessary to pay any tax imposed by section 511 or any section of chapter 42 of the Code except section 4940, are to be included in the assets described in subparagraph (1)(i) of this paragraph.

(4) *Valuation of assets.—(i) Certain securities.—(a)* For purposes of subparagraph (1)(i) of this paragraph, a private foundation may use any reasonable method to determine the fair market value on a monthly basis of securities for which market quotations are readily available, as long as such method is consistently used. For purposes of this subparagraph, market quotations are readily available if a security is:

(1) Listed on the New York Stock Exchange, the American Stock Exchange, or any city or regional exchange in which quotations appear on a daily basis, including foreign securities listed on a recognized foreign national or regional exchange;

(2) Regularly traded in the national or regional over-the-counter market, for which published quotations are available; or

(3) Locally traded, for which quotations can readily be obtained from established brokerage firms.

(b) For purposes of this subdivision, commonly accepted methods of valuation must be used in making an appraisal. Valuations made in accordance with the principles stated in the regulations under section 2031 constitute acceptable methods of valuation. This paragraph (c)(4)(i)(b) applies only for taxable years beginning before January 1, 1976. See section 4942(e)(2)(B) and paragraph (c)(4)(i)(c) of this section for special valuation rules that apply for subsequent taxable years.

(c) For purposes of this subdivision (i) and with respect to taxable years beginning after December 31, 1975, if the private foun-

dation can show that the value of securities determined on the basis of market quotations as provided by subdivision (i)(a) does not reflect the fair market value thereof because—

(1) The securities constitute a block of securities so large in relation to the volume of actual sales on the existing market that it could not be liquidated in a reasonable time without depressing the market,

(2) The securities are securities in a closely held corporation and sales are few or of a sporadic nature, and/or

(3) The sale of the securities would result in a forced or distress sale because the securities could not be offered to the public for sale without first being registered under the Securities Act of 1933 or because of other factors,

then the price at which the securities could be sold as such outside the usual market, as through an underwriter, may be a more accurate indication of value than market quotations. On the other hand, if the securities to be valued represent a controlling interest, either actual or effective, in a going business, the price at which other lots change hands may have little relation to the true value of the securities. No decrease in the fair market value of any given class of securities determined on the basis of market quotations as provided by subdivision (i)(a) shall be allowed except as authorized by this subdivision, and no such decrease shall in the aggregate exceed 10 percent of the fair market value of such class of securities so determined on the basis of market quotations and without regard to this subdivision.

(d) In the case of securities described in subdivision (i)(a) of this subparagraph, which are held in trust for, or on behalf of, a foundation by a bank or other financial institution which values such securities periodically by use of a computer, a foundation may determine the correct value of such securities by use of such computer pricing system, provided the Commissioner has accepted such computer pricing system as a valid method for valuing securities for Federal estate tax purposes.

(e) This subdivision may be illustrated by the following examples:

*Example (1).* U, a private foundation, owns 1,000 shares of the stock of M Corporation. M stock is regularly traded on the New York Stock Exchange. U consistently follows a practice of valuing its 1,000 shares of M stock on the last trading day of each month based upon the quoted closing price for M stock. U's method of valuing its M Corporation stock is permissible under the rules contained in subdivision (i)(a) of this subparagraph.

*Example (2).* Assume the facts as stated in example (1), except that U consistently follows a practice of valuing its 1,000 shares of M stock by taking the mean of the closing prices for M stock on the first and last trading days of each month and the trading day nearest the 15th day of each month. U's method of valuing its M stock is permissible under the rules contained in subdivision (i)(a) of this subparagraph.

*Example (3).* Assume the facts as stated in example (1), except that U consistently follows a practice of valuing its M stock by taking the mean of the highest and lowest quoted prices for the stock on the last trading day of each month. U's method of valuing its M stock is permissible under the rules contained in subdivision (1)[(i)](a) of this subparagraph.

*Example (4).* V, a private foundation, owns 1,000 shares of the stock of N Corporation. N stock is regularly traded in the national over-the-counter market and published quotations of the bid and asked prices for the stock are available. V consistently follows a practice of valuing its 1,000 shares of N stock on the first trading day of each month by taking the mean of the bid and asked prices on that day. V's method of valuing its N Corporation stock is permissible under the rules contained in subdivision (i)(a) of this subparagraph.

*Example (5).* W, a private foundation, owns 1,000 shares of the stock of O Corporation. O stock is locally traded and quotations can readily be obtained from established brokerage firms. W consistently follows a practice of valuing its O stock on the 15th day of each month by obtaining a bona fide quotation of bid and asked prices for the stock from an established brokerage firm and taking the mean of such prices on that day. If a quotation is unavailable on the regular valuation date, W values its O stock based upon a bona fide quotation on the first day thereafter on which such a quotation is available. W's method of valuing its O Corporation stock is permissible under the rules contained in subdivision (i)(a) of this subparagraph.

(ii) *Cash.*—In order to determine the amount of a foundation's cash balances, the foundation shall value its cash on a monthly basis by averaging the amount of cash on hand as of the first day of each month and as of the last day of each month.

(iii) *Common trust funds.*—If a private foundation owns a participating interest in a common trust fund (as defined in section 584) established and administered under a plan providing for the periodic valuation of participating interests during the fund's taxable year and the reporting of such valuations to participants, the value of the foundation's interest in the common trust fund based upon the average of the valuations reported to the foundation during its taxable year will ordinarily constitute an acceptable method of valuation.

(iv) *Other assets.—(a)* Except as otherwise provided in subdivision (iv)(*b*) of this subparagraph, the fair market value of assets other than those described in subdivisions (i) through (iii) of this subparagraph shall be determined annually. Thus, the fair market value of securities other than those described in subdivision (i) of this subparagraph shall be determined in accordance with this subdivision (*a*). If, however, a private foundation owns voting stock of an issuer of unlisted securities and has, or together with disqualified persons or another private foundation has, effective control of the issuer (within the meaning of § 53.4943-3(b)(3)(ii)), then to the extent that the issuer's assets consist of shares of listed securities issues, such assets shall be valued monthly on the basis of market quotations or in accordance with section 4942(e)(2)(B), if applicable. Thus, for example, if a private foundation and a disqualified person together own all of the unlisted voting stock of a holding company which in turn holds a portfolio of securities of issues which are listed on the New York Stock Exchange, in determining the net worth of the holding company, the underlying portfolio securities are to be valued monthly by reference to market quotations for their issues unless a decrease in such value is authorized in accordance with section 4942(e)(2)(B). Such determination may be made by employees of the private foundation or by any other person, without regard to whether such person is a disqualified person with respect to the foundation. A valuation made pursuant to the provisions of this subdivision, if accepted by the Commissioner, shall be valid only for the taxable year for which it is made. A new valuation made in accordance with these provisions is required for the succeeding taxable year.

(*b*) If the requirements of this subdivision are met, the fair market value of any interest in real property, including any improvements thereon, may be determined on a five-year basis. Such value must be determined by means of a certified, independent appraisal made in writing by a qualified person who is neither a disqualified person with respect to, nor an employee of, the private foundation. The appraisal is certified only if it contains a statement at the end thereof to the effect that, in the opinion of the appraiser, the values placed on the assets appraised were determined in accordance with valuation principles regularly employed in making appraisals of such property using all reasonable valuation methods. The foundation shall retain a copy of the independent appraisal for its records. If a valuation made pursuant to the provisions of this subdivision in fact falls within the range of reasonable values for the appraised property, such valuation may be used by the foundation for the taxable year for which the valuation is made and for each of the succeeding four taxable years. Any valuation made pursuant to the provisions of this subdivision may be replaced during the five-year period by a subsequent five-year valuation made in accordance with the rules set forth in this subdivision, or with an annual valuation made in accordance with subdivision (iv)(*a*) of this subparagraph, and the most recent such valuation of such assets shall be used in computing the foundation's minimum investment return. In the case of a foundation organized before May 27, 1969, a valuation made in accordance with this subdivision applicable to the foundation's first taxable year beginning after December 31, 1972 and the four succeeding taxable years must be made no later than the last day of such first taxable year. In the case of a foundation organized after May 26, 1969, a valuation made in accordance with this subdivision applicable to the foundation's first taxable year beginning after February 5, 1973, and the succeeding four taxable years must be made no later than the last day of such first taxable year. Any subsequent valuation made in accordance with this subdivision must be made no later than the last day of the first taxable year for which such new valuation is applicable. A valuation, if properly made in accordance with the rules set forth in this subdivision, will not be disturbed by the Commissioner during the five-year period for which it applies even if the actual fair market value of such property changes during such period.

(*c*) For purposes of this subdivision, commonly accepted methods of valuation must be used in making an appraisal. Valuations made in accordance with the principles stated in the regulations under section 2031 constitute acceptable methods of valuation. The term "appraisal," as used in this subdivision, means a determination of fair market value and is not to be construed in a technical sense peculiar to particular property or interests therein, such as, for example, mineral interests in real property.

(v) *Definition of "securities".*—For purposes of this subparagraph, the term "securities" includes, but it is not limited to, common and preferred stocks, bonds, and mutual fund shares.

(vi) *Valuation date.—(a)* In the case of an asset which is required to be valued on an annual basis as provided in subdivision (iv) (*a*) of this subparagraph, such asset may be valued as of any day in the private foundation's taxable year to which such valuation applies, provided the foundation follows a consistent practice of valuing such asset as of such date in all taxable years.

(*b*) A valuation described in subdivision (iv) (*b*) of this subparagraph may be made as of any day in the first taxable year of the private foundation to which such valuation is to be applied.

(vii) *Assets held for less than a taxable year.*—For purposes of this paragraph, any asset described in subparagraph (1)(i) of this paragraph which is held by a foundation for only part of a taxable year shall be taken into account for purposes of determining the foundation's minimum investment return for such taxable year by multiplying the fair market value of such asset (as determined pursuant to this subparagraph) by a fraction, the numerator of which is the number of days in such taxable year that the foundation held such asset and the denominator of which is the number of days in such taxable year.

(5) *Applicable percentage.*—(i) *In general.*—For purposes of paragraph (c)(1)(ii) of this section, except as provided in paragraph (c)(5)(ii) or (iii) of this section, the applicable percentage is:

(*a*) Six percent for a taxable year beginning in 1970 or 1971;

(*b*) Five and a half percent for a taxable year beginning in 1972;

(*c*) Five and one-quarter percent for a taxable year beginning in 1973;

(*d*) Six percent for a taxable year beginning in 1974 or 1975; and

(*e*) Five percent for taxable years beginning after Dec. 31, 1975.

(ii) *Transitional rule.*—In the case of organizations organized before May 27, 1969 (including organizations deemed to be so organized by virtue of the provisions of paragraph (e)(2) of this section), section 4942 shall, for all purposes other than the determination of the minimum investment return under section 4942(j)(3)(B)(ii), for taxable years—

(*a*) Beginning before January 1, 1972, apply without regard to section 4942(e),

(*b*) Beginning in 1972, apply with an applicable percentage of 4¹/₈ percent,

(*c*) Beginning in 1973, apply with an applicable percentage of 4³/₈ percent, and

(*d*) Beginning in 1974, apply with an applicable percentage of 5¹/₂ percent.

(iii) *Short taxable periods.*—In any case in which a taxable year referred to in this subparagraph is a period less than 12 months, the applicable percentage to be applied to the amount determined under the provisions of subparagraph (1) of this paragraph shall be equal to the applicable percentage for the calendar year in which the short taxable period began multiplied by a fraction, the numerator of which is the number of days in such short taxable period and the denominator of which is 365.

(d) *Adjusted net income.*—(1) *Definition.*—For purposes of paragraph (b) of this section, the term "adjusted net income" means the excess (if any) of—

(i) The gross income for the taxable year (including gross income from any unrelated trade or business) determined with the income modifications provided by subparagaph (2) of this paragraph, over

(ii) The sum of the deductions (including deductions directly connected with the carrying on of any unrelated trade or business), determined with the deduction modifications provided by subparagraph (4) of this paragraph, which would be allowed to a corporation subject to the tax imposed by section 11 for the taxable year.

In computing the income includible under this paragraph as gross income and the deductions allowable under this paragraph from such income, the principles of subtitle A of the Code shall apply except to the extent such principles conflict with section 4942 and the regulations thereunder (without regard to this sentence). Except as otherwise provided in this paragraph, no exclusions or deductions from gross income or credits against tax are allowable under this paragraph. For purposes of subdivision (i) of this subparagraph, the term "gross income" does not include gifts, grants, or contributions received by the private foundation but does include income from a functionally related business (as defined in paragraph (c)(3)(iii) of this section).

(2) *Income modifications.*—The income modifications referred to in subparagraph (1)(i) of this paragraph are as follows:

(i) Section 103 (relating to interest on certain governmental obligations) shall not apply. Hence, interest which would have been excluded from gross income by section 103 shall be included in gross income.

(ii) Capital gains and losses from the sale or other disposition of property shall be taken into account only in an amount equal to any net short-term capital gain (as defined in section 1222(5)) for the taxable year. Long-term capital gain or loss is not included in the computation of adjusted net income. Similarly, net section 1231 gains shall be excluded from the computation of adjusted net income. However, net section 1231 losses shall be included in the computation of adjusted net income, if such losses are otherwise described in subparagraph (1)(ii) of this paragraph. Any net short-term capital loss for a given taxable year shall not be taken into account in computing adjusted net income for such year or in computing net short-term capital gain for purposes of determining adjusted net income for prior or future taxable years regardless of whether the foundation is a corporation or a trust.

(iii) The following amounts shall be included in gross income for the taxable year—

(a) Amounts received or accrued as repayments of amounts which were taken into account as a qualifying distribution within the meaning of paragraph (a)(2)(i) of § 53.4942(a)-3 for any taxable year;

(b) Notwithstanding subdivision (ii) of this subparagraph, gross amounts received or accrued from the sale or other disposition of property to the extent that the acquisition of such property was taken into account as a qualifying distribution (within the meaning of paragraph (a)(2)(ii) of § 53.4942(a)-3) for any taxable year; and

(c) Any amount set aside under paragraph (b) of § 53.4942(a)-3 to the extent it is determined that such amount is not necessary for the purposes for which it was set aside.

(iv) Any distribution received by a private foundation from a disqualified person in redemption of stock held by such private foundation if a business enterprise shall be treated as not essentially equivalent to a dividend under section 302(b)(1) if all of the following conditions are satisfied:

(a) Such redemption is of stock which was owned by a private foundation on May 26, 1969 (or which is acquired by a private foundation under the terms of a trust which was irrevocable on May 26, 1969, or under the terms of a will executed on or before such date which are in effect on such date and at all times thereafter);

(b) Such foundation is required to dispose of such property in order not to be liable for tax under section 4943 (relating to taxes on excess business holdings) applied, in the case of a disposition before January 1, 1975, without taking section 4943(c)(4) into account; and

(c) Such foundation receives in return an amount which equals or exceeds the fair market value of such property at the time of such disposition or at the time a contract for such disposition was previously executed in a transaction which would not constitute a prohibited transaction (within the meaning of section 503(b) or the corresponding provisions of prior law).

(v) If, as of the date of distribution of property for purposes described in section 170(c)(1) or (2)(B), the fair market value of such property exceeds its adjusted basis, such excess shall not be deemed an amount includible in gross income.

(vi) The income received by a private foundation from an estate during the period of administration of such estate shall not be included in such foundation's gross income, unless, due to a prolonged period of administration, such estate is considered terminated for Federal income tax purposes by operation of paragraph (a) of § 1.641(b)-3 of this chapter (Income Tax Regulations).

(vii) Distributions received by a private foundation from a trust created and funded by another person shall not be included in the foundation's gross income. However, with respect to distributions from certain trusts described in section 4947(a)(2), see paragraph (b)(2) of this section.

(viii) Gross income shall include all amounts derived from, or in connection with, property held by the foundation, even though the fair market value of such property may not be included in such foundation's assets for purposes of determining minimum investment return by operation of paragraph (c)(3) of this section.

(ix) Gross income shall include amounts treated in a preceding taxable year as a "qualifying distribution" by operation of paragraph (c) of § 53.4942(a)-3 where such amounts are not redistributed by the close of the donee organization's succeeding taxable year in accordance with the rules prescribed in such paragraph (c). In such cases, such amounts shall be included in the donor foundation's gross income for such foundation's first taxable year beginning after the close of the donee organization's first taxable year following the donee organization's taxable year of receipt.

(x) For taxable years ending after October 4, 1976, section 4942(f)(2)(D) states that section 483 (relating to imputed interest on deferred payments) does not apply to payments made pursuant to a binding contract entered into in a taxable year beginning before January 1, 1970. Amounts that are not treated as imputed interest because of section 4942(f)(2)(D) and this subdivision will represent gain or loss from the sale of property. If the gain or loss is long term capital gain or loss, section 4942(f)(2)(B) excludes the gain or loss from the computation of the foundation's gross income. If, in a taxable year beginning after December 31, 1969, there is a substantial change in the terms of a contract entered into in a taxable year beginning before January 1, 1970, then any payment made pursuant to the changed contract is not considered a payment made pursuant to a contract entered into in a taxable year beginning before January 1, 1970. Whether or not a change in the terms of a contract (for example, a change relating to time of payment, sales price, or obligations under the contract) is a substantial change is determined by applying the rules under section 483 and § 1.483-1(b)(4). As used in this subdivision, a binding contract includes an irrevocable written option.

(3) *Adjusted basis.*—(i) *In general.*—For purposes of subparagraph (2)(ii) of this paragraph, the adjusted basis for purposes of determining gain from the sale or other disposition of property shall be determined in accordance with the rules set forth in subdivision (ii) of this subparagraph and the adjusted basis for purposes of determining loss from such disposition shall be determined in accordance with the rules set forth in subdivision (iii) of this subparagraph. Further, the provisions of this subparagraph do not apply for any purpose other than for purposes of subparagraph (2)(ii) of this paragraph. For example, the determination of gain pursuant to the provisions of section 341 is determined without regard to this subparagraph.

(ii) *Gain from sale or other disposition.*—The adjusted basis for purposes of determining gain from the sale or other disposition of property shall be the greater of:

(a) The fair market value of such property on December 31, 1969, plus or minus all adjustments after December 31, 1969, and before the date of sale or other disposition under the rules of Part II, subchapter O, chapter 1 of the Code, provided that the property was held by the private foundation on December 31, 1969, and continuously thereafter to such date of sale or other disposition; or

(b) The adjusted basis as determined under the rules of Part II, subchapter O, chapter 1 of the Code, subject to the provisions of section 4940(c)(3)(B) and the regulations thereunder (and without regard to section 362(c)). With respect to assets acquired prior to December 31, 1969, which were subject to depreciation or depletion, for purposes of determining the adjustments to be made to basis between the date of acquisition and December 31, 1969, an amount equal to straight-line depreciation or cost depletion shall be taken into account. In addition, in determining such adjustments to basis, if any other adjustments would have been made during such period (such as a change in useful life based upon additional data or a change in facts), such adjustments shall also be taken into account.

(iii) *Loss from sale or other disposition.*—For purposes of determining loss from the sale or other disposition of property, adjusted basis as determined in subdivision (ii)(b) of this subparagraph shall apply.

(iv) *Examples.*—The provisions of this subparagraph may be illustrated by the following examples:

*Example (1).* A private foundation, which uses the cash receipts and disbursements method of accounting, purchased certain depreciable real property on December 1, 1969. On December 31, 1969, the fair market value of such property was $100,000 and its adjusted basis (determined under the provisions of this subparagraph) was $102,000. The property was sold on January 2, 1970, for $105,000. Because fair market value on December 31, 1969, $100,000, is less than the adjusted basis as determined by Part II, subchapter O, chapter 1 of the Code, $102,000, a short-term gain of $3,000 is recognized (*i.e.,* sale price of $105,000 less the greater of the two possible bases) for purposes of subparagraph (2)(ii) of this paragraph.

*Example (2).* Assume the facts as stated in example (1), except that the sale price was $95,000. Because the sale price was $7,000 less than the adjusted basis for loss ($102,000 as determined by the application of subdivision (iii) of this subparagraph), there is a capital loss of $7,000 which may be deducted against short-term capital gains for 1970 (if any) in determining net short-term capital gain.

*Example (3).* A private foundation, which uses the cash receipts and disbursements method of accounting, purchased unimproved land on December 1, 1969. On December 31, 1969, the fair market value of such property was $110,000 and its adjusted basis (determined under the provisions of this subparagraph) was $102,000. The property was sold on January 2, 1970, for $105,000. Since the fair market value on December 31, 1969, $110,000, exceeds the adjusted basis as determined by Part II, subchapter O, chapter 1 of the Code,

$102,000, such fair market value will be used for purposes of determining gain. However, because the adjusted basis for purposes of determining gain exceeds the sale price, there is no gain. Furthermore, because the adjusted basis for purposes of determining loss, $102,000, is less than the sale price, there is no loss.

(4) *Deduction modifications.*—(i) *In general.*—For purposes of computing adjusted net income under subparagraph (1) of this paragraph, no deduction shall be allowed other than all the ordinary and necessary expenses paid or incurred for the production or collection of gross income or for the management, conservation, or maintenance of property held for the production of such income, except as provided in subdivision (ii) of this subparagraph. Such expenses include that portion of a private foundation's operating expenses which is paid or incurred for the production or collection of gross income. Operating expenses include compensation of officers, other salaries and wages of employees, interest, rent, and taxes. Where only a portion of the property produces (or is held for the production of) income subject to the provisions of section 4942, and the remainder of the property is used for charitable, educational, or other similar exempt purposes, the deductions allowed by this subparagraph shall be apportioned between the exempt and non-exempt uses. Similarly, where the deductions with respect to property used for a charitable, educational, or other similar exempt purpose exceed the income derived from such property, such excess shall not be allowed as a deduction, but may be treated as a qualifying distribution described in paragraph (a)(2)(ii) of § 53.4942(a)-3. Furthermore, this subdivision does not allow deductions which are not paid or incurred for the purposes herein prescribed. Thus, for example, the deductions prescribed by the following sections are not allowable: (*a*) The charitable contributions deduction prescribed under sections 170 and 642(c); (*b*) the net operating loss deduction prescribed under section 172; and (*c*) the special deductions prescribed under Part VIII, subchapter B, chapter 1 of the Code.

(ii) *Special rules.*—For purposes of computing adjusted net income under subparagraph (1) of this paragraph: (*a*) The allowances for depreciation and depletion as determined under section 4940(c)(3)(B) and the regulations thereunder shall be taken into account, and (*b*) section 265 (relating to expenses and interest relating to tax-exempt interest) shall not apply.

(e) *Certain transitional rules.*—(1) *In general.*—In the case of organizations organized before May 27, 1969, section 4942 shall—

(i) Not apply to an organization to the extent its income is required to be accumulated pursuant to the mandatory terms (as in effect on May 26, 1969, and at all times thereafter) of an instrument executed before May 27, 1969, with respect to the transfer of income producing property to such organization, except that section 4942 shall apply to such organization if the organization would have been denied exemption had section 504(a) not been repealed, or would have had its deductions under section 642(c) limited had section 681(c) not been repealed. In applying the preceding sentence, in addition to the limitations contained in section 504(a) or 681(c) before its repeal, section 504(a)(1) or 681(c)(1) shall be treated as not applying to an organization to the extent its income is required to be accumulated pursuant to the mandatory terms (as in effect on January 1, 1951, and at all times thereafter) of an instrument executed before January 1, 1951, with respect to the transfer of income producing property to such organization before such date, if such transfer was irrevocable on such date; and

(ii) Not apply to an organization which is prohibited by its governing instrument or other instrument from distributing capital or corpus to the extent the requirements of section 4942 are inconsistent with such prohibition.

(2) *Certain existing organizations.*—For purposes of this section, an organization will be deemed to be organized prior to May 27, 1969, if it is either a testamentary trust created under the will of an individual who died prior to such date or an inter vivos trust which was in existence and irrevocable prior to such date, even though it is not funded until after May 26, 1969. Similarly, a split-interest trust, as described in section 4947(a)(2) (without regard to section 4947(a)(2)(C)), which became irrevocable prior to May 27, 1969, and which is treated as a private foundation under section 4947(a)(1) subsequent to such date, likewise shall be treated as an organization organized prior to such date. See section 507(b)(2) and the regulations thereunder with respect to the applicability of transitional rules where there has been a merger of two or more private foundations or a reorganization of a private foundation.

(3) *Limitation.*—With respect to taxable years beginning after December 31, 1971, subparagraph (1)(i) and (ii) of this paragraph shall apply only for taxable years during which there is pending any judicial proceeding by the private foundation which is necessary to reform, or to excuse such foundation from compliance with, its

governing instrument or any other instrument (as in effect on May 26, 1969) in order to comply with the provisions of section 4942, and in the case of subparagraph (1)(i) of this paragraph for all taxable years following the taxable year in which such judicial proceeding is terminated during which the governing instrument or any other instrument does not permit compliance with such provisions. Thus, the exception described in subparagraph (1)(ii) of this paragraph applies after 1971 only for taxable years during which such judicial proceeding is pending. Accordingly, beginning with the first taxable year following the taxable year in which such judicial proceeding is terminated, such foundation will be required to meet the requirements of section 4942 and the regulations thereunder (and be subject to the taxes provided upon failure to do so) except to the extent such foundation is required to accumulate income as described in subparagraph (1)(i) of this paragraph, even if the governing instrument continues to prohibit invasion of capital or corpus. In any case where a foundation's governing instrument or any other instrument requires accumulation of income as described in subparagraph (1)(i) of this paragraph beginning with the first taxable year following the taxable year in which such judicial proceeding is terminated, the distributable amount (as defined in paragraph (b) of this section) for such foundation shall be reduced by the amount of the income required to be accumulated. Therefore, if the foundation's adjusted net income for any taxable year equals or exceeds its minimum investment return for such year, the accumulation provision will be given full effect. However, if the minimum investment return exceeds the adjusted net income for any taxable year, the foundation will be required to distribute such excess for such year. For purposes of this paragraph, a judicial proceeding will be treated as pending only if the foundation is diligently pursuing its judicial remedies and there is no unreasonable delay in such proceeding for which the private foundation is responsible.

(4) *Examples.*—The provisions of this paragraph may be illustrated by the following examples:

*Example (1).* X, a private foundation organized in 1930, is required by the mandatory terms of its governing instrument to accumulate 25 percent of its adjusted net income and to add such accumulations to corpus. The instrument also prohibits distribution of corpus for any purpose. On July 13, 1971, X instituted an action in the appropriate State court to reform the instrument by deleting the accumulation and corpus provisions described above. If the court's final order reforms the accumulation provision to allow distributions of income sufficient to avoid the imposition of a tax under section 4942, then section 4942 applies to X, regardless of the court's action with respect to the corpus provision. However, if the court rules that the accumulation provision may not be reformed, section 4942 applies to X only to the extent provided for in subparagraph (3) of this paragraph, regardless of the court's action with respect to the corpus provision.

*Example (2).* Private foundation Y was created by the will of A who died in 1940. Y's governing instrument requires that 40 percent of Y's adjusted net income be added to corpus each year. In an action commenced prior to December 31, 1971, a court of competent jurisdiction ruled that this accumulation provision must be complied with. In Y's succeeding taxable year its adjusted net income is $120,000, and its minimum investment return is $140,000. Thus, Y is required to accumulate $48,000 (40 percent of $120,000) and shall be allowed to do so. Therefore, Y's distributable amount for such taxable year shall be the greater of its adjusted net income ($120,000) or its minimum investment return ($140,000), reduced by the amount of the income required to be accumulated ($48,000) and the taxes imposed by subtitle A of the Code and section 4940 and increased by any trust distributions described in paragraph (b)(2) of this section. Accordingly, Y's distributable amount for such taxable year is $92,000 ($140,000 reduced by $48,000), before other adjustments. If Y's minimum investment return had been $120,000 instead of $140,000, its distributable amount for such taxable year would have been $72,000 ($120,000 reduced by $48,000), before other adjustments. Similarly, if Y's minimum investment return had been $100,000 instead of $140,000, its distributable amount for such taxable year would also have been $72,000, before other adjustments. [Reg. § 53.4942(a)-2.]

☐ [*T.D. 7256, 2-2-73. Amended by T.D. 7486, 5-12-77, T.D. 7594, 2-5-79, T.D. 7610, 4-10-79, T.D. 7715, 8-25-80, T.D. 7849, 11-9-82 and T.D. 7878, 3-21-83.*]

**[Reg. § 53.4942(a)-3]**

**§ 53.4942(a)-3. Qualifying distributions defined.**—(a) *In general.*—(1) *Distributions generally.*—For purposes of section 4942 and the regulations thereunder, the amount of a qualifying distribution of property (as defined in subparagraph(2) of this paragraph) is the fair market value of such property as of the date such qualifying distribution is made. The amount of an organization's qualifying distributions will be determined solely on the cash receipts and disbursements method of accounting described in section 466(c)(1).

(2) *Definition.*—The term "qualifying distribution" means:

(i) Any amount (including program related investments, as defined in section 4944(c), and reasonable and necessary administrative expenses) paid to accomplish one or more purposes described in section 170(c)(1) or (2)(B), other than any contribution to:

(*a*) A private foundation which is not an operating foundation (as defined in section 4942(j)(3)), except as provided in paragraph (c) of this section;

(*b*) An organization controlled (directly or indirectly) by the contributing private foundation or one or more disqualified persons with respect to such foundation, except as provided in paragraph (c) of this section; or

(*c*) An organization described in section 4942(g)(4)(A)(i) or (ii), if paid by a private foundation that is not an operating foundation;

(ii) Any amount paid to acquire an asset used (or held for use) directly in carrying out one or more purposes described in section 170(c)(1) or (2)(B). See paragraph (c)(3) of § 53.4942(a)-2 for the definition of "used (or held for use)"; or

(iii) Any amount set aside within the meaning of paragraph (b) of this section.

(3) *Control.*—For purposes of subparagraph (2)(i)(*b*) of this paragraph, an organization is "controlled" by a foundation or one or more disqualified persons with respect to the foundation if any of such persons may, by aggregating their votes or positions of authority, require the donee organization to make an expenditure, or prevent the donee organization from making an expenditure, regardless of the method by which the control is exercised or exercisable. "Control" of a donee organization is determined without regard to any conditions imposed upon the donee as part of the distribution or any other restrictions accompanying the distribution as to the manner in which the distribution is to be used, unless such conditions or restrictions are described in paragraph (a)(8) of § 1.507-2 of this chapter (Income Tax Regulations). In general, it is the donee, not the distribution, which must be "controlled" by the distributing private foundation for the provisions of subparagraph (2)(i)(*b*) of this paragraph to apply. Thus, the furnishing of support to an organization and the consequent imposition of budgetary procedures upon that organization with respect to such support shall not in itself be treated as subjecting that organization to the distributing foundation's control within the meaning of this subparagraph. Such "budgetary procedures" include expenditure responsibility requirements under section 4945(d)(4). The "controlled" organization need not be a private foundation; it may be any type of exempt or nonexempt organization including a school, hospital, operating foundation, or social welfare organization.

(4) *Borrowed funds.*—(i) *In general.*—For purposes of this paragraph, if a private foundation borrows money in a particular taxable year to make expenditures for a specific charitable, educational, or other similar purpose, a qualifying distribution out of such borrowed funds will, except as otherwise provided in subdivision (ii) of this subparagraph, be deemed to have been made only at the time that such borrowed funds are actually distributed for such exempt purpose.

(ii) *Funds borrowed before 1970.*—(*a*) If a private foundation has borrowed money in a taxable year beginning before January 1, 1970, or subsequently borrows money pursuant to a written commitment which was binding as of the last day of such taxable year, to make expenditures for a specific charitable, educational, or other similar exempt purpose, if such borrowed funds are in fact expended for such purpose in any taxable year, and if such loan is thereafter repaid, in whole or in part, in a taxable year beginning after December 31, 1969, then, at the election of the foundation as provided in subdivision (ii) (*b*) of this subparagraph, a qualifying distribution will be deemed to have been made at such time or times that such loan principal is so repaid rather than at the earlier time that the borrowed funds were actually distributed for such exempt purpose.

(*b*) The election described in subdivision (ii)(*a*) of this subparagraph is to be made by attaching a statement to the form the private foundation is required to file under section 6033 for the first taxable year beginning after December 31, 1969 in which a repayment of loan principal is made. Such statement shall be made a part of such form and shall be attached to such form in each succeeding taxable year in which any repayment of loan principal is made. The statement shall set forth the name and address of the lender, the amount borrowed, the specific use made of such borrowed funds, and the private foundation's election to treat repayments of loan principal as qualifying distributions.

(iii) *Interest.*—Any payment of interest with respect to a loan described in subdivision (i) or (ii) of this subparagraph shall be treated as a deduction under paragraph (d)(1)(ii) of § 53.4942(a)-2 in the taxable year in which it is made.

(5) *Changes in use of an asset.*—If an asset not used (or held for use) directly in carrying out one or more purposes described in section 170(c)(1) or (2)(B) is subsequently converted to such a use, the foundation may treat such conversion as a qualifying distribution. The amount of such qualifying distribution shall be the fair market value of the converted asset as of the date of its conversion. For purposes of the preceding sentence, fair market value shall be determined by making a valuation of the converted asset as of the date of its conversion in accordance with the rules set forth in paragraph (c)(4) of § 53.4942(a)-2.

(6) *Certain foreign organizations.*—(i) *In general.*—A distribution for purposes described in section 170(c)(2)(B) to a foreign organization, which has not received a ruling or determination letter that it is an organization described in section 509(a)(1), (a)(2), or (a)(3) or in section 4942 (j)(3), will be treated as a distribution made to an organization described in section 509(a)(1), (a)(2), or (a)(3) (other than an organization described in section 4942(g)(4)(A)(i) or (ii)) or in section 4942(j)(3) if the distributing foundation has made a good faith determination that the donee organization is an organization described in section 509(a)(1), (a)(2), or (a)(3) (other than an organization described in section 4942(g)(4)(A)(i) or (ii)) or in section 4942(j)(3). A determination ordinarily will be considered a good faith determination if the determination is based on current written advice received from a qualified tax practitioner concluding that the donee is an organization described in section 509(a)(1), (a)(2), or (a)(3) (other than an organization described in section 4942(g)(4)(A)(i) or (ii)) or in section 4942(j)(3), and if the foundation reasonably relied in good faith on the written advice in accordance with the requirements of § 1.6664-4(c)(1) of this chapter. The written advice must set forth sufficient facts concerning the operations and support of the donee organization for the Internal Revenue Service to determine that the donee organization would be likely to qualify as an organization described in section 509(a)(1), (a)(2), or (a)(3) (other than an organization described in section 4942(g)(4)(A)(i) or (ii)) or in section 4942(j)(3) as of the date of the written advice. For purposes of this section, except as provided in the next sentence, written advice will be considered current if, as of the date of distribution, the relevant law on which the advice is based has not changed since the date of the written advice and the factual information on which the advice is based is from the donee's current or prior taxable year (or annual accounting period if the donee does not have a taxable year for United States federal tax purposes). Written advice that a donee met the public support test under section 170(b)(1)(A)(vi) or section 509(a)(2) for a test period of five years will be treated as current for purposes of distributions to the donee during the two taxable years (or, as applicable, annual accounting periods) of the donee immediately following the end of the five-year test period.

(ii) *Definitions.*—For purposes of this paragraph (a)(6)—

(*a*) The term "foreign organization" means any organization that is not described in section 170(c)(2)(A).

(*b*) The term "qualified tax practitioner" means an attorney, a certified public accountant, or an enrolled agent, within the meaning of 31 CFR 10.2 and 10.3, who is subject to the requirements in 31 CFR part 10.

(7) *Payment of tax.*—The payment of any tax imposed under chapter 42 of the Code shall not be treated as a qualifying distribution.

(8) *Examples.*—The provisions of this paragraph may be illustrated by the following examples:

*Example (1).* M, a private foundation which uses the calendar year as the taxable year, makes the following payments in 1970: (i) a payment of $44,000 to five employees for conducting a foundation program of educational grants for research and study; (ii) $20,000 for various items of overhead, 10 percent of which is attributable to the activities of the employees mentioned in payment (i) of this example and the other 90 percent of which is attributable to administrative expenses which were not paid to accomplish any section 170(c)(1) or (2)(B) purpose; and (iii) a $100,000 general purpose grant paid to an educational institution described in section 170(b)(1)(A)(ii) which is not controlled by M or any disqualified persons with respect to M. Payments (i) and (ii) of this example are qualifying distributions to the extent of $46,000 ($44,000 of salaries and 10 percent of the overhead, both of which are reasonable administrative expenses paid to accomplish section 170(c)(1) or (2)(B) purposes). Payment (iii) of this example is also a qualifying distribution, since it is a contribution for section 170(c)(2)(B) purposes to an organization which is not described in subparagraph (2)(i)(*a*) or (*b*) of this paragraph. The other

90 percent of payment (ii) of this example may constitute items of deduction under paragraph (d)(1)(ii) of §53.4942(a)-2 if such items otherwise qualify under such paragraph.

*Example (2).* On February 21, 1972, N, a private foundation which uses the calendar year as the taxable year, pays $500,000 for real property on which it plans to build hospital facilities to be used for medical care and education. The real property produces no income and the hospital facilities will not be constructed until 1974 according to the set-aside plan submitted to and approved by the Commissioner pursuant to paragraph (b) of this section. The purchase of the land is a qualifying distribution under subparagraph (2)(ii) of this paragraph. If, however, the property were used to produce rental income for more than a reasonable period of time before construction of the hospital is begun, then as of the time such rental use becomes unreasonable (i) such purchase would no longer constitute a qualifying distribution under subparagraph (2)(ii) of this paragraph and (ii) the amount of the qualifying distribution would be included in N's gross income. See paragraphs (c)(3)(i) and (d)(2)(iii)(*b*) of §53.4942(a)-2.

*Example (3).* In 1971, X, a private foundation engaged in holding paintings and exhibiting them to the public, purchases an additional building to be used to exhibit the paintings. Such expenditure is a qualifying distribution under subparagraph (2)(ii) of this paragraph. In 1975, X sells the building. Under paragraph (d)(2)(iii)(*b*) of §53.4942(a)-2, all of the proceeds of the sale (less direct costs of the sale) are included in X's gross income for 1975.

*Example (4).* In January 1969, M, a private foundation which uses the calendar year as the taxable year, borrows $10 million to give to N, a private college, for the construction of a science center. M borrowed the money from X, a commercial bank. M is to repay X at the rate of $1.1 million per year ($1 million principal plus $0.1 million interest) for 10 years beginning in January, 1973. M distributed $5 million of the borrowed funds to N in February 1969, and the other $5 million in March 1970. M files a statement with the form it is required to file under section 6033 for 1973 which contains the information required by subparagraph (4)(ii)(*b*) of this paragraph. Pursuant to M's election, each repayment of loan principal constitutes a qualifying distribution in the year of repayment. Accordingly, the distribution of $5 million to N in March 1970 will not be treated as a qualifying distribution. Each payment of interest ($0.1 million annually) with respect to M's loan from X is treated as a deduction under paragraph (d)(1)(ii) of §53.4942(a)-2 in the taxable year in which it is made.

*Example (5).* Private foundation Y engages in providing care for the aged. Y makes a distribution of cash to H, a hospital described in section 170(b)(1)(A)(iii) which is not controlled by Y or any disqualified person with respect to Y. The distribution is made subject to the conditions that H will invest the money as a separate fund which will bear a name commemorating the creator of Y and will use the income from such fund only for H's exempt hospital purposes which relate to care for the aged. Under these circumstances, the distribution from Y to H is a qualifying distribution pursuant to subparagraph (2)(i) of this paragraph.

(b) *Certain set-asides.*—(1) *In general.*—An amount set aside for a specific project that is for one or more of the purposes described in section 170(c)(1) or (2)(B) may be treated as a qualifying distribution in the year in which set aside (but not in the year in which actually paid), if the requirements of section 4942(g)(2) and this paragraph (b) are satisfied. The requirements of this paragraph (b) are satisfied if the private foundation establishes to the satisfaction of the Commissioner that the amount set aside will be paid for the specific project within 60 months after it is set aside, and

(i) The set-aside satisfies the suitability test described in subparagraph (2) of this paragraph, or

(ii) With respect to a set-aside made in a taxable year beginning after December 31, 1974, the private foundation satisfies the cash distribution test described in subparagraph (3) of this paragraph.

If the suitability test or cash distribution test is otherwise satisfied, the 60 month period for paying the amount set aside may, for good cause shown, be extended by the Commissioner.

(2) *Suitability test.*—The suitability test is satisfied if the private foundation establishes to the satisfaction of the Commissioner that the specific project for which the amount is set aside is one that can be better accomplished by the set-aside than by the immediate payment of funds. Specific projects than can be better accomplished by the use of a set-aside include, but are not limited to, projects in which relatively long-term grants or expenditures must be made in order to assure the continuity of particular charitable projects or program-related investments (as defined in section 4944(c)) or where grants are made as part of a matching-grant program. Such projects include, for example, a plan to erect a building to house the direct charitable,

educational, or other similar exempt activity of the private foundation (such as a museum building in which paintings are to be hung), even though the exact location and architectural plans have not been finalized; a plan to purchase an additional group of paintings offered for sale only as a unit that requires an expenditure of more than one year's income; or a plan to fund a specific research program that is of such magnitude as to require an accumulation of funds before beginning the research, even though not all of the details of the program have been finalized.

(3) *Cash distribution test; in general.*—The cash distribution test is satisfied if—

(i) The specific project for which the amount is set aside will not be completed before the end of the taxable year in which the set-aside is made,

(ii) The private foundation actually distributes, in cash or its equivalent and for one or more of the purposes described in section 170(c)(1) or (2)(B), the "start-up period minimum amount" described in subparagraph (4) of this paragraph during the private foundation's start-up period, and

(iii) The private foundation actually distributes, in cash or its equivalent and for one or more of the purposes described in section 170(c)(1) or (2)(B), the "full-payment period minimum amount" described in subparagraph (5) of this paragraph in each taxable year of the private foundation's full-payment period.

For purposes of the cash distribution test, an amount set aside will be treated as distributed in the year in which actually paid and not in the year in which set aside.

(4) *Minimum distribution required during start-up period.*—(i) *Start-up period.*—For private foundations created before January 1, 1972, the start-up period is the four taxable years immediately preceding the taxable year beginning in calendar year 1976. For private foundations created after December 31, 1971 (or for organizations that first become private foundations after that date), the start-up period is the four taxable years following the taxable year in which the private foundation was created (or otherwise became a private foundation). For purposes of this subparagraph (4), a private foundation will be considered "created" in the taxable year in which the private foundation's distributable amount (as determined under section 4942(d)) first exceeds $500.

(ii) *Start-up period minimum amount.*—The amount that a private foundation must actually distribute in cash or its equivalent during the private foundation's start-up period is not less than the sum of—

(*a*) Twenty percent of the private foundation's distributable amount (as determined under section 4942(d)) for the first taxable year of the start-up period,

(*b*) Forty percent of the private foundation's distributable amount for the second taxable year of the start-up period,

(*c*) Sixty percent of the private foundation's distributable amount for the third taxable year of the start-up period, and

(*d*) Eighty percent of the private foundation's distributable amount for the fourth taxable year of the start-up period.

(iii) *Timing of distributions.*—The requirement that a private foundation distribute the start-up period minimum amount during the start-up period is a requirement that such amount be distributed before the end of the start-up period, and is not a requirement that any portion of such amount be distributed in any one taxable year of the start-up period.

(iv) *Distribution actually made during start-up period.*—In general, only a distribution actually made during the start-up period is taken into account in determining whether a private foundation has distributed the start-up period minimum amount. However, in the case of a private foundation created after December 31, 1971 (or an organization that first became a private foundation after that date), a distribution actually made during the taxable year in which the foundation was created (the year immediately preceding the first taxable year of the private foundation's start-up period) may be treated as a distribution actually made during the start-up period. In addition, a distribution actually made by a private foundation within 5½ months after the end of the start-up period will be treated as a distribution actually made during the start-up period if—

(*a*) The private foundation was unable to determine the distributable amount for the fourth taxable year of the start-up period until after the end of such period, and

(*b*) The private foundation actually made distributions prior to the end of the start-up period based upon a reasonable estimate of the private foundation's distributable amount for the fourth taxable year of the start-up period.

(v) *Examples.*—The provisions of this subparagraph (4) may be illustrated by the following examples:

*Example (1).* F, a private foundation created on January 1, 1975, uses the calendar year as its taxable year. The start-up period for F is January 1, 1976 through December 31, 1979. F has distributable amounts under section 4942(d) for taxable years 1976 through 1979 in the following amounts: 1976, $100,000; 1977, $120,000; 1978, $150,000; 1979, $200,000. F's start-up period minimum amount is the sum of the following amounts: 20% of $100,000 ($20,000); 40% of $120,000 ($48,000); 60% of $150,000 ($90,000); and 80% of $200,000 ($160,000); which equals $318,000. Thus F is required to actually distribute at least $318,000 in cash or its equivalent during the start-up period.

*Example (2).* F, a private foundation created in 1969, uses the calendar year as its taxable year. F's start-up period is the calendar years 1972 through 1975. F makes two cash distributions in 1972. The first distribution is made on account of a set-aside made in 1969. Under section 4942(g), that distribution is treated as a qualifying distribution made in 1969. The second distribution is treated under section 4942(h) as made out of F's undistributed income for 1971. In addition, F makes a cash distribution in 1976 that is treated under section 4942(h) as made out of F's undistributed income for 1975. In determining whether F has distributed its start-up period minimum amount within the start-up period, the 1972 distributions are both taken into account because they were actually made during F's start-up period. The 1976 distribution is not taken into account, however, because that distribution was not actually made during F's start-up period.

(5) *Minimum distribution required during full-payment period.*—(i) *Full-payment period.*—A private foundation's full-payment period includes each taxable year that begins after the end of the private foundation's start-up period.

(ii) *Full-payment period minimum amount.*—The amount that a private foundation must actually distribute in cash or its equivalent in a taxable year of the private foundation's full-payment period is not less than 100 percent of the private foundation's distributable amount determined under section 4942(d) (without regard to section 4942(i)) with respect to the taxable year.

(iii) *Carryover of distributions in excess of full-payment period minimum amount.*—If, in a taxable year beginning after December 31, 1975, a private foundation distributes an amount in excess of the full-payment period minimum amount for the taxable year, the excess shall be used to reduce the full-payment period minimum amount in the taxable years in the adjustment period. The amount of the excess distribution used to reduce the full-payment period minimum amount in each successive taxable year of the adjustment period shall be equal to the amount of such excess less the sum of the full-payment period minimum amounts for all prior taxable years in the adjustment period to which the excess was previously applied. The taxable years in the adjustment period are the five taxable years immediately following the taxable year in which the excess distribution is made. Any distribution in excess of the full-payment period minimum amount made during a taxable year of the adjustment period shall not be taken into account under this subparagraph (iii) until any earlier excess has been completely applied against full-payment period minimum amounts during its adjustment period.

(iv) *Distributions actually made during a taxable year.*—Except as described in subdivision (ii) of subparagraph (6), only a distribution actually made during a taxable year of the full-payment period is taken into account in determining whether a private foundation has distributed the full-payment period minimum amount for such year.

(v) *Examples.*—The provisions of this subparagraph (5) may be illustrated by the following examples:

*Example (1).* F, a private foundation created on January 1, 1973, uses the calendar year as its taxable year. F has a start-up period of January 1, 1974, through December 31, 1977, and a full-payment period that includes every taxable year beginning after December 31, 1977. F's distributable amount (as determined under section 4942(d)) for 1978 is $500,000. Thus, F's full-payment period minimum amount for 1978 is $500,000. During 1978 F distributes $100,000 in cash to Charity X and $400,000 in cash to Charity Y on account of a set-aside made in 1973. F has distributed its full-payment period minimum amount for 1978 because it has made actual cash distributions during that year which total $500,000. However, F has made qualifying distributions (as determined under section 4942(g)) with respect to 1978 of only $100,000. In order to avoid liability for the tax on undistributed income under section 4942(a), F must distribute or set aside an additional $400,000 before January 1, 1980.

*Example (2).* Assume the facts as stated in Example (1) except that in 1978 F makes cash distributions totaling $600,000. Since the total cash distributions made in 1978 ($600,000) exceed the full-payment period minimum amount for 1978 ($500,000), there exists a $100,000 excess which must be used by F to reduce its full-payment period minimum amounts for the years 1979-1983 (the taxable years

in the adjustment period with respect to the 1978 excess). Therefore, if F's distributable amount (as determined under section 4942(d)) for 1979 is $500,000, F's full-payment period minimum amount for 1979 is $400,000 ($500,000 – $100,000).

(6) *Failure to distribute minimum amounts.*—(i) *In general.*—If a private foundation fails to actually distribute the start-up period minimum amount during the start-up period or, except as described in subdivision (ii) of this subparagraph (6), if a private foundation fails to actually distribute the full-payment period minimum amount during a taxable year of the full-payment period, then any set-aside made by the private foundation during the start-up period (if the failure relates to the start-up period) or during the taxable year (if the failure relates to the full-payment period) that was not approved by the Commissioner under the suitability test described in subparagraph (2) of this paragraph will not be treated as a qualifying distribution. Further, any set-aside made after the year of such a failure to so distribute a minimum amount will be treated as a qualifying distribution only if the Commissioner approves the set-aside under the suitability test. In any case in which a set-aside ceases to be treated as a qualifying distribution as a result of a failure to distribute the full-payment period minimum amount, a private foundation may be assessed a deficiency under section 4942(a) within the period described in section 6501(n)(3).

(ii) *Correction of certain failures to distribute.*—If a private foundation's failure to distribute the full-payment period minimum amount during a taxable year of the full-payment period was not willful and was due to reasonable cause, the private foundation may correct the failure to so distribute. Correction will be achieved if the private foundation distributes within the correction period cash or its equivalent in an amount not less than the difference between the full-payment period minimum amount for the taxable year and the amount actually distributed during the taxable year. The correction period is the correction period as defined in section 4962(e), determined with respect to the earliest occurring taxable event (as defined in section 4962(e)(2)(A)) that would result if the failure to distribute a full-payment period minimum amount were not corrected. The additional distribution will be treated for purposes of subparagraph (5) of this paragraph as made during the taxable year with respect to which the failure occurred. If a private foundation fails to distribute the full-payment period minimum amount during a taxable year of the full-payment period because such amount can be determined only after the end of the taxable year, no "willful failure to distribute" the full-payment period minimum amount will occur if the private foundation makes an additional distribution within 5¹/₂ months after the end of the taxable year.

(7) *Approval and information requirements.*—(i) *Suitability test.*—If an amount is set aside under the suitability test of section 4942(g)(2)(B)(i) and subparagraph (2) of this paragraph, the private foundation must apply for the Commissioner's approval of the set-aside before the end of the taxable year in which the amount is set aside. The Commissioner will either approve or disapprove the set-aside in writing. An otherwise proper set-aside will not be treated as a qualifying distribution under this paragraph (b) with respect to a taxable year if the Commissioner's approval is not sought before the end of the taxable year in which the amount is actually set aside. To obtain approval by the Commissioner for a set-aside under the suitability test, the private foundation must write to Commissioner of Internal Revenue, Attention: OP:E:EO:T, 1111 Constitution Avenue, N.W., Washington, D.C. 20224, and include—

(a) A statement describing the nature and purposes of the specific project and the amount of the set-aside for which approval is requested;

(b) A statement describing the amounts and approximate dates of any planned additions to the set-aside after its initial establishment;

(c) A statement of the reasons why the project can be better accomplished by a set-aside than by the immediate payment of funds;

(d) A detailed description of the project, including estimated costs, sources of any future funds expected to be used for completion of the project, and the location or locations (general or specific) of any physical facilities to be acquired or constructed as part of the project; and

(e) A statement by an appropriate foundation manager (as defined in section 4946(b)) that the amounts to be set aside will actually be paid for the specific project within a specified period of time that ends not more than 60 months after the date of the first set-aside, or a statement showing good cause why the period for paying the amount set aside should be extended (including a showing that the proposed project could not be divided into two or more projects covering periods of no more than 60 months each) and setting forth the extension of time required.

Reg. §53.4942(a)-3(b)(7)(i)(e)

(ii) *Cash distribution test.*—If an amount is set aside under the cash distribution test of section 4942(g)(2)(B)(ii) and subparagraphs (3), (4), and (5) of this paragraph, then for taxable years ending after April 2, 1984, the private foundation must submit an attachment with the return required by section 6033 for the taxable year in which the amount is set aside and for certain subsequent taxable years. For the taxable year in which the amount is set aside the attachment must include—

(*a*) A statement describing the nature and purposes of the specific project for which amounts are to be set aside;

(*b*) A statement that the amounts set aside for the specific project will actually be paid for the specific project within a specified period of time that ends not more than 60 months after the date of the set-aside;

(*c*) A statement that the project will not be completed before the end of the taxable year of the private foundation in which the set-aside is made;

(*d*) A statement showing the distributable amounts determined under section 4942(d) for any past taxable years in the private foundation's start-up and full-payment periods; and

(*e*) A statement showing the aggregate amount of actual payments made in cash or its equivalent, for purposes described in section 170(c)(1) or (2)(B), during each taxable year in the private foundation's start-up and full-payment periods. This statement should include a detailed description of any payments that are to be treated, pursuant to the rules of subparagraphs (4)(iv) and (6)(ii) of this paragraph (b), as distributed during a taxable year prior to the taxable year in which such payments were actually made and, in addition, should explain the circumstances that justify the application of those rules.

For the five taxable years following the taxable year in which the amount is set aside (or, if longer, for each taxable year in the extended period for paying the amount set aside), the attachment must include the statements required by (*d*) and (*e*) of this subdivision (ii). The submission of the statement required by (*b*) of this subdivision (ii) will satisfy the requirement of section 4942(g)(2)(B) and subparagraph (1) of this paragraph (b) that the private foundation establish to the satisfaction of the Commissioner that the amount set aside will be paid for the specific project within 60 months after it is set aside.

(8) *Evidence of set-aside.*—A set-aside that is approved by the Commissioner or which satisfies the cash distribution test shall be evidenced by the entry of a dollar amount on the books and records of a private foundation as a pledge or obligation to be paid at a future date or dates. Any amount which is set aside shall be taken into account for purposes of determining the private foundation's minimum investment return under §53.4942(a)-2(c)(1), and any income attributable to such set-aside shall be taken into account in computing adjusted net income under §53.4942(a)-2(d).

(9) *Contingent set-aside.*—In the event a private foundation is involved in litigation and may not distribute assets or income because of a court order, the private foundation may (except as provided in §53.4942(a)-2(e)(1)(i) or (ii)) seek and obtain a set-aside for a purpose described in §53.4942(a)-3(a)(2). The amount to be set aside shall be equal to that portion of the private foundation's distributable amount which is attributable to the assets or income that are held pursuant to court order and which, but for the court order precluding the distribution of such assets or income, would have been distributed. In the event that the litigation encompasses more than one taxable year, the private foundation may seek additional contingent set-asides. Such amounts must actually be distributed by the last day of the taxable year following the taxable year in which the litigation is terminated. Amounts not distributed by the close of the appropriate taxable year shall be treated as described in §53.4942(a)-2(d)(2)(iii)(c) for the succeeding taxable year.

(c) *Certain contributions to section 501(c)(3) organizations.*—(1) *In general.*—For purposes of this section, the term "qualifying distribution" includes (in the year in which it is paid) a contribution to an exempt organization described in section 501(c)(3) and described in paragraph (a)(2)(i)(*a*) or (*b*) of this section if—

(i) Not later than the close of the first taxable year after the donee organization's taxable year in which such contribution is received, such donee organization makes a distribution equal to the full amount of such contribution and such distribution is a qualifying distribution (within the meaning of paragraph (a) of this section, without regard to this paragraph) which is treated under paragraph (d) of this section as a distribution out of corpus (or would be so treated if such section 501(c)(3) organization were a private foundation which is not an operating foundation); and

(ii) The private foundation making the contribution obtains adequate records or other sufficient evidence from such donee organization (such as a statement by an appropriate officer, director, or

trustee of such donee organization) showing (except as otherwise provided in this subparagraph) (*a*) that the qualifying distribution described in subdivision (i) of this subparagraph has been made by such organization, (*b*) the name and addresses of the recipients of such distribution and the amount received by each, and (*c*) that the distribution is treated as a distribution out of corpus under graph (d) of this section (or would be so treated if the donee organization were a private foundation which is not an operating foundation).

Where a distribution is for an administrative expense which is part of a section 170(c)(1) or (2)(B) expenditure or is part of another section 170(c)(1) or (2)(B) expenditure that cannot reasonably be separately accounted for, the provisions of subdivision (ii) of this subparagraph may be satisfied by the submission by the donee organization of a statement setting forth the general purpose for which such expenditure was made and that the amount was distributed as a qualifying distribution described in subdivision (ii)(*c*) of this subparagraph.

(2) *Distribution requirements.*—(i) In order for a donee organization to meet the distribution requirements of subparagraph (1)(i) of this paragraph, it must, not later than the close of the first taxable year after its taxable year in which any contributions are received, distribute (within the meaning of this subparagraph) an amount equal in value to the contributions received in such prior taxable year and have no remaining undistributed income for such prior taxable year. In the event that a donee organization redistributes less than an amount equal to the total contributions from donor organizations which are required to be redistributed by such donee organization by the close of the first taxable year following the taxable year in which such contributions were received, amounts treated as redistributions of such contributions shall be deemed to have been made pro rata out of all such contributions, regardless of any earmarking or identification made by such donee organization with respect to the source of such distributions. See paragraph (d)(2)(ix) of §53.4942(a)-2 for the treatment of amounts deemed not to have so redistributed. For purposes of this paragraph, the term "contributions" means all contributions, whether of cash or property, and the fair market value of contributed property determined as of the date of the contribution must be used in determining whether an amount equal in value to the contributions received has been redistributed.

(ii) For purposes of this paragraph, the characterization of qualifying distributions made during the taxable year (i.e., whether out of the prior year's undistributed income, the current year's undistributed income, or corpus) is to be made as of the close of the taxable year in question, except to the extent that a different characterization is effected by means of the election provided for by paragraph (d)(2) of this section or by subdivision (iv) of this subparagraph. Once it is determined that a qualifying distribution is attributable to corpus, such distribution will first be charged to distributions which are required to be redistributed under this paragraph.

(iii) All amounts contributed to a specific exempt organization described in section 501(c)(3) and in paragraph (a)(2)(i)(*a*) or (*b*) of this section within any one taxable year of such organization shall be treated (with respect to the contributing private foundation) as one "contribution". If subparagraph (1)(i) or (ii) of this paragraph is not completely satisfied with respect to such contribution within the meaning of such subparagraph, only that portion of such contribution which was redistributed (within the meaning of subparagraph (1)(i) and (ii) of this paragraph) shall be treated as a qualifying distribution.

(iv) In order to satisfy distribution requirements under section 170(b)(1)(E)(ii) or this paragraph, a donee organization may elect to treat as a current distribution out of corpus any amount distributed in a prior taxable year which was treated as a distribution out of corpus under paragraph (d)(1)(iii) of this section provided that (*a*) such amount has not been availed of for any other purpose, such as a carryover under paragraph (e) of this section or a redistribution under this paragraph for a prior year, (*b*) such corpus distribution occurred within the preceding 5 years, and (*c*) such amount is not later availed of for any other purpose. Such election must be made by attaching a statement to the return the foundation is required to file under section 6033 with respect to the taxable year for which such election is to apply. Such statement must contain a declaration by an appropriate foundation manager (within the meaning of section 4946(b)(1)) that the foundation is making an election under this subdivision and it must specify that the distribution was treated under paragraph (d)(1)(iii) of this section as a distribution out of corpus in a designated prior taxable year (or years).

(3) *Examples.*—The provisions of subparagraphs (1) and (2) of this paragraph may be illustrated by the following examples. It is assumed in these examples that all private foundations described use the calendar year as the taxable year.

*Example (1).* In 1972 M, a private foundation, makes a contribution out of 1971 income to X, another private foundation which is not an operating foundation. The contribution is the only one received by X in 1972. In 1973 X makes a qualifying distribution to an art museum maintained by an operating foundation in an amount equal to the amount of the contribution received from M. X also distributes all of its undistributed income for 1972 and 1973 for other purposes described in section 170(c)(2)(B). Under the provisions of paragraph (d) of this section, such distribution to the museum is treated as a distribution out of corpus. Thus, M's contribution to X is a qualifying distribution out of M's 1971 income provided M obtains adequate records or other sufficient evidence from X showing the nature and amount of the distribution made by X, the identity of the recipient, and the fact that the distribution is treated as made out of corpus. If X's qualifying distributions during 1973 had been equal only to M's contribution to X and X's undistributed income for 1972, X could have made an election under paragraph (d)(2) of this section to treat the amount distributed in excess of its 1972 undistributed income as a distribution out of corpus and in that manner satisfied the requirements of this paragraph.

*Example (2).* Assume the facts stated in example (1), except that X is a private college described in section 170(b)(1)(A)(ii) which is controlled by disqualified persons with respect to M and that the records which X furnishes to M show that the distribution would have been treated as made out of corpus if X were a private nonoperating foundation. Under these circumstances, result is the same as in example (1).

*Example (3).* Assume the facts stated in example (1), except that X makes a distribution to the museum equal only to one-half of the contribution from M, that the remainder of such contribution is added to X's funds and used to pay charitable administrative expenses, and that the records obtained by M from X are not sufficient to show the amounts distributed or the identities of the recipients of the distributions. The contribution by M to X will be a qualifying distribution only to the extent that M can obtain (i) other sufficient evidence (such as statements from officers or employees of X or from the museum) showing the facts required by subparagraph (1)(ii)(*a*), (*b*), and (*c*) of this paragraph and (ii) a statement from X setting forth that the remainder of the contribution was used for charitable administrative expenses which constituted qualifying distributions described in paragraph (a)(2)(i) of this section.

*Example (4).* X and Y are private nonoperating foundations. A is an exempt organization which is not described in section 501(c)(3) but which supervises and conducts a program described in section 170(c)(2)(B). Y, but not X, controls A within the meaning of paragraph (a)(3) of this section. In 1972, X and Y each makes a grant to A of $100, specifically designated for use in the operation of A's section 170(c)(2)(B) program. X has made a qualifying distribution to A because the distribution is one described in paragraph (a)(2)(i) of this section. However, because A is controlled by Y, Y's grant of $100 to A does not constitute a qualifying distribution within the meaning of such paragraph (a)(2)(i). Furthermore, because A is not an exempt organization described in section 501(c)(3), Y's grant to A does not constitute a qualifying distribution by operation of the provisions of this paragraph.

*Example (5).* N, a private nonoperating foundation, had distributable amounts of $100 in 1970 and $125 in 1971. In 1970 N received total contributions of $540: $150 from Y, a public charity; $70 from Z, a private foundation; $140 from Q, a private foundation, subject to the requirement that N earmark the amount and distribute it before distributing Z's contribution; and, $180 from R, also a private foundation. However, R specifically instructed that such contribution did not have to be redistributed because R already had made enough qualifying distributions to avoid all section 4942 taxes. N is not controlled by Y, Z, Q, or R, and N made no qualifying distributions in 1970. By the close of 1971, N had made qualifying distributions of $420, earmarking $140 as having been a distribution of Q's contribution, but had made no election under paragraph (d)(2) of this section to have any amount distributed which was in excess of N's 1970 undistributed income treated as distributed out of corpus. Therefore, the first $225 of qualifying distributions made in 1971 (the sum of $100 and $125, N's distributable amounts for 1970 and 1971, respectively) are treated as amounts described in paragraph (d)(1)(i) and (ii) of this section. Since Y's contribution is a contribution from a public charity and does not have to be "redistributed" and since R specifically instructed N that its contribution need not be "redistributed", the remaining $195 of qualifying distributions will be treated as distributed pro rata from Z's and Q's contributions, regardless of N's earmarking. Accordingly, of Z's original qualifying distribution of $70 only $65 ($195 multiplied by $70, Z's contribution, over $210, the total ($70 plus $140) of Z's and Q's contributions) will be treated as redistributed by N. Similarly, of Q's original qualifying distribution of $140 only $130 ($195 multiplied by $140 over $210) will be treated as redistributed by N. Thus, Z's gross income for 1972 will be increased by $5 ($70 less the $65 actually redistributed), and Q's gross income for 1972 will be increased by $10 ($140 less the $130 actually redistributed).

(4) *Limitation.*—A contribution by a private foundation to a donee organization which the donee uses to make payments to another organization (the secondary donee) shall not be regarded as a contribution by the private foundation to the secondary donee if the distributing foundation does not earmark the use of the contribution for any named secondary donee and does not retain power to cause the selection of the secondary donee by the organization to which such foundation has made the contribution. For purposes of this subparagraph, a contribution described herein shall not be regarded as a contribution by the foundation to the secondary donee even though such foundation has reason to believe that certain organizations would derive benefits from such contribution so long as the original donee organization exercises control, in fact, over the selection process and actually makes the selection completely independently of such foundation.

(5) *Transitional rule.*—(i) For purposes of this paragraph, a contribution to a private foundation which is not an operating foundation and which is not controlled (directly or indirectly) by the distributing foundation or one or more disqualified persons with respect to the distributing foundation will be treated as a contribution to an operating foundation if—

(*a*) Such contribution is made pursuant to a written commitment which was binding on May 26, 1969, and at all times thereafter,

(*b*) Such contribution is made for one or more of the purposes described in section 170(c)(1) or (2)(B), and

(*c*) Such contribution is to be paid out to the donee private foundation on or before December 31, 1974.

(ii) For purposes of this subparagraph, a written commitment will be considered to have been binding prior to May 27, 1969, only if the amount and nature of the contribution and the name of the donee foundation were entered in the records of the distributing foundation, or were otherwise adequately evidenced, prior to May 27, 1969, or notice of the contribution was communicated in writing to such donee prior to May 27, 1969.

(d) *Treatment of qualifying distributions.*—(1) *In general.*—Except as provided in subparagraph (2) of this paragraph, any qualifying distribution made during a taxable year shall be treated as made—

(i) First out of the undistributed income (as defined in paragraph (a) of §53.4942(a)-2) of the immediately preceding taxable year (if the private foundation was subject to the initial excise tax imposed by section 4942(a) for such preceding taxable year) to the extent thereof;

(ii) Second out of the undistributed income for the taxable year to the extent thereof; and

(iii) Then out of corpus.

(2) *Election.*—In the case of any qualifying distribution which (under subparagraph (1) of this paragraph) is not treated as made out of the undistributed income of the immediately preceding taxable year, the foundation may elect to treat any portion of such distribution as made out of the undistributed income of a designated prior taxable year or out of corpus. Such election must be made by filing a statement with the Commissioner during the taxable year in which such qualifying distribution is made or by attaching a statement to the return the foundation is required to file under section 6033 with respect to the taxable year in which such qualifying distribution was made. Such statement must contain a declaration by an appropriate foundation manager (within the meaning of section 4946(b)(1)) that the foundation is making an election under this subparagraph, and it must specify whether the distribution is made out of the undistributed income of a designated prior taxable year (or years) or is made out of corpus. In any case where the election described in this subparagraph is made during the taxable year in which the qualifying distribution is made, such election may be revoked in whole or in part by filing a statement with the Commissioner during such taxable year revoking such election in whole or in part or by attaching a statement to the return the foundation is required to file under section 6033 with respect to the taxable year in which the qualifying distribution was made revoking such election in whole or in part. Such statement must contain a declaration by an appropriate foundation manager (within the meaning of section 4946(b)(1)) that the foundation is revoking an election under this subparagraph in whole or in part, and it must specify the election or part thereof being revoked.

(3) *Examples.*—The provisions of this paragraph may be illustrated by the following examples:

*Example (1).* M, a private foundation which was created in 1968 and which uses the calendar year as the taxable year, has distributable amounts and qualifying distributions for 1970 through 1976 as follows:

| Year | 1970 | 1971 | 1972 | 1973 | 1974 | 1975 | 1976 |
|---|---|---|---|---|---|---|---|
| Distributable amount | $100 | $100 | $100 | $100 | $100 | $100 | $100 |
| Qualifying distribution | $0 | $100 | $250 | $100 | $100 | $100 | $100 |

In 1971 the qualifying distribution of $100 is treated under subparagraph (1)(i) of this paragraph as made out of the $100 of undistributed income for 1970. The qualifying distribution of $250 in 1972 is treated as made: (i) $100 out of the undistributed income for 1971 under subparagraph (1)(i) of this paragraph; (ii) $100 out of the undistributed income for 1972 under subparagraph (1)(ii) of this paragraph; and (iii) $50 out of corpus in 1972 under subparagraph (1)(iii) of this paragraph. The qualifying distribution of $100 in each of the years 1973 through 1976 is treated as made out of the undistributed income for each of those respective years under subparagraph (1)(ii) of this paragraph. See paragraph (e) of this section for rules relating to the carryover of qualifying distributions out of corpus.

*Example (2).* M, a private foundation which uses the calendar year as the taxable year, has undistributed income of $300 for 1981, $200 for 1982, and $400 for 1983. On January 14, 1983, M makes its first qualifying distribution in 1983 when it sets aside (within the meaning of paragraph (b) of this section) $700 for construction of a hospital. On February 24, 1983 a notice of deficiency with respect to the excise taxes imposed by section 4942(a) and (b) in regard to M's undistributed income for 1981 is mailed to M under section 6212(a). M notifies the Commissioner in writing on March 24, 1983, that it is making an election under subparagraph (2) of this paragraph to have its distribution of January 14th applied first against its undistributed income for 1982, next against its undistributed income for 1981, and last against its undistributed income for 1983. Thus, $200 of the $700 qualifying distribution is treated as made out of the undistributed income for 1982; $300, out of undistributed income for 1981; and $200 ($700 less the sum of $200 and $300), out of the undistributed income for 1983. Thus, an initial excise tax of $45 (15 percent of $300) is imposed under section 4942 (a). Since M made the election described above, the $300 (treated as distributed out of undistributed income for 1981) corrects (within the meaning of section 4963(d)(2)) the taxable act because the undistributed income for 1981 is reduced to zero. Furthermore, correction is effected within the correction period (as defined in section 4963(e)(1) and §53.4963-1(e)). Therefore, under the provisions of section 4961(a), the additional tax imposed by section 4942(b) will not be assessed.

(e) *Carryover of excess qualifying distributions.*—(1) *In general.*—If in any taxable year for which an organization is subject to the initial excise tax imposed by section 4942(a) there is created an excess of qualifying distributions (as determined under subparagraph (2) of this paragraph), such excess may be used to reduce distributable amounts in any taxable year of the adjustment period (as defined [in] subparagraph (3) of this paragraph). For purposes of section 4942,

including paragraph (d) of this section, the distributable amount for a taxable year in the adjustment period shall be reduced to the extent of the lesser of (i) the excess of qualifying distributions made in prior taxable years to which such adjustment period applies or (ii) the remaining undistributed income at the close of such taxable year after applying any qualifying distributions made in such taxable year to the distributable amount for such taxable year (determined without regard to this paragraph). If during any taxable year of the adjustment period there is created another excess of qualifying distributions, such excess shall not be taken into account until any earlier excess of qualifying distributions has been completely applied against distributable amounts during its adjustment period.

(2) *Excess qualifying distributions.*—An excess of qualifying distributions is created for any taxable year beginning after December 31, 1969, if—

(i) The total qualifying distributions treated (under paragraph (d) of this section) as made out of the undistributed income for such taxable year or as made out of corpus with respect to such taxable year (other than amounts distributed by an organization in satisfaction of section 170(b)(1)(E)(ii) or paragraph (c) of this section, or applied to a prior taxable year by operation of the elections contained in paragraphs (c)(2)(iv) and (d)(2) of this section), exceeds

(ii) The distributable amount for such taxable year (determined without regard to this paragraph).

(3) *Adjustment period.*—For purposes of this paragraph, the taxable years in the adjustment period are the five taxable years immediately following the taxable year in which the excess of qualifying distributions is created. Thus, an excess (within the meaning of subparagraph (2) of this paragraph) for any one taxable year can not be carried over beyond the succeeding five taxable years. However, if during any taxable year in the adjustment period an organization ceases to be subject to the initial excise tax imposed by section 4942(a), any portion of the excess of qualifying distributions, which prior to such taxable year has not been applied against distributable amounts, may not be carried over to such taxable year or subsequent taxable years in the adjustment period, even if during any of such taxable years the organization again becomes subject to the initial excise tax imposed by section 4942(a).

(4) *Examples.*—The provisions of this paragraph may be illustrated by the following examples:

*Example (1).* (i) F, a private foundation which was created in 1967 and which uses the calendar year as the taxable year, has distributable amounts and qualifying distributions for 1970 through 1976 as follows:

| Year | 1970 | 1971 | 1972 | 1973 | 1974 | 1975 | 1976 |
|---|---|---|---|---|---|---|---|
| Distributable amount | $100 | $100 | $100 | $100 | $100 | $100 | $100 |
| Qualifying distribution | $0 | $250 | $70 | $140 | $60 | $75 | $105 |

(ii) The qualifying distributions made in 1971 will be treated under paragraph (d) of this section as $100 made out of the undistributed income for 1970, then as $100 made out of the undistributed income for 1971, and finally as $50 out of corpus in 1971. Since the total qualifying distributions for 1971 ($150) exceed the distributable amount for 1971 ($100), there exists a $50 excess of qualifying distributions which F may use to reduce its distributable amounts for the years 1972 through 1976 (the taxable years in the adjustment period with respect to the 1971 excess). Therefore, the $100 distributable amount for 1972 is reduced by $30 (the lesser of the 1971 excess ($50) and the remaining undistributed income at the close of 1972 ($30), after the qualifying distributions of $70 for 1972 were applied to the original distributable amount for 1972 of $100). Since the distributable amount for 1972 was reduced to $70, there is no remaining undistributed income for 1972. Accordingly, the qualifying distributions made in 1973 will be treated as $100 made out of the undistributed income for 1973 and as $40 out of corpus in 1973. Since this amount ($140) exceeds the distributable amount for 1973 ($100), there exists a $40 excess which F may use to reduce its distributable amounts for the years 1974 through 1978 (the taxable years in the adjustment period with respect to the 1973 excess). However, in accordance with subparagraph (1) of this paragraph such excess may not be used to reduce F's distributable amounts for the years 1974 through 1976 until the excess created in 1971 has been completely applied against distributable amounts during such years. The distributable amount for 1974 is reduced by $40 (the lesser of the unused portion of the 1971 excess ($20) plus the 1973 excess ($40) and the remaining undistributed income at the close of 1974 ($40), after the

qualifying distributions of $60 for 1974 were applied to the original distributable amount for 1974 of $100). The distributable amount for 1975 is reduced by $20 (the lesser of the unused portion of the 1973 excess of qualifying distributions ($20) and the remaining undistributed income at the close of 1975 ($25), after the qualifying distributions of $75 for 1975 were applied to the original distributable amount for 1975 of $100). Consequently, qualifying distributions made in 1976 will be treated as made first out of the $5 of remaining undistributed income for 1975 and then as $100 made out of the undistributed income for 1976.

*Example (2).* Assume the facts as stated in example (1), except that in 1974 F receives a contribution of $300 from G, a private foundation which controls F (within the meaning of paragraph (a)(3) of this section), and F distributes such contribution in 1975 in satisfaction of paragraph (c) of this section. Under these circumstances, there would be no excess of qualifying distributions for 1975 with respect to such distribution, since such distribution is excluded from the computation of an excess of qualifying distributions by operation of subparagraph (2)(i) of this paragraph.

*Example (3).* Assume the facts as stated in example (1), except that in 1972 F is treated as an operating foundation (as such term is defined in section 4942(j)(3)). In accordance with subparagraph (3) of this paragraph since F is not subject to the initial excise tax imposed by section 4942(a) for 1972, the 1971 excess can not be carried forward to 1972 or any subsequent year in the adjustment period with respect to the 1971 excess, even if F is subsequently treated as a private nonoperating foundation for any year during the period 1973 through 1976.

(f) *Effective/applicability date and transition relief.*—Paragraphs (a)(2)(i) and (a)(6) of this section are effective on and apply with respect to distributions made after September 25, 2015. However, foundations may continue to rely on the provisions of paragraph (a)(6) of this section as contained in 26 CFR part 53, revised April 1, 2015, with respect to distributions made on or before December 24, 2015 pursuant to a good faith determination made in accordance with such provisions. Also, foundations may continue to rely on the provisions of paragraph (a)(6) of this section as contained in 26 CFR part 53, revised April 1, 2015, with respect to distributions pursuant to a written commitment made on or before September 25, 2015 and pursuant to a good faith determination made on or before such date in accordance with such provisions if the committed amount is distributed within five years of such date. [Reg. § 53.4942(a)-3.]

☐ [*T.D. 7256, 2-7-73. Amended by T.D. 7486, 5-12-77, T.D. 7849, 11-9-82, T.D. 7938, 1-30-84 T.D. 8084, 5-1-86 and T.D. 9740, 9-23-2015.*]

### [Reg. § 53.4942(b)-1]

**§ 53.4942(b)-1. Operating foundations.**—(a) *Operating foundation defined.*—(1) *In general.*—For purposes of section 4942 and the regulations thereunder, the term "operating foundation" means any private foundation which, in addition to satisfying the assets test, the endowment test or the support test set forth in § 53.4942(b)-2(a), (b) and (c), makes qualifying distributions (within the meaning of § 53.4942(a)-3(a)(2)) directly for the active conduct of activities constituting its charitable, educational, or other similar exempt purpose equal in value to—

(i) For taxable years beginning before January 1, 1982, substantially all of the foundation's adjusted net income (as defined in § 53.4942(a)-2(d)); and

(ii) For taxable years beginning after December 31, 1981, substantially all of the lesser of the foundation's adjusted net income (as defined in § 53.4942(a)-2(d)) or minimum investment return (as defined in § 53.4942(a)-2(c)). If the foundation's qualifying distributions exceed its minimum investment return (but are less than the foundation's adjusted net income) substantially all of such qualifying distributions must be made directly for the active conduct of activities constituting its charitable, educational or other similar exempt purpose. However, if the foundation's minimum investment return is less than its adjusted net income and the foundation's qualifying distributions equal or exceed such adjusted net income, only that portion of the qualifying distributions equal to substantially all of the foundation's adjusted net income must be made directly for the active conduct of activities constituting its charitable, educational or other similar exempt purpose.

(2) *Certain elderly care facilities described in section 4942(j)(6).*—(i) *In general.*—For purposes of the distribution requirements of section 4942 (but no other provision of the Internal Revenue Code) and for taxable years beginning after December 31, 1969, the term "operating foundation" includes a private foundation which—

(A) On or before May 26, 1969, and continuously thereafter to the close of the taxable year, operates and maintains, as its principal functional purpose, residential facilities for the long-term care, comfort, maintenance, or education of permanently and totally disabled persons, elderly persons, needy widows, or children, and

(B) Satisfies the endowment test set forth in § 53.4942(b)-2(b).

(ii) *Principal functional purpose.*—For purposes of section 4942(j)(6) and this subparagraph (2), an organization's "principal functional purpose" is operating and maintaining residential facilities for the long-term care, comfort, maintenance, or education of permanently and totally disabled persons, elderly persons, needy widows, or children, if it is organized for the principal purpose of operating and maintaining such residential facilities and is primarily engaged directly in the operation and maintenance of those facilities. An organization will be treated as being primarily engaged directly in the operation and maintenance of the described residential facilities if at least 50% of the qualifying distributions (as defined in § 53.4942(a)-3(a)(2)) normally made by the organization are expended for the operation and maintenance of the facilities.

(b) *Active conduct of activities constituting the exempt purpose.*—(1) *In general.*—For purposes of this section, except as provided in subparagraph (2) or (3) of this paragraph, qualifying distributions are not made by a foundation "directly for the active conduct of activities constituting its charitable, educational, or other similar exempt purpose" unless such qualifying distributions are used by the foundation itself, rather than by or through one or more grantee organizations which receive such qualifying distributions directly or indirectly from such foundation. Thus, grants made to other organizations to assist them in conducting activities which help to accomplish their charitable, educational, or other similar exempt purpose are considered an indirect, rather than direct, means of carrying out activities constituting the charitable, educational, or other similar exempt purpose of the grantor foundation, regardless of the fact that the exempt activities of the grantee organization may assist the grantor foundation in carrying out its own exempt activities. However, amounts paid to acquire or maintain assets which are used directly in the conduct of the foundation's exempt activities, such as the operating assets of a museum, public park, or historic site, are considered direct expenditures for the active conduct of the foundation's exempt activities. Likewise, administrative expenses (such as staff salaries and traveling expenses) and other operating costs necessary to conduct the foundation's exempt activities (regardless of whether they are "directly for the active conduct" of such exempt activities) shall be treated as qualifying distributions expended directly for the active conduct of such exempt activities if such expenses and costs are reasonable in amount. Conversely, administrative expenses and operating costs which are not attributable to exempt activities, such as expenses in connection with the production of investment income, are not treated as such qualifying distributions. Expenses attributable to both exempt and nonexempt activities shall be allocated to each such activity on a reasonable and consistently applied basis. Any amount set aside by a foundation for a specific project, such as the acquisition and restoration, or construction, of additional buildings or facilities which are to be used by the foundation directly for the active conduct of the foundation's exempt activities, shall be deemed to be qualifying distributions expended directly for the active conduct of the foundation's exempt activities if the initial setting aside of the funds constitutes a set-aside within the meaning of paragraph (b) of § 53.4942(a)-3.

(2) *Payments to individual beneficiaries.*—(i) *In general.*—If a foundation makes or awards grants, scholarships, or other payments to individual beneficiaries (including program related investment within the meaning of section 4944(c) made to individuals or corporate enterprises) to support active programs conducted to carry out the foundation's charitable, educational, or other similar exempt purpose, such grants, scholarships, or other payments will be treated as qualifying distributions made directly for the active conduct of exempt activities for purposes of paragraph (a) of this section only if the foundation, apart from the making or awarding of the grants, scholarships, or other payments, otherwise maintains some significant involvement (as defined in subdivision (ii) of this subparagraph) in the active programs in support of which such grants, scholarships, or other payments were made or awarded. Whether the making or awarding of grants, scholarships, or other payments constitutes qualifying distributions made directly for the active conduct of the foundation's exempt activities is to be determined on the basis of the facts and circumstances of each particular case. The test applied is a qualitative, rather than a strictly quantitative, one. Therefore, if the foundation maintains a significant involvement (as defined in subdivision (ii) of this subparagraph) it will not fail to meet the general rule of subparagraph (1) of this paragraph solely because more of its funds are devoted to the making or awarding of grants, scholarships, or other payments than to the active programs which such grants, scholarships, or other payments support. However, if a foundation does no more than select, screen, and investigate applicants for grants or scholarships, pursuant to which the recipients perform their work or studies alone or exclusively under the direction of some other organization, such grants or scholarships will not be treated as qualifying distributions made directly for the active conduct of the foundation's exempt activities. The administrative expenses of such screening and investigation (as opposed to the grants or scholarships themselves) may be treated as qualifying distributions made directly for the active conduct of the foundation's exempt activities.

(ii) *Definition.*—For purposes of this subparagraph, a foundation will be considered as maintaining a "significant involvement" in a charitable, educational, or other similar exempt activity in connection with which grants, scholarships, or other payments are made or awarded if—

(A) An exempt purpose of the foundation is the relief of poverty or human distress, and its exempt activities are designed to ameliorate conditions among a poor or distressed class of persons or in an area subject to poverty or national disaster (such as providing food or clothing to indigents or residents of a disaster area), the making or awarding of the grants or other payments to accomplish such exempt purpose is direct and without the assistance of an intervening organization or agency, and the foundation maintains a salaried or voluntary staff of administrators, researchers, or other personnel who supervise and direct the activities described in this subdivision (A) on a continuing basis; or

(B) The foundation has developed some specialized skills, expertise, or involvement in a particular discipline or substantive area (such as scientific or medical research, social work, education, or the social sciences), it maintains a salaried staff of administrators, researchers, or other personnel who supervise or conduct programs or activities which support and advance the foundation's work in its particular area of interest, and, as a part of such programs or activities, the foundation makes or awards grants, scholarships, or other payments to individuals to encourage and further their involvement in the foundation's particular area of interest and in some segment of the programs or activities carried on by the foundation (such as grants under which the recipients, in addition to independent study, attend classes, seminars, or conferences sponsored or conducted by the foundation, or grants to engage in social work or scientific research projects which are under the general direction and supervision of the foundation).

(3) *Payment of section 4940 tax.*—For purposes of section 4942(j)(3)(A) and (B)(ii), payment of the tax imposed upon a foundation under section 4940 shall be considered a qualifying distribution which is made directly for the active conduct of activities constituting the foundation's charitable, educational, or other similar exempt purpose.

(c) *Substantially all.*—For purposes of this section, the term "substantially all" shall mean 85 percent or more. Thus, if a foundation makes qualifying distributions directly for the active conduct of activities constituting its charitable, educational, or other similar exempt purpose in an amount equal to at least 85 percent of its adjusted net income, it will be considered as satisfying the income test described in this section even if it makes grants to organizations or engages in other activities with the remainder of its adjusted net income and with other funds. In determining whether the amount of qualifying distributions made directly for the active conduct of such exempt activities equals at least 85 percent of a foundation's adjusted net income, a foundation is not required to trace the source of such expenditures to determine whether they were derived from income or from contributions.

(d) *Examples.*—The provisions of this section may be illustrated by the following examples. It is assumed that none of the organizations described in these examples is described in section 509(a)(1), (2), or (3).

*Example (1).* N, an exempt museum described in section 501(c)(3), was founded by the gift of an endowment from a single contributor. N uses 90 percent of its adjusted net income to operate the museum. If N satisfies one of the tests set forth in §53.4942(b)-2 it may be classified as an operating foundation since substantially all of the qualifying distributions made by N are used directly for the active conduct of N's exempt activities within the meaning of paragraph (b)(1) of this section.

*Example (2).* M, an exempt organization described in section 501(c)(3), was created to improve conditions in a particular urban ghetto. M receives its funds primarily from a limited number of wealthy contributors interested in helping carry out its exempt purpose. M's program consists of making a survey of the problems of the ghetto to determine the areas in which its funds may be applied most effectively. Approximately 10 percent of M's adjusted net income is used to conduct this survey. The balance of its income is used to make grants to other nonprofit organizations doing work in the ghetto in those areas determined to have the greatest likelihood of resulting in improved conditions. Under these circumstances, since only 10 percent of M's adjusted net income may be considered as constituting qualifying distributions made directly for the active conduct of M's exempt activities, M cannot qualify as an operating foundation.

*Example (3).* Assume the facts as stated in example (2), except that M uses the remaining 90 percent of its adjusted net income for the following purposes: (1) M maintains a salaried staff of social workers and researchers who analyze its surveys and make recommendations as to methods for improving ghetto conditions; (2) M makes grants to independent social scientists who assist in these analyses and recommendations; (3) M publishes periodic reports indicating the results of its surveys and recommendations; (4) M makes grants to social workers and others who act as advisors to nonprofit organizations, as well as small business enterprises, functioning in the community (these advisors acting under the general direction of M attempt to implement M's recommendations through their advice and assistance to the nonprofit organizations and small business enterprises); and (5) M makes grants to other social scientists who study and report on the success of the various enterprises which attempt to implement M's recommendations. Under these circumstances, M satisfies the requirements of paragraph (b)(2) of this section, and the various grants it makes constitute qualifying distributions made directly for the active conduct of its exempt activities. Thus, if M satisfies one of the tests set forth in §53.4942(b)-2 it may be classified as an operating foundation.

*Example (4).* P, an exempt educational organization described in section 501(c)(3), was created for the purpose of training teachers for institutions of higher education. Each year P awards a substantial number of fellowships to students for graduate study leading to-

wards their M.A. or Ph. D. degrees. The applicants for these fellowships are carefully screened by P's staff, and only those applicants who indicate a strong interest in teaching in colleges or universities are chosen. P publishes and circulates various pamphlets encouraging a development of interests in college teaching and describing its fellowships. P also conducts annual summer seminars which are attended by its fellowship recipients, its staff, consultants and other interested parties. The purpose of these seminars is to foster and encourage the development of college teaching. P publishes a report of the seminar proceedings along with related studies written by those who attended. Despite the fact that a substantial portion of P's adjusted net income is devoted to granting fellowships, its commitment to encouraging individuals to become teachers at institutions of higher learning, its maintenance of a staff and programs designed to further this purpose, and the granting of fellowships to encourage involvement both in its own seminars and in its exempt purpose indicate a significant involvement by P beyond the mere granting of fellowships. Thus, the fellowship grants made by P constitute qualifying distributions made directly for the active conduct of P's exempt activities within the meaning of paragraph (b)(2) of this section.

*Example (5).* Q, an exempt organization described in section 501(c)(3), is composed of professional organizations interested in different branches of one academic discipline. Q trains its own professional staff, conducts its own program of research, selects research topics, screens and investigates grant recipients, makes grants to those selected, and sets up and conducts conferences and seminars for the grantees. Q has particular knowledge and skill in the given discipline, carries on activities to advance its study of that discipline, and makes grants to individuals to enable them to participate in activities which it conducts in carrying out its exempt purpose. Under these circumstances, Q's grants constitute qualifying distributions made directly for the active conduct of Q's exempt activities within the meaning of paragraph (b)(2) of this section.

*Example (6).* R, an exempt medical research organization described in section 501(c)(3), was created to study and perform research concerning heart disease. R has its own research center in which it carries on a broad number of research projects in the field of heart disease with its own professional staff. Physicians and scientists who are interested in special projects in this area present the plans for their projects to R. The directors of R study these plans and decide if the project is feasible and will further the work being done by R. If it is, R makes a grant to the individual to enable him to carry out his project, either at R's facilities or elsewhere. Reports of the progress of the project are made periodically to R, and R exercises a certain amount of supervision over the project. The resulting findings of these projects are usually published by R. Under these circumstances, the grants made by R constitute qualifying distributions made directly for the active conduct of R's exempt activities within the meaning of paragraph (b)(2) of this section.

*Example (7).* S, an exempt organization described in section 501(c)(3), maintains a large library of manuscripts and other historical reference material relating to the history and development of the region in which the collection is located. S makes a limited number of annual grants to enable post-doctoral scholars and doctoral candidates to use its library. Sometimes S obtains the right to publish the scholar's work, although this is not a prerequisite to the receipt of a grant. The primary criterion for selection of grant recipients is the usefulness of the library's resources to the applicant's field of study. Under these circumstances, the grants made by S constitute qualifying distributions made directly for the active conduct of S's exempt activities within the meaning of paragraph (b)(2) of this section.

*Example (8).* T, an exempt charitable organization described in section 501(c)(3), was created by the members of one family for the purpose of relieving poverty and human suffering. T has a large salaried staff of employees who operate offices in various areas throughout the country. Its employees make gifts of foods and clothing to poor persons in the area serviced by each office. On occasion, T also provides temporary relief in the form of food and clothing to persons in areas stricken by natural disasters. If conditions improve in one poverty area, T transfers the resources of the office in that area to another poverty area. Under these circumstances, the gifts of food and clothing made by T constitute qualifying distributions made directly for the active conduct of T's exempt activities within the meaning of paragraph (b)(2) of this section.

*Example (9).* U, an exempt scientific organization described in section 501(c)(3), was created for the principal purpose of studying the effects of early childhood brain damage. U conducts an active and continuous research program in this area through a salaried staff of scientists and physicians. As part of its research program, U awards scholarships to young people suffering mild brain damage to enable them to attend special schools equipped to handle such problems. The recipients are periodically tested to determine the effect of such schooling upon them. Under these circumstances, the scholarships awarded by U constitute qualifying distributions made directly for the active conduct of U's exempt activities within the meaning of paragraph (b)(2) of this section.

*Example (10).* O, an exempt charitable organization described in section 501(c)(3), was created for the purpose of giving scholarships to children of the employees of X Corporation who meet the standards set by O. O not only screens and investigates each applicant to make sure that he complies with the academic and financial requirements set for scholarship recipients, but also administers an examination which each applicant must take—90 percent of O's adjusted net income is used in awarding these scholarships to the chosen applicants. O does not conduct any activities of an educational nature on its own. Under these circumstances, O is not using substantially all of its adjusted net income directly for the active conduct of its exempt activities within the meaning of paragraph (b) of this section. Thus, O is not an operating foundation because it fails to satisfy the income test set forth in paragraph (a) of this section. [Reg. § 53.4942(b)-1.]

☐ [*T.D. 7249, 12-29-72. Amended by T.D. 7718, 9-3-80 and T.D. 7878, 3-21-83.*]

### [Reg. § 53.4942(b)-2]

**§ 53.4942(b)-2. Alternative tests.**—(a) *Assets test.*—(1) *In general.*—A private foundation will satisfy the assets test under the provisions of this paragraph if substantially more than half of the foundation's assets:

(i) Are devoted directly (A) to the active conduct of activities constituting the foundation's charitable, educational, or other similar exempt purpose, (B) to functionally related businesses (as defined in paragraph (c)(3)(iii) of § 53.4942(a)-2), or (C) to any combination thereof;

(ii) Are stock of a corporation which is controlled by the foundation (within the meaning of section 368(c)) and substantially all the assets of which (within the meaning of paragraph (c) of § 53.4942(b)-1) are so devoted; or

(iii) Are in part assets which are described in subdivision (i) of this subparagraph and in part stock which is described in subdivision (ii) of this subparagraph.

(2) *Qualifying assets.*—(i) *In general.*—For purposes of subparagraph (1) of this paragraph, an asset is "devoted directly to the active conduct of activities constituting the foundation's charitable, educational, or other similar exempt purpose" only if the asset is actually used by the foundation directly for the active conduct of activities constituting its charitable, educational, or other similar exempt purpose. Thus, such assets as real estate, physical facilities or objects (such as museum assets, classroom fixtures and equipment, and research facilities), and intangible assets (such as patents, copyrights and trademarks) will be considered qualifying assets for purposes of this paragraph to the extent they are used directly for the active conduct of the foundation's exempt activities. However, assets which are held for the production of income, for investment, or for some other similar use (for example, stocks, bonds, interest-bearing notes, endowment funds, or, generally, leased real estate) are not devoted directly to the active conduct of the foundation's exempt activities, even though the income derived from such assets is used to carry out such exempt activities. Whether an asset is held for the production of income, for investment, or for some other similar use rather than being used for the active conduct of the foundation's exempt activities is a question of fact. For example, an office building used for the purpose of providing offices for employees engaged in the management of endowment funds of the foundation is not devoted to the active conduct of the foundation's exempt activities. However, where property is used both for exempt purposes and for other purposes, if such exempt use represents 95 percent or more of the total use, such property shall be considered to be used exclusively for an exempt purpose. Property acquired by a foundation to be used in carrying out the foundation's exempt purpose may be considered as devoted directly to the active conduct of such purpose even though the property, in whole or in part, is leased for a limited period of time during which arrangements are made for its conversion to the use for which it was acquired, provided such income-producing use of the property does not exceed a reasonable period of time. Generally, one year shall be deemed to be a reasonable period of time for purposes of the immediately preceding sentence. Similarly, where property is leased by a foundation in carrying out its exempt purpose and where the rental income derived from such property by the foundation is less than the amount which would be required to be charged in order to recover the cost of purchase and maintenance of such property (taking into account the deductions permitted by paragraph (d)(4) of § 53.4942(a)-2), such property shall be considered devoted directly to the active conduct of the foundation's exempt activities.

(ii) *Limitations.*—(A) Assets which are held for the purpose of extending credit or making funds available to members of a charitable class (including any interest in a program related-investment,

except as provided in paragraph (b)(2) of § 53.4942(b)-1) are not considered assets devoted directly to the active conduct of activities constituting the foundation's charitable, educational, or other similar exempt purpose. For example, assets which are set aside in special reserve accounts to guarantee student loans made by lending institutions will not be considered assets devoted directly to the active conduct of the foundation's exempt activities.

(B) Any amount set aside by a foundation within the meaning of paragraph (b)(1) of § 53.4942(b)-1 shall not be treated as an asset devoted directly to the active conduct of the foundation's exempt activities.

(3) *Assets held for less than a taxable year.*—For purposes of this paragraph, any asset which is held by a foundation for part of a taxable year shall be taken into account for such taxable year by multiplying the fair market value of such asset (as determined pursuant to subparagraph (4) of this paragraph) by a fraction, the numerator of which is the number of days in such taxable year that the foundation held such asset and the denominator of which is the number of days in such taxable year.

(4) *Valuation.*—For purposes of this paragraph, all assets shall be valued at their fair market value. Fair market value shall be determined in accordance with the rules set forth in paragraph (c)(4) of § 53.4942(a)-2, except in the case of assets which are devoted directly to the active conduct of the foundation's exempt activities and for which neither a ready market nor standard valuation methods exist (such as historical objects or buildings, certain works of art, and botanical gardens). In such cases, the historical cost (unadjusted for depreciation) shall be considered equal to fair market value unless the foundation demonstrates that fair market value is other than cost. In any case in which the foundation so demonstrates that the fair market value of an asset is other than historical cost, such substituted valuation may be used for the taxable year for which such new valuation is demonstrated and for each of the succeeding four taxable years if the valuation methods and procedures prescribed by paragraph (c)(4)(iv)(B) of § 53.4942(a)-2 are followed.

(5) *Substantially more than half.*—For purposes of this paragraph, the term "substantially more than half" shall mean 65 percent or more.

(6) *Examples.*—The provisions of this paragraph may be illustrated by the following examples. It is assumed that none of the organizations described in these examples is described in section 509(a)(1), (2), or (3).

*Example (1).* W, an exempt organization described in section 501(c)(3), is devoted to the maintenance and operation of a historic area for the benefit of the general public. W has acquired and erected facilities for lodging and other visitor accommodations in such area, which W operates through a wholly owned, separately incorporated, taxable entity. These facilities comprise substantially all of the subsidiary's assets. The operation of such accommodations constitutes a functionally related business within the meaning of paragraph (c)(3)(iii) of § 53.4942(a)-2. Under these circumstances, the stock of the subsidiary will be considered as part of W's assets which may be taken into account by W in determining whether it satisfies the assets test described in this paragraph.

*Example (2).* M, an exempt conservation organization described in section 501(c)(3), is devoted to acquiring, preserving, and otherwise making available for public use geographically diversified areas of natural beauty. M has acquired and erected facilities for lodging and other visitor accommodations in national park areas. The operation of such accommodations constitutes a functionally related business within the meaning of paragraph (c)(3)(iii) of § 53.4942(a)-2. Therefore, M's assets which are directly devoted to such visitor accommodations may be taken into account by M in determining whether it satisfies the assets test described in this paragraph.

*Example (3).* P, an exempt organization described in section 501(c)(3), is devoted to acquiring and restoring historic houses. To insure that the restored houses will be kept in the restored condition, and to make the houses more readily available for public display, P rents the houses rather than sells them once they have been restored. The rental income derived by P is substantially less than the amount which would be required to be charged in order to recover the cost of purchase, restoration, and maintenance of such houses. Therefore, such houses may be taken into account by P in determining whether it satisfies the assets test described in this paragraph.

*Example (4).* Z, an exempt organization described in section 501(c)(3), is devoted to improving the public's understanding of Renaissance art. Z's principal assets are a number of paintings of this period which it circulates on an active and continuing basis to museums and schools for public display. These paintings constitute 80 percent of Z's assets. Under these circumstances, although Z does not have a building in which it displays these paintings, such paintings are devoted directly to the active conduct of activities constituting Z's exempt purpose. Therefore, Z has satisfied the assets test described in this paragraph.

(b) *Endowment test.*—(1) *In general.*—A foundation will satisfy the endowment test under the provisions of this paragraph if it normally makes qualifying distributions (within the meaning of paragraph (a)(2) of §53.4942(a)-3) directly for the active conduct of activities constituting its charitable, educational, or other similar exempt purpose in an amount not less than two-thirds of its minimum investment return (as defined in paragraph (c) of §53.4942(a)-2). In determining whether the amount of such qualifying distributions is not less than an amount equal to two-thirds of the foundation's minimum investment return, the foundation is not required to trace the source of such expenditures to determine whether they were derived from investment income or from contributions.

(2) *Definitions.*—For purposes of this paragraph, the phrase "directly for the active conduct of activities constituting the foundation's charitable, educational, or other similar exempt purpose" shall have the same meaning as in paragraph (b) of §53.4942(b)-1.

(3) *Example.*—This paragraph may be illustrated by the following example:

*Example.* X, an exempt organization described in section 501(c)(3) and not described in section 509(a)(1), (2), or (3), was created on July 15, 1970. X uses the cash receipts and disbursements method of accounting. For 1971, the fair market value of X's assets not described in paragraph (c)(2) or (3) of §53.4942(a)-2 is $400,000. X makes qualifying distributions for 1971 directly for the active conduct of its exempt activities of $17,000. For 1971 two-thirds of X's minimum investment return is $16,000 (6 percent × $400,000 = $24,000; $2/3$ × $24,000 = $16,000). Under these circumstances, X has satisfied the endowment test described in this paragraph for 1971. However, if X's qualifying distributions for 1971 directly for the active conduct of its exempt activities were only $15,000, X would not satisfy the endowment test for 1971, unless the fair market value of its assets not described in paragraph (c)(2) or (3) of §53.4942(a)-2 were no greater than $375,000 (6 percent × $375,000 = $22,500; $2/3$ × $22,500 = $15,000).

(c) *Support test.*—(1) *In general.*—A foundation will satisfy the support test under the provisions of this paragraph if:

(i) Substantially all of its support (other than gross investment income as defined in section 509(e)) is normally received from the general public and from five or more exempt organizations which are not described in section 4946(a)(1)(H) with respect to each other or the recipient foundation;

(ii) Not more than 25 percent of its support (other than gross investment income) is normally received from any one such exempt organization; and

(iii) Not more than half of its support is normally received from gross investment income.

(2) *Definitions and special rules.*—For purposes of this paragraph—

(i) *Support.*—The term "support" shall have the same meaning as in section 509(d).

(ii) *Substantially all.*—The term "substantially all" shall have the same meaning as in paragraph (c) of §53.4942(b)-1.

(iii) *Support from exempt organizations.*—The support received from any one exempt organization may be counted towards satisfaction of the support test described in this paragraph only if the foundation receives support from no fewer than five exempt organizations. For example, a foundation which normally receives 20 percent of its support (other than gross investment income) from each of five exempt organizations may qualify under this paragraph even though it receives no support from the general public. However, if a foundation normally received 10 percent of its support from each of three exempt organizations and the balance of its support from sources other than exempt organizations, such support could not be taken into account in determining whether the foundation had satisfied the support test set forth in this paragraph.

(iv) *Support from the general public.*—"Support" received from an individual, or from a trust or corporation (other than an exempt organization), shall be taken into account as support from the general public only to the extent that the total amount of the support received from any such individual, trust, or corporation during the period for determining the normal sources of the foundation's support (as set forth in §53.4942(b)-3) does not exceed one percent of the foundation's total support (other than gross investment income) for such period. In applying this one-percent limitation, all support received by the foundation from any one person and from any other person or persons standing in a relationship to such person which is described in section 4946(a)(1)(C) through (G) and the regulations

thereunder shall be treated as received from one person. For purposes of this paragraph, support received from a governmental unit described in section 170(c)(1) shall be treated as support received from the general public, but shall not be subject to the one-percent limitation. [Reg. §53.4942(b)-2.]

☐ [*T.D. 7249, 12-29-72.*]

## [Reg. §53.4942(b)-3]

**§53.4942(b)-3. Determination of compliance with operating foundation tests.**—(a) *In general.*—A foundation may satisfy the income test and either the assets, endowment, or support test by satisfying such tests for any three taxable years during a four-year period consisting of the taxable year in question and the three immediately preceding taxable years or on the basis of an aggregation of all pertinent amounts of income or assets held, received, or distributed during such four-year period. A foundation may not use one method for satisfying the income test described in paragraph (a) of §53.4942(b)-1 and another for satisfying either the assets, endowment, or support test described in §53.4942(b)-2. Thus, if a foundation satisfies the income test on the three-out-of-four-year basis for a particular taxable year, it may not use the aggregation method for satisfying either the assets, endowment, or support test for such particular taxable year. However, the fact that a foundation has chosen one method for satisfying the tests under §§53.4942(b)-1 and 53.4942(b)-2 for one taxable year will not preclude it from satisfying such tests for a subsequent taxable year by the alternate method. If a foundation fails to satisfy the income test and either the assets, endowment, or support test for a particular taxable year under either the three-out-of-four-year method or the aggregation method, it shall be treated as a nonoperating foundation for such taxable year and for all subsequent taxable years until it satisfies the tests set forth in §§53.4942(b)-1 and 53.4942(b)-2 for a taxable year occurring after the taxable year in which it was treated as a non-operating foundation.

(b) *New organizations.*—(1) *In general.*—Except as provided in subparagraph (2) of this paragraph, an organization organized after December 31, 1969, will be treated as an operating foundation only if it has satisfied the tests set forth in §§53.4942(b)-1 and 53.4942(b)-2 for its first taxable year of existence. If an organization satisfies such tests for its first taxable year, it will be treated as an operating foundation from the beginning of such taxable year. If such is the case, the organization will be treated as an operating foundation for its second and third taxable years of existence only if it satisfies the tests set forth in §§53.4942(b)-1 and 53.4942(b)-2 by the aggregation method for all such taxable years that it has been in existence.

(2) *Special rule.*—An organization organized after December 31, 1969, will be treated as an operating foundation prior to the end of its first taxable year if such organization has made a good faith determination that it is likely to satisfy the income test set forth in paragraph (a) of §53.4942(b)-1 and one of the tests set forth in §53.4942(b)-2 for such first taxable year pursuant to subparagraph (1) of this paragraph. Such a "good faith determination" ordinarily will be considered as made where the determination is based on an affidavit or opinion of counsel of such organization that such requirements will be satisfied. Such an affidavit or opinion must set forth sufficient facts concerning the operations and support of such organization for the Commissioner to be able to determine that such organization is likely to satisfy such requirements. An organization which, pursuant to this subparagraph, has been treated as an operating foundation for its first taxable year, but actually fails to qualify as an operating foundation under subparagraph (1) of this paragraph for such taxable year, will be treated as a private foundation which is not an operating foundation as of the first day of its second taxable year for purposes of making any determination under the internal revenue laws with respect to such organization. The preceding sentence shall not apply if such organization establishes to the satisfaction of the Commissioner that it is likely to qualify as an operating foundation on the basis of its second, third and fourth taxable years. Thus, if such an organization fails to qualify as an operating foundation in its second, third, and fourth taxable year after having failed in its first taxable year, it will be treated as a private foundation which is not an operating foundation as of the first day of such second, third or fourth taxable year in which it fails to qualify as an operating foundation, except as otherwise provided by paragraph (d) of this section. Such status as a private foundation which is not an operating foundation will continue until such time as the organization is able to satisfy the tests set forth in §§53.4942(b)-1 and 53.4942(b)-2 by either the three-out-of-four-year method or the aggregation method. For the status of grants or contributions made to such an organzation with respect to sections 170 and 4942, see paragraph (d) of this section.

(c) *Transitional rule for existing organizations.*—An organization organized before December 31, 1969 (including organizations deemed to be so organized by virtue of the principles of paragraph (e)(2) of

§ 53.4942(a)-2), but which is unable to satisfy the tests under §§ 53.4942(b)-1 and 53.4942(b)-2 for its first taxable year beginning after December 31, 1969 on the basis of its operations for taxable years prior to such taxable year by either the three-out-of-four-year method or the aggregation method, will be treated as a new organization for purposes of paragraph (b) of this section only if:

(1) The organization changes its methods of operation prior to its first taxable year beginning after December 31, 1972 to conform to the requirements of §§ 53.4942(b)-1 and 53.4942(b)-2;

(2) The organization has made a good faith determination (within the meaning of paragraph (b)(2) of the section) that it is likely to satisfy the tests set forth in §§ 53.4942(b)-1 and 53.4942(b)-2 prior to its first taxable year beginning after December 31, 1972 on the basis of its income or assets held, received, or distributed during its taxable years beginning in 1970 through 1972; and

(3) Such good faith determination is attached to the return the organization is required to file under section 6033 for its taxable year beginning in 1972.

(d) *Treatment of contributions.*—(1) *In general.*—The status of grants or contributions made to an operating foundation with respect to sections 170 and 4942 will not be affected until notice of change of status of such organization is made to the public (such as by publication in the Internal Revenue Bulletin), unless the grant or contribution was made after:

(i) The act or failure to act that resulted in the organization's inability to satisfy the requirements of §§ 53.4942(b)-1 and 53.4942(b)-2, and the grantor or contributor was responsible for, or was aware of, such act or failure to act, or

(ii) The grantor or contributor acquired knowledge that the Commissioner has given notice to such organization that it would be deleted from classification as an operating foundation.

(2) *Exception.*—For purposes of subparagraph (1)(i) of this paragraph, a grantor or contributor will not be considered to be responsible for, or aware of, the act or failure to act that resulted in the grantee organization's inability to satisy the requirements of §§ 53.4942(b)-1 and 53.4942(b)-2 if such grantor or contributor has made his grant or contribution in reliance upon a written statement by the grantee organization that such grant or contribution would not result in the inability of such grantee organization to qualify as an operating foundation. Such a statement must be signed by a foundation manager (as defined in section 4946(b)) of the grantee organization and must set forth sufficient facts concerning the operations and support of such grantee organization to assure a reasonably prudent man that his grant or contribution will not result in the grantee organization's inability to qualify as an operating foundation. [Reg. § 53.4942(b)-3.]

☐ [T.D. 7249, 12-29-72.]

**[Reg. § 53.4943-1]**

**§ 53.4943-1. General rule; purpose.**—Generally, under section 4943, the combined holdings of a private foundation and all disqualified persons (as defined in section 4946(a)) in any corporation conducting a business which is not substantially related (aside from the need of the foundation for income or funds or the use it makes of the profits derived) to the exempt purposes of the foundation are limited to 20 percent of the voting stock in such corporation. In addition, the combined holdings of a private foundation and all disqualified persons in any unincorporated business (other than a sole proprietorship) which is not substantially related (aside from the need of the foundation for income or funds or the use it makes of the profits derived) to the exempt purposes of such foundation are limited to 20 percent of the beneficial or profits interest in such business. In the case of a sole proprietorship which is not substantially related (within the meaning of the preceding sentence), section 4943 provides that a private foundation shall have no permitted holdings. These general provisions are subject to a number of exceptions and special provisions which will be described in following sections. [Reg. § 53.4943-1.]

☐ [T.D. 7946, 7-5-77.]

**[Reg. § 53.4943-2]**

**§ 53.4943-2. Imposition of tax on excess business holdings of private foundations.**—(a) *Imposition of initial tax.*—(1) *In general.*—(i) *Initial tax.*—Section 4943(a)(1) imposes an initial excise tax (the "initial tax") on the excess business holdings of a private foundation for each taxable year of the foundation which ends during the taxable period defined in section 4943(d)(2). The amount of such tax is equal to 5 percent of the total value of all the private foundation's excess business holdings in each of its business enterprises. In determining the value of the excess business holdings of the foundation subject to tax under section 4943, the rules set forth in §§ 20.2031-1 through 20.2031-3 of this chapter (Estate Tax Regulations) shall apply.

(ii) *Disposition of certain excess business holdings within ninety days.*—In any case in which a private foundation acquires excess business holdings, other than as a result of a purchase by the foundation, the foundation shall not be subject to the taxes imposed by section 4943, but only if it disposes of an amount of its holdings so that it no longer has such excess business holdings within 90 days from the date on which it knows, or has reason to know, of the event which caused it to have such excess business holdings. Similarly, a private foundation shall not be subject to the taxes imposed by section 4943 because of its purchase of holdings where it did not know, or have reason to know of prior acquisitions by disqualified persons, but only if the foundation disposes of its excess holdings within the 90-day period described previously, and its purchase would not have created excess business holding but for such prior acquisitions by disqualified persons. In determining whether for purposes of this (ii) the foundation has disposed of such excess business holdings during such 90-day period, any disposition of holdings by a disqualified person during such period shall be disregarded.

(iii) *Extension of ninety day period.*—The period described in paragraph (a)(1)(ii) of this section, during which no tax shall be imposed under section 4943, shall be extended to include the period during which a foundation is prevented by federal or state securities laws from disposing of such excess business holdings.

(iv) *Effect of disposition subject to material restrictions.*—If a private foundation disposes of an interest in a business enterprise but imposes any material restrictions or conditions that prevent the transferee from freely and effectively using or disposing of the transferred interest, then the transferor foundation will be treated as owning such interest until all such restrictions or conditions are eliminated (regardless of whether the transferee is treated for other purposes of the Code as owning such interest from the date of the transfer). However, a restriction or condition imposed in compliance with federal or state securities laws, or in accordance with the terms or conditions of the gift or bequest through which such interest was acquired by the foundation, shall not be considered a material restriction or condition imposed by a private foundation.

(v) *Foundation knowledge of acquisitions made by disqualified persons.*—(A) For purposes of paragraph (a)(1)(ii) of this section, whether a private foundation will be treated as knowing, or having reason to know, of the acquisition of holdings by a disqualified person will depend on the facts and circumstances of each case. Factors which will be considered relevant to a determination that a private foundation did not know or had no reason to know of an acquisition are: the fact that it did not discover acquisitions made by disqualified persons through the use of procedures reasonably calculated to discover such holdings; the diversity of foundation holdings; and the existence of large numbers of disqualified persons who have little or no contact with the foundation or its managers.

(B) The provisions of paragraph (a)(1)(v)(A) of this section may be illustrated by the following example:

*Example.* By the fifteenth day of the fifth month after the close of each taxable year, the F Foundation sends to each foundation manager, substantial contributor, person holding more than a 20% interest (as described in section 4946(a)(1)(C)) in a substantial contributor, and foundation described in section 4946(a)(1)(H), a questionnaire asking such persons to list all holdings, actual or constructive, in each business enterprise in which F had holdings during the taxable year in excess of those permitted by the 2 percent *de minimis* rule of section 4943(c)(2)(C). In preparing the list of such enterprises, F takes into account its constructive holdings only if, during the taxable year, F (along with all related foundations described in section 4946(a)(1)(H)) owned over 2% of the voting stock, profits interest or beneficial interest in the entity actually owning the holdings constructively held by F. The questionnaire asks each such person to list the holdings in such enterprises of any persons who, because of their relationship to such disqualified person, were themselves disqualified persons (*i.e.*, members of the family (as defined in section 4946(d)), and any corporations, partnerships, trusts and estates described in section 4946(a)(1)(E) through (G) in which such person, or members of his family, had an interest. The questionnaire asks that constructive holdings be listed only if, during the taxable year, the disqualified person owned over 2% of the voting stock, profits interests or beneficial interest in the entity actually owning the holdings constructively held by such person. (Thus a disqualified person owning less than 2% of a mutual fund is not required to list his attributed share of all the securities in the portfolio of the fund.) If no response to the questionnaire is received, the foundation seeks the information requested by the questionnaire by mailing a second (but not a third) questionnaire. If a questionnaire which is returned to the foundation indicates that certain information was unavailable to the person completing the questionnaire, the foundation seeks that information directly. For example, if a disqualified person indicates that he could not find out whether a corporation described in section 4946(a)(1)(E) had holdings in the enterprise listed in the questionnaire, the foundation seeks to obtain this information directly from the corporation by mailing it a questionnaire. In such a case, F may be found not to have reason to know of the acquisition of holdings by a disqualified person.

(vi) *Holdings acquired other than by purchase.*—See section 4943(c)(6) and §53.4943-6 for rules relating to the acquisition of certain holdings other than by purchase by the foundation or a disqualified person.

(2) *Special rules.*—In applying subparagraph (1) of this paragraph, the tax imposed by section 4943(a)(1)—

(i) Shall be imposed on the last day of the private foundation's taxable year, but

(ii) The amount of such tax and the value of the excess business holdings subject to such tax shall be determined with respect to the foundation's holdings (based upon voting power, profits or beneficial interest, or value, whichever is applicable) in any business enterprise as of that day during the foundation's taxable year when the foundation's excess holdings in such enterprise were the greatest.

In applying subdivision (ii) of this subparagraph, if a foundation's excess business holdings in a business enterprise which constitute such foundation's greatest excess holdings in such enterprise for any taxable year are maintained for 2 or more days during such taxable year, the value of such excess holdings which is subject to tax under section 4943(a)(1) shall be the greatest value of such excess holdings in such enterprise as of any day on which such greatest excess holdings are maintained during such taxable year.

(3) *Examples.*—The provisions of this paragraph may be illustrated by the following examples:

*Example (1).* Y is a private foundation reporting on a calendar year basis. On January 1, 1973, Y has 20 shares of common stock in corporation N, of which five shares constitute excess business holdings. On June 1, 1973, Y disposes of such five shares; however, because of additional acquisitions of N common stock on such date by disqualified persons with respect to Y, the remaining 15 shares of N common stock held by Y now constitute excess business holdings. There are no further acquisitions or dispositions of N common stock during 1973 by Y or its disqualified persons. Although Y's greatest holdings in N during 1973 are held between January 1, 1973, and May 31, 1973, Y's greatest excess holdings in N during 1973 are held between June 1, 1973, and December 31, 1973. Therefore, the tax specified in section 4943(a)(1) shall be computed on the basis of the greatest value of such greatest excess holdings as of any day between June 1 and December 31, 1973.

*Example (2).* X is a private foundation reporting on a calendar year basis. On January 1, 1972, X has 100 shares of common stock in M corporation which are excess business holdings. On such date each share of M common stock has a fair market value of $100. On February 28, 1972, in an effort to dispose of such excess business holdings, X sells 70 shares of M common stock for $120 per share (the fair market value of each share on such date) to A, an individual who is not a disqualified person within the meaning of section 4946(a). The value of $120 per share is the highest fair market value between January 1 and February 28, 1972. X disposes of no more stock in M for the remainder of calendar year 1972. On December 31, 1972, the fair market value of each share of M common stock is $80. X calculates its tax on its excess business holdings in M for 1972 as follows:

| | |
|---|---|
| 100 shares of M common stock times $120 fair market value per share as of Feb. 28, 1972 | $12,000 |
| $12,000 multiplied by rate of tax (percent) . . . | 5 |
| Amount of tax on X foundation's excess business holdings for 1972 . . . . . . . . . . . . . . . . | $ 600 |

*Example (3).* Assume the same facts as in Example (2) except that the sale of X to A occurs on January 7, 1973, when the fair market value of each share of M corporation common stock equals $70. A value of $100 per share is the highest fair market value of the M common stock between January 1 and January 7, 1973. On May 9, 1973, X for the first time has excess business holdings in N corporation in the form of 200 shares of N common stock. The value per share of N common stock on May 9, 1973, equals $200. X makes no disposition of the N common stock during 1973, and the value of each share of N common stock as of December 31, 1973 equals $250 (the highest value of N common stock during 1973). X calculates its tax on its excess business holdings in both M and N for 1973 as follows:

| | |
|---|---|
| 100 shares of M common stock times $100 fair market value per share . . . . . . . . . . . | $10,000 |
| 200 shares of N common stock times $250 fair market value per share . . . . . . . . . . . . | $50,000 |
| Total . . . . . . . . . . . . . . . . . . . . . | $60,000 |

| | |
|---|---|
| $60,000 multiplied by rate of tax (percent) . . . . | 5 |
| Amount of tax on X foundation's excess business holdings for 1973 . . . . . . . . . . . . . . . . . | $3,000 |

(b) *Additional tax.*—In any case in which the initial tax is imposed under section 4943(a) with respect to the holdings of a private foundation in any business enterprise, if, at the close of the taxable period (as defined in section 4943(d)(2) and §53.4943-9) with respect to such holdings the foundation still has excess business holdings in such enterprise, there is imposed a tax under section 4943(b) equal to 200 percent of the value of such excess holdings as of the last day of the taxable period. [Reg. §53.4943-2.]

□ [T.D. 7496, 7-5-77. *Amended by T.D. 8084, 5-1-86.*]

**[Reg. §53.4943-3]**

**§53.4943-3. Determination of excess business holdings.**—(a) *Excess business holdings.*—(1) *In general.*—For purposes of section 4943, the term "excess business holdings" means, with respect to the holdings of any private foundation in any business enterprise (as described in section 4943(d)(4)), the amount of stock or other interest in the enterprise which, except as provided in §53.4943-2(a)(1), the foundation, or a disqualified person, would have to dispose of, or cause the disposition of, to a person other than a disqualified person (as defined in section 4946(a)) in order for the remaining holdings of the foundation in such enterprise to be permitted holdings (as defined in paragraphs (b) and (c) of this section). If a private foundation is required by section 4943 and the regulations thereunder to dispose of certain shares of a class of stock in a particular period of time and other shares of the same class of stock in a shorter period of time, any stock disposed of shall be charged first against those dispositions which must be made in such shorter period.

(2) *Example.*—The provisions of this paragraph may be illustrated by the following example:

*Example.* Corporation X has outstanding 100 shares of voting stock, with each share entitling the holder thereof to one vote. F, a private foundation, possesses 20 shares of X voting stock representing 20 percent of the voting power in X. Assume that the permitted holdings of F in X under paragraph (b)(1) of this section are 11 percent of the voting stock in X. F, therefore, possesses voting stock in X representing a percentage of voting stock in excess of the percentage permitted by such paragraph. Such excess percentage is 9 percent of the voting stock in X, determined by subtracting the percentage of voting stock representing the permitted holdings of F in X (i.e., 11 percent) from the percentage of voting stock held by F in X (i.e., 20 percent) (20%−11%=9%). The excess business holdings of F in X are an amount of voting stock representing such excess percentage, or 9 shares of X voting stock (9 percent of 100).

(b) *Permitted holdings in an incorporated business enterprise.*—(1) *In general.*—(i) *Permitted holdings defined.*—Except as otherwise provided in section 4943(c)(2) and (4), the permitted holdings of any private foundation in an incorporated business enterprise (including a real estate investment trust, as defined in section 856) are—

(A) 20 percent of the voting stock in such enterprise reduced (but not below zero) by

(B) The percentage of voting stock in such enterprise actually or constructively owned by all disqualified persons.

(ii) *Voting stock.*—For purposes of this section, the percentage of voting stock held by any person in a corporation is normally determined by reference to the power of stock to vote for the election of directors, with treasury stock and stock which is authorized but unissued being disregarded. Thus, for example, if a private foundation holds 20 percent of the shares of one class of stock in a corporation, which class is entitled to elect three directors, and such foundation holds no stock in the other class of stock, which is entitled to elect five directors, such foundation shall be treated as holding 7.5 percent of the voting stock because the class of stock it holds has 37.5 percent of such voting power, by reason of being able to elect three of the eight directors, and the foundation holds one-fifth of the shares of such class (20 percent of 37.5 percent is 7.5 percent). The fact that extraordinary corporate action (*e.g.*, charter or by-law amendments) by a corporation may require the favorable vote of more than a majority of the directors, or of the outstanding voting stock, of such corporation shall not alter the determination of voting power of stock in such corporation in accordance with the two preceding sentences.

(2) *Nonvoting stock as permitted holdings.*—(i) *In general.*—In addition to those holdings permitted by paragraph (b)(1) of this section, the permitted holdings of a private foundation in an incorporated business enterprise shall include any share of nonvoting stock in such enterprise held by the foundation in any case in which all disqualified persons hold, actually or constructively, no more than 20 percent (35 percent where third persons have effective control as defined in paragraph (b)(3)(ii) of this section) of the voting stock in

such enterprise. All equity interests which do not have voting power attributable to them shall, for purposes of section 4943, be classified as nonvoting stock. For this purpose, evidences of indebtedness (including convertible indebtedness), and warrants and other options or rights to acquire stock shall not be considered equity interests.

(ii) *Stock with contingent voting rights and convertible nonvoting stock.*—Stock carrying voting rights which will vest only when conditions, the occurrence of which are indeterminate, have been met, such as preferred stock which gains such voting rights only if no dividends are paid thereon, will be treated as nonvoting stock until the conditions have occurred which cause the voting rights to vest. When such rights vest, the stock will be treated as voting stock that was acquired other than by purchase, but only if the private foundation or disqualified persons had no control over whether the conditions would occur. Similarly, nonvoting stock which may be converted into voting stock will not be treated as voting stock until such conversion occurs. For special rules where stock is acquired other than by purchase, see section 4943(c)(6) and the regulations thereunder.

(iii) *Example.*—The provisions of this paragraph (2) may be illustrated by the following example:

*Example.* Assume that F, a private foundation, holds 10 percent of the single class of voting stock of corporation X, and owns 20 shares of nonvoting stock in X. Assume further that A and B, the only disqualified persons with respect to F, hold 10 percent of the voting stock of X. Under the provisions of paragraph (b)(1) of this section, the 10 percent of X voting stock held by F will be classified as permitted holdings of F in X since 20 percent less the percentage of voting stock held by A and B in X is 10 percent. In addition, under the provisions of this (2), the 20 shares of X nonvoting stock will qualify as permitted holdings of F in X since the percentage of voting stock held by A and B in X is no greater than 20 percent.

(3) *Thirty-five-percent rule where third person has effective control of enterprise.*—(i) *In general.*—Except as provided in section 4943(c)(4), paragraph (b)(1) of this section shall be applied by substituting 35 percent for 20 percent if—

(A) The private foundation and all disqualified persons together do not hold, actually or constructively, more than 35 percent of the voting stock in the business enterprise, and

(B) The foundation establishes to the satisfaction of the Commissioner that effective control (as defined in paragraph (b)(3)(ii) of this section) of the business enterprise is in one or more persons (other than the foundation itself) who are not disqualified persons.

(ii) *"Effective control" defined.*—For purposes of this subparagraph, the term "effective control" means the possession, directly or indirectly, of the power to direct or cause the direction of the management and policies of a business enterprise, whether through the ownership of voting stock, the use of voting trusts, or contractual arrangements, or otherwise. It is the reality of control which is decisive and not its form or the means by which it is exercisable. Thus, where a minority interest held by individuals who are not disqualified persons has historically elected the majority of a corporation's directors, effective control is in the hands of those individuals.

(4) *Two percent de minimis rule.*—(i) *In general.*—Under section 4943(c)(2)(C), a private foundation is not treated as having excess business holdings in any incorporated business enterprise in which it (together with all other private foundations (including trusts described in section 4947(a)(2)) which are described in section 4946(a)(1)(H)) actually or constructively owns not more than 2 percent of the voting stock and not more than 2 percent in value of all outstanding shares of all classes of stock. If, however, the private foundation, together with all other private foundations which are described in section 4946(a)(1)(H), actually or constructively owns more than 2 percent of either the voting stock or the value of the outstanding shares of all classes of stock in any incorporated business enterprise, all the stock in such business enterprise classified as excess business holding under section 4943 is treated as excess business holdings. For purposes of this paragraph, any stock owned by a private foundation which is treated as held by a disqualified person under section 4943(c)(4)(B), (5), or (6) shall be treated as actually owned by the private foundation. See paragraph (b)(1) of §53.4941(d)-4 for the determination of excess business holdings without regard to section 4943(c)(2)(C) for purposes of applying section 101(C)(2)(B) of the Tax Reform Act of 1969 (83 Stat. 533).

(ii) *Examples.*—The provisions of this subparagraph may be illustrated by the following examples:

*Example (1).* F, a private foundation, owns 1 percent of the single class of voting stock and 1 percent in value of all the outstanding shares of all classes of stock in X corporation. No other private

foundation described in section 4946(a)(1)(H) owns any stock in X. All of the stock owned by F in X would be excess business holdings under section 4943(c)(1) if section 4943(c)(2)(C) were inapplicable. F owns no other shares of stock in X. Since F owns no more than 2 percent of the voting stock and no more than 2 percent in value of all outstanding shares of all classes of stock in X, under section 4943(c)(2)(C) none of the stock in X owned by F is treated as excess business holdings.

*Example (2).* Assume the facts as stated in Example (1), except that F and T, a controlled private foundation under section 4946(a)(1)(H), together own 1 percent of all the voting stock and 1 percent in value of all the outstanding shares of all classes of stock in X. All of the stock in X owned by F and T would be excess business holdings under section 4943(c)(1) if section 4943(c)(2)(C) were inapplicable. Since F and T together own no more than 2 percent of the voting stock and no more than 2 percent in value of all outstanding shares of all classes of stock in X, under section 4943(c)(2)(C) none of the stock in X owned by either F or T is treated as excess business holdings.

*Example (3).* Assume the facts as stated in Example (1), except that F owns 3 percent of the voting stock in X, 2 percent of which is treated as held by P, a disqualified person of F, under section 4943(c)(4)(B). Under subdivision (i) of this subparagraph, the 2 percent of the stock in X owned by F which is treated as held by P under section 4943(c)(4)(B) is treated as actually owned by F for purposes of section 4943(c)(2)(C). Consequently, all of the X stock owned by F is treated as excess business holdings under section 4943(c)(2)(C). However, only 1 percent of the stock in X is subject to tax under section 4943(a), since the other 2 percent is treated as owned by a disqualified person under section 4943(c)(4)(B) for purposes of determining the tax upon F under section 4943(a).

(c) *Permitted holdings in an unincorporated business enterprise.*—(1) *In general.*—The permitted holdings of a private foundation in any business enterprise which is not incorporated shall, subject to the provisions of subparagraphs (2), (3), and (4) of this paragraph, be determined under the principles of paragraph (b) of this section.

(2) *Partnership or joint venture.*—In the case of a partnership (including a limited partnership) or joint venture, the terms "profits interest" and "capital interest" shall be substituted for "voting stock" and "nonvoting stock," respectively, wherever those terms appear in paragraph (b) of this section. The interest in profits of such foundation (or such disqualified person) shall be determined in the same manner as its distributive share of partnership taxable income. See section 704(b) (relating to the determination of the distributive share by the income or loss ratio) and the regulations thereunder. In the absence of a provision in the partnership agreement, the capital interest of such foundation (or such disqualified person) in a partnership shall be determined on the basis of its interest in the assets of the partnership which would be distributable to such foundation (or such disqualified person) upon its withdrawal from the partnership, or upon liquidation of the partnership, whichever is the greater.

(3) *Sole proprietorship.*—For purposes of section 4943, a private foundation shall have no permitted holdings in a sole proprietorship. In the case of a transfer by a private foundation of a portion of a sole proprietorship, see paragraph (c)(2) of this section (relating to permitted holdings in partnerships). For the treatment of a private foundation's ownership of a sole proprietorship prior to May 26, 1969, see §53.4943-4.

(4) *Trusts and other unincorporated business enterprises.*—(i) *In general.*—In the case of any unincorporated business enterprise which is not described in paragraph (c)(2) or (3) of this section, the term "beneficial interest" shall be substituted for "voting stock" wherever the term appears in paragraph (b) of this section. Any and all references to nonvoting stock in paragraph (b) of this section shall be inapplicable with respect to any unincorporated business enterprise described in this subparagraph.

(ii) *Trusts.*—For purposes of section 4943, the beneficial interest of a private foundation or any disqualified person in a trust shall be the beneficial remainder interest of such foundation or person determined as provided in paragraph (b) of §53.4943-8.

(iii) *Other unincorporated business enterprises.*—For purposes of section 4943, the beneficial interest of a private foundation or any disqualified person in an unincorporated business enterprise (other than a trust or an enterprise described in paragraph (c)(2) or (3) of this section) includes any right to receive a portion of distributions of profits of such enterprise, and, if the portion of distributions is not fixed by an agreement among the participants, any right to receive a portion of the assets (if any) upon liquidation of the enterprise, except as a creditor or employee. For purposes of this subparagraph, a right to receive distributions of profits includes a right to receive any amount from such profits (other than as a creditor or employee), whether as a sum certain or as a portion of profits realized by the enterprise. Where there is no agreement fixing the rights of the participants in such enterprise, the interest of such foundation (or such disqualified person) in such enterprise shall be determined by dividing the amount of all equity investments or contributions to the capital of the enterprise made or obligated to be made by such foundation (or such disqualified person) by the amount of all equity investments or contributions to capital made or obligated to be made by all participants in the enterprise.

(i) Determination of voting stock percentages:

| | |
|---|---|
| (a) Total number of outstanding votes in X | 100 |
| (b) Total number of votes in X held by F | 30 |
| (c) Total number of votes in X held by A and B | 10 |
| (d) Percentage of voting stock in X held by F (item (b) divided by item (a)) (percent) | 30 |
| (e) Percentage of voting stock in X held by A and B (item (c) divided by item (a)) (percent) | 10 |

(ii) Determination of permitted holdings of voting stock:

| | |
|---|---|
| (a) Percentage of voting stock in X held by A and B (percent) | 10 |
| (b) Permitted holdings of voting stock by F in X (20% less item (a)) (percent) | 10 |

(iii) Determination of excess business holdings:

| | |
|---|---|
| (a) Percentage of voting stock in X held by F (percent) | 30 |
| (b) Permitted holdings of voting stock by F in X (percent) | 10 |
| (c) Item (a) less item (b) (percent) | 20 |
| (d) Excess business holdings of F in X (i.e., an amount of X voting stock representing a percentage of voting stock equivalent to that in item (c)) (shares) | 20 |

*Example (2).* F, a private foundation, is a partner in P partnership. In addition, A and B, the only disqualified persons with respect to F, are partners in P. The partnership agreement of P contains no provisions regarding the sharing of profits by, and the respective capital interests of, the partners.

(i) Assume that, under section 704(b), F's distributive share of P taxable income is determined to be 20 percent. In addition, assume that under such section, A and B are determined to have a 4-percent distributive share each of P taxable income. Accordingly, F holds a 20-percent profits interest in P, and A and B hold an 8-percent profits interest in P. Assuming that the provisions of section 4943(c)(2)(B) do not apply, the permitted holdings of F in P are 12 percent of the profits interest in P, determined by subtracting the percentage of the profits interest held by A and B in P (i.e., 8 percent) from 20 percent. (20 percent – 8 percent = 12 percent.) F, therefore, holds a percentage of the profits interest in P in excess of the percentage permitted by § 53.4943-3(b)(1). The excess business holdings of F in P are a percentage of the profits interest in P equivalent to such excess percentage, or 8 percent of the profits interest in P, determined by subtracting the permitted holdings of F in P (i.e., 12 percent) from the percentage of the profits interest held by F in P (i.e., 20 percent) (20 percent – 12 percent = 8 percent).

(ii) Assume that, under the partnership agreement, F would be entitled to a distribution of 20 percent of P's assets upon F's withdrawal from P and to a distribution of 30 percent of P's assets upon the liquidation of P. F, therefore, holds a 30-percent capital interest in P; that is, the greater of the percentage of the assets of P distributable to F upon F's withdrawal from P, or the percentage of such assets distributable to F upon the liquidation of P. Since the percentage of the profits interest held by A and B in P is less than 20 percent, such 30-percent capital interest will be included in the permitted holdings of F in P. [Reg. § 53.4943-3.]

☐ [*T.D. 7496, 7-5-77.*]

**[Reg. § 53.4943-4]**

**§ 53.4943-4. Present holdings.**—(a) *Introduction.*—(1) *Section 4943(c)(4) in general.*—(i) Paragraph(4) of section 4943(c) prescribes transition rules for a private foundation which, but for such paragraph, would have excess business holdings on May 26, 1969. Section 4943(c)(4) provides such a foundation with protection from the initial tax on excess business holdings in two ways. First, the entire interest of such a foundation in any business enterprise in which such a foundation, but for section 4943(c)(4), would have had excess business holdings on May 26, 1969, is treated under section 4943(c)(4)(B) as held by disqualified persons for a certain period of time (the "first phase"). The effect of such treatment is to prevent a private foundation from being subject to the initial tax with respect to its May 26, 1969, interest during the first phase holding period and also to prevent the foundation from purchasing any additional business holdings in such business enterprise during such period (unless the combined holdings of the foundation and all disqualified persons fall below the 20 percent (or 35 percent, if applicable) figure prescribed by section 4943(c)(2)). Second, section 4943(c)(4)(A)(i) initially increases the percentage of permitted holdings of such a foundation to a percentage equal to the difference between—

(A) The percentage of combined holdings of the foundation and all disqualified persons in such business enterprise on May 26, 1969 (subject to a 50 percent maximum), and

(B) The percentage of holdings of all disqualified persons.

(d) *Examples.*—The provisions of this section may be illustrated by the following examples:

*Example (1).* Corporation X has outstanding 100 shares of voting stock, with each share entitling the holder thereof to one vote. Assume that F, a private foundation, possesses 30 shares of X voting stock, and that A and B, the only disqualified persons with respect to F, together own 10 shares of X voting stock. The excess business holdings of F in X are 20 shares of X voting stock, determined as follows:

The percentage referred to in paragraph (a)(1)(i)(A) of this section is referred to in this section as the "substituted level". This "substituted level" is then reduced by the "downward ratchet rule" prescribed by section 4943(c)(4)(A)(ii) and paragraph (d)(3) of this section for certain dispositions by such foundation or by disqualified persons. The primary purpose of the substituted level is to indicate what the permitted holdings in such business enterprise will be immediately after the expiration of the first phase holding period. Thereafter, the permitted holdings of a private foundation itself are further limited to a maximum 25 percent interest in such business enterprise by section 4943(c)(4)(D) as soon as the combined holdings of all disqualified persons in such business enterprise exceed 2 percent (of the voting stock). If the combined holdings of all disqualified persons at no time exceed 2 percent (of the voting stock) during the 15 years following the first phase (the "second phase"), then the substituted level is reduced to a 35 percent maximum after the second phase.

(ii) Paragraph (a)(1)(i) of this section may be illustrated by the following example:

*Example.* On May 26, 1969, private foundation P held a 5 percent interest in corporation X (voting stock and value). On such date disqualified persons held a 16 percent interest in X (voting stock and value). Assume that except for section 4943(c)(4), P would have had a 1 percent interest in X which would have constituted excess business holdings. Therefore, section 4943(c)(4)(B) applies and P's 5 percent interest in X is treated as held by a disqualified person during the 10-year period beginning May 26, 1969. Since the entire 21 percent held by P and disqualified persons is now treated as held by disqualified persons, P's substituted level is 21 percent and its permitted holdings are zero (21% – 21%). However, P has no excess business holdings in X, because during the 10-year period P is not treated as holding such interest. The only change in the interest in X occurs on January 2, 1972, when P disposes of 2 percent of its interest in X to A, an unrelated person. Since the interest held by P and all disqualified persons (21% – 2% = 19%) has decreased below 20 percent, P's substituted level is reduced to 20 percent and its permitted holdings are 1 percent (20% – 19%) on such date. Therefore, if the other interests in X do not change, P will not have excess business holdings if P purchases no more than an additional 1 percent interest in X.

(2) *Interaction of provisions of section 4943(c)(4), (5), and (6).*—During the first phase, a private foundation may acquire additional interests in a business enterprise, other than by purchase, which are entitled to be treated as held by disqualified persons for varying holding periods under section 4943(c)(5) or (6) (relating respectively to certain holdings acquired pursuant to the terms of a trust or will in effect on May 26, 1969, and to the 5-year period to dispose of certain gifts, bequests, etc.). In any case, holdings which the private foundation disposes of shall be charged first against those holdings which it must dispose of in the shortest period in order to avoid the initial tax thereon. Further, acquisitions of a private foundation under a pre-May 27, 1969, will or trust described in section 4943(c)(5) are treated in a manner similar to the treatment of interests actually held by a private foundation on May 26, 1969. See §§ 53.4943-5 and 53.4943-6.

(b) *Present holdings in general.*—(1) Section 4943(c)(4)(B) provides that any interest in a business enterprise held by a private foundation on May 26, 1969, if the foundation on such date has excess business holdings (determined without regard to section 4943(c)(4)), shall (while held by the foundation) be treated as held by a disqualified person during a first phase. Therefore, no interest of a private foundation shall be treated as held by a disqualified person under section 4943(c)(4)(B) and this section unless:

(i) The private foundation was an entity (not including a revocable trust) in existence on May 26, 1969, even though it was not then treated as a private foundation under section 509 or section 4947;

(ii) Such interest was actually or constructively owned by such entity on such date; and

(iii) Without regard to section 4943(c)(4) such entity had on such date an interest (considered in connection with the interests actually or constructively owned by all disqualified persons with respect to such entity on that date in the same business enterprise, determined as if the entity were then a private foundation) which exceeded the permitted holdings prescribed by section 4943(c)(2) or (3).

(See, however, section 4943(c)(5) and § 53.4943-5 for similar treatment for certain interests acquired by a private foundation under the terms of a trust or a will which were in effect on May 26, 1969.) If a private foundation owns an interest described by section 4943(c)(4)(B), then the length of the first phrase for such an interest is prescribed by paragraph (c) of this section and shall not be affected by any interest acquired by the private foundation or any disqualified person in such business enterprise after May 26, 1969. In addition, the amount of permitted holdings in such business enterprise is prescribed by paragraph (d) of this section. An interest constructively held by a private foundation (or a disqualified person) on May 26, 1969, shall not cease to be an interest to which section 4943(c)(4) applies merely because it is later distributed to such foundation (or to such disqualified person). Nor shall an interest directly held by a private foundation (or disqualified person) on May 26, 1969, cease to be treated as an interest to which section 4943(c)(4) applies to the extent it remains actually or constructively held by such foundation (or such disqualified person) upon transfer of such interest, such as upon the incorporation of a sole proprietorship.

(2) The provisions of this paragraph may be illustrated by the following example:

*Example.* A, a nonprofit research organization described in section 501(c)(3), was organized in 1966. On May 26, 1969, A held 50 percent of the stock of corporation B. For its taxable years 1970, 1971, and 1972, A is classified as an organization described in section 509(a)(2). However, for 1973 and subsequent years, A fails to satisfy the gross investment income limitation of section 509(a)(2)(B), and is thus classified as a private foundation. In such a case, section 4943(c)(4) applies, and a disqualified person shall be treated as holding A's stock in B during a first phase that begins on May 26, 1969.

(c) *First phase holding periods.*—(1) *In general.*—If, on May 26, 1969, a private foundation has excess business holdings in any business enterprise (determined with regard to the 20 or 35 percent permitted holdings of section 4943(c)(2)), then all interests which such foundation holds, actually or constructively, in such enterprise on May 26, 1969, shall (while held by such foundation) be deemed held by a disqualified person during the following periods:

(i) The 20-year period beginning on May 26, 1969, if the private foundation holds, actually or constructively, more than 95 percent of the voting stock (or more than a 95 percent profits or beneficial interest in the case of an unincorporated enterprise) in such enterprise on such date;

(ii) Except as provided in paragraph (c)(1)(i) of this section, the 15-year period beginning on May 26, 1969, if the private foundation and all disqualified persons hold, actually or constructively on such date, more than 75 percent of the voting stock (or more than a 75 percent profits or beneficial interest in the case of any unincorporated enterprise) or 75 percent of the value of all outstanding shares of all classes of stock in such enterprise (or more than a 75 percent profits and capital interest in the case of a partnership or joint venture); or

(iii) The 10-year period beginning on May 26, 1969, in any case not described in paragraph (c)(1)(i) or (ii) of this section. The 20-year, 15-year, or 10-year period described in this subdivision (whichever applies) shall, for purposes of section 4943 and this section, be known as the "first phase".

(2) *Sole proprietorships.*—The 20-year period described in paragraph (c)(1) of this section shall apply with respect to any interest which a private foundation holds in a sole proprietorship on May 26, 1969. See paragraph (b) of this section for the effect of converting such an enterprise to a corporate, partnership, or other form.

(3) *Suspension of first-phase periods.*—The 20-year, 15-year, or 10-year period described in paragraph (c)(1) of this section shall be suspended during the pendency of any judicial proceeding which is brought and diligently litigated by the private foundation and which is necessary to reform, or to excuse the foundation from compliance

with, its governing instrument or any other instrument (as in effect on May 26, 1969) in order to allow disposition of any excess business holdings held by the foundation on May 26, 1969.

(4) *Election to shorten the period during which certain holdings of private foundations are treated as held by disqualified persons.*—If, on May 26, 1969, the combined holdings of a private foundation and all disqualified persons in any one business enterprise are such as to make applicable the 15-year period referred to in paragraph (c)(1)(ii) of this section, and if, on such date, the foundation's holdings do not exceed 95 percent of the voting stock in such enterprise, then such 15-year period is shortened to the 10-year period referred to in paragraph (c)(1)(iii), if at any time before January 1, 1971, one or more individuals—

(i) Who are substantial contributors (as described in section 507(d)(2)), or members of the family within the meaning of section 4946(d) of one or more substantial contributors, to such private foundation, and

(ii) Who on May 26, 1969, held in the aggregate more than 15 percent of the voting stock in the enterprise,
made an election in the manner described in 26 CFR 143.6 (rev. as of Apr. 1, 1974).

(5) *Examples.*—The provisions of this paragraph (c) may be illustrated by the following examples:

*Example (1).* Assume that F, a private foundation, owns, on May 26, 1969, 50 shares of voting stock in corporation X representing 50 percent of the voting power in X and 25 percent of the value of all outstanding shares of all classes of stock in X. Assume further that A and B, the only disqualified persons with respect to F, own five shares each of voting stock in X on such date. The 10 shares of voting stock in X owned by A and B together represent 10 percent of the voting power in X and 5 percent of the value of all outstanding shares of all classes of stock in X. Under the provisions of § 53.4943-3, the excess business holdings of F in X (determined without regard to section 4943(c)(4)) as of such date are, therefore, 40 percent of X voting stock. Accordingly, since the combined holdings of F, A, and B in X are, on such date, less than 75 percent of the voting stock in X and less than 75 percent of the value of all outstanding shares of all classes of stock in X, under the provisions of section 4943(c)(4)(B)(iii), all holdings of F in X (i.e., 50 percent of X voting stock) will be treated as held by a disqualified person through May 25, 1979.

*Example (2).* Assume the facts as stated in Example (1), except that F, on December 15, 1969, purchases an additional 10 shares of voting stock in X respresenting 10 percent of X voting power. Assume, further, that there were no other transactions in the stock in X during 1969. While the 50 percent of X voting stock held by F on May 26, 1969, will be deemed held by a disqualified person through May 25, 1979, the additional 10 shares of X voting stock acquired by purchase by F on December 15, 1969, will not be deemed to be so held. Accordingly, since, under the provisions of § 53.4943-3, such 10 shares represent excess business holding of F in X, such 10 shares will be subject to the imposition of tax under the provisions of section 4943(a).

*Example (3).* Assume the facts as stated in Example (1), except that F, on December 15, 1971, acquires an additional 10 shares of voting stock in X (representing 10 percent of X voting power) under the terms of a will which was executed before May 26, 1969, to which section 4943(c)(5) applies. While the 50 percent of X voting stock held by F on May 26, 1969, will be deemed held by a disqualified person through May 25, 1979, the additional 10 percent of X voting stock acquired by F on December 15, 1971, will, under the provisions of section 4943(c)(5), be deemed held by a disqualified person through December 14, 1981. See § 53.4943-5.

*Example (4).* Assume that F, a private foundation, owns on May 26, 1969, 50 shares of voting stock in corporation Y representing 50 percent of the voting power in Y. Assume further that C and D, the only disqualified persons with respect to F, own on such date 15 shares each of Y voting stock and that the 30 shares of Y voting stock owned by C and D together represent 30 percent of the voting power in Y. Under the provisions of § 53.4943-3 the excess business holdings of F in Y (determined without regard to section 4943(c)(4)) as of such date are, therefore, 50 percent of Y voting stock. Accordingly, since the combined holdings of F, C, and D in Y represent, on such date, more than 75 percent of the voting stock in Y, under the provisions of section 4943(c)(4)(B)(ii), all holdings of F in Y, (i.e., 50 percent of Y voting stock) will be treated as held by a disqualified person through May 25, 1984.

*Example (5).* M, a private foundation, owns on May 26, 1969, sole proprietorship S. Since, under the provisions of § 53.5954-3, M's ownership of S constitutes excess business holdings (determined without regard to section 4943(c)(4)) as of May 26, 1969, and since M's interest in S is greater than 95 percent on such date, under the provisions of this paragraph a disqualified person will be treated as the owner of S for the 20-year period beginning on such date. If S is later incorporated, that percentage of the interest in S retained by M, even though less than a 95-percent interest, shall continue to be treated as held by a disqualified person through May 25, 1989.

*Example (6).* A and B, individuals, together own on May 26, 1969, 40 shares of voting stock in corporation X representing 40 percent of the voting power in X and 20 percent of the value of all outstanding shares of all classes of stock in X. A and B are both disqualified persons with respect to F, a private foundation, which owns no stock in X on May 26, 1969. On January 1, 1973, A and B donate the 40 shares of X voting stock held by them to F. Since F had no excess business holdings on May 26, 1969, section 4943(c)(4) does not apply. See however, section 4943(c)(6) and § 53.4943-6.

*Example (7).* Assume the facts as stated in Example (6), except that F, on May 26, 1969, owns 50 shares of voting stock in X, representing 50 percent of the voting power in X and 25 percent of the value of all outstanding shares of all classes of stock in X. Under the provisions of this paragraph, the 50 shares of X voting stock held by F on May 26, 1969 shall be treated in accordance with the provisions of section 4943(c)(4), while the 40 shares of X voting stock acquired by F on January 1, 1973 shall be treated in accordance with the provisions of section 4943(c)(6). See § 53.4943-6.

(d) *Permitted holdings under section 4943(c)(4).*—(1) *In general.*—The permitted holdings of a private foundation to which section 4943(c)(4) applies in a business enterprise shall be as follows:

(i) The excess of the substituted combined voting level over the disqualified person voting level, and separately,

(ii) The excess of the substituted combined value level over the disqualified person value level.

(2) *Definitions.*—For purposes of paragraph (d) of this section—

(i) The term "disqualified person voting level" on any given date means the percentage of voting stock held by all disqualified persons together on such date (including stock deemed held by such a person by reason of section 4943(c)(4), (5), or (6)).

(ii) The term "disqualified person value level" on any given date means the percentage of the total value of all outstanding shares of all classes of stock in a business enterprise held by all disqualified persons together on such date (including stock deemed held by such a person by reason of section 4943(c)(4), (5), or (6)).

(iii) The term "foundation voting level" prior to the second phase is equal to zero. After the first phase, such term on any given date means the lowest percentage of voting stock held by a private foundation (without regard to section 4943(c)(4)(B)) in a business enterprise on May 26, 1969, and at all times thereafter up to such date. See section 4943(c)(5) and § 53.4943-5 for the effect of interests acquired pursuant to the terms of certain wills or trusts in effect on May 26, 1969.

(iv) The term "foundation value level" prior to the second phase is equal to zero. After the first phase, such term on any given date means the lowest percentage of the total value of all outstanding shares of all classes of stock held by a private foundation (without regard to section 4943(c)(4)(B)) in a business enterprise on May 26, 1969, and at all times thereafter up to such date. See section 4943(c)(5) and § 53.4943-5 for the effect of interests acquired pursuant to the terms of certain wills or trusts in effect on May 26, 1969.

(v) The term "substituted combined voting level" means the lowest percentage to which the sum of the foundation voting level plus the disqualified person voting level has been reduced since May 26, 1969, by paragraph (d)(4) of this section (the "downward ratchet rule"), subject to the following modifications:

(A) In no event shall such substituted level exceed 50 percent; and

(B) Such substituted level shall be increased (but not above 50 percent) in accordance with section 4943(c)(5) and § 53.4943-5 for certain interests acquired by such foundation pursuant to the terms of a will or trust in effect on May 26, 1969.

(vi) The term "substituted combined value level" means the lowest percentage to which the sum of the foundation value level plus the disqualified person value level has been reduced since May 26, 1969, by paragraph (d)(4) of this section (the "downward ratchet rule"), subject to the following modifications:

(A) In no event shall such substituted level exceed 50 percent; and

(B) Such substituted level shall be increased (but not above 50 percent) in accordance with section 4943(c)(5) and § 53.4943-5 for certain interests acquired by such foundation pursuant to the terms of a will or trust in effect on May 26, 1969.

(vii) In the case of an interest in a partnership or joint venture, definitions (i) through (iv) of this subparagraph shall be applied by substituting "profit interests" for "voting stock" and "all partnership interests" for "all outstanding shares of all classes of stock."

(viii) In the case of an interest in a business enterprise other than a corporation, partnership or joint venture, definitions (i)

through (iv) of this subparagraph shall be applied by substituting "beneficial remainder interests" for "voting stock" and "all beneficial remainder interests" for "all outstanding shares of all classes of stock."

(ix) Each level defined in paragraph (d)(2)(iii), (iv), (v), and (vi) as of any date shall be carried over to the subsequent date subject to any adjustments prescribed for such level.

(3) *Permitted holdings—First phase.*—Since during the first phase the substituted combined voting level generally does not exceed the disqualified person voting level, and the substituted combined value level generally does not exceed the disqualified person value level, the permitted holdings during the first phase are generally equal to zero. The permitted holdings during the first phase exceed zero only where the 20 percent (or 35 percent) limitation on the downward ratchet rule contained in paragraph (d)(4)(ii)(B) of this section applies.

(4) *Downward ratchet rule.*—(i) *In general.*—Except as provided in paragraph (d)(4)(ii) of this section and section 4943(c)(5)—

(A) *Scope of rule.*—In general, when the percentage of the holdings in a business enterprise held by a private foundation and all disqualified persons together to which section 4943(c)(4) applies decreases, or when the percentage of the holdings of the private foundation alone in such business enterprise decreases, such holdings may not be increased (except as provided under section 4943(c)(5) or (6)). This so-called "downward ratchet rule" is designed to prevent the private foundation from purchasing additional holdings in the business enterprise until the substituted combined voting level is reduced to the 20-percent (or 35 percent) figure prescribed by section 4943(c)(2).

(B) *Levels affected.*—Under the downward ratchet rule any decrease after May 26, 1969, in the percentage of holdings comprising either the substituted combined voting level, the substituted combined value level, the foundation voting level or the foundation value level shall cause the respective level to be decreased to such decreased percentage for purposes of determining the foundation's permitted holdings.

(C) *Implementation of reductions.*—Thus, if at any time the sum of the foundation voting level and the disqualified person voting level is less than the immediately preceding substituted combined voting level, the substituted level shall be decreased so that it equals such sum. For example, if on May 26, 1969, a foundation and all disqualified persons together have holdings in a business enterprise equal to 50 percent, on such date the substituted combined voting level and the disqualified person voting level equal 50 percent (since such holdings of the foundation are treated as held by a disqualified person). If the private foundation or a disqualified person on May 27, 1969, sold 2 percent of such holdings to a nondisqualified person, the disqualified person voting level would be decreased to 48 percent (50% – 2%), causing the substituted combined voting level to be decreased to 48 percent. As a further example, assume that on May 26, 1969, a foundation and all disqualified persons together have holdings in a business enterprise equal to 50 percent, and when the first phase expires on May 26, 1979, the substituted combined voting level is still 50 percent, the foundation voting level is 10 percent, and the disqualified person voting level is 40 percent. If a disqualified person thereafter sells 2 percent to a nondisqualified person so that the sum of the disqualified person voting level (40% – 2% = 38%) and the foundation voting level (10%) equals 48 percent (38% + 10%), then the substituted combined voting level is decreased to 48 percent. Similarly, if at any time the sum of the foundation value level and the disqualified person value level is less than the immediately preceding substituted combined value level, the substituted combined value level shall be decreased so that it equals such sum.

(D) *Restrictions on increases in levels.*—In addition, none of the four levels referred to in paragraph (d)(4)(i)(B) of this section may be adjusted upward to reflect any increase in the holdings comprising such level, except as provided in section 4943(c)(5) and § 53.4943-5. As a result, any transfer of May 26, 1969, holdings from a disqualified person to a private foundation shall not increase the foundation voting level or the foundation value level (unless the transfer qualifies under section 4943(c)(5)), and thus may reduce the substituted combined value level (and, where appropriate, the substituted combined voting level). Thus, in the last preceding example, if the disqualified person, instead of selling the 2 percent interest to a nondisqualified person, had sold such interest to the foundation, the substituted combined voting level would still be reduced to 48 percent, since the disqualified person voting level would be reduced by 2 percent (to 38%) but the foundation voting level would not be increased by 2 percent (remaining at 10%). However, any transfer of May 26, 1969, holdings from a private foundation to a disqualified person under section 101(1)(2)(B) of the Tax Reform Act of 1969, shall reduce the foundation value level (and, where appropriate, the foundation voting level), but will not reduce the substituted combined value level or the substituted combined voting level. The disqualified person voting level and disqualified person value level are correspondingly increased, not being limited to interests held since May 26, 1969. In addition, a transfer of May 26, 1969, holdings from one disqualified person to another, for example, by bequest, shall not reduce the substituted combined voting level nor the substituted combined value level.

(ii) *Exceptions.*—(A) *One percent de minimis rule.*—If after May 26, 1969, there are one or more decreases in the holdings comprising any of the four levels referred to in paragraph (d)(4)(i)(B) of this section during such taxable year of a private foundation, and if such decreases are attributable to issuances of stock (or such issuances coupled with redemptions), then, unless the aggregate of such decreases equals or exceeds 1 percent, the determination of whether there is a decrease in such level for purposes of this paragraph (d)(4) shall be made only at the close of such taxable year. If, however, the aggregate of such decreases equals or exceeds 1 percent, such level shall be decreased at that time as if the previous sentence had never applied.

(B) *Twenty percent (or 35 percent) floor.*—In no event shall the downward ratchet rule contained in paragraph (d)(4)(i) of this section decrease the substituted combined voting level or the substituted combined value level below 20 percent, or, for purposes of section 4943(c)(2)(B), below 35 percent.

(iii) *Special rules.*—(A) *Change of foundation managers.*—In the case of a foundation manager (as defined in section 4946(b)) who on May 26, 1969, owns holdings in a business enterprise and who is replaced by another foundation manager, the decrease in the substituted combined voting or value levels shall be limited to the excess, if any, of the departing foundation manager's holdings over his successor's holdings.

(B) *Termination of private foundation status under section 507.*—If an organization gives the notification described in section 507(b)(1)(B)(ii) of the commencement of a 60-month termination period and fails to meet the requirements of section 509(a)(1), (2) or (3) for the entire period, then such organization will be treated as a private foundation during the entire 60-month period for purposes of this paragraph (d)(4) and section 4946(a)(1)(H). For example, X, a private foundation gives notification of the commencement of a 60-month termination commencing on January 1, 1972. X and Y, another private foundation, are effectively controlled by the same persons within the meaning of section 4946(a)(1)(H). X and Y hold 25 percent each of the voting stock of Z corporation on May 26, 1969, so that the substituted combined voting level for X or Y is 50 percent on such date. If X meets the requirements of section 509(a)(1), (2), or (3) for the entire 60-month period, section 4946(a)(1)(H) is inapplicable to X, and, under the downward ratchet rule, the substituted combined voting level for Y is decreased to 25 percent. On the other hand, if X meets the requirements of section 509(a)(2) for its taxable years 1972 and 1973, but fails to meet the requirements of section 509(a)(1), (2), or (3) in 1974, 1975, and 1976, then solely for purposes of section 4943(c)(4)(A)(ii) and this paragraph (d)(4), X will be treated as a disqualified person with respect to Y, and Y will be treated as a disqualified person with respect to X, for taxable years 1972 through 1976 pursuant to section 4946(a)(1)(H). Thus, for purposes of section 4943(c)(4)(A)(ii), the substituted combined voting level for X or Y will not be decreased by reason of the fact that X was attempting to terminate under section 507(b)(1)(B), and assuming no other transactions, such level will remain at 50 percent.

(iv) *Examples.*—The provisions of this paragraph (d)(4) may be illustrated by the following examples:

*Example (1).* F, a private foundation, owns on May 26, 1969, 50 shares of voting stock in corporation X respresenting 50 percent of the voting stock in X and 25 percent of the value of all outstanding shares of all classes of stock in X. A and B, the only disqualified persons with respect to F, together own, on such date, 2 shares of voting stock in X representing 2 percent of the voting stock in X and 1 percent of the value of all outstanding shares of all classes of stock in X. In addition, on such date, F owns 30 shares of nonvoting stock in X, representing 30 percent of the value of all outstanding shares of all classes of stock in X, and A and B together own 15 shares of nonvoting stock in X representing 15 percent of the value of all outstanding shares of all classes of stock in X. The provisions of section 4943(c)(4)(B)(iii) apply and during the 10-year period beginning on May 26, 1969, a disqualified person is deemed to hold all interests of F in X. Assume that on February 1, 1972, F sells to C, an unrelated individual, 12 shares of voting stock in X representing 12 percent of the voting stock in X and 6 percent of the value of all outstanding shares of all classes of stock in X.

(i) Beginning on May 26, 1969, the disqualified person voting level is 52 percent, the foundation voting level is zero, and the substituted combined voting level is 50 percent; the disqualified person value level is 71 percent, the foundation value level is zero, and the substituted combined value level is 50 percent.

(ii) Beginning on February 1, 1972, the disqualified person voting level is 40 percent (52% − 12%), the foundation voting level is zero, and the substituted combined voting level is 40 percent; the disqualified person value level is 65 percent (71% − 6%), the foundation value level is zero and the substituted combined value level is 50 percent.

*Example (2).* F, a private foundation on the calendar year basis, holds, on May 26, 1969, 30 percent of the voting stock in corporation Y. C and D, the only disqualified persons with respect to F, together hold, on such date, 10 percent of the voting stock in Y. The provisions of section 4943(c)(4)(B)(iii) apply with respect to F, and disqualified persons are deemed to hold all interests of F in Y for the 10-year period beginning on May 26, 1969, so that the substituted combined voting level as of such date is 40 percent. On February 1, 1973, a stock issuance by Y causes the combined holdings of voting power by F, C, and D in Y to decrease by 0.3 percent. On June 1, 1973, another such issuance causes such combined holdings to decrease by 0.5 percent. In September 1, 1973, an unrelated stock redemption by Y causes such combined holdings to increase by 0.4 percent. Under this paragraph the determination whether there is a decrease in the substituted combined voting level for purposes of the downward ratchet rule shall not be made before January 1, 1974, since the aggregate of the decreases occurring on February 1 and June 1 of 1973 is less than 1 percent (0.3% + 0.5%). Therefore, the substituted combined voting level as of January 1, 1974, is 39.6 percent (40% − [(0.3% + 0.5%) − 0.4%]).

*Example (3).* Assume the facts as stated in Example (2), except that, on October 1, 1973, a stock issuance by Y causes the combined holdings of voting power by F, C, and D in Y to decrease by 0.3 percent. Since the aggregate of the decreases occurring on February 1, June 1, and October 1, of 1973 exceeds 1 percent, the determination whether there is a decrease in the substituted combined voting level shall be made as of October 1, 1973. At that time the substituted combined voting level shall be reduced to 39.2 percent (40% − 0.3% − 0.5%), the lowest actual combined holdings during the period that the *de minimis* rule was in effect.

(5) *Permitted holdings—Second phase.*—(i) *In general.*—For purposes of section 4943 and this section, the term "second phase" means the 15-year period immediately following the first phase. Upon the expiration of the first phase with respect to an interest to which section 4943(c)(4) applies, such interest shall no longer be treated as held by a disqualified person under section 4943(c)(4)(B). During the second phase, the manner of determining the permitted holdings of a private foundation to which section 4943(c)(4) applies shall be the same as applicable to the first phase, except that a 25 percent maximum shall apply under certain conditions specified in paragraph (d)(5)(ii) of this section. For these purposes the substituted combined voting level and the substituted combined value level in effect for the foundation at the end of the first phase shall be carried over to the second phase. The substituted levels are carried over because although there is a decrease in the disqualified person levels (since holdings are no longer treated as held by disqualified persons under section 4943(c)(4)(B)), a corresponding increase in the foundation levels occurs. For example, if a private foundation on May 26, 1969, held 10 percent of the voting stock in a corporation and disqualified persons held 40 percent of the voting stock, both the disqualified person voting level and the substituted combined voting level equal 50 percent (10% + 40%). Assuming no transactions during the first phase, on May 26, 1979, the disqualified person voting level would be decreased to 40 percent (50% − 10%), but the foundation voting level would be increased to 10 percent so that the substituted combined voting level would remain at 50 percent. In addition, the downward ratchet rule of paragraph (d)(4) of this section shall continue to apply, to prevent the foundation and disqualified persons from purchasing any additional interest in the same enterprise until the substituted combined voting level decreases below 20 percent.

(ii) *25 percent maximum on foundation holdings.*—If, or as soon as, the disqualified person voting level exceeds 2 percent after the expiration of the first phase, the permitted holdings shall not thereafter exceed 25 percent of the voting stock or 25 percent of the value of all outstanding shares of all classes of stock, even though the holdings of the foundation and all disqualified persons combined do not exceed the substituted level. Solely for purposes of determining whether the 25 percent limitation of this subdivision (ii) applies, the disqualified person voting level shall not be treated as exceeding 2 percent solely as a result of the holdings of a private foundation which are treated as held by a disqualified person by reason of section 4943(c)(5) or (6). For example, where under the constructive ownership rules for trusts in §53.4943-8(b), a private foundation is deemed to own more than 2 percent of the voting stock of a business enterprise but such stock is treated as held by a disqualified person under section 4943(c)(5), the determination of the substituted percentage for permitted holdings in the second phase will be as if the foundation owned the stock held by the trust. Similarly, where a private foundation is the only remainder beneficiary of a trust that is a disqualified person under section 4946(a)(1)(H), the disqualified person voting level shall not be treated as exceeding 2 percent solely as a result of the holdings of such a trust.

(6) *Permitted holdings—Third phase.*—For purposes of section 4943 and this section, the term "third phase" means the entire period following the second phase. During the third phase the manner of determining the permitted holdings of a private foundation to which section 4943(c)(4) applies shall be the same as applicable to the second phase under paragraph (d)(5) of this section (including the carryover of levels from the earlier phase). However, if the 25 percent limit of paragraph (d)(5)(ii) of this section never applied during the second phase, the substituted combined voting level and the substituted combined value level each shall not exceed 35 percent during the third phase.

(7) *Examples.*—The provisions of this paragraph may be illustrated by the following examples:

*Example (1).* F, a private foundation, owns, on May 26, 1969, 30 shares of voting stock in corporation Z representing 30 percent of the voting power in Z and 15 percent of the value of all outstanding shares of all classes of stock in Z, and owns, on such date, 10 shares of nonvoting stock in Z representing 10 percent of the value of all outstanding shares of all classes of stock in Z. E and G, the only disqualified persons with respect to F, own, on such date, 5 shares each of nonvoting stock in Z. The 10 shares of nonvoting stock in Z owned by E and G together represent 10 percent of the value of all outstanding shares of all classes of stock in Z. Assume further that F cannot meet the requirements for the 35 percent test of section 4943(c)(2)(B). For purposes of applying section 4943(c)(4)(B) and this paragraph, F has excess business holdings in Z (determined without regard to section 4943(c)(4)), because under section 4943(c)(2)(A) F's permitted holdings are 20 percent (20% – 0%) of the voting stock since disqualified persons have no holdings of voting stock. Therefore, section 4943(c)(4)(B) and this paragraph apply, and a disqualified person is treated as holding F's shares of both voting and nonvoting stock in Z for the 10-year period through May 25, 1979. Thus, since all holdings by F in Z are treated as held by a disqualified person during the first phase, F cannot be subject to tax under section 4943(a) on its May 26, 1969, holdings prior to the termination of the first phase, regardless of whether or not disqualified persons purchase additional shares of Z during the first phase.

*Example (2).* Assume the same facts as in Example (1), and further assume that there were no transactions in the stock of Z during the first phase (May 26, 1969 through May 25, 1979). During the first phase the permitted holdings by F in Z for both the voting stock and the value is zero. The disqualified person voting level and the substituted combined voting level are each 30 percent, and the disqualified person value level and the substituted combined value level are each 35 percent (15% + 10% + 10%). The substituted levels are carried over into the second phase. The disqualified person voting level on May 26, 1979, the beginning of the second phase, is zero, because the voting shares held by F are no longer treated as held by a disqualified person. Therefore, F's permitted holdings on such date are 30 percent of the voting stock, because such percentage is equal to the excess of the substituted combined voting level (30%) over the disqualified person voting level (0%). The disqualified person value level on May 26, 1979, is 10 percent, because the voting and nonvoting shares held by F are no longer treated as held by a disqualified person. Therefore, F's permitted holdings on such date are 25 percent of the value of Z stock, because such percentage is equal to the excess of the substituted combined value level (35%) over the disqualified person value level (10%) as of such date.

*Example (3).* Assume the facts as stated in Example (2), except that E and G acquire, on February 1, 1970, 10 shares of Z voting stock representing 10 percent of the voting power in Z and 5 percent of the value of all outstanding shares of all classes of stock in Z. During the first phase such permitted holdings remain zero, and prior to May 25, 1979, the substituted combined voting level and substituted combined value level remain 30 and 35 percent, respectively, because such levels may not be increased by acquisitions by disqualified persons. However, the disqualified person voting level and the disqualified person value level are each increased to 40 percent (30% + 10%) and 40 percent (35% + 5%) respectively. During the first phase the excess of the disqualified person voting level over the substituted combined voting level (40% – 30%) and the excess of the disqualified person value level over the substituted combined value level (40% – 35%) indicate how much stock F must dispose of during the first

phase to avoid the initial tax when it expires. On May 25, 1979, the last day of the first phase, F disposes of 12 shares of Z voting stock, representing 12 percent of the voting power in Z and 6 percent of the value of all such outstanding shares. The disposition by F reduces the interest F owns to 18 percent (30% – 12%) of the voting power, and 19 percent (25% – 6%) of the value of all outstanding shares of all classes of stock, in Z. Since the disqualified person voting level decreases to 28 percent (40% – 12%), the substituted combined voting level as of May 25, 1979, accordingly is decreased to 28 percent under the downward ratchet rule. Similarly, the substituted combined value level is decreased to 34 percent, as the disqualified person value level as of such date is 34 percent (40% – 6%). On May 26, 1979, the disqualified person voting level is 10 percent (28% – 18%), and the disqualified person value level is 15 percent (34% – 19%), since the shares owned by F are no longer treated as held by a disqualified person as of such date. Accordingly, on May 26, 1979, the permitted holdings by F in Z are 18 percent of the voting power in Z, because such percentage is equal to the excess of the substituted combined voting level (28%) over the disqualified person voting level (10%) as of such date. Similarly, the permitted holdings of F in Z by value are 19 percent (34% – 15%). If F had not disposed of the 12 shares, then on May 26, 1979, F's permitted holdings in voting power and value would be 20 percent (30% – 10%) and 20 percent (35% – 15%), respectively.

*Example (4).* F, a private foundation, owns on May 26, 1969, 35 shares of voting stock in corporation Y representing 35 percent of the voting stock in Y and 17.5 percent of the value of all classes of stock in Y, and owns on such date 45 shares of nonvoting stock representing 22.5 percent of the value of all outstanding shares of all classes of stock in Y. No disqualified person with respect to F owns, on such date, any stock in Y. Assume further that Y cannot meet the requirements of the 35 percent test of section 4943(c)(2)(B). For purposes of applying section 4943(c)(4)(B) and this paragraph, F has excess business holdings in Y (determined without regard to section 4943(c)(4)), because under section 4943(c)(2)(A) F's permitted holdings are 20 percent (20% – 0%) of the voting stock since disqualified persons have no holdings of voting stock. Therefore, section 4943(c)(4)(B) and this paragraph apply, and a disqualified person is treated as holding F's shares of both voting and nonvoting stock in Y for the 10-year period through May 25, 1979. During the first phase the permitted holdings by F in Y of both the voting stock and of value are zero. The disqualified person voting level and the substituted combined voting level are each 35 percent, and the disqualified person value level and the substituted combined value level are each 40 percent (17.5% + 22.5%). The substituted levels are carried over into the second phase. The disqualified person voting level and value level on May 26, 1979, are both zero, because the shares held by F are no longer treated as held by a disqualified person. Therefore, F's permitted holdings on such date are 35 percent of the voting power (35% – 0%) and 40 percent of the value (40% – 0%). Assume that on February 1, 1981, A, a disqualified person, acquires 6 percent of the voting stock in Y representing 3 percent of the value of all outstanding shares of all classes of stock in Y. The permitted holdings by F in Z on February 1, 1981, are thus reduced to 25 percent of the voting stock (the lesser of the separate 25% second phase limitation or 29% (35% substituted combined voting level minus 6% disqualified person voting level)) and 25 percent of the value (the lesser of the separate 25% second phase limitation or 37% (40% substituted combined value level minus 3% disqualified person value level)). But see paragraph (d)(8) of this section for limitations on restrictions with respect to nonvoting stock.

*Example (5).* Assume the same facts as in Example (4) except that A does not acquire the 6 shares of voting stock until February 1, 1996 (in the third phase), rather on February 1, 1981. Thus, F's permitted holdings in Y would remain at 35 percent of the voting stock and 40 percent of the value during the second phase, which expired on May 25, 1994. Assume that on May 25, 1994, the last day of the second phase, F disposes of 10 shares of nonvoting stock representing 5 percent of the value of all outstanding shares in Y to meet the 35 percent third phase limit. In accordance with the downward ratchet rule, the substituted combined value level and F's permitted holdings in Y would be reduced to 35 percent of value. On February 1, 1996, F's permitted holdings in Y would be reduced to 25 percent of the voting stock (the lesser of the separate 25% third phase limitation or 29% (35% substituted combined voting level minus 6% disqualified person level)) and 25 percent of the value (the lesser of the separate 25% third phase limitation or 32% (35% substituted combined value level minus 3% disqualified person value level)). But see paragraph (d)(8) of this section for limitations on restrictions with respect to nonvoting stock.

(8) *Special rule where all holdings are permitted under section 4943(c)(2).*—(i) Since section 4943(c)(4) and this paragraph provide transitional rules for foundations which would otherwise have had excess business holdings on May 26, 1969, no holdings shall cease to

be permitted holdings under this paragraph where such holdings would be permitted holdings under section 4943(c)(2) and §53.4943-3. Thus, for example, where the substituted voting level has been reduced to 20 percent, the provisions of §53.4943-3(b)(2) concerning nonvoting stock as permitted holdings generally apply.

(ii) The provisions of this paragraph (d)(8) may be illustrated by the following example:

*Example.* (A) F, a private foundation, owns, on May 26, 1969, 40 shares of voting stock in corporation X respresenting 40 percent of the voting stock in X and 20 percent of the value of all outstanding shares of all classes of stock in X, and owns, on such date, 60 shares of nonvoting stock in X, representing 30 percent of the value of all outstanding shares of all classes of stock in X. A, the only disqualified person with respect to F, owns, on such date, 10 shares of voting stock in X, representing 10 percent of the voting stock in X and 5 percent of the value of all outstanding shares of all classes of stock in X. Under section 4943(c)(4)(B)(iii), a disqualified person is deemed the owner of all holdings by F in X for the 10-year period beginning on May 26, 1969.

(B) Assume that the only transaction in X stock during the first phase is the disposition of 30 shares of voting stock by F on May 1, 1975. The voting stock held by F is permitted holdings under §53.4943-3 and under such section since all disqualified persons together do not own more than 20 percent of the voting stock in X, all nonvoting stock held by F shall also be treated as permitted holdings. Therefore, all the stock held by F is permitted holdings.

(C) Assume that on May 1, 1975, F had disposed of only 15 shares of voting stock and also had disposed of 35 shares of nonvoting stock. On May 26, 1979, at the beginning of the second phase, this paragraph (d)(8) would not apply since F would have excess business holdings under §53.4943-3. Under the provisions of this section, the permitted holdings by F in X on such date are 25 percent of the voting stock (35% substituted combined voting level minus 10% disqualified person voting level) and 25 percent of the value (30% substituted combined value level minus 5% disqualified person value level).

(9) *Special rule for certain private foundations.*—In the case of a private foundation—

(i) Which was incorporated before January 1, 1951;

(ii) Substantially all of the assets of which on May 26, 1969, consisted of more than 90 percent of the stock of an incorporated business enterprise which is licensed and regulated, the sales or contracts of which are regulated, and the professional representatives of which are licensed, by State regulatory agencies in at least 10 States;

(iii) Which acquired such stock solely by gift, devise, or bequest;

(iv) Which does not purchase any stock or other interest in such enterprise after May 26, 1969, and does not acquire any stock or other interest in any other business enterprise which constitutes excess business holdings under §53.4943-3; and

(v) Which, in the last 5 taxable years ending on or before December 31, 1970, expended substantially all of its adjusted net income (as defined in section 4942(f)) for the purpose or function for which it is organized and operated;

paragraph (d)(1) through (5) of this section (permitted holdings during the first and second phase) shall be applied with respect to the holdings of such foundation in such incorporated business enterprise by substituting "51 percent" for "50 percent," and section 4943(c)(4)(D) (third phase) shall not apply with respect to such holdings. For purposes of the preceding sentence, stock of such enterprise in a trust created before May 27, 1969, of which the foundation is the remainder beneficiary shall be deemed to be held by such foundation on May 26, 1969, if such foundation held (without regard to such trust) more than 20 percent of the stock of such enterprise on May 26, 1969.

(10) *Special rule for changes in the relative values of stock of different classes.*—(i) In the case of a corporation that has more than one class of stock outstanding, if the percentage of value held by the private foundation, its disqualified persons, or both, increases over a period of time solely as a result of changes in the relative values of the stock of different classes, then the foundation value level, the disqualified person value level, and the substituted combined value level, as defined in paragraph (d)(2) of this section, shall be adjusted to reflect such increase. An increase in the percentage of value held shall not be considered to have occurred solely as a result of changes in the relative values of the stock of different classes if:

(A) There has been any increase during the period in the percentage of any class of stock held by the private foundation, its disqualified persons, or both, or

(B) There has been any issuance, redemption, or purchase by the issuing corporation of any stock during the period.

See §53.4943-6(d) for rules relating to increases caused by readjustments.

(ii) *Example.*—The provisions of this paragraph (b)[d](10) may be illustrated by the following example:

*Example.* (i) At all times since May 26, 1969, F, a private foundation, has held 25% (500,000 shares) of the outstanding class of voting stock of X corporation. No disqualified person with respect to F holds any voting stock of X. In addition X has had outstanding since May 26, 1969, a class of non-voting preferred stock, none of which is held by F or a disqualified person. X is an active business corporation and third parties do not have effective control of X. On May 26, 1969, the voting stock (2 million shares outstanding) was trading for $5 a share on the New York Stock Exchange. The non-voting preferred stock, not publicly traded, was valued at $1 million. The total value of all outstanding stock was $11 million ($10 million voting stock plus $1 million non-voting preferred). On May 26, 1969, F held 22.73% of the value of X's outstanding stock ($2.5 million/$11 million).

(ii) On October 31, 1982, X's voting stock is trading for $20 a share and the nonvoting stock is valued at $3 million. At all times during the period May 26, 1969, through October 31, 1982, F has held 25 percent of the voting stock and none of the nonvoting stock of X. No stock of X is owned by disqualified persons. No stock of X has been issued, redeemed or purchased by X during this period. On October 13, 1982, the total value of X's outstanding stock is $43 million ($40 million voting stock and $3 million nonvoting stock) and F holds 23.26 percent of the value of X's outstanding stock ($10 million/$43 million). F's foundation value level and the substituted combined value level are increased from 22.73 percent to 23.26 percent to reflect this change.

(iii) On November 1, 1982, X corporation distributes the stock of Y corporation, a wholly-owned subsidiary, to X's shareholders. Y is a business enterprise. Under this paragraph (d)(10), all of F's stock in X is permitted holdings under section 4943(c)(4) even though the percentage of value held by F has increased from 22.73 percent on May 26, 1969, to 23.26 percent on November 1, 1982. F's permitted holdings in Y will be determined by reference to F's permitted holdings in X under §53.4943-7. Therefore, assuming no prohibited transaction occurs, F's permitted holdings in Y stock equal 25 percent of Y's voting stock and, separately, 23.26 percent of the value of all of Y's outstanding stock. [Reg. §53.4943-4.]

☐ [*T.D. 7496, 7-5-77. Amended by T.D. 7944, 2-21-84.*]

### [Reg. §53.4943-5]

**§53.4943-5. Present holdings acquired by trust or a will.**— (a) *Interests to which section 4943(c)(5) applies.*—(1) *In general.*—Section 4943(c)(5) provides that section 4943(c)(4) (other than the 20-year first phase holding period) applies to an interest in a business enterprise acquired after May 26, 1969 by a private foundation under the terms of a trust which was irrevocable on May 26, 1969, or under the terms of a will executed on or before May 26, 1969, which were in effect on May 26, 1969, and at all times thereafter, as if such interest were held on May 26, 1969. However the first phase holding period prescribed by §53.4943-4(c)(1)(ii) or (iii) shall commence for such an interest on the date of distribution to the foundation. Unlike section 4943(c)(4) and §53.4943-4, section 4943(c)(5) and this section treat only the interest so acquired (and not the entire interest held by the foundation in such enterprise on the date of distribution) as held by a disqualified person during a first phase holding period. (See, however, section 4943(c)(6) and paragraph (b)(2) of §53.4943-6 for the treatment of other holdings of the foundation in the same enterprise if an interest to which section 4943(c)(5) applies is acquired from a person who was not a disqualified person prior to the acquisition.) In addition, section 4943(c)(5) and this section shall not apply if after the acquisition of such an interest the foundation would not have excess business holdings (determined without regard to section 4943(c)(4), (5), or (6)).

(2) *After-acquired interests.*—Section 4943(c)(5) and this section shall not apply to any interest acquired after May 26, 1969, by an estate or trust, other than by reason of the death of the decedent. For example, where a foundation is a residuary beneficiary under the terms of a will executed before May 26, 1969, and the residue of the estate consists of cash, then stock subsequently purchased with this cash for distribution to the foundation will not be treated as an interest acquired under the terms of a will executed on or before May 26, 1969.

(3) *Certain revocable trusts.*—If an interest in a business enterprise actually passes to a private foundation under a trust which would have met the tests referred to in paragraph (a)(1) of this section but for the fact that the trust was revocable (even though it was not in fact revoked) and such interest would have passed to such foundation under a will that meets those tests but for the fact that the

grantor died without having revoked the trust, then for purposes of section 4943(c)(5) and this section, such an interest shall be treated as having been acquired by the foundation under the will.

(4) *Modification of will.*—(i) *In general.*—For purposes of section 4943(c)(5) and this section, an amendment or republication of a will which was executed on or before May 26, 1969, does not prevent any interest in a business enterprise which was to pass under the terms (which were in effect on May 26, 1969, and at all times thereafter) of such will from being treated as a present holding under section 4943(c)(4) or (5)—

(A) Solely because there is a reduction in the interest in the business enterprise which the foundation was to receive under the terms of the will (for example, if the foundation is to receive the residuary estate, and if one class of stock is disposed of by the decedent during his lifetime or by a subsequent codicil);

(B) Solely because such amendment or republication is necessary in order to comply with section 508(e) and the regulations thereunder;

(C) Solely because there is a change in the executor of the will; or

(D) Solely because of any other change which does not otherwise change the rights of the foundation with respect to such interest in the business enterprise.

However, if under such amendment or republication there is an increase in the interest in the business enterprise which the foundation was to receive under the terms of the will in effect on May 26, 1969, such increase shall not be treated as present holdings under section 4943(c)(4) or (5). Under such circumstances the interest which would have been acquired before such increase shall remain present holdings. See section 4943(c)(6) and § 53.4943-6 with respect to the treatment of such increase in holdings of a private foundation.

(ii) *Examples.*—The provisions of this paragraph (a)(4) may be illustrated by the following examples:

*Example (1).* On May 9, 1985, A modifies by codicil his will which was in effect on May 26, 1969, and was unchanged until such modification. The purpose of the codicil was, in the event of A's death, to increase the number of shares in X Corporation that would pass to the W foundation from 70 percent of all the voting power and value to 80 percent. Under these facts, if A dies without further modifying the terms of the will which apply to W's interest in X, section 4943(c)(5) will apply to 70 percent of the X voting power and value and section 4943(c)(6) will apply to 10 percent of the X voting power and value, since 10 percent of the X voting power and value would not pass under a provision of the will which was in effect on May 26, 1969, and at all times thereafter. Accordingly, if the stock is distributed to W on July 6, 1988, then, assuming that on May 26, 1969, W and all disqualified persons owned less than 75% of the voting stock in X, an amount of such stock representing 70 percent of X voting power and value shall be treated as held by a disqualified person through July 5, 1998, and an amount of such stock representing 10 percent of X voting power and value shall be treated as held by a disqualified person through July 5, 1993.

*Example (2).* Assume the facts as stated in Example (1), except that the sole purpose of the codicil was to change the executor of the will. Under paragraph (a)(4)(i) of this section, such codicil will not prevent the X voting stock which was bequeathed to W from being treated as held by a disqualified person through July 5, 1998.

(b) *Holding periods.*—(1) *In general.*—An interest to which section 4943(c)(5) applies shall be entitled to a 15-year holding period starting on the date of distribution only if the interests actually or constructively owned by a private foundation and all disqualified persons on May 26, 1969, in a business enterprise exceed 75 percent of the voting stock (or of the profits or beneficial interest) or 75 percent of the value of all outstanding shares of all classes of stock (or of the profits and capital interest) in such enterprise. For purposes of the preceding sentence, interests held by the foundation on May 26, 1969, shall be deemed to include an interest to which section 4943(c)(5) applies and which has been acquired (on or before the date of distribution for the interest in question) from a person who was not a disqualified person on May 26, 1969. Therefore, if under the terms of a will in effect on May 26, 1969, and at all times thereafter, a private foundation is created on July 1, 1975, and receives 76 percent of the voting stock of a business enterprise on that date, such stock shall be treated as held by a disqualified person until June 30, 1990. Any interest to which section 4943(c)(5) applies but which is not entitled to a 15-year holding period shall be entitled to a 10-year holding period starting on the date of distribution. For purposes of this paragraph the date of distribution shall be deemed to occur no later than the date on which the trust or estate is considered to be terminated under § 1.641(b)-3 of this chapter (Income Tax Regulations).

(2) *Constructive ownership prior to date of distribution.*—To the extent that an interest to which section 4943(c)(5) applies is constructively held by a private foundation under section 4943(d)(1) and § 53.4943-8 prior to the date of distribution, it shall be treated as held by a disqualified person prior to such date by reason of section 4943(c)(5). In addition, in the case of a foundation's interest in a trust which was irrevocable on May 26, 1969, and to which both sections 4943(c)(4) and (c)(5) apply, the first phase holding period for such interest shall end with whichever such period under section 4943(c)(4) or (5) ends later. For example, if under the terms of such a trust, 96 percent of the voting stock in a business enterprise was constructively held by a private foundation on May 26, 1969, and was distributed to such foundation on June 30, 1970, such interest is entitled to a 20-year holding period beginning on May 26, 1969.

(c) *Permitted holdings.*—(1) *In general.*—The permitted holdings of a private foundation which has an interest in a business enterprise to which section 4943(c)(5) applies shall be determined in accordance with the rules of paragraph (d) of § 53.4943-4. The levels referred to in such paragraph shall be adjusted to take into account the acquisition of such an interest as if it were treated as held by a disqualified person from May 26, 1969, until the date of acquisition. See also § 53.4943-6(b)(2) for the special rule for interests held by a private foundation at the time it acquires a section 4943(c)(5) interest from a nondisqualified person. Thus, for example, if on June 30, 1975, the disqualified person voting level and the substituted combined voting level in corporation X with respect to foundation F are 45 percent, and a nondisqualified person's 10 percent voting interest in X is acquired by F on July 1, 1975, in a transaction to which section 4943(c)(5) applies, the above-mentioned levels shall be increased to 55 and 50 percent respectively, on July 1, 1975. However, if such interest had been acquired from a person who was a disqualified person on May 26, 1969, rather than from a nondisqualified person, no adjustments in such levels would have taken place on July 1, 1975. In such a case, though, at the beginning of the second phase on July 1, 1985, the foundation voting level would be increased by 10 percent, and the disqualified person voting level decreased by 10 percent (assuming that none of the acquired stock had been disposed of prior to such date).

(2) *Separate phases.*—The phases for each interest to which section 4943(c)(5) applies start independently from those for any other interest of the foundation in the same enterprise to which section 4943(c)(4) or (5) applies. Therefore, until an interest enters its own second phase, the 25 percent limit described in paragraph (d)(5) of § 53.4943-4 shall not apply to such interest since such interest (and any subsequently acquired section 4943(c)(5) interest in the first phase) is still treated as held by a disqualified person for purposes of that 25 percent limit. In addition, if such an interest enters its second phase and at such time all disqualified persons together do not have holdings in excess of 2 percent of the voting stock in the same business enterprise, then the 25 percent limit of section 4943(c)(4)(D)(i) shall not then apply to such interest, even though such limit may have been applicable to an interest with an earlier second phase. Moreover, the 35 percent limit of section 4943(c)(4)(D)(ii) shall cause only interests which have entered the third phase to become excess business holdings, taking into account, however, interests in prior phases in determining the holdings subject to such limit.

(3) *Examples.*—The provisions of this paragraph may be illustrated by the following examples: (After each example is a chart setting forth the chronological changes in the various levels referred to in paragraph (d) of § 53.4943-4.)

*Example (1).* On May 26, 1969, F, a private foundation, owns no stock in M Corporation, and A, a disqualified person owns 40 percent of the voting stock (voting power and value) in M. A dies on May 1, 1971, leaving 30 percent of the voting stock in M to F and leaving the other 10 percent to a disqualified person. Distribution is made on June 1, 1972, and assume that section 4943(c)(5) applies. No transactions in the stock of M, other than those described in this example, occur. On May 26, 1969, the substituted combined voting level is 40 percent, the disqualified person voting level is deemed to be 40 percent, and the permitted holdings by F in M is deemed to be 0 percent (40% – 40%). On May 1, 1971 (the date that F acquired the M stock by reason of its constructive ownership of A's estate), the various levels remain unchanged. On May 1, 1971, the 30 percent interest is treated as held by a disqualified person for a period extending through May 31, 1982. On June 1, 1981, F disposes of 6 percent of the voting stock to a nondisqualified person. The substituted combined voting level and the disqualified person voting level thereby are reduced to 34 percent (40% – 6%) each. On June 1, 1982, at the beginning of the second phase, the foundation voting level increases to 24 percent (30% – 6%) and the disqualified person voting level is reduced to 10 percent (34% – 24%). The substituted combined voting level as of June 1, 1982, remains at 34 percent. The permitted holdings as of such date are 24 percent (34% – 10%). If F had not disposed of any holdings prior to June 1, 1982, F's permitted holdings would have been 25 percent, the lesser of 25 percent (the limitation of section 4943(c)(4)(D)(i)), or 30 percent (40% – 10%). Since on such date the 30 percent interest would no longer have been treated as held by a disqualified person, F would have had excess business holdings of 5 percent (30% – 25%).

| Date | F owns | Interest treated as held by dis-qualified person | Disquali-fied per-sons own | Foundation voting level | Substituted combined voting level | Disqualified person voting level | Permitted holdings | Comments |
|---|---|---|---|---|---|---|---|---|
| 5/26/69 | 0% | 0% | 40% | 0% | 40% | 40% | 0% | |
| 5/1/71 | +30% | +30% | –30% | | | | | A dies. |
| Do. | 30% | 30% | 10% | 0% | 40% | 40% | 0% | |
| 6/1/72 | 30% | 30% | 10% | 0% | 40% | 40% | 0% | Distribution. |
| 6/1/81 | – 6% | – 6% | | | – 6% | – 6% | | F sells 6%. |
| 6/1/81 | 24% | 24% | 10% | 0% | 34% | 34% | 0% | |
| 6/1/82 | –24% | | | +24% | | –24% | +24% | |
| Do. | 24% | 0% | 10% | 24% | 34% | 10% | 24% | 2d phase begins. |

*Example (2).* (i) On May 26, 1969, F, a private foundation, owns 30 percent of the voting stock of N Corporation (voting power and value) and disqualified persons own 20 percent of the voting stock of N Corporation. On May 1, 1971, B, a disqualified person, dies leaving 15 percent of the voting stock to F. Assume that distribution was made on June 1, 1972, and that section 4943(c)(5) applies. On May 26, 1969, the substituted combined voting level and the disqualified person voting levels are each 50 percent and the permitted holdings are 0 percent (50% – 50%). On May 1, 1971, and June 1, 1972, these levels remain unchanged. On May 1, 1971, the 15 percent interest is treated as held by a disqualified person for a period extending through May 31, 1982.

(ii) On July 1, 1978, F sells 6 percent of the F stock to a nondisqualified person, thereby reducing the disqualified person voting level and the substituted combined voting level to 44 percent (50% – 6%). On May 26, 1979, at the beginning of the second phase for F's 1969 holdings, the foundation voting level is 24 percent (30% – 6%), the substituted combined voting level is still 44 percent, and the disqualified person voting level is 20 percent (44% – 24%). The permitted holdings are 24 percent (44% – 20%). In addition F's 24 percent holdings do not exceed the 25 percent limitation of section 4943(c)(4)(D)(i) and paragraph (d)(5)(ii) of § 53.4943-4.

(iii) On August 1, 1981, F sells 16 percent of the N stock to a nondisqualified person, thereby reducing the foundation voting level to 8 percent (24% – 16%), and reducing the substituted combined voting level to 28 percent (44% – 16%). The disqualified person voting level remains at 20 percent. On June 1, 1982, at the beginning of the second phase for F's holdings acquired by will, the substituted combined voting level is still 28 percent, the foundation voting level is 23 percent (8% + 15%), the disqualified person voting level is 5 percent (20% – 15%), and the permitted holdings are 23 percent (28% – 5%).

(iv) If F had not disposed of the 6 percent on July 1, 1978, then on May 26, 1979, at the beginning of the second phase for F's 1969 holdings, F's permitted holdings would have been 25 percent, the lesser of 25 percent (the limitation of section 4943(c)(4)(D)(i)), or 30 percent (50% – 20%). Since F's 30 percent interest would no longer have been treated as held by a disqualified person on May 26, 1979, F would have had excess business holdings of 5 percent (30% – 25%). Similarly, if F had not disposed of the 16 percent interest on August 1, 1981 (but had disposed of the 6 percent interest), on July 1, 1982, at the beginning of the second phase for F's holdings acquired by will, F's permitted holdings would have been 25 percent, the lesser of 25 percent (under section 4943(c)(4)(D)(i)), or 39 percent (44% – 5%). Since as of such date F's entire holdings of 39 percent would no longer have been treated as held by a disqualified person, F would have had excess business holdings of 14 percent (39% – 25%).

| Date | F owns | F's interest 1969 | F's interest 1971 | Interest treated as held by dis-qualified person | Disquali-fied per-sons own | Foun-dation voting level | Substi-tuted com-bined voting level | Disquali-fied per-son voting level | Permitted holdings | Comments |
|---|---|---|---|---|---|---|---|---|---|---|
| 5/26/69 | 30% | 30% | | 30% | 20% | 0% | 50% | 50% | 0% | |
| 5/1/71 | +15% | | +15% | +15% | –15% | | | | | B dies |
| 5/1/71 | 45% | 30% | 15% | 45% | 5% | 0% | 50% | 50% | 0% | |
| 6/1/72 | 45% | 30% | 15% | 45% | 5% | 0% | 50% | 50% | 0% | Distribution |
| 7/1/78 | – 6% | – 6% | | – 6% | | | – 6% | – 6% | | F sells 6% |
| 7/1/78 | 39% | 24% | 15% | 39% | 5% | 0% | 44% | 44% | 0% | |
| 5/26/79 | | | | –24% | | +24% | | –24% | +24% | 2nd phase for 24% |
| 5/26/79 | 39% | 24% | 15% | 15% | 5% | 24% | 44% | 20% | 24% | |
| 8/1/81 | –16% | –16% | | | | –16% | –16% | | –16% | F sells 16% |
| 8/1/81 | 23% | 8% | 15% | 15% | 5% | 8% | 28% | 20% | 8% | |
| 7/1/82 | | | | –15% | | +15% | | –15% | +15% | All in 2nd phase |
| 7/1/82 | 23% | 8% | 15% | 0% | 5% | 23% | 28% | 5% | 23% | |

*Example (3).* (i) On May 26, 1969, F, a private foundation owns 5 percent of the voting stock of O Corporation (voting power and value), and disqualified persons own 45 percent of the voting stock. C, a disqualified person, dies on May 1, 1971, and leaves 41 percent of the voting stock of O to F. Assume that distribution is made on June 1, 1972, and that section 4943(c)(5) applies. On May 26, 1969, the substituted combined voting level and the disqualified person voting level are 50 percent and the permitted holdings are 0 percent (50% – 50%). On May 1, 1971, and June 1, 1972, the various levels remain unchanged. On May 1, 1971, the 41 percent interest is treated as held by a disqualified person for a period extending through May 31, 1982. On May 26, 1979, at the beginning of the second phase for F's 1969 holdings of 5 percent, the 5 percent is no longer treated as held by a disqualified person, the foundation voting level is 5 percent, the disqualified person voting level is reduced to 45 percent (50% – 5%), and the substituted combined voting level remains at 50 percent. On such date F's permitted holdings are 5 percent (50% – 45%). Since the 41 percent interest is treated as held by a disqualified person, the interest treated as held by F (5%) does not exceed the 25 percent limitation of section 4943(c)(4)(D)(i).

(ii) On August 1, 1981, F sells 22 percent of the O stock to a nondisqualified person, thereby reducing the foundation voting level to 0 percent. Since the reductions are first applied to the 1969 holdings of 5 percent, 17 percent (22% – 5%) applies to the 41 percent interest, reducing such interest to 24 percent (41% – 17%), and reducing the disqualified person voting level to 28 percent (45% – 17%). The substituted combined voting level is reduced to 28 percent (0% + 28%). On June 1, 1982, at the beginning of the second phase for F's holdings acquired by will, the substituted combined voting level remains at 28 percent, the foundation voting level is 24 percent the disqualified person voting level is reduced to 4 percent (28% – 24%).

(iii) If F had not disposed of the 22 percent interest prior to June 1, 1982, F's permitted holdings would have been 25 percent, the lesser of 25 percent (under section 4943(c)(4)(D)(i)), or 46 percent (50% – 4%). Since as of such date, F's entire holdings of 46 percent would no longer have been treated as held by a disqualified person, F would have had excess business holdings of 21 percent (46% – 25%).

| Date | F owns | F's interest 1969 | F's interest 1971 | Interest treated as held by disqualified person | Disqualified persons own | Foundation voting level | Substituted combined voting level | Disqualified person voting level | Permitted holdings | Comments |
|---|---|---|---|---|---|---|---|---|---|---|
| 5/26/69 | 5% | 5% | | 5% | 45% | 0% | 50% | 50% | 0% | |
| 5/1/71 | +41% | | +41% | +41% | −41% | | | | | C dies |
| 5/1/71 | 46% | 5% | 41% | 46% | 4% | 0% | 50% | 50% | 0% | |
| 6/1/72 | 46% | 5% | 41% | 46% | 4% | 0% | 50% | 50% | 0% | Distribution |
| 5/26/79 | | | | − 5% | | + 5% | | − 5% | + 5% | 2nd phase for 5% |
| 5/26/79 | 46% | 5% | 41% | 41% | 4% | 5% | 50% | 45% | 5% | |
| 8/1/81 | −22% | − 5% | −17% | −17% | | − 5% | −22% | −17% | − 5% | F sells 22% |
| 8/1/81 | 24% | 0% | 24% | 24% | 4% | 0% | 28% | 28% | 0% | |
| 6/1/82 | | | | −24% | | +24% | | −24% | +24% | 2nd phase for 24% |
| 6/1/82 | 24% | 0% | 24% | 0% | 4% | 24% | 28% | 4% | 24% | |

Example (4). (i) On May 26, 1969, F, a private foundation, owns 30 percent of the voting stock in P Corporation (voting power and value), and disqualified persons own 20 percent. On May 1, 1971, D, a disqualified person, dies leaving 18 percent of the voting stock to F. Assume that distribution was made on June 1, 1972, and that section 4943(c)(5) applies. On May 26, 1969, the substituted combined voting level and the disqualified person voting level are each 50 percent and the permitted holdings are 0 percent (50% – 50%). On May 1, 1971, and June 1, 1972, these levels remain unchanged. On May 1, 1971, the 18 percent interest is treated as held by a disqualified person for a period extending through May 31, 1982. On May 26, 1979, the foundation voting level increases to 30 percent, the disqualified person voting level decreases to 20 percent (50% – 30%), and the permitted holdings are 30 percent (50% – 20%). On June 1, 1982, the foundation voting level increases to 48 percent, the disqualified person voting level decreases to 2 percent and the permitted holdings are 48 percent (50% – 2%). Since at no time during the second phase for F's 1969 holdings did all disqualified persons together have holdings in excess of 2 percent of the voting stock of P, the 25 percent limitation of section 4943(c)(4)(D)(i) did not apply to F's 1969 holdings.

(ii) On July 1, 1993, F disposes of 16 percent of the stock in P, thereby reducing the substituted combined voting level to 34 percent (50% – 16%), and reducing the permitted holdings to 32 percent (34% – 2%). If F had not disposed of the 16 percent of the stock of P prior to May 26, 1994, on such date, under section 4943(c)(4)(D)(ii), F's substituted combined voting level for its 1969 holdings would have been 35 percent, and the permitted holdings would have been 33 percent (35% – 2%). Since none of F's holdings of 48 percent would have been treated as held by a disqualified person on such date (the beginning of the third phase for F's 1969 holdings), F would have had excess business holdings of 15 percent, the lesser of 30 percent (F's 1969 holdings in the third phase), or 15 percent (the excess of F's 48 percent holdings over the permitted holdings of 33 percent).

| Date | F owns | F's interest 1969 | F's interest 1971 | Interest treated as held by disqualified person | Disqualified persons own | Foundation voting level | Substituted combined voting level | Disqualified person voting level | Permitted holdings | Comments |
|---|---|---|---|---|---|---|---|---|---|---|
| 5/26/69 | 30% | 30% | | 30% | 20% | 0% | 50% | 50% | 0% | |
| 5/1/71 | +18% | | +18% | +18% | −18% | | | | | D dies |
| 5/1/71 | 48% | 30% | 18% | 48% | 2% | 0% | 50% | 50% | 0% | |
| 6/1/72 | 48% | 30% | 18% | 48% | 2% | 0% | 50% | 50% | 0% | Distribution |
| 5/26/79 | | | | −30% | | +30% | | −30% | +30% | 2nd phase for 30% |
| 5/26/79 | 48% | 30% | 18% | 18% | 2% | 30% | 50% | 20% | 30% | |
| 6/1/82 | | | | −18% | | +18% | | −18% | +18% | 2nd phase for 18% |
| 6/1/82 | 48% | 30% | 18% | 0% | 2% | 48% | 50% | 2% | 48% | |
| 7/1/93 | −16% | −16% | | | | −16% | −16% | | −16% | F disposes of 16% |
| 7/1/93 | 32% | 14% | 18% | 0% | 2% | 32% | 34% | 2% | 32% | |
| 5/26/94 | 32% | 14% | 18% | 0% | 2% | 32% | 34% | 2% | 32% | 3rd phase for 14% |
| 6/1/97 | 32% | 14% | 18% | 0% | 2% | 32% | 34% | 2% | 32% | 3rd phase for 18% |

Example (5). (i) On May 26, 1969, F, a private foundation, owns 5 percent of the voting stock in Q Corporation (voting power and value), and disqualified persons own 45 percent. On May 1, 1971, E, a disqualified person, dies leaving 43 percent of the voting stock to F. Assume that distribution was made on June 1, 1972, and that section 4943(c)(5) applies. On May 26, 1969, the substituted combined voting level and the disqualified person voting level are each 50 percent and the permitted holdings are 0 percent (50% – 50%). On May 1, 1971, and June 1, 1972, these levels remain unchanged. On May 1, 1971, the 43 percent interest is treated as held by a disqualified person for a period extending through May 31, 1982. On May 26, 1979, the foundation voting level increases to 5 percent, the disqualified person voting level decreases to 45 percent, and the permitted holdings are 5 percent (50% – 45%). On June 1, 1982, the foundation voting level increases to 48 percent, the disqualified person voting level decreases to 2 percent, and the permitted holdings are 48 percent (50% – 2%). At no time during the second phase for F's 1969 holdings did all disqualified persons together have holdings in excess of 2 percent of the voting stock of Q. Therefore, the 25 percent limitation of section 4943(c)(4)(D)(i) did not apply.

(ii) On July 1, 1993, F sells 6 percent of the stock in Q to a nondisqualified person. This reduces the substituted combined voting level to 44 percent and reduces the permitted holdings to 42 percent (44% – 2%). If F had not disposed of the 6 percent of the stock in 1993, on May 26, 1994, at the beginning of the third phase for F's 1969 holdings, F would have had 5 percent excess business holdings. The excess business holdings are 5 percent because although the excess business holdings computed for the third phase are 15 percent (the excess of F's actual holdings (48%) over the permitted holdings of 33 percent (35% – 2%)), only 5 percent of the holdings are in this phase and subject to the 35 percent combined holdings limitation.

(iii) On July 1, 1995, F sells 10 percent of the stock in Q, thereby reducing the substituted combined voting level to 34 percent and reducing the permitted holdings to 32 percent (34% – 2%). If F had not disposed of the 10 percent of the stock, on June 1, 1997, at the beginning of the third phase for F's acquired holdings, F would have had 9 percent excess business holdings (the excess of F's total holdings in the third phase (42%) over the permitted holdings of 33 percent (35% – 2%)).

| Date | F owns | F's interest 1969 | F's interest 1971 | Interest treated as held by disqualified person | Disqualified persons own | Foundation voting level | Substituted combined voting level | Disqualified person voting level | Permitted holdings | Comments |
|---|---|---|---|---|---|---|---|---|---|---|
| 5/26/69 | 5% | 5% | | 5% | 45% | 0% | 50% | 50% | 0% | |
| 5/1/71 | +43% | | +43% | +43% | −43% | | | | | E dies |
| 5/1/71 | 48% | 5% | 43% | 48% | 2% | 0% | 50% | 50% | 0% | |
| 6/1/72 | 48% | 5% | 43% | 48% | 2% | 0% | 50% | 50% | 0% | Distribution |
| 5/26/79 | | | | − 5% | | + 5% | | − 5% | + 5% | 2nd phase for 5% |

Reg. §53.4943-5(c)(3)

| Date | F owns | F's interest 1969 | F's interest 1971 | Interest treated as held by disqualified person | Disqualified persons own | Foundation voting level | Substituted combined voting level | Disqualified person voting level | Permitted holdings | Comments |
|---|---|---|---|---|---|---|---|---|---|---|
| 5/26/79 | 48% | 5% | 43% | 43% | 2% | 5% | 50% | 45% | 5% | |
| 6/1/82 | | | | −43% | | +43% | | −43% | +43% | 2nd phase for 43% |
| 6/1/82 | 48% | 5% | 43% | 0% | 2% | 48% | 50% | 2% | 48% | |
| 7/1/93 | − 6% | − 5% | − 1% | | | − 6% | − 6% | | − 6% | F sells 6% |
| 7/1/93 | 42% | 0% | 42% | 0% | 2% | 42% | 44% | 2% | 42% | |
| 7/1/95 | −10% | | −10% | | | −10% | −10% | | −10% | F sells 10% |
| 7/1/95 | 32 | 0% | 32% | 0% | 2% | 32% | 34% | 2% | 32% | |
| 6/1/97 | 32% | 0% | 32% | 0% | 2% | 32% | 34% | 2% | 32% | 3rd phase for 32% |

*Example (6).* (i) On May 26, 1969, F, a private foundation, owns 30 percent of the voting stock in R Corporation (voting power and value), and disqualified persons own 20 percent. On August 1, 1978, F disposes of 6 percent of the stock to a nondisqualified person. On May 1, 1981, G, a disqualified person, dies leaving 15 percent of the voting stock to F. Assume that distribution was made on June 1, 1982, and that section 4943(c)(5) applies. On May 26, 1969, the substituted combined voting level and the disqualified person voting level are each 50 percent, and the permitted holdings are 0 percent (50% − 50%). On August 1, 1978, these levels decrease to 44 percent (50% − 6%). On May 26, 1979, the foundation voting level increases to 24 percent (30% − 6%), the disqualified person voting level decreases to 20 percent (44% − 24%), and the permitted holdings are 24 percent (44% − 20%). If F had not disposed of the 6 percent of the stock prior to May 26, 1979, on May 26, 1979, the beginning of the second phase for F's 1969 holdings, F's permitted holdings would have been 25 percent, the lesser of 25 percent (under section 4943(c)(4)(W)(i)) or 30 percent (50% − 20%). Since the 30 percent interest would no longer have been treated as held by a disqualified person on such a date, F would have had excess business holdings of 5 percent (30% − 25%).

(ii) On May 1, 1981, and June 1, 1982 (assuming F had disposed of the 6 percent holdings), the foundation voting level, the disqualified person voting level, the substituted combined voting level and permitted holdings remain respectively 24 percent, 20 percent, 44 percent and 24 percent. On May 1, 1981, the 15 percent interest is treated as held by a disqualified person for a period extending through May 31, 1992. On July 1, 1991, F sells 16 percent of the voting stock in R to a nondisqualified person, thereby reducing the substituted combined voting level to 28 percent (44% − 16%), and reducing the foundation voting level to 8 percent (24% − 16%). The disqualified person voting level remains at 20 percent. On June 1, 1992, at the beginning of the second phase of F's holdings acquired by will, the substituted combined voting level remains at 28 percent, the foundation voting level increases to 23 percent (8% + 15%) and the disqualified person voting level decreases to 5 percent (20% − 15%). The permitted holdings on such date are 23 percent (28% − 5%). If F had not disposed of the 16 percent interest prior to June 1, 1992, F's permitted holdings would have been 25 percent, the lesser of 25 percent (under section 4943(c)(4)(D)(i)) or 39 percent (44% − 5%). Since as of such date, F's entire holdings of 39 percent would no longer have been treated as held by a disqualified person, F would have had excess business holdings of 14 percent (39% − 25%).

| Date | F owns | F's interest 1969 | F's interest 1981 | Interest treated as held by disqualified person | Disqualified persons own | Foundation voting level | Substituted combined voting level | Disqualified person voting level | Permitted holdings | Comments |
|---|---|---|---|---|---|---|---|---|---|---|
| 5/26/69 | 30% | 30% | | 30% | 20% | 0% | 50% | 50% | 0% | |
| 8/1/78 | − 6% | − 6% | | − 6% | | | − 6% | − 6% | | F disposes of 6% |
| 8/1/78 | 24% | 24% | | 24% | 20% | 0% | 44% | 44% | 0% | |
| 5/26/79 | | | | −24% | | +24% | | −24% | +24% | 2nd phase for 24% |
| 5/26/79 | 24% | 24% | | 0% | 20% | 24% | 44% | 20% | 24% | |
| 5/1/81 | +15% | | +15% | +15% | −15% | | | | | G dies |
| 5/1/81 | 39% | 24% | 15% | 15% | 5% | 24% | 44% | 20% | 24% | |
| 6/1/82 | 39% | 24% | 15% | 15% | 5% | 24% | 44% | 20% | 24% | Distribution |
| 7/1/91 | −16% | −16% | | | | −16% | −16% | | −16% | F disposes of 16% |
| 7/1/91 | 23% | 8% | 15% | 15% | 5% | 8% | 28% | 20% | 8% | |
| 6/1/92 | | | | −15% | | +15% | | −15% | +15% | 2nd phase of 15% |
| 6/1/92 | 23% | 8% | 15% | 0% | 5% | 23% | 28% | 5% | 23% | |

*Example (7).* (i) On May 26, 1969, F, a private foundation, owns 5 percent of the voting stock in S Corporation (voting power and value), and disqualified persons own 45 percent. On May 1, 1980, H, a disqualified person, dies leaving 41 percent of the voting stock to F. Assume that distribution is made on June 1, 1981, and that section 4943(c)(5) applies. On May 26, 1969, the substituted combined voting level and disqualified person voting levels are each 50 percent. On May 26, 1979, the disqualified person voting level decreases to 45 percent, the foundation voting level increases to 5 percent, and the permitted holdings are 5 percent (50% − 45%). On May 1, 1980, and June 1, 1981, the levels remain the same. Since the 41 percent holdings are treated as held by a disqualified person for the period beginning on May 1, 1980, and extending through May 31, 1991, F's remaining holdings of 5 percent do not exceed the 25 percent limitation of section 4943(c)(4)(D)(i).

(ii) On August 1, 1990, F sells 22 percent of the voting stock of S to a nondisqualified person, reducing the 5 percent foundation vot-

ing level to zero, leaving 17 percent (22% − 5%) to reduce the disqualified person voting level to 28 percent (45% − 17%) so that the substituted combined voting level equals 28 percent (50% − 22%). On June 1, 1991, the beginning of the second phase for the remaining 24 percent (41% − 17%) of F's holdings acquired by will, the foundation voting level increases from zero to 24 percent, the disqualified person voting level decreases to 4 percent (28% − 24%), the substituted combined voting level remains at 28 percent, and the permitted holdings equal 24 percent (28% − 4%).

(iii) If F had not disposed of the 22 percent holdings prior to June 1, 1991, F's permitted holdings would have been 25 percent, the lesser of 25 percent (under section 4943 (c)(4)(D)(i)) or 46 percent (50% − 4%). Since as of such date, F's entire holdings of 46 percent would no longer have been treated as held by a disqualified person, F would have had excess business holdings of 21 percent (46% − 25%).

| Date | F owns | F's interest 1969 | F's interest 1980 | Interest treated as held by disqualified person | Disqualified persons own | Foundation voting level | Substituted combined voting level | Disqualified person voting level | Permitted holdings | Comments |
|---|---|---|---|---|---|---|---|---|---|---|
| 5/26/69 | 5% | 5% | | 5% | 45% | 0% | 50% | 50% | 0% | |
| 5/26/69 | | | | − 5% | | + 5% | | − 5% | + 5% | 2nd phase for 5% |
| 5/26/69 | 5% | 5% | | 0% | 45% | 5% | 50% | 45% | 5% | |

| Date | F owns | F's interest 1969 | F's interest 1980 | Interest treated as held by disqualified person | Disqualified persons own | Foundation voting level | Substituted combined voting level | Disqualified person voting level | Permitted holdings | Comments |
|---|---|---|---|---|---|---|---|---|---|---|
| 5/1/80 | +41% | | +41% | +41% | −41% | | | | | H dies |
| 5/1/80 | 46% | 5% | 41% | 41% | 4% | 5% | 50% | 45% | 5% | |
| 6/1/81 | 46% | 5% | 41% | 41% | 4% | 5% | 50% | 45% | 5% | Distribution |
| 8/1/90 | −22% | −5% | −17% | −17% | | −5% | −22% | −17% | −5% | F disposes of 22% |
| 8/1/90 | 24% | 0% | 24% | 24% | 4% | 0% | 28% | 28% | 0% | |
| 6/1/91 | | | | −24% | | +24% | | −24% | +24% | 2nd phase for 24% |
| 6/1/91 | 24% | 0% | 24% | 0% | 4% | 24% | 28% | 4% | 24% | |

[Reg. § 53.4943-5.]

☐ [T.D. 7496, 7-5-77.]

### [Reg. § 53.4943-6]

**§ 53.4943-6. Five-year period to dispose of gifts, bequests, etc.—** (a) *In general.*—(1) *Application.*—(i) Paragraph (6) of section 4943(c) prescribes transition rules for a private foundation, which, but for such paragraph, would have excess business holdings as a result of a change in the holdings in a business enterprise after May 26, 1969 (other than by purchase by such private foundation or by a disqualified person) to the extent that section 4943(c)(5) (relating to certain holdings acquired under a pre-May 27, 1969, will or trust) does not apply.

(ii) Subparagraph (A) of section 4943(c)(6) applies where, immediately prior to a change in holdings described in paragraph (a)(1)(i) of this section, the foundation has no excess business holdings in such enterprise (determined without regard to section 4943(c)(4), (5), or (6)). In such a case, the entire interest of the foundation in such enterprise (immediately after such change) shall (while held by the foundation) be treated as held by a disqualified person (rather than by the foundation) during the five-year period beginning on the date of such change.

(iii) Subparagraph (B) of section 4943(c)(6) applies where the foundation has excess business holdings in such enterprise (determined without regard to section 4943(c)(4), (5), or (6)) immediately prior to a change in holdings described in paragraph (a)(1)(i) of this section. In such a case, the interest of the foundation in such enterprise (immediately after such change) shall (while held by the foundation) be treated as held by a disqualified person (rather than by the foundation) during the five-year period beginning on the date of such change, except that if and as soon as any holdings in such enterprise become excess business holdings during such period (determined without regard to such change (and the resulting application of section 4943(c)(6) to the foundation's interest in such enterprise)), such holdings shall no longer be treated as held by a disqualified person under this section, but shall constitute excess business holdings subject to the initial tax. In applying the preceding sentence, if holdings of the foundation which (but for such change in holdings (and the resulting application of section 4943(c)(6) to the foundation's interest in such enterprise)) would be subject to the 25 percent limit prescribed by section 4943(c)(4)(D) after the expiration of the first phase, such holdings shall be treated as subject to such percentage limitation for purposes of determining excess business holdings. For example, if a private foundation in 1978 has present holdings of 28 percent in a business enterprise to which section 4943(c)(4) applies, and such holdings would exceed the 25 percent limit of section 4943(c)(4)(D)(i) on May 26, 1979, a gift of 5 percent to the foundation in 1978 of an interest in such enterprise shall not prevent the 3 percent (28% − 25%) excess over the 25 percent limit from constituting excess business holdings on May 26, 1979, if on such date disqualified persons hold more than a 2 percent interest in such enterprise (and no other transaction has taken place).

(2) *Acquisitions that are not purchases.*—Section 4943(c)(6) does not apply if a change in holdings in a business enterprise is the result of a purchase by the private foundation or a disqualified person. For purposes of subparagraph (a) of this paragraph, the term "purchase" shall not include any acquisition by gift, devise, bequest, legacy, or intestate succession. Paragraph (d) of this section provides rules for the treatment of increases in holdings received in a readjustment (as defined in § 53.4943-7(d)(1)).

(3) *Examples.*—The provisions of paragraph (a) of this section may be illustrated by the following examples:

*Example (1).* On January 4, 1985, A, an individual, makes a contribution to F, a private foundation, of 200 shares of X Corporation common stock. Assume that F had no X stock before January 4, 1985, and under section 4943(c)(1) the receipt of the X stock by F would cause some or all of the 200 shares of the X stock to be classified as excess business holdings. Under the provisions of section 4943(c)(6)(A) and this paragraph (a), since the contribution of the X stock to F is a gift and not a purchase, the X stock in F's hands is treated as held by disqualified persons and not by F through January 3, 1990.

*Example (2).* Assume the facts as stated in Example (1) except that F receives the X stock as a bequest pursuant to the terms of A's will executed on April 1, 1980. A dies on June 3, 1984, and the stock is distributed to F on February 16, 1985. As in Example (1), the bequest of X to F is not a purchase under this paragraph (a). Consequently, the X stock in F's hands is treated as held by disqualified persons and not by F through February 15, 1990.

*Example (3).* On February 1, 1980, F, a private foundation, owns 15 percent of the voting stock of X Corporation, and disqualified persons own 4 percent of the voting stock of X Corporation. On February 2, 1980, B, a nondisqualified person, contributes 8 percent of the voting stock of X to F in a transaction to which section 4943(c)(5) does not apply. Assuming that the 35 percent limit of section 4943(c)(2)(B) does not apply under the provisions of section 4943(c)(6)(A) and paragraph (a) of this section the 23 percent voting stock owned by F on such date is treated as held by a disqualified person through February 1, 1985, since F would have had excess business holdings of 7 percent as a result of the contribution (23% actual holdings less 16% (20% − 4%) permitted holdings). On March 1, 1984, C, another nondisqualified person, contributes 6 percent of the voting stock of X Corporation to F. But for this second contribution and the resulting application of section 4943(c)(6) to F's interest in X, F would have excess business holdings of 7 percent (23% − 16%) within the five-year period beginning on the date of such contribution. Accordingly, under section 4943(c)(6)(B) and paragraph (a) of this section, all 29 percent (6% + 23%) of the stock held by F on March 1, 1984, will be treated as held by a disqualified person until March 1, 1989, except that 7 percent will cease to be so treated on February 2, 1985. If prior to February 2, 1985, no further transactions occurred in the stock of X, F would have excess business holdings of 7 percent subject to the initial tax, since the amount still treated as held by disqualified persons (29% − 7%) plus the amount actually held by disqualified persons (4%) already exceed 20 percent.

(b) *Special rules for acquisitions by will or trust.*—(1) *In general.*—In the case of an acquisition of holdings in a business enterprise by a private foundation pursuant to the terms of a will or trust, the five-year period described in section 4943(c)(6) and in this section shall not commence until the date on which the distribution of such holdings from the estate or trust to the foundation occurs. See § 53.4943-5(b)(1) for rules relating to the determination of the date of distribution under the terms of a will or trust. For purposes of this subparagraph, holdings in a business enterprise will not be treated as acquired by a private foundation pursuant to the terms of a will where the holdings in the business enterprise were not held by the decedent. Thus, in the case of after-acquired property, this subparagraph shall not apply, the five-year period described in section 4943(c)(6) and this section shall commence on the date of acquisition of such holdings by the estate, and such five-year period may expire prior to the date of distribution of such holdings from the estate. To the extent that an interest to which section 4943(c)(6) and this paragraph (b)(1) apply is constructively held by a private foundation under section 4943(d)(1) and § 53.4943-8 prior to the date of distribution, it shall be treated as held by a disqualified person prior to such date by reason of section 4943(c)(6). See § 53.4943-8 for rules relating to constructive holdings held in an estate or trust for the benefit of the foundation.

(2) *Special rule for section 4943(c)(5) interests acquired from a nondisqualified person.*—(i) In the case of holdings of a private foundation in a business enterprise to which section 4943(c)(5) (relating to certain holdings acquired under a pre-May 27, 1969, will or trust) applies which are acquired from a nondisqualified person, the interest of the foundation in such enterprise (immediately after such acquisition) shall (while held by the foundation) be treated as held by a disqualified person (rather than the foundation) under section 4943(c)(6)(B) and paragraph (a)(1)(iii) of this section from the date of acquisition until the end of the fifth year following the date of distribution of

such holdings. Thereafter, only the holdings to which section 4943(c)(5) and §53.4943-5(a)(1) apply shall continue to be treated as held by a disqualified person until the end of the first phase with respect thereto.

(ii) The provisions of paragraph (b)(2)(i) of this section may be illustrated by the following examples:

*Example (1).* On May 26, 1969, F, a private foundation, owns 5 percent of the voting stock of Corporation X and no disqualified persons own any stock in X. On June 30, 1977, a nondisqualified person bequeaths to F 33 percent of the voting stock in X to which section 4943(c)(5) applies. This 33 percent interest is distributed to F on August 17, 1978. Under section 4943(c)(6)(A) the entire 38 percent (5% + 33%) of the X voting stock shall be treated as held by a disqualified person from June 30, 1977 (the date the 33 percent interest is contructively acquired by F) until August 17, 1983 (five years after the date of distribution of the 33 percent interest to F). However, assuming that the 35 percent limit of section 4943(c)(2)(B) does not apply, the substituted combined voting level on June 30, 1977 is only 33 percent because there was no interest to which section 4943(c)(4) or (5) applied immediately before that date and thus there was no substituted combined voting level at that time. In that case, since the 3-phase holding period is only available for the interest acquired by will (33%) under section 4943(c)(5), the substituted combined voting level on June 30, 1977 is only 33 percent, not 38 percent. Assuming that the substituted combined voting level remains 33 percent at all relevant times, and prior to August 17, 1983, no further transactions occur in the stock of X, F on that date would have excess business holdings of 5 percent subject to the initial tax. The amount treated as held by disqualified persons at that time (33%) would equal the substituted combined voting level at that time (33%), and thus permitted holdings would be zero. Under section 4943(c)(5) the 33 percent interest will continue to be treated as held by a disqualified person until August 17, 1988 (10 years after the date of distribution).

*Example (2).* On May 26, 1969, F, a private foundation, owns 29 percent of the stock (voting power and value) of Corporation X, and on June 30, 1977, a nondisqualified person bequeaths to F 23 percent of the stock (voting power and value) in X to which section 4943(c)(5) does apply. This 23 percent interest is distributed to F on August 17, 1978. Disqualified persons hold no stock of X. Although the substituted combined voting and value levels cannot exceed 50 percent on May 26, 1979 (at the start of the second phase with respect to the 29 percent interest), under section 4943(c)(6)(B) the entire 52 percent (29% + 23%) of the X voting stock shall be treated as held by a disqualified person from June 30, 1977 (the date the 23% interest is constructively acquired by F) until August 17, 1983 (five years after the date of distribution of the 23% interest to F). On June 1, 1980, during such second phase, D, a disqualified person, purchases 3 percent of the X stock (voting power and value). On such date, but for the acquisition by F of the 23 percent interest, F would have had excess business holdings of 4 percent. The purchase by D of more than 2 percent of the voting stock of X causes the 25 percent limit of section 4943(c)(4)(D)(i) to apply to the 29 percent interest (29% − 25% = 4%). Thus, on June 1, 1980, 4 percent of the X voting stock held by F since May 27, 1969, shall cease to be treated as held by a disqualified person under section 4943(c)(6)(B) and become excess business holdings subject to the initial tax. See §53.4943-2(a)(1)(ii) for the 90-day period in which to dispose of these excess business holdings resulting from the purchase by the disqualified person.

(c) *Exceptions.*—(1) Section 4943(c)(6) and this section shall not apply to any transfer of holdings in a business enterprise by one private foundation to another private foundation which is related to the first foundation within the meaning of section 4946(a)(1)(H).

(2) Section 4943(c)(6) and this section shall not apply to an increase in the holdings of a private foundation in a business enterprise that is part of a plan whereby disqualified persons will purchase additional holdings in the same enterprise during the five-year period beginning on the date of such change, *e.g.*, to maintain control of such enterprise, since such increase shall be treated as caused in part by the purchase of such additional holdings.

(3) The purchase of holdings by an entity whose holdings are treated as constructively owned by a foundation, its disqualified persons, or both, under section 4943(d)(1) shall be treated as a purchase by a disqualified person if the foundation, its disqualified persons or both have effective control of the entity or otherwise can control the purchase. For example, if a foundation is the beneficiary of a specific bequest of $20,000 and its consent is required for the estate to make a purchase using such cash, then a purchase by the estate using such cash would be treated as a purchase by a disqualified person. Similarly, if an executor of an estate is a disqualified person with respect to a private foundation, any purchase by the estate would be treated as a purchase by a disqualified person.

(4) If a private foundation, its disqualified persons, or both, hold an interest in specific property under the terms of a will or trust, and

if the private foundation, its disqualified persons, or both, consent or otherwise agree to the substitution of holdings in a business enterprise for such specific property, such holdings shall be treated as required by purchase by a disqualified person. For example, if a private foundation is the beneficiary of a specific bequest of $20,000 and the private foundation agrees to accept certain of the estate's holdings in a business enterprise in satisfaction of such specific bequest, such holdings will be treated as acquired by purchase by a disqualified person even if such holdings were held by the decedent.

(d) *Readjustments and distributions.*—(1) *General rule.*—Except as otherwise provided in subparagraph (2) of this paragraph, any increase in holdings in a business enterprise that is the result of a readjustment (as defined in §53.4943-7(d)(1)) shall be treated as acquired other than by purchase. However, holdings that are attributable to holdings owned by the private foundation that would have been excess business holdings except for the fact that such holdings were treated as held by a disqualified person prior to the readjustment shall in no event be treated as held by a disqualified person after the date on which the holdings to which the change is attributable would have ceased to be treated as held by a disqualified person.

(2) *Exceptions.*—Any increase in holdings in a business enterprise that is the result of a readjustment (as defined in §53.4943-7(d)(1)), including any change resulting from application of the rule in §53.4943-8(c)(3), shall be treated as occurring by purchase by a disqualified person:

(i) To the extent the increase is attributable to holdings that were excess business holdings prior to the readjustment, and separately

(ii) To the full extent of the increase if the readjustment includes a prohibited transaction, unless the foundation establishes to the satisfaction of the Commissioner that effective control of all parties to the transaction was, at the time of the transaction, in one or more persons (other than the foundation) who are not disqualified persons with respect to the foundation. See §53.4943-7(d)(2) for the definition of prohibited transaction.

(3) *Section 4943(c)(6) holdings.*—If, immediately prior to a readjustment (as defined in §53.4943-7(d)(1)), a private foundation has holdings in a business enterprise that are treated under section 4943(c)(6) as held by a disqualified person, then any holdings in a business enterprise that are received in the readjustment in exchange for such section 4943(c)(6) holdings shall be treated as the holdings surrendered in the exchange to the same extent as provided in §53.4943-7 with respect to exchanges involving holdings to which section 4943(c)(4) or (5) applies. Rules similar to those in §53.4943-7(a)(2) shall be applied to determine when holdings are treated as surrendered or received in a readjustment for purposes of this paragraph.

(4) *Redemption by a corporation that is a disqualified person.*—If a foundation holds an interest in a corporation that is a disqualified person, an increase in the holdings of the private foundation, its disqualified persons, or both, as a result of a redemption or a purchase of stock of the disqualified person corporation by such corporation shall not be treated as acquired by purchase by a disqualified person based solely on the status of the corporation as a disqualified person.

(5) *One percent rule for redemptions.*—If the holdings of a foundation, its disqualified persons, or both, in a business enterprise are increased as a result of one or more redemptions during any taxable year then, unless the aggregate of such increases equals or exceeds one percent of the outstanding voting stock or one percent of the value of all outstanding shares of all classes of stock, the determination of whether such increases cause the foundation to have excess business holdings shall be made only at the close of the private foundation's taxable year. The five-year period described in section 4943(c)(6) or the 90-day period described in §53.4943-2(a)(1)(ii), whichever is applicable, shall begin on the last day of such taxable year. If, however, the aggregate of such increases equals or exceeds one percent of the outstanding voting stock or one percent of the value of all outstanding shares of all classes of stock, the determination of whether such increases cause the foundation to have excess business holdings shall be made, and the applicable five-year or 90-day period shall begin, as of the date the increases, in the aggregate, equal or exceed one percent.

(6) *Examples.*—The provisions of this paragraph are illustrated in §53.4943-7(f) and by the following examples:

*Example (1).* (i) F, a private foundation, holds 20% of the voting stock of X corporation, an active business enterprise. No disqualified person with respect to F holds any X stock. In 1980, X redeems 10% of its outstanding shares, increasing F's holdings to 22% of the X stock. Assume the redemption by X is not a prohibited transaction.

(ii) All of F's holdings before the redemption are permitted holdings under section 4943(c)(2). There is no effective control of X by third parties so that 35% permitted holdings rule is inapplicable. F's holdings after the redemption exceed the permitted holdings under section 4943(c)(2) (20%). Because the increase is attributable to stock that was permitted holdings prior to the readjustment, and the readjustment does not involve a prohibited transaction, the 2% increase in F's holdings of X stock is treated as acquired other than by purchase. Therefore, under section 4943(c)(6) and this section, F will have 5 years from the date of the redemption to dispose of the 2% excess.

*Example (2).* (i) Assume the same facts as in *Example (1)* except that the 20% of X stock held by F was donated by X corporation, was worth more than $5,000 and represented 20% of the contributions received by the foundation through the end of the taxable year in which the gift of stock was made.

(ii) X corporation is a disqualified person with respect to F under section 4946(a)(1)(A). Under subparagraph (4), the redemption of X stock is not treated as a purchase by a disqualified person merely because X is a disqualified person with respect to F. Therefore the rules of this paragraph apply as if the redemption were made by a corporation which is not a disqualified person. The analysis and result are the same as in *Example (1).*

*Example (3).* (i) On May 1, 1990, F, a private foundation, received a donation of 40% of the stock of X corporation, a business enterprise. Neither F nor any disqualified person with respect to F holds any other interest in X. On June 1, 1992, the X corporation redeemed F's 40% interest in exchange for 100% of the stock of Y corporation, a wholly-owned subsidiary of X. Assume the redemption by X is not a prohibited transaction.

(ii) Under section 4943(c)(6), the X stock acquired by gift is treated as held by disqualified persons through April 30, 1995. Under subparagraph (3) of this paragraph (d), 40% of the 100% interest in Y received in exchange for F's 40% interest in X is treated as F's 40% interest in X and is therefore treated as held by disqualified persons through April 30, 1995. In addition, under subparagraph (1) of this paragraph (d), the 60% interest in Y that represents an increase in holdings above the 40% held before the readjustment will be treated as acquired other than by purchase. However, F's 20% interest in X in excess of the 20% permitted holdings under 4943(c)(2) would have been excess business holdings if such interest had not been treated as held by a disqualified person on June 1, 1992. Therefore, to the extent of a 30% interest in Y (*i.e.,* the portion of the increased holdings in Y attributable to F's 20% holdings in X) the increased holdings will be treated as held by disqualified persons only through April 30, 1995, since this is the latest date on which F's original 40% interest in X would have been treated as held by disqualified persons. The remaining 30% interest in Y will be treated as held by disqualified persons for five years from the date of the exchange (through May 31, 1997).

(e) *Constructive holdings.*—Any change in holdings in a business enterprise that occurs because a corporation ceases to be actively engaged in a trade or business, thus causing its holdings to be constructively owned by its shareholders, shall be treated as acquired other than by purchase.

(f) *Certain transactions treated as purchases; cross references.*—For the application of section 4943(c)(6) to holdings that were not an interest in a business enterprise when acquired but that subsequently become holdings in a business enterprise, see §53.4943-10(d)(2). [Reg. §53.4943-6.]

☐ [*T.D. 7496, 7-5-77. Amended by T.D. 7944, 2-21-84.*]

**[Reg. §53.4943-7]**

**§53.4943-7. Special rules for readjustments involving grandfathered holdings.**—(a) *General rules.*—(1) *Readjustments.*— Except to the extent provided in paragraph (b) of this section, if a private foundation, its disqualified persons, or both together have holdings in a corporation to which section 4943(c)(4) or (5) applies, stock of a corporation received by the foundation, its disqualified persons, or both together in a readjustment(as defined in paragraph (d)(1) of this section) in exchange for such holdings to which section 4943(c)(4) or (5) applies shall be treated, for purposes of section 4943(c)(4) or (5), as the stock surrendered in the exchange.

(2) *No exchange necessary.*—Paragraph (a)(1) of this section shall apply to all readjustments even if no exchange occurs. For purposes of this section, all stock held (directly or indirectly) before a readjustment in any corporation involved in the readjustment shall be treated as stock surrendered in the readjustment and all stock held (directly or indirectly) after the readjustment in any corporation involved in the readjustment shall be treated as stock received in the readjustment in exchange for the stock treated as surrendered.

(b) *Exceptions and limitations.*—(1) *Limitation on increases in percentage of voting stock.*—(i) If the percentage of voting stock in a business enterprise owned (directly or indirectly) by a private foundation by reason of its ownership of stock received in an exchange described in paragraph (a) of this section exceeds the greatest percentage of voting stock in any business enterprise owned (directly or indirectly) by the private foundation prior to such exchange by reason of its ownership of the stock surrendered by it in the exchange, then—

(A) That portion of the stock received by the private foundation in the exchange which represents such excess is to be treated as an increase in the holdings of the private foundation in accordance with §53.4943-6(d), and

(B) Only the remaining portion of the stock received by the private foundation in the exchange shall be treated as the stock surrendered by the private foundation in the exchange.

(ii) If the sum of the percentage of voting stock in a business enterprise owned (directly or indirectly) by disqualified persons by reason of their ownership of stock received in an exchange described in paragraph (a) of this section plus the percentage of voting stock in the business enterprise owned (directly or indirectly) by the private foundation by reason of its ownership of stock received in the exchange and treated as the stock surrendered under paragraph (b)(1)(i) of this section exceeds the greatest percentage of voting stock in any business enterprise owned (directly or indirectly) by the private foundation and its disqualified person in combination by reason of their ownership of the stock surrendered by them in the exchange, then—

(A) That portion of the stock received by the disqualified persons in the exchange which represents such excess is to be treated as an increase in the holdings of the disqualified persons in accordance with §53.4943-6(d), and

(B) Only the remaining portion of the stock received by the disqualified persons in the exchange is to be treated as the stock surrendered by the disqualified persons in the exchange.

(2) *Limitation on increase in percentage of value.*—(i) If the percentage of value of all outstanding shares of all classes of stock in a business enterprise owned (directly or indirectly) by a private foundation by reason of its ownership of stock received in an exchange described in paragraph (a) of this section exceeds the greatest percentage of such value in any business enterprise owned (directly or indirectly) by the private foundation prior to such exchange by reason of its ownership of the stock surrendered by it in the exchange, then—

(A) That portion of the stock received by the private foundation in the exchange which represents such excess is to be treated as an increase in the holdings of the private foundation in accordance with §53.4943-6(d), and

(B) Only the remaining portion of the stock received by the private foundation in the exchange shall be treated as the stock surrendered by the private foundation in the exchange.

(ii) If the sum of the percentage of value of all outstanding shares of all classes of stock in a business enterprise owned (directly or indirectly) by disqualified persons by reason of their ownership of stock received in an exchange described in paragraph (a) of this section plus the percentage of such value in the business enterprise owned (directly or indirectly) by the private foundation by reason of its ownership of stock received in the exchange and treated as the stock surrendered under paragraph (b)(2)(i) of this section exceeds the greatest percentage of such value in any business enterprise owned (directly or indirectly) by the private foundation and its disqualified persons in combination prior to the exchange by reason of their ownership of the stock surrendered by them in the exchange, then—

(A) That portion of the stock received by the disqualified persons in the exchange which represents such excess is to be treated as an increase in the holdings of the disqualified persons in accordance with §53.4943-6(d), and

(B) Only the remaining portion of the stock received by the disqualified persons in the exchange is to be treated as the stock surrendered by the disqualified persons in the exchange.

(3) *Increases in percentage of both voting stock and value.*—(i) If, as the result of an exchange described in paragraph (a) of this section, a private foundation has excesses determined under both paragraphs (b)(1)(i) and (b)(2)(i) of this section, then—

(A) That portion of the stock received by the private foundation in the exchange that represents the larger excess is to be treated as an increase in the holdings of the private foundation in accordance with §53.4943-6(d), and

(B) Only the remaining portion of the stock received by the private foundation in the exchange is to be treated as the stock surrendered by the private foundation in the exchange.

(ii) If as the result of an exchange described in paragraph (a) of this section, disqualified persons have excesses determined under both paragraphs (b)(1)(ii) and (b)(2)(ii) of this section, then—

(A) That portion of the stock received by the disqualified persons in the exchange that represents the larger excess is to be treated as an increase in the holdings of the disqualified persons in accordance with § 53.4943-6(d), and

(B) Only the remaining portion of the stock received by disqualified persons in the exchange is to be treated as the stock surrendered by disqualified persons in the exchange.

(4) *Exception for prohibited transactions.*—If a readjustment includes a prohibited transaction, as defined in paragraph (d)(2) of this section, then this paragraph shall be applied substituting, for purposes of paragraph (b)(1) and (b)(2), the lowest percentage of voting power or value owned prior to the exchange in any business enterprise involved in the readjustment to which the exchange relates for the greatest percentage of voting power or value in any business enterprise owned by reason of ownership of the stock surrendered in the exchange.

(5) *Voting and value levels.*—After an exchange described in paragraph (a) of this section, the private foundation voting and value levels, and the substituted combined voting and value levels (as defined in § 53.4943-4(d)(2)) shall be the lesser of each respective level immediately prior to the exchange with respect to the stock surrendered in the exchange and each such respective level determined immediately after the exchange by taking into account only the stock received in the exchange that is treated under this paragraph as the stock surrendered in the exchange. If the stock of more than one corporation is surrendered in exchange for stock of one corporation, the highest of each voting or value level determined immediately prior to the exchange with respect to the stock of the corporations surrendered in the exchange shall be treated as such level immediately prior to the exchange.

(6) *Determination of phases.*—(i) *In general.*—Stock received in an exchange described in paragraph (a) of this section that is treated as stock surrendered in the exchange under this paragraph shall be treated as subject to the same first, second, and third phases that were applicable to the stock surrendered for it. For purposes of determining the applicable phases, stock received in an exchange shall be treated as received in exchange for particular holdings of stock surrendered based on the terms of the exchange. Where only a portion of the stock received is treated as the stock surrendered, such portion of the stock received shall be treated as exchanged for particular holdings of stock surrendered in the same proportions as the total stock received was exchanged for particular holdings of stock surrendered. For example, if 20 shares of X stock owned by a private foundation, subject to a first phase beginning on January 1, 1978 and ending on December 31, 1987, are exchanged for 20 shares of Y stock, and 40 shares of X stock owned by the private foundation, subject to a first phase beginning on June 1, 1980 and ending on May 31, 1990, are exchanged for 40 shares of Y stock, then $^1/_3$ of the Y stock received by the private foundation is treated as received in exchanged [sic] for X stock having the January 1, 1978—December 31, 1987 first phase and $^2/_3$ of the Y stock received by the private foundation is treated as received in exchange for the X stock having the June 1, 1980—May 31, 1990 first phase. If only 30 shares of the Y stock received by the private foundation are treated as the stock surrendered, then $^1/_3$ (10 Y shares) will be subject to the January 1, 1978—December 31, 1987 first phase and $^2/_3$ (20 Y shares) will be subject to the June 1, 1980—May 31, 1990 first phase.

(ii) *Transitional rule.*—In any case in which holdings subject to section 4943(c)(4) or 4943(c)(5) have been consolidated prior to May 22, 1984, then the longest first phase applicable to any of the holdings surrendered in the consolidation shall be applied to the holdings received by the foundation in the consolidation that are treated as the holdings surrendered in the consolidation. For purposes of this clause, a consolidation is any readjustment that results in a reduction in the number of entities in which the foundation has direct holdings.

(c) *Plan to dispose of excess business holdings.*—(1) Notwithstanding § 53.4943-4(d)(4)(i)(D) (relating to restrictions on increases in levels) and paragraphs (a) and (b) of this section, if a readjustment occurs under an approved plan to dispose of stock to which section 4943(c)(4) or (5) applies, in order to meet the requirements of section 4943(c)(4) (*i.e.*, to meet the reduced limits that will be applicable after the first phase holding period described in § 53.4943-4(c)) or to meet the requirements of section 4943(c)(2), all of the stock received in the readjustment shall be treated as held by disqualified persons through the end of the longest first phase holding period applicable to stock surrendered in the readjustment. The foundation and substituted combined voting and value levels shall not be increased on account of the readjustment.

(2) For purposes of this paragraph, a plan is an approved plan only if it is approved by the Commissioner and may be subject to such conditions as the Commissioner determines. A plan must be approved prior to any exchange or distribution pursuant to the plan except for a showing of good cause such as a business emergency.

(d) *Definitions.*—(1) *Readjustments.*—For purposes of this section, the term "readjustment" includes, but is not limited to—

(i) A merger or consolidation;

(ii) A recapitalization;

(iii) An acquisition of stock or assets;

(iv) A transfer of assets;

(v) A change in identity, form, or place of organization, however effected;

(vi) A redemption;

(vii) A distribution of assets or of stock, including a distribution to which section 301, 302, 331, or 355 applies or a distribution of stock of the distributing corporation.

(2) *Prohibited transaction.*—A prohibited transaction is any transaction involving a private foundation that has holdings in a business enterprise which—

(i) Acquires stock (or similar interest in the case of an unincorporated entity) or assets of a business enterprise or redeems its own stock (or similar interest in the case of an unincorporated entity) using cash or other property transferred to the acquiring business enterprise (*e.g.*, as a contribution to capital) by the private foundation, its disqualified persons, or both;

(ii) Acquires stock (or similar interest in the case of an unincorporated entity) or assets of a business enterprise or redeems its own stock (or similar interest in the case of an unincorporated entity) using the proceeds of a loan made to, or guaranteed by, the private foundation, its disqualified persons, or both;

(iii) Acquires 40 percent or more of the voting stock (or similar interest in the case of an unincorporated entity), 40 percent or more of the value of all outstanding shares of all classes of stock (or similar interest in the case of an unincorporated entity), or 40 percent or more of the assets of a business enterprise if the acquiring business enterprise's net assets used in its trade or business prior to such acquisition are insubstantial when compared to the net assets acquired or when compared to the net assets of the business enterprise, the stock (or similar interest in the case of an unincorporated entity) of which was acquired. For this purpose, an insubstantial ratio means a ratio that is 15% or less; or

(iv) Is used as a device to acquire or expand excess business holdings. The determination of whether a business enterprise is used as a device to acquire or expand excess business holdings shall be determined based on all the facts and circumstances. A business enterprise shall be presumed to have been used as a device to acquire or expand excess business holdings if it acquires 40 percent or more of the voting stock (or similar interest in the case of an unincorporated entity), 40 percent or more of the value of all outstanding shares of all classes of stock (or similar interest in the case of an unincorporated entity), or 40 percent or more of the assets of a business enterprise if the consideration for the acquisition consists primarily of nonvoting stock (or similar interest in the case of an unincorporated entity) of the acquiring business enterprise.

(3) *Corporation involved in a readjustment.*—A corporation shall be treated as involved in a readjustment if, as part of the readjustment, any stock of the corporation is issued or redeemed, or any stock or assets of the corporation are distributed, exchanged, purchased, sold, acquired, or otherwise transferred.

(e) *Application to unincorporated business enterprise.*—The rules of this section shall apply equally to partnerships and other unincorporated business enterprises, applying the rules and substitutions provided in § 53.4943-3(c)(2), (3), and (4).

(f) *Examples.*—The provisions of this section and § 53.4943-6(d) are illustrated by the following examples, which assume no prohibited transactions are involved unless otherwise stated:

*Example (1).* (i) F, a private foundation, has owned 80% of the one outstanding class of stock of X corporation since 1965. The X stock is subject to section 4943(c)(4) with a first phase ending on May 25, 1984. On January 1, 1982, X merges with Y corporation to form Z corporation. X, Y and Z are active business corporations. F owns no Y stock. No disqualified person with respect to F owns any stock in X, Y, or Z. After the merger, F owns 25% of the one outstanding class of Z stock. Third parties do not control Z so that the 35% permitted holdings rule under section 4943(c)(2) is inapplicable.

(ii) F's percentages of voting power and value in Z after the merger (25%) are less than F's percentages of voting power and value in X before the merger (80%). Therefore, under paragraph (a)(1) of this section, all of F's holdings in Z are treated as the X stock surrendered. Therefore, the Z stock is treated as subject to section 4943(c)(4) with a first phase ending on May 25, 1984. Under the downward ratchet of paragraph (a)(5) of this section, the foundation voting and value levels and the substituted combined voting and value levels are reduced to 25%.

*Example (2).* (i) F, a private foundation, owns 100% of the one outstanding class of stock in X corporation and 30% of the one outstanding class of stock in Y corporation. F has held this stock continuously since 1960, and no disqualified person has ever owned any stock in X or Y. Under section 4943(c)(4), F's holdings in X are treated as held by disqualified persons through the end of the first phase on May 25, 1989, and F's holdings in Y are permitted holdings during the second phase, which began on May 26, 1979. On January 1, 1985, X and Y consolidate, forming a new corporation Z. In the consolidation, F acquires 50% of the one class of outstanding stock of Z, 40% in exchange for F's 100% interest in X and 10% in exchange for F's 30% interest in Y. Unrelated parties hold the remaining 50% of Z.

(ii) F's percentages of voting power and value in Z after the merger (50%) are less than F's percentages of voting power and value in X before the merger (100%). Thus, under paragraph (a)(1) of this section, the 50% interest in Z held by F is treated as the stock surrendered in the exchange for purposes of section 4943(c)(4). Under paragraph (b)(6) of this section, the 10% interest in Z received for the Y stock is subject to the same second phase period as the surrendered Y stock. The 40% interest in Z received for the X stock is subject to the same first phase period as the surrendered X stock.

*Example (3).* (i) F, a private foundation, owns 50% of the one class of outstanding stock in X corporation which F has held continuously since 1935. No disqualified person with respect to F owns any stock in X. Neither F nor any disqualified person with respect to F owns any stock in Y corporation. On July 1, 1982, X and Y enter into an agreement to consolidate their businesses in a reorganization to which section 368(a)(1)(A) will apply. As a result of the contemplated consolidation, F will own 60% of the voting stock in Z, the resulting corporation. In addition, parties unrelated to F will own the remaining 40% of the Z voting stock and 100% of a new issue of nonvoting preferred stock in Z. Assume for purposes of this example, that the 60% of the voting stock to be held by F in Z will represent 50% of the fair market value of the outstanding Z stock.

(ii) Under the provisions of paragraph (b)(1) of this section, that portion of the Z stock held by F which represents a percentage of voting power equivalent to that held by F in X immediately prior to the consolidation (i.e., 50%) will be treated as the X stock held by F on May 26, 1969, for purposes of section 4943(c)(4). Therefore, 50% of the Y stock will be treated as subject to a second phase ending on May 25, 1994. The remaining portion of the Z voting stock held by F (10%) is subject to the provisions of §53.4943-6(d)(1). F will have five years from the date of the merger in which to dispose of 10% of the Z stock without incurring the tax on excess business holdings.

*Example (4).* (i) F, a private foundation, owns 80% of the one class of outstanding stock in X corporation, an active business corporation. F has held this stock continuously since 1960 and no disqualified person with respect to F owns any stock in X. X has two operating divisions, one which manufactures shoes and the other which manufactures refrigerators. On January 1, 1978, in a section 351(a) exchange, X transferred all of the assets of its shoe manufacturing division to Y, a corporation which X has formed for this purpose, and receives 100% of the stock of Y so that Y is a wholly-owned subsidiary of X. X then transfers all of the Y stock to F in exchange for all of F's holdings of X stock in a distribution to which section 355 applies.

(ii) Under paragraph (b)(1) of this section, 80% of the Y stock is treated as the X stock surrendered in the exchange for purposes of section 4943(c)(4). The 80% is treated under §53.4943-4(c) as held by disqualified persons through May 25, 1984, which constitutes the 15-year first phase holding period applicable to the 80% holding in X. The 80% of the Y stock must be reduced to the permitted holdings allowed during the second and third phase as provided by section 4943(c)(4)(D) in the same manner as F's holdings of X stock would have had to have been reduced.

(iii) Under §53.4943-6(d)(1), the remaining 20% of Y stock is treated as held by a disqualified person for five years from the date of the exchange. F will have five years from the date of the exchange in which to dispose of 20% of the Y stock without incurring the tax on excess business holdings.

*Example (5).* (i) X corporation, an active business corporation, has outstanding 1,000 shares of one class of stock, of which 600 shares have been held by F1, a private foundation; 100 shares have been held by F2, another private foundation; and 100 shares have been held by D, a disqualified person with respect to both F1 and F2. Unrelated parties hold the remaining 200 shares. F1 and F2 are disqualified persons with respect to each other under section 4946(a)(1)(H). Thus, F1 holds 60% of the X stock (600/1000); F2 and D each hold 10% (100/1000); and the foundation group (F1, F2 and D) holds 80% of X (800/1000). The holdings of F1 and F2 were acquired

on January 1, 1980 pursuant to a pre-1969 will and are subject to section 4943(c)(5). There have been no changes in holdings since January 1, 1980.

(ii) On January 1, 1985, pursuant to a plan to dispose of excess business holdings approved by the Commissioner under paragraph (c) of this section, X redeems for cash the 600 shares held by F1. After the redemption, D and F2 each hold 25% of X (100/400). F1 no longer holds any X stocks. The foundation group's holdings (F1, F2 and D) have decreased from 80% to 50% while holdings of unrelated parties have increased from 20% to 50%. At the same time F2's and D's holdings each have increased from 10% to 25%.

(iii) Notwithstanding the increase in F2's and D's holdings, under paragraph (c) of this section, all of the X stock held by F2 will be treated as held by a disqualified person through the end of the first phase (December 31, 1994). However, the foundation voting and value levels do not increase. Therefore, after the end of the first phase, F2's holdings in X may not exceed 10 percent (if the combined holdings of F1, F2 and D exceed the permitted holdings under section 4943(c)(2)).

*Example (6).* (i) X corporation, an active business corporation, has outstanding 1,000 shares of its one class of stock. Since 1960, 100 shares (10%) have been held by F, a private foundation, and 350 shares (35%) have been held by D, a disqualified person with respect to F. All of the stock held by F is permitted holdings under section 4943(c)(4) and the substituted combined voting and value levels are 45% (10% + 35%). Because of disagreements concerning management of X between D and A, an unrelated party who holds 300 shares (30%) of the X stock, X redeems all of A's shares on December 1, 1981.

(ii) After the redemption, F holds 14.3% (100/700) of the X stock and D holds 50% (350/700), for combined holdings of 64.3%. Because the combined holdings exceed the substituted combined voting level (45%) by more than F's entire holdings, all of the F stock is excess business holdings. However, all of F's stock will be treated as acquired other than by purchase under §53.4943-6(d)(1) and therefore will be treated under section 4943(c)(6) and this section, as held by a disqualified person for five years from the date of the redemption (through November 30, 1986). If the combined holdings of F and its disqualified person are reduced to 45 percent by the end of the five year period, F may retain a portion of its holdings in X (limited to no more than the foundation voting and value level of 10 percent).

*Example (7).* Assume the same facts as in *Example (6)*, except that D loaned the money to X that was used to redeem A's shares. Under these facts, the increased holdings result from a prohibited transaction described in paragraph (d)(2) of this section. Therefore, all of F's stock will be treated as acquired by purchase by a disqualified person under §53.4943-6(d)(2). F will have 90 days after the redemption in which to dispose of its holdings or to reduce its holdings and the combined holdings to the levels held prior to the redemption as discussed in *Example (6)*.

*Example (8).* (i) F, a private foundation, has held 100% of the outstanding stock of X corporation since 1960. F also holds 15% of the voting stock of Y corporation. Both X and Y are active business corporations. X has $1 million in net assets used in its trade or business and Y has $6.7 million used in its trade or business. On June 1, 1985, Y is merged into X. After the merger F holds 25% of the voting stock of X. No person other than F controls X after the merger.

(ii) Because more than 40% of Y was acquired and the net assets of X, the acquiring corporation, used in its trade or business prior to the merger represent less than 15% of the net assets of Y used in its trade or business, the merger is a prohibited transaction described in paragraph (d)(2)(iii). Therefore, only 15% of the stock of X is treated, pursuant to paragraph (b), as the stock held by F prior to the redemption. F's holding of 5% (the excess of F's 25% holdings over the 20% permitted holdings in X (determined under section 4943(c)(2)) are treated as purchased by a disqualified person pursuant to §53.4943-6(d)(2). F will have 90 days after June 1, 1985, in which to dispose of the 5% excess holdings. [Reg. §53.4943-7.]

☐ [*T.D.* 7944, 2-21-84.]

**[Reg. §53.4943-8]**

**§53.4943-8. Business holdings; constructive ownership.—** (a) *Constructive ownership.—*(1) *In general.—*For purposes of section 4943, in computing the holdings in a business enterprise of a private foundation, or a disqualified person (as defined in section 4946), any stock or other interest owned, directly or indirectly, by or for a corporation, partnership, estate or trust shall be considered as being owned proportionately by or for its shareholders, partners, or beneficiaries except as otherwise provided in paragraphs (b), (c) and (d) of this section. Any interest in a business enterprise actually or constructively owned by a shareholder of a corporation, a partner of a partnership, or a beneficiary of an estate or trust shall not be considered as constructively held by the corporation, partnership, trust or estate. Further, if any corporation, partnership, estate or trust has a warrant or other option to acquire an interest in a business enterprise, such interest is not deemed to be constructively owned by such entity until the option is exercised. (See paragraph (b)(2) of §53.4943-3 for rules that options are not stock for purposes of determining excess business holdings.)

(2) *Powers of appointment.*—Any interest in business enterprise over which a foundation or a disqualified person has a power of appointment exercisable in favor of the foundation or a disqualified person shall be considered owned by the foundation or disqualified person holding such power of appointment.

(3) *Determination of extent of constructive ownership.*—If an interest in a business enterprise owned by a corporation is constructively owned by a shareholder, each shareholder's proportion of ownership is generally computed on the basis of the voting stock each shareholder has in the corporation. In determining holdings permitted under section 4943(c)(4) and (5), each shareholder's proportion of ownership in the business enterprise shall also be computed on the basis of value, taking into account both voting and nonvoting stock held by the shareholder.

(4) *Nonvoting stock.*—If a private foundation, its disqualified persons, or both, own (directly or constructively) nonvoting stock of a parent corporation, the holdings of which are treated as constructively owned by its shareholders by reason of section 4943(d)(1) and this section, such nonvoting stock shall be treated as nonvoting stock of any corporation in which the parent corporation holds an interest for purposes of the limitation on the holding of nonvoting stock under section 4943(c)(2)(A) and §53.4943-3(b)(2).

(5) *Interests held by certain disqualified persons.*—In the case of an entity that is a disqualified person (other than an entity described in section 4946(a)(1)(H)), the holdings of which are treated as constructively owned by its shareholders, partners, or beneficiaries, for purposes of determining the total holdings of disqualified persons the holdings of the entity shall be considered held by a disqualified person only to the extent such holdings are treated as constructively owned by disqualified persons who are shareholders, partners, or beneficiaries of the entity. In the case of an entity described in section 4946(a)(1)(H) or an entity, the holdings of which are not treated as constructively owned by its shareholders, partners, or beneficiaries, all holdings of such entity shall be treated as held by a disqualified person if and only if the entity itself is a disqualified person.

(b) *Estates and trusts.*—(1) *In general.*—Any interest actually or constructively owned by an estate or trust is deemed constructively owned, in the case of an estate, by its beneficiaries or, in the case of a trust, by its remainder beneficiaries except as provided in paragraphs (b)(2), (3) and (4) of this section (relating to certain split-interest trusts described in section 4947(a)(2), to trusts of qualified pension, profit-sharing, and stock bonus plans described in section 401(a) and to revocable trusts). Thus, if a trust owns 100 percent of the stock of a corporation A, and if, on an actuarial basis, W's life interest in the trust is 15 percent, Y's life interest is 25 percent, and Z's remainder interest is 60 percent, under this paragraph (b), Z will be considered to be the owner of 100 percent of the stock of corporation A. See §53.4943-4, §53.4943-5 and §53.4943-6 for rules relating to certain actual or constructive holdings of a foundation being treated as held by a disqualified person. For the treatment of certain property acquired by an estate or trust after May 26, 1969, see paragraph (a)(2) of §53.4943-5.

(2) *Split-interest trusts.*—(i) *Amounts transferred in trust after May 26, 1969.*—In the case of an interest in a business enterprise which was transferred to a trust described in section 4947(a)(2) after May 26, 1969, for the benefit of a private foundation, no portion of such interest shall be considered as owned by the private foundation—

(A) If the foundation holds only an income interest in the trust, or

(B) If the foundation holds only a remainder interest in the trust (unless the foundation can exercise primary investment discretion with respect to such interest)

until such trust ceases to be so described. See section 4947(a)(2) and (b)(3) and the regulations thereunder for rules relating to such trusts. See also sections 4946(a)(1)(G) and (H) and the regulations thereunder for rules relating to when a trust described in this paragraph (b)(2) is itself a disqualified person.

(ii) *Amounts transferred in trust on or before May 26, 1969.*—In the case of an interest in a business enterprise which was transferred to a trust described in section 4947(a)(2) (without regard to section 4947(a)(2)(C)) on or before May 26, 1969, for the benefit of a private foundation, no portion of such interest shall be considered as owned by the foundation until it is actually distributed to the foundation or until the trust ceases to be so described. See section 4943(c)(5) and §53.4943-5 for rules relating to certain trusts which were irrevocable on May 26, 1969.

(3) *Employee benefit trusts.*—An interest in a business enterprise owned by a trust described in section 401(a) (pension and profit-sharing plans) shall not be considered as owned by its beneficiaries, unless disqualified persons (within the meaning of section 4946) control the investment of the trust assets.

(4) *Revocable trusts.*—An interest in a business enterprise owned by a revocable trust shall be treated as owned by the grantor of such trust.

(5) *Estates.*—For purposes of applying section 4943(d)(1) to estates, the term "beneficiary" includes any person (including a private foundation) entitled to receive property of a decedent pursuant to a will or pursuant to laws of descent and distribution. However, a person shall no longer be considered a beneficiary of an estate when all the property to which he is entitled has been received by him, when he no longer has a claim against the estate and when there is only a remote possibility that it will be necessary for the estate to seek the return of property or to seek payment from him by contribution or otherwise to satisfy claims against the estate or expenses of administration. When pursuant to the preceding sentence, a person (including a private foundation) ceases to be a beneficiary, stock or another interest in a business enterprise owned by the estate shall not thereafter be considered owned by such person. If any person is the constructive owner of an interest in a business enterprise actually held by an estate, the date of death of the testator or decedent intestate shall be the first day on which such person shall be considered a constructive owner of such interest. See §53.4943-5 for rules relating to wills executed on or before May 26, 1969.

(c) *Corporation actively engaged in a trade or business.*—(1) *In general.*—Except as provided in paragraphs (c)(2) and (3) of this section, any interest (whether or not in a separate entity) owned by a corporation which is actively engaged in a trade or business shall not be deemed to be constructively owned by such corporation's shareholders.

(2) *Actively engaged in a trade or business.*—For purposes of paragraph (c)(1) of this section—

(i) A corporation shall not be considered to be actively engaged in a trade or business if the corporation is not a business enterprise by reason of section 4943(d)(3)(A) or (B) and §53.4943-10(b) or (c);

(ii) In the case of a corporation which owns passive holdings and is actively engaged in a trade or business, such corporation shall not be considered to be actively engaged in a trade or business if the net assets used in such trade or business are insubstantial when compared to passive holdings.

(3) *Exceptions.*—If a corporation has been involved in a prohibited transaction, any interest in a business enterprise owned by such corporation shall be treated as constructively owned by its shareholders, whether or not such corporation is actively engaged in a trade or business. For a definition of prohibited transaction, see §53.4943-7(d)(2).

(4) *Affiliated group.*—In applying this paragraph to the common parent in an affiliated group (as defined in §53.4943-10(c)(3)(ii)), the assets and activities of the affiliated group shall be treated as the assets and activities of the common parent.

(d) *Partnerships.*—Any interest in a business enterprise which is owned by a partnership shall be deemed to be constructively owned by the partners in such partnerships.

(e) *Examples.*—The provisions of this section are illustrated by the following examples.

*Example (1).* F, a private foundation, directly owns voting stock of X, a holding company described in section 4943(d)(3)(B). That stock represents 40% of the voting power in X and 20% of the value of all outstanding shares of all classes of stock in X. F also owns nonvoting stock in X that represents 10% of the value of all outstanding shares of all classes of stock in X. D, a disqualified person, owns voting stock of X that represents 40% of the voting power in X and 20% of the value. D does not own any nonvoting stock in X. X corporation's only holding is stock of Y corporation. The Y voting stock held by X represents 50% of the voting power in Y and 25% of the value of all outstanding shares of all classes of stock in Y. X also owns nonvoting stock in Y that represents 25% of the value of all outstanding shares of all classes of stock in Y. Under paragraph (a)(3) of this section, F and D each constructively owns 20% of the voting power in Y through their voting interest in X (40% of X's 50% in Y). F also constructively owns 15% of the value of all outstanding shares of all classes of stock in Y through F's interest in X (F's 30% of the value of X multiplied by X's 50% of the value of Y), while D constructively owns 10% of the value of Y (D's 20% of the value of X multiplied by X's 50% of the value of Y).

*Example (2).* (i) F, a private foundation, owns 50% of the one class of nonvoting stock of X corporation, a corporation described in section 4943(d)(3)(B) and paragraph (c)(2)(i) above. D, a disqualified person with respect to F as described in section 4946(a)(1)(A), owns 40% of the one class of voting stock of X. X corporation is a disqualified person with respect to F because D owns more than 35% of the voting of X. (See section 4946(a)(1)(E).) On January 1, 1980, X purchases for cash 40% of the only class of stock of Y corporation, a retail clothing store, from unrelated third parties.

(ii) Under paragraph (a)(4) of this section, F is treated as owning nonvoting stock of Y. Although X is a disqualified person, its holdings are not treated as held by disqualified persons except as constructive holdings. Therefore, the "deemed" nonvoting stock in Y is a permitted holding because D, a disqualified person with respect to F, constructively owns only 16% of the voting stock of Y (less than 20% permitted under section 4943(c)(2)).

*Example (3).* (i) The facts are the same as in *Example (2)*, except that X purchases 100% of the stock of Y corporation. Under paragraph (a)(4) of this section, F is treated as owning nonvoting stock of Y. The "deemed" nonvoting stock in Y is not a permitted holding because D, a disqualified person with respect to F, constructively owns 40% of the voting stock of Y.

*Example (4).* (i) D, a disqualified person with respect to F, owns 40% of the one class of stock in X corporation, an active business. X is a disqualified person with respect to F. X acquires 40% of the voting stock in Y corporation. Under paragraph (a)(5) of this section, the holdings of X in Y are treated as held by a disqualified person. F cannot hold any Y stock, voting or nonvoting. [Reg. §53.4943-8.]

☐ [T.D. 7496, 7-5-77. Amended by T.D. 7944, 2-21-84.]

### [Reg. §53.4943-9]

**§53.4943-9. Business holdings; certain periods.**—(a) *Taxable period.*—(1) *In general.*—For purposes of section 4943, the term "taxable period" means, with respect to any excess business holdings of a private foundation in a business enterprise, the period beginning with the first day on which there are such excess business holdings and ending on the earliest of:

(i) The date of mailing of a notice of deficiency under section 6212 with respect to the tax imposed on the holdings by section 4943(a);

(ii) The date on which the excess is eliminated; or

(iii) The date on which the tax imposed by section 4943(a) is assessed.

For example, M, a private foundation, first has excess business holdings in X, a corporation, on February 5, 1972. A notice of deficiency is mailed under section 6212 to M on June 1, 1974. With respect to M's excess business holdings in X, the taxable period begins on February 5, 1972, and ends on June 1, 1974.

(2) *Special rule.*—Where a notice of deficiency referred to in subparagraph (1)(i) of this paragraph is not mailed because there is a waiver of the restrictions on assessment and collection of a deficiency, or because the deficiency is paid, the date of filing of the waiver or the date of such payment, respectively, shall be treated as the end of the taxable period.

(3) *Suspension of taxable period for 90 days.*—In any case in which a private foundation has excess business holdings solely because of the acquisition of an interest in a business enterprise to which paragraph (a)(1)(ii) or (iii) of §53.4943-2 applies, the taxable period described in paragraph (a) of this section shall be suspended for the 90-day period (as extended) starting with the date on which the foundation knows or has reason to know of the acquisition, provided that at the end of such period the foundation has disposed of such excess holdings.

(b) *Cross reference.*—For rules relating to taxable events that are corrected within the correction period, defined in section 4963(e), see section 4961(a) and the regulations thereunder.

(c) *Correction.*—For purposes of section 4943, correction shall be considered as made when no interest in the enterprise held by the foundation is classified as an excess business holding under section 4943(c)(1). In any case where the private foundation has excess business holdings which are constructively held for it under section 4943(c)(1), correction shall be considered made when either a corporation, partnership, estate, or trust in which holdings in such enterprise are constructively held for the foundation or a disqualified person, the foundation itself, or a disqualified person disposes of a sufficient interest in the enterprise so that no interest in the enterprise held by the foundation is classified as excess business holdings under section 4943(c)(1). [Reg. §53.4943-9.]

☐ [T.D. 7496, 7-5-77. Amended by T.D. 8084, 5-1-86.]

### [Reg. §53.4943-10]

**§53.4943-10. Business enterprise; definition.**—(a) *In general.*—(1) Except as provided in paragraph (b) or (c) of this section, under section 4943(d)(4) the term "business enterprise" includes the active conduct of a trade or business, including any activity which is regularly carried on for the production of income from the sale of goods or the performance of services and which constitutes an unrelated trade or business under section 513. For purposes of the preceding sentence, where an activity carried on for profit constitutes an unrelated trade or business, no part of such trade or business shall be excluded from the classification of a business enterprise merely because it does not result in a profit.

(2) Notwithstanding paragraph (a)(1) of this section, a bond or other evidence of indebtedness does not constitute a holding in a business enterprise unless such bond or evidence of indebtedness is otherwise determined to be an equitable interest in such enterprise. Similarly, a leasehold interest in real property does not constitute an interest in a business enterprise, even though rent payable under such lease is dependent, in whole or in part, upon the income or profits derived by another from such property, unless such leasehold interest constitutes an interest in the income or profits of an unrelated trade or business under section 513.

(b) *Certain program-related activities.*—For purposes of section 4943(d)(4) the term "business enterprise" does not include a functionally related business as defined in section 4942(j)(5). See §53.4942(a)-2(c)(3)(iii). In addition, business holdings do not include program-related investments (such as investments in small businesses in central cities or in corporations to assist in neighborhood renovation) as defined in section 4944(c) and the regulations thereunder.

(c) *Income derived from passive sources.*—(1) *In general.*—For purposes of section 4943(d)(4), the term "business enterprise" does not include a trade or business at least 95 percent of the gross income of which is derived from passive sources; except that if in the taxable year in question less than 95 percent of the income of a trade or business is from passive sources, the foundation may, in applying this 95 percent test, substitute for the passive source gross income in such taxable year the average gross income from passive sources for the 10 taxable years immediately preceding the taxable year in question (or for such shorter period as the entity has been in existence). Thus, stock in a passive holding company is not to be considered a holding in a business enterprise even if the company is controlled by the foundation. Instead, the foundation is treated as owning its proportionate share of any interests in a business enterprise held by such company under section 4943(d)(1).

(2) *Gross income from passive sources.*—Gross income from passive sources, for purposes of this paragraph, includes the items excluded by sections 512(b)(1) (relating to dividends, interest, and annuities), 512(b)(2) (relating to royalties), 512(b)(3) (relating to rent) and 512(b)(5) (relating to gains or losses from the disposition of certain property). Any income classified as passive under this paragraph does not lose its character merely because section 512(b)(4) or 514 (relating to unrelated debt-financed income) applies to such income. In addition, income from passive sources includes income from the sale of goods (including charges or costs passed on at cost to purchasers of such goods or income received in settlement of a dispute concerning or in lieu of the exercise of the right to sell such goods) if the seller does not manufacture, produce, physically receive or deliver, negotiate sales of, or maintain inventories in such goods. Thus, for example, where a corporation purchases a product under a contract with the manufacturer, resells it under contract at a uniform markup in price, and does not physically handle the product, the income derived from that markup meets the definition of passive income for purposes of this paragraph. On the other hand, income from individually negotiated sales, such as those made by a broker, would not meet such definition even if the broker did not physically handle the goods.

(3) *Affiliated group.*—(i) For a common parent corporation in an affiliated group, substitute "consolidated gross income" in subparagraph (1) of this paragraph.

(ii) For purposes of this section, the term "affiliated group" shall have the same meaning as in section 1504(a), without regard to section 1504(b) through (e).

(iii) Section 53.4943-11(d) provides a transitional rule for certain parent corporations.

(d) *Application of section 4943(c)(6).*—(1) *Program related activities.*—If a private foundation holds an interest which is not an interest in a business enterprise because of paragraph (b) of this section (relating to program related activities), and such interest later becomes an interest in a business enterprise solely by reason of failing to meet the requirements of such paragraph (b), such interest will then be subject to section 4943(c)(6) (regardless of when it was originally acquired) and will be treated as having been acquired other than by purchase for purposes of section 4943(c)(6).

(2) *Passive holdings, etc.*—(i) Except as provided in subdivision (ii), if a private foundation holds an interest that is not an interest in a business enterprise, and the interest later becomes an interest in a business enterprise (other than by reason of a readjustment as defined in §53.4943-7(d)(1)), the interest will be treated as having been acquired by purchase by a disqualified person at the time the interest becomes an interest in a business enterprise. The treatment of an interest that becomes an interest in a business enterprise by reason of a readjustment shall be determined under §53.4943-6 and §53.4943-7.

(ii) If a private foundation establishes that the events which caused an interest not originally a business enterprise to become a business enterprise were not effectively controlled by the private foundation, then such interest shall be treated as acquired other than by purchase from the time of the change for purposes of section 4943(c)(6).

(iii) See §53.4943-3(b)(4)(ii) for the definition of effective control.

(e) *Sole proprietorship.*—For purposes of section 4943 and the regulations thereunder, the term "sole proprietorship" means any business enterprise (as defined in paragraphs (a), (b), and (c)) of this section—

(1) Which is actually and directly owned by a private foundation,

(2) In which the foundation has a 100 percent equity interest, and

(3) Which is not held by a corporation, trust, or other business entity for such foundation.

A foundation may be considered to own a sole proprietorship even though the foundation is itself a corporation or a trust. However, a sole proprietorship which is owned by a foundation shall cease to be treated as a sole proprietorship when the foundation no longer has a 100-percent interest in the equity of the business enterprise. Thus, if and when a foundation sells a 10-percent interest in a sole proprietorship, such business enterprise shall be treated as a partnership under section 4943 and the regulations thereunder. [Reg. §53.4943-10.]

☐ *[T.D. 7496, 7-5-77. Amended by T.D. 7944, 2-21-84.]*

**[Reg. §53.4943-11]**

**§53.4943-11. Effective/applicability date.**—(a) *In general.*—Section 4943 and §§53.4943-1 through 53.4943-11 shall take effect for taxable years beginning after December 31, 1969, except as otherwise provided by such sections.

(b) *Special transitional rule.*—In the case of any acquisition of excess holdings prior to February 2, 1973, section 4943(a)(1) shall not apply if correction occurs (within the meaning of paragraph (c) of §53.4943-9) within a period ending 90 days after July 5, 1977, extended (prior to the expiration of the original period) by any period which the Commissioner determines is reasonable and necessary (within the meaning of paragraph (b) of §53.4943-9) to bring about such correction.

(c) *Special transitional rule for aquisition by will, etc.*—(i) The rule in §53.4943-6(b)(1) whereby holdings not held by a decedent are not treated as acquired under a will shall not apply to acquisitions of after-acquired property of a decedent's estate occurring on or before May 22, 1984.

(ii) The rule in §53.4943-6(b)(1) treating a purchase by an estate as a purchase by a disqualified person where the executor is a disqualified person shall not apply to purchases occurring on or before May 22, 1984.

(d) *Special transitional rule for affiliated groups.*—If on or before May 22, 1984, a foundation holds an interest in a common parent corporation in an affiliated group, as defined in §53.4943-10(c)(3)(ii), the foundation may elect to have both §53.4943-8(c)(4) and §53.4943-10(c)(3) not apply to such common parent corporation. No election may be made to have only one section not apply. Such election shall be made by the governing body of the private foundation at any time prior to February 22, 1985.

(e) *Special transitional rule for changes to a business enterprise.*—Any interest that is not an interest in a business enterprise which becomes an interest in a business enterprise under §53.4943-10(d)(2) prior to May 22, 1984, will be treated as having been acquired other than by purchase for purposes of section 4943(c)(6).

(f) *Special transitional rule for private foundations that qualified as Type III supporting organizations before August 17, 2006.*—The present holdings of a private foundation that qualified as a Type III supporting organization under section 509(a)(3) immediately before August 17,

2006, and that was reclassified as a private foundation under section 509(a) on or after August 17, 2006, solely as a result of the rules enacted by section 1241 of the Pension Protection Act of 2006, Public Law 109-280 (120 Stat. 780), will be determined using the same rules that apply to Type III supporting organizations under section 4943(f)(7).

(g) *Special transitional rule for Type III supporting organizations created as trusts before November 20, 1970.*—A trust that qualifies as a Type III supporting organization under section 509(a)(3) and meets the requirements of §1.509(a)-4(i)(9) of this chapter will be treated as a "functionally integrated Type III supporting organization" for purposes of section 4943(f)(3)(A). [Reg. §53.4943-11.]

☐ *[T.D. 7496, 7-5-77. Amended by T.D. 7944, 2-21-84 and T.D. 9605, 12-21-2012.]*

**[Reg. §53.4944-1]**

**§53.4944-1. Initial taxes.**—(a) *On the private foundation.*—(1) *In general.*—If a private foundation(as defined in section 509) invests any amount in such a manner as to jeopardize the carrying out of any of its exempt purposes, section 4944(a)(1) of the Code imposes an excise tax on the making of such investment. This tax is to be paid by the private foundation and is at the rate of 5 percent of the amount so invested for each taxable year (or part thereof) in the taxable period (as defined in section 4944(e)(1)). The tax imposed by section 4944(a)(1) and this paragraph shall apply to investments of either income or principal.

(2) *Jeopardizing investments.*—(i) Except as provided in section 4944(c), §53.4944-3, §53.4944-6(a), and subdivision (ii) of this subparagraph, an investment shall be considered to jeopardize the carrying out of the exempt purposes of a private foundation if it is determined that the foundation managers, in making such investment, have failed to exercise ordinary business care and prudence, under the facts and circumstances prevailing at the time of making the investment, in providing for the long- and short-term financial needs of the foundation to carry out its exempt purposes. In the exercise of the requisite standard of care and prudence the foundation managers may take into account the expected return (including both income and appreciation of capital), the risks of rising and falling price levels, and the need for diversification within the investment portfolio (for example, with respect to type of security, type of industry, maturity of company, degree of risk and potential for return). The determination whether the investment of a particular amount jeopardizes the carrying out of the exempt purposes of a foundation shall be made on an investment by investment basis, in each case taking into account the foundation's portfolio as a whole. No category of investments shall be treated as a *per se* violation of section 4944. However, the following are examples of types or methods of investment which will be closely scrutinized to determine whether the foundation managers have met the requisite standard of care and prudence: Trading in securities on margin, trading in commodity futures, investments in working interests in oil and gas wells, the purchase of "puts" and "calls," and "straddles," the purchase of warrants, and selling short. The determination whether the investment of any amount jeopardizes the carrying out of a foundation's exempt purposes is to be made as of the time that the foundation makes the investment and not subsequently on the basis of hindsight. Therefore, once it has been ascertained that an investment does not jeopardize the carrying out of a foundation's exempt purposes, the investment shall never be considered to jeopardize the carrying out of such purposes, even though, as a result of such investment, the foundation subsequently realizes a loss. The provisions of section 4944 and the regulations thereunder shall not exempt or relieve any person from compliance with any Federal or State law imposing any obligation, duty, responsibility, or other standard of conduct with respect to the operation or administration of an organization or trust to which section 4944 applies. Nor shall any State law exempt or relieve any person from any obligation, duty, responsibility, or other standard of conduct provided in section 4944 and the regulations thereunder.

(ii)*(a)* Section 4944 shall not apply to an investment made by any person which is later gratuitously transferred to a private foundation. If such foundation furnishes any consideration to such person upon the transfer, the foundation will be treated as having made an investment (within the meaning of section 4944(a)(1)) in the amount of such consideration.

*(b)* Section 4944 shall not apply to an investment which is acquired by a private foundation solely as a result of a corporate reorganization within the meaning of section 368(a).

(iii) For purposes of section 4944, a private foundation which, after December 31, 1969, changes the form or terms of an investment (regardless of whether subdivision (ii) of this subparagraph applies to such investment), will be considered to have entered into a new investment on the date of such change, except as provided in subdivision (ii)(b) of this subparagraph. Accordingly, a determination, under subdivision (i) of this subparagraph, whether such change in the investment jeopardizes the carrying out of the foundation's exempt purposes shall be made at such time.

(iv) It is not intended that the taxes imposed under chapter 42 be exclusive. For example, if a foundation purchases a sole proprietorship in a business enterprise within the meaning of section 4943(d)(4), in addition to tax under section 4943, the foundation may be liable for tax under section 4944 if the investment jeopardizes the carrying out of any of its exempt purposes.

(b) *On the management.*—(1) *In general.*—In any case in which a tax is imposed by section 4944(a)(1) and paragraph (a) of this section, section 4944(a)(2) of the Code imposes on the participation of any foundation manager in the making of the investment, knowing that it is jeopardizing the carrying out of any of the foundation's exempt purposes, a tax equal to 5 percent of the amount so invested for each taxable year of the foundation (or part thereof) in the taxable period (as defined in section 4944(e)(1)), subject to the provisions of section 4944(d) and §53.4944-4, unless such participation is not willful and is due to reasonable cause. The tax imposed under section 4944(a)(2) shall be paid by the foundation manager.

(2) *Definitions and special rules.*—(i) *Knowing.*—For purposes of section 4944, a foundation manager shall be considered to have participated in the making of an investment "knowing" that it is jeopardizing the carrying out of any of the foundation's exempt purposes only if—

(a) He has actual knowledge of sufficient facts so that, based solely upon such facts, such investment would be a jeopardizing investment under paragraph (a)(2) of this section,

(b) He is aware that such an investment under these circumstances may violate the provisions of federal tax law governing jeopardizing investments, and

(c) He negligently fails to make reasonable attempts to ascertain whether the investment is a jeopardizing investment, or he is in fact aware that it is such an investment.

For purposes of this part and chapter 42, the term "knowing" does not mean "having reason to know". However, evidence tending to show that a foundation manager has reason to know of a particular fact or particular rule is relevant in determining whether he had actual knowledge of such fact or rule. Thus, for example, evidence tending to show that a foundation manager has reason to know of sufficient facts so that, based solely upon such facts, an investment would be a jeopardizing investment is relevant in determining whether he has actual knowledge of such facts.

(ii) *Willful.*—A foundation manager's participation in a jeopardizing investment is willful if it is voluntary, conscious, and intentional. No motive to avoid the restrictions of the law or the incurrence of any tax is necessary to make such participation willful. However, a foundation manager's participation in a jeopardizing investment is not willful if he does not know that it is a jeopardizing investment under paragraph (a)(2) of this section.

(iii) *Due to reasonable cause.*—A foundation manager's actions are due to reasonable cause if he has exercised his responsibility on behalf of the foundation with ordinary business care and prudence.

(iv) *Participation.*—The participation of any foundation manager in the making of an investment shall consist of any manifestation of approval of the investment.

(v) *Advice of counsel.*—If a foundation manager, after full disclosure of the factual situation to legal counsel (including house counsel), relies on the advice of such counsel expressed in a reasoned written legal opinion that a particular investment would not jeopardize the carrying out of any of the foundation's exempt purposes (because, as a matter of law, the investment is excepted from such classification, for example, as a program-related investment under section 4944(c)), then although such investment is subsequently held to be a jeopardizing investment under paragraph (a)(2) of this section, the foundation manager's participation in such investment will ordinarily not be considered "knowing" or "willful" and will ordinarily be considered "due to reasonable cause" within the meaning of section 4944(a)(2). In addition, if a foundation manager, after full disclosure of the factual situation to qualified investment counsel, relies on the advice of such counsel, such advice being derived in a manner consistent with generally accepted practices of persons who are such a qualified investment counsel and being expressed in writing that a particular investment will provide for the long-and short-term financial needs of the foundation under paragraph (a)(2) of this section, then although such investment is subsequently held not to provide for such long- and short-term financial needs, the foundation manager's participation in failing to provide for such

long- and short-term financial needs will ordinarily not be considered "knowing" or "willful" and will ordinarily be considered "due to reasonable cause" within the meaning of section 4944(a)(2). For purposes of this subdivision, a written legal opinion will be considered "reasoned" even if it reaches a conclusion which is subsequently determined to be incorrect so long as such opinion addresses itself to the facts and applicable law. However, a written legal opinion will not be considered "reasoned" if it does nothing more than recite the facts and express a conclusion. However, the absence of advice of legal counsel or qualified investment counsel with respect to the investment shall not, by itself, give rise to any inference that a foundation manager participated in such investment knowingly, willfully, or without reasonable cause.

(vi) *Cross reference.*—For provisions relating to the burden of proof in cases involving the issue whether a foundation manager has knowingly participated in the making of a jeopardizing investment, see section 7454(b).

(c) *Examples.*—The provisions of this section may be illustrated by the following examples:

*Example (1).* A is a foundation manager of B, a private foundation with assets of $100,000. A approves the following three investments by B after taking into account with respect to each of them B's portfolio as a whole: (1) an investment of $5,000 in the common stock of corporation X; (2) an investment of $10,000 in the common stock of corporation Y; and (3) an investment of $8,000 in the common stock of corporation Z. Corporation X has been in business a considerable time, its record of earnings is good and there is no reason to anticipate a diminution of its earnings. Corporation Y has a promising product, has had earnings in some years and substantial losses in others, has never paid a dividend, and is widely reported in investment advisory services as seriously undercapitalized. Corporation Z has been in business a short period of time and manufactures a product that is new, is not sold by others, and must compete with a well-established alternative product that serves the same purpose. Z's stock is classified as a high-risk investment by most investment advisory services with the possibility of substantial long-term appreciation but with little prospect of a current return. A has studied the records of the three corporations and knows the foregoing facts. In each case the price per share of common stock purchased by B is favorable to B. Under the standards of paragraph (a)(2)(i) of this section, the investment of $10,000 in the common stock of Y and the investment of $8,000 in the common stock of Z may be classified as jeopardizing investments, while the investment of $5,000 in the common stock of X will not be so classified. B would then be liable for an initial tax of $500 (*i.e.,* 5% of $10,000) for each year (or part thereof) in the taxable period for the investment in Y, and an initial tax of $400 (*i.e.,* 5% of $8,000) for each year (or part thereof) in the taxable period for the investment in Z. Further, A had actual knowledge that the investments in the common stock of Y and Z were jeopardizing investments and would be, therefore, liable for the same amount of initial taxes as B.

*Example (2).* Assume the facts as stated in Example (1), except that: (1) in the case of corporation Y, B's investment will be made for new stock to be issued by Y and there is reason to anticipate that B's investment, together with investments required by B to be made concurrently with its own, will satisfy the capital needs of corporation Y and will thereby overcome the difficulties that have resulted in Y's uneven earnings record; and (2) in the case of corporation Z, the management has a demonstrated capacity for getting new businesses started successfully and Z has received substantial orders for its new product. Under the standards of paragraph (a)(2)(i) of this section, neither the investment in Y nor the investment in Z will be classified as a jeopardizing investment and neither A nor B will be liable for an initial tax on either of such investments.

*Example (3).* D is a foundation manager of E, a private foundation with assets of $200,000. D was hired by E to manage E's investments after a careful review of D's training, experience and record in the field of investment management and advice indicated to E that D was well qualified to provide professional investment advice in the management of E's investment assets. D, after careful research into how best to diversify E's investments, provide for E's long-term financial needs, and protect against the effects of long-term inflation, decides to allocate a portion of E's investment assets to unimproved real estate in selected areas of the country where population patterns and economic factors strongly indicate continuing growth at a rapid rate. D determines that the short-term financial needs of E can be met through E's other investments. Under the standards of paragraph (a)(2)(i) of this section, the investment of a portion of E's investment assets in unimproved real estate will not be classified as a jeopardizing investment and neither D nor E will be liable for an initial tax on such investment. [Reg. §53.4944-1.]

☐ [*T.D. 7240, 12-28-72. Amended by T.D. 7299, 12-21-73.*]

**[Reg. § 53.4944-2]**

**§ 53.4944-2. Additional taxes.**—(a) *On the private foundation.*—Section 4944(b)(1) of the Code imposes an excise tax in any case in which an initial tax is imposed by section 4944(a)(1) and § 53.4944-1(a) on the making of a jeopardizing investment by a private foundation and such investment is not removed from jeopardy within the taxable period (as defined in section 4944(e)(1)). The tax imposed under section 4944(b)(1) is to be paid by the private foundation and is at the rate of 25 percent of the amount of the investment. This tax shall be imposed upon the portion of the investment which has not been removed from jeopardy within the taxable period.

(b) *On the management.*—Section 4944(b)(2) of the Code imposes an excise tax in any case in which an additional tax is imposed by section 4944(b)(1) and paragraph (a) of this section and a foundation manager has refused to agree to part or all of the removal of the investment from jeopardy. The tax imposed under section 4944(b)(2) is at the rate of 5 percent of the amount of the investment, subject to the provisions of section 4944(d) and § 53.4944-4. This tax is to be paid by any foundation manager who has refused to agree to the removal of part or all of the investment from jeopardy, and shall be imposed upon the portion of the investment which has not been removed from jeopardy within the taxable period.

(c) *Examples.*—The provisions of this section may be illustrated by the following examples:

*Example (1).* X is a foundation manager of Y, a private foundation. On the advice of X, Y invests $5,000 in the common stock of corporation M. Assume that both X and Y are liable for the taxes imposed by section 4944(a) on the making of the investment. Assume further that no part of the investment is removed from jeopardy within the taxable period and that X refused to agree to such removal. Y will be liable for an additional tax of $1,250 (*i.e.*, $5,000 × 25%). X will be liable for an additional tax of $250 (*i.e.*, $5,000 × 5%).

*Example (2).* Assume the facts as stated in Example (1), except that X is not liable for the tax imposed by section 4944(a)(2) for his participation in the making of the investment, because such participation was not willful and was due to reasonable cause. X will nonetheless be liable for the tax of $250 imposed by section 4944(b)(2) since an additional tax has been imposed upon Y and since X refused to agree to the removal of the investment from jeopardy.

*Example (3).* Assume the facts as stated in Example (1), except that Y removes $2,000 of the investment from jeopardy within the taxable period, with X refusing to agree to the removal from jeopardy of the remaining $3,000 of such investment. Y will be liable for an additional tax of $750, imposed upon the portion of the investment which has not been removed from jeopardy within the taxable period (*i.e.*, $3,000 × 25%). Further, X will be liable for an additional tax of $150, also imposed upon the same portion of the investment (*i.e.*, $3,000 × 5%). [Reg. § 53.4944-2.]

☐ [*T.D. 7240, 12-28-72. Amended by T.D. 8084, 5-1-86.*]

**[Reg. § 53.4944-3]**

**§ 53.4944-3. Exception for program-related investments.**—(a) *In general.*—(1) For purposes of section 4944 and § § 53.4944-1 through 53.4944-6, a "program-related investment" shall not be classified as an investment which jeopardizes the carrying out of the exempt purposes of a private foundation. A "program-related investment" is an investment which possesses the following characteristics:

(i) The primary purpose of the investment is to accomplish one or more of the purposes described in section 170(c)(2)(B);

(ii) No significant purpose of the investment is the production of income or the appreciation of property; and

(iii) No purpose of the investment is to accomplish one or more of the purposes described in section 170(c)(2)(D).

(2)(i) An investment shall be considered as made primarily to accomplish one or more of the purposes described in section 170(c)(2)(B) if it significantly furthers the accomplishment of the private foundation's exempt activities and if the investment would not have been made but for such relationship between the investment and the accomplishment of the foundation's exempt activities. For purposes of section 4944 and § § 53.4944-1 through 53.4944-6, the term "purposes described in section 170(c)(2)(B)" shall be treated as including purposes described in section 170(c)(2)(B) whether or not carried out by organizations described in section 170(c).

(ii) An investment in an activity described in section 4942(j)(4)(B) and the regulations thereunder shall be considered, for purposes of this paragraph, as made primarily to accomplish one or more of the purposes described in section 170(c)(2)(B).

(iii) In determining whether a significant purpose of an investment is the production of income or the appreciation of property, it shall be relevant whether investors solely engaged in the investment for profit would be likely to make the investment on the same terms as the private foundation. However, the fact that an invest-

ment produces significant income or capital appreciation shall not, in the absence of other factors, be conclusive evidence of a significant purpose involving the production of income or the appreciation of property.

(iv) An investment shall not be considered as made to accomplish one or more of the purposes described in section 170(c)(2)(D) if the recipient of the investment appears before, or communicates to, any legislative body with respect to legislation or proposed legislation of direct interest to such recipient, provided that the expense of engaging in such activities would qualify as a deduction under section 162.

(3)(i) Once it has been determined that an investment is "program-related" it shall not cease to qualify as a "program-related investment" provided that changes, if any, in the form or terms of the investment are made primarily for exempt purposes and not for any significant purpose involving the production of income or the appreciation of property. A change made in the form or terms of a program-related investment for the prudent protection of the foundation's investment shall not ordinarily cause the investment to cease to qualify as program-related. Under certain conditions, a program-related investment may cease to be program-related because of a critical change in circumstances, as, for example, where it is serving an illegal purpose or the private purpose of the foundation or its managers. For purposes of the preceding sentence, an investment which ceases to be program-related because of a critical change in circumstances shall in no event subject the foundation making the investment to the tax imposed by section 4944(a)(1) before the thirtieth day after the date on which such foundation (or any of its managers) has actual knowledge of such critical change in circumstances.

(ii) If a private foundation changes the form or terms of an investment, and if, as a result of the application of subdivision (i) of this subparagraph, such investment no longer qualifies as program-related, the determination whether the investment jeopardizes the carrying out of exempt purposes shall be made pursuant to the provisions of § 53.4944-1(a)(2).

(b) *Examples.*—The provisions of this section may be illustrated by the following examples:

*Example (1).* X is a small business enterprise located in a deteriorated urban area and owned by members of an economically disadvantaged minority group. Conventional sources of funds are unwilling or unable to provide funds to X on terms it considers economically feasible. Y, a private foundation, makes a loan to X bearing interest below the market rate for commercial loans of comparable risk. Y's primary purpose for making the loan is to encourage the economic development of such minority groups. The loan has no significant purpose involving the production of income or the appreciation of property. The loan significantly furthers the accomplishment of Y's exempt activities and would not have been made but for such relationship between the loan and Y's exempt activities. Accordingly, the loan is a program-related investment even though Y may earn income from the investment in an amount comparable to or higher than earnings from conventional portfolio investments.

*Example (2).* Assume the facts as stated in Example (1), except that after the date of execution of the loan Y extends the due date of the loan. The extension is granted in order to permit X to achieve greater financial stability before it is required to repay the loan. Since the change in the terms of the loan is made primarily for exempt purposes and not for any significant purpose involving the production of income or the appreciation of property, the loan shall continue to qualify as a program-related investment.

*Example (3).* X is a small business enterprise located in a deteriorated urban area and owned by members of an economically disadvantaged minority group. Conventional sources of funds are unwilling to provide funds to X at reasonable interest rates unless it increases the amount of its equity capital. Consequently, Y, a private foundation, purchases shares of X's common stock. Y's primary purpose in purchasing the stock is to encourage the economic development of such minority group, and no significant purpose involves the production of income or the appreciation of property. The investment significantly furthers the accomplishment of Y's exempt activities and would not have been made but for such relationship between the investment and Y's exempt activities. Accordingly, the purchase of the common stock is a program-related investment, even though Y may realize a profit if X is successful and the common stock appreciates in value.

*Example (4).* X is a business enterprise which is not owned by low-income persons or minority group members, but the continued operation of X is important to the economic well-being of a deteriorated urban area because X employs a substantial number of low-income persons from such area. Conventional sources of funds are unwilling or unable to provide funds to X at reasonable rates. Y, a private foundation, makes a loan to X at an interest rate below the market rate for commercial loans of comparable risk. The loan is made pursuant to a program run by Y to assist low-income persons by providing increased economic opportunities and to prevent community deterioration. No significant purpose of the loan involves the production of income or the appreciation of property. The investment significantly furthers the accomplishment of Y's exempt activities and would not have been made but for such relationship between the loan and Y's exempt activities. Accordingly, the loan is a program-related investment.

*Example (5).* X is a business enterprise which is financially secure and the stock of which is listed and traded on a national exchange. Y, a private foundation, makes a loan to X at an interest rate below the market rate in order to induce X to establish a new plant in a deteriorated urban area which, because of the high risks involved, X would be unwilling to establish absent such inducement. The loan is made pursuant to a program run by Y to enhance the economic development of the area by, for example, providing employment opportunities for low-income persons at the new plant, and no significant purpose involves the production of income or the appreciation of property. The loan significantly furthers the accomplishment of Y's exempt activities and would not have been made but for such relationship between the loan and Y's exempt activities. Accordingly, even though X is large and established, the investment is program-related.

*Example (6).* X is a business enterprise which is owned by a non-profit community development corporation. When fully operational, X will market agricultural products, thereby providing a marketing outlet for low-income farmers in a depressed rural area. Y, a private foundation, makes a loan to X bearing interest at a rate less than the rate charged by financial institutions which have agreed to lend funds to X if Y makes the loan. The loan is made pursuant to a program run by Y to encourage economic redevelopment of depressed areas, and no significant purpose involves the production of income or the appreciation of property. The loan significantly furthers the accomplishment of Y's exempt activities and would not have been made but for such relationship between the loan and Y's exempt activities. Accordingly, the loan is a program-related investment.

*Example (7).* X, a private foundation, invests $100,000 in the common stock of corporation M. The dividends received from such investment are later applied by X in furtherance of its exempt purposes. Although there is a relationship between the return on the investment and the accomplishment of X's exempt activities, there is no relationship between the investment *per se* and such accomplishment. Therefore, the investment cannot be considered as made primarily to accomplish one or more of the purposes described in section 170(c)(2)(B) and cannot qualify as program-related.

*Example (8).* S, a private foundation, makes an investment in T, a business corporation, which qualifies as a program-related investment under section 4944(c) at the time it is made. All of T's voting stock is owned by S. T experiences financial and management problems which, in the judgment of the foundation, require changes in management, in financial structure or in the form of the investment. The following three methods of resolving the problems appear feasible to S, but each of the three methods would result in reduction of the exempt purposes for which the program-related investment was initially made:

(a) *Sale of stock or assets.* The foundation sells its stock to an unrelated person. Payment is made in part at the time of sale; the balance is payable over an extended term of years with interest on the amount outstanding. The foundation receives a purchase-money mortgage.

(b) *Lease.* The corporation leases its assets for a term of years to an unrelated person, with an option in the lessee to buy the assets. If the option is exercised, the terms of payment are to be similar to those described in (a) of this example.

(c) *Management contract.* The corporation enters into a management contract which gives broad operating authority to one or more unrelated persons for a term of years. The foundation and the unrelated persons are obligated to contribute toward working capital requirements. The unrelated persons will be compensated by a fixed fee or a share of profits, and they will receive an option to buy the stock held by S or the assets of the corporation. If the option is exercised, the terms of payment are to be similar to those described in (a) of this example.

Each of the three methods involves a change in the form or terms of a program-related investment for the prudent protection of the foundation's investment. Thus, under §53.4944-3(a)(3)(i), none of the three transactions (nor any debt instruments or other obligations held by S as a result of engaging in one of these transactions) would cause the investment to cease to qualify as program-related.

*Example (9).* X is a socially and economically disadvantaged individual. Y, a private foundation, makes an interest-free loan to X for the primary purpose of enabling X to attend college. The loan has no significant purpose involving the production of income or the appre-

ciation of property. The loan significantly furthers the accomplishment of Y's exempt activities and would not have been made but for such relationship between the loan and Y's exempt activities. Accordingly, the loan is a program-related investment.

*Example (10).* Y, a private foundation, makes a high-risk investment in low-income housing, the indebtedness with respect to which is insured by the Federal Housing Administration. Y's primary purpose in making the investment is to finance the purchase, rehabilitation, and construction of housing for low-income persons. The investment has no significant purpose involving the production of income or the appreciation of property. The investment significantly furthers the accomplishment of Y's exempt activities and would not have been made but for such relationship between the investment and Y's exempt activities. Accordingly, the investment is program-related.

*Example 11.* X is a business enterprise that researches and develops new drugs. X's research demonstrates that a vaccine can be developed within ten years to prevent a disease that predominantly affects poor individuals in developing countries. However, neither X nor other commercial enterprises like X will devote their resources to develop the vaccine because the potential return on investment is significantly less than required by X or other commercial enterprises to undertake a project to develop new drugs. Y, a private foundation, enters into an investment agreement with X in order to induce X to develop the vaccine. Pursuant to the investment agreement, Y purchases shares of the common stock of S, a subsidiary corporation that X establishes to research and develop the vaccine. The agreement requires S to distribute the vaccine to poor individuals in developing countries at a price that is affordable to the affected population, although, the agreement does not preclude S from selling the vaccine to other individuals at a market rate. The agreement also requires S to publish the research results, disclosing substantially all information about the results that would be useful to the interested public. S agrees that the publication of its research results will be made as promptly after the completion of the research as is reasonably possible without jeopardizing S's right to secure patents necessary to protect its ownership or control of the results of the research. The expected rate of return on Y's investment in S is less than the expected market rate of return for an investment of similar risk. Y's primary purpose in making the investment is to fund scientific research in the public interest. No significant purpose of the investment involves the production of income or the appreciation of property. The investment significantly furthers the accomplishment of Y's exempt activities and would not have been made but for such relationship between the investment and Y's exempt activities. Accordingly, Y's purchase of the common stock of S is a program-related investment.

*Example 12.* Q, a developing country, produces a substantial amount of recyclable solid waste materials that are currently disposed of in landfills and by incineration, contributing significantly to environmental deterioration in Q. X is a new business enterprise located in Q. X's only activity will be collecting recyclable solid waste materials in Q and delivering those materials to recycling centers that are inaccessible to a majority of the population. If successful, the recycling collection business would prevent pollution in Q caused by the usual disposition of solid waste materials. X has obtained funding from only a few commercial investors who are concerned about the environmental impact of solid waste disposal. Although X made substantial efforts to procure additional funding, X has not been able to obtain sufficient funding because the expected rate of return is significantly less than the acceptable rate of return on an investment of this type. Because X has been unable to attract additional investors on the same terms as the initial investors, Y, a private foundation, enters into an investment agreement with X to purchase shares of X's common stock on the same terms as X's initial investors. Although there is a high risk associated with the investment in X, there is also the potential for a high rate of return if X is successful in the recycling business in Q. Y's primary purpose in making the investment is to combat environmental deterioration. No significant purpose of the investment involves the production of income or the appreciation of property. The investment significantly furthers the accomplishment of Y's exempt activities and would not have been made but for such relationship between the investment and Y's exempt activities. Accordingly, Y's purchase of the X common stock is a program-related investment.

*Example 13.* Assume the facts as stated in *Example 12*, except that X offers Y shares of X's common stock in order to induce Y to make a below-market rate loan to X. X previously made the same offer to a number of commercial investors. These investors were unwilling to provide loans to X on such terms because the expected return on the combined package of stock and debt was below the expected market return for such a package based on the level of risk involved, and they were also unwilling to provide loans on other terms X considers economically feasible. Y accepts the stock and makes the loan on the same terms that X offered to the commercial investors. Y's primary purpose in making the investment is to combat environmental deterioration. No significant purpose of the investment involves the production of income or the appreciation of property. The investment significantly furthers the accomplishment of Y's exempt activities and would not have been made but for such relationship between the investment and Y's exempt activities. Accordingly, the loan accompanied by the acceptance of common stock is a program-related investment.

*Example 14*. X is a business enterprise located in V, a rural area in State Z. X employs a large number of poor individuals in V. A natural disaster occurs in V, causing significant damage to the area. The business operations of X are harmed because of damage to X's equipment and buildings. X has insufficient funds to continue its business operations and conventional sources of funds are unwilling or unable to provide loans to X on terms it considers economically feasible. In order to enable X to continue its business operations, Y, a private foundation, makes a loan to X bearing interest below the market rate for commercial loans of comparable risk. Y's primary purpose in making the loan is to provide relief to the poor and distressed. No significant purpose of the loan involves the production of income or the appreciation of property. The loan significantly furthers the accomplishment of Y's exempt activities and would not have been made but for such relationship between the loan and Y's exempt activities. Accordingly, the loan is a program-related investment.

*Example 15*. Y, a private foundation, makes loans bearing interest below the market rate for commercial loans of comparable risk to poor individuals who live in W, a developing country, to enable them to start small businesses such as a roadside fruit stand. Conventional sources of funds were unwilling or unable to provide such loans on terms they consider economically feasible. Y's primary purpose in making the loans is to provide relief to the poor and distressed. No significant purpose of the loans involves the production of income or the appreciation of property. The loans significantly further the accomplishment of Y's exempt activities and would not have been made but for such relationship between the loans and Y's exempt activities. Accordingly, the loans to the poor individuals who live in W are program-related investments.

*Example 16*. X is a limited liability company treated as a partnership for federal income tax purposes. X purchases coffee from poor farmers residing in a developing country, either directly or through farmer-owned cooperatives. To fund the provision of efficient water management, crop cultivation, pest management, and farm management training to the poor farmers by X, Y, a private foundation, makes a loan to X bearing interest below the market rate for commercial loans of comparable risk. The loan agreement requires X to use the proceeds from the loan to provide the training to the poor farmers. X would not provide such training to the poor farmers absent the loan. Y's primary purpose in making the loan is to educate poor farmers about advanced agricultural methods. No significant purpose of the loan involves the production of income or the appreciation of property. The loan significantly furthers the accomplishment of Y's exempt activities and would not have been made but for such relationship between the loan and Y's exempt activities. Accordingly, the loan is a program-related investment.

*Example 17*. X is a social welfare organization that is recognized as an organization described in section 501(c)(4). X was formed to develop and encourage interest in painting, sculpture, and other art forms by, among other things, conducting weekly community art exhibits. X needs to purchase a large exhibition space to accommodate the demand for exhibition space within the community. Conventional sources of funds are unwilling or unable to provide funds to X on terms it considers economically feasible. Y, a private foundation, makes a loan to X at an interest rate below the market rate for commercial loans of comparable risk to fund the purchase of the new space. Y's primary purpose in making the loan is to promote the arts. No significant purpose of the loan involves the production of income or the appreciation of property. The loan significantly furthers the accomplishment of Y's exempt activities and would not have been made but for such relationship between the loan and Y's exempt activities. Accordingly, the loan is a program-related investment.

*Example 18*. X is a non-profit corporation that provides child care services in a low-income neighborhood, enabling many residents of the neighborhood to be gainfully employed. X meets the requirements of section 501(k) and is recognized as an organization described in section 501(c)(3). X's current child care facility has reached capacity and has a long waiting list. X has determined that the demand for its services warrants the construction of a new child care facility in the same neighborhood. X is unable to obtain a loan from conventional sources of funds including B, a commercial bank because of X's credit record. Pursuant to a deposit agreement, Y, a private foundation, deposits $h in B, and B lends an identical amount to X to construct the new child care facility. The deposit agreement requires Y to keep $h on deposit with B during the term of X's loan and provides that if X defaults on the loan, B may deduct the amount

of the default from the deposit. To facilitate B's access to the funds in the event of default, the agreement requires that the funds be invested in instruments that allow B to access them readily. The deposit agreement also provides that Y will earn interest at a rate of t% on the deposit. The t% rate is substantially less than Y could otherwise earn on this sum of money, if Y invested it elsewhere. The loan agreement between B and X requires X to use the proceeds from the loan to construct the new child care facility. Y's primary purpose in making the deposit is to further its educational purposes by enabling X to provide child care services within the meaning of section 501(k). No significant purpose of the deposit involves the production of income or the appreciation of property. The deposit significantly furthers the accomplishment of Y's exempt activities and would not have been made but for such relationship between the deposit and Y's exempt activities. Accordingly, the deposit is a program-related investment.

*Example 19*. Assume the same facts as stated in *Example 18*, except that instead of making a deposit of $h into B, Y enters into a guarantee agreement with B. The guarantee agreement provides that if X defaults on the loan, Y will repay the balance due on the loan to B. B was unwilling to make the loan to X in the absence of Y's guarantee. X must use the proceeds from the loan to construct the new child care facility. At the same time, X and Y enter into a reimbursement agreement whereby X agrees to reimburse Y for any and all amounts paid to B under the guarantee agreement. The signed guarantee and reimbursement agreements together constitute a "guarantee and reimbursement arrangement." Y's primary purpose in entering into the guarantee and reimbursement arrangement is to further Y's educational purposes. No significant purpose of the guarantee and reimbursement arrangement involves the production of income or the appreciation of property. The guarantee and reimbursement arrangement significantly furthers the accomplishment of Y's exempt activities and would not have been made but for such relationship between the guarantee and reimbursement arrangement and Y's exempt activities. Accordingly, the guarantee and reimbursement arrangement is a program-related investment.

(c) *Effective/applicability date*.—Paragraphs (a)(2)(ii) and (b), *Examples 11* through *19* of this section, apply on or after April 25, 2016. [Reg. § 53.4944-3.]

☐ [*T.D. 7240*, 12-28-72. *Amended by T.D. 9762*, 4-21-2016.]

## [Reg. § 53.4944-4]

**§ 53.4944-4. Special rules.**—(a) *Joint and several liability.*—In any case where more than one foundation manager is liable for the tax imposed under section 4944(a)(2) or (b)(2) with respect to any one jeopardizing investment, all such foundation managers shall be jointly and severally liable for the tax imposed under each such paragraph with respect to such investment.

(b) *Limits on liability for management.*—With respect to any one jeopardizing investment, the maximum aggregate amount of tax collectible under section 4944(a)(2) from all foundation managers shall not exceed $5,000, and the maximum aggregate amount of tax collectible under section 4944(b)(2) from all foundation managers shall not exceed $10,000.

(c) *Examples.*—The provisions of this section may be illustrated by the following examples:

*Example (1)*. A, B, and C are foundation managers of X, a private foundation. Assume that A, B, and C are liable for both initial and additional taxes under sections 4944(a)(2) and 4944(b)(2), respectively, for the following investments by X: an investment of $5,000 in the common stock of corporation M, and an investment of $10,000 in the common stock of corporation N. A, B, and C will be jointly and severally liable for the following initial taxes under section 4944(a)(2): a tax of $250 (*i.e.*, 5% of $5,000) for each year (or part thereof) in the taxable period (as defined in section 4944(e)(1)) for the investment in M, and a tax of $500 (*i.e.*, 5% of $10,000) for each year (or part thereof) in the taxable period for the investment in N. Further, A, B, and C will be jointly and severally liable for the following additional taxes under section 4944(b)(2): a tax of $250 (*i.e.*, 5% of $5,000) for the investment in M, and a tax of $500 (*i.e.*, 5% of $10,000) for the investment in N.

*Example (2)*. Assume the facts as stated in Example (1), except that X has invested $500,000 in the common stock of M, and $1,000,000 in the common stock of N. A, B, and C will be jointly and severally liable for the following initial taxes under section 4944(a)(2): a tax of $5,000 for the investment in M and a tax of $5,000 for the investment in N. Further, A, B, and C will be jointly and severally liable for the following additional taxes under section 4944(b)(2): a tax of $10,000 for the investment in M, and a tax of $10,000 for the investment in N. [Reg. § 53.4944-4.]

☐ [*T.D. 7240*, 12-28-72.]

**[Reg. §53.4944-5]**

**§53.4944-5. Definitions.**—(a) *Taxable period.*—(1) *In general.*—For purposes of section 4944, the term "taxable period" means, with respect to any investment which jeopardizes the carrying out of a private foundation's exempt purposes, the period beginning with the date on which the amount is so invested and ending on the earliest of:

(i) The date of mailing of a notice of deficiency under section 6212 with respect to the tax imposed on the making of the investment by section 4944(a)(1);

(ii) The date on which the amount invested is removed from jeopardy; or

(iii) The date on which the tax imposed by section 4944(a)(1) is assessed.

(2) *Special rule.*—Where a notice of deficiency referred to in subparagraph (1)(i) of this paragraph is not mailed because there is a waiver of the restrictions on assessment and collection of a deficiency, or because the deficiency is paid, the date of filing of the waiver or the date of such payment, respectively, shall be treated as the end of the taxable period.

(b) *Removal from jeopardy.*—An investment which jeopardizes the carrying out of a private foundation's exempt purposes shall be considered to be removed from jeopardy when—

(1) The foundation sells or otherwise disposes of the investment, and

(2) The proceeds of such sale or other disposition are not themselves investments which jeopardize the carrying out of such foundation's exempt purposes.

A change by a private foundation in the form or terms of a jeopardizing investment shall result in the removal of the investment from jeopardy if, after such change, the investment no longer jeopardizes the carrying out of such foundation's exempt purposes. For purposes of section 4944, the making by a private foundation of one jeopardizing investment and a subsequent exchange by the foundation of such investment for another jeopardizing investment will be treated as only one jeopardizing investment, except as provided in §53.4944-6(b) and (c). For the treatment of a jeopardizing investment which is removed from jeopardy or otherwise transferred by a private foundation by the making of a grant or by bargain-sale, see sections 4941 and 4945 and the regulations thereunder. A jeopardizing investment cannot be removed from jeopardy by a transfer from a private foundation to another private foundation which is related to the transferor foundation within the meaning of section 4946(a)(1)(H)(i) or (ii), unless the investment is a program-related investment in the hands of the transferee foundation.

(c) *Examples.*—The provisions of this section may be illustrated by the following examples:

*Example (1).* X, a private foundation on the calendar year basis, makes a $1,000 jeopardizing investment on January 1, 1970. X thereafter sells the investment for $1,000 on January 3, 1971. The taxable period is from January 1, 1970, to January 3, 1971. X will be liable for an initial tax of $100, that is, a tax of 5 percent of the amount of the investment for each year (or part thereof) in the taxable period.

*Example (2).* Assume that both C and D are investments which jeopardize exempt purposes. X, a private foundation, purchases C in 1971 and later exchanges C for D. Such exchange does not constitute a removal of C from jeopardy. In addition, no new taxable period will arise with respect to D, since, for purposes of section 4944, only one jeopardizing investment has been made.

*Example (3).* Assume the facts as stated in Example (2), except that X sells C for cash and later reinvests such cash in D. Two separate investments jeopardizing exempt purposes have resulted. Since the cash received in the interim is not of a jeopardizing nature, the amount invested in C has been removed from jeopardy and, thus, the taxable period with respect to C has been terminated. The subsequent reinvestment of such cash in D gives rise to a new taxable period with respect to D.

(d) *Cross reference.*—For rules relating to taxable events that are corrected within the correction period, defined in section 4963(e), see section 4961(a) and the regulations thereunder. [Reg. §53.4944-5.]

☐ [*T.D. 7240, 12-28-72. Amended by T.D. 8084, 5-1-86.*]

**[Reg. §53.4944-6]**

**§53.4944-6. Special rules for investments made prior to January 1, 1970.**—(a) Except as provided in paragraph (b) or (c) of this section, an investment made by a private foundation prior to January 1, 1970, shall not be subject to the provisions of section 4944.

(b) If the form or terms of an investment made by a private foundation prior to January 1, 1970, are changed (other than as described in paragraph (c) of this section) on or after such date, the provisions of §53.4944-1(a)(2)(iii) shall apply with respect to such investment.

(c) In the case of an investment made by a private foundation prior to January 1, 1970, which is exchanged on or after such date for another investment, for purposes of section 4944 the foundation will be considered to have made a new investment on the date of such exchange, unless the post-1969 investment is described in §53.4944-1(a)(2)(ii)(b). Accordingly, a determination, under §53.4944-1(a)(2)(i), whether the investment jeopardizes the carrying out of the foundation's exempt purposes shall be made as such time. [Reg. §53.4944-6.]

☐ [*T.D. 7240, 12-28-72.*]

**[Reg. §53.4945-1]**

**§53.4945-1. Taxes on taxable expenditures.**—(a) *Imposition of initial taxes.*—(1) *Tax on private foundation.*—Section 4945(a)(1) of the Code imposes an excise tax on each taxable expenditure(as defined in section 4945(d)) of a private foundation. This tax is to be paid by the private foundation and is at the rate of 10 percent of the amount of each taxable expenditure.

(2) *Tax on foundation manager.*—(i) *In general.*—Section 4945(a)(2) of the Code imposes, under certain circumstances, an excise tax on the agreement of any foundation manager to the making of a taxable expenditure by a private foundation. This tax is imposed only in cases in which the following circumstances are present:

(a) A tax is imposed by section 4945(a)(1),

(b) Such foundation manager knows that the expenditure to which he agrees is a taxable expenditure, and

(c) Such agreement is willful and is not due to reasonable cause. However, the tax with respect to any particular expenditure applies only to the agreement of those foundation managers who are authorized to approve, or to exercise discretion in recommending approval of, the making of the expenditure by the foundation and to those foundation managers who are members of a group (such as the foundation's board of directors or trustees) which is so authorized. For the definition of the term "foundation manager", see section 4946(b) and the regulations thereunder.

(ii) *Agreement.*—The agreement of any foundation manager to the making of a taxable expenditure shall consist of any manifestation of approval of the expenditure which is sufficient to constitute an exercise of the foundation manager's authority to approve, or to exercise discretion in recommending approval of, the making of the expenditure by the foundation, whether or not such manifestation of approval is the final or decisive approval on behalf of the foundation.

(iii) *Knowing.*—For purposes of section 4945, a foundation manager shall be considered to have agreed to an expenditure "knowing" that it is a taxable expenditure only if—

(a) He has actual knowledge of sufficient facts so that, based solely upon such facts, such expenditure would be a taxable expenditure,

(b) He is aware that such an expenditure under these circumstances may violate the provisions of federal tax law governing taxable expenditures, and

(c) He negligently fails to make reasonable attempts to ascertain whether the expenditure is a taxable expenditure, or he is in fact aware that it is such an expenditure.

For purposes of this part and chapter 42, the term "knowing" does not mean "having reason to know". However, evidence tending to show that a foundation manager has reason to know of a particular fact or particular rule is relevant in determining whether he had actual knowledge of such fact or rule. Thus, for example, evidence tending to show that a foundation manager has reason to know of sufficient facts so that, based solely upon such facts, an expenditure would be a taxable expenditure is relevant in determining whether he has actual knowledge of such facts.

(iv) *Willful.*—A foundation manager's agreement to a taxable expenditure is willful if it is voluntary, conscious, and intentional. No motive to avoid the restrictions of the law or the incurrence of any tax is necessary to make an agreement willful. However, a foundation manager's agreement to a taxable expenditure is not willful if he does not know that it is a taxable expenditure.

(v) *Due to reasonable cause.*—A foundation manager's actions are due to reasonable cause if he has exercised his responsibility on behalf of the foundation with ordinary business care and prudence.

(vi) *Advice of counsel.*—If a foundation manager, after full disclosure of the factual situation to legal counsel (including house counsel), relies on the advice of such counsel expressed in a reasoned written legal opinion that an expenditure is not a taxable expenditure under section 4945 (or that expenditures conforming to certain guidelines are not taxable expenditures), although such expenditure is subsequently held to be a taxable expenditure (or that certain proposed reporting procedures with respect to an expenditure will satisfy the tests of section 4945(h), although such procedures are subsequently held not to satisfy such section), the foundation manager's agreement to such expenditure (or to grants made with provisions for such reporting procedures which are taxable solely because of such inadequate reporting procedures) will ordinarily not be considered "knowing" or "willful" and will ordinarily be considered "due to reasonable cause" within the meaning of section 4945(a)(2). For purposes of the subdivision, a written legal opinion will be considered "reasoned" even if it reaches a conclusion which is subsequently determined to be incorrect so long as such opinion addresses itself to the facts and applicable law. However, a written legal opinion will not be considered "reasoned" if it does nothing more than recite the facts and express a conclusion. However, the absence of advice of counsel with respect to an expenditure shall not, by itself, give rise to any inference that a foundation manager agreed to the making of the expenditure knowingly, willfully, or without reasonable cause.

(vii) *Rate and incidence of tax.*—The tax imposed under section 4945(a)(2) is at the rate of 2¹/₂ percent of the amount of each taxable expenditure to which the foundation manager has agreed. This tax shall be paid by the foundation manager.

(viii) *Cross reference.*—For provisions relating to the burden of proof in cases involving the issue whether a foundation manager has knowingly agreed to the making of a taxable expenditure, see section 7454(b).

(b) *Imposition of additional taxes.*—(1) *Taxes on private foundation.*—Section 4945(b)(1) of the Code imposes an excise tax in any case in which an initial tax is imposed under section 4945(a)(1) on a taxable expenditure of a private foundation and the expenditure is not corrected within the taxable period (as defined in section 4945(i)(2)). The tax imposed under section 4945(b)(1) is to be paid by the private foundation and is at the rate of 100 percent of the amount of each taxable expenditure.

(2) *Tax on foundation manager.*—Section 4945(b)(2) of the Code imposes an excise tax in any case in which a tax is imposed under section 4945(b)(1) and a foundation manager has refused to agree to part or all of the correction of the taxable expenditure. The tax imposed under section 4945(b)(2) is at the rate of 50 percent of the amount of the taxable expenditure. This tax is to be paid by any foundation manager who has refused to agree to part or all of the correction of the taxable expenditure.

(c) *Special rules.*—(1) *Joint and several liability.*—In any case where more than one foundation manager is liable for the tax imposed under section 4945(a)(2) or (b)(2) with respect to the making of a taxable expenditure, all such foundation managers shall be jointly and severally liable for the tax imposed under such paragraph with respect to such taxable expenditure.

(2) *Limits on liability for management.*—The maximum aggregate amount of tax collectible under section 4945(a)(2) from all foundation managers with respect to any one taxable expenditure shall be $5,000, and the maximum aggregate amount of tax collectible under section 4945(b)(2) from all foundation managers with respect to any one taxable expenditure shall be $10,000.

(3) *Examples.*—The provisions of this paragraph may be illustrated by the following examples:

*Example (1).* A, B, and C comprise the board of directors of Foundation M. They vote unanimously in favor of a grant of $100,000 to D, a business associate of each of the directors. The grant is to be used by D for travel and educational purposes and is not made in accordance with the requirements of section 4945(g). Each director knows that D was selected as the recipient of the grant solely because of his friendship with the directors and is aware that some grants made for travel, study, or other similar purposes may be taxable expenditures. Also, none of the directors makes any attempt to consult counsel, or to otherwise determine, whether this grant is a taxable expenditure. Initial taxes are imposed under paragraphs (1) and (2) of section 4945(a). The tax to be paid by the foundation is $10,000 (10 percent of $100,000). The tax to be paid by the board of directors is $2,500 (2¹/₂ percent of $100,000). A, B, and C are jointly and severally liable for this $2,500 and this sum may be collected by the Service from any one of them.

*Example (2).* Assume the same facts as in example (1). Further assume that within the taxable period A makes a motion to correct the taxable expenditure at a meeting of the board of directors. The motion is defeated by a two-to-one vote, A voting for the motion and B and C voting against it. In these circumstances an additional tax is imposed on the private foundation in the amount of $100,000 (100

percent of $100,000). The additional tax imposed on B and C is $10,000 (50 percent of $100,000 subject to a maximum of $10,000). B and C are jointly and severally liable for the $10,000, and this sum may be collected by the Service from either of them.

(d) *Correction.*—(1) *In general.*—Except as provided in paragraph (d)(2) or (3) of this section, correction of a taxable expenditure shall be accomplished by recovering part or all of the expenditure to the extent recovery is possible, and, where full recovery cannot be accomplished, by any additional corrective action which the Commissioner may prescribe. Such additional corrective action is to be determined by circumstances of each particular case and may include the following:

(i) Requiring that any unpaid funds due the grantee be withheld;

(ii) Requiring that no further grants be made to the particular grantee;

(iii) In addition to other reports that are required, requiring periodic (*e.g.,* quarterly) reports from the foundation with respect to all expenditures of the foundation (such reports shall be equivalent in detail to the reports required by section 4945(h)(3) and §53.4945-5(d));

(iv) Requiring improved methods of exercising expenditure responsibility;

(v) Requiring improved methods of selecting recipients of individual grants; and

(vi) Requiring such other measures as the Commissioner may prescribe in a particular case.

The foundation making the expenditure shall not be under any obligation to attempt to recover the expenditure by legal action if such action would in all probability not result in the satisfaction of execution on a judgment.

(2) *Correction for inadequate reporting.*—If the expenditure is taxable only because of a failure to obtain a full and complete report as required by section 4945(h)(2) or because of a failure to make a full and detailed report as required by section 4945(h)(3), correction may be accomplished by obtaining or making the report in question. In addition, if the expenditure is taxable only because of a failure to obtain a full and complete report as required by section 4945(h)(2) and an investigation indicates that no grant funds have been diverted to any use not in furtherance of a purpose specified in the grant, correction may be accomplished by exerting all reasonable efforts to obtain the report in question and reporting the failure to the Internal Revenue Service, even though the report is not finally obtained.

(3) *Correction for failure to obtain advance approval.*—Where an expenditure is taxable under section 4945(d)(3) only because of a failure to obtain advance approval of procedures with respect to grants as required by section 4945(g), correction may be accomplished by obtaining approval of the grant making procedures and establishing to the satisfaction of the Commissioner that:

(i) no grant funds have been diverted to any use not in furtherance of a purpose specified in the grant;

(ii) the grant making procedures instituted would have been approved if advance approval of such procedures had been properly requested; and

(iii) where advance approval of grant making procedures is subsequently required, such approval will be properly requested.

(e) *Certain periods.*—(1) *Taxable period.*—For purposes of section 4945, the term "taxable period" means, with respect to any taxable expenditure, the period beginning with the date on which the taxable expenditure occurs and ending on the earlier of:

(i) The date of mailing of a notice of deficiency under section 6212 with respect to the tax imposed on taxable expenditures by section 4945(a)(1); or

(ii) The date on which the tax imposed by section 4945(a)(1) is assessed.

(2) *Cross reference.*—For rules relating to taxable events that are corrected within the correction period, defined in section 4963(e), see section 4961(a) and the regulations thereunder. [Reg. §53.4945-1.]

☐ [*T.D. 7215, 10-30-72. Amended by T.D. 7299, 12-21-73, T.D. 7527, 12-23-77 and T.D. 8084, 5-1-86.*]

**[Reg. §53.4945-2]**

**§53.4945-2. Propaganda influencing legislation.**—(a) *Propaganda influencing legislation, etc.*—(1) *In general.*—Under section 4945(d)(1) the term "taxable expenditure" includes any amount paid or incurred by a private foundation to carry on propaganda, or otherwise to attempt, to influence legislation. An expenditure is an attempt to influence legislation if it is for a direct or grass roots lobbying communication, as defined in §56.4911-2 (without reference to §§56.4911-2(b)(3) and 56.4911-2(c) and §56.4911-3. See, however, paragraph (d) of this section for exceptions to the general rule of this paragraph (a)(1).

(2) *Expenditures for membership communications.*—Section 56.4911-5, which provides special rules for electing public charities' communications with their members, does not apply to private foundations. Thus, whether a private foundation's communications with its members (assuming it has any) are lobbying communications is determined solely under §56.4911-2 and without reference to §56.4911-5. However, where a private foundation makes a grant to an electing public charity, §56.4911-5 applies to the electing public charity's communications with its own members. Therefore, in the limited context of determining whether a private foundation's grant to an electing public charity is a taxable expenditure under section 4945, the §56.4911-5 membership rules apply. For example, if the grant is specifically earmarked for a communication from the electing public charity to its members and the communication is, because of §56.4911-5, a nonlobbying communication, the grant is not a taxable expenditure under section 4945.

(3) *Jointly funded projects.*—A private foundation will not be treated as having paid or incurred any amount to attempt to influence legislation merely because it makes a grant to a another organization upon the condition that the recipient obtain a matching support appropriation from a governmental body. In addition, a private foundation will not be treated as having made taxable expenditures of amounts paid or incurred in carrying on discussions with officials of governmental bodies provided that:

(i) The subject of such discussions is a program which is jointly funded by the foundation and the government or is a new program which may be jointly funded by the foundation and the government,

(ii) The discussions are undertaken for the purpose of exchanging data and information on the subject matter of the program, and

(iii) Such discussions are not undertaken by foundation managers in order to make any direct attempt to persuade governmental officials or employees to take particular positions on specific legislative issues other than such program.

(4) *Certain expenditures by recipients of program-related investments.*—Any amount paid or incurred by a recipient of a program-related investment (as defined in §53.4944-3) in connection with an appearance before, or communication with, any legislative body with respect to legislation or proposed legislation of direct interest to such recipient shall not be attributed to the investing foundation, if—

(i) The foundation does not earmark its funds to be used for any activities described in section 4945(d)(1) and

(ii) A deduction under section 162 is allowable to the recipient for such amount.

(5) *Grants to public organizations.*—(i) *In general.*—A grant by a private foundation to an organization described in section 509(a)(1), (2) or (3) does not constitute a taxable expenditure by the foundation under section 4945(d), other than under section 4945(d)(1), if the grant by the private foundation is not earmarked to be used for any activity described in section 4945(d)(2) or (5), is not earmarked to be used in a manner which would violate section 4945(d)(3) or (4), and there does not exist an agreement, oral or written, whereby the grantor foundation may cause the grantee to engage in any such prohibited activity or to select the recipient to which the grant is to be devoted. For purposes of this paragraph (a)(5)(i), a grant by a private foundation is earmarked if the grant is given pursuant to an agreement, oral or written, that the grant will be used for specific purposes. For the expenditure responsibility requirements with respect to organizations other than those described in section 509(a)(1), (2), or (3), see §53.4945-5. For rules for determining whether grants to public charities are taxable expenditures under section 4945(d)(1), see paragraphs (a)(2), (a)(6) and (a)(7) of this section.

(ii) *Certain "public" organizations.*—For purposes of this section, an organization shall be considered a section 509(a)(1) organization if it is treated as such under subparagraph (4) of §53.4945-5(a).

(6) *Grants to public organizations that attempt to influence legislation.*—(i) *General support grant.*—A general support grant by a private foundation to an organization described in section 509(a)(1), (2), or (3) (a "public charity" for purposes of paragraphs (a)(6) and (a)(7) of this section) does not constitute a taxable expenditure under section 4945(d)(1) to the extent that the grant is not earmarked, within the meaning of §53.4945-2(a)(5)(i), to be used in an attempt to influence legislation. The preceding sentence applies without regard to whether the public charity has made the election under section 501(h).

(ii) *Specific project grant.*—A grant by a private foundation to fund a specific project of a public charity is not a taxable expenditure by the foundation under section 4945(d)(1) to the extent that—

(A) The grant is not earmarked, within the meaning of §53.4945-2(a)(5)(i), to be used in an attempt to influence legislation, and

(B) The amount of the grant, together with other grants by the same private foundation for the same project for the same year, does not exceed the amount budgeted, for the year of the grant, by the grantee organization for activities of the project that are not attempts to influence legislation. If the grant is for more than one year, the preceding sentence applies to each year of the grant with the amount of the grant measured by the amount actually disbursed by the private foundation in each year or divided equally between years, at the option of the private foundation. The same method of measuring the annual amount must be used in all years of a grant. This paragraph (a)(6)(ii) applies without regard to whether the public charity has made the election under section 501(h).

(iii) *Reliance upon grantee's budget.*—For purposes of determining the amount budgeted by a prospective grantee for specific project activities that are not attempts to influence legislation under paragraph (a)(6)(ii) of this section, a private foundation may rely on budget documents or other sufficient evidence supplied by the grantee organization (such as a signed statement by an authorized officer, director or trustee of such grantee organization) showing the proposed budget of the specific project, unless the private foundation doubts or, in light of all the facts and circumstances, reasonably should doubt the accuracy or reliability of the documents.

(7) *Grants to organizations that cease to be described in 501(c)(3).*—(i) *Not taxable expenditure; conditions.*—A grant to a public charity (as defined in paragraph (a)(6)(i) of this section) that thereafter ceases to be an organization described in section 501(c)(3) by reason of its attempts to influence legislation is not a taxable expenditure if—

(A) The grant meets the requirements of paragraph (a)(6) of this section,

(B) The recipient organization had received a ruling or determination letter, or an advance ruling or determination letter, that it is described in sections 501(c)(3) and 509(a),

(C) Notice of a change in the recipient organization's status has not been made to the public (such as by publication in the Internal Revenue Bulletin), and the private foundation has not acquired knowledge that the Internal Revenue Service has given notice to the recipient organization that it will be deleted from such status, and

(D) The recipient organization is not controlled directly or indirectly by the private foundation. A recipient organization is controlled by a private foundation for this purpose if the private foundation and disqualified persons (defined in section 4946(a)(1)(A) through (H)) with reference to the private foundation, by aggregating their votes or positions of authority, can cause or prevent action on legislative issues by the recipient.

(ii) *Examples.*—The provisions of paragraphs (a)(6) and (a)(7) of this section are illustrated by the following examples:

*Example (1).* W, a private foundation, makes a general support grant to Z, a public charity described in section 509(a)(1). Z informs W that, as an insubstantial portion of its activities, Z attempts to influence the State legislature with regard to changes in the mental health laws. The use of the grant is not earmarked by W to be used in a manner that would violate section 4945(d)(1). Even if the grant is subsequently devoted by Z to its legislative activities, the grant by W is not a taxable expenditure under section 4945(d).

*Example (2).* X, a private foundation, makes a specific project grant to Y University for the purpose of conducting research on the potential environmental effects of certain pesticides. X does not earmark the grant for any purpose that would violate section 4945(d)(1) and there is no oral or written agreement or understanding whereby X may cause Y to engage in any activity described in section 4945(d)(1), (2), or (5), or to select any recipient to which the grant may be devoted. Further, X determines, based on budget information supplied by Y, that Y's budget for the project does not contain any amount for attempts to influence legislation. X has no reason to doubt the accuracy or reliability of the budget information. Y uses most of the funds for the research project; however, Y expends a portion of the grant funds to send a representative to testify at Congressional hearings on a specific bill proposing certain pesticide control measures. The portion of the grant funds expended with respect to the Congressional hearings is not treated as a taxable expenditure by X under section 4945(d)(1).

*Example (3).* M, a private foundation, makes a specific project grant of $150,000 to P, a public charity described in section 509(a)(1). In requesting the grant from M, P stated that the total budgeted cost of the project is $200,000, and that of this amount $20,000 is allocated to attempts to influence legislation related to the project. M relies on the budget figures provided by P in determining the amount P will spend on influencing legislation and M has no reason to doubt the accuracy or reliability of P's budget figures. In making the grant, M did not earmark any of the funds from the grant to be used for attempts to influence legislation. M's grant of $150,000 to P will not constitute a taxable expenditure under section 4945(d)(1) because M did not earmark any of the funds for attempts to influence legislation and because the amount of its grant ($150,000) does not exceed the amount allocated to specific project activities that are not attempts to influence legislation ($200,000 − $20,000 = $180,000).

*Example (4).* Assume the same facts as in example (3), except that M's grant letter to P provides that M has the right to renegotiate the terms of the grant if there is a substantial deviation from those terms. This additional fact does not make M's grant a taxable expenditure under section 4945(d)(1).

*Example (5).* Assume the same facts as in example (3), except that M made a specific project grant of $200,000 to P. Part of M's grant of $200,000 will constitute a taxable expenditure under section 4945(d)(1). The amount of the grant ($200,000) exceeds by $20,000 the amount P allocated to specific project activities that are not attempts to influence legislation ($180,000). M has made a taxable expenditure of $20,000.

*Example (6).* Assume the same facts as in [in]example (3), except that M made a specific project grant of $180,000, and received from P an enforceable commitment that grant funds would not be used in connection with attempts to influence legislation. M's grant is not a taxable expenditure under section 4945(d)(1).

*Example (7).* Assume the same facts as in example (3), except that M directed P to hire A, an individual, to expend $20,000 from the grant to engage in direct lobbying (within the meaning of § 56.4911-2(b)) and grass roots lobbying (within the meaning of § 56.4911-2(c)). P does not expend any other grant funds for lobbying activities. The $20,000 that is earmarked for direct lobbying and grass roots lobbying is a taxable expenditure under section 4945(d)(1).

*Example (8).* R, a public charity described in section 509(a)(1), requested N, a private foundation, to make a general purpose grant to it to aid R in carrying out its exempt purpose. In making this request, R notified N that it had elected the expenditure test under section 501(h) and that it expected to attempt to influence legislation in areas related to its exempt purpose. Since its formation, R generally has had exempt purpose expenditures (as defined in § 56.4911-4) in excess of $7,000,000 in each of its taxable years, and has budgeted in excess of $7,000,000 of exempt purpose expenditures for the year of the grant. N made a grant of $200,000 to R. N did not earmark the funds for R's attempt to influence legislation. The general purpose grant by N does not constitute a taxable expenditure under section 4945(d)(1).

*Example (9).* Assume the same facts as in example (8), except that N learns that R has had excess lobbying expenditures (within the meaning of § 56.4911-1(b)) in some prior years. N also learns that in no year has [sic] R's lobbying or grass roots expenditures (within the meaning of § 56.4911-2(a) and (c)) exceeded the corresponding ceiling amount (within the meaning of § 1.501(h)-3(c)(3) and (6)). N then makes the grant to R. After receiving the grant, R spends a large portion of its funds on influencing legislation and, as a consequence, is denied exemption from tax, as an organization described in section 501(c)(3), under section 501(h) and § 1.501(h)-3. No disqualified person with respect to N controlled, in whole or in part, R's attempts to influence legislation. The general purpose grant will not constitute a taxable expenditure under section 4945(d)(1).

*Example (10).* X, a private foundation, makes a specific project grant to Y, a public charity described in section 509(a). In requesting the grant, Y stated that it planned to use the funds to purchase a computer for purposes of computerizing its research files and that the grant will not be used to influence legislation. Two years after X makes the grant, X discovers that Y has also used the computer for purposes of maintaining and updating the mailing list for Y's lobbying newsletter. Because X did not earmark any of the grant funds to be used for attempts to influence legislation and because X had no reason to doubt the accuracy or reliability of Y's documents representing that the grant would not be used to influence legislation, X's grant is not treated as a taxable expenditure.

*Example (11).* G, a private foundation, makes a specific project grant of $300,000 to L, a public charity described in section 509(a)(1) for a three-year specific project studying child care problems. L provides budget material indicating that the specific project will expend $200,000 in each of three years. L's budget materials indicate that attempts to influence legislation will amount to $10,000 in the first year, $20,000 in the second year and $100,000 in the third year. G intends to pay its $300,000 grant over three years as follows: $200,000 in the first year, $50,000 in the second year and $50,000 in the third year. The amount of the grant actually disbursed by G in the first year of the grant exceeds the nonlobbying expenditures of L in that

year. However, because the amount of the grant in each of the three years, when divided equally among the three years ($100,000 for each year), is not more than the nonlobbying expenditures of L on the specific project for any of the three years, none of the grant is treated as a taxable expenditure under section 4945(d)(1).

*Example (12).* P, a private foundation, makes a $120,000 specific project grant to C, a public charity described in section 509(a) for a three-year project. P intends to pay its grant to C in three equal annual installments of $40,000. C provides budget material indicating that the specific project will expend $100,000 in each of three years. C's budget materials, which P reasonably does not doubt, indicate that the project's attempts to influence legislation will amount to $50,000 in each of the three years. After P pays the first annual installment to C, but before P pays the second installment to C, reliable information comes to P's attention that C has spent $90,000 of the project's $100,000 first-year budget on attempts to influence legislation. This information causes P to doubt the accuracy and reliability of C's budget materials. Because of the information, P does not pay the second-year installment to C. P's payment of the first installment of $40,000 is not a taxable expenditure under section 4945(d)(1) because the grant in the first year is not more than the nonlobbying expenditures C projected in its budget materials that P reasonably did not doubt.

*Example (13).* Assume the same facts as in example (12), except that P pays the second-year installment of $40,000 to C. In the project's second year, C once again spends $90,000 of the project's $100,000 annual budget in attempts to influence legislation. Because P doubts or reasonably should doubt the accuracy or reliability of C's budget materials when P makes the second-year grant payment, P may not rely upon C's budget documents at that time. Accordingly, although none of the $40,000 paid in the first installment is a taxable expenditure, only $10,000 ($100,000 minus $90,000) of the second-year grant payment is not a taxable expenditure. The remaining $30,000 of the second installment is a taxable expenditure within the meaning of section 4945(d)(1).

*Example (14).* B, a private foundation, makes a specific project grant to C, a public charity described in section 509(a), of $40,000 for the purpose of conducting a study on the effectiveness of seat belts in preventing traffic deaths. B did not earmark any of the grant for attempts to influence legislation. In requesting the grant from B, C submitted a budget of $100,000 for the project. The budget contained expenses for postage and mailing, computer time, advertising, consulting services, salaries, printing, advertising, and similar categories of expenses. C also submitted to B a statement, signed by an officer of C, that 30% of the budgeted funds would be devoted to attempts to influence legislation within the meaning of section 4945. B has no reason to doubt the accuracy of the budget figures or the statement. B may rely on the budget figures and signed statement provided by C in determining the amount C will spend on influencing legislation. B's grant to C will not constitute a taxable expenditure under section 4945(d)(1), because the amount of the grant does not exceed the amount allocated to specific project activities that are not attempts to influence legislation.

(b) [Reserved]

(c) [Reserved]

(d) *Exceptions.*—(1) *Nonpartisan analysis, study, or research.*—(i) *In general.*—A communication is not a lobbying communication, for purposes of § 53.4945-2(a)(1), if the communication constitutes engaging in nonpartisan analysis, study or research and making available to the general public or a segment or members thereof or to governmental bodies, officials, or employees the results of such work. Accordingly, an expenditure for such a communication does not constitute a taxable expenditure under section 4945(d)(1) and § 53.4945-2(a)(1).

(ii) *Nonpartisan analysis, study, or research.*—For purposes of section 4945(e), "nonpartisan analysis, study, or research" means an independent and objective exposition of a particular subject matter, including any activity that is "educational" within the meaning of § 1.501(c)(3)-1(d)(3). Thus, "nonpartisan analysis, study, or research" may advocate a particular position or viewpoint so long as there is a sufficiently full and fair exposition of the pertinent facts to enable the public or an individual to form an independent opinion or conclusion. On the other hand, the mere presentation of unsupported opinion does not qualify as "nonpartisan analysis, study, or research".

(iii) *Presentation as part of a series.*—Normally, whether a publication or broadcast qualifies as "nonpartisan analysis, study, or research" will be determined on a presentation-by-presentation basis. However, if a publication or broadcast is one of a series prepared or supported by a private foundation and the series as a whole meets the standards of subdivision (ii) of this subparagraph, then any individual publication or broadcast within the series will not result in a taxable expenditure even though such individual broadcast or publication does not, by itself, meet the standards of subdivision (ii) of this subparagraph. Whether a broadcast or publication is considered part of a series will ordinarily depend on all the facts and circumstances of each particular situation. However, with respect to broadcast activities, all broadcasts within any period of 6 consecutive months will ordinarily be eligible to be considered as part of a series. If a private foundation times or channels a part of a series which is described in this subdivision in a manner designed to influence the general public or the action of a legislative body with respect to a specific legislative proposal in violation of section 4945(d)(1), the expenses of preparing and distributing such part of the analysis, study, or research will be a taxable expenditure under this section.

(iv) *Making available results of analysis, study, or research.*—A private foundation may choose any suitable means, including oral or written presentations, to distribute the results of its nonpartisan analysis, study, or research, with or without charge. Such means include distribution of reprints of speeches, articles and reports (including the report required under section 6056); presentation of information through conferences, meetings and discussions; and dissemination to the news media, including radio, television and newspapers, and to other public forums. For purposes of this paragraph (d)(1)(iv), such communications may not be limited to, or be directed toward, persons who are interested solely in one side of a particular issue.

(v) *Subsequent lobbying use of certain analysis, study or research.*—(A) *In general.*—Even though certain analysis, study or research is initially within the exception for nonpartisan analysis, study or research, subsequent use of that analysis, study or research for grass roots lobbying may cause that analysis, study or research to be treated as a grass roots lobbying communication that is not within the exception for nonpartisan analysis, study, or research. This paragraph (d)(1)(v) of this section does not cause any analysis, study or research to be considered a direct lobbying communication. For rules regarding when analysis, study or research is treated as a grass roots lobbying communication that is not within the scope of the exception for nonpartisan analysis, study or research, see § 56.4911-2(b)(2)(v).

(B) *Special rule for grants to public charities.*—This paragraph (d)(1)(v)(B) of this section applies where a public charity uses a private foundation grant to finance, in whole or in part, a nonlobbying communication that is subsequently used in lobbying, causing the public charity's expenditures for the communication to be treated as lobbying expenditures under the subsequent use rule. In such a case, the private foundation's grant will ordinarily not be characterized as a lobbying expenditure by virtue of the subsequent use rule. The only situations where the private foundation's grant will be treated as a lobbying expenditure under the subsequent use rule are where the private foundation's primary purpose in making the grant to the public charity was for lobbying or where, at the time of making the grant, the private foundation knows (or in light of all the facts and circumstances reasonably should know) that the public charity's primary purpose in preparing the communication to be funded by the grant is for use in lobbying.

(vi) *Directly encouraging action by recipients of a communication.*—A communication that reflects a view on specific legislation is not within the nonpartisan analysis, study or research exception of this § 53.4945-2(d)(1) if the communication directly encourages the recipient to take action with respect to such legislation. For purposes of this section, a communication directly encourages the recipient to take action with respect to legislation if the communication is described in one or more of § 56.4911-2(b)(2)(iii)(A) through (C). As described in § 56.4911-2(b)(2)(iv), a communication would encourage the recipient to take action with respect to legislation, but not *directly* encourage such action, if the communication does no more than specifically identify one or more legislators who will vote on the legislation as: opposing the communication's view with respect to the legislation; being undecided with respect to the legislation; being the recipient's representative in the legislature; or being a member of the legislative committee or subcommittee that will consider the legislation.

(vii) *Examples.*—The provisions of this paragraph may be illustrated by the following examples:

*Example (1).* M, a private foundation, establishes a research project to collect information for the purpose of showing the dangers of the use of pesticides in raising crops. The information collected includes data with respect to proposed legislation, pending before several State legislatures, which would ban the use of pesticides. The project takes favorable positions on such legislation without producing a sufficiently full and fair exposition of the pertinent facts to enable the public or an individual to form an independent opinion or conclusion on the pros and cons of the use of pesticides. This project is not within the exception for nonpartisan analysis, study, or re-

search because it is designed to present information merely on one side of the legislative controversy.

*Example (2).* N, a private foundation, establishes a research project to collect information concerning the dangers of the use of pesticides in raising crops for the ostensible purpose of examining and reporting information as to the pros and cons of the use of pesticides in raising crops. The information is collected and distributed in the form of a published report which analyzes the effects and costs of the use and nonuse of various pesticides under various conditions on humans, animals and crops. The report also presents the advantages, disadvantages, and economic cost of allowing the continued use of pesticides unabated, of controlling the use of pesticides, and of developing alternatives to pesticides. Even if the report sets forth conclusions that the disadvantages as a result of using pesticides are greater than the advantages of using pesticides and that prompt legislative regulation of the use of pesticides is needed, the project is within the exception for nonpartisan analysis, study or research since it is designed to present information on both sides of the legislative controversy and presents a sufficiently full and fair exposition of the pertinent facts to enable the public or an individual to form an independent opinion or conclusion.

*Example (3).* O, a private foundation, establishes a research project to collect information on the presence or absence of disease in humans from eating food grown with pesticides and the presence or absence of disease in humans from eating food not grown with pesticides. As part of the research project, O hires a consultant who prepares a "fact sheet" which calls for the curtailment of the use of pesticides and which addresses itself to the merits of several specific legislative proposals to curtail the use of pesticides in raising crops which are currently pending before State Legislatures. The "fact sheet" presents reports of experimental evidence tending to support its conclusions but omits any reference to reports of experimental evidence tending to dispute its conclusions. O distributes ten thousand copies to citizens' groups. Expenditures by O in connection with this work of the consultant are not within the exception for nonpartisan analysis, study, or research.

*Example (4).* P publishes a bi-monthly newsletter to collect and report all published materials, ongoing research, and new developments with regard to the use of pesticides in raising crops. The newsletter also includes notices of proposed pesticide legislation with impartial summaries of the provisions and debates on such legislation. The newsletter does not encourage recipients to take action with respect to such legislation, but is designed to present information on both sides of the legislative controversy and does present such information fully and fairly. It is within the exception for nonpartisan analysis, study, or research.

*Example (5).* X is satisfied that A, a member of the faculty of Y University, is exceptionally well qualified to undertake a project involving a comprehensive study of the effects of pesticides on crop yields. Consequently, X makes a grant to A to underwrite the cost of the study and of the preparation of a book on the effect of pesticides on crop yields. X does not take any position on the issues or control the content of A's output. A produces a book which concludes that the use of pesticides often has a favorable effect on crop yields, and on that basis argues against pending bills which would ban the use of pesticides. A's book contains a sufficiently full and fair exposition of the pertinent facts, including known or potential disadvantages of the use of pesticides, to enable the public or an individual to form an independent opinion or conclusion as to whether pesticides should be banned as provided in the pending bills. The book does not directly encourage readers to take action with respect to the pending bills. Consequently, the book is within the exception for nonpartisan analysis, study, or research.

*Example (6).* Assume the same facts as Example (2), except that, instead of issuing a report, X presents within a period of 6 consecutive months a two-program television series relating to the pesticide issue. The first program contains information, arguments, and conclusions favoring legislation to restrict the use of pesticides. The second program contains information, arguments, and conclusions opposing legislation to restrict the use of pesticides. The programs are broadcast within 6 months of each other during commensurate periods of prime time. X's programs are within the exception for nonpartisan analysis, study, or research. Although neither program individually could be regarded as nonpartisan, the series of two programs constitutes a balanced presentation.

*Example (7).* Assume the same facts as Example (6), except that X arranged for televising the program favoring legislation to restrict the use of pesticides at 8:00 p.m. on a Thursday evening and for televising the program opposing such legislation at 7:00 a.m. on a Sunday morning. X's presentation is not within the exception for nonpartisan analysis, study, or research, since X disseminated its information in a manner prejudicial to one side of the legislative controversy.

*Example (8).* Organization Z researches, writes, prints and distributes a study on the use and effects of pesticide X. A bill is pending in the U.S. Senate to ban the use of pesticide X. Z's study leads to the conclusion that pesticide X is extremely harmful and that the bill pending in the U.S. Senate is an appropriate and much needed remedy to solve the problems caused by pesticide X. The study contains a sufficiently full and fair exposition of the pertinent facts, including known or potential advantages of the use of pesticide X, to enable the public or an individual to form an independent opinion or conclusion as to whether pesticides should be banned as provided in the pending bills. In its analysis of the pending bill, the study names certain undecided Senators on the Senate committee considering the bill. Although the study meets the three part test for determining whether a communication is a grass roots lobbying communication, the study is within the exception for nonpartisan analysis, study or research, because it does not directly encourage recipients of the communication to urge a legislator to opppose the bill.

*Example (9).* Assume the same facts as in Example (8), except that, after stating support for the pending bill, the study concludes: "You should write to the undecided commitee members to support this crucial bill." The study is not within the exception for nonpartisan analysis, study or research because it directly encourages the recipients to urge a legislator to support a specific piece of legislation.

*Example (10).* Organization X plans to conduct a lobbying campaign with respect to illegal drug use in the United States. It incurs $5,000 in expenses to conduct research and prepare an extensive report primarily for use in the lobbying campaign. Although the detailed report discusses specific pending legislation and reaches the conclusion that the legislation would reduce illegal drug use, the report contains a sufficiently full and fair exposition of the pertinent facts to enable the public or an indiviual to form an independent conclusion regarding the effect of the legislation. The report does not encourage readers to contact legislators regarding the legislation. Accordingly, the report does not, in and of itself, constitute a lobbying communication.

Copies of the report are available to the public at X's office, but X does not actively distribute the report or otherwise seek to make the contents of the report available to the general public. Whether or not X's distribution is sufficient to meet the requirement in §53.4945-2(d)(1)(iv) that a nonpartisan communication be made available, X's distribution is not substantial (for purposes of §§53.4945-2(d)(1)(v) and 56.4911-2(b)(2)(v) in light of all of the facts and circumstances, including the normal distribution pattern of similar nonpartisan reports. X then mails copies of the report, along with a letter, to 10,000 individuals on X's mailing list. In the letter, X requests that individuals contact legislators urging passage of the legislation discussed in the report. Because X's research and report were primarily undertaken by X for lobbying purposes and X did not make a substantial distribution of the report (without an accompanying lobbying message) prior to or contemporaneously with the use of the report in lobbying, the report is a grass roots lobbying communication that is not within the exception for nonpartisan analysis, study or research. Thus, the expenditures for preparing and mailing both the report and the letter are taxable expenditures under section 4945.

*Example (11).* Assume the same facts as in Example (10), except that before using the report in the lobbying campaign, X sends the research and report (without an accompanying lobbying message) to universities and newspapers. At the same time, X also advertises the availability of the report in its newsletter. This distribution is similar in scope to the normal distribution pattern of similar nonpartisan reports. In light of all of the facts and circumstances, X's distribution of the report is substantial. Because of X's substantial distribution of the report, X's primary purpose will be considered to be other than for use in lobbying and the report will not be considered a grass roots lobbying communication. Accordingly, only the expenditures for copying and mailing the report to the 10,000 individuals on X's mailing list, as well as for preparing and mailing the letter, are expenditures for grass roots lobbying communications, and are thus taxable expenditures under section 4945.

*Example (12).* Organization M pays for a bumper sticker that reads: "STOP ABORTION: Vote *NO* on Prop. X!" M also pays for a 30-second television advertisement and a billboard that similarly advocate opposition to Prop. X. In light of the limited scope of the communications, none of the communications is within the exception for nonpartisan analysis, study or research. First, none of the communications rises to the level of analysis, study or research. Second, none of the communications is nonpartisan because none contains a sufficiently full and fair exposition of the pertinent facts to enable the public or an individual to form an independent opinion or conclusion. Thus, each communication is a lobbying communication.

(2) *Technical advice or assistance.*—(i) *In general.*—Amounts paid or incurred in connection with providing technical advice or assistance to a governmental body, a governmental committee, or a subdivision of either of the foregoing, in response to a written request by such body, committee, or subdivision do not constitute taxable expenditures for purposes of this section. Under this exception, the request for assistance or advice must be made in the name of the requesting governmental body, committee or subdivision rather than an individual member thereof. Similarly, the response to such request must be available to every member of the requesting body, committee or subdivision. For example, in the case of a written response to a request for technical advice or assistance from a Congressional committee, the response will be considered available to every member of the requesting committee if the response is submitted to the person making such request in the name of the committee and it is made clear that the response is for the use of all the members of the committee.

(ii) *Nature of technical advice or assistance.*—"Technical advice or assistance" may be given as a result of knowledge or skill in a given area. Because such assistance or advice may be given only at the express request of a governmental body, committee or subdivision, the oral or written presentation of such assistance or advice need not qualify as nonpartisan analysis, study or research. The offering of opinions or recommendations will ordinarily qualify under this exception only if such opinions or recommendations are specifically requested by the governmental body, committee or subdivision or are directly related to the materials so requested.

(iii) *Examples.* The provisions of this subparagraph may be illustrated by the following examples:

*Example (1).* A Congressional committee is studying the feasibility of legislation to provide funds for scholarships to United States students attending schools abroad. X, a private foundation which has engaged in a private scholarship program of this type, is asked, in writing, by the committee to describe the manner in which it selects candidates for its program. X's response disclosing its methods of selection constitutes technical advice or assistance.

*Example (2).* Assume the same facts as Example (1), except that X's response not only includes a description of its own grant-making procedures, but also its views regarding the wisdom of adopting such a program. Since such views are directly related to the subject matter of the request for technical advice or assistance, expenditures paid or incurred with respect to the presentation of such views would not constitute taxable expenditures. However, expenditures paid or incurred with respect to a response which is not directly related to the subject matter of the request for technical advice or assistance would constitute taxable expenditures unless the presentation can qualify as the making available of nonpartisan analysis, study or research.

*Example (3).* Assume the same facts as in Example (1), except that X is requested, in addition, to give any views it considers relevant. A response to this request giving opinions which are relevant to the committee's consideration of the scholarship program but which are not necessarily directly related to X's scholarship program, such as discussions of alternative scholarship programs and their relative merits, would qualify as "technical advice or assistance", and expenditures paid or incurred with respect to such response would not constitute taxable expenditures.

*Example (4).* A, an official of the State Department, makes a written request in his official capacity for information from Foundation Y relating to the economic development of Country M and for the opinions of Y as to the proper position of the United States in pending negotiations with M concerning a proposed treaty involving a program of economic and technical aid to M. Y's furnishing of such information and opinions constitutes technical advice or assistance.

*Example (5).* In response to a telephone inquiry from Senator X's staff, organization B sends Senator X a report concluding that the Senate should not advise and consent to the nomination of Z to serve as a Supreme Court Justice. Because the request was not in writing, and also because the request was not from the Senate itself or from a committee or subcommittee, B's report is not within the scope of the exception for responses to requests for technical advice. Accordingly, B's report is a lobbying communication unless the report is within the scope of the exception for nonpartisan analysis, study or research.

*Example (6).* Assume the same facts as in Example (5), except that B's report is sent in response to a written request that Senator X sends to B. The request from Senator X is a request from the Senator as an individual member of the Senate rather than from the Senate itself or from a committee or subcommittee. Accordingly, B's report is not within the scope of the exception for responses to requests for technical advice and is a lobbying communication unless the report is within the scope of the exception for nonpartisan analysis, study or research.

*Example (7).* Assume the same facts as in Example (6), except that B's report is sent in response to a written request from the Senate committee that is considering the nomination for an evaluation of the nominee's legal writings and a recommendation as to whether the candidate is or is not qualified to serve on the Supreme Court. The

(3) *Decisions affecting the powers, duties, etc., of a private foundation.*—(i) *In general.*—Paragraph (c) of this section does not apply to any amount paid or incurred in connection with an appearance before, or communication with, any legislative body with respect to a possible decision of such body which might affect the existence of the private foundation, its powers and duties, its tax-exempt status, or the deductibility of contributions to such foundation. Under this exception, a foundation may communicate with the entire legislative body, committees or subcommittees of such legislative body, individual congressmen or legislators, members of their staffs, or representatives of the executive branch, who are involved in the legislative process, if such communication is limited to the prescribed subjects. Similarly, the foundation may make expenditures in order to initiate legislation if such legislation concerns only matters which might affect the existence of the private foundation, its powers and duties, its tax-exempt status, or the deductibility of contributions to such foundation.

(ii) *Examples.* The provisions of this subparagraph may be illustrated by the following examples:

*Example (1).* A bill is being considered by Congress which would, if enacted, restrict the power of a private foundation to engage in transactions with certain related persons. Under the proposed bill a private foundation would lose its exemption from taxation if it engages in such transactions. W, a private foundation, writes to the Congressional committee considering the bill, arguing that the enactment of such a bill would not be advisable, and subsequently appears before such committee to make its arguments. In addition, W requests that the Congressional committee consider modification of the 2 percent *de minimis* rule of section 4943(c)(2)(C). Expenditures paid or incurred with respect to such submissions do not constitute taxable expenditures since they are made with respect to a possible decision of Congress which might affect the existence of the private foundation, its powers and duties, its tax-exempt status, or the deduction of contributions to such foundation.

*Example (2).* A bill being considered in a State legislature is designed to implement the requirements of section 508(e) of the Internal Revenue Code of 1954. Under such section, a private foundation is required to make certain amendments to its governing instrument. X, a private foundation, makes a submission to the legislature which proposes alternative measures which might be taken in lieu of the proposed bill. X also arranges to have its president contact certain State legislators with regard to this bill. Expenditures paid or incurred in making such submission and in contacting the State legislators do not constitute taxable expenditures since they are made with respect to a possible decision of such State legislature which might affect the existence of the private foundation, its powers and duties, its tax-exempt status, or the deduction of contributions to such foundation.

*Example (3).* A bill is being considered by a State legislature under which the State would assume certain responsibilities for nursing care of the aged. Y, a private foundation which hitherto has engaged in such activities, appears before the State legislature and contends that such activities can be better performed by privately supported organizations. Expenditures paid or incurred with respect to such appearance are not made with respect to possible decisions of the State legislature which might affect the existence of the private foundation, its powers and duties, its tax-exempt status, or the deduction of contributions to such foundation, but rather merely affect the scope of the private foundation's future activities.

*Example (4).* A State legislature is considering the annual appropriations bill. Z, a private foundation which had hitherto performed contract research for the State, appears before the appropriations committee in order to attempt to persuade the committee of the advisability of continuing the program. Expenditures paid or incurred with respect to such appearance are not made with respect to possible decisions of the State legislature which might affect the existence of the private foundation, its powers and duties, its tax-exempt status, or the deduction of contributions to such foundation, but rather merely affect the scope of the private foundation's future activities.

(4) *Examinations and discussions of broad social, economic, and similar problems.*—Examinations and discussions of broad social, economic, and similar problems are neither direct lobbying communications under § 56.4911-2(b)(1) nor grass roots lobbying communications under § 56.4911-2(b)(2) even if the problems are of the type with which government would be expected to deal ultimately. Thus, under § 56.4911-2(b)(1) and (2), lobbying communications do not include public discussion, or communications with members of legislative bodies or governmental employees, the general subject of which is also the subject of legislation before a legislative body, so long as such discussion does not address itself to the merits of a specific legislative proposal and so long as such discussion does not directly encourage recipients with respect to legislation. For example, this paragraph (d)(4) excludes from grass roots lobbying under § 56.4911-2(b)(2) an organization's discussions of problems such as environmental pollution or population growth that are being considered by Congress and various State legislatures, but only where the discussions are not directly addressed to specific legislation being considered, and only where the discussions do not directly encourage recipients of the communication to contact a legislator, an employee of a legislative body, or a government official or employee who may participate in the formulation of legislation. [Reg. § 53.4945-2.]

☐ [*T.D. 7215, 10-30-72. Amended by T.D. 8308, 8-30-90.*]

**[Reg. § 53.4945-3]**

**§ 53.4945-3. Influencing elections and carrying on voter registration drives.**—(a) *Expenditures to influence elections or carry on voter registration drives.*—(1) *In general.*—Under section 4945(d)(2), the term "taxable expenditure" includes any amount paid or incurred by a private foundation to influence the outcome of any specific public election or to carry on, directly or indirectly, any voter registration drive, unless such amount is paid or incurred by an organization described in section 4945(f). However, for treatment of non-earmarked grants to public organizations, see § 53.4945-2(a)(5) and for treatment of certain earmarked grants to organizations described in section 4945(f), see paragraph (b)(2) of this section.

(2) *Influencing the outcome of a specific public election.*—For purposes of this section, an organization shall be considered to be influencing the outcome of any specific public election if it participates or intervenes, directly or indirectly, in any political campaign on behalf of or in opposition to any candidate for public office. The term "candidate for public office" means an individual who offers himself, or is proposed by others, as a contestant for an elective public office, whether such office be national, State or local. Activities which constitute participation or intervention in a political campaign on behalf of or in opposition to a candidate include, but are not limited to:

(i) Publishing or distributing written or printed statements or making oral statements on behalf of or in opposition to such a candidate;

(ii) Paying salaries or expenses of campaign workers; and

(iii) Conducting or paying the expenses of conducting a voter registration drive limited to the geographic area covered by the campaign.

(b) *Nonpartisan activities carried on by certain organizations.*—(1) *In general.*—If an organization meets the requirements described in section 4945(f), an amount paid or incurred by such organization shall not be considered a taxable expenditure even though the use of such amount is otherwise described in section 4945(d)(2). Such requirements are:

(i) The organization is described in section 501(c)(3) and exempt from taxation under section 501(a);

(ii) The activities of the organization are nonpartisan, are not confined to one specific election period, and are carried on in five or more States;

(iii) The organization expends at least 85 percent of its income directly for the active conduct (within the meaning of section 4942(j)(3) and the regulations thereunder) of the activities constituting the purpose or function for which it is organized and operated;

(iv) The organization receives at least 85 percent of its support (other than gross investment income as defined in section 509(e)) from exempt organizations, the general public, governmental units described in section 170(c)(1), or any combination of the foregoing; the organization does not receive more than 25 percent of its support (other than gross investment income) from any one exempt organization (for this purpose treating private foundations which are described in section 4946(a)(1)(H) with respect to each other as one exempt organization); and not more than half of the support of the organization is received from gross investment income; and

(v) Contributions to the organization for voter registration drives are not subject to conditions that they may be used only in specified States, possessions of the United States, or political subdivisions or other areas of any of the foregoing, or the District of Columbia, or that they may be used in only one specific election period.

(2) *Grants to section 4945(f) organizations.*—If a private foundation makes a grant to an organization described in section 4945(f) (whether or not such grantee is a private foundation as defined in section 509(a)), such grant will not be treated as a taxable expenditure under section 4945(d)(2) or (4). Even if a grant to such an organization is earmarked for voter registration purposes generally, such a grant will not be treated as a taxable expenditure under section

4945(d)(2) or (4) as long as such earmarking does not violate section 4945(f)(5).

(3) *Period for determining support.*—(i) *In general.*—The determination whether an organization meets the support test in section 4945(f)(4) for any taxable year is to be made by aggregating all amounts of support received by the organization during the taxable year and the immediately preceding four taxable years. However, the support received in any taxable year which begins before January 1, 1970, shall be excluded.

(ii) *New organizations and organizations with no preceding taxable years beginning after December 31, 1969.*—Except as provided in subparagraph (4) of this paragraph, in the case of a new organization or an organization with no taxable years that begin after December 31, 1969, and immediately precede the taxable year in question, the requirements of the support test in section 4945(f)(4) will be considered as met for the taxable year if such requirements are met by the end of the taxable year.

(iii) *Organization with three or fewer preceding taxable years.*—In the case of an organization which has been in existence for at least one but fewer than four preceding taxable years beginning after December 31, 1969, the determination whether such organization meets the requirements of the support test in section 4945(f)(4) for the taxable year is to be made by taking into account all the support received by such organization during the taxable year and during each preceding taxable year beginning after December 31, 1969.

(4) *Advance rulings.*—An organization will be given an advance ruling that it is an organization described in section 4945(f) for its first taxable year of operation beginning after [insert date these final regulations are filed by the Office of the Federal Register] or for its first taxable year of operation beginning after December 31, 1969, if it submits evidence establishing that it can reasonably be expected to meet the tests under section 4945(f) for such taxable year. An organization which, pursuant to this subparagraph, has been treated as an organization described in section 4945(f) for a taxable year (without withdrawal of such treatment by notification from the Internal Revenue Service during such year), but which actually fails to meet the requirements of section 4945(f) for such taxable year, will not be treated as an organization described in section 4945(f) as of the first day of its next taxable year (for purposes of making any determination under the internal revenue laws with respect to such organization) and until such time as the organization does meet the requirements of section 4945(f). For purposes of section 4945, the status of grants or contributions with respect to grantors or contributors to such organization will not be affected until notice of change of status of such organization is made to the public (such as by publication in the Internal Revenue Bulletin). The preceding sentence shall not apply, however, if the grantor or contributor was responsible for, or was aware of, the fact that the organization did not satisfy section 4945(f) at the end of the taxable year with respect to which the organization had obtained an advance ruling or a determination letter that it was a section 4945(f) organization, or acquired knowledge that the Internal Revenue Service had given notice to such organization that it would be deleted from classification as a section 4945(f) organization. [Reg. § 53.4945-3.]

□ [*T.D. 7215, 10-30-72.*]

### [Reg. § 53.4945-4]

**§ 53.4945-4. Grants to individuals.**—(a) *Grants to individuals.*—(1) *In general.*—Under section 4945(d)(3) the term "taxable expenditure" includes any amount paid or incurred by a private foundation as a grant to an individual for travel, study, or other similar purposes by such individual unless the grant satisfies the requirements of section 4945(g). Grants to individuals which are not taxable expenditures because made in accordance with the requirements of section 4945(g) may result in the imposition of excise taxes under other provisions of chapter 42.

(2) *"Grants" defined.*—For purposes of section 4945, the term "grants" shall include, but is not limited to, such expenditures as scholarships, fellowships, internships, prizes, and awards. Grants shall also include loans for purposes described in section 170(c)(2)(B) and "program related investments" (such as investments in small businesses in central cities or in businesses which assist in neighborhood renovation). Similarly, "grants" include such expenditures as payments to exempt organizations to be used in furtherance of such recipient organizations' exempt purposes whether or not such payments are solicited by such recipient organizations. Conversely, "grants" do not ordinarily include salaries or other compensation to employees. For example, "grants" do not ordinarily include educational payments to employees which are includible in the employees' incomes pursuant to section 61. In addition, "grants" do not ordinarily include payments (including salaries, consultants' fees and reimbursement for travel expenses such as transportation, board, and lodging) to persons (regardless of whether such persons are individuals) for personal services in assisting a foundation in planning, evaluating or developing projects or areas of program activity by consulting, advising, or participating in conferences organized by the foundation.

(3) *Requirements for individual grants.*—(i) *Grants for other than section 4945(d)(3) purposes.*—A grant to an individual for purposes other than those described in section 4945(d)(3) is not a taxable expenditure within the meaning of section 4945(d)(3). For example, if a foundation makes grants to indigent individuals to enable them to purchase furniture, such grants are not taxable expenditures within the meaning of section 4945(d)(3) even if the requirements of section 4945(g) are not met.

(ii) *Grants for section 4945(d)(3) purposes.*—Under section 4945(g), a grant to an individual for travel, study, or other similar purposes is not a "taxable expenditure" only if:

(a) The grant is awarded on an objective and nondiscriminatory basis (within the meaning of paragraph (b) of this section);

(b) The grant is made pursuant to a procedure approved in advance by the Commissioner; and

(c) It is demonstrated to the satisfaction of the Commissioner that:

(1) The grant constitutes a scholarship or fellowship grant which is excluded from gross income under section 117(a) and is to be utilized for study at an educational institution described in section 151(e)(4);

(2) The grant constitutes a prize or award which is excluded from gross income under section 74(b), and the recipient of such prize or award is selected from the general public (within the meaning of section 4941(d)(2)(G)(i) and the regulations thereunder); or

(3) The purpose of the grant is to achieve a specific objective, produce a report or other similar product, or improve or enhance a literary, artistic, musical, scientific, teaching, or other similar capacity, skill, or talent of the grantee.

If a grant is made to an individual for a purpose described in section 4945(g)(3) and such grant otherwise meets the requirements of section 4945(g), such grant shall not be treated as a taxable expenditure even if it is a scholarship or a fellowship grant which is not excludable from income under section 117 or if it is a prize or award which is includible in income under section 74.

(iii) *Renewals.*—A renewal of a grant which satisfied the requirements of subdivision (ii) of this subparagraph shall not be treated as a grant to an individual which is subject to the requirements of this section, if—

(a) The grantor has no information indicating that the original grant is being used for any purpose other than that for which it was made,

(b) Any reports due at the time of the renewal decision pursuant to the terms of the original grant have been furnished, and

(c) Any additional criteria and procedures for renewal are objective and nondiscriminatory.

For purposes of this section, an extension of the period over which a grant is to be paid shall not itself be regarded as a grant or a renewal of a grant.

(4) *Certain designated grants.*—(i) *In general.*—A grant by a private foundation to another organization, which the grantee organization uses to make payments to an individual for purposes described in section 4945(d)(3), shall not be regarded as a grant by the private foundation to the individual grantee if the foundation does not earmark the use of the grant for any named individual and there does not exist an agreement, oral or written, whereby such grantor foundation may cause the selection of the individual grantee by the grantee organization. For purposes of this subparagraph, a grant described herein shall not be regarded as a grant by the foundation to an individual grantee even though such foundation has reason to believe that certain individuals would derive benefits from such grant so long as the grantee organization exercises control, in fact, over the selection process and actually makes the selection completely independently of the private foundation.

(ii) *Certain grants to "public charities".*—A grant by a private foundation to an organization described in section 509(a)(1), (2), or (3), which the grantee organization uses to make payments to an individual for purposes described in section 4945(d)(3), shall not be regarded as a grant by the private foundation to the individual grantee (regardless of the application of subdivision (i) of this subparagraph) if the grant is made for a project which is to be undertaken under the supervision of the section 509(a)(1), (2), or (3) organization and such grantee organization controls the selection of the individual grantee. This subdivision shall apply regardless of whether the name of the individual grantee was first proposed by the private foundation, but only if there is an objective manifestation of the section 509(a)(1), (2), or (3) organization's control over the selection process, although the selection need not be made completely independently of the private foundation. For purposes of this subdivision, an organization shall be considered a section 509(a)(1) organization if it is treated as such under subparagraph (4) of § 53.4945-5(a).

(iii) *Grants to governmental agencies.*—If a private foundation makes a grant to an organization described in section 170(c)(1) (regardless of whether it is described in section 501(c)(3)) and such grant is earmarked for use by an individual for purposes described in section 4945(d)(3), such grant is not subject to the requirements of section 4945(d)(3) and (g) and this section (regardless of the application of subdivision (i) of this subparagraph) if the section 170(c)(1) organization satisfies the Commissioner in advance that its grant-making program:

(a) Is in furtherance of a purpose described in section 170(c)(2)(B),

(b) Requires that the individual grantee submit reports to it which would satisfy paragraph (c)(3) of this section, and

(c) Requires that the organization investigate jeopardized grants in a manner substantially similar to that described in paragraph (c)(4) of this section.

(iv) *Examples.*—The provisions of this subparagraph may be illustrated by the following examples:

*Example (1).* M, a university described in section 170(b)(1)(A)(ii), requests that P, a private foundation, grant it $100,000 to enable M to obtain the services of a particular scientist for a research project in a special field of biochemistry in which he has exceptional qualifications and competence. P, after determining that the project deserves support, makes the grant to M to enable it to obtain the services of this scientist. M is authorized to keep the funds even if it is unsuccessful in attempting to employ the scientist. Under these circumstances P will not be treated as having made a grant to the individual scientist for purposes of section 4945(d)(3) and (g), since the requirements of subdivision (i) of this subparagraph have been satisfied. Even if M were not authorized to keep the funds if it is unsuccessful in attempting to employ the scientist, P would not be treated as having made a grant to the individual scientist for purposes of section 4945(d)(3) and (g), since it is clear from the facts and circumstances that the selection of the particular scientist was made by M and thus the requirements of subdivision (ii) of this subparagraph would have been satisfied.

*Example (2).* Assume the same facts as Example (1), except that there are a number of scientists who are qualified to administer the research project, P suggests the name of the particular scientist to be employed by M, and M is not authorized to keep the funds if it is unsuccessful in attempting to employ the particular scientist. For purposes of section 4945(d)(3) and (g), P will be treated as having made a grant to the individual scientist whose name it suggested, since it is clear from the facts and circumstances that selection of the particular scientist was made by P.

*Example (3).* X, a private foundation, is aware of the exceptional research facilities at Y University, an organization described in section 170(b)(1)(A)(ii). Officials of X approach officials of Y with an offer to give Y a grant of $100,000 if Y will engage an adequately qualified physicist to conduct a specific research project. Y's officials accept this proposal, and it is agreed that Y will administer the funds. After examining the qualifications of several research physicists, the officials of Y agree that A, whose name was first suggested by officials of X and who first suggested the specific research project to X, is uniquely qualified to conduct the project. X's grant letter provides that X has the right to renegotiate the terms of the grant if there is a substantial deviation from such terms, such as breakdown of Y's research facilities or termination of the conduct of the project by an adequately qualified physicist. Under these circumstances, X will not be treated as having made a grant to A for purposes of section 4945(d)(3) and (g), since the requirements of subdivision (ii) of this subparagraph have been satisfied.

*Example (4).* Professor A, a scholar employed by University Y, an organization described in section 170(b)(1)(A)(ii), approaches Foundation X to determine the availability of grant funds for a particular research project supervised or conducted by Professor A relevant to the program interests of Foundation X. After learning that Foundation X would be willing to consider the project if University Y were to submit the project to X, Professor A submits his proposal to the appropriate administrator of University Y. After making a determination that it should assume responsibility for the project, that Professor A is qualified to conduct the project, and that his participation would be consistent with his other faculty duties, University Y formally adopts the grant proposal and submits it to Foundation X. The grant is made to University Y which, under the terms of the grant, is responsible for the expenditure of the grant funds and the

grant project. In such a case, and even if Foundation X retains the right to renegotiate the terms of the grant if the project ceases to be conducted by Professor A, the grant shall not be regarded as a grant by Foundation X to Professor A since University Y has retained control over the selection process within the meaning of subdivision (ii) of this subparagraph.

(5) *Earmarked grants to individuals.*—A grant by a private foundation to an individual, which meets the requirements of section 4945(d)(3) and (g), is a taxable expenditure by such foundation under section 4945(d) only if—

(i) The grant is earmarked to be used for any activity described in section 4945(d)(1), (2), or (5), or is earmarked to be used in a manner which would violate section 4945(d)(3) or (4),

(ii) There is an agreement, oral or written, whereby such grantor foundation may cause the grantee to engage in any such prohibited activity and such grant is in fact used in a manner which violates section 4945(d), or

(iii) The grant is made for a purpose other than a purpose described in section 170(c)(2)(B).

For purposes of this subparagraph, a grant by a private foundation is earmarked if such grant is given pursuant to an agreement, oral or written, that the grant will be used for specific purposes.

(b) *Selection of grantees on "an objective and nondiscriminatory basis".*—(1) *In general.*—For purposes of this section, in order for a foundation to establish that its grants to individuals are made on an objective and nondiscriminatory basis, the grants must be awarded in accordance with a program which, if it were a substantial part of the foundation's activities, would be consistent with:

(i) The existence of the foundation's exempt status under section 501(c)(3);

(ii) The allowance of deductions to individuals under section 170 for contributions to the granting foundation; and

(iii) The requirements of subparagraphs (2), (3), and (4) of this paragraph.

(2) *Candidates for grants.*—Ordinarily, selection of grantees on an objective and nondiscriminatory basis requires that the group from which grantees are selected be chosen on the basis of criteria reasonably related to the purposes of the grant. Furthermore, the group must be sufficiently broad so that the giving of grants to members of such group would be considered to fulfill a purpose described in section 170(c)(2)(B). Thus, ordinarily the group must be sufficiently large to constitute a charitable class. However, selection from a group is not necessary where taking into account the purposes of the grant, one or several persons are selected because they are exceptionally qualified to carry out these purposes or it is otherwise evident that the selection is particularly calculated to effectuate the charitable purpose of the grant rather than to benefit particular persons or a particular class of persons. Therefore, consistent with the requirements of this subparagraph, the foundation may impose reasonable restrictions on the group of potential grantees. For example, selection of a qualified research scientist to work on a particular project does not violate the requirements of section 4945(d)(3) merely because the foundation selects him from a group of three scientists who are experts in that field.

(3) *Selection from within group of potential grantees.*—The criteria used in selecting grant recipients from the potential grantees should be related to the purpose of the grant. Thus, for example, proper criteria for selecting scholarship recipients might include (but are not limited to) the following: prior academic performance; performance on tests designed to measure ability and aptitude for college work; recommendations from instructors; financial need; and the conclusions which the selection committee might draw from a personal interview as to the individual's motivation, character, ability and potential.

(4) *Persons making selections.*—The person or group of persons who select recipients of grants should not be in a position to derive a private benefit, directly or indirectly, if certain potential grantees are selected over others.

(5) *Examples.*—The provisions of this paragraph may be illustrated by the following examples:

*Example (1).* X Company employs 100,000 people of whom 1,000 are classified by the company as executives. The company has organized the X Company Foundation which, as its sole activity, provides 100 four-year college scholarships per year for children of the company's employees. Children of all employees (other than disqualified persons with respect to the foundation) who have worked for the X Company for at least two years are eligible to apply for these scholarships. In previous years, the number of children eligible to apply for such scholarships has averaged 2,000 per year. Selection of scholarship recipients from among the applicants is made by three prominent educators, who have no connection (other than as members of the selection committee) with the company, the foundation or any of the employees of the company. The selections are made on the basis of the applicants' prior academic performance, performance on certain tests designed to measure ability and aptitude for college work, and financial need. No disproportionate number of scholarships has been granted to relatives of executives of X Company. Under these circumstances, the operation of the scholarship program by the X Company Foundation: (1) is consistent with the existence of the foundation's exempt status under section 501(c)(3) and with the allowance of deductions under section 170 for contributions to the foundation; (2) utilizes objective and nondiscriminatory criteria in selecting scholarship recipients from among the applicants; and (3) utilizes a selection committee which appears likely to make objective and nondiscriminatory selections of grant recipients.

*Example (2).* Assume the same facts as Example (1), except that the foundation establishes a program to provide 20 college scholarships per year for members of a certain ethnic minority. All members of this minority group (other than disqualified persons with respect to the foundation) living in State Z are eligible to apply for these scholarships. It is estimated that at least 400 persons will be eligible to apply for these scholarships each year. Under these circumstances, the operation of this scholarship program by the foundation: (1) is consistent with the existence of the foundation's exempt status under section 501(c)(3) and with the allowance of deductions under section 170 for contributions to the foundation; (2) utilizes objective and nondiscriminatory criteria in selecting scholarship recipients from among the applicants; and (3) utilizes a selection committee which appears likely to make objective and nondiscriminatory selections of grant recipients.

(c) *Requirements of a proper procedure.*—(1) *In general.*—Section 4945(g) requires that grants to individuals must be made pursuant to a procedure approved in advance. To secure such approval, a private foundation must demonstrate to the satisfaction of the Commissioner that—

(i) Its grant procedure includes an objective and nondiscriminatory selection process (as described in paragraph (b) of this section);

(ii) Such procedure is reasonably calculated to result in performance by grantees of the activities that the grants are intended to finance; and

(iii) The foundation plans to obtain reports to determine whether the grantees have performed the activities that the grants are intended to finance.

No single procedure or set of procedures is required. Procedures may vary depending upon such factors as the size of the foundation, the amount and purpose of the grants and whether one or more recipients are involved.

(2) *Supervision of scholarship and fellowship grants.*—Except as provided in subparagraph (5) of this paragraph, with respect to any scholarship or fellowship grants, a private foundation must make arrangements to receive a report of the grantee's courses taken (if any) and grades received (if any) in each academic period. Such a report must be verified by the educational institution attended by the grantee and must be obtained at least once a year. In cases of grantees whose study at an educational institution does not involve the taking of courses but only the preparation of research papers or projects, such as the writing of a doctoral thesis, the foundation must receive a brief report on the progress of the paper or project at least once a year. Such a report must be approved by the faculty member supervising the grantee or by another appropriate university official. Upon completion of a grantee's study at an educational institution, a final report must also be obtained.

(3) *Grants described in section 4945(g)(3).*—With respect to a grant made under section 4945(g)(3), the private foundation shall require reports on the use of the funds and the progress made by the grantee toward achieving the purposes for which the grant was made. Such reports must be made at least once a year. Upon completion of the undertaking for which the grant was made, a final report must be made describing the grantee's accomplishments with respect to the grant and accounting for the funds received under such grant.

(4) *Investigation of jeopardized grants.*—(i) Where the reports submitted under this paragraph or other information (including the failure to submit such reports) indicates that all or any part of a grant is not being used in furtherance of the purposes of such grant, the foundation is under a duty to investigate. While conducting its investigation, the foundation must withhold further payments to the extent possible until any delinquent reports required by this paragraph have been submitted and where required by subdivision (ii) or (iii) of this subparagraph.

(ii) In cases in which the grantor foundation determines that any part of a grant has been used for improper purposes and the grantee has not previously diverted grant funds to any use not in furtherance of a purpose specified in the grant, the foundation will not be treated as having made a taxable expenditure solely because of the diversion so long as the foundation—

(a) Is taking all reasonable and appropriate steps either to recover the grant funds or to insure the restoration of the diverted funds and the dedication (consistent with the requirements of (b)(1) and (2) of this subdivision) of other grant funds held by the grantee to the purposes being financed by the grant, and

(b) Withholds any further payments to the grantee after the grantor becomes aware that a diversion may have taken place (hereinafter referred to as "further payments") until it has—

(1) Received the grantee's assurances that future diversions will not occur, and

(2) Required the grantee to take extraordinary precautions to prevent future diversions from occurring.

If a foundation is treated as having made a taxable expenditure under this subparagraph in a case to which this subdivision applies, then unless the foundation meets the requirements of (a) of this subdivision the amount of the taxable expenditure shall be the amount of the diversion plus the amount of any further payments to the same grantee. However, if the foundation complies with the requirements of (a) of this subdivision but not the requirements of (b) of this subdivision, the amount of the taxable expenditure shall be the amount of such further payments.

(iii) In cases where a grantee has previously diverted funds received from a grantor foundation, and the grantor foundation determines that any part of a grant has again been used for improper purposes, the foundation will not be treated as having made a taxable expenditure solely by reason of such diversion so long as the foundation—

(a) Is taking all reasonable and appropriate steps to recover the grant funds or to insure the restoration of the funds and the dedication (consistent with the requirements of (b)(2) and (3) of this subdivision) of other grant funds held by the grantee to the purposes being financed by the grant, and

(b) Withholds further payments until—

(1) Such funds are in fact so recovered or restored,

(2) It has received the grantee's assurances that future diversions will not occur, and

(3) It requires the grantee to take extraordinary precautions to prevent future diversions from occurring.

If a foundation is treated as having made a taxable expenditure under this subparagraph in a case to which this subdivision applies, then unless the foundation meets the requirements of (a) of this subdivision, the amount of the taxable expenditure shall be the amount of the diversion plus the amount of any further payments to the same grantee. However, if the foundation complies with the requirements of (a) of this subdivision, but fails to withhold further payments until the requirements of (b) of this subdivision are met, the amount of the taxable expenditure shall be the amount of such further payments.

(iv) The phrase "all reasonable and appropriate steps" in subdivisions (ii) and (iii) of this subparagraph includes legal action where appropriate but need not include legal action if such action would in all probability not result in the satisfaction of execution on a judgment.

(5) *Supervision of certain scholarship and fellowship grants.*—Subparagraphs (2) and (4) of this paragraph shall be considered satisfied with respect to scholarship or fellowship grants under the following circumstances:

(i) The scholarship or fellowship grants are described in section 4945(g)(1);

(ii) The grantor foundation pays the scholarship or fellowship grants to an educational institution described in section 151(e)(4); and

(iii) Such educational institution agrees to use the grant funds to defray the recipient's expenses or to pay the funds (or a portion thereof) to the recipient only if the recipient is enrolled at such educational institution and his standing at such educational institution is consistent with the purposes and conditions of the grant.

(6) *Retention of records.*—A private foundation shall retain records pertaining to all grants to individuals for purposes described in section 4945(d)(3). Such records shall include:

(i) All information the foundation secures to evaluate the qualification of potential grantees;

(ii) Identification of grantees (including any relationship of any grantee to the foundation sufficient to make such grantee a disqualified person of the private foundation within the meaning of section 4946(a)(1));

(iii) Specification of the amount and purpose of each grant; and

(iv) The follow-up information which the foundation obtains in complying with subparagraphs (2), (3) and (4) of this paragraph.

(7) *Example.*—The provisions of paragraphs (b) and (c) of this section may be illustrated by the following example:

*Example.* The X Foundation grants ten scholarships each year to graduates of high schools in its area to permit the recipients to attend college. It makes the availability of its scholarships known by oral or written communications each year to the principals of three major high schools in the area. The foundation obtains information from each high school on the academic qualifications, background, and financial need of applicants. It requires that each applicant be recommended by two of his teachers or by the principal of his high school. All application forms are reviewed by the foundation officer responsible for making the awards and scholarships are granted on the basis of the academic qualifications and financial need of the grantees. The foundation obtains annual reports on the academic performance of the scholarship recipient from the college or university which he attends. It maintains a file on each scholarship awarded, including the original application, recommendations, a record of the action taken on the application, and the reports on the recipient from the institution which he attends. The described procedures of the X Foundation for the making of grants to individuals qualify for Internal Revenue Service approval under section 4945(g). Furthermore, if the X Foundation's scholarship program meets the requirements of subparagraph (5) of this paragraph, X Foundation will not have to obtain reports on the academic performance of the scholarship recipients.

(d) *Submission of grant procedure.*—(1) *Contents of request for approval of grant procedures.*—A request for advance approval of a foundation's grant procedures must fully describe the foundation's procedures for awarding grants and for ascertaining that such grants are used for the proper purposes. The approval procedure does not contemplate specific approval of particular grant programs but instead one-time approval of a system of standards, procedures, and follow-up designed to result in grants which meet the requirements of section 4945(g). Thus, such approval shall apply to a subsequent grant program as long as the procedures under which it is conducted do not differ materially from those described in the request to the Commissioner. The request must contain the following items:

(i) A statement describing the selection process. Such statement shall be sufficiently detailed for the Commissioner to determine whether the grants are made on an objective and nondiscriminatory basis under paragraph (b) of this section.

(ii) A description of the terms and conditions under which the foundation ordinarily makes such grants, which is sufficient to enable the Commissioner to determine whether the grants awarded under such procedures would meet the requirements of paragraph (1), (2), or (3) of section 4945(g).

(iii) A detailed description of the private foundation's procedure for exercising supervision over grants, as described in paragraph (c)(2) and (3) of this section.

(iv) A description of the foundation's procedures for review of grantee reports, for investigation where diversion of grant funds from their proper purposes is indicated, and for recovery of diverted grant funds, as described in paragraph (c)(4) of this section.

(2) *Place of submission.*—Request for approval of grant procedures shall be submitted to the District Director.

(3) *Internal Revenue Service action on request for approval of grant procedures.*—If, by the 45th day after a request for approval of grant procedures has been properly submitted to the Internal Revenue Service, the organization has not been notified that such procedures are not acceptable, such procedures shall be considered as approved from the date of submission until receipt of actual notice from the Internal Revenue Service that such procedures do not meet the requirements of this section. If a grant to an individual for a purpose described in section 4945(d)(3) is made after notification to the organization by the Internal Revenue Service that the procedures under which the grant is made are not acceptable, such grant is a taxable expenditure under this section.

(e) *Effective dates.*—(1) *In general.*—This section shall apply to all grants to individuals for travel, study or other similar purposes which are made by private foundations more than 90 days after October 30, 1972.

(2) *Transitional rules.*—(i) *Grants committed prior to January 1, 1970.*—Section 4945(d)(3) and (g) and this section shall not apply to a grant for section 170(c)(2)(B) purposes made on or after January 1, 1970, if the grant was made pursuant to a commitment entered into prior to such date, but only if such commitment was made in accordance with the foundation's usual practices and is reasonable in amount in light of the purposes of the grant. For purposes of this subdivision, a commitment will be considered entered into prior to

January 1, 1970, if prior to such date, the amount and nature of the payments to be made and the name of the payee were entered on the records of the payor, or were otherwise adequately evidenced, or the notice of the payment to be received was communicated to the payee in writing.

(ii) *Grants awarded on or after January 1, 1970.*—In the case of a grant awarded on or after January 1, 1970, but prior to the expiration of 90 days after October 30, 1972, and paid within 48 months after the award of such grant, the requirements of section 4945(g) that an individual grant be awarded on an objective and nondiscriminatory basis pursuant to a procedure approved in advance by the Commissioner are deemed satisfied if the grantor utilizes any procedure in good faith in awarding a grant to an individual which, in fact, is reasonably calculated to provide objectivity and nondiscrimination in the awarding of such grant and to result in a grant which complies with the conditions of section 4945(g)(1), (2) or (3). [Reg. § 53.4945-4.]

☐ [T.D. 7215, 10-30-72.]

**[Reg. § 53.4945-5]**

**§ 53.4945-5. Grants to organizations.**—(a) *Grants to nonpublic organizations.*—(1) *In general.*—Under section 4945(d)(4) the term "taxable expenditure" includes any amount paid or incurred by a private foundation as a grant to an organization (other than an organization described in section 509(a)(1), (a)(2), or (a)(3) (other than an organization described in section 4942(g)(4)(A)(i) or (ii)) or in section 4940(d)(2)), unless the private foundation exercises expenditure responsibility with respect to such grant in accordance with section 4945(h). However, the granting foundation does not have to exercise expenditure responsibility with respect to amounts granted to organizations described in section 4945(f).

(2) *"Grants" described.*—For a description of the term "grants", see § 53.4945-4(a)(2).

(3) *Section 509(a)(1), (2), and (3) organizations.*—See section 508(b) and the regulations thereunder for rules relating to when a grantor may rely on a potential grantee's characterization of its status as set forth in the notice described in section 508(b).

(4) *Certain "public" organizations.*—For purposes of this section, an organization will be treated as a section 509(a)(1) organization if:

(i) It qualifies as such under paragraph (a) of § 1.509(a)-2 of this chapter;

(ii) It is an organization described in section 170(c)(1) or 511(a)(2)(B), even if it is not described in section 501(c)(3); or

(iii) It is a foreign government, or any agency or instrumentality thereof, or an international organization designated as such by Executive Order under 22 U.S.C. 288, even if it is not described in section 501(c)(3).

However, any grant to an organization referred to in this subparagraph must be made exclusively for charitable purposes as described in section 170(c)(2)(B).

(5) *Certain foreign organizations.*—(i) *In general.*—If a private foundation makes a grant to a foreign organization, which does not have a ruling or determination letter that it is an organization described in section 509(a)(1), (a)(2), or (a)(3) or in section 4940(d)(2), the grant will nonetheless be treated as a grant made to an organization described in section 509(a)(1), (a)(2), or (a)(3) (other than an organization described in section 4942(g)(4)(A)(i) or (ii)) or in section 4940(d)(2) if the grantor private foundation has made a good faith determination that the grantee organization is an organization described in section 509(a)(1), (a)(2), or (a)(3) (other than an organization described in section 4942(g)(4)(A)(i) or (ii)) or in section 4940(d)(2). A determination ordinarily will be considered a good faith determination if the determination is based on current written advice received from a qualified tax practitioner concluding that the grantee is an organization described in section 509(a)(1), (a)(2), or (a)(3) (other than an organization described in section 4942(g)(4)(A)(i) or (ii)) or in section 4940(d)(2), and if the foundation reasonably relied in good faith on the written advice in accordance with the requirements of § 1.6664-4(c)(1) of this chapter. The written advice must set forth sufficient facts concerning the operations and support of the grantee organization for the Internal Revenue Service to determine that the grantee organization would be likely to qualify as an organization described in section 509(a)(1), (a)(2), or (a)(3) (other than an organization described in section 4942(g)(4)(A)(i) or (ii)) or in section 4940(d)(2) as of the date of the written advice. For purposes of these rules, except as provided in the next sentence, written advice will be considered current if, as of the date of the grant payment, the relevant law on which the advice is based has not changed since the date of the written advice and the factual information on which the advice is based is from the grantee's current or prior taxable year (or annual accounting period if the grantee does not have a taxable year for United States federal tax purposes). Written advice that a grantee

met the public support test under section 170(b)(1)(A)(vi) or section 509(a)(2) for a test period of five years will be treated as current for purposes of grant payments to the grantee during the two taxable years (or, as applicable, annual accounting periods) of the grantee immediately following the end of the five-year test period. See paragraphs (b)(5) and (6) of this section for additional rules relating to foreign organizations.

(ii) *Definitions.*—For purposes of this paragraph (a)(5)—

(*a*) The term "foreign organization" means any organization that is not described in section 170(c)(2)(A).

(*b*) The term "qualified tax practitioner" means an attorney, a certified public accountant, or an enrolled agent, within the meaning of 31 CFR 10.2 and 10.3, who is subject to the requirements in 31 CFR part 10.

(6) *Certain earmarked grants.*—(i) *In general.*—A grant by a private foundation to a grantee organization which the grantee organization uses to make payments to another organization (the secondary grantee) shall not be regarded as a grant by the private foundation to the secondary grantee if the foundation does not earmark the use of the grant for any named secondary grantee and there does not exist an agreement, oral or written, whereby such grantor foundation may cause the selection of the secondary grantee by the organization to which it has given the grant. For purposes of this subdivision, a grant described herein shall not be regarded as a grant by the foundation to the secondary grantee even though such foundation has reason to believe that certain organizations would derive benefits from such grant so long as the original grantee organization exercises control, in fact, over the selection process and actually makes the selection completely independently of the private foundation.

(ii) *To governmental agencies.*—If a private foundation makes a grant to an organization described in section 170(c)(1) and such grant is earmarked for use by another organization, the granting foundation need not exercise expenditure responsibility with respect to such grant if the section 170(c)(1) organization satisfies the Commissioner in advance that:

(*a*) Its grantmaking program is in furtherance of a purpose described in section 170(c)(2)(B), and

(*b*) The section 170(c)(1) organization exercises "expenditure responsibility" in a manner that would satisfy this section if it applied to such section 170(c)(1) organization. However, with respect to such grant, the granting foundation must make the reports required by section 4945(h)(3) and paragraph (d) of this section, unless such grant is earmarked for use by an organization described in section 509(a)(1), (a)(2), or (a)(3) (other than an organization described in section 4942(g)(4)(A)(i) or (ii)), or in section 4940(d)(2).

(b) *Expenditure responsibility.*—(1) *In general.*—A private foundation is not an insurer of the activity of the organization to which it makes a grant. Thus, satisfaction of the requirements of sections 4945(d)(4) and (h) and of subparagraph (3) or (4) of this paragraph, will ordinarily mean the grantor foundation will not have violated section 4945(d)(1) or (2). A private foundation will be considered to be exercising "expenditure responsibility" under section 4945(h) as long as it exerts all reasonable efforts and establishes adequate procedures—

(i) To see that the grant is spent solely for the purpose for which made,

(ii) To obtain full and complete reports from the grantee on how the funds are spent, and

(iii) To make full and detailed reports with respect to such expenditures to the Commissioner.

In cases in which pursuant to paragraph (a)(6) of this section a grant is considered made to a secondary grantee rather than the primary grantee, the grantor foundation's obligation to obtain reports from the grantee pursuant to section 4945(h)(2) and this section will be satisfied if appropriate reports are obtained from the secondary grantee. For rules relating to expenditure responsibility with respect to transfers of assets described in section 507(b)(2), see section 507(b)(2) and the regulations thereunder.

(2) *Pre-grant inquiry.*—(i) Before making a grant to an organization with respect to which expenditure responsibility must be exercised under this section, a private foundation should conduct a limited inquiry concerning the potential grantee. Such inquiry should be complete enough to give a reasonable man assurance that the grantee will use the grant for the proper purposes. The inquiry should concern itself with matters such as: (*a*) the identity, prior history and experience (if any) of the grantee organization and its managers; and (*b*) any knowledge which the private foundation has (based on prior experience or otherwise) of, or other information which is readily available concerning, the management, activities, and practices of the grantee organization. The scope of the inquiry might be expected to vary from case to case depending upon the size

and purpose of the grant, the period over which it is to be paid, and the prior experience which the grantor has had with respect to the capacity of the grantee to use the grant for the proper purposes. For example, if the grantee has made proper use of all prior grants to it by the grantor and filed the required reports substantiating such use, no further pre-grant inquiry will ordinarily be necessary. Similarly, in the case of an organization, such as a trust described in section 4947(a)(2), which is required by the terms of its governing instrument to make payments to a specified organization exempt from taxation under section 501(a), a less extensive pre-grant inquiry is required than in the case of a private foundation possessing discretion with respect to the distribution of funds.

(ii) The provisions of this subparagraph may be illustrated by the following examples:

*Example (1).* Officials of M, a newly established organization which is described in section 501(c)(4), request a grant from X Foundation to be used for a proposed program to combat drug abuse by establishing neighborhood clinics in certain ghetto areas of a city. Before making a grant to M, X makes an inquiry concerning the identity, prior history and experience of the officials of M. X obtains information pertaining to the officials of M from references supplied by these officials. Since one of the references indicated that A, an official of M, has an arrest record, police records are also checked and A's probation officer is interviewed. The inquiry also shows M has no previous history of administering grants and that the officials of M have had no experience in administering programs of this nature. However, in the opinion of X's managers, M's officials (including A who appears to be fully rehabilitated after having been convicted of a narcotics violation several years ago) are well qualified to conduct this program since they are members of the communities in which the clinics are to be established and are more likely to be trusted by drug users in these communities than are outsiders. Under these circumstances X has complied with the requirements of this subparagraph and a grant to M for its proposed program will not be treated as a taxable expenditure solely because of the operation of this subparagraph.

*Example (2).* Foundation Y wishes to make a grant to Foundation R for use in R's scholarship program. Y has made similar grants to R annually for the last several years and knows that R's managers have observed the terms of the previous grants and have made all requested reports with respect to such grants. No changes in R's management have occurred during the past several years. Under these circumstances, Y has enough information to have such assurance as a reasonable man would require that the grant to R will be used for proper purposes. Consequently, Y is under no obligation to make any further pre-grant inquiry pursuant to this subparagraph.

*Example (3).* S Foundation requests a grant from Z Foundation for use in S's program of providing medical research fellowships. S has been engaged in this program for several years and has received large numbers of grants from other foundations. Z's managers know that the reputations of S and of S's officials are good. Z's managers also have been advised by managers of W Foundation that W had recently made a grant to S and that W's managers were satisfied that such grant has been used for the purposes for which it was made. Under these circumstances Z has enough information to have such assurance as a reasonable man would require that the grant to S will be used for proper purposes. Consequently, Z is under no obligation to make any further pre-grant inquiry pursuant to this subparagraph.

(3) *Terms of grants.*—Except as provided in subparagraph (4) of this paragraph, in order to meet the expenditure responsibility requirements of section 4945(h), a private foundation must require that each grant to an organization, with respect to which expenditure responsibility must be exercised under this section, be made subject to a written commitment signed by an appropriate officer, director or trustee of the grantee organization. Such commitment must include an agreement by the grantee—

(i) To repay any portion of the amount granted which is not used for the purposes of the grant,

(ii) To submit full and complete annual reports on the matter in which the funds are spent and the progress made in accomplishing the purposes of the grant, except as provided in paragraph (c)(2) of this section,

(iii) To maintain records of receipts and expenditures and to make its books and records available to the grantor at reasonable times, and

(iv) Not to use any of the funds—

(*a*) To carry on propaganda, or otherwise to attempt, to influence legislation (within the meaning of section 4945(d)(1)),

(*b*) To influence the outcome of any specific public election, or to carry on, directly or indirectly, any voter registration drive (within the meaning of section 4945(d)(2)),

(*c*) To make any grant which does not comply with the requirements of section 4945(d)(3) or (4), or *(d)* To undertake any activity for any purpose other than one specified in section 170(c)(2)(B).

The agreement must also clearly specify the purposes of the grant. Such purposes may include contributing for capital endowment, for the purchase of capital equipment, or for general support provided that neither the grants nor the income therefrom may be used for purposes other than those described in section 170(c)(2)(B).

(4) *Terms of program-related investments.*—In order to meet the expenditure responsibility requirements of section 4945(h), with regard to the making of a program-related investment (as defined in section 4944 and the regulations thereunder), a private foundation must require that each such investment with respect to which expenditure responsibility must be exercised under section 4945(d)(4) and (h) and this section be made subject to a written commitment signed by an appropriate officer, director or trustee of the recipient organization. Such commitment must specify the purpose of the investment and must include an agreement by the organization—

(i) To use all the funds received from the private foundation (as determined under paragraph (c)(3) of this section) only for the purposes of the investment and to repay any portion not used for such purposes, provided that, with respect to equity investments, such repayment shall be made only to the extent permitted by applicable law concerning distributions to holders of equity interests,

(ii) At least once a year during the existence of the program-related investment, to submit full and complete financial reports of the type ordinarily required by commercial investors under similar circumstances and a statement that it has complied with the terms of the investment,

(iii) To maintain books and records adequate to provide information ordinarily required by commercial investors under similar circumstances and to make such books and records available to the private foundation at reasonable times, and

(iv) Not to use any of the funds—

*(a)* To carry on propaganda, or otherwise to attempt, to influence legislation (within the meaning of section 4945(d)(1)),

*(b)* To influence the outcome of any specific public election, or to carry on, directly or indirectly, any voter registration drive (within the meaning of section 4945(d)(2)), or

*(c)* With respect to any recipient which is a private foundation (as defined in section 509(a)), to make any grant which does not comply with the requirements of section 4945(d)(3) or (4).

(5) *Certain grants to foreign organizations.*—With respect to a grant to a foreign organization (other than an organization described in section 509(a)(1), (a)(2), or (a)(3) (other than an organization described in section 4942(g)(4)(A)(i) or (ii)) or in section 4940(d)(2) or treated as so described pursuant to paragraph (a)(4) or (5) of this section), paragraph (b)(3)(iv) or (b)(4)(iv) of this section shall be deemed satisfied if the agreement referred to in paragraph (b)(3) or (4) of this section imposes restrictions on the use of the grant substantially equivalent to the limitations imposed on a domestic private foundation under section 4945(d). Such restrictions may be phrased in appropriate terms under foreign law or custom and ordinarily will be considered sufficient if an affidavit or opinion of counsel (of the grantor or grantee) or written advice of a qualified tax practitioner is obtained stating that, under foreign law or custom, the agreement imposes restrictions on the use of the grant substantially equivalent to the restrictions imposed on a domestic private foundation under paragraph (b)(3) or (4) of this section.

(6) *Special rules for grants by foreign private foundations.*—With respect to activities in jurisdictions other than those described in section 170(c)(2)(A), the failure of a foreign private foundation which is described in section 4948(b) to comply with subparagraph (3) or (4) of this paragraph with respect to a grant to an organization shall not constitute an act or failure to act which is a prohibited transaction (within the meaning of section 4948(c)(2)).

(7) *Expenditure responsibility with respect to certain transfers of assets described in section 507.*—(i) *Transfers of assets described in section 507(b)(2).*—For rules relating to the extent to which the expenditure responsibility rules contained in sections 4945(d)(4) and (h) and this section apply to transfers of assets described in section 507(b)(2), see §§ 1.507-3(a)(7), 1.507-3(a)(8)(ii)(*f*), and 1.507-3(a)(9).

(ii) *Certain other transfers of assets.*—For rules relating to the extent to which the expenditure responsibility rules contained in sections 4945(d)(4) and (h) and this section apply to certain other transfers of assets described in § 1.507-3(b), see § 1.507-3(b) of this chapter.

(8) *Restrictions on grants (other than program-related investments) to organizations not described in section 501(c)(3).*—For other restrictions on certain grants (other than program-related investments) to organizations which are not described in section 501(c)(3), see § 53.4945-6(c).

(c) *Reports from grantees.*—(1) *In general.*—In the case of grants described in section 4945(d)(4), except as provided in subparagraph (2) of this paragraph, the granting private foundation shall require reports on the use of the funds, compliance with the terms of the grant, and the progress made by the grantee toward achieving the purposes for which the grant was made. The grantee shall make such reports as of the end of its annual accounting period within which the grant or any portion thereof is received and all such subsequent periods until the grant funds are expended in full or the grant is otherwise terminated. Such reports shall be furnished to the grantor within a reasonable period of time after the close of the annual accounting period of the grantee for which such reports are made. Within a reasonable period of time after the close of its annual accounting period during which the use of the grant funds is completed, the grantee must make a final report with respect to all expenditures made from such funds (including salaries, travel, and supplies) and indicating the progress made toward the goals of the grant. The grantor need not conduct any independent verification of such reports unless it has reason to doubt their accuracy or reliability.

(2) *Capital endowment grants to exempt private foundations.*—If a private foundation makes a grant described in section 4945(d)(4) to a private foundation which is exempt from taxation under section 501(a) for endowment, for the purchase of capital equipment, or for other capital purposes, the grantor foundation shall require reports from the grantee on the use of the principal and the income (if any) from the grant funds. The grantee shall make such reports annually for its taxable year in which the grant was made and the immediately succeeding two taxable years. Only if it is reasonably apparent to the grantor that, before the end of such second succeeding taxable year, neither the principal, the income from the grant funds, nor the equipment purchased with the grant funds has been used for any purpose which would result in liability for tax under section 4945(d), the grantor may then allow such reports to be discontinued.

(3) *Grantees' accounting and record-keeping procedures.*—(i) A private foundation grantee exempt from taxation under section 501(a) (or the recipient of a program-related investment) need not segregate grant funds physically nor separately account for such funds on its books unless the grantor requires such treatment of the grant funds. If such a grantee neither physically segregates grant funds nor establishes separate accounts on its books, grants received within a given taxable year beginning after December 31, 1969, shall be deemed, for purposes of section 4945, to be expended before grants received in a succeeding taxable year. In such case expenditures of grants received within any such taxable year shall be prorated among all such grants. In accounting for grant expenditures, private foundations may make the necessary computations on a cumulative annual basis (or, where appropriate, as of the date for which the computations are made). The rules set forth in the preceding three sentences shall apply to the extent they are consistent with the available records of the grantee and with the grantee's treatment of qualifying distributions under section 4942(h) and the regulations thereunder. The records of expenditures, as well as copies of the reports submitted to the grantor, must be kept for at least 4 years after completion of the use of the grant funds.

(ii) For rules relating to accounting and record-keeping requirements for grantees other than those described in subdivision (i) of this subparagraph, see §§ 53.4945-5(b)(8) and 53.4945-6(c).

(4) *Reliance on information supplied by grantee.*—A private foundation exercising expenditure responsibility with respect to its grants may rely on adequate records or other sufficient evidence supplied by the grantee organization (such as a statement by an appropriate officer, director or trustee of such grantee organization) showing, to the extent applicable, the information which the grantor must report to the Internal Revenue Service in accordance with paragraph (d)(2) of this section.

(d) *Reporting to Internal Revenue Service by grantor.*—(1) *In general.*—To satisfy the report-making requirements of section 4945(h)(3), a granting foundation must provide the required information on its annual information return, required to be filed by section 6033, for each taxable year with respect to each grant made during the taxable year which is subject to the expenditure responsibility requirements of section 4945(h). Such information must also be provided on such return with respect to each grant subject to such requirements upon which any amount or any report is outstanding at any time during the taxable year. However, with respect to any grant made for endowment or other capital purposes, the grantor must provide the required information only for any taxable year for which the grantor must require a report from the grantee under paragraph (c)(2) of this section. The requirements of this subparagraph with respect to any grant may be satisfied by submission with the foundation's information return of a report received from the grantee, if the information required by subparagraph (2) of this paragraph is contained in such report.

(2) *Contents of report.*—The report required by this paragraph shall include the following information:

(i) The name and address of the grantee,

(ii) The date and amount of the grant,

(iii) The purpose of the grant,

(iv) The amounts expended by the grantee (based upon the most recent report received from the grantee),

(v) Whether the grantee has diverted any portion of the funds (or the income therefrom in the case of an endowment grant) from the purpose of the grant (to the knowledge of the grantor),

(vi) The dates of any reports received from the grantee, and

(vii) The date and results of any verification of the grantee's reports undertaken pursuant to and to the extent required under paragraph (c)(1) of this section by the grantor or by others at the direction of the grantor.

(3) *Record-keeping requirements.*—In addition to the information included on the information return, a granting foundation shall make available to the Internal Revenue Service at the foundation's principal office each of the following items:

(i) A copy of the agreement covering each "expenditure responsibility" grant made during the taxable year,

(ii) A copy of each report received during the taxable year from each grantee on any "expenditure responsibility" grant, and

(iii) A copy of each report made by the grantor's personnel or independent auditors of any audits or other investigations made during the taxable year with respect to any "expenditure responsibility" grant.

(4) *Reports received after the close of grantor's accounting year.*—Data contained in reports required by this paragraph, which reports are received by a private foundation after the close of its accounting year but before the due date of its information return for that year need not be reported on such return, but may be reported on the grantor's information return for the year in which such reports are received from the grantee.

(e) *Violations of expenditure responsibility requirements.*—(1) *Diversions by grantee.*—(i) Any diversion of grant funds (including the income therefrom in the case of an endowment grant) by the grantee to any use not in furtherance of a purpose specified in the grant may result in the diverted portion of such grant being treated as a taxable expenditure of the grantor under section 4945(d)(4). However, for purposes of this section, the fact that a grantee does not use any portion of the grant funds as indicated in the original budget projection shall not be treated as a diversion if the use to which the funds are committed is consistent with the purpose of the grant as stated in the grant agreement and does not result in a violation of the terms of such agreement required to be included by paragraph (b)(3) or (b)(4) of this section.

(ii) In any event, a grantor will not be treated as having made a taxable expenditure under section 4945(d)(4) solely by reason of a diversion by the grantee, if the grantor has complied with subdivision (iii)(a) and (b) or (iv)(a) and (b) of this subparagraph, whichever is applicable.

(iii) In cases in which the grantor foundation determines that any part of a grant has been used for improper purposes and the grantee has not previously diverted grant funds, the foundation will not be treated as having made a taxable expenditure solely by reason of the diversion so long as the foundation—

(a) Is taking all reasonable and appropriate steps either to recover the grant funds or to insure the restoration of the diverted funds and the dedication (consistent with the requirements of (b)(1) and (2) of this subdivision) of the other grant funds held by the grantee to the purposes being financed by the grant, and

(b) Withholds any further payments to the grantee after the grantor becomes aware that a diversion may have taken place (hereinafter referred to as "further payments") until it has—

(1) Received the grantee's assurances that future diversions will not occur, and

(2) Required the grantee to take extraordinary precautions to prevent future diversions from occurring.

If a foundation is treated as having made a taxable expenditure under this subparagraph in a case to which this subdivision applies, then unless the foundation meets the requirements of (a) of this subdivision the amount of the taxable expenditure shall be the amount of the diversion (for example, the income diverted in the case of an endowment grant, or the rental value of capital equipment for the period of time for which diverted) plus the amount of any further payments to the same grantee. However, if the foundation complies with the requirements of (a) of this subdivision but not the require-

ments of (b) of this subdivision, the amount of the taxable expenditures shall be the amount of such further payments.

(iv) In cases where a grantee has previously diverted funds received from a grantor foundation, and the grantor foundation determines that any part of a grant has again been used for improper purposes, the foundation will not be treated as having made a taxable expenditure solely by reason of such diversion so long as the foundation—

(a) Is taking all reasonable and appropriate steps to recover the grant funds or to insure the restoration of the diverted funds and the dedication (consistent with the requirements of (b)(2) and (3) of this subdivision) of other grant funds held by the grantee to the purposes being financed by the grant, except that if, in fact, some or all of the diverted funds are not so restored or recovered, then the foundation must take all reasonable and appropriate steps to recover all of the grant funds, and

(b) Withholds further payments until—

(1) Such funds are in fact so recovered or restored,

(2) It has received the grantee's assurances that future diversions will not occur, and

(3) It requires the grantee to take extraordinary precautions to prevent future diversions from occurring.

If a foundation is treated as having made a taxable expenditure under this subparagraph in a case to which this subdivision applies, then unless the foundation meets the requirements of (a) of this subdivision, the amount of the taxable expenditure shall be the amount of the diversion plus the amount of any further payments to the same grantee. However, if the foundation complies with the requirements of (a) of this subdivision, but fails to withhold further payments until the requirements of (b) of this subdivision are met, the amount of the taxable expenditure shall be the amount of such further payments.

(v) The phrase "all reasonable and appropriate steps" (as used in subdivisions (iii) and (iv) of this subparagraph) includes legal action where appropriate but need not include legal action if such action would in all probability not result in the satisfaction of execution on a judgment.

(2) *Grantee's failure to make reports.*—A failure by the grantee to make the reports required by paragraph (c) of this section (or the making of inadequate reports) shall result in the grant's being treated as a taxable expenditure by the grantor unless the grantor:

(i) Has made the grant in accordance with paragraph (b) of this section,

(ii) Has complied with the reporting requirements contained in paragraph (d) of this section,

(iii) Makes a reasonable effort to obtain the required report, and

(iv) Withholds all future payments on this grant and on any other grant to the same grantee until such report is furnished.

(3) *Violations by the grantor.*—In addition to the situations described in subparagraphs (1) and (2) of this paragraph, a grant which is subject to the expenditure responsibility requirements of section 4945(h) will be considered a taxable expenditure of the granting foundation if the grantor—

(i) Fails to make a pre-grant inquiry as described in paragraph (b)(2) of this section,

(ii) Fails to make the grant in accordance with a procedure consistent with the requirements of paragraph (b)(3) or (4) of this section, or

(iii) Fails to report to the Internal Revenue Service as provided in paragraph (d) of this section.

(f) *Effective dates.*—(1) *In general.*—This section shall apply to all grants which are subject to the expenditure responsibility requirements of section 4945(d)(4) and (h) and which are made by private foundations more than 90 days after October 30, 1972.

(2) *Transitional rules.*—(i) *Certain grants awarded prior to May 27, 1969.*—Section 4945(d)(4) and (h) and this section shall not apply to a grant to a private foundation which is not controlled, directly or indirectly, by the grantor foundation or one or more disqualified persons (as defined in section 4946) with respect to the grantor foundation, provided that such grant—

(a) Is made pursuant to a written commitment which was binding on May 26, 1969, and at all times thereafter,

(b) Is made for one or more of the purposes described in section 170(c)(2)(B), and

(c) Is to be paid out to such grantee foundation on or before December 31, 1974.

(ii) *Grants or expenditures committed prior to January 1, 1970.*—Except as provided in paragraph (e)(2)(i) of § 53.4945-4, section 4945 shall not apply to a grant or an expenditure for section 170(c)(2)(B)

**Reg. § 53.4945-5(f)(2)(ii)**

purposes made on or after January 1, 1970, if the grant or expenditure was made pursuant to a commitment entered into prior to such date, but only if (in the case of a grant or an expenditure other than an unlimited general-purpose grant to an organization) such commitment is reasonable in amount in light of the purposes of the grant. For purposes of this subdivision, a commitment will be considered entered into prior to January 1, 1970, if prior to such date, the amount and nature of the payments to be made and the name of the payee were entered on the records of the payor, or were otherwise adequately evidenced, or the notice of the payment to be received was communicated to the payee in writing.

(iii) *Grants awarded on or after January 1, 1970.*—Paragraphs (b), (c), and (d) of this section shall not apply to grants awarded on or after January 1, 1970, but prior to the expiration of 90 days after October 30, 1972, if the grantor has made reasonable efforts, and has established adequate procedures such as a prudent man would adopt in managing his own property, to see that the grant is spent solely for the purpose for which made, to obtain full and complete reports from the grantee on how the funds are spent, and to make full and detailed reports with respect to such grant to the Commissioner. With respect to any return filed with the Internal Revenue Service before the expiration of 90 days after October 30, 1972, the grantor may treat reports which satisfy the requirements of the statement to be attached to Form 4720 for the year 1970 under "Specific Instructions—Question B" (items (1) through (5)) as satisfying the grantor reporting requirements with respect to "expenditure responsibility" grants. In the case of a private foundation required to file an annual return for a taxable year ending after January 1, 1970, and before December 31, 1970, the reporting requirements imposed by section 4945(h)(3) for such period shall be regarded as satisfied if such reports are made on the annual return for its first taxable year beginning after December 31, 1969.

(3) *Effective/applicability date of paragraphs (a)(1), (a)(5), (a)(6)(ii), and (b)(5) and transition relief.*—Paragraphs (a)(1), (a)(5), (a)(6)(ii), and (b)(5) of this section are effective on and apply with respect to grants paid after September 25, 2015. However, foundations may continue to rely on paragraph (a)(5) as contained in 26 CFR part 53, revised April 1, 2015, with respect to grants paid on or before December 24, 2015 pursuant to a good faith determination made in accordance with such provisions. Also, foundations may continue to rely on paragraph (a)(5) as contained in 26 CFR part 53, revised April 1, 2015, with respect to grants paid pursuant to a written commitment made on or before September 25, 2015 and pursuant to a good faith determination made on or before such date in accordance with such provisions if the committed amount is paid out within five years of such date. [Reg. § 53.4945-5.]

☐ [*T.D. 7215, 10-30-72. Amended by T.D. 7233, 12-20-72 T.D. 7290, 11-16-73 and T.D. 9740, 9-23-2015.*]

### [Reg. § 53.4945-6]

**§ 53.4945-6. Expenditures for noncharitable purposes.**—(a) *In general.*—Under section 4945(d)(5) the term "taxable expenditure" includes any amount paid or incurred by a private foundation for any purpose other than one specified in section 170(c)(2)(B). Thus, ordinarily only an expenditure for an activity which, if it were a substantial part of the organization's total activities, would cause loss of tax exemption is a taxable expenditure under section 4945(d)(5). For purposes of this section and §§ 53.4945-1 through 53.4945-5, the term "purposes described in section 170(c)(2)(B)" shall be treated as including purposes described in section 170(c)(2)(B) whether or not carried out by an organization described in section 170(c).

(b) *Particular expenditures.*—(1) The following types of expenditures ordinarily will not be treated as taxable expenditures under section 4945(d)(5):

(i) Expenditures to acquire investments entered into for the purpose of obtaining income or funds to be used in furtherance of purposes described in section 170(c)(2)(B),

(ii) Reasonable expenses with respect to investments described in subdivision (i) of this subparagraph,

(iii) Payment of taxes,

(iv) Any expenses which qualify as deductions in the computation of unrelated business income tax under section 511,

(v) Any payment which constitutes a qualifying distribution under section 4942(g) or an allowable deduction under section 4940,

(vi) Reasonable expenditures to evaluate, acquire, modify, and dispose of program-related investments, or

(vii) Business expenditures by the recipient of a program-related investment.

(2) Conversely, any expenditures for unreasonable administrative expenses, including compensation, consultant fees, and other fees for services rendered, will ordinarily be taxable expenditures

under section 4945(d)(5) unless the foundation can demonstrate that such expenses were paid or incurred in the good faith belief that they were reasonable and that the payment or incurrence of such expenses in such amounts was consistent with ordinary business care and prudence. The determination of whether an expenditure is unreasonable shall depend upon the facts and circumstances of the particular case.

(c) *Grants to "noncharitable" organizations.*—(1) *In general.*—Since a private foundation cannot make an expenditure for a purpose other than a purpose described in section 170(c)(2)(B), a private foundation may not make a grant to an organization other than an organization described in section 501(c)(3) unless

(i) The making of the grant itself constitutes a direct charitable act or the making of a program-related investment, or

(ii) Through compliance with the requirements of subparagraph (2) of this paragraph, the grantor is reasonably assured that the grant will be used exclusively for purposes described in section 170(c)(2)(B).

For purposes of this paragraph, an organization treated as a section 509(a)(1) organization under § 53.4945-5(a)(4) shall be treated as an organization described in section 501(c)(3).

(2) *Grants other than transfers of assets described in § 1.507-3(c)(1).*—(i) If a private foundation makes a grant which is not a transfer of assets pursuant to any liquidation, merger, redemption, recapitalization, or other adjustment, organization or reorganization to any organization other than an organization described in section 501(c)(3) (except an organization described in section 509(a)(4)), the grantor is reasonably assured (within the meaning of subparagraph (1)(ii) of this paragraph) that the grant will be used exclusively for purposes described in section 170(c)(2)(B) only if the grantee organization agrees to maintain and, during the period in which any portion of such grant funds remain unexpended, does continuously maintain the grant funds (or other assets transferred) in a separate fund dedicated to one or more purposes described in section 170(c)(2)(B). The grantor of a grant described in this paragraph must also comply with the expenditure responsibility provisions contained in sections 4945(d) and (h) and § 53.4945-5.

(ii) For purposes of this paragraph, a foreign organization which does not have a ruling or determination letter that it is an organization described in section 501(c)(3) (other than section 509(a)(4)) will be treated as an organization described in section 501(c)(3) (other than section 509(a)(4)) if in the reasonable judgment of a foundation manager of the transferor private foundation, the grantee organization is an organization described in section 501(c)(3) (other than section 509(a)(4)). The term "reasonable judgment" shall be given its generally accepted legal sense within the outlines developed by judicial decisions in the law of trusts.

(3) *Transfers of assets described in § 1.507-3(c)(1).*—If a private foundation makes a transfer of assets (other than a transfer described in subparagraph (1)(i) of this paragraph) pursuant to any liquidation, merger, redemption, recapitalization, or other adjustment, organization, or reorganization to any person, the transferred assets will not be considered used exclusively for purposes described in section 170(c)(2)(B) unless the assets are transferred to a fund or organization described in section 501(c)(3) (other than an organization described in section 509(a)(4)) or treated as so described under section 4947(a)(1). [Reg. § 53.4945-6.]

☐ [*T.D. 7215, 10-30-72. Amended by T.D. 7233, 12-20-72.*]

### [Reg. § 53.4946-1]

**§ 53.4946-1. Definitions and special rules.**—(a) *Disqualified person.*—(1) For purposes of chapter 42 and the regulations thereunder, the following are disqualified persons with respect to a private foundation—

(i) All substantial contributors to the foundation, as defined in section 507(d)(2) and the regulations thereunder,

(ii) All foundation managers of the foundation as defined in section 4946(b)(1) and paragraph (f)(1)(i) of this section,

(iii) An owner of more than 20 percent of—

  (a) The total combined voting power of a corporation,

  (b) The profits interest of a partnership,

  (c) The beneficial interest of a trust or unincorporated enterprise, which is (during such ownership) a substantial contributor to the foundation, as defined in section 507(d)(2) and the regulations thereunder,

(iv) A member of the family, as defined in section 4946(d) and paragraph (h) of this section, of any of the individuals described in subdivision (i), (ii), or (iii) of this subparagraph,

(v) A corporation of which more than 35 percent of the total combined voting power is owned by persons described in subdivision (i), (ii), (iii), or (iv) of this subparagraph,

(vi) A partnership of which more than 35 percent of the profits interest is owned by persons described in subdivision (i), (ii), (iii), or (iv) of this subparagraph, and

(vii) A trust, estate, or unincorporated enterprise of which more than 35 percent of the beneficial interest is owned by persons described in subdivision (i), (ii), (iii), or (iv) of this subparagraph.

(2) For purposes of subparagraphs (1)(iii)(*b*) and (vi) of this paragraph, the profits interest of a partner shall be equal to his distributive share of income of the partnership, as determined under section 707(b)(3) and the regulations thereunder as modified by section 4946(a)(4).

(3) For purposes of subparagraph (1)(iii)(*c*) and (vii) of this paragraph, the beneficial interest in an unincorporated enterprise (other than a trust or estate) includes any right to receive a portion of distributions from profits of such enterprise, and, if the portion of distributions is not fixed by an agreement among the participants, any right to receive a portion of the assets (if any) upon liquidation of the enterprise, except as a creditor or employee. For purposes of this subparagraph, a right to receive distributions of profits includes a right to receive any amount from such profits other than as creditor or employee, whether as a sum certain or as a portion of profits realized by the enterprise. Where there is no agreement fixing the rights of the participants in such enterprise, the fraction of the respective interests of each participant in such enterprise shall be determined by dividing the amount of all investments or contributions to the capital of the enterprise made or obligated to be made by such participant by the amount of all investments or contributions to capital made or obligated to be made by all of them.

(4) For purposes of subparagraph (1)(iii)(*c*) and (vii) of this paragraph, a person's beneficial interest in a trust shall be determined in proportion to the actuarial interest of such person in the trust.

(5) For purposes of subparagraph (1)(iii)(*a*) and (v) of this paragraph, the term "combined voting power" includes voting power represented by holdings of voting stock, actual or constructive (under section 4946(a)(3)), but does not include voting rights held only as a director or trustee.

(6) For purposes of subparagraph (1)(iii)(*a*) and (v) of this paragraph, the term "voting power" includes outstanding voting power and does not include voting power obtainable but not obtained, such as, for example, voting power obtainable by converting securities or nonvoting stock into voting stock or by exercising warrants or options to obtain voting stock, and voting power which will vest in preferred stockholders only if and when the corporation has failed to pay preferred dividends for a specified period of time or has otherwise failed to meet specified requirements. Similarly, for purposes of subparagraph (1) (iii) (*b*) and (*c*), (vi), and (vii) of this paragraph, the terms "profits interest" and "beneficial interest" include any such interest that is outstanding, but do not include any such interest that is obtainable but has not been obtained.

(7) For purposes of sections 170(b)(1)(E)(iii), 507(d)(1), 508(d), 509(a)(1) and (3), and chapter 42, the term "disqualified person" shall not include an organization which is described in section 509(a)(1), (2), or (3), or any other organization which is wholly owned by such section 509(a)(1), (2), or (3) organization.

(8) For purposes of section 4941 only, the term "disqualified person" shall not include any organization which is described in section 501(c)(3) (other than an organization described in section 509(a)(4)).

(b) *Section 4943.*—(1) For purposes of section 4943 only, the term "disqualified person" includes a private foundation—

(i) Which is effectively controlled (within the meaning of §1.482-1(a)(3) of this chapter), directly or indirectly, by the same person or persons (other than a bank, trust company, or similar organization acting only as a foundation manager) who control the private foundation in question, or

(ii) Substantially all the contributions to which were made, directly or indirectly, by persons described in subdivision (i), (ii), (iii), or (iv) of paragraph (a)(1) of this section who made, directly or indirectly, substantially all of the contributions to the private foundation in question.

(2) For purposes of subparagraph (1)(ii) of this paragraph, one or more persons will be considered to have made substantially all of the contributions to a private foundation, if such persons have contributed or bequeathed at least 85 percent (and each such person has contributed or bequeathed at least 2 percent) of the total contributions and bequests (within the meaning of section 507(d)(2) and the regulations thereunder) which have been received by such private foundation during its entire existence.

(3) *Examples.*—The provisions of this paragraph may be illustrated by the following examples:

*Example (1).* A, a private foundation, has a board of directors made up of X, Y, Z, M, N, and O. Foundation B's board of directors is made up of Y, M, N, and O. The board of directors in each case has plenary power to determine the manner in which the foundation is operated. For purposes of section 4943, foundation A is a disqualified person with respect to foundation B, and foundation B is a disqualified person with respect to foundation A.

*Example (2).* Private foundation A has received contributions of $100,000 throughout its existence: $35,000 from X, $51,000 from Y (who is X's father), and $14,000 from Z (an unrelated person). Private foundation B has received $100,000 in contributions during its existence: $50,000 from X and $50,000 from W, X's wife.

For purposes of section 4943, private foundation A is a disqualified person with respect to private foundation B, and private foundation B is a disqualified person with respect to private foundation A.

(c) *Section 4941.*—For purposes of section 4941, a government official, as defined in section 4946(c) and paragraph (g) of this section, is a disqualified person.

(d) *Attribution of stockholdings.*—(1) For purposes of paragraph (a)(1)(iii)(*a*) and (v) of this section, indirect stockholdings shall be taken into account under section 267(c) and the regulations thereunder. However, for purposes of this paragraph—

(i) Section 267(c)(4) shall be treated as though it provided that the members of the family of an individual are the members within the meaning of section 4946(d) and paragraph (h) of this section; and

(ii) Any stockholdings which have been counted once (whether by reason of actual or constructive ownership) in applying section 4946(a)(1)(E) shall not be counted a second time.

For purposes of paragraph (a)(1)(v) of this section, section 267(c) shall be applied without regard to section 267(c)(3), and stock constructively owned by an individual by reason of the application of section 267(c)(2) shall not be treated as owned by him if he is described in section 4946(a)(1)(D) but not also in section 4946(a)(1)(A), (B), or (C).

(2) *Examples.*—The provisions of this paragraph may be illustrated by the following examples:

*Example (1).* D is a substantial contributor to private foundation Y. D owns 20 percent of the outstanding stock of corporation P. E, D's wife, owns none of the outstanding stock of P. F, E's father, owns 10 percent of the outstanding stock of P. E. is treated under section 507(d)(2) as a substantial contributor to Y. E is also treated under section 267(c)(2) as owning both D's 20 percent and F's 10 percent of P, but E is treated as owning nothing for purposes of section 4946(a)(1)(E) because D's 20 percent and F's 10 percent have already been taken into account once (because of their actual ownership of the stock of P) for such purposes. Hence, corporation P is not a disqualified person under section 4946(a)(1)(E) with respect to private foundation Y because persons described in section 4946(a)(1)(A), (B), (C), and (D) own only 30 percent of the stock of P.

*Example (2).* I, a substantial contributor to private foundation X, is the son of J. I owns 100 percent of the stock of corporation R, which in turn owns 18 percent of the stock of corporation S. J owns 18 percent of the stock of S. I constructively owns 36 percent of the stock of S (J's 18 percent plus R's 18 percent). Both J's actual holdings and R's actual holdings are counted in determining I's constructive holdings because this does not result in counting either of the holdings more than once for purposes of section 4946(a)(1)(E). Therefore, S is a disqualified person with respect to private foundation X, since I, a substantial contributor, constructively owns more than 35 percent of S's stock.

(e) *Attribution of profits or beneficial interests.*—(1) For purposes of paragraph (a)(1)(iii)(*b*), (iii)(*c*), (vi), and (vii) of this section, ownership of profits or beneficial interests shall be taken into account as though such ownership related to stockholdings, if such stockholdings would be taken into account under section 267(c) and the regulations thereunder, except that section 267(c)(3) shall not apply to attribute the ownership of one partner to another solely by reason of such partner relationship. However, for purposes of this paragraph—

(i) Section 267(c)(4) shall be treated as though it provided that the members of the family of an individual are the members within the meaning of section 4946(d) and paragraph (h) of this section; and

(ii) Any profits interest or beneficial interest which has been counted once (whether by reason of actual or constructive ownership) in applying section 4946(a)(1)(F) or (G) shall not be counted a second time.

For purposes of paragraph (a)(1)(vi) and (vii) of this section, profits or beneficial interests constructively owned by an individual by reason of the application of section 267(c)(2) shall not be treated as owned by him if he is described in section 4946(a)(1)(D) but not in section 4946(a)(1)(A), (B) or (C).

(2) *Example.*—The provisions of this paragraph may be illustrated by the following example:

*Example.* Partnership S is a substantial contributor to private foundation X. Trust T, of which G is sole beneficiary, owns 12 percent of the profits interest of S. G's husband, H, owns 10 percent of the profits interest of S. H is a disqualified person with respect to X (under section 4946(a)(1)(C)) because he is considered to own 22 percent of the profits interest of S (10 percent actual ownership, plus G's 12 percent constructively under section 267(c)(2)). G is a disqualified person with respect to X (under section 4946(a)(1)(C)) because she is considered to own 22 percent of the profits interest of S (12 percent constructively by reason of her beneficial interest in trust T, plus 10 percent constructively under section 267(c)(2) by reason of being a member of the family of H).

(f) *Foundation manager.*—(1) For purposes of chapter 42 and the regulations thereunder, the term "foundation manager" means—

(i) An officer, director, or trustee of a foundation (or a person having powers or responsibilities similar to those of officers, directors, or trustees of the foundation), and

(ii) With respect to any act or failure to act, any employee of the foundation having final authority or responsibility (either officially or effectively) with respect to such act or failure to act.

(2) For purposes of subparagraph (1)(i) of this paragraph, a person shall be considered an officer of a foundation if—

(i) He is specifically so designated under the certificate of incorporation, by-laws, or other constitutive documents of the foundation; or

(ii) He regularly exercises general authority to make administrative or policy decisions on behalf of the foundation.

With respect to any act or failure to act, any person described in subdivision (ii) of this subparagraph who has authority merely to recommend particular administrative or policy decisions, but not to implement them without approval of a superior, is not an officer. Moreover, such independent contractors as attorneys, accountants, and investment managers and advisors, acting in their capacities as such, are not officers within the meaning of subparagraph (1)(i) of this paragraph.

(3) For purposes of subparagraph (1)(ii) of this paragraph, an individual rendering services to a private foundation shall be considered an employee of the foundation only if he is an employee within the meaning of section 3121(d)(2).

(4) Since the definition of the term "disqualified person" contained in section 4946(a)(1)(B) incorporates only so much of the definition of the term "foundation manager" as is found in section 4946(b)(1) and subparagraph (1)(i) of this paragraph, any references, in section 4946 and this section, to "disqualified persons" do not constitute references to persons who are "foundation managers" solely by reason of the definition of that term contained in section 4946(b)(2) and subparagraph (1)(ii) of this paragraph.

(g) *Government official.*—(1) *In general.*—Except as provided in subparagraph (3) of this paragraph, for purposes of section 4941 and paragraph (c) of this section, the term "government official" means, with respect to an act of self-dealing described in section 4941, an individual who, at the time of such act, is described in subdivision (i), (ii), (iii), (iv), or (v) of this subparagraph (other than a "special Government employee" as defined in 18 U.S.C. 202(a)):

(i)*(a)* An individual who holds an elective public office in the executive or legislative branch of the Government of the United States.

(b) An individual who holds an office in the executive or judicial branch of the Government of the United States, appointment to which was made by the President.

(ii) An individual who holds a position in the executive, legislative or judicial branch of the Government of the United States—

(a) Which is listed in schedule C of rule VI of the Civil Service Rules, or

(b) The compensation for which is equal to or greater than the lowest rate prescribed for GS-16 of the General Schedule under 5 U.S.C. 5332.

(iii) An individual who holds a position under the House of Representatives or the Senate of the United States, as an employee of either of such bodies, who receives gross compensation therefrom at an annual rate of $15,000 or more.

(iv) The holder of an elective or appointive public office in the executive, legislative, or judicial branch of the government of a State, possession of the United States, or political subdivision or other area of any of the foregoing, or of the District of Columbia, for which the gross compensation is at an annual rate of $15,000 or more, who is described in subparagraph (2) of this paragraph.

(v) The holder of a position as personal or executive assistant or secretary to any individual described in subdivision (i), (ii), (iii) or (iv) of this subparagraph.

(2) *Public office.*—(i) *Definition.*—In defining the term "public office" for purposes of section 4946(c)(5) and subparagraph (1)(iv) of this paragraph, such term must be distinguished from mere public employment. Although holding a public office is one form of public employment, not every position in the employ of a State or other governmental subdivision (as described in section 4946(c)(5)) constitutes a "public office." Although a determination whether a public employee holds a public office depends on the facts and circumstances of the case, the essential element is whether a significant part of the activities of a public employee is the independent performance of policymaking functions. In applying this subparagraph, several factors may be considered as indications that a position in the executive, legislative, or judicial branch of the government of a State, possession of the United States, or political subdivision or other area of any of the foregoing, or of the District of Columbia, constitutes a "public office." Among such factors to be considered in addition to that set forth above, are that the office is created by the Congress, a State constitution, or the State legislature, or by a municipality or other governmental body pursuant to authority conferred by the Congress, State constitution, or State legislature, and the powers conferred on the office and the duties to be discharged by such office are defined either directly or indirectly by the Congress, State constitution, or State legislature, or through legislative authority.

(ii) *Illustrations.*—The following are illustrations of positions of public employment which do not involve policymaking functions within the meaning of subdivision (i) of this subparagraph and which are thus not a "public office" for purposes of section 4946(c)(5) and subparagraph (1)(iv) of this paragraph:

(a) The chancellor, president, provost, dean, and other officers of a State university who are appointed, elected, or otherwise hired by a State Board of Regents or equivalent public body and who are subject to the direction and supervision of such body;

(b) Professors, instructors, and other members of the faculty of a State educational institution who are appointed, elected, or otherwise hired by the officers of the institution or by the State Board of Regents or equivalent public body;

(c) The superintendent of public schools and other public school officials who are appointed, elected, or otherwise hired by a Board of Education or equivalent public body and who are subject to the direction and supervision of such body;

(d) Public school teachers who are appointed, elected, or otherwise hired by the superintendent of public schools or by a Board of Education or equivalent public body;

(e) Physicians, nurses, and other professional person associated with public hospitals and State boards of health who are appointed, elected, or otherwise hired by the governing board or officers of such hospitals or agencies; and

(f) Members of police and fire departments, except for those department heads who, under the facts and circumstances of the case, independently perform policymaking functions as a significant part of their activities.

(3) *Certain government officials on leave of absence.*—For purposes of this paragraph, an individual who is otherwise described in section 4946(c) and this paragraph who was on leave of absence without pay on December 31, 1969, from his position or office pursuant to a commitment entered into on or before such date to engage in certain activities for which he is paid by one or more private foundations, is not to be treated as holding such position or office for any continuous period after December 31, 1969, and prior to January 1, 1971, during which such individual remains on leave of absence to engage in the same activities for which he is paid by such foundations. For purposes of this subparagraph, a commitment is considered entered into on or before December 31, 1969, if on or before such date, the amount and nature of the payments to be made and the name of the individual receiving such payments were entered on the records of the payor, or were otherwise adequately evidenced, or the notice of the payment to be received was communicated to the payee orally or in writing.

(h) *Members of the family.*—For purposes of this section, the members of the family of an individual include only—

(1) His spouse,

(2) His ancestors,

(3) His lineal descendants, and

(4) Spouses of his lineal descendants.

For example, a brother or sister of an individual is not a member of his family for purposes of this section. However, for example, the wife of a grandchild of an individual is a member of his family for such purposes. For purposes of this paragraph, a legally adopted child of an individual shall be treated as a child of such individual by blood. [Reg. § 53.4946-1.]

☐ [*T.D.* 7241, 12-28-71.]

[Reg. §53.4947-1]

**§53.4947-1. Application of tax.**—(a) *In general.*—Section 4947 subjects trusts which are not exempt from taxation under section 501(a), all or part of the unexpired interests in which are devoted to one or more of the purposes described in section 170(c)(2)(B), and which have amounts in trust for which a deduction was allowed under section 170, 545(b)(2), 556(b)(2), 642(c), 2055, 2106(a)(2), or 2522 to the same requirements and restrictions as are imposed on private foundations. The basic purpose of section 4947 is to prevent these trusts from being used to avoid the requirements and restrictions applicable to private foundations. For purposes of this section, a trust shall be presumed (in the absence of proof to the contrary) to have amounts in trust for which a deduction was allowed under section 170, 545(b)(2), 556(b)(2), 642(c), 2055, 2106(a)(2), or 2522 if a deduction would have been allowable under one of these sections. Also for purposes of this section and §53.4947-2, the term "purposes described in section 170(c)(2)(B)" shall be treated as including purposes described in section 170(c)(1).

(b) *Charitable trusts.*—(1) *General rule.*—(i) For purposes of this section and §53.4947-2, a "charitable trust," within the meaning of section 4947(a)(1), is a trust which is not exempt from taxation under section 501(a), all of the unexpired interests in which are devoted to one or more of the purposes described in section 170(c)(2)(B), and for which a deduction was allowed under section 170, 545(b)(2), 556(b)(2), 642(c), 2055, 2106(a)(2) or 2522 (or the corresponding provisions of prior law). A trust is one for which a deduction was allowed under section 642(c), within the meaning of section 4947(a)(1), once a deduction is allowed under section 642(c) to the trust for any amount paid or permanently set aside. (See section 642(c) and §1.642-4 for the limitation on such deduction in certain cases.) A charitable trust (as defined in this paragraph) shall be treated as an organization described in section 501(c)(3) and, if it is determined under section 509 that the trust is a private foundation, then Part II of subchapter F of chapter 1 of the Code (other than section 508(a), (b) and (c)) and chapter 42 shall apply to the trust. However, the charitable trust is not treated as an organization described in section 501(c)(3) for purposes of exemption from taxation under section 501(a). Thus, the trust is subject to the excise tax on its investment income under section 4940(b) rather than the tax imposed by section 4940(a). For purposes of satisfying the organizational test described in §1.501(c)(3)-1(b) when a charitable trust seeks an exemption from taxation under section 501(a), a charitable trust (as defined in this paragraph) shall be considered organized on the day it first becomes subject to section 4947(a)(1). However, for purposes of the special and transitional rules in sections 4940(c)(4)(B), 4942(f)(4), 4943(c)(4)(A)(i) and (B) and section 101(1)(2)(A), (B), (C), and (D), and (1)(3) of the Tax Reform Act of 1969, a charitable trust (as defined in this paragraph) shall be considered organized on the first day it has amounts in trust for which a deduction was allowed (within the meaning of paragraph (a) of this section) under section 170, 545(b)(2), 556(b)(2), 642(c), 2055, 2106(a)(2), or 2522. Thus, under this rule, a trust may be treated as a private foundation in existence on a date governing one of the applicable special and transitional rules even though the trust did not otherwise become subject to the provisions of chapter 42 until a later date.

(ii) The provisions of paragraph (b)(1) of this section may be illustrated by the following examples:

*Example (1).* On January 30, 1970, X creates an inter vivos trust under which M receives 50 percent and N receives 50 percent of the trust's income for 10 years, and upon the termination of which, at the end of the 10-year period, the corpus is to be distributed to O. M, N and O are all organizations described in section 501(c)(3) and X is allowed a deduction under section 170 for the value of all interests placed in trust. The trustees of the trust do not give notice to the Internal Revenue Service under the provisions of section 508(a), and the trust will therefore not be exempt from taxation under section 501(a). The trust is a charitable trust within the meaning of section 4947(a)(1) from the date of its creation.

*Example (2).* On March 1, 1971, Y creates a charitable remainder annuity trust described in section 664(d)(1) under which Z, Y's son, receives $10,000 per year for life, remainder to be held in trust for P, an organization described in section 501(c)(3). Y is allowed a deduction under section 170 for the present value of the remainder interest to P. During Z's lifetime, the trust is a split-interest trust described in section 4947(a)(2) and paragraph (c) of this section. Upon the death of Z, all unexpired interests (consisting of P's remainder interest) will be devoted to section 170(c)(2)(B) purposes. Except as provided in §53.4947-1(b)(2)(iv) (relating to a reasonable period of settlement) the trust will be treated as a charitable trust within the meaning of section 4947(a)(1) from the date of the death of Z unless the trustees of the trust apply for recognition of section 501(c)(3) status under the provisions of section 508(a).

(2) *Scope of application of section 4947(a)(1).*—(i) *In general.*—Subject to paragraph (b)(2)(ii) through (vii) of this section, section 4947(a)(1) applies to nonexempt trusts in which all unexpired interests are charitable. For purposes of this section, the term "charitable" when used to describe an interest or beneficiary refers to the purposes described in section 170(c)(2)(B). An estate from which the executor or administrator is required to distribute all of the net assets in trust to such beneficiaries will not be considered a charitable trust under section 4947(a)(1) during the period of estate administration or settlement, except as provided in paragraph (b)(2)(ii) of this section. A charitable trust created by will shall be considered a charitable trust under section 4947(a)(1) as of the date of death of the decedent-grantor, except as provided in paragraph (b)(2)(v) of this section (relating to trusts which wind up). For the circumstances under which segregated amounts are treated as charitable trusts, see §53.4947-1(c)(3)(iii).

(ii) *Estates.*—(A) When an estate from which the executor or administrator is required to distribute all of the net assets in trust for charitable beneficiaries, or free of trust to such beneficiaries, is considered terminated for Federal income tax purposes under §1.641(b)-3 (a), then the estate will be treated as a charitable trust under section 4947(a)(1) between the date on which the estate is considered terminated under §1.641(b)-3 (a) and the date final distribution of all of the net assets is made to or for the benefit of the charitable beneficiaries. This (ii) does not affect the determination of the tax liability under subtitle A of the beneficiaries of the estates.

(B) The provisions of this (ii) may be illustrated by the following example:

*Example.* X bequeaths his entire estate, including 100 percent of the stock of a wholly-owned corporation, to M, an organization described in section 501(c)(3), under a will which gives his executor authority to hold the stock and manage the corporation for a period of up to 10 years for the benefit of M prior to its ultimate disposition. A deduction for the charitable bequest was allowed to X's estate under section 2055. The executor is vested with a full range of powers, including the power of sale. Upon the death of X, his executor distributes X's assets to M except for the stock of the corporation, which he holds for 5 years prior to its disposition. The continued holding of the stock of the corporation by the executor after the expiration of a reasonable time for performance of all the ordinary duties of administration causes the estate to be considered terminated for Federal income tax purposes pursuant to §1.641(b)-3 (a) and thereby subjects it to the provisions of section 4947(a)(1) from the date of such termination to the date of final disposition of the stock of the corporation.

(iii) *Certain split-interest trusts which wind up.*—A split-interest trust (as defined in paragraph (c) of this section) in which all of the unexpired interests are charitable remainder interests and in which the charitable beneficiaries have become entitled to distributions of corpus in trust or free of trust shall continue to be treated as a split-interest trust under section 4947(a)(2) until the date on which final distribution of all of the net assets is made. However, if after the expiration of any intervening interests the trust is considered terminated for Federal income tax purposes under §1.641(b)-3 (b), then the trust will be treated as a charitable trust under section 4947(a)(1), rather than a split-interest trust under section 4947(a)(2), between the date on which the trust is considered terminated under §1.641(b)-3 (b) and the date on which such final distribution of all of the net assets is made to or for the benefit of the charitable remainder beneficiaries. This (iii) does not affect the determination of the tax liability under subtitle A of the beneficiaries of the trusts.

(iv) *Split-interest trusts which become charitable trusts.*—(A) A split-interest trust (as defined in paragraph (c) of this section) in which all of the unexpired interests are charitable remainder interests and in which some or all of the charitable beneficiaries are not entitled to distributions of corpus within the meaning of paragraph (b)(2)(iii) of this section shall continue to be treated as a split-interest trust under section 4947(a)(2) rather than a charitable trust under section 4947(a)(1) for a reasonable period of settlement after the expiration of the noncharitable interest. Thus, a split-interest trust which under its terms is to continue to hold assets for charitable beneficiaries after the expiration of the noncharitable interest rather than distributing them as in paragraph (b)(2)(iii) of this section is given a reasonable period of settlement before being treated as a charitable trust. For purposes of this paragraph, the term "reasonable period of settlement" means that period reasonably required (or if shorter, actually required) by the trustee to perform the ordinary duties of administration necessary for the settlement of the trust. These duties include, for example, the collection of assets, the payment of debts, taxes, and distributions, and the determination of the rights of the subsequent beneficiaries.

(B) This (iv) may be illustrated by the following example:

*Example.* On January 15, 1971, A creates a charitable remainder annuity trust described in section 664(d)(1) under which the trustees are required to distribute $10,000 a year to B, A's wife, for life, remainder to be held in trust for the use of M, an organization described in section 501(c)(3). A is allowed a deduction under section 170 for the amount of the charitable interest, and the trust is, therefore, treated as a split-interest trust under section 4947(a)(2) from the date of its creation. B dies on February 10, 1975. On April 15, 1975, the trustees complete performance of the ordinary duties of administration necessary for the settlement of the trust brought about by the death of B. These duties include, for example, an accounting for and payment to the estate of B of amounts accrued by B while alive during 1975. However, the trustees do not distribute the corpus to M by April 15, 1975. The trust shall continue to be treated as a split-interest trust under section 4947(a)(2) until April 15, 1975. After April 15, 1975, the trust shall be treated as a charitable trust under section 4947(a)(1).

(v) *Certain revocable and testamentary trusts which wind up.*—A revocable trust that becomes irrevocable upon the death of the decedent-grantor, or a trust created by will, from which the trustee is required to distribute all of the net assets in trust for or free of trust to charitable beneficiaries is not considered a charitable trust under section 4947(a)(1) for a reasonable period of settlement (within the meaning of paragraph (b)(2)(iv) of this section) after becoming irrevocable. After that period the trust is considered a charitable trust under section 4947(a)(1).

(vi) *Revocable trusts which become charitable trusts.*—A revocable trust that becomes irrevocable upon the death of the decedent-grantor in which all of the unexpired interests are charitable and under the terms of the governing instrument of which the trustee is required to hold some or all of the net assets in trust after becoming irrevocable solely for charitable beneficiaries is not considered a trust under section 4947(a)(1) for a reasonable period of settlement (within the meaning of paragraph (b)(2)(iv) of this section) after becoming irrevocable except that section 4941 may apply if the requirements of § 53.4941(d)-1(b)(3) are not met. After that period, the trust is considered a charitable trust under section 4947(a)(1).

(vii) *Trust devoted to 170(c) purposes.*—(A) A trust all of the unexpired interests in which are devoted to section 170(c)(3) or (5) purposes together with section 170(c)(2)(B) purposes shall be considered a charitable trust except that payments under the terms of the governing instrument to an organization described in section 170(c)(3) or (5) shall not be considered a violation of section 4945(d)(5) or any other provisions of chapter 42 and shall be considered qualifying distributions under section 4942.

(B) *Example.*—The application of paragraph (b)(2)(vii) of this section may be illustrated by the following example:

*Example.* On January 30, 1970, H creates an *inter vivos* trust under the terms of the governing instrument of which M, an organization described in section 170(c)(3), and N, an organization described in section 501(c)(3), are each to receive 50 percent of the income for a period of 10 years. At the end of the 10-year period, the corpus is to be distributed to O, an organization also described in section 501(c)(3). H is allowed a deduction under section 170 for the value of all interests placed in trust. The payments to M and N do not constitute a violation of section 4945(d)(5) or any other provision of chapter 42 and constitute qualifying distributions under section 4942. However, except as provided in the previous sentence, the trust shall be considered a charitable trust.

(3) *Charitable trusts described in section 509(a)(3).*—For purposes of section 509(a)(3)(A), a charitable trust shall be treated as if organized on the day on which it first becomes subject to section 4947(a)(1). However, for purposes of applying § § 1.509(a)-4(d)(2)(iv)(a), and 1.509(a)-4(i)(1)(ii) and (iii)(c) the previous relationship between the charitable trust and the section 509(a)(1) or (2) organizations it benefits or supports may be considered. If the charitable trust otherwise meets the requirements of section 509(a)(3), it may obtain recognition of its status as a section 509(a)(3) organization by requesting a ruling from the Internal Revenue Service. For the special rules pertaining to the application of the organizational test to organizations terminating their private foundation status under the 12-month or 60-month termination period provided under section 507(b)(1)(B) by becoming "public" under section 509(a)(3), see the regulations under section 507(b)(1).

(c) *Split-interest trusts.*—(1) *General rule.*—(i) *Definition.*—For purposes of this section and § 53.4947-2, a "split-interest trust," within the meaning of section 4947(a)(2), is a trust which is not exempt from taxation under section 501(a), not all of the unexpired interests in which are devoted to one or more of the purposes described in section 170(c)(2)(B), and which has amounts in trust for which a deduction was allowed (within the meaning of paragraph (a) of this

section) under section 170, 545(b)(2), 556(b)(2), 642(c), 2055, 2106(a)(2), or 2522. A trust is one which has amounts in trust for which a deduction was allowed under section 642(c) within the meaning of section 4947(a)(2) once a deduction is allowed under section 642(c) to the trust for any amount permanently set aside. This (i) also includes any trust which is not treated as a charitable trust by operation of paragraph (b)(2)(iii) or (iv) of this section (relating to split-interest trusts in the process of winding up or during a reasonable period of settlement). Section 4947(a)(1) shall apply to a trust described in this (i) (without regard to section 4947(a)(2)(A), (B), or (C)) from the first date upon which the provisions of paragraph (b)(2)(iii) or (iv) of this section are satisfied. For the circumstances under which a trust all of the unexpired interests in which are devoted to section 170(c)(3) or (5) purposes together with section 170(c)(2)(B) purposes is considered a charitable trust, see § 53.4947-1(b)(2)(vii).

(ii) *Applicability of statutory rules.*—A split-interest trust is subject to the provisions of section 507 (except as provided in paragraph (e) of this section), 508(e) (to the extent applicable to a split-interest trust), 4941, 4943 (except as provided in section 4947(b)(3)), 4944 (except as provided in section 4947(b)(3)), and 4945 in the same manner as if such trust were a private foundation.

(iii) *Special rules.*—A newly created trust shall, for purposes of section 4947(a)(2), be treated as having amounts in trust for which a deduction was allowed under section 170, 545(b)(2), 556(b)(2), 642(c), 2055, 2106(a)(2), or 2522 from the date of its creation, even if a deduction was allowed for such amounts only at a later date. For purposes of this (iii), the date of creation of a charitable remainder trust shall be determined by applying the rules in § 1.664-1(a)(4).

(2) *Exception for amounts payable to income beneficiaries.*—(i) Under section 4947(a)(2)(A), paragraph (c)(1)(ii) of this section does not apply to any amounts payable under the terms of a split-interest trust to income beneficiaries unless a deduction was allowed under section 170(f)(2)(B), 2055(e)(2)(B), or 2522(c)(2)(B) with respect to income interest of any such beneficiary. See § 1.170A-6(c), § 20.2055-2(e)(2), and § 25.2522(c)-3(c)(2) for rules regarding the allowance of these deductions. However, section 4947(a)(2)(A) does not apply when the value of all interests in property transferred in trust are deductible under section 170, 545(b)(2), 556(b)(2), 642(c), 2055, 2106(a)(2), or 2522.

(ii) The application of this subparagraph may be illustrated by the following examples:

*Example (1).* H creates a charitable remainder unitrust (described in section 664(d)(2)) which is required annually to pay W, H's wife, 5 percent of the net fair market value of the trust assets, valued annually, for her life; and to pay the remainder to Y, a section 501(c)(3) organization. A deduction under section 170(f)(2)(A) was allowed with respect to the remainder interest of Y. Under section 4947(a)(2)(A), each annual amount which becomes payable to W during her life is not subject to paragraph (c)(1)(ii) of this section on or after the date upon which it becomes so payable and the payment of each amount to W is not an act of self-dealing under section 4941(d)(1) and does not violate any other provision of chapter 42. However, except as provided in the preceding sentence, the trust is subject to paragraph (c)(1)(ii) of this section in the same manner as any other split-interest trust.

*Example (2).* H bequeaths the residue of his estate in trust for the benefit of S, his son, and Y, an organization described in section 501(c)(3). A guaranteed annuity interest of $10,000 is to be paid to S for 20 years. A guaranteed annuity interest of $5,000 which meets the requirements contained in § 20.2055-2(e)(2)(v)(a) is also to be paid to Y for 20 years. Upon termination of the 20-year term, the corpus is to be distributed to Z, another organization described in section 501(c)(3). The trust is a charitable remainder annuity trust as described in section 664(d)(1) and the regulations thereunder, and a deduction under section 2055(e)(2)(A) was allowed with respect to the remainder interest of Z. A deduction was also allowed under section 2055(e)(2)(B) with respect to the guaranteed annuity interest of Y. The assets in the trust are not segregated under section 4947(a)(2)(B) and paragraph (c)(3) of this section. Under section 4947(a)(2)(A), each payment of $10,000 to S is not subject to section 4947(a)(2) and paragraph (c)(1)(ii) of this section. The payment of each amount to S is not an act of self-dealing under section 4941(d)(1) and does not violate any other provision of chapter 42. However, except as provided in the preceding sentence, the trust is subject to section 4947(a)(2) and paragraph (c)(1)(ii) of this section in the same manner as any other split-interest trust.

*Example (3).* H creates a trust under which the trustees are required to pay over an annuity interest of $20,000 to W, H's wife, for her life. A guaranteed annuity interest of $10,000 which meets the requirements contained in § 25.2522(c)-3 (c)(2)(v) is also to be paid to X, an organization described in section 501(c)(3), for the life of W. Upon the death of W, the corpus of the trust, which consists of office buildings M and N, is to be distributed to S, H's son. He received a deduction under section 2522(c)(2)(B) for the value of X's income interest in the trust. The assets in the trust are not segregated under section 4947(a)(2)(B) and paragraph (c)(3) of this section. Under section 4947(a)(2)(A), each payment of $20,000 to W is not subject to section 4947(a)(2) and paragraph (c)(1)(ii) of this section. The payment of each amount to W is not an act of self-dealing under section 4941(d)(1) and does not violate any other provision of chapter 42. However, except as provided in the preceding sentence, the trust is subject to paragraph (c)(1)(ii) of this section in the same manner as any other split-interest trust. See example (1) of paragraph (c)(3)(v) of this section for the application of section 4947(a)(2)(B) to a similar trust where the trustees segregate the assets of the trust.

(3) *Exception for certain segregated amounts.*—(i) *In general.*—Under section 4947(a)(2)(B), paragraph (c)(1)(ii) of this section does not apply to assets held in trust (together with the income and capital gains derived from the assets), which are segregated from other assets held in trust for which a deduction was allowed for an income or remainder interest under section 170, 545(b)(2), 556(b)(2), 642(c), 2055, 2106(a)(2), or 2522.

(ii) *Segregation of amounts.*—Amounts will generally be considered segregated (within the meaning of section 4947(a)(2)(B)) if:

(A) assets with respect to which no deduction was allowed (for an income or remainder interest) under section 170, 545(b)(2), 556(b)(2), 642(c), 2055, 2106(a)(2), or 2522, are separately accounted for under section 4947(a)(3) and paragraph (c)(4) of this section from assets for which such a deduction was allowed for any income or remainder interest and,

(B) by reason of the separate accounting the trust can be treated as two separate trusts, one of which is devoted exclusively to noncharitable income and remainder interests and the other of which is a charitable trust described in section 4947(a)(1) or a split-interest trust described in section 4947(a)(2).

Under these circumstances, only the "trust" which is devoted exclusively to noncharitable income and remainder interests will be considered a segregated amount which, under section 4947(a)(2)(B), is not subject to section 4947(a)(2) and paragraph (c)(1)(ii) of this section.

(iii) *Exclusively charitable amounts.*—If, under section 4947(a)(2)(B),

(A) an amount held in trust which is devoted exclusively to noncharitable income and remainder interests is segregated from

(B) an amount held in trust which is devoted exclusively to charitable income and remainder interests,

then for purposes of this section the amount described in paragraph (c)(3)(iii)(B) of this section will be treated as a charitable trust which is subject to the provisions of section 4947(a)(1).

(iv) *Charitable and noncharitable amounts.*—If, under section 4947(a)(2)(B),

(A) an amount held in trust which is devoted exclusively to noncharitable income and remainder interests is segregated from

(B) an amount held in trust which is devoted to both charitable income or remainder interests and noncharitable income or remainder interests,

then for purposes of this section the amount described in paragraph (c)(3)(iv)(B) of this section will be treated as a split-interest trust which is subject to the provisions of section 4947(a)(2).

(v) *Examples.*—The application of paragraph (c)(3) of this section may be illustrated by the following examples:

*Example (1).* H creates a trust under which the trustees are required to pay over annually 5 percent of the net fair market value of M building, valued annually, to W, H's wife, for life, remainder to S, H's son. The other asset in the trust is N building, with respect to which the trustees are required to pay over annually 5 percent of the net fair market value of the building, valued annually, to X, a section 501(c)(3) organization, for a period of 15 years, remainder to S. Each asset is separately accounted for under section 4947(a)(3) and paragraph (c)(4) of this section. H received a deduction under section 2522 for the value of X's income interest in N building. Under these circumstances, M building is considered segregated (within the meaning of section 4947(a)(2)(B)) from N building and is not subject to section 4947(a)(2). The remainder interest of S in N building is not considered segregated from the income interest of X in N building, since both are interests in the same asset. N building is considered held in a split-interest trust which is subject to section 4947(a)(2) and paragraph (c)(1)(ii) of this section.

*Example (2).* H transfers $50,000 in trust to pay $2,500 per year to Z, a section 501(c)(3) organization, for a term of 20 years, remainder to S, H's son. H is allowed a deduction under section 2522 for the present value of Z's income interest. The income interest of Z in the trust asset cannot be segregated (within the meaning of section

4947(a)(2)(B)) from the remainder interest of S since both are interests in the same asset. Therefore, the entire trust is subject to section 4947(a)(2) and paragraph (c)(1)(ii) of this section.

(4) *Accounting for segregated amounts.*—(i) *General rule.*—Under section 4947(a)(2)(B), a trust with respect to which amounts are segregated within the meaning of paragraph (c)(3) of this section must separately account for the various income, deduction, and other items properly attributable to each segregated amount in the books of account and separately account to each of the beneficiaries of the trust.

(ii) *Method.*—Separate accounting shall be made—

(A) According to the method regularly employed by the trust, if the method is reasonable, and

(B) In all other cases in a manner which, in the opinion of the Commissioner, is reasonable.

A method of separate accounting will be considered "regularly employed" by a trust when the method has been consistently followed in prior taxable years or when a trust which has never before maintained segregated amounts initiates a reasonable method of separate accounting for its segregated amounts and consistently follows such method thereafter. The trust shall keep permanent records and other data relating to the segregated amounts as are necessary to enable the district director to determine the correctness of the application of the rules prescribed in paragraph (c)(3) and (4) of this section.

(5) *Amounts transferred in trust before May 27, 1969.*—(i) *General rule.*—Under section 4947(a)(2)(C), paragraph (c)(1)(ii) of this section does not apply to any amounts transferred in trust before May 27, 1969. For purposes of this (5), an amount shall be considered to be transferred in trust only when the transfer is one which meets the requirements for the allowance of a deduction under section 170, 545(b)(2), 556(b)(2), 642(c), 2055, 2106(a)(2), or 2522 (or the corresponding provisions of prior law). Income and capital gains which are derived at any time from amounts transferred in trust before May 27, 1969, shall also be excluded from the application of paragraph (c)(1)(ii) of this section. If an asset which was transferred in trust before May 27, 1969, is sold or exchanged after May 26, 1969, any asset received by the trust upon the sale or exchange shall be treated as an asset which was transferred in trust before May 27, 1969.

(ii) *Requirement for separate accounting for amounts transferred in trust before May 27, 1969.*—If:

(A) Amounts are transferred in trust after May 26, 1969, and the trust to which the amounts are transferred also contains

(B) Amounts transferred in trust before May 27, 1969,

the general rule of paragraph (c)(5)(i) of this section applicable to the amounts described in paragraph (c)(5)(ii)(B) of this section will apply only if the amounts described in paragraph (c)(5)(ii)(A) of this section (together with all income and capital gains derived therefrom) are separately accounted for (within the meaning of paragraph (c)(4) of this section) from the amounts described in paragraph (c)(5)(ii)(B) of this section, together with all income and capital gains derived therefrom. For the application of section 508(e) to a trust with respect to which amounts were transferred both before and after May 27, 1969, see section 508(e) and the regulations thereunder.

(iii) *Exception for certain testamentary trusts.*—(A) Amounts transferred in trust before May 27, 1969 include amounts transferred in trust after May 26, 1969 when the transfer is made under the terms of a testamentary trust created by the will of a decedent who died before May 27, 1969, (regardless of whether the executors or the testamentary trustees are required to execute testamentary trusts by court order under applicable local law). Amounts transferred in trust before May 27, 1969, also include amounts transferred to a testamentary trust created by the will of a decedent who died after May 26, 1969 if the will was executed before May 27, 1969 and no dispositive provision of the will was amended (within the meaning of § 20.2055-2(e)(4) and (5)) by the decedent by codicil or otherwise, after May 26, 1969, and the decedent was on May 27, 1969, and at all times thereafter under a mental disability (as defined in § 1.642(c)-2(b)(3)(ii)) to amend the will by codicil or otherwise.

(B) The provisions of this (iii) may be illustrated by the following example:

*Example.* X executed a will in 1960 which provided for the creation of a testamentary trust which meets the description of a split-interest trust under section 4947(a)(2). X died on April 15, 1969. Under the provisions of his will, the probate court permitted certain property in X's estate to be transferred to the testamentary trust at fixed intervals over a period of two years during the administration of the estate. Section 4947(a)(2) does not apply to any amount described in this example, including the amounts transferred after May 26, 1969, because, for purposes of section 4947(a)(2)(C), each such transfer will be treated as an amount transferred in trust before May 27, 1969, within the meaning of section 4947(a)(2)(C).

Reg. §53.4947-1(c)(5)(iii)(B)

(6) *Scope of application of section 4947(a)(2).*—(i) *In general.*—Subject to paragraph (c)(6)(ii), (iii), and (iv) of this section, section 4947(a)(2) applies to trusts in which some but not all unexpired interests are charitable. An estate from which the executor or administrator is required to distribute all of the net assets in trust or free of trust to both charitable and noncharitable beneficiaries will not be considered to be a split-interest trust under section 4947(a)(2) during the period of estate administration or settlement, except as provided in paragraph (c)(6)(ii) of this section. A split-interest trust created by will shall be considered a split-interest trust under section 4947(a)(2) as of the date of death of the decedent-grantor, except as provided in paragraph (c)(6)(iv) of this section.

(ii) *Estates.*—(A) When an estate from which the executor or administrator is required to distribute all of the net assets in trust or free of trust to both charitable and noncharitable beneficiaries is considered terminated for Federal income tax purposes under §1.641(b)-3 (a), then the estate will be treated as a split-interest trust under section 4947(a)(2) (or a charitable trust under section 4947(a)(1), if applicable) between the date on which the estate is considered terminated under §1.641(b)-3 (a) and the date on which final distribution of the net assets to the last remaining charitable beneficiary is made. This (ii) does not affect the determination of the tax liability under subtitle A of either charitable or noncharitable beneficiaries of the estates.

(B) The provisions of this (ii) may be illustrated by the following example:

*Example.* X dies on January 15, 1973 and bequeaths $10,000 to M, an organization described in section 501(c)(3), and the residue of his estate to W, his wife. A deduction for the charitable bequest was allowed to X's estate under section 2055. Substantially all of X's estate consists of 100 percent of the stock of a wholly owned corporation, certain liquid assets such as marketable stocks and securities and bank accounts, and X's home, automobile, and other personal property. X's will gives the executor a full range of powers, including the power to sell the stock of the wholly owned corporation. After the death of X, his executor continues to manage the wholly owned corporation while attempting to sell the stock of the corporation. During this period, the executor makes no distributions to M. On May 24, 1978, the Internal Revenue Service determines under §1.641(b)-3(a) that the administration of the estate has been unduly prolonged and the estate is considered terminated as of that date for Federal income tax purposes. X's estate will be treated as a split-interest trust described in section 4947(a)(2) between May 24, 1978 and the date on which the $10,000 bequest to M is satisfied. X's estate will therefore be subject to the applicable private foundation provisions during that period and, for example, a sale of the house by the estate to any disqualified person (as defined in section 4946) will be an act of self-dealing under section 4941.

(iii) *Revocable trusts which become split-interest trusts.*—A revocable trust that becomes irrevocable upon the death of the decedent-grantor under the terms of the governing instrument of which the trustee is required to hold some or all of its net assets in trust after becoming irrevocable for both charitable and noncharitable beneficiaries is not considered a split-interest trust under section 4947(a)(2) for a reasonable period of settlement after becoming irrevocable except that section 4941 may apply if the requirements of §53.4941(d)-1(b)(3) are not met.

After that period, the trust is considered a split-interest trust under section 4947(a)(2). For purposes of this (iii), the term "reasonable period of settlement" means that period reasonably required (or if shorter, actually required) by the trustee to perform the ordinary duties of administration necessary for the settlement of the trust. These duties include, for example, the collection of assets, the payment of debts, taxes, and distributions, and the determination of rights of the subsequent beneficiaries.

(iv) *Certain revocable and testamentary trusts which wind up.*—A revocable trust that becomes irrevocable upon the death of the decedent-grantor, or a trust created by will, from which the trustee is required to distribute all of the net assets in trust or free of trust to both charitable and noncharitable beneficiaries is not considered a split-interest trust under section 4947(a)(2) for a reasonable period of settlement (within the meaning of paragraph (c)(6)(iii) of this section) after becoming irrevocable. After that period, the trust is considered a split-interest trust under section 4947(a)(2) (or a charitable trust under section 4947(a)(1), if applicable).

(d) *Cross references; Governing instrument requirements and charitable deduction limitations.*—For the application of section 642(c)(6) (relating to section 170 limitations on charitable deductions of non-exempt private foundation trusts) to a trust described in section 4947(a)(1), see §1.642(c)-4. For the denial of a deduction under section 170, 545(b)(2), 556(b)(2), 642(c), 2055, 2106(a)(2), or 2522 for a gift, a bequest, or an amount paid to (and the denial of a deduction under

section 642(c) for an amount set aside in) a trust described in section 4947(a)(1) or (2) that fails to meet the applicable governing instrument requirements of section 508(e) by the end of the taxable year of the trust, see section 508(d)(2) and §1.508-2(b). Since a charitable remainder trust (as defined in section 664) is not exempt under section 501(a), it is subject to section 4947(a)(2), and thus to the governing instrument requirements of section 508(e) to the extent they are applicable.

(e) *Application of section 507(a).*—(1) *General rule.*—The provisions of section 507(a) shall not apply to a trust described in section 4947(a)(1) or (2) by reason of any payment to a beneficiary that is directed by the terms of the governing instrument of the trust and is not discretionary with the trustee or, in the case of a discretionary payment, by reason of, or following, the expiration of the last remaining charitable interest in the trust.

(2) *Examples.*—The provisions of this (e) may be illustrated by the following examples:

*Example (1).* H creates a section 4947(a)(1) trust under which the income is to be paid for 15 years to R, a section 501(c)(3) organization. Upon the expiration of 15 years, the trust is to terminate and distribute all of its assets to S, another section 501(c)(3) organization. Distribution of the corpus of the trust to S will not be considered a termination of the trust's private foundation status within the meaning of section 507(a).

*Example (2).* H creates a trust under which X, a section 501(c)(3) organization, receives $20,000 per year for a period of 20 years, remainder to S, H's son. H is allowed a deduction under section 2522 for the present value of X's interest.

When the final payment to X has been made at the end of the 20-year period in accordance with the terms of the trust, the provisions of section 4947(a)(2) will cease to apply to the trust because the trust no longer retains any amounts for which the deduction under section 2522 was allowed. However, the final payment to X will not be considered a termination of the trust's private foundation status within the meaning of section 507(a).

*Example (3).* J creates a charitable remainder annuity trust described in section 664(d)(1) under which S, J's son, receives $10,000 per year for life, remainder to be distributed outright to P, an organization described in section 501(c)(3). J is allowed a deduction under section 170 for the value of the remainder interest placed in trust for the benefit of P, and the provisions of section 4947(a)(2) apply to the trust. At the death of S, the trust will terminate and all assets will be distributed to P. However, such final distribution to P will not be considered a termination of the trust's private foundation status within the meaning of section 507(a). [Reg. §53.4947-1.]

☐ [T.D. 7431, 8-20-76.]

## [Reg. §53.4947-2]

§53.4947-2. **Special rules.**—(a) *Limit to segregated amounts.*—If any amounts held in trust are segregated within the meaning of §53.4947-1(c)(3), the value of the net assets for purposes of section 507(c)(2) and (g) shall be limited to the segregated amounts with respect to which a deduction under section 170, 545(b)(2), 556(b)(2), 642(c), 2055, 2106(a)(2), or 2522 was allowed. See the regulations under section 507(c)(2) and (g).

(b) *Applicability of sections 4943 and 4944 to split-interest trusts.*—(1) *General rule.*—Under section 4947(b)(3), sections 4943 and 4944 do not apply to a split-interest trust described in section 4947(a)(2) if:

(i) all the income interest (and none of the remainder interest) of the trust is devoted solely to one or more of the purposes described in section 170(c)(2)(B) and all amounts in the trust for which a deduction was allowed under section 170, 545(b)(2), 556(b)(2), 642(c), 2055, 2106(a)(2), or 2522 have an aggregated value (at the time for which the deduction was allowed) of not more than 60 percent of the aggregate fair market value of all amounts in the trust (after the payment of estate taxes and all other liabilities), or

(ii) a deduction was allowed under section 170, 545(b)(2), 556(b)(2), 642(c), 2055, 2106(a)(2) or 2522 for amounts payable under the terms of the trust to every remainder beneficiary, but not to any income beneficiary.

This (1) shall apply to a trust described in paragraph (b)(1)(ii) of this section only if all amounts payable under the terms of the trust to every remainder beneficiary are to be devoted solely to one or more of the purposes described in section 170(c)(2)(B). After the expiration of all income interests in a trust described in paragraph (b)(1)(ii) of this section, the trust shall become subject to section 4947(a)(1) under §53.4947-1(b)(2), and section 4947(b)(3) shall no longer apply to the trust. A pooled income fund described in section 642(c)(5) will generally meet the requirements of paragraph (b)(1)(ii) of this section, as will a charitable remainder trust described in section 664(d)(1), if in either case it does not make payments to any income beneficiary described in section 170(c).

(2) *Definitions.*—(i) For purposes of section 4947(b)(3)(A), the term "income interest" shall include an interest in property transferred in trust which is in the form of a guaranteed annuity interest or unitrust interest as described in §1.170A-6(c), §20.2055-2(e)(2) or §25.2522(c)-3(c)(2) and the term "remainder interest" shall include an interest which succeeds an "income interest" within the meaning of this (i).

(ii) For purposes of section 4947(b)(3)(B), the term "income beneficiary" shall include a recipient of payments described in section 642(c)(5)(F) from a pooled income fund, payments described in section 664(d)(1)(A) from a charitable remainder annuity trust, or payments described in section 664(d)(2)(A) or (3) from a charitable remainder unitrust. The term "remainder beneficiary" shall include a beneficiary of a remainder interest described in section 642(c)(5) or 664(d)(1)(C) or (2)(C).

(c) *Effective date.*—Except as otherwise provided in §§53.4947-1 and 53.4947-2 and the regulations under sections 508(d) and (e), §§53.4947-1 and 53.4947-2 shall take effect on January 1, 1970. [Reg. §53.4947-2.]

☐ [*T.D. 7431,* 8-20-76.]

### [Reg. §53.4948-1]

**§53.4948-1. Application of taxes and denial of exemption with respect to certain foreign organizations.**—(a) *Tax on income of certain foreign organizations.*—(1) In lieu of the tax imposed by section 4940 and the regulations thereunder, there is hereby imposed for each taxable year beginning after December 31, 1969, on the gross investment income (within the meaning of section 4940(c)(2) and the regulations thereunder) derived from sources within the United States (within the meaning of section 861 and the regulations thereunder) by every foreign organization which is a private foundation (within the meaning of section 509 and the regulations thereunder) and exempt from taxation under section 501(a) for the taxable year a tax equal to 4 percent of such income, except as provided in subparagraph (3) of this paragraph. The tax (if any) will be reported on the form the foundation is required to file under section 6033 for the taxable year, and will be paid annually at the time prescribed for filing such annual return (determined without regard to any extension of time for filing). For purposes of this section, the term "foreign organization" means any organization which is not described in section 170(c)(2)(A).

(2) With respect to the deduction and withholding of tax imposed by section 4948(a), see section 1443(b) and the regulations thereunder.

(3) Whenever there exists a tax treaty between the United States and a foreign country, and a foreign private foundation subject to section 4948(a) is a resident of such country or is otherwise entitled to the benefits of such treaty (whether or not such benefits are available to all residents), if the treaty provides that any item or items (or all items with respect to an organization exempt from income taxation) of gross investment income (within the meaning of section 4940(c)(2)) shall be exempt from income tax, such item or items shall not be taken into account by such foundation in computing the tax to be imposed under section 4948(a) for any taxable year for which the treaty is effective.

(b) *Certain sections inapplicable.*—Section 507 (relating to termination of private foundation status), section 508 (relating to special rules with respect to section 501(c)(3) organizations), and chapter 42 (other than section 4948) of the Code shall not apply to any foreign organization which from the date of its creation has received at least 85 percent of its support (as defined in section 509(d), other than section 509(d)(4)) from sources outside the United States. For purposes of this paragraph, gifts, grants, contributions, or membership fees directly or indirectly from a United States person (as defined in section 7701(a)(30)) are from sources within the United States.

(c) *Denial of exemption to foreign organizations engaged in prohibited transactions.*—(1) *In general.*—A foreign private foundation described in section 4948(b) and paragraph (b) of this section shall not be exempt from taxation under section 501(a) if it has engaged in a prohibited transaction (within the meaning of subparagraph (2) of this paragraph) after December 31, 1969.

(2) *Prohibited transactions.*—(i) For purposes of this section, the term "prohibited transaction" means any act or failure to act (other than with respect to section 4942(e), relating to minimum investment return) which would subject a foreign private foundation described in paragraph (b) of this section, or a disqualified person (as defined in section 4946) with respect thereto, to liability for a penalty under section 6684 (relating to assessable penalties with respect to liability for tax under chapter 42) or a tax under section 507 (relating to termination of private foundation status) if such foreign private foundation were a domestic private foundation.

(ii) For purposes of subdivision (i) of this subparagraph—

(*a*) Approval by an appropriate foreign government of grants by the foreign private foundation to individuals is sufficient to satisfy the requirements of section 4945(g) and the regulations thereunder.

(*b*) In determining whether a grantee of the foreign organization is a private foundation which is not an operating foundation for purposes of section 4942(g)(1)(A)(ii) or is an organization which is not described in section 509(a)(1), (2), or (3) for purposes of section 4945(d)(4) and (h), a determination made by such foreign organization will be accepted if such determination is made in good faith after a reasonable effort to identify the status of its grantee.

(iii) For purposes of subdivision (i) of this subparagraph, in order for an act or failure to act (without regard to section 4942(e)) to be treated as a prohibited transaction under section 4948(c)(2) by reason of the application of section 6684(1), there must have been a prior act or failure to act (without regard to section 4942(e)), which—

(*a*) Would have resulted in liability for tax under chapter 42 (other than section 4940 or 4948(a)) if the foreign private foundation had been a domestic private foundation, and

(*b*) Had been the subject of a warning from the Commissioner that a second act or failure to act (without regard to section 4942(e)) would result in a prohibited transaction.

The second act or failure to act (with respect to which a warning described in subparagraph (3)(i) of this paragraph is given) need not be related to the prior act or failure to act with respect to which a warning from the Commissioner was given under (*b*) of this subdivision.

(3) *Taxable years affected.*—(i) Except as provided in subdivision (ii) of this subparagraph, a foreign private foundation described in paragraph (b) of this section shall be denied exemption from taxation under section 501(a) by reason of subparagraph (1) of this paragraph for all taxable years beginning with the taxable year during which it is notified by the Commissioner that it has engaged in a prohibited transaction. The Commissioner shall publish such notice in the FEDERAL REGISTER on the day on which he so notifies such foreign private foundation. In the case of an act or failure to act (without regard to section 4942(e)) which would result in a penalty under section 6684(1) if the foreign private foundation were a domestic private foundation, before giving notice under this subdivision the Commissioner shall warn such foreign private foundation that such act or failure to act may be treated as a prohibited transaction. However, such act or failure to act will not be treated as a prohibited transaction if it is corrected (within the meaning of chapter 42 and the regulations thereunder) within 90 days after the making of such warning.

(ii)(*a*) Any foreign private foundation described in paragraph (b) of this section which is denied exemption from taxation under section 501(a) by reason of subparagraph (1) of this paragraph may, with respect to the second taxable year following the taxable year in which notice is given under subdivision (i) of this subparagraph (or any taxable year subsequent to such second taxable year), file a request for exemption from taxation under section 501(a) on Form 1023. In addition to the information generally required of an organization requesting exemption as an organization described in section 501(a), a request under this subdivision must contain or have attached to it a written declaration, made under the penalties of perjury, by a principal officer of such organization authorized to make such declaration, that the organization will not knowingly again engage in a prohibited transaction.

(*b*) If the Commissioner is satisfied that such organization will not knowingly again engage in a prohibited transaction and that the organization has satisfied all other requirements under section 501, the organization will be so notified in writing. In such case the organization shall not, with respect to taxable years beginning with the taxable year with respect to which a request under this subdivision is filed, be denied exemption from taxation under section 501(a) by reason of any prohibited transaction which was engaged in before the date on which notice was given under subdivision (i) of this subparagraph. Section 4948(c) provides that an organization denied exemption under such section will not be exempt from taxation under section 501(a) for the taxable year in which notice of loss of exemption is given and at least one immediately subsequent taxable year.

(d) *Disallowance of certain charitable deductions.*—No gift, bequest, legacy, devise, or transfer shall be allowed as a deduction under section 170, 545(b)(2), 556(b)(2), 642(c), 2055, 2106(a)(2), or 2522, if made:

(1) To a foreign private foundation described in paragraph (b) of this section after the date on which the Commissioner publishes notice under paragraph (c)(3)(i) of this section that he has notified such organization that it has engaged in a prohibited transaction, and

(2) In a taxable year of such organization for which it is not exempt from taxation under section 501(a) by reason of paragraph (c)(1) of this section.

For purposes of this paragraph, a bequest, legacy, devise, or transfer under section 2055 or 2106(a)(2) shall be treated as made on the date of death of the decedent. For example, assume that an individual gives money to a foreign private foundation described in section 4948(b) in January 1970, January 1971, and January 1972. The organization has a taxable year from June 1 through May 31. In February 1970, notice is duly published that the foreign organization has engaged in a prohibited transaction. In December 1970, the organiza-

tion duly submits a request for exemption under paragraph (c)(3)(ii)(a) of this section which is granted for the taxable year ending May 31, 1972. The January 1970 gift is allowable as a deduction under section 2522 since it was made before the notice (February 1970). The January 1971 gift is not allowable as a deduction because the taxable year ending May 31, 1971, is a nonexempt year (the first taxable year subsequent to the taxable year of the notice) for the foreign organization. The January 1972 gift is allowable as a deduction under section 2522 because the taxable year ending May 31, 1972, is an exempt year for the organization. [Reg. § 53.4948-1.]

☐ [T.D. 7218, 11-9-72.]

# BLACK LUNG BENEFIT TRUSTS

**[Reg. § 53.4951-1]**

**§ 53.4951-1. Black lung trusts—taxes on self-dealing.**—(a) *In general.*—Section 4951 contains provisions that correspond to provisions of section 4941 (relating to taxes on foundation self-dealing) and section 4946 (relating to definitions and special rules). Regulations and rulings under these corresponding provisions apply to section 4951 where appropriate.

(b) *Transfer of property to trust.*—A transfer of personal property without consideration to a trust for which a deduction is allowable under section 192 does not constitute a sale or exchange for purposes of section 4951 unless the property is subject to a mortgage or similar lien within section 4951(d)(2)(A). The transfer to a trust of a note or other evidence of indebtedness constitutes an extension of credit to the obligor for purposes of section 4951(d)(1)(B).

(c) *Deposits.*—A time or demand deposit made with a bank or credit union that is a trustee or other disqualified person with respect to a trust constitutes a lending of money for purposes of section 4951(d)(1)(B) even though the deposit is of a kind generally authorized for investments by the trust.

(d) *Trustee.*—The term "trustee" as used in section 4951(e)(5)(B) includes any person having powers or responsibilities with respect to a trust similar to those of trustees.

(e) *Misallocation of insurance premium.*—Under section 501(c)(21)(A)(ii) and § 1.501(c)(21)-1(d), a trust may pay a portion of a premium for insurance which covers both black lung liabilities and other liabilities, so long as the requirements of section 501(c)(21)(A)(i)

concerning allocation of the total premium are met. However, if an insurance company misallocates the total premium in a manner which benefits a disqualified person, the amount of misallocation constitutes a use of trust assets for the benefit of the disqualified person within section 4951(d)(1)(D). For these purposes, it is irrelevant whether the combination of insurance is sold under one policy or more than one policy.

(f) *Effective date.*—Section 4951 applies with respect to acts that occur after December 31, 1977, in and for trust taxable years beginning after December 31, 1977. [Reg. § 53.4951-1.]

☐ [T.D. 7644, 9-6-79.]

**[Reg. § 53.4952-1]**

**§ 53.4952-1. Black lung trusts—taxes on taxable expenditures.**—(a) *In general.*—Section 4952 contains provisions that generally correspond to provisions of section 4945 (relating to taxes on taxable expenditures by private foundations) and section 4946 (relating to definitions and special rules). Regulations and rulings under these corresponding provisions apply to section 4952 where appropriate. See section 4952(e)(1) for the definition of "correction".

(b) *Unauthorized investments.*—The term "taxable expenditure" in section 4952(d) includes an investment that is not authorized under section 501(c)(21)(B)(ii).

(c) *Effective date.*—Section 4952 applies with respect to expenditures made after December 31, 1977, in and for trust taxable years beginning after December 31, 1977. [Reg. § 53.4952-1.]

☐ [T.D. 7644, 9-6-79.]

# TAXES ON POLITICAL EXPENDITURES

**[Reg. § 53.4955-1]**

**§ 53.4955-1. Tax on political expenditures.**—(a) *Relationship between section 4955 excise taxes and substantive standards for exemption under section 501(c)(3).*—The excise taxes imposed by section 4955 do not affect the substantive standards for tax exemption under section 501(c)(3). under which an organization is described in section 501(c)(3) only if it does not participate or intervene in any political campaign on behalf of any candidate for public office.

(b) *Imposition of initial taxes on organization managers.*—(1) *In general.*—The excise tax under section 4955(a)(2) on the agreement of any organization manager to the making of a political expenditure by a section 501(c)(3) organization is imposed only in cases where—

(i) A tax is imposed by section 4955(a)(1);

(ii) The organization manager knows that the expenditure to which the manager agrees is a political expenditure; and

(iii) The agreement is willful and is not due to reasonable cause.

(2) *Type of organization managers covered.*—(i) *In general.*—The tax under section 4955(a)(2) is imposed only on those organization managers who are authorized to approve, or to exercise discretion in recommending approval of, the making of the expenditure by the organization and on those organization managers who are members of a group (such as the organization's board of directors or trustees) which is so authorized.

(ii) *Officer.*—For purposes of section 4955(f)(2)(A), a person is an officer of an organization if—

(A) That person is specifically so designated under the certificate of incorporation, bylaws, or other constitutive documents of the foundation; or

(B) That person regularly exercises general authority to make administrative or policy decisions on behalf of the organization. Independent contractors, acting in a capacity as attorneys, ac-

countants, and investment managers and advisors, are not officers. With respect to any expenditure, any person described in this paragraph (b)(2)(ii)(B) who has authority merely to recommend particular administrative or policy decisions, but not to implement them without approval of a superior, is not an officer.

(iii) *Employee.*—For purposes of section 4955(f)(2)(B), an individual rendering services to an organization is an employee of the organization only if that individual is an employee within the meaning of section 3121(d)(2). With respect to any expenditure, an employee (other than an officer, director, or trustee of the organization) is described in section 4955(f)(2)(B) only if he or she has final authority or responsibility (either officially or effectively) with respect to such expenditure.

(3) *Type of agreement required.*—An organization manager agrees to the making of a political expenditure if the manager manifests approval of the expenditure which is sufficient to constitute an exercise of the organization manager's authority to approve, or to exercise discretion in recommending approval of, the making of the expenditure by the organization. The manifestation of approval need not be the final or decisive approval on behalf of the organization.

(4) Knowing—

(i) *General rule.*—For purposes of section 4955, an organization manager is considered to have agreed to an expenditure *knowing* that it is a political expenditure only if—

(A) The manager has actual knowledge of sufficient facts so that, based solely upon these facts, the expenditure would be a political expenditure;

(B) The manager is aware that such an expenditure under these circumstances may violate the provisions of federal tax law governing political expenditures; and

(C) The manager negligently fails to make reasonable attempts to ascertain whether the expenditure is a political expenditure, or the manager is aware that it is a political expenditure.

(ii) *Amplification of general rule.*—For purposes of section 4955, knowing does not mean having reason to know. However, evidence tending to show that an organization manager has reason to know of a particular fact or particular rule is relevant in determining whether the manager had actual knowledge of the fact or rule. Thus, for example, evidence tending to show that an organization manager has reason to know of sufficient facts so that, based solely upon those facts, an expenditure would be a political expenditure is relevant in determining whether the manager has actual knowledge of the facts.

(5) *Willful.*—An organization manager's agreement to a political expenditure is willful if it is voluntary, conscious, and intentional. No motive to avoid the restrictions of the law or the incurrence of any tax is necessary to make an agreement willful. However, an organization manager's agreement to a political expenditure is not willful if the manager does not know that it is a political expenditure.

(6) *Due to reasonable cause.*—An organization manager's actions are due to reasonable cause if the manager has exercised his or her responsibility on behalf of the organization with ordinary business care and prudence.

(7) *Advice of counsel.*—An organization manager's agreement to an expenditure is ordinarily not considered knowing or willful and is ordinarily considered due to reasonable cause if the manager, after full disclosure of the factual situation to legal counsel (including house counsel), relies on the advice of counsel expressed in a reasoned written legal opinion that an expenditure is not a political expenditure under section 4955 (or that expenditures conforming to certain guidelines are not political expenditures). For this purpose, a written legal opinion is considered reasoned even if it reaches a conclusion which is subsequently determined to be incorrect, so long as the opinion addresses itself to the facts and applicable law. A written legal opinion is not considered reasoned if it does nothing more than recite the facts and express a conclusion. However, the absence of advice of counsel with respect to an expenditure does not, by itself, give rise to any inference that an organization manager agreed to the making of the expenditure knowingly, willfully, or without reasonable cause.

(8) *Cross reference.*—For provisions relating to the burden of proof in cases involving the issue of whether an organization manager has knowingly agreed to the making of a political expenditure, see section 7454(b).

(c) Amplification of political expenditure definition

(1) *General rule.*—Any expenditure that would cause an organization that makes the expenditure to be classified as an action organization by reason of § 1.501(c)(3)-1(c)(3)(iii) of this chapter is a political expenditure within the meaning of section 4955(d)(1).

(2) *Other political expenditures.*—(i) For purposes of section 4955(d)(2), an organization is effectively controlled by a candidate or prospective candidate only if the individual has a continuing, substantial involvement in the day-to-day operations or management of the organization. An organization is not effectively controlled by a candidate or a prospective candidate merely because it is affiliated with the candidate, or merely because the candidate knows the directors, officers, or employees of the organization. The effectively controlled test is not met merely because the organization carries on its research, study, or other educational activities with respect to subject matter or issues in which the individual is interested or with which the individual is associated.

(ii) For purposes of section 4955(d)(2), a determination of whether the primary purpose of an organization is promoting the candidacy or prospective candidacy of an individual for public office is made on the basis of all the facts and circumstances. The factors to be considered include whether the surveys, studies, materials, etc. prepared by the organization are made available only to the candidate or are made available to the general public; and whether the organization pays for speeches and travel expenses for only one individual, or for speeches or travel expenses of several persons. The fact that a candidate or prospective candidate utilizes studies, papers, materials, etc., prepared by the organization (such as in a speech by the candidate) is not to be considered as a factor indicating that the organization has a purpose of promoting the candidacy or prospective candidacy of that individual where such studies, papers, materials, etc. are not made available only to that individual.

(iii) Expenditures for voter registration, voter turnout, or voter education constitute other expenses, treated as political expenditures by reason of section 4955(d)(2)(E), only if the expenditures violate the prohibition on political activity provided in section 501(c)(3).

(d) *Abatement, refund, or no assessment of initial tax.*—No initial (first-tier) tax will be imposed under section 4955(a), or the initial tax will be abated or refunded, if the organization or an organization manager establishes to the satisfaction of the IRS that—

(1) The political expenditure was not willful and flagrant; and

(2) The political expenditure was corrected.

(e) Correction.—(1) *Recovery of Expenditure.*—For purposes of section 4955(f)(3) and this section, correction of a political expenditure is accomplished by recovering part or all of the expenditure to the extent recovery is possible, and, where full recovery cannot be accomplished, by any additional corrective action which the Commissioner may prescribe. The organization making the political expenditure is not under any obligation to attempt to recover the expenditure by legal action if the action would in all probability not result in the satisfaction of execution on a judgment.

(2) *Establishing safeguards.*—Correction of a political expenditure must also involve the establishment of sufficient safeguards to prevent future political expenditures by the organization. The determination of whether safeguards are sufficient to prevent future political expenditures by the organization is made by the District Director.

(f) *Effective date.*—This section is effective December 5, 1995. [Reg. § 53.4955-1.]

☐ [*T.D.* 8628, 12-4-95.]

# EXCESS BENEFIT TRANSACTIONS

## [Reg. § 53.4958-0]

**§ 53.4958-0. Table of contents.**—This section lists the major captions contained in § § 53.4958-1 through 53.4958-8.

(2) Certain foreign organizations.

§53.4958-3 *Definition of disqualified person.*
(a) In general.
  (1) Scope of definition.
  (2) Transition rule for lookback period.
(b) Statutory categories of disqualified persons.
  (1) Family members.
  (2) Thirty-five percent controlled entities.
    (i) In general.
    (ii) Combined voting power.
    (iii) Constructive ownership rules.
      (A) Stockholdings.
      (B) Profits or beneficial interest.
(c) Persons having substantial influence.
  (1) Voting members of the governing body.
  (2) Presidents, chief executive officers, or chief operating officers.
  (3) Treasurers and chief financial officers.
  (4) Persons with a material financial interest in a provider-sponsored organization.
(d) Persons deemed not to have substantial influence.
  (1) Tax-exempt organizations described in section 501(c)(3).
  (2) Certain section 501(c)(4) organizations.
  (3) Employees receiving economic benefits of less than a specified amount in a taxable year.
(e) Facts and circumstances govern in all other cases.
  (1) In general.
  (2) Facts and circumstances tending to show substantial influence.
  (3) Facts and circumstances tending to show no substantial influence.
(f) Affiliated organizations.
(g) Examples.

§53.4958-4 *Excess benefit transaction.*
(a) Definition of excess benefit transaction.
  (1) In general.
  (2) Economic benefit provided indirectly.
    (i) In general.
    (ii) Through a controlled entity.
      (A) In general.
      (B) Definition of control.
        *(1)* In general.
        *(2)* Constructive ownership.
    (iii) Through an intermediary.
    (iv) Examples.
  (3) Exception for fixed payments made pursuant to an initial contract.
    (i) In general.
    (ii) Fixed payment.
      (A) In general.
      (B) Special rules.
    (iii) Initial contract.
    (iv) Substantial performance required.
    (v) Treatment as a new contract.
    (vi) Evaluation of non-fixed payments.
    (vii) Examples.
  (4) Certain economic benefits disregarded for purposes of section 4958.
    (i) Nontaxable fringe benefits.
    (ii) Expense reimbursement payments pursuant to accountable plans.
    (iii) Certain economic benefits provided to a volunteer for the organization.
    (iv) Certain economic benefits provided to a member of, or donor to, the organization.
    (v) Economic benefits provided to a charitable beneficiary.
    (vi) Certain economic benefits provided to a governmental unit.
  (5) Exception for certain payments made pursuant to an exemption granted by the Department of Labor under ERISA.
(b) Valuation standards.
  (1) In general.
    (i) Fair market value of property.
    (ii) Reasonable compensation.
      (A) In general.
      (B) Items included in determining the value of compensation for purposes of determining reasonableness under section 4958.
      (C) Inclusion in compensation for reasonableness determination does not govern income tax treatment.

(2) Timing of reasonableness determination.
  (i) In general.
  (ii) Treatment as a new contract.
  (iii) Examples.
(c) Establishing intent to treat economic benefit as consideration for the performance of services.
  (1) In general.
  (2) Nontaxable benefits.
  (3) Contemporaneous substantiation.
    (i) Reporting of benefit.
      (A) In general.
      (B) Failure to report due to reasonable cause.
    (ii) Other written contemporaneous evidence.
  (4) Examples.

§53.4958-5 *Transaction in which the amount of the economic benefit is determined in whole or in part by the revenues of one or more activities of the organization.*—[Reserved]

§53.4958-6 *Rebuttable presumption that a transaction is not an excess benefit transaction.*
(a) In general.
(b) Rebutting the presumption.
(c) Requirements for invoking rebuttable presumption.
  (1) Approval by an authorized body.
    (i) In general.
    (ii) Individuals not included on authorized body.
    (iii) Absence of conflict of interest.
  (2) Appropriate data as to comparability.
    (i) In general.
    (ii) Special rule for compensation paid by small organizations.
    (iii) Application of special rule for small organizations.
    (iv) Examples.
  (3) Documentation.
(d) No presumption with respect to non-fixed payments until amounts are determined.
  (1) In general.
  (2) Special rule for certain non-fixed payments subject to a cap.
(e) No inference from absence of presumption.
(f) Period of reliance on rebuttable presumption.

§53.4958-7 *Correction.*
(a) In general.
(b) Form of correction.
  (1) Cash or cash equivalents.
  (2) Anti-abuse rule.
  (3) Special rule relating to nonqualified deferred compensation.
  (4) Return of specific property.
    (i) In general.
    (ii) Payment not equal to correction amount.
    (iii) Disqualified person may not participate in decision.
(c) Correction amount.
(d) Correction where contract has been partially performed.
(e) Correction in the case of an applicable tax-exempt organization that has ceased to exist, or is no longer tax-exempt.
  (1) In general.
  (2) Section 501(c)(3) organizations.
  (3) Section 501(c)(4) organizations.
(f) Examples.

§53.4958-8 *Special rules.*
(a) Substantive requirements for exemption still apply.
(b) Interaction between section 4958 and section 7611 rules for church tax inquiries and examinations.
(c) Other substantiation requirements.
[Reg. §53.4958-0.]
☐ [*T.D.* 8978, 1-22-2002.]

### [Reg. §53.4958-1]

**§53.4958-1. Taxes on excess benefit transactions.**—(a) *In general.*—Section 4958 imposes excise taxes on each excess benefit transaction (as defined in section 4958(c) and §53.4958-4) between an applicable tax-exempt organization (as defined in section 4958(e) and §53.4958-2) and a disqualified person (as defined in section 4958(f)(1) and §53.4958-3). A disqualified person who receives an excess benefit from an excess benefit transaction is liable for payment of a section 4958(a)(1) excise tax equal to 25 percent of the excess benefit. If an initial tax is imposed by section 4958(a)(1) on an excess benefit transaction and the transaction is not corrected (as defined in section

4958(f)(6) and §53.4958-7) within the taxable period (as defined in section 4958(f)(5) and paragraph (c)(2)(ii) of this section), then any disqualified person who received an excess benefit from the excess benefit transaction on which the initial tax was imposed is liable for an additional tax of 200 percent of the excess benefit. An organization manager (as defined in section 4958(f)(2) and paragraph (d) of this section) who participates in an excess benefit transaction, knowing that it was such a transaction, is liable for payment of a section 4958(a)(2) excise tax equal to 10 percent of the excess benefit, unless the participation was not willful and was due to reasonable cause. If an organization manager also receives an excess benefit from an excess benefit transaction, the manager may be liable for both taxes imposed by section 4958(a).

(b) *Excess benefit defined.*—An excess benefit is the amount by which the value of the economic benefit provided by an applicable tax-exempt organization directly or indirectly to or for the use of any disqualified person exceeds the value of the consideration (including the performance of services) received for providing such benefit.

(c) *Taxes paid by disqualified person.*—(1) *Initial tax.*—Section 4958(a)(1) imposes a tax equal to 25 percent of the excess benefit on each excess benefit transaction. The section 4958(a)(1) tax shall be paid by any disqualified person who received an excess benefit from that excess benefit transaction. With respect to any excess benefit transaction, if more than one disqualified person is liable for the tax imposed by section 4958(a)(1), all such persons are jointly and severally liable for that tax.

(2) *Additional tax on disqualified person.*—(i) *In general.*—Section 4958(b) imposes a tax equal to 200 percent of the excess benefit in any case in which section 4958(a)(1) imposes a 25-percent tax on an excess benefit transaction and the transaction is not corrected (as defined in section 4958(f)(6) and §53.4958-7) within the taxable period (as defined in section 4958(f)(5) and paragraph (c)(2)(ii) of this section). If a disqualified person makes a payment of less than the full correction amount under the rules of §53.4958-7, the 200-percent tax is imposed only on the unpaid portion of the correction amount (as described in §53.4958-7(c)). The tax imposed by section 4958(b) is payable by any disqualified person who received an excess benefit from the excess benefit transaction on which the initial tax was imposed by section 4958(a)(1). With respect to any excess benefit transaction, if more than one disqualified person is liable for the tax imposed by section 4958(b), all such persons are jointly and severally liable for that tax.

(ii) *Taxable period.*—*Taxable period* means, with respect to any excess benefit transaction, the period beginning with the date on which the transaction occurs and ending on the earlier of—

(A) The date of mailing a notice of deficiency under section 6212 with respect to the section 4958(a)(1) tax; or

(B) The date on which the tax imposed by section 4958(a)(1) is assessed.

(iii) *Abatement if correction during the correction period.*—For rules relating to abatement of taxes on excess benefit transactions that are corrected within the correction period, as defined in section 4963(e), see sections 4961(a), 4962(a), and the regulations thereunder. The abatement rules of section 4961 specifically provide for a 90-day correction period after the date of mailing a notice of deficiency under section 6212 with respect to the section 4958(b) 200-percent tax. If the excess benefit is corrected during that correction period, the 200-percent tax imposed shall not be assessed, and if assessed the assessment shall be abated, and if collected shall be credited or refunded as an overpayment. For special rules relating to abatement of the 25-percent tax, see section 4962.

(d) *Tax paid by organization managers.*—(1) *In general.*—In any case in which section 4958(a)(1) imposes a tax, section 4958(a)(2) imposes a tax equal to 10 percent of the excess benefit on the participation of any organization manager who knowingly participated in the excess benefit transaction, unless such participation was not willful and was due to reasonable cause. Any organization manager who so participated in the excess benefit transaction must pay the tax.

(2) *Organization manager defined.*—(i) *In general.*—An organization manager is, with respect to any applicable tax-exempt organization, any officer, director, or trustee of such organization, or any individual having powers or responsibilities similar to those of officers, directors, or trustees of the organization, regardless of title. A person is an officer of an organization if that person—

(A) Is specifically so designated under the certificate of incorporation, by-laws, or other constitutive documents of the organization; or

(B) Regularly exercises general authority to make administrative or policy decisions on behalf of the organization. A contractor who acts solely in a capacity as an attorney, accountant, or investment manager or advisor, is not an officer. For purposes of this

paragraph (d)(2)(i)(B), any person who has authority merely to recommend particular administrative or policy decisions, but not to implement them without approval of a superior, is not an officer.

(ii) *Special rule for certain committee members.*—An individual who is not an officer, director, or trustee, yet serves on a committee of the governing body of an applicable tax-exempt organization (or as a designee of the governing body described in §53.4958-6(c)(1)) that is attempting to invoke the rebuttable presumption of reasonableness described in §53.4958-6 based on the committee's (or designee's) actions, is an organization manager for purposes of the tax imposed by section 4958(a)(2).

(3) *Participation.*—For purposes of section 4958(a)(2) and this paragraph (d), participation includes silence or inaction on the part of an organization manager where the manager is under a duty to speak or act, as well as any affirmative action by such manager. An organization manager is not considered to have participated in an excess benefit transaction, however, where the manager has opposed the transaction in a manner consistent with the fulfillment of the manager's responsibilities to the applicable tax-exempt organization.

(4) *Knowing.*—(i) *In general.*—For purposes of section 4958(a)(2) and this paragraph (d), a manager participates in a transaction knowingly only if the person—

(A) Has actual knowledge of sufficient facts so that, based solely upon those facts, such transaction would be an excess benefit transaction;

(B) Is aware that such a transaction under these circumstances may violate the provisions of Federal tax law governing excess benefit transactions; and

(C) Negligently fails to make reasonable attempts to ascertain whether the transaction is an excess benefit transaction, or the manager is in fact aware that it is such a transaction.

(ii) *Amplification of general rule.*—*Knowing* does not mean having reason to know. However, evidence tending to show that a manager has reason to know of a particular fact or particular rule is relevant in determining whether the manager had actual knowledge of such a fact or rule. Thus, for example, evidence tending to show that a manager has reason to know of sufficient facts so that, based solely upon such facts, a transaction would be an excess benefit transaction is relevant in determining whether the manager has actual knowledge of such facts.

(iii) *Reliance on professional advice.*—An organization manager's participation in a transaction is ordinarily not considered knowing within the meaning of section 4958(a)(2), even though the transaction is subsequently held to be an excess benefit transaction, to the extent that, after full disclosure of the factual situation to an appropriate professional, the organization manager relies on a reasoned written opinion of that professional with respect to elements of the transaction within the professional's expertise. For purposes of section 4958(a)(2) and this paragraph (d), a written opinion is reasoned even though it reaches a conclusion that is subsequently determined to be incorrect so long as the opinion addresses itself to the facts and the applicable standards. However, a written opinion is not reasoned if it does nothing more than recite the facts and express a conclusion. The absence of a written opinion of an appropriate professional with respect to a transaction shall not, by itself, however, give rise to any inference that an organization manager participated in the transaction knowingly. For purposes of this paragraph, appropriate professionals on whose written opinion an organization manager may rely, are limited to—

(A) Legal counsel, including in-house counsel;

(B) Certified public accountants or accounting firms with expertise regarding the relevant tax law matters; and

(C) Independent valuation experts who—

(1) Hold themselves out to the public as appraisers or compensation consultants;

(2) Perform the relevant valuations on a regular basis;

(3) Are qualified to make valuations of the type of property or services involved; and

(4) Include in the written opinion a certification that the requirements of paragraphs (d)(4)(iii)(C)(1) through (3) of this section are met.

(iv) *Satisfaction of rebuttable presumption of reasonableness.*—An organization manager's participation in a transaction is ordinarily not considered knowing within the meaning of section 4958(a)(2), even though the transaction is subsequently held to be an excess benefit transaction, if the appropriate authorized body has met the requirements of §53.4958-6(a) with respect to the transaction.

(5) *Willful.*—For purposes of section 4958(a)(2) and this paragraph (d), participation by an organization manager is willful if it is voluntary, conscious, and intentional. No motive to avoid the restric-

tions of the law or the incurrence of any tax is necessary to make the participation willful. However, participation by an organization manager is not willful if the manager does not know that the transaction in which the manager is participating is an excess benefit transaction.

(6) *Due to reasonable cause.*—An organization manager's participation is due to reasonable cause if the manager has exercised responsibility on behalf of the organization with ordinary business care and prudence.

(7) *Limits on liability for management.*—The maximum aggregate amount of tax collectible under section 4958(a)(2) and this paragraph (d) from organization managers with respect to any one excess benefit transaction is $10,000.

(8) *Joint and several liability.*—In any case where more than one person is liable for a tax imposed by section 4958(a)(2), all such persons shall be jointly and severally liable for the taxes imposed under section 4958(a)(2) with respect to that excess benefit transaction.

(9) *Burden of proof.*—For provisions relating to the burden of proof in cases involving the issue of whether an organization manager has knowingly participated in an excess benefit transaction, see section 7454(b) and §301.7454-2 of this chapter. In these cases, the Commissioner bears the burden of proof.

(e) *Date of occurrence.*—(1) *In general.*—Except as otherwise provided, an excess benefit transaction occurs on the date on which the disqualified person receives the economic benefit for Federal income tax purposes. When a single contractual arrangement provides for a series of compensation or other payments to (or for the use of) a disqualified person over the course of the disqualified person's taxable year (or part of a taxable year), any excess benefit transaction with respect to these aggregate payments is deemed to occur on the last day of the taxable year (or if the payments continue for part of the year, the date of the last payment in the series).

(2) *Special rules.*—In the case of benefits provided pursuant to a qualified pension, profit-sharing, or stock bonus plan, the transaction occurs on the date the benefit is vested. In the case of a transfer of property that is subject to a substantial risk of forfeiture or in the case of rights to future compensation or property (including benefits under a nonqualified deferred compensation plan), the transaction occurs on the date the property, or the rights to future compensation or property, is not subject to a substantial risk of forfeiture. However, where the disqualified person elects to include an amount in gross income in the taxable year of transfer pursuant to section 83(b), the general rule of paragraph (e)(1) of this section applies to the property with respect to which the section 83(b) election is made. Any excess benefit transaction with respect to benefits under a deferred compensation plan which vest during any taxable year of the disqualified person is deemed to occur on the last day of such taxable year. For the rules governing the timing of the reasonableness determination for deferred, contingent, and certain other noncash compensation, see §53.4958-4(b)(2).

(3) *Statute of limitations rules.*—See sections 6501(e)(3) and (l) and the regulations thereunder for statute of limitations rules as they apply to section 4958 excise taxes.

(f) *Effective date for imposition of taxes.*—(1) *In general.*—The section 4958 taxes imposed on excess benefit transactions or on participation in excess benefit transactions apply to transactions occurring on or after September 14, 1995.

(2) *Existing binding contracts.*—The section 4958 taxes do not apply to any transaction occurring pursuant to a written contract that was binding on September 13, 1995, and at all times thereafter before the transaction occurs. A written binding contract that is terminable or subject to cancellation by the applicable tax-exempt organization without the disqualified person's consent (including as the result of a breach of contract by the disqualified person) and without substantial penalty to the organization, is no longer treated as a binding contract as of the earliest date that any such termination or cancellation, if made, would be effective. If a binding written contract is materially changed, it is treated as a new contract entered into as of the date the material change is effective. A material change includes an extension or renewal of the contract (other than an extension or renewal that results from the person contracting with the applicable tax-exempt organization unilaterally exercising an option expressly granted by the contract), or a more than incidental change to any payment under the contract. [Reg. §53.4958-1.]

☐ [*T.D.* 8978, 1-22-2002.]

**[Reg. §53.4958-2]**

**§53.4958-2. Definition of applicable tax-exempt organization.**—(a) *Organizations described in section 501(c)(3) or (4) and exempt from tax under section 501(a).*—(1) *In general.*—An applicable tax-exempt organization is any organization that, without regard to any excess benefit, would be described in section 501(c)(3) or (4) and exempt from tax under section 501(a). An applicable tax-exempt organization also includes any organization that was described in section 501(c)(3) or (4) and was exempt from tax under section 501(a) at any time during a five-year period ending on the date of an excess benefit transaction (the lookback period).

(2) *Exceptions from definition of applicable tax-exempt organization.*—(i) *Private foundation.*—A private foundation as defined in section 509(a) is not an applicable tax-exempt organization for section 4958 purposes.

(ii) *Governmental unit or affiliate.*—A governmental unit or an affiliate of a governmental unit is not an applicable tax-exempt organization for section 4958 purposes if it is—

(A) Exempt from (or not subject to) taxation without regard to section 501(a); or

(B) Relieved from filing an annual return pursuant to the authority of §1.6033-2(g)(6).

(3) *Organizations described in section 501(c)(3).*—An organization is described in section 501(c)(3) for purposes of section 4958 only if the organization—

(i) Provides the notice described in section 508; or

(ii) Is described in section 501(c)(3) and specifically is excluded from the requirements of section 508 by that section.

(4) *Organizations described in section 501(c)(4).*—An organization is described in section 501(c)(4) for purposes of section 4958 only if the organization—

(i) Has applied for and received recognition from the Internal Revenue Service as an organization described in section 501(c)(4); or

(ii) Has filed an application for recognition under section 501(c)(4) with the Internal Revenue Service, has filed an annual information return as a section 501(c)(4) organization under the Internal Revenue Code or regulations promulgated thereunder, or has otherwise held itself out as being described in section 501(c)(4) and exempt from tax under section 501(a).

(5) *Effect of non-recognition or revocation of exempt status.*—An organization is not described in paragraph (a)(3) or (4) of this section during any period covered by a final determination or adjudication that the organization is not exempt from tax under section 501(a) as an organization described in section 501(c)(3) or (4), so long as that determination or adjudication is not based upon participation in inurement or one or more excess benefit transactions. However, the organization may be an applicable tax-exempt organization for that period as a result of the five-year lookback period described in paragraph (a)(1) of this section.

(6) *Examples.*—The following examples illustrate the principles of this section, which defines an applicable tax-exempt organization for purposes of section 4958:

*Example 1.* O is a nonprofit corporation formed under state law. O filed its application for recognition of exemption under section 501(c)(3) within the time prescribed under section 508(a). In its application, O described its plans for purchasing property from some of its directors at prices that would exceed fair market value. After reviewing the application, the IRS determined that because of the proposed property purchase transactions, O failed to establish that it met the requirements for an organization described in section 501(c)(3). Accordingly, the IRS denied O's application. While O's application was pending, O engaged in the purchase transactions described in its application at prices that exceeded the fair market values of the properties. Although these transactions would constitute excess benefit transactions under section 4958, because the IRS never recognized O as an organization described in section 501(c)(3), O was never an applicable tax-exempt organization under section 4958. Therefore, these transactions are not subject to the excise taxes provided in section 4958.

*Example 2.* O is a nonprofit corporation formed under state law. O files its application for recognition of exemption under section 501(c)(3) within the time prescribed under section 508(a). The IRS issues a favorable determination letter in Year 1 that recognizes O as an organization described in section 501(c)(3). Subsequently, in Year 5 of O's operations, O engages in certain transactions that constitute excess benefit transactions under section 4958 and violate the proscription against inurement under section 501(c)(3) and §1.501(c)(3)-1(c)(2). The IRS examines the Form 990, "Return of Organization Exempt From Income Tax", that O filed for Year 5. After considering all the relevant facts and circumstances in accordance with §1.501(c)(3)-1(f), the IRS concludes that O is no longer described in section 501(c)(3) effective in Year 5. The IRS does not examine the Forms 990 that O filed for its first four years of operations and, accordingly, does not revoke O's exempt status for those years. Although O's tax-exempt status is revoked effective in Year 5, under the *lookback* rules in paragraph (a)(1) of this section and §53.4958-3(a)(1) of this chapter, during the five-year period prior to the excess benefit transactions that occurred in Year 5, O was an applicable tax-exempt organization and O's directors were disqualified persons as to O. Therefore, the transactions between O and its directors during Year 5 are subject to the applicable excise taxes provided in section 4958.

(b) *Special rules.*—(1) *Transition rule for lookback period.*—In the case of any excess benefit transaction occurring before September 14, 2000, the lookback period described in paragraph (a)(1) of this section begins on September 14, 1995, and ends on the date of the transaction.

(2) *Certain foreign organizations.*—A foreign organization, recognized by the Internal Revenue Service or by treaty, that receives substantially all of its support (other than gross investment income) from sources outside of the United States is not an organization described in section 501(c)(3) or (4) for purposes of section 4958. [Reg. §53.4958-2.]

☐ [*T.D. 8978, 1-22-2002 and T.D. 9390, 3-27-08.*]

### [Reg. §53.4958-3]

**§53.4958-3. Definition of disqualified person.**—(a) *In general.*—(1) *Scope of definition.*—Section 4958(f)(1) defines *disqualified person*, with respect to any transaction, as any person who was in a position to exercise substantial influence over the affairs of an applicable tax-exempt organization at any time during the five-year period ending on the date of the transaction (the lookback period). Paragraph (b) of this section describes persons who are defined to be disqualified persons under the statute, including certain family members of an individual in a position to exercise substantial influence, and certain 35-percent controlled entities. Paragraph (c) of this section describes persons in a position to exercise substantial influence over the affairs of an applicable tax-exempt organization by virtue of their powers and responsibilities or certain interests they hold. Paragraph (d) of this section describes persons deemed not to be in a position to exercise substantial influence. Whether any person who is not described in paragraph (b), (c) or (d) of this section is a disqualified person with respect to a transaction for purposes of section 4958 is based on all relevant facts and circumstances, as described in paragraph (e) of this section. Paragraph (f) of this section describes special rules for affiliated organizations. Examples in paragraph (g) of this section illustrate these categories of persons.

(2) *Transition rule for lookback period.*—In the case of any excess benefit transaction occurring before September 14, 2000, the lookback period described in paragraph (a)(1) of this section begins on September 14, 1995, and ends on the date of the transaction.

(b) *Statutory categories of disqualified persons.*—(1) *Family members.*—A person is a disqualified person with respect to any transaction with an applicable tax-exempt organization if the person is a member of the family of a person who is a disqualified person described in paragraph (a) of this section (other than as a result of this paragraph) with respect to any transaction with the same organization. For purposes of the following sentence, a legally adopted child of an individual is treated as a child of such individual by blood. A person's family is limited to—

(i) Spouse;

(ii) Brothers or sisters (by whole or half blood);

(iii) Spouses of brothers or sisters (by whole or half blood);

(iv) Ancestors;

(v) Children;

(vi) Grandchildren;

(vii) Great grandchildren; and

(viii) Spouses of children, grandchildren, and great grandchildren.

(2) *Thirty-five percent controlled entities.*—(i) *In general.*—A person is a disqualified person with respect to any transaction with an applicable tax-exempt organization if the person is a 35-percent controlled entity. A 35-percent controlled entity is—

(A) A corporation in which persons described in this section (except in paragraphs (b)(2) and (d) of this section) own more than 35 percent of the combined voting power;

(B) A partnership in which persons described in this section (except in paragraphs (b)(2) and (d) of this section) own more than 35 percent of the profits interest; or

(C) A trust or estate in which persons described in this section (except in paragraphs (b)(2) and (d) of this section) own more than 35 percent of the beneficial interest.

(ii) *Combined voting power.*—For purposes of this paragraph (b)(2), combined voting power includes voting power represented by holdings of voting stock, direct or indirect, but does not include voting rights held only as a director, trustee, or other fiduciary.

(iii) *Constructive ownership rules.*—(A) *Stockholdings.*—For purposes of section 4958(f)(3) and this paragraph (b)(2), indirect stock-holdings are taken into account as under section 267(c), except that in applying section 267(c)(4), the family of an individual shall include the members of the family specified in section 4958(f)(4) and paragraph (b)(1) of this section.

(B) *Profits or beneficial interest.*—For purposes of section 4958(f)(3) and this paragraph (b)(2), the ownership of profits or beneficial interests shall be determined in accordance with the rules for constructive ownership of stock provided in section 267(c) (other than section 267(c)(3)), except that in applying section 267(c)(4), the family of an individual shall include the members of the family specified in section 4958(f)(4) and paragraph (b)(1) of this section.

(c) *Persons having substantial influence.*—A person who holds any of the following powers, responsibilities, or interests is in a position to exercise substantial influence over the affairs of an applicable tax-exempt organization:

(1) *Voting members of the governing body.*—This category includes any individual serving on the governing body of the organization who is entitled to vote on any matter over which the governing body has authority.

(2) *Presidents, chief executive officers, or chief operating officers.*—This category includes any person who, regardless of title, has ultimate responsibility for implementing the decisions of the governing body or for supervising the management, administration, or operation of the organization. A person who serves as president, chief executive officer, or chief operating officer has this ultimate responsibility unless the person demonstrates otherwise. If this ultimate responsibility resides with two or more individuals (e.g., co-presidents), who may exercise such responsibility in concert or individually, then each individual is in a position to exercise substantial influence over the affairs of the organization.

(3) *Treasurers and chief financial officers.*—This category includes any person who, regardless of title, has ultimate responsibility for managing the finances of the organization. A person who serves as treasurer or chief financial officer has this ultimate responsibility unless the person demonstrates otherwise. If this ultimate responsibility resides with two or more individuals who may exercise the responsibility in concert or individually, then each individual is in a position to exercise substantial influence over the affairs of the organization.

(4) *Persons with a material financial interest in a provider-sponsored organization.*—For purposes of section 4958, if a hospital that participates in a provider-sponsored organization (as defined in section 1855(e) of the Social Security Act, 42 U.S.C. 1395w-25) is an applicable tax-exempt organization, then any person with a material financial interest (within the meaning of section 501(o)) in the provider-sponsored organization has substantial influence with respect to the hospital.

(d) *Persons deemed not to have substantial influence.*—A person is deemed not to be in a position to exercise substantial influence over the affairs of an applicable tax-exempt organization if that person is described in one of the following categories:

(1) *Tax-exempt organizations described in section 501(c)(3).*—This category includes any organization described in section 501(c)(3) and exempt from tax under section 501(a).

(2) *Certain section 501(c)(4) organizations.*—Only with respect to an applicable tax-exempt organization described in section 501(c)(4) and §53.4958-2(a)(4), this category includes any other organization so described.

(3) *Employees receiving economic benefits of less than a specified amount in a taxable year.*—This category includes, for the taxable year in which benefits are provided, any full-or part-time employee of the applicable tax-exempt organization who—

(i) Receives economic benefits, directly or indirectly from the organization, of less than the amount referenced for a highly compensated employee in section 414(q)(1)(B)(i);

(ii) Is not described in paragraph (b) or (c) of this section with respect to the organization; and

(iii) Is not a substantial contributor to the organization within the meaning of section 507(d)(2)(A), taking into account only contributions received by the organization during its current taxable year and the four preceding taxable years.

(e) *Facts and circumstances govern in all other cases.*—(1) *In general.*— Whether a person who is not described in paragraph (b), (c) or (d) of this section is a disqualified person depends upon all relevant facts and circumstances.

(2) *Facts and circumstances tending to show substantial influence.*— Facts and circumstances tending to show that a person has substantial influence over the affairs of an organization include, but are not limited to, the following—

(i) The person founded the organization;

(ii) The person is a substantial contributor to the organization (within the meaning of section 507(d)(2)(A)), taking into account only contributions received by the organization during its current taxable year and the four preceding taxable years;

(iii) The person's compensation is primarily based on revenues derived from activities of the organization, or of a particular department or function of the organization, that the person controls;

(iv) The person has or shares authority to control or determine a substantial portion of the organization's capital expenditures, operating budget, or compensation for employees;

(v) The person manages a discrete segment or activity of the organization that represents a substantial portion of the activities, assets, income, or expenses of the organization, as compared to the organization as a whole;

(vi) The person owns a controlling interest (measured by either vote or value) in a corporation, partnership, or trust that is a disqualified person; or

(vii) The person is a non-stock organization controlled, directly or indirectly, by one or more disqualified persons.

(3) *Facts and circumstances tending to show no substantial influence.*—Facts and circumstances tending to show that a person does not have substantial influence over the affairs of an organization include, but are not limited to, the following—

(i) The person has taken a bona fide vow of poverty as an employee, agent, or on behalf, of a religious organization;

(ii) The person is a contractor (such as an attorney, accountant, or investment manager or advisor) whose sole relationship to the organization is providing professional advice (without having decision-making authority) with respect to transactions from which the contractor will not economically benefit either directly or indirectly (aside from customary fees received for the professional advice rendered);

(iii) The direct supervisor of the individual is not a disqualified person;

(iv) The person does not participate in any management decisions affecting the organization as a whole or a discrete segment or activity of the organization that represents a substantial portion of the activities, assets, income, or expenses of the organization, as compared to the organization as a whole; or

(v) Any preferential treatment a person receives based on the size of that person's contribution is also offered to all other donors making a comparable contribution as part of a solicitation intended to attract a substantial number of contributions.

(f) *Affiliated organizations.*—In the case of multiple organizations affiliated by common control or governing documents, the determination of whether a person does or does not have substantial influence shall be made separately for each applicable tax-exempt organization. A person may be a disqualified person with respect to transactions with more than one applicable tax-exempt organization.

(g) *Examples.*—The following examples illustrate the principles of this section. A finding that a person is a disqualified person in the following examples does not indicate that an excess benefit transaction has occurred. If a person is a disqualified person, the rules of section 4958(c) and §53.4958-4 apply to determine whether an excess benefit transaction has occurred. The examples are as follows:

*Example 1.* N, an artist by profession, works part-time at R, a local museum. In the first taxable year in which R employs N, R pays N a salary and provides no additional benefits to N except for free admission to the museum, a benefit R provides to all of its employees and volunteers. The total economic benefits N receives from R during the taxable year are less than the amount referenced for a highly compensated employee in section 414(q)(1)(B)(i). The part-time job constitutes N's only relationship with R. N is not related to any other disqualified person with respect to R. N is deemed not to be in a position to exercise substantial influence over the affairs of R. Therefore, N is not a disqualified person with respect to R in that year.

*Example 2.* The facts are the same as in *Example 1*, except that in addition to the salary that R pays N for N's services during the

taxable year, R also purchases one of N's paintings for $x. The total of N's salary plus $x exceeds the amount referenced for highly compensated employees in section 414(q)(1)(B)(i). Consequently, whether N is in a position to exercise substantial influence over the affairs of R for that taxable year depends upon all of the relevant facts and circumstances.

*Example 3.* Q is a member of K, a section 501(c)(3) organization with a broad-based public membership. Members of K are entitled to vote only with respect to the annual election of directors and the approval of major organizational transactions such as a merger or dissolution. Q is not related to any other disqualified person of K. Q has no other relationship to K besides being a member of K and occasionally making modest donations to K. Whether Q is a disqualified person is determined by all relevant facts and circumstances. Q's voting rights, which are the same as granted to all members of K, do not place Q in a position to exercise substantial influence over K. Under these facts and circumstances, Q is not a disqualified person with respect K.

*Example 4.* E is the headmaster of Z, a school that is an applicable tax-exempt organization for purposes of section 4958. E reports to Z's board of trustees and has ultimate responsibility for supervising Z's day-to-day operations. For example, E can hire faculty members and staff, make changes to the school's curriculum and discipline students without specific board approval. Because E has ultimate responsibility for supervising the operation of Z, E is in a position to exercise substantial influence over the affairs of Z. Therefore, E is a disqualified person with respect to Z.

*Example 5.* Y is an applicable tax-exempt organization for purposes of section 4958 that decides to use bingo games as a method of generating revenue. Y enters into a contract with B, a company that operates bingo games. Under the contract, B manages the promotion and operation of the bingo activity, provides all necessary staff, equipment, and services, and pays Y *q* percent of the revenue from this activity. B retains the balance of the proceeds. Y provides no goods or services in connection with the bingo operation other than the use of its hall for the bingo games. The annual gross revenue earned from the bingo games represents more than half of Y's total annual revenue. B's compensation is primarily based on revenues from an activity B controls. B also manages a discrete activity of Y that represents a substantial portion of Y's income compared to the organization as a whole. Under these facts and circumstances, B is in a position to exercise substantial influence over the affairs of Y. Therefore, B is a disqualified person with respect to Y.

*Example 6.* The facts are the same as in *Example 5*, with the additional fact that P owns a majority of the stock of B and is actively involved in managing B. Because P owns a controlling interest (measured by either vote or value) in and actively manages B, P is also in a position to exercise substantial influence over the affairs of Y. Therefore, under these facts and circumstances, P is a disqualified person with respect to Y.

*Example 7.* A, an applicable tax-exempt organization for purposes of section 4958, owns and operates one acute care hospital. B, a for-profit corporation, owns and operates a number of hospitals. A and B form C, a limited liability company. In exchange for proportional ownership interests, A contributes its hospital, and B contributes other assets, to C. All of A's assets then consist of its membership interest in C. A continues to be operated for exempt purposes based almost exclusively on the activities it conducts through C. C enters into a management agreement with a management company, M, to provide day to day management services to C. Subject to supervision by C's board, M is given broad discretion to manage C's day to day operation and has ultimate responsibility for supervising the management of the hospital. Because M has ultimate responsibility for supervising the management of the hospital operated by C, A's ownership interest in C is its primary asset, and C's activities form the basis for A's continued exemption as an organization described in section 501(c)(3), M is in a position to exercise substantial influence over the affairs of A. Therefore, M is a disqualified person with respect to A.

*Example 8.* T is a large university and an applicable tax-exempt organization for purposes of section 4958. L is the dean of the College of Law of T, a substantial source of revenue for T, including contributions from alumni and foundations. L is not related to any other disqualified person of T. L does not serve on T's governing body or have ultimate responsibility for managing the university as whole. However, as dean of the College of Law, L plays a key role in faculty hiring and determines a substantial portion of the capital expenditures and operating budget of the College of Law. L's compensation is greater than the amount referenced for a highly compensated employee in section 414(q)(1)(B)(i) in the year benefits are provided. L's management of a discrete segment of T that represents a substantial portion of the income of T (as compared to T as a whole) places L in a position to exercise substantial influence over the affairs of T. Under these facts and circumstances L is a disqualified person with respect to T.

*Example 9.* S chairs a small academic department in the College of Arts and Sciences of the same university T described in *Example 8.* S is not related to any other disqualified person of T. S does not serve on T's governing body or as an officer of T. As department chair, S supervises faculty in the department, approves the course curriculum, and oversees the operating budget for the department. S's compensation is greater than the amount referenced for a highly compensated employee in section 414(q)(1)(B)(i) in the year benefits are provided. Even though S manages the department, that department does not represent a substantial portion of T's activities, assets, income, expenses, or operating budget. Therefore, S does not participate in any management decisions affecting either T as a whole, or a discrete segment or activity of T that represents a substantial portion of its activities, assets, income, or expenses. Under these facts and circumstances, S does not have substantial influence over the affairs of T, and therefore S is not a disqualified person with respect to T.

*Example 10.* U is a large acute-care hospital that is an applicable tax-exempt organization for purposes of section 4958. U employs X as a radiologist. X gives instructions to staff with respect to the radiology work X conducts, but X does not supervise other U employees or manage any substantial part of U's operations. X's compensation is primarily in the form of a fixed salary. In addition, X is eligible to receive an incentive award based on revenues of the radiology department. X's compensation is greater than the amount referenced for a highly compensated employee in section 414(q)(1)(B)(i) in the year benefits are provided. X is not related to any other disqualified person of U. X does not serve on U's governing body or as an officer of U. Although U participates in a provider-sponsored organization (as defined in section 1855(e) of the Social Security Act), X does not have a material financial interest in that organization. X does not receive compensation primarily based on revenues derived from activities of U that X controls. X does not participate in any management decisions affecting either U as a whole or a discrete segment of U that represents a substantial portion of its activities, assets, income, or expenses. Under these facts and circumstances, X does not have substantial influence over the affairs of U, and therefore X is not a disqualified person with respect to U.

*Example 11.* W is a cardiologist and head of the cardiology department of the same hospital U described in *Example 10.* The cardiology department is a major source of patients admitted to U and consequently represents a substantial portion of U's income, as compared to U as a whole. W does not serve on U's governing board or as an officer of U. W does not have a material financial interest in the provider-sponsored organization (as defined in section 1855(e) of the Social Security Act) in which U participates. W receives a salary and retirement and welfare benefits fixed by a three-year renewable employment contract with U. W's compensation is greater than the amount referenced for a highly compensated employee in section 414(q)(1)(B)(i) in the year benefits are provided. As department head, W manages the cardiology department and has authority to allocate the budget for that department, which includes authority to distribute incentive bonuses among cardiologists according to criteria that W has authority to set. W's management of a discrete segment of U that represents a substantial portion of its income and activities (as compared to U as a whole) places W in a position to exercise substantial influence over the affairs of U. Under these facts and circumstances, W is a disqualified person with respect to U.

*Example 12.* M is a museum that is an applicable tax-exempt organization for purposes of section 4958. D provides accounting services and tax advice to M as a contractor in return for a fee. D has no other relationship with M and is not related to any disqualified person of M. D does not provide professional advice with respect to any transaction from which D might economically benefit either directly or indirectly (aside from fees received for the professional advice rendered). Because D's sole relationship to M is providing professional advice (without having decision-making authority) with respect to transactions from which D will not economically benefit either directly or indirectly (aside from customary fees received for the professional advice rendered), under these facts and circumstances, D is not a disqualified person with respect to M.

*Example 13.* F is a repertory theater company that is an applicable tax-exempt organization for purposes of section 4958. F holds a fund-raising campaign to pay for the construction of a new theater. J is a regular subscriber to F's productions who has made modest gifts to F in the past. J has no relationship to F other than as a subscriber and contributor. F solicits contributions as part of a broad public campaign intended to attract a large number of donors, including a substantial number of donors making large gifts. In its solicitations for contributions, F promises to invite all contributors giving $z or more to a special opening production and party held at the new theater. These contributors are also given a special number to call in F's office to reserve tickets for performances, make ticket exchanges, and make other special arrangements for their convenience. J makes a contribution of $z to F, which makes J a substantial contributor within the meaning of section 507(d)(2)(A), taking into account only contributions received by F during its current and the four preceding taxable years. J receives the benefits described in F's solicitation. Because F offers the same benefit to all donors of $z or more, the preferential treatment that J receives does not indicate that J is in a position to exercise substantial influence over the affairs of the organization. Therefore, under these facts and circumstances, J is not a disqualified person with respect to F.
[Reg. § 53.4958-3.]

☐ [*T.D. 8978*, 1-22-2002.]

**[Reg. § 53.4958-4]**

**§ 53.4958-4. Excess benefit transaction.**—(a) *Definition of excess benefit transaction.*—(1) *In general.*—An *excess benefit transaction* means any transaction in which an economic benefit is provided by an applicable tax-exempt organization directly or indirectly to or for the use of any disqualified person, and the value of the economic benefit provided exceeds the value of the consideration(including the performance of services) received for providing the benefit. Subject to the limitations of paragraph (c) of this section (relating to the treatment of economic benefits as compensation for the performance of services), to determine whether an excess benefit transaction has occurred, all consideration and benefits (except disregarded benefits described in paragraph (a)(4) of this section) exchanged between a disqualified person and the applicable tax-exempt organization and all entities the organization controls(within the meaning of paragraph (a)(2)(ii)(B) of this section) are taken into account. For example, in determining the reasonableness of compensation that is paid (or vests, or is no longer subject to a substantial risk of forfeiture) in one year, services performed in prior years may be taken into account. The rules of this section apply to all transactions with disqualified persons, regardless of whether the amount of the benefit provided is determined, in whole or in part, by the revenues of one or more activities of the organization. For rules regarding valuation standards, see paragraph (b) of this section. For the requirement that an applicable tax-exempt organization clearly indicate its intent to treat a benefit as compensation for services when paid, see paragraph (c) of this section.

(2) *Economic benefit provided indirectly.*—(i) *In general.*—A transaction that would be an excess benefit transaction if the applicable tax-exempt organization engaged in it directly with a disqualified person is likewise an excess benefit transaction when it is accomplished indirectly. An applicable tax-exempt organization may provide an excess benefit indirectly to a disqualified person through a controlled entity or through an intermediary, as described in paragraphs (a)(2)(ii) and (iii) of this section, respectively.

(ii) *Through a controlled entity.*—(A) *In general.*—An applicable tax-exempt organization may provide an excess benefit indirectly through the use of one or more entities it controls. For purposes of section 4958, economic benefits provided by a controlled entity will be treated as provided by the applicable tax-exempt organization.

(B) *Definition of control.*—(1) *In general.*—For purposes of this paragraph, *control* by an applicable tax-exempt organization means—

(*i*) In the case of a stock corporation, ownership (by vote or value) of more than 50 percent of the stock in such corporation;

(*ii*) In the case of a partnership, ownership of more than 50 percent of the profits interests or capital interests in the partnership;

(*iii*) In the case of a nonstock organization (i.e., an entity in which no person holds a proprietary interest), that at least 50 percent of the directors or trustees of the organization are either representatives (including trustees, directors, agents, or employees) of, or directly or indirectly controlled by, an applicable tax-exempt organization; or

(*iv*) In the case of any other entity, ownership of more than 50 percent of the beneficial interest in the entity.

(2) *Constructive ownership.*—Section 318 (relating to constructive ownership of stock) shall apply for purposes of determining ownership of stock in a corporation. Similar principles shall apply for purposes of determining ownership of interests in any other entity.

(iii) *Through an intermediary.*—An applicable tax-exempt organization may provide an excess benefit indirectly through an intermediary. An intermediary is any person (including an individual or a taxable or tax-exempt entity) who participates in a transaction with one or more disqualified persons of an applicable tax-exempt organization. For purposes of section 4958, economic benefits provided by an intermediary will be treated as provided by the applicable tax-exempt organization when—

(A) An applicable tax-exempt organization provides an economic benefit to an intermediary; and

(B) In connection with the receipt of the benefit by the intermediary—

(1) There is evidence of an oral or written agreement or understanding that the intermediary will provide economic benefits to or for the use of a disqualified person; or

(2) The intermediary provides economic benefits to or for the use of a disqualified person without a significant business purpose or exempt purpose of its own.

(iv) *Examples.*—The following examples illustrate when economic benefits are provided indirectly under the rules of this paragraph (a)(2):

*Example 1.* K is an applicable tax-exempt organization for purposes of section 4958. L is a wholly-owned taxable subsidiary of K. J is employed by K, and is a disqualified person with respect to K. K pays J an annual salary of $ *12m*, and reports that amount as compensation during calendar year 2001. Although J only performed services for K for nine months of 2001, J performed equivalent services for L during the remaining three months of 2001. Taking into account all of the economic benefits K provided to J, and all of the services J performed for K and L, $12m does not exceed the fair market value of the services J performed for K and L during 2001. Therefore, under these facts, K does not provide an excess benefit to J directly or indirectly.

*Example 2.* F is an applicable tax-exempt organization for purposes of section 4958. D is an entity controlled by F within the meaning of paragraph (a)(2)(ii)(B) of this section. T is the chief executive officer (CEO) of F. As CEO, T is responsible for overseeing the activities of F. T's duties as CEO make him a disqualified person with respect to F. T's compensation package with F represents the maximum reasonable compensation for T's services as CEO. Thus, any additional economic benefits that F provides to T without T providing additional consideration constitute an excess benefit. D contracts with T to provide enumerated consulting services to D. However, the contract does not require T to perform any additional services for D that T is not already obligated to perform as F's chief executive officer. Therefore, any payment to T pursuant to the consulting contract with D represents an indirect excess benefit that F provides through a controlled entity, even if F, D, or T treats the additional payment to T as compensation.

*Example 3.* P is an applicable tax-exempt organization for purposes of section 4958. S is a taxable entity controlled by P within the meaning of paragraph (a)(2)(ii)(B) of this section. V is the chief executive officer of S, for which S pays V $*w* in salary and benefits. V also serves as a voting member of P's governing body. Consequently, V is a disqualified person with respect to P. P provides V with $*x* representing compensation for the services V provides P as a member of its governing body. Although $*x* represents reasonable compensation for the services V provides directly to P as a member of its governing body, the total compensation of $*w* + $*x* exceeds reasonable compensation for the services V provides to P and S collectively. Therefore, the portion of total compensation that exceeds reasonable compensation is an excess benefit provided to V.

*Example 4.* G is an applicable tax-exempt organization for section 4958 purposes. F is a disqualified person who was last employed by G in a position of substantial influence three years ago. H is an entity engaged in scientific research and is unrelated to either F or G. G makes a grant to H to fund a research position. H subsequently advertises for qualified candidates for the research position. F is among several highly qualified candidates who apply for the research position. H hires F. There was no evidence of an oral or written agreement or understanding with G that H will use G's grant to provide economic benefits to or for the use of F. Although G provided economic benefits to H, and in connection with the receipt of such benefits, H will provide economic benefits to or for the use of F, H acted with a significant business purpose or exempt purpose of its own. Under these facts, G did not provide an economic benefit to F indirectly through the use of an intermediary.

(3) *Exception for fixed payments made pursuant to an initial contract.*—(i) *In general.*—Except as provided in paragraph (a)(3)(iv) of this section, section 4958 does not apply to any fixed payment made to a person pursuant to an initial contract.

(ii) *Fixed payment.*—(A) *In general.*—For purposes of paragraph (a)(3)(i) of this section, *fixed payment* means an amount of cash or other property specified in the contract, or determined by a fixed formula specified in the contract, which is to be paid or transferred in exchange for the provision of specified services or property. A fixed formula may incorporate an amount that depends upon future specified events or contingencies, provided that no person exercises discretion when calculating the amount of a payment or deciding whether to make a payment (such as a bonus). A specified event or contingency may include the amount of revenues generated ·by (or other objective measure of) one or more activities of the applicable tax-exempt organization. A fixed payment does not include any

amount paid to a person under a reimbursement (or similar) arrangement where discretion is exercised by any person with respect to the amount of expenses incurred or reimbursed.

(B) *Special rules.*—Amounts payable pursuant to a qualified pension, profit-sharing, or stock bonus plan under section 401(a), or pursuant to an employee benefit program that is subject to and satisfies coverage and nondiscrimination rules under the Internal Revenue Code (e.g., sections 127 and 137), other than nondiscrimination rules under section 9802, are treated as fixed payments for purposes of this section, regardless of the applicable tax-exempt organization's discretion with respect to the plan or program. The fact that a person contracting with an applicable tax-exempt organization is expressly granted the choice whether to accept or reject any economic benefit is disregarded in determining whether the benefit constitutes a fixed payment for purposes of this paragraph.

(iii) *Initial contract.*—For purposes of paragraph (a)(3)(i) of this section, *initial contract* means a binding written contract between an applicable tax-exempt organization and a person who was not a disqualified person within the meaning of section 4958(f)(1) and § 53.4958-3 immediately prior to entering into the contract.

(iv) *Substantial performance required.*—Paragraph (a)(3)(i) of this section does not apply to any fixed payment made pursuant to the initial contract during any taxable year of the person contracting with the applicable tax-exempt organization if the person fails to perform substantially the person's obligations under the initial contract during that year.

(v) *Treatment as a new contract.*—A written binding contract that provides that the contract is terminable or subject to cancellation by the applicable tax-exempt organization (other than as a result of a lack of substantial performance by the disqualified person, as described in paragraph (a)(3)(iv) of this section) without the other party's consent and without substantial penalty to the organization is treated as a new contract as of the earliest date that any such termination or cancellation, if made, would be effective. Additionally, if the parties make a material change to a contract, it is treated as a new contract as of the date the material change is effective. A material change includes an extension or renewal of the contract (other than an extension or renewal that results from the person contracting with the applicable tax-exempt organization unilaterally exercising an option expressly granted by the contract), or a more than incidental change to any amount payable under the contract. The new contract is tested under paragraph (a)(3)(iii) of this section to determine whether it is an initial contract for purposes of this section.

(vi) *Evaluation of non-fixed payments.*—Any payment that is not a fixed payment (within the meaning of paragraph (a)(3)(ii) of this section) is evaluated to determine whether it constitutes an excess benefit transaction under section 4958. In making this determination, all payments and consideration exchanged between the parties are taken into account, including any fixed payments made pursuant to an initial contract with respect to which section 4958 does not apply.

(vii) *Examples.*—The following examples illustrate the rules governing fixed payments made pursuant to an initial contract. Unless otherwise stated, assume that the person contracting with the applicable tax-exempt organization has performed substantially the person's obligations under the contract with respect to the payment. The examples are as follows:

*Example 1.* T is an applicable tax-exempt organization for purposes of section 4958. On January 1, 2002, T hires S as its chief financial officer by entering into a five-year written employment contract with S. S was not a disqualified person within the meaning of section 4958(f)(1) and § 53.4958-3 immediately prior to entering into the January 1, 2002, contract (initial contract). S's duties and responsibilities under the contract make S a disqualified person with respect to T (see § 53.4958-3(c)(3)). Under the initial contract, T agrees to pay S an annual salary of $200,000, payable in monthly installments. The contract provides that, beginning in 2003, S's annual salary will be adjusted by the increase in the Consumer Price Index (CPI) for the prior year. Section 4958 does not apply because S's compensation under the contract is a fixed payment pursuant to an initial contract within the meaning of paragraph (a)(3) of this section. Thus, for section 4958 purposes, it is unnecessary to evaluate whether any portion of the compensation paid to S pursuant to the initial contract is an excess benefit transaction.

*Example 2.* The facts are the same as in *Example 1*, except that the initial contract provides that, in addition to a base salary of $200,000, T may pay S an annual performance-based bonus. The contract provides that T's governing body will determine the amount of the annual bonus as of the end of each year during the term of the contract, based on the board's evaluation of S's performance, but the bonus cannot exceed $100,000 per year. Unlike the base salary portion of S's compensation, the bonus portion of S's compensation is not a fixed payment pursuant to an initial contract, because the governing body has discretion over the amount, if any, of the bonus payment. Section 4958 does not apply to payment of the $200,000 base salary (as adjusted for inflation), because it is a fixed payment pursuant to an initial contract within the meaning of paragraph (a)(3) of this section. By contrast, the annual bonuses that may be paid to S under the initial contract are not protected by the initial contract exception. Therefore, each bonus payment will be evaluated under section 4958, taking into account all payments and consideration exchanged between the parties.

*Example 3.* The facts are the same as in *Example 1*, except that in 2003, T changes its payroll system, such that T makes biweekly, rather than monthly, salary payments to its employees. Beginning in 2003, T also grants its employees an additional two days of paid vacation each year. Neither change is a material change to S's initial contract within the meaning of paragraph (a)(3)(v) of this section. Therefore, section 4958 does not apply to the base salary payments to S due to the initial contract exception.

*Example 4.* The facts are the same as in *Example 1*, except that on January 1, 2003, S becomes the chief executive officer of T and a new chief financial officer is hired. At the same time, T's board of directors approves an increase in S's annual base salary from $200,000 to $240,000, effective on that day. These changes in S's employment relationship constitute material changes of the initial contract within the meaning of paragraph (a)(3)(v) of this section. As a result, S is treated as entering into a new contract with T on January 1, 2003, at which time S is a disqualified person within the meaning of section 4958(f)(1) and § 53.4958-3. T's payments to S made pursuant to the new contract will be evaluated under section 4958, taking into account all payments and consideration exchanged between the parties.

*Example 5.* J is a performing arts organization and an applicable tax-exempt organization for purposes of section 4958. J hires W to become the chief executive officer of J. W was not a disqualified person within the meaning of section 4958(f)(1) and § 53.4958-3 immediately prior to entering into the employment contract with J. As a result of this employment contract, W's duties and responsibilities make W a disqualified person with respect to J (see § 53.4958-3(c)(2)). Under the contract, J will pay W $x (a specified amount) plus a bonus equal to 2 percent of the total season subscription sales that exceed $100z. The $x base salary is a fixed payment pursuant to an initial contract within the meaning of paragraph (a)(3) of this section. The bonus payment is also a fixed payment pursuant to an initial contract within the meaning of paragraph (a)(3) of this section, because no person exercises discretion when calculating the amount of the bonus payment or deciding whether the bonus will be paid. Therefore, section 4958 does not apply to any of J's payments to W pursuant to the employment contract due to the initial contract exception.

*Example 6.* Hospital B is an applicable tax-exempt organization for purposes of section 4958. Hospital B hires E as its chief operating officer. E was not a disqualified person within the meaning of section 4958(f)(1) and § 53.4958-3 immediately prior to entering into the employment contract with Hospital B. As a result of this employment contract, E's duties and responsibilities make E a disqualified person with respect to Hospital B (see § 53.4958-3(c)(2)). E's initial employment contract provides that E will have authority to enter into hospital management arrangements on behalf of Hospital B. In E's personal capacity, E owns more than 35 percent of the combined voting power of Company X. Consequently, at the time E becomes a disqualified person with respect to B, Company X also becomes a disqualified person with respect to B (see § 53.4958-3(b)(2)(i)(A)). E, acting on behalf of Hospital B as chief operating officer, enters into a contract with Company X under which Company X will provide billing and collection services to Hospital B. The initial contract exception of paragraph (a)(3)(i) of this section does not apply to the billing and collection services contract, because at the time that this contractual arrangement was entered into, Company X was a disqualified person with respect to Hospital B. Although E's employment contract (which is an initial contract) authorizes E to enter into hospital management arrangements on behalf of Hospital B, the payments made to Company X are not made pursuant to E's employment contract, but rather are made by Hospital B pursuant to a separate contractual arrangement with Company X. Therefore, even if payments made to Company X under the billing and collection services contract are fixed payments (within the meaning of paragraph (a)(3)(ii) of this section), section 4958 nonetheless applies to payments made by Hospital B to Company X because the billing and collection services contract itself does not constitute an initial contract under paragraph (a)(3)(iii) of this section. Accordingly, all payments made to Company X under the billing and collection services contract will be evaluated under section 4958.

*Example 7.* Hospital C, an applicable tax-exempt organization, enters into a contract with Company Y, under which Company Y will provide a wide range of hospital management services to Hospital C. Upon entering into this contractual arrangement, Company Y becomes a disqualified person with respect to Hospital C. The contract provides that Hospital C will pay Company Y a management fee of $x$ percent of adjusted gross revenue (i.e., gross revenue increased by the cost of charity care provided to indigents) annually for a five-year period. The management services contract specifies the cost accounting system and the standards for *indigents* to be used in calculating the cost of charity care. The cost accounting system objectively defines the direct and indirect costs of all health care goods and services provided as charity care. Because Company Y was not a disqualified person with respect to Hospital C immediately before entering into the management services contract, that contract is an initial contract within the meaning of paragraph (a)(3)(iii) of this section. The annual management fee paid to Company Y is determined by a fixed formula specified in the contract, and is therefore a fixed payment within the meaning of paragraph (a)(3)(ii) of this section. Accordingly, section 4958 does not apply to the annual management fee due to the initial contract exception.

*Example 8.* The facts are the same as in *Example 7*, except that the management services contract also provides that Hospital C will reimburse Company Y on a monthly basis for certain expenses incurred by Company Y that are attributable to management services provided to Hospital C (e.g., legal fees and travel expenses). Although the management fee itself is a fixed payment not subject to section 4958, the reimbursement payments that Hospital C makes to Company Y for the various expenses covered by the contract are not fixed payments within the meaning of paragraph (a)(3)(ii) of this section, because Company Y exercises discretion with respect to the amount of expenses incurred. Therefore, any reimbursement payments that Hospital C pays pursuant to the contract will be evaluated under section 4958.

*Example 9.* X, an applicable tax-exempt organization for purposes of section 4958, hires C to conduct scientific research. On January 1, 2003, C enters into a three-year written employment contract with X (initial contract). Under the terms of the contract, C is required to work full-time at X's laboratory for a fixed annual salary of $90,000. Immediately prior to entering into the employment contract, C was not a disqualified person within the meaning of section 4958(f)(1) and § 53.4958-3, nor did C become a disqualified person pursuant to the initial contract. However, two years after joining X, C marries D, who is the child of X's president. As D's spouse, C is a disqualified person within the meaning of section 4958(f)(1) and § 53.4958-3 with respect to X. Nonetheless, section 4958 does not apply to X's salary payments to C due to the initial contract exception.

*Example 10.* The facts are the same as in *Example 9*, except that the initial contract included a below-market loan provision under which C has the unilateral right to borrow up to a specified dollar amount from X at a specified interest rate for a specified term. After C's marriage to D, C borrows money from X to purchase a home under the terms of the initial contract. Section 4958 does not apply to X's loan to C due to the initial contract exception.

*Example 11.* The facts are the same as in *Example 9*, except that after C's marriage to D, C works only sporadically at the laboratory, and performs no other services for X. Notwithstanding that X fails to perform substantially C's obligations under the initial contract, X does not exercise its right to terminate the initial contract for nonperformance and continues to pay full salary to C. Pursuant to paragraph (a)(3)(iv) of this section, the initial contract exception does not apply to any payments made pursuant to the initial contract during any taxable year of C in which C fails to perform substantially C's obligations under the initial contract.

(4) *Certain economic benefits disregarded for purposes of section 4958.*—The following economic benefits are disregarded for purposes of section 4958—

(i) *Nontaxable fringe benefits.*—An economic benefit that is excluded from income under section 132, except any liability insurance premium, payment, or reimbursement that must be taken into account under paragraph (b)(1)(ii)(B)(2) of this section;

(ii) *Expense reimbursement payments pursuant to accountable plans.*—Amounts paid under reimbursement arrangements that meet the requirements of § 1.62-2(c) of this chapter;

(iii) *Certain economic benefits provided to a volunteer for the organization.*—An economic benefit provided to a volunteer for the organization if the benefit is provided to the general public in exchange for a membership fee or contribution of $75 or less per year;

(iv) *Certain economic benefits provided to a member of, or donor to, the organization.*—An economic benefit provided to a member of an organization solely on account of the payment of a membership fee, or to a donor solely on account of a contribution for which a deduction is allowable under section 170 (charitable contribution), regardless of whether the donor is eligible to claim the deduction, if—

(A) Any non-disqualified person paying a membership fee or making a charitable contribution above a specified amount to the organization is given the option of receiving substantially the same economic benefit; and

(B) The disqualified person and a significant number of non-disqualified persons make a payment or charitable contribution of at least the specified amount;

(v) *Economic benefits provided to a charitable beneficiary.*—An economic benefit provided to a person solely because the person is a member of a charitable class that the applicable tax-exempt organization intends to benefit as part of the accomplishment of the organization's exempt purpose; and

(vi) *Certain economic benefits provided to a governmental unit.*— Any transfer of an economic benefit to or for the use of a governmental unit defined in section 170(c)(1), if the transfer is for exclusively public purposes.

(5) *Exception for certain payments made pursuant to an exemption granted by the Department of Labor under ERISA.*—Section 4958 does not apply to any payment made pursuant to, and in accordance with, a final individual prohibited transaction exemption issued by the Department of Labor under section 408(a) of the Employee Retirement Income Security Act of 1974 (88 Stat. 854) (ERISA) with respect to a transaction involving a plan (as defined in section 3(3) of ERISA) that is an applicable tax exempt organization.

(b) *Valuation standards.*—(1) *In general.*—This section provides rules for determining the value of economic benefits for purposes of section 4958.

(i) *Fair market value of property.*—The value of property, including the right to use property, for purposes of section 4958 is the fair market value (i.e., the price at which property or the right to use property would change hands between a willing buyer and a willing seller, neither being under any compulsion to buy, sell or transfer property or the right to use property, and both having reasonable knowledge of relevant facts).

(ii) *Reasonable compensation.*—(A) *In general.*—The value of services is the amount that would ordinarily be paid for like services by like enterprises (whether taxable or tax-exempt) under like circumstances (i.e., reasonable compensation). Section 162 standards apply in determining reasonableness of compensation, taking into account the aggregate benefits (other than any benefits specifically disregarded under paragraph (a)(4) of this section) provided to a person and the rate at which any deferred compensation accrues. The fact that a compensation arrangement is subject to a cap is a relevant factor in determining the reasonableness of compensation. The fact that a State or local legislative or agency body or court has authorized or approved a particular compensation package paid to a disqualified person is not determinative of the reasonableness of compensation for purposes of section 4958.

(B) *Items included in determining the value of compensation for purposes of determining reasonableness under section 4958.*—Except for economic benefits that are disregarded for purposes of section 4958 under paragraph (a)(4) of this section, compensation for purposes of determining reasonableness under section 4958 includes all economic benefits provided by an applicable tax-exempt organization in exchange for the performance of services. These benefits include, but are not limited to—

(1) All forms of cash and noncash compensation, including salary, fees, bonuses, severance payments, and deferred and noncash compensation described in § 53.4958-1(e)(2);

(2) Unless excludable from income as a *de minimis* fringe benefit pursuant to section 132(a)(4), the payment of liability insurance premiums for, or the payment or reimbursement by the organization of—

(i) Any penalty, tax, or expense of correction owed under section 4958;

(ii) Any expense not reasonably incurred by the person in connection with a civil judicial or civil administrative proceeding arising out of the person's performance of services on behalf of the applicable tax-exempt organization; or

(iii) Any expense resulting from an act or failure to act with respect to which the person has acted willfully and without reasonable cause; and

(3) All other compensatory benefits, whether or not included in gross income for income tax purposes, including payments to welfare benefit plans, such as plans providing medical, dental, life insurance, severance pay, and disability benefits, and both taxable and nontaxable fringe benefits (other than fringe benefits described in section 132), including expense allowances or reimbursements

(other than expense reimbursements pursuant to an accountable plan that meets the requirements of § 1.62-2(c)), and the economic benefit of a below-market loan (within the meaning of section 7872(e)(1)). (For this purpose, the economic benefit of a below-market loan is the amount deemed transferred to the disqualified person under section 7872(a) or (b), regardless of whether section 7872 otherwise applies to the loan).

(C) *Inclusion in compensation for reasonableness determination does not govern income tax treatment.*—The determination of whether any item listed in paragraph (b)(1)(ii)(B) of this section is included in the disqualified person's gross income for income tax purposes is made on the basis of the provisions of chapter 1 of Subtitle A of the Internal Revenue Code, without regard to whether the item is taken into account for purposes of determining reasonableness of compensation under section 4958.

(2) *Timing of reasonableness determination.*—(i) *In general.*—The facts and circumstances to be taken into consideration in determining reasonableness of a fixed payment (within the meaning of paragraph (a)(3)(ii) of this section) are those existing on the date the parties enter into the contract pursuant to which the payment is made. However, in the event of substantial non-performance, reasonableness is determined based on all facts and circumstances, up to and including circumstances as of the date of payment. In the case of any payment that is not a fixed payment under a contract, reasonableness is determined based on all facts and circumstances, up to and including circumstances as of the date of payment. In no event shall circumstances existing at the date when the payment is questioned be considered in making a determination of the reasonableness of the payment. These general timing rules also apply to property subject to a substantial risk of forfeiture. Therefore, if the property subject to a substantial risk of forfeiture satisfies the definition of fixed payment (within the meaning of paragraph (a)(3)(ii) of this section), reasonableness is determined at the time the parties enter into the contract providing for the transfer of the property. If the property is not a fixed payment, then reasonableness is determined based on all facts and circumstances up to and including circumstances as of the date of payment.

(ii) *Treatment as a new contract.*—For purposes of paragraph (b)(2)(i) of this section, a written binding contract that provides that the contract is terminable or subject to cancellation by the applicable tax-exempt organization without the other party's consent and without substantial penalty to the organization is treated as a new contract as of the earliest date that any such termination or cancellation, if made, would be effective. Additionally, if the parties make a material change to a contract (within the meaning of paragraph (a)(3)(v) of this section), it is treated as a new contract as of the date the material change is effective.

(iii) *Examples.*—The following examples illustrate the timing of the reasonableness determination under the rules of this paragraph (b)(2):

*Example 1.* G is an applicable tax-exempt organization for purposes of section 4958. H is an employee of G and a disqualified person with respect to G. H's new multi-year employment contract provides for payment of a salary and provision of specific benefits pursuant to a qualified pension plan under section 401(a) and an accident and health plan that meets the requirements of section 105(h)(2). The contract provides that H's salary will be adjusted by the increase in the Consumer Price Index (CPI) for the prior year. The contributions G makes to the qualified pension plan are equal to the maximum amount G is permitted to contribute under the rules applicable to qualified plans. Under these facts, all items comprising H's total compensation are treated as fixed payments within the meaning of paragraph (a)(3)(ii) of this section. Therefore, the reasonableness of H's compensation is determined based on the circumstances existing at the time G and H enter into the employment contract.

*Example 2.* The facts are the same as in *Example 1*, except that the multi-year employment contract provides, in addition, that G will transfer title to a car to H under the condition that if H fails to complete *x* years of service with G, title to the car will be forfeited back to G. All relevant information about the type of car to be provided (including the make, model, and year) is included in the contract. Although ultimate vesting of title to the car is contingent on H continuing to work for G for *x* years, the amount of property to be vested (i.e., the type of car) is specified in the contract, and no person exercises discretion regarding the type of property or whether H will retain title to the property at the time of vesting. Under these facts, the car is a fixed payment within the meaning of paragraph (a)(3)(ii) of this section. Therefore, the reasonableness of H's compensation, including the value of the car, is determined based on the circumstances existing at the time G and H enter into the employment contract.

*Example 3.* N is an applicable tax-exempt organization for purposes of section 4958. On January 2, N's governing body enters into a new one-year employment contract with K, its executive director, who is a disqualified person with respect to N. The contract provides that K will receive a specified amount of salary, contributions to a qualified pension plan under section 401(a), and other benefits pursuant to a section 125 cafeteria plan. In addition, the contract provides that N's governing body may, in its discretion, declare a bonus to be paid to K at any time during the year covered by the contract. K's salary and other specified benefits constitute fixed payments within the meaning of paragraph (a)(3)(ii) of this section. Therefore, the reasonableness of those economic benefits is determined on the date when the contract was made. However, because the bonus payment is not a fixed payment within the meaning of paragraph (a)(3)(ii) of this section, the determination of whether any bonus awarded to N is reasonable must be made based on all facts and circumstances (including all payments and consideration exchanged between the parties), up to and including circumstances as of the date of payment of the bonus.

(c) *Establishing intent to treat economic benefit as consideration for the performance of services.*—(1) *In general.*—An economic benefit is not treated as consideration for the performance of services unless the organization providing the benefit clearly indicates its intent to treat the benefit as compensation when the benefit is paid. Except as provided in paragraph (c)(2) of this section, an applicable tax-exempt organization (or entity controlled by an applicable tax-exempt organization, within the meaning of paragraph (a)(2)(ii)(B) of this section) is treated as clearly indicating its intent to provide an economic benefit as compensation for services only if the organization provides written substantiation that is contemporaneous with the transfer of the economic benefit at issue. If an organization fails to provide this contemporaneous substantiation, any services provided by the disqualified person will not be treated as provided in consideration for the economic benefit for purposes of determining the reasonableness of the transaction. In no event shall an economic benefit that a disqualified person obtains by theft or fraud be treated as consideration for the performance of services.

(2) *Nontaxable benefits.*—For purposes of section 4958(c)(1)(A) and this section, an applicable tax-exempt organization is not required to indicate its intent to provide an economic benefit as compensation for services if the economic benefit is excluded from the disqualified person's gross income for income tax purposes on the basis of the provisions of chapter 1 of Subtitle A of the Internal Revenue Code. Examples of these benefits include, but are not limited to, employer-provided health benefits and contributions to a qualified pension, profit-sharing, or stock bonus plan under section 401(a), and benefits described in sections 127 and 137. However, except for economic benefits that are disregarded for purposes of section 4958 under paragraph (a)(4) of this section, all compensatory benefits (regardless of the Federal income tax treatment) provided by an organization in exchange for the performance of services are taken into account in determining the reasonableness of a person's compensation for purposes of section 4958.

(3) *Contemporaneous substantiation.*—(i) *Reporting of benefit.*—(A) *In general.*—An applicable tax-exempt organization provides contemporaneous written substantiation of its intent to provide an economic benefit as compensation if—

(1) The organization reports the economic benefit as compensation on an original Federal tax information return with respect to the payment (e.g., Form W-2, "Wage and Tax Statement", or Form 1099, "Miscellaneous Income") or with respect to the organization (e.g., Form 990, "Return of Organization Exempt From Income Tax"), or on an amended Federal tax information return filed prior to the commencement of an Internal Revenue Service examination of the applicable tax-exempt organization or the disqualified person for the taxable year in which the transaction occurred (as determined under § 53.4958-1(e)); or

(2) The recipient disqualified person reports the benefit as income on the person's original Federal tax return (e.g., Form 1040, "U.S. Individual Income Tax Return"), or on the person's amended Federal tax return filed prior to the earlier of the following dates—

(i) Commencement of an Internal Revenue Service examination described in paragraph (c)(3)(i)(A)(1) of this section; or

(ii) The first documentation in writing by the Internal Revenue Service of a potential excess benefit transaction involving either the applicable tax-exempt organization or the disqualified person.

(B) *Failure to report due to reasonable cause.*—If an applicable tax-exempt organization's failure to report an economic benefit as required under the Internal Revenue Code is due to reasonable cause (within the meaning of § 301.6724-1 of this chapter), then the organi-

zation will be treated as having clearly indicated its intent to provide an economic benefit as compensation for services. To show that its failure to report an economic benefit that should have been reported on an information return was due to reasonable cause, an applicable tax-exempt organization must establish that there were significant mitigating factors with respect to its failure to report (as described in § 301.6724-1(b) of this chapter), or the failure arose from events beyond the organization's control (as described in § 301.6724-1(c) of this chapter), and that the organization acted in a responsible manner both before and after the failure occurred (as described in § 301.6724-1(d) of this chapter).

(ii) *Other written contemporaneous evidence.*—In addition, other written contemporaneous evidence may be used to demonstrate that the appropriate decision-making body or an officer authorized to approve compensation approved a transfer as compensation for services in accordance with established procedures, including but not limited to—

(A) An approved written employment contract executed on or before the date of the transfer;

(B) Documentation satisfying the requirements of § 53.4958-6(a)(3) indicating that an authorized body approved the transfer as compensation for services on or before the date of the transfer; or

(C) Written evidence that was in existence on or before the due date of the applicable Federal tax return described in paragraph (c)(3)(i)(A)(1) or (2) of this section (including extensions but not amendments), of a reasonable belief by the applicable tax-exempt organization that a benefit was a nontaxable benefit as defined in paragraph (c)(2) of this section.

(4) *Examples.*—The following examples illustrate the requirement that an organization contemporaneously substantiate its intent to provide an economic benefit as compensation for services, as defined in paragraph (c) of this section:

*Example 1.* G is an applicable tax-exempt organization for purposes of section 4958. G hires an individual contractor, P, who is also the child of a disqualified person of G, to design a computer program for it. G executes a contract with P for that purpose in accordance with G's established procedures, and pays P $1,000 during the year pursuant to the contract. Before January 31 of the next year, G reports the full amount paid to P under the contract on a Form 1099 filed with the Internal Revenue Service. G will be treated as providing contemporaneous written substantiation of its intent to provide the $1,000 paid to P as compensation for the services P performed under the contract by virtue of either the Form 1099 filed with the Internal Revenue Service reporting the amount, or by virtue of the written contract executed between G and P.

*Example 2.* G is an applicable tax-exempt organization for purposes of section 4958. D is the chief operating officer of G, and a disqualified person with respect to G. D receives a bonus at the end of the year. G's accounting department determines that the bonus is to be reported on D's Form W-2. Due to events beyond G's control, the bonus is not reflected on D's Form W-2. As a result, D fails to report the bonus on D's individual income tax return. G acts to amend Forms W-2 affected as soon as G is made aware of the error during an Internal Revenue Service examination. G's failure to report the bonus on an information return issued to D arose from events beyond G's control, and G acted in a responsible manner both before and after the failure occurred. Thus, because G had reasonable cause (within the meaning § 301.6724-1 of this chapter) for failing to report D's bonus, G will be treated as providing contemporaneous written substantiation of its intent to provide the bonus as compensation for services when paid.

*Example 3.* H is an applicable tax-exempt organization and J is a disqualified person with respect to H. J's written employment agreement provides for a fixed salary of $y. J's duties include soliciting funds for various programs of H. H raises a large portion of its funds in a major metropolitan area. Accordingly, H maintains an apartment there in order to provide a place to entertain potential donors. H makes the apartment available exclusively to J to assist in the fundraising. J's written employment contract does not mention the use of the apartment. H obtains the written opinion of a benefits compensation expert that the rental value of the apartment is not includable in J's income by reason of section 119, based on the expectation that the apartment will be used for fundraising activities. Consequently, H does not report the rental value of the apartment on J's Form W-2, which otherwise correctly reports J's taxable compensation. J does not report the rental value of the apartment on J's individual Form 1040. Later, the Internal Revenue Service correctly determines that the requirements of section 119 were not satisfied. Because of the written expert opinion, H has written evidence of its reasonable belief that use of the apartment was a nontaxable benefit as defined in paragraph (c)(2) of this section. That evidence was in existence on or before the due date of the applicable Federal tax return. Therefore,

H has demonstrated its intent to treat the use of the apartment as compensation for services performed by J.

[Reg. § 53.4958-4.]

☐ [*T.D. 8978*, 1-22-2002 (*corrected* 3-18-2002).]

**[Reg. § 53.4958-5]**

**§ 53.4958-5. Transaction in which the amount of the economic benefit is determined in whole or in part by the revenues of one or more activities of the organization.—[Reserved]**

☐ [*T.D. 8978*, 1-22-2002.]

**[Reg. § 53.4958-6]**

**§ 53.4958-6. Rebuttable presumption that a transaction is not an excess benefit transaction.**—(a) *In general.*—Payments under a compensation arrangement are presumed to be reasonable, and a transfer of property, or the right to use property, is presumed to be at fair market value, if the following conditions are satisfied—

(1) The compensation arrangement or the terms of the property transfer are approved in advance by an authorized body of the applicable tax-exempt organization (or an entity controlled by the organization with the meaning of § 53.4958-4(a)(2)(ii)(B)) composed entirely of individuals who do not have a conflict of interest (within the meaning of paragraph (c)(1)(iii) of this section) with respect to the compensation arrangement or property transfer, as described in paragraph (c)(1) of this section;

(2) The authorized body obtained and relied upon appropriate data as to comparability prior to making its determination, as described in paragraph (c)(2) of this section; and

(3) The authorized body adequately documented the basis for its determination concurrently with making that determination, as described in paragraph (c)(3) of this section.

(b) *Rebutting the presumption.*—If the three requirements of paragraph (a) of this section are satisfied, then the Internal Revenue Service may rebut the presumption that arises under paragraph (a) of this section only if it develops sufficient contrary evidence to rebut the probative value of the comparability data relied upon by the authorized body. With respect to any fixed payment (within the meaning of § 53.4958-4(a)(3)(ii)), rebuttal evidence is limited to evidence relating to facts and circumstances existing on the date the parties enter into the contract pursuant to which the payment is made (except in the event of substantial nonperformance). With respect to all other payments (including non-fixed payments subject to a cap, as described in paragraph (d)(2) of this section), rebuttal evidence may include facts and circumstances up to and including the date of payment. See § 53.4958-4(b)(2)(i).

(c) *Requirements for invoking rebuttable presumption.*—(1) *Approval by an authorized body.*—An authorized body means—

(A) The governing body (i.e., the board of directors, board of trustees, or equivalent controlling body) of the organization;

(B) A committee of the governing body, which may be composed of any individuals permitted under State law to serve on such a committee, to the extent that the committee is permitted by State law to act on behalf of the governing body; or

(C) To the extent permitted under State law, other parties authorized by the governing body of the organization to act on its behalf by following procedures specified by the governing body in approving compensation arrangements or property transfers.

(ii) *Individuals not included on authorized body.*—For purposes of determining whether the requirements of paragraph (a) of this section have been met with respect to a specific compensation arrangement or property transfer, an individual is not included on the authorized body when it is reviewing a transaction if that individual meets with other members only to answer questions, and otherwise recuses himself or herself from the meeting and is not present during debate and voting on the compensation arrangement or property transfer.

(iii) *Absence of conflict of interest.*—A member of the authorized body does not have a conflict of interest with respect to a compensation arrangement or property transfer only if the member—

(A) Is not a disqualified person participating in or economically benefitting from the compensation arrangement or property transfer, and is not a member of the family of any such disqualified person, as described in section 4958(f)(4) or § 53.4958-3(b)(1);

(B) Is not in an employment relationship subject to the direction or control of any disqualified person participating in or economically benefitting from the compensation arrangement or property transfer;

(C) Does not receive compensation or other payments subject to approval by any disqualified person participating in or eco-

nomically benefitting from the compensation arrangement or property transfer;

(D) Has no material financial interest affected by the compensation arrangement or property transfer; and

(E) Does not approve a transaction providing economic benefits to any disqualified person participating in the compensation arrangement or property transfer, who in turn has approved or will approve a transaction providing economic benefits to the member.

(2) *Appropriate data as to comparability.*—(i) *In general.*—An authorized body has appropriate data as to comparability if, given the knowledge and expertise of its members, it has information sufficient to determine whether, under the standards set forth in § 53.4958-4(b), the compensation arrangement in its entirety is reasonable or the property transfer is at fair market value. In the case of compensation, relevant information includes, but is not limited to, compensation levels paid by similarly situated organizations, both taxable and tax-exempt, for functionally comparable positions; the availability of similar services in the geographic area of the applicable tax-exempt organization; current compensation surveys compiled by independent firms; and actual written offers from similar institutions competing for the services of the disqualified person. In the case of property, relevant information includes, but is not limited to, current independent appraisals of the value of all property to be transferred; and offers received as part of an open and competitive bidding process.

(ii) *Special rule for compensation paid by small organizations.*—For organizations with annual gross receipts (including contributions) of less than $1 million reviewing compensation arrangements, the authorized body will be considered to have appropriate data as to comparability if it has data on compensation paid by three comparable organizations in the same or similar communities for similar services. No inference is intended with respect to whether circumstances falling outside this safe harbor will meet the requirement with respect to the collection of appropriate data.

(iii) *Application of special rule for small organizations.*—For purposes of determining whether the special rule for small organizations described in paragraph (c)(2)(ii) of this section applies, an organization may calculate its annual gross receipts based on an average of its gross receipts during the three prior taxable years. If any applicable tax-exempt organization is controlled by or controls another entity (as defined in § 53.4958-4(a)(2)(ii)(B)), the annual gross receipts of such organizations must be aggregated to determine applicability of the special rule stated in paragraph (c)(2)(ii) of this section.

(iv) *Examples.*—The following examples illustrate the rules for appropriate data as to comparability for purposes of invoking the rebuttable presumption of reasonableness described in this section. In all examples, compensation refers to the aggregate value of all benefits provided in exchange for services. The examples are as follows:

*Example 1.* Z is a university that is an applicable tax-exempt organization for purposes of section 4958. Z is negotiating a new contract with Q, its president, because the old contract will expire at the end of the year. In setting Q's compensation for its president at $600x per annum, the executive committee of the Board of Trustees relies solely on a national survey of compensation for university presidents that indicates university presidents receive annual compensation in the range of $100x to $700x; this survey does not divide its data by any criteria, such as the number of students served by the institution, annual revenues, academic ranking, or geographic location. Although many members of the executive committee have significant business experience, none of the members has any particular expertise in higher education compensation matters. Given the failure of the survey to provide information specific to universities comparable to Z, and because no other information was presented, the executive committee's decision with respect to Q's compensation was not based upon appropriate data as to comparability.

*Example 2.* The facts are the same as *Example 1*, except that the national compensation survey divides the data regarding compensation for university presidents into categories based on various university-specific factors, including the size of the institution (in terms of the number of students it serves and the amount of its revenues) and geographic area. The survey data shows that university presidents at institutions comparable to and in the same geographic area as Z receive annual compensation in the range of $200x to $300x. The executive committee of the Board of Trustees of Z relies on the survey data and its evaluation of Q's many years of service as a tenured professor and high-ranking university official at Z in setting Q's compensation at $275x annually. The data relied upon by the executive committee constitutes appropriate data as to comparability.

*Example 3.* X is a tax-exempt hospital that is an applicable tax-exempt organization for purposes of section 4958. Before renewing the contracts of X's chief executive officer and chief financial officer, X's governing board commissioned a customized compensation survey from an independent firm that specializes in consulting on issues related to executive placement and compensation. The survey covered executives with comparable responsibilities at a significant number of taxable and tax-exempt hospitals. The survey data are sorted by a number of different variables, including the size of the hospitals and the nature of the services they provide, the level of experience and specific responsibilities of the executives, and the composition of the annual compensation packages. The board members were provided with the survey results, a detailed written analysis comparing the hospital's executives to those covered by the survey, and an opportunity to ask questions of a member of the firm that prepared the survey. The survey, as prepared and presented to X's board, constitutes appropriate data as to comparability.

*Example 4.* The facts are the same as *Example 3,* except that one year later, X is negotiating a new contract with its chief executive officer. The governing board of X obtains information indicating that the relevant market conditions have not changed materially, and possesses no other information indicating that the results of the prior year's survey are no longer valid. Therefore, X may continue to rely on the independent compensation survey prepared for the prior year in setting annual compensation under the new contract.

*Example 5.* W is a local repertory theater and an applicable tax-exempt organization for purposes of section 4958. W has had annual gross receipts ranging from $400,000 to $800,000 over its past three taxable years. In determining the next year's compensation for W's artistic director, the board of directors of W relies on data compiled from a telephone survey of three other unrelated performing arts organizations of similar size in similar communities. A member of the board drafts a brief written summary of the annual compensation information obtained from this informal survey. The annual compensation information obtained in the telephone survey is appropriate data as to comparability.

(3) *Documentation.*—(i) For a decision to be documented adequately, the written or electronic records of the authorized body must note—

(A) The terms of the transaction that was approved and the date it was approved;

(B) The members of the authorized body who were present during debate on the transaction that was approved and those who voted on it;

(C) The comparability data obtained and relied upon by the authorized body and how the data was obtained; and

(D) Any actions taken with respect to consideration of the transaction by anyone who is otherwise a member of the authorized body but who had a conflict of interest with respect to the transaction.

(ii) If the authorized body determines that reasonable compensation for a specific arrangement or fair market value in a specific property transfer is higher or lower than the range of comparability data obtained, the authorized body must record the basis for its determination. For a decision to be documented concurrently, records must be prepared before the later of the next meeting of the authorized body or 60 days after the final action or actions of the authorized body are taken. Records must be reviewed and approved by the authorized body as reasonable, accurate and complete within a reasonable time period thereafter.

(d) *No presumption with respect to non-fixed payments until amounts are determined.*—(1) *In general.*—Except as provided in paragraph (d)(2) of this section, in the case of a payment that is not a fixed payment (within the meaning of §53.4958-4(a)(3)(ii)), the rebuttable presumption of this section arises only after the exact amount of the payment is determined, or a fixed formula for calculating the payment is specified, and the three requirements for the presumption under paragraph (a) of this section subsequently are satisfied. See §53.4958-4(b)(2)(i).

(2) *Special rule for certain non-fixed payments subject to a cap.*—If the authorized body approves an employment contract with a disqualified person that includes a non-fixed payment (such as a discretionary bonus) subject to a specified cap, the authorized body may establish a rebuttable presumption with respect to the non-fixed payment at the time the employment contract is entered into if—

(i) Prior to approving the contract, the authorized body obtains appropriate comparability data indicating that a fixed payment of up to a certain amount to the particular disqualified person would represent reasonable compensation;

(ii) The maximum amount payable under the contract (taking into account both fixed and non-fixed payments) does not exceed the amount referred to in paragraph (d)(2)(i) of this section; and

(iii) The other requirements for the rebuttable presumption of reasonableness under paragraph (a) of this section are satisfied.

(e) *No inference from absence of presumption.*—The fact that a transaction between an applicable tax-exempt organization and a disquali-

fied person is not subject to the presumption described in this section neither creates any inference that the transaction is an excess benefit transaction, nor exempts or relieves any person from compliance with any Federal or state law imposing any obligation, duty, responsibility, or other standard of conduct with respect to the operation or administration of any applicable tax-exempt organization.

(f) *Period of reliance on rebuttable presumption.*—Except as provided in paragraph (d) of this section with respect to non-fixed payments, the rebuttable presumption applies to all payments made or transactions completed in accordance with a contract, provided that the provisions of paragraph (a) of this section were met at the time the parties entered into the contract. [Reg. §53.4958-6.]

☐ [T.D. 8978, 1-22-2002.]

### [Reg. §53.4958-7]

**§53.4958-7. Correction.**—(a) *In general.*—An excess benefit transaction is corrected by undoing the excess benefit to the extent possible, and taking any additional measures necessary to place the applicable tax-exempt organization involved in the excess benefit transaction in a financial position not worse than that in which it would be if the disqualified person were dealing under the highest fiduciary standards. Paragraph (b) of this section describes the acceptable forms of correction. Paragraph (c) of this section defines the correction amount. Paragraph (d) of this section describes correction where a contract has been partially performed. Paragraph (e) of this section describes correction where the applicable tax-exempt organization involved in the transaction has ceased to exist or is no longer tax-exempt. Paragraph(f) of this section provides examples illustrating correction.

(b) *Form of correction.*—(1) *Cash or cash equivalents.*—Except as provided in paragraphs (b)(3) and (4) of this section, a disqualified person corrects an excess benefit only by making a payment in cash or cash equivalents, excluding payment by a promissory note, to the applicable tax-exempt organization equal to the correction amount, as defined in paragraph (c) of this section.

(2) *Anti-abuse rule.*—A disqualified person will not satisfy the requirements of paragraph (b)(1) of this section if the Commissioner determines that the disqualified person engaged in one or more transactions with the applicable tax-exempt organization to circumvent the requirements of this correction section, and as a result, the disqualified person effectively transferred property other than cash or cash equivalents.

(3) *Special rule relating to nonqualified deferred compensation.*—If an excess benefit transaction results, in whole or in part, from the vesting (as described in §53.4958-1(e)(2)) of benefits provided under a nonqualified deferred compensation plan, then, to the extent that such benefits have not yet been distributed to the disqualified person, the disqualified person may correct the portion of the excess benefit resulting from the undistributed deferred compensation by relinquishing any right to receive the excess portion of the undistributed deferred compensation (including any earnings thereon).

(4) *Return of specific property.*—(i) *In general.*—A disqualified person may, with the agreement of the applicable tax-exempt organization, make a payment by returning specific property previously transferred in the excess benefit transaction. In this case, the disqualified person is treated as making a payment equal to the lesser of—

(A) The fair market value of the property determined on the date the property is returned to the organization; or

(B) The fair market value of the property on the date the excess benefit transaction occurred.

(ii) *Payment not equal to correction amount.*—If the payment described in paragraph (b)(4)(i) of this section is less than the correction amount (as described in paragraph (c) of this section), the disqualified person must make an additional cash payment to the organization equal to the difference. Conversely, if the payment described in paragraph (b)(4)(i) of this section exceeds the correction amount (as described in paragraph (c) of this section), the organization may make a cash payment to the disqualified person equal to the difference.

(iii) *Disqualified person may not participate in decision.*—Any disqualified person who received an excess benefit from the excess benefit transaction may not participate in the applicable tax-exempt organization's decision whether to accept the return of specific property under paragraph (b)(4)(i) of this section.

(c) *Correction amount.*—The correction amount with respect to an excess benefit transaction equals the sum of the excess benefit (as defined in §53.4958-1(b)) and interest on the excess benefit. The amount of the interest charge for purposes of this section is determined by multiplying the excess benefit by an interest rate, compounded annually, for the period from the date the excess benefit transaction occurred (as defined in §53.4958-1(e)) to the date of correction. The interest rate used for this purpose must be a rate that equals or exceeds the applicable Federal rate (AFR), compounded annually, for the month in which the transaction occurred. The period from the date the excess benefit transaction occurred to the date of correction is used to determine whether the appropriate AFR is the Federal short-term rate, the Federal mid-term rate, or the Federal long-term rate. See section 1274(d)(1)(A).

(d) *Correction where contract has been partially performed.*—If the excess benefit transaction arises under a contract that has been partially performed, termination of the contractual relationship between the organization and the disqualified person is not required in order to correct. However, the parties may need to modify the terms of any ongoing contract to avoid future excess benefit transactions.

(e) *Correction in the case of an applicable tax-exempt organization that has ceased to exist, or is no longer tax-exempt.*—(1) *In general.*—A disqualified person must correct an excess benefit transaction in accordance with this paragraph where the applicable tax-exempt organization that engaged in the transaction no longer exists or is no longer described in section 501(c)(3) or (4) and exempt from tax under section 501(a).

(2) *Section 501(c)(3) organizations.*—In the case of an excess benefit transaction with a section 501(c)(3) applicable tax-exempt organization, the disqualified person must pay the correction amount, as defined in paragraph (c) of this section, to another organization described in section 501(c)(3) and exempt from tax under section 501(a) in accordance with the dissolution clause contained in the constitutive documents of the applicable tax-exempt organization involved in the excess benefit transaction, provided that—

(i) The organization receiving the correction amount is described in section 170(b)(1)(A) (other than in section 170(b)(1)(A)(vii) and (viii)) and has been in existence and so described for a continuous period of at least 60 calendar months ending on the correction date;

(ii) The disqualified person is not also a disqualified person (as defined in §53.4958-3) with respect to the organization receiving the correction amount; and

(iii) The organization receiving the correction amount does not allow the disqualified person (or persons described in §53.4958-3(b) with respect to that person) to make or recommend any grants or distributions by the organization.

(3) *Section 501(c)(4) organizations.*—In the case of an excess benefit transaction with a section 501(c)(4) applicable tax-exempt organization, the disqualified person must pay the correction amount, as defined in paragraph (c) of this section, to a successor section 501(c)(4) organization or, if no tax-exempt successor, to any organization described in section 501(c)(3) or (4) and exempt from tax under section 501(a), provided that the requirements of paragraphs (e)(2)(i) through (iii) of this section are satisfied (except that the requirement that the organization receiving the correction amount is described in section 170(b)(1)(A) (other than in section 170(b)(1)(A)(vii) and (viii)) shall not apply if the organization is described in section 501(c)(4)).

(f) *Examples.*—The following examples illustrate the principles of this section describing the requirements of correction:

*Example 1.* W is an applicable tax-exempt organization for purposes of section 4958. D is a disqualified person with respect to W. W employed D in 1999 and made payments totaling $12t to D as compensation throughout the taxable year. The fair market value of D's services in 1999 was $7t. Thus, D received excess compensation in the amount of $5t, the excess benefit for purposes of section 4958. In accordance with §53.4958-1(e)(1), the excess benefit transaction with respect to the series of compensatory payments during 1999 is deemed to occur on December 31, 1999, the last day of D's taxable year. In order to correct the excess benefit transaction on June 30, 2002, D must pay W, in cash or cash equivalents, excluding payment with a promissory note, $5t (the excess benefit) plus interest on $5t for the period from the date the excess benefit transaction occurred to the date of correction (i.e., December 31, 1999, to June 30, 2002). Because this period is not more than three years, the interest rate D must use to determine the interest on the excess benefit must equal or exceed the short-term AFR, compounded annually, for December, 1999 (5.74%, compounded annually).

*Example 2.* X is an applicable tax-exempt organization for purposes of section 4958. B is a disqualified person with respect to X. On January 1, 2000, B paid X $6v for Property F. Property F had a fair market value of $10v on January 1, 2000. Thus, the sales transaction on that date provided an excess benefit to B in the amount of $4v. In order to correct the excess benefit on July 5, 2005, B pays X, in cash or cash equivalents, excluding payment with a promissory note, $4v (the excess benefit) plus interest on $4v for the period from the date

the excess benefit transaction occurred to the date of correction (i.e., January 1, 2000, to July 5, 2005). Because this period is over three but not over nine years, the interest rate B must use to determine the interest on the excess benefit must equal or exceed the mid-term AFR, compounded annually, for January, 2000 (6.21%, compounded annually).

*Example 3.* The facts are the same as in *Example 2*, except that B offers to return Property F. X agrees to accept the return of Property F, a decision in which B does not participate. Property F has declined in value since the date of the excess benefit transaction. On July 5, 2005, the property has a fair market value of $9v. For purposes of correction, B's return of Property F to X is treated as a payment of $9v, the fair market value of the property determined on the date the property is returned to the organization. If $9v is greater than the correction amount ($4v plus interest on $4v at a rate that equals or exceeds 6.21%, compounded annually, for the period from January 1, 2000, to July 5, 2005), then X may make a cash payment to B equal to the difference.

*Example 4.* The facts are the same as in *Example 3*, except that Property F has increased in value since January 1, 2000, the date the excess benefit transaction occurred, and on July 5, 2005, has a fair market value of $13v. For purposes of correction, B's return of Property F to X is treated as a payment of $10v, the fair market value of the property on the date the excess benefit transaction occurred. If $10v is greater than the correction amount ($4v plus interest on $4v at a rate that equals or exceeds 6.21%, compounded annually, for the period from January 1, 2000, to July 5, 2005), then X may make a cash payment to B equal to the difference.

*Example 5.* The facts are the same as in *Example 2*. Assume that the correction amount B paid X in cash on July 5, 2005, was $5.58v. On July 4, 2005, X loaned $5.58v to B, in exchange for a promissory note signed by B in the amount of $5.58v, payable with interest at a future date. These facts indicate that B engaged in the loan transaction to circumvent the requirement of this section that (except as provided in paragraph (b)(3) or (4) of this section), the correction amount must be paid only in cash or cash equivalents. As a result, the Commissioner may determine that B effectively transferred property other than cash or cash equivalents, and therefore did not satisfy the correction requirements of this section.
[Reg. §53.4958-7.]

☐ [T.D. 8978, 1-22-2002.]

**[Reg. §53.4958-8]**

**§53.4958-8. Special rules.**—(a) *Substantive requirements for exemption still apply.*—Section 4958 does not affect the substantive standards for tax exemption under section 501(c)(3) or (4), including the requirements that the organization be organized and operated exclusively for exempt purposes, and that no part of its net earnings inure to the benefit of any private shareholder or individual. Thus, regardless of whether a particular transaction is subject to excise taxes under section 4958, existing principles and rules may be implicated, such as the limitation on private benefit. For example, transactions that are not subject to section 4958 because of the initial contract exception described in §53.4958-4(a)(3) may, under certain circumstances, jeopardize the organization's tax-exempt status.

(b) *Interaction between section 4958 and section 7611 rules for church tax inquiries and examinations.*—The procedures of section 7611 will be used in initiating and conducting any inquiry or examination into whether an excess benefit transaction has occurred between a church and a disqualified person. For purposes of this rule, the reasonable belief required to initiate a church tax inquiry is satisfied if there is a reasonable belief that a section 4958 tax is due from a disqualified person with respect to a transaction involving a church. See §301.7611-1 Q&A 19 of this chapter.

(c) *Other substantiation requirements.*—These regulations, in §53.4958-4(c)(3), set forth specific substantiation rules. Compliance with the specific substantiation rules of that section does not relieve applicable tax-exempt organizations of other rules and requirements of the Internal Revenue Code, regulations, Revenue Rulings, and other guidance issued by the Internal Revenue Service (including the substantiation rules of sections 162 and 274, or §1.6001-1(a) and (c) of this chapter). [Reg. §53.4958-8.]

☐ [T.D. 8978, 1-22-2002.]

**[Reg. §53.4959-1]**

**§53.4959-1. Taxes on failures by hospital organizations to meet section 501(r)(3).**—(a) *Excise tax for failure to meet the section 501(r)(3) requirements.*—(1) *In general.*—If a hospital organization (as defined in §1.501(r)-1(b)(18)) fails to meet the requirements of section 501(r)(3) separately with respect to a hospital facility it operates in any taxable year, there is imposed on the hospital organization a tax equal to $50,000. If a hospital organization operates multiple hospital facilities and fails to meet the requirements of section 501(r)(3) with respect to more than one facility it operates, the $50,000 tax is imposed on the hospital organization separately for each hospital facility's failure. The tax is imposed for each taxable year that a hospital facility fails to meet the requirements of section 501(r)(3).

(2) *Examples.*—The following examples illustrate this paragraph (a):

*Example 1.* (i) U is a hospital organization that operates only one hospital facility, V. In Year 1, V conducts a community health needs assessment (CHNA) and adopts an implementation strategy to meet the health needs identified through the CHNA. In Years 2 and 3, V does not conduct a CHNA. V fails to conduct a CHNA by the last day of Year 4. Accordingly, U has failed to meet the requirements of section 501(r)(3) with respect to V in Year 4 because V has failed to conduct a CHNA in Years 2, 3, and 4. U is subject to a tax equal to $50,000 for Year 4.

(ii) V also fails to conduct a CHNA by the last day of Year 5. Accordingly, U has failed to meet the requirements of section 501(r)(3) with respect to V in Year 5 because V has failed to conduct a CHNA in Years 3, 4, and 5. U is subject to a tax equal to $50,000 for Year 5.

*Example 2.* P is a hospital organization that operates only one hospital facility, Q. In Year 1, Q conducts a CHNA and adopts an implementation strategy to meet the health needs identified through the CHNA. In Years 2 and 3, Q does not conduct a CHNA. In Year 4, Q conducts a CHNA but does not adopt an implementation strategy to meet the health needs identified through that CHNA by the 15th day of the fifth month of Year 5. Accordingly, P has failed to meet the requirements of section 501(r)(3) with respect to Q in Year 4 because Q has failed to adopt an implementation strategy by the 15th day of the fifth month after the end of the taxable year in which Q conducted its CHNA. P is subject to a tax equal to $50,000 for Year 4.

*Example 3.* R is a hospital organization that operates two hospital facilities, S and T. In Year 1, S and T each conduct a CHNA and adopt an implementation strategy to meet the health needs identified through the CHNA. In Years 2 and 3, S and T do not conduct a CHNA. S and T each fail to conduct a CHNA by the last day of Year 4. Accordingly, R has failed to meet the requirements of section 501(r)(3) with respect to both S and T in Year 4. R is subject to a tax equal to $100,000 ($50,000 for S's failure plus $50,000 for T's failure) for Year 4.

(b) *Interaction with other provisions.*—(1) *Correction.*—Unless a hospital organization's failure to meet the requirements of section 501(r)(3) involves an omission or error that is described in and corrected in accordance with §1.501(r)-2(b) (and is thus not considered a failure), a failure to meet the requirements of section 501(r)(3) will result in a tax being imposed on the organization under this section, notwithstanding the organization's correction and disclosure of the failure in accordance with the guidance described in §1.501(r)-2(c).

(2) *Interaction with other taxes.*—The tax imposed by this section is in addition to any tax imposed by §1.501(r)-2(d) or as a result of revocation of a hospital organization's section 501(c)(3) status.

(c) *Effective/applicability date.*—Paragraph (a) of this section applies on and after December 29, 2014. [Reg. §53.4959-1.]

☐ [*T.D. 9708*, 12-29-2014 (*corrected* 3-10-2015).]

**[Reg. §53.4960-0]**

**§53.4960-0. Table of contents.**

(i) In general.

(ii) Allocation of remuneration for medical services and non-medical services.

(iii) Examples.

(b) Source of payment.

(1) Remuneration paid by third parties for employment by an employer.

(2) Remuneration paid by a related organization for employment by the related organization.

(c) Applicable year in which remuneration is treated as paid.

(1) In general.

(2) Vested remuneration.

(3) Change in related status during the year.

(d) Amount of remuneration treated as paid.

(1) In general.

(2) Earnings and losses on previously paid remuneration.

(i) In general.

(ii) Previously paid remuneration.

(A) New covered employee.

(B) Existing covered employee.

(iii) Earnings.

(iv) Losses.

(v) Net earnings.

(vi) Net losses.

(3) Remuneration paid for a taxable year before the employee becomes a covered employee.

(i) In general.

(ii) Examples.

(e) Calculation of present value.

(1) In general.

(2) Treatment of future payment amount as present value for certain amounts.

(f) Examples.

§ 53.4960-3 Determination of whether there is a parachute payment

(a) Parachute payment.

(1) In general.

(2) Exclusions.

(i) Certain qualified plans.

(ii) Certain annuity contracts.

(iii) Compensation for medical services.

(iv) Payments to non-HCEs.

(3) Determination of HCEs for purposes of the exclusion from parachute payments.

(b) Payment in the nature of compensation.

(1) In general.

(2) Consideration paid by covered employee.

(c) When payment is considered to be made.

(1) In general.

(2) Transfers of section 83 property.

(3) Stock options.

(d) Payment contingent on an employee's separation from employment.

(1) In general.

(2) Employment agreements.

(i) In general.

(ii) Example.

(3) Noncompetition agreements.

(4) Payment of amounts previously included in income or excess remuneration.

(5) Window programs.

(6) Anti-abuse provision.

(e) Involuntary separation from employment.

(1) In general.

(2) Separation from employment for good reason.

(i) In general.

(ii) Material negative change required.

(iii) Deemed material negative change.

(A) Material diminution of compensation.

(B) Material diminution of responsibility.

(C) Material diminution of authority of a supervisor.

(D) Material diminution of a location.

(E) Material change of location.

(F) Other material breach.

(3) Separation from employment.

(f) Accelerated payment or accelerated vesting resulting **from an** involuntary separation from employment.

(1) In general.

(2) Nonvested payments subject to a non-service vesting condition.

(3) Vested payments.

(4) Nonvested payments subject to a service vesting condition.

(i) In general.

(A) Vesting trigger.

(B) Vesting condition.

(C) Services condition.

(ii) Value of the lapse of the obligation to continue to perform services.

(iii) Accelerated vesting of equity compensation.

(5) Application to benefits under a nonqualified deferred compensation plan.

(6) Present value.

(7) Examples.

(g) Three-times-base-amount test for parachute payments.

(1) In general.

(2) Examples.

(h) Calculating present value.

(1) In general.

(2) Deferred payments.

(3) Health care.

(i) Discount rate.

(j) Present value of a payment to be made in the future that is contingent on an uncertain future event or condition.

(1) Treatment based on the estimated probability of payment.

(2) Correction of incorrect estimates.

(3) Initial option value estimate.

(4) Examples.

(k) Base amount.

(1) In general.

(2) Short or incomplete taxable years.

(3) Excludable fringe benefits.

(4) Section 83(b) income.

(l) Base period.

(1) In general.

(2) Determination of base amount if employee separates from employment in the year hired.

(3) Examples.

§ 53.4960-4 Liability for tax on excess remuneration and excess parachute payments

(a) Liability, reporting, and payment of excise taxes.

(1) Liability.

(2) Reporting and payment.

(3) Arrangements between an ATEO and a related organization.

(4) Certain foreign related organizations.

(5) [Reserved].

(b) Amounts subject to tax.

(1) Excess remuneration.

(i) In general.

(ii) Exclusion for excess parachute payments.

(2) Excess parachute payment.

(c) Calculation of liability for tax on excess remuneration.

(1) In general.

(2) Calculation if liability is allocated from more than one ATEO with respect to an individual.

(3) Calculation if liability is allocated from an ATEO with a short applicable year.

(4) Examples.

(d) Calculation of liability for excess parachute payments.

(1) In general.

(2) Computation of excess parachute payments.

(3) Reallocation when the payment is disproportionate to base amount.

(4) Election to prepay tax.

(5) Liability after a redetermination of total parachute payments.

(6) Examples.

§ 53.4960-5 [Reserved]

§ 53.4960-6 Applicability date

(a) General applicability date.

(b) [Reserved].

[Reg. § 53.4960-0.]

☐ [*T.D. 9938, 1-15-2021 (corrected 5-4-2021).*]

### [Reg. § 53.4960-1]

**§ 53.4960-1. Scope and definitions.**—(a) *Scope.*—This section provides definitions for purposes of section 4960, this section, and §§ 53.4960-2 through 53.4960-6. Section 53.4960-2 provides definitions and rules for determining the amount of remuneration paid for a taxable year. Section 53.4960-3 provides definitions and rules for determining whether a parachute payment is paid. Section 53.4960-4 provides definitions and rules for calculating the amount of excess remuneration paid for a taxable year, excess parachute payments paid in a taxable year, and liability for the excise tax. Section 53.4960-5 is reserved for rules on the coordination of sections 4960 and 162(m). Section 53.4960-6 provides rules regarding the applicability date for the regulations in §§ 53.4960-1 through 53.4960-5. The rules and definitions provided in this section through § 53.4960-6 apply solely for purposes of section 4960 unless specified otherwise.

(b) *Applicable tax-exempt organization.*—(1) *In general.*—Applicable tax-exempt organization or ATEO means any organization that is one of the following types of organizations:

(i) *Section 501(a) organization.*—The organization is exempt from taxation under section 501(a) (except as provided in paragraph (b)(2) or (b)(3) of this section);

(ii) *Section 521 farmers' cooperative.*—The organization is a farmers' cooperative organization described in section 521(b)(1);

(iii) *Section 115(1) organization.*—The organization has income excluded from taxation under section 115(1); or

(iv) *Section 527 political organization.*—The organization is a political organization described in section 527(e)(1).

(2) *Certain foreign organizations.*—Any foreign organization described in section 4948(b) that either is exempt from tax under section 501(a) or is a taxable private foundation (section 4948(b) organization) is not an ATEO. A foreign organization is an organization not created or organized in the United States or in any possession thereof, or under the law of the United States, any State, the District of Columbia, or any possession of the United States. See section 4948(b) and § 53.4948-1. For purposes of this paragraph (b)(2) and the application of section 4960 to a taxable year, an organization's status as a section 4948(b) organization is determined at the end of its taxable year.

(c) *Applicable year.*—(1) *In general.*—Applicable year means the calendar year ending with or within the ATEO's taxable year. See § 53.4960-4 regarding how an ATEO's applicable year affects the liability of related organizations.

(2) *Examples.*—The following examples illustrate the rules of paragraph (c)(1) of this section.

(i) *Example 1 (Calendar year taxpayer).*—(A) *Facts.* ATEO 1 uses the calendar year as its taxable year and became an ATEO before 2022.

(B) *Conclusion.* ATEO 1's applicable year for its 2022 taxable year is the period from January 1, 2022, through December 31, 2022 (that is, the 2022 calendar year).

(ii) *Example 2 (Fiscal year taxpayer).*—(A) *Facts.* ATEO 2 uses a taxable year that starts July 1 and ends June 30 and became an ATEO before 2022.

(B) *Conclusion.* ATEO 2's applicable year for the taxable year beginning July 1, 2022, and ending June 30, 2023, is the 2022 calendar year.

(3) *Short applicable years.*—(i) *In general.*—An ATEO may have an applicable year that does not span the entire calendar year for the initial taxable year that the organization is an ATEO or for the taxable year in which the taxpayer ceases to be an ATEO. The beginning and end dates of the applicable year in the case of an ATEO's change in status depend on when the change in status occurs.

(ii) *Initial year of ATEO status.*—For the taxable year in which an ATEO first becomes an ATEO, *applicable year* means the period beginning on the date the ATEO first becomes an ATEO and ending on the last day of the calendar year ending with or within such taxable year (or, if earlier, the date of termination of ATEO status, as described in paragraph (c)(3)(ii)(A) of this section). If the taxable year in which an ATEO first becomes an ATEO ends before the end of the calendar year in which the ATEO first becomes an ATEO, then there is no applicable year for the ATEO's first taxable year; however, for the ATEO's next taxable year, *applicable year* means the period beginning on the date the ATEO first becomes an ATEO and ending on December 31 of the calendar year (or, if earlier, the date of termination of ATEO status, as described in paragraph (c)(3)(ii)(A) of this section).

(iii) *Year of termination of ATEO status.*—(A) *Termination on or before the close of the calendar year ending with or within the taxable year of termination.*—If an ATEO has a termination of ATEO status during the taxable year and the termination of ATEO status occurs on or before the close of the calendar year ending with or within such taxable year, then, for the taxable year of termination of ATEO status, applicable year means the period starting January 1 of the calendar year of the termination of ATEO status and ending on the date of the termination of ATEO status.

(B) *Termination after the close of the calendar year ending in the taxable year of termination.*—If an ATEO has a termination of ATEO status during the taxable year and the termination of ATEO status occurs after the close of the calendar year ending within such taxable year, then, for the taxable year of the termination of ATEO status, *applicable year* means both the calendar year ending within such taxable year and the period beginning January 1 of the calendar year of the termination of ATEO status and ending on the date of the termination of ATEO status. Both such applicable years are treated as separate applicable years. See § 53.4960-4(b)(2)(ii) for rules regarding calculation of the tax in the event there are multiple applicable years associated with a taxable year.

(4) *Examples.*—The following examples illustrate the rules of paragraph (c)(3) of this section. For purposes of these examples, assume any entity referred to as "ATEO" is an ATEO and any entity referred to as "CORP" is not an ATEO.

(i) *Example 1 (Taxable year of formation ending after December 31).*—(A) *Facts.* ATEO 1, ATEO 2, and CORP 1 are related organizations that all use a taxable year that starts July 1 and ends June 30. ATEO 1 is recognized as a section 501(c)(3) organization by the IRS on May 8, 2023, effective as of October 1, 2022. ATEO 2 became an ATEO in 2017.

(B) *Conclusion (ATEO 1).* ATEO 1's applicable year for the taxable year beginning October 1, 2022, and ending June 30, 2023, is the period beginning October 1, 2022, and ending December 31, 2022. For purposes of determining the amount of remuneration paid by ATEO 1 and all related organizations for ATEO 1's taxable year beginning October 1, 2022, and ending June 30, 2023, (including for purposes of determining ATEO 1's covered employees), only remuneration paid between October 1, 2022, and December 31, 2022, is taken into account. Thus, any remuneration paid by ATEO 1, ATEO 2, and CORP 1 before October 1, 2022, is disregarded for purposes of ATEO 1's applicable year associated with its initial taxable year.

(C) *Conclusion (ATEO 2).* ATEO 2's applicable year for its taxable year beginning July 1, 2022, and ending June 30, 2023, is the 2022 calendar year. Thus, any remuneration paid by ATEO 1, ATEO 2, and CORP 1 during the 2022 calendar year is taken into account for purposes of determining ATEO 2's covered employees and remuneration paid for ATEO 2's taxable year ending June 30, 2023.

(ii) *Example 2 (Taxable year of formation ending before December 31).*—(A) *Facts.* Assume the same facts as in paragraph (c)(4)(i)(A) of this section (Example 1), except that ATEO 1 is recognized as a section 501(c)(3) organization effective as of March 15, 2023.

(B) *Conclusion.* ATEO 1 has no applicable year for the taxable year starting March 15, 2023, and ending June 30, 2023, because no calendar year ends (or termination of ATEO status occurs) with or within the taxable year. ATEO 1's applicable year for the taxable year ending June 30, 2024, is the period beginning March 15, 2023, and ending December 31, 2023. For purposes of determining the amount of remuneration paid by ATEO 1 and all related organizations for ATEO 1's taxable year ending June 30, 2024 (including for purposes of determining ATEO 1's covered employees), only remuneration paid between March 15, 2023, and December 31, 2023, is taken into account. The conclusion for ATEO 2 is the same as in paragraph (c)(4)(i)(C) of this section (Example 1).

(iii) *Example 3 (Termination before the close of the calendar year ending in the taxable year of termination).*—(A) *Facts.* Assume the same facts as in paragraph (c)(4)(i)(A) of this section (Example 1). In addition, ATEO 1 has a termination of ATEO status on September 30, 2024.

(B) *Conclusion.* For ATEO 1's taxable year beginning July 1, 2024, and ending September 30, 2024, ATEO 1's applicable year is the period beginning January 1, 2024, and ending September 30, 2024.

(iv) *Example 4 (Termination after the close of the calendar year ending in the taxable year of termination).*—(A) *Facts.* Assume the same facts as in paragraph (c)(4)(i)(A) of this section (Example 1). In addition, ATEO 1 has a termination of ATEO status on March 31, 2025.

(B) *Conclusion.* For ATEO 1's taxable year beginning July 1, 2024, and ending March 31, 2025, ATEO 1 has two applicable years: the 2024 calendar year, and the period beginning on January 1, 2025, and ending on March 31, 2025.

(d) *Covered employee.*—(1) *In general.*—For each taxable year, *covered employee* means any individual who is one of the five highest-compensated employees of the ATEO for the taxable year or was a covered employee of the ATEO (or any predecessor) for any preceding taxable year beginning after December 31, 2016.

(2) *Five highest-compensated employees.*—(i) *In general.*—Except as otherwise provided in this paragraph (d)(2), an individual is one of an ATEO's five highest-compensated employees for the taxable year

if the individual is among the five employees of the ATEO with the highest amount of remuneration paid during the applicable year, as determined under § 53.4960-2. However, remuneration for which the deduction is disallowed by reason of section 162(m) is taken into account for purposes of determining an ATEO's five highest-compensated employees. The five highest-compensated employees of an ATEO for the taxable year are identified on the basis of the total remuneration paid during the applicable year to the employee for services performed as an employee of the ATEO or any related organization. An ATEO may have fewer than five highest-compensated employees for a taxable year if it has fewer than five employees other than employees who are disregarded under paragraphs (d)(2)(ii) through (iv) of this section. For purposes of this paragraph (d)(2), a grant of a legally binding right (within the meaning of § 1.409A-1(b)) to vested remuneration is considered to be remuneration paid as of the date of grant, as described in § 53.4960-2(c)(2), and a person or governmental entity is considered to grant a legally binding right to nonvested remuneration if the person or governmental entity grants a legally binding right to remuneration that is not vested within the meaning of § 53.4960-2(c)(2). An employee is disregarded for purposes of determining an ATEO's five highest-compensated employees for a taxable year if, during the applicable year, neither the ATEO nor any related organization paid remuneration or granted a legally binding right to nonvested remuneration to the individual for services the individual performed as an employee of the ATEO or any related organization.

(ii) *Limited hours exception.*—(A) *In general.*—An individual is disregarded for purposes of determining an ATEO's five highest-compensated employees for a taxable year if all of the following requirements are met:

(1) *Remuneration requirement.*—Neither the ATEO nor any related ATEO paid remuneration or granted a legally binding right to nonvested remuneration to the individual for services the individual performed as an employee of the ATEO during the applicable year; and

(2) *Hours of service requirement.*—The individual performed services as an employee of the ATEO and all related ATEOs for no more than 10 percent of the total hours the individual worked as an employee of the ATEO and any related organizations during the applicable year. An ATEO may instead make this determination based on the total days the individual worked as an employee of the ATEO and all related ATEOs as a percentage of the total days worked as an employee of the ATEO and all related organizations, provided that for purposes of the calculation, any day that the individual worked at least one hour as an employee of the ATEO or a related ATEO is treated as a day worked as an employee of the ATEO and not for any other organization.

(B) *Certain payments disregarded.*—For purposes of paragraph (d)(2)(ii)(A)(1) of this section, a payment of remuneration made to the individual by a related organization that is an employer of the individual and for which the related organization is neither entitled to reimbursement by the ATEO nor entitled to any other consideration from the ATEO is not considered remuneration paid by the ATEO under § 53.4960-2(b)(1), and a payment of remuneration made to the individual by a related organization is not treated as remuneration paid by the ATEO under § 53.4960-2(b)(2).

(C) *Safe harbor.*—For purposes of paragraph (d)(2)(ii)(A)(2) of this section, an individual is treated as having performed services as an employee of the ATEO and all related ATEOs for no more than 10 percent of the total hours the individual worked as an employee of the ATEO and all related organizations during the applicable year if the employee performed no more than 100 hours of service as an employee of the ATEO and all related ATEOs during the applicable year.

(iii) *Nonexempt funds exception.*—(A) *In general.*—An individual is disregarded for purposes of determining an ATEO's five highest-compensated employees for a taxable year if all the following requirements are met:

(1) *Remuneration requirement.*—Neither the ATEO, nor any related ATEO, nor any taxable related organization controlled by the ATEO, or by one or more related ATEOs, either alone or together with the ATEO, paid remuneration or granted a legally binding right to nonvested remuneration to the individual for services the individual performed as an employee of an ATEO during the applicable year and the preceding applicable year. For this purpose, whether a taxable related organization is controlled by the ATEO (or one or more related ATEOs) is determined without regard to paragraph (i)(2)(vii)(B)(2) of this section and without regard to section 318(a)(3) for purposes of applying paragraph (i)(2)(vii)(A) of this section, so that an interest in a corporation or nonstock entity is not attributed

downward in determining control of the corporation or nonstock entity;

(2) *Hours of service requirement.*—The individual performed services as an employee of the ATEO and any related ATEOs for not more than 50 percent of the total hours worked as an employee of the ATEO and any related organizations during the applicable year and the preceding applicable year. An ATEO may instead make this determination based on the total days the individual worked as an employee of the ATEO and all related ATEOs as a percentage of the total days worked as an employee of the ATEO and all related organizations, provided that for purposes of the calculation, any day that the individual worked at least one hour as an employee of the ATEO or a related ATEO is treated as a day worked as an employee of the ATEO and not for any other organization; and

(3) *Related organizations requirement.*—No related organization that paid remuneration or granted a legally binding right to nonvested remuneration to the individual during the applicable year and the preceding applicable year provided services for a fee to the ATEO, to any related ATEO, or to any taxable related organization controlled by the ATEO or by one or more related ATEOs, either alone or together with the ATEO, during the applicable year and the preceding applicable year. For purposes of this paragraph (d)(2)(iii)(A)(3), whether a taxable related organization is controlled by the ATEO (or one or more related ATEOs) is determined without regard to paragraph (i)(2)(vii)(B)(2) of this section and without regard to section 318(a)(3) for purposes of applying paragraph (i)(2)(vii)(A) of this section, so that an interest in a corporation or nonstock entity is not attributed downward in determining control of the corporation or nonstock entity.

(B) *Certain payments disregarded.*—For purposes of paragraph (d)(2)(iii)(A)(1) of this section, a payment of remuneration made to an individual by a related organization that is an employer of the individual and for which the related organization is neither entitled to reimbursement by the ATEO nor entitled to any other consideration from the ATEO is not considered remuneration paid by the ATEO under § 53.4960-2(b)(1) and a payment of remuneration made to the individual by a related organization is not treated as paid by the ATEO under § 53.4960-2(b)(2).

(iv) *Limited services exception.*—An individual is disregarded for purposes of determining an ATEO's five highest-compensated employees for a taxable year even though the ATEO paid remuneration to the individual if, disregarding § 53.4960-2(b)(2), all of the following requirements are met:

(A) *Remuneration requirement.*—The ATEO did not pay 10 percent or more of the individual's total remuneration for services performed as an employee of the ATEO and all related organizations during the applicable year; and

(B) *Related ATEO requirement.*—The ATEO had at least one related ATEO during the applicable year and one of the following conditions applies:

(1) *Ten percent remuneration condition.*—A related ATEO paid at least 10 percent of the remuneration paid by the ATEO and any related organizations during the applicable year; or

(2) *Less remuneration condition.*—No related ATEO paid at least 10 percent of the total remuneration paid by the ATEO and any related organizations and the ATEO paid less remuneration to the individual than at least one related ATEO during the applicable year.

(3) *Examples.*—The following examples illustrate the rules of this paragraph (d). For purposes of these examples, assume any entity referred to as "ATEO" is an ATEO, any entity referred to as "CORP" is not an ATEO and is not a publicly held company within the meaning of section 162(m)(2) unless otherwise stated, and each taxpayer uses the calendar year as its taxable year.

(i) *Example 1 (Employee of two related ATEOs).*—(A) *Facts*. ATEO 1 and ATEO 2 are related organizations and have no other related organizations. Both employ Employee A during calendar year 2022 and pay remuneration to Employee A for Employee A's services. During 2022, Employee A performed services for 1,000 hours as an employee of ATEO 1 and 1,000 hours as an employee of ATEO 2.

(B) *Conclusion*. Employee A may be a covered employee of both ATEO 1 and ATEO 2 as one of the five highest-compensated employees for taxable year 2022 under paragraph (d)(2)(i) of this section because the exceptions in paragraphs (d)(2)(ii) through (iv) of this section do not apply. Because they are related organizations, ATEO 1 and ATEO 2 must each include the remuneration paid to Employee A by the other during each of their applicable years in determining their respective five highest-compensated employees for taxable year 2022.

(ii) *Example 2 (Employee of an ATEO and a related non-ATEO).*— (A) *Facts.* Assume the same facts as in paragraph (d)(3)(i) of this section *(Example 1)*, except that ATEO 1 is instead CORP 1.

(B) *Conclusion (CORP 1).* For taxable year 2022, CORP 1 is not an ATEO and therefore does not need to identify covered employees.

(C) *Conclusion (ATEO 2).* Employee A may be a covered employee of ATEO 2 as one of its five highest-compensated employees for taxable year 2022 under paragraph (d)(2)(i) of this section because no exception in paragraphs (d)(2)(ii) through (iv) of this section applies. ATEO 2 must include the remuneration paid to Employee A by CORP 1 during its applicable year in determining ATEO 2's five highest-compensated employees for taxable year 2022.

(iii) *Example 3 (Amounts for which a deduction is disallowed under section 162(m) are taken into account for purposes of determining the five highest-compensated employees).*—(A) *Facts.* CORP 2 is a publicly held corporation within the meaning of section 162(m)(2) and is a related organization of ATEO 3. ATEO 3 is a corporation that is part of CORP 2's affiliated group (as defined in section 1504, without regard to section 1504(b)) and has no other related organizations. Employee B is a covered employee (as defined in section 162(m)(3)) of CORP 2 and an employee of ATEO 3. In 2022, CORP 2 paid Employee B $8 million of remuneration for services provided as an employee of CORP 2 and ATEO 3 paid Employee B $500,000 of remuneration for services provided as an employee of ATEO 3. $7.5 million of the remuneration is compensation for which a deduction is disallowed pursuant to section 162(m)(1).

(B) *Conclusion.* The $7.5 million of remuneration for which a deduction is disallowed under section 162(m)(1) is taken into account for purposes of determining ATEO 3's five highest-compensated employees. Thus, ATEO 3 is treated as paying Employee B $8.5 million of remuneration for purposes of determining its five highest-compensated employees.

(iv) *Example 4 (Employee disregarded due to receiving no remuneration).*—(A) *Facts.* Employee C is an officer of ATEO 4 who performs more than minor services for ATEO 4. In 2022, neither ATEO 4 nor any related organization paid remuneration or granted a legally binding right to any nonvested remuneration to Employee C. ATEO 4 paid premiums for insurance for liability arising from Employee C's service with ATEO 4, which is properly treated as a working condition fringe benefit excluded from gross income under §1.132-5.

(B) *Conclusion.* Even though Employee C is an employee of ATEO 4, Employee C is disregarded for purposes of determining ATEO 4's five highest-compensated employees for taxable year 2022 under paragraph (d)(2)(i) of this section because neither ATEO 4 nor any related organization paid Employee C any remuneration (nor did they grant a legally binding right to nonvested remuneration) in applicable year 2022. The working condition fringe benefit is not wages within the meaning of section 3401(a), as provided in section 3401(a)(19), and thus is not remuneration within the meaning of §53.4960-2(a).

(v) *Example 5 (Limited hours exception).*—(A) *Facts.* ATEO 5 and CORP 3 are related organizations. ATEO 5 has no other related organizations. Employee D is an employee of CORP 3. As part of Employee D's duties at CORP 3, Employee D serves as an officer of ATEO 5. Only CORP 3 paid remuneration (or granted a legally binding right to nonvested remuneration) to Employee D and ATEO 5 did not reimburse CORP 3 for any portion of Employee D's remuneration in any manner. During 2022, Employee D provided services as an employee for 2,000 hours to CORP 3 and 200 hours to ATEO 5.

(B) *Conclusion.* Even though Employee D is an employee of ATEO 5 because Employee D provided more than minor services as an officer, Employee D is disregarded for purposes of determining ATEO 5's five highest-compensated employees for taxable year 2022. Employee D is disregarded under paragraph (d)(2)(ii) of this section because only CORP 3 paid Employee D any remuneration or granted a legally binding right to nonvested remuneration in applicable year 2022 and Employee D provided services as an employee of ATEO 5 for 200 hours, which is not more than ten percent of the 2,200 total hours (2,000 + 200 = 2,200) worked as an employee of ATEO 5 and all related organizations.

(vi) *Example 6 (Limited hours exception).*—(A) *Facts.* Assume the same facts as in paragraph (d)(3)(v) of this section *(Example 5)*, except that ATEO 5 also provides a reasonable allowance for expenses incurred by Employee D in executing Employee D's duties as an officer of ATEO 5, which is properly excluded from gross income under an accountable plan described in §1.62-2.

(B) *Conclusion.* The conclusion is the same as in paragraph (d)(3)(v)(B) of this section *(Example 5)*. Specifically, even though Employee D is an employee of ATEO 5 because Employee D provided more than minor services for ATEO 5, Employee D is disregarded for purposes of determining ATEO 5's five highest-compensated employees for taxable year 2022 under paragraph (d)(2)(ii) of this section because the expense allowance under the accountable plan is excluded from wages within the meaning of section 3401(a), as provided in §31.3401(a)-4, and thus is not remuneration within the meaning of §53.4960-2(a).

(vii) *Example 7 (No exception applies due to source of payment).*— (A) *Facts.* Assume the same facts as in paragraph (d)(3)(v) of this section *(Example 5)*, except that ATEO 5 has a contractual arrangement with CORP 3 to reimburse CORP 3 for the hours of service Employee D provides to ATEO 5 during applicable year 2022 by paying an amount equal to the total remuneration received by Employee D from both ATEO 5 and CORP 3, multiplied by a fraction equal to the hours of service Employee D provided ATEO 5 over Employee D's total hours of service to both ATEO 5 and CORP 3.

(B) *Conclusion.* Employee D may be one of ATEO 5's five highest-compensated employees for taxable year 2022 under paragraph (d)(2)(i) of this section because the exceptions in paragraphs (d)(2)(ii) through (iv) of this section do not apply. Pursuant to the contractual arrangement between CORP 3 and ATEO 5, ATEO 5 reimburses CORP 3 for a portion of Employee D's remuneration during applicable year 2022; thus, the exceptions under paragraphs (d)(2)(ii) and (iii) of this section do not apply. Further, while ATEO 5 paid Employee D less than 10 percent of the total remuneration from ATEO 5 and all related organizations (200 hours of service to ATEO 5 / 2,200 hours of service to ATEO 5 and all related organizations = 9 percent), it had no related ATEO; thus, the limited services exception under paragraph (d)(2)(iv) of this section does not apply.

(viii) *Example 8 (Nonexempt funds exception for part-time services).*—(A) *Facts.* ATEO 6 and CORP 4 are related organizations. ATEO 6 has no other related organizations and does not control CORP 4. During applicable year 2022, Employee E provided 2,000 hours of services as an employee of CORP 4 and 0 hours of services as an employee of ATEO 6; during applicable year 2023, Employee E provided 1,100 hours of services as an employee of CORP 4 and 900 hours of services as an employee of ATEO 6; during applicable year 2024, Employee E provided 1,100 hours of services as an employee of CORP 4 and 900 hours of services as an employee of ATEO 6. ATEO 6 neither paid any remuneration to Employee E nor paid a fee for services to CORP 4 during any applicable year. No exception under paragraphs (d)(2)(i), (ii), or (iv) applies to Employee E.

(B) *Conclusion (2023).* Employee E is disregarded for purposes of determining ATEO 6's five highest-compensated employees for taxable year 2023 under paragraph (d)(2)(iii) of this section because for applicable years 2022 and 2023, Employee E provided services as an employee of ATEO 6 for not more than 50 percent of the total hours Employee E provided services as an employee of ATEO 6 and CORP 4 (900 hours / 4,000 hours), and ATEO 6 neither paid any remuneration to Employee E nor paid a fee for services to CORP 4 during applicable years 2022 and 2023.

(C) *Conclusion (2024).* Employee E is disregarded for purposes of determining ATEO 6's five highest-compensated employees for taxable year 2024 under paragraph (d)(2)(iii) of this section because for applicable years 2023 and 2024, Employee E provided services as an employee of ATEO 6 for not more than 50 percent of the total hours Employee E provided services as an employee of ATEO 6 and CORP 4 (1,800 hours / 4,000 hours), and ATEO 6 neither paid any remuneration to Employee E nor paid a fee for services to CORP 4 during applicable years 2023 and 2024.

(ix) *Example 9 (Nonexempt funds for full-time services in one applicable year).*—(A) *Facts.* Assume the same facts as in paragraph (d)(3)(viii) of this section *(Example 8)*, except that during applicable year 2022, Employee E provided services as an employee for 2,000 hours to CORP 4 and for 0 hours to ATEO 6; during applicable year 2023, Employee E provided services as an employee for 0 hours to CORP 4 and 2,000 hours to ATEO 6; and during applicable year 2024, Employee E resumes employment with CORP 4 so that Employee E provided services as an employee for 2,000 hours to CORP 4 and 0 hours to ATEO 6.

(B) *Conclusion (2023).* Employee E is disregarded for purposes of determining ATEO 6's five highest-compensated employees for taxable year 2023 under paragraph (d)(2)(iii) of this section because for applicable years 2022 and 2023, Employee E provided services as an employee of ATEO 6 for not more than 50 percent of the total hours Employee E provided services as an employee of ATEO 6 and CORP 4 (2,000 hours / 4,000 hours), and ATEO 6 neither paid any remuneration to Employee E nor paid a fee for services to CORP 4 during applicable years 2022 and 2023.

(C) *Conclusion (2024).* Employee E is disregarded for purposes of determining ATEO 6's five highest-compensated employees for taxable year 2024 under paragraph (d)(2)(iii) of this section because for applicable years 2023 and 2024, Employee E provided services as an employee of ATEO 6 for not more than 50 percent of the total hours Employee E provided services as an employee of ATEO 6 and CORP 4 (2,000 hours / 4,000 hours for ATEO 6 and CORP 4), and ATEO 6 neither paid any remuneration to Employee E nor paid a fee for services to CORP 4 during applicable years 2023 and 2024.

(x) *Example 10 (Nonexempt funds exception for full-time services across two applicable years).*—(A) *Facts.* Assume the same facts as in paragraph (d)(3)(viii)(A) of this section *(Example 8)*, except that during applicable year 2022, Employee E provided services as an employee for 2,000 hours to CORP 4 and for 0 hours to ATEO 6; during applicable year 2023, Employee E provided services as an employee for 600 hours to CORP 4 and for 1,400 hours to ATEO 6; and during applicable year 2024, Employee E provided services as an employee for 1,400 hours to CORP 4 and for 600 hours to ATEO 6.

(B) *Conclusion (2023).* Employee E is disregarded for purposes of determining ATEO 6's five highest-compensated employees for taxable year 2023 under paragraph (d)(2)(iii) of this section because for applicable years 2022 and 2023, Employee E provided services as an employee of ATEO 6 for not more than 50 percent of the total hours Employee E provided services as an employee of ATEO 6 and CORP 4 (1,400 hours / 4,000 hours), and ATEO 6 neither paid any remuneration to Employee E, nor paid a fee for services to CORP 4 during applicable years 2022 and 2023.

(C) *Conclusion (2024).* Employee E is disregarded for purposes of determining ATEO 6's five highest-compensated employees for taxable year 2024 under paragraph (d)(2)(iii) of this section because for applicable years 2023 and 2024, Employee E provided services as an employee of ATEO 6 for not more than 50 percent of the total hours Employee E provided services as an employee of ATEO 6 and CORP 4 (2,000 hours / 4,000 hours), and ATEO 6 neither paid any remuneration to Employee E, nor paid a fee for services to CORP 4 during applicable years 2023 and 2024.

(xi) *Example 11 (Failure under the nonexempt funds exception).*—(A) *Facts.* Assume the same facts as in paragraph (d)(3)(viii)(A) of this section *(Example 8)*, except that during applicable year 2022, Employee E provided services as an employee for 2,000 hours to CORP 4 and for 0 hours to ATEO 6; during applicable year 2023, Employee E provided services as an employee for 600 hours to CORP 4 and for 1,400 hours to ATEO 6; and during applicable year 2024, Employee E provided services as an employee for 1,300 hours to CORP 4 and for 700 hours to ATEO 6.

(B) *Conclusion (2023).* Employee E is disregarded for purposes of determining ATEO 6's five highest-compensated employees for taxable year 2023 under paragraph (d)(2)(iii) of this section because for applicable years 2022 and 2023, Employee E provided services as an employee of ATEO 6 for less than 50 percent of the total hours Employee E provided services as an employee of ATEO 6 and CORP 4 (1,400 hours / 4,000 hours), and ATEO 6 neither paid any remuneration to Employee E, nor paid a fee for services to CORP 4 during applicable years 2022 and 2023.

(C) *Conclusion (2024).* Employee E may be a covered employee of ATEO 6 as one of its five highest-compensated employees for taxable year 2024 because the requirements under paragraph (d)(2)(iii) are not met and no other exception applies. For applicable years 2023 and 2024, Employee E provided services as an employee of ATEO 6 for more than 50 percent of the total hours Employee E provided services as an employee of ATEO 6 and CORP 4 (2,100 hours / 4,000 hours).

(xii) *Example 12 (Limited services exception).*—(A) *Facts.* ATEO 7, ATEO 8, ATEO 9, and ATEO 10 are a group of related organizations, none of which have any other related organizations. During 2022, Employee F is an employee of ATEO 7, ATEO 8, ATEO 9, and ATEO 10. During applicable year 2022, ATEO 7 paid 5 percent of Employee F's remuneration, ATEO 8 paid 10 percent of Employee F's remuneration, ATEO 9 paid 25 percent of Employee F's remuneration, and ATEO 10 paid 60 percent of Employee F's remuneration. No exception under paragraph (d)(2)(i), (ii), or (iii) applies to Employee F for any of ATEO 7, ATEO 8, ATEO 9, or ATEO 10.

(B) *Conclusion (ATEO 7).* Employee F is disregarded for purposes of determining ATEO 7's five highest-compensated employees for taxable year 2022 under paragraph (d)(2)(iv) of this section because ATEO 7 paid less than 10 percent of Employee F's total remuneration from ATEO 7 and all related organizations during applicable year 2022, and another related ATEO paid at least 10 percent of that total remuneration.

(C) *Conclusion (ATEO 8, ATEO 9, and ATEO 10).* Employee F may be a covered employee of ATEO 8, ATEO 9, and ATEO 10 as one of their respective five highest-compensated employees for their taxable years 2022 because each of those ATEOs paid 10 percent or more of Employee F's remuneration during the 2022 applicable year. Thus, the limited services exception under paragraph (d)(2)(iv) of this section does not apply.

(xiii) *Example 13 (Limited services exception if no ATEO paid at least 10 percent of remuneration).*—(A) *Facts.* Assume the same facts as in paragraph (d)(3)(xii) of this section *(Example 12)*, except that for applicable year 2022, ATEO 7 paid 6 percent of F's remuneration, ATEO 8, ATEO 9, and ATEO 10 each paid 5 percent of Employee F's remuneration, and Employee F also works as an employee of CORP 5, a related organization of ATEO 7, ATEO 8, ATEO 9, and ATEO 10 that paid 79 percent of Employee F's remuneration for applicable year 2022.

(B) *Conclusion (ATEO 7).* Employee F may be one of ATEO 7's five highest-compensated employees for taxable year 2022. Although ATEO 7 did not pay Employee F 10 percent or more of the total remuneration paid by ATEO 7 and all of its related organizations, no related ATEO paid more than 10 percent of Employee F's remuneration, and ATEO 7 did not pay less remuneration to Employee F than at least one related ATEO. Thus, the limited services exception under paragraph (d)(2)(iv) of this section does not apply, and Employee F may be one of ATEO 7's five highest-compensated employees because ATEO 7 paid Employee F more remuneration than any other related ATEO.

(C) *Conclusion (ATEO 8, ATEO 9, and ATEO 10).* Employee F is disregarded for purposes of determining the five highest-compensated employees of ATEO 8, ATEO 9, and ATEO 10 for taxable year 2022 under paragraph (d)(2)(iv) of this section because none paid 10 percent or more of Employee F's total remuneration, each had no related ATEO that paid at least 10 percent of Employee F's total remuneration, and each paid less remuneration than at least one related ATEO (ATEO 7).

(e) *Employee.*—(1) *In general.*—*Employee* means an employee as defined in section 3401(c) and § 31.3401(c)-1. Section 31.3401(c)-1 generally defines an employee as any individual performing services if the relationship between the individual and the person for whom the individual performs services is the legal relationship of employer and employee. As set forth in § 31.3401(c)-1, this includes common law employees, as well as officers and employees of government entities, whether or not elected. An employee generally also includes an officer of a corporation, but an officer of a corporation who as such does not perform any services or performs only minor services and who neither receives, nor is entitled to receive, any remuneration is not considered to be an employee of the corporation solely due to the individual's status as an officer of the corporation. Whether an individual is an employee depends on the facts and circumstances.

(2) *Directors.*—A director of a corporation (or an individual holding a substantially similar position in a corporation or other entity) in the individual's capacity as such is not an employee of the corporation. See § 31.3401(c)-1(f).

(3) *Trustees.*—The principles of paragraph (e)(2) of this section apply by analogy to a trustee of any arrangement classified as a trust for Federal tax purposes in § 301.7701-4(a).

(f) *Employer.*—(1) *In general.*—*Employer* means an employer within the meaning of section 3401(d), without regard to section 3401(d)(1) or (2), meaning generally the person or governmental entity for whom the services were performed as an employee. Whether a person or governmental entity is the employer depends on the facts and circumstances, but a person does not cease to be the employer through use of a payroll agent under section 3504, a common paymaster under section 3121(s), a person described in section 3401(d)(1) or (2), a certified professional employer organization under section 7705, or any similar arrangement.

(2) *Disregarded entities.*—In the case of a disregarded entity described in § 301.7701-3, § 301.7701-2(c)(2)(iv) does not apply; thus, the sole owner of the disregarded entity is treated as the employer of any individual performing services as an employee of the disregarded entity.

(g) *Medical services.*—(1) *Medical and veterinary services.*—(i) *In general.*—*Medical services* means services directly performed by a licensed medical professional (as defined in paragraph (g)(2) of this section) for the diagnosis, cure, mitigation, treatment, or prevention of disease in humans or animals; services provided for the purpose of affecting any structure or function of the human or animal body; and other services integral to providing such medical services. For purposes of section 4960, teaching and research services are not medical services except to the extent that they involve the services performed to directly diagnose, cure, mitigate, treat, or prevent disease or affect a structure or function of the body. Administrative services may be integral to directly providing medical services. For example, documenting the care and condition of a patient is integral to providing medical services, as is accompanying another licensed professional as a supervisor while that medical professional provides medical services. However, managing an organization's operations, including scheduling, staffing, appraising employee performance, and other similar functions that may relate to a particular medical professional or professionals who perform medical services, is not integral to providing medical services. See §53.4960-2(a)(2)(ii) for rules regarding allocating remuneration paid to a medical professional who performs both medical services and other services.

(ii) *Examples.*—The following examples illustrate the rules of this paragraph (g):

(A) *Example 1 (Administrative tasks that are integral to providing medical services).*—(1) *Facts.* Employee A is a doctor who is licensed to practice medicine in the state in which Employee A's place of employment is located. In the course of Employee A's practice, Employee A treats patients and performs some closely-related administrative tasks, such as examining and updating patient records.

(2) *Conclusion.* Employee A's administrative tasks are integral to providing medical services and thus are medical services.

(B) *Example 2 (Administrative tasks that are not integral to providing medical services).*—(1) *Facts.* Assume the same facts as in paragraph (g)(1)(ii)(A)(*1*) of this section (Example 1), except that Employee A also performs additional administrative tasks such as analyzing the budget, authorizing capital expenditures, and managing human resources for the organization by which Employee A is employed.

(2) *Conclusion.* Employee A's additional administrative tasks are not integral to providing medical services and thus are not medical services.

(C) *Example 3 (Teaching duties that are and are not medical services).*—(1) *Facts.* Employee B is a medical doctor who is licensed to practice medicine in the state in which her place of employment, a university hospital, is located. Employee B's duties include overseeing and teaching a group of resident physicians who have restricted licenses to practice medicine. Those duties include supervising and instructing the resident physicians while they treat patients and instruction in a classroom setting.

(2) *Conclusion.* Employee B's supervision and instruction of resident physicians during the course of patient treatment are necessary for the treatment, and thus are medical services. Employee B's classroom instruction is not necessary for patient treatment, and thus is not medical services.

(D) *Example 4 (Research services that are and are not medical services).*—(1) *Facts.* Employee C is a licensed medical doctor who is employed to work on a research trial. Employee C provides an experimental treatment to patients afflicted by a disease and performs certain closely-related administrative tasks that ordinarily are performed by a medical professional in a course of patient treatment. As part of the research trial, Employee C also compiles and analyzes patient results and prepares reports and articles that would not ordinarily be prepared by a medical professional in the course of patient treatment.

(2) *Conclusion.* Employee C's services that are ordinarily performed by a medical professional in a course of treatment, including closely-related administrative tasks, are medical services. Because the compilation and analysis of patient results and the formulation of reports and articles are neither services ordinarily performed by a medical professional in a course of treatment nor necessary for such treatment, these services are not medical services.

(2) *Definition of licensed medical professional.*—*Licensed medical professional* means an individual who is licensed under applicable state or local law to perform medical services, including as a doctor, nurse, nurse practitioner, dentist, veterinarian, or other licensed medical professional.

(h) *Predecessor.*—(1) *Asset acquisitions.*—If an ATEO (acquiror) acquires at least 80 percent of the operating assets or total assets (determined by fair market value on the date of acquisition) of another ATEO (target), then the target is a predecessor of the acquiror. For an acquisition of assets that occurs over time, only assets acquired within a 12-month period are taken into account to determine whether at least 80 percent of the target's operating assets or total assets were acquired. However, this 12-month period is extended to include any continuous period that ends or begins on any day during which the acquiror has an arrangement to acquire directly or indirectly, assets of the target. Additions to the assets of target made as part of a plan or arrangement to avoid the application of this subsection to acquiror's purchase of target's assets are disregarded in applying this paragraph. This paragraph (h)(1) applies for purposes of determining whether an employee is a covered employee under paragraph (d)(1) of this section only with respect to a covered employee of the target who commences the performance of services for the acquiror (or a related organization with respect to the acquiror) within the period beginning 12 months before and ending

12 months after the date of the transaction as defined in paragraph (h)(7) of this section.

(2) *Corporate reorganizations.*—A predecessor of an ATEO includes another separate ATEO the stock or assets of which are acquired in a corporate reorganization as defined in section 368(a)(1)(A), (C), (D), (E), (F), or (G)(including by reason of section 368(a)(2)).

(3) *Predecessor change of form or of place of organization.*—An ATEO that restructured by changing its organizational form or place of organization (or both) is a predecessor of the restructured ATEO.

(4) *ATEO that becomes a non-ATEO.*—(i) *General rule.*—An organization is a predecessor of an ATEO if it ceases to be an ATEO and then again becomes an ATEO effective on or before the predecessor end date. The *predecessor end date* is the date that is 36 months following the date that the organization's Federal information return under section 6033 (or, for an ATEO described in paragraph (b)(1)(ii) or (iii) of this section, its Federal income tax return under section 6011(a)) is due (or would be due if the organization were required to file), excluding any extension, for the last taxable year for which the organization previously was an ATEO. If the organization becomes an ATEO again effective after the predecessor end date, then the former ATEO is treated as a separate organization that is not a predecessor of the current ATEO.

(ii) *Intervening changes or entities.*—If an ATEO that ceases to be an ATEO (former ATEO) would be treated as a predecessor to an organization that becomes an ATEO before the predecessor end date (successor ATEO), and if the former ATEO would be treated as a predecessor to each intervening entity (if such intervening entities had been ATEOs) under the rules of this paragraph (h), then the former ATEO is a predecessor of the successor ATEO. For example, if ATEO 1 loses its tax-exempt status and then merges into Corporation X, Corporation X then merges into Corporation Y, and Corporation Y becomes an ATEO before the predecessor end date, then ATEO 1 is a predecessor of Corporation Y.

(5) *Predecessor of a predecessor.*—A reference to a predecessor includes any predecessor or predecessors of such predecessor, as determined under these rules.

(6) *Elections under sections 336(e) and 338.*—For purposes of this paragraph (h), when an ATEO organized as a corporation makes an election to treat as an asset purchase either the sale, exchange, or distribution of stock pursuant to regulations under section 336(e) or the purchase of stock pursuant to regulations under section 338, the corporation that issued the stock is treated as the same corporation both before and after such transaction.

(7) *Date of transaction.*—For purposes of this paragraph (h), the date that a transaction is treated as having occurred is the date on which all events necessary to complete the transaction described in the relevant provision have occurred.

(i) *Related organization.*—(1) *In general.*—*Related organization* means any person or governmental entity, domestic or foreign, that meets any of the following tests:

(i) *Controls or controlled by test.*—The person or governmental entity controls, or is controlled by, the ATEO;

(ii) *Controlled by same persons test.*—The person or governmental entity is controlled by one or more persons that control the ATEO;

(iii) *Supported organization test.*—The person or governmental entity is a supported organization (as defined in section 509(f)(3)) with respect to the ATEO;

(iv) *Supporting organization test.*—The person or governmental entity is a supporting organization described in section 509(a)(3) with respect to the ATEO; or

(v) *VEBA test.*—With regard to an ATEO that is a voluntary employees' beneficiary association (VEBA) described in section 501(c)(9), the person or governmental entity establishes, maintains, or makes contributions to such VEBA.

(2) *Control.*—(i) *In general.*—Control may be direct or indirect. For rules concerning application of the principles of section 318 in applying this paragraph (i)(2), see paragraph (i)(2)(vii) of this section.

(ii) *Stock corporation.*—A person or governmental entity controls a stock corporation if it owns (by vote or value) more than 50 percent of the stock in the stock corporation.

(iii) *Partnership.*—A person or governmental entity controls a partnership if it owns more than 50 percent of the profits interests or capital interests in the partnership, determined in accordance with the rules and principles of § 1.706-1(b)(4)(ii) for a partner's interest in the profits of a partnership and § 1.706-1(b)(4)(iii) for a partner's interest in the capital of a partnership.

(iv) *Trust.*—A person or governmental entity controls a trust if it owns more than 50 percent of the beneficial interests in the trust, determined by actuarial value.

(v) *Nonstock organization.*—(A) *In general.*—A person or governmental entity controls a nonstock organization if more than 50 percent of the trustees or directors of the nonstock organization are either representatives of, or directly or indirectly controlled by, the person or governmental entity. A *nonstock organization* is a nonprofit organization or other organization without owners and includes a governmental entity.

(B) *Control of a trustee or director of a nonstock organization.*— A person or governmental entity controls a trustee or director of the nonstock organization if the person or governmental entity has the power (either at will or at regular intervals) to remove such trustee or director and designate a new one.

(C) *Representatives.*—Trustees, directors, officers, employees, or agents of a person or governmental entity are deemed representatives of the person or governmental entity. However, an employee of a person or governmental entity (other than a trustee, director, or officer, or an employee who possesses at least the authority commonly exercised by an officer) who is a director or trustee of a nonstock organization (or acting in that capacity) will not be treated as a representative of the person or governmental entity if the employee does not act as a representative of the person or governmental entity and that fact is reported in the form and manner prescribed by the Commissioner in forms and instructions.

(vi) *Brother-sister related organizations.*—Under paragraph (i)(1)(ii) of this section, an organization is a related organization with respect to an ATEO if one or more persons control both the ATEO and the other organization. In the case of control by multiple persons, the control tests described in this paragraph (i)(2) of this section apply to the persons as a group. For example, if 1,000 individuals who are members of both ATEO 1 and ATEO 2 elect a majority of the board members of each organization, then ATEO 1 and ATEO 2 are related to each other because the same group of 1,000 persons controls both ATEO 1 and ATEO 2.

(vii) *Section 318 principles.*—(A) *In general.*—Section 318 (relating to constructive ownership of stock) applies in determining ownership of stock in a corporation. The principles of section 318 also apply for purposes of determining ownership of interests in a partnership or in a trust with beneficial interests. For example, applying the principles of section 318(a)(1)(A), an individual is considered to own the partnership interest or trust interest owned, directly or indirectly, by or for the family members specified in such section.

(B) *Nonstock organizations.*—(1) *Attribution of ownership interest from a nonstock organization to a controlling person.*—If a person or governmental entity controls a nonstock organization, the person or governmental entity is treated as owning a percentage of the stock (or partnership interest or beneficial interest in a trust) owned by the nonstock organization in accordance with the percentage of trustees or directors of the nonstock organization that are representatives of, or directly or indirectly controlled by, the person or governmental entity.

(2) *Attribution of ownership interest from a controlling person to a nonstock organization.*—If a person or governmental entity controls a nonstock organization, the nonstock organization is treated as owning a percentage of the stock (or partnership interest or beneficial interest in a trust) owned by the person or governmental entity in accordance with the percentage of trustees or directors of the nonstock organization that are representatives of, or directly or indirectly controlled by, the person or governmental entity.

(3) *Indirect control of a nonstock organization through another nonstock organization.*—If a person or governmental entity controls one nonstock organization that controls a second nonstock organization, the person or governmental entity is treated as controlling the second nonstock organization if the product of the percentage of trustees or directors of the first nonstock organization that are representatives of, or directly or indirectly controlled by, the person or governmental entity, multiplied by the percentage of trustees or directors of the second nonstock organization that are representatives of, or directly or indirectly controlled by, the person or governmental entity or first nonstock organization, exceeds 50 percent. Similar principles apply to successive tiers of nonstock organizations.

(4) *Attribution of control of nonstock organization to family member.*—An individual's control of a nonstock organization or of a

trustee or director of a nonstock organization is attributed to the members of the individual's family (as set forth in section 318(a)(1) and the regulations thereunder), subject to the limitation of section 318(a)(5)(B) and the regulations thereunder.

(3) *Examples.*—The following examples illustrate the principles of this paragraph (i). For purposes of these examples, assume any entity referred to as "ATEO" is an ATEO and any entity referred to as "CORP" is not an ATEO.

(i) *Example 1 (Related through a chain of control).*—(A) *Facts.* ATEO 1, ATEO 2, and ATEO 3 are nonstock organizations. ATEO 3 owns 80 percent of the stock (by value) of corporation CORP 1. Eighty percent of ATEO 2's directors are representatives of ATEO 1. In addition, 80 percent of ATEO 3's directors are representatives of ATEO 1.

(B) *Conclusion.* ATEO 1 is a related organization with respect to ATEO 2 (and vice versa) because more than 50 percent of ATEO 2's directors are representatives of ATEO 1; thus, ATEO 1 controls ATEO 2. Based on the same analysis, ATEO 1 is also a related organization with respect to ATEO 3 (and vice versa). CORP 1 is a related organization with respect to ATEO 3 because, as the owner of more than 50 percent of CORP 1's stock, ATEO 3 controls CORP 1. Applying the principles of section 318, ATEO 1 is deemed to own 64 percent of the stock of CORP 1 (80 percent of ATEO 3's stock in CORP 1). Thus, CORP 1 is a related organization with respect to ATEO 1 because ATEO 1 controls CORP 1. ATEO 2 is a related organization with respect to ATEO 3, ATEO 3 is a related organization with respect to ATEO 2, and CORP 1 is a related organization with respect to ATEO 2 because ATEO 2, ATEO 3, and CORP 1 are all controlled by the same person (ATEO 1).

(ii) *Example 2 (Not related through a chain of control).*—(A) *Facts.* ATEO 4, ATEO 5, and ATEO 6 are nonstock organizations. Sixty percent of ATEO 5's directors are representatives of ATEO 4. In addition, 60 percent of ATEO 6's directors are representatives of ATEO 5, but none are representatives of ATEO 4.

(B) *Conclusion.* ATEO 4 is a related organization with respect to ATEO 5 (and vice versa) because more than 50 percent of ATEO 5's directors are representatives of ATEO 4; thus, ATEO 4 controls ATEO 5. Based on the same analysis, ATEO 6 is a related organization with respect to ATEO 5 (and vice versa). Applying the principles of section 318, ATEO 4 is deemed to control 36 percent of ATEO 6's directors (60 percent of ATEO 5's 60 percent control over ATEO 6). Because less than 50 percent of ATEO 6's directors are representatives of ATEO 4, and absent any facts suggesting that ATEO 4 directly or indirectly controls ATEO 6, ATEO 4 and ATEO 6 are not related organizations with respect to each other. [Reg. § 53.4960-1.]

☐ [*T.D.* 9938, 1-15-2021.]

**[Reg. § 53.4960-2]**

**§ 53.4960-2. Determination of remuneration paid for a taxable year.**—(a) *Remuneration.*—(1) *In general.*—For purposes of section 4960, *remuneration* means any amount that is wages as defined in section 3401(a), excluding any designated Roth contribution (as defined in section 402A(c)) and including any amount required to be included in gross income under section 457(f). Remuneration includes amounts includible in gross income as compensation for services as an employee pursuant to a below-market loan described in section 7872(c)(1)(B)(i) (compensation-related loans) but does not include amounts excepted by section 7872(c)(3) ($10,000 de minimis exception). For example, see § 1.7872-15(e)(1)(i). Director's fees paid by a corporation to a director of the corporation are not remuneration, provided that if the director is also an employee of the corporation, the director's fees are excluded from remuneration only to the extent that they do not exceed fees paid to a director who is not an employee of the corporation or any related organization or, if there is no such director, they do not exceed reasonable director's fees. Remuneration does not include any amount that vested or was paid by a taxpayer before the start of the taxpayer's first taxable year that began on or after January 1, 2018.

(2) *Exclusion of remuneration for medical services.*—(i) *In general.*— Remuneration does not include the portion of any remuneration paid to a licensed medical professional that is for the performance of medical services by such professional.

(ii) *Allocation of remuneration for medical services and non-medical services.*—If, during an applicable year, an employer pays a covered employee remuneration for providing both medical services and non-medical services, the employer must make a reasonable, good faith allocation between the remuneration for medical services and the remuneration for non-medical services. For example, if a medical doctor receives current remuneration (or vests in remuneration under a deferred compensation plan) for providing medical services and administrative or management services, the employer must make a reasonable, good faith allocation between the remuneration for the medical services and the remuneration for the administrative or management services. For this purpose, if an employment agreement or similar written arrangement sets forth the remuneration to be paid for particular services, that allocation of remuneration applies unless the facts and circumstances demonstrate that the amount allocated to medical services is unreasonable for those services or that the allocation was established for purposes of avoiding application of the excise tax under section 4960. If some or all of the remuneration is not reasonably allocated in an employment agreement or similar arrangement, an employer may use any reasonable allocation method. For example, an employer may use a representative sample of records, such as patient, insurance, and Medicare/Medicaid billing records or internal time reporting mechanisms to determine the time spent providing medical services, and then allocate remuneration to medical services in the proportion such time bears to the total hours the employee worked for the employer (and any related employer) for purposes of making a reasonable allocation of remuneration. Similarly, if some or all of the remuneration is not reasonably allocated in an employment agreement or other similar arrangement, an employer may use salaries or other remuneration paid by the employer or similarly situated employers for duties comparable to those the employee performs (for example, hospital administrator and physician) for purposes of making a reasonable allocation between remuneration for providing medical services and for providing non-medical services.

(iii) *Examples.*—The following examples illustrate the rules of this paragraph (a)(2). For purposes of these examples, assume any entity referred to as "ATEO" is an ATEO.

(A) *Example 1 (Allocation based on employment agreement).*— (1) *Facts.* Employee A is a covered employee of ATEO 1. Employee A is a licensed medical professional who provides patient care services for ATEO 1 and also provides management and administrative services to ATEO 1 as the manager of a medical practice group within ATEO 1. The employment agreement between ATEO 1 and Employee A specifies that of Employee A's salary, 30 percent is allocable to Employee A's services as manager of the medical practice group and 70 percent is allocable to Employee A's services as a medical professional providing patient care services. The facts regarding Employee A's employment indicate the employment agreement provides a reasonable allocation and that the allocation was not established for purposes of avoiding application of the excise tax.

(2) *Conclusion.* Consistent with Employee A's employment agreement, ATEO 1 must allocate 30 percent of Employee A's salary to the provision of non-medical services and 70 percent of Employee A's salary to the provision of medical services. Accordingly, only the 30 percent portion of Employee A's salary allocated to the other, non-medical services is remuneration for purposes of paragraph (a) of this section.

(B) *Example 2 (Allocation based on billing records).*—(1) *Facts.* Assume the same facts as in paragraph (a)(2)(iii)(A) of this section (Example 1), except that the employment agreement does not allocate Employee A's salary between medical and non-medical services performed by Employee A. Based on a representative sample of insurance and Medicare billing records, as well as time reports that Employee A submits to ATEO 1, ATEO 1 determines that Employee A spends 50 percent of her work hours providing patient care and 50 percent of her work hours performing administrative and management services. ATEO 1 allocates 50 percent of Employee A's remuneration to medical services.

(2) *Conclusion.* ATEO 1's allocation of Employee A's salary is a reasonable, good faith allocation. Accordingly, only the 50 percent portion of Employee A's remuneration allocated to the non-medical services is remuneration for purposes of paragraph (a) of this section.

(b) *Source of payment.*—For purposes of this section, the determination of the source of a payment of remuneration may involve the application of one or both of two separate rules described in this paragraph (b). Paragraph (b)(1) of this section addresses payments by a third party for services performed as an employee of a separate employer entity, while paragraph (b)(2) of this section addresses the application of section 4960(c)(4)(A) to treat certain remuneration paid by a related organization (after application of paragraph (b)(1) of this section, if applicable) as paid by the ATEO.

(1) *Remuneration paid by a third party for employment by an employer.*—Remuneration paid (or a grant of a legally binding right to nonvested remuneration) by a third-party payor (whether a related organization, payroll agent, agent designated under section 3504, certified professional employer organization under section 7705, or other entity) during an applicable year for services performed as an employee of an employer is remuneration paid (or payable) by the employer, except as otherwise provided in §53.4960-1(d)(2)(ii) and (iii).

(2) *Remuneration paid by a related organization for employment by the related organization.*—Pursuant to section 4960(c)(4)(A), remuneration paid (or a grant of a legally binding right to nonvested remuneration) by a related organization to an ATEO's employee during an applicable year for services performed as an employee of the related organization is treated as remuneration paid (or payable) by the ATEO, except as otherwise provided in §53.4960-1(d)(2)(ii) and (iii).

(c) *Applicable year in which remuneration is treated as paid.*—(1) *In general.*—Remuneration that is a regular wage within the meaning of §31.3402(g)-1(a)(1)(ii) is treated as paid on the date it is actually or constructively paid and all other remuneration is treated as paid on the first date on which the remuneration is vested.

(2) *Vested remuneration.*—Remuneration is *vested* if it is not subject to a substantial risk of forfeiture within the meaning of section 457(f)(3)(B) (regardless of whether the arrangement under which the remuneration is to be paid is deferred compensation described in section 457(f) or 409A). In general, an amount is subject to a substantial risk of forfeiture if entitlement to the amount is conditioned on the future performance of substantial services or upon the occurrence of a condition that is related to a purpose of the remuneration if the possibility of forfeiture is substantial. Except as provided in paragraph (c)(1) of this section, remuneration that is never subject to a substantial risk of forfeiture is considered paid on the first date the service provider has a legally binding right to the payment. For purposes of this section, a *plan* means a plan within the meaning of §1.409A-1(c), an *account balance plan* means an account balance plan within the meaning of §1.409A-1(c)(2)(i)(A), and a *nonaccount balance plan* means a nonaccount balance plan within the meaning of §1.409A-1(c)(2)(i)(C). Net earnings on previously paid remuneration (described in paragraph (d)(2) of this section) that are not subject to a substantial risk of forfeiture are vested (and, thus, treated as paid) at the earlier of the date actually or constructively paid to the employee or the close of the applicable year in which they accrue. For example, the present value of a principal amount accrued to an employee's account under an account balance plan (under which the earnings and losses attributed to the account are based solely on a predetermined actual investment as determined under §31.3121(v)(2)-1(d)(2)(i)(B) or a reasonable market interest rate) is treated as paid on the date vested, but the present value of any net earnings subsequently accrued on that amount (the increase in value due to the predetermined actual investment or a reasonable market interest rate) is treated as paid at the close of the applicable year in which they accrue. Similarly, while the present value of an amount accrued under a nonaccount balance (including earnings that accrued while the amount was nonvested) is treated as paid on the date it is first vested, the present value of the net earnings on that amount (the increase in the present value) is treated as paid at the close of the applicable year in which they accrue.

(3) *Change in related status during the year.*—If a taxpayer becomes or ceases to be a related organization with respect to an ATEO during an applicable year, then only the remuneration paid by the taxpayer to an employee with respect to services performed as an employee of the related organization during the portion of the applicable year during which the employer is a related organization is treated as paid by the ATEO. If an amount is treated as paid due to vesting in the year the taxpayer becomes or ceases to be a related organization with respect to the ATEO, then the amount is treated as paid by the ATEO only if the amount becomes vested during the portion of the applicable year that the taxpayer is a related organization with respect to the ATEO.

(d) *Amount of remuneration treated as paid.*—(1) *In general.*—For each applicable year, the amount of remuneration treated as paid by the employer to a covered employee is the sum of regular wages within the meaning of §31.3402(g)-1(a)(1)(ii) actually or constructively paid during the applicable year and the present value (as determined under paragraph (e) of this section) of all other remuneration that vested during the applicable year. The amount of remuneration that vests during an applicable year is determined on an employer-by-employer basis with respect to each covered employee.

(2) *Earnings and losses on previously paid remuneration.*—(i) *In general.*—The amount of net earnings or losses on previously paid remuneration paid by an employer is determined on an employee-by-employee basis, such that amounts accrued with regard to one employee do not affect amounts accrued with regard to a different employee. Similarly, losses accrued on previously paid remuneration from one employer do not offset earnings accrued on previously paid remuneration from another employer. The amount of net earnings or losses on previously paid remuneration paid by the employer is determined on a net aggregate basis for all plans maintained by the

employer in which the employee participates for each applicable year. For example, losses under an account balance plan may offset earnings under a nonaccount balance plan for the same applicable year maintained by the same employer for the same employee.

(ii) *Previously paid remuneration.*—(A) *New covered employee.*— For an individual who was not a covered employee for any prior applicable year, *previously paid remuneration* means, for the applicable year for which the individual becomes a covered employee, the present value of vested remuneration that was not actually or constructively paid or otherwise includible in the employee's gross income before the start of the applicable year plus any remuneration that vested during the applicable year but that is not actually or constructively paid or otherwise includible in the employee's gross income before the close of the applicable year.

(B) *Existing covered employee.*—For an individual who was a covered employee for any prior applicable year, *previously paid remuneration* means, for each applicable year, the amount of remuneration that the employer treated as paid in the applicable year or for a prior applicable year but that is not actually or constructively paid or otherwise includible in the employee's gross income before the close of the applicable year. Actual or constructive payment or another event causing an amount of previously paid remuneration to be includible in the employee's gross income thus reduces the amount of previously paid remuneration.

(iii) *Earnings.*—*Earnings* means any increase in the vested present value of previously paid remuneration as of the close of the applicable year, regardless of whether the plan denominates the increase as earnings. For example, an increase in the vested account balance of a nonqualified deferred compensation plan based solely on the investment return of a predetermined actual investment (and disregarding any additional contributions) constitutes earnings. Similarly, an increase in the vested present value of a benefit under a nonqualified nonaccount balance plan due solely to the passage of time (and disregarding any additional benefit accruals) constitutes earnings. However, an increase in an account balance of a nonqualified deferred compensation plan due to a salary reduction contribution or an employer contribution does not constitute earnings (and therefore may not be offset with losses). Likewise, an increase in the benefit under a nonaccount balance plan due to an additional year of service or an increase in compensation that is reflected in a benefit formula does not constitute earnings.

(iv) *Losses.*—*Losses* means any decrease in the vested present value of previously paid remuneration as of the close of the applicable year, regardless of whether the plan denominates that decrease as losses.

(v) *Net earnings.*—*Net earnings* means, for each applicable year, the amount (if any) by which the earnings accrued for the applicable year on previously paid remuneration exceeds the sum of the losses accrued on previously paid remuneration for the applicable year and any net losses carried forward from a previous taxable year.

(vi) *Net losses.*—*Net losses* means, for each applicable year, the amount (if any) by which the sum of the losses accrued on previously paid remuneration for the applicable year and any net losses carried forward from a previous taxable year exceed the earnings accrued for the applicable year on previously paid remuneration. Losses may only be used to offset earnings and thus do not reduce the remuneration treated as paid for an applicable year except to the extent of the earnings accrued for that applicable year. However, with regard to a covered employee, an employer may carry net losses forward to the next applicable year and offset vested earnings for purposes of determining net earnings or losses for that subsequent applicable year. For example, if a covered employee who participates in a nonaccount balance plan and an account balance plan vests in an amount of earnings under the nonaccount balance plan and has losses under the account balance plan that exceed the vested earnings treated as remuneration under the nonaccount balance plan, those excess losses are carried forward to the next applicable year and offset vested earnings for purposes of determining net earnings or losses for that applicable year. If, for the next applicable year, there are not sufficient earnings to offset the entire amount of losses carried forward from the previous year (and any additional losses), the offset process repeats for each subsequent applicable year until there are sufficient earnings for the applicable year to offset any remaining losses carried forward.

(3) *Remuneration paid for a taxable year before the employee becomes a covered employee.*—(i) *In general.*—In accordance with the payment timing rules of paragraph (c) of this section, any remuneration that is vested but is not actually or constructively paid or otherwise includible in an employee's gross income as of the close of the applicable

year for the taxable year immediately preceding the taxable year in which the employee first becomes a covered employee of an ATEO is treated as previously paid remuneration for the taxable year in which the employee first becomes a covered employee. Net losses on this previously paid remuneration from any preceding applicable year do not carry forward to subsequent applicable years. However, net earnings and losses that vest on such previously paid remuneration in subsequent applicable years are treated as remuneration paid for a taxable year for which the employee is a covered employee.

(ii) *Examples.*—The following examples illustrate the rules of this paragraph (d)(3). For purposes of these examples, assume any organization described as "ATEO" is an ATEO.

(A) *Example 1 (Earnings on pre-covered employee remuneration).*—(1) *Facts.* ATEO 1 uses a taxable year beginning July 1 and ending June 30. Employee A becomes a covered employee of ATEO 1 for the taxable year beginning July 1, 2023, and ending June 30, 2024. During the 2022 applicable year, Employee A vests in $1 million of nonqualified deferred compensation. As of December 31, 2022, the present value of the amount deferred under the plan is $1.1 million. During the 2023 applicable year, ATEO 1 pays Employee A $1 million in regular wages. The present value as of December 31, 2023, of Employee A's nonqualified deferred compensation is $1.3 million.

(2) *Conclusion (Taxable year beginning July 1, 2022, and ending June 30, 2023).* ATEO 1 pays Employee A $1.1 million of remuneration in the 2022 applicable year. This is comprised of $1 million of vested nonqualified deferred compensation, and $100,000 of earnings, all of which is treated as paid for the taxable year beginning July 1, 2022, and ending June 30, 2023.

(3) *Conclusion (Taxable year beginning July 1, 2023, and ending June 30, 2024).* ATEO 1 pays Employee A $1.2 million of remuneration in the 2023 applicable year. This is comprised of $1 million regular wages and $200,000 of earnings ($1.3 million present value as of December 31, 2023, minus $1.1 million previously paid remuneration as of December 31, 2022).

(B) *Example 2 (Losses on pre-covered employee remuneration).*— (1) *Facts.* Assume the same facts as in paragraph (d)(3)(ii)(A) of this section (Example 1), except that the present value of the nonqualified deferred compensation as of December 31, 2022, is $900,000.

(2) *Conclusion (Taxable year beginning July 1, 2022, and ending June 30, 2023).* ATEO 1 pays Employee A $1 million of remuneration in the 2022 applicable year. This is comprised of $1 million of vested nonqualified deferred compensation. The present value of all vested deferred compensation as of December 31 of the 2022 applicable year ($900,000) is treated as previously paid remuneration for the next applicable year (as Employee A is a covered employee for the next taxable year). The $100,000 of losses accrued while Employee A was not a covered employee do not carry forward to the next applicable year.

(3) *Conclusion (Taxable year beginning July 1, 2023, and ending June 30, 2024).* ATEO 1 pays Employee A $1.4 million of remuneration in the 2023 applicable year. This is comprised of $1 million cash and $400,000 of earnings ($1.3 million present value as of December 31, 2023, minus $900,000 previously paid remuneration).

(e) *Calculation of present value.*—(1) *In general.*—The employer must determine present value using reasonable actuarial assumptions regarding the amount, time, and probability that a payment will be made. For this purpose, a discount for the probability that an employee will die before commencement of benefit payments is permitted, but only to the extent that benefits will be forfeited upon death. The present value may not be discounted for the probability that payments will not be made (or will be reduced) because of the unfunded status of the plan; the risk associated with any deemed or actual investment of amounts deferred under the plan; the risk that the employer, the trustee, or another party will be unwilling or unable to pay; the possibility of future plan amendments; the possibility of a future change in the law; or similar risks or contingencies. The present value of the right to future payments as of the vesting date includes any earnings that have accrued as of the vesting date that are not previously paid remuneration.

(2) *Treatment of future payment amount as present value for certain amounts.*—For purposes of determining the present value of remuneration that is scheduled to be actually or constructively paid within 90 days of vesting, the employer may treat the future amount that is to be paid as the present value at vesting.

(f) *Examples.*—The following examples illustrate the rules of this section. For purposes of these examples, assume any entity referred to as "ATEO" is an ATEO, any entity referred to as "CORP" is not an ATEO, and all taxpayers use the calendar year as their taxable year.

(1) *Example 1 (Account balance plan).*—(i) *Facts.* Employee A is a covered employee of ATEO 1. Employee A participates in a nonquali-

fied deferred compensation plan (the NQDC plan) in which the account balance is adjusted based on the investment returns on predetermined actual investments. On January 1, 2022, ATEO 1 credits $100,000 to Employee A's account under the plan, subject to the requirement that Employee A remain employed through June 30, 2024. On June 30, 2024, the vested account balance is $110,000. Due to earnings or losses on the account balance, the closing account balance on each of the following dates is: $115,000 on December 31, 2024, $120,000 on December 31, 2025, $100,000 on December 31, 2026, and $110,000 on December 31, 2027. During 2028, Employee A defers an additional $10,000 under the plan, all of which is vested at the time of deferral. On December 31, 2028, the closing account balance is $125,000. In 2029, ATEO 1 pays $10,000 to Employee A under the plan. On December 31, 2029, the closing account balance is $135,000 due to earnings on the account balance.

(ii) *Conclusion (2022 and 2023 applicable years—nonvested amounts).* For 2022 and 2023, ATEO 1 is not treated as paying Employee A any remuneration attributable to Employee A's participation in the NQDC plan because the amount deferred under the plan remains subject to a substantial risk of forfeiture within the meaning of section 457(f)(3)(B).

(iii) *Conclusion (2024 applicable year—amounts in year of vesting).* For 2024, ATEO 1 is treated as paying Employee A $115,000 of remuneration attributable to Employee A's participation in the NQDC plan, including $110,000 of remuneration on June 30, 2024, when the amount becomes vested, and an additional $5,000 of remuneration on December 31, 2024, which is earnings on the previously paid remuneration ($110,000).

(iv) *Conclusion (2025 applicable year—earnings).* For 2025, ATEO 1 is treated as paying Employee A $5,000 of remuneration attributable to Employee A's participation in the NQDC plan, which is the additional earnings on the previously paid remuneration ($115,000) as of December 31, 2025.

(v) *Conclusion (2026 applicable year—losses).* For 2026, ATEO 1 is not treated as paying Employee A any remuneration attributable to Employee A's participation in the NQDC plan because the present value of the previously paid remuneration ($120,000) decreased to $100,000 as of December 31, 2026. The $20,000 loss for 2026 does not reduce any amount previously treated as remuneration but is available for carryover to subsequent taxable years to offset earnings.

(vi) *Conclusion (2027 applicable year—recovery of losses).* For 2027, ATEO 1 is not treated as paying Employee A any remuneration attributable to Employee A's participation in the NQDC plan because the present value of the previously paid remuneration ($120,000) was $110,000 as of December 31, 2027. Due to increases on the account balance, ATEO 1 recovers $10,000 of the $20,000 of losses carried over from 2026. The net losses as of December 31, 2027, are $10,000, and none of the $10,000 in earnings during 2027 is treated as remuneration paid in 2027.

(vii) *Conclusion (2028 applicable year—no recovery of losses against additional deferrals of compensation).* For 2028, ATEO 1 is treated as paying Employee A $10,000 of remuneration attributable to Employee A's participation in the NQDC plan. The additional $10,000 deferral is vested and thus is treated as remuneration paid on the date credited to Employee A's account. This credit increases the amount of previously paid remuneration from $120,000 to $130,000. Additionally, due to earnings, ATEO 1 recovers $5,000 of the $10,000 loss carried over from 2027, none of which was remuneration paid for 2028, so that as of December 31, 2028, the net loss available for carryover to 2029 is $5,000.

(viii) *Conclusion (2029 applicable year—distributions, recovery of remainder of losses through earnings and additional earnings).* For 2029, ATEO 1 is treated as paying Employee A $15,000 of remuneration attributable to Employee A's participation in the NQDC plan. The $10,000 payment reduces the amount of previously paid remuneration (from $130,000 to $120,000) and the account balance (from $125,000 to $115,000). The present value of the vested account balance increases by $20,000 (from $115,000 to $135,000) as of December 31, 2029. Therefore, due to earnings, ATEO 1 recovers the remaining $5,000 loss carried over from 2028 (the difference between the $120,000 previously paid remuneration before earnings and the $115,000 account balance before earnings) and is treated as paying Employee A an additional $15,000 of remuneration as earnings (the difference between the $135,000 account balance after earnings and the $120,000 previously paid remuneration after loss recovery).

(2) *Example 2 (Nonaccount balance plan with earnings).—(i) Facts.* ATEO 2 and CORP 2 are related organizations. Employee B is a covered employee of ATEO 2 and is also employed by CORP 2. On January 1, 2022, CORP 2 and Employee B enter into an agreement under which CORP 2 will pay Employee B $100,000 on December 31, 2025, if B remains employed by CORP 2 through January 1, 2024. Employee B remains employed by CORP 2 through January 1, 2024. On January 1, 2024, the present value based on reasonable actuarial assumptions of the $100,000 to be paid on December 31, 2025, is $75,000. On December 31, 2024, the present value of the $100,000 future payment increases to $85,000 due solely to the passage of time. On December 31, 2025, CORP 2 pays Employee B $100,000.

(ii) *Conclusion (2022 and 2023 applicable years—nonvested amounts).* For 2022 and 2023, CORP 2 is not treated as paying Employee B any remuneration attributable to the agreement because the amount deferred under the agreement remains subject to a substantial risk of forfeiture within the meaning of section 457(f)(3)(B).

(iii) *Conclusion (2024 applicable year—amounts in year of vesting).* For 2024, CORP 2 is treated as paying Employee B $75,000 of remuneration attributable to the agreement on January 1, 2024, which is the present value on that date of the $100,000 payable on December 31, 2025. In addition, CORP 2 is treated as paying Employee B $10,000 of remuneration attributable to the agreement on December 31, 2024, which is earnings based on the increase in the present value of the previously paid remuneration (from $75,000 to $85,000) as of December 31, 2024.

(iv) *Conclusion (2025 applicable year—earnings and distribution of previously paid remuneration).* For 2025, CORP 2 is treated as paying Employee B $15,000 in remuneration attributable to the agreement on December 31, 2025, which is earnings based on the increase in the present value of the previously paid remuneration (from $85,000 to $100,000) as of December 31, 2025. In addition, the $100,000 payment is treated as reducing the amount of previously paid remuneration ($100,000) to zero.

(3) *Example 3 (Treatment of amount payable as present value at vesting).—(i) Facts.* Employee C is a covered employee of ATEO 3. Under an agreement between ATEO 3 and Employee C, ATEO 3 agrees to pay Employee C $100,000 two months after the date Employee C meets a specified performance goal that is a substantial risk of forfeiture within the meaning of section 457(f)(3)(B). Employee C meets the performance goal on November 30, 2022, and ATEO 3 pays Employee C $100,000 on January 31, 2023. In accordance with § 53.4960-2(e)(2), because the payment is to be made within 90 days of vesting, ATEO 3 elects to treat the full payment amount as the amount of remuneration paid at vesting.

(ii) *Conclusion (2022 applicable year—election to treat amount payable within 90 days as paid at vesting).* For taxable year 2022, ATEO 3 is treated as paying Employee C $100,000 of remuneration attributable to the agreement. Employee C vests in the $100,000 payment in 2022 upon meeting the performance goal. Under the general rule, ATEO 3 would be treated as paying for the taxable year 2022 the present value as of November 30, 2022, of $100,000 payable on January 31, 2023 (two months after the date of vesting), with adjustments to the present value as of the end of the year. However, because ATEO 3 elected to treat the full $100,000 amount payable within 90 days of vesting as the remuneration paid, the $100,000 payable to Employee C in 2023 is treated as remuneration paid in 2022 (and no additional amount related to the $100,000 paid on January 31, 2023, is treated as remuneration paid in 2023).

(4) *Example 4 (Aggregation of remuneration from related organizations).—(i) Facts.* Employee D is a covered employee of ATEO 4 and also an employee of CORP 4 and CORP 5. ATEO 4, CORP 4, and CORP 5 are related organizations. ATEO 4, CORP 4, and CORP 5 each pay Employee D $200,000 of salary during 2022 and 2023. On January 1, 2022, ATEO 4 promises to pay Employee D $120,000 on December 31, 2023, under a nonaccount balance plan, the right to which is vested and the present value of which is $100,000 on January 1, 2022. On January 1, 2022, CORP 4 and CORP 5 each contribute $100,000 on Employee D's behalf to account balance plans of CORP 4 and CORP 5, respectively, under which all amounts deferred are vested. On December 31, 2022, the present value of the amounts deferred under the ATEO 4 plan is $110,000, the present value of the amounts deferred under the CORP 4 plan is $120,000, and the present value of the amounts deferred under the CORP 5 plan maintained is $90,000. On December 31, 2023, the present value of the amounts deferred under the ATEO 4 plan is $120,000, the present value of the amounts deferred under the CORP 4 plan is $130,000, and the present value of the amounts deferred under the CORP 5 plan is $110,000.

(ii) *Conclusion (2022 applicable year).* For 2022, before aggregation of remuneration paid by related organizations, ATEO 4 is treated as paying Employee D $310,000 of remuneration ($200,000 salary + $100,000 upon vesting of deferred amounts + $10,000 net earnings on vested deferred amounts). CORP 4 is treated as paying Employee D $320,000 of remuneration ($200,000 salary + $100,000 upon vesting of deferred amounts + $20,000 net earnings on vested deferred amounts). CORP 5 is treated as paying Employee D $300,000 of remuneration ($200,000 salary + $100,000 upon vesting of deferred amounts) and has $10,000 of net losses on vested deferred amounts, which are carried forward to 2023. Thus, ATEO 4 is treated as paying $930,000 of remuneration to Employee D for the applicable year.

(iii) *Conclusion (2023 applicable year)*. For 2023, before aggregation of remuneration paid by related organizations, ATEO 4 is treated as paying Employee D $210,000 of remuneration ($200,000 salary + $10,000 earnings on previously paid remuneration). CORP 4 is treated as paying Employee D $210,000 of remuneration ($200,000 salary + $10,000 net earnings on previously paid remuneration). CORP 5 is treated as paying Employee D $210,000 of remuneration ($200,000 salary + $10,000 net earnings on previously paid remuneration after taking into account the loss carryforward). Thus, ATEO 4 is treated as paying $630,000 of remuneration to Employee D for the applicable year.

(5) *Example 5 (Treatment of regular wages for a pay period spanning applicable years)*.—(i) *Facts*. ATEO 5 pays its employees' salaries in accordance with a two-week payroll period that begins Sunday of the first week and ends Saturday of the second week. Payment occurs the Friday following the end of the payroll period. The last payroll period of 2023 ends on December 31, 2023. For the last payroll period, Employee E earns $8,000 of salary. In addition, ATEO 5 awards Employee E a $10,000 bonus that vests on December 31, 2023. ATEO 5 pays Employee E $18,000 on Friday, January 5, 2024, reflecting Employee E's salary for the last payroll period of 2023 and the bonus, the right to which vested on December 31, 2023.

(ii) *Conclusion (Regular wages)*. The $8,000 of salary is regular wages within the meaning of § 31.3402(g)-1-a(1)(ii) because it is an amount paid at a periodic rate for the current payroll period. Thus, $8,000 is treated as remuneration paid on January 5, 2024 (when it is actually or constructively paid), and, therefore, is treated as remuneration paid in ATEO 5's 2024 applicable year.

(iii) *Conclusion (Amounts other than regular wages)*. The $10,000 bonus is not regular wages within the meaning of § 31.3402(g)-1(a)(1)(ii) because it is not an amount paid at a periodic rate for the current payroll period. Thus, $10,000 is treated as remuneration paid on December 31, 2023 (when it is vested) and, therefore, is treated as remuneration paid in ATEO 5's 2023 applicable year. [Reg. § 53.4960-2.]

☐ [*T.D. 9938*, 1-15-2021.]

### [Reg. § 53.4960-3]

**§ 53.4960-3. Determination of whether there is a parachute payment.**—(a) *Parachute payment*.—(1) *In general*.—Except as otherwise provided in paragraph (a)(2) of this section (relating to payments excluded from the definition of a parachute payment), *parachute payment* means any payment in the nature of compensation made by an ATEO (or a predecessor of the ATEO) or a related organization to (or for the benefit of) a covered employee if the payment is contingent on the employee's separation from employment with the employer, and the aggregate present value of the payments in the nature of compensation to (or for the benefit of) the individual that are contingent on the separation equals or exceeds an amount equal to 3-times the base amount.

(2) *Exclusions*.—The following payments are not parachute payments:

(i) *Certain qualified plans*.—A payment that is a contribution to or a distribution from a plan described in section 401(a) that includes a trust exempt from tax under section 501(a), an annuity plan described in section 403(a), a simplified employee pension (as defined in section 408(k)), or a simple retirement account described in section 408(p);

(ii) *Certain annuity contracts*.—A payment made under or to an annuity contract described in section 403(b) or a plan described in section 457(b);

(iii) *Compensation for medical services*.—A payment made to a licensed medical professional for the performance of medical services performed by such professional; and

(iv) *Payments to non-HCEs*.—A payment made to an individual who is not a highly compensated employee (HCE) as defined in paragraph (a)(3) of this section.

(3) *Determination of HCEs for purposes of the exclusion from parachute payments*.—For purposes of this section, *highly compensated employee* or *HCE* means, with regard to an ATEO that maintains a qualified retirement plan or other employee benefit plan described in § 1.414(q)-1T, Q/A–1, any person who is a highly compensated employee within the meaning of section 414(q) and, with regard to an ATEO that does not maintain such a plan, any person who would be a highly compensated employee within the meaning of section 414(q) if the ATEO did maintain such a plan. For purposes of determining the group of highly compensated employees for a determination year, consistent with § 1.414(q)-1T, Q/A–14(a)(1), the determination year calculation is made on the basis of the applicable plan year under § 1.414(q)-1T, Q/A–14(a)(2) of the plan or other entity for

which a determination is made, and the look-back year calculation is made on the basis of the 12-month period immediately preceding that year. For an ATEO that does not maintain a plan described in § 1.414(q)-1T, Q/A–1, the rules are applied by analogy, substituting the calendar year for the plan year. Thus, for example, in 2022, an ATEO that does not maintain such a plan must use its employees' 2021 annual compensation (as defined in § 1.414(q)-1T, Q/A–13, including any of the safe harbor definitions if applied consistently to all employees) to determine which employees are HCEs for 2022, if any, for purposes of section 4960. If an employee is an HCE at the time of separation from employment, then for purposes of section 4960 any parachute payment that is contingent on the separation from employment (as defined in paragraph (d) of this section) is treated as paid to an HCE so that the exception from the term parachute payment under paragraph (a)(2)(iv) of this section does not apply, even if the payment occurs during one or more later taxable years (that is, taxable years after the taxable year during which the employee separated from employment).

(b) *Payment in the nature of compensation*.—(1) *In general*.—Any payment—in whatever form—is a payment in the nature of compensation if the payment arises out of an employment relationship, including holding oneself out as available to perform services or refraining from performing services. Thus, for example, a payment made under a covenant not to compete or a similar arrangement is a payment in the nature of compensation. A payment in the nature of compensation includes (but is not limited to) wages and salary, bonuses, severance pay, fringe benefits, life insurance, pension benefits, and other deferred compensation (including any amount characterized by the parties as interest or earnings thereon). A payment in the nature of compensation also includes cash when paid, the value of the right to receive cash, the value of accelerated vesting, or a transfer of property. The vesting of an option, stock appreciation right, or similar form of compensation as a result of a covered employee's separation from employment is a payment in the nature of compensation. However, a payment in the nature of compensation does not include attorney's fees or court costs paid or incurred in connection with the payment of any parachute payment or a reasonable rate of interest accrued on any amount during the period the parties contest whether a parachute payment will be made.

(2) *Consideration paid by covered employee*.—Any payment in the nature of compensation is reduced by the amount of any money or the fair market value of any property (owned by the covered employee without restriction) that is (or will be) transferred by the covered employee in exchange for the payment.

(c) *When payment is considered to be made*.—(1) *In general*.—A payment in the nature of compensation is considered made in the taxable year in which it is includible in the covered employee's gross income or, in the case of fringe benefits and other benefits that are excludable from income, in the taxable year the benefits are received. In the case of taxable non-cash fringe benefits provided in a calendar year, payment is considered made on the date or dates the employer chooses, but no later than December 31 of the calendar year in which the benefits are provided, except that when the fringe benefit is the transfer of personal property (either tangible or intangible) of a kind normally held for investment or the transfer of real property, payment is considered made on the actual date of transfer. If the fringe benefit is neither a transfer of personal property nor a transfer of real property, the employer may, in its discretion, treat the value of the benefit actually provided during the last two months of the calendar year as paid during the subsequent calendar year. However, an employer that treats the value of a benefit paid during the last two months of a calendar year as paid during the subsequent calendar year under this rule must treat the value of that fringe benefit as paid during the subsequent calendar year with respect to all employees who receive it.

(2) *Transfers of section 83 property*.—A transfer of property in connection with the performance of services that is subject to section 83 is considered a payment made in the taxable year in which the property is transferred or would be includible in the gross income of the covered employee under section 83, disregarding any election made by the employee under section 83(b) or (i). Thus, in general, such a payment is considered made at the later of the date the property is transferred (as defined in § 1.83-3(a)) to the covered employee or the date the property becomes substantially vested (as defined in § 1.83-3(b) and (j)). The amount of the payment is the compensation as determined under section 83, disregarding any amount includible in income pursuant to an election made by an employee under section 83(b).

(3) *Stock options*.—An option (including an option to which section 421 applies) is treated as property that is transferred when the option becomes vested (regardless of whether the option has a readily ascertainable fair market value as defined in § 1.83-7(b)). For

purposes of determining the timing and amount of any payment related to the option, the principles of §1.280G–1, Q/A–13 and any method prescribed by the Commissioner in published guidance of general applicability under §601.601(d)(2) apply.

(d) *Payment contingent on an employee's separation from employment.*—(1) *In general.*—A payment is contingent on an employee's separation from employment if the facts and circumstances indicate that the employer would not make the payment in the absence of the employee's involuntary separation from employment. A payment generally would be made in the absence of the employee's involuntary separation from employment if it is substantially certain at the time of the involuntary separation from employment that the payment would be made whether or not the involuntary separation occurred. A payment the right to which is not subject to a substantial risk of forfeiture within the meaning of section 457(f)(3)(B) at the time of an involuntary separation from employment generally is a payment that would have been made in the absence of an involuntary separation from employment (and is therefore not contingent on a separation from employment), except that the increased value of an accelerated payment of a vested amount described in paragraph (f)(3) of this section resulting from an involuntary separation from employment is not treated as a payment that would have been made in the absence of an involuntary separation from employment. A payment the right to which is no longer subject to a substantial risk of forfeiture within the meaning of section 457(f)(3)(B) as a result of an involuntary separation from employment, including a payment the vesting of which is accelerated due to the separation from employment as described in paragraph (f)(3) of this section, is not treated as a payment that would have been made in the absence of an involuntary separation from employment (and thus is contingent on a separation from employment). A payment does not fail to be contingent on a separation from employment merely because the payment is conditioned upon the execution of a release of claims, noncompetition or nondisclosure provisions, or other similar requirements. See paragraph (d)(3) of this section for the treatment of a payment made pursuant to a covenant not to compete. If, after an involuntary separation from employment, the former employee continues to provide certain services as a nonemployee, payments for services rendered as a nonemployee are not payments that are contingent on a separation from employment to the extent those payments are reasonable and are not made on account of the involuntary separation from employment. Whether services are performed as an employee or nonemployee depends upon all the facts and circumstances. See §53.4960-1(e). For rules on determining whether payments are reasonable compensation for services, the rules of §1.280G–1, Q/A–40 through Q/A–42 (excluding Q/A–40(b) and Q/A–42(b)), and Q/A–44 are applied by analogy (substituting involuntary separation from employment for change in ownership or control).

(2) *Employment agreements.*—(i) *In general.*—If a covered employee involuntarily separates from employment before the end of a contract term and is paid damages for breach of contract pursuant to an employment agreement, the payment of damages is treated as a payment that is contingent on a separation from employment. An *employment agreement* is an agreement between an employee and employer that describes, among other things, the amount of compensation or remuneration payable to the employee for services performed during the term of the agreement.

(ii) *Example.*—The following example illustrates the rules of this paragraph (d)(2). For purposes of this example, assume any entity referred to as "ATEO" is an ATEO.

(A) *Example.*—(1) *Facts.* Employee A, a covered employee, has a 3-year employment agreement with ATEO 1. Under the agreement, Employee A will receive a salary of $200,000 for the first year and, for each succeeding year, an annual salary that is $100,000 more than the previous year. The agreement provides that, in the event of A's involuntary separation from employment without cause, Employee A will receive the remaining salary due under the agreement. At the beginning of the second year of the agreement, ATEO 1 involuntarily terminates Employee A's employment without cause and pays Employee A $700,000 representing the remaining salary due under the employment agreement ($300,000 for the second year of the agreement plus $400,000 for the third year of the agreement).

(2) *Conclusion.* The $700,000 payment is treated as a payment that is contingent on a separation from employment.

(3) *Noncompetition agreements.*—A payment under an agreement requiring a covered employee to refrain from performing services (for example, a covenant not to compete) is a payment that is contingent on a separation from employment if the payment would not have been made in the absence of an involuntary separation from employment. For example, a payment contingent on compliance in whole or in part with a covenant not to compete negotiated as part of

a severance arrangement arising from an involuntary separation from employment is contingent on a separation from employment. Similarly, one or more payments contingent on compliance in whole or in part with a covenant not to compete not negotiated as part of a severance arrangement arising from an involuntary separation from employment but that provides for a payment specific to an involuntary separation from employment (and not voluntary separation from employment) is contingent on a separation from employment. Payments made under an agreement requiring a covered employee to refrain from performing services that are contingent on separation from employment are not treated as paid in exchange for the performance of services and are not excluded from parachute payments.

(4) *Payment of amounts previously included in income or excess remuneration.*—Actual or constructive payment of an amount that was previously included in gross income of the employee is not a payment contingent on a separation from employment. For example, payment of an amount included in income under section 457(f)(1)(A) due to the lapsing of a substantial risk of forfeiture on a date before the separation from employment generally is not a payment that is contingent on a separation from employment, even if the amount is paid in cash or otherwise to the employee because of the separation from employment. In addition, actual or constructive receipt of an amount treated as excess remuneration under §53.4960-4(b)(1) is not a payment that is contingent on a separation from employment (and thus is not a parachute payment), even if the amount is paid to the employee because of the separation from employment.

(5) *Window programs.*—A payment under a window program is contingent on a separation from employment. A *window program* is a program established by an employer in connection with an impending separation from employment to provide separation pay if the program is made available by the employer for a limited period of time (no longer than 12 months) to employees who separate from employment during that period or to employees who separate from service during that period under specified circumstances. A payment made under a window program is treated as a payment that is contingent on an employee's separation from employment notwithstanding that the employee may not have had an involuntary separation from employment.

(6) *Anti-abuse provision.*—Notwithstanding paragraphs (d)(1) through (5) of this section, if the facts and circumstances demonstrate that either the vesting or the payment of an amount (whether before or after an employee's involuntary separation from employment) would not have occurred but for the involuntary nature of the separation from employment, the payment of the amount is contingent on a separation from employment. For example, an employer's exercise of discretion to accelerate vesting of an amount shortly before an involuntary separation from employment may indicate that the acceleration of vesting was due to the involuntary nature of the separation from employment and was therefore contingent on the employee's separation from employment. Similarly, payment of an amount in excess of an amount otherwise payable (for example, increased salary), shortly before or after an involuntary separation from employment, may indicate that the amount was paid because the separation was involuntary and was therefore contingent on the employee's separation from employment. If an ATEO becomes a predecessor as a result of a reorganization or other transaction described in §53.4960-1(h), any payment to an employee by a successor organization that is contingent on the employee's separation from employment with the predecessor ATEO is treated as paid by the predecessor ATEO.

(e) *Involuntary separation from employment.*—(1) *In general.*—*Involuntary separation from employment* means a separation from employment due to the independent exercise of the employer's unilateral authority to terminate the employee's services, other than due to the employee's implicit or explicit request, if the employee was willing and able to continue performing services as an employee. An involuntary separation from employment may include an employer's failure to renew a contract at the time the contract expires, provided that the employee was willing and able to execute a new contract providing terms and conditions substantially similar to those in the expiring contract and to continue providing services. The determination of whether a separation from employment is involuntary is based on all the facts and circumstances.

(2) *Separation from employment for good reason.*—(i) *In general.*—Notwithstanding paragraph (e)(1) of this section, an employee's voluntary separation from employment is treated as an involuntary separation from employment if the separation occurs under certain bona fide conditions (referred to herein as a separation from employment for good reason).

(ii) *Material negative change required.*—A separation from employment for good reason is treated as an involuntary separation from employment if the relevant facts and circumstances demonstrate that it was the result of unilateral employer action that caused a material negative change to the employee's relationship with the employer. Factors that may provide evidence of such a material negative change include a material reduction in the duties to be performed, a material negative change in the conditions under which the duties are to be performed, or a material reduction in the compensation to be received for performing such services.

(iii) *Deemed material negative change.*—An involuntary separation from employment due to a material negative change is deemed to occur if the separation from employment occurs within 2 years following the initial existence of one or more of the following conditions arising without the consent of the employee:

(A) *Material diminution of compensation.*—A material diminution in the employee's base compensation;

(B) *Material diminution of responsibility.*—A material diminution in the employee's authority, duties, or responsibilities;

(C) *Material diminution of authority of supervisor.*—A material diminution in the authority, duties, or responsibilities of the supervisor to whom the employee is required to report, including a requirement that an employee report to a corporate officer or employee instead of reporting directly to the board of directors (or similar governing body) of an organization;

(D) *Material diminution of budget.*—A material diminution in the budget over which the employee retains authority;

(E) *Material change of location.*—A material change in the geographic location at which the employee must perform services; or

(F) *Other material breach.*—Any other action or inaction that constitutes a material breach by the employer of the agreement under which the employee provides services.

(3) *Separation from employment.*—Except as otherwise provided in this paragraph, separation from employment has the same meaning as separation from service as defined in § 1.409A-1(h). Pursuant to § 1.409A-1(h), an employee generally separates from employment with the employer if the employee dies, retires, or otherwise has a termination of employment with the employer or experiences a sufficient reduction in the level of services provided to the employer. For purposes of applying the rules regarding reductions in the level of services set forth in the definition of termination of employment in § 1.409A-1(h)(1)(ii), the rules are modified for purposes of this paragraph such that an employer may not set the level of the anticipated reduction in future services that will give rise to a separation from employment, meaning that the default percentages set forth in § 1.409A-1(h)(1)(ii) apply in all circumstances. Thus, an anticipated reduction of the level of service of less than 50 percent is not treated as a separation from employment, an anticipated reduction of more than 80 percent is treated as a separation from employment, and the treatment of an anticipated reduction between those two levels is determined based on the facts and circumstances. The measurement of the anticipated reduction of the level of service is based on the average level of service for the prior 36 months (or shorter period for an employee employed for less than 36 months). In addition, an employee's separation from employment is determined without regard to § 1.409A-1(h)(2) and (5) (application to independent contractors), since, for purposes of this section, only an employee may have a separation from employment, and a change from bona fide employee status to bona fide independent contractor status is also a separation from employment. See § 53.4960-2(a)(1) regarding the treatment of an employee who also serves as a director of a corporation (or in a substantially similar position). The definition of separation from employment also incorporates the rules under § 1.409A-1(h)(1)(i) (addressing leaves of absence, including military leaves of absence), § 1.409A-1(h)(4) (addressing asset purchase transactions), and § 1.409A-1(h)(6) (addressing employees participating in collectively bargained plans covering multiple employers). The definition further incorporates the rules of § 1.409A-1(h)(3), under which an employee separates from employment only if the employee has a separation from employment with the employer and all employers that would be considered a single employer under section 414(b) and (c), except that the "at least 80 percent" rule under section 414(b) and (c) is used, rather than replacing it with "at least 50 percent." However, for purposes of determining whether there has been a separation from employment, a purported ongoing employment relationship between a covered employee and an ATEO or a related organization is disregarded if the facts and circumstances demonstrate that the purported employment relationship is not bona fide, or the primary purpose of the establishment or continuation of the relationship is avoidance of the application of section 4960.

(f) *Accelerated payment or accelerated vesting resulting from an involuntary separation from employment.*—(1) *In general.*—If a payment or the lapse of a substantial risk of forfeiture is accelerated as a result of an involuntary separation from employment, generally only the value due to the acceleration of payment or vesting is treated as contingent on a separation from employment, as described in paragraphs (f)(3) and (4) of this section, except as otherwise provided in this paragraph (f). For purposes of this paragraph (f), the terms *vested* and *substantial risk of forfeiture* have the same meaning as provided in § 53.4960-2(c)(2).

(2) *Nonvested payments subject to a non-service vesting condition.*—If (without regard to a separation from employment) vesting of a payment would depend on an event other than the performance of services, such as the attainment of a performance goal, and that vesting event does not occur prior to the employee's separation from employment and the payment vests due to the employee's involuntary separation from employment, the full amount of the payment is treated as contingent on the separation from employment.

(3) *Vested payments.*—If an involuntary separation from employment accelerates actual or constructive payment of an amount that previously vested without regard to the separation, the portion of the payment, if any, that is contingent on the separation from employment is the amount by which the present value of the accelerated payment exceeds the present value of the payment absent the acceleration. The payment of an amount otherwise due upon a separation from employment (whether voluntary or involuntary) is not treated as an acceleration of the payment unless the payment timing was accelerated due to the involuntary nature of the separation from employment. If the value of the payment absent the acceleration is not reasonably ascertainable, and the acceleration of the payment does not significantly increase the present value of the payment absent the acceleration, the present value of the payment absent the acceleration is the amount of the accelerated payment (so the amount contingent on the separation from employment is zero). If the present value of the payment absent the acceleration is not reasonably ascertainable but the acceleration significantly increases the present value of the payment, the future value of the payment contingent on the separation from employment is treated as equal to the amount of the accelerated payment. For purposes of this paragraph (f)(3), the acceleration of a payment by 90 days or less is not treated as significantly increasing the present value of the payment. For rules on determining present value, see paragraph (f)(6) and paragraphs (h), (i) and (j) of this section.

(4) *Nonvested payments subject to a service vesting condition.*—(i) *In general.*—If an involuntary separation from employment accelerates vesting of a payment, the portion of the payment that is contingent on separation from employment is the amount described in paragraph (f)(3) of this section (if any) plus the value of the lapse of the obligation to continue to perform services described in paragraph (f)(4)(ii) of this section (but the amount cannot exceed the amount of the accelerated payment, or, if the payment is not accelerated, the present value of the payment), to the extent that all of the following conditions are satisfied with respect to the payment:

(A) *Vesting trigger.*—The payment vests as a result of an involuntary separation from employment;

(B) *Vesting condition.*—Disregarding the involuntary separation from employment, the vesting of the payment was contingent only on the continued performance of services for the employer for a specified period of time; and

(C) *Services condition.*—The payment is attributable, at least in part, to the performance of services before the date the payment is made or becomes certain to be made.

(ii) *Value of the lapse of the obligation to continue to perform services.*—The value of the lapse of the obligation to continue to perform services is one percent of the amount of the accelerated payment multiplied by the number of full months between the date that the employee's right to receive the payment is vested and the date that, absent the acceleration, the payment would have been vested. This paragraph (f)(4)(ii) applies to the accelerated vesting of a payment in the nature of compensation even if the time when the payment is made is not accelerated. In that case, the value of the lapse of the obligation to continue to perform services is one percent of the present value of the future payment multiplied by the number of full months between the date that the individual's right to receive the payment is vested and the date that, absent the acceleration, the payment would have been vested.

(iii) *Accelerated vesting of equity compensation.*—For purposes of this paragraph (f)(4), the acceleration of the vesting of a stock option or stock appreciation right (or similar arrangement) or the lapse of a restriction on restricted stock or a restricted stock unit (or a similar arrangement) is considered to significantly increase the value of the payment.

(5) *Application to benefits under a nonqualified deferred compensation plan.*—In the case of a payment of benefits under a nonqualified deferred compensation plan, paragraph (f)(3) of this section applies to the extent benefits under the plan are vested without regard to the involuntary separation from employment, but the payment of benefits is accelerated due to the involuntary separation from employment. Paragraph (f)(4) of this section applies to the extent benefits under the plan are subject to the conditions described in paragraph (f)(4)(i) of this section. For any other payment of benefits under a nonqualified deferred compensation plan (such as a contribution made due to the employee's involuntary separation from employment), the full amount of the payment is contingent on the employee's separation from employment.

(6) *Present value.*—For purposes of this paragraph (f), the present value of a payment is determined based on the payment date absent the acceleration and the date on which the accelerated payment is scheduled to be made. The amount that is treated as contingent on the separation from employment is the amount by which the present value of the accelerated payment exceeds the present value of the payment absent the acceleration.

(7) *Examples.*—See § 1.280G Q/A–24(f) for examples that may be applied by analogy to illustrate the rules of this paragraph (f).

(g) *Three-times-base-amount test for parachute payments.*—(1) *In general.*—To determine whether payments in the nature of compensation made to a covered employee that are contingent on the covered employee separating from employment with the ATEO are parachute payments, the aggregate present value of the payments must be compared to the individual's base amount. To do this, the aggregate present value of all payments in the nature of compensation that are made or to be made to (or for the benefit of) the same covered employee by an ATEO (or any predecessor of the ATEO) or related organization and that are contingent on the separation from employment must be determined. If this aggregate present value equals or exceeds the amount equal to 3-times the individual's base amount, the payments are parachute payments. If this aggregate present value is less than the amount equal to 3-times the individual's base amount, the payments are not parachute payments. See paragraphs (f)(6), (h), (i), and (j) of this section for rules on determining present value.

(2) *Examples.*—The following examples illustrate the rules of this paragraph (g). For purposes of these examples, assume any entity referred to as "ATEO" is an ATEO.

(i) *Example 1 (Parachute payment).*—(A) *Facts.* Employee A is a covered employee and an HCE of ATEO 1. Employee A's base amount is $200,000. Payments in the nature of compensation that are contingent on a separation from employment with ATEO 1 totaling $800,000 are made to Employee A on the date of Employee A's separation from employment.

(B) *Conclusion.* The payments are parachute payments because they have an aggregate present value at the time of the separation from employment of $800,000, which is at least equal to 3-times Employee A's base amount of $200,000 (3 x $200,000 = $600,000).

(ii) *Example 2 (No parachute payment).*—(A) *Facts.* Assume the same facts as in paragraph (g)(2)(i) of this section (Example 1), except that the payments contingent on Employee A's separation from employment total $580,000.

(B) *Conclusion.* Because the aggregate present value of the payments ($580,000) is not at least equal to 3-times Employee A's base amount ($600,000), the payments are not parachute payments.

(h) *Calculating present value.*—(1) *In general.*—Except as otherwise provided in this paragraph (h), for purposes of determining if a payment contingent on a separation from employment exceeds 3-times the base amount, the present value of a payment is determined as of the date of the separation from employment or, if the payment is made prior to that date, the date on which the payment is made.

(2) *Deferred payments.*—For purposes of determining whether a payment is a parachute payment, if a payment in the nature of compensation is the right to receive payments in a year (or years) subsequent to the year of the separation from employment, the value of the payment is the present value of the payment (or payments) calculated on the basis of reasonable actuarial assumptions and using the applicable discount rate for the present value calculation that is determined in accordance with paragraph (i) of this section.

(3) *Health care.*—If the payment in the nature of compensation is an obligation to provide health care (including an obligation to purchase or provide health insurance), then, for purposes of this paragraph (h) and for applying the 3-times-base-amount test under paragraph (g) of this section, the present value of the obligation is calculated in accordance with generally accepted accounting principles. For purposes of paragraph (g) of this section and this paragraph (h), the obligation to provide health care is permitted to be measured by projecting the cost of premiums for health care insurance, even if no health care insurance is actually purchased. If the obligation to provide health care is made in coordination with a health care plan that the employer makes available to a group, then the premiums used for purposes of this paragraph (h)(3) may be the allocable portion of group premiums.

(i) *Discount rate.*—Present value generally is determined by using a discount rate equal to 120 percent of the applicable Federal rate (determined under section 1274(d) and the regulations in part 1 under section 1274(d)), compounded semiannually. The applicable Federal rate to be used is the Federal rate that is in effect on the date as of which the present value is determined, using the period until the payment is expected to be made as the term of the debt instrument under section 1274(d). See paragraph (h) of this section for rules with respect to the date as of which the present value is determined. However, for any payment, the employer and the covered employee may elect to use the applicable Federal rate that is in effect on the date on which the parties entered into the contract that provides for the payment if that election is set forth in writing in the contract.

(j) *Present value of a payment to be made in the future that is contingent on an uncertain future event or condition.*—(1) *Treatment based on the estimated probability of payment.*—In certain cases, it may be necessary to apply the 3-times-base-amount test to a payment that is contingent on separation from employment at a time when the aggregate present value of all the payments is uncertain because the time, amount, or right to receive one or more of the payments is also contingent on the occurrence of an uncertain future event or condition. In that case, the employer must reasonably estimate whether it will make the payment. If the employer reasonably estimates there is a 50-percent or greater probability that it will make the payment, the full amount of the payment is considered for purposes of the 3-times-base-amount test and the allocation of the base amount. If the employer reasonably estimates there is a less than 50-percent probability that the payment will be made, the payment is not considered for either purpose.

(2) *Correction of incorrect estimates.*—If an ATEO later determines that an estimate it made under paragraph (j)(1) of this section was incorrect, it must reapply the 3-times-base-amount test to reflect the actual time and amount of the payment. In reapplying the 3-times-base-amount test (and, if necessary, reallocating the base amount), the ATEO must determine the aggregate present value of payments paid or to be paid as of the date described in paragraph (h) of this section using the discount rate described in paragraph (i) of this section. This redetermination may affect the amount of any excess parachute payment for a prior taxable year. However, if, based on the application of the 3-times-base-amount test without regard to the payment described in this paragraph (j), an ATEO has determined it will pay an employee an excess parachute payment or payments, then the 3-times-base-amount test does not have to be reapplied when a payment described in this paragraph (j) is made (or becomes certain to be made) if no base amount is allocated to that payment under § 53.4960-4(d)(5).

(3) *Initial option value estimate.*—To the extent provided in published guidance of general applicability under § 601.601(d)(2), an initial estimate of the value of an option subject to paragraph (c) of this section is permitted to be made, with the valuation subsequently redetermined and the 3-times-base-amount test reapplied. Until guidance is published under section 4960, published guidance of general applicability described in § 601.601(d)(2) that is issued under section 280G applies by analogy.

(4) *Examples.*—See § 1.280G-1, Q/A–33(d) for examples that may be applied by analogy to illustrate the rules of this paragraph (j).

(k) *Base amount.*—(1) *In general.*—A covered employee's base amount is the average annual compensation for services performed as an employee of the ATEO (including compensation for services performed for a predecessor of the ATEO), and/or, if applicable, a related organization, with respect to which there has been a separation from employment, if the compensation was includible in the gross income of the individual for taxable years in the base period (including amounts that were excluded under section 911) or that would have been includible in the individual's gross income if the individual had been a United States citizen or resident. See paragraph (l) of this section for the definition of base period and for examples of base amount computations.

(2) *Short or incomplete taxable years.*—If the base period of a covered employee includes a short taxable year or less than all of a taxable year of the employee, compensation for the short or incomplete taxable year must be annualized before determining the average annual compensation for the base period. In annualizing compensation, the frequency with which payments are expected to be made over an annual period must be taken into account. Thus, any amount of compensation for a short or incomplete taxable year that represents a payment that will not be made more often than once per year is not annualized.

(3) *Excludable fringe benefits.*—Because the base amount includes only compensation that is includible in gross income, the base amount does not include certain items that may constitute parachute payments. For example, payments in the form of excludable fringe benefits or excludable health care benefits are not included in the base amount but may be treated as parachute payments.

(4) *Section 83(b) income.*—The base amount includes the amount of compensation included in income under section 83(b) during the base period.

(l) *Base period.*—(1) *In general.*—The base period of a covered employee is the covered employee's 5 most-recent taxable years ending before the date on which the separation from employment occurs. However, if the covered employee was not an employee of the ATEO for this entire 5-year period, the individual's base period is the portion of the 5-year period during which the covered employee performed services for the ATEO, a predecessor, or a related organization.

(2) *Determination of base amount if employee separates from employment in the year hired.*—If a covered employee commences services as an employee and experiences a separation from employment in the same taxable year, the covered employee's base amount is the annualized compensation for services performed for the ATEO (or a predecessor or related organization) that was not contingent on the separation from employment and either was includible in the employee's gross income for that portion of the employee's taxable year prior to the employee's separation from employment (including amounts that were excluded under section 911) or would have been includible in the employee's gross income if the employee had been a United States citizen or resident.

(3) *Examples.*—The following examples illustrate the rules of paragraph (k) of this section and this paragraph (l). For purposes of these examples, assume any entity referred to as "ATEO" is an ATEO, any entity referred to as "CORP" is not an ATEO, and all employees are HCEs of their respective employers.

(i) *Example 1 (Calculation with salary deferrals).*—(A) *Facts.* Employee A, a covered employee of ATEO 1, receives an annual salary of $500,000 per year during the 5-year base period. Employee A defers $100,000 of salary each year under a nonqualified deferred compensation plan (none of which is includible in Employee A's income until paid in cash to Employee A).

(B) *Conclusion.* Employee A's base amount is $400,000 (($400,000 x 5) / 5).

(ii) *Example 2 (Calculation for less-than-5-year base period).*—(A) *Facts.* Employee B, a covered employee of ATEO 1, was employed by ATEO 1 for 2 years and 4 months preceding the year in which Employee B separates from employment. Employee B's compensation includible in gross income was $100,000 for the 4-month period, $420,000 for the first full year, and $450,000 for the second full year.

(B) *Conclusion.* Employee B's base amount is $390,000 (((3 x $100,000) + $420,000 + $450,000) / 3). Any compensation Employee B receives in the year of separation from employment is not included in the base amount calculation.

(iii) *Example 3 (Calculation for less-than-5-year base period with signing bonus).*—(A) *Facts.* Assume the same facts as in paragraph (l)(3)(ii)(A) of this section (Example 2), except that Employee B also received a $60,000 signing bonus when Employee B's employment with ATEO 1 commenced at the beginning of the 4-month period.

(B) *Conclusion.* Employee B's base amount is $410,000 ((($60,000 + (3 x $100,000)) + $420,000 + $450,000) / 3). Pursuant to paragraph (k)(2) of this section, because the bonus is a payment that will not be paid more often than once per year, the bonus is not taken into account in annualizing Employee B's compensation for the 4-month period.

(iv) *Example 4 (Effect of non-employee compensation).*—(A) *Facts.* Employee C, a covered employee of ATEO 1, was not an employee of ATEO 1 for the full 5-year base period. In 2024 and 2025, Employee C is only a director of ATEO 1 and receives $30,000 per year for services as a director. On January 1, 2026, Employee C becomes an officer and

covered employee of ATEO 1. Employee C's includible compensation for services as an officer of ATEO 1 is $250,000 for each of 2026 and 2027, and $300,000 for 2028. In 2028, Employee C separates from employment with ATEO 1.

(B) *Conclusion.* Employee C's base amount is $250,000 ((2 x $250,000) / 2). The $30,000 of director's fees paid to Employee C in each of 2024 and 2025 is not included in Employee C's base amount calculation because it was not for services performed as an employee of ATEO 1. [Reg. § 53.4960-3.]

☐ [*T.D.* 9938, 1-15-2021.]

**[Reg. § 53.4960-4]**

**§ 53.4960-4. Liability for tax on excess remuneration and excess parachute payments.**—(a) *Liability, reporting, and payment of excise taxes.*—(1) *Liability.*—For each taxable year, with respect to each covered employee, the taxpayer is liable for tax at the rate imposed under section 11 on the sum of the excess remuneration allocated to the taxpayer under paragraph (c) of this section and, if the taxpayer is an ATEO, any excess parachute payment paid by the taxpayer or a predecessor during the taxable year.

(2) *Reporting and payment.*—The excise tax imposed by section 4960 is reported as provided in § § 53.6011-1(b) and 53.6071-1(i) and paid in the form and manner prescribed by the Commissioner.

(3) *Arrangements between an ATEO and a related organization.*—Calculation of, and liability for, the excise tax imposed by section 4960 is separate from, and unaffected by, any arrangement that an ATEO and any related organization may have for bearing the cost of any liability for the excise tax imposed by section 4960.

(4) *Certain foreign related organizations.*—A related organization that is a foreign organization described in section 4948(b) that either is exempt from tax under section 501(a) or is a taxable private foundation (section 4948(b) related organization) is not liable for the excise tax imposed by section 4960. A foreign organization is an organization not created or organized in the United States or in any possession thereof, or under the law of the United States, any State, the District of Columbia, or any possession of the United States. See section 4948(b) and § 53.4948-1. For purposes of this paragraph (a)(4) and the application of section 4960 to a taxable year, an organization's status as a section 4948(b) related organization is determined at the end of its taxable year. However, remuneration that the section 4948(b) related organization pays to a covered employee of an ATEO must be taken into account by the ATEO and other related organizations for purposes of section 4960 generally, including for purposes of determining the five highest-compensated employees and the total remuneration paid to a covered employee. For example, if an ATEO and its related organization that is a section 4948(b) related organization each paid $600,000 remuneration to a covered employee during the applicable year, then the related organization would not be liable for the tax that would otherwise be allocable to it, and the ATEO would be liable for tax on $100,000 (50 percent of the $200,000 excess remuneration paid to the employee).

(5) [Reserved].

(b) *Amounts subject to tax.*—(1) *Excess remuneration.*—(i) *In general.*—Excess remuneration means the amount of remuneration paid by an ATEO to any covered employee during an applicable year in excess of $1 million, as determined under § 53.4960-2.

(ii) *Exclusion for excess parachute payments.*—Excess remuneration does not include any amount that is an excess parachute payment as defined in paragraph (b)(2) of this section.

(2) *Excess parachute payment.*—Excess parachute payment means an amount equal to the excess (if any) of the amount of any parachute payment paid by an ATEO, a predecessor of the ATEO, or a related organization, or on behalf of any such person, during the taxable year over the portion of the base amount allocated to such payment.

(c) *Calculation of liability for tax on excess remuneration.*—(1) *In general.*—For each taxable year, an employer is liable for the tax on excess remuneration paid in the applicable year ending with or within the employer's taxable year. If, for the taxable year, remuneration paid during an applicable year by an ATEO or one or more related organizations to a covered employee is taken into account in determining the tax imposed on excess remuneration for that taxable year, then each employer is liable for the tax in an amount that bears the same ratio to the total tax determined under section 4960(a) as the amount of remuneration paid by the employer to the covered employee (including remuneration paid by the employer as described in § 53.4960-2(b)(1), but disregarding remuneration treated as paid by the employer under § 53.4960-2(b)(2)), bears to the total amount of remuneration paid by the ATEO under § 53.4960-2 (including remuneration treated as paid by the ATEO under § 53.4960-2(b)(2)).

(2) *Calculation if liability is allocated from more than one ATEO with regard to an individual.*—If liability for the tax on excess remuneration is allocated to an employer from more than one ATEO in a taxable year with regard to an individual that is a covered employee of each ATEO, then the employer is liable for the tax only in the capacity in which it is liable for the greatest amount of the tax with respect to that individual for the taxable year. For example, assume ATEO 1 is a related organization to both ATEO 2 and ATEO 3 and pays excess remuneration to Employee D, and Employee D is a covered employee of ATEO 1, ATEO 2, and ATEO 3. In this case, ATEO 1's liability for the tax on excess remuneration to Employee D is the highest of its liability as an ATEO, as a related organization to ATEO 2, or as a related organization to ATEO 3.

(3) *Calculation if liability is allocated from an ATEO with a short applicable year.*—If liability for the tax on excess remuneration paid to an individual is allocated to an employer from an ATEO with a short applicable year under § 53.4960-1(c)(3), then the liability with respect to the excess remuneration paid to that individual is allocated in accordance with the principles of this paragraph (c) adjusted as necessary to avoid, to the extent possible, duplication of application of the excise tax. The Commissioner may provide additional guidance of general applicability, published in the Internal Revenue Bulletin (see § 601.601(d)(2) of this chapter), on the application of this paragraph (c)(3) to particular circumstances, including circumstances involving an ATEO with a short applicable year that has one or more related organizations and the ATEO's short applicable year and the preceding applicable year both end with or within the related organization's taxable year, such that the ATEO and related organizations are liable for the tax for multiple applicable years ending with or within the employer's taxable year.

(4) *Examples.*—The following examples illustrate the rules of this paragraph (c). For purposes of these examples, assume that the rate of excise tax under section 4960 is 21 percent, that any entity that is referred to as "ATEO" is an ATEO, that any entity referred to as "CORP" is not an ATEO and is not a publicly held corporation within the meaning of section 162(m)(2) or a covered health insurance provider within the meaning of section 162(m)(6)(C), that no related organization is a section 4948(b) related organization, all taxpayers use the calendar year as their taxable year unless otherwise stated, and that no parachute payments are made in any of the years at issue.

(i) *Example 1 (Remuneration from multiple employers).*—(A) *Facts.* ATEO 1 and CORP 1 are related organizations. Employee A is a covered employee of ATEO 1 and an employee of CORP 1. In the 2022 applicable year, ATEO 1 pays Employee A $1.2 million of remuneration, and CORP 1 pays A $800,000 of remuneration. Remuneration paid by each employer is for services performed by Employee A solely as an employee of that employer.

(B) *Conclusion.* For the 2022 taxable year, ATEO 1 is treated as paying Employee A $2 million of remuneration, $1 million of which is excess remuneration. The total excise tax is $210,000 (21 percent x $1 million). ATEO 1 paid 3/5 of Employee A's total remuneration ($1.2 million / $2 million); thus, ATEO 1 is liable for 3/5 of the excise tax, which is $126,000. CORP 1 paid 2/5 of Employee A's total remuneration ($800,000 / $2 million); thus, CORP 1 is liable for 2/5 of the excise tax, which is $84,000.

(ii) *Example 2 (Application when taxpayers have different taxable years).*—(A) *Facts.* Assume the same facts as in paragraph (c)(4)(i) of this section (*Example 1*), except that CORP 2 uses a taxable year beginning July 1 and ending June 30.

(B) *Conclusion.* The conclusion is the same as the conclusion in paragraph (c)(4)(i) of this section (*Example 1*), except that ATEO 1 is liable for the tax for its taxable year starting January 1, 2022, and ending December 31, 2022, and CORP 1 is liable for the tax for its taxable year beginning July 1, 2022, and ending June 30, 2023 (the taxable year with or within which ATEO 1's 2022 applicable year ends).

(iii) *Example 3 (Multiple liabilities for same applicable year due to multiple ATEOs).*—(A) *Facts.* The following facts are all with respect to the 2023 applicable year: ATEO 5 owns 60 percent of the stock of CORP 2. Sixty percent of ATEO 4's directors are representatives of ATEO 3. In addition, 60 percent of ATEO 5's directors are representatives of ATEO 4, but none are representatives of ATEO 3. Employee B is a covered employee of ATEO 3, ATEO 4, and ATEO 5 and is an employee of CORP 2. ATEO 3, ATEO 4, ATEO 5, and CORP 2 each pay Employee B $1.2 million of remuneration in the applicable year. ATEO 4's related organizations are ATEO 3 and ATEO 5. ATEO 3's only related organization is ATEO 4. ATEO 5's related organizations are ATEO 4 and CORP 2.

(B) *Calculation (ATEO 3).* Under ATEO 3's calculation as an ATEO for the 2023 applicable year, ATEO 3 is treated as paying Employee B a total of $2.4 million in remuneration ($1.2 million from ATEO 3 + $1.2 million from ATEO 4). The total excise tax is $294,000 (21 percent X $1.4 million). ATEO 3 and ATEO 4 each paid 1/2 of Employee B's total remuneration ($1.2 million / $2.4 million); thus, under ATEO 3's calculation, ATEO 3 and ATEO 4 each would be liable for 1/2 of the excise tax, which is $147,000.

(C) *Calculation (ATEO 4).* Under ATEO 4's calculation as an ATEO for the 2023 applicable year, ATEO 4 is treated as paying Employee B a total of $3.6 million in remuneration for the 2022 applicable year ($1.2 million from ATEO 3 + $1.2 million from ATEO 4 + $1.2 million from ATEO 5). The total excise tax is $546,000 (21 percent X $2.6 million). ATEO 3, ATEO 4, and ATEO 5 each paid 1/3 of the total remuneration to Employee B ($1.2 million / $3.6 million); thus, under ATEO 4's calculation, ATEO 3, ATEO 4, and ATEO 5 each would be liable for 1/3 of the excise tax, which is $182,000.

(D) *Calculation (ATEO 5).* Under ATEO 5's calculation as an ATEO for the 2023 applicable year, ATEO 5 is treated as paying Employee B a total of $3.6 million in remuneration ($1.2 million from ATEO 4 + $1.2 million from ATEO 5 + $1.2 million from CORP 2). The total excise tax is $546,000 (21 percent X $2.6 million). ATEO 4, ATEO 5, and CORP 2 each paid 1/3 of the total remuneration to Employee B ($1.2 million / $3.6 million); thus, under ATEO 5's calculation, ATEO 4, ATEO 5, and CORP 2 each would be liable for 1/3 of the excise tax, which is $182,000.

(E) *Conclusion (Liability of ATEO 3).* For the 2023 applicable year, ATEO 3 is liable for $182,000 of excise tax as a related organization under ATEO 4's calculation, which is greater than the $147,000 of excise tax under ATEO 3's own calculation. Thus, ATEO 3's excise tax liability with respect to Employee B is $182,000 for its 2023 taxable year.

(F) *Conclusion (Liability of ATEO 4).* For the 2023 applicable year, ATEO 4 is liable as a related organization for $147,000 of excise tax according to ATEO 3's calculation, for $182,000 according to ATEO 4's own calculation, and for $182,000 according to ATEO 5's calculation. Thus, ATEO 4's excise tax liability with respect to Employee B is $182,000 for its 2023 taxable year.

(G) *Conclusion (Liability of ATEO 5).* For the 2023 applicable year, ATEO 5 is liable as a related organization for $182,000 of excise tax under ATEO 4's calculation, and is liable for $182,000 of excise tax under ATEO 5's own calculation. Thus, ATEO 5's excise tax liability with respect to Employee B is $182,000 for its 2023 taxable year.

(H) *Conclusion (Liability of CORP 2).* For the 2023 applicable year, CORP 2 is liable as a related organization for $182,000 of excise tax according to ATEO 5's calculation only. Thus, CORP 2's excise tax liability with respect to Employee B is $182,000 for its 2023 taxable year.

(d) *Calculation of liability for excess parachute payments.*—(1) *In general.*—Except as provided in paragraph (d)(3) of this section, only excess parachute payments made by or on behalf of an ATEO are subject to tax under this section. However, parachute payments made by related organizations that are not made by or on behalf of an ATEO are taken into account for purposes of determining the total amount of excess parachute payments.

(2) *Computation of excess parachute payments.*—(i) *Calculation.*—The amount of an excess parachute payment is the excess of the amount of any parachute payment made by an ATEO, a predecessor of the ATEO, or a related organization, or on behalf of any such person, over the portion of the covered employee's base amount that is allocated to the payment. The portion of the base amount allocated to any parachute payment is the amount that bears the same ratio to the base amount as the present value of the parachute payment bears to the aggregate present value of all parachute payments made or to be made to (or for the benefit of) the same covered employee. Thus, the portion of the base amount allocated to any parachute payment is determined by multiplying the base amount by a fraction, the numerator of which is the present value of the parachute payment and the denominator of which is the aggregate present value of all parachute payments.

(ii) *Examples.*—The following examples illustrate the rules of this paragraph (d)(2). For purposes of these examples, assume any entity referred to as "ATEO" is an ATEO and all employees are HCEs of their respective employers.

(A) *Example 1 (Compensation from related organizations).*—(1) *Facts.* ATEO 1 and ATEO 2 are related organizations. Employee A is a covered employee of ATEO 1 and an employee of ATEO 2 who has an involuntary separation from employment with ATEO 1 and ATEO 2. Employee A's base amount is $200,000 with respect to ATEO 1 and $400,000 with respect to ATEO 2. A receives $1 million from ATEO 1 contingent upon Employee A's involuntary separation from employment from ATEO 1 and $1 million from ATEO 2 contingent upon Employee A's involuntary separation from employment from ATEO 2.

(2) *Conclusion.* Employee A has a base amount of $600,000 ($200,000 + $400,000). The two $1 million payments are parachute payments because their aggregate present value is at least 3-times Employee A's base amount (3 x $600,000 = $1.8 million). The portion of the base amount allocated to each parachute payment is $300,000 (($1 million / $2 million) x $600,000). Thus, the amount of each excess parachute payment is $700,000 ($1 million – $300,000).

(B) *Example 2 (Multiple parachute payments).*—(1) *Facts.* Employee B is a covered employee of ATEO 3 with a base amount of $200,000 who is entitled to receive two parachute payments: one of $200,000 and the other of $900,000. The $200,000 payment is made upon separation from employment, and the $900,000 payment is to be made on a date in a future taxable year. The present value of the $900,000 payment is $800,000 as of the date of the separation from employment.

(2) *Conclusion.* The portion of the base amount allocated to the first payment is $40,000 (($200,000 present value of the parachute payment / $1 million present value of all parachute payments) x $200,000 total base amount) and the portion of the base amount allocated to the second payment is $160,000 (($800,000 present value of the parachute payment / $1 million present value of all parachute payments) x $200,000 total base amount). Thus, the amount of the first excess parachute payment is $160,000 ($200,000 – $40,000) and that the amount of the second excess parachute payment is $740,000 ($900,000 – $160,000).

(3) *Reallocation when the payment is disproportionate to base amount.*—In accordance with section 4960(d), the Commissioner may treat a parachute payment as paid by an ATEO if the facts and circumstances indicate that the ATEO and other payors of parachute payments structured the payments in a manner primarily to avoid liability under section 4960. For example, if an ATEO would otherwise be treated as paying a portion of an excess parachute payment in an amount that is materially lower in proportion to the total excess parachute payment than the proportion that the amount of average annual compensation paid by the ATEO (or any predecessor) during the base period bears to the total average annual compensation paid by the ATEO (or any predecessor) and any related organization (or organizations), and the lower amount is offset by payments from a non-ATEO or an unrelated ATEO, this may indicate that that the parachute payments were structured in a manner primarily to avoid liability under section 4960.

(4) *Election to prepay tax.*—An ATEO may prepay the excise tax under paragraph (a)(1) of this section on any excess parachute payment for the taxable year of the separation from employment or any later taxable year before the taxable year in which the parachute payment is actually or constructively paid. However, an employer may not prepay the excise tax on a payment to be made in cash if the present value of the payment is not reasonably ascertainable under § 31.3121(v)(2)-1(e)(4) or on a payment related to health coverage. Any prepayment must be based on the present value of the excise tax that would be due for the taxable year in which the employer will pay the excess parachute payment, and be calculated using the discount rate equal to 120 percent of the applicable Federal rate (determined under section 1274(d) and the regulations in part 1 under section 1274) and the tax rate in effect under section 11 for the year in which the excise tax is paid. For purposes of projecting the future value of a payment that provides for interest to be credited at a variable interest rate, the employer may make a reasonable assumption regarding the variable rate. An employer is not required to adjust the excise tax paid merely because the actual future interest rates are not the same as the rate used for purposes of projecting the future value of the payment.

(5) *Liability after a redetermination of total parachute payments.*—If an ATEO determines that an estimate made under § 53.4960-3(j)(1) was incorrect, it must reapply the 3-times-base-amount test to reflect the actual time and amount of the payment. In reapplying the 3-times-base-amount test (and, if necessary, reallocating the base amount), the ATEO must determine the correct base amount allocable to any parachute payment paid in the taxable year. See § 1.280G-1, Q/A-33(d) for examples that may be applied by analogy to illustrate the rules of this paragraph (d)(5).

(6) *Examples.*—The following examples illustrate the rules of this paragraph (d). For purposes of these examples, assume any entity referred to as "ATEO" is an ATEO, any entity referred to as "CORP" is not an ATEO, and all employees are HCEs of their respective employers.

(i) *Example 1 (Excess parachute payment paid by a non-ATEO).*—(A) *Facts.* ATEO 1 and CORP 1 are related organizations that are treated as the same employer for purposes of § 53.4960-3(e)(3) (defining separation from employment) and are both calendar year taxpayers. For 2022 through 2026, ATEO 1 and CORP 1 each pay Employee A $250,000 of compensation per year for services performed as an employee of each organization ($500,000 total per year). In 2027, ATEO 1 and CORP 1 each pay Employee A $1 million payment ($2 million total) that is contingent on Employee A's separation from employment with both ATEO 1 and CORP 1, all of which is remuneration, and no other compensation. Employee A is a covered employee of ATEO 1 in 2027.

(B) *Conclusion.* Employee A's base amount in 2027 is $500,000 (Employee A's average annual compensation from both ATEO 1 and CORP 1 for the previous 5 years). ATEO 1 makes a parachute payment of $2 million in 2027, the amount paid by both ATEO 1 and CORP 1 that is contingent on Employee A's separation from employment with ATEO 1 and all organizations that are treated as the same employer under § 53.4960-3(e)(3). Employee A's $2 million payment exceeds 3-times the base amount ($1.5 million). ATEO 1 makes a $1.5 million excess parachute payment (the amount by which $2 million exceeds the $500,000 base amount). However, ATEO 1 is liable for tax only on the excess parachute payment paid by ATEO 1 ($1 million parachute payment – $250,000 base amount = $750,000) that is subject to tax under § 53.4960-4(a). CORP 1 is not liable for tax under § 53.4960-4(a) in 2027.

(ii) *Example 2 (Election to prepay tax on excess parachute payments and effect on excess remuneration).*—(A) *Facts.* Employee B is a covered employee of ATEO 2 with a base amount of $200,000 who is entitled to receive two parachute payments, one of $200,000 and the other of $900,000. The $200,000 payment is made upon separation from employment, and the $900,000 payment is to be made on a date in a future taxable year. The present value of the $900,000 payment is $800,000 as of the date of the separation from employment. ATEO 2 elects to prepay the excise tax on the $900,000 future parachute payment (of which $740,000 is an excess parachute payment). The tax rate under section 11 is 21 percent for the taxable year the excise tax is paid and, using a discount rate determined under § 53.4960-3(i), the present value of the $155,400 ($740,000 x 21 percent) excise tax on the $740,000 future excess parachute payment is $140,000.

(B) *Conclusion.* The excess parachute payment is thus $800,000 ($200,000 plus $800,000 present value of the $900,000 future payment, less $200,000 base amount), with $40,000 of the base amount allocable to the $200,000 payment and $160,000 of the base amount allocable to the $900,000 payment. To prepay the excise tax on the $740,000 future excess parachute payment, the employer must satisfy its $140,000 obligation under section 4960 with respect to the future payment, in addition to the $33,600 excise tax ($160,000 x 21 percent) on the $160,000 excess parachute payment made upon separation from employment. For purposes of determining the amount of excess remuneration (if any) under section 4960(a)(1), the amount of remuneration paid by the employer to the covered employee for the taxable year of the separation from employment is reduced by the $900,000 of total excess parachute payments ($160,000 + $740,000). [Reg. § 53.4960-4.]

☐ [*T.D.* 9938, 1-15-2021.]

### [Reg. § 53.4960-5]

**§ 53.4960-5. [Reserved].**

☐ [*T.D.* 9938, 1-15-2021.]

### [Reg. § 53.4960-6]

**§ 53.4960-6. Applicability date.**—(a) *General applicability date.*—Sections 53.4960-0 through 53.4960-4 apply to taxable years beginning after December 31, 2021. Taxpayers may choose to apply § § 53.4960-0 through 53.4960-4 to taxable years beginning after December 31, 2017, and on or before December 31, 2021, provided the taxpayer applies § § 53.4960-0 through 53.4960-4 in their entirety and in a consistent manner.

(b) [Reserved]. [Reg. § 53.4960-6.]

☐ [*T.D.* 9938, 1-15-2021.]

# ABATEMENT OF FIRST AND SECOND TIER TAXES

### [Reg. § 53.4961-1]

**§ 53.4961-1. Abatement of second tier taxes for correction within correction period.**—If any taxable event is corrected during the correction period for the event, then any second tier tax imposed with respect to the event shall not be assessed. If the tax has been assessed, it shall be abated. If the tax has been collected, it shall be credited or refunded as an overpayment. For purposes of this section, the tax imposed includes interest, additions to the tax and additional amounts. For definitions of the terms "second tier tax," "taxable event," "correct," and "correction period," see §53.4963-1. [Reg. §53.4961-1.]

☐ [*T.D. 8084, 5-1-86.*]

### [Reg. §53.4961-2]

**§53.4961-2. Court proceedings to determine liability for second tier tax.**—(a) *Introduction.*—Under section 4961(b) and (c), the period of limitations on collection may be suspended and assessment or collection of first or second tier tax may be prohibited during the pendency of administrative and judicial proceedings conducted to determine a taxpayer s liability for second tier tax. This section provides rules relating to the suspension of the limitations period and the prohibitions on assessment and collection. In addition, this section describes the administrative and judicial proceedings to which these rules apply.

(b) *Initial proceeding.*—(1) *Defined.*—For purposes of subpart K, an initial proceeding means a proceeding described in subparagraph (2) or (3).

(2) *Tax Court proceeding before assessment* A proceeding is described in this subparagraph (2) if it is a proceeding with respect to the taxpayer's liability for second tier tax and is commenced in accordance with section 6213(a).

(3) *Refund proceeding commenced before correction period ends.*—A proceeding is described in this subparagraph (3) if it is a proceeding commenced under section 7422, in accordance with the provisions of §53.4963-1(e)(4) and (5) (relating to prerequisites to extension of the correction period during certain refund proceedings), and with respect to the taxpayer's liability for second tier tax.

(c) *Supplemental proceeding.*—(1) *Jurisdiction.*—If a determination in an initial proceeding that a taxpayer is liable for a second tier tax has become final, the court in which the initial proceeding was commenced shall have jurisdiction to conduct any necessary supplemental proceeding to determine whether the taxable event was corrected during the correction period.

(2) *Time for beginning proceeding.*—The time for beginning a supplemental proceeding begins on the day after a determination in an initial proceeding becomes final and ends on the 96th day after the last day of the correction period.

(d) *Restriction on assessment during Tax Court proceeding.*—If a supplemental proceeding described in section 4961(b) and §53.4961-2(c) is commenced in the Tax Court, the provisions of the second and third sentences of section 6213(a) and the first and third sentences of §301.6213-1(a)(2) apply with respect to a deficiency in second tier tax until the decision of the Tax Court in the supplemental proceeding is final.

(e) *Suspension of period of collection for second tier tax.*—(1) *Scope.*—Except as provided in subparagraph (6), this paragraph (e) applies to the second tier tax assessed with respect to a taxable event if a claim described in subparagraph (2) is filed.

(2) *Claim for refund.*—A claim for refund is described in this subparagraph (2) if, no later than 90 days after the day on which the second tier tax is assessed with respect to a taxable event, the taxpayer—

(i) Pays the full amount of first tier tax for the taxable period, and

(ii) Files a claim for refund of the amount paid.

(3) *Collection prohibited.*—No levy or proceeding in court for the collection of the second tier tax shall be made, begun, or prosecuted until the end of the collection prohibition period described in subparagraph (5). Notwithstanding section 7421(a), the collection by levy or proceeding may be enjoined during the collection prohibition period by a proceeding in the proper court.

(4) *Suspension of running of period of limitation on collection.*—With respect to a second tier tax to which this paragraph (e) applies, the running of the period of limitations provided in section 6502 (relating to collection of tax by levy or by a proceeding in court) shall be suspended for the collection prohibition period described in subparagraph (5).

(5) *Collection prohibition period.*—The collection prohibition period begins on the day the second tier tax is assessed and ends on the latest of:

(i) The day a decision in a refund proceeding commenced before the 91st day after denial of the claim described in subpara-

graph (2) of this paragraph (including any supplemental proceeding under §53.4961-2(c)) becomes final;

(ii) The 90th day after the claim referred to in subparagraph (2) is denied; or

(iii) The 90th day after the second tier tax is assessed.

(6) *Jeopardy collection.*—If the Secretary makes a finding that the collection of the second tier tax is in jeopardy, nothing in this paragraph (e) shall prevent the immediate collection of such tax.

(f) *Finality.*—(1) *Tax Court proceeding.*—For purposes of this subpart K, section 7481 applies in determining when a decision in a Tax Court proceeding becomes final.

(2) *Refund proceeding.*—For purposes of this subpart K, §301.7422-1 applies in determining when a decision in a refund proceeding becomes final. [Reg. §53.4961-2.]

☐ [*T.D. 8084, 5-1-86.*]

### [Reg. §53.4963-1]

**§53.4963-1. Definitions.**—(a) *First tier tax.*—For purposes of this subpart K, the term "first tier tax" means any tax imposed by subsection (a) of section 4941, 4942, 4943, 4944, 4945, 4951, 4952, 4955, 4958, 4966, 4967, 4971, or 4975. A first tier tax may also be referred to as an "initial tax" in parts 53 and 54.

(b) *Second tier tax.*—For purposes of this subpart K, the term "second tier tax" means any tax imposed by subsection (b) of section 4941, 4942, 4943, 4944, 4945, 4951, 4952, 4955, 4958, 4971, or 4975. A second tier tax may also be referred to as an "additional tax" in parts 53 and 54.

(c) *Taxable event.*—For purposes of this subpart K, the term "taxable event" means any act, or failure to act, giving rise to liability for tax under section 4941, 4942, 4943, 4944, 4945, 4951, 4952, 4955, 4958, 4966, 4967, 4971, or 4975.

(d) *Correct.*—(1) *In general.*—Except as provided in subparagraph (2), the term "correct" has the same meaning for purposes of this subpart K as in the section which imposes the second tier tax or the regulations thereunder.

(2) *Special rules.*—The term "correct" means—

(i) For a second tier tax imposed by section 4942(b), reducing the amount of the undistributed income to zero,

(ii) For a second tier tax imposed by section 4943(b), reducing the amount of the excess business holdings to zero, and

(iii) For a second tier tax imposed by section 4944(b), removing the investment from jeopardy.

(e) *Correction period.*—(1) *In general.*—The correction period with respect to any taxable event shall begin with the date on which the taxable event occurs and shall end 90 days after the date of mailing of a notice of deficiency under section 6212 with respect to the second tier tax imposed with respect to the taxable event.

(2) *Extensions of correction period.*—The correction period referred to in subparagraph (1) of this paragraph shall be extended by any period in which a deficiency cannot be assessed under section 6213(a). In addition, the correction period referred to in subparagraph (1) of this paragraph (e) shall be extended in accordance with subparagraphs (3), (4), and (5) of this paragraph except that subparagraph (4) or (5) shall not operate to extend a correction period with respect to which a taxpayer has filed a petition with the United States Tax Court for redetermination of a deficiency within the time prescribed by section 6213(a).

(3) *Extensions by Commissioner.*—The correction period referred to in subparagraph (1) of this paragraph may be extended by any period which the Commissioner determines is reasonable and necessary to bring about correction (including, for taxes imposed by section 4975, equitable relief sought by the Secretary of Labor) of the taxable event. The Commissioner ordinarily will not extend the correction period unless the following factors are present:

(i) The taxpayer on whom the second tier tax is imposed, the Secretary of Labor (for taxes imposed by section 4975), or an appropriate State officer (as defined in section 6104(c)(2)) is actively seeking in good faith to correct the taxable event;

(ii) Adequate corrective action cannot reasonably be expected to result during the unextended correction period;

(iii) For taxes imposed by section 4975, the Secretary of Labor requests the extension because subdivision (ii) applies; and

(iv) For taxes imposed by chapter 42 (other than taxes imposed by section 4940), the taxable event appears to have been an isolated occurrence so that it appears unlikely that similar taxable events will occur in the future.

(4) *Extension for payment of first tier tax.*—If, within the unextended correction period, the taxpayer pays the full amount of the first tier tax imposed with respect to the taxable event the Commissioner shall extend the correction period to the later of—

(i) Ninety days after the payment of the first tier tax, or

(ii) The last day of the correction period determined without regard to this paragraph.

(5) *Extensions for filing claim for refund or refund suit.*—If prior to the expiration of the correction period (including extensions) a claim for refund is filed with respect to payment of the full amount of the first tier tax imposed with respect to the taxable event, the Commissioner shall extend the correction period during the pendency of the claim plus an additional 90 days. If within that time a suit or proceeding referred to in section 7422(g) with respect to the claim is filed, the Commissioner shall extend the correction period until the determination in the suit for refund (determined without regard to a supplemental proceeding under section 4961(b)) is final, determined under § 301.7422-2(a).

(6) *End of correction period if waiver accepted.*—If the notice of deficiency referred to in paragraph (1) is not mailed because there is a waiver of the restrictions on assessment and collection of the deficiency or because the deficiency is paid, the correction period will end with the end of the collection prohibition period described in § 53.4961-2(e)(5).

(7) *Date on which taxable event occurs.*—For purposes of subparagraph (1), the taxable event shall be treated as occurring—

(i) Under section 4942, on the first day of the taxable year for which there is undistributed income,

(ii) Under section 4943, on the first day on which there are excess business holdings,

(iii) Under section 4971, on the last day of the plan year in which there is an accumulated funding deficiency, and

(iv) In all other cases, the date on which the event occurred.

(f) *Effective date.*—The provisions of this subpart K are effective with respect to second tier taxes assessed after December 24,1980. The preceding sentence shall not be construed to permit the assessment of a tax in a case to which, on December 24,1980, the doctrine of res judicata applied. [Reg. § 53.4963-1.]

☐ [*T.D. 8084, 5-1-86. Amended by T.D. 8628, 12-4-95, T.D. 8920, 1-9-2001 and T.D. 9855, 4-5-2019.*]

# TAX SHELTER TRANSACTIONS

### [Reg. § 53.4965-1]

**§ 53.4965-1. Overview.**—(a) *Entity-level excise tax.*—Section 4965 imposes two excise taxes with respect to certain tax shelter transactions to which tax-exempt entities are parties. Section 4965(a)(1) imposes an entity-level excise tax on certain tax-exempt entities that are parties to "prohibited tax shelter transactions," as defined in section 4965(e). See § 53.4965-2 for the discussion of covered tax-exempt entities. See § 53.4965-3 for the definition of prohibited tax shelter transactions. See § 53.4965-4 for the definition of tax-exempt party to a prohibited tax shelter transaction. The entity-level excise tax under section 4965(a)(1) is imposed on a specified percentage of the entity's net income or proceeds that are attributable to the transaction for the relevant tax year (or a period within that tax year). The rate of tax depends on whether the entity knew or had reason to know that the transaction was a prohibited tax shelter transaction at the time the entity became a party to the transaction. See § 53.4965-7(a) for the discussion of the entity-level excise tax under section 4965(a)(1). See § 53.4965-6 for the discussion of "knowing or having reason to know." See § 53.4965-8 for the definition of net income and proceeds and the standard for allocating net income and proceeds that are attributable to a prohibited tax shelter transaction to various periods.

(b) *Manager-level excise tax.*—Section 4965(a)(2) imposes a manager-level excise tax on "entity managers," as defined in section 4965(d), of tax-exempt entities who approve the entity as a party (or otherwise cause the entity to be a party) to a prohibited tax shelter transaction and know or have reason to know, at the time the tax-exempt entity enters into the transaction, that the transaction is a prohibited tax shelter transaction. See § 53.4965-5 for the definition of entity manager and the meaning of "approving or otherwise causing," and § 53.4965-6 for the discussion of "knowing or having reason to know." See § 53.4965-7(b) for the discussion of the manager-level excise tax under section 4965(a)(2).

(c) *Effective/applicability dates.*—See § 53.4965-9 for the discussion of the relevant effective and applicability dates. [Reg. § 53.4965-1.]

☐ [*T.D. 9492, 7-2-2010.*]

### [Reg. § 53.4965-2]

**§ 53.4965-2. Covered tax-exempt entities.**—(a) *In general.*—Under section 4965(c), the term "tax-exempt entity" refers to entities that are described in sections 501(c), 501(d), or 170(c) (other than the United States), Indian tribal governments (within the meaning of section 7701(a)(40)), and tax-qualified pension plans, individual retirement arrangements and similar tax-favored savings arrangements that are described in sections 4979(e)(1), (2) or (3), 529, 457(b), or 4973(a). The tax-exempt entities referred to in section 4965(c) are divided into two broad categories, non-plan entities and plan entities.

(b) *Non-plan entities.*—Non-plan entities are—

(1) Entities described in section 501(c);

(2) Religious or apostolic associations or corporations described in section 501(d);

(3) Entities described in section 170(c), including states, possessions of the United States, the District of Columbia, political subdivisions of states and political subdivisions of possessions of the United States (but not including the United States); and

(4) Indian tribal governments within the meaning of section 7701(a)(40).

(c) *Plan entities.*—Plan entities are—

(1) Entities described in section 4979(e)(1) (qualified plans under section 401(a), including qualified cash or deferred arrangements under section 401(k) (including a section 401(k) plan that allows designated Roth contributions));

(2) Entities described in section 4979(e)(2) (annuity plans described in section 403(a));

(3) Entities described in section 4979(e)(3) (annuity contracts described in section 403(b), including a section 403(b) arrangement that allows Roth contributions);

(4) Qualified tuition programs described in section 529;

(5) Eligible deferred compensation plans under section 457(b) that are maintained by a governmental employer as defined in section 457(e)(1)(A);

(6) Arrangements described in section 4973(a) which include—

(i) Individual retirement plans defined in section 408(a) and (b), including—

(A) Simplified employee pensions (SEPs) under section 408(k);

(B) Simple individual retirement accounts (SIMPLEs) under section 408(p);

(C) Deemed individual retirement accounts or annuities (IRAs) qualified under a qualified plan (deemed IRAs) under section 408(q); and

(D) Roth IRAs under section 408A.

(ii) Arrangements described in section 220(d) (Archer Medical Savings Accounts (MSAs));

(iii) Arrangements described in section 403(b)(7) (custodial accounts treated as annuity contracts);

(iv) Arrangements described in section 530 (Coverdell education savings accounts); and

(v) Arrangements described in section 223(d) (health savings accounts (HSAs)).

(d) *Effective/applicability dates.*—See § 53.4965-9 for the discussion of the relevant effective and applicability dates. [Reg. § 53.4965-2.]

☐ [*T.D. 9492, 7-2-2010 (corrected 8-3-2010).*]

### [Reg. § 53.4965-3]

**§ 53.4965-3. Prohibited tax shelter transactions.**—(a) *In general.*—Under section 4965(e), the term *prohibited tax shelter transaction* means—

(1) Listed transactions within the meaning of section 6707A(c)(2), including subsequently listed transactions described in paragraph (b) of this section; and

(2) Prohibited reportable transactions, which consist of the following reportable transactions within the meaning of section 6707A(c)(1)—

(i) Confidential transactions, as described in § 1.6011-4(b)(3) of this chapter; or

(ii) Transactions with contractual protection, as described in § 1.6011-4(b)(4) of this chapter.

(b) *Subsequently listed transactions.*—A subsequently listed transaction for purposes of section 4965 is a transaction that is identified by the Secretary as a listed transaction after the tax-exempt entity has entered into the transaction and that was not a prohibited reportable transaction (within the meaning of section 4965(e)(1)(C) and paragraph (a)(2) of this section) at the time the entity entered into the transaction.

(c) *Cross-reference.*—The determination of whether a transaction is a listed transaction or a prohibited reportable transaction for section 4965 purposes shall be made under the law applicable to section 6707A(c)(1) and (c)(2).

(d) *Effective/applicability dates.*—See §53.4965-9 for the discussion of the relevant effective and applicability dates. [Reg. §53.4965-3.]

☐ [T.D. 9492, 7-2-2010.]

**[Reg. §53.4965-4]**

**§53.4965-4. Definition of tax-exempt party to a prohibited tax shelter transaction.**—(a) *In general.*—For purposes of sections 4965 and 6033(a)(2), a tax-exempt entity is a party to a prohibited tax shelter transaction if the entity—

(1) Facilitates a prohibited tax shelter transaction by reason of its tax-exempt, tax indifferent or tax-favored status; or

(2) Is identified in published guidance, by type, class or role, as a party to a prohibited tax shelter transaction.

(b) Published guidance may identify which tax-exempt entities, by type, class or role, will not be treated as a party to a prohibited tax shelter transaction.

(c) *Example.*—The following example illustrates the principle of paragraph (a)(1) of this section:

*Example.* A tax-exempt entity enters into a transaction (Transaction A) with an S corporation. Transaction A is the same as or substantially similar to the transaction identified by the Secretary as a listed transaction in Notice 2004-30 (2004-1 CB 828). The tax-exempt entity's role in Transaction A is similar to the role of the tax-exempt party, as described in Notice 2004-30. Under the terms of the transaction, as described in Notice 2004-30, the tax-exempt entity receives the S corporation stock and purports to aid the S corporation and its shareholders in avoiding taxable income. The tax-exempt entity facilitates Transaction A by reason of its tax-exempt, tax indifferent or tax-favored status. Accordingly, the tax-exempt entity is a party to Transaction A for purposes of sections 4965 and 6033(a)(2). See §601.601(d)(2)(ii)(b) of this chapter.

(d) *Effective/applicability dates.*—See §53.4965-9 for the discussion of the relevant effective and applicability dates. [Reg. §53.4965-4.]

☐ [T.D. 9492, 7-2-2010.]

**[Reg. §53.4965-5]**

**§53.4965-5. Entity managers and related definitions.**—(a) *Entity manager of a non-plan entity.*—(1) *In general.*—Under section 4965(d)(1), an *entity manager of a non-plan entity* is—

(i) A person with the authority or responsibility similar to that exercised by an officer, director, or trustee of an organization (that is, the non-plan entity); and

(ii) With respect to any act, the person who has final authority or responsibility (either individually or as a member of a collective body) with respect to such act.

(2) *Definition of officer.*—For purposes of paragraph (a)(1)(i) of this section, a person is considered to be an officer of the non-plan entity (or to have similar authority or responsibility) if the person—

(i) Is specifically designated as such under the certificate of incorporation, bylaws, or other constitutive documents of the non-plan entity; or

(ii) Regularly exercises general authority to make administrative or policy decisions on behalf of the non-plan entity.

(3) *Exception for acts requiring approval by a superior.*—With respect to any act, any person is not described in paragraph (a)(2)(ii) of this section if the person has authority merely to recommend particular administrative or policy decisions, but not to implement them without approval of a superior.

(4) *Delegation of authority.*—A person is an entity manager of a non-plan entity within the meaning of paragraph (a)(1)(ii) of this section if, with respect to any prohibited tax shelter transaction, such person has been delegated final authority or responsibility with respect to such transaction (including by transaction type or dollar amount) by a person described in paragraph (a)(1)(i) of this section or the governing board of the entity. For example, an investment manager is an entity manager with respect to a prohibited tax shelter transaction if the non-plan entity's governing body delegated to the investment manager the final authority to make certain investment decisions and, in the exercise of that authority, the manager commit-

ted the entity to the transaction. To be considered an entity manager of a non-plan entity within the meaning of paragraph (a)(1)(ii) of this section, a person need not be an employee of the entity. A person is not described in paragraph (a)(1)(ii) of this section if the person is merely implementing a decision made by a superior.

(b) *Entity manager of a plan entity.*—(1) *In general.*—Under section 4965(d)(2), an *entity manager of a plan entity* is the person who approves or otherwise causes the entity to be a party to the prohibited tax shelter transaction.

(2) *Special rule for plan participants and beneficiaries who have investment elections.*—(i) *Fully self-directed plans or arrangements.*—In the case of a fully self-directed qualified plan, IRA, or other savings arrangement (including a case where a plan participant or beneficiary is given a list of prohibited investments, such as collectibles), if the plan participant or beneficiary selected a certain investment and, therefore, approved the plan entity to become a party to a prohibited tax shelter transaction, the plan participant or the beneficiary is an entity manager.

(ii) *Plans or arrangements with limited investment options.*—In the case of a qualified plan, IRA, or other savings arrangement where a plan participant or beneficiary is offered a limited number of investment options from which to choose, the person responsible for determining the pre-selected investment options is an entity manager and the plan participant or the beneficiary generally is not an entity manager.

(c) *Meaning of "approves or otherwise causes".*—(1) *In general.*—A person is treated as approving or otherwise causing a tax-exempt entity to become a party to a prohibited tax shelter transaction if the person has the authority to commit the entity to the transaction, either individually or as a member of a collective body, and the person exercises that authority.

(2) *Collective bodies.*—If a person shares the authority described in paragraph (c)(1) of this section as a member of a collective body (for example, board of trustees or committee), the person will be considered to have exercised such authority if the person voted in favor of the entity becoming a party to the transaction. However, a member of the collective body will not be treated as having exercised the authority described in paragraph (c)(1) of this section if he or she voted against a resolution that constituted approval or an act that caused the tax-exempt entity to be a party to a prohibited tax shelter transaction, abstained from voting for such approval, or otherwise failed to vote in favor of such approval.

(3) *Exceptions.*—(i) *Successor in interest.*—If a tax-exempt entity that is a party to a prohibited tax shelter transaction is dissolved, liquidated, or merged into a successor entity, an entity manager of the successor entity will not, solely by reason of the reorganization, be treated as approving or otherwise causing the successor entity to become a party to a prohibited tax shelter transaction, provided that the reorganization of the tax-exempt entity does not result in a material change to the terms of the transaction. For purposes of this paragraph (c)(3)(i), a material change includes an extension or renewal of the agreement (other than an extension or renewal that results from another party to the transaction unilaterally exercising an option granted by the agreement) or a more than incidental change to any payment under the agreement. A change for the sole purpose of substituting the successor entity for the original tax-exempt party is not a material change.

(ii) *Exercise or nonexercise of options.*—Nonexercise of an option pursuant to a transaction involving the tax-exempt entity generally will not constitute an act of approving or causing the entity to be a party to the transaction. If, pursuant to a transaction involving the tax-exempt entity, the entity manager exercises an option (such as a repurchase option), the entity manager will not be subject to the entity manager-level tax if the exercise of the option does not result in the tax-exempt entity becoming a party to a second transaction that is a prohibited tax shelter transaction.

(4) *Example.*—The following example illustrates the principles of paragraph (c)(3)(ii) of this section:

*Example.* In a sale-in, lease-out (SILO) transaction described in Notice 2005-13 (2005-1 CB 630), X, which is a non-plan entity, has purported to sell property to Y, a taxable entity and lease it back for a term of years. At the end of the basic lease term, X has the option of "repurchasing" the property from Y for a predetermined purchase price, with funds that have been set aside at the inception of the transaction for that purpose. The entity manager, by deciding to exercise or not exercise the "repurchase" option is not approving or otherwise causing the non-plan entity to become a party to a second prohibited tax shelter transaction. See §601.601(d)(2)(ii)(b) of this chapter.

(5) *Coordination with the reason-to-know standard.*—The determination that an entity manager approved or caused a tax-exempt entity to be a party to a prohibited tax shelter transaction, by itself, does not establish liability for the section 4965(a)(2) tax. For rules on determining whether an entity manager knew or had reason to know that the transaction was a prohibited tax shelter transaction, see §53.4965-6(b).

(d) *Effective/applicability dates.*—See §53.4965-9 for the discussion of the relevant effective and applicability dates. [Reg. §53.4965-5.]

□ [*T.D. 9492, 7-2-2010 (corrected 8-3-2010).*]

### [Reg. §53.4965-6]

**§53.4965-6. Meaning of "knows or has reason to know".—**
(a) *Attribution to the entity.*—An entity will be treated as knowing or having reason to know for section 4965 purposes if one or more of its entity managers knew or had reason to know that the transaction was a prohibited tax shelter transaction at the time the entity manager(s) approved the entity as (or otherwise caused the entity to be) a party to the transaction. The entity shall be attributed the knowledge or reason to know of any entity manager described in §53.4965-5(a)(1)(i) even if that entity manager does not approve the entity as (or otherwise cause the entity to be) a party to the transaction.

(b) *Determining whether an entity manager knew or had reason to know.*—(1) *In general.*—Whether an entity manager knew or had reason to know that a transaction is a prohibited tax shelter transaction is based on all facts and circumstances. In order for an entity manager to know or have reason to know that a transaction is a prohibited tax shelter transaction, the entity manager must have knowledge of sufficient facts that would lead a reasonable person to conclude that the transaction is a prohibited tax shelter transaction. An entity manager will be considered to have "reason to know" if a reasonable person in the entity manager's circumstances would conclude that the transaction was a prohibited tax shelter transaction based on all the facts reasonably available to the manager at the time of approving the entity as (or otherwise causing the entity to be) a party to the transaction. Factors that will be considered in determining whether a reasonable person in the entity manager's circumstances would conclude that the transaction was a prohibited tax shelter transaction include, but are not limited to—

(i) The presence of tax shelter indicia (see paragraph (b)(2) of this section);

(ii) Whether the entity manager received a disclosure statement prior to the consummation of the transaction indicating that the transaction may be a prohibited tax shelter transaction (see paragraph (b)(3) of this section); and

(iii) Whether the entity manager made appropriate inquiries into the transaction (see paragraph (b)(4) of this section).

(2) *Tax-shelter indicia.*—The presence of indicia that a transaction is a tax shelter will be treated as an indication that the entity manager knew or had reason to know that the transaction was a prohibited tax shelter transaction. Tax shelter indicia include but are not limited to—

(i) The transaction is extraordinary for the entity considering prior investment activity;

(ii) The transaction promises an economic return for the organization that is exceptional considering the amount invested by, the participation of, or the absence of risk to the organization; or

(iii) The transaction is of significant size relative to the receipts of the entity.

(3) *Effect of disclosure statements.*—Receipt by an entity manager of a statement, including a statement described in section 6011(g), in advance of a transaction that the transaction may be a prohibited tax shelter transaction (or a statement that a partnership, hedge fund or other investment conduit may engage in a prohibited tax shelter transaction in the future) is a factor relevant in the determination of whether the entity manager knew or had reason to know that the transaction is a prohibited transaction. However, an entity manager will not be treated as knowing or having reason to know that the transaction was a prohibited tax shelter transaction solely because the entity manager receives such a disclosure.

(4) *Appropriate inquiries.*—What inquiries are appropriate will be determined from the facts and circumstances of each case. For example, if one or more tax shelter indicia are present or if an entity manager receives a disclosure statement described in paragraph (b)(3) of this section, an entity manager has a responsibility to inquire further whether the transaction is a prohibited tax shelter transaction.

(c) *Reliance on professional advice.*—(1) *In general.*—An entity manager is not required to obtain the advice of a professional tax advisor to establish that the entity manager made appropriate inquiries.

Moreover, not seeking professional advice, by itself, shall not give rise to an inference that the entity manager had reason to know that a transaction is a prohibited tax shelter transaction.

(2) *Reliance on written opinion of professional tax advisor.*—An entity manager may establish that he or she did not have a reason to know that a transaction was a prohibited tax shelter transaction at the time the tax-exempt entity entered into the transaction if the entity manager reasonably, and in good faith, relied on the written opinion of a professional tax advisor. Reliance on the written opinion of a professional tax advisor establishes that the entity manager did not have reason to know if, taking into account all the facts and circumstances, the reliance was reasonable and the entity manager acted in good faith. For example, the entity manager's education, sophistication, and business experience will be relevant in determining whether the reliance was reasonable and made in good faith. In no event will an entity manager be considered to have reasonably relied in good faith on an opinion unless the requirements of this paragraph (c)(2) are satisfied. The fact that these requirements are satisfied, however, will not necessarily establish that the entity manager reasonably relied on the opinion in good faith. For example, reliance may not be reasonable or in good faith if the entity manager knew, or reasonably should have known, that the advisor lacked knowledge in the relevant aspects of Federal tax law.

(i) *All facts and circumstances considered.*—The advice must be based upon all pertinent facts and circumstances and the law as it relates to those facts and circumstances. The requirements of this paragraph (c)(2) are not satisfied if the entity manager fails to disclose a fact that it knows, or reasonably should know, is relevant to determining whether the transaction is a prohibited tax shelter transaction.

(ii) *No unreasonable assumptions.*—The advice must not be based on unreasonable factual or legal assumptions (including assumptions as to future events) and must not unreasonably rely on the representations, statements, findings, or agreements of the entity manager or any other person (including another party to the transaction or a material advisor within the meaning of sections 6111 and 6112).

(iii) *"More likely than not" opinion.*—The written opinion of the professional tax advisor must apply the appropriate law to the facts and, based on this analysis, must conclude that the transaction was not a prohibited tax shelter transaction at a "more likely than not" level of certainty at the time the entity manager approved the entity (or otherwise caused the entity) to be a party to the transaction.

(3) *Special rule.*—An entity manager's reliance on a written opinion of a professional tax advisor will not be considered reasonable if the advisor is, or is related to a person who is, a material advisor with respect to the transaction within the meaning of sections 6111 and 6112.

(d) *Subsequently listed transactions.*—An entity manager will not be treated as knowing or having reason to know that a transaction (other than a prohibited reportable transaction as defined in section 4965(e)(1)(C) and §53.4965-3(a)(2)) is a prohibited tax shelter transaction if the entity enters into the transaction before the date on which the transaction is identified by the Secretary as a listed transaction.

(e) *Effective/applicability dates.*—See §53.4965-9 for the discussion of the relevant effective and applicability dates. [Reg. §53.4965-6.]

□ [*T.D. 9492, 7-2-2010.*]

### [Reg. §53.4965-7]

**§53.4965-7. Taxes on prohibited tax shelter transactions.—**
(a) *Entity-level taxes.*—(1) *In general.*—Entity-level excise taxes apply to non-plan entities (as defined in §53.4965-2(b)) that are parties to prohibited tax shelter transactions.

(i) *Prohibited tax shelter transactions other than subsequently listed transactions.*—(A) *Amount of tax if the entity did not know and did not have reason to know.*—If the tax-exempt entity did not know and did not have reason to know that the transaction was a prohibited tax shelter transaction at the time the entity entered into the transaction, the tax is the highest rate of tax under section 11 multiplied by the greater of—

(1) The entity's net income with respect to the prohibited tax shelter transaction (after taking into account any tax imposed by Subtitle D, other than by this section, with respect to such transaction) for the taxable year; or

(2) 75 percent of the proceeds received by the entity for the taxable year that are attributable to such transaction.

(B) *Amount of tax if the entity knew or had reason to know.*—If the tax-exempt entity knew or had reason to know that the transaction was a prohibited tax shelter transaction at the time the entity entered into the transaction, the tax is the greater of—

*(1)* 100 percent of the entity's net income with respect to the transaction (after taking into account any tax imposed by Subtitle D, other than by this section, with respect to such transaction) for the taxable year; or

*(2)* 75 percent of the proceeds received by the entity for the taxable year that are attributable to such transaction.

(ii) *Subsequently listed transactions.*—(A) *In general.*—In the case of a subsequently listed transaction (as defined in section 4965(e)(2) and § 53.4965-3(b)), the tax-exempt entity's income and proceeds attributable to the transaction are allocated between the period before the transaction became listed and the period beginning on the date the transaction became listed. See § 53.4965-8 for the standard for allocating net income or proceeds to various periods. The tax for each taxable year is the highest rate of tax under section 11 multiplied by the greater of—

*(1)* The entity's net income with respect to the subsequently listed transaction (after taking into account any tax imposed by Subtitle D, other than by this section, with respect to such transaction) for the taxable year that is allocable to the period beginning on the later of the date such transaction is identified by the Secretary as a listed transaction or the first day of the taxable year; or

*(2)* 75 percent of the proceeds received by the entity for the taxable year that are attributable to such transaction and allocable to the period beginning on the later of the date such transaction is identified by the Secretary as a listed transaction or the first day of the taxable year.

(B) *No increase in tax.*—The 100 percent tax under section 4965(b)(1)(B) and § 53.4965-7(a)(1)(i)(B) does not apply to any subsequently listed transaction (as defined in section 4965(e)(2) and § 53.4965-3(b)) entered into by a tax-exempt entity before the date on which the transaction is identified by the Secretary as a listed transaction.

(2) *Taxable year.*—The excise tax imposed under section 4965(a)(1) applies for the taxable year in which the entity becomes a party to the prohibited tax shelter transaction and any subsequent taxable year for which the entity has net income or proceeds attributable to the transaction. A taxable year for tax-exempt entities is the calendar year or fiscal year, as applicable, depending on the basis on which the tax-exempt entity keeps its books for Federal income tax purposes. If a tax-exempt entity has not established a taxable year for Federal income tax purposes, the entity's taxable year for the purpose of determining the amount and timing of net income and proceeds attributable to a prohibited tax shelter transaction will be deemed to be the annual period the entity uses in keeping its books and records.

(b) *Manager-level taxes.*—(1) *Amount of tax.*—If any entity manager approved or otherwise caused the tax-exempt entity to become a party to a prohibited tax shelter transaction and knew or had reason to know that the transaction was a prohibited tax shelter transaction, such entity manager is liable for the $20,000 tax. See § 53.4965-5(d) for the meaning of approved or otherwise caused. See § 53.4965-6 for the meaning of knew or had reason to know.

(2) *Timing of the entity manager tax.*—If a tax-exempt entity enters into a prohibited tax shelter transaction during a taxable year of an entity manager, then the entity manager that approved or otherwise caused the tax-exempt entity to become a party to the transaction is liable for the entity manager tax for that taxable year if the entity manager knew or had reason to know that the transaction was a prohibited tax shelter transaction.

(3) *Example.*—The application of paragraph (b)(2) of this section is illustrated by the following example:

*Example.* The entity manager's taxable year is the calendar year. On December 1, 2006, the entity manager approved or otherwise caused the tax-exempt entity to become a party to a transaction that the entity manager knew or had reason to know was a prohibited tax shelter transaction. The tax-exempt entity entered into the transaction on January 31, 2007. The entity manager is liable for the entity manager level tax for the entity manager's 2007 taxable year, during which the tax-exempt entity entered into the prohibited tax shelter transaction.

(4) *Separate liability.*—If more than one entity manager approved or caused a tax-exempt entity to become a party to a prohibited tax shelter transaction while knowing (or having reason to know) that the transaction was a prohibited tax shelter transaction, then each such entity manager is separately (that is, not jointly and severally) liable for the entity manager-level tax with respect to the transaction.

(c) *Effective/applicability dates.*—See § 53.4965-9 for the discussion of the relevant effective and applicability dates. [Reg. § 53.4965-7.]

☐ [T.D. 9492, 7-2-2010.]

**[Reg. § 53.4965-8]**

**§ 53.4965-8. Definition of net income and proceeds and standard for allocating net income or proceeds to various periods.**—(a) *In general.*—For purposes of section 4965(a), the amount and the timing of the net income and proceeds attributable to the prohibited tax shelter transaction will be computed in a manner consistent with the substance of the transaction. In determining the substance of listed transactions, the IRS will look to, among other items, the listing guidance and any subsequent guidance published in the Internal Revenue Bulletin relating to the transaction.

(b) *Definition of net income and proceeds.*—(1) *Net income.*—A tax-exempt entity's net income attributable to a prohibited tax shelter transaction is its gross income derived from the transaction reduced by those deductions that are attributable to the transaction and that would be allowed by chapter 1 of the Internal Revenue Code if the tax-exempt entity were treated as a taxable entity for this purpose, and further reduced by taxes imposed by Subtitle D, other than by this section, with respect to the transaction.

(2) *Proceeds.*—(i) *Tax-exempt entities that facilitate the transaction by reason of their tax-exempt, tax indifferent or tax-favored status.*—Solely for purposes of section 4965, in the case of a tax-exempt entity that is a party to the transaction by reason of § 53.4965-4(a)(1) of this chapter, the term *proceeds* means the gross amount of the tax-exempt entity's consideration for facilitating the transaction, not reduced for any costs or expenses attributable to the transaction. Published guidance with respect to a particular prohibited tax shelter transaction may designate additional amounts as proceeds from the transaction for section 4965 purposes.

(ii) *Treatment of gifts and contributions.*—To the extent not otherwise included in the definition of proceeds in paragraph (b)(2)(i) of this section, any amount that is a gift or a contribution to a tax-exempt entity and is attributable to a prohibited tax shelter transaction will be treated as proceeds for section 4965 purposes, unreduced by any associated expenses.

(c) *Allocation of net income and proceeds.*—(1) *In general.*—For purposes of section 4965(a), the net income and proceeds attributable to a prohibited tax shelter transaction must be allocated in a manner consistent with the tax-exempt entity's established method of accounting for Federal income tax purposes. If the tax-exempt entity has not established a method of accounting for Federal income tax purposes, solely for purposes of section 4965(a) the tax-exempt entity must use the cash receipts and disbursements method of accounting (cash method) provided for in section 446 of the Internal Revenue Code to determine the amount and timing of net income and proceeds attributable to a prohibited tax shelter transaction.

(2) *Special rule.*—If a tax-exempt entity has established a method of accounting other than the cash method, the tax-exempt entity may nevertheless use the cash method of accounting to determine the amount of the net income and proceeds—

(i) Attributable to a prohibited tax shelter transaction entered into prior to the effective date of section 4965(a) tax and allocable to pre- and post-effective date periods; or

(ii) Attributable to a subsequently listed transaction and allocable to pre- and post-listing periods.

(d) *Transition year rules.*—In the case of the taxable year that includes August 16, 2006 (the transition year), the IRS will treat the period beginning on the first day of the transition year and ending on August 15, 2006, and the period beginning on August 16, 2006, and ending on the last day of the transition year as short taxable years. This treatment is solely for purposes of allocating net income or proceeds under section 4965. The tax-exempt entity continues to file tax returns for the full taxable year, does not file tax returns with respect to these deemed short taxable years and does not otherwise take the short taxable years into account for Federal tax purposes. Accordingly, the net income or proceeds that are properly allocated to the transition year in accordance with this section will be treated as allocable to the period—

(1) Ending on or before August 15, 2006 (and accordingly not subject to tax under section 4965(a)) to the extent such net income or proceeds would have been properly taken into account in accordance with this section by the tax-exempt entity in the deemed short year ending on August 15, 2006; and

(2) Beginning after August 15, 2006 (and accordingly subject to tax under section 4965(a)) to the extent such income or proceeds would have been properly taken into account in accordance with this

section by the tax-exempt entity in the short year beginning August 16, 2006.

(e) *Allocation to pre- and post-listing periods.*—If a transaction other than a prohibited reportable transaction (as defined in section 4965(e)(1)(C) and § 53.4965-3(a)(2)) to which the tax-exempt entity is a party is subsequently identified in published guidance as a listed transaction during a taxable year of the entity (the listing year) in which it has net income or proceeds attributable to the transaction, the net income or proceeds are allocated between the pre- and post-listing periods. The IRS will treat the period beginning on the first day of the listing year and ending on the day immediately preceding the date of the listing, and the period beginning on the date of the listing and ending on the last day of the listing year as short taxable years. This treatment is solely for purposes of allocating net income or proceeds under section 4965. The tax-exempt entity continues to file tax returns for the full taxable year, does not file tax returns with respect to these deemed short taxable years and does not otherwise take the short taxable years into account for Federal tax purposes. Accordingly, the net income or proceeds that are properly allocated to the listing year in accordance with this section will be treated as allocable to the period—

(1) Ending before the date of the listing (and accordingly not subject to tax under section 4965(a)) to the extent such net income or proceeds would have been properly taken into account in accordance with this section by the tax-exempt entity in the deemed short year ending on the day immediately preceding the date of the listing; and

(2) Beginning on the date of the listing (and accordingly subject to tax under section 4965(a)) to the extent such income or proceeds would have been properly taken into account in accordance with this section by the tax-exempt entity in the short year beginning on the date of the listing.

(f) *Examples.*—The following examples illustrate the allocation rules of this section:

*Example 1.* (i) In 1999, X, a calendar year non-plan entity using the cash method of accounting, entered into a lease-in/lease-out transaction (LILO) substantially similar to the transaction described in Notice 2000-15 (2000-1 CB 826) (describing Rev. Rul. 99-14 (1999-1 CB 835), superseded by Rev. Rul. 2002-69 (2002-2 CB 760)). In 1999, X purported to lease property to Y pursuant to a "head lease," and Y purported to lease the property back to X pursuant to a "sublease" of a shorter term. In form, X received $268M as an advance payment of head lease rent. Of this amount, $200M had been, in form, financed by a nonrecourse loan obtained by Y. X deposited the $200M with a "debt payment undertaker." This served to defease both a portion of X's rent obligation under its sublease and Y's repayment obligation under the nonrecourse loan. Of the remainder of the $268M advance head lease rent payment, X deposited $54M with an "equity payment undertaker." This served to defease the remainder of X's rent obligation under the sublease as well as the exercise price of X's end-of-sublease term purchase option. This amount inures to the benefit of Y and enables Y to recover its investment in the transaction and a return on that investment. In substance, the $54M is a loan from Y to X. X retained the remaining $14M of the advance head lease rent payment. In substance, this represents a fee for X's participation in the transaction. See § 601.601(d)(2)(ii)(b) of this chapter.

(ii) According to the substance of the transaction, the head lease, sublease and nonrecourse debt will be ignored for Federal income tax purposes. Therefore, any net income or proceeds resulting from these elements of the transaction will not be considered net income or proceeds attributable to the LILO transaction for purposes of section 4965(a). The $54M deemed loan from Y to X and the $14M fee are not ignored for Federal income tax purposes.

(iii) Under X's established cash basis method of accounting, any net income received in 1999 and attributable to the LILO transaction is allocated to X's December 31, 1999, tax year for purposes of section 4965. The $14M fee received in 1999, which constitutes proceeds of the transaction, is likewise allocated to that tax year. Because the 1999 tax year is before the effective date of the section 4965 tax, X will not be subject to any excise tax under section 4965 for the amounts received in 1999.

(iv) Any earnings on the amount deposited with the equity payment undertaker that constitute gross income to X will be reduced by X's original issue discount deductions with respect to the deemed loan from Y, in determining X's net income from the transaction.

*Example 2.* B, a non-plan entity using the cash method of accounting, has an annual accounting period that ends on December 31, 2006. B entered into a prohibited tax shelter transaction on March 15, 2006. On that date, B received a payment of $600,000 as a fee for its involvement in the transaction. B received no other proceeds or income attributable to this transaction in 2006. Under B's method of accounting, the payment received by B on March 15, 2006, is taken into account in the deemed short year ending on August 15, 2006. Accordingly, solely for purposes of section 4965, the payment is

treated as allocable solely to the period ending on or before August 15, 2006, and is not subject to the excise tax imposed by section 4965(a).

*Example 3.* The facts are the same as in *Example 2*, except that B received an additional payment of $400,000 on September 30, 2006. Under B's method of accounting, the payment received by B on September 30, 2006, is taken into account in the deemed short year beginning on August 16, 2006. Accordingly, solely for purposes of section 4965, the $400,000 payment is treated as allocable to the period beginning after August 15, 2006, and is subject to the excise tax imposed by section 4965(a).

*Example 4.* C, a non-plan entity using the cash method of accounting, has an annual accounting period that ends on December 31. C entered into a prohibited tax shelter transaction on May 1, 2005. On March 15, 2007, C received a payment of $580,000 attributable to the transaction. On June 1, 2007, the transaction is identified by the IRS in published guidance as a listed transaction. On June 15, 2007, C received an additional payment of $400,000 attributable to the transaction. Under C's method of accounting, the payments received on March 15, 2007, and June 15, 2007, are taken into account in 2007. The IRS will treat the period beginning on January 1, 2007, and ending on May 31, 2007, and the period beginning on June 1, 2007, and ending on December 31, 2007, as short taxable years. The payment received by C on March 15, 2007, is taken into account in the deemed short year ending on May 31, 2007. Accordingly, solely for purposes of section 4965, the payment is treated as allocable solely to the pre-listing period, and is not subject to the excise tax imposed by section 4965(a). The payment received by C on June 15, 2007, is taken into account in the deemed short year beginning on June 1, 2007. Accordingly, solely for purposes of section 4965, the payment is treated as allocable to the post-listing period, and is subject to the excise tax imposed by section 4965(a).

(g) *Effective/applicability dates.*—See § 53.4965-9 for the discussion of the relevant effective and applicability dates. [Reg. § 53.4965-8.]

☐ [*T.D. 9492, 7-2-2010 (corrected 8-3-2010).*]

**[Reg. § 53.4965-9]**

**§ 53.4965-9. Effective/applicability dates.**—(a) *In general.*—The taxes under section 4965(a) and § 53.4965-7 are effective for taxable years ending after May 17, 2006, with respect to transactions entered into before, on or after that date, except that no tax under section 4965(a) applies with respect to income or proceeds that are properly allocable to any period ending on or before August 15, 2006.

(b) *Applicability of the regulations.*—As of July 6, 2010, except as provided in paragraph (c) of this section, §§ 53.4965-1 through 53.4965-8 of this chapter will apply to taxable years ending after July 6, 2007. A tax-exempt entity may rely on the provisions of §§ 53.4965-1 through 53.4965-8 for taxable years ending on or before July 6, 2007.

(c) *Effective/applicability date with respect to certain knowing transactions.*—(1) *Entity-level tax.*—The 100 percent tax under section 4965(b)(1)(B) and § 53.4965-7(a)(1)(i)(B) does not apply to prohibited tax shelter transactions entered into by a tax-exempt entity on or before May 17, 2006.

(2) *Manager-level tax.*—The IRS will not assert that an entity manager who approved or caused a tax-exempt entity to become a party to a prohibited tax shelter transaction is liable for the entity manager tax under section 4965(b)(2) and § 53.4965-7(b)(1) with respect to the transaction if the tax-exempt entity entered into such transaction prior to May 17, 2006. [Reg. § 53.4965-9.]

☐ [*T.D. 9492, 7-2-2010.*]

**[Reg. § 53.4968-1]**

**§ 53.4968-1. Excise tax based on investment income of certain private colleges and universities.**—(a) *Excise tax on the investment income of certain private colleges and universities.*—For taxable years beginning after December 31, 2017, section 4968 of the Internal Revenue Code (Code) imposes a tax equal to 1.4 percent of the net investment income (as defined in section 4968(c) and § 53.4968-2) of an applicable educational institution (as defined in section 4968(b)(1) and paragraph (b)(1) of this section).

(b) *Definitions.*—The definitions in this paragraph (b) apply for purposes of section 4968 and §§ 53.4968-1 through 53.4968-4.

(1) *Applicable educational institution.*—The term *applicable educational institution* means any eligible educational institution (as defined in section 25A(f)(2) of the Code and § 1.25A-2(b) of this chapter)—

(i) That had at least 500 tuition-paying students during the preceding taxable year;

(ii) More than 50 percent of whose tuition-paying students are located in the United States;

(iii) That is not described in the first sentence of section 511(a)(2)(B) of the Code (relating to state colleges and universities); and

(iv) The aggregate fair market value of the assets of which at the end of such preceding taxable year (other than those assets that are used directly in carrying out the institution's exempt purpose) is at least $500,000 per student.

(2) *Student.*—The term *student* means a person who is enrolled and attending a course for academic credit from the institution and who is being charged tuition at a rate that is commensurate with the tuition rate charged to students enrolled for a degree. The number of students of an educational institution (including for purposes of determining the number of students at a particular location) is based on the daily average number of full-time students (with part-time students taken into account on a full-time student equivalent basis). The standards for determining part-time students, full-time students, full-time equivalents, and daily average are determined by each educational institution. However, the standards may not be lower than the minimum applicable standards established by the Department of Education under the Higher Education Act of 1965 (20 U.S.C. 1088), as amended.

(3) *Tuition-paying.*—(i) *In general.*—The term *tuition-paying* means the payment of any tuition or fees required for the enrollment or attendance of a student for a course of instruction at an educational institution. Tuition and fees do not include payment for supplies or equipment required during a specific course once a student is enrolled in and attending the course, or payment for room and board or other personal living expenses.

(ii) *Treatment of a comprehensive or bundled fee.*—If a student is required to pay a fee (such as a comprehensive fee or a bundled fee) to an educational institution that combines charges for tuition with charges for personal expenses such as room and board, the student is a tuition-paying student.

(iii) *Scholarships, grants, and work study programs.*—Whether a student is tuition-paying is determined after taking into account any scholarships and grants provided directly by the educational institution or by the Federal government or any state or local government, and after application of any work study programs operated directly by the institution. Scholarships and grants provided by non-governmental third parties, even if administered by the institution, are considered payments of tuition on behalf of the student. Accordingly, a student will be considered a tuition-paying student if payment of tuition or a fee is required for the enrollment or attendance of the student for courses of instruction after the application of any scholarships offered directly by the institution, any work study program operated directly by the institution, and any grants and scholarships provided by the Federal government or any state or local government.

(4) *Located in the United States.*—A student is *located in the United States* if the student resided in the United States for at least a portion of the time the student attended the educational institution during the institution's preceding taxable year. Whether a student resided in the United States in any given year can be determined using any reasonable method, as long as that method is consistently applied.

(5) *Assets used directly in carrying out an institution's exempt purpose.*—(i) *In general.*—Except as provided in paragraph (b)(5)(iv) of this section, an asset is *used directly in carrying out an educational institution's exempt purpose* only if the asset is actually used directly by the institution in carrying out its exempt purpose. Whether an asset is used directly by the institution to carry out its exempt purpose is determined based on all the facts and circumstances. If property is used for an exempt purpose and for other purposes, and the exempt use represents 95 percent or more of the total use, the property is considered to be used exclusively for an exempt purpose. If the exempt use of such property represents less than 95 percent of the total use, the institution must make a reasonable allocation between such exempt and nonexempt uses.

(ii) *Illustrations.*—Examples of assets that are used directly in carrying out an institution's exempt purpose include, but are not limited to, the following—

(A) Administrative assets, such as office equipment and supplies used by the institution directly in the administration of its exempt activities;

(B) Real estate or the portion of any building used by the institution directly in its exempt activities;

(C) Physical property such as paintings or other works of art owned by the institution that are on public display (or held for public display), fixtures and equipment in classrooms, research facilities and related equipment that under the facts and circumstances serve a useful purpose in the conduct of the institution's exempt activities;

(D) The reasonable cash balance, determined using any reasonable method, necessary to cover current operating and administrative expenses and other normal and current disbursements directly connected with the educational institution's exempt activities. For this purpose, a reasonable method would include calculating an amount equal to three months of operating expenses allocable to program services, calculated by dividing annual functional expenses allocable to program services by four. A larger amount may be a reasonable cash balance for this purpose if, under the facts and circumstances, a larger amount is established to be necessary to cover administrative expenses and other normal disbursements directly connected with the institution's exempt activity.

(E) Any property the educational institution leases to other persons at no cost (or at a nominal rent) to the lessee in furtherance of the institution's exempt purposes; and

(F) Patents, copyrights, and other intellectual property and intangible property to the extent that income from those assets is excluded from net investment income by § 53.4968-2(b)(2)(iii).

(iii) *Assets not used directly.*—The following assets are examples of assets not used directly in carrying out an institution's exempt purpose—

(A) Assets that are held for the production of income or for investment (for example, stocks, bonds, interest-bearing notes, endowment funds, or leased real estate not described in paragraph (b)(5)(ii)(E) of this section), even if the income from such assets is used to carry out such exempt purpose; and

(B) Property (such as offices and equipment) used for the purpose of managing the institution's endowment funds.

(iv) *Assets of related organizations.*—An asset of a related organization that is treated as an asset of an educational institution by section 4968(d) and § 53.4968-3(c) and that is used directly in carrying out an educational institution's exempt purpose, or that is used directly in carrying out the exempt purpose of a related organization that is described in section 501(c)(3), is considered used directly by the educational institution in carrying out its exempt purpose.

(v) *Valuation of assets not used directly in carrying out an institution's exempt purpose.*—(A) *In general.*—The values of assets not used directly in carrying out an educational institution's exempt purpose are determined under the rules of section 4942(e) and § 53.4942(a)-2(c)(4), as modified by paragraph (b)(5)(v)(B) of this section.

(B) *Modifications.*—In applying the rules of § 53.4942(a)-2(c)(4), an educational institution must—

(1) Substitute "educational institution" for "private foundation" or "foundation" every place they appear; and

(2) Make such adjustments as are reasonable and necessary to obtain the fair market value of any and all assets as of the last day of the preceding taxable year, rather than as of any other times permitted or required by § 53.4942(a)-2(c)(4). [Reg. § 53.4968-1.]

☐ [*T.D.* 9917, 10-14-2020.]

### [Reg. § 53.4968-2]

**§ 53.4968-2. Net investment income.**—(a) *Net investment income.*—(1) *In general.*—For taxable years beginning after December 31, 2017, section 4968(a) of the Internal Revenue Code (Code) imposes a 1.4 percent excise tax on the net investment income (as defined in section 4968(c) and this section) of an applicable educational institution and on certain amounts of net investment income of certain related organizations, as described in section 4968(d) and § 53.4968-3. For purposes of this section, net investment income is determined under rules similar to the rules of section 4940(c) of the Code. Thus, net investment income generally is the amount by which the sum of the gross investment income (as defined in paragraph (b) of this section) and the capital gain net income (as defined in paragraph (d) of this section) exceeds the deductions allowed by paragraph (c) of this section. Except to the extent inconsistent with the provisions of this section, net investment income is determined under the principles of subtitle A of the Code.

(2) *Tax-exempt income.*—For purposes of this section, net investment income is determined by applying section 103 of the Code (relating to State and local bonds) and section 265 of the Code (relating to expenses and interest relating to tax-exempt income).

(b) *Gross investment income.*—(1) *In general.*—For purposes of this section and except as provided in paragraph (b)(2) of this section, the term *gross investment income* means the gross amounts of income from interest, dividends, rents, payments with respect to securities loans (as defined in section 512(a)(5) of the Code), and royalties, but not including any such income to the extent included in computing the tax imposed by section 511 of the Code. Such term also includes income from sources similar to those in the preceding sentence. In general, gross investment income includes the items of investment income described in § 1.512(b)-1(a) of this chapter.

(2) *Exceptions.*—The following items of income are excluded from the definition of gross investment income:

(i) Interest income from a student loan that was made by the applicable educational institution or a related organization to a student of the applicable educational institution in connection with the student's attendance at the institution;

(ii) Rental income from the provision of housing by the applicable educational institution or a related organization to students of the applicable educational institution and from housing for faculty and staff if the housing is provided contingent on their roles as faculty or staff of the applicable educational institution; and

(iii) Royalty income that is derived from patents, copyrights, and other intellectual property and intangible property to the extent those assets resulted from the work of student(s) or faculty member(s) in their capacities as such with the applicable educational institution. However, neither royalty income from trademarks on the institution's logo or name nor royalty income from intellectual property donated or sold to the institution is excluded from gross investment income under this rule.

(c) *Deductions.*—(1) *In general.*—For purposes of computing net investment income—

(i) There is allowed as a deduction from gross investment income all the ordinary and necessary expenses paid or incurred for the production or collection of gross investment income or for the management, conservation, or maintenance of property held for the production of such income, determined with the modifications set forth in paragraph (c)(2) of this section. Taxes paid or incurred under section 4968 are not paid or incurred for the production or collection of gross investment income. Allowable expenses include that portion of an applicable educational institution's operating expenses that is paid or incurred for the production or collection of gross investment income. An applicable educational institution's operating expenses include compensation of officers, other salaries and wages of employees, outside professional fees, interest, and rent and taxes on property used in the applicable educational institution's operations. Where an applicable educational institution's officers or employees engage in activities on behalf of the institution for both activities that generate net investment income and for activities that do not generate net investment income, compensation and salaries paid to such officers or employees must be allocated between the activities that generate net investment income and for activities that do not generate net investment income.

(ii) Where only a portion of property produces, or is held for the production of, income subject to the section 4968 excise tax, and the remainder of the property is used for other purposes, the deductions allowed by this paragraph must be apportioned between the taxable and other uses.

(iii) No amount is allowable as a deduction under this section to the extent it is paid or incurred for purposes other than those described in paragraph (c)(1)(i) of this section. Thus, for example, the charitable deductions prescribed under sections 170 and 642(c) of the Code; the net operating loss deduction prescribed under section 172; and the special deductions prescribed under part VIII of subchapter B of chapter 1 of the Code are not allowable.

(2) *Deduction modifications.*—The following modifications must be made in determining deductions otherwise allowable under this paragraph (c):

(i) The depreciation deduction is allowed, but only on the basis of the straight-line method provided in section 168(b)(3) and without regard to section 168(b)(1) and (2).

(ii) The depletion deduction is allowed, but such deduction is determined without regard to sections 613 and 613A of the Code, relating to percentage depletion.

(iii) The basis to be used for purposes of the deduction allowed for depreciation or depletion is the basis determined under the rules of part II of subchapter O of chapter 1 of the Code (part II of subchapter O), subject to the modifications found in paragraphs (c)(2)(i) and (ii) of this section (relating to depreciation and depletion), and without regard to § 53.4968-2(d)(2) (relating to the basis for determining gain for property held on December 31, 2017, and continuously thereafter to the date of disposition), or section 362(c) of the Code (relating to certain special basis rules regarding contributions of capital to corporations). Thus, an applicable educational institution must reduce the cost or other substituted or transferred basis by an amount equal to the straight-line depreciation or cost depletion, without regard to whether the applicable educational institution deducted such depreciation or depletion during the period prior to

its first taxable year beginning after December 31, 2017. However, where an applicable educational institution has previously taken depreciation or depletion deductions in excess of the amount which would have been taken had the straight-line or cost method been employed, such excess depreciation or depletion also is taken into account to reduce basis. If the facts necessary to determine the basis of property in the hands of the donor or the last preceding owner by whom it was not acquired by gift are unknown to the applicable educational institution, then the original basis to the applicable educational institution of such property is determined under the rules of § 1.1015-1(a)(3) of this chapter.

(iv) The deduction for expenses paid or incurred in any taxable year for the production of gross investment income earned as an incident to a charitable function can be no greater than the income earned from such function which is includible as gross investment income for such year. For example, where rental income incidentally is realized in a year from historic buildings held open to the public, deductions for amounts paid or incurred in that year for the production of such income is limited to the amount of rental income includible as gross investment income for the year.

(d) *Capital gains and losses.*—(1) *In general.*—In determining capital gain net income for purposes of the tax imposed by section 4968—

(i) *Interaction with section 511.*—No gain or loss from the sale or other disposition of property is taken into account to the extent that such gain or loss is taken into account for purposes of computing the tax imposed by section 511.

(ii) *Sales or other dispositions of exempt use property.*—To the extent that property is used by the educational institution for its exempt purposes, capital gain from the sale or exchange of the portion of that property that is used by the educational institution for its exempt purposes is disregarded;

(iii) *Sales of donated property.*—(A) *In general.*—Any appreciation in the value of donated property that occurred prior to the date of its donation to the institution is disregarded.

(B) *Date of donation.*—The date of donation is determined under the timing rules of § 1.170A-1(b) of this chapter.

(C) *Value on the date of donation.*—The value of the donated property on the date of donation is determined under the valuation rules of § 1.170A-1(c) of this chapter; and

(iv) *Capital losses.*—Net losses from sales or other dispositions of property by one related organization (or by the applicable educational institution) reduce (but not below zero) net gains from such sales or other dispositions by other related organizations (or by the applicable educational institution). Should overall net losses from sales or other dispositions of property exceed gains from sales or other dispositions of such property during the same taxable year, such excess may not be deducted from gross investment income in any taxable year, nor may such excess be used to reduce gains in prior taxable years. However, capital loss carryovers are allowed and may be deducted from capital gains in a future year.

(2) *Basis.*—(i) *For purposes of calculating gain from the sale or other disposition of property other than a partnership interest.*—Subject to the modifications of paragraphs (c)(2)(i) and (ii) of this section (referring to the modifications relating to deductions against gross investment income) and without regard to section 362(c), the basis for purposes of determining gain from the sale or other disposition of property (other than a partnership interest) for purposes of determining capital gain net income for purposes of the tax imposed by section 4968 is the greater of—

(A) Fair market value on December 31, 2017, plus or minus all adjustments after December 31, 2017, and before the date of disposition under the rules of part II of subchapter O, provided that the property was held by the applicable educational institution on December 31, 2017, and continuously thereafter to the date of disposition, or

(B) Basis as determined under the rules of part II of subchapter O.

(ii) *For purposes of determining a distributive share of gain from the sale or other disposition of a partnership asset.*—For purposes of determining an applicable educational institution's share of gain upon the sale or other disposition of a partnership asset, the applicable educational institution's basis in each such partnership asset generally is determined under the rules of subchapter K of chapter 1 of the Code (subchapter K). However, see paragraph (d)(3) of this section.

(iii) *For purposes of determining gain on the sale or other disposition of a partnership interest.*—For purposes of determining an applicable educational institution's gain upon the sale or other disposition of all or a portion of a partnership interest, the applicable educational institution's basis in such partnership interest is generally determined under the rules of subchapter K, subject to the special rules in paragraph (d)(3) of this section.

(iv) *For purposes of calculating loss.*—Subject to the modifications of paragraphs (c)(2)(i) and (ii) of this section (referring to the modifications relating to deductions against gross investment income) and without regard to section 362(c), basis as determined in paragraph (d)(2)(i)(B) of this section applies for purposes of determining loss. For purposes of determining loss from the sale or other disposition of a partnership interest, basis is determined under the rules of subchapter K.

(3) *Special rules regarding partnership interests and partnership assets.*—(i) *Reduction of distributive share of capital gain net income from a partnership.*—For purposes of computing net investment income, an applicable educational institution reduces the amount of its distributive share of capital gain net income from a partnership by the least of—

(A) The applicable educational institution's share of applicable capital gain (as defined in paragraph (d)(3)(iii)(A) of this section) from such partnership;

(B) One-third of the applicable educational institution's unadjusted step-up (as defined in paragraph (d)(3)(iii)(B) of this section) for such partnership; or

(C) The applicable educational institution's adjusted step-up (as defined in paragraph (d)(3)(iii)(C) of this section) for such partnership.

(ii) *Reduction of capital gain net income from a sale or other disposition of all or a portion of a partnership interest.*—For purposes of computing net investment income, an applicable educational institution reduces the amount of its capital gain net income upon the sale or other disposition of all or a portion of a partnership interest by an amount that bears the same relation to the applicable educational institution's adjusted step-up (as defined in paragraph (d)(3)(iii)(C) of this section) for such partnership as the fair market value of the transferred portion of the interest bears to the fair market value of the applicable educational institution's entire interest in such partnership before the sale or other disposition.

(iii) *Definitions.*—For purposes of this section –

(A) *Applicable capital gain.*—For an applicable educational institution's first taxable year beginning after December 31, 2017, the term *applicable capital gain* means an applicable educational institution's share of both short-term and long-term capital gains and losses subject to section 4968 from a partnership. For subsequent taxable years, applicable capital gain does not include an applicable educational institution's share of short-term capital gains and losses subject to section 4968 from a partnership. For purposes of this paragraph, applicable capital gain is not less than zero.

(B) *Unadjusted step-up.*—An applicable educational institution computes an *unadjusted step-up* for each partnership interest it held on December 31, 2017. The unadjusted step-up for a partnership interest equals the excess, if any, of the fair market value of such partnership interest on December 31, 2017, over the adjusted basis of such partnership interest on December 31, 2017.

(C) *Adjusted step-up.*—An applicable educational institution computes an *adjusted step-up* for each partnership interest it held on December 31, 2017. The adjusted step-up for a partnership interest equals the unadjusted step-up for such partnership, reduced by the amount of any capital gain net income reduction pursuant to paragraphs (d)(3)(i) and (ii) of this section for such partnership.

(4) *Examples.*—The following examples illustrate paragraph (d)(3) of this section. Unless stated otherwise in the examples, partners have no tax items other than those listed in the example. With respect to partnerships, all allocations are in accordance with section 704(b) and the regulations under section 704(b) in part 1 of this chapter (Income Tax Regulations).

(i) *Example 1.*—(A) *Facts.* University (U), an applicable educational institution, is a partner in partnership PRS. On December 31, 2017, U's PRS interest had a fair market value of $130 and tax basis of $100. In 2018, U's share of capital gain net income from PRS is $5, which is comprised of $20 of gain from the sale of capital asset X and ($15) of loss from the sale of capital asset Y. Further, such $5 of capital gain net income is applicable capital gain (as defined in paragraph (d)(3)(iii)(A) of this section).

(B) *Analysis.* U has an unadjusted step-up (as defined in paragraph (d)(3)(iii)(B) of this section) for PRS of $30 ($130 fair market value - $100 tax basis on December 31, 2017). Pursuant to paragraph (d)(3)(i) of this section, for purposes of computing its net investment income, U reduces the amount of its capital gain net income from PRS by $5, which is the least of: U's share of applicable capital gain

from PRS ($5); or one-third of U's unadjusted step-up for PRS ($10); or U's adjusted step-up for PRS ($30). Thus, U reduces its $5 of capital gain net income allocated from PRS by $5, resulting in U having $0 of capital gain net income in 2018 for purposes of section 4968. As a result, U's adjusted step-up for PRS for subsequent taxable years is reduced to $25 ($30 - $5) pursuant to paragraph (d)(4)(iii)(C) of this section. Pursuant to section 705, the $5 of gain allocated to U increases U's tax basis in its PRS interest to $105.

(ii) *Example 2.*—(A) *Facts.* The facts are the same as in paragraph (d)(4)(i)(A) of this section (Example 1). In 2019, U sells its entire interest in PRS for $130, which, immediately prior to the sale, had a tax basis of $105. As a result, U has $25 of capital gain from the sale of its PRS interest.

(B) *Analysis.* Pursuant to paragraph (d)(3)(iii) of this section, for purposes of computing its net investment income, U reduces its capital gain net income resulting from the sale of its entire PRS interest by $25, which is the amount that bears the same relation to U's adjusted step-up for PRS ($25) as the fair market value of the transferred portion of PRS ($130) bears to the fair market value of the U's entire interest in PRS before the sale or other disposition ($130). Thus, U reduces its $25 of capital gain net income from the sale of its PRS interest by $25, resulting in U having $0 of capital gain net income in 2019 for purposes of section 4968.

(iii) *Example 3.*—(A) *Facts.* The facts are the same as in paragraph (d)(4)(i)(A) of this section (Example 1). In 2019, U's share of capital gain net income from PRS is $15, which is comprised of $15 of gain from the sale of capital asset Z. Further, such $15 of capital gain net income is applicable capital gain (as defined in paragraph (d)(3)(iii)(A) of this section).

(B) *Analysis.* Pursuant to paragraph (d)(3)(i) of this section, for purposes of computing its net investment income, U reduces the amount of its capital gain net income from PRS by $10, which is the least of: U's share of applicable capital gain from PRS ($15); or one-third of U's unadjusted step-up for PRS ($10); or U's adjusted step-up for PRS ($25, computed as $30 of unadjusted step-up, less $5 of capital gain net income reduced in 2018 pursuant to paragraph (d)(3)(i) of this section). Thus, U reduces its $15 of capital gain net income allocated from PRS by $10, resulting in U having $5 of capital gain net income in 2019 for purposes of section 4968. As a result, U's adjusted step-up for PRS is reduced for subsequent taxable years to $15 ($25 - $10) pursuant to paragraph (d)(3)(iii)(C) of this section. Pursuant to section 705, the $15 of gain allocated to U increases U's tax basis in its PRS interest to $120. [Reg. § 53.4968-2.]

☐ [*T.D.* 9917, 10-14-2020.]

### [Reg. § 53.4968-3]

**§ 53.4968-3. Related organizations.**—(a) *Definition of related organization.*—(1) *In general.*—For purposes of section 4968(d) of the Internal Revenue Code (Code) and § § 53.4968-1 through 53.4968-4, except as provided in paragraph (a)(2) of this section, the term *related organization* means, with respect to an educational institution, any organization that—

(i) Controls such institution;

(ii) Is controlled by such institution;

(iii) Is controlled by one or more persons that also control such institution;

(iv) Is a supported organization (as defined in section 509(f)(3) of the Code) with respect to such institution during the taxable year; or

(v) Is a supporting organization (as described in section 509(a)(3)) with respect to such institution during the taxable year.

(2) *Organizations not considered related organizations.*—For purposes of section 4968(d) and § § 53.4968-1 through 53.4968-4, the term *related organization* does not include any organization that is—

(i) A taxable corporation;

(ii) A taxable trust, including a non-grantor charitable lead trust (except to the extent the trust is controlled by the educational institution as described in paragraph (b)(2)(ii) of this section);

(iii) A grantor charitable lead trust;

(iv) A charitable remainder trust;

(v) A partnership, S corporation (as defined in section 1361(a)(1) of the Code), or other pass-through entity that is generally not subject to Federal income tax, the income of which is taxable to its partners or other interest holders; or

(vi) A decedent's estate.

(3) *Employee benefit plans or arrangements.*—A trust or similar funding vehicle of an employee benefit plan or arrangement, such as a section 501(a) trust funding a section 401(a) qualified retirement plan, or an annuity contract funding a section 403(b) plan, or a section 419(e) welfare benefit fund (including a voluntary employees' beneficiary association under section 501(c)(9)) funding a welfare

benefit plan, will not be treated as a related organization and its assets will not be treated as the assets of the educational institution or of a related organization. A trust or other funding vehicle of an unfunded employee benefit plan of an educational institution or a related organization, such as a grantor trust described in section 671 et seq., used in connection with a section 457(b) plan or an arrangement subject to section 457(f), will be treated as a related organization for purposes of section 4968(d) and its assets will be treated as the assets of the educational institution or of a related organization, but the assets are not considered "used directly in carrying out the institution's exempt purpose" for purposes of section 4968(b)(1)(D). For purposes of determining whether the employee benefit plan of an educational institution is funded or unfunded, the educational institution and all of its related organizations are treated as a single sponsor and payor of the benefits.

(b) *Control.*—(1) *Controls such institution.*—For purposes of section 4968(d) and §§ 53.4968-1 through 53.4968-4, an organization controls an educational institution if—

(i) The organization owns (by vote or value) more than 50 percent of the voting and non-voting stock or membership interest of the educational institution; or

(ii) The organization (or one or more of its managers, directors, officers, trustees, or employees, acting only in those capacities) can—

(A) Appoint or elect (which must include the power to remove and replace) more than 50 percent of the members of the educational institution's governing body (such as directors, officers, or trustees), or otherwise has the ongoing power to appoint or elect more than 50 percent of such members with reasonable frequency;

(B) Require the educational institution to make an expenditure (or prevent the educational institution from making an expenditure); or

(C) Require the educational institution to perform any act that significantly affects its operations (or prevent it from performing such an act).

(2) *Is controlled by such institution.*—For purposes of section 4968(d) and §§ 53.4968-1 through 53.4968-4, an organization is controlled by an educational institution:

(i) *Tax-exempt corporation.*—In the case of a corporation recognized as exempt from income tax under section 501(a), if the educational institution owns (by vote or value) more than 50 percent of the voting and nonvoting stock or membership interest of the corporation.

(ii) *Trust.*—(A) *In general.*—In the case of a trust—

(1) If the educational institution is substantially the sole permissible trust beneficiary or appointee of both income and principal, whether or not the timing of the distribution is subject to the trustee's discretion;

(2) If the trust is a pooled income fund described in sections 642(c)(3) and 642(c)(5);

(3) If, but only to the extent that, the assets of the trust were contributed to the trust by the educational institution (or by a person controlled by the educational institution); or

(4) If, but only to the extent that, the educational institution (or person controlled by the educational institution) has the right to demand (or can otherwise cause) a distribution of principal from the trust to the educational institution (or a person controlled by the educational institution).

(B) *Person controlled by the educational organization.*—For purposes of this paragraph (b)(2)(ii), a person is controlled by an educational institution if the educational institution has the power to remove and replace such person or otherwise controls the person under one of the tests described in § 53.4968-3(b)(2)(i), (ii), or (iii), with similar principles applying for purposes of determining control of any other form of entity.

(iii) *Nonstock organization.*—In the case of a nonstock organization, if the educational institution (or one or more of its managers, directors, officers, trustees, or employees, acting only in those capacities) can—

(A) Appoint or elect (which must include the power to remove and replace) more than 50 percent of the members of the organization's governing body (such as directors, officers, or trustees), or otherwise has an ongoing power to appoint or elect more than 50 percent of such members with reasonable frequency);

(B) Require the organization to make an expenditure (or prevent the organization from making an expenditure); or

(C) Require the organization to perform any act that significantly affects its operations (or prevent it from performing such an act).

(3) *Is controlled by one or more persons that also control such institution.*—For purposes of section 4968(d) and this section, an organization (other than one described in paragraph (a)(2) of this section) is controlled by one or more persons that also control the educational institution if more than 50 percent of the members of the governing body of the other organization are directly or indirectly controlled by persons that comprise more than 50 percent of the members of the governing body of the educational institution.

(4) *Constructive ownership.*—The principles of section 318(a)(2) (relating to ownership attribution from partnerships, estates, trusts, and corporations) apply for purposes of determining ownership of stock in a corporation, and similar principles apply for purposes of determining ownership of an interest in any other entity.

(5) *Method of control.*—Control includes control by aggregating votes or positions of authority (including by veto power), but applies regardless of the method by which the control is exercised or exercisable.

(c) *Organization described in section 509(a)(3) during the taxable year with respect to the educational institution.*—A section 509(a)(3) organization is a supporting organization *with respect to* an educational institution only if the supporting organization meets the organizational, operational, and relationship tests of section 509(a)(3)(B) and § 1.509(a)-4 of this chapter with respect to the educational institution.

(d) *Assets and net investment income of related organizations.*—(1) *In general.*—A related organization's assets and net investment income are taken into account both in determining whether an institution is an applicable educational institution and in computing the net investment income of an applicable educational institution. For purposes of determining the aggregate fair market value of the assets and net investment income of an educational institution, the assets and net investment income of all related organizations are treated as the assets and net investment income, respectively, of the institution, unless an exception provided in paragraph (d)(2) of this section or the exception provided in § 53.4968-1(b)(5)(iv) (relating to assets used directly in carrying out an exempt purpose) applies. In cases in which an organization is a related organization with respect to an educational institution under more than one definition of this § 53.4968-3, then the rule that attributes the largest amount of assets and net investment income of the related organization to the educational institution must be applied.

(2) *Exceptions.*—For purposes of section 4968 and this paragraph (d)(2)—

(i) *No amount is taken into account with respect to more than one educational institution.*—In determining the aggregate fair market value of the assets and net investment income of an educational institution, assets and net investment income of a related organization are not taken into account with respect to more than one educational institution. Thus, in any case in which an organization is a related organization with respect to more than one educational institution, the assets and net investment income of the related organization must be allocated between or among the educational institutions as to which the organization is a related organization, subject to paragraph (d)(2)(ii) of this section. The educational institution must make such allocation in a reasonable manner, taking into account all facts and circumstances, that is consistent across all related organizations.

(ii) *Assets and net investment income that are not intended or available for the use or benefit of the educational institution.*—(A) *In general.*—Unless a related organization is controlled by the educational institution or is a supporting organization described in section 509(a)(3) with respect to such institution for the taxable year, assets and net investment income of a related organization that are not intended or available for the use or benefit of the educational institution are not taken into account by that educational institution.

(B) *Determining whether assets and net investment income of a related organization are intended or available for the use or benefit of an educational institution.*—If a related organization controls the educational institution, is controlled by one or more persons that also control such institution (but is not described in section 509(a)(3) with respect to the educational institution for the taxable year), or is a supported organization (as defined in section 509(f)(3)) during the taxable year with respect to the educational institution, then the related organization's assets and net investment income are taken into account as assets and net investment income of the educational institution only to the extent the assets and net investment income are intended or available for the use or benefit of that educational institution. Assets and net investment income of a related organization are intended or available for the use or benefit of an educational institution if such assets and net investment income are specifically earmarked or restricted for the benefit of, or otherwise are fairly attributable to, the educational institution. For example, assets are fairly attributable to the educational institution if they have been affirmatively designated or appropriated for the educational institution to draw upon at will. Conversely, assets and net investment income of a related organization are not intended or available for the use or benefit of an educational institution if such assets and net investment income are specifically earmarked or restricted for another entity or for unrelated purposes or otherwise are not fairly attributable to the educational institution. The assets and net investment income of a related organization must be allocated between those intended or available for the use or benefit of an educational institution and those not intended or not available for the use or benefit of that same educational institution. The educational institution must make such allocation in a reasonable manner, taking into account all facts and circumstances, that is consistent across all related organizations.

(C) *Related organizations that are controlled by the educational institution or that are supporting organizations (as described in section 509(a)(3)) with respect to the educational institution during the taxable year.*—(1) *In general.*—If a related organization is controlled, as defined in paragraph (b)(2) of this section, by an educational institution, or is a supporting organization with respect to the educational institution during the taxable year, as defined in paragraph (c) of this section, the assets and net investment income of the related organization are taken into account as assets and net investment income of the educational institution regardless of whether those assets and net investment income are earmarked or restricted for the benefit of, or otherwise are fairly attributable to, the educational institution and even if they are specifically earmarked or restricted for another entity or for unrelated purposes or otherwise are not fairly attributable to the educational institution, subject to paragraph (d)(2)(ii)(C)(2) of this section. However, see §§ 53.4968-1(b)(2)(ii)(A)(3) and (4) regarding trusts that are controlled related organizations only to the extent assets of the trust were contributed to the trust by the educational institution (or by a person controlled by the educational institution), or only to the extent the educational institution (or person controlled by the educational institution) has the right to demand (or can otherwise cause) a distribution of principal from the trust to the educational institution (or a person controlled by the educational institution). *See also* § 53.4968-1(b)(5)(iv) for rules relating to when assets of a related organization are deemed to be used directly in carrying out the institution's exempt purpose.

(2) *Special rule for Type III supporting organizations with respect to an educational institution as of December 31, 2017.*—An educational institution with a related organization that was a Type III supporting organization with respect to the educational institution on December 31, 2017, takes into account only the assets and net investment income of such Type III supporting organization that are intended or available for the use or benefit of, or otherwise are fairly attributable to, the educational institution, as described in paragraph (d)(2)(ii)(B) of this section. An educational institution may determine whether the assets and net investment income of such a Type III supporting organization are intended or available for the use or benefit of, or otherwise are fairly attributable to, the educational institution using any reasonable method. A method that attributes to an educational institution assets and net investment income of a supporting organization that specifically are earmarked for the educational institution, are restricted for the benefit of the educational institution, or otherwise are fairly attributable to the educational institution (such as those that have been affirmatively designated or appropriated for the educational institution or made available for the educational institution to draw upon at will) will be deemed to be reasonable.

(3) *Determining assets of related organizations.*—To determine which assets of a related organization are included by an educational institution under section 4968(b)(1)(D) for a particular year, an educational institution determines which organizations are related organizations, as defined in section 4968(d)(2) and § 53.4968-3, as of the end of the educational institution's preceding taxable year, and values the relevant assets on that date.

(4) *Determining net investment income of related organizations.*—To determine the amount of net investment income of a related organization that is included by the applicable educational institution in calculating the tax imposed by section 4968(a) for a particular taxable year, an applicable educational institution determines which organizations are related organizations, as defined in section 4968(d)(2) and § 53.4968-3, as of the end of that taxable year of the applicable educational institution and includes the net investment income from each related organization's taxable year that ends with or within that same taxable year of the applicable educational institution. If an organization became a related organization after the beginning of the applicable educational institution's taxable year, then the applicable educational institution includes the organization's net investment income for the portion of the year that the organization was a related organization, using any reasonable method. [Reg. § 53.4968-3.]

☐ [*T.D.* 9917, 10-14-2020.]

**[Reg. § 53.4968-4]**

**§ 53.4968-4. Applicability date.**—The rules of §§ 53.4968-1 through 53.4968-4 apply to taxable years of an educational institution beginning after October 15, 2020. [Reg. § 53.4968-4.]

☐ [*T.D.* 9917, 10-14-2020.]

# Qualified Pension, Etc., Plans

See p. 20,601 for regulations not amended to reflect law changes

**[Reg. § 54.4971-1]**

**§ 54.4971-1. General rules relating to excise tax on failure to meet minimum funding standards.**—

(a) [Reserved]

(b) [Reserved]

(c) *Additional tax.*—Section 4971(b) imposes an excise tax in any case in which an initial tax is imposed under section 4971(a) on an accumulated funding deficiency and the accumulated funding deficiency is not corrected within the taxable period (as defined in section 4971(c)(3)). The additional tax is 100 percent of the accumulated funding deficiency to the extent not corrected.

(d) [Reserved]

(e) *Definition of taxable period.*—(1) *In general.*—For purposes of any accumulated funding deficiency, the term "taxable period" means the period beginning with the end of the plan year in which there is an accumulated funding deficiency and ending on the earlier of:

(i) The date of mailing of a notice of deficiency under section 6212 with respect to the tax imposed by section 4971(a), or

(ii) The date on which the tax imposed by section 4971(a) is assessed.

(2) *Special rule.*—Where a notice of deficiency referred to in paragraph (e)(1)(i) of this section is not mailed because a waiver of the restrictions on assessment and collection of a deficiency has been accepted or because the deficiency is paid, the date of filing of the waiver or the date of such payment, respectively, shall be treated as the end of the taxable period. [Reg. § 54.4971-1.]

☐ [*T.D.* 8084, 5-1-86.]

**[Reg. § 54.4971(c)-1]**

**§ 54.4971(c)-1. Taxes on failure to meet minimum funding standards; definitions.**—(a) *In general.*—This section sets forth definitions that apply for purposes of applying the rules of section 4971.

(b) *Accumulated funding deficiency.*—(1) *Multiemployer plans.*—With respect to a multiemployer plan defined in section 414(f), the term *accumulated funding deficiency* has the meaning given to that term by section 431. A plan's accumulated funding deficiency for a plan year takes into account all charges and credits to the funding standard account under section 412 for plan years before the first plan year for which section 431 applies to the plan.

(2) *CSEC plans.*—With respect to a CSEC plan (that is, a plan that fits within the definition of a CSEC plan in section 414(y) for plan years beginning on or after January 1, 2014 and for which the election under section 414(y)(3)(A) has not been made), the term *accumulated funding deficiency* means the CSEC accumulated funding deficiency determined under section 433. A plan's CSEC accumulated funding deficiency for a plan year takes into account all charges and credits to the funding standard account under section 412 for plan years before the first plan year for which section 433 applies to the plan.

(c) *Unpaid minimum required contribution.*—(1) *In general.*—The term *unpaid minimum required contribution* means, with respect to any plan year, the portion of the minimum required contribution under section 430 for the plan year for which contributions have not been made on or before the due date for the plan year under section 430(j)(1). The unpaid minimum required contribution is determined after taking into account the interest adjustment to contributions under §1.430(j)-1(b)(4) and any offsets from use of the funding balances under §1.430(f)-1(d).

(2) *Accumulated funding deficiency for pre-effective plan year.*—For purposes of this section, a plan's accumulated funding deficiency under section 412 for the pre-effective plan year is treated as an unpaid minimum required contribution for that plan year until correction is made under the rules of paragraph (d)(2) of this section.

(d) *Correct.*—(1) *Accumulated funding deficiency.*—With respect to an accumulated funding deficiency for a plan year that is described in paragraph (b) of this section, the term *correct* means to contribute, to or under the plan, the amount necessary to reduce the accumulated funding deficiency as of the end of that plan year to zero. To reduce the deficiency to zero, the contribution must include interest at the plan's valuation interest rate for the period between the end of that plan year and the date of the contribution (determined taking into account the rules of section 431(c)(8) or section 433(c)(9), as applicable).

(2) *Unpaid minimum required contribution.*—(i) *In general.*—With respect to an unpaid minimum required contribution for a plan year, the term *correct* means to contribute, to or under the plan, an amount that, when discounted to the valuation date for the plan year for which the unpaid minimum required contribution is due at the appropriate rate of interest, equals or exceeds the unpaid minimum required contribution. For this purpose, the appropriate rate of interest is the plan's effective interest rate for the plan year for which the unpaid minimum required contribution is due except to the extent that the payments are subject to additional interest as provided under section 430(j)(3) or (4).

(ii) *Pre-PPA accumulated funding deficiency.*—With respect to the accumulated funding deficiency under section 412 for the pre-effective plan year that is described in paragraph (c)(2) of this section, the term *correct* means to contribute, to or under the plan, the amount of that accumulated funding deficiency increased with interest from the end of the pre-effective plan year to the date of the contribution at the plan's valuation interest rate for the pre-effective plan year.

(iii) *Ordering rule.*—For purposes of section 4971 and this section, a contribution is attributable first to the earliest plan year of any unpaid minimum required contribution for which correction has not yet been made.

(3) *Corrective action of certain retroactive plan amendments.*—Certain retroactive plan amendments that meet the requirements of section 412(d)(2) may reduce the minimum required contribution for a plan year, which would reduce the accumulated funding deficiency or the amount of the unpaid minimum required contribution for a plan year.

(e) *Taxable period.*—(1) *In general.*—The term *taxable period* means the period beginning with the end of the plan year in which there is an accumulated funding deficiency or unpaid minimum required contribution, whichever is applicable, and ending on the earlier of:

(i) The date of mailing of a notice of deficiency under section 6212 with respect to the tax imposed by section 4971(a); or

(ii) The date on which the tax imposed by section 4971(a) is assessed.

(2) *Special rule.*—Where a notice of deficiency referred to in paragraph (e)(1)(i) of this section is not mailed because a waiver of the restrictions on assessment and collection of a deficiency has been accepted or because the deficiency is paid, the date of filing of the waiver or the date of such payment, respectively, is treated as the end of the taxable period.

(f) *Single-employer plan.*—The term *single-employer plan* means a plan to which the minimum funding requirements of section 412 apply that is not a multiemployer plan as described in section 414(f). The term *single-employer plan* includes a multiple employer plan to which section 413(c) applies, other than a CSEC plan as described in paragraph (b)(2) of this section.

(g) *Examples.*—The following examples illustrate the rules of this section.

*Example 1.* (i) Plan A, a single-employer defined benefit plan, has a calendar year plan year and a January 1 valuation date. The sponsor of Plan A has a calendar taxable year. Plan A has no funding shortfall as of January 1, 2008, and Plan A has no unpaid minimum required contributions for 2008 or any earlier plan year. The minimum required contribution for the 2009 plan year is $250,000. The plan sponsor makes one contribution for 2009 on July 1, 2009 in the amount of $200,000, and the sponsor does not make an election to use the prefunding balance or funding standard carryover balance to offset the minimum required contribution for 2009. The effective interest rate for Plan A for the 2009 plan year is 5.90%.

(ii) The contribution paid July 1, 2009 is discounted for 6 months (to the valuation date) at the effective interest rate ($200,000 ÷ $1.0590^{(6/12)} = $194,349). The unpaid minimum required contribution for the 2009 plan year is $250,000 minus $194,349, or $55,651. The excise tax due under section 4971(a) is 10% of the unpaid minimum required contribution, or $5,565.

*Example 2.* (i) The facts are the same as in *Example 1.* The plan sponsor makes an additional contribution of $175,000 on December 31, 2010.

(ii) Under the ordering rule in paragraph (d)(2)(iii) of this section, the contribution made on December 31, 2010 is applied first to correct the unpaid minimum required contribution for 2009. The portion of the contribution paid December 31, 2010 that is required to eliminate the unpaid minimum required contribution for 2009 (taking into account the 2009 effective interest rate for the 24 months between January 1, 2009 and the payment date of December 31, 2010), is $55,651 multiplied by $1.059^{(24/12)}$ or $62,412. The remaining payment of $112,588 ($175,000 minus $62,412) is applied to the contribution required for the 2010 plan year.

*Example 3.* (i) Plan B, a single-employer defined benefit plan, has a calendar year plan year. The sponsor of Plan B has a calendar taxable year. Plan B has an accumulated funding deficiency of $100,000 as of December 31, 2007, including additional interest due to late required installments during 2007. The valuation interest rate for the 2007 plan year is 7.5%.

(ii) In accordance with paragraph (c)(2) of this section, the accumulated funding deficiency under section 412 as of December 31, 2007 is considered an unpaid minimum required contribution until it is corrected. Pursuant to paragraph (d)(2)(ii) of this section, the amount needed to correct that accumulated funding deficiency is $100,000 plus interest at the valuation interest rate of 7.5% for the period between December 31, 2007 and the date of payment of the contribution.

(iii) The funding shortfall as of January 1, 2008 is calculated as the difference between the funding target and the value of assets as of that date. The assets are not adjusted by the amount of the accumulated funding deficiency. The fact that the contribution was not made for the 2007 plan year means that the January 1, 2008 funding shortfall is larger than it would have been otherwise.

*Example 4.* (i) The facts are the same as in *Example 3.* The minimum required contribution for the 2008 plan year is $125,000, but the plan sponsor does not make any required contributions for 2008.

(ii) The total unpaid minimum required contribution as of December 31, 2008 is the sum of the $100,000 accumulated funding deficiency under section 412 from 2007 and the $125,000 unpaid minimum required contribution for 2008, or $225,000. The section 4971(a) excise tax applies to the aggregate unpaid minimum required contributions for all plan years that remain unpaid as of the end of 2008. In this case, there is an unpaid minimum required contribution of $100,000 for the 2007 plan year and an unpaid minimum required contribution of $125,000 for the 2008 plan year. The section 4971(a) excise tax is 10% of the aggregate of those unpaid amounts, $22,500.

*Example 5.* (i) The facts are the same as in *Example 4*, except that the plan sponsor makes a contribution of $150,000 on December 31, 2008. No additional contributions are paid through September 15, 2009. Required installments of $25,000 each are due April 15, 2008, July 15, 2008, October 15, 2008, and January 15, 2009. Plan B's effective interest rate for the 2008 plan year is 5.75%.

(ii) In accordance with paragraph (c)(2) of this section, the accumulated funding deficiency under section 412 as of December 31, 2007 is treated as an unpaid minimum required contribution until it is corrected.

(iii) The December 31, 2008 contribution is first applied to the 2007 accumulated funding deficiency under section 412 that is treated as an unpaid minimum required contribution. Accordingly, the amount needed to correct the 2007 unpaid minimum required contribution ($100,000 multiplied by 1.075, or $107,500) is applied to eliminate this unpaid minimum required contribution for the 2007 plan year.

(iv) The remaining $42,500 December 31, 2008 contribution ($150,000 minus $107,500) is then applied to the 2008 minimum required contribution. This amount is first allocated to the required installment due April 15, 2008. In accordance with §1.430(j)-1(b)(4)(ii) of this chapter, the adjustment for interest on late required installments is increased by 5 percentage points for the period of underpayment. Therefore, $25,000 of the remaining December 31, 2008 contribution is discounted using an interest rate of 10.75% for the $8^{1}/_2$-month period between the payment date of December 31, 2008 and the required installment due date of April 15, 2008, and at the 5.75% effective interest rate for the $3^{1}/_2$ months between April 15, 2008 and January 1, 2008. This portion of the December 31, 2008 contribution results in an adjusted amount of $22,880 (that is, $25,000 ÷ $1.1075^{(8.5/12)}$ ÷ $1.0575^{(3.5/12)}$) as of January 1, 2008.

(v) The remaining December 31, 2008 contribution is then applied to the required installment due July 15, 2008. The $17,500 balance of the December 31, 2008 contribution ($150,000 minus $107,500 minus $25,000) is paid after the due date for the second required installment. Accordingly, the remaining $17,500 contribution is adjusted using an interest rate of 10.75% for the $5^1/2$-month period between the payment date of December 31, 2008 and the required installment due date of July 15, 2008, and at the 5.75% effective interest rate for the $6^1/2$ months between July 15, 2008 and January 1, 2008. This portion of the December 31, 2008 contribution results in an adjusted amount of $16,202 (that is, $17,500 ÷ $1.1075^{(5.5/12)}$ ÷ $1.0575^{(6.5/12)}$) as of January 1, 2008.

(vi) The remaining unpaid minimum required contribution for 2008 is $125,000 minus the interest-adjusted amounts of $22,880 and $16,202 applied towards the 2008 minimum required contribution as determined in paragraphs (iv) and (v) of this *Example 5*. This results in an unpaid minimum required contribution of $85,918 for 2008. The section 4971(a) excise tax is 10% of the unpaid minimum required contribution, or $8,592.

*Example 6.* (i) Plan C, a single-employer defined benefit plan, has a calendar year plan year and a January 1 valuation date, and has no funding standard carryover balance or prefunding balance as of January 1, 2008. Plan C's sponsor has a calendar taxable year. The minimum required contributions for Plan C are $100,000 for the 2008 plan year, $110,000 for the 2009 plan year, $125,000 for the 2010 plan year, and $135,000 for the 2011 plan year. No contributions for these plan years are made until September 15, 2012, at which time the plan sponsor contributes $273,000 (which is exactly enough to correct the unpaid minimum required contributions for the 2008 and 2009 plan years).

(ii) The excise tax under section 4971(a) for the 2008 taxable year is 10% of the aggregate unpaid minimum required contributions for all plan years remaining unpaid as of the end of any plan year ending within the 2008 taxable year. Accordingly, the excise tax for the 2008 taxable year is $10,000 (that is, 10% of $100,000). The excise tax for the 2009 taxable year is $21,000 (that is, 10% of the sum of $100,000 and $110,000) and the excise tax for the 2010 taxable year is $33,500 (that is, 10% of the sum of $100,000, $110,000, and $125,000).

(iii) The contribution made on September 15, 2012 is applied to correct the unpaid minimum required contributions for the 2008 and 2009 plan years by the deadline for making contributions for the 2011 plan year. Therefore, the excise tax under section 4971(a) for the 2011 taxable year is based only on the remaining unpaid minimum required contributions for the 2010 and 2011 plan years, or $26,000 (that is, 10% of the sum of $125,000 and $135,000).

(iv) The plan sponsor may also be required to pay an excise tax of 100% under section 4971(b), if the unpaid minimum required contributions are not corrected by the end of the taxable period.

(h) *Effective/applicability dates and transition rules.*—(1) *Statutory effective date.*—(i) *In general.*—In general, the amendments made to section 4971 by section 114 of the Pension Protection Act of 2006, Public Law 109-280, 120 Stat. 780 (2006), as amended (PPA '06), apply to taxable years beginning on or after January 1, 2008, but only with respect to a plan year that—

(A) Begins on or after January 1, 2008; and

(B) Ends with or within any such taxable year.

(ii) *Plans with delayed PPA '06 effective dates.*—In the case of a plan for which the effective date of section 430 for purposes of determining the minimum required contribution is delayed in accordance with sections 104 through 106 of PPA '06, the amendments made to section 4971 by section 114 of PPA '06 apply to taxable years beginning on or after January 1, 2008, but only with respect to a plan year—

(A) To which section 430 applies to determine the minimum required contribution of the plan; and

(B) That ends with or within any such taxable year.

(2) *Effective date of regulations.*—This section is effective for taxable years beginning on or after the statutory effective date described in paragraph (h)(1) of this section, but in no event does this section apply to taxable years ending before April 15, 2008.

(3) *Pre-effective plan year.*—For purposes of this section, the pre-effective plan year for a plan is the plan year described in §1.430(a)-1(h)(5) of this chapter. Thus, except for plans with a delayed effective date under paragraph (h)(1)(ii) of this section, the pre-effective plan year for a plan is the last plan year beginning before January 1, 2008. [Reg. §54.4971(c)-1.]

☐ [*T.D.* 9732, 9-8-2015.]

### [Reg. §54.4974-1]

**§54.4974-1. Excise tax on accumulations in individual retirement accounts or annuities.**—(a) *General rule.*—A tax equal to 50 percent of the amount by which the minimum amount required to be distributed from an individual retirement account or annuity described in

section 408 during the taxable year of the payee under paragraph (b) of this section exceeds the amount actually distributed during the taxable year is imposed by section 4974 on the payee.

(b) *Minimum amount required to be distributed.*—For purposes of this section, the minimum amount required to be distributed is the amount required under §1.408-2(b)(6)(v) to be distributed in the taxable year described in paragraph (a) of this section.

(c) *Examples.*—The application of this section may be illustrated by the following examples.

*Example (1).* In 1975, the minimum amount required to be distributed under §1.408-2(b)(6)(v) to A under his individual retirement account is $100. Only $60 is actually distributed to A in 1975. Under section 4974, A would have an excise tax liability of $20 [50% of ($100–60)].

*Example (2).* Although no distribution is required under §1.408-2(b)(6)(v) to be made in 1986, H, a married individual born on February 1, 1921, who has established and maintained an individual retirement account decides to begin receiving distributions from the account beginning in 1986. H's wife, W, was born on March 6, 1921. H and W are calendar year taxpayers. H decides to receive his interest in the account over the joint life and last survivor expectancy of himself and his wife. On January 1, 1986, the balance in H's account is $10,000; H and W, based on their nearest birthdates, are 65; and the joint life and last survivor expectancy of H and his wife is 22.0 years (see Table II of §1.72-9). His annual payments during the following years (none of which were required) were determined by dividing the balance in the account on the first day of each year by the joint life and last survivor expectancy reduced by the number of whole years elapsed since the distributions were to commence.

| Date | Life expectancy minus whole years elapsed | Account balance at beginning of each year | Annual payment |
|---|---|---|---|
| 1-1-86 | 22.0 | $10,000 | $455 |
| 1-1-87 | 21.0 | $10,118 | $482 |
| 1-1-88 | 20.0 | $10,214 | $511 |
| 1-1-89 | 19.0 | $10,285 | $541 |
| 1-1-90 | 18.0 | $10,329 | $574 |
| 1-1-91 | 17.0 | $10,340 | $608 |

For 1986, 1987, 1989, and 1990, the amount required to be distributed under §1.408-2(b)(6)(v) is zero. Thus, H would have no excise tax liability under section 4974 for these years. In 1991, the year H attains age $70^1/2$, the amount required to be distributed from the account under §1.408-2(b)(6)(v) is $565, determined by dividing $10,340 (the account balance as of January 1, 1991) by 18.3 years (the joint life and last survivor expectancy of H and W, assuming they are both still living, as of January 1, 1991). If W should die after December 31, 1990, the joint life and last survivor expectancy determined on January 1, 1991 (18.3 years) would not be redetermined. Because the amount distributed from the account in 1991 ($608) exceeds the amount required to be distributed from the account in 1991 ($565), H has no excise tax liability under section 4974 for 1991.

*Example (3).* Assume the same facts as in example (2) except that W dies in 1988. For 1988, 1989, and 1990, the amount required to be distributed under §1.408-2(b)(6)(v) is zero. Thus, H would have no excise tax liability under section 4974 for these years. In 1991, the amount required to be distributed under §1.408-2(b)(6)(v) is $855, determined by dividing $10,340 (the account balance as of January 1, 1991) by 12.1 years (the life expectancy of H as of January 1, 1991). Because the amount distributed from the account in 1991 ($608) is less than the amount required to be distributed from the account in 1991 ($855), H has an excise tax liability of $123.50 under section 4974 for 1991 [50% of ($855–$608)]. [Reg. §54.4974-1.]

☐ [*T.D.* 7714, 8-7-80.]

### [Reg. §54.4974-2]

**§54.4974-2. Excise tax on accumulations in qualified retirement plans.**—

Q-1. Is any tax imposed on a payee under any qualified retirement plan or any eligible deferred compensation plan (as defined in section 457(b)) to whom an amount is required to be distributed for a taxable year if the amount distributed during the taxable year is less than the required minimum distribution?

A-1. Yes, if the amount distributed to a payee under any qualified retirement plan or any eligible deferred compensation plan (as defined in section 457(b)) for a calendar year is less than the required minimum distribution for such year, an excise tax is imposed on such payee under section 4974 for the taxable year beginning with or within the calendar year during which the amount is required to be distributed. The tax is equal to 50 percent of the amount by which such required minimum distribution exceeds the actual amount distributed during the calendar year. Section 4974 provides that this tax shall be paid by the payee. For purposes of section 4974, the term *required minimum distribution* means the minimum distribution amount required to be distributed pursuant to section 401(a)(9),

403(b)(10), 408(a)(6), 408(b)(3), or 457(d)(2), as the case may be, and the regulations thereunder. Except as otherwise provided in A-6 of this section, the required minimum distribution for a calendar year is the required minimum distribution amount required to be distributed during the calendar year. A-6 of this section provides a special rule for amounts required to be distributed by an employee's (or individual's) required beginning date.

Q-2. For purposes of section 4974, what is a qualified retirement plan?

A-2. For purposes of section 4974, each of the following is a qualified retirement plan—

(a) A plan described in section 401(a) which includes a trust exempt from tax under section 501(a);

(b) An annuity plan described in section 403(a);

(c) An annuity contract, custodial account, or retirement income account described in section 403(b);

(d) An individual retirement account described in section 408(a) (including a Roth IRA described in section 408A);

(e) An individual retirement annuity described in section 408(b) (including a Roth IRA described in section 408A); or

(f) Any other plan, contract, account, or annuity that, at any time, has been treated as a plan, account, or annuity described in paragraphs (a) through (e) of this A-2, whether or not such plan, contract, account, or annuity currently satisfies the applicable requirements for such treatment.

Q-3. If a payee's interest under a qualified retirement plan is in the form of an individual account, how is the required minimum distribution for a given calendar year determined for purposes of section 4974?

A-3. (a) *General rule.* If a payee's interest under a qualified retirement plan is in the form of an individual account and distribution of such account is not being made under an annuity contract purchased in accordance with A-4 of § 1.401(a)(9)-6, the amount of the required minimum distribution for any calendar year for purposes of section 4974 is the required minimum distribution amount required to be distributed for such calendar year in order to satisfy the minimum distribution requirements in § 1.401(a)(9)-5 as provided in the following (whichever is applicable)—

(1) Section 401(a)(9) and §§ 1.401(a)(9)-1 through 1.401(a)(9)-5 and 1.401(a)(9)-7 through 1.401(a)(9)-9 in the case of a plan described in section 401(a) which includes a trust exempt under section 501(a) or an annuity plan described in section 403(a);

(2) Section 403(b)(10) and § 1.403(b)-6(e) (in the case of an annuity contract, custodial account, or retirement income account described in section 403(b));

(3) Section 408(a)(6) or (b)(3) and § 1.408-8 (in the case of an individual retirement account or annuity described in section 408(a) or (b)); or

(4) Section 457(d) in the case of an eligible deferred compensation plan (as defined in section 457(b)).

(b) *Default provisions.* Unless otherwise provided under the qualified retirement plan (or, if applicable, the governing instrument of the qualified retirement plan), the default provisions in A-4(a) of § 1.401(a)(9)-3 apply in determining the required minimum distribution for purposes of section 4974.

(c) *Five-year rule.* If the 5-year rule in section 401(a)(9)(B)(ii) applies to the distribution to a payee, no amount is required to be distributed for any calendar year to satisfy the applicable enumerated section in paragraph (a) of this A-3 until the calendar year which contains the date 5 years after the date of the employee's death. For the calendar year which contains the date 5 years after the employee's death, the required minimum distribution amount required to be distributed to satisfy the applicable enumerated section is the payee's entire remaining interest in the qualified retirement plan.

Q-4. If a payee's interest in a qualified retirement plan is being distributed in the form of an annuity, how is the amount of the required minimum distribution determined for purposes of section 4974?

A-4. If a payee's interest in a qualified retirement plan is being distributed in the form of an annuity (either directly from the plan, in the case of a defined benefit plan, or under an annuity contract purchased from an insurance company), the amount of the required minimum distribution for purposes of section 4974 will be determined as follows:

(a) *Permissible annuity distribution option.* A permissible annuity distribution option is an annuity contract (or, in the case of annuity distributions from a defined benefit plan, a distribution option) which specifically provides for distributions which, if made as provided, would for every calendar year equal or exceed the minimum distribution amount required to be distributed to satisfy the applicable section enumerated in paragraph (a) of A-2 of this section for every calendar year. If the annuity contract (or, in the case of annuity distributions from a defined benefit plan, a distribution option) under which distributions to the payee are being made is a permissi-

ble annuity distribution option, the required minimum distribution for a given calendar year will equal the amount which the annuity contract (or distribution option) provides is to be distributed for that calendar year.

(b) *Impermissible annuity distribution option.* An impermissible annuity distribution option is an annuity contract (or, in the case of annuity distributions from a defined benefit plan, a distribution option) under which distributions to the payee are being made that specifically provides for distributions which, if made as provided, would for any calendar year be less than the minimum distribution amount required to be distributed to satisfy the applicable section enumerated in paragraph (a) of A-3 of this section. If the annuity contract (or, in the case of annuity distributions from a defined benefit plan, the distribution option) under which distributions to the payee are being made is an impermissible annuity distribution option, the required minimum distribution for each calendar year will be determined as follows:

(1) If the qualified retirement plan under which distributions are being made is a defined benefit plan, the minimum distribution amount required to be distributed each year will be the amount which would have been distributed under the plan if the distribution option under which distributions to the payee were being made was the following permissible annuity distribution option:

(i) In the case of distributions commencing before the death of the employee, if there is a designated beneficiary under the impermissible annuity distribution option for purposes of section 401(a)(9), the permissible annuity distribution option is the joint and survivor annuity option under the plan for the lives of the employee and the designated beneficiary that provides for the greatest level amount payable to the employee determined on an annual basis. If the plan does not provide such an option or there is no designated beneficiary under the impermissible distribution option for purposes of section 401(a)(9), the permissible annuity distribution option is the life annuity option under the plan payable for the life of the employee in level amounts with no survivor benefit.

(ii) In the case of distributions commencing after the death of the employee, if there is a designated beneficiary under the impermissible annuity distribution option for purposes of section 401(a)(9), the permissible annuity distribution option is the life annuity option under the plan payable for the life of the designated beneficiary in level amounts. If there is no designated beneficiary, the 5-year rule in section 401(a)(9)(B)(ii) applies. See paragraph (b)(3) of this A-4. The determination of whether or not there is a designated beneficiary and the determination of which designated beneficiary's life is to be used in the case of multiple beneficiaries will be made in accordance with § 1.401(a)(9)-4 and A-7 of § 1.401(a)(9)-5. If the defined benefit plan does not provide for distribution in the form of the applicable permissible distribution option, the required minimum distribution for each calendar year will be an amount as determined by the Commissioner.

(2) If the qualified retirement plan under which distributions are being made is a defined contribution plan and the impermissible annuity distribution option is an annuity contract purchased from an insurance company, the minimum distribution amount required to be distributed each year will be the amount that would have been distributed in the form of an annuity contract under the permissible annuity distribution option under the plan determined in accordance with paragraph (b)(1) of this A-4 for defined benefit plans. If the defined contribution plan does not provide the applicable permissible annuity distribution option, the required minimum distribution for each calendar year will be the amount that would have been distributed under an annuity described in paragraph (b)(2)(i) or (ii) of this A-4 purchased with the employee's or individual's account used to purchase the annuity contract that is the impermissible annuity distribution option.

(i) In the case of distributions commencing before the death of the employee, if there is a designated beneficiary under the impermissible annuity distribution option for purposes of section 401(a)(9), the annuity is a joint and survivor annuity for the lives of the employee and the designated beneficiary which provides level annual payments and which would have been a permissible annuity distribution option. However, the amount of the periodic payment which would have been payable to the survivor will be the applicable percentage under the table in A-2(c) of § 1.401(a)(9)-6 of the amount of the periodic payment which would have been payable to the employee or individual. If there is no designated beneficiary under the impermissible distribution option for purposes of section 401(a)(9), the annuity is a life annuity for the life of the employee with no survivor benefit which provides level annual payments and which would have been a permissible annuity distribution option.

(ii) In the case of a distribution commencing after the death of the employee, if there is a designated beneficiary under the impermissible annuity distribution option for purposes of section 401(a)(9), the annuity option is a life annuity for the life of the designated beneficiary which provides level annual payments and which would have been a permissible annuity distribution option. If there is no designated beneficiary, the 5-year rule in section 401(a)(9)(B)(ii) applies. See paragraph (b)(3) of this A-4. The amount of the payments under the annuity contract will be determined using the interest rate and actuarial tables prescribed under section 7520 determined using the date determined under A-3 of §1.401(a)(9)-3 when distributions are required to commence and using the age of the beneficiary as of the beneficiary's birthday in the calendar year that contains that date. The determination of whether or not there is a designated beneficiary and the determination of which designated beneficiary's life is to be used in the case of multiple beneficiaries will be made in accordance with §1.401(a)(9)-4 and A-7 of §1.401(a)(9)-5.

(3) If the 5-year rule in section 401(a)(9)(B)(ii) applies to the distribution to the payee under the contract (or distribution option), no amount is required to be distributed to satisfy the applicable enumerated section in paragraph (a) of this A-4 until the calendar year which contains the date 5 years after the date of the employee's death. For the calendar year which contains the date 5 years after the employee's death, the required minimum distribution amount required to be distributed to satisfy the applicable enumerated section is the payee's entire remaining interest in the annuity contract (or under the plan in the case of distributions from a defined benefit plan).

(4) If the plan provides that the required beginning date for purposes of section 401(a)(9) for all employees is April 1 of the calendar year following the calendar year in which the employee attained age 70½ in accordance with paragraph A-2(e) of §1.401(a)(9)-2, the required minimum distribution for each calendar year for an employee who is not a 5-percent owner for purposes of this section will be the lesser of the amount determined based on the required beginning date as set forth in A-2(a) of §1.401(a)(9)-2 or the required beginning date under the plan. Thus, for example, if an employee dies after attaining age 70½, but before April 1 of the calendar year following the calendar year in which the employee retired, and there is no designated beneficiary as of September 30 of the year following the employee's year of death, required minimum distributions for calendar years after the calendar year containing the employee's date of death may be based on either the applicable distribution period provided under either the 5-year rule of A-1 of §1.401(a)(9)-3 or the employee's remaining life expectancy as set forth in A-5(c)(3) of §1.401(a)(9)-5.

Q-5. If there is any remaining benefit with respect to an employee (or IRA owner) after any calendar year in which the entire remaining benefit is required to be distributed under section 401(a)(9), what is the amount of the required minimum distribution for each calendar year subsequent to such calendar year?

A-5. If there is any remaining benefit with respect to an employee (or IRA owner) after the calendar year in which the entire remaining benefit is required to be distributed, the required minimum distribution for each calendar year subsequent to such calendar year is the entire remaining benefit.

Q-6. With respect to which calendar year is the excise tax under section 4974 imposed in the case in which the amount not distributed is an amount required to be distributed by April 1 of a calendar year (by the employee's or individual's required beginning date)?

A-6. In the case in which the amount not paid is an amount required to be paid by April 1 of a calendar year, such amount is a required minimum distribution for the previous calendar year, i.e., for the employee's or the individual's first distribution calendar year. However, the excise tax under section 4974 is imposed for the calendar year containing the last day by which the amount is required to be distributed, i.e., the calendar year containing the employee's or individual's required beginning date, even though the preceding calendar year is the calendar year for which the amount is required to be distributed. There is also a required minimum distribution for the calendar year which contains the employee's or individual's required beginning date. Such distribution is also required to be made during the calendar year which contains the employee's or individual's required beginning date.

Q-7. Are there any circumstances when the excise tax under section 4974 for a taxable year may be waived?

A-7. (a) *Reasonable cause.* The tax under section 4974(a) may be waived if the payee described in section 4974(a) establishes to the satisfaction of the Commissioner the following—

(1) The shortfall described in section 4974(a) in the amount distributed in any taxable year was due to reasonable error; and

(2) Reasonable steps are being taken to remedy the shortfall.

(b) *Automatic waiver.* The tax under section 4974 will be automatically waived, unless the Commissioner determines otherwise, if—

(1) The payee described in section 4974(a) is an individual who is the sole beneficiary and whose required minimum distribution amount for a calendar year is determined under the life expectancy rule described in §1.401(a)(9)-3 A-3 in the case of an employee's or

individual's death before the employee's or individual's required beginning date; and

(2) The employee's or individual's entire benefit to which that beneficiary is entitled is distributed by the end of the fifth calendar year following the calendar year that contains the employee's or individual's date of death. [Reg. §54.4974-2.]

☐ [*T.D. 8987, 4-16-2002 (corrected 5-20-2002). Amended by T.D. 9130, 6-14-2004 and T.D. 9340, 7-23-2007.*]

### [Reg. §54.4975-1]

**§54.4975-1. General rules relating to excise tax on prohibited transactions.**—(a) *Scope.*—This section provides general rules for the imposition of the excise taxes on prohibited transactions.

(b) *Initial tax.*—Section 4975(a) imposes an initial tax on each prohibited transaction. The initial tax is 5 percent of the amount involved with respect to the prohibited transaction for each year (or part thereof) in the taxable period.

(c) *Additional tax.*—Section 4975(b) imposes an excise tax in any case in which an initial tax is imposed under section 4975(a) on a prohibited transaction and the prohibited transaction is not corrected within the taxable period (as defined in paragraph (d) of this section). The additional tax is 100 percent of the amount involved with respect to the prohibited transaction.

(d) *Taxable period.*—(1) *In general.*—For purposes of any prohibited transaction, the term "taxable period" means the period beginning with the date on which the prohibited transaction occurs and ending on the earliest of:

(i) The date of mailing of a notice of deficiency under section 6212 with respect to the tax imposed by section 4975(a);

(ii) The date on which correction of the prohibited transaction is completed; or

(iii) The date on which the tax imposed by section 4975(a) is assessed.

(2) *Special rule.*—Where a notice of deficiency referred to in paragraph (d)(1)(i) of this section is not mailed because a waiver of the restrictions on assessment and collection of a deficiency has been accepted or because the deficiency is paid, the date of filing of the waiver or the date of such payment, respectively, shall be treated as the end of the taxable period. [Reg. §54.4975-1.]

☐ [*T.D. 8084, 5-1-86.*]

### [Reg. §54.4975-6]

**§54.4975-6. Statutory exemptions for office space or services and certain transactions involving financial institutions.**—(a) *Exemption for office space or services.*—(1) *In general.*—Section 4975(d)(2) exempts from the excise taxes imposed by section 4975 payment by a plan to a disqualified person, including a fiduciary, for office space or any service (or a combination of services), if (i) such office space or service is necessary for the establishment or operation of the plan; (ii) such office space or service is furnished under a contract or arrangement which is reasonable; and (iii) no more than reasonable compensation is paid for such office space or service. However, section 4975(d)(2) does not contain an exemption for acts described in section 4975(c)(1)(E) (relating to fiduciaries dealing with the income or assets of plans in their own interest or for their own account) or acts described in section 4975(c)(1)(F) (relating to fiduciaries receiving consideration for their own personal account from any party dealing with a plan in connection with a transaction involving the income or assets of the plan). Such acts are separate transactions not described in section 4975(d)(2). See §§54.4975-6(a)(5) and 54.4975-6(a)(6) for guidance as to whether transactions relating to the furnishing of office space or services by fiduciaries to plans involve acts described in section 4975(c)(1)(E).

Section 4975(d)(2) does not contain an exemption from other provisions of the Code, such as section 401, or other provisions of law which may impose requirements or restrictions relating to the transactions which are exempt under section 4975(d)(2). See, for example, the general fiduciary responsibility provisions of section 404 of the Employee Retirement Income Security Act of 1974 (the Act) (88 Stat. 877). The provisions of section 4975(d)(2) are further limited by the flush language at the end of section 4975(d) (relating to transactions with owner-employees and related persons).

(2) *Necessary service.*—A service is necessary for the establishment or operation of a plan within the meaning of section 4975(d)(2) and §54.4975-6(a)(1)(i) if the service is appropriate and helpful to the plan obtaining the service in carrying out the purposes for which the plan is established or maintained. A person providing such a service to a plan (or a person who is a disqualified person solely by reason of a relationship to such a service provider described in section 4975(e)(2)(F), (G), (H), or (I)) may furnish goods which are necessary

for the establishment or operation of the plan in the course of, and incidental to, the furnishing of such service to the plan.

(3) *Reasonable contract or arrangement.*—No contract or arrangement is reasonable within the meaning of section 4975(d)(2) and §54.4975-6(a)(1)(ii) if it does not permit termination by the plan without penalty to the plan on reasonably short notice under the circumstances to prevent the plan from becoming locked into an arrangement that has become disadvantageous. A long-term lease which may be terminated prior to its expiration (without penalty to the plan) on reasonably short notice under the circumstances is not generally an unreasonable arrangement merely because of its long term. A provision in a contract or other arrangement which reasonably compensates the service provider or lessor for loss upon early termination of the contract, arrangement or lease is not a penalty. For example, a minimal fee in a service contract which is charged to allow recoupment of reasonable start-up costs is not a penalty.

Similarly, a provision in a lease for a termination fee that covers reasonably foreseeable expenses related to the vacancy and reletting of the office space upon early termination of the lease is not a penalty. Such a provision does not reasonably compensate for loss if it provides for payments in excess of actual loss or if it fails to require mitigation of damages.

(4) *Reasonable compensation.*—Section 4975(d)(2) and §54.4975-6(a)(1)(iii) permit a plan to pay a disqualified person reasonable compensation for the provision of office space or services described in section 4975(d)(2). Paragraph (e) of this section contains regulations relating to what constitutes reasonable compensation for the provision of services.

(5) *Transactions with fiduciaries.*—(i) *In general.*—If the furnishing of office space or a service involves an act described in section 4975(c)(1)(E) or (F) (relating to acts involving conflicts of interest by fiduciaries), such an act constitutes a separate transaction which is not exempt under section 4975(d)(2). The prohibitions of sections 4975(c)(1)(E) and (F) supplement the other prohibitions of section 4975(c)(1) by imposing on disqualified persons who are fiduciaries a duty of undivided loyalty to the plans for which they act. These prohibitions are imposed upon fiduciaries to deter them from exercising the authority, control, or responsibility which makes such persons fiduciaries when they have interests which may conflict with the interests of the plans for which they act. In such cases, the fiduciaries have interests in the transactions which may affect the exercise of their best judgment as fiduciaries. Thus, a fiduciary may not use the authority, control, or responsibility which makes such person a fiduciary to cause a plan to pay an additional fee to such fiduciary (or to a person in which such fiduciary has an interest which may affect the exercise of such fiduciary's best judgment as a fiduciary) to provide a service. Nor may a fiduciary use such authority, control, or responsibility to cause a plan to enter into a transaction involving plan assets whereby such fiduciary (or a person in which such fiduciary has an interest which may affect the exercise of such fiduciary's best judgment as a fiduciary) will receive consideration from a third party in connection with such transaction.

A person in which a fiduciary has an interest which may affect the exercise of such fiduciary's best judgment as a fiduciary includes, for example, a person who is a disqualified person by reason of a relationship to such fiduciary described in section 4975(e)(2)(E), (F), (G), (H), or (I).

(ii) *Transactions not described in section 4975(c)(1)(E).*—A fiduciary does not engage in an act described in section 4975(c)(1)(E) if the fiduciary does not use any of the authority, control or responsibility which makes such person a fiduciary to cause a plan to pay additional fees for a service furnished by such fiduciary or to pay a fee for a service furnished by a person in which such fiduciary has an interest which may affect the exercise of such fiduciary's best judgment as a fiduciary. This may occur, for example, when one fiduciary is retained on behalf of a plan by a second fiduciary to provide a service for an additional fee. However, because the authority, control or responsibility which makes a person a fiduciary may be exercised "in effect" as well as in form, mere approval of the transaction by a second fiduciary does not mean that the first fiduciary has not used any of the authority, control or responsibility which makes such person a fiduciary to cause the plan to pay the first fiduciary an additional fee for a service.

(iii) *Services without compensation.*—If a fiduciary provides services to a plan without the receipt of compensation or other consideration (other than reimbursement of direct expenses properly and actually incurred in the performance of such services within the meaning of paragraph (e)(4) of this section), the provision of such services does not, in and of itself, constitute an act described in section 4975(c)(1)(E) or (F). The allowance of a deduction to an employer under section 162 or 212 for the expense incurred in

furnishing office space or services to a plan established or maintained by such employer does not constitute compensation or other consideration.

(6) *Examples.*—The provisions of §54.4975-6(a)(5) may be illustrated by the following examples:

*Example (1).* E, an employer whose employees are covered by plan P, is a fiduciary of P. I is a professional investment adviser in which E has no interest which may affect the exercise of E's best judgment as a fiduciary. E causes P to retain I to provide certain kinds of investment advisory services of a type which causes I to be a fiduciary of P under section 4975(e)(3)(B). Thereafter, I proposes to perform for additional fees portfolio evaluation services in addition to the services currently provided. The provision of such services is arranged by I and approved on behalf of the plan by E. I has not engaged in an act described in section 4975(c)(1)(E), because I did not use any of the authority, control or responsibility which makes I a fiduciary (the provision of investment advisory services) to cause the plan to pay I additional fees for the provision of the portfolio evaluation services. E has not engaged in an act which is described in section 4975(c)(1)(E). E, as the fiduciary who has the responsibility to be prudent in his selection and retention of I and the other investment advisers of the plan, has an interest in the purchase by the plan of portfolio evaluation services. However, such an interest is not an interest which may affect the exercise of E's best judgment as a fiduciary.

*Example (2).* D, a trustee of plan P with discretion over the management and disposition of plan assets, relies on the advice of C, a consultant to P, as to the investment of plan assets, thereby making C a fiduciary of the plan. On January 1, 1978, C recommends to D that the plan purchase an insurance policy from U, an insurance company which is not a disqualified person with respect to P. C thoroughly explains the reasons for the recommendation and makes a full disclosure concerning the fact that C will receive a commission from U upon the purchase of the policy by P. D considers the recommendation and approves the purchase of the policy by P. C receives a commission. Under such circumstances, C has engaged in an act described in section 4975(c)(1)(E) (as well as section 4975(c)(1)(F)) because C is in fact exercising the authority, control or responsibility which makes C a fiduciary to cause the plan to purchase the policy. However, the transaction is exempt from the prohibited transaction provisions of section 4975(c)(1) if the requirements of Prohibited Transaction Exemption 77-9 are met.

*Example (3).* Assume the same facts as in Example (2) except that the nature of C's relationship with the plan is not such that C is a fiduciary of P. The purchase of the insurance policy does not involve an act described in section 4975(c)(1)(E) or (F), because such sections only apply to acts by fiduciaries.

*Example (4).* E, an employer whose employees are covered by plan P, is a fiduciary with respect to P. A, who is not a disqualified person with respect to P, persuades E that the plan needs the services of a professional investment adviser and that A should be hired to provide the investment advice. Accordingly, E causes P to hire A to provide investment advice of the type which makes A a fiduciary under §54.4975-9(c)(1)(ii)(B). Prior to the expiration of A's first contract with P, A persuades E to cause P to renew A's contract with P to provide the same services for additional fees in view of the increased costs in providing such services. During the period of A's second contract, A provides additional investment advice services for which no additional charge is made. Prior to the expiration of A's second contract, A persuades E to cause P to renew his contract for additional fees in view of the additional services A is providing. A has not engaged in an act described in section 4975(c)(1)(E), because A has not used any of the authority, control or responsibility which makes A a fiduciary (the provision of investment advice) to cause the plan to pay additional fees for A's services.

*Example (5).* F, a trustee of plan P with discretion over the management and disposition of plan assets, retains C to provide administrative services to P of the type which makes C a fiduciary under section 4975(e)(3)(C). Thereafter, C retains F to provide, for additional fees, actuarial and various kinds of administrative services in addition to the services F is currently providing to P. Both F and C have engaged in an act described in section 4975(c)(1)(E). F, regardless of any intent which he may have had at the time he retained C, has engaged in such an act because F has, in effect, exercised the authority, control or responsibility which makes F a fiduciary to cause the plan to pay F additional fees for the services. C, whose continued employment by P depends on F, has also engaged in such an act, because C has an interest in the transaction which might affect the exercise of C's best judgment as a fiduciary. As a result, C has dealt with plan assets in his own interest under section 4975(c)(1)(E).

*Example (6).* F, a fiduciary of plan P with discretionary authority respecting the management of P, retains S, the son of F, to provide for a fee various kinds of administrative services necessary for the operation of the plan. F has engaged in an act described in section

4975(c)(1)(E), because S is a person in whom F has an interest which may affect the exercise of F's best judgment as a fiduciary. Such act is not exempt under section 4975(d)(2) irrespective of whether the provision of the services by S is exempt.

*Example (7).* T, one of the trustees of plan P, is president of bank B. The bank proposes to provide administrative services to P for a fee. T physically absents himself from all consideration of B's proposal and does not otherwise exercise any of the authority, control or responsibility which makes T a fiduciary to cause the plan to retain B. The other trustees decide to retain B. T has not engaged in an act described in section 4975(c)(1)(E). Further, the other trustees have not engaged in an act described in section 4975(c)(1)(E) merely because T is on the board of trustees of P. This fact alone would not make them have an interest in the transaction which might affect the exercise of their best judgment as fiduciaries.

(b) *Exemption for bank deposits.*—(1) *In general.*—Section 4975(d)(4) exempts from the excise taxes imposed by section 4975 investment of all or a part of a plan's assets in deposits bearing a reasonable rate of interest in a bank or similar financial institution supervised by the United States or a State, even though such bank or similar financial institution is a fiduciary or other disqualified person with respect to the plan, if the conditions of either § 54.4975-6(b)(2) or § 54.4975-6(b)(3) are met. Section 4975(d)(4) provides an exemption from section 4975(c)(1)(E) (relating to fiduciaries dealing with the income or assets of plans in their own interest or for their own account), as well as sections 4975(c)(1)(A) throught (D), because section 4975(d)(4) contemplates a bank or similar financial institution causing a plan for which it acts as a fiduciary to invest plan assets in its own deposits if the requirements of section 4975(d)(4) are met. However, it does not provide an exemption from section 4975(c)(1)(F) (relating to fiduciaries receiving consideration for their own personal account from any party dealing with a plan in connection with a transaction involving the income or assets of the plan). The receipt of such consideration is a separate transaction not described in the exemption. Section 4975(d)(4) does not contain an exemption from other provisions of the Code, such as section 401, or other provisions of law which may impose requirements or restrictions relating to the transactions which are exempt under section 4975(d)(4). See, for example, the general fiduciary responsibility provisions of section 404 of the Act. The provisions of section 4975(d)(4) are further limited by the flush language at the end of section 4975(d) (relating to transactions with owner-employees and related persons).

(2) *Plan covering own employees.*—Such investment may be made if the plan is one which covers only the employees of the bank or similar financial institution, the employees of any of its affiliates, or the employees of both.

(3) *Other plans.*—(i) *General rule.*—Such investment may be made if the investment is expressly authorized by a provision of the plan or trust instrument or if the investment is expressly authorized (or made) by a fiduciary of the plan (other than the bank or similar financial institution or any of its affiliates) who has authority to make such investments, or to instruct the trustee or other fiduciary with respect to investments, and who has no interest in the transaction which may affect the exercise of such authorizing fiduciary's best judgment as a fiduciary so as to cause such authorization to constitute an act described in section 4975(c)(1)(E) or (F). Any authorization to make investments contained in a plan or trust instrument will satisfy the requirement of express authorization for investments made prior to November 1, 1977.

Effective November 1, 1977, in the case of a bank or similar financial institution that invests plan assets in deposits in itself or its affiliates under an authorization contained in a plan or trust instrument, such authorization must name such bank or similar financial institution and must state that such bank or similar financial institution may make investments in deposits which bear a reasonable rate of interest in itself (or in an affiliate).

(ii) *Example.*—B, a bank, is the trustee of plan P's assets. The trust instruments give the trustee the right to invest plan assets in its discretion. B invests in the certificates of deposit of bank C, which is a fiduciary of the plan by virtue of performing certain custodial and administrative services. The authorization is sufficient for the plan to make such investment under section 4975(d)(4). Further, such authorization would suffice to allow B to make investments in deposits in itself prior to November 1, 1977. However, subsequent to October 31, 1977, B may not invest in deposits in itself, unless the plan or trust instrument specifically authorizes it to invest in deposits of B.

(4) *Definitions.*—(i) The term "bank or similar financial institution" includes a bank (as defined in section 581), a domestic building and loan association (as defined in section 7701(a)(19)), and a credit union (as defined in section 101(6) of the Federal Credit Union Act).

(ii) A person is an affiliate of a bank or similar financial institution if such person and such bank or similar financial institution would be treated as members of the same controlled group of corporations or as members of two or more trades or businesses under common control within the meaning of section 414(b) or (c) and the regulations thereunder.

(iii) The term "deposits" includes any account, temporary or otherwise, upon which a reasonable rate of interest is paid, including a certificate of deposit issued by a bank or similar financial institution.

(c) *Exemption for ancillary bank services.*—(1) *In general.*—Section 4975(d)(6) exempts from the excise taxes imposed by section 4975 the provision of certain ancillary services by a bank or similar financial institution (as defined in § 54.4975-6(b)(4)(i)) supervised by the United States or a State to a plan for which it acts as a fiduciary if the conditions in § 54.4975-6(c)(2) are met. Such ancillary services include services which do not meet the requirements of section 4975(d)(2), because the provision of such services involves an act described in section 4975(c)(1)(E) (relating to fiduciaries dealing with the income or assets of plans in their own interest or for their own account) by the fiduciary bank or similar financial institution. Section 4975(d)(6) provides an exemption from section 4975(c)(1)(E), because section 4975(d)(6) contemplates the provision of such ancillary services without the approval of a second fiduciary (as described in § 54.4975-6(a)(5)(ii)) if the conditions of § 54.4975-6(c)(2) are met. Thus, for example, plan assets held by a fiduciary bank which are reasonably expected to be needed to satisfy current plan expenses may be placed by the bank in a non-interest-bearing checking account in the bank if the conditions of § 54.4975-6(c)(2) are met, notwithstanding the provisions of section 4975(d)(4) (relating to investments in bank deposits). However, section 4975(d)(6) does not provide an exemption for an act described in section 4975(c)(1)(F) (relating to fiduciaries receiving consideration for their own personal account from any party dealing with a plan in connection with a transaction involving the income or assets of the plan). The receipt of such consideration is a separate transaction not described in section 4975(d)(6). Section 4975(d)(6) does not contain an exemption from other provisions of the Code, such as section 401, or other provisions of law which may impose requirements or restrictions relating to the transactions which are exempt under section 4975(d)(6). See, for example, the general fiduciary responsibility provisions of section 404 of the Act. The provisions of section 4975(d)(6) are further limited by the flush language at the end of section 4975(d) (relating to transactions with owner-employees and related persons).

(2) *Conditions.*—Such service must be provided:

(i) At not more than reasonable compensation;

(ii) Under adequate internal safeguards which assure that the provision of such service is consistent with sound banking and financial practice, as determined by Federal or State supervisory authority; and

(iii) Only to the extent that such service is subject to specific guidelines issued by the bank or similar financial institution which meet the requirements of § 54.4975-6(c)(3).

(3) *Specific guidelines.*—[Reserved]

(d) *Exemption for services as a fiduciary.*—[Reserved]

(e) *Compensation for services.*—(1) *In general.*—Section 4975(d)(2) refers to the payment of reasonable compensation by a plan to a disqualified person for services rendered to the plan. Section 4975(d)(10) and §§ 54.4975-6(e)(2) through 54.4975-6(e)(5) clarify what constitutes reasonable compensation for such services.

(2) *General rule.*—Generally, whether compensation is "reasonable" under sections 4975(d)(2) and (10) depends on the particular facts and circumstances of each case.

(3) *Payments to certain fiduciaries.*—Under sections 4975(d)(2) and (10), the term "reasonable compensation" does not include any compensation to a fiduciary who is already receiving full-time pay from an employer or association of employers (any of whose employees are participants in the plan) or from an employee organization (any of whose members are participants in the plan), except for the reimbursement of direct expenses properly and actually incurred and not otherwise reimbursed. The restrictions of this paragraph (e)(3) do not apply to a disqualified person who is not a fiduciary.

(4) *Certain expenses not direct expenses.*—An expense is not a direct expense to the extent it would have been sustained had the service not been provided or if it represents an allocable portion of overhead costs.

(5) *Expense advances.*—Under sections 4975(d)(2) and (10), the term "reasonable compensation", as applied to a fiduciary or an employee of a plan, includes an advance to such a fiduciary or

employee by the plan to cover direct expenses to be properly and actually incurred by such person in the performance of such person's duties with the plan if:

(i) The amount of such advance is reasonable with respect to the amount of the direct expense which is likely to be properly and actually incurred in the immediate future (such as during the next month); and

(ii) The fiduciary or employee accounts to the plan at the end of the period covered by the advance for the expenses properly and actually incurred.

(6) *Excessive compensation.*—Under sections 4975(d)(2) and (10), any compensation which would be considered excessive under § 1.162-7 (relating to compensation for personal services which constitutes an ordinary and necessary trade or business expense) will not be "reasonable compensation". Depending upon the facts and circumstances of the particular situation, compensation which is not excessive under § 1.162-7 may, nevertheless, not be "reasonable compensation" within the meaning of sections 4975(d)(2) and (10). [Reg. § 54.4975-6.]

☐ [*T.D. 7491, 6-13-77.*]

### [Reg. § 54.4975-7]

**§ 54.4975-7. Other statutory exemptions.**—(a) [Reserved]

(b) *Loans to employee stock ownership plans*—

(1) *Definitions.*—When used in this paragraph (b) and § 54.4975-11, the terms listed below have the following meanings:

(i) *ESOP.*—The term "ESOP" refers to an employee stock ownership plan that meets the requirements of section 4975(e)(7) and § 54.4975-11. It is not synonymous with "stock bonus plan." A stock bonus plan must, however, be an ESOP to engage in an exempt loan. The qualification of an ESOP under section 401(a) and § 54.4975-11 will not be adversely affected merely because it engages in a non-exempt loan.

(ii) *Loan.*—The term "loan" refers to a loan made to an ESOP by a disqualified person or a loan to an ESOP which is guaranteed by a disqualified person. It includes a direct loan of cash, a purchase-money transaction, and an assumption of the obligation of an ESOP. "Guarantee" includes an unsecured guarantee and the use of assets of a disqualified person as collateral for a loan, even though the use of assets may not be a guarantee under applicable state law. An amendment of a loan in order to qualify as an exempt loan is not a refinancing of the loan or the making of another loan.

(iii) *Exempt loan.*—The term "exempt loan" refers to a loan that satisfies the provisions of this paragraph (b). A "non-exempt loan" is one that fails to satisfy such provisions.

(iv) *Publicly traded.*—The term "publicly traded" refers to a security that is listed on a national securities exchange registered under section 6 of the Securities Exchange Act of 1934 (15 U.S.C. 78f) or that is quoted on a system sponsored by a national securities association registered under section 15A(b) of the Securities Exchange Act (15 U.S.C. 78o).

(v) *Qualifying employer security.*—The term "qualifying employer security" refers to a security described in § 54.4975-12.

(2) *Statutory exemption.*—(i) *Scope.*—Section 4975(d)(3) provides an exemption from the excise tax imposed under section 4975(a) and (b) by reason of section 4975(c)(1)(A) through (E). Section 4975(d)(3) does not provide an exemption from the imposition of such tax by reason of section 4975(c)(1)(F), relating to fiduciaries receiving consideration for their own personal account from any party dealing with a plan in connection with a transaction involving the income or assets of the plan.

(ii) *Special scrutiny of transaction.*—The exemption under section 4975(d)(3) includes within its scope certain transactions in which the potential for self-dealing by fiduciaries exists and in which the interests of fiduciaries may conflict with the interests of participants. To guard against these potential abuses, the Internal Revenue Service will subject these transactions to special scrutiny to ensure that they are primarily for the benefit of participants and their beneficiaries. Although the transactions need not be arranged and approved by an independent fiduciary, fiduciaries are cautioned to exercise scrupulously their discretion in approving them. For example, fiduciaries should be prepared to demonstrate compliance with the net effect test and the arm's-length standard under paragraph (b)(3)(ii) and (iii) of this section. Also, fiduciaries should determine that the transaction is truly arranged primarily in the interest of participants and their beneficiaries rather than, for example, in the interest of certain selling shareholders.

(3) *Primary benefit requirement.*—(i) *In general.*—An exempt loan must be primarily for the benefit of the ESOP participants and their beneficiaries. All the surrounding facts and circumstances, including those described in paragraph (b)(3)(ii) and (iii) of this section, will be considered in determining whether the loan satisfies this requirement. However, no loan will satisfy the requirement unless it satisfies the requirements of paragraph (b)(4), (5), and (6) of this section.

(ii) *Net effect on plan assets.*—At the time that a loan is made, the interest rate for the loan and the price of securities to be acquired with the loan proceeds should not be such that plan assets might be drained off.

(iii) *Arm's-length standard.*—The terms of a loan, whether or not between independent parties, must, at the same time the loan is made, be at least as favorable to the ESOP as the terms of a comparable loan resulting from arm's-length negotiations between independent parties.

(4) *Use of loan proceeds.*—The proceeds of an exempt loan must be used within a reasonable time after their receipt by the borrowing ESOP only for any or all of the following purposes:

(i) To acquire qualifying employer securities.

(ii) To repay such loan.

(iii) To repay a prior exempt loan. A new loan, the proceeds of which are so used, must satisfy the provisions of this paragraph (b). Except as provided in paragraph (b)(9) and (10) of this section or as otherwise required by applicable law, no security acquired with the proceeds of an exempt loan may be subject to a put, call, or other option, or buy-sell or similar arrangement while held by and when distributed from a plan, whether or not the plan is then an ESOP.

(5) *Liability and collateral of ESOP for loan.*—An exempt loan must be without recourse against the ESOP. Furthermore, the only assets of the ESOP that may be given as collateral on an exempt loan are qualifying employer securities of two classes: those acquired with the proceeds of the loan and those that were used as collateral on a prior exempt loan repaid with the proceeds of the current exempt loan. No person entitled to payment under the exempt loan shall have any right to assets of the ESOP other than:

(i) Collateral given for the loan,

(ii) Contributions (other than contributions of employer securities) that are made under and ESOP to meet its obligations under the loan, and

(iii) Earnings attributable to such collateral and the investment of such contributions.

The payments made with respect to an exempt loan by the ESOP during a plan year must not exceed an amount equal to the sum of such contributions and earnings received during or prior to the year less such payments in prior years. Such contributions and earnings must be accounted for separately in the books of account of the ESOP until the loan is repaid.

(6) *Default.*—In the event of default upon an exempt loan, the value of plan assets transferred in satisfaction of the loan must not exceed the amount of default. If the lender is a disqualified person, a loan must provide for a transfer of plan assets upon default only upon and to the extent of the failure of the plan to meet the payment schedule of the loan. For purposes of this subparagraph (6), the making of a guarantee does not make a person a lender.

(7) *Reasonable rate of interest.*—The interest rate of a loan must not be in excess of a reasonable rate of interest. All relevant factors will be considered in determining a reasonable rate of interest, including the amount and duration of the loan, the security and guarantee (if any) involved, the credit standing of the ESOP and the guarantor (if any), and the interest rate prevailing for comparable loans. When these factors are considered, a variable interest rate may be reasonable.

(8) *Release from encumbrance.*—(i) *General rule.*—In general, an exempt loan must provide for the release from encumbrance under this subdivision (i) of plan assets used as collateral for the loan. For each plan year during the duration of the loan, the number of securities released must equal the number of encumbered securities held immediately before release for the current plan year multiplied by a fraction. The numerator of the fraction is the amount of principal and interest paid for the year. The denominator of the fraction is the sum of the numerator plus the principal and interest to be paid for all future years. See § 54.4975-7(b)(8)(iv). The number of future years under the loan must be definitely ascertainable and must be determined without taking into account any possible extensions or renewal periods. If the interest rate under the loan is variable, the interest to be paid in future years must be computed by using the interest rate applicable as of the end of the plan year. If collateral includes more than one class of securities, the number of securities of

each class to be released for a plan year must be determined by applying the same fraction to each class.

(ii) *Special rule.*—A loan will not fail to be exempt merely because the number of securities to be released from encumbrance is determined solely with reference to principal payments. However, if release is determined with reference to principal payments only, the following three additional rules apply. The first rule is that the loan must provide for annual payments of principal and interest at a cumulative rate that is not less rapid at any time than level annual payments of such amounts for 10 years. The second rule is that interest included in any payment is disregarded only to the extent that it would be determined to be interest under standard loan amortization tables. The third rule is that this subdivision (ii) is not applicable from the time that, by reason of a renewal, extension, or refinancing, the sum of the expired duration of the exempt loan, the renewal period, the extension period, and the duration of a new exempt loan exceeds 10 years.

(iii) *Caution against plan disqualification.*—Under an exempt loan, the number of securities released from encumbrance may vary from year to year. The release of securities depends upon certain employer contributions and earnings under the ESOP. Under § 54.4975-11(d)(2) actual allocations to participants' accounts are based upon assets withdrawn from the suspense account. Nevertheless, for purposes of applying the limitations under section 415 to these allocations, under § 54.4975-11(a)(8)(ii) contributions used by the ESOP to pay the loan are treated as annual additions to participants' accounts. Therefore, particular caution must be exercised to avoid exceeding the maximum annual additions under section 415. At the same time, release from encumbrance in annual varying numbers may reflect a failure on the part of the employer to make substantial and recurring contributions to the ESOP which will lead to loss of qualification under section 401(a). The Internal Revenue Service will observe closely the operation of ESOP's that release encumbered securities in varying annual amounts, particularly those that provide for the deferral of loan payments or for balloon payments.

(iv) *Illustration.*—The general rule under paragraph (b)(8)(i) of this section operates as illustrated in the following example:

*Example.* Corporation X establishes an ESOP that borrows $750,000 from a bank. X guarantees the loan, which is for 15 years at 5% interest and is payable in level annual amounts of $72,256.72. Total payments on the loan are $1,083,850.80. The ESOP uses the entire loan proceeds to acquire 15,000 shares of X stock which is used as collateral for the loan. The number of securities to be released for the first year is 1,000 shares, i.e., 15,000 shares × $72,256.72/$1,083,850.80 = 15,000 shares × 1/15. The number of securities to be released for the second year is 1,000 shares, i.e., 14,000 shares × $72,256.72/$1,011,594.08 = 14,000 shares × 1/14. If all loan payments are made as originally scheduled, the number of securities released in each succeeding year of the loan will also be 1,000.

(9) *Right of first refusal.*—Qualifying employer securities acquired with proceeds of an exempt loan may, but need not, be subject to a right of first refusal. However, any such right must meet the requirements of this subparagraph (9). Securities subject to such right must be stock or an equity security, or a debt security convertible into stock or an equity security. Also, the securities must not be publicly traded at the time the right may be exercised. The right of first refusal must be in favor of the employer, the ESOP, or both in any order of priority. The selling price and other terms under the right must not be less favorable to the seller than the greater of the value of the security determined under § 54.4975-11(d)(5), or the purchase price and other terms offered by a buyer, other than the employer or the ESOP, making a good faith offer to purchase the security. The right of first refusal must lapse no later than 14 days after the security holder gives written notice to the holder of the right that an offer by a third party to purchase the security has been received.

(10) *Put option.*—A qualifying employer security acquired with the proceeds of an exempt loan by an ESOP after September 30, 1976, must be subject to a put option if it is not publicly traded when distributed or if it is subject to a trading limitation when distributed. For purposes of this subparagraph (10), a "trading limitation" on a security is a restriction under any Federal or state securities law, any regulation thereunder, or an agreement, not prohibited by this paragraph (b), affecting the security which would make the security not as freely tradable as one not subject to such restriction. The put option must be exercisable only by a participant, by the participant's donees, or by a person (including an estate or its distributee) to whom the security passes by reason of a participant's death. (Under this subparagraph (10), "participant" means a participant and beneficiaries of the participant under the ESOP.) The put option must permit a participant to put the security to the employer. Under no

circumstances may the put option bind the ESOP. However, it may grant the ESOP an option to assume the rights and obligations of the employer at the time that the put option is exercised. If it is known at the time a loan is made that Federal or state law will be violated by the employer's honoring such put option, the put option must permit the security to be put, in a manner consistent with such law, to a third party (e.g., an affiliate of the employer or a shareholder other than the ESOP) that has substantial net worth at the time the loan is made and whose net worth is reasonably expected to remain substantial.

(11) *Duration of put option.*—(i) *General rule.*—A put option must be exercisable at least during a 15-month period which begins on the date the security subject to the put option is distributed by the ESOP.

(ii) *Special rule.*—In the case of a security that is publicly traded without restriction when distributed but ceases to be so traded within 15 months after distribution, the employer must notify each security holder in writing on or before the tenth day after the date the security ceases to be so traded that for the remainder of the 15-month period the security is subject to a put option. The number of days between such tenth day and the date on which notice is actually given, if later than the tenth day, must be added to the duration of the put option. The notice must inform distributees of the terms of the put options that they are to hold. Such terms must satisfy the requirements of paragraph (b)(10) through (12) of this section.

(12) *Other put option provisions.*—(i) *Manner of exercise.*—A put option is exercised by the holder notifying the employer in writing that the put option is being exercised.

(ii) *Time excluded from duration of put option.*—The period during which a put option is exercisable does not include any time when a distributee is unable to exercise it because the party bound by the put option is prohibited from honoring it by applicable Federal or state law.

(iii) *Price.*—The price at which a put option must be exercisable is the value of the security, determined under § 54.4975-11(d)(5).

(iv) *Payment terms.*—The provisions for payment under a put option must be reasonable. The deferral of payment is reasonable if adequate security and a reasonable interest rate are provided for any credit extended and if the cumulative payments at any time are no less than the aggregate of reasonable periodic payments as of such time. Periodic payments are reasonable if annual installments, beginning with 30 days after the date the put option is exercised, are substantially equal. Generally, the payment period may not end more than 5 years after the date the put option is exercised. However, it may be extended to a date no later than the earlier of 10 years from the date the put option is exercised or the date the proceeds of the loan used by the ESOP to acquire the security subject to the put option are entirely repaid.

(v) *Payment restrictions.*—Payment under a put option may be restricted by the terms of a loan, including one used to acquire a security subject to a put option, made before November 1, 1977. Otherwise, payment under a put option must not be restricted by the provisions of a loan or any other arrangement, including the terms of the employer's articles of incorporation, unless so required by applicable state law.

(13) *Other terms of loan.*—An exempt loan must be for a specific term. Such loan may not be payable at the demand of any person, except in the case of default.

(14) *Status of plan as ESOP.*—To be exempt, a loan must be made to a plan that is an ESOP at the time of such loan. However, a loan to a plan formally designated as an ESOP at the time of the loan that fails to be an ESOP because it does not comply with section 401(a) of the Code or § 54.4975-11 will be exempt as of the time of such loan if the plan is amended retroactively under section 401(b) or § 54.4975-11(a)(4).

(15) *Special rules for certain loans.*—(i) *Loans made before January 1, 1976.*—A loan made before January 1, 1976, or made afterwards under a binding agreement in effect on January 1, 1976 (or under renewals permitted by the terms of the agreement on that date) is exempt for the entire period of the loan if it otherwise satisfies the provisions of this paragraph (b) for such period, even though it does not satisfy the following provisions of this section: the last sentence of paragraph (b)(4) and all of paragraph (b)(5), (6), (8)(i) and (ii), and (9) through (13), inclusive.

(ii) *Loans made after December 31, 1975, but before November 1, 1977.*—A loan made after December 31, 1975, but before November 1, 1977 or made afterwards under a binding agreement in effect on November 1, 1977 (or under renewals permitted by the terms of the agreement on that date) is exempt for the entire period of the loan if it otherwise satisfies the provisions of this paragraph (b) for such period even though it does not satisfy the following provisions of this section: paragraph (b)(6) and (9) and the three additional rules listed in paragraph (b)(8)(ii).

(iii) *Release rule.*—Notwithstanding paragraph (b)(15)(i) and (ii) of this section, if the proceeds of a loan are used to acquire securities after November 1, 1977, the loan must comply by such date with the provisions of paragraph (b)(8) of this section.

(iv) *Default rule.*—Notwithstanding paragraph (b)(15)(i) and (ii) of this section, a loan by a disqualified person other than a guarantor must meet the requirements of paragraph (b)(6) of this section. A loan will meet these requirements if it is retroactively amended before November 1, 1977 to meet these requirements.

(v) *Put option rule.*—With respect to a security distributed before November 1, 1977, the put option provisions of paragraph (b)(10), (11), and (12) of this section will be deemed satisfied as of the date the security is distributed if by December 31, 1977, the security is subject to a put option satisfying such provisions. For purposes of satisfying such provisions, the security will be deemed distributed on the date the put option is issued. However, the put option provisions need not be satisfied with respect to a security that is not owned on November 1, 1977 by a person in whose hands a put option must be exercisable. [Reg. § 54.4975-7.]

☐ [T.D. 7506, 8-30-77.]

### [Reg. § 54.4975-9]

**§ 54.4975-9. Definition of "Fiduciary".**—(a) [Reserved]
(b) [Reserved]

(c) *Investment advice.*—(1) A person shall be deemed to be rendering "investment advice" to an employee benefit plan, within the meaning of section 4975(e)(3)(B) and this paragraph, only if:

(i) Such person renders advice to the plan as to the value of securities or other property, or makes recommendations as to the advisability of investing in, purchasing, or selling securities or other property; and

(ii) Such person either directly or indirectly (e.g., through or together with any affiliate)—

(A) Has discretionary authority or control, whether or not pursuant to agreement, arrangement or understanding, with respect to purchasing or selling securities or other property for the plan; or

(B) Renders any advice described in paragraph (c)(1)(i) of this section on a regular basis to the plan pursuant to a mutual agreement, arrangement or understanding, written or otherwise, between such person and the plan or a fiduciary with respect to the plan, that such services will serve as a primary basis for investment decisions with respect to plan assets, and that such person will render individualized investment advice to the plan based on the particular needs of the plan regarding such matters as, among other things, investment policies or strategy, overall portfolio composition, or diversification of plan investments.

(2) A person who is a fiduciary with respect to a plan by reason of rendering investment advice (as defined in paragraph (c)(1) of this section) for a fee or other compensation, direct or indirect, with respect to any moneys or other property of such plan, or having any authority or responsibility to do so, shall not be deemed to be a fiduciary regarding any assets of the plan with respect to which such person does not have any discretionary authority, discretionary control or discretionary responsibility, does not exercise any authority or control, does not render investment advice (as defined in paragraph (c)(1) of this section) for a fee or other compensation, and does not have any authority or responsibility to render such investment advice, provided that nothing in this paragraph shall be deemed to:

(i) Exempt such person from the provisions of section 405(a) of the Employee Retirement Income Security Act of 1974 concerning liability for fiduciary breaches by other fiduciaries with respect to any assets of the plan; or

(ii) Exclude such person from the definition of the term "disqualified person" (as set forth in section 4975(e)(2)) with respect to any assets of the plan.

(d) *Execution of securities transactions.*—(1) A person who is a broker or dealer registered under the Securities Exchange Act of 1934, a reporting dealer who makes primary markets in securities of the United States Government or of an agency of the United States Government and reports daily to the Federal Reserve Bank of New York its positions with respect to such securities and borrowings thereon, or a bank supervised by the United States or a State, shall not be deemed to be a fiduciary, within the meaning of section 4975(e)(3), with respect to an employee benefit plan solely because such person executes transactions for the purchase or sale of securi-

ties on behalf of such plan in the ordinary course of its business as a broker, dealer, or bank, pursuant to instructions of a fiduciary with respect to such plan, if:

(i) Neither the fiduciary nor any affiliate of such fiduciary is such broker, dealer, or bank; and

(ii) The instructions specify (A) the security to be purchased or sold, (B) a price range within which such security is to be purchased or sold, or, if such security is issued by an open-end investment company registered under the Investment Company Act of 1940 (15 U.S.C. 80a-1, et seq.), a price which is determined in accordance with Rule 22c-1 under the Investment Company Act of 1940 (17 CFR 270.22c-1), (C) a time span during which such security may be purchased or sold (not to exceed five business days), and (D) the minimum or maximum quantity of such security which may be purchased or sold within such price range, or, in the case of a security issued by an open-end investment company registered under the Investment Company Act of 1940, the minimum or maximum quantity of such security which may be purchased or sold, or the value of such security in dollar amount which may be purchased or sold, at the price referred to in paragraph (d)(1)(ii)(B) of this section.

(2) A person who is a broker-dealer, reporting dealer, or bank which is a fiduciary with respect to an employee benefit plan solely by reason of the possession or exercise of discretionary authority or discretionary control in the management of the plan or the management or disposition of plan assets in connection with the execution of a transaction for the purchase or sale of securities on behalf of such plan which fails to comply with the provisions of paragraph (d)(1) of this section, shall not be deemed to be a fiduciary regarding any assets of the plan with respect to which such broker-dealer, reporting dealer or bank does not have any discretionary authority, discretionary control or discretionary responsibility, does not exercise any authority or control, does not render investment advice (as defined in paragraph (c)(1) of this section) for a fee or other compensation, and does not have any authority or responsibility to render such investment advice, provided that nothing in this paragraph shall be deemed to:

(i) Exempt such broker-dealer, reporting dealer, or bank from the provisions of section 405(a) of the Employee Retirement Income Security Act of 1974 concerning liability for fiduciary breaches by other fiduciaries with respect to any assets of the plan; or

(ii) Exclude such broker-dealer, reporting dealer, or bank from the definition of the term "disqualified person" (as set forth in section 4975(e)(2)) with respect to any assets of the plan.

(e) *Affiliate and control.*—(1) For purposes of paragraphs (c) and (d) of this section, an "affiliate" of a person shall include:

(i) Any person directly or indirectly, through one or more intermediaries, controlling, controlled by, or under common control with such person;

(ii) Any officer, director, partner, employee or relative (as defined in section 4975(e)(6)) of such person; and

(iii) Any corporation or partnership of which such person is an officer, director or partner.

(2) For purposes of this paragraph, the term "control" means the power to exercise a controlling influence over the management or policies of a person other than an individual. [Reg. § 54.4975-9.]

☐ [T.D. 7386, 10-28-75.]

### [Reg. § 54.4975-11]

**§ 54.4975-11. "ESOP" requirements.**—(a) *In general.*—(1) *Type of plan.*—To be an "ESOP" (employee stock ownership plan), a plan described in section 4975(e)(7)(A) must meet the requirements of this section. See section 4975(e)(7)(B).

(2) *Designation as ESOP.*—To be an ESOP, a plan must be formally designated as such in the plan document.

(3) *Continuing loan provisions under plan.*—(i) *Creation of protections and rights.*—The terms of an ESOP must formally provide participants with certain protections and rights with respect to plan assets acquired with the proceeds of an exempt loan. These protections and rights are those referred to in the third sentence of § 54.4975-7(b)(4), relating to put, call, or other options and to buy-sell or similar arrangements, and in § 54.4975-7(b)(10), (11), and (12), relating to put options.

(ii) *"Nonterminable" protections and rights.*—The terms of an ESOP must also formally provide that these protections and rights are nonterminable. Thus, if a plan holds or has distributed securities acquired with the proceeds of an exempt loan and either the loan is repaid or the plan ceases to be an ESOP, these protections and rights must continue to exist under the terms of the plan. However, the protections and rights will not fail to be nonterminable merely because they are not exercisable under § 54.4975-7(b)(11) and (12)(ii).

For example, if, after a plan ceases to be an ESOP, securities acquired with the proceeds of an exempt loan cease to be publicly traded, the 15-month period prescribed by §54.4975-7(b)(11) includes the time when the securities are publicly traded.

(iii) *No incorporation by reference of protections and rights.*—The formal requirements of paragraph (a)(3)(i) and (ii) of this section must be set forth in the plan. Mere reference to the third sentence of §54.4975-7(b)(4) and to the provisions of §54.4975-7(b)(10), (11), and (12) is not sufficient.

(iv) *Certain remedial amendments.*—Notwithstanding the limits under paragraph (a)(4) and (10) of this section on the retroactive effect of plan amendments, a remedial plan amendment adopted before December 31, 1979, to meet the requirements of paragraph (a)(3)(i) and (ii) of this section is retroactively effective as of the later of the date on which the plan was designated as an ESOP or November 1, 1977.

(4) *Retroactive amendment.*—A plan meets the requirements of this section as of the date that it is designated as an ESOP if it is amended retroactively to meet, and in fact does meet, such requirements at any of the following times:

(i) 12 months after the date on which the plan is designated as an ESOP;

(ii) 90 days after a determination letter is issued with respect to the qualification of the plan as an ESOP under this section, but only if the determination is requested by the time in paragraph (a)(4)(i) of this section; or

(iii) A later date approved by the district director.

(5) *Addition to other plan.*—An ESOP may form a portion of a plan the balance of which includes a qualified pension, profit-sharing, or stock bonus plan which is not an ESOP. A reference to an ESOP includes an ESOP that forms a portion of another plan.

(6) *Conversion of existing plan to an ESOP.*—If an existing pension, profit-sharing, or stock bonus plan is converted into an ESOP, the requirements of section 404 of the Employee Retirement Income Security Act of 1974 (ERISA) (88 Stat. 877), relating to fiduciary duties, and section 401(a) of the Code, relating to requirements for plans established for the exclusive benefit of employees, apply to such conversion. A conversion may constitute a termination of an existing plan. For definition of a termination, see the regulations under section 411(d)(3) of the Code and section 4041(f) of ERISA.

(7) *Certain arrangements barred.*—(i) *Buy-sell agreements.*—An arrangement involving an ESOP that creates a put option must not provide for the issuance of put options other than as provided under §54.4975-7(b)(10), (11), and (12). Also, as ESOP must not otherwise obligate itself to acquire securities from a particular security holder at an indefinite time determined upon the happening of an event such as the death of the holder.

(ii) *Integrated plans.*—A plan designated as an ESOP after November 1, 1977, must not be integrated directly or indirectly with contributions or benefits under Title II of the Social Security Act or any other State or Federal law. ESOP's established and integrated before such date may remain integrated. However, such plans must not be amended to increase the integration level or the integration percentage. Such plans may in operation continue to increase the level of integration if under the plan such increase is limited by reference to a criterion existing apart from the plan.

(8) *Effect of certain ESOP provisions on section 401(a) status.*—(i) *Exempt loan requirements.*—An ESOP will not fail to meet the requirements of section 401(a)(2) merely because it gives plan assets as collateral for an exempt loan under §54.4975-7(b)(5) or uses plan assets under §54.4975-7(b)(6) to repay an exempt loan in the event of default.

(ii) *Individual annual contribution limitation.*—An ESOP will not fail to meet the requirements of section 401(a)(16) merely because annual additions under section 415(c) are calculated with respect to employer contributions used to repay an exempt loan rather than with respect to securities allocated to participants.

(iii) *Income pass-through.*—An ESOP will not fail to meet the requirements of section 401(a) merely because it provides for the current payment of income under paragraph (f)(3) of this section.

(9) *Transitional rules for ESOP's established before November 1, 1977.*—A plan established before November 1, 1977 that otherwise satisfies the provisions of this section constitutes an ESOP if it is amended by December 31, 1977, to comply from November 1, 1977 with this section even though before November 1, 1977 the plan did not satisfy paragraphs (c) and (d)(2), (4), and (5) of this section.

(10) *Additional transitional rules.*—Notwithstanding paragraph (a)(9) of this section, a plan established before November 1, 1977 that otherwise satisfies the provisions of this section constitutes an ESOP if by December 31, 1977, it is amended to comply from November 1, 1977 with this section even though before such date the plan did not satisfy the following provisions of this section:

(i) Paragraph (a)(3) and (8)(iii);

(ii) The last sentence of paragraph (d)(3); and

(iii) Paragraph (f)(3).

(b) *Plan designed to invest primarily in qualifying employer securities.*—A plan constitutes an ESOP only if the plan specifically states that it is designed to invest primarily in qualifying employer securities. Thus, a stock bonus plan or a money purchase pension plan constituting an ESOP may invest part of its assets in other than qualifying employer securities. Such plan will be treated the same as other stock bonus plans or money purchase pension plans qualified under section 401(a) with respect to those investments.

(c) *Suspense account.*—All assets acquired by an ESOP with the proceeds of an exempt loan under section 4975(d)(3) must be added to and maintained in a suspense account. They are to be withdrawn from the suspense account by applying §54.4975-7(b)(8) and (15) as if all securities in the suspense account were encumbered. Such assets acquired before November 1, 1977, must be withdrawn by applying §54.4975-7(b)(8) or the provision of the loan that controls release from encumbrance. Assets in such suspense accounts are assets of the ESOP. Thus, for example, such assets are subject to section 401(a)(2).

(d) *Allocations to accounts of participants.*—(1) *In general.*—Except as provided in this section, amounts contributed to an ESOP must be allocated as provided under §1.401-1(b)(ii) and (iii) of this chapter, and securities acquired by an ESOP must be accounted for as provided under §1.402(a)-1(b)(2)(ii) of this chapter.

(2) *Assets withdrawn from suspense account.*—As of the end of each plan year, the ESOP must consistently allocate to the participants' accounts non-monetary units representing participants' interests in assets withdrawn from the suspense account.

(3) *Income.*—Income with respect to securities acquired with the proceeds of an exempt loan must be allocated as income of the plan except to the extent that the ESOP provides for the use of income from such securities to repay the loan. Certain income may be distributed currently under paragraph (f)(3) of this section.

(4) *Forfeitures.*—If a portion of a participant's account is forfeited, qualifying employer securities allocated under paragraph (d)(2) of this section must be forfeited only after other assets. If interests in more than one class of qualifying employer securities have been allocated to the participant's account, the participant must be treated as forfeiting the same proportion of each such class.

(5) *Valuation.*—For purposes of §54.4975-7(b)(9) and (12) and this section, valuations must be made in good faith and based on all relevant factors for determining the fair market value of securities. In the case of a transaction between a plan and a disqualified person, value must be determined as of the date of the transaction. For all other purposes under this subparagraph (5), value must be determined as of the most recent valuation date under the plan. An independent appraisal will not in itself be a good faith determination of value in the case of a transaction between a plan and a disqualified person. However, in other cases, a determination of fair market value based on at least an annual appraisal independently arrived at by a person who customarily makes such appraisals and who is independent of any party to a transaction under §54.4975-7(b)(9) and (12) will be deemed to be a good faith determination of value.

(e) *Multiple plans.*—(1) *General rule.*—An ESOP may not be considered together with another plan for purposes of applying section 401(a)(4) and (5) or section 410(b) unless—

(i) The ESOP and such other plan exist on November 1, 1977, or

(ii) Paragraph (e)(2) of this section is satisfied.

(2) *Special rule for combined ESOP's.*—Two or more ESOP's, one or more of which does not exist on November 1, 1977, may be considered together for purposes of applying section 401(a)(4) and (5) or section 410(b) only if the proportion of qualifying employer securities to total plan assets is substantially the same for each ESOP and—

(i) The qualifying employer securities held by all ESOP's are all of the same class; or

(ii) The ratios of each class held to all such securities held is substantially the same for each plan.

(3) *Amended coverage, contribution, or benefit structure.*—For purposes of paragraph (e)(1)(i) of this section, if the coverage, contribu-

**Reg. §54.4975-11(e)(3)**

tion, or benefit structure of a plan that exists on November 1, 1977 is amended after that date, as of the effective date of the amendment, the plan is no longer considered to be a plan that exists on November 1, 1977.

(f) *Distribution.*—(1) *In general.*—Except as provided in paragraph (f)(2) and (3) of this section, with respect to distributions, a portion of an ESOP consisting of a stock bonus plan or a money purchase pension plan is not to be distinguished from other such plans under section 401(a). Thus, for example, benefits distributable from the portion of an ESOP consisting of a stock bonus plan are distributable only in stock of the employer. Also, benefits distributable from the money-purchase portion of the ESOP may be, but are not required to be, distributable in qualifying employer securities.

(2) *Exempt loan proceeds.*—If securities acquired with the proceeds of an exempt loan available for distribution consist of more than one class, a distributee must receive substantially the same proportion of each such class. However, as indicated in paragraph (f)(1) of this section, benefits distributable from the portion of an ESOP consisting of a stock bonus plan are distributable only in stock of the employer.

(3) *Income.*—Income paid with respect to qualifying employer securities acquired by an ESOP in taxable years beginning after December 31, 1974, may be distributed at any time after receipt by the plan to participants on whose behalf such securities have been allocated. However, under an ESOP that is a stock bonus plan, income held by the plan for a 2-year period or longer must be distributed under the general rules described in paragraph (f)(1) of this section. (See the last sentence of section 803(h), Tax Reform Act of 1976). [Reg. § 54.4975-11.]

☐ *[T.D. 7506, 8-30-77. Amended by T.D. 7571, 11-16-78.]*

**[Reg. § 54.4975-12]**

**§ 54.4975-12. Definition of the term "qualifying employer security".**—(a) *In general.*—For purposes of section 4975(e)(8) and this section, the term "qualifying employer security" means an employer security which is:

(1) Stock or otherwise an equity security, or

(2) A bond, debenture, note, or certificate or other evidence of indebtedness which is described in paragraphs (1), (2), and (3) of section 503(e).

(b) *Special rule.*—In determining whether a bond, debenture, note, or certificate or other evidence of indebtedness is described in paragraphs (1), (2), and (3) of section 503(e), any organization described in section 401(a) shall be treated as an organization subject to the provisions of section 503. [Reg. § 54.4975-12.]

☐ *[T.D. 7506, 8-30-77.]*

**[Reg. § 141.4975-13]**

**§ 141.4975-13. Definition of "amount involved" and "correction." (Temporary).**—Until superseded by permanent regulations under sections 4975(f), (4) and (5), § 53.4941(e)-1 of this chapter (Foundation Excise Tax Regulations) will be controlling to the extent such regulations describe terms appearing both in section 4941(e) and section 4975(f). [Temporary Reg. § 141.4975-13.]

☐ *[T.D. 7425, 8-5-76. Amended by T.D. 8084, 5-1-86.]*

**[Reg. § 54.4975-14]**

**§ 54.4975-14. Election to pay an excise tax for certain pre-1975 prohibited transactions.**—(a) *In general.*—Section 2003(c)(1)(B) of the Employee Retirement Income Security Act of 1974 (88 Stat. 978) provides an election to pay an excise tax by certain persons involved prior to 1975 in prohibited transactions within the meaning of section 503(b) or (g).

(b) *Effect of election.*—If a valid election is made under this section with respect to a particular transaction, any loss of exemption under section 501(a) because of a prohibited transaction within the meaning of section 503(b) or (g) shall not apply. Instead, the person who made the election referred to in this section shall be subject to the taxes which would have been imposed by section 4975(a) or (b) as though section 4975 had imposed a tax in respect of the transaction. (However, section 4975(f)(1), relating to joint and several liability, shall not apply to any person who has not made an election under this section, and interest for late payment of tax shall not begin to accrue until after the date of the election.) Such an election is irrevocable. However, the making of the election does not affect the application of section 6501 for purposes of assessment and collection of tax and section 6511 for purposes of filing a claim for credit or refund with respect to taxpayers and to taxable years of taxpayers whose tax liability is or may be affected by reason of the nonapplication of a denial of exempt status.

(c) *Method of election.*—A person shall make the election referred to in this section by filing the form issued for such purpose by the Internal Revenue Service, including therein the information required by such form and the instructions issued with respect thereto, and by paying the tax which the taxpayer indicates is due at the time the return is filed. To be valid the election must be made prior to the later of December 6, 1976, or 120 days after the date of notification referred to in § 1.503(a)-1(b) of this chapter (Income Tax Regulations), relating to loss of exemption for certain prohibited transactions. If there has been no notification of loss of exemption, the election may be made at any time. However, these limitations do not preclude an agreement between the disqualified person and the district director to extend the time within which the election is permitted.

(d) *Computation of section 4975 excise tax.*—To the extent applicable, and solely for purposes associated with the payment of a section 4975 excise tax under the election referred to in this section, § 53.4941(e)-1 of this chapter (Foundation Excise Tax Regulations) is controlling. [Reg. § 54.4975-14.]

☐ *[T.D. 7489, 5-26-77.]*

**[Reg. § 54.4975-15]**

**§ 54.4975-15. Other transitional rules.**—(a) [Reserved]

(b) [Reserved]

(c) [Reserved]

(d) *Provision of certain services until June 30, 1977.*—(1) *In general.*—Section 2003(c)(2)(D) of the Employee Retirement Income Security Act of 1974 (the Act) (88 Stat. 979) provides that section 4975 shall not apply to the provision of services before June 30, 1977, between a plan and a disqualified person if the three requirements contained in section 2003(c)(2)(D) of the Act are met. The first requirement is that such services must be provided either (i) under a binding contract in effect on July 1, 1974 (or pursuant to a renewal or modification of such contract); or (ii) by a disqualified person who ordinarily and customarily furnished such services on June 30, 1974. The second requirement is that the services be provided on terms that remain at least as favorable to the plan as an arm's-length transaction with an unrelated party would be. For this purpose, such services are provided on terms that remain at least as favorable to the plan as an arm's-length transaction with an unrelated party would be if, at the time of execution (or renewal) of such binding contract, the contract (or renewal) is on terms at least as favorable to the plan as an arm's-length transaction with an unrelated party would be. However, if in a normal commercial setting an unrelated party in the position of the plan could be expected to insist upon a renegotiation or termination of a binding contract, the plan must so act. Thus, for example, if a disqualified person provides services to a plan on a month-to-month basis, and a party in the position of the plan could be expected to renegotiate the price paid under such contract because of a decline in the fair market value of such services, the plan must so act in order to avoid participation in a prohibited transaction. The third requirement is that the provision of services must not be, or have been, at the time of such provision a prohibited transaction within the meaning of section 503(b) or the corresponding provisions of prior law. If these three requirements are met, section 4975 will apply neither to services provided before June 30, 1977 (both to customers to whom such services were being provided on June 30, 1974, and to new customers) nor to the receipt of compensation therefor. Thus, if these three requirements are met, section 4975 will not apply until June 30, 1977, to the provision of services to a plan by a disqualified person (including a fiduciary) even if such services could not be furnished pursuant to the exemption provisions of sections 4975(d)(2) or (6) and § 54.4975-6. For example, if the three requirements of section 2003(c)(2)(D) of the Act are met, a person serving as fiduciary to a plan who already receives full-time pay from an employer or an association of employers, whose employees are participants in such plan, or from an employee organization whose members are participants in such plan, may continue to receive reasonable compensation from the plan for services rendered to the plan before June 30, 1977. Similarly, until June 30, 1977, a plan consultant who may be a fiduciary because of the nature of the consultative and administrative services being provided may, if these three requirements are met, continue to cause the sale of insurance to the plan and continue to receive commissions for such sales from the insurance company writing the policy. Further, if the three requirements of section 2003(c)(2)(D) of the Act are met, a securities broker-dealer who renders investment advice to a plan for a fee, thereby becoming a fiduciary, may furnish other services to the plan, such as brokerage services, and receives compensation therefor. Also, if a registered representative of such a broker-dealer were a fiduciary, the registered representative may receive compensation, including commissions, for brokerage services performed before June 30, 1977.

(2) *Persons deemed to be June 30, 1974, service providers.*—A disqualified person with respect to a plan which did not, on June 30, 1974, ordinarily and customarily furnish a particular service, will nevertheless be considered to have ordinarily and customarily furnished such service on June 30, 1974, for purposes of this section and section 2003(c)(2)(D) of the Act, if either of the following conditions are met:

(i) At least 50 percent of the outstanding beneficial interests of such disqualified person are owned directly or through one or more intermediaries by the same person or persons who owned, directly or through one or more intermediaries, at least 50 percent of the outstanding beneficial interests of a person who ordinarily and customarily furnished such service on June 30, 1974; or

(ii) Control or the power to exercise a controlling influence over the management and policies of such disqualified person is possessed, directly or through one or more intermediaries, by the same person or persons who possessed, directly or through one or more intermediaries, control or the power to exercise a controlling influence over the management and policies of a person who ordinarily and customarily furnished such service on June 30, 1974. For purposes of this paragraph (d)(2) a person shall be deemed to be an "intermediary" of another person if at least 50 percent of the outstanding beneficial interests of such person are owned by such other person, directly or indirectly, or if such other person controls or has the power to exercise a controlling influence over the management and policies of such person.

(3) *Examples.*—The principles of § 54.4975-15(d)(2) may be illustrated by the following examples.

*Example (1).* A owns 50 percent of the outstanding beneficial interest of ABC Partnership which ordinarily and customarily furnished certain services on June 30, 1974. On July 2, 1974, ABC Partnership was incorporated into ABC Corporation with one class of stock outstanding. A owns 50 percent of the shares of such stock. ABC Corporation furnishes the same services that were furnished by ABC Partnership on June 30, 1974. ABC Corporation will be deemed to have ordinarily and customarily furnished such services on June 30, 1974, for purposes of section 2003(c)(2)(D) of the Act.

*Example (2).* A and B together own 100 percent of the beneficial interests of AB Partnership, which ordinarily and customarily furnished certain services on June 30, 1974. On September 1, 1974, AB Partnership was incorporated into AB Corporation with one class of stock outstanding. A and B each own 20 percent of such outstanding class of stock and together have control over the management and policies of AB Corporation. AB Corporation furnishes the same services that were furnished by AB Partnership on June 30, 1974. AB Corporation will be deemed to have ordinarily and customarily furnished such services on June 30, 1974, for purposes of section 2003(c)(2)(D) of the Act.

*Example (3).* On June 30, 1974, M Corporation was ordinarily and customarily furnishing certain services. On that date, X, Y and Z together owned 50 percent of all classes of the outstanding shares of M Corporation. On January 28, 1975, all of the shareholders of M Corporation exchanged their shares in M Corporation for shares of a new N Corporation. As a result of that exchange, X, Y and Z together own 50 percent of the common stock of N Corporation, the only class of N Corporation stock outstanding after the exchange. N Corporation furnishes the services formerly furnished by M Corporation. N Corporation will be deemed to have ordinarily and customarily furnished such services on June 30, 1974, for purposes of section 2003(c)(2)(D) of the Act.

*Example (4).* I Corporation ordinarily and customarily furnished certain services on June 30, 1974. On November 3, 1975, I corporation organizes a wholly owned subsidiary, S Corporation, which furnishes the same services ordinarily and customarily furnished by I Corporation on June 30, 1974. S Corporation will be deemed to have ordinarily and customarily furnished such services on June 30, 1974, for purposes of section 2003(c)(2)(D) of the Act.

*Example (5).* X Corporation, wholly-owned and controlled by A, ordinarily and customarily furnished certain services on June 30, 1974. Y Corporation did not perform such services on that date. On January 2, 1976, X Corporation is merged into Y Corporation and, although A received less than 50 percent of the total outstanding shares of Y Corporation, after such merger A has control over the management and policies of Y Corporation. Y Corporation furnishes the same services that were formerly furnished by X Corporation. Y Corporation will be deemed to have ordinarily and customarily furnished such services on June 30, 1974, for purposes of section 2003(c)(2)(D) of the Act. [Reg. § 54.4975-15.]

☐ [*T.D.* 7491, 6-21-77.]

[Reg. § 54.4976-1T]

## § 54.4976-1T. Questions and answers relating to taxes with respect to welfare benefit funds. (Temporary)

Q-1: What does section 4976 provide?

A-1: Section 4976 imposes a tax on employers who provide disqualified benefits through a welfare benefit fund. The tax imposed is equal to 100 percent of the disqualified benefit.

Q-2: What constitutes a disqualified benefit?

A-2: A disqualified benefit is (a) any post-retirement medical or life insurance benefit provided with respect to a key employee (as defined in section 419A(d)(3)) through a welfare benefit fund if a separate account is required to be established for such employee under section 419A(d) and the cost for such coverage is not charged against or paid from such separate account; (b) any post-retirement medical or life insurance benefit provided through a welfare benefit fund with respect to an individual in whose favor discrimination is prohibited unless the plan of which the fund is a part meets the requirements of section 505(b) with respect to that benefit; and (c) any portion of the fund which reverts to the benefit of the employer. A post-retirement medical or life insurance benefit provided with respect to a key employee will not constitute a disqualified benefit even though such benefit is not provided through a separate account if the cost of such benefit is paid by the employer in the taxable year in which the benefit is provided and there is not (and there is not required to be) a separate account with an outstanding credit balance maintained for the key employee.

Q-3: What is the effective date of section 4976?

A-3: (a) Generally, section 4976 applies to disqualified benefits provided by a welfare benefit fund after December 31, 1985. However, a disqualified benefit, as defined in section 4976(b)(1) or (2), is not subject to section 4976(a) if it is provided from "existing reserves for post-retirement medical or life insurance benefits" that are within the transition rule set forth in section 512(a)(3)(E)(iii) and Q&A-4 of § 1.512(a)-5T (or would be if such transition rule applied to such welfare benefit fund). For example, if a welfare benefit fund in existence on July 18, 1984, provides an individual in whose favor discrimination is prohibited with a post-retirement life insurance benefit after December 31, 1985, that does not meet the requirements of section 505(b) and if the welfare benefit fund received no contributions after July 18, 1984, then the disqualified benefit provided by the fund is not subject to section 4976(a).

(b) A welfare benefit fund will be able to avoid the application of section 4976(b)(1) and (2) if the employer withdraws from such fund, before April 7, 1986, any amounts that are not attributable to "existing reserves for post-retirement medical or life insurance benefits" because they were neither actually set aside nor treated as actually set aside under Q&A-4 of § 1.512(a)-5T, on July 18, 1984. The employer making such a withdrawal must include the amount in income for the first taxable year ending after July 18, 1984, or, to the extent that the withdrawn amount is attributable to the following taxable year, for such following taxable year. Such a withdrawal will not be treated as an impermissible distribution or reversion under section 501(c)(9), and will not be treated as a disqualified benefit under section 4976(b)(3). Of course, to the extent that the welfare benefit fund contains amounts that are attributable to "existing reserves" but are not within the transition rule set forth in Q&A-4 of § 1.512(a)-5T (as applied to welfare benefit funds), for example, because such amounts exceed the amounts that could have been accumulated under the principles set forth in Revenue Rulings 69-382, 1969-2 C.B. 28; 69-478, 1969-2 C.B. 29; and 73-599, 1973-2 C.B. 40, the fund will not be able to avoid the application of section 4976(b)(1) and (2) under this paragraph.

(c) In the case of a plan which is maintained pursuant to one or more collective bargaining agreements (1) between employee representatives and one or more employers and (2) which are in effect on July 1, 1985 (or ratified on or before that date), the provision does not apply to disqualified benefits provided in years beginning before the termination of the last of the collective bargaining agreements pursuant to which the plan is maintained (determined without regard to any extension of the contract agreed to after July 1, 1985). For purposes of the preceding sentence, any plan amendment made pursuant to a collective bargaining agreement relating to the plan which amends the plan solely to conform to any requirement added under section 511 of the Tax Reform Act 1984 (i.e., requirements under sections 419, 419A, 512(a)(3)(E), and 4976) shall not be treated as a termination of such collective bargaining agreement. [Temporary Reg. § 54.4976-1T.]

☐ [*T.D.* 8073, 1-29-86.]

[Reg. § 54.4977-1T]

## § 54.4977-1T. Questions and answers relating to the election concerning lines of business in existence on January 1, 1984 (Temporary).—The following questions and answers relate to the election by

employers under section 4977 of the Internal Revenue Code of 1954, as added by section 531(e)(1) of the Tax Reform Act of 1984 (98 Stat. 886), to treat all employees of any line of business in existence on January 1, 1984, as employees of one of those lines of business for purposes of section 132(a)(1) and (2):

Q-1: What does section 4977 provide with respect to the exclusion from gross income of certain fringe benefits?

A-1: In general, section 4977 provides an elective grandfather rule that allows an employer under certain circumstances to treat employees of all lines of business which were in existence on January 1, 1984, as employees of one of those lines of business for purposes of section 132(a)(1) and (2), but not for purposes of section 132(g)(2).

Q-2: Under what circumstances does the elective grandfather rule of section 4977 apply?

A-2: If—

(a) an election under section 4977 is in effect with respect to an employer for any calendar year, and

(b) on and after January 1, 1984, at least 85 percent of the employees of the employer in all of its lines of business which existed on January 1, 1984, were entitled to employee discounts or services provided by the employer in one line of business,

then all employees of any line of business of the employer which was in existence on January 1, 1984, are treated, for purposes of section 132(a)(1) and (2) (but not for purposes of section 132(g)(2)) as employees of the one line of business referred to in (b) of this Q/A-2.

Q-3: How does an employer make the election provided for in section 4977?

A-3: An employer must file a statement with the director of the service center with which the employer's tax returns are filed. The statement must indicate that the employer is electing to apply the provisions of section 4977 to one or more of the employer's lines of business and must contain the following information:

(a) The employer's name, address, and taxpayer identification number;

(b) A description of all of the employer's lines of business in existence on January 1, 1984; and

(c) For each line of business which is to have as an employee for purposes of section 132(a)(1) and (2) an individual who but for the election under section 4977 would not be treated as an employee for purposes of section 132(a)(1) and (2)—

(1) a description of the no-additional-cost service or qualified employee discount (including, with respect to discounts, the percentage discount) to be offered to employees pursuant to section 4977 in such line of business, and

(2) with respect to employees in all of the employer's lines of business in existence on January 1, 1984, the number of such employees and the number entitled to the described fringe benefit. Such numbers may be determined as of a date which does not precede the date the election is filed by more than 30 days.

Q-4: In order to make a timely section 4977 election, when must an employer file the election statement?

A-4: Except as otherwise provided in the second sentence of this answer, the employer must file the election statement before the end of the calendar year preceding the year for which the election is to apply. For calendar year 1985, however, the employer has until March 31, 1985, to file the election statement. However, the Commissioner may, in his discretion, extend the March 31, 1985 deadline to a later date.

Q-5: Does section 4977 apply to all calendar years following the calendar year in which the election is made?

A-5: Yes, unless the employer revokes the election.

Q-6: When is a revocation effective?

A-6: A revocation is effective with respect to the calendar year following the calendar year in which it is filed.

Q-7: If an employer does not make a timely section 4977 election with respect to 1985, will the employer be entitled to make an election with respect to any subsequent year?

A-7: No.

Q-8: If an employer revokes a section 4977 election, is the employer entitled to elect the application of section 4977 for subsequent years?

A-8: No. [Temporary Reg. § 54.4977-1T.]

☐ [T.D. 8004, 1-2-85.]

### [Reg. § 54.4978-1T]

**§ 54.4978-1T. Questions and answers relating to the tax on certain dispositions by employee stock ownership plans and certain cooperatives (Temporary).**

Q-1: What does section 4978 provide?

A-1: Section 4978 imposes a tax (as determined under section 4978(b) and Q&A-2 of this section) on the amount realized on the disposition of any qualified securities, if:

(a) An employee stock ownership plan or eligible worker-owned cooperative acquires any qualified securities in a sale to which section 1042 applies;

(b) Such plan or cooperative disposes of any qualified securities during the 3-year period after the date on which any qualified securities were acquired in the sale to which section 1042 applies; and

(c) Either (1) the percentage of the total outstanding shares of the class of employer securities of which the disposed qualified securities are a part held by such plan or cooperative after such disposition is less than the percentage of the total outstanding shares of such class of employer securities held immediately after the sale to which section 1042 applies, or (2) the value of the employer securities held by such plan or cooperative immediately after such disposition is less than 30 percent of the total value of all employer securities outstanding at that time. For purposes of this section, the following terms have the same meanings given to such terms by the identified provisions: "employee stock ownership plan" (section 4975(e)(7)); "qualified securities" (section 1042(b)(1)); "eligible worker-owned cooperative" (section 1042(b)(2)); "employer securities" (section 409(l)). For purposes of determining what constitutes a disposition to which section 4978 applies, see Q&A-3 of this section.

Q-2: What is the amount of tax imposed under section 4978?

A-2: Section 4978 imposes a tax of 10 percent of the amount realized on the disposition of qualified securities. The amount realized that is subject to tax under section 4978 shall not exceed that portion of the amount realized that is allocable to qualified securities acquired within the 3-year period prior to the date of disposition and to which section 1042 applied ("restricted qualified securities"). In determining the amount realized (except as otherwise provided in Q&A-3 of this section), any disposition of employer securities with respect to which the condition contained in provision (c) of Q&A-1 is met shall be treated, first, as a disposition of restricted qualified securities (on a first in, first out basis) and, thereafter, as a disposition of any other employer securities. Thus, for example, if a plan disposes of more employer securities than the number of restricted qualified securities held by the plan at that time and immediately after such disposition the value of the employer securities held by the plan is less than 30 percent of the total value of all outstanding employer securities, the portion of the total amount realized that is allocable to restricted qualified securities subject to tax under section 4978 is determined by multiplying the total amount realized on the disposition by a fraction, the numerator of which is the total value of restricted qualified securities included in the disposition and the denominator of which is the total value of employer securities in the disposition.

Q-3: What constitutes a "disposition" under section 4978?

A-3: (a) Under section 4978, the term "disposition" includes any sale, exchange, or distribution. However, in the case of any exchange of qualified securities for stock of another corporation in any reorganization described in section 368(a)(1), such exchange shall not be treated as a disposition for purposes of section 4978.

(b) Section 4978 shall not apply to any disposition of qualified securities which is made by reason of:

(1) The death of the employee;

(2) The retirement of the employee after the employee has attained 59 1/2 years of age;

(3) The disability of the employee (within the meaning of section 72(m)(5)); or

(4) The separation of the employee from service for any period which results in a 1-year break in service (within the meaning of section 411(a)(6)(A)).

Any disposition of employer securities within this paragraph and any disposition of employer securities with respect to which the condition contained in provision (c) of Q&A-1 of this section is not met shall be treated, first, as a disposition of securities that are not restricted qualified securities and, thereafter, as a disposition of restricted qualified securities (on a first-in, first-out basis).

(c) If restricted qualified securities held by an employee stock ownership plan or eligible worker-owned cooperative no longer meet the definition of qualified securities ("old restricted qualified securities") as a result of a transaction changing (1) the status of a corporation as an employer, or as a member of a controlled group of corporations including the employer, or (2) the existence of employer securities of the type described in section 409(l)(1), the disposition of such securities shall not be treated as a disposition of restricted qualified securities to which the tax under section 4978 is imposed if, within 90 days after such disposition, securities meeting the requirements of section 409(l) ("new restricted qualified securities") that are of equal value to the old restricted qualified securities (at the time of the disposition of the old restricted qualified securities) are substituted for such old restricted qualified securities. However, for purposes of determining the tax imposed under section 4978, old restricted qualified securities shall not be treated as if they retained their status as restricted qualified securities and new restricted qualified securities derived from the disposition of old restricted qualified securities pursuant to the preceding sentence shall be treated as restricted qualified securities for the remaining portion of the period during which the disposition of the old restricted qualified securities would have been subject to tax under section 4978.

Q-4: To whom does the tax under section 4978 apply?

A-4: The tax under section 4978 is imposed on the domestic corporation (or corporations) or the eligible worker-owned cooperative that made the written statement of consent as described in section 1042(a)(2)(B) and Q&A-2 of §1.1042-1T with respect to the disposition of the restricted qualified securities.

Q-5: When does section 4978, as enacted by the Tax Reform Act of 1984, become effective?

A-5: Section 4978 applies to the disposition of qualified securities acquired in a sale to which section 1042 applies. See Q&A-6 of §1.1042-1T for the effective date of section 1042. [Temporary Reg. §54.4978-1T.]

☐ [T.D. 8073, 1-29-86.]

### [Reg. §54.4979-0]

**§54.4979-0. Excise tax on certain excess contributions and excess aggregate contributions; table of contents.**—This section contains the captions that appear in §54.4979-1.

*§54.4979-1. Excise tax on certain excess contributions and excess aggregate contributions.*

(a) In general.
　(1) General rule.
　(2) Liability for tax.
　(3) Due date and form for payment of tax.
　(4) Special rule for simplified employee pensions.
(b) Definitions.
　(1) Excess aggregate contributions.
　(2) Excess contributions.
　(3) Plan.
(c) No tax when excess distributed within 2¹/₂ months of close of year or additional employer contributions made.
　(1) General rule.
　(2) Tax treatment of distributions.
　(3) Income.
　(4) Example.
(d) Effective date.
　(1) General rule.
　(2) Section 403(b) annuity contracts.
　(3) Collectively bargained plans and plans of state or local governments.
　(4) Plan years beginning before January 1, 1992.
[Reg. §54.4979-0.]

☐ [T.D. 8357, 8-8-91. *Amended by* T.D. 8581, 12-22-94.]

### [Reg. §54.4979-1]

**§54.4979-1. Excise tax on certain excess contributions and excess aggregate contributions.**—(a) *In general.*—(1) *General rule.*—In the case of any plan (as defined in paragraph (b)(3) of this section), there is imposed a tax for the employer's taxable year equal to 10 percent of the sum of:

　(i) Any excess contributions under a plan for the plan year ending in the taxable year; and

　(ii) Any excess aggregate contributions under the plan for the plan year ending in the taxable year.

(2) *Liability for tax.*—The tax imposed by paragraph (a)(1) of this section is to be paid by the employer. In the case of a collectively bargained plan to which section 413(b) applies, all employers who are parties to the collective bargaining agreement and whose employees are participants in the plan are jointly and severally liable for the tax.

(3) *Due date and form for payment of tax.*—(i) The tax described in paragraph (a)(1) of this section is due on the last day of the 15th month after the close of the plan year to which the excess contributions or excess aggregate contributions relate.

　(ii) An employer that owes the tax described in paragraph (a)(1) of this section must file the form prescribed by the Commissioner for the payment of the tax.

(4) *Special rule for simplified employee pensions.*—(i) An employer that maintains a simplified employee pension (SEP) as defined in section 408(k) that accepts elective contributions is exempt from the tax of section 4979 and paragraph (a)(1) of this section if it notifies its employees of the fact and tax consequences of excess contributions within 2¹/₂ months following the plan year for which excess contri-

butions are made. The notification must meet the standards of paragraph (a)(4)(ii) of this section.

　(ii) The employer's notification to each affected employee of the excess SEP contributions must specifically state, in a manner calculated to be understood by the average plan participant: the amount of the excess contributions attributable to that employee's elective deferrals; the calendar year for which the excess contributions were made; that the excess contributions are includible in the affected employee's gross income for the specified calendar year; and that failure to withdraw the excess contributions and income attributable thereto by the due date (plus extensions) for filing the affected employee's tax return for the preceding calendar year may result in significant penalties.

　(iii) If an employer does not notify its employees by the last day of the 12-month period following the year of excess SEP contributions, the SEP will no longer be considered to meet the requirements of section 408(k)(6).

(b) *Definitions.*—The following is a list of terms and definitions to be used for purposes of section 4979 and this section:

　(1) *Excess aggregate contributions.*—The term "excess aggregate contribution" has the meaning set forth in §1.401(m)-5 of this Chapter. For purposes of determining excess aggregate contributions under an annuity contract described in section 403(b), the contract is treated as a plan described in section 401(a).

　(2) *Excess contributions.*—The term "excess contributions" has the meaning set forth in sections 401(k)(8)(B), 408(k)(6)(C)(ii), and 501(c)(18). See, e.g., §1.401(k)-6 of this Chapter.

　(3) *Plan.*—The term "plan" means:
　　(i) A plan described in section 401(a) that includes a trust exempt from tax under section 501(a);
　　(ii) Any annuity plan described in section 403(a);
　　(iii) Any annuity contract described in section 403(b);
　　(iv) A simplified employee pension of an employer that satisfies the requirements of section 408(k); and
　　(v) A plan described in section 501(c)(18).
The term includes any plan that at any time has been determined by the Secretary to be one of the types of plans described in this paragraph (b)(3).

(c) *No tax when excess distributed within 2¹/₂ months of close of year or additional employer contributions made.*—(1) *General rule.*—No tax is imposed under this section on any excess contribution or excess aggregate contribution, as the case may be, to the extent the contribution (together with any income allocable thereto) is corrected before the close of the first 2¹/₂ months of the following plan year (6 months in the case of a plan that includes an eligible automatic contribution arrangement within the meaning of section 414(w)). The extension to 6 months applies to a distribution of excess contributions or excess aggregate contributions for a plan year beginning on or after January 1, 2010, only where all the eligible NHCEs and eligible HCEs (both as defined in §1.401(k)-6 of this Chapter) are covered employees under an eligible automatic contribution arrangement within the meaning of section 414(w) for the entire plan year (or the portion of the plan year that the eligible NHCEs and eligible HCEs are eligible employees under the plan)). Qualified nonelective contributions and qualified matching contributions taken into account under §1.401(k)-2(a)(6) of this Chapter or qualified nonelective contributions or elective contributions taken into account under §1.401(m)-2(a)(6) of this Chapter for a plan year may permit a plan to avoid excess contributions or excess aggregate contributions, respectively, even if made after the close of the 2¹/₂ month (or 6 month) period for distributing excess contributions or excess aggregate contributions without the excise tax. See §1.401(k)-2(b)(1)(i) and (5)(i) of this Chapter for methods to avoid excess contributions, and §1.401(m)-2(b)(1)(i) of the Chapter for methods to avoid excess aggregate contributions.

(2) *Tax treatment of distributions.*—See §1.401(k)-2(b)(3)(ii) and (2)(vi) of this Chapter for rules for determining the tax consequences to a participant of a distribution or recharacterization of excess contributions and income allocable thereto, including a special rule for de minimis distributions. See §1.401(m)-2(b)(2)(vi) of this Chapter for rules for determining the tax consequences to a participant of a distribution of excess aggregate contributions and income allocable thereto.

(3) *Income.*—See §1.401(k)-2(b)(2)(iv) of this Chapter for rules for determining income allocable to excess contributions. See §1.401(m)-2(b)(2)(iv) of this Chapter for rules for determining income allocable to excess aggregate contributions.

(4) *Example.*—The provisions of this paragraph (c) are illustrated by the following example.

*Example.* (i) Employer X maintains Plan Y, a calendar year profit-sharing plan that includes a qualified cash or deferred arrangement. Under the plan, failure to satisfy the actual deferral percentage test may only be corrected by distributing the excess contributions or making qualified nonelective contributions (QNECs).

(ii) On December 31, 1990, X determines that Y does not satisfy the actual deferral percentage test for the 1990 plan year, and that excess contributions for the year equal $5,000. On March 1, 1991, Y distributes $2,000 of these excess contributions. On May 30, 1991, X distributes another $2,000 of excess contributions. On December 17, 1991, X contributes QNECs for certain nonhighly compensated employees, thereby eliminating the remainder of the excess contributions for 1990.

(iii) X has incurred a tax liability under section 4979 for 1990 equal to 10 percent of the excess contributions that were in the plan as of December 31, 1990. However, this tax is not imposed on the $2,000 distributed on March 1, 1991, or the amount corrected by QNECs. X must pay an excise tax of $200, 10 percent of the $2,000 of excess contributions distributed after March 15, 1991. This tax must be paid by March 31, 1992.

(d) *Effective date.*—(1) *General rule.*—Except as provided in paragraphs (d)(2) through (4), this section is effective for plan years beginning after December 31, 1986.

(2) *Section 403(b) annuity contracts.*—In the case of an annuity contract under section 403(b), this section applies to plan years beginning after December 31, 1988.

(3) *Collectively bargained plans and plans of state or local governments.*—For plan years beginning before January 1, 1993, the provisions of this section do not apply to a collectively bargained plan that automatically satisfies the requirements of section 410(b). See §§ 1.401(a)(4)-1(c)(5) and 1.410(b)-2(b)(7) of this chapter. In the case of a plan (including a collectively bargained plan) maintained by a state or local government, the provisions of this section do not apply for plan years beginning before the later of January 1, 1996, or 90 days after the opening of the first legislative session beginning on or after January 1, 1996, of the governing body with authority to amend the plan, if that body does not meet continuously. For purposes of this paragraph (d)(3), the term *governing body with authority to amend the plan* means the legislature, board, commission, council, or other governing body with authority to amend the plan.

(4) *Plan years beginning before January 1, 1992.*—For plan years beginning before January 1, 1992, a reasonable interpretation of the rules set forth in section 4979, as in effect during those years, may be relied upon in determining whether the excise tax is due for those years. [Reg. § 54.4979-1.]

☐ [T.D. 8357, 8-8-91. *Amended by T.D.* 8581, 12-22-94; *T.D.* 9169, 12-28-2004 *and T.D.* 9447, 2-23-2009.]

### [Reg. § 54.4980B-0]

**§ 54.4980B-0. Table of contents.**—This section contains first a list of the section headings and then a list of the questions in each section in §§ 54.4980B-1 through 54.4980B-10.

LIST OF QUESTIONS

*§ 54.4980B-1 COBRA in general.*
Q-1: What are the health care continuation coverage requirements contained in section 4980B of the Internal Revenue Code and in ERISA?
Q-2: What standard applies for topics not addressed in §§ 54-4980B-1 through 54.4980B-10?

*§ 54.4980B-2 Plans that must comply.*
Q-1: For purposes of section 4980B, what is a group health plan?
Q-2: For purposes of section 4980B, what is the employer?
Q-3: What is a multiemployer plan?
Q-4: What group health plans are subject to COBRA?
Q-5: What is a small-employer plan?
Q-6: How is the number of group health plans that an employer or employee organization maintains determined?

Q-7: What is the plan year?
Q-8: How do the COBRA continuation coverage requirements apply to cafeteria plans and other flexible benefit arrangements?
Q-9: What is the effect of a group health plan's failure to comply with the requirements of section 4980B(f)?
Q-10: Who is liable for the excise tax if a group health plan fails to comply with the requirements of section 4980B(f)?
Q-11: If a person is liable for the excise tax under section 4980B, what form must the person file and what is the due date for the filing and payment of the excise tax?

*§ 54.4980B-3 Qualified beneficiaries.*
Q-1: Who is a qualified beneficiary?
Q-2: Who is an employee and who is a covered employee?
Q-3: Who are the similarly situated nonCOBRA beneficiaries?

*§ 54.4980B-4 Qualifying events.*
Q-1: What is a qualifying event?
Q-2: Are the facts surrounding a termination of employment (such as whether it was voluntary or involuntary) relevant in determining whether the termination of employment is a qualifying event?

*§ 54.4980B-5 COBRA continuation coverage.*
Q-1: What is COBRA continuation coverage?
Q-2: What deductibles apply if COBRA continuation coverage is elected?
Q-3: How do a plan's limits apply to COBRA continuation coverage?
Q-4: Can a qualified beneficiary who elects COBRA continuation coverage ever change from the coverage received by that individual immediately before the qualifying event?
Q-5: Aside from open enrollment periods, can a qualified beneficiary who has elected COBRA continuation coverage choose to cover individuals (such as newborn children, adopted children, or new spouses) who join the qualified beneficiary's family on or after the date of the qualifying event?

*§ 54.4980B-6 Electing COBRA continuation coverage.*
Q-1: What is the election period and how long must it last?
Q-2: Is a covered employee or qualified beneficiary responsible for informing the plan administrator of the occurrence of a qualifying event?
Q-3: During the election period and before the qualified beneficiary has made a election, must coverage be provided?
Q-4: Is a waiver before the end of the election period effective to end a qualified beneficiary's election rights?
Q-5: Can an employer or employee organization withhold money or other benefits owed to a qualified beneficiary until the qualified beneficiary either waives COBRA continuation coverage, elects and pays for such coverage, or allows the election period to expire?
Q-6: Can each qualified beneficiary make an independent election under COBRA?

*§ 54.4980B-7 Duration of COBRA continuation coverage.*
Q-1: How long must COBRA continuation coverage be made available to a qualified beneficiary?
Q-2: When may a plan terminate a qualified beneficiary's COBRA continuation coverage due to coverage under another group health plan?
Q-3: When may a plan terminate a qualified beneficiary's COBRA continuation coverage due to the qualified beneficiary's entitlement to Medicare benefits?
Q-4: When does the maximum coverage period end?
Q-5: How does a qualified beneficiary become entitled to a disability extension?
Q-6: Under what circumstances can the maximum coverage period be expanded?
Q-7: If health coverage is provided to a qualified beneficiary after a qualifying event without regard to COBRA continuation coverage (for example, as a result of state or local law, the Uniformed Services Employment and Reemployment Rights Act of 1994 (38 U.S.C. 4315), industry practice, a collective bargaining agreement, severance agreement, or plan procedure), will such alternative coverage extend the maximum coverage period?
Q-8: Must a qualified beneficiary be given the right to enroll in a conversion health plan at the end of the maximum coverage period for COBRA continuation coverage?

*§ 54.4980B-8 Paying for COBRA continuation coverage.*
Q-1: Can a group health plan require payment for COBRA continuation coverage?
Q-2: When is the applicable premium determined and when can a group health plan increase the amount it requires to be paid for COBRA continuation coverage?

Q-3: Must a plan allow payment for COBRA continuation coverage to be made in monthly installments?

Q-4: Is a plan required to allow a qualified beneficiary to choose to have the first payment for COBRA continuation coverage applied prospectively only?

Q-5: What is timely payment for COBRA continuation coverage?

*§ 54.4980B-9 Business reorganizations and employer withdrawals from multiemployer plans.*

Q-1: For purposes of this section, what are a business reorganization, a stock sale, and an asset sale?

Q-2: In the case of a stock sale, what are the selling group, the acquired organization, and the buying group?

Q-3: In the case of an asset sale, what are the selling group and the buying group?

Q-4: Who is an M & A qualified beneficiary?

Q-5: In the case of a stock sale, is the sale a qualifying event with respect to a covered employee who is employed by the acquired organization before the sale and who continues to be employed by the acquired organization after the sale, or with respect to the spouse or dependent children of such a covered employee?

Q-6: In the case of an asset sale, is the sale a qualifying event with respect to a covered employee whose employment immediately before the sale was associated with the purchased assets, or with respect to the spouse or dependent children of such a covered employee who are covered under a group health plan of the selling group immediately before the sale?

Q-7: In a business reorganization, are the buying group and the selling group permitted to allocate by contract the responsibility to make COBRA continuation coverage available to M & A qualified beneficiaries?

Q-8: Which group health plan has the obligation to make COBRA continuation coverage available to M & A qualified beneficiaries in a business reorganization?

Q-9: Can the cessation of contributions by an employer to a multiemployer group health plan be a qualifying event?

Q-10: If an employer stops contributing to a multiemployer group health plan, does the multiemployer plan have the obligation to make COBRA continuation coverage available to a qualified beneficiary who was receiving coverage under the multiemployer plan on the day before the cessation of contributions and who is, or whose qualifying event occurred in connection with, a covered employee whose last employment prior to the qualifying event was with the employer that has stopped contributing to the multiemployer plan?

*§ 54.4980B-10 Interaction of FMLA and COBRA.*

Q-1: In what circumstances does a qualifying event occur if an employee does not return from leave taken under FMLA?

Q-2: If a qualifying event described in Q & A-1 of this section occurs; when does it occur, and how is the maximum coverage period measured?

Q-3: If an employee fails to pay the employee portion of premiums for coverage under a group health plan during FMLA leave or declines coverage under a group health plan during FMLA leave, does this affect the determination of whether or when the employee has experienced a qualifying event?

Q-4: Is the application of the rules in Q & A-1 through Q & A-3 of this section affected by a requirement of state or local law to provide a period of coverage longer than that required under FMLA?

Q-5: May COBRA continuation coverage be conditioned upon reimbursement of the premiums paid by the employer for coverage under a group health plan during FMLA leave?

[Reg. § 54.4980B-0.]

☐ [*T.D.* 8812, 2-2-99. *Amended by T.D.* 8928, 1-9-2001 *and T.D.* 9457, 9-4-2009.]

**[Reg. § 54.4980B-1]**

**§ 54.4980B-1. COBRA in general.**—The COBRA continuation coverage requirements are described in general in the following questions-and-answers:

Q-1: What are the health care continuation coverage requirements contained in section 4980B of the Internal Revenue Code and in ERISA?

A-1: (a) Section 4980B provides generally that a group health plan must offer each qualified beneficiary who would otherwise lose coverage under the plan as a result of a qualifying event an opportunity to elect, within the election period, continuation coverage under the plan. The continuation coverage requirements were added to section 162 by the Consolidated Omnibus Budget Reconciliation Act of 1985 (COBRA), Public Law 99-272 (100 Stat. 222), and moved to section 4980B by the Technical and Miscellaneous Revenue Act of 1988, Public Law 100-647 (102 Stat. 3342). Continuation coverage required under section 4980B is referred to in §§ 54.4980B-1 through 54.4980B-10 as COBRA continuation coverage.

(b) COBRA also added parallel continuation coverage requirements to Part 6 of Subtitle B of Title I of the Employee Retirement Income Security Act of 1974 (ERISA) (29 U.S.C. 1161-1168), which is administered by the U.S. Department of Labor. If a plan does not comply with the COBRA continuation coverage requirements, the Internal Revenue Code imposes an excise tax on the employer maintaining the plan (or on the plan itself), whereas ERISA gives certain parties—including qualified beneficiaries who are participants or beneficiaries within the meaning of Title I of ERISA, as well as the Department of Labor—the right to file a lawsuit to redress the noncompliance. The rules in §§ 54.4980B-1 through 54.4980B-10 apply for purposes of section 4980B and generally also for purposes of the COBRA continuation coverage requirements in Title I of ERISA. However, certain provisions of the COBRA continuation coverage requirements (such as the definitions of group health plan, employee, and employer) are not identical in the Internal Revenue Code and Title I of ERISA. In those cases in which the statutory language is not identical, the rules in §§ 54.4980B-1 through 54.4980B-10 nonetheless apply to the COBRA continuation coverage requirements of Title I of ERISA, except to the extent those rules are inconsistent with the statutory language of Title I of ERISA.

(c) A group health plan that is subject to section 4980B (or the parallel provisions under ERISA) is referred to as being subject to COBRA. (See Q&A-4 of § 54.4980B-2.) A qualified beneficiary can be required to pay for COBRA continuation coverage. The term *qualified beneficiary* is defined in Q&A-1 of § 54.4980B-3. The term *qualifying event* is defined in Q&A-1 of § 54.4980B-4. COBRA continuation coverage is described in § 54.4980B-5. The election procedures are described in § 54.4980B-6. Duration of COBRA continuation coverage is addressed in § 54.4980B-7, and payment for COBRA continuation coverage is addressed in § 54.4980B-8. Section 54.4980B-9 contains special rules for how COBRA applies in connection with business reorganizations and employer withdrawals from a multiemployer plan, and § 54.4980B-10 addresses how COBRA applies for individuals who take leave under the Family and Medical Leave Act of 1993. Unless the context indicates otherwise, any reference in §§ 54.4980B-1 through § 54.4980B-10 to COBRA refers to section 4980B (as amended) and to the parallel provisions of ERISA.

Q-2: What standard applies for topics not addressed in §§ 54.4980B-1 through 54.4980B-10?

A-2: For purposes of section 4980B, for topics relating to the COBRA continuation coverage requirements of section 4980B that are not addressed in §§ 54.4980B-1 through 54.4980B-10 (such as methods for calculating the applicable premium), plans and employers must operate in good faith compliance with a reasonable interpretation of the statutory requirements in section 4980B.

[Reg. § 54.4980B-1.]

☐ [*T.D.* 8812, 2-2-99 (corrected 3-24-99). *Amended by T.D.* 8928, 1-9-2001.]

**[Reg. § 54.4980B-2]**

**§ 54.4980B-2. Plans that must comply.**—The following questions-and-answers apply in determining which plans must comply with the COBRA continuation coverage requirements:

Q-1: For purposes of section 4980B, what is a group health plan?

A-1: (a) For purposes of section 4980B, a group health plan is a plan maintained by an employer or employee organization to provide health care to individuals who have an employment-related connection to the employer or employee organization or to their families. Individuals who have an employment-related connection to the employer or employee organization consist of employees, former employees, the employer, and others associated or formerly associated with the employer or employee organization in a business relationship (including members of a union who are not currently employees). Health care is provided under a plan whether provided directly or through insurance, reimbursement, or otherwise, and whether or not provided through an on-site facility (except as set forth in paragraph (d) of this Q & A-1), or through a cafeteria plan (as defined in section 125) or other flexible benefit arrangement. (See paragraphs (b) through (e) in Q & A-8 of this section for rules regarding the application of the COBRA continuation coverage requirements to certain health flexible spending arrangements.) For purposes of this Q & A-1, insurance includes not only group insurance policies but also one or more individual insurance policies in any arrangement that involves the provision of health care to two or more employees. A plan maintained by an employer or employee organization is any plan of, or contributed to (directly or indirectly) by, an employer or employee organization. Thus, a group health plan is maintained by an employer or employee organization even if the employer or employee organization does not contribute to it if coverage under the plan would not be available at the same cost to an individual but for the individual's employment-related connection to the employer or employee organization. These rules are further explained in paragraphs (b) through (d) of this Q & A-1. An exception for qualified long-term care services is set forth in paragraph (e) of this Q & A-1, and for medical savings accounts in paragraph (f) of this Q & A-1. See Q & A-6 of this section for rules to determine the number of group health plans that an employer or employee organization maintains.

(b) For purposes of §§ 54.4980B-1 through 54.4980B-10, *health care* has the same meaning as *medical care* under section 213(d). Thus, health care generally includes the diagnosis, cure, mitigation, treatment, or prevention of disease, and any other undertaking for the purpose of affecting any structure or function of the body. Health care also includes transportation primarily for and essential to health care as described in the preceding sentence. However, health care does not include anything that is merely beneficial to the general health of an individual, such as a vacation. Thus, if an employer or employee organization maintains a program that furthers general good health, but the program does not relate to the relief or alleviation of health or medical problems and is generally accessible to and used by employees without regard to their physical condition or state of health, that program is not considered a program that provides health care and so is not a group health plan. For example, if an employer maintains a spa, swimming pool, gymnasium, or other exercise/fitness program or facility that is normally accessible to and used by employees for reasons other than relief of health or medical problems, such a facility does not constitute a program that provides health care and thus is not a group health plan. In contrast, if an employer maintains a drug or alcohol treatment program or a health clinic, or any other facility or program that is intended to relieve or alleviate a physical condition or health problem, the facility or program is considered to be the provision of health care and so is considered a group health plan.

(c) Whether a benefit provided to employees constitutes health care is not affected by whether the benefit is excludable from income under section 132 (relating to certain fringe benefits). For example, if a department store provides its employees discounted prices on all merchandise, including health care items such as drugs or eyeglasses, the mere fact that the discounted prices also apply to health care items will not cause the program to be a plan providing health care, so long as the discount program would normally be accessible to and used by employees without regard to health needs or physical condition. If, however, the employer maintaining the discount program is a health clinic, so that the program is used exclusively by employees with health or medical needs, the program is considered to be a plan providing health care and so is considered to be a group health plan.

(d) The provision of health care at a facility that is located on the premises of an employer or employee organization does not constitute a group health plan if—

(1) The health care consists primarily of first aid that is provided during the employer's working hours for treatment of a health condition, illness, or injury that occurs during those working hours;

(2) The health care is available only to current employees; and

(3) Employees are not charged for the use of the facility.

(e) A plan does not constitute a group health plan subject to COBRA if substantially all of the coverage provided under the plan is for qualified long-term care services (as defined in section 7702B(c)). For this purpose, a plan is permitted to use any reasonable method in determining whether substantially all of the coverage provided under the plan is for qualified long-term care services.

(f) Under section 106(b)(5), amounts contributed by an employer to a medical savings account (as defined in section 220(d)) are not considered part of a group health plan subject to COBRA. Thus, a plan is not required to make COBRA continuation coverage available with respect to amounts contributed by an employer to a medical savings account. A high deductible health plan does not fail to be a group health plan subject to COBRA merely because it covers a medical savings account holder.

Q-2: For purposes of section 4980B, what is the employer?

A-2: (a) For purposes of section 4980B, employer refers to—

(1) A person for whom services are performed;

(2) Any other person that is a member of a group described in section 414(b), (c), (m), or (o) that includes a person described in paragraph (a)(1) of this Q & A-2; and

(3) Any successor of a person described in paragraph (a)(1) or (2) of this Q & A-2.

(b) An employer is a successor employer if it results from a consolidation, merger, or similar restructuring of the employer or if it is a mere continuation of the employer. See paragraph (c) in Q & A-8 of § 54.4980B-9 for rules describing the circumstances in which a purchaser of substantial assets is a successor employer to the employer selling the assets.

Q-3: What is a multiemployer plan?

A-3: For purposes of §§ 54.4980B-1 through 54.4980B-10, a multiemployer plan is a plan to which more than one employer is required to contribute, that is maintained pursuant to one or more collective bargaining agreements between one or more employee

organizations and more than one employer, and that satisfies such other requirements as the Secretary of Labor may prescribe by regulation. Whenever reference is made in §§ 54.4980B-1 through 54.4980B-10 to a plan of or maintained by an employer or employee organization, the reference includes a multiemployer plan.

Q-4: What group health plans are subject to COBRA?

A-4: (a) All group health plans are subject to COBRA except group health plans described in paragraph (b) of this Q&A-4. Group health plans described in paragraph (b) of this Q&A-4 are referred to in §§ 54.4980B-1 through 54.4980B-10 as excepted from COBRA.

(b) The following group health plans are excepted from COBRA—

(1) Small-employer plans (see Q&A-5 of this section);

(2) Church plans (within the meaning of section 414(e)); and

(3) Governmental plans (within the meaning of section 414(d)).

(c) The COBRA continuation coverage requirements generally do not apply to group health plans that are excepted from COBRA. However, a small-employer plan otherwise excepted from COBRA is nonetheless subject to COBRA with respect to qualified beneficiaries who experience a qualifying event during a period when the plan is not a small-employer plan (see paragraph (g) of Q&A-5 of this section).

(d) Although governmental plans are not subject to the COBRA continuation coverage requirements, group health plans maintained by state or local governments are generally subject to parallel continuation coverage requirements that were added by section 10003 of COBRA to the Public Health Service Act (42 U.S.C. 300bb-1 through 300bb-8), which is administered by the U.S. Department of Health and Human Services. Federal employees and their family members covered under the Federal Employees Health Benefit Program are covered by generally similar, but not parallel, temporary continuation of coverage provisions enacted by the Federal Employees Health Benefits Amendments Act of 1988. See 5 U.S.C. 8905a.

Q-5: What is a small-employer plan?

A-5: (a) Except in the case of a multiemployer plan, a *small-employer plan* is a group health plan maintained by an employer (within the meaning of Q&A-2 of this section) that normally employed fewer than 20 employees (within the meaning of paragraph (c) of this Q&A-5) during the preceding calendar year. In the case of a multiemployer plan, a *small-employer plan* is a group health plan under which each of the employers contributing to the plan for a calendar year normally employed fewer than 20 employees during the preceding calendar year. See Q & A-6 of this section for rules to determine the number of plans that an employer or employee organization maintains. The rules of this paragraph (a) are illustrated in the following example:

*Example.* (i) Corporation S employs 12 employees, all of whom work and reside in the United States. S maintains a group health plan for its employees and their families. S is a wholly-owned subsidiary of P. In the previous calendar year, the controlled group of corporations including P and S employed more than 19 employees, although the only employees in the United States of the controlled group that includes P and S are the 12 employees of S.

(ii) Under § 1.414(b)-1 of this chapter, foreign corporations are not excluded from membership in a controlled group of corporations. Consequently, the group health plan maintained by S is not a small-employer plan during the current calendar year because the controlled group including S normally employed at least 20 employees in the preceding calendar year.

(b) An employer is considered to have normally employed fewer than 20 employees during a particular calendar year if, and only if, it had fewer than 20 employees on at least 50 percent of its typical business days during that year.

(c) All full-time and part-time common law employees of an employer are taken into account in determining whether an employer had fewer than 20 employees; however, an individual who is not a common law employee of the employer is not taken into account. Thus, the following individuals are not counted as employees for purposes of this Q&A-5 even though they are referred to as employees for all other purposes of §§ 54.4980B-1 through 54.4980B-10—

(1) Self-employed individuals (within the meaning of section 401(c)(1));

(2) Independent contractors (and their employees and independent contractors); and

(3) Directors (in the case of a corporation).

(d) In determining the number of the employees of an employer, each full-time employee is counted as one employee and each part-time employee is counted as a fraction of an employee, determined in accordance with paragraph (e) of this Q & A-5.

(e) An employer may determine the number of its employees on a daily basis or a pay period basis. The basis used by the employer must be used with respect to all employees of the employer and must be used for the entire year for which the number of employees is being determined. If an employer determines the number of its employees on a daily basis, it must determine the actual number of full-time employees on each typical business day and the actual number of part-time employees and the hours worked by each of those part-time employees on each typical business day. Each full-time employee counts as one employee on each typical business day and each part-time employee counts as a fraction, with the numerator of the fraction equal to the number of hours worked by that employee and the denominator equal to the number of hours that must be worked on a typical business day in order to be considered a full-time employee. If an employer determines the number of its employees on a pay period basis, it must determine the actual number of full-time employees employed during that pay period and the actual number of part-time employees employed and the hours worked by each of those part-time employees during the pay period. For each day of that pay period, each full-time employee counts as one employee and each part-time employee counts as a fraction, with the numerator of the fraction equal to the number of hours worked by that employee during that pay period and the denominator equal to the number of hours that must be worked during that pay period in order to be considered a full-time employee. The determination of the number of hours required to be considered a full-time employee is based upon the employer's employment practices, except that in no event may the hours required to be considered a full-time employee exceed eight hours for any day or 40 hours for any week.

(f) In the case of a multiemployer plan, the determination of whether the plan is a small-employer plan on any particular date depends on which employers are contributing to the plan on that date and on the workforce of those employers during the preceding calendar year. If a plan that is otherwise subject to COBRA ceases to be a small-employer plan because of the addition during a calendar year of an employer that did not normally employ fewer than 20 employees on a typical business day during the preceding calendar year, the plan ceases to be excepted from COBRA immediately upon the addition of the new employer. In contrast, if the plan ceases to be a small-employer plan by reason of an increase during a calendar year in the workforce of an employer contributing to the plan, the plan ceases to be excepted from COBRA on the January 1 immediately following the calendar year in which the employer's workforce increased.

(g) A small-employer plan is generally excepted from COBRA. If, however, a plan that has been subject to COBRA (that is, was not a small-employer plan) becomes a small-employer plan, the plan remains subject to COBRA for qualifying events that occurred during the period when the plan was subject to COBRA. The rules of this paragraph (g) are illustrated by the following examples:

*Example 1.* An employer maintains a group health plan. The employer employed 20 employees on more than 50 percent of its working days during 2001, and consequently the plan is not excepted from COBRA during 2002. Employee *E* resigns and does not work for the employer after January 31, 2002. Under the terms of the plan, *E* is no longer eligible for coverage upon the effective date of the resignation, that is, February 1, 2002. The employer does not hire a replacement for *E*. *E* timely elects and pays for COBRA continuation coverage. The employer employs 19 employees for the remainder of 2002, and consequently the plan is not subject to COBRA in 2003. The plan must nevertheless continue to make COBRA continuation coverage available to *E* during 2003 until the obligation to make COBRA continuation coverage available ceases under the rules of § 54.4980B-7. The obligation could continue until August 1, 2003, the date that is 18 months after the date of *E*'s qualifying event, or longer if *E* is eligible for a disability extension.

*Example 2.* The facts are the same as in *Example 1*. The employer continues to employ 19 employees throughout 2003 and 2004 and consequently the plan continues to be excepted from COBRA during 2004 and 2005. Spouse *S* is covered under the plan because *S* is married to one of the employer's employees. On April 1, 2002, *S* is divorced from that employee and ceases to be eligible for coverage under the plan. The plan is subject to COBRA during 2002 because *X* normally employed 20 employees during 2001. *S* timely notifies the plan administrator of the divorce and timely elects and pays for COBRA continuation coverage. Even though the plan is generally excepted from COBRA during 2003, 2004, and 2005, it must nevertheless continue to make COBRA continuation coverage available to *S* during those years until the obligation to make COBRA continuation coverage available ceases under the rules of § 54.4980B-7. The obligation could continue until April 1, 2005, the date that is 36 months after the date of *S*'s qualifying event.

*Example 3.* The facts are the same as in *Example 2*. *C* is a dependent child of one of the employer's employees and is covered under the plan. A dependent child is no longer eligible for coverage under the plan upon the attainment of age 23. *C* attains age 23 on November 16, 2005. The plan is excepted from COBRA with respect to *C* during 2005 because the employer normally employed fewer than 20 employees during 2004. Consequently, the plan is not obligated to make COBRA continuation coverage available to *C* (and would not be

obligated to make COBRA continuation coverage available to *C* even if the plan later became subject to COBRA again).

Q-6: How is the number of group health plans that an employer or employee organization maintains determined?

A-6: (a) The rules of this Q & A-6 apply in determining the number of group health plans that an employer or employee organization maintains. All references elsewhere in § § 54.4980B-1 through 54.4980B-10 to a group health plan are references to a group health plan as determined under Q & A-1 of this section and this Q & A-6. Except as provided in paragraph (b) or (c) of this Q & A-6, all health care benefits, other than benefits for qualified long-term care services (as defined in section 7702B(c)), provided by a corporation, partnership, or other entity or trade or business, or by an employee organization, constitute one group health plan, unless—

(1) It is clear from the instruments governing an arrangement or arrangements to provide health care benefits that the benefits are being provided under separate plans; and

(2) The arrangement or arrangements are operated pursuant to such instruments as separate plans.

(b) A multiemployer plan and a nonmultiemployer plan are always separate plans.

(c) If a principal purpose of establishing separate plans is to evade any requirement of law, then the separate plans will be considered a single plan to the extent necessary to prevent the evasion.

(d) The significance of treating an arrangement as two or more separate group health plans is illustrated by the following examples:

*Example 1.* (i) Employer *X* maintains a single group health plan, which provides major medical and prescription drug benefits. Employer *Y* maintains two group health plans; one provides major medical benefits and the other provides prescription drug benefits.

(ii) *X*'s plan could comply with the COBRA continuation coverage requirements by giving a qualified beneficiary experiencing a qualifying event with respect to *X*'s plan the choice of either electing both major medical and prescription drug benefits or not receiving any COBRA continuation coverage under *X*'s plan. By contrast, for *Y*'s plans to comply with the COBRA continuation coverage requirements, a qualified beneficiary experiencing a qualifying event with respect to each of *Y*'s plans must be given the choice of electing COBRA continuation coverage under either the major medical plan or the prescription drug plan or both.

*Example 2.* If a joint board of trustees administers one multiemployer plan, that plan will fail to qualify for the small-employer plan exception if any one of the employers whose employees are covered under the plan normally employed 20 or more employees during the preceding calendar year. However, if the joint board of trustees maintains two or more multiemployer plans, then the exception would be available with respect to each of those plans in which each of the employers whose employees are covered under the plan normally employed fewer than 20 employees during the preceding calendar year.

Q-7: What is the plan year?

A-7: (a) The *plan year* is the year that is designated as the plan year in the plan documents.

(b) If the plan documents do not designate a plan year (or if there are no plan documents), then the plan year is determined in accordance with this paragraph (b).

(1) The plan year is the deductible/limit year used under the plan.

(2) If the plan does not impose deductibles or limits on an annual basis, then the plan year is the policy year.

(3) If the plan does not impose deductibles or limits on an annual basis, and either the plan is not insured or the insurance policy is not renewed on an annual basis, then the plan year is the employer's taxable year.

(4) In any other case, the plan year is the calendar year.

Q-8: How do the COBRA continuation coverage requirements apply to cafeteria plans and other flexible benefit arrangements?

A-8: (a)(1) The provision of health care benefits does not fail to be a group health plan merely because those benefits are offered under a cafeteria plan (as defined in section 125) or under any other arrangement under which an employee is offered a choice between health care benefits and other taxable or nontaxable benefits. However, the COBRA continuation coverage requirements apply only to the type and level of coverage under the cafeteria plan or other flexible benefit arrangement that a qualified beneficiary is actually receiving on the day before the qualifying event. See paragraphs (b) through (e) of this Q & A-8 for rules limiting the obligations of certain health flexible spending arrangements.

(2) The rules of this paragraph (a) are illustrated by the following example:

*Example*: (i) Under the terms of a cafeteria plan, employees can choose among life insurance coverage, membership in a health maintenance organization (HMO), coverage for medical expenses under an indemnity arrangement, and cash compensation. Of these available choices, the HMO and the indemnity arrangement are the arrangements providing health care. The instruments governing the HMO and indemnity arrangements indicate that they are separate group health plans. These group health plans are subject to COBRA. The employer does not provide any group health plan outside of the cafeteria plan. *B* and *C* are unmarried employees. *B* has chosen the life insurance coverage, and *C* has chosen the indemnity arrangement.

(ii) *B* does not have to be offered COBRA continuation coverage upon terminating employment, nor is a subsequent open enrollment period for active employees required to be made available to *B*. However, if *C* terminates employment and the termination constitutes a qualifying event, *C* must be offered an opportunity to elect COBRA continuation coverage under the indemnity arrangement. If *C* makes such an election and an open enrollment period for active employees occurs while *C* is still receiving the COBRA continuation coverage, *C* must be offered the opportunity to switch from the indemnity arrangement to the HMO (but not to the life insurance coverage because that does not constitute coverage provided under a group health plan).

(b) If a health flexible spending arrangement (health FSA), within the meaning of section 106(c)(2), satisfies the two conditions in paragraph (c) of this Q & A-8 for a plan year, the obligation of the health FSA to make COBRA continuation coverage available to a qualified beneficiary who experiences a qualifying event in that plan year is limited in accordance with paragraphs (d) and (e) of this Q & A-8, as illustrated by an example in paragraph (f) of this Q & A-8. To the extent that a health FSA is obligated to make COBRA continuation coverage available to a qualified beneficiary, the health FSA must comply with all the applicable rules of §§ 54.4980B-1 through 54.4980B-10, including the rules of Q & A-3 in § 54.498OB-5 (relating to limits).

(c) The conditions of this paragraph (c) are satisfied if—

(1) Benefits provided under the health FSA are excepted benefits within the meaning of sections 9831 and 9832; and

(2) The maximum amount that the health FSA can require to be paid for a year of COBRA continuation coverage under Q & A-1 of § 54.4980B-8 equals or exceeds the maximum benefit available under the health FSA for the year.

(d) If the conditions in paragraph (c) of this Q & A-8 are satisfied for a plan year, then the health FSA is not obligated to make COBRA continuation coverage available for any subsequent plan year to any qualified beneficiary who experiences a qualifying event during that plan year.

(e) If the conditions in paragraph (c) of this Q & A-8 are satisfied for a plan year, the health FSA is not obligated to make COBRA continuation coverage available for that plan year to any qualified beneficiary who experiences a qualifying event during that plan year unless, as of the date of the qualifying event, the qualified beneficiary can become entitled to receive during the remainder of the plan year a benefit that exceeds the maximum amount that the health FSA is permitted to require to be paid for COBRA continuation coverage for the remainder of the plan year. In determining the amount of the benefit that a qualified beneficiary can become entitled to receive during the remainder of the plan year, the health FSA may deduct from the maximum benefit available to that qualified beneficiary for the year (based on the election made under the health FSA for that qualified beneficiary before the date of the qualifying event) any reimbursable claims submitted to the health FSA for that plan year before the date of the qualifying event.

(f) The rules of paragraphs (b), (c), (d), and (e) of this Q & A-8 are illustrated by the following example:

*Example.* (i) An employer maintains a group health plan providing major medical benefits and a group health plan that is a health FSA, and the plan year for each plan is the calendar year. Both the plan providing major medical benefits and the health FSA are subject to COBRA. Under the health FSA, during an open season before the beginning of each calendar year, employees can elect to reduce their compensation during the upcoming year by up to $1200 per year and have that same amount contributed to a health flexible spending account. The employer contributes an additional amount to the account equal to the employee's salary reduction election for the year. Thus, the maximum amount available to an employee under the health FSA for a year is two times the amount of the employee's salary reduction election for the year. This amount may be paid to the employee during the year as reimbursement for health expenses not covered by the employer's major medical plan (such as deductibles, copayments, prescription drugs, or eyeglasses). The employer determined, in accordance with section 4980B(f)(4), that a reasonable estimate of the cost of providing coverage for similarly situated nonCOBRA beneficiaries for 2002 under this health FSA is equal to two times their salary reduction election for 2002 and, thus, that two times the salary reduction election is the applicable premium for 2002.

(ii) Because the employer provides major medical benefits under another group health plan, and because the maximum benefit that any employee can receive under the health FSA is not greater than two times the employee's salary reduction election for the plan year, benefits under this health FSA are excepted benefits within the meaning of sections 9831 and 9832. Thus, the first condition of paragraph (c) of this Q & A-8 is satisfied for the year. The maximum amount that a plan can require to be paid for coverage (outside of coverage required to be made available due to a disability extension) under Q & A-1 of § 54.4980B-8 is 102 percent of the applicable premium. Thus, the maximum amount that the health FSA can require to be paid for coverage for the 2002 plan year is 2.04 times the employee's salary reduction election for the plan year. Because the maximum benefit available under the health FSA is 2.0 times the employee's salary reduction election for the year, the maximum benefit available under the health FSA for the year is less than the maximum amount that the health FSA can require to be paid for coverage for the year. Thus, the second condition in paragraph (c) of this Q & A-8 is also satisfied for the 2002 plan year. Because both conditions in paragraph (c) of this Q & A-8 are satisfied for 2002, with respect to any qualifying event occurring in 2002, the health FSA is not obligated to make COBRA continuation coverage available for any year after 2002.

(iii) Whether the health FSA is obligated to make COBRA continuation coverage available in 2002 to a qualified beneficiary with respect to a qualifying event that occurs in 2002 depends upon the maximum benefit that would be available to the qualified beneficiary under COBRA continuation coverage for that plan year. *Case 1*: Employee *B* has elected to reduce *B*'s salary by $1200 for 2002. Thus, the maximum benefit that *B* can become entitled to receive under the health FSA during the entire year is $2400. *B* experiences a qualifying event that is the termination of *B*'s employment on May 31, 2002. As of that date, *B* had submitted $300 of reimbursable expenses under the health FSA. Thus, the maximum benefit that *B* could become entitled to receive for the remainder of 2002 is $2100. The maximum amount that the health FSA can require to be paid for COBRA continuation coverage for the remainder of 2002 is 102 percent times 1/12 of the applicable premium for 2002 times the number of months remaining in 2002 after the date of the qualifying event. In *B*'s case, the maximum amount that the health FSA can require to be paid for COBRA continuation coverage for 2002 is 2.04 times $1200, or $2448. One-twelfth of $2448 is $204. Because seven months remain in the plan year, the maximum amount that the health FSA can require to be paid for *B*'s coverage for the remainder of the year is seven times $204, or $1428. Because $1428 is less than the maximum benefit that *B* could become entitled to receive for the remainder of the year ($2100), the health FSA is required to make COBRA continuation coverage available to *B* for the remainder of 2002 (but not for any subsequent year).

(iv) *Case 2*: The facts are the same as in *Case 1* except that *B* had submitted $1000 of reimbursable expenses as of the date of the qualifying event. In that case, the maximum benefit available to *B* for the remainder of the year would be $1400 instead of $2100. Because the maximum amount that the health FSA can require to be paid for *B*'s coverage is $1428, and because the $1400 maximum benefit for the remainder of the year does not exceed $1428, the health FSA is not obligated to make COBRA continuation coverage available to *B* in 2002 (or any later year). (Of course, the administrator of the health FSA is permitted to make COBRA continuation coverage available to every qualified beneficiary in the year that the qualified beneficiary's qualifying event occurs in order to avoid having to determine the maximum benefit available for each qualified beneficiary for the remainder of the plan year.)

Q-9: What is the effect of a group health plan's failure to comply with the requirements of section 4980B(f)?

A-9: Under section 4980B(a), if a group health plan subject to COBRA fails to comply with section 4980B(f), an excise tax is imposed. Moreover, non-tax remedies may be available if the plan fails to comply with the parallel requirements in ERISA, which are administered by the Department of Labor.

Q-10: Who is liable for the excise tax if a group health plan fails to comply with the requirements of section 4980B(f)?

A-10: (a) In general, the excise tax is imposed on the employer maintaining the plan, except that in the case of a multiemployer plan (see Q & A-3 of this section for a definition of multiemployer plan) the excise tax is imposed on the plan.

(b) In certain circumstances, the excise tax is also imposed on a person involved with the provision of benefits under the plan (other than in the capacity of an employee), such as an insurer providing benefits under the plan or a third party administrator administering claims under the plan. In general, such a person will be liable for the excise tax if the person assumes, under a legally enforceable written agreement, the responsibility for performing the act to which the failure to comply with the COBRA continuation coverage requirements relates. Such a person will be liable for the excise tax notwithstanding the absence of a written agreement assuming responsibility for complying with COBRA if the person provides coverage under the plan to a similarly situated nonCOBRA beneficiary (see Q&A-3 of §54.4980B-3 for a definition of similarly situated nonCOBRA beneficiaries) and the employer or plan administrator submits a written request to the person to provide to a qualified beneficiary the same coverage that the person provides to the similarly situated nonCOBRA beneficiary. If the person providing coverage under the plan to a similarly situated nonCOBRA beneficiary is the plan administrator and the qualifying event is a divorce or legal separation or a dependent child's ceasing to be covered under the generally applicable requirements of the plan, the plan administrator will also be liable for the excise tax if the qualified beneficiary submits a written request for coverage.

Q-11: If a person is liable for the excise tax under section 4980B, what form must the person file and what is the due date for the filing and payment of the excise tax?

A-11: (a) *In general.* See §§54.6011-2 and 54.6151-1.

(b) *Due date for filing of return by employers or other persons responsible for benefits under a group health plan.* See §54.6071-1(a)(1).

(c) *Due date for filing of return by multiemployer plans.* See §54.6071-1(a)(2).

(d) *Effective/applicability date.* In the case of an employer or other person mentioned in paragraph (b) of this Q & A-11, the rules in this Q & A-11 are effective for taxable years beginning on or after January 1, 2010. In the case of a plan mentioned in paragraph (c) of this Q & A-11, the rules in this Q & A-11 are effective for plan years beginning on or after January 1, 2010.

[Reg. §54.4980B-2.]

☐ [*T.D. 8812, 2-2-99. Amended by T.D. 8928, 1-9-2001 and T.D. 9457, 9-4-2009.*]

## [Reg. §54.4980B-3]

**§54.4980B-3. Qualified beneficiaries.**—The determination of who is a qualified beneficiary, an employee, or a covered employee, and of who are the similarly situated nonCOBRA beneficiaries is addressed in the following questions-and-answers:

Q-1: Who is a qualified beneficiary?

A-1: (a)(1) Except as set forth in paragraphs (c) through (f) of this Q&A-1, a qualified beneficiary is—

(i) Any individual who, on the day before a qualifying event, is covered under a group health plan by virtue of being on that day either a covered employee, the spouse of a covered employee, or a dependent child of the covered employee; or

(ii) Any child who is born to or placed for adoption with a covered employee during a period of COBRA continuation coverage.

(2) In the case of a qualifying event that is the bankruptcy of the employer, a covered employee who had retired on or before the date of substantial elimination of group health plan coverage is also a qualified beneficiary, as is any spouse, surviving spouse, or dependent child of such a covered employee if, on the day before the bankruptcy qualifying event, the spouse, surviving spouse, or dependent child is a beneficiary under the plan.

(3) In general, an individual (other than a child who is born to or placed for adoption with a covered employee during a period of COBRA continuation coverage) who is not covered under a plan on the day before the qualifying event cannot be a qualified beneficiary with respect to that qualifying event, and the reason for the individual's lack of actual coverage (such as the individual's having declined participation in the plan or failed to satisfy the plan's conditions for participation) is not relevant for this purpose. However, if the individual is denied or not offered coverage under a plan under circumstances in which the denial or failure to offer constitutes a violation of applicable law (such as the Americans with Disabilities Act, 42 U.S.C. 12101-12213, the special enrollment rules of section 9801, or the requirements of section 9802 prohibiting discrimination in eligibility to enroll in a group health plan based on health status), then, for purposes of §§54.4980B-1 through 54.4980B-10, the individual will be considered to have had the coverage that was wrongfully denied or not offered.

(4) Paragraph (b) of this Q&A-1 describes how certain family members are not qualified beneficiaries even if they become covered under the plan; paragraphs (c), (d), and (e) of this Q&A-1 place limits on the general rules of this paragraph (a) concerning who is a qualified beneficiary; paragraph (f) of this Q&A-1 provides when an individual who has been a qualified beneficiary ceases to be a qualified beneficiary; paragraph (g) of this Q&A-1 defines *placed for adoption*; and paragraph (h) of this Q&A-1 contains examples.

(b) In contrast to a child who is born to or placed for adoption with a covered employee during a period of COBRA continuation coverage, an individual who marries any qualified beneficiary on or after the date of the qualifying event and a newborn or adopted child

(other than one born to or placed for adoption with a covered employee) are not qualified beneficiaries by virtue of the marriage, birth, or placement for adoption or by virtue of the individual's status as the spouse or the child's status as a dependent of the qualified beneficiary. These new family members do not themselves become qualified beneficiaries even if they become covered under the plan. (For situations in which a plan is required to make coverage available to new family members of a qualified beneficiary who is receiving COBRA continuation coverage, see Q&A-5 of §54.4980B-5, paragraph (c) in Q&A-4 of §54.4980B-5, and section 9801(f)(2).)

(c) An individual is not a qualified beneficiary if, on the day before the qualifying event referred to in paragraph (a) of this Q&A-1, the individual is covered under the group health plan by reason of another individual's election of COBRA continuation coverage and is not already a qualified beneficiary by reason of a prior qualifying event.

(d) A covered employee can be a qualified beneficiary only in connection with a qualifying event that is the termination, or reduction of hours, of the covered employee's employment, or that is the bankruptcy of the employer.

(e) An individual is not a qualified beneficiary if the individual's status as a covered employee is attributable to a period in which the individual was a nonresident alien who received from the individual's employer no earned income (within the meaning of section 911(d)(2)) that constituted income from sources within the United States (within the meaning of section 861(a)(3)). If, pursuant to the preceding sentence, an individual is not a qualified beneficiary, then a spouse or dependent child of the individual is not considered a qualified beneficiary by virtue of the relationship to the individual.

(f) A qualified beneficiary who does not elect COBRA continuation coverage in connection with a qualifying event ceases to be a qualified beneficiary at the end of the election period (see Q&A-1 of §54.4980B-6). Thus, for example, if such a former qualified beneficiary is later added to a covered employee's coverage (e.g., during an open enrollment period) and then another qualifying event occurs with respect to the covered employee, the former qualified beneficiary does not become a qualified beneficiary by reason of the second qualifying event. If a covered employee who is a qualified beneficiary does not elect COBRA continuation coverage during the election period, then any child born to or placed for adoption with the covered employee on or after the date of the qualifying event is not a qualified beneficiary. Once a plan's obligation to make COBRA continuation coverage available to an individual who has been a qualified beneficiary ceases under the rules of §54.4980B-7, the individual ceases to be a qualified beneficiary.

(g) For purposes of §§54.4980B-1 through 54.4980B-10, *placement for adoption* or *being placed for adoption* means the assumption and retention by the covered employee of a legal obligation for total or partial support of a child in anticipation of the adoption of the child. The child's placement for adoption with the covered employee terminates upon the termination of the legal obligation for total or partial support. A child who is immediately adopted by the covered employee without a preceding placement for adoption is considered to be placed for adoption on the date of the adoption.

(h) The rules of this Q&A-1 are illustrated by the following examples:

*Example 1.* (i) B is a single employee who voluntarily terminates employment and elects COBRA continuation coverage under a group health plan. To comply with the requirements of section 9801(f), the plan permits a covered employee who marries to have her or his spouse covered under the plan. One month after electing COBRA continuation coverage, B marries and chooses to have B's spouse covered under the plan.

(ii) B's spouse is not a qualified beneficiary. Thus, if B dies during the period of COBRA continuation coverage, the plan does not have to offer B's surviving spouse an opportunity to elect COBRA continuation coverage.

*Example 2.* (i) C is a married employee who terminates employment. C elects COBRA continuation coverage for C but not C's spouse, and C's spouse declines to elect such coverage. C's spouse thus ceases to be a qualified beneficiary. At the next open enrollment period, C adds the spouse as a beneficiary under the plan.

(ii) The addition of the spouse during the open enrollment period does not make the spouse a qualified beneficiary. The plan thus will not have to offer the spouse an opportunity to elect COBRA continuation coverage upon a later divorce from or death of C.

*Example 3.* (i) Under the terms of a group health plan, a covered employee's child, upon attaining age 19, ceases to be a dependent eligible for coverage.

(ii) At that time, the child must be offered an opportunity to elect COBRA continuation coverage. If the child elects COBRA continuation coverage, the child marries during the period of the COBRA continuation coverage, and the child's spouse becomes covered under the group health plan, the child's spouse is not a qualified beneficiary.

*Example 4.* (i) *D* is a single employee who, upon retirement, is given the opportunity to elect COBRA continuation coverage but declines it in favor of an alternative offer of 12 months of employer-paid retiree health benefits. At the end of the election period, *D* ceases to be a qualified beneficiary and will not have to be given another opportunity to elect COBRA continuation coverage (at the end of those 12 months or at any other time). *D* marries *E* during the period of retiree health coverage and, under the terms of that coverage, *E* becomes covered under the plan.

(ii) If a divorce from or death of *D* will result in *E*'s losing coverage, *E* will be a qualified beneficiary because *E*'s coverage under the plan on the day before the qualifying event (that is, the divorce or death) will have been by reason of *D*'s acceptance of 12 months of employer-paid coverage after the prior qualifying event (*D*'s retirement) rather than by reason of an election of COBRA continuation coverage.

*Example 5.* (i) The facts are the same as in *Example 4*, except that, under the terms of the plan, the divorce or death does not cause *E* to lose coverage so that *E* continues to be covered for the balance of the original 12-month period.

(ii) *E* does not have to be allowed to elect COBRA continuation coverage because the loss of coverage at the end of the 12-month period is not caused by the divorce or death, and thus the divorce or death does not constitute a qualifying event. See Q&A-1 of §54.4980B-4.

Q-2: Who is an employee and who is a covered employee?

A-2: (a)(1) For purposes of §§54.4980B-1 through 54.4980B-10 (except for purposes of Q&A-5 in §54.4980B-2, relating to the exception from COBRA for plans maintained by an employer with fewer than 20 employees), an *employee* is any individual who is eligible to be covered under a group health plan by virtue of the performance of services for the employer maintaining the plan or by virtue of membership in the employee organization maintaining the plan. Thus, for purposes of §§54.4980B-1 through 54.4980B-10 (except for purposes of Q&A-5 in §54.4980B-2), the following individuals are employees if their relationship to the employer maintaining the plan makes them eligible to be covered under the plan—

(i) Self-employed individuals (within the meaning of section 401(c)(1));

(ii) Independent contractors (and their employees and independent contractors); and

(iii) Directors (in the case of a corporation).

(2) Similarly, whenever reference is made in §§54.4980B-1 through 54.4980B-10 (except in Q&A-5 of §54.4980B-2) to an employment relationship (such as by referring to the termination of employment of an employee or to an employee's being employed by an employer), the reference includes the relationship of those individuals who are employees within the meaning of this paragraph (a). See paragraph (c) in Q&A-5 of §54.4980B-2 for a narrower meaning of employee solely for purposes of Q&A-5 of §54.4980B-2.

(b) For purposes of §§54.4980B-1 through 54.4980B-10, a *covered employee* is any individual who is (or was) provided coverage under a group health plan (other than a plan that is excepted from COBRA on the date of the qualifying event; see Q&A-4 of §54.4980B-2) by virtue of being or having been an employee. For example, a retiree or former employee who is covered by a group health plan is a covered employee if the coverage results in whole or in part from her or his previous employment. An employee (or former employee) who is merely eligible for coverage under a group health plan is generally not a covered employee if the employee (or former employee) is not actually covered under the plan. In general, the reason for the employee's (or former employee's) lack of actual coverage (such as having declined participation in the plan or having failed to satisfy the plan's conditions for participation) is not relevant for this purpose. However, if the employee (or former employee) is denied or not offered coverage under circumstances in which the denial or failure to offer constitutes a violation of applicable law (such as the Americans with Disabilities Act, 42 U.S.C. 12101 through 12213, the special enrollment rules of section 9801, or the requirements of section 9802 prohibiting discrimination in eligibility to enroll in a group health plan based on health status), then, for purposes of §§54.4980B-1 through 54.4980B-10, the employee (or former employee) will be considered to have had the coverage that was wrongfully denied or not offered.

Q-3: Who are the similarly situated nonCOBRA beneficiaries?

A-3: For purposes of §§54.4980B-1 through 54.4980B-10, *similarly situated nonCOBRA beneficiaries* means the group of covered employees, spouses of covered employees, or dependent children of covered employees receiving coverage under a group health plan maintained by the employer or employee organization who are receiving that coverage for a reason other than the rights provided under the COBRA continuation coverage requirements and who, based on all

of the facts and circumstances, are most similarly situated to the situation of the qualified beneficiary immediately before the qualifying event.

[Reg. §54.4980B-3.]

☐ [*T.D. 8812, 2-2-99. Amended by T.D. 8928, 1-9-2001.*]

### [Reg. §54.4980B-4]

**§54.4980B-4. Qualifying events.**—The determination of what constitutes a qualifying event is addressed in the following questions-and-answers:

Q-1: What is a qualifying event?

A-1: (a) A *qualifying event* is an event that satisfies paragraphs (b), (c), and (d) of this Q&A-1. Paragraph (e) of this Q&A-1 further explains a reduction of hours of employment, paragraph (f) of this Q&A-1 describes the treatment of children born to or placed for adoption with a covered employee during a period of COBRA continuation coverage, and paragraph (g) of this Q&A-1 contains examples. See Q & A-1 through Q & A-3 of §54.4980B-10 for special rules in the case of leave taken under the Family and Medical Leave Act of 1993 (29 U.S.C. 2601-2619).

(b) An event satisfies this paragraph (b) if the event is any of the following—

(1) The death of a covered employee;

(2) The termination (other than by reason of the employee's gross misconduct), or reduction of hours, of a covered employee's employment;

(3) The divorce or legal separation of a covered employee from the employee's spouse;

(4) A covered employee's becoming entitled to Medicare benefits under Title XVIII of the Social Security Act (42 U.S.C. 1395-1395ggg);

(5) A dependent child's ceasing to be a dependent child of a covered employee under the generally applicable requirements of the plan; or

(6) A proceeding in bankruptcy under Title 11 of the United States Code with respect to an employer from whose employment a covered employee retired at any time.

(c) An event satisfies this paragraph (c) if, under the terms of the group health plan, the event causes the covered employee, or the spouse or a dependent child of the covered employee, to lose coverage under the plan. For this purpose, to *lose coverage* means to cease to be covered under the same terms and conditions as in effect immediately before the qualifying event. Any increase in the premium or contribution that must be paid by a covered employee (or the spouse or dependent child of a covered employee) for coverage under a group health plan that results from the occurrence of one of the events listed in paragraph (b) of the Q&A-1 is a loss of coverage. In the case of an event that is the bankruptcy of the employer, *lose coverage* also means any substantial elimination of coverage under the plan, occurring within 12 months before or after the date the bankruptcy proceeding commences, for a covered employee who had retired on or before the date of the substantial elimination of group health plan coverage or for any spouse, surviving spouse, or dependent child of such a covered employee if, on the day before the bankruptcy qualifying event, the spouse, surviving spouse, or dependent child is a beneficiary under the plan. For purposes of this paragraph (c), a loss of coverage need not occur immediately after the event, so long as the loss of coverage occurs before the end of the maximum coverage period (see Q&A-4 and Q&A-6 of §54.4980B-7). However, if neither the covered employee nor the spouse or a dependent child of the covered employee loses coverage before the end of what would be the maximum coverage period, the event does not satisfy this paragraph (c). If coverage is reduced or eliminated in anticipation of an event (for example, an employer's eliminating an employee's coverage in anticipation of the termination of the employee's employment, or an employee's eliminating the coverage of the employee's spouse in anticipation of a divorce or legal separation), the reduction or elimination is disregarded in determining whether the event causes a loss of coverage.

(d) An event satisfies this paragraph (d) if it occurs while the plan is subject to COBRA. Thus, an event will not satisfy this paragraph (d) if it occurs while the plan is excepted from COBRA (see Q&A-4 of §54.4980B-2). Even if the plan later becomes subject to COBRA, it is not required to make COBRA continuation coverage available to anyone whose coverage ends as a result of an event during a year in which the plan is excepted from COBRA. For example, if a group health plan is excepted from COBRA as a small-employer plan during the year 2001 (see Q&A-5 of §54.4980B-2) and an employee terminates employment on December 31, 2001, the termination is not a qualifying event and the plan is not required to permit the employee to elect COBRA continuation coverage. This is the case even if the plan ceases to be a small-employer plan as of January 1, 2002. Also, the same result will follow even if the employee is given three months of coverage beyond December 31 (that is, through March of 2002), because there will be no qualifying event as of the termination of coverage in March. However, if the employee's spouse is initially provided with the three-month coverage through March 2002, but the spouse divorces the employee before the end of the three months and loses coverage as a result of the divorce, the divorce will constitute a qualifying event during 2002 and so entitle the spouse to elect COBRA continuation coverage. See Q&A-7 of § 54.4980B-7 regarding the maximum coverage period in such a case.

(e) A reduction of hours of a covered employee's employment occurs whenever there is a decrease in the hours that a covered employee is required to work or actually works, but only if the decrease is not accompanied by an immediate termination of employment. This is true regardless of whether the covered employee continues to perform services following the reduction of hours of employment. For example, an absence from work due to disability, a temporary layoff, or any other reason (other than due to leave that is FMLA leave; see § 54.4980B-10) is a reduction of hours of a covered employee's employment if there is not an immediate termination of employment. If a group health plan measures eligibility for the coverage of employees by the number of hours worked in a given time period, such as the preceding month or quarter, and an employee covered under the plan fails to work the minimum number of hours during that time period, the failure to work the minimum number of required hours is a reduction of hours of that covered employee's employment.

(f) The qualifying event of a qualified beneficiary who is a child born to or placed for adoption with a covered employee during a period of COBRA continuation coverage is the qualifying event giving rise to the period of COBRA continuation coverage during which the child is born or placed for adoption. If a second qualifying event has occurred before the child is born or placed for adoption (such as the death of the covered employee), then the second qualifying event also applies to the newborn or adopted child. See Q&A-6 of § 54.4980B-7.

(g) The rules of this Q&A-1 are illustrated by the following examples, in each of which the group health plan is subject to COBRA:

*Example 1.* (i) An employee who is covered by a group health plan terminates employment (other than by reason of the employee's gross misconduct) and, beginning with the day after the last day of employment, is given 3 months of employer-paid coverage under the same terms and conditions as before that date. At the end of the three months, the coverage terminates.

(ii) The loss of coverage at the end of the three months results from the termination of employment and, thus, the termination of employment is a qualifying event.

*Example 2.* (i) An employee who is covered by a group health plan retires (which is a termination of employment other than by reason of the employee's gross misconduct) and, upon retirement, is required to pay an increased amount for the same group health coverage that the employee had before retirement.

(ii) The increase in the premium or contribution required for coverage is a loss of coverage under paragraph (c) of this Q&A-1 and, thus, the retirement is a qualifying event.

*Example 3.* (i) An employee and the employee's spouse are covered under an employer's group health plan. The employee retires and is given identical coverage for life. However, the plan provides that the spousal coverage will not be continued beyond six months unless a higher premium for the spouse is paid to the plan.

(ii) The requirement for the spouse to pay a higher premium at the end of the six months is a loss of coverage under paragraph (c) of this Q&A-1. Thus, the retirement is a qualifying event and the spouse must be given an opportunity to elect COBRA continuation coverage.

*Example 4.* (i) F is a covered employee who is married to G, and both are covered under a group health plan maintained by F's employer. F and G are divorced. Under the terms of the plan, the divorce causes G to lose coverage. The divorce is a qualifying event, and G elects COBRA continuation coverage, remarries during the period of COBRA continuation coverage, and G's new spouse becomes covered under the plan. (See Q&A-5 in § 54.4980B-5, paragraph (c) in Q&A-4 of § 54.4980B-5, and section 9801(f)(2).) G dies. Under the terms of the plan, the death causes G's new spouse to lose coverage under the plan.

(ii) G's death is not a qualifying event because G is not a covered employee.

*Example 5.* (i) An employer maintains a group health plan for both active employees and retired employees (and their families). The coverage for active employees and retired employees is identical, and the employer does not require retirees to pay more for coverage than active employees. The plan does not make COBRA continuation coverage available when an employee retires (and is not required to because the retired employee has not lost coverage under the plan). The employer amends the plan to eliminate coverage for retired employees effective January 1, 2002. On that date, several retired employees (and their spouses and dependent children) have been covered under the plan since their retirement for less than the maxi-

mum coverage period that would apply to them in connection with their retirement.

(ii) The elimination of retiree coverage under these circumstances is a deferred loss of coverage for those retirees (and their spouses and dependent children) under paragraph (c) of this Q&A-1 and, thus, the retirement is a qualifying event. The plan must make COBRA continuation coverage available to them for the balance of the maximum coverage period that applies to them in connection with their retirement.

Q-2: Are the facts surrounding a termination of employment (such as whether it was voluntary or involuntary) relevant in determining whether the termination of employment is a qualifying event?

A-2: Apart from facts constituting gross misconduct, the facts surrounding the termination or reduction of hours are irrelevant in determining whether a qualifying event has occurred. Thus, it does not matter whether the employee voluntarily terminated or was discharged. For example, a strike or a lockout is a termination or reduction of hours that constitutes a qualifying event if the strike or lockout results in a loss of coverage as described in paragraph (c) of Q&A-1 of this section. Similarly, a layoff that results in such a loss of coverage is a qualifying event.

[Reg. § 54.4980B-4.]

☐ [T.D. 8812, 2-2-99. *Amended by T.D. 8928, 1-9-2001.*]

### [Reg. § 54.4980B-5]

**§ 54.4980B-5. COBRA continuation coverage.**—The following questions-and-answers address the requirements for coverage to constitute COBRA continuation coverage:

Q-1: What is COBRA continuation coverage?

A-1: (a) If a qualifying event occurs, each qualified beneficiary (other than a qualified beneficiary for whom the qualifying event will not result in any immediate or deferred loss of coverage) must be offered an opportunity to elect to receive the group health plan coverage that is provided to similarly situated nonCOBRA beneficiaries (ordinarily, the same coverage that the qualified beneficiary had on the day before the qualifying event). See Q & A-3 of § 54.4980B-3 for the definition of similarly situated nonCOBRA beneficiaries. This coverage is COBRA continuation coverage. If coverage is modified for similarly situated nonCOBRA beneficiaries, then the coverage made available to qualified beneficiaries is modified in the same way. If the continuation coverage offered differs in any way from the coverage made available to similarly situated nonCOBRA beneficiaries, the coverage offered does not constitute COBRA continuation coverage and the group health plan is not in compliance with COBRA unless other coverage that does constitute COBRA continuation coverage is also offered. Any elimination or reduction of coverage in anticipation of an event described in paragraph (b) of Q & A-1 of § 54.4980B-4 is disregarded for purposes of this Q & A-1 and for purposes of any other reference in §§ 54.4980B-1 through 54.4980B-10 to coverage in effect immediately before (or on the day before) a qualifying event. COBRA continuation coverage must not be conditioned upon, or discriminate on the basis of lack of, evidence of insurability.

(b) In the case of a qualified beneficiary who is a child born to or placed for adoption with a covered employee during a period of COBRA continuation coverage, the child is generally entitled to elect immediately to have the same coverage that dependent children of active employees receive under the benefit packages under which the covered employee has coverage at the time of the birth or placement for adoption. Such a child would be entitled to elect coverage different from that elected by the covered employee during the next available open enrollment period under the plan. See Q&A-4 of this section.

Q-2: What deductibles apply if COBRA continuation coverage is elected?

A-2: (a) Qualified beneficiaries electing COBRA continuation coverage generally are subject to the same deductibles as similarly situated nonCOBRA beneficiaries. If a qualified beneficiary's COBRA continuation coverage begins before the end of a period prescribed for accumulating amounts toward deductibles, the qualified beneficiary must retain credit for expenses incurred toward those deductibles before the beginning of COBRA continuation coverage as though the qualifying event had not occurred. The specific application of this rule depends on the type of deductible, as set forth in paragraphs (b) through (d) of this Q&A-2. Special rules are set forth in paragraph (e) of this Q&A-2, and examples appear in paragraph (f) of this Q&A-2.

(b) If a deductible is computed separately for each individual receiving coverage under the plan, each individual's remaining deductible amount (if any) on the date COBRA continuation coverage begins is equal to that individual's remaining deductible amount immediately before that date.

(c) If a deductible is computed on a family basis, the remaining deductible for the family on the date that COBRA continuation coverage begins depends on the members of the family electing

COBRA continuation coverage. In computing the family deductible that remains on the date COBRA continuation coverage begins, only the expenses of those family members receiving COBRA continuation coverage need be taken into account. If the qualifying event results in there being more than one family unit (for example, because of a divorce), the family deductible may be computed separately for each resulting family unit based on the members in each unit. These rules apply regardless of whether the plan provides that the family deductible is an alternative to individual deductibles or an additional requirement.

(d) Deductibles that are not described in paragraph (b) or (c) of this Q&A-2 must be treated in a manner consistent with the principles set forth in those paragraphs.

(e) If a deductible is computed on the basis of a covered employee's compensation instead of being a fixed dollar amount and the employee remains employed during the period of COBRA continuation coverage, the plan is permitted to choose whether to apply the deductible by treating the employee's compensation as continuing without change for the duration of the COBRA continuation coverage at the level that was used to compute the deductible in effect immediately before the COBRA continuation coverage began, or to apply the deductible by taking the employee's actual compensation into account. In applying a deductible that is computed on the basis of the covered employee's compensation instead of being a fixed dollar amount, for periods of COBRA continuation coverage in which the employee is not employed by the employer, the plan is required to compute the deductible by treating the employee's compensation as continuing without change for the duration of the COBRA continuation coverage either at the level that was used to compute the deductible in effect immediately before the COBRA continuation coverage began or at the level that was used to compute the deductible in effect immediately before the employee's employment was terminated.

(f) The rules of this Q&A-2 are illustrated by the following examples; in each example, deductibles under the plan are determined on a calendar year basis:

*Example 1.* (i) A group health plan applies a separate $100 annual deductible to each individual it covers. The plan provides that the spouse and dependent children of a covered employee will lose coverage on the last day of the month after the month of the covered employee's death. A covered employee dies on June 11, 2001. The spouse and the two dependent children elect COBRA continuation coverage, which will begin on August 1, 2001. As of July 31, 2001, the spouse has incurred $80 of covered expenses, the older child has incurred no covered expenses, and the younger one has incurred $120 of covered expenses (and therefore has already satisfied the deductible).

(ii) At the beginning of COBRA continuation coverage on August 1, the spouse has a remaining deductible of $20, the older child still has the full $100 deductible, and the younger one has no further deductible.

*Example 2.* (i) A group health plan applies a separate $200 annual deductible to each individual it covers, except that each family member is treated as having satisfied the individual deductible once the family has incurred $500 of covered expenses during the year. The plan provides that upon the divorce of a covered employee, coverage will end immediately for the employee's spouse and any children who do not remain in the employee's custody. A covered employee with four dependent children is divorced, the spouse obtains custody of the two oldest children, and the spouse and those children all elect COBRA continuation coverage to begin immediately. The family had accumulated $420 of covered expenses before the divorce, as follows: $70 by each parent, $200 by the oldest child, $80 by the youngest child, and none by the other two children.

(ii) The resulting family consisting of the spouse and the two oldest children accumulated a total of $270 of covered expenses, and thus the remaining deductible for that family could be as high as $230 (because the plan would not have to count the incurred expenses of the covered employee and the youngest child). The remaining deductible for the resulting family consisting of the covered employee and the two youngest children is not subject to the rules of this Q&A-2 because their coverage is not COBRA continuation coverage.

*Example 3.* Each year a group health plan pays 70 percent of the cost of an individual's psychotherapy after that individual's first three visits during the year. A qualified beneficiary whose election of COBRA continuation coverage takes effect beginning August 1, 2001 and who has already made two visits as of that date need only pay for one more visit before the plan must begin to pay 70 percent of the cost of the remaining visits during 2001.

*Example 4.* (i) A group health plan has a $250 annual deductible per covered individual. The plan provides that if the deductible is not satisfied in a particular year, expenses incurred during October through December of that year are credited toward satisfaction of the deductible in the next year. A qualified beneficiary who has incurred

covered expenses of $150 from January through September of 2001 and $40 during October elects COBRA continuation coverage beginning November 1, 2001.

(ii) The remaining deductible amount for this qualified beneficiary is $60 at the beginning of the COBRA continuation coverage. If this individual incurs covered expenses of $50 in November and December of 2001 combined (so that the $250 deductible for 2001 is not satisfied), the $90 incurred from October through December of 2001 are credited toward satisfaction of the deductible amount for 2002.

Q-3: How do a plan's limits apply to COBRA continuation coverage?

A-3: (a) Limits are treated in the same way as deductibles (see Q&A-2 of this section). This rule applies both to limits on plan benefits (such as a maximum number of hospital days or dollar amount of reimbursable expenses) and limits on out-of-pocket expenses (such as a limit on copayments, a limit on deductibles plus copayments, or a catastrophic limit). This rule applies equally to annual and lifetime limits and applies equally to limits on specific benefits and limits on benefits in the aggregate under the plan.

(b) The rule of this Q&A-3 is illustrated by the following examples; in each example limits are determined on a calendar year basis:

*Example 1.* (i) A group health plan pays for a maximum of 150 days of hospital confinement per individual per year. A covered employee who has had 20 days of hospital confinement as of May 1, 2001 terminates employment and elects COBRA continuation coverage as of that date.

(ii) During the remainder of the year 2001 the plan need only pay for a maximum of 130 days of hospital confinement for this individual.

*Example 2.* (i) A group health plan reimburses a maximum of $20,000 of covered expenses per family per year, and the same $20,000 limit applies to unmarried covered employees. A covered employee and spouse who have no children divorce on May 1, 2001, and the spouse elects COBRA continuation coverage as of that date. In 2001, the employee had incurred $5,000 of expenses and the spouse had incurred $8,000 before May 1.

(ii) The plan can limit its reimbursement of the amount of expenses incurred by the spouse on and after May 1 for the remainder of the year to $12,000 ($20,000 – $8,000 = $12,000). The remaining limit for the employee is not subject to the rules of this Q&A-3 because the employee's coverage is not COBRA continuation coverage.

*Example 3.* (i) A group health plan pays for 80 percent of covered expenses after satisfaction of a $100-per-individual deductible, and the plan pays for 100 percent of covered expenses after a family has incurred out-of-pocket costs of $2,000. The plan provides that upon the divorce of a covered employee, coverage will end immediately for the employee's spouse and any children who do not remain in the employee's custody. An employee and spouse with three dependent children divorce on June 1, 2001, and one of the children remains with the employee. The spouse elects COBRA continuation coverage as of that date for the spouse and the other two children. During January through May of 2001, the spouse incurred $600 of covered expenses and each of the two children in the spouse's custody after the divorce incurred covered expenses of $1,100. This resulted in total out-of-pocket costs for these three individuals of $800 ($300 total for the three deductibles, plus $500 for 20 percent of the other $2,500 in incurred expenses [$600 + $1,100 + $1,100 = $2,800; $2,800 – $300 = $2,500]).

(ii) For the remainder of 2001, the resulting family consisting of the spouse and two children has an out-of-pocket limit of $1,200 ($2,000 – $800 = $1,200). The remaining out-of-pocket limit for the resulting family consisting of the employee and one child is not subject to the rules of this Q&A-3 because their coverage is not COBRA continuation coverage.

Q-4: Can a qualified beneficiary who elects COBRA continuation coverage ever change from the coverage received by that individual immediately before the qualifying event?

A-4: (a) In general, a qualified beneficiary need only be given an opportunity to continue the coverage that she or he was receiving immediately before the qualifying event. This is true regardless of whether the coverage received by the qualified beneficiary before the qualifying event ceases to be of value to the qualified beneficiary, such as in the case of a qualified beneficiary covered under a region-specific health maintenance organization (HMO) who leaves the HMO's service region. The only situations in which a qualified beneficiary must be allowed to change from the coverage received immediately before the qualifying event are as set forth in paragraphs (b) and (c) of this Q&A-4 and in Q&A-1 of this section (regarding changes to or elimination of the coverage provided to similarly situated nonCOBRA beneficiaries).

(b) If a qualified beneficiary participates in a region-specific benefit package (such as an HMO or an on-site clinic) that will not service her or his health needs in the area to which she or he is relocating (regardless of the reason for the relocation), the qualified beneficiary must be given, within a reasonable period after requesting other coverage, an opportunity to elect alternative coverage that the employer or employee organization makes available to active employees. If the employer or employee organization makes group health plan coverage available to similarly situated nonCOBRA beneficiaries that can be extended in the area to which the qualified beneficiary is relocating, then that coverage is the alternative coverage that must be made available to the relocating qualified beneficiary. If the employer or employee organization does not make group health plan coverage available to similarly situated nonCOBRA beneficiaries that can be extended in the area to which the qualified beneficiary is relocating but makes coverage available to other employees that can be extended in that area, then the coverage made available to those other employees must be made available to the relocating qualified beneficiary. The effective date of the alternative coverage must be not later than the date of the qualified beneficiary's relocation, or, if later, the first day of the month following the month in which the qualified beneficiary requests the alternative coverage. However, the employer or employee organization is not required to make any other coverage available to the relocating qualified beneficiary if the only coverage the employer or employee organization makes available to active employees is not available in the area to which the qualified beneficiary relocates (because all such coverage is region-specific and does not service individuals in that area).

(c) If an employer or employee organization makes an open enrollment period available to similarly situated active employees with respect to whom a qualifying event has not occurred, the same open enrollment period rights must be made available to each qualified beneficiary receiving COBRA continuation coverage. An open enrollment period means a period during which an employee covered under a plan can choose to be covered under another group health plan or under another benefit package within the same plan, or to add or eliminate coverage of family members.

(d) The rules of this Q&A-4 are illustrated by the following examples:

*Example 1.* (i) *E* is an employee who works for an employer that maintains several group health plans. Under the terms of the plans, if an employee chooses to cover any family members under a plan, all family members must be covered by the same plan and that plan must be the same as the plan covering the employee. Immediately before *E*'s termination of employment (for reasons other than gross misconduct), *E* is covered along with *E*'s spouse and children by a plan. The coverage under that plan will end as a result of the termination of employment.

(ii) Upon *E*'s termination of employment, each of the four family members is a qualified beneficiary. Even though the employer maintains various other plans and options, it is not necessary for the qualified beneficiaries to be allowed to switch to a new plan when *E* terminates employment.

(iii) COBRA continuation coverage is elected for each of the four family members. Three months after *E*'s termination of employment there is an open enrollment period during which similarly situated active employees are offered an opportunity to choose to be covered under a new plan or to add or eliminate family coverage.

(iv) During the open enrollment period, each of the four qualified beneficiaries must be offered the opportunity to switch to another plan (as though each qualified beneficiary were an individual employee). For example, each member of *E*'s family could choose coverage under a separate plan, even though the family members of employed individuals could not choose coverage under separate plans. Of course, if each family member chooses COBRA continuation coverage under a separate plan, the plan can require payment for each family member that is based on the applicable premium for individual coverage under that separate plan. See Q&A-1 of §54.4980B-8.

*Example 2.* (i) The facts are the same as in *Example 1*, except that *E*'s family members are not covered under *E*'s group health plan when *E* terminates employment.

(ii) Although the family members do not have to be given an opportunity to elect COBRA continuation coverage, *E* must be allowed to add them to *E*'s COBRA continuation coverage during the open enrollment period. This is true even though the family members are not, and cannot become, qualified beneficiaries (see Q&A-1 of §54.4980B-3).

Q-5: Aside from open enrollment periods, can a qualified beneficiary who has elected COBRA continuation coverage choose to cover individuals (such as newborn children, adopted children, or new spouses) who join the qualified beneficiary's family on or after the date of the qualifying event?

A-5: (a) Yes. Under section 9801, employees eligible to participate in a group health plan (whether or not participating), as well as former employees participating in a plan (referred to in those rules as participants), are entitled to special enrollment rights for certain family members upon the loss of other group health plan coverage or upon the acquisition by the employee or participant of a new spouse or of a new dependent through birth, adoption, or placement for adoption, if certain requirements are satisfied. Employees not participating in the plan also can obtain rights for self-enrollment under those rules. Once a qualified beneficiary is receiving COBRA continuation coverage (that is, has timely elected and made timely payment for COBRA continuation coverage), the qualified beneficiary has the same right to enroll family members under those special enrollment rules as if the qualified beneficiary were an employee or participant within the meaning of those rules. However, neither a qualified beneficiary who is not receiving COBRA continuation coverage nor a former qualified beneficiary has any special enrollment rights under those rules.

(b) In addition to the special enrollment rights described in paragraph (a) of this Q&A-5, if the plan covering the qualified beneficiary provides that new family members of active employees can become covered (either automatically or upon an appropriate election) before the next open enrollment period, then the same right must be extended to the new family members of a qualified beneficiary.

(c) If the addition of a new family member will result in a higher applicable premium (for example, if the qualified beneficiary was previously receiving COBRA continuation coverage as an individual, or if the applicable premium for family coverage depends on family size), the plan can require the payment of a correspondingly higher amount for the COBRA continuation coverage. See Q&A-1 of §54.4980B-8.

(d) The right to add new family members under this Q&A-5 is in addition to the rights that newborn and adopted children of covered employees may have as qualified beneficiaries; see Q&A-1 in §54.4980B-3.

[Reg. §54.4980B-5.]

☐ *[T.D. 8812, 2-2-99. Amended by T.D. 8928, 1-9-2001.]*

**[Reg. §54.4980B-6]**

**§54.4980B-6. Electing COBRA continuation coverage.**—The following questions-and-answers address the manner in which COBRA continuation coverage is elected:

Q-1: What is the election period and how long must it last?

A-1: (a) A group health plan can condition the availability of COBRA continuation coverage upon the timely election of such coverage. An election of COBRA continuation coverage is a timely election if it is made during the election period. The election period must begin not later than the date the qualified beneficiary would lose coverage on account of the qualifying event. (See paragraph (c) of Q&A-1 of §54.4980B-4 for the meaning of *lose coverage*.) The election period must not end before the date that is 60 days after the later of—

(1) The date the qualified beneficiary would lose coverage on account of the qualifying event; or

(2) The date notice is provided to the qualified beneficiary of her or his right to elect COBRA continuation coverage.

(b) An election is considered to be made on the date it is sent to the plan administrator.

(c) The rules of this Q&A-1 are illustrated by the following example:

*Example.* (i) An unmarried employee without children who is receiving employer-paid coverage under a group health plan voluntarily terminates employment on June 1, 2001. The employee is not disabled at the time of the termination of employment nor at any time thereafter, and the plan does not provide for the extension of the required periods (as is permitted under paragraph (b) of Q & A-4 of §54.4980B-7).

(ii) *Case 1:* If the plan provides that the employer-paid coverage ends immediately upon the termination of employment, the election period must begin not later than June 1, 2001, and must not end earlier than July 31, 2001. If notice of the right to elect COBRA continuation coverage is not provided to the employee until June 15, 2001, the election period must not end earlier than August 14, 2001.

(iii) *Case 2:* If the plan provides that the employer-paid coverage does not end until 6 months after the termination of employment, the employee does not lose coverage until December 1, 2001. The election period can therefore begin as late as December 1, 2001, and must not end before January 30, 2002.

(iv) *Case 3:* If employer-paid coverage for 6 months after the termination of employment is offered only to those qualified beneficiaries who waive COBRA continuation coverage, the employee loses coverage on June 1, 2001, so the election period is the same as in Case 1. The difference between Case 2 and Case 3 is that in Case 2 the employee can receive 6 months of employer-paid coverage and then elect to pay for up to an additional 12 months of COBRA continuation coverage, while in Case 3 the employee must choose between 6 months of employer-paid coverage and paying for up to 18 months of COBRA continuation coverage. In all three cases, COBRA continuation coverage need not be provided for more than 18 months after the termination of employment (see Q & A-4 of §54.4980B-7), and in certain circumstances might be provided for a shorter period (see Q & A-1 of §54.4980B-7).

Q-2: Is a covered employee or qualified beneficiary responsible for informing the plan administrator of the occurrence of a qualifying event?

A-2: (a) In general, the employer or plan administrator must determine when a qualifying event has occurred. However, each covered employee or qualified beneficiary is responsible for notifying the plan administrator of the occurrence of a qualifying event that is either a dependent child's ceasing to be a dependent child under the generally applicable requirements of the plan or a divorce or legal separation of a covered employee. The group health plan is not required to offer the qualified beneficiary an opportunity to elect COBRA continuation coverage if the notice is not provided to the plan administrator within 60 days after the later of—

(1) The date of the qualifying event; or

(2) The date the qualified beneficiary would lose coverage on account of the qualifying event.

(b) For purposes of this Q&A-2, if more than one qualified beneficiary would lose coverage on account of a divorce or legal separation of a covered employee, a timely notice of the divorce or legal separation that is provided by the covered employee or any one of those qualified beneficiaries will be sufficient to preserve the election rights of all of the qualified beneficiaries.

Q-3: During the election period and before the qualified beneficiary has made an election, must coverage be provided?

A-3: (a) In general, each qualified beneficiary has until 60 days after the later of the date the qualifying event would cause her or him to lose coverage or the date notice is provided to the qualified beneficiary of her or his right to elect COBRA continuation coverage to decide whether to elect COBRA continuation coverage. If the election is made during that period, coverage must be provided from the date that coverage would otherwise have been lost (but see Q&A-4 of this section). This can be accomplished as described in paragraph (b) or (c) of this Q&A-3.

(b) In the case of an indemnity or reimbursement arrangement, the employer or employee organization can provide for plan coverage during the election period or, if the plan allows retroactive reinstatement, the employer or employee organization can terminate the coverage of the qualified beneficiary and reinstate her or him when the election (and, if applicable, payment for the coverage) is made. Claims incurred by a qualified beneficiary during the election period do not have to be paid before the election (and, if applicable, payment for the coverage) is made. If a provider of health care (such as a physician, hospital, or pharmacy) contacts the plan to confirm coverage of a qualified beneficiary during the election period, the plan must give a complete response to the health care provider about the qualified beneficiary's COBRA continuation coverage rights during the election period. For example, if the plan provides coverage during the election period but cancels coverage retroactively if COBRA continuation coverage is not elected, then the plan must inform a provider that a qualified beneficiary for whom coverage has not been elected is covered but that the coverage is subject to retroactive termination. Similarly, if the plan cancels coverage but then retroactively reinstates it once COBRA continuation coverage is elected, then the plan must inform the provider that the qualified beneficiary currently does not have coverage but will have coverage retroactively to the date coverage was lost if COBRA continuation coverage is elected. (See paragraph (c) of Q&A-5 in §54.4980B-8 for similar rules that a plan must follow in confirming coverage during a period when the plan has not received payment but that is still within the grace period for a qualified beneficiary for whom COBRA continuation coverage has been elected.)

(c)(1) In the case of a group health plan that provides health services (such as a health maintenance organization or a walk-in clinic), the plan can require with respect to a qualified beneficiary who has not elected and paid for COBRA continuation coverage that the qualified beneficiary choose between—

(i) Electing and paying for the coverage; or

(ii) Paying the reasonable and customary charge for the plan's services, but only if a qualified beneficiary who chooses to pay for the services will be reimbursed for that payment within 30 days after the election of COBRA continuation coverage (and, if applicable, the payment of any balance due for the coverage).

(2) In the alternative, the plan can provide continued coverage and treat the qualified beneficiary's use of the facility as a constructive election. In such a case, the qualified beneficiary is obligated to pay any applicable charge for the coverage, but only if the qualified beneficiary is informed that use of the facility will be a constructive election before using the facility.

Q-4: Is a waiver before the end of the election period effective to end a qualified beneficiary's election rights?

A-4: If, during the election period, a qualified beneficiary waives COBRA continuation coverage, the waiver can be revoked at any time before the end of the election period. Revocation of the waiver is an election of COBRA continuation coverage. However, if a waiver of COBRA continuation coverage is later revoked, coverage need not be provided retroactively (that is, from the date of the loss of coverage until the waiver is revoked). Waivers and revocations of waivers are considered made on the date they are sent to the employer, employee organization, or plan administrator, as applicable.

Q-5: Can an employer or employee organization withhold money or other benefits owed to a qualified beneficiary until the qualified beneficiary either waives COBRA continuation coverage, elects and pays for such coverage, or allows the election period to expire?

A-5: No. An employer, and an employee organization, must not withhold anything to which a qualified beneficiary is otherwise entitled (by operation of law or other agreement) in order to compel payment for COBRA continuation coverage or to coerce the qualified beneficiary to give up rights to COBRA continuation coverage (including the right to use the full election period to decide whether to elect such coverage). Such a withholding constitutes a failure to comply with the COBRA continuation coverage requirements. Furthermore, any purported waiver obtained by means of such a withholding is invalid.

Q-6: Can each qualified beneficiary make an independent election under COBRA?

A-6: Yes. Each qualified beneficiary (including a child who is born to or placed for adoption with a covered employee during a period of COBRA continuation coverage) must be offered the opportunity to make an independent election to receive COBRA continuation coverage. If the plan allows similarly situated active employees with respect to whom a qualifying event has not occurred to choose among several options during an open enrollment period (for example, to switch to another group health plan or to another benefit package under the same group health plan), then each qualified beneficiary must also be offered an independent election to choose during an open enrollment period among the options made available to similarly situated active employees with respect to whom a qualifying event has not occurred. If a qualified beneficiary who is either a covered employee or the spouse of a covered employee elects COBRA continuation coverage and the election does not specify whether the election is for self- only coverage, the election is deemed to include an election of COBRA continuation coverage on behalf of all other qualified beneficiaries with respect to that qualifying event. An election on behalf of a minor child can be made by the child's parent or legal guardian. An election on behalf of a qualified beneficiary who is incapacitated or dies can be made by the legal representative of the qualified beneficiary or the qualified beneficiary's estate, as determined under applicable state law, or by the spouse of the qualified beneficiary. (See also Q&A-5 of §54.4980B-7 relating to the independent right of each qualified beneficiary with respect to the same qualifying event to receive COBRA continuation coverage during the disability extension.) The rules of this Q&A-6 are illustrated by the following examples; in each example each group health plan is subject to COBRA:

*Example 1.* (i) Employee *H* and *H*'s spouse are covered under a group health plan immediately before *H*'s termination of employment (for reasons other than gross misconduct). Coverage under the plan will end as a result of the termination of employment.

(ii) Upon *H*'s termination of employment, both *H* and *H*'s spouse are qualified beneficiaries and each must be allowed to elect COBRA continuation coverage. Thus, *H* might elect COBRA continuation coverage while the spouse declines to elect such coverage, or *H* might elect COBRA continuation coverage for both of them. In contrast, *H* cannot decline COBRA continuation coverage on behalf of *H*'s spouse. Thus, if *H* does not elect COBRA continuation coverage on behalf of the spouse, the spouse must still be allowed to elect COBRA continuation coverage.

*Example 2.* (i) An employer maintains a group health plan under which all employees receive employer-paid coverage. Employees can arrange to cover their families by paying an additional amount. The employer also maintains a cafeteria plan, under which one of the options is to pay part or all of the employee share of the cost for family coverage under the group health plan. Thus, an employee might pay for family coverage under the group health plan partly with before-tax dollars and partly with after-tax dollars.

(ii) If an employee's family is receiving coverage under the group health plan when a qualifying event occurs, each of the qualified beneficiaries must be offered an opportunity to elect COBRA continuation coverage, regardless of how that qualified beneficiary's coverage was paid for before the qualifying event.

[Reg. §54.4980B-6.]

☐ [*T.D. 8812, 2-2-99. Amended by T.D. 8928, 1-9-2001.*]

[Reg. § 54.4980B-7]

**§ 54.4980B-7. Duration of COBRA continuation coverage.**—The following questions-and-answers address the duration of COBRA continuation coverage:

Q-1: How long must COBRA continuation coverage be made available to a qualified beneficiary?

A-1: (a) Except for an interruption of coverage in connection with a waiver, as described in Q & A-4 of § 54.4980B-6, COBRA continuation coverage that has been elected for a qualified beneficiary must extend for at least the period beginning on the date of the qualifying event and ending not before the earliest of the following dates—

(1) The last day of the maximum coverage period (see Q & A-4 of this section);

(2) The first day for which timely payment is not made to the plan with respect to the qualified beneficiary (see Q & A-5 in § 54.4980B-8);

(3) The date upon which the employer or employee organization ceases to provide any group health plan (including successor plans) to any employee;

(4) The date, after the date of the election, upon which the qualified beneficiary first becomes covered under any other group health plan, as described in Q & A-2 of this section;

(5) The date, after the date of the election, upon which the qualified beneficiary first becomes entitled to Medicare benefits, as described in Q & A-3 of this section; and

(6) In the case of a qualified beneficiary entitled to a disability extension (see Q & A-5 of this section), the later of—

(i) Either 29 months after the date of the qualifying event, or the first day of the month that is more than 30 days after the date of a final determination under Title II or XVI of the Social Security Act (42 U.S.C. 401-433 or 1381-1385) that the disabled qualified beneficiary whose disability resulted in the qualified beneficiary's being entitled to the disability extension is no longer disabled, whichever is earlier; or

(ii) The end of the maximum coverage period that applies to the qualified beneficiary without regard to the disability extension.

(b) However, a group health plan can terminate for cause the coverage of a qualified beneficiary receiving COBRA continuation coverage on the same basis that the plan terminates for cause the coverage of similarly situated nonCOBRA beneficiaries. For example, if a group health plan terminates the coverage of active employees for the submission of a fraudulent claim, then the coverage of a qualified beneficiary can also be terminated for the submission of a fraudulent claim. Notwithstanding the preceding two sentences, the coverage of a qualified beneficiary can be terminated for failure to make timely payment to the plan only if payment is not timely under the rules of Q&A-5 in § 54.4980B-8.

(c) In the case of an individual who is not a qualified beneficiary and who is receiving coverage under a group health plan solely because of the individual's relationship to a qualified beneficiary, if the plan's obligation to make COBRA continuation coverage available to the qualified beneficiary ceases under this section, the plan is not obligated to make coverage available to the individual who is not a qualified beneficiary.

Q-2: When may a plan terminate a qualified beneficiary's COBRA continuation coverage due to coverage under another group health plan?

A-2: (a) If a qualified beneficiary first becomes covered under another group health plan (including for this purpose any group health plan of a governmental employer or employee organization) after the date on which COBRA continuation coverage is elected for the qualified beneficiary and the other coverage satisfies the requirements of paragraphs (b), (c), and (d) of this Q&A-2, then the plan may terminate the qualified beneficiary's COBRA continuation coverage upon the date on which the qualified beneficiary first becomes covered under the other group health plan (even if the other coverage is less valuable to the qualified beneficiary). By contrast, if a qualified beneficiary first becomes covered under another group health plan on or before the date on which COBRA continuation coverage is elected, then the other coverage cannot be a basis for terminating the qualified beneficiary's COBRA continuation coverage.

(b) The requirement of this paragraph (b) is satisfied if the qualified beneficiary is actually covered, rather than merely eligible to be covered, under the other group health plan.

(c) The requirement of this paragraph (c) is satisfied if the other group health plan is a plan that is not maintained by the employer or employee organization that maintains the plan under which COBRA continuation coverage must otherwise be made available.

(d) The requirement of this paragraph (d) is satisfied if the other group health plan does not contain any exclusion or limitation with respect to any preexisting condition of the qualified beneficiary (other than such an exclusion or limitation that does not apply to, or is satisfied by, the qualified beneficiary by reason of the provisions in section 9801 (relating to limitations on preexisting condition exclusion periods in group health plans)).

(e) The rules of this Q&A-2 are illustrated by the following examples:

*Example 1.* (i) Employer X maintains a group health plan subject to COBRA. C is an employee covered under the plan. C is also covered under a group health plan maintained by Employer Y, the employer of C's spouse. C terminates employment (for reasons other than gross misconduct), and the termination of employment causes C to lose coverage under X's plan (and, thus, is a qualifying event). C elects to receive COBRA continuation coverage under X's plan.

(ii) Under these facts, X's plan cannot terminate C's COBRA continuation coverage on the basis of C's coverage under Y's plan.

*Example 2.* (i) Employer W maintains a group health plan subject to COBRA. D is an employee covered under the plan. D terminates employment (for reasons other than gross misconduct), and the termination of employment causes D to lose coverage under W's plan (and, thus, is a qualifying event). D elects to receive COBRA continuation coverage under W's plan. Later D becomes employed by Employer V and is covered under V's group health plan. D's coverage under V's plan is not subject to any exclusion or limitation with respect to any preexisting condition of D.

(ii) Under these facts, W can terminate D's COBRA continuation coverage on the date D becomes covered under V's plan.

*Example 3.* (i) The facts are the same as in *Example 2*, except that D becomes employed by V and becomes covered under V's group health plan before D elects COBRA continuation coverage under W's plan.

(ii) Because the termination of employment is a qualifying event, D must be offered COBRA continuation coverage under W's plan, and W is not permitted to terminate D's COBRA continuation coverage on account of D's coverage under V's plan because D first became covered under V's plan before COBRA continuation coverage was elected for D.

Q-3: When may a plan terminate a qualified beneficiary's COBRA continuation coverage due to the qualified beneficiary's entitlement to Medicare benefits?

A-3: (a) If a qualified beneficiary first becomes entitled to Medicare benefits under Title XVIII of the Social Security Act (42 U.S.C. 1395-1395ggg) after the date on which COBRA continuation coverage is elected for the qualified beneficiary, then the plan may terminate the qualified beneficiary's COBRA continuation coverage upon the date on which the qualified beneficiary becomes so entitled. By contrast, if a qualified beneficiary first becomes entitled to Medicare benefits on or before the date that COBRA continuation coverage is elected, then the qualified beneficiary's entitlement to Medicare benefits cannot be a basis for terminating the qualified beneficiary's COBRA continuation coverage.

(b) A qualified beneficiary becomes entitled to Medicare benefits upon the effective date of enrollment in either part A or B, whichever occurs earlier. Thus, merely being eligible to enroll in Medicare does not constitute being entitled to Medicare benefits.

Q-4: When does the maximum coverage period end?

A-4: (a) Except as otherwise provided in this Q & A-4, the maximum coverage period ends 36 months after the qualifying event. The maximum coverage period for a qualified beneficiary who is a child born to or placed for adoption with a covered employee during a period of COBRA continuation coverage is the maximum coverage period for the qualifying event giving rise to the period of COBRA continuation coverage during which the child was born or placed for adoption. Paragraph (b) of this Q & A-4 describes the starting point from which the end of the maximum coverage period is measured. The date that the maximum coverage period ends is described in paragraph (c) of this Q & A-4 in a case where the qualifying event is a termination of employment or reduction of hours of employment, in paragraph (d) of this Q & A-4 in a case where a covered employee becomes entitled to Medicare benefits under Title XVIII of the Social Security Act (42 U.S.C. 1395-1395ggg) before experiencing a qualifying event that is a termination of employment or reduction of hours of employment, and in paragraph (e) of this Q & A-4 in the case of a qualifying event that is the bankruptcy of the employer. See Q & A-8 of § 54.4980B-2 for limitations that apply to certain health flexible spending arrangements. See also Q & A-6 of this section in the case of multiple qualifying events. Nothing in §§ 54.4980B-1 through 54.4980B-10 prohibits a group health plan from providing coverage that continues beyond the end of the maximum coverage period.

(b)(1) The end of the maximum coverage period is measured from the date of the qualifying event even if the qualifying event does not result in a loss of coverage under the plan until a later date. If, however, coverage under the plan is lost at a later date and the plan provides for the extension of the required periods, then the maximum coverage period is measured from the date when coverage is lost. A plan provides for the extension of the required periods if it provides both—

(i) That the 30-day notice period (during which the employer is required to notify the plan administrator of the occurrence of certain qualifying events such as the death of the covered employee or the termination of employment or reduction of hours of employment of the covered employee) begins on the date of the loss of coverage rather than on the date of the qualifying event; and

(ii) That the end of the maximum coverage period is measured from the date of the loss of coverage rather than from the date of the qualifying event.

(2) In the case of a plan that provides for the extension of the required periods, whenever the rules of §§ 54.4980B-1 through 54.4980B-10 refer to the measurement of a period from the date of the qualifying event, those rules apply in such a case by measuring the period instead from the date of the loss of coverage.

(c) In the case of a qualifying event that is a termination of employment or reduction of hours of employment, the maximum coverage period ends 18 months after the qualifying event if there is no disability extension, and 29 months after the qualifying event if there is a disability extension. See Q & A-5 of this section for rules to determine if there is a disability extension. If there is a disability extension and the disabled qualified beneficiary is later determined to no longer be disabled, then a plan may terminate the COBRA continuation coverage of an affected qualified beneficiary before the end of the disability extension; see paragraph (a)(6) in Q & A-1 of this section.

(d)(1) If a covered employee becomes entitled to Medicare benefits under Title XVIII of the Social Security Act (42 U.S.C. 1395-1395ggg) before experiencing a qualifying event that is a termination of employment or reduction of hours of employment, the maximum coverage period for qualified beneficiaries other than the covered employee ends on the later of—

(i) 36 months after the date the covered employee became entitled to Medicare benefits; or

(ii) 18 months (or 29 months, if there is a disability extension) after the date of the covered employee's termination of employment or reduction of hours of employment.

(2) See paragraph (b) of Q & A-3 of this section regarding the determination of when a covered employee becomes entitled to Medicare benefits.

(e) In the case of a qualifying event that is the bankruptcy of the employer, the maximum coverage period for a qualified beneficiary who is the retired covered employee ends on the date of the retired covered employee's death. The maximum coverage period for a qualified beneficiary who is the spouse, surviving spouse, or dependent child of the retired covered employee ends on the earlier of—

(1) The date of the qualified beneficiary's death; or

(2) The date that is 36 months after the death of the retired covered employee.

Q-5: How does a qualified beneficiary become entitled to a disability extension?

A-5: (a) A qualified beneficiary becomes entitled to a disability extension if the requirements of paragraphs (b), (c), and (d) of this Q&A-5 are satisfied with respect to the qualified beneficiary. If the disability extension applies with respect to a qualifying event, it applies with respect to each qualified beneficiary entitled to COBRA continuation coverage because of that qualifying event. Thus, for example, the 29-month maximum coverage period applies to each qualified beneficiary who is not disabled as well as to the qualified beneficiary who is disabled, and it applies independently with respect to each of the qualified beneficiaries. See Q&A-1 in § 54.4980B-8, which permits a plan to require payment of an increased amount during the disability extension.

(b) The requirement of this paragraph (b) is satisfied if a qualifying event occurs that is a termination, or reduction of hours, of a covered employee's employment.

(c) The requirement of this paragraph (c) is satisfied if an individual (whether or not the covered employee) who is a qualified beneficiary in connection with the qualifying event described in paragraph (b) of this Q&A-5 is determined under Title II or XVI of the Social Security Act (42 U.S.C. 401-433 or 1381-1385) to have been disabled at any time during the first 60 days of COBRA continuation coverage. For this purpose, the period of the first 60 days of COBRA continuation coverage is measured from the date of the qualifying event described in paragraph (b) of this Q & A-5 (except that if a loss of coverage would occur at a later date in the absence of an election for COBRA continuation coverage and if the plan provides for the extension of the required periods (as described in paragraph (b) of Q & A-4 of this section) then the period of the first 60 days of COBRA continuation coverage is measured from the date on which the coverage would be lost). However, in the case of a qualified beneficiary who is a child born to or placed for adoption with a covered employee during a period of COBRA continuation coverage, the period of the first 60 days of COBRA continuation coverage is measured from the date of birth or placement for adoption. For purposes of this

paragraph (c), an individual is determined to be disabled within the first 60 days of COBRA continuation coverage if the individual has been determined under Title II or XVI of the Social Security Act to have been disabled before the first day of COBRA continuation coverage and has not been determined to be no longer disabled at any time between the date of that disability determination and the first day of COBRA continuation coverage.

(d) The requirement of this paragraph (d) is satisfied if any of the qualified beneficiaries affected by the qualifying event described in paragraph (b) of this Q&A-5 provides notice to the plan administrator of the disability determination on a date that is both within 60 days after the date the determination is issued and before the end of the original 18-month maximum coverage period that applies to the qualifying event.

Q-6: Under what circumstances can the maximum coverage period be expanded?

A-6: (a) The maximum coverage period can be expanded if the requirements of Q&A-5 of this section (relating to the disability extension) or paragraph (b) of this Q&A-6 are satisfied.

(b) The requirements of this paragraph (b) are satisfied if a qualifying event that gives rise to an 18-month maximum coverage period (or a 29-month maximum coverage period in the case of a disability extension) is followed, within that 18-month period (or within that 29-month period, in the case of a disability extension), by a second qualifying event (for example, a death or a divorce) that gives rise to a 36-month maximum coverage period. (Thus, a termination of employment following a qualifying event that is a reduction of hours of employment cannot be a second qualifying event that expands the maximum coverage period; the bankruptcy of an employer also cannot be a second qualifying event that expands the maximum coverage period.) In such a case, the original 18-month period (or 29-month period, in the case of a disability extension) is expanded to 36 months, but only for those individuals who were qualified beneficiaries under the group health plan in connection with the first qualifying event and who are still qualified beneficiaries at the time of the second qualifying event. No qualifying event (other than a qualifying event that is the bankruptcy of the employer) can give rise to a maximum coverage period that ends more than 36 months after the date of the first qualifying event (or more than 36 months after the date of the loss of coverage, in the case of a plan that provides for the extension of the required periods; see paragraph (b) in Q & A-4 of this section). For example, if an employee covered by a group health plan that is subject to COBRA terminates employment (for reasons other than gross misconduct) on December 31, 2000, the termination is a qualifying event giving rise to a maximum coverage period that extends for 18 months to June 30, 2002. If the employee dies after the employee and the employee's spouse and dependent children have elected COBRA continuation coverage and on or before June 30, 2002, the spouse and dependent children (except anyone among them whose COBRA continuation coverage had already ended for some other reason) will be able to receive COBRA continuation coverage through December 31, 2003. See Q & A-8(b) of § 54.4980B-2 for a special rule that applies to certain health flexible spending arrangements.

Q-7: If health coverage is provided to a qualified beneficiary after a qualifying event without regard to COBRA continuation coverage (for example, as a result of state or local law, the Uniformed Services Employment and Reemployment Rights Act of 1994 (38 U.S.C. 4315), industry practice, a collective bargaining agreement, severance agreement, or plan procedure), will such alternative coverage extend the maximum coverage period?

A-7: (a) No. The end of the maximum coverage period is measured solely as described in Q&A-4 and Q&A-6 of this section, which is generally from the date of the qualifying event.

(b) If the alternative coverage does not satisfy all the requirements for COBRA continuation coverage, or if the amount that the group health plan requires to be paid for the alternative coverage is greater than the amount required to be paid by similarly situated nonCOBRA beneficiaries for the coverage that the qualified beneficiary can elect to receive as COBRA continuation coverage, the plan covering the qualified beneficiary immediately before the qualifying event must offer the qualified beneficiary receiving the alternative coverage the opportunity to elect COBRA continuation coverage. See Q&A-1 of § 54.4980B-6.

(c) If an individual rejects COBRA continuation coverage in favor of alternative coverage, then, at the expiration of the alternative coverage period, the individual need not be offered a COBRA election. However, if the individual receiving alternative coverage is a covered employee and the spouse or a dependent child of the individual would lose that alternative coverage as a result of a qualifying event (such as the death of the covered employee), the spouse or dependent child must be given an opportunity to elect to continue that alternative coverage, with a maximum coverage period of 36 months measured from the date of that qualifying event.

Q-8: Must a qualified beneficiary be given the right to enroll in a conversion health plan at the end of the maximum coverage period for COBRA continuation coverage?

A-8: If a qualified beneficiary's COBRA continuation coverage under a group health plan ends as a result of the expiration of the maximum coverage period, the group health plan must, during the 180-day period that ends on that expiration date, provide the qualified beneficiary the option of enrolling under a conversion health plan if such an option is otherwise generally available to similarly situated nonCOBRA beneficiaries under the group health plan. If such a conversion option is not otherwise generally available, it need not be made available to qualified beneficiaries.

[Reg. § 54.4980B-7.]

☐ [*T.D. 8812, 2-2-99. Amended by T.D. 8928, 1-9-2001.*]

### [Reg. § 54.4980B-8]

**§ 54.4980B-8. Paying for COBRA continuation coverage.**—The following questions-and-answers address paying for COBRA continuation coverage:

Q-1: Can a group health plan require payment for COBRA continuation coverage?

A-1: (a) Yes. For any period of COBRA continuation coverage, a group health plan can require the payment of an amount that does not exceed 102 percent of the applicable premium for that period. (See paragraph (b) of this Q&A-1 for a rule permitting a plan to require payment of an increased amount due to the disability extension.) The *applicable premium* is defined in section 4980B(f)(4). A group health plan can terminate a qualified beneficiary's COBRA continuation coverage as of the first day of any period for which timely payment is not made to the plan with respect to that qualified beneficiary (see Q&A-1 of § 54.4980B-7). For the meaning of *timely payment*, see Q&A-5 of this section.

(b) A group health plan is permitted to require the payment of an amount that does not exceed 150 percent of the applicable premium for any period of COBRA continuation coverage covering a disabled qualified beneficiary (for example, whether single or family coverage) if the coverage would not be required to be made available in the absence of a disability extension. (See Q&A-5 of § 54.4980B-7 for rules to determine whether a qualified beneficiary is entitled to a disability extension.) A plan is not permitted to require the payment of an amount that exceeds 102 percent of the applicable premium for any period of COBRA continuation coverage to which a qualified beneficiary is entitled without regard to the disability extension. Thus, if a qualified beneficiary entitled to a disability extension experiences a second qualifying event within the original 18-month maximum coverage period, then the plan is not permitted to require the payment of an amount that exceeds 102 percent of the applicable premium for any period of COBRA continuation coverage. By contrast, if a qualified beneficiary entitled to a disability extension experiences a second qualifying event after the end of the original 18-month maximum coverage period, then the plan may require the payment of an amount that is up to 150 percent of the applicable premium for the remainder of the period of COBRA continuation coverage (that is, from the beginning of the 19th month through the end of the 36th month) as long as the disabled qualified beneficiary is included in that coverage. The rules of this paragraph (b) are illustrated by the following examples; in each example the group health plan is subject to COBRA:

*Example 1.* (i) An employer maintains a group health plan. The plan determines the cost of covering individuals under the plan by reference to two categories, individual coverage and family coverage, and the applicable premium is determined for those two categories. An employee and members of the employee's family are covered under the plan. The employee experiences a qualifying event that is the termination of the employee's employment. The employee's family qualifies for the disability extension because of the disability of the employee's spouse. (Timely notice of the disability is provided to the plan administrator.) Timely payment of the amount required by the plan for COBRA continuation coverage for the family (which does not exceed 102 percent of the cost of family coverage under the plan) was made to the plan with respect to the employee's family for the first 18 months of COBRA continuation coverage, and the disabled spouse and the rest of the family continue to receive COBRA continuation coverage through the 29th month.

(ii) Under these facts, the plan may require payment of up to 150 percent of the applicable premium for family coverage in order for the family to receive COBRA continuation coverage from the 19th month through the 29th month. If the plan determined the cost of coverage by reference to three categories (such as employee, employee-plus-one-dependent, employee-plus-two-or- more-dependents) or more than three categories, instead of two categories, the plan could still require, from the 19th month through the 29th month

of COBRA continuation coverage, the payment of 150 percent of the cost of coverage for the category of coverage that included the disabled spouse.

*Example 2.* (i) The facts are the same as in *Example 1*, except that only the covered employee elects and pays for the first 18 months of COBRA continuation coverage.

(ii) Even though the employee's disabled spouse does not elect or pay for COBRA continuation coverage, the employee satisfies the requirements for the disability extension to apply with respect to the employee's qualifying event. Under these facts, the plan may not require the payment of more than 102 percent of the applicable premium for individual coverage for the entire period of the employee's COBRA continuation coverage, including the period from the 19th month through the 29th month. If COBRA continuation coverage had been elected and paid for with respect to other nondisabled members of the employee's family, then the plan could not require the payment of more than 102 percent of the applicable premium for family coverage (or for any other appropriate category of coverage that might apply to that group of qualified beneficiaries under the plan, such as employee-plus-one-dependent or employee-plus-two-or-more-dependents) for those family members to continue their coverage from the 19th month through the 29th month.

(c) A group health plan does not fail to comply with section 9802(b) (which generally prohibits an individual from being charged, on the basis of health status, a higher premium than that charged for similarly situated individuals enrolled in the plan) with respect to a qualified beneficiary entitled to the disability extension merely because the plan requires payment of an amount permitted under paragraph (b) of this Q & A-1.

Q-2: When is the applicable premium determined and when can a group health plan increase the amount it requires to be paid for COBRA continuation coverage?

A-2: (a) The applicable premium for each determination period must be computed and fixed by a group health plan before the determination period begins. A determination period is any 12-month period selected by the plan, but it must be applied consistently from year to year. The determination period is a single period for any benefit package. Thus, each qualified beneficiary does not have a separate determination period beginning on the date (or anniversaries of the date) that COBRA continuation coverage begins for that qualified beneficiary.

(b) During a determination period, a plan can increase the amount it requires to be paid for a qualified beneficiary's COBRA continuation coverage only in the following three cases:

(1) The plan has previously charged less than the maximum amount permitted under Q&A-1 of this section and the increased amount required to be paid does not exceed the maximum amount permitted under Q&A-1 of this section;

(2) The increase occurs during the disability extension and the increased amount required to be paid does not exceed the maximum amount permitted under paragraph (b) of Q&A-1 of this section; or

(3) A qualified beneficiary changes the coverage being received (see paragraph (c) of this Q&A-2 for rules on how the amount the plan requires to be paid may or must change when a qualified beneficiary changes the coverage being received).

(c) If a plan allows similarly situated active employees who have not experienced a qualifying event to change the coverage they are receiving, then the plan must also allow each qualified beneficiary to change the coverage being received on the same terms as the similarly situated active employees. (See Q&A-4 in § 54.4980B-5.) If a qualified beneficiary changes coverage from one benefit package (or a group of benefit packages) to another benefit package (or another group of benefit packages), or adds or eliminates coverage for family members, then the following rules apply. If the change in coverage is to a benefit package, group of benefit packages, or coverage unit (such as family coverage, self-plus-one-dependent, or self-plus-two-or-more-dependents) for which the applicable premium is higher, then the plan may increase the amount that it requires to be paid for COBRA continuation coverage to an amount that does not exceed the amount permitted under Q&A-1 of this section as applied to the new coverage. If the change in coverage is to a benefit package, group of benefit packages, or coverage unit (such as individual or self-plus-one- dependent) for which the applicable premium is lower, then the plan cannot require the payment of an amount that exceeds the amount permitted under Q&A-1 of this section as applied to the new coverage.

Q-3: Must a plan allow payment for COBRA continuation coverage to be made in monthly installments?

A-3: Yes. A group health plan must allow payment for COBRA continuation coverage to be made in monthly installments. A group health plan is permitted to also allow the alternative of payment for COBRA continuation coverage being made at other intervals (for example, weekly, quarterly, or semiannually).

Q-4: Is a plan required to allow a qualified beneficiary to choose to have the first payment for COBRA continuation coverage applied prospectively only?

A-4: No. A plan is permitted to apply the first payment for COBRA continuation coverage to the period of coverage beginning immediately after the date on which coverage under the plan would have been lost on account of the qualifying event. Of course, if the group health plan allows a qualified beneficiary to waive COBRA continuation coverage for any period before electing to receive COBRA continuation coverage, the first payment is not applied to the period of the waiver.

Q-5: What is timely payment for COBRA continuation coverage?

A-5: (a) Except as provided in this paragraph (a) or in paragraph (b) or (d) of this Q&A-5, timely payment for a period of COBRA continuation coverage under a group health plan means payment that is made to the plan by the date that is 30 days after the first day of that period. Payment that is made to the plan by a later date is also considered timely payment if either—

(1) Under the terms of the plan, covered employees or qualified beneficiaries are allowed until that later date to pay for their coverage for the period; or

(2) Under the terms of an arrangement between the employer or employee organization and an insurance company, health maintenance organization, or other entity that provides plan benefits on the employer's or employee organization's behalf, the employer or employee organization is allowed until that later date to pay for coverage of similarly situated nonCOBRA beneficiaries for the period.

(b) Notwithstanding paragraph (a) of this Q&A-5, a plan cannot require payment for any period of COBRA continuation coverage for a qualified beneficiary earlier than 45 days after the date on which the election of COBRA continuation coverage is made for that qualified beneficiary.

(c) If, after COBRA continuation coverage has been elected for a qualified beneficiary, a provider of health care (such as a physician, hospital, or pharmacy) contacts the plan to confirm coverage of a qualified beneficiary for a period for which the plan has not yet received payment, the plan must give a complete response to the health care provider about the qualified beneficiary's COBRA continuation coverage rights, if any, described in paragraphs (a), (b), and (d) of this Q&A-5. For example, if the plan provides coverage during the 30- and 45-day grace periods described in paragraphs (a) and (b) of this Q&A-5 but cancels coverage retroactively if payment is not made by the end of the applicable grace period, then the plan must inform a provider with respect to a qualified beneficiary for whom payment has not been received that the qualified beneficiary is covered but that the coverage is subject to retroactive termination if timely payment is not made. Similarly, if the plan cancels coverage if it has not received payment by the first day of a period of coverage but retroactively reinstates coverage if payment is made by the end of the grace period for that period of coverage, then the plan must inform the provider that the qualified beneficiary currently does not have coverage but will have coverage retroactively to the first date of the period if timely payment is made. (See paragraph (b) of Q&A-3 in §54.4980B-6 for similar rules that the plan must follow in confirming coverage during the election period.)

(d) If timely payment is made to the plan in an amount that is not significantly less than the amount the plan requires to be paid for a period of coverage, then the amount paid is deemed to satisfy the plan's requirement for the amount that must be paid, unless the plan notifies the qualified beneficiary of the amount of the deficiency and grants a reasonable period of time for payment of the deficiency to be made. For this purpose, as a safe harbor, 30 days after the date the notice is provided is deemed to be a reasonable period of time. An amount is not significantly less than the amount the plan requires to be paid for a period of coverage if and only if the shortfall is no greater than the lesser of the following two amounts:

(1) Fifty dollars (or such other amount as the Commissioner may provide in a revenue ruling, notice, or other guidance published in the Internal Revenue Bulletin (see §601.601(d)(2)(ii) of this chapter)); or

(2) 10 percent of the amount the plan requires to be paid.

(e) Payment is considered made on the date on which it is sent to the plan.

[Reg. §54.4980B-8.]

☐ [T.D. 8812, 2-2-99. Amended by T.D. 8928, 1-9-2001.]

### [Reg. §54.4980B-9]

**§54.4980B-9. Business reorganizations and employer withdrawals from multiemployer plans.**—The following questions-and-answers address who has the obligation to make COBRA continuation coverage available to affected qualified beneficiaries in the context of business reorganizations and employer withdrawals from multiemployer plans:

Q-1: For purposes of this section, what are a business reorganization, a stock sale, and an asset sale?

A-1: For purposes of this section:

(a) A *business reorganization* is a stock sale or an asset sale.

(b) A *stock sale* is a transfer of stock in a corporation that causes the corporation to become a different employer or a member of a different employer. (See Q & A-2 of §54.4980B-2, which defines *employer* to include all members of a controlled group of corporations.) Thus, for example, a sale or distribution of stock in a corporation that causes the corporation to cease to be a member of one controlled group of corporations, whether or not it becomes a member of another controlled group of corporations, is a stock sale.

(c) An *asset sale* is a transfer of substantial assets, such as a plant or division or substantially all the assets of a trade or business.

(d) The rules of §1.414(b)-1 of this chapter apply in determining what constitutes a controlled group of corporations, and the rules of §§1.414(c)-1 through 1.41(c)-5 of this chapter apply in determining what constitutes a group of trades or businesses under common control.

Q-2: In the case of a stock sale, what are the selling group, the acquired organization, and the buying group?

A-2: In the case of a stock sale—

(a) The *selling group* is the controlled group of corporations, or the group of trades or businesses under common control, of which a corporation ceases to be a member as a result of the stock sale;

(b) The *acquired organization* is the corporation that ceases to be a member of the selling group as a result of the stock sale; and

(c) The *buying group* is the controlled group of corporations, or the group of trades or businesses under common control, of which the acquired organization becomes a member as a result of the stock sale. If the acquired organization does not become a member of such a group, the *buying group* is the acquired organization.

Q-3: In the case of an asset sale, what are the selling group and the buying group?

A-3: In the case of an asset sale—

(a) The *selling group* is the controlled group of corporations or the group of trades or businesses under common control that includes the corporation or other trade or business that is selling the assets; and

(b) The *buying group* is the controlled group of corporations or the group of trades or businesses under common control that includes the corporation or other trade or business that is buying the assets.

Q-4: Who is an M & A qualified beneficiary?

A-4: (a) Asset sales: In the case of an asset sale, an individual is an M & A qualified beneficiary if the individual is a qualified beneficiary whose qualifying event occurred prior to or in connection with the sale and who is, or whose qualifying event occurred in connection with, a covered employee whose last employment prior to the qualifying event was associated with the assets being sold.

(b) Stock sales: In the case of a stock sale, an individual is an M & A qualified beneficiary if the individual is a qualified beneficiary whose qualifying event occurred prior to or in connection with the sale and who is, or whose qualifying event occurred in connection with, a covered employee whose last employment prior to the qualifying event was with the acquired organization.

(c) In the case of a qualified beneficiary who has experienced more than one qualifying event with respect to her or his current right to COBRA continuation coverage, the qualifying event referred to in paragraphs (a) and (b) of this Q & A-4 is the first qualifying event.

Q-5: In the case of a stock sale, is the sale a qualifying event with respect to a covered employee who is employed by the acquired organization before the sale and who continues to be employed by the acquired organization after the sale, or with respect to the spouse or dependent children of such a covered employee?

A-5: No. A covered employee who continues to be employed by the acquired organization after the sale does not experience a termination of employment as a result of the sale. Accordingly, the sale is not a qualifying event with respect to the covered employee, or with respect to the covered employee's spouse or dependent children, regardless of whether they are provided with group health coverage after the sale, and neither the covered employee, nor the covered employee's spouse or dependent children, become qualified beneficiaries as a result of the sale.

Q-6: In the case of an asset sale, is the sale a qualifying event with respect to a covered employee whose employment immediately before the sale was associated with the purchased assets, or with respect to the spouse or dependent children of such a covered employee who are covered under a group health plan of the selling group immediately before the sale?

A-6: (a) Yes, unless—

(1) The buying group is a successor employer under paragraph (c) of Q & A-8 of this section or Q & A-2 of §54.4980B-2, and the covered

employee is employed by the buying group immediately after the sale; or

(2) The covered employee (or the spouse or any dependent child of the covered employee) does not lose coverage (within the meaning of paragraph (c) in Q & A-1 of § 54.4980B-4) under a group health plan of the selling group after the sale.

(b) Unless the conditions in paragraph (a)(1) or (2) of this Q & A-6 are satisfied, such a covered employee experiences a termination of employment with the selling group as a result of the asset sale, regardless of whether the covered employee is employed by the buying group or whether the covered employee's employment is associated with the purchased assets after the sale. Accordingly, the covered employee, and the spouse and dependent children of the covered employee who lose coverage under a plan of the selling group in connection with the sale, are M & A qualified beneficiaries in connection with the sale.

Q-7: In a business reorganization, are the buying group and the selling group permitted to allocate by contract the responsibility to make COBRA continuation coverage available to M & A qualified beneficiaries?

A-7: Yes. Nothing in this section prohibits a selling group and a buying group from allocating to one or the other of the parties in a purchase agreement the responsibility to provide the coverage required under §§ 54.4980B-1 through 54.4980B-10. However, if and to the extent that the party assigned this responsibility under the terms of the contract fails to perform, the party who has the obligation under Q & A-8 of this section to make COBRA continuation coverage available to M & A qualified beneficiaries continues to have that obligation.

Q-8: Which group health plan has the obligation to make COBRA continuation coverage available to M & A qualified beneficiaries in a business reorganization?

A-8: (a) In the case of a business reorganization (whether a stock sale or an asset sale), so long as the selling group maintains a group health plan after the sale, a group health plan maintained by the selling group has the obligation to make COBRA continuation coverage available to M & A qualified beneficiaries with respect to that sale. This Q & A-8 prescribes rules for cases in which the selling group ceases to provide any group health plan to any employee in connection with the sale. Paragraph (b) of this Q & A-8 contains these rules for stock sales, and paragraph (c) of this Q & A-8 contains these rules for asset sales. Neither a stock sale nor an asset sale has any effect on the COBRA continuation coverage requirements applicable to any group health plan for any period before the sale.

(b)(1) In the case of a stock sale, if the selling group ceases to provide any group health plan to any employee in connection with the sale, a group health plan maintained by the buying group has the obligation to make COBRA continuation coverage available to M & A qualified beneficiaries with respect to that stock sale. A group health plan of the buying group has this obligation beginning on the later of the following two dates and continuing as long as the buying group continues to maintain a group health plan (but subject to the rules in § 54.4980B-7, relating to the duration of COBRA continuation coverage)—

(i) The date the selling group ceases to provide any group health plan to any employee; or

(ii) The date of the stock sale.

(2) The determination of whether the selling group's cessation of providing any group health plan to any employee is in connection with the stock sale is based on all of the relevant facts and circumstances. A group health plan of the buying group does not, as a result of the stock sale, have an obligation to make COBRA continuation coverage available to those qualified beneficiaries of the selling group who are not M & A qualified beneficiaries with respect to that sale.

(c)(1) In the case of an asset sale, if the selling group ceases to provide any group health plan to any employee in connection with the sale and if the buying group continues the business operations associated with the assets purchased from the selling group without interruption or substantial change, then the buying group is a successor employer to the selling group in connection with that asset sale. A buying group does not fail to be a successor employer in connection with an asset sale merely because the asset sale takes place in connection with a proceeding in bankruptcy under Title 11 of the United States Code. If the buying group is a successor employer, a group health plan maintained by the buying group has the obligation to make COBRA continuation coverage available to M & A qualified beneficiaries with respect to that asset sale. A group health plan of the buying group has this obligation beginning on the later of the following two dates and continuing as long as the buying group continues to maintain a group health plan (but subject to the rules in § 54.4980B-7, relating to the duration of COBRA continuation coverage)—

(i) The date the selling group ceases to provide any group health plan to any employee; or

(ii) The date of the asset sale.

(2) The determination of whether the selling group's cessation of providing any group health plan to any employee is in connection with the asset sale is based on all of the relevant facts and circumstances. A group health plan of the buying group does not, as a result of the asset sale, have an obligation to make COBRA continuation coverage available to those qualified beneficiaries of the selling group who are not M & A qualified beneficiaries with respect to that sale.

(d) The rules of Q & A-1 through Q & A-7 of this section and this Q & A-8 are illustrated by the following examples; in each example, each group health plan is subject to COBRA:

*Stock Sale Examples*

*Example 1.* (i) Selling Group S consists of three corporations, *A*, *B*, and *C*. Buying Group *P* consists of two corporations, *D* and *E*. *P* enters into a contract to purchase all the stock of *C* from *S* effective July 1, 2002. Before the sale of *C*, *S* maintains a single group health plan for the employees of *A*, *B*, and *C* (and their families). *P* maintains a single group health plan for the employees of *D* and *E* (and their families). Effective July 1, 2002, the employees of *C* (and their families) become covered under *P*'s plan. On June 30, 2002, there are 48 qualified beneficiaries receiving COBRA continuation coverage under *S*'s plan, 15 of whom are M & A qualified beneficiaries with respect to the sale of *C*. (The other 33 qualified beneficiaries had qualifying events in connection with a covered employee whose last employment before the qualifying event was with either *A* or *B*.)

(ii) Under these facts, *S*'s plan continues to have the obligation to make COBRA continuation coverage available to the 15 M & A qualified beneficiaries under *S*'s plan after the sale of *C* to *P*. The employees who continue in employment with *C* do not experience a qualifying event by virtue of *P*'s acquisition of *C*. If they experience a qualifying event after the sale, then the group health plan of *P* has the obligation to make COBRA continuation coverage available to them.

*Example 2.* (i) Selling Group *S* consists of three corporations, *A*, *B*, and *C*. Each of *A*, *B*, and *C* maintains a group health plan for its employees (and their families). Buying Group *P* consists of two corporations, *D* and *E*. *P* enters into a contract to purchase all of the stock of *C* from *S* effective July 1, 2002. As of June 30, 2002, there are 14 qualified beneficiaries receiving COBRA continuation coverage under *C*'s plan. *C* continues to employ all of its employees and continues to maintain its group health plan after being acquired by *P* on July 1, 2002.

(ii) Under these facts, *C* is an acquired organization and the 14 qualified beneficiaries under *C*'s plan are M & A qualified beneficiaries. A group health plan of *S* (that is, either the plan maintained by *A* or the plan maintained by *B*) has the obligation to make COBRA continuation coverage available to the 14 M & A qualified beneficiaries. *S* and *P* could negotiate. to have *C*'s plan continue to make COBRA continuation coverage available to the 14 M & A qualified beneficiaries. In such a case, neither *A*'s plan nor *B*'s plan would make COBRA continuation coverage available to the 14 M & A qualified beneficiaries unless *C*'s plan failed to fulfill its contractual responsibility to make COBRA continuation coverage available to the M & A qualified beneficiaries. *C*'s employees (and their spouses and dependent children) do not experience a qualifying even in connection with *P*'s acquisition of *C*, and consequently no plan maintained by either *P* or *S* has any obligation to make COBRA continuation coverage available to *C*'s employees (or their spouses or dependent children) in connection with the transfer of stock in *C* from *S* to *P*.

*Example 3.* (i) The facts are the same as in *Example 2*, except that *C* ceases to employ two employees on June 30, 2002, and those two employees never become covered under *P*'s plan.

(ii) Under these facts, the two employees experience a qualifying event on June 30, 2002 because their termination of employment causes a loss of group health coverage. A group health plan of *S* (that is, either the plan maintained by *A* or the plan maintained by *B*) has the obligation to make COBRA continuation coverage available to the two employees (and to any spouse or dependent child of the two employees who loses coverage under *C*'s plan in connection with the termination of employment of the two employees) because they are M & A qualified beneficiaries with respect to the sale of *C*.

*Example 4.* (i) Selling Group *S* consists of three corporations, *A*, *B*, and *C*. Buying Group *P* consists of two corporations, *D* and *E*. *P* enters into a contract to purchase all of the stock of *C* from *S* effective July 1, 2002. Before the sale of *C*, *S* maintains a single group health plan for the employees of *A*. *B*. and *C* (and their families). *P* maintains a single group health plan for the employees of *D* and *E* (and their families). Effective July 1, 2002, the employees of *C* (and their families) become covered under *P*'s plan. On June 30, 2002, there are 25 qualified beneficiaries receiving COBRA continuation coverage under *S*'s plan, 20 of whom are M & A qualified beneficiaries with respect to the sale of C. (The other five qualified beneficiaries had qualifying events in connection with a covered employee whose last employment before the qualifying event was with either A or B.) S terminates its group health plan effective June 30, 2002 and begins to liquidate the assets of A and B and to lay off the employees of A and B.

(ii) Under these facts, S ceases to provide a group health plan to any employee in connection with the sale of C to P. Thus, beginning July 1, 2002 P's plan has the obligation to make COBRA continuation coverage available to the 20 M & A qualified beneficiaries, but P is not obligated to make COBRA continuation coverage available to the other 5 qualified beneficiaries with respect to S's plan as of June 30, 2002 or to any of the employees of A or B whose employment is terminated by S (or to any of those employees' spouses or dependent children).

*Asset Sale Examples*

*Example 5.* (i) Selling Group S provides group health plan coverage to employees at each of its operating divisions. S sells the assets of one of its divisions to Buying Group P. Under the terms of the group health plan covering the employees at the division being sold, their coverage will end on the date of the sale. P hires all but one of those employees, gives them the same positions that they had with S before the sale, and provides them with coverage under a group health plan. Immediately before the sale, there are two qualified beneficiaries receiving COBRA continuation coverage under a group health plan of S whose qualifying events occurred in connection with a covered employee whose last employment prior to the qualifying event was associated with the assets sold to P.

(ii) These two qualified beneficiaries are M & A qualified beneficiaries with respect to the asset sale to P. Under these facts, a group health plan of S retains the obligation to make COBRA continuation coverage available to these two M & A qualified beneficiaries. In addition, the one employee P does not hire as well as all of the employees P hires (and the spouses and dependent children of these employees) who were covered under a group health plan of S on the day before the sale are M & A qualified beneficiaries with respect to the sale. A group health plan of S also has the obligation to make COBRA continuation coverage available to these M & A qualified beneficiaries.

*Example 6.* (i) Selling Group S provides group health plan coverage to employees at each of its operating divisions. S sells substantially all of the assets of all of its divisions to Buying Group P, and S ceases to provide any group health plan to any employee on the date of the sale. P hires all but one of S's employees on the date of the asset sale by S, gives those employees the same positions that they had with S before the sale, and continues the business operations of those divisions without substantial change or interruption. P provides these employees with coverage under a group health plan. Immediately before the sale, there are 10 qualified beneficiaries receiving COBRA continuation coverage under a group health plan of S whose qualifying events occurred in connection with a covered employee whose last employment prior to the qualifying event was associated with the assets sold to P.

(ii) These 10 qualified beneficiaries are M & A qualified beneficiaries with respect to the asset sale to P. Under these facts, P is a successor employer described in paragraph (c) of this Q & A-8. Thus, a group health plan of P has the obligation to make COBRA continuation coverage available to these 10 M & A qualified beneficiaries.

(iii) The one employee that P does not hire and the family members of that employee are also M & A qualified beneficiaries with respect to the sale. A group health plan of P also has the obligation to make COBRA continuation coverage available to these M & A qualified beneficiaries.

(iv) The employees who continue in employment in connection with the asset sale (and their family members) and who were covered under a group health plan of S on the day before the sale are not M & A qualified beneficiaries because P is a successor employer to S in connection with the asset sale. Thus, no group health plan of P has any obligation to make COBRA continuation coverage available to these continuing employees with respect to the qualifying event that resulted from their losing coverage under S's plan in connection with the asset sale.

*Example 7.* (i) Selling Group S provides group health plan coverage to employees at each of its two operating divisions. S sells the assets of one of its divisions to Buying Group P1. Under the terms of the group health plan covering the employees at the division being sold, their coverage will end on the date of the sale. P1 hires all but one of those employees, gives them the same positions that they had with S before the sale, and provides them with coverage under a group health plan.

(ii) Under these facts, a group health plan of S has the obligation to make COBRA continuation coverage available to M & A qualified beneficiaries with respect to the sale to P1. (If an M & A qualified beneficiary first became covered under P1's plan after electing CO-

BRA continuation coverage under S's plan, then S's plan could terminate the COBRA continuation coverage once the M & A qualified beneficiary became covered under P1's plan, provided that the remaining conditions of Q & A-2 of § 54.49890B-7 were satisfied.)

(iii) Several months after the sale to P1, S sells the assets of its remaining division to Buying Group P2 and S ceases to provide any group health plan to any employee on the date of that sale. Thus, under Q & A-1 of § 54.4980B-7, S ceases to have an obligation to make COBRA continuation coverage available to any qualified beneficiary on the date of the sale to P2. P1 and P2 are unrelated organizations.

(iv) Even if it was foreseeable that S would sell its remaining division to an unrelated third party after the sale to P1, under these facts the cessation of S to provide any group health plan to any employee on the date of the sale to P2 is not in connection with the asset sale to P1. Thus, even after the date S ceases to provide any group health plan to any employee, no group health plan of P1. has any obligation to make COBRA continuation coverage available to M & A qualified beneficiaries with respect to the asset sale to P1 by S. If P2 is a successor employer under the rules of paragraph (c) of this Q & A-8 and maintains one or more group health plans after the sale, then a group health plan of P2 would have an obligation to make COBRA continuation coverage available to M & A qualified beneficiaries with respect to the asset sale to P2 by S (but in such a case employees of S before the sale who continued working for P2 after the sale would not be M & A qualified beneficiaries). However, even in such a case, no group health plan of P2 would have an obligation to make COBRA continuation coverage available to M & A qualified beneficiaries with respect to the asset sale to P1 by S. Thus, under these facts, after S has ceased to provide any group health plan to any employee, no plan has an obligation to make COBRA continuation coverage available to M & A qualified beneficiaries with respect to the asset sale to P1.

*Example 8.* (i) Selling Group S provides group health plan coverage to employees at each of its operating divisions. S sells substantially all of the assets of all of its divisions to Buying Group P. P hires most of S's employees on the date of the purchase of S's assets, retains those employees in the same positions that they had with S before the purchase, and continues the business operations of those divisions without substantial change or interruption. P provides these employees with coverage under a group health plan. S continues to employ a few employees for the principal purpose of winding up the affairs of S in preparation for liquidation. S continues to provide coverage under a group health plan to these few remaining employees for several weeks after the date of the sale and then ceases to provide any group health plan to any employee.

(ii) Under these facts, the cessation by S to provide any group health plan to any employee is in connection with the asset sale to P. Because of this, and because P continued the business operations associated with those assets without substantial change or interruption, P is a successor employer to S with respect to the asset sale. Thus, a group health plan of P has the obligation to make COBRA continuation coverage available to M & A qualified beneficiaries with respect to the sale beginning on the date that S ceases to provide any group health plan to any employee. (A group health plan of S retains this obligation for the several weeks after the date of the sale until S ceases to provide any group health plan to any employee.)

Q-9: Can the cessation of contributions by an employer to a multiemployer group health plan be a qualifying event?

A-9: The cessation of contributions by an employer to a multiemployer group health plan is not itself a qualifying event, even though the cessation of contributions may cause current employees (and their spouses and dependent children) to lose coverage under the multiemployer plan. An event coinciding with the employer's cessation of contributions (such as a reduction of hours of employment in the case of striking employees) will constitute a qualifying event if it otherwise satisfies the requirements of Q & A-1 of § 54.4980B-4.

Q-10: If an employer stops contributing to a multiemployer group health plan, does the multiemployer plan have the obligation to make COBRA continuation coverage available to a qualified beneficiary who was receiving coverage under the multiemployer plan on the day before the cessation of contributions and who is, or whose qualifying event occurred in connection with, a covered employee whose last employment prior to the qualifying event was with the employer that has stopped contributing to the multiemployer plan?

A-10: (a) In general, yes. (See Q & A-3 of § 54.4980B-2 for a definition of *multiemployer plan*.) If, however, the employer that stops contributing to the multiemployer plan makes group health plan coverage available to (or starts contributing to another multiemployer plan that is a group health plan with respect to) a class of the employer's employees formerly covered under the multiemployer plan, the plan maintained by the employer (or the other multiemployer plan), from that date forward, has the obligation to make COBRA continuation coverage available to any qualified beneficiary who was receiving coverage under the multiemployer plan on the day before the cessation of contributions and who is, or whose qualifying event occurred in connection with, a covered employee whose last employment prior to the qualifying event was with the employer.

(b) The rules of Q & A-9 of this section and this Q & A-10 are illustrated by the following examples; in each example, each group health plan is subject to COBRA:

*Example 1.* (i) Employer Z employs a class of employees covered by a collective bargaining agreement and participating in multiemployer group health plan M. As required by the collective bargaining agreement, Z has been making contributions to M. Z experiences financial difficulties and stops making contributions to M but continues to employ all of the employees covered by the collective bargaining agreement. Z's cessation of contributions to M causes those employees (and their spouses and dependent children) to lose coverage under M. Z does not make group health plan coverage available to any of the employees covered by the collective bargaining agreement.

(ii) After Z stops contributing to M, M continues to have the obligation to make COBRA continuation coverage available to any qualified beneficiary who experienced a qualifying event that preceded or coincided with the cessation of contributions to M and whose coverage under M on the day before the qualifying event was due to an employment affiliation with Z. The loss of coverage under M for those employees of Z who continue in employment (and the loss of coverage for their spouses and dependent children) does not constitute a qualifying event.

*Example 2.* (i) The facts are the same as in *Example 1* except that B, one of the employees covered under M before Z stops contributing to M, is transferred into management. Z maintains a group health plan for managers and B becomes eligible for coverage under the plan on the day of B's transfer.

(ii) Under these facts, Z does not make group health plan coverage available to a class of employees formerly covered under M after B becomes eligible under Z's group health plan for managers. Accordingly, M continues to have the obligation to make COBRA continuation coverage available to any qualified beneficiary who experienced a qualifying event that preceded or coincided with the cessation of contributions to M and whose coverage under M on the day before the qualifying event was due to an employment affiliation with Z.

*Example 3.* (i) Employer Y employs two classes of employees— skilled and unskilled laborers— covered by a collective bargaining agreement and participating in multiemployer group health plan M. As required by the collective bargaining agreement, Y has been making contributions to M. Y stops making contributions to M but continues to employ all the employees covered by the collective bargaining agreement. Y's cessation of contributions to M causes those employees (and their spouses and dependent children) to lose coverage under M. Y makes group health plan coverage available to the skilled laborers immediately after their coverage ceases under M, but Y does not make group health plan coverage available to any of the unskilled laborers.

(ii) Under these facts, because Y makes group health plan coverage available to a class of employees previously covered under M immediately after both classes of employees lose coverage under M, Y alone has the obligation to make COBRA continuation coverage available to any qualified beneficiary who experienced a qualifying event that preceded or coincided with the cessation of contributions to M and whose coverage under M on the day before the qualifying event was due to an employment affiliation with Y, regardless of whether the employment affiliation was as a skilled or unskilled laborer. However, the loss of coverage under M for those employees of Y who continue in employment (and the loss of coverage for their spouses and dependent children) does not constitute a qualifying event.

*Example 4.* (i) Employer X employs a class of employees covered by a collective bargaining agreement and participating in multiemployer group health plan M. As required by the collective bargaining agreement, X has been making contributions to M. X experiences financial difficulties and is forced into bankruptcy by its creditors. X continues to employ all of the employees covered by the collective bargaining agreement. X also continues to make contributions to M until the current collective bargaining agreement expires, on June 30, 2001, and then X stops making contributions to M. X's employees (and their spouses and dependent children) lose coverage under M effective July 1, 2001. X does not enter into another collective bargaining agreement covering the class of employees covered by the expired collective bargaining agreement. Effective September 1, 2001, X establishes a group health plan covering the class of employees formerly covered by the collective bargaining agreement. The group health plan also covers their spouses and dependent children.

(ii) Under these facts, M has the obligation to make COBRA continuation coverage available from July 1, 2001 until August 31, 2001, and the group health plan established by X has the obligation

to make COBRA continuation coverage available from September 1, 2001 until the obligation ends (see Q & A-1 of § 54.4980B-7) to any qualified beneficiary who experienced a qualifying event that preceded or coincided with the cessation of contributions to M and whose coverage under M on the day before the qualifying event was due to an employment affiliation with X. The loss of coverage under M for those employees of X who continue in employment (and the loss of coverage for their spouses and dependent children) does not constitute a qualifying event.

*Example 5.* (i) Employer W employs a class of employees covered by a collective bargaining agreement and participating in multiemployer group health plan M. As required by the collective bargaining agreement, W has been making contributions to M. The employees covered by the collective bargaining agreement vote to decertify their current employee representative effective January 1, 2002 and vote to certify a new employee representative effective the same date. As a consequence, on January 1, 2002 they cease to be covered under M and commence to be covered under multiemployer group health plan N.

(ii) Effective January 1, 2002, N has the obligation to make COBRA continuation coverage available to any qualified beneficiary who experienced a qualifying event that preceded or coincided with the cessation of contributions to M and whose coverage under M on the day before the qualifying event was due to an employment affiliation with W. The loss of coverage under M for those employees of W who continue in employment (and the loss of coverage for their spouses and dependent children) does not constitute a qualifying event. [Reg. § 54.4980B-9.]

☐ [T.D. 8928, 1-9-2001.]

**[Reg. § 54.4980B-10]**

**§ 54.4980B-10. Interaction of FMLA and COBRA.**—The following questions-and-answers address how the taking of leave under the Family and Medical Leave Act of 1993 (FMLA) (29 U.S.C. 2601-2619) affects the COBRA continuation coverage requirements:

Q-1: In what circumstances does a qualifying event occur if an employee does not return from leave taken under FMLA?

A-1: (a) The taking of leave under FMLA does not constitute a qualifying event. A qualifying event under Q & A-1 of § 54.4980B-4 occurs, however, if—

(1) An employee (or the spouse or a dependent child of the employee) is covered on the day before the first day of FMLA leave (or becomes covered during the FMLA leave) under a group health plan of the employee's employer;

(2) The employee does not return to employment with the employer at the end of the FMLA leave; and

(3) The employee (or the spouse or a dependent child of the employee) would, in the absence of COBRA continuation coverage, lose coverage under the group health plan before the end of the maximum coverage period.

(b) However, the satisfaction of the three conditions in paragraph (a) of this Q & A-1 does not constitute a qualifying event if the employer eliminates, on or before the last day of the employee's FMLA leave, coverage under a group health plan for the class of employees (while continuing to employ that class of employees) to which the employee would have belonged if the employee had not taken FMLA leave.

Q-2: If a qualifying event described in Q & A-1 of this section occurs, when does it occur, and how is the maximum coverage period measured?

A-2: A qualifying event described in Q & A-1 of this section occurs on the last day of FMLA leave. (The determination of when FMLA leave ends is not made under the rules of this section. See the FMLA regulations, 29 CFR Part 825 (§ § 825.100-825.800).) The maximum coverage period (see Q & A-4 of § 54.4980B-7) is measured from the date of the qualifying event (that is, the last day of FMLA leave). If, however, coverage under the group health plan is lost at a later date and the plan provides for the extension of the required periods (see paragraph (b) of Q & A-4 of § 54.4980B-7), then the maximum coverage period is measured from the date when coverage is lost. The rules of this Q & A-2 are illustrated by the following examples:

*Example 1.* (i) Employee B is covered under the group health plan of Employer X on January 31, 2001. B takes FMLA leave beginning February 1, 2001. B's last day of FMLA leave is 12 weeks later, on April 25, 2001, and B does not return to work with X at the end of the FMLA leave. If B does not elect COBRA continuation coverage, B will not be covered under the group health plan of X as of April 26, 2001.

(ii) B experiences a qualifying event on April 25, 2001, and the maximum coverage period is measured from that date. (This is the case even if, for part or all of the FMLA leave, B fails to pay the employee portion of premiums for coverage under the group health plan of X and is not covered under X's plan. See Q & A-3 of this section.)

*Example 2.* (i) Employee *C* and *C*'s spouse are covered under the group health plan of Employer *Y* on August 15, 2001. *C* takes FMLA leave beginning August 16, 2001. *C* informs *Y* less than 12 weeks later, on September 28, 2001, that *C* will not be returning to work. Under the FMLA regulations, 29 CFR Part 825 (§§ 825.100-825.800), *C*'s last day of FMLA leave is September 28, 2001. *C* does not return to work with *Y* at the end of the FMLA leave. If *C* and *C*'s spouse do not elect COBRA continuation coverage, they will not be covered under the group health plan of *Y* as of September 29, 2001.

(ii) *C* and *C*'s spouse experience a qualifying event on September 28, 2001, and the maximum coverage period (generally 18 months) is measured from that date. (This is the case even if, for part or all of the FMLA leave, *C* fails to pay the employee portion of premiums for coverage under the group health plan of *Y* and *C* or *C*'s spouse is not covered under *Y*'s plan. See Q & A-3 of this section.)

Q-3: If an employee fails to pay the employee portion of premiums for coverage under a group health plan during FMLA leave or declines coverage under a group health plan during FMLA leave, does this affect the determination of whether or when the employee has experienced a qualifying event?

A-3: No. Any lapse of coverage under a group health plan during FMLA leave is irrelevant in determining whether a set of circumstances constitutes a qualifying event under Q & A-1 of this section or when such a qualifying event occurs under Q & A-2 of this section.

Q-4: Is the application of the rules in Q & A-1 through Q & A-3 of this section affected by a requirement of state or local law to provide a period of coverage longer than that required under FMLA?

A-4: No. Any state or local law that requires coverage under a group health plan to be maintained during a leave of absence for a period longer than that required under FMLA (for example, for 16 weeks of leave rather than for the 12 weeks required under FMLA) is disregarded for purposes of determining when a qualifying event occurs under Q & A-1 through Q & A-3 of this section.

Q-5: May COBRA continuation coverage be conditioned upon reimbursement of the premiums paid by the employer for coverage under a group health plan during FMLA leave?

A-5: No. The U.S. Department of Labor has published rules describing the circumstances in which an employer may recover premiums it pays to maintain coverage, including family coverage, under a group health plan during FMLA leave from an employee who fails to return from leave. See 29 CFR 825.213. Even if recovery of premiums is permitted under 29 CFR 825.213, the right to COBRA continuation coverage cannot be conditioned upon the employee's reimbursement of the employer for premiums the employer paid to maintain coverage under a group health plan during FMLA leave. [Reg. § 54.4980B-10.]

☐ [*T.D.* 8928, 1-9-2001.]

### [Reg. § 54.4980D-1]

**§ 54.4980D-1. Requirement of return and time for filing of the excise tax under section 4980D.**

Q-1: If a person is liable for the excise tax under section 4980D, what form must the person file and what is the due date for the filing and payment of the excise tax?

A-1: (a) *In general.* See §§ 54.6011-2 and 54.6151-1.

(b) *Due date for filing of return by employers.* See § 54.6071-1(b)(1).

(c) *Due date for filing of return by multiemployer plans or multiple employer health plans.* See § 54.6071-1(b)(2).

(d) *Effective/applicability date.* In the case of an employer or other person mentioned in paragraph (b) of this Q & A-1, the rules in this Q & A-1 are effective for taxable years beginning on or after January 1, 2010. In the case of a plan mentioned in paragraph (c) of this Q & A-1, the rules in this Q & A-1 are effective for plan years beginning on or after January 1, 2010. [Reg. § 54.4980D-1.]

☐ [*T.D.* 9457, 9-4-2009.]

### [Reg. § 54.4980E-1]

**§ 54.4980E-1. Requirement of return and time for filing of the excise tax under section 4980E.**

Q-1: If a person is liable for the excise tax under section 4980E, what form must the person file and what is the due date for the filing and payment of the excise tax?

A-1: (a) *In general.* See §§ 54.6011-2, 54.6151-1 and 54.6071-1(c).

(b) *Effective/applicability date.* The rules in this Q & A-1 are effective for plan years beginning on or after January 1, 2010. [Reg. § 54.4980E-1.]

☐ [*T.D.* 9457, 9-4-2009.]

### [Reg. § 54.4980F-1]

**§ 54.4980F-1. Notice requirements for certain pension plan amendments significantly reducing the rate of future benefit ac-**

**crual.**—The following questions and answers concern the notification requirements imposed by 4980F of the Internal Revenue Code and section 204(h) of ERISA relating to a plan amendment of an applicable pension plan that significantly reduces the rate of future benefit accrual or that eliminates or significantly reduces an early retirement benefit or retirement-type subsidy.

List of Questions

Q-1. What are the notice requirements of section 4980F(e) of the Internal Revenue Code and section 204(h) of ERISA?

Q-2. What are the differences between section 4980F and section 204(h)?

Q-3. What is an "applicable pension plan" to which section 4980F and section 204(h) apply?

Q-4. What is "section 204(h) notice" and what is a "section 204(h) amendment"?

Q-5. For which amendments is section 204(h) notice required?

Q-6. What is an amendment that reduces the rate of future benefit accrual or reduces an early retirement benefit or retirement-type subsidy for purposes of determining whether section 204(h) notice is required?

Q-7. What plan provisions are taken into account in determining whether an amendment is a section 204(h) amendment?

Q-8. What is the basic principle used in determining whether a reduction in the rate of future benefit accrual or a reduction in an early retirement benefit or retirement-type subsidy is significant for purposes of section 4980F and section 204(h)?

Q-9. When must section 204(h) notice be provided?

Q-10. To whom must section 204(h) notice be provided?

Q-11. What information is required to be provided in a section 204(h) notice?

Q-12. What special rules apply if participants can choose between the old and new benefit formulas?

Q-13. How may section 204(h) notice be provided?

Q-14. What are the consequences if a plan administrator fails to provide section 204(h) notice?

Q-15. What are some of the rules that apply with respect to the excise tax under section 4980F?

Q-16. How do section 4980F and section 204(h) apply when a business is sold?

Q-17. How are amendments to cease accruals and terminate a plan treated under section 4980F and section 204(h)?

Q-18. What are the effective dates of section 4980F, section 204(h), as amended by EGTRRA, and these regulations?

Questions and Answers

Q-1. What are the notice requirements of section 4980F(e) of the Internal Revenue Code and section 204(h) of ERISA?

A-1. (a) *Requirements of Internal Revenue Code section 4980F(e) and ERISA section 204(h).* Section 4980F of the Internal Revenue Code (section 4980F) and section 204(h) of the Employee Retirement Income Security Act of 1974, as amended (ERISA), 29 U.S.C. 1054(h) (section 204(h)) each generally requires notice of an amendment to an applicable pension plan that either provides for a significant reduction in the rate of future benefit accrual or that eliminates or significantly reduces an early retirement benefit or retirement-type subsidy. The notice is required to be provided to plan participants and alternate payees who are applicable individuals (as defined in Q&A-10 of this section), to certain employee organizations, and to contributing employers under a multiemployer plan (as described in Q&A-10(a) of this section). The plan administrator must generally provide the notice before the effective date of the plan amendment. Q&A-9 of this section sets forth the time frames for providing notice, Q&A-11 of this section sets forth the content requirements for the notice, and Q&A-12 of this section contains special rules for cases in which participants can choose between the old and new benefit formulas.

(b) *Other notice requirements.* Other provisions of law may require that certain parties be notified of a plan amendment. See, for example, sections 102 and 104 of ERISA, and the regulations thereunder, for requirements relating to summary plan descriptions and summaries of material modifications.

Q-2. What are the differences between section 4980F and section 204(h)?

A-2. The notice requirements of section 4980F generally are parallel to the notice requirements of section 204(h), as amended by the Economic Growth and Tax Relief Reconciliation Act of 2001, Public Law 107-16 (115 Stat. 38) (2001) (EGTRRA). However, the consequences of the failure to satisfy the requirements of the two provisions differ: section 4980F imposes an excise tax on a failure to satisfy the notice requirements, while section 204(h)(6), as amended by EGTRRA, contains a special rule with respect to an egregious failure to satisfy the notice requirements. See Q&A-14 and Q&A-15 of this section. Except to the extent specifically indicated, these regulations apply both to section 4980F and to section 204(h).

Q-3. What is an "applicable pension plan" to which section 4980F and section 204(h) apply?

A-3. (a) *In general*. Section 4980F and section 204(h) apply to an applicable pension plan. For purposes of section 4980F, an *applicable pension plan* means a defined benefit plan qualifying under section 401(a) or 403(a) of the Internal Revenue Code, or an individual account plan that is subject to the funding standards of section 412 of the Internal Revenue Code. For purposes of section 204(h), an *applicable pension plan* means a defined benefit plan that is subject to part 2 of subtitle B of title I of ERISA, or an individual account plan that is subject to such part 2 and to the funding standards of section 412 of the Internal Revenue Code. Accordingly, individual account plans that are not subject to the funding standards of section 412 of the Internal Revenue Code, such as profit-sharing and stock bonus plans and contracts under section 403(b) of the Internal Revenue Code, are not applicable pension plans to which section 4980F or section 204(h) apply. Similarly, a defined benefit plan that neither qualifies under section 401(a) or 403(a) of the Internal Revenue Code nor is subject to part 2 of subtitle B of title 1 of ERISA is not an applicable pension plan. Further, neither a governmental plan (within the meaning of section 414(d) of the Internal Revenue Code), nor a church plan (within the meaning of section 414(e) of the Internal Revenue Code) with respect to which no election has been made under section 410(d) of the Internal Revenue Code is an applicable pension plan.

(b) *Section 204(h) notice not required for small plans covering no employees*. Section 204(h) notice is not required for a plan under which no employees are participants covered under the plan, as described in § 2510.3-3(b) of the Department of Labor regulations, and which has fewer than 100 participants.

Q-4. What is "section 204(h) notice" and what is a "section 204(h) amendment"?

A-4. (a) *Section 204(h) notice* is notice that complies with section 4980F(e) of the Internal Revenue Code, section 204(h)(1) of ERISA, and this section.

(b) A *section 204(h) amendment* is an amendment for which section 204(h) notice is required under this section.

Q-5. For which amendments is section 204(h) notice required?

A-5. (a) *Significant reduction in the rate of future benefit accrual*. Section 204(h) notice is required for an amendment to an applicable pension plan that provides for a significant reduction in the rate of future benefit accrual.

(b) *Early retirement benefits and retirement- type subsidies*. Section 204(h) notice is also required for an amendment to an applicable pension plan that provides for the significant reduction of an early retirement benefit or retirement-type subsidy. For purposes of this section, *early retirement benefit* and *retirement-type subsidy* mean early retirement benefits and retirement-type subsidies within the meaning of section 411(d)(6)(B)(i).

(c) *Elimination or cessation of benefits*. For purposes of this section, the terms *reduce* or *reduction* include eliminate or cease or elimination or cessation.

(d) *Delegation of authority to Commissioner*. The Commissioner may provide in revenue rulings, notices, or other guidance published in the Internal Revenue Bulletin (see § 601.601(d)(2) of this chapter) that section 204(h) notice need not be provided for plan amendments otherwise described in paragraph (a) or (b) of this Q&A-5 that the Commissioner determines to be necessary or appropriate, as a result of changes in the law, to maintain compliance with the requirements of the Internal Revenue Code (including requirements for tax qualification), ERISA, or other applicable federal law.

Q-6. What is an amendment that reduces the rate of future benefit accrual or reduces an early retirement benefit or retirement-type subsidy for purposes of determining whether section 204(h) notice is required?

A-6. (a) *In general*. For purposes of determining whether section 204(h) notice is required, an amendment reduces the rate of future benefit accrual or reduces an early retirement benefit or retirement-type subsidy only as provided in paragraph (b) or (c) of this Q&A-6.

(b) *Reduction in rate of future benefit accrual*—(1) *Defined benefit plans*. For purposes of section 4980F and section 204(h), an amendment to a defined benefit plan reduces the rate of future benefit accrual only if it is reasonably expected that the amendment will reduce the amount of the future annual benefit commencing at normal retirement age (or at actual retirement age, if later) for benefits accuring for a year. For this purpose, the annual benefit commencing at normal retirement age is the benefit payable in the form in which the terms of the plan express the accrued benefit (or, in the case of a plan in which the accrued benefit is not expressed in the form of an annual benefit commencing at normal retirement age, the benefit payable in the form of a single life annuity commencing at normal retirement age that is the actuarial equivalent of the accrued benefit expressed under the terms of the plan, as determined in accordance with section 411(c)(3) of the Internal Revenue Code).

(2) *Individual account plans*. For purposes of section 4980F and section 204(h), an amendment to an individual account plan reduces the rate of future benefit accrual only if it is reasonably expected that the amendment will reduce the amount of contributions or forfeitures allocated for any future year. Changes in the investments or investment options under an individual account plan are not taken into account for this purpose.

(3) *Determination of rate of future benefit accrual*. The rate of future benefit accrual for purposes of this paragraph (b) is determined without regard to optional forms of benefit within the meaning of § 1.411(d)-4, Q&A-1(b) of this chapter (other than the annual benefit described in paragraph (b)(1) of this Q&A-6). The rate of future benefit accrual is also determined without regard to ancillary benefits and other rights or features as defined in § 1.401(a)(4)-4(e) of this chapter.

(c) *Reduction of early retirement benefits or retirement-type subsidies*. For purposes of section 4980F and section 204(h), an amendment reduces an early retirement benefit or retirement-type subsidy only if it is reasonably expected that the amendment will eliminate or reduce an early retirement benefit or retirement-type subsidy.

Q-7. What plan provisions are taken into account in determining whether an amendment is a section 204(h) amendment?

A-7. (a) *Plan provisions taken into account*— (1) *In general*. All plan provisions that may affect the rate of future benefit accrual, early retirement benefits, or retirement-type subsidies of participants or alternate payees must be taken into account in determining whether an amendment is a section 204(h) amendment. For example, plan provisions that may affect the rate of future benefit accrual include the dollar amount or percentage of compensation on which benefit accruals are based; the definition of service or compensation taken into account in determining an employee's benefit accrual; the method of determining average compensation for calculating benefit accruals; the definition of normal retirement age in a defined benefit plan; the exclusion of current participants from future participation; benefit offset provisions; minimum benefit provisions; the formula for determining the amount of contributions and forfeitures allocated to participants' accounts in an individual account plan; in the case of a plan using permitted disparity under section 401(I) of the Internal Revenue Code, the amount of disparity between the excess benefit percentage or excess contribution percentage and the base benefit percentage or base contribution percentage (all as defined in section 401(I) of the Internal Revenue Code); and the actuarial assumptions used to determine contributions under a target benefit plan (as defined in § 1.401(a)(4)-8(b)(3)(i) of this chapter). Plan provisions that may affect early retirement benefits or retirement-type subsidies include the right to receive payment of benefits after severance from employment and before normal retirement age and actuarial factors used in determining optional forms for distribution of retirement benefits.

(2) *Provisions incorporated by reference in plan*. If all or a part of a plan's rate of future benefit accrual, or an early retirement benefit or retirement-type subsidy provided under the plan, depends on provisions in another document that are referenced in the plan document, a change in the provisions of the other document is an amendment of the plan.

(b) *Plan provisions not taken into account*—(1) *In general*. Plan provisions that do not affect the rate of future benefit accrual of participants or alternate payees are not taken into account in determining whether there has been a reduction in the rate of future benefit accrual.

(2) *Interaction with section 411(d)(6)*. Any benefit that is not a section 411(d)(6) protected benefit as described in § § 1.411(d)-3(g)(14) and 1.411(d)-4, Q&A-1(d) of this chapter, or that is a section 411(d)(6) protected benefit that may be eliminated or reduced as permitted under § 1.411(d)-3(c), (d), or (f), or under § 1.411(d)-4, Q&A-2(a)(2), (a)(3), (b)(1), or (b)(2)(ii) through (b)(2)(xi) of this chapter, is not taken into account in determining whether an amendment is a section 204(h) amendment. Thus, for example, provisions relating to the right to make after-tax deferrals are not taken into account.

(c) *Examples*. The following examples illustrate the rules in this Q&A-7:

*Example 1*. (i) *Facts*. A defined benefit plan provides a normal retirement benefit equal to 50% of highest 5-year average pay multiplied by a fraction (not in excess of one), the numerator of which equals the number of years of participation in the plan and the denominator of which is 20. A plan amendment is adopted that changes the numerator or denominator of that fraction.

(ii) *Conclusion*. The plan amendment must be taken into account in determining whether there has been a reduction in the rate of future benefit accrual.

*Example 2*. (i) *Facts*. Plan C is a multiemployer defined benefit plan subject to several collective bargaining agreements. The specific benefit formula under Plan C that applies to an employee depends on the hourly rate of contribution of the employee's employer, which is set forth in the provisions of the collective bargaining agreements that are referenced in the Plan C document. Collective Bargaining Agreement A between Employer B and the union representing employees of Employer B is renegotiated to provide that the hourly contribution rate for an employee of B who is subject to the Collective Bargaining Agreement A will decrease. That decrease will result in a decrease in the rate of future benefit accrual for employees of B.

(ii) *Conclusion.* Under paragraph (a)(2) of this Q&A-7, the change to Collective Bargaining Agreement A is a plan amendment that is a section 204(h) amendment if the reduction in the rate of future benefit accrual is significant.

Q-8. What is the basic principle used in determining whether a reduction in the rate of future benefit accrual or a reduction in an early retirement benefit or retirement-type subsidy is significant for purposes of section 4980F and section 204(h)?

A-8. (a) *General rule.* Whether an amendment reducing the rate of future benefit accrual or eliminating or reducing an early retirement benefit or retirement-type subsidy provides for a reduction that is significant for purposes of section 4980F (and section 204(h) of ERISA) is determined based on reasonable expectations taking into account the relevant facts and circumstances at the time the amendment is adopted, or, if earlier, at the effective date of the amendment.

(b) *Application for determining significant reduction in the rate of future benefit accrual.* For a defined benefit plan, the determination of whether an amendment provides for a significant reduction in the rate of future benefit accrual is made by comparing the amount of the annual benefit commencing at normal retirement age (or at actual retirement age, if later), as determined under Q&A-6(b)(1) of this section, under the terms of the plan as amended with the amount of the annual benefit commencing at normal retirement age (or at actual retirement age, if later), as determined under Q&A-6(b)(1) of this section, under the terms of the plan prior to amendment. For an individual account plan, the determination of whether an amendment provides for a significant reduction in the rate of future benefit accrual is made in accordance with Q&A-6(b)(2) of this section by comparing the amounts to be allocated in the future to participants' accounts under the terms of the plan as amended with the amounts to be allocated in the future to participants' accounts under the terms of the plan prior to amendment. An amendment to convert a money purchase pension plan to a profit-sharing or other individual account plan that is not subject to section 412 of the Internal Revenue Code is, in all cases, deemed to be an amendment that provides for a significant reduction in the rate of future benefit accrual.

(c) *Application to certain amendments reducing early retirement benefits or retirement-type subsidies.* Section 204(h) notice is not required for an amendment that reduces an early retirement benefit or retirement-type subsidy if the amendment is permitted under the third sentence of section 411(d)(6)(B) of the Internal Revenue Code and paragraphs (c), (d), and (f) of §1.411(d)-3 of this chapter (relating to the elimination or reduction of benefits or subsidies which create significant burdens or complexities for the plan and plan participants unless the amendment adversely affects the rights of any participant in a more than de minimis manner). However, in determining whether an amendment reducing a retirement-type subsidy constitutes a significant reduction because it reduces a retirement-type subsidy as permitted under §1.411(d)-3(e)(6) of this chapter, the amendment is treated in the same manner as an amendment that limits the retirement-type subsidy to benefits that accrue before the applicable amendment date (as defined at §1.411(d)-3(g)(4) of this chapter) with respect to each participant or alternate payee to whom the reduction is reasonably expected to apply.

(d) *Plan amendments reflecting a change in statutorily mandated minimum present value rules.* If a defined benefit plan offers a distribution to which the minimum present value rules of section 417(e)(3) apply (other than a payment to which section 411(a)(13)(A) applies) and the plan is amended to reflect the changes to the applicable interest rate and applicable mortality table in section 417(e)(3) made by the Pension Protection Act of 2006, Public Law 109-780 (120 Stat. 780) (PPA '06) (and no change is made in the dates on which the payment will be made), no section 204(h) notice is required to be provided.

(e) *Examples.* The following examples illustrate the rules in this Q&A-8:

*Example 1.* (i) *Facts.* Pension Plan A is a defined benefit plan that provides a rate of benefit accrual of 1% of highest-5 years' pay multiplied by years of service, payable annually for life commencing at normal retirement age (or at actual retirement age, if later). An amendment to Plan A is adopted on August 1, 2009, effective January 1, 2010, to provide that any participant who separates from service after December 31, 2009, and before January 1, 2015, will have the same number of years of service he or she would have had if his or her service continued to December 31, 2014.

(ii) *Conclusion.* In this example, the effective date of the plan amendment is January 1, 2010. While the amendment will result in a reduction in the annual rate of future benefit accrual from 2011

through 2014 (because, under the amendment, benefits based upon an additional 5 years of service accrue on January 1, 2010, and no additional service is credited after January 1, 2010 until January 1, 2015), the amendment does not result in a reduction that is significant because the amount of the annual benefit commencing at normal retirement age (or at actual retirement age, if later) under the terms of the plan as amended is not under any conditions less than the amount of the annual benefit commencing at normal retirement age (or at actual retirement age, if later) to which any participant would have been entitled under the terms of the plan had the amendment not been made.

*Example 2.* (i) *Facts.* The facts are the same as in *Example 1*, except that the 2009 amendment does not alter the plan provisions relating to a participant's number of years of service, but instead amends the plan's provisions relating to early retirement benefits. Before the amendment, the plan provides for distributions before normal retirement age to be actuarially reduced, but, if a participant retires after attainment of age 55 and completion of 10 years of service, the applicable early retirement reduction factor is 3% per year for the years between the ages 65 and 62 and 6% per year for the ages from 62 to 55. The amendment changes these provisions so that an actuarial reduction applies in all cases, but, in accordance with section 411(d)(6)(B), provides that no participant's early retirement benefit will be less than the amount provided under the plan as in effect on December 31, 2009 with respect to service before January 1, 2010. For participant X, the reduction is significant.

(ii) *Conclusion.* The amendment will result in a reduction in a retirement-type subsidy provided under Plan A (i.e., Plan A's early retirement subsidy). Section 204(h) notice must be provided to participant X and any other participant for whom the reduction is significant and the notice must be provided at least 45 days before January 1, 2010 (or by such other date as may apply under Q&A-9 of this section).

*Example 3.* (i) *Facts.* The facts are the same as in *Example 2*, except that, for participant X, the change does not go into effect for any annuity commencement date before January 1, 2011. Participant X continues employment through January 1, 2011.

(ii) *Conclusion.* The conclusion is the same as in *Example 2*. Taking into account the rule in the second sentence of Q&A-8(c) of this section, the reduction that occurs for participant X on January 1, 2011, is treated as the same reduction that occurs under *Example 2*. Accordingly, assuming that the reduction is significant, section 204(h) notice must be provided to participant X at least 45 days before the January 1, 2010 effective date of the amendment (or by such other date as may apply under Q&A-9 of this section).

Q-9. When must section 204(h) notice be provided?

A-9. (a) *45-day general rule.* Except as otherwise provided in this Q&A-9, section 204(h) notice must be provided at least 45 days before the effective date of any section 204(h) amendment. See paragraph (e) of this Q&A-9 for special rules for amendments permitting participant choice.

(b) *15-day rule for small plans.* Except for amendments described in paragraphs (d)(2) and (g) of this Q&A-9, section 204(h) notice must be provided at least 15 days before the effective date of any section 204(h) amendment in the case of a small plan. For purposes of this section, a small plan is a plan that the plan administrator reasonably expects to have, on the effective date of the section 204(h) amendment, fewer than 100 participants who have an accrued benefit under the plan.

(c) *15-day rule for multiemployer plans.* Except for amendments described in paragraphs (d)(2) and (g) of this Q&A-9, section 204(h) notice must be provided at least 15 days before the effective date of any section 204(h) amendment in the case of a multiemployer plan. For purposes of this section, a multiemployer plan means a multiemployer plan as defined in section 414(f) of the Internal Revenue Code.

(d) *Special timing rule for business transactions—(1) 15-day rule for section 204(h) amendment in connection with an acquisition or disposition.* Except for amendments described in paragraphs (d)(2) and (g) of this Q&A-9, if a section 204(h) amendment is adopted in connection with an acquisition or disposition, section 204(h) notice must be provided at least 15 days before the effective date of the section 204(h) amendment.

(2) *Later notice permitted for a section 204(h) amendment significantly reducing early retirement benefit or retirement-type subsidies in connection with certain plan transfers, mergers, or consolidations.* If a section 204(h) amendment is adopted with respect to liabilities that are transferred to another plan in connection with a transfer, merger, or consolidation of assets or liabilities as described in section 414(l) of the Internal Revenue Code and §1.414(l)-1 of this chapter, the amendment is adopted in connection with an acquisition or disposition, and the amendment significantly reduces an early retirement benefit or retirement-type subsidy, but does not significantly reduce the rate of future benefit accrual, then section 204(h) notice must be provided no

later than 30 days after the effective date of the section 204(h) amendment.

(3) *Definition of acquisition or disposition.* For purposes of this paragraph (d), see § 1.410(b)-2(f) of this chapter for the definition of acquisition or disposition.

(e) *Timing rule for amendments permitting participant choice.* In general, section 204(h) notice of a section 204(h) amendment that provides applicable individuals with a choice between the old and the new benefit formulas (as described in Q&A-12 of this section) must be provided in accordance with the time period applicable under paragraphs (a) through (d) of this Q&A-9. See Q&A-12 of this section for additional guidance regarding section 204(h) notice in connection with participant choice.

(f) *Special timing rule for certain plans maintained by commercial airlines.* See section 402 of PPA '06 for a special rule that applies to certain plans maintained by an employer that is a commercial passenger airline or the principal business of which is providing catering services to a commercial passenger airline. Under this special rule, section 204(h) notice must be provided at least 15 days before the effective date of the amendment.

(g) *Special timing rules relating to certain section 204(h) amendments that reduce section 411(d)(6) protected benefits*—(1) *Plan amendments permitted to reduce prior accruals.* This paragraph (g) generally provides special rules with respect to a plan amendment that would not violate section 411(d)(6) even if the amendment were to reduce section 411(d)(6) protected benefits, which are limited to accrued benefits that are attributable to service before the applicable amendment date. For example, this paragraph (g) applies to amendments that are permitted to be effective retroactively under section 412(d)(2) of the Code (section 412(c)(8) for plan years beginning before January 1, 2008), section 418D of the Code, section 418E of the Code, section 4281 of ERISA, or section 1107 of PPA '06. See, generally, § 1.411(d)-3(a)(1).

(2) *General timing rule for amendments to which this paragraph (g) applies.* For an amendment to which this paragraph (g) applies, the amendment is effective on the first date on which the plan is operated as if the amendment were in effect. Thus, except as otherwise provided in this paragraph (g), a section 204(h) notice for an amendment to which paragraph (a) of this section applies that is adopted after the effective date of the amendment must be provided, with respect to any applicable individual, at least 45 days before (or such other date as may apply under paragraph (b), (c), (d), or (f) of this Q&A-9) the date the amendment is put into operational effect.

(3) *Special rules for section 204(h) notices provided in connection with other disclosure requirements*—(i) *In general.* Notwithstanding the requirements in this Q&A-9 and Q&A-11 of this section, if a plan provides one of the notices in paragraph (g)(3)(ii) of this Q&A-9, in accordance with the applicable timing and content rules for such notice, the plan is treated as timely providing a section 204(h) notice with respect to a section 204(h) amendment.

(ii) *Notice requirements.* The notices in this paragraph (g)(3)(ii) are—

(A) A notice required under any revenue ruling, notice, or other guidance published under the authority of the Commissioner in the Internal Revenue Bulletin to affected parties in connection with a retroactive plan amendment described in section 412(d)(2) (section 412(c)(8) for plan years beginning before January 1, 2008);

(B) A notice required under section 101(j) of ERISA if an amendment is adopted to comply with the benefit limitation requirements of section 206(g) of ERISA (section 436 of the Code);

(C) A notice required under section 432(b)(3)(D) of the Code for an amendment adopted to comply with the benefit restrictions under section 432(f)(2);

(D) A notice required under section 418D, or section 4244A(b) of ERISA, for an amendment that reduces or eliminates accrued benefits attributable to employer contributions with respect to a multiemployer plan in reorganization;

(E) A notice required under section 418E, or section 4245(e) of ERISA, relating to the effects of the insolvency status for a multiemployer plan; and

(F) A notice required under section 4281 of ERISA for an amendment of a multiemployer plan reducing benefits pursuant to section 4281(c) of ERISA.

(4) *Delegation of authority to Commissioner.* The Commissioner may provide special rules under section 4980F, in revenue rulings, notices, or other guidance published in the Internal Revenue Bulletin (see § 601.601(d)(2)(ii)(*b*) of this chapter), that the Commissioner determines to be necessary or appropriate with respect to a section 204(h) amendment—

(A) That applies to benefits accrued before the applicable amendment date but that does not violate section 411(d)(6); or

(B) For which there is a required notice relating to a reduction in benefits and such notice has timing and content requirements similar to a section 204(h) notice with respect to a significant reduction in the rate of future benefit accruals.

Q-10. To whom must section 204(h) notice be provided?

A-10. (a) *In general.* Section 204(h) notice must be provided to each applicable individual, to each employee organization representing participants who are applicable individuals, and, for plan years beginning after December 31, 2007, to each employer that has an obligation to contribute (within the meaning of section 4212(a) of ERISA) to a multiemployer plan. A special rule is provided in paragraph (d) of this Q&A-10.

(b) *Applicable individual.* Applicable individual means each participant in the plan, and any alternate payee, whose rate of future benefit accrual under the plan is reasonably expected to be significantly reduced, or for whom an early retirement benefit or retirement-type subsidy under the plan may reasonably be expected to be significantly reduced, by the section 204(h) amendment. The determination is made with respect to individuals who are reasonably expected to be participants or alternate payees in the plan at the effective date of the section 204(h) amendment.

(c) *Alternate payee.* Alternate payee means a beneficiary who is an alternate payee (within the meaning of section 414(p)(8) of the Internal Revenue Code) under an applicable qualified domestic relations order (within the meaning of section 414(p)(1)(A) of the Internal Revenue Code).

(d) *Designees.* Section 204(h) notice may be provided to a person designated in writing by an applicable individual or by an employee organization representing participants who are applicable individuals, instead of being provided to that applicable individual or employee organization. Any designation of a representative made through an electronic method that satisfies standards similar to those of Q&A-13(c)(1) of this section satisfies the requirement that a designation be in writing.

(e) *Facts and circumstances test.* Whether a participant or alternate payee is an applicable individual is determined on a typical business day that is reasonably proximate to the time the section 204(h) notice is provided (or at the latest date for providing section 204(h) notice, if earlier), based on all relevant facts and circumstances.

(f) *Examples.* The following examples illustrate the rules in this Q&A-10:

*Example 1.* (i) *Facts.* A defined benefit plan requires an individual to complete 1 year of service to become a participant who can accrue benefits, and participants cease to accrue benefits under the plan at severance from employment with the employer. There are no alternate payees and employees are not represented by an employee organization. On November 18, 2004, the plan is amended effective as of January 1, 2005, to reduce significantly the rate of future benefit accrual. Section 204(h) notice is provided on November 1, 2004.

(ii) *Conclusion.* Section 204(h) notice is only required to be provided to individuals who, based on the facts and circumstances on November 1, 2004, are reasonably expected to have completed at least 1 year of service and to be employed by the employer on January 1, 2005.

*Example 2.* (i) *Facts.* The facts are the same as in *Example 1*, except that the sole effect of the plan amendment is to alter the pre-amendment plan provisions under which benefits payable to an employee who retires after 20 or more years of service are unreduced for commencement before normal retirement age. The amendment requires 30 or more years of service in order for benefits commencing before normal retirement age to be unreduced, but the amendment only applies for future benefit accruals.

(ii) *Conclusion.* Section 204(h) notice is only required to be provided to individuals who, on January 1, 2005, have completed at least 1 year of service but less than 30 years of service, are employed by the employer, have not attained normal retirement age, and will have completed 20 or more years of service before normal retirement age if their employment continues to normal retirement age.

*Example 3.* (i) *Facts.* A plan is amended to reduce significantly the rate of future benefit accrual for all current employees who are participants. Based on the facts and circumstances, it is reasonable to expect that the amendment will not reduce the rate of future benefit accrual of former employees who are currently receiving benefits or of former employees who are entitled to deferred vested benefits.

(ii) *Conclusion.* The plan administrator is not required to provide section 204(h) notice to any former employees.

*Example 4.* (i) *Facts.* The facts are the same as in *Example 3*, except that the plan covers two groups of alternate payees. The alternate payees in the first group are entitled to a certain percentage or portion of the former spouse's accrued benefit and, for this purpose, the accrued benefit is determined at the time the former spouse begins receiving retirement benefits under the plan. The alternate payees in the second group are entitled to a certain percentage or portion of the former spouse's accrued benefit and, for this purpose, the accrued benefit was determined at the time the qualified domestic relations order was issued by the court.

(ii) *Conclusion.* It is reasonable to expect that the benefits to be received by the second group of alternate payees will not be affected by any reduction in a former spouse's rate of future benefit accrual.

Accordingly, the plan administrator is not required to provide section 204(h) notice to the alternate payees in the second group.

*Example 5.* (i) *Facts.* A plan covers hourly employees and salaried employees. The plan provides the same rate of benefit accrual for both groups. The employer amends the plan to reduce significantly the rate of future benefit accrual of the salaried employees only. At that time, it is reasonable to expect that only a small percentage of hourly employees will become salaried in the future.

(ii) *Conclusion.* The plan administrator is not required to provide section 204(h) notice to the participants who are currently hourly employees.

*Example 6.* (i) *Facts.* A plan covers employees in Division M and employees in Division N. The plan provides the same rate of benefit accrual for both groups. The employer amends the plan to reduce significantly the rate of future benefit accrual of employees in Division M. At that time, it is reasonable to expect that in the future only a small percentage of employees in Division N will be transferred to Division M.

(ii) *Conclusion.* The plan administrator is not required to provide section 204(h) notice to the participants who are employees in Division N.

*Example 7.* (i) *Facts.* The facts are the same facts as in *Example 6,* except that at the time the amendment is adopted, it is expected that thereafter Division N will be merged into Division M in connection with a corporate reorganization (and the employees in Division N will become subject to the plan's amended benefit formula applicable to the employees in Division M).

(ii) *Conclusion.* In this case, the plan administrator must provide section 204(h) notice to the participants who are employees in Division M and to the participants who are employees in Division N.

*Example 8.* (i) *Facts.* A plan is amended to reduce significantly the rate of future benefit accrual for all current employees who are participants. The plan amendment will be effective on January 1, 2004. The plan will provide the notice to applicable individuals on October 31, 2003. In determining which current employees are applicable individuals, the plan administrator determines that October 1, 2003, is a typical business day that is reasonably proximate to the time the section 204(h) notice is provided.

(ii) *Conclusion.* In this case, October 1, 2003 is a typical business day that satisfies the requirements of Q&A-10(e) of this section.

Q-11. What information is required to be provided in a section 204(h) notice?

A-11. (a) *Explanation of notice requirements*— (1) *In general.* Section 204(h) notice must include sufficient information to allow applicable individuals to understand the effect of the plan amendment. In order to satisfy this rule, a plan administrator providing section 204(h) notice must generally satisfy paragraphs (a)(2), (a)(3), (a)(4), (a)(5), and (a)(6) of this Q&A-11. See paragraph (g)(3) of Q&A-9 of this section for special rules relating to section 204(h) notices provided in connection with certain other written notices. See also paragraph (g)(4) of Q&A-9 of this section for a delegation of authority to the Commissioner to provide special rules.

(2) *Information in section 204(h) notice.* The information in a section 204(h) notice must be written in a manner calculated to be understood by the average plan participant and to apprise the applicable individual of the significance of the notice.

(3) *Required narrative description of amendment*—(i) *Reduction in rate of future benefit accrual.* In the case of an amendment reducing the rate of future benefit accrual, the notice must include a description of the benefit or allocation formula prior to the amendment, a description of the benefit or allocation formula under the plan as amended, and the effective date of the amendment.

(ii) *Reduction in early retirement benefit or retirement-type subsidy.* In the case of an amendment that reduces an early retirement benefit or retirement-type subsidy (other than as a result of an amendment reducing the rate of future benefit accrual), the notice must describe how the early retirement benefit or retirement-type subsidy is calculated from the accrued benefit before the amendment, how the early retirement benefit or retirement-type subsidy is calculated from the accrued benefit after the amendment, and the effective date of the amendment. For example, if, for a plan with a normal retirement age of 65, the change is from an unreduced normal retirement benefit at age 55 to an unreduced normal retirement benefit at age 60 for benefits accrued in the future, with an actuarial reduction to apply for benefits accrued in the future to the extent that the early retirement benefit begins before age 60, the notice must state the change and specify the factors that apply in calculating the actuarial reduction (for example, a 5% per year reduction applies for early retirement before age 60).

(4) *Sufficient information to determine the approximate magnitude of reduction*—(i) *General rule*—(A) Section 204(h) notice must include sufficient information for each applicable individual to determine the approximate magnitude of the expected reduction for that individual. Thus, in any case in which it is not reasonable to expect that the

approximate magnitude of the reduction for each applicable individual will be reasonably apparent from the description of the amendment provided in accordance with paragraph (a)(3) of this Q&A-11, further information is required. The further information may be provided by furnishing additional narrative information or in other information that satisfies this paragraph of this section.

(B) To the extent any expected reduction is not uniformly applicable to all participants, the notice must either identify the general classes of participants to whom the reduction is expected to apply, or by some other method include sufficient information to allow each applicable individual receiving the notice to determine which reductions are expected to apply to that individual.

(ii) *Illustrative examples*—(A) *Requirement generally.* The requirement to include sufficient information for each applicable individual to determine the approximate magnitude of the expected reduction for that individual under (a)(4)(i)(A) of this Q&A-11 is deemed satisfied if the notice includes one or more illustrative examples showing the approximate magnitude of the reduction in the examples, as provided in this paragraph (a)(4)(ii). Illustrative examples are in any event required to be provided for any change from a traditional defined benefit formula to a cash balance formula or a change that results in a period of time during which there are no accruals (or minimal accruals) with regard to normal retirement benefits or an early retirement subsidy (a wear-away period).

(B) *Examples must bound the range of reductions.* Where an amendment results in reductions that vary (either among participants, as would occur for an amendment converting a traditional defined benefit formula to a cash balance formula, or over time as to any individual participant, as would occur for an amendment that results in a wear-away period), the illustrative example(s) provided in accordance with this paragraph (a)(4)(ii) must show the approximate range of the reductions. However, any reductions that are likely to occur in only a de minimis number of cases are not required to be taken into account in determining the range of the reductions if a narrative statement is included to that effect and examples are provided that show the approximate range of the reductions in other cases. Amendments for which the maximum reduction occurs under identifiable circumstances, with proportionately smaller reductions in other cases, may be illustrated by one example illustrating the maximum reduction, with a statement that smaller reductions also occur. Further, assuming that the reduction varies from small to large depending on service or other factors, two illustrative examples may be provided showing the smallest likely reduction and the largest likely reduction.

(C) *Assumptions used in examples.* The examples provided under this paragraph (a)(4)(ii) are not required to be based on any particular form of payment (such as a life annuity or a single sum), but may be based on whatever form appropriately illustrates the reduction. The examples generally may be based on any reasonable assumptions (for example, assumptions relating to the representative participant's age, years of service, and compensation, along with any interest rate and mortality table used in the illustrations, as well as salary scale assumptions used in the illustrations for amendments that alter the compensation taken into account under the plan), but the section 204(h) notice must identify those assumptions. However, if a plan's benefit provisions include a factor that varies over time (such as a variable interest rate), the determination of whether an amendment is reasonably expected to result in a wear-away period must be based on the value of the factor applicable under the plan at a time that is reasonably close to the date section 204(h) notice is provided, and any wear-away period that is solely a result of a future change in the variable factor may be disregarded. For example, to determine whether a wear-away occurs as a result of a section 204(h) amendment that converts a defined benefit plan to a cash balance pension plan that will credit interest based on a variable interest factor specified in the plan, the future interest credits must be projected based on the interest rate applicable under the variable factor at the time section 204(h) notice is provided.

(D) *Individual statements.* This paragraph (a)(4)(ii) may be satisfied by providing a statement to each applicable individual projecting what that individual's future benefits are reasonably expected to be at various future dates and what that individual's future benefits would have been under the terms of the plan as in effect before the section 204(h) amendment, provided that the statement includes the same information required for examples under paragraphs (a)(4)(ii)(A) through (C) of this Q&A-11, including showing the approximate range of the reductions for the individual if the reductions vary over time and identification of the assumptions used in the projections.

(5) *No false or misleading information.* A section 204(h) notice may not include materially false or misleading information or omit information so as to cause the information provided to be misleading).

(6) *Additional information when reduction not uniform*—(i) *In general.* If an amendment by its terms affects different classes of participants

differently (e.g., one new benefit formula will apply to Division A and another to Division B), then the requirements of paragraph (a) of this Q&A-11 apply separately with respect to each such general class of participants. In addition, the notice must include sufficient information to enable an applicable individual who is a participant to understand which class he or she is a member of.

(ii) *Option for different section 204(h) notices.* If a section 204(h) amendment affects different classes of applicable individuals differently, the plan administrator may provide to differently affected classes of applicable individuals a section 204(h) notice appropriate to those individuals. Such section 204(h) notice may omit information that does not apply to the applicable individuals to whom it is furnished, but must identify the class or classes of applicable individuals to whom it is provided.

(b) *Examples.* The following examples illustrate the requirements paragraph (a) of this Q&A-11. In each example, it is assumed that the actual notice provided is written in a manner calculated to be understood by the average plan participant and to apprise the applicable individual of the significance of the notice in accordance with paragraph (a)(2) of this Q&A-11. The examples are as follows:

*Example 1.* (i) *Facts.* Plan A provides that a participant is entitled to a normal retirement benefit of 2% of the participant's average pay over the 3 consecutive years for which the average is the highest (highest average pay) multiplied by years of service. Plan A is amended to provide that, effective January 1, 2004, the normal retirement benefit will be 2% of the participant's highest average pay multiplied by years of service before the effective date, plus 1% of the participant's highest average pay multiplied by years of service after the effective date. The plan administrator provides notice that states: "Under the Plan's current benefit formula, a participant's normal retirement benefit is 2% of the participant's average pay over the 3 consecutive years for which the average is the highest multiplied by the participant's years of service. This formula is being changed by a plan amendment. Under the Plan as amended, a participant's normal retirement benefit will be the sum of 2% of the participant's average pay over the 3 consecutive years for which the average is the highest multiplied by years of service before the January 1, 2004 effective date, plus 1% of the participant's average pay over the 3 consecutive years for which the average is the highest multiplied by the participant's years of service after December 31, 2003. This change is effective on January 1, 2004." The notice does not contain any additional information.

(ii) *Conclusion.* The notice satisfies the requirements of paragraph (a) of this Q&A-11.

*Example 2.* (i) *Facts.* Plan B provides that a participant is entitled to a normal retirement benefit at age 64 of 2.2% of the participant's career average pay multiplied by years of service. Plan B is amended to cease all accruals, effective January 1, 2004. The plan administrator provides notice that includes a description of the old benefit formula, a statement that, after December 31, 2003, no participant will earn any further accruals, and the effective date of the amendment. The notice does not contain any additional information.

(ii) *Conclusion.* The notice satisfies the requirements of paragraph (a) of this Q&A-11.

*Example 3.* (i) *Facts.* Plan C provides that a participant is entitled to a normal retirement benefit at age 65 of 2% of career average compensation multiplied by years of service. Plan C is amended to provide that the normal retirement benefit will be 1% of average pay over the 3 consecutive years for which the average is the highest multiplied by years of service. The amendment only applies to accruals for years of service after the amendment, so that each employee's accrued benefit is equal to the sum of the benefit accrued as of the effective date of the amendment plus the accrued benefit equal to the new formula applied to years of service beginning on or after the effective date. The plan administrator provides notice that describes the old and new benefit formulas and also explains that for an individual whose compensation increases over the individual's career such that the individual's highest 3-year average exceeds the individual's career average, the reduction will be less or there may be no reduction. The notice does not contain any additional information.

(ii) *Conclusion.* The notice satisfies the requirements of paragraph (a) of this Q&A-11.

*Example 4.* (i) *Facts.* (A) Plan D is a defined benefit pension plan under which each participant accrues a normal retirement benefit, as a life annuity beginning at the normal retirement age of 65, equal to the participant's number of years of service multiplied by 1.5 percent multiplied by the participant's average pay over the 3 consecutive years for which the average is the highest. Plan D provides early retirement benefits for former employees beginning at or after age 55 in the form of an early retirement annuity that is actuarially equivalent to the normal retirement benefit, with the reduction for early commencement based on reasonable actuarial assumptions that are specified in Plan D. Plan D provides for the suspension of benefits of participants who continue in employment beyond normal

retirement age, in accordance with section 203(a)(3)(B) of ERISA and regulations thereunder issued by the Department of Labor. The pension of a participant who retires after age 65 is calculated under the same normal retirement benefit formula, but is based on the participant's service credit and highest 3-year pay at the time of late retirement with any appropriate actuarial increases.

(B) Plan D is amended, effective July 1, 2005, to change the formula for all future accruals to a cash balance formula under which the opening account balance for each participant on July 1, 2005, is zero, hypothetical pay credits equal to 5 percent of pay are credited to the account thereafter, and hypothetical interest is credited monthly based on the applicable interest rate under section 417(e)(3) of the Internal Revenue Code at the beginning of the quarter. Any participant who terminates employment with vested benefits can receive an actuarially equivalent annuity (based on the same reasonable actuarial assumptions that are specified in Plan D) commencing at any time after termination of employment and before the plan's normal retirement age of 65. The benefit resulting from the hypothetical account balance is in addition to the benefit accrued before July 1, 2005 (taking into account only service and highest 3-year pay before July 1, 2005), so that it is reasonably expected that no wear-away period will result from the amendment. The plan administrator expects that, as a general rule, depending on future pay increases and future interest rates, the rate of future benefit accrual after the conversion is higher for participants who accrue benefits before approximately age 50 and after approximately age 70, but is lower for participants who accrue benefits between approximately age 50 and age 70.

(C) The plan administrator of Plan D announces the conversion to a cash balance formula on May 16, 2005. The announcement is delivered to all participants and includes a written notice that describes the old formula, the new formula, and the effective date.

(D) In addition, the notice states that the Plan D formula before the conversion provided a normal retirement benefit equal to the product of a participant's number of years of service multiplied by 1.5 percent multiplied by the participant's average pay over the 3 years for which the average is the highest (highest 3-year pay). The notice includes an example showing the normal retirement benefit that will be accrued after June 30, 2005 for a participant who is age 49 with 10 years of service at the time of the conversion. The plan administrator reasonably believes that such a participant is representative of the participants whose rate of future benefit accrual will be reduced as a result of the amendment. The example estimates that, if the participant continues employment to age 65, the participant's normal retirement benefit for service from age 49 to age 65 will be $657 per month for life. The example assumes that the participant's pay is $50,000 at age 49. The example states that the estimated $657 monthly pension accrues over the 16-year period from age 49 to age 65 and that, based on assumed future pay increases, this amount annually would be 9.1 percent of the participant's highest 3-year pay at age 65, which over the 16 years from age 49 to age 65 averages 0.57 percent per year multiplied by the participant's highest 3-year pay. The example also states that the sum of the monthly annuity accrued before the conversion in the 10-year period from age 39 to age 49 plus the $657 monthly annuity estimated to be accrued over the 16-year period from age 49 to age 65 is $1,235 and that, based on assumed future increases in pay, this would be 17.1 percent of the participant's highest 3-year pay at age 65, which over the employee's career from age 39 to age 65 averages 0.66 percent per year multiplied by the participant's highest 3-year pay. The notice also includes two other examples with similar information, one of which is intended to show the circumstances in which a small reduction may occur and the other of which shows the largest reduction that the plan administrator thinks is likely to occur. The notice states that the estimates are based on the assumption that pay increases annually after June 30, 2005, at a 4 percent rate. The notice also specifies that the applicable interest rate under section 417(e) for hypothetical interest credits after June 30, 2005 is assumed to be 6 percent, which is the section 417(e) of the Internal Revenue Code applicable interest rate under the plan for 2005.

(ii) *Conclusion.* The information in the notice, as described in paragraph (i)(C) and (i)(D) of this *Example 4*, satisfies the requirements of paragraph (a)(3) of this Q&A-11 with respect to applicable individuals who are participants. The requirements of paragraph (a)(4) of this Q&A-11 are satisfied because, as noted in paragraph (i)(D) of this *Example 4*, the notice describes the old formula and describes the estimated future accruals under the new formula in terms that can be readily compared to the old formula, i.e., the notice states that the estimated $657 monthly pension accrued over the 16-year period from age 49 to age 65 averages 0.57 percent of the participant's highest 3-year pay at age 65. The requirement in paragraph (a)(4)(ii) of this Q&A-11 that the examples include sufficient information to be able to determine the approximate magnitude of the reduction would also be satisfied if the notice instead directly stated the amount of the monthly pension that would have accrued over the 16-year period from age 49 to age 65 under the old formula.

*Example 5.* (i) *Facts.* The facts are the same as in *Example 4,* except that, under the plan as in effect before the amendment, the early retirement pension for a participant who terminates employment after age 55 with at least 20 years of service is equal to the normal retirement benefit without reduction from age 65 to age 62 and reduced by only 5 percent per year for each year before age 62. As a result, early retirement benefits for such a participant constitute a retirement-type subsidy. The plan as in effect after the amendment provides an early retirement benefit equal to the sum of the early retirement benefit payable under the plan as in effect before the amendment taking into account only service and highest 3-year pay before July 1, 2005, plus an early retirement annuity that is actuarially equivalent to the account balance for service after June 30, 2005. The notice provided by the plan administrator describes the old early retirement annuity, the new early retirement annuity, and the effective date. The notice includes an estimate of the early retirement annuity payable to the illustrated participant for service after the conversion if the participant were to retire at age 59 (which the plan administrator believes is a typical early retirement age) and elect to begin receiving an immediate early retirement annuity. The example states that the normal retirement benefit expected to be payable at age 65 as a result of service from age 49 to age 59 is $434 per month for life beginning at age 65 and that the early retirement annuity expected to be payable as a result of service from age 49 to age 59 is $270 per month for life beginning at age 59. The example states that the monthly early retirement annuity of $270 is 38 percent less than the monthly normal retirement benefit of $434, whereas a 15 percent reduction would have applied under the plan as in effect before the amendment. The notice also includes similar information for examples that show the smallest and largest reduction that the plan administrator thinks is likely to occur in the early retirement benefit. The notice also specifies the applicable interest rate, mortality table, and salary scale used in the example to calculate the early retirement reductions.

(ii) *Conclusion.* The information in the notice, as described in paragraphs (i)(C) and (D) of *Example 4* and paragraph (i) of this *Example 5,* satisfies the requirements of paragraph (a)(3) of this Q&A-11 with respect to applicable individuals who are participants. The requirements of paragraph (a)(4) of this Q&A-11 are satisfied because, as noted in paragraph (i) of this *Example 5,* the notice describes the early retirement subsidy under the old formula and describes the estimated early retirement pension under the new formula in terms that can be readily compared to the old formula, i.e., the notice states that the monthly early retirement pension of $270 is 38 percent less than the monthly normal retirement benefit of $434, whereas a 15 percent reduction would have applied under the plan as in effect before the amendment. The requirements of paragraph (a)(4)(ii) of this Q&A-11 that the examples include sufficient information to be able to determine the approximate magnitude of the reduction would also be satisfied if the notice instead directly stated the amount of the monthly early retirement pension that would be payable at age 59 under the old formula.

Q-12. What special rules apply if participants can choose between the old and new benefit formulas?

A-12. In any case in which an applicable individual can choose between the benefit formula (including any early retirement benefit or retirement-type subsidy) in effect before the section 204(h) amendment (old formula) or the benefit formula in effect after the section 204(h) amendment (new formula), section 204(h) notice has not been provided unless the applicable individual has been provided the information required under Q&A-11 of this section, and has also been provided sufficient information to enable the individual to make an informed choice between the old and new benefit formulas. The information required under Q&A-11 of this section must be provided by the date otherwise required under Q&A-9 of this section. The information sufficient to enable the individual to make an informed choice must be provided within a period that is reasonably contemporaneous with the date by which the individual is required to make his or her choice and that allows sufficient advance notice to enable the individual to understand and consider the additional information before making that choice.

Q-13. How may section 204(h) notice be provided?

A-13. (a) *Delivering section 204(h) notice.* A plan administrator (including a person acting on behalf of the plan administrator, such as the employer or plan trustee) must provide section 204(h) notice through a method that results in actual receipt of the notice or the plan administrator must take appropriate and necessary measures reasonably calculated to ensure that the method for providing section 204(h) notice results in actual receipt of the notice. Section 204(h) notice must be provided either in the form of a paper document or in an electronic form that satisfies the requirements of paragraph (c) of this Q&A-13. First class mail to the last known address of the party is an acceptable delivery method. Likewise, hand delivery is accept-

able. However, the posting of notice is not considered provision of section 204(h) notice. Section 204(h) notice may be enclosed with or combined with other notice provided by the employer or plan administrator (for example, a notice of intent to terminate under title IV of ERISA). Except as provided in paragraph (c) of this Q&A-13, a section 204(h) notice is deemed to have been provided on a date if it has been provided by the end of that day. When notice is delivered by first class mail, the notice is considered provided as of the date of the United States postmark stamped on the cover in which the document is mailed.

(b) *Example.* The following example illustrates the provisions of paragraph (a) of this Q&A-13:

*Example.* (i) *Facts.* Plan A is amended to reduce significantly the rate of future benefit accrual effective January 1, 2005. Under Q&A-9 of this section, section 204(h) notice is required to be provided at least 45 days before the effective date of the amendment. The plan administrator causes section 204(h) notice to be mailed to all affected participants. The mailing is postmarked November 16, 2004.

(ii) *Conclusion.* Because section 204(h) notice is given 45 days before the effective date of the plan amendment, it satisfies the timing requirement of Q&A-9 of this section.

(c) *New technologies*—(1) *General rule.* A section 204(h) notice may be provided to an applicable individual through an electronic method (other than an oral communication or a recording of an oral communication), provided that all of the following requirements are satisfied:

(i) Either the notice is actually received by the applicable individual or the plan administrator takes appropriate and necessary measures reasonably calculated to ensure that the method for providing section 204(h) notice results in actual receipt of the notice by the applicable individual.

(ii) The section 204(h) notice is delivered using an electronic medium (other than an oral communication or a recording of an oral communication) under an electronic system that satisfies the applicable notice requirements of § 1.401(a)-21.

(iii) *Special effective date.* For plan years beginning prior to January 1, 2007, Q&A-13 of this section, as it appeared in the April 1, 2006 edition of 26 CFR part 1, applies.

(2) *Examples.* The following examples illustrate the requirement in paragraph (c)(1)(i) of this Q&A-13. In these examples, it is assumed that the notice satisfies the requirements in paragraphs (c)(1)(ii) of this section. The examples are as follows:

*Example 1.* (i) *Facts.* On July 1, 2003, M, a plan administrator of Company N's plan, sends notice intended to constitute section 204(h) notice to A, an employee of Company N and a participant in the plan. The notice is sent through e-mail to A's e-mail address on Company N's electronic information system. Accessing Company N's electronic information system is not an integral part of A's duties. M sends the e-mail with a request for a computer-generated notification that the message was received and opened. M receives notification indicating that the e-mail was received and opened by A on July 9, 2003.

(ii) *Conclusion.* With respect to A, although M has failed to take appropriate and necessary measures reasonably calculated to ensure that the method for providing section 204(h) notice results in actual receipt of the notice, M satisfies the requirement of paragraph (c)(1)(i) of this Q&A-13 on July 9, 2003, which is when A actually receives the notice.

*Example 2.* (i) *Facts.* On August 1, 2003, O, a plan administrator of Company P's plan, sends a notice intended to constitute section 204(h) notice of ERISA to B, who is an employee of Company P and a participant in Company P's plan. The notice is sent through e-mail to B's e-mail address on Company P's electronic information system. B has the ability to effectively access electronic documents from B's e-mail address on Company P's electronic information system and accessing the system is an integral part of B's duties.

(ii) *Conclusion.* Because access to the system is an integral part of B's duties, O has taken appropriate and necessary measures reasonably calculated to ensure that the method for providing section 204(h) notice results in actual receipt of the notice. Thus, regardless of whether B actually accesses B's email on that date, O satisfies the requirement of paragraph (c)(1)(i) of this Q&A-13 on August 1, 2003, with respect to B.

Q-14. What are the consequences if a plan administrator fails to provide section 204(h) notice?

A-14. (a) *Egregious failures*—(1) *Effect of egregious failure to provide section 204(h) notice.* Section 204(h)(6)(A) of ERISA provides that, in the case of any egregious failure to meet the notice requirements with respect to any plan amendment, the plan provisions are applied so that all applicable individuals are entitled to the greater of the benefit to which they would have been entitled without regard to the amendment, or the benefit under the plan with regard to the amendment. For a special rule applicable in the case of a plan termination, see Q&A-17(b) of this section.

Reg. §54.4980F-1

(2) *Definition of egregious failure.* For purposes of section 204(h) of ERISA and this Q&A-14, there is an egregious failure to meet the notice requirements if a failure to provide required notice is within the control of the plan sponsor and is either an intentional failure or a failure, whether or not intentional, to provide most of the individuals with most of the information they are entitled to receive. For this purpose, an intentional failure includes any failure to promptly provide the required notice or information after the plan administrator discovers an unintentional failure to meet the requirements. A failure to give section 204(h) notice is deemed not to be egregious if the plan administrator reasonably determines, taking into account section 4980F, section 204(h), these regulations, other administrative pronouncements, and relevant facts and circumstances, that the reduction in the rate of future benefit accrual resulting from an amendment is not significant (as described in Q&A-8 of this section), or that an amendment does not significantly reduce an early retirement benefit or retirement-type subsidy.

(3) *Example.* The following example illustrates the provisions of this paragraph (a):

*Example.* (i) *Facts.* Plan A is amended to reduce significantly the rate of future benefit accrual effective January 1, 2003. Section 204(h) notice is required to be provided 45 days before January 1, 2003. Timely section 204(h) notice is provided to all applicable individuals (and to each employee organization representing participants who are applicable individuals), except that the employer intentionally fails to provide section 204(h) notice to certain participants until May 16, 2003.

(ii) *Conclusion.* The failure to provide section 204(h) notice is egregious. Accordingly, for the period from January 1, 2003 through June 30, 2003 (which is the date that is 45 days after May 16, 2003), all participants and alternate payees are entitled to the greater of the benefit to which they would have been entitled under Plan A as in effect before the amendment or the benefit under the plan as amended.

(b) *Effect of non-egregious failure to provide section 204(h) notice.* If an egregious failure has not occurred, the amendment with respect to which section 204(h) notice is required may become effective with respect to all applicable individuals. However, see section 502 of ERISA for civil enforcement remedies. Thus, where there is a failure, whether or not egregious, to provide section 204(h) notice in accordance with this section, individuals may have recourse under section 502 of ERISA.

(c) *Excise taxes.* See section 4980F and Q&A-15 of this section for excise taxes that may apply to a failure to notify applicable individuals of a pension plan amendment that provides for a significant reduction in the rate of future benefit accrual or eliminates or significantly reduces an early retirement benefit or retirement-type subsidy, regardless of whether or not the failure is egregious.

Q-15. What are some of the rules that apply with respect to the excise tax under section 4980F?

A-15. (a) *Person responsible for excise tax.* In the case of a plan other than a multiemployer plan, the employer is responsible for reporting and paying the excise tax. In the case of a multiemployer plan, the plan is responsible for reporting and paying the excise tax.

(b) *Excise tax inapplicable in certain cases.* Under section 4980F(c)(1) of the Internal Revenue Code, no excise tax is imposed on a failure for any period during which it is established to the satisfaction of the Commissioner that the employer (or other person responsible for the tax) exercised reasonable dilligence, but did not know that the failure existed. Under section 4980F(c)(2) of the Internal Revenue Code, no excise tax applies to a failure to provide section 204(h) notice if the employer (or other person responsible for the tax) exercised reasonable diligence and corrects the failure within 30 days after the employer (or other person responsible for the tax) first knew, or exercising reasonable diligence would have known, that such failure existed. For purposes of section 4980F(c)(1) of the Internal Revenue Code, a person has exercised reasonable diligence, but did not know that the failure existed if and only if—

(1) The person exercised reasonable diligence in attempting to deliver section 204(h) notice to applicable individuals by the latest date permitted under this section; and

(2) At the latest date permitted for delivery of section 204(h) notice, the person reasonably believes that section 204(h) notice was actually delivered to each applicable individual by that date.

(c) *Example.* The following example illustrates the provisions of paragraph (b) of this Q&A-15:

*Example.* (i) *Facts.* Plan A is amended to reduce significantly the rate of future benefit accrual. The employer sends out a section 204(h) notice to all affected participants and other applicable individuals and to any employee organization representing applicable individuals, including actual delivery by hand to employees at worksites and by first-class mail for any other applicable individual and to any employee organization representing applicable individuals. However, although the employer exercises reasonable diligence in seeking

to deliver the notice, the notice is not delivered to any participants at one worksite due to a failure of an overnight delivery service to provide the notice to appropriate personnel at that site for them to timely hand deliver the notice to affected employees. The error is discovered when the employer subsequently calls to confirm delivery. Appropriate section 204(h) notice is then promptly delivered to all affected participants at the worksite.

(ii) *Conclusion.* Because the employer exercised reasonable diligence, but did not know that a failure existed, no excise tax applies, assuming that participants at the worksite receive section 204(h) notice within 30 days after the employer first knew, or exercising reasonable diligence would have known, that the failure occurred.

Q-16. How do section 4980F and section 204(h) apply when a business is sold?

A-16. (a) *Generally.* Whether section 204(h) notice is required in connection with the sale of a business depends on whether a plan amendment is adopted that significantly reduces the rate of future benefit accrual or significantly reduces an early retirement benefit or retirement-type subsidy.

(b) *Examples.* The following examples illustrate the rules of this Q&A-16:

*Example 1.* (i) *Facts.* Corporation Q maintains Plan A, a defined benefit plan that covers all employees of Corporation Q, including employees in its Division M. Plan A provides that participating employees cease to accrue benefits when they cease to be employees of Corporation Q. On January 1, 2006, Corporation Q sells all of the assets of Division M to Corporation R. Corporation R maintains Plan B, which covers all of the employees of Corporation R. Under the sale agreement, employees of Division M become employees of Corporation R on the date of the sale (and cease to be employees of Corporation Q), Corporation Q continues to maintain Plan A following the sale, and the employees of Division M become participants in Plan B.

(ii) *Conclusion.* No section 204(h) notice is required because no plan amendment was adopted that reduced the rate of future benefit accrual. The employees of Division M who become employees of Corporation R ceased to accrue benefits under Plan A because their employment with Corporation Q terminated.

*Example 2.* (i) *Facts.* Subsidiary Y is a wholly owned subsidiary of Corporation S. Subsidiary Y maintains Plan C, a defined benefit plan that covers employees of Subsidiary Y. Corporation S sells all of the stock of Subsidiary Y to Corporation T. At the effective date of the sale of the stock of Subsidiary Y, in accordance with the sale agreement between Corporation S and Corporation T, Subsidiary Y amends Plan C so that all benefit accruals cease.

(ii) *Conclusion.* Section 204(h) notice is required to be provided because Subsidiary Y adopted a plan amendment that significantly reduced the rate of future benefit accrual in Plan C.

*Example 3.* (i) *Facts.* As a result of an acquisition, Corporation U maintains two defined benefit plans: Plan D covers employees of Division N and Plan E covers the rest of the employees of Corporation U. Plan E provides a significantly lower rate of future benefit accrual than Plan D. Plan D is merged with Plan E, and all of the employees of Corporation U will accrue benefits under the merged plan in accordance with the benefit formula of former Plan E.

(ii) *Conclusion.* Section 204(h) notice is required.

*Example 4.* (i) *Facts.* The facts are the same as in *Example 3*, except that the rate of future benefit accrual in Plan E is not significantly lower. In addition, Plan D has a retirement-type subsidy that Plan E does not have and the Plan D employees' rights to the subsidy under the merged plan are limited to benefits accrued before the merger.

(ii) *Conclusion.* Section 204(h) notice is required for any participants or beneficiaries for whom the reduction in the retirement-type subsidy is significant (and for any employee organization representing such participants).

*Example 5.* (i) *Facts.* Corporation V maintains several plans, including Plan F, which covers employees of Division P. Plan F provides that participating employees cease to accrue further benefits under the plan when they cease to be employees of Corporation V. Corporation V sells all of the assets of Division P to Corporation W, which maintains Plan G for its employees. Plan G provides a significantly lower rate of future benefit accrual than Plan F. Plan F is merged with Plan G as part of the sale, and employees of Division P who become employees of Corporation W will accrue benefits under the merged plan in accordance with the benefit formula of former Plan G.

(ii) *Conclusion.* No section 204(h) notice is required because no plan amendment was adopted that reduces the rate of future benefit accrual or eliminates or significantly reduces an early retirement benefit or retirement-type subsidy. Under the terms of Plan F as in effect prior to the merger, employees of Division P cease to accrue any further benefits (including benefits with respect to early retirement benefits and any retirement-type subsidy) under Plan F after the date of the sale because their employment with Corporation V terminated.

Q-17. How are amendments to cease accruals and terminate a plan treated under section 4980F and section 204(h)?

A-17. (a) *General rule*—(1) *Rule.* An amendment providing for the cessation of benefit accruals on a specified future date and for the termination of a plan is subject to section 4980F and section 204(h).

(2) *Example.* The following example illustrates the rule of paragraph (a)(1) of this Q&A-17:

*Example.* (i) *Facts.* An employer adopts an amendment that provides for the cessation of benefit accruals under a defined benefit plan on December 31, 2003, and for the termination of the plan pursuant to title IV of ERISA as of a proposed termination date that is also December 31, 2003. As part of the notice of intent to terminate required under title IV in order to terminate the plan, the plan administrator gives section 204(h) notice of the amendment ceasing accruals, which states that benefit accruals will cease "on December 31, 2003 whether or not the plan is terminated on that date." However, because all the requirements of title IV for a plan termination are not satisfied, the plan cannot be terminated until a date that is later than December 31, 2003.

(ii) *Conclusion.* Nonetheless, because section 204(h) notice was given stating that the plan was amended to cease accruals on December 31, 2003, section 204(h) does not prevent the amendment to cease accruals from being effective on December 31, 2003. The result would be the same had the section 204(h) notice informed the participants that the plan was amended to provide for a proposed termination date of December 31, 2003 and to provide that "benefit accruals will cease on the proposed termination date whether or not the plan is terminated on that date." However, neither section 4980F nor section 204(h) would be satisfied with respect to the December 31, 2003 effective date if the section 204(h) notice had merely stated that benefit accruals would cease, "on the termination date" or "on the proposed termination date."

(3) *Additional requirements under title IV of ERISA.* See 29 CFR 4041.23(b)(4) and 4041.43(b)(5) for special rules applicable to plans terminating under title IV of ERISA.

(b) *Terminations in accordance with title IV of ERISA.* A plan that is terminated in accordance with title IV of ERISA is deemed to have satisfied section 4980F and section 204(h) not later than the termination date (or date of termination, as applicable) established under section 4048 of ERISA. Accordingly, neither section 4980F nor section 204(h) would in any event require that any additional benefits accrue after the effective date of the termination.

(c) *Amendment effective before termination date of a plan subject to title IV of ERISA.* To the extent that an amendment providing for a significant reduction in the rate of future benefit accrual or a significant reduction in an early retirement benefit or retirement-type subsidy has an effective date that is earlier than the termination date (or date of termination, as applicable) established under section 4048 of ERISA, that amendment is subject to section 4980F and section 204(h). Accordingly, the plan administrator must provide section 204(h) notice (either separately, with, or as part of the notice of intent to terminate) with respect to such an amendment.

Q-18. What are the effective dates of section 4980F, section 204(h), as amended by EGTRRA, and these regulations?

A-18. (a) *Statutory effective date*—(1) *General rule.* Section 4980F and section 204(h), as amended by EGTRRA, apply to plan amendments taking effect on or after June 7, 2001 (statutory effective date), which is the date of enactment of EGTRRA.

(2) *Transition rule.* For amendments applying after the statutory effective date in paragraph (a)(1) of this Q&A-18 and prior to the regulatory effective date in paragraph (c) of this Q&A-18, the requirements of section 4980F(e)(2) and (3) of the Internal Revenue Code and section 204(h), as amended by EGTRRA, are treated as satisfied if the plan administrator makes a reasonable, good faith effort to comply with those requirements.

(3) *Special notice rule*—(i) *In general.* Notwithstanding Q&A-9 of this section, section 204(h) notice is not required by section 4980F(e) of the Internal Revenue Code or section 204(h), as amended by EGTRRA, to be provided prior to September 7, 2001 (the date that is three months after the date of enactment of EGTRRA).

(ii) *Reasonable notice.* The requirements of section 4980F and section 204(h), as amended by EGTRRA, do not apply to any plan amendment that takes effect on or after June 7, 2001 if, before April 25, 2001, notice was provided to participants and beneficiaries adversely affected by the plan amendment (and their representatives) which was reasonably expected to notify them of the nature and effective date of the plan amendment. For purposes of this paragraph (a)(3)(ii), notice that complies with § 1.411(d)-6 of this chapter, as it appeared in the April 1, 2001 edition of 26 CFR part 1, is deemed to be notice which was reasonably expected to notify participants and beneficiaries adversely affected by the plan amendment (and their representatives) of the nature and effective date of the plan amendment.

(4) *Special effective date for certain section 204(h) amendments made by plans of commercial airlines.* Section 402 of PPA '06 applies to section

204(h) amendments adopted in plan years ending after August 17, 2006.

(5) *Special effective date for rule relating to contributing employers.* Section 502(c) of PPA '06, which amended section 4980F(e)(1) of the Internal Revenue Code, applies to section 204(h) amendments adopted in plan years beginning after December 31, 2007.

(b) *Regulatory effective date*—(1) *General effective date.* Except as otherwise provided in this paragraph (b) of this section, Q&A-1 through Q&A-18 of this section apply to amendments with an effective date that is on or after September 1, 2003.

(2) *Effective date for Q&A-7(a)(2).* Q&A-7(a)(2) of this section applies to amendments with an effective date that is on or after January 1, 2004.

(3) *Effective dates for Q&A-9(g)(1), (g)(3), and (g)(4)*—(i) *General effective date.* Except as otherwise provided in Q&A-18(b)(3)(ii) or (b)(3)(iii) of this section, Q&A-9(g)(1), (g)(3), and (g)(4) of this section apply to amendments that are effective on or after January 1, 2008.

(ii) *Effective dates for Q&A-9(g)(2) and Q&A-7(b).* Except as otherwise provided in Q&A-18(b)(3)(iii) of this section, Q&A-9(g)(2) and Q&A-7(b) of this section apply to section 204(h) amendments adopted in plan years beginning after July 1, 2008.

(iii) *Special rules for section 204(h) amendments to an applicable defined benefit plan.* Except as otherwise provided in paragraph (b)(3)(i) or (b)(3)(ii) of this Q&A-18, with respect to any section 204(h) notice provided in connection with a section 204(h) amendment to an applicable defined benefit plan within the meaning of section 411(a)(13)(C)(i) to limit distributions as permitted under section 411(a)(13)(A) for distributions made after August 17, 2006, that is made pursuant to section 701 of PPA '06, paragraphs (g)(1) and (g)(2) of Q&A-9 of this section apply to amendments that are effective after December 21, 2006. For such an amendment that is effective not later than December 31, 2008, section 204(h) notice does not fail to be timely if the notice is provided at least 30 days, rather than 45 days, before the date that the amendment is first effective.

(c) *Amendments taking effect prior to June 7, 2001.* For rules applicable to amendments taking effect prior to June 7, 2001, see § 1.411(d)-6 of this chapter, as it appeared in the April 1, 2001 edition of 26 CFR part 1. [Reg. § 54.4980F-1.]

☐ [*T.D. 9052*, 4-8-2003 (*corrected* 5-6-2003). *Amended by T.D. 9219*, 8-11-2005; *T.D. 9294*, 10-19-2006 *and T.D. 9472*, 11-23-2009.]

### [Reg. § 54.4980G-0]

**§ 54.4980G-0. Table of contents.**—This section contains the questions for § § 54.4980G-1, 54.4980G-2, 54.4980G-3, 54.4980G-4, and 54.4980G-5.

*§ 54.4980G-1 Failure of employer to make comparable health savings account contributions.*

Q-1: What are the comparability rules that apply to employer contributions to Health Savings Accounts (HSAs)?

Q-2: What are the categories of HDHP coverage for purposes of applying the comparability rules?

Q-3: What is the testing period for making comparable contributions to employees' HSAs?

Q-4: How is the excise tax computed if employer contributions do not satisfy the comparability rules for a calendar year?

*§ 54.4980G-2 Employer contribution defined.*

Q-1: Do the comparability rules apply to amounts rolled over from an employee's HSA or Archer Medical Savings Account (Archer MSA)?

Q-2: If an employee requests that his or her employer deduct after-tax amounts from the employee's compensation and forward these amounts as employee contributions to the employee's HSA, do the comparability rules apply to these amounts?

*§ 54.4980G-3 Definition of employee for comparability testing.*

Q-1: Do the comparability rules apply to contributions that an employer makes to the HSAs of independent contractors or self-employed individuals?

Q-2: May a sole proprietor who is an eligible individual contribute to his or her own HSA without contributing to the HSAs of his or her employees who are eligible individuals?

Q-3: Do the comparability rules apply to contributions by a partnership to a partner's HSA?

Q-4: How are members of controlled groups treated when applying the comparability rules?

Q-5: What are the categories of employees for comparability testing?

Q-6: Are employees who are included in a unit of employees covered by a collective bargaining agreement comparable participating employees?

Q-7: Is an employer permitted to make comparable contributions only to the HSAs of comparable participating employees who have coverage under the employer's HDHP?

Q-8: If an employee and his or her spouse are eligible individuals who work for the same employer and one employee-spouse has family coverage for both employees under the employer's HDHP, must the employer make comparable contributions to the HSAs of both employees?

Q-9: Does an employer that makes HSA contributions only for one class of non-collectively bargained employees who are eligible individuals, but not for another class of non-collectively bargained employees who are eligible individuals (for example, management v. non-management) satisfy the requirement that the employer make comparable contributions?

Q-10: If an employer contributes to the HSAs of former employees who are eligible individuals, do the comparability rules apply to these contributions?

Q-11: Is an employer permitted to make comparable contributions only to the HSAs of comparable participating former employees who have coverage under the employer's HDHP?

Q-12: If an employer contributes only to the HSAs of former employees who are eligible individuals with coverage under the employer's HDHP, must the employer make comparable contributions to the HSAs of former employees who are eligible individuals with coverage under the employer's HDHP because of an election under a COBRA continuation provision (as defined in section 9832(d)(1))?

Q-13: How do the comparability rules apply if some employees have HSAs and other employees have Archer MSAs?

§ 54.4980G-4 *Calculating comparable contributions.*

Q-1: What are comparable contributions?

Q-2: How does an employer comply with the comparability rules when some non-collectively bargained employees who are eligible individuals do not work for the employer during the entire calendar year?

Q-3: How do the comparability rules apply to employer contributions to employees' HSAs if some non-collectively bargained employees work full-time during the entire calendar year, and other non-collectively bargained employees work full-time for less than the entire calendar year?

Q-4: May an employer make contributions for the entire year to the HSAs of its employees who are eligible individuals at the beginning of the calendar year (i.e., on a pre-funded basis) instead of contributing on a pay-as-you-go or on a look-back basis?

Q-5: Must an employer use the same contribution method as described in Q & A-2 and Q & A-4 of this section for all employees for any month during the calendar year?

Q-6: How does an employer comply with the comparability rules if an employee has not established an HSA at the time the employer contributes to its employees' HSAs?

Q-7: If an employer bases its contributions on a percentage of the HDHP deductible, how is the correct percentage or dollar amount computed?

Q-8: Does an employer that contributes to the HSA of each comparable participating employee in an amount equal to the employee's HSA contribution or a percentage of the employee's HSA contribution (matching contributions) satisfy the rule that all comparable participating employees receive comparable contributions?

Q-9: If an employer conditions contributions by the employer to an employee's HSA on an employee's participation in health assessments, disease management programs or wellness programs and makes the same contributions available to all employees who participate in the programs, do the contributions satisfy the comparability rules?

Q-10: If an employer makes additional contributions to the HSAs of all comparable participating employees who have attained a specified age or who have worked for the employer for a specified number of years, do the contributions satisfy the comparability rules?

Q-11: If an employer makes additional contributions to the HSAs of all comparable participating employees who are eligible to make the additional contributions (HSA catch-up contributions) under section 223(b)(3), do the contributions satisfy the comparability rules?

Q-12: If an employer's contributions to an employee's HSA result in non-comparable contributions, may the employer recoup the excess amount from the employee's HSA?

Q-13: What constitutes a reasonable interest rate for purposes of making comparable contributions?

Q-14: How does an employer comply with the comparability rules if an employee has not established an HSA by December 31st?

Q-15: For any calendar year, may an employer accelerate part or all of its contributions for the entire year to the HSAs of employees who have incurred, during the calendar year, qualified medical expenses (as defined in section 223(d)(2)) exceeding the employer's cumulative HSA contributions at that time?

Q-16: What is the effective date for the rules in Q & A-14 and Q & A-15 of this section?

§ 54.4980G-5 *HSA comparability rules and cafeteria plans and waiver of excise tax.*

Q-1: If an employer makes contributions through a section 125 cafeteria plan to the HSA of each employee who is an eligible individual, are the contributions subject to the comparability rules?

Q-2: If an employer makes contributions through a cafeteria plan to the HSA of each employee who is an eligible individual in an amount equal to the amount of the employee's HSA contribution or a percentage of the amount of the employee's HSA contribution (i.e., matching contributions), are the contributions subject to the section 4980G comparability rules?

Q-3: If under the employer's cafeteria plan, employees who are eligible individuals and who participate in health assessments, disease management programs or wellness programs receive an employer contribution to an HSA and the employees have the right to elect to make pre-tax salary reduction contributions to their HSAs, are the contributions subject to the comparability rules?

Q-4: May all or part of the excise tax imposed under section 4980G be waived?

[Reg. § 54.4980G-0.]

☐ [*T.D. 9277, 7-28-2006 (corrected 9-12-2006). Amended by T.D. 9393, 4-16-2008.*]

### [Reg. § 54.4980G-1]

**§ 54.4980G-1. Failure of employer to make comparable health savings account contributions.**

Q-1: What are the comparability rules that apply to employer contributions to Health Savings Accounts (HSAs)?

A-1: If an employer makes contributions to any employee's HSA, the employer must make comparable contributions to the HSAs of all comparable participating employees. See Q & A-1 in § 54.4980G-4 for the definition of comparable contributions. Comparable participating employees are eligible individuals (as defined in section 223(c)(1)) who are in the same category of employees and who have the same category of high deductible health plan (HDHP) coverage. See sections 4980G(b) and 4980E(d)(3). See section 223(c)(2) and (g) for the definition of an HDHP. See also Q & A-5 in § 54.4980G-3 for the categories of employees and Q & A-2 of this section for the categories of HDHP coverage. But see Q & A-6 in § 54.4980G-3 for treatment of collectively bargained employees and Q & A-1 in § 54.4980G-6 for the rules allowing larger comparable contributions to nonhighly compensated employees.

Q-2: What are the categories of HDHP coverage for purposes of applying the comparability rules?

A-2: (a) *In general.* Generally, the categories of coverage are self-only HDHP coverage and family HDHP coverage. Family HDHP coverage means any coverage other than self-only HDHP coverage. The comparability rules apply separately to self-only HDHP coverage and family HDHP coverage. In addition, if an HDHP has family coverage options meeting the descriptions listed in paragraph (b) of this Q & A-2, each such coverage option may be treated as a separate category of coverage and the comparability rules may be applied separately to each category. However, if the HDHP has more than one category that provides coverage for the same number of individuals, all such categories are treated as a single category for purposes of the comparability rules. Thus, the categories of "employee plus spouse" and "employee plus dependent," each providing coverage for two individuals, are treated as the single category "self plus one" for comparability purposes. See, however, the final sentence of paragraph (a) of Q & A-1 of § 54.4980G-4 for a special rule that applies if different amounts are contributed for different categories of family coverage. See also § 54.4980G-6 for the rules allowing larger comparable contributions to nonhighly compensated employees.

(b) *HDHP Family coverage categories.* The coverage categories are—

(1) Self plus one;

(2) Self plus two; and

(3) Self plus three or more.

(c) *Examples.* The rules of this Q & A-2 are illustrated by the following examples:

*Example 1.* Employer A maintains an HDHP and contributes to the HSAs of eligible employees who elect coverage under the HDHP. The HDHP has self-only coverage and family coverage. Thus, the categories of coverage are self-only and family coverage. Employer A contributes $750 to the HSA of each eligible employee with self-only HDHP coverage and $1,000 to the HSA of each eligible employee with family HDHP coverage. Employer A's contributions satisfy the comparability rules.

*Example 2.* (i) Employer B maintains an HDHP and contributes to the HSAs of eligible employees who elect coverage under the HDHP, The HDHP has the following coverage options:

(A) Self-only;

(B) Self plus spouse;

(C) Self plus dependent;

(D) Self plus spouse plus one dependent;

(E) Self plus two dependents; and

(F) Self plus spouse and two or more dependents.

(ii) The self plus spouse category and the self plus dependent category constitute the same category of HDHP coverage (self plus one) and Employer B must make the same comparable contributions to the HSAs of all eligible individuals who are in either the self plus spouse category of HDHP coverage or the self plus dependent category of HDHP coverage. Likewise, the self plus spouse plus one dependent category and the self plus two dependents category constitute the same category of HDHP coverage (self plus two) and Employer B must make the same comparable contributions to the HSAs of all eligible individuals who are in either the self plus spouse plus one dependent category of HDHP coverage or the self plus two dependents category of HDHP coverage.

*Example 3.* (i) Employer C maintains an HDHP and contributes to the HSAs of eligible employees who elect coverage under the HDHP. The HDHP has the following coverage options:

(A) Self-only;

(B) Self plus one;

(C) Self plus two; and

(D) Self plus three or more.

(ii) Employer C contributes $500 to the HSA of each eligible employee with self-only HDHP coverage, $750 to the HSA of each eligible employee with self plus one HDHP coverage, $900 to the HSA of each eligible employee with self plus two HDHP coverage and $1,000 to the HSA of each eligible employee with self plus three or more HDHP coverage. Employer C's contributions satisfy the comparability rules.

Q-3: What is the testing period for making comparable contributions to employees' HSAs?

A-3: To satisfy the comparability rules, an employer must make comparable contributions for the calendar year to the HSAs of employees who are comparable participating employees. See section 4980G(a). See Q & A-3 and Q & A-4 in §54.4980G-4 for a discussion of HSA contribution methods.

Q-4: How is the excise tax computed if employer contributions do not satisfy the comparability rules for a calendar year?

A-4: (a) *Computation of tax.* If employer contributions do not satisfy the comparability rules for a calendar year, the employer is subject to an excise tax equal to 35% of the aggregate amount contributed by the employer to HSAs for that period.

(b) *Example.* The following example illustrates the rules in paragraph (a) of this Q & A-4:

*Example.* During the 2007 calendar year, Employer D has 8 employees who are eligible individuals with self-only coverage under an HDHP provided by Employer D. The deductible for the HDHP is $2,000. For the 2007 calendar year, Employer D contributes $2,000 each to the HSAs of two employees and $1,000 each to the HSAs of the other six employees, for total HSA contributions of $10,000. Employer D's contributions do not satisfy the comparability rules. Therefore, Employer D is subject to an excise tax of $3,500 (35% of $10,000) for its failure to make comparable contributions to its employees' HSAs.

Q-5: If a person is liable for the excise tax under section 4980G, what form must the person file and what is the due date for the filing and payment of the excise tax?

A-5: (a) *In general.* §§ 54.6011-2, 54.6151-1 and 54.6071-1(d).

(b) *Effective/applicability date.* The rules in this Q & A-5 are effective for employer contributions made for calendar years beginning on or after January 1, 2010.

[Reg. §54.4980G-1.]

☐ [*T.D. 9277, 7-28-2006. Amended by T.D. 9457, 9-4-2009.*]

### [Reg. §54.4980G-2]

### §54.4980G-2. Employer contribution defined.

Q-1: Do the comparability rules apply to amounts rolled over from an employee's HSA or Archer Medical Savings Account (Archer MSA)?

A-1: No. The comparability rules do not apply to amounts rolled over from an employee's HSA or Archer MSA.

Q-2: If an employee requests that his or her employer deduct after-tax amounts from the employee's compensation and forward these amounts as employee contributions to the employee's HSA, do the comparability rules apply to these amounts?

A-2: No. Section 106(d) provides that amounts contributed by an employer to an eligible employee's HSA shall be treated as employer-provided coverage for medical expenses and are excludible from the employee's gross income up to the limit in section 223(b). After-tax employee contributions to an HSA are not subject to the comparability rules because they are not employer contributions under section 106(d).

[Reg. §54.4980G-2.]

☐ [*T.D. 9277, 7-28-2006.*]

### [Reg. §54.4980G-3]

### §54.4980G-3. Failure of employer to make comparable health savings account contributions.

Q-1: Do the comparability rules apply to contributions that an employer makes to the HSAs of independent contractors or self-employed individuals?

A-1: No. The comparability rules apply only to contributions that an employer makes to the HSAs of employees.

Q-2: May a sole proprietor who is an eligible individual contribute to his or her own HSA without contributing to the HSAs of his or her employees who are eligible individuals?

A-2: (a) *Sole proprietor not an employee.* Yes. The comparability rules apply only to contributions made by an employer to the HSAs of employees. Because a sole proprietor is not an employee, the comparability rules do not apply to contributions the sole proprietor makes to his or her own HSA. However, if a sole proprietor contributes to any employee's HSA, the sole proprietor must make comparable contributions to the HSAs of all comparable participating employees. In determining whether the comparability rules are satisfied, contributions that a sole proprietor makes to his or her own HSA are not taken into account.

(b) *Example.* The following example illustrates the rules in paragraph (a) of this Q & A-2:

*Example.* In a calendar year, B, a sole proprietor is an eligible individual and contributes $1,000 to B's own HSA. B also contributes $500 for the same calendar year to the HSA of each employee who is an eligible individual. The comparability rules are not violated by B's $1,000 contribution to B's own HSA.

Q-3: Do the comparability rules apply to contributions by a partnership to a partner's HSA?

A-3: (a) *Partner not an employee.* No. Contributions by a partnership to a bona fide partner's HSA are not subject to the comparability rules because the contributions are not contributions by an employer to the HSA of an employee. The contributions are treated as either guaranteed payments under section 707(c) or distributions under section 731. However, if a partnership contributes to the HSAs of any employee who is not a partner, the partnership must make comparable contributions to the HSAs of all comparable participating employees.

(b) *Example.* The following example illustrates the rules in paragraph (a) of this Q & A-3:

*Example.* (i) Partnership X is a limited partnership with three equal individual partners, A (a general partner), B (a limited partner), and C (a limited partner). C is to be paid $300 annually for services rendered to Partnership X in her capacity as a partner without regard to partnership income (a section 707(c) guaranteed payment). D and E are the only employees of Partnership X and are not partners in Partnership X. A, B, C, D, and E are eligible individuals and each has an HSA. During Partnership X's Year 1 taxable year, which is also a calendar year, Partnership X makes the following contributions—

(A) A $300 contribution to each of A's and B's HSAs which are treated as section 731 distributions to A and B;

(B) A $300 contribution to C's HSA in lieu of paying C the guaranteed payment directly; and

(c) A $200 contribution to each of D's and E's HSAs, who are comparable participating employees.

(ii) Partnership X's contributions to A's and B's HSAs are section 731 distributions, which are treated as cash distributions. Partnership X's contribution to C's HSA is treated as a guaranteed payment under section 707(c). The contribution is not excludible from C's gross income under section 106(d) because the contribution is treated as a distributive share of partnership income for purposes of all Code sections other than sections 61(a) and 162(a), and a guaranteed payment to a partner is not treated as compensation to an employee. Thus, Partnership X's contributions to the HSAs of A, B, and C are not subject to the comparability rules. Partnership X's contributions to D's and E's HSAs are subject to the comparability rules because D and E are employees of Partnership X and are not partners in Partnership X. Partnership X's contributions satisfy the comparability rules.

Q-4: How are members of controlled groups treated when applying the comparability rules?

A-4: All persons or entities treated as a single employer under section 414 (b), (c), (m), or (o) are treated as one employer. See sections 4980G(b) and 4980E(e).

Q-5: What are the categories of employees for comparability testing?

A-5: (a) *Categories.* The categories of employees for comparability testing are as follows (but see Q & A-6 of this section for the treatment of collectively bargained employees and Q & A-1 of

§ 54.4980G-6 for a special rule for contributions made to the HSAs of nonhighly compensated employees)—

  (1) Current full-time employees;

  (2) Current part-time employees; and

  (3) Former employees (except for former employees with coverage under the employer's HDHP because of an election under a COBRA continuation provision (as defined in section 9832(d)(1)).

(b) *Part-time and full-time employees.* For purposes of section 4980G, part-time employees are customarily employed for fewer than 30 hours per week and full-time employees are customarily employed for 30 or more hours per week. See sections 4980G(b) and 4980E(d)(4)(A) and (B).

(c) *In general.* Except as provided in Q & A-6 of this section, the categories of employees in paragraph (a) of this Q & A-5 are the exclusive categories of employees for comparability testing. An employer must make comparable contributions to the HSAs of all comparable participating employees (eligible individuals who are in the same category of employees with the same category of HDHP coverage) during the calendar year without regard to any classification other than these categories. For example, full-time eligible employees with self-only HDHP coverage and part-time eligible employees with self-only HDHP coverage are separate categories of employees and different amounts can be contributed to the HSAs for each of these categories. But see § 54.4980G-6 for a special rule for contributions made to the HSAs of nonhighly compensated employees.

Q-6: Are employees who are included in a unit of employees covered by a collective bargaining agreement comparable participating employees?

A-6: (a) *In general.* No. Collectively bargained employees who are covered by a bona fide collective bargaining agreement between employee representatives and one or more employers are not comparable participating employees, if health benefits were the subject of good faith bargaining between such employee representatives and such employer or employers. Former employees covered by a collective bargaining agreement also are not comparable participating employees.

(b) *Examples.* The following examples illustrate the rules in paragraph (a) of this Q & A-6. The examples read as follows:

*Example 1.* Employer A offers its employees an HDHP with a $1,500 deductible for self-only coverage. Employer A has collectively bargained and non-collectively bargained employees. The collectively bargained employees are covered by a collective bargaining agreement under which health benefits were bargained in good faith. In the 2007 calendar year, Employer A contributes $500 to the HSAs of all eligible non-collectively bargained employees with self-only coverage under Employer A's HDHP. Employer A does not contribute to the HSAs of the collectively bargained employees. Employer A's contributions to the HSAs of non-collectively bargained employees satisfy the comparability rules. The comparability rules do not apply to collectively bargained employees.

*Example 2.* Employer B offers its employees an HDHP with a $1,500 deductible for self-only coverage. Employer B has collectively bargained and non-collectively bargained employees. The collectively bargained employees are covered by a collective bargaining agreement under which health benefits were bargained in good faith. In the 2007 calendar year and in accordance with the terms of the collective bargaining agreement, Employer B contributes to the HSAs of all eligible collectively bargained employees. Employer B does not contribute to the HSAs of the non-collectively bargained employees. Employer B's contributions to the HSAs of collectively bargained employees are not subject to the comparability rules because the comparability rules do not apply to collectively bargained employees. Accordingly, Employer B's failure to contribute to the HSAs of the non-collectively bargained employees does not violate the comparability rules.

*Example 3.* Employer C has two units of collectively bargained employees - unit Q and unit R - each covered by a collective bargaining agreement under which health benefits were bargained in good faith. In the 2007 calendar year and in accordance with the terms of the collective bargaining agreement, Employer C contributes to the HSAs of all eligible collectively bargained employees in unit Q. In accordance with the terms of the collective bargaining agreement, Employer C makes no HSA contributions for collectively bargained employees in unit R. Employer C's contributions to the HSAs of collectively bargained employees are not subject to the comparability rules because the comparability rules do not apply to collectively bargained employees.

*Example 4.* Employer D has a unit of collectively bargained employees that are covered by a collective bargaining agreement under which health benefits were bargained in good faith. In accordance with the terms of the collective bargaining agreement, Employer D contributes an amount equal to a specified number of cents per hour for each hour worked to the HSAs of all eligible collectively bar-

gained employees. Employer D's contributions to the HSAs of collectively bargained employees are not subject to the comparability rules because the comparability rules do not apply to collectively bargained employees.

Q-7: Is an employer permitted to make comparable contributions only to the HSAs of comparable participating employees who have coverage under the employer's HDHP?

A-7: (a) *Employer-provided HDHP coverage.* If during a calendar year, an employer contributes to the HSA of any employee who is an eligible individual covered under an HDHP provided by the employer, the employer is required to make comparable contributions to the HSAs of all comparable participating employees with coverage under any HDHP provided by the employer. An employer that contributes only to the HSAs of employees who are eligible individuals with coverage under the employer's HDHP is not required to make comparable contributions to HSAs of employees who are eligible individuals but are not covered under the employer's HDHP.

(b) *Non-employer provided HDHP coverage.* An employer that contributes to the HSA of any employee who is an eligible individual with coverage under any HDHP that is not an HDHP provided by the employer, must make comparable contributions to the HSAs of all comparable participating employees whether or not covered under the employer's HDHP. An employer that makes a reasonable good faith effort to identify all comparable participating employees with non-employer provided HDHP coverage and makes comparable contributions to the HSAs of such employees satisfies the requirements in paragraph (b) of this Q & A-7.

(c) *Examples.* The following examples illustrate the rules in this Q & A-7. None of the employees in the following examples are covered by a collective bargaining agreement. The examples read as follows:

*Example 1.* In a calendar year, Employer E offers an HDHP to its full-time employees. Most full-time employees are covered under Employer E's HDHP and Employer E makes comparable contributions only to these employees' HSAs. Employee W, a full-time employee of Employer E and an eligible individual, is covered under an HDHP provided by the employer of W's spouse and not under Employer E's HDHP. Employer E is not required to make comparable contributions to W's HSA.

*Example 2.* In a calendar year, Employer F does not offer an HDHP. Several full-time employees of Employer F, who are eligible individuals, have HSAs. Employer F contributes to these employees' HSAs. Employer F must make comparable contributions to the HSAs of all full-time employees who are eligible individuals.

*Example 3.* In a calendar year, Employer G offers an HDHP to its full-time employees. Most full-time employees are covered under Employer G's HDHP and Employer G makes comparable contributions to these employees' HSAs and also to the HSAs of full-time employees who are eligible individuals and who are not covered under Employer G's HDHP. Employee S, a full-time employee of Employer G and a comparable participating employee, is covered under an HDHP provided by the employer of S's spouse and not under Employer G's HDHP. Employer G must make comparable contributions to S's HSA.

Q-8: If an employee and his or her spouse are eligible individuals who work for the same employer and one employee-spouse has family coverage for both employees under the employer's HDHP, must the employer make comparable contributions to the HSAs of both employees?

A-8: (a) *In general.* If the employer makes contributions only to the HSAs of employees who are eligible individuals covered under its HDHP where only one employee-spouse has family coverage for both employees under the employer's HDHP, the employer is not required to contribute to the HSAs of both employee-spouses. The employer is required to contribute to the HSA of the employee-spouse with coverage under the employer's HDHP, but is not required to contribute to the HSA of the employee-spouse covered under the employer's HDHP by virtue of his or her spouse's coverage. However, if the employer contributes to the HSA of any employee who is an eligible individual with coverage under an HDHP that is not an HDHP provided by the employer, the employer must make comparable contributions to the HSAs of both employee-spouses if they are both eligible individuals. If an employer is required to contribute to the HSAs of both employee-spouses, the employer is not required to contribute amounts in excess of the annual contribution limits in section 223(b).

(b) *Examples.* The following examples illustrate the rules in paragraph (a) of this Q & A-8. None of the employees in the following examples are covered by a collective bargaining agreement. The examples read as follows:

*Example 1.* In a calendar year, Employer H offers an HDHP to its full-time employees. Most full-time employees are covered under Employer H's HDHP and Employer H makes comparable contributions only to these employees' HSAs. T and U are a married couple. Employee T, who is a full-time employee of Employer H and an eligible individual, has family coverage under Employer H's HDHP for T and T's spouse. Employee U, who is also a full-time employee of Employer H and an eligible individual, does not have coverage under Employer H's HDHP except as the spouse of Employee T. Employer H is required to make comparable contributions to T's HSA, but is not required to make comparable contributions to U's HSA.

*Example 2.* In a calendar year, Employer J offers an HDHP to its full-time employees. Most full-time employees are covered under Employer J's HDHP and Employer J makes comparable contributions to these employees' HSAs and to the HSAs of full-time employees who are eligible individuals but are not covered under Employer J's HDHP. R and S are a married couple. Employee S, who is a full-time employee of Employer J and an eligible individual, has family coverage under Employer J's HDHP for S and S's spouse. Employee R, who is also a full-time employee of Employer J and an eligible individual, does not have coverage under Employer J's HDHP except as the spouse of Employee S. Employer J must make comparable contributions to S's HSA and to R's HSA.

Q-9: Does an employer that makes HSA contributions only for one class of non-collectively bargained employees who are eligible individuals, but not for another class of non-collectively bargained employees who are eligible individuals (for example, management v. non-management) satisfy the requirement that the employer make comparable contributions?

A-9: (a) *Different classes of employees.* No. If the two classes of employees are comparable participating employees, the comparability rules are not satisfied. The only categories of employees for comparability purposes are current full-time employees, current part-time employees, and former employees. Collectively bargained employees are not comparable participating employees. But see Q & A-1 in § 54.4980G-5 on contributions made through a cafeteria plan. See § 54.4980G-6 for a special rule for contributions made to the HSAs of nonhighly compensated employees.

(b) *Examples.* The following examples illustrate the rules in paragraph (a) of this Q & A-9. None of the employees in the following examples are covered by a collective bargaining agreement. The examples read as follows:

*Example 1.* In a calendar year, Employer K maintains an HDHP covering all management and non-management employees. Employer K contributes to the HSAs of non-management employees who are eligible individuals covered under its HDHP. Employer K does not contribute to the HSAs of its management employees who are eligible individuals covered under its HDHP. The comparability rules are not satisfied.

*Example 2.* All of Employer L's employees are located in city X and city Y. In a calendar year, Employer L maintains an HDHP for all employees working in city X only. Employer L does not maintain an HDHP for its employees working in city Y. Employer L contributes $500 to the HSAs of city X employees who are eligible individuals with coverage under its HDHP. Employer L does not contribute to the HSAs of any of its city Y employees. The comparability rules are satisfied because none of the employees in city Y are covered under an HDHP of Employer L. (However, if any employees in city Y were covered by an HDHP of Employer L, Employer L could not fail to contribute to their HSAs merely because they work in a different city.)

*Example 3.* Employer M has two divisions - division N and division O. In a calendar year, Employer M maintains an HDHP for employees working in division N and division O. Employer M contributes to the HSAs of division N employees who are eligible individuals with coverage under its HDHP. Employer M does not contribute to the HSAs of division O employees who are eligible individuals covered under its HDHP. The comparability rules are not satisfied.

Q-10: If an employer contributes to the HSAs of former employees who are eligible individuals, do the comparability rules apply to these contributions?

A-10: (a) *Former employees.* Yes. The comparability rules apply to contributions an employer makes to former employees' HSAs. Therefore, if an employer contributes to any former employee's HSA, it must make comparable contributions to the HSAs of all comparable participating former employees (former employees who are eligible individuals with the same category of HDHP coverage). However, an employer is not required to make comparable contributions to the HSAs of former employees with coverage under the employer's HDHP because of an election under a COBRA continuation provision (as defined in section 9832(d)(1)). See Q & A-5 and Q & A-12 of this section. The comparability rules apply separately to former employees because they are a separate category of covered employee. See Q & A-5 of this section. Also, former employees who were covered by a collective bargaining agreement immediately before termination of

employment are not comparable participating employees. See Q & A-6 of this section.

(b) *Locating former employees.* An employer making comparable contributions to former employees must take reasonable actions to locate any missing comparable participating former employees. In general, such actions include the use of certified mail, the Internal Revenue Service Letter Forwarding Program or the Social Security Administration's Letter Forwarding Service.

(c) *Examples.* The following examples illustrate the rules in paragraph (a) of this Q & A-10. None of the employees in the following examples are covered by a collective bargaining agreement. The examples read as follows:

*Example 1.* In a calendar year, Employer N contributes $1,000 for the calendar year to the HSA of each current employee who is an eligible individual with coverage under any HDHP. Employer N does not contribute to the HSA of any former employee who is an eligible individual. Employer N's contributions satisfy the comparability rules.

*Example 2.* In a calendar year, Employer O contributes to the HSAs of current employees and former employees who are eligible individuals covered under any HDHP. Employer O contributes $750 to the HSA of each current employee with self-only HDHP coverage and $1,000 to the HSA of each current employee with family HDHP coverage. Employer O also contributes $300 to the HSA of each former employee with self-only HDHP coverage and $400 to the HSA of each former employee with family HDHP coverage. Employer O's contributions satisfy the comparability rules.

Q-11: Is an employer permitted to make comparable contributions only to the HSAs of comparable participating former employees who have coverage under the employer's HDHP?

A-11: If during a calendar year, an employer contributes to the HSA of any former employee who is an eligible individual covered under an HDHP provided by the employer, the employer is required to make comparable contributions to the HSAs of all former employees who are comparable participating former employees with coverage under any HDHP provided by the employer. An employer that contributes only to the HSAs of former employees who are eligible individuals with coverage under the employer's HDHP is not required to make comparable contributions to the HSAs of former employees who are eligible individuals and who are not covered under the employer's HDHP. However, an employer that contributes to the HSA of any former employee who is an eligible individual with coverage under an HDHP that is not an HDHP of the employer, must make comparable contributions to the HSAs of all former employees who are eligible individuals whether or not covered under an HDHP of the employer.

Q-12: If an employer contributes only to the HSAs of former employees who are eligible individuals with coverage under the employer's HDHP, must the employer make comparable contributions to the HSAs of former employees who are eligible individuals with coverage under the employer's HDHP because of an election under a COBRA continuation provision (as defined in section 9832(d)(1))?

A-12: No. An employer that contributes only to the HSAs of former employees who are eligible individuals with coverage under the employer's HDHP is not required to make comparable contributions to the HSAs of former employees who are eligible individuals with coverage under the employer's HDHP because of an election under a COBRA continuation provision (as defined in section 9832(d)(1)).

Q-13: How do the comparability rules apply if some employees have HSAs and other employees have Archer MSAs?

A-13: (a) *HSAs and Archer MSAs.* The comparability rules apply separately to employees who have HSAs and employees who have Archer MSAs. However, if an employee has both an HSA and an Archer MSA, the employer may contribute to either the HSA or the Archer MSA, but not to both.

(b) *Example.* The following example illustrates the rules in paragraph (a) of this Q & A-13:

*Example.* In a calendar year, Employer P contributes $600 to the Archer MSA of each employee who is an eligible individual and who has an Archer MSA. Employer P contributes $500 for the calendar year to the HSA of each employee who is an eligible individual and who has an HSA. If an employee has both an Archer MSA and an HSA, Employer P contributes to the employee's Archer MSA and not to the employee's HSA. Employee X has an Archer MSA and an HSA. Employer P contributes $600 for the calendar year to X's Archer MSA but does not contribute to X's HSA. Employer P's contributions satisfy the comparability rules.

[Reg. § 54.4980G-3.]

☐ [*T.D. 9277, 7-28-2006. Amended by T.D. 9457, 9-4-2009.*]

[Reg. § 54.4980G-4]

## § 54.4980G-4. Calculating comparable contributions.

Q-1: What are comparable contributions?

A-1: (a) *Definition*. Contributions are comparable if, for each month in a calendar year, the contributions are either the same amount or the same percentage of the deductible under the HDHP for employees who are eligible individuals with the same category of coverage on the first day of that month. Employees with self-only HDHP coverage are tested separately from employees with family HDHP coverage. Similarly, employees with different categories of family HDHP coverage may be tested separately. See Q & A-2 in § 54.4980G-1. An employer is not required to contribute the same amount or the same percentage of the deductible for employees who are eligible individuals with one category of HDHP coverage that it contributes for employees who are eligible individuals with a different category of HDHP coverage. For example, an employer that satisfies the comparability rules by contributing the same amount to the HSAs of all employees who are eligible individuals with family HDHP coverage is not required to contribute any amount to the HSAs of employees who are eligible individuals with self-only HDHP coverage, or to contribute the same percentage of the self-only HDHP deductible as the amount contributed with respect to family HDHP coverage. However, the contribution with respect to the self plus two category may not be less than the contribution with respect to the self plus one category and the contribution with respect to the self plus three or more category may not be less than the contribution with respect to the self plus two category. But see Q & A-1 of § 54.4980G-6 for a special rule for contributions made to the HSAs of nonhighly compensated employees.

(b) *Examples*. The following examples illustrate the rules in paragraph (a) of this Q & A-1. None of the employees in the following examples are covered by a collective bargaining agreement. The examples read as follows:

*Example 1*. In the 2007 calendar year, Employer A offers its full-time employees three health plans, including an HDHP with self-only coverage and a $2,000 deductible. Employer A contributes $1,000 for the calendar year to the HSA of each employee who is an eligible individual electing the self-only HDHP coverage. Employer A makes no HSA contributions for employees with family HDHP coverage or for employees who do not elect the employer's self-only HDHP. Employer A's HSA contributions satisfy the comparability rules.

*Example 2*. In the 2007 calendar year, Employer B offers its employees an HDHP with a $3,000 deductible for self-only coverage and a $4,000 deductible for family coverage. Employer B contributes $1,000 for the calendar year to the HSA of each employee who is an eligible individual electing the self-only HDHP coverage. Employer B contributes $2,000 for the calendar year to the HSA of each employee who is an eligible individual electing the family HDHP coverage. Employer B's HSA contributions satisfy the comparability rules.

*Example 3*. In the 2007 calendar year, Employer C offers its employees an HDHP with a $1,500 deductible for self-only coverage and a $3,000 deductible for family coverage. Employer C contributes $1,000 for the calendar year to the HSA of each employee who is an eligible individual electing the self-only HDHP coverage. Employer C contributes $1,000 for the calendar year to the HSA of each employee who is an eligible individual electing the family HDHP coverage. Employer C's HSA contributions satisfy the comparability rules.

*Example 4*. In the 2007 calendar year, Employer D offers its employees an HDHP with a $1,500 deductible for self-only coverage and a $3,000 deductible for family coverage. Employer D contributes $1,500 for the calendar year to the HSA of each employee who is an eligible individual electing the self-only HDHP coverage. Employer D contributes $1,000 for the calendar year to the HSA of each employee who is an eligible individual electing the family HDHP coverage. Employer D's HSA contributions satisfy the comparability rules.

*Example 5*. (i) In the 2007 calendar year, Employer E maintains two HDHPs. Plan A has a $2,000 deductible for self-only coverage and a $4,000 deductible for family coverage. Plan B has a $2,500 deductible for self-only coverage and a $4,500 deductible for family coverage. For the calendar year, Employer E makes contributions to the HSA of each full-time employee who is an eligible individual covered under Plan A of $600 for self-only coverage and $1,000 for family coverage. Employer E satisfies the comparability rules, if it makes either of the following contributions for the 2007 calendar year to the HSA of each full-time employee who is an eligible individual covered under Plan B—

(A) $600 for each full-time employee with self-only coverage and $1,000 for each full-time employee with family coverage; or

(B) $750 for each employee with self-only coverage and $1,125 for each employee with family coverage (the same percentage of the deductible Employer E contributes for full-time employees covered under Plan A, 30% of the deductible for self-only coverage and 25% of the deductible for family coverage).

(ii) Employer E also makes contributions to the HSA of each part-time employee who is an eligible individual covered under Plan A of $300 for self-only coverage and $500 for family coverage. Employer E satisfies the comparability rules, if it makes either of the following contributions for the 2007 calendar year to the HSA of each part-time employee who is an eligible individual covered under Plan B—

(A) $300 for each part-time employee with self-only coverage and $500 for each part-time employee with family coverage; or

(B) $375 for each part-time employee with self-only coverage and $563 for each part-time employee with family coverage (the same percentage of the deductible Employer E contributes for part-time employees covered under Plan A, 15% of the deductible for self-only coverage and 12.5% of the deductible for family coverage).

*Example 6*. (i) In the 2007 calendar year, Employer F maintains an HDHP. The HDHP has the following coverage options—

(A) A $2,500 deductible for self-only coverage;

(B) A $3,500 deductible for self plus one dependent (self plus one);

(C) A $3,500 deductible for self plus spouse (self plus one);

(D) A $3,500 deductible for self plus spouse and one dependent (self plus two); and

(E) A $3,500 deductible for self plus spouse and two or more dependents (self plus three or more).

(ii) Employer F makes the following contributions for the calendar year to the HSA of each full-time employee who is an eligible individual covered under the HDHP—

(A) $750 for self-only coverage;

(B) $1,000 for self plus one dependent;

(C) $1,000 for self plus spouse;

(D) $1,500 for self plus spouse and one dependent; and

(E) $2,000 for self plus spouse and two or more dependents.

(iii) Employer F's HSA contributions satisfy the comparability rules.

*Example 7*. (i) In a calendar year, Employer G offers its employees an HDHP and a health flexible spending arrangement (health FSA). The health FSA reimburses employees for medical expenses as defined in section 213(d). Some of Employer G's employees have coverage under the HDHP and the health FSA, some have coverage under the HDHP and their spouse's FSA, and some have coverage under the HDHP and are enrolled in Medicare. For the calendar year, Employer G contributes $500 to the HSA of each employee who is an eligible individual. No contributions are made to the HSAs of employees who have coverage under Employer G's health FSA or under a spouse's health FSA or who are enrolled in Medicare.

(ii) The employees who have coverage under a health FSA (whether Employer H's or their spouse's FSA) or who are covered under Medicare are not eligible individuals. Specifically, the employees who have coverage under the health FSA or under a spouse's health FSA are not comparable participating employees because they are not eligible individuals under section 223(c)(1). Similarly, the employees who are enrolled in Medicare are not comparable participating employees because they are not eligible individuals under section 223(b)(7) and (c)(1). Therefore, employees who have coverage under the health FSA or under a spouse's health FSA and employees who are enrolled in Medicare are excluded from comparability testing. See sections 4980G(b) and 4980E. Employer G's contributions satisfy the comparability rules.

Q-2: How does an employer comply with the comparability rules when some non-collectively bargained employees who are eligible individuals do not work for the employer during the entire calendar year?

A-2: (a) *In general*. In determining whether the comparability rules are satisfied, an employer must take into account all full-time and part-time employees who were employees and eligible individuals for any month during the calendar year. (Full-time and part-time employees are tested separately. See Q & A-5 in § 54.4980G-3.) There are two methods to comply with the comparability rules when some employees who are eligible individuals do not work for the employer during the entire calendar year; contributions may be made on a pay-as-you-go basis or on a look-back basis. See Q & A-9 through Q & A-11 in § 54.4980G-3 for the rules regarding comparable contributions to the HSAs of former employees.

(b) *Contributions on a pay-as-you-go basis*. An employer may comply with the comparability rules by contributing amounts at one or more dates during the calendar year to the HSAs of employees who are eligible individuals as of the first day of the month, if contributions are the same amount or the same percentage of the HDHP deductible for employees who are eligible individuals as of the first day of the month with the same category of coverage and are made at the same time. Contributions made at the employer's usual payroll interval for different groups of employees are considered to be made at the same time. For example, if salaried employees are paid monthly and hourly employees are paid bi-weekly, an employer may contribute to the HSAs of hourly employees on a bi-weekly basis and to the HSAs of salaried employees on a monthly basis. An employer may change the amount that it contributes to the HSAs of employees at any point. However, the changed contribution amounts must satisfy the comparability rules.

(c) *Examples.* The following examples illustrate the rules in paragraph (b) of this Q & A-2: The examples read as follows:

*Example 1.* (i) Beginning on January 1st, Employer H contributes $50 per month on the first day of each month to the HSA of each employee who is an eligible individual on that date. Employer H does not contribute to the HSAs of former employees. In mid-March of the same year, Employee X, an eligible individual, terminates employment after Employer H has contributed $150 to X's HSA. After X terminates employment, Employer H does not contribute additional amounts to X's HSA. In mid-April of the same year, Employer H hires Employee Y, an eligible individual, and contributes $50 to Y's HSA in May and $50 in June. Effective in July of the same year, Employer H stops contributing to the HSAs of all employees and makes no contributions to the HSA of any employee for the months of July through December. In August, Employer H hires Employee Z, an eligible individual. Employer H does not contribute to Z's HSA. After Z is hired, Employer H does not hire additional employees. As of the end of the calendar year, Employer H has made the following HSA contributions to its employees' HSAs—

(A) Employer H contributed $150 to X's HSA;

(B) Employer H contributed $100 to Y's HSA;

(C) Employer H did not contribute to Z's HSA; and

(D) Employer H contributed $300 to the HSA of each employee who was an eligible individual and employed by Employer J from January through June.

(ii) Employer H's contributions satisfy the comparability rules.

*Example 2.* In a calendar year, Employer J offers its employees an HDHP and contributes on a monthly pay-as-you-go basis to the HSAs of employees who are eligible individuals with coverage under Employer J's HDHP. In the calendar year, Employer J contributes $50 per month to the HSA of each of employee with self-only HDHP coverage and $100 per month to the HSA of each employee with family HDHP coverage. From January 1st through March 31st of the calendar year, Employee X is an eligible individual with self-only HDHP coverage. From April 1st through December 31st of the calendar year, X is an eligible individual with family HDHP coverage. For the months of January, February and March of the calendar year, Employer J contributes $50 per month to X's HSA. For the remaining months of the calendar year, Employer J contributes $100 per month to X's HSA. Employer J's contributions to X's HSA satisfy the comparibility rules.

(d) *Contributions on a look-back basis.* An employer may also satisfy the comparability rules by determining comparable contributions for the calendar year at the end of the calendar year, taking into account all employees who were eligible individuals for any month during the calendar year and contributing the same percentage of the HDHP deductible or the same dollar amount to the HSAs of all employees with the same category of coverage for that month.

(e) *Examples.* The following examples illustrate the rules in paragraph (d) of this Q & A-2. The examples read as follows:

*Example 1.* In a calendar year, Employer K offers its employees an HDHP and contributes on a look-back basis to the HSAs of employees who are eligible individuals with coverage under Employer K's HDHP. Employer K contributes $600 ($50 per month) for the calendar year to the HSA of each employee with self-only HDHP coverage and $1,200 ($100 per month) for the calendar year to the HSA of each employee with family HDHP coverage. From January 1st through June 30th of the calendar year, Employee Y is an eligible individual with family HDHP coverage. From July 1st through December 31st, Y is an eligible individual with self-only HDHP coverage. Employer K contributes $900 on a look-back basis for the calendar year to Y's HSA ($100 per month for the months of January through June and $50 per month for the months of July through December). Employer K's contributions to Y's HSA satisfy the comparability rules.

*Example 2.* On December 31st, Employer L contributes $50 per month on a look-back basis to each employee's HSA for each month in the calendar year that the employee was an eligible individual. In mid-March of the same year, Employee T, an eligible individual, terminated employment. In mid-April of the same year, Employer L hired Employee U, who becomes an eligible individual as of May 1st and works for Employer L through December 31st. On December 31st, Employer L contributes $150 to Employee T's HSA and $400 to Employee U's HSA. Employer L's contributions satisfy the comparability rules.

(f) *Periods and dates for making contributions.* With both the pay-as-you go method and the look-back method, an employer may establish, on a reasonable and consistent basis, periods for which contributions will be made (for example, a quarterly period covering three consecutive months in a calendar year) and the dates on which such contributions will be made for that designated period (for example, the first day of the quarter or the last day of the quarter in the case of an employer who has established a quarterly period for making contributions). An employer that makes contributions on a pay-as-you-go basis for a period covering more than one month will not fail to satisfy the comparability rules because an employee who terminates employment prior to the end of the period for which contributions were made has received more contributions on a monthly basis than employees who have worked the entire period. In addition, an employer that makes contributions on a pay-as-you-go basis for a period covering more than one month must make HSA contributions for any comparable participating employees hired after the date of initial funding for that period.

(g) *Example.* The following example illustrates the rules in paragraph (f) of this Q & A-2:

*Example.* Employer M has established, on a reasonable and consistent basis, a quarterly period for making contributions to the HSAs of eligible employees on a pay-as-you-go basis. Beginning on January 1st, Employer M contributes $150 for the first three months of the calendar year to the HSA of each employee who is an eligible individual on that date. On January 15th, Employee V, an eligible individual, terminated employment after Employer M has contributed $150 to V's HSA. On January 15th, Employer M hired Employee W, who becomes an eligible individual as of February 1st. On April 1st, Employer M has contributed $100 to W's HSA for the two months (February and March) in the quarter period that Employee W was an eligible employee. Employer M's contributions satisfy the comparability rules.

(h) *Maximum contribution permitted for all employees who are eligible individuals during the last month of the taxable year.* An employer may contribute up to the maximum annual contribution amount for the calendar year (based on the employees' HDHP coverage) to the HSAs of all employees who are eligible individuals on the first day of the last month of the employees' taxable year, including employees who worked for the employer for less than the entire calendar year and employees who became eligible individuals after January 1st of the calendar year. For example, such contribution may be made on behalf of an eligible individual who is hired after January 1st or an employee who becomes an eligible individual after January 1st. Employers are not required to provide more than a pro-rata contribution based on the number of months that an individual was an eligible individual and employed by the employer during the year. However, if an employer contributes more than a pro-rata amount for the calendar year to the HSA of any eligible individual who is hired after January 1st of the calendar year or any employee who becomes an eligible individual any time after January 1st of the calendar year, the employer must contribute that same amount on an equal and uniform basis to the HSAs of all comparable participating employees (as defined in Q & A-1 in § 54.4980G-1) who are hired or become eligible individuals after January 1st of the calendar year. Likewise, if an employer contributes the maximum annual contribution amount for the calendar year to the HSA of any eligible individual who is hired after January 1st of the calendar year or any employee who becomes an eligible individual any time after January 1st of the calendar year, the employer must contribute the maximum annual contribution amount on an equal and uniform basis to the HSAs of all comparable participating employees (as defined in Q & A-1 in § 54.4980G-1) who are hired or become eligible individuals after January 1st of the calendar year. An employer who makes the maximum calendar year contribution or more than a pro-rata contribution to the HSAs of employees who become eligible individuals after the first day of the calendar year or eligible individuals who are hired after the first day of the calendar year will not fail to satisfy comparability merely because some employees will have received more contributions on a monthly basis than employees who worked the entire calendar year.

(i) *Examples.* The following examples illustrate the rules in paragraph (h) in this Q & A-2. In the following examples, no contributions are made through a section 125 cafeteria plan and none of the employees are covered by a collective bargaining agreement.

*Example 1.* On January 1, 2010, Employer Q contributes $1,000 for the calendar year to the HSAs of employees who are eligible individuals with family HDHP coverage. In mid-March of the same year, Employer Q hires Employee A, an eligible individual with family HDHP coverage. On April 1, 2010, Employer Q contributes $1,000 to the HSA of Employee A. In September of the same year, Employee B becomes an eligible individual with family HDHP coverage. On October 1, 2010, Employer G contributes $1,000 to the HSA of Employee B. Employer Q does not make any other contributions for the 2010 calendar year. Employer Q's contributions satisfy the comparability rules.

*Example 2.* For the 2010 calendar year, Employer R only has two employees, Employee C and Employee D. Employee C, an eligible individual with family HDHP coverage, works for Employer R for the entire calendar year. Employee D, an eligible individual with family HDHP coverage works for Employer R from July 1st through December 31st. Employer R contributes $1,200 for the calendar year to the HSA of Employee C and $600 to the HSA of Employee D. Employer R does not make any other contributions for the 2010 calendar year. Employer R's contributions satisfy the comparability rules.

(j) *Effective/applicability date.* The rules in paragraphs (h) and (i) of Q & A-2 are effective for employer contributions made for calendar years beginning on or after January 1, 2010.

Q-3: How do the comparability rules apply to employer contributions to employees' HSAs if some non-collectively bargained employees work full-time during the entire calendar year, and other non-collectively bargained employees work full-time for less than the entire calendar year?

A-3: Employer contributions to the HSAs of employees who work full-time for less than twelve months satisfy the comparability rules if the contribution amount is comparable when determined on a month-to-month basis. For example, if the employer contributes $240 to the HSA of each full-time employee who works the entire calendar year, the employer must contribute $60 to the HSA of each full-time employee who works on the first day of each three months of the calendar year. The rules set forth in this Q & A-2 apply to employer contributions made on a pay-as-you-go basis or on a look-back basis as described in Q & A-3 of this section. See sections 4980G(b) and 4980E(d)(2)(B).

Q-4: May an employer make contributions for the entire year to the HSAs of its employees who are eligible individuals at the beginning of the calendar year (on a pre-funded basis) instead of contributing on a pay-as-you-go or on a look-back basis?

A-4: (a) *Contributions on a pre-funded basis.* Yes. An employer may make contributions for the entire year to the HSAs of its employees who are eligible individuals at the beginning of the calendar year. An employer that pre-funds the HSAs of its employees will not fail to satisfy the comparability rules because an employee who terminates employment prior to the end of the calendar year has received more contributions on a monthly basis than employees who work the entire calendar year. See Q & A-12 of this section. Under section 223(d)(1)(E), an account beneficiary's interest in an HSA is nonforfeitable. An employer must make comparable contributions for all employees who are comparable participating employees for any month during the calendar year, including employees who are eligible individuals hired after the date of initial funding. An employer that makes HSA contributions on a pre-funded basis may also contribute on a pre-funded basis to the HSAs of employees who are eligible individuals hired after the date of initial funding. Alternatively, an employer that has pre-funded the HSAs of comparable participating employees may contribute to the HSAs of employees who are eligible individuals hired after the date of initial funding on a pay-as-you-go basis or on a look-back basis. An employer that makes HSA contributions on a pre-funded basis must use the same contribution method for all employees who are eligible individuals hired after the date of initial funding.

(b) *Example.* The following example illustrates the rules in paragraph (a) of this Q & A-4:

*Example.* (i) On January 1, Employer N contributes $1,200 for the calendar year on a pre-funded basis to the HSA of each employee who is an eligible individual. In mid-May, Employer N hires Employee B, who becomes an eligible individual as of June 1st. Therefore, Employer N is required to make comparable contributions to B's HSA beginning in June. Employer N satisfies the comparability rules with respect to contributions to B's HSA if it makes HSA contributions in any one of the following ways—

(A) Pre-funding B's HSA by contributing $700 to B's HSA;

(B) Contributing $100 per month on a pay-as-you-go basis to B's HSA; or

(C) Contributing to B's HSA at the end of the calendar year taking into account each month that B was an eligible individual and employed by Employer M.

(ii) If Employer M hires additional employees who are eligible individuals after initial funding, it must use the same contribution method for these employees that it used to contribute to B's HSA.

Q-5: Must an employer use the same contribution method as described in Q & A-2 and Q & A-4 of this section for all employees who were comparable participating employees for any month during the calendar year?

A-5: Yes. If an employer makes comparable HSA contributions on a pay-as-you-go basis, it must do so for each employee who is a comparable participating employee as of the first day of the month. If an employer makes comparable contributions on a look-back basis, it must do so for each employee who was a comparable participating employee for any month during the calendar year. If an employer makes HSA contributions on a pre-funded basis, it must do so for all employees who are comparable participating employees at the beginning of the calendar year and must make comparable HSA contributions for all employees who are comparable participating employees for any month during the calendar year, including employees who

are eligible individuals hired after the date of initial funding. See Q & A-4 of this section for rules regarding contributions for employees hired after initial funding.

Q-6: How does an employer comply with the comparability rules if an employee has not established an HSA at the time the employer contributes to its employees' HSAs?

A-6: (a) *Employee has not established an HSA at the time the employer funds its employees' HSAs.* If an employee has not established an HSA at the time the employer funds its employees' HSAs, the employer complies with the comparability rules by contributing comparable amounts plus reasonable interest to the employee's HSA when the employee establishes the HSA, taking into account each month that the employee was a comparable participating employee. See Q & A-13 of this section for rules regarding reasonable interest.

(b) *Example.* The following example illustrates the rules in paragraph (a) of this Q & A-6:

*Example.* Beginning on January 1st, Employer O contributes $500 per calendar year on a pay-as-you-go basis to the HSA of each employee who is an eligible individual. Employee C is an eligible individual during the entire calendar year but does not establish an HSA until March. Notwithstanding C's delay in establishing an HSA, Employer O must make up the missed HSA contributions plus reasonable interest for January and February by April 15th of the following calendar year.

Q-7: If an employer bases its contributions on a percentage of the HDHP deductible, how is the correct percentage or dollar amount computed?

A-7: (a) *Computing HSA contributions.* The correct percentage is determined by rounding to the nearest 1/100th of a percentage point and the dollar amount is determined by rounding to the nearest whole dollar.

(b) *Example.* The following example illustrates the rules in paragraph (a) of this Q & A-7:

*Example.* In this *Example,* assume that each HDHP provided by Employer P satisfies the definition of an HDHP for the 2007 calendar year. In the 2007 calendar year, Employer P maintains two HDHPs. Plan A has a deductible of $3,000 for self-only coverage. Employer P contributes $1,000 for the calendar year to the HSA of each employee covered under Plan A. Plan B has a deductible of $3,500 for self-only coverage. Employer P satisfies the comparability rules if it makes either of the following contributions for the 2007 calendar year to the HSA of each employee who is an eligible individual with self-only coverage under Plan B—

(i) $1,000; or

(ii) $1,167 (33.33% of the deductible rounded to the nearest whole dollar amount).

Q-8: Does an employer that contributes to the HSA of each comparable participating employee in an amount equal to the employee's HSA contribution or a percentage of the employee's HSA contribution (matching contributions) satisfy the rule that all comparable participating employees receive comparable contributions?

A-8: No. If all comparable participating employees do not contribute the same amount to their HSAs and, consequently, do not receive comparable contributions to their HSAs, the comparability rules are not satisfied, notwithstanding that the employer offers to make available the same contribution amount to each comparable participating employee. But see Q & A-1 in § 54.4980G-5 on contributions to HSAs made through a cafeteria plan.

Q-9: If an employer conditions contributions by the employer to an employee's HSA on an employee's participation in health assessments, disease management programs or wellness programs and makes the same contributions available to all employees who participate in the programs, do the contributions satisfy the comparability rules?

A-9: No. If all comparable participating employees do not elect to participate in all the programs and consequently, all comparable participating employees do not receive comparable contributions to their HSAs, the employer contributions fail to satisfy the comparability rules. But see Q & A-1 in § 54.4980G-5 on contributions made to HSAs through a cafeteria plan.

Q-10: If an employer makes additional contributions to the HSAs of all comparable participating employees who have attained a specified age or who have worked for the employer for a specified number of years, do the contributions satisfy the comparability rules?

A-10: No. If all comparable participating employees do not meet the age or length of service requirement, all comparable participating employees do not receive comparable contributions to their HSAs and the employer contributions fail to satisfy the comparability rules.

Q-11: If an employer makes additional contributions to the HSAs of all comparable participating employees who are eligible to make the additional contributions (HSA catch-up contributions) under section 223(b)(3), do the contributions satisfy the comparability rules?

A-11: No. If all comparable participating employees are not eligible to make the additional HSA contributions under section 223(b)(3), all comparable participating employees do not receive comparable contributions to their HSAs, and the employer contributions fail to satisfy the comparability rules.

Q-12: If an employer's contributions to an employee's HSA result in non-comparable contributions, may the employer recoup the excess amount from the employee's HSA?

A-12: No. An employer may not recoup from an employee's HSA any portion of the employer's contribution to the employee's HSA. Under section 223(d)(1)(E), an account beneficiary's interest in an HSA is nonforfeitable. However, an employer may make additional HSA contributions to satisfy the comparability rules. An employer may contribute up until April 15th following the calendar year in which the non-comparable contributions were made. An employer that makes additional HSA contributions to correct non-comparable contributions must also contribute reasonable interest. However, an employer is not required to contribute amounts in excess of the annual contribution limits in section 223(b). See Q & A-13 of this section for rules regarding reasonable interest.

Q-13: What constitutes a reasonable interest rate for purposes of making comparable contributions?

A-13: The determination of whether a rate of interest used by an employer is reasonable will be based on all of the facts and circumstances. If an employer calculates interest using the Federal short-term rate as determined by the Secretary in accordance with section 1274(d), the employer is deemed to use a reasonable interest rate.

Q-14: Does an employer fail to satisfy the comparability rules for a calendar year if the employer fails to make contributions with respect to eligible employees because the employee has not established an HSA or because the employer does not know that the employee has established an HSA?

A-14: (a) *In general.* An employer will not fail to satisfy the comparability rules for a calendar year (Year 1) merely because the employer fails to make contributions with respect to an eligible employee because the employee has not established an HSA or because the employer does not know that the employee has established an HSA, if —

(1) The employer provides timely written notice to all such eligible employees that it will make comparable contributions for Year 1 for eligible employees who, by the last day of February of the following calendar year (Year 2), both establish an HSA and notify the employer (in accordance with a procedure specified in the notice) that they have established an HSA; and

(2) For each such eligible employee who establishes an HSA and so notifies the employer on or before the last day of February of Year 2, the employer contributes to the HSA for Year 1 comparable amounts (taking into account each month that the employee was a comparable participating employee) plus reasonable interest by April 15th of Year 2.

(b) *Notice.* The notice described in paragraph (a) of this Q & A-14 must be provided to each eligible employee who has not established an HSA by December 31 of Year 1 or if the employer does not know if the employee established an HSA. The employer may provide the notice to other employees as well. However, if an employee has earlier notified the employer that he or she has established an HSA, or if the employer has previously made contributions to that employee's HSA, the employer may not condition making comparable contributions on receipt of any additional notice from that employee. For each calendar year, a notice is deemed to be timely if the employer provides the notice no earlier than 90 days before the first HSA employer contribution for that calendar year and no later than January 15 of the following calendar year.

(c) *Model notice.* Employers may use the following sample language as a basis in preparing their own notices.

**Notice to Employees Regarding Employer Contributions to HSAs:**

This notice explains how you may be eligible to receive contributions from [employer] if you are covered by a High Deductible Health Plan (HDHP). [Employer] provides contributions to the Health Savings Account (HSA) of each employee who is [insert employer's eligibility requirements for HSA contributions] ("eligible employee"). If you are an eligible employee, you must do the following in order to receive an employer contribution:

(1) establish an HSA on or before the last day in February of [insert year after the year for which the contribution is being made] and;

(2) notify [insert name and contact information for appropriate person to be contacted] of your HSA account information on or before the last day in February of [insert year after year for which the contribution is being made]. [Specify the HSA account information that the employee must provide (e.g., account number, name and address of trustee or custodian, etc.) and the method by which the employee must provide this account information (e.g., in writing, by e-mail, on a certain form, etc.)].

If you establish your HSA on or before the last day of February in [insert year after year for which the contribution is being made] and notify [employer] of your HSA account information, you will receive your HSA contributions, plus reasonable interest, for [insert year for which contribution is being made] by April 15 of [insert year after year for which contribution is being made]. If, however, you do not establish your HSA or you do not notify us of your HSA account information by the deadline, then we are not required to make any contributions to your HSA for [insert applicable year]. You may notify us that you have established an HSA by sending an [e-mail or] a written notice to [insert name, title and, if applicable, e-mail address]. If you have any questions about this notice, you can contact [insert name and title] at [insert telephone number or other contact information].

(e) *Electronic delivery.* An employer may furnish the notice required under this section electronically in accordance with § 1.401(a)-21 of this chapter.

(f) *Examples.* The following examples illustrate the rules in this Q & A-14:

*Example 1.* In a calendar year, Employer Q contributes to the HSAs of current employees who are eligible individuals covered under any HDHP. For the 2009 calendar year, Employer Q contributes $50 per month on the first day of each month, beginning January 1st, to the HSA of each employee who is an eligible employee on that date. For the 2009 calendar year, Employer Q provides written notice satisfying the content requirements of this Q & A-14 on October 16, 2008 to all employees regarding the availability of HSA contributions for eligible employees. For eligible employees who are hired after October 16, 2008, Employer Q provides such a notice no later than January 15, 2010. Employer Q's notice satisfies the notice timing requirements in paragraph (a)(1) of this Q & A-14.

*Example 2.* Employer R's written cafeteria plan permits employees to elect to make pre-tax salary reduction contributions to their HSAs. Employees making this election have the right to receive cash or other taxable benefits in lieu of their HSA pretax contribution. Employer R automatically contributes a non-elective matching contribution to the HSA of each employee who makes a pre-tax HSA contribution. Because Employer R's HSA contributions are made through the cafeteria plan, the comparability requirements do not apply to the HSA contributions made by Employer R. Consequently, Employer R is not required to provide written notice to its employees regarding the availability of this matching HSA contribution. See Q & A-1 in 54.4980G- 5 for treatment of HSA contributions made through a cafeteria plan.

*Example 3.* In a calendar year, Employer S maintains an HDHP and only contributes to the HSAs of eligible employees who elect coverage under its HDHP. For the 2009 calendar year, Employer S employs ten eligible employees and all ten employees have elected coverage under Employer S's HDHP and have established HSAs. For the 2009 calendar year, Employer S makes comparable contributions to the HSAs of all ten employees. Employer S satisfies the comparability rules. Thus, Employer S is not required to provide written notice to its employees regarding the availability of HSA contributions for eligible employees.

*Example 4.* In a calendar year, Employer T contributes to the HSAs of current full-time employees with family coverage under any HDHP. For the 2009 calendar year, Employer T provides timely written notice satisfying the content requirements of this section to all employees regardless of HDHP coverage. Employer T makes identical monthly contributions to all eligible employees (meaning full time employees with family HDHP coverage) that establish HSAs. Employer T contributes comparable amounts (taking into account each month that the employee was a comparable participating employee) plus reasonable interest to the HSAs of the eligible employees that establish HSAs and provide the necessary information after the end of the year but on or before the last day of February, 2010. Employer T makes no contribution to the HSAs of employees that do not establish an HSA or that do not provide the necessary information on or before the last day of February, 2010. Employer T satisfies the comparability requirements.

*Example 5.* For the 2009 calendar year, Employer V contributes to the HSAs of current full time employees with family coverage under any HDHP. Employer V has 500 current full time employees. As of the date for Employer V's first HSA contribution for the 2009 calendar year, 450 eligible employees have established HSAs. Employer V provides timely written notice satisfying the content requirements of this section only to those 50 eligible employees who have not established HSAs. Employer V makes identical quarterly contributions to the 450 eligible employees who established HSAs. By April 15, 2010, Employer V contributes comparable amounts to the other eligible employees who establish HSAs and provide the necessary information on or before the last day of February, 2010. Employer V makes no contribution to the HSAs of eligible employees that do not establish an HSA or that do not provide the necessary information on or before the last day of February, 2010. Employer V satisfies the comparability rules.

Q-15: For any calendar year, may an employer accelerate part or all of its contributions for the entire year to the HSAs of employees who have incurred, during the calendar year, qualified medical expenses (as defined in section 223(d)(2)) exceeding the employer's cumulative HSA contributions at that time?

A-15: (a) *In general.* Yes. For any calendar year, an employer may accelerate part or all of its contributions for the entire year to the HSAs of employees who have incurred, during the calendar year, qualified medical expenses exceeding the employer's cumulative HSA contributions at that time. If an employer accelerates contributions to the HSA of any such eligible employee, all accelerated contributions must be available throughout the calendar year on an equal and uniform basis to all such eligible employees. Employers must establish reasonable uniform methods and requirements for accelerated contributions and the determination of medical expenses.

(b) *Satisfying comparability.* An employer that accelerates contributions to the HSAs of its employees will not fail to satisfy the comparability rules because employees who incur qualifying medical expenses exceeding the employer's cumulative HSA contributions at that time have received more contributions in a given period than comparable employees who do not incur such expenses, provided that all comparable employees receive the same amount or the same percentage for the calendar year. Also, an employer that accelerates contributions to the HSAs of its employees will not fail to satisfy the comparability rules because an employee who terminates employment prior to the end of the calendar year has received more contributions on a monthly basis than employees who work the entire calendar year. An employer is not required to contribute reasonable interest on either accelerated or non-accelerated HSA contributions. But see Q & A-6 and Q & A-12 of this section for when reasonable interest must be paid.

Q-16: What is the effective date for the rules in Q & A-14 and Q & A-15 of this section?

A-16: These regulations apply to employer contributions made for calendar years beginning on or after January 1, 2009.
[Reg. § 54.4980G-4.]

☐ [*T.D. 9277, 7-28-2006 (corrected 9-12-2006). Amended by T.D. 9393, 4-16-2008 and T.D. 9457, 9-4-2009.*]

## [Reg. § 54.4980G-5]

### § 54.4980G-5. HSA comparability rules and cafeteria plans and waiver of excise tax.

Q-1: If an employer makes contributions through a section 125 cafeteria plan to the HSA of each employee who is an eligible individual, are the contributions subject to the comparability rules?

A-1: (a) *In general.* No. The comparability rules do not apply to HSA contributions that an employer makes through a section 125 cafeteria plan. However, contributions to an HSA made through a cafeteria plan are subject to the section 125 nondiscrimination rules (eligibility rules, contributions and benefits tests and key employee concentration tests). See section 125(b), (c) and (g) and the regulations thereunder.

(b) *Contributions made through a section 125 cafeteria plan.* Employer contributions to employees' HSAs are made through a section 125 cafeteria plan and are subject to the section 125 cafeteria plan nondiscrimination rules and not the comparability rules if under the written cafeteria plan, the employees have the right to elect to receive cash or other taxable benefits in lieu of all or a portion of an HSA contribution (meaning that all or a portion of the HSA contributions are available as pre-tax salary reduction amounts), regardless of whether an employee actually elects to contribute any amount to the HSA by salary reduction.

Q-2: If an employer makes contributions through a cafeteria plan to the HSA of each employee who is an eligible individual in an amount equal to the amount of the employee's HSA contribution or a percentage of the amount of the employee's HSA contribution (matching contributions), are the contributions subject to the section 4980G comparability rules?

A-2: No. The comparability rules do not apply to HSA contributions that an employer makes through a section 125 cafeteria plan. Thus, where matching contributions are made by an employer through a cafeteria plan, the contributions are not subject to the comparability rules of section 4980G. However, contributions, including matching contributions, to an HSA made under a cafeteria plan are subject to the section 125 nondiscrimination rules (eligibility rules, contributions and benefits tests and key employee concentration tests). See Q & A-1 of this section.

Q-3: If under the employer's cafeteria plan, employees who are eligible individuals and who participate in health assessments, disease management programs or wellness programs receive an employer contribution to an HSA and the employees have the right to

elect to make pre-tax salary reduction contributions to their HSAs, are the contributions subject to the comparability rules?

A-3: (a) *In general.* No. The comparability rules do not apply to employer contributions to an HSA made through a cafeteria plan. See Q & A-1 of this section.

(b) *Examples.* The following examples illustrate the rules in this § 54.4980G-5. The examples read as follows:

*Example 1.* Employer A's written cafeteria plan permits employees to elect to make pre-tax salary reduction contributions to their HSAs. Employees making this election have the right to receive cash or other taxable benefits in lieu of their HSA pre-tax contribution. The section 125 cafeteria plan nondiscrimination rules and not the comparability rules apply because the HSA contributions are made through the cafeteria plan.

*Example 2.* Employer B's written cafeteria plan permits employees to elect to make pre-tax salary reduction contributions to their HSAs. Employees making this election have the right to receive cash or other taxable benefits in lieu of their HSA pre-tax contribution. Employer B automatically contributes a non-elective matching contribution or seed money to the HSA of each employee who makes a pre-tax HSA contribution. The section 125 cafeteria plan nondiscrimination rules and not the comparability rules apply to Employer B's HSA contributions because the HSA contributions are made through the cafeteria plan.

*Example 3.* Employer C's written cafeteria plan permits employees to elect to make pre-tax salary reduction contributions to their HSAs. Employees making this election have the right to receive cash or other taxable benefits in lieu of their HSA pre-tax contribution. Employer C makes a non-elective contribution to the HSAs of all employees who complete a health risk assessment and participate in Employer C's wellness program. Employees do not have the right to receive cash or other taxable benefits in lieu of Employer C's non-elective contribution. The section 125 cafeteria plan nondiscrimination rules and not the comparability rules apply to Employer C's HSA contributions because the HSA contributions are made through the cafeteria plan.

*Example 4.* Employer D's written cafeteria plan permits employees to elect to make pre-tax salary reduction contributions to their HSAs. Employees making this election have the right to receive cash or other taxable benefits in lieu of their HSA pre-tax contribution. Employees participating in the plan who are eligible individuals receive automatic employer contributions to their HSAs. Employees make no election with respect to Employer D's contribution and do not have the right to receive cash or other taxable benefits in lieu of Employer D's contribution, but are permitted to make their own pre-tax salary reduction contributions to fund their HSAs. The section 125 cafeteria plan nondiscrimination rules and not the comparability rules apply to Employer D's HSA contributions because the HSA contributions are made through the cafeteria plan.

Q-4: May all or part of the excise tax imposed under section 4980G be waived?

A-4: In the case of a failure which is due to reasonable cause and not to willful neglect, all or a portion of the excise tax imposed under section 4980G may be waived to the extent that the payment of the tax would be excessive relative to the failure involved. See sections 4980G(b) and 4980E(c).
[Reg. § 54.4980G-5.]

☐ [*T.D. 9277, 7-28-2006.*]

## [Reg. § 54.4980G-6]

### § 54.4980G-6. Special rule for contributions made to the HSAs of nonhighly compensated employees.

Q-1: May an employer make larger contributions to the HSAs of nonhighly compensated employees than to the HSAs of highly compensated employees?

A-1: Yes. Employers may make larger HSA contributions for nonhighly compensated employees who are comparable participating employees than for highly compensated employees who are comparable participating employees. See Q & A-1 in § 54.4980G-1 for the definition of comparable participating employee. For purposes of this section, highly compensated employee is defined under section 414(q). Nonhighly compensated employees are employees that are not highly compensated employees. The comparability rules continue to apply with respect to contributions to the HSAs of all nonhighly compensated employees. Employers must make comparable contributions for the calendar year to the HSA of each nonhighly compensated employee who is a comparable participating employee.

Q-2: May an employer make larger contributions to the HSAs of highly compensated employees than to the HSAs of nonhighly compensated employees?

A-2: (a) *In general.* No. Employer contributions to HSAs for highly compensated employees who are comparable participating employees may not be larger than employer HSA contributions for nonhighly compensated employees who are comparable participating employees. The comparability rules continue to apply with respect to contributions to the HSAs of all highly compensated employees. Employers must make comparable contributions for the calendar year to the HSA of each highly compensated comparable participating employee. See Q & A-1 in § 54.4980G-1 for the definition of comparable participating employee.

(b) *Examples.* The following examples illustrate the rules in Q & A-1 and Q & A-2 of this section. No contributions are made through a section 125 cafeteria plan and none of the employees in the following examples are covered by a collective bargaining agreement. All of the employees in the following examples have the same HDHP deductible for the same category of coverage.

*Example 1.* In 2010, Employer A contributes $1,000 for the calendar year to the HSA of each full-time nonhighly compensated employee who is an eligible individual with self-only HDHP coverage. Employer A makes no contribution to the HSA of any full-time highly compensated employee who is an eligible individual with self-only HDHP coverage. Employer A's HSA contributions for calendar year 2010 satisfy the comparability rules.

*Example 2.* In 2010, Employer B contributes $2,000 for the calendar year to the HSA of each full-time nonhighly compensated employee who is an eligible individual with self-only HDHP coverage. Employer B also contributes $1,000 for the calendar year to the HSA of each full-time highly compensated employee who is an eligible individual with self-only HDHP coverage. Employer B's HSA contributions for calendar year 2010 satisfy the comparability rules.

*Example 3.* In 2010, Employer C contributes $1,000 for the calendar year to the HSA of each full-time nonhighly compensated employee who is an eligible individual with self-only HDHP coverage. Employer C contributes $2,000 for the calendar year to the HSA of each full-time highly compensated employee who is an eligible individual with self-only HDHP coverage. Employer C's HSA contributions for calendar year 2010 do not satisfy the comparability rules.

*Example 4.* In 2010, Employer D contributes $1,000 for the calendar year to the HSA of each full-time nonhighly compensated employee who is an eligible individual with self-only HDHP coverage. Employer D also contributes $1,000 to the HSA of each full-time highly compensated employee who is an eligible individual with self-only HDHP coverage. In addition, the employer contributes an additional $500 to the HSA of each nonhighly compensated employee who participates in a wellness program. The nonhighly compensated employees did not receive comparable contributions, and, therefore, Employer D's HSA contributions for calendar year 2010 do not satisfy the comparability rules.

*Example 5.* In 2010, Employer E contributes $1,000 for the calendar year to the HSA of each full-time non-management nonhighly compensated employee who is an eligible individual with family HDHP coverage. Employer E also contributes $500 for the calendar year to the HSA of each full-time management nonhighly compensated employee who is an eligible individual with family HDHP coverage. The nonhighly compensated employees did not receive comparable contributions, and, therefore, Employer E's HSA contributions for calendar year 2010 do not satisfy the comparability rules.

Q-3: May an employer make larger HSA contributions for employees with self plus two HDHP coverage than employees with self plus one HDHP coverage even if the employees with self plus two are all highly compensated employees and the employees with self plus one are all nonhighly compensated employees?

A-3: (a) Yes. Q & A-1 in § 54.4980G-4 provides that an employer's contribution with respect to the self plus two category of HDHP coverage may not be less than the contribution with respect to the self plus one category and the contribution with respect to the self plus three or more category may not be less than the contribution with respect to the self plus two category. Therefore, the comparability rules are not violated if an employer makes a larger HSA contribution for the self plus two category of HDHP coverage than to self plus one coverage, even if the employees with self plus two coverage are all highly compensated employees and the employees with self plus one coverage are all nonhighly compensated employees. Likewise, the comparability rules are not violated if an employer makes a larger HSA contribution for the self plus three category of HDHP coverage than to self plus two coverage, even if the employees with self plus three coverage are all highly compensated employees and the employees with self plus two coverage are all nonhighly compensated employees.

(b) *Example.* The following example illustrates the rules in paragraph (a) of this Q & A-3. In the following example, no contributions are made through a section 125 cafeteria plan and none of the employees are covered by a collective bargaining agreement.

*Example.* In 2010, Employer F contributes $1,000 for the calendar year to the HSA of each full-time employee who is an eligible individual with self plus one HDHP coverage. Employer F contributes $1,500 for the calendar year to the HSA of each employee who is an eligible individual with self plus two HDHP coverage. The deductible for both the self plus one HDHP and the self plus two HDHP is $2,000. Employee A, an eligible individual, is a nonhighly compensated employee with self plus one coverage. Employee B, an eligible individual, is a highly compensated employee with self plus two coverage. For the 2010 calendar year, Employer F contributes $1,000 to Employee A's HSA and $1,500 to Employee B's HSA. Employer F's HSA contributions satisfy the comparability rules.

Q-4: What is the effective date for the rules in this section?

A-4: The rules in this section are effective for employer contributions made for calendar years beginning on or after January 1, 2010. [Reg. § 54.4980G-6.]

☐ [*T.D.* 9457, 9-4-2009.]

**[Reg. § 54.4980G-7]**

**§ 54.4980G-7. Special comparability rules for qualified HSA distributions contributed to HSAs on or after December 20, 2006 and before January 1, 2012.**

Q-1: How do the comparability rules of section 4980G apply to qualified HSA distributions under section 106(e)(2)?

A-1: The comparability rules of section 4980G do not apply to amounts contributed to employee HSAs through qualified HSA distributions. However, in order to satisfy the comparability rules, if an employer offers qualified HSA distributions, as defined in section 106(e)(2), to any employee who is an eligible individual covered under any HDHP, the employer must offer qualified HSA distributions to all employees who are eligible individuals covered under any HDHP. However, if an employer offers qualified HSA distributions only to employees who are eligible individuals covered under the employer's HDHP, the employer is not required to offer qualified HSA distributions to employees who are eligible individuals but are not covered under the employer's HDHP.

Q-2: What is the effective date for the rules in this section?

A-2: The rules in this section are effective for are effective for employer contributions made for calendar years beginning on or after January 1, 2010. [Reg. § 54.4980G-7.]

☐ [*T.D.* 9457, 9-4-2009.]

**[Reg. § 54.4980H-0]**

**§ 54.4980H-0. Table of contents.**—This section lists the table of contents for §§ 54.4980H-1 through 54.4980H-6.

*§ 54.4980H-1 Definitions.*

(37) Qualified health plan.
(38) Seasonal employee.
(39) Seasonal worker.
(40) Section 1411 certification.
(41) Section 4980H(a) applicable payment amount.
(42) Section 4980H(b) applicable payment amount.
(43) Self-only coverage.
(44) Special unpaid leave.
(45) Stability period.
(46) Standard measurement period.
(47) Start date.
(48) United States.
(49) Variable hour employee.
(50) Week.
(b) Effective/applicability date.

*§ 54.4980H-2 Applicable large employer and applicable large employer member.*
(a) In general.
(b) Determining applicable large employer status.
(1) In general.
(2) Seasonal worker exception.
(3) Employers not in existence in preceding calendar year.
(4) Special rules for government entities, churches, and conventions and associations of churches.
(5) Transition rule for an employer's first year as an applicable large employer.
(c) Full-time equivalent employees (FTEs).
(1) In general.
(2) Calculating the number of FTEs.
(d) Examples.
(e) Additional guidance.
(f) Effective/applicability date.

*§ 54.4980H-3 Determining full-time employees.*
(a) In general.
(b) Hours of service.
(1) In general.
(2) Hourly employees calculation.
(3) Non-hourly employees calculation.
(c) Monthly measurement method.
(1) In general.
(2) Employee first otherwise eligible for an offer of coverage.
(3) Use of weekly periods.
(4) Employees rehired after termination of employment or resuming service after other absence.
(5) Examples.
(d) Look-back measurement method.
(1) Ongoing employees.
(2) New non-variable hour, new non-seasonal and new non-part-time employees.
(3) New variable hour employees, new seasonal employees, and new part-time employees.
(4) Transition from new variable hour employee, new seasonal employee, or new part-time employee to ongoing employee.
(5) Examples.
(6) Employees rehired after termination of employment or resuming service after other absence.
(e) Use of the look-back measurement method and the monthly measurement method for different categories of employees.
(f) Changes in employment status resulting in a change in full-time employee determination method.
(1) Change in employment status from a position to which a look-back measurement method applies to a position to which the monthly measurement method applies, or vice versa.
(2) Special rule for certain employees to whom minimum value coverage has been continuously offered.
(g) Nonpayment or late payment of premiums.
(h) Additional guidance.
(i) Effective/applicability date.

*§ 54.4980H-4 Assessable payments under section 4980H(a).*
(a) In general.
(b) Offer of coverage.
(1) In general.
(2) Offer of coverage on behalf of another entity.
(c) Partial calendar month.
(d) Application to applicable large employer member.
(e) Allocated reduction of 30 full-time employees.
(f) Example.
(g) Additional guidance.
(h) Effective/applicability date.

*§ 54.4980H-5 Assessable payments under section 4980H(b).*

(a) In general.
(b) Offer of coverage.
(c) Partial calendar month.
(d) Applicability to applicable large employer member.
(e) Affordability.
(1) In general.
(2) Affordability safe harbors for section 4980H(b) purposes.
(f) Additional guidance.
(g) Effective/applicability date.

*§ 54.4980H-6 Administration and procedure.*
(a) In general.
(b) Effective/applicability date.
[Reg. § 54.4980H-0.]

☐ *[T.D. 9655, 2-10-2014.]*

### [Reg. § 54.4980H-1]

**§ 54.4980H-1. Definitions.**—(a) *Definitions.*—The definitions in this section apply only for purposes of this section and §§ 54.4980H-2 through 54.4980H-6.

(1) *Administrative period.*—The term *administrative period* means an optional period, selected by an applicable large employer member, of no longer than 90 days beginning immediately following the end of a measurement period and ending immediately before the start of the associated stability period. The administrative period also includes the period between a new employee's start date and the beginning of the initial measurement period, if the initial measurement period does not begin on the employee's start date.

(2) *Advance credit payment.*—The term *advance credit payment* means an advance payment of the premium tax credit as provided in Affordable Care Act section 1412 (42 U.S.C. 18082).

(3) *Affordable Care Act.*—The term *Affordable Care Act* means the Patient Protection and Affordable Care Act, Public Law 111-148 (124 Stat. 119 (2010)), and the Health Care and Education Reconciliation Act of 2010, Public Law 111-152 (124 Stat. 1029 (2010)), as amended by the Medicare and Medicaid Extenders Act of 2010, Public Law 111-309 (124 Stat. 3285 (2010)), the Comprehensive 1099 Taxpayer Protection and Repayment of Exchange Subsidy Overpayments Act of 2011, Public Law 112-9 (125 Stat. 36 (2011)), the Department of Defense and Full-Year Continuing Appropriations Act, 2011, Public Law 112-10 (125 Stat. 38 (2011)), and the 3% Withholding Repeal and Job Creation Act, Public Law 112-56 (125 Stat. 711 (2011)).

(4) *Applicable large employer.*—The term *applicable large employer* means, with respect to a calendar year, an employer that employed an average of at least 50 full-time employees (including full-time equivalent employees) on business days during the preceding calendar year. For rules relating to the determination of applicable large employer status, see § 54.4980H-2.

(5) *Applicable large employer member.*—The term *applicable large employer member* means a person that, together with one or more other persons, is treated as a single employer that is an applicable large employer. For this purpose, if a person, together with one or more other persons, is treated as a single employer that is an applicable large employer on any day of a calendar month, that person is an applicable large employer member for that calendar month. If the applicable large employer comprises one person, that one person is the applicable large employer member. An applicable large employer member does not include a person that is not an employer or only an employer of employees with no hours of service for the calendar year. For rules for government entities, and churches, or conventions or associations of churches, see § 54.4980H-2(b)(4).

(6) *Applicable premium tax credit.*—The term *applicable premium tax credit* means any premium tax credit that is allowed or paid under section 36B and any advance payment of such credit.

(7) *Bona fide volunteer.*—The term *bona fide volunteer* means an employee of a government entity or an organization described in section 501(c) that is exempt from taxation under section 501(a) whose only compensation from that entity or organization is in the form of—

(i) Reimbursement for (or reasonable allowance for) reasonable expenses incurred in the performance of services by volunteers, or

(ii) Reasonable benefits (including length of service awards), and nominal fees, customarily paid by similar entities in connection with the performance of services by volunteers.

(8) *Calendar month.*—The term *calendar month* means one of the 12 full months named in the calendar, such as January, February, or March.

(9) *Church or a convention or association of churches.*—The term *church or a convention or association of churches* has the same meaning as provided in § 1.170A-9(b).

(10) *Collective bargaining agreement.*—The term *collective bargaining agreement* means an agreement that the Secretary of Labor determines to be a collective bargaining agreement, provided that the health benefits provided under the collective bargaining agreement are the subject of good faith bargaining between employee representatives and one or more employers, and the agreement between employee representatives and one or more employers satisfies section 7701(a)(46).

(11) *Cost-sharing reduction.*—The term *cost-sharing reduction* means a cost-sharing reduction and any advance payment of the reduction as defined under section 1402 of the Affordable Care Act and 45 CFR 155.20.

(12) *Dependent.*—The term *dependent* means a child (as defined in section 152(f)(1) but excluding a stepson, stepdaughter or an eligible foster child (and excluding any individual who is excluded from the definition of dependent under section 152 by operation of section 152(b)(3))) of an employee who has not attained age 26. A child attains age 26 on the 26th anniversary of the date the child was born. A child is a dependent for purposes of section 4980H for the entire calendar month during which he or she attains age 26. Absent knowledge to the contrary, applicable large employer members may rely on an employee's representation about that employee's children and the ages of those children. The term *dependent* does not include the spouse of an employee.

(13) *Educational organization.*—The term *educational organization* means an entity described in § 1.170A-9(c)(1), whether or not described in section 501(c)(3) and tax-exempt under section 501(a). Thus, the term *educational organization* includes taxable entities, tax-exempt entities and government entities.

(14) *Eligible employer-sponsored plan.*—The term *eligible employer-sponsored plan* has the same meaning as provided under section 5000A(f)(2) and the regulations thereunder and any other applicable guidance.

(15) *Employee.*—The term *employee* means an individual who is an employee under the common-law standard. See § 31.3401(c)-1(b). For purposes of this paragraph (a)(15), a leased employee (as defined in section 414(n)(2)), a sole proprietor, a partner in a partnership, a 2-percent S corporation shareholder, or a worker described in section 3508 is not an employee.

(16) *Employer.*—The term *employer* means the person that is the employer of an employee under the common-law standard. See § 31.3121(d)-1(c). For purposes of determining whether an employer is an applicable large employer, all persons treated as a single employer under section 414(b), (c), (m), or (o) are treated as a single employer. Thus, all employees of a controlled group of entities under section 414(b) or (c), an affiliated service group under section 414(m), or an entity in an arrangement described under section 414(o), are taken into account in determining whether the members of the controlled group or affiliated service group together are an applicable large employer. For purposes of determining applicable large employer status, the term *employer* also includes a predecessor employer (see paragraph (a)(36) of this section) and a successor employer.

(17) *Employment break period.*—The term *employment break period* means a period of at least four consecutive weeks (disregarding special unpaid leave), measured in weeks, during which an employee of an educational organization is not credited with hours of service for an applicable large employer.

(18) *Exchange.*—The term *Exchange* means an Exchange as defined in 45 CFR 155.20.

(19) *Federal poverty line.*—The term *federal poverty line* means for a plan year any of the poverty guidelines (updated periodically in the **Federal Register** by the Secretary of Health and Human Services under the authority of 42 U.S.C. 9902(2)) in effect within six months before the first day of the plan year of the applicable large employer member's health plan, as selected by the applicable large employer member.

(20) *Form W-2 wages.*—The term *Form W-2 wages* with respect to an employee refers to the amount of wages as defined under section 3401(a) for the applicable calendar year (required to be reported in Box 1 of the Form W-2 (Wage and Tax Statement)) received from an applicable large employer.

(21) *Full-time employee.*—(i) *In general.*—The term *full-time employee* means, with respect to a calendar month, an employee who is employed an average of at least 30 hours of service per week with an employer. For rules on the determination of whether an employee is a full-time employee, including a description of the look-back measurement method and the monthly measurement method, see § 54.4980H-3. The look-back measurement method for identifying full-time employees is available only for purposes of determining and computing liability under section 4980H and not for the purpose of determining status as an applicable large employer under § 54.4980H-2.

(ii) *Monthly equivalency.*—Except as otherwise provided in paragraph (a)(21)(iii) of this section, 130 hours of service in a calendar month is treated as the monthly equivalent of at least 30 hours of service per week, and this 130 hours of service monthly equivalency applies for both the look-back measurement method and the monthly measurement method for determining full-time employee status.

(iii) *Determination of full-time employee status using weekly rule under the monthly measurement method.*—Under the optional weekly rule set forth in § 54.4980H-3(c)(3), full-time employee status for certain calendar months is based on hours of service over four weekly periods and for certain other calendar months is based on hours of service over five weekly periods. With respect to a month with four weekly periods, an employee with at least 120 hours of service is a full-time employee, and with respect to a month with five weekly periods, an employee with at least 150 hours of service is a full-time employee. For purposes of this rule, the seven continuous calendar days that constitute a week (for example Sunday through Saturday) must be consistently applied for all calendar months of the calendar year.

(22) *Full-time equivalent employee (FTE).*—The term *full-time equivalent employee,* or *FTE,* means a combination of employees, each of whom individually is not treated as a full-time employee because he or she is not employed on average at least 30 hours of service per week with an employer, who, in combination, are counted as the equivalent of a full-time employee solely for purposes of determining whether the employer is an applicable large employer. For rules on the method for determining the number of an employer's full-time equivalent employees, or FTEs, see § 54.4980H-2(c).

(23) *Government entity.*—The term *government entity* means the government of the United States, any State or political subdivision thereof, any Indian tribal government (as defined in section 7701(a)(40)) or subdivision of an Indian tribal government (determined in accordance with section 7871(d)), or any agency or instrumentality of any of the foregoing.

(24) *Hour of service.*—(i) *In general.*—The term *hour of service* means each hour for which an employee is paid, or entitled to payment, for the performance of duties for the employer; and each hour for which an employee is paid, or entitled to payment by the employer for a period of time during which no duties are performed due to vacation, holiday, illness, incapacity (including disability), layoff, jury duty, military duty or leave of absence (as defined in 29 CFR 2530.200b-2(a)). For the rules for determining an employee's hours of service, see § 54.4980H-3.

(ii) *Excluded hours.*—(A) *Bona fide volunteers.*—The term *hour of service* does not include any hour for services performed as a bona fide volunteer.

(B) *Work-study program.*—The term *hour of service* does not include any hour for services to the extent those services are performed as part of a Federal Work-Study Program as defined under 34 CFR 675 or a substantially similar program of a State or political subdivision thereof.

(C) *Services outside the United States.*—The term *hour of service* does not include any hour for services to the extent the compensation for those services constitutes income from sources without the United States (within the meaning of sections 861 through 863 and the regulations thereunder).

(iii) *Service for other applicable large employer members.*—In determining hours of service and status as a full-time employee for all purposes under section 4980H, an hour of service for one applicable large employer member is treated as an hour of service for all other applicable large employer members for all periods during which the applicable large employer members are part of the same group of employers forming an applicable large employer.

(25) *Initial measurement period.*—The term *initial measurement period* means a period selected by an applicable large employer member of at least three consecutive months but not more than 12 consecutive months used by the applicable large employer as part of the look-back measurement method in § 54.4980H-3(d).

(26) *Limited non-assessment period for certain employees.*—References to the *limited non-assessment period for certain employees* refers to

the limited period during which an employer will not be subject to an assessable payment under section 4980H(a), and in certain cases section 4980H(b), with respect to an employee as set forth in—

(i) Section 54.4980H-2(b)(5) (regarding the transition rule for an employer's first year as an applicable large employer),

(ii) Section 54.4980H-3(c)(2) (regarding the application of section 4980H for the three full calendar month period beginning with the first full calendar month in which an employee is first otherwise eligible for an offer of coverage under the monthly measurement method),

(iii) Section 54.4980H-3(d)(2)(iii) (regarding the application of section 4980H during the initial three full calendar months of employment for an employee reasonably expected to be a full-time employee at the start date, under the look-back measurement method),

(iv) Section 54.4980H-3(d)(3)(iii) (regarding the application of section 4980H during the initial measurement period to a new variable hour employee, seasonal employee or part-time employee determined to be employed on average at least 30 hours of service per week, under the look-back measurement method),

(v) Section 54.4980H-3(d)(3)(vii) (regarding the application of section 4980H following an employee's change in employment status to a full-time employee during the initial measurement period, under the look-back measurement method), and

(vi) Section 54.4980H-4(c) and §54.4980H-5(c) (regarding the application of section 4980H to the calendar month in which an employee's start date occurs on a day other than the first day of the calendar month).

(27) *Minimum essential coverage.*—The term *minimum essential coverage*, or *MEC*, has the same meaning as provided in section 5000A(f) and any regulations or other guidance thereunder.

(28) *Minimum value.*—The term *minimum value* has the same meaning as provided in section 36B(c)(2)(C)(ii) and any regulations or other guidance thereunder.

(29) *Month.*—The term *month* means—

(i) A *calendar month* as defined in paragraph (a)(8) of this section, or

(ii) The period that begins on any date following the first day of a calendar month and that ends on the immediately preceding date in the immediately following calendar month (for example, from February 2 to March 1 or from December 15 to January 14).

(30) *New employee.*—Under the look-back measurement method, the term *new employee* means an employee who has been employed by an applicable large employer for less than one complete standard measurement period; for treatment of the employee as a new employee or continuing employee under the look-back measurement method following a period for which no hours of service are earned, see the rehire and continuing employee rules at §54.4980H-3(d)(6). Under the monthly measurement method, the term *new employee* means an employee who either has not previously been employed by the applicable large employer or has previously been employed by the applicable large employer but is treated as a new employee under the rehire and continuing employee rules at §54.4980H-3(c)(4).

(31) *Ongoing employee.*—The term *ongoing employee* means an employee who has been employed by an applicable large employer member for at least one complete standard measurement period. For the treatment of an ongoing employee as a new employee or continuing employee following a period for which no hours of service are earned, see the rehire and continuing employee rules at §54.4980H-3(d)(6).

(32) *Part-time employee.*—The term *part-time employee* means a new employee who the applicable large employer member reasonably expects to be employed on average less than 30 hours of service per week during the initial measurement period, based on the facts and circumstances at the employee's start date. Whether an employer's determination that a new employee is a part-time employee is reasonable is based on the facts and circumstances at the employee's start date. Factors to consider in determining a new employee's full-time employee status are set forth in §54.4980H-3(d)(2)(ii).

(33) *Period of employment.*—The term *period of employment* means the period of time beginning on the first date for which an employee is credited with an hour of service for an applicable large employer (including any member of that applicable large employer) and ending on the last date on which the employee is credited with an hour of service for that applicable large employer, both dates inclusive. An employee may have one or more periods of employment with the same applicable large employer.

(34) *Person.*—The term *person* has the same meaning as provided in section 7701(a)(1) and the regulations thereunder.

(35) *Plan year.*—A *plan year* must be twelve consecutive months, unless a short plan year of less than twelve consecutive months is permitted for a valid business purpose. A *plan year* is permitted to begin on any day of a year and must end on the preceding day in the immediately following year (for example, a plan year that begins on October 15, 2015, must end on October 14, 2016). A calendar year *plan year* is a period of twelve consecutive months beginning on January 1 and ending on December 31 of the same calendar year. Once established, a plan year is effective for the first plan year and for all subsequent plan years, unless changed, provided that such change will only be recognized if made for a valid business purpose. A change in the plan year is not permitted if a principal purpose of the change in plan year is to circumvent the rules of section 4980H or these regulations.

(36) *Predecessor employer.*—[Reserved]

(37) *Qualified health plan.*—The term *qualified health plan* means a qualified health plan as defined in Affordable Care Act section 1301(a) (42 U.S.C. 18021(a)), but does not include a catastrophic plan described in Affordable Care Act section 1302(e) (42 U.S.C. 18022(e)).

(38) *Seasonal employee.*—The term *seasonal employee* means an employee who is hired into a position for which the customary annual employment is six months or less.

(39) *Seasonal worker.*—The term *seasonal worker* means a worker who performs labor or services on a seasonal basis as defined by the Secretary of Labor, including (but not limited to) workers covered by 29 CFR 500.20(s)(1), and retail workers employed exclusively during holiday seasons. Employers may apply a reasonable, good faith interpretation of the term *seasonal worker* and a reasonable good faith interpretation of 29 CFR 500.20(s)(1) (including as applied by analogy to workers and employment positions not otherwise covered under 29 CFR 500.20(s)(1)).

(40) *Section 1411 Certification.*—The term *Section 1411 Certification* means the certification received as part of the process established by the Secretary of Health and Human Services under which an employee is certified to the employer under section 1411 of the Affordable Care Act as having enrolled for a calendar month in a qualified health plan with respect to which an applicable premium tax credit or cost-sharing reduction is allowed or paid with respect to the employee.

(41) *Section 4980H(a) applicable payment amount.*—The term *section 4980H(a) applicable payment amount* means, with respect to any calendar month, 1/12 of $2,000, adjusted for inflation in accordance with section 4980H(c)(5) and any applicable guidance thereunder.

(42) *Section 4980H(b) applicable payment amount.*—The term *section 4980H(b) applicable payment amount* means, with respect to any calendar month, 1/12 of $3,000, adjusted for inflation in accordance with section 4980H(c)(5) and any applicable guidance thereunder.

(43) *Self-only coverage.*—The term *self-only coverage* means health insurance coverage provided to only one individual, generally the employee.

(44) *Special unpaid leave.*—The term *special unpaid leave* means—

(i) Unpaid leave that is subject to the Family and Medical Leave Act of 1993 (FMLA), Public Law 103-3, 29 U.S.C. 2601 et seq.;

(ii) Unpaid leave that is subject to the Uniformed Services Employment and Reemployment Rights Act of 1994 (USERRA), Public Law 103-353, 38 U.S.C. 4301 et seq.; or

(iii) Unpaid leave on account of jury duty.

(45) *Stability period.*—The term *stability period* means a period selected by an applicable large employer member that immediately follows, and is associated with, a standard measurement period or an initial measurement period (and, if elected by the employer, the administrative period associated with that standard measurement period or initial measurement period), and is used by the applicable large employer member as part of the look-back measurement method in §54.4980H-3(d).

(46) *Standard measurement period.*—The term *standard measurement period* means a period of at least three but not more than 12 consecutive months that is used by an applicable large employer member as part of the look-back measurement method in §54.4980H-3(d). See §54.4980H-3(d)(1)(ii) for rules on the use of payroll periods that include the beginning and end dates of the measurement period.

(47) *Start date.*—The term *start date* means the first date on which an employee is required to be credited with an hour of service with

an employer. For rules relating to when, following a period for which an employee does not earn an hour of service, that employee may be treated as a new employee with a new start date rather than a continuing employee, see the rehire and continuing employee rules at §54.4980H–3(c)(4) and §54.4980H–3(d)(6).

(48) *United States.*—The term *United States* means United States as defined in section 7701(a)(9).

(49) *Variable hour employee-.*—(i) *In general.*—The term *variable hour employee* means an employee if, based on the facts and circumstances at the employee's start date, the applicable large employer member cannot determine whether the employee is reasonably expected to be employed on average at least 30 hours of service per week during the initial measurement period because the employee's hours are variable or otherwise uncertain.

(ii) *Factors.*—(A) *In general.*—Factors to consider in determining whether it can be determined that the employee is reasonably expected to be (or reasonably expected not to be) employed on average at least 30 hours of service per week during the initial measurement period include, but are not limited to, whether the employee is replacing an employee who was a full-time employee or a variable hour employee, the extent to which the hours of service of employees in the same or comparable positions have actually varied above and below an average of 30 hours of service per week during recent measurement periods, and whether the job was advertised, or otherwise communicated to the new employee or otherwise documented (for example, through a contract or job description) as requiring hours of service that would average at least 30 hours of service per week, less than 30 hours of service per week, or may vary above and below an average of 30 hours of service per week. These factors are only relevant for a particular new employee if the employer has no reason to anticipate that the facts and circumstances related to that new employee will be different. In all cases, no single factor is determinative. For purposes of determining whether an employee is a variable hour employee, the applicable large employer member may not take into account the likelihood that the employee may terminate employment with the applicable large employer (including any member of the applicable large employer) before the end of the initial measurement period.

(B) *Additional factors for an employee hired by an employer for temporary placement at an unrelated entity.*—In the case of an individual who, under all the facts and circumstances, is the employee of an entity (referred to solely for purposes of this paragraph (a)(49) as a "temporary staffing firm") that hired such individual for temporary placement at an unrelated entity that is not the common law employer, additional factors to consider to determine whether the employee is reasonably expected to be (or reasonably expected not to be) employed by the temporary staffing firm on average at least 30 hours of service per week during the initial measurement period include, but are not limited to, whether other employees in the same position of employment with the temporary staffing firm, as part of their continuing employment, retain the right to reject temporary placements that the temporary staffing firm offers the employee; typically have periods during which no offer of temporary placement is made; typically are offered temporary placements for differing periods of time; and typically are offered temporary placements that do not extend beyond 13 weeks.

(C) *Educational organizations.*—An employer that is an educational organization cannot take into account the potential for, or likelihood of, an employment break period in determining its expectation of future hours of service.

(iii) *Application only for look-back measurement method.*—The term *variable hour employee* is used as a category of employees under the look-back measurement method and is not relevant to the monthly measurement method.

(50) *Week.*—The term *week* means any period of seven consecutive calendar days applied consistently by the applicable large employer member.

(b) *Effective/applicability date.*—This section is applicable for periods after December 31, 2014. [Reg. §54.4980H–1.]

☐ [*T.D.* 9655, 2-10-2014.]

**[Reg. §54.4980H-2]**

**§54.4980H-2. Applicable large employer and applicable large employer member.**—(a) *In general.*—Section 4980H applies to an applicable large employer and to all of the applicable large employer members that comprise that applicable large employer.

(b) *Determining applicable large employer status.*—(1) *In general.*—An employer's status as an applicable large employer for a calendar year

is determined by taking the sum of the total number of full-time employees (including any seasonal workers) for each calendar month in the preceding calendar year and the total number of FTEs (including any seasonal workers) for each calendar month in the preceding calendar year, and dividing by 12. The result, if not a whole number, is then rounded to the next lowest whole number. If the result of this calculation is less than 50, the employer is not an applicable large employer for the current calendar year. If the result of this calculation is 50 or more, the employer is an applicable large employer for the current calendar year, unless the seasonal worker exception in paragraph (b)(2) of this section applies.

(2) *Seasonal worker exception.*—If the sum of an employer's full-time employees and FTEs exceeds 50 for 120 days or less during the preceding calendar year, and the employees in excess of 50 who were employed during that period of no more than 120 days are seasonal workers, the employer is not considered to employ more than 50 full-time employees (including FTEs) and the employer is not an applicable large employer for the current calendar year. In the case of an employer that was not in existence on any business day during the preceding calendar year, if the employer reasonably expects that the sum of its full-time employees and FTEs for the current calendar year will exceed 50 for 120 days or less during the calendar year, and that the employees in excess of 50 who will be employed during that period of no more than 120 days will be seasonal workers, the employer is not an applicable large employer for the current calendar year. For purposes of this paragraph (b)(2) only, four calendar months may be treated as the equivalent of 120 days. The four calendar months and the 120 days are not required to be consecutive.

(3) *Employers not in existence in preceding calendar year.*—An employer not in existence throughout the preceding calendar year is an applicable large employer for the current calendar year if the employer is reasonably expected to employ an average of at least 50 full-time employees (taking into account FTEs) on business days during the current calendar year and it actually employs an average of at least 50 full-time employees (taking into account FTEs) on business days during the calendar year. An employer is treated as not having been in existence throughout the prior calendar year only if the employer was not in existence on any business day in the prior calendar year. See paragraph (b)(2) of this section for the application of the seasonal worker exception to employers not in existence in the preceding calendar year.

(4) *Special rules for government entities, churches, and conventions and associations of churches.*—[Reserved]

(5) *Transition rule for an employer's first year as an applicable large employer.*—With respect to an employee who was not offered coverage by the employer at any point during the prior calendar year, if the applicable large employer offers coverage to the employee on or before April 1 of the first calendar year for which the employer is an applicable large employer, the employer will not be subject to an assessable payment under section 4980H by reason of its failure to offer coverage to the employee for January through March of that year, provided that this relief applies only with respect to potential liability under section 4980H(b) (for January through March of the first calendar year for which the employer is an applicable large employer) if the coverage offered by April 1 provides minimum value. If the employer does not offer coverage to the employee by April 1, the employer may be subject to a section 4980H(a) assessable payment with respect January through March of the first calendar year for which the employer is an applicable large employer in addition to any later calendar months for which coverage was not offered. If the employer offers coverage to the employee by April 1 that does not provided minimum value, the employer may be subject to a section 4980H(b) assessable payment with respect to the employee for January through March of the first calendar year for which the employer is an applicable large employer in addition to any later calendar months for which coverage does not provide minimum value or is not affordable. This rule applies only during the first year that an employer is an applicable large employer (and would not apply if, for example, the employer falls below the 50 full-time employee (plus FTE) threshold for a subsequent calendar year and then increases employment and becomes an applicable large employer again).

(c) *Full-time equivalent employees (FTEs).*—(1) *In general.*—In determining whether an employer is an applicable large employer, the number of FTEs it employed during the preceding calendar year is taken into account. All employees (including seasonal workers) who were not employed on average at least 30 hours of service per week for a calendar month in the preceding calendar year are included in calculating the employer's FTEs for that calendar month.

(2) *Calculating the number of FTEs.*—The number of FTEs for each calendar month in the preceding calendar year is determined by

calculating the aggregate number of hours of service for that calendar month for employees who were not full-time employees (but not more than 120 hours of service for any employee) and dividing that number by 120. In determining the number of FTEs for each calendar month, fractions are taken into account; an employer may round the number of FTEs for each calendar month to the nearest one hundredth.

(d) *Examples.*—The following examples illustrate the rules of paragraphs (a) through (c) of this section. In these examples, hours of service are computed following the rules set forth in §54.4980H-3, and references to years refer to calendar years unless otherwise specified. The employers in *Example 2* through *Example 6* are each the sole applicable large employer member of the applicable large employer, as determined under section 414(b), (c), (m), and (o).

*Example 1 (Applicable large employer/controlled group).* (i) *Facts.* For all of 2015 and 2016, Corporation Z owns 100 percent of all classes of stock of Corporation Y and Corporation X. Corporation Z has no employees at any time in 2015. For every calendar month in 2015, Corporation Y has 40 full-time employees and Corporation X has 60 full-time employees. Corporations Z, Y, and X are a controlled group of corporations under section 414(b).

(ii) *Conclusion.* Because Corporations Z, Y and X have a combined total of 100 full-time employees during 2015, Corporations Z, Y, and X together are an applicable large employer for 2016. Each of Corporations Z, Y and X is an applicable large employer member for 2016.

*Example 2 (Applicable large employer with FTEs).* (i) *Facts.* During each calendar month of 2015, Employer W has 20 full-time employees each of whom averages 35 hours of service per week, 40 employees each of whom averages 90 hours of service per calendar month, and no seasonal workers.

(ii) *Conclusion.* Each of the 20 employees who average 35 hours of service per week count as one full-time employee for each calendar month. To determine the number of FTEs for each calendar month, the total hours of service of the employees who are not full-time employees (but not more than 120 hours of service per employee) are aggregated and divided by 120. The result is that the employer has 30 FTEs for each calendar month ($40 \times 90 = 3,600$, and $3,600 \div 120 = 30$). Because Employer W has 50 full-time employees (the sum of 20 full-time employees and 30 FTEs) during each calendar month in 2015, and because the seasonal worker exception is not applicable, Employer W is an applicable large employer for 2016.

*Example 3 (Seasonal worker exception).* (i) *Facts.* During 2015, Employer V has 40 full-time employees for the entire calendar year, none of whom are seasonal workers. In addition, Employer V also has 80 seasonal workers who are full-time employees and who work for Employer V from September through December 2015. Employer V has no FTEs during 2015.

(ii) *Conclusion.* Before applying the seasonal worker exception, Employer V has 40 full-time employees during each of eight calendar months of 2015, and 120 full-time employees during each of four calendar months of 2015, resulting in an average of 66.67 full-time employees for the year. However, Employer V's workforce exceeded 50 full-time employees (counting seasonal workers) for no more than four calendar months (treated as the equivalent of 120 days) in calendar year 2015, and the number of full-time employees would be less than 50 during those months if seasonal workers were disregarded. Accordingly, because after application of the seasonal worker exception described in paragraph (b)(2) of this section Employer V is not considered to employ more than 50 full-time employees, Employer V is not an applicable large employer for 2016.

*Example 4 (Seasonal workers and other FTEs).* (i) *Facts.* Same facts as *Example 3*, except that Employer V has 20 FTEs in August, some of whom are seasonal workers.

(ii) *Conclusion.* The seasonal worker exception described in paragraph (b)(2) of this section does not apply if the number of an employer's full-time employees (including seasonal workers) and FTEs exceeds 50 for more than 120 days during the calendar year. Because Employer V has at least 50 full-time employees for a period greater than four calendar months (treated as the equivalent of 120 days) during 2015, the exception described in paragraph (b)(2) of this section does not apply. Employer V averaged 68 full-time employees in 2015: $[(40 \times 7) + (60 \times 1) + (120 \times 4)] \div 12 = 68.33$, and accordingly, Employer V is an applicable large employer for calendar year 2016.

*Example 5 (New employer).* (i) *Facts.* Corporation S is incorporated on January 1, 2016. On January 1, 2016, Corporation S has three employees. However, prior to incorporation, Corporation S's owners purchased a factory intended to open within two calendar months of incorporation and to employ approximately 100 full-time employees. By March 15, 2016, Corporation S has more than 75 full-time employees.

(ii) *Conclusion.* Because Corporation S can reasonably be expected to employ on average at least 50 full-time employees on business days during 2016, and actually employs an average of at least 50 full-time employees on business days during 2016, Corporation S is an applicable large employer (and an applicable large employer member) for calendar year 2016.

*Example 6 (First year as applicable large employer).* (i) *Facts.* As of January 1, 2015, Employer R has been in existence for several years and did not average 50 or more full-time employees (including FTEs) on business days during 2014. Employer R averages 50 or more full-time employees on business days during 2015, so that for 2016 Employer R is an applicable large employer, for the first time. For all the calendar months of 2016, Employer R has the same 60 full-time employees. Employer R offered 20 of those full-time employees healthcare coverage during 2015, and offered those same employees coverage providing minimum value for 2016. With respect to the 40 full-time employees who were not offered coverage during 2015, Employer R offers coverage providing minimum value for calendar months April 2016 through December 2016.

(ii) *Conclusion.* For the 40 full-time employees not offered coverage during 2015 and offered coverage providing minimum value for the calendar months April 2016 through December 2016, the failure to offer coverage during the calendar months January 2016 through March 2016 will not result in an assessable payment under section 4980H with respect to those employees for those three calendar months. For those same 40 full-time employees, the offer of coverage during the calendar months April 2016 through December 2016 may result in an assessable payment under section 4980H(b) with respect to any employee for any calendar month for which the offer is not affordable and for which Employer R has received a Section 1411 Certification. For the other 20 full-time employees, the offer of coverage during 2016 may result in an assessable payment under section 4980H(b) for any calendar month if the offer is not affordable and Employer R has received a Section 1411 Certification with respect to the employee who received the offer of coverage. For all calendar months of 2016, Employer R will not be subject to an assessable payment under section 4980H(a).

(e) *Additional guidance.*—With respect to an employer's status as an applicable large employer, the Commissioner may prescribe additional guidance of general applicability, published in the Internal Revenue Bulletin (see §601.601(d)(2)(ii)(b) of this chapter).

(f) *Effective/applicability date.*—This section is applicable for periods after December 31, 2014. [Reg. §54.4980H-2.]

☐ [*T.D. 9655*, 2-10-2014.]

**[Reg. §54.4980H-3]**

**§54.4980H-3. Determining full-time employees.**—(a) *In general.*—This section sets forth the rules for determining hours of service and status as a full-time employee for purposes of section 4980H. These regulations provide two methods for determining full-time employee status—the monthly measurement method, set forth in paragraph (c) of this section, and the look-back measurement method, set forth in paragraph (d) of this section. The monthly measurement method applies for purposes of determining and calculating liability under section 4980H(a) and (b), as well as, with respect to paragraph (c)(1) of this section, determination of applicable large employer status (except with respect to the weekly rule under the monthly measurement method). The look-back measurement method applies solely for purposes of determining and calculating liability under section 4980H(a) and (b) (and not for purposes of determining status as an applicable large employer). See §54.4980H-1(a)(21) for the definition of full-time employee. The rules set forth in this section prescribe the minimum standards for determining status as a full-time employee for purposes of section 4980H; treatment of additional employees as full-time employees for other purposes does not affect section 4980H liability if those employees are not full-time employees under the look-back measurement method or the monthly measurement method.

(b) *Hours of service.*—(1) *In general.*—The following rules on the calculation of hours of service apply for purposes of applying both the look-back measurement method and the monthly measurement method.

(2) *Hourly employees calculation.*—Under the look-back measurement method and the monthly measurement method, for employees paid on an hourly basis, an employer must calculate actual hours of service from records of hours worked and hours for which payment is made or due.

(3) *Non-hourly employees calculation.*—(i) *In general.*—Except as otherwise provided, under the look-back measurement method and the monthly measurement method, for employees paid on a non-hourly basis, an employer must calculate hours of service by using one of the following methods:

(A) Using actual hours of service from records of hours worked and hours for which payment is made or due;

(B) Using a days-worked equivalency whereby the employee is credited with eight hours of service for each day for which the employee would be required to be credited with at least one hour of service in accordance with paragraph (b)(2) of this section; or

(C) Using a weeks-worked equivalency whereby the employee is credited with 40 hours of service for each week for which the employee would be required to be credited with at least one hour of service in accordance with paragraph (b)(2) of this section.

(ii) *Change in method.*—An employer must use one of the three methods in paragraph (b)(3)(i) of this section for calculating the hours of service for non-hourly employees. An employer is not required to use the same method for all non-hourly employees, and may apply different methods for different categories of non-hourly employees, provided the categories are reasonable and consistently applied. Similarly, an applicable large employer member is not required to apply the same methods as other applicable large employer members of the same applicable large employer for the same or different categories of non-hourly employees, provided that in each case the categories are reasonable and consistently applied by the applicable large employer member. An employer may change the method of calculating the hours of service of non-hourly employees (or of one or more categories of non-hourly employees) for each calendar year.

(iii) *Prohibited use of equivalencies.*—The number of hours of service calculated using the days-worked or weeks-worked equivalency must reflect generally the hours actually worked and the hours for which payment is made or due. An employer is not permitted to use the days-worked equivalency or the weeks-worked equivalency if the result is to substantially understate an employee's hours of service in a manner that would cause that employee not to be treated as a full-time employee, or if the result is to understate the hours of service of a substantial number of employees (even if no particular employee's hours of service are understated substantially and even if the understatement would not cause the employee to not be treated as a full-time employee). For example, as to the former, an employer may not use a days-worked equivalency in the case of an employee who generally works three 10-hour days per week, because the equivalency would substantially understate the employee's hours of service as 24 hours of service per week, which would result in the employee being treated as not a full-time employee.

(c) *Monthly measurement method.*—(1) *In general.*—Under the monthly measurement method, an applicable large employer member determines each employee's status as a full-time employee by counting the employee's hours of service for each calendar month. See §54.4980H-1(a)(21) for the definition of full-time employee. This paragraph (c)(1) (except with respect to the weekly rule) applies for purposes of the determination of status as an applicable large employer; paragraphs (c)(2) through (4) of this section do not apply for purposes of the determination of status as an applicable large employer. For rules regarding the use of the look-back measurement method and the monthly measurement method for different categories of employees, see paragraph (e) of this section.

(2) *Employee first otherwise eligible for an offer of coverage.*—The rule in this paragraph (c)(2) applies with respect to an employee who, in a calendar month, first becomes otherwise eligible to be offered coverage under a group health plan of an employer using the monthly measurement method with respect to that employee. For purposes of this paragraph (c)(2), an employee is otherwise eligible to be offered coverage under a group health plan for a calendar month if, pursuant to the terms of the plan as in effect for that calendar month, the employee meets all conditions to be offered coverage under the plan for that calendar month, other than the completion of a waiting period, within the meaning of §54.9801-2, and an employee is first otherwise eligible if the employee has not previously been eligible or otherwise eligible for an offer of coverage under a group health plan of the employer during the employee's period of employment. An employer is not subject to an assessable payment under section 4980H(a) with respect to an employee for each calendar month during the period of three full calendar months beginning with the first full calendar month in which the employee is otherwise eligible for an offer of coverage under a group health plan of the employer, provided that the employee is offered coverage no later than the first day of the first calendar month immediately following the three-month period if the employee is still employed on that day. If the coverage for which the employee is otherwise eligible during the three-month period, and which the employee actually is offered on the day following that three-month period if still employed, provides minimum value, the employer also will not be subject to an assessable payment under section 4980H(b) with respect to that employee for the three-month period. This rule cannot apply more than once per period of employment of an employee. If an employee terminates employment and returns under circum-

stances that would constitute a rehire as set forth in paragraph (c)(4) of this section, the rule in this paragraph (c)(2) may apply again.

(3) *Use of weekly periods.*—With respect to a category of employees for whom an employer uses the monthly measurement method, an employer may determine full-time employee status for a calendar month based on hours of service over a period that:

(i) begins on the first day of the week that includes the first day of the calendar month, provided that the period over which hours of service are measured does not include the week in which falls the last day of the calendar month (unless that week ends with the last day of the calendar month, in which case it is included); or

(ii) begins on the first day of the week immediately subsequent to the week that includes the first day of the calendar month (unless the week begins on the first day of the calendar month, in which case it is included), provided the period over which hours of service are measured includes the week in which falls the last day of the calendar month.

(4) *Employees rehired after termination of employment or resuming service after other absence.*—(i) *Treatment as a new employee after a period of absence for employees of employers other than educational organizations.*—Except as provided in paragraph (c)(4)(ii) of this section (related to rules for employers that are educational organizations), an employee who resumes providing services to (or is otherwise credited with an hour of service for) an applicable large employer after a period during which the individual was not credited with any hours of service may be treated as having terminated employment and having been rehired, and therefore may be treated as a new employee upon the resumption of services only if the employee did not have an hour of service for the applicable large employer for a period of at least 13 consecutive weeks immediately preceding the resumption of services. The rule set forth in this paragraph (c)(4)(i) applies solely for the purpose of determining whether the employee, upon the resumption of services, is treated as a new employee or as a continuing employee, and does not determine whether the employee is treated as a continuing full-time employee (for example, an employee on leave) or a terminated employee for some or all of the period during which no hours of service are credited.

(ii) *Treatment as a new employee after a period of absence for employees of educational organizations.*—With respect to an employer that is an educational organization, an employee who resumes providing services to (or is otherwise credited with an hour of service for) an applicable large employer after a period during which the individual was not credited with any hours of service may be treated as having terminated employment and having been rehired, and therefore may be treated as a new employee upon the resumption of services, only if the employee did not have an hour of service for the applicable large employer for a period of at least 26 consecutive weeks immediately preceding the resumption of services. The rule set forth in this paragraph (c)(4)(ii) applies solely for the purpose of determining whether the employee, upon the resumption of services, is treated as a new employee or as a continuing employee, and does not determine whether the employee is treated as a continuing full-time employee (for example, an employee on leave) or a terminated employee for some or all of the period during which no hours of service are credited.

(iii) *Averaging method for special unpaid leave and employment break periods.*—The averaging method for periods of special unpaid leave and employment break periods does not apply under the monthly measurement method, regardless of whether the employer is (or is not) an educational organization.

(iv) *Treatment of continuing employee.*—The rule set forth in paragraph (c)(2) of this section applies to an employee treated as a continuing employee in the same way that it applies to an employee who has not experienced a period with no hours of service. A continuing employee treated as a full-time employee is treated as offered coverage upon resumption of services if the employee is offered coverage as of the first day that employee is credited with an hour of service, or, if later, as soon as administratively practicable. For this purpose, offering coverage by no later than the first day of the calendar month following resumption of services is deemed to be as soon as administratively practicable.

(v) *Rule of parity.*—For purposes of determining the period after which an employee may be treated as having terminated employment and having been rehired, an applicable large employer may choose a period, measured in weeks, of at least four consecutive weeks during which the employee was not credited with any hours of service that exceeds the number of weeks of that employee's period of employment with the applicable large employer immediately preceding the period that is shorter than 13 weeks (for an employee of an educational organization employer, a period that is shorter than 26 weeks).

(vi) *International transfers.*—An employer may treat an employee as having terminated employment if the employee transfers to a position at the same applicable large employer (including a different applicable large employer member that is part of the same applicable large employer) if the position is anticipated to continue indefinitely or for at least 12 months and if substantially all of the compensation will constitute income from sources without the United States (within the meaning of sections 861 through 863 and the regulations thereunder). With respect to an employee transferring from a position that was anticipated to continue indefinitely or for at least 12 months and in which substantially all of the compensation for the hours of service constitutes income from sources without the United States (within the meaning of sections 861 through 863 and the regulations thereunder) to a position at the same applicable large employer (including a different applicable large employer member that is part of the same applicable large employer) with respect to which substantially all of the compensation will constitute U.S. source income, the employer may treat that employee as a new hire to the extent consistent with the rules related to rehired employees as set forth in paragraph (c)(4) of this section.

(5) *Examples.*—The following examples illustrate the rules of paragraphs (c)(1) through (4) of this section. In each example, the employer is an applicable large employer with 200 full-time employees (including FTEs) that uses the monthly measurement method to identify full-time employees and offers coverage only to employees who are full-time employees (and their dependents).

*Example 1 (Monthly measurement method - employee first otherwise eligible for an offer of coverage).* (i) *Facts.* Employer Z uses the monthly measurement method. Employer Z hires Employee A on January 1, 2016. For each calendar month in 2016, Employee A averages 20 hours of service per week and is not eligible (or otherwise eligible) for an offer of coverage under the group health plan of Employer Z. Effective January 1, 2017, Employee A is promoted to a position that is eligible for an offer of coverage under a group health plan of Employer Z, following completion of a 90-day waiting period. For January 2017 through March 2017, Employee A meets all of the conditions for eligibility under the group health plan, other than completion of the waiting period. The coverage that would have been offered to Employee A under the terms of the plan, but for the waiting period, during those three months would have provided minimum value. Effective April 1, 2017, Employer Z offers Employee A coverage that provides minimum value. Employee A averages 40 hours of service per week for each calendar month in 2017.

(ii) *Conclusion.* Because Employer Z offers minimum value coverage to Employee A no later than the first day following the period of three full calendar months beginning with the first full calendar month in which Employee A is otherwise eligible for an offer of coverage under a group health plan of Employer Z, Employer Z is not subject to an assessable payment for January 2017 through March 2017 under section 4980H by reason of its failure to offer coverage to Employee A during those months. For calendar months after March 2017, an offer of minimum value coverage may result in an assessable payment under section 4980H(b) with respect to Employee A for any month for which the offer is not affordable and for which Employer Z has received a Section 1411 Certification. Employer Z is not subject to an assessable payment under section 4980H by reason of its failure to offer coverage to Employee A during each month of 2016 because for each month of 2016, Employee A was not a full-time employee.

*Example 2 (Rehire rules under monthly measurement method for employers that are not educational organizations).* (i) *Facts.* Same as *Example 1,* except that Employee A has zero hours of service during a nine week period of unpaid leave (that constitutes special unpaid leave) beginning on June 25, 2017, and ending on August 26, 2017. As a result of the nine week period during which Employee A has zero hours of service, Employee A averages less than 30 hours of service per week for July 2017 and August 2017. Employee A averages more than 30 hours of service per week for each month between and including September 2017 through December 2017. Employer Z does not use the rule of parity, set forth in paragraph (c)(4)(v) of this section, and Employer Z is not an educational organization.

(ii) *Conclusion.* Because Employee A resumes providing services for Employer Z after a period during which the employee was not credited with any hours of service of less than 13 consecutive weeks, Employer Z may not treat Employee A as having terminated employment and having been rehired. Therefore, Employer Z may not treat Employee A as a new employee upon the resumption of services, and, accordingly, Employer Z may not apply the rule set forth in paragraph (c)(2) of this section. Although the nine consecutive weeks of zero hours of service constitute special unpaid leave, the averaging method for periods of special unpaid leave does not apply under the monthly measurement method. Therefore, Employer Z may treat Employee A as a non-full-time employee for July 2017 and August 2017.

*Example 3 (Use of weekly rule).* (i) *Facts.* Employer Y uses the monthly measurement method in combination with the weekly rule for purposes of determining whether an employee is a full-time employee for a particular calendar month. For purposes of applying the weekly rule, Employer Y uses the period of Sunday through Saturday as a week and includes the week that includes the first day of a calendar month and excludes the week that includes the last day of a calendar month (except in any case in which the last day of the calendar month occurs on a Saturday). Employer Y measures hours of service for the five weeks from Sunday, December 27, 2015, through Saturday, January 30, 2016, to determine an employee's full-time employee status for January 2016, for the four weeks from Sunday, January 31, 2016, through Saturday, February 27, 2016, to determine an employee's status for February 2016, and the four weeks from Sunday, February 28, 2016, through Saturday, March 26, 2016, to determine an employee's status for March 2016. For January 2016, Employer Y treats an employee as a full-time employee if the employee has at least 150 hours of service (30 hours per week × 5 weeks). For February 2016 and March 2016, Employer Y treats an employee as a full-time employee if the employee has at least 120 hours of service (30 hours per week × 4 weeks).

(ii) *Conclusion.* Employer Y has correctly applied the weekly rule as part of the monthly measurement method for determining each employee's status as a full-time employee for the months January, February, and March 2016.

(d) *Look-back measurement method.*—(1) *Ongoing employees.*—(i) *In general.*—Under the look-back measurement method for ongoing employees, an applicable large employer determines each ongoing employee's full-time employee status by looking back at the standard measurement period. The applicable large employer member determines the months in which the standard measurement period starts and ends, provided that the determination must be made on a uniform and consistent basis for all employees in the same category (see paragraph (d)(1)(v) of this section for a list of permissible categories). For example, if an applicable large employer member chooses a standard measurement period of 12 months, the applicable large employer member could choose to make it the calendar year, a non-calendar plan year, or a different 12-month period, such as one that ends shortly before the start of the plan's annual open enrollment period. If the applicable large employer member determines that an employee was employed on average at least 30 hours of service per week during the standard measurement period, then the applicable large employer member must treat the employee as a full-time employee during a subsequent stability period, regardless of the employee's number of hours of service during the stability period, so long as he or she remains an employee.

(ii) *Use of payroll periods.*—For payroll periods that are one week, two weeks, or semi-monthly in duration, an employer is permitted to treat as a measurement period a period that ends on the last day of the payroll period preceding the payroll period that includes the date that would otherwise be the last day of the measurement period, provided that the measurement period begins on the first day of the payroll period that includes the date that would otherwise be the first day of the measurement period. An employer may also treat as a measurement period a period that begins on the first day of the payroll period that follows the payroll period that includes the date that would otherwise be the first day of the measurement period, provided that the measurement period ends on the last day of the payroll period that includes the date that would otherwise be the last day of the measurement period. For example, an employer using the calendar year as a measurement period could exclude the entire payroll period that included January 1 (the beginning of the year) if it included the entire payroll period that included December 31 (the end of that same year), or, alternatively, could exclude the entire payroll period that included December 31 of a calendar year if it included the entire payroll period that included January 1 of that calendar year.

(iii) *Employee determined to be employed an average of at least 30 hours of service per week.*—An employee who was employed on average at least 30 hours of service per week during the standard measurement period must be treated as a full-time employee for a stability period that begins immediately after the standard measurement period and any applicable administrative period. The stability period must be at least six consecutive calendar months but no shorter in duration than the standard measurement period.

(iv) *Employee determined not to be employed on average at least 30 hours of service per week.*—If an employee was not employed an average of at least 30 hours of service per week during the standard measurement period, the applicable large employer member may treat the employee as not a full-time employee during the stability period that follows, but is not longer than, the standard measurement period. The stability period must begin immediately after the end of the measurement period and any applicable administrative period.

(v) *Permissible employee categories.*—Different applicable large employer members of the same applicable large employer may use measurement periods and stability periods that differ either in length or in their starting or ending dates. In addition, subject to the rules governing the relationship between the length of the measurement period and the stability period, applicable large employer members may use measurement periods and stability periods that differ either in length or in their starting and ending dates for—

(A) Collectively bargained employees and non-collectively bargained employees,

(B) Each group of collectively bargained employees covered by a separate collective bargaining agreement,

(C) Salaried employees and hourly employees, and

(D) Employees whose primary places of employment are in different States.

(vi) *Optional administrative period.*—An applicable large employer member may provide for an administrative period that begins immediately after the end of a standard measurement period and that ends immediately before the associated stability period; however, any administrative period between the standard measurement period and the stability period for ongoing employees may neither reduce nor lengthen the measurement period or the stability period. The administrative period following the standard measurement period may last up to 90 days. To prevent this administrative period from creating a period during which coverage is not available, the administrative period must overlap with the prior stability period, so that, during any such administrative period applicable to ongoing employees following a standard measurement period, ongoing employees who are enrolled in coverage because of their status as full-time employees based on a prior measurement period must continue to be covered through the administrative period. Applicable large employer members may use administrative periods that differ in length for the categories of employees identified in paragraph (d)(1)(v) of this section.

(vii) *Change in employment status.*—Except as provided in paragraph (f)(2) of this section, if an ongoing employee experiences a change in employment status before the end of a stability period, the change will not affect the application of the classification of the employee as a full-time employee (or not a full-time employee) for the remaining portion of the stability period. For example, if an ongoing employee in a certain position of employment is not treated as a full-time employee during a stability period because the employee's hours of service during the prior measurement period were insufficient for full-time-employee treatment, and the employee experiences a change in employment status that involves an increased level of hours of service, the treatment of the employee as a non-full-time employee during the remainder of the stability period is unaffected. Similarly, if an ongoing employee in a certain position of employment is treated as a full-time employee during a stability period because the employee's hours of service during the prior measurement period were sufficient for full-time-employee treatment, and the employee experiences a change in employment status that involves a lower level of hours of service, the treatment of the employee as a full-time employee during the remainder of the stability period is unaffected.

(viii) *Example.*—The following example illustrates the application of paragraph (d)(1) of this section:

(A) *Facts.*—Employer Z is an applicable large employer member and computes hours of service following the rules in this paragraph (d)(1). Employer Z chooses to use a 12-month stability period that begins January 1 and a 12-month standard measurement period that begins October 15. Consistent with the terms of Employer Z's group health plan, only employees classified as full-time employees using the look-back measurement method are eligible for coverage. Employer Z chooses to use an administrative period between the end of the standard measurement period (October 14) and the beginning of the stability period (January 1) to determine which employees were employed on average 30 hours of service per week during the measurement period, notify them of their eligibility for the plan for the calendar year beginning on January 1 and of the coverage available under the plan, answer questions and collect materials from employees, and enroll those employees who elect coverage in the plan. Previously-determined full-time employees already enrolled in coverage continue to be offered coverage through the administrative period. Employee A and Employee B have been employed by Employer Z for several years, continuously from their start date. Employee A was employed on average 30 hours of service per week during the standard measurement period that begins October 15, 2015, and ends October 14, 2016, and for all prior standard measure-

ment periods. Employee B also was employed on average 30 hours of service per week for all prior standard measurement periods, but averaged less than 30 hours of service per week during the standard measurement period that begins October 15, 2015, and ends October 14, 2016.

(B) *Conclusions.*—Because Employee A was employed for the entire standard measurement period that begins October 15, 2015, and ends October 14, 2016, Employee A is an ongoing employee with respect to the stability period running from January 1, 2017, through December 31, 2017. Because Employee A was employed on average 30 hours of service per week during that standard measurement period, Employee A is offered coverage for the entire 2017 stability period (including the administrative period from October 15, 2017, through December 31, 2017). Because Employee A was employed on average 30 hours of service per week during the prior standard measurement period, Employee A is offered coverage for the entire 2016 stability period and, if enrolled, would continue such coverage during the administrative period from October 15, 2016, through December 31, 2016. Because Employee B was employed for the entire standard measurement period that begins October 15, 2015, and ends October 14, 2016, Employee B is also an ongoing employee with respect to the stability period in 2017. Because Employee B was not a full-time employee based on hours of service during this standard measurement period, Employee B is not offered coverage for the stability period in 2017 (including the administrative period from October 15, 2017, through December 31, 2017). However, because Employee B was employed on average 30 hours of service per week during the prior standard measurement period, Employee B is offered coverage through the end of the 2016 stability period and, if enrolled, would continue such coverage during the administrative period from October 15, 2016, through December 31, 2016. Employer Z complies with the standards of paragraph (d)(1) of this section because the standard measurement period is no longer than 12 months, the stability period for ongoing employees who are full-time employees based on hours of service during the standard measurement period is not shorter than the standard measurement period, the stability period for ongoing employees who are not full-time employees based on hours of service during the standard measurement period is no longer than the standard measurement period, and the administrative period is no longer than 90 days.

(2) *New non-variable hour, new non-seasonal and new non-part-time employees.*—(i) *In general.*—For a new employee who is reasonably expected at the employee's start date to be a full-time employee (and is not a seasonal employee), an applicable large employer member determines such employee's status as a full-time employee based on the employee's hours of service for each calendar month. If the employee's hours of service for the calendar month equal or exceed an average of 30 hours of service per week, the employee is a full-time employee for that calendar month. Once a new employee who is reasonably expected at the employee's start date to be a full-time employee (and is not a seasonal employee) becomes an ongoing employee, the rules set forth in paragraph (d)(1) of this section apply for determining full-time employee status.

(ii) *Factors for determining full-time employee status.*—Whether an employer's determination that a new employee (who is not a seasonal employee) is a full-time employee or is not a full-time employee is reasonable is based on the facts and circumstances at the employee's start date. Factors to consider in determining whether a new employee who is not a seasonal employee is reasonably expected at the employee's start date to be a full-time employee include, but are not limited to, whether the employee is replacing an employee who was (or was not) a full-time employee, the extent to which hours of service of ongoing employees in the same or comparable positions have varied above and below an average of 30 hours of service per week during recent measurement periods, and whether the job was advertised, or otherwise communicated to the new hire or otherwise documented (for example, through a contract or job description), as requiring hours of service that would average 30 (or more) hours of service per week or less than 30 hours of service per week. In all cases, no single factor is determinative. An educational organization employer cannot take into account the potential for, or likelihood of, an employment break period in determining its expectation of future hours of service.

(iii) *Application of section 4980H to initial full three calendar months of employment.*—Notwithstanding paragraph (d)(2)(i) of this section, with respect to an employee who is reasonably expected at his or her start date to be a full-time employee (and is not a seasonal employee), the employer will not be subject to an assessable payment under section 4980H(a) for any calendar month of the three-month period beginning with the first day of the first full calendar month of employment if, for the calendar month, the employee is otherwise eligible for an offer of coverage under a group health plan of the employer, provided that the employee is offered coverage by the employer no later than the first day of the fourth full calendar month of employment if the employee is still employed on that day. If the offer of coverage for which the employee is otherwise eligible during the first three full calendar months of employment, and which the employee actually is offered by the first day of the fourth month if still employed, provides minimum value, the employer also will not be subject to an assessable payment under section 4980H(b) with respect to that employee for the first three full calendar months of employment. For purposes of this paragraph (d)(2)(iii), an employee is otherwise eligible to be offered coverage under a group health plan for a calendar month if, pursuant to the terms of the plan as in effect for that calendar month, the employee meets all conditions to be offered coverage under the plan for that calendar month, other than the completion of a waiting period, within the meaning of § 54.9801-2.

(3) *New variable hour employees, new seasonal employees, and new part-time employees.*—(i) *In general.*—For new variable hour employees, new seasonal employees, and new part-time employees, applicable large employer members are permitted to determine whether the new employee is a full-time employee using an initial measurement period of no less than three consecutive months and no more than 12 consecutive months (as selected by the applicable large employer member) that begins on the employee's start date or on any date up to and including the first day of the first calendar month following the employee's start date (or on the first day of the first payroll period starting on or after the employee's start date, if later, as set forth in paragraph (d)(3)(ii) of this section). The applicable large employer member measures the new employee's hours of service during the initial measurement period and determines whether the employee was employed on average at least 30 hours of service per week during this period. The stability period for such employees must be the same length as the stability period for ongoing employees.

(ii) *Use of payroll periods.*—An applicable large employer member may apply the payroll period rule set forth in paragraph (d)(1)(ii) of this section for purposes of determining an initial measurement period, provided that the initial measurement period must begin on the start date or any date during the period beginning with the employee's start date and ending with the later of the first day of the first calendar month following the employee's start date and the first day of the first payroll period that starts after the employee's start date. As set forth in paragraph (d)(1)(ii) of this section, the use of payroll periods for purposes of determining the initial measurement period applies for payroll periods that are one week, two weeks, or semi-monthly in duration.

(iii) *Employees determined to be employed on average at least 30 hours of service per week.*—If a new variable hour employee, new seasonal employee, or new part-time employee has on average at least 30 hours of service per week during the initial measurement period, the applicable large employer member must treat the employee as a full-time employee during the stability period that begins after the initial measurement period (and any associated administrative period). The stability period must be a period of at least six consecutive calendar months that is no shorter in duration than the initial measurement period. The stability period must begin immediately after the end of the measurement period and any applicable administrative period. With respect to an employee who has on average at least 30 hours of service per week during the initial measurement period, the employer will not be subject to an assessable payment under section 4980H(a) for any calendar month during the initial measurement period and any associated administrative period if, for the calendar month, the employee is otherwise eligible for an offer of coverage under a group health plan of the employer, provided that the employee is offered coverage by the employer no later than the first day of the associated stability period if the employee is still employed on that day. If the offer of coverage for which the employee is otherwise eligible during the initial measurement period, and which the employee actually is offered by the first day of the stability period if still employed, provides minimum value, the employer also will not be subject to an assessable payment under section 4980H(b) with respect to that employee during the initial measurement period and any associated administrative period. For purposes of this paragraph (d)(3)(iii), an employee is otherwise eligible to be offered coverage under a group health plan for a month if, pursuant to the terms of the plan as in effect for that calendar month, the employee meets all conditions to be offered coverage under the plan for that month, other than the completion of a waiting period, within the meaning of § 54.9801-2.

(iv) *Employees determined not to be employed on average at least 30 hours of service per week.*—If a new variable hour employee, new seasonal employee, or new part-time employee does not have on

average at least 30 hours of service per week during the initial measurement period, the applicable large employer member may treat the employee as not a full-time employee during the stability period that follows the initial measurement period. Except as provided in paragraph (d)(4)(iv) of this section, the stability period for such employees must not be more than one month longer than the initial measurement period and must not exceed the remainder of the first entire standard measurement period (plus any associated administrative period) for which a variable hour employee, seasonal employee, or part-time employee has been employed. The stability period must begin immediately after the end of the measurement period and any applicable administrative period.

(v) *Permissible differences in measurement or stability periods for different categories of employees.*—Subject to the rules governing the relationship between the length of the measurement period and the stability period, with respect to a new variable hour employee, new seasonal employee, or new part-time employee, applicable large employer members may use measurement periods and stability periods that differ either in length or in their starting and ending dates for the categories of employees identified in paragraph (d)(1)(v) of this section.

(vi) *Optional administrative period.*—(A) *In general.*—Subject to the limits in paragraph (d)(3)(vi)(B) of this section, an applicable large employer member may apply an administrative period in connection with an initial measurement period and before the start of the stability period. This administrative period must not exceed 90 days in total. For this purpose, the administrative period includes all periods between the start date of a new variable hour employee, new seasonal employee, or new part-time employee and the date the employee is first offered coverage under the applicable large employer member's group health plan, other than the initial measurement period. Thus, for example, if the applicable large employer member begins the initial measurement period on the first day of the first month following a new employee's start date, the period between the employee's start date and the first day of the next month must be taken into account in applying the 90-day limit on the administrative period. Similarly, if there is a period between the end of the initial measurement period and the date the employee is first offered coverage under the plan, that period must be taken into account in applying the 90-day limit on the administrative period. Applicable large employer members may use administrative periods that differ in length for the categories of employees identified in paragraph (d)(1)(v) of this section.

(B) *Limit on combined length of initial measurement period and administrative period.*—In addition to the specific limits on the initial measurement period (which must not exceed 12 months) and the administrative period (which must not exceed 90 days), there is a limit on the combined length of the initial measurement period and the administrative period applicable to a new variable hour employee, new seasonal employee, or new part-time employee. Specifically, the initial measurement period and administrative period together cannot extend beyond the last day of the first calendar month beginning on or after the first anniversary of the employee's start date. For example, if an applicable large employer member uses a 12-month initial measurement period for a new variable hour employee, and begins that initial measurement period on the first day of the first calendar month following the employee's start date, the period between the end of the initial measurement period and the offer of coverage to a new variable hour employee who is a full-time employee based on hours of service during the initial measurement period must not exceed one month.

(vii) *Change in employment status during the initial measurement period.*—(A) *In general.*—If a new variable hour employee, new seasonal employee, or new part-time employee experiences a change in employment status before the end of the initial measurement period such that, if the employee had begun employment in the new position or status, the employee would have reasonably been expected to be employed on average at least 30 hours of service per week (or, if applicable, would not have been a seasonal employee and would have been expected to be employed on average at least 30 hours of service per week), the rules set forth in the remainder of this paragraph (d)(3)(vii) apply. With respect to an employee described in this paragraph (d)(3)(vii) and subject to the rules in the next sentence, the employer will not be subject to an assessable payment under section 4980H for the period before the first day of the fourth full calendar month following the change in employment status (or, if earlier and the employee averages 30 or more hours of service per week during the initial measurement period, the first day of the first month following the end of the initial measurement period (including any optional administrative period associated with the initial measurement period)). An employer will not be subject to an assessable payment under section 4980H(a) with respect to an employee described in this paragraph (d)(3)(vii) for any calendar month during the period described in the prior sentence if, for the calendar month, the employee is otherwise eligible for an offer of coverage under a group health plan of the employer, provided that the employee is offered coverage by the employer no later than the end of the period described in the prior sentence if the employee is still employed on that date; if the offer of coverage for which the employee is otherwise eligible during the period described in the prior sentence, and which the employee is actually offered by the first day after the end of that period if still employed, provides minimum value, the employer also will not be subject to an assessable payment under section 4980H(b) with respect to that employee during that period. For purposes of this paragraph (d)(3)(vii), an employee is otherwise eligible to be offered coverage under a group health plan for a calendar month if, pursuant to the terms of the plan as in effect for that calendar month, the employee meets all conditions to be offered coverage under the plan for that calendar month, other than the completion of a waiting period, within the meaning of § 54.9801-2.

(B) *Example.*—The following example illustrates the provisions of paragraph (d)(3)(vii) of this section. In the following example, the applicable large employer member has 200 full-time employees and offers all of its full-time employees (and their dependents) the opportunity to enroll in minimum essential coverage under an eligible employer-sponsored plan. The coverage is affordable within the meaning of section 36B(c)(2)(C)(i) (or is treated as affordable under one of the affordability safe harbors described in § 54.4980H-5) and provides minimum value.

*Example (Change in employment status from variable hour employee to full-time employee).* (i) *Facts.* For new variable hour employees, Employer Z uses a 12-month initial measurement period that begins on the start date and applies an administrative period from the end of the initial measurement period through the end of the first calendar month beginning on or after the end of the initial measurement period. For new variable hour employees, Employer Z offers coverage no later than the first day of the fourteenth month after the start date if an employee averages 30 or more hours of service per week during the initial measurement period. Employer Z hires Employee A on May 10, 2015. Employee A's initial measurement period runs from May 10, 2015, through May 9, 2016, with the optional administrative period ending June 30, 2016. At Employee A's May 10, 2015, start date, Employee A is a variable hour employee. On September 15, 2015, Employer Z promotes Employee A to a position that can reasonably be expected to average at least 30 hours of service per week. For October 2015 through December 2015, Employee A is otherwise eligible for an offer of coverage that provides minimum value, and, on January 1, 2016, Employee A is offered coverage by the employer that provides minimum value.

(ii) *Conclusion.* Employer Z will not be subject to an assessable payment under section 4980H(a) with respect to Employee A for October 2015, November 2015, or December 2015, because for each of those months Employee A is otherwise eligible for an offer of coverage and because Employee A is offered coverage by January 1, 2016 (the date that is the earlier of the first day of the fourth calendar month following the change in employment status (January 1, 2016) or the first day of the calendar month after the end of the initial measurement period plus the optional administrative period (July 1, 2016)). Because the coverage offered on January 1, 2016, provides minimum value, Employer Z also will not be subject to an assessable payment under section 4980H(b) with respect to Employee A for October 2015, November 2015, or December 2015.

(4) *Transition from new variable hour employee, new seasonal employee, or new part-time employee to ongoing employee.*—(i) *In general.*—Once a new variable hour employee, new seasonal employee, or new part-time employee has been employed for an entire standard measurement period, the applicable large employer member must test the employee for full-time employee status, beginning with that standard measurement period, at the same time and under the same conditions as apply to other ongoing employees. Accordingly, for example, an applicable large employer member with a calendar year standard measurement period that also uses a one-year initial measurement period beginning on the employee's start date would test a new employee whose start date is April 12 for full-time employee status first based on the initial measurement period (April 12 of the year including the start date through April 11 of the following year) and again based on the calendar year standard measurement period (if the employee continues in employment for that entire standard measurement period) beginning on January 1 of the year after the start date.

(ii) *Employee determined to be employed an average of at least 30 hours of service per week.*—An employee who was employed an average of at least 30 hours of service per week during an initial measurement period or standard measurement period must be treated as a full-time employee for the entire associated stability period. This is

the case even if the employee was employed an average of at least 30 hours of service per week during the initial measurement period but was not employed an average of at least 30 hours of service per week during the overlapping or immediately following standard measurement period. In that case, the applicable large employer member may treat the employee as not a full-time employee only after the end of the stability period associated with the initial measurement period. Thereafter, the applicable large employer member must determine the employee's status as a full-time employee in the same manner as it determines such status in the case of its other ongoing employees as described in paragraph (d)(1) of this section.

(iii) *Employee determined not to be employed an average of at least 30 hours of service per week.*—If the employee was not employed an average of at least 30 hours of service per week during the initial measurement period, but was employed at least 30 hours of service per week during the overlapping or immediately following standard measurement period, the employee must be treated as a full-time employee for the entire stability period that corresponds to that standard measurement period (even if that stability period begins before the end of the stability period associated with the initial measurement period). Thereafter, the applicable large employer member must determine the employee's status as a full-time employee in the same manner as it determines such status in the case of its other ongoing employees as described in paragraph (d)(1) of this section.

(iv) *Treatment during periods between stability periods.*—If there is a period between the end of the stability period associated with the initial measurement period and the beginning of the stability period associated with the first full standard measurement period during which an employee is employed, the treatment as a full-time employee or not a full-time employee that applies during the stability period associated with the initial measurement period continues to apply until the beginning of the stability period associated with the first full standard measurement period during which the employee is employed.

(5) *Examples.*—The following examples illustrate the look-back measurement methods described in paragraphs (d)(1), (d)(3) and (d)(4) of this section. In all of the following examples, the applicable large employer member has 200 full-time employees and offers all of its full-time employees (and their dependents) the opportunity to enroll in minimum essential coverage under an eligible employer-sponsored plan. The coverage is affordable within the meaning of section 36B(c)(2)(C)(i) (or is treated as affordable coverage under one of the affordability safe harbors described in § 54.4980H-5) and provides minimum value. In *Example 1* through *Example 8*, the new employee is a new variable hour employee, and the employer has chosen to use a 12-month standard measurement period for ongoing employees starting October 15 and a 12-month stability period associated with that standard measurement period starting January 1. (Thus, during the administrative period from October 15 through December 31 of each calendar year, the employer continues to offer coverage to employees who qualified for coverage for that entire calendar year based upon having an average of at least 30 hours of service per week during the prior standard measurement period.) In *Example 9* and *Example 10*, the new employee is a new variable hour employee, and the employer uses a six-month standard measurement period, starting each May 1 and November 1, with six-month stability periods associated with those standard measurement periods starting January 1 and July 1. In *Example 12, Example 13,* and *Example 14*, the employer is in the trade or business of providing temporary workers to numerous clients that are unrelated to the employer and to one another; the employer is the common law employer of the temporary workers based on all of the facts and circumstances; the employer offers health plan coverage only to full-time employees (including temporary workers who are full-time employees) and their dependents; and the employer uses a 12-month initial measurement period for new variable hour employees that begins on the start date and applies an administrative period from the end of the initial measurement period through the end of the first calendar month beginning after the end of the initial measurement period.

*Example 1 (12-Month initial measurement period followed by 1+ partial month administrative period).* (i) *Facts.* For new variable hour employees, Employer Z uses a 12-month initial measurement period that begins on the start date and applies an administrative period from the end of the initial measurement period through the end of the first calendar month beginning on or after the end of the initial measurement period. Employer Z hires Employee A on May 10, 2015. Employee A's initial measurement period runs from May 10, 2015, through May 9, 2016. Employee A has an average of 30 hours of service per week during this initial measurement period. Employer Z offers coverage that provides minimum value to Employee A for a stability period that runs from July 1, 2016, through June 30, 2017. For each calendar month during the period beginning with June 2015 and ending with June 2016, Employee A is otherwise eligible for an offer of coverage with respect to the coverage that is offered to Employee A on July 1, 2016.

(ii) *Conclusion.* Employer Z uses an initial measurement period that does not exceed 12 months; an administrative period totaling not more than 90 days; and a combined initial measurement period and administrative period that does not last beyond the final day of the first calendar month beginning on or after the one-year anniversary of Employee A's start date. Accordingly, Employer Z complies with the standards for the initial measurement period and stability periods for a new variable hour employee. Employer Z will not be subject to an assessable payment under section 4980H(a) with respect to Employee A for any calendar month from June 2015 through June 2016 because, for each month during that period, Employee A is otherwise eligible for an offer of coverage and because coverage is offered no later than the end of the initial measurement period plus the associated administrative period (July 1, 2016). Employer Z will not be subject to an assessable payment under section 4980H(b) with respect to Employee A for any calendar month from June 2015 through June 2016 because the coverage Employer Z offers to Employee A provides minimum value. Employer Z will not be subject to an assessable payment under section 4980H(a) or (b) with respect to Employee A for May 2015 because an applicable large employer member is not subject to an assessable payment under section 4980H with respect to an employee for the calendar month in which falls the employee's start date if the start date is on a date other than the first day of the calendar month. Employer Z must test Employee A again based on the period from October 15, 2015, through October 14, 2016 (Employer Z's first standard measurement period that begins after Employee A's start date).

*Example 2 (11-Month initial measurement period followed by 2+ partial month administrative period).* (i) *Facts.* Same as *Example 1*, except that Employer Z uses an 11-month initial measurement period that begins on the start date and applies an administrative period from the end of the initial measurement period until the end of the second calendar month beginning after the end of the initial measurement period. Employee A's initial measurement period runs from May 10, 2015, through April 9, 2016. The administrative period associated with Employee A's initial measurement period ends on June 30, 2016. Employee A has an average of 30 hours of service per week during this initial measurement period.

(ii) *Conclusion.* Same as *Example 1*.

*Example 3 (11-Month initial measurement period preceded by partial month administrative period and followed by 2-month administrative period).* (i) *Facts.* Same as *Example 1*, except that Employer Z uses an 11-month initial measurement period that begins on the first day of the first calendar month beginning after the start date and applies an administrative period that runs from the end of the initial measurement period through the end of the second calendar month beginning on or after the end of the initial measurement period. Employee A's initial measurement period runs from June 1, 2015, through April 30, 2016. The administrative period associated with Employee A's initial measurement period ends on June 30, 2016. Employee A has an average of 30 hours of service per week during this initial measurement period.

(ii) *Conclusion.* Same as *Example 1*.

*Example 4 (12-Month initial measurement period preceded by partial month administrative period and followed by 2-month administrative period).* (i) *Facts.* For new variable hour employees, Employer Z uses a 12-month initial measurement period that begins on the first day of the first month following the start date and applies an administrative period that runs from the end of the initial measurement period through the end of the second calendar month beginning on or after the end of the initial measurement period. Employer Z hires Employee A on May 10, 2015. Employee A's initial measurement period runs from June 1, 2015, through May 31, 2016. Employee A has an average of 30 hours of service per week during this initial measurement period. Employer Z offers coverage to Employee A for a stability period that runs from August 1, 2016, through July 31, 2017.

(ii) *Conclusion.* Employer Z does not satisfy the standards for the look-back measurement method in paragraph (d)(3)(vi)(B) of this section because the combination of the initial partial month delay, the 12-month initial measurement period, and the two month administrative period means that the coverage offered to Employee A does not become effective until after the first day of the second calendar month following the first anniversary of Employee A's start date. Accordingly, Employer Z is potentially subject to an assessable payment under section 4980H for each full calendar month during the initial measurement period and associated administrative period.

*Example 5 (Continuous full-time employee).* (i) *Facts.* Same as *Example 1*; in addition, Employer Z tests Employee A again based on Employee A's hours of service from October 15, 2015, through October 14, 2016 (Employer Z's first standard measurement period that begins after Employee A's start date), determines that Employee A

has an average of 30 hours of service per week during that period, and offers Employee A coverage for July 1, 2017, through December 31, 2017. (Employee A already has an offer of coverage for the period of January 1, 2017, through June 30, 2017, because that period is covered by the initial stability period following the initial measurement period, during which Employee A was determined to be a full-time employee.)

(ii) *Conclusion.* Employer Z is not subject to any payment under section 4980H for any calendar month during 2017 with respect to Employee A.

*Example 6 (Initially full-time employee, becomes non-full-time employee).* (i) *Facts.* Same as *Example 1*; in addition, Employer Z tests Employee A again based on Employee A's hours of service from October 15, 2015, through October 14, 2016 (Employer Z's first standard measurement period that begins after Employee A's start date), and determines that Employee A has an average of 28 hours of service per week during that period. Employer Z continues to offer coverage to Employee A through June 30, 2017 (the end of the stability period based on the initial measurement period during which Employee A was determined to be a full-time employee), but does not offer coverage to Employee A for the period of July 1, 2017, through December 31, 2017.

(ii) *Conclusion.* Employer Z is not subject to any payment under section 4980H for any calendar month during 2017 with respect to Employee A.

*Example 7 (Initially non-full-time employee).* (i) *Facts.* Same as *Example 1*, except that Employee A has an average of 28 hours of service per week during the initial measurement period (May 10, 2015, through May 9, 2016), and Employer Z does not offer coverage to Employee A for any calendar month in 2016.

(ii) *Conclusion.* From Employee A's start date through the end of 2016, Employer Z is not subject to any payment under section 4980H with respect to Employee A, because Employer Z complies with the standards for the measurement and stability periods for a new variable hour employee with respect to Employee A and because under those standards, Employee A is not a full-time employee for any month during 2016.

*Example 8 (Initially non-full-time employee, becomes full-time employee).* (i) *Facts.* Same as *Example 7*; in addition, Employer Z tests Employee A again based on Employee A's hours of service from October 15, 2015, through October 14, 2016 (Employer Z's first standard measurement period that begins after Employee A's start date), determines that Employee A has an average of 30 hours of service per week during this standard measurement period, and offers coverage to Employee A for 2017.

(ii) *Conclusion.* Employer Z is not subject to any payment under section 4980H for any calendar month during 2017 with respect to Employee A.

*Example 9 (Initially full-time employee).* (i) *Facts.* For new variable hour employees, Employer Y uses a six-month initial measurement period that begins on the start date and applies an administrative period that runs from the end of the initial measurement period through the end of the first full calendar month beginning after the end of the initial measurement period. Employer Y hires Employee B on May 10, 2015. Employee B's initial measurement period runs from May 10, 2015, through November 9, 2015, during which Employee B has an average of 30 hours of service per week. Employer Y offers coverage that provides minimum value to Employee B for a stability period that runs from January 1, 2016, through June 30, 2016. For each calendar month during the period from June 2015 through December 2015, Employee B is otherwise eligible for an offer of coverage with respect to the coverage that is offered to Employee B on January 1, 2016.

(ii) *Conclusion.* Employer Y uses an initial measurement period that does not exceed 12 months; an administrative period totaling not more than 90 days; and a combined initial measurement period and administrative period that does not extend beyond the final day of the first calendar month beginning on or after the one-year anniversary of Employee B's start date. Employer Y complies with the standards for the measurement and stability periods for a new variable hour employee with respect to Employee B. Employer Y is not subject to an assessable payment under section 4980H(a) with respect to Employee B for any calendar month from June 2015 through December 2015 because, for each month during that period, Employee B is otherwise eligible for an offer of coverage and because Employee B is offered coverage no later than the end of the initial measurement period plus the associated administrative period (January 1, 2016). Employer Y is not subject to an assessable payment under section 4980H(b) with respect to Employee B for any calendar month from June 2015 through December 2015 because the coverage Employer Y offers to Employee B no later than January 1, 2016, provides minimum value. Employer Y is not subject to an assessable payment under section 4980H(a) or (b) with respect to Employee B for May 2015 because an applicable large employer member is not subject to an assessable payment under section 4980H with respect to an employee for the calendar month in which falls the employee's start date if the start date is on a date other than the first day of the calendar month. Employer Y must test Employee B again based on Employee B's hours of service during the period from November 1, 2015, through April 30, 2016 (Employer Y's first standard measurement period that begins after Employee B's start date).

*Example 10 (Initially full-time employee, becomes non-full-time employee).* (i) *Facts.* Same as *Example 9*; in addition, Employer Y tests Employee B again based on Employee B's hours of service during the period from November 1, 2015, through April 30, 2016 (Employer Y's first standard measurement period that begins after Employee B's start date), during which period Employee B has an average of 28 hours of service per week. Employer Y continues to offer coverage to Employee B through June 30, 2016 (the end of the initial stability period based on the initial measurement period during which Employee B has an average of 30 hours of service per week), but does not offer coverage to Employee B from July 1, 2016, through December 31, 2016.

(ii) *Conclusion.* Employer Y is not subject to any payment under section 4980H with respect to Employee B for any calendar month during 2016.

*Example 11 (Seasonal employee, 12-month initial measurement period; 1+ partial month administrative period).* (i) *Facts.* Employer X offers health plan coverage only to full-time employees (and their dependents). Employer X uses a 12-month initial measurement period for new seasonal employees that begins on the start date and applies an administrative period from the end of the initial measurement period through the end of the first calendar month beginning after the end of the initial measurement period. Employer X hires Employee C, a ski instructor, on November 15, 2015, with an anticipated season during which Employee C will work running through March 15, 2016. Employee C's initial measurement period runs from November 15, 2015, through November 14, 2016.

(ii) *Conclusion.* Employer X determines that Employee C is a seasonal employee because Employee C is hired into a position for which the customary annual employment is six months or less. Accordingly, Employer X may treat Employee C as a seasonal employee during the initial measurement period.

*Example 12 (Variable hour employee; temporary staffing firm).* (i) *Facts.* Employer W hires Employee D on January 1, 2015, in a position under which Employer W will offer assignments to Employee D to provide services in temporary placements at clients of Employer W, and employees of Employer W in the same position as Employee D, as part of their continuing employment, retain the right to reject an offer of placement. Employees of Employer W in the same position of employment as Employee D typically perform services for a particular client for 40 hours of service per week for a period of less than 13 weeks, and for each employee there are typically periods in a calendar year during which Employer W does not have an assignment to offer the employee. At the time Employee D is hired by Employer W, Employer W has no reason to anticipate that Employee D's position of employment will differ from the typical employee in the same position.

(ii) *Conclusion.* Employer W cannot determine whether Employee D is reasonably expected to average at least 30 hours of service per week for the 12-month initial measurement period. Accordingly, Employer W may treat Employee D as a variable hour employee during the initial measurement period.

*Example 13 (Variable hour employee; temporary staffing firm).* (i) *Facts.* Employer V hires Employee E on January 1, 2015, in a position under which Employer V will offer assignments to Employee E to provide services in temporary placements at clients of Employer V. Employees of Employer V in the same position of employment as Employee E typically are offered assignments of varying hours of service per week (so that some weeks of the assignment typically result in more than 30 hours of service per week and other weeks of the assignment typically result in less than 30 hours of service per week). Although a typical employee in the same position of employment as Employee E rarely fails to have an offer of an assignment for any period during the calendar year, employees of Employer V in the same position of employment, as part of their continuing employment, retain the right to reject an offer of placement, and typically refuse one or more offers of placement and do not perform services for periods ranging from four to twelve weeks during a calendar year. At the time Employee E is hired by Employer V, Employer V has no reason to anticipate that Employee E's position of employment will differ from the typical employee in the same position.

(ii) *Conclusion.* Employer V cannot determine whether Employee E is reasonably expected to average at least 30 hours of service per week for the 12-month initial measurement period. Accordingly, Employer V may treat Employee E as a variable hour employee during the initial measurement period.

*Example 14 (Variable hour employee; temporary staffing firm).* (i) *Facts.* Employer T hires Employee F on January 1, 2015, in a position under which Employer T will offer assignments to Employee F to provide services in temporary placements at clients of Employer T. Employees of Employer T in the same position typically are offered assignments of 40 or more hours of service per week for periods expected to last for periods of three months to 12 months, subject to a request for renewal by the client. Employees of Employer T in similar positions to Employee F are typically offered and take new positions immediately upon cessation of a placement. At the time Employee F is hired by Employer T, Employer T has no reason to anticipate that Employee F's position of employment will differ from the typical employee in the same position.

(ii) *Conclusion.* Employer T must assume that Employee F will be employed by Employer T and available for an offer of temporary placement for the entire initial measurement period. Under that assumption, Employer T would reasonably determine that Employee F is reasonably expected to average at least 30 hours of service per week for the 12-month initial measurement period. Accordingly, Employer T may not treat Employee F as a variable hour employee during the initial measurement period.

*Example 15 (Variable hour employee).* (i) *Facts.* Employee G is hired on an hourly basis by Employer S to fill in for employees who are absent and to provide additional staffing at peak times. Employer S expects that Employee G will average 30 hours of service per week or more for Employee G's first few months of employment, while assigned to a specific project, but also reasonably expects that the assignments will be of unpredictable duration, that there will be periods of unpredictable duration between assignments, that the hours per week required by subsequent assignments will vary, and that Employee G will not necessarily be available for all assignments.

(ii) *Conclusion.* Employer S cannot determine whether Employee G is reasonably expected to average at least 30 hours of service per week for the initial measurement period. Accordingly, Employer S may treat Employee G as a variable hour employee during the initial measurement period.

*Example 16 (Period between initial stability period and standard stability period).* (i) *Facts.* Employer R uses an 11-month initial measurement period for new variable hour, new seasonal, and new part-time employees with an administrative period that lasts from the end of the initial measurement period through the last day of the first calendar month beginning on or after the first anniversary of the employee's start date. Employer R uses a standard measurement period of October 15 through October 14, and an administrative period of October 15 through December 31. Employee H is hired as a variable hour employee on October 20, 2015, with an initial measurement period of October 20, 2015, through September 19, 2016, and an administrative period lasting through November 30, 2016. Employee H is a full-time employee based on the hours of service in the initial measurement period, and Employee H's stability period for the initial measurement period is December 1, 2016, through November 30, 2017. Employee H's first full standard measurement period begins on October 15, 2016, with an associated stability period beginning on January 1, 2018. The standard measurement period beginning on October 15, 2015, does not apply to Employee H because Employee H is not hired until October 20, 2015.

(ii) *Conclusion.* For the period after the stability period associated with the initial measurement period and before the stability period associated with Employee H's first full standard measurement period (that is December 1, 2017, through December 31, 2017), Employer R must treat Employee H as a full-time employee because the treatment as a full-time employee (or not a full-time employee) that applies during the stability period associated with the initial measurement period continues to apply until the beginning of the stability period associated with the first full standard measurement period during which the employee is employed.

(6) *Employees rehired after termination of employment or resuming service after other absence.*—(i) *Treatment as a new employee after a period of absence for employers of employers other than educational organizations.*—(A) *In general.*—The rules in this paragraph (d)(6)(i) apply to employers that are not educational organizations. For rules relating to employers that are educational organizations, see paragraph (d)(6)(ii) of this section. An employee who resumes providing services to (or is otherwise credited with an hour of service for) an applicable large employer that is not an educational organization after a period during which the employee was not credited with any hours of service may be treated as having terminated employment and having been rehired, and therefore may be treated as a new employee upon the resumption of services, only if the employee did not have an hour of service for the applicable large employer for a period of at least 13 consecutive weeks immediately preceding the resumption of services. The rule set forth in this paragraph (d)(6)(i) applies solely for the purpose of determining whether the employee, upon the resumption of services, is treated as a new employee or as a

continuing employee, and does not determine whether the employee is treated as a continuing full-time employee or a terminated employee during the period during which no hours of service are credited.

(B) *Averaging method for special unpaid leave.*—For purposes of applying the look-back measurement method described in paragraph (d) of this section to an employee who is not treated as a new employee under paragraph (d)(6)(i) of this section, the employer determines the employee's average hours of service for a measurement period by computing the average after excluding any special unpaid leave during that measurement period and by using that average as the average for the entire measurement period. Alternatively, for purposes of determining the employee's average hours of service for the measurement period, the employer may choose to treat the employee as credited with hours of service for any periods of special unpaid leave during that measurement period at a rate equal to the average weekly rate at which the employee was credited with hours of service during the weeks in the measurement period that are not part of a period of special unpaid leave. There is no limit on the number of hours of service required to be excluded or credited (as the case may be) with respect to special unpaid leave. For purposes of this paragraph (d)(6)(i)(B), in computing the average weekly rate, employers are permitted to use any reasonable method if applied on a consistent basis. In addition, if an employee's average weekly rate under this paragraph (d)(6)(i)(B) is computed for a measurement period and that measurement period is shorter than six months, the six-month period ending with the close of the measurement period is used to compute the average hours of service.

(C) *Averaging rules for employment break periods for employers other than educational organizations.*—The averaging rule for employment break periods described in paragraph (d)(6)(ii)(B) of this section applies only to educational organizations and does not apply to other employers.

(ii) *Treatment as a new employee after a period of absence for employees of employers that are educational organizations.*—(A) *In general.*—The rules of this paragraph (d)(6)(ii) apply only to employers that are educational institutions. An employee who resumes providing services to (or is otherwise credited with an hour of service for) an applicable large employer that is an educational organization after a period during which the employee was not credited with any hours of service may be treated as having terminated employment and having been rehired, and therefore may be treated as a new employee upon the resumption of services, only if the employee did not have an hour of service for the applicable large employer for a period of at least 26 consecutive weeks immediately preceding the resumption of services. The rule set forth in this paragraph (d)(6)(ii)(A) applies solely for the purpose of determining whether the employee, upon the resumption of services, is treated as a new employee or as a continuing employee, and does not determine whether the employee is treated as a continuing full-time employee or a terminated employee during the period during which no hours of service are credited.

(B) *Averaging method for special unpaid leave and employment break periods.*—For purposes of applying the look-back measurement method described in paragraph (d) of this section to an employee who is not treated as a new employee under paragraph (d)(6)(ii)(A) of this section, an educational organization employer determines the employee's average hours of service for a measurement period by computing the average after excluding any special unpaid leave and any employment break period during that measurement period and by using that average as the average for the entire measurement period. Alternatively, for purposes of determining the employee's average hours of service for the measurement period, the employer may choose to treat the employee as credited with hours of service for any periods of special unpaid leave and any employment break period during that measurement period at a rate equal to the average weekly rate at which the employee was credited with hours of service during the weeks in the measurement period that are not part of a period of special unpaid leave or an employment break period. Notwithstanding the preceding two sentences, no more than 501 hours of service during employment break periods in a calendar year are required to be excluded (under the first sentence) or credited (under the second sentence) by an educational organization, provided that this 501-hour limit does not apply to hours of service required to be excluded or credited in respect of special unpaid leave. In applying the preceding sentence, an employer that uses the method described in the first sentence of this paragraph (d)(6)(ii)(B) determines the number of hours excluded by multiplying the average weekly rate for the measurement period (determined as in the second sentence of this paragraph (d)(6)(ii)(B)) by the number of weeks in the employment break period. For purposes of this paragraph (d)(6)(ii)(B), in computing the average weekly rate, employers are permitted to use any reasonable method if applied on a consistent basis. In addition, if an employee's average weekly rate under this paragraph (d)(6)(ii)(B) is being computed for a measurement period and that measurement period is shorter than six months, the six-month period ending with the close of the measurement period is used to compute the average hours of service.

(iii) *Treatment of continuing employee.*—Under the look-back measurement method, an employee treated as a continuing employee retains, upon resumption of services, the status that employee had with respect to the application of any stability period (for example, if the continuing employee returns during a stability period in which the employee is treated as a full-time employee, the employee is treated as a full-time employee upon return and through the end of that stability period). For purposes of the preceding sentence, a continuing employee treated as a full-time employee is treated as offered coverage upon resumption of services if the employee is offered coverage as of the first day that employee is credited with an hour of service, or, if later, as soon as administratively practicable. For this purpose, offering coverage by no later than the first day of the calendar month following resumption of services is deemed to be as soon as administratively practicable. If a continuing employee returns during a stability period in which the employee is treated as a full-time employee and the employer previously made the employee an offer of coverage with respect to the entire stability period and the employee declined the offer, the employer will continue to be treated as having offered coverage for that stability period and the employer need not make a new offer of coverage for the remainder of the ongoing stability period due to the employee's resumption of services.

(iv) *Rule of parity.*—For purposes of determining the period after which an employee may be treated as having terminated employment and having been rehired, an applicable large employer may choose a period, measured in weeks, of at least four consecutive weeks during which the employee was not credited with any hours of service that exceeds the number of weeks of that employee's period of employment with the applicable large employer immediately preceding the period and that is shorter than 13 weeks (for an employee of an educational organization employer, a period that is shorter than 26 weeks). For purposes of the preceding sentence, the duration of the immediately preceding period of employment is determined after application to that period of employment of the averaging methods described in paragraphs (d)(6)(i)(B) and (d)(6)(ii)(B) of this section (relating to employment break periods and special unpaid leave), if applicable.

(v) *International transfers.*—An employer may treat an employee as having terminated employment if the employee transfers to a position at the same applicable large employer (including a different applicable large employer member that is part of the same applicable large employer) if the position is anticipated to continue indefinitely or for at least 12 months and if substantially all of the compensation will constitute income from sources without the United States (within the meaning of sections 861 through 863 and the regulations thereunder). With respect to an employee transferring from a position that was anticipated to continue indefinitely or for at least 12 months and in which substantially all of the compensation for the hours of service constitutes income from sources without the United States (within the meaning of sections 861 through 863 and the regulations thereunder) to a position at the same applicable large employer (including a different applicable large employer member that is part of the same applicable large employer) with respect to which substantially all of the compensation will constitute U.S. source income, the employer may treat that employee as a new hire to the extent consistent with the rules related to rehired employees in paragraph (d)(6) of this section.

(vi) *Anti-abuse rule.*—For purposes of this paragraph (d)(6), any hour of service is disregarded if the hour of service is credited, or the services giving rise to the crediting of the hour of service are requested or required of the employee, for a purpose of avoiding or undermining the application of the employee rehire rules under paragraph (d)(6) of this section, or the application of the averaging method for employment break periods under paragraph (d)(6)(ii)(B) of this section. For example, if an employee of an educational organization would otherwise have a period with no hours of service to which the rules under paragraph (d)(6)(ii)(B) of this section would apply, but for the employer's request or requirement that the employee perform one or more hours of service for a purpose of avoiding the application of those rules, any such hours of service for the week are disregarded, and the rules under paragraph (d)(6)(ii)(B) of this section will apply.

(vii) *Examples.*—The following examples illustrate the provisions of paragraph (d)(6) of this section. All employers in these examples are applicable large employer members with 200 full-time employees (including full-time equivalent employees), each is in a different applicable large employer group, and each determines full-time employee status under the look-back measurement method. None of the periods during which an employee is not credited with an hour of service for an employer involve special unpaid leave or the employee being credited with hours of service for any applicable large employer member in the same applicable large employer as the employer.

*Example 1.* (i) *Facts.* As of April 1, 2015, Employee A has been an employee of Employer Z (which is not an educational organization) for 10 years. On April 1, 2015, Employee A terminates employment and is not credited with an hour of service until June 1, 2015, when Employer Z rehires Employee A and Employee A continues as an employee through December 31, 2015, which is the close of the measurement period as applied by Employer Z.

(ii) *Conclusion.* Because the period for which Employee A is not credited with any hours of service is not longer than Employee A's prior period of employment and is less than 13 weeks, Employee A is not treated as having terminated employment and been rehired for purposes of determining whether Employee A is treated as a new employee upon resumption of services. Therefore, Employee A's hours of service prior to termination are required to be taken into account for purposes of the measurement period, and Employee A's period with no hours of service is taken into account as a period of zero hours of service during the measurement period.

*Example 2.* (i) *Facts.* Same facts as *Example 1*, except that Employee A is rehired on December 1, 2015.

(ii) *Conclusion.* Because the period during which Employee A is not credited with an hour of service for Employer Z exceeds 13 weeks, Employee A is treated as having terminated employment on April 1, 2015, and having been rehired as a new employee on December 1, 2015, for purposes of determining Employee A's full-time employee status. Because Employee A is treated as a new employee, Employee A's hours of service prior to termination are not taken into account for purposes of the measurement period, and the period between termination and rehire with no hours of service is not taken into account in the new measurement period that begins after the employee is rehired.

*Example 3.* (i) *Facts.* Employee B is employed by Employer Y, an educational organization. Employee B is employed for 38 hours of service per week on average from September 7, 2014, through May 23, 2015, and then does not provide services (and is not otherwise credited with an hour of service) during the summer break when the school is generally not in session. Employee B resumes providing services for Employer Y on September 7, 2015, when the new school year begins.

(ii) *Conclusion.* Because the period from May 24, 2015 through September 5, 2015 (a total of 15 weeks), during which Employee B is not credited with an hour of service does not exceed 26 weeks, and also does not exceed the number of weeks of Employee B's immediately preceding period of employment, Employee B is not treated as having terminated employment on May 24, 2015, and having been rehired on September 6, 2015. Also, for purposes of determining Employee B's average hours of service per week for the measurement period, Employee B is credited, under the averaging method for employment break periods applicable to educational organizations, as having an average of 38 hours of service per week for the 15 weeks between May 24, 2015 and September 5, 2015, during which Employee B otherwise was credited with no hours of service. However, Employer Y is not required to credit more than 501 hours of service for the employment break period (15 weeks x 38 hours = 570 hours).

*Example 4.* (i) *Facts.* Same facts as *Example 3*, except that Employee B does not resume providing services for Employer Y until December 5, 2015.

(ii) *Conclusion.* Because the period from May 24, 2015 through December 5, 2015, exceeds 26 weeks, Employee B may be treated as having terminated employment on May 24, 2015, and having been rehired on December 5, 2015. Because Employee B is treated as a new employee on December 5, 2015, Employee B's hours of service prior to termination are not taken into account for purposes of the measurement period, and the period between termination and rehire with no hours of service is not taken into account in the new measurement period that begins after Employee B is rehired. The averaging method for employment break periods applicable to educational organizations does not apply because Employee B is treated as a new employee rather than a continuing employee as of the date of resumption of services.

(e) *Use of the look-back measurement method and the monthly measurement method for different categories of employees.*—Different applicable large employer members of the same applicable large employer may use different methods of determining full-time employee status (that is, either the monthly measurement method or the look-back measurement method). In addition, an applicable large employer member may use either the monthly measurement method or the look-

back measurement method for each of the categories of employees set forth in paragraphs (d)(1)(v) and (d)(3)(v) of this section, and is not required to use the same method for all categories.

(f) *Changes in employment status resulting in a change in full-time employee determination method.*—(1) *Change in employment status from a position to which a look-back measurement method applies to a position to which the monthly measurement method applies, or vice versa.*—(i) *Change from look-back measurement method to monthly measurement method.*—For an employee transferring from a position under which the look-back measurement method is used to determine the employee's status as a full-time employee, to a position under which the monthly measurement method is used to determine the employee's status as a full-time employee, the following rules apply:

(A) For an employee who at the time of the change of position is in a stability period under which the employee is treated as a full-time employee, the employer must continue to treat the employee as a full-time employee through the end of the stability period;

(B) For an employee who at the time of the change of position is in a stability period under which the employee is not treated as a full-time employee, the employer may continue to treat the employee as not a full-time employee through the end of the stability period, or may apply the monthly measurement method set forth in paragraph (c) of this section through the end of the stability period beginning with any calendar month including the calendar month in which the change in employment status occurs or any subsequent calendar month;

(C) For the stability period associated with the measurement period during which the change in employment status occurs, the employer must treat the employee as a full-time employee for any calendar month during which the employee either would be treated as a full-time employee under the stability period that would have applied based on the measurement period in which the change in employment status occurred or would be treated as a full-time employee under the monthly measurement method; and

(D) For any calendar month subsequent to the stability period identified in paragraph (f)(1)(i)(C) of this section, the monthly measurement method applies for determination of the employee's status as a full-time employee.

(ii) *Change from monthly measurement method to look-back measurement method.*—For an employee who is transferring from a position under which the monthly measurement method is used to determine the employee's status as a full-time employee, to a position under which a look-back measurement method is used to determine the employee's status as a full-time employee, the following rules apply:

(A) For the remainder of the applicable stability period during which the change in employment status occurs, the employer must continue to use the monthly measurement method to determine the employee's status as a full-time employee unless the employee's hours of service prior to the change in employment status would have resulted in the employee being treated as a full-time employee during the stability period in which the change in employment status occurs, in which case the employer must treat the employee as a full-time employee for that stability period;

(B) For the applicable stability period following the measurement period during which the change in employment status occurs, the employer must treat the employee as a full-time employee for any calendar month during which the employee either would be treated as a full-time employee based on the measurement period during which the change in employment status occurs or would be treated as a full-time employee under the monthly measurement method; and

(C) For any calendar month subsequent to the stability period identified in paragraph (f)(1)(ii)(B) of this section, the look-back measurement method applies for determination of the employee's status as a full-time employee.

(iii) *Examples.*—The following examples illustrate the rules of this paragraph (f). In each example, the employer is an applicable large employer with 200 full-time employees (including FTEs). For each example, the employer uses the monthly measurement method for determining whether a salaried employee is a full-time employee, and the look-back measurement method for determining whether an hourly employee is a full-time employee with a measurement period from October 15 through October 14 of the following calendar year, and a stability period from January 1 through December 31. In each case, the relevant employee has been employed continuously for several years.

*Example 1 (Look-back measurement method to monthly measurement method).* Employee A is an hourly employee. Based on Employee A's hours of service from October 15, 2015, through October 14, 2016, Employee A is treated as a full-time employee from January

1, 2017, through December 31, 2017. On July 1, 2017, Employee A transfers from a position as an hourly employee to a position as a salaried employee. For the months July 2017 through December 2017, Employee A must be treated as a full-time employee. Employee A is employed for hours of service from October 15, 2016, through October 14, 2017, such that under the applicable look-back measurement method Employee A would be treated as a full-time employee for the period of January 1, 2018, through December 31, 2018. Accordingly, Employee A must be treated as a full-time employee for the calendar year 2018. For calendar year 2019, the determination of whether Employee A is a full-time employee is made under the monthly measurement method.

*Example 2 (Look-back measurement method to monthly measurement method).* Same facts as *Example 1*, except that based on Employee A's hours of service from October 15, 2015, through October 14, 2016, Employee A is not treated as a full-time employee from January 1, 2017, through December 31, 2017. For the months July 2017 through December 2017, Employer Z may either treat Employee A as not a full-time employee or apply the monthly measurement method to determine Employee A's status as a full-time employee. Employee A is employed for hours of service from October 15, 2016, through October 14, 2017, such that under the applicable look-back measurement method Employee A would be treated as a full-time employee for the period of January 1, 2018, through December 31, 2018. Employee A must be treated as a full-time employee for the calendar year 2018. For calendar year 2019, the determination of whether Employee A is a full-time employee is made under the monthly measurement method.

*Example 3 (Look-back measurement method to monthly measurement method).* Same facts as *Example 1*, except that Employee A is employed for hours of service from October 15, 2016, through October 14, 2017, such that under the applicable look-back measurement method Employee A would not be treated as a full-time employee for the period of January 1, 2018, through December 31, 2018. For the calendar year 2018, Employer Z must treat Employee A as a full-time employee only for calendar months during which Employee A would be a full-time employee under the monthly measurement method. For calendar year 2019, the determination of whether Employee A is a full-time employee is made under the monthly measurement method.

*Example 4 (Monthly measurement method to look-back measurement method).* Employee B is a salaried employee of Employer Y. On July 1, 2017, Employee B transfers to an hourly employee position. Based on Employee B's hours of service from October 15, 2015, through October 14, 2016, Employee B would have been treated as a full-time employee for the stability period from January 1, 2017, through December 31, 2017, had the look-back measurement method applicable to hourly employees applied to Employee B for the entire stability period. For the calendar months January 2017 through June 2017 (prior to Employee B's change to hourly employee status), Employee B's status as a full-time employee is determined using the monthly measurement method. For the calendar months July 2017 through December 2017, Employer Y must treat Employee B as a full-time employee because Employee B would have been treated as a full-time employee during that portion of the stability period had the look-back measurement method applied to Employee B for that entire stability period. Employee B is employed for hours of service from October 15, 2016, through October 14, 2017, such that under the applicable look-back measurement method Employee B would be treated as a full-time employee for the period January 1, 2018, through December 31, 2018. Accordingly, Employee B must be treated as a full-time employee for the calendar year 2018. For calendar year 2019, the determination of whether Employee B is a full-time employee is made under the applicable look-back measurement method.

*Example 5 (Monthly measurement method to look-back measurement method).* Same facts as *Example 4*, except that based on Employee B's hours of service from October 15, 2015, through October 14, 2016, Employee B would not have been treated as a full-time employee from January 1, 2017, through December 31, 2017. For the calendar months of 2017, Employer Y applies the monthly measurement method to determine Employee B's status as a full-time employee. Employee B is employed for hours of service from October 15, 2016, through October 14, 2017, such that under the applicable look-back measurement method Employee B would be treated as a full-time employee for the period January 1, 2018, through December 31, 2018. Accordingly, Employee B must be treated as a full-time employee for the calendar year 2018. For calendar year 2019, the determination of whether Employee B is a full-time employee is made under the applicable look-back measurement method.

*Example 6 (Monthly measurement method to look-back measurement method).* Same facts as *Example 4*, except that Employee B is employed for hours of service from October 15, 2016, through October 14, 2017, such that under the applicable look-back measurement method Employee B would not be treated as a full-time employee for

the period of January 1, 2018, through December 31, 2018. For the calendar year 2018, Employer Y must treat Employee B as a full-time employee only for calendar months during which Employee B would be a full-time employee under the monthly measurement method.

(2) *Special rule for certain employees to whom minimum value coverage has been continuously offered.*—(i) *In general.*—Notwithstanding the rules in paragraphs (e) and (f) of this section, an employer using the look-back measurement method to determine the full-time employee status of an employee may apply the monthly measurement method to that employee beginning on the first day of the fourth full calendar month following the calendar month in which the employee experiences a change in employment status such that, if the employee had begun employment in the new position or status, the employee would have reasonably been expected not to be employed on average at least 30 hours of service per week (for example, the employee has changed to a part-time position of only 20 hours of service per week). This rule only applies with respect to an employee to whom the applicable large employer member offered minimum value coverage by the first day of the calendar month following the employee's initial three full calendar months of employment through the calendar month in which the change in employment status described in this paragraph (f)(2) occurs, and only if the employee actually averages less than 30 hours of service per week for each of the three full calendar months following the change in employment status. For the three full calendar months between the employee's change in employment status and the application of the monthly measurement method, the employee's full-time employee status is determined based on the employee's status during the applicable stability period(s). Under this rule, an employer may apply the monthly measurement method to an employee even if the employer does not apply the monthly measurement method to the other employees in the same category of employees under paragraph (d)(1)(v) or (d)(3)(v) of this section (for example, under this method an employer could apply the monthly measurement method to an hourly employee, even if the employer uses the look-back measurement method to determine full-time employee status of all other hourly employees). The employer may continue to apply the monthly measurement method through the end of the first full measurement period (and any associated administrative period) that would have applied had the employee remained under the applicable look-back measurement method.

(ii) *Examples.*—The following examples illustrate the rule of paragraphs (f)(2) of this section. In each example, the employer is an applicable large employer with 200 full-time employees (including FTEs).

*Example 1 (New variable hour employee, no delay in coverage, becomes non-full-time employee).* (i) *Facts.* Employer Z, an applicable large employer, uses the look-back measurement method to determine the full-time employee status for all of its employees. On May 10, 2015, Employer Z hired Employee A who is a variable hour employee. Although Employee A is a new variable hour employee, so that Employer Z could wait until the end of an initial measurement period to offer coverage to Employee A without an assessable payment under section 4980H with respect to Employee A, Employer Z offers coverage that provides minimum value to Employee A on September 1, 2015. For its ongoing employees, Employer Z has chosen to use a 12-month standard measurement period starting October 15 and a 12-month stability period associated with that standard measurement period starting January 1. Employee A continues in employment with Employer Z for over five years and averages more than 30 hours of service per week for all measurement periods through the measurement period ending October 14, 2020. On February 12, 2021, Employee A experiences a change in position of employment with Employer Z to a position under which Employer Z reasonably expects Employee A to average less than 30 hours of service per week. For the calendar months after February 2021, Employee A averages less than 30 hours of service per week. Employer Z offered Employee A coverage that provided minimum value continuously from September 1, 2015, through May 31, 2021. Effective June 1, 2021, Employer Z elects to apply the monthly measurement method to determine Employee A's status as a full-time employee for the remainder of the stability period ending December 31, 2021, and the calendar year 2022 (which is through the end of the first full measurement period following the change in employment status plus the associated administrative period). Applying the stability period beginning January 1, 2021, Employer Z treats Employee A as a full-time employee for each calendar month from January 2021 through May 2021. Applying the monthly measurement method, for each calendar month from June 2021 through December 2022, Employer Z treats Employee A as not a full-time employee.

(ii) *Conclusion.* Because Employer Z offered coverage that provided minimum value to Employee A from no later than the first day of the fourth full calendar month following Employee A's start date through the calendar month in which the change in employment status occurred, and because Employee A did not average 30 hours of service per week for any of the three calendar months immediately following Employee A's change in employment status to an employee not reasonably expected to average 30 hours of service per week, Employer Z may use the monthly measurement method to determine the full-time employee status of Employee A beginning on the first day of the fourth month following the change in employment status (June 1, 2021) through the end of the first full measurement period (plus any associated administrative period) immediately following the change in employment status (December 31, 2022). Because Employee A did not average at least 30 hours of service per week for any calendar month from June 2021 through December 2022, Employer Z has properly treated Employee A as not a full-time employee for those calendar months.

*Example 2 (New full-time employee, no delay in coverage, becomes non-full-time employee).* (i) *Facts.* Same facts as *Example 1*, except that at Employee A's start date, Employer Z reasonably expects that Employee A will average at least 30 hours of service per week. Accordingly, Employer Z offers coverage to Employee A beginning on September 1, 2015, and offers coverage continuously to Employee A for all calendar months through May 2021.

(ii) *Conclusion.* Same as *Example 1*.

(g) *Nonpayment or late payment of premiums.*—An applicable large employer member will not be treated as failing to offer to a full-time employee (and his or her dependents) the opportunity to enroll in minimum essential coverage under an eligible employer-sponsored plan for an employee whose coverage under the plan is terminated during the coverage period solely due to the employee failing to make a timely payment of the employee portion of the premium. This treatment continues only through the end of the coverage period (typically the plan year). For this purpose, the rules in § 54.4980B-8, Q&A-5(a), (c), (d) and (e) apply under this section to the payment for coverage with respect to a full-time employee in the same manner that they apply to payment for COBRA continuation coverage under § 54.4980B-8.

(h) *Additional guidance.*—With respect to the determination of full-time employee status, including determination of hours of service, the Commissioner may prescribe additional guidance of general applicability, published in the Internal Revenue Bulletin (see § 601.601(d)(2)(ii)(b) of this chapter).

(i) *Effective/applicability date.*—This section is applicable for periods after December 31, 2014. [Reg. § 54.4980H-3.]

☐ [T.D. 9655, 2-10-2014.]

**[Reg. § 54.4980H-4]**

**§ 54.4980H-4. Assessable payments under section 4980H(a).**— (a) *In general.*—If an applicable large employer member fails to offer to its full-time employees (and their dependents) the opportunity to enroll in minimum essential coverage under an eligible employer-sponsored plan for any calendar month, and the applicable large employer member has received a Section 1411 Certification with respect to at least one full-time employee, an assessable payment is imposed. For the calendar month, the applicable large employer member will owe an assessable payment equal to the product of the section 4980H(a) applicable payment amount and the number of full-time employees of the applicable large employer member (other than employees in a limited non-assessment period for certain employees and as adjusted in accordance with paragraph (e) of this section). For purposes of this paragraph (a), an applicable large employer member is treated as offering such coverage to its full-time employees (and their dependents) for a calendar month if, for that month, it offers such coverage to all but five percent (or, if greater, five) of its full-time employees (provided that an employee is treated as having been offered coverage only if the employer also offers coverage to that employee's dependents). For purposes of the preceding sentence, an employee in a limited non-assessment period for certain employees is not included in the calculation.

(b) *Offer of coverage.*—(1) *In general.*—An applicable large employer member will not be treated as having made an offer of coverage to a full-time employee for a plan year if the employee does not have an effective opportunity to elect to enroll in the coverage at least once with respect to the plan year, or does not have an effective opportunity to decline to enroll if the coverage offered does not provide minimum value or requires an employee contribution for any calendar month of more than 9.5 percent of a monthly amount determined as the federal poverty line for a single individual for the applicable calendar year, divided by 12. For this purpose, the applicable federal poverty line is the federal poverty line for the 48 contiguous states and the District of Columbia. Whether an employee

has an effective opportunity to enroll or to decline to enroll is determined based on all the relevant facts and circumstances, including adequacy of notice of the availability of the offer of coverage, the period of time during which acceptance of the offer of coverage may be made, and any other conditions on the offer. An employee's election of coverage from a prior year that continues for the next plan year unless the employee affirmatively elects to opt out of the plan constitutes an offer of coverage for purposes of section 4980H.

(2) *Offer of coverage on behalf of another entity.*—For purposes of section 4980H, an offer of coverage by one applicable large employer member to an employee for a calendar month is treated as an offer of coverage by all applicable large employer members for that calendar month. In addition, an offer of coverage made to an employee on behalf of a contributing employer under a multiemployer or single employer Taft-Hartley plan or multiple employer welfare arrangement (MEWA) is treated as made by the employer. For an offer of coverage to an employee performing services for an employer that is a client of a staffing firm, in cases in which the staffing firm is not the common law employer of the individual and the staffing firm makes an offer of coverage to the employee on behalf of the client employer under a plan established or maintained by the staffing firm, the offer is treated as made by the client employer for purposes of section 4980H only if the fee the client employer would pay to the staffing firm for an employee enrolled in health coverage under the plan is higher than the fee the client employer would pay the staffing firm for the same employee if that employee did not enroll in health coverage under the plan.

(c) *Partial calendar month.*—If an applicable large employer member fails to offer coverage to a full-time employee for any day of a calendar month, that employee is treated as not offered coverage during that entire month, regardless of whether the employer uses the payroll period rule set forth in § 54.4980H-3(d)(1)(ii) or the weekly rule set forth in § 54.4980H-3(c)(3) to determine full-time employee status for the calendar month. However, in a calendar month in which the employment of a full-time employee terminates, if the employee would have been offered coverage for the entire calendar month had the employee been employed for the entire calendar month, the employee is treated as having been offered coverage for that entire calendar month. In addition, an applicable large employer member is not subject to an assessable payment under section 4980H with respect to an employee for the calendar month in which the employee's start date occurs if the start date is on a date other than the first day of the calendar month, and, in addition, with respect to the calendar month in which the start date occurs, such an employee is not included for purposes of the calculation of any potential liability under section 4980H(a).

(d) *Application to applicable large employer member.*—The liability for an assessable payment under section 4980H(a) for a calendar month with respect to a full-time employee applies solely to the applicable large employer member that was the employer of that employee for that calendar month. For an employee who was an employee of more than one applicable large employer member of the same applicable large employer during a calendar month, the liability for the assessable payment under section 4980H(a) for a calendar month applies to the applicable large employer member for whom the employee has the greatest number of hours of service for that calendar month (if the employee has an equal number of hours of service for two or more applicable large employer members of the same applicable large employer for the calendar month, those applicable large employer members can treat one of those members as the employer of that employee for that calendar month for purposes of this section, and if the members do not select one member, or select in an inconsistent manner, the IRS will select a member to be treated as the employer of that employee for purposes of the assessable payment determination). For a calendar month, an applicable large employer member may be liable for an assessable payment under section 4980H(a) or under section 4980H(b), but will not be liable for an assessable payment under both section 4980H(a) and section 4980H(b).

(e) *Allocated reduction of 30 full-time employees.*—For purposes of the liability calculation under paragraph (a) of this section, with respect to each calendar month, an applicable large employer member's number of full-time employees is reduced by that member's allocable share of 30. The applicable large employer member's allocation is equal to 30 allocated ratably among all members of the applicable large employer on the basis of the number of full-time employees employed by each applicable large employer member during the calendar month (after application of the rules of paragraph (d) of this section addressing employees who work for more than one applicable large employer member during a calendar month). If an applicable large employer member's total allocation is not a whole number, the allocation is rounded to the next highest whole number. This rounding rule may result in the aggregate reduction for the entire group of applicable large employer members exceeding 30.

(f) *Example.*—The following example illustrates the provisions of paragraphs (a) and (e) of this section.

*Example.* (i) *Facts.* Applicable large employer member Z and applicable large employer member Y are the two members of an applicable large employer. Applicable large employer member Z employs 40 full-time employees in each calendar month of 2017. Applicable large employer member Y employs 35 full-time employees in each calendar month of 2017. Assume that for 2017, the applicable payment amount for a calendar month is $2,000 divided by 12. Applicable large employer member Z does not sponsor an eligible employer-sponsored plan for any calendar month of 2017, and receives a Section 1411 Certification for 2017 with respect to at least one of its full-time employees. Applicable large employer member Y sponsors an eligible employer-sponsored plan under which all of its full-time employees are eligible for minimum essential coverage.

(ii) *Conclusion.* Pursuant to section 4980H(a) and this section, applicable large employer member Z is subject to an assessable payment under section 4980H(a) for 2017 of $48,000, which is equal to 24 × $2,000 (40 full-time employees reduced by 16 (its allocable share of the 30-employee offset (($40/75) × 30 = 16)) and then multiplied by $2,000). Applicable large employer member Y is not subject to an assessable payment under section 4980H(a) for 2017.

(g) *Additional guidance.*—With respect to assessable payments under section 4980H(a), the Commissioner may prescribe additional guidance of general applicability, published in the Internal Revenue Bulletin (see § 601.601(d)(2)(ii)(b) of this chapter).

(h) *Effective/applicability date.*—This section is applicable for periods after December 31, 2014. [Reg. § 54.4980H-4.]

☐ [T.D. 9655, 2-10-2014.]

## [Reg. § 54.4980H-5]

§ 54.4980H-5. **Assessable payments under section 4980H(b).**—(a) *In general.*—If an applicable large employer member offers to its full-time employees (and their dependents) the opportunity to enroll in minimum essential coverage under an eligible employer-sponsored plan for any calendar month (including an offer of coverage to all but five percent or less (or, if greater, five or less) of its full-time employees (provided that an employee is treated as having been offered coverage only if the employer also offers coverage to that employee's dependents)) and the applicable large employer member has received a Section 1411 Certification with respect to one or more full-time employees of the applicable large employer member, then there is imposed on the applicable large employer member an assessable payment equal to the product of the number of full-time employees of the applicable large employer member for which it has received a Section 1411 Certification (minus the number of those employees in a limited non-assessment period for certain employees and the number of other employees who were offered the opportunity to enroll in minimum essential coverage under an eligible employer-sponsored plan that satisfied minimum value and met one or more of the affordability safe harbors described in paragraph (e) of this section) and the section 4980H(b) applicable payment amount. Notwithstanding the foregoing, the aggregate amount of assessable payment determined under this paragraph (a) with respect to all employees of an applicable large employer member for any calendar month may not exceed the product of the section 4980H(a) applicable payment amount and the number of full-time employees of the applicable large employer member during that calendar month (reduced by the applicable large employer member's ratable allocation of the 30 employee reduction under § 54.4980H-4(e)).

(b) *Offer of coverage.*—For purposes of this section, the same rules with respect to an offer of coverage for purposes of section 4980H(a) apply. See § 54.4980H-4.

(c) *Partial calendar month.*—If an applicable large employer member fails to offer coverage to a full-time employee for any day of a calendar month, that employee is treated as not offered coverage during that entire month, regardless of whether the employer uses the payroll period rule set forth in § 54.4980H-3(d)(1)(ii) or the weekly rule set forth in § 54.4980H-3(c)(3) to determine full-time employee status for the calendar month. However, in a calendar month in which a full-time employee's employment terminates, if the employee would have been offered coverage if the employee had been employed for the entire month, the employee is treated as having been offered coverage during that month. Also, an applicable large employer member is not subject to an assessable payment under section 4980H with respect to an employee for the calendar month in which the employee's start date occurs if the start date is on a date other than the first day of the calendar month.

(d) *Applicability to applicable large employer member.*—The liability for an assessable payment under section 4980H(b) for a calendar month with respect to a full-time employee applies solely to the applicable large employer member that was the employer of that employee for that calendar month. For an employee who was a full-time employee of more than one applicable large employer member during that calendar month, the liability for the assessable payment under section 4980H(b) for a calendar month applies to the applicable large employer member for whom the employee has the greatest number of hours of service for that calendar month (if the employee has an equal number of hours of service for two or more applicable large employer members for the calendar month, those applicable large employer members can treat one of those members as the employer of that employee for that calendar month for purposes of this paragraph (d), and if the members do not select one member, or select in an inconsistent manner, the IRS will select a member to be treated as the employer of that employee for purposes of the assessable payment determination). For a calendar month, an applicable large employer member may be liable for an assessable payment under section 4980H(a) or under section 4980H(b), but will not be liable for an assessable payment under both section 4980H(a) and section 4980H(b).

(e) *Affordability.*—(1) *In general.*—An employee who is offered coverage by an applicable large employer member may be eligible for an applicable premium tax credit or cost-sharing reduction if that offer of coverage is not affordable within the meaning of section 36B(c)(2)(C)(i) and the regulations thereunder.

(2) *Affordability safe harbors for section 4980H(b) purposes.*—The affordability safe harbors set forth in paragraph (e)(2)(ii) through (iv) of this section apply solely for purposes of section 4980H(b), so that an applicable large employer member that offers minimum essential coverage providing minimum value will not be subject to an assessable payment under section 4980H(b) with respect to any employee receiving the applicable premium tax credit or cost-sharing reduction for a period for which the coverage is determined to be affordable under the requirements of an affordability safe harbor. This rule applies even if the applicable large employer member's offer of coverage that meets the requirements of an affordability safe harbor is not affordable for a particular employee under section 36B(c)(2)(C)(i) and an applicable premium tax credit or cost-sharing reduction is allowed or paid with respect to that employee.

(i) *Conditions of using an affordability safe harbor.*—An applicable large employer member may use one or more of the affordability safe harbors described in this paragraph (e)(2) only if the employer offers its full-time employees and their dependents the opportunity to enroll in minimum essential coverage under an eligible employer-sponsored plan that provides minimum value with respect to the self-only coverage offered to the employee. Use of any of the safe harbors is optional for an applicable large employer member, and an applicable large employer member may choose to apply the safe harbors for any reasonable category of employees, provided it does so on a uniform and consistent basis for all employees in a category. Reasonable categories generally include specified job categories, nature of compensation (hourly or salary), geographic location, and similar bona fide business criteria. An enumeration of employees by name or other specific criteria having substantially the same effect as an enumeration by name is not considered a reasonable category.

(ii) *Form W-2 safe harbor-.*—(A) *Full-year offer of coverage.*—An employer will not be subject to an assessable payment under section 4980H(b) with respect to a full-time employee if that employee's required contribution for the calendar year for the employer's lowest cost self-only coverage that provides minimum value during the entire calendar year (excluding COBRA or other continuation coverage except with respect to an active employee eligible for continuation coverage) does not exceed 9.5 percent of that employee's Form W-2 wages from the employer (and any other member of the same applicable large employer that also pays wages to that employee) for the calendar year. Application of this safe harbor is determined after the end of the calendar year and on an employee-by-employee basis, taking into account the Form W-2 wages and the required employee contribution for that year. In addition, to qualify for this safe harbor, the employee's required contribution must remain a consistent amount or percentage of all Form W-2 wages during the calendar year (or during the plan year for plans with non-calendar year plan years) so that an applicable large employer member is not permitted to make discretionary adjustments to the required employee contribution for a pay period. A periodic contribution that is based on a consistent percentage of all Form W-2 wages may be subject to a dollar limit specified by the employer.

(B) *Adjustment for partial-year offer of coverage.*—For an employee not offered coverage for an entire calendar year, the Form W-2 safe harbor is applied by adjusting the Form W-2 wages to reflect the period for which coverage was offered, then determining whether the employee's required contribution for the employer's lowest cost self-only coverage that provides minimum value, totaled for the periods during which coverage was offered, does not exceed 9.5 percent of the adjusted amount of Form W-2 wages. To adjust Form W-2 wages for this purpose, the Form W-2 wages are multiplied by a fraction equal to the number of calendar months for which coverage was offered over the number of calendar months in the employee's period of employment with the employer during the calendar year. For this purpose, if coverage is offered during at least one day during the calendar month, or the employee is employed for at least one day during the calendar month, the entire calendar month is counted in determining the applicable fraction.

(iii) *Rate of pay safe harbor.*—An applicable large employer member satisfies the rate of pay safe harbor with respect to an hourly employee for a calendar month if the employee's required contribution for the calendar month for the applicable large employer member's lowest cost self-only coverage that provides minimum value does not exceed 9.5 percent of an amount equal to 130 hours multiplied by the lower of the employee's hourly rate of pay as of the first day of the coverage period (generally the first day of the plan year) or the employee's lowest hourly rate of pay during the calendar month. An applicable large employer member satisfies the rate of pay safe harbor with respect to a non-hourly employee for a calendar month if the employee's required contribution for the calendar month for the applicable large employer member's lowest cost self-only coverage that provides minimum value does not exceed 9.5 percent of the employee's monthly salary, as of the first day of the coverage period (instead of 130 multiplied by the hourly rate of pay); provided that if the monthly salary is reduced, including due to a reduction in work hours, the safe harbor is not available, and, solely for purposes of this paragraph (e)(2)(iii), an applicable large employer member may use any reasonable method for converting payroll periods to monthly salary. For this purpose, if coverage is offered during at least one day during the calendar month, the entire calendar month is counted both for purposes of determining the assumed income for the calendar month and for determining the employee's share of the premium for the calendar month.

(iv) *Federal poverty line safe harbor.*—An applicable large employer member satisfies the federal poverty line safe harbor with respect to an employee for a calendar month if the employee's required contribution for the calendar month for the applicable large employer member's lowest cost self-only coverage that provides minimum value does not exceed 9.5 percent of a monthly amount determined as the federal poverty line for a single individual for the applicable calendar year, divided by 12. For this purpose, if coverage is offered during at least one day during the calendar month, the entire calendar month is counted both for purposes of determining the monthly amount for the calendar month and for determining the employee's share of the premium for the calendar month. For this purpose, the applicable federal poverty line is the federal poverty line for the State in which the employee is employed.

(v) *Examples.*—The following examples illustrate the application of the affordability safe harbors described in this paragraph (e)(2). In each example, each employer is an applicable large employer member with 200 full-time employees (including full-time equivalent employees).

*Example 1 (Form W-2 wages safe harbor).* (i) *Facts.* Employee A is employed by Employer Z consistently from January 1, 2015, through December 31, 2015. In addition, Employer Z offers Employee A and his dependents minimum essential coverage during that period that provides minimum value. The employee contribution for self-only coverage is $100 per calendar month, or $1,200 for the calendar year. For 2015, Employee A's Form W-2 wages with respect to employment with Employer Z are $24,000.

(ii) *Conclusion.* Because the employee contribution for 2015 is less than 9.5 percent of Employee A's Form W-2 wages for 2015, the coverage offered is treated as affordable with respect to Employee A for 2015 ($1,200 is 5 percent of $24,000).

*Example 2 (Form W-2 wages safe harbor).* (i) *Facts.* Employee B is employed by Employer Y from January 1, 2015, through September 30, 2015. In addition, Employer Y offers Employee B and his dependents minimum essential coverage during that period that provides minimum value. The employee contribution for self-only coverage is $100 per calendar month, or $900 for Employee B's period of employment. For 2015, Employee B's Form W-2 wages with respect to employment with Employer Y are $18,000. For purposes of applying the affordability safe harbor, the Form W-2 wages are multiplied by 9/9 (9 calendar months of coverage offered over 9 months of employment during the calendar year) or 1. Accordingly, affordability is determined by comparing the adjusted Form W-2 wages ($18,000) to the employee contribution for the period for which coverage was offered ($900).

(ii) *Conclusion.* Because the employee contribution for 2015 is less than 9.5 percent of Employee B's adjusted Form W-2 wages for 2015, the coverage offered is treated as affordable with respect to Employee B for 2015 ($900 is 5 percent of $18,000).

*Example 3 (Form W-2 wages safe harbor).* (i) *Facts.* Employee C is employed by Employer X from May 15, 2015, through December 31, 2015. In addition, Employer X offers Employee C and her dependents minimum essential coverage during the period from August 1, 2015, through December 31, 2015, that provides minimum value. The employee contribution for self-only coverage is $100 per calendar month, or $500 for Employee C's period of employment. For 2015, Employee C's Form W-2 wages with respect to employment with Employer X are $15,000. For purposes of applying the affordability safe harbor, the Form W-2 wages are multiplied by 5/8 (5 calendar months of coverage offered over 8 months of employment during the calendar year). Accordingly, affordability is determined by comparing the adjusted Form W-2 wages ($9,375 or $15,000 × 5/8) to the employee contribution for the period for which coverage was offered ($500).

(ii) *Conclusion.* Because the employee contribution of $500 is less than 9.5 percent of $9,375 (Employee C's adjusted Form W-2 wages for 2015), the coverage offered is treated as affordable with respect to Employee C for 2015 ($500 is 5.33 percent of $9,375).

*Example 4 (Rate of pay safe harbor).* (i) *Facts.* Employer W offers its full-time employees and their dependents minimum essential coverage that provides minimum value. For the 2016 calendar year, Employer W is using the rate of pay safe harbor to establish premium contribution amounts for full-time employees paid at a rate of $7.25 per hour (the minimum wage in Employer W's jurisdiction) for each calendar month of the entire 2016 calendar year. Employer W can apply the affordability safe harbor by using an assumed monthly income amount that is based on an assumed 130 hours of service multiplied by $7.25 per hour ($942.50 per calendar month). To satisfy the safe harbor, Employer W would set the employee monthly contribution amount at a rate that does not exceed 9.5 percent of the assumed monthly income of $942.50. Employer W sets the employee contribution for self-only coverage at $85 per calendar month for 2016.

(ii) *Conclusion.* Because $85 is less than 9.5 percent of the employee's assumed monthly income at a $7.25 rate of pay, the coverage offered is treated as affordable under the rate of pay safe harbor for each calendar month of 2016 ($85 is 9.01 percent of $942.50).

*Example 5 (Rate of pay safe harbor).* (i) *Facts.* Employee E is employed by Employer V from May 1, 2015, through December 31, 2015. Employer V offers Employee E and her dependents minimum essential coverage from May 1, 2015, through December 31, 2015, that provides minimum value. The employee contribution for self-only coverage is $100 per calendar month. From May 1, 2015, through October 31, 2015, Employee E is paid at a rate of $10 per hour. From November 1, 2015, through December 31, 2015, Employee E is paid at a rate of $12 per hour. For purposes of applying the affordability safe harbor for the calendar months May 2015 through October 2015, Employer V may assume that Employee E earned $1,300 per calendar month (130 hours of service multiplied by $10 (which is the lower of the employee's hourly rate of pay at the beginning of the coverage period ($10) and the lowest hourly rate of pay for the calendar month ($10)). Accordingly, affordability is determined by comparing the assumed income ($1,300 per month) to the employee contribution ($100 per calendar month). For the calendar months November 2015 through December 2015, Employer V may assume that Employee E earned $1,300 per calendar month (130 hours of service multiplied by $10 (which is the lower of the employee's hourly rate of pay at the beginning of the coverage period ($10) and the lowest hourly rate of pay for the calendar month ($12)). Accordingly, affordability is determined by comparing the assumed income ($1,300 per month) to the employee contribution ($100 per calendar month).

(ii) *Conclusion.* Because $100 is less than 9.5 percent of Employee E's assumed monthly income for each calendar month from May 2015 through December 2015, the coverage offered is treated as affordable with respect to Employee E for May 2015 through December 2015 ($100 is 7.69 percent of $1,300).

*Example 6 (Federal poverty line safe harbor).* (i) *Facts.* Employee F is employed by Employer T from January 1, 2015, through December 31, 2015. In addition, Employer T offers Employee F and his dependents minimum essential coverage during that period that provides minimum value. Employer T uses the look-back measurement method. Under that measurement method as applied by Employer T, Employee F is treated as a full-time employee for the entire calendar year 2015. Employee F is regularly credited with 35 hours of service per week but is credited with only 20 hours of service during the month of March 2015 and only 15 hours of service during the month of August 2015. Assume for this purpose that the federal poverty line for 2015 for an individual is $11,670. With respect to Employee F,

Employer T sets the monthly employee contribution for employee single-only coverage for each calendar month of 2015 at $92.39 (9.5 percent of $11,670, divided by 12).

(ii) *Conclusion.* Regardless of Employee F's actual wages for any calendar month in 2015, including the months of March 2015 and August 2015, when Employee F has lower wages because of significantly lower hours of service, the coverage under the plan is treated as affordable with respect to Employee F, because the employee contribution does not exceed 9.5 percent of the federal poverty line.

(f) *Additional guidance.*—With respect to assessable payments under section 4980H(b), including the determination of whether an offer of coverage is affordable for purposes of section 4980H, the Commissioner may prescribe additional guidance of general applica-

bility, published in the Internal Revenue Bulletin (see § 601.601(d)(2)(ii)(b) of this chapter).

(g) *Effective/applicability date.*—This section is applicable for periods after December 31, 2014. [Reg. § 54.4980H-5.]

☐ [T.D. 9655, 2-10-2014.]

### [Reg. § 54.4980H-6]

**§ 54.4980H-6. Administration and procedure.**—(a) *In general.*—[Reserved]

(b) *Effective/applicability date.*—This section is applicable for periods after December 31, 2014. [Reg. § 54.4980H-6.]

☐ [T.D. 9655, 2-10-2014.]

# Qualified Investment Entities

See p. 20,601 for regulations not amended to reflect law changes

### [Reg. § 55.4981-1]

**§ 55.4981-1. [Reserved].**

☐ [T.D. 7767, 2-3-81. *Amended by T.D. 7936, 1-17-84, and T.D. 8180,* 2-29-88. *Removed and reserved by T.D. 9849, 3-11-2019.*]

### [Reg. § 55.4981-2]

**§ 55.4981-2. Imposition of excise tax with respect to certain undistributed income of real estate investment trusts; calendar years beginning after December 31, 1986.**—Section 4981, as amended by the Tax Reform Act of 1986, imposes an excise tax on a real estate investment trust in the amount of four percent of the excess, if any, of the required distribution for a calendar year over the distributed amount for such calendar year. Section 4981, as so amended, applies

only to calendar years that begin after December 31, 1986. [Reg. § 55.4981-2.]

☐ [T.D. 8180, 2-29-88. *Amended by T.D. 9849, 3-11-2019.*]

### [Reg. § 55.4982-1]

**§ 55.4982-1. Imposition of excise tax on undistributed income of regulated investment companies.**—Section 4982 imposes an excise tax on a regulated investment company in the amount of four percent of the excess, if any, of the required distribution for a calendar year over the distributed amount for such calendar year. Section 4982 applies only to calendar years beginning after December 31, 1986. [Reg. § 55.4982-1.]

☐ [T.D. 8180, 2-29-88.]

# Maintenance of Minimum Essential Coverage

See p. 20,601 for regulations not amended to reflect law changes

### [Reg. § 1.5000A-0]

**§ 1.5000A-0. Table of contents.**—This section lists the captions contained in §§ 1.5000A-1 through 1.5000A-5.

(3) Individuals eligible for coverage under eligible employer-sponsored plans.
    (i) Eligibility.
        (A) In general.
        (B) Multiple eligibility.
        (C) Special rule for post-employment coverage.
    (ii) Required contribution for individuals eligible for coverage under an eligible employersponsored plan.
        (A) Employees.
        (B) Individuals related to employees.
        (C) Required contribution for part-year period.
        (D) Employer contributions to health reimbursement arrangements.
        (E) Wellness program incentives.
    (iii) Examples.
(4) Individuals ineligible for coverage under eligible employer-sponsored plans.
    (i) Eligibility for coverage other than an eligible employer-sponsored plan.
    (ii) Required contribution for individuals ineligible for coverage under eligible employersponsored plans.
        (A) In general.
        (B) Applicable plan.
          (1) In general.
          (2) Lowest cost bronze plan does not cover all individuals included in the taxpayer's nonexempt family.
             (i) In general.
             (ii) Optional simplified method for applicable plan identification.
        (C) Wellness program incentives.
        (D) Credit allowable under section 36B.
        (E) Required contribution for part-year period.
    (iii) Examples.
(f) Household income below filing threshold.
    (1) In general.
    (2) Applicable filing threshold.
        (i) In general.
        (ii) Certain dependents.
    (3) Manner of claiming the exemption.
(g) Members of Indian tribes.
(h) Individuals with hardship exemption certification.
    (1) In general.
    (2) Hardship exemption certification.
    (3) Hardship exemption without hardship exemption certification.
(i) [Reserved]
(j) Individuals with certain short coverage gaps.
    (1) In general.
    (2) Short coverage gap.
        (i) In general.
        (ii) Coordination with other exemptions.
        (iii) More than one short coverage gap during calendar year.
    (3) Continuous period.
        (i) In general.
        (ii) Continuous period straddling more than one taxable year.
    (4) Examples.

**§ 1.5000A-4 Computation of shared responsibility payment.**
(a) In general.
(b) Monthly penalty amount.
    (1) In general.
    (2) Flat dollar amount.
        (i) In general.
        (ii) Applicable dollar amount.
        (iii) Special applicable dollar amount for individuals under age 18.
        (iv) Indexing of applicable dollar amount.
    (3) Excess income amount.
        (i) In general.
        (ii) Income percentage.
(c) Monthly national average bronze plan premium.
(d) Examples.

**§ 1.5000A-5 Administration and procedure.**
(a) In general.
(b) Special rules.
    (1) Waiver of criminal penalties.
    (2) Limitations on liens and levies.
    (3) Authority to offset against overpayment.
(c) Effective/applicability date. [Reg. § 1.5000A-0.]

☐ [*T.D.* 9632, 8-27-2013 (*corrected* 12-24-2013) and T.D. 9705, 11-21-2014.]

**Reg. § 1.5000A-1**

**[Reg. § 1.5000A-1]**

**§ 1.5000A-1. Maintenance of minimum essential coverage and liability for the shared responsibility payment.**—(a) *In general.*—For each month during the taxable year, a nonexempt individual must have minimum essential coverage or pay the shared responsibility payment. For a month, a nonexempt individual is an individual in existence for the entire month who is not an exempt individual described in § 1.5000A-3.

(b) *Coverage under minimum essential coverage.*—(1) *In general.*—An individual has minimum essential coverage for a month in which the individual is enrolled in and entitled to receive benefits under a program or plan identified as minimum essential coverage in § 1.5000A-2 for at least one day in the month.

    (2) *Special rule for United States citizens or residents residing outside the United States or residents of territories.*—An individual is treated as having minimum essential coverage for a month—
        (i) If the month occurs during any period described in section 911(d)(1)(A) or section 911(d)(1)(B) that is applicable to the individual; or
        (ii) If, for the month, the individual is a bona fide resident of a possession of the United States (as determined under section 937(a)).

(c) *Liability for shared responsibility payment.*—(1) *In general.*—A taxpayer is liable for the shared responsibility payment for a month for which—
    (i) The taxpayer is a nonexempt individual without minimum essential coverage; or
    (ii) A nonexempt individual for whom the taxpayer is liable under paragraph (c)(2) or (c)(3) of this section does not have minimum essential coverage.

    (2) *Liability for dependents.*—(i) *In general.*—For a month when a nonexempt individual does not have minimum essential coverage, if the nonexempt individual is a dependent (as defined in section 152) of another individual for the other individual's taxable year including that month, the other individual is liable for the shared responsibility payment attributable to the dependent's lack of coverage. An individual is a dependent of a taxpayer for a taxable year if the individual satisfies the definition of dependent under section 152, regardless of whether the taxpayer claims the individual as a dependent on a Federal income tax return for the taxable year. If an individual may be claimed as a dependent by more than one taxpayer in the same calendar year, the taxpayer who properly claims the individual as a dependent for the taxable year is liable for the shared responsibility payment attributable to the individual. If more than one taxpayer may claim an individual as a dependent in the same calendar year but no one claims the individual as a dependent, the taxpayer with priority under the rules of section 152 to claim the individual as a dependent is liable for the shared responsibility payment for the individual.

        (ii) *Special rules for dependents adopted or placed in foster care during the taxable year.*—(A) *Taxpayers adopting an individual.*—If a taxpayer adopts a nonexempt dependent (or accepts a nonexempt dependent who is an eligible foster child as defined in section 152(f)(1)(C)) during the taxable year and is otherwise liable for the nonexempt dependent under paragraph (c)(2)(i) of this section, the taxpayer is liable under paragraph (c)(2)(i) of this section for the nonexempt dependent only for the full months in the taxable year that follow the month in which the adoption or acceptance occurs.

        (B) *Taxpayers placing an individual for adoption.*—If a taxpayer who is otherwise liable for a nonexempt dependent under paragraph (c)(2)(i) of this section places (or, by operation of law, must place) the nonexempt dependent for adoption or foster care during the taxable year, the taxpayer is liable under paragraph (c)(2)(i) of this section for the nonexempt dependent only for the full months in the taxable year that precede the month in which the adoption or foster care placement occurs.

        (C) *Examples.*—The following examples illustrate the provisions of this paragraph (c)(2)(ii). In each example the taxpayer's taxable year is a calendar year.
        *Example 1. Taxpayers adopting a child.* (i) E and F, married individuals filing a joint return, initiate proceedings for the legal adoption of a 2-year old child, G, in January 2016. On May 15, 2016, G becomes the adopted child (within the meaning of section 152(f)(1)(B)) of E and F, and resides with them for the remainder of 2016. Prior to the adoption, G resides with H, an unmarried individual, with H providing all of G's support. For 2016 G meets all requirements under section 152 to be E and F's dependent, and not H's dependent.
        (ii) Under paragraph (c)(2) of this section, E and F are not liable for a shared responsibility payment attributable to G for Janu-

ary through May of 2016, but are liable for a shared responsibility payment attributable to G, if any, for June through December of 2016. H is not liable for a shared responsibility payment attributable to G for any month in 2016, because G is not H's dependent for 2016 under section 152.

*Example 2. Taxpayers placing a child for adoption.* (i) The facts are the same as *Example 1*, except the legal adoption occurs on August 15, 2016, and, for 2016, G meets all requirements under section 152 to be H's dependent, and not E and F's dependent.

(ii) Under paragraph (c)(2) of this section, H is liable for a shared responsibility payment attributable to G, if any, for January through July of 2016, but is not liable for a shared responsibility payment attributable to G for August through December of 2016. E and F are not liable for a shared responsibility payment attributable to G for any month in 2016, because G is not E and F's dependent for 2016 under section 152.

(3) *Liability of individuals filing a joint return.*—Married individuals (within the meaning of section 7703) who file a joint return for a taxable year are jointly liable for any shared responsibility payment for a month included in the taxable year.

(d) *Definitions.*—The definitions in this paragraph (d) apply to this section and §§ 1.5000A-2 through 1.5000A-5.

(1) *Affordable Care Act.*—*Affordable Care Act* refers to the Patient Protection and Affordable Care Act, Public Law 111-148 (124 Stat. 119 (2010)), and the Health Care and Education Reconciliation Act of 2010, Public Law 111-152 (124 Stat. 1029 (2010)), as amended.

(2) *Employee.*—*Employee* includes former employees.

(3) *Exchange.*—*Exchange* has the same meaning as in 45 CFR 155.20.

(4) *Family.*—A taxpayer's family means the individuals for whom the taxpayer properly claims a deduction for a personal exemption under section 151 for the taxable year.

(5) *Family coverage.*—*Family coverage* means health insurance that covers more than one individual.

(6) *Group health insurance coverage.*—*Group health insurance coverage* has the same meaning as in section 2791(b)(4) of the Public Health Service Act (42 U.S.C. 300gg-91(b)(4)).

(7) *Group health plan.*—*Group health plan* has the same meaning as in section 2791(a)(1) of the Public Health Service Act (42 U.S.C. 300gg-91(a)(1)).

(8) *Health insurance coverage.*—*Health insurance coverage* has the same meaning as in section 2791(b)(1) of the Public Health Service Act (42 U.S.C. 300gg-91(b)(1)).

(9) *Health insurance issuer.*—*Health insurance issuer* has the same meaning as in section 2791(b)(2) of the Public Health Service Act (42 U.S.C. 300gg-91(b)(2)).

(10) *Household income.*—(i) *In general.*—*Household income* means the sum of—

(A) A taxpayer's modified adjusted gross income; and

(B) The aggregate modified adjusted gross income of all other individuals who—

*(1)* Are included in the taxpayer's family under paragraph (d)(4) of this section; and

*(2)* Are required to file a Federal income tax return for the taxable year.

(ii) *Modified adjusted gross income.*—*Modified adjusted gross income* means adjusted gross income (within the meaning of section 62) increased by—

(A) Amounts excluded from gross income under section 911; and

(B) Tax-exempt interest the taxpayer receives or accrues during the taxable year.

(11) *Individual market.*—*Individual market* has the same meaning as in section 1304(a)(2) of the Affordable Care Act (42 U.S.C. 18024(a)(2)).

(12) *Large and small group market.*—*Large group market* and *small group market* have the same meanings as in section 1304(a)(3) of the Affordable Care Act (42 U.S.C. 18024(a)(3)).

(13) *Month.*—*Month* means calendar month.

(14) *Qualified health plan.*—*Qualified health plan* has the same meaning as in section 1301(a) of the Affordable Care Act (42 U.S.C. 18021(a)).

(15) *Rating area.*—*Rating area* has the same meaning as in § 1.36B-1(n).

(16) *Self-only coverage.*—*Self-only coverage* means health insurance that covers one individual.

(17) *Shared responsibility family.*—*Shared responsibility family* means, for a month, all nonexempt individuals for whom the taxpayer (and the taxpayer's spouse, if the taxpayer is married and files a joint return with the spouse) is liable for the shared responsibility payment under paragraph (c) of this section.

(18) *State.*—*State* means each of the 50 states and the District of Columbia. [Reg. § 1.5000A-1.]

☐ [*T.D.* 9632, 8-27-2013 (*corrected* 12-24-2013).]

## [Reg. § 1.5000A-2]

**§ 1.5000A-2. Minimum essential coverage.**—(a) *In general.*—*Minimum essential coverage* means coverage under a government-sponsored program (described in paragraph (b) of this section), an eligible employer-sponsored plan (described in paragraph (c) of this section), a plan in the individual market (described in paragraph (d) of this section), a grandfathered health plan (described in paragraph (e) of this section), or other health benefits coverage (described in paragraph (f) of this section). Minimum essential coverage does not include coverage described in paragraph (g) of this section. All terms defined in this section apply for purposes of this section and § 1.5000A-1 and §§ 1.5000A-3 through 1.5000A-5.

(b) *Government-sponsored program.*—(1) *In general.*—Except as provided in paragraph (2), *government-sponsored program* means any of the following:

(i) *Medicare.*—The Medicare program under part A of Title XVIII of the Social Security Act (42 U.S.C.1395c and following sections);

(ii) *Medicaid.*—The Medicaid program under Title XIX of the Social Security Act (42 U.S.C. 1396 and following sections);

(iii) *Children's Health Insurance Program.*—The Children's Health Insurance Program (CHIP) under Title XXI of the Social Security Act (42 U.S.C 1397aa and following sections);

(iv) *TRICARE.*—Medical coverage under chapter 55 of Title 10, U.S.C., including coverage under the TRICARE program;

(v) *Veterans programs.*—The following health care programs under chapter 17 or 18 of Title 38, U.S.C.:

(A) The medical benefits package authorized for eligible veterans under 38 U.S.C. 1710 and 38 U.S.C. 1705;

(B) The Civilian Health and Medical Program of the Department of Veterans Affairs (CHAMPVA) authorized under 38 U.S.C. 1781; and

(C) The comprehensive health care program authorized under 38 U.S.C. 1803 and 38 U.S.C. 1821 for certain children of Vietnam Veterans and Veterans of covered service in Korea who are suffering from spina bifida.

(vi) *Peace Corp program.*—A health plan under section 2504(e) of Title 22, U.S.C. (relating to Peace Corps volunteers); and

(vii) *Nonappropriated Fund Health Benefits Program.*—The Nonappropriated Fund Health Benefits Program of the Department of Defense, established under section 349 of the National Defense Authorization Act for Fiscal Year 1995 (Public Law No. 103-337; 10 U.S.C. 1587 note).

(2) *Certain health care coverage not minimum essential coverage under a government-sponsored program.*—Government-sponsored program does not mean any of the following:

(i) Optional coverage of family planning services under section 1902(a)(10)(A)(ii)(XXI) of the Social Security Act (42 U.S.C. 1396a(a)(10)(A)(ii)(XXI));

(ii) Optional coverage of tuberculosis-related services under section 1902(a)(10)(A)(ii)(XII) of the Social Security Act (42 U.S.C. 1396a(a)(10)(A)(ii)(XII));

(iii) Coverage of pregnancy-related services under section 1902(a)(10)(A)(i)(IV) and (a)(10)(A)(ii)(IX) of the Social Security Act (42 U.S.C. 1396a(a)(10)(A)(i)(IV), (a)(10)(A)(ii)(IX));

(iv) Coverage limited to treatment of emergency medical conditions in accordance with 8 U.S.C. 1611(b)(1)(A), as authorized by section 1903(v) of the Social Security Act (42 U.S.C. 1396b(v));

(v) Coverage for medically needy individuals under section 1902(a)(10)(C) of the Social Security Act (42 U.S.C. 1396a(a)(10)(C)) and 42 CFR 435.300 and following sections;

(vi) Coverage authorized under section 1115(a) of the Social Security Act (42 U.S.C. 1315(a));

(vii) Coverage under section 1079(a), 1086(c)(1), or 1086(d)(1) of title 10, U.S.C., that is solely limited to space available care in a facility of the uniformed services for individuals excluded from TRICARE coverage for care from private sector providers; and

(viii) Coverage under sections 1074a and 1074b of title 10, U.S.C., for an injury, illness, or disease incurred or aggravated in the line of duty for individuals who are not on active duty.

(c) *Eligible employer-sponsored plan.*—(1) *In general.*—*Eligible employer-sponsored plan* means, with respect to any employee:

(i) Group health insurance coverage offered by, or on behalf of, an employer to the employee that is—

(A) A governmental plan (within the meaning of section 2791(d)(8) of the Public Health Service Act (42 U.S.C.300gg-91(d)(8)));

(B) Any other plan or coverage offered in the small or large group market within a State; or

(C) A grandfathered health plan (within the meaning of paragraph (e) of this section) offered in a group market; or

(ii) A self-insured group health plan under which coverage is offered by, or on behalf of, an employer to the employee.

(2) *Government-sponsored program generally not an eligible employer-sponsored plan.*—Except for the program identified in paragraph (b)(1)(vii) of this section, a government-sponsored program described in paragraph (b) of this section is not an eligible employer-sponsored plan.

(d) *Plan in the individual market.*—(1) *In general.*—*Plan in the individual market* means health insurance coverage offered to individuals in the individual market within a state, other than short-term limited duration insurance within the meaning of section 2791(b)(5) of the Public Health Service Act (42 U.S.C. 300gg-91(b)(5)).

(2) *Qualified health plan offered by an Exchange.*—A qualified health plan offered by an Exchange is a plan in the individual market. If a territory of the United States elects to establish an Exchange under section 1323(a)(1) and (b) of the Affordable Care Act (42 U.S.C. 18043(a)(1), (b)), a qualified health plan offered by that Exchange is a plan in the individual market.

(e) *Grandfathered health plan.*—*Grandfathered health plan* means any group health plan or group health insurance coverage to which section 1251 of the Affordable Care Act (42 U.S.C. 18011) applies.

(f) *Other coverage that qualifies as minimum essential coverage.*—Minimum essential coverage includes any plan or arrangement recognized by the Secretary of Health and Human Services, in coordination with the Secretary of the Treasury, as minimum essential coverage.

(g) *Excepted benefits not minimum essential coverage.*—Minimum essential coverage does not include any coverage that consists solely of excepted benefits described in section 2791(c)(1), (c)(2), (c)(3), or (c)(4) of the Public Health Service Act (42 U.S.C. §300gg-91(c)). [Reg. §1.5000A-2.]

☐ [*T.D.* 9632, 8-27-2013 (*corrected* 12-24-2013) and T.D. 9705, 11-21-2014.]

### [Reg. §1.5000A-3]

**§1.5000A-3. Exempt individuals.**—(a) *Members of recognized religious sects.*—(1) *In general.*—An individual is an exempt individual for a month that includes a day on which the individual has in effect a religious conscience exemption certification described in paragraph (a)(2) of this section.

(2) *Exemption certification.*—A religious conscience exemption certification is issued by an Exchange in accordance with the requirements of section 1311(d)(4)(H) of the Affordable Care Act (42 U.S.C. 18031(d)(4)(H)), 45 CFR 155.605(c), and 45 CFR 155.615(b) and certifies that an individual is—

(i) A member of a recognized religious sect or division of the sect that is described in section 1402(g)(1); and

(ii) An adherent of established tenets or teachings of the sect or division as described in that section.

(b) *Member of health care sharing ministries.*—(1) *In general.*—An individual is an exempt individual for a month that includes a day on which the individual is a member of a health care sharing ministry.

(2) *Health care sharing ministry.*—For purposes of this section, *health care sharing ministry* means an organization—

(i) That is described in section 501(c)(3) and is exempt from tax under section 501(a);

(ii) Members of which share a common set of ethical or religious beliefs and share medical expenses among themselves in accor-

dance with those beliefs and without regard to the state in which a member resides or is employed;

(iii) Members of which retain membership even after they develop a medical condition;

(iv) That (or a predecessor of which) has been in existence at all times since December 31, 1999;

(v) Members of which have shared medical expenses continuously and without interruption since at least December 31, 1999; and

(vi) That conducts an annual audit performed by an independent certified public accounting firm in accordance with generally accepted accounting principles and makes the annual audit report available to the public upon request.

(c) *Exempt noncitizens.*—(1) *In general.*—An individual is an exempt individual for a month that the individual is an exempt noncitizen.

(2) *Exempt noncitizens.*—For purposes of this section, an individual is an exempt noncitizen for a month if the individual—

(i) Is not a U.S. citizen or U.S. national for any day during the month; and

(ii) Is either—

(A) A nonresident alien (within the meaning of section 7701(b)(1)(B)) for the taxable year that includes the month; or

(B) An individual who is not lawfully present (within the meaning of 45 CFR 155.20) on any day in the month.

(d) *Incarcerated individuals.*—(1) *In general.*—An individual is an exempt individual for a month that includes a day on which the individual is incarcerated.

(2) *Incarcerated.*—For purposes of this section, the term *incarcerated* means confined, after the disposition of charges, in a jail, prison, or similar penal institution or correctional facility.

(e) *Individuals with no affordable coverage.*—(1) *In general.*—An individual is an exempt individual for a month in which the individual lacks affordable coverage. For purposes of this paragraph (e), an individual lacks affordable coverage in a month if the individual's required contribution (determined on an annual basis) for minimum essential coverage for the month exceeds the required contribution percentage (as defined in paragraph (e)(2) of this section) of the individual's household income. For purposes of this paragraph (e), an individual's household income is increased by any amount of the required contribution made through a salary reduction arrangement that is excluded from gross income.

(2) *Required contribution percentage.*—(i) *In general.*—Except as provided in paragraph (e)(2)(ii) of this section, the required contribution percentage is 8 percent.

(ii) *Indexing.*—For plan years beginning in any calendar year after 2014, the required contribution percentage is the percentage determined by the Department of Health and Human Services that reflects the excess of the rate of premium growth between the preceding calendar year and 2013 over the rate of income growth for the period.

(iii) *Plan year.*—For purposes of this paragraph (e), *plan year* means the eligible employer-sponsored plan's regular 12-month coverage period, or for a new employee or an individual who enrolls during a special enrollment period, the remainder of a 12-month coverage period.

(3) *Individuals eligible for coverage under eligible employer-sponsored plans.*—(i) *Eligibility.*—(A) *In general.*—Except as provided in paragraph (e)(3)(i)(B) of this section, an employee or related individual (as defined in paragraph (e)(3)(ii)(B) of this section) is treated as eligible for coverage under an eligible employer-sponsored plan for a month during a plan year if the employee or related individual could have enrolled in the plan for any day in that month during an open or special enrollment period, regardless of whether the employee or related individual is eligible for any other type of minimum essential coverage.

(B) *Multiple eligibility.*—For purposes of this paragraph (e)(3), an employee eligible for coverage under an eligible employer-sponsored plan offered by the employee's employer is not treated as eligible as a related individual for coverage under an eligible employer-sponsored plan (for example, an eligible employer-sponsored plan offered by the employer of the employee's spouse) for any month included in the plan year of the eligible employer-sponsored plan offered by the employee's employer.

(C) *Special rule for post-employment coverage.*—A former employee or an individual related to a former employee, who may enroll in continuation coverage required under Federal law or a state law that provides comparable continuation coverage, or in retiree coverage under an eligible employer-sponsored plan, is eligible for coverage under an eligible employer-sponsored plan only if the individual enrolls in the coverage.

(ii) *Required contribution for individuals eligible for coverage under an eligible employer-sponsored plan.*—(A) *Employees.*—In the case of an employee who is eligible to purchase coverage under an eligible employer-sponsored plan sponsored by the employee's employer, the required contribution is the portion of the annual premium that the employee would pay (whether through salary reduction or otherwise) for the lowest cost self-only coverage.

(B) *Individuals related to employees.*—In the case of an individual who is eligible for coverage under an eligible employer-sponsored plan because of a relationship to an employee and for whom a personal exemption deduction under section 151 is claimed on the employee's Federal income tax return (related individual), the required contribution is the portion of the annual premium that the employee would pay (whether through salary reduction or otherwise) for the lowest cost family coverage that would cover the employee and all related individuals who are included in the employee's family and are not otherwise exempt under § 1.5000A-3.

(C) *Required contribution for part-year period.*—For each individual described in paragraph (e)(3)(ii)(A) or (e)(3)(ii)(B) of this section, affordability under this paragraph (e)(3) is determined separately for each employment period that is less than a full calendar year or for the portions of an employer's plan year that fall in different taxable years of the individual. Coverage under an eligible employer-sponsored plan is affordable for a part-year period if the annualized required contribution for self-only coverage (in the case of the employee) or family coverage (in the case of a related individual) under the plan for the part-year period does not exceed the required contribution percentage of the individual's household income for the taxable year. The annualized required contribution is the required contribution determined under paragraph (e)(3)(ii)(A) or (e)(3)(ii)(B) of this section for the part-year period times a fraction, the numerator of which is 12 and the denominator of which is the number of months in the part-year period during the individual's taxable year. Only full calendar months are included in the computation under this paragraph (e)(3)(ii)(C).

(D) *Employer contributions to health reimbursement arrangements.*—Amounts newly made available for the current plan year under a health reimbursement arrangement that an employee may use to pay premiums, or may use to pay cost-sharing or benefits not covered by the primary plan in addition to premiums, are counted toward the employee's required contribution if the health reimbursement arrangement would be integrated, as that term is used in Notice 2013-54 (2013-40 IRB 287) or in any successor published guidance (see § 601.601(d) of this chapter), with an eligible employer-sponsored plan for an employee enrolled in the plan. The eligible employer-sponsored plan and the health reimbursement arrangement must be offered by the same employer. Employer contributions to a health reimbursement arrangement count toward an employee's required contribution only to the extent the amount of the annual contribution is required under the terms of the plan or otherwise determinable within a reasonable time before the employee must decide whether to enroll in the eligible employer-sponsored plan.

(E) *Employer contributions to cafeteria plans.*—Amounts made available for the current plan year under a cafeteria plan, within the meaning of section 125, are taken into account in determining an employee's or a related individual's required contribution if:

(1) The employee may not opt to receive the amount as a taxable benefit;

(2) The employee may use the amount to pay for minimum essential coverage; and

(3) The employee may use the amount exclusively to pay for medical care, within the meaning of section 213.

(F) *Wellness program incentives.*—Nondiscriminatory wellness program incentives, within the meaning of § 54.9802-1(f) of this chapter, offered by an eligible employer-sponsored plan that affect premiums are treated as earned in determining an employee's required contribution for purposes of affordability of an eligible employer-sponsored plan to the extent the incentives relate exclusively to tobacco use. Wellness program incentives that do not relate to tobacco use or that include a component unrelated to tobacco use are treated as not earned for this purpose. For purposes of this section, the term *wellness program incentive* has the same meaning as the term *reward* in § 54.9802-1(f)(1)(i) of this chapter.

(G) *Opt-out arrangements.*—[Reserved]

(iii) *Examples.*—The following examples illustrate the application of this paragraph (e)(3). Unless stated otherwise, in each exam-

ple, each individual's taxable year is a calendar year, the individual is ineligible for any other exemptions described in this section for a month, the rate of premium growth has not exceeded the rate of income growth since 2013, and the individual's employer offers a single plan that uses a calendar plan year and is an eligible employer-sponsored plan as described in § 1.5000A-2(c).

*Example 1. Unmarried employee with no dependents.* Taxpayer A is an unmarried individual with no dependents. In November 2015, A is eligible to enroll in self-only coverage under a plan offered by A's employer for calendar year 2016. If A enrolls in the coverage, A is required to pay $5,000 of the total annual premium. In 2016, A's household income is $60,000. Under paragraph (e)(3)(ii)(A) of this section, A's required contribution is $5,000, the portion of the annual premium A pays for self-only coverage. Under paragraph (e)(1) of this section, A lacks affordable coverage for 2016 because A's required contribution ($5,000) is greater than 8% of A's household income ($4,800).

*Example 2. Married employee with dependents.* Taxpayers B and C are married and file a joint return for 2016. B and C have two children, D and E. In November 2015, B is eligible to enroll in self-only coverage under a plan offered by B's employer for calendar year 2016 at a cost of $5,000 to B. C, D, and E are eligible to enroll in family coverage under the same plan for 2016 at a cost of $20,000 to B. B, C, D, and E's household income for 2016 is $90,000. Under paragraph (e)(3)(ii)(A) of this section, B's required contribution is B's share of the cost for self-only coverage, $5,000. Under paragraph (e)(1) of this section, B has affordable coverage for 2016 because B's required contribution ($5,000) does not exceed 8% of B's household income ($7,200). Under paragraph (e)(3)(ii)(B) of this section, the required contribution for C, D, and E is B's share of the cost for family coverage, $20,000. Under paragraph (e)(1) of this section, C, D, and E lack affordable coverage for 2016 because their required contribution ($20,000) exceeds 8% of their household income ($7,200).

*Example 3. Plan year is a fiscal year.* (i) Taxpayer F is an unmarried individual with no dependents. In June 2015, F is eligible to enroll in self-only coverage under a plan offered by F's employer for the period July 2015 through June 2016 at a cost to F of $4,750. In June 2016, F is eligible to enroll in self-only coverage under a plan offered by F's employer for the period July 2016 through June 2017 at a cost to F of $5,000. In 2016, F's household income is $60,000.

(ii) Under paragraph (e)(3)(ii)(C) of this section, F's annualized required contribution for the period January 2016 through June 2016 is $4,750 ($2,375 paid for premiums in 2016 × 12/6). Under paragraph (e)(1) of this section, F has affordable coverage for January 2016 through June 2016 because F's annualized required contribution ($4,750) does not exceed 8% of F's household income ($4,800).

(iii) Under paragraph (e)(3)(ii)(C) of this section, F's annualized required contribution for the period July 2016 to December 2016 is $5,000 ($2,500 paid for premiums in 2016 × 12/6). Under paragraph (e)(1) of this section, F lacks affordable coverage for July 2016 through December 2016 because F's annualized required contribution ($5,000) exceeds 8% of F's household income ($4,800).

*Example 4. Eligibility for coverage under an eligible employer-sponsored plan and under government sponsored coverage.* Taxpayer G is unmarried and has one child, H. In November 2015, H is eligible to enroll in family coverage under a plan offered by G's employer for 2016. H is also eligible to enroll in the CHIP program for 2016. Under paragraph (e)(3)(i) of this section, H is treated as eligible for coverage under an eligible employer-sponsored plan for each month in 2016, notwithstanding that H is eligible to enroll in government sponsored coverage for the same period.

(4) *Individuals ineligible for coverage under eligible employer-sponsored plans.*—(i) *Eligibility for coverage other than an eligible employer-sponsored plan.*—An individual is treated as ineligible for coverage under an eligible employer-sponsored plan for a month that is not described in paragraph (e)(3)(i) of this section.

(ii) *Required contribution for individuals ineligible for coverage under eligible employer-sponsored plans.*—(A) *In general.*—In the case of an individual who is ineligible for coverage under an eligible employer-sponsored plan, the required contribution is the premium for the applicable plan, reduced by the maximum amount of any credit allowable under section 36B for the taxable year, determined as if the individual was covered for the entire taxable year by a qualified health plan offered through the Exchange serving the rating area where the individual resides.

(B) *Applicable plan.*—(1) *In general.*—Except as provided in paragraph (e)(4)(ii)(B)(2) of this section, *applicable plan* means the single lowest cost bronze plan available in the individual market through the Exchange serving the rating area in which the individual resides (without regard to whether the individual purchased a qualified health plan through the Exchange) that would cover all individuals in the individual's nonexempt family. For purposes of this paragraph (e)(4), an individual's *nonexempt family* means the family (as defined in §1.5000A-1(d)(4)) that includes the individual, excluding any family members who are otherwise exempt under section 1.5000A-3 or are treated as eligible for coverage under an eligible employer-sponsored plan under paragraph (e)(3)(i) of this section. The premium for the applicable plan takes into account rating factors (for example, an individual's age or tobacco use) that an Exchange would use to determine the cost of coverage.

(2) *Lowest cost bronze plan does not cover all individuals included in the taxpayer's nonexempt family.—(i) In general.*—If the Exchange serving the rating area where the individual resides does not offer a single bronze plan covering all individuals included in the individual's nonexempt family, the premium for the applicable plan is the sum of the premiums for the lowest cost bronze plans that are offered through the Exchanges serving the rating areas where one or more of the individuals reside that would cover in the aggregate all the individuals in the individual's nonexempt family. For instance, coverage offered through the Exchange in a rating area might not cover a family member living in different rating area or a single policy might not cover all the members in a taxpayer's household.

(ii) *Optional simplified method for applicable plan identification.*—[Reserved]

(C) *Wellness program incentives.*—[Reserved]

(D) *Credit allowable under section 36B.*—For purposes of paragraph (e)(4)(ii)(A) of this section, *maximum amount of any credit allowable under section 36B* means the maximum amount of credit that would be allowable to the individual, or to the taxpayer who can properly claim the individual as a dependent, under section 36B if all members of the individual's nonexempt family enrolled in a qualified health plan through the Exchange serving the rating area where the individual resides.

(E) *Required contribution for part-year period.*—For each individual, affordability under paragraph (e)(4) of this section is determined separately for each period described in paragraph (e)(4)(ii)(E) of this section that is less than a 12-month period. Coverage under a plan is affordable for a part-year period if the annualized required contribution for coverage under the plan for the part-year period does not exceed the required contribution percentage of the individual's household income for the taxable year. The annualized required contribution is the required contribution determined under paragraph (e)(4)(ii)(A) of this section for the part-year period times a fraction, the numerator of which is 12 and the denominator of which is the number of months in the part-year period during the individual's taxable year. Only full calendar months are included in the computation under this paragraph (e)(4)(ii)(D).

(iii) *Examples.*—The following examples illustrate the provisions of this paragraph (e)(4). Unless stated otherwise, in each example the taxpayer's taxable year is a calendar year, the rate of premium growth has not exceeded the rate of income growth since 2013, and the taxpayer is ineligible for any of the exemptions described in paragraphs (a) through (d) and (f) through (j) of this section for a month.

*Example 1. Unmarried individual with no dependents.* (i) Taxpayer G is an unmarried individual with no dependents. G is ineligible to enroll in any minimum essential coverage other than coverage in the individual market for all months in 2016. The annual premium for the lowest cost bronze self-only plan in G's rating area (G's applicable plan) is $5,000. The adjusted annual premium for the second lowest cost silver self-only plan in G's rating area (G's applicable benchmark plan within the meaning of §1.36B-3(f)) is $5,500. In 2016 G's household income is $40,000, which is 358% of the Federal poverty line for G's family size for the taxable year.

(ii) Under paragraph (e)(4)(ii)(C) of this section, the credit allowable under section 36B is determined pursuant to section 36B. With household income at 358% of the Federal poverty line, G's applicable percentage is 9.5. Because each month in 2016 is a coverage month (within the meaning of §1.36B-3(c)), G's maximum credit allowable under section 36B is the excess of G's premium for the applicable benchmark plan over the product of G's household income and G's applicable percentage ($1,700). Therefore, under paragraph (e)(4)(ii)(A) of this section, G's required contribution is $3,300. Under paragraph (e)(1) of this section, G lacks affordable coverage for 2016 because G's required contribution ($3,300) exceeds 8% of G's household income ($3,200).

*Example 2. Family.* (i) In 2016 Taxpayers M and N are married and file a joint return. M and N have two children, P and Q. M, N, P, and Q are ineligible to enroll in minimum essential coverage other than coverage in the individual market for a month in 2016. The annual premium for M, N, P, and Q's applicable plan is $20,000. The adjusted annual premium for M, N, P, and Q's applicable benchmark plan (within the meaning of §1.36B-3(f)) is $25,000. M and N's

household income is $80,000, which is 347% of the Federal poverty line for a family size of 4 for the taxable year.

(ii) Under paragraph (e)(4)(ii)(C) of this section, the credit allowable under section 36B is determined pursuant to section 36B. With household income at 347% of the Federal poverty line, the applicable percentage is 9.5. Because each month in 2016 is a coverage month (within the meaning of §1.36B-3(c)), the maximum credit allowable under section 36B is the excess of the premium for the applicable benchmark plan over the product of the household income and the applicable percentage ($17,400). Therefore, under paragraph (e)(4)(ii)(A) of this section, the required contribution for M, N, P, and Q is $2,600. Under paragraph (e)(1) of this section, M, N, P, and Q have affordable coverage for 2016 because their required contribution ($2,600) does not exceed 8% of their household income ($6,400).

*Example 3. Family with some members eligible for government-sponsored coverage.* (i) In 2016 Taxpayers U and V are married and file a joint return. U and V have two children, W and X. U and V are ineligible to enroll in minimum essential coverage other than coverage in the individual market for all months in 2016; however, W and X are eligible for coverage under CHIP for 2016. The annual premium for U, V, W, and X's applicable plan is $20,000. The adjusted annual premium for the second lowest cost silver plan that would cover U and V (the applicable benchmark plan within the meaning of §1.36B-3(f)) is $12,500. U and V's household income is $50,000, which is 217% of the Federal poverty line for a family size of 4 for the taxable year. W and X do not enroll in CHIP coverage.

(ii) Under paragraph (e)(4)(ii)(C) of this section, the credit allowable under section 36B is determined pursuant to section 36B. With household income at 217% of the Federal poverty line, the applicable percentage is 6.89. Each month in 2016 is a coverage month (within the meaning of §1.36B-3(c)) for U and V, but no months in 2016 are coverage months for W and X because they are eligible for CHIP coverage. The maximum credit allowable under section 36B is the excess of the premium for the applicable benchmark plan over the product of the household income and the applicable percentage ($9,055). Therefore, under paragraph (e)(4)(ii)(A) of this section, the required contribution is $10,945. Under paragraph (e)(1) of this section, U, V, W, and X lack affordable coverage for 2016 because their required contribution ($10,945) exceeds 8% of their household income ($4,000).

*Example 4. Family with some members enrolled in government-sponsored minimum essential coverage.* The facts are the same as *Example 3*, except W and X enroll in CHIP coverage on January 1, 2016. Under paragraph (e)(4)(ii)(B), U, V, W, and X are members of U and V's nonexempt family for 2016. Therefore, the annual premium for the applicable plan is the same as in *Example 3* ($20,000). The maximum credit allowable under section 36B is also the same as in *Example 3* ($9,055). Under paragraph (e)(4)(ii)(A) of this section, the required contribution is $10,945. Under paragraph (e)(1) of this section, U and V lack affordable coverage for 2016 because their required contribution ($10,945) exceeds 8% of their household income ($4,000).

(f) *Household income below filing threshold.—(1) In general.*—An individual is an exempt individual for any taxable year for which the individual's household income is less than the applicable filing threshold.

(2) *Applicable filing threshold.—(i) In general.*—For purposes of this section, *applicable filing threshold* means the amount of gross income that would trigger an individual's requirement to file a Federal income tax return under section 6012(a)(1).

(ii) *Certain dependents.*—The applicable filing threshold for an individual who is properly claimed as a dependent by another taxpayer is equal to the other taxpayer's applicable filing threshold.

(3) *Manner of claiming the exemption.*—A taxpayer is not required to file a Federal income tax return solely to claim the exemption described in this paragraph (f). If a taxpayer has a household income below the applicable filing threshold and nevertheless files a Federal income tax return, the taxpayer may claim the exemption described in this paragraph (f) on the return.

(g) *Members of Indian tribes.*—An individual is an exempt individual for a month that includes a day on which the individual is a member of an Indian tribe. For purposes of this section, *Indian tribe* means a group or community described in section 45A(c)(6).

(h) *Individuals with hardship exemption certification.—(1) In general.*—Except as provided in paragraph (h)(3) of this section, an individual is an exempt individual for a month that includes a day on which the individual has in effect a hardship exemption certification described in paragraph (h)(2) of this section.

(2) *Hardship exemption certification.*—A hardship exemption certification is issued by an Exchange under section 1311(d)(4)(H) of the Affordable Care Act (42 U.S.C. 18031(d)(4)(H)), 45 CFR 155.605(g)(1), (g)(2), (g)(4) and (g)(6), 45 CFR 155.610(i), and 45 CFR 155.615(f), and certifies that an individual has suffered a hardship (as that term is defined in 45 CFR 155.605(g)) affecting the capability to obtain minimum essential coverage.

(3) *Hardship exemption without hardship exemption certification.*—An individual may claim an exemption without obtaining a hardship exemption certification described in paragraph (h)(2) of this section for any month that includes a day on which the individual meets the requirements of any hardship for which:

(i) The Secretary of HHS issues guidance of general applicability describing the hardship and indicating that an exemption for such hardship can be claimed on a Federal income tax return pursuant to guidance published by the Secretary; and

(ii) The Secretary issues published guidance of general applicability, see §601.601(d)(2) of this chapter, allowing an individual to claim the hardship exemption on a return without obtaining a hardship exemption from an Exchange.

(i) [Reserved]

(j) *Individuals with certain short coverage gaps.*—(1) *In general.*—An individual is an exempt individual for a month the last day of which is included in a short coverage gap.

(2) *Short coverage gap.*—(i) *In general.*—Short coverage gap means a continuous period of less than three months in which the individual is not covered under minimum essential coverage. If the individual does not have minimum essential coverage for a continuous period of three or more months, none of the months included in the continuous period are treated as included in a short coverage gap.

(ii) *Coordination with other exemptions.*—For purposes of this paragraph (j), an individual is treated as having minimum essential coverage for a month in which an individual is exempt under any of paragraphs (a) through (h) of this section.

(iii) *More than one short coverage gap during calendar year.*—If a calendar year includes more than one short coverage gap, the exemption provided by this paragraph (j) only applies to the earliest short coverage gap.

(3) *Continuous period.*—(i) *In general.*—Except as provided in paragraph (j)(3)(ii) of this section, the number of months included in a continuous period is determined without regard to the calendar years in which months included in that period occur. For purposes of paragraph (j) of this section, a continuous period begins no earlier than January 1, 2014.

(ii) *Continuous period straddling more than one taxable year.*—If an individual does not have minimum essential coverage for a continuous period that begins in one taxable year and ends in the next, for purposes of applying this paragraph (j) to the first taxable year, the months in the second taxable year included in the continuous period are disregarded. For purposes of applying this paragraph (j) to the second taxable year, the months in the first taxable year included in the continuous period are taken into account.

(4) *Examples.*—The following examples illustrate the provisions of this paragraph (j). Unless stated otherwise, in each example the taxpayer's taxable year is a calendar year and the taxpayer is ineligible for any of the exemptions described in paragraphs (a) through (h) of this section for a month.

*Example 1. Short coverage gap.* Taxpayer D has minimum essential coverage in 2016 from January 1 through March 2. After March 2, D does not have minimum essential coverage until D enrolls in an eligible employer-sponsored plan effective June 15. Under §1.5000A-1(b), for purposes of section 5000A, D has minimum essential coverage for January, February, March, and June through December. D's continuous period without coverage is 2 months, April and May. April and May constitute a short coverage gap under paragraph (j)(2)(i) of this section.

*Example 2. Continuous period of 3 months or more.* The facts are the same as in *Example 1*, except D's coverage is not effective until July 1. D's continuous period without coverage is 3 months, April, May, and June. Under paragraph (j)(2)(i) of this section, April, May, and June are not included in a short coverage gap.

*Example 3. Short coverage gap following exempt period.* Taxpayer E is incarcerated from January 1 through June 2. E enrolls in an eligible employer-sponsored plan effective September 15. Under paragraph (d) of this section, E is exempt for the period January through June. Under paragraph (j)(2)(ii) of this section, E is treated as having minimum essential coverage for this period, and E's continuous period without minimum essential coverage is 2 months, July and

August. July and August constitute a short coverage gap under paragraph (j)(2)(i) of this section.

*Example 4. Continuous period covering more than one taxable year.* Taxpayer F, an unmarried individual with no dependents, has minimum essential coverage for the period January 1 through October 15, 2016. F is without coverage until February 15, 2017. F files his Federal income tax return for 2016 on March 10, 2017. Under paragraph (j)(3)(ii) of this section, November and December of 2016 are treated as a short coverage gap. However, November and December of 2016 are included in the continuous period that includes January 2017. The continuous period for 2017 is not less than 3 months and, therefore, January is not a part of a short coverage gap.

*Example 5. Enrollment following loss of coverage.* The facts are the same as in *Example 4* except F loses coverage on June 15, 2017. F enrolls in minimum essential coverage effective September 15, 2017. The continuous period without minimum essential coverage in July and August of 2017 is two months and, therefore, is a short coverage gap. Because January 2017 was not part of a short coverage gap, the earliest short coverage gap occurring in 2017 is the gap that includes July and August.

*Example 6. Multiple coverage gaps.* (i) The facts are the same as in *Example 5* except F has minimum essential coverage for November 2016. Under paragraph (j)(3)(ii) of this section, December 2016 is treated as a short coverage gap.

(ii) December 2016 is included in the continuous period that includes January 2017. This continuous period is two months and, therefore, January 2017 is the earliest month in 2017 that is included in a short coverage gap. Under paragraph (j)(2)(iii) of this section, the exemption under this paragraph (j) applies only to January 2017. Thus, the continuous period without minimum essential coverage in July and August of 2017 is not a short coverage gap. [Reg. §1.5000A-3.]

☐ [*T.D. 9632,* 8-27-2013 (*corrected* 12-24-2013). Amended by T.D. 9705, 11-21-2014 *and T.D. 9804,* 12-14-2016.]

[**Reg. §1.5000A-4**]

**§1.5000A-4. Computation of shared responsibility payment.**—(a) *In general.*—For each taxable year, the shared responsibility payment imposed on a taxpayer in accordance with §1.5000A-1(c) is the lesser of—

(1) The sum of the monthly penalty amounts; or

(2) The sum of the monthly national average bronze plan premiums for the shared responsibility family.

(b) *Monthly penalty amount.*—(1) *In general.*—Monthly penalty amount means, for a month that a nonexempt individual is not covered under minimum essential coverage, 1/12 multiplied by the greater of—

(i) The flat dollar amount; or

(ii) The excess income amount.

(2) *Flat dollar amount.*—(i) *In general.*—Flat dollar amount means the lesser of—

(A) The sum of the applicable dollar amounts for all individuals included in the taxpayer's shared responsibility family; or

(B) 300 percent of the applicable dollar amount (determined without regard to paragraph (b)(2)(iii) of this section) for the calendar year with or within which the taxable year ends.

(ii) *Applicable dollar amount.*—Except as provided in paragraphs (b)(2)(iii) and (b)(2)(iv) of this section, the applicable dollar amount is—

(A) $95 in 2014;

(B) $325 in 2015; or

(C) $695 in 2016.

(iii) *Special applicable dollar amount for individuals under age 18.*—If an individual has not attained the age of 18 before the first day of a month, the applicable dollar amount for the individual is equal to one-half of the applicable dollar amount (as expressed in paragraph (b)(2)(ii) of this section) for the calendar year in which the month occurs. For purposes of this paragraph (b)(2)(iii), an individual attains the age of 18 on the anniversary of the date when the individual was born. For example, an individual born on March 1, 1999, attains the age of 18 on March 1, 2017.

(iv) *Indexing of applicable dollar amount.*—In any calendar year after 2016, the applicable dollar amount is $695 as increased by the product of $695 and the cost-of-living adjustment determined under section 1(f)(3) for the calendar year. For purposes of this paragraph (b)(2)(iv), the cost-of-living adjustment is determined by substituting "calendar year 2015" for "calendar year 1992" in section 1(f)(3)(B). If any increase under this paragraph (b)(2)(iv) is not a multiple of $50, the increase is rounded down to the next lowest multiple of $50.

(3) *Excess income amount.*—(i) *In general.*—*Excess income amount* means the product of—

(A) The excess of the taxpayer's household income over the taxpayer's applicable filing threshold (as defined in § 1.5000A-3(f)(2)); and

(B) The income percentage.

(ii) *Income percentage.*—For purposes of this section, *income percentage* means—

(A) 1.0 percent for taxable years beginning in 2013;

(B) 1.0 percent for taxable years beginning in 2014;

(C) 2.0 percent for taxable years beginning in 2015; or

(D) 2.5 percent for taxable years beginning after 2015.

(c) *Monthly national average bronze plan premium.*—*Monthly national average bronze plan premium* means, for a month for which a shared responsibility payment is imposed, 1/12 of the annual national average premium for qualified health plans that have a bronze level of coverage, would provide coverage for the taxpayer's shared responsibility family members who do not have minimum essential coverage for the month, and are offered through Exchanges for plan years beginning in the calendar year with or within which the taxable year ends.

(d) *Examples.*—The following examples illustrate the provisions of this section. In each example the taxpayer's taxable year is a calendar year and all members of the taxpayer's shared responsibility family are ineligible for any of the exemptions described in § 1.5000A-3 for a month.

*Example 1. Unmarried taxpayer without minimum essential coverage.* (i) In 2016, Taxpayer G is an unmarried individual with no dependents. G does not have minimum essential coverage for any month in 2016. G's household income is $120,000. G's applicable filing threshold is $12,000. The annual national average bronze plan premium for G is $5,000.

(ii) For each month in 2016, under paragraph (b)(2)(ii) of this section, G's applicable dollar amount is $695. Under paragraph (b)(2)(i) of this section, G's flat dollar amount is $695 (the lesser of $695 and $2,085 ($695 × 3)). Under paragraph (b)(3) of this section, G's excess income amount is $2,700 (($120,000 - $12,000) × 0.025). Therefore, under paragraph (b)(1) of this section, the monthly penalty amount is $225 (the greater of $58 ($695/12) or $225 ($2,700/12)).

(iii) The sum of the monthly penalty amounts is $2,700 ($225 × 12). The sum of the monthly national average bronze plan premiums is $5,000 ($5,000/12 × 12). Therefore, under paragraph (a) of this section, the shared responsibility payment imposed on G for 2016 is $2,700 (the lesser of $2,700 or $5,000).

*Example 2. Part-year coverage.* The facts are the same as in *Example 1*, except G has minimum essential coverage for January through June. The sum of the monthly penalty amounts is $1,350 ($225 × 6). The sum of the monthly national average bronze plan premiums is $2,500 ($5,000/12 × 6). Therefore, under paragraph (a) of this section, the shared responsibility payment imposed on G for 2016 is $1,350 (the lesser of $1,350 or $2,500).

*Example 3. Family without minimum essential coverage.* (i) In 2016, Taxpayers H and J are married and file a joint return. H and J have three children: K, age 21, L, age 15, and M, age 10. No member of the family has minimum essential coverage for any month in 2016. H and J's household income is $250,000. H and J's applicable filing threshold is $24,000. The annual national average bronze plan premium for a family of 5 (3 adults, 2 children) is $15,000.

(ii) For each month in 2016, under paragraphs (b)(2)(ii) and (b)(2)(iii) of this section, the applicable dollar amount is $2,780 (($695 × 3 adults) + (($695/2) × 2 children)). Under paragraph (b)(2)(i) of this section, the flat dollar amount is $2,085 (the lesser of $2,780 and $2,085 ($695 × 3)). Under paragraph (b)(3) of this section, the excess income amount is $5,650 (($250,000 - $24,000) × 0.025). Therefore, under paragraph (b)(1) of this section, the monthly penalty amount is $470.83 (the greater of $173.75 ($2,085/12) or $470.83 ($5,650/12)).

(iii) The sum of the monthly penalty amounts is $5,650 ($470.83 × 12). The sum of the monthly national average bronze plan premiums is $15,000 ($15,000/12 × 12). Therefore, under paragraph (a) of this section, the shared responsibility payment imposed on H and J for 2016 is $5,650 (the lesser of $5,650 or $15,000).

*Example 4. Change in shared responsibility family during the year.* (i) The facts are the same as in *Example 3*, except J has minimum essential coverage for January through June. The annual national average bronze plan premium for a family of 4 (2 adults, 2 children) is $10,000.

(ii) For the period January through June 2016, under paragraphs (b)(2)(ii) and (b)(2)(iii) of this section the applicable dollar amount is $2,085 (($695 × 2 adults) + (($695/2) × 2 children)). Under paragraph (b)(2)(i) of this section, the flat dollar amount is $2,085 (the lesser of $2,085 or $2,085 ($695 × 3)).

(iii) For the period July through December 2016, the applicable dollar amount is $2,780 (($695 × 3 adults) + (($695/2) × 2 children)). Under paragraph (b)(2) of this section, the flat dollar amount is $2,085 (the lesser of $2,780 or $2,085 ($695 × 3)). Under paragraph (b)(3) of this section, the excess income amount is $5,650 (($250,000 - $24,000) × 0.025). Therefore, under paragraph (b)(1) of this section, for January through June the monthly penalty amount is $470.83 (the greater of $173.75 ($2,085/12) or $470.83 ($5,650/12)). The monthly penalty amount for July through December is $470.83 (the greater of $173.75 ($2,085/12) or $470.83 ($5,650/12)).

(iv) The sum of the monthly penalty amounts is $5,650 ($470.83 × 12). The sum of the monthly national average bronze plan premiums is $12,500 ((($10,000/12) × 6) + (($15,000/12) × 6))). Therefore, under paragraph (a) of this section, the shared responsibility payment imposed on H and J for 2016 is $5,650 (the lesser of $5,650 or $12,500).

*Example 5. Eighteenth birthday during the year.* (i) In 2016 Taxpayers S and T are married and file a joint return. S and T have one child, U, who turns 18 years old on June 28. S, T, and U do not enroll in, and as a result are not eligible to receive benefits under, affordable employer-sponsored coverage offered by T's employer for 2016. S and T's household income is $60,000. S and T's applicable filing threshold is $24,000. The annual national average bronze plan premium for a family of 3 (2 adults, 1 child) is $11,000.

(ii) For the period January through June 2016, under paragraphs (b)(2)(ii) and (b)(2)(iii) of this section, the applicable dollar amount is $1,737.50 (($695 × 2 adults) + ($695/2) × 1 child)). Under paragraph (b)(2) of this section, the flat dollar amount is $1,737.50 (the lesser of $1,737.50 or $2,085 ($695 × 3)).

(iii) For the period July through December 2016, the applicable dollar amount is $2,085 ($695 × 3). Under paragraph (b)(2)(i) of this section, the flat dollar amount is $2,085 (the lesser of $2,085 or $2,085 ($695 x 3)). Under paragraph (b)(3) of this section, the excess income amount is $900 (($60,000 - $24,000) × 0.025). Therefore, under paragraph (b)(1) of this section, for January through June the monthly penalty amount is $144.79 (the greater of $144.79 ($1,737.50/12) or $75 ($900/12)). The monthly penalty amount for July through December is $173.75 (the greater of $173.75 ($2,085/12) or $75 ($900/12)).

(iv) The sum of the monthly penalty amounts is $1,911.24 (($144.79 × 6) + ($173.75 × 6)). The sum of the monthly national average bronze plan premiums is $11,000 ($11,000/12 × 12). Therefore, under paragraph (a) of this section, the shared responsibility payment imposed on S and T for 2016 is $1,911.24 (the lesser of $1,911.24 or $11,000). [Reg. § 1.5000A-4.]

☐ [T.D. 9632, 8-27-2013 (*corrected* 12-24-2013) and T.D. 9705, 11-21-2014.]

### [Reg. § 1.5000A-5]

§ 1.5000A-5. **Administration and procedure.**—(a) *In general.*—A taxpayer's liability for the shared responsibility payment for a month must be reported on the taxpayer's Federal income tax return for the taxable year that includes the month. The period of limitations for assessing the shared responsibility payment is the same as that prescribed by section 6501 for the taxable year to which the Federal income tax return on which the shared responsibility payment is to be reported relates. The shared responsibility payment is payable upon notice and demand by the Secretary, and except as provided in paragraph (b) of this section, is assessed and collected in the same manner as an assessable penalty under subchapter B of chapter 68 of the Internal Revenue Code. The shared responsibility payment is not subject to deficiency procedures of subchapter B of chapter 63 of the Internal Revenue Code. Interest on this payment accrues in accordance with the rules in section 6601.

(b) *Special rules.*—Notwithstanding any other provision of law—

(1) *Waiver of criminal penalties.*—In the case of a failure by a taxpayer to timely pay the shared responsibility payment, the taxpayer is not subject to criminal prosecution or penalty for the failure.

(2) *Limitations on liens and levies.*—If a taxpayer fails to pay the shared responsibility payment imposed by this section and §§ 1.5000A-1 through 1.5000A-4, the Secretary will not file notice of lien on any property of the taxpayer, or levy on any property of the taxpayer for the failure.

(3) *Authority to offset against overpayment.*—Nothing in this section prohibits the Secretary from offsetting any liability for the shared responsibility payment against any overpayment due the taxpayer, in accordance with section 6402(a) and its corresponding regulations.

(c) *Effective/applicability date.*—This section and §§ 1.5000A-1 through 1.5000A-4 apply for months beginning after December 31, 2013. [Reg. § 1.5000A-5.]

☐ [T.D. 9632, 8-27-2013.]

# Cosmetic Services

**See p. 20,601 for regulations not amended to reflect law changes**

[Reg. §49.5000B-1]

**§49.5000B-1. Indoor tanning services.**—(a) *Overview.*—This section provides rules for the tax imposed by section 5000B on any indoor tanning service.

(b) *Imposition of tax.*—(1) *General rule.*—Tax is imposed by section 5000B at the time of payment for any indoor tanning service.

(2) *Undesignated payment cards—In general.*—Payment for indoor tanning services is made when an undesignated payment card is redeemed, in whole or in part, to pay for indoor tanning services (and not when a payment is made to purchase the undesignated payment card).

(c) *Definitions.*—(1) The term *indoor tanning service* means a service employing any electronic product designed to incorporate one or more ultraviolet lamps and intended for the irradiation of an individual by ultraviolet radiation, with wavelengths in air between 200 and 400 nanometers, to induce skin tanning. The term does not include phototherapy service performed by, and on the premises of, a licensed medical professional (such as a dermatologist, psychologist, or registered nurse).

(2) The term *other goods and services* includes, but is not limited to, protective eyewear, footwear, towels, and tanning lotions; manicures, pedicures, and other cosmetic or spa treatments; and access to sport or exercise facilities.

(3) The term *phototherapy service* means a service that exposes an individual to specific wavelengths of light for the treatment of—

(i) Dermatological conditions (such as acne, psoriasis, and eczema);

(ii) Sleep disorders;

(iii) Seasonal affective disorder or other psychiatric disorder;

(iv) Neonatal jaundice;

(v) Wound healing; or

(vi) Other medical condition determined by a licensed medical professional to be treatable by exposing the individual to specific wavelengths of light.

(4) The term *provider* means a person that provides an indoor tanning service as defined in paragraph (c)(1) of this section.

(5) The term *qualified physical fitness facility* means a facility—

(i) In which the predominant business or activity is providing equipment and services to its members for purposes of exercise and physical fitness (determined by taking into consideration all of the facts and circumstances, such as the cost of the equipment, variety of services offered, actual usage of services by customers, revenue generated by different services, and how the entity holds itself out to the public through advertising or other means);

(ii) In which providing indoor tanning services is not a substantial part of the business or activity; and

(iii) That does not sell indoor tanning services for a fee to the public or otherwise offer different pricing options to its members based in whole or in part on access to indoor tanning services.

(6) The term *undesignated payment card* means a gift certificate, gift card, or similar item that can be redeemed for goods or services that may, but do not necessarily, include indoor tanning services.

(d) *Application of tax.*—(1) *Tax on total amount paid for indoor tanning services.*—(i) *In general.*—The tax is imposed on the total amount paid for indoor tanning services, including any amount paid by insurance. The total amount paid is presumed to include the tax if the tax is not separately stated.

(ii) *Free services and reduced rates.*—The tax does not apply to indoor tanning services that are provided free of charge. Indoor tanning services are provided free of charge if no one pays anything of value to the provider of the service for the indoor tanning service. Thus, for example, tax is not imposed on the redemption of a promotional coupon for indoor tanning services if the coupon is provided at no cost and at no obligation to purchase anything. If indoor tanning services are provided at a reduced rate, the tax applies to the amount actually paid for the services.

(iii) *Bonus points.*—The redemption of benefits such as "bonus points" under a loyalty program or similar program or promotion is not a payment for indoor tanning services. Thus, for example, in a promotion that entitles a customer to a "free" tan with the purchase of four tans, tax is not imposed on the redemption of the fifth tan because the amount paid for the four tans included a reduced price for the fifth tan.

(iv) *Other fees.*—Fees for starting, joining, registering, enrolling, and similar fees paid to a provider to join a monthly (or other periodic) membership program that provides indoor tanning services are amounts paid for indoor tanning services. Similarly, amounts paid to a provider that temporarily suspend a periodic membership program are amounts paid for indoor tanning services.

(2) *Charges for other goods and services; tanning services separately stated.*—If a payment covers charges for indoor tanning services as well as other goods and services, the charges for other goods and services may be excluded in computing the tax payable on the amount paid, if the charges—

(i) Are separable (regardless of the manner of invoicing the charges);

(ii) Do not exceed the fair market value of such other goods and services; and

(iii) Are shown in the exact amounts in the provider's records pertaining to the indoor tanning services charge.

(3) *Charges for other goods and services; tanning services bundled.*—This paragraph (d)(3) applies if paragraph (d)(2) of this section does not apply. If a provider offers indoor tanning services (whether of a specified or unlimited amount, including "free" or reduced-rate indoor tanning services) bundled with other goods and services, the payment for the bundled services includes an amount paid for indoor tanning services. The tax applies to that portion of the amount paid to the provider that is reasonably attributable to indoor tanning services. The amount reasonably attributable to indoor tanning services may be determined by—

(i) Applying to the total amount paid a ratio determined by comparing—

(A) The provider's charge for indoor tanning services not in bundled services or, if the provider only charges for indoor tanning services as part of bundled services, the fair market value of similar indoor tanning services (based on the amount charged by comparable providers in the same geographic area); to

(B) The charge determined in paragraph (d)(3)(i)(A) of this section plus the provider's charge for the other goods and services in the bundled services or, if the provider only charges for other goods and services as part of bundled services, the fair market value of similar goods and services (based on the amount charged by comparable providers in the same geographic area); or

(ii) Any other method allowed in guidance published in the Internal Revenue Bulletin.

(4) *Exemption; qualified physical fitness facilities.*—No portion of a payment to a qualified physical fitness facility (within the meaning of paragraph (c)(5) of this section) that includes access to indoor tanning services is treated as a payment for indoor tanning services.

(e) *Person liable for the tax.*—(1) *General rule.*—The person who pays for the indoor tanning service is deemed to be the person on whom the service is performed for purposes of collecting the tax. Thus, the person paying for the indoor tanning service is liable for the tax at the time of payment.

(2) *Undesignated payment cards.*—(i) *In general.*—In the case of a payment made with an undesignated payment card (as defined in paragraph (c)(6) of this section), the person who redeems the card, in whole or in part, to pay specifically for indoor tanning services is the person who pays for the indoor tanning services. Thus, the person who redeems an undesignated payment card, in whole or in part, to pay specifically for indoor tanning services is liable for the tax at the time such payment is made (as described in paragraph (b)(2) of this section).

(ii) *Alternative treatment.*—The Treasury Department and IRS may provide additional options for the treatment of undesignated payment cards in guidance published in the Internal Revenue Bulletin.

(3) *Tax not collected at time of payment.*—If the person paying for the indoor tanning services does not pay the tax to the person receiving the payment for the services at the time of payment for the services, the person receiving the payment is liable for the tax.

(f) *Persons receiving payment must collect tax.*—Every person receiving a payment for indoor tanning services on which a tax is imposed under this section must collect the amount of the tax from the person making that payment.

(g) *Examples.*—The following examples illustrate the application of section 5000B and this section.

*Example 1: Imposition of tax; general rule.* (i) P is a nail salon that also provides indoor tanning service incidental to its primary business of providing nail salon services. P advertises a price of $15.00 (exclusive of the tax imposed by section 5000B) for one 10-minute indoor tanning service. During a period when the tax is 10 percent of the amount paid, P calculates the section 5000B tax on $15.00 as provided by paragraph (d)(1) of this section. Thus, the tax is $1.50 ($15.00 X 10%). The person paying for the service is liable for the tax when that person pays for the services. If P does not collect the tax from the person at the time of the payment for the services, P is liable for the tax.

(ii) The facts are the same as in paragraph (i) of this example except that P's advertised price of $15.00 includes the tanning tax. In this case, the tax is $1.36 ($15.00 X 10%/110%) under the second sentence of paragraph (d)(1) of this section.

*Example 2: Charges for other goods and services; tanning services separately stated.* P provides indoor tanning services and other goods and services. On July 1, 2013, A, an individual, pays P for one 10-minute indoor tanning service and one pair of protective eyewear. P charges $15.00 for the 10-minute indoor tanning service and $2.00 for a pair of protective eyewear. The $2.00 charge for the protective eyewear does not exceed its fair market value. The invoice from P is $17.00 (exclusive of the tax imposed by section 5000B) and separately states the cost of the protective eyewear. Because the cost of the protective eyewear is separately stated, P calculates the section 5000B tax on $15.00 as provided by paragraph (d)(2) of this section. A is liable for the tax when A pays for the services. If P does not collect the tax from A at the time A pays for the services, P is liable for the tax.

*Example 3: Charges for other goods and services; tanning services bundled.* P provides indoor tanning services and other goods and services and offers bundled services. On July 1, 2013, A, an individual, buys bundled service from P that includes 10 swimming lessons, the use of towels while on P's premises, one pair of protective eyewear, and 2 "free" 10-minute indoor tanning service. P charges $252.00 (exclusive of the tax imposed by section 5000B) for the bundled services. If these services are purchased separately, P charges (exclusive of the tax imposed by section 5000B) $25.00 per swimming lesson, $15.00 for a 10-minute indoor tanning service, $2.00 for the protective eyewear, and does not charge for the use of towels while on P's premises. As determined under paragraph (d)(3) of this section, the section 5000B tax applies to the amount reasonably attributable to the indoor tanning service, which is $26.81 (($30.00/$282.00) x $252.00).

*Example 4: Person liable for the tax.* On July 1, 2013, A buys bundled services (described in *Example 3*) from P as a gift for B. Under paragraph (e)(1) of this section, A is deemed to be the person on whom the indoor tanning services are performed for purposes of collecting the tax. Therefore, under paragraph (b)(1) of this section, A is liable for the tax when A pays for the services. The tax will be computed under the rules of paragraph (d)(3) of this section. If A does not pay the tax at the time A pays for the services, P is liable for the tax.

*Example 5: Undesignated payment cards.* (i) P operates a spa that provides a variety of cosmetic goods and services, including indoor tanning services. On July 1, 2013, A buys a gift certificate in the amount of $100.00 from P as a gift for B. The gift certificate may be redeemed by B for B's choice among several services offered by P, including indoor tanning services. On July 15, 2013, B partially redeems the gift certificate to pay for one 10-minute indoor tanning service.

(ii) Under paragraph (b)(2) of this section, a payment for indoor tanning services is made, and the tax under section 5000B is imposed, on July 15, 2013, when B partially redeems the gift certificate to pay for one indoor tanning service. Under paragraph (e)(2) of this section, B is the person who pays for the indoor tanning services. Therefore, B is liable for the tax, computed under the rules of paragraph (d) of this section, and pays the tax by permitting P to debit the amount of the tax from the balance of the gift certificate or by paying the amount of the tax to P in cash. If B does not pay the tax at the time B partially redeems the gift certificate to pay for the indoor tanning services, P is liable for the tax.

*Example 6: Charges for other goods and services; tanning services bundled; amount attributable to tanning services.* On July 1, 2013, A pays $1,000.00 (exclusive of the tax imposed by section 5000B) to spa P for the right to use the following equipment and services during the month of July: up to four massages or facials, unlimited use of a sauna, steam room, showers, and towel service, and unlimited indoor tanning services. If the services are purchased separately, P charges (exclusive of the tax imposed by section 5000B) $150.00 for unlimited indoor tanning services during the month of July, and $900.00 for the other equipment and services during the month of July, not including indoor tanning services. Under paragraph (b) of this section, A has made a payment for indoor tanning services and the tax will be computed under the rules of paragraph (d)(3) of this section. As determined under paragraph (d)(3) of this section, the section 5000B tax applies to the amount reasonably attributable to the indoor tanning services, which is $142.86 (($150.00/$1050.00) x $1000.00). If A does not pay the tax at the time A pays for the bundled services, P is liable for the tax.

*Example 7: Payments to qualified physical fitness facilities.* P operates a fullservice gym facility that offers fitness classes, multiple exercise machines (such as treadmills, stationary bicycles, weight training machines, and free weights), and has as its predominant business providing these facilities, equipment, and services to members for purposes of exercise and physical fitness. P provides its members with access to indoor tanning services, comprised of two tanning beds that meet the definition of indoor tanning services under paragraph (c)(1) of this section. P generally charges its members a fee for monthly usage of its facilities, equipment, and services, but also offers short-term or free trial memberships and allows non-members to purchase individual or a series of exercise classes. P does not charge any fee for the indoor tanning services, does not offer indoor tanning services separately from its other services, and has no membership tier or category that differs from others based on access to the indoor tanning services. P holds itself out to the public through advertising and marketing as providing equipment and services to improve physical fitness. On July 1, 2013, A pays a membership fee to P in return for use of P's facility during the month of July. Under paragraph (d)(4) of this section, no portion of A's membership fee payment is treated as a payment made for indoor tanning services, because A is a qualified physical fitness facility under paragraph (c)(5) of this section. Therefore, no liability for tax arises under section 5000B.

(h) *Effective/applicability date.*—This section applies to amounts paid on or after June 11, 2013. For rules that apply before that date, see 26 CFR part 49 (revised as of April 1, 2013). [Reg. § 49.5000B-1.]

☐ [*T.D. 9621, 6-10-2013.*]

# Tax on Certain Foreign Procurement

**[Reg. § 1.5000C-0]**

**§ 1.5000C-0. Outline of regulation provisions for section 5000C.**—This section lists the captions contained in §§ 1.5000C-1 through 1.5000C-7.

*§ 1.5000C-1 Tax on specified Federal procurement payments.*

(a) Overview.

(b) Imposition of tax.

(c) Definitions.

(d) Exemptions.

(1) Simplified acquisitions.

(2) Emergency acquisitions.

(3) Certain personal service contracts.

(4) Certain foreign humanitarian assistance contracts.

(5) Certain international agreements.

(6) Goods manufactured or produced or services provided in the United States.

(7) Goods manufactured or produced or services provided in a country that is a party to an international procurement agreement.

(e) Country in which goods are manufactured or produced or services provided.

(1) Goods manufactured or produced.

(2) Provision of services.

(3) Allocation of total contract price to determine the nonexempt amount.

(4) Reduction or elimination of withholding by an acquiring agency.

*§ 1.5000C-2 Withholding on specified Federal procurement payments.*

(a) In general.

(b) Steps in determining the obligation to withhold under section 5000C.

(1) Determine whether the payment is pursuant to a contract for goods or services.

(2) Determine whether the payment is made pursuant to a contract with a U.S. person.

(3) Determine whether the payment is for purchases under the simplified acquisition procedures.

(4) Determine whether the payment is for emergency acquisitions.

(5) Determine whether the payment is for personal services under the simplified acquisition threshold.

(6) Determine whether the payment is pursuant to a foreign humanitarian assistance contract.

(7) Determine whether the foreign contracting party is entitled to relief pursuant to an international agreement.

(8) Determine whether the contract is for goods manufactured or produced or services provided in the United States or in a foreign country that is a party to an international procurement agreement.

(9) Compute amounts to withhold.

(10) Deposit and report amounts withheld.

(c) Determining whether the contracting party is a U.S. person.

(1) In general.

(2) Determination based on Taxpayer Identification Number (TIN).

(3) Determination based on the Form W-9.

(4) Contracting party treated as a foreign contracting party.

(d) Withholding when a foreign contracting party submits a Section 5000C Certificate.

(1) In general.

(2) Exemption for a foreign contracting party entitled to the benefit of relief pursuant to certain international agreements.

(3) Exemption when goods are manufactured or produced or services provided in the United States, or in a foreign country that is a party to an international procurement agreement.

(4) Information required for Section 5000C Certificate.

(5) Validity period of Section 5000C Certificate.

(6) Change in circumstances.

(7) Form W-14.

(8) Time for submitting Section 5000C Certificate.

(e) Offset for underwithholding or overwithholding.

(1) In general.

(2) Underwithholding.

(3) Overwithholding.

*§ 1.5000C-3 Payment and returns of tax withheld by the acquiring agency.*

(a) In general.

(b) Deposit rules.

(1) Acquiring agency with a chapter 3 deposit requirement treats amounts withheld as under chapter 3.

(2) Acquiring agency with no chapter 3 filing obligation deposits its withheld amounts monthly.

(c) Return requirements.

(1) In general.

(2) Classified or confidential contracts.

(d) Special arrangement for certain contracts.

*§ 1.5000C-4 Requirement for the foreign contracting party to file a return and pay tax, and procedures for the contracting party to seek a refund.*

(a) In general.

(b) Tax obligation of foreign contracting party independent of withholding.

(c) Return of tax by the foreign contracting party.

(d) Time and manner of paying tax.

(e) Refund requests when amount withheld exceeds tax liability.

*§ 1.5000C-5 Anti-abuse rule.*

*§ 1.5000C-6 Examples.*

*§ 1.5000C-7 Effective/applicability date.* [Reg. § 1.5000C-0.]

☐ *[T.D. 9782, 8-17-2016.]*

### [Reg. § 1.5000C-1]

**§ 1.5000C-1. Tax on specified Federal procurement payments.—** (a) *Overview.*—This section provides definitions and general rules relating to the imposition of, and exemption from, the tax on specified Federal procurement payments under section 5000C. Section 1.5000C-2 provides rules concerning withholding under section 5000C(d)(1), including the steps that must be taken to determine the obligation to withhold and whether an exemption from withholding applies. Section 1.5000C-3 provides the time and manner for depositing the amounts withheld under section 5000C and the related reporting requirements. Section 1.5000C-4 contains the rules that apply to a foreign contracting party that must pay and report the tax under section 5000C when the tax obligation under section 5000C is not fully satisfied by withholding, as well as procedures by which a contracting party may seek a refund when the amount withheld exceeds its tax liability under section 5000C. Section 1.5000C-5 contains an anti-abuse rule. Section 1.5000C-6 contains examples illustrating the principles of § § 1.5000C-1 through 1.5000C-4. Finally, § 1.5000C-7 contains the effective/applicability date for § § 1.5000C-1 through 1.5000C-7.

(b) *Imposition of tax.*—Except as otherwise provided, section 5000C imposes on any foreign contracting party a tax equal to 2 percent of the amount of a specified Federal procurement payment. In general, the tax imposed under section 5000C applies to specified Federal procurement payments received pursuant to contracts entered into on and after January 2, 2011. Specified Federal procurement payments received by a nominee or agent on behalf of a contracting party are considered to be received by that contracting party. The tax imposed under section 5000C is to be applied in a manner consistent with U.S. obligations under international agreements. Payments for the purchase or lease of land or an interest in land are not subject to the tax imposed under section 5000C.

(c) *Definitions.*—Solely for purposes of section 5000C and § § 1.5000C-1 through 1.5000C-7, the following definitions apply:

(1) The term *acquiring agency* means the U.S. government department, agency, independent establishment, or corporation described in paragraph (c)(7) of this section that is a party to the contract. To the extent that a U.S. government department or agency, other than the acquiring agency, is making the payments pursuant to the contract, that department or agency is also considered to be the acquiring agency.

(2) The term *contract* has the same meaning as provided in 48 CFR 2.101, and thus does not include a grant agreement or a cooperative agreement within the meaning of 31 U.S.C. 6304 and 6305, respectively. A contract may include an agreement that is not executed under the Federal Acquisition Regulations (FAR), 48 CFR Chapter 1.

(3) The term *contract ratio* refers to the nonexempt amount over the total contract price.

(4) The term *contracting party* means any person that is a party to a contract with the U.S. government that is entered into on or after January 2, 2011. See § 1.5000C-1(b) for situations involving a nominee or agent.

(5) The term *foreign contracting party* means a contracting party that is a foreign person.

(6) The term *foreign person* means any person other than a United States person (as defined in section 7701(a)(30)).

(7) The term *Government of the United States* or *U.S. government* means the executive departments specified in 5 U.S.C. 101, the military departments specified in 5 U.S.C. 102, the independent establishments specified in 5 U.S.C. 104(1), and wholly owned government corporations specified in 31 U.S.C. 9101(3). Unless otherwise specified in 5 U.S.C. 101, 102, or 104(1), or 31 U.S.C. 9101(3), the term Government of the United States or U.S. government does not include any quasi-governmental entities or instrumentalities of the U.S. government.

(8) The term *international procurement agreement* means the World Trade Organization Government Procurement Agreement within the meaning of 48 CFR 25.400(a)(1) and any free trade agreement to which the United States is a party that includes government procurement obligations that provide appropriate competitive government procurement opportunities to U.S. goods, services, and suppliers. A party to an international procurement agreement is a signatory to the agreement and does not include a country that is merely an observer with respect to the agreement.

(9) The term *nonexempt amount* means the portion of the contract price allocated to nonexempt goods and nonexempt services.

(10) The term *nonexempt goods* means goods manufactured or produced in a foreign country that is not a party to an international procurement agreement with the United States.

(11) The term *nonexempt services* means services provided in a foreign country that is not a party to an international procurement agreement with the United States.

(12) The term *outlying areas* has the same meaning as set forth in 48 CFR 2.101(b), which includes Puerto Rico, the Northern Mariana Islands, American Samoa, Guam, the Virgin Islands, Baker Island, Howland Island, Jarvis Island, Johnston Atoll, Kingman Reef, Midway Islands, Navassa Island, Palmyra Atoll, and Wake Atoll.

(13) The term *qualified income tax treaty* means a U.S. income tax treaty in force that contains a nondiscrimination provision that applies to the tax imposed under section 5000C and prohibits taxation that is more burdensome on a foreign national than a U.S. national (or in the case of certain income tax treaties, taxation that is more burdensome on a foreign citizen than a U.S. citizen), regardless of its residence.

(14) The term *Section 5000C Certificate* means a written statement that includes the information described in § 1.5000C-2(d) that the foreign contracting party submits to an acquiring agency for the purposes of demonstrating that the foreign contracting party is eligible for certain exemptions from withholding (in whole or in part) under section 5000C with respect to a contract. The term may also include any form that the Internal Revenue Service may prescribe as a substitute for the Section 5000C Certificate, such as Form W-14, "Certificate of Foreign Contracting Party Receiving Federal Procurement Payments."

(15) The term *specified Federal procurement payment* means any payment made pursuant to a contract with a foreign contracting party that is for goods manufactured or produced or services provided in a foreign country that is not a party to an international

procurement agreement with the United States. For purposes of the prior sentence, a foreign country does not include an outlying area.

(16) The term *Taxpayer Identification Number* or *TIN* means the identifying number assigned to a person under section 6109, as defined in section 7701(a)(41).

(17) The term *total contract price* means the total cost to the U.S. Government of the goods and services procured under a contract and paid to the contracting party.

(d) *Exemptions.*—The tax imposed under paragraph (b) of this section does not apply to the payments made in the following situations. For the exemptions in paragraphs (d)(5), (6) and (7) of this section, see § 1.5000C-2(d) for the procedures to eliminate withholding by an acquiring agency.

(1) *Simplified acquisitions.*—Payments for purchases under the simplified acquisition procedures that do not exceed the simplified acquisition threshold as described in 48 CFR 2.101.

(2) *Emergency acquisitions.*—Payments made pursuant to a contract if the contract is—

(i) Awarded under the "unusual and compelling urgency" authority of 48 CFR 6.302-2, or

(ii) Entered into under the emergency acquisition flexibilities as defined in 48 CFR part 18.

(3) *Certain personal service contracts.*—Payments for services provided by, and under contracts with, a single individual in which the payments do not (and will not) exceed on an annual calendar year basis the simplified acquisition threshold as described in 48 CFR 2.101 for all years of the contract. Payments that satisfy this exemption remain exempt if the contract is later renegotiated so that future payments under the contract do not meet this exemption.

(4) *Certain foreign humanitarian assistance contracts.*—Payments made by the U.S. government pursuant to a contract with a foreign contracting party to obtain goods or services described in or authorized under 7 U.S.C. 1691, *et seq.*, 22 U.S.C. 2151, *et seq.*, 22 U.S.C 2601 *et seq.*, 22 U.S.C. 5801 *et seq.*, 22 U.S.C. 5401 *et seq.*, 10 U.S.C. 402, 10 U.S.C. 404, 10 U.S.C. 407, 10 U.S.C. 2557, and 10 U.S.C. 2561, if the acquiring agency determines that the payment is for the purpose of providing foreign humanitarian assistance.

(5) *Certain international agreements.*—Payments made by the U.S. government pursuant to a contract with a foreign contracting party when the payments are entitled to relief from the tax imposed under section 5000C pursuant to an international agreement with the United States, including relief pursuant to a nondiscrimination provision of a qualified income tax treaty, because the foreign contracting party is entitled to the benefit of that provision.

(6) *Goods manufactured or produced or services provided in the United States.*—A payment made pursuant to a contract to the extent that the payment is for goods manufactured or produced or services provided in the United States.

(7) *Goods manufactured or produced or services provided in a country that is a party to an international procurement agreement.*—A payment made pursuant to a contract to the extent the payment is for goods manufactured or produced or services provided in a country that is a party to an international procurement agreement, as defined in paragraph (c)(8) of this section.

(e) *Country in which goods are manufactured or produced or services provided.*—(1) *Goods manufactured or produced.*—Solely for purposes of section 5000C, goods are manufactured or produced in the country (or countries)—

(i) Where property has been substantially transformed into the goods that are procured pursuant to a contract; or

(ii) Where there has been assembly or conversion of component parts (involving activities that are substantial in nature and generally considered to constitute the manufacture or production of property) into the final product that constitutes the goods procured pursuant to a contract.

(2) *Provision of services.*—Solely for purposes of section 5000C, services are considered to be provided in the country where the individuals performing the services are physically located when they perform their duties pursuant to the contract.

(3) *Allocation of total contract price to determine the nonexempt amount.*—If, pursuant to a contract, goods are manufactured or produced, or services are provided, in multiple countries and only a portion of the goods manufactured or produced, or the services provided, pursuant to the contract are nonexempt goods or nonexempt services, a foreign contracting party may use a reasonable allocation method to determine the nonexempt amount. A reasonable allocation method would include taking into account the proportionate costs (including the cost of labor and raw materials) incurred to

manufacture or produce the goods in each country, or taking into account the proportionate costs incurred to provide the services in each country.

(4) *Reduction or elimination of withholding by an acquiring agency.*—For procedures to reduce or eliminate withholding by an acquiring agency based on where goods are manufactured or produced or where services are provided, including as a result of an allocation under this paragraph (e), see § 1.5000C-2(d). [Reg. § 1.5000C-1.]

☐ [*T.D. 9782, 8-17-2016.*]

### [Reg. § 1.5000C-2]

**§ 1.5000C-2. Withholding on specified Federal procurement payments.**—(a) *In general.*—Except as otherwise provided in this section, every acquiring agency making a specified Federal procurement payment on which tax is imposed under section 5000C and §§ 1.5000C-1 through 1.5000C-7 must deduct and withhold an amount equal to 2 percent of the payment. For rules relating to the liability of a foreign contracting party with respect to specified Federal procurement payments not fully withheld upon at source, see § 1.5000C-4. An acquiring agency may rely upon any information furnished by a contracting party under this section unless the acquiring agency has reason to know that the information is incorrect or unreliable. An acquiring agency has reason to know that the information is incorrect or unreliable if it has knowledge of relevant facts or statements contained in the submitted information such that a reasonably prudent person in the position of the acquiring agency would know that the information provided is incorrect or unreliable.

(b) *Steps in determining the obligation to withhold under section 5000C.*—An acquiring agency generally determines its obligation to withhold under section 5000C according to the steps described in this paragraph (b). See, however, paragraph (e) of this section for situations in which withholding may be increased in the case of underwithholding, or may be decreased in the case of overwithholding.

(1) *Determine whether the payment is pursuant to a contract for goods or services.*—The acquiring agency determines whether it is making a payment pursuant to a contract for goods or services. To the extent that the acquiring agency is making a payment for any other purpose, it does not have an obligation to withhold under section 5000C on the payment.

(2) *Determine whether the payment is made pursuant to a contract with a U.S. person.*—The acquiring agency determines whether the payment is made pursuant to a contract with a person considered to be a United States person (U.S. person) in accordance with paragraph (c) of this section. If the other contracting party is a U.S. person, the acquiring agency does not have an obligation to withhold under section 5000C on the payment.

(3) *Determine whether the payment is for purchases under the simplified acquisition procedures.*—The acquiring agency determines whether the payment is for purchases under the simplified acquisitions procedures that do not exceed the simplified acquisition threshold as described in 48 CFR 2.101. If it is, the acquiring agency does not have an obligation to withhold under section 5000C on the payment.

(4) *Determine whether the payment is for emergency acquisitions.*—The acquiring agency determines whether the payment is made for certain emergency acquisitions within the meaning of § 1.5000C-1(d)(2). If it is, the acquiring agency does not have an obligation to withhold under section 5000C on the payment.

(5) *Determine whether the payment is for personal services under the simplified acquisition threshold.*—The acquiring agency determines whether payments for services under contracts with a single individual do not exceed the simplified acquisition threshold as described in 48 CFR 2.101 on an annual basis for all years of the contract. If that is the case, the acquiring agency does not have an obligation to withhold under section 5000C on the payment.

(6) *Determine whether the payment is pursuant to a foreign humanitarian assistance contract.*—The acquiring agency determines whether the payment is made pursuant to a foreign humanitarian assistance contract described in § 1.5000C-1(d)(4). If it is, the acquiring agency does not have an obligation to withhold under section 5000C on the payment.

(7) *Determine whether the foreign contracting party is entitled to relief pursuant to an international agreement.*—If the foreign contracting party submits a Section 5000C Certificate in accordance with paragraph (d) of this section representing that the foreign contracting party is entitled to relief from the tax imposed under section 5000C pursuant to an international agreement with the United States (such as relief pursuant to the nondiscrimination provision of a qualified income tax treaty), the acquiring agency does not have an obligation to withhold under section 5000C on the payment.

(8) *Determine whether the contract is for goods manufactured or produced or services provided in the United States or in a foreign country that is a party to an international procurement agreement.*—If the foreign contracting party submits a Section 5000C Certificate in accordance with paragraph (d) of this section that represents that the contract is for goods manufactured or produced or services provided in the United States, or in a foreign country that is a party to an international procurement agreement, the acquiring agency does not have an obligation to withhold. If the Section 5000C Certificate provides that payments under the contract are only partially exempt from withholding under section 5000C, the acquiring agency must withhold to the extent described in paragraph (b)(8) of this section.

(9) *Compute amounts to withhold.*—If, after evaluating each step described in this paragraph (b), the acquiring agency determines that it has an obligation to withhold, the acquiring agency computes the amount of withholding by multiplying the amount of the payment by 2 percent, unless the foreign contracting party has provided a Section 5000C Certificate or the payment is only in part for goods or services. In cases in which the Section 5000C Certificate demonstrates that the exemption in Step 8 applies, the acquiring agency generally computes the amount of withholding by multiplying the amount of the payment by the contract ratio provided on the most recent Section 5000C Certificate, the product of which is multiplied by 2 percent. However, in cases in which the exemption in Step 8 applies and the requirements of paragraph (d)(4)(iii)(B)(2) of this section are met, the acquiring agency computes the amount of withholding based on the payment for the specifically identified items, which may be identified by the contract line item number, or CLIN. In the case in which the payment is only in part for goods or services, the acquiring agency reduces the amount of the payment subject to the tax to the extent it is for something other than goods or services. The acquiring agency withholds the computed amount from the payment.

(10) *Deposit and report amounts withheld.*—The acquiring agency deposits and reports the amounts determined in the prior step in accordance with § 1.5000C-3.

(c) *Determining whether the contracting party is a U.S. person.*—(1) *In general.*—An acquiring agency must rely on the provisions of this paragraph (c) to determine the status of the contracting party as a U.S. person for purposes of withholding under section 5000C.

(2) *Determination based on Taxpayer Identification Number (TIN).*—An acquiring agency must treat a contracting party as a U.S. person if the U.S. government information system (such as the System for Award Management (SAM)) indicates that the contracting party is a corporation (for example, because the name listed in SAM contains the term "Corporation," "Inc.," or "Corp.") and that it has a TIN that begins with two digits other than "98" (a limited liability company or LLC is not treated as a corporation for purposes of this paragraph (c)(2)). Further, an acquiring agency must treat a contracting party as a U.S. person if the acquiring agency has access to a U.S. government information system that indicates that the contracting party is an individual with a TIN that begins with a digit other than "9".

(3) *Determination based on the Form W-9.*—An acquiring agency must treat a contracting party as a U.S. person if the person has submitted to it a valid Form W-9, "Request for Taxpayer Identification Number (TIN) and Certificate" (or valid substitute form described in § 31.3406(h)-3(c)(2) of this chapter), signed under penalties of perjury.

(4) *Contracting party treated as a foreign contracting party.*—If an acquiring agency cannot determine that a contracting party is a U.S. person based on application of paragraph (c)(2) or (3) of this section, then the contracting party is treated as a foreign contracting party for purposes of this section.

(d) *Withholding when a foreign contracting party submits a Section 5000C Certificate.*—(1) *In general.*—Unless the acquiring agency has reason to know that the information is incorrect or unreliable, the acquiring agency may rely on a claim that a foreign contracting party is entitled to an exemption (in whole or in part) from withholding on payments pursuant to a contract if the foreign contracting party provides a Section 5000C Certificate to the acquiring agency as prescribed in this paragraph (d). When a Section 5000C Certificate is furnished, the acquiring agency does not withhold, or must reduce the amount of withholding, on payments made to a foreign person if the certificate establishes that the foreign person is wholly or partially exempt from withholding. An acquiring agency may establish a system for a foreign contracting party to electronically furnish a Section 5000C Certificate.

(2) *Exemption for a foreign contracting party entitled to the benefit of relief pursuant to certain international agreements.*—An acquiring agency does not withhold on payments pursuant to a contract with a foreign contracting party when the payment is entitled to relief from

the tax imposed under section 5000C pursuant to an international agreement, including relief pursuant to a nondiscrimination provision of a qualified income tax treaty, because the foreign contracting party is entitled to the benefit of that agreement and the foreign contracting party has submitted a Section 5000C Certificate that includes all of the information described in paragraphs (d)(4)(i) and (ii) of this section.

(3) *Exemption when goods are manufactured or produced or services provided in the United States, or in a foreign country that is a party to an international procurement agreement.*—An acquiring agency does not withhold on payments pursuant to a contract with a foreign contracting party to the extent that the payments are for goods manufactured or produced or services provided in the United States or in a foreign country that is a party to an international procurement agreement with the United States, provided that the foreign contracting party has submitted a Section 5000C Certificate that includes all of the information described in paragraphs (d)(4)(i) and (iii) of this section. If the Section 5000C Certificate provides that the payment is only partially exempt from withholding under section 5000C, the acquiring agency must withhold to the extent that the payment is not exempt.

(4) *Information required for Section 5000C Certificate.*—(i) *In general.*—The Section 5000C Certificate must be signed under penalties of perjury by the foreign contracting party and contain—

(A) The name of the foreign contracting party, country of organization (if applicable), and permanent residence address of the foreign contracting party;

(B) The mailing address of the foreign contracting party (if different than the permanent residence address);

(C) The TIN assigned to the foreign contracting party (if any);

(D) The identifying or reference number on the contract (if known);

(E) The name and address of the acquiring agency;

(F) A statement that the person signing the Section 5000C Certificate is the foreign contracting party listed in paragraph (d)(4)(i)(A) of this section (or is authorized to sign on behalf of the foreign contracting party);

(G) A statement that the foreign contracting party is not acting as an agent or nominee for another foreign person with respect to the goods manufactured or produced or services provided under the contract;

(H) A statement that the foreign contracting party agrees to pay an amount equal to any tax (including any applicable penalties and interest) due under section 5000C that the acquiring agency does not withhold under section 5000C;

(I) A statement that the foreign contracting party acknowledges and understands the rules in § 1.5000C-4 relating to procedural obligations related to section 5000C; and

(J) A statement that the foreign contracting party has not engaged in a transaction (or series of transactions) with a principal purpose of avoiding the tax imposed under section 5000C as defined in § 1.5000C-5.

(ii) *Additional information required for claiming an exemption based on certain international agreements with the United States.*—In addition to the information required by paragraph (d)(4)(i) of this section, a foreign contracting party claiming an exemption from withholding in reliance on a provision of an international agreement with the United States, including a qualified income tax treaty, must provide—

(A) The name of the international agreement under which the foreign contracting party is claiming benefits;

(B) The specific provision of the international agreement relied upon (for example, the nondiscrimination article of a qualified income tax treaty); and

(C) The basis on which it is entitled to the benefits of that provision (for example, because the foreign contracting party is a corporation organized in a foreign country that has in force a qualified income tax treaty with the United States that covers all nationals, regardless of their residence).

(iii) *Additional required information for claiming exemption based on country where goods are manufactured or services provided.*—(A) *In general.*—In addition to the information required by paragraph (d)(4)(i) of this section, a foreign contracting party claiming an exemption from withholding (in whole or in part) because payments will be pursuant to a contract for goods manufactured or produced or services provided in the United States, or a foreign country that is party to an international procurement agreement, must describe on the Section 5000C Certificate the relevant goods or services and the country (or countries) in which they are manufactured or produced, or are provided, and must include the name of the international procurement agreement or agreements (if relevant).

(B) *Information on allocation to exempt and nonexempt amounts.*—*(1) In general.*—In situations in which a foreign contracting party claims the exemption in paragraph (d)(3) of this section with respect to only a portion of the payments received under the contract, the Section 5000C Certificate must include an explanation of the method used by the foreign contracting party to allocate the total contract price among the countries, as described in § 1.5000C-1(e)(3), if applicable. In general, the Section 5000C Certificate also must include the total contract price and the nonexempt amount; however, when necessary, an estimate of the total contract price or the nonexempt amount may be used. For example, total contract price may be estimated when a Section 5000C Certificate is being completed with respect to payments to be made pursuant to a cost-reimbursement contract that is paid on the basis of actual incurred costs and the total amount of such costs is not known at the time the certificate is provided.

(2) *Specific identification of exempt items.*—If agreed to by the acquiring agency, the Section 5000C Certificate may identify specific exempt and nonexempt amounts. For example, specific contract line items (such as a contract line item number or CLIN) identified in the contract may be listed on the Section 5000C Certificate as exempt and nonexempt amounts (in whole or in part), as applicable. When this paragraph applies, and whether or not the contract identifies exempt and nonexempt amounts, a foreign contracting party must provide the information required by paragraphs (d)(4)(iii)(A) and (d)(4)(iii)(B)(1) of this section, on the Section 5000C Certificate to explain why the contract line items are eligible for an exemption; however, the foreign contracting party is not required to include information about the total contract price under this paragraph. In these circumstances, only one Section 5000C Certificate is required to be provided identifying the exempt and nonexempt contract line items that relate to the contract (for example, a spreadsheet may be attached to the Section 5000C Certificate that identifies the contract line items with an explanation for the treatment as exempt or nonexempt).

(5) *Validity period of Section 5000C Certificate.*—Except as otherwise provided in paragraph (d)(6) of this section, the Section 5000C Certificate is valid for the term of the contract.

(6) *Change in circumstances.*—A foreign contracting party must submit a revised Section 5000C Certificate within 30 days of a change in circumstances that causes the information in a Section 5000C Certificate held by the acquiring agency to be incorrect with respect to the acquiring agency's determination of whether to withhold or the amount of withholding under Section 5000C. An acquiring agency must request a new Section 5000C Certificate from a contracting party in circumstances in which it knows (or has reason to know) that a previously submitted Section 5000C Certificate becomes incorrect or unreliable. An acquiring agency may request an updated Section 5000C Certificate at any time, including when other documentation is required under the contract, such as the annual representations and certifications required in 48 CFR 4.1201. *See* § 1.5000C-6, *Example 6*, for an illustration of this paragraph (6).

(7) *Form W-14.*—A foreign contracting party may choose to use Form W-14, "Certificate of Foreign Contracting Party Receiving Federal Procurement Payments" (or other form that the IRS may prescribe), as its Section 5000C Certificate, provided that it includes all the necessary information required by this paragraph (d).

(8) *Time for submitting Section 5000C Certificate.*—A contracting party must submit the Section 5000C Certificate (such as Form W-14 or Form W-9) as early as practicable (for example, when the offer for the contract is submitted to the U.S. government). In all cases, however, the Section 5000C Certificate must be submitted to the acquiring agency no later than the date of execution of the contract.

(e) *Offset for underwithholding or overwithholding.*—*(1) In general.*—If the foreign contracting party discovers that amounts withheld on prior payments either were insufficient or in excess of the amount required to satisfy its tax liability under section 5000C, the foreign contracting party may request the acquiring agency to increase or decrease the amount of withholding on future payments for which withholding is required under section 5000C. The request must be in writing, signed under penalties of perjury, contain the amount by which the foreign contracting party requests to increase or decrease future amounts withheld under section 5000C, and explain the reason for the request. The request may be submitted in conjunction with an original or updated Section 5000C Certificate.

(2) *Underwithholding.*—Upon receipt of a request described in paragraph (e)(1) of this section, acquiring agencies may increase the amount of withholding under this paragraph to correct underwithholding only if the payment for which the increase is applied is otherwise subject to withholding under section 5000C and made before the date that Form 1042, "Annual Withholding Tax Return for

U.S. Source Income of Foreign Persons," is required to be filed (not including extensions) with respect to the payment for which the underwithholding occurred. Amounts withheld under this paragraph must be deposited and reported in the time and manner as prescribed by § 1.5000C-3. *See* § 1.5000C-4 for procedures for a foreign contracting party that must pay tax due when its tax liability under section 5000C was not fully satisfied by withholding by an acquiring agency.

(3) *Overwithholding.*—Upon receipt of a request described in paragraph (e)(1) of this section, acquiring agencies may decrease the amount of withholding on subsequent payments made to the foreign contracting party that are otherwise subject to withholding under section 5000C provided that the payment for which the decrease is applied is made on or before the date on which Form 1042, "Annual Withholding Tax Return for U.S. Source Income of Foreign Persons," is required to be filed (not including extensions) with respect to the payment for which the overwithholding occurred. *See* § 1.5000C-4(e) for procedures for foreign contracting parties to file a claim for refund for the overwithheld amount under section 5000C. [Reg. § 1.5000C-2.]

☐ [*T.D. 9782, 8-17-2016.*]

## [Reg. § 1.5000C-3]

**§ 1.5000C-3. Payment and returns of tax withheld by the acquiring agency.**—(a) *In general.*—This section provides administrative procedures that acquiring agencies must follow to satisfy their obligations to deposit and report amounts withheld under § 1.5000C-2. An acquiring agency with a section 5000C withholding obligation must increase the amount it deducts and withholds under chapter 3 for fixed or determinable annual or periodical income (FDAP income) by the amount it must withhold under § 1.5000C-2. Accordingly, this section generally applies the administrative provisions of chapter 3 for FDAP income relating to the deposit, payment, and reporting for amounts withheld under § 1.5000C-2, and contains some variation from those provisions to take into account the nature of the tax imposed under section 5000C.

(b) *Deposit rules.*—*(1) Acquiring agency with a chapter 3 deposit requirement treats amounts withheld as under chapter 3.*—If an acquiring agency has a chapter 3 deposit obligation for a period, it must treat any amount withheld under § 1.5000C-2 as an additional amount of tax withheld under chapter 3 for purposes of the deposit rules of § 1.6302-2. Thus, depending on the combined amount withheld under chapter 3 and § 1.5000C-2, an acquiring agency subject to this paragraph (b)(1) must make monthly deposits, quarter-monthly deposits, or annual deposits under the rules in § 1.6302-2. To the extent provided in forms, instructions, or publications prescribed by the Internal Revenue Service (IRS), acquiring agencies must deposit all withheld amounts by *electronic funds transfer*, as that term is defined in § 31.6302-1(h)(4)(i) of this chapter.

(2) *Acquiring agency with no chapter 3 filing obligation deposits withheld amounts monthly.*—If an acquiring agency has no chapter 3 deposit obligation to which the deposit rules of § 1.6302-2 apply for a calendar month, it must make monthly deposits of the amounts withheld under the rules in this paragraph (b)(2). Thus, an acquiring agency with no chapter 3 deposit obligations and that has withheld any amount under § 1.5000C-2 during any calendar month must deposit that amount by the 15th day of the month following the payment. To the extent provided in forms, instructions, or publications prescribed by the Internal Revenue Service (IRS), acquiring agencies must deposit all withheld amounts by *electronic funds transfer*, as that term is defined in § 31.6302-1(h)(4)(i) of this chapter.

(c) *Return requirements.*—*(1) In general.*—Except as provided in paragraph (c)(2) of this section, an acquiring agency that withholds an amount pursuant to section 5000C generally must file Form 1042-S, "Foreign Person's U.S. Source Income Subject to Withholding," and Form 1042, "Annual Withholding Tax Return for U.S. Source Income of Foreign Persons," each year, or other such forms as the IRS may prescribe, to report information related to amounts withheld under section 5000C. The acquiring agency must prepare a Form 1042-S for each contracting party reporting the amount withheld under section 5000C for the preceding calendar year. The Form 1042 must show the aggregate amounts withheld under section 5000C that were required to be reported on Forms 1042-S (including those amounts withheld under section 5000C for which a Form 1042-S is not required to be filed pursuant to paragraph (c)(2) of this section). The Form 1042 must also include the information required by the form and accompanying instructions. Further, any forms required under this paragraph (c) are due at the same time, at the same place, and eligible for the same extended due dates and may be amended in the same manner as Form 1042 and Form 1042-S (or such other forms as the IRS may prescribe related to chapter 3). The acquiring agency must furnish a copy of the Form 1042-S (or such other form as the IRS may prescribe for the same purpose) to the contracting party for whom the form is prepared on or before March 15 of the calendar year following the year in which the amount subject to reporting under section 5000C was paid. It must be filed with a transmittal form as provided in the instructions for Form 1042-S and to the transmittal form. Section 5000C Certificates or other statements or information as prescribed by § 1.5000C-2 that are provided to the acquiring agency are not required to be attached to the Form 1042 filed with the IRS. However, an acquiring agency that is required to file Form 1042 must retain a copy of Form 1042, Form 1042-S, the Section 5000C Certificates, or other statements or information prescribed by § 1.5000C-2 for at least three years from the original due date of Form 1042 or the date it was filed, whichever is later. An acquiring agency that is not required to file Form 1042 must retain any Section 5000C Certificates or other statements or information as prescribed by § 1.5000C-2 for at least three years from the date the Form 1042 would have been due had the acquiring agency had an obligation to file.

(2) *Classified or confidential contracts.*—An acquiring agency is not required to report information otherwise required by this section on Form 1042-S for payments made pursuant to classified or confidential contracts (as described in section 6050M(e)(3)), unless the acquiring agency determines that the information reported on the Form 1042-S does not compromise the safeguarding of classified information or national security.

(d) *Special arrangement for certain contracts.*—In limited circumstances, the IRS may authorize the amount otherwise required to be withheld under section 5000C to be deposited in the time and manner mutually agreed upon by the acquiring agency and the foreign contracting party. In these circumstances, the IRS may in its sole discretion also modify any reporting or return requirements of the acquiring agency or the foreign contracting party. [Reg. § 1.5000C-3.]

☐ [*T.D.* 9782, 8-17-2016.]

### [Reg. § 1.5000C-4]

**§ 1.5000C-4. Requirement for the foreign contracting party to file a return and pay tax, and procedures for the contracting party to seek a refund.**—(a) *In general.*—For purposes of subtitle F of the Internal Revenue Code ("Procedure and Administration"), the tax imposed under section 5000C on foreign persons is treated as a tax imposed under subtitle A. Except as provided elsewhere in the regulations under section 5000C, forms, or accompanying instructions, the tax imposed on foreign contracting parties under section 5000C is administered in a manner similar to gross basis income taxes. This section provides procedures that a foreign contracting party must follow to satisfy its obligations to report and deposit tax due under § 1.5000C-1 as well as procedures for contracting parties to seek a refund of amounts overwithheld.

(b) *Tax obligation of foreign contracting party independent of withholding.*—A foreign contracting party subject to tax under section 5000C and § 1.5000C-1 through 1.5000C-7 remains liable for the tax unless its tax obligation was fully satisfied by withholding by an acquiring agency in accordance with § § 1.5000C-2 and 1.5000C-3.

(c) *Return of tax by the foreign contracting party.*—If the tax liability under § 1.5000C-1 relating to a payment is not fully satisfied by withholding in accordance with § § 1.5000C-2 and 1.5000C-3 (including as a result of the use of an estimated nonexempt amount or estimated total contract price in computing the contract ratio), a foreign contracting party subject to tax under § 1.5000C-1 during a calendar year must make a return of tax on, for example, Form 1120-F, "U.S. Income Tax Return of a Foreign Corporation," or such other form as the Internal Revenue Service (IRS) may prescribe to report the amount of tax due under section 5000C (required return). A foreign contracting party with no other U.S. tax filing obligation other than with respect to its liability for the tax imposed under section 5000C must file its required return on or before the fifteenth day of the sixth month following the close of its taxable year. The required return must include the information required by the form and accompanying instructions. The required return must be filed at the place and time (including any extension of time to file) provided by the form and accompanying instructions. Penalties for failure to file contained in Subtitle F can apply to foreign contracting parties who fail to file the required return. A foreign contracting party must attach copies of all Forms 1042-S, "Foreign Person's U.S. Source Income Subject to Withholding," received from acquiring agencies (if any) to the required return.

(d) *Time and manner of paying tax.*—A foreign contracting party must pay the tax imposed under section 5000C in the manner provided and in the time prescribed in the required return and accompanying instructions. In general, the foreign contracting party must pay the tax at the time that the required return is due, excluding extensions. To the extent provided in forms, instructions, or publications prescribed by the IRS, each foreign contracting party must deposit tax due under section 5000C by *electronic funds transfer,* as that term is defined in § 31.6302-1(h)(4)(i) of this chapter. A foreign contracting party that fails to pay tax in the time and manner prescribed in this section (or under forms, instructions, or publications prescribed by the IRS under this section) may be subject to penalties and interest under Subtitle F.

(e) *Refund requests when amount withheld exceeds tax liability.*—After taking into account any offsets pursuant to § 1.5000C-2(e)(3), if the acquiring agency has overwithheld amounts under section 5000C and has made a deposit of the amounts under § 1.5000C-3(b), the contracting party may claim a refund of the amount overwithheld pursuant to the procedures described in chapter 65. The contracting party's claim for refund must meet the requirements of section 6402 and the regulations thereunder, as applicable, and must be filed before the expiration of the period of limitations on refund in section 6511 and the regulations thereunder. In general, the contracting party making a refund claim must file the required return to claim a refund, stating the grounds upon which the claim is based. A Section 5000C Certificate and a copy of the Form 1042-S received from the acquiring agency must be attached to the required return. For purposes of this section, an amount is overwithheld if the amount withheld from the payment pursuant to section 5000C and § § 1.5000C-1 through 1.5000C-7 exceeds the contracting party's tax liability under § 1.5000C-1, regardless of whether the overwithholding was in error or appeared correct when it occurred. A U.S. person may seek a refund under this paragraph (e) even if it was treated as a foreign person under the rules in § 1.5000C-2 (for example, because it neither had a taxpayer identification number on file in the System for Award Management nor submitted Form W-9, "Request for Taxpayer Identification Number (TIN) and Certification," to the acquiring agency). [Reg. § 1.5000C-4.]

☐ [*T.D.* 9782, 8-17-2016.]

### [Reg. § 1.5000C-5]

**§ 1.5000C-5. Anti-abuse rule.**—If a foreign person engages in a transaction (or series of transactions) with a principal purpose of avoiding the tax imposed under section 5000C, the transaction (or series of transactions) may be disregarded or the arrangement may be recharacterized (including disregarding an intermediate entity), in accordance with its substance. If this section applies, the foreign person remains liable for any tax (including any tax obligation unsatisfied as a result of underwithholding) and the Internal Revenue Service retains all other rights and remedies under any applicable law available to collect any tax imposed on the foreign contracting party by section 5000C. [Reg. § 1.5000C-5.]

☐ [*T.D.* 9782, 8-17-2016.]

### [Reg. § 1.5000C-6]

**§ 1.5000C-6. Examples.**—The rules of § § 1.5000C-1 through 1.5000C-4 are illustrated by the following examples. For purposes of the examples: All contracts are executed with acquiring agencies on or after January 2, 2011, and are for the provision of either goods or services; none of the exemptions described in § 1.5000C-1(d) apply, unless otherwise explicitly stated; the acquiring agencies have no other withholding obligations under chapter 3 of the Code and have no other contracts subject to section 5000C; the foreign contracting parties do not have any U.S. source income or a U.S. tax return filing obligation other than a tax return filing obligation that arises based on the facts described in the particular example; and none of the contracts are classified or confidential contracts as described in section 6050M(e)(3).

*Example 1. U.S. person not subject to tax; no withholding.* (i) *Facts.* Company A Inc., a domestic corporation and the contracting party, enters into a contract with Agency L, the acquiring agency. Before making its first payment under the contract (for example, on the date of execution of the contract), pursuant to the first step in § 1.5000C-2(b), Agency L determines that the contract will be for services. Under the second step, Agency L reviews Company A Inc.'s record in the System for Award Management (SAM) and determines that Company A is a corporation and is considered to be a U.S. person because Agency L's records demonstrate that Company A Inc. is a business entity treated as a corporation for tax purposes that has a TIN that does not begin with "98."

(ii) *Analysis.* Company A Inc. is a U.S. person and thus is not subject to the tax under section 5000C. Moreover, because Company A Inc. is a corporation for tax purposes that has a TIN that does not begin with "98," Agency L is able to determine that it has no obligation to withhold any amounts under section 5000C on the payment made to Company A Inc. For purposes of section 5000C, Company A Inc. could also establish that it is a U.S. person by providing a Form W-9, "Request for Taxpayer Identification Number (TIN) and Certification," to Agency L. Company A Inc. does not need to file a Section 5000C Certificate to demonstrate its eligibility for an exemption from withholding.

*Example 2. Foreign national entitled to the benefit of a nondiscrimination provision of a treaty; no withholding.* (i) *Facts.* Company B, a foreign contracting party and a national of Country T, provides goods to Agency M, the acquiring agency. Company B determines that it is exempt from tax under section 5000C because it is entitled to the benefit of the nondiscrimination article of a qualified income tax treaty between the United States and Country T. Company B submits a Section 5000C Certificate to Agency M when the contract is executed. Company B uses Form W-14, "Certificate of Foreign Contracting Party Receiving Federal Procurement Payments," and properly fills the relevant sections stating the name of the treaty, the specific article relied upon, and the basis on which it is entitled to the benefits of that article. Following the steps in § 1.5000C-2, Agency M determines that the nondiscrimination provision of the Country T-United States income tax treaty applies to exempt Company B from the tax imposed under section 5000C. Agency M makes one lump sum payment of $50 million to Company B pursuant to the contract.

(ii) *Analysis.* Company B has no liability for tax under section 5000C because it is entitled to the benefit of a nondiscrimination article of a qualified income tax treaty. Because Company B submitted a Section 5000C Certificate meeting the requirements in § 1.5000C-2 and Agency M does not have reason to know that the submitted information is incorrect or unreliable, Agency M is not required to withhold under section 5000C. Agency M must retain the Section 5000C Certificate for at least three years pursuant to § 1.5000C-3(c)(1) from the due date for the Form 1042 (if it were required).

*Example 3. Foreign treaty beneficiary does not submit Section 5000C Certificate; withholding required.* (i) *Facts.* The facts are the same as in *Example 2*, except that Company B does not submit a Section 5000C Certificate to Agency M before Agency M makes the $50 million payment.

(ii) *Analysis.* Company B is not subject to tax under section 5000C, but Agency M must nevertheless withhold on the payment made to Company B because Agency M did not receive a Section 5000C Certificate from Company B in the time and manner required pursuant to § 1.5000C-2(d). Agency M must withhold $1 million (2 percent of $50 million) on the payment, and deposit that amount under the rules in § 1.5000C-3 no later than the 15th day of the month following the month in which the payment was made. Agency M must also complete Forms 1042, "Annual Withholding Tax Return for U.S. Source Income of Foreign Persons," and 1042-S, "Foreign Person's U.S. Source Income Subject to Withholding," on or before the date specified on those forms and the accompanying instructions. Agency M must furnish copies of Form 1042-S to Company B. Agency M must retain a copy of the Form 1042 and the Form 1042-S for 3 years from the due date for the Form 1042 pursuant to § 1.5000C-3(c)(1). As Company B is not liable for the tax, it may later file a claim for refund pursuant to the procedures described in chapter 65.

*Example 4. Foreign contracting party partially exempt from tax under section 5000C when goods are manufactured in different countries.* (i) *Facts.* Company C, a foreign contracting party, provides goods to Agency N in 2015. The terms of the contract require that payment be made to Company C by Agency N in two $5 million installments in 2015. Company C has a TIN that begins with "98" and is not entitled to relief pursuant to an international agreement with the United States, such as relief pursuant to a nondiscrimination provision of a qualified income tax treaty. Some of the goods are manufactured in Country R, which is a party to an international procurement agreement with the United States, with the remainder being manufactured in Country S, a country that is not a party to an international procurement agreement with the United States. Company C uses a reasonable allocation method based on the information available to it at the time in accordance with § 1.5000C-1(e)(3) to estimate that $3 million is the nonexempt amount that is allocated to the goods produced in Country S. Company C submits a valid and complete Section 5000C Certificate to Agency N in the time and manner required by § § 1.5000C-1 through 1.5000C-7 that provides that the nonexempt amount is $3 million. In 2015, Agency N pays Company C in two installments pursuant to the terms of the contract.

(ii) *Analysis.* Using a reasonable allocation method to determine the estimated nonexempt amount, Company C determines that pursuant

to section 5000C and § § 1.5000C-1 through 1.5000C-7, tax of $30,000 (2 percent of the $5 million payment, or $100,000 multiplied by a fraction, the numerator of which is the estimated nonexempt amount, $3 million, and the denominator of which is the estimated total contract price, or $10 million) is imposed on each payment made to Company C. Because Company C has timely submitted a Section 5000C Certificate explaining the basis for this allocation, Agency N withholds $30,000 on each payment made to Company C. Agency N must deposit each $30,000 withholding tax under the rules in § 1.5000C-3 no later than the 15th day of the month following the month in which each payment is made. Agency N must also complete Forms 1042 and 1042-S and furnish copies of Form 1042-S to Company C. Agency N must retain a copy of the Form 1042 and the Form 1042-S for at least three years from the due date for the Form 1042 pursuant to § 1.5000C-3(c)(1). Provided that Agency N properly withholds on the nonexempt portion as required under section 5000C and § § 1.5000C-1 through 1.5000C-7 and that Company C's estimate of the nonexempt amount is the actual nonexempt amount, Company C does not have an additional tax liability or a U.S. tax return filing obligation as a result of receiving the payments.

*Example 5. Foreign contracting party liable for additional tax under Section 5000C not fully withheld upon due to errors on the Section 5000C Certificate.* (i) *Facts.* The facts are the same as in *Example 4*, except that the Section 5000C Certificate submitted to Agency N by Company C erroneously provides that the estimated nonexempt amount is $1.5 million instead of $3 million. As a result, Agency N only withholds $15,000 (2 percent of the $5 million payment multiplied by a fraction (the numerator of which is the estimated nonexempt amount stated on the Section 5000C Certificate, $1.5 million, and the denominator of which is the estimated total contract price, or $10 million)) on each payment made to Company C. Agency N neither discovered nor had reason to know that the information on the Section 5000C Certificate was incorrect or unreliable. After both payments have been made and after the filing due date for Form 1042 for 2015, Company C determines that the estimated nonexempt amount should have been stated as $3 million on the Section 5000C Certificate.

(ii) *Analysis.* The tax imposed under section 5000C on Company C as a result of the receipt of specified Federal procurement payments is $60,000 and this amount has not been fully satisfied by withholding by Agency N. Accordingly, Company C must remit additional tax of $30,000 ($60,000 tax liability less $30,000 amounts already withheld by Agency N) and file its required return, a Form 1120-F, "U.S. Income Tax Return of a Foreign Corporation," for 2015 to report this tax liability, as required by § 1.5000C-4. Company C must explain its corrected allocation method in its Form 1120-F. Company C must also attach a copy of the Form 1042-S it received from Agency N to Form 1120-F.

*Example 6. Foreign contracting party submits revised Section 5000C Certificate due to change in circumstances.* (i) *Facts.* The facts are the same as in *Example 4*, except that, after the first payment, Company C changes its business so that all of the goods manufactured with respect to the second payment are manufactured in Country R. Prior to the second payment, Company C submits a revised Section 5000C Certificate indicating this change in circumstance pursuant to § 1.5000C-2(d)(6).

(ii) *Analysis.* Agency N withholds $30,000 on the first payment made to Company C and does not withhold on the second payment. Company C does not have an additional tax liability or a U.S. tax return filing obligation as a result of receiving the payments. [Reg. § 1.5000C-6.]

☐ [*T.D.* 9782, 8-17-2016.]

### [Reg. § 1.5000C-7]

**§ 1.5000C-7. Effective/applicability date.**—Section 5000C applies to specified Federal procurement payments received pursuant to contracts entered into on and after January 2, 2011. Sections 1.5000C-1 through 1.5000C-7 apply on and after November 16, 2016. Contracting parties and acquiring agencies may rely upon the rules in the regulations before such date. If a foreign contracting party fully satisfies its tax and filing obligations under section 5000C with respect to any payments received in tax years ending before November 16, 2016 on or before the later of November 16, 2016 or the due date for the foreign person's income tax return for the year in which the payment was received in a manner consistent with the final regulations, penalties will not be asserted on the foreign contracting parties with respect to those payments or returns. [Reg. § 1.5000C-7.]

☐ [*T.D.* 9782, 8-17-2016.]

# Branded Prescription Drug Fee

See p. 20,601 for regulations not amended to reflect law changes

## [Reg. § 51.1]

**§ 51.1. Overview.**—(a) The regulations in this part 51 are designated "Branded Prescription Drug Fee Regulations."

(b) The regulations in this part 51 provide guidance on the annual fee imposed on covered entities engaged in the business of manufacturing or importing branded prescription drugs by section 9008 of the Patient Protection and Affordable Care Act (ACA), Public Law 111-148 (124 Stat. 119 (2010)), as amended by section 1404 of the Health Care and Education Reconciliation Act of 2010 (HCERA), Public Law 111-152 (124 Stat. 1029 (2010)). All references in these regulations to section 9008 are references to section 9008 of the ACA, as amended by section 1404 of HCERA. Unless otherwise indicated, all other section references are to sections in the Internal Revenue Code. All references to "fee" in these regulations are references to the fee imposed by section 9008.

(c) Section 9008(b)(4) sets an applicable fee amount for each year, beginning with 2011, that will be apportioned among covered entities with aggregate branded prescription drug sales of over $5 million to government programs or pursuant to coverage under such programs. Generally, each covered entity is liable for a fee in each fee year that is based on its sales of branded prescription drugs in the sales year that corresponds to the fee year in an amount determined by the Internal Revenue Service (IRS) under the rules of this part. [Reg. § 51.1.]

☐ [T.D. 9684, 7-24-2014.]

## [Reg. § 51.2]

**§ 51.2. Explanation of terms.**—(a) *In general.*—This section explains the terms used in this part for purposes of the fee imposed by section 9008 on branded prescription drugs.

(b) *Agencies.*—The term *Agencies* means—

(1) The Centers for Medicare and Medicaid Services of the Department of Health and Human Services (CMS);

(2) The Department of Veterans Affairs (VA); and

(3) The Department of Defense (DOD).

(c) *Branded prescription drug.*—(1) *In general.*—The term *branded prescription drug* means—

(i) Any prescription drug the application for which was submitted under section 505(b) of the Federal Food, Drug, and Cosmetic Act (21 U.S.C. 355(b)) (FFDCA); or

(ii) Any biological product the license for which was submitted under section 351(a) of the Public Health Service Act (42 U.S.C. 262(a)).

(2) *Prescription drug.*—The term *prescription drug* means any drug that is subject to section 503(b) of the FFDCA.

(d) *Branded prescription drug sales.*—The term *branded prescription drug sales* means sales of branded prescription drugs to any government program or pursuant to coverage under any such government program. However, the term does not include sales of orphan drugs.

(e) *Covered entity.*—(1) *In general.*—The term *covered entity* means any manufacturer or importer with gross receipts from branded prescription drug sales including—

(i) A single-person covered entity; or

(ii) A controlled group.

(2) *Single-person covered entity.*—The term *single-person covered entity* means a covered entity that is not affiliated with a controlled group.

(3) *Controlled group.*—The term *controlled group* means a group of two or more persons, including at least one person that is a covered entity, that is treated as a single employer under section 52(a), 52(b), 414(m), or 414(o).

(4) *Special rules for controlled groups.*—For purposes of paragraph (e)(3) of this section (related to controlled groups)—

(i) A foreign entity subject to tax under section 881 is included within a group under section 52(a) or 52(b); and

(ii) A person is treated as being a member of a controlled group if it is a member of the group on the end of the day on December 31st of the sales year.

(5) *Covered entity status.*—(i) *Rule.*—An entity's status as a covered entity begins in the first fee year in which the entity has branded prescription drug sales and continues each subsequent fee year until there are no remaining branded prescription drug sales for that entity to be taken into account as described in § 51.5(c) or used to calculate the adjustment amount described in § 51.5(e).

(ii) *Example.*—The following example illustrates the rule of paragraph (e)(5)(i) of this section:

(A) *Facts.*—Entity A is a manufacturer with gross receipts of more than $5 million from branded prescription drugs sales in 2011. Entity A does not have any gross receipts from branded prescription drug sales before or after 2011.

(B) *Analysis.*—Entity A is a covered entity beginning in 2011 because it had gross receipts from branded prescription drug sales in 2011. For the 2011 fee year, Entity A does not owe a fee because the 2011 fee is based on sales data from the 2009 sales year. For the 2012 fee year, Entity A does not owe a fee because the 2012 fee is based on sales data from the 2010 sales year. Entity A continues to be a covered entity for the 2012 fee year because its branded prescription drug sales from the 2011 sales year have not yet been taken into account as described in § 51.5(c) and used to calculate the adjustment amount described in § 51.5(e). For the 2013 fee year, Entity A continues to be a covered entity because a portion of its branded prescription drug sales from the 2011 sales year are taken into account as described in § 51.5(c) for purposes of computing the 2013 fee. For the 2013 fee year, Entity A is also liable for the adjustment amount described in § 51.5(e) for the difference between its 2012 fee computed using sales data from the 2010 sales year, which is $0, and what the 2012 fee would have been using sales data from the 2011 sales year. For the 2014 fee year, Entity A continues to be a covered entity because a portion of its branded prescription drug sales for the 2011 sales year are used to calculate the adjustment amount described in § 51.5(e). Therefore, for the 2014 fee year, Entity A will receive an adjustment amount for the difference between its 2013 fee computed using sales data from the 2011 sales year, and what the 2013 fee would have been using sales data from the 2012 sales year, which is $0. After the 2014 fee year, there are no remaining branded prescription drug sales to be taken into account as described in § 51.5(c) or used to calculate the adjustment amount described in § 51.5(e) for Entity A. Accordingly, Entity A is not a covered entity after the 2014 fee year.

(f) *Designated entity.*—(1) *In general.*—The term *designated entity* means the person within a controlled group that is designated to act for the controlled group regarding the fee by—

(i) Filing Form 8947, "Report of Branded Prescription Drug Information";

(ii) Receiving IRS communications about the fee for the group;

(iii) Filing an error report for the group, if applicable, as described in § 51.7; and

(iv) Paying the fee to the government.

(2) *Selection of designated entity.*—(i) *Controlled group selection of a designated entity.*—Except as provided in paragraph (f)(2)(ii) of this section, the controlled group may select a person as the designated entity by filing Form 8947 in accordance with the form instructions. The designated entity must state under penalties of perjury that all members of the controlled group have consented to the selection of the designated entity. The designated entity must maintain a record of all member consents. Each member of a controlled group must maintain a record of its consent to the controlled group's selection of the designated entity.

(ii) *Requirement for affiliated groups; agent for the group.*—If the controlled group, without regard to foreign corporations included under section 9008(d)(2)(B), is also an affiliated group whose common parent files a consolidated return for federal income tax purposes, the designated entity is the agent for the group (within the meaning of § 1.1502-77 of this title).

(iii) *IRS selection of a designated entity.*—Except as provided in paragraph (f)(2)(ii) of this section, if a controlled group does not select a designated entity as provided in paragraph (f)(2)(i) of this section, the IRS will select a member of the controlled group as the designated entity for the controlled group. If the IRS selects the designated entity, then all members of that controlled group will be deemed to have consented to the IRS's selection of the designated entity.

(g) *Fee year.*—The term *fee year* means the calendar year in which the fee for a particular sales year must be paid to the government.

(h) *Government programs.*—The term *government programs* (collectively "Programs"), means—

(1) The Medicare Part B program;

(2) The Medicare Part D program;

(3) The Medicaid program;

(4) Any program under which branded prescription drugs are procured by the Department of Veterans Affairs;

(5) Any program under which branded prescription drugs are procured by the Department of Defense; and

(6) The TRICARE retail pharmacy program.

(i) *Manufacturer or importer.*—The term *manufacturer or importer* means the person identified in the Labeler Code of the National Drug Code (NDC) for a branded prescription drug.

(j) *NDC.*—The term *NDC* means the National Drug Code. The NDC is a unique identifier that is assigned to all drug products approved by the Food and Drug Administration (FDA), including a branded prescription drug. The Labeler Code is the first five numeric characters of the NDC or the first six numeric characters when the available five-character code combinations are exhausted.

(k) *Orphan drugs.*—(1) *In general.*—Except as provided in paragraph (k)(2) of this section, the term *orphan drug* means any branded prescription drug for which any person claimed a section 45C credit and that credit was allowed for any taxable year.

(2) *Exclusions.*—The term *orphan drug* does not include—

(i) Any drug for which there has been a final assessment or court order disallowing the full section 45C credit taken for the drug; or

(ii) Any drug for any sales year after the calendar year in which the FDA approved the drug for marketing for any indication other than the treatment of a rare disease or condition for which a section 45C credit was allowed, regardless of whether a section 45C credit was allowed for the drug before, in the same year as, or after this FDA designation.

(3) *FDA marketing approval for treatment of another rare disease or condition.*—If a drug has prior FDA marketing approval for the treatment of a rare disease or condition for which a section 45C credit was allowed, and the FDA subsequently gives the drug marketing approval for the treatment of another rare disease or condition for which another section 45C credit was also allowed, the drug retains its status as an orphan drug provided the FDA has never approved the drug for marketing for any indication other than the treatment of a rare disease or condition for which a section 45C credit was allowed.

(4) *Examples.*—The following examples illustrate the rules of this paragraph (k):

*Example 1: Allowance of section 45C credit and later FDA marketing approval of drug for an indication other than the treatment of a rare disease or condition.* (i) *Facts.* Drug A is a branded prescription drug that was not on the market before 2011. In 2011, a covered entity claimed a section 45C credit for its qualified clinical testing expenses related to Drug A. There was no final IRS assessment or court order that disallowed the full credit for Drug A. In 2012, the FDA approved Drug A for marketing for an indication other than the treatment of the rare disease or condition for which the section 45C credit was allowed and this indication was not for another rare disease or condition for which a section 45C was allowed.

(ii) *Analysis.* In 2011 and 2012, Drug A is an orphan drug because: first, it was a branded prescription drug for which a person claimed a section 45C credit and for which that credit was allowed for a taxable year; second, there was not a final assessment or court order disallowing the full credit taken for the drug; and third, before 2012, the FDA did not approve the drug for marketing for any indication other than the treatment of a rare disease or condition for which a section 45C credit was allowed. However, Drug A is not an orphan drug for the 2013 sales year or later sales years because in 2012 the FDA approved Drug A for marketing for an indication other than the treatment of the rare disease or condition for which the section 45C credit was allowed and this indication was not for treatment of another rare disease or condition for which a section 45C credit was allowed.

*Example 2: FDA marketing approval of drug for an indication other than the treatment of a rare disease or condition and later allowance of section 45C credit.* (i) *Facts.* Drug B is a branded prescription drug that was not on the market before 2011. In 2011, FDA approved Drug B for marketing for the treatment of a rare disease or condition and also approved Drug B for marketing for an indication other than the treatment of a rare disease or condition. In 2012, a covered entity claimed a section 45C credit for its qualified clinical testing expenses related to Drug B. There was no final IRS assessment or court order that disallowed the full credit for Drug B.

(ii) *Analysis.* In 2011, Drug B is not an orphan drug because no section 45C credit was allowed and because the FDA approved Drug B for an indication other than the treatment of a rare disease or condition. In 2012, although the covered entity was allowed a section 45C credit for its qualified clinical testing expenses related to Drug B and there was no final IRS assessment or court order that disallowed the full credit, Drug B still is not an orphan drug because the FDA had approved the drug in 2011 for marketing for an indication other

than the treatment of a rare disease or condition for which a section 45C credit was allowed in 2012. Thus, Drug B is not an orphan drug for the 2012 sales year or later sales years.

*Example 3: Allowance of section 45C credit and subsequent allowance of section 45C credit with no intervening FDA marketing approval of drug for an indication other than the treatment of a rare disease or condition for which a section 45C credit was allowed.* (i) *Facts.* Drug C is a branded prescription drug that was not on the market before 2010. In 2010, a covered entity claimed a section 45C credit for its qualified clinical testing expenses related to Drug C. In 2012, a covered entity claimed an additional section 45C credit for its qualified clinical testing expenses related to Drug C for marketing for the treatment of a rare disease or condition different than the one for which the section 45C credit was claimed in 2010. There was no final IRS assessment or court order that disallowed the full credit for Drug C in 2010 or 2012. The FDA has not approved Drug C for an indication other than the treatment of a rare disease or condition for which a section 45C was allowed.

(ii) *Analysis.* In 2010 and 2011, Drug C is an orphan drug because: first, it was a branded prescription drug for which a person claimed a section 45C credit and for which that credit was allowed for a taxable year; second, there was not a final assessment or court order disallowing the full credit taken for the drug; and third, FDA had not approved the drug for marketing for any indication other than the treatment of a rare disease or condition for which a section 45C credit was allowed. In 2012, Drug C retains its orphan drug status because another section 45C credit was allowed and the FDA did not approve Drug C for marketing for any indication other than the treatment of another rare disease or condition for which a section 45C credit was allowed. Thus, Drug C is an orphan drug for the 2013 sales year.

(l) *Sales taken into account.*—The term *sales taken into account* means branded prescription drug sales after application of the percentage adjustment table in section 9008(b)(2) (relating to annual sales less than $400,000,001). See § 51.5(a)(3).

(m) *Sales year.*—The term *sales year* means the second calendar year preceding the fee year. Thus, for example, for the fee year of 2014, the sales year is 2012. [Reg. § 51.2.]

☐ [*T.D. 9684, 7-24-2014. Amended by T.D. 9823, 7-24-2017.*]

**[Reg. § 51.3]**

**§ 51.3. Information requested from covered entities.**—(a) *In general.*—Annually, each covered entity may submit a completed Form 8947, "Report of Branded Prescription Drug Information," in accordance with the instructions for the form. Generally, the form solicits information from covered entities on NDCs, orphan drugs, designated entities, rebates, and other information specified by the form or its instructions.

(b) *Due date.*—Form 8947 must be filed by the date prescribed in guidance in the Internal Revenue Bulletin. [Reg. § 51.3.]

☐ [*T.D. 9684, 7-24-2014.*]

**[Reg. § 51.4]**

**§ 51.4. Information provided by the Agencies.**—(a) *In general.*—For each sales year, the IRS will compile a list of branded prescription drugs by NDC using the data submitted on Forms 8947 and in error reports submitted as part of the dispute resolution process (described in § 51.7) and, after applying appropriate due diligence, will provide this list to the Agencies. The Agencies will provide data to the IRS on branded prescription drug sales that occurred during the sales year by Program and NDC. The Agencies will provide data for use in preparing the preliminary fee calculation (described in §§ 51.5 and 51.6) and may revise or supplement that data following review of error reports submitted as part of the dispute resolution process. The calculation methodology for calculating the sales amounts for each Program, including any reasonable estimation techniques and assumptions that the Agencies expect to use, is described in this section.

(b) *Medicare Part D.*—(1) *In general.*—CMS will determine branded prescription drug sales under Medicare Part D by aggregating the ingredient cost reported in the "Ingredient Cost Paid" field on the Prescription Drug Event (PDE) records at the NDC level, reduced by discounts, rebates, and other price concessions provided by the covered entity, for each sales year. CMS will only include PDE data that Part D sponsors have submitted by the PDE submission deadline (within 6 months after the end of the sales year) and that CMS has approved for inclusion in the Part D payment reconciliation.

(2) *Discounts, rebates, and other price concessions.*—(i) *In general.*—For purposes of paragraph (b)(1) of this section, the term *discounts, rebates, and other price concessions* means:

(A) Any direct and indirect remuneration (DIR) (within the meaning of paragraph (b)(2)(ii) of this section), which includes any DIR reported on the PDE records at the 3 point of sale and any DIR reported on a Detailed DIR Report (within the meaning of a paragraph (b)(2)(iii) of this section); and

    (B) Any coverage gap discount amount (within the meaning of paragraph (b)(2)(iv) of this section).

    (ii) *Direct and indirect remuneration.*—For purposes of paragraph (b)(2)(i)(A) of this section, the term *direct and indirect remuneration* (DIR) has the same meaning as found in the definition of *actually paid* in 42 CFR 423.308.

    (iii) *Detailed DIR Report.*—For purposes of paragraph (b)(2)(i)(A) of this section, the term *Detailed DIR Report* means the report containing any DIR (within the meaning of paragraph (b)(2)(ii) of this section) that is collected yearly from Part D sponsors at the NDC level.

    (iv) *Coverage gap discount amount.*—For purposes of paragraph (b)(2)(i)(B) of this section, the term *coverage gap discount amount* means a 50-percent manufactured-paid discount on certain drugs under the Coverage Gap Discount Program described in section 1860D-14A of the Social Security Act.

| HCPCS | NDC | Part B amount |
|---|---|---|
| J9876 | 12345-6789-01 | $789,000 |
| | 12345-6789-02 | 0 |
| | 12345-6789-03 | 0 |
| | 12345-6800-80 | 0 |
| | 12345-6800-90 | 0 |

    (3) *HCPCS code; single entity.*—For each HCPCS code consisting solely and exclusively of branded prescription drugs (as identified by their respective NDCs) manufactured by a single entity, CMS will multiply the annual weighted ASP by the total number of allowed billing units paid during the sales year to determine the total sales for all NDCs associated with the HCPCS code attributed to Medicare Part B.

    (4) *HCPCS code; multiple manufacturers and/or multiple drugs.*—(i) *Step one.*—For each HCPCS code consisting of a mixture of branded prescription drugs made by different manufacturers and/or a mixture of branded prescription and generic drugs, CMS will determine—

    (A) The annual weighted ASP for the HCPCS code;

    (B) The total number of allowed billing units paid by Medicare Part B for each HCPCS code during the sales year;

    (C) The names of the entities engaged in manufacturing each NDC assigned to the HCPCS code; and

    (D) Those entities (if any) identified in paragraph (c)(4)(i)(C) of this section that are manufacturing branded prescription drugs assigned to the HCPCS code.

    (ii) *Step two.*—Using the information from paragraph (c)(4)(i) of this section, CMS will then do the following:

    (A) Calculate the proportion of sales, expressed as a percentage, attributed to each NDC assigned to the HCPCS code by determining the percentage of total sales reported to CMS by each manufacturer of NDC(s) that are assigned to the HCPCS code. For example, if HCPCS code JXXXX contains three drugs with a total of $310,000 sales reported by manufacturers to CMS for the sales year, and $100,000 was reported for Drug A, $200,000 was reported for Drug B, and $10,000 was reported for Drug C, the proportion of sales attributed to each NDC will be 32.26 percent for Drug A, 64.52 percent for Drug B, and 3.22 percent for Drug C; and

    (B) For each NDC, multiply the product of the annual weighted ASP and the total allowed billing units paid by Medicare Part B for the HCPCS code by the proportion of sales calculated in paragraph (c)(4)(ii)(A) of this section to determine the sales reportable to the IRS (that is, percentage x (annual weighted ASP x allowed units) = total sales reported to IRS for the NDC). The sales for each manufacturer's NDCs assigned to a HCPCS code are summed and the total sales for each manufacturer's NDCs in a HCPCS code will be reported to the IRS.

    (5) *HCPCS code; unable to establish a reliable proportion of sales.*—If CMS is unable to establish a reliable proportion of sales attributable to each NDC assigned to the HCPCS code using the method described in paragraph (c)(4)(ii)(A) of this section, CMS will use Medicare Part D utilization percentages in lieu of the proportion of sales determined under paragraph (c)(4)(ii)(A) of this section to perform the calculation described in paragraph (c)(4)(ii)(B) of this section.

    (c) *Medicare Part B.*—(1) *In general.*—CMS will determine branded prescription drug sales under Medicare Part B using the following two data sources:

    (i) CMS will use data reported by manufacturers pursuant to section 1847A(c) of the Social Security Act to calculate the annual weighted average sales price (ASP) for each Healthcare Common Procedure Coding System (HCPCS) code for the sales year.

    (ii) CMS will use the Medicare Part B National Summary Data File located at http://www.cms.gov/NonIdentifiableDataFiles/03_PartBNationalSummaryDataFile.asp to obtain the number of allowed billing units per HCPCS code for claims incurred during the sales year.

    (2) *Calculation.*—(i) *In general.*—Using the data described in paragraph (c)(1) of this section, CMS will determine branded prescription drugs sales under Medicare Part B as described in paragraphs (c)(3), (4), and (5) of this section. CMS reports sales amounts per HCPCS billing code, not per NDC. Therefore, a covered entity's total Part B sales amounts for all NDCs in a given HCPCS billing code appears under only one NDC in each HCPCS billing code and the covered entity's remaining NDCs in the HCPCS billing code are listed with a sales amount of zero.

    (ii) *Example of a Part B sales report:*

    (d) *Medicaid.*—(1) CMS will determine the branded prescription drug sales for Medicaid as the per-unit Average Manufacturer Price (AMP) less the Unit Rebate Amounts (URA) that CMS calculates based on manufacturer-reported pricing data multiplied by the number of units reported billed by states to manufacturers. This data will be based on the data reported to CMS for the sales year by covered entities and the states for drugs paid for by the states in the Medicaid Drug Rebate Program for the sales year. The data will include all branded prescription drug units for which the states bill rebates to covered entities under the Medicaid Drug Rebate Program. This program includes, but is not limited to, units paid for under various health care plans such as fee for service, managed care organizations, and drugs administered in a non-retail setting such as drugs administered in a physician's office, clinic, hospital or other setting. The Medicaid Drug Rebate Program's calculated branded prescription drug fee does not include state-only pharmaceutical program sales or rebates.

    (2) For any covered entity identified in the first five (or six) digits of an NDC during any of the four quarters of a sales year, CMS will use the following methodology to derive the sales figures that account for third-party payers, such as Medicare Part B:

    (i) Report total dollars per NDC for AMP minus URA multiplied by the units reported by a state or states.

    (ii) Determine the percentage of the total amount reimbursed that is the Medicaid amount of that reimbursement. For example, if the total amount reimbursed is $100,000, and the Medicaid amount reimbursed is $20,000, then the percentage is 20 percent.

    (iii) Multiply the percentage of the Medicaid amount of that reimbursement (in the example in paragraph (d)(2)(ii) of this section, 20 percent) by the dollar figure derived from paragraph (d)(2)(i) of this section (AMP minus URA multiplied by units) to get the new adjusted sales dollar totals.

    (e) *Department of Veterans Affairs.*—VA will determine branded prescription drug sales to VA by providing, by NDC, the total amount paid (net of refunds and rebates, when they are associated with a specific NDC) for each branded prescription drug procured by VA for its beneficiaries during the sales year. For this purpose, a drug is procured on the invoice (billing) date. The basis of this information will be national procurement data reported during the sales year by VA's Pharmaceutical Prime Vendor to the VA Pharmacy Benefits Management Service and National Acquisition Center. VA sales data includes the Industrial Funding Fee and the Cost Recovery Fee because these amounts are part of the price VA pays to its Pharmaceutical Prime Vendor to procure a drug.

    (f) *Department of Defense.*—DOD will determine branded prescription drug sales to DOD (for DOD programs other than the TRICARE retail pharmacy program) by providing, by Labeler Code, the manufacturer's name, the NDC, brand name, and the amount paid (net of rebates and or refunds) for each branded prescription drug procured by DOD (for DOD programs other than the TRICARE retail pharmacy program) during the sales year. For DOD programs other than the TRICARE retail pharmacy program, a drug is procured based upon the date it was ordered. DOD includes the Industrial Funding Fee and the Cost Recovery Fee in its drug sales data because these amounts are part of the price DOD pays to procure a drug.

(g) *TRICARE.*—DOD will determine branded prescription drug sales to DOD for the TRICARE retail pharmacy program by providing, by Labeler Code, the manufacturer's name, the NDC, brand name, and the amount paid (net of rebates or refunds) for each branded prescription drug procured by DOD through the TRICARE retail pharmacy program during the sales year. For the TRICARE retail pharmacy program, a drug is procured based upon the date it was dispensed. The amount paid is based on the submitted ingredient cost paid, aggregated by NDC, for eligible TRICARE retail pharmacy claims submitted during the program year, minus any refunds or rebates for the corresponding claims. [Reg. § 51.4.]

☐ [T.D. 9684, 7-24-2014 (*corrected* 9-25-2014).]

**[Reg. § 51.5]**

**§ 51.5. Fee calculation.**—(a) *Fee components.*—(1) *In general.*—For every fee year, the IRS will calculate a covered entity's total fee as described in this section. The IRS will determine a covered entity's total fee by applying, if applicable, the adjustment amount described in paragraph (e) of this section to the entity's allocated fee described in paragraph (d) of this section.

(2) *Calculation of branded prescription drug sales.*—Each covered entity's allocated fee for any fee year is equal to an amount that bears the same ratio to the applicable amount as the covered entity's branded prescription drug sales taken into account during the sales year bears to the aggregate branded prescription drug sales of all covered entities taken into account during the sales year.

(3) *Applicable amount.*—The applicable amounts for fee years are—

| Fee year | Applicable amount |
|---|---|
| 2011 | $2,500,000,000 |
| 2012 | $2,800,000,000 |
| 2013 | $2,800,000,000 |
| 2014 | $3,000,000,000 |
| 2015 | $3,000,000,000 |
| 2016 | $3,000,000,000 |
| 2017 | $4,000,000,000 |
| 2018 | $4,100,000,000 |
| 2019 and thereafter | $2,800,000,000 |

(4) *Sales taken into account.*—A covered entity's branded prescription drug sales taken into account during any calendar year are as follows:

| Covered entity's branded prescription drug sales during the calendar year that are: | Percentage of branded prescription drug sales taken into account is |
|---|---|
| Not more than $5,000,000 | 0 percent |
| More than $5,000,000 but not more than $125,000,000 | 10 percent |
| More than $125,000,000 but not more than $225,000,000 | 40 percent |
| More than $225,000,000 but not more than $400,000,000 | 75 percent |
| More than $400,000,000 | 100 percent |

(b) *Determination of branded prescription drug sales.*—The IRS will compile each covered entity's branded prescription drug sales for each Program by NDC. Each NDC will be attributed to the covered entity identified in the Labeler Code as of the end of the day on December 31st of the sales year. For a covered entity that is a controlled group, this includes all NDCs in which a member of the covered entity is identified. For this purpose, the IRS may revise the list of NDCs as a result of information received in the dispute resolution process, and the data the IRS uses to produce the final fee calculation will include any revisions provided by the Agencies at the completion of the dispute resolution process. Each covered entity's branded prescription drug sales will be reduced by its Medicaid state supplemental rebate amounts in the following manner. If CMS has Medicaid state supplemental rebate information for a sales year, CMS will report to the IRS branded prescription drug sales for Medicaid net of Medicaid state supplemental rebates. If CMS does not have complete Medicaid state supplemental rebate information for a sales year, the IRS will reduce the branded prescription drug sales that CMS reported for Medicaid by Medicaid state supplemental rebates reported by the covered entities on Form 8947.

(c) *Determination of sales taken into account.*—(1) For each sales year and for each covered entity, the IRS will calculate sales taken into account. The resulting number is the numerator of the ratio described in paragraph (d)(1) of this section.

(2) For each sales year, the IRS will calculate the aggregate branded prescription drug sales taken into account for all covered entities. The resulting number is the denominator of the ratio described in paragraph (d)(2) of this section.

(d) *Allocated fee calculation.*—For each covered entity for each fee year, the IRS will calculate the entity's allocated fee by multiplying the applicable amount from paragraph (a)(2) of this section by a fraction—

(1) The numerator of which is the covered entity's branded prescription drug sales taken into account during the sales year (described in paragraph (c)(1) of this section); and

(2) The denominator of which is the aggregate branded prescription drug sales taken into account for all covered entities during the same year (described in paragraph (c)(2) of this section).

(e) *Adjustment amount.*—(1) *In general.*—In addition to the allocated fee computed under paragraph (d) of this section, the IRS will also automatically calculate for each covered entity an adjustment amount. An adjustment amount reflects the difference between the allocated fee determined for the covered entity in the immediately preceding fee year, using data from the second calendar year preceding that fee year, and what the allocated fee would have been for that entity for the immediately preceding fee year using data from the calendar year immediately preceding that fee year. For example, for 2014, the adjustment amount for a covered entity will be the difference between the entity's 2013 allocated fee, using 2011 data, and what the 2013 allocated fee would have been using 2012 data. Although the adjustment reflects a revision of the prior year's fee based on data from the year immediately preceding the prior fee year, the adjustment is only taken into account by adding it to or subtracting it from the allocated fee computed under paragraph (d) of this section for the current fee year to arrive at the total fee for the current fee year. An adjustment amount is treated as a component of the current year's fee. For purposes of section 6601, any increase in the allocated fee computed under paragraph (d) of this section for the current fee year resulting from any adjustment amount, along with the remainder of the fee, is treated as a fee liability due on the due date for the current year's fee. For purposes of sections 6511 and 6611, any adjustment amount that decreases the allocated fee computed under paragraph (d) of this section for the current fee year is treated as a payment towards the current fee liability made on the due date of the current fee year.

(2) *Amounts paid to a covered entity because of an adjustment amount.*—If a covered entity's adjustment amount reduces the fee computed under paragraph (d) of this section below zero and results in an amount due to the covered entity for the fee year, the IRS will pay this amount due to the covered entity. A covered entity does not

file Form 843, Claim for Refund and Request for Abatement, to receive this amount owed to a covered entity. [Reg. §51.5.]

☐ [*T.D.* 9684, 7-24-2014.]

### [Reg. §51.6]

**§51.6. Notice of preliminary fee calculation.**—(a) *Content of notice.*—For each sales year, the IRS will make a preliminary calculation of the fee for each covered entity as described in §51.5. The IRS will notify each covered entity of its preliminary fee calculation for that sales year. The notification to a covered entity of its preliminary fee calculation will include—

(1) The covered entity's allocated fee;

(2) The covered entity's branded prescription drug sales, by NDC, by Program;

(3) The covered entity's branded prescription drug sales taken into account after application of §51.5(a)(4);

(4) The aggregate branded prescription drug sales taken into account for all covered entities;

(5) The covered entity's adjustment amount calculated as described in §51.5(e); and

(6) A reference to the fee dispute resolution procedures set forth in guidance published in the Internal Revenue Bulletin.

(b) *Time of notice.*—The IRS will send each covered entity notice of its preliminary fee calculation by the date prescribed in guidance published in the Internal Revenue Bulletin. [Reg. §51.6.]

☐ [*T.D.* 9684, 7-24-2014.]

### [Reg. §51.7]

**§51.7. Dispute resolution process.**—(a) *In general.*—Upon receipt of its preliminary fee calculation, each covered entity will have an opportunity to dispute this calculation by submitting to the IRS an error report as described in this section. The IRS will provide its final determination with respect to error reports no later than the time the IRS provides a covered entity with a final fee calculation.

(b) *Error report information.*—To assert that there have been one or more errors in the drug sales data reported by a Program, the mathematical calculation of the fee, the rebate data, the listing of an NDC for an orphan drug, or any other error, a covered entity must submit an error report with each asserted error reported on a separate line. The report must include the following information—

(1) Entity name, address, and Employer Identification Number (EIN) as previously reported on the Form 8947;

(2) The name, telephone number, fax number, and e-mail address (if available) of one or more employees or representatives of the entity with whom the IRS may discuss the claimed errors. If the representative is not an employee of the covered entity who is authorized under section 6103 or designated on Form 8947 to discuss the information reported on Form 8947 with the IRS, a Form 2848, "Power of Attorney and Declaration of Representative," must be filed with the error report;

(3) For an error in the drug sales data reported by a Program, the name of the Program that reported the data, the NDC, the specific amount of sales data disputed, the proposed corrected amount, an explanation of why the Agency should use the proposed corrected data instead, and documentation of any Program drug sales data or other information used to establish the existence of any errors.

(4) For a mathematical calculation error, the specific calculation element(s) that the entity disputes and its proposed corrected calculation;

(5) For a rebate data error, the NDC for the drug to which it relates; a discussion of whether the data used in the preliminary fee calculation matches previously reported Form 8947 data on rebates; and, if the data used in the preliminary fee calculation does match the Form 8947 data, an explanation of why the Form 8947 data was erroneous and why the IRS should use the proposed corrected data instead;

(6) For the listing of an NDC for an orphan drug, the name and NDC of the orphan drug; a discussion of whether the data used in the preliminary fee calculation matches previously reported Form 8947 data on orphan drugs; and, if the data used in the preliminary fee calculation does match the Form 8947 data, an explanation of why the Form 8947 data was erroneous and why the IRS should use the proposed corrected data instead;

(7) For any other asserted error, an explanation of the nature of the error, how the error affects the fee calculation, an explanation of how the entity established that an error occurred, the proposed correction to the error, and an explanation of why the IRS or Agency should use the proposed corrected data instead;

(8) If an entity is using data to establish the existence of an error and that data was not reported on Form 8947 or contained in the notification of the preliminary fee calculation, a description of what the data is, how the entity acquired the data, and who maintains it; and

(9) Documentation of any rebate and orphan drug data, or other information used to establish the existence of any errors.

(c) *Form, manner, and timing of submission.*—Each covered entity must submit its error report(s) in the form and manner that is prescribed in guidance published in the Internal Revenue Bulletin. This guidance will also prescribe the date by which each covered entity must submit its report(s).

(d) *Finality.*—A covered entity must assert any basis for contesting its preliminary fee calculation during the dispute resolution period. In the interest of providing finality to the fee calculation process, the IRS will not accept an error report after the end of the dispute resolution period or alter the final fee calculation on the basis of information provided after the end of the dispute resolution period. [Reg. §51.7.]

☐ [*T.D.* 9684, 7-24-2014.]

### [Reg. §51.8]

**§51.8. Notification and payment of fee.**—(a) *Notification of final fee calculation.*—No later than August 31st of each fee year, the IRS will send each covered entity its final fee calculation for that year. In any fee year, the IRS will base its final fee calculation on data provided to it by the Agencies as adjusted pursuant to the dispute resolution process. The notification to a covered entity of its final fee calculation will include—

(1) The covered entity's allocated fee;

(2) The covered entity's adjustment amount calculated as described in §51.5;

(3) The covered entity's branded prescription drug sales, by NDC, by Program;

(4) The covered entity's branded prescription drug sales taken into account after application of §51.5(a)(4);

(5) The aggregate branded prescription drug sales taken into account for all covered entities; and

(6) The final determination with respect to error reports.

(b) *Differences in preliminary fee calculation and final fee calculation.*—A covered entity's final fee calculation may differ from the covered entity's preliminary fee calculation because of changes made pursuant to the dispute resolution process described in §51.7. Even if a covered entity did not file an error report described in §51.7, a covered entity's final fee may differ from a covered entity's preliminary fee because of a change in data reported by the Agencies after resolution of error reports, including a change in the aggregate prescription drug sales figure. A change in aggregate prescription drug sales data can affect each covered entity's fee because each covered entity's fee is a fraction of the aggregate fee collected from all covered entities. A covered entity's final fee may also differ from its preliminary fee calculation because the data used in the preliminary fee calculation may have contained inaccurate branded prescription drug sales information that was corrected or updated at the conclusion of the dispute resolution process.

(c) *Payment of final fee.*—Each covered entity must pay its final fee by September 30th of the fee year. For a controlled group, the payment must be made using the designated entity's EIN as reported on Form 8947. The fee must be paid by electronic funds transfer as required by §51.6302-1. There is no tax return to be filed for the fee.

(d) *Joint and several liability.*—In the case of a controlled group that is liable for the fee, all members of the controlled group are jointly and severally liable for the fee. Accordingly, if a controlled group's fee is not paid, the IRS will separately assess each member of the group for the full amount of the controlled group's fee. [Reg. §51.8.]

☐ [*T.D.* 9684, 7-24-2014.]

### [Reg. §51.9]

**§51.9. Tax treatment of fee.**—(a) *Treatment as an excise tax.*—The fee imposed by section 9008 is treated as an excise tax for purposes of subtitle F of the Internal Revenue Code (Code) (sections 6001-7874). Thus, references in subtitle F to "taxes imposed by this title," "internal revenue tax," and similar references, are also references to the fee imposed by section 9008. For example, the fee imposed by section 9008 is assessed (section 6201), collected (sections 6301, 6321, and 6331), enforced (section 7402 and 7403), subject to examination and summons (section 7602), and subject to confidentiality rules (section 6103) in the same manner as taxes imposed by the Code.

(b) *Deficiency procedures.*—The deficiency procedures of sections 6211-6216 do not apply to the fee imposed by section 9008.

(c) *Limitation on assessment.*—The IRS must assess the amount of the fee for any fee year within three years of September 30th of that fee year.

(d) *Application of section 275.*—The fee is treated as a tax described in section 275(a)(6) (relating to taxes for which no deduction is allowed). [Reg. §51.9.]

☐ *[T.D. 9684, 7-24-2014.]*

**[Reg. §51.10]**

**§51.10. Refund claims.**—Any claim for a refund of the fee must be made by the person that paid the fee to the government and must be made on Form 843, "Claim for Refund and Request for Abatement," in accordance with the instructions for that form. [Reg. §51.10.]

☐ *[T.D. 9684, 7-24-2014.]*

**[Reg. §51.11]**

**§51.11. Applicability date.**—(a) Except as otherwise provided in this section, §§51.1 through 51.10 apply on and after July 28, 2014.

(b) Section 51.2(e)(3) applies on and after July 24, 2017. [Reg. §51.11.]

☐ *[T.D. 9684, 7-24-2014. Amended by T.D. 9823, 7-24-2017.]*

# Health Insurance Providers Fee

See p. 20,601 for regulations not amended to reflect law changes

**[Reg. §57.1]**

**§57.1. Overview.**—(a) The regulations in this part are designated "Health Insurance Providers Fee Regulations."

(b) The regulations in this part provide guidance on the annual fee imposed on covered entities engaged in the business of providing health insurance by section 9010 of the Patient Protection and Affordable Care Act (PPACA), Public Law 111-148 (124 Stat. 119 (2010)), as amended by section 10905 of PPACA, and as further amended by section 1406 of the Health Care and Education Reconciliation Act of 2010, Public Law 111-152 (124 Stat. 1029 (2010)) (collectively, the Affordable Care Act or ACA). All references to section 9010 in this part 57 are references to section 9010 of the ACA. Unless otherwise indicated, all other references to subtitles, chapters, subchapters, and sections are references to subtitles, chapters, subchapters and sections in the Internal Revenue Code and the related regulations.

(c) Section 9010(e)(1) sets an applicable fee amount for each year, beginning with 2014, that will be apportioned among covered entities with aggregate net premiums written over $25 million for health insurance for United States health risks. Generally, each covered entity is liable for a fee in each fee year that is based on its net premiums written during the data year in an amount determined by the Internal Revenue Service (IRS) under the rules of this part. [Reg. §57.1.]

☐ *[T.D. 9643, 11-26-2013.]*

**[Reg. §57.2]**

**§57.2. Explanation of terms.**—(a) *In general.*—This section explains the terms used in this part 57 for purposes of the fee.

(b) *Covered entity.*—(1) *In general.*—Except as provided in paragraph (b)(2) of this section, the term *covered entity* means any entity with net premiums written for health insurance for United States health risks in the fee year if the entity is—

(i) A health insurance issuer within the meaning of section 9832(b)(2), defined in section 9832(b)(2) as an insurance company, insurance service, or insurance organization that is licensed to engage in the business of insurance in a State and that is subject to State law that regulates insurance (within the meaning of section 514(b)(2) of the Employee Retirement Income Security Act of 1974 (ERISA));

(ii) A health maintenance organization within the meaning of section 9832(b)(3), defined in section 9832(b)(3) as—

(A) A Federally qualified health maintenance organization (as defined in section 1301(a) of the Public Health Service Act);

(B) An organization recognized under State law as a health maintenance organization; or

(C) A similar organization regulated under State law for solvency in the same manner and to the same extent as such a health maintenance organization;

(iii) An insurance company subject to tax under part I or II of subchapter L, or that would be subject to tax under part I or II of subchapter L but for the entity being exempt from tax under section 501(a);

(iv) An entity that provides health insurance under Medicare Advantage, Medicare Part D, or Medicaid; or

(v) A multiple employer welfare arrangement (MEWA), within the meaning of section 3(40) of ERISA, to the extent not fully insured, provided that for this purpose a covered entity does not include a MEWA that with respect to the plan year ending with or within the section 9010 data year satisfies the requirements to be exempt from reporting under 29 CFR 2520.101-2(c)(2)(ii)(A), (B), or (C).

(2) *Exclusions.*—(i) *Self-insured employer.*—The term *covered entity* does not include any entity (including a voluntary employees' beneficiary association under section 501(c)(9) (VEBA)) that is part of a self-insured employer plan to the extent that such entity self-insures its employees' health risks. The term *self-insured employer* means an employer that sponsors a self-insured medical reimbursement plan within the meaning of §1.105-11(b)(1)(i) of this chapter. Self-insured medical reimbursement plans include plans that do not involve shifting risk to an unrelated third party as described in §1.105-11(b)(1)(ii) of this chapter. A self-insured medical reimbursement plan may use an insurance company or other third party to provide administrative or bookkeeping functions. For purposes of this section, the term *self-insured employer* does not include a MEWA.

(ii) *Governmental entity.*—The term *covered entity* does not include any governmental entity. For this purpose, the term *governmental entity* means—

(A) The government of the United States;

(B) Any State or a political subdivision thereof (as defined for purposes of section 103) including, for example, a State health department or a State insurance commission;

(C) Any Indian tribal government (as defined in section 7701(a)(40)) or a subdivision thereof (determined in accordance with section 7871(d)); or

(D) Any agency or instrumentality of any of the foregoing.

(iii) *Certain nonprofit corporations.*—The term *covered entity* does not include any entity—

(A) That is incorporated as a nonprofit corporation under a State law;

(B) No part of the net earnings of which inures to the benefit of any private shareholder or individual (within the meaning of §§1.501(a)-1(c) and 1.501(c)(3)-1(c)(2) of this chapter);

(C) No substantial part of the activities of which is carrying on propaganda, or otherwise attempting, to influence legislation (within the meaning of §1.501(c)(3)-1(c)(3)(ii) of this chapter) (or which is described in section 501(h)(3) and is not denied exemption under section 501(a) by reason of section 501(h));

(D) That does not participate in, or intervene in (including the publishing or distributing of statements), any political campaign on behalf of (or in opposition to) any candidate for public office (within the meaning of §1.501(c)(3)-1(c)(3)(iii) of this chapter); and

(E) More than 80 percent of the gross revenues of which is received from government programs that target low-income, elderly, or disabled populations under titles XVIII, XIX, and XXI of the Social Security Act.

(iv) *Certain voluntary employees' beneficiary associations (VEBAs).*—The term *covered entity* does not include any entity that is described in section 501(c)(9) that is established by an entity (other than by an employer or employers) for purposes of providing health care benefits. This exclusion applies to a VEBA that is established by a union or established pursuant to a collective bargaining agreement and having a joint board of trustees (such as in the case of a multiemployer plan within the meaning of section 3(37) of ERISA or a single-employer plan described in section 302(c)(5) of the Labor Management Relations Act, 29 U.S.C. 186(c)(5)). This exclusion does not apply to a MEWA.

(3) *Application of exclusions.*—(i) *Test year.*—An entity qualifies for an exclusion described in paragraphs (b)(2)(i) through (iv) of this section if it so qualifies in its test year. The term *test year* means either the entire data year or the entire fee year.

(ii) *Consistency rule.*—For purposes of paragraph (b)(3)(i) of this section, an entity must use the same test year as it used in its first fee year beginning after December 31, 2014, and in each subsequent fee year. Thus, for example, if an entity used the 2014 data year as its test year for the 2015 fee year, that entity must use the data year as its test year for each subsequent fee year.

(iii) *Special rule for fee year as test year.*—For purposes of paragraph (b)(3) of this section, any entity that uses the fee year as its test year but ultimately does not qualify for an exclusion described in paragraphs (b)(2)(i) through (iv) of this section for that entire fee year must use the data year as its test year for each subsequent fee year.

(4) *State.*—Solely for purposes of paragraph (b) of this section, the term *State* means any of the 50 States, the District of Columbia, or any of the possessions of the United States, including American Samoa, Guam, the Northern Mariana Islands, Puerto Rico, and the Virgin Islands.

(c) *Controlled groups.*—(1) *In general.*—The term *controlled group* means a group of two or more persons, including at least one person that is a covered entity, that is treated as a single employer under section 52(a), 52(b), 414(m), or 414(o).

(2) *Treatment of controlled group.*—A controlled group (as defined in paragraph (c)(1) of this section) is treated as a single covered entity for purposes of the fee.

(3) *Special rules.*—For purposes of paragraph (c)(1) of this section (related to controlled groups)—

(i) A foreign entity subject to tax under section 881 is included within a controlled group under section 52(a) or (b); and

(ii) A person is treated as being a member of the controlled group if it is a member of the group at the end of the day on December 31st of the data year. However, a person's net premiums written are included in net premiums written for the controlled group only if the person would qualify as a covered entity in the fee year if the person were not a member of the controlled group.

(d) *Data year.*—The term *data year* means the calendar year immediately before the fee year. Thus, for example, 2013 is the data year for fee year 2014.

(e) *Designated entity.*—(1) *In general.*—The term *designated entity* means the person within a controlled group that is designated to act on behalf of the controlled group regarding the fee with respect to—

(i) Filing Form 8963, "Report of Health Insurance Provider Information";

(ii) Receiving IRS communications about the fee for the group;

(iii) Filing a corrected Form 8963 for the group, if applicable, as described in § 57.6; and

(iv) Paying the fee for the group to the government.

(2) *Selection of designated entity.*—(i) *In general.*—Except as provided in paragraph (e)(2)(ii) of this section, each controlled group must select a designated entity by having that entity file the Form 8963 in accordance with the form instructions. The designated entity must state under penalties of perjury that all persons that provide health insurance for United States health risks that are members of the group have consented to the selection of the designated entity. Each member of a controlled group must maintain a record of its consent to the controlled group's selection of the designated entity. The designated entity must maintain a record of all member consents.

(ii) *Requirement for consolidated groups; common parent.*—If a controlled group, without regard to foreign corporations included under section 9010(c)(3)(B), is also an affiliated group the common parent of which files a consolidated return for Federal income tax purposes, the designated entity is the agent for the group (within the meaning of § 1.1502-77 of this chapter) for the data year.

(iii) *Failure to select a designated entity.*—Excepted as provided in paragraph (e)(2)(ii) of this section, if a controlled group fails to select a designated entity as provided in paragraph (e)(2)(i) of this section, then the IRS will select a member of the controlled group to be the designated entity. If the IRS selects the designated entity, then all members of the controlled group that provide health insurance for a United States health risk will be deemed to have consented to the IRS's selection of the designated entity.

(f) *Fee.*—The term *fee* means the fee imposed by section 9010 on each covered entity engaged in the business of providing health insurance.

(g) *Fee year.*—The term *fee year* means the calendar year in which the fee must be paid to the government. The first fee year is 2014.

(h) *Health insurance.*—(1) *In general.*—Except as provided in paragraph (h)(2) of this section, the term *health insurance* generally has the same meaning as the term *health insurance coverage* in section 9832(b)(1)(A), defined to mean benefits consisting of medical care (provided directly, through insurance or reimbursement, or otherwise) under any hospital or medical service policy or certificate, hospital or medical service plan contract, or health maintenance organization contract, when these benefits are offered by an entity that is one of the types of entities described in paragraph (b)(1)(i) through (b)(1)(v) of this section. The term *health insurance* includes limited scope dental and vision benefits under section 9832(c)(2)(A) and retiree-only health insurance.

(2) *Exclusions.*—The term *health insurance* does not include—

(i) Coverage only for accident, or disability income insurance, or any combination thereof, within the meaning of section 9832(c)(1)(A);

(ii) Coverage issued as a supplement to liability insurance within the meaning of section 9832(c)(1)(B);

(iii) Liability insurance, including general liability insurance and automobile liability insurance, within the meaning of section 9832(c)(1)(C);

(iv) Workers' compensation or similar insurance within the meaning of section 9832(c)(1)(D);

(v) Automobile medical payment insurance within the meaning of section 9832(c)(1)(E);

(vi) Credit-only insurance within the meaning of section 9832(c)(1)(F);

(vii) Coverage for on-site medical clinics within the meaning of section 9832(c)(1)(G);

(viii) Other insurance coverage that is similar to the insurance coverage in paragraph (h)(2)(i) through (vii) of this section under which benefits for medical care are secondary or incidental to other insurance benefits, within the meaning of section 9832(c)(1)(H), to the extent such insurance coverage is specified in regulations under section 9832(c)(1)(H);

(ix) Benefits for long-term care, nursing home care, home health care, community-based care, or any combination thereof, within the meaning of section 9832(c)(2)(B), and such other similar, limited benefits to the extent such benefits are specified in regulations under section 9832(c)(2)(C);

(x) Coverage only for a specified disease or illness within the meaning of section 9832(c)(3)(A);

(xi) Hospital indemnity or other fixed indemnity insurance within the meaning of section 9832(c)(3)(B);

(xii) Medicare supplemental health insurance (as defined under section 1882(g)(1) of the Social Security Act), coverage supplemental to the coverage provided under chapter 55 of title 10, United States Code, and similar supplemental coverage provided to coverage under a group health plan, within the meaning of section 9832(c)(4);

(xiii) Coverage under an employee assistance plan, a disease management plan, or a wellness plan, if the benefits provided under the plan constitute excepted benefits under section 9832(c)(2) (or do not otherwise provide benefits consisting of health insurance under paragraph (h)(1) of this section);

(xiv) Student administrative health fee arrangements, as defined in paragraph (h)(3);

(xv) Travel insurance, as defined in paragraph (h)(4) of this section; or

(xvi) Indemnity reinsurance, as defined in paragraph (h)(5)(i) of this section.

(3) *Student administrative health fee arrangement.*—For purposes of paragraph (h)(2)(xiv) of this section, the term *student administrative health fee arrangement* means an arrangement under which an educational institution, other than through an insured arrangement, charges student administrative health fees to students on a periodic basis to help cover the cost of student health clinic operations and care delivery (regardless of whether the student uses the clinic and regardless of whether the student purchases any available student health insurance coverage).

(4) *Travel insurance.*—For purposes of paragraph (h)(2)(xv) of this section, the term *travel insurance* means insurance coverage for personal risks incident to planned travel, which may include, but is not limited to, interruption or cancellation of trip or event, loss of baggage or personal effects, damages to accommodations or rental vehicles, and sickness, accident, disability, or death occurring during travel, provided that the health benefits are not offered on a stand-alone basis and are incidental to other coverage. For this purpose, the term *travel insurance* does not include major medical plans that provide comprehensive medical protection for travelers with trips lasting 6 months or longer, including, for example, those working overseas as an expatriate or military personnel being deployed.

(5) *Reinsurance.*—(i) *Indemnity reinsurance.*—For purposes of paragraphs (h)(2)(xvi) and (k) of this section, the term *indemnity reinsurance* means an agreement between one or more reinsuring companies and a covered entity under which—

(A) The reinsuring company agrees to accept, and to indemnify the issuing company for, all or part of the risk of loss under policies specified in the agreement; and

(B) The covered entity retains its liability to, and its contractual relationship with, the individuals whose health risks are insured under the policies specified in the agreement.

(ii) *Assumption reinsurance.*—For purposes of paragraph (k) of this section, the term *assumption reinsurance* means reinsurance for which there is a novation and the reinsurer takes over the entire risk of loss pursuant to a new contract.

(i) *Located in the United States.*—The term *located in the United States* means present in the United States (within the meaning of paragraph (m) of this section) under section 7701(b)(7) (for presence in the 50 States and the District of Columbia) or § 1.937-1(c)(3)(i) of this chapter (for presence in a possession of the United States).

(j) *NAIC.*—The term *NAIC* means the National Association of Insurance Commissioners.

(k) *Net premiums written.*—The term *net premiums written* means premiums written, including reinsurance premiums written, reduced by reinsurance ceded, and reduced by ceding commissions and medical loss ratio (MLR) rebates with respect to the data year. For this purpose, MLR rebates are computed on an accrual basis in determining net premiums written. Because indemnity reinsurance within the meaning of paragraph (h)(5)(i) of this section is not health insurance under paragraph (h)(1) of this section, the term *net premiums written* does not include premiums written for indemnity reinsurance and is not reduced by indemnity reinsurance ceded. However, in the case of assumption reinsurance within the meaning of paragraph (h)(5)(ii) of this section, the term *net premiums written* does include premiums written for assumption reinsurance and is reduced by assumption reinsurance premiums ceded.

(l) *SHCE.*—The term *SHCE* means the Supplemental Health Care Exhibit. The SHCE is a form published by the NAIC that most covered entities are required to file annually under State law.

(m) *United States.*—For purposes of paragraph (i) of this section, the term *United States* means the 50 States, the District of Columbia, and any possession of the United States, including American Samoa, Guam, the Northern Mariana Islands, Puerto Rico, and the Virgin Islands.

(n) *United States health risk.*—The term *United States health risk* means the health risk of any individual who is—

(1) A United States citizen;

(2) A resident of the United States (within the meaning of section 7701(b)(1)(A)); or

(3) Located in the United States (within the meaning of paragraph (i) of this section) during the period such individual is so located. [Reg. § 57.2.]

☐ *[T.D. 9643, 11-26-2013. Amended by T.D. 9711, 2-23-2015 and T.D. 9830, 2-22-2018.]*

### [Reg. § 57.3]

**§ 57.3. Reporting requirements and associated penalties.**—(a) *Reporting requirement.*—(1) *In general.*—Annually, each covered entity, including each controlled group that is treated as a single covered entity, must report its net premiums written for health insurance of United States health risks during the data year to the IRS by April 15th of the fee year on Form 8963, "Report of Health Insurance Provider Information," in accordance with the instructions for the form. A covered entity that has net premiums written during the data year is subject to this reporting requirement even if it does not have any amount taken into account as described in § 57.4(a)(4). If an entity is not in the business of providing health insurance for any United States health risk in the fee year, it is not a covered entity and does not have to report.

(2) *Manner of reporting.*—(i) *In general.*—The IRS may provide rules in guidance published in the Internal Revenue Bulletin for the manner of reporting by a covered entity under this section, including rules for reporting by a designated entity on behalf of a controlled group that is treated as a single covered entity.

(ii) *Electronic Filing Required.*—Any Form 8963 (including corrected forms) filed pursuant to paragraph (a)(1) of this section and reporting more than $25 million in net premiums written must be filed electronically in accordance with the instructions to the form. If a Form 8963 or corrected Form 8963 is required to be filed electronically under this paragraph (a)(2)(ii), any subsequently filed Form 8963 filed for the same fee year must also be filed electronically. For purposes of § 57.3(b), any Form 8963 required to be filed electroni-

cally under this section will not be considered filed unless it is filed electronically.

(3) *Disclosure of reported information.*—Pursuant to section 9010(g)(4), the information reported on each original and corrected Form 8963 will be open for public inspection or available upon request.

(b) *Penalties.*—(1) *Failure to report.*—(i) *In general.*—A covered entity that fails to timely submit a report containing the information required by paragraph (a) of this section is liable for a failure to report penalty in the amount described in paragraph (b)(1)(ii) of this section in addition to its fee liability and any other applicable penalty, unless the failure is due to reasonable cause as defined in paragraph (b)(1)(iii) of this section.

(ii) *Amount.*—The amount of the failure to report penalty described in paragraph (b)(1)(i) of this section is—

(A) $10,000, plus

(B) The lesser of—

(1) An amount equal to $1,000 multiplied by the number of days during which such failure continues; or

(2) The amount of the covered entity's fee for which the report was required.

(iii) *Reasonable cause.*—The failure to report penalty described in paragraph (b)(1)(i) of this section is waived if the failure is due to reasonable cause. A failure is due to reasonable cause if the covered entity exercised ordinary business care and prudence and was nevertheless unable to submit the report within the prescribed time. In determining whether the covered entity was unable to submit the report timely despite the exercise of ordinary business care and prudence, the IRS will consider all the facts and circumstances surrounding the failure to submit the report.

(iv) *Treatment of penalty.*—The failure to report penalty described in this paragraph (b)(1)—

(A) Is treated as a penalty under subtitle F;

(B) Must be paid on notice and demand by the IRS and in the same manner as a tax under the Internal Revenue Code; and

(C) Is a penalty for which only civil actions for refund under procedures of subtitle F apply.

(2) *Accuracy-related penalty.*—(i) *In general.*—A covered entity that understates its net premiums written for health insurance of United States health risks in the report required under paragraph (a)(1) of this section is liable for an accuracy-related penalty in the amount described in paragraph (b)(2)(ii) of this section, in addition to its fee liability and any other applicable penalty.

(ii) *Amount.*—The amount of the accuracy-related penalty described in paragraph (b)(2)(i) of this section is the excess of—

(A) The amount of the covered entity's fee for the fee year that the IRS determines should have been paid in the absence of any understatement; over

(B) The amount of the covered entity's fee for the fee year that the IRS determined based on the understatement.

(iii) *Understatement.*—An understatement of a covered entity's net premiums written for health insurance of United States health risks is the difference between the amount of net premiums written that the covered entity reported and the amount of net premiums written that the IRS determines the covered entity should have reported.

(iv) *Treatment of penalty.*—The accuracy-related penalty is subject to the provisions of subtitle F that apply to assessable penalties imposed under chapter 68.

(3) *Controlled groups.*—Each member of a controlled group that is required to provide information to the controlled group's designated entity for purposes of the report required to be submitted by the designated entity on behalf of the controlled group is jointly and severally liable for any penalties described in this paragraph (b) for any reporting failures by the designated entity. [Reg. § 57.3.]

☐ *[T.D. 9643, 11-26-2013. Amended by T.D. 9881, 11-8-2019.]*

### [Reg. § 57.4]

**§ 57.4. Fee calculation.**—(a) *Fee components.*—(1) *In general.*—For every fee year, the IRS will calculate a covered entity's allocated fee as described in this section.

(2) *Calculation of net premiums written.*—Each covered entity's allocated fee for any fee year is equal to an amount that bears the same ratio to the applicable amount as the covered entity's net premiums written for health insurance of United States health risks during the data year taken into account bears to the aggregate net

premiums written for health insurance of United States health risks of all covered entities during the data year taken into account.

(3) *Applicable amount.*—The applicable amounts for fee years are—

| Fee year | Applicable amount |
|---|---|
| 2014 | $ 8,000,000,000 |
| 2015 | $ 11,300,000,000 |
| 2016 | $ 11,300,000,000 |
| 2017 | $ 13,900,000,000 |
| 2018 | $ 14,300,000,000 |
| 2019 and thereafter | The applicable amount in the preceding fee year increased by the rate of premium growth (within the meaning of section 36B(b)(3)(A)(ii)). |

(4) *Net premiums written taken into account.*—(i) *In general.*—A covered entity's net premiums written for health insurance of United States health risks during any data year are taken into account as follows:

| Covered entity's net premiums written during the data year that are: | Percentage of net premiums written taken into account is: |
|---|---|
| Not more than $25,000,000 | 0 |
| More than $25,000,000 but not more than $50,000,000 | 50 |
| More than $50,000,000 | 100 |

(ii) *Controlled groups.*—In the case of a controlled group, paragraph (a)(4)(i) of this section applies to all net premiums written for health insurance of United States health risks during the data year, in the aggregate, of the entire controlled group, except that any net premiums written by any member of the controlled group that is a nonprofit corporation meeting the requirements of § 57.2(b)(2)(iii) or a voluntary employees' beneficiary association meeting the requirements of § 57.2(b)(2)(iv) are not taken into account.

(iii) *Partial exclusion for certain exempt activities.*—After the application of paragraph (a)(4)(i) of this section, if the covered entity (or any member of a controlled group treated as a single covered entity) is exempt from Federal income tax under section 501(a) and is described in section 501(c)(3), (4), (26), or (29) as of December 31st of the data year, then only 50 percent of its remaining net premiums written for health insurance of United States health risks that are attributable to its exempt activities (and not to activities of an unrelated trade or business as defined in section 513) during the data year are taken into account. If an entity to which this partial exclusion applies is a member of a controlled group, then the partial exclusion applies to that entity after first applying paragraph (a)(4)(i) on a pro rata basis to all members of the controlled group.

(b) *Determination of net premiums written.*—(1) *In general.*—The IRS will determine net premiums written for health insurance of United States health risks for each covered entity based on the Form 8963, "Report of Health Insurance Provider Information," submitted by each covered entity, together with any other source of information available to the IRS. Other sources of information that the IRS may use to determine net premiums written for each covered entity include the SHCE, which supplements the annual statement filed with the NAIC pursuant to State law, the annual statement itself or the Accident and Health Policy Experience filed with the NAIC, the MLR Annual Reporting Form filed with the Center for Medicare & Medicaid Services' Center for Consumer Information and Insurance Oversight of the U.S. Department of Health and Human Services, or any similar statements filed with the NAIC, with any State government, or with the Federal government pursuant to applicable State or Federal requirements.

(2) *Presumption for United States health risks.*—For any covered entity that files the SHCE with the NAIC, the entire amount reported on the SHCE as direct premiums written will be considered to be for health insurance of United States health risks as described in § 57.2(n) (subject to any applicable exclusions for amounts that are not health insurance as described in § 57.2(h)(2)) unless the covered entity can demonstrate otherwise.

(c) *Determination of amounts taken into account.*—(1) For each fee year and for each covered entity, the IRS will calculate the net premiums written for health insurance of United States health risks taken into account during the data year. The resulting number is the numerator of the fraction described in paragraph (d)(1) of this section.

(2) For each fee year, the IRS will calculate the aggregate net premiums written for health insurance of United States health risks taken into account for all covered entities during the data year. The resulting number is the denominator of the fraction described in paragraph (d)(2) of this section.

(d) *Allocated fee calculated.*—For each covered entity for each fee year, the IRS will calculate the covered entity's allocated fee by multiplying the applicable amount from paragraph (a)(3) of this section by a fraction—

(1) The numerator of which is the covered entity's net premiums written for health insurance of United States health risks during the data year taken into account (described in paragraph (c)(1) of this section); and

(2) The denominator of which is the aggregate net premiums written for health insurance of United States health risks for all covered entities during the data year taken into account (described in paragraph (c)(2) of this section). [Reg. § 57.4.]

☐ [*T.D.* 9643, 11-26-2013.]

**[Reg. § 57.5]**

**§ 57.5. Notice of preliminary fee calculation.**—(a) *Content of notice.*—Each fee year, the IRS will make a preliminary calculation of the fee for each covered entity as described in § 57.4. The IRS will notify each covered entity of its preliminary fee calculation for that fee year. The notification to a covered entity of its preliminary fee calculation will include—

(1) The covered entity's allocated fee;

(2) The covered entity's net premiums written for health insurance of United States health risks;

(3) The covered entity's net premiums written for health insurance of United States health risks taken into account after the application of § 57.4(a)(4);

(4) The aggregate net premiums written for health insurance of United States health risks taken into account for all covered entities; and

(5) Instructions for how to submit a corrected Form 8963, "Report of Health Insurance Provider Information," to correct any errors through the error correction process.

(b) *Timing of notice.*—The IRS will specify in other guidance published in the Internal Revenue Bulletin the date by which it will send each covered entity a notice of its preliminary fee calculation. [Reg. § 57.5.]

☐ [*T.D.* 9643, 11-26-2013.]

**[Reg. § 57.6]**

**§ 57.6. Error correction process.**—(a) *In general.*—Upon receipt of its preliminary fee calculation, each covered entity must review this calculation during the error correction period. If the covered entity identifies one or more errors in its preliminary fee calculation, the covered entity must timely submit to the IRS a corrected Form 8963, "Report of Health Insurance Provider Information," during the error correction period. The corrected Form 8963 will replace the original Form 8963 for all purposes, including for the purpose of determining whether an accuracy-related penalty applies, except that a covered entity remains subject to the failure to report penalty if it fails to timely submit the original Form 8963. In the case of a controlled group, if the preliminary fee calculation for the controlled group contains one or more errors, the corrected Form 8963 must include all of the required information for the entire controlled group, including members that do not have corrections.

(b) *Time and manner.*—The IRS will specify in other guidance published in the Internal Revenue Bulletin the time and manner by which a covered entity must submit a corrected Form 8963. The IRS will provide its final determination regarding the covered entity's submission no later than the time the IRS provides a covered entity with a final fee calculation.

(c) *Finality.*—Covered entities must assert any basis for contesting their preliminary fee calculation during the error correction period. In the interest of providing finality to the fee calculation process, the IRS will not accept a corrected Form 8963 after the end of the error correction period or alter final fee calculations on the basis of information provided after the end of the error correction period. [Reg. § 57.6.]

☐ [*T.D.* 9643, 11-26-2013.]

**[Reg. § 57.7]**

**§ 57.7. Notification and fee payment.**—(a) *Content of notice.*—Each fee year, the IRS will make a final calculation of the fee for each covered entity as described in § 57.4. The IRS will base its final fee calculation on each covered entity's original or corrected Form 8963, "Report of Health Insurance Provider Information," as adjusted by other sources of information described in § 57.4(b)(1). The notification to a covered entity of its final fee calculation will include-

(1) The covered entity's allocated fee;

(2) The covered entity's net premiums written for health insurance of United States health risks;

(3) The covered entity's net premiums written for health insurance of United States health risks taken into account after the application of § 57.4(a)(4);

(4) The aggregate net premiums written for health insurance of United States health risks taken into account for all covered entities; and

(5) The final determination on the covered entity's corrected Form 8963, "Report of Health Insurance Provider Information," if any.

(b) *Timing of notice.*—The IRS will send each covered entity a notice of its final fee calculation by August 31st of the fee year.

(c) *Differences in preliminary fee calculation and final calculation.*—A covered entity's final fee calculation may differ from the covered entity's preliminary fee calculation because of changes made pursuant to the error correction process described in § 57.6 or because the IRS discovered additional information relevant to the fee calculation through other information sources as described in § 57.4(b)(1). Even if a covered entity did not file a corrected Form 8963 described in § 57.6, a covered entity's final fee may differ from a covered entity's preliminary fee because of information discovered about that covered entity through other information sources. In addition, a change in aggregate net premiums written for health insurance of United States health risks can affect every covered entity's fee because each covered entity's fee is equal to a fraction of the aggregate fee collected from all covered entities.

(d) *Payment of final fee.*—Each covered entity must pay its final fee by September 30th of the fee year. For a controlled group, the payment must be made using the designated entity's Employer Identification Number as reported on Form 8963. The fee must be paid by electronic funds transfer as required by § 57.6302-1. There is no tax return to be filed with the payment of the fee.

(e) *Controlled groups.*—In the case of a controlled group that is liable for the fee, all members of the controlled group are jointly and severally liable for the fee. Accordingly, if a controlled group's fee is not paid, the IRS may separately assess each member of the controlled group for the full amount of the controlled group's fee. [Reg. § 57.7.]

☐ [*T.D.* 9643, 11-26-2013.]

### [Reg. § 57.8]

**§ 57.8. Tax treatment of fee.**—(a) *Treatment as an excise tax.*—The fee is treated as an excise tax for purposes of subtitle F (sections 6001-7874). Thus, references in subtitle F to "taxes imposed by this title," "internal revenue tax," and similar references, are also references to the fee. For example, the fee is assessed (section 6201), collected (sections 6301, 6321, and 6331), enforced (section 7602), and subject to examination and summons (section 7602) in the same manner as taxes imposed by the Code.

(b) *Deficiency procedures.*—The deficiency procedures of sections 6211-6216 do not apply to the fee.

(c) *Limitation on assessment.*—The IRS must assess the amount of the fee for any fee year within three years of September 30th of that fee year.

(d) *Application of section 275.*—The fee is treated as a tax described in section 275(a)(6) (relating to taxes for which no deduction is allowed). [Reg. § 57.8.]

☐ [*T.D.* 9643, 11-26-2013.]

### [Reg. § 57.9]

**§ 57.9. Refund claims.**—Any claim for a refund of the fee must be made by the entity that paid the fee to the government and must be made on Form 843, "Claim for Refund and Request for Abatement," in accordance with the instructions for that form. [Reg. § 57.9.]

☐ [*T.D.* 9643, 11-26-2013.]

### [Reg. § 57.10]

**§ 57.10. Applicability date.**—(a) Except as provided in paragraphs (b) and (c) of this section, § § 57.1 through 57.9 apply to any fee that is due on or after September 30, 2014.

(b) *Paragraphs (b)(3) and (c)(3)(ii) of § 57.2.*—Paragraphs (b)(3) and (c)(3)(ii) of § 57.2 apply on February 22, 2018.

(c) Section 57.3(a)(2)(ii) applies to Forms 8963, including corrected Forms 8963, filed after December 31, 2019. [Reg. § 57.10.]

☐ [*T.D.* 9643, 11-26-2013. *Amended by T.D.* 9711, 2-23-2015, *T.D.* 9830, 2-22-2018 *and T.D.* 9881, 11-8-2019.]

# ALCOHOL, TOBACCO, AND CERTAIN OTHER EXCISE TAXES

## Greenmail

See p. 20,601 for regulations not amended to reflect law changes

### [Reg. § 156.5881-1]

**§ 156.5881-1. Imposition of excise tax on greenmail.**—(a) *In general.*—Section 5881 of the Code imposes a tax equal to 50 percent of the gain or other income realized by any person on the receipt of greenmail, whether or not the gain or other income is recognized.

(b) *Transactions occurring on or after March 31, 1988.*—For transactions occurring on or after March 31, 1988, greenmail is defined as any consideration transferred by a corporation (or any person acting in concert with the corporation) to directly or indirectly acquire stock of the corporation from any shareholder if:

(1) The transferring shareholder has held the stock (as determined under section 1223) for less than two years before entering into the agreement to transfer the stock,

(2) The shareholder, any person acting in concert with the shareholder, or any person related to the shareholder or to a person acting in concert with the shareholder made or threatened to make a public tender offer for stock of the corporation at some time during the two-

year period ending on the date of the acquisition of the stock by the corporation, and

(3) The acquisition is pursuant to an offer that was not made on the same terms to all shareholders.

(c) *Transactions occurring before March 31, 1988.*—For transactions occurring before March 31, 1988, greenmail has the same meaning as in paragraph (b) of this section, except that it does not include any consideration transferred by any person acting in concert with the corporation described in that paragraph.

(d) *Effective date.*—Generally, section 5881 of the Code applies to consideration received after December 22, 1987, in taxable years ending after that date. However, section 5881 does not apply to any acquisition of stock pursuant to a written binding contract in effect on December 15, 1987, and at all times thereafter before the acquisition. [Reg. § 156.5881-1.]

☐ [*T.D.* 8379, 12-17-91.]

## Structured Settlement Factoring Transactions

See p. 20,601 for regulations not amended to reflect law changes

### [Reg. § 157.5891-1]

**§ 157.5891-1. Imposition of excise tax on structured settlement factoring transactions.**—(a) *In general.*—Section 5891 imposes on any person who acquires, directly or indirectly, structured settlement payment rights in a structured settlement factoring transaction a tax equal to 40 percent of the factoring discount with respect to such factoring transaction.

(b) *Exceptions for certain approved transactions.*—(1) *In general.*—The excise tax shall not apply to a structured settlement factoring transac-

tion if the transfer of structured settlement payment rights is approved in advance in a qualified order.

(2) *Qualified order dispositive.*—A qualified order shall be treated as dispositive for purposes of this exception.

(c) *Definitions.*—(1) *Applicable state statute* means—

(i) A statute that is enacted by the state in which the payee of the structured settlement is domiciled and provides for the entry of an order, judgment, or decree described in paragraph (c)(4)(i) of this section; or

(ii) If there is no such statute, a statute that—

(A) Is enacted by the state in which either the party to the structured settlement (including an assignee under a qualified assignment under section 130) or the person issuing the funding asset for the structured settlement is domiciled or has its principal place of business; and

(B) Provides for the entry of such an order, judgment, or decree.

(2) *Applicable state court* means, with respect to any applicable state statute, a court of the state that enacted such statute. If the payee of the structured settlement is not domiciled in the state that enacted the statute, the term also includes a court of the state in which the payee is domiciled.

(3) *Factoring discount* means an amount equal to the excess of—

(i) The aggregate undiscounted amount of structured settlement payments being acquired in the structured settlement factoring transaction; over

(ii) The total amount actually paid by the acquirer to the person from whom such structured settlement payments are acquired.

(4) *Qualified order* means a final order, judgment, or decree that—

(i) Finds that the transfer of structured settlement payment rights does not contravene any Federal or state statute, or the order of any court or responsible administrative authority, and is in the best interest of the payee, taking into account the welfare and support of the payee's dependents; and

(ii) Is issued under the authority of an applicable state statute by an applicable state court, or is issued by the responsible administrative authority (if any) which has exclusive jurisdiction over the underlying action or proceeding which was resolved by means of the structured settlement.

(5) *Responsible administrative authority* means the administrative authority that had jurisdiction over the underlying action or proceeding that was resolved by means of the structured settlement.

(6) *State* includes the Commonwealth of Puerto Rico and any possession of the United States.

(7) *Structured settlement* means an arrangement—

(i) that is established by—

(A) Suit or agreement for the periodic payment of damages excludable from the gross income of the recipient under section 104(a)(2); or

(B) Agreement for the periodic payment of compensation under any workers' compensation law excludable from the gross income of the recipient under section 104(a)(1); and

(ii) Under which the periodic payments are—

(A) Of the character described in section 130(c)(2)(A) and (B); and

(B) Payable by a person who is a party to the suit or agreement or to the workers' compensation claim or by a person who has assumed the liability for such periodic payments under a qualified assignment in accordance with section 130.

(8) *Structured settlement factoring transaction* means a transfer of structured settlement payment rights (including portions of structured settlement payments) made for consideration by means of sale, assignment, pledge, or other form of encumbrance or alienation for consideration other than—

(i) The creation or perfection of a security interest in structured settlement payment rights under a blanket security agreement entered into with an insured depository institution in the absence of any action to redirect the structured settlement payments to such institution (or agent or successor thereof) or otherwise to enforce such blanket security interest as against the structured settlement payment rights; or

(ii) A subsequent transfer of structured settlement payment rights acquired in a structured settlement factoring transaction.

(9) *Structured settlement payment rights* means rights to receive payments under a structured settlement.

(d) *Coordination with other provisions of the Internal Revenue Code.*— (1) *In general.*—If the applicable requirements of sections 72, 104(a)(1), 104(a)(2), 130, and 461(h) were satisfied at the time the structured settlement involving structured settlement payment rights was entered into, the subsequent occurrence of a structured settlement factoring transaction shall not affect the application of the provisions of such sections to the parties to the structured settlement (including an assignee under a qualified assignment under section 130) in any taxable year.

(2) *No withholding of tax.*—The provisions of section 3405 regarding withholding of tax shall not apply to the person making the payments in the event of a structured settlement factoring transaction.

(e) *Effective dates.*—This section applies to structured settlement factoring transactions entered into on or after July 8, 2004. For structured settlement factoring transactions entered into before July 8, 2004, see §157.5891-1T of this chapter (2003-1 C.B. 564. See §601.601(d)(2) of this chapter.), as it appeared in the April 1, 2003, edition of 26 CFR part 157. [Reg. §157.5891-1.]

☐ [*T.D.* 9134, 7-7-2004.]

**[The next page is 64,601.]**

# PROCEDURE AND ADMINISTRATION

## Information and Returns

## RETURNS AND RECORDS

## Records, Statements and Special Returns

See p. 20,601 for regulations not amended to reflect law changes

### [Reg. §1.6001-1]

**§1.6001-1. Records.**—(a) *In general.*—Except as provided in paragraph (b) of this section, any person subject to tax under subtitle A of the Code (including a qualified State individual income tax which is treated pursuant to section 6361(a) as if it were imposed by chapter 1 of subtitle A), or any person required to file a return of information with respect to income, shall keep such permanent books of account or records, including inventories, as are sufficient to establish the amount of gross income, deductions, credits, or other matters required to be shown by such person in any return of such tax or information.

(b) *Farmers and wage-earners.*—Individuals deriving gross income from the business of farming, and individuals whose gross income includes salaries, wages, or similar compensation for personal services rendered, are required with respect to such income to keep such records as will enable the district director to determine the correct amount of income subject to the tax. It is not necessary, however, that with respect to such income individuals keep the books of account or records required by paragraph (a) of this section. For rules with respect to the records to be kept in substantiation of traveling and other business expenses of employees, see §1.162-17.

(c) *Exempt organizations.*—In addition to such permanent books and records as are required by paragraph (a) of this section with respect to the tax imposed by section 511 on unrelated business income of certain exempt organizations, every organization exempt from tax under section 501(a) shall keep such permanent books of account or records, including inventories, as are sufficient to show specifically the items of gross income, receipts and disbursements. Such organizations shall also keep such books and records as are required to substantiate the information required by section 6033. See section 6033 and §§1.6033-1 through -3.

(d) *Notice by district director requiring returns, statements, or the keeping of records.*—The district director may require any person, by notice served upon him, to make such returns, render such statements, or keep such specific records as will enable the district director to determine whether or not such person is liable for tax under subtitle A of the Code, including qualified State individual income taxes, which are treated pursuant to section 6361(a) as if they were imposed by chapter 1 of subtitle A.

(e) *Retention of records.*—The books or records required by this section shall be kept at all times available for inspection by authorized internal revenue officers or employees, and shall be retained so long as the contents thereof may become material in the administration of any internal revenue law [Reg. §1.6001-1.]

☐ [*T.D.* 6364, 2-13-59. *Amended by T.D.* 7122, 6-7-71; *T.D.* 7577, 12-19-78 *and T.D.* 8308, 8-30-90.]

### [Reg. §20.6001-1]

**§20.6001-1. Persons required to keep records and render statements.**—(a) It is the duty of the executor to keep such complete and detailed records of the affairs of the estate for which he acts as will enable the district director to determine accurately the amount of the estate tax liability. All documents and vouchers used in preparing the estate tax return (§20.6018-1) shall be retained by the executor so as to be available for inspection whenever required.

(b) In addition to filing an estate tax return (see §20.6018-1) and, if applicable, a preliminary notice (see §20.6036-1), the executor shall furnish such supplemental data as may be necessary to establish the correct estate tax. It is therefore the duty of the executor (1) to furnish, upon requests, copies of any documents in his possession (or on file in any court having jurisdiction over the estate) relating to the estate, appraisal lists of any items included in the gross estate, copies of balance sheets or other financial statements obtainable by him relating to the value of stock, and any other information obtainable by him that may be found necessary in the determination of the tax, and (2) to render any written statement, containing a declaration that it is made under penalties of perjury, of facts within his knowledge which the district director may require for the purpose of determining whether a tax liability exists and, if so, the extent thereof. Failure to comply with such a request will render the executor liable to

penalties (see section 7269), and proceedings may be instituted in the proper court of the United States to secure compliance therewith (see section 7604).

(c) Persons having possession or control of any records or documents containing or supposed to contain any information concerning the estate, or having knowledge of or information about any fact or facts which have a material bearing upon the liability, or the extent of liability, of the estate for the estate tax, shall, upon request of the district director, make disclosure thereof. Failure on the part of any person to comply with such request will render him liable to penalties (section 7269), and compliance with the request may be enforced in the proper court of the United States (section 7604).

(d) Upon notification from the Internal Revenue Service, a corporation (organized or created in the United States) or its transfer agent is required to furnish the following information pertaining to stocks or bonds registered in the name of a nonresident decedent (regardless of citizenship): (1) The name of the decedent as registered; (2) the date of the decedent's death; (3) the decedent's residence and his place of death; (4) the names and addresses of executors, attorneys, or other representatives of the estate, within and without the United States; and (5) a description of the securities, the number of shares or bonds and the par values thereof. [Reg. §20.6001-1.]

☐ [*T.D.* 6296, 6-23-58. *Amended by T.D.* 7238, 12-28-72.]

### [Reg. §25.6001-1]

**§25.6001-1. Records required to be kept.**—(a) *In general.*—Every person subject to taxation under chapter 12 of the Internal Revenue Code of 1954 shall for the purpose of determining the total amount of his gifts, keep such permanent books of account or records as are necessary to establish the amount of his total gifts (limited as provided by section 2503(b)), together with the deductions allowable in determining the amount of his taxable gifts, and the other information required to be shown in a gift tax return. All documents and vouchers used in preparing the gift tax return (see §25.6019-1) shall be retained by the donor so as to be available for inspection whenever required.

(b) *Supplemental data.*—In order that the Internal Revenue Service may determine the correct tax the donor shall furnish such supplemental data as may be deemed necessary by the Internal Revenue Service. It is, therefore, the duty of the donor to furnish, upon request, copies of all documents relating to his gift or gifts, appraisal lists of any items included in the total amount of gifts, copies of balance sheets or other financial statements obtainable by him relating to the value of stock constituting the gift, and any other information obtainable by him that may be necessary in the determination of the tax. See section 2512 and the regulations issued thereunder. For every policy of life insurance listed on the return, the donor must procure a statement from the insurance company on Form 712 and file it with the internal revenue officer with whom the return is filed. If specifically requested by an internal revenue officer, the insurance company shall file this statement direct with the internal revenue officer. [Reg. §25.6001-1.]

☐ [*T.D.* 6334, 11-14-58. *Amended by T.D.* 7012, 5-14-69 *and T.D.* 7517, 11-11-77.]

### [Reg. §31.6001-1]

**§31.6001-1. Records in general.**—(a) *Form of records.*—The records required by the regulations in this part shall be kept accurately, but no particular form is required for keeping the records. Such forms and systems of accounting shall be used as will enable the district director to ascertain whether liability for tax is incurred and, if so, the amount thereof.

(b) *Copies of returns, schedules, and statements.*—Every person who is required, by the regulations in this part or by instructions applicable to any form prescribed thereunder, to keep any copy of any return, schedule, statement, or other document, shall keep such copy as a part of his records.

(c) *Records of claimants.*—Any person (including an employee) who, pursuant to the regulations in this part, claims a refund, credit, or abatement, shall keep a complete and detailed record with respect to the tax, interest, addition to the tax, additional amount, or assessable penalty to which the claim relates. Such record shall include any records required of the claimant by paragraph (b) of this section and by §§ 31.6001-2 to 31.6001-5, inclusive, which relate to the claim.

(d) *Records of employees.*—While not mandatory (except in the case of claims), it is advisable for each employee to keep permanent, accurate records showing the name and address of each employer for whom he performs services as an employee, the dates of beginning and termination of such services, the information with respect to himself which is required by the regulations in this subpart to be kept by employers, and the receipts furnished in accordance with the provisions of § 31.6051-1.

(e) *Place and period for keeping records.*—(1) All records required by the regulations in this part shall be kept, by the person required to keep them, at one or more convenient and safe locations accessible to internal revenue officers, and shall at all times be available for inspection by such officers.

(2) Except as otherwise provided in the following sentence, every person required by the regulations in this part to keep records in respect of a tax (whether or not such person incurs liability for such tax) shall maintain such records for at least four years after the due date of such tax for the return period to which the records relate, or the date such tax is paid, whichever is the later. The records of claimants required by paragraph (c) of this section shall be maintained for a period of at least four years after the date the claim is filed.

(f) *Cross references.*—See §§ 31.6001-2 to 31.6001-5, inclusive, for additional records required with respect to the Federal Insurance Contributions Act, the Railroad Retirement Tax Act, the Federal Unemployment Tax Act, and the collection of income tax at source on wages, respectively. [Reg. § 31.6001-1.]

☐ [*T.D. 6354, 1-13-59.*]

### [Reg. § 41.6001-1]

**§ 41.6001-1. Records.**—(a) *Records to be kept.*—Every person in whose name a highway motor vehicle having a taxable gross weight of at least 55,000 pounds is registered or required to be registered at any time during the taxable period shall keep records sufficient to enable the Commissioner to determine whether such person is liable for the tax and, if so, the amount thereof. See § 41.4482(b)-1 for the definition of taxable gross weight. Such records shall show with respect to each such vehicle:

(1) A description of the vehicle (including serial number or manufacturer's number) in sufficient detail to permit positive identification of the vehicle.

(2) The weight of the loads carried by the vehicle in such form as is required under the laws of any State in which the vehicle is registered or required to be registered, in order to permit verification of such vehicle's taxable gross weight.

(3) The date on which such person acquired such vehicle and the name and address of the person from whom the vehicle was acquired.

(4) The first month of each taxable period in which occurred a taxable use of each such vehicle while the vehicle was registered in the name of such person; information showing whether such vehicle was operated, while registered in the name of such person, in any prior month in such taxable period; and if such vehicle was so operated, evidence establishing that such operation was not a taxable use.

(5) The date of sale or other transfer to another of any such vehicle, together with the name and address of the person to whom transferred.

(6) In the case of any such vehicle disposed of otherwise than by sale or other transfer (including disposition by theft or destruction), the date and method of disposition of the vehicle.

(7) In the case of a secondhand highway motor vehicle acquired at any time in the taxable period, evidence showing whether there was a prior taxable use in such taxable period of the highway motor vehicle (see paragraph (b) of § 41.4481-2) or whether there was a suspension of tax in effect (see § 41.4483-3).

(8) A copy of each return, schedule, statement, or other document filed, pursuant to the regulations in this part or in accordance with the instructions applicable to any form prescribed thereunder, by the person required to keep such records.

(b) *Transit systems.*—Every person engaged in the operation of a transit system who claims exemption from tax with respect to a transit-type bus shall keep records sufficient to show, with respect to each taxable period, whether it meets the 60-percent passenger fare revenue test (see paragraph (e) of § 41.4483-2) for the period prescribed as the test period (see paragraph (c) of § 41.4483-2) for such system for such taxable period.

(c) *Exemption for vehicles used 5,000 miles or less.*—The owner of a highway motor vehicle who reasonably expects the vehicle to be exempt from the tax under section 4481(a) by reason of § 41.4483-3(c) for a given taxable period shall keep records which indicate the reason that the use of the vehicle is not expected to exceed 5,000 miles on public highways.

(d) *Records of claimants.*—Any person claiming refund, credit, or abatement of the tax, interest, additional amount, addition to the tax, or assessable penalty, shall keep a complete and detailed record with respect to the claim.

(e) *Place and period for keeping records.*—(1) All records required by the regulations in this part shall be kept, by the person required to keep them, at a convenient and safe location within the United States which is accessible to internal revenue officers. Such records shall at all times be available for inspection by such officers. If such person has a principal place of business in the United States, the records shall be kept at such place of business.

(2) Records required by paragraph (a) of this section shall be maintained for a period of at least 3 years after the date the tax becomes due or the date the tax is paid, whichever is the later. Records required by paragraphs (b) and (c) of this section shall be maintained for a period of at least 3 years after the end of the taxable period for which such exemption applies. Records required by paragraph (d) of this section (including any record required by paragraphs (a), (b), or (c) of this section which relates to a claim) shall be maintained for a period of at least 3 years after the date the claim is filed. [Reg. § 41.6001-1.]

☐ [*T.D. 6216, 12-6-56. Amended by T.D. 6743, 6-22-64 and T.D. 8027, 5-23-85; T.D. 8879, 3-30-2000 and T.D. 9698, 10-28-2014.*]

### [Reg. § 44.6001-1]

**§ 44.6001-1. Record requirements.**—(a) *In general.*—(1) In addition to all other records required pursuant to § 44.4403-1, every person required to pay tax under section 4401 shall keep such records as will clearly show as to each day's operation:

(i) Separately, the gross amount of wagers—

(a) Accepted directly by the taxpayer or at any registered place of business of the taxpayer (other than laid-off wagers),

(b) Accepted for his account by agents at any place other than a registered place of business of the taxpayer (other than laid-off wagers), and

(c) Accepted as laid-off wagers from persons subject to the tax on wagers;

(ii) With respect to wagers laid off with others, the name, address, and registration number of each person with whom the laid-off wagers were placed, and the gross amount laid off with each such person, showing separately the gross amount of laid-off wagers with respect to each event, contest, or other wagering medium, as, for example, the gross amount laid off on each horse in a race; and

(iii) The gross amount of tax collected from or charged to bettors as a separate item.

(2) If a taxpayer has any agents or employees receiving wagers on his behalf, he shall maintain a separate record showing the name and address of each agent or employee, the period of employment, and the number of the special tax stamp issued to each such agent or employee.

(3) A duplicate copy of each return required by § 44.6011(a)-1 shall be retained as part of the taxpayer's records.

(b) *Records of agent or employee.*—Every person who is engaged in receiving for or on behalf of another person (at any place other than a registered place of business of such other person) wagers of a type subject to the tax imposed by section 4401 shall keep a record showing for each day (1) the gross amount of such wagers received by him, (2) the amount, if any, retained as a commission or as compensation for receiving such wagers, and (3) the amount turned over to the person on whose behalf the wagers were received, and the name and address of such person.

(c) *Record of claimants.*—Any person claiming a credit or refund shall keep a complete and detailed record of each overpayment and of each laid-off wager for which credit is taken or refund is claimed, including a copy of the certificate required under paragraph (d) of § 44.6419-2.

(d) *Place for keeping records.*—Every person required to pay the tax imposed by section 4401 shall keep or cause to be kept, at his office or principal place of business, or, if he has no office or principal place of business, at his residence or some other convenient or safe location, all such records as are required pursuant to paragraphs (a) and (c) of this section and §§ 44.4403 and 44.4403-1.

(e) *Period for retaining records.*—All records required by the regulations in this part shall at all times be available for inspection by internal revenue officers. Records required by § 44.4403-1 and by paragraph (a) of this section shall be maintained for a period of at least three years from the date the tax became due. Records required by paragraph (b) of this section shall be maintained for a period of at least three years from the date the wager was received. Records required by paragraph (c) of this section shall be maintained for a period of at least three years from the date any credit is taken or refund is claimed. [Reg. § 44.6001-1.]

☐ [*T.D.* 6370, 4-4-59. *Amended by T.D.* 6568, 8-15-61.]

#### [Reg. § 53.6001-1]

**§ 53.6001-1. Notice or regulations requiring records, statements, and special returns.**—(a) *In general.*—Any person subject to tax under chapter 42, Subtitle D, of the Code shall keep such complete and detailed records as are sufficient to enable the district director to determine accurately the amount of liability under chapter 42.

(b) *Notice by district director requiring returns, statements, or the keeping of records.*—The district director may require any person, by notice served upon him, to make such returns, render such statements, or keep such specific records as will enable the district director to determine whether or not such person is liable for tax under chapter 42.

(c) *Retention of records.*—The records required by this section shall be kept at all times available for inspection by authorized internal revenue officers or employees, and shall be retained so long as the contents thereof may become material in the administration of any internal revenue law. [Reg. § 53.6001-1.]

☐ [*T.D.* 7368, 7-15-75.]

#### [Reg. § 55.6001-1]

**§ 55.6001-1. Notice or regulations requiring records, statements and special returns.**—(a) *In general.*—Any person subject to tax under chapter 44 of the Code shall keep such complete and detailed records as are sufficient to enable the district director to determine accurately the amount of liability under chapter 44.

(b) *Notice by district director requiring returns, statements, or the keeping of records.*—The district director may require any person, by notice served upon him, to make such returns, render such statements, or keep such specific records as will enable the district director to determine whether or not such person is liable for tax under chapter 44.

(c) *Retention of records.*—The records required by this section shall be kept at all times available for inspection by authorized internal revenue officers or employees, and shall be retained so long as the contents thereof may become material in the administration of any internal revenue law. [Reg. § 55.6001-1.]

☐ [*T.D.* 7767, 2-3-81.]

#### [Reg. § 56.6001-1]

**§ 56.6001-1. Notice or regulations requiring records, statements, and special returns.**—(a) *In general.*—The provisions of § 53.6001-1 shall apply to any person subject to tax under chapter 41, Subtitle D, of the Code, by treating each reference to chapter 42 in § 53.6001-1 as a reference to chapter 41.

(b) *Cross references.*—See § 56.4911-6 for general information on records of lobbying expenditures. See § § 56.4911-9(d) and 56.4911-10(f) for information that members of an affiliated group and a limited affiliated group, respectively, are to provide to other members of the group and to the Internal Revenue Service. [Reg. § 56.6001-1.]

☐ [*T.D.* 8308, 8-30-90.]

#### [Reg. § 156.6001-1]

**§ 156.6001-1. Notice or regulations requiring records, statements, and special returns.**—(a) *In general.*—Any person subject to tax under chapter 54 (Greenmail) of the Code shall keep such complete and detailed records as are sufficient to enable the district director to determine accurately the amount of liability under chapter 54.

(b) *Notice by district director requiring returns, statements, or the keeping of records.*—The district director may require any person, by notice served upon him, to make such returns, render such statements, or keep such specific records as will enable the district director to determine whether or not the person is liable for tax under chapter 54 of the Code.

(c) *Retention of records.*—The records required by this section shall be kept at all times available for inspection by authorized internal revenue officers or employees, and shall be retained so long as the contents thereof may become material in the administration of any internal revenue law. [Reg. § 156.6001-1.]

☐ [*T.D.* 8379, 12-17-91.]

#### [Reg. § 157.6001-1]

**§ 157.6001-1. Records, statements, and special returns.**—(a) *In general.*—Any person subject to tax under chapter 55 (Structured Settlement Factoring Transactions) of the Internal Revenue Code must keep such complete and detailed records as are sufficient to enable the Internal Revenue Service (IRS) to determine accurately the amount of liability under chapter 55.

(b) *Notice by the IRS requiring returns, statements, or the keeping of records.*—The IRS may require any person, by notice served upon him, to make such returns, render such statements, or keep such specific records as will enable the IRS to determine whether or not the person is liable for tax under chapter 55.

(c) *Retention of records.*—The records required by this section must be kept at all times available for inspection by the IRS, and shall be retained so long as the contents thereof may become material in the administration of any internal revenue law. [Reg. § 157.6001-1.]

☐ [*T.D.* 9134, 7-7-2004.]

#### [Reg. § 301.6001-1]

**§ 301.6001-1. Notice or regulations requiring records, statements, and special returns.**—For provisions requiring records, statements, and special returns, see the regulations relating to the particular tax. [Reg. § 301.6001-1.]

☐ [*T.D.* 6498, 10-24-60.]

#### [Reg. § 1.6001-2]

**§ 1.6001-2. Returns.**—For rules relating to returns required to be made by every individual, estate or trust which is liable for one or more qualified State individual income taxes as defined in section 6362 for a taxable year, see paragraph (b) of § 301.6361-1 of this chapter (Regulations on Procedure and Administration). [Reg. § 1.6001-2.]

☐ [*T.D.* 7577, 12-19-78.]

#### [Reg. § 31.6001-2]

**§ 31.6001-2. Additional records under Federal Insurance Contributions Act.**—(a) *In general.*—(1) Every employer liable for tax under the Federal Insurance Contributions Act shall keep records of all remuneration, whether in cash or in a medium other than cash, paid to his employees after 1954 for services (other than agricultural labor which constitutes or is deemed to constitute employment, domestic service in a private home of the employer, or service not in the course of the employer's trade or business) performed for him after 1936. Such records shall show with respect to each employee receiving such remuneration—

(i) The name, address, and account number of the employee and such additional information with respect to the employee as is required by paragraph (c) of § 31.6011(b)-2 when the employee does not advise the employer what his account number and name are as shown on an account number card issued to the employee by the Social Security Administration.

(ii) The total amount and date of each payment of remuneration (including any sum withheld therefrom as tax or for any other reason) and the period of services covered by such payment.

(iii) The amount of each such remuneration payment which constitutes wages subject to tax. See § § 31.3121(a)-1 to 31.3121(a)(12)-1, inclusive.

(iv) The amount of employee tax, or any amount equivalent to employee tax, collected with respect to such payment, and, if collected at a time other than the time such payment was made, the date collected. See paragraph (b) of § 31.3102-1 for provisions relating to collection of amounts equivalent to employee tax.

(v) If the total remuneration payment (subdivision (ii) of this subparagraph) and the amount thereof which is taxable (subdivision (iii) of this subparagraph) are not equal, the reason therefor.

(2) Every employer shall keep records of the details of each adjustment or settlement of taxes under the Federal Insurance Contributions Act made pursuant to the regulations in this part. The employer shall keep as a part of his records a copy of each statement furnished pursuant to paragraph (c) of § 31.6011(a)-1.

(3) Every employer shall keep records of all remuneration in the form of tips received by his employees after 1965 in the course of their employment and reported to him pursuant to section 6053(a). The employer shall keep as part of his records employee statements of tips furnished him pursuant to section 6053(a) (unless the information disclosed by such statements is recorded on another document retained by the employer pursuant to subparagraph (1) of this para-

graph) and copies of employer statements furnished employees pursuant to section 6053(b).

(b) *Agricultural labor, domestic service, and service not in the course of employer's trade or business.*—(1) Every employer who pays cash remuneration after 1954 for the performance for him after 1950 of agricultural labor which constitutes or is deemed to constitute employment, of domestic, service in a private home of the employer not on a farm operated for profit, or of service not in the course of his trade or business shall keep records of all such cash remuneration with respect to which he incurs, or expects to incur, liability for the taxes imposed by the Federal Insurance Contributions Act, or with respect to which amounts equivalent to employee tax are deducted pursuant to section 3102(a). See §§ 31.3101-3, 31.3111-3, and 31.3121(a)-2 for provisions relating, respectively, to the liability for employee tax which is incurred when wages are received, the liability for employer tax which is incurred when wages are paid, and the time when wages are paid and received. Such records shall show with respect to each employee receiving such cash remuneration—

(i) The name of the employee.

(ii) The account number of each employee to whom wages for such services are paid, within the meaning of § 31.3121(a)-2, and such additional information as is required by paragraph (c) of § 31.6011(b)-2 when the employee does not advise the employer what his account number and name are as shown on an account number card issued to the employee by the Social Security Administration.

(iii) The amount of such cash remuneration paid to the employee (including any sum withheld therefrom as tax or for any other reason) for agricultural labor which constitutes or is deemed to constitute employment, for domestic service in a private home of the employer not on a farm operated for profit, or for service not in the course of the employer's trade or business; the calendar month in which such cash remuneration was paid; and the character of the services for which such cash remuneration was paid. When the employer incurs liability for the taxes imposed by the Federal Insurance Contributions Act with respect to any such cash remuneration which he did not previously expect would be subject to the taxes, the amount of any such cash remuneration not previously made a matter of record shall be determined by the employer to the best of his knowledge and belief.

(iv) The amount of employee tax, or any amount equivalent to employee tax, collected with respect to such cash remuneration and the calendar month in which collected. See paragraph (b) of § 31.3102-1 for provisions relating to collection of amounts equivalent to employee tax.

(v) To the extent material to a determination of tax liability, the number of days during each calendar year after 1956 on which agricultural labor which constitutes or is deemed to constitute employment is performed by the employee for cash remuneration computed on a time basis.

(2) Every person to whom a "crew leader", as that term is defined in section 3121(i), furnishes individuals for the performance of agricultural labor after December 31, 1958, shall keep records of the name; permanent mailing address, or if none, present address; and identification number, if any, of such "crew leader". [Reg. § 31.6001-2.]

☐ [T.D. 6516, 12-20-60. Amended by T.D. 7001, 1-23-69.]

**[Reg. § 41.6001-2]**

**§ 41.6001-2. Proof of payment for state registration purposes.**—(a) *In general.*—This section sets forth the circumstances under which a State must require proof of payment of the tax imposed by section 4481(a), and the required manner in which such proof of payment is to be received by the State as a condition of issuing a registration for a highway motor vehicle. A State must either comply with the provisions of this section or, in the alternative, comply with such other rules regarding the satisfaction of this proof of payment requirement as may be prescribed by the Commissioner (by Revenue Procedure or otherwise), in order to avoid a reduction of Federal-aid highway funds apportioned under 23 U.S.C. 104(b)(4). For purposes of this section, the rules of section 7502 and § 301.7502-1 of this chapter (relating to timely mailing treated as timely filing) determine when an application for registration is considered to be received by a State.

(b) *Proof of payment required.*—(1) *In general.*—A State to which an application is made to register a highway motor vehicle must receive from the registrant proof of payment of the tax imposed by section 4481(a) (or proof of suspension of such tax under § 41.4483-3) unless otherwise provided in this paragraph (b)(1), or paragraph (b)(2) or (5) of this section. See paragraph (c) of this section for the meaning of "proof of payment". Such proof of payment must be received by the State before the State issues a registration for such vehicle unless the State is using a system of registration provided in paragraph (b)(3) of

this section. The term "proof of payment", when used in this section, shall be considered to refer in appropriate cases to proof of suspension of the tax imposed by section 4481(a). Except as provided in paragraph (b)(4) of this section, any proof of payment presented to a State must relate to tax paid (or suspended under § 41.4483-3) for the taxable period which includes the date that the State receives the application for registration. A "base state" must be presented proof of payment when issuing an "apportioned plate" under the International Registration Plan (IRP) (or similar agreement) for a highway motor vehicle, but no proof of payment of the tax imposed by section 4481(a) is required to be presented to the other states for which the vehicle is proportionally registered and which are listed on the IRP cab card issued by the base state. Further, a State is not required to receive proof of payment in order to issue special temporary travel permits which allow a vehicle to, (i) operate in a State in which the vehicle is not registered (including proportional or prorate registration), (ii) operate at more than the State's maximum statutory weight limit, or (iii) operate at more than the weight that the vehicle is registered in a State. Further, a State may register a highway motor vehicle without proof of payment if the person registering the vehicle presents the original or a photocopy of a bill of sale (or other document evidencing transfer) indicating that the vehicle was purchased by the owner either as a new or used vehicle during the preceding 60 days before the date that the State receives the application for registration of such vehicle.

(ii) [Reserved].

(2) *States required to receive proof of payment with respect to vehicles subject to tax.*—(i) *Registration in States that register vehicles on the basis of gross weight.*—A State that registers vehicles on the basis of gross weight must require proof of payment with respect to any highway motor vehicle that has a declared gross weight in that State of 55,000 pounds or more. If no declaration of a specific gross weight is made with respect to a highway motor vehicle registered on the basis of gross weight, then the State must require proof of payment with respect to such vehicle if the minimum weight of the registered weight category for such vehicle is 55,000 pounds or more. No such proof of payment is required for any vehicle that does not have a declared gross weight in that State of 55,000 pounds or more.

(ii) *Registration in States that register vehicles other than on the basis of gross weight.*—A State that registers vehicles other than on the basis of gross weight must require proof of payment in order to register a highway motor vehicle unless the State receives a written statement stating that during the taxable period which includes the date on which the State receives the application for registration, such vehicle had a taxable gross weight of less than 55,000 pounds. The written statement must state the number of vehicles being registered that have a taxable gross weight of less than 55,000 pounds and must be signed by the person registering the vehicles. A State may register a highway motor vehicle without receiving either proof of payment or a written statement as described above if such vehicle has an unladen weight of 8,000 pounds or less. However, the State must require proof of payment when issuing a "base plate" registration for a vehicle if a gross weight declaration of 55,000 pounds or more is made to the State with respect to such vehicle in order to proportionally register the vehicle in another State under the IRP.

(iii) *State may require additional proof.*—Nothing contained in this section shall prohibit a State from refusing to register a highway motor vehicle without additional proof that the vehicle is not subject to tax under section 4481(a) even though the person registering the vehicle submits a written statement declaring that the taxable gross weight of such vehicle is less than 55,000 pounds.

(3) *Suspension registration system.*—A State may issue a registration with respect to any or all highway motor vehicles subject to tax under section 4481(a) without receiving proof of payment if such vehicles are registered under a "suspension" registration system. Registration of a vehicle subject to tax under a suspension system must be on the condition that, (i) the State receive proof of payment with respect to such vehicle no later than 4 months (or any lesser time to be determined by the State) after the beginning of the vehicle's registration period, and (ii) the State's system provides for the automatic suspension (*e.g.*, through the use of computer-generated notices) of such vehicle's registration if no proof of payment is received within the required time. Following such a suspension of registration, the State must not allow the vehicle to be registered until valid proof of payment is received. A State may either register all vehicles subject to tax under section 4481(a) in the manner described in this paragraph (b)(3) or adopt this manner of registration only in situations which the State deems appropriate. A State that registers vehicles other than on the basis of gross weight may also register vehicles not subject to tax under a suspension registration system for purposes of receiving the written statement described in paragraph (b)(2)(ii).

(4) *Registration during certain months.*—In the case of a highway motor vehicle subject to tax under section 4481(a) for which a State receives an application for registration during the months of July, August or September, proof of payment for the immediately preceding taxable period may be used to verify payment of the tax imposed by section 4481(a).

(ii) [Reserved].

(5) *Registration in a State several times during the taxable period.*—A State is required to receive proof of payment with respect to a highway motor vehicle subject to tax under section 4481(a) only once

during a taxable period. Thus, in the case of a State that allows a highway motor vehicle to be registered on a quarterly basis, rather than annually, proof of payment will be required to be presented to the State only once during the taxable period. The State may designate any one of the four quarterly registration periods as the time for submitting proof of payment.

(6) *Proof of payment records.*—See 23 CFR Part 669 for a description of the supporting documentation and records that will be required by the Federal Highway Administration (FHWA) in order to allow the FHWA to verify that the State is in compliance with the rules of this section.

⤘→ *Caution: Reg. §41.6001-2(c), below, prior to amendment by T.D. 9698, applies before July 1, 2015.*

(c) *Proof of payment.*—(1) *In general.*—(i) The proof of payment required in paragraph (b) of this section shall consist of a receipted Schedule 1 (Form 2290) that is returned by the Internal Revenue Service to a taxpayer who files a return of tax under section 4481(a) and pays the amount of tax (or installment thereof) due with such return. A photocopy of such receipted Schedule 1 shall also serve as proof of payment. Such Schedule 1 shall serve as proof of suspension of such tax under § 41.4483-3 for the number of vehicles entered in that part of the Schedule 1 designated for vehicles for which tax has been suspended. Except as provided in paragraph (c)(1)(ii) of this section, the vehicle identification number of the vehicle being registered must appear on the Schedule 1 (or an attached page) in order for the Schedule 1 to be a valid proof of payment for such vehicle.

(ii) With respect to taxable periods beginning before July 1, 2000, if a receipted Schedule 1 is submitted as proof of payment for the registration of one or more highway motor vehicles and—

(A)*(1)* The total of the number of vehicles on such Schedule 1 for which tax has not been suspended under § 41.4483-3 exceeds 21, or

*(2)* The total of the number of vehicles on such Schedule 1 for which tax has been suspended under § 41.4483-3 exceeds 9, and

(B) The name of the taxpayer appearing on such Schedule 1 is one of the names in which such vehicles are sought to be registered, such Schedule 1 shall be accepted as proof of payment in support of the registration of a number of vehicles equal to or less than such total and a list of the vehicles (or their vehicle identification numbers) is not required as part of such proof of payment.

(iii) With respect to taxable periods beginning before July 1, 2000, if a Schedule 1 which does not include a list of vehicle identification numbers is submitted as proof of payment for the registration

of one or more highway motor vehicles and the name of the taxpayer appearing on such Schedule 1 is not one of the names in which such vehicles are sought to be registered then such Schedule 1 shall be accepted as proof of payment in support of the registration of a number of vehicles equal to or less than the total number of vehicles on such Schedule 1 provided the Schedule 1 is accompanied by a written statement executed by the taxpayer. Such written statement shall contain the vehicle identification numbers of the vehicles sought to be registered and a statement that the tax under section 4481(a) has been paid with respect to such vehicles for the taxable period. The statement must be signed by the taxpayer whose name appears on the Schedule 1.

(2) *Acceptable substitute for receipted Schedule 1.*—(i) *General rule.*—For purposes of this section, a State shall accept as proof of payment a photocopy of the Form 2290 (with the Schedule 1 attached) which was filed with the Internal Revenue Service for the vehicle being registered with sufficient documentation of payment of tax due at the time the Form 2290 was filed (such as a photocopy of both sides of a cancelled check). This substitute proof of payment may be used to register a vehicle when, for example, the receipted Schedule 1 has been lost, or when at the time required for registration of a vehicle, a receipted Schedule 1 has not been received by a taxpayer who has filed a Form 2290 with respect to such vehicle. The rules of paragraph (c)(1)(ii) of this section regarding the circumstances in which a list of vehicle identification numbers is not required as part of a valid proof of payment, apply to a non-receipted Schedule 1 received by a State with a Form 2290 as a substitute proof of payment under this paragraph (c)(2).

(ii) [Reserved]. For further guidance, see § 41.6001-2T(c)(2)(ii).

⤘→ *Caution: Reg. §41.6001-2(c), below, as amended by T.D. 9698, applies on or after July 1, 2015.*

(c) *Proof of payment.*—(1) *In general.*—The proof of payment required in paragraph (b) of this section consists of a receipted Schedule 1 (Form 2290 "Heavy Highway Vehicle Use Tax Return") that is returned by the Internal Revenue Service, by mail or electronically, to a taxpayer that files a return of tax under section 4481(a), meets the requirements of § 41.6011(a)-1, and pays the amount of tax due with such return. A photocopy of such receipted Schedule 1 also serves as proof of payment. Such Schedule 1 serves as proof of suspension of such tax under § 41.4483-3 for the number of vehicles entered in that part of the Schedule 1 designated for vehicles for which tax has been suspended. The vehicle identification number of the vehicle being registered must appear on the Schedule 1 (or an attached page) in order for the Schedule 1 to be a valid proof of payment for such vehicle.

(2) *Acceptable substitute for receipted Schedule 1.*—For purposes of this section, a State must accept as proof of payment a photocopy of the Form 2290 (with the Schedule 1 attached) that was filed with the Internal Revenue Service for the vehicle being registered with sufficient documentation of payment of tax due at the time the Form 2290 was filed (such as a photocopy of both sides of a cancelled check). This substitute proof of payment may be used to register a vehicle when, for example, the receipted Schedule 1 has been lost, or when at the time required for registration of a vehicle, a receipted Schedule 1 has not been received by a taxpayer who has filed a Form 2290 with respect to such vehicle.

(d) *Examples.*—The application of this section may be illustrated by the following examples:

*Example (1).* A applies to register a 3-axle single unit truck in State R, a member of the International Registration Plan, on November 1, 1985. State R registers vehicles based on unladen weight. At the same time, A applies for a proportional registration under the IRP to use the truck in State S. State S does not register vehicles on the basis of unladen weight. For purposes of the proportional registration in State S, A declares the gross weight of his truck at 50,000 pounds. A does not register the truck in any other states. A's truck has a taxable gross weight, as determined under § 41.4482(b)-1, of less than 55,000 pounds and therefore is not subject to tax under section 4481(a). A submits a written statement along with his application for registra-

tion in State R. The written statement states that A's vehicle has a taxable gross weight of less than 55,000 pounds and is signed by A. State R may register A's truck and issue a proportional registration for A to use his truck in State S without receiving proof of payment.

*Example (2).* Assume the same facts as in example (1) except that A applies for proportional registration under the IRP in State S and declares the truck to have a gross weight of 60,000 pounds. The taxable gross weight of A's truck, as determined under § 41.4482(b)-1 is 60,000 pounds. State R may not register A's truck unless it receives proof of payment within the meaning of paragraph (c) of this section.

*Example (3).* On October 10, 1985, C applies to register 9 vehicles in State U and declares the gross weight of each vehicle to be 70,000 pounds. C has not applied for registration in any other states. At the time of applying for registration, C presents a photocopy of a receipted Schedule 1 (Form 2290) that shows a total of 9 vehicles which are subject to tax under section 4481(a) and for which tax is not suspended under § 41.4483-3(a). The vehicle identification numbers of the vehicles that C is seeking to register must be listed on the Schedule 1 in order for State U to register the vehicles.

(e) *Effective/applicability date.*—Paragraph (c) of this section applies to registrations of highway motor vehicles pursuant to applications that are received by a State on or after July 1, 2015. The rules of section 7502 and § 301.7502-1 of this chapter (relating to timely mailing treated as timely filing) determine when an application for registration is considered to be received by a State. For rules applicable to applications before that date, see 26 CFR 41.6001-2 (revised as of April 1, 2014). [Reg. § 41.6001-2.]

☐ [*T.D. 8027, 5-23-85. Amended by T.D. 8879, 3-30-2000; T.D. 9537, 7-15-2011 and T.D. 9698 10-28-2014.*]

**[Reg. §31.6001-3]**

**§31.6001-3. Additional records under Railroad Retirement Tax Act.**—(a) *Records of employers.*—(1) Every employer liable for tax under the Railroad Retirement Tax Act shall keep records of all remuneration (whether in money or in something which may be used in lieu of money), other than tips, paid to his employees after 1954 for services rendered to him (including "time lost") after 1954. Such records shall show with respect to each employee—

(i) The name and address of the employee.

(ii) The total amount and date of each payment of remuneration to the employee (including any sum withheld therefrom as tax or for any other reason) and the period of service (including any period of absence from active service) covered by such payment.

(iii) The amount of such remuneration payment with respect to which the tax is imposed.

(iv) The amount of employee tax collected with respect to such payment, and, if collected at a time other than the time such payment was made, the date collected.

(v) If the total payment of remuneration (paragraph (a)(1)(ii) of this section) and the amount thereof with respect to which the tax is imposed (paragraph (a)(1)(iii) of this section) are not equal, the reason therefor.

(2) The employer shall keep records of the details of each adjustment or settlement of taxes under the Railroad Retirement Tax Act made pursuant to the regulations in this part.

(b) *Records of employee representatives.*—Every individual liable for employee representative tax under the Railroad Retirement Tax Act shall keep records of all remuneration (whether in money or in something which may be used in lieu of money) paid to him after 1954 for services rendered (including "time lost") by him as an employee representative after 1954. Such records shall show—

(1) The name and address of each employee organization employing him.

(2) The total amount and date of each payment of remuneration for services rendered as an employee representative (including any sum withheld therefrom as tax or for any other reason) and the period of service (including any period of absence from active service) covered by such payment.

(3) The amount of such remuneration payment with respect to which the employee representative tax is imposed.

(4) If the total payment of remuneration (paragraph (a)(2) of this section) and the amount thereof with respect to which the employee representative tax is imposed (paragraph (a)(3) of this section) are not equal, the reason therefor. [Reg. §31.6001-3.]

### [Reg. §41.6001-3]

**§41.6001-3. Proof of payment for entry into the United States.**—(a) *In general.*—(1) Except as otherwise provided in paragraph (a)(2) of this section, proof of payment of the tax imposed by section 4481(a) must be presented to United States Customs officials with respect to any highway motor vehicle subject to the tax imposed by section 4481(a) that has a base for registration purposes in a contiguous foreign country upon entry of such vehicle into the United States during any taxable period to which this section applies. Such proof of payment must relate to tax paid (or suspended under §41.4483-3) for the taxable period that includes the date of entry into the United States. See paragraph (c) of this section for the definition of the term "proof of payment."

(2) No proof of payment is required upon entry of a highway motor vehicle described in paragraph (a)(1) of this section into the United States if, as of the date of such entry, the period of time for filing a return of the tax imposed on such vehicle by section 4481(a) for the taxable period that includes the date of such entry has not expired and a written declaration is presented to United States Customs officials. Such declaration must state that, as of the date of such entry, the period of time for filing a return of the tax imposed on such vehicle by section 4481(a) for the taxable period that includes the date of such entry has not expired. The written declaration must include (1) the name, address, and taxpayer identification number of the person liable under §41.4481-2 for the tax imposed on such vehicle; (2) the vehicle identification number of such vehicle; (3) the date on which such vehicle was first used on the public highways in the United States during the taxable period (or a statement that the current entry is the first use on the public highways in the United States during the taxable period); (4) an acknowledgement by the person liable for the tax imposed on such vehicle that the willful use of the declaration to evade or defeat the tax otherwise applicable under section 4481(a) will subject such person to a fine or imprisonment or both; and (5) the signature of the person liable for the tax imposed on such vehicle. A copy of the written declaration shall be retained in the records of the person liable for the tax imposed on such vehicle under the rules of §41.6001-1. See §41.6071(a)-1 for rules regarding the time for filing a return of the tax imposed by section 4481(a).

(b) *Failure to provide proof of payment.*—If, upon attempting to enter the United States, the operator of a highway motor vehicle described in paragraph (a) of this section is unable to present proof of payment of the tax imposed by section 4481(a), or documentation described in paragraph (a)(2) of this section, with respect to such vehicle, then such vehicle may be denied entry into the United States.

(c) *Proof of payment.*—(1) *In general.*—For purposes of this section, the proof of payment required in paragraph (a) of this section shall consist of a receipted Schedule 1 (Form 2290) that is returned by the Internal Revenue Service to a taxpayer that files a return of tax under section 4481(a) and pays the amount of tax (or installment thereof) due with such return. A photocopy of such receipted Schedule 1 shall also serve as proof of payment. Such proof of payment shall also serve as proof of suspension of the tax under §41.4483-3 for the number of vehicles entered in that part of the Schedule 1 designated for vehicles for which tax has been suspended. The vehicle identification number of any vehicle for which a return is being filed, whether tax is being paid with respect to such vehicle or tax is suspended on such vehicle, must appear on the Schedule 1 (or an attached page) in order for the Schedule 1 to be a valid proof of payment for such vehicle.

(2) *Acceptable substitute for receipted Schedule 1.*—For purposes of this section, a photocopy of the Form 2290 (with the Schedule 1 attached) that is filed with the Internal Revenue Service for a vehicle being entered into the United States with sufficient documentation of payment of tax due at the time the Form 2290 is filed (such as a photocopy of both sides of a cancelled check) shall be accepted as proof of payment. No documentation of payment of tax is required with the substitute proof of payment if at the time the Form 2290 is filed the tax imposed by section 4481(a) is suspended under §41.4483-3 with respect to the vehicle entering the United States. This substitute proof of payment may be used to enter a vehicle into the United States when, for example, the receipted Schedule 1 has been lost, or if the taxpayer that filed a Form 2290 with respect to such vehicle has not received a receipted Schedule 1 at the time such vehicle enters the United States.

(d) *Taxable periods to which this section applies.*—This section shall apply to any taxable period beginning on or after July 1, 1987. [Reg. §41.6001-3.]

☐ [*T.D. 8159, 9-3-87. Amended by T.D. 8177, 3-3-88.*]

### [Reg. §31.6001-4]

**§31.6001-4. Additional records under Federal Unemployment Tax Act.**—(a) *Records of employers.*—Every employer liable for tax under the Federal Unemployment Tax Act for any calendar year shall, with respect to each such year, keep such records as are necessary to establish—

(1) The total amount of remuneration (including any sum withheld therefrom as tax or for any other reason) paid to his employees during the calendar year for services performed after 1938.

(2) The amount of such remuneration which constitutes wages subject to the tax. See §31.3306(b)-1 through §31.3306(b)(8)-1.

(3) The amount of contributions paid by him into each State unemployment fund, with respect to services subject to the law of such State, showing separately (i) payments made and neither deducted nor to be deducted from the remuneration of his employees, and (ii) payments made and deducted or to be deducted from the remuneration of his employees.

(4) The information required to be shown on the prescribed return and the extent to which the employer is liable for the tax.

(5) If the total remuneration paid (subparagraph (1) of this paragraph) and the amount thereof which is subject to the tax (subparagraph (2) of this paragraph) are not equal, the reason therefor.

(6) To the extent material to a determination of tax liability, the dates, in each calendar quarter, on which each employee performed services not in the course of the employer's trade or business, and the amount of cash remuneration paid at any time for such services performed within such quarter. See §31.3306(c)(3)-1.
The term "remuneration," as used in this paragraph, includes all payments whether in cash or in a medium other than cash, except that the term does not include payments in a medium other than cash for services not in the course of the employer's trade or business. See §31.3306(b)(7)-1.

(b) *Records of persons who are not employers.*—Any person who employs individuals in employment (see §31.3306(c)-1 to §31.3306(c)-3, inclusive) during any calendar year but who considers that he is not an employer subject to the tax (see §31.3306(a)-1) shall, with respect to each such year, be prepared to establish by proper records (including, where necessary, records of the number of employees employed each day) that he is not an employer subject to the tax. [Reg. §31.6001-4.]

☐ [*T.D. 6516, 12-20-60. Amended by T.D. 6658, 6-27-63.*]

### [Reg. §31.6001-5]

**§31.6001-5. Additional records in connection with collection of income tax at source on wages.**—(a) Every employer required under section 3402 to deduct and withhold income tax upon the wages of employees shall keep records of all remuneration paid to (including tips reported by) such employees. Such records shall show with respect to each employee—

(1) The name and address of the employee, and, after December 31, 1962, the account number of the employee.

(2) The total amount and date of each payment of remuneration (including any sum withheld therefrom as tax or for any other reason) and the period of services covered by such payment.

(3) The amount of such remuneration payment which constitutes wages subject to withholding.

(4) The amount of tax collected with respect to such remuneration payment and, if collected at a time other than the time such payment was made, the date collected.

(5) If the total remuneration payment (subparagraph (2) of this paragraph) and the amount thereof which is taxable (subparagraph (3) of this paragraph) are not equal, the reason therefor.

(6) Copies of any statements furnished by the employee pursuant to paragraph (b)(12) of §31.3401(a)-1 of Subpart E of the regulations in this part (relating to permanent residents of the Virgin Islands).

(7) Copies of any statements furnished by the employee pursuant to §§31.3401(a)(6)-1 and 31.3401(a)(7)-1, relating to nonresident alien individuals.

(8) Copies of any statements furnished by the employee pursuant to §31.3401(a)(8)(A)-1 of Subpart E of the regulations in this part (relating to residence or physical presence in a foreign country).

(9) Copies of any statements furnished by the employee pursuant to §31.3401(a)(8)(C)-1 of Subpart E of the regulations in this part (relating to citizens resident in Puerto Rico).

(10) The fair market value and date of each payment of noncash remuneration, made to an employee after August 9, 1955, for services performed as a retail commission salesman, with respect to which no income tax is withheld by reason of §31.3402(j)-1 of Subpart E of the regulations in this part.

[Subparagraph (11) was deleted by T.D. 7888.—CCH.]

(12) In the case of the employer for whom services are performed, with respect to payments made directly by him after December 31, 1955, under an accident or health plan (as defined in section 105 and the regulations thereunder)—

(i) The beginning and ending dates of each period of absence from work for which any such payment was made; and

(ii) Sufficient information to establish the amount and weekly rate of each such payment.

(13) The withholding exemption certificates (Forms W-4 and W-4E) filed with the employer by the employee.

(14) The agreement, if any, between the employer and the employee for the withholding of additional amounts of tax pursuant to §31.3402(i)-1 of Subpart E of the regulations in this part.

(15) To the extent material to a determination of tax liability, the dates, in each calendar quarter, on which the employee performed services not in the course of the employer's trade or business, and the amount of cash remuneration paid at any time for such services performed within such quarter. See §31.3401(a)(4)-1 of Subpart E of the regulations in this part.

(16) In the case of tips received by an employee after 1965 in the course of his employment, copies of any statements furnished by the employee pursuant to section 6053(a) unless the information disclosed by such statements is recorded on another document retained by the employer pursuant to the provisions of this paragraph.

(17) Any request of an employee under section 3402(h)(3) and §31.3402(h)(3)-1 to have the amount of tax to be withheld from his wages computed on the basis of his cumulative wages, and any notice of revocation thereof.

The term "remuneration," as used in this paragraph, includes all payments whether in cash or in a medium other than cash, except that the term does not include payments in a medium other than cash for services not in the course of the employer's trade or business, and does not include tips received by an employee in any medium other than cash or in cash if such tips amount to less than $20 for any calendar month. See §§31.3401(a)(11)-1 and 31.3401(a)(16)-1, respectively.

(b) The employer shall keep records of the details of each adjustment or settlement of income tax withheld under section 3402 made pursuant to the regulations in this part. [Reg. §31.6001-5.]

□ [T.D. 6155, 12-29-55 and T.D. 6354, 1-13-59. Amended by T.D. 6606, 8-24-62; T.D. 6908, 12-30-66; T.D. 7001, 1-17-69; T.D. 7048, 6-23-70; T.D. 7053, 7-20-70 and T.D. 7888, 4-22-83.]

**[Reg. §31.6001-6]**

**§31.6001-6. Notice by district director requiring returns, statements, or the keeping of records.**—The district director may require any person, by notice served upon him, to make such returns, render such statements, or keep such specific records as will enable the district director to determine whether or not such person is liable for any of the taxes to which the regulations in this part have application. [Reg. §31.6001-6.]

□ [T.D. 6472, 6-22-60.]

## Tax Returns or Statements

**[Reg. §1.6011-1]**

**§1.6011-1. General requirement of return, statement, or list.**—(a) General rule.—Every person subject to any tax, or required to collect any tax, under subtitle A of the Code, shall make such returns or statements as are required by the regulations in this chapter. The return or statement shall include therein the information required by the applicable regulations or forms.

(b) Use of prescribed forms.—Copies of the prescribed return forms will so far as possible be furnished taxpayers by district directors. A taxpayer will not be excused from making a return, however, by the fact that no return form has been furnished to him. Taxpayers not supplied with the proper forms should make application therefor to the district director in ample time to have their returns prepared, verified, and filed on or before the due date with the internal revenue office where such returns are required to be filed. Each taxpayer should carefully prepare his return and set forth fully and clearly the information required to be included therein. Returns which have not been so prepared will not be accepted as meeting the requirements of the Code. In the absence of a prescribed form, a statement made by a taxpayer disclosing his gross income and the deductions therefrom may be accepted as a tentative return, and, if filed within the prescribed time, the statement so made will relieve the taxpayer from liability for the addition to tax imposed for the delinquent filing of the return, provided that without unnecessary delay such a tentative return is supplemented by a return made on the proper form.

(c) Tax withheld on nonresident aliens and foreign corporations.—For requirements respecting the return of the tax required to be withheld under chapter 3 of the Code on nonresident aliens and foreign corporations and tax-free covenant bonds, see §1.1461-2. [Reg. §1.6011-1.]

□ [T.D. 6364, 2-13-59. Amended by T.D. 6922, 6-16-67.]

**[Reg. §20.6011-1]**

**§20.6011-1. General requirement of return, statement, or list.**—(a) General rule.—Every person made liable for any tax imposed by subtitle B of the Code shall make such returns or statements as are required by the regulations in this part. The return or statement shall include therein the information required by the applicable regulations or forms.

(b) Use of prescribed forms.—Copies of the forms prescribed by §§20.6018-1 and 20.6036-1 may be obtained from district directors. The fact that an executor has not been furnished with copies of these forms will not excuse him from making a return or, if applicable, from filing a preliminary notice. Application for a form shall be made to the district director in ample time for the executor to have the form prepared, verified, and filed with the appropriate internal revenue office on or before the date prescribed for the filing thereof (see §§20.6071-1 and 20.6075-1). The executor shall carefully prepare the return and, if applicable, the preliminary notice so as to set forth fully and clearly the data called for therein. A return or, if applicable, a preliminary notice which has not been so prepared will not be accepted as meeting the requirements of §§20.6018-1 through 20.6018-4 and §20.6036-1. [Reg. §20.6011-1.]

□ [T.D. 6296, 6-23-58. Amended by T.D. 7238, 12-28-72.]

**[Reg. §25.6011-1]**

**§25.6011-1. General requirement of return, statement, or list.**—(a) General rule.—Every person made liable for any tax imposed by chapter 12 of the Code shall make such returns or statements as are required by the regulations in this part. The return or statement shall include therein the information required by the applicable regulations or forms.

(b) Use of prescribed forms.—Copies of the forms prescribed by paragraph (b) of §25.6001-1 and §25.6019-1 may be obtained from district directors and directors of service centers. The fact that a person required to file a form has not been furnished with copies of a form will not excuse him from the making of a gift tax return, or from the furnishing of the evidence for which the forms are to be used. Application for a form should be made to the district director or director of a service center in ample time to enable the person whose duty it is to file the form to have the form prepared, verified, and filed on or before the date prescribed for the filing thereof. [Reg. § 25.6011-1.]

☐ *[T.D. 6334, 11-14-58. Amended by T.D. 7012, 5-14-69.]*

### [Reg. § 53.6011-1]

**§ 53.6011-1. General requirement of return, statement, or list.—** (a) Every private foundation liable for tax under section 4940 or 4948(a) shall file an annual return with respect to such tax on the form prescribed by the Internal Revenue Service for such purpose and shall include therein the information required by such form and the instructions issued with respect thereto.

(b) Every person (including a governmental entity) liable for tax imposed by sections 4941(a), 4942(a), 4943(a), 4944(a), 4945(a), 4955(a), 4958(a), 4959, 4960(a), 4965(a), 4966(a), 4967(a), or 4968(a), and every private foundation and every trust described in section 4947(a)(2) which has engaged in an act of self-dealing (as defined in section 4941(d)) (other than an act giving rise to no tax under section 4941(a)) shall file an annual return on Form 4720, "Return of Certain Excise Taxes Under Chapters 41 and 42 of the Internal Revenue Code," and shall include therein the information required by such form and the instructions issued with respect thereto. In the case of any tax imposed by sections 4941(a), 4942(a), 4943(a), and 4944(a), the annual return shall be filed with respect to each act (or failure to act) for each year (or part thereof) in the taxable period (as defined in sections 4941(e)(1), 4942(j)(1), 4943(d)(2), and 4944(e)(1)). In the case of a tax imposed by section 4945(a), 4955(a), 4958(a), 4960(a), 4965(a), 4966(a), or 4967(a), the annual return shall be filed with respect to each act for the year in which such act giving rise to liability occurred. In the case of a tax imposed by section 4959 on a hospital organization (as defined in § 1.501(r)-1(b)(18)), the annual return must include the required information for each of the organization's hospital facilities that failed to meet the requirements of section 501(r)(3) for the taxable year.

(c) If a Form 4720 is filed by a private foundation or trust described in section 4947(a)(2) with respect to a transaction to which other persons are required to file under paragraph (b) of this section, such persons may by their signature designate such organization's Form 4720 (to the extent applicable) as their return for purposes of compliance with this paragraph. However, this paragraph shall not apply to a person whose taxable year is other than the taxable year of the foundation or trust.

(d) For taxable years ending on or after December 31, 1975, every trust described in section 4947(a)(2) which is subject to any of the provisions of Chapter 42 as if it were a private foundation shall file an annual return on Form 5227. For taxable years beginning after December 31, 1980, every trust described in section 4947(a)(1) which is a private foundation shall file an annual return on Form 990-PF.

(e) For taxable years beginning after December 31, 1977, every person liable for tax under section 4951, 4952, or 4953 (relating to taxes on self-dealing, taxable expenditures, and excess contributions involving black lung benefit trusts) shall file an annual return with respect to the tax on the form prescribed by the Internal Revenue Service for that purpose. The person liable for the tax shall include the information required by the form and its related instructions. [Reg. § 53.6011-1.]

☐ *[T.D. 7368, 7-15-75. Amended by T.D. 7407, 3-3-76; T.D. 7838, 10-5-82; T.D. 8026, 5-17-85; T.D. 8628, 12-4-95; T.D. 8705, 12-31-96; T.D. 9334, 7-5-2007; T.D. 9629, 8-14-2013, T.D. 9708, 12-29-2014 and T.D. 9855, 4-5-2019.]*

### [Reg. § 54.6011-1]

**§ 54.6011-1. General requirement of return, statement, or list.—** (a) *Minimum funding standards or excess contributions for self-employed individuals and section 403(b)(7)(A) custodial accounts.*—Any employer or individual liable for tax under section 4971, 4972 or 4973(a)(2) (for a custodial account under section 403(b)(7)(A)) shall file an annual return on Form 5330 and shall include therein the information required by such form and the instructions issued with respect thereto.

(b) *Tax on prohibited transactions.*—Every disqualified person (as defined in section 4975(e)(2)) liable for the tax imposed under section 4975(a) with respect to a prohibited transaction shall file an annual return on Form 5330 and shall include therein the information required by such form and the instructions issued with respect thereto. The annual return on Form 5330 shall be filed with respect to each prohibited transaction and for each taxable year (or part thereof) of the disqualified person in the taxable period (as defined in section

4975(f)(2)) beginning on the date on which such prohibited transaction occurs.

(c) *Entity manager tax on prohibited tax shelter transactions.*—(1) *In general.*—Any entity manager of a tax-exempt entity described in section 4965(c)(4), (c)(5), (c)(6), or (c)(7) who is liable for tax under section 4965(a)(2) shall file a return on Form 5330, "Return of Excise Taxes Related to Employee Benefit Plans," on or before the 15th day of the fifth month following the close of such entity manager's taxable year during which the entity entered into the prohibited tax shelter transaction, and shall include therein the information required by such form and the instructions issued with respect thereto.

(2) *Transition rule.*—A Form 5330, "Return of Excise Taxes Related to Employee Benefit Plans," for an excise tax under section 4965 that was due on or before October 4, 2007, will be deemed to have been filed on the due date if it was filed by October 4, 2007, and if the section 4965 tax that was required to be reported on that Form 5330 was paid by October 4, 2007.

(d) *Effective/applicability date.*—Paragraph (c) of this section is applicable on July 6, 2007. [Reg. § 54.6011-1.]

☐ *[T.D. 7838, 10-5-82. Amended by T.D. 9334, 7-5-2007 and T.D. 9492, 7-2-2010 (corrected 8-3-2010).]*

### [Reg. § 54.6011-1T]

**§ 54.6011-1T. General requirement of return, statement, or list (temporary).**—(a) *Tax on reversions of qualified plan assets to employer.*—Every employer liable for the tax imposed under section 4980(a) with respect to an employer reversion (as defined in section 4980(c)(2)) shall file a quarterly return on Form 5330 and shall include therein the information required by such form and the instructions issued with respect thereto. The quarterly return on Form 5330 shall be filed with respect to employer reversions from each qualified plan (as defined in section 4980(c)(1)).

(b) *[Reserved].*
[Temporary Reg. § 54.6011-1T.]

☐ *[T.D. 8133, 4-1-87. Amended by T.D. 9334, 7-5-2007 (corrected 8-15-2007) and T.D. 9492, 7-2-2010.]*

### [Reg. § 54.6011-2]

**§ 54.6011-2. General requirement of return, statement, or list.**—Effective for any Form 8928 that is due on or after January 1, 2010, any person liable for tax under section 4980B, 4980D, 4980E, or 4980G of the Code shall file a return with respect to the tax on Form 8928. The return must include the information required by Form 8928 and the instructions issued with respect to it. [Reg. § 54.6011-2.]

☐ *[T.D. 9457, 9-4-2009.]*

### [Reg. § 55.6011-1]

**§ 55.6011-1. General requirement of return, statement, or list.**—Every person liable for tax under Chapter 44 shall file an annual return with respect to the tax on the form prescribed by the Internal Revenue Service for such purpose and shall include therein the information required by the form and the instructions issued with respect thereto. For calendar years beginning after December 31, 1986, the return, which must be made on a calendar year basis, shall be filed by a real estate investment trust on Form 8612 and by a regulated investment company on Form 8613. [Reg. § 55.6011-1.]

☐ *[T.D. 7767, 2-3-81. Amended by T.D. 8180, 2-29-88.]*

### [Reg. § 56.6011-1]

**§ 56.6011-1. General requirement of return, statement, or list.**—Every organization liable for the tax imposed by section 4911(a) shall file an annual return with respect to the tax on the form prescribed by the Internal Revenue Service for that purpose and shall include therein the information required by the form and its instructions. [Reg. § 56.6011-1.]

☐ *[T.D. 8308, 8-30-90.]*

### [Reg. § 156.6011-1]

**§ 156.6011-1. General requirement of return, statement or list.**—Every person liable for tax under section 5881 of the Code shall file a return with respect to the tax on the form prescribed by the Internal Revenue Service (Form 8725). Each such person shall include therein the information required by the form and the instructions issued with respect thereto. [Reg. § 156.6011-1.]

☐ *[T.D. 8379, 12-17-91.]*

### [Reg. § 157.6011-1]

**§ 157.6011-1. General requirement of return, statement, or list.**—Every person liable for tax under section 5891 must file a return with respect to the tax in accordance with the forms and instructions provided by the Internal Revenue Service. [Reg. § 157.6011-1.]

☐ [*T.D. 9134, 7-7-2004.*]

### [Reg. § 301.6011-1]

**§ 301.6011-1. General requirement of return, statement or list.—** (a) For provisions requiring returns, statements, or lists, see the regulations relating to the particular tax.

(b) The Internal Revenue Service may prescribe in forms, instructions, or other appropriate guidance the information or documentation required to be included with any return or any statement required to be made or other document required to be furnished under any provision of the internal revenue laws or regulations. [Reg. § 301.6011-1.]

☐ [*T.D. 9040, 1-30-2003.*]

### [Reg. § 1.6011-2]

**§ 1.6011-2. Returns, etc., of DISC's and former DISC's.—** (a) *Records and information.*—Every DISC and former DISC (as defined in section 992(a)) must comply with section 6001 and the regulations thereunder, relating to required records, statements, and special returns. Thus, for example, a DISC is required to maintain the books of account or records described in § 1.6001-1(a). In addition, every DISC must furnish to each of its shareholders on or before the last day of the second month following the close of the taxable year of the DISC a copy of Schedule K (Form 1120-DISC) disclosing the amounts of actual distributions and deemed distributions from the DISC to such shareholder for the taxable year of the DISC. In the case of a deficiency distribution to meet qualification requirements, see § 1.992-3(a)(4) for requirements that distribution be designated in the form of a communication sent to a shareholder and service center at the time of distribution.

(b) *Returns.*—(1) *Requirement of return.*—Every DISC (as defined in section 992(a)(1)) shall make a return of income. A former DISC (as defined in section 992(a)(3)) shall also make a return of income in addition to any other return required. The return required of a DISC or former DISC under this section shall be made on Form 1120-DISC. The provisions of § 1.6011-1 shall apply with respect to a DISC and former DISC. A former DISC should indicate clearly on Form 1120-DISC that it is making a return of income as a former DISC (for example, by labeling at the top of the Form 1120-DISC "Former DISC"). In the case of a former DISC, those items on the form which pertain to the computation of taxable income shall not be completed, but Schedules J, K, L, and M must be completed. Except as otherwise specifically provided in the Code or regulations, the return of a DISC or former DISC is considered to be an income tax return.

(2) *Existence of DISC.*—A corporation which is a DISC and which is in existence during any portion of a taxable year is required to make a return for that fractional part of its taxable year during which it was in existence. [Reg. § 1.6011-2.]

☐ [*T.D. 7533, 2-14-78.*]

### [Reg. § 301.6011-2]

**§ 301.6011-2. Required use of magnetic media.—** (a) *Meaning of terms.*—The following definitions apply for purposes of this section:

(1) *Magnetic media.*—The term *magnetic media* means any media permitted under applicable regulations, revenue procedures or publications, or, in the case of returns filed with the Social Security Administration, Social Security Administration publications. These generally include magnetic tape, tape cartridge, and diskette, as well as other media (such as electronic filing) specifically permitted under the applicable regulations, procedures, or publications.

(2) *Machine-readable paper form.*—The term "machine-readable paper form" means—

(i) Optical-scan paper form; or

(ii) Any other machine-readable paper form permitted under applicable regulations, revenue procedures, or Social Security Administration publications.

(3) *Person.*—The term "person" includes any person that is required to file a return that is described in paragraph (b) of this section. Thus, the term "person" includes the United States, a State, the District of Columbia, a foreign government, a political subdivision of a State or of a foreign government, or an international organization. In addition, in the case of an affiliated group of corporations filing a consolidated return, each member of the affiliated group is a separate person.

(b) *Returns required on magnetic media.*—(1) If the use of Form 1042-S, 1094 series, 1095-B, 1095-C, 1098, 1098-E, 1098-T, 1099 series, 5498 series, 8027, W-2G, or other form treated as a form specified in

this paragraph (b)(1) is required by the applicable regulations or revenue procedures for the purpose of making an information return, the information required by the form must be submitted on magnetic media, except as otherwise provided in paragraph (c) of this section. Returns on magnetic media must be made in accordance with applicable revenue procedures or publications (see § 601.601(d)(2)(ii)(*b*) of this chapter). Pursuant to these procedures, the consent of the Commissioner of Internal Revenue (or other authorized officer or employee of the Internal Revenue Service) to a magnetic medium must be obtained by submitting Form 4419 (Application for Filing Information Returns Magnetically/Electronically) prior to submitting a return described in this paragraph (b)(1) on the magnetic medium.

(2) If the use of Form W-2 (Wage and Tax Statement), Form 499R-2/W-2PR (Withholding Statement (Puerto Rico)), Form W-2VI (U.S. Virgin Islands Wage and Tax Statement), Form W-2GU (Guam Wage and Tax Statement), Form W-2AS (American Samoa Wage and Tax Statement), or other form treated as a form specified in this paragraph (b)(2) is required for the purpose of making an information return, the information required by the form must be submitted on magnetic media, except as otherwise provided in paragraph (c) of this section. Returns described in this paragraph (b)(2) must be made in accordance with applicable Social Security Administration procedures or publications (which may be obtained from the local office of the Social Security Administration).

(3) The Commissioner may prescribe by revenue procedure that additional forms are treated, for purposes of this section, as forms specified in paragraph (b)(1) or (b)(2) of this section.

(c) *Exceptions.*—(1) *Low-volume filers/250-threshold.*—(i) *In general.*—No person is required to file information returns on magnetic media unless the person is required to file 250 or more returns during the calendar year. Persons filing fewer than 250 returns during the calendar year may make the returns on the prescribed paper form, or, alternatively, such persons may make returns on magnetic media in accordance with paragraph (b) of this section.

(ii) *Machine-readable forms.*—Returns made on a paper form under this paragraph (c)(1) shall be machine-readable if applicable revenue procedures provide for a machine-readable paper form.

(iii) *No aggregation.*—Each type of information return described in paragraphs (b)(1) and (2) of this section is considered a separate return for purposes of this paragraph (c)(1). Therefore, the 250-threshold applies separately to each type of form required to be filed.

(iv) *Examples.*—The provisions of paragraph (c)(1)(iii) of this section are illustrated by the following examples:

*Example 1.* For the calendar year ending December 31, 1998, Company X is required to file 200 returns on Form 1099-INT and 350 returns on Form 1099-MISC. Company X is not required to file Forms 1099-INT on magnetic media but is required to file Forms 1099-MISC on magnetic media.

*Example 2.* During the calendar year ending December 31, 1998, Company Y has 275 employees in Puerto Rico and 50 employees in American Samoa. Company Y is required to file Forms 499R-2/W-2PR on magnetic media but is not required to file Forms W-2AS on magnetic media.

*Example 3.* For the calendar year ending December 31, 1998, Company Z files 300 original returns on Form 1099-DIV and later files 70 corrected returns on Form 1099-DIV. Company Z is required to file the original returns on magnetic media. However, Company Z is not required to file the corrected returns on magnetic media because the corrected returns fall under the 250-threshold. See § 301.6721-1(a)(2)(ii).

(2) *Waiver.*—(i) The Commissioner may waive the requirements of this section if hardship is shown in a request for waiver filed in accordance with this paragraph (c)(2)(i). The principal factor in determining hardship will be the amount, if any, by which the cost of filing the information returns in accordance with this section exceeds the cost of filing the returns on other media. Notwithstanding the foregoing, if an employer is required to make a final return on Form 941, or a variation thereof, and expedited filing of Forms W-2, Forms 499R-2/W-2PR, Forms W-2VI, Forms W-2GU, or Form W-2AS is required, the unavailability of the specifications for magnetic media filing will be treated as creating a hardship (see § 31.6071(a)-1(a)(3)(ii) of this chapter). A request for waiver must be made in accordance with applicable revenue procedures or publications (see § 601.601(d)(2)(ii)(*b*) of this chapter). Pursuant to these procedures, a request for waiver should be filed at least 45 days before the due date of the information return in order for the Service to have adequate time to respond to the request for waiver. The waiver will specify the type of information return and the period to which it applies and will be subject to such terms and conditions regarding the method of reporting as may be prescribed by the Commissioner.

(ii) The Commissioner may prescribe rules that supplement the provisions of paragraph (c)(2)(i) of this section.

(d) *Paper form returns.*—Returns submitted on paper forms (whether or not machine-readable) permitted under paragraph (c) of this section shall be in accordance with applicable Internal Revenue Service or Social Security Administration procedures.

(e) *Applicability of current procedures.*—Until procedures are prescribed which further implement the mandatory filing on magnetic media provided by this section, a return to which this section applies shall be made in the manner and shall be subject to the requirements and conditions (including the requirement of applying for consent to the magnetic medium) prescribed in the regulations, revenue procedures and Social Security Administration publications relating to the filing of such return on magnetic media.

(f) *Failure to file.*—If a person fails to file an information return on magnetic media when required to do so by this section, the person is deemed to have failed to file the return. In addition, if a person making returns on a paper form under paragraph (c) of this section fails to file a return on machine-readable paper form when required to do so by this section, the person is deemed to have failed to file the return. See sections 6652, 6693, and 6721 for penalties for failure to file certain returns. See also section 6724 and the regulations under section 6721 for the specific rules and limitations regarding the penalty imposed under section 6721 for failure to file on magnetic media.

(g) *Effective dates.*—(1) Except as otherwise provided in paragraph (g)(2) or (3) of this section, this section applies to returns required to be filed after December 31, 1986.

(2) Paragraphs (a)(1), (b)(1), (b)(2), (c)(1)(i), (c)(1)(iii), (c)(1)(iv), (c)(2), (d), (e), and (f) of this section are effective for information returns required to be filed after December 31, 1996. For information returns required to be filed after December 31, 1989, and before January 1, 1997, see section 6011(e).

(3) This section applies to returns on Forms 1098-E, "Student Loan Interest Statement," and 1098-T, "Tuition Statement," filed after December 31, 2003. [Reg. § 301.6011-2.]

☐ [*T.D.* 8081, 3-20-86. *Amended by T.D.* 8097, 8-25-86; *T.D.* 8140, 5-15-87; *T.D.* 8636, 12-20-95; *T.D.* 8772, 6-29-98; *T.D.* 8992, 4-26-2002; *T.D.* 9029, 12-18-2002, *T.D.* 9660, 3-5-2014, *T.D.* 9804, 12-14-2016 *and T.D.* 9923, 11-18-2020.]

### [Reg. § 1.6011-3]

**§1.6011-3. Requirement of statement from payees of certain gambling winnings.**—(a) *General rule.*—Except as provided in paragraph (c) of this section, any person receiving a payment with respect to a wager in a sweepstakes, wagering pool, lottery, or other wagering transaction (including a parimutuel pool with respect to horse races, dog races, or jai alai) shall make a statement to the payer of such winnings upon the payer's demand. Such statements shall accompany the payer's return made with respect to the payment as required pursuant to section 3402(q) or 6041, as the case may be.

(b) *Contents of statement.*—The statement referred to in paragraph (a) shall contain information (in addition to that required under section 6041 (c)) as to the amount, if any, of winnings from identical wagers to which the recipient is entitled. If any person other than the recipient is entitled to all or a portion of the payment, the statement shall also include information as to the amount, if any, of winnings from identical wagers to which each such person is entitled. The statement shall be provided on Form W-2G or, if persons other than the recipient are entitled to all or a portion of such payment, on Form 5754.

(c) *Exception.*—The requirement of paragraph (a) of this section does not apply with respect to any payment of winnings—

(i) From a slot machine play, or a bingo or keno game,

(ii) Which is subject to withholding under section 3402(q) without regard to the existence of winnings from identical wagers, or

(iii) For which no return of information under section 6041 is required of the payer.

(d) *Meaning of terms.*—For purposes of this section, the terms "sweepstakes", "wagering pool", "lottery," "other wagering transaction" and "identical wagers" shall have the same meaning as ascribed to them under § 31.3402(q)-1. [Reg. § 1.6011-3.]

☐ [*T.D.* 7919, 10-11-83.]

### [Reg. § 301.6011-3]

**§ 301.6011-3. Required use of magnetic media for partnership returns.**—(a) *Partnership returns required on magnetic media.*—If a partnership with more than 100 partners is required to file a partnership return pursuant to § 1.6031(a)-1 of this chapter, the information re-

quired by the applicable forms and schedules must be filed on magnetic media, except as otherwise provided in paragraph (b) of this section. Returns filed on magnetic media must be made in accordance with applicable revenue procedures or publications. In prescribing revenue procedures or publications, the Commissioner may determine that partnerships will be required to use any one form of magnetic media filing. For example, the Commissioner may determine that partnerships with more than 100 partners must file their partnership returns electronically. In filing its return, a partnership must register to participate in the magnetic media filing program in the manner prescribed by the Internal Revenue Service in applicable revenue procedures or publications.

(b) *Waiver.*—The Commissioner may waive the requirements of this section if hardship is shown in a request for waiver filed in accordance with this paragraph (b). A determination of hardship will be based upon all of the facts and circumstances. One factor in determining hardship will be the reasonableness of the incremental cost to the partnership of complying with the magnetic media filing requirements. Other factors, such as equipment breakdowns or destruction of magnetic media filing equipment, also may be considered. A request for waiver must be made in accordance with applicable revenue procedures or publications. The waiver will specify the type of partnership return and the period to which it applies. The waiver will also be subject to such terms and conditions regarding the method of filing as may be prescribed by the Commissioner.

(c) *Failure to file.*—If a partnership fails to file a partnership return on magnetic media in the manner required and when required to do so by this section, the partnership will be deemed to have failed to file the return in the manner prescribed for purposes of the information return penalty under section 6721. See § 301.6724-1(c)(3) for rules regarding the waiver of penalties for undue economic hardship relating to filing returns on magnetic media.

(d) *Meaning of terms.*—The following definitions apply for purposes of this section:

(1) *Magnetic media.*—The term *magnetic media* means any magnetic media permitted under applicable regulations, revenue procedures, or publications. These generally include magnetic tape, tape cartridge, and diskette, as well as other media (such as electronic filing) specifically permitted under the applicable regulations, procedures, or publications.

(2) *Partnership.*—The term *partnership* means a partnership as defined in § 1.761-1(a) of this chapter.

(3) *Partner.*—The term *partner* means a member of a partnership as defined in section 7701(a)(2).

(4) *Partnership return.*—The term *partnership return* means a form in Series 1065 (including Form 1065, U.S. Partnership Return of Income, and Form 1065-B, U.S. Return of Income for Electing Large Partnerships), along with the corresponding Schedules K-1 and all other related forms and schedules that are required to be attached to the Series 1065 form.

(5) *Partnerships with more than 100 partners.*—A partnership has more than 100 partners if, over the course of the partnership's taxable year, the partnership had more than 100 partners, regardless of whether a partner was a partner for the entire year or whether the partnership had over 100 partners on any particular day in the year. For purposes of this paragraph (d)(5), however, only those persons having a direct interest in the partnership must be considered partners for purposes of determining the number of partners during the partnership's taxable year.

(e) *Examples.*—The following examples illustrate the provisions of paragraph (d)(5) of this section. In the examples, the partnerships utilize the calendar year, and the taxable year in question is 2000:

*Example 1.* Partnership P had five general partners and 90 limited partners on January 1, 2000. On March 15, 2000, 10 more limited partners acquired an interest in P. On September 29, 2000, the 10 newest partners sold their individual partnership interests to C, a corporation which was one of the original 90 limited partners. On December 31, 2000, P had the same five general partners and 90 limited partners it had on January 1, 2000. P had a total of 105 partners over the course of partnership taxable year 2000. Therefore, P must file its 2000 partnership return on magnetic media.

*Example 2.* Partnership Q is a general partnership that had 95 partners on January 1, 2000. On March 15, 2000, 10 partners sold their individual partnership interests to corporation D, which was not previously a partner in Q. On September 29, 2000, corporation D sold one-half of its partnership interest in equal shares to five individuals, who were not previously partners in Q. On December 31, 2000, Q had a total of 91 partners, and on no date in the year did Q have more than 100 partners. Over the course of the year, however, Q had

101 partners. Therefore, Q must file its 2000 partnership return on magnetic media.

*Example 3.* Partnership G is a general partnership with 100 partners on January 1, 2000. There are no new partners added to G in 2000. One of G's partners, A, is a partnership with 53 partners. A is one partner, regardless of the number of partners A has. Therefore, G has 100 partners and is not required to file its 2000 partnership return on magnetic media.

(f) *Effective date.*—In general, this section applies to partnership returns for taxable years ending on or after December 31, 2000. However, electing large partnerships under section 775 and partnerships using foreign addresses on their Series 1065 forms are not required to file using magnetic media for taxable years ending before January 1, 2001. [Reg. § 301.6011-3.]

☐ [*T.D. 8843, 11-10-99.*]

### [Reg. § 1.6011-4]

**§ 1.6011-4. Requirement of statement disclosing participation in certain transactions by taxpayers.**—(a) *In general.*—Every taxpayer that has participated, as described in paragraph (c)(3) of this section, in a reportable transaction within the meaning of paragraph (b) of this section and who is required to file a tax return must file within the time prescribed in paragraph (e) of this section a disclosure statement in the form prescribed by paragraph (d) of this section. The fact that a transaction is a reportable transaction shall not affect the legal determination of whether the taxpayer's treatment of the transaction is proper.

(b) *Reportable transactions.*—(1) *In general.*—A reportable transaction is a transaction described in any of the paragraphs (b)(2) through (7) of this section. The term transaction includes all of the factual elements relevant to the expected tax treatment of any investment, entity, plan, or arrangement, and includes any series of steps carried out as part of a plan.

(2) *Listed transactions.*—A listed transaction is a transaction that is the same as or substantially similar to one of the types of transactions that the Internal Revenue Service (IRS) has determined to be a tax avoidance transaction and identified by notice, regulation, or other form of published guidance as a listed transaction.

(3) *Confidential transactions.*—(i) *In general.*—A confidential transaction is a transaction that is offered to a taxpayer under conditions of confidentiality and for which the taxpayer has paid an advisor a minimum fee.

(ii) *Conditions of confidentiality.*—A transaction is considered to be offered to a taxpayer under conditions of confidentiality if the advisor who is paid the minimum fee places a limitation on disclosure by the taxpayer of the tax treatment or tax structure of the transaction and the limitation on disclosure protects the confidentiality of that advisor's tax strategies. A transaction is treated as confidential even if the conditions of confidentiality are not legally binding on the taxpayer. A claim that a transaction is proprietary or exclusive is not treated as a limitation on disclosure if the advisor confirms to the taxpayer that there is no limitation on disclosure of the tax treatment or tax structure of the transaction.

(iii) *Minimum fee.*—For purposes of this paragraph (b)(3), the minimum fee is—

(A) $250,000 for a transaction if the taxpayer is a corporation;

(B) $50,000 for all other transactions unless the taxpayer is a partnership or trust, all of the owners or beneficiaries of which are corporations (looking through any partners or beneficiaries that are themselves partnerships or trusts), in which case the minimum fee is $250,000.

(iv) *Determination of minimum fee.*—For purposes of this paragraph (b)(3), in determining the minimum fee, all fees for a tax strategy or for services for advice (whether or not tax advice) or for the implementation of a transaction are taken into account. Fees include consideration in whatever form paid, whether in cash or in kind, for services to analyze the transaction (whether or not related to the tax consequences of the transaction), for services to implement the transaction, for services to document the transaction, and for services to prepare tax returns to the extent return preparation fees are unreasonable in light of the facts and circumstances. For purposes of this paragraph (b)(3), a taxpayer also is treated as paying fees to an advisor if the taxpayer knows or should know that the amount it pays will be paid indirectly to the advisor, such as through a referral fee or fee-sharing arrangement. A fee does not include amounts paid to a person, including an advisor, in that person's capacity as a party to the transaction. For example, a fee does not include reasonable charges for the use of capital or the sale or use of property. The IRS will scrutinize carefully all of the facts and circumstances in deter-mining whether consideration received in connection with a confidential transaction constitutes fees.

(v) *Related parties.*—For purposes of this paragraph (b)(3), persons who bear a relationship to each other as described in section 267(b) or 707(b) will be treated as the same person.

(4) *Transactions with contractual protection.*—(i) *In general.*—A transaction with contractual protection is a transaction for which the taxpayer or a related party (as described in section 267(b) or 707(b)) has the right to a full or partial refund of fees (as described in paragraph (b)(4)(ii) of this section) if all or part of the intended tax consequences from the transaction are not sustained. A transaction with contractual protection also is a transaction for which fees (as described in paragraph (b)(4)(ii) of this section) are contingent on the taxpayer's realization of tax benefits from the transaction. All the facts and circumstances relating to the transaction will be considered when determining whether a fee is refundable or contingent, including the right to reimbursements of amounts that the parties to the transaction have not designated as fees or any agreement to provide services without reasonable compensation.

(ii) *Fees.*—Paragraph (b)(4)(i) of this section only applies with respect to fees paid by or on behalf of the taxpayer or a related party to any person who makes or provides a statement, oral or written, to the taxpayer or related party (or for whose benefit a statement is made or provided to the taxpayer or related party) as to the potential tax consequences that may result from the transaction.

(iii) *Exceptions.*—(A) *Termination of transaction.*—A transaction is not considered to have contractual protection solely because a party to the transaction has the right to terminate the transaction upon the happening of an event affecting the taxation of one or more parties to the transaction.

(B) *Previously reported transaction.*—If a person makes or provides a statement to a taxpayer as to the potential tax consequences that may result from a transaction only after the taxpayer has entered into the transaction and reported the consequences of the transaction on a filed tax return, and the person has not previously received fees from the taxpayer relating to the transaction, then any refundable or contingent fees are not taken into account in determining whether the transaction has contractual protection. This paragraph (b)(4) does not provide any substantive rules regarding when a person may charge refundable or contingent fees with respect to a transaction. See Circular 230, 31 CFR Part 10, for the regulations governing practice before the IRS.

(5) *Loss transactions.*—(i) *In general.*—A loss transaction is any transaction resulting in the taxpayer claiming a loss under section 165 of at least—

(A) $10 million in any single taxable year or $20 million in any combination of taxable years for corporations;

(B) $10 million in any single taxable year or $20 million in any combination of taxable years for partnerships that have only corporations as partners (looking through any partners that are themselves partnerships), whether or not any losses flow through to one or more partners; or

(C) $2 million in any single taxable year or $4 million in any combination of taxable years for all other partnerships, whether or not any losses flow through to one or more partners;

(D) $2 million in any single taxable year or $4 million in any combination of taxable years for individuals, S corporations, or trusts, whether or not any losses flow through to one or more shareholders or beneficiaries; or

(E) $50,000 in any single taxable year for individuals or trusts, whether or not the loss flows through from an S corporation or partnership, if the loss arises with respect to a section 988 transaction (as defined in section 988(c)(1) relating to foreign currency transactions).

(ii) *Cumulative losses.*—In determining whether a transaction results in a taxpayer claiming a loss that meets the threshold amounts over a combination of taxable years as described in paragraph (b)(5)(i) of this section, only losses claimed in the taxable year that the transaction is entered into and the five succeeding taxable years are combined.

(iii) *Section 165 loss.*—(A) For purposes of this paragraph (b)(5)(i) of this section, in determining the thresholds in paragraph (b)(5)(i) of this section, the amount of a section 165 loss is adjusted for any salvage value and for any insurance or other compensation received. See § 1.165-1(c)(4). However, a section 165 loss does not take into account offsetting gains, or other income or limitations. For example, a section 165 loss does not take into account the limitation in section 165(d) (relating to wagering losses) or the limitations in sections 165(f), 1211, and 1212 (relating to capital losses). The full amount of a section 165 loss is taken into account for the year in which the loss is sustained, regardless of whether all or part of the loss enters into the computation of a net operating loss under section 172 or a net capital loss under section 1212 that is a carryback or carryover to another year. A section 165 loss does not include any portion of a loss, attributable to a capital loss carryback or carryover from another year, that is treated as a deemed capital loss under section 1212.

(B) For purposes of this section, a section 165 loss includes an amount deductible pursuant to a provision that treats a transaction as a sale or other disposition, or otherwise results in a deduction under section 165. A section 165 loss includes, for example, a loss resulting from a sale or exchange of a partnership interest under section 741 and a loss resulting from a section 988 transaction.

(6) *Transactions of interest.*—A transaction of interest is a transaction that is the same as or substantially similar to one of the types of transactions that the IRS has identified by notice, regulation, or other form of published guidance as a transaction of interest.

(7) *[Reserved].*

(8) *Exceptions.*—(i) *In general.*—A transaction will not be considered a reportable transaction, or will be excluded from any individual category of reportable transaction under paragraphs (b)(3) through (7) of this section, if the Commissioner makes a determination by published guidance that the transaction is not subject to the reporting requirements of this section. The Commissioner may make a determination by individual letter ruling under paragraph (f) of this section that an individual letter ruling request on a specific transaction satisfies the reporting requirements of this section with regard to that transaction for the taxpayer who requests the individual letter ruling.

(ii) *Special rule for RICs.*—For purposes of this section, a regulated investment company (RIC) as defined in section 851 or an investment vehicle that is owned 95 percent or more by one or more RICs at all times during the course of the transaction is not required to disclose a transaction that is described in any of paragraphs (b)(3) through (5) and (b)(7) of this section unless the transaction is also a listed transaction or a transaction of interest.

(c) *Definitions.*—For purposes of this section, the following definitions apply:

(1) *Taxpayer.*—The term *taxpayer* means any person described in section 7701(a)(1), including S corporations. Except as otherwise specifically provided in this section, the term *taxpayer* also includes an affiliated group of corporations that joins in the filing of a consolidated return under section 1501.

(2) *Corporation.*—When used specifically in this section, the term *corporation* means an entity that is required to file a return for a taxable year on any 1120 series form, or successor form, excluding S corporations.

(3) *Participation.*—(i) *In general.*—(A) *Listed transactions.*—A taxpayer has participated in a listed transaction if the taxpayer's tax return reflects tax consequences or a tax strategy described in the published guidance that lists the transaction under paragraph (b)(2) of this section. A taxpayer also has participated in a listed transaction if the taxpayer knows or has reason to know that the taxpayer's tax benefits are derived directly or indirectly from tax consequences or a tax strategy described in published guidance that lists a transaction under paragraph (b)(2) of this section. Published guidance may identify other types or classes of persons that will be treated as participants in a listed transaction. Published guidance also may identify types or classes of persons that will not be treated as participants in a listed transaction.

(B) *Confidential transactions.*—A taxpayer has participated in a confidential transaction if the taxpayer's tax return reflects a tax benefit from the transaction and the taxpayer's disclosure of the tax treatment or tax structure of the transaction is limited in the manner described in paragraph (b)(3) of this section. If a partnership's, S corporation's or trust's disclosure is limited, and the partner's, shareholder's, or beneficiary's disclosure is not limited, then the partnership, S corporation, or trust, and not the partner, shareholder, or beneficiary, has participated in the confidential transaction.

(C) *Transactions with contractual protection.*—A taxpayer has participated in a transaction with contractual protection if the taxpayer's tax return reflects a tax benefit from the transaction and, as described in paragraph (b)(4) of this section, the taxpayer has the right to the full or partial refund of fees or the fees are contingent. If a partnership, S corporation, or trust has the right to a full or partial refund of fees or has a contingent fee arrangement, and the partner, shareholder, or beneficiary does not individually have the right to the refund of fees or a contingent fee arrangement, then the partner-

ship, S corporation, or trust, and not the partner, shareholder, or beneficiary, has participated in the transaction with contractual protection.

(D) *Loss transactions.*—A taxpayer has participated in a loss transaction if the taxpayer's tax return reflects a section 165 loss and the amount of the section 165 loss equals or exceeds the threshold amount applicable to the taxpayer as described in paragraph (b)(5)(i) of this section. If a taxpayer is a partner in a partnership, shareholder in an S corporation, or beneficiary of a trust and a section 165 loss as described in paragraph (b)(5) of this section flows through the entity to the taxpayer (disregarding netting at the entity level), the taxpayer has participated in a loss transaction if the taxpayer's tax return reflects a section 165 loss and the amount of the section 165 loss that flows through to the taxpayer equals or exceeds the threshold amounts applicable to the taxpayer as described in paragraph (b)(5)(i) of this section. For this purpose, a tax return is deemed to reflect the full amount of a section 165 loss described in paragraph (b)(5) of this section allocable to the taxpayer under this paragraph (c)(3)(i)(D), regardless of whether all or part of the loss enters into the computation of a net operating loss under section 172 or net capital loss under section 1212 that the taxpayer may carry back or carry over to another year.

(E) *Transactions of interest.*—A taxpayer has participated in a transaction of interest if the taxpayer is one of the types or classes of persons identified as participants in the transaction in the published guidance describing the transaction of interest.

(F) *[Reserved].*

(G) *Shareholders of foreign corporations.*—(1) *In general.*—A reporting shareholder of a foreign corporation participates in a transaction described in paragraphs (b)(2) through (5) and (b)(7) of this section if the foreign corporation would be considered to participate in the transaction under the rules of this paragraph (c)(3) if it were a domestic corporation filing a tax return that reflects the items from the transaction. A reporting shareholder of a foreign corporation participates in a transaction described in paragraph (b)(6) of this section only if the published guidance identifying the transaction includes the reporting shareholder among the types or classes of persons identified as participants. A reporting shareholder (and any successor in interest) is considered to participate in a transaction under this paragraph (c)(3)(i)(G) only for its first taxable year with or within which ends the first taxable year of the foreign corporation in which the foreign corporation participates in the transaction, and for the reporting shareholder's five succeeding taxable years.

(2) *Reporting shareholder.*—The term *reporting shareholder* means a United States shareholder (as defined in section 951(b)) in a controlled foreign corporation (as defined in section 957) or a 10 percent shareholder (by vote or value) of a qualified electing fund (as defined in section 1295).

(ii) *Examples.*—The following examples illustrate the provisions of paragraph (c)(3)(i) of this section:

*Example 1.* Notice 2003-55 (2003-2 CB 395), which modified and superseded Notice 95-53 (1995-2 CB 334) (see § 601.601(d)(2) of this chapter), describes a lease stripping transaction in which one party (the transferor) assigns the right to receive future payments under a lease of tangible property and treats the amount realized from the assignment as its current income. The transferor later transfers the property subject to the lease in a transaction intended to qualify as a transferred basis transaction, for example, a transaction described in section 351. The transferee corporation claims the deductions associated with the high basis property subject to the lease. The transferor's and transferee corporation's tax returns reflect tax positions described in Notice 2003-55. Therefore, the transferor and transferee corporation have participated in the listed transaction. In the section 351 transaction, the transferor will have received stock with low value and high basis from the transferee corporation. If the transferor subsequently transfers the high basis/low value stock to a taxpayer in another transaction intended to qualify as a transferred basis transaction and the taxpayer uses the stock to generate a loss, and if the taxpayer knows or has reason to know that the tax loss claimed was derived indirectly from the lease stripping transaction, then the taxpayer has participated in the listed transaction. Accordingly, the taxpayer must disclose the transaction and the manner of the taxpayer's participation in the transaction under the rules of this section. For purposes of this example, if a bank lends money to the transferor, transferee corporation, or taxpayer for use in their transactions, the bank has not participated in the listed transaction because the bank's tax return does not reflect tax consequences or a tax strategy described in the listing notice (nor does the bank's tax return reflect a tax benefit derived from tax consequences or a tax strategy described in the listing notice) nor is the bank described as a participant in the listing notice.

*Example 2.* XYZ is a limited liability company treated as a partnership for tax purposes. X, Y, and Z are members of XYZ. X is an individual, Y is an S corporation, and Z is a partnership. XYZ enters into a confidential transaction under paragraph (b)(3) of this section. XYZ and X are bound by the confidentiality agreement, but Y and Z are not bound by the agreement. As a result of the transaction, XYZ, X, Y, and Z all reflect a tax benefit on their tax returns. Because XYZ's and X's disclosure of the tax treatment and tax structure are limited in the manner described in paragraph (b)(3) of this section and their tax returns reflect a tax benefit from the transaction, both XYZ and X have participated in the confidential transaction. Neither Y nor Z has participated in the confidential transaction because they are not subject to the confidentiality agreement.

*Example 3.* P, a corporation, has an 80% partnership interest in PS, and S, an individual, has a 20% partnership interest in PS. P, S, and PS are calendar year taxpayers. In 2006, PS enters into a transaction and incurs a section 165 loss (that does not meet any of the exceptions to a section 165 loss identified in published guidance) of $12 million and offsetting gain of $3 million. On PS' 2006 tax return, PS includes the section 165 loss and the corresponding gain. PS must disclose the transaction under this section because PS' section 165 loss of $12 million is equal to or greater than $2 million. P is allocated $9.6 million of the section 165 loss and $2.4 million of the offsetting gain. P does not have to disclose the transaction under this section because P's section 165 loss of $9.6 million is not equal to or greater than $10 million. S is allocated $2.4 million of the section 165 loss and $600,000 of the offsetting gain. S must disclose the transaction under this section because S's section 165 loss of $2.4 million is equal to or greater than $2 million.

(4) *Substantially similar.*—The term *substantially similar* includes any transaction that is expected to obtain the same or similar types of tax consequences and that is either factually similar or based on the same or similar tax strategy. Receipt of an opinion regarding the tax consequences of the transaction is not relevant to the determination of whether the transaction is the same as or substantially similar to another transaction. Further, the term *substantially similar* must be broadly construed in favor of disclosure. For example, a transaction may be substantially similar to a listed transaction even though it involves different entities or uses different Internal Revenue Code provisions. (See for example, Notice 2003-54 (2003-2 CB 363), describing a transaction substantially similar to the transactions in Notice 2002-50 (2002-2 CB 98), and Notice 2002-65 (2002-2 CB 690).) The following examples illustrate situations where a transaction is the same as or substantially similar to a listed transaction under paragraph (b)(2) of this section. (Such transactions may also be reportable transactions under paragraphs (b)(3) through (7) of this section.) See § 601.601(d)(2)(ii)(*b*) of this chapter. The following examples illustrate the provisions of this paragraph (c)(4):

*Example 1.* Notice 2000-44 (2000-2 CB 255) (see § 601.601(d)(2)(ii)(*b*) of this chapter), sets forth a listed transaction involving offsetting options transferred to a partnership where the taxpayer claims basis in the partnership for the cost of the purchased options but does not adjust basis under section 752 as a result of the partnership's assumption of the taxpayer's obligation with respect to the options. Transactions using short sales, futures, derivatives or any other type of offsetting obligations to inflate basis in a partnership interest would be the same as or substantially similar to the transaction described in Notice 2000-44. Moreover, use of the inflated basis in the partnership interest to diminish gain that would otherwise be recognized on the transfer of a partnership asset would also be the same as or substantially similar to the transaction described in Notice 2000-44. See § 601.601(d)(2)(ii)(b).

*Example 2.* Notice 2001-16 (2001-1 CB 730) (see § 601.601(d)(2)(ii)(*b*) of this chapter), sets forth a listed transaction involving a seller (X) who desires to sell stock of a corporation (T), an intermediary corporation (M), and a buyer (Y) who desires to purchase the assets (and not the stock) of T. M agrees to facilitate the sale to prevent the recognition of the gain that T would otherwise report. Notice 2001-16 describes M as a member of a consolidated group that has a loss within the group or as a party not subject to tax. Transactions utilizing different intermediaries to prevent the recognition of gain would be the same as or substantially similar to the transaction described in Notice 2001-16. An example is a transaction in which M is a corporation that does not file a consolidated return but which buys T stock, liquidates T, sells assets of T to Y, and offsets the gain on the sale of those assets with currently generated losses. See § 601.601(d)(2)(ii)(*b*).

(5) *Tax.*—The term *tax* means Federal income tax.

(6) *Tax benefit.*—A tax benefit includes deductions, exclusions from gross income, nonrecognition of gain, tax credits, adjustments (or the absence of adjustments) to the basis of property, status as an entity exempt from Federal income taxation, and any other tax

consequences that may reduce a taxpayer's Federal income tax liability by affecting the amount, timing, character, or source of any item of income, gain, expense, loss, or credit.

(7) *Tax return.*—The term *tax return* means a Federal income tax return and a Federal information return.

(8) *Tax treatment.*—The tax treatment of a transaction is the purported or claimed Federal income tax treatment of the transaction.

(9) *Tax structure.*—The tax structure of a transaction is any fact that may be relevant to understanding the purported or claimed Federal income tax treatment of the transaction.

(d) *Form and content of disclosure statement.*—A taxpayer required to file a disclosure statement under this section must file a completed Form 8886, "Reportable Transaction Disclosure Statement" (or a successor form), in accordance with this paragraph (d) and the instructions to the form. The Form 8886 (or a successor form) is the disclosure statement required under this section. The form must be attached to the appropriate tax return(s) as provided in paragraph (e) of this section. If a copy of a disclosure statement is required to be sent to the Office of Tax Shelter Analysis (OTSA) under paragraph (e) of this section, it must be sent in accordance with the instructions to the form. To be considered complete, the information provided on the form must describe the expected tax treatment and all potential tax benefits expected to result from the transaction, describe any tax result protection (as defined in § 301.6111-3(c)(12) of this chapter) with respect to the transaction, and identify and describe the transaction in sufficient detail for the IRS to be able to understand the tax structure of the reportable transaction and the identity of all parties involved in the transaction. An incomplete Form 8886 (or a successor form) containing a statement that information will be provided upon request is not considered a complete disclosure statement. If the form is not completed in accordance with the provisions in this paragraph (d) and the instructions to the form, the taxpayer will not be considered to have complied with the disclosure requirements of this section. If a taxpayer receives one or more reportable transaction numbers for a reportable transaction, the taxpayer must include the reportable transaction number(s) on the Form 8886 (or a successor form). See § 301.6111-3(d)(2) of this chapter.

(e) *Time of providing disclosure.*—(1) *In general.*—The disclosure statement for a reportable transaction must be attached to the taxpayer's tax return for each taxable year for which a taxpayer participates in a reportable transaction. In addition, a disclosure statement for a reportable transaction must be attached to each amended return that reflects a taxpayer's participation in a reportable transaction. A copy of the disclosure statement must be sent to OTSA at the same time that any disclosure statement is first filed by the taxpayer pertaining to a particular reportable transaction. If a reportable transaction results in a loss which is carried back to a prior year, the disclosure statement for the reportable transaction must be attached to the taxpayer's application for tentative refund or amended tax return for that prior year. In the case of a taxpayer that is a partnership, an S corporation, or a trust, the disclosure statement for a reportable transaction must be attached to the partnership, S corporation, or trust's tax return for each taxable year in which the partnership, S corporation, or trust participates in the transaction under the rules of paragraph (c)(3)(i) of this section. If a taxpayer who is a partner in a partnership, a shareholder in an S corporation, or a beneficiary of a trust receives a timely Schedule K-1 less than 10 calendar days before the due date of the taxpayer's return (including extensions) and, based on receipt of the timely Schedule K-1, the taxpayer determines that the taxpayer participated in a reportable transaction within the meaning of paragraph (c)(3) of this section, the disclosure statement will not be considered late if the taxpayer discloses the reportable transaction by filing a disclosure statement with OTSA within 60 calendar days after the due date of the taxpayer's return (including extensions). The Commissioner in his discretion may issue in published guidance other provisions for disclosure under § 1.6011-4.

(2) *Special rules.*—(i) *Listed transactions and transactions of interest.*—In general, if a transaction becomes a listed transaction or a transaction of interest after the filing of a taxpayer's tax return (including an amended return) reflecting the taxpayer's participation in the listed transaction or transaction of interest and before the end of the period of limitations for assessment of tax for any taxable year in which the taxpayer participated in the listed transaction or transaction of interest, then a disclosure statement must be filed, regardless of whether the taxpayer participated in the transaction in the year the transaction became a listed transaction or a transaction of interest, with OTSA within 90 calendar days after the date on which the transaction became a listed transaction or a transaction of interest. The Commissioner also may determine the time for disclosure of

listed transactions and transactions of interest in the published guidance identifying the transaction.

(ii) *Loss transactions.*—If a transaction becomes a loss transaction because the losses equal or exceed the threshold amounts as described in paragraph (b)(5)(i) of this section, a disclosure statement must be filed as an attachment to the taxpayer=s tax return for the first taxable year in which the threshold amount is reached and to any subsequent tax return that reflects any amount of section 165 loss from the transaction.

(3) *Multiple disclosures.*—The taxpayer must disclose the transaction in the time and manner provided for under the provisions of this section regardless of whether the taxpayer also plans to disclose the transaction under other published guidance, for example, § 1.6662-3(c)(2).

(4) *Example.*—The following example illustrates the application of this paragraph (e):

*Example.* In January of 2008, F, a calendar year taxpayer, enters into a transaction that at the time is not a listed transaction and is not a transaction described in any of the paragraphs (b)(3) through (7) of this section. All the tax benefits from the transaction are reported on F's 2008 tax return filed timely in April 2009. On May 2, 2011, the IRS publishes a notice identifying the transaction as a listed transaction described in paragraph (b)(2) of this section. Upon issuance of the May 2, 2011 notice, the transaction becomes a reportable transaction described in paragraph (b) of this section. The period of limitations on assessment for F's 2008 taxable year is still open. F is required to file Form 8886 for the transaction with OTSA within 90 calendar days after May 2, 2011.

(f) *Rulings and protective disclosures.*—(1) *Rulings.*—If a taxpayer requests a ruling on the merits of a specific transaction on or before the date that disclosure would otherwise be required under this section, and receives a favorable ruling as to the transaction, the disclosure rules under this section will be deemed to have been satisfied by that taxpayer with regard to that transaction, so long as the request fully discloses all relevant facts relating to the transaction which would otherwise be required to be disclosed under this section. If a taxpayer requests a ruling as to whether a specific transaction is a reportable transaction on or before the date that disclosure would otherwise be required under this section, the Commissioner in his discretion may determine that the submission satisfies the disclosure rules under this section for the taxpayer requesting the ruling for that transaction if the request fully discloses all relevant facts relating to the transaction which would otherwise be required to be disclosed under this section. The potential obligation of the taxpayer to disclose the transaction under this section will not be suspended during the period that the ruling request is pending.

(2) *Protective disclosures.*—If a taxpayer is uncertain whether a transaction must be disclosed under this section, the taxpayer may disclose the transaction in accordance with the requirements of this section and comply with all the provisions of this section, and indicate on the disclosure statement that the disclosure statement is being filed on a protective basis. The IRS will not treat disclosure statements filed on a protective basis any differently than other disclosure statements filed under this section. For a protective disclosure to be effective, the taxpayer must comply with these disclosure regulations by providing to the IRS all information requested by the IRS under this section.

(g) *Retention of documents.*—(1) In accordance with the instructions to Form 8886 (or a successor form), the taxpayer must retain a copy of all documents and other records related to a transaction subject to disclosure under this section that are material to an understanding of the tax treatment or tax structure of the transaction. The documents must be retained until the expiration of the statute of limitations applicable to the final taxable year for which disclosure of the transaction was required under this section. (This document retention requirement is in addition to any document retention requirements that section 6001 generally imposes on the taxpayer.) The documents may include the following:

(i) Marketing materials related to the transaction;

(ii) Written analyses used in decision-making related to the transaction;

(iii) Correspondence and agreements between the taxpayer and any advisor, lender, or other party to the reportable transaction that relate to the transaction;

(iv) Documents discussing, referring to, or demonstrating the purported or claimed tax benefits arising from the reportable transaction; and documents, if any, referring to the business purposes for the reportable transaction.

(2) A taxpayer is not required to retain earlier drafts of a document if the taxpayer retains a copy of the final document (or, if there is no final document, the most recent draft of the document) and the final document (or most recent draft) contains all the information in the earlier drafts of the document that is material to an understanding of the purported tax treatment or tax structure of the transaction.

(h) *Effective/applicability date.*—(1) *In general.*—This section applies to transactions entered into on or after August 3, 2007. However, this section applies to transactions of interest entered into on or after November 2, 2006. Paragraph (f)(1) of this section applies to ruling requests received on or after November 1, 2006. Otherwise, the rules that apply with respect to transactions entered into before August 3, 2007, are contained in § 1.6011-4 in effect prior to August 3, 2007. (See 26 CFR part 1 revised as of April 1, 2007).

(2) *[Reserved].*
[Reg. § 1.6011-4.]

□ [*T.D. 9046, 2-28-2003. Amended by T.D. 9108, 12-29-2003; T.D. 9295, 11-1-2006 and T.D. 9350, 7-31-2007 (corrected 5-10-2010).*]

### [Reg. § 20.6011-4]

**§ 20.6011-4. Requirement of statement disclosing participation in certain transactions by taxpayers.**—(a) *In general.*—If a transaction is identified as a *listed transaction* or a *transaction of interest* as defined in § 1.6011-4 of this chapter by the Commissioner in published guidance (see § 601.601(d)(2)(ii)(b) of this chapter), and the listed transaction or transaction of interest involves an estate tax under chapter 11 of subtitle B of the Internal Revenue Code, the transaction must be disclosed in the manner stated in such published guidance.

(b) *Effective/applicability date.*—This section applies to listed transactions entered into on or after January 1, 2003. This section applies to transactions of interest entered into on or after November 2, 2006. [Reg. § 20.6011-4.]

□ [*T.D. 9046, 2-28-2003. Amended by T.D. 9350, 7-31-2007.*]

### [Reg. § 25.6011-4]

**§ 25.6011-4. Requirement of statement disclosing participation in certain transactions by taxpayers.**—(a) *In general.*—If a transaction is identified as a *listed transaction* or a *transaction of interest* as defined in § 1.6011-4 of this chapter by the Commissioner in published guidance (see § 601.601(d)(2)(ii)(b) of this chapter), and the listed transaction or transaction of interest involves a gift tax under chapter 12 of subtitle B of the Internal Revenue Code, the transaction must be disclosed in the manner stated in such published guidance.

(b) *Effective/applicability date.*—This section applies to listed transactions entered into on or after January 1, 2003. This section applies to transactions of interest entered into on or after November 2, 2006. [Reg. § 25.6011-4.]

□ [*T.D. 9046, 2-28-2003. Amended by T.D. 9350, 7-31-2007.*]

### [Reg. § 26.6011-4]

**§ 26.6011-4. Requirement of statement disclosing participation in certain transactions by taxpayers.**—(a) *In general.*—If a transaction is identified as a *listed transaction* or a *transaction of interest* as defined in § 1.6011-4 of this chapter by the Commissioner in published guidance, and the listed transaction or transaction of interest involves a tax on generation-skipping transfers under chapter 13 of subtitle B of the Internal Revenue Code, the transaction must be disclosed in the manner stated in such published guidance.

(b) *Effective/applicability date.*—This section applies to listed transactions and transactions of interest entered into on or after November 14, 2011. [Reg. § 26.6011-4.]

□ [*T.D. 9556, 11-10-2011.*]

### [Reg. § 31.6011-4]

**§ 31.6011-4. Requirement of statement disclosing participation in certain transactions by taxpayers.**—(a) *In general.*—If a transaction is identified as a *listed transaction* or a *transaction of interest* as defined in § 1.6011-4 of this chapter by the Commissioner in published guidance (see § 601.601(d)(2)(ii)(b) of this chapter), and the listed transaction or transaction of interest involves an employment tax under chapters 21 through 25 of subtitle C of the Internal Revenue Code, the transaction must be disclosed in the manner stated in such published guidance.

(b) *Effective/applicability date.*—This section applies to listed transactions entered into on or after January 1, 2003. This section applies to transactions of interest entered into on or after November 2, 2006. [Reg. § 31.6011-4.]

□ [*T.D. 9046, 2-28-2003. Amended by T.D. 9350, 7-31-2007.*]

### [Reg. § 53.6011-4]

**§ 53.6011-4. Requirement of statement disclosing participation in certain transactions by taxpayers.**—(a) *In general.*—If a transaction is identified as a *listed transaction* or a *transaction of interest* as defined in §1.6011-4 of this chapter by the Commissioner in published guidance (see §601.601(d)(2)(ii)(*b*) of this chapter), and the listed transaction or transaction of interest involves an excise tax under chapter 42 of subtitle D of the Internal Revenue Code (relating to private foundations and certain other tax-exempt organizations), the transaction must be disclosed in the manner stated in such published guidance.

(b) *Effective/applicability date.*—This section applies to listed transactions entered into on or after January 1, 2003. This section applies to transactions of interest entered into on or after November 2, 2006. [Reg. §53.6011–4.]

☐ [*T.D.* 9046, 2-28-2003. *Amended by T.D.* 9350, 7-31-2007.]

### [Reg. §54.6011-4]

**§54.6011-4. Requirement of statement disclosing participation in certain transactions by taxpayers.**—(a) *In general.*—If a transaction is identified as a *listed transaction* or a *transaction of interest* as defined in §1.6011-4 of this chapter by the Commissioner in published guidance (see §601.601(d)(2)(ii)(*b*) of this chapter), and the listed transaction or transaction of interest involves an excise tax under chapter 43 of subtitle D of the Internal Revenue Code (relating to qualified pension, etc., plans) the transaction must be disclosed in the manner stated in such published guidance.

(b) *Effective/applicability date.*—This section applies to listed transactions entered into on or after January 1, 2003. This section applies to transactions of interest entered into on or after November 2, 2006. [Reg. §54.6011–4.]

☐ [*T.D.* 9046, 2-28-2003. *Amended by T.D.* 9350, 7-31-2007.]

### [Reg. §56.6011-4]

**§56.6011-4. Requirement of statement disclosing participation in certain transactions by taxpayers.**—(a) *In general.*—If a transaction is identified as a *listed transaction* or a *transaction of interest* as defined in §1.6011-4 of this chapter by the Commissioner in published guidance (see §601.601(d)(2) of this chapter), and the listed transaction or transaction of interest involves an excise tax under chapter 41 of subtitle D of the Internal Revenue Code (relating to public charities), the transaction must be disclosed in the manner stated in such published guidance.

(b) *Effective/applicability date.*—This section applies to listed transactions entered into on or after January 1, 2003. This section applies to transactions of interest entered into on or after November 2, 2006. [Reg. §56.6011–4.]

☐ [*T.D.* 9046, 2-28-2003. *Amended by T.D.* 9350, 7-31-2007.]

### [Reg. §1.6011-5]

**§1.6011-5. Required use of magnetic media for corporate income tax returns.**—The return of a corporation that is required to be filed on magnetic media under §301.6011-5 of this chapter must be filed in accordance with Internal Revenue Service revenue procedures, publications, forms, or instructions, including those posted electronically. (See §601.601(d)(2) of this chapter). [Reg. §1.6011-5.]

☐ [*T.D.* 9363, 11-9-2007.]

### [Reg. §301.6011-5]

**§301.6011-5. Required use of magnetic media for corporate income tax returns.**—(a) *Corporate income tax returns required on magnetic media.*—(1) A corporation required to file a corporate income tax return on Form 1120, "U.S. Corporation Income Tax Return," under §1.6012-2 of this chapter must file its corporate income tax return on magnetic media if the corporation is required by the Internal Revenue Code or regulations to file at least 250 returns during the calendar year. Returns filed on magnetic media must be made in accordance with applicable revenue procedures, publications, forms, or instructions. In prescribing revenue procedures, publications, forms, or instructions, the Commissioner may direct the type of magnetic media filing. (See §601.601(d)(2) of this chapter).

(2) All members of a controlled group of corporations must file their corporate income tax returns on magnetic media if the aggregate number of returns required to be filed by the controlled group of corporations is at least 250.

(b) *Waiver.*—The Commissioner may grant waivers of the requirements of this section in cases of undue hardship. A request for waiver must be made in accordance with applicable revenue procedures or publications. The waiver also will be subject to the terms and conditions regarding the method of filing as may be prescribed by the Commissioner.

(c) *Failure to file.*—If a corporation fails to file a corporate income tax return on magnetic media when required to do so by this section,

the corporation is deemed to have failed to file the return. (See section 6651 for the addition to tax for failure to file a return). In determining whether there is reasonable cause for failure to file the return, §301.6651-1(c) and rules similar to the rules in §301.6724-1(c)(3) (undue economic hardship related to filing information returns on magnetic media) will apply.

(d) *Meaning of terms.*—The following definitions apply for purposes of this section:

(1) *Magnetic media.*—The term *magnetic media* means any magnetic media permitted under applicable regulations, revenue procedures, or publications. These generally include magnetic tape, tape cartridge, and diskette, as well as other media, such as electronic filing, specifically permitted under the applicable regulations, procedures, publications, forms, or instructions. (See §601.601(d)(2) of this chapter).

(2) *Corporation.*—The term *corporation* means a corporation as defined in section 7701(a)(3).

(3) *Controlled group of corporations.*—The term *controlled group of corporations* means a group of corporations as defined in section 1563(a).

(4) *Corporate income tax return.*—The term *corporate income tax return* means a Form 1120, "U.S. Corporation Income Tax Return," along with all other related forms, schedules, and statements that are required to be attached to the Form 1120, and all members of the Form 1120 series of returns, including amended and superseding returns.

(5) *Determination of 250 returns.*—For purposes of this section, a corporation or controlled group of corporations is required to file at least 250 returns if, during the calendar year ending with or within the taxable year of the corporation or the controlled group, the corporation or the controlled group is required to file at least 250 returns of any type, including information returns (for example, Forms W-2, Forms 1099), income tax returns, employment tax returns, and excise tax returns. In the case of a short year return, a corporation is required to file at least 250 returns if, during the calendar year which includes the short taxable year of the corporation, the corporation is required to file at least 250 returns of any type, including information returns (for example, Forms W-2, Forms 1099), income tax returns, employment tax returns, and excise tax returns. If the corporation is a member of a controlled group, the determination of the number of returns includes all returns required to be filed by all members of the controlled group during the calendar year ending with or within the taxable year of the controlled group.

(e) *Example.*—The following example illustrates the provisions of paragraph (d)(5) of this section:

*Example.* The taxable year of Corporation X, a fiscal year taxpayer with assets in excess of $10 million, ends on September 30. During the calendar year ending December 31, 2007, X was required to file one Form 1120, "U.S. Corporation Income Tax Return," 100 Forms W-2, "Wage and Tax Statement," 146 Forms 1099-DIV, "Dividends and Distributions," one Form 940, "Employer's Annual Federal Unemployment (FUTA) Tax Return," and four Forms 941, "Employer's Quarterly Federal Tax Return." Because X is required to file 252 returns during the calendar year that ended within its taxable year ending September 30, 2008, X is required to file its Form 1120 electronically for its taxable year ending September 30, 2008.

(f) *Effective/applicability dates.*—This section applies to corporate income tax returns for corporations that report total assets at the end of the corporation's taxable year that equal or exceed $10 million on Schedule L of their Form 1120, for taxable years ending on or after December 31, 2006, except for the application of the short year rules in paragraph (d)(5) of this section, which is applicable for taxable years ending on or after November 13, 2007. [Reg. §301.6011-5.]

☐ [*T.D.* 9363, 11-9-2007.]

### [Reg. §1.6011-6]

**§1.6011-6. [Reserved]**
☐ [*T.D.* 9518, 3-28-2011.]

### [Reg. §301.6011-6]

**§301.6011-6. Statement of series and series organizations.**—**[Reserved]**.
☐ [*T.D.* 9518, 3-28-2011.]

### [Reg. §1.6011-7]

**§1.6011-7. Specified tax return preparers required to file individual income tax returns using magnetic media.**—Individual income tax returns that are required to be filed on magnetic media by tax return preparers under section 6011(e)(3) and §301.6011-7 of this chapter must be filed in accordance with Internal Revenue Service regulations, revenue procedures, revenue rulings, publications, forms or instructions, including those posted electronically. [Reg. §1.6011-7.]

☐ [T.D. 9518, 3-28-2011.]

### [Reg. §301.6011-7]

**§301.6011-7. Specified tax return preparers required to file individual income tax returns using magnetic media.**—(a) *Definitions.*—(1) *Magnetic media.*—For purposes of this section, the term *magnetic media* has the same meaning as in §301.6011-2(a)(1).

(2) *Individual income tax return.*—The term *individual income tax return* means any return of tax imposed by subtitle A on individuals, estates, and trusts.

(3) *Specified tax return preparer.*—The term *specified tax return preparer* means any person who is a tax return preparer, as defined in section 7701(a)(36) and §301.7701-15, unless that person reasonably expects to file 10 or fewer individual income tax returns in a calendar year. If a person who is a tax return preparer is a member of a firm, that person is a specified tax return preparer unless the person's firm members in the aggregate reasonably expect to file 10 or fewer individual income tax returns in a calendar year. Solely for the 2011 calendar year, a person will not be considered a specified tax return preparer if that person reasonably expects, or if the person is a member of a firm, the firm's members in the aggregate reasonably expect, to file fewer than 100 individual income tax returns in the 2011 calendar year. Solely for purposes of this section, a person is considered a member of a firm if the person is an employee, agent, member, partner, shareholder, or other equity holder of the firm.

(4) *File or Filed.*—(i) For purposes of section 6011(e)(3) and these regulations only, an individual income tax return is considered to be "filed" by a tax return preparer or a specified tax return preparer if the preparer submits the individual income tax return to the IRS on the taxpayer's behalf, either electronically (by e-file or other magnetic media) or in non-electronic (paper) form. Submission of an individual income tax return by a tax return preparer or a specified tax return preparer in non-electronic form includes the transmission, sending, mailing or otherwise delivering of the paper individual income tax return to the IRS by the preparer, any member, employee, or agent of the preparer, or any member, employee, or agent of the preparer's firm.

(ii) An individual income tax return will not be considered to be filed, as defined in paragraph (a)(4)(i) of this section, by a tax return preparer or specified tax return preparer if the tax return preparer or specified tax return preparer who prepared the return obtains, on or prior to the date the individual income tax return is filed, a handsigned and dated statement from the taxpayer (by either spouse if a joint return) that states the taxpayer chooses to file the individual income tax return in paper format, and that the taxpayer, and not the preparer, will submit the paper individual income tax return to the IRS. The IRS may provide guidance through forms, instructions or other appropriate guidance regarding how tax return preparers and specified tax return preparers can document a taxpayer's choice to file an individual income tax return in paper format.

(iii) The rules contained in this section do not alter or affect a taxpayer's obligation to file returns under any other provision of law. The definition of file or filed by a tax return preparer or specified tax return preparer contained in paragraph (a)(4)(i) of this section applies only for the purposes of section 6011(e)(3) and these regulations and does not apply for any other purpose under any other provision of law.

(b) *Magnetic media filing requirement.*—Except as provided in paragraphs (a)(4)(ii) and (c) of this section, any individual income tax return prepared by a specified tax return preparer in a calendar year must be filed on magnetic media if the return is filed by the specified tax return preparer.

(c) *Exclusions.*—The following exclusions apply to the magnetic media filing requirement in this section:

(1) *Undue hardship waiver.*—The IRS may grant a waiver of the requirement of this section in cases of undue hardship. An undue hardship waiver may be granted upon application by a specified tax return preparer consistent with instructions provided in published guidance and as prescribed in relevant forms and instructions. A determination of undue hardship will be based upon all facts and circumstances. The undue hardship waiver provided to a specified tax return preparer may apply to a series or class of individual income tax returns or for a specified period of time, subject to the

terms and conditions regarding the method of filing prescribed in such waiver.

(2) *Administrative exemptions.*—The IRS may provide administrative exemptions from the requirement of this section for certain classes of specified tax return preparers, or regarding certain types of individual income tax returns, as the IRS determines necessary to promote effective and efficient tax administration. The IRS may provide administrative exemptions and any criteria or procedures necessary to claim an administrative exemption through forms, instructions, or other appropriate guidance.

(d) *Reasonably expect to file.*—(1) *In general.*—The determination of whether a tax return preparer reasonably expects, or if the preparer is a member of a firm, the firm's members in the aggregate reasonably expect, to file 10 or fewer individual income tax returns (or, in the case of the 2011 calendar year, fewer than 100 individual income tax returns) is made by adding together all of the individual income tax returns the tax return preparer and, if the preparer is a member of a firm, the firm's members reasonably expect to prepare and file in the calendar year. In making this determination, individual income tax returns that the tax return preparer reasonably expects will not be subject to the magnetic media filing requirement under paragraph (a)(4)(ii) of this section or are excluded from the requirement under (c)(2) of this section are not to be counted. Individual income tax returns excluded from the magnetic media filing requirement under paragraph (c)(1) of this section are to be counted for purposes of making this determination.

(2) *Time for making determination of reasonable expectations.*—The determination regarding reasonable expectations is made separately for each calendar year in order to ascertain whether the magnetic media filing requirement applies to a tax return preparer for that year. For each calendar year, the determination of whether a tax return preparer and the preparer's firm reasonably expect to file 10 or fewer individual income tax returns (or, in the case of the 2011 calendar year, fewer than 100 individual income tax returns) is made based on all relevant, objective, and demonstrable facts and circumstances prior to the time the tax return preparer and the preparer's firm first file an individual income tax return during the calendar year.

(e) *Examples.*—The following examples illustrate the rules of paragraphs (a) through (d) of this section.

*Example 1.* Tax Return Preparer A is an accountant who recently graduated from college with an accounting degree and has opened his own practice. A has not prepared individual income tax returns for compensation in the past and does not plan to focus his practice on individual income tax return preparation. A intends instead to focus his practice on providing specialized accounting services to certain health care service providers. A has no plans to, and does not, employ or engage any other tax return preparers. A estimates that he may be asked by some clients to prepare and file their individual income tax returns for compensation, but A expects that the number of people who do ask him to provide this service will be no more than seven in 2012. In fact, A actually prepares and files six paper Forms 1040 (U.S. Individual Income Tax Return) in 2012. Due to a growing client base, and based upon his experience in 2012, A expects that the number of individual income tax returns he will prepare and file in 2013 will at least double, estimating he will prepare and file 12 Form 1040 returns in 2013. A does not qualify as a specified tax return preparer for 2012 because A reasonably expects to file 10 or fewer returns (seven) in 2012. Consequently, A is not required to electronically file the individual income tax returns he prepares and files in 2012. A's expectation is reasonable based on his business projections, individual income tax return filing history, and staffing decisions. A is a specified tax return preparer in 2013, however, because based on those same factors A reasonably expects to file more than 10 individual income tax returns (12) during that calendar year. A, therefore, must electronically file all individual income tax returns that A prepares and files in 2013 that are not otherwise excluded from the electronic filing requirement.

*Example 2.* Same facts as in *Example 1*, except three of Tax Return Preparer A's clients specifically chose to have A prepare their individual income tax returns in paper format in 2012 with the clients mailing their respective returns to the IRS. A expects that these three clients will similarly choose to have him prepare their returns in paper format in 2013, with the clients being responsible for mailing their returns to the IRS. A is not required to electronically file these three returns in 2013 because the taxpayers chose to file their returns in paper format. A obtained a hand-signed and dated statement from each of those taxpayers, indicating that they chose to file their returns in paper format. These three individual income tax returns are not counted in determining how many individual income tax returns A reasonably expects to file in 2013. Because the total number of individual income tax returns A reasonably expects to file in 2013 (nine) does not exceed 10, A is not a specified tax return preparer for calendar year 2013, and A is not required to electronically file any individual income tax return that he prepares and files in 2013.

*Example 3.* Tax Return Preparer B is a solo general practice attorney in a small county. Her practice includes the preparation of wills and assisting executors in administering estates. As part of her practice, B infrequently prepares and files Forms 1041 (U.S. Income Tax Return for Estates and Trusts) for executors. In the past three years, she prepared and filed an average of five Forms 1041 each year and never exceeded more than seven Forms 1041 in any year. Based on B's prior experience and her estimate for 2012, made prior to the time she first files an individual income tax return in 2012, she reasonably expects to prepare and file no more than five Forms 1041 in 2012. Due to the unforeseen deaths of several of her clients in late 2011, B actually prepares and files 12 Forms 1041 in 2012. B does not find out about these deaths until after she has already filed the first Form 1041 in 2012 for another client. B is not required to electronically file these returns in 2012. She does not qualify as a specified tax return preparer for calendar year 2012 because prior to the time she filed the first Form 1041 in 2012, she reasonably expected to file 10 or fewer individual income tax returns in 2012.

*Example 4.* Same facts as *Example 3*, except, in addition to the five Forms 1041 that she expects to prepare and file in 2012, Tax Return Preparer B also expects to prepare and file 10 paper Forms 1040 (U.S. Individual Income Tax Return) in 2012, based upon the requests that she has received from some of her clients. Because the total number of individual income tax returns B reasonably expects to file in 2012 (fifteen) exceeds 10, B is a specified tax return preparer for calendar year 2012, and B must electronically file all individual income tax returns that B prepares and files in 2012 that are not otherwise excluded from the electronic filing requirement.

*Example 5.* Firm X consists of two tax return preparers, Tax Return Preparer C who owns Firm X, and Tax Return Preparer D who is employed by C in Firm X. Based upon the firm's experience over the past three years, C and D reasonably expect to file nine and ten individual income tax returns for compensation, respectively, in 2012. Both C and D must electronically file the individual income tax returns that they prepare in 2012, unless the returns are otherwise excluded from the electronic filing requirement, because they are members of the same firm and the aggregated total of individual income tax returns that they reasonably expect to file in 2012 (nineteen), exceeds 10 individual income tax returns.

(f) *Additional guidance.*—The IRS may implement the requirements of this section through additional guidance, including by revenue procedures, notices, publications, forms and instructions, including those issued electronically.

(g) *Effective /applicability date.*—This section is effective on March 30, 2011, and applicable to individual income tax returns filed after December 31, 2010. [Reg. § 301.6011-7.]

☐ [*T.D.* 9518, 3-28-2011.]

**[Reg. § 1.6011-8]**

**§ 1.6011-8. Requirement of income tax return for taxpayers who claim the premium tax credit under section 36B.**—(a) *Requirement of return.*—Except as otherwise provided in this paragraph (a), a taxpayer who receives the benefit of advance payments of the premium tax credit (advance credit payments) under section 36B must file an income tax return for that taxable year on or before the due date for the return (including extensions of time for filing) and reconcile the advance credit payments. However, if advance credit payments are made for coverage of an individual who is not included in any taxpayer's family, as defined in § 1.36B-1(d), the taxpayer who attested to the Exchange to the intention to include such individual in the taxpayer's family as part of the advance credit payment eligibility determination for coverage of the individual must file a tax return and reconcile the advance credit payments.

(b) *Applicability dates.*—(1) *In general.*—Except as provided in paragraph (b)(2) of this section, paragraph (a) of this section applies for taxable years ending on or after December 31, 2020.

(2) *Prior periods.*—Paragraph (a) of this section as contained in 26 CFR part 1 edition revised as of April 1, 2016, applies to taxable years ending after December 31, 2013, and beginning before January 1, 2017. Paragraph (a) of this section as contained in 26 CFR part 1 edition revised as of April 1, 2020, applies to taxable years beginning after December 31, 2016, and ending before December 31, 2020. [Reg. § 1.6011-8.]

☐ [*T.D.* 9590, 5-18-2012. *Amended by T.D.* 9745, 12-16-2015, *T.D.* 9804, 12-14-2016 *and T.D.* 9912, 11-27-2020.]

**[Reg. § 31.6011(a)-1]**

**§ 31.6011(a)-1. Returns under Federal Insurance Contributions Act.**—(a) *Requirement.*—(1) *In general.*—Except as otherwise provided in paragraphs (a)(3) and (a)(5) of this section and in § 31.6011(a)-5 every employer is required to make a return for the first calendar quarter in which the employer pays wages, other than wages for agricultural labor, subject to the tax imposed by the Federal Insurance Contributions Act, and is required to make a return for each subsequent calendar quarter (whether or not wages are paid therein) until the employer has filed a final return in accordance with § 31.6011(a)-6. Except as otherwise provided in § 31.6011(a)-8 and in paragraphs (a)(3), (a)(4), and (a)(5) of this section, Form 941, "Employer's QUARTERLY Federal Tax Return," is the form prescribed for making the return required by this paragraph (a)(1). Such return shall not include wages for agricultural labor required to be reported on any return prescribed by paragraph (a)(2) of this section. The return shall include wages received by an employee in the form of tips only to the extent of the tips reported by the employee to the employer in a written statement furnished to the employer pursuant to section 6053(a).

(2) *Employers of agricultural workers.*—Every employer who pays wages for agricultural labor with respect to taxes imposed by the Federal Insurance Contributions Act must make a return for the first calendar year in which the employer pays such wages and for each subsequent calendar year (whether or not wages are paid) until the employer has filed a final return in accordance with § 31.6011(a)-6. Form 943, "Employer's Annual Federal Tax Return for Agricultural Employees," is the form prescribed for making the annual return required by this section, except that, if the employer's principal place of business is in Puerto Rico, or if the employer has employees who are subject to income tax withholding for Puerto Rico, the return must be made on Form 943-PR, "Planilla para la Declaración ANUAL de la Contribución Federal del Patrono de Empleados Agrícolas." However, Form 943 is the form prescribed for making such return in the case of every employer of agricultural workers who is required pursuant to § 31.6011(a)-4 to make a return of income tax withheld from wages.

(3) *Employers of domestic workers.*—Schedule H (Form 1040), "Household Employment Taxes," is the form prescribed for use by every employer in making a return as required under paragraph (a)(1) of this section in respect of wages, as defined in the Federal Insurance Contributions Act, paid by the employer in any calendar year for domestic service as defined in section 3510. Schedule H (Form 1040) is generally filed as an attachment to an income tax return; however, if the employer does not otherwise have an obligation to file an income tax return, Schedule H (Form 1040) may be filed as a separate return. If, however, the employer is required under paragraph (a)(1) of this section to make a return on Form 941, "Employer's QUARTERLY Federal Tax Return," or under paragraph (a)(2) of this section to make a return on Form 943, "Employer's Annual Federal Tax Return For Agricultural Employees," or under paragraph (a)(5) of this section to make a return on Form 944, "Employer's ANNUAL Federal Tax Return," the employer may choose instead to report wages with respect to domestic workers on such Form 941, Form 943, or Form 944. If such wages are also included on Form 941, Form 943, or Form 944, the employer must also include Federal unemployment tax for the employee(s) on Form 940, "Employer's Annual Federal Unemployment (FUTA) Tax Return," under the provisions of § 31.6011(a)-3.

(4) *Employers in Puerto Rico, the U.S. Virgin Islands, Guam, American Samoa, or the Commonwealth of the Northern Mariana Islands.*—Except as otherwise provided in paragraph (a)(5), Form 941-PR, "Planilla para la Declaracion Federal TRIMESTRAL del Patrono," is the form prescribed for use in making the return required under paragraph (a)(1) of this section in the case of every employer whose principal place of business is in Puerto Rico, or if the employer has employees who are subject to income tax withholding for Puerto Rico. Except as otherwise provided in paragraph (a)(5), Form 941-SS, "Employer's QUARTERLY Federal Tax Return (American Samoa, Guam, the Commonwealth of the Northern Mariana Islands, and the U.S. Virgin Islands)," is the form prescribed for use in making the return required under paragraph (a)(1) of this section in the case of every employer whose principal place of business is in the U.S. Virgin Islands, Guam, American Samoa, or the Commonwealth of the Northern Mariana Islands, or if the employer has employees who are subject to income tax withholding for these U.S. possessions. Form 941 (or Form 944, as described under paragraph (a)(5) of this section, if the IRS notified the employer that Form 944 must be filed in lieu of Form 941) is the form prescribed for making the return in the case of every employer who is required pursuant to § 31.6011(a)-4 to make a return of income tax withheld from wages.

(5) *Employers in the Employers' Annual Federal Tax Program (Form 944).*—(i) *In general.*—Employers notified of their qualification for the Employers' Annual Federal Tax Program (Form 944) are required to file Form 944, "Employer's ANNUAL Federal Tax Return," instead of Form 941 (or Form 941-SS or Form 941-PR under paragraph (a)(4) of this section) to make a return as required by paragraph (a)(1) of this section. Upon proper request by the employer, the IRS will notify employers in writing of their qualification for the Employers' Annual Federal Tax Program (Form 944). The IRS will notify employers when they no longer qualify for the Employers' Annual Federal Tax Program (Form 944) and must file Forms 941 instead. Qualified employers are those with an estimated annual employment tax liability (that is, social security, Medicare, and withheld Federal income taxes) of $1,000 or less for the entire calendar year, except employers required under—

    (A) Paragraph (a)(2) of this section to make a return on Form 943, "Employer's Annual Federal Tax Return For Agricultural Employees"; or

    (B) Paragraph (a)(3) of this section to make a return on Schedule H (Form 1040), "Household Employment Taxes."

    (ii) *Requests to opt in or opt out of the Employers' Annual Federal Tax Program (Form 944).*—The IRS has established procedures in Revenue Procedure 2009-51 published in the Internal Revenue Bulletin for employers to follow to request to participate in the Employers' Annual Federal Tax Program (Form 944) (to opt in) and to request to be removed from the Employers' Annual Federal Tax Program (Form 944) after becoming a participant in order to file Forms 941 instead (to opt out). The IRS will notify employers that their filing requirements have changed to Form 944 or Forms 941. Employers must follow the procedures in Revenue Procedure 2009-51 or its successor to request to opt in or opt out of the Employers' Annual Federal Tax Program (Form 944).

(b) *When to report wages.*—Wages with respect to which taxes are imposed by the Federal Insurance Contributions Act shall be reported in the return of such taxes required under this section or §31.6011(a)-5 for the return period in which they are actually paid unless they were constructively paid in a prior return period, in which case such wages shall be reported only in the return for such prior period. However, if such wages are deemed to be paid in a later return period, they shall be reported only in the return for such later period. See §31.3121(a)-2 relating to the time when wages are paid or deemed to be paid.

(c) *Adjustments and refunds.*—For rules applicable to adjustments and refunds of employment taxes, see sections 6205, 6402, 6413, and 6414, and the applicable regulations.

(d) *Returns by employees in respect of tips.*—If—

    (1) An employee, during a calendar year, is paid wages in the form of tips which are subject to the tax under section 3101, and

    (2) Any portion of the tax under section 3101 in respect of such wages can not be collected by the employer from wages (exclusive of tips) of such employee or from funds turned over by the employee to the employer,

the employee shall make a return for the calendar year in respect of the employee tax not collected by the employer. Except as otherwise provided in this subparagraph, the return shall be made on Form 1040. The form to be used by residents of the Virgin Islands, Guam, or American Samoa is Form 1040SS. In the case of a resident of Puerto Rico who is not required to make a return of income under section 6012(a), the form to be used is Form 1040SS, except that Form 1040PR shall be used if it is furnished by the Internal Revenue Service to such resident for use in lieu of Form 1040SS.

(e) *Time and place for filing returns.*—For provisions relating to the time and place for filing returns, see §§31.6071(a)-1 and 31.6091-1, respectively.

(f) *Wages paid in nonconvertible foreign currency.*—For provisions relating to returns filed by certain employers who pay wages in nonconvertible foreign currency, see §301.6316-7 of this chapter (Regulations on Procedure and Administration).

(g) *Returns by employees in respect of Additional Medicare Tax.*—An employee who is paid wages, as defined in section 3121(a), subject to the tax under section 3101(b)(2)(Additional Medicare Tax), must make a return for the taxable year in respect of such tax. The return shall be made on Form 1040, "U.S. Individual Income Tax Return." The form to be used by residents of the U.S. Virgin Islands, Guam, American Samoa, or the Northern Mariana Islands is Form 1040-SS, "U.S. Self-Employment Tax Return (Including Additional Child Tax Credit for Bona Fide Residents of Puerto Rico)." The form to be used by residents of Puerto Rico is either Form 1040-SS or Form 1040-PR, "Planilla para la Declaración de la Contribución Federal sobre el Trabajo por Cuenta Propia (Incluyendo el Crédito Tributario Adicional por Hijos para Residentes Bona Fide de Puerto Rico)."

(h) *Effective/applicability dates.*—Paragraphs (a)(1) and (a)(5)(i) of this section apply to taxable years beginning on or after December 30, 2008. Paragraph (a)(4) of this section applies to taxable years beginning on or after January 1, 2012. Paragraph (a)(5)(ii) of this section applies to taxable years beginning on or after January 1, 2010. The rules of paragraph (a)(1) of this section that apply to taxable years beginning before December 30, 2008, are contained in §31.6011(a)-1 as in effect prior to December 30, 2008. The rules of paragraph (a)(4) of this section that apply to taxable years beginning before January 1, 2012, are contained in §31.6011(a)-1 as in effect prior to January 1, 2012. The rules of paragraph (a)(5)(ii) of this section that apply to taxable years beginning before January 1, 2010, but on or after December 30, 2008, are contained in §31.6011(a)-1T as in effect on or after December 30, 2008. The rules of paragraph (a)(5) of this section that apply to taxable years beginning before December 30, 2008, are contained in §31.6011(a)-1T as in effect prior to December 30, 2008. Paragraph (g) of this section applies to taxable years beginning on or after November 29, 2013. [Reg. §31.6011(a)-1.]

☐ [*T.D.* 6516, 12-20-60. *Amended by T.D.* 7001, 1-17-69; *T.D.* 7200, 8-15-72; *T.D.* 7351, 4-16-75; *T.D.* 7396, 1-12-76; *T.D.* 9239, 12-30-2005; *T.D.* 9405, 6-30-2008; *T.D.* 9440, 12-24-2008; *T.D.* 9566, 12-9-2011 *and T.D.* 9645, 11-26-2013 (*corrected* 1-28-2014).]

## [Reg. §31.6011(a)-2]

**§31.6011(a)-2. Returns under Railroad Retirement Tax Act.**— (a) *Requirement.*—(1) *Employers.*—Every employer shall make a return for the first return period after 1954 within which compensation taxable under the Railroad Retirement Tax Act is paid to his employee or employees for services rendered after 1954, and for each subsequent return period (whether or not taxable compensation is paid therein) until he has filed a final return in accordance with §31.6011(a)-6. For calendar years after 1975, the return period shall be the calendar year; for calendar years prior to 1976, the return period shall be the calendar quarter. Form CT-1 is the form prescibed for making the return required under this paragraph. One original and a duplicate of each return on Form CT-1 shall be filed with the director of the service center.

    (2) *Employee representatives.*—Every employee representative shall make a return for the first calendar quarter after 1954 within which he is paid taxable compensation for services rendered after 1954 as an employee representative, and for each subsequent calendar quarter (whether or not he is paid taxable compensation therein) until he has filed a final return in accordance with §31.6011(a)-6. Form CT-2 is the form prescribed for making the return required under this subparagraph. One original and a duplicate of each return on Form CT-2 shall be filed with the director of the service center.

(b) *When to report compensation.*—(1) *In general.*—Except as otherwise provided in subparagraph (2) of this paragraph, compensation taxable under the Railroad Retirement Tax Act shall be reported in the return required under this section for the period in which it is deemed, under paragraph (d) of §31.3231(e)-1 to be paid, unless under such section the compensation may be deemed to be paid in more than one return period, in which case it shall be reported only in the return for the first return period in which it is deemed to be paid.

    (2) *Pre-1976 returns of employers required by State law to pay compensation on weekly basis.*—(i) *In general.*—If any employer is required by the laws of any State to pay compensation weekly in any calendar year prior to 1976, the return of tax with respect to such compensation may, at the election of such employer, cover all payroll weeks which, or the major part of which, fall within the period for which a return of tax is required by paragraph (a)(1) of this section. This provision shall not apply, however, to any payroll week which falls in two calendar years. Any employer who elects to file a return as provided in this subparagraph shall notify the district director in writing of such election and shall include therein a statement setting forth the facts which entitle him to make the election. Such notice shall be in duplicate and shall be attached to the original and duplicate of the return for the first period to which such election applies. Any election so made shall be binding upon the employer with respect to all reurns subsequently made by him until the director of the service center authorizes or directs the employer to make a return on a different basis. For the purpose of determining the time when compensation is deemed to be paid in accordance with paragraph (d) of §31.3231(e)-1 and of determining the due date of a return in accordance with paragraph (b) of §31.6071(a)-1, the calendar month following the period covered by the return of an employer making such election is the same calendar month which would be determinative for such purposes if the employer had not made the election.

(ii) *Prior elections.*—An election made by an employer, pursuant to the provisions of 26 CFR (1939) 410.501(b) (Regulations 100) or of 26 CFR (1939) 411.601(b) (Regulations 114), which is in force and effect at the time the employer makes his first return under this section shall satisfy the requirements of paragraph (b)(2)(i) of this section with respect to the making of an election and shall be binding upon the employer with respect to all returns made by him under this section until the director of the service center authorizes or directs the employer to make a return on a different basis.

(iii) *Example.*—Employer X is required by State law to pay his employees within 6 days after the compensation is earned. In compliance with the State law, employer X, for services rendered to him for the payroll week of June 27 to July 2, 1955, pays his employees on the last-named date. June 1955 is the last month of a period for which a return of tax is required by paragraph (a)(1) of this section. Employer X may elect to include in the return required by paragraph (a)(1) of this section for the period April 1 to June 30, 1955, the compensation paid to his employees for the payroll week of June 27 to July 2, 1955, inclusive, although the compensation for July 1 and 2 falls within another period for which a return is required by paragraph (a)(1) of this section. If, in this example, the payroll week ended on July 5, 1955, the compensation paid for the payroll week of June 29 to July 5 would be included in the return period in which July falls although the compensation earned for June 29 and 30 fell in a prior return period under the general rule.

(c) *Time and place for filing returns.*—For provisions relating to the time and place for filing returns, see §§ 31.6071(a)-1 and 31.6091-1, respectively.

(d) *Returns by employees and employee representatives in respect of Additional Medicare Tax.*—An employee or employee representative who is paid compensation, as defined in section 3231(e), subject to the tax under sections 3201(a) (as calculated under section 3101(b)(2)) or section 3211(a) (as calculated under section 3101(b)(2)) (Additional Medicare Tax), must make a return for the taxable year in respect of such tax. The return shall be made on Form 1040, "U.S. Individual Income Tax Return." The form to be used by residents of the U.S. Virgin Islands, Guam, American Samoa, or the Northern Mariana Islands is Form 1040-SS, "U.S. Self-Employment Tax Return (Including Additional Child Tax Credit for Bona Fide Residents of Puerto Rico)." The form to be used by residents of Puerto Rico is either Form 1040-SS or Form 1040-PR, "Planilla para la Declaración de la Contribución Federal sobre el Trabajo por Cuenta Propia (Incluyendo el Crédito Tributario Adicional por Hijos para Residentes Bona Fide de Puerto Rico)."

(e) *Effective/applicability date.*—Paragraph (d) of this section applies to taxable years beginning on or after November 29, 2013. [Reg. § 31.6011(a)-2.]

☐ [*T.D.* 6516, 12-20-60. *Amended by T.D.* 7396, 1-13-76 *and T.D.* 9645, 11-26-2013.]

**[Reg. § 31.6011(a)-3]**

**§ 31.6011(a)-3. Returns under Federal Unemployment Tax Act.**— (a) *Requirement.*—Every person shall make a return of tax under the Federal Unemployment Tax Act for each calendar year with respect to which he is an employer as defined in § 31.3306(a)-1. Except as otherwise provided in § 31.6011(a)-8, Form 940 is the form prescribed for use in making the return.

(b) *When to report wages.*—Wages taxable under the Federal Unemployment Tax Act shall be reported in the return required under this section for the return period in which they are actually paid unless they were constructively paid in a prior return period, in which case such wages shall be reported only in the return for such prior period.

(c) *Time and place for filing returns.*—For provisions relating to the time and place for filing returns, see §§ 31.6071(a)-1 and 31.6091-1, respectively. [Reg. § 31.6011(a)-3.]

☐ [*T.D.* 6516, 12-20-60. *Amended by T.D.* 7200, 8-15-72.]

**[Reg. § 31.6011(a)-4]**

**§ 31.6011(a)-4. Returns of income tax withheld.**—(a) *Withheld from wages.*—(1) *In general.*—Except as otherwise provided in paragraphs (a)(2), (a)(3), (a)(4), and (b) of this section, and in § 31.6011(a)-5, every person required to make a return of income tax withheld from wages pursuant to section 3402 shall make a return for the first calendar quarter in which the person is required to deduct and withhold such tax and for each subsequent calendar quarter, whether or not wages are paid therein, until the person has filed a final return in accordance with § 31.6011(a)-6. Except as otherwise provided in paragraphs (a)(2), (a)(3), (a)(4), and (b) of this section, and in § 31.6011(a)-8, Form 941, "Employer's QUARTERLY Federal

Tax Return," is the form prescribed for making the return required under this paragraph (a)(1).

(2) *Wages paid for domestic service.*—Schedule H (Form 1040), "Household Employment Taxes," is the form prescribed for making the return required under paragraph (a)(1) of this section with respect to income tax withheld, pursuant to an agreement under section 3402(p), from wages paid for domestic service as defined in section 3510. Schedule H (Form 1040) is generally filed as an attachment to an income tax return; however, if the employer does not otherwise have an obligation to file an income tax return, Schedule H (Form 1040) may be filed as a separate return. The preceding sentence shall not apply in the case of an employer who has chosen under § 31.6011(a)-1(a)(3) to use Form 941, "Employer's QUARTERLY Federal Tax Return," Form 943, "Employer's Annual Tax Return for Agricultural Employees," or Form 944, "Employer's ANNUAL Federal Tax Return," as the return with respect to such payments for purposes of the Federal Insurance Contributions Act. For the requirements relating for Schedule H (Form 1040) with respect to qualified State individual income taxes, see § 301.6361-1(d)(3)(iv).

(3) *Wages paid for agricultural labor.*—Every person shall make a return of income tax withheld, pursuant to an agreement under section 3402(p), from wages paid for agricultural labor for the first calendar year in which he is required (by reason of such agreement) to deduct and withhold such tax and for each subsequent calendar year (whether or not wages for agricultural labor are paid therein) until he has filed a final return in accordance with § 31.6011(a)-6. Form 943 is the form prescribed for making the return required under this subparagraph. For the requirements relating to Form 943 with respect to qualified State individual income taxes, see paragraph (d)(3)(iv) of § 301.6361-1.

(4) *Employers in the Employers' Annual Federal Tax Program (Form 944).*—(i) *In general.*—Employers notified of their qualification for the Employers' Annual Federal Tax Program (Form 944) are required to file Form 944, "Employer's ANNUAL Federal Tax Return," instead of Form 941 to make a return of income tax withheld from wages pursuant to section 3402. Upon proper request by the employer, the IRS will notify employers in writing of their qualification for the Employers' Annual Federal Tax Program (Form 944). The IRS will notify employers when they no longer qualify for the Employers' Annual Federal Tax Program (Form 944) and must file Forms 941 instead. Qualified employers are those with an estimated annual employment tax liability (that is, social security, Medicare, and withheld federal income taxes) of $1,000 or less for the entire calendar year, except employers required under—

(A) Paragraph (a)(3) of this section to make a return on Form 943, "Employer's Annual Federal Tax Return For Agricultural Employees"; or

(B) Paragraph (a)(2) of this section to make a return on Schedule H (Form 1040), "Household Employment Taxes."

(ii) *Request to opt in or opt out of the Employers' Annual Federal Tax Program (Form 944).*—The IRS established procedures in Revenue Procedure 2009-51 published in the Internal Revenue Bulletin for employers to follow to request to participate in the Employers' Annual Federal Tax Program (Form 944) (to opt in) and to request to be removed from the Employers' Annual Federal Tax Program (Form 944) after becoming a participant in order to file Forms 941 instead (to opt out). The IRS will notify employers that their filing requirements have changed to Form 944 or Forms 941. Employers must follow the procedures in Revenue Procedure 2009-51 or its successor to opt in or opt out of the Employers' Annual Federal Tax Program (Form 944).

(b) *Withheld from nonpayroll payments.*—Every person required to withhold tax from nonpayroll payments for calendar year 1994 must make a return for calendar year 1994 and for any subsequent calendar year in which the person is required to withhold such tax until the person makes a final return in accordance with § 31.6011(a)-6. Every person not required to withhold tax from nonpayroll payments for calendar year 1994 must make a return for the first calendar year after 1994 in which the person is required to withhold such tax and for any subsequent calendar year in which the person is required to withhold such tax until the person makes a final return in accordance with § 31.6011(a)-6. Form 945, Annual Return of Withheld Federal Income Tax, is the form prescribed for making the return required under this paragraph (b). Nonpayroll payments are—

(1) Certain gambling winnings subject to withholding under section 3402(q);

(2) Retirement pay for services in the Armed Forces of the United States subject to withholding under section 3402;

(3) Certain annuities as described in section 3402(o)(1)(B);

(4) Pensions, annuities, IRAs, and certain other deferred income subject to withholding under section 3405; and

(5) Reportable payments subject to backup withholding under section 3406.

(c) *Time and place for filing returns.*—For provisions relating to the time and place for filing returns, see §§ 31.6071(a)-1 and 31.6091-1, respectively.

(d) *Effective/applicability dates.*—Paragraphs (a)(1) and (a)(4)(i) of this section apply to taxable years beginning on or after December 30, 2008. Paragraph (a)(4)(ii) of this section applies to taxable years beginning on or after January 1, 2010. The rules of paragraph (a)(1) of this section that apply to taxable years beginning before December 30, 2008, are contained in § 31.6011(a)-4 as in effect prior to December 30, 2008. The rules of paragraph (a)(4)(ii) of this section that apply to taxable years beginning before January 1, 2010, but on or after December 30, 2008, are contained in § 31.6011(a)-4T as in effect on or after December 30, 2008. The rules of paragraph (a)(4) of this section that apply to taxable years beginning before December 30, 2008, are contained in § 31.6011(a)-4T as in effect prior to December 30, 2008. [Reg. § 31.6011(a)-4.]

☐ [*T.D. 6354, 1-13-59. Amended by T.D. 7096, 3-17-71; T.D. 7200, 8-15-72; T.D. 7351, 4-16-75; T.D. 7577, 12-19-78; T.D. 7580, 12-20-78; T.D. 8504, 12-22-93; T.D. 8624, 10-13-95; T.D. 8672, 5-29-96; T.D. 9239, 12-30-2005; T.D. 9405, 6-30-2008; T.D. 9440, 12-24-2008; T.D. 9524, 5-6-2011, T.D. 9566, 12-9-2011 and T.D. 9586, 4-24-2012.*]

### [Reg. § 31.6011(a)-5]

**§ 31.6011(a)-5. Monthly returns.**—(a) *In general.*—(1) *Requirement.*—The provisions of this section are applicable in respect of the taxes reportable on returns required pursuant to § 31.6011(a)-1 or § 31.6011(a)-4. An employer (or other person) who is required by § 31.6011(a)-1 or § 31.6011(a)-4 to make quarterly or annual returns on any such form shall, in lieu of making such quarterly or annual returns, make returns of such taxes in accordance with the provisions of this section if the employer is so notified in writing by the IRS. Every employer (or other person) notified by the IRS shall make a return for the calendar month in which the notice is received, for each of the prior calendar months in the return period, and for each calendar month afterwards (whether or not wages are paid in any such month) until the employer has filed a final return or is required to make quarterly or annual returns pursuant to notification as provided in paragraph (a)(2) of this section. Each return required under this section shall be made on the form prescribed for making the return which would otherwise be required of the employer (or other person) under the provisions of § 31.6011(a)-1 or § 31.6011(a)-4, except that, if some other form is furnished by the IRS for use in lieu of such prescribed form, the return shall be made on such other prescribed form. The IRS may notify any employer (or other person)—

(i) Who by reason of notification as provided in § 301.7512-1, is required to comply with the provisions of such § 301.7512-1; or

(ii) Who failed to—

(A) Make any return required pursuant to § 31.6011(a)-1 or § 31.6011(a)-4;

(B) Pay tax reportable on any such form; or

(C) Deposit any such tax as required under the provisions of § 31.6302-1.

(2) *Termination of requirement.*—The IRS, in its discretion, may notify the employer in writing that the employer shall discontinue the filing of monthly returns under this section. If the employer is so notified, the IRS will provide the employer with instructions for filing the final monthly return. Afterwards, the employer shall make quarterly or annual returns in accordance with the provisions of § 31.6011(a)-1 or § 31.6011(a)-4.

(b) *Information returns on Form W-3 and Social Security Administration copies of Form W-2.*—See § 31.6051-2 for requirements with respect to information returns on Form W-3 and Social Security Administration copies of Form W-2.

(c) *Time and place for filing returns.*—For provisions relating to the time and place for filing returns, see §§ 31.6071(a)-1 and 31.6091-1, respectively. [Reg. § 31.6011(a)-5.]

☐ [*T.D. 6354, 1-13-59. Amended by T.D. 7351, 4-16-75; T.D. 7580, 12-20-78; T.D. 8637, 12-20-95; T.D. 9061, 6-10-2003 and T.D. 9405, 6-30-2008.*]

### [Reg. § 31.6011(a)-6]

**§ 31.6011(a)-6. Final returns.**—(a) *In general.*—(1) *Federal Insurance Contributions Act; income tax withheld from wages and nonpayroll payments.*—An employer (or other person) who is required to make a return on a particular form pursuant to § 31.6011(a)-1, § 31.6011(a)-4,

or § 31.6011(a)-5, and who in any return period ceases to pay wages or nonpayroll payments in respect of which he is required to make a return on that form, must make the return for the period as a final return. Each return made as a final return shall be marked "Final return" by the person filing the return. Every such person filing a final return (other than a final return on Form 942 or Form 943) must furnish information showing the date of the last payment of wages (as defined in section 3121(a) or section 3401(a)), and, if appropriate, the date of the last payment of nonpayroll payments defined in § 31.6011(a)-4(b). If (i) for any return period an employer makes a final return on a particular form, and (ii) after the close of such period the employer pays wages, as defined in section 3121(a) or section 3401(a), in respect of which the same or a different return form is prescribed, such employer shall make returns on the appropriate return form. For example, if an employer who has filed a final return on Form 941 pays wages only for domestic service in his private home not on a farm operated for profit, the employer is required to make returns on Form 942 in respect of such wages.

(2) *Railroad Retirement Tax Act.*—(i) *Form CT-1.*—An employer required to make returns on Form CT-1 who in any return period ceases to pay taxable compensation shall make the return on Form CT-1 for such period as a final return. Such return shall be marked "Final return" by the person filing the return, and such person shall furnish information showing the date of the last payment of taxable compensation. An employer who has only temporarily ceased to pay taxable compensation shall continue to file returns on Form CT-1.

(ii) *Form CT-2.*—An employee representative required to make returns on Form CT-2 who in any calendar quarter ceases to be paid taxable compensation for services as an employee representative shall make the return on Form CT-2 for such quarter as a final return. Such return shall be marked "Final return" by the person filing the return, and such person shall furnish information showing the date of the last payment of taxable compensation. An employee representative who only temporarily ceases to be paid taxable compensation for services as an employee representative shall continue to file returns on Form CT-2.

(3) *Federal Unemployment Tax Act.*—An employer required to make a return on Form 940 for a calendar year in which he ceases to be an employer, as defined in § 31.3306(a)-1, because of the discontinuance, sale, or other transfer of his business, shall make such return as a final return. Such return shall be marked "Final return" by the person filing the return.

(b) *Statement to accompany final return.*—There shall be executed as a part of each final return, except in the case of a final return on Form 942, a statement showing the address at which the records required by the regulations in this part will be kept, the name of the person keeping such records, and, if the business of an employer has been sold or otherwise transferred to another person, the name and address of such person and the date on which such sale or other transfer took place. If no such sale or transfer occurred or the employer does not know the name of the person to whom the business was sold or transferred, that fact should be included in the statement. Such statement shall include any information required by this section as to the date of the last payment of wages or compensation. If the statement is executed as a part of a final return on Form CT-1 or Form CT-2, such statement shall be furnished in duplicate.

(c) *Time and place for filing returns.*—For provisions relating to the time and place for filing returns, see §§ 31.6071(a)-1 and 31.6091-1, respectively. [Reg. § 31.6011(a)-6.]

☐ [*T.D. 6354, 1-13-59. Amended by T.D. 7396, 1-12-76 and T.D. 8637, 12-20-95.*]

### [Reg. § 31.6011(a)-7]

**§ 31.6011(a)-7. Execution of returns.**—(a) *In general.*—Each return required under the regulations in this part, together with any prescribed copies or supporting data, shall be filled in and disposed of in accordance with the forms, instructions, and regulations applicable thereto. The return shall be carefully prepared so as fully and accurately to set forth the data required to be furnished therein. Returns which have not been so prepared will not be accepted as meeting the requirements of the regulations in this part. The return may be made by an agent in the name of the person required to make the return if an acceptable power of attorney is filed with the district director and if such return includes all taxes required to be reported by such person on such return for the period covered by the return. Only one return on any one prescribed form for a return period shall be filed by or for a taxpayer. Any supplemental return made on such form in accordance with § 31.6205-1 shall constitute a part of the return which it supplements. Except as may be provided under procedures authorized by the Commissioner with respect to taxes imposed by the Railroad Retirement Tax Act, consolidated returns of two or more employers are not permitted, as for example, returns of a parent and a subsidiary corporation. For provisions relating to the filing of returns of the taxes imposed by the Federal Insurance Contributions Act and of income tax withheld under section 3402 in the case of governmental employers, see § 31.3122 and § 31.3404-1.

(b) *Use of prescribed forms.*—(1) *In general.*—Copies of the prescribed return forms will so far as possible be regularly furnished taxpayers by the Internal Revenue Service. A taxpayer will not be excused from making a return, however, by the fact that no return form has been furnished to him. Taxpayers not supplied with the proper forms should make application therefor to an internal revenue office in ample time to have their returns prepared, verified, and filed on or before the due date with the internal revenue office with which they are required to file their returns. See § § 31.6071(a)-1 and 31.6091-1, relating, respectively, to the time and place for filing returns. In the absence of a prescribed return form, a statement made by a taxpayer disclosing the aggregate amount of wages or compensation reportable on such form for the period in respect of which a return is required and the amount of taxes due may be accepted as a tentative return. If filed within the prescribed time, the statement so made will relieve the taxpayer from liability for the addition to tax imposed for the delinquent filing of the return, provided that without unnecessary delay such tentative return is supplemented by a return made on the proper form. For additions to the tax in case of failure to file a return within the prescribed time, see the provisions of § 301.6651-1 of this chapter (Regulations on Procedure and Administration).

(2) *Permission for use of magnetic tape.*—In any case where the use of Form W-2 is required for the purpose of making a return or reporting information, such requirement may be satisfied by submitting the information required by such form on magnetic tape or other approved media, provided that the prior consent of the Commissioner of Social Security (or other authorized officer or employee thereof) has been obtained.

(c) *Signing and verification.*—For provisions relating to the signing of returns, see § 31.6061-1. For provisions relating to the verifying of returns, see § 31.6065(a)-1.

(d) *Reporting of identifying numbers.*—For provisions relating to the reporting of identifying numbers on returns required under the regulations in this part, see § 31.6109-1. [Reg. § 31.6011(a)-7.]

□ *[T.D. 6354, 1-13-59. Amended by T.D. 6472, 6-22-60; T.D. 6606, 8-24-62; T.D. 6883, 5-2-66; T.D. 7276, 5-4-73; T.D. 7396, 1-12-76 and T.D. 7580, 12-20-78.]*

### [Reg. § 31.6011(a)-8]

**§ 31.6011(a)-8. Composite return in lieu of specified form.**—The Commissioner may authorize the use, at the option of the employer, of a composite return in lieu of any form specified in this part for use by an employer, subject to such conditions, limitations, and special rules governing the preparation, execution, filing, and correction thereof as the Commissioner may deem appropriate. Such composite return shall consist of a form prescribed by the Commissioner and an attachment or attachments of magnetic tape or other approved media. Notwithstanding any provisions in this part to the contrary, a single form and attachment may comprise the returns of more than one employer. To the extent that the use of a composite return has been authorized by the Commissioner, references in this part to a specific form for use by the employer shall be deemed to refer also to a composite return under this section. [Reg. § 31.6011(a)-8.]

□ *[T.D. 7200, 8-15-72.]*

### [Reg. § 31.6011(a)-9]

**§ 31.6011(a)-9. Instructions to forms control as to which form is to be used.**—Notwithstanding provisions in this part which specify the use of a particular form for a return or other document required by this part, the use of a different form may be required by the latter form's instructions. In such case, the latter form shall be completed in accordance with its instructions. [Reg. § 31.6011(a)-9.]

□ *[T.D. 7351, 4-16-75.]*

### [Reg. § 31.6011(a)-10]

**§ 31.6011(a)-10. Instructions to forms may waive filing requirement in case of no liability tax returns.**—Notwithstanding provisions in this part which require that a tax return be filed, the instructions to the form on which a return of tax is otherwise required by this part to be made may waive such requirement with respect to a particular class or classes of no liability tax returns. Returns in a class for which such requirement has been so waived need not be made. [Reg. § 31.6011(a)-10.]

□ *[T.D. 8229, 9-14-88.]*

### [Reg. § 40.0-1]

**§ 40.0-1. Introduction.**—(a) *In general.*—The regulations in this part 40 are designated "Excise Tax Procedural Regulations." The regulations set forth administrative provisions relating to the excise taxes imposed by chapters 31, 32, 33, 34, 36, 38, 39, and 49 (except for the chapter 32 tax imposed by section 4181 (firearms tax) and the chapter 36 taxes imposed by sections 4461 (harbor maintenance tax) and 4481 (heavy vehicle use tax)), and to floor stocks taxes imposed on articles subject to any of these taxes. Chapter 31 relates to retail excise taxes; chapter 32 to manufacturers' excise taxes; chapter 33 to taxes imposed on communications services and air transportation; chapter 34 to taxes imposed on certain insurance policies; chapter 36 to taxes imposed on transportation by water; chapter 38 to environmental taxes; chapter 39 to taxes imposed on registration-required obligations; and chapter 49 to taxes imposed on indoor tanning services. References in this part to "taxes" also include references to the fees imposed by sections 4375 and 4376. See parts 43, 46, 48, 49, and 52 of this chapter for regulations relating to the imposition of tax.

(b) *References to forms.*—Any reference to a form in this part is also a reference to any other form designated for the same use by the Commissioner after October 22, 1992.

(c) *Definition of semimonthly period.*—The term "semimonthly period" means the first 15 days of a calendar month (the "first semimonthly period") or the portion of a calendar month following the 15th day of the month (the "second semimonthly period").

(d) *Person.*—For purposes of this part, each business unit that has, or is required to have, a separate employer identification number is treated as a separate person. Thus, business units (for example, a parent corporation and a subsidiary corporation, a partner and the partner's partnership, or the various members of a consolidated group), each of which has, or is required to have, a different employer identification number, are separate persons.

(e) *Applicability date.*—(1) *Paragraphs (a), (b), and (c) of this section.*—Paragraphs (a), (b), and (c) of this section apply to returns for periods beginning after March 31, 2013. For rules that apply before that date, *see* 26 CFR part 40, revised as of April 1, 2012.

(2) *Paragraph (d) of this section.*—Paragraph (d) of this section applies to returns for periods beginning on or after January 19, 2021. For rules that apply before that date, *see* 26 CFR part 40, revised as of April 1, 2020. [Reg. § 40.0-1.]

□ *[T.D. 8442, 10-21-92. Amended by T.D. 8887, 6-7-2000; T.D. 8963, 8-8-2001; T.D. 9486, 6-11-2010; T.D. 9602, 12-5-2012 T.D. 9621, 6-10-2013 and T.D. 9948, 1-14-2021.]*

### [Reg. § 40.6011(a)-1]

**§ 40.6011(a)-1. Returns.**—(a) *In general.*—(1) *Return required.*—The return of any tax to which this part 40 applies must be made on Form 720, *Quarterly Federal Excise Tax Return,* according to the instructions applicable to the form. The requirement for filing a return under this part 40 applies separately to each tax listed by IRS Number on Form 720. Except as provided in this paragraph (a)(1), an entry must be made on the line for the IRS Number in order to file a return of the tax corresponding to that number. The entry on an IRS Number line of the word "none," "zero," or comparable entry clearly indicating a denial of liability constitutes a return of that tax. The entry of the word "none" across the return or in the summary portion, provided it clearly indicates a denial of liability for all taxes, constitutes a return of all taxes listed on Form 720.

(2) *Period covered by return.*—(i) *In general.*—Except as provided in paragraphs (b) and (c) of this section, the return must be made for a period of one calendar quarter. A return must be filed for the first calendar quarter in which liability for tax is incurred (or in which tax must be collected and paid over) and for each subsequent calendar quarter, whether or not liability is incurred (or tax must be collected and paid over) during that subsequent quarter, until a final return under § 40.6011(a)-2 is filed. In the case of one-time filings (as defined in § 40.6011(a)-2(b)) and returns of floor stocks taxes under § 40.6011(a)-2(c), a first return is also a final return.

(ii) *First return.*—A person's return is a first return if the person was not required under this part 40 to file a return (other than a final return) for the preceding period.

(iii) *Floor stocks tax return.*—A return reporting liability for a floor stocks tax described in § 40.0-1(a) is a return for the calendar quarter in which the tax payment is due and not the calendar quarter in which the liability for tax is incurred.

(3) *Person required to file the return.*—Except in the case of a tax required to be collected and paid over, the person incurring liability for tax must file the return. In the case of a tax required to be

collected and paid over, the person required to collect the tax (and not the person incurring liability) must file the return.

(b) *Monthly and semimonthly returns.*—(1) *In general.*—If the district director determines that any person that is required under this section to file returns has failed to comply in a timely manner with the requirements of this part 40 relating to returns, payments, and deposits of tax, that person will be required, if so notified in writing by the district director, to make a return for a monthly or semimonthly period (as defined in § 40.0-1(c)). Each person so notified by the district director must make a return for the calendar month or semimonthly period in which the notice is received and for each calendar month or semimonthly period thereafter until the person has filed a final return or until the person is notified by the district director to resume making quarterly returns.

(2) *Certain persons liable for tax on taxable fuel.*—The district director may require a person to make a return of tax for a monthly or semimonthly period in the manner prescribed in paragraph (b)(1) of this section if the person—

(i) Is a bonded registrant (as defined in § 48.4101-1(b) of this chapter) at any time during the period;

(ii) has been registered under section 4101 for less than one year at the beginning of the period;

(iii) Meets the acceptable risk test of § 48.4101-1(f)(3) of this chapter by reason of § 48.4101-1(f)(3)(i)(B) of this chapter at any time during the period;

(iv) Has failed to comply with the applicable provisions of § 48.4101-1(h) of this chapter (relating to the terms and conditions of registration);

(v) Is liable for tax under § 48.4082-4(a) of this chapter (relating to the back-up tax on diesel fuel and kerosene) at any time during the period; or

(vi) Is liable for tax under section 4081 (relating to the tax on taxable fuel) at any time during the period and is not registered under section 4101 at that time.

(c) *Fees on health insurance policies and self-insured health plans.*—(1) *In general.*—A return that reports liability imposed by section 4375 or 4376 is a return for policies or plans with policy or plan years ending in the previous calendar year, and, for issuers that determine the average number of lives covered under a policy for purposes of section 4375 using the member months method under § 46.4375-1(c)(2)(v) or the state form method under § 46.4375-1(c)(2)(vi) of this chapter, the return is for all policies in effect during the previous calendar year. The second sentence of paragraph (a)(2)(i) of this section (relating to filing quarterly returns regardless of whether liability is incurred) does not apply to a person that files a Form 720, "Quarterly Federal Excise Tax Return," only to report liability imposed by section 4375 or 4376.

(2) *Applicability date.*—This paragraph (c) applies to returns that report liability imposed by section 4375 or 4376. [Reg. § 40.6011(a)-1.]

☐ [*T.D.* 8442, 10-21-92. *Amended by T.D.* 8659, 3-13-96; *T.D.* 8685, 11-8-96; *T.D.* 8748, 12-31-97; *T.D.* 8879, 3-30-2000; *T.D.* 8887, 6-7-2000; *T.D.* 8963, 8-8-2001 *and T.D.* 9602, 12-5-2012.]

### [Reg. § 41.6011(a)-1]

**§ 41.6011(a)-1. Returns.**—(a) *In general.*—(1) A person that is liable for tax under § 41.4481-2(a)(1)(i)(A), (B), or (C) must file a return for the taxable period with respect to the tax imposed by section 4481.

(2) A person that is liable for tax under § 41.4481-2(a)(1)(i)(D) must file a return for a taxable period with respect to the tax imposed by section 4481 if the Commissioner notifies the person that the tax for the taxable period has not been paid in full.

(3) A transferee of a vehicle that receives a statement described in the first sentence of § 41.4483-3(f) must file a return with the statement attached.

(4) A person that is liable for tax under § 41.4481-2(a)(1)(i)(A), (B), (C), or (D), after taking into account the modification required under § 41.4481-2(a)(2), is treated as liable for tax by the same provision of § 41.4481-2(a)(1)(i) for purposes of this section and must file a return.

(b) *Form 2290.*—The return required under paragraph (a) of this section is Form 2290, "Heavy Highway Vehicle Use Tax Return," or such other return as the Commissioner may prescribe. The return is made in accordance with the instructions applicable to the form.

(c) *Required use of electronic filing.*—(1) *In general.*—A person that files any return reporting 25 or more vehicles must file the return electronically, as prescribed by the Commissioner. For this purpose, the number of vehicles reported on a return is the total number of vehicles for which tax is reported and does not include vehicles for which a suspension of tax is claimed.

(2) *Examples.*—The application of this paragraph (c) may be illustrated by the following examples:

*Example* 1. A has 100 vehicles registered in its name, all of which have a taxable gross weight in excess of 55,000 pounds. Seventy-five of the vehicles are in use on July 1. Twenty-five are in dead storage as described in § 41.4482(c)-1(c). The vehicles in dead storage are not in use and they are not listed on the Schedule 1. A files Form 2290 electronically for the 75 vehicles in use on July 1 and receives a receipted Schedule 1. On August 23 of the same calendar year, A uses the remaining 25 vehicles. A does not file Form 2290 electronically but uses a paper Form 2290. A has failed to meet the requirements of section 4481(e) for the remaining 25 vehicles.

*Example* 2. Assume the same facts as in *Example* 1 except that on August 23, A uses 15 of the vehicles that were not used in July. The remaining 10 vehicles are not used in August. A does not file Form 2290 electronically but uses a paper Form 2290. A has correctly filed a return as required by section 4481(e).

(d) *Effective/applicability date.*—Paragraphs (a)(4) and (c) of this section apply to returns filed on and after July 1, 2015. For rules applicable before that date, see 26 CFR 41.6011(a)-1 (revised as of April 1, 2014). [Reg. § 41.6011(a)-1.]

☐ [*T.D.* 6216. *Amended by T.D.* 6743, 6-22-64; *T.D.* 8879, 3-30-2000 *and T.D.* 9698, 10-28-2014.]

### [Reg. § 44.6011(a)-1]

**§ 44.6011(a)-1. Returns.**—(a) *In general.*—Every person required to pay the tax on wagers imposed by section 4401 of the Code shall make for each month, from the daily records required by § § 44.4403-1 and 44.6001-1, a return on Form 730 in accordance with the instructions and regulations applicable thereto. A return shall be made for each month whether or not liability has been incurred for that month. If the taxpayer ceases operations which make him liable for the tax, the last return shall be marked "Final Return".

(b) *Return on Form 11-C.*—Every person required to pay the special tax imposed by section 4411 shall make a return on Form 11-C in accordance with the instructions and regulations applicable thereto. [Reg. § 44.6011(a)-1.]

☐ [*T.D.* 6370, 4-4-59.]

### [Reg. § 46.6011(a)-1]

**§ 46.6011(a)-1. Returns.**—(a) *In general.*—Liability for tax imposed under section 4371, 4501(a) or 4701 shall be reported on Form 720. Except as provided in paragraph (b) of this section, a return on Form 720 shall be filed for a period of one calendar quarter. Every person required to make a return on Form 720 for a return period ended December 31, 1954, shall make a return for each subsequent calendar quarter, month, or semimonthly period (whether or not liability was incurred for any tax reportable on such return for such return period) until he has filed a final return in accordance with § 46.6011(a)-2. Every person not required to make a return on Form 720 for a return period ended December 31, 1954, shall make a return for the first calendar quarter thereafter in which he incurs liability for tax imposed under section 4371, 4501(a) or 4701 and shall make a return for each subsequent calendar quarter, month, or semimonthly period until he has filed a final return in accordance with § 46.6011(a)-2.

(b) *Monthly and semimonthly returns.*—(1) *Requirement.*—If the district director determines that any taxpayer who is required to make deposit of taxes under the provisions of § 46.6302(c)-1 has failed to make deposits of such taxes, such taxpayer shall be required, if so notified in writing by the district director, to file a monthly or semimonthly return on Form 720, except that, if some other form is furnished by the district director for use in lieu of Form 720, the return shall be made on such other form. Every person so notified by the district director shall make a return for the calendar month or semimonthly period (as defined in § 46.6302(c)-1(b)(1)) in which the notice is received and for each calendar month or semimonthly period thereafter until he has filed a final return or is required to make returns on the basis of a different return period pursuant to notification as provided in subparagraph (2) of this paragraph.

(2) *Change of requirement.*—The district director, in his discretion, may notify the taxpayer in writing that he is required to make a quarterly or monthly return, if he has been filing returns for a semimonthly period, or is required to make a quarterly or semimonthly return, if he has been filing monthly returns.

(3) *Return for period change takes effect.*—If a taxpayer who has been filing quarterly returns receives notice to file a monthly or semimonthly return or a taxpayer who has been filing monthly returns receives notice to file a semimonthly return, the first return required pursuant to the notice shall be made for the month or semimonthly period in which the notice is received and all prior

months or semimonthly periods which are not includible in a prior period for which the taxpayer is required to file a return. If a taxpayer who has been filing monthly or semimonthly returns receives notice to file a quarterly return, the last month or semimonthly period for which a return shall be made is the last month or semimonthly period of the calendar quarter in which such notice is received. If a taxpayer who has been filing semimonthly returns receives notice to file a monthly return, the last semimonthly period for which a return shall be made is the last semimonthly period of the month in which such notice is received.

(c) *Signing and verification of returns.*—For provisions relating to the signing and verification of returns, see §§46.6061-1 and 46.6065, respectively.

(d) *Time and place for filing returns.*—For provisions relating to the time and place for filing returns, see §§46.6071(a)-1 and 46.6091-1, respectively. [Reg. §46.6011(a)-1.]

☐ [*T.D. 6461, 5-6-60. Amended by T.D. 6915, 3-29-67; T.D. 7023, 1-21-70 and T.D. 8102, 9-19-86.*]

### [Reg. §49.6011(a)-1]

**§49.6011(a)-1. Returns.**—(a) *In general.*—Liability for tax imposed under chapter 33 of the Code shall be reported on Form 720. Except as provided in paragraph (b) of this section, a return on Form 720 shall be filed for a period of one calendar quarter. Every person required to make a return on Form 720 for the return period ended December 31, 1958, shall make a return for each subsequent calendar quarter, month, or semimonthly period (whether or not liability was incurred for any tax reportable on the return for such return period) until he has filed a final return in accordance with §49.6011(a)-2. Every person not required to make a return on Form 720 for the return period ended December 31, 1958, shall make a return for the first calendar quarter thereafter in which he incurs liability for tax imposed under chapter 33, and shall make a return for each subsequent calendar quarter, month, or semimonthly period until he has filed a final return in accordance with §49.6011(a)-2. Each return required under the regulations in this part, together with any prescribed copies, records, or supporting data, shall be filled in and disposed of in accordance with the forms, instructions, and regulations applicable thereto.

(b) *Monthly and semimonthly returns.*—(1) *Requirement.*—If the district director determines that any person who is required to make deposit of taxes under the provisions of §49.6302(c)-1 has failed to make deposits of such taxes, such person shall be required, if so notified in writing by the district director, to file a monthly or semimonthly return on Form 720, except that, if some other form is furnished by the district director for use in lieu of Form 720, the return shall be made on such other form. Every person so notified by the district director shall make a return for the calendar month or semimonthly period (as defined in §49.6302(c)-1 (b)) in which the notice is received and for each calendar month or semimonthly period thereafter until he has filed a final return or is required to make returns on the basis of a different return period pursuant to notification as provided in subparagraph (2) of this paragraph.

(2) *Change of requirement.*—The district director, in his discretion, may notify the person in writing that he is required to make a quarterly or monthly return, if he has been filing returns for a semimonthly period, or is required to make a quarterly or semimonthly return, if he has been filing monthly returns.

(3) *Return for period change takes effect.*—If a person who has been filing quarterly returns receives notice to file a monthly or semimonthly return or a person who has been filing monthly returns receives notice to file a semimonthly return, the first return required pursuant to the notice shall be made for the month or semimonthly period in which the notice is received and all prior months or semimonthly periods which are not includible in a prior period for which the person is required to file a return. If a person who has been filing monthly or semimonthly returns receives notice to file a quarterly return, the last month or semimonthly period for which a return shall be made is the last month or semimonthly period of the calendar quarter in which such notice is received. If a person who has been filing semimonthly returns receives notice to file a monthly return, the last semimonthly period for which a return shall be made is the last semimonthly period of the month in which such notice is received. [Reg. §49.6011(a)-1.]

☐ [*T.D. 6915, 3-28-67.*]

### [Reg. §40.6011(a)-2]

**§40.6011(a)-2. Final returns.**—(a) *In general.*—(1) *Permanent cessation of operations.*—Any person that is required under §40.6011(a)-1 to make returns and that permanently ceases all operations with respect to which liability for tax was incurred (or with respect to which tax had to be collected and paid over) must make a final return in accordance with the instructions applicable to the form on which the return is made. A person does not make a final return if only a temporary or partial cessation of such operations occurs and must continue to file returns as required under §40.6011(a)-1.

(2) *Change in law without cessation of operations.*—Any person that is required under §40.6011(a)-1 to make returns must make a final return in accordance with the instructions applicable to the form on which the return is made if, by reason of a change in law, that person is no longer liable for any tax (or, in the case of a collected tax, is no longer responsible for collecting and paying over any tax). For example, if the tax on a product is changed from a retail tax to a manufacturers tax, a retailer formerly liable for the tax but now buying the product tax-paid from its supplier must make a final return (assuming that the retailer has no other tax liability reportable on the return).

(b) *Special rule for one-time filings.*—(1) *In general.*—A first return is also a final return if it is a one-time filing. A return is a one-time filing if the person reporting tax does not engage in any activity with respect to which tax is reportable on the return in the course of a trade or business.

(2) *Deposits not required.*—See §40.6302(c)-1(e)(2) for a rule providing that no deposit of taxes reported on a one-time filing is required.

(c) *Special rule for floor stocks taxes.*—A first return reporting only floor stocks taxes under this part 40 is also a final return. [Reg. §40.6011(a)-2.]

☐ [*T.D. 8442, 10-21-92. Amended by T.D. 8685, 11-8-96 and T.D. 8963, 8-8-2001.*]

### [Reg. §46.6011(a)-2]

**§46.6011(a)-2. Final returns.**—(a) *In general.*—Any person who is required to make a return on Form 720 pursuant to §46.6011(a)-1, and who in any return period ceases operations in respect of which he is required to make a return on such form, shall make such return for such period as a final return. Each return made as a final return shall be marked "Final Return" by the person filing the return. A person who has only temporarily ceased to incur liability for tax required to be reported on Form 720, because of temporary or seasonal suspension of his business or for other reasons, shall not make a final return but shall continue to file returns.

(b) *Statement to accompany final return.*—There shall be executed as a part of each final return a statement showing the address at which the records required by the regulations in this part will be kept, the name of the person keeping such records, and, if the business of a taxpayer has been sold or otherwise transferred to another person, the name and address of such person and the date on which such sale or transfer took place. If no such sale or transfer occurred or the taxpayer does not know the name of the person to whom the business was sold or transferred, that fact should be included in the statement. [Reg. §46.6011(a)-2.]

☐ [*T.D. 6461, 5-6-60.*]

### [Reg. §49.6011(a)-2]

**§49.6011(a)-2. Final returns.**—(a) *In general.*—Any person who is required to make a return on Form 720 pursuant to §49.6011(a)-1, and who in any return period ceases operations in respect of which he is required to make a return on such form, shall make his return for that period as a final return. Each return made as a final return shall be marked "Final Return" by the person filing the return. A person who has only temporarily ceased to incur liability for tax required to be reported on Form 720, because of temporary or seasonal suspension of his business or for other reasons, shall not make a final return but shall continue to file returns.

(b) *Statement to accompany final return.*—There shall be executed as a part of each final return a statement showing the address at which the records required by the regulations in this part will be kept, the name of the person keeping such records, and, if the business of a person required to make a return on Form 720 has been sold or otherwise transferred to another person, the name and address of such other person and the date on which the sale or transfer took place. If no sale or transfer occurred or the person required to make a return on Form 720 does not know the name of the person to whom the business was sold or transferred, that fact should be included in the statement. [Reg. §49.6011(a)-2.]

☐ [*T.D. 6915, 3-28-67.*]

## [Reg. §31.6011(b)-1]

**§31.6011(b)-1. Employers' identification numbers.—**
(a) *Requirement of application.*—(1) *In general.*—(i) *Before October 1, 1962.*—Except as provided in paragraph (b) of this section, every employer who on any day after December 31, 1954, and before October 1, 1962, has in his employ one or more individuals in employment for wages subject to the taxes imposed by the Federal Insurance Contributions Act, but who prior to such day neither has been assigned an identification number nor has applied therefor, shall make an application on Form SS-4 for an identification number.

(ii) *On or after October 1, 1962.*—Except as provided in paragraph (b) of this section, every employer who on any day after September 30, 1962, has in his employ one or more individuals in employment for wages which are subject to the taxes imposed by the Federal Insurance Contributions Act or which are subject to the withholding of income tax from wages under section 3402, but who prior to such day neither has been assigned an identification number nor has applied therefor, shall make an application on Form SS-4 for an identification number.

(iii) *Method of application.*—The application, together with any supplementary statement, shall be prepared in accordance with the form, instructions, and regulations applicable thereto, and shall set forth fully and clearly the data therein called for. Form SS-4 may be obtained from any district director or director of a service center or any district office of the Social Security Administration. The application shall be filed with the internal revenue officer designated in the instructions applicable to Form SS-4, or with the nearest district office of the Social Security Administration. The application shall be signed by (*a*) the individual, if the employer is an individual; (*b*) the president, vice president, or other principal officer, if the employer is a corporation; (*c*) a responsible and duly authorized member or officer having knowledge of its affairs, if the employer is a partnership or other unincorporated organization; or (*d*) the fiduciary, if the employer is a trust or estate. An identification number will be assigned to the employer in due course upon the basis of the information reported on the application required under this section.

(2) *Time for filing Form SS-4.*—The application for an identification number shall be filed on or before the seventh day after the first payment of wages to which reference is made in subparagraph (1) of this paragraph. For provisions relating to the time when wages are paid, see §31.3121(a)-2 and paragraph (b) of §31.3402(a)-1.

(b) *Employers who are assigned identification numbers without application.*—An identification number may be assigned, without application by the employer, in the case of an employer who has in his employ only employees who are engaged exclusively in the performance of domestic service in his private home not on a farm operated for profit (see §31.3121(a)(7)-1). If an identification number is so assigned, the employer is not required to make an application on Form SS-4 for the number.

(c) *Crew leaders.*—Any person who, as a crew leader within the meaning of section 3121(o), furnishes individuals to perform agricultural labor for another person shall, on or before the first date on which he furnishes such individuals to perform such labor for such other person, advise such other person of his name, permanent mailing address, or if none, present address, and identification number, if any.

(d) *Use of identification number.*—The identification number assigned to an employer (other than a household employer referred to in paragraph (b) of this section) shall be shown in the employer's records, and shall be shown in his claims to the extent required by the applicable forms, regulations, and instructions. For provisions relating to the inclusion of identification numbers in returns, statements on Form W-2, and depositary receipts, see §31.6109-1. [Reg. §31.6011(b)-1.]

☐ [*T.D. 6354, 1-13-59. Amended by T.D. 6606, 8-24-62 and T.D. 7012, 5-14-89.*]

## [Reg. §31.6011(b)-2]

**§31.6011(b)-2. Employees' account numbers.—**(a) *Requirement of application.*—(1) *In general.*—(i) *Before November 1, 1962.*—Every employee who on any day after December 31, 1954, and before November 1, 1962, is in employment for wages subject to the taxes imposed by the Federal Insurance Contributions Act, but who prior to such day has neither secured an account number nor made application therefor, shall make an application on Form SS-5 for an account number.

(ii) *On or after November 1, 1962.*—Every employee who on any day after October 31, 1962, is in employment for wages which are subject to the taxes imposed by the Federal Insurance Contributions Act or which are subject to the withholding of income tax from wages under section 3402, but who prior to such day has neither secured an account number nor made application therefor, shall make an application on Form SS-5 for an account number.

(iii) *Method of application.*—The application shall be prepared in accordance with the form, instructions, and regulations applicable thereto, and shall set forth fully and clearly the data therein called for. The employee shall file the application with any district office of the Social Security Administration or, if the employee is not working within the United States, with the district office of the Social Security Administration at Baltimore, Maryland. Form SS-5 may be obtained from any district office of the Social Security Administration or from any district director. An account number will be assigned to the employee by the Social Security Administration in due course upon the basis of information reported on the application required under this section. A card showing the name and account number of the employee to whom an account number has been assigned will be furnished to the employee by the Social Security Administration.

(2) *Time for filing Form SS-5.*—The application shall be filed on or before the seventh day after the occurrence of the first day of employment to which reference is made in subparagraph (1) of this paragraph, unless the employee leaves the employ of his employer before such seventh day, in which case the application shall be filed on or before the date on which the employee leaves the employ of his employer.

(3) *Changes and corrections.*—Any employee may have his account number changed at any time by applying to a district office of the Social Security Administration and showing good reasons for a change. With that exception, only one account number will be assigned to an employee. Any employee whose name is changed by marriage or otherwise, or who has stated incorrect information on Form SS-5, should report such change or correction to a district office of the Social Security Administration. Copies of the form for making such reports may be obtained from any district office of the Administration.

(b) *Duties of employee with respect to his account number.*—(1) *Information to be furnished to employer.*—An employee shall, on the day on which he enters the employ of any employer for wages, comply with the provisions of subdivision (i), (ii), (iii), or (iv) of this subparagraph, except that, if the employee's services for the employer consist solely of agricultural labor, domestic service in a private home of the employer not on a farm operated for profit, or service not in the course of the employer's trade or business, the employee shall comply with such provisions on the first day on which wages are paid to him by such employer, within the meaning of §31.3121(a)-2:

(i) *Employee who has account number card.*—If the employee has been issued an account number card by the Social Security Administration and has the card available, the employee shall show it to the employer.

(ii) *Employee who has number but card not available.*—If the employee does not have available the account number card issued to him by the Social Security Administration but knows what his account number is, and what his name is, exactly as shown on such card, the employee shall advise the employer of such number and name. Care must be exercised that the employer is correctly advised of such number and name.

(iii) *Employee who has receipt acknowledging application.*—If the employee does not have an account number card but has available a receipt issued to him by an office of the Social Security Administration acknowledging that an application for an account number has been received, the employee shall show such receipt to the employer.

(iv) *Employee who is unable to furnish number or receipt.*—If an employee is unable to comply with the requirement of subdivision (i), (ii), or (iii) of this subparagraph, the employee shall furnish to the employer a statement in writing, signed by the employee, setting forth the date of the statement, the employee's full name, present address, date and place of birth, father's full name, mother's full name before marriage, and the employee's sex, including a statement as to whether the employee has previously filed an application on Form SS-5 and, if so, the date and place of such filing. The information required by this subdivision shall be furnished on Form SS-5, if a copy of Form SS-5 is available. The furnishing of such a Form SS-5 or other statement by the employee to the employer does not relieve the employee of his obligation to make an application on Form SS-5 and file it with a district office of the Social Security Administration as required by paragraph (a) of this section. The foregoing provisions of this subdivision are not applicable to an employee engaged exclusively in the performance of domestic service in a private home of his employer not on a farm operated for profit, or in the performance of agricultural labor, if the services are performed for an employer other than an employer required to file returns of the taxes imposed by the Federal Insurance Contributions Act with the office of the United States Internal Revenue Service in Puerto Rico. However, such employee shall advise the employer of his full name and present address.

For provisions relating to the duties of an employer when furnished the information required by subdivision (i), (ii), (iii), or (iv) of this subparagraph, see paragraph (c) of this section.

(2) *Additional information to be furnished by employee to employer.*— Every employee who, on the day on which he is required to comply with subdivision (i), (ii), (iii), or (iv) of subparagraph (1) of this paragraph, has an account number card but for any reason does not show such card to the employer on such day shall promptly thereafter show the card to the employer. An employee who does not have an account number card on such day shall, upon receipt of an account number card from the Social Security Administration, promptly show such card to the employer, if he is still in the employ of that employer. If the employee has left the employ of the employer when the employee receives an account number card from the Social Security Administration, he shall promptly advise the employer of his account number and name exactly as shown on such card. The account number originally assigned to an employee (or the number as changed in accordance with paragraph (a)(3) of this section) shall be used by the employee as required by this paragraph even though he enters the employ of other employers.

(3) *Furnishing of account number by employee to employer.*—See §31.6109-1 for additional provisions relating to the furnishing of an account number by the employee to his employer.

(c) *Duties of employer with respect to employees' account numbers.*— (1) *Employee who shows account number.*—Upon being shown the account number card issued to an employee by the Social Security Administration, the employer shall enter the account number and name, exactly as shown on the card, in the employer's records, returns, statements for employees, and claims to the extent required by the applicable forms, regulations, and instructions.

(2) *Employee who does not show account number card.*—With respect to an employee who, on the day on which he is required to comply with subdivision (i), (ii), (iii), or (iv) of paragraph (b)(1) of this section, does not show the employer an account number card issued to the employee by the Social Security Administration, the employer shall request such employee to show him such card. If the card is not shown, the employer shall comply with the applicable provisions of subdivision (i), (ii), (iii), (iv), or (v) of this subparagraph:

(i) *Employee who has not applied for account number.*—If the employee has not been assigned an account number and has not made application therefor with a district office of the Social Security Administration, the employer shall inform the employee of his duties under this section.

(ii) *Employee who has account number.*—If the employee advises the employer of his number and name as shown on his account number card, as provided in paragraph (b)(1)(ii) of this section, the employer shall enter such number and name in his records.

(iii) *Employee who has receipt for application.*—If the employee shows the employer, as provided in paragraph (b)(1)(iii) of this section, a receipt issued to him by an office of the Social Security Administration acknowledging that an application for an account number has been received from the employee, the employer shall enter in his records with respect to such employee the name and address of the employee exactly as shown on the receipt, the expiration date of the receipt, and the address of the issuing office. The receipt shall be retained by the employee.

(iv) *Employee who furnishes Form SS-5 or statement.*—If the employee furnishes information to the employer as provided in paragraph (b)(1)(iv) of this section, the employer shall retain such information for use as provided in subparagraph (3)(ii) of this paragraph.

(v) *Household or agricultural employees.*—If the employee advises the employer of his full name and present address in accordance with those provisions of paragraph (b)(1)(iv) of this section which are applicable in the case of employees engaged exclusively in the performance of domestic service in a private home of the employer not on a farm operated for profit, or agricultural labor, the employer shall enter such name and address in his records.

(3) *Account number unknown when return is filed.*—In any case in which the employee's account number is for any reason unknown to the employer at the time the employer's return is filed for any return

period with respect to which the employer is required to report the wages paid to such employee—

(i) *If employee has shown receipt for application.*—If the employee has shown to the employer, as provided in paragraph (b)(1)(iii) of this section, a receipt issued to him by an office of the Social Security Administration acknowledging that an application for an account number has been received from the employee, the employer shall enter on the return, with the entry with respect to the employee, the name and address of the employee exactly as shown on the receipt, the expiration date of the receipt, and the address of the issuing office.

(ii) *If employee furnished Form SS-5 or statement.*—If the employee has furnished information to the employer as provided in paragraph (b)(1)(iv) of this section, the employer shall prepare a copy of the Form SS-5 or statement furnished by the employee and attach the copy to the return.

(iii) *If employee did not furnish receipt, Form SS-5, or statement.*— If neither subdivision (i) nor (ii) of this subparagraph is applicable, the employer shall, except as provided in subparagraph (4) of this paragraph, attach to the return a Form SS-5 or statement, signed by the employer, setting forth as fully and clearly as practicable the employee's full name, his present or last known address, date and place of birth, father's full name, mother's full name before marriage, the employee's sex, and a statement as to whether an application for an account number has previously been filed by the employee and, if so, the date and place of such filing. The employer shall also insert in such Form SS-5 or statement an explanation of why he has not secured from the employee the information referred to in paragraph (b)(1)(iv) of this section, and shall insert the word "Employer" as part of his signature.

(4) *Household or agricultural employees.*—The provisions of subparagraph (3)(iii) of this paragraph are not applicable with respect to an employee engaged exclusively in the performance of domestic service in a private home of his employer not on a farm operated for profit, or in the performance of agricultural labor, if the services are performed for an employer other than an employer required to file returns of the taxes imposed by the Federal Insurance Contributions Act with the office of the United States Internal Revenue Service in Puerto Rico. If any such employee has not furnished to the employer the information required by paragraph (b)(1)(i), (ii), or (iii) of this section prior to the time the employer's return is filed for any return period with respect to which the employer is required to report wages paid to such employee, the employer shall enter the word "Unknown" in the account number column of the return and (i) file with the return a statement showing the employee's full name and present or last known address, or (ii) enter such address on the return form immediately below the name of the employee.

(5) *Where to obtain Form SS-5.*—Employers may obtain copies of Form SS-5 from any district office of the Social Security Administration or from any district director.

(6) *Prospective employees.*—While not mandatory, it is suggested that the employer advise any prospective employee who does not have an account number of the requirements of paragraphs (a) and (b) of this section. [Reg. §31.6011(b)-2.]

☐[T.D. 6354, 1-13-59. Amended by T.D. 6606, 8-24-62.]

### [Reg. §301.6011(g)-1]

§301.6011(g)-1. **Disclosure by taxable party to the tax-exempt entity.**—(a) *Requirement of disclosure.*—(1) *In general.*—Except as provided in paragraph (d)(2) of this section, any taxable party (as defined in paragraph (c) of this section) to a prohibited tax shelter transaction (as defined in section 4965(e) and §53.4965-3 of this chapter) must disclose by statement to each tax-exempt entity (as defined in section 4965(c) and §53.4965-2 of this chapter) that the taxable party knows or has reason to know is a party to such transaction (as defined in paragraph (b) of this section) that the transaction is a prohibited tax shelter transaction.

(2) *Determining whether a taxable party knows or has reason to know.*—Whether a taxable party knows or has reason to know that a tax-exempt entity is a party to a prohibited tax shelter transaction is based on all the facts and circumstances. If the taxable party knows or has reason to know that a prohibited tax shelter transaction involves a tax-exempt, tax indifferent or tax-favored entity, relevant factors for determining whether the taxable party knows or has reason to know that a specific tax-exempt entity is a party to the transaction include—

(i) The extent of the efforts made to determine whether a tax-exempt entity is facilitating the transaction by reason of its tax-exempt, tax indifferent or tax-favored status (or is identified in published guidance, by type, class or role, as a party to the transaction); and

(ii) If a tax-exempt entity is facilitating the transaction by reason of its tax-exempt, tax indifferent or tax-favored status (or is identified in published guidance, by type, class or role, as a party to the transaction), the extent of the efforts made to determine the identity of the tax-exempt entity.

(b) *Definition of tax-exempt party to a prohibited tax shelter transaction.*—For purposes of section 6011(g), a tax-exempt entity is a party to a prohibited tax shelter transaction if the entity is defined as such under § 53.4965-4 of this chapter.

(c) *Definition of taxable party.*—(1) *In general.*—For purposes of this section, the term *taxable party* means—

(i) A person who has entered into and participates or expects to participate in the transaction under § § 1.6011-4(c)(3)(i)(A), (B), or (C), 20.6011-4, 25.6011-4, 31.6011-4, 53.6011-4, 54.6011-4, or 56.6011-4 of this chapter; or

(ii) A person who is designated as a taxable party by the Secretary in published guidance.

(2) *Special rules.*—(i) *Certain listed transactions.*—If a transaction that was otherwise not a prohibited tax shelter transaction becomes a listed transaction after the filing of a person's tax return (including an amended return) reflecting either tax consequences or a tax strategy described in the published guidance listing the transaction (or a tax benefit derived from tax consequences or a tax strategy described in the published guidance listing the transaction), the person is a taxable party beginning on the date the transaction is described as a listed transaction in published guidance.

(ii) *Persons designated as non-parties.*—Published guidance may identify which persons, by type, class or role, will not be treated as a party to a prohibited tax shelter transaction for purposes of section 6011(g).

(d) *Time for providing disclosure statement.*—(1) *In general.*—A taxable party to a prohibited tax shelter transaction must make the disclosure required by this section to each tax-exempt entity that the taxable party knows or has reason to know is a party to the transaction within 60 days after the last to occur of—

(i) The date the person becomes a taxable party to the transaction within the meaning of paragraph (c) of this section;

(ii) The date the taxable party knows or has reason to know that the tax-exempt entity is a party to the transaction within the meaning of paragraph (b) of this section; or

(iii) July 6, 2010.

(2) *Termination of a disclosure obligation.*—A person shall not be required to provide the disclosure otherwise required by this section if the person does not know or have reason to know that the tax-exempt entity is a party to the transaction within the meaning of paragraph (b) of this section on or before the first date on which the transaction is required to be disclosed by the person under § § 1.6011-4, 20.6011-4, 25.6011-4, 31.6011-4, 53.6011-4, 54.6011-4, or 56.6011-4 of this chapter.

(3) Disclosure is not required with respect to any prohibited tax shelter transaction entered into by a tax-exempt entity on or before May 17, 2006.

(e) *Frequency of disclosure.*—One disclosure statement is required per tax-exempt entity per transaction. See paragraph (h) of this section for rules relating to designation agreements.

(f) *Form and content of disclosure statement.*—The statement disclosing to the tax-exempt entity that the transaction is a prohibited tax shelter transaction must be a written statement that—

(1) Identifies the type of prohibited tax shelter transaction (including the published guidance citation for a listed transaction); and

(2) States that the tax-exempt entity's involvement in the transaction may subject either it or its entity manager(s) or both to excise taxes under section 4965 and to disclosure obligations under section 6033(a) of the Internal Revenue Code.

(g) *To whom disclosure is made.*—The disclosure statement must be provided—

(1) In the case of a non-plan entity as defined in § 53.4965-2(b) of this chapter, to—

(i) Any entity manager of the tax-exempt entity with authority or responsibility similar to that exercised by an officer, director or trustee of an organization; or

(ii) If a person described in paragraph (g)(1)(i) of this section is not known, to the primary contact on the transaction.

(2) In the case of a plan entity as defined in § 53.4965-2(c) of this chapter, including a fully self-directed qualified plan, IRA, or other savings arrangement, to any entity manager of the plan entity who

approved or otherwise caused the entity to become a party to the prohibited tax shelter transaction.

(h) *Designation agreements.*—If more than one taxable party is required to disclose a prohibited tax shelter transaction under this section, the taxable parties may designate by written agreement a single taxable party to disclose the transaction. The transaction must then be disclosed in accordance with this section. The designation of one taxable party to disclose the transaction does not relieve the other taxable parties of their obligation to disclose the transaction to a tax-exempt entity that is a party to the transaction in accordance with this section, if the designated taxable party fails to disclose the transaction to the tax-exempt entity in a timely manner.

(i) *Penalty for failure to provide disclosure statement.*—See section 6707A for the penalty applicable to the failure to disclose a prohibited tax shelter transaction in accordance with this section.

(j) *Effective date/applicability date.*—This section will apply with respect to transactions entered into by a tax-exempt entity after May 17, 2006. [Reg. § 301.6011(g)-1.]

☐ [T.D. 9492, 7-2-2010.]

**[Reg. § 1.6012-1]**

**§ 1.6012-1. Individuals required to make returns of income.**— (a) *Individual citizen or resident.*—(1) *In general.*—Except as provided in subparagraph (2) of this paragraph, an income tax return must be filed by every individual for each taxable year beginning before January 1, 1973, during which he receives $600 or more of gross income, and for each taxable year beginning after December 31, 1972, during which he receives $750 or more of gross income, if such individual is—

(i) A citizen of the United States, whether residing at home or abroad,

(ii) A resident of the United States even though not a citizen thereof, or

(iii) An alien bona fide resident of Puerto Rico or any section 931 possession, as defined in § 1.931-1(c)(1), during the entire taxable year.

(2) *Special rules.*—(i) For taxable years beginning before January 1, 1970, an individual who is described in subparagraph (1) of this paragraph and who has attained the age of 65 before the close of his taxable year must file an income tax return only if he receives $1,200 or more of gross income during his taxable year.

(ii) For taxable years beginning after December 31, 1969, and before January 1, 1973, an individual described in subparagraph (1) of this paragraph (other than an individual referred to in section 142(b))—

(a) Who is not married (as determined by applying section 143(a) and the regulations thereunder) must file an income tax return only if he receives $1,700 or more of gross income during his taxable year, except that if such an individual has attained the age of 65 before the close of his taxable year an income tax return must be filed by such individual only if he receives $2,300 or more of gross income during his taxable year.

(b) Who is entitled to make a joint return under section 6013 and the regulations thereunder must file an income tax return only if his gross income received during his taxable year, when combined with the gross income of his spouse received during his taxable year, is $2,300 or more. However, if such individual or his spouse has attained the age of 65 before the close of the taxable year an income tax return must be filed by such individual only if their combined gross income is $2,900 or more. If both the individual and his spouse have attained the age of 65 before the close of the taxable year such return must be filed only if their combined gross income is $3,500 or more. However, this subdivision (ii)(b) shall not apply if the individual and his spouse did not have the same household as their home at the close of their taxable year, if such spouse files a separate return for a taxable year which includes any part of such individual's taxable year,

or if any other taxpayer is entitled to an exemption for such individual or his spouse under section 151(e) for such other taxpayer's taxable year beginning in the calendar year in which such individual's taxable year begins. For example, a married student more than half of whose support is furnished by his father must file an income tax return if he receives $600 or more of gross income during his taxable year.

(iii) For taxable years beginning after December 31, 1972, an individual described in subparagraph (1) of this paragraph (other than an individual referred to in section 142(b))—

(a) Who is not married (as determined by applying section 143(a) and the regulations thereunder) must file an income tax return only if he receives $1,750 or more of gross income during his taxable year, except that if such an individual has attained the age of 65 before the close of his taxable year an income tax return must be filed by such individual only if he receives $2,500 or more of gross income during his taxable year.

(b) Who is entitled to make a joint return under section 6013 and the regulations thereunder must file an income tax return only if his gross income received during his taxable year, when combined with the gross income of his spouse received during his taxable year, is $2,500 or more. However, if such individual or his spouse has attained the age of 65 before the close of the taxable year an income tax return must be filed by such individual only if their combined gross income is $3,250 or more. If both the individual and his spouse attain the age of 65 before the close of the taxable year such return must be filed only if their combined gross income is $4,000 or more. However, this subdivision (iii)(b) shall not apply if the individual and his spouse did not have the same household as their home at the close of their taxable year, if such spouse files a separate return for a taxable year which includes any part of such individual's taxable year, or if any other taxpayer is entitled to an exemption for the taxpayer or his spouse under section 151(e) for such other taxpayer's taxable year beginning in the calendar year in which such individual's taxable year begins. For example, a married student more than half of whose support is furnished by his father must file an income tax return if he receives $750 or more of gross income during the taxable year.

(iv) For purposes of section 6012(a)(1)(A)(ii) and subdivisions (ii)(b) and (iii)(b) of this subparagraph, an individual and his spouse are considered to have the same household as their home at the close of a taxable year if the same household constituted the principal place of abode of both the individual and his spouse at the close of such taxable year (or on the date of death, if the individual or his spouse died within the taxable year). The individual and his spouse will be considered to have the same household as their home at the close of the taxable year notwithstanding a temporary absence from the household due to special circumstances, as, for example, in the case of a nonpermanent failure on the part of the individual and his spouse to have a common abode by reason of illness, education, business, vacation, or military service. For example, A, a calendar-year individual under 65 years of age, is married to B, also under 65 years of age, and is a member of the Armed Forces of the United States. During 1970 A is transferred to an overseas base. A and B give up their home, which they had jointly occupied until that time; B moves to the home of her parents for the duration of A's absence. They fully intend to set up a new joint household upon A's return. Neither A nor B must file a return for 1970 if their combined gross income for the year is less than $2,300 and if no other taxpayer is entitled to a dependency exemption for A or B under section 151(e).

(v) In the case of a short taxable year referred to in section 443(a)(1), an individual described in subparagraph (1) of this paragraph shall file an income tax return if his gross income received during such short taxable year equals or exceeds his own personal exemption allowed by section 151(b) (prorated as provided in section 443(c)) and, when applicable, his additional exemption for age 65 or more allowed by section 151(c)(1) (prorated as provided in section 443(c)).

(vi) For rules relating to returns required to be made by every individual who is liable for one or more qualified State individual income taxes, as defined in section 6362, for a taxable year, see paragraph (b) of § 301.6361-1 of this chapter (Regulations on Procedure and Administration).

(vii) For taxable years beginning after December 31, 1978, an individual who receives payments during the calendar year in which the taxable year begins under section 3507 (relating to advance payment of earned income credit) must file an income tax return.

(viii) For rules relating to returns required of taxpayers who receive advance payments of the premium tax credit under section 36B, see § 1.6011-8(a).

(3) *Earned income from without the United States and gain from sale of residence.*—For the purpose of determining whether an income tax return must be filed for any taxable year beginning after December 31, 1957, gross income shall be computed without regard to the exclusion provided for in section 911 (relating to earned income from sources without the United States). For the purpose of determining whether an income tax return must be filed for any taxable year ending after December 31, 1963, gross income shall be computed without regard to the exclusion provided for in section 121 (relating to sale of residence by individual who has attained age 65). In the case of an individual claiming an exclusion under section 121, he shall attach Form 2119 to the return required under this paragraph and in the case of an individual claiming an exclusion under section 911, he shall attach Form 2555 to the return required under this paragraph.

(4) *Return of income of minor.*—A minor is subject to the same requirements and elections for making returns of income as are other individuals. Thus, for example, for a taxable year beginning after December 31, 1972, a return must be made by or for a minor who has an aggregate of $1,750 of gross income from funds held in trust for him and from his personal services, regardless of the amount of his taxable income. The return of a minor must be made by the minor himself or must be made for him by his guardian or other person charged with the care of the minor's person or property. See paragraph (b)(3) of § 1.6012-3. See § 1.73-1 for inclusion in the minor's gross income of amounts received for his personal services. For the amount of tax which is considered to have been properly assessed against the parent, if not paid by the child, see section 6201(c) and paragraph (c) of § 301.6201-1 of this chapter (Regulations on Procedure and Administration).

(5) *Returns made by agents.*—The return of income may be made by an agent if, by reason of disease or injury, the person liable for the making of the return is unable to make it. The return may also be made by an agent if the taxpayer is unable to make the return by reason of continuous absence from the United States (including Puerto Rico as if a part of the United States) for a period of at least 60 days prior to the date prescribed by law for making the return. In addition, a return may be made by an agent if the taxpayer requests permission, in writing, of the district director for the internal revenue district in which is located the legal residence or principal place of business of the person liable for the making of the return, and such district director determines that good cause exists for permitting the return to be so made. However, assistance in the preparation of the return may be rendered under any circumstances. Whenever a return is made by an agent it must be accompanied by a power of attorney (or copy thereof) authorizing him to represent his principal in making, executing, or filing the return. A Form 2848, when properly completed, is sufficient. In addition, where one spouse is physically unable by reason of disease or injury to sign a joint return, the other spouse may, with the oral consent of the one who is incapacitated, sign the incapacitated spouse's name in the proper place on the return followed by the words "By .......... Husband (or Wife)," and by the signature of the signing spouse in his own right, provided that a dated statement signed by the spouse who is signing the return is attached to and made a part of the return stating—

(i) The name of the return being filed,

(ii) The taxable year,

(iii) The reason for the inability of the spouse who is incapacitated to sign the return, and

(iv) That the spouse who is incapacitated consented to the signing of the return.

The taxpayer and his agent, if any, are responsible for the return as made and incur liability for the penalties provided for erroneous, false, or fraudulent returns.

(6) *Form of return.*—Form 1040 is prescribed for general use in making the return required under this paragraph. Form 1040A is an optional short form which, in accordance with paragraph (a)(7) of this section, may be used by certain taxpayers. A taxpayer otherwise entitled to use Form 1040A as his return for any taxable year may not make his return on such form if he elects not to take the standard deduction provided in section 141, and in such case he must make his return on Form 1040. For taxable years beginning before January 1, 1970, a taxpayer entitled under section 6014 and § 1.6014-1 to elect not to show his tax on his return must, if he desires to exercise such election, make his return on Form 1040A. Form 1040W is an optional short form which, in accordance with paragraph (a)(8) of this section, may be used only with respect to taxable years beginning after December 31, 1958 and ending before December 31, 1961.

(7)(i) *Use of Form 1040A.*—Form 1040A may be filed only by those individuals entitled to use such form as provided by and in accordance with the instructions for such form.

(ii) *Computation and payment of tax.*—Unless a taxpayer is entitled to elect under section 6014 and § 1.6014-1 not to show the tax on Form 1040A and does so elect, he shall compute and show on his return on Form 1040A the amount of the tax imposed by subtitle A of the Code and shall, without notice and demand therefor, pay any unpaid balance of such tax not later than the date fixed for filing the return.

(iii) *Change of election to use Form 1040A.*—A taxpayer who has elected to make his return on Form 1040A may change such election. Such change of election shall be within the time and subject to the conditions prescribed in section 144(b) and § 1.144-2 relating to change of election to take, or not to take the standard deduction.

(iv) *Status benefits not allowable.*—The status of a taxpayer as head of household as defined in section 1(b)(2), or as a surviving spouse, as defined in section 2(b), shall not be considered in determining the tax liability of a taxpayer filing Form 1040A.

(8) *Use of Form 1040W for certain taxable years.*—(i) *In general.*—An individual may use Form 1040W as his return for any taxable year beginning after December 31, 1958, and ending before December 31, 1961, in which the gross income of the individual, regardless of the amount thereof—

(a) Consists entirely of remuneration for personal services performed as an employee (whether or not such remuneration constitutes wages as defined in section 3401(a)), dividends, or interest, and

(b) Does not include more than $200 from dividends and interest.

For purposes of determining whether gross income from dividends and interest exceeds $200, dividends from domestic corporations are taken into account to the extent that they are includible in gross income. For purposes of this subparagraph, any reference to Form 1040 in §§ 1.4-2, 1.142-1, and 1.144-1 and this section shall also be deemed a reference to Form 1040W.

(ii) *Change of election to use Form 1040W.*—A taxpayer who has elected to make his return on Form 1040W may change such election. Such change of election shall be within the time and subject to the conditions prescribed in section 144(b) and § 1.144-2, relating to change of election to take, or not to take, the standard deduction.

(iii) *Joint return of husband and wife on Form 1040W.*—A husband and wife, eligible under section 6013 and the regulations thereunder to file a joint return for the taxable year, may, subject to the provisions of this subparagraph, make a joint return on Form 1040W for any taxable year beginning after December 31, 1958, and ending before December 31, 1961, in which the aggregate gross income of the spouses (regardless of amount) consists entirely of remuneration for personal services performed as an employee (whether or not such remuneration constitutes wages as defined in section 3401(a)), dividends, or interest, and does not include more than $200 from dividends and interest. For purposes of determining whether gross income from sources to which the $200 limitation applies exceeds such amount in cases where both spouses receive dividends from domestic corporations, the amount of such dividends received by each spouse is taken into account to the extent that such dividends are includible in gross income. See section 116 and §§ 1.116-1 and 1.116-2. If a joint return is made by husband and wife on Form 1040W, the liability for the tax shall be joint and several.

(9) *Items of tax preference.*—For a taxable year ending after December 31, 1969, an individual shall attach Form 4625 to the return required by this paragraph if during the year the individual—

(i) has items of tax preference (described in section 57) in excess of its minimum tax exemption (determined under § 1.58-1) or

(ii) uses a net operating loss carryover from a prior taxable year in which it deferred minimum tax under section 56(b).

(b) *Return of nonresident alien individual.*—(1) *Requirement of return.*—(i) *In general.*—Except as otherwise provided in subparagraph (2) of this paragraph, every nonresident alien individual (other than one treated as a resident under section 6013(g) or (h)) who is engaged in trade or business in the United States at any time during the taxable year or who has income which is subject to taxation under subtitle A of the Code shall make a return on Form 1040NR. For this purpose it is immaterial that the gross income for the taxable year is less than the minimum amount specified in section 6012(a) for making a return. Thus, a nonresident alien individual who is engaged in a trade or business in the United States at any time during the taxable year is required to file a return on Form 1040NR even though (a) he has no income which is effectively connected with the conduct of a trade or business in the United States, (b) he has no income from sources within the United States, or (c) his income is exempt from income tax by reason of an income tax convention or any section of the Code. However, if the nonresident alien individual has no gross income for the taxable year, he is not required to complete the return schedules but must attach a statement to the return indicating the nature of any exclusions claimed and the amount of such exclusions to the extent such amounts are readily determinable.

(ii) *Treaty income.*—If the gross income of a nonresident alien individual includes treaty income, as defined in paragraph (b)(1) of § 1.871-12, a statement shall be attached to the return on Form 1040NR showing with respect to that income—

(a) The amounts of tax withheld,

(b) The names and post office addresses of withholding agents, and

(c) Such other information as may be required by the return form, or by the instructions issued with respect to the form, to show the taxpayer's entitlement to the reduced rate of tax under the tax convention.

(2) *Exceptions.*—(i) *Return not required when tax is fully paid at source.*—A nonresident alien individual (other than one treated as a resident under section 6013(g) or (h)) who at no time during the taxable year is engaged in a trade or business in the United States is not required to make a return for the taxable year if his tax liability for the taxable year is fully satisfied by the withholding of tax at source under chapter 3 of the Code. This subdivision does not apply to a nonresident alien individual who has income for the taxable year which is treated under section 871(c) or (d) and § 1.871-9 (relating to students or trainees) or § 1.871-10 (relating to real property income) as income which is effectively connected for the taxable year with the conduct of a trade or business in the United States by that individual, or to a nonresident alien individual making a claim under § 301.6402-3 of this chapter (Procedure and Administration Regulations) for the refund of an overpayment of tax for the taxable year. In addition, this subdivision does not apply to a nonresident alien individual who has income for the taxable year that is treated under section 871(b)(1) as effectively connected with the conduct of a trade or business within the United States by reason of the operation of section 897. For purposes of this subdivision, some of the items of income from sources within the United States upon which the tax liability will not have been fully satisfied by the withholding of tax at source under chapter 3 of the Code are:

(a) Interest upon so-called tax-free covenant bonds upon which, in accordance with section 1451 and § 1.1451-1, a tax of only 2 percent is required to be withheld at the source,

(b) In the case of bonds or other evidences of indebtedness issued after September 28, 1965, amounts described in section 871(a)(1)(C),

(c) Capital gains described in section 871(a)(2) and paragraph (d) of § 1.871-7, and

(d) Accrued interest received in connection with the sale of bonds between interest dates, which, in accordance with paragraph (h) of § 1.1441-4, is not subject to withholding of tax at the source.

(ii) *Return of individual for taxable year of change of U.S. citizenship or residence.*—(a) If an alien individual becomes a citizen or resident of the United States during the taxable year and is a citizen or resident of the United States on the last day of such year, he must make a return of Form 1040 for the taxable year. However, a separate schedule is required to be attached to this return to show the income tax computation for the part of the taxable year during which the alien was neither a citizen nor resident of the United States, unless an election under section 6013(g) or (h) is in effect for the alien. A Form 1040NR, clearly marked "Statement" across the top, may be used as such a separate schedule.

(b) If an individual abandons his U.S. citizenship or residence during the taxable year and is not a citizen or resident of the United States on the last day of such year, he must make a return on Form 1040NR for the taxable year, even if an election under section 6013(g) was in effect for the taxable year preceding the year of abandonment. However, a separate schedule is required to be attached to this return to show the income tax computation for the part of the taxable year during which the individual was a citizen or resident of the United States. A Form 1040, clearly marked "Statement" across the top, may be used as such a separate schedule.

(c) A return is required under this subdivision (ii) only if the individual is otherwise required to make a return for the taxable year.

(iii) *Beneficiaries of estates or trusts.*—A nonresident alien individual who is a beneficiary of an estate or trust which is engaged in trade or business in the United States is not required to make a return for the taxable year merely because he is deemed to be engaged in trade or business within the United States under section 875(2). However, such nonresident alien beneficiary will be required to make a return if he otherwise satisfies the conditions of subparagraph (1)(i) of this paragraph for making a return.

(iv) *Certain alien residents of Puerto Rico.*—This paragraph does not apply to a nonresident alien individual who is a bona fide resident of Puerto Rico during the taxable year. See section 876 and paragraph (a)(1)(iii) of this section.

(3) *Representative or agent for nonresident alien individual.*—(i) *Cases where power of attorney is not required.*—The responsible representative or agent within the United States of a nonresident alien individual shall make on behalf of his nonresident alien principal a return of, and shall pay the tax on, all income coming within his control as representative or agent which is subject to the income tax under subtitle A of the Code. The agency appointment will determine how completely the agent is substituted for the principal for tax purposes. Any person who collects interest or dividends on deposited securities of a nonresident alien individual, executes ownership certificates in connection therewith, or sells such securities under special instructions shall not be deemed merely by reason of such acts to be the responsible representative or agent of the nonresident alien individual. If the responsible representative or agent does not

have a specific power of attorney from the nonresident alien individual to file a return in his behalf, the return shall be accompanied by a statement to the effect that the representative or agent does not possess specific power of attorney to file a return for such individual but that the return is being filed in accordance with the provisions of this subdivision.

(ii) *Cases where power of attorney is required.*—Whenever a return of income of a nonresident alien individual is made by an agent acting under a duly authorized power of attorney for that purpose, the return shall be accompanied by the power of attorney in proper form, or a copy thereof, specifically authorizing him to represent his principal in making, executing, and filing the income tax return. Form 2848 may be used for this purpose. The agent, as well as the taxpayer, may incur liability for the penalties provided for erroneous, false, or fraudulent returns. For the requirements regarding signing of returns, see § 1.6061-1. The rules of paragraph (e) of § 601.504 of this chapter (Statement of Procedural Rules) shall apply under this subparagraph in determining whether a copy of a power of attorney must be certified.

(iii) *Limitation.*—A return of income shall be required under this subparagraph only if the nonresident alien individual is otherwise required to make a return in accordance with this paragraph.

(4) *Disallowance of deductions and credits.*—For provisions disallowing deductions and credits when a return of income has not been filed by or on behalf of a nonresident alien individual, see section 874(a) and the regulations thereunder.

(5) *Effective date.*—This paragraph shall apply for taxable years beginning after December 31, 1966, except that it shall not be applied to require (i) the filing of a return for any taxable year ending before January 1, 1974, which, pursuant to instructions applicable to the return, is not required to be filed or (ii) the amendment of a return for such a taxable year which, pursuant to such instructions, is required to be filed. For corresponding rules applicable to taxable years beginning before January 1, 1967, see 26 CFR 1.6012-1(b) (Rev. as of Jan. 1, 1967).

(c) *Cross reference.*—For returns by fiduciaries for individuals, estates, and trusts, see § 1.6012-3. [Reg. § 1.6012-1.]

☐ [T.D. 6364, 2-13-59. *Amended by T.D. 6455, 3-1-60; T.D. 6533, 1-18-61; T.D. 6581, 12-5-61; T.D. 6777, 12-15-64; T.D. 6817, 4-7-65; T.D. 6856, 10-19-65; T.D. 6885, 6-1-66; T.D. 7069, 11-10-70; T.D. 7269, 4-12-73; T.D. 7274, 5-4-73; T.D. 7332, 12-20-74; T.D. 7564, 9-11-78; T.D. 7577, 12-19-78; T.D. 7670, 1-30-80; T.D. 7683, 3-12-80; T.D. 8000, 12-26-84; T.D. 8113, 12-18-86, T.D. 9391, 4-4-2008, and T.D. 9590, 5-18-2012.]*

### [Reg. § 301.6012-1]

**§ 301.6012-1. Persons required to make returns of income.**—For provisions with respect to persons required to make returns of income, see §§ 1.6012-1 to 1.6012-4, inclusive, of this chapter (Income Tax Regulations). [Reg. § 301.6012-1.]

☐ [T.D. 6498, 10-24-60.]

### [Reg. § 1.6012-2]

**§ 1.6012-2. Corporations required to make returns of income.**—(a) *In general.*—(1) *Requirement of return.*—Except as provided in paragraphs (e) and (g)(1) of this section with respect to charitable and other organizations having unrelated business income and to certain foreign corporations, respectively, every corporation, as defined in section 7701(a)(3), subject to taxation under subtitle A of the Code shall make a return of income regardless of whether it has taxable income or regardless of the amount of its gross income.

(2) *Existence of corporation.*—A corporation in existence during any portion of a taxable year is required to make a return. If a corporation was not in existence throughout an annual accounting period (either calendar year or fiscal year), the corporation is required to make a return for that fractional part of a year during which it was in existence. A corporation is not in existence after it ceases business and dissolves, retaining no assets, whether or not under State law it may thereafter be treated as continuing as a corporation for certain limited purposes connected with winding up its affairs, such as for the purpose of suing and being sued. If the corporation has valuable claims for which it will bring suit during this period, it has retained assets and therefore continues in existence. A corporation does not go out of existence if it is turned over to receivers or trustees who continue to operate it. If a corporation has received a charter but has never perfected its organization and has transacted no business and has no income from any source, it may upon presentation of the facts to the district director be relieved from the necessity of making a return. In the absence of a proper showing of such facts to the district director, a corporation will be required to make a return.

(3) *Form of return.*—The return required of a corporation under this section shall be made on Form 1120 unless the corporation is of a type for which a special form is prescribed. The special forms of returns and schedules required of particular types of corporations are set forth in paragraphs (b) to (g), inclusive, of this section.

(4) *Disclosure of uncertain tax positions.*—A corporation required to make a return under this section shall attach Schedule UTP, Uncertain Tax Position Statement, or any successor form, to such return, in accordance with forms, instructions, or other appropriate guidance provided by the IRS.

(5) *Effective/applicability date.*—Paragraph (a)(4) of this section applies to returns filed for tax years beginning on or after January 1, 2010.

(b) *Personal holding companies.*—A personal holding company, as defined in section 542, including a foreign corporation within the definition of such section, shall attach Schedule PH, Computation of U.S. Personal Holding Company Tax, to the return required by paragraph (a) or (g), as the case may be, of this section.

(c) *Insurance companies.*—(1) *Domestic life insurance companies.*—(i) *In general.*—A life insurance company subject to tax under section 801 shall make a return on Form 1120-L, "U.S. Life Insurance Company Income Tax Return." Except as provided in paragraph (c)(4) of this section, such company shall file with its return—

(A) A copy of its annual statement which shows the reserves used by the company in computing the taxable income reported on its return; and

(B) A copy of Schedule A (real estate) and of Schedule D (bonds and stocks), or any successor thereto, of such annual statement.

(ii) *Mutual savings banks.*—Mutual savings banks conducting life insurance business and meeting the requirements of section 594 are subject to partial tax computed on Form 1120, "U.S. Corporation Income Tax Return," and partial tax computed on Form 1120-L. The Form 1120-L is attached as a schedule to Form 1120, together with the annual statement and schedules required to be filed with Form 1120-L.

(2) *Domestic nonlife insurance companies.*—Every domestic insurance company other than a life insurance company shall make a return on Form 1120-PC, "U.S. Property and Casualty Insurance Company Income Tax Return." This includes organizations described in section 501(m)(1) that provide commercial-type insurance and organizations described in section 833. Except as provided in paragraph (c)(4) of this section, such company shall file with its return a copy of its annual statement (or a pro forma annual statement), including the underwriting and investment exhibit (or any successor thereto) for the year covered by such return.

(3) *Foreign insurance companies.*—The provisions of paragraphs (c)(1) and (c)(2) of this section concerning the returns and statements of insurance companies subject to tax under section 801 or section 831 also apply to foreign insurance companies subject to tax under those sections, except that the copy of the annual statement required to be submitted with the return shall, in the case of a foreign insurance company that is not required to file an annual statement, be a copy of the pro forma annual statement relating to the United States business of such company.

(4) *Special rule for insurance companies filing their Federal income tax returns electronically.*—If an insurance company described in paragraph (c)(1), (2), or (3) of this section files its Federal income tax return electronically, it must include on or with such return its annual statement (or pro forma annual statement), or a portion thereof, as and to the extent required by forms or instructions. If the full annual statement is not required to be included with the return, such statement must be available at all times for inspection by authorized Internal Revenue Service officers or employees and retained for so long as such statements may be material in the administration of any internal revenue law. See § 1.6001-1(e).

(5) *Definition.*—For purposes of this section, the term annual statement means the annual statement, the form of which is approved by the National Association of Insurance Commissioners (NAIC), which is filed by an insurance company for the year with the insurance departments of States, Territories, and the District of Columbia. The term annual statement also includes a pro forma annual statement if the insurance company is not required to file the NAIC annual statement.

(d) *Affiliated groups.*—For the forms to be used by affiliated corporations filing a consolidated return, see § 1.1502-75.

(e) *Charitable and other organizations with unrelated business income.*—Every organization described in section 511(a)(2) which is subject to the tax imposed by section 511(a)(1) on its unrelated business taxable income shall make a return on Form 990-T for each taxable year if it has gross income, included in computing unrelated business taxable income for such taxable year, of $1,000 or more. The filing of a return of unrelated business income does not relieve the organization of the duty of filing other required returns.

(f) *Subchapter T cooperatives.*—(1) *In general.*—For taxable years ending on or after December 31, 2007, a cooperative organization described in section 1381 (including a farmers' cooperative exempt from tax under section 521) is required to make a return, whether or not it has taxable income and regardless of the amount of its gross income, on Form 1120-C, "U.S. Income Tax Return for Cooperative Associations," or such other form as may be designated by the Commissioner.

(2) *Farmers' cooperatives.*—For taxable years ending before December 31, 2007, a farmers' cooperative organization described in section 521(b)(1) (including a farmers' cooperative that is not exempt from tax under section 521) is required to make a return on Form 990-C, "Farmers' Cooperative Association Income Tax Return."

(3) *Effective/applicability date.*—This paragraph (f) is applicable on or after July 13, 2007.

(g) *Returns by foreign corporations.*—(1) *Requirement of return.*—(i) *In general.*—Except as otherwise provided in subparagraph (2) of this paragraph, every foreign corporation which is engaged in trade or business in the United States at any time during the taxable year or which has income which is subject to taxation under subtitle A of the Code (relating to income taxes) shall make a return on Form 1120-F. Thus, for example, a foreign corporation which is engaged in trade or business in the United States at any time during the taxable year is required to file a return on Form 1120-F even though (*a*) it has no income which is effectively connected with the conduct of a trade or business in the United States, (*b*) it has no income from sources within the United States, or (*c*) its income is exempt from income tax by reason of an income tax convention or any section of the Code. However, if the foreign corporation has no gross income for the taxable year, it is not required to complete the return schedules but must attach a statement to the return indicating the nature of any exclusions claimed and the amount of such exclusions to the extent such amounts are readily determinable.

(ii) *Treaty income.*—If the gross income of a foreign corporation includes treaty income, as defined in paragraph (b)(1) of § 1.871-12, a statement shall be attached to the return on Form 1120-F showing with respect to that income—

(*a*) The amounts of tax withheld,

(*b*) The names and post office addresses of withholding agents, and

(*c*) Such other information as may be required by the return form or by the instructions issued with respect to the form, to show the taxpayer's entitlement to the reduced rate of tax under the tax convention.

(iii) *Balance sheet and reconciliation of income.*—At the election of the taxpayer, the balance sheets and reconciliation of income, as shown on Form 1120-F, may be limited to—

(*a*) The assets of the corporation located in the United States and to its other assets used in the trade or business conducted in the United States, and

(*b*) Its income effectively connected with the conduct of a trade or business in the United States and its other income from sources within the United States.

(2) *Exceptions.*—(i) *Return not required when tax is fully paid at source.*—(*a*) *In general.*—A foreign corporation which at no time during the taxable year is engaged in a trade or business in the United States is not required to make a return for the taxable year if its tax liability for the taxable year is fully satisfied by the withholding of tax at source under chapter 3 of the Code. For purposes of this subdivision, some of the items of income from sources within the United States upon which the tax liability will not have been fully satisfied by the withholding of tax at source under chapter 3 of the Code are:

(*1*) Interest upon so-called tax-free covenant bonds upon which, in accordance with section 1451 and § 1.1451-1, a tax of only 2 percent is required to be withheld at source,

(*2*) In the case of bonds or other evidence of indebtedness issued after September 25, 1965, amounts described in section 881(a)(3),

(*3*) Accrued interest received in connection with the sale of bonds between interest dates, which, in accordance with paragraph (h) of § 1.1441-4, is not subject to withholding of tax at source.

(*b*) *Corporations not included.*—This subdivision (i) shall not apply—

(*1*) To a foreign corporation which has income for the taxable year which is treated under section 882(d) or (e) and § 1.882-2 as income which is effectively connected for the taxable year with the conduct of a trade or business in the United States by that corporation,

(*2*) To a foreign corporation making a claim under § 301.6402-3 of this chapter (Procedure and Administration Regulations) for the refund of an overpayment of tax for the taxable year, or

(*3*) To a foreign corporation described in paragraph (c)(2)(i) of § 1.532-1 whose accumulated taxable income for the taxable year is determined under paragraph (b)(2) of § 1.535-1.

(ii) *Beneficiaries of estates or trusts.*—A foreign corporation which is a beneficiary of an estate or trust which is engaged in trade or business in the United States is not required to make a return for the taxable year merely because it is deemed to be engaged in trade or business within the United States under section 875(2). However, such foreign corporation will be required to make a return if it otherwise satisfies the conditions of subparagraph (1)(i) of this paragraph for making a return.

(iii) *Special returns and schedules.*—The provisions of paragraphs (b) through (f) of this section shall apply to a foreign corporation except that a foreign corporation which is an insurance company to which paragraph (c)(3) of this section applies shall make a return on Form 1120-F and not on Form 1120. If a foreign corporation which is an insurance company to which paragraph (c)(1) or (2) of this section applies has income for the taxable year from sources within the United States which is not effectively connected for that year with the conduct of a trade or business in the United States by that corporation, the corporation shall attach to its return on Form 1120L or 1120M, as the case may be, a separate schedule showing the nature and amount of the items of such income, the rate of tax applicable thereto, and the amount of tax withheld therefrom under chapter 3 of the code.

(3) *Representative or agent for foreign corporation.*—(i) *Cases where power of attorney is not required.*—The responsible representative or agent within the United States of a foreign corporation shall make on behalf of his principal a return of, and shall pay the tax on, all income coming within his control as representative or agent which is subject to the income tax under subtitle A of the code. The agency appointment will determine how completely the agent is substituted for the principal for tax purposes. Any person who collects interest or dividends on deposited securities of a foreign corporation, executes ownership certificates in connection therewith, or sells such securities under special instructions shall not be deemed merely by reason of such acts to be the responsible representative or agent of the foreign corporation. If the responsible representative or agent does not have a specific power of attorney from the foreign corporation to file a return in its behalf, the return shall be accompanied by a statement to the effect that the representative or agent does not possess specific power of attorney to file a return for such corporation but that the return is being filed in accordance with the provisions of this subdivision.

(ii) *Cases where power of attorney is required.*—Whenever a return of income of a foreign corporation is made by an agent acting under a duly authorized power of attorney for that purpose, the return shall be accompanied by the power of attorney in proper form, or a copy thereof specifically authorizing him to represent his principal in making, executing, and filing the income tax return. Form 2848 may be used for this purpose. The agent, as well as the taxpayer, may incur liability for the penalties provided for erroneous, false, or fraudulent returns. For the requirements regarding signing of returns, see § 1.6062-1. The rules of paragraph (e) of § 601.504 of this chapter (Statement of Procedural Rules) shall apply under this subparagraph in determining whether a copy of a power of attorney must be certified.

(iii) *Limitation.*—A return of income shall be required under this subparagraph only if the foreign corporation is otherwise required to make a return in accordance with this paragraph.

(4) *Disallowance of deductions and credits.*—For provisions disallowing deductions and credits when a return of income has not been filed by or on behalf of a foreign corporation, see section 882(c)(2) and the regulations thereunder, and paragraph (b)(2) and (3) of § 1.535-1.

(5) *Effective date.*—This paragraph shall apply for taxable years beginning after December 31, 1966, except that it shall not be applied to require (i) the filing of a return for any taxable year ending before January 1, 1974, which, pursuant to instructions applicable to the return, is not required to be filed or (ii) the amendment of a return for such a taxable year which, pursuant to such instructions, is required to be filed. For corresponding rules applicable to taxable years beginning before January 1, 1967, see 26 CFR 1.6012-2(g) (Rev. as of Jan. 1, 1967).

(h) *Electing small business corporations.*—An electing small business corporation, whether or not subject to the tax imposed by section 1378, shall make a return on Form 1120-S. See also section 6037 and the regulations thereunder.

(i) *Hospital organizations with noncompliant hospital facilities.*—Every hospital organization (as defined in §1.501(r)-1(b)(18)) that is subject to the tax imposed by §1.501(r)-2(d) shall make a return on Form 990-T. The filing of a return to pay the tax described in §1.501(r)-2(d) does not relieve the organization of the duty of filing other required returns.

(j) *Items of tax preference.*—(1) *In general.*—Every corporation required to make a return under this section and having items of tax preference (described in section 57 and the regulations thereunder) in any amount shall file the required form relating to such items as part of such return.

(2) *Organizations with unrelated business income and foreign corporations.*—Regardless of the provisions of paragraphs (e) and (g) of this section, any organization described in either such paragraph having items of tax preference (described in section 57 and the regulations thereunder) in any amount entering into the computation of unrelated business income is required to make a return on form 990-T or form 1120F, respectively, and to attach the required form as part of such return.

(k) *Other provisions.*—For returns by fiduciaries or corporations, see §1.6012-3. For information returns by corporations regarding payments of dividends, see §§1.6042-1 through 1.6042-3, inclusive; regarding corporate dissolutions or liquidations, see §1.6043-1; regarding distributions in liquidation, see §1.6043-2; regarding payments of patronage dividends, see §§1.6044-1 through 1.6044-4, inclusive; and regarding certain payments of interest, see §§1.6049-1 and 1.6049-1. For returns as to formation or reorganization of foreign corporations, see §§1.6046-1 through 1.6046-3, inclusive.

(l) *Applicability date.*—Paragraph (c) of this section applies to any taxable year beginning after October 13, 2020. For taxable years beginning on or before October 13, 2020, see paragraph (c) of this section as contained in 26 CFR part 1 in effect on April 1, 2020. [Reg. §1.6012-2.]

☐ [*T.D. 6364, 2-13-59. Amended by T.D. 6427, 12-2-59; T.D. 6523, 12-28-60; T.D. 6533, 1-18-61; T.D. 6628, 12-27-62; T.D. 6960, 6-24-68; T.D. 7244, 12-29-72; T.D. 7293, 11-27-73; T.D. 7332, 12-20-74; T.D. 7564, 9-11-78; T.D. 7579, 12-19-78; T.D. 7838, 10-5-82; T.D. 9264, 5-26-2006; T.D. 9329, 6-13-2007; T.D. 9336, 7-27-2007; T.D. 9510, 12-13-2010, T.D. 9708, 12-29-2014, T.D. 9849, 3-11-2019 and T.D. 9911, 10-9-2020.*]

### [Reg. §1.6012-3]

**§1.6012-3. Returns by fiduciaries.**—(a) *For estates and trusts.*—(1) *In general.*—Every fiduciary, or at least one of the joint fiduciaries, must make a return of income on form 1041 (or by use of a composite return pursuant to §1.6012-5) and attach the required form if the estate or trust has items of tax preference (as defined in section 57 and the regulations thereunder) in any amount—

(i) For each estate for which he acts if the gross income of such estate for the taxable year is $600 or more;

(ii) For each trust for which he acts, except a trust exempt under section 501(a), if such trust has for the taxable year any taxable income, or has for the taxable year gross income of $600 or more regardless of the amount of taxable income; and

(iii) For each estate and each trust for which he acts, except a trust exempt under section 501(a), regardless of the amount of income for the taxable year, if any beneficiary of such estate or trust is a nonresident alien.

(iv) For each trust electing to be taxed as, or as part of, an estate under section 645 for which a trustee acts, and for each related estate joining in a section 645 election for which an executor acts, if the aggregate gross income of the electing trust(s) and related estate, if any, joining in the election for the taxable year is $600 or more. (For the respective filing requirements of the trustee of each electing trust and executor of any related estate, see §1.645-1).

(2) *Wills and trust instruments.*—At the request of the Internal Revenue Service, a copy of the will or trust instrument (including any amendments), accompanied by a written declaration of the fiduciary under the penalties of perjury that it is a true and complete copy, shall be filed together with a statement by the fiduciary indicating the provisions of the will or trust instrument (including any amendments) which, in the fiduciary's opinion, determine the extent to which the income of the estate or trust is taxable to the estate or trust, the beneficiaries, or the grantor, respectively.

(3) *Domiciliary and ancillary representatives.*—In the case of an estate required to file a return under subparagraph (1) of this paragraph, having both domiciliary and ancillary representatives, the domiciliary and ancillary representatives must each file a return on Form 1041. The domiciliary representative is required to include in the return rendered by him as such domiciliary representative the entire income of the estate. The return of the ancillary representative shall be filed with the district director for his internal revenue district and shall show the name and address of the domiciliary representative, the amount of gross income received by the ancillary representative, and the deductions to be claimed against such income, including any amount of income properly paid or credited by the ancillary representative to any legatee, heir, or other beneficiary. If the ancillary representative for the estate of a nonresident alien is a citizen or resident of the United States, and the domiciliary representative is a nonresident alien, such ancillary representative is required to render the return otherwise required of the domiciliary representative.

(4) *Two or more trusts.*—A trustee of two or more trusts must make a separate return for each trust, even though such trusts were created by the same grantor for the same beneficiary or beneficiaries.

(5) *Trusts with unrelated business income.*—Every fiduciary for a trust described in section 511(b)(2) which is subject to the tax on its unrelated business taxable income by section 511(b)(1) shall make a return on Form 990-T for each taxable year if the trust has gross income, included in computing unrelated business taxable income for such taxable year, of $1,000 or more. The filing of a return of unrelated business income does not relieve the fiduciary of such trusts from the duty of filing other required returns.

(6) *Charitable remainder trusts.*—Every fiduciary for a charitable remainder annuity trust (as defined in §1.664-2) or a charitable remainder unitrust (as defined in §1.664-3) shall make a return on Form 1041-B for each taxable year of the trust even though it is nonexempt because it has unrelated business taxable income. The return on Form 1041-B shall be made in accordance with the instructions for the form and shall be filed with the designated Internal Revenue office on or before the 15th day of the fourth month following the close of the taxable year of the trust. A copy of the instrument governing the trust, accompanied by a written declaration of the fiduciary under the penalties of perjury that it is a true and complete copy, shall be attached to the return for the first taxable year of the trust.

(7) *Certain trusts described in section 4947(a)(1).*—For taxable years beginning after December 31, 1980, in the case of a trust described in section 4947(a)(1) which has no taxable income for a taxable year, the filing requirements of Section 6012 and this section shall be satisfied by the filing, pursuant to §53.6011-1 of this chapter (Foundation Excise Tax Regulations) and §1.6033-2(a), by the fiduciary of such trust of—

(i) Form 990-PF if such trust is treated as a private foundation, or

(ii) Form 990 if such trust is not treated as a private foundation.

When the provisions of this paragraph (7) are met, the fiduciary shall not be required to file Form 1041.

(8) *Estates and trusts liable for qualified tax.*—In the case of an estate or trust which is liable for one or more qualified State individual income taxes, as defined in section 6362, for a taxable year, see paragraph (b) of §301.6361-1 of this chapter (Regulations on Procedure and Administration) for rules relating to returns required to be made.

(9) *A trust any portion of which is treated as owned by the grantor or another person pursuant to sections 671 through 678.*—In the case of a trust any portion of which is treated as owned by the grantor or another person under the provisions of subpart E (section 671 and following) part I, subchapter J, chapter 1 of the Internal Revenue Code see §1.671-4.

(10) *Hospital organizations organized as trusts with noncompliant hospital facilities.*—Every fiduciary for a hospital organization (as defined in §1.501(r)-1(b)(18)) organized as a trust described in section

511(b)(2) that is subject to the tax imposed by §1.501(r)-2(d) shall make a return on Form 990-T. The filing of a return to pay the tax described in §1.501(r)-2(d) does not relieve the organization of the duty of filing other required returns.

(b) *For other persons.*—(1) *Decedents.*—The executor or administrator of the estate of a decedent, or other person charged with the property of a decedent, shall make the return of income required in respect of such decedent. For the decedent's taxable year which ends with the date of his death, the return shall cover the period during which he was alive. For the filing of returns of income for citizens and alien residents of the United States, and alien residents of Puerto Rico, see paragraph (a) of §1.6012-1. For the filing of a joint return after death of spouse, see paragraph (d) of §1.6013-1.

(2) *Nonresident alien individuals.*—(i) *In general.*—A resident or domestic fiduciary or other person charged with the care of the person or property of a nonresident alien individual shall make a return for that individual and pay the tax unless—

(a) The nonresident alien individual makes a return of, and pays the tax on, his income for the taxable year,

(b) A responsible representative or agent in the United States of the nonresident alien individual makes a return of, and pays the tax on, the income of such alien individual for the taxable year, or

(c) The nonresident alien individual has appointed a person in the United States to act as his agent for the purpose of making a return of income and, if such fiduciary is required to file a Form 1041 for an estate or trust of which such alien individual is a beneficiary, such fiduciary attaches a copy of the agency appointment to his return on Form 1041.

(ii) *Income to be returned.*—A return of income shall be required under this subparagraph only if the nonresident alien individual is otherwise required to make a return in accordance with paragraph (b) of §1.6012-1. The provisions of that paragraph shall apply in determining the form of return to be used and the income to be returned.

(iii) *Disallowance of deductions and credits.*—For provisions disallowing deductions and credits when a return of income has not been filed by or on behalf of a nonresident alien individual, see section 874 and the regulations thereunder.

(iv) *Alien resident of Puerto Rico.*—This subparagraph shall not apply to the return of a nonresident alien individual who is a bona fide resident of Puerto Rico during the entire taxable year. See §1.876-1.

(v) *Cross reference.*—For requirements of withholding tax at source on nonresident alien individuals and of returns with respect to such withheld taxes, see §§1.1441-1 to 1.1465-1, inclusive.

(3) *Persons under a disability.*—A fiduciary acting as the guardian of a minor, or as the guardian or committee of an insane person, must make the return of income required in respect of such person unless, in the case of a minor, the minor himself makes the return or causes it to be made.

(4) *Corporations.*—A receiver, trustee in dissolution, trustee in bankruptcy, or assignee, who, by order of a court of competent jurisdiction, by operation of law or otherwise, has possession of or holds title to all or substantially all the property or business of a corporation, shall make the return of income for such corporation in the same manner and form as corporations are required to make such returns. Such return shall be filed whether or not the receiver, trustee, or assignee is operating the property or business of the corporation. A receiver in charge of only a small part of the property of a corporation, such as a receiver in mortgage foreclosure proceedings involving merely a small portion of its property, need not make the return of income. See also §1.6041-1, relating to returns regarding information at source; §§1.6042-1 to 1.6042-3, inclusive, relating to returns regarding payments of dividends; §§1.6044-1 to 1.6044-4, inclusive, relating to returns regarding payments of patronage dividends; §§1.6049-1 and 1.6049-2, relating to returns regarding certain payments of interest.

(5) *Individuals in receivership.*—A receiver who stands in the place of an individual must make the return of income required in respect of such individual. A receiver of only part of the property of an individual need not file a return, and the individual must make his own return.

(c) *Joint fiduciaries.*—In the case of joint fiduciaries, a return is required to be made by only one of such fiduciaries. A return made by one of joint fiduciaries shall contain a statement that the fiduciary has sufficient knowledge of the affairs of the person for whom the return is made to enable him to make the return, and that the return is, to the best of his knowledge and belief, true and correct.

(d) *Other provisions.*—For the definition of the term "fiduciary", see section 7701(a)(6) and the regulations thereunder. For information returns required to be made by fiduciaries under section 6041, see §1.6041-1. As to further duties and liabilities of fiduciaries, see section 6903 and §301.6903-1 of this chapter (Regulations on Procedure and Administration). [Reg. §1.6012-3.]

☐ [*T.D. 6031, 7-8-58 and T.D. 6364, 2-13-59. Amended by T.D. 6628,* 12-27-62; *T.D. 6972,* 9-11-68; *T.D. 7200,* 8-15-72; *T.D. 7202,* 8-22-72; *T.D. 7332,* 12-20-74; *T.D. 7407,* 3-3-76; *T.D. 7564,* 9-11-78; *T.D. 7577,* 12-19-78; *T.D. 7608,* 4-3-79; *T.D. 7796,* 11-23-81; *T.D. 7838,* 10-5-82; *T.D. 8026,* 5-17-85; *T.D. 8633,* 12-20-95; *T.D. 9032, 12-23-2002 and T.D.* 9708, 12-29-2014.]

### [Reg. §1.6012-4]

**§1.6012-4. Miscellaneous returns.**—For returns by regulated investment companies of tax on undistributed capital gain designated for special treatment under section 852(b)(3)(D), see §1.852-9. For returns with respect to tax withheld on nonresident aliens and foreign corporations and on tax-free covenant bonds, see §§1.1461-1 to 1.1465-1, inclusive. For the requirement of an annual report by persons completing a Government contract, see 26 CFR (1939) 17.16 (Treasury Decision 4906, approved June 23, 1939), and 26 CFR (1939) 16.15 (Treasury Decision 4909, approved June 28, 1939), as made applicable to section 1471 of the 1954 Code by Treasury Decision 6091, approved August 16, 1954 (19 F.R. 5167, C.B. 1954-2, 47). See also §1.1471-1. [Reg. §1.6012-4.]

☐ [*T.D. 6364, 2-13-59. Amended by T.D. 7332, 12-20-74 and T.D. 9849,* 3-11-2019.]

### [Reg. §1.6012-5]

**§1.6012-5. Composite return in lieu of specified form.**—The Commissioner may authorize the use, at the option of a person required to make a return, of a composite return in lieu of any form specified in this part for use by such a person, subject to such conditions, limitations, and special rules governing the preparation, execution, filing, and correction thereof as the Commissioner may deem appropriate. Such composite return shall consist of a form prescribed by the Commissioner and an attachment or attachments of magnetic tape or other approved media. Notwithstanding any provisions in this part to the contrary, a single form and attachment may comprise the returns of more than one such person. To the extent that the use of a composite return has been authorized by the Commissioner, references in this part to a specific form for use by such a person shall be deemed to refer also to a composite return under this section. [Reg. §1.6012-5.]

☐ [*T.D. 7200, 8-15-72.*]

### [Reg. §1.6012-6]

**§1.6012-6. Returns by political organizations.**—(a) *Requirement of return.*—(1) *In general.*—For taxable years beginning after December 31, 1974, every political organization described in section 527(e)(1), and every fund described in section 527(f)(3) or section 527(g), and every organization described in section 501(c) and exempt from taxation under section 501(a) shall, if a tax is imposed on such an organization or fund by section 527(b), make a return of income on or before the fifteenth day of the fourth month following the close of the taxable year.

(2) *Taxable years beginning after December 31, 1971, and before January 1, 1975.*—For taxable years beginning after December 31, 1971, and before January 1, 1975, any political organization which would be described in section 527(e)(1) if such section applied to such years shall not be required to make a return if such organization would not be required to make a return under paragraph (a)(1) of this section.

(b) *Form of return.*—The return required by an organization or fund upon which a tax is imposed by section 527(b) shall be made on Form 1120-POL.

(c) *Applicability date.*—This section applies to returns filed on or after January 30, 2020. Section 1.6012-6T (as contained in 26 CFR part 1, revised April 2019) applies to returns filed before January 30, 2020. [Reg. §1.6012-6.]

☐ [*T.D. 7516, 11-1-77. Amended by T.D. 9821, 7-18-2017 and T.D.* 9892, 1-29-2020.]

### [Reg. §1.6013-1]

**§1.6013-1. Joint returns.**—(a) *In general.*—(1) A husband and wife may elect to make a joint return under section 6013(a) even though one of the spouses has no gross income or deductions. For rules for determining whether individuals occupy the status of husband and wife for purposes of filing a joint return, see paragraph (a) of §1.6013-4. For any taxable year with respect to which a joint return has been filed, separate returns shall not be made by the spouses after the time for filing the return of either has expired. See, however, paragraph (d)(5) of this section for the right of an executor to file a late separate return for a deceased spouse and thereby disaffirm a timely joint return made by the surviving spouse.

(2) A joint return of a husband and wife (if not made by an agent of one or both spouses) shall be signed by both spouses. The provisions of paragraph (a)(5) of §1.6012-1, relating to returns made by agents, shall apply where one spouse signs a return as agent for the other, or where a third party signs a return as agent for one or both spouses.

(b) *Nonresident alien.*—A joint return shall not be made if either the husband or wife at any time during the taxable year is a nonresident alien, unless an election is in effect for the taxable year under section 6013(g) or (h) and the regulations thereunder.

(c) *Different taxable years.*—Except as otherwise provided in this section, a husband and wife shall not file a joint return if they have different taxable years.

(d) *Joint return after death.*—(1) Section 6013(a)(2) provides that a joint return may be made for the survivor and the deceased spouse or for both deceased spouses if the taxable years of such spouses begin on the same day and end on different days only because of the death of either or both. Thus, if a husband and wife make their returns on a calendar year basis, and the wife dies on August 1, 1956, a joint return may be made with respect to the calendar year 1956 of the husband and the taxable year of the wife beginning on January 1, 1956, and ending with her death on August 1, 1956. Similarly, if husband and wife both make their returns on the basis of a fiscal year beginning on July 1 and the wife dies on October 1, 1956, a joint return may be made with respect to the fiscal year of the husband beginning on July 1, 1956, and ending on June 30, 1957, and with respect to the taxable year of the wife beginning on July 1, 1956, and ending with her death on October 1, 1956.

(2) The provision allowing a joint return to be made for the taxable year in which the death of either or both spouses occurs is subject to two limitations. The first limitation is that if the surviving spouse remarries before the close of his taxable year, he shall not make a joint return with the first spouse who died during the taxable year. In such a case, however, the surviving spouse may make a joint return with his new spouse provided the other requirements with respect to the filing of a joint return are met. The second limitation is that the surviving spouse shall not make a joint return with the deceased spouse if the taxable year of either spouse is a fractional part of the year under section 443(a)(1) resulting from a change of accounting period. For example, if a husband and wife make their returns on the calendar year basis and the wife dies on March 1, 1956, and thereafter the husband receives permission to change his annual accounting period to a fiscal year beginning July 1, 1956, no joint return shall be made for the short taxable year ending June 30, 1956. Similarly, if a husband and wife who make their returns on a calendar year basis receive permission to change to a fiscal year beginning July 1, 1956, and the wife dies on June 1, 1956, no joint return shall be made for the short taxable year ending June 30, 1956.

(3) Section 6013(a)(3) provides for the method of making a joint return in the case of the death of one spouse or both spouses. The general rule is that, in the case of the death of one spouse, or of both spouses, the joint return with respect to the decedent may be made only by his executor or administrator, as defined in paragraph (c) of §1.6013-4. An exception is made to this general rule whereby, in the case of the death of one spouse, the joint return may be made by the surviving spouse with respect to both him and the decedent if all the following conditions exist:

(i) No return has been made by the decedent for the taxable year in respect of which the joint return is made;

(ii) No executor or administrator has been appointed at or before the time of making such joint return; and

(iii) No executor or administrator is appointed before the last day prescribed by law for filing the return of the surviving spouse.

These conditions are to be applied with respect to the return for each of the taxable years of the decedent for which a joint return may be made if more than one such taxable year is involved. Thus, in the case of husband and wife on the calendar year basis, if the wife dies in February 1957, a joint return for the husband and wife for 1956 may be made if the conditions set forth in this subparagraph are satisfied with respect to such return. A joint return also may be made by the survivor for both himself and the deceased spouse for the calendar year 1957 if it is separately determined that the conditions set forth in this subparagraph are satisfied with respect to the return for such year. If, however, the deceased spouse should, prior to her death, make a return for 1956, the surviving spouse may not thereafter make a joint return for himself and the deceased spouse for 1956.

(4) If an executor or administrator is appointed at or before the time of making the joint return or before the last day prescribed by law for filing the return of the surviving spouse, the surviving spouse cannot make a joint return for himself and the deceased spouse whether or not a separate return for the deceased spouse is made by such executor or administrator. In such a case, any return made solely by the surviving spouse shall be treated as his separate return. The joint return, if one is to be made, must be made by both the surviving spouse and the executor or administrator. In determining whether an executor or administrator is appointed before the last day prescribed by law for filing the return of the surviving spouse, an extension of time for making the return is included.

(5) If the surviving spouse makes the joint return provided for in subparagraph (3) of this paragraph and thereafter an executor or administrator of the decedent is appointed, the executor or administrator may disaffirm such joint return. This disaffirmance, in order to be effective, must be made within one year after the last day prescribed by law for filing the return of the surviving spouse (including any extension of time for filing such return) and must be made in the form of a separate return for the taxable year of the decedent with respect to which the joint return was made. In the event of such proper disaffirmance the return made by the survivor shall constitute his separate return, that is, the joint return made by him shall be treated as his return and the tax thereon shall be computed by excluding all items properly includible in the return of the deceased spouse. The separate return made by the executor or administrator shall constitute the return of the deceased spouse for the taxable year.

(6) The time allowed the executor or administrator to disaffirm the joint return by the making of a separate return does not establish a new due date for the return of the deceased spouse. Accordingly, the provisions of sections 6651 and 6601, relating to delinquent returns and delinquency in payment of tax, are applicable to such return made by the executor in disaffirmance of the joint return.

(e) *Return of surviving spouse treated as joint return.*—For provisions relating to the treatment of the return of a surviving spouse as a joint return for each of the next two taxable years following the year of the death of the spouse, see section 2 and §1.2-2. [Reg. §1.6013-1.]

☐ [*T.D. 6364, 2-13-59. Amended by T.D. 7274, 5-4-73 and T.D. 7670, 1-30-80.]*

### [Reg. §301.6013-1]

**§301.6013-1. Joint returns of income tax by husband and wife.**— For provisions with respect to joint returns of income tax by husband and wife, see §§1.6013-1 to 1.6013-7, inclusive, of this chapter (Income Tax Regulations). [Reg. §301.6013-1.]

☐ [*T.D. 6498, 10-24-60. Amended by T.D. 7670, 1-30-80.]*

### [Reg. §1.6013-2]

**§1.6013-2. Joint return after filing separate return.**—(a) *In general.*—(1) Where an individual has filed a separate return for a taxable year for which a joint return could have been made by him and his spouse under section 6013(a), and the time prescribed by law for filing the return for such taxable year has expired, such individual and his spouse may, under conditions hereinafter set forth, make a joint return for such taxable year. The joint return filed pursuant to section 6013(b) shall constitute the return of the husband and wife for such year, and all payments, credits, refunds, or other repayments, made or allowed with respect to the separate return of either spouse are to be taken into account in determining the extent to which the tax based on the joint return has been paid.

(2) If a joint return is made under section 6013(b), any election, other than the election to file a separate return, made by either spouse in his separate return for the taxable year with respect to the treatment of any income, deduction, or credit of such spouse shall not be changed in the making of the joint return where such election would have been irrevocable if the joint return had not been made. Thus, if one spouse has made an irrevocable election to adopt and use the last-in, first-out inventory method under section 472, this election may not be changed upon making the joint return under section 6013(b).

(3) A joint return made under section 6013(b) after the death of either spouse shall, with respect to the decedent, be made only by his executor or administrator. Thus, where no executor or administrator has been appointed, a joint return cannot be made under section 6013(b).

(4) A nonresident alien treated as a resident under section 6013(g) or (h) for any taxable year ending on or after December 31, 1975, but before December 31, 1978, and the alien's United States citizen or resident spouse may file a joint return for that taxable year, even though one or both of the spouses have previously filed separate returns for that taxable year. In this case, the rule in paragraph (a)(3) of this section does not apply.

(b) *Limitations with respect to making of election.*—A joint return shall not be made under section 6013(b)(1) with respect to a taxable year—

(1) Beginning on or before July 30, 1996, unless there is paid in full at or before the time of the filing of the joint return the amount shown as tax upon such joint return; or

(2) After the expiration of three years from the last day prescribed by law for filing the return for such taxable year determined without regard to any extension of time granted to either spouse; or

(3) After there has been mailed to either spouse, with respect to such taxable year, a notice of deficiency under section 6212, if the spouse, as to such notice, files a petition with the Tax Court of the United States within the time prescribed in section 6213; or

(4) After either spouse has commenced a suit in any court for the recovery of any part of the tax for such taxable year; or

(5) After either spouse has entered into a closing agreement under section 7121 with respect to such taxable year, or after any civil or criminal case arising against either spouse with respect to such taxable year has been compromised under section 7122.

(c) *When return deemed filed; assessment and collection; credit or refund.*—(1) For the purpose of section 6501, relating to the period of limitations upon assessment and collection, and section 6651, relating to delinquent returns, a joint return made under section 6013(b) shall be deemed to have been filed, giving due regard to any extension of time granted to either spouse, on the following date:

(i) Where both spouses filed separate returns, prior to making the joint return under section 6013(b), on the date the last separate return of either spouse was filed for the taxable year, but not earlier than the last date prescribed by law for the filing of the return of either spouse;

(ii) Where only one spouse was required and did file a return prior to the making of the joint return under section 6013(b), on the date of the filing of the separate return, but not earlier than the last day prescribed by law for the filing of such return; or

(iii) Where both spouses were required to file a return, but only one spouse did so file, on the date of the filing of the joint return under section 6013(b).

(2) For the purpose of section 6511, relating to refunds and credits, a joint return made under section 6013(b) shall be deemed to have been filed on the last date prescribed by law for filing the return for such taxable year, determined without regard to any extension of time granted to either spouse for filing the return or paying the tax.

(d) *Additional time for assessment.*—In the case of a joint return made under section 6013 (b), the period of limitations provided in sections 6501 and 6502 shall not be less than one year after the date of the actual filing of such joint return. The expiration of the one year is to be determined without regard to the rules provided in paragraph (c)(1) of this section, relating to the application of sections 6501 and 6651 with respect to a joint return made under section 6013(b).

(e) *Additions to the tax and penalties.*—(1) Where the amount shown as the tax by the husband and wife on a joint return made under section 6013(b) exceeds the aggregate of the amounts shown as tax on the separate return of each spouse, and such excess is attributable to negligence, intentional disregard of rules and regulations, or fraud at the time of the making of such separate return, there shall be assessed, collected, and paid in the same manner as if it were a deficiency an additional amount as provided by the following:

(i) If any part of such excess is attributable to negligence, or intentional disregard of rules and regulations, at the time of the making of such separate return, but without any intent to defraud, this additional amount shall be 5 percent of the total amount of the excess.

(ii) If any part of such excess is attributable to fraud with intent to evade tax at the time of the making of such separate return, this additional amount shall be 50 percent of the total amount of the excess. The latter addition is in lieu of the 50 percent addition to the tax provided in section 6653(b).

(2) For purposes of section 7206(1) and (2) and section 7207 (relating to criminal penalties in the case of fraudulent returns), the term "return" includes a separate return filed by a spouse with respect to a taxable year for which a joint return is made under section 6013(b) after the filing of a separate return. [Reg. § 1.6013-2.]

☐ [*T.D. 6364, 2-13-59. Amended by T.D. 7670, 1-30-80 and T.D. 8725, 7-21-97.*]

### [Reg. § 1.6013-3]

**§1.6013-3. Treatment of joint return after death of either spouse.**—For purposes of section 21 (relating to change in rates during a taxable year), section 443 (relating to returns for a period of less than 12 months), and section 7851(a)(1)(A) (relating to the applicability of certain provisions of the Internal Revenue Code of 1954 and the Internal Revenue Code of 1939), where the husband and wife have different taxable years because of death of either spouse, the

joint return shall be treated as if the taxable years of both ended on the date of the closing of the surviving spouse's taxable year. Thus, in cases where the Internal Revenue Code of 1939 otherwise would apply to the taxable year of the decedent spouse and the Internal Revenue Code of 1954 would apply to the taxable year of the surviving spouse, this provision makes the Internal Revenue Code of 1954 applicable to the taxable years of both spouses if a joint return is filed. [Reg. § 1.6013-3.]

☐ [*T.D. 6364, 2-13-59.*]

### [Reg. §1.6013-4]

**§1.6013-4. Applicable rules.**—(a) *Status as husband and wife.*—For the purpose of filing a joint return under section 6013, the status as husband and wife of two individuals having taxable years beginning on the same day shall be determined—

(1) If the taxable year of each individual is the same, as of the close of such year; and

(2) If the close of the taxable year is different by reason of the death of one spouse, as of the time of such death.

An individual legally separated from his spouse under a decree of divorce or of separate maintenance shall not be considered as married. However, the mere fact that spouses have not lived together during the course of the taxable year shall not prohibit them from making a joint return. A husband and wife who are separated under an interlocutory decree of divorce retain the relationship of husband and wife until the decree becomes final. The fact that the taxpayer and his spouse are divorced or legally separated at any time after the close of the taxable year shall not deprive them of their right to file a joint return for such taxable year under section 6013.

(b) *Computation of income, deductions, and tax.*—If a joint return is made, the gross income and adjusted gross income of husband and wife on the joint return are computed in an aggregate amount and the deductions allowed and the taxable income are likewise computed on an aggregate basis. Deductions limited to a percentage of the adjusted gross income, such as the deduction for charitable, etc., contributions and gifts, under section 170, will be allowed with reference to such aggregate adjusted gross income. A similar rule is applied in the case of the limitation of section 1211(b) on the allowance of losses resulting from the sale or exchange of capital assets (see §1.1211-1). Although there are two taxpayers on a joint return, there is only one taxable income. The tax on the joint return shall be computed on the aggregate income and the liability with respect to the tax shall be joint and several. For computation of tax in the case of a joint return, see §1.2-1. For tax in the case of a joint return of husband and wife electing to pay the optional tax under section 3, see §1.3-1. For the election not to show on a joint return the amount of tax due in connection therewith, see paragraph (c) of §1.6014-1 and paragraph (d) of §1.6014-2. For separate computations of the self-employment tax of each spouse on a joint return, see paragraph (b) of §1.6017-1.

(c) *Definition of executor or administrator.*—For purposes of section 6013 the term "executor or administrator" means the person who is actually appointed to such office and not a person who is merely in charge of the property of the decedent.

(d) *Return signed under duress.*—If an individual asserts and establishes that he or she signed a return under duress, the return is not a joint return. The individual who signed such return under duress is not jointly and severally liable for the tax shown on the return or any deficiency in tax with respect to the return. The return is adjusted to reflect only the tax liability of the individual who voluntarily signed the return, and the liability is determined at the applicable rates in section 1(d) for married individuals filing separate returns. Section 6212 applies to the assessment of any deficiency in tax on such return. [Reg. § 1.6013-4.]

☐ [*T.D. 6364, 2-13-59. Amended by T.D. 7102, 3-23-71 and T.D. 9003, 7-17-2002.*]

### [Reg. §1.6013-6]

**§1.6013-6. Election to treat nonresident alien individual as resident of the United States.**—(a) *Election for special treatment.*—(1) *In general.*—Two individuals who are husband and wife at the close of a taxable year ending on or after December 31, 1975, may make an election under this section for that taxable year if, at the close of that year, one spouse is a citizen or resident of the United States and the other spouse is a nonresident alien. The effect of the election is that each spouse is treated as a resident of the United States for purposes of chapters 1, 5, and 24 and sections 6012, 6013, 6072, and 6091 of the Code for the entire taxable year. An election made under this section is in effect for the taxable year for which made and for all subsequent years of the husband and wife, except—

(i) Any taxable year for which the election is suspended, as described in paragraph (a)(3) of this section, and

(ii) Any taxable year for which the election is terminated in accordance with paragraph (b) of this section and all subsequent taxable years.

A husband and wife may not make an election if an election previously made under this section by either spouse has been terminated under paragraph (b) of this section.

(2) *Particular rules.*—(i) As used in paragraph (a)(3) of this section, the term "United States spouse" means any married individual who is a citizen or resident of the United States at any time during a taxable year.

(ii) An individual's residence is determined by application of the principles of §§ 301.7701(b)-1 through 301.7701(b)-9 of this chapter relating to what constitutes residence in the United States by an alien individual.

(iii) Whether two individuals are married at the close of a taxable year is determined by application of the rules in § 1.6013-4(a).

(iv) The provisions of section 879 and the regulations thereunder shall not apply for any taxable year for which an election under this section is in effect.

(v) An individual who makes an election under this section may not, for United States income tax purposes, claim under any United States income tax treaty not to be a U.S. resident. The relationship of U.S. income tax treaties and the election under this section is illustrated by the following example.

*Example.* H, a U.S. citizen, is married to W, a nonresident alien of the United States and a domiciliary of country X. H and W maintain their only permanent home in country X. W receives both U.S. source and country X source interest during the taxable year. The interest is not effectively connected with a permanent establishment or a fixed base in any country. H and W make the section 6013(g) election. Under article ii (1) of the United States—country X Income Tax Convention interest derived and beneficially owned by a resident of one contracting state is exempt from tax in the other contracting state. Article 4(1) of the treaty provides that an individual is a resident of a contracting state if subject to tax in that country by reason of the individual's domicile, residence, or citizenship. Under article 4(1) of the treaty, W is a resident of country X by virtue of her domicile in country X and also of the United States by virtue of the section 6013(g) election. Article 4(2) of the treaty provides that if an individual is a resident of both the United States and country X by reason of article 4(1), the individual shall be deemed to be a resident of the contracting state in which he or she has a permanent home available. Because W's sole permanent home is in country X, under article 4(2) of the treaty W is treated as a resident of country X for purposes of the treaty. Because W has elected under section 6013(g) to be treated as a U.S. resident (and thus to be taxed on worldwide income), W may not, for U.S. income tax purposes, claim under the treaty not to be a U.S. resident. W, therefore, is subject to U.S. income tax on the interest. For purposes of country X income tax, W is considered a resident of country X under the treaty.

(3) *Suspension of election.*—(i) An election made under this section is suspended and is not in effect for a taxable year subsequent to the first taxable year for which made if neither spouse is a United States spouse during that subsequent taxable year. Thus, for example, the election is in suspense if both spouses are nonresident aliens for the entire taxable year.

(ii) If either spouse dies during any taxable year for which the election under this section is in effect, other than the first taxable year for which the election is to be in effect, the taxable year shall include, solely for purposes of this paragraph (a)(3), only those days during the taxable year on which both spouses are alive. Thus, for example, if the United States spouse dies during the taxable year, the election is not suspended for that year even if the surviving nonresident alien spouse never acquires United States citizenship or residency. Similarly, if the nonresident alien spouse dies during the taxable year, the election is not suspended for that year even if the surviving United States spouse subsequently abandons United States citizenship or residency. However, if neither spouse was a United States spouse at any time during the period of the taxable year when both spouses were alive, the election is suspended for that year even if the surviving spouse subsequently acquires United States citizenship or residency. For the effect of the death of either spouse on the status of the election in subsequent taxable years, see paragraph (b)(2) of this section.

(4) *Time and manner of making an election.*—(i) A husband and wife shall make the election under this section by attaching a statement to a joint return for the first taxable year for which the election is to be in effect. The election must be made before the expiration of the period prescribed by section 6511(a) (or section 6511(c) if the period is extended by agreement) for making a claim for credit or refund. If either or both spouses die after the close of the taxable year but before the joint return is filed, the election may be made by the

executor, administrator, or other person charged with the property of the deceased spouse. If the election is made with a joint amended return, the amended return should be made on Form 1040 or 1040A, the word "Amended" should be written clearly on the front of the return, and an amended return also must be filed for each subsequent taxable year as to which a return previously has been filed by either spouse.

(ii) The statement must contain a declaration that the election is being made and that the requirements of paragraph (a)(1) of this section are met for the taxable year. The statement must also contain the name, address, and taxpayer identifying number of each spouse. If the election is being made on behalf of a deceased spouse, the statement must contain the name and address of the executor, administrator, or other person making the election on behalf of the deceased spouse. The statement must be signed by both persons making the election.

(b) *Termination of election.*—(1) *Revocation.*—(i) An election under this section shall terminate if either spouse revokes the election. An election that is revoked terminates as of the first taxable year for which the last day prescribed by section 6072(a) and 6081(a) for filing the return of tax has not yet occurred.

(ii) Revocation of the election is made by filing a statement of revocation in the following manner. If the spouse revoking the election is required to file a return under section 6012, the statement is filed by attaching it to the return for the first taxable year to which the revocation applies. If the spouse revoking the election is not required to file a return under section 6012, but files a claim for refund under section 6511, the statement is filed by attaching it to the claim for refund. If the spouse revoking the election is not required to file a return and does not file a claim for refund, the statement is filed by submitting it to the service center director with whom was filed the most recent joint return of the spouses. The revocation may, if the revoking spouse dies after the close of the first taxable year to which the revocation applies but before the return, claim for refund, or statement of revocation is filed, be made by the executor, administrator or other person charged with the property of the deceased spouse.

(iii) A revocation of the election is effective as of a particular taxable year if it is filed on or before the last day prescribed by section 6072(a) and 6081(a) for filing the return of tax for that taxable year. However, the revocation is not final until that last day.

(iv) The statement of revocation must contain a declaration that the election under this section is being revoked. The statement must also contain the name, address, and taxpayer identifying number of each spouse. If the revocation is being made on behalf of a deceased spouse, the statement must contain the name and address of the executor, administrator, or other person revoking the election on behalf of the deceased spouse. The statement must also include a list of the States, foreign countries, and possessions of the United States which have community property laws and in which—

(A) Each spouse is domiciled, or

(B) Real property is located from which either of the spouses receives income.

The statement must be signed by the person revoking the election.

(2) *Death.*—An election under this section shall terminate if either spouse dies. An election that terminates on account of death terminates as of the first taxable year of the surviving spouse following the taxable year in which the death occurred. However, if the surviving spouse is a citizen or resident of the United States who is entitled to the benefits of section 2, the election terminates as of the first taxable year following the last taxable year for which the surviving spouse is entitled to the benefits of section 2. If both spouses die within the same taxable year, the election terminates as of the first day after the close of the taxable year in which the deaths occurred.

(3) *Legal separation.*—An election under this section terminates if the spouses legally separate under a decree of divorce or of separate maintenance. An election that terminates on account of legal separation terminates as of the close of the taxable year preceding the taxable year in which the separation occurs. The rules in § 1.6013-4(a) are relevant in determining whether two spouses are legally separated.

(4) *Inadequate records.*—An election under this section may be terminated by the Commissioner if it is determined that either spouse has failed to keep adequate records. An election that is terminated on account of inadequate records terminates as of the close of the taxable year preceding the taxable year for which the Commissioner determines that the election should be terminated. Adequate records are the books, records, and other information reasonably necessary to ascertain the amount of liability for taxes under chapters 1, 5, and 24 of the code of either spouse for the taxable year. Adequate records also include the granting of access to the books and records.

(c) *Illustrations.*—The application of this section is illustrated by the following examples. In each case the individual's taxable year is the calendar year and the spouses are not legally separated.

*Example (1).* W, a U.S. citizen for the entire taxable year 1979, is married to H, a nonresident alien individual. W and H may make the section 6013(g) election for 1979 by filing the statement of election with a joint return. If W and H make the election, income from sources within and without the United States received by W and H in 1979 and subsequent years must be included in gross income for each taxable year unless the election later is terminated or suspended. While W and H must file a joint return for 1979, joint or separate returns may be filed for subsequent years.

*Example (2).* H and W are husband and wife and are both nonresident alien individuals. In June 1980 H becomes a U.S. resident and remains a resident for the balance of the year. H and W may make the section 6013(g) election for 1980. If H and W make the election, income from sources within and without the United States received by H and W for the entire taxable year 1980 and subsequent years must be included in gross income for each taxable year, unless the election later is terminated or suspended.

*Example (3).* W, a U.S. resident on December 31, 1981, is married to H, a nonresident alien. W and H make the section 6013(g) election and file joint returns for 1981 and succeeding years. On January 10, 1987, W becomes a nonresident alien. H has remained a nonresident alien. W and H may file a joint return or separate returns for 1987. As neither W nor H is a U.S. resident at any time during 1988, their election is suspended for 1988. If W and H have U.S. source or foreign source income effectively connected with the conduct of a U.S. trade or business in 1988, they must file separate returns as nonresident aliens. W becomes a U.S. resident again on January 5, 1990. Their election no longer is in suspense. Income from sources within and without the United States received by W or H in the years their election is not suspended must be included in gross income for each taxable year.

*Example (4).* H, a U.S. citizen for the entire taxable year 1979, is married to W, who is not a U.S. citizen. While W believes that she is a U.S. resident, H and W make the section 6013(g) election for 1979 to cover the possibility that later it would be determined that she is a nonresident alien during 1979. The election for 1979 will not be considered evidence that W was a nonresident alien in prior years. Income from sources within and without the United States received by H and W in 1979 and subsequent years must be included in gross income for each taxable year, unless the election later is terminated or suspended. [Reg. §1.6013-6.]

☐ [*T.D. 7670, 1-30-80. Amended by T.D. 7842, 11-2-85 and T.D. 8411, 4-24-92.*]

### [Reg. §1.6013-7]

**§1.6013-7. Joint return for year in which nonresident alien becomes resident of the United States.**—(a) *Election for special treatment.*—(1) *In general.*—Two individuals who are husband and wife at the close of a taxable year ending on or after December 31, 1975, may make an election under this section for that taxable year if one spouse is a citizen or resident of the United States on the last day of that taxable year and the other spouse is a nonresident alien at the beginning of that taxable year and a citizen or resident of the United States at the close of that taxable year. Two married individuals who are nonresident aliens at the beginning of a taxable year and who are U.S. citizens or residents on the last day of that taxable year qualify for the election. The effect of the election is that each spouse is treated as a resident of the United States for purposes of chapters 1, 5, and 24 and sections 6012, 6013, 6072, and 6091 of the Code for all of that taxable year. A husband and wife may not make an election if an election has previously been made under this section by either spouse.

(2) *Particular rules.*—The rules in subdivisions (ii) through (v) of §1.6013-6(a)(2) are applicable to this section.

(3) *Time and manner of making an election.*—A husband and wife shall make the election under this section in accordance with the rules in §1.6013-6(a)(4).

(b) *Section 6013(g) election in effect.*—If an election under section 6013(g) is in effect for a year subsequent to the first taxable year for which made and during that subsequent year the husband and wife meet the requirements of section 6013(h) and paragraph (a)(1) of this section, then the election under section 6013(g) shall apply to that subsequent taxable year. A separate election under section 6013(h) is not required for that subsequent taxable year. [Reg. §1.6013-7.]

☐ [*T.D. 7670, 1-30-80.*]

### [Reg. §301.6014-1]

**§301.6014-1. Income tax return—Tax not computed by taxpayer.**—For provisions relating to the election not to show on an

income tax return the amount of tax due in connection therewith, see §§1.6014-1 and 1.6014-2 of this chapter (Income Tax Regulations). [Reg. §301.6014-1.]

☐ [*T.D. 6498, 10-24-60. Amended by T.D. 7102, 3-23-71.*]

### [Reg. §1.6014-2]

**§1.6014-2. Tax not computed by taxpayer for taxable years beginning after December 31, 1969.**—(a) *In general.*—An individual subject to the tax imposed by section 1 of the Code may, in accordance with the instructions applicable to the income tax return to be filed, elect, for any taxable year beginning after December 31, 1969, not to show on his income tax return for such year the amount of tax due in connection with such return.

(b) *Restriction on making an election.*—The election pursuant to this section shall not be made by an individual who does not file his return (or amended return) making such election on or before the date prescribed in section 6072(a) for the filing of the original return (determined without regard to any extension of time).

(c) *Effect of election.*—(1) A taxpayer who, in accordance with the provisions of this section, elects not to show the tax on his income tax return is not required to pay the unpaid balance of such tax at the time he files the return. In such case, the tax will be computed for the taxpayer by the Internal Revenue Service, and a notice will be mailed to the taxpayer stating the amount of tax due. Where it is determined that a refund of tax is due, the Internal Revenue Service will send such refund to the taxpayer. See paragraph (c) of §301.6402-3 of this chapter (Regulations on Procedure and Administration). The computation of tax by the Internal Revenue Service shall be treated for purposes of this chapter as if made by the taxpayer, and such computation or the issuance of a notice or refund pursuant thereto shall not relieve the taxpayer of liability for any deficiency (although the deficiency is based upon an amount of tax different from that computed for the taxpayer by the Internal Revenue Service) or affect the rights of the Internal Revenue Service with respect to any subsequent audit or other review of the taxpayer's return.

(2) Where the election provided for in this section is made by a taxpayer who takes the standard deduction and who has adjusted gross income of less than $10,000, such election constitutes an election to pay the tax imposed by section 3.

(3) A taxpayer who makes an election under section 6014 shall not be precluded from claiming—

(i) Status as a head of household or a surviving spouse;

(ii) The credit under section 31 (relating to tax withheld on wages);

(iii) The credit under section 37 (relating to retirement income);

(iv) The credit under section 38 (relating to investment in certain depreciable property);

(v) The credit under section 39 (relating to certain uses of gasoline and lubricating oil);

(vi) The credit under section 41 (relating to contributions to candidates for public office);

(vii) The credit under section 42 (relating to personal exemptions);

(viii) The credit under section 43 (relating to earned income);

(ix) The credit under section 44 (relating to purchase of new principal residence); or

(x) The credit under section 45 (relating to overpayments of tax).

(d) *Joint returns.*—(1) A husband and wife who file a joint return may elect not to show the tax on such return in accordance with the rules prescribed in paragraphs (a) and (b) of this section.

(2) The tax computed for a husband and wife who elect pursuant to this section not to show their tax on their joint income tax return shall be the lesser of the following amounts:

(i) A tax computed as though the return of income constituted a joint return, or

(ii) If sufficient information is provided for the taxable income of each spouse to be determined, a tax computed as though the return of income constituted the separate returns of the spouses.

(e) *Married individuals filing separate returns.*—This section shall apply to married individuals filing separate returns unless otherwise provided in the instructions accompanying a return. The instructions may require the taxpayer to attach to his return a statement to the effect that his tax and the tax of his spouse were determined in accordance with the rules of sections 141(d) and 142(a).

(f) *Revocation of election.*—An election pursuant to this section may be revoked on an amended return (whether such return is filed before or after the date prescribed in section 6072(a) for filing the original return). [Reg. §1.6014-2.]

☐ [*T.D. 7102, 3-23-71. Amended by T.D. 7298, 12-21-73 and T.D. 7391, 12-1-75.*]

### [Reg. §1.6015-0]

**§1.6015-0. Table of contents.**—This section lists captions contained in §§1.6015-1 through 1.6015-9.

  ☐ [*T.D. 9003, 7-17-2002.*]

### [Reg. §1.6015-1]

**§1.6015-1. Relief from joint and several liability on a joint return.**—(a) *In general.*—(1) An individual who qualifies and elects under section 6013 to file a joint Federal income tax return with another individual is jointly and severally liable for the joint Federal income tax liabilities for that year. A spouse or former spouse may be relieved of joint and several liability for Federal income tax for that year under the following three relief provisions:

  (i) Innocent spouse relief under §1.6015-2.
  (ii) Allocation of deficiency under §1.6015-3.
  (iii) Equitable relief under §1.6015-4.

(2) A requesting spouse may submit a single claim electing relief under both or either §§1.6015-2 and 1.6015-3, and requesting relief under §1.6015-4. However, equitable relief under §1.6015-4 is available only to a requesting spouse who fails to qualify for relief under §§1.6015-2 and 1.6015-3. If a requesting spouse elects the application of either §1.6015-2 or 1.6015-3, the Internal Revenue Service will consider whether relief is appropriate under the other elective provision and, to the extent relief is unavailable under either, under §1.6015-4. If a requesting spouse seeks relief only under §1.6015-4, the Secretary may not grant relief under §1.6015-2 or 1.6015-3 in the absence of an affirmative election made by the requesting spouse under either of those sections. If in the course of reviewing a request for relief only under §1.6015-4, the IRS determines that the requesting spouse may qualify for relief under §1.6015-2 or 1.6015-3 instead of §1.6015-4, the Internal Revenue Service will correspond with the requesting spouse to see if the requesting spouse would like to amend his or her request to elect the application of §1.6015-2 or 1.6015-3. If the requesting spouse chooses to amend the claim for relief, the requesting spouse must submit an affirmative election under §1.6015-2 or 1.6015-3. The amended claim for relief will relate

back to the original claim for purposes of determining the timeliness of the claim.

(3) Relief is not available for liabilities that are required to be reported on a joint Federal income tax return but are not income taxes imposed under Subtitle A of the Internal Revenue Code (e.g., domestic service employment taxes under section 3510).

(b) *Duress.*—For rules relating to the treatment of returns signed under duress, see § 1.6013-4(d).

(c) *Prior closing agreement or offer in compromise.*—(1) *In general.*—A requesting spouse is not entitled to relief from joint and several liability under § 1.6015-2, 1.6015-3, or 1.6015-4 for any tax year for which the requesting spouse has entered into a closing agreement with the Commissioner that disposes of the same liability that is the subject of the claim for relief. In addition, a requesting spouse is not entitled to relief from joint and several liability under § 1.6015-2, 1.6015-3, or 1.6015-4 for any tax year for which the requesting spouse has entered into an offer in compromise with the Commissioner. For rules relating to the effect of closing agreements and offers in compromise, see sections 7121 and 7122, and the regulations thereunder.

(2) *Exception for agreements relating to TEFRA partnership proceedings.*—The rule in paragraph (c)(1) of this section regarding the unavailability of relief from joint and several liability when the liability to which the claim for relief relates was the subject of a prior closing agreement entered into by the requesting spouse, shall not apply to an agreement described in section 6224(c) with respect to partnership items (or any penalty, addition to tax, or additional amount that relates to adjustments to partnership items) that is entered into while the requesting spouse is a party to a pending partnership-level proceeding conducted under the provisions of subchapter C of chapter 63 of subtitle F of the Internal Revenue Code (TEFRA partnership proceeding). If, however, a requesting spouse enters into a closing agreement pertaining to any penalty, addition to tax, or additional amount that relates to adjustments to partnership items, at a time when the requesting spouse is not a party to a pending TEFRA partnership proceeding (e.g., in connection with an affected items proceeding), then the provisions of paragraph (c)(1) shall apply. Similarly, if a requesting spouse enters into a closing agreement with respect to both partnership items (including affected items) and nonpartnership items, while the requesting spouse is a party to a pending TEFRA partnership proceeding, the provisions of paragraph (c)(1) shall apply to the portion of the closing agreement that relates to nonpartnership items and the provisions of this paragraph (c)(2) shall apply to the remainder of the closing agreement.

(3) *Examples.*—The following examples illustrate the rules of this paragraph (c):

*Example 1.* H and W file joint returns for taxable years 2002-2004, on which they claim losses attributable to H's limited partnership interest in Partnership A. In January 2006, the Internal Revenue Service commences an audit under the provisions of subchapter C of chapter 63 of subtitle F of the Internal Revenue Code (TEFRA partnership proceeding) regarding Partnership A's 2002-2004 taxable years, and sends H and W a notice under section 6223(a)(1). In September 2007, H files a bankruptcy petition under chapter 7 of the Bankruptcy Code and receives a discharge in April 2008. In August 2008, H and W enter into a closing agreement with the Internal Revenue Service, in which H and W agree to the disallowance of some of the claimed losses from Partnership A for taxable years 2002 through 2007. W may not later claim relief from joint and several liability under section 6015 as to the disallowed losses attributable to Partnership A for taxable years 2002 to 2007. This is because at the time W entered into the closing agreement, H's partnership items attributable to Partnership A had converted to nonpartnership items as a result of H's filing of the bankruptcy petition. The conversion of H's items also terminated W's status as a partner in the TEFRA partnership proceeding regarding Partnership A. Consequently, the closing agreement did not pertain to partnership items and W was not a party to a pending partnership-level proceeding regarding Partnership A when she entered into the closing agreement. Accordingly, the exception in paragraph (c)(2) of this section for agreements relating to TEFRA partnership proceedings does not apply.

*Example 2.* H and W file a joint return for taxable year 2002, on which they claim $25,000 in losses attributable to H's general partnership interest in Partnership B. In November 2003, the Service proposes a deficiency in tax relating to H's and W's 2002 joint return arising from omitted taxable interest income in the amount of $2,000 that is attributable to H. In July 2005, the Internal Revenue Service commences a TEFRA partnership proceeding regarding Partnership B's 2002 and 2003 taxable years, and sends H and W a notice under section 6223(a)(1). In March 2006, H and W enter into a closing agreement with the Service. The closing agreement provides for the disallowance of the claimed losses from Partnership B in excess of

H's and W's out-of-pocket expenditures relating to Partnership B for taxable year 2002 and any subsequent year(s) in which H and W claimed losses from Partnership B. In addition, H and W agree to the imposition of the accuracy-related penalty under section 6662 with respect to the disallowed losses attributable to partnership B. In the closing agreement, H and W also agree to the deficiency resulting from the omitted interest income for taxable year 2002. W may not later claim relief from joint and several liability under section 6015 as to the deficiency in tax attributable to the omitted income of $2,000 for taxable year 2002, because this portion of the closing agreement pertains to nonpartnership items. In contrast, W may claim relief from joint and several liability as to the disallowed losses and accuracy-related penalty attributable to Partnership B for taxable year 2002 or any subsequent year(s). This is because this portion of the closing agreement pertains to partnership and affected items and was entered into at a time when W was a party to the pending partnership-level proceeding regarding Partnership B. Consequently, W never had the opportunity to raise the innocent spouse defense in the course of that TEFRA partnership proceeding. (See § 1.6015-5(b)(5) relating to premature claims).

(d) *Fraudulent scheme.*—If the Secretary establishes that a spouse transferred assets to the other spouse as part of a fraudulent scheme, relief is not available under section 6015, and section 6013(d)(3) applies to the return. For purposes of this section, a fraudulent scheme includes a scheme to defraud the Service or another third party, including, but not limited to, creditors, ex-spouses, and business partners.

(e) *Res judicata and collateral estoppel.*—A requesting spouse is barred from relief from joint and several liability under section 6015 by res judicata for any tax year for which a court of competent jurisdiction has rendered a final decision on the requesting spouse's tax liability if relief under section 6015 was at issue in the prior proceeding, or if the requesting spouse meaningfully participated in that proceeding and could have raised relief under section 6015. A requesting spouse has not meaningfully participated in a prior proceeding if, due to the effective date of section 6015, relief under section 6015 was not available in that proceeding. Also, any final decisions rendered by a court of competent jurisdiction regarding issues relevant to section 6015 are conclusive and the requesting spouse may be collaterally estopped from relitigating those issues.

(f) *Community property laws.*—(1) *In general.*—In determining whether relief is available under § 1.6015-2, 1.6015-3, or 1.6015-4, items of income, credits, and deductions are generally allocated to the spouses without regard to the operation of community property laws. An erroneous item is attributed to the individual whose activities gave rise to such item. See § 1.6015-3(d)(2).

(2) *Example.*—The following example illustrates the rule of this paragraph (f):

*Example.* (i) H and W are married and have lived in State A (a community property state) since 1987. On April 15, 2003, H and W file a joint Federal income tax return for the 2002 taxable year. In August 2005, the Internal Revenue Service proposes a $17,000 deficiency with respect to the 2002 joint return. A portion of the deficiency is attributable to $20,000 of H's unreported interest income from his individual bank account. The remainder of the deficiency is attributable to $30,000 of W's disallowed business expense deductions. Under the laws of State A, H and W each own 1/2 of all income earned and property acquired during the marriage.

(ii) In November 2005, H and W divorce and W timely elects to allocate the deficiency. Even though the laws of State A provide that 1/2 of the interest income is W's, for purposes of relief under this section, the $20,000 unreported interest income is allocable to H, and the $30,000 disallowed deduction is allocable to W. The community property laws of State A are not considered in allocating items for this purpose.

(g) *Scope of this section and § § 1.6015-2 through 1.6015-9.*—This section and § § 1.6015-2 through 1.6015-9 do not apply to any portion of a liability for any taxable year for which a claim for credit or refund is barred by operation of law or rule of law.

(h) *Definitions.*—(1) *Requesting spouse.*—A requesting spouse is an individual who filed a joint return and elects relief from Federal income tax liability arising from that return under § 1.6015-2 or 1.6015-3, or requests relief from Federal income tax liability arising from that return under § 1.6015-4.

(2) *Nonrequesting spouse.*—A nonrequesting spouse is the individual with whom the requesting spouse filed the joint return for the year for which relief from liability is sought.

(3) *Item.*—An item is that which is required to be separately listed on an individual income tax return or any required attach-

ments. Items include, but are not limited to, gross income, deductions, credits, and basis.

(4) *Erroneous item.*—An erroneous item is any item resulting in an understatement or deficiency in tax to the extent that such item is omitted from, or improperly reported (including improperly characterized) on an individual income tax return. For example, unreported income from an investment asset resulting in an understatement or deficiency in tax is an erroneous item. Similarly, ordinary income that is improperly reported as capital gain resulting in an understatement or deficiency in tax is also an erroneous item. In addition, a deduction for an expense that is personal in nature that results in an understatement or deficiency in tax is an erroneous item of deduction. An erroneous item is also an improperly reported item that affects the liability on other returns (e.g., an improper net operating loss that is carried back to a prior year's return). Penalties and interest are not erroneous items. Rather, relief from penalties and interest will generally be determined based on the proportion of the total erroneous items from which the requesting spouse is relieved. If a penalty relates to a particular erroneous item, see §1.6015-3(d)(4)(iv)(B).

(5) *Election or request.*—A qualifying election under §1.6015-2 or 1.6015-3, or request under §1.6015-4, is the first timely claim for relief from joint and several liability for the tax year for which relief is sought. A qualifying election also includes a requesting spouse's second election to seek relief from joint and several liability for the same tax year under §1.6015-3 when the additional qualifications of paragraphs (h)(5)(i) and (ii) of this section are met—

(i) The requesting spouse did not qualify for relief under §1.6015-3 when the Internal Revenue Service considered the first election solely because the qualifications of §1.6015-3(a) were not satisfied; and

(ii) At the time of the second election, the qualifications for relief under §1.6015-3(a) are satisfied.

(i) [Reserved]

(j) *Transferee liability.*—(1) *In general.*—The relief provisions of section 6015 do not negate liability that arises under the operation of other laws. Therefore, a requesting spouse who is relieved of joint and several liability under §1.6015-2, 1.6015-3, or 1.6015-4 may nevertheless remain liable for the unpaid tax (including additions to tax, penalties, and interest) to the extent provided by Federal or state transferee liability or property laws. For the rules regarding the liability of transferees, see sections 6901 through 6904 and the regulations thereunder. In addition, the requesting spouse's property may be subject to collection under Federal or state property laws.

(2) *Example.*—The following example illustrates the rule of this paragraph (j):

*Example.* H and W timely file their 1998 joint income tax return on April 15, 1999. H dies in March 2000, and the executor of H's will transfers all of the estate's assets to W. In July 2001, the Internal Revenue Service assesses a deficiency for the 1998 return. The items giving rise to the deficiency are attributable to H. W is relieved of the liability under section 6015, and H's estate remains solely liable. The Internal Revenue Service may seek to collect the deficiency from W to the extent permitted under Federal or state transferee liability or property laws.

[Reg. §1.6015-1.]

☐ [*T.D.* 9003, 7-17-2002.]

### [Reg. §1.6015-2]

**§1.6015-2. Relief from liability applicable to all qualifying joint filers.**—(a) *In general.*—A requesting spouse may be relieved of joint and several liability for tax (including additions to tax, penalties, and interest) from an understatement for a taxable year under this section if the requesting spouse elects the application of this section in accordance with §§1.6015-1(h)(5) and 1.6015-5, and—

(1) A joint return was filed for the taxable year;

(2) On the return there is an understatement attributable to erroneous items of the nonrequesting spouse;

(3) The requesting spouse establishes that in signing the return he or she did not know and had no reason to know of the understatement; and

(4) It is inequitable to hold the requesting spouse liable for the deficiency attributable to the understatement.

(b) *Understatement.*—The term *understatement* has the meaning given to such term by section 6662(d)(2)(A) and the regulations thereunder.

(c) *Knowledge or reason to know.*—A requesting spouse has knowledge or reason to know of an understatement if he or she actually knew of the understatement, or if a reasonable person in similar circumstances would have known of the understatement. For rules

relating to a requesting spouse's actual knowledge, see §1.6015-3(c)(2). All of the facts and circumstances are considered in determining whether a requesting spouse had reason to know of an understatement. The facts and circumstances that are considered include, but are not limited to, the nature of the erroneous item and the amount of the erroneous item relative to other items; the couple's financial situation; the requesting spouse's educational background and business experience; the extent of the requesting spouse's participation in the activity that resulted in the erroneous item; whether the requesting spouse failed to inquire, at or before the time the return was signed, about items on the return or omitted from the return that a reasonable person would question; and whether the erroneous item represented a departure from a recurring pattern reflected in prior years' returns (e.g., omitted income from an investment regularly reported on prior years' returns).

(d) *Inequity.*—All of the facts and circumstances are considered in determining whether it is inequitable to hold a requesting spouse jointly and severally liable for an understatement. One relevant factor for this purpose is whether the requesting spouse significantly benefitted, directly or indirectly, from the understatement. A significant benefit is any benefit in excess of normal support. Evidence of direct or indirect benefit may consist of transfers of property or rights to property, including transfers that may be received several years after the year of the understatement. Thus, for example, if a requesting spouse receives property (including life insurance proceeds) from the nonrequesting spouse that is beyond normal support and traceable to items omitted from gross income that are attributable to the nonrequesting spouse, the requesting spouse will be considered to have received significant benefit from those items. Other factors that may also be taken into account, if the situation warrants, include the fact that the requesting spouse has been deserted by the nonrequesting spouse, the fact that the spouses have been divorced or separated, or that the requesting spouse received benefit on the return from the understatement. For guidance concerning the criteria to be used in determining whether it is inequitable to hold a requesting spouse jointly and severally liable under this section, see Rev. Proc. 2000-15 (2000-1 C.B. 447), or other guidance published by the Treasury and IRS (see §601.601(d)(2) of this chapter).

(e) *Partial relief.*—(1) *In general.*—If a requesting spouse had no knowledge or reason to know of only a portion of an erroneous item, the requesting spouse may be relieved of the liability attributable to that portion of that item, if all other requirements are met with respect to that portion.

(2) *Example.*—The following example illustrates the rules of this paragraph (e):

*Example.* H and W are married and file their 2004 joint income tax return in March 2005. In April 2006, H is convicted of embezzling $2 million from his employer during 2004. H kept all of his embezzlement income in an individual bank account, and he used most of the funds to support his gambling habit. H and W had a joint bank account into which H and W deposited all of their reported income. Each month during 2004, H transferred an additional $10,000 from the individual account to H and W's joint bank account. W paid the household expenses using this joint account, and regularly received the bank statements relating to the account. W had no knowledge or reason to know of H's embezzling activities. However, W did have knowledge and reason to know of $120,000 of the $2 million of H's embezzlement income at the time she signed the joint return because that amount passed through the couple's joint bank account. Therefore, W may be relieved of the liability arising from $1,880,000 of the unreported embezzlement income, but she may not be relieved of the liability for the deficiency arising from $120,000 of the unreported embezzlement income of which she knew and had reason to know.

[Reg. §1.6015-2.]

☐ [*T.D.* 9003, 7-17-2002.]

### [Reg. §1.6015-3]

**§1.6015-3. Allocation of deficiency for individuals who are no longer married, are legally separated, or are not members of the same household.**—(a) *Election to allocate deficiency.*—A requesting spouse may elect to allocate a deficiency if, as defined in paragraph (b) of this section, the requesting spouse is divorced, widowed, or legally separated, or has not been a member of the same household as the nonrequesting spouse at any time during the 12-month period ending on the date an election for relief is filed. For purposes of this section, the marital status of a deceased requesting spouse will be determined on the earlier of the date of the election or the date of death in accordance with section 7703(a)(1). Subject to the restrictions of paragraph (c) of this section, an eligible requesting spouse who elects the application of this section in accordance with §§1.6015-1(h)(5) and 1.6015-5 generally may be relieved of joint and several liability for the portion of any deficiency that is allocated to the nonrequesting spouse pursuant to the allocation methods set forth in paragraph(d) of this section. Relief may be available to both spouses filing the joint return if each spouse is eligible for and elects the application of this section.

(b) *Definitions.*—(1) *Divorced.*—A determination of whether a requesting spouse is divorced for purposes of this section will be made in accordance with section 7703 and the regulations thereunder. Such determination will be made as of the date the election is filed.

(2) *Legally separated.*—A determination of whether a requesting spouse is legally separated for purposes of this section will be made in accordance with section 7703 and the regulations thereunder. Such determination will be made as of the date the election is filed.

(3) *Members of the same household.*—(i) *Temporary absences.*—A requesting spouse and a nonrequesting spouse are considered members of the same household during either spouse's temporary absences from the household if it is reasonable to assume that the absent spouse will return to the household, and the household or a substantially equivalent household is maintained in anticipation of such return. Examples of temporary absences may include, but are not limited to, absence due to incarceration, illness, business, vacation, military service, or education.

(ii) *Separate dwellings.*—A husband and wife who reside in the same dwelling are considered members of the same household. In addition, a husband and wife who reside in two separate dwellings are considered members of the same household if the spouses are not estranged or one spouse is temporarily absent from the other's household within the meaning of paragraph (b)(3)(i) of this section.

(c) *Limitations.*—(1) *No refunds.*—Relief under this section is only available for unpaid liabilities resulting from understatements of liability. Refunds are not authorized under this section.

(2) *Actual knowledge.*—(i) *In general.*—If, under section 6015(c)(3)(C), the Secretary demonstrates that, at the time the return was signed, the requesting spouse had actual knowledge of an erroneous item that is allocable to the nonrequesting spouse, the election to allocate the deficiency attributable to that item is invalid, and the requesting spouse remains liable for the portion of the deficiency attributable to that item. The Service, having both the burden of production and the burden of persuasion, must establish, by a preponderance of the evidence, that the requesting spouse had actual knowledge of the erroneous item in order to invalidate the election.

(A) *Omitted income.*—In the case of omitted income, knowledge of the item includes knowledge of the receipt of the income. For example, assume W received $5,000 of dividend income from her investment in X Co. but did not report it on the joint return. H knew that W received $5,000 of dividend income from X Co. that year. H had actual knowledge of the erroneous item (i.e., $5,000 of unreported dividend income from X Co.), and no relief is available under this section for the deficiency attributable to the dividend income from X Co. This rule applies equally in situations where the other spouse has unreported income although the spouse does not have an actual receipt of cash (e.g., dividend reinvestment or a distributive share from a flow-through entity shown on Schedule K-1, "Partner's Share of Income, Credits, Deductions, etc.").

(B) *Deduction or credit.*—(1) *Erroneous deductions in general.*—In the case of an erroneous deduction or credit, knowledge of the item means knowledge of the facts that made the item not allowable as a deduction or credit.

(2) *Fictitious or inflated deduction.*—If a deduction is fictitious or inflated, the IRS must establish that the requesting spouse actually knew that the expenditure was not incurred, or not incurred to that extent.

(ii) *Partial knowledge.*—If a requesting spouse had actual knowledge of only a portion of an erroneous item, then relief is not available for that portion of the erroneous item. For example, if H knew that W received $1,000 of dividend income and did not know that W received an additional $4,000 of dividend income, relief would not be available for the portion of the deficiency attributable to the $1,000 of dividend income of which H had actual knowledge. A requesting spouse's actual knowledge of the proper tax treatment of an item is not relevant for purposes of demonstrating that the requesting spouse had actual knowledge of an erroneous item. For example, assume H did not know W's dividend income from X Co. was taxable, but knew that W received the dividend income. Relief is not available under this section. In addition, a requesting spouse's knowledge of how an erroneous item was treated on the tax return is not relevant to a determination of whether the requesting spouse had actual knowledge of the item. For example, assume that H knew of W's dividend income, but H failed to review the completed return

and did not know that W omitted the dividend income from the return. Relief is not available under this section.

(iii) *Knowledge of the source not sufficient.*—Knowledge of the source of an erroneous item is not sufficient to establish actual knowledge. For example, assume H knew that W owned X Co. stock, but H did not know that X Co. paid dividends to W that year. H's knowledge of W's ownership in X Co. is not sufficient to establish that H had actual knowledge of the dividend income from X Co. In addition, a requesting spouse's actual knowledge may not be inferred when the requesting spouse merely had reason to know of the erroneous item. Even if H's knowledge of W's ownership interest in X Co. indicates a reason to know of the dividend income, actual knowledge of such dividend income cannot be inferred from H's reason to know. Similarly, the IRS need not establish that a requesting spouse knew of the source of an erroneous item in order to establish that the requesting spouse had actual knowledge of the item itself. For example, assume H knew that W received $1,000, but he did not know the source of the $1,000. W and H omit the $1,000 from their joint return. H has actual knowledge of the item giving rise to the deficiency ($1,000), and relief is not available under this section.

(iv) *Factors supporting actual knowledge.*—To demonstrate that a requesting spouse had actual knowledge of an erroneous item at the time the return was signed, the IRS may rely upon all of the facts and circumstances. One factor that may be relied upon in demonstrating that a requesting spouse had actual knowledge of an erroneous item is whether the requesting spouse made a deliberate effort to avoid learning about the item in order to be shielded from liability. This factor, together with all other facts and circumstances, may demonstrate that the requesting spouse had actual knowledge of the item, and the requesting spouse's election would be invalid with respect to that entire item. Another factor that may be relied upon in demonstrating that a requesting spouse had actual knowledge of an erroneous item is whether the requesting spouse and the nonrequesting spouse jointly owned the property that resulted in the erroneous item. Joint ownership is a factor supporting a finding that the requesting spouse had actual knowledge of an erroneous item. For purposes of this paragraph, a requesting spouse will not be considered to have had an ownership interest in an item based solely on the operation of community property law. Rather, a requesting spouse who resided in a community property state at the time the return was signed will be considered to have had an ownership interest in an item only if the requesting spouse's name appeared on the ownership documents, or there otherwise is an indication that the requesting spouse asserted dominion and control over the item. For example, assume H and W live in State A, a community property state. After their marriage, H opens a bank account in his name. Under the operation of the community property laws of State A, W owns 1/2 of the bank account. However, W does not have an ownership interest in the account for purposes of this paragraph (c)(2)(iv) because the account is not held in her name and there is no other indication that she asserted dominion and control over the item.

(v) *Abuse exception.*—If the requesting spouse establishes that he or she was the victim of domestic abuse prior to the time the return was signed, and that, as a result of the prior abuse, the requesting spouse did not challenge the treatment of any items on the return for fear of the nonrequesting spouse's retaliation, the limitation on actual knowledge in this paragraph (c) will not apply. However, if the requesting spouse involuntarily executed the return, the requesting spouse may choose to establish that the return was signed under duress. In such a case, § 1.6013-4(d) applies.

(3) *Disqualified asset transfers.*—(i) *In general.*—The portion of the deficiency for which a requesting spouse is liable is increased (up to the entire amount of the deficiency) by the value of any disqualified asset that was transferred to the requesting spouse. For purposes of this paragraph (c)(3), the value of a disqualified asset is the fair market value of the asset on the date of the transfer.

(ii) *Disqualified asset defined.*—A disqualified asset is any property or right to property that was transferred from the nonrequesting spouse to the requesting spouse if the principal purpose of the transfer was the avoidance of tax or payment of tax (including additions to tax, penalties, and interest).

(iii) *Presumption.*—Any asset transferred from the nonrequesting spouse to the requesting spouse during the 12-month period before the mailing date of the first letter of proposed deficiency (e.g., a 30-day letter or, if no 30-day letter is mailed, a notice of deficiency) is presumed to be a disqualified asset. The presumption also applies to any asset that is transferred from the nonrequesting spouse to the requesting spouse after the mailing date of the first letter of proposed deficiency. The presumption does not apply, however, if the requesting spouse establishes that the asset was transferred pursuant to a decree of divorce or separate maintenance or a written instrument incident to such a decree. If the presumption does not apply, but the Internal Revenue Service can establish that the purpose of the transfer was the avoidance of tax or payment of tax, the asset will be disqualified, and its value will be added to the amount of the deficiency for which the requesting spouse remains liable. If the presumption applies, a requesting spouse may still rebut the presumption by establishing that the principal purpose of the transfer was not the avoidance of tax or payment of tax.

(4) *Examples.*—The following examples illustrate the rules in this paragraph (c):

*Example 1. Actual knowledge of an erroneous item.* (i) H and W file their 2001 joint Federal income tax return on April 15, 2002. On the return, H and W report W's self-employment income, but they do not report W's self-employment tax on that income. H and W divorce in July 2003. In August 2003, H and W receive a 30-day letter from the Internal Revenue Service proposing a deficiency with respect to W's unreported self-employment tax on the 2001 return. On November 4, 2003, H files an election to allocate the deficiency to W. The erroneous item is the self-employment income, and it is allocable to W. H knows that W earned income in 2001 as a self-employed musician, but he does not know that self-employment tax must be reported on and paid with a joint return.

(ii) H's election to allocate the deficiency to W is invalid because, at the time H signed the joint return, H had actual knowledge of W's self-employment income. The fact that H was unaware of the tax consequences of that income (i.e., that an individual is required to pay self-employment tax on that income) is not relevant.

*Example 2. Actual knowledge not inferred from a requesting spouse's reason to know.* (i) H has long been an avid gambler. H supports his gambling habit and keeps all of his gambling winnings in an individual bank account, held solely in his name. W knows about H's gambling habit and that he keeps a separate bank account, but she does not know whether he has any winnings because H does not tell her, and she does not otherwise know of H's bank account transactions. H and W file their 2001 joint Federal income tax return on April 15, 2002. On October 31, 2003, H and W receive a 30-day letter proposing a $100,000 deficiency relating to H's unreported gambling income. In February 2003, H and W divorce, and in March 2004, W files an election under section 6015(c) to allocate the $100,000 deficiency to H.

(ii) While W may have had reason to know of the gambling income because she knew of H's gambling habit and separate account, W did not have actual knowledge of the erroneous item (i.e., the gambling winnings). The Internal Revenue Service may not infer actual knowledge from W's reason to know of the income. Therefore, W's election to allocate the $100,000 deficiency to H is valid.

*Example 3. Actual knowledge and failure to review return.* (i) H and W are legally separated. In February 1999, W signs a blank joint Federal income tax return for 1998 and gives it to H to fill out. The return was timely filed on April 15, 1999. In September 2001, H and W receive a 30-day letter proposing a deficiency relating to $100,000 of unreported dividend income received by H with respect to stock of ABC Co. owned by H. W knew that H received the $100,000 dividend payment in August 1998, but she did not know whether H reported that payment on the joint return.

(ii) On January 30, 2002, W files an election to allocate the deficiency from the 1998 return to H. W claims she did not review the completed joint return, and therefore, she had no actual knowledge that there was an understatement of the dividend income. W's election to allocate the deficiency to H is invalid because she had actual knowledge of the erroneous item (dividend income from ABC Co.) at the time she signed the return. The fact that W signed a blank return is irrelevant. The result would be the same if W had not reviewed the completed return or if W had reviewed the completed return and had not noticed that the item was omitted.

*Example 4. Actual knowledge of an erroneous item of income.* (i) H and W are legally separated. In June 2004, a deficiency is proposed with respect to H's and W's 2002 joint Federal income tax return that is attributable to $30,000 of unreported income from H's plumbing business that should have been reported on a Schedule C. No Schedule C was attached to the return. At the time W signed the return, W knew that H had a plumbing business but did not know whether H received any income from the business. W's election to allocate to H the deficiency attributable to the $30,000 of unreported plumbing income is valid.

(ii) Assume the same facts as in paragraph (i) of this *Example 5* except that, at the time W signed the return, W knew that H received $20,000 of plumbing income. W's election to allocate to H the deficiency attributable to the $20,000 of unreported plumbing income (of which W had actual knowledge) is invalid. W's election to allocate to H the deficiency attributable to the $10,000 of unreported plumbing income (of which W did not have actual knowledge) is valid.

(iii) Assume the same facts as in paragraph (i) of this *Example 5* except that, at the time W signed the return, W did not know the exact amount of H's plumbing income. W did know, however, that H received at least $8,000 of plumbing income. W's election to allocate to H the deficiency attributable to $8,000 of unreported plumbing income (of which W had actual knowledge) is invalid. W's election to allocate to H the deficiency attributable to the remaining $22,000 of unreported plumbing income (of which W did not have actual knowledge) is valid.

(iv) Assume the same facts as in paragraph (i) of this *Example 5* except that H reported $26,000 of plumbing income on the return and omitted $4,000 of plumbing income from the return. At the time W signed the return, W knew that H was a plumber, but she did not know that H earned more than $26,000 that year. W's election to allocate to H the deficiency attributable to the $4,000 of unreported plumbing income is valid because she did not have actual knowledge that H received plumbing income in excess of $26,000.

(v) Assume the same facts as in paragraph (i) of this *Example 5* except that H reported only $20,000 of plumbing income on the return and omitted $10,000 of plumbing income from the return. At the time W signed the return, W knew that H earned at least $26,000 that year as a plumber. However, W did not know that, in reality, H earned $30,000 that year as a plumber. W's election to allocate to H the deficiency attributable to the $6,000 of unreported plumbing income (of which W had actual knowledge) is invalid. W's election to allocate to H the deficiency attributable to the $4,000 of unreported plumbing income (of which W did not have actual knowledge) is valid.

*Example 5. Actual knowledge of a deduction that is an erroneous item.* (i) H and W are legally separated. In February 2005, a deficiency is asserted with respect to their 2002 joint Federal income tax return. The deficiency is attributable to a disallowed $1,000 deduction for medical expenses H claimed he incurred. At the time W signed the return, W knew that H had not incurred any medical expenses. W's election to allocate to H the deficiency attributable to the disallowed medical expense deduction is invalid because W had actual knowledge that H had not incurred any medical expenses.

(ii) Assume the same facts as in paragraph (i) of this *Example 6* except that, at the time W signed the return, W did not know whether H had incurred any medical expenses. W's election to allocate to H the deficiency attributable to the disallowed medical expense deduction is valid because she did not have actual knowledge that H had not incurred any medical expenses.

(iii) Assume the same facts as in paragraph (i) of this *Example 6* except that the Internal Revenue Service disallowed $400 of the $1,000 medical expense deduction. At the time W signed the return, W knew that H had incurred some medical expenses but did not know the exact amount. W's election to allocate to H the deficiency attributable to the disallowed medical expense deduction is valid because she did not have actual knowledge that H had not incurred medical expenses (in excess of the floor amount under section 213(a)) of more than $600.

(iv) Assume the same facts as in paragraph (i) of this *Example 6* except that H claims a medical expense deduction of $10,000 and the Internal Revenue Service disallows $9,600. At the time W signed the return, W knew H had incurred some medical expenses but did not know the exact amount. W also knew that H incurred medical expenses (in excess of the floor amount under section 213(a)) of no more than $1,000. W's election to allocate to H the deficiency attributable to the portion of the overstated deduction of which she had actual knowledge ($9,000) is invalid. W's election to allocate the deficiency attributable to the portion of the overstated deduction of which she had no knowledge ($600) is valid.

*Example 6. Disqualified asset presumption.* (i) H and W are divorced. In May 1999, W transfers $20,000 to H, and in April 2000, H and W receive a 30-day letter proposing a $40,000 deficiency on their 1998 joint Federal income tax return. The liability remains unpaid, and in October 2000, H elects to allocate the deficiency under this section. Seventy-five percent of the net amount of erroneous items are allocable to W, and 25% of the net amount of erroneous items are allocable to H.

(ii) In accordance with the proportionate allocation method (see paragraph (d)(4) of this section), H proposes that $30,000 of the deficiency be allocated to W and $10,000 be allocated to himself. H submits a signed statement providing that the principal purpose of the $20,000 transfer was not the avoidance of tax or payment of tax, but he does not submit any documentation indicating the reason for the transfer. H has not overcome the presumption that the $20,000 was a disqualified asset. Therefore, the portion of the deficiency for which H is liable ($10,000) is increased by the value of the disqualified asset ($20,000). H is relieved of liability for $10,000 of the $30,000 deficiency allocated to W, and remains jointly and severally liable for the remaining $30,000 of the deficiency (assuming that H does not qualify for relief under any other provision).

*Example 7. Disqualified asset presumption inapplicable.* On May 1, 2001, H and W receive a 30-day letter regarding a proposed deficiency on their 1999 joint Federal income tax return relating to unreported capital gain from H's sale of his investment in Z stock. W had no actual knowledge of the stock sale. The deficiency is assessed in November 2001, and in December 2001, H and W divorce. According to a decree of divorce, H must transfer 1/2 of his interest in mutual fund A to W. The transfer takes place in February 2002. In August 2002, W elects to allocate the deficiency to H. Although the transfer of 1/2 of H's interest in mutual fund A took place after the 30-day letter was mailed, the mutual fund interest is not presumed to be a disqualified asset because the transfer of H's interest in the fund was made pursuant to a decree of divorce.

*Example 8. Overcoming the disqualified asset presumption.* (i) H and W are married for 25 years. Every September, on W's birthday, H gives W a gift of $500. On February 28, 2002, H and W receive a 30-day letter from the Internal Revenue Service relating to their 1998 joint individual Federal income tax return. The deficiency relates to H's Schedule C business, and W had no knowledge of the items giving rise to the deficiency. H and W are legally separated in June 2003, and, despite the separation, H continues to give W $500 each year for her birthday. H is not required to give such amounts pursuant to a decree of divorce or separate maintenance.

(ii) On January 27, 2004, W files an election to allocate the deficiency to H. The $1,500 transferred from H to W from February 28, 2001 (a year before the 30-day letter was mailed) to the present is presumed disqualified. However, W may overcome the presumption that such amounts were disqualified by establishing that such amounts were birthday gifts from H and that she has received such gifts during their entire marriage. Such facts would show that the amounts were not transferred for the purpose of avoidance of tax or payment of tax.

(d) *Allocation.*—(1) *In general.*—(i) An election to allocate a deficiency limits the requesting spouse's liability to that portion of the deficiency allocated to the requesting spouse pursuant to this section.

(ii) Only a requesting spouse may receive relief. A nonrequesting spouse who does not also elect relief under this section remains liable for the entire amount of the deficiency. Even if both spouses elect to allocate a deficiency under this section, there may be a portion of the deficiency that is not allocable, for which both spouses remain jointly and severally liable.

(2) *Allocation of erroneous items.*—For purposes of allocating a deficiency under this section, erroneous items are generally allocated to the spouses as if separate returns were filed, subject to the following four exceptions:

(i) *Benefit on the return.*—An erroneous item that would otherwise be allocated to the nonrequesting spouse is allocated to the requesting spouse to the extent that the requesting spouse received a tax benefit on the joint return.

$$X = (\text{deficiency}) \quad \times \quad \frac{\text{net amount of erroneous items allocable to the spouse}}{\text{net amount of all erroneous items}}$$

where X=the portion of the deficiency allocable to the spouse.

(B) The proportionate allocation applies to any portion of the deficiency other than—

(1) Any portion of the deficiency attributable to erroneous items allocable to the nonrequesting spouse of which the requesting spouse had actual knowledge;

(2) Any portion of the deficiency attributable to separate treatment items (as defined in paragraph (d)(4)(ii) of this section);

(3) Any portion of the deficiency relating to the liability of a child (as defined in paragraph (d)(4)(iii) of this section) of the requesting spouse or nonrequesting spouse;

(4) Any portion of the deficiency attributable to alternative minimum tax under section 55;

(5) Any portion of the deficiency attributable to accuracyrelated or fraud penalties;

(6) Any portion of the deficiency allocated pursuant to alternative allocation methods authorized under paragraph (d)(6) of this section.

(ii) *Separate treatment items.*—Any portion of a deficiency that is attributable to an item allocable solely to one spouse and that results from the disallowance of a credit, or a tax or an addition to tax (other than tax imposed by section 1 or section 55) that is required to be included with a joint return (a separate treatment item) is allocated separately to that spouse. If such credit or tax is attributable in whole or in part to both spouses, then the IRS will determine on a case by case basis how such item will be allocated. Once the proportionate allocation is made, the liability for the requesting spouse's

(ii) *Fraud.*—The Internal Revenue Service may allocate any item between the spouses if the Internal Revenue Service establishes that the allocation is appropriate due to fraud by one or both spouses.

(iii) *Erroneous items of income.*—Erroneous items of income are allocated to the spouse who was the source of the income. Wage income is allocated to the spouse who performed the services producing such wages. Items of business or investment income are allocated to the spouse who owned the business or investment. If both spouses owned an interest in the business or investment, the erroneous item of income is generally allocated between the spouses in proportion to each spouse's ownership interest in the business or investment, subject to the limitations of paragraph (c) of this section. In the absence of clear and convincing evidence supporting a different allocation, an erroneous income item relating to an asset that the spouses owned jointly is generally allocated 50% to each spouse, subject to the limitations in paragraph (c) of this section and the exceptions in paragraph (c)(2)(iv) of this section. For rules regarding the effect of community property laws, see §1.6015-1(f) and paragraph (c)(2)(iv) of this section.

(iv) *Erroneous deduction items.*—Erroneous deductions related to a business or investment are allocated to the spouse who owned the business or investment. If both spouses owned an interest in the business or investment, an erroneous deduction item is generally allocated between the spouses in proportion to each spouse's ownership interest in the business or investment. In the absence of clear and convincing evidence supporting a different allocation, an erroneous deduction item relating to an asset that the spouses owned jointly is generally allocated 50% to each spouse, subject to the limitations in paragraph (c) of this section and the exceptions in paragraph (d)(4) of this section. Deduction items unrelated to a business or investment are also generally allocated 50% to each spouse, unless the evidence shows that a different allocation is appropriate.

(3) *Burden of proof.*—Except for establishing actual knowledge under paragraph (c)(2) of this section, the requesting spouse must prove that all of the qualifications for making an election under this section are satisfied and that none of the limitations (including the limitation relating to transfers of disqualified assets) apply. The requesting spouse must also establish the proper allocation of the erroneous items.

(4) *General allocation method.*—(i) *Proportionate allocation.*—(A) The portion of a deficiency allocable to a spouse is the amount that bears the same ratio to the deficiency as the net amount of erroneous items allocable to the spouse bears to the net amount of all erroneous items. This calculation may be expressed as follows:

separate treatment items is added to the requesting spouse's share of the liability.

(iii) *Child's liability.*—Any portion of a deficiency relating to the liability of a child of the requesting and nonrequesting spouse is allocated jointly to both spouses. For purposes of this paragraph, a child does not include the taxpayer's stepson or stepdaughter, unless such child was legally adopted by the taxpayer. If the child is the child of only one of the spouses, and the other spouse had not legally adopted such child, any portion of a deficiency relating to the liability of such child is allocated solely to the parent spouse.

(iv) *Allocation of certain items.*—(A) *Alternative minimum tax.*—Any portion of a deficiency relating to the alternative minimum tax under section 55 will be allocated appropriately.

(B) *Accuracy-related and fraud penalties.*—Any accuracyrelated or fraud penalties under section 6662 or 6663 are allocated to the spouse whose item generated the penalty.

(5) *Examples.*—The following examples illustrate the rules of this paragraph (d). In each example, assume that the requesting spouse or spouses qualify to elect to allocate the deficiency, that any election is timely made, and that the deficiency remains unpaid. In addition, unless otherwise stated, assume that neither spouse has actual knowledge of the erroneous items allocable to the other spouse. The examples are as follows:

*Example 1. Allocation of erroneous items.* (i) H and W file a 2003 joint Federal income tax return on April 15, 2004. On April 28, 2006, a deficiency is assessed with respect to their 2003 return. Three erroneous items give rise to the deficiency—

(A) Unreported interest income, of which W had actual knowledge, from H's and W's joint bank account;

(B) A disallowed business expense deduction on H's Schedule C; and

(C) A disallowed Lifetime Learning Credit for W's postsecondary education, paid for by W.

(ii) H and W divorce in May 2006, and in September 2006, W timely elects to allocate the deficiency. The erroneous items are allocable as follows:

(A) The interest income would be allocated 1/2 to H and 1/2 to W, except that W has actual knowledge of it. Therefore, W's election to allocate the portion of the deficiency attributable to this item is invalid, and W remains jointly and severally liable for it.

(B) The business expense deduction is allocable to H.

| W's items | |
| --- | --- |
| $40,000 | charitable deduction |
| $40,000 | interest deduction |
| $80,000 | |

(iii) The ratio of erroneous items allocable to W to the total erroneous items is 2/3 ($80,000/$120,000). W's liability is limited to $36,000 of the deficiency (2/3 of $54,000). The Internal Revenue Service may collect up to $36,000 from W and up to $54,000 from H (the total amount collected, however, may not exceed $54,000). If H also made an election, there would be no remaining joint and several liability, and the Internal Revenue Service would be permitted to collect $36,000 from W and $18,000 from H.

*Example 3. Proportionate allocation with joint erroneous item.* (i) On September 4, 2001, W elects to allocate a $3,000 deficiency for the 1998 tax year to H. Three erroneous items give rise to the deficiency—

(A) Unreported interest in the amount of $4,000 from a joint bank account;

| H's items |
| --- |
| $2,000 business deduction |
| Total allocable items: $8,000 |

(iii) The ratio of erroneous items allocable to W to the total erroneous items is 3/4 ($6,000/$8,000). W's liability is limited to $1,500 of the deficiency (3/4 of $2,000) allocated to her. The Internal Revenue Service may collect up to $2,500 from W (3/4 of the total allocated deficiency plus $1,000 of the deficiency attributable to the joint bank account interest) and up to $3,000 from H (the total amount collected, however, cannot exceed $3,000).

(iv) Assume H also elects to allocate the 1998 deficiency. H is relieved of liability for 3/4 of the deficiency, which is allocated to W. H's relief totals $1,500 (3/4 of $2,000). H remains liable for $1,500 of the deficiency (1/4 of the allocated deficiency plus $1,000 of the deficiency attributable to the joint bank account interest).

*Example 4. Separate treatment items (STIs).* (i) On September 1, 2006, a $28,000 deficiency is assessed with respect to H's and W's 2003 joint return. The deficiency is the result of 4 erroneous items—

(A) A disallowed Lifetime Learning Credit of $2,000 attributable to H;

| W's share of allocable items |
| --- |
| 3/4 ($24,000/$32,000) |

(v) W's liability for the portion of the deficiency subject to proportionate allocation is limited to $9,000 (3/4 of $12,000) and H's liability for such portion is limited to $3,000 (1/4 of $12,000).

| W's share of total deficiency | |
| --- | --- |
| $9,000 allocated deficiency | |
| $14,000 self-employment tax | |
| $23,000 | |

(vii) Therefore, W's liability is limited to $23,000 and H's liability is limited to $5,000.

*Example 5. Requesting spouse receives a benefit on the joint return from the nonrequesting spouse's erroneous item.* (i) In 2001, H reports gross income of $4,000 from his business on Schedule C, and W reports $50,000 of wage income. On their 2001 joint Federal income tax return, H deducts $20,000 of business expenses resulting in a net loss from his business of $16,000. H and W divorce in September 2002, and on May 22, 2003, a $5,200 deficiency is assessed with respect to their 2001 joint return. W elects to allocate the deficiency. The deficiency on the joint return results from a disallowance of all of H's $20,000 of deductions.

(ii) Since H used only $4,000 of the disallowed deductions to offset gross income from his business, W benefitted from the other $16,000 of the disallowed deductions used to offset her wage income. Therefore, $4,000 of the disallowed deductions are allocable to H and

(C) The Lifetime Learning Credit is allocable to W.

*Example 2. Proportionate allocation.* (i) W and H timely file their 2001 joint Federal income tax return on April 15, 2002. On August 16, 2004, a $54,000 deficiency is assessed with respect to their 2001 joint return. H and W divorce on October 14, 2004, and W timely elects to allocate the deficiency. Five erroneous items give rise to the deficiency—

(A) A disallowed $15,000 business deduction allocable to H;

(B) $20,000 of unreported income allocable to H;

(C) A disallowed $5,000 deduction for educational expense allocable to H;

(D) A disallowed $40,000 charitable contribution deduction allocable to W; and

(E) A disallowed $40,000 interest deduction allocable to W.

(ii) In total, there are $120,000 worth of erroneous items, of which $80,000 are attributable to W and $40,000 are attributable to H.

| H's items | |
| --- | --- |
| $15,000 | business deduction |
| $20,000 | unreported income |
| $5,000 | education deduction |
| $40,000 | |

(B) A disallowed deduction for business expenses in the amount of $2,000 attributable to H's business; and

(C) Unreported wage income in the amount of $6,000 attributable to W's second job.

(ii) The erroneous items total $12,000. Generally, income, deductions, or credits from jointly held property that are erroneous items are allocable 50% to each spouse. However, in this case, both spouses had actual knowledge of the unreported interest income. Therefore, W's election to allocate the portion of the deficiency attributable to this item is invalid, and W and H remain jointly and severally liable for this portion. Assume that this portion is $1,000. W may allocate the remaining $2,000 of the deficiency.

| W's items |
| --- |
| $6,000 wage income |

(B) A disallowed business expense deduction of $8,000 attributable to H;

(C) Unreported income of $24,000 attributable to W; and

(D) Unreported self-employment tax of $14,000 attributable to W.

(ii) H and W both elect to allocate the deficiency.

(iii) The $2,000 Lifetime Learning Credit and the $14,000 self-employment tax are STIs totaling $16,000. The amount of erroneous items included in computing the proportionate allocation ratio is $32,000 ($24,000 unreported income and $8,000 disallowed business expense deduction). The amount of the deficiency subject to proportionate allocation is reduced by the amount of STIs ($28,000 − $16,000 = $12,000).

(iv) Of the $32,000 of proportionate allocation items, $24,000 is allocable to W, and $8,000 is allocable to H.

| H's share of allocable items |
| --- |
| 1/4 ($8,000/$32,000) |

(vi) After the proportionate allocation is completed, the amount of the STIs is added to each spouse's allocated share of the deficiency.

| H's share of total deficiency | |
| --- | --- |
| $3,000 allocated deficiency | |
| $2,000 Lifetime Learning Credit | |
| $5,000 | |

$16,000 of the disallowed deductions are allocable to W. W's liability is limited to $4,160 (4/5 of $5,200). If H also elected to allocate the deficiency, H's election to allocate the $4,160 of the deficiency to W would be invalid because H had actual knowledge of the erroneous items.

*Example 6. Calculation of requesting spouse's benefit on the joint return when the nonrequesting spouse's erroneous item is partially disallowed.* Assume the same facts as in Example 6, except that H deducts $18,000 for business expenses on the joint return, of which $16,000 are disallowed. Since H used only $2,000 of the $16,000 disallowed deductions to offset gross income from his business, W received benefit on the return from the other $14,000 of the disallowed deductions used to offset her wage income. Therefore, $2,000 of the disallowed deductions are allocable to H and $14,000 of the disallowed deductions are allocable to W. W's liability is limited to $4,550 (7/8 of $5,200).

(6) *Alternative allocation methods.*—(i) *Allocation based on applicable tax rates.*—If a deficiency arises from two or more erroneous items that are subject to tax at different rates (e.g., ordinary income and capital gain items), the deficiency will be allocated after first separating the erroneous items into categories according to their applicable tax rate. After all erroneous items are categorized, a separate allocation is made with respect to each tax rate category using the proportionate allocation method of paragraph (d)(4) of this section.

(ii) *Allocation methods provided in subsequent published guidance.*—Additional alternative methods for allocating erroneous items under section 6015(c) may be prescribed by the Treasury and IRS in subsequent revenue rulings, revenue procedures, or other appropriate guidance.

(iii) *Example.*—The following example illustrates the rules of this paragraph (d)(6):

*Example. Allocation based on applicable tax rates.* H and W timely file their 1998 joint Federal income tax return. H and W divorce in 1999. On July 13, 2001, a $5,100 deficiency is assessed with respect to H's and W's 1998 return. Of this deficiency, $2,000 results from unreported capital gain of $6,000 that is attributable to W and $4,000 of capital gain that is attributable to H (both gains being subject to tax at the 20% marginal rate). The remaining $3,100 of the deficiency is attributable to $10,000 of unreported dividend income of H that is subject to tax at a marginal rate of 31%. H and W both timely elect to allocate the deficiency, and qualify under this section to do so. There are erroneous items subject to different tax rates; thus, the alternative allocation method of this paragraph (d)(6) applies. The three erroneous items are first categorized according to their applicable tax rates, then allocated. Of the total amount of 20% tax rate items ($10,000), 60% is allocable to W and 40% is allocable to H. Therefore, 60% of the $2,000 deficiency attributable to these items (or $1,200) is allocated to W. The remaining 40% of this portion of the deficiency ($800) is allocated to H. The only 31% tax rate item is allocable to H. Accordingly, H is liable for $3,900 of the deficiency ($800+$3,100), and W is liable for the remaining $1,200.

[Reg. § 1.6015-3.]

□ [T.D. 9003, 7-17-2002.]

### [Reg. § 1.6015-4]

**§ 1.6015-4. Equitable relief.**—(a) A requesting spouse who files a joint return for which a liability remains unpaid and who does not qualify for full relief under § 1.6015-2 or 1.6015-3 may request equitable relief under this section. The Internal Revenue Service has the discretion to grant equitable relief from joint and several liability to a requesting spouse when, considering all of the facts and circumstances, it would be inequitable to hold the requesting spouse jointly and severally liable.

(b) This section may not be used to circumvent the limitation of § 1.6015-3(c)(1) (i.e., no refunds under § 1.6015-3). Therefore, relief is not available under this section to obtain a refund of liabilities already paid, for which the requesting spouse would otherwise qualify for relief under § 1.6015-3.

(c) For guidance concerning the criteria to be used in determining whether it is inequitable to hold a requesting spouse jointly and severally liable under this section, see Rev. Proc. 2000-15 (2000-1 C.B. 447), or other guidance published by the Treasury and IRS (see § 601.601(d)(2) of this chapter). [Reg. § 1.6015-4.]

□ [T.D. 9003, 7-17-2002.]

### [Reg. § 1.6015-5]

**§ 1.6015-5. Time and manner for requesting relief.**—(a) *Requesting relief.*—To elect the application of § 1.6015-2 or 1.6015-3, or to request equitable relief under § 1.6015-4, a requesting spouse must file Form 8857, "Request for Innocent Spouse Relief" (or other specified form); submit a written statement containing the same information required on Form 8857, which is signed under penalties of perjury; or submit information in the manner prescribed by the Treasury and IRS in forms, relevant revenue rulings, revenue procedures, or other published guidance (see § 601.601(d)(2) of this chapter).

(b) *Time period for filing a request for relief.*—(1) *In general.*—To elect the application of § 1.6015-2 or 1.6015-3, or to request equitable relief under § 1.6015-4, a requesting spouse must file Form 8857 or other similar statement with the Internal Revenue Service no later than two years from the date of the first collection activity against the requesting spouse after July 22, 1998, with respect to the joint tax liability.

(2) *Definitions.*—(i) *Collection activity.*—For purposes of this paragraph (b), collection activity means a section 6330 notice; an offset of an overpayment of the requesting spouse against a liability under section 6402; the filing of a suit by the United States against the requesting spouse for the collection of the joint tax liability; or the

filing of a claim by the United States in a court proceeding in which the requesting spouse is a party or which involves property of the requesting spouse. Collection activity does not include a notice of deficiency; the filing of a Notice of Federal Tax Lien; or a demand for payment of tax. The term *property of the requesting spouse*, for purposes of this paragraph (b), means property in which the requesting spouse has an ownership interest (other than solely through the operation of community property laws), including property owned jointly with the nonrequesting spouse.

(ii) *Section 6330 notice.*—A section 6330 notice refers to the notice sent, pursuant to section 6330, providing taxpayers notice of the Service's intent to levy and of their right to a collection due process (CDP) hearing.

(3) *Requests for relief made before commencement of collection activity.*—An election or request for relief may be made before collection activity has commenced. For example, an election or request for relief may be made in connection with an audit or examination of the joint return or a demand for payment, or pursuant to the CDP hearing procedures under section 6320 in connection with the filing of a Notice of Federal Tax Lien. For more information on the rules regarding collection due process for liens, see the Treasury regulations under section 6320. However, no request for relief may be made before the date specified in paragraph (b)(5) of this section.

(4) *Examples.*—The following examples illustrate the rules of this paragraph (b):

*Example 1.* On January 11, 2000, a section 6330 notice is mailed to H and W regarding their 1997 joint Federal income tax liability. The Internal Revenue Service levies on W's employer on June 5, 2000. The Internal Revenue Service levies on H's employer on July 10, 2000. An election or request for relief must be made by January 11, 2002, which is two years after the Internal Revenue Service sent the section 6330 notice.

*Example 2.* The Internal Revenue Service offsets an overpayment against a joint liability for 1995 on January 12, 1998. The offset only partially satisfies the liability. The Internal Revenue Service takes no other collection actions. On July 24, 2001, W elects relief with respect to the unpaid portion of the 1995 liability. W's election is timely because the Internal Revenue Service has not taken any collection activity after July 22, 1998; therefore, the two-year period has not commenced.

*Example 3.* Assume the same facts as in *Example 2*, except that the Internal Revenue Service sends a section 6330 notice on January 22, 1999. W's election is untimely because it is filed more than two years after the first collection activity after July 22, 1998.

*Example 4.* H and W do not remit full payment with their timely filed joint Federal income tax return for the 1989 tax year. No collection activity is taken after July 22, 1998, until the United States files a suit against both H and W to reduce the tax assessment to judgment and to foreclose the tax lien on their jointly-held business property on July 1, 1999. H elects relief on October 2, 2000. The election is timely because it is made within two years of the filing of a collection suit by the United States against H.

*Example 5.* W files a Chapter 7 bankruptcy petition on July 10, 2000. On September 5, 2000, the United States files a proof of claim for her joint 1998 income tax liability. W elects relief with respect to the 1998 liability on August 20, 2002. The election is timely because it is made within two years of the date the United States filed the proof of claim in W's bankruptcy case.

(5) *Premature requests for relief.*—The Internal Revenue Service will not consider premature claims for relief under § 1.6015-2, 1.6015-3, or 1.6015-4. A premature claim is a claim for relief that is filed for a tax year prior to the receipt of a notification of an audit or a letter or notice from the IRS indicating that there may be an outstanding liability with regard to that year. Such notices or letters do not include notices issued pursuant to section 6223 relating to TEFRA partnership proceedings. A premature claim is not considered an election or request under § 1.6015-1(h)(5).

(c) *Effect of a final administrative determination.*—(1) *In general.*—A requesting spouse is entitled to only one final administrative determination of relief under § 1.6015-1 for a given assessment, unless the requesting spouse properly submits a second request for relief that is described in § 1.6015-1(h)(5).

(2) *Example.*—The following example illustrates the rule of this paragraph (c):

*Example.* In January 2001, W becomes a limited partner in partnership P, and in February 2001, she starts her own business from which she earns $100,000 of net income for the year. H and W file a joint return for tax year 2001, on which they claim $20,000 in losses from their investment in P, and they omit W's self-employment tax. In March 2003, the Internal Revenue Service commences an audit under the provisions of subchapter C of chapter 63 of subtitle F of the

Internal Revenue Code (TEFRA partnership proceeding) and sends H and W a notice under section 6223(a)(1). In September 2003, the Internal Revenue Service audits H's and W's 2001 joint return regarding the omitted self-employment tax. H may file a claim for relief from joint and several liability for the self-employment tax liability because he has received a notification of an audit indicating that there may be an outstanding liability on the joint return. However, his claim for relief regarding the TEFRA partnership proceeding is premature under paragraph (b)(5) of this section. H will have to wait until the Internal Revenue Service sends him a notice of computational adjustment or assesses the liability resulting from the TEFRA partnership proceeding before he files a claim for relief with respect to any such liability. The assessment relating to the TEFRA partnership proceeding is separate from the assessment for the self-employment tax; therefore, H's subsequent claim for relief for the liability from the TEFRA partnership proceeding is not precluded by his previous claim for relief from the self-employment tax liability under this paragraph (c).
[Reg. § 1.6015-5.]

☐ [*T.D. 9003, 7-17-2002 (corrected 8-23-2002).*]

### [Reg. § 1.6015-6]

**§ 1.6015-6. Nonrequesting spouse's notice and opportunity to participate in administrative proceedings.**—(a) *In general.*—(1) When the Internal Revenue Service receives an election under § 1.6015-2 or 1.6015-3, or a request for relief under § 1.6015-4, the Internal Revenue Service must send a notice to the nonrequesting spouse's last known address that informs the nonrequesting spouse of the requesting spouse's claim for relief. For further guidance regarding the definition of last known address, see § 301.6212-2 of this chapter. The notice must provide the nonrequesting spouse with an opportunity to submit any information that should be considered in determining whether the requesting spouse should be granted relief from joint and several liability. A nonrequesting spouse is not required to submit information under this section. Upon the request of either spouse, the Internal Revenue Service will share with one spouse the information submitted by the other spouse, unless such information would impair tax administration.

(2) The Internal Revenue Service must notify the nonrequesting spouse of the Service's preliminary and final determinations with respect to the requesting spouse's claim for relief under section 6015.

(b) *Information submitted.*—The Internal Revenue Service will consider all of the information (as relevant to each particular relief provision) that the nonrequesting spouse submits in determining whether relief from joint and several liability is appropriate, including information relating to the following—

(1) The legal status of the requesting and nonrequesting spouses' marriage;

(2) The extent of the requesting spouse's knowledge of the erroneous items or underpayment;

(3) The extent of the requesting spouse's knowledge or participation in the family business or financial affairs;

(4) The requesting spouse's education level;

(5) The extent to which the requesting spouse benefitted from the erroneous items;

(6) Any asset transfers between the spouses;

(7) Any indication of fraud on the part of either spouse;

(8) Whether it would be inequitable, within the meaning of §§ 1.6015-2(d) and 1.6015-4, to hold the requesting spouse jointly and severally liable for the outstanding liability;

(9) The allocation or ownership of items giving rise to the deficiency; and

(10) Anything else that may be relevant to the determination of whether relief from joint and several liability should be granted.

(c) *Effect of opportunity to participate.*—The failure to submit information pursuant to paragraph (b) of this section does not affect the nonrequesting spouse's ability to seek relief from joint and several liability for the same tax year. However, information that the nonrequesting spouse submits pursuant to paragraph (b) of this section is relevant in determining whether relief from joint and several liability is appropriate for the nonrequesting spouse should the nonrequesting spouse also submit an application for relief. [Reg. § 1.6015-6.]

☐ [*T.D. 9003, 7-17-2002.*]

### [Reg. § 1.6015-7]

**§ 1.6015-7. Tax Court review.**—(a) *In general.*—Requesting spouses may petition the Tax Court to review the denial of relief under § 1.6015-1.

(b) *Time period for petitioning the Tax Court.*—Pursuant to section 6015(e), the requesting spouse may petition the Tax Court to review a denial of relief under § 1.6015-1 within 90 days after the date notice of the Service's final determination is mailed by certified or registered mail (90-day period). If the IRS does not mail the requesting spouse a final determination letter within 6 months of the date the requesting spouse files an election under § 1.6015-2 or 1.6015-3, the requesting spouse may petition the Tax Court to review the election at any time after the expiration of the 6-month period, and before the expiration of the 90-day period. The Tax Court also may review a claim for relief if Tax Court jurisdiction has been acquired under another section of the Internal Revenue Code such as section 6213(a) or 6330(d).

(c) *Restrictions on collection and suspension of the running of the period of limitations.*—(1) *Restrictions on collection under § 1.6015-2 or 1.6015-3.*—Unless the Internal Revenue Service determines that collection will be jeopardized by delay, no levy or proceeding in court shall be made, begun, or prosecuted against a requesting spouse electing the application of § 1.6015-2 or 1.6015-3 for the collection of any assessment to which the election relates until the expiration of the 90-day period described in paragraph (b) of this section, or if a petition is filed with the Tax Court, until the decision of the Tax Court becomes final under section 7481. For more information regarding the date on which a decision of the Tax Court becomes final, see section 7481 and the regulations thereunder. Notwithstanding the above, if the requesting spouse appeals the Tax Court's decision, the Internal Revenue Service may resume collection of the liability from the requesting spouse on the date the requesting spouse files the notice of appeal, unless the requesting spouse files an appeal bond pursuant to the rules of section 7485. Jeopardy under this paragraph (c)(1) means conditions exist that would require an assessment under section 6851 or 6861 and the regulations thereunder.

(2) *Waiver of the restrictions on collection.*—A requesting spouse may, at any time (regardless of whether a notice of the Service's final determination of relief is mailed), waive the restrictions on collection in paragraph (c)(1) of this section.

(3) *Suspension of the running of the period of limitations.*—(i) *Relief under § 1.6015-2 or 1.6015-3.*—The running of the period of limitations in section 6502 on collection against the requesting spouse of the assessment to which an election under § 1.6015-2 or 1.6015-3 relates is suspended for the period during which the Internal Revenue Service is prohibited by paragraph (c)(1) of this section from collecting by levy or a proceeding in court and for 60 days thereafter. However, if the requesting spouse signs a waiver of the restrictions on collection in accordance with paragraph (c)(2) of this section, the suspension of the period of limitations in section 6502 on collection against the requesting spouse will terminate on the date that is 60 days after the date the waiver is filed with the Internal Revenue Service.

(ii) *Relief under § 1.6015-4.*—If a requesting spouse seeks only equitable relief under § 1.6015-4, the restrictions on collection of paragraph (c)(1) of this section do not apply. Accordingly, the request for relief does not suspend the running of the period of limitations on collection.

(4) *Definitions.*—(i) *Levy.*—For purposes of this paragraph (c), levy means an administrative levy or seizure described by section 6331.

(ii) *Proceedings in court.*—For purposes of this paragraph (c), proceedings in court means suits filed by the United States for the collection of Federal tax. Proceedings in court does not refer to the filing of pleadings and claims and other participation by the Internal Revenue Service or the United States in suits not filed by the United States, including Tax Court cases, refund suits, and bankruptcy cases.

(iii) *Assessment to which the election relates.*—For purposes of this paragraph (c), the assessment to which the election relates is the entire assessment of the deficiency to which the election relates, even if the election is made with respect to only part of that deficiency. [Reg. § 1.6015-7.]

☐ [*T.D. 9003, 7-17-2002.*]

### [Reg. § 1.6015-8]

**§ 1.6015-8. Applicable liabilities.**—(a) *In general.*—Section 6015 applies to liabilities that arise after July 22, 1998, and to liabilities that arose prior to July 22, 1998, that were not paid on or before July 22, 1998.

(b) *Liabilities paid on or before July 22, 1998.*—A requesting spouse seeking relief from joint and several liability for amounts paid on or before July 22, 1998, must request relief under section 6013(e) and the regulations thereunder.

(c) *Examples.*—The following examples illustrate the rules of this section:

*Example 1.* H and W file a joint Federal income tax return for 1995 on April 15, 1996. There is an understatement on the return attributable to an omission of H's wage income. On October 15, 1998, H and W receive a 30-day letter proposing a deficiency on the 1995 joint return. W pays the outstanding liability in full on November 30, 1998. In March 1999, W files Form 8857, requesting relief from joint and several liability under section 6015(b). Although W's liability arose prior to July 22, 1998, it was unpaid as of that date. Therefore, section 6015 is applicable.

*Example 2.* H and W file their 1995 joint Federal income tax return on April 15, 1996. On October 14, 1997, a deficiency of $5,000 is assessed regarding a disallowed business expense deduction attributable to H. On June 30, 1998, the Internal Revenue Service levies on the $3,000 in W's bank account in partial satisfaction of the outstanding liability. On August 31, 1998, W files a request for relief from joint and several liability. The liability arose prior to July 22, 1998. Section 6015 is applicable to the $2,000 that remained unpaid as of July 22, 1998, and section 6013(e) is applicable to the $3,000 that was paid prior to July 22, 1998.
[Reg. § 1.6015-8.]

☐ [*T.D. 9003, 7-17-2002.*]

**[Reg. § 1.6015-9]**

**§ 1.6015-9. Effective date.**—Sections 1.6015-0 through 1.6015-9 are applicable for all elections under § 1.6015-2 or 1.6015-3 or any requests for relief under § 1.6015-4 filed on or afte July 18, 2002. [Reg. § 1.6015-9.]

☐ [*T.D. 9003, 7-17-2002.*]

**[Reg. § 1.6017-1]**

**§ 1.6017-1. Self-employment tax returns.**—(a) *In general.*—(1) Every individual, other than a nonresident alien, having net earnings from self-employment, as defined in section 1402, of $400 or more for the taxable year shall make a return of such earnings. For purposes of this section, an individual who is a resident of the Virgin Islands, Puerto Rico, or (for any taxable year beginning after 1960) Guam or American Samoa is not to be considered a nonresident alien individual. See paragraph(d) of § 1.1402(b)-1. A return is required under this section if an individual has self-employment income, as defined in section 1402(b), even though he may not be required to make a return under section 6012 for purposes of the tax imposed by section 1 or 3. Provisions applicable to returns under section 6012(a) shall be applicable to returns under this section.

(2) Except as otherwise provided in this subparagraph, the return required by this section shall be made on Form 1040. The form to be used by residents of the Virgin Islands, Guam, or American Samoa is Form 1040SS. In the case of a resident of Puerto Rico who is not required to make a return of income under section 6012(a), the form to be used is Form 1040SS, except that Form 1040PR shall be used if it is furnished by the Internal Revenue Service to such resident for use in lieu of Form 1040SS.

(b) *Joint returns.*—(1) In the case of a husband and wife filing a joint return under section 6013, the tax on self-employment income is computed on the separate self-employment income of each spouse, and not on the aggregate of the two amounts. The requirement of section 6013(d)(3) that in the case of a joint return the tax is computed on the aggregate income of the spouses is not applicable with respect to the tax on self-employment income. Where the husband and wife each has net earnings from self-employment of $400 or more, it will be necessary for each to complete separate schedules of the computation of self-employment tax with respect to the net earnings of each spouse, despite the fact that a joint return is filed. If the net earnings from self-employment of either the husband or the wife are less than $400, such net earnings are not subject to the tax on self-employment income, even though they must be shown on the joint return for purposes of the tax imposed by section 1 or 3.

(2) Except as otherwise expressly provided, section 6013 is applicable to the return of the tax on self-employment income; therefore, the liability with respect to such tax in the case of a joint return is joint and several.

(c) *Social security account numbers.*—(1) Every individual making a return of net earnings from self-employment for any period commencing before January 1, 1962, is required to show thereon his social security account number, or, if he has no such account number, to make application therefor on Form SS-5 before filing such return. However, the failure to apply for or receive a social security account number will not excuse the individual from the requirement that he file such return on or before the due date thereof. Form SS-5 may be obtained from any district office of the Social Security Administration or from any district director. The application shall be filed with a district office of the Social Security Administration or, in the case of an individual not in the United States, with the district office of the Social Security Administration at Baltimore, Maryland. An individual who has previously secured a social security account number as

an employee shall use that account number on his return of net earnings from self-employment.

(2) For provisions applicable to the securing of identifying numbers and the reporting thereof on returns and schedules for periods commencing after December 31, 1961, see § 1.6109-1.

(d) *Declaration of estimated tax with respect to taxable years beginning after December 31, 1966.*—For taxable years beginning after December 31, 1966, section 6015 provides that the term "estimated tax" includes the amount which an individual estimates as the amount of self-employment tax imposed by chapter 2 for the taxable year. Thus, individuals upon whom self-employment tax is imposed by section 1401 must make a declaration of estimated tax if they meet the requirements of section 6015(a), except as otherwise provided under section 6015(i). [Reg. § 1.6017-1.]

☐ [*T.D. 6364, 2-13-59. Amended by T.D. 6691, 12-2-63 and T.D. 7427, 8-9-76.*]

**[Reg. § 301.6017-1]**

**§ 301.6017-1. Self-employment tax returns.**—For provisions relating to the requirement of self-employment tax returns, see § 1.6017-1 of this chapter (Income Tax Regulations). [Reg. § 301.6017-1.]

☐ [*T.D. 6498, 10-24-60.*]

**[Reg. § 20.6018-1]**

**§ 20.6018-1. Returns.**—(a) *Estates of citizens or residents.*—A return must be filed on Form 706 for the estate of every citizen or resident of the United States whose gross estate exceeded $60,000 in value on the date of his death. The value of the gross estate at the date of death governs with respect to the filing of the return regardless of whether the value of the gross estate is, at the executor's election, finally determined as of a date subsequent to the date of death pursuant to the provisions of section 2032. Duplicate copies of the return are not required to be filed. For the contents of the return, see § 20.6018-3.

(b) *Estates of nonresidents not citizens.*—(1) *In general.*—Except as provided in subparagraph (2) of this paragraph, a return must be filed on Form 706 or Form 706NA for the estate of every nonresident not a citizen of the United States if the value of that part of the gross estate situated in the United States on the date of his death exceeded $30,000 in the case of a decedent dying on or after November 14, 1966, or $2,000 in the case of a decedent dying before November 14, 1966. Under certain conditions the return may be made only on Form 706. See the instructions on Form 706NA for circumstances under which that form may not be used. Duplicate copies of the return are not required to be filed. For the contents of the return, see § 20.6018-3. For the determination of the gross estate situated in the United States, see § § 20.2103-1 and 20.2104-1.

(2) *Certain estates of decedents dying on or after November 14, 1966.*—In the case of an estate of a nonresident not a citizen of the United States dying on or after November 14, 1966—

(i) *Transfers subject to the tax imposed by section 2107(a).*—If the transfer of the estate is subject to the tax imposed by section 2107(a) (relating to expatriation to avoid tax), any amounts includible in the decedent's gross estate under section 2107(b) are to be added to the value on the date of his death of that part of his gross estate situated in the United States, for purposes of determining under subparagraph (1) of this paragraph whether his gross estate exceeded $30,000 on the date of his death.

(ii) *Transfers subject to a Presidential proclamation.*—If the transfer of the estate is subject to tax pursuant to a Presidential proclamation made under section 2108(a) (relating to Presidential proclamations of the application of pre-1967 estate tax provisions), the return must be filed on Form 706 or Form 706NA if the value on the date of the decedent's death of that part of his gross estate situated in the United States exceeded $2,000.

(c) *Place for filing.*—See § 20.6091-1 for the place where the return shall be filed.

(d) *Time for filing.*—See § 20.6075-1 for the time for filing the return. [Reg. § 20.6018-1.]

☐ [*T.D. 7296, 12-11-73.*]

**[Reg. § 20.6018-2]**

**§ 20.6018-2. Returns; person required to file return.**—It is required that the duly qualified executor or administrator shall file the return. If there is more than one executor or administrator, the return must be made jointly by all. If there is no executor or administrator appointed, qualified and acting within the United States, every person in actual or constructive possession of any property of the decedent situated in the United States is constituted an executor for purposes of the tax (see § 20.2203-1), and is required to make and file a return. If in any case the executor is unable to make a complete return as to any part of the gross estate, he is required to give all the information he has as to such property, including a full description, and the name of every person holding a legal or beneficial interest in the property. If the executor is unable to make a return as to any property, every person holding a legal or beneficial interest therein shall, upon notice from the district director, make a return as to that part of the gross estate. For delinquency penalty for failure to file return, see section 6651 and § 301.6651-1 of this chapter (Regulations on Procedure and Administration). For criminal penalties for failure to file a return and filing a false or fraudulent return, see sections 7203, 7206, 7207, and 7269. [Reg. § 20.6018-2.]

☐ [T.D. 6296, 6-23-58.]

## [Reg. § 20.6018-3]

§ 20.6018-3. Returns; contents of returns.—(a) *Citizens or residents.*—The return of an estate of a decedent who was a citizen or resident of the United States at the time of his death must contain an itemized inventory by schedule of the property constituting the gross estate and lists of the deductions under the proper schedules. The return shall set forth (1) the value of the gross estate (see §§ 20.2031-1 through 20.2044-1), (2) the deductions claimed (see §§ 20.2052-1 through 20.2056(e)-3), (3) the taxable estate (see § 20.2051-1), and (4) the gross estate tax, reduced by any credits (see §§ 20.2011-1 through 20.2014-6) against the tax. In listing upon the return the property constituting the gross estate (other than household and personal effects for which see § 20.2031-6), the description of it shall be such that the property may be readily identified for the purpose of verifying the value placed on it by the executor.

(b) *Nonresidents not citizens.*—The return of an estate of a decedent who was not a citizen or resident of the United States at the time of his death must contain the following information: (1) An itemized list of that part of the gross estate situated in the United States (see §§ 20.2103-1 and 20.2104-1); (2) in the case of an estate the transfer of which is subject to the tax imposed by section 2107(a) (relating to expatriation to avoid tax), a list of any amounts with respect to stock in a foreign corporation which are includible in the gross estate under section 2107(b), together with an explanation of how the amounts were determined; (3) an itemized list of any deductions claimed (see §§ 20.2106-1 and 20.2106-2); (4) the amount of the taxable estate (see § 20.2106-1); and (5) the gross estate tax, reduced by any credits against the tax (see § 20.2102-1). For the disallowance of certain deductions if the return does not disclose that part of the gross estate not situated in the United States, see §§ 20.2106-1 and 20.2106-2.

(c) *Provisions applicable to returns described in paragraphs (a) and (b) of this section.*—(1) A legal description shall be given of each parcel of real estate, and, if located in a city, the name of the street and number, its area, and, if improved, a short statement of the character of the improvements.

(2) A description of bonds shall include the number held, principal amount, name of obligor, date of maturity, rate of interest, date or dates on which interest is payable, series number if there is more than one issue, and the principal exchange upon which listed, or the principal business office of the obligor, if unlisted. A description of stocks, shall include number of shares, whether common or preferred, and, if preferred, what issue, par value, quotation at which returned, exact name of corporation, and, if the stock is unlisted, the location of the principal business office and State in which incorporated and the date of incorporation, or if the stock is listed, the principal exchange upon which sold. A description of notes shall include name of maker, date on which given, date of maturity, amount of principal, amount of principal unpaid, rate of interest and whether simple or compound, date to which interest has been paid and amount of unpaid interest. A description of the seller's interest in land contracts shall include name of buyer, date of contract, description of property, sale price, initial payment, amounts of installment payments, unpaid balance of principal and accrued interest, interest rate and date prior to decedent's death to which interest had been paid.

(3) A description of bank accounts shall disclose the name and address of depository, amount on deposit, whether a checking, savings, or a time-deposit account, rate of interest, if any payable, amount of interest accrued and payable, and serial number. A description of life insurance shall give the name of the insurer, number of policy, name of the beneficiary, and the amount of the proceeds.

(4) In describing an annuity, the name and address of the grantor of the annuity shall be given, or, if the annuity is payable out of a trust or other funds, such a description as will fully identify it. If the annuity is payable for a term of years, the duration of the term and the date on which it began shall be given, and if payable for the life of a person other than the decedent, the date of birth of such person

shall be stated. If the executor has not included in the gross estate the full value of an annuity or other payment described in section 2039, he shall nevertheless fully describe the annuity and state its total purchase price and the amount of the contribution made by each person (including the decedent's employer) toward the purchase price. If the executor believes that any part of the annuity or other payment is excludable from the gross estate under the provisions of section 2039, or for any other reason, he shall state in the return the reason for his belief.

(5) Judgments should be described by giving the title of the cause and the name of the court in which rendered, date of judgment, name and address of the judgment debtor, amount of judgment, and rate of interest to which subject, and by stating whether any payments have been made thereon, and, if so, when and in what amounts.

(6) If, pursuant to section 2032, the executor elects to have the estate valued at a date or dates subsequent to the time of the decedent's death, there must be set forth on the return: (i) An itemized description of all property included in the gross estate on the date of the decedent's death, together with the value of each item as of that date; (ii) an itemized disclosure of all distributions, sales, exchanges, and other dispositions of any property during the 6-month (1 year, if the decedent died on or before December 31, 1970) period after the date of the decedent's death, together with the dates thereof; and (iii) the value of each item of property in accordance with the provisions of section 2032 (see § 20.2032-1). Interest and rents accrued at the date of the decedent's death and dividends declared to stockholders of record on or before the date of the decedent's death and not collected at that date are to be shown separately. (See also paragraph (e) of § 20.6018-4 with respect to documents required to be filed with the return.)

(7) All transfers made by the decedent within 3 years before the date of his death of a value of $1,000 or more and all transfers (other than outright transfers not in trust) made by the decedent at any time during his life of a value of $5,000 or more, except bona fide sales for an adequate and full consideration in money or money's worth, must be disclosed in the return, whether or not the executor regards the transfers as subject to the tax. If the executor believes that such a transfer is not subject to the tax, a brief statement of the pertinent facts shall be made. [Reg. § 20.6018-3.]

☐ [T.D. 7238, 12-28-72 and T.D. 7295, 12-11-73.]

## [Reg. § 20.6018-4]

§ 20.6018-4. Returns; documents to accompany the return.—(a) A certified copy of the will, if the decedent died testate, must be submitted with the return, together with copies of such other documents as are required in Form 706 and in the applicable sections of these regulations. There may also be filed copies of any documents which the executor may desire to submit in explanation of the return.

(b) In the case of an estate of a nonresident citizen, the executor shall also file the following documents with the return: (1) A copy of any inventory of property and schedule of liabilities, claims against the estate and expenses of administration filed with the foreign court of probate jurisdiction, certified by a proper official of the court; and (2) a copy of any return filed under any applicable foreign inheritance, estate, legacy, or succession tax act, certified by a proper official of the foreign tax department.

(c) In the case of an estate of a nonresident not a citizen of the United States, the executor must also file with the return, but only if deductions are claimed or the transfer of the estate is subject to the tax imposed by section 2107(a) (relating to expatriation to avoid tax), a copy of the inventory of property filed under the foreign death duty act; or, if no such inventory was filed, a certified copy of the inventory filed with the foreign court of probate jurisdiction.

(d) For every policy of life insurance listed on the return, the executor must procure a statement, on Form 712, by the company issuing the policy and file it with the return.

(e) If, pursuant to section 2032, the executor elects to have the estate valued at a date or dates subsequent to the time of the decedent's death, the executor shall file with the return evidence in support of any statements made by him in the return as to distributions, sales, exchanges, or other dispositions of property during the 6-month (1 year, if the decedent died on or before December 31, 1970) period which followed the decedent's death. If the court having jurisdiction over the estate makes an order or decree of distribution during that period, a certified copy thereof must be submitted as part of the evidence. The district director, or the director of a service center, may require the submission of such additional evidence as is deemed necessary.

(f) In any case where a transfer, by trust or otherwise, was made by a written instrument, a copy thereof shall be filed with the return if (1) the property is included in the gross estate, or (2) the executor pursuant to the provisions of paragraph (c)(7) of § 20.6018-3 has made a disclosure of the transfer on the return but has not included its value in the gross estate in the belief that it is not so includible. If the written instrument is of public record, the copy shall be certified, or if it is not of record, the copy shall be verified. If the decedent was a nonresident not a citizen at the time of his death, the copy may be either certified or verified.

(g) If the executor contends that the value of property transferred by the decedent within a period of three years ending with the date of the decedent's death should not be included in the gross estate because he considers that the transfer was not made in contemplation of death, he shall file with the return (1) a copy of the death certificate, and (2) a statement, containing a declaration that it is made under the penalties of perjury, of all the material facts and circumstances, including those directly or indirectly indicating the decedent's motive in making the transfer and his mental and physical condition at that time. However, this data need not be furnished with respect to transfers of less than $1,000 in value unless requested by the district director. [Reg. §20.6018-4.]

☐ [T.D. 6296, 6-23-58. Amended by T.D. 7238, 12-28-72 and T.D. 7296, 12-11-73.]

### [Reg. §25.6019-1]

**§25.6019-1. Persons required to file returns.**—(a) *Gifts made after December 31, 1981.*—Subject to section 2523(i)(2), an individual citizen or resident of the United States who in any calendar year beginning after December 31, 1981, makes any transfer by gift other than a transfer that, under section 2503(b) or (e) (relating, respectively, to certain gifts of $10,000 per donee and the exclusion for payment of certain educational and medical expenses), is not included in the total amount of gifts for that year, or a transfer of an interest with respect to which a marital deduction is allowed for the value of the entire interest under section 2523 (other than a marital deduction allowed by reason of section 2523(f), regarding qualified terminable interest property for which a return must be filed in order to make the election under that section), must file a gift tax return on Form 709 for that calendar year.

(b) *Gifts made after December 31, 1976, and before January 1, 1982.*—An individual citizen or resident of the United States who makes a transfer by gift within any calendar year beginning after December 31, 1976, and before January 1, 1982, must file a gift tax return on Form 709 for any calendar quarter in which the sum of the taxable gifts made during that calendar quarter, plus all other taxable gifts made during the year (for which a return has not yet been required to be filed), exceeds $25,000. If the aggregate transfers made in a calendar year after 1976 and before 1982 that must be reported do not exceed $25,000, only one return must be filed for the calendar year and it must be filed by the due date for a fourth quarter gift tax return (April 15).

(c) *Gifts made after December 31, 1970, and before January 1, 1977.*—An individual citizen or resident of the United States who makes a transfer by gift within any calendar year beginning after December 31, 1970, and before January 1, 1977, must file a gift tax return on Form 709 for the calendar quarter in which any portion of the value of the gift, or any portion of the sum of the values of the gifts to such donee during that calendar year, is not excluded from the total amount of taxable gifts for that year, and must also make a return for any subsequent quarter within the same taxable year in which any additional gift is made to the same donee.

(d) *Gifts by nonresident alien donors.*—The rules contained in paragraphs (a) through (c) of this section also apply to a nonresident not a citizen of the United States provided that, under section 2501(a)(1) and §25.2511-3, the transfer is subject to the gift tax.

(e) *Miscellaneous provisions.*—Only individuals are required to file returns and not trusts, estates, partnerships, or corporations. Duplicate copies of the return are not required to be filed. See §§25.6075-1 and 25.6091-1 for the time and place for filing the gift tax return. For delinquency penalties for failure to file or pay the tax, see section 6651 and §301.6651-1 of this chapter (Procedure and Administration Regulations). For criminal penalties for failure to file a return and filing a false or fraudulent return, see sections 7203, 7206, and 7207.

(f) *Return required even if no tax due.*—The return is required even though, because of the deduction authorized by section 2522 (charitable deduction) or the unified credit under section 2505, no tax may be payable on the transfer.

(g) *Deceased donor.*—If the donor dies before filing his return, the executor of his will or the administrator of his estate shall file the return. If the donor becomes legally incompetent before filing his return, his guardian or committee shall file the return.

(h) *Ratification of return.*—The return shall not be made by an agent unless by reason of illness, absence, or nonresidence, the person liable for the return is unable to make it within the time prescribed.

Mere convenience is not sufficient reason for authorizing an agent to make the return. If by reason of illness, absence or nonresidence, a return is made by an agent, the return must be ratified by the donor or other person liable for its filing within a reasonable time after such person becomes able to do so. If the return filed by the agent is not so ratified, it will not be considered the return required by the statute. Supplemental data may be submitted at the time of ratification. The ratification may be in the form of a statement executed under the penalties of perjury and filed with the internal revenue officer with whom the return was filed, showing specifically that the return made by the agent has been carefully examined and that the person signing ratifies the return as the donor's. If a return is signed by an agent, a statement fully explaining the inability of the donor must accompany the return. [Reg. §25.6019-1.]

☐ [T.D. 6334, 11-14-58. Amended by T.D. 7012, 5-14-69; T.D. 7238, 12-28-72 and T.D. 8522, 2-28-94.]

### [Reg. §25.6019-2]

**§25.6019-2. Returns required in case of consent under section 2513.**—Except as otherwise provided in this section, the provisions of §25.6019-1 (other than paragraph (d) of §25.6019-1) apply with respect to the filing of a gift tax return or returns in the case of a husband and wife who consent (see §25.2513-1) to the application of section 2513. If both spouses are (without regard to the provisions of section 2513) required under the provisions of §25.6019-1 to file returns, returns must be filed by both spouses. If only one of the consenting spouses is (without regard to the provisions of section 2513) required under §25.6019-1 to file a return, a return must be filed by that spouse. In the latter case if, after giving effect to the provisions of section 2513, the other spouse is considered to have made a gift not excluded from the total amount of such other spouse's gifts for the taxable year by reason of section 2503(b) or (e) (relating, respectively, to certain gifts of $10,000 per donee and the exclusion for certain educational or medical expenses), a return must also be filed by such other spouse. Thus, if during a calendar year beginning after December 31, 1981, the first spouse made a gift of $18,000 to a child (the gift not being either a future interest in property or an amount excluded under section 2503(e)) and the other spouse made no gifts, only the first spouse is required to file a return for that calendar year. However, if the other spouse had made a gift in excess of $2,000 to the same child during the same calendar year or if the gift made by the first spouse had amounted to $21,000, each spouse would be required to file a return if the consent is signified as provided in section 2513. [Reg. §25.6019-2.]

☐ [T.D. 6334, 11-14-58. Amended by T.D. 7238, 12-28-72 and T.D. 8522, 2-28-94.]

### [Reg. §25.6019-3]

**§25.6019-3. Contents of return.**—(a) *In general.*—The return must set forth each gift made during the calendar year (or calendar quarter with respect to gifts made after December 31, 1970, and before January 1, 1982) that under sections 2511 through 2515 is to be included in computing taxable gifts; the deductions claimed and allowable under sections 2521 through 2524; and the taxable gifts made for each of the preceding reporting periods. (See §25.2504-1.) In addition the return shall set forth the fair market value of all gifts not made in money, including gifts resulting from sales and exchanges of property made for less than full and adequate consideration in money or money's worth, giving, as of the date of the sale or exchange, both the fair market value of the property sold or exchanged and the fair market value of the consideration received by the donor. If a donor contends that his retained power over property renders the gift incomplete (see §25.2511-2) and hence not subject to tax as of the calendar quarter or calendar year of the initial transfer, the transaction should be disclosed in the return for the calendar quarter or calendar year of the initial transfer and evidence showing all relevant facts, including a copy of the instrument of transfer, shall be submitted with the return. The instructions printed on the return should be carefully followed. A certified or verified copy of each document required by the instructions printed on the return form shall be filed with the return. Any additional documents the donor may desire to submit may be submitted with the return.

(b) *Disclosure of transfers coming within provisions of section 2516.*—Section 2516 provides that certain transfers of property pursuant to written property settlements between husband and wife are deemed to be transfers for full and adequate consideration in money or money's worth if divorce occurs within 2 years. In any case where a husband and wife enter into a written agreement of the type contemplated by section 2516 and the final decree of divorce is not granted on or before the due date for the filing of a gift tax return for the calendar year (or calendar quarter with respect to periods beginning after December 31, 1970, and ending before January 1, 1982) in which the agreement became effective (see §25.6075-1), then, except to the extent §25.6019-1 provides otherwise, the transfer must be disclosed by the transferor upon a gift tax return filed for the calendar year (or calendar quarter) in which the agreement becomes effective, and a copy of the agreement must be attached to the return. In addition, a certified copy of the final divorce decree shall be furnished the internal revenue officer with whom the return was filed not later than 60 days after the divorce is granted. Pending receipt of evidence that the final decree of divorce has been granted (but in no event for a period of more than 2 years from the effective date of the agreement), the transfer will tentatively be treated as made for a full and adequate consideration in money or money's worth. [Reg. § 25.6019-3.]

☐ [T.D. 6334, 11-14-58. *Amended by T.D. 7012, 5-14-69; T.D. 7238, 12-28-72 and T.D. 8522, 2-28-94.*]

### [Reg. § 25.6019-4]

**§25.6019-4. Description of property listed on return.**—The properties comprising the gifts made during the calendar year (or calendar quarter with respect to gifts made after December 31, 1970, and before January 1, 1982) must be listed on the return and described in a manner that they may be readily identified. Thus, there should be given for each parcel of real estate a legal description, its area, a short statement of the character of any improvements, and, if located in a city, the name of the street and number. Description of bonds shall include the number transferred, principal amount, name of obligor, date of maturity, rate of interest, date or dates on which interest is payable, series number where there is more than one issue, and the principal exchange upon which listed, or the principal business office of the obligor, if unlisted. Description of stocks shall include number of shares, whether common or preferred, and, if preferred, what issue thereof, par value, quotation at which returned, exact name of corporation, and, if the stock is unlisted, the location of the principal business office, the State in which incorporated and the date of incorporation, or if the stock is listed, the principal exchange upon which sold. Description of notes shall include name of maker, date on which given, date of maturity, amount of principal, amount of principal unpaid, rate of interest and whether simple or compound, and date to which interest has been paid. If the gift or property includes accrued income thereon to the date of the gift, the amount of such accrued income shall be separately set forth. Description of the seller's interest in land contracts transferred shall include name of buyer, date of contract, description of property, sale price, initial payment, amounts of installment payments, unpaid balance of principal, interest rate, and date prior to gift to which interest has been paid. Description of life insurance policies shall show the name of the insurer and the number of the policy. In describing an annuity, the name and address of the issuing company shall be given, or, if payable out of a trust or other fund, such a description as will fully identify the trust or fund. If the annuity is payable for a term of years, the duration of the term and the date on which it began shall be given, and if payable for the life of any person, the date of birth of that person shall be stated. Judgments shall be described by giving the title of the cause and the name of the court in which rendered, date of judgment, name and address of judgment debtor, amount of judgment, rate of interest to which subject, and by stating whether any payments have been made thereon, and, if so, when and in what amounts. [Reg. § 25.6019-4.]

☐ [T.D. 6334, 11-14-58. *Amended by T.D. 7238, 12-28-72 and T.D. 8522, 2-28-94.*]

### [Reg. § 301.6020-1]

**§301.6020-1. Returns prepared or executed by the Commissioner or other internal revenue officers.**—(a) *Preparation of returns.*—(1) *In general.*—If any person required by the Internal Revenue Code (Code) or by the regulations to make a return fails to make such return, it may be prepared by the Commissioner or other authorized Internal Revenue Officer or employee provided such person consents to disclose all information necessary for the preparation of such return. The return upon being signed by the person required to make it shall be received by the Commissioner as the return of such person.

(2) *Responsibility of person for whom return is prepared.*—A person for whom a return is prepared in accordance with paragraph (a)(1) of this section shall for all legal purposes remain responsible for the correctness of the return to the same extent as if the return had been prepared by him.

(b) *Execution of returns.*—(1) *In general.*—If any person required by the Code or by the regulations to make a return (other than a declaration of estimated tax required under section 6654 or 6655) fails to make such return at the time prescribed therefore, or makes, willfully or otherwise, a false, fraudulent or frivolous return, the Commissioner or other authorized Internal Revenue Officer or employee shall make such return from his own knowledge and from such information as he can obtain through testimony or otherwise. The Commissioner or other authorized Internal Revenue Officer or

employee may make the return by gathering information and making computations through electronic, automated or other means to make a determination of the taxpayer's tax liability.

(2) *Form of the return.*—A document (or set of documents) signed by the Commissioner or other authorized Internal Revenue Officer or employee shall be a return for a person described in paragraph (b)(1) of this section if the document (or set of documents) identifies the taxpayer by name and taxpayer identification number, contains sufficient information from which to compute the taxpayer's tax liability, and purports to be a return. A Form 13496, "IRC Section 6020(b) Certification," or any other form that an authorized Internal Revenue Officer or employee signs and uses to identify a set of documents containing the information set forth in this paragraph as a section 6020(b) return, and the documents identified, constitute a return under section 6020(b). A return may be signed by the name or title of an Internal Revenue Officer or employee being handwritten, stamped, typed, printed or otherwise mechanically affixed to the return, so long as that name or title was placed on the document to signify that the Internal Revenue Officer or employee adopted the document as a return for the taxpayer. The document and signature may be in written or electronic form.

(3) *Status of returns.*—Any return made in accordance with paragraph (b)(1) of this section and signed by the Commissioner or other authorized Internal Revenue Officer or employee shall be good and sufficient for all legal purposes except insofar as any Federal statute expressly provides otherwise. Furthermore, the return shall be treated as the return filed by the taxpayer for purposes of determining the amount of the addition to tax under sections 6651(a)(2) and (3).

(4) *Deficiency procedures.*—For deficiency procedures in the case of income, estate, and gift taxes, see §§ 6211 through 6216, inclusive, and §§ 301.6211-1 through 301.6215-1, inclusive.

(5) *Employment status procedures.*—For pre-assessment procedures in employment taxes cases involving worker classification, see section 7436 (proceedings for determination of employment status).

(6) *Examples.*—The application of this paragraph (b) is illustrated by the following examples:

*Example 1.* Individual A, a calendar-year taxpayer, fails to file his 2003 return. Employee X, an Internal Revenue Service (IRS) employee, opens an examination related to A's 2003 taxable year. At the end of the examination, X completes a Form 13496, "IRC Section 6020(b) Certification," and attached to it the documents listed on the form. Those documents explain examination changes and provide sufficient information to compute A's tax liability. The Form 13496 provides that the IRS employee identified on the form certifies that the attached pages constitute a return under section 6020(b). When X signs the certification package, the package constitutes a return under paragraph (b) of this section because the package identifies A by name, contains A's taxpayer identifying number (TIN), has sufficient information to compute A's tax liability, and contains a statement stating that it constitutes a return under section 6020(b). In addition, the IRS will determine the amount of the additions to tax under section 6651(a)(2) by treating the section 6020(b) return as the return filed by the taxpayer. Likewise, the IRS will determine the amount of any addition to tax under section 6651(a)(3), which arises only after notice and demand for payment, by treating the section 6020(b) return as the return filed by the taxpayer.

*Example 2.* Same facts as in *Example 1*, except that, after performing the examination, X does not compile any examination documents together as a related set of documents. X also does not sign and complete the Form 13496 nor associate the forms explaining examination changes with any other document. Because X did not sign any document stating that it constitutes a return under section 6020(b) and the documents otherwise do not purport to be a section 6020(b) return, the documents do not constitute a return under section 6020(b). Therefore, the IRS cannot determine the section 6651(a)(2) addition to tax against nonfiler A for A's 2003 taxable year on the basis of those documents.

*Example 3.* Individual C, a calendar-year taxpayer, fails to file his 2003 return. The IRS determines through its automated internal matching programs that C received reportable income and failed to file a return. The Service, again through its automated systems, generates a Letter 2566, "30 Day Proposed Assessment (SFR-01) 910 SC/CG." This letter contains C's name, TIN, and has sufficient information to compute C's tax liability. Contemporaneous with the creation of the Letter 2566, the IRS, through its automated system, electronically creates and stores a certification stating that the electronic data contained as part of C's account constitutes a valid return under section 6020(b) as of that date. Further, the electronic data includes the signature of the IRS employee authorized to sign the section 6020(b) return upon its creation. Although the signature is stored electronically, it can appear as a printed name when the IRS requests a paper copy of the certification. The electronically created information, signature, and certification is a return under section 6020(b). The IRS will treat that return as the return filed by the taxpayer in determining the amount of the section 6651(a)(2) addition to tax with respect to C's 2003 taxable year. Likewise, the IRS will determine the amount of any addition to tax under section 6651(a)(3), which arises only after notice and demand for payment, by treating the section 6020(b) return as the return filed by the taxpayer.

*Example 4.* Corporation M, a quarterly taxpayer, fails to file a Form 941, "Employer's Quarterly Federal Tax Return," for the second quarter of 2004. Q, a IRS employee authorized to sign returns under section 6020(b), prepares a Form 941 by hand, stating Corporation M's name, address, and TIN. Q completes the Form 941 by entering line item amounts, including the tax due, and then signs the document. The Form 941 that Q prepared and signed constitutes a section 6020(b) return because the Form 941 purports to be a return under section 6020(b), the form contains M's name and TIN, and it includes sufficient information to compute M's tax liability for the second quarter of 2004.

(c) *Cross references.*—(1) For provisions that a return executed by the Commissioner or other authorized internal revenue officer or employee will not start the running of the period of limitations on assessment and collection, see section 6501(b)(3) and § 301.6501(b)-1(e).

(2) For determining the period of limitations on collection after assessment of a liability on a return executed by the Commissioner or other authorized internal revenue officer or employee, see section 6502 and § 301.6502-1.

(3) For additions to the tax and additional amounts for failure to file returns, see section 6651 and § 301.6651-1, and section 6652 and § 301.6652-1, respectively.

(4) For additions to the tax for failure to pay tax, see section 6651 and § 301.6651-1.

(5) For criminal penalties for willful failure to make returns, see sections 7201, 7202 and 7203.

(6) For criminal penalties for willfully making false or fraudulent returns, see sections 7206 and 7207.

(7) For civil penalties for filing frivolous income tax returns, see section 6702.

(8) For authority to examine books and witnesses, see section 7602 and § 301.7602-1.

(d) *Effective/Applicability date.*—This section is applicable on February 20, 2008. [Reg. § 301.6020-1.]

☐ [T.D. 9380, 2-19-2008.]

### [Reg. § 301.6021-1]

**§ 301.6021-1. Listing by district directors of taxable objects owned by nonresidents of internal revenue districts.**—Whenever there are in any internal revenue district any articles subject to tax, which are not owned or possessed by or under the care or control of any person within such district, and of which no list has been transmitted to the district director, as required by law or by regulations prescribed pursuant to law, the district director, or other authorized internal revenue officer or employee, shall enter the premises where such articles are situated, shall make such inspection of the articles as may be necessary, and shall make lists of the same according to the forms prescribed. Such lists, being subscribed by the district director or other authorized internal revenue officer or employee, shall be sufficient lists of such articles for all purposes. [Reg. § 301.6021-1.]

☐ [T.D. 6498, 10-24-60.]

### [Reg. § 1.6031(a)-1]

**§ 1.6031(a)-1. Return of partnership income.**—(a) *Domestic partnerships.*—(1) *Return required.*—Except as provided in paragraphs (a)(3) and (c) of this section, every domestic partnership must file a return of partnership income under section 6031 (partnership return) for each taxable year on the form prescribed for the partnership return. The partnership return must be filed for the taxable year of the partnership regardless of the taxable years of the partners. For taxable years of a partnership and of a partner, see section 706 and § 1.706-1. For the rules governing partnership statements to partners and nominees, see § 1.6031(b)-1T. For the rules requiring the disclosure of certain transactions, see § 1.6011-4T.

(2) *Content of return.*—The partnership return must contain the information required by the prescribed form and the accompanying instructions.

(3) *Special rule.*—(i) A partnership that has no income, deductions, or credits for federal income tax purposes for a taxable year is not required to file a partnership return for that year.

(ii) The Commissioner may, in guidance published in the Internal Revenue Bulletin (see § 601.601(d)(2)(ii)(b) of this chapter), provide for an exception to partnership reporting under section 6031 and for conditions for the exception, if all or substantially all of a partnership's income is derived from the holding or disposition of tax-exempt obligations (as defined in section 1275(a)(3) and § 1.1275-1(e)) or shares in a regulated investment company (as defined in section 851(a)) that pays exempt-interest dividends (as defined in section 852(b)(5)).

(4) *Failure to file.*—For the consequences of a failure to comply with the requirements of section 6031(a) and this paragraph (a), see sections 6229(a), 6231(f), 6698, and 7203.

(b) *Foreign partnerships.*—(1) *General rule.*—(i) *Filing requirement.*— A foreign partnership is not required to file a partnership return, if the foreign partnership does not have gross income that is (or is treated as) effectively connected with the conduct of a trade or business within the United States (ECI) and does not have gross income (including gains) derived from sources within the United States (U.S.-source income). Except as provided in paragraphs (b)(2) and (3) of this section, a foreign partnership that has ECI or has U.S.-source income that is not ECI must file a partnership return for its taxable year in accordance with the rules for domestic partnerships in paragraph (a) of this section.

(ii) *Special rule.*—For purposes of this paragraph (b)(1) and paragraph (b)(3)(iii) of this section, a foreign partnership will not be considered to have derived income from sources within the United States solely because a U.S. partner marks to market his pro rata share of PFIC stock held by the foreign partnership pursuant to an election under section 1296.

(2) *Foreign partnerships with de minimis U.S.-source income and de minimis U.S. partners.*—A foreign partnership (other than a withholding foreign partnership, as defined in § 1.1441-5(c)(2)(i)) that has $20,000 or less of U.S.-source income and has no ECI during its taxable year is not required to file a partnership return if, at no time during the partnership taxable year, one percent or more of any item of partnership income, gain, loss, deduction, or credit is allocable in the aggregate to direct United States partners. The United States partners must directly report their shares of the allocable items of partnership income, gain, loss, deduction, and credit.

(3) *Filing obligations for certain other foreign partnerships with no ECI.*—(i) *General requirements for modified filing obligations.*—A foreign partnership will be subject to the modified filing obligations in paragraphs (b)(3)(ii) and (iii) of this section if, in addition to satisfying the requirements contained in paragraph 5(b)(3)(ii) and (iii) of this section—

(A) The partnership is not a withholding foreign partnership as defined in § 1.1441-5(c)(2)(i);

(B) Forms 1042 and 1042-S are filed by the partnership with respect to the amounts subject to reporting under § 1.1461-1(b) and (c), unless the partnership is not required to file such returns under § 1.1461-1(b)(2) and (c)(4), in which case Forms 1042 and 1042-S must be filed by another withholding agent or agents; and

(C) The tax liability of the partners with respect to such amounts has been fully satisfied by the withholding of tax at the source, if applicable, under chapter 3 of the Internal Revenue Code.

(ii) *Foreign partnerships with U.S.-source income but no U.S. partners.*—A foreign partnership that has U.S.-source income is not required to file a partnership return if the partnership has no ECI and no United States partners at any time during the partnership's taxable year.

(iii) *Foreign partnerships with U.S.-source income and U.S. partners.*—Except as provided in paragraph (b)(2) of this section, a foreign partnership with one or more United States partners that has U.S.-source income but no ECI must file a partnership return. However, such a foreign partnership need not file Statements of Partner's Share of Income, Credit, Deduction, Etc. (Schedules K-1) for any partners other than its direct United States partners and its passthrough partners (whether U.S. or foreign) through which United States partners hold an interest in the foreign partnership. Schedules K-1 that are not excepted from filing under this paragraph (b)(3)(iii) must contain the same information required of a domestic partnership filing under paragraph (a) of this section.

(4) *Information or returns required of partners who are United States persons.*—(i) *In general.*—If a United States person is a partner in a partnership that is not required to file a partnership return, the district director or director of the relevant service center may require that person to render the statements or provide the information necessary to verify the accuracy of the reporting by that person of any items of partnership income, gain, loss, deduction, or credit.

(ii) *Controlled foreign partnerships.*—Certain United States persons who are partners in a foreign partnership controlled (within the meaning of section 6038(e)(1)) by United States persons may be required to provide information with respect to the partnership under section 6038.

(5) *Certain partnership elections.*—For a partnership that is not otherwise required to file a partnership return, if an election that can only be made by the partnership under section 703 (affecting the computation of taxable income derived from a partnership) is to be made by or for the partnership, a return on the form prescribed for the partnership return must be filed for the partnership. Unless otherwise provided in the form or the accompanying instructions, a return filed solely to make an election need only contain a written statement citing paragraph (b)(5)(ii) of this section, listing the name and address of the partnership making the election, and clearly identifying the specific election being made. A return filed under paragraph (b)(5)(ii) of this section solely to make an election is not a partnership return. Thus, such a return is not a return filed under section 6031(a) for purposes of sections 6501 (except regarding the specific election issue), 6231(a)(1)(A), and 6233. The return must be signed by—

(i) Each partner that is a partner in the partnership at the time the election is made; or

(ii) Any partner of the partnership who is authorized (under local law or the partnership's organizational documents) to make the election and who represents to having such authorization under penalties of perjury.

(6) *Exclusion for certain organizations.*—The return requirement of section 6031 and this section does not apply to the International Telecommunications Satellite Organization, the International Maritime Satellite Organization, or any organization that is a successor of either.

(7) *Filing obligation for certain partners of certain foreign partnerships with respect to base erosion payments.*—If a foreign partnership is not required to file a partnership return and the foreign partnership has made a payment or accrual that is treated as a base erosion payment of a partner as provided in § 1.59A-7(c), a partner in the foreign partnership who is a person required to file a Form 8991 (or successor) must include the information necessary to report those base erosion payments and base erosion tax benefits on Form 8991 (or successor) in accordance with the related instructions. A partner with a Form 8991 (or successor) filing requirement who is a partner in a foreign partnership that is not required to file a partnership return must obtain the necessary information to report any base erosion payments on Form 8991 (or successor) from the foreign partnership or from any other reliable records of these payments. This paragraph does not apply to any partner described in § 1.59A-7(d)(2).

(c) *Partnerships excluded from the application of subchapter K of the Internal Revenue Code.*—(1) *Wholly excluded.*—(i) *Year of election.*—An eligible partnership as described in § 1.761-2(a) that elects to be excluded from all the provisions of subchapter K of chapter 1 of the Internal Revenue Code in the manner specified by § 1.761-2(b)(2)(i) must timely file the form prescribed for the partnership return for the taxable year for which the election is made. In lieu of the information otherwise required, the return must contain or be accompanied by the information required by § 1.761-2(b)(2)(i).

(ii) *Subsequent years.*—Except as otherwise provided in paragraph (c)(1)(i) of this section, an eligible partnership that elects to be wholly excluded from the application of subchapter K is not required to file a partnership return.

(2) *Deemed excluded.*—An eligible partnership that is deemed to have elected exclusion from the application of subchapter K beginning with its first taxable year, as specified in § 1.761-2(b)(2)(ii), is not required to file a partnership return.

(d) *Definitions.*—(1) *Partnership.*—For the meaning of the term *partnership*, see § 1.761-1(a).

(2) *United States person.*—In applying this section, a United States person is a person described in section 7701(a)(30); the government of the United States, a State, or the District of Columbia (including an agency or instrumentality thereof); or a corporation created or organized in Guam, the Commonwealth of Northern Mariana Islands, the U.S. Virgin Islands, and American Samoa, if the requirements of section 881(b)(1)(A), (B), and (C) are met for such corporation. The term does not include an alien individual who is a resident of Puerto Rico, Guam, the Commonwealth of Northern Mariana Islands, the U.S. Virgin Islands, or American Samoa, as determined under § 301.7701(b)-1(d) of this chapter.

(3) *United States partner.*—In applying this section, a United States partner is any United States person who holds a direct or indirect interest in the partnership.

(4) *Indirect interest.*—An indirect interest is any interest held through one or more passthrough partners, as defined in section 6231(a)(9).

(e) *Procedural requirements.*—(1) *Place for filing.*—The return of a partnership must be filed with the service center prescribed in the relevant IRS revenue procedure, publication, form, or instructions to the form (see § 601.601(d)(2)).

(2) *Time for filing.*—The return of a partnership must be filed on or before the date prescribed by section 6072(b).

(3) *Magnetic media filing.*—For magnetic media filing requirements with respect to partnerships, see section 6011(e)(2) and the regulations thereunder.

(f)(1) *Applicability date.*—This section applies to returns filed on or after January 30, 2020. Section 1.6031(a)-1T (as contained in 26 CFR part 1, revised April 2019) applies to returns filed before January 30, 2020.

(2) *Applicability date.*—Paragraph (b)(7) of this section applies to taxable years ending on or after October 9, 2020. [Reg. § 1.6031(a)-1.]

☐ [*T.D.* 8841, 11-10-99. *Amended by T.D.* 9000, 6-14-2002; *T.D.* 9094, 11-5-2003; *T.D.* 9123, 4-30-2004; *T.D.* 9177, 2-10-2005; *T.D.* 9821, 7-18-2017; *T.D.* 9892, 1-29-2020 *and T.D.* 9910, 10-8-2020.]

**[Reg. § 301.6031(a)-1]**

**§ 301.6031(a)-1. Return of partnership income.**—For provisions relating to the requirement of returns of partnership income, see § 1.6031(a)-1 of this chapter. [Reg. § 301.6031(a)-1.]

☐ [*T.D.* 8841, 11-10-99.]

**[Reg. § 1.6031(b)-1T]**

**§ 1.6031(b)-1T. Statements to partners (temporary).**—(a) *Statement required to be furnished to partners.*—(1) *In general.*—Except as provided in this paragraph (a)(1) and paragraph (a)(2)(ii) of this section, any partnership required under section 6031(a) and the regulations thereunder to file a partnership return for a taxable year shall furnish to every person who was a partner (within the meaning of section 7701(a)(2)) at any time during the taxable year a written statement containing the information described in paragraph (a)(3) of this section. This section shall not apply to a real estate mortgage investment conduit (REMIC) treated as a partnership under subtitle F of the Code by reason of section 860F(e). For the reporting requirements applicable to REMICs see § 1.6031(b)-2T.

(2) *Special rules applicable to partnership interests held by nominees.*—(i) *Statements furnished to nominees.*—For any partnership taxable year beginning after October 22, 1986, a partnership shall provide a person that holds (directly or indirectly) an interest in such partnership as a nominee on behalf of another person at any time during such year with a statement under paragraph (a)(1) of this section with respect to such interest if—

(A) Such nominee has not furnished the statement required under § 1.6031(c)-1T(a)(1)(i) to the partnership with respect to such other person;

(B) Such nominee either holds legal title to such partnership interest in its own name or is identified in a statement provided to the partnership pursuant to § 1.6031(c)-1T(a)(1)(i) by another nominee as the person on whose behalf such other nominee holds such interest; and

(C) Such nominee is not a person described in § 1.6031(c)-1T(a)(2) (relating to the special rule for clearing agencies). In such case, the partnership shall assume, for purposes of this section, that the nominee is the beneficial owner of the partnership interest.

(ii) *Statements not required to be furnished to partners holding partnership interests through nominees.*—A partnership shall not be required to furnish a statement under paragraph (a)(1) of this section to a partner with respect to any portion of such partner's interest in the partnership that is owned through a nominee if—

(A) Such nominee has not furnished (or is not required to furnish under § 1.6031(c)-1T(a)(2)), a statement to the partnership under § 1.6031(c)-1T(a)(1)(i) with respect to such partner; and

(B) Such partner has not furnished (or is not required to furnish) a statement to the partnership under § 1.6031(c)-1T(a)(3), with respect to such interest in the partnership.

(3) *Contents of statement.*—The statement required under paragraph (a)(1) of this section shall include the following information:

(i) The partner's distributive share of partnership income, gain, loss, deduction, or credit required to be shown on the partnership return (or, for taxable years beginning before January 1, 1987, the partner's distributive share of partnership income, gain, loss, deduction, or credit shown on the partnership return); and

(ii) To the extent provided by form or the accompanying instructions, any additional information that may be required to apply particular provisions of subtitle A of the Code to the partner with respect to items related to the partnership.

(b) *Time for furnishing statement.*—The statement required to be furnished by the partnership under paragraph (a)(1) of this section shall be furnished on or before the day on which the partnership return for that taxable year is required to be filed (determined with regard to extensions). For partnership returns the due date for which (determined without regard to extensions) is before January 1, 1987, the statement required to be furnished by the partnership under paragraph (a)(1) of this section shall be furnished on or before the day on which the partnership return is filed.

(c) *Statement may be provided to agent.*—If a partner designates another person, such as an attorney or an investment advisor, as the partner's (or nominee's) agent in dealing with the partnership, the partnership may provide the statement required under paragraph (a)(1) of this section with respect to such partner to such other person instead of the partner.

(d) *Penalties.*—For penalties for failure to comply with the requirements of section 6031(b) and paragraph (a) of this section, see section 6722(a).

(e) *Effective date.*—Except as otherwise provided in this section, the provisions of this section apply to partnership taxable years beginning after September 3, 1982. [Temporary Reg. § 1.6031(b)-1T.]

☐ [*T.D.* 8225, 9-6-88.]

### [Reg. § 1.6031(b)-2T]

**§ 1.6031(b)-2T. REMIC reporting requirements(temporary).—[Reserved].—**

### [Reg. § 1.6031(c)-1T]

**§ 1.6031(c)-1T. Nominee reporting of partnership information (temporary).**—(a) *Statements required to be furnished to partnership.*—(1) *Statement from nominee.*—(i) *In general.*—Except as otherwise provided in this section, any person who holds, directly or indirectly, an interest in a partnership (required under section 6031(a) and the regulations thereunder to file a partnership return for a taxable year) as a nominee on behalf of another person at any time during the partnership taxable year shall furnish to the partnership a written statement (or statements) for that taxable year with respect to such other person containing the information described in paragraph (a)(1)(ii) of this section.

(ii) *Contents of statement.*—The statement required under paragraph (a)(1)(i) of this section shall, except as otherwise provided in paragraph (a)(4) of this section, include the following information:

(A) The name, address, and taxpayer identification number of the nominee;

(B) The name, address, and taxpayer identification number of such other person;

(C) Whether such other person is—

(*1*) A person that is not a United States person;

(*2*) A foreign government, an international organization, or any wholly-owned agency or instrumentality of either of the foregoing; or

(*3*) A tax-exempt entity (within the meaning of section 168(h)(2));

(D) A description of any interest in the partnership held by the nominee on behalf of such other person at the beginning of the partnership taxable year;

(E) A description of any interest in the partnership that the nominee acquires (within the meaning of paragraph (g)(1) of this section) on behalf of such other person during the partnership taxable year, the method of acquisition (e.g., purchase, exchange, acquisition at death, gift, or commencement of nominee relationship) and acquisition cost (within the meaning of paragraph (g)(2) of this section) of such interest, and the date of the acquisition of such interest; and

(F) A description of any interest in the partnership that the nominee transfers (within the meaning of paragraph (g)(5) of this section) on behalf of such other person during the partnership taxable year, the net proceeds from the transfer (within the meaning of paragraph (g)(6) of this section) of such interest, and the date of the transfer of such interest.

A description of a partnership interest must include sufficient detail to enable the partnership to furnish to such other person the statement required under § 1.6031(b)-1T(a).

(2) *Special rule for clearing agencies.*—A clearing agency registered pursuant to the provisions of section 17A of the Securities Exchange Act of 1934 (or its nominee) that holds an interest in a partnership as a nominee on behalf of another person shall not be required to furnish any statement described in paragraph (a)(1)(i) of this section with respect to such interest.

(3) *Special rule for brokers and financial institutions.*—(i) *Additional statement required.*—Any broker (within the meaning of paragraph (g)(3) of this section) or financial institution (within the meaning of paragraph (g)(4) of this section) that holds an interest in a partnership indirectly through a nominee described in paragraph (a)(2) of this section at any time during a partnership taxable year shall furnish (in addition to any statement (or statements) required under paragraph (a)(1)(i) of this section) to the partnership a written statement (or statements) containing the information described in paragraph (a)(3)(ii) of this section with respect to any interest in such partnership that it holds (directly or indirectly) for its own account at any time during such partnership taxable year.

(ii) *Contents of statement.*—The statement required under paragraph (a)(3)(i) of this section shall, except as otherwise provided in paragraph (a)(4) of this section, include the following information:

(A) The name, address, and taxpayer identification number of the broker or financial institution;

(B) Whether such broker or financial institution is a person that is not a United States person;

(C) A description of any interest in the partnership held by the broker or financial institution for its own account at the beginning of the partnership taxable year;

(D) A description of any interest in the partnership that the broker or financial institution acquires for its own account during the partnership taxable year, the method of acquisition and acquisition cost of such interest, and the date of the acquisition of such interest; and

(E) A description of any interest in the partnership that the broker or financial institution transfers for its own account during the partnership taxable year, the net proceeds from the transfer of such interest, and the date of the transfer of such interest.

A description of a partnership interest held by a broker or financial institution for its own account must include sufficient detail to enable the partnership to furnish to the broker or financial institution the statement required under § 1.6031(b)-1T(a).

(4) *Exception.*—(i) *In general.*—Except as otherwise provided in this paragraph (a)(4), any statement required under paragraph (a)(1)(i) or (3)(i) of this section for a taxable year is not required to include—

(A) That part of the information described in paragraph (a)(1)(ii)(E) and (3)(ii)(D) of this section regarding the method of acquisition and acquisition cost; or

(B) That part of the information described in paragraph (a)(1)(ii)(F) and (3)(ii)(E) of this section regarding the net proceeds from the transfer;

to the extent that, prior to the beginning of the partnership taxable year, the partnership has provided the nominee with a written statement that the nominee need not provide such information to the partnership, and the partnership has not modified or revoked such statement. For purposes of the preceding sentence, the modification or revocation of a statement furnished to a nominee is effective for a partnership taxable year if and only if the partnership notifies the nominee of such modification or revocation by a written statement more than 60 days before the beginning of the partnership taxable year. The nominee shall retain a copy of any statement that is furnished to it by the partnership under this paragraph (a)(4) in the nominee's records so long as the contents thereof may become material in the administration of any internal revenue law.

(ii) *Effect of election under section 754.*—Paragraph (a)(4)(i)(A) of this section shall not apply to a partnership taxable year if—

(A) The partnership has an election in effect under section 754 (relating to optional adjustment to basis of partnership property) for such taxable year; and

(B) The nominee knows or has reason to know of such election more than 60 days before the beginning of such taxable year.

(5) *Examples.*—The following examples illustrate the application of this paragraph (a):

*Example (1).* B, a broker, holds 50 units of interest in Partnership P, a calendar year partnership, in street name for customer A, the beneficial owner. B holds the units on behalf of A at all times during 1989. B must furnish a statement to P for calendar year 1989 under paragraph (a)(1)(i) of this section that includes the information required under paragraph (a)(1)(ii)(A) through (D) of this section. The description of the partnership interest held by B on A's behalf on January 1, 1989, must identify the number of units of P held by B on A's behalf at that time (50), and the class of the partnership interest (including the Committee on Uniform Security Identification Procedures (CUSIP) number of the partnership interest, if known).

*Example (2)*. The facts are the same as in example (1), except that pursuant to A's instructions, B sells 25 of A's units of interest in P on August 1, 1989, receiving net proceeds from the transfer of $500. In addition to the information described in example (1), the statement that B must furnish to P must include the class of the partnership interest transferred (including the CUSIP number of the partnership interest, if known), the number of units transferred (25), the net proceeds from the transfer ($500), and the date of the transfer (August 1, 1989).

*Example (3)*. The facts are the same as in example (1), except that A is not the beneficial owner, but rather holds the units as a nominee on behalf of C, the beneficial owner, at all times during 1989. In addition to the statement that B must furnish to P (as described in Example (1) of this paragraph (a)(5)), A must furnish a statement to P for calendar year 1989 under paragraph (a)(1)(i) of this section that includes the information required under paragraph (a)(1)(ii)(A) through (D) of this section. If both A and B provide P with the statement required under paragraph (a)(1)(i) of this section, P must provide C with the statement required under § 1.6031(b)-1T(a)(1).

(b) *Time for furnishing statements.*—A nominee may furnish to the partnership any statement required under paragraph (a) of this section annually, quarterly, monthly, or on any other basis, provided that all statements required to be furnished under paragraph (a) of this section for a partnership taxable year shall be furnished on or before the last day of the first month following the close of such partnership taxable year.

(c) *Use of magnetic media.*—A nominee required to furnish a written statement under paragraph (a) of this section, may, in lieu of furnishing such written statement, furnish the required information on magnetic tape or by other media if the partnership and the nominee so agree.

(d) *Use of single document.*—Any person who holds interests in a partnership as a nominee on behalf of more than one other person during the partnership taxable year may, in lieu of furnishing to the partnership a separate statement for each such other person, furnish to the partnership a single document which includes, for each such other person, the information described in paragraph (a)(1)(ii) of this section. To the extent that a single document is used, references in this section to the statement required under paragraph (a)(1)(i) of this section shall be deemed to refer also to the information included in a single document under this paragraph (d).

(e) *Retention of information.*—The nominee shall retain a copy of any statement that is furnished to the partnership under this section in the nominee's records so long as the contents thereof may become material in the administration of any internal revenue law.

(f) *Use of agent.*—If a partnership has designated another person, such as a clearing organization, as the partnership's agent for purposes of receiving the statements required under paragraph (a) of this section, such statements may be furnished to that other person instead of the partnership. If a nominee has designated another person as its agent for purposes of furnishing to the partnership (or its agent) the statements required under paragraph (a) of this section, that other person may furnish such statements to the partnership (or its agent) on behalf of the nominee.

(g) *Meaning of terms.*—For purposes of this section, the following terms have the meanings set forth below:

(1) The term "acquires" means—

(i) A purchase or other acquisition of a partnership interest; or

(ii) The commencement of a nominee relationship, including the substitution of one nominee for another.

(2) The term "acquisition cost" means the sum of any money paid and the fair market value of any property (other than money) transferred to acquire a partnership interest increased by any expenses paid or incurred with respect to the acquisition (such as broker's fees or commissions).

(3) The term "broker" shall have the meaning set forth in paragraph (a)(1) of § 1.6045-1.

(4) The term "financial institution" means a financial institution such as a bank, mutual savings bank, savings and loan association, building and loan association, cooperative bank, homestead association, credit union, industrial loan association or bank, or other similar organization.

(5) The term "transfer" means—

(i) A sale, exchange, or other disposition of a partnership interest; or

(ii) The termination of a nominee relationship, including the substitution of one nominee for another.

(6) The term "net proceeds from the transfer" means the sum of any money and the fair market value of any property (other than money) received in connection with a transfer of a partnership interest reduced by any expenses paid or incurred with respect to the transfer (such as broker's fees or commissions).

(7) The term "person" includes the United States, a State, the District of Columbia, a foreign government, a political subdivision of a State or foreign government, or an international organization.

(h) *Statement required by nominees that do not comply with § 1.6031(c)-1T(a).*—(1) *In general.*—Any person that—

(i) Holds an interest in a partnership as a nominee (other than a nominee described in paragraph (a)(3) of this section) on behalf of another person at any time during the partnership taxable year;

(ii) Does not furnish to such partnership the statement required under paragraph (a)(1)(i) of this section for such other person with respect to such interest in the partnership; and

(iii) Receives from such partnership the statement described in paragraph (a)(1) of § 1.6031(b)-1T with respect to such interest in the partnership;

shall furnish to such other person a written statement containing the information described in paragraph (h)(2) of this section with respect to such interest in the partnership.

(2) *Contents of statement.*—The statement required under paragraph (h)(1) of this section shall contain the following information:

(i) The distributive share of partnership income, gain, loss, deduction, or credit required to be shown on the partnership return that is allocable to such interest in the partnership; and

(ii) Any additional information that may be required to apply particular provisions of subtitle A of the Code to the beneficial owner of such interest in the partnership in connection with items related to the partnership.

(3) *Time for furnishing statements.*—A nominee shall furnish the statement required under paragraph (h)(1) of this section within 30 days after receiving the statement described in paragraph (a) of § 1.6031(b)-1T.

(i) *REMICs.*—This section shall not apply with respect to any interest in a real estate mortgage investment conduit (REMIC) treated as a partnership under subtitle F of the Code by reason of section 860F(e). For the nominee reporting requirements with respect to REMICs see § 1.6031(c)-2T.

(j) *Penalties.*—[Reserved].

(k) *Effective date.*—(1) *In general.*—Except as otherwise provided in paragraph (k)(2) of this section, the provisions of this section shall apply to partnership taxable years beginning after October 22, 1986.

(2) *Transitional rule for taxable years beginning before January 1, 1989.*—For partnership taxable years beginning before January 1, 1989,—

(i) Any statement that a nominee is required to furnish to a partnership under paragraph (a)(1) of this section shall not be required to include the following information:

(A) The information described in paragraph (a)(1)(ii)(C) of this section;

(B) That part of the information described in paragraph (a)(1)(ii)(E) of this section regarding the method of acquisition and acquisition cost of a partnership interest; or

(C) That part of the information described in paragraph (a)(1)(ii)(F) of this section regarding the net proceeds from the transfer of a partnership interest.

(ii) A broker or financial institution shall not be required to furnish the additional statement described in paragraph (a)(3)(i) of this section. [Temporary Reg. § 1.6031(c)-1T.]

☐ [*T.D. 8225, 9-6-88.*]

### [Reg. § 1.6031(c)-2T]

**§ 1.6031(c)-2T. Nominee reporting of REMIC information (temporary).**—[Reserved]

### [Reg. § 1.6032-1]

**§ 1.6032-1. Returns of banks with respect to common trust funds.**—(a) Every bank (as defined in section 581) maintaining a common trust fund shall make a return of income of the common trust fund, regardless of the amount of its taxable income. Member banks of an affiliated group that serve as co-trustees with respect to a common trust fund must act jointly in making a return for the fund.

If a bank maintains more than one common trust fund, a separate return shall be made for each. No particular form is prescribed for making the return under this section, but Form 1065 may be used if it is designated by the bank as the return of a common trust fund. The return shall be made for the taxable year of the common trust fund and shall be filed on or before the date prescribed by section 6072(b) with the service center prescribed in the relevant Internal Revenue Service revenue procedure, publication, form, or instructions to the form (see § 601.601(d)(2) of this chapter). Such return shall state specifically with respect to the fund the items of gross income and the deductions allowed by subtitle A of the Internal Revenue Code, shall include each participant's name and address, the participant's proportionate share of taxable income or net loss (exclusive of gains and losses from sales or exchanges of capital assets), the participant's proportionate share of gains and losses from sales or exchanges of capital assets, and the participant's share of items which enter into the determination of the tax imposed by section 56. See §§ 1.584-2 and 1.58-5. If the common trust fund is maintained by two or more banks that are members of the same affiliated group, the return must also identify the member bank in the group that has contributed each participant's property or money to the fund. A copy of the plan of the common trust fund must be filed with the return. If, however, a copy of such plan has once been filed with a return, it need not again be filed if the return contains a statement showing when and where it was filed. If the plan is amended in any way after such copy has been filed, a copy of the amendment must be filed with the return for the taxable year in which the amendment was made. For the signing of a return of a bank with respect to common trust funds, see § 1.6062-1, relating to the manner prescribed for the signing of a return of a corporation.

(b) This section applies to returns filed on or after January 30, 2020. Section 1.6032-1T (as contained in 26 CFR part 1, revised April 2019) applies to taxable years beginning before January 30, 2020. [Reg. § 1.6032-1.]

☐ [*T.D.* 6364, 2-13-59. *Amended by T.D.* 7564, 9-11-78, *T.D.* 7935, 1-12-84, *T.D.* 9821, 7-18-2017 *and T.D.* 9892, 1-29-2020.]

### [Reg. § 301.6032-1]

**§ 301.6032-1. Returns of banks with respect to common trust funds.**—For provisions relating to requirement of returns of banks with respect to common trust funds, see § 1.6032-1 of this chapter (Income Tax Regulations). [Reg. § 301.6032-1.]

☐ [*T.D.* 6498, 10-24-60.]

### [Reg. § 1.6033-1]

**§ 1.6033-1. Returns by exempt organizations; taxable years beginning before January 1, 1970.**—[The text of Reg. § 1.6033-1, relating to returns by exempt organizations for taxable years beginning before 1970, is no longer reproduced by CCH. Present rules are contained in Reg. § 1.6033-2.]

### [Reg. § 301.6033-1]

**§ 301.6033-1. Returns by exempt organizations.**—For provisions relating to the requirement of returns by exempt organizations, see § 1.6033-1 of this chapter (Income Tax Regulations). [Reg. § 301.6033-1.]

☐ [*T.D.* 6498, 10-24-60.]

### [Reg. § 1.6033-2]

**§ 1.6033-2. Returns by exempt organizations and returns by certain nonexempt organizations.**—(a) *In general.*—(1) Except as provided in section 6033(a)(3) and paragraph (g) of this section, every organization exempt from taxation under section 501(a) shall file an annual information return specifically setting forth its items of gross income, gross receipts and disbursements, and such other information as may be prescribed in the instructions, issued with respect to the return. Except as provided in paragraph (d) of this section, such return shall be filed annually regardless of whether such organization is chartered by, or affiliated or associated with, any central, parent, or other organization.

(2)(i) Except as otherwise provided in this paragraph and paragraph (g) of this section, every organization exempt from taxation under section 501(a), and required to file a return under section 6033 and this section (including, for taxable years ending before December 31, 1972, private foundations, as defined in section 509(a)), other than an organization described in section 401(a) or 501(d), shall file its annual return on Form 990. For taxable years ending on or after December 31, 1972, every private foundation shall file Form 990-PF as its annual information return. For taxable years beginning after December 31, 1977, every section 501(c)(21) black lung trust shall file an annual information return on Form 990-BL or any other form prescribed by the Internal Revenue Service for that purpose.

(ii) Subject to paragraph (a)(1) of this section, the information generally required to be furnished by an organization exempt under section 501(a) is:

(A) Its gross income for the year. For this purpose, gross income includes tax-exempt income, but does not include contributions, gifts, grants, and similar amounts received. Whether an item constitutes a contribution, gift, grant, or similar amount depends upon all the surrounding facts and circumstances. The computation of gross income shall be made by subtracting the cost of goods sold from all receipts other than gross contributions, gifts, grants and similar amounts received and nonincludible dues and assessments from members and affiliates.

(B) To the extent not included in gross income, its dues and assessments from members and affiliates for the year.

(C) Its expenses incurred within the year attributable to gross income.

(D) Its disbursements (including prior years' accumulations) made within the year for the purposes for which it is exempt.

(E) A balance sheet showing its assets, liabilities, and net worth as of the beginning and end of such year. Detailed information relating to the assets, liabilities, and net worth shall be furnished on the schedule provided for this purpose on the return required by this section. Such schedule shall be supplemented by attachments where appropriate.

(F) The total of the contributions, gifts, grants, and similar amounts received by it during the taxable year, and, in the case of an organization described in section 501(c)(3), the names and addresses of all persons that contributed, bequeathed, or devised $5,000 or more (in money or other property) during the taxable year. In the case of a private foundation (as defined in section 509(a)), the names and addresses of all persons who became substantial contributors (as defined in section 507(d)(2)) during the taxable year shall be furnished. In addition, for its first taxable year beginning after December 31, 1969, each private foundation shall furnish the names and addresses of all persons who became substantial contributors before such taxable year. For special rules with respect to contributors and donors, see paragraph (a)(2)(iii) of this section.

(G) The names and addresses of all officers, directors, or trustees (or any person having responsibilities or powers similar to those of officers, directors or trustees) of the organization, and, in the case of a private foundation, all persons who are foundation managers, within the meaning of section 4946(b)(1). Organizations must also attach a schedule showing the names and addresses and/or total numbers of key employees, highly compensated employees, and independent contractors as prescribed by publication, form, or instructions.

(H) A schedule showing the compensation and other payments made to each person whose name is required to be listed pursuant to paragraph (a)(2)(ii)(G) of this section during the calendar year ending within the organization's annual accounting period, or during such other period as prescribed by publication, form, or instructions.

(I) For any taxable year ending on or after December 31, 1971, such information as is required by Forms 4848 and 4849 and, only with respect to any such taxable year ending before December 31, 1972, such information as is required by Form 2950. Such forms are required by this section to be filed by an organization exempt from tax under section 501(a) which is an employer who maintains a funded pension or annuity plan for its employees. See paragraph (g) of this section for exceptions from filing. Form 4849 need not be filed by the organization if the fiduciary for the plan has given written notification to the organization that such form will be filed as an attachment to Form 990-P filed by the fiduciary. Form 4848 (and Form 4849 if required to be filed by the organization) shall be filed as a separate return on or before the due date for Form 990. For rules relating to the extension of time for filing, see section 6081 and the regulations thereunder and the instructions for Form 4848. A central organization which files Form 990 as a group return under paragraph (d) of this section may also file Form 4848 as a group return. The rules provided by paragraph (d) of this section with respect to a group return filed on Form 990 shall apply to a group return filed on Form 4848. Unless otherwise expressly provided therein, an authorization to include a local organization in a group for purposes of filing Form 990 as a group return shall be treated as an authorization to include such local organization in a group for purposes of filing Form 4848 as a group return. A group return on Form 4848 shall be filed in accordance with this section and the instructions to Form 4848 and shall be considered the return of each local organization included therein. In addition to the information required to be furnished by Forms 4848 and 4849, the district director may require any further information that he considers necessary to determine qualification of the plan under section 401 or the taxability under section 403(b) of a beneficiary under an annuity purchased by a section 501(c)(3) organization.

(J) In the case of a private foundation liable for tax imposed under Chapter 42, such information as is required by Form 4720.

(K) In the case of an organization described in section 501(c)(3), the respective amounts (if any) of the taxes imposed on the organization, or any organization manager of the organization, during the taxable year under any of the following provisions (and the respective amounts (if any) of reimbursements paid by the organization during the taxable year with respect to taxes imposed on any such organization manager under any of such provisions):

(1) Section 4911 (relating to tax on excess expenditures to influence legislation);

(2) Section 4912 (relating to tax on disqualifying lobbying expenditures of certain organizations); and

(3) Section 4955 (relating to taxes on political expenditures of section 501(c)(3) organizations), except to the extent that, by reason of section 4962, the taxes imposed under such section are not required to be paid or are credited or refunded.

(L) In the case of organizations described in section 501(c)(3), (4), or (29), the respective amounts (if any) of—

(1) The taxes imposed with respect to the organization on any organization manager, or any disqualified person, during the taxable year under section 4958 (relating to taxes on excess benefit transactions); and

(2) Reimbursements paid by the organization during the taxable year with respect to taxes imposed under such section, except to the extent that, by reason of section 4962, the taxes imposed under such section are not required to be paid or are credited or refunded.

(M) Its lobbying expenditures, grass roots expenditures, exempt purpose expenditures, lobbying nontaxable amount, and grass roots nontaxable amount for the taxable year and for prior taxable years that are base years (within the meaning of § 1.501(h)-3(c)(7)), if the organization has an election under section 501(h) in effect for the taxable year. An organization that is a member of an affiliated group of organizations (as defined in § 56.4911-7(e)) but that is not a member of a limited affiliated group (as defined in § 56.4911-10(b)) shall report this information based on the expenditures of all members of the group during the taxable year of the group that ends with or within the member's taxable year and for prior taxable years of the group that are base years (within the meaning of § 56.4911-9(b)). For additional information required to be furnished by members of an affiliated group of organizations, and by controlling members in a limited affiliated group, see § § 56.4911-9(d) and 56.4911-10(f)(1), respectively.

(N) In the case of a hospital organization (as defined in § 1.501(r)-1(b)(18)) described in section 501(c)(3) during the taxable year—

(1) A copy of its audited financial statements for the taxable year (or, in the case of an organization the financial statements of which are included in consolidated financial statements with other organizations, such consolidated financial statements);

(2) Either a copy of the most recently adopted implementation strategy, within the meaning of § 1.501(r)-3(c), for each hospital facility it operates or the URL of each Web page where it has made each such implementation strategy widely available on a Web site within the meaning of § 1.501(r)-1(b)(29) along with or as part of the report documenting the community health needs assessment (CHNA) to which the implementation strategy relates;

(3) For each hospital facility it operates, a description of the actions taken during the taxable year to address the significant health needs identified through its most recently conducted CHNA, within the meaning of § 1.501(r)-3(b), or, if no actions were taken with respect to one or more of these health needs, the reason(s) why no actions were taken; and

(4) The amount of the excise tax imposed on the organization under section 4959 during the taxable year.

(iii) *Special rules.*—In providing the names and addresses of contributors and donors under paragraph (a)(2)(ii)(F) of this section:

(A) An organization described in section 501(c)(3) which meets the 33⅓ percent-of-support test of the regulations under section 170 (b)(1)(A)(vi) (without regard to whether such organization otherwise qualifies as an organization described in section 170(b)(1)(A)) is required to provide the name and address of a person who contributed, bequeathed, or devised $5,000 or more during the year only if his amount is in excess of 2 percent of the total contributions, bequests and devises received by the organization during the year.

(B) An organization other than a private foundation is required to report only the names and addresses of contributors of whom it has actual knowledge. For instance, an organization need not require an employer who withholds contributions from the compensation of employees and pays over to the organization periodically the total amounts withheld, to specify the amounts paid over with respect to a particular employee. In such case, unless the organization has actual knowledge that a particular employee gave more than $5,000 (and in excess of 2 percent if paragraph (a)(2)(iii)(A) of this section is applicable), the organization need report only the name and address of the employer, and the total amount paid over by the employer.

(C) Separate and independent gifts made by one person in a particular year need be aggregated to determine whether his contributions and bequests exceed $5,000 (and are in excess of 2 percent if paragraph (a)(2)(iii)(A) of this section is applicable), only if such gifts are of $1,000 or more.

(D)(1) Organizations described in section 501(c)(7), (8), or (10) that receive contributions or bequests to be used exclusively for purposes described in section 170(c)(4), 2055(a)(3), or 2522(a)(3), must attach a schedule with respect to all gifts that aggregate more than $1,000 from any one person showing the total amount of the contributions or bequests from each such person, the specific purpose or purposes for which such amount was received, and the specific use or uses to which such amount was put. In the case of an amount set aside for such purposes, the organization shall indicate the manner in which such amount is held (for instance, whether such amount is commingled with amounts held for other purposes). If the contribution or bequest was transferred to another organization, the schedule must include the name of the transferee organization, a description of the nature of such organization, and a description of the relationship between the transferee and transferor organizations.

(2) For taxable years beginning after December 31, 1970, such organizations must also attach a statement showing the total dollar amount of contributions and bequests received for such purposes which are $1,000 or less.

(iv) *Listing of States.*—A private foundation is required to attach to its return required by this section a list of all States—

(A) to which the organization reports in any fashion concerning its organization, assets, or activities, or

(B) with which the organization has registered (or which it has otherwise notified in any manner) that it intends to be, or is, a charitable organization or a holder of property devoted to a charitable purpose.

(3)(i) For taxable years beginning after December 31, 1969, and ending before December 31, 1971, every employee's trust described in section 401(a) which is exempt from taxation under section 501(a) shall file an annual return on Form 990-P. The return shall include the information required by paragraph (b)(5)(ii) of § 1.401-1. For such years, in addition, the trust must file the information required to be filed by the employer pursuant to the provisions of § 1.404(a)-2, unless the employer has notified the trustee in writing that he has filed or will timely file such information. If the trustee has received such notification from the employer, then such notification, or a copy thereof, shall be retained by the trust as a part of its records.

(ii) For taxable years ending on or after December 31, 1971, and before December 31, 1975, every employee's trust described in section 401(a) which is exempt from taxation under section 501(a) shall file an annual return on Form 990-P. The trust shall furnish such information as is required by such form and the instructions issued with respect thereto.

(4) For taxable years beginning after December 31, 1980, trusts described in section 4947(a)(1) and nonexempt private foundations shall comply with the requirements of section 6033 and this section in the same manner as organizations described in section 501(c)(3) which are exempt from tax under section 501(a). This section shall be applied for taxable years beginning after December 31, 1980 as if trusts described in section 4947(a)(1) and nonexempt private foundations were described in section 501(c)(3). Therefore, for purposes of this section, all references to exempt organizations shall include section 4947(a)(1) trusts and nonexempt private foundations and all references to private foundations shall include section 4947(a)(1) trusts that would be private foundations if they were described in section 501(c)(3) and all nonexempt private foundations. Similarly, for purposes of paragraph (a)(2)(ii)(D) of this section, the purposes for which a section 4947(a)(1) trust or a nonexempt private foundation is organized shall be treated as the purposes for which it is exempt. For purposes of this section, the term "nonexempt private foundation" means a taxable organization (other than a section 4947(a)(1) trust) that is a private foundation. See section 509(b) and § 1.509(b)-1. See also section 642(c)(6) and § 1.642(c)-4.

(5) Political organizations, as defined by section 527(e)(1), that have gross receipts of $25,000 or more for the taxable year (or in the case of a qualified State or local political organization, as defined in section 527(e)(5), that has gross receipts of $100,000 or more for the taxable year) generally must comply with the requirements of section 6033 and this section in the same manner as organizations exempt from tax under section 501(a), except to the extent that the Commissioner may modify such requirements through forms, instructions to forms, or guidance published in the Internal Revenue Bulletin as appropriate for carrying out the purposes of section 527. For the

purposes of this section, all references to organizations exempt from tax under section 501(a) shall include political organizations referred to in section 6033(g), other than those referred to in section 6033(g)(3) and except to the extent the Commissioner exercises discretion under section 6033(g)(4). This discretion may be exercised through forms, instructions to forms, or guidance published in the Internal Revenue Bulletin. In addition to the reporting requirements applicable to organizations exempt under section 501(a), such political organizations generally must report the names and addresses of all persons that contributed, bequeathed, or devised $5,000 or more (in money or other property) during the taxable year.

(6) Each controlling organization (within the meaning of section 512(b)(13)) that is subject to the requirements of section 6033(a) shall include on its annual return such information required by that return regarding—

(i) Any interest, annuities, royalties, or rents received from each controlled entity (within the meaning of section 512(b)(13));

(ii) Any loans made to each such controlled entity; and

(iii) Any transfers of funds between such controlling organization and each such controlled entity.

(7) Every organization described in section 4966(d)(1) shall, on its annual return for the taxable year—

(i) List the total number of donor advised funds (as defined in section 4966(d)(2)) it owns at the end of such taxable year;

(ii) Report the aggregate value of assets held in such funds at the end of such taxable year; and

(iii) Report the aggregate contributions to and grants made from such funds during such taxable year.

(8) Every organization described in section 509(a)(3) shall, on its annual return—

(i) List the supported organizations (as defined in section 509(f)(3)) with respect to which such organization provides support;

(ii) Specify whether the organization meets the requirements of clause (i), (ii), or (iii) of section 509(a)(3)(B); and

(iii) Certify that the organization meets the requirements of section 509(a)(3)(C).

(b) *Accounting period for filing return.*—A return required by this section shall be on the basis of the established annual accounting period of the organization. If the organization has no such established accounting period, such return shall be on the basis of the calendar year.

(c) *Returns when exempt status not established.*—An organization claiming an exempt status under section 501(a) prior to the establishment of such exempt status under section 501 and § 1.501(a)-1, shall file a return required by this section in accordance with the instructions applicable thereto. In such case the organization must indicate on such return that it is being filed in the belief that the organization is exempt under section 501(a), but that the Internal Revenue Service has not yet recognized such exemption.

(d) *Group returns.*—(1) A central, parent, or like organization (referred to in this paragraph as "central organization"), exempt under section 501(a) and described in section 501(c) (other than a private foundation), although required to file a separate annual return for itself under section 6033 and paragraph (a) of this section, may file annually, in addition to such separate annual return, a group return on Form 990. Such group return may be filed for two or more of the local organizations, chapters, or the like (referred to in this paragraph as "local organizations") which are (i) affiliated with such central organization at the close of its annual accounting period, (ii) subject to the general supervision or control of the central organization, and (iii) exempt from taxation under the same paragraph of section 501(c) of the Code, although the local organizations are not necessarily exempt under the paragraph under which the central organization is exempt. Such group return may not be filed for a local organization which is a private foundation.

(2)(i) The filing of the group return shall be in lieu of the filing of a separate return by each of the local organizations included in the group return. The group return shall include only those local organizations which in writing have authorized the central organization to include them in the group return, and which have made and filed, with the central organization, their statements, specifically stating their items of gross income, receipts, and disbursements, and such other information relating to them as is required to be stated in the group return. Such an authorization and statement by a local organization shall be made under the penalties of perjury, shall be signed by a duly authorized officer of the local organization in his official capacity, and shall contain the following statement, or a statement of like import: "I hereby declare under the penalties of perjury that this authorization (including any accompanying schedules and statements) has been examined by me and to the best of my knowledge and belief is true, correct and complete and made in good faith." Such authorization and statement with respect to a local organization

shall be retained by the central organization until the expiration of six years after the last taxable year for which a group return filed by such central organization includes such local organization.

(ii) There shall be attached to the group return and made a part thereof a schedule showing the name, address, and employer identification number of each of the local organizations and the total number thereof included in such return, and a schedule showing the name, address, and employer identification number of each of the local organizations and the total number thereof not included in the group return.

(3) The group return shall be on the basis of the established annual accounting period of the central organization. Where such central organization has no established annual accounting period, such return shall be on the basis of the calendar year. The same income, receipts, and disbursements of a local organization shall not be included in more than one group return.

(4) The group return shall be filed in accordance with these regulations and the instructions issued with respect to Form 990, and shall be considered the return of each local organization included therein. The tax exempt status of a local organization must be established under a group exemption letter issued to the central organization before a group return including the local organization will be considered as the return of the local organization. See § 1.501(a)-1 for requirements for establishing a tax-exempt status.

(5) In providing the information required by paragraphs (a)(2)(ii)(F), (G), and (H) of this section, such information may be provided:

(i) with respect to the central or parent organization on its Form 990, and with respect to the local organizations on separate schedules attached to the group return for the year, or

(ii) on a consolidated basis for all the local organizations and the central or parent organization on the group return.

Such information need be provided only with respect to those local organizations which are not excepted from filing under the provisions of paragraph (g) of this section. A central or parent organization shall indicate whether it has provided such information in the manner described in paragraphs (d)(5)(i) or (ii) of this section, and may not change the manner in which it provides such information without the consent of the Commissioner.

(e) *Time and place for filing.*—The annual return required by this section shall be filed on or before the 15th day of the fifth month following the close of the period for which the return is required to be filed. The annual return on Form 1065 required to be filed by a religious or apostolic association or corporation shall be filed on or before the date prescribed by section 6072(b). Each such return shall be filed in accordance with the instructions applicable thereto.

(f) *Penalties and additions to tax.*—For penalties and additions to tax for failure to file a return and filing a false or fraudulent return, see sections 6652, 7203, 7206 and 7207.

(g) *Organizations not required to file annual returns.*—(1) Annual returns required by this section are not required to be filed by an organization exempt from taxation under section 501(a) which is—

(i) A church, an interchurch organization of local units of a church, a convention or association of churches, or an integrated auxiliary of a church (as defined in paragraph (h) of this section);

(ii) An exclusively religious activity of any religious order;

(iii) Except as provided in paragraph (g)(1)(viii) of this section, an organization described in section 501(c) (other than a private foundation or a supporting organization described in section 509(a)(3)) the gross receipts of which in each taxable year are normally not more than $50,000 (as described in paragraph (g)(3) of this section);

(iv) A mission society (other than an organization described in section 509(a)(3)) sponsored by or affiliated with one or more churches or church denominations, more than one-half of the activities of which society are conducted in, or directed at persons in foreign countries;

(v) A State institution, the income of which is excluded from gross income under section 115(a);

(vi) An organization described in section 501(c)(1);

(vii) An educational organization (below college level) that is described in section 170(b)(1)(A)(ii), that has a program of a general academic nature, and that is affiliated (within the meaning of paragraph (h)(2) of this section) with a church or operated by a religious order; or

(viii) A foreign organization (described in paragraph (k)(1) of this section) or a United States possession organization (described in paragraph (k)(2) of this section) (other than a private foundation or a supporting organization described in section 509(a)(3))—

(A) The gross receipts of which in each taxable year from sources within the United States (as determined under paragraph (k)(3) of this section) are normally not more than $50,000 (as described in paragraph (g)(3) of this section); and

(B) That has no significant activity (including lobbying and political activity and the operation of a trade or business, but excluding investment activity) in the United States.

(2) The provisions of section 6033(a) relieving certain specified types of organizations exempt from taxation under section 501(a) from filing annual returns do not abridge or impair in any way the powers and authority of district directors or directors of service centers provided for in other provisions of the Code and in regulations thereunder to require the filing of returns or notices by such organizations. See section 6001 and § 1.6001-1.

(3) For purposes of paragraphs (g)(1)(iii) and (viii) of this section, the gross receipts (as defined in paragraph (g)(4) of this section) of an organization are normally not more than $50,000 if:

(i) In the case of an organization that has been in existence for 1 year or less, the organization has received, or donors have pledged to give, gross receipts of $75,000 or less during the first taxable year of the organization;

(ii) In the case of an organization that has been in existence for more than one but less than 3 years, the average of the gross receipts received by the organization in its first 2 taxable years is $60,000 or less; and

(iii) In the case of an organization that has been in existence for 3 years or more, the average of the gross receipts received by the organization in the immediately preceding 3 taxable years, including the year for which the return would be required to be filed, is $50,000 or less.

(4) For purposes of this paragraph and paragraph (a)(2) of this section, "gross receipts" means the gross amount received by the organization during its annual accounting period from all sources without reduction for any costs or expenses including, for example, cost of goods or assets sold, cost of operations, or expenses of earning, raising, or collecting such amounts. Thus "gross receipts" includes, but is not limited to, (i) the gross amount received as contributions, gifts, grants, and similar amounts without reduction for the expenses of raising and collecting such amounts, (ii) the gross amount received as dues or assessments from members or affiliated organizations without reduction for expenses attributable to the receipt of such amounts, (iii) gross sales or receipts from business activities (including business activities unrelated to the purpose for which the organization qualifies for exemption, the net income or loss from which may be required to be reported on Form 990-T), (iv) the gross amount received from the sale of assets without reduction for cost or other basis and expenses of sale, and (v) the gross amount received as investment income, such as interest, dividends, rents, and royalties.

(5) An organization that is not required to file an annual return by virtue of paragraphs (g)(1)(iii) and (viii) of this section must submit an annual electronic notification as described in section 6033(i). See § 1.6033-6.

(6) The Commissioner may relieve any organization or class of organizations (other than an organization described in section 509(a)(3)) from filing, in whole or in part the annual return required by this section where he determines that such returns are not necessary for the efficient administration of the internal revenue laws. This discretion may be exercised through forms, instructions to forms, or guidance published in the Internal Revenue Bulletin.

(h) *Integrated auxiliary.*—(1) *In general.*—For purposes of this title, the term *integrated auxiliary of a church* means an organization that is—

(i) Described both in sections 501(c)(3) and 509(a)(1), (2), or (3);

(ii) Affiliated with a church or a convention or association of churches; and

(iii) Internally supported.

(2) *Affiliation.*—An organization is affiliated with a church or a convention or association of churches, for purposes of paragraph (h)(1)(ii) of this section, if—

(i) The organization is covered by a group exemption letter issued under applicable administrative procedures, (such as Rev. Proc. 80-27 (1980-1 C.B. 677); See § 601.601(a)(2)(ii)(*b*)), to a church or a convention or association of churches;

(ii) The organization is operated, supervised, or controlled by or in connection with (as defined in § 1.509(a)-4) a church or a convention or association of churches; or

(iii) Relevant facts and circumstances show that it is so affiliated.

(3) *Facts and circumstances.*—For purposes of paragraph (h)(2)(iii) of this section, relevant facts and circumstances that indicate an organization is affiliated with a church or a convention or association of churches include the following factors. However, the absence of one or more of the following factors does not necessarily preclude classification of an organization as being affiliated with a church or a convention or association of churches—

(i) The organization's enabling instrument (corporate charter, trust instrument, articles of association, constitution or similar document) or by-laws affirm that the organization shares common religious doctrines, principles, disciplines, or practices with a church or a convention or association of churches;

(ii) A church or a convention or association of churches has the authority to appoint or remove, or to control the appointment or removal of, at least one of the organization's officers or directors;

(iii) The corporate name of the organization indicates an institutional relationship with a church or a convention or association of churches;

(iv) The organization reports at least annually on its financial and general operations to a church or a convention or association of churches;

(v) An institutional relationship between the organization and a church or a convention or association of churches is affirmed by the church, or convention or association of churches, or a designee thereof; and

(vi) In the event of dissolution, the organization's assets are required to be distributed to a church or a convention or association of churches, or to an affiliate thereof within the meaning of this paragraph (h).

(4) *Internal support.*—An organization is internally supported, for purposes of paragraph (h)(1)(iii) of this section, unless it both—

(i) Offers admissions, goods, services or facilities for sale, other than on an incidental basis, to the general public (except goods, services, or facilities sold at a nominal charge or for an insubstantial portion of the cost); and

(ii) Normally receives more than 50 percent of its support from a combination of governmental sources, public solicitation of contributions, and receipts from the sale of admissions, goods, performance of services, or furnishing of facilities in activities that are not unrelated trades or businesses.

(5) *Special rule.*—Men's and women's organizations, seminaries, mission societies, and youth groups that satisfy paragraphs (h)(1)(i) and (ii) of this section are integrated auxiliaries of a church regardless of whether such an organization meets the internal support requirement under paragraph (h)(1)(iii) of this section.

(6) *Effective date.*—This paragraph (h) applies for returns filed for taxable years beginning after December 31, 1969. For returns filed for taxable years beginning after December 31, 1969 but beginning before December 20, 1995, the definition for the term *integrated auxiliary of a church* set forth in § 1.6033-2(g)(5) (as contained in the 26 CFR edition revised as of April 1, 1995) may be used as an alternative definition to such term set forth in this paragraph (h).

(7) *Examples of internal support.*—The internal support test of this paragraph (h) is illustrated by the following examples, in each of which it is assumed that the organization's provision of goods and services does not constitute an unrelated trade or business:

*Example 1.* Organization A is described in sections 501(c)(3) and 509(a)(2) and is affiliated (within the meaning of this paragraph (h)) with a church. Organization A publishes a weekly newspaper as its only activity. On an incidental basis, some copies of Organization A's publication are sold to nonmembers of the church with which it is affiliated. Organization A advertises for subscriptions at places of worship of the church. Organization A is internally supported, regardless of its sources of financial support, because it does not offer admissions, goods, services, or facilities for sale, other than on an incidental basis, to the general public. Organization A is an integrated auxiliary.

*Example 2.* Organization B is a retirement home described in sections 501(c)(3) and 509(a)(2). Organization B is affiliated (within the meaning of this paragraph (h)) with a church. Admission to Organization B is open to all members of the community for a fee. Organization B advertises in publications of general distribution appealing to the elderly and maintains its name on non-denominational listings of available retirement homes. Therefore, Organization B offers its services for sale to the general public on more than an incidental basis. Organization B receives a cash contribution of $50,000 annually from the church. Fees received by Organization B from its residents total $100,000 annually. Organization B does not receive any government support or contributions from the general public. Total support is $150,000 ($100,000 + $50,000), and $100,000 of that total is from receipts from the performance of services (66-2/3% of total support). Therefore, Organization B receives more than 50 percent of its support from receipts from the performance of services. Organization B is not internally supported and is not an integrated auxiliary.

*Example 3.* Organization C is a hospital that is described in sections 501(c)(3) and 509(a)(1). Organization C is affiliated (within the meaning of this paragraph (h)) with a church. Organization C is open to all persons in need of hospital care in the community, although most of Organization C's patients are members of the same denomination as the church with which Organization C is affiliated. Organization C maintains its name on hospital listings used by the general public, and participating doctors are allowed to admit all patients. Therefore, Organization C offers its services for sale to the general public on more than an incidental basis. Organization C annually receives $250,000 in support from the church, $1,000,000 in payments from patients and third party payors (including Medicare, Medicaid and other insurers) for patient care, $100,000 in contributions from the public, $100,000 in grants from the federal government (other than Medicare and Medicaid payments) and $50,000 in investment income. Total support is $1,500,000 ($250,000 + $1,000,000 + $100,000 + $100,000 + $50,000), and $1,200,000 ($1,000,000 + $100,000 + $100,000) of that total is support from receipts from the performance of services, government sources, and public contributions (80% of total support). Therefore, Organization C receives more than 50 percent of its support from receipts from the performance of services, government sources, and public contributions. Organization C is not internally supported and is not an integrated auxiliary.

(i) *Records, statements, and other returns of tax-exempt organizations.*—(1) An organization that is exempt from taxation under section 501(a) and is not required to file annually an information return required by this section shall immediately notify in writing Exempt Organizations Determinations, at an address prescribed by publication (including publication on the Internal Revenue Service website), of any changes in its character, operations, or purpose for which it was originally created.

(2) Every organization which is exempt from tax, whether or not it is required to file an annual information return, shall submit such additional information as may be required by the Internal Revenue Service for the purpose of inquiring into its exempt status and administering the provisions of subchapter F (section 501 and following), chapter 1 of subtitle A of the Code, section 6033, and chapter 42 of subtitle D of the Code. See section 6001 and § 1.6001-1 with respect to the authority of the district directors or directors of service centers to require such additional information and with respect to the books of accounts or records to be kept by such organizations.

(3) An organization which has established its exemption from taxation under section 501(a), including an organization which is relieved under section 6033 and this section from filing annual returns of information, is not relieved of the duty of filing other returns of information. See, for example, sections 6041, 6043, 6051, 6057, 6058 and the regulations thereunder.

(j) *Unrelated business tax returns.*—In addition to the foregoing requirements of this section, certain organizations otherwise exempt from tax under section 501(a) which are subject to tax on unrelated business taxable income are also required to file returns on Form 990-T. See paragraph (e) of § 1.6012-2 and paragraph (a)(5) of § 1.6012-3 for requirements with respect to such returns.

(k) *Foreign organizations and United States possession organizations.*—(1) *Foreign organization.*—For purposes of this section, a *foreign organization* is any organization not described in section 170(c)(2)(A).

(2) *United States possession organization.*—For purposes of this section, a *United States possession organization* is any organization created or organized in a possession of the United States.

(3) *Source of funds.*—For purposes of paragraph (g)(1)(viii) of this section, the source of an organization's gross receipts from gifts, grants, contributions or membership fees is determined by applying the rules found in § 53.4948-1(b) of this chapter. For purposes of paragraph (g)(1)(viii) of this section, the source of an organization's gross receipts other than gifts, grants, contributions, and membership fees is determined by applying the rules in sections 861 through 865 and the regulations in this part issued under section 861 through 865. For purposes of applying this paragraph (k)(3) regarding United States possession organizations, a United States person does not include individuals who are *bona fide* residents of a United States possession.

(l) *Applicability date.*—(1) *Generally.*—This section applies to returns filed on or after January 30, 2020. Section 1.6033-2T (as contained in 26 CFR part 1, revised April 2019) applies to returns filed before January 30, 2020.

(2) Paragraphs (a)(2)(ii)(F), (a)(2)(iii)(D)(*1*), (g)(1)(iii) and (viii), and (g)(3) of this section apply to annual information returns filed after May 28, 2020. Under section 7805(b)(7) an organization may choose to apply the paragraphs listed in this paragraph (l)(2) to returns filed after September 6, 2019. [Reg. § 1.6033-2.]

☐ [*T.D.* 7122, 6-7-71. *Amended by T.D.* 7168, 3-8-72; *T.D.* 7223, 11-20-72; *T.D.* 7290, 11-16-73; *T.D.* 7454, 12-29-76; *T.D.* 7551, 7-3-78; *T.D.* 7785, 7-27-81; *T.D.* 7838, 10-5-82; *T.D.* 8026, 5-17-85; *T.D.* 8308, 8-30-90; *T.D.* 8640, 12-19-95; *T.D.* 9423, 9-8-2008; *T.D.* 9549, 9-7-2011, *T.D.* 9708, 12-29-2014 (*corrected* 5-1-2015), *T.D.* 9821, 7-18-2017, *T.D.* 9892, 1-29-2020 *and T.D.* 9898, 5-26-2020.]

**[Reg. § 1.6033-3]**

**§ 1.6033-3. Additional provisions relating to private foundations.**—(a) *In general.*—The foundation managers (as defined in section 4946(b)) of every organization (including a trust described in section 4947(a)(1)) which is (or is treated as) a private foundation (as defined in section 509) the assets of which are at least $5,000 at any time during a taxable year shall include the following information on its annual return in addition to that information required under § 1.6033-2(a):

(1) An itemized statement of its securities and all other assets at the close of the year, showing both book and market value,

(2) An itemized list of all grants and contributions made or approved for future payment during the year, showing the amount of each such grant or contribution, the name and address of the recipient (other than a recipient who is not a disqualified person and who receives, from the foundation, grants to indigent or needy persons that, in the aggregate, do not exceed $1,000 during the year), any relationship between any individual recipient and the foundation's managers or substantial contributors, and a concise statement of the purpose of each such grant or contribution,

(3) The address of the principal office of the foundation and (if different) of the place where its books and records are maintained,

(4) The names and addresses of its foundation managers (within the meaning of section 4946(b)), that are substantial contributors (within the meaning of section 507(d)(2)) or that own 10 percent or more of the stock of any corporation of which the foundation owns 10 percent or more of the stock, or corresponding interests in partnerships or other entities, in which the foundation has a 10 percent or greater interest.

For purposes of subparagraph (2) of this paragraph, the business address of an individual grant recipient or foundation manager may be used by the foundation in its annual return in lieu of the home address of such recipient or manager, and the term "relationship" shall include, but is not limited to, any case in which an individual recipient of a grant or contribution by a private foundation is (i) a member of the family (as defined in section 4946(d)) of a substantial contributor or foundation manager of such foundation, (ii) a partner of such substantial contributor or foundation manager, or (iii) an employee of such substantial contributor or foundation manager or of an organization which is effectively controlled (within the meaning of section 4946(a)(1)(H)(i) and the regulations thereunder), directly or indirectly, by one or more such substantial contributors or foundation managers.

(b) *Notice to public of availability of annual return.*—A copy of the notice required by section 6104(d) (relating to public inspection of private foundations' annual returns), and proof of publication thereof, shall be filed with the annual return required by § 1.6033-2(a). A copy of such notice as published, and a statement signed by a foundation manager stating that such notice was published, setting forth the date of publication and the publication in which it appeared, shall be sufficient proof of publication for purposes of this paragraph.

(c) *Special rules.*—(1) *Furnishing of copies to State officers.*—The foundation managers of a private foundation shall furnish a copy of the annual return required by section 6033 and § 1.6033-2 to the Attorney General of:

(i) each State which the foundation is required to list on its return pursuant to § 1.6033-2(a)(2)(iv),

(ii) the State in which is located the principal office of the foundation, and

(iii) the State in which the foundation was incorporated or created.

The annual return shall be sent to each Attorney General described in paragraph (c)(1)(i), (ii), or (iii) of this section at the same time as it is sent to the Internal Revenue Service. Upon request the foundation managers shall also furnish a copy of the annual return to the Attorney General or other appropriate State officer (within the meaning of section 6104(c)(2)) of any state. The foundation managers shall attach to each copy of the annual return sent to State officers under this subparagraph a copy of the Form 4720, if any, filed by the foundation for the year.

(2) *Cross-reference.*—For additional rules with respect to private foundations' returns and the public inspection of such returns, see section 6104(d) and the regulations thereunder.

(d) *Special rules for certain foreign organizations.*—The provisions of paragraphs (b) and (c) of this section shall not apply with respect to an organization described in section 4948(b). The foundation managers of such organizations are not required to publish notice of availability of the annual return for inspection, to make the annual return available at the principal office of the foundation for public inspection under section 6104(d), or to send copies of the annual return to State officers.

(e) *Effective date.*—The provisions of this section shall apply with respect to returns filed for taxable years beginning after December 31, 1980. [Reg. § 1.6033-3.]

☐ [*T.D.* 8026, 5-17-85.]

### [Reg. § 1.6033-4]

**§ 1.6033-4. Required use of magnetic media for returns by organizations required to file returns under section 6033.**—The return of an organization that is required to be filed on magnetic media under § 301.6033-4 of this chapter must be filed in accordance with Internal Revenue Service revenue procedures, publications, forms, or instructions, including those posted electronically. (See § 601.601(d)(2) of this chapter). [Reg. § 1.6033-4.]

☐ [*T.D.* 9363, 11-9-2007.]

### [Reg. § 301.6033-4]

**§ 301.6033-4. Required use of magnetic media for returns by organizations required to file returns under section 6033.**—(a) *Returns by organizations required to file returns under section 6033 on magnetic media.*—An organization required to file a return under section 6033 on Form 990, "Return of Organization Exempt from Income Tax," or Form 990-PF, "Return of Private Foundation or Section 4947(a)(1) Trust Treated as a Private Foundation," must file its Form 990 or 990-PF on magnetic media if the organization is required by the Internal Revenue Code or regulations to file at least 250 returns during the calendar year ending with or within its taxable year. Returns filed on magnetic media must be made in accordance with applicable revenue procedures, publications, forms, or instructions. In prescribing revenue procedures, publications, forms, or instructions, the Commissioner may direct the type of magnetic media filing. (See § 601.601(d)(2) of this chapter).

(b) *Waiver.*—The Commissioner may grant waivers of the requirements of this section in cases of undue hardship. A request for waiver must be made in accordance with applicable revenue procedures or publications. The waiver also will be subject to the terms and conditions regarding the method of filing as may be prescribed by the Commissioner.

(c) *Failure to file.*—If an organization required to file a return under section 6033 fails to file an information return on magnetic media when required to do so by this section, the organization is deemed to have failed to file the return. (See section 6652 for the addition to tax for failure to file a return.) In determining whether there is reasonable cause for failure to file the return, § 301.6652-2(f) and rules similar to the rules in § 301.6724-1(c)(3) (undue economic hardship related to filing information returns on magnetic media) will apply.

(d) *Meaning of terms.*—The following definitions apply for purposes of this section:

(1) *Magnetic media.*—The term *magnetic media* means any magnetic media permitted under applicable regulations, revenue procedures, or publications. These generally include magnetic tape, tape cartridge, and diskette, as well as other media, such as electronic filing, specifically permitted under the applicable regulations, procedures, publications, forms or instructions. (See § 601.601(d)(2) of this chapter).

(2) *Return required under section 6033.*—The term *return required under section 6033* means a Form 990, "Return of Organization Exempt from Income Tax," and Form 990-PF, "Return of Private Foundation or Section 4947(a)(1) Trust Treated as a Private Foundation," along with all other related forms, schedules, and statements that are required to be attached to the Form 990 or Form 990-PF, and all members of the Form 990 series of returns, including amended and superseding returns.

(3) *Determination of 250 returns.*—For purposes of this section, an organization is required to file at least 250 returns if, during the calendar year ending with or within the taxable year of the organization, the organization is required to file at least 250 returns of any type, including information returns (for example, Forms W-2, Forms 1099), income tax returns, employment tax returns, and excise tax returns. In the case of a short year return, an organization is required to file at least 250 returns if, during the calendar year which includes the short taxable year of the organization, the organization is re-

quired to file at least 250 returns of any type, including information returns (for example, Forms W-2, Forms 1099), income tax returns, employment tax returns, and excise tax returns.

(e) *Example.*—The following example illustrates the provisions of paragraph (d)(3) of this section. In the example, the organization is a calendar year taxpayer:

*Example.* In 2006, Organization T, with total assets in excess of $10 million, is required to file one Form 990, "Return of Organization Exempt from Income Tax," 200 Forms W-2, "Wage and Tax Statement," one Form 940, "Employer's Annual Federal Unemployment (FUTA) Tax Return," four Forms 941, "Employer's Quarterly Federal Tax Return," and 60 Forms 1099-MISC, "Miscellaneous Income." Because T is required to file 266 returns during the calendar year, T must file its 2006 Form 990 electronically.

(f) *Effective/applicability dates.*—This section applies to any organization required to file Form 990 for a taxable year ending on or after December 31, 2006, that has total assets as of the end of the taxable year of $10 million or more. This section applies to any organization required to file Form 990-PF for taxable years ending on or after December 31, 2006, except for the application of the short year rules in paragraph (d)(3) of this section, which is applicable for taxable years ending on or after November 13, 2007. [Reg. § 301.6033-4.]

☐ [*T.D.* 9363, 11-9-2007.]

### [Reg. § 1.6033-5]

**§ 1.6033-5. Disclosure by tax-exempt entities that are parties to certain reportable transactions.**—(a) *In general.*—Every tax-exempt entity (as defined in section 4965(c)) shall file with the IRS on Form 8886-T, "Disclosure by Tax-Exempt Entity Regarding Prohibited Tax Shelter Transaction" (or a successor form), in accordance with this section and the instructions to the form, a disclosure of—

(1) Such entity's being a party (as defined in § 53.4965-4 of this chapter) to a prohibited tax shelter transaction (as defined in section 4965(e)); and

(2) The identity of any other party (whether taxable or tax-exempt) to such transaction that is known to the tax-exempt entity.

(b) *Frequency of disclosure.*—A single disclosure is required for each prohibited tax shelter transaction.

(c) *By whom disclosure is made.*—(1) *Tax-exempt entities referred to in section 4965(c)(1), (2) or (3).*—In the case of tax-exempt entities referred to in section 4965(c)(1), (2) or (3), the disclosure required by this section must be made by the entity.

(2) *Tax-exempt entities referred to in section 4965(c)(4), (5), (6) or (7).*—In the case of tax-exempt entities referred to in section 4965(c)(4), (5), (6) or (7), including a fully self-directed qualified plan, IRA, or other savings arrangement, the disclosure required by this section must be made by the entity manager (as defined in section 4965(d)(2)) of the entity.

(d) *Time and place for filing.*—(1) *In general.*—The disclosure required by this section shall be filed on or before May 15 of the calendar year following the close of the calendar year during which the tax-exempt entity entered into the prohibited tax shelter transaction.

(2) *Subsequently listed transactions.*—In the case of subsequently listed transactions (as defined in section 4965(e)(2)), the disclosure required by this section shall be filed on or before May 15 of the calendar year following the close of the calendar year during which the transaction was identified by the Secretary as a listed transaction.

(3) *Transition rule.*—If a tax-exempt entity entered into a prohibited tax shelter transaction after May 17, 2006, and before January 1, 2007, the disclosure required by this section shall be filed on or before November 2, 2007.

(4) *No disclosure.*—Disclosure is not required with respect to any prohibited tax shelter transaction entered into by a tax-exempt entity on or before May 17, 2006.

(e) *Penalty for failure to provide disclosure statement.*—See section 6652(c)(3) for the penalty applicable to the failure to disclose a prohibited tax shelter transaction in accordance with this section.

(f) *Effective date/applicability date.*—This section applies with respect to transactions entered into by a tax-exempt entity after May 17, 2006. [Reg. § 1.6033-5.]

☐ [*T.D.* 9492, 7-2-2010.]

### [Reg. § 301.6033-5]

**§ 301.6033-5. Disclosure by tax-exempt entities that are parties to certain reportable transactions.**—(a) *In general.*—For provisions relating to the requirement of the disclosure by a tax-exempt entity that it is a party to certain reportable transactions, see § 1.6033-5 of this chapter (Income Tax Regulations).

(b) *Effective date/applicability date.*—This section applies with respect to transactions entered into by a tax-exempt entity after May 17, 2006. [Reg. § 301.6033-5.]

☐ [T.D. 9492, 7-2-2010.]

### [Reg. § 1.6033-6]

**§ 1.6033-6. Notification requirement for entities not required to file an annual information return under section 6033(a)(1) (taxable years beginning after December 31, 2006).**—(a) *In general.*—Except as otherwise provided in this paragraph, every organization exempt from taxation under section 501(a) that is not required to file a return described in § 1.6033-2(a)(2), other than an organization described in section 401(a) or 501(d), shall submit annually, in electronic form, a notification setting forth the items described in paragraph (c) of this section and such other information as may be prescribed in the instructions and publications issued with respect to the notification.

(b) *Organizations not required to submit annual electronic notification.*—(1) An organization exempt from taxation under section 501(a) that is required to file or files an annual information return under section 6033(a)(1) shall not submit an annual electronic notification under section 6033(i). This includes the following types of organizations:

(i) Any organization included in a group return for that year under § 1.6033-2(d).

(ii) All private foundations required to file under § 1.6033-2(a)(2)(i) Form 990-PF, "Return of Private Foundation or Section 4947(a)(1) Nonexempt Charitable Trust Treated as a Private Foundation."

(iii) Section 509(a)(3) supporting organizations required to file under § 1.6033-2(a)(2)(i) Form 990, "Return of Organization Exempt From Income Tax," or Form 990-EZ, "Short Form Return of Organization Exempt From Income Tax."

(iv) A section 501(c)(21) black lung trust required to file under § 1.6033-2(a)(2)(i) Form 990-BL, "Information and Initial Excise Tax Return for Black Lung Benefit Trusts and Certain Related Persons."

(v) Any organization that is required to file or files an annual information return under section 6033(a)(1) on any other form prescribed by the Internal Revenue Service for that purpose.

(2) An organization exempt from taxation under section 501(a) that is not required to file a return under section 6033(a)(1) is also not required to submit an annual electronic notification under section 6033(i). This includes the following types of organizations:

(i) A church, an interchurch organization of local units of a church, a convention or association of churches, or an integrated auxiliary of a church (as defined in § 1.6033-2(h)).

(ii) An exclusively religious activity of any religious order.

(iii) A mission society sponsored by or affiliated with one or more churches or church denominations, more than one-half of the activities of which society are conducted in, or directed at persons in, foreign countries.

(iv) An educational organization (below college level) described in section 170(b)(1)(A)(ii), that has a program of a general academic nature, and that is affiliated (within the meaning of § 1.6033-2(h)(2)) with a church or operated by a religious order.

(v) A State institution, the income of which is excluded from gross income under section 115(a).

(vi) An organization described in section 501(c)(1).

(vii) An organization that is a governmental unit or an affiliate of a governmental unit exempt from Federal income tax under section 501(a).

(3) If an organization exempt from taxation under section 501(a) is not described in paragraph (b)(1) or (2) of this section, the organization must submit an annual electronic notification. Thus, a black lung trust that normally has gross receipts of $25,000 or less is not required to file Form 990-BL but is required to submit an annual electronic notification. A section 509(a)(3) supporting organization of a religious organization that normally has gross receipts of $5,000 or less is not required to file Form 990 or Form 990-EZ but is required to submit an annual electronic notification.

(c) *Additional notification requirements.*—(1) *In general.*—Any organization described in paragraph (a) of this section shall submit an annual electronic notification described in section 6033(i)(1). The annual electronic notification shall—

(i) Be in electronic form; and

(ii) Set forth—

(A) The legal name of the organization;

(B) Any name under which the organization operates or does business;

(C) The organization's mailing address and Internet Web site address (if any);

(D) The organization's taxpayer identification number;

(E) The name and address of a principal officer;

(F) Evidence of the continuing basis for the organization's exemption from the filing requirements under section 6033(a)(1); and

(G) Additional information necessary to process the notification.

(2) The mailing address required by section 6033(i)(1)(C) and submitted in the annual electronic notification shall be the organization's last known address as provided by § 301.6212-2(a) of this chapter. This last known address may be updated as provided under § 301.6212-2 of this chapter, or by clear and concise notification. The Internal Revenue Service will use this last known address as the organization's address of record and will direct all mailings to this address.

(3) By submitting the annual electronic notification described in paragraph (c)(1) of this section, an organization acknowledges that it is not required to file a return under section 6033(a) because its annual gross receipts are not normally in excess of $25,000. In order to make this determination, the organization must keep records that enable it to calculate its gross receipts. All organizations are required to maintain records under section 6001. These records will provide evidence of the continuing basis for the organization's exemption from the filing requirements under section 6033(a)(1).

(4) If an organization that is required to submit an annual electronic notification files a complete Form 990 or Form 990-EZ, the annual electronic notification requirement shall be deemed satisfied. The annual electronic notification requirement is not satisfied if the Form 990 or Form 990-EZ contains only those items of information that would have been required by submitting the notification in electronic form. Also, the filing of a complete Form 990 or Form 990-EZ, rather than the submission of an annual electronic notification, is the filing of a return that starts the period of limitations for assessment under section 6501(g)(2).

(d) *No effect on other filing requirements.*—An organization that is relieved from filing an information return under section 6033(a) is still subject to the requirements of § § 1.6033-2(i) and (j), concerning: notice regarding changes in character, operations, or purpose; provision of additional information; duty to file other returns of information; and duty to file unrelated business tax returns. If an organization is required to file an unrelated business tax return, Form 990-T, "Exempt Organization Business Income Tax Return," the filing of that return does not relieve the organization from the requirement of submitting an annual electronic notification under section 6033(i).

(e) *Accounting period for submitting annual electronic notification.*—An annual electronic notification required by this section shall be on the basis of the established annual accounting period of the organization. If the organization has no established accounting period, the annual electronic notification shall be on the basis of the calendar year.

(f) *Time and place for submitting annual electronic notification.*—The annual electronic notification required by this section shall be submitted on or before the 15th day of the fifth calendar month following the close of the period for which the notification is required to be submitted. Thus, an organization with an accounting period ending December 31, 2007, is required to submit an annual electronic notification by May 15, 2008. The notification shall be submitted in accordance with instructions and publications, including those provided at the Internal Revenue Service Web site for exempt organizations.

(g) *Effective/applicability date.*—These regulations are applicable to annual periods beginning after 2006. [Reg. § 1.6033-6.]

☐ [T.D. 9454, 7-22-2009.]

### [Reg. § 1.6034-1]

**§ 1.6034-1. Information returns required of trusts described in section 4947(a) or claiming charitable or other deductions under section 642(c).**—(a) *In general.*—Every trust (other than a trust described in paragraph (b) of this section) claiming a charitable or other deduction under section 642(c) for the taxable year shall file, with respect to such taxable year, a return of information on Form 1041-A. In addition, for taxable years beginning after December 31, 1969, every trust (other than a trust described in paragraph (b) of this section) described in section 4947(a)(2) (including trusts described in section 664) shall file such return for each taxable year, unless all transfers in trust occurred before May 27, 1969. The return shall set forth the name and address of the trust and the following information concerning the trust in such detail as is prescribed by the form or in the instructions issued with respect to such form:

(1) The amount of the charitable or other deduction taken under section 642(c) for the taxable year (and, for taxable years beginning

prior to January 1, 1970, showing separately for each class of activity for which disbursements were made (or amounts were permanently set aside) the amounts which, during such year, were paid out (or which were permanently set aside) for charitable or other purposes under section 642(c));

(2) The amount paid out during the taxable year which represents amounts permanently set aside in prior years for which charitable or other deductions have been taken under section 642(c), and separately listing for each class of activity, for which disbursements were made, the total amount paid out;

(3) The amount for which charitable or other deductions have been taken in prior years under section 642(c) and which had not been paid out at the beginning of the taxable year;

(4)(i) The amount paid out of principal in the taxable year for charitable, etc., purposes, and separately listing for each such class of activity, for which disbursements were made, the total amount paid out;

(ii) The total amount paid out of principal in prior years for charitable, etc., purposes;

(5) The gross income of the trust for the taxable year and the expenses attributable thereto, in sufficient detail to show the different categories of income and of expense; and

(6) A balance sheet showing the assets, liabilities, and net worth of the trust as of the beginning of the taxable year.

(b) *Exceptions.*—(1) *In general.*—A trust is not required to file a Form 1041-A for any taxable year with respect to which the trustee is required by the terms of the governing instrument and applicable local law to distribute currently all of the income of the trust. For this purpose, the income of the trust shall be determined in accordance with section 643(b) and §§ 1.643(b)-1 and 1.643(b)-2.

(2) *Trusts described in section 4947(a)(1).*—For taxable years beginning after December 31, 1980, a trust described in section 4947(a)(1) is not required to file a Form 1041-A.

(c) *Time and place for filing return.*—The return on Form 1041-A shall be filed on or before the 15th day of the 4th month following the close of the taxable year of the trust, with the internal revenue officer designated by the instructions applicable to such form. For extensions of time for filing returns under this section, see § 1.6081-1.

(d) *Other provisions.*—For publicity of information on Form 1041-A, see section 6104 and the regulations thereunder in Part 301 of this chapter. For provisions relating to penalties for failure to file a return required by this section, see section 6652(d). For the criminal penalties for a willful failure to file a return and filing a false or fraudulent return, see sections 7203, 7206, and 7207. [Reg. § 1.6034-1.]

☐ [*T.D.* 6364, 2-13-59. *Amended by T.D.* 7012, 5-14-69; *T.D.* 7563, 9-8-78 *and T.D.* 8026, 5-17-85.]

### [Reg. § 301.6034-1]

**§ 301.6034-1. Returns by trusts described in section 4947(a)(2) or claiming charitable or other deductions under section 642(c).**—For provisions relating to the requirement of returns by trusts described in section 4947(a)(2) or claiming charitable or other deductions under section 642(c), see § 1.6034-1 of this chapter (Income Tax Regulations). [Reg. § 301.6034-1.]

☐ [*T.D.* 6498, 10-24-60. *Amended by T.D.* 7563, 9-8-78 *and T.D.* 8026, 5-17-85.]

### [Reg. § 1.6035-1]

**§ 1.6035-1. [Reserved].**

☐ [*T.D.* 6364, 2-13-59. *Amended by T.D.* 7322, 8-23-74; *T.D.* 7517, 11-11-77; *T.D.* 7557, 8-4-78; *T.D.* 8028, 6-3-85 *and T.D.* 8573, 12-13-94. *Removed and reserved by T.D.* 9849, 3-11-2019.]

### [Reg. § 1.6035-2]

**§ 1.6035-2. Transitional relief.**—(a) *Statements due before June 30, 2016.*—Executors and other persons required to file or furnish a statement under section 6035(a)(1) or (2) after July 31, 2015 and before June 30, 2016, need not have done so until June 30, 2016.

(b) *Applicability Date.*—This section is applicable to executors and other persons who file a return required by section 6018(a) or (b) after July 31, 2015. [Reg. § 1.6035-2.]

☐ [*T.D.* 6364, 2-13-59. *Amended by T.D.* 7322, 8-23-74, *T.D.* 8028, 6-3-85 *and T.D.* 9797, 12-1-2016.]

### [Reg. § 1.6036-1]

**§ 1.6036-1. Notice of qualification as executor or receiver.**—For provisions relating to the notice required of fiduciaries, see the regulations under section 6036 contained in Part 301 of this chapter (Regulations on Procedure and Administration). [Reg. § 1.6036-1.]

☐ [*T.D.* 6455, 3-1-60.]

### [Reg. § 20.6036-1]

**§ 20.6036-1. Notice of qualification as executor.**—(a) *Preliminary notice for estates of decedents dying before January 1, 1971.*—(1) A preliminary notice must be filed on Form 704 for the estate of every citizen or resident of the United States whose gross estate exceeded $60,000 in value on the date of his death.

(2) In the case of a nonresident not a citizen of the United States dying on or after November 14, 1966—

(i) Subject to the provisions of subdivisions (ii) and (iii) of this subparagraph, a preliminary notice must be filed on Form 705 if that part of the decedent's gross estate situated in the United States exceeded $30,000 in value on the date of his death (see §§ 20.2103-1 and 20.2104-1).

(ii) If the transfer of the estate is subject to the tax imposed by section 2107(a) (relating to expatriation to avoid tax), any amounts includible in the decedent's gross estate under section 2107(b) are to be added to the value on the date of his death of that part of his gross estate situated in the United States, for purposes of determining under subdivision (i) of this subparagraph whether his gross estate exceeded $30,000 in value on the date of his death.

(iii) If the transfer of the estate is subject to tax pursuant to a Presidential proclamation made under section 2108(a) (relating to Presidential proclamations of the application of pre-1967 estate tax provisions), a preliminary notice must be filed on Form 705 if the value on the date of the decedent's death of that part of his gross estate situated in the United States exceeded $2,000.

(3) A preliminary notice must be filed on Form 705 for the estate of every nonresident not a citizen of the United States dying before November 14, 1966, if the value on the date of his death of that part of his gross estate situated in the United States exceeded $2,000.

(4) The value of the gross estate on the date of death governs with respect to the requirement for filing the preliminary notice irrespective of whether the value of the gross estate is, at the executor's election, finally determined pursuant to the provisions of section 2032 as of a date subsequent to the date of death. If there is doubt as to whether the gross estate exceeds $60,000, $30,000, or $2,000, as the case may be, the notice shall be filed as a matter of precaution in order to avoid the possibility of penalties attaching.

(5) The primary purpose of the preliminary notice is to advise the Internal Revenue Service of the existence of taxable estates, and filing shall not be delayed beyond the period provided for in § 20.6071-1 merely because of uncertainty as to the exact value of the assets. The estimate of the gross estate called for by the notice shall be the best approximation of value which can be made within the time allowed. Duplicate copies of the preliminary notice are not required to be filed.

(6) For criminal penalties for failure to file a notice and filing a false or fraudulent notice, see sections 7203, 7207, and 7269. See § 20.6091-1 for the place for filing the notice. See § 20.6071-1 for the time for filing the notice.

(b) *Persons required to file.*—In the case of an estate of a citizen or resident of the United States described in paragraph (a) of this section, the preliminary notice must be filed by the duly qualified executor or administrator, or if none qualifies within 2 months after the decedent's death, by every person in actual or constructive possession of any property of the decedent at or after the time of the decedent's death. The signature of one executor or administrator on the preliminary notice is sufficient. In the case of a nonresident not a citizen, the notice must be filed by every duly qualified executor or administrator within the United States, or if none qualifies within 2 months after the decedent's death, by every person in actual or constructive possession of any property of the decedent at or after the time of the decedent's death. [Reg. § 20.6036-1.]

☐ [*T.D.* 6296, 6-23-58. *Amended by T.D.* 7238, 12-28-72 *and T.D.* 7296, 12-11-73.]

### [Reg. § 301.6036-1]

**§ 301.6036-1. Notice required of executor or of receiver or other like fiduciary.**—(a) *Receivers and other like fiduciaries.*—(1) *Exemption for bankruptcy proceedings.*—(i) A bankruptcy trustee, debtor in possession or other like fiduciary in a bankruptcy proceeding is not required by this section to give notice of appointment, qualification or authorization to act to the Secretary or his delegate. (However, see the notice requirements under the Bankruptcy Rules.)

(ii) Paragraph (a)(1)(i) of this section is effective for appointments, qualifications and authorizations to act made on or after January 29, 1988. For appointments, qualifications and authorizations to act made before the foregoing date, 26 CFR 301.6036-1(a)(1) and (4)(i) (revised as of April 1, 1986) apply.

(2) *Proceedings other than bankruptcy.*—A receiver in a receivership proceeding or a similar fiduciary in any proceeding (including a fiduciary in aid of foreclosure), designated by order of any court of the United States or of any State or Territory or of the District of Columbia as in control of all or substantially all the assets of a debtor or other party to such proceeding shall, on, or within 10 days of, the date of his appointment or authorization to act, give notice thereof in writing to the district director for the internal revenue district in which the debtor, or such other party, is or was required to make returns. Moreover, any fiduciary in aid of foreclosure not appointed by order of any such court, if he takes possession of all or substantially all the assets of the debtor, shall, on, or within 10 days of, the date of his taking possession, give notice thereof in writing to such district director.

(3) *Assignment for benefit of creditors.*—An assignee for the benefit of a creditor or creditors shall, on, or within 10 days of, the date of an assignment, give notice thereof in writing to the district director for the internal revenue district in which the debtor is or was required to make returns. For purposes of this subparagraph, an assignee for the benefit of creditors shall be any person who, by authority of law, by the order of any court, by oral or written agreement, or in any other manner acquires control or possession of or title to all or substantially all the assets of a debtor, and who under such acquisition is authorized to use, reassign, sell, or in any manner dispose of such assets so that the proceeds from the use, sale, or other disposition may be paid to or may inure directly or indirectly to the benefit of a creditor or creditors of such debtor.

(4) *Contents of notice.*—(i) *Proceedings other than bankruptcy.*—The written notice required under paragraph (a)(2) of this section shall contain—

(a) The name and address of the person making such notice and the date of his appointment or of his taking possession of the assets of the debtor or other person whose assets are controlled,

(b) The name, address, and, for notices filed after December 20, 1972, the taxpayer identification number of the debtor or other person whose assets are controlled, and

(c) In the case of a court proceeding—

(1) The name and location of the court in which the proceedings are pending,

(2) The date on which such proceedings were instituted,

(3) The number under which such proceedings are docketed, and

(4) When possible, the date, time, and place of any hearing, meeting of creditors, or other scheduled action with respect to such proceedings.

(ii) *Assignment for benefit of creditors.*—The written notice required under subparagraph (3) of this paragraph shall contain—

(a) The name and address of, and the date the asset or assets were assigned to, the assignee,

(b) The name, address, and, for notices filed after December 20, 1972, the taxpayer identification number of the debtor whose assets were assigned,

(c) A brief description of the assets assigned,

(d) An explanation of the action expected to be taken with respect to such assets, and

(e) When possible, the date, time, and place of any hearing, meeting of creditors, sale, or other scheduled action with respect to such assets.

(iii) The notice required by this section shall be sent to the attention of the Chief, Special Procedures Staff, of the District office to which it is required to be sent.

(b) *Executors, administrators, and persons in possession of property of decedent.*—For provisions relating to the requirement of filing, by an executor, administrator, or person in possession of property of a decedent, of a preliminary notice in the case of the estate of a decedent dying before January 1, 1971, see §20.6036-1 of this chapter (Estate Tax Regulations).

(c) *Notice of fiduciary relationship.*—When a notice is required under §301.6903-1 of a person acting in fiduciary capacity and is also required of such person under this section, notice given in accordance with the provisions of this section shall be considered as complying with both sections.

(d) *Suspension of period on assessment.*—For suspension of the running of the period of limitations on the making of assessments from the date a proceeding is instituted to a date 30 days after receipt of notice from a fiduciary in any proceeding under the Bankruptcy Act or from a receiver in any other court proceeding, see section 6872 and §301.6872-1.

(e) *Applicability.*—Except as provided in paragraph (a)(1)(ii) of this section, the provisions of this section shall apply to those persons referred to in this section whose appointments, authorizations, or assignments occur on or after the date of the publication of these regulations in the Federal Register as a Treasury decision.

(f) *Cross references.*—(1) For criminal penalty for willful failure to supply information, see section 7203.

(2) For criminal penalties for willfully making false or fraudulent statements, see sections 7206 and 7207.

(3) For time for performance of acts where the last day falls on a Saturday, Sunday, or legal holiday, see section 7503 and §301.7503-1 [Reg. §301.6036-1.]

□ [*T.D. 6517, 12-20-60. Amended by T.D. 7222, 11-20-72; T.D. 7238, 12-28-72 and T.D. 8172, 1-28-88.*]

**[Reg. §20.6036-2]**

**§20.6036-2. Notice of qualification as executor of estate of decedent dying after 1970.**—In the case of the estate of a decedent dying after December 31, 1970, no special notice of qualification as executor of an estate is required to be filed. The requirement of section 6036 for notification of qualification as executor of an estate shall be satisfied by the filing of the estate tax return required by section 6018 and the regulations thereunder. [Reg. §20.6036-2.]

□ [*T.D. 7238, 12-28-72.*]

**[Reg. §1.6037-1]**

**§1.6037-1. Return of electing small business corporation.**—(a) *In general.*—Every small business corporation (as defined in section 1371(a)) which has made an election under section 1372(a) not to be subject to the tax imposed by chapter 1 of the Code shall file, with respect to each taxable year for which the election is in effect, a return of income on Form 1120-S. The return shall set forth the items of gross income and the deductions allowable in computing taxable income as required by the return form or in the instructions issued with respect thereto and shall be signed in accordance with section 6062 by the person authorized to sign a return. The return shall also set forth the following information concerning the electing small business corporation:

(1) The names and addresses of all persons owning stock in the corporation at any time during the taxable year;

(2) The number of shares of stock owned by each shareholder at all times during the taxable year;

(3) The amount of money and other property distributed by the corporation during the taxable year to each shareholder;

(4) The date of each distribution of money and other property; and

(5) Such other information as is required by the form or by the instructions issued with respect to such form.

(b) *Time and place for filing return.*—The return shall be filed on or before the 15th day of the third month following the close of the taxable year with the internal revenue officer designated in the instructions applicable to Form 1120-S. (See section 6072.)

(c) *Other provisions.*—The return on Form 1120-S will be treated as a return filed by the corporation under section 6012, relating to persons required to make returns of income, for purposes of the provisions of chapter 66 of the Code, relating to limitations. Thus, for example, the period of limitation on assessment and collection of any corporate tax found to be due upon a subsequent determination that the corporation was not entitled to the benefits of subchapter S, chapter 1 of the Code, will run from the date of filing the return under section 6037, or from the date prescribed for filing such return, whichever is the later. For the rules requiring the disclosure of certain transactions, see §1.6011-4T.

(d) *Penalties.*—For criminal penalties for failure to file a return, supply information, or pay tax, and for filing a false or fraudulent return, statement, or other document, see sections 7203, 7206, and 7207. [Reg. §1.6037-1.]

□ [*T.D. 6432, 12-18-59. Amended by T.D. 7012, 5-14-69 and T.D. 9000, 6-14-2002.*]

**[Reg. §301.6037-1]**

**§301.6037-1. Return of electing small business corporation.**—For provisions relating to requirement of return of electing small business corporation, see §1.6037-1 of this chapter (Income Tax Regulations). [Reg. §301.6037-1.]

□ [*T.D. 6498, 10-24-60.*]

**[Reg. §1.6037-2]**

**§1.6037-2. Required use of magnetic media for income tax returns of electing small business corporations.**—The return of an electing small business corporation that is required to be filed on magnetic media under §301.6037-2 of this chapter must be filed in accordance with Internal Revenue Service revenue procedures, publications, forms, or instructions, including those posted electronically. (See §601.601(d)(2) of this chapter). [Reg. §1.6037-2.]

☐ [*T.D. 9363, 11-9-2007.*]

[Reg. §301.6037-2]

**§301.6037-2. Required use of magnetic media for returns of electing small business corporation.**—(a) *Returns of electing small business corporation required on magnetic media.*—An electing small business corporation required to file an electing small business return on Form 1120S, "U.S. Income Tax Return for an S Corporation," under §1.6037-1 of this chapter must file its Form 1120S on magnetic media if the small business corporation is required by the Internal Revenue Code and regulations to file at least 250 returns during the calendar year ending with or within its taxable year. Returns filed on magnetic media must be made in accordance with applicable revenue procedures, publications, forms, or instructions. In prescribing revenue procedures, publications, forms, or instructions, the Commissioner may direct the type of magnetic media filing. (See §601.601(d)(2) of this chapter).

(b) *Waiver.*—The Commissioner may grant waivers of the requirements of this section in cases of undue hardship. A request for waiver must be made in accordance with applicable revenue procedures or publications. The waiver also will be subject to the terms and conditions regarding the method of filing as may be prescribed by the Commissioner.

(c) *Failure to file.*—If an electing small business corporation fails to file a return on magnetic media when required to do so by this section, the corporation is deemed to have failed to file the return. (See section 6651 for the addition to tax for failure to file a return.) In determining whether there is reasonable cause for failure to file the return, §301.6651-1(c) and rules similar to the rules in §301.6724-1(c)(3) (undue economic hardship related to filing information returns on magnetic media) will apply.

(d) *Meaning of terms.*—The following definitions apply for purposes of this section:

(1) *Magnetic media.*—The term *magnetic media* means any magnetic media permitted under applicable regulations, revenue procedures, or publications. These generally include magnetic tape, tape cartridge, and diskette, as well as other media, such as electronic filing, specifically permitted under the applicable regulations, procedures, publications, forms, or instructions. (See §601.601(d)(2) of this chapter).

(2) *Corporation.*—The term *corporation* means a corporation as defined in section 7701(a)(3).

(3) *Electing small business corporation return.*—The term *electing small business corporation return* means a Form 1120S, "U.S. Income Tax Return for an S Corporation," along with all other related forms, schedules, and statements that are required to be attached to the Form 1120S, and all members of the Form 1120S series of returns, including amended and superseding returns.

(4) *Electing small business corporation.*—The term *electing small business corporation* means an S corporation as defined in section 1361(a)(1).

(5) *Determination of 250 returns.*—For purposes of this section, a corporation is required to file at least 250 returns if, during the calendar year ending with or within the taxable year of the corporation, the corporation is required to file at least 250 returns of any type, including information returns (for example, Forms W-2, Forms 1099), income tax returns, employment tax returns, and excise tax returns. In the case of a short year return, a corporation is required to file at least 250 returns if, during the calendar year which includes the short taxable year of the corporation, the corporation is required to file at least 250 returns of any type, including information returns (for example, Forms W-2, Forms 1099), income tax returns, employment tax returns, and excise tax returns.

(e) *Example.*—The following example illustrates the provisions of paragraph (d)(5) of this section. In the example, the corporation is a calendar year taxpayer:

*Example.* In 2007, Corporation S, an electing small business corporation with assets in excess of $10 million, is required to file one Form 1120S, "U.S. Corporation Income Tax Return," 100 Forms W-2, "Wage and Tax Statement," 146 Forms 1099-DIV, "Dividends and Distributions," one Form 940, "Employer's Annual Federal Unemployment (FUTA) Tax Return," and four Forms 941, "Employer's Quarterly Federal Tax Return." Because S is required to file 252 returns during

the calendar year, S is required to file its 2007 Form 1120S electronically.

(f) *Effective/applicability dates.*—This section applies to returns of electing small business corporations that report total assets at the end of the corporation's taxable year that equal or exceed $10 million on Schedule L of Form 1120S for taxable years ending on or after December 31, 2006, except for the application of the short year rules in paragraph (d)(5) of this section, which is applicable for taxable years ending on or after November 13, 2007. [Reg. §301.6037-2.]

☐ [*T.D. 9363, 11-9-2007.*]

[Reg. §301.6038-1]

**§301.6038-1. Information returns required of United States persons with respect to certain foreign corporations.**—For provisions relating to information returns required of United States persons with respect to certain foreign corporations, see §§1.6038-1 and 1.6038-2 of this chapter (Income Tax Regulations). [Reg. §301.6038-1.]

☐ [*T.D. 6555, 3-14-61. Amended by T.D. 6700, 1-6-64.*]

[Reg. §1.6038-2]

**§1.6038-2. Information returns required of United States persons with respect to annual accounting periods of certain foreign corporations.**—(a) *Requirement of return.*—Every U.S. person shall make a separate annual information return with respect to each annual accounting period (described in paragraph (e) of this section) of each foreign corporation which that person controls (as defined in paragraph (b) of this section) at any time during such annual accounting period.

(1) Form 2952, "Information Return with Respect to Controlled Foreign Corporations," if such taxable year ends before December 31, 1982;

(2) Form 5471, "Information Return of U.S. Persons with Respect to Certain Foreign Corporations," if such taxable year ends on or after December 31, 1983; or

(3) Either Form 5471 or Form 2952 if such taxable year ends on or after December 31, 1982 and before December 31, 1963.

(b) *Control.*—A person shall be deemed to be in control of a foreign corporation if at any time during that person's taxable year it owns stock possessing more than 50 percent of the total combined voting power of all classes of stock entitled to vote, or more than 50 percent of the total value of shares of all classes of stock of the foreign corporation. A person in control of a corporation which, in turn, owns more than 50 percent of the combined voting power, or of the value, of all classes of stock of another corporation is also treated as being in control of such other corporation. The provisions of this paragraph may be illustrated by the following example:

*Example.* Corporation A owns 51 percent of the voting stock in Corporation B. Corporation B owns 51 percent of the voting stock in Corporation C. Corporation C in turn owns 51 percent of the voting stock in Corporation D. Corporation D is controlled by Corporation A.

(c) *Attribution rules.*—For the purpose of determining control of domestic or foreign corporations the constructive ownership rules of section 318(a) shall apply except that:

(1) Stock owned by or for a partner or a beneficiary of an estate or trust shall not be considered owned by the partnership, estate, or trust when the effect is to consider a United States person as owning stock owned by a person who is not a United States person;

(2) A corporation will not be considered as owning stock owned by or for a 50 percent or more shareholder when the effect is to consider a United States person as owning stock owned by a person who is not a United States person; and

(3) If 10 percent or more in value of the stock in a corporation is owned, directly or indirectly, by or for any person, section 318(a)(2)(C) shall apply.

The constructive ownership rules of section 318(a) apply only for purposes of determining control as defined in paragraph (b) of this section.

(d) *U.S. person.*—(1) *In general.*—For purposes of section 6038 and this section, the term *United States person* has the meaning assigned to it by section 7701(a)(30), except as provided in paragraphs (d)(2) and (3) of this section.

(2) *Special rule for individuals residing in certain possessions.*—(i) With respect to an individual who is a bona fide resident of Puerto Rico, the term United States person has the meaning assigned to it by §1.957-3 except that the rules of §1.937-2(g)(1) will apply.

(ii) With respect to an individual who is a bona fide resident of any section 931 possession, as defined in §1.931-1(c)(1), the term United States person has the meaning assigned to it by §1.957-3.

(3) *Special rule for certain nonresident aliens.*—An individual for whom an election under section 6013(g) or (h) is in effect will, subject to the exceptions contained in paragraph (d)(2) of this section, be considered a United States person for purposes of section 6038 and this section.

(e) *Period covered by return.*—The information required under paragraphs (f) and (g) of this section with respect to a foreign corporation shall be furnished for the annual accounting period of the foreign corporation ending with or within the United States person's taxable year. For purposes of this section, the annual accounting period of a foreign corporation is the annual period on the basis of which that corporation regularly computes its income in keeping its books. In the case of a specified foreign corporation (as defined in section 898), the taxable year of such corporation shall be treated as its annual accounting period. The term *annual accounting period* may refer to a period of less than one year, where, for example, the foreign income, war profits, and excess profits taxes are determined on the basis of an accounting period of less than one year as described in section 902(c)(5). If more than one annual accounting period ends with or within the United States person's taxable year, separate annual information returns shall be submitted for each annual accounting period.

(f) *Contents of return.*—The return on Form 5471 shall contain so much of the following information, and in such form or manner, as the form shall prescribe with respect to each foreign corporation:

(1) The name, address, and employer identification number, if any, of the corporation;

(2) The principal place of business of the corporation;

(3) The date of incorporation and the country under whose laws incorporated;

(4) The name and address of the foreign corporation's statutory or resident agent in the country of incorporation;

(5) The name, address, and identifying number of any branch office or agent of the foreign corporation located in the United States;

(6) The name and address of the person (or persons) having custody of the books of account and records of the foreign corporation, and the location of such books and records if different from such address;

(7) The nature of the corporation's business and the principal places where conducted;

(8) As regards the outstanding stock of the corporation—

(i) A description of each class of the corporation's stock, and

(ii) The number of shares of each class outstanding at the beginning and end of the annual accounting period;

(9) A list showing the name, address, and identifying number of, and the number of shares of each class of the corporation's stock held by, each United States person who is a shareholder owning at any time during the annual acounting period 5 percent or more in value of any class of the corporation's outstanding stock;

(10) For the annual accounting period, the amount of the corporation's:

(i) Current earnings and profits;

(ii) Foreign income, war profits, and excess profits taxes paid or accrued;

(iii) Distributions out of current earnings and profits for the period;

(iv) Distributions other than those described in paragraph (f)(10)(iii) of this section and the source thereof; and

(v) For Forms 5471 filed for taxable years ending after December 15, 1990, such earnings and profits information as the form shall prescribe, including post-1986 undistributed earnings described in section 902(c)(1), pre-1987 amounts, total earnings and profits, and previously taxed earnings and profits described in section 959(c); and

(11) *Transactions with certain related parties.*—(i) A summary showing the total amount of each of the following types of transactions of the corporation, which took place during the annual accounting period, with the person required to file this return, any other corporation or partnership controlled by that person, or any United States person owning at the time of the transaction 10 percent or more in value of any class of stock outstanding of the foreign corporation, or of any corporation controlling that foreign corporation—

(A) Sales and purchases of stock in trade;

(B) Sales and purchases of tangible property other than stock in trade;

(C) Sales and purchases of patents, inventions, models, or designs (whether or not patented), copyrights, trademarks, secret formulas or processes, or any other similar property rights;

(D) Compensation paid and compensation received for the rendition of technical, managerial, engineering, construction, scientific, or like services;

(E) Commissions paid and commissions received;

(F) Rents and royalties paid and rents and royalties received;

(G) Amounts loaned and amounts borrowed (except open accounts resulting from sales and purchases reported under other items listed in this paragraph (f)(11) that arise and are collected in full in the ordinary course of business);

(H) Dividends paid and dividends received;

(I) Interest paid and interest received; and

(J) Premiums paid and premiums received for insurance or reinsurance.

(ii) *Special rule for banks.*—For purposes of this paragraph (f)(11), if the United States person is a bank, as defined in section 581, or is controlled within the meaning of section 368(c) by a bank, the term transactions shall not, as to a corporation with respect to which a return is filed, include banking transactions entered into on behalf of customers; in any event, however, deposits in accounts between a foreign corporation, controlled (within the meaning of paragraph (b) of this section) by a United States person, and a person described in this paragraph (f)(11) and withdrawals from such accounts shall be summarized by reporting end-of-month balances.

(12) *Accrued payments and receipts.*—For purposes of the required summary under paragraph (f)(11) of this section, a corporation that uses an accrual method of accounting shall use accrued payments and accrued receipts for purposes of computing the total amount of each of the types of transactions listed.

(13) *Amounts involving hybrid transactions or hybrid entities under section 267A.*—If for the annual accounting period, the corporation pays or accrues interest or royalties for which a deduction is disallowed under section 267A and the regulations in this part under section 267A of the Internal Revenue Code, then Form 5471 (or successor form) must contain such information about the disallowance in the form and manner and to the extent prescribed by the form, instruction, publication, or other guidance.

(14) *Hybrid dividends under section 245A(e).*—If for the annual accounting period, the corporation pays or receives a hybrid dividend or a tiered hybrid dividend under section 245A(e) and the regulations in this part under section 245A(e) of the Internal Revenue Code, then Form 5471 (or successor form) must contain such information about the hybrid dividend or tiered hybrid dividend in the form and manner and to the extent prescribed by the form, instruction, publication, or other guidance. Form 5471 (or successor form) must also contain any other information relating to the rules of section 245A(e) and the regulations in this part under section 245A(e) of the Internal Revenue Code (including information related to a specified owner's hybrid deduction account), as prescribed by the form, instruction, publication, or other guidance.

(15) *Information reporting under section 250.*—If the person required to file Form 5471 (or any successor form) claims a deduction under section 250(a) that is determined, in whole or part, by reference to its foreign-derived intangible income, and any amount required to be reported under paragraph (f)(11) of this section is included in its computation of foreign-derived deduction eligible income, such person will provide on Form 5471 (or any successor form) such information that is prescribed by the form, instructions to the form, publication, or other guidance published in the Internal Revenue Bulletin.

(16) *Amounts related to extraordinary dispositions and extraordinary reductions.*—The corporation must report the information in the form and manner and to the extent prescribed by the form, instructions to the form, publication, or other guidance published in the Internal Revenue Bulletin if any of the following conditions are met during the corporation's annual accounting period—

(i) The corporation distributes or receives a dividend that gives rise to an ineligible amount (as defined in §1.245A-5(i)(12)), a tiered extraordinary disposition amount (as defined in §1.245A-5(i)(25)), or a tiered extraordinary reduction amount (as defined in §1.245A-5(i)(26);

(ii) A section 245A shareholder with respect to the corporation has an extraordinary disposition account (as defined in §1.245A-5(i)(6)); or

(iii) The corporation would have been deemed to have undertaken an extraordinary disposition (as defined in §1.245A-5(i)(5)) but for the application of §1.245A-5(c)(3)(ii)(C)(2).

(17) *Reporting of disqualified basis and disqualified payments.*—If for the annual accounting period of a corporation it holds an item of property having disqualified basis within the meaning of §1.951A-3(h)(2)(ii) or §1.951A-2(c)(5), or incurs an item of deduction or loss related to a disqualified payment (within the meaning of §1.951A-2(c)(6)(ii)(A), then Form 5471 (or successor form) must contain such information about the disqualified basis, or such informa-

tion relating to the disqualified payment, in the form and manner and to the extent prescribed by the form, instructions to the form, publication, or other guidance published in the Internal Revenue Bulletin.

(18) *Adjustments to extraordinary disposition accounts and disqualified basis.*—If for the annual accounting period a section 245A shareholder of the corporation reduces its extraordinary disposition account pursuant to §1.245A-7(c) or §1.245A-8(c), as applicable, or the corporation reduces the disqualified basis in an item of specified property pursuant to §1.245A-7(b) or §1.245A-8(b), as applicable, then Form 5471 (or a successor form) must contain such information about the reduction to the extraordinary disposition account or disqualified basis, as applicable, in the form and manner and to the extent prescribed by the form, instructions to the form, publication, or other guidance published in the Internal Revenue Bulletin.

(g) *Financial statements.*—The following information with respect to the foreign corporation shall be attached to and filed as part of the return required by this section. Forms 5471 filed after September 30, 1991, shall contain this information in such form or manner as the form shall prescribe with respect to each foreign corporation:

(1) A statement of the corporation's profit and loss for the annual accounting period;

(2) A balance sheet as of the end of the annual accounting period of the corporation showing—

    (i) The corporation's assets;

    (ii) The corporation's liabilities; and

    (iii) The corporation's net worth; and

(3) An analysis of changes in the corporation's surplus accounts during the annual accounting period including both opening and closing balances.

The information listed in this paragraph (g) shall be prepared in conformity with generally accepted accounting principles, and in such detail as is customary for the corporation's accounting records.

(h) *Method of reporting.*—Except as provided in this paragraph (h), all amounts furnished under paragraphs (f) and (g) of this section shall be expressed in United States dollars with a statement of the exchange rates used. The following rules shall apply for taxable years ending after December 31, 1994, with respect to returns filed after December 31, 1995. All amounts furnished under paragraph (g) of this section shall be expressed in United States dollars computed and translated in conformity with United States generally accepted accounting principles. Amounts furnished under paragraph (g)(1) of this section shall also be furnished in the foreign corporation's functional currency as required on the form. Earnings and profits amounts furnished under paragraphs (f)(10)(i), (iii), (iv), and (v) of this section shall be expressed in the foreign corporation's functional currency except to the extent the form requires specific items to be translated into United States dollars. Tax amounts furnished under paragraph (f)(10)(ii) of this section shall be furnished in the foreign currency in which the taxes are payable and in United States dollars translated in accordance with section 986(a). All amounts furnished under paragraph (f)(11) of this section shall be expressed in U.S. dollars translated from functional currency at the weighted average exchange rate for the year as defined in §1.989(b)-1. The foreign corporation's functional currency is determined under section 985. All statements submitted on or with the return required under this section shall be rendered in the English language.

(i) *Time and place for filing return.*—Returns on Form 5471 required under paragraph (a) of this section shall be filed with the United States person's income tax return on or before the date required by law for the filing of that person's income tax return. Directors of Field Operations and Field Directors are authorized to grant reasonable extensions of time for filing returns on Form 5471 in accordance with the applicable provisions of §1.6081-1 of this chapter. An application for an extension of time for filing a return of income shall also be considered as an application for an extension of time for filing returns on Form 5471.

(j) *Two or more persons required to submit the same information.*—(1) *Return jointly made.*—If two or more persons are required to furnish information with respect to the same foreign corporation for the same period, such persons may, in lieu of making separate returns, jointly make one return. Such joint return shall be filed with the income tax return of any one of the persons making such joint return.

(2) *Persons excepted from furnishing information.*—(i) *Conditions.*—Any person required to furnish information under this section with respect to a foreign corporation need not furnish that information provided all of the following conditions are met:

    (A) Such person does not directly own an interest in the foreign corporation;

(B) Such person is required to furnish the information solely by reason of attribution of stock ownership from a United States person under paragraph (c) of this section; and

    (C) The person from whom the stock ownership is attributed furnishes all of the information required under this section of the person to whom the stock ownership is attributed. (For a rule regarding attribution from a nonresident alien, see paragraph (l) of this section).

(ii) If an individual who is a United States person required to furnish information with respect to a foreign corporation under section 6038 is entitled under a treaty to be treated as a nonresident of the United States, and if the individual claims this treaty benefit, and if there are no other United States persons that are required to furnish information under section 6038 with respect to the foreign corporation, then the individual may satisfy the requirements of paragraphs (f)(10), (f)(11), (g), and (h) of this section by filing the audited foreign financial statements of the foreign corporation with the individual's return required under section 6038.

(iii) *Illustrations.*—The rule of this paragraph (j)(2) is illustrated by the following examples:

*Example (1).* A, a U.S. person owns 100 percent of the stock of M, a domestic corporation. A also owns 100 percent of the stock of N, a foreign corporation organized under the laws of foreign country Y. A, in filing the information return required by this section with respect to N Corporation, in fact furnishes all of the information required of M Corporation with respect to N Corporation. M Corporation need not file the information.

*Example (2).* X, a domestic corporation owns 100 percent of the stock of Y, a domestic corporation, Y Corporation owns 100 percent of the stock of Z, a foreign corporation. X Corporation is not excused by this paragraph (j)(2) from filing information with respect to Z Corporation because X Corporation is deemed to control Z Corporation under the provisions of paragraph (b) of this section without recourse to the attribution rules in paragraph (c) of this section.

(3) *Statement required.*—Any United States person required to furnish information under this section with his return who does not do so by reason of the provisions of paragraph (j)(1) of this section shall file a statement with his income tax return indicating that such requirement has been (or will be) satisfied and identifying the return with which the information was or will be filed and the place of filing.

(k) *Failure to furnish information.*—(1) *Dollar amount penalty.*—(i) *In general.*—If any person required to file Form 5471 under section 6038 and this section fails to furnish any information described in paragraphs (f) and (g) of this section within the time prescribed by paragraph (i) of this section, such person shall pay a penalty of $10,000 for each annual accounting period of each foreign corporation with respect to which such failure occurs.

(ii) *Increase in penalty for continued failure after notification.*—If a failure described in paragraph (k)(1)(i) of this section continues for more than 90 days after the date on which the Director of Field Operations, Area Director, or Director of Compliance Campus Operations mails notice of such failure to the person required to file Form 5471, such person shall pay a penalty of $10,000, in addition to the penalty imposed by section 6038(b)(1) and paragraph (k)(1)(i) of this section, for each 30-day period (or a fraction of) during which such failure continues after such 90-day period has expired. The additional penalty imposed by section 6038(b)(2) and this paragraph (k)(1)(ii) shall be limited to a maximum of $50,000 for each failure.

(2) *Penalty of reducing foreign tax credit.*—(i) *Effect on foreign tax credit.*—Failure of a United States person to furnish, in accordance with the provisions of this section, any return of any information in any return, required to be filed for a taxable year under authority of section 6038 on or before the date prescribed in paragraph (i) of this section may affect the application of section 901 as provided in paragraph (k)(2)(ii) of this section and may affect the application of sections 902 and 960 as provided in paragraph (k)(2)(iii) of this section. Such failure may affect the application of sections 902 and 960 to any such United States person which is a corporation or to any person who acquires from any other person any portion (but only to the extent of such portion) of the interest of such other person in any such foreign corporation.

(ii) *Application of section 901.*—In the application of section 901 to a United States person referred to in paragraph (k)(2)(i) of this section, the amount of taxes paid or deemed paid by such person for any taxable year, with or within which the annual accounting period of a foreign corporation for which such person failed to furnish information required under this section ended, may be reduced by 10 percent. However, no tax reduced under paragraph (k)(2)(iii) of this section or deemed paid under section 904(c) shall be reduced under the provisions of this paragraph (k)(2)(ii).

(iii) *Application of sections 902 and 960.*—In the application of sections 902 and 960 to a United States person referred to in paragraph (k)(2)(i) of this section for any taxable year, the amount of taxes paid or deemed paid by each foreign corporation for the accounting period or periods for which such person was required for the taxable year of the failure to furnish information under this section may be reduced by 10 percent. The 10-percent reduction is not limited to the taxes paid or deemed paid by the foreign corporation with respect to which there is a failure to file information but may apply to the taxes paid or deemed paid by all foreign corporations controlled by that person. In applying subsections (a) and (b) of section 902, and in applying subsection (a) of section 960, the reduction provided by this paragraph (k)(2) shall not apply for purposes of determining the amount of accumulated profits in excess of income, war profits, and excess profits taxes.

(iv) *Reduction for continued failure after notice.*—(A) If the failure referred to in paragraph (k)(2)(i) of this section continues for more than 90 days after the date on which the Director of Field Operations mails notice of such failure to such United States person, then the amount of the reduction referred to in paragraph (k)(2)(ii) and (iii) of this section may be 10 percent plus an additional 5 percent for each 3-month period, or fraction thereof, during which such failure continues after the expiration of such 90-day period.

(B) No taxes shall be reduced under this paragraph (k)(2) more than once for the same failure. Taxes paid by a foreign corporation when once reduced for a failure shall not be reduced again for the same failure in their status as taxes deemed paid by a corporate shareholder. Where a failure continues, each additional periodic 5-percent reduction, referred to in paragraph (k)(2)(iv)(A) of this section, shall be considered as part of the one reduction.

(v) *Limitation on reduction of foreign tax credit.*—The amount of the reduction under this paragraph (k)(2) for each failure to furnish information with respect to a foreign corporation as required under this section shall not exceed the greater of:

(A) $10,000, or

(B) The income of the foreign corporation for its annual accounting period with respect to which the failure occurs. For purposes of this section if a person is required to furnish information with respect to more than one foreign corporation, controlled (within the meaning of paragraph (b) of this section) by that person, each failure to submit information for each such corporation constitutes a separate failure.

(vi) *Offset for dollar amount penalty imposed.*—The total amount of the reduction or reductions which, but for this paragraph (k)(2)(vi), may be made under this paragraph (k)(2) with respect to any separate failure, shall not exceed the maximum amount of such reductions which may be imposed, reduced (but not below zero) by

the amount of the dollar amount penalty imposed by paragraph (k)(1) of this section with respect to such separate failure.

(3) *Reasonable cause.*—(i) For purposes of section 6038(b) and (c) and this section, the time prescribed for furnishing information under paragraph (i) of this section, and the beginning of the 90-day period after mailing of notice by the Director of Field Operations under paragraph (k)(1)(ii) and (k)(2)(iv)(A) of this section, shall be treated as being not earlier than the last day on which reasonable cause existed for failure to furnish the information.

(ii) To show that reasonable cause existed for failure to furnish information as required by section 6038 and this section, the person required to report such information must make an affirmative showing of all facts alleged as reasonable cause for such failure in a written statement containing a declaration that it is made under the penalties of perjury. The statement must be filed with the district director for the district or the director of the service center where the return is required to be filed. The district director or the director of the service center shall determine whether the failure to furnish information was due to reasonable cause, and if so, the period of time for which such reasonable cause existed. In the case of a return that has been filed as required by this section except for an omission of, or error with respect to, some of the information required, if the person who filed the return establishes to the satisfaction of the district director or the director of the service center that the person has substantially complied with this section, then the omission or error shall not constitute a failure under this section.

(4) *Other penalties.*—The information required by section 6038 and this section must be furnished even though there are no foreign taxes which would be reduced under the provisions of this section, and even though the information required may not affect the amount of any tax due under the Internal Revenue Code. For criminal penalties for failure to file a return and filing a false or fraudulent return, see sections 7203, 7206, and 7207 of the Code.

(5) *Illustrations.*—The provisions of this paragraph may be illustrated by the following examples.

*Example (1).* M, a domestic corporation owns 100 percent of the stock of N, a foreign corporation. Both M and N use the calendar year as a taxable year and annual accounting period, and all of the following events occur in or with respect to the 1980 taxable year. The dividend from N is the only dividend from a foreign corporation received by M during the taxable year, and the foreign taxes listed are the only foreign taxes paid or deemed paid by M and N for the taxable year. On March 15, 1981, M filed its income tax return and paid its income tax, but M did not file Form 2952 with respect to N's 1980 annual accounting period. On June 1, 1961, the district director mailed notice to M of M's failure to file Form 2952 with respect to N. On November 30, 1981, M filed a complete Form 2952 with respect to N's 1980 annual accounting period.

| | | |
|---|---|---:|
| (a) | Gains, profits, and income of N | $100,000 |
| (b) | Foreign tax paid by N with respect to such gains, profits, and income | 40,000 |
| (c) | Deduction of foreign tax paid by N (for purposes of M's section 902 deemed paid credit) resulting from M's failure to file information with respect to N as required under section 6038(a) and this section: failure to file within the time prescribed in paragraph (i) of this section, 10-percent reduction; continued failure for one additional 3-month period after 90-day period after notice mailed, 5-percent reduction; total reduction, 15 percent ($40,000 times 15 percent) | 6,000 |
| (d) | Foreign tax paid by N after section 6038(c)(1)(B) reduction | 34,000 |
| (e) | Dividend paid by N to M | 45,000 |
| (f) | Accumulated profits of N as defined in section 902(c)(1) (determined without regard to the section 6038(c)(1)(B) reduction) | 100,000 |
| (g) | Accumulated profits of N as described in section 902(a) (determined without regard to the section 6038(c)(1)(B) reduction) | 60,000 |
| (h) | For purposes of section 902 credit, M is deemed to have paid the same proportion of foreign taxes paid (reduced as provided under section 6038(c)) with respect to the accumulated profits described in section 902(a) (determined without regard to the reduction provided under section 6038(c)) as the amount of the dividend (determined without regard to section 78) bears to such amount of accumulated profits | 25,500 |

$$(45,000 \div 60,000) \times 34,000 = 25,500$$

M must include $25,500 in gross income as a dividend under the provisions of section 78 of the Code. This example illustrates that the reductions in foreign taxes paid by the foreign corporation provided under section 8038(c) are taken into account in determining the amount included in gross income of the domestic corporation under section 78 of the Code as foreign taxes deemed paid, but such reductions are not taken into account in computing accumulated profits for purposes of determining the portion of foreign taxes deemed paid with respect to a particular dividend. The dollar amount penalty imposed by section 8038(b) and paragraph (k)(1) of this section does not apply with respect to information for annual accounting periods ending before September 4, 1982, and therefore does not apply to M with respect to M's failure to file Form 2952 in this example.

*Example (2).* The facts are the same as in example (1) except that all of the events occur in or with respect to the 1982 taxable year. On March 15, 1983, M filed its income tax return and paid its income tax, but M did not file Form 2952 or Form 5471 with respect to N's 1982 annual accounting period. On June 1, 1983, the district director mailed notice to M of M's failure to file Form 2952 or Form 5471 with respect to N. On November 30, 1983, M filed a complete Form 5471 with respect to N's 1982 annual accounting period. Under paragraph (k)(1)(i) of this section, M is subject to a penalty of $1,000. Under paragraph (k)(1)(ii) of this section, that penalty is increased by $4,000 because the failure continued for 92 days (three full 30-day periods and a fraction of a fourth 30-day period) after the end of the 90-day period following mailing of the notice by the district director, bringing M's dollar amount penalty under paragraph (k)(1) of this section to $5,000. For purpose of determining the foreign tax credit available to M, there may be imposed a reduction of foreign tax paid by N of $6,000, which would be the total of reductions under paragraph (k)(2) of this section with respect to M's failure to file under section 6038 for N's 1982 annual accounting period, before application of paragraph (k)(2)(vi) of this section. Under said paragraph (k)(2)(vi), the amount of the foreign tax reduction imposed is reduced by the amount of the dollar amount penalty, leaving a foreign tax reduction penalty of $1,000 which may be imposed in addition to the $5,000 dollar amount penalty. If imposed, the $1,000 tax reduction would then be applied in the calculation of taxes deemed paid by M under section 902 as in example (1), item (c), (d), and (h).

*Example 3.* A, a US person, owns 100 percent of the stock of FC. On April 15, 2008, A timely filed its 2007 income tax return but did not file Form 5471 with respect to FC's 2007 annual accounting period. On June 1, 2008, the Director of Field Operations mailed a notice to A of A's failure to file Form 5471 for 2007 with respect to FC. On August 1, 2008, A submits a written statement asserting facts for reasonable cause for failure to file the 2007 Form 5471 for FC. Based on A's statement and discussions with A, the Director of Field Operations agrees that A had reasonable cause for failure to file FC's 2007 Form 5471 and determined that it is reasonable for A to file FC's 2007 Form 5471 by September 15, 2008. The time prescribed for furnishing information under paragraph (i) of this section is September 15, 2008, and the 90-day period described under paragraphs (k)(1)(ii) and (k)(2)(iv)(A) of this section begins on that same date. Thus, if A files a completed Form 5471 by September 15, 2008, A is not subject to the penalties under paragraphs (k)(1) and (k)(2) of this section. If A does not file a completed Form 5471 by December 14, 2008, in addition to the penalties under paragraphs (k)(1) and (k)(2) of this section, A will also be subject to the penalties for continued failure under paragraphs (k)(1)(ii) and (k)(2)(iv)(A) of this section.

*Example 4.* The facts are the same as in Example 3 except A submits the written statement to the Director before a notice of failure to furnish information is mailed to A. The notice is mailed to A on September 7, 2008. Under these facts, the time prescribed for furnishing information under paragraph (i) of this section is September 15, 2008, and the 90-day period after mailing of notice of failure under paragraphs (k)(1)(ii) and (k)(2)(iv)(A) of this section begins on that same date.

(l) *Other persons excepted from filing.*—For tax years of foreign corporations ending on or after December 29, 1999, any person required to furnish information under this section with respect to a foreign corporation does not have to furnish that information if the following conditions are met—

(1) Such person does not own a direct or indirect interest in the foreign corporation; and

(2) Such person is required to furnish information solely by reason of attribution of stock ownership from a nonresident alien(s) under paragraph (c) of this section.

(m) *Applicability dates.*—(1) *In general.*—This section applies to taxable years of foreign corporations beginning on or after October 3, 2018. See 26 CFR 1.6038-2 (revised as of April 1, 2018) for rules applicable to taxable years of foreign corporations beginning before such date.

(2) *Special rule for paragraph (f)(16) of this section.*—Paragraph (f)(16) of this section applies with respect to information for annual accounting periods to which § 1.245A-5 applies.

(3) *Rules relating to certain hybrid arrangements.*—Paragraphs (f)(13) and (14) of this section apply with respect to information for annual accounting periods beginning on or after December 20, 2018.

(4) Paragraph (f)(15) of this section applies with respect to information for annual accounting periods beginning on or after March 4, 2019.

(5) *Special rule for paragraphs (f)(17) and (18) of this section.*—Paragraphs (f)(17) and (18) of this section apply with respect to information for annual accounting periods beginning after December 1, 2020. In addition, as provided in § 1.245A-11(b), paragraph (f)(18) of this section applies with respect to information for an annual accounting period that includes a taxable year for which a taxpayer has chosen to apply §§ 1.245A-6 through 1.245A-11 pursuant to § 1.245A-11(b). [Reg. § 1.6038-2.]

☐ [T.D. 6621, 11-30-62. *Amended by T.D. 6969, 8-22-68; T.D. 6997, 1-17-69; T.D. 8040, 7-23-85; T.D. 8573, 12-13-94; T.D. 8733, 10-6-97; T.D. 8850, 12-27-99; T.D. 9194, 4-6-2005; T.D. 9268, 6-20-2006; T.D. 9338, 7-12-2007; T.D. 9391, 4-4-2008, T.D. 9650, 12-30-2013; T.D. 9806, 12-27-2016; T.D. 9866, 6-14-2019; T.D. 9896, 4-7-2020; T.D. 9901, 7-9-2020, T.D. 9909, 8-21-2020 and T.D. 9934, 11-25-2020.]*

[Reg. § 1.6038-3]

**§ 1.6038-3. Information returns required of certain United States persons with respect to controlled foreign partnerships (CFPs).**—(a) *Persons required to make return.*—(1) *Controlling fifty-percent partners.*—The term *controlling fifty-percent partner* means a United States person that controlled (as defined in paragraph (b)(1) of this section) the foreign partnership at any time during the partnership's tax year (as defined in paragraph (b)(8) of this section). Except as provided in paragraph (c), (d), or (e) of this section, for each tax year of a foreign partnership during which the partnership has one or more controlling fifty-percent partners, each controlling fifty-percent partner must complete and file Form 8865, "Return of U.S. Persons With Respect To Certain Foreign Partnerships," containing the information described in paragraph (g) of this section.

(2) *Controlling ten-percent partners.*—If at any point during a foreign partnership's tax year (as defined in paragraph (b)(8) of this section) a United States person owned a ten- percent or greater interest in the partnership while the partnership was controlled by United States persons owning ten-percent or greater interests, such United States person is a controlling ten-percent partner. See paragraph (b)(1) of this section for the definition of control. However, a United States person is not a controlling ten-percent partner with respect to a particular foreign partnership for a particular tax year of the foreign partnership if at any point during that year the partnership had a controlling fifty-percent partner, as defined in paragraph (a)(1) of this section. Except as provided in paragraph (c), (d), or (e) of this section, for each tax year of a partnership during which the partnership has controlling ten-percent partners, each controlling ten-percent partner must complete and file Form 8865 containing the information described in paragraph (g)(1) of this section.

(3) *Separate returns for each partnership.*—A United States person required to report under this paragraph (a) must file a separate Form 8865 for each foreign partnership with respect to which the person is a controlling fifty-percent partner or a controlling ten-percent partner.

(b) *Ownership determinations and definitions.*—(1) *Control.*—Control of a foreign partnership is ownership of more than a fifty-percent interest in the partnership.

(2) *Fifty-percent interest.*—A fifty-percent interest in a partnership is an interest equal to fifty percent of the capital interest in such partnership, an interest equal to fifty percent of the profits interest in such partnership, or an interest to which fifty percent of the deductions or losses of such partnership are allocated.

(3) *Ten-percent interest.*—A ten-percent interest in a partnership is an interest equal to ten percent of the capital interest in such partnership, an interest equal to ten percent of the profits interest in such partnership, or an interest to which ten percent of the deductions or losses of such partnership are allocated.

(4) *Constructive ownership rules.*—For purposes of determining an interest in a partnership, the constructive ownership rules of section 267(c) (other than section 267(c)(3)) apply, taking into account that such rules refer to corporations and not to partnerships. However, an interest will be attributed from a nonresident alien under the family attribution rules of section 267(c)(2) and (4) only if the person to whom the interest is attributed owns a direct or indirect (under the rules of 267(c)(1) or (5)) interest in the foreign partnership.

(5) *Determination of amount of interest.*—Whether a person owns a fifty-percent interest, or a ten-percent interest, as described in paragraphs (b)(2) and (3) of this section, is determined for each tax year of the foreign partnership by reference to the agreement of the partners relating to such interests during that tax year.

(6) *Definition of United States person.*—The term *United States person* is defined in section 7701(a)(30).

(7) *Definition of a foreign partnership.*—A foreign partnership is a partnership described in section 7701(a)(5).

(8) *Tax year of a foreign partnership.*—The tax year of a foreign partnership is determined under section 706.

(9) *Examples.*—The rules of paragraph (a) of this section and this paragraph (b) are illustrated by the following examples:

*Example 1. Sole U.S. partner does not own more than a fifty-percent interest.* No United States person owns any interest (directly or constructively) in *FPS*, a foreign partnership whose tax year under section 706 is the calendar year. On January 1, 2001, *US*, a United States person with the calendar year as its tax year, contributes property to *FPS* in exchange for a 40% interest in a section 721 transaction. No United States persons acquire directly or constructively any other interests in *FPS* during *FPS*'s 2001 tax year. *US* is not a controlling fifty-percent partner during *FPS*'s 2001 tax year. *US* did not own during that tax year, either directly or constructively, more than a 50% interest in the partnership under paragraphs (b)(2) and (4) of this section. Also, *US* is not a controlling ten-percent partner; although *US* owned a 10% or greater interest, *US* persons owning at least 10% interests did not control *FPS*. Therefore, *US* does not have to file with its 2001 income tax return a Form 8865 with respect to *FPS* under section 6038. (But see section 6038B for the reporting obligations of *US* with respect to its transfer of property to *FPS* and section 6046A for the reporting obligation of *US* with respect to its acquisition of an interest in *FPS*. See also §1.6046A-1(f)(1) regarding the overlap between sections 6038B and 6046A).

*Example 2. Controlling ten-percent partners.* Assume the same facts as in *Example 1.* In addition, on January 1, 2002, *US1*, a United States person unrelated to *US* and a calendar year taxpayer, purchases a 15% interest in *FPS* from a foreign partner of *FPS*. Neither *US* nor *US1* is a controlling fifty-percent partner during *FPS*'s 2002 tax year because neither one owns more than a 50% percent interest in *FPS* during that year. However, *US* and *US1* are controlling ten-percent partners for that year because each owns at least a 10% interest (*US* owns a 40% interest and *US1* owns a 15% interest) and together they control *FPS* because collectively they own more than a 50% interest in *FPS*. As controlling ten-percent partners, under section 6038, each is required to file a Form 8865 with its 2002 income tax return. (*US1* must also report its acquisition of the 15% interest in *FPS* under section 6046A on its Form 8865 filed with its 2002 income tax return.)

*Example 3. Constructive ownership rules.* Assume the same facts as in *Example 2.* In addition, on January 1, 2003, *US2*, a United States person and the brother of *US*, purchases 50% of the stock of *FC*, a foreign corporation. *FC* owns a 20% interest in *FPS*. Thus, under sections 6038(e)(3) and 267(c)(1), *US2* indirectly owns a 10% interest in *FPS* (10% is *US2*'s proportionate share of *FC*'s 20% interest in *FPS*), and under sections 6038(e)(3) and 267(c)(2), *US2* is attributed *US*'s 40% interest. Additionally, *US* directly owns a 40% interest in *FPS* and is attributed *US2*'s 10% interest pursuant to section 6038(e)(3) and section 267(c)(2). Therefore, *US2* is considered to own a 50% interest (10% indirectly and 40% from *US*) in *FPS*, and *US* is considered to own a 50% interest in *FPS* (40% directly and 10% from *US2*). *FPS* has no controlling fifty-percent partners, because neither *US*, *US1*, nor *US2*, owns a greater than 50% interest. However, *US*, *US1*, and *US2* are each controlling ten-percent partners and each must file Form 8865 pursuant to section 6038 for *FPS*'s 2003 tax year ending December 31, 2003. Each must attach Form 8865 to its tax return for its 2003 tax year.

*Example 4. Controlling fifty-percent partners.* Assume the same facts as in *Example 3.* In addition, on June 1, 2004, *US* acquires an additional 1% direct interest in *FPS*. *US* is now a controlling fifty-percent partner of *FPS*, because *US* owns a 41% interest directly and a 10% interest constructively from *US2*. *US2* is also a controlling fifty-percent partner, because *US2* owns 10% indirectly and 41% constructively from *US*. Both *US* and *US2* are required to file Form 8865 containing all the information required to be submitted by controlling fifty-percent partners. (But see paragraph (c)(1) of this section, which contains filing exceptions when there are multiple controlling fifty-percent partners). *US1* is no longer a controlling ten-percent partner because *FPS* now has at least one controlling fifty-percent partner, and *US1* does not qualify as a controlling fifty-percent partner. Therefore, *US1* is not required to file Form 8865 under section 6038.

*Example 5. Constructive ownership from a nonresident alien.* *US*, a United States person, does not own directly or constructively an interest in *FPS*, a foreign partnership. The tax year of *FPS* is the calendar year. *NRA*, a nonresident alien, is the mother of *US*. In 2002, *NRA* acquires a 55% interest in *FPS*. Because *US* owns neither a direct nor a constructive interest in *FPS* under sections 6038(e)(3) and 267(c)(1) or (5), *NRA*'s interest is not attributed to *US* under sections 6038(e)(3) and 267(c)(2). If in 2003 *NRA* becomes a United States person, *NRA*'s interest will be attributed to *US*. However, *US* is excused from filing Form 8865 if *US* satisfies the requirements of the constructive owners exception in paragraph (c)(2) of this section. In 2003, *NRA* is a controlling fifty-percent partner and must file a Form 8865 under section 6038 for *FPS*'s 2003 tax year.

(c) *Exceptions when more than one United States person is required to file Form 8865 pursuant to section 6038.*—(1) *Multiple controlling fifty-percent partners.*—(i) *In general.*—If, with respect to the same foreign partnership for the same tax year, more than one United States person is a controlling fifty-percent partner, then in lieu of each controlling fifty-percent partner filing a separate Form 8865, only one Form 8865 from one of the controlling fifty-percent partners is required, provided all of the requirements of paragraph (c)(1)(ii) of this section are satisfied. A person that is a controlling fifty-percent partner solely because of an interest to which deductions or losses are allocated may file the single return only if there is no United States

person that is a controlling fifty-percent partner by reason of an interest in capital or profits.

(ii) *Requirements.*—(A) The person undertaking the filing obligation must file Form 8865 with that person's income tax return in the manner provided by Form 8865 and the accompanying instructions. The return must contain all of the information that would have been required to be reported by this section if each controlling fifty-percent partner had filed its own Form 8865.

(B) Any controlling fifty-percent partner not filing Form 8865 must file with its income tax return a statement titled "Controlled Foreign Partnership Reporting" containing the following information—

(1) A statement that the person qualified as a controlling fifty-percent partner, but is not submitting Form 8865 pursuant to the multiple controlling fifty-percent partners exception;

(2) The name, address, and taxpayer identification number (if any) of the foreign partnership of which the person qualified as a controlling fifty-percent partner;

(3) A representation that the filing requirement has been or will be satisfied;

(4) The name and address of the person filing the single return;

(5) The Internal Revenue Service Center where the single return is required to be filed; and

(6) Any additional information that Form 8865 and the accompanying instructions require.

(iii) *Penalties.*—If the requirements listed in paragraph (c)(1)(ii) of this section are not satisfied, a United States person that did not file a Form 8865 pursuant to this paragraph will be subject to the penalties in paragraph (k) of this section, unless the reasonable cause provision in paragraph (k)(4) of this section is satisfied.

(2) *Certain constructive owners excepted from furnishing information.*—(i) *In general.*—A United States person that does not own a direct interest in the foreign partnership and that is required to file Form 8865 under this section solely by reason of constructive ownership from a United States person(s) pursuant to paragraph (b)(4) of this section (an indirect partner) is not required to file Form 8865 if all of the requirements listed in paragraph (c)(2)(ii) of this section are met.

(ii) *Requirements.*—(A) The United States person(s) whose interest the indirect partner constructively owns reports all the information such person(s) is required to submit under this section, unless such person also is required to file solely by reason of constructive ownership from a United States person(s) pursuant to paragraph (b)(4) of this section, or another person reports the information pursuant to paragraph (c)(1) of this section.

(B) The indirect partner files with its income tax return a statement titled "Controlled Foreign Partnership Reporting" containing the following information—

(1) A representation that the indirect partner was required to file Form 8865, but is not doing so pursuant to the constructive owners exception;

(2) The names and addresses of the United States persons whose interests the indirect partner constructively owns;

(3) The name and address of the foreign partnership with respect to which the indirect partner would have had to have filed Form 8865 but for this exception; and

(4) Any additional information that Form 8865 and the accompanying instructions require.

(iii) *Penalties.*—A United States person that pursuant to this paragraph (c)(2) does not file a return will be subject to the penalties in paragraph (k) of this section if the requirements listed in paragraph (c)(2)(ii) are not satisfied, unless such failure is due to reasonable cause, as defined in paragraph (k)(4) of this section.

(iv) *Overlap with multiple controlling fifty-percent partners exception.*—(A) If a United States person qualifies for both the exception in paragraph (c)(1) of this section and the exception in this paragraph (c)(2), such person may only utilize the multiple controlling fifty-percent partners exception in paragraph (c)(1) of this section to avoid filing Form 8865.

(B) *Example.*—The following example illustrates the operation of this paragraph (c)(2)(iv):

*Example.* *US* is a U.S. citizen. *US* owns 100% of the stock of *DC*, a domestic corporation. *DC* owns a 60% direct interest in *FPS*, a foreign partnership. *DC* and *US* are the only U.S. persons that own interests directly or constructively in *FPS*. *DC* owns directly a greater than 50% interest in *FPS*. *US* constructively owns *DC*'s interest pursuant to sections 6038(e)(3) and 267(c)(1). Therefore, both *DC* and

*US* are controlling fifty-percent partners. *US* qualifies for both the exception in paragraph (c)(1) of this section (multiple controlling fifty-percent partners) and the exception in paragraph (c)(2) of this section (constructive owner exception). *US* may only utilize the paragraph (c)(1) exception to avoid its filing obligation. Accordingly, *DC* may file a single Form 8865 on behalf of *US* and itself. However, that form must contain all the information that would have been submitted had *DC* and *US* each submitted a separate Form 8865.

(3) *Members of an affiliated group of corporations filing a consolidated return.*—If one or more members of an affiliated group of corporations filing a consolidated return are required under section 6038 to file a Form 8865 for a particular foreign partnership, the common parent corporation may file one Form 8865 on behalf of all of the members of the group required to report under section 6038. Except with respect to group members who also qualify under the exception in paragraph (c)(2) of this section, the Form 8865 must contain all the information that would have been required to be submitted if each group member were required to file its own Form 8865.

(d) *Exception for certain trusts.*—Trusts relating to state and local government employee retirement plans are not required to report under this section, unless the instructions to Form 8865 provide otherwise.

(e) *Reporting under this section not required with respect to partnerships excluded from the application of subchapter K.*—The reporting requirements of this section will not apply to any United States person in respect of an eligible partnership as described in §1.761-2(a) if such partnership has validly elected to be excluded from all of the provisions of subchapter K of chapter 1 of the Internal Revenue Code in the manner specified in §1.761-2(b)(2)(i), or such partnership is deemed to have elected to be excluded from all of the provisions of subchapter K of chapter 1 of the Internal Revenue Code in accordance with the provisions of §1.761-2(b)(2)(ii).

(f) *Period covered by return.*—The information required under this section must be furnished for the tax year of the foreign partnership ending with or within the United States person's tax year. See section 706 for rules regarding tax years of partnerships.

(g) *Contents of return.*—(1) *Information required to be submitted by controlling fifty-percent partners and controlling ten-percent partners.*—All controlling fifty-percent partners and all controlling ten-percent partners must submit the following information on Form 8865 in the form and manner and to the extent prescribed by Form 8865 and its instructions—

(i) The name, address, and taxpayer identification number (if any) of the foreign partnership of which the person qualified as a controlling fifty-percent partner or a controlling ten-percent partner;

(ii) A statement of the income, gain, losses, deductions and credits allocated to the direct interest in the partnership of the person reporting under section 6038;

(iii) A list of all partnerships (foreign or domestic) in which the foreign partnership owned a direct interest, or owned a constructive interest of ten percent of more under the rules of section 267(c)(1) or (5), during the partnership's tax year for which the Form 8865 is being filed;

(iv) Information about all foreign entities that were disregarded as entities separate from their owner under §§301.7701-2 and 301.7701-3 that were owned by the foreign partnership during the partnership's tax year for which the Form 8865 is being filed;

(v) A summary of the transactions that took place during the partnership's tax year between the partnership and the person filing the return, between the partnership and any other partnership of which the person filing the return is a controlling fifty-percent partner, and between the partnership and any corporation controlled (under section 6038(e)(2) and the regulations thereunder) by the person filing the return; and

(vi) Any other information that Form 8865 or its accompanying instructions require to be submitted.

(2) *Additional information required to be submitted by controlling fifty-percent partners.*—In addition to the information required pursuant to paragraph (g)(1) of this section, controlling fifty-percent partners must also submit the following information in the form and manner and to the extent required by Form 8865 and its instructions—

(i) A list of the names, addresses and tax identification numbers (if any) of each United States person that owned a direct interest of ten percent or more in the partnership during the partnership's tax year, and of each United States and foreign person whose interests in the partnership the controlling fifty-percent partner constructively owned under paragraph (b)(4) of this section during the partnership's tax year;

(ii) A list of transactions between the partnership and any United States person owning at the time of the transaction at least a 10-percent direct interest (as defined in paragraph (b)(3) of this section) in the foreign partnership;

(iii) A statement of the aggregate of the partners' distributive shares of items of income, gain, losses, deductions and credits;

(iv) A statement of income, gain, losses, deductions and credits allocated to each United States person holding a direct interest in the foreign partnership of ten percent or more; and

(v) Any other information Form 8865 or its accompanying instructions require controlling fifty-percent partners to submit.

(3) *Amounts involving hybrid transactions or hybrid entities under section 267A.*—In addition to the information required pursuant to paragraphs (g)(1) and (2) of this section, if, during the partnership's taxable year for which the Form 8865 is being filed, the partnership paid or accrued interest or royalties for which a deduction is disallowed under section 267A and the regulations in this part under section 267A, the controlling fifty-percent partners must provide information about the disallowance in the form and manner and to the extent prescribed by Form 8865 (or successor form), instruction, publication, or other guidance.

(4) *Additional information required to be submitted by a controlling ten-percent or a controlling fifty-percent partner that has a deduction under section 250 by reason of FDII.*—In addition to the information required pursuant to paragraphs (g)(1), (2), and (3) of this section, if, with respect to the partnership's tax year for which the Form 8865 is being filed, a controlling ten-percent partner or a controlling fifty-percent partner has a deduction under section 250 (by reason of having foreign-derived intangible income), determined, in whole or in part, by reference to the income, assets, or activities of the partnership, or transactions between the controlling-ten percent partner or controlling fifty-percent partner and the partnership, the controlling ten-percent partner or controlling fifty-percent partner must provide its share of the partnership's gross DEI, gross FDDEI, deductions that are properly allocable to the partnership's gross DEI and gross FD-DEI, and partnership QBAI (as those terms are defined in the section 250 regulations) in the form and manner and to the extent prescribed by Form 8865 (or any successor form), instructions to the form, publication, or other guidance published in the Internal Revenue Bulletin. To the extent that the partnership amounts described in the previous sentence cannot be determined, the controlling ten-percent partner or controlling fifty-percent partner must provide its share of the partnership's attributes that the partner uses to determine the partner's gross DEI, gross FDDEI, deductions that are properly allocable to the partner's gross DEI and gross FDDEI, and the partner's adjusted bases in partnership specified tangible property.

(h) *Method of reporting.*—Except as otherwise provided on Form 8865 or the accompanying instructions, all amounts required to be furnished on Form 8865 must be expressed in United States dollars. All statements required on or with Form 8865 pursuant to this section must be in English.

(i) *Time and place for filing return.*—(1) *In general.*—Form 8865 must be filed with the United States person's income tax return on or before the due date (including extensions) of that return. If the United States person is not required to file an income tax return for its tax year with which or within which the foreign partnership's tax year ends, but is required to file an information return for that year (for example, Form 1065, "U.S. Partnership Return of Income," or Form 990, "Return of Organization Exempt from Income Tax"), the Form 8865 must be filed with the United States person's information return filed on or before the due date (including extensions) of that return.

(2) *Duplicate return.*—If required by the instructions to Form 8865, a duplicate Form 8865 (including attachments and schedules) must also be filed.

(j) *Overlap with section 6031.*—A partner may be required to file Form 8865 under this section and the foreign partnership in which it is a partner may also be required to file a Form 1065 or Form 1065-B under section 6031(e) for the same partnership tax year. For cases where a United States person is a controlling fifty-percent partner or a controlling ten-percent partner with respect to a foreign partnership, and that foreign partnership completes and files Form 1065 or Form 1065-B, the instructions for Form 8865 will specify the filing requirements that address this overlap in reporting obligations.

(k) *Failure to comply with reporting requirement.*—(1) *In general.*—Any United States person required to file Form 8865 under Section 6038 and this section that fails to comply (as defined in paragraph (k)(2) of this section) with the reporting requirements of this section, will be subject to the penalties described in paragraph (k)(3) of this section.

(2) *Failure to comply.*—A failure to comply is separately determined for each foreign partnership for which a United States person has a section 6038 reporting obligation. A failure to comply with the requirements of section 6038 includes the following—

(i) The failure to report at the proper time and in the proper manner any information required to be reported under the rules of this section; or

(ii) The provision of false or inaccurate information in purported compliance with the requirements of this section.

(3) *Penalties.*—A United States person that fails to comply (as defined in paragraph (k)(2) of this section) with the reporting requirements of this section must pay the following penalties, subject to the reasonable cause exception in paragraph (k)(4) of this section:

(i) *Dollar amount penalty.*—(A) *$10,000 penalty.*—A penalty of $10,000 shall be imposed for each tax year of each foreign partnership with respect to which a failure to comply occurs.

(B) *Increase in penalty.*—If a failure to comply with the applicable reporting requirements of section 6038 and this section continues for more than 90 days after the date on which the Commissioner or the Commissioner's delegate mails notice of the failure to the United States person required to file Form 8865, the person must pay an additional penalty of $10,000 for each 30-day period (or fraction thereof) during which the failure continues after the 90-day period has expired.

(C) *Limitation.*—The additional penalty imposed on any United States person by section 6038(b)(2) and paragraph (k)(3)(i)(B) of this section is limited to a maximum of $50,000 for each partnership for each tax year with respect to which the failure occurs.

(ii) *Penalty of reducing foreign tax credit.*—(A) *Effect on foreign tax credit.*—Failure to comply with the reporting requirements of section 6038 and this section may cause a reduction of foreign tax credits under section 901 (taxes of foreign countries and of possessions of the United States). In applying section 901 to a United States person for any tax year with or within which its foreign partnership's tax year ended, the amount of taxes paid (and deemed paid under sections 902 and 960) by the United States person will be reduced by 10 percent if the person fails to comply. However, no tax deemed paid under section 904(c) will be reduced under the provisions of this paragraph (k)(3)(ii).

(B) *Reduction for continued failure.*—If a failure to comply with the reporting requirements of section 6038 and this section continues for more than 90 days after the date on which the Commissioner or the Commissioner's delegate mails notice of the failure to the person required to file Form 8865, then the amount of the reduction in paragraph (k)(3)(ii)(A) of this section will be 10 percent, plus an additional 5 percent for each 3-month period (or fraction thereof) during which the failure continues after the 90-day period has expired.

(C) *Limitation on reduction.*—The amount of the reduction under paragraphs (k)(3)(ii)(A) and (B) of this section for each failure to furnish information required under this section will not exceed the greater of $10,000, or the gross income of the foreign partnership for its tax year with respect to which the failure occurred.

(D) *Offset for dollar amount penalty imposed.*—The total amount of the reduction which, but for this paragraph (k)(3)(ii)(D), may be made under this paragraph (k)(3)(ii) with respect to any separate failure, may not exceed the maximum amount of the reductions that may be imposed, reduced (but not below zero) by the dollar amount penalty imposed by paragraph (k)(3)(i) of this section with respect to the failure.

(4) *Reasonable cause limitation.*—The time prescribed for filing a complete Form 8865, and the beginning of the 90-day period after the Commissioner or the Commissioner's delegate mails notice under paragraphs (k)(3)(i)(B) and (ii)(B) of this section, will be treated as being not earlier than the last day on which reasonable cause existed for failure to furnish the information. The United States person may show reasonable cause by providing a written statement to the Commissioner's delegate having jurisdiction over the person's return to which the Form 8865 should have been attached, setting forth the reasons for the failure to comply. Whether a failure to comply was due to reasonable cause will be determined by the Commissioner, or the Commissioner's delegate, under all the facts and circumstances.

(5) *Statute of limitations.*—For exceptions to the limitations on assessment in the event of a failure to provide information under section 6038, see section 6501(c)(8).

(l) *Applicability dates.*—Except as otherwise provided, this section shall apply for tax years of a foreign partnership ending on or after December 31, 2000. For tax years of a foreign partnership ending before December 23, 2002, see §1.6038-3(j) in effect prior to the amendments made by T.D. 9033 (see 26 CFR part 1 revised April 1, 2002). Paragraph (g)(3) of this section applies for taxable years of a foreign partnership beginning on or after December 20, 2018. Paragraph (g)(4) of this section applies for tax years of a foreign partnership beginning on or after March 4, 2019. [Reg. §1.6038-3.]

☐ [*T.D.* 8850, 12-27-99. *Amended by T.D.* 9033, 12-20-2002; *T.D.* 9065, 6-30-2003; *T.D.* 9896, 4-7-2020 *and T.D.* 9901, 7-9-2020.]

### [Reg. §1.6038-4]

**§1.6038-4. Information returns required of certain United States persons with respect to such person's U.S. multinational enterprise group.**—(a) *Requirement of return.*—Except as provided in paragraph (h) of this section, every ultimate parent entity of a U.S. multinational enterprise (MNE) group must make an annual return on Form 8975, *Country-by-Country Report*, setting forth the information described in paragraph (d) of this section, and any other information required by Form 8975, with respect to the reporting period described in paragraph (c) of this section.

(b) *Definitions.*—(1) *Ultimate parent entity of a U.S. MNE group.*—An ultimate parent entity of a U.S. MNE group is a U.S. business entity that:

(i) Owns directly or indirectly a sufficient interest in one or more other business entities, at least one of which is organized or tax resident in a tax jurisdiction other than the United States, such that the U.S. business entity is required to consolidate the accounts of the other business entities with its own accounts under U.S. generally accepted accounting principles, or would be so required if equity interests in the U.S. business entity were publicly traded on a U.S. securities exchange; and

(ii) Is not owned directly or indirectly by another business entity that consolidates the accounts of such U.S. business entity with its own accounts under generally accepted accounting principles in the other business entity's tax jurisdiction of residence, or would be so required if equity interests in the other business entity were traded on a public securities exchange in its tax jurisdiction of residence.

(2) *Business entity.*—For purposes of this section, a business entity generally is any entity recognized for federal tax purposes that is not properly classified as a trust under §301.7701-4 of this chapter. However, any grantor trust within the meaning of section 671, all or a portion of which is owned by a person other an individual, is a business entity for purposes of this section. Additionally, the term business entity includes any entity with a single owner that may be disregarded as an entity separate from its owner under §301.7701-3 of this chapter and a permanent establishment, as defined in paragraph (b)(3) of this section, that prepares financial statements separate from those of its owner for financial reporting, regulatory, tax reporting, or internal management control purposes. A business entity does not include a decedent's estate or a bankruptcy estate described in section 1398.

(3) *Permanent establishment.*—For purposes of this section, the term permanent establishment includes:

(i) A branch or business establishment of a constituent entity in a tax jurisdiction that is treated as a permanent establishment under an income tax convention to which that tax jurisdiction is a party;

(ii) A branch or business establishment of a constituent entity that is liable to tax in the tax jurisdiction in which it is located pursuant to the domestic law of such tax jurisdiction; or

(iii) A branch or business establishment of a constituent entity that is treated in the same manner for tax purposes as an entity separate from its owner by the owner's tax jurisdiction of residence.

(4) *U.S. business entity.*—A U.S. business entity is a business entity that is organized or has its tax jurisdiction of residence in the United States. For purposes of this section, foreign insurance companies that elect to be treated as domestic corporations under section 953(d) are U.S. business entities that have their tax jurisdiction of residence in the United States.

(5) *U.S. MNE group.*—A U.S. MNE group comprises the ultimate parent entity of a U.S. MNE group as defined in paragraph (b)(1) of this section and all of the business entities required to consolidate their accounts with the ultimate parent entity's accounts under U.S. generally accepted accounting principles, or that would be so required if equity interests in the ultimate parent entity were publicly traded on a U.S. securities exchange, regardless of whether any such business entities could be excluded from consolidation solely on size or materiality grounds.

(6) *Constituent entity.*—With respect to a U.S. MNE group, a constituent entity is any separate business entity of such U.S. MNE

group, except that the term constituent entity does not include a foreign corporation or foreign partnership for which the ultimate parent entity is not required to furnish information under section 6038(a) (determined without regard to §§ 1.6038-2(j) and 1.6038-3(c)) or any permanent establishment of such foreign corporation or foreign partnership.

(7) *Tax jurisdiction.*—For purposes of this section, a tax jurisdiction is a country or a jurisdiction that is not a country but that has fiscal autonomy. For purposes of this section, a U.S. territory or possession of the United States is considered to have fiscal autonomy.

(8) *Tax jurisdiction of residence.*—A business entity is considered a resident in a tax jurisdiction if, under the laws of that tax jurisdiction, the business entity is liable to tax therein based on place of management, place of organization, or another similar criterion. A business entity will not be considered a resident in a tax jurisdiction if the business entity is liable to tax in such tax jurisdiction only by reason of a tax imposed by reference to gross amounts of income without any reduction for expenses, provided such tax applies only with respect to income from sources in such tax jurisdiction or capital situated in such tax jurisdiction. If a business entity is resident in more than one tax jurisdiction, then the applicable income tax convention rules, if any, should be applied to determine the business entity's tax jurisdiction of residence. If a business entity is resident in more than one tax jurisdiction and no applicable income tax convention exists between those tax jurisdictions, or if the applicable income tax convention provides that the determination of residence is based on a determination by the competent authorities of the relevant tax jurisdictions and no such determination has been made, the business entity's tax jurisdiction of residence is the tax jurisdiction of the business entity's place of effective management determined in accordance with Article 4 of the Organisation for Economic Co-operation and Development Model Tax Convention on Income and on Capital 2014, or as provided by Form 8975. A corporation that is organized or managed in a tax jurisdiction that does not impose an income tax on corporations will be treated as resident in that tax jurisdiction, unless such corporation is treated as resident in another tax jurisdiction under another provision of this section. The tax jurisdiction of residence of a permanent establishment is the jurisdiction in which the permanent establishment is located. If a business entity does not have a tax jurisdiction of residence, then solely for purposes of paragraph (b)(1) of this section, the tax jurisdiction of residence is the business entity's country of organization.

(9) *Applicable financial statements.*—An applicable financial statement is a certified audited financial statement that is accompanied by a report of an independent certified public accountant or similarly qualified independent professional that is used for purposes of reporting to shareholders, partners, or similar persons; for purposes of reporting to creditors in connection with securing or maintaining financing; or for any other substantial non-tax purpose.

(10) *U.S. territory or possession of the United States.*—The term U.S. territory or possession of the United States means American Samoa, Guam, the Northern Mariana Islands, Puerto Rico, or the U.S. Virgin Islands.

(11) *U.S. territory ultimate parent entity.*—A U.S. territory ultimate parent entity is a business entity organized in a U.S. territory or possession of the United States that controls (as defined in section 6038(e)) a U.S. business entity and that is not owned directly or indirectly by another business entity that consolidates the accounts of the U.S. territory ultimate parent entity with its accounts under generally accepted accounting principles in the other business entity's tax jurisdiction of residence, or would be so required if equity interests in the other business entity were traded on a public securities exchange in its tax jurisdiction of residence.

(c) *Reporting period.*—The reporting period covered by Form 8975 is the period of the ultimate parent entity's applicable financial statement prepared for the 12-month period (or a 52-53 week period described in section 441(f)) that ends with or within the ultimate parent entity's taxable year. If the ultimate parent entity does not prepare an annual applicable financial statement, then the reporting period covered by Form 8975 is the 12-month period (or a 52-53 week period described in section 441(f)) that ends on the last day of the ultimate parent entity's taxable year.

(d) *Contents of return.*—(1) *Constituent entity information.*—The return on Form 8975 must contain so much of the following information with respect to each constituent entity of the U.S. MNE group, and in such form or manner, as Form 8975 prescribes:

(i) The complete legal name of the constituent entity;

(ii) The tax jurisdiction, if any, in which the constituent entity is resident for tax purposes;

(iii) The tax jurisdiction in which the constituent entity is organized or incorporated (if different from the tax jurisdiction of residence);

(iv) The tax identification number, if any, used for the constituent entity by the tax administration of the constituent entity's tax jurisdiction of residence; and

(v) The main business activity or activities of the constituent entity.

(2) *Tax jurisdiction of residence information.*—The return on Form 8975 must contain so much of the following information with respect to each tax jurisdiction in which one or more constituent entities of a U.S. MNE group is resident, presented as an aggregate of the information for the constituent entities resident in each tax jurisdiction, and in such form or manner, as Form 8975 prescribes:

(i) Revenues generated from transactions with other constituent entities;

(ii) Revenues not generated from transactions with other constituent entities;

(iii) Profit or loss before income tax;

(iv) Total income tax paid on a cash basis to all tax jurisdictions, and any taxes withheld on payments received by the constituent entities;

(v) Total accrued tax expense recorded on taxable profits or losses, reflecting only operations in the relevant annual period and excluding deferred taxes or provisions for uncertain tax liabilities;

(vi) Stated capital, except that the stated capital of a permanent establishment must be reported in the tax jurisdiction of residence of the legal entity of which it is a permanent establishment unless there is a defined capital requirement in the permanent establishment tax jurisdiction for regulatory purposes;

(vii) Total accumulated earnings, except that accumulated earnings of a permanent establishment must be reported by the legal entity of which it is a permanent establishment;

(viii) Total number of employees on a full-time equivalent basis; and

(ix) Net book value of tangible assets, which, for purposes of this section, does not include cash or cash equivalents, intangibles, or financial assets.

(3) *Special rules.*—(i) *Constituent entity with no tax jurisdiction of residence.*—The information listed in paragraph (d)(2) of this section also must be provided, in the aggregate, for any constituent entity or entities that have no tax jurisdiction of residence. In addition, if a constituent entity is an owner of a constituent entity that does not have a jurisdiction of tax residence, then the owner's share of such entity's revenues and profits will be aggregated with the information for the owner's tax jurisdiction of residence.

(ii) *Definition of revenue.*—For purposes of this section, the term revenue includes all amounts of revenue, including revenue from sales of inventory and property, services, royalties, interest, and premiums. The term revenue does not include payments received from other constituent entities that are treated as dividends in the payor's tax jurisdiction of residence. Distributions and remittances from partnerships and other fiscally transparent entities and permanent establishments that are constituent entities are not considered revenue of the recipient-owner. The term revenue also does not include imputed earnings or deemed dividends received from other constituent entities that are taken into account solely for tax purposes and that otherwise would be included as revenue by a constituent entity. With respect to a constituent entity that is an organization exempt from taxation under section 501(a) because it is an organization described in section 501(c), 501(d), or 401(a), a state college or university described in section 511(a)(2)(B), a plan described in section 403(b) or 457(b), an individual retirement plan or annuity as defined in section 7701(a)(37), a qualified tuition program described in section 529, a qualified ABLE program described in section 529A, or a Coverdell education savings account described in section 530, the term revenue includes only revenue that is reflected in unrelated business taxable income as defined in section 512.

(iii) *Number of employees.*—For purposes of this section, the number of employees on a full-time equivalent basis may be reported as of the end of the accounting period, on the basis of average employment levels for the annual accounting period, or on any other reasonable basis consistently applied across tax jurisdictions and from year to year. Independent contractors participating in the ordinary operating activities of a constituent entity may be reported as employees of such constituent entity. Reasonable rounding or approximation of the number of employees is permissible, provided that such rounding or approximation does not materially distort the relative distribution of employees across the various tax jurisdictions. Consistent approaches should be applied from year to year and across entities.

(iv) *Income tax paid and accrued tax expense of permanent establishment.*—In the case of a constituent entity that is a permanent establishment, the amount of income tax paid and the amount of accrued tax expense referred to in paragraphs (d)(2)(iv) and (v) of this section should not include the income tax paid or tax expense accrued by the business entity of which the permanent establishment would be a part, but for the third sentence of paragraph (b)(2) of this section, in that business entity's tax jurisdiction of residence on the income derived by the permanent establishment.

(v) *Certain transportation income.*—If a constituent entity of a U.S. MNE group derives income from international transportation or transportation in inland waterways that is covered by income tax convention provisions that are specific to such income and under which the taxing rights on such income are allocated exclusively to one tax jurisdiction, then the U.S. MNE group should report the information required under paragraph (d)(2) of this section with respect to such income for the tax jurisdiction to which the relevant income tax convention provisions allocate these taxing rights.

(e) *Reporting of financial amounts.*—(1) *Reporting in U.S. dollars required.*—All amounts furnished under paragraph (d)(2) of this section, other than paragraph (d)(2)(viii) of this section, must be expressed in U.S. dollars. If an exchange rate is used other than in accordance with U.S. generally accepted accounting principles for conversion to U.S. dollars, the exchange rate must be indicated.

(2) *Sources of financial amounts.*—All amounts furnished under paragraph (d)(2) of this section, other than paragraph (d)(2)(viii) of this section, should be based on applicable financial statements, books and records maintained with respect to the constituent entity, regulatory financial statements, or records used for tax reporting or internal management control purposes for an annual period of each constituent entity ending with or within the period described in paragraph (c) of this section.

(f) *Time and manner for filing.*—Returns on Form 8975 required under paragraph (a) of this section for a reporting period must be filed with the ultimate parent entity's income tax return for the taxable year, in or with which the reporting period ends, on or before the due date (including extensions) for filing that person's income tax return or as otherwise prescribed by Form 8975.

(g) *Maintenance of records.*—The U.S. person filing Form 8975 as an ultimate parent entity of a U.S. MNE group must maintain records to support the information provided on Form 8975. However, the U.S. person is not required to create and maintain records that reconcile the amounts provided on Form 8975 with the tax returns of any tax jurisdiction or applicable financial statements.

(h) *Exceptions to furnishing information.*—An ultimate parent entity of a U.S. MNE group is not required to report information under this section for the reporting period described in paragraph (c) of this section if the annual revenue of the U.S. MNE group for the immediately preceding reporting period was less than $850,000,000.

(i) [Reserved]

(j) *U.S. territories and possessions of the United States.*—A U.S. territory ultimate parent entity may designate a U.S. business entity that it controls (as defined in section 6038(e)) to file Form 8975 on the U.S. territory ultimate parent entity's behalf with respect to such U.S. territory ultimate parent entity and the business entities that would be required to consolidate their accounts with such U.S. territory ultimate parent entity under U.S. generally accepted accounting principles, or would be so required if equity interests in the U.S. territory ultimate parent entity were publicly traded on a U.S. securities exchange.

(k) *Applicability dates.*—The rules of this section apply to reporting periods of ultimate parent entities of U.S. MNE groups that begin on or after the first day of a taxable year of the ultimate parent entity that begins on or after June 30, 2016. [Reg. § 1.6038-4.]

□ [*T.D. 9773, 6-29-2016 (corrected 9-16-2016).*]

### [Reg. § 1.6038-5]

**§ 1.6038-5. Information returns required of certain United States persons to report amounts determined with respect to certain foreign corporations for global intangible low-taxed income (GILTI) purposes.**—(a) *Requirement of return.*—Except as provided in paragraph (d) of this section, each United States person who is a United States shareholder (as defined in section 951(b)) of any controlled foreign corporation (as defined in section 957) must make an annual return on Form 8992, "U.S. Shareholder Calculation of Global Intangible Low-Taxed Income (GILTI)," (or successor form) for each U.S. shareholder inclusion year (as defined in § 1.951A-1(f)(7)) setting forth the information with respect to each such controlled foreign corporation, in such form and manner, as Form 8992 (or successor form) prescribes.

(b) *Time and manner for filing.*—Returns on Form 8992 (or successor form) required under paragraph (a) of this section for a taxable year must be filed with the United States person's income tax return on or before the due date (taking into account extensions) for filing that person's income tax return.

(c) *Failure to furnish information.*—(1) *Penalties.*—If any person required to file Form 8992 (or successor form) under section 6038 and this section fails to furnish the information prescribed on Form 8992 within the time prescribed by paragraph (b) of this section, the penalties imposed by section 6038(b) and (c) apply.

(2) *Increase in penalty.*—If a failure described in paragraph (c)(1) of this section continues for more than 90 days after the date on which the Director of Field Operations, Area Director, or Director of Compliance Campus Operations mails notice of such failure to the person required to file Form 8992, such person shall pay a penalty of $10,000, in addition to the penalty imposed by section 6038(b)(1), for each 30-day period (or a fraction of) during which such failure continues after such 90-day period has expired. The additional penalty imposed by section 6038(b)(2) and this paragraph (c)(2) shall be limited to a maximum of $50,000 for each failure.

(3) *Reasonable cause.*—(i) For purposes of section 6038(b) and (c) and this section, the time prescribed for furnishing information under paragraph (b) of this section, and the beginning of the 90-day period after mailing of notice by the director under paragraph (c)(2) of this section, shall be treated as being not earlier than the last day on which reasonable cause existed for failure to furnish the information.

(ii) To show that reasonable cause existed for failure to furnish information as required by section 6038 and this section, the person required to report such information must make an affirmative showing of all facts alleged as reasonable cause for such failure in a written statement containing a declaration that it is made under the penalties of perjury. The statement must be filed with the director where the return is required to be filed. The director shall determine whether the failure to furnish information was due to reasonable cause, and if so, the period of time for which such reasonable cause existed. In the case of a return that has been filed as required by this section except for an omission of, or error with respect to, some of the information required, if the person who filed the return establishes to the satisfaction of the director that the person has substantially complied with this section, then the omission or error shall not constitute a failure under this section.

(d) *Exception from filing requirement.*—Any United States person that does not own, within the meaning of section 958(a), stock of a controlled foreign corporation in which the United States person is a United States shareholder for a taxable year is not required to file Form 8992. For this purpose, whether a U.S. person owns, within the meaning of section 958(a), stock of a controlled foreign corporation is determined under § 1.951A-1(e).

(e) *Applicability date.*—This section applies to taxable years of controlled foreign corporations beginning on or after October 3, 2018. [Reg. § 1.6038-5.]

□ [*T.D. 9866, 6-14-2019.* ]

### [Reg. § 1.6038A-0]

**§ 1.6038A-0. Table of contents.**—This section lists the captions that appear in the regulations under section 6038A.

(1) Attribution under section 318.
(2) Attribution of transactions with related parties engaged in by a partnership.
(f) Foreign person.
(g) Foreign related party.
(h) Small corporation exception.
(i) Safe harbor for reporting corporations with related party transactions of *de minimis* value.
(1) In general.
(2) Aggregate value of gross payments made or received.
(j) Related reporting corporations.
(k) Consolidated return groups.
(1) Required information.
(2) Maintenance of records and authorization of agent.
(3) Monetary penalties.
(l) District Director.
(m) Examples.
(n) Effective dates.
(1) Section 1.6038A-1.
(2) Section 1.6038A-2.
(3) Section 1.6038A-3.
(4) Section 1.6038A-4.
(5) Section 1.6038A-5.
(6) Section 1.6038A-6.
(7) Section 1.6038A-7.

§1.6038A-2. *Requirement of return.*
(a) Form 5472 required.
(1) In general.
(2) Reportable transaction.
(b) Contents of return.
(1) Reporting corporation.
(2) Related party.
(3) Foreign related party transactions for which only monetary consideration is paid or received by the reporting corporation.
(4) Foreign related party transactions involving nonmonetary consideration or less than full consideration.
(5) Additional information.
(6) Reasonable estimate.
(i) Estimate within 25 percent of actual amount.
(ii) Other estimates.
(7) Small amounts.
(8) Accrued payments and receipts.
(9) Examples.
(c) Method of reporting.
(d) Time and place for filing returns.
(e) Untimely filed return.
(f) Exceptions.
(1) No reportable transactions.
(2) Transactions solely with a domestic reporting corporation.
(3) Transactions with a corporation subject to reporting under section 6038.
(4) Transactions with a foreign sales corporation.
(g) Filing Form 5472 when transactions with related parties engaged in by a partnership are attributed to a reporting corporation.
(h) Effective dates for certain reporting corporations.

§1.6038A-3. *Record maintenance.*
(a) General maintenance requirements.
(1) Section 6001 and section 6038A.
(2) Safe harbor.
(3) Examples.
(b) Other maintenance requirements.
(1) Indirectly related records.
(2) Foreign related party or third-party maintenance.
(3) Translation of records.
(4) Exception for foreign governments.
(c) Specific records to be maintained for safe harbor.
(1) In general.
(2) Descriptions of categories of documents to be maintained.
(i) Original entry books and transaction records.
(ii) Profit and loss statements.
(iii) Pricing documents.
(iv) Foreign country and third-party filings.
(v) Ownership and capital structure records.
(vi) Records of loans, services, and other non-sales transactions.
(3) Material profit and loss statements.
(4) Existing records test.
(5) Significant industry segment test.

(i) In general.
(ii) Form of the statements.
(iii) Special rule for component sales.
(iv) Level of specificity required.
(v) Examples.
(6) High profit test.
(i) In general.
(ii) Return on assets test.
(iii) Additional rules.
(7) Definitions.
(i) U.S.-connected products or services.
(ii) Industry segment.
(iii) Gross revenue of an industry segment.
(iv) Identifiable assets of an industry segment.
(v) Operating profit of an industry segment.
(vi) Product.
(vii) Related products or services.
(viii) Model.
(ix) Product line.
(8) Example.
(i) Facts.
(ii) Existing records test.
(iii) Significant industry segments.
(iv) High profit test.
(v) Material profit and loss statements.
(d) Liability for certain partnership record maintenance.
(e) Agreements with the District Director or the Assistant Commissioner (International).
(1) In general.
(2) Content of agreement.
(i) In general.
(ii) Significant industry segment test.
(iii) Example.
(3) Circumstances of agreement.
(4) Agreement as part of APA process.
(f) U.S. maintenance.
(1) General rule.
(2) Non-U.S. maintenance requirements.
(3) Prior taxable years.
(4) Scheduled production for high volume or other reasons.
(5) Required U.S. maintenance.
(g) Period of retention.
(h) Application of record maintenance rules to banks and other financial institutions. [Reserved]
(i) Effective dates.

§1.6038A-4. *Monetary penalty.*
(a) Imposition of monetary penalty.
(1) In general.
(2) Liability for certain partnership transactions.
(3) Calculation of monetary penalty.
(b) Reasonable cause.
(1) In general.
(2) Affirmative showing required.
(i) In general.
(ii) Small corporations.
(iii) Facts and circumstances taken into account.
(c) Failure to maintain records or to cause another to maintain records.
(d) Increase in penalty where failure continues after notification.
(1) In general.
(2) Additional penalty for another failure.
(3) Cessation of accrual.
(4) Continued failures.
(e) Other penalties.
(f) Examples.
Example (1)—Failure to file Form 5472.
Example (2)—Failure to maintain records.
(g) Effective dates.

§1.6038A-5. *Authorization of agent.*
(a) Failure to authorize.
(b) Authorization by related party.
(1) In general.
(2) Authorization for prior years.
(c) Foreign affiliated groups.
(1) In general.
(2) Application of noncompliance penalty adjustment.
(d) Legal effect of authorization of agent.
(1) Agent for purposes of commencing judicial proceedings.

(2) Foreign related party found where reporting corporation found.

  (e) Successors in interest.

  (f) Deemed compliance.

    (1) In general.

    (2) Reason to know.

    (3) Effect of deemed compliance.

  (g) Effective dates.

§ 1.6038A-6. Failure to furnish information.

  (a) In general.

  (b) Coordination with treaties.

  (c) Enforcement proceeding not required.

  (d) *De minimis* failure.

  (e) Suspension of statute of limitations.

  (f) Effective dates.

§ 1.6038A-7. Noncompliance.

  (a) In general.

  (b) Determination of the amount.

  (c) Separate application.

  (d) Effective dates. [Reg. § 1.6038A-0.]

□ [*T.D. 8353,* 6-14-91. Amended by *T.D. 9796,* 12-12-2016.]

### [Reg. § 1.6038A-1]

**§ 1.6038A-1. General requirements and definitions.**—(a) *Purpose and scope.*—This section and §§ 1.6038A-2 through 1.6038A-7 provide rules for certain foreign-owned U.S. corporations and foreign corporations engaged in trade or business within the United States (reporting corporations) relating to information that must be furnished, records that must be maintained, and the authorization of the reporting corporation to act as agent for related foreign persons for purposes of sections 7602, 7603, and 7604 that must be executed. Section 6038A(a) and this section require that a reporting corporation furnish certain information annually and maintain certain records relating to transactions between the reporting corporation and certain related parties. This section also provides definitions of terms used in section 6038A. Section 1.6038A-2 provides guidance concerning the information to be submitted and the filing of the required return. Section 1.6038A-3 provides guidance concerning the maintenance of records. Section 1.6038A-4 provides guidance concerning the application of the monetary penalty for the failure either to furnish information or to maintain records. Section 1.6038A-5 provides guidance concerning the authorization of an agent for purposes of sections 7602, 7603, and 7604. Section 1.6038A-6 provides guidance concerning the failure to furnish information requested by a summons. Finally, § 1.6038A-7 provides guidance concerning the application of the noncompliance penalty for failure by the related party to authorize an agent or by the reporting corporation to substantially comply with a summons.

(b) *In general.*—A reporting corporation must furnish the information described in § 1.6038A-2 by filing an annual information return (Form 5472 or any successor), and must maintain records as described in § 1.6038A-3.

(c) *Reporting corporation.*—(1) *In general.*—For purposes of section 6038A, a reporting corporation is either a domestic corporation that is 25-percent foreign-owned as defined in paragraph (c)(2) of this section, or a foreign corporation that is 25-percent foreign-owned and engaged in trade or business within the United States. After November 4, 1990, a foreign corporation engaged in a trade or business within the United States at any time during a taxable year is a reporting corporation. *See* section 6038C. A domestic business entity that is wholly owned by one foreign person and that is otherwise classified under § 301.7701-3(b)(1)(ii) of this chapter as disregarded as an entity separate from its owner is treated as an entity separate from its owner and classified as a domestic corporation for purposes of section 6038A. *See* § 301.7701-2(c)(2)(vi) of this chapter.

(2) *25-percent foreign-owned.*—A corporation is 25-percent foreign-owned if it has at least one direct or indirect 25-percent foreign shareholder at any time during the taxable year.

(3) *25-percent foreign shareholder.*—(i) *In general.*—A foreign person is a 25-percent foreign shareholder of a corporation if the person owns at least 25 percent of—

    (A) The total voting power of all classes of stock of the corporation entitled to vote, or

    (B) The total value of all classes of stock of the corporation.

  (ii) *Total voting power and value.*—In determining whether one foreign person owns 25 percent of the total voting power of all classes of stock of a corporation entitled to vote or 25 percent of the total value of all classes of stock of a corporation, consideration will be given to all the facts and circumstances of each case, under

principles similar to § 1.957-1(b)(2) (consideration of arrangements to shift formal voting power away from a foreign person).

  (iii) *Direct 25-percent foreign shareholder.*—A foreign person is a direct 25-percent foreign shareholder if it owns directly at least 25 percent of the stock of the reporting corporation, either by vote or by value.

  (iv) *Indirect 25-percent foreign shareholder.*—A foreign person is an indirect 25-percent foreign shareholder if it owns indirectly (or under the attribution rules of section 318 is considered to own indirectly) at least 25 percent of the stock of the reporting corporation, either by vote or by value.

(4) *Application to prior open years.*—For taxable years beginning before July 11, 1989, the definition of a reporting corporation under this paragraph applies in determining whether a foreign-owned corporation is a reporting corporation. An examination may be reopened if the statute of limitations period for that taxable year has not expired. A taxable year may not be reopened under section 6038A for examination purposes if the taxable year is open under section 6511 only for purposes of the carryback of net operating losses or net capital losses.

(5) *Exceptions.*—(i) *Treaty country residents having no permanent establishment.*—A foreign corporation that has no permanent establishment in the United States under an applicable income tax convention is not a reporting corporation for purposes of section 6038A and this section. Accordingly, such a foreign corporation is not subject to §§ 1.6038A-2, 1.6038A-3, and 1.6038A-5. It must timely and fully provide the required notice to the Commissioner under section 6114. See section 6114 and the regulations thereunder for the notice that such a corporation must file and the applicable penalties for failure to file such notice.

  (ii) *Qualified exempt shipping income.*—A foreign corporation whose gross income is exempt from U.S. taxation under section 883 is not a reporting corporation provided that it timely and fully complies with the reporting requirements required to claim such exemption. In the event that such a corporation does not timely and fully comply with the reporting requirements under sections 887 and 883, it will be a reporting corporation subject to section 6038A, including the application of the monetary penalty for failure to file required information.

  (iii) *Status as foreign related party.*—Nothing in this paragraph affects the determination of whether a person is a foreign related party as defined in paragraph (g) of this section.

(d) *Related party.*—The term "related party" means—

  (1) Any direct or indirect 25-percent foreign shareholder of the reporting corporation,

  (2) Any person who is related within the meaning of sections 267(b) or 707(b)(1) to the reporting corporation or to a 25-percent foreign shareholder of the reporting corporation, or

  (3) Any other person who is related to the reporting corporation within the meaning of section 482 and the regulations thereunder. However, the term "related party" does not include any corporation filing a consolidated federal income tax return with the reporting corporation.

(e) *Attribution rules.*—(1) *Attribution under section 318.*—For purposes of determining whether a corporation is 25-percent foreign-owned and whether a person is a related party under section 6038A, the constructive ownership rules of section 318 shall apply, and the attribution rules of section 267(c) also shall apply to the extent they attribute ownership to persons to whom section 318 does not attribute ownership. However, "10 percent" shall be substituted for "50 percent" in section 318(a)(2)(C), and section 318(a)(3)(A), (B), and (C) shall not be applied so as to consider a U.S. person as owning stock that is owned by a person who is not a U.S. person. Additionally, section 318(a)(3)(C) and § 1.318-1(b) shall not be applied so as to consider a U.S. corporation as being a reporting corporation if, but for the application of such sections, the U.S. corporation would not be 25-percent foreign owned.

  (2) *Attribution of transactions with related parties engaged in by a partnership.*—The transactions in which a domestic or foreign partnership engages shall be attributed to any reporting corporation whose interest in the capital or profits of the partnership, either directly or indirectly, combined with the interests of all related parties of the reporting corporation partner, equals 25 percent or more of the total partnership interests. Attribution of such transactions shall be made only to the extent of the partnership interest held by that reporting corporation partner. *See* sections 875 and 702(a) and the regulations thereunder. (Attribution shall not be made, however, of transactions directly between the partnership and a reporting corporation.) Accordingly, a reporting corporation partner that is deemed

to engage in transactions with related parties under this rule is subject to the information reporting requirements of §1.6038A-2, to the record maintenance requirements of §1.6038A-3, to the monetary penalty under §1.6038A-4, to the requirement of authorization of agent under §1.6038A-5, to the rules of §1.6038A-6 relating to the requirement to produce records, and to the noncompliance penalty adjustment under §1.6038A-7.

(f) *Foreign person.*—For purposes of section 6038A, a foreign person is—

(1) Any individual who is not a citizen or resident of the United States, but not including any individual for whom an election under section 6013(g) or (h) (relating to an election to file a joint return) is in effect;

(2) Any individual who is a citizen of any possession of the United States and who is not otherwise a citizen or resident of the United States;

(3) Any partnership, association, company, or corporation that is not created or organized in the United States or under the law of the United States or any State thereof;

(4) Any foreign trust or foreign estate, as defined in section 7701(a)(31); or

(5) Any foreign government (or agency or instrumentality thereof). To the extent that a foreign government is engaged in the conduct of commercial activity as defined under section 892 and the regulations thereunder, it will be treated as a foreign person under section 6038A and this section only for purposes of the information reporting requirements of §1.6038A-2. A foreign government will not be treated as a foreign related party for purposes of §§1.6038A-3 and 1.6038A-5.

For purposes of section 6038A, a possession of the United States shall be considered to be a foreign country.

(g) *Foreign related party.*—A foreign related party is a foreign person as defined under paragraph (f) of this section that is also a related party as defined under paragraph (d) of this section.

(h) *Small corporation exception.*—A reporting corporation (other than an entity that is a reporting corporation as a result of being treated as a corporation under §301.7701-2(c)(2)(vi) of this chapter) that has less than $10,000,000 in U.S. gross receipts for a taxable year is not subject to §§1.6038A-3 and 1.6038A-5 for that taxable year. Such a corporation, however, remains subject to the information reporting requirements of §1.6038A-2 and the general record maintenance requirements of section 6001. For purposes of this paragraph, U.S. gross receipts includes all amounts received or accrued to the extent that such amounts are taken into account for the determination and computation of the gross income of the corporation. For purposes of this test, the U.S. gross receipts of all related reporting corporations shall be aggregated.

(i) *Safe harbor for reporting corporations with related party transactions of de minimis value.*—(1) *In general.*—A reporting corporation (other than an entity that is a reporting corporation as a result of being treated as a corporation under §301.7701-2(c)(2)(vi) of this chapter) is not subject to §§1.6038A-3 and 1.6038A-5 for any taxable year in which the aggregate value of all gross payments it makes to and receives from foreign related parties with respect to related party transactions (including monetary consideration, nonmonetary consideration, and the value of transactions involving less than full consideration) is not more than $5,000,000 and is less than 10 percent of its U.S. gross income. Such a corporation, however, remains subject to the information reporting requirements of §1.6038A-2 and the general record maintenance requirements of section 6001. For purposes of this paragraph, U.S. gross income means the gross income reportable by the reporting corporation (or the aggregate gross income reportable by all related reporting corporations) for U.S. income tax purposes. Gross payments made to or received from foreign related parties cannot be netted; rather, the gross payments made to and received from foreign related parties are to be aggregated. Thus, for example, if a reporting corporation receives $4,700,000 of gross payments from a related party and makes $500,000 of gross payments to the same related party, it has aggregate gross payments of $5,200,000, and, therefore, does not qualify for the safe harbor under this paragraph.

(2) *Aggregate value of gross payments made or received.*—The aggregate value of gross payments made to (or received from) a foreign related party with respect to foreign related party transactions is determined by totaling the dollar amounts of foreign related party transactions as described in §1.6038A-2(b)(3) and (4) on all Forms 5472 filed by the reporting corporation or related reporting corporations.

(j) *Related reporting corporations.*—A reporting corporation is related to another reporting corporation if it is related to that other

reporting corporation under the principles described in paragraphs (d) and (e) of this section.

(k) *Consolidated return groups.*—(1) *Required information.*—If a reporting corporation is a member of an affiliated group for which a U.S. consolidated income tax return is filed, the return requirement of §1.6038A-2 may be satisfied by filing a consolidated Form 5472. The common parent, as identified on Form 851, must attach a schedule to the consolidated Form 5472 stating which members of the U.S. affiliated group are reporting corporations under section 6038A, and which of those are joining in the consolidated Form 5472. The schedule must provide the name, address, and taxpayer identification number of each member whose transactions are included on the consolidated Form 5472. A member is not required to join in filing a consolidated Form 5472 merely because other members of the group choose to file one or more Forms 5472 on a consolidated basis.

(2) *Maintenance of records and authorization of agent.*—Either the common parent or the principal operating company of an affiliated group filing a consolidated income tax return may be authorized under §1.6038A-5 to act as the agent for foreign related persons engaged in transactions with members of the group solely for purposes of section 7602, 7603, and 7604 under section 6038A(e)(1) and §1.6038A-5. Each member of the group, however, must maintain the records required under section 6038A(a) and §1.6038A-3 relating to its related party transactions.

(3) *Monetary penalties.*—The common parent (or principal operating company) and all reporting corporations that join in the filing of a consolidated Form 5472 are liable jointly and severally for penalties for failure to file Form 5472 and for failure to maintain records under section 6038A(d) and §1.6038A-4(e). *See* §1.1502-77(a) regarding the scope of agency of the common parent corporation.

(l) *District Director.*—For purposes of the regulations under section 6038A, the term "District Director" means any District Director, or the Assistant Commissioner (International) when performing duties similar to those of a District Director with respect to any person over which the Assistant Commissioner (International) has appropriate jurisdiction.

(m) *Examples.*—The following examples illustrate the rules of this section.

*Example 1.* P, a U.S. partnership that is engaged in a U.S. trade or business, is 75 percent owned by FC1, a foreign corporation that, in turn, is wholly owned by another foreign corporation, FC2. The remaining 25 percent of P is owned by Corp, a domestic corporation, that is wholly owned by FC3. P engages in transactions solely with FC2 and FC3. These transactions are attributed to FC1 and Corp. Under section 875, FC1 is considered as being engaged in a U.S. trade or business. For purposes of section 6038A and this section, FC1 and Corp are reporting corporations and must report their pro rata shares of the value of the transactions with FC2 and FC3. Thus, Corp must report 25 percent of P's transactions with FC3 and FC1 must report 75 percent of P's transactions with FC2.

*Example 2.* FC2 and FC3 are both foreign corporations that are wholly owned by FC1, also a foreign corporation. FC2 engages in a trade or business in the United States through a branch. The branch engages in related party transactions with FC1. FC2 is a reporting corporation. FC3 is a foreign related party. FC1 is a direct 25-percent foreign shareholder of both FC2 and FC3. Neither FC1 nor FC3 is a reporting corporation.

*Example 3.* FC1 owns 25 percent of total voting power in each of FC2 and FC3. FC2 and FC3 each own 20 percent of the total voting power of Corp, a domestic corporation. The remaining stock of Corp is owned by an unrelated domestic corporation. Neither FC2 nor FC3 is engaged in a U.S. trade or business. Under section 318(a)(2)(C) and paragraph (e) of this section, FC1 constructively owns its proportionate share of the stock of Corp owned directly by FC2 and FC3. Thus, FC1 is treated as constructively owning five percent of Corp through each of FC2 and FC3 or a total of 10 percent of the Corp stock. Consequently, Corp is not a reporting corporation because no 25 percent shareholder exists.

*Example 4.* FP owns 100 percent of FC1 which, in turn, owns 100 percent of FC2. FC2 owns 100 percent of FC3 which owns 100 percent of RC. FP, FC1, and FC2 are indirect 25-percent foreign shareholders of RC, and FC3 is a direct 25-percent foreign shareholder.

*Example 5.* FP owns 100 percent of USS, a U.S. corporation, and 25 percent of FS, a foreign corporation. The remaining 75 percent of FS is publicly owned by numerous small shareholders. Sales transactions occur between USS and FS. Applying the rules of this section, USS is a reporting corporation. It is determined that USS and FS are each controlled by FP under section 482 and the regulations thereunder. Therefore, FS is related to USS within the meaning of section 482 and is a related party to USS. Accordingly, the sales transactions between USS and FS are subject to section 6038A.

*Example 6.* The facts are the same as in *Example 5*, except that the remaining 75 percent of FS is owned by one shareholder that is unrelated to the FP group and it is determined that FS is not controlled by FP for purposes of section 482. Under these facts, FS is not a related party of either FP or USS. Accordingly, section 6038A does not apply to the sales transactions between FS and USS.

*Example 7.* P, a U.S. multinational, is a holding company that wholly owns X, a U.S. operating company, which in turn wholly owns FS, a controlled foreign corporation. Applying the rule of section 318(a)(3)(C), FS is deemed to own the stock of X that is actually held by P. However, under the rules of paragraph (e) of this section, X will not be a reporting corporation by reason of section 318.

(n) *Effective dates.*—(1) *Section 1.6038A-1.*—Paragraphs (c) (relating to the definition of a reporting corporation), (d) (relating to the definition of a related party), (e)(1) (relating to the application of section 318), and (f) (relating to the definition of a foreign person) of this section are effective for taxable years beginning after July 10, 1989. The remaining paragraphs of this section are effective December 10, 1990, without regard to when the taxable year began. However, §1.6038A-1 as it applies to entities that are reporting corporations as a result of being treated as a corporation under §301.7701-2(c)(2)(vi) of this chapter applies to taxable years of such reporting corporations beginning after December 31, 2016, and ending on or after December 13, 2017.

(2) *Section 1.6038A-2.*—(i) *In general.*—Section 1.6038A-2 (relating to the requirement to file Form 5472) generally applies for taxable years beginning after July 10, 1989. However, §1.6038A-2 as it applies to reporting corporations whose sole trade or business in the United States is a banking, financing, or similar business as defined in §1.864-4(c)(5)(i) applies for taxable years beginning after December 10, 1990. Section 1.6038A-2(d) applies for taxable years ending on or after June 10, 2011. For taxable years ending on or after June 10, 2011, but before December 24, 2014, see §1.6038A-2(e) as contained in 26 CFR part 1 revised as of April 1, 2014. Section 1.6038A-2 as it applies to entities that are reporting corporations as a result of being treated as a corporation under §301.7701-2(c)(2)(vi) of this chapter applies to taxable years of such reporting corporations beginning after December 31, 2016, and ending on or after December 13, 2017. Section 1.6038A-2(a)(3), (b)(6), and (b)(7) apply to taxable years ending on or after December 17, 2018. However, taxpayers may apply these final regulations in their entirety for taxable years ending before December 17, 2018.

(ii) *Transition rule.*—No penalty under sections 6038A(d) or 6038C(c) will apply to a failure solely under §1.6038A-2(a)(3), (b)(6), or (b)(7) that is corrected by March 6, 2020.

(3) *Section 1.6038A-4.*—Section 1.6038A-4 (relating to the monetary penalty) is generally effective for taxable years beginning after July 10, 1989, for the failure to file Form 5472. For the failure to maintain records or the failure to produce documents under §1.6038A-4(f)(2), the section is effective December 10, 1990, without regard to when the taxable year to which the records relate began. For taxable years ending on or before December 31, 2017, see §1.6038A-4 as contained in 26 CFR part 1 revised as of April 1, 2018.

(4) *Section 1.6038A-5.*—Section 1.6038A-5 (relating to the authorization of agent requirement) is effective December 10, 1990, without regard to when the taxable year to which the records relate began.

(5) *Section 1.6038A-6.*—Section 1.6038A-6 (relating to the failure to furnish information under a summons) is effective November 6, 1990, without regard to when the taxable year to which the summons relates began.

(6) *Section 1.6038A-7.*—Section 1.6038A-7 (relating to the noncompliance penalty adjustment) is effective December 10, 1990, without regard to when the taxable year began. [Reg. §1.6038A-1.]

☐ [T.D. 8353, 6-14-91. *Amended by T.D. 9161, 9-14-2004; T.D. 9456, 7-31-2009; T.D. 9529, 6-9-2011; T.D. 9667, 6-5-2014, T.D. 9707, 12-23-2014, T.D. 9796, 12-12-2016 and T.D. 9885, 12-2-2019.]*

### [Reg. §1.6038A-2]

**§1.6038A-2. Requirement of return.**—(a) *Forms required.*—(1) *Form 5472.*—Each reporting corporation as defined in §1.6038A-1(c) (or members of an affiliated group filing together as described in §1.6038A-1(k)) shall make a separate annual information return on Form 5472 with respect to each related party as defined in §1.6038A-1(d) with which the reporting corporation(or any group member joining in a consolidated Form 5472) has had any reportable transaction during the taxable year. The information required by section 6038A and this section must be furnished even though it may not affect the amount of any tax due under the Code.

(2) *Reportable transaction.*—A reportable transaction is any transaction of the types listed in paragraphs (b)(3) and (4) of this section, and, in the case of a reporting corporation that is an applicable taxpayer, as defined under §1.59A-2(b), any other arrangement that, to prevent avoidance of the purposes of section 59A, is identified on Form 5472 as a reportable transaction. However, except as the Secretary may prescribe otherwise for an applicable taxpayer, the transaction is not a reportable transaction if neither party to the transaction is a United States person as defined in section 7701(a)(30) (which, for purposes of section 6038A, includes an entity that is a reporting corporation as a result of being treated as a corporation under §301.7701-2(c)(2)(vi) of this chapter) and the transaction—

(i) Will not generate in any taxable year gross income from sources within the United States or income effectively connected, or treated as effectively connected, with the conduct of a trade or business within the United States, and

(ii) Will not generate in any taxable year any expense, loss, or other deduction that is allocable or apportionable to such income.

(3) *Form 8991.*—Each reporting corporation that is an applicable taxpayer, as defined under §1.59A-2(b), must make an annual information return on Form 8991. The obligation of an applicable taxpayer to report on Form 8991 does not depend on applicability of tax under section 59A or obligation to file Form 5472.

(b) *Contents of return.*—(1) *Reporting corporation.*—Form 5472 must provide the following information in the manner the form prescribes with respect to each reporting corporation:

(i) Its name, address (including mailing code), and U.S. taxpayer identification number; each country in which the reporting corporation files an income tax return as a resident under the tax laws of that country; its country or countries of organization, and incorporation; its total assets for U.S. reporting corporation; the places where it conducts its business; and its principal business activity.

(ii) The name, address, and U.S. taxpayer identification number, if applicable, of all its direct and indirect foreign shareholders (for an indirect 25-percent foreign shareholder, explain the attribution of ownership); whether any 25-percent foreign shareholder is a surrogate foreign corporation under section 7874(a)(2)(B) or a member of an expanded affiliated group as defined in section 7874(c)(1); each country in which each 25-percent foreign shareholder files an income tax return as a resident under the tax laws of that country; the places where each 25-percent shareholder conducts its business; and the country or countries of organization, citizenship, and incorporation of each 25-percent foreign shareholder.

(iii) The number of Forms 5472 filed for the taxable year and the aggregate value in U.S. dollars of gross payments as defined in §1.6038A-1(h)(2) made with respect to all foreign related party transactions reported on all Forms 5472.

(2) *Related party.*—The reporting corporation must provide information on Form 5472, set forth in the manner the form prescribes, about each related party, whether foreign or domestic, with which the reporting corporation had a transaction of the types described in paragraphs (b) (3) and (4) of this section during its taxable year, including the following information:

(i) The name, U.S. taxpayer identification number, if applicable, and address of the related party.

(ii) The nature of the related party's business and the principal place or places where it conducts its business.

(iii) Each country in which the related party files an income tax return as a resident under the tax laws of that country.

(iv) The relationship of the reporting corporation to the related party (including, to the extent the form may prescribe, any intermediate relationships).

(3) *Foreign related party transactions for which only monetary consideration is paid or received by the reporting corporation.*—If the related party is a foreign person, the reporting corporation must set forth on Form 5472 the dollar amounts of all reportable transactions for which monetary consideration (including U.S. and foreign currency) was the sole consideration paid or received during the taxable year of the reporting corporation. The total amount of such transactions, as well as the separate amounts for each type of transaction described below, and, to the extent the form may prescribe, any further description, categorization, or listing of transactions within these types, must be reported on Form 5472, in the manner the form or its instructions may prescribe. Where actual amounts are not determinable, a reasonable estimate (as described in paragraph (b)(6) of this section) is permitted. The types of transactions described in this paragraph are:

(i) Sales and purchases of stock in trade (inventory);

(ii) Sales and purchases of tangible property other than stock in trade;

(iii) Rents and royalties paid and received (other than amounts reported under paragraph (b)(3)(iv) of this section);

(iv) Sales, purchases, and amounts paid and received as consideration for the use of all intangible property, including (but not limited to) copyrights, designs, formulas, inventions, models, patents, processes, trademarks, and other similar intangible property rights;

(v) Consideration paid and received for technical, managerial, engineering, construction, scientific, or other services;

(vi) Commissions paid and received;

(vii) Amounts loaned and borrowed (except open accounts resulting from sales and purchases reported under other items listed in this paragraph (b)(3) that arise and are collected in full in the ordinary course of business), to be reported as monthly averages or outstanding balances at the beginning and end of the taxable year, as the form shall prescribe;

(viii) Interest paid and received;

(ix) Premiums paid and received for insurance and reinsurance;

(x) Other amounts paid or received not specifically identified in this paragraph (b)(3) to the extent that such amounts are taken into account for the determination and computation of the taxable income of the reporting corporation; and

(xi) With respect to an entity that is a reporting corporation as a result of being treated as a corporation under § 301.7701-2(c)(2)(vi) of this chapter, any other transaction as defined by § 1.482-1(i)(7), such as amounts paid or received in connection with the formation, dissolution, acquisition and disposition of the entity, including contributions to and distributions from the entity.

(4) *Foreign related party transactions involving nonmonetary consideration or less than full consideration.*—If the related party is a foreign person, the reporting corporation must provide on Form 5472 a description of any reportable transaction, or group of reportable transactions, listed in paragraph (b)(3) of this section, for which any part of the consideration paid or received was not monetary consideration, or for which less than full consideration was paid or received. A description required under paragraph (b)(4) of this section shall include sufficient information from which to determine the nature and approximate monetary value of the transaction or group of transactions, and shall include:

(i) A description of all property (including monetary consideration), rights, or obligations transferred from the reporting corporation to the foreign related party and from the foreign related party to the reporting corporation;

(ii) A description of all services performed by the reporting corporation for the foreign related party and by the foreign related party for the reporting corporation; and

(iii) A reasonable estimate of the fair market value of all properties and services exchanged, if possible, or some other reasonable indicator of value.

If, for any transaction, the entire consideration received includes both tangible and intangible property and the consideration paid is solely monetary consideration, the transaction should be reported under paragraph (b)(3) of this section if the intangible property was related and incidental to the transfer of the tangible property (for example, a right to warranty services.)

(5) *Additional information.*—In addition to the information required under paragraphs (b)(3) and (4) of this section, a reporting corporation must provide on Form 5472, in the manner the form prescribes, the following information:

(i) If the reporting corporation imports goods from a foreign related party, whether the costs taken into account in computing the basis or inventory cost of such goods are greater than the costs taken into account in computing the valuation of the goods for customs purposes, adjusted pursuant to section 1059A and the regulations thereunder, and if so, the reasons for the difference.

(ii) If the costs taken into account in computing the basis or inventory cost of such goods are greater than the costs taken into account in computing the valuation of the goods for customs purposes, whether the documents supporting the reporting corporation's treatment of the items set forth in paragraph (b)(5)(i) of this section are in existence and available in the United States at the time Form 5472 is filed.

(iii) If, for the taxable year, a reporting corporation pays or accrues interest or royalties for which a deduction is disallowed under section 267A and the regulations in this part under section 267A, then the reporting corporation must provide such information about the disallowance in the form and manner and to the extent prescribed by Form 5472 (or successor form), instruction, publication, or other guidance.

(iv) If, for the taxable year, the reporting corporation has a deduction under section 250 (by reason of having foreign-derived intangible income) with respect to any amount required to be reported under paragraph (b)(3) or (4) of this section, the reporting corporation will provide on Form 5472 (or any successor form) such information about the deduction in the form and manner and to the extent prescribed by Form 5472 (or any successor form), instructions to the form, publication, or other guidance published in the Internal Revenue Bulletin.

(6) *Compilation of reportable transactions across multiple related parties.*—A reporting corporation must, to the extent and in the manner Form 5472 or its instructions may prescribe, include a schedule tabulating information with respect to related parties for which the reporting corporation is required to file Forms 5472. The schedule will not require information (beyond totaling) that is not required for the individual Forms 5472. The schedule may include the following:

(i) The identity and status of the related parties;

(ii) The reporting corporation's relationship to the related parties;

(iii) The reporting corporation's reportable transactions with the related parties; and

(iv) Other items required to be reported on Form 5472.

(7) *Information on Form 5472 and Form 8991 regarding base erosion payments.*—If any reporting corporation is an applicable taxpayer, as defined under § 1.59A-2(b), it must report the information required by Form 8991 and by any Form 5472 it is required to file (including the information required by their accompanying instructions), regarding:

(i) Determination of whether a taxpayer is an applicable taxpayer;

(ii) Computation of base erosion minimum tax amount, including computation of regular tax liability as adjusted for purposes of computing base erosion minimum tax amount;

(iii) Computation of modified taxable income;

(iv) Base erosion tax benefits;

(v) Base erosion percentage calculation;

(vi) Base erosion payments;

(vii) Amounts with respect to services as described in § 1.59A-3(b)(3)(i), including a breakdown of the amount of the total services cost and any mark-up component;

(viii) Arrangements or transactions described in § 1.59A-9;

(ix) Any qualified derivative payment, including:

(A) The aggregate amount of qualified derivative payments for the taxable year; and

(B) A representation that all payments satisfy the requirements of § 1.59A-6(b)(2); and

(x) Any other information necessary to carry out section 59A.

(8) *Reasonable estimate.*—(i) *Estimate within 25 percent of actual amount.*—Any amount reported under this section is considered to be a reasonable estimate if it is at least 75 percent and not more than 125 percent of the actual amount.

(ii) *Other estimates.*—If any amount reported under this paragraph (b) of this section fails to meet the reasonable estimate test of paragraph (b)(6)(i) of this section, the reporting corporation nevertheless may show that such amount is a reasonable estimate by making an affirmative showing of relevant facts and circumstances in a written statement containing a declaration that it is made under the penalties of perjury. The District Director shall determine whether the amount reported was a reasonable estimate.

(9) *Small amounts.*—If any actual amount required under this section does not exceed $50,000, the amount may be reported as "$50,000 or less."

(10) *Accrued payments and receipts.*—For purposes of this section, a reporting corporation that uses an accrual method of accounting shall use accrued payments and accrued receipts for purposes of computing the total amount of each of the types of transactions listed in this section.

(11) *Examples.*—The following examples illustrate the application of paragraph (b)(3) of this section:

*Example 1.* (i) In year 1, W, a foreign corporation, forms and contributes assets to X, a domestic limited liability company that does not elect to be treated as a corporation under § 301.7701-3(c) of this chapter. In year 2, W contributes funds to X. In year 3, X makes a payment to W. In year 4, X, in liquidation, distributes its assets to W.

(ii) In accordance with § 301.7701-3(b)(1)(ii) of this chapter, X is disregarded as an entity separate from W. In accordance with § 301.7701-2(c)(2)(vi) of this chapter, X is treated as an entity separate from W and classified as a domestic corporation for purposes of section 6038A. In accordance with paragraphs (a)(2) and (b)(3) of this section, each of the transactions in years 1 through 4 is a reportable transaction with respect to X. Therefore, X has a section 6038A reporting and record maintenance requirement for each of those years.

Example 2. (i) The facts are the same as in *Example 1* of this paragraph (b)(9) except that, in year 1, W also forms and contributes assets to Y, another domestic limited liability company that does not elect to be treated as a corporation under § 301.7701-3(c) of this chapter. In year 1, X and Y form and contribute assets to Z, another domestic limited liability company that does not elect to be treated as a corporation under § 301.7701-3(c) of this chapter. In year 2, X transfers funds to Z. In year 3, Z makes a payment to Y. In year 4, Z distributes its assets to X and Y in liquidation.

(ii) In accordance with § 301.7701-3(b)(1)(ii) of this chapter, Y and Z are disregarded as entities separate from each other, W, and X. In accordance with § 301.7701-2(c)(2)(vi) of this chapter, Y, Z and X are treated as entities separate from each other and W, and are classified as domestic corporations for purposes of section 6038A. In accordance with paragraph (b)(3) of this section, each of the transactions in years 1 through 4 involving Z is a reportable transaction with respect to Z. Similarly, W's contribution to Y and Y's contribution to Z in year 1, the payment to Y in year 3, and the distribution to Y in year 4 are reportable transactions with respect to Y. Moreover, X's contribution to Z in Year 1, X's funds transfer to Z in year 2, and the distribution to X in year 4 are reportable transactions with respect to X. Therefore, Z has a section 6038A reporting and record maintenance requirement for years 1 through 4; Y has a section 6038A reporting and record maintenance requirement for years 1, 3, and 4; and X has a section 6038A reporting and record maintenance requirement in years 1, 2, and 4 in addition to its section 6038A reporting and record maintenance described in *Example 1* of this paragraph (b)(9).

(c) *Method of reporting.*—All statements required on or with the Form 5472 or Form 8991 under this section and § 1.6038A-5 must be in the English language. All amounts required to be reported under paragraph (b) of this section must be expressed in United States currency, with a statement of the exchange rates used, and, to the extent the forms may require, must indicate the method by which the amount of a reportable transaction or item was determined.

(d) *Time for filing returns.*—A Form 5472 and Form 8991 required under this section must be filed with the reporting corporation's income tax return for the taxable year by the due date (including extensions) of that return. In the case of an entity that is a reporting corporation as a result of being treated as a corporation under § 301.7701-2(c)(2)(vi) of this chapter, Form 5472 must be filed at such time and in such manner as the Commissioner may prescribe in forms or instructions.

(e) *Exceptions.*—(1) *No reportable transactions.*—A reporting corporation is not required to file Form 5472 if it has no transactions of the types listed in paragraphs (b)(3) and (4) of this section during the taxable year with any related party.

(2) *Transactions solely with a domestic reporting corporation.*—If all of a foreign reporting corporation's reportable transactions are with one or more related domestic reporting corporations that are not members of the same affiliated group, the foreign reporting corporation shall furnish on Form 5472 only the information required under paragraphs (b)(1) and (2) of this section, if the domestic reporting corporations provide the information required under paragraphs (b)(3) through (5) of this section. Such a foreign reporting corporation nonetheless is subject to the record maintenance requirements of § 1.6038A-3 and the requirements of §§ 1.6038A-5 and 1.6038A-6. The name, address, and taxpayer identification number of each domestic reporting corporation that provided such information must be indicated on Form 5472 in the space provided for the information under paragraphs (b)(1) and (2) of this section.

(3) *Transactions with a corporation subject to reporting under section 6038.*—A reporting corporation (other than an entity that is a reporting corporation as a result of being treated as a corporation under § 301.7701-2(c)(2)(vi) of this chapter) is not required to make a return of information on Form 5472 with respect to a related foreign corporation for a taxable year for which a U.S. person that controls the foreign related corporation makes a return of information on Form 5471 that is required under section 6038 and this section, if that return contains information required under § 1.6038-2(f)(11) with respect to the reportable transactions between the reporting corporation and the related corporation for that taxable year. Such a reporting corporation also is not subject to §§ 1.6038A-3 and 1.6038A-5. It remains subject to the general record maintenance requirements of section 6001.

(4) *Transactions with a foreign sales corporation.*—A reporting corporation (other than an entity that is a reporting corporation as a result of being treated as a corporation under § 301.7701-2(c)(2)(vi) of this chapter) is not required to make a return of information on Form

5472 with respect to a related corporation that qualifies as a foreign sales corporation for a taxable year for which the foreign sales corporation files Form 1120-FSC.

(f) *Filing Form 5472 when transactions with related parties engaged in by a partnership are attributed to a reporting corporation.*—If transactions engaged in by a partnership are attributed under § 1.6038A-1(e)(2) to a reporting corporation, the reporting corporation need report on Form 5472 only the percentage of the value of the transaction or transactions equal to the percentage of its partnership interest. Thus, for example, if a partnership buys $1000 of widgets from the foreign parent of a reporting corporation whose partnership interest in the partnership equals 50 percent of the partnership interests (and the remaining 50 percent is held by unrelated parties), the reporting corporation must report $500 of purchases from a foreign related party on Form 5472.

(g) *Effective/applicability date.*—Except as otherwise provided, for applicability dates for this section for certain reporting corporations, see § 1.6038A-1(n). Paragraph (b)(10) of this section applies with respect to information for annual accounting periods beginning on or after June 21, 2006. Paragraph (b)(7)(ix) of this section applies to taxable years beginning on or after June 7, 2021. Before these final regulations are applicable, a taxpayer will be treated as satisfying the reporting requirement described in § 1.59A-6(b)(2) only to the extent that it reports the aggregate amount of qualified derivative payments on Form 8991. *See* § 1.59A-6(b)(2)(iv) (transition period for qualified derivative payment reporting). Paragraph (b)(5)(iii) of this section applies with respect to information for annual accounting periods beginning on or after December 20, 2018. Paragraph (b)(5)(iv) of this section applies with respect to information for annual accounting periods beginning on or after March 4, 2019. [Reg. § 1.6038A-2.]

☐ [*T.D.* 8353, 6-14-91. *Amended by T.D.* 9113, 2-6-2004; *T.D.* 9161, 9-14-2004; *T.D.* 9268, 6-20-2006; *T.D.* 9338, 7-12-2007; *T.D.* 9529, 6-9-2011; *T.D.* 9667, 6-5-2014; *T.D.* 9707, 12-23-2014; *T.D.* 9796, 12-12-2016; *T.D.* 9885, 12-2-2019 (corrected 2-18-2020); *T.D.* 9896, 4-7-2020 and T.D. 9901, 7-9-2020.]

**[Reg. § 1.6038A-3]**

**§ 1.6038A-3. Record maintenance.**—(a) *General maintenance requirements.*—(1) *Section 6001 and section 6038A.*—A reporting corporation must keep the permanent books of account or records as required by section 6001 that are sufficient to establish the correctness of the federal income tax return of the corporation, including information, documents, or records ("records") to the extent they may be relevant to determine the correct U.S. tax treatment of transactions with related parties. Under section 6001, the District Director may require any person to make such returns, render such statements, or keep such specific records as will enable the District Director to determine whether or not that person is liable for any of the taxes to which the regulations under Part I have application. *See* section 6001 and the regulations thereunder. Such records must be permanent, accurate, and complete, and must clearly establish income, deductions, and credits. Additionally, in appropriate cases, such records include sufficient relevant cost data from which a profit and loss statement may be prepared for products or services transferred between a reporting corporation and its foreign related parties. This requirement includes records of the reporting corporation itself, as well as to records of any foreign related party that may be relevant to determine the correct U.S. tax treatment of transactions between the reporting corporation and foreign related parties. The relevance of such records with respect to related party transactions shall be determined upon the basis of all the facts and circumstances. Section 6038A and this section provide detailed guidance regarding the required maintenance of records with respect to such transactions and specify penalties for noncompliance. Banks and other financial institutions shall follow the specific record maintenance rules described in paragraph (h) of this section.

(2) *Safe harbor.*—A safe harbor for record maintenance is provided under paragraph (c) of this section, which sets forth detailed guidance concerning the types of records to be maintained with respect to related party transactions. The safe harbor consists of an all-inclusive list of record types that could be relevant to different taxpayers under a variety of facts and circumstances. It does not constitute a checklist of records that every reporting corporation must maintain or that generally should be requested by the Service. A specific reporting corporation is required to maintain, and the Service will request, only those records enumerated in the safe harbor (including material profit and loss statements) that may be relevant to its business or industry and to the correct U.S. tax treatment of its transactions with its foreign related parties. Accordingly, not every item listed in the safe harbor must be maintained by every reporting corporation. A corporation that maintains or causes another person to maintain the records listed in paragraph (c)(2) of this

section that may be relevant to its foreign related party transactions and to its business or industry will be deemed to have met the record maintenance requirements of section 6038A.

(3) *Examples.*—The following examples illustrate the rules of this paragraph.

*Example 1.* RC, a U.S. reporting corporation, is owned by two shareholders, F and P. F is a foreign corporation that owns 30 percent of the stock of RC. P is a domestic corporation that owns the remaining 70 percent. RC purchases tangible property from F; however, the only potential audit issue with respect to these transactions is their treatment under section 482. It is determined that F does not in fact control RC and the two corporations do not constitute a group of "controlled taxpayers" for purposes of section 482 and the regulations thereunder. There are no other reportable transactions between RC and F. Under §1.6038A-1(g), F is a foreign related party with respect to RC. Accordingly, RC is required to report its purchases of property from F under the reporting requirements of §1.6038A-2. Nevertheless, because section 482 is not applicable to the transactions between RC and F, the records created by F with respect to its sales to RC are not relevant for purposes of determining the correct tax treatment of these transactions. RC is required to maintain its own records of these transactions under the requirements of section 6001, but the transactions are not subject to the record maintenance requirements of this section. If, however, on audit it is determined that F does control RC, all records relevant to determining the arm's length consideration for the tangible property under section 482 will be subject to these requirements.

*Example 2.* FP, a foreign person, owns 30 percent of the stock of RC, a reporting corporation. The remaining 70 percent of RC stock is held by persons that are not 25-percent foreign shareholders. It is determined that FP is related to RC within the meaning of section 482 and the regulations thereunder. The only transactions between FP and RC are FP's capital contributions, dividends paid from RC to FP, and loans from FP to RC. Under section 6001, RC is required to maintain all documentation necessary to establish the U.S. tax treatment of the capital contributions, dividends, and loans. RC is not required to maintain records in other categories listed in paragraph (c)(3) of this section because they are not relevant to the transactions between FP and RC. Records of FP not related to these transactions are not subject to the record maintenance requirements under section 6038A(a) and this section.

*Example 3.* G, a foreign multinational group, creates Sub, a wholly-owned U.S. subsidiary, in order to purchase tangible property from unrelated parties in the United States and resell such property to G. The property purchased by Sub is either used in G's business or resold to other unrelated parties by G. Sub's sole function is to act as a buyer for G and these purchases are the only transactions that G has with any U.S. affiliates. Under all the facts and circumstances of this case, it is determined that an analysis of the group's worldwide profit attributable to the property it purchases from Sub is not relevant for purposes of determining the tax treatment of the sales from Sub to G. Therefore, the records with respect to the profitability of G are not subject to the record maintenance requirements of this section. However, all records related to the appropriate method under section 482 for determining an arm's-length consideration for the property sold by Sub to G are subject to the record maintenance requirements of this section.

*Example 4.* S, a U.S. reporting corporation, provides computer consulting services for its foreign parent, X. Based on the application of section 482 and the regulations, it is determined that the cost of services plus method, as described in §1.482-9(e), will provide the most reliable measure of an arm's length result, based on the facts and circumstances of the controlled transaction between S and X. S is required to maintain records to permit verification upon audit of the comparable transactional costs (as described in §1.482-9(e)(2)(iii)) used to calculate the arm's length price. Based on the facts and circumstances, if it is determined that X's records are relevant to determine the correct U.S. tax treatment of the controlled transaction between S and X, the record maintenance requirements under section 6038A(a) and this section will be applicable to the records of X.

(b) *Other maintenance requirements.*—(1) *Indirectly related records.*— This section applies to records that are directly or indirectly related to transactions between the reporting corporation and any foreign related parties. An example of records that are indirectly related to such transactions is records possessed by a foreign subsidiary of a foreign related party that document the raw material or component costs of a product that is manufactured or assembled by the subsidiary and sold as a finished product by the foreign related party to the reporting corporation.

(2) *Foreign related party or third-party maintenance.*—If records that are required to be maintained under this section are in the control of a foreign related party, the records may be obtained or compiled (if not already in the possession of the foreign related party or already

compiled) under the direction of the reporting corporation and then maintained by the reporting corporation, the foreign related party, or a third party. Thus, for example, a foreign related party may either itself maintain such records outside the United States or permit a third party to maintain such records outside the United States, provided that the conditions described in paragraph (f) of this section are met. Upon a request for such records by the Service, a foreign related party or third party may make arrangements with the District Director to furnish the records directly, rather than through the reporting corporation.

(3) *Translation of records.*—When records are provided to the Service under a request for production, any portion of such records must be translated into the English language within 30 days of a request for translation of that portion by the District Director. To the extent that any requested documents are identical to documents that have already been translated, an explanation of how such documents are identical instead may be provided. An extension of this time period may be requested under paragraph (f)(4) of this section. Appropriate extensions will be liberally granted for translation requests where circumstances warrant. If a good faith effort is made to translate accurately the requested documents within the specified time period, the reporting corporation will not be subject to the penalties in §§1.6038A-4 and 1.6038A-7.

(4) *Exception for foreign governments.*—A foreign government is not subject to the obligation to maintain records under this section.

(5) *Records relating to conduit financing arrangements.*—See §1.881-4 relating to conduit financing arrangements.

(c) *Specific records to be maintained for safe harbor.*—(1) *In general.*— A reporting corporation that maintains or causes another person to maintain the records specified in this paragraph (c) that are relevant to its business or industry and to the correct U.S. tax treatment of its transactions with its foreign related parties will be deemed to have met the record maintenance requirements of this section. This paragraph provides general descriptions of the categories of records to be maintained; the particular title or label applied by a reporting corporation or related party does not control. Functional equivalents of the specified documents are acceptable. Record maintenance in accordance with this safe harbor, however, requires only the maintenance of types of documents described in paragraph (c)(2) of this section that are directly or indirectly related to transactions between the reporting corporation and any foreign related party. Additionally, to the extent the reporting corporation establishes that records in a particular category are not applicable to the industry or business of the reporting corporation and any foreign related party, maintenance of such records is not required under this paragraph. Record maintenance in accordance with this paragraph (c) generally does not require the original creation of records that are ordinarily not created by the reporting corporation or its related parties. (If, however, a document that is actually created is described in this paragraph (c), it is to be maintained even if the document is not of the type ordinarily created by the reporting corporation or its related parties.) There are two exceptions to the rule. First, basic accounting records that are sufficient to document the U.S. tax effects of transactions between related parties must be created and retained, if they do not otherwise exist. Second, records sufficient to produce material profit and loss statements as described in paragraphs (c)(2)(ii) and (3) of this section that are relevant for determining the U.S. tax treatment of transactions between the reporting corporation and foreign related parties must be created if such records are not ordinarily maintained. All internal records storage and retrieval systems used for each taxable year must be retained.

(2) *Descriptions of categories of documents to be maintained.*—The following records must be maintained in order to satisfy this paragraph (c) to the extent they may be relevant to determine the correct U.S. tax treatment of transactions between the reporting corporation and any foreign related party.

(i) *Original entry books and transaction records.*—This category includes books and records of original entry or their functional equivalents, however designated or labelled, that are relevant to transactions between any foreign related party and the reporting corporation. Examples include, but are not limited to, general ledgers, sales journals, purchase order books, cash receipts books, cash disbursement books, canceled checks and bank statements, workpapers, sales contracts, and purchase invoices. Descriptive material to explicate entries in the foregoing types of records, such as a chart of accounts or an accounting policy manual, is included in this category.

(ii) *Profit and loss statements.*—This category includes records from which the reporting corporation can compile and supply, within a reasonable time, material profit and loss statements of the reporting corporation and all related parties as defined in §1.6038A-1(d) the "related party group") that reflect profit or loss of the related party group attributable to U.S.-connected products or services as defined in paragraph (c)(7)(i) of this section. The determination of whether a profit and loss statement is material is made under the rules provided in paragraph (c)(3) of this section. The material profit and loss statements described in this paragraph (c)(2)(ii) must reflect the consolidated revenue and expenses of all members of the related party group. Thus, records in this category include the documentation of the cost of raw materials used by a related party to manufacture finished goods that are then sold by another related party to the reporting corporation. The records should be kept under U.S. generally accepted accounting principles if they are ordinarily maintained in such manner; if not, an explanation of the material differences between the accounting principles used and U.S. generally accepted accounting principles must be made available. The statements need not reflect tracing of the actual costs borne by the group with respect to its U.S.-connected products or services; rather, any reasonable method may be used to allocate the group's worldwide costs to the revenues generated by the sales of those products or services. An explanation of the methods used to allocate specific items to a particular profit and loss statement must be made available. The explanation of material differences between accounting principles and the explanation of allocation methods must be sufficient to permit a comparison of the profitability of the group to that of the reporting corporation attributable to the provision of U.S.-connected products or services.

(iii) *Pricing documents.*—This category includes all documents relevant to establishing the appropriate price or rate for transactions between the reporting corporation and any foreign related party. Examples include, but are not limited to, documents related to transactions involving the same or similar products or services entered into by the reporting corporation or a foreign related party with related and unrelated parties; shipping and export documents; commission agreements; documents relating to production or assembly facilities; third-party and intercompany purchase invoices; manuals, specifications, and similar documents relating to or describing the performance of functions conducted at particular locations; intercompany correspondence discussing any instructions or assistance relating to such transactions provided to the reporting corporations by the related foreign person (or vice versa); intercompany and intracompany correspondence concerning the price or the negotiation of the price used in such transactions; documents related to the value and ownership of intangibles used or developed by the reporting corporation or the foreign related party; documents related to cost of goods sold and other expenses; and documents related to direct and indirect selling, and general and administrative expenses (for example, relating to advertising, sales promotions, or warranties).

(iv) *Foreign country and third party filings.*—This category includes financial and other documents relevant to transactions between a reporting corporation and any foreign related party filed with or prepared for any foreign government entity, any independent commission, or any financial institution.

(v) *Ownership and capital structure records.*—This category includes records or charts showing the relationship between the reporting corporation and the foreign related party; the location, ownership, and status (for example, joint venture, partnership, branch, or division) of all entities and offices directly or indirectly involved in the transactions between the reporting corporation and any foreign related party; a worldwide organization chart; records showing the management structure of all foreign affiliates; and loan documents, agreements, and other documents relating to any transfer of the stock of the reporting corporation that results in the change of the status of a foreign person as a foreign related party.

(vi) *Records of loans, services, and other non-sales transactions.*—This category includes relevant documents relating to loans (including all deposits by one foreign related party or reporting corporation with an unrelated party and a subsequent loan by that unrelated party to a foreign related party or reporting corporation that is in substance a direct loan between a reporting corporation and a foreign related party); guarantees of a foreign related party of debts of the reporting corporation, and vice versa; hedging arrangements or other risk shifting or currency risk shifting arrangements involving the reporting corporation and any foreign related party; security agreements between the reporting corporation and any foreign related party; research and development expense allocations between any foreign related party and the reporting corporation; service transactions between any foreign related party and the reporting corporation, including, for example, a description of the allocation of charges for management services, time or travel records, or allocation studies; import and export transactions between a reporting corporation and

any foreign related party; the registration of patents and copyrights with respect to transactions between the reporting corporation and any foreign related party; and documents regarding lawsuits in foreign countries that relate to such transactions between a reporting corporation and any foreign related party (for example, product liability suits for U.S. products).

(vii) *Records relating to conduit financing arrangements.*—See §1.881-4 relating to conduit financing arrangements.

(3) *Material profit and loss statements.*—For purposes of paragraph (c)(2)(ii) of this section, the determination of whether a profit and loss statement is material will be made according to the following rules. An agreement between the reporting corporation and the District Director as described in paragraph (e) of this section may identify material profit and loss statements of the related party group and describe the items to be included in any profit and loss statements for which records are to be maintained to satisfy the requirements of paragraph (c)(2)(ii) of this section. In the absence of such an agreement, a profit and loss statement will be material if it meets any of the following tests: the existing records test described in paragraph (c)(4) of this section, the significant industry segment test described in paragraph (c)(5) of this section, or the high profit test described in paragraph (c)(6) of this section.

(4) *Existing records test.*—A profit and loss statement is material under the existing records test described in this paragraph (c)(4) if any member of the related party group creates or compiles such statement in the course of its business operations and the statement reflects the profit or loss of the related party group attributable to the provision of U.S.-connected products or services (regardless of whether the profit and loss attributable to U.S.-connected products or services is shown separately or included within the calculation of aggregate figures on the statement). For example, a profit and loss statement is described in this paragraph if it was produced for internal accounting or management purposes, or for disclosure to shareholders, financial institutions, government agencies, or any other persons. Such existing statements and the records from which they were compiled (to the extent such records relate to profit and loss attributable to U.S.-connected products or services) are subject to the record maintenance requirements described in paragraph (c)(2)(ii) of this section.

(5) *Significant industry segment test.*—(i) *In general.*—A profit and loss statement is material under the significant industry segment test described in this paragraph (c)(5) if—

(A) The statement reflects the profit or loss of the related party group attributable to the group's provision of U.S.-connected products or services within a single industry segment (as defined in paragraph (c)(7)(ii) of this section);

(B) The worldwide gross revenue attributable to such industry segment is 10 percent or more of the worldwide gross revenue attributable to the group's combined industry segments; and

(C) The amount of gross revenue earned by the group from the provision of U.S.-connected products or services within such industry segment is $25 million or more in the taxable year.

(ii) *Form of the statements.*—Profit and loss statements compiled for the group's provision of U.S.-connected products or services in each significant industry segment must reflect revenues and expenses attributable to the operations in such segment by all members of the related party group. Statements may show each related party's revenues and expenses separately, or may be prepared in a consolidated format. Any reasonable method may be used to allocate the group's worldwide costs within the industry segment to the U.S.-connected products or services within that segment. An explanation of the methods used to prepare consolidated statements and to allocate specific items to a particular profit and loss statement must be made available, and the records from which the consolidations and allocations were prepared must be maintained.

(iii) *Special rule for component sales.*—Where the U.S.-connected products or services consist of components that are incorporated into other products or services before sale to customers, the portion of the total gross revenue derived from sales of the finished products or services attributable to the components may be determined on the basis of relative costs of production. Thus, where relevant for determining whether the $25 million threshold in paragraph (c)(5)(i)(C) of this section has been met, the amount of gross revenue derived by the related party group from the provision of the finished products or services may be reduced by multiplying it by a fraction, the numerator of which is the costs of production of the related party group attributable to the component products or services that constitute U.S.-connected products or services and the denominator of which is the costs of production of the related party group attributable to the finished products in which such components are incorporated.

(iv) *Level of specificity required.*—In applying the significant industry segment test of this paragraph (c)(5), groups of related products and services must be chosen to provide a reasonable level of specificity that results in the greatest number of separate significant industry segments in comparison to other possible classifications. This determination must be made on the basis of the particular facts presented by the operations of the related party group. The following rules, however, provide general guidelines for making such classifications. First, the related party group's operations that involve the provision of U.S.-connected products should be grouped into product lines. The rules of this paragraph (c)(5) should then be applied to determine if any such product line would, standing alone, constitute a significant industry segment when compared to the related party group's operations as a whole. Any significant industry segments determined at the level of product lines should be further segregated, and tested for significant industry segments, at the level of separate products. Finally, any significant industry segments determined at the level of separate products should be segregated, and tested for significant industry segments, at the level of separate models. Similar principles should be applied in classifying and testing types of services. A profit and loss statement reflecting the related party group's provision of any product or service (or group of products or services as classified under these rules) that constitutes a significant industry segment will be considered material for purposes of this paragraph (c)(5). For definitions of the terms "product", "related products or services", "model", and "product line", see paragraph (c)(7) of this section.

(v) *Examples.*—The rules for determining reasonable levels of specificity for significant industry segments may be illustrated by the following examples.

*Example 1.* A related party group is engaged in the manufacture and worldwide sales of automobiles and aftermarket parts. The group's operations within the categories of "automobiles" and "aftermarket parts" are each sufficient to constitute significant industry segments for the group under the rules of this paragraph (c)(5). No narrower classification of aftermarket parts results in any significant industry segments. Automobiles produced by the group are generally classified for marketing purposes by trade names; aggregating groups of automobiles by these trade names results in three significant industry segments, those for trade names A, B, and C. Finally, two car models sold under the trade name A ("A1" and "A2") and one car model sold under the trade name B ("B3"), produce sufficient revenue to constitute significant industry segments. Such classifications into trade names and car models are generally used in the related party group's industry; moreover, different types of classifications would produce fewer significant industry segments. Accordingly, a reasonable level of specificity for this related party group's industry segments would be eight categories of products consisting of "automobiles", "aftermarket parts", "A", "B", "C", "A1", "A2", and "B3".

*Example 2.* A related party group is engaged in manufacturing electronic goods that are distributed at retail in the United States by the reporting corporation. The group sells three types of products in the United States: televisions, radios, and video cassette recorders (VCRs). Each of these three broad product areas constitutes a significant industry segment for the group as a whole. VCRs can be further segregated by price into high-end and low-end models, and the provision of each constitutes a significant industry segment for the group. Revenues from only one VCR model, model number VCRX-10, are sufficiently large to make the provision of that model a significant industry segment. With respect to televisions, the group normally accounts for these products by size. Using this classification, portable televisions, medium-sized televisions, and consoles each constitute significant industry segments. Narrower classifications by television model numbers result in no additional significant industry segments. Finally, a single radio product line, those sold under the trade name R, produces sufficient revenue to constitute a significant industry segment, but no other radio models or product groups are large enough to constitute a significant industry segment. In each case, these classifications conform to normal business practices in the industry and result in the greatest possible number of significant industry segments for this related party group. Accordingly, a reasonable level of specificity for this related party group's industry segments would include the ten categories consisting of "VCRs", "high-end VCRs", "low-end VCRs", "model number VCRX-10", "televisions", "portable televisions", "medium-sized televisions", "console televisions", "radios", and "radio trade name R".

(6) *High profit test.*—(i) *In general.*—A profit and loss statement is material under the high profit test described in this paragraph (c)(6) if—

(A) The statement reflects the profit or loss of the related party group attributable to the group's provision of U.S.-connected

products or services within a single industry segment (as defined in paragraph (c)(7)(ii) of this section);

(B) The amount of gross revenue earned by the group from the provision of U.S.-connected products or services within such industry segment is $100 million or more in the taxable year; and

(C) The return on assets test described in paragraph (c)(6)(ii) of this section is satisfied with respect to the products and services attributable to such segment.

Accordingly, a significant industry segment (as determined under paragraph (c)(5) of this section) must be divided into any narrower industry segments that meet the high profit test of this paragraph (c)(6), even if such narrower segments would not, standing alone, meet the significant industry segment test of paragraph (c)(5) of this section.

(ii) *Return on assets test.*—An industry segment meets the return on assets test if the rate of return on assets earned by the related party group on its worldwide operations within this industry segment exceeds 15 percent, and is at least 200 percent of the return on assets earned by the group in all industry segments combined. For purposes of this paragraph, the rate of return on assets earned by an industry segment is determined by dividing that segment's operating profit (as defined in paragraph (c)(7)(v) of this section) by its identifiable assets (as defined in paragraph (c)(7)(iv) of this section).

(iii) *Additional rules.*—The rules in paragraphs (c)(5)(ii) through (iv) of this section describing the application of the significant industry segment test shall apply in a similar manner for purposes of the high profit test.

(7) *Definitions.*—The following definitions apply for purposes of paragraphs (c)(2)(ii), (c)(5), and (c)(6) of this section.

(i) *U.S.-connected products or services.*—The term "U.S.-connected products or services" means products or services that are imported to or exported from the United States by transfers between the reporting corporation and any of its foreign related parties.

(ii) *Industry segment.*—An industry segment is a segment of the related party group's combined operations that is engaged in providing a product or service or a group of related products or services (as defined in paragraph (c)(7)(vii) of this section) primarily to customers that are not members of the related party group.

(iii) *Gross revenue of an industry segment.*—Gross revenue of an industry segment includes receipts (prior to reduction for cost of goods sold) both from sales to customers outside of the related party group and from sales or transfers to other industry segments within the related party group (but does not include sales or transfers between members of the related party group within the same industry segment). Interest from sources outside the related party group and interest earned on trade receivables between industry segments is included in gross revenue if the asset on which the interest is earned is included among the industry segment's identifiable assets, but interest earned on advances or loans to other industry segments is not included.

(iv) *Identifiable assets of an industry segment.*—The identifiable assets of an industry segment are those tangible and intangible assets of the related party group that are used by the industry segment, including assets that are used exclusively by that industry segment and an allocated portion of assets used jointly by two or more industry segments. The value of an identifiable asset may be determined using any reasonable method (such as book value or fair market value) applied consistently. Any allocation of assets among industry segments must be made on a reasonable basis, and a description of such basis must be provided. Assets of an industry segment that transfers products or services to another industry segment shall not be allocated to the receiving segment. Assets that represent part of the related party group's investment in an industry segment, such as goodwill, shall be included in the industry segment's identifiable assets. Assets maintained for general corporate purposes (that is, those not used in the operations of any industry segment) shall not be allocated to industry segments.

(v) *Operating profit of an industry segment.*—The operating profit of an industry segment is its gross revenue (as defined in paragraph (c)(7)(iii) of this section) minus all operating expenses. None of the following shall be added or deducted in computing the operating profit of an industry segment: revenue earned at the corporate level and not derived from the operations of any industry segment; general corporate expenses; interest expense; domestic and foreign income taxes; and other extraordinary items not reflecting the ongoing business operations of the industry segment.

(vi) *Product.*—The term "product" means an item of property (or combination of component parts) that is the result of a production process, is primarily sold to unrelated parties (or incorporated by the related party group into other products sold to unrelated parties), and performs a specific function.

(vii) *Related products or services.*—The term "related products or services" means groupings of products and types of services that reflect reasonable accounting, marketing, or other business practices within the industries in which the related party group operates.

(viii) *Model.*—The term "model" means a classification of products that incorporate particular components, options, styles, and any other unique features resulting in product differentiation. Examples of models are electronic products that are sold or accounted for under a single model number and automobiles sold under a single model name.

(ix) *Product line.*—The term "product line" means a group of products that are aggregated into a single classification for accounting, marketing, or other business purposes. Examples of product lines are groups of products that perform similar functions; products that are marketed under the same trade names, brand names, or trademarks; and products that are related economically (that is, having similar rates of profitability, similar degrees of risk, and similar opportunities for growth).

(8) *Example.*—The application of the rules for determining material profit and loss statements under paragraphs (c)(4) through (7) of this section is illustrated by the following example.

*Example. (i) Facts.* A multinational enterprise manufactures 50 different agricultural and chemical products that are sold through Sub1, its wholly owned U.S. subsidiary, and other subsidiaries located in foreign countries. The parent company of the enterprise, P, is a foreign corporation. The corporations participating in the enterprise form a related party group, and Sub1 is a reporting corporation for purposes of section 6038A. Under the facts and circumstances of this case, an analysis of the group's worldwide profit attributable to its products sold in the U.S. is relevant for determining an arm's length consideration under section 482 for the transfers of goods between Sub1 and its foreign affiliates.

(ii) *Existing records test.* For management purposes, the group prepares profit and loss statements that are segmented by sales in different geographic markets. One of these statements shows the combined worldwide profitability of the group. Another statement shows the profitability of the group attributable to its North American sales. Both of these profit and loss statements reflect aggregate figures that include sales to unrelated parties of products that have been transferred from P and other group members to Sub1 (that is, the group's "U.S.-connected products"). The two statements meet the existing records test described in paragraph (c)(4) of this section.

(iii) *Significant industry segments.* The group's worldwide gross revenue in all industry segments is $2 billion. An analysis of the group's 50 products demonstrates that they are reasonably grouped into eight industry segments (each of which earns roughly $250 million in worldwide gross revenue). Segments 1 through 6 relate to agricultural products and Segments 7 and 8 relate to other chemical products. More specific categories would result in groupings that generate less than 10 percent of the group's worldwide gross revenue (that is, less than $200 million each); these narrower categories would thus fail the gross revenue percentage test of paragraph (c)(5)(i)(B) of this section. The gross revenue in each of the eight segments from the sale to unrelated parties of U.S.-connected products is as follows: $180 million for Segment 1; $30 million for Segment 2; and less than $25 million for each of Segments 3 through 8. Under the $25 million threshold test of paragraph (c)(5)(i)(C) of this section, the group's significant industry segments are thus limited to Segments 1 and 2. In addition, the combined operations of the group related to agricultural products (encompassing Segments 1 through 6 on an aggregated basis), constitute a single significant industry segment.

(iv) *High profit test.* One highly profitable product line within Segment 1, HPPL, accounts for $120 million gross revenue from Sub1's domestic sales of U.S.-connected products (and thus exceeds the $100 million gross revenue threshold in paragraph (c)(6)(i)(B) of this section). The return on the identifiable assets attributable to the HPPL product line is 85 percent, which is more than 15 percent and more than twice the return on assets earned by the group from its worldwide operations in its combined industry segments. The group's industry segment for HPPL thus meets the high profit test described in paragraph (c)(6) of this section.

(v) *Material Profit and Loss Statements.* The group's material profit and loss statements consist of statements for combined worldwide sales and North American sales (under the existing records test); Segment 1, Segment 2, and aggregated Segments 1-6 (under the significant industry segment test); and HPPL (under the high profit test). Under paragraph (c) of this section, Sub1 is required to retain the combined worldwide sales and North American sales profit and loss statements and to maintain sufficient records so that it can compile and supply upon request statements of the group's profit-

ability from sales of its U.S.-connected products within Segment 1, Segment 2, aggregated Segments 1-6, and HPPL. These records need not be in the possession of Sub1 and may be kept under the control of and produced by P or any third party. The statements for Segment 1, Segment 2, aggregated Segments 1-6, and HPPL do not require tracing of actual costs to the U.S.-connected products; rather, these statements may be prepared by using any reasonable method to allocate a portion of the industry segment's overall operating costs to the sales of U.S.-connected products within that segment.

(d) *Liability for certain partnership record maintenance.*—A reporting corporation to which transactions engaged in by a partnership are attributed under § 1.6038A-1(e)(2) is subject to the record maintenance requirements of this section to the extent of the transactions so attributed.

(e) *Agreements with the District Director.*—(1) *In general.*—The District Director who has audit jurisdiction over the reporting corporation may negotiate and enter into an agreement with a reporting corporation that establishes the records the reporting corporation must maintain or cause another to maintain, how the records must be maintained, the period of retention for the records, and by whom the records must be maintained in order to satisfy the reporting corporation's obligations under this section.

(2) *Content of agreement.*—(i) *In general.*—The agreement may include provisions relating to the authorization of agent requirement, the record maintenance requirement, and the production and translation time periods that vary the rules contained in these regulations under section 6038A. The District Director will generally require a reporting corporation to maintain only those records specified under the safe harbor provisions of paragraph (c) of this section that permit an adequate audit of the income tax return of the reporting corporation and to provide such authorizations of agent that permit adequate access to such records. In most instances, required record maintenance for a particular reporting corporation under a negotiated agreement will be less than the broad range of records described under the safe harbor provisions. Additionally, a provision specifying the effective date and the expiration date of the agreement that may vary the effective date of the regulations may be included.

(ii) *Significant industry segment test.*—A District Director may determine which industry segment profit and loss statements are material for purposes of requiring the maintenance of records (under either paragraph (a)(1) of this section or the safe harbor described in paragraph (a)(2) of this section). The industry segments that the District Director determines are material need not be the industry segments that meet the significant industry segment test under paragraph (c)(5) of this section or the high profit test under paragraph (c)(6) of this section. For this purpose, a reporting corporation will be required to maintain only those records from which profit and loss statements for the related party group may be constructed with respect to industry segments identified by the District Director. To the extent that existing profit and loss statements are similar in scope and level of detail to statements for industry segments that would otherwise be described under the tests of paragraphs (c)(5) and (6) of this section, the District Director shall accept the existing statements instead of the statements that would otherwise be required under paragraphs (c)(5) and (6) of this section.

(iii) *Example.*—The following example illustrates the rules of paragraph (e)(2)(ii) of this section.

*Example.* The District Director determines that RC, a reporting corporation that is a manufacturer of related chemical products, has two industry segments, Segment 1 and Segment 2. While both industry segments meet the significant industry segment test of paragraph (c)(5) of this section, Segment 1 has a relatively low volume of sales to foreign related parties. Additionally, Segment 1 consists of products that produce only a small profit margin because the product is generic and other companies also sell the product. The District Director enters into an agreement with RC that requires only records from which a profit and loss statement for the related party group can be constructed for Segment 2. Therefore, RC is not required to maintain records for Segment 1 from which a profit and loss statement for the related party group can be constructed. The other record maintenance requirements under this section apply, however.

(3) *Circumstances of agreement.*—The District Director generally will enter into an agreement under this paragraph (e) upon request by the reporting corporation when the District Director believes that the District has or can obtain sufficient knowledge of the business or industry of the reporting corporation to limit the record maintenance requirement to particular documents.

(4) *Agreement as part of APA process.*—An agreement with a reporting corporation under this paragraph (e) may be entered into as a part of the Advance Pricing Agreement (APA) process at any time

during the APA process, insofar as the agreement relates to the subject matter of the APA.

(f) *U.S. maintenance.*—(1) *General rule.*—Records that must be maintained under this section must be maintained within the United States, unless the conditions described in paragraph (f)(2) of this section are met.

(2) *Non-U.S. maintenance requirements.*—A reporting corporation may maintain outside the United States records not ordinarily maintained in the United States but required to be maintained in the United States under this section. However, the reporting corporation must either:

(i) Deliver to the Service the original documents (or duplicates) requested within 60 days of the request by the Service for such records and provide translations of such documents within 30 days of a request for translations of specific documents; or

(ii) Move the original documents (or duplicates) requested to the United States within 60 days of the request of the Service for such records; provide the Service with an index to the requested records, the name and address of a custodian located within the United States having control over the records, and the address where the records are located within 60 days of the Service's request for the records; and continue to maintain the records within the United States throughout the period of retention described in paragraph (g) of this section. For summons procedures with respect to records that have been moved to the United States, see sections 6038A(e), 7602, 7603, and 7604.

With respect to any material profit and loss statements required to be created (either under paragraph (c) of this section or under an agreement with the District Director), unless otherwise specified, "120 days" shall be substituted for "60 days" in this paragraph (f)(2), and labels and text with respect to such statements must be in the English language.

(3) *Prior taxable years.*—The non-U.S. maintenance requirements described in paragraph (f)(2) of this section apply to records located outside the United States that were in existence on or after March 20, 1990, without regard to the taxable year to which such records relate.

(4) *Scheduled production for high volume or other reasons.*—Upon a written request, for good cause shown, the District Director may grant an extension of the time for the production or translation of the requested documents. Such requests should be made within 30 days of the request for records by the Service. If an extension is needed because of the volume of records requested or the amount of translation requested, the District Director may allow production or translation to be scheduled over a period of time so that not all records need be produced or translated at the same time.

(5) *Required U.S. maintenance.*—The District Director (with the concurrence of the Assistant Commissioner (International)), may require, for cause, the maintenance within the United States of any records specified in paragraph (f)(1) of this section. Such a requirement will be imposed only if there exists a clear pattern of failure to maintain or timely produce the required records. The assessment of a monetary penalty under section 6038A(d) and § 1.6038A-4 for failure to maintain records is not necessarily sufficient to require the maintenance of records within the United States.

(g) *Period of retention.*—Records required to be maintained by section 6038A(a) and this section shall be kept as long as they may be relevant or material to determining the correct tax treatment of any transaction between the reporting corporation and a related party, but in no case less than the applicable statute of limitations on assessment and collection with respect to the taxable year in which the transaction or item to which the records relate affects the U.S. tax liability of the reporting corporation. *See* section 6001 and the regulations thereunder.

(h) *Application of record maintenance rules to banks and other financial institutions.*—[Reserved].

(i) *Effective/applicability date.*—(1) *In general.*—This section is generally applicable on December 10, 1990. However, records described in this section in existence on or after March 20, 1990, must be maintained, without regard to when the taxable year to which the records relate began. Paragraph (a)(3) *Example 4* of this section is generally applicable for taxable years beginning after July 31, 2009.

(2) *Election to apply regulation to earlier taxable years.*—A person may elect to apply the provisions of paragraph (a)(3) *Example 4* of this section to earlier taxable years in accordance with the rules set forth in § 1.482-9(n)(2). [Reg. § 1.6038A-3.]

☐ [*T.D.* 8353, 6-14-91. *Amended by T.D.* 8611, 8-10-95; *T.D.* 9278, 7-31-2006 *and T.D.* 9456, 7-31-2009.]

**[Reg. § 1.6038A-4]**

**§ 1.6038A-4. Monetary penalty.**—(a) *Imposition of monetary penalty.*—(1) *In general.*—If a reporting corporation fails to furnish the information described in § 1.6038A-2 within the time and manner prescribed in § 1.6038A-2(d), fails to maintain or cause another to maintain records as required by § 1.6038A-3, or (in the case of records maintained outside the United States) fails to meet the non-U.S. record maintenance requirements within the applicable time prescribed in § 1.6038A-3(f), a penalty of $25,000 shall be assessed for each taxable year with respect to which such failure occurs. The filing of a substantially incomplete Form 5472 constitutes a failure to file Form 5472. Where, however, the information described in § 1.6038A-2(b)(3) through Reg. § (5) is not required to be reported, a Form 5472 filed without such information is not a substantially incomplete Form 5472.

(2) *Liability for certain partnership transactions.*—A reporting corporation to which transactions engaged in by a partnership are attributed under § 1.6038A-1(e)(2) is subject to the rules of this section to the extent failures occur with respect to the partnership transactions so attributed.

(3) *Calculation of monetary penalty.*—If a reporting corporation fails to maintain records as required by § 1.6038A-3 of transactions with multiple related parties, the monetary penalty may be assessed for each failure to maintain records with respect to each related party. The monetary penalty, however, shall be imposed on a reporting corporation only once for a taxable year with respect to each related party for a failure to furnish the information required on Form 5472, for a failure to maintain or cause another to maintain records, or for a failure to comply with the non-U.S. maintenance requirements described in § 1.6038A-3(f). An additional penalty for another failure may be imposed, however, under the rules of paragraph (d)(2) of this section. Thus, unless such failures continue after notification as described in paragraph (d) of this section, the maximum penalty under this paragraph with respect to each related party for all such failures in a taxable year is $25,000. The members of a group of corporations filing a consolidated return are jointly and severally liable for any monetary penalty that may be imposed under this section.

(b) *Reasonable cause.*—(1) *In general.*—Certain failures may be excused for reasonable cause, including not timely filing Form 5472, not maintaining or causing another to maintain records as required by § 1.6038A-3, and not complying with the non-U.S. maintenance requirements described in § 1.6038A-3(f). If an affirmative showing is made that the taxpayer acted in good faith and there is reasonable cause for a failure that results in the assessment of the monetary penalty, the period during which reasonable cause exists shall be treated as beginning on the day reasonable cause is established and ending not earlier than the last day on which reasonable cause existed for any such failure. Additionally, the beginning of the 90-day period after mailing of a notice by the District Director or the Director of an Internal Revenue Service Center of a failure described in paragraph (d) of this section shall be treated as not earlier than the last day on which reasonable cause existed.

(2) *Affirmative showing required.*—(i) *In general.*—To show that reasonable cause exists for purposes of paragraph (b)(1) of this section, the reporting corporation must make an affirmative showing of all the facts alleged as reasonable cause for the failure in a written statement containing a declaration that it is made under penalties of perjury. The statement must be filed with the District Director (in the case of failure to maintain or furnish requested information permitted to be maintained outside the United States within the time required under § 1.6038A-3(f) or a failure to file Form 5472) or the Director of the Internal Revenue Service Center where the Form 5472 is required to be filed (in the case of failure to file Form 5472). The District Director or the Director of the Internal Revenue Service Center where the Form 5472 is required to be filed, as appropriate, shall determine whether the failure was due to reasonable cause, and if so, the period of time for which reasonable cause existed. If a return has been filed as required by § 1.6038A-2 or records have been maintained as required by § 1.6038A-3, except for an omission of, or error with respect to, some of the information required or a record to be maintained, the omission or error shall not constitute a failure for purposes of section 6038A(d) if the reporting corporation that filed the return establishes to the satisfaction of the District Director or the Director of the Internal Revenue Service Center that it has substantially complied with the filing of Form 5472 or the requirement to maintain records.

(ii) *Small corporations.*—The District Director shall apply the reasonable cause exception liberally in the case of a small corporation that had no knowledge of the requirements imposed by section 6038A; has limited presence in and contact with the United States; and promptly and fully complies with all requests by the District

Director to file Form 5472, and to furnish books, records, or other materials relevant to the reportable transaction. A small corporation is a corporation whose gross receipts for a taxable year are $20,000,000 or less.

(iii) *Facts and circumstances taken into account.*—The determination of whether a taxpayer acted with reasonable cause and in good faith is made on a case-by-case basis, taking into account all pertinent facts and circumstances. Circumstances that may indicate reasonable cause and good faith include an honest misunderstanding of fact or law that is reasonable in light of the experience and knowledge of the taxpayer. Isolated computational or transcriptional errors generally are not inconsistent with reasonable cause and good faith. Reliance upon an information return or on the advice of a professional (such as an attorney or accountant) does not necessarily demonstrate reasonable cause and good faith. Similarly, reasonable cause and good faith is not necessarily indicated by reliance on facts that, unknown to the taxpayer, are incorrect. Reliance on an information return, professional advice or other facts, however, constitutes reasonable cause and good faith if, under all the circumstances, the reliance was reasonable. A taxpayer, for example, may have reasonable cause for not filing a Form 5472 or for not maintaining records under section 6038A if the taxpayer has a reasonable belief that it is not owned by a 25-percent foreign shareholder. A reasonable belief means that the taxpayer does not know or has no reason to know that it is owned by a 25-percent foreign shareholder. For example, a reporting corporation would not know or have reason to know that it is owned by a 25-percent foreign shareholder if its belief that it is not so owned is consistent with other information reported or otherwise furnished to or known by the reporting corporation. A taxpayer may have reasonable cause for not treating a foreign corporation as a related party for purposes of section 6038A where the foreign corporation is a related party solely by reason of §1.6038A-1(d)(3) (under the principles of section 482), and the taxpayer had a reasonable belief that its relationship with the foreign corporation did not meet the standards for related parties under section 482.

(c) *Failure to maintain records or to cause another to maintain records.*— A failure to maintain records or to cause another to maintain records is determined by the District Director upon the basis of the reporting corporation's overall compliance (including compliance with the non-U.S. maintenance requirements under §1.6038A-3(f)(2)) with the record maintenance requirements. It is not an item-by-item determination. Thus, for example, a failure to maintain a single or small number of items may not constitute a failure for purposes of section 6038A(d), unless the item or items are essential to the correct determination of transactions between the reporting corporation and any foreign related parties. The District Director shall notify the reporting corporation in writing of any determination that it has failed to comply with the record maintenance requirement.

(d) *Increase in penalty where failure continues after notification.*— (1) *In general.*—If any failure described in this section continues for more than 90 days after the day on which the District Director or the Director of the Internal Revenue Service Center where the Form 5472 is required to be filed mails notice of the failure to the reporting corporation, the reporting corporation shall pay a penalty (in addition to the penalty described in paragraph (a) of this section) of $25,000 with respect to each related party for which a failure occurs for each 30-day period during which the failure continues after the expiration of the 90-day period. Any uncompleted fraction of a 30-day period shall count as a 30-day period for purposes of this paragraph (d).

(2) *Additional penalty for another failure.*—An additional penalty for a taxable year may be imposed, however, if at a time subsequent to the time of the imposition of the monetary penalty described in paragraph (a) of this section, a second failure is determined and the second failure continues after notification under paragraph (d)(1) of this section. Thus, if a taxpayer fails to file Form 5472 and is assessed a monetary penalty and later, upon audit, is determined to have failed to maintain records, an additional penalty for the failure to maintain records may be assessed under the rules of this paragraph if the failure to maintain records continues after notification under this paragraph.

(3) *Cessation of accrual.*—The monetary penalty will cease to accrue if the reporting corporation either files Form 5472 (in the case of a failure to file Form 5472), furnishes information to substantially complete Form 5472, or demonstrates compliance with respect to the maintenance of records (in the case of a failure to maintain records) for the taxable year in which the examination occurs and subsequent years to the satisfaction of the District Director. The monetary penalty also will cease to accrue if requested information, documents, or records, kept outside the United States under the requirements of §1.6038A-3(f) and not produced within the time specified are pro-

duced or moved to the United States under the rules of paragraph (f)(2)(ii) of this section.

(4) *Continued failures.*—If a failure under this section relating to a taxable year beginning before July 11, 1989 occurs, and if the failure continues following 90 days after the notice of failure under this paragraph is sent, the amount of the additional penalty to be assessed under this paragraph is $25,000 for each 30-day period beginning after November 5, 1990, during which the failure continues. There is no limitation on the amount of the monetary penalty that may be assessed after November 5, 1990.

(e) *Other penalties.*—For criminal penalties for failure to file a return and filing a false or fraudulent return, see sections 7203 and 7206 of the Code. For the penalty relating to an underpayment of tax, see section 6662.

(f) *Examples.*—The following examples illustrate the rules of this section.

(1) *Example 1—Failure to file Form 5472.* Corp X, a U.S. reporting corporation, engages in related party transactions with FC. Corp X does not timely file a Form 5472 or maintain records relating to the transactions with FC for Year 1 or subsequent years. The Service Center with which Corp X files its income tax return imposes a $25,000 penalty for each of Years 1, 2, and 3 under section 6038A(d) and this section for failure to provide information as required on Form 5472 and mails a notice of failure to provide information. Corp X does not file Form 5472. Ninety days following the mailing of the notice of failure to Corp X an additional penalty of $25,000 is imposed. On the 135th day following the mailing of the notice of failure, Corp X files Form 5472 for Years 1, 2, and 3. The total penalty owed by Corp X for Year 1 is $75,000 ($25,000 for not timely filing Form 5472, $25,000 for the first 30-day period following the expiration of the 90-day period, and $25,000 for the fraction of the second 30-day period). The penalty for Years 2 and 3 for the failure to file Form 5472 is also $75,000 for each year, calculated in the same manner as for Year 1. The total penalty for failure to file Form 5472 for Years 1, 2, and 3 is $225,000.

(2) *Example 2—Failure to maintain records.* Assume the same facts as in *Example 1.* In Year 5, Corp X is audited for Years 1 through 3. Corp X has not been maintaining records relating to the transactions with FC. The District Director issues a notice of failure to maintain records. Corp X has already been subject to the monetary penalty of $25,000 for each of Years 1, 2, and 3 for failure to file Form 5472 and, therefore, a monetary penalty under paragraph (a) of this section for failure to maintain records is not assessed. However, an additional penalty is assessed after the 90th day following the mailing of the notice of failure to maintain records. Corp X develops a record maintenance system as required by section 6038A and §1.6038A-3. On the 180th day following the mailing of the notice of failure to maintain records, Corp X demonstrates to the satisfaction of the District Director that the newly developed record maintenance system will comply with the requirements of §1.6038A-3 and the increase in the monetary penalty after notification ceases to accrue. The additional penalty for failure to maintain records is $75,000. An additional penalty of $75,000 per year is assessed for each of years 2 and 3 for the failure to maintain records for a total of $225,000.

(g) *Effective dates.*—For effective dates for this section, see §1.6038A-1(n). [Reg. §1.6038A-4.]

☐ [T.D. 8353, 6-14-91. *Amended by T.D. 9707, 12-23-2014 and T.D. 9885, 12-2-2019.*]

**[Reg. §1.6038A-5]**

**§1.6038A-5. Authorization of agent.**—(a) *Failure to authorize.*— The rules of §1.6038A-7 shall apply to any transaction between a foreign related party and a reporting corporation (including any transaction engaged in by a partnership that is attributed to the reporting corporation under §1.6038A-1(e)(2)), unless the foreign related party authorizes (in the manner described in paragraph (b) of this section) the reporting corporation to act as its limited agent solely for purposes of sections 7602, 7603, and 7604 with respect to any request by the Service to examine records or produce testimony that may be relevant to the tax treatment of such a transaction or with respect to any summons by the Service for such records or testimony. The fact that a reporting corporation is authorized to act as an agent for a foreign related party is to be disregarded for purposes of determining whether the foreign related party either has a trade or business in the United States for purposes of the Code or a permanent establishment or fixed base in the United States for purposes of an income tax treaty.

(b) *Authorization by related party.*—(1) *In general.*—Upon request by the Service, a foreign related party shall authorize as its agent (solely for purposes of sections 7602, 7603, and 7604) the reporting corporation with which it engages in transactions. The authorization must be signed by the foreign related party or an officer of the foreign related party possessing the authority to authorize an agent for purposes of Rule 4 of the Federal Rules of Civil Procedure. The reporting corporation will accept this appointment by providing a statement to that effect, signed by an officer of the reporting corporation possessing the authority to accept such an appointment. The agency shall be effective at all times. For taxable years beginning after July 10, 1989, the authorization and acceptance must be provided to the Service within 30 days of a request by the Service to the reporting corporation for such an authorization. The authorization must contain a heading and statement as set forth below. A foreign government is not subject to the authorization of agent requirement.

## AUTHORIZATION OF AGENT

"[Name of foreign related party] hereby expressly authorizes [name of reporting corporation] to act as its agent solely for purposes of sections 7602, 7603, and 7604 of the Internal Revenue Code with respect to any request to examine records or produce testimony that may be relevant to the U.S. income tax treatment of any transaction between [name of the above-named foreign related party] and [name of reporting corporation] or with respect to any summons for such records or testimony.

_____     _____     _____

Signature of or for [name of foreign related party]     (Title)     (Date)
(If signed by a corporate officer, partner, or fiduciary on behalf of a foreign related party: I certify that I have the authority to execute this authorization of agent to act on behalf of [name of foreign related party]).

_____

Type or print your name below if signing for a foreign related party that is not an individual.

_____

[Name of reporting corporation] accepts this appointment to act as agent for [name of foreign related party] for the above purpose.

_____     _____     _____

Signature for [Name of Reporting Corporation]     (Title)     (Date)
I certify that I have the authority to accept this appointment to act as agent on behalf of [name of foreign related party] and agree to accept service of process for the above purposes.
Type or print your name below.

(2) *Authorization for prior years.*—A foreign related party shall authorize a reporting corporation to act as its agent with respect to taxable years for which a Form 5472 is required to be filed prior to the date on which the final regulations under section 6038A are published by providing the above executed authorization of agent within 30 days of a request by the Service for such an authorization.

(c) *Foreign affiliated groups.*—(1) *In general.*—A foreign corporation that has effective legal authority to make the authorization of agent under paragraph (b) of this section on behalf of any group of foreign related parties may execute such an authorization for any members of the group. A single authorization may be made on a consolidated basis. In such a case, the common parent must attach a schedule to the authorization of agent stating which members of the group would otherwise be required to separately authorize the reporting corporation as agent. The schedule must provide the name, address, relationship to the reporting corporation, and U.S. taxpayer identification number, if applicable, of each member.

(2) *Application of noncompliance penalty adjustment.*—In circumstances where a consolidated authorization of agent has been executed, if the agency authorization for any member of the group is not legally effective for purposes of sections 7602, 7603, and 7604, the noncompliance penalty adjustment under section 6038A(e) and §1.6038A-7 shall apply.

(d) *Legal effect of authorization of agent.*—The legal consequences of a foreign related party authorizing a reporting corporation to act as its agent for purposes of sections 7602, 7603, and 7604 of the Code are as follows.

(1) *Agent for purposes of commencing judicial proceedings.*—A reporting corporation that is authorized by a foreign related party to act as its agent for purposes of sections 7602, 7603, and 7604 (including service of process) is also the agent of the foreign related party for purposes of—

(i) The filing of a petition to quash under section 6038A(e)(4)(A) or a petition to review an Internal Revenue Service determination of noncompliance under section 6038A(e)(4)(B), and

(ii) The commencement of a judicial proceeding to enforce a summons under section 7604, whether commenced in conjunction with a petition to quash under section 6038A(e)(4)(A) or commenced as a separate proceeding in the federal district court for the district in which the person to whom the summons is issued resides or is found.

(2) *Foreign related party found where reporting corporation found.*—For any purposes relating to sections 7602, 7603, or 7604 (including service of process), a foreign related party that authorizes a reporting corporation to act on its behalf under section 6038A(e)(1) and this section may be found anywhere where the reporting corporation has residence or is found.

(e) *Successors in interest.*—A successor in interest to a related party must execute the authorization of agent as described in paragraph (b) of this section.

(f) *Deemed compliance.*—(1) *In general.*—In exceptional circumstances, the District Director may treat a reporting corporation as authorized to act as agent for a related party for purposes of sections 7602, 7603, and 7604 in the absence of an actual agency appointment by the foreign related party, in circumstances where the actual absence of an appointment is reasonable. Factors to be considered include—

(i) If neither the reporting corporation nor the other party to the transaction knew or had reason to know that the two parties were related at the time of the transaction, and

(ii) The extent to which the taxpayer establishes to the satisfaction of the District Director that all transactions between the reporting corporation and the related party were on arm's length terms and did not involve the participation of any known related party.

(2) *Reason to know.*—Whether the reporting corporation or other party had reason to know that the two parties were related at the time of the transaction will be determined by all the facts and circumstances.

(3) *Effect of deemed compliance.*—If a reporting corporation is deemed under this paragraph (f) to have been authorized to act as an agent for a foreign related party for purposes of section 7602, 7603, and 7604, such deemed compliance is applicable only for that particular transaction and other reportable transactions entered into prior to the time when the reporting corporation knew or had reason to know that the related party, in fact, was related. The noncompliance rule of §1.6038A-7 shall apply to any transaction subsequent to that time with the same related party, unless the related party actually authorizes the reporting corporation to act as its agent under paragraph (a) of this section. In addition, the record maintenance requirements of §1.6038A-3 will apply to all subsequent transactions and, with respect to prior transactions, will apply to relevant records in existence at the time the relationship was discovered.

(g) *Effective dates.*—For effective dates for this section, see §1.6038A-1(n). [Reg. §1.6038A-5.]

☐ [*T.D.* 8353, 6-14-91.]

### [Reg. §1.6038A-6]

**§1.6038A-6. Failure to furnish information.**—(a) *In general.*—The rules of §1.6038A-7 may be applied with respect to a transaction between a foreign related party and the reporting corporation (including any transaction engaged in by a partnership that is attributed to the reporting corporation under §1.6038A-1(e)(2)) if a summons is issued to the reporting corporation to produce any records or testimony, either directly or as agent for such related party, to determine the correct treatment under Title 1 of the Code of such a transaction between the reporting corporation and the related party; and if—

(1)(i) The summons is not quashed in a proceeding, if any, begun under section 6038A(e)(4) and is not determined to be invalid in a proceeding, if any, begun under section 7604 to enforce such summons; and

(ii) The reporting corporation does not substantially and timely comply with the summons, and the District Director has sent by certified or registered mail a notice under section 6038A(e)(2)(C) to the reporting corporation that it has not so complied; or

(2) The reporting corporation fails to maintain or to cause another to maintain records as required by §1.6038A-3, and by reason of that failure, the summons is quashed in a proceeding under section 6038A(e)(4) or in a proceeding begun under section 7604 to enforce the summons, or the reporting corporation is not able to provide the records requested in the summons.

(b) *Coordination with treaties.*—Where records of a related party are obtainable on a timely and efficient basis under information exchange procedures provided under a tax treaty or tax information exchange agreement (TIEA), the Service generally will make use of such procedures before issuing a summons. The absence or pendency of a treaty or TIEA request may not be asserted as grounds for refusing to comply with a summons or as a defense against the assertion of the noncompliance penalty adjustment under §1.6038A-7. For purposes of this paragraph, information is available on a timely and efficient basis if it can be obtained within 180 days of the request.

(c) *Enforcement proceeding not required.*—The District Director is not required to begin an enforcement proceeding to enforce the summons in order to apply the rules of §1.6038A-7.

(d) *De minimis failure.*—Where a reporting corporation's failure to comply with the requirement to furnish information under this section is *de minimis*, the District Director, in the exercise of discretion, may choose not to apply the noncompliance penalty. Thus, for example, in cases where a particular document or group of documents is not furnished upon request or summons, the District Director (in the District Director's sole discretion) may choose not to apply the noncompliance penalty if the District Director deems the document or documents not to have significant or sufficient value in the determination of the correctness of the tax treatment of the related party transaction.

(e) *Suspension of statute of limitations.*—If the reporting corporation brings an action under section 6038A(e)(4)(A) (proceeding to quash) or (e)(4)(B) (review of secretarial determination of noncompliance), the running of any period of limitation under section 6501 (relating to assessment and collection of tax) or under section 6531 (relating to criminal prosecutions) for the taxable year or years to which the summons that is the subject of such proceeding relates shall be suspended for the period during which such proceeding, and appeals therein, are pending. In no event shall any such period expire before the 90th day after the day on which there is a final determination in such proceeding.

(f) *Effective dates.*—For effective dates for this section, see §1.6038A-1(n). [Reg. §1.6038A-6.]

☐ [T.D. 8353, 6-14-91.]

### [Reg. §1.6038A-7]

**§1.6038A-7. Noncompliance.**—(a) *In general.*—In the case of any failure described in §1.6038A-5 or §1.6038A-6, the rules of this §1.6038A-7 apply to the reporting corporation. In such a case—

(1) The amount of the deduction allowed under subtitle A for any amount paid or incurred by the reporting corporation to the related party in connection with such transaction, and

(2) The cost to the reporting corporation of any property acquired in such transaction from the related party or transferred by such corporation in such transaction to the related party, may be determined by the District Director.

(b) *Determination of the amount.*—The amount of the deduction or the cost to the reporting corporation shall be the amount determined by the District Director (in the District Director's sole discretion) from the District Director's own knowledge or from such information as the District Director may choose to obtain through testimony or otherwise. The District Director shall consider any information or materials that have been submitted by the reporting corporation or a foreign related party. The District Director, however, may disregard any information, documents, or records submitted by the reporting corporation or the related party if (in the District Director's sole discretion) the District Director deems that they are insufficiently probative of the relevant facts.

(c) *Separate application.*—If the noncompliance penalty of this section applies with respect to transactions with a related party of the reporting corporation, it will not be applied with respect to any other related parties of the reporting corporation solely upon the basis of that failure. Thus, for example, if a reporting corporation engages in transactions with related party A and related party B, and the reporting corporation does not respond to a summons for records related to the transactions between the reporting corporation and related party A, the noncompliance penalty imposed as a result of such failure will not apply to the transactions between the reporting corporation and related party B. If a separate summons is issued for records relating to the transactions between the reporting corporation and related party B and the reporting corporation does not produce such records, the noncompliance penalty may be applied to those transactions.

(d) *Effective dates.*—For effective dates for this section, see §1.6038A-1(n). [Reg. §1.6038A-7.]

☐ [T.D. 8353, 6-14-91.]

⟫⟫→ *Caution: The Treasury Department has identified Reg. §1.6038B-1, as amended by T.D. 9803, as a significant tax regulation that imposes an undue financial burden on U.S. taxpayers and/or adds undue complexity to the federal tax laws, pursuant to Executive Order 13789 (issued April 21, 2017) (Notice 2017-38, I.R.B. 2017-30). In a subsequent report, issued October 4, 2017, Treasury recommended planned actions that would reduce the burden of these regulations.*

### [Reg. §1.6038B-1]

**§1.6038B-1. Reporting of certain transfers to foreign corporations.**—(a) *Purpose and scope.*—This section sets forth information reporting requirements under section 6038B concerning certain transfers of property to foreign corporations. Paragraph (b) of this section provides general rules explaining when and how to carry out the reporting required under section 6038B with respect to the transfers to foreign corporations. Paragraph (c) of this section and §1.6038B-1T(d) specify the information that is required to be reported with respect to certain transfers of property that are described in section 6038B(a)(1)(A) and 367(d), respectively. Section 1.6038B-1(e) describes the filing requirements for property transfers described in section 367(e). Paragraph (f) of this section sets forth the consequences of a failure to comply with the requirements of section 6038B and this section. For effective dates, see paragraph (g) of this section. For rules regarding transfers to foreign partnerships, see section 6038B(a)(1)(B) and any regulations thereunder.

(b) *Time and manner of reporting.*—(1) *In general.*—(i) *Reporting procedure.*—Except for stock or securities qualifying under the special reporting rule of §1.6038B-1(b)(2), and certain exchanges described in section 354 or 356 (listed below), any U.S. person that makes a transfer described in section 6038B(a)(1)(A), 367(d) or (e), is required to report pursuant to section 6038B and the rules of §1.6038B-1 and must attach the required information to Form 926, "Return by a U.S. Transferor of Property to a Foreign Corporation." In addition, if the U.S. person files a statement under §1.367(a)-3(d)(2)(vi)(C), a gain recognition agreement under §1.367(a)-8, or a liquidation document under §1.367(e)-2(b), such person must comply in all material respects with the requirements of such section pursuant to the terms of the statement, gain recognition agreement, or liquidation document, as applicable, in order to satisfy a reporting obligation under section 6038B. For special rules regarding cash transfers made in tax years beginning after February 5, 1999, see paragraphs (b)(3) and (g) of this section. For purposes of determining a U.S. transferor that is subject to section 6038B, the rules of §§1.367(a)-1(c) and 1.367(a)-3(d) shall apply with respect to a transfer described in section 367(a), and the rules of §1.367(a)-1(c) shall apply with respect to a transfer described in section 367(d). Additionally, if in an exchange described in section 354 or 356, a U.S. person exchanges stock or securities of a foreign corporation in a reorganization described in section 368(a)(1)(E), or a U.S. person exchanges stock or securities of a domestic or foreign corporation pursuant to an asset reorganization described in section 368(a)(1) (involving a transfer of assets under section 361) that is not treated as an indirect stock transfer under §1.367(a)-3(d), then the U.S. person exchanging stock or securities is not required to report under section 6038B. Notwithstanding any statement to the contrary on Form 926, the form and attachments must be attached to, and filed by the due date (including extensions) of the transferor's income tax return for the taxable year that includes the date of the transfer (as defined in §1.6038B-1T(b)(4)). For taxable years beginning before January 1, 2003, any attachment to Form 926 required under the rules of this section is filed subject to the transferor's declaration under penalties of perjury on Form 926 that the information submitted is true, correct and complete to the best of the transferor's knowledge and belief. For taxable years beginning after December 31, 2002,

Form 926 and any attachments shall be verified by signing the income tax return with which the form and attachments are filed.

(ii) *Reporting by corporate transferor.*—For transfers by corporations in taxable years beginning before January 1, 2003, Form 926 must be signed by an authorized officer of the corporation if the transferor is not a member of an affiliated group under section 1504(a)(1) that files a consolidated Federal income tax return and by an authorized officer of the common parent corporation if the transferor is a member of such an affiliated group. For transfers by corporations in taxable years beginning after December 31, 2002, Form 926 shall be verified by signing the income tax return to which the form is attached.

(iii) *Transfers of jointly-owned property.*—If two or more persons transfer jointly-owned property to a foreign corporation in a transfer with respect to which a notice is required under this section, then each person must report with respect to the particular interest transferred, specifying the nature and extent of the interest. However, a husband and wife who jointly file a single Federal income tax return may file a single Form 926 with their tax return.

(2) *Exceptions and special rules for transfers of stock or securities under section 367(a).*—(i) *Transfers on or after July 20, 1998.*—A U.S. person that transfers stock or securities on or after July 20, 1998 in a transaction described in section 6038B(a)(1)(A) will be considered to have satisfied the reporting requirement under section 6038B and paragraph (b)(1) of this section if either—

(A) The U.S. transferor owned less than 5 percent of both the total voting power and the total value of the transferee foreign corporation immediately after the transfer (taking into account the attribution rules of section 318 as modified by section 958(b)), and either:

(1) The U.S. transferor qualified for nonrecognition treatment with respect to the transfer (i.e., the transfer was not taxable under §§ 1.367(a)-3(b) or (c)); or

(2) The U.S. transferor is a tax-exempt entity and the income was not unrelated business income; or

(3) The transfer was taxable to the U.S. transferor under § 1.367(a)-3(c), and such person properly reported the income from the transfer on its timely-filed (including extensions) Federal income tax return for the taxable year that includes the date of the transfer; or

(4) The transfer is considered to be to a foreign corporation solely by reason of § 1.83-6(d)(1) and the fair market value of the property transferred did not exceed $100,000; or

(B) The U.S. transferor owned 5 percent or more of the total voting power or the total value of the transferee foreign corporation immediately after the transfer (taking into account the attribution rules of section 318 as modified by section 958(b)) and either:

(1) Except as provided in paragraph (b)(2)(iii) of this section, the U.S. transferor (or one or more successors) filed an initial gain recognition agreement under § 1.367(a)-8, and filed Form 926 in accordance with paragraph (b)(2)(iv) of this section; or

(2) The transferor is a tax-exempt entity and the income was not unrelated business income; or

(3) The transferor properly reported the income from the transfer on its timely-filed (including extensions) Federal income tax return for the taxable year that includes the date of the transfer; or

(4) The transfer is considered to be to a foreign corporation solely by reason of § 1.83-6(d)(1) and the fair market value of the property transferred did not exceed $100,000.

(ii) *Transfers before July 20, 1998.*—With respect to transfers occurring after December 16, 1987, and prior to July 20, 1998, a U.S. transferor that transferred U.S. or foreign stock or securities in a transfer described in section 367(a) is not subject to section 6038B if such person is described in paragraph (b)(2)(i)(A) of this section.

(iii) *Timely filed initial gain recognition agreement.*—Paragraph (b)(2)(i)(B)(1) of this section will not apply unless the initial gain recognition agreement is timely filed as determined under § 1.367(a)-8(d)(1), but for purposes of this section, determined without regard to § 1.367(a)-8(p). However, see paragraph (f)(3) of this section for certain relief that may be available.

(iv) *Satisfaction of section 6038B reporting if a gain recognition agreement is timely filed.*—If the U.S. transferor is described in paragraph (b)(2)(i)(B)(1) of this section and is not otherwise required to file a Form 926 with respect to a transfer of assets other than the stock or securities to the transferee foreign corporation, the requirements of this section are satisfied with respect to the transfer of the stock or securities by completing Part I and Part II of Form 926, noting on the Form 926 that a gain recognition agreement is being filed pursuant to § 1.367(a)-8; reporting on the Form 926 the fair market value, adjusted tax basis, and gain recognized with respect to the transferred stock or

securities; submitting on the Form 926 any other information that Form 926, its accompanying instructions, or other applicable guidance require to be submitted with respect to the transfer of the stock or securities; and attaching a signed copy of the Form 926 to its timely filed U.S. income tax return (including extensions) for the year of the transfer. If the U.S. transferor is required to file Form 926 with respect to a transfer of assets in addition to the stock or securities, the requirements of this section are satisfied with respect to the transfer of the stock or securities by noting on the Form 926 that a gain recognition agreement is being filed pursuant to § 1.367(a)-8; reporting on the Form 926 the fair market value, adjusted tax basis, and gain recognized with respect to the transferred stock or securities; and submitting on the Form 926 any other information that Form 926, its accompanying instructions, or other applicable guidance require to be submitted with respect to the transfer of the stock or securities.

(3) *Special rule for transfers of cash.*—A U.S. person that transfers cash to a foreign corporation in a transfer described in section 6038B(a)(1)(A) must report the transfer if—

(i) Immediately after the transfer such person holds directly, indirectly, or by attribution (determined under the rules of section 318(a), as modified by section 6038(e)(2)) at least 10 percent of the total voting power or the total value of the foreign corporation; or

(ii) The amount of cash transferred by such person or any related person (determined under section 267(b)(1) through (3) and (10) through (12)) to such foreign corporation during the 12-month period ending on the date of the transfer exceeds $100,000.

(4) [Reserved]. For further guidance, see § 1.6038B-1T(b)(4).

(c) *Information required with respect to transfers described in section 6038B(a)(1)(A).*—A United States person that transfers property to a foreign corporation in an exchange described in section 6038B(a)(1)(A) (including cash transferred in taxable years beginning after February 5, 1999, and other unappreciated property) must provide the following information, in paragraphs labeled to correspond with the number or letter set forth in this paragraph (c) and § 1.6038B-1T(c)(1) through (5). If a particular item is not applicable to the subject transfer, the taxpayer must list its heading and state that it is not applicable. For special rules applicable to transfers of stock or securities, see paragraph (b)(2)(ii) of this section.

(1) through (4) introductory text [Reserved]. For further guidance, see § 1.6038B-1T(c)(1) through (4) introductory text.

(i) *Active business property.*—Describe any transferred property that qualifies under § 1.367(a)-2(a)(2). Provide here a general description of the business conducted (or to be conducted) by the transferee, including the location of the business, the number of its employees, the nature of the business, and copies of the most recently prepared balance sheet and profit and loss statement. Property listed within this category may be identified by general type. For example, upon the transfer of the assets of a manufacturing operation, a reasonable description of the property to be used in the business might include the categories of office equipment and supplies, computers and related equipment, motor vehicles, and several major categories of manufacturing equipment. However, any property that is includible in both paragraphs (c)(4)(i) and (iii) of this section (property subject to depreciation recapture under § 1.367(a)-4(a)) must be identified in the manner required in paragraph (c)(4)(iii) of this section. If property is considered to be transferred for use in the active conduct of a trade or business under a special rule in paragraph (e), (f), or (g) of § 1.367(a)-2, specify the applicable rule and provide information supporting the application of the rule.

(ii) *Stock or securities.*—Describe any transferred stock or securities, including the class or type, amount, and characteristics of the transferred stock or securities, as well as the name, address, place of incorporation, and general description of the corporation issuing the stock or securities.

(iii) *Depreciated property.*—Describe any property that is subject to depreciation recapture under § 1.367(a)-4(a). Property within this category must be separately identified to the same extent as was required for purposes of the previously claimed depreciation deduction. Specify with respect to each such asset the relevant recapture provision, the number of months that such property was in use within the United States, the total number of months the property was in use, the fair market value of the property, a schedule of the depreciation deduction taken with respect to the property, and a calculation of the amount of depreciation required to be recaptured.

(iv) *Property not transferred for use in the active conduct of a trade or business.*—Describe any property that is eligible property, as defined in § 1.367(a)-2(b) taking into account the application of § 1.367(a)-2(c), that was transferred to the foreign corporation but not for use in the active conduct of a trade or business outside the United

States (and was therefore not listed under paragraph (c)(4)(i) of this section).

(v) *Property transferred under compulsion.*—If property qualifies for the exception of §1.367(a)-2(a)(2) under the rules of paragraph (h) of that section, provide information supporting the claimed application of such exception.

(vi) *Certain ineligible property.*—Describe any property that is described in §1.367(a)-2(c) and that therefore cannot qualify under §1.367(a)-2(a)(2) regardless of its use in the active conduct of a trade or business outside of the United States. The description must be divided into the relevant categories, as follows:

(A) *Inventory, etc.*—Property described in §1.367(a)-2(c)(1);

(B) *Installment obligations, etc.*—Property described in §1.367(a)-2(c)(2);

(C) *Foreign currency, etc.*—Property described in §1.367(a)-2(c)(3); and

(D) *Leased property.*—Property described in §1.367(a)-2(c)(4).

(vii) *Other property that is ineligible property.*—Describe any property, other than property described in §1.367(a)-2(c), that cannot qualify under §1.367(a)-2(a)(2) regardless of its use in the active conduct of a trade or business outside of the United States and that is not subject to the rules of section 367(d) under §1.367(a)-1(b)(5) (treatment of certain property as subject to section 367(d)). Each item of property must be separately identified.

(viii) [Reserved]. For further guidance, see §1.6038B-1T(c)(4)(viii).

(5) *Transfer of foreign branch with previously deducted losses.*—If the property transferred is property of a foreign branch with previously deducted losses subject to §§1.367(a)-6 and -6T, provide the following information:

(i) through (iv) [Reserved]. For further information, see §1.6038B-1T(c)(5)(i) through (iv).

(6) *Transfers subject to section 367(a)(5).*—(i) *In general.*—This paragraph (c)(6) applies to a domestic corporation (U.S. transferor) that transfers section 367(a) property (as defined in §1.367(a)-7(f)(10)) to a foreign corporation in a section 361 exchange (as defined in §1.367(a)-7(f)(8)) and to which the provisions of §1.367(a)-7(c) apply. Paragraph (c)(6)(ii) of this section establishes the time and manner for the U.S. transferor to elect to apply the provisions of §1.367(a)-7(c). Paragraph (c)(6)(iii) of this section establishes the manner for the U.S. transferor to satisfy the requirement of §1.367(a)-7(c)(4).

(ii) *Election.*—The U.S. transferor elects to apply the provisions of §1.367(a)-7(c) by including a statement entitled, "ELECTION TO APPLY EXCEPTION UNDER §1.367(a)-7(c)," with its timely filed return (within the meaning of §1.367(a)-7(f)(12)) for the taxable year during which the reorganization occurs and that includes the information described in paragraphs (c)(6)(ii)(A), (c)(6)(ii)(B), (c)(6)(ii)(C), (c)(6)(ii)(D), (c)(6)(ii)(E), (c)(6)(ii)(F), (c)(6)(ii)(G), and (c)(6)(ii)(H) of this section. See §1.367(a)-7(c)(5)(ii) for the statement required to be filed by a control group member (as defined in §1.367(a)-7(f)(1)) or final distributee (as defined in §1.367(a)-7(d)).

(A) The name and taxpayer identification number (if any) of each control group member and final distributee (if any), the foreign acquiring corporation, and in the case of a triangular reorganization (within the meaning of §1.358-6(b)(2)) the corporation that controls the foreign acquiring corporation, and the ownership interest percentage (as defined in §1.367(a)-7(f)(7)) in the U.S. transferor of each control group member.

(B) A calculation of the gain recognized (if any) by the U.S. transferor under §1.367(a)-7(c)(2)(i) and (c)(2)(ii), and the basis adjustments (if any) required to be made by each control group member under §1.367(a)-7(c)(3).

(C) The date on which the U.S. transferor and each control group member or final distributee entered into the written agreement described in §1.367(a)-7(c)(5)(iv).

(D) The amount of any deductible liability (as defined by §1.367(a)-7(f)(2)).

(E) The fair market value (as defined by §1.367(a)-7(f)(3)) of property transferred to the foreign acquiring corporation in the section 361 exchange.

(F) The inside basis (as defined by §1.367(a)-7(f)(4)).

(G) The inside gain (as defined by §1.367(a)-7(f)(5)).

(H) The section 367(a) percentage (as defined by §1.367(a)-7(f)(9)).

(iii) *Agreement to amend U.S. transferor's tax return.*—The U.S. transferor complies with the requirement of §1.367(a)-7(c)(4)(i) by attaching a statement to its timely filed return (within the meaning of §1.367(a)-7(f)(12)) for the taxable year in which the reorganization occurs, entitled "STATEMENT UNDER §1.367(a)-7(c)(4) FOR TRANSFERS OF ASSETS TO A FOREIGN CORPORATION IN A SECTION 361 EXCHANGE." The statement must certify that if a significant amount of the section 367(a) property received by the foreign acquiring corporation from the U.S. transferor in the section 361 exchange is disposed of, directly or indirectly, in one or more related transactions described in paragraph (c)(6)(iii)(B) of this section occurring within the sixty (60) month period that begins on the date of distribution or transfer (within the meaning of §1.381(b)-1(b)), then the exception provided in §1.367(a)-7(c) will not apply to the section 361 exchange. Accordingly, the U.S. transferor will recognize the gain realized but not recognized in the section 361 exchange, computed as if the exception provided in §1.367(a)-7(c) had never applied. A U.S. income tax return (or amended U.S. income tax return, as the case may be) for the year in which the reorganization occurred reporting the gain must be filed. If the section 361 exchange occurs in connection with a triangular reorganization (within the meaning of §1.358-6(b)(2)) and the corporation that controls the foreign acquiring corporation is foreign, an indirect disposition of the section 367(a) property includes the disposition by such controlling foreign corporation of the stock of the foreign acquiring corporation.

(A) *Disposition of a significant amount.*—(1) *General rule.*—Except as provided in paragraphs (c)(6)(iii)(A)(2) and (c)(6)(iii)(A)(3) of this section, for purposes of this paragraph (c)(6)(iii), a disposition of a significant amount occurs if, in one or more related transactions, the foreign acquiring corporation disposes of an amount of the section 367(a) property received from the U.S. transferor in the section 361 exchange that is greater than 40 percent of the fair market value of all of the section 367(a) property transferred in the section 361 exchange.

(2) *Exception for certain nonrecognition exchanges.*—Section 367(a) property that is subsequently transferred (retransferred property) pursuant to a nonrecognition provision is not treated as disposed of for purposes of paragraph (c)(6)(iii)(A)(1) of this section, provided such transfer satisfies, and is treated in a manner consistent with the principles underlying §1.367(a)-8(k). Thus, for example, if section 367(a) property is subsequently transferred to a foreign corporation in exchange solely for stock in a transaction described in section 351, such retransferred property is not treated as disposed of for purposes of paragraph (c)(6)(iii)(A)(1) of this section; in such a case, however, a subsequent disposition of either the retransferred property by the transferee foreign corporation, or of the stock of the transferee foreign corporation received in exchange for the retransferred property, is subject to the provisions of paragraph (c)(6)(iii)(A)(1) of this section.

(3) *Exception for dispositions occurring in the ordinary course of business.*—Dispositions of section 367(a) property described in section 1221(a)(2) occurring in the ordinary course of business of the foreign acquiring corporation are not treated as disposed of for purposes of paragraph (c)(6)(iii)(A)(1) of this section.

(B) *Gain recognition transaction.*—(1) *General rule.*—A transaction is described in this paragraph (c)(6)(iii)(B) if the transaction is entered into with a principal purpose of avoiding the U.S. tax that would have been imposed on the U.S. transferor on the disposition of the property transferred to the foreign acquiring corporation in the section 361 exchange. A disposition may have a principal purpose of tax avoidance even if the tax avoidance purpose is outweighed by other purposes when taken together.

(2) *Presumptive tax avoidance.*—For purposes of this paragraph (c)(6)(iii)(B), the principal purpose of the foreign acquiring corporation's disposition of a significant amount of the section 367(a) property within the two-year period that begins on the date of distribution or transfer (within the meaning of §1.381(b)-1(b)) (whether in a recognition or nonrecognition transaction) will be presumed to be the avoidance of the U.S. tax that would have been imposed on the U.S. transferor on the disposition of the property transferred to the foreign acquiring corporation in the section 361 exchange. However, this presumption will not apply if it is demonstrated to the satisfaction of the Director of Field Operations, Large Business & International (or any successor to the roles and responsibilities of such person (Director) that the avoidance of U.S. tax was not a principal purpose of the disposition.

(3) *Interest.*—If additional tax is required to be paid as a result of a transaction described in paragraph (c)(6)(iii)(B) of this section, then interest must be paid on that amount at rates determined under section 6621 with respect to the period between the date

prescribed for filing the U.S. transferor's income tax return for the year in which the reorganization occurs and the date on which the additional tax for that year is paid.

(d)(1) through (1)(iii) [Reserved]. For further guidance, see § 1.6038B-1T(d)(1) through (1)(iii).

(iv) *Intangible property transferred.*—Provide a description of the intangible property transferred, including its adjusted basis. Generally, each item of intangible property must be separately identified, including intangible property described in § 1.367(d)-1(g)(2)(i). Identify all property that is subject to the rules of section 367(d) under § 1.367(a)-1(b)(5) (treatment of certain property as subject to section 367(d)). Describe any property for which the income required to be taken into account under section 367(d) and the regulations thereunder will be recognized over a 20-year period pursuant to § 1.367(d)-1(c)(3)(ii). Estimate the anticipated income or cost reductions attributable to the intangible property's use beyond the 20-year period.

(v)–(vi) [Reserved]. For further guidance, see § 1.6038B-1T(d)(1)(v) through (1)(vi).

(vii) *Coordination with loss rules.*—List any intangible property subject to section 367(d) the transfer of which also gives rise to the recognition of gain under section 904(f)(3) or § § 1.367(a)-6 or -6T. Provide a calculation of the gain required to be recognized with respect to such property, in accordance with the provisions of § 1.367(d)-1(g)(3).

(d)(1)(viii) through (d)(2) [Reserved]. For further guidance, see § 1.6038B-1T(d)(1)(viii) through (d)(2).

(e) *Transfers subject to section 367(e).*—(1) *In general.*—If a domestic corporation (distributing corporation) makes a distribution described in section 367(e)(1) or section 367(e)(2), the distributing corporation must comply with the reporting requirements of this paragraph (e). Unless otherwise provided in this section, a distributing corporation making a distribution described in sections 367(e)(1) or 367(e)(2) must file a Form 926, "Return by a U.S. Transferor of Property to a Foreign Corporation (under section 367)," as amended and modified by this section.

(2) *Reporting requirements for section 367(e)(1) distributions of domestic controlled corporations.*—A domestic distributing corporation making a distribution of the stock or securities of a domestic corporation under section 355 is not required to file a Form 926, as described in paragraph (e)(1) of this section, and shall have no other reporting requirements under section 6038B.

(3) *Reporting requirements for section 367(e)(1) distributions of foreign controlled corporations.*—If the distributing corporation makes a section 355 distribution of the stock or securities of a foreign controlled corporation to distributee shareholders who are not qualified U.S. persons, as defined in § 1.367(e)-1(b)(1), then the distributing corporation shall complete Part 1 of the Form 926 and attach a signed copy of such form to its U.S. income tax return for the year of the distribution. The distributing corporation shall also attach to its U.S. income tax return for the year of distribution a statement signed under the penalties of perjury entitled, "Addendum to Form 926." The addendum shall contain a brief description of the transaction, state the number of shares distributed to distributees who are not qualified U.S. persons (applying the rules contained in § 1.367(e)-1(d)), and state the basis and fair market value of the distributed stock or securities (including a list stating the amounts that were distributed to distributees who were not qualified U.S. persons and distributees who were qualified U.S. persons).

(4) *Reporting rules for section 367(e)(2) distributions by domestic liquidating corporations.*—(i) *General rule.*—Except as provided in paragraph (e)(4)(ii) of this section, if the distributing corporation makes a distribution of property in complete liquidation under section 332 to a foreign distributee corporation that meets the stock ownership requirements of section 332(b) with respect to the stock of the distributing corporation, then the distributing corporation must complete a Form 926 and attach a signed copy of such form to its timely filed U.S. income tax return (including extensions) for the taxable years that include one or more liquidating distributions. The property description contained in Part III of the Form 926 must contain a description, including the adjusted tax basis and fair market value, of all property distributed by the distributing corporation (regardless of whether the distribution of the property qualifies for nonrecognition treatment). The description must also identify the items of property for which nonrecognition treatment is claimed under § 1.367(e)-2(b)(2)(ii) or (iii), as applicable.

(ii) *Special rule.*—Except as provided in paragraph (e)(4)(iii) of this section, if the distributing corporation distributes items of property that will be used by the foreign distributee corporation in the conduct of a trade or business in the United States and the distributing corporation does not recognize gain or loss on such distribution under § 1.367(e)-2(b)(2)(i) with respect to such property, then the distributing corporation may satisfy the requirements of this section by completing Part I and Part II of Form 926, noting in Part III that the information required by Form 926 is contained in a statement required by § 1.367(e)-2(b)(2)(i)(C)(2), and attaching a signed copy of Form 926 to its timely filed U.S. income tax return (including extensions) for each taxable year that includes one or more distributions in liquidation. In addition, if the distributing corporation distributes stock of a domestic subsidiary corporation and does not recognize gain or loss on such distribution under § 1.367(e)-2(b)(2)(iii) with respect to such stock, then the distributing corporation may satisfy the requirements of this section by completing Part I and Part II of Form 926, noting in Part III that the information required by Form 926 is contained in a statement required by § 1.367(e)-2(b)(2)(iii)(D), and attaching a signed copy of Form 926 to its timely filed U.S. income tax return (including extensions) for the taxable years that include one or more distributions of domestic subsidiary stock.

(iii) *Properly filed statement.*—Paragraph (e)(4)(ii) will not apply if there is a failure to file an initial liquidation document as determined under § 1.367(e)-2(e)(3)(i), determined without regard to § 1.367(e)-2(f). However, see paragraph (f)(3) of this section for certain relief that may be available.

(f) *Failure to comply with reporting requirements.*—(1) *Consequences of failure.*—If a U.S. person is required to file a notice (or otherwise comply) under paragraph (b) of this section and fails to comply with the applicable requirements of section 6038B and this section, then with respect to the particular property as to which there was a failure to comply—

(i) The U.S. person shall pay a penalty under section 6038B(b)(1) equal to 10 percent of the fair market value of the transferred property at the time of the exchange, but in no event shall the penalty exceed $100,000 unless the failure with respect to such exchange was due to intentional disregard (described under paragraph (g)(4) of this section); and

(ii) The period of limitations on assessment of tax upon the transfer of that property does not expire before the date which is 3 years after the date on which the Secretary is furnished the information required to be reported under this section. See section 6501(c)(8) and any regulations thereunder.

(2) *Failure to comply.*—A failure to comply with the requirements of section 6038B is—

(i) The failure to report at the proper time and in the proper manner any material information required to be reported under the rules of this section; or

(ii) The provision of false or inaccurate information in purported compliance with the requirements of this section. Thus, a transferor that timely files Form 926 with the attachments required under the rules of this section shall, nevertheless, have failed to comply if, for example, the transferor reports therein that property will be used in the active conduct of a trade or business outside of the United States, but in fact the property continues to be used in a trade or business within the United States.

(iii) With respect to an initial gain recognition agreement filed under § 1.367(a)-8, a failure to comply as determined under § 1.367(a)-8(j)(8), but for purposes of this section, determined without regard to the application of § 1.367(a)-8(p).

(iv) With respect to an initial liquidation document filed under § 1.367(e)-2(b)(2), a failure to comply as determined under § 1.367(e)-2(e)(4)(i), but for purposes of this section, determined without regard to the application of § 1.367(e)-2(f).

(3) *Reasonable cause for failure to comply.*—(i) *Request for relief.*—If the U.S. transferor fails to comply with any requirement of section 6038B and this section, the failure shall be deemed not to have occurred if the U.S. transferor is able to demonstrate that the failure was due to reasonable cause and not willful neglect using the procedure set forth in paragraph (f)(3)(ii) of this section. Whether the failure to timely comply was due to reasonable cause and not willful neglect will be determined by the Director of Field Operations, Cross Border Activities Practice Area of Large Business & International (Director) based on all the facts and circumstances.

(ii) *Procedures for establishing that a failure to timely comply was due to reasonable cause and not willful neglect.*—(A) *Time of submission.*—A U.S. transferor's statement that the failure to timely comply was due to reasonable cause and not willful neglect will be considered only if, promptly after the U.S. transferor becomes aware of the failure, an amended return is filed for the taxable year to which the failure relates that includes the information that should have been included with the original return for such taxable year or that otherwise complies with the rules of this section, and that includes a written statement explaining the reasons for the failure to timely comply.

(B) *Notice requirement.*—In addition to the requirements of paragraph (f)(3)(ii)(A) of this section, the U.S. transferor must comply with the notice requirements of this paragraph (f)(3)(ii)(B). If any taxable year of the U.S. transferor is under examination when the amended return is filed, a copy of the amended return and any information required to be included with such return must be delivered to the Internal Revenue Service personnel conducting the examination. If no taxable year of the U.S. transferor is under examination when the amended return is filed, a copy of the amended return and any information required to be included with such return must be delivered to the Director.

(4) *Definition of intentional disregard.*—If the transferor fails to qualify for the exception under paragraph (f)(3) of this section and if the taxpayer knew of the rule or regulation that was disregarded, the failure will be considered an intentional disregard of section 6038B, and the monetary penalty under paragraph (f)(1)(ii) of this section will not be limited to $100,000. See § 1.6662-3(b)(2).

(g) *Effective/applicability dates.*—(1) This section applies to transfers occurring on or after July 20, 1998, except as provided in paragraphs (g)(2) through (g)(7) of this section, and except for transfers of cash made in tax years beginning on or before February 5, 1999 (which are not required to be reported under section 6038B), and transfers described in paragraph (e) of this section (which applies to transfers that are subject to §§ 1.367(e)-1(f) and 1.367(e)-2(e)). See § 1.6038B-1T for transfers occurring prior to July 20, 1998. See also § 1.6038B-1T(e) in effect prior to August 9, 1999, (as contained in 26 CFR part 1 revised April 1, 1999) for transfers described in section 367(e) that are not subject to §§ 1.367(e)-1(f) and 1.367(e)-2(e).

(2) The rules of paragraph (b)(1)(i) of this section as they apply to section 368(a)(1)(A) reorganizations (including reorganizations described in section 368(a)(2)(D) or (E)) apply to transfers occurring on or after January 23, 2006.

(3) The rules of paragraph (b)(1)(i) of this section that provide an exception from reporting under section 6038B for transfers of stock or securities in a section 354 or 356 exchange, pursuant to a section 368(a)(1)(G) reorganization that is not treated as an indirect stock transfer under § 1.367(a)-3(d), apply to transfers occurring on or after January 23, 2006.

(4) The rules of paragraph (b)(1)(i) of this section that provide an exception from reporting under section 6038B for transfers of stock in a section 354 or 356 exchange, pursuant to a section 368(a)(1)(E) reorganization or an asset reorganization under section 368(a)(1) that is not treated as an indirect stock transfer under § 1.367(a)-3(d), apply to transfers occurring on or after January 23, 2006. The rules of paragraph (b)(1)(i) of this section that provide an exception from reporting under section 6038B for transfers of securities in a section 354 or 356 exchange, pursuant to section 368(a)(1)(E) reorganization or an asset reorganization under section 368(a)(1) that is not treated as an indirect stock transfer under § 1.367(a)-3(d), apply only to transfers occurring after January 5, 2005 (although taxpayers may apply such provision to transfers of securities occurring on or after July 20, 1998 and on or before January 5, 2005 if done consistently to all transactions). See § 1.6038-1T(b)(i), as contained in 26 CFR Part 1 revised as of April 1, 2005, for transfers occurring prior to the effective dates described in paragraphs (g)(2) through (4) of this section.

(5) Paragraphs (c)(6) and (f)(3) of this section apply to transfers occurring on or after April 18, 2013. For guidance with respect to paragraphs (c)(6) and (f)(3) of this section before April 18, 2013, see 26 CFR part 1 revised as of April 1, 2012.

(6) The second sentence of paragraph (b)(1)(i) and paragraphs (b)(2)(i)(B)(1), (b)(2)(iii), (b)(2)(iv), (c), (e)(4), (f)(2)(iii), and (f)(2)(iv) of this section will apply to transfers for which documents are required to be filed on or after November 19, 2014, as well as to transfers that are the subject of requests for relief submitted on or after November 19, 2014. The second sentence of paragraph (b)(1)(i) and paragraphs (b)(2)(i)(B)(1), (b)(2)(iii), (b)(2)(iv), (c), and (f)(2)(iii) of this section will also apply to any transfer that is the subject of a request for relief submitted pursuant to § 1.367(a)-8(r)(3).

(7) Paragraphs (c)(4)(i) through (vii), (c)(5), and (d)(1)(iv) and (vii) of this section apply to transfers occurring on or after September 14, 2015, and to transfers occurring before September 14, 2015, resulting from entity classification elections made under § 301.7701-3 that are filed on or after September 14, 2015. For guidance with respect to paragraphs (c)(4), (c)(5), and (d)(1) of this section before this section is applicable, see §§ 1.6038B-1 and 1.6038B-1T as contained in 26 CFR part 1 revised as of April 1, 2016. [Reg. § 1.6038B-1.]

☐ [T.D. 8770, 6-18-98 (*corrected* 3-31-99). *Amended by* T.D. 8817, 2-4-99 (*corrected* 3-31-99); T.D. 8834, 8-6-99; T.D. 8850, 12-27-99; T.D. 9100, 12-18-2003; T.D. 9243, 1-23-2006; T.D. 9300, 12-7-2006; T.D. 9614, 3-18-2013, T.D. 9704, 11-18-2014 (*corrected* 1-2-2015), T.D. 9760, 3-18-2016 *and* T.D. 9803, 12-15-2016.]

**⫸→ *Caution: The Treasury Department has identified Temporary Reg. §1.6038B-1T, as amended by T.D. 9803, as a significant tax regulation that imposes an undue financial burden on U.S. taxpayers and/or adds undue complexity to the federal tax laws, pursuant to Executive Order 13789 (issued April 21, 2017) (Notice 2017-38, I.R.B. 2017-30). In a subsequent report, issued October 4, 2017, Treasury recommended planned actions that would reduce the burden of these regulations.***

### [Reg. § 1.6038B-1T]

**§ 1.6038B-1T. Reporting of certain transactions to foreign corporations (temporary).**—(a) through (b)(3) [*Reserved*].—For further guidance, see § 1.6038B-1(a) through (b)(3).

(4) *Date of transfer.*—(i) *In general.*—For purposes of this section, the date of a transfer described in section 367 is the first date on which title to, possession of, or rights to the use of stock, securities, or other property passes pursuant to the plan for purposes of subtitle A of the Internal Revenue Code. A transfer will not be considered to begin with a decision of a board of directors or similar action unless the transaction otherwise takes effect for purposes of subtitle A of the Internal Revenue Code on that date.

(ii) *Termination of section 1504(d) election.*—A transfer deemed to occur as a result of the termination of an election under section 1504(d) will be considered to occur on the date the contiguous country corporation first fails to continue to qualify for the election under section 1504(d). The rule of this paragraph (b)(3)(ii) is illustrated by the following example.

*Example.* Domestic corporation W previously made a valid election under section 1504(d) to have its Mexican subsidiary S treated as a domestic corporation. On August 1, 1986, W disposes of its right, title, and interest in 10 percent of the stock of S by selling such stock to an unrelated United States person who is not a director of S. S first fails to continue to qualify for the election under section 1504(d) on August 1, 1986, since on such date it ceases to be directly or indirectly wholly owned or controlled by W. The constructive transfer of assets from "domestic" corporation S to Mexican corporation S is considered to occur on that date.

(iii) *Change in classification.*—A transfer deemed to occur as a result of a change in classification of an entity caused by a change in the governing documents, articles, or agreements of the entity (as described in § 1.367(a)-1T(c)(6)) will be considered to occur on the date that such changes take effect for purposes of subtitle A of the Internal Revenue Code.

(iv) *U.S. resident under section 6013(g) or (h).*—A transfer made by an alien individual who is considered to be a U.S resident by reason of a timely election under section 6013(g) or (h) will be considered to occur, for purposes of this section (but not for purposes of section 367), on the later of—

(A) The date on which the election under section 6013(g) or (h) is made; or

(B) The date on which the transfer would otherwise be considered to occur under the rules of this paragraph (b)(3).

The rule of this paragraph (b)(3)(iv) is illustrated by the following example.

*Example.* D is a nonresident alien individual who is married to a United States citizen. On March 1, 1986, D transfers property to a foreign corporation in an exchange described in section 351. On April 15, 1987, D and the spouse timely file with their tax return for the taxable year ended December 31, 1986, an election under section 6013(g) for D to be treated as a United States resident. The election is effective on January 1, 1986. For purposes of section 6038B, the transfer described in section 367(a) made by D in connection with the section 351 exchange is considered to occur on April 15, 1987, the date on which the timely election was made under section 6013(g).

(c) Introductory text [Reserved]. For further guidance, see § 1.6038B-1(c).

(1) *Transferor.*—Provide the name, U.S. taxpayer identification number, and address of the U.S. person making the transfer.

(2) *Transfer.*—Provide the following information concerning the transfer:

(i) Name, U.S. taxpayer identification number (if any), address, and country of incorporation of transferee foreign corporation;

(ii) A general description of the transfer, and any wider transaction of which it forms a part, including a chronology of the transfers involved and an identification of the other parties to the transaction to the extent known.

(3) *Consideration received.*—Provide a description of the consideration received by the U.S. person making the transfer, including its estimated fair market value and, in the case of stock or securities, the class or type, amount, and characteristics of the interest received.

(4) *Property transferred.*—Provide a description of the property transferred. The description must be divided into the following categories, and must include the estimated fair market value and adjusted basis of the property, as well as any additional information specified below.

(i) through (c)(5) introductory text [Reserved].

(i) *Branch operation.*—Describe the foreign branch the property of which is transferred, in accordance with the definition of §1.367(a)-6T(g).

(ii) *Branch property.*—Describe the property of the foreign branch, including its adjusted basis and fair market value. For this purpose property must be identified with reasonable particularity, but may be identified by category rather than listing every asset separately. Substantially similar property may be listed together for this purpose, and property of minor value may be grouped into functional categories. For example, a reasonable description of the property of a business office might include the following categories: word processing or data processing equipment, other office equipment and furniture, and office supplies.

(iii) *Previously deducted losses.*—Set forth a detailed calculation of the sum of the losses incurred by the foreign branch before the transfer, and a detailed calculation of any reduction of such losses, in accordance with §1.367(a)-6T(d) and (e).

(iv) *Character of gain.*—Set forth a statement of the character of the gain required to be recognized, in accordance with §1.367(a)-6T(c)(1).

(6) [Reserved]. For further guidance, see §1.6038B-1(c)(6).

(d) *Transfers subject to section 367(d).*—(1) *Initial transfer.*—A U.S. person that transfers intangible property to a foreign corporation in an exchange described in section 351 or 361 must provide the following information in paragraphs labelled to correspond with the number or letter set forth below. If a particular item is not applicable to the subject transfer, list its heading and state that it is not applicable. The information required by subdivisions (i) through (iii) need only be provided if such information was not otherwise provided under paragraph (c) of this section. (Note that the U.S. transferor may subsequently be required to file another return under paragraph (d)(2) of this section.)

(i) *Transferor.*—Provide the name, U.S. taxpayer identification number, and address of the U.S. person making the transfer.

(ii) *Transfer.*—Provide information concerning the transfer, including:

(A) Name, U.S. taxpayer identification number (if any), address, and country of incorporation of the transferee foreign corporation;

(B) A general description of the transfer, and any wider transaction of which it forms a part, including a chronology of the transfers involved and an identification of the other parties to the transaction to the extent known.

(iii) *Consideration received.*—Provide a description of the consideration received by the U.S. person making the transfer, including its estimated fair market value and, in the case of stock or securities, the class or type, amount, and characteristics of the interest received.

(iv) [Reserved].

(v) *Annual payment.*—Provide and explain the calculation of the annual deemed payment for the use of the intangible property required to be recognized by the transferor under the rules of section 367(d).

(vi) *Election to treat as sale.*—List any intangible with respect to which an election is being made under §1.367(d)-1T(g)(2) to treat the transfer as a sale. Include the fair market value of the intangible on the date of the transfer and a calculation of the gain required to be recognized in the year of the transfer by reason of the election.

(vii) [Reserved].

(viii) *Other intangibles.*—Describe any intangible property sold or licensed by the transferor to the transferee foreign corporation, and set forth the general terms of each sale or license.

(2) *Subsequent transfers.*—If a U.S. person transfers intangible property to a foreign corporation in an exchange described in section 351 or 361, and at any time thereafter (within the useful life of the intangible property) either that U.S. person disposes of the stock of the transferee foreign corporation or the transferee foreign corporation disposes of the transferred intangible, then the U.S. person must provide the following information in paragraphs labelled to correspond with the number or letter set forth below. The information required by subdivisions (i) and (ii) need only be provided if such information was not otherwise provided in the same return, pursuant to paragraph (c) or (d)(1) of this section. For purposes of determining the date on which a return under this subparagraph (2) is required to be filed, the date of transfer is the date of the subsequent transfer of stock or intangible property.

(i) *Transferor.*—Provide the name, U.S. taxpayer identification number, and address of the U.S. person making the transfer.

(ii) *Initial transfer.*—Provide the following information concerning the initial transfer:

(A) The date of the transfer;

(B) The name, U.S. taxpayer identification number (if any), address, and country of incorporation of the transferee foreign corporation; and

(C) A general description of the transfer and any wider transaction of which it formed a part.

(iii) *Subsequent transfer.*—Provide the following information concerning the subsequent transfer:

(A) A general description of the subsequent transfer and any wider transaction of which it forms a part;

(B) A calculation of any gain required to be recognized by the U.S. person under the rules of §1.367(d)-1T(d) through (f); and

(C) The name, address, and identifying number of each person that under the rules of §1.367(d)-1T(e) or (f) will be considered to receive contingent annual payments for the use of the intangible property.

(e) [Reserved]For further guidance, see §1.6038B-1(e).

(f)(1) through (f)(2) [Reserved].—For further guidance, see §1.6038B-1(f)(1) through (f)(2).

(3) [Reserved.]

(f)(4) [Reserved]. For further guidance, see §1.6038B-1T(f)(4).

(g) *Effective date.*—This section applies to transfers occurring after December 31, 1984. See §1.6038B-1T(a) through (b)(2), (c) introductory text, and (f) (26 CFR part 1, revised April 1, 1998) for transfers occurring prior to July 20, 1998. See §1.6038B-1 for transfers occurring on or after July 20, 1998. [Temporary Reg. §1.6038B-1T.]

☐ [*T.D. 8087, 5-15-86. Amended by T.D. 8682, 8-9-96; T.D. 8770, 6-18-98; T.D. 8834, 8-6-99; T.D. 9100, 12-18-2003 (corrected 2-2-2004); T.D. 9243, 1-23-2006; T.D. 9300, 12-7-2006; T.D. 9615, 3-18-2013, T.D. 9760, 3-18-2016 and T.D. 9803, 12-15-2016.*]

### [Reg. §1.6038B-2]

**§1.6038B-2. Reporting of certain transfers to foreign partnerships.**—(a) *Reporting requirements.*—(1) *Requirement to report transfers.*—A United States person that transfers property to a foreign partnership in a contribution described in section 721 (including section 721(b)) must report that transfer on Form 8865 "Information Return of U.S. Persons With Respect To Certain Foreign Partnerships" pursuant to section 6038B and the rules of this section, if—

(i) Immediately after the transfer, the United States person owns, directly, indirectly, or by attribution, at least a 10-percent interest in the partnership, as defined in section 6038(e)(3)(C) and the regulations thereunder;

(ii) The value of the property transferred, when added to the value of any other property transferred in a section 721 contribution by such person (or any related person) to the partnership during the 12-month period ending on the date of the transfer, exceeds $100,000; or

(iii) The United States person is a U.S. transferor (as defined in §1.721(c)-1(b)(18)) that makes a gain deferral contribution and is required to report under §1.721(c)-6(b)(2). The reporting required under this paragraph (a) includes the annual reporting required by §1.721(c)-6(b)(3). For purposes of applying this paragraph (a)(1)(iii) to partnerships formed on or after January 18, 2017, a domestic partnership is treated as a foreign partnership pursuant to section 7701(a)(4).

(2) *Indirect transfer through a domestic partnership.*—For purposes of this section, if a domestic partnership transfers property to a foreign partnership in a section 721 transaction, the domestic partnership's partners shall be considered to have transferred a proportionate share of the property to the foreign partnership. However, if the domestic partnership properly reports all of the information required under this section with respect to the contribution, no partner of the transferor partnership, whether direct or indirect (through tiers of

partnerships), is also required to report under this section. For illustrations of this rule, see *Examples 4* and *5* of paragraph (a)(7) of this section.

(3) *Indirect transfer through a foreign partnership.*—Solely for purposes of this section, if a foreign partnership transfers section 721(c) property (as defined in §1.721(c)-1(b)(15)) to another foreign partnership in a transfer described in §1.721(c)-3(d) (tiered-partnership rules), then the transferor foreign partnership's partners will be considered to have transferred a proportionate share of the property to the foreign partnership.

(4) *Requirement to report dispositions.*—(i) *In general.*—If a United States person was required to report a transfer to a foreign partnership of appreciated property under paragraph (a)(1) or (2) of this section, and the foreign partnership disposes of the property while such United States person remains a direct or indirect partner, that United States person must report the disposition by filing Form 8865. The form must be attached to, and filed by the due date (including extensions) of, the United States person's income tax return for the year in which the disposition occurred.

(ii) *Disposition of contributed property in nonrecognition transaction.*—If a foreign partnership disposes of contributed appreciated property in a nonrecognition transaction and substituted basis property is received in exchange, and the substituted basis property has built-in gain under §1.704-3(a)(8), the original transferor is not required to report the disposition. However, the transferor must report the disposition of the substituted basis property in the same manner as provided for the contributed property.

(5) *Time for filing Form 8865.*—The Form 8865 on which a transfer is reported must be attached to the transferor's timely filed (including extensions) income tax return for the tax year that includes the date of the transfer. If the person required to report under this section is not required to file an income tax return for its tax year during which the transfer occurred, but is required to file an information return for that year (for example, Form 1065, "U.S. Partnership Return of Income," or Form 990, "Return of Organization Exempt from Income Tax"), the person should attach the Form 8865 to its information return.

(6) *Returns to be made.*—(i) *Separate returns for each partnership.*— If a United States person transfers property reportable under this section to more than one foreign partnership in a taxable year, the United States person must submit a separate Form 8865 for each partnership.

(ii) *Duplicate form to be filed.*—If required by the instructions accompanying Form 8865, a duplicate Form 8865 (including attachments and schedules) must also be filed by the due date for submitting the original Form 8865 under paragraph (a)(5)(i) or (ii) of this section, as applicable.

(7) *Examples.*—The application of this paragraph (a) may be illustrated by the following examples:

*Example 1.* On November 1, 2001, *US*, a United States person that uses the calendar year as its taxable year, contributes $200,000 to *FP*, a foreign partnership, in a transaction subject to section 721. After the contribution, *US* owns a 5% interest in *FP*. *US* must report the contribution by filing Form 8865 for its taxable year ending December 31, 2001. On March 1, 2002, *US* makes a $40,000 section 721 contribution to *FP*, after which *US* owns a 6% interest in *FP*. *US* must report the $40,000 contribution by filing Form 8865 for its taxable year ending December 31, 2002, because the contribution, when added to the value of the other property contributed by *US* to *FP* during the 12-month period ending on the date of the transfer, exceeds $100,000.

*Example 2.* F, a nonresident alien, is the brother of *US*, a United States person. F owns a 15% interest in *FP*, a foreign partnership. *US* contributes $99,000 to *FP*, in exchange for a 1-percent partnership interest. Under sections 6038(e)(3)(C) and 267(c)(2), *US* is considered to own at least a 10-percent interest in *FP* and, therefore, *US* must report the $99,000 contribution under this section.

*Example 3.* *US*, a United States person, owns 40 percent of *FC*, a foreign corporation. *FC* owns a 20-percent interest in *FP*, a foreign partnership. Under section 267(c)(1), *US* is considered to own 8 percent of *FP* due to its ownership of *FC*. *US* contributes $50,000 to *FP* in exchange for a 5-percent partnership interest. Immediately after the contribution, *US* is considered to own at least a 10-percent interest in *FP* and, therefore, must report the $50,000 contribution under this section.

*Example 4.* *US*, a United States person, owns a 60-percent interest in *USP*, a domestic partnership. On March 1, 2001, *USP* contributes $200,000 to *FP*, a foreign partnership, in exchange for a 5-percent partnership interest. Under paragraph (a)(2) of this section, *US* is considered as having contributed $120,000 to *FP* ($200,000 × 60%).

However, under paragraph (a)(2), if *USP* properly reports the contribution to *FP*, *US* is not required to report its $120,000 contribution. If *US* directly contributes $5,000 to *FP* on June 10, 2001, *US* must report the $5,000 contribution because *US* is considered to have contributed more than $100,000 to *FP* in the 12-month period ending on the date of the $5,000 contribution.

*Example 5.* *US*, a United States person, owns an 80-percent interest in *USP*, a domestic partnership. USP owns an 80-percent interest in *USP1*, a domestic partnership. On March 1, 2001, *USP1* contributes $200,000 to *FP*, a foreign partnership, in exchange for a 3-percent partnership interest. Under paragraph (a)(2) of this section, *USP* is considered to have contributed $160,000 ($200,000 × 80%) to *FP*. *US* is considered to have contributed $128,000 to *FP* ($200,000 × 80% × 80%). However, if *USP1* reports the transfer of the $200,000 to *FP*, neither *US* nor *USP* are required to report under this section the amounts they are considered to have contributed. Additionally, regardless of whether *USP1* reports the $200,000 contribution, if *USP* reports the $160,000 contribution it is considered to have made, *US* does not have to report under this section the $128,000 contribution *US* is considered to have made.

(b) *Transfers by trusts relating to state and local government employee retirement plans.*—Trusts relating to state and local government employee retirement plans are not required to report transfers under this section, unless otherwise specified in the instructions to Form 8865.

(c) *Information required with respect to transfers of property.*—With respect to transfers required to be reported under paragraph (a)(1) or (2) of this section, the return must contain information in such form or manner as Form 8865 (and its accompanying instructions) prescribes with respect to reportable events, including—

(1) The name, address, and U.S. taxpayer identification number of the United States person making the transfer;

(2) The name, U.S. taxpayer identification number (if any), and address of the transferee foreign partnership, and the type of entity and country under whose laws the partnership was created or organized;

(3) A general description of the transfer, and of any wider transaction of which it forms a part, including the date of transfer;

(4) The names and addresses of the other partners in the foreign partnership, unless the transfer is solely of cash and the transferor holds less than a ten-percent interest in the transferee foreign partnership immediately after the transfer. However, for tax years of U.S. persons beginning on or after January 1, 2000, the person reporting pursuant to section 6038B (the transferor) must provide the names and addresses of each United States person that owned a ten-percent or greater direct interest in the foreign partnership during the transferor's tax year in which the transfer occurred, and the names and addresses of any other United States or foreign persons that were direct partners in the foreign partnership during that tax year and that were related to the transferor during that tax year. See paragraph (i)(4) of this section for the definition of a related person;

(5) A description of the partnership interest received by the United States person, including a change in partnership interest;

(6) A separate description of each item of contributed property that is appreciated property subject to the allocation rules of section 704(c) (except to the extent that the property is permitted to be aggregated in making allocations under section 704(c)), or is intangible property, including its estimated fair market value and adjusted basis;

(7) A description of other contributed property, not specified in paragraph (c)(6) of this section, aggregated by the following categories (with, in each case, a brief description of the property)—

(i) Stock in trade of the transferor (inventory);

(ii) Tangible property (other than stock in trade) used in a trade or business of the transferor;

(iii) Cash;

(iv) Stock, notes receivable and payable, and other securities; and

(v) Other property;

(8) With respect to reporting required under §1.721(c)-6(b)(2) and paragraph (a)(1)(iii) of this section with regard to a gain deferral contribution, the information required by §1.721(c)-6(b)(2); and

(9) With respect to section 721(c) property for which reporting is required under §1.721(c)-6(b)(3) and paragraph (a)(1)(iii) of this section, the information required by §1.721(c)-6(b)(3).

(d) *Information required with respect to dispositions of property.*—In respect of dispositions required to be reported under paragraph (a)(4) of this section, the return must contain information in such form or manner as Form 8865 (and its accompanying instructions) prescribes with respect to reportable events, including—

(1) The date and manner of disposition;

(2) The gain and depreciation recapture amounts, if any, realized by the partnership; and

(3) Any such amounts allocated to the United States person.

(e) *Method of reporting.*—Except as otherwise provided on Form 8865, or the accompanying instructions, all amounts reported as required under this section must be expressed in United States currency, with a statement of the exchange rates used. All statements required on or with Form 8865 pursuant to this section must be in the English language.

(f) *Reporting under this section not required of partnerships excluded from the application of subchapter K.*—(1) *Election to be wholly excluded.*—The reporting requirements of this section will not apply to any United States person in respect of an eligible partnership as described in § 1.761-2(a), if such partnership has validly elected to be excluded from all of the provisions of subchapter K of chapter 1 of the Internal Revenue Code in the manner specified in § 1.761-2(b)(2)(i).

(2) *Deemed excluded.*—The reporting requirements of this section will not apply to any United States person in respect of an eligible partnership as described in § 1.761-2(a), if such partnership is validly deemed to have elected to be excluded from all of the provisions of subchapter K of chapter 1 of the Internal Revenue Code in accordance with the provisions of § 1.761-2(b)(2)(ii).

(g) *Deemed contributions.*—Deemed contributions resulting from IRS-initiated section 482 adjustments are not required to be reported under section 6038B. However, taxpayers must report deemed contributions resulting from taxpayer-initiated adjustments. Such information will be furnished timely if filed by the due date, including extensions, for filing the taxpayer's income tax return for the year in which the adjustment is made.

(h) *Failure to comply with reporting requirements.*—(1) *Consequences of a failure.*—If a United States person is required to file a return under paragraph (a) of this section and fails to comply with the reporting requirements of section 6038B and this section, or Reg. § 1.721(c)-6, then that person is subject to the following penalties:

(i) The United States person is subject to a penalty equal to 10 percent of the fair market value of the property at the time of the contribution. Such penalty with respect to a particular transfer is limited to $100,000, unless the failure to comply with respect to such transfer was due to intentional disregard.

(ii) The United States person must recognize gain (reduced by the amount of any gain recognized, with respect to that property, by the transferor after the transfer) as if the contributed property had been sold for fair market value at the time of the contribution. Adjustments to the basis of the partnership's assets and any relevant partner's interest as a result of gain being recognized under this provision will be made as though the gain was recognized in the year in which the failure to report was finally determined.

(2) *Failure to comply.*—A failure to comply with the requirements of section 6038B includes—

(i) The failure to report at the proper time and in the proper manner any information required to be reported under the rules of this section; and

(ii) The provision of false or inaccurate information in purported compliance with the requirements of this section.

(3) *Reasonable cause exception.*—Under section 6038B(c)(2) and this section, the provisions of paragraph (h)(1) of this section will not apply if the United States person shows, in a timely manner, that a failure to comply was due to reasonable cause and not willful neglect. A United States person's statement that the failure to comply was due to reasonable cause and not willful neglect will be considered timely only if, promptly after the United States person becomes aware of the failure, an amended return is filed for the taxable year to which the failure relates that includes the information that should have been included with the original return for such taxable year or that otherwise complies with the rules of this section, and that includes a written statement explaining the reasons for the failure to comply. If any taxable year of the United States person is under examination when the amended return is filed, a copy of the amended return must be delivered to the Internal Revenue Service personnel conducting the examination when the amended return is filed. If no taxable year of the United States person is under examination when the amended return is filed, a copy of the amended return must be delivered to the Director of Field Operations, Cross Border Activities Practice Area of Large Business & International (or any successor to the roles and responsibilities of such position, as appropriate) (Director). Whether a failure to comply was due to reasonable cause and not willful neglect will be determined by the Director under all the facts and circumstances.

(4) *Statute of limitations.*—For exceptions to the limitations on assessment in the event of a failure to provide information under section 6038B, see section 6501(c)(8).

(i) *Definitions.*—(1) *Appreciated property.*—Appreciated property is property that has a fair market value in excess of basis.

(2) *Domestic partnership.*—A domestic partnership is a partnership described in section 7701(a)(4).

(3) *Foreign partnership.*—A foreign partnership is a partnership described in section 7701(a)(5).

(4) *Related person.*—Persons are related persons if they bear a relationship described in section 267(b)(1) through (3) or (10) through (12), after application of section 267(c) (except for (c)(3)), or in section 707(b)(1)(B).

(5) *Substituted basis property.*—Substituted basis property is property described in section 7701(a)(42).

(6) *Taxpayer-initiated adjustment.*—A taxpayer-initiated adjustment is a section 482 adjustment that is made by the taxpayer pursuant to § 1.482-1(a)(3).

(7) *United States person.*—A United States person is a person described in section 7701(a)(30).

(j) *Effective dates.*—(1) *In general.*—Except as otherwise provided in this section, this section applies to transfers made on or after January 1, 1998. However, for a transfer made on or after January 1, 1998, but before January 1, 1999, the filing requirements of this section may be satisfied by—

(i) Filing a Form 8865 with the taxpayer's income tax return (including a partnership return of income) for the first taxable year beginning on or after January 1, 1999; or

(ii) Filing a Form 926 (modified to reflect that the transferee is a partnership, not a corporation) with the taxpayer's income tax return (including a partnership return of income) for the taxable year in which the transfer occurred.

(2) *Transfers made between August 5, 1997 and January 1, 1998.*—A United States person that made a transfer of property between August 5, 1997, and January 1, 1998, that is required to be reported under section 6038B may satisfy its reporting requirement by reporting in accordance with the provisions of this section or in accordance with the provisions of Notice 98-17 (1998-11 IRB 6) (see § 601.601(d)(2) of this chapter).

(3) *Special rule for transfers made before January 1, 2000.*—Even if not reported in accordance with the rules provided in paragraph (a)(5) of this section, or paragraph (j)(1) or (2) of this section, a transfer that occurred before January 1, 2000 will nevertheless be considered timely reported if the transferor reports it on a Form 8865 attached to an amended tax return for the transferor's tax year in which the transfer occurred, provided such amended return is filed no later than September 15, 2000.

(4) *Transfers of section 721(c) property.*—Paragraph (c)(8) of this section applies to transfers occurring on or after August 6, 2015, and to transfers that occurred before August 6, 2015 resulting from an entity classification election made under § 301.7701-3 of this chapter that was effective on or before August 6, 2015 but was filed on or after August 6, 2015. Paragraphs (a)(1)(iii), (a)(3), and (c)(9) of this section apply to transfers occurring on or after January 18, 2017, and to transfers that occurred before January 18, 2017 resulting from entity classification elections made under § 301.7701-3 of this chapter that were effective on or before January 18, 2017 but were filed on or after January 18, 2017.

(5) *Reasonable cause exception.*—Paragraph (h)(3) of this section applies to all requests for relief for transfers of property to partnerships filed on or after January 18, 2017. [Reg. § 1.6038B-2.]

☐ [*T.D.* 8817, 2-4-99 (*corrected* 3-31-99). *Amended by T.D.* 8850, 12-27-99, *T.D.* 9814, 1-18-2017 *and T.D.* 9891, 1-17-2020.]

### [Reg. § 1.6038D-0]

**§ 1.6038D-0. Outline of regulation provisions.**—This section lists the table of contents for § § 1.6038D-1 through 1.6038D-8. [Reg. § 1.6038D-0.]

☐ [*T.D.* 9706, 12-11-2014. *Amended by T.D.* 9752, 2-22-2016.]

### [Reg. § 1.6038D-1]

**§ 1.6038D-1. Reporting with respect to specified foreign financial assets, definition of terms.**—(a) *In general.*—The following definitions apply for purposes of section 6038D and the regulations—

(1) *Specified person.*—The term *specified person* means a specified individual or a specified domestic entity.

(2) *Specified individual.*—The term *specified individual* means an individual who is a—

(i) U.S. citizen;

(ii) Resident alien of the United States for any portion of the taxable year;

(iii) Nonresident alien for whom an election under section 6013(g) or (h) is in effect; or

(iv) Nonresident alien who is a bona fide resident of Puerto Rico or a section 931 possession (as defined in §1.931-1(c)(1)).

(3) *Resident alien.*—The term *resident alien* has the meaning set forth in section 7701(b) and §§301.7701(b)-1 through 301.7701(b)-9 of this chapter.

(4) *Bona fide resident of a U.S. possession.*—The term *bona fide resident of a U.S. possession* means an individual who is a "bona fide resident" under section 937(a) and §1.937-1.

(5) *U.S. possession.*—The term *U.S. possession* means American Samoa, Guam, the Northern Mariana Islands, Puerto Rico, or the U.S. Virgin Islands.

(6) *Specified foreign financial asset.*—The term *specified foreign financial asset* has the meaning set forth in §1.6038D-3.

(7) *Financial account.*—The term *financial account* has the meaning set forth in §1.1471-5(b), provided, however, that the exclusions of retirement and pension accounts and non-retirement savings accounts under §1.1471-5(b)(2)(i) and retirement and pension accounts, non-retirement savings accounts, and accounts satisfying similar conditions in an applicable Model 1 IGA or Model 2 IGA under §1.1471-5(b)(2)(vi) shall not apply (see the section 6038D coordination rule in §1.1471-5(b)(2)(i)(D)). See §1.6038D-3(a)(2) relating to financial accounts maintained by a financial institution that is organized under the laws of a U.S. possession.

(8) *Financial institution.*—The term *financial institution* has the meaning set forth in section 1471(d)(5) and the regulations thereunder.

(9) *Foreign financial institution.*—The term *foreign financial institution* has the meaning set forth in §1.1471-5(d).

(10) *Foreign entity.*—The term *foreign entity* has the meaning set forth in §1.1473-1(e).

(11) *Annual return.*—The term *annual return* means an annual federal income tax return of a specified individual or an annual federal income tax return or information return of a specified domestic entity filed with the Internal Revenue Service under section 876, 6011, 6012, 6013, 6031, or 6037, and the regulations.

(12) *Specified domestic entity.*—The term *specified domestic entity* has the meaning set forth in §1.6038D-6.

(13) *Model 1 IGA* and *Model 2 IGA.*—The terms *Model 1 IGA* and *Model 2 IGA* have the meanings set forth in §1.1471-1(b)(78) and (79), respectively.

(b) *Effective/applicability dates.*—(1) *In general.*—Except as otherwise provided in this paragraph (b), this section applies to taxable years ending after December 19, 2011. Taxpayers may elect to apply the rules of this section to taxable years ending prior to December 19, 2011.

(2) *Financial accounts.*—For purposes of applying the financial account definition in §1.6038D-1(a)(7), the treatment under §1.1471-5(b)(2)(vi) of retirement and pension accounts, non-retirement savings accounts, and accounts satisfying similar conditions in an applicable Model 1 IGA or Model 2 IGA (see §1.1471-1(b)(78) and (79)) as financial accounts for purposes of the reporting required under section 6038D and §1.6038D-2(a) shall apply to taxable years beginning after December 12, 2014. [Reg. §1.6038D-1.]

☐ [*T.D. 9706, 12-11-2014. Amended by T.D. 9752, 2-22-2016.*]

**[Reg. §1.6038D-2]**

**§1.6038D-2. Requirement to report specified foreign financial assets.**—(a) *Reporting requirement.*—(1) *In general.*—Except as otherwise provided, a specified person that has any interest in a specified foreign financial asset during the taxable year must attach Form 8938, "Statement of Specified Foreign Financial Assets," to that specified person's annual return for the taxable year to report the information required by section 6038D and §1.6038D-4 if the aggregate value of all such assets exceeds—

(i) $50,000 on the last day of the taxable year; or

(ii) $75,000 at any time during the taxable year.

(2) *Special rule for married specified individuals filing a joint annual return.*—Except as provided in paragraph (a)(4) of this section, married specified individuals who file a joint annual return for the taxable year must attach a single Form 8938 to their joint annual return for the taxable year to report the information required by section 6038D and §1.6038D-4 if the aggregate value of all of the specified foreign financial assets in which either married specified individual has an interest exceeds—

(i) $100,000 on the last day of the taxable year; or

(ii) $150,000 at any time during the taxable year.

(3) *Special rule for certain specified individuals living abroad.*—Except as provided in paragraph (a)(4) of this section, a specified individual who is a qualified individual under section 911(d)(1) for the taxable year must attach a Form 8938 to his or her annual return for the taxable year to report the information required by section 6038D and §1.6038D-4 if the aggregate value of the specified foreign financial assets in which the specified individual has an interest exceeds—

(i) $200,000 on the last day of the taxable year; or

(ii) $300,000 at any time during the taxable year.

(4) *Special rule for married specified individuals filing a joint annual return and living abroad.*—A specified individual who is a qualified individual under section 911(d)(1) for the taxable year and the qualified individual's spouse who file a joint annual return for the taxable year must attach a single Form 8938 to their return for the taxable year to report the information required by section 6038D and §1.6038D-4 if the aggregate value of the all of the specified foreign financial assets in which either married individual has an interest exceeds—

(i) $400,000 on the last day of the taxable year; or

(ii) $600,000 at any time during the taxable year.

(5) *Assets with no positive value.*—A specified foreign financial asset is subject to reporting even if the specified foreign financial asset does not have a positive value. See §1.6038D-5(b)(3) to determine the maximum value of a specified foreign financial asset that does not have a positive value during the taxable year.

(6) *Aggregate value calculation in case of specified foreign financial asset excluded from reporting.*—(i) *Specified individual.*—The value of any specified foreign financial asset in which a specified individual has an interest and that is excluded from reporting on Form 8938 pursuant to §1.6038D-7(a) (concerning certain assets reported on another form) is included for purposes of determining the aggregate value of specified foreign financial assets. The value of any specified foreign financial asset in which a specified individual has an interest and that is excluded from reporting under §1.6038D-7(b) (concerning assets held by certain domestic trusts) or §1.6038D-7(c) (concerning certain assets owned by a bona fide resident of a U.S. possession) is excluded for purposes of determining the aggregate value of specified foreign financial assets.

(ii) *Specified domestic entity.*—The value of any specified foreign financial asset in which a specified domestic entity has an interest and that is excluded from reporting on Form 8938 pursuant to §1.6038D-7(a) (concerning certain assets reported on another form) is excluded for purposes of determining the aggregate value of specified foreign financial assets. For purposes of determining the aggregate value of specified foreign financial assets, a specified domestic entity that is a corporation or partnership and that has an interest in any specified foreign financial asset is treated as owning all the specified foreign financial assets (excluding specified foreign financial assets excluded from reporting on Form 8938 pursuant to §1.6038D-7(a)) held by all domestic corporations and domestic partnerships that are closely held by the same specified individual as determined under §1.6038D-6(b)(2).

(7) *Form 8938 filed with annual return.*—(i) *General rule.*—A specified person, including a specified individual who is a bona fide resident of a U.S. possession, is not required to file Form 8938 with respect to a taxable year if the specified person is not required to file an annual return with the Internal Revenue Service with respect to such taxable year.

(ii) *Consolidated returns.*—If a specified domestic entity is a member of an affiliated group of corporations that files a consolidated income tax return, the Form 8938 of the specified domestic entity must be filed with the affiliated group's annual return.

(8) *Reporting required regardless of tax result.*—The Form 8938 required by section 6038D and this section must be furnished by a specified person even if none of the specified foreign financial assets that must be reported affect the specified person's tax liability under the Internal Revenue Code for the taxable year.

(9) *Reporting period.*—The reporting period covered by Form 8938 is the specified person's taxable year, except the reporting period for a specified person that is a specified individual for less than an entire taxable year is the portion of the taxable year that the specified person is a specified individual.

(10) *Successor forms.*—References to Form 8938 include any successor form.

(b) *Interest in a specified foreign financial asset.*—(1) *In general.*—A specified person has an interest in a specified foreign financial asset if any income, gains, losses, deductions, credits, gross proceeds, or distributions attributable to the holding or disposition of the specified foreign financial asset are or would be required to be reported, included, or otherwise reflected by the specified person on an annual return. A specified person has an interest in a specified foreign financial asset even if no income, gains, losses, deductions, credits, gross proceeds, or distributions are attributable to the holding or disposition of the specified foreign financial asset for the taxable year.

(2) *Property transferred in connection with the performance of services.*—A specified person that is transferred property in connection with the performance of personal services is first considered to have an interest in the property for purposes of section 6038D on the first date that the property is substantially vested (within the meaning of §1.83-3(b)) or, in the case of property with respect to which a specified person makes a valid election under section 83(b), on the date of transfer of the property.

(3) *Special rule for parent making election under section 1(g)(7).*—A parent who makes an election under section 1(g)(7) to include certain unearned income of a child in the parent's gross income has an interest in any specified foreign financial asset held by the child for the purposes of section 6038D and the regulations.

(4) *Entities.*—(i) *In general.*—Except as provided in this paragraph (b)(4), a specified person is not treated as having an interest in any specified foreign financial assets held by a corporation, partnership, trust, or estate solely as a result of the specified person's status as a shareholder, partner, or beneficiary of such entity.

(ii) *Specified foreign financial assets held by certain trusts.*—A specified person that is treated as the owner of a trust or any portion of a trust under sections 671 through 679, other than a domestic liquidating trust under §301.7701-4(d) of this chapter created pursuant to a court order issued in a bankruptcy under Chapter 7 (11 U.S.C. 701 *et seq.*) or a confirmed plan under Chapter 11 (11 U.S.C. 1101 *et seq.*) of the Bankruptcy Code, or a domestic widely held fixed investment trust under §1.671-5, is treated as having an interest in any specified foreign financial assets held by the trust or the portion of the trust.

(iii) *Specified foreign financial assets held by a disregarded entity.*—A specified person that owns a foreign or domestic entity that is disregarded as an entity separate from its owner as described in §301.7701-2 of this chapter (a disregarded entity) is treated as having an interest in any specified foreign financial assets held by the disregarded entity.

(iv) *Interest in a foreign trust or foreign estate.*—See §1.6038D-3(c) to determine whether an interest in a foreign trust or foreign estate is a specified foreign financial asset. See §1.6038D-5(f) to determine the maximum value of an interest in a foreign trust or foreign estate.

(c) *Special rules for joint interests.*—(1) *In general.*—(i) *Determining aggregate value of assets.*—Except as otherwise provided in this paragraph (c), each specified person that is a joint owner of a specified foreign financial asset (whether with a spouse or other person) must include the entire value of the specified foreign financial asset (and not the value of the specified person's interest) for purposes of determining whether the aggregate value of the specified person's specified foreign financial assets exceeds the reporting thresholds set forth in §1.6038D-2(a).

(ii) *Reporting maximum value.*—Except as provided in paragraph (d) of this section, a specified person that is a joint owner of a specified foreign financial asset must report the entire value of each jointly owned specified foreign financial asset on Form 8938.

(2) *Aggregate asset value for married specified individuals filing a joint annual return.*—Married specified individuals who file a joint annual return must include the value of each specified foreign financial asset that they jointly own or in which both have an interest under paragraph (b)(1) of this section only once in determining whether the aggregate value of all of the specified foreign financial assets in which either married specified individual has an interest exceeds the reporting thresholds set forth in §1.6038D-2(a).

(3) *Aggregate asset value for married specified individual filing a separate annual return.*—(i) *Both spouses are specified individuals.*—If a married specified individual files a separate annual return and his or her spouse is a specified individual, the married specified individual must include one-half of the value of a specified foreign financial asset that the married specified individual jointly owns with his or her spouse in determining whether the married specified individual has an interest in specified foreign financial assets the aggregate value of which exceeds the reporting thresholds set forth in §1.6038D-2(a).

(ii) *One spouse is not a specified individual.*—If a married specified individual files a separate annual return and his or her spouse is not a specified individual, the married specified individual must include the entire value of a specified foreign financial asset that the married specified individual jointly owns with his or her spouse in determining whether the married specified individual has an interest in specified foreign financial assets the aggregate value of which exceeds the reporting thresholds set forth in §1.6038D-2(a).

(d) *Annual return filed by a married specified individual.*—(1) *Joint annual return.*—Married specified individuals who file a joint annual return must file a single Form 8938 to fulfill their reporting requirements under section 6038D and §1.6038D-2(a). The single Form 8938 must report all of the specified foreign financial assets in which either married specified individual has an interest. If both married specified individuals jointly own a specified foreign financial asset or if they have an interest in a specified foreign financial asset under paragraph (b)(1) of this section, the asset must be reported only once on the single Form 8938 filed for the taxable year.

(2) *Separate annual return.*—A married specified individual who files a separate annual return for the taxable year must fulfill the reporting requirements under section 6038D and §1.6038D-2(a) by filing a separate Form 8938 with his or her return that reports all of the specified foreign financial assets in which the married specified individual has an interest, including each of the assets jointly owned with the married specified individual's spouse or with another person. If both of the spouses are specified individuals, each specified individual must report the entire value of each specified foreign financial asset that the spouses jointly own on Form 8938, not the value taken into account under paragraph (c)(3)(i) of this section for purposes of applying the applicable reporting thresholds.

(e) *Special rules for dual resident taxpayers.*—(1) *In general.*—Subject to the provisions of paragraphs (e)(2) and (3) of this section, a specified individual is not required to report specified foreign financial assets on Form 8938 for a taxable year or any portion of a taxable year that the individual is a dual resident taxpayer (within the meaning of §301.7701(b)-7(a)(1) of this chapter) who is treated as a nonresident alien pursuant to §301.7701(b)-7 of this chapter for purposes of computing his or her U.S. tax liability with respect to the portion of the taxable year the individual is considered a dual resident taxpayer.

(2) *Dual resident taxpayer filing as a nonresident alien at end of taxable year.*—If a specified individual to whom this paragraph (e) applies computes his or her U.S. income tax liability as a nonresident alien on the last day of the taxable year and complies with the filing requirements of §301.7701(b)-7(b) and (c) of this chapter and, in particular, such individual timely files with the Internal Revenue Service Form 1040NR, "U.S. Nonresident Alien Income Tax Return," or Form 1040NR-EZ, "U.S. Income Tax Return for Certain Nonresident Aliens With No Dependents," as applicable, and attaches thereto Form 8833, "Treaty-Based Return Position Disclosure Under Section 6114 or 7701(b)," such individual will not be required to report specified foreign financial assets on Form 8938 with respect to the portion of the taxable year covered by Form 1040NR (or Form 1040NR-EZ).

(3) *Dual resident taxpayer filing as resident alien at end of taxable year.*—If a specified individual to whom this paragraph (e) applies computes his or her U.S. income tax liability as a resident alien on the last day of the taxable year and complies with the filing requirements of §1.6012-1(b)(2)(ii)(a) and, in particular, such individual timely files with the Internal Revenue Service Form 1040, "U.S. Individual Income Tax Return," or Form 1040EZ, "Income Tax Return for Single and Joint Filers With No Dependents," as applicable, and attaches a properly completed Form 8833 to the schedule required by §1.6012-1(b)(2)(ii)(a), such individual will not be required to report specified foreign financial assets on Form 8938 with respect to the portion of the individual's taxable year reflected on the schedule to such Form 1040 or Form 1040EZ required by §1.6012-1(b)(2)(ii)(a).

(f) *Example.*—The following example illustrates the application of paragraph (c) of this section:

*Example.* (1) *Facts.* Two married specified individuals, H and W, jointly own a specified foreign financial asset with a value of $90,000 at all times during the taxable year. H separately has an interest in a specified foreign financial asset with a value of $10,000 at all times during the taxable year. W separately has an interest in a specified foreign financial asset with a value of $1,000 at all times during the taxable year.

(2) *Filing requirement.*—(i) *Married specified individuals filing separate annual returns.* If H and W file separate annual returns, the aggregate value of the specified foreign financial assets in which H has an interest at the end of the taxable year is $55,000, comprising one-half of the value of the jointly owned asset, $45,000, and the value of H's separately owned specified foreign financial asset, $10,000. The aggregate value of the specified foreign financial assets in which W has an interest at the end of the taxable year is $46,000, comprising one-half of the value of the jointly owned asset, $45,000, and the value of W's separately owned specified foreign financial asset, $1,000. H must file Form 8938 with his annual return for the taxable year because the aggregate value of the specified foreign financial assets in which H has an interest exceeds the applicable reporting threshold ($50,000) set forth in § 1.6038D-2(a)(1). H must report the maximum value of the entire jointly owned asset, $90,000, and the maximum value of the separately owned asset, $10,000. See § 1.6038D-5(b) regarding the maximum value of a jointly owned specified foreign financial asset to be reported by a specified person, including a married specified individual, that is a joint owner of an asset. The aggregate value of the specified foreign financial assets in which W has an interest, $46,000, does not exceed the applicable reporting threshold set forth in § 1.6038D-2(a)(1). W is not required to file Form 8938 with her separate annual return.

(ii) *Married specified individuals filing a joint annual return.* If H and W file a joint annual return, they must file a single Form 8938 with their joint annual return for the taxable year because the aggregate value of all of the specified foreign financial assets in which either H or W have an interest ($90,000 (included only once), $10,000, and $1000, or $101,000) exceeds the applicable reporting threshold ($100,000) set forth in § 1.6038D-2(a)(2). The single Form 8938 must report the maximum value of the jointly owned specified foreign financial asset, $90,000, and the maximum value of the specified foreign financial assets separately owned by H and W, $10,000 and $1,000, respectively.

(g) *Effective/applicability dates.*—This section, with the exception of § 1.6038D-2(a)(6)(ii), applies to taxable years ending after December 19, 2011. Section 1.6038D-2(a)(6)(ii) applies to taxable years beginning after December 31, 2015. Taxpayers may elect to apply the rules of this section, with the exception of § 1.6038D-2(a)(6)(ii), to taxable years ending on or prior to December 19, 2011. [Reg. § 1.6038D-2.]

☐ [*T.D.* 9706, 12-11-2014. *Amended by T.D.* 9752, 2-22-2016.]

**[Reg. § 1.6038D-3]**

**§ 1.6038D-3. Specified foreign financial assets.**—(a) *Financial accounts.*—(1) *In general.*—Except as otherwise provided in this section, a specified foreign financial asset includes any financial account maintained by a foreign financial institution. An asset held in a financial account maintained by a foreign financial institution is not required to be separately reported on Form 8938, "Statement of Specified Foreign Financial Assets."

(2) *Financial account in a U.S. possession.*—A specified foreign financial asset includes a financial account maintained by a financial institution that is organized under the laws of a U.S. possession.

(3) *Excepted financial accounts.*—(i) *Accounts maintained by U.S. payors.*—A financial account maintained by a U.S. payor as defined in § 1.6049-5(c)(5)(i) (including assets held in such an account) is not a specified foreign financial asset for purposes of section 6038D and the regulations.

(ii) *Mark-to-market election under section 475.*—A financial account is not a specified foreign financial asset if the rules of section 475(a) apply to all of the holdings in the account or an election under section 475(e) or (f) is made with respect to all of the holdings in the account.

(b) *Other specified foreign financial assets.*—(1) *In general.*—Except as otherwise provided in this section, a specified foreign financial asset includes any of the following assets that are not financial accounts and that are held for investment and not held in an account maintained by a financial institution—

(i) Stock or securities issued by a person other than a United States person (including stock or securities issued by a person organized under the laws of a U.S. possession);

(ii) A financial instrument or contract that has an issuer or counterparty which is other than a United States person (including a

financial instrument or contract issued by a person organized under the laws of a U.S. possession); and

(iii) An interest in a foreign entity.

(2) *Mark-to-market election under section 475.*—An asset is not a specified foreign financial asset if the rules of section 475(a) apply to the asset or an election under section 475(e) or (f) is made with respect to the asset.

(3) *Held for investment.*—An asset is held for investment for purposes of section 6038D and the regulations if that asset is not used in, or held for use in, the conduct of a trade or business of a specified person.

(4) *Trade-or-business test.*—For purposes of section 6038D and the regulations, an asset is used in, or held for use in, the conduct of a trade or business and not held for investment if the asset is—

(i) Held for the principal purpose of promoting the present conduct of the trade or business;

(ii) Acquired and held in the ordinary course of the trade or business, as, for example, in the case of an account or note receivable arising from that trade or business; or

(iii) Otherwise held in a direct relationship to the trade or business as determined under paragraph (b)(5) of this section.

(5) *Direct relationship between holding an asset and a trade or business.*—(i) *In general.*—In determining whether an asset is held in a direct relationship to the conduct of a trade or business by a specified person, principal consideration will be given to whether the asset is needed in the trade or business of the specified person. An asset shall be considered needed in the trade or business, for this purpose, only if the asset is held to meet the present needs of that trade or business and not its anticipated future needs. An asset shall be considered as needed in the trade or business if, for example, the asset is held to meet the operating expenses of the trade or business. Conversely, an asset shall be considered as not needed in the trade or business if, for example, the asset is held for the purpose of providing for future diversification into a new trade or business, future plant replacement, or future business contingencies. Stock is never considered used or held for use in a trade or business for purposes of applying this test.

(ii) *Presumption of direct relationship.*—An asset will be treated as held in a direct relationship to the conduct of a trade or business of a specified person if—

(A) The asset was acquired with funds generated by the trade or business of the specified person or the affiliated group of the specified person, if any;

(B) The income from the asset is retained or reinvested in the trade or business; and

(C) Personnel who are actively involved in the conduct of the trade or business exercise significant management and control over the investment of such asset.

(c) *Special rule for interests in foreign trusts and foreign estates.*—An interest in a foreign trust or a foreign estate is not a specified foreign financial asset of a specified person unless the person knows, or has reason to know based on readily accessible information, of the interest. Receipt of a distribution from the foreign trust or foreign estate constitutes actual knowledge for this purpose.

(d) *Examples.*—Examples of assets other than financial accounts that may be considered other specified foreign financial assets include, but are not limited to—

(1) Stock issued by a foreign corporation;

(2) A capital or profits interest in a foreign partnership;

(3) A note, bond, debenture, or other form of indebtedness issued by a foreign person;

(4) An interest in a foreign trust;

(5) An interest rate swap, currency swap, basis swap, interest rate cap, interest rate floor, commodity swap, equity swap, equity index swap, credit default swap, or similar agreement with a foreign counterparty; and

(6) Any option or other derivative instrument with respect to any of the items listed as examples in this paragraph or with respect to any currency or commodity that is entered into with a foreign counterparty or issuer.

(e) *Effective/applicability dates.*—This section applies to taxable years ending after December 19, 2011. Taxpayers may elect to apply the rules of this section to taxable years ending prior to December 19, 2011. [Reg. § 1.6038D-3.]

☐ [*T.D.* 9706, 12-11-2014.]

**[Reg. § 1.6038D-4]**

**§ 1.6038D-4. Information required to be reported.**—(a) *Required information.*—The following information must be reported on Form

8938, "Statement of Specified Foreign Financial Assets," with respect to each specified foreign financial asset:

(1) In the case of a financial account, the name and address of the foreign financial institution with which the account is maintained and the account number of the financial account;

(2) In the case of stock or securities, the name and address of the issuer, and information that identifies the class or issue of which the stock or security is a part;

(3) In the case of a financial instrument or contract, information that identifies the financial instrument or contract, including the names and addresses of all issuers and counterparties;

(4) In the case of an interest in a foreign entity, information that identifies the interest, including the name and address of the foreign entity in which the interest is held;

(5) The maximum value of the specified foreign financial asset during the portion of the taxable year in which the specified person has an interest in the asset;

(6) In the case of a financial account that is a depository account as defined in § 1.1471-5(b)(3)(i) or a custodial account as defined in § 1.1471-5(b)(3)(ii), whether the account was opened or closed during the taxable year;

(7) The date, if any, on which the specified foreign financial asset, other than a financial account that is a depository account as defined in § 1.1471-5(b)(3)(i) or a custodial account as defined in § 1.1471-5(b)(3)(ii), was either acquired or disposed of (or both) during the taxable year;

(8) The amount of any income, gain, loss, deduction, or credit recognized for the taxable year with respect to the reported specified foreign financial asset, and the schedule, form, or return filed with the Internal Revenue Service on which the income, gain, loss, deduction, or credit, if any, is reported or included by the specified person;

(9) The foreign currency in which the account is maintained or the asset is denominated, the foreign currency exchange rate and, if the source of such rate is other than as described in § 1.6038D-5(c)(1), the source of the rate used to determine the specified foreign financial asset's U.S. dollar value, including maximum value;

(10) For any specified foreign financial asset excepted from reporting on Form 8938 under § 1.6038D-7(a), the specified person must report the number of Forms 3520, "Annual Return To Report Transactions With Foreign Trusts and Receipt of Certain Foreign Gifts," Forms 3520-A, "Annual Information Return of Foreign Trust With a U.S. Owner," Forms 5471, "Information Return of U.S. Persons With Respect To Certain Foreign Corporations," Forms 8621, "Return by a Shareholder of a Passive Foreign Investment Company or a Qualified Electing Fund," Forms 8865, "Return of U.S. Persons With Respect To Certain Foreign Partnerships," and, solely for taxable years beginning after March 18, 2010, and ending on or before December 31, 2013, Forms 8891, "U.S. Information Return for Beneficiaries of Certain Canadian Registered Retirement Plans," or such other form under Title 26 of the United States Code identified by the Secretary under § 1.6038D-7(a), timely filed with the Internal Revenue Service on which excepted foreign financial assets are reported or reflected for the taxable year; and

(11) Such other information as may be required by Form 8938 or its instructions or other guidance.

(b) *Effective/applicability dates.*—This section applies to taxable years ending after December 19, 2011. Taxpayers may elect to apply the rules of this section to taxable years ending prior to December 19, 2011. [Reg. § 1.6038D-4.]

☐ [T.D. 9706, 12-11-2014.]

**[Reg. § 1.6038D-5]**

**§ 1.6038D-5. Valuation guidelines.**—(a) *Fair market value.*—Except as provided in paragraphs (c) and (e) of this section, the value of a specified foreign financial asset for purposes of determining the aggregate value of specified foreign financial assets held by a specified person and the maximum value of a specified foreign financial asset required to be reported on Form 8938, "Statement of Specified Foreign Financial Assets," is the asset's fair market value.

(b) *Valuation of assets.*—(1) *Maximum value.*—Except as provided in this section, the maximum value of a specified foreign financial asset means a reasonable estimate of the asset's maximum fair market value during the taxable year.

(2) *U.S. dollars.*—For purposes of determining the aggregate value of specified foreign financial assets in which a specified person has an interest and determining the maximum value of a specified foreign financial asset, the value of a specified foreign financial asset denominated in a foreign currency during the taxable year must be determined in the foreign currency and then converted to U.S. dollars.

(3) *Asset with no positive value.*—If the maximum fair market value of a specified foreign financial asset is zero or less than zero, then the asset's value is treated as zero for purposes of determining the aggregate value of specified foreign financial assets in which a specified person has an interest, and the maximum value of the specified foreign financial asset is zero for purposes of reporting under § 1.6038D-4(a)(5).

(c) *Foreign currency conversion.*—(1) *In general.*—Except as provided in paragraphs (c)(2) and (d) of this section, the U.S. Treasury Department's Bureau of the Fiscal Service foreign currency exchange rate is to be used to convert the value of a specified foreign financial asset into U.S. dollars for purposes of determining the aggregate value of specified foreign financial assets in which a specified person has an interest and determining the maximum value of a specified foreign financial asset.

(2) *Other publicly available exchange rate.*—If no U.S. Treasury Department Bureau of the Fiscal Service foreign currency exchange rate is available for a particular currency, another publicly available foreign currency exchange rate may be used to convert the value of a specified foreign financial asset into U.S. dollars. In such case, the source of the foreign currency exchange rate must be disclosed on Form 8938.

(3) *Currency exchange rate.*—In converting the currency of a foreign country, the foreign currency exchange rate applicable for converting the currency into U.S. dollars (that is, to purchase U.S. dollars) must be used.

(4) *Determination date.*—In converting the currency of a foreign country into U.S. dollars for purposes of determining the maximum value of a specified foreign financial asset and determining the aggregate value of specified foreign financial assets in which a specified person has an interest, the applicable foreign currency exchange rate is the rate on the last day of the taxable year of the specified person, even if the specified person sold or otherwise disposed of a specified foreign financial asset prior to the last day of such year.

(d) *Financial accounts.*—A specified person may rely upon periodic account statements that are provided at least annually by or on behalf of a financial institution maintaining an account, including the foreign currency conversion reflected in those statements, to determine the financial account's maximum value unless the specified person has actual knowledge, or reason to know based on readily accessible information, that the statements do not reflect a reasonable estimate of the maximum account value during the taxable year.

(e) *Asset held in a financial account.*—The value of an asset held in a financial account maintained by a foreign financial institution is included in determining the value of that financial account for purposes of § 1.6038D-5(a).

(f) *Other specified foreign financial assets.*—(1) *General rule.*—Except as provided in paragraphs (f)(2) and (3) of this section, for specified foreign financial assets that are not financial accounts and that are held for investment and not held in an account maintained by a financial institution, a specified person may use the value of the asset as of the last day of the taxable year on which the specified person has an interest in the asset as the maximum value of that asset, unless the specified person has actual knowledge, or reason to know based on readily accessible information, that the value does not reflect a reasonable estimate of the maximum value of the asset during the taxable year.

(2) *Interests in trusts that are specified foreign financial assets.*—(i) *Maximum value.*—If a specified person is a beneficiary of a foreign trust, the maximum value of the specified person's interest in the trust is the sum of-

(A) The fair market value, determined as of the last day of the taxable year, of all of the currency or other property distributed from the foreign trust during the taxable year to the specified person as a beneficiary; and

(B) The value, determined as of the last day of the taxable year, of the specified person's right as a beneficiary to receive mandatory distributions from the foreign trust as determined under section 7520.

(ii) *Reporting threshold.*—For purposes of determining the aggregate value of specified foreign financial assets in which a specified person has an interest, if the specified person does not know, or have reason to know based on readily accessible information, the fair market value of the person's interest in a foreign trust during the taxable year, the value to be included in determining the aggregate value of the specified foreign financial assets is the maximum value of the specified person's interest in the foreign trust under paragraph (f)(2)(i) of this section.

(3) *Interests in estates, pension plans, and deferred compensation plans.*—(i) *Maximum value.*—The maximum value of a specified person's interest in a foreign estate, foreign pension plan, or foreign deferred compensation plan is the fair market value, determined as of the last day of the taxable year, of the specified person's beneficial interest in the assets of the foreign estate, foreign pension plan, or foreign deferred compensation plan. If the specified person does not know, or have reason to know based on readily accessible information, such fair market value, the maximum value to be reported is the fair market value, determined as of the last day of the taxable year, of the currency and other property distributed during the taxable year to the specified person as a beneficiary or participant.

(ii) *Reporting threshold.*—For purposes of determining the aggregate value of specified foreign financial assets in which a specified person has an interest, if the specified person does not know, or have reason to know based on readily accessible information, the fair market value of the person's interest in a foreign estate, foreign pension plan, or foreign deferred compensation plan during the taxable year, the value to be included in determining the aggregate value of the specified foreign financial assets is the fair market value, determined as of the last day of the taxable year, of the currency and other property distributed during the taxable year to the specified person as a beneficiary or participant.

(g) *Effective/applicability dates.*—This section applies to taxable years ending after December 19, 2011. Taxpayers may elect to apply the rules of this section to taxable years ending prior to December 19, 2011. [Reg. § 1.6038D-5.]

☐ [*T.D. 9706, 12-11-2014.*]

### [Reg. § 1.6038D-6]

**§ 1.6038D-6. Specified domestic entities.**—(a) *Specified domestic entity.*—A specified domestic entity is a domestic corporation, a domestic partnership, or a trust described in section 7701(a)(30)(E), if such corporation, partnership, or trust is formed or availed of for purposes of holding, directly or indirectly, specified foreign financial assets. Whether a domestic corporation, a domestic partnership, or a trust described in section 7701(a)(30)(E) is a specified domestic entity is determined annually.

(b) *Corporations and partnerships.*—(1) *Formed or availed of.*—Except as otherwise provided in paragraph (d) of this section, a domestic corporation or a domestic partnership is formed or availed of for purposes of holding, directly or indirectly, specified foreign financial assets if and only if—

(i) The corporation or partnership is closely held by a specified individual as determined under paragraph (b)(2) of this section; and

(ii) At least 50 percent of the corporation's or partnership's gross income for the taxable year is passive income or at least 50 percent of the assets held by the corporation or partnership for the taxable year are assets that produce or are held for the production of passive income as determined under paragraph (b)(3) of this section (passive assets). For purposes of this paragraph (b)(1)(ii), the percentage of passive assets held by a corporation or partnership for a taxable year is the weighted average percentage of passive assets (weighted by total assets and measured quarterly), and the value of assets of a corporation or partnership is the fair market value of the assets or the book value of the assets that is reflected on the corporation's or partnership's balance sheet (as determined under either a U.S. or an international financial accounting standard).

(2) *Closely held.*—(i) *Domestic corporation.*—A domestic corporation is closely held by a specified individual if at least 80 percent of the total combined voting power of all classes of stock of the corporation entitled to vote, or at least 80 percent of the total value of the stock of the corporation, is owned, directly, indirectly, or constructively, by a specified individual on the last day of the corporation's taxable year.

(ii) *Domestic partnership.*—A partnership is closely held by a specified individual if at least 80 percent of the capital or profits interest in the partnership is held, directly, indirectly, or constructively, by a specified individual on the last day of the partnership's taxable year.

(iii) *Constructive ownership.*—For purposes of this paragraph (b)(2), sections 267(c) and (e)(3) apply for the purpose of determining the constructive ownership of a specified individual in a corporation or partnership, except that section 267(c)(4) is applied as if the family of an individual includes the spouses of the individual's family members.

(3) *Determination of passive income and assets.*—(i) *Definition of passive income.*—Except as provided in paragraph (b)(3)(ii) of this

section, for purposes of paragraph (b)(1)(ii) of this section, passive income means the portion of gross income that consists of—

(A) Dividends, including substitute dividends;

(B) Interest;

(C) Income equivalent to interest, including substitute interest;

(D) Rents and royalties, other than rents and royalties derived in the active conduct of a trade or business conducted, at least in part, by employees of the corporation or partnership;

(E) Annuities;

(F) The excess of gains over losses from the sale or exchange of property that gives rise to passive income described in paragraphs (b)(3)(i)(A) through (b)(3)(i)(E) of this section;

(G) The excess of gains over losses from transactions (including futures, forwards, and similar transactions) in any commodity, but not including—

(*1*) Any commodity hedging transaction described in section 954(c)(5)(A), determined by treating the corporation or partnership as a controlled foreign corporation; or

(*2*) Active business gains or losses from the sale of commodities, but only if substantially all the corporation or partnership's commodities are property described in paragraph (1), (2), or (8) of section 1221(a);

(H) The excess of foreign currency gains over foreign currency losses (as defined in section 988(b)) attributable to any section 988 transaction; and

(I) Net income from notional principal contracts as defined in § 1.446-3(c)(1).

(ii) *Exception from passive income treatment for dealers.*—Notwithstanding paragraph (b)(3)(i) of this section, in the case of a corporation or partnership that regularly acts as a dealer in property described in paragraph (b)(3)(i)(F) of this section (referring to the sale or exchange of property that gives rise to passive income), forward contracts, option contracts, or similar financial instruments (including notional principal contracts and all instruments referenced to commodities), the term passive income does not include—

(A) Any item of income or gain (other than any dividends or interest) from any transaction (including hedging transactions and transactions involving physical settlement) entered into in the ordinary course of such dealer's trade or business as such a dealer; and

(B) If such dealer is a dealer in securities (within the meaning of section 475(c)(2)), any income from any transaction entered into in the ordinary course of such trade or business as a dealer in securities.

(iii) *Related entities.*—For purposes of applying the passive income and asset thresholds of paragraph (b)(1)(ii) of this section, all domestic corporations and domestic partnerships that are closely held by the same specified individual as determined under paragraph (b)(2) of this section and that are connected through stock or partnership interest ownership with a common parent corporation or partnership are treated as owning the combined assets and receiving the combined income of all members of that group. For purposes of the preceding sentence, assets relating to any contract, equity, or debt existing between members of such a group, as well as any items of gross income arising under or from such contract, equity, or debt, are eliminated. A domestic corporation or a domestic partnership is considered connected through stock or partnership interest ownership with a common parent corporation or partnership if stock representing at least 80 percent of the total combined voting power of all classes of stock of the corporation entitled to vote or of the value of such corporation, or partnership interests representing at least 80 percent of the profits interests or capital interests of such partnership, in each case other than stock of or partnership interests in the common parent, is owned by one or more of the other connected corporations, connected partnerships, or the common parent.

(4) *Examples.*—The following examples illustrate the application of this section:

*Example 1. Closely held and constructive ownership.* (i) *Facts.* DC1 is a domestic corporation the total value of the stock of which is owned 60% by A, a specified individual, 30% by B, a member of A's family for purposes of section 267(c)(2) who is not a specified individual, and 10% by FC1, a foreign corporation. DC1 owns 90% of the total value of the stock of DC2, a domestic corporation. FC2, a foreign corporation, owns 10% of DC2. Neither A nor B owns, directly, indirectly, or constructively, any stock in FC1 or FC2.

(ii) *Closely held ownership determination.* A is considered to own 90% and 81% of the total value of DC1 and DC2, respectively, by application of the rules of section 267(c) and this section. DC1 and DC2 are closely held by A within the meaning of paragraph (b)(2) of this section because A, a specified individual, is considered to own more than 80% of their total value.

*Example 2. Application of aggregation rule and reporting threshold.* (i) *Facts.* L is a specified individual. In Year X, L wholly owns DC1, a domestic corporation, and also owns a 90% capital interest in DP, a domestic partnership. DC1 owns 80% of the sole class of stock of DC2, a domestic corporation. DC1 has no assets other than its interest in DC2. DC2's only assets are assets that produce passive income, with a maximum value in Year X of $40,000 on October 12. DC2's assets are comprised in relevant part of specified foreign financial assets with a maximum value in Year X of $15,000 on October 12. DP's only assets are assets that produce passive income and that are specified foreign financial assets with a maximum value of $90,000 in Year X on October 12.

(ii) *Specified domestic entity status*—(A) *DC1 and DC2.* DC1 and DC2 are closely held by a specified individual for purposes of paragraph (b)(2) of this section. DC1 and DC2 are considered related entities that are connected through stock ownership with a common parent corporation under paragraph (b)(3)(iii) of this section, because DC1 and DC2 are closely held by L, and DC2 is connected with DC1 through DC1's ownership of stock of DC2 representing at least 80% of the voting power or value of DC2. As a result, for purposes of applying paragraph (b)(1)(ii) of this section, each of DC1 and DC2 is considered as owning the combined assets, and receiving the combined income, of both DC1 and DC2; however, DC1's equity interest in DC2 is disregarded for this purpose under paragraph (b)(3)(iii) of this section. Therefore, DC1 and DC2 each satisfies the passive asset threshold of paragraph (b)(1)(ii) of this section, because 100 percent of each company's assets is passive. DC1 and DC2 are specified domestic entities for Year X.

(B) *DP.* DP is closely held by a specified individual for purposes of paragraph (b)(2) of this section. DP is not considered a related entity with DC1 and DC2 under paragraph (b)(3)(iii) of this section, because DC1 and DP are not owned by a common parent corporation or partnership. As a result, whether the passive income or passive asset threshold of paragraph (b)(1)(ii) of this section is met with respect to DP is determined solely by reference to DP's separately earned passive income and separately held passive assets. DP holds only passive assets during Year X and therefore satisfies paragraph (b)(1)(ii) of this section. DP is a specified domestic entity for Year X.

(iii) *Reporting requirements*—(A) *DC1.* Under § 1.6038D-2(a)(6)(ii), DC1 is not treated as owning the specified foreign financial assets held by DC2 and DP for purposes of applying the reporting threshold of § 1.6038D-2(a)(1), because DC1 does not have an interest in any specified foreign financial assets. DC1 is not required to file Form 8938 because DC1 does not satisfy the reporting threshold of § 1.6038D-2(a)(1).

(B) *DC2 and DP.* Under § 1.6038D-3, DC2 and DP each has an interest in specified foreign financial assets. For purposes of applying the reporting threshold of § 1.6038D-2(a)(1), § 1.6038D-2(a)(6)(ii) provides that DC2 is treated as owning in addition to its own assets the assets of DP, and DP is treated as owning in addition to its own assets the assets of DC2. As a result, DC2 and DP each satisfies the reporting threshold of § 1.6038D-2(a)(1), because the value of the specified foreign financial assets each is considered as owning for purposes of § 1.6038D-2(a)(1) is $105,000 on October 12, Year X, which exceeds DC2's and DP's $75,000 reporting threshold. DC2 and DP must each file Form 8938 for Year X to report their respective specified foreign financial assets in which they have an interest and disclose their maximum values as provided in § 1.6038D-4 ($15,000 in the case of DC2 and $90,000 in the case of DP).

*Example 3. Application of aggregation rule and entity with an active trade or business.* (i) *Facts.* The facts are the same as in *Example 2,* except that DC2 also owns an active business. The assets attributable to the business are not passive assets and constitute at least 60% of the value of DC2's assets at all times during Year X. The income from the business is not passive income and constitutes at least 60% of the gross income generated by DC2 in Year X.

(ii) *Specified domestic entity status*—(A) *DC1 and DC2.* DC1 and DC2 are considered related entities that are connected through stock ownership with a common parent corporation under paragraph (b)(3)(iii) of this section because DC1 and DC2 are closely held by L, and DC2 is connected with DC1 though DC1's ownership of stock of DC2 representing at least 80% of the voting power or value of DC2. As a result, for purposes of applying paragraph (b)(1)(ii) of this section, each of DC1 and DC2 is treated as owning the combined assets, and receiving the combined income, of both DC1 and DC2; however, DC1's equity interest in DC2 is disregarded for this purpose under paragraph (b)(3)(iii) of this section. As a result, no more than 40 percent of the value of DC1's and DC2's assets at all times during Year X are passive and no more than 40 percent of DC1's and DC2's gross income for Year X is passive. DC1 and DC2 do not satisfy the passive income or passive asset threshold in paragraph (b)(1)(ii) of this section for Year X. DC1 and DC2 are not specified domestic entities for Year X.

(B) *DP.* For the reasons described in paragraph (ii)(B) of *Example 2,* DP is a specified domestic entity for Year X.

(iii) *Reporting requirements*—(A) *DC1 and DC2.* DC1 and DC2 are not specified domestic entities for Year X, and are not required to file Form 8938.

(B) *DP.* Under § 1.6038D-3, DP has an interest in specified foreign financial assets. Under § 1.6038D-2(a)(6)(ii), DP is treated as owning in addition to its own assets the assets of DC2. As a result, DP satisfies the reporting threshold of § 1.6038D-2(a)(1) because the value of the specified foreign financial assets it is considered to own for purposes of § 1.6038D-2(a)(1) is $105,000 on October 12, Year X, which exceeds DP's $75,000 reporting threshold. DP must file Form 8938 for Year X to report the specified foreign financial assets in which it has an interest and disclose their maximum values as provided in § 1.6038D-4, which is $90,000.

(c) *Domestic trusts.*—Except as otherwise provided in paragraph (d) of this section, a trust described in section 7701(a)(30)(E) is formed or availed of for purposes of holding, directly or indirectly, specified foreign financial assets if and only if the trust has one or more specified persons as a current beneficiary. The term current beneficiary means, with respect to the taxable year, any person who at any time during such taxable year is entitled to, or at the discretion of any person may receive, a distribution from the principal or income of the trust (determined without regard to any power of appointment to the extent that such power remains unexercised at the end of the taxable year). The term current beneficiary also includes any holder of a general power of appointment, whether or not exercised, that was exercisable at any time during the taxable year, but does not include any holder of a general power of appointment that is exercisable only on the death of the holder.

(d) *Excepted domestic entities.*—An entity is not considered to be a specified domestic entity if the entity is—

(1) *Certain persons described in section 1473(3).*—An entity, except for a trust that is exempt from tax under section 664(c), that is excepted from the definition of the term "specified United States person" under section 1473(3) and the regulations issued under that section;

(2) *Certain domestic trusts.*—A trust described in section 7701(a)(30)(E) provided that the trustee of the trust—

(i) Has supervisory authority over or fiduciary obligations with regard to the specified foreign financial assets held by the trust;

(ii) Timely files (including any applicable extensions) annual returns and information returns on behalf of the trust; and

(iii) Is —

(A) A bank that is examined by the Office of the Comptroller of the Currency, the Board of Governors of the Federal Reserve System, the Federal Deposit Insurance Corporation, or the National Credit Union Administration;

(B) A financial institution that is registered with and regulated or examined by the Securities and Exchange Commission; or

(C) A domestic corporation described in section 1473(3)(A) or (B), and the regulations issued with respect to those provisions.

(3) *Domestic trusts owned by one or more specified persons.*—A trust described in section 7701(a)(30)(E) to the extent such trust or any portion thereof is treated as owned by one or more specified persons under sections 671 through 678 and the regulations issued under those sections.

(e) *Effective/applicability dates.*—This section applies to taxable years beginning after December 31, 2015. [Reg. § 1.6038D-6.]

☐ [*T.D. 9706, 12-11-2014. Amended by T.D. 9752, 2-22-2016.*]

### [Reg. § 1.6038D-7]

**§ 1.6038D-7. Exceptions from the reporting of certain assets under Section 6038D.**—(a) *Elimination of duplicative reporting of assets.*—(1) *In general.*—A specified person is not required to report a specified foreign financial asset on Form 8938, "Statement of Specified Foreign Financial Assets," if the specified person—

(i) Reports the asset on at least one of the following forms timely filed with the Internal Revenue Service for the taxable year—

(A) Form 3520, "Annual Return To Report Transactions With Foreign Trusts and Receipt of Certain Foreign Gifts" (in the case of a specified person that is the beneficiary of a foreign trust);

(B) Form 5471, "Information Return of U.S. Persons With Respect To Certain Foreign Corporations";

(C) Form 8621, "Return by a Shareholder of a Passive Foreign Investment Company or Qualified Electing Fund";

(D) Form 8865, "Return of U.S. Persons With Respect To Certain Foreign Partnerships";

(E) For taxable years beginning after March 18, 2010, and ending on or before December 31, 2013, Form 8891, "U.S. Information Return for Beneficiaries of Certain Canadian Registered Retirement Plans"; or

(F) Any other form under Title 26 of the United States Code timely filed with the Internal Revenue Service and identified for this purpose by the Secretary in regulations or other guidance; and

(ii) Reports on Form 8938 the filing of the form on which the asset is reported.

(2) *Foreign grantor trusts.*—A specified person that is treated as an owner of a foreign trust or any portion of a foreign trust under sections 671 through 679 is not required to report any specified foreign financial assets held by the foreign trust on Form 8938, provided—

(i) The specified person reports the trust on a Form 3520 timely filed with the Internal Revenue Service for the taxable year;

(ii) The trust timely files Form 3520-A, "Annual Information Return of Foreign Trust With a U.S. Owner," with the Internal Revenue Service for the taxable year; and

(iii) The Form 8938 filed by the specified person for the taxable year reports the filing of the Form 3520 and Form 3520-A.

(3) *Joint Form 5471 or Form 8865 filing.*—A specified person that is included as part of a joint Form 5471 filing pursuant to § 1.6038-2(j) or a joint Form 8865 filing pursuant to § 1.6038-3(c) and who notifies the Internal Revenue Service as required by § 1.6038-2(i) or § 1.6038D-(3)(c) will be considered to have filed a Form 5471 or Form 8865 for purposes of paragraph (a)(1) of this section.

(b) *Owner of certain trusts.*—A specified person that is treated as an owner of any portion of a domestic trust under sections 671 through 678 is not required to file Form 8938 to report any specified foreign financial asset held by the trust if the trust is—

(1) A widely-held fixed investment trust under § 1.671-5; or

(2) A liquidating trust within the meaning of § 301.7701-4(d) of this chapter that is created pursuant to a court order issued in a bankruptcy under Chapter 7 (11 U.S.C. 701 *et seq.*) or a confirmed plan under Chapter 11 (11 U.S.C. 1101 *et seq.*) of the Bankruptcy Code.

(c) *Special rules for bona fide residents of a U.S. possession.*—A specified individual who is a bona fide resident of a U.S. possession is not required to include the following specified foreign financial assets in the determination of the aggregate value of his or her specified foreign financial assets and, if required to file Form 8938 with the Internal Revenue Service, is not required to report the following specified foreign financial assets:

(1) A financial account maintained by a financial institution organized under the laws of the U.S. possession of which the specified individual is a bona fide resident;

(2) A financial account maintained by a branch of a financial institution not organized under the laws of the U.S. possession of which the specified individual is a bona fide resident, if the branch is subject to the same tax and information reporting requirements applicable to a financial institution organized under the laws of the U.S. possession;

(3) Stock or securities issued by an entity organized under the laws of the U.S. possession of which the specified individual is a bona fide resident;

(4) An interest in an entity organized under the laws of the U.S. possession of which the specified individual is a bona fide resident; and

(5) A financial instrument or contract held for investment, provided each issuer or counterparty that is not a United States person is—

(i) An entity organized under the laws of the U.S. possession of which the specified individual is a bona fide resident; or

(ii) A bona fide resident of the U.S. possession of which the specified individual is a bona fide resident.

(d) *Effective/applicability dates.*—This section applies to taxable years ending after December 19, 2011. Taxpayers may elect to apply the rules of this section to taxable years ending prior to December 19, 2011. [Reg. § 1.6038D-7.]

☐ [*T.D. 9706*, 12-11-2014.]

**[Reg. § 1.6038D-8]**

**§ 1.6038D-8. Specified domestic entities.**—(a) *In general.*—If a specified person fails to file a Form 8938, "Statement of Specified Foreign Financial Assets," that includes the information required by section 6038D(c) and § 1.6038D-4 with respect to any taxable year at the time and in the manner described in section 6038D(a) and § 1.6038D-2, a penalty of $10,000 will apply to that specified person.

(b) *Married specified individuals filing a joint annual return.*—Married specified individuals who file a joint annual return and fail to file a required Form 8938 that includes the information required by section 6038D(c) and § 1.6038D-4 with respect to any taxable year at the time and in the manner described in section 6038D(a) and § 1.6038D-2 are subject to penalties under this section as if the married specified individuals are a single specified individual. The liability of married specified individuals who file a joint annual return with respect to any penalties under this section is joint and several.

(c) *Increase in penalty.*—If any failure to comply with the applicable reporting requirement of section 6038D and the regulations continues for more than 90 days after the day on which the Commissioner or his delegate mails a notice of the failure to the specified person required to file the Form 8938, the specified person is required to pay an additional penalty of $10,000 for each 30-day period (or fraction thereof) during which the failure continues after the 90-day period has expired. The additional penalty imposed by section 6038D(d)(2) and this paragraph (c) is limited to a maximum of $50,000 for each such failure.

(d) *Presumption of aggregate value.*—For the purpose of assessing penalties imposed under section 6038D(d), if the Commissioner or his delegate determines that a specified person has an interest in one or more specified foreign financial assets and the specified person does not provide sufficient information to demonstrate the aggregate value of the assets upon request by the Commissioner or his delegate, then the aggregate value of the assets is treated as being in excess of the applicable reporting threshold set forth in § 1.6038D-2(a).

(e) *Reasonable cause exception.*—(1) *In general.*—If the failure to report the information required in section 6038D(c) and § 1.6038D-4 is shown to be due to reasonable cause and not due to willful neglect, no penalty will be imposed under section 6038D(d) or this section.

(2) *Affirmative showing required.*—In order to show that the failure to report the information required in section 6038D(c) and § 1.6038D-4 is due to reasonable cause and not due to willful neglect for purposes of section 6038D(g) and this section, the specified person must make an affirmative showing of all the facts alleged as reasonable cause for the failure to disclose.

(3) *Facts and circumstances taken into account.*—The determination of whether a failure to disclose a specified foreign financial asset on Form 8938 was due to reasonable cause and not due to willful neglect is made on a case-by-case basis, taking into account all pertinent facts and circumstances. The fact that a foreign jurisdiction would impose a civil or criminal penalty on the specified person (or any other person) for disclosing the required information is not reasonable cause.

(f) *Penalties for underpayments attributable to undisclosed foreign financial assets.*—(1) *Accuracy-related penalty.*—For application of the accuracy-related penalty in the case of any portion of an underpayment attributable to any undisclosed foreign financial asset understatement, see section 6662(j).

(2) *Criminal penalties.*—In addition to other penalties, failure to comply with the reporting requirements of section 6038D and the regulations, or any underpayment related to such failure, may result in criminal penalties under sections 7201, 7203, 7206, et seq., or other provisions of Federal law.

(g) *Effective/applicability dates.*—This section applies to taxable years ending after December 19, 2011. Taxpayers may elect to apply the rules of this section to taxable years ending prior to December 19, 2011. [Reg. § 1.6038D-8.]

☐ [*T.D. 9706*, 12-11-2014.]

**[Reg. § 1.6039-1]**

**§ 1.6039-1. Returns required in connection with certain options.**—(a) *Requirement of return with respect to incentive stock options under section 6039(a)(1).*—(1) Every corporation which in any calendar year transfers to any person a share of stock pursuant to such person's exercise of an incentive stock option shall, for such calendar year, file a return with respect to each transfer made during such year. This return must include the following information—

(i) The name, address, and employer identification number of the corporation transferring the stock;

(ii) If other than the corporation identified in paragraph (a)(1)(i) of this section, the name, address and employer identification number of the corporation whose stock is being transferred;

(iii) The name, address, and identifying number of the person to whom the share or shares of stock were transferred pursuant to the exercise of the option;

(iv) The date the option was granted to the person;

(v) The exercise price per share;

(vi) The date the option was exercised by the person;

(vii) The fair market value of a share of stock on the date the option was exercised by the person; and

(viii) The number of shares of stock transferred to the person pursuant to the exercise of the option.

(2) Each return required by this paragraph (a) shall be made on Form 3921, Exercise of an Incentive Stock Option Under Section 422(b) (or its designated successor) and shall be filed in such manner as provided in the instructions thereto.

(b) *Requirement of return with respect to stock purchased under an employee stock purchase plan under section 6039(a)(2).*—(1) Every corporation which in any calendar year records, or has by its agent recorded, a transfer of the legal title of a share of stock acquired by the transferor (person who acquires the shares pursuant to the exercise of the option) pursuant to the transferor's exercise of an option granted under an employee stock purchase plan as described in section 423(c) and where the exercise price is less than 100 percent of the value of the stock on date of grant or is not fixed or determinable on the date of the grant, shall, for such calendar year, file a return with respect each transfer made during such year. This return must include the following information—

(i) The name, address, and identifying number of the transferor;

(ii) The name, address and employer identification number of the corporation whose stock is being transferred;

(iii) The date the option was granted to the transferor;

(iv) The fair market value of the stock on the date the option was granted;

(v) The actual exercise price paid per share;

(vi) The exercise price per share determined as if the option were exercised on the date the option was granted to the transferor (to be provided only if the exercise price per share is not fixed or determinable on the date the option was granted);

(vii) The date the option was exercised by the transferor;

(viii) The fair market value of the stock on the date the option was exercised by the transferor;

(ix) The date the legal title of the shares was transferred by the transferor (see paragraph (b)(3) of this section); and

(x) The number of shares to which legal title was transferred by the transferor.

(2) Each return required by this paragraph (b) shall be made on Form 3922, Transfer of Stock Acquired Through an Employee Stock Purchase Plan Under Section 423(c) (or its designated successor) and shall be filed in such manner as provided in the instructions thereto.

(3) A return is required by reason of a transfer described in section 6039(a)(2) only with respect to the first transfer of legal title of the shares by the transferor, including the first transfer of legal title to a recognized broker or financial institution. If a contractual agreement exists or is entered into with a recognized broker or financial institution pursuant to which shares acquired upon exercise of the option will be immediately deposited into a brokerage account established on behalf of the transferor, then the deposit of shares by the transferor into the brokerage account following the exercise of the option is the first transfer of legal title of the shares acquired by the transferor, and the corporation is only required to file a return relating to such transfer of legal title.

(4) Every corporation that transfers any share of stock pursuant to the exercise of an option described in this paragraph shall identify such stock in a manner sufficient to enable the accurate reporting of the transfer of legal title to such shares. Such identification may be accomplished by assigning to the certificates of stock issued pursuant to the exercise of such options a special serial number or color.

(c) *Time for filing returns.*—Each return required by this section for a calendar year must be filed in accordance with the guidelines and procedures set forth in the instructions to Form 3921 and Form 3922.

(d) *Penalty.*—For provisions relating to the penalty applicable to the failure to file a return under this section, see section 6721.

(e) *Exception to return requirements of section 6039(a) for certain nonresident aliens.*—(1) *Return requirement under section 6039(a)(1).*—The return requirement of section 6039(a)(1) is not applicable to the exercise of an incentive stock option by an employee who is a nonresident alien (as defined in section 7701(b)) and to whom the corporation is not required to provide a Form W-2, Wage and Tax Statement (or its designated successor) for any calendar year within the time period beginning with the first day of the calendar year in which the option was granted to the employee and ending on the last day of the calendar year in which the employee exercised the option.

(2) *Return requirement under section 6039(a)(2).*—The return requirement of section 6039(a)(2) is not applicable to the first transfer of

legal title of a share of stock by an employee who is a nonresident alien (as defined in section 7701(b)) and to whom the corporation is not required to provide a Form W-2 for any calendar year within the time period beginning with the first day of the calendar year in which the option was granted to the employee and ending on the last day of the calendar year in which the employee first transferred legal title to shares acquired under the option as described in paragraph (b)(3) of this section.

(3) For purposes of this paragraph (e), the term *corporation* is defined in section 7701(a) and includes, but is not limited to, the corporation issuing the stock, a related corporation of the corporation, any agent of the corporation, any party distributing shares of stock or other payments in connection with the plan (for example, a brokerage firm), and any party in control of the payment of remuneration for employment to the employee.

(f) *Effective/applicability date.*—(1) *In general.*—This section is effective on November 17, 2009. This section will apply as of January 1, 2007.

(2) *Transition period.*—Taxpayers are not required to comply with the return requirements of paragraphs (a) and (b) of this section for stock transfers that occur during the 2007, 2008 and 2009 calendar years. [Reg. § 1.6039-1.]

[T.D. 9144, 8-2-2004 (corrected 10-15-2004). Amended by T.D. 9470, 11-16-2009.]

### [Reg. § 301.6039-1]

§ 301.6039-1. Information returns and statements required in connection with certain options.—For provisions relating to information returns and statements required in connection with certain options, see §§ 1.6039-1 and 1.6039-2 of this chapter (Income Tax Regulations). [Reg. § 301.6039-1.]

☐ [T.D. 7275, 5-4-73.]

### [Reg. § 1.6039-2]

§ 1.6039-2. Statements to persons with respect to whom information is reported.—(a) *Requirement of statement with respect to incentive stock options under section 6039(b).*—(1) Every corporation filing a return under § 1.6039-1(a) shall furnish to each person whose name is set forth in such return a written statement with respect to the transfer or transfers made to such person during such year. This statement must include the information described in § 1.6039-1(a)(1).

(2) Each statement required by this paragraph (a) to be furnished to any person must be furnished to such person on Form 3921, Exercise of an Incentive Stock Option Under Section 422(b) (or its designated successor) and be delivered at such time and in such manner as provided in the instructions thereto.

(b) *Requirement of statement with respect to stock purchased under an employee stock purchase plan under section 6039(b).*—(1) Every corporation filing a return under § 1.6039-1(b) shall furnish to each person whose name is set forth in such return a written statement with respect to the transfer or transfers made by such person during such year. This statement must include the information described in § 1.6039-1(b)(1).

(2) Each statement required by this paragraph (b) to be furnished to any person must be furnished to such person on Form 3922, Transfer of Stock Acquired Through an Employee Stock Purchase Plan Under Section 423(c) (or its designated successor) and be delivered at such time and in such manner as provided in the instructions thereto.

(3) If the statement required by this paragraph is made by the authorized transfer agent of the corporation, it is deemed to have been made by the corporation. The term *transfer agent*, as used in this section, means any designee authorized to keep the stock ownership records of a corporation and to record a transfer of title of the stock of such corporation on behalf of such corporation.

(c) *Time for furnishing statements.*—(1) *In general.*—Each statement required by this section to be furnished to any person for a calendar year must be furnished to such person on or before January 31 of the year following the year for which the statement is required. However, for a statement required to be furnished after December 31, 2008, the February 15 due date under section 6045 applies to the statement if the statement is furnished in a consolidated reporting statement under section 6045. See §§ 1.6045-1(k)(3), 1.6045-2(d)(2), 1.6045-3(e)(2), 1.6045-4(m)(3), and 1.6045-5(a)(3)(ii).

(2) *Extension of time.*—An extension of time to furnish statements required by this section may be granted in accordance with the guidelines and procedures set forth in the instructions to Form 3921 and Form 3922.

(d) *Penalty.*—For provisions relating to the penalty applicable to the failure to furnish a statement under this section, see section 6722.

(e) *Effective/applicability date.*—(1) *In general.*—This section is effective on November 17, 2009. This section will apply as of January 1, 2007.

(2) *Reliance and transition period.*—Notwithstanding § 1.6039-1(f), corporations must furnish information statements to employees in accordance with this section for stock transfers that are subject to § 1.6039-1(a) and (b), and occur during the 2007, 2008 and 2009 calendar years. For purposes of furnishing information statements for stock transfers that occur during the 2007 or 2008 calendar years, taxpayers may rely on § 1.6039-1 of the 2004 final regulations (69 FR 46401) or § 1.6039-2 of the 2008 proposed regulations (REG-103146-08) (73 FR 40999). For purposes of furnishing information statements for stock transfers that occur during the 2009 calendar year, taxpayers may rely on § 1.6039-1 of the 2004 final regulations (69 FR 46401), § 1.6039-2 of the 2008 proposed regulations (REG-103146-08) (73 FR 40999), or this section. [Reg. § 1.6039-2.]

[*T.D.* 9470, 11-16-2009 (*corrected* 12-22-2009). *Amended by T.D.* 9504, 10-12-2010.]

### [Reg. § 301.6039E-1]

**§ 301.6039E-1. Information reporting by passport applicants.**—(a) *In general.*—Every individual who applies for a U.S. passport or the renewal of a passport (passport applicant), other than a passport for use in diplomatic, military, or other official U.S. government business, shall include with his or her passport application the information described in paragraph (b)(1) of this section in the time and manner described in paragraph (b)(2) of this section.

(b) *Required information.*—(1) *In general.*—The information required under paragraph (a) of this section shall include the following information:

(i) The passport applicant's full name and, if applicable, previous name;

(ii) The passport applicant's permanent address and, if different, mailing address;

(iii) The passport applicant's taxpayer identifying number (TIN), if such a number has been issued to the passport applicant. A TIN means the individual's social security number (SSN) issued by the Social Security Administration. A passport applicant who does not have an SSN must enter zeros in the appropriate space on the passport application; and

(iv) The passport applicant's date of birth.

(2) *Time and manner for furnishing information.*—A passport applicant must provide the information required by this section with his or her passport application, whether by personal appearance or mail, to the Department of State (including United States Embassies and Consular posts abroad).

(c) *Penalties.*—(1) *In general.*—If the information required by paragraph (b)(1) of this section is incomplete or incorrect, or the information is not filed in the time and manner described in paragraph (b)(2) of this section, then the passport applicant may be subject to a penalty equal to $500 per application. Before assessing a penalty under this section, the IRS will provide to the passport applicant written notice of the potential assessment of the $500 penalty, requesting the information being sought, and offering the applicant an opportunity to explain why the information was not provided with the passport application. A passport applicant has 60 days from the date of the notice of the potential assessment of the penalty (90 days from such date if the notice is addressed to an applicant outside the United States) to respond to the notice. If the passport applicant demonstrates to the satisfaction of the Commissioner (or the Commissioner's delegate) that the failure is due to reasonable cause and not due to willful neglect, after considering all the surrounding circumstances, then the IRS will not assess the penalty.

(2) *Example.*—The following example illustrates the provisions of paragraph (c) of this section.

*Example.* C, a citizen of the United States, makes an error in supplying information on his passport application. Based on the nature of the error and C's timely response to correct the error after being contacted by the IRS, the Commissioner concludes that the mistake is due to reasonable cause and not due to willful neglect. Accordingly, no penalty is assessed.

(d) *Effective/applicability date.*—This section applies to passport applications submitted after July 18, 2014. [Reg. § 301.6039E-1.]

☐ [*T.D.* 9679, 7-17-2014.]

### [Reg. § 1.6039I-1]

**§ 1.6039I-1. Reporting of certain employer-owned life insurance contracts.**—(a) *Requirement to report.*—Section 6039I requires every taxpayer that is an applicable policyholder owning one or more employer-owned life insurance contracts issued after August 17, 2006, to file a return showing the following information for each year the contracts are owned—

(1) The number of employees of the applicable policyholder at the end of the year;

(2) The number of such employees insured under such contracts at the end of the year;

(3) The total amount of insurance in force at the end of the year under such contracts;

(4) The name, address, and taxpayer identification number of the applicable policyholder and the type of business in which the policyholder is engaged; and

(5) That the applicable policyholder has a valid consent for each insured employee (or, if all such consents are not obtained, the number of insured employees for whom such consent was not obtained).

(b) *Time and manner of reporting.*—Applicable policyholders owning one or more employer-owned life insurance contracts issued after August 17, 2006, must provide the information required under § 6039I by attaching Form 8925, "Report of Employer-Owned Life Insurance Contracts", to the policyholder's income tax return by the due date of that return, or by filing such other form at such time and in such manner as the Commissioner may in the future prescribe.

(c) *Effective/applicability date.*—These regulations are applicable for tax years ending after November 6, 2008. [Reg. § 1.6039I-1.]

☐ [*T.D.* 9431, 11-5-2008.]

### [Reg. § 1.6041-1]

**§ 1.6041-1. Return of information as to payments of $600 or more.**—(a) *General rule.*—(1) *Information returns required.*—(i) *Payments required to be reported.*—Except as otherwise provided in §§ 1.6041-3 and 1.6041-4, every person engaged in a trade or business shall make an information return for each calendar year with respect to payments it makes during the calendar year in the course of its trade or business to another person of fixed or determinable income described in paragraph (a)(1)(i)(A) or (B) of this section. For purposes of the regulations under this section, the person described in this paragraph (a)(1)(i) is a payor.

(A) Salaries, wages, commissions, fees, and other forms of compensation for services rendered aggregating $600 or more.

(B) Interest (including original issue discount), rents, royalties, annuities, pensions, and other gains, profits, and income aggregating $600 or more.

(ii) *Information returns required under other provisions of the Internal Revenue Code.*—The payments described in paragraphs (a)(1)(i)(A) and (B) of this section shall not include any payments of amounts with respect to which an information return is required by, or may be required under authority of, section 6042(a) (relating to dividends), section 6043(a)(2) (relating to distributions in liquidation), section 6044(a) (relating to patronage dividends), section 6045 (relating to brokers' transactions with customers and certain other transactions), sections 6049(a)(1) and (2) (relating to interest), section 6050N(a) (relating to royalties), or section 6050P(a) or (b) (relating to cancellation of indebtedness). For information returns required under section 6045(f) (relating to payments to attorneys), see special rules in §§ 1.6041-1(a)(1)(iii) and 1.6045-5(c)(4). For payment card transactions (as described in § 1.6050W-1(b)) and third party network transactions (as defined in § 1.6050W-1(c)) required to be reported on information returns required under section 6050W (relating to payment card and third party network transactions), see special rules in § 1.6041-1(a)(1)(iv).

(iii) *Information returns required under section 6045(f) on or after January 1, 2007.*—For payments made on or after January 1, 2007 to which section 6045(f) (relating to payments to attorneys) applies, the following rules apply. Not withstanding the provisions of paragraph (a)(1)(ii) of this section, payments to an attorney that are described in paragraph (a)(1)(i) of this section but which otherwise would be reportable under section 6045(f) are reported under section 6041 and this section and not section 6045(f). This exception applies only if the payments are reportable with respect to the same payee under both sections. Thus, a person who, in the course of a trade or business, pays $600 of taxable damages to a claimant by paying that amount to the claimant's attorney is required to file an information return under section 6041 with respect to the claimant, as well as another information return under section 6045(f) with respect to the claimant's attorney. For provisions relating to information reporting for payments to attorneys, see § 1.6045-5.

(iv) *Information returns required under section 6050W for calendar years beginning after December 31, 2010.*—For payments made by payment card (as defined in § 1.6050W-1(b)(3)) or through a third party payment network (as defined in § 1.6050W-1(c)(3)) after December

31, 2010, that are required to be reported on an information return under section 6050W (relating to payment card and third party network transactions), the following rule applies. Transactions that are described in paragraph (a)(1)(ii) of this section that otherwise would be subject to reporting under both sections 6041 and 6050W are reported under section 6050W and not section 6041. For provisions relating to information reporting for payment card and third party network transactions, see §1.6050W-1. Solely for purposes of this paragraph, the de minimis threshold for third party network transactions in §1.6050W-1(c)(4) is disregarded in determining whether the transaction is subject to reporting under section 6050W.

(v) *Examples.*—The provisions of paragraph (a)(1)(iv) of this section are illustrated by the following examples:

*Example 1.* Restaurant owner A, in the course of business, pays $600 of fixed or determinable income to B, a repairman, by credit card. B is one of a network of unrelated persons that has agreed to accept A's credit card as payment under an agreement that provides standards and mechanisms for settling the transactions between a merchant acquiring bank and the persons who accept the cards. Merchant acquiring bank Y is responsible for making the payment to B. Under paragraph (a)(1)(iv) of this section, A, as payor, is not required to file an information return under section 6041 with respect to the transaction because Y, as the payment settlement entity for the payment card transaction, is required to file an information return under section 6050W.

*Example 2.* Restaurant owner A, in the course of business, pays $600 of fixed or determinable income to B, a repairman, through a third party payment network. B is one of a substantial number of persons who have established accounts with Y, a third party settlement organization that provides standards and mechanisms for settling the transactions and guarantees payments to those persons for goods or services purchased through the network. Y is responsible for making the payment to B. Under paragraph (a)(1)(iv) of this section, A, as payor, is not required to file an information return under section 6041 with respect to the transaction because the transaction is a third party network transaction that is subject to reporting under section 6050W. Solely for purposes of determining whether A is eligible for relief from reporting under section 6041, the de minimis threshold for third party network transactions in §1.6050W-1(c)(4) is disregarded.

(2) *Prescribed form.*—The return required by subparagraph (1) of this paragraph shall be made on Forms 1096 and 1099 except that (i) the return with respect to distributions to beneficiaries of a trust or of an estate shall be made on Form 1041, and (ii) the return with respect to certain payments of compensation to an employee by his employer shall be made on Forms W-3 and W-2 under the provisions of §1.6041-2 (relating to return of information as to payments to employees). Where Form 1099 is required to be filed under this section, a separate Form 1099 shall be furnished for each person to whom payments described in subdivision (i), (ii), or (iii) of subparagraph (1) of this paragraph are made. For time and place for filing Forms 1096 and 1099, see §1.6041-6. For the requirement to submit the information required by Form 1099 on magnetic media for payments after December 31, 1983, see section 6011(e) and §301.6011-2 of this chapter (Procedure and Administration Regulations).

(b) *Persons engaged in trade or business.*—(1) *In general.*—The term "all persons engaged in a trade or business", as used in section 6041(a), includes not only those so engaged for gain or profit, but also organizations the activities of which are not for the purpose of gain or profit. Thus, the term includes the organizations referred to in sections 401(a), 501(c), 501(d) and 521 and in paragraph (i) of this section. On the other hand, section 6041(a) applies only to payments in the course of trade or business; hence it does not apply to an amount paid by the proprietor of a business to a physician for medical services rendered by the physician to the proprietor's child.

(2) *Special rule for REMICs.*—For purposes of chapter 1 subtitle F, chapter 61A, part IIIB, the terms "all persons engaged in a trade or business" and "any service-recipient engaged in a trade or business" includes a real estate mortgage investment conduit or REMIC (as defined in section 860D).

(c) *Fixed or determinable income.*—Income is fixed when it is to be paid in amounts definitely predetermined. Income is determinable whenever there is a basis of calculation by which the amount to be paid may be ascertained. The income need not be paid annually or at regular intervals. The fact that the payments may be increased or decreased in accordance with the happening of an event does not for purposes of this section make the payments any the less determinable. A payment made jointly to two or more payees may be fixed and determinable income to one payee even though the payment is not fixed and determinable income to another payee. For example, property insurance proceeds paid jointly to the owner of damaged property and to a contractor that repairs the property may be fixed and determinable income to the contractor but not fixed and determinable income to the owner, and should be reported to the contractor. A salesman working by the month for a commission on sales which is paid or credited monthly receives determinable income.

(d) *Payments specifically included.*—(1) *In general.*—Amounts paid in respect of life insurance, endowment, or annuity contracts are required to be reported in returns of information under this section—

(i) Unless the payment is made in respect of a life insurance or endowment contract by reason of the death of the insured and is not required to be reported by paragraph (b) of §1.6041-2,

(ii) Unless the payment is made by reason of the surrender prior to maturity or lapse of a policy, other than a policy which was purchased (*a*) by a trust described in section 401(a) which is exempt from tax under section 501(a), (*b*) as part of a plan described in section 403(a), or (*c*) by an employer described in section 403(b)(1)(A),

(iii) Unless the payment is interest as defined in §1.6049-2 and is made after December 31, 1962,

(iv) Unless the payment is a payment with respect to which a return is required by §1.6047-1, relating to employee retirement plans covering owner-employees,

(v) Unless the payment is payment with respect to which a return is required by §1.6052-1, relating to payment of wages in the form of group-term life insurance.

(2) *Professional fees.*—Fees for professional services paid to attorneys, physicians, and members of other professions are required to be reported in returns of information if paid by persons engaged in a trade or business and paid in the course of such trade or business.

(3) *Prizes and awards.*—Amounts paid as prizes and awards that are required to be included in gross income under section 74 and §1.74-1 when paid in the course of a trade or business are required to be reported in returns of information under this section.

(4) *Disability payments.*—Amounts paid as disability payments under section 105(d) are required to be reported in returns of information under this section.

(5) *Notional principal contracts.*—Except as provided in paragraphs (b)(5)(i) and (ii) of this section, amounts paid after December 31, 2000, with respect to notional principal contracts referred to in §1.863-7 or 1.988-2(e) to persons who are not described in §1.6049-4(c)(1)(ii) are required to be reported in returns of information under this section. The amount required to be reported under this paragraph (d)(5) is limited to the amount of cash paid from the notional principal contract as described in §1.446-3(d). A non-periodic payment is reportable for the year in which an actual payment is made. Any amount of interest determined under the provisions of §1.446-3(g)(4) (dealing with interest in the case of a significant non-periodic payment) is reportable under this paragraph (d)(5) and not under section 6049 (see §1.6049-5(b)(15)). See §1.6041-4(a)(4) for reporting exceptions regarding payments to foreign persons. See, however, §1.1461-1(c)(1) for reporting amounts described under this paragraph (d)(5) that are paid to foreign persons. The provisions of §1.6049-5(d) shall apply for determining whether a payment with respect to a notional principal contract is made to a foreign person. See §1.6049-4(a) for a definition of payor. For purposes of this paragraph (d)(5), a payor includes a middleman defined in §1.6049-4(f)(4).

(i) An amount paid with respect to a notional principal contract is not required to be reported if the amount is paid by a non-U.S. payor or a non-U.S. middleman and is paid and received outside the United States (as defined in §1.6049-4(f)(16)).

(ii) An amount paid with respect to a notional principal contract is not required to be reported if the amount is paid by a payor that has no actual knowledge that the payee is a U.S. person and is paid and received outside the United States (as defined in §1.6049-4(f)(16)), and the payor is—

(A) A U.S. payor or U.S. middleman that is not a U.S. person (such as a controlled foreign corporation defined in section 957(a) or certain foreign corporations or foreign partnerships engaged in a U.S. trade or business); or

(B) A foreign branch of a U.S. bank. See §1.6049-5(c)(5) for a definition of a U.S. payor, a U.S. middleman, a non-U.S. payor, and a non-U.S. middleman.

(e) *Payment made on behalf of another person.*—(1) *In general.*—A person that makes a payment in the course of its trade or business on behalf of another person is the payor that must make a return of information under this section with respect to that payment if the payment is described in paragraph (a) of this section and, under all the facts and circumstances, that person—

(i) Performs management or oversight functions in connection with the payment (this would exclude, for example, a person who performs mere administrative or ministerial functions such as writing checks at another's direction); or

(ii) Has a significant economic interest in the payment (i.e., an economic interest that would be compromised if the payment were not made, such as by creation of a mechanic's lien on property to which the payment relates, or a loss of collateral).

(2) *Determination of payor obligated to report.*—If two or more persons meet the requirements for making a return of information with respect to a payment, as set forth in paragraph (e)(1) of this section, the person obligated to report the payment is the person closest in the chain to the payee, unless the parties agree in writing that one of the other parties meeting the requirements set forth in paragraph (e)(1) of this section will report the payment.

(3) *Special rule for payment by employee to employer.*—Notwithstanding the provisions of paragraph (e)(1) of this section, an employee acting in the course of his employment who makes a payment to his employer on behalf of another person is not required to make a return of information with respect to that payment.

(4) *Optional method to report.*—A person that makes a payment on behalf of another person but is not required to make an information return under paragraph (e)(1) of this section may elect to do so pursuant to the procedures established by the Commissioner. See, e.g., Rev. Proc. 84-33 (1984-1 C.B. 502) (optional method for a paying agent to report and deposit amounts withheld for payors under the statutory provisions of backup withholding) (see § 601.601(d)(2) of this chapter).

(5) *Examples.*—The provisions of this paragraph (e) are illustrated by the following examples:

*Example 1.* Bank B provides financing to C, a real estate developer, for a construction project. B makes disbursements from the account for labor, materials, services, and other expenses related to the construction project. In connection with the payments, B performs the following functions: approves payments to the general contractor or subcontractors; ensures that loan proceeds are properly applied and that all approved bills are properly paid to avoid mechanics' or materialmen's liens; conducts site inspections to determine whether work has been completed (but does not check the quality of the work). B is performing management or oversight functions in connection with the payments and is subject to the information reporting requirements of section 6041 with respect to payments.

*Example 2.* Mortgage company D holds a mortgage on business property owned by E. When the property is damaged by a storm, E's insurance company issues a check payable to both D and E in settlement of E's claim. Pursuant to the contract between D and E, D holds the insurance proceeds in an escrow account and makes disbursements, according to E's instructions, to contractors and subcontractors performing repairs on the property. D is not performing management or oversight functions, but D has a significant economic interest in the payments because the purpose of the arrangement is to ensure that property on which D holds a mortgage is repaired or replaced. D is subject to the information reporting requirements of section 6041 with respect to the payments to contractors.

*Example 3.* Settlement agent F provides real estate closing services to real estate brokers and agents. F deposits money received from the buyer or lender in an escrow account and makes payments from the account to real estate agents or brokers, appraisers, land surveyors, building inspectors, or similar service providers according to the provisions of the real estate contract and written instructions from the lender. F may also make disbursements pursuant to oral instructions of the seller or purchaser at closing. F is not performing management or oversight functions and does not have a significant economic interest in the payments, and is not subject to the information reporting requirements of section 6041. For the rules relating to F's obligation to report the gross proceeds of the sale, see section 6045(e) and § 1.6045-4.

*Example 4.* Assume the same facts as in *Example 3.* In addition, the seller instructs F to hire a contractor to perform repairs on the property. F selects the contractor, negotiates the cost, monitors the progress of the project, and inspects the work to ensure it complies with the contract. With respect to the payments to the contractor, F is performing management or oversight functions and is subject to the information reporting requirements of section 6041.

*Example 5.* G is a rental agent who manages certain rental property on behalf of property owner H. G finds tenants, arranges leases, collects rent, responds to tenant inquiries regarding maintenance, and hires and makes payments to repairmen. G subtracts her commission and any maintenance payments from rental payments and remits the remainder to H. With respect to payments to repairmen, G is performing management or oversight functions and is subject to

the information reporting requirements of section 6041. With respect to the payment of rent to H, G is subject to the information reporting requirements of section 6041 regardless of whether she performs management or oversight functions or has a significant economic interest in the payment. See § 1.6041-3(d) for rules relating to rental agents. See § 1.6041-1(f) to determine the amount that G should report to H as rent.

*Example 6.* Literary agent J receives a payment from publisher L of fees earned by J's client, author K. J deposits the payment into a bank account in J's name. From time to time and as directed by K, J makes payments from these funds to attorneys, managers, and other third parties for services rendered to K. After subtracting J's commission, J pays K the net amount. J does not order or direct the provision of services by the third parties to K, and J exercises no discretion in making the payments to the third parties or to K. J is not performing management or oversight functions and does not have a significant economic interest in the payments and is not subject to the information reporting requirements of section 6041 in connection with the payments to K or to the third parties. For the rules relating to L's obligation to report the payment of the fees to K, see paragraphs (a)(1)(i) and (f) of this section. For the rules relating to K's obligation to report the payment of the commission to J and the payments to the third parties for services, see paragraphs (a)(1)(i) and (d)(2) of this section.

*Example 7.* Attorney P deposits into a client trust fund a settlement payment from R, the defendant in a breach of contract action for lost profits in which P represented plaintiff Q. P makes payments from the client trust fund to service providers such as expert witnesses and private investigators for expenses incurred in the litigation. P decides whom to hire, negotiates the amount of payment, and determines that the services have been satisfactorily performed. In the event of a dispute with a service provider, P withholds payment until the dispute is settled. With respect to payments to the service providers, P is performing management or oversight functions and is subject to the information reporting requirements of section 6041.

*Example 8.* Assume the same facts as in *Example 7.* In addition, assume that after paying the service providers and deducting his legal fee, P pays Q the remaining funds that P had received from the settlement with R. With respect to the payment to Q, P is not performing management or oversight functions, does not have a significant economic interest in the payment, and is not subject to the information reporting requirements of section 6041. For the rules relating to R's obligation to report the payment of the settlement proceeds to P, see section 6045(f) and the regulations thereunder. For the rules relating to R's obligation to report the payment of the settlement proceeds to Q, see paragraphs (a)(1)(i) and (f) of this section. For the rules relating to Q's obligation to report the payment of attorney fees to P, see paragraphs (a)(1)(i) and (d)(2) of this section.

*Example 9.* Medical insurer S operates as the administrator of a health care program under a contract with a state. S makes payments of government funds to health care providers who provide care to eligible patients. S receives and reviews claims submitted by patients or health care providers, determines if the claims meet all the requirements of the program (e.g., that the care is authorized and that the patients are eligible beneficiaries), and determines the amount of payment. S is performing management or oversight functions and is subject to the information reporting requirements of section 6041 with respect to the payments.

*Example 10.* Race track employee T holds deposits made by horse owner U in a special escrow account in U's name. U enters into a contract with jockey V to ride U's horse in a race at the track. As directed by U, T pays V the fee for riding U's horse from U's escrow account. T is not performing management or oversight functions, does not have a significant economic interest in the payment, and is not subject to the information reporting requirements of section 6041. For the rules relating to U's obligation to report the payment of the fee to V, see paragraph (a)(1)(i) of this section.

*Example 11.* X is a certified public accountant employed by Firm Y, and is not a partner. Client Z pays X directly for accounting services. X remits the amount received to Y, as required by the terms of his employment. X does not have any reporting obligation with respect to the payment to Y. For the rules relating to Z's obligation to report the payment to Y for services, see paragraphs (a)(1)(i) and (d)(2) of this section.

*Example 12.* Bank contracts with Title Company with respect to the disbursement of funds on a construction loan. Pursuant to their arrangement, the contractor sends draw requests to Title Company, which inspects the work, verifies the amount requested, and then sends the draw request to Bank with supporting documents. Bank pays Title Company the amount of the draw request, and Title Company insures Bank against any loss if it cannot obtain the necessary lien waivers. Bank has a significant economic interest in the payment as a mortgagee, and Title Company exercises management or oversight over the payment. Since Title Company is closest in the chain to the contractor, Title Company should report the payment, unless the parties agree in writing that Bank will report the payment.

(f) *Amount to be reported when fees, expenses or commissions are deducted.*—(1) *In general.*—The amount to be reported as paid to a payee is the amount includible in the gross income of the payee (which in many cases will be the gross amount of the payment or payments before fees, commissions, expenses, or other amounts owed by the payee to another person have been deducted), whether the payment is made jointly or separately to the payee and another person. The Commissioner may, by guidance published in the Internal Revenue Bulletin, illustrate the circumstances under which the gross amount or less than the gross amount may be reported.

(2) *Examples.*—The provisions of this paragraph (f) are illustrated by the following examples:

*Example 1.* Attorney P represents client Q in a breach of contract action for lost profits against defendant R. R settles the case for $100,000 damages and $40,000 for attorney fees. Under applicable law, the full $140,000 is includible in Q's gross taxable income. R issues a check payable to P and Q in the amount of $140,000. R is required to make an information return reporting a payment to Q in the amount of $140,000. For the rules with respect to R's obligation to report the payment to P, see section 6045(f) and the regulations thereunder.

*Example 2.* Assume the same facts as in *Example 1*, except that R issues a check to Q for $100,000 and a separate check to P for $40,000. R is required to make an information return reporting a payment to Q in the amount of $140,000. For the rules with respect to R's obligation to report the payment to P, see section 6045(f) and the regulations thereunder.

(g) *Payment made in medium other than cash.*—If any payment required to be reported on Form 1099 is made in property other than money, the fair market value of the property at the time of payment is the amount to be included on such form.

(h) *When payment deemed made.*—For purposes of a return of information, an amount is deemed to have been paid when it is credited or set apart to a person without any substantial limitation or restriction as to the time or manner of payment or condition upon which payment is to be made, and is made available to him so that it may be drawn at any time, and its receipt brought within his own control and disposition.

(i) *Payments made by United States or a State.*—Information returns on—

(1) Forms 1096 and 1099 and

(2) Forms W-3 and W-2 (when made under the provisions of §1.6041-2)

of payments made by the United States or a State, or political subdivision thereof, or the District of Columbia, or any agency or instrumentality of any one or more of the foregoing, shall be made by the officer or employee of the United States, or of such State, or political subdivision, or of the District of Columbia, or of such agency or instrumentality, as the case may be, having control of such payments or by the officer or employee appropriately designated to make such returns.

(j) *Effective/applicability date.*—This section applies to payments made on or after January 6, 2017. (For payments made after June 30, 2014, and before January 6, 2017, see this section as in effect and contained in 26 CFR part 1, as revised April 1, 2016. For payments made after December 31, 2010, and before July 1, 2014, see this section as in effect and contained in 26 CFR part 1, as revised April 1, 2013.) [Reg. §1.6041-1.]

☐ [T.D. 6364, 2-13-59. *Amended by T.D.* 6628, 12-27-62; *T.D.* 6677, 9-16-63; *T.D.* 6888, 7-5-66; *T.D.* 7284, 8-2-73; *T.D.* 7580, 12-20-78; *T.D.* 7888, 4-22-83; *T.D.* 8458, 12-23-92; *T.D.* 8734, 10-6-97 (T.D. 8804 delayed the effective date of T.D. 8734 from January 1, 1999, to January 1, 2000; T.D. 8856 further delayed the effective date of T.D. 8734 until January 1, 2001); *T.D.* 8804, 12-30-98 (*corrected* 3-8-99); *T.D.* 8881, 5-15-2000; *T.D.* 9010, 7-25-2002; *T.D.* 9270, 7-12-2006 (*corrected* 8-15-2006); *T.D.* 9496, 8-13-2010, *T.D.* 9658, 2-28-2014 (*corrected* 6-30-2014 *and T.D.* 9808, 12-30-2016).]

**[Reg. §301.6041-1]**

**§301.6041-1. Returns of information regarding certain payments.**—For provisions relating to the requirement of returns of information regarding certain payments see §§1.6041-1 to 1.6041-6, inclusive, of this chapter (Income Tax Regulations). [Reg. §301.6041-1.]

☐ [T.D. 6498, 10-24-60.]

**[Reg. §1.6041-2]**

**§1.6041-2. Return of information as to payments to employees.**—(a)(1) *In general.*—Wages, as defined in section 3401, paid to an employee are required to be reported on Form W-2. See section 6011 and the Employment Tax Regulations thereunder. All other payments of compensation, including the cash value of payments made in any medium other than cash, to an employee by his employer in the course of the trade or business of the employer must also be reported on Form W-2 if the total of such payments and the amount of the employee's wages (as defined in section 3401), if any, required to be reported on Form W-2 aggregates $600 or more in a calendar year. For example, if a payment of $700 was made to an employee and $400 thereof represents wages subject to withholding under section 3402 and the remaining $300 represents compensation not subject to withholding, such wages and compensation must both be reported on Form W-2. A separate Form W-2 shall be furnished for each employee for whom a return must be made. At the election of the employer, components of amounts required to be reported on Form W-2 pursuant to the provisions of this subparagraph may be reported on more than one Form W-2.

(2) *Transmittal form.*—The transmittal form for a return on Form W-2 made pursuant to the provisions of subparagraph (1) of this paragraph shall be Form W-3. In a case where an employer must file a Form W-3 under this paragraph and also under §31.6011(a)-4 or §31.6011(a)-5 of this chapter (Employment Tax Regulations), the Form W-3 filed under such §31.6011(a)-4 or §31.6011(a)-5 shall also be used as the transmittal form for a return on Form W-2 made pursuant to the provisions of this paragraph.

(3) *Time for filing.*—(i) *General rule.*—In a case where an employer must file Forms W-3 and W-2 under this paragraph and also under §31.6011(a)-4 or §31.6011(a)-5 of this chapter (Employment Tax Regulations), the time for filing such forms under this paragraph shall be the same as the time (including extensions thereof) for filing such forms under §31.6011(a)-4 or §31.6011(a)-5.

(ii) *Exception.*—In a case where an employer is not required to file Forms W-3 and W-2 under §31.6011(a)-4 or §31.6011(a)-5 of this chapter, returns on Forms W-3 and W-2 required under this paragraph (a) for any calendar year shall be filed on or before January 31 of the following year.

(iii) *Cross reference.*—For extensions of time for filing returns, see section 6081 and the regulations thereunder.

(4) *Place for filing.*—The returns on Forms W-3 and W-2 required under this paragraph shall be filed pursuant to the rules contained in §31.6091-1 of this chapter (Employment Tax Regulations), relating to the place for filing certain returns.

(5) *Statement for employees.*—An employer required under this paragraph (a) to file Form W-2 with respect to an employee is also required under sections 6041(d) and 6051 to furnish a written statement to the employee. This written statement must be furnished on Form W-2 in accordance with section 6051 and the regulations.

(b) *Distributions under employees' trust or plan.*—(1) Amounts which are—

(i) Distributed or made available to a beneficiary, and to which section 402 (relating to employees' trusts) or section 403 (relating to employee annuity plans) applies, or

(ii) Described in section 72(m)(3)(B),

shall be reported on Forms 1096 and 1099 to the extent such amounts are includible in the gross income of such beneficiary if the amounts so includible aggregate $600 or more in any calendar year. In addition, every trust described in section 501(c)(17) which makes one or more payments (including separation and sick and accident benefits) totaling $600 or more in 1 year to an individual must file an annual information return on Form 1096, accompanied by a statement on Form 1099, for each such individual. Payments made by an employer or a person other than the trustee of the trust should not be considered in determining whether the $600 minimum has been paid by the trustee. The provisions of this subparagraph shall not be applicable to payments of supplemental unemployment compensation benefits made after December 31, 1970, which are treated as if they were wages for purposes of section 3401(a). Such amounts are required to be reported on Forms W-3 and W-2. See paragraph (b)(14) of §31.3401(a)-1 of this chapter (Employment Tax Regulations).

(2) Any amount with respect to which a statement is required by §1.6047-1, relating to employee retirement plans covering owner-employees, shall not be included in amounts required to be reported under section 6041.

(c) *Payments to foreign persons.*—See §1.6041-4 for reporting exemptions regarding payments to foreign persons. See §1.6049-5(d) for determining whether a payment is made to a foreign person.

(d) *Applicability date.*—This section applies to returns filed on or after January 30, 2020. Section 1.6041-2T (as contained in 26 CFR part 1, revised April 2019) applies to returns filed before January 30, 2020. [Reg. § 1.6041-2.]

☐ [*T.D. 6364,* 2-13-59. *Amended by T.D. 6677,* 9-16-63; *T.D. 6972,* 9-11-68; *T.D. 7068,* 11-10-70; *T.D. 7284,* 8-2-73; *T.D. 7580,* 12-20-78; *T.D. 8734,* 10-6-97 (T.D. 8804 delayed the effective date of T.D. 8734 from January 1, 1999, to January 1, 2000; T.D. 8856 further delayed the effective date of T.D. 8734 until January 1, 2001); *T.D. 8895,* 8-17-2000, *T.D. 9114,* 2-13-2004, *T.D. 9821,* 7-18-2017 *and T.D. 9892,* 1-29-2020.]

### [Reg. § 1.6041-3]

**§ 1.6041-3. Payments for which no return of information is required under section 6041.**—Returns of information are not required under section 6041 and §§ 1.6041-1 and 1.6041-2 for payments described in paragraphs (a) through (q) of this section. See § 1.6041-4 for reporting exemptions regarding payments to foreign persons.

(a) Payments of income required to be reported on Forms 1120-S, 941, W-2, and W-3, (however, see § 1.6041-2(a) with respect to Forms W-2 and W-3).

(b) Payments by a broker to his customer (but for reporting requirements as to certain of such payments, see sections 6042, 6045, and 6049 and the regulations thereunder in this part).

(c) Payments of bills for merchandise, telegrams, telephone, freight, storage, and similar charges.

(d) Payments of rent made to rental agents (but the agent is required to report payments of rent to the landlord in accordance with § 1.6041-1(a)(1)(i)(B) and (2)).

(e) Payments representing earned income for services rendered without the United States made to a citizen of the United States, if it is reasonable to believe that such amounts will be excluded from gross income under the provisions of section 911 and the regulations thereunder.

(f) Compensation and profits paid or distributed by a partnership to the individual partners (but for reporting requirements, see § 1.6031-1).

(g) Payments of commissions to general agents by fire insurance companies or other companies insuring property, except when specifically directed by the Commissioner to be filed.

(h)(1) *In general.*—Payments made under reimbursement or other expense allowance arrangements that meet the requirements of section 62(c) of the Code and § 1.62-2, that do not exceed the amount of the expenses substantiated (i.e., amounts which are treated as paid under an accountable plan), and that are received by an employee on or after January 1, 1989, with respect to expenses paid or incurred on or after January 1, 1989.

(2) *Transition rule.*—Payments made under reimbursement or other expense allowance arrangements that are received by an employee on or after January 1, 1989, but prior to July 1, 1990, to the extent that the employee is required to account (within the meaning of the term "account" as set forth in § 1.162-17(b)(4) or 1.274-5T(f)(4), whichever is applicable) and does so account to the payor for such expenses, provided the payor has made a reasonable, good faith effort to comply with the requirements of section 62(c). In general, compliance with the provisions of this section, as in effect for payments made under reimbursement or other expense allowance arrangements that were received by an employee before January 1, 1989, with respect to expenses paid or incurred before January 1, 1989, will constitute such reasonable good faith compliance. In no event, however, will reasonable good faith compliance exist if a payor fails to report payments made under an arrangement (other than a per diem or mileage allowance type arrangement) under which an employee is not required to substantiate expenses paid or incurred or is not required to return amounts in excess of the substantiated expenses.

(i) Payments of interest on obligations of the United States, or a State, Territory, or political subdivision thereof, or the District of Columbia, or any agency or instrumentality of any one or more of the foregoing (but for requirements for reporting certain such payments by the United States or any agency or instrumentality thereof, see §§ 1.1461-1 to 1.1461-3, inclusive).

(j) Payments of interest on corporate bonds (but for reporting requirements as to payments of interest on certain corporate bonds, see § 1.6049-5).

(k) Amounts paid as an allowance or reimbursement for traveling or other bona fide ordinary and necessary expenses, including an allowance for meals and lodging or a per diem allowance in lieu of subsistence, to persons in the service of an international organization (without regard to whether there is a requirement to account for such amounts) if—

(1) The organization is designated as an international organization by the President of the United States in Executive Orders issued pursuant to 22 U.S.C. 288, and

(2) The organization has immunity with respect to the inviolability of its archives pursuant to an international agreement having full force and effect in the United States;

(l) A payment to an informer as an award, fee, or reward for information relating to criminal activity, but only if such payment is made by the United States, a State, Territory, or political subdivision thereof, or the District of Columbia, or any agency or instrumentality of any one or more of the foregoing, or, with respect to payments made after December 31, 1987, by an organization that is described in section 501(c)(3) and that makes such payments in furtherance of a charitable purpose to lessen the burdens of government within the meaning of § 1.501(c)(3)-1(d)(2).

(m) On and after September 9, 1968, payments by a person carrying on the banking business of interest on a deposit evidenced by a negotiable time certificate of deposit (but for reporting requirements as to payments made after December 31, 1962, of interest on certain deposits, see section 6049 and the regulations thereunder in this part); and

(n) Payments to individuals as scholarships or fellowship grants within the meaning of section 117(b)(1), whether or not "qualified scholarships" as described in section 117(b). This exception does not apply to any amount of a scholarship or fellowship grant that represents payment for services within the meaning of section 117(c). Instead, these amounts are required to be reported as wages on Form W-2. See § 1.1461-1(c) for applicable reporting requirements for amounts paid to foreign persons.

(o) Per diem of certain alien trainees described under section 1441(c)(6).

(p) Payments made to the following persons:

(1) A corporation described in § 1.6049-4(c)(1)(ii)(A), except with respect to payments made to a corporation after December 31, 1997 for attorneys' fees, and except a corporation engaged in providing medical and health care services or engaged in the billing and collecting of payments in respect to the providing of medical and health care services. However, no reporting is required where payment is made to a hospital or extended care facility described in section 501(c)(3) which is exempt from taxation under section 501(a) or to a hospital or extended care facility owned and operated by the United States, a State, the District of Columbia, a possession of the United States, or a political subdivision, agency or instrumentality of any of the foregoing. For reporting requirements as to payments by cooperatives, and to certain other payments, see sections 6042, 6044, and 6049 and the regulations thereunder in this part.

(2) An organization exempt from taxation under section 501(a), as described in § 1.6049-4(c)(1)(ii)(B)(*1*), or an individual retirement plan, as described in § 1.6049-4(c)(1)(ii)(C).

(3) The United States, as described in § 1.6049-4(c)(1)(ii)(D).

(4) A State, the District of Columbia, a possession of the United States, or any political subdivision of any of the foregoing, as described in § 1.6049-4(c)(1)(ii)(E).

(5) A foreign government or political subdivision of a foreign government, as described in § 1.6049-4(c)(1)(ii)(F).

(6) An international organization, as described in § 1.6049-4(c)(1)(ii)(G).

(7) A foreign central bank of issue, as described in § 1.6049-4(c)(1)(ii)(H) and the Bank for International Settlements.

(8) Any wholly owned agency or instrumentality of any person described in paragraph (p)(2), (3), (4), (5), (6), or (7) of this section. [Reg. § 1.6041-3.]

☐ [*T.D. 6364,* 2-13-59. *Amended by T.D. 6628,* 12-27-62; *T.D. 6966,* 8-7-68; *T.D. 7000,* 1-17-69; *T.D. 7119,* 6-1-71; *T.D. 7284,* 8-2-73; *T.D. 8151,* 8-13-87; *T.D. 8193,* 4-12-88; *T.D. 8276,* 12-7-89; *T.D. 8324,* 12-14-90; *T.D. 8734,* 10-6-97 (T.D. 8804 delayed the effective date of T.D. 8734 from January 1, 1999, to January 1, 2000; T.D. 8856 further delayed the effective date of T.D. 8734 until January 1, 2001); *T.D. 8804,* 12-30-98; *T.D. 9010,* 7-25-2002 *and T.D. 9270,* 7-12-2006.]

### [Reg. § 1.6041-4]

**§ 1.6041-4. Foreign-related items and other exceptions.**—(a) *Exempted foreign-related items.*—(1) Returns of information are not required for payments that a payor can, prior to payment, reliably associate with documentation upon which it may rely to treat as made to a foreign beneficial owner in accordance with § 1.1441-1(e)(1)(ii) or as made to a foreign payee in accordance with § 1.6049-5(d)(1) or presumed to be made to a foreign payee under § 1.6049-5(d)(2), (3), (4), or (5). Returns of information are also not required for a payment that a payor or middleman can, prior to payment, reliably associate with documentation upon which it may rely to treat as made to a foreign intermediary or flow-through entity in accordance with § 1.1441-1(b) if it obtains from the intermediary or flow-through entity a withholding statement described in §1.6049-5(b)(14) that allocates the payment to a chapter 4 withholding rate pool (as defined in §1.6049-4(f)(5)) or specific payees to which withholding applies under chapter 4. Payments excepted from reporting under this paragraph (a)(1) may be reportable, for purposes of chapter 3 of the Internal Revenue Code (Code), under §1.1461-1(b) and (c) and, for purposes of chapter 4 of the Code, under §1.1474-1(d)(2). The provisions in §1.6049-5(c) regarding documentation of foreign status shall apply for purposes of this paragraph (a)(1). The provisions in §1.6049-5(c)(5) regarding the definitions of U.S. payor and non-U.S. payor shall also apply for purposes of this paragraph (a)(1). See §1.1441-1(b)(3)(iii)(B) and (C) for special payee rules regarding scholarships, grants, pensions, annuities, etc. The provisions of §1.1441-1 shall apply by substituting the term "payor" for the term "withholding agent" and without regard to the fact that the provisions apply only to amounts subject to withholding under chapter 3 of the Code and the regulations under that chapter.

(2) Returns of information are not required for payments of amounts from sources outside the United States (determined under the provisions of part I, subchapter N, chapter 1 of the Code and the regulations under those provisions) paid by a non-U.S. payor or non-U.S. middleman and that are paid and received outside the United States. For a definition of non-U.S. payor and non-U.S. middleman, see §1.6049-5(c)(5). For circumstances in which an amount is considered to be paid and received outside the United States, see §1.6049-4(f)(16).

(3) If a foreign intermediary, as described in §1.1441-1(c)(13), or a U.S. branch that is not treated as a U.S. person receives a payment from a payor, which payment the payor can reliably associate with a valid withholding certificate described in §1.1441-1(e)(3)(ii) or (iii), or §1.1441-1(e)(3)(v), respectively, furnished by such intermediary or branch, then the intermediary or branch is not required to report such payment when it, in turn, pays the amount, unless, and to the extent, the intermediary or branch knows that the payment is required to be reported under this section and was not so reported. For example, if a U.S. branch described in §1.1441-1(b)(2)(iv) fails to provide information regarding U.S. persons that are not exempt from reporting under §1.6041-3(q) to the person from whom the U.S. branch receives the payment, the U.S. branch must report the payment on an information return. See, however, paragraph (a)(7) of this section for when reporting under section 6041is coordinated with reporting under chapter 4 of the Code or an applicable IGA (as defined in §1.6049-4(f)(7)). The exception described in this paragraph (a)(3) for amounts paid by a foreign intermediary shall not apply to a qualified intermediary that assumes reporting responsibility under chapter 61 of the Code with respect to amounts reportable under the agreement described in §1.1441-1(e)(5)(iii).

(4) Returns of information are not required for amounts paid with respect to notional principal contracts referred to in §1.863-7 or 1.988-2(e) which the payor may treat as effectively connected income of a foreign payee under the provisions of §1.1441-4(a)(3) or if the payee provides a representation in a master agreement that governs the transactions in notional principal contracts between the parties (for example, an International Swap and Derivatives Association (ISDA) Agreement, including the Schedule thereto) or in the confirmation on the particular notional principal contract transaction that the counterparty is a foreign person. See, however, §1.1461-1(c)(2)(i) for applicable reporting requirements.

(5) Returns of information are not required for the period that the amounts paid represent assets blocked as described in §1.1441-2(e)(3). The exemption in this paragraph (a)(5) shall terminate when payment is deemed to occur in accordance with the provisions of §1.1441-2(e)(3).

(6) For rules concerning direct sellers, see §1.6041A-1(d)(3)(i)(C).

(7) Returns of information are not required for payments with respect to which a return is not required by applying the rules of §1.6049-4(c)(4) (by substituting the term "a payment subject to reporting under section 6041" for the term "an interest payment").

(b) *Joint owners.*—Amounts paid to joint owners for which a certificate or documentation is required as a condition for being exempt from reporting under paragraph (a) of this section are presumed made to U.S. payees who are not exempt recipients if, prior to payment, the payor or middleman cannot reliably associate the payment either with a Form W-9 furnished by one of the joint owners in the manner required in §§31.3406(d)-1 through 31.3406(d)-5, or with documentation described in paragraph (a)(1) of this section furnished by each joint owner upon which the payor or middleman can rely to treat each joint owner as a foreign payee or foreign beneficial owner. However, in the case of a withholdable payment (as defined in §1.6049-4(f)(15)) made to joint payees, if any joint payee does not appear to be an individual, the payment is presumed made to a foreign payee that is a nonparticipating FFI (as defined in §1.1471-1(b)(82)). See §1.1471-3(f)(7).

(c) *Conversion into United States dollars of amounts paid in foreign currency.*—For rules concerning foreign currency conversion, see §1.6049-4(d)(3)(i).

(d) *Effective/applicability date.*—This section applies to payments made on or after January 6, 2017. (For payments made after June 30, 2014, and before January 6, 2017, see this section as in effect and contained in 26 CFR part 1, as revised April 1, 2016. For payments made after December 31, 2002, and before July 1, 2014, see this section as in effect and contained in 26 CFR part 1, as revised April 1, 2013.) [Reg. §1.6041-4.]

☐ [*T.D.* 6364, 2-13-59. *Amended by T.D.* 8734, 10-6-97; *T.D.* 8804, 12-30-98; *T.D.* 8856, 12-29-99; *T.D.* 8881, 5-15-2000, *T.D.* 9658, 2-28-2014 *and T.D.* 9808, 12-30-2016.]

**[Reg. §1.6041-5]**

**§1.6041-5. Information as to actual owner.**—When a person receiving a payment described in section 6041 is not the actual owner of the income received, the name and address of the actual owner shall be furnished upon demand of the person paying the income, and in default of compliance with such demand the payee becomes liable for the penalties provided. See section 7203. [Reg. §1.6041-5.]

☐ [*T.D.* 6364, 2-13-59.]

**[Reg. §1.6041-6]**

**§1.6041-6. Returns made on Forms 1096 and 1099 under section 6041; contents and time and place for filing.**—(a) *In general.*—Except as provided in paragraph (b) of this section, returns made under section 6041 on Forms 1096 and 1099 for any calendar year shall be filed on or before February 28 (March 31 if filed electronically) of the following year with any of the Internal Revenue Service Centers, the addresses of which are listed in the instructions for such forms. The name and address of the person making the payment and the name and address of the recipient of the payment shall be stated on Form 1099. If the present address of the recipient is not available, the last known post office address must be given. See section 6109 and the regulations in part 301 of this title under section 6109 for rules requiring the inclusion of identifying numbers in Form 1099.

(b) *Exception.*—Returns made on Form 1099 reporting nonemployee compensation shall be filed on or before January 31 of the year following the calendar year to which such returns relate.

(c) *Applicability date.*—This section applies to returns filed on or after January 30, 2020. Section 1.6041-6T (as contained in 26 CFR part 1, revised April 2019) applies to returns filed before January 30, 2020. [Reg. §1.6041-6.]

☐ [*T.D.* 6364, 2-13-59. *Amended by T.D.* 6628, 12-27-62; *T.D.* 7284, 8-2-73, *T.D.* 8895, 8-17-2000, *T.D.* 9821, 7-18-2017 *and T.D.* 9892, 1-29-2020.]

**[Reg. §1.6041-7]**

**§1.6041-7. Magnetic media requirement.**—(a) *General.*—For rules relating to permission to submit the information required by Form 1099 or W-2 on magnetic tape or other media, see §1.9101-1. See also paragraph (b)(2) of §31.6011(a)-7 of this chapter (Employment Tax Regulations) for additional rules relating to Form W-2. High-volume filers of information returns must file their returns on magnetic media. See section 6011(e) and §301.6011-2 of this chapter (Procedure and Administration Regulations) for the requirements for filing on magnetic media.

(b) *Returns on magnetic tape by departments of health care carriers.*—(1) For calendar years beginning on or after January 1, 1971, a health care carrier, or an agent thereof, making payment of fees or other compensation to providers of medical and health care services, may make a separate return on magnetic tape for each separate department within a specific line of such carrier's business, so long as all of such returns taken together contain all of the information required by section 6041 with respect to each provider of medical and health care services to whom such health care carrier makes payments aggregating $600 or more during the calendar year. Examples of separate departments within a specific line of such carrier's business (such as health and accident insurance) include, but are not limited to, separate departments to process claims of individual and group policyholders; and separate departments established along geographic lines.

(2) For purposes of this paragraph, the term "health care carrier" means any person making health care payments: (i) In exchange for the payment of a premium, (ii) in accordance with an employee benefit program, or (iii) in connection with a government-sponsored health care program. [Reg. §1.6041-7.]

☐ [*T.D.* 6883, 5-2-66. *Amended by T.D.* 7106, 4-2-71 *and T.D.* 8734, 10-6-97 (*T.D.* 8804 delayed the effective date of T.D. 8734 from

January 1, 1999, to January 1, 2000; T.D. 8856 further delayed the effective date of T.D. 8734 until January 1, 2001).]

### [Reg. §1.6041-8]

**§1.6041-8. Cross-reference to penalties.**—For provisions relating to the penalty provided for failure to file timely a correct information return required under section 6041(a) or (b), see §301.6721-1 of this chapter (Procedure and Administration Regulations). For provisions relating to the penalty provided for failure to furnish timely a correct payee statement required under section 6041(d), see §301.6722-1 of this chapter. See §301.6724-1 of this chapter for the waiver of a penalty if the failure is due to reasonable cause and is not due to willful neglect. [Reg. §1.6041-8.]

☐ [*T.D. 8734*, 10-6-97 (T.D. 8804 delayed the effective date of T.D. 8734 from January 1, 1999, to January 1, 2000; T.D. 8856 further delayed the effective date of T.D. 8734 until January 1, 2001).]

### [Reg. §1.6041-9]

**§1.6041-9. Coordination with reporting rules for widely held fixed investment trusts under §1.671-5.**—See §1.671-5 for the reporting rules for widely held fixed investment trusts (WHFIT) (as defined under that section). For purposes of section 6041, middlemen and trustees of WHFITs are deemed to have management and oversight functions in connection with payments made by the WHFIT. [Reg. §1.6041-9.]

☐ [*T.D. 9241*, 1-23-2006.]

### [Reg. §1.6041-10]

**§1.6041-10. Return of information as to payments of winnings from bingo, keno, and slot machine play.**—(a) *In general.*—Every person engaged in a trade or business (as defined in §1.6041-1(b)) and who, in the course of such trade or business, makes a payment of reportable gambling winnings (defined in paragraph (b)(1) of this section) must make an information return with respect to such payment. Unless the provisions of paragraph (g) of this section (regarding aggregate reporting) apply, a separate information return is required with respect to each payment of reportable gambling winnings.

(b) *Definitions.*—(1) *Reportable gambling winnings.*—(i) For purposes of this section, the term reportable gambling winnings is defined as follows:

(A) For bingo, the term "reportable gambling winnings" means winnings of $1,200 or more from one bingo game, without reduction for the amount wagered. All winnings received from all wagers made during one bingo game are combined (for example, all winnings from all cards played during one bingo game are combined).

(B) For keno, the term "reportable gambling winnings" means winnings of $1,500 or more from one keno game reduced by the amount wagered on the same keno game. All winnings received from all wagers made during one keno game are combined (for example, all winnings from all "ways" on a multi-way keno ticket are combined).

(C) For slot machine play, the term "reportable gambling winnings" means winnings of $1,200 or more from one slot machine play, without reduction for the amount wagered.

(ii) Winnings and wagers from different types of games are not combined to determine if the reporting threshold is satisfied. Bingo, keno, and slot machine play are different types of games.

(iii) Winnings include the fair market value of a payment in any medium other than cash.

(iv) The amount wagered in the case of a free play is zero.

(2) *Information reporting period.*—(i) *In general.*—For purposes of paragraph (g) of this section, the "information reporting period" begins when a patron places the first wager on a particular type of game at a gaming establishment, as defined in paragraph (b)(2)(iv) of this section, and ends when the patron places his or her last wager on the same type of game at the same gaming establishment before the end of the "information reporting period." An information reporting period is a 24-hour period. A payor may select a calendar day (as defined in paragraph (b)(2)(ii) of this section) or a gaming day (as defined in paragraph (b)(2)(iii) of this section) as the information reporting period for purposes of the aggregate reporting method in paragraph (g) of this section. For purposes of this paragraph (b)(2), time is determined by the time zone of the location where the patron places the wager. A payor must use the same information reporting period (a calendar day or gaming day) to report all "reportable gambling winnings" paid during the calendar year. Once selected, a payor may not change its information reporting period during a calendar year. Any changes to a payor's information reporting period from one calendar year to another must be implemented on January 1.

(ii) *Calendar day.*—A calendar day is determined with reference to a period beginning at 12 a.m. and ending no later than 11:59 p.m. of the same calendar day.

(iii) *Gaming day.*—(A) *In general.*—A gaming day is a 24-hour period other than a calendar day (as defined in paragraph (b)(2)(ii) of this section) selected by the payor, subject to the special rules for December 31 and January 1 in paragraphs (b)(2)(iii)(B) and (C) of this section.

(B) *Special rule for December 31.*—For purposes of paragraph (b)(2)(iii) of this section, the gaming day that begins on December 31 of any calendar year ends at 11:59 p.m. on December 31, regardless of the time on December 31 on which that gaming day began.

(C) *Special rule for January 1.*—For purposes of paragraph (b)(2)(iii) of this section, the gaming day of January 1 begins at 12:00 a.m. on January 1, regardless of the time and calendar day on which that gaming day ends, and may extend beyond 24 hours.

(iv) *Gaming establishment.*—For purposes of this section, a gaming establishment is a business entity of a payor of reportable gambling winnings with respect to bingo, keno, or slot machine play, and includes all gaming establishments owned by such payor using the same employer identification number (EIN) issued to such payor in accordance with section 6109.

(v) *Examples.*—The following examples illustrate the provisions of paragraph (b)(2) of this section.

*Example 1.* Casino R uses the aggregate reporting method under paragraph (g) of this section to report certain reportable gambling winnings. For other regulatory purposes, Casino R uses a gaming day that begins at 3 a.m. and ends at 2:59 a.m. the following calendar day. Casino R chooses to use its gaming day as its information reporting period for purposes of paragraph (b)(2) of this section during Year 1. Accordingly, the information reporting period for purposes of paragraph (g) of this section for each day during Year 1 begins at 3 a.m. and ends at 2:59 a.m. the following day. The information reporting period for December 31 of Year 1 begins at 3 a.m. on December 31 of Year 1 and ends at 11:59 p.m. on December 31 of Year 1. The information reporting period for January 1 of Year 2 begins at 12 a.m. on January 1 of Year 2 and ends at 2:59 a.m. on January 2 of Year 2.

*Example 2.* The facts are the same as Example 1, except Casino R uses a calendar day as its information reporting period for purposes of paragraph (b)(2) of this section during Year 1. Accordingly, the information reporting period for purpose of paragraph (g) of this section for each day during Year 1 begins at 12 a.m. and ends at 11:59 p.m. on the same day.

*Example 3.* Casino R uses the aggregate reporting method under paragraph (g) of this section to report certain reportable gambling winnings. For other regulatory purposes, Casino R uses a gaming day that begins at 9:00 p.m. and ends at 8:59 p.m. the following calendar day. Casino R chooses to use its gaming day as its information reporting period for purposes of paragraph (b)(2) of this section during Year 1. Accordingly, the information reporting period for purposes of paragraph (g) of this section for each day during Year 1 begins at 9:00 p.m. and ends at 8:59 p.m. the following day. The information reporting period for December 31 of Year 1 begins at 9:00 p.m. on December 30 and ends at 8:59 p.m. on December 31. A second information reporting period for December 31 then begins at 9:00 p.m. on December 31 and ends at 11:59 p.m. on December 31. The information reporting period for January 1 of Year 2 begins at 12:00 a.m. on January 1 and ends at 8:59 p.m. on January 1 of Year 2.

*Example 4.* Casino R uses the aggregate reporting method under paragraph (g) of this section to report certain reportable gambling winnings. In Year 1, Casino R chooses to use a "gaming day" that begins at 3 a.m. and ends at 2:59 a.m. the following day as its information reporting period. During the course of Year 1, Casino R decides that it would like to change its information reporting period to instead begin at 5 a.m. and end at 4:59 a.m. the following day. Casino R must wait until January 1 of Year 2 to implement such a change. On January 1 of Year 2, Casino R's information reporting period will begin at 12 a.m. and end at 4:59 a.m. on January 2. On December 31 of Year 2, Casino R's information reporting period will begin at 5 a.m. and end at 11:59 p.m.

(3) *Slot machine.*—The term "slot machine" means a device that, by application of the element of chance, may deliver, or entitle the person playing or operating the device to receive cash, premiums, merchandise, or tokens whether or not the device is operated by insertion of a coin, token, or similar object.

(c) *Prescribed form; time and place for filing the return.*—The return described in paragraph (a) of this section is a Form W-2G, "Certain Gambling Winnings." The Form W-2G must be filed with the appropriate Internal Revenue Service location designated in the instructions to the form on or before February 28 (March 31, if filed electronically) of the year following the calendar year in which the reportable gambling winnings were paid. See section 6011 and § 1.6011-2 for requirements to file electronically.

(d) *Information included on the return.*—(1) *In general.*—Each return required by paragraph (a) of this section must contain:

(i) The name, address, and taxpayer identification number of the payor;

(ii) The name, address, and taxpayer identification number of the payee;

(iii) A general description of the two types of identification (as described in paragraph (e) of this section), one of which must have the payee's photograph on it (except in the case of tribal member identification cards in certain circumstances as described in paragraph (d)(2) of this section) that the payor relied on to verify the payee's name, address, and taxpayer identification number;

(iv) The date and amount of payment;

(v) The type of wagering transaction (bingo, keno, or slot machine play);

(vi) In the case of a bingo or keno game, any number, color, or other designation assigned to the game for which the payment is made;

(vii) In the case of slot machine play, the identification number of the slot machine(s) (for example, location and asset number);

(viii) Any other information required by the forms, instructions, revenue procedures, or other applicable guidance published in the Internal Revenue Bulletin.

(2) *Special rule for tribal member identification cards.*—A tribal member identification card need not contain the payee's photograph to meet the identification requirement described in paragraph (d)(1)(iii) of this section if:

(i) The payee is a member of a federally recognized Indian tribe;

(ii) The payee presents the payor with a tribal member identification card issued by a federally recognized Indian tribe stating that the payee is a member of such tribe; and

(iii) The payor is a gaming establishment (as described in paragraph (b)(2)(iv) of this section) owned or licensed (in accordance with 25 U.S.C. 2710) by the tribal government that issued the tribal member identification card referred to in (d)(2)(ii).

(3) *Special rule for optional aggregate reporting method.*—In the case of aggregate reporting under paragraph (g) of this section, the amount of the payment in paragraph (d)(1)(iv) of this section is the aggregate amount of payments of reportable gambling winnings from the same type of game (bingo, keno, or slot machine play) made to the same payee during the same information reporting period (as defined in paragraph (b)(2) of this section). Unless otherwise provided in forms, instructions, or other guidance, in the case of aggregate reporting under paragraph (g) of this section, the information required by paragraphs (d)(1)(v) through (viii) of this section must be maintained by the payor as described in paragraph (g)(3) of this section.

(e) *Identification.*—The following items are treated as identification for purposes of paragraph (d)(1)(iii) of this section—

(1) Government-issued identification (for example, a driver's license, passport, social security card, military identification card, tribal member identification card issued by a federally recognized Indian tribe, or voter registration card) in the name of the payee; and

(2) A Form W-9, "Request for Taxpayer Identification Number and Certification," signed by the payee, that includes the payee's name, address, taxpayer identification number, and other information required by the form. A Form W-9 is not acceptable for this purpose if the payee has modified the form (other than pursuant to instructions to the form) or if the payee has deleted the jurat or other similar provisions by which the payee certifies or affirms the correctness of the statements contained on the form.

(f) *Furnishing a statement to the payee.*—Every payor required to make a return under paragraph (a) of this section must also make and furnish to each payee, with respect to each payment of reportable gambling winnings, a written statement that contains the information that is required to be included on the return under paragraph (d) of this section. The payor must furnish the statement to the payee on or before January 31st of the year following the calendar year in which payment of the reportable gambling winnings is made. The statement will be considered furnished to the payee if it is provided to the payee at the time of payment or if it is mailed to the payee on or before January 31st of the year following the calendar year in which payment was made.

(g) *Aggregate reporting of bingo, keno, and slot machine winnings.*— (1) *In general.*—In lieu of filing a separate information return for each payment of reportable gambling winnings as required by paragraph (a) of this section, a payor may use the aggregate reporting method (defined in paragraph (g)(2) of this section) to report reportable gambling winnings from bingo, keno, or slot machine play. A payor using the aggregate reporting method to file information returns under paragraph (a) of this section must also furnish statements to the payee under paragraph (f) of this section using the aggregate reporting method.

(2) *Aggregate reporting method defined.*—(i) The aggregate reporting method is a method of reporting more than one payment of reportable gambling winnings from the same type of game (bingo, keno, or slot machine play) made to the same payee during the same information reporting period (as defined in this paragraph (b)(2) of this section) on one information return or statement.

(ii) A payor may use the aggregate reporting method for payments to some payees and not others, at its own discretion. In addition, with respect to a single payee, the payor may use the aggregate reporting method to report winnings from one type of game, but not for winnings from another type of game.

(iii) Failure to report some reportable gambling winnings from a particular type of game during one information reporting period to a particular payee under the aggregate reporting method (for whatever reason, including because the winnings are not permitted to be reported using the aggregate reporting method under paragraph (g)(4) of this section) will not disqualify the payor from using the aggregate reporting method to report other reportable gambling winnings from that type of game during that information reporting period to that payee. The payor may stop using the aggregate reporting method for a particular payee or for all payees before the end of the payor's information reporting period for any reason.

(3) *Recordkeeping under the aggregate reporting method.*—A payor using the aggregate reporting method must maintain a record of every payment of reportable gambling winnings from the same type of game made to the same payee during the information reporting period that will be reported using the aggregate reporting method. Every individual that the payor has determined is responsible for an entry in the record must confirm the information in the entry by signing the record in a manner that will enable the signature to be associated with the relevant entry. Each payment of a reportable gambling winning made to the same payee and reported under the aggregate reporting method must have its own entry in the record, however, the information required by paragraphs (d)(1)(i) through (iii) of this section is not required to be recorded more than one time per information reporting period. A payor that uses the aggregate reporting method must retain a copy of the record in its files. The record (which may be electronic provided the requirements set forth in forms, instructions, or guidance published in the Internal Revenue Bulletin are met) must include the following information about each payment:

(i) The payee's signature confirming the information in the record;

(ii) The information required under paragraph (d) of this section;

(iii) The time of the win resulting in the reportable gambling winnings;

(iv) The total amount of reportable gambling winnings with respect to all payments to the payee during the information reporting period;

(v) The amount of reportable gambling winnings with respect to each particular payment;

(vi) The method of payment to the payee (for example, cash, check, voucher, credit, token, or chips); and

(vii) The name and unique identification number of the individual who the payor has determined is responsible for ensuring that the entry with respect to the reportable gambling winnings (including the general description of two types of identification used to verify the payee's name, address, and taxpayer identification number) is complete and accurate and who is authorized to perform that function by the applicable gaming regulatory control authority. Such individual may or may not be the same individual who prepared the entry.

(4) *When the aggregate reporting method may not be used.*—A payor cannot use the aggregate reporting method if—

(i) The payment is to a foreign person, as described in section 1.6041-10(h);

(ii) The payor knows or has reason to know that the person making the wager is not the person entitled to the winnings or is not the only person entitled to the winnings (regardless of whether the person making the wager furnishes a Form 5754, "Statement by Person(s) Receiving Gambling Winnings"); or

(iii) Backup withholding under section 3406(a) applies to the payment.

(5) *Examples.*—The following examples illustrate the provisions of this section. For each example, assume that for purposes of the aggregate reporting method in paragraph (g) of this section, Casino R's "information reporting period" for all calendar years is a gaming day that begins at 3 a.m. and ends at 2:59 a.m. the following day (except for January 1 and December 31) and that individuals C, D, and E are U.S. persons.

*Example 1.* On Day 1, between 7 a.m. and 4 p.m., C places five wagers at casino R on five different slot machines. The first two wagers result in no win. The third wager results in a $1,500 win. The fourth wager results in a $2,500 win. The fifth wager results in an $800 win:

(i) Under paragraph (b)(1)(i)(C) of this section, there are reportable gambling winnings from the slot machine play of $4,000 ($1,500 + $2,500). The $800 win is not a reportable gambling winning from slot machine play because it does not equal or exceed the $1,200 threshold.

(ii) Because all of the amounts were won on the same type of game (even though each of the winnings occurred on different machines) during the same information reporting period, R is permitted to use the aggregate reporting method under this paragraph (g). If R decides not to use the aggregate reporting method, a separate Form W-2G would have to be filed and furnished for the payment of reportable gambling winnings of $1,500 and for the payment of reportable gambling winnings of $2,500. However, if R decides to use the aggregate reporting method, R may report total reportable gambling winnings from slot machine play of $4,000 ($1,500 + $2,500) on one Form W-2G.

*Example 2.* Assume the same facts as *Example 1*, except that in addition to the winnings described in *Example 1*, at 5 a.m. on Day 2, C wins $3,250 from one slot machine play at casino R. Even though C played the same type of game (slot machine play) on Day 1 and Day 2, under paragraph (b)(2) of this section, the win at 5 a.m. on Day 2 is a win during a separate information reporting period. Under paragraph (g)(2)(i) of this section, the $3,250 of reportable gambling winnings on Day 2 cannot be aggregated with the reportable gambling winnings of $4,000 from Day 1 on a single Form W-2G. Accordingly, if R uses the aggregate reporting method, R must file two Forms W-2G with respect to C's reportable gambling winnings on Day 1 and Day 2. R must report $4,000 of reportable gambling winnings from slot machine play paid to C on Day 1 on the first Form W-2G, and $3,250 of reportable gambling winnings from slot machine play paid to C on Day 2 on the second Form W-2G.

*Example 3.* On December 31 of Year 1 at 4:00 p.m., C wins $10,000 from one slot machine play at casino R. At 12:30 a.m. on January 1 of Year 2, C wins $4,000 from one slot machine play at casino R. Under paragraphs (b)(2)(iii)(B) and (C) of this section, the win at 4 p.m. on December 31 of Year 1 and the win at 12:30 a.m. on January 1 of Year 2 are wins during different information reporting periods. Under paragraph (g)(2)(i) of this section, the $4,000 of reportable gambling winnings on January 1 cannot be aggregated with the reportable gambling winnings of $10,000 from December 31 on a single Form W-2G. Accordingly, if R uses the aggregate reporting method, R must file two Forms W-2G with respect to C's reportable gambling winnings on Day 1 and Day 2. R must report $10,000 of reportable gambling winnings from slot machine play paid to C on December 31 on the first Form W-2G and $4,000 of reportable gambling winnings from slot machine play paid to C on January 1 on the second Form W-2G.

*Example 4.* Assume the same facts as example 3, except that C also wins $5,000 from one slot machine play at 3:30 p.m. on January 1 and $7,000 from one slot machine play at 1:30 a.m. on January 2. Under the special rule of paragraph (b)(2)(iii) of this section, the "information reporting period" begins at 12:00 a.m. on January 1 and extends until the start of the next information reporting period, in this case 2:59 a.m. on January 2. Under paragraph (b)(1)(C) of this section, Casino R will pay C a total of $26,000 ($10,000 + $4,000 + $5,000 + $7,000) in reportable gambling winnings; however, $10,000 must be reported in Year 1, and $16,000 must be reported in Year 2. Because all of the amounts won in Year 2 were won on the same type of game and during the same information reporting period, R is permitted to use the aggregate reporting method under this paragraph (g). If R decides to use the aggregate reporting method, R may report $10,000 of reportable gambling winnings from slot machine play paid to C on December 31 on the first Form W-2G and $16,000 of total reportable gambling winnings from slot machine play paid to C on January 1 on the second Form W-2G.

*Example 5.* At 2 p.m. on Day 1, D won $2,000 (after reducing the amount of the win by the amount wagered) playing one keno game at casino R. D provides R with his driver's license. The driver's license has D's photograph on it, as well as D's name and address. The driver's license does not include D's social security number. D cannot remember his social security number and has no other identi-

fication at the time with his social security number on it. D does not provide R with his social security number before R pays the winnings to D. Because D cannot remember his social security number, D cannot complete and sign a Form W-9. R deducts and withholds $560 (28 percent of $2,000) under the backup withholding provisions of section 3406(a) and pays the remaining $1,440 in winnings to D. D returns to casino R and at 6 p.m. on Day 1 wins $1,500 (after reducing the amount of the win by the amount wagered) in one keno game. D provides R with his driver's license as well as D's social security card. R generally uses the aggregate reporting method and in all cases where it is used, R complies with the requirements of this paragraph (g). At 8 p.m. and 10 p.m. on Day 1, D wins an additional $1,800 and $1,700 (after reducing the amount of the win by the amount wagered), respectively, from two different keno games. For each of these two wins, an employee of R obtains the information from D required by this paragraph (g):

(i) Under paragraph (b)(1)(i)(B) of this section, each of D's wins from the four games of keno on Day 1 ($2,000, $1,500, $1,800, and $1,700) are reportable gambling winnings. Because D's first win on Day 1 was at 2 p.m. and D's last win on Day 1 was at 10 p.m., all of D's reportable gambling winnings from keno are won during the same information reporting period. Because R satisfies the requirements of paragraph (g)(2)(i), R may use the aggregate reporting method to report D's reportable gambling winnings from keno. However, pursuant to paragraph (g)(4)(iii) of this section, the $2,000 payment made to D at 2 p.m. cannot be reported under the aggregate reporting method because that payment was subject to backup withholding. Accordingly, if R uses the aggregate reporting method under this paragraph (g), R will have to file two Forms W-2G with respect to D's reportable gambling winnings from keno on Day 1. On the first Form W-2G, R will report $2,000 of reportable gambling winnings and $560 of backup withholding with respect to the 2 p.m. win from keno, and, on the second Form W-2G, R will report $5,000 of reportable gambling winnings from keno (representing the three payments of $1,500, $1,800, and $1,700 that D won between 6 p.m. and 10 p.m. on Day 1).

*Example 6.* In one information reporting period on Day 1, E won five reportable gambling winnings from five different bingo games at a casino R. R generally uses the aggregate reporting method and in all cases where it is used, R complies with the requirements of this paragraph (g). Although E signed the entry in the record R maintains for payment of the first four reportable gambling winnings, E refuses to sign the entry in the record for the fifth payment of reportable gambling winnings. R may use the aggregate reporting method for the first four payments of reportable gambling winnings to E. However, because the entry in the record for the fifth payment of reportable gambling winnings does not include E's signature, as required by paragraph (g)(3)(i) of this section, that payment may not be reported under the aggregate reporting method. Accordingly, if R uses the aggregate reporting method under paragraph (g) of this section, R must prepare two Forms W-2G as follows: On the first Form W-2G, R must report the first four payments of reportable gambling winnings from bingo made to E on Day 1. On the second Form W-2G, R must report the fifth payment of reportable gambling winnings from bingo made to E on Day 1.

(h) *Payments to foreign persons.*—See § 1.6041-4 regarding payments to foreign persons. See § 1.6049-5(d) for determining whether the payee is a foreign person.

(i) *Effective/applicability date.*—Section 1.6041-10(b)(2), concerning payor-selected "information reporting periods," applies to payments of reportable gambling winnings from bingo, keno, or slot machine play made on or after January 1 of the year following the date these regulations are published in the **Federal Register**. All other sections contained herein apply to payments of reportable gambling winnings from bingo, keno, or slot machine play made on or after December 30, 2016.

(j) *Cross-references for certain gambling winnings.*—For provisions relating to backup withholding for winnings from bingo, keno, and slot machine play and other reportable gambling winnings, see § 31.3406(g)-2(d). For provisions relating to withholding and reporting for gambling winnings from lotteries, sweepstakes, wagering pools, and other wagering transactions, including a wagering transaction in a parimutuel pool with respect to horse races, dog races, or jai alai, see § 31.3402(q)-1. [Reg. § 1.6041-10.]

☐ [*T.D. 9807, 12-29-2016.*]

### [Reg. § 1.6041A-1]

**§ 1.6041A-1. Returns regarding payments of remuneration for services and certain direct sales.**—(a) through (c) [Reserved].

(d) *Exceptions to return requirement.*—[Reserved].
    (1) and (2) [Reserved].

(3) *Foreign transactions.*—(i) *In general.*—No return shall be required under section 6041A with respect to payments described in this paragraph (d)(3).

(A) Returns of information are not required for payments that a payor can, prior to payment, associate with documentation upon which it may rely to treat as made to a foreign beneficial owner in accordance with § 1.1441-1(e)(1)(ii) or as made to a foreign payee in accordance with § 1.6049-5(d)(1) or presumed to be made to a foreign payee under § 1.6049-5(d)(2), (3), (4), or (5). However, such payments may be reportable under § 1.1461-1(b) and (c). For purposes of this paragraph (d)(3)(i)(A), the provisions in § 1.6049-5(c) (regarding rules applicable to documentation of foreign status and definition of U.S. payor and non-U.S. payor) shall apply. The provisions of § 1.1441-1 shall apply by substituting the term *payor* for the term *withholding agent.*

(B) Returns of information are not required for payments of remuneration for services from sources outside the United States (determined under the provisions of part I, subchapter N, chapter 1 of the Internal Revenue Code and the regulations under those provisions) if payments are made outside the United States by a non-U.S. payor or non U.S. middleman. For a definition of non U.S. payor or non-U.S. middleman, see § 1.6049-5(c)(5). For circumstances in which a payment is considered to be made outside the United States, see § 1.6049-5(e).

(C) Returns of information are not required under sections 6041 or 6041A for amounts paid outside of the United States (within the meaning of § 1.6049-5(e)) as remuneration for services as a direct seller (within the meaning of section 3508) performed outside the United States or for sales described in section 6041A(b) made outside of the United States of consumer products for resale outside of the United States.

(ii) *Payor.*—The term *payor* has the same meaning as described in § 1.6049-4(a)(2).

(iii) *Joint owners.*—Amounts paid to joint owners for which a certificate or documentation is required as a condition for being exempt from reporting under paragraph (d)(3)(i) of this section are presumed made to U.S. payees who are not exempt recipients if, prior to payment, the payor or middleman cannot reliably associate the payment either with a Form W-9 furnished by one of the joint owners in the manner required in § § 31.3406(d)-1 through 31.3406(d)-5 of this chapter, or with documentation described in paragraph (d)(3)(i)(A) of this section furnished by each joint owner upon which it can rely to treat each joint owner as a foreign payee or foreign beneficial owner.

(iv) *Conversion into United States dollars of amounts paid in foreign currency.*—For rules concerning foreign currency conversion, see § 1.6049-4(d)(3)(i).

(v) *Effective date.*—The provisions of this paragraph (d)(3) apply to payments made after December 31, 2000.

(4) *Information returns required under section 6050W for calendar years beginning after December 31, 2010.*—(i) For payments made by payment card (as defined in § 1.6050W-1(b)(3)) or through a third party payment network (as defined in § 1.6050W-1(c)(3)) after December 31, 2010, that are required to be reported on an information return under section 6050W (relating to payment card and third party network transactions), the following rule applies. Transactions that otherwise would be reportable under both sections 6041A(a) and 6050W are reported under section 6050W and not section 6041A(a). For provisions relating to information reporting for payment card transactions and third party network transactions, see § 1.6050W-1. Solely for purposes of this paragraph, the de minimis threshold for third party network transactions in § 1.6050W-1(c)(4) is disregarded in determining whether the transaction is subject to reporting under section 6050W.

(ii) *Examples.*—The provisions of paragraph (d)(4) of this section are illustrated by the following examples:

*Example 1.* Service-recipient A, in the course of its business, pays remuneration of $600 to service provider B by credit card for services performed by B. B is one of a network of unrelated persons that has agreed to accept A's credit card as payment under an agreement that provides standards and mechanisms for settling the transactions between a merchant acquiring bank and the persons who accept the cards. Merchant acquiring bank Y is responsible for making the payment to B. Under paragraph (d)(4)(i) of this section, A is not required to file an information return under section 6041A(a) with respect to the transaction because Y, as the payment settlement entity for the payment card transaction, is required to file an information return under section 6050W.

*Example 2.* Service-recipient A, in the course of business, pays $600 of fixed or determinable income to B, a repairman, through a third party payment network. B is one of a substantial number of persons who have established accounts with Y, a third party settlement organization that provides standards and mechanisms for settling the transactions and guarantees payments to those persons for goods or services purchased through the network. Y is responsible for making the payment to B. Under paragraph (d)(4)(i) of this section, A is not required to file an information return under section 6041A(a) with respect to the transaction because the transaction is a third party network transaction that is subject to reporting under section 6050W. Solely for purposes of determining whether the transaction is subject to reporting under section 6050W, the de minimis threshold for third party network transactions in § 1.6050W-1(c)(4) is disregarded.

(iii) *Effective/applicability date.*—Paragraph (d)(4) of this section applies to payments made by payment card or through a third party payment network after December 31, 2010.

(e) [Reserved].

(f) *Statements to be furnished to persons with respect to whom information is required to be furnished.*—(1) [Reserved].

(2) *Time for furnishing statement.*—[Reserved].

(3) *Contents of statement.*—[Reserved].

(g) [Reserved].

(h) *Cross-reference to penalties.*—For provisions relating to the penalty provided for failure to file timely a correct information return required under section 6041A(a) or (b), see § 301.6721-1 of this chapter (Procedure and Administration Regulations). For provisions relating to the penalty provided for failure to furnish timely a correct payee statement required under section 6041A(e), see § 301.6722-1 of this chapter. See § 301.6724-1 of this chapter for the waiver of a penalty if the failure is due to reasonable cause and is not due to willful neglect. [Reg. § 1.6041A-1.]

☐ [*T.D.* 8734, 10-6-97. *Amended by T.D.* 8804, 12-30-98; *T.D.* 8856, 12-29-99; *T.D.* 8881, 5-15-2000 *and T.D.* 9496, 8-13-2010.]

**[Reg. § 301.6042-1]**

**§ 301.6042-1. Returns of information regarding payments of dividends and corporate earnings and profits.**—For provisions relating to the requirement of returns of information regarding payments of dividends and corporate earnings and profits, see § § 1.6042-1 to 1.6042-4, inclusive, of this chapter (Income Tax Regulations). [Reg. § 301.6042-1.]

☐ [*T.D.* 6498, 10-24-60. *Amended by T.D.* 6700, 1-6-64.]

**[Reg. § 1.6042-2]**

**§ 1.6042-2. Returns of information as to dividends paid.**—(a) *Requirement of reporting.*—(1) An information return on Form 1099 shall be made under section 6042(a) by—

(i) Every person who makes a payment of dividends (as defined in § 1.6042-3) to any other person during a calendar year. The information return shall show the aggregate amount of the dividends, the name, address, and taxpayer identifying number of the person to whom paid, the amount of tax deducted and withheld under section 3406 from the dividends, if any, and such other information as required by the forms. An information return is generally not required if the amount of dividends paid to the other person during the calendar year aggregates less than $10 or if the payment is made to a person who is an exempt recipient described in § 1.6049-4(c)(1)(ii) unless the payor backup withholds under section 3406 on such payment (because, for example, the payee has failed to furnish a Form W-9), in which case the payor must make a return under this section, unless the payor refunds the amount withheld pursuant to § 31.6413(a)-3 of this chapter. Further, a return of information is not required under this section for—

(A) Payments with respect to which a return is not required by applying the rules of § 1.6049-4(c)(4) (by substituting the term "dividend" for the term "interest"); or

(B) Payments made by a paying agent on behalf of a corporation described in section 1297(a) with respect to a shareholder of the corporation if—

(1) The paying agent obtains from the corporation a written certification signed by a person authorized to sign on behalf of the corporation, that states that the corporation is described in section 1297(a) for each calendar year during which the paying agent relies on the provisions of paragraph (a)(1)(i)(B) of this section, and the paying agent has no reason to know the written certification is unreliable or incorrect;

(2) The paying agent identifies, prior to payment, the corporation as a participating FFI (including a reporting Model 2 FFI) (as defined in § 1.6049-4(f)(10) or (14), respectively), or reporting Model 1 FFI (as defined in § 1.6049-4(f)(13)), in accordance with the requirements of § 1.1471-3(d)(4) (substituting the terms "paying

agent" and "corporation" for the terms "withholding agent" and "payee," respectively) and validates that status annually;

(3) The paying agent obtains a written certification representing that the corporation shall report the payment as part of its reporting obligations under chapter 4 of the Code or an applicable IGA (as defined in §1.6049-4(f)(7)) with respect to its U.S. accounts and provided the paying agent does not know that the corporation is not reporting the payment as required. The paying agent may rely on the written certification until there is a change in circumstances or the paying agent knows or has reason to know that the statement is unreliable or incorrect. A paying agent that knows that the corporation is not reporting the payment as required under chapter 4 of the Code or an applicable IGA (as defined in §1.6049-4(f)(7)) must report all payments reportable under this section that it makes during the year in which it obtains such knowledge; and

(4) The paying agent is not also acting in its capacity as a custodian, nominee, or other agent of the payee with respect to the payments.

(ii) Every person, except to the extent that he acts as a nominee described in paragraph (a)(1)(iii) of this section, who receives payments of dividends as a nominee on behalf of another person shall make a return of information under this section for the calendar year of the payment. The information return shall show the aggregate amount of the dividends, the name, address, and taxpayer identification number of the person on whose behalf the dividends are received, the amount of tax deducted and withheld under section 3406 from the dividends, if any, and such other information as required by the forms. An information return is generally not required if the amount of the dividends received on behalf of the other person during the calendar year aggregates less than $10. However, a return of information is not required under this section if—

(A) The record owner is, pursuant to section 6012(a)(3) or (4) and §1.6012-3, required to file a fiduciary return on Form 1041 that is filed for the estate or trust disclosing the name, address, and identifying number of both the record owner and actual owner and furnishes Form K-1 to each actual owner containing the information required to be shown on the form, including amounts withheld under section 3406;

(B) The record owner is a nominee of a banking institution or trust company exercising trust powers, and such banking institution or trust company is, pursuant to section 6012(a)(3) or (4) and §1.6012-3, required to file a fiduciary return on Form 1041 that is filed for the estate or trust disclosing the name, address, and identifying number of both the record owner and the actual owner and furnishes Form K-1 to each actual owner containing the information required to be shown on the form, including amounts withheld under section 3406; or

(C) The record owner is a banking institution or trust company exercising trust powers, or a nominee thereof, and the actual owner is an organization exempt from taxation under section 501(a) for which such banking institution or trust company files an annual return but only if the name, address, and identifying number of the record owner are included on or with the annual return filed for the tax exempt organization).

(iii) Every person who is a nominee acting as a custodian of a unit investment trust described in section 851(f)(1) and paragraph (d) of §1.851-7 who, during a calendar year after 1968, receives payments of dividends in such capacity, shall make an information return on Forms 1096 and 1099, for such calendar year showing the information required by such forms and instructions thereto and the name, address, and identifying number of the nominee identified as such. This subdivision shall not apply if the regulated investment company agrees with the nominee to satisfy the requirements of section 6042 and the regulations thereunder with respect to each holder of an interest in the unit investment trust whose shares are being held by the nominee as custodian and within the time limit for furnishing statements prescribed by §1.6042-4, files with the Internal Revenue Service office where such company's return is to be filed for the taxable year, a statement that the holders of the unit investment trust with whom the agreement was made have been directly notified by the regulated investment company. Such statement shall include the name, sponsor, and custodian of each unit investment trust whose holders have been directly notified. The nominee's requirements under this subdivision shall be deemed met if the regulated investment company transmits a copy of such statement to the nominee within such period; provided, however, if the regulated investment company fails or is unable to satisfy the requirements of section 6042 with respect to the holders of interest in the unit investment trust, it shall so notify the Internal Revenue Service within 45 days following the close of its taxable year. The custodian shall, upon notice by the Internal Revenue Service that the regulated investment company has failed to comply with the agreement, satisfy the requirements of this subdivision within 30 days of such notice.

(2) *Definitions.*—The term "person" when used in this section does not include the United States, a State, the District of Columbia, a foreign government, a political subdivision of a State or of a foreign government, or an international organization. Therefore, dividends paid by or to one of these entities need not be reported. For purposes of this section, a person who receives a dividend shall be considered to have received it as a nominee if he is not the actual owner of such dividend and if he was required under §1.6109-1 to furnish his identifying number to the payer of the dividend (or would have been so required if the total of such dividends for the year had been $10 or more), and such number was (or would have been) required to be included on an information return filed by the payer with respect to the dividend. However, a person shall not be considered to be a nominee as to any portion of a dividend which is actually owned by another person whose name is also shown on the information return filed by the payer or nominee with respect to such dividend. Thus, in the case of a stock jointly owned by a husband and wife, the husband will not be considered as receiving any portion of a dividend on that stock as a nominee for his wife if his wife's name is included on the information return filed by the payer with respect to the dividend.

(3) *Determination of person to whom a dividend is paid or for whom it is received.*—For purposes of applying the provisions of this section, the person whose identifying number is required to be included by the payer of a dividend on an information return with respect to such dividend shall be considered the person to whom the dividend is paid. In the case of a dividend received by a nominee on behalf of another person, the person whose identifying number is required to be included on an information return made by the nominee with respect to such dividend shall be considered the person on whose behalf such dividend is received by the nominee. Thus, in the case of a dividend made payable to a person other than the record owner of the stock with respect to which the dividend is paid, the record owner of the stock shall be considered the person to whom the dividend is paid for purposes of applying the reporting requirements in this section, since his identifying number is required to be included on the information return filed under this section by the payer of the dividend. Similarly, if a stockbroker receives a dividend on stock held in street name for the joint account of a husband and wife, the dividend is considered as received on behalf of the husband since his identifying number should be shown on the information return filed by the nominee under this section. Thus, if the wife has a separate account with the same stockbroker, any dividends received by the stockbroker for her separate account should not be aggregated with the dividends received for the joint account for purposes of information reporting. For regulations relating to the use of identifying numbers, see §1.6109-1.

(4) *Inclusion of other payments.*—The Form 1099 filed by any person with respect to payments of dividends to another person during a calendar year may, at the election of the maker, include other payments made by him to such other person during such year which are required to be reported on Form 1099. Similarly, the Form 1099 filed by a nominee with respect to payments of dividends received by him on behalf of any other person during a calendar year may include payments of interest received by him on behalf of such person during such year which are required to be reported on Form 1099.

(b) *When payment deemed made.*—For purposes of a return of information, an amount is deemed to have been paid when it is credited or set apart to a person without any substantial limitation or restriction as to the time or manner of payment or condition upon which payment is to be made, and is made available to him so that it may be drawn at any time, and its receipt brought within his own control and disposition.

(c) *Time and place for filing.*—The returns required under this section for any calendar year shall be filed after September 30 of such year, but not before the payer's final payment for the year, and on or before February 28 (March 31 if filed electronically) of the following year with any of the Internal Revenue Service Centers, the addresses of which are listed in the instructions for Form 1096. For extensions of time for filing returns under this section, see §1.6081-1.

(d) *Cross-reference to penalty.*—For provisions relating to the penalty provided for failure to file timely a correct information return required under section 6042(a), see §301.6721-1 of this chapter (Procedure and Administration Regulations). See §301.6724-1 of this chapter for the waiver of a penalty if the failure is due to reasonable cause and is not due to willful neglect.

(e) *Magnetic media requirement.*—For rules relating to permission to submit the information required by Form 1087 or 1099 on magnetic tape or other media, see §1.9101-1. For the requirement to submit the information required by Form 1099 on magnetic media for payments after December 31, 1983, see section 6011(e) and §301.6011-2 of this chapter (Procedure and Administration Regulations).

(f) *Effective/applicability date.*—This section applies to payments made on or after January 6, 2017. (For payments made after June 30, 2014, and before January 6, 2017, see this section as in effect and contained in 26 CFR part 1, as revised April 1, 2016. For payments made after December 31, 2000, and before July 1, 2014, see this section as in effect and contained in 26 CFR part 1, as revised April 1, 2013.) [Reg. §1.6042-2.]

☐ [*T.D.* 6628, 12-27-62. *Amended by T.D.* 6677, 9-16-63; *T.D.* 6879, 3-7-66; *T.D.* 6883, 5-2-66; *T.D.* 6891, 8-3-66; *T.D.* 7000, 1-17-69; *T.D.* 7187, 7-5-72; *T.D.* 8734, 10-6-97 (T.D. 8804 delayed the effective date of T.D. 8734 from January 1, 1999, to January 1, 2000; T.D. 8856 further delayed the effective date of T.D. 8734 until January 1, 2001; *T.D.* 8804, 12-30-98 (*corrected* 3-8-99); *T.D.* 8895, 8-17-2000, *T.D.* 9658, 2-28-2014 *and T.D.* 9808, 12-30-2016.]

### [Reg. §1.6042-3]

**§1.6042-3. Dividends subject to reporting.**—(a) *In general.*—Except as provided in paragraph (b) of this section, the term *dividend* for purposes of this section and §§1.6042-2 and 1.6042-4 means the amounts described in the following paragraphs (a)(1) through (3) of this section—

(1) Any distribution made by a corporation to its shareholders which is a dividend as defined in section 316; and

(2) Any payment made by a stockbroker to any person as a substitute for a dividend. Such a payment includes any payment made in lieu of a dividend to a person whose stock has been borrowed. See §1.6045-2(h) for coordination of the reporting requirements under sections 6042 and 6045(d) with respect to such payments; and

(3) A distribution from a regulated investment company (irrespective of the fact that any part of the distribution may not represent ordinary income (i.e., may, for example, represent a capital gain dividend as defined in section 852(b)(3)(C)).

(b) *Exceptions.*—(1) *In general.*—For purposes of §§1.6042-2 and 1.6042-4, the amounts described in paragraphs (b)(1)(i) through (vii) of this section are not dividends.

(i) Amounts paid by an insurance company to a policyholder, other than a dividend upon its capital stock.

(ii) Payments (however denominated) by a mutual savings bank, savings and loan association, or similar organization, in respect of deposits, investment certificates, or withdrawable or repurchasable shares. See, however, section 6049 and the regulations under that section for provisions requiring reporting of these payments.

(iii) Distributions or payments that a payor can, prior to payment, reliably associate with documentation upon which it may rely to treat as made to a foreign beneficial owner in accordance with §1.1441-1(e)(1)(ii) or as made to a foreign payee in accordance with §1.6049-5(d)(1) or presumed to be made to a foreign payee under §1.6049-5(d)(2), (3), (4), or (5). Returns of information are also not required for payments that a payor or middleman can, prior to payment, reliably associate with documentation upon which it may rely to treat as made to a foreign intermediary in accordance with §1.1441-1(b) if it obtains from the intermediary entity a withholding statement (described in §1.6049-5(b)(14)) that allocates the payment to a chapter 4 withholding rate pool (as defined in §1.6049-4(f)(5)) or to specific payees to which withholding under chapter 4 applies. Payments excepted from reporting under this paragraph (b)(1)(iii) may be reportable, for purposes of chapter 3 of the Internal Revenue Code (Code), under §1.1461-1(b) and (c) or, for chapter 4 purposes, under §1.1474-1(d)(2). The provisions in §1.6049-5(c) regarding documentation of foreign status shall apply for purposes of this paragraph (b)(1)(iii). The provisions in §1.6049-5(c) regarding definitions of U.S. payor and non-U.S. payor shall also apply for purposes of this paragraph (b)(1)(iii). The provisions of §1.1441-1 shall apply by substituting the term *payor* for the term *withholding agent* and without regard to the fact that the provisions apply only to amounts subject to withholding under chapter 3 of the Code.

(iv) Distributions or payments from sources outside the United States (as determined under the provisions of part I, subchapter N, chapter 1 of the Code and the regulations under those provisions) that are paid by a non-U.S. payor or non-U.S. middleman and that are paid and received outside the United States. For a definition of non-U.S. payor and non-U.S. middleman, see §1.6049-5(c)(5). For circumstances in which an amount is considered to be paid and received outside the United States, see §1.6049-4(f)(16).

(v) Distributions or payments for the period that the amounts represent assets blocked as described in §1.1441-2(e)(3). The exemption in this paragraph (b)(1)(v) shall terminate when payment is deemed to occur in accordance with the rules of §1.1441-2(e)(3).

(vi) If a foreign intermediary, as described in §1.1441-1(c)(13), or a U.S. branch that is not treated as a U.S. person receives a payment from a payor, which payment the payor can reliably associate with a valid withholding certificate described in §1.1441-1(e)(3)(ii) or (iii), or §1.1441-1(e)(3)(v), respectively, furnished by such intermediary or branch, then the intermediary or branch is not required to report such payment when it, in turn, pays the amount, unless, and to the extent, the intermediary or branch knows that the payment is required to be reported under this section and was not so reported. For example, if a U.S. branch described in §1.1441-1(b)(2)(iv) fails to provide information regarding U.S. persons that are not exempt from reporting under §1.6049-4(c)(1)(ii) to the person from whom the U.S. branch receives the payment, the amount paid by the U.S. branch to such person is a dividend. See, however, §1.6042-2(a)(1)(i)(A) for when reporting under section 6042 is coordinated with reporting under chapter 4 of the Code or an applicable IGA (as defined in §1.6049-4(f)(7)). The exception of this paragraph (b)(1)(vi) for amounts paid by a foreign intermediary shall not apply to a qualified intermediary that assumes reporting responsibility under chapter 61 of the Code with respect to amounts reportable under the agreement described in §1.1441-1(e)(5)(iii).

(vii) With respect to amounts paid or credited after December 31, 1982, any amount paid or credited to any person described in §1.6049-4(c)(1)(ii), unless a tax is withheld under section 3406 and is not refunded by the payor in accordance with §31.6413(a)-3 of this chapter (Employment Tax Regulations).

(2) *Payor.*—The term *payor* has the same meaning as described in §1.6049-4(a)(2).

(3) *Joint owners.*—Amounts paid to joint owners for which a certificate or documentation is required as a condition for being exempt from reporting under this paragraph (b) are presumed made to U.S. payees who are not exempt recipients if, prior to payment, the payor or middleman cannot reliably associate the payment either with a Form W-9 furnished by one of the joint owners in the manner required in §§31.3406(d)-1 through 31.3406(d)-5 of this chapter, or with documentation described in paragraph (b)(1)(iii) of this section furnished by each joint owner upon which it can rely to treat each joint owner as a foreign payee or foreign beneficial owner. However in the case of a withholdable payment (as defined in §1.6049-4(f)(15)) made to joint payees, if any such joint payee does not appear to be an individual, the payment is presumed made to a foreign payee that is a nonparticipating FFI (as defined in §1.1471-1(b)(82)). See §1.1471-3(f)(7). For purposes of applying this paragraph (b)(3), the grace period described in §1.6049-5(d)(2)(ii) shall apply only if each payee qualifies for such grace period.

(4) *Conversion into United States dollars of amounts paid in foreign currency.*—For rules concerning foreign currency conversion, see §1.6049-4(d)(3)(i).

(c) *Special rule.*—If a person makes a payment which may be a dividend, or if a nominee receives a payment which may be a dividend, but such person or nominee is unable to determine the portion of the payment which is a dividend (as defined in paragraphs (a) and (b) of this section) at the time he files his return under §1.6042-2, he shall, for purposes of such section treat the entire amount of such payment as a dividend.

(d) *Effective/applicability date.*—This section applies on or after January 6, 2017. (For payments made after June 30, 2014, and before January 6, 2017, see this section as in effect and contained in 26 CFR part 1, as revised April 1, 2016. For payments made after December 31, 2000, and before July 1, 2014, see this section as in effect and contained in 26 CFR part 1, as revised April 1, 2013). [Reg. §1.6042-3.]

☐ [*T.D.* 6628, 12-27-62. *Amended by T.D.* 6908, 12-30-66; *T.D.* 7987, 10-23-84; *T.D.* 8029, 6-4-85; *T.D.* 8734, 10-6-97; *T.D.* 8804, 12-30-98; *T.D.* 8856, 12-29-99; *T.D.* 8881, 5-15-2000, *T.D.* 9658, 2-28-2014 *and T.D.* 9808, 12-30-2016.]

### [Reg. §1.6042-4]

**§1.6042-4. Statement to recipients of dividend payments.**—(a) *Requirement.*—A person required to make an information return under section 6042(a)(1) and §1.6042-2 must furnish a statement to each recipient whose identifying number is required to be shown on the related information return for dividend payments.

(b) *Form and content of the statement.*—The statement required by paragraph (a) of this section must be either the official Form 1099 prescribed by the Internal Revenue Service for the respective calendar year or an acceptable substitute statement that contains provisions that are substantially similar to those of the official Form 1099 for the respective calendar year. For further guidance on how to prepare an acceptable substitute statement, see Rev. Proc. 2012-38, 2012-48 IRB 575, also published as Publication 1179, "General Rules and Specifications for Substitute Forms 1096, 1098, 1099, 5498, and Certain Other Information Returns," or any successor guidance. An IRS truncated taxpayer identifying number (TTIN) may be used as the identifying number of the recipient. For provisions relating to the use of TTINs, see § 301.6109-4 of this chapter (Procedure and Administration Regulations).

(c) *Aggregation of payments.*—A payor may aggregate on one Form 1099 all payments made to a recipient with respect to each separate account during a calendar year.

(d) *Manner of providing statements to recipients.*—(1) *In general.*—The Form 1099, or acceptable substitute statement, must be provided to the recipient either in person or by first-class mail to the recipient's last known address in a statement mailing.

(2) *Statement mailing requirement.*—The mailing required under section 6042(c) of a Form 1099 to a payee-recipient must qualify as a statement mailing. A statement mailing must contain the required Form 1099 or acceptable substitute statement (written statement) and must comply with enclosure and envelope restrictions.

(i) *Enclosure restrictions.*—To qualify as a statement mailing, the mailing cannot contain any enclosures except those listed in this paragraph (d)(2)(i). Moreover, no promotional or advertising material is permitted in the mailing of the written statement. Even a *de minimis* amount of promotional or advertising material violates the statement mailing requirement. However, a logo on the envelope containing the written statement and on nontax enclosures described in paragraph (d)(2)(i)(A) through (D) of this section does not violate the written statement requirement. The written statement required under section 6042(c) and paragraph (a) of this section may be perforated to a check or to a statement of the recipient-payee's specific account with the payor described in paragraph (d)(2)(i)(A) or (C) of this section. The enclosure to which the written statement is perforated must contain, in a bold and conspicuous type, the legend: "Important Tax Return Document Attached." The enclosures permitted in a mailing are limited to—

(A) A check with respect to the account reported on the written statement;

(B) A letter explaining why a check with respect to such account is not enclosed with the written statement (for example, because a dividend has not been declared payable);

(C) A statement of the taxpayer-recipient's specific account with the payor if payments on such account are reflected on the written statement;

(D) A letter limited to an explanation of the tax consequences of the information set forth on the enclosed written statement;

(E) Payee statements related to other Forms 1099, Form 1098, and Form 5498 (or the account balance on a Form 5498), Forms W-2 and W-2G; and

(F) Any document concerning the solicitation of the Form W-9, as described in § 31.3406(h)-3(a) of this chapter, or of the Form W-8 as described in § 1.1441-1(e)(1).

(ii) *Envelope and delivery restrictions.*—(A) *Envelope restrictions.*—The outside of the envelope in which the written statement is mailed and each nontax enclosure enclosed in the envelope must contain, in a bold and conspicuous type, the legend: "Important Tax Return Document Enclosed." For purposes of this paragraph (d)(2)(ii), a nontax enclosure is any item listed in paragraphs (d)(2)(i)(A) through (C) of this section. However, a payor is not required to include the legend on the outside of an envelope containing only the enclosures in paragraph (d)(2)(i)(D) through (F) of this section.

(B) *Delivery restrictions.*—The requirement to provide the written statement in person or by first-class mail may be satisfied by sending the written statement and any enclosures described in paragraph (d)(2)(i) of this section by intra-office mail, provided that intra-office mail is used by the payor in sending account activity, balance information, and other correspondence to the payee. If a payor does not personally deliver the written statement (i.e., the Form 1099 or its acceptable substitute) to the recipient or mail it to the recipient in a statement mailing as described in this paragraph (d), the payor is considered to have failed to mail the statement required under section 6042(c) and will be subject to the penalty under section 6722.

(e) *Time for furnishing statements.*—(1) *In general.*—Each statement required by section 6042(c) and this section to be furnished to any person for a calendar year must be furnished to such person after November 30 of the year and on or before January 31 (February 10 in the case of a nominee filing under § 1.6042-2(a)(1)(iii)) of the following year, but no statement may be furnished before the final dividend for the calendar year has been paid. However, the statement may be furnished at any time after April 30 if it is furnished with the

final dividend for the calendar year. For a statement required to be furnished after December 31, 2008, the February 15 due date under section 6045 applies to the statement if the statement is furnished in a consolidated reporting statement under section 6045. *See* §§ 1.6045-1(k)(3), 1.6045-2(d)(2), 1.6045-3(e)(2), 1.6045-4(m)(3), and 1.6045-5(a)(3)(ii).

(2) *Extensions of time.*—For good cause upon written application of the person required to furnish statements under this section, the Director, Martinsburg Computing Center, may grant an extension of time not exceeding 30 days in which to furnish such statements. The application must be addressed to the Director, Martinsburg Computing Center, and must contain a full recital of the reasons for requesting the extension to aid the Director in determining the period of the extension, if any, that will be granted. Such a request in the form of a letter to the Director, Martinsburg Computing Center, signed by the applicant will suffice as an application. The application must be filed on or before the date prescribed in paragraph (e)(1) of this section.

(3) *Last day for furnishing statement.*—For provisions relating to the time for performance of an act when the last day prescribed for performance falls on Saturday, Sunday, or a legal holiday, see section 7503 and § 301.7503-1 of this chapter (Regulations on Procedure and Administration).

(f) *Cross-reference to penalty.*—For provisions relating to the penalty provided for failure to furnish timely a correct payee statement required under section 6042(c), see § 301.6722-1 of this chapter (Procedure and Administration Regulations). See § 301.6724-1 of this chapter for the waiver of a penalty if the failure is due to reasonable cause and is not due to willful neglect.

(g) *Effective/applicability date.*—This section is effective for payee statements due after December 31, 1995, without regard to extensions. The amendments to paragraph (b) are effective for payee statements due after December 31, 2014. For payee statements due before January 1, 2015, § 1.6042-4(b) (as contained in 26 CFR part 1, revised April 2013) shall apply. [Reg. § 1.6042-4.]

☐ [*T.D.* 6628, 12-27-62. *Amended by T.D.* 6879, 3-7-66; *T.D.* 7187, 7-5-72; *T.D.* 7624, 5-29-79; *T.D.* 8637, 12-20-95; *T.D.* 8734, 10-6-97 (*T.D.* 8804 delayed the effective date of *T.D.* 8734 from January 1, 1999, to January 1, 2000; *T.D.* 8856 further delayed the effective date of *T.D.* 8734 until January 1, 2001); *T.D.* 9504, 10-12-2010 *and T.D.* 9675, 7-14-2014.]

### [Reg. § 1.6042-5]

**§ 1.6042-5. Coordination with reporting rules for widely held fixed investment trusts under § 1.671-5.**—See § 1.671-5 for the reporting rules for widely held fixed investment trusts (as defined under that section). [Reg. § 1.6042-5.]

☐ [*T.D.* 9241, 1-23-2006.]

### [Reg. § 1.6043-1]

**§ 1.6043-1. Return regarding corporate dissolution or liquidation.**—(a) *Requirement of returns.*—Within 30 days after the adoption of any resolution or plan for or in respect of the dissolution of a corporation or the liquidation of the whole or any part of its capital stock, the corporation shall file a return on Form 966, containing the information required by paragraph (b) of this section and by such form. Such return shall be filed with the district director for the district in which the income tax return of the corporation is filed. Further, if after the filing of a Form 966 there is an amendment of or supplement to the resolution or plan, an additional Form 966, based on the resolution or plan as amended or supplemented, must be filed within 30 days after the adoption of such amendment or supplement. A return must be filed under section 6043 and this section in respect of a liquidation whether or not any part of the gain or loss to the shareholders upon the liquidation is recognized under the provisions of section 1002.

(b) *Contents of return.*—(1) *In general.*—There shall be attached to and made a part of the return required by section 6043 and paragraph (a) of this section a certified copy of the resolution or plan, together with any amendments thereof or supplements thereto, and such return shall in addition contain the following information:

(i) The name and address of the corporation;

(ii) The place and date of incorporation;

(iii) The date of the adoption of the resolution or plan and the dates of any amendments thereof or supplements thereto; and

(iv) The internal revenue district in which the last income tax return of the corporation was filed and the taxable year covered thereby.

(2) *Returns in respect of amendments or supplements.*—If a return has been filed pursuant to section 6043 and this section, any additional return made necessary by an amendment of or a supplement

to the resolution or plan will be deemed sufficient if it gives the date the prior return was filed and contains a duly certified copy of the amendment or supplement and all other information required by this section and by Form 966 which was not given in the prior return. [Reg. § 1.6043-1.]

☐ [*T.D. 6364, 2-13-59. Amended by T.D. 6949, 4-8-68 and T.D. 7926, 12-15-83.*]

### [Reg. § 301.6043-1]

**§ 301.6043-1. Returns regarding liquidation, dissolution, termination, or contraction.**—For provisions relating to the requirement of returns of information regarding liquidations, dissolutions, terminations, or contractions, see § § 1.6043-1, 1.6043-2, and 1.6043-3 of this chapter(Income Tax Regulations). [Reg. § 301.6043-1.]

☐ [*T.D. 6498, 10-24-60. Amended by T.D. 7563, 9-8-73.*]

### [Reg. § 1.6043-2]

**§ 1.6043-2. Return of information respecting distributions in liquidation.**—(a) Unless the distribution is one in respect of which information is required to be filed pursuant to § 1.332-6(a), 1.368-3(a), or 1.1081-11, every corporation making any distribution of $600 or more during a calendar year to any shareholder in liquidation of the whole or any part of its capital stock shall file a return of information on Forms 1096 and 1099, giving all the information required by such form and by the regulations in this part. A separate Form 1099 must be prepared for each shareholder to whom such distribution was made, showing the name and address of such shareholder, the number and class of shares owned by him in liquidation of which such distribution was made, and the total amount distributed to him on each class of stock. If the amount distributed to such shareholder on any class of stock consisted in whole or in part of property other than money, the return on such form shall in addition show the amount of money distributed, if any, and shall list separately each class of property other than money distributed, giving a description of the property in each such class and a statement of its fair market value at the time of the distribution. Such forms, accompanied by transmittal Form 1096 showing the number of Forms 1099 filed therewith, shall be filed on or before February 28 (March 31 if filed electronically) of the year following the calendar year in which such distribution was made with any of the Internal Revenue Service Centers, the addresses of which are listed in the instructions for Form 1096.

(b) If the distribution is in complete liquidation of a domestic corporation pursuant to a plan of liquidation in accordance with which all the capital stock of the corporation is cancelled or redeemed, and the transfer of all property under the liquidation occurs within some one calendar month pursuant to section 333, and any shareholder claims the benefit of such section, the return on Form 1096 shall show:

(1) The amount of earnings and profits of the corporation accumulated after February 28, 1913, determined as of the close of such calendar month, without diminution by reason of distributions made during such calendar month, but including in such computation all items of income and expense accrued up to the date on which the transfer of all the property under the liquidation is completed;

(2) The ratable share of such earnings and profits of each share of stock canceled or redeemed in the liquidation;

(3) The date and circumstances of the acquisition by the corporation of any stock or securities distributed to shareholders in the liquidation;

(4) If the liquidation is pursuant to section 333(g), a schedule showing the amount of earnings and profits to which the corporation has succeeded after December 31, 1963, pursuant to any corporate reorganization or pursuant to a liquidation to which section 332 applies, except earnings and profits which on December 31, 1963, constituted earnings and profits of a corporation referred to in section 333(g)(3), and except earnings and profits which were earned after such date by a corporation referred to in section 333(g)(3); and

(5) If the liquidation occurs after December 31, 1966, and is pursuant to section 333(g)(2), the amount of earnings and profits of the corporation accumulated after February 28, 1913, and before January 1, 1967, and the ratable share of such earnings and profits of each share of stock canceled or redeemed in the liquidation. [Reg. § 1.6043-2.]

☐ [*T.D. 6464, 2-13-59. Amended by T.D. 6949, 4-8-68; T.D. 8734, 10-6-97 (T.D. 8804 and T.D. 8856 delayed the effective date of T.D. 8734); T.D. 8804, 12-30-98; T.D. 8895, 8-17-2000; T.D. 9264, 5-26-2006 and T.D. 9329, 6-13-2007.*]

### [Reg. § 1.6043-3]

**§ 1.6043-3. Return regarding liquidation, dissolution, termination, or substantial contraction of organizations exempt from taxation under section 501(a).**—(a) *In general.*—(1) *Requirement to provide information.*—Except as provided in paragraph (b) of this section, for

taxable years beginning after December 31, 1969, every organization which for any of its last 5 taxable years preceding any liquidation, dissolution, termination, or substantial contraction of the organization was exempt from taxation under section 501(a) shall provide the information with respect to such liquidation, dissolution, termination, or substantial contraction required by the instructions accompanying the organization's annual return of information. The information required by this section shall be provided with, and at the time prescribed for filing, the organization's annual return of information for the period during which any liquidation, dissolution (or the adoption of a resolution or plan for the dissolution or liquidation in whole or part), termination or substantial contraction occurred with respect to the organization. An organization which is no longer exempt from taxation under section 501 (a) shall use the annual return of information it would have been required to file when the organization was exempt.

(2) *Transitional rule.*—In the case of an annual return of information of an organization which was filed before September 11, 1978, if the organization had failed to provide the information with such return in accordance with paragraph (a)(1) of this section, the organization may comply with this section by providing the information with the organization's first annual return of information filed after such date.

(b) *Exceptions.*—The following organizations are not required to provide the information under paragraph (a) of this section:

(1) Churches, their integrated auxiliaries, or conventions or associations of churches;

(2) Any organization which is not a private foundation (as defined in section 509(a)) and the gross receipts of which in each taxable year are normally not more than $5,000;

(3) Any organization which has terminated its private foundation status under section 507(b)(1)(B) with respect to a liquidation, dissolution, termination, or substantial contraction which is in connection with the termination under section 507(b)(1)(B);

(4) Any organization described in section 401(a) if the employer who established such organization files a return which provides the information under paragraph (a) of this section;

(5) Any organization described in section 501(c)(1) and any corporation described in section 501(c)(2) which holds title to property for such 501(c)(1) organizations;

(6) Any organization described in section 501(c)(14)(A) subject to a group exemption letter issued to a state regulatory body; and

(7) Any subordinate unit of a central organization (other than a private foundation) which established its exempt status under the group ruling procedure of regulations § 601.201(n)(7), if the central or parent organization files an annual information return for the group in accordance with § 1.6033-2(d); and

(8) Any organization no longer exempt from taxation under section 501(a) and that during the period of its exemption under such section was not an organization described in section 501(c)(3), a corporation described in section 501(c)(2) that held title to property for an organization described in section 501(c)(3), or an organization described in such other section as prescribed by publication, form, or instructions.

(9) The Commissioner may relieve any organization or class of organizations from filing the return required by section 6043(b) of this section, where it is determined that such information is not necessary for the efficient administration of the internal revenue laws.

(c) *Penalties.*—For provisions relating to the penalty provided for failure to furnish any information required by this section, see section 6652(d) and the regulations thereunder.

(d) *Definitions.*—(1) For the definition of the term "normally" as used in paragraph (b)(2) of this section, see § 1.6033-2(g)(3).

(2) For the definition of the term "integrated auxiliaries" as used in paragraph (b)(1) of this section, see § 1.6033-2(h).

(3) For returns filed for taxable years beginning before January 1, 2008, for purposes of this section the definition of the term "substantial contraction" set forth in § 1.6043-3(d)(1) (as contained in 26 CFR part 1 revised April 1, 2008) may be used.

(e) *Effective/applicability date.*—(1) *Generally.*—The provisions of this section shall apply with respect to returns filed for taxable years beginning after December 31, 1969.

(2) Paragraphs (b)(8) and (d) of this section shall apply for taxable years beginning on or after January 1, 2008. For taxable years beginning before January 1, 2008, § § 1.6043-3(b)(8) and 1.6043-3(d) (as contained in 26 CFR part 1 revised April 1, 2008) shall apply. [Reg. § 1.6043-3.]

☐ [*T.D. 7563, 9-8-78. Amended by T.D. 9423, 9-8-2008 and T.D. 9549, 9-7-2011.*]

**[Reg. §1.6043-4]**

**§1.6043-4. Information returns relating to certain acquisitions of control and changes in capital structure.**—(a) *Information returns for an acquisition of control or a substantial change in capital structure.*—(1) *General rule.*—If there is an acquisition of control (as defined in paragraph (c) of this section) or a substantial change in the capital structure (as defined in paragraph (d) of this section) of a domestic corporation (reporting corporation), the reporting corporation must file a completed Form 8806, "Information Return for Acquisition of Control or Substantial Change in Capital Structure," in accordance with the instructions to that form. The Form 8806 will request information with respect to the following and such other information specified in the instructions:

(i) *Reporting corporation.*—The name, address, and taxpayer identification number (TIN) of the reporting corporation

(ii) *Common parent, if any, of the reporting corporation.*—If the reporting corporation was a subsidiary member of an affiliated group filing a consolidated return immediately prior to the acquisition of control or the substantial change in capital structure, the name, address, and TIN of the common parent of that affiliated group.

(iii) *Acquiring corporation.*—The name, address and TIN of any corporation that acquired control of the reporting corporation within the meaning of paragraph (c) of this section or combined with or received assets from the reporting corporation pursuant to a substantial change in capital structure within the meaning of paragraph (d) of this section (acquiring corporation) and whether the acquiring corporation was newly formed prior to its involvement in the transaction.

(iv) *Information about acquisition of control or substantial change in capital structure.*

(A) A description of the transaction or transactions that gave rise to the acquisition of control or the substantial change in capital structure of the corporation;

(B) The date or dates of the transaction or transactions that gave rise to the acquisition of control or the substantial change in capital structure; and

(C) A description of and a statement of the fair market value of any stock and other property, if any, provided to the reporting corporation's shareholders in exchange for their stock.

(2) *Consent election.*—Form 8806 will provide the reporting corporation with the ability to elect to permit the Internal Revenue Service (IRS) to publish information that will inform brokers of the transaction and enable brokers to satisfy their reporting obligations under §1.6045-3. The information to be published, whether on the IRS website or in an IRS publication, would be limited to the name and address of the corporation, the date of the transaction, a description of the shares affected by the transaction, and the amount of cash and the fair market value of stock or other property provided to each class of shareholders in exchange for a share.

(3) *Time for making return.*—Form 8806 must be filed on or before the 45th day following the acquisition of control or substantial change in capital structure of the corporation, or, if earlier, on or before January 5th of the year following the calendar year in which the acquisition of control or substantial change in capital structure occurs.

(4) *Exception where transaction is reported under section 6043(a).*—No reporting is required under this paragraph (a) with respect to a transaction for which information is required to be reported pursuant to section 6043(a), provided the transaction is properly reported in accordance with that section.

(5) *Exception where shareholders are exempt recipients.*—No reporting is required under this paragraph (a) if the reporting corporation reasonably determines that all of its shareholders who receive cash, stock, or other property pursuant to the acquisition of control or substantial change in capital structure are exempt recipients under paragraph (b)(5) of this section.

(b) *Information returns regarding shareholders.*—(1) *General rule.*—A corporation that is required to file Form 8806 pursuant to paragraph (a)(1) of this section shall file a return of information on Forms 1096, "Annual Summary and Transmittal of U.S. Information Returns," and 1099-CAP, "Changes in Corporate Control and Capital Structure," with respect to each shareholder of record in the corporation (before or after the acquisition of control or the substantial change in capital structure) who receives cash, stock, or other property pursuant to the acquisition of control or the substantial change in capital structure and who is not an exempt recipient as defined in paragraph (b)(5) of this section. A corporation is not required to file a Form 1096

or 1099-CAP with respect to a clearing organization if the corporation makes the election described in paragraph (a)(2) of this section.

(2) *Time for making information returns.*—Forms 1096 and 1099-CAP must be filed on or before February 28 (March 31 if filed electronically) of the year following the calendar year in which the acquisition of control or the substantial change in capital structure occurs.

(3) *Contents of return.*—A separate Form 1099-CAP must be filed with respect to amounts received by each shareholder (who is not an exempt recipient as defined in paragraph (b)(5) of this section). The Form 1099-CAP will request information with respect to the following and such other information as may be specified in the instructions:

(i) The name, address, telephone number and TIN of the reporting corporation;

(ii) The name, address and TIN of the shareholder;

(iii) The number and class of shares in the reporting corporation exchanged by the shareholder; and

(iv) The aggregate amount of cash and the fair market value of any stock or other property provided to the shareholder in exchange for its stock.

(4) *Furnishing of forms to shareholders.*—The Form 1099-CAP filed with respect to each shareholder must be furnished to such shareholder on or before January 31 of the year following the calendar year in which the shareholder receives cash, stock, or other property as part of the acquisition of control or the substantial change in capital structure. The Form 1099-CAP filed with respect to a clearing organization must be furnished to the clearing organization on or before January 5th of the year following the calendar year in which the acquisition of control or substantial change in capital structure occurred. A Form 1099-CAP is not required to be furnished to a clearing organization if the reporting corporation makes the election described in paragraph (a)(2) of this section. An IRS truncated taxpayer identifying number (TTIN) may be used as the identifying number of the shareholder in lieu of the identifying number appearing on the Form 1099-CAP filed with the Internal Revenue Service. For provisions relating to the use of TTINs, see §301.6109-4 of this chapter (Procedure and Administration Regulations).

(5) *Exempt recipients.*—A corporation is not required to file a Form 1099-CAP pursuant to this paragraph (b) with respect to any of the following shareholders that is not a clearing organization:

(i) Any shareholder who receives stock in an exchange that is not subject to gain recognition under section 367(a) and the regulations.

(ii) Any shareholder if the corporation reasonably determines that the total amount of cash and the fair market value of stock and other property received by the shareholder does not exceed $1,000.

(iii) Any shareholder described in paragraphs (b)(5)(iii)(A) through (M) of this section if the corporation has actual knowledge that the shareholder is described in one of paragraphs (b)(5)(iii)(A) through (M) of this section or if the corporation has a properly completed exemption certificate from the shareholder (as provided in §31.3406(h)-3 of this chapter). The corporation also may treat a shareholder as described in paragraphs (b)(5)(iii)(A) through (M) of this section based on the applicable indicators described in §1.6049-4(c)(1)(ii).

(A) A corporation, as described in §1.6049-4(c)(1)(ii)(A) (except for corporations for which an election under section 1362(a) is in effect).

(B) a tax-exempt organization, as described in §1.6049-4(c)(1)(ii)(B)(*1*).

(C) An individual retirement plan, as described in §1.6049-4(c)(1)(ii)(C).

(D) The United States, as described in §1.6049-4(c)(1)(ii)(D).

(E) A state, as described in §1.6049-4(c)(1)(ii)(E).

(F) A foreign government, as described in §1.6049-4(c)(1)(ii)(F).

(G) An international organization, as described in §1.6049-4(c)(1)(ii)(G).

(H) A foreign central bank of issue, as described in §1.6049-4(c)(1)(ii)(H).

(I) A securities or commodities dealer, as described in §1.6049-4(c)(1)(ii)(I).

(J) A real estate investment trust, as described in §1.6049-4(c)(1)(ii)(J).

(K) An entity registered under the Investment Company Act of 1940 (15 U.S.C. 80a-1), as described in §1.6049-4(c)(1)(ii)(K).

(L) A common trust fund, as described in §1.6049-4(c)(1)(ii)(L).

(M) A financial institution such as a bank, mutual savings bank, savings and loan association, building and loan association, cooperative bank, homestead association, credit union, industrial loan association or bank, or other similar organization.

(iv) Any shareholder that the corporation, prior to the transaction, associates with documentation upon which the corporation may rely in order to treat payments to the shareholder as made to a foreign beneficial owner in accordance with §1.1441-1(e)(1)(ii) or as made to a foreign payee in accordance with §1.6049-5(d)(1) or presumed to be made to a foreign payee under §1.6049-5(d)(2) or (3). For purposes of this paragraph (b)(5)(iv), the provisions in §1.6049-5(c) (regarding rules applicable to documentation of foreign status and definition of U.S. payor and non-U.S. payor) shall apply. The provisions of §1.1441-1 shall apply by using the terms "corporation" and "shareholder" in place of the terms "withholding agent" and "payee" and without regard to the fact that the provisions apply only to amounts subject to withholding under chapter 3 of the Internal Revenue Code. The provisions of §1.6049-5(d) shall apply by using the terms "corporation" and "shareholder" in place of the terms "payor" and "payee". Nothing in this paragraph (b)(5)(iv) shall be construed to relieve a corporation of its withholding obligations under section 1441.

(v) Any shareholder if, on January 31 of the year following the calendar year in which the shareholder receives cash, stock, or other property, the corporation did not know and did not have reason to know that the shareholder received such cash, stock, or other property in a transaction or series of related transactions that would result in an acquisition of control or a substantial change in capital structure within the meaning of this section.

(6) *Coordination with other sections.*—In general, no reporting is required under this paragraph (b) with respect to amounts that are required to be reported under sections 6042 or 6045, unless the corporation knows or has reason to know that such amounts are not properly reported in accordance with those sections. A corporation must satisfy the requirements under this paragraph (b) with respect to any shareholder of record that is a clearing organization.

(c) *Acquisition of control of a corporation.*—(1) *In general.*—For purposes of this section, an acquisition of control of a corporation (first corporation) occurs if, in a transaction or series of related transactions—

(i) Before an acquisition of stock of the first corporation (directly or indirectly) by a second corporation, the second corporation does not have control of the first corporation;

(ii) After the acquisition, the second corporation has control of the first corporation;

(iii) The fair market value of the stock acquired in the transaction and in any related transactions as of the date or dates on which such stock was acquired is $100 million or more;

(iv) The shareholders of the first corporation receive stock or other property pursuant to the acquisition; and

(v) The first corporation or any shareholder of the first corporation is required to recognize gain (if any) under section 367(a) and the regulations, as a result of the transaction.

(2) *Control.*—For purposes of this section, control is determined in accordance with the first sentence of section 304(c)(1). For these purposes the rules of section 318 as modified by the rules of section 958(b) shall apply in determining the ownership of stock.

(d) *Substantial change in capital structure of a corporation.*—(1) *In general.*—A corporation has a substantial change in capital structure if it has a change in capital structure (as defined in paragraph (d)(2) of this section) and the amount of any cash and the fair market value of any property (including stock) provided to the shareholders of such corporation pursuant to the change in capital structure, as of the date or dates on which the cash or other property is provided, is $100 million or more.

(2) *Change in capital structure.*—For purposes of this section, a corporation has a change in capital structure if—

(i) The corporation in a transaction or series of transactions—

(A) Merges, consolidates or otherwise combines with another corporation or transfers all or substantially all of its assets to one or more corporations;

(B) Transfers all or part of its assets to another corporation in a title 11 or similar case and, in pursuance of the plan, distributes stock or securities of that corporation; or

(C) (C) Changes its identity, form or place of organization; and

(ii) The corporation or any shareholder is required to recognize gain (if any) under section 367(a) and the regulations, as a result of the transaction.

(e) *Reporting by successor entity.*—If a corporation (transferor) transfers all or substantially all of its assets to another entity (transferee) in a transaction that constitutes a substantial change in the capital structure of transferor, transferor must satisfy the reporting obligations in paragraph (a) and (b) of this section. If transferor does not satisfy one or both of those reporting obligations, then transferee must do so. If neither transferor nor transferee satisfies the reporting obligations in paragraphs (a) and (b) of this section, then transferor and transferee shall be jointly and severally liable for any applicable penalties (see paragraph (g) of this section).

(f) *Receipt of property.*—For purposes of this section, a shareholder is treated as receiving property (or as having property provided to it) pursuant to an acquisition of control or a substantial change in capital structure if a liability of the shareholder is assumed in the transaction and, as a result of the transaction, an amount is realized by the shareholder from the sale or exchange of stock.

(g) *Penalties for failure to file.*—For penalties for failure to file as required under this section, see section 6652(l). The information returns required to be filed under paragraphs (a) and (b) of this section shall be treated as one return for purposes of section 6652(l) and, accordingly, the penalty shall not exceed $500 for each day the failure continues (up to a maximum of $100,000) with respect to any acquisition of control or any substantial change in capital structure. Failure to file as required under this section also includes the failure to satisfy the requirement to file on magnetic media as required by section 6011(e) and §1.6011-2. In addition, criminal penalties under sections 7203, 7206 and 7207 may apply in appropriate cases.

(h) *Examples.*—The following examples illustrate the application of the rules of this section. For purposes of these examples, assume the transaction is not reported under sections 6042, 6043(a), or 6045, unless otherwise specified, and assume that the fair market value of the consideration provided to the shareholders exceeds $100 million. The examples are as follows:

*Example 1.* The shareholders of X, a domestic corporation and parent of an affiliated group, exchange their X stock for stock in Y, a foreign corporation, pursuant to sections 351 and 354. After the transaction, Y owns all the outstanding X stock. Assume that, under section 367(a) and the regulations, the X shareholders must recognize gain (if any) on the exchange of their stock. Because the transaction results in an acquisition of control of X, X must comply with the rules in paragraphs (a) and (b) of this section. X must file Form 8806 reporting the transaction. X must also file a Form 1099-CAP with respect to each shareholder who is not an exempt recipient showing the fair market value of the Y stock received by that shareholder, and X must furnish a copy of the Form 1099-CAP to that shareholder. If X elects on the Form 8806 to permit the IRS to publish information regarding the transaction, X is not required to file or furnish Forms 1099-CAP with respect to shareholders that are clearing organizations.

*Example 2.* The facts are the same as in *Example 1*, except X hires a transfer agent to effectuate the exchange. The transfer agent is treated as a broker under section 6045 and is required to report the fair market value of the Y stock received by X's shareholders under §1.6045-3. Under paragraph (b)(6) of this section, X is not required to file information returns under paragraph (b) of this section with respect to a shareholder of record, unless X knows or has reason to know that the transfer agent does not satisfy its information reporting obligation under §1.6045-3 with respect to that shareholder. Thus, if the transfer agent satisfies its information reporting requirements under §1.6045-3 with respect to shareholder I, an individual who receives X stock, X is not required to file a Form 1099-CAP with respect to I. Conversely, if the transfer agent does not have an information reporting obligation under §1.6045-3 with respect to one of X's shareholders of record (for example, a clearing organization that is an exempt recipient under §1.6045-3(b)(2)), or if X knows or has reason to know that the transfer agent has not satisfied its information reporting requirement with respect to a shareholder, then X must provide a Form 1099-CAP to that shareholder.

(i) *Effective/applicability date.*—This section applies to transactions occurring after December 5, 2005. The amendments to paragraph (b)(4) are effective for any Form 1099-CAP required to be furnished after December 31, 2014. For any Form 1099-CAP required to be furnished before January 1, 2015, §1.6043-4(b) (as contained in 26 CFR part 1, revised April 2013) shall apply. [Reg. §1.6043-4.]

☐ [*T.D. 9230, 12-2-2005. Amended by T.D. 9675, 7-14-2014.*]

**Reg. §1.6043-4(i)**

»»→ *Caution: Temporary Reg. §1.6043-4T, below, was removed by T.D. 9230, but it remains outstanding with respect to transactions not covered by Reg. §1.6043-4 while the IRS considers additional information reporting requirements under Code Secs. 6043(c), 6043A and 6045.*

[Reg. §1.6043-4T]

§1.6043-4T. Information returns relating to certain acquisitions of control and changes in capital structure (temporary).—(a) *Information returns for an acquisition of control or a substantial change in capital structure.*—(1) *General rule.*—If there is an acquisition of control (as defined in paragraph (c) of this section) or a substantial change in the capital structure (as defined in paragraph (d) of this section) of a domestic corporation (reporting corporation), the reporting corporation must file a completed Form 8806, "Information Return for Acquisition of Control or Substantial Change in Capital Structure," in accordance with the instructions to that form. Form 8806 will request the information required in paragraphs (a)(1)(i) through (vi) of this section and any other information specified in the instructions.

(i) *Reporting corporation.*—Provide the name, address, and taxpayer identification number (TIN) of the reporting corporation.

(ii) *Common parent, if any, of the reporting corporation.*—If the reporting corporation was a subsidiary member of an affiliated group filing a consolidated return immediately prior to the acquisition of control or the substantial change in capital structure, provide the name, address, and TIN of the common parent of that affiliated group.

(iii) *Acquiring corporation.*—Provide the name, address and TIN of any corporation that acquired control of the reporting corporation within the meaning of paragraph (c) of this section or combined with or received assets from the reporting corporation pursuant to a substantial change in capital structure within the meaning of paragraph (d) of this section (acquiring corporation). State whether the acquiring corporation is foreign (as defined in section 7701(a)(5)) or is a dual resident corporation (as defined in §1.1503-2(c)(2)). In either case, state whether the acquiring corporation was newly formed prior to its involvement in the transaction.

(iv) *Common parent, if any, of acquiring corporation.*—If the acquiring corporation named in paragraph (a)(1)(iii) of this section was a subsidiary member of an affiliated group filing a consolidated return immediately prior to the acquisition of control or the substantial change in capital structure, provide the name, address, and TIN of the common parent of that affiliated group.

(v) *Information about acquisition of control or substantial change in capital structure.*—Provide—

(A) A description of the transaction or transactions that gave rise to the acquisition of control or the substantial change in capital structure of the corporation;

(B) The date or dates of the transaction or transactions that gave rise to the acquisition of control or the substantial change in capital structure;

(C) A description of and a statement of the fair market value of any stock provided to the reporting corporation's shareholders in exchange for their stock if the reporting corporation reasonably determines that the shareholders are not required to recognize gain (if any) from the receipt of such stock for U.S. federal income tax purposes; and

(D) A statement of the amount of cash plus the fair market value of any property (including stock if the reporting corporation reasonably determines that its shareholders would be required to recognize gain (if any) on the receipt of such stock, but excluding stock described in paragraph (a)(1)(v)(C) of this section) provided to the reporting corporation's shareholders in exchange for each share of their stock.

(2) *Consent election.*—Form 8806 will provide the reporting corporation with the ability to elect to permit the IRS to publish information that will inform brokers of the transaction and enable brokers to satisfy their reporting obligations under §1.6045-3T. The information to be published, on the IRS website and/or in an IRS publication, would be limited to the name and address of the corporation, the date of the transaction, a description of the shares affected by the transaction, and the amount of cash and the fair market value of any property (excluding stock described in paragraph (a)(1)(v)(C) of this section) provided to each class of shareholders in exchange for a share.

(3) *Time for making return.*—(i) *In general.*—Form 8806 must be filed on or before the 45Th day following the acquisition of control or substantial change in capital structure of the corporation, or, if earlier, on or before January 5th of the year following the calendar year in which the acquisition of control or substantial change in capital structure occurs.

(ii) *Transition rule.*—If an acquisition of control or a substantial change in capital structure of a corporation occurs after December 31, 2002, and before December 29, 2003, Form 8806 must be filed on or before January 5, 2004.

(4) *Exception where transaction is reported under section 6043(a).*—No reporting is required under paragraph (a) of this section with respect to a transaction for which information is required to be reported pursuant to section 6043(a), provided the transaction is properly reported in accordance with that section.

(5) *Exception where shareholders are exempt recipients.*—No reporting is required under paragraph (a) of this section if the reporting corporation reasonably determines that all of its shareholders who receive cash, stock or other property pursuant to the acquisition of control or substantial change in capital structure are exempt recipients under paragraph (b)(5) of this section.

(b) *Information returns regarding shareholders.*—(1) *General rule.*—A corporation that is required to file Form 8806 pursuant to paragraph (a)(1) of this section shall file a return of information on Forms 1096, "Annual Summary and Transmittal of U.S. Information Returns," and 1099-CAP, "Changes in Corporate Control and Capital Structure," with respect to each shareholder of record in the corporation (before or after the acquisition of control or the substantial change in capital structure) who receives cash, stock, or other property pursuant to the acquisition of control or the substantial change in capital structure and who is not an exempt recipient as defined in paragraph (b)(5) of this section. A corporation is not required to file a Form 1096 or 1099-CAP with respect to a clearing organization if the corporation makes the election described in paragraph (a)(2) of this section.

(2) *Time for making information returns.*—Forms 1096 and 1099-CAP must be filed on or before February 28 (March 31 if filed electronically) of the year following the calendar year in which the acquisition of control or the substantial change in capital structure occurs.

(3) *Contents of return.*—A separate Form 1099-CAP must be filed with respect to amounts received by each shareholder (who is not an exempt recipient as defined in paragraph (b)(5) of this section) showing—

(i) The name, address, telephone number and TIN of the reporting corporation;

(ii) The name, address and TIN of the shareholder;

(iii) The number and class of shares in the reporting corporation exchanged by the shareholder;

(iv) The aggregate amount of cash and the fair market value of any stock (other than stock described in paragraph (a)(1)(v)(C) of this section) or other property provided to the shareholder in exchange for its stock; and

(v) Such other information as may be required by the instructions to Form 1099-CAP.

(4) *Furnishing of forms to shareholders.*—The Form 1099-CAP filed with respect to each shareholder must be furnished to such shareholder on or before January 31 of the year following the calendar year in which the shareholder receives cash, stock, or other property as part of the acquisition of control or the substantial change in capital structure. The Form 1099-CAP filed with respect to a clearing organization must be furnished to the clearing organization on or before January 5th of the year following the calendar year in which the acquisition of control or substantial change in capital structure occurred. A Form 1099-CAP is not required to be furnished to a clearing organization if the reporting corporation makes the election described in paragraph (a)(2) of this section.

(5) *Exempt recipients.*—A corporation is not required to file a Form 1099-CAP pursuant to this paragraph (b) of this section with respect to any of the following shareholders that is not a clearing organization:

(i) Any shareholder who receives solely stock described in paragraph (a)(1)(v)(C) of this section in exchange for its stock in the corporation.

(ii) Any shareholder who is required to recognize gain (if any) as a result of the receipt of cash, stock, or other property if the corporation reasonably determines that the amount of such cash plus the fair market value of such stock and other property does not exceed $1,000. Stock described in paragraph (a)(1)(v)(C) of this section is not taken into account for purposes of this paragraph (b)(5)(ii).

(iii) Any shareholder described in paragraphs (b)(5)(iii)(A) through (M) of this section if the corporation has actual knowledge that the shareholder is described in one of paragraphs (b)(5)(iii)(A) through (M) of this section or if the corporation has a properly

>>>→ *Caution: Temporary Reg. §1.6043-4T, below, was removed by T.D. 9230, but it remains outstanding with respect to transactions not covered by Reg. §1.6043-4 while the IRS considers additional information reporting requirements under Code Secs. 6043(c), 6043A and 6045.*

completed exemption certificate from the shareholder (as provided in §31.3406(h)-3 of this chapter). The corporation also may treat a shareholder as described in paragraphs (b)(5)(iii)(A) through (M) of this section based on the applicable indicators described in §1.6049-4(c)(1)(ii).

(A) A corporation, as described in section §1.6049-4(c)(1)(ii)(A)(except for corporations for which an election under section 1362(a) is in effect).

(B) A tax-exempt organization, as described in §1.6049-4(c)(1)(ii)(B)(1).

(C) An individual retirement plan, as described in §1.6049-4(c)(1)(ii)(C).

(D) The United States, as described in §1.6049-4(c)(1)(ii)(D).

(E) A state, as described in §1.6049-4(c)(1)(ii)(E).

(F) A foreign government, as described in §1.6049-4(c)(1)(ii)(F).

(G) An international organization, as described in §1.6049-4(c)(1)(ii)(G).

(H) A foreign central bank of issue, as described in §1.6049-4(c)(1)(ii)(H).

(I) A securities or commodities dealer, as described in §1.6049-4(c)(1)(ii)(I).

(J) A real estate investment trust, as described in §1.6049-4(c)(1)(ii)(J).

(K) An entity registered under the Investment Company Act of 1940 (15 U.S.C. 80a-1), as described in §1.6049-4(c)(1)(ii)(K).

(L) A common trust fund, as described in §1.6049-4(c)(1)(ii)(L).

(M) A financial institution such as a bank, mutual savings bank, savings and loan association, building and loan association, cooperative bank, homestead association, credit union, industrial loan association or bank, or other similar organization.

(iv) Any shareholder that the corporation, prior to the transaction, associates with documentation upon which the corporation may rely in order to treat payments to the shareholder as made to a foreign beneficial owner in accordance with §1.1441-1(e)(1)(ii) or as made to a foreign payee in accordance with §1.6049-5(d)(1) or presumed to be made to a foreign payee under §1.6049-5(d)(2) or (3). For purposes of this paragraph (b)(5)(iv), the provisions in §1.6049-5(c) (regarding rules applicable to documentation of foreign status and definition of U.S. payor and non-U.S. payor) shall apply. The provisions of §1.1441-1 shall apply by using the terms *corporation* and *shareholder* in place of the terms *withholding agent* and *payee* and without regard to the fact that the provisions apply only to amounts subject to withholding under chapter 3 of the Internal Revenue Code. The provisions of §1.6049-5(d) shall apply by using the terms *corporation* and *shareholder* in place of the terms *payor* and *payee*. Nothing in this paragraph (b)(5)(iv) shall be construed to relieve a corporation of its withholding obligations under section 1441.

(v) Any shareholder if, on January 31 of the year following the calendar year in which the shareholder receives cash, stock, or other property, the corporation did not know and did not have reason to know that the shareholder received such cash, stock, or other property in a transaction or series of related transactions that would result in an acquisition of control or a substantial change in capital structure.

(6) *Coordination with other sections.*—In general, no reporting is required under paragraph (b) of this section with respect to amounts that are required to be reported under section 6042 or section 6045, unless the corporation knows or has reason to know that such amounts are not properly reported in accordance with those sections. A corporation must satisfy the requirements under paragraph (b) of this section with respect to any shareholder of record that is a clearing organization.

(c) *Acquisition of control of a corporation.*—(1) *In general.*—For purposes of this section, an acquisition of control of a corporation (first corporation) occurs if, in a transaction or series of related transactions, either—

(i) Stock representing control of the first corporation is distributed by a second corporation to shareholders of the second corporation and the fair market value of such stock on the date of distribution is $100,000,000 or more; or

(ii)(A) Before an acquisition of stock of the first corporation (directly or indirectly) by a second corporation, the second corporation does not have control of the first corporation;

(B) After the acquisition, the second corporation has control of the first corporation;

(C) The fair market value of the stock acquired in the transaction and in any related transactions as of the date or dates on which such stock was acquired is $100,000,000 or more; and

(D) The shareholders of the first corporation (determined without applying the constructive ownership rule of section 318(a)) receive cash, stock, or other property pursuant to the acquisition.

(2) *Control.*—For purposes of this section, control is determined in accordance with the first sentence of section 304(c)(1).

(3) *Constructive ownership.*—(i) Except as otherwise provided in this section, the constructive ownership rules of section 318(a) (except for section 318(a)(4), providing for constructive ownership through an option to acquire stock), modified as provided in section 304(c)(3)(B), shall apply for determining whether there has been an acquisition of control.

(ii) The determination of whether there has been an acquisition of control shall be made without regard to whether the person or persons from whom control was acquired retain indirect control of the first corporation under section 318(a).

(iii) For purposes of paragraph (c)(1)(ii) of this section, section 318(a) shall not apply to cause a second corporation to be treated as owning, before an acquisition of stock in a first corporation (directly or indirectly) by the second corporation, any stock that is acquired in the first corporation. For example, if the shareholders of a domestic corporation form a new holding company and then transfer their shares in the domestic corporation to the new holding company, the new holding company shall not be treated as having control of the domestic corporation before the acquisition. The new holding company acquires control of the domestic corporation as a result of the transfer. Similarly, if the shareholders of a domestic parent corporation transfer their shares in the parent corporation to a subsidiary of the parent in exchange for shares in the subsidiary, the subsidiary shall not be treated as having control of the parent before the transaction. The subsidiary acquires control of the parent as a result of the transfer.

(4) *Corporation includes group.*—For purposes of this paragraph (c), if two or more corporations act pursuant to a plan or arrangement with respect to acquisitions of stock, such corporations will be treated as one corporation for purposes of this section. Whether two or more corporations act pursuant to a plan or arrangement depends on the facts and circumstances.

(5) *Section 338 election.*—For purposes of this paragraph (c), an acquisition of stock of a corporation with respect to which an election under section 338 is made is treated as an acquisition of stock (and not as an acquisition of the assets of such corporation).

(d) *Substantial change in capital structure of a corporation.*—(1) *In general.*—A corporation has a substantial change in capital structure if it has a change in capital structure (as defined in paragraph (d)(2) of this section) and the amount of any cash and the fair market value of any property (including stock) provided to the shareholders of such corporation pursuant to the change in capital structure, as of the date or dates on which the cash or other property is provided, is $100,000,000 or more.

(2) *Change in capital structure.*—For purposes of this section, a corporation has a change in capital structure if the corporation in a transaction or series of transactions—

(i) Undergoes a recapitalization with respect to its stock;

(ii) Redeems its stock (including deemed redemptions);

(iii) Merges, consolidates or otherwise combines with another corporation or transfers all or substantially all of its assets to one or more corporations;

(iv) Transfers all or part of its assets to another corporation in a title 11 or similar case and, in pursuance of the plan, distributes stock or securities of that corporation; or

(v) Changes its identity, form or place of organization.

(e) *Reporting by successor entity.*—If a corporation (transferor) transfers all or substantially all of its assets to another entity (transferee) in a transaction that constitutes a substantial change in the capital structure of transferor, transferor must satisfy the reporting obligations in paragraph (a) or (b) of this section. If transferor does not satisfy the reporting obligations in paragraph (a) or (b) of this section, then transferee must satisfy those reporting obligations. If neither transferor nor transferee satisfies the reporting obligations in paragraphs (a) and (b) of this section, then transferor and transferee shall be jointly and severally liable for any applicable penalties (see paragraph (g) of this section).

(f) *Receipt of property.*—For purposes of this section, a shareholder is treated as receiving property (or as having property provided to it) pursuant to an acquisition of control or a substantial change in capital structure if a liability of the shareholder is assumed in the

**Reg. §1.6043-4T(f)**

>>>→ *Caution: Temporary Reg. §1.6043-4T, below, was removed by T.D. 9230, but it remains outstanding with respect to transactions not covered by Reg. §1.6043-4 while the IRS considers additional information reporting requirements under Code Secs. 6043(c), 6043A and 6045.*

transaction and, as a result of the transaction, an amount is realized by the shareholder from the sale or exchange of stock.

(g) *Penalties for failure to file.*—For penalties for failure to file as required under this section, see section 6652(1). The information returns required to be filed under paragraphs (a) and (b) of this section shall be treated as one return for purposes of section 6652(1) and, accordingly, the penalty shall not exceed $500 for each day the failure continues (up to a maximum of $100,000) with respect to any acquisition of control or any substantial change in capital structure. Failure to file as required under this section also includes the requirement to file on magnetic media as required by section 6011(e) and §1.6011-2. In addition, criminal penalties under sections 7203, 7206 and 7207 may apply in appropriate cases.

(h) *Examples.*—The following examples illustrate the application of the rules of this section. For purposes of these examples, assume the transaction is not reported under sections 6042, 6043(a) or 6045, unless otherwise specified, and assume that the fair market value of the consideration provided to the shareholders exceeds $100,000,000. The examples are as follows:

*Example 1.* The shareholders of X, a domestic corporation and parent of an affiliated group, exchange their X stock for stock in Y, a newly-formed foreign holding corporation. After the transaction, Y owns all the outstanding X stock. The X shareholders must recognize gain (if any) on the exchange of their stock as a result of the application of section 367(a). Because the transaction results in an acquisition of control of X, X must comply with the rules in paragraphs (a) and (b) of this section. X must file Form 8806 reporting the transaction. X must also file a Form 1099-CAP with respect to each shareholder who is not an exempt recipient showing the fair market value of the Y stock received by that shareholder, and X must furnish a copy of the Form 1099-CAP to that shareholder. If X elects on the Form 8806 to permit the IRS to publish information regarding the transaction, X is not required to file or furnish Forms 1099-CAP with respect to shareholders that are clearing organizations.

*Example 2.* C, a domestic corporation, and parent of an affiliated group merges into D, an unrelated domestic corporation. Pursuant to the transaction, the C shareholders exchange their C stock for D stock or for a combination of short term notes and D stock. The transaction does not satisfy the requirements of section 368, and the C shareholders must recognize gain (if any) on the exchange. Because the transaction results in a substantial change in the capital structure of C, C (or D as the successor to C) must comply with the rules in paragraphs (a) and (b) of this section. C must file Form 8806. C (or D as the successor to C) also must file a Form 1099-CAP with respect to each shareholder who is not an exempt recipient showing the fair market value of the short term notes and the fair market value of the D stock provided to that shareholder. In addition, C (or D) must furnish a copy of the Form 1099-CAP to that shareholder.

*Example 3.* (i) The facts are the same as in *Example 2,* except that C reasonably determines that—

(A) The transaction satisfies the requirements of section 368;

(B) The C shareholders who exchange their C stock solely for D stock will not be required to recognize gain (if any) on the exchange; and

(C) The C shareholders who exchange their C stock for a combination of short term notes and D stock will be required to recognize gain (if any) on the exchange solely with respect to the receipt of the short term notes.

(ii) C is required to file Form 8806 under paragraph (a) of this section. C (or D as the successor to C) must also comply with the rules in paragraph (b) of this section. With respect to each shareholder who receives a combination of short term notes and D stock, and who is not an exempt recipient, C (or D) must file a Form 1099-CAP showing the fair market value of the short term notes provided to the shareholder, and C (or D) must furnish a copy of the Form 1099-CAP to that shareholder. The Form 1099-CAP should not show the fair market value of the D stock provided to the shareholder. C and D are not required to file and furnish Forms 1099-CAP with respect to shareholders who receive only D stock in exchange for their C stock.

*Example 4.* The facts are the same as in *Example 3,* except C hires a transfer agent to effectuate the exchange. The transfer agent is treated as a broker under section 6045 and is required to report the fair market value of the short term notes provided to C's shareholders under §1.6045-3T. Under paragraph (b)(6) of this section, C and D are not required to file information returns under paragraph (b) of this section with respect to a shareholder of record, unless C or D knows or has reason to know that the transfer agent does not satisfy its information reporting obligation under §1.6045-3T with respect to that shareholder. Thus, if the transfer agent satisfies its information

reporting requirements under §1.6045-3T with respect to shareholder I, an individual who receives both D stock and short term notes, C and D are not required to file a Form 1099-CAP with respect to I. Conversely, if the transfer agent does not have an information reporting obligation under §1.6045-3T with respect to one of C's shareholder's of record (for example, a clearing organization that is an exempt recipient under §1.6045-3T(b)(ii)), or if C or D knows or has reason to know that the transfer agent has not satisfied its information reporting requirement with respect to a shareholder, then C (or D) must provide a Form 1099-CAP to that shareholder.

(i) *Effective date.*—This section applies to any acquisition of control and any substantial change in capital structure occurring after December 31, 2001, if the reporting corporation or any shareholder is required to recognize gain (if any) as a result of the application of section 367(a) as a result of the transaction. However, paragraphs (a) through (h) of this section apply to acquisitions of control and substantial changes in capital structure occurring after December 31, 2002, if the reporting corporation or any shareholder is required to recognize gain (if any) as a result of the application of section 367(a) as a result of the transaction. For transactions prior to January 1, 2003, see §1.6043-4T as published in 26 CFR Part 1 (revised as of April 1, 2003). This section expires on November 14, 2005. [Temporary Reg. §1.6043-4T.]

☐ [T.D. 9022, 11-13-2002 (*corrected* 2-5-2003). *Amended by T.D. 9101,* 12-29-2003. *Removed by T.D. 9230,* 12-2-2005.]

### [Reg. §301.6044-1]

**§301.6044-1. Returns of information regarding payments of patronage dividends.**—For provisions relating to the requirement of returns of information regarding payments of patronage dividends, see §§1.6044-1 to 1.6044-5, inclusive, of this chapter (Income Tax Regulations). [Reg. §301.6044-1.]

☐ [T.D. 6498, 10-24-60. *Amended by T.D. 6700,* 1-6-64.]

### [Reg. §1.6044-2]

**§1.6044-2. Returns of information as to payments of patronage dividends.**—(a) *Requirement of reporting.*—(1) *In general.*—Except as provided in §1.6044-4, every organization described in paragraph (b) of this section which makes payments with respect to patronage occurring on or after the first day of the first taxable year of the organization beginning after December 31, 1962, of amounts described in §1.6044-3 aggregating $10 or more to any person during any calendar year shall make an information return on Forms 1096 and 1099 for the calendar year showing the aggregate amount of such payments, the name and address of the person to whom paid, the total of such payments for all persons, and such other information as is required by the forms. The organization is required to make an information return regardless of the amount of the payment if tax imposed by section 3406 is required to be withheld. Thus, in the case of any amount subject to backup withholding under section 3406 and not refunded by the payor before the due date of the information return in accordance with the regulations under section 3406, an information return shall be made even if the payment is not generally reportable because it is made to an exempt recipient described in §1.6049-4(c)(1)(ii) or the amount paid during the calendar year to the recipient aggregates less than $10.

(2) *Definitions.*—The term "person" when used in this section does not include the United States, a State, the District of Columbia, a foreign government, a political subdivision of a State or of a foreign government, or an international organization. Therefore, payment of amounts described in §1.6044-3 to one of these entities need not be reported.

(3) *Determination of person to whom a patronage dividend is paid.*—For purposes of applying the provisions of this section, the person whose identifying number is required to be included by the cooperative on an information return with respect to a patronage dividend shall be considered the person to whom such dividend is paid. For regulations relating to the use of identifying numbers, see §1.6109-1.

(4) *Inclusion of other payments.*—The Form 1099 filed by an organization with respect to payments of patronage dividends made to any person during a calendar year may, at the election of the organization, include other payments made by it to such person during such year which are required to be reported on Form 1099.

(b) *Organizations subject to reporting requirement.*—The organizations subject to the reporting requirements of paragraph (a) of this section are—

(1) Any organization exempt from tax under section 521 (relating to exemption of farmers' cooperatives from tax), and

(2) Any corporation operating on a cooperative basis other than an organization—

(i) Which is exempt from tax under chapter 1 (other than section 521), or

(ii) Which is subject to the provisions of part II of subchapter H of chapter 1 (relating to mutual savings banks, etc.), or subchapter L of chapter 1 (relating to insurance companies), or

(iii) Which is engaged in furnishing electric energy, or providing telephone service, to persons in rural areas.

(c) *When payment deemed made.*—For purposes of this section, money or other property (except written notices of allocation) is deemed to have been paid when it is credited or set apart to a person without any substantial limitation or restriction as to the time or manner of payment or condition upon which payment is to be made, and is made available to him so that it may be drawn at any time, and its receipt brought within his own control and disposition. A written notice of allocation is considered to have been paid when it is issued by the organization to the distributee. Similarly, a qualified check (as defined in section 1388(d)(4)) is considered to have been paid when it is issued to the distributee.

(d) *Time and place for filing.*—The return required under this section on Forms 1096 and 1099 for any calendar year shall be filed after September 30 of such year, but not before the payer's final payment for the year, and on or before February 28 (March 31 if filed electronically) of the following year, with any of the Internal Revenue Service Centers, the addresses of which are listed in the instructions for such forms. For extensions of time for filing returns under this section, see § 1.6081-1.

(e) *Cross-reference to penalty.*—For provisions relating to the penalty provided for failure to file timely a correct information return required under section 6044(a), see § 301.6721-1 of this chapter (Procedure and Administration Regulations). See § 301.6724-1 of this chapter for the waiver of a penalty if the failure is due to reasonable cause and is not due to willful neglect.

(f) *Magnetic media requirement.*—For the requirement to submit the information required by Form 1099 on magnetic media for payments after December 31, 1983, see section 6011(e) and § 301.6011-2 of this chapter (Procedure and Administration Regulations). For rules relating to permission to submit the information required by Form 1099 on magnetic tape or other media, see § 1.9101-1. [Reg. § 1.6044-2.]

☐ [*T.D. 6628, 12-27-62. Amended by T.D. 6677, 9-16-63; T.D. 6879, 3-7-66; T.D. 6883, 5-2-66; T.D. 8734, 10-6-97 (T.D. 8804 delayed the effective date of T.D. 8734 from January 1, 1999, to January 1, 2000; T.D. 8856 further delayed the effective date of T.D. 8734 until January 1, 2001) and T.D. 8895, 8-17-2000.*]

### [Reg. § 1.6044-3]

**§ 1.6044-3. Amounts subject to reporting.**—(a) *In general.*—Except as provided in paragraph (c) of this section, the amounts subject to reporting under § 1.6044-2 are—

(1) Payments by all organizations subject to such reporting requirements of—

(i) Patronage dividends (as defined in section 1388(a)) paid in money, qualified written notices of allocation (as defined in section 1388(c)), or other property (except nonqualified written notices of allocation as defined in section 1388(d)); and

(ii) Amounts described in section 1382(b)(2) (relating to redemption of nonqualified written notices of allocation previously paid as patronage dividends) paid in money or property (except written notices of allocation); and

(2) Payments by farmers' cooperatives exempt from tax under section 521 of—

(i) Amounts described in section 1382(c)(2)(A) (relating to distributions with respect to earnings derived from sources other than patronage) paid in money, qualified written notices of allocation, or other property (except nonqualified written notices of allocation); and

(ii) Amounts described in section 1382(c)(2)(B) (relating to redemption of nonqualified written notices of allocation previously paid as distributions with respect to earnings derived from sources other than patronage) paid in money or other property (except written notices of allocation).

(b) *Special rules.*—(1) If an organization makes a distribution consisting in whole or in part of a written notice of allocation and a qualified check and, at the time it files its return under § 1.6044-2, is unable to determine whether such written notice of allocation and such check constitute nonqualified written notices of allocation, such organization shall for purposes of such return treat such written notice of allocation as a qualified written notice of allocation and such qualified check as a payment in money.

(2) An amount described in paragraph (a) of this section is subject to reporting even though the organization paying such amount is allowed no deduction for it because it was not paid within the time prescribed in section 1382. Thus, a patronage dividend of $25 paid by a marketing cooperative must be reported even though it is paid after the end of the payment period (see section 1382(d)) for the organization's taxable year in which the patronage occurred.

(c) *Exceptions.*—An amount described in paragraph (a) of this section does not include—

(1) Any amount described in § 1.6042-3(b); or

(2) With respect to amounts paid or credited after December 31, 1982, any amount paid or credited to any person described in § 1.6049-4(c)(1)(ii).

(d) *Determination of amount paid.*—For purposes of § 1.6044-2 and this section, in determining the amount of any payment subject to reporting under paragraph (a) of this section—

(1) Property (other than a qualified written notice of allocation) shall be taken into account at its fair market value, and

(2) A qualified written notice of allocation shall be taken into account at its stated dollar amount. [Reg. § 1.6044-3.]

☐ [*T.D. 6628, 12-27-62. Amended by T.D. 8734, 10-6-97 (T.D. 8804 delayed the effective date of T.D. 8734 from January 1, 1999, to January 1, 2000; T.D. 8856 further delayed the effective date of T.D. 8734 until January 1, 2001).*]

### [Reg. § 1.6044-4]

**§ 1.6044-4. Exemption for certain consumer cooperatives.**—(a) *In general.*—(1) *Determination of exemption.*—Exemption from the reporting requirements of § 1.6044-2 shall, upon application therefor, be granted by the district director to any cooperative which he determines is primarily engaged in selling at retail goods or services of a type which is generally for personal, living, or family use. A cooperative is not exempt from the reporting requirements merely because it is an organization of a type to which section 6044(c) and this section relate. In order for the exemption from reporting to apply, it is necessary that the cooperative file an application in accordance with this section and obtain a determination of exemption.

(2) *Basis of exemption.*—For a cooperative to qualify for the exemption from reporting provided by section 6044(c) and this section 85 percent of its gross receipts for the preceding taxable year, or 85 percent of its aggregate gross receipts for the preceding three taxable years, must have been derived from the sale at retail of goods or services of a type which is generally for personal, living, or family use. In determining whether an item is of a type that is generally for personal, living, or family use, an item which may be purchased either for such use or for business use and which when acquired for business purposes is generally purchased at wholesale will, when sold by a cooperative at retail, be treated as goods or services of a type generally for personal, living, or family use.

(3) *Period of exemption.*—A determination of exemption from reporting shall apply beginning with the payments made during the calendar year in which the determination is made and shall automatically cease to be effective beginning with payments made after the close of the first taxable year of the cooperative in which less than 70 percent of its gross receipts is derived from the sale at retail of goods or services of a type which is generally for personal, living, or family use.

(b) *Application for exemption.*—Application for exemption from the reporting requirements of section 6044 shall be made on Form 3491, and shall be filed with the district director for the internal revenue district in which the cooperative has its principal place of business. [Reg. § 1.6044-4.]

☐ [*T.D. 6628, 12-27-62.*]

### [Reg. § 1.6044-5]

**§ 1.6044-5. Statements to recipients of patronage dividends.**—(a) *Requirement.*—A person required to make an information return under section 6044(a)(1) and § 1.6044-2 must furnish a statement to each recipient whose identifying number is required to be shown on the related information return for patronage dividends paid.

(b) *Form, manner, and time for providing statements to recipients.*—The statement required by paragraph (a) of this section must be either the official Form 1099 prescribed by the Internal Revenue Service for the respective calendar year or an acceptable substitute statement. The rules under § 1.6042-4 (relating to statements with respect to dividends) apply comparably in determining the form of an acceptable substitute statement permitted by this section. Those rules also apply for purposes of determining the manner of and time for providing the Form 1099 or its acceptable substitute to a recipient under this section. However, each Form 1099 or acceptable substitute statement required by this section must be furnished on or before January 31 of the following year, but no statement may be furnished before the final payment has been made for the calendar year. For a statement required to be furnished after December 31, 2008, the February 15 due date under section 6045 applies to the statement if the statement is furnished in a consolidated reporting statement under section 6045. *See* §§ 1.6045-1(k)(3), 1.6045-2(d)(2), 1.6045-3(e)(2), 1.6045-4(m)(3), and 1.6045-5(a)(3)(ii). An IRS truncated taxpayer identifying number (TTIN) may be used as the identifying number of the recipient in lieu of the identifying number appearing on the corresponding information return filed with the Internal Revenue Service. For provisions relating to the use of TTINs, see § 301.6109-4 of this chapter (Procedure and Administration Regulations).

(c) *Cross-reference to penalty.*—For provisions relating to the penalty provided for failure to furnish timely a correct payee statement required under section 6044(e), see § 301.6722-1 of this chapter (Procedure and Administration Regulations). See § 301.6724-1 of this chapter for the waiver of a penalty if the failure is due to reasonable cause and is not due to willful neglect.

(d) *Effective/applicability date.*—This section is effective for payee statements due after December 31, 1995, without regard to extensions. The amendments to paragraph (b) are effective for payee statements due after December 31, 2014. For payee statements due before January 1, 2015, § 1.6044-5(b) (as contained in 26 CFR part 1, revised April 2013) shall apply. [Reg. § 1.6044-5.]

☐ [*T.D.* 6628, 12-27-62. *Amended by T.D.* 6879, 3-7-66; *T.D.* 7529, 12-27-77; *T.D.* 8637, 12-20-95; *T.D.* 8734, 10-6-97 (*T.D.* 8804 delayed the effective date of *T.D.* 8734 from January 1, 1999, to January 1, 2000; *T.D.* 8856 further delayed the effective date of *T.D.* 8734 until January 1, 2001); *T.D.* 9504, 10-12-2010 and *T.D.* 9675, 7-14-2014.]

### [Reg. § 1.6045-1]

**§ 1.6045-1. Returns of information of brokers and barter exchanges.**—(a) *Definitions.*—The following definitions apply for purposes of this section and § 1.6045-2:

(1) The term *broker* means any person (other than a person who is required to report a transaction under section 6043), U.S. or foreign, that, in the ordinary course of a trade or business during the calendar year, stands ready to effect sales to be made by others. A broker includes an obligor that regularly issues and retires its own debt obligations or a corporation that regularly redeems its own stock. However, with respect to a sale (including a redemption or retirement) effected at an office outside the United States, a broker includes only a person described as a U.S. payor or U.S. middleman in § 1.6049-5(c)(5). In addition, a broker does not include an international organization described in § 1.6049-4(c)(1)(ii)(G) that redeems or retires an obligation of which it is the issuer.

(2) The term "customer" means, with respect to a sale effected by a broker, the person (other than such broker) that makes the sale, if the broker acts as—

(i) An agent for such person in the sale;

(ii) A principal in the sale; or

(iii) The participant in the sale responsible for paying to such person or crediting to such person's account the gross proceeds on the sale.

(3) The term "security" means—

(i) A share of stock in a corporation (foreign or domestic);

(ii) An interest in a trust;

(iii) An interest in a partnership;

(iv) A debt obligation;

(v) An interest in or right to purchase any of the foregoing in connection with the issuance thereof from the issuer or an agent of the issuer or from an underwriter that purchases any of the foregoing from the issuer;

(vi) An interest in a security described in paragraph (a)(3)(i) or (iv) of this section (but not including executory contracts that require delivery of such type of security);

(vii) An option described in paragraph (m)(2) of this section; or

(viii) A securities futures contract.

(4) The term "barter exchange" means any person with members or clients that contract either with each other or with such person to trade or barter property or services either directly or through such person. The term does not include arrangements that provide solely for the informal exchange of similar services on a noncommercial basis.

(5) The term "commodity" means—

(i) Any type of personal property or an interest therein (other than securities as defined in paragraph (a)(3)), the trading of regulated futures contracts in which has been approved by the Commodity Futures Trading Commission;

(ii) Lead, palm oil, rapeseed, tea, tin, or an interest in any of the foregoing; or

(iii) Any other personal property or an interest therein that is of a type the Secretary determines is to be treated as a "commodity" under this section, from and after the date specified in a notice of such determination published in the Federal Register.

(6) The term "regulated futures contract" means a regulated futures contract within the meaning of section 1256(b).

(7) The term "forward contract" means—

(i) An executory contract that requires delivery of a commodity in exchange for cash and which contract is not a regulated futures contract; or

(ii) An executory contract that requires delivery of personal property or an interest therein in exchange for cash, or a cash settlement contract, if such executory contract or cash settlement contract is of a type the Secretary determines is to be treated as a "forward contract" under this section, from and after the date specified in a notice of such determination published in the Federal Register.

(8) The term *closing transaction* means a lapse, expiration, settlement, abandonment, or other termination of a position. For purposes of the preceding sentence, a position includes a right or an obligation under a forward contract, a regulated futures contract, a securities futures contract, or an option.

(9) The term *sale* means any disposition of securities, commodities, options, regulated futures contracts, securities futures contracts, or forward contracts, and includes redemptions of stock, retirements of debt instruments (including a partial retirement attributable to a principal payment received on or after January 1, 2014), and enterings into short sales, but only to the extent any of these actions are conducted for cash. In the case of an option, a regulated futures contract, a securities futures contract, or a forward contract, a sale includes any closing transaction. When a closing transaction for a contract described in section 1256(b)(1)(A) involves making or taking delivery, there are two sales, one resulting in profit or loss on the contract, and a separate sale on the delivery. When a closing transaction for a contract described in section 988(c)(5) involves making delivery, there are two sales, one resulting in profit or loss on the contract, and a separate sale on the delivery. For purposes of the preceding sentence, a broker may assume that any customer's functional currency is the U.S. dollar. When a closing transaction in a forward contract involves making or taking delivery, the broker may treat the delivery as a sale without separating the profit or loss on the contract from the profit or loss on the delivery, except that taking delivery for United States dollars is not a sale. The term *sale* does not include entering into a contract that requires delivery of personal property or an interest therein, the initial grant or purchase of an option, or the exercise of a purchased call option for physical delivery (except for a contract described in section 988(c)(5)). For purposes of this section only, a constructive sale under section 1259 and a mark to fair market value under section 475 or 1296 are not sales.

(10) The term "effect" means, with respect to a sale, to act as—

(i) An agent for a party in the sale wherein the nature of the agency is such that the agent ordinarily would know the gross proceeds from the sale; or

(ii) A principal in such sale.

Acting as an agent or principal with respect to grants or purchases of options, exercises of call options, or enterings into contracts that require delivery of personal property or an interest therein is not of itself effecting a sale. A broker that has on its books a forward contract under which delivery is made effects such delivery.

(11) The term "foreign currency" means currency of a foreign country.

(12) The term "cash" means United States dollars or any convertible foreign currency.

(13) The term *person* includes any governmental unit and any agency or instrumentality thereof.

(14) The term *specified security* means:

(i) Any share of stock (or any interest treated as stock, including, for example, an American Depositary Receipt) in an entity organized as, or treated for Federal tax purposes as, a corporation, either foreign or domestic (provided that, solely for purposes of this paragraph (a)(14)(i), a security classified as stock by the issuer is treated as stock, and if the issuer has not classified the security, the security is not treated as stock unless the broker knows that the security is reasonably classified as stock under general Federal tax principles);

(ii) Any debt instrument described in paragraph (a)(17) of this section, other than a debt instrument subject to section 1272(a)(6) (certain interests in or mortgages held by a REMIC, certain other debt instruments with payments subject to acceleration, and pools of debt instruments the yield on which may be affected by prepayments) or a short-term obligation described in section 1272(a)(2)(C);

(iii) Any option described in paragraph (m)(2) of this section; or

(iv) Any securities futures contract.

(15) The term *covered security* means a specified security described in this paragraph (a)(15).

(i) *In general.*—Except as provided in paragraph (a)(15)(iv) of this section, the following securities are covered securities:

(A) A specified security described in paragraph (a)(14)(i) of this section acquired for cash in an account on or after January 1, 2011, except stock for which the average basis method is available under § 1.1012-1(e).

(B) Stock for which the average basis method is available under § 1.1012-1(e) acquired for cash in an account on or after January 1, 2012.

(C) A specified security described in paragraphs (a)(14)(ii) and (n)(2)(i) of this section (not including the debt instruments described in paragraph (n)(2)(ii) of this section) acquired for cash in an account on or after January 1, 2014.

(D) A specified security described in paragraphs (a)(14)(ii) and (n)(3) of this section acquired for cash in an account on or after January 1, 2016.

(E) An option described in paragraph (a)(14)(iii) of this section granted or acquired for cash in an account on or after January 1, 2014.

(F) A securities futures contract described in paragraph (a)(14)(iv) of this section entered into in an account on or after January 1, 2014.

(G) A specified security transferred to an account if the broker or other custodian of the account receives a transfer statement (as described in § 1.6045A-1 reporting the security as a covered security.

(ii) *Acquired in an account.*—For purposes of this paragraph (a)(15), a security is considered acquired in a customer's account at a broker or custodian if the security is acquired by the customer's broker or custodian or acquired by another broker and delivered to the customer's broker or custodian. Acquiring a security in an account includes granting an option and entering into a short sale.

(iii) *Corporate actions and other events.*—For purposes of this paragraph (a)(15), a security acquired due to a stock dividend, stock split, reorganization, redemption, stock conversion, recapitalization, corporate division, or other similar action is considered acquired for cash in an account.

(iv) *Exceptions.*—Notwithstanding paragraph (a)(15)(i) of this section, the following securities are not covered securities:

(A) Stock acquired in 2011 that is transferred to a dividend reinvestment plan (as described in § 1.1012-1(e)(6) in 2011. However, a covered security acquired in 2011 that is transferred to a dividend reinvestment plan after 2011 remains a covered security.

(B) A security acquired through an event described in paragraph (a)(15)(iii) of this section if the basis of the acquired security is determined from the basis of a noncovered security.

(C) A security that is excepted at the time of its acquisition from reporting under paragraph (c)(3) or (g) of this section. However, a broker cannot treat a security as acquired by an exempt foreign person under paragraph (g)(1)(i) of this section at the time of acquisition if, at that time, the broker knows or should have known (including by reason of information that the broker is required to collect under section 1471 or 1472) that the customer is not a foreign person.

(D) A security for which reporting under this section is required by § 1.6049-5(d)(3)(ii) (certain securities owned by a foreign intermediary or flow-through entity).

(16) The term *noncovered security* means any security that is not a covered security.

(17) For purposes of this section, the terms *debt instrument, bond, debt obligation,* and *obligation* mean a debt instrument as defined in § 1.1275-1(d) and any instrument or position that is treated as a debt instrument under a specific provision of the Internal Revenue Code (for example, a regular interest in a REMIC as defined in section 860G(a)(1) and § 1.860G-1). Solely for purposes of this section, a security classified as debt by the issuer is treated as debt. If the issuer has not classified the security, the security is not treated as debt unless the broker knows that the security is reasonably classified as debt under general Federal tax principles or that the instrument or position is treated as a debt instrument under a specific provision of the Internal Revenue Code.

(18) For purposes of this section, the term *securities futures contract* means a contract described in section 1234B(c) whose underlying asset is described in paragraph (a)(14)(i) of this section and which is entered into on or after January 1, 2014.

(b) *Examples.*—The following examples illustrate the definitions in paragraph (a):

*Example 1.* The following persons generally are brokers within the meaning of paragraph (a)(1):

(i) A mutual fund, an underwriter of the mutual fund, or an agent for the mutual fund, any of which stands ready to redeem or repurchase shares in such mutual fund.

(ii) A professional custodian (such as a bank) that regularly arranges sales for custodial accounts pursuant to instructions from the owner of the property.

(iii) A depository trust or other person that regularly acts as an escrow agent in corporate acquisitions, if the nature of the activities of the agent is such that the agent ordinarily would know the gross proceeds from sales.

(iv) A stock transfer agent for a corporation, which agent records transfers of stock in such corporation, if the nature of the activities of the agent is such that the agent ordinarily would know the gross proceeds from sales.

(v) A dividend reinvestment agent for a corporation that stands ready to purchase or redeem shares.

*Example 2.* The following persons are not brokers within the meaning of paragraph (a)(1) in the absence of additional facts that indicate the person is a broker:

(i) A stock transfer agent for a corporation, which agent daily records transfers of stock in such corporation, if the nature of the activities of the agent is such that the agent ordinarily would not know the gross proceeds from sales.

(ii) A person (such as a stock exchange) that merely provides facilities in which others effect sales.

(iii) An escrow agent or nominee if such agency is not in the ordinary course of a trade or business.

(iv) An escrow agent, otherwise a broker, which agent effects no sales other than such transactions as are incidental to the purpose of the escrow (such as sales to collect on collateral).

(v) A floor broker on a commodities exchange, which broker maintains no records with respect to the terms of sales.

(vi) A corporation that issues and retires long-term debt on an irregular basis.

(vii) A clearing organization.

*Example 3.* A, B, and C belong to a carpool in which they commute to and from work. Every third day, each member of the carpool provides transportation for the other two members. Because the carpool arrangement provides solely for the informal exchange of similar services on a noncommercial basis, the carpool is not a barter exchange within the meaning of paragraph (a)(4).

*Example 4.* X is an organization whose members include retail merchants, wholesale merchants, and persons in the trade or business of performing services. X's members exchange property and services among themselves using credits on the books of X as a medium of exchange. Each exchange through X is reflected on the books of X by crediting the account of the member providing property or services and debiting the account of the member receiving such property or services. X also provides information to its members concerning property and services available for exchange through X. X charges its members a commission on each transaction in which credits on its books are used as a medium of exchange. X is a barter exchange within the meaning of paragraph (a)(4) of this section.

*Example 5.* A warehouse receipt is an interest in personal property for purposes of paragraph (a). Consequently, a warehouse receipt for a quantity of lead is a commodity under paragraph (a)(5)(ii). Similarly, an executory contract that requires delivery of a warehouse receipt for a quantity of lead is a forward contract under paragraph (a)(7)(ii).

*Example 6.* The only customers of a depository trust acting as an escrow agent in corporate acquisitions, which trust is a broker, are shareholders to whom the trust makes payments or shareholders for whom the trust is acting as an agent.

*Example 7.* The only customers of a stock transfer agent, which agent is a broker, are shareholders to whom the agent makes payments or shareholders for whom the agent is acting as an agent.

*Example 8.* D, an individual not otherwise exempt from reporting, is the holder of an obligation issued by P, a corporation. R, a broker, acting as an agent for P, retires such obligation held by D. Such obligor payments from R represent obligor payments by P. (See paragraph (c)(3)(v)). D, the person to whom the gross proceeds are paid or credited by R, is the customer of R.

*Example 9.* E, an individual not otherwise exempt from reporting, maintains an account with S, a broker. On June 1, 2012, E instructs S to purchase stock that is a specified security for cash. S places an order to purchase the stock with T, another broker. E does not maintain an account with T. T executes the purchase. Custody of the purchased stock is transferred to E's account at S. Under paragraph (a)(15)(ii) of this section, the stock is considered acquired for cash in

E's account at S. Because the stock is acquired on or after January 1, 2012, under paragraph (a)(15)(i) of this section, it is a covered security.

*Example 10.* F, an individual not otherwise exempt from reporting, is granted 100 shares of stock in F's employer by F's employer. Because F does not acquire the stock for cash or through a transfer to an account with a transfer statement (as described in §1.6045A-1, under paragraph (a)(15) of this section, the stock is not a covered security.

*Example 11.* G, an individual not otherwise exempt from reporting, owns 400 shares of stock in Q, a corporation, in an account with U, a broker. Of the 400 shares, 100 are covered securities and 300 are noncovered securities. Q takes a corporate action to split its stock in a 2-for-1 split. After the stock split, G owns 800 shares of stock. Because the adjusted basis of 600 of the 800 shares that G owns is determined from the basis of noncovered securities, under paragraphs (a)(15)(iii) and (a)(15)(iv)(B) of this section, these 600 shares are not covered securities and the remaining 200 shares are covered securities.

(c) *Reporting by brokers.*—(1) *Requirement of reporting.*—Any broker shall, except as otherwise provided, report in the manner prescribed in this section.1

(2) *Sales required to be reported.*—Except as provided in paragraphs (c)(3), (c)(5), and (g) of this section, a broker is required to make a return of information for each sale by a customer of the broker if, in the ordinary course of a trade or business in which the broker stands ready to effect sales to be made by others, the broker effects the sale or closes the short position opened by the sale.

(3) *Exceptions.*—(i) *Sales effected for exempt recipients.*—(A) *In general.*—No return of information is required with respect to a sale effected for a customer that is an exempt recipient under paragraph (c)(3)(i)(B) of this section.

(B) *Exempt recipient defined.*—The term *exempt recipient* means—

(1) A corporation as defined in section 7701(a)(3), whether domestic or foreign, except that this exclusion does not apply to sales of covered securities acquired on or after January 1, 2012, by an S corporation as defined in section 1361(a);

(2) An organization exempt from taxation under section 501(a) or an individual retirement plan;

(3) The United States or a State, the District of Columbia, a possession of the United States, a political subdivision of any of the foregoing, a wholly owned agency or instrumentality of any one or more of the foregoing, or a pool or partnership composed exclusively of any of the foregoing;

(4) A foreign government, a political subdivision thereof, an international organization, or any wholly owned agency or instrumentality of the foregoing;

(5) A foreign central bank of issue as defined in §1.895-1(b)(1) (i.e., a bank that is by law or government sanction the principal authority, other than the government itself, issuing instruments intended to circulate as currency);

(6) A dealer in securities or commodities registered as such under the laws of the United States or a State;

(7) A futures commission merchant registered as such with the Commodity Futures Trading Commission;

(8) A real estate investment trust (as defined in section 856);

(9) An entity registered at all times during the taxable year under the Investment Company Act of 1940 (15 U.S.C. 80a-1, et seq.);

(10) A common trust fund (as defined in section 584(a)); or

(11) A financial institution such as a bank, mutual savings bank, savings and loan association, building and loan association, cooperative bank, homestead association, credit union, industrial loan association or bank, or other similar organization.

(C) *Exemption certificate.*—(1) *In general.*—Except as provided in paragraph (c)(3)(i)(C)(2) of this section, a broker may treat a person described in paragraph (c)(3)(i)(B) of this section as an exempt recipient based on a properly completed exemption certificate (as provided in §31.3406(h)-3 of this chapter); the broker's actual knowledge that the customer is a person described in paragraph (c)(3)(i)(B) of this section; or the applicable indicators described in §1.6049-4(c)(1)(ii)(A) through (M). A broker may require an exempt recipient to file a properly completed exemption certificate and may treat an exempt recipient that fails to do so as a recipient that is not exempt.

(2) *Limitation for corporate customers.*—For sales of covered securities acquired on or after January 1, 2012, a broker may not treat a customer as an exempt recipient described in paragraph

(c)(3)(i)(B)(1) of this section based on the indicators of corporate status described in §1.6049-4(c)(1)(ii)(A). However, for sales of all securities, a broker may treat a customer as an exempt recipient if one of the following applies:

(i) The name of the customer contains the term "insurance company," "indemnity company," "reinsurance company," or "assurance company."

(ii) The name of the customer indicates that it is an entity listed as a per se corporation under §301.7701-2(b)(8)(i) of this chapter.

(iii) The broker receives a properly completed exemption certificate (as provided in §31.3406(h)-3 of this chapter) that asserts that the customer is not an S corporation as defined in section 1361(a).

(iv) The broker receives a withholding certificate described in §1.1441-1(e)(2)(i) that includes a certification that the person whose name is on the certificate is a foreign corporation.

(ii) *Excepted sales.*—No return of information is required with respect to a sale effected by a broker for a customer if the sale is an excepted sale. For this purpose, a sale is an excepted sale if it is—

(A) So designated by the Internal Revenue Service in a revenue ruling or revenue procedure (see §601.601(d)(2) of this chapter); or

(B) A sale with respect to which a return is not required by applying the rules of §1.6049-4(c)(4) (by substituting the term "a sale subject to reporting under section 6045" for the term "an interest payment").

(iii) *Multiple brokers.*—If a broker is instructed to initiate a sale by a person that is an exempt recipient described in paragraph (c)(3)(i)(B)(6), (7), or (11) of this section, no return of information is required with respect to the sale by that broker. In a redemption of stock or retirement of securities, only the broker responsible for paying the holder redeemed or retired, or crediting the gross proceeds on the sale to that holder's account, is required to report the sale.

(iv) *Cash on delivery transactions.*—In the case of a sale of securities through a cash on delivery account, a delivery versus payment account, or other similar account or transaction, only the broker that receives the gross proceeds from the sale against delivery of the securities sold is required to report the sale. If, however, the broker's customer is another broker (second-party broker) that is an exempt recipient, then only the second-party broker is required to report the sale.

(v) *Fiduciaries and partnerships.*—No return of information is required with respect to a sale effected by a custodian or trustee in its capacity as such or a redemption of a partnership interest by a partnership, provided the sale is otherwise reported by the custodian or trustee on a properly filed Form 1041, or the redemption is otherwise reported by the partnership on a properly filed Form 1065, and all Schedule K-1 reporting requirements are satisfied.

(vi) *Money market funds.*—(A) *In general.*—No return of information is required with respect to a sale of shares in a regulated investment company that is permitted to hold itself out to investors as a money market fund under Rule 2a-7 under the Investment Company Act of 1940 (17 CFR 270.2a-7).

(B) *Effective/applicability date.*—Paragraph (c)(3)(vi)(A) of this section applies to sales of shares in calendar years beginning on or after July 8, 2016. Taxpayers and brokers (as defined in §1.6045-1(a)(1)), however, may rely on paragraph (c)(3)(vi)(A) of this section for sales of shares in calendar years beginning before July 8, 2016.

(vii) *Obligor payments on certain obligations.*—No return of information is required with respect to payments representing obligor payments on—

(A) Nontransferable obligations (including savings bonds, savings accounts, checking accounts, and NOW accounts);

(B) Obligations as to which the entire gross proceeds are reported by the broker on Form 1099 under provisions of the Internal Revenue Code other than section 6045 (including stripped coupons issued prior to July 1, 1982); or

(C) Retirement of short-term obligations (i.e., obligations with a fixed maturity date not exceeding 1 year from the date of issue) that have original issue discount, as defined in section 1273(a)(1), with or without application of the de minimis rule. The preceding sentence does not apply to a debt instrument issued on or after January 1, 2014. For a short-term obligation issued on or after January 1, 2014, see paragraph (c)(3)(xiii) of this section.

(D) Demand obligations that also are callable by the obligor and that have no premium or discount. The preceding sentence does not apply to a debt instrument issued on or after January 1, 2014.

(viii) *Foreign currency.*—No return of information is required with respect to a sale of foreign currency other than a sale pursuant to a forward contract or regulated futures contract that requires delivery of foreign currency.

(ix) *Fractional share.*—No return of information is required with respect to a sale of a fractional share of stock if the gross proceeds on the sale of the fractional share are less than $20.

(x) *Certain retirements.*—No return of information is required from an issuer or its agent with respect to the retirement of book entry or registered form obligations as to which the relevant books and records indicate that no interim transfers have occurred. The preceding sentence does not apply to a debt instrument issued on or after January 1, 2014.

(xi) *Short sales.*—(A) *In general.*—A broker may not make a return of information under this section for a short sale of a security entered into on or after January 1, 2011, until the year a customer delivers a security to satisfy the short sale obligation. The return must be made without regard to the constructive sale rule in section 1259 or to section 1233(h). In general, the broker must report on a single return the information required by paragraph (d)(2)(i) of this section for the short sale except that the broker must report the date the short sale was closed in lieu of the sale date. In applying paragraph (d)(2)(i) of this section, the broker must report the relevant information regarding the security sold to open the short sale and the adjusted basis of the security delivered to close the short sale and whether any gain or loss on the closing of the short sale is long-term or short-term (within the meaning of section 1222).

(B) *Short sale closed by delivery of a noncovered security.*—A broker is not required to report adjusted basis and whether any gain or loss on the closing of the short sale is long-term or short-term if the short sale is closed by delivery of a noncovered security and the return so indicates. A broker that chooses to report this information is not subject to penalties under section 6721 or 6722 for failure to report this information correctly if the broker indicates on the return that the short sale was closed by delivery of a noncovered security.

(C) *Short sale obligation transferred to another account.*—If a short sale obligation is satisfied by delivery of a security transferred into a customer's account accompanied by a transfer statement (as described in §1.6045A-1(b)(7)) indicating that the security was borrowed, the broker receiving custody of the security may not file a return of information under this section. The receiving broker must furnish a statement to the transferor that reports the amount of gross proceeds received from the short sale, the date of the sale, the quantity of shares, units, or amounts sold, and the Committee on Uniform Security Identification Procedures (CUSIP) number of the sold security (if applicable) or other security identifier number that the Secretary may designate by publication in the **Federal Register** or in the Internal Revenue Bulletin (see §601.601(d)(2) of this chapter). The statement to the transferor also must include the transfer date, the name and contact information of the receiving broker, the name and contact information of the transferor, and sufficient information to identify the customer. If the customer subsequently closes the short sale obligation in the transferor's account with nonborrowed securities, the transferor must make the return of information required by this section. In that event, the transferor must take into account the information furnished under this paragraph (c)(3)(xi)(C) on the return unless the transferor knows that the information furnished under this paragraph is incorrect or incomplete. A failure to report correct information that arises solely from this reliance is deemed to be due to reasonable cause for purposes of penalties under sections 6721 and 6722. *See* §301.6724-1(a)(1) of this chapter.

(xii) *Cross reference.*—For an exception for certain sales of agricultural commodities and certificates issued by the Commodity Credit Corporation after January 1, 1993, see paragraph (c)(7) of this section.

(xiii) *Short-term obligations issued on or after January 1, 2014.*—No return of information is required under this section with respect to a sale (including a retirement) of a short-term obligation, as described in section 1272(a)(2)(C), that is issued on or after January 1, 2014.

(xiv) *Certain redemptions.*—No return of information is required under this section for payments made by a stock transfer agent (as described in §1.6045-1(b)(iv)) with respect to a redemption of stock of a corporation described in section 1297(a) with respect to a shareholder in the corporation if—

(A) The stock transfer agent obtains from the corporation a written certification signed by a person authorized to sign on behalf of the corporation, that states that the corporation is described in section 1297(a) for each calendar year during which the stock transfer agent relies on the provisions of paragraph (c)(3)(xiv) of this section,

and the stock transfer agent has no reason to know that the written certification is unreliable or incorrect;

(B) The stock transfer agent identifies, prior to payment, the corporation as a participating FFI (including a reporting Model 2 FFI (as defined in §1.6049-4(f)(10) or (f)(14), respectively), or reporting Model 1 FFI (as defined in §1.6049-4(f)(13)), in accordance with the requirements of §1.1471-3(d)(4) (substituting the terms "stock transfer agent" and "corporation" for the terms "withholding agent" and "payee," respectively) and validates that status annually;

(C) The stock transfer agent obtains a written certification representing that the corporation shall report the payment as part of its account holder reporting obligations under chapter 4 of the Code or an applicable IGA (as defined in §1.6049-4(f)(7)) and provided the stock transfer agent does not know that the corporation is not reporting the payment as required. The paying agent may rely on the written certification until there is a change in circumstances or the paying agent knows or has reason to know that the statement is unreliable or incorrect. A stock transfer agent that knows that the corporation is not reporting the payment as required under chapter 4 of the Code or an applicable IGA must report all payments reportable under this section that it makes during the year in which it obtains such knowledge; and

(D) The stock transfer agent is not also acting in its capacity as a custodian, nominee, or other agent of the payee with respect to the payment.

(4) *Examples.*—The following examples illustrate the application of the rules in paragraph (c)(3) of this section:

*Example 1.* P, an individual who is not an exempt recipient, places an order with B, a person generally known in the investment community to be a federally registered broker/dealer, to effect a sale of P's stock in a publicly traded corporation. B, in turn, places an order to sell the stock with C, a second broker, who will execute the sale. B discloses to C the identity of the customer placing the order. C is not required to make a return of information with respect to the sale because C was instructed by B, an exempt recipient as defined in paragraph (c)(3)(i)(B)(6) of this section, to initiate the sale. B is required to make a return of information with respect to the sale because P is B's customer and is not an exempt recipient.

*Example 2.* Assume the same facts as in *Example 1* except that B has an omnibus account with C so that B does not disclose to C whether the transaction is for a customer of B or for B's own account. C is not required to make a return of information with respect to the sale because C was instructed by B, an exempt recipient as defined in paragraph (c)(3)(i)(B)(6) of this section, to initiate the sale. B is required to make a return of information with respect to the sale because P is B's customer and is not an exempt recipient.

*Example 3.* D, an individual who is not an exempt recipient, enters into a cash on delivery stock transaction by instructing K, a federally registered broker/dealer, to sell stock owned by D, and to deliver the proceeds to L, a custodian bank. Concurrently with the above instructions, D instructs L to deliver D's stock to K (or K's designee) against delivery of the proceeds from K. The records of both K and L with respect to this transaction show an account in the name of D. Pursuant to paragraph (h)(1) of this section, D is considered the customer of K and L. Under paragraph (c)(3)(iv) of this section, K is not required to make a return of information with respect to the sale because K will pay the gross proceeds to L against delivery of the securities sold. L is required to make a return of information with respect to the sale because D is L's customer and is not an exempt recipient.

*Example 4.* Assume the same facts as in *Example 3* except that E, a federally registered investment advisor, instructs K to sell stock owned by D and to deliver the proceeds to L. Concurrently with the above instructions, E instructs L to deliver D's stock to K (or K's designee) against delivery of the proceeds from K. The records of both K and L with respect to the transaction show an account in the name of D. Pursuant to paragraph (h)(1) of this section, D is considered the customer of K and L. Under paragraph (c)(3)(iv) of this section, K is not required to make a return of information with respect to the sale because K will pay the gross proceeds to L against delivery of the securities sold. L is required to make a return of information with respect to the sale because D is L's customer and is not an exempt recipient.

*Example 5.* Assume the same facts as in *Example 4* except that the records of both K and L with respect to the transaction show an account in the name of E. Pursuant to paragraph (h)(1) of this section, E is considered the customer of K and L. Under paragraph (c)(3)(iv) of this section, K is not required to make a return of information with respect to the sale because K will pay the gross proceeds to L against delivery of the securities sold. L is required to make a return of information with respect to the sale because E is L's customer and is not an exempt recipient. E is required to make a return of information with respect to the sale because D is E's customer and is not an exempt recipient.

*Example 6.* F, an individual who is not an exempt recipient, owns bonds that are held by G, a federally registered broker/dealer, in an account for F with G designated as nominee for F. Upon the retirement of the bonds, the gross proceeds are automatically credited to the account of F. G is required to make a return of information with respect to the retirement because G is the broker responsible for making payments of the gross proceeds to F.

*Example 7.* On June 24, 2010, H, an individual who is not an exempt recipient, opens a short sale of stock in an account with M, a broker. Because the short sale is entered into before January 1, 2011, paragraph (c)(3)(xi) of this section does not apply. Under paragraphs (c)(2) and (j) of this section, M must make a return of information for the year of the sale regardless of when the short sale is closed.

*Example 8.* (i) On August 25, 2011, H opens a short sale of stock in an account with M, a broker. H closes the short sale with M on January 25, 2012, by purchasing stock of the same corporation in the account in which H opened the short sale and delivering the stock to satisfy H's short sale obligation. The stock H purchased is a covered security.

(ii) Because the short sale is entered into on or after January 1, 2011, under paragraphs (c)(2) and (c)(3)(xi) of this section, the broker closing the short sale must make a return of information reporting the sale for the year in which the short sale is closed. Thus, M is required to report the sale for 2012. M must report on a single return the relevant information for the sold stock, the adjusted basis of the purchased stock, and whether any gain or loss on the closing of the short sale is long-term or short-term (within the meaning of section 1222). Thus, M must report the information about the short sale opening and closing transactions on a single return for taxable year 2012.

*Example 9.* (i) Assume the same facts as in *Example 8* except that H also has an account with N, a broker, and satisfies the short sale obligation with M by borrowing stock of the same corporation from N and transferring custody of the borrowed stock from N to M. N indicates on the transfer statement that the transferred stock was borrowed in accordance with §1.6045A-1(b)(7).

(ii) Under paragraph (c)(3)(xi)(C) of this section, M may not file the return of information required under this section. M must furnish a statement to N that reports the gross proceeds from the short sale on August 25, 2011, the date of the sale, the quantity of shares sold, the CUSIP number or other security identifier number of the sold stock, the transfer date, the name and contact information of M and N, and information identifying H such as H's name and the account number from which H transferred the borrowed stock.

(iii) N must report the gross proceeds from the short sale, the date the short sale was closed, the adjusted basis of the stock acquired to close the short sale, and whether any gain or loss on the closing of the short sale is long-term or short-term (within the meaning of section 1222) on the return of information N is required to file under paragraph (c)(2) of this section when H closes the short sale in the account with N.

(5) *Form of reporting for regulated futures contracts.*—(i) *In general.*—A broker effecting closing transactions in regulated futures contracts shall report information with respect to regulated futures contracts solely in the manner prescribed in this paragraph (c)(5). In the case of a sale that involves making a delivery pursuant to a regulated futures contract, only the profit or loss on the contract is reported as a transaction with respect to regulated futures contracts under this paragraph (c)(5); such sales are, however, subject to reporting under paragraph (d)(2). The information required under this paragraph (c)(5) must be reported on a calendar year basis, unless the broker is advised in writing by an account's owner that the owner's taxable year is other than a calendar year and the broker elects to report with respect to regulated futures contracts in such account on the basis of the owner's taxable year. The following information must be reported as required by Form 1099 with respect to regulated futures contracts held in a customer's account:

(A) The name, address, and taxpayer identification number of the customer.

(B) The net realized profit or loss from all regulated futures contracts closed during the calendar year.

(C) The net unrealized profit or loss in all open regulated futures contracts at the end of the preceding calendar year.

(D) The net unrealized profit or loss in all open regulated futures contracts at the end of the calendar year.

(E) The aggregate profit or loss from regulated futures contracts $((b) + (d) - (c))$ $[((B) + (D) - (C))]$.

(F) Any other information required by Form 1099.

See 17 CFR 1.33. For this purpose, the end of a year is the close of business of the last day of such year. In reporting under this paragraph (c)(5), the broker shall make such adjustments for commissions that have actually been paid and for option premiums as are consistent with the books of the broker. No additional returns of information with respect to regulated futures contracts so reported are required.

(ii) *Determination of profit or loss from foreign currency contracts.*—A broker effecting a closing transaction in foreign currency contracts (as defined in section 1256(g)) shall report information with respect to such contracts in the manner prescribed in paragraph (c)(5)(i) of this section. If a foreign currency contract is closed by making or taking delivery, the net realized profit or loss for purposes of paragraph (c)(5)(i)(B) of this section is determined by comparing the contract price to the spot price for the contract currency at the time and place specified in the contract. If a foreign currency contract is closed by entry into an offsetting contract, the net realized profit or loss for purposes of paragraph (c)(5)(i)(B) of this section is determined by comparing the contract price to the price of the offsetting contract. The net unrealized profit or loss in a foreign currency contract for purposes of paragraphs (c)(5)(i)(C) and (D) of this section is determined by comparing the contract price to the broker's price for similar contracts at the close of business of the relevant year.

(iii) *Examples.*—The following examples illustrate the application of the rules in this paragraph (c)(5):

*Example 1.* On October 30, 1984, A, an individual who is a calendar year taxpayer not otherwise exempt from reporting, buys one March 1985 put on Treasury Bond futures (i.e. A purchases an option to enter into a short regulated futures contract of $100,000 face value U.S. Treasury bonds). A pays $500 for the option. On December 19, 1984, A, through B, exercises the option and enters into the futures contract. On February 15, 1985, A, through B, enters into a closing transaction with respect to the futures contract. These are A's only transactions in the account. Since B's books list A's regulated futures contract on December 31, 1984, B must report for A, for 1984, the unrealized profit or loss in the contract as of December 31, 1984. For 1985, B will report the same amount for A as the unrealized profit or loss at the beginning of 1985. The return of information for 1985 will also include the gain or loss from the contract in the net realized profit or loss from all regulated futures contracts sales during 1985.

*Example 2.* The facts are the same as in Example (1) except that A does not enter into the closing transaction, but instead, on March 20, 1985, B informs A that A will make delivery under the contract. On March 22, 1985, A does so; consequently, A becomes entitled to the gross proceeds. B enters the closing transaction on its books on March 20, 1985. In addition to the return[s] of information required by paragraph (c)(5), as described in Example (1), B must report the March 22, 1985 delivery as a separate transaction. B may use as the sale date for the delivery either March 20, 1985, the date the transaction is entered on the books of B, or March 22, 1985, the date A becomes entitled to the gross proceeds. B may not deduct the $500 premium from the gross proceeds with respect to the March 22, 1985 delivery.

*Example 3.* The facts are the same as in Example (2) except that A buys a call on Treasury bond futures and takes delivery. B will supply the returns of information required by paragraph (c)(5), as described in Example (1). B is not required to make a return of information with respect to A's taking delivery.

*Example 4.* C, an individual who is a calendar year taxpayer not otherwise exempt from reporting, has an account with D, a broker. C trades both regulated futures contracts and forward contracts through C's account with D. D must report C's regulated futures contracts on an annual basis as required by paragraph (c)(5). With respect to C's forward contracts, D may elect to use the calendar month, quarter, or year as D's reporting period as provided in paragraph (c)(6).

(6) *Reporting periods and filing groups.*—(i) *Reporting period.*—(A) *In general.*—A broker may elect to use the calendar month, quarter, or year as the broker's reporting period. A broker may separately elect a reporting period for each filing group.

(B) *Election.*—For each calendar year, a broker shall elect a reporting period by filing Forms 1096 and 1099 in the manner elected. A different reporting period may be subsequently elected by filing in the manner subsequently elected, provided no duplication of reported transactions results.

(ii) *Filing group.*—(A) *In general.*—A broker may elect to group customers or customer accounts by office, branch, department or other method of operational classification and separately file Forms 1096 and 1099 for each filing group.

(B) *Election.*—For each calendar year, a broker shall elect filing groups by filing Forms 1096 and 1099 in the manner elected. Different filing groups may be subsequently elected by filing in the manner subsequently elected, provided no duplication of reported transactions results.

(iii) *Example.*—The following example illustrates the rules of this paragraph (c)(6):

*Example.* The A department of C, a broker, files a separate report for each month of 1984, whereas the B department of C files one report for all of 1984. C makes no other reports or returns of information under section 6045 for 1984. C has thereby elected two filing groups for 1984, the A department and the B department. The A department has the calendar month as its 1984 reporting period, whereas the B department has the calendar year as its 1984 reporting period. The same result would occur if A and B were offices or branches of C.

(7) *Exception for certain sales of agricultural commodities and commodity certificates.*—(i) *Agricultural commodities.*—No return of information is required under section 6045 for a spot or forward sale of an agricultural commodity. This paragraph (c)(7)(i) does not except from reporting sales of agricultural commodities pursuant to regulated futures contracts, sales of derivative interests in agricultural commodities, or sales described in paragraph (c)(7)(iii) of this section.

(ii) *Commodity Credit Corporation certificates.*—Except as otherwise provided in a revenue ruling or revenue procedure, no return of information is required under section 6045 with respect to a sale of a commodity certificate issued by the Commodity Credit Corporation under 7 CFR 1470.4 (1990).

(iii) *Sales involving designated warehouses.*—Paragraph (c)(7)(i) of this section does not apply to any sale involving a warehouse receipt for an agricultural commodity issued by a designated warehouse for an agricultural commodity of the type for which the warehouse is a designated warehouse.

(iv) *Definitions.*—For purposes of this paragraph (c)(7):

(A) *Agricultural commodity.*—An "agricultural commodity" includes, but is not limited to, a commodity within the meaning of paragraph (a)(5) of this section that is a grain, feed, livestock, meat, oil seed, timber, or fiber.

(B) *Spot sale.*—A spot sale is a sale that results in the substantially contemporaneous delivery of a commodity.

(C) *Forward sale.*—A forward sale is a sale pursuant to a forward contract within the meaning of paragraph (a)(7) of this section.

(D) *Designated warehouse.*—A designated warehouse is a warehouse, depository, or other similar entity, designated by a commodity exchange under 7 CFR 1.43 (1992), in which or out of which a particular type of agricultural commodity is deliverable in satisfaction of a regulated futures contract.

(d) *Information required.*—(1) *In general.*—A broker that is required to make a return of information under paragraph (c) of this section during a reporting period is required to report for each filing group on a separate Form 1096, "Annual Summary and Transmittal of U.S. Information Returns," or any successor form, the information required by the form in the manner and number of copies required by the form.

(2) *Transactional reporting.*—(i) *Required information.*—Except as provided in paragraph (c)(5) of this section, for each sale for which a broker is required to make a return of information under this section, the broker must report on Form 1099-B, "Proceeds From Broker and Barter Exchange Transactions," or any successor form the name, address, and taxpayer identification number of the customer, the property sold, the CUSIP number of the security sold (if applicable) or other security identifier number that the Secretary may designate by publication in the **Federal Register** or in the Internal Revenue Bulletin (*see* § 601.601(d)(2) of this chapter), the adjusted basis of the security sold, whether any gain or loss with respect to the security sold is long-term or short-term (within the meaning of section 1222), the gross proceeds of the sale, the sale date, and other information required by the form in the manner and number of copies required by the form. In addition, for a sale of a covered security on or after January 1, 2014, a broker must report on Form 1099-B whether any gain or loss is ordinary. See paragraph (m) of this section for additional rules related to options and paragraph (n) of this section for additional rules related to debt instruments.

(ii) *Specific identification of securities.*—Except as provided in § 1.1012-1(e)(7)(ii), for a specified security described in paragraph (a)(14)(i) of this section sold on or after January 1, 2011, or for a specified security described in paragraph (a)(14)(ii) of this section sold on or after January 1, 2014, a broker must report a sale of less than the entire position in an account of a specified security that was acquired on different dates or at different prices consistently with a customer's adequate and timely identification of the security to be sold. *See* § 1.1012-1(c). If the customer does not provide an adequate

and timely identification for the sale, the broker must first report the sale of securities in the account for which the broker does not know the acquisition or purchase date followed by the earliest securities purchased or acquired, whether covered securities or noncovered securities.

(iii) *Sales of noncovered securities.*—A broker is not required to report adjusted basis and the character of any gain or loss for the sale of a noncovered security if the return identifies the sale as a sale of a noncovered security. A broker that chooses to report this information for a noncovered security is not subject to penalties under section 6721 or 6722 for failure to report this information correctly if the return identifies the sale as a sale of a noncovered security. For purposes of this paragraph (d)(2)(iii), a broker must treat a security for which a broker makes the singleaccount election described in § 1.1012-1(e)(11)(i) as a covered security.

(iv) *Information from other parties and other accounts.*—(A) *Transfer and issuer statements.*—When reporting a sale of a covered security, a broker must take into account all information, other than the classification of the security (such as stock), furnished on a transfer statement (as described in § 1.6045A-1 and all information furnished or deemed furnished on an issuer statement (as described in § 1.6045B-1, unless the statement is incomplete or the broker has actual knowledge that it is incorrect. A broker may treat a customer as a minority shareholder when taking the information on an issuer statement into account unless the broker knows that the customer is a majority shareholder and the issuer statement reports the action's effect on the basis of majority shareholders. A failure to report correct information that arises solely from reliance on information furnished on a transfer statement or issuer statement is deemed to be due to reasonable cause for purposes of penalties under sections 6721 and 6722. *See* § 301.6724-1(a)(1) of this chapter.

(B) *Other information.*—A broker is permitted, but not required, to take into account information about a covered security other than what is furnished on a transfer statement or issuer statement, including any information the broker has about securities held by the same customer in other accounts with the broker. For purposes of penalties under sections 6721 and 6722, a broker that takes into account information received from a customer or third party other than information furnished on a transfer statement or issuer statement is deemed to have relied upon this information in good faith if the broker neither knows nor has reason to know that the information is incorrect. See § 301.6724-1(c)(6) of this chapter.

(v) *Failure to receive a complete transfer statement.*—A broker that has not received a complete transfer statement as required under § 1.6045A-1(a)(3) for a transfer of a specified security must request a complete statement from the applicable person effecting the transfer unless, under § 1.6045A-1(a), the transferor has no duty to furnish a transfer statement for the transfer. The broker is only required to make this request once. If the broker does not receive a complete transfer statement after requesting it, the broker may treat the security as a noncovered security upon its subsequent sale or transfer. A transfer statement for a covered security is complete if, in the view of the receiving broker, it provides sufficient information to comply with this section when reporting the sale of the security. A transfer statement for a noncovered security is complete if it indicates that the security is a noncovered security.

(vi) *Reporting by other parties after a sale.*—(A) *Transfer statements.*—If a broker receives a transfer statement indicating that a security is a covered security after the broker reports the sale of the security, the broker must file a corrected return within thirty days of receiving the statement unless the broker reported the required information on the original return consistently with the transfer statement.

(B) *Issuer statements.*—If a broker receives or is deemed to receive an issuer statement after the broker reports the sale of a covered security, the broker must file a corrected return within thirty days of receiving the issuer statement unless the broker reported the required information on the original return consistently with the issuer statement.

(C) *Exception.*—A broker is not required to file a corrected return under this paragraph (d)(2)(vi) if the broker receives the transfer statement or issuer statement more than three years after the broker filed the return.

(vii) *Examples.*—The following examples illustrate the rules of this paragraph (d)(2):

*Example 1.* (i) On February 22, 2012, K sells 100 shares of stock of C, a corporation, at a loss in an account held with F, a broker. On March 15, 2012, K purchases 100 shares of C stock for cash in an account with G, a different broker. Because K acquires the stock purchased on March 15, 2012, for cash in an account after January 1,

2012, under paragraph (a)(15) of this section, the stock is a covered security. K asks G to increase K's adjusted basis in the stock to account for the application of the wash sale rules under section 1091 to the loss transaction in the account held with F.

(ii) Under paragraph (d)(2)(iv)(B) of this section, G is not required to take into account the information provided by K when subsequently reporting the adjusted basis and whether any gain or loss on the sale is long-term or short-term. If G chooses to take this information into account, under paragraph (d)(2)(iv)(B) of this section, G is deemed to have relied upon the information received from K in good faith for purposes of penalties under sections 6721 and 6722 if G neither knows nor has reason to know that the information provided by K is incorrect.

*Example 2.* (i) L purchases shares of stock of a single corporation in an account with F, a broker, on April 17, 1969, April 17, 2012, April 17, 2013, and April 17, 2014. In January 2015, L sells all the stock.

(ii) Under paragraph (d)(2)(i) of this section, F must separately report the gross proceeds and adjusted basis attributable to the stock purchased in 2014, for which the gain or loss on the sale is short-term, and the combined gross proceeds and adjusted basis attributable to the stock purchased in 2012 and 2013, for which the gain or loss on the sale is long-term. Under paragraph (d)(2)(iii) of this section, F must also separately report the gross proceeds attributable to the stock purchased in 1969 as the sale of noncovered securities in order to avoid treatment of this sale as the sale of covered securities.

(3) *Sales between interest payment dates.*—For each sale of a debt instrument prior to maturity with respect to which a broker is required to make a return of information under this section, a broker must show separately on Form 1099 the amount of accrued and unpaid qualified stated interest as of the sale date that must be reported by the customer as interest income under § 1.61-7(d). *See* § 1.1273-1(c) for the definition of qualified stated interest. Such interest information must be shown in the manner and at the time required by Form 1099 and section 6049.

(4) *Sale date.*—With respect to sales of property that are reportable under this section, a broker must report a sale as occurring on the date the sale is entered on the books of the broker.

(5) *Gross proceeds.*—For purposes of this section, *gross proceeds* on a sale are the total amount paid to the customer or credited to the customer's account as a result of the sale reduced by the amount of any qualified stated interest reported under paragraph (d)(3) of this section and increased by any amount not paid or credited by reason of repayment of margin loans. In the case of a closing transaction (other than a closing transaction related to an option) that results in a loss, gross proceeds are the amount debited from the customer's account. For sales before January 1, 2014, a broker may, but is not required to, reduce gross proceeds by the amount of commissions and transfer taxes, provided the treatment chosen is consistent with the books of the broker. For sales on or after January 1, 2014, a broker must reduce gross proceeds by the amount of commissions and transfer taxes related to the sale of the security. For securities sold pursuant to the exercise of an option granted or acquired before January 1, 2014, a broker may, but is not required to, take the option premiums into account in determining the gross proceeds of the securities sold, provided the treatment chosen is consistent with the books of the broker. For securities sold pursuant to the exercise of an option granted or acquired on or after January 1, 2014, or for the treatment of an option granted or acquired on or after January 1, 2014, see paragraph (m) of this section. A broker must report the gross proceeds of identical stock (within the meaning of § 1.1012-1(e)(4) by averaging the proceeds of each share if the stock is sold at separate times on the same calendar day in executing a single trade order and the broker executing the trade provides a single confirmation to the customer that reports an aggregate total price or an average price per share. However, a broker may not average the proceeds if the customer notifies the broker in writing of an intent to determine the proceeds of the stock by the actual proceeds per share and the broker receives the notification by January 15 of the calendar year following the year of the sale. A broker may extend the January 15 deadline but not beyond the due date for filing the return required under this section.

(6) *Adjusted basis.*—(i) *In general.*—For purposes of this section, the adjusted basis of a security is determined from the initial basis under paragraph (d)(6)(ii) of this section as of the date the security is acquired in an account, increased by the commissions and transfer taxes related to its sale to the extent not accounted for in gross proceeds as described in paragraph (d)(5) of this section. A broker is not required to consider transactions or events occurring outside the account except for an organizational action taken by an issuer during the period the broker holds custody of the security (beginning with

the date that the broker receives a transferred security) reported on an issuer statement (as described in § 1.6045B-1) furnished or deemed furnished to the broker. Except as otherwise provided in paragraph (n) of this section, a broker is not required to consider customer elections. For rules related to the adjusted basis of a debt instrument, see paragraph (n) of this section.

(ii) *Initial basis.*—(A) *Cost basis.*—For a security acquired for cash, the initial basis generally is the total amount of cash paid by the customer or credited against the customer's account for the security, increased by the commissions and transfer taxes related to its acquisition. A broker may, but is not required to, take option premiums into account in determining the initial basis of securities purchased or acquired pursuant to the exercise of an option granted or acquired before January 1, 2014. For rules related to options granted or acquired on or after January 1, 2014, see paragraph (m) of this section. A broker may, but is not required to, increase initial basis for income recognized upon the exercise of a compensatory option or the vesting or exercise of other equity-based compensation arrangements, granted or acquired before January 1, 2014. A broker may not increase initial basis for income recognized upon the exercise of a compensatory option or the vesting or exercise of other equity-based compensation arrangements, granted or acquired on or after January 1, 2014. A broker must report the basis of identical stock (within the meaning of § 1.1012-1(e)(4) by averaging the basis of each share if the stock is purchased at separate times on the same calendar day in executing a single trade order and the broker executing the trade provides a single confirmation to the customer that reports an aggregate total price or an average price per share. However, a broker may not average the basis if the customer timely notifies the broker in writing of an intent to determine the basis of the stock by the actual cost per share in accordance with § 1.1012-1(c)(1)(ii).

(B) *Basis of transferred securities.*—(1) *In general.*—The initial basis of a security transferred to an account is generally the basis reported on the transfer statement (as described in § 1.6045A-1.

(2) *Securities acquired by gift.*—If a transfer statement indicates that the security is acquired as a gift, a broker must apply the relevant basis rules for property acquired by gift in determining the initial basis, but is not required to adjust basis for gift tax. A broker must treat the initial basis as equal to the gross proceeds from the sale determined under paragraph (d)(5) of this section if the relevant basis rules for property acquired by gift prevent recognizing both gain and loss, or if the relevant basis rules treat the initial basis of the security as its fair market value as of the date of the gift and the broker neither knows nor can readily ascertain this value. If the transfer statement did not report a date for the gift, the broker must treat the settlement date for the transfer as the date of the gift.

(iii) *Adjustments for wash sales.*—(A) *In general.*—A broker must apply the wash sale rules under section 1091 if both the sale and purchase transactions are of covered securities with the same CUSIP number or other security identifier number that the Secretary may designate by publication in the **Federal Register** or in the Internal Revenue Bulletin (*see* § 601.601(d)(2) of this chapter). When reporting the sale transaction that triggered the wash sale, the broker must report the amount of loss that is disallowed by section 1091 in addition to gross proceeds and adjusted basis. The broker must increase the basis of the purchased security by the amount of loss disallowed on the sale transaction.

(B) *Securities in different accounts.*—A broker is not required to apply paragraph (d)(6)(iii)(A) of this section if the securities are purchased and sold from different accounts, if the purchased security is transferred to another account before the wash sale, or if the securities are treated as held in separate accounts under § 1.1012-1(e). A security is not purchased in an account if it is purchased in another account and transferred into the account.

(C) *Effect of election under section 475(f)(1).*—A broker is not required to apply paragraph (d)(6)(iii)(A) of this section to securities in an account if a customer has in writing both informed the broker that the customer has made a valid and timely election under section 475(f)(1) and identified the account as solely containing securities subject to the election. For purposes of this paragraph (d)(6)(iii)(C), a writing may be in electronic format. If a customer subsequently informs a broker that the election no longer applies to the customer or the account, the broker must prospectively apply paragraph (d)(6)(iii)(A) of this section but is not required to apply paragraph (d)(6)(iii)(A) of this section for the period covered by the customer's prior instruction to the broker. A taxpayer that is not a trader in securities within the meaning of section 475(f)(1) does not become a trader in securities, or create an inference that it is a trader in securities, by notifying a broker that it has made a valid and timely election under section 475(f)(1).

(D) *Reporting at or near the time of sale.*—If a wash sale occurs after a broker has completed a return or statement reporting a sale of a covered security, the broker must redetermine adjusted basis under this paragraph (d)(6)(iii) and, if the return or statement included information inconsistent with this redetermination, correct the return or statement by the applicable original due date set forth in this section for the return or statement.

(iv) *Certain adjustments not taken into account.*—A broker is not required to apply section 1259 (regarding constructive sales), section 475 (regarding the mark-to-market method of accounting), section 1296 (regarding the mark-to-market method of accounting for marketable stock in a passive foreign investment company), or section 1092 (regarding straddles) when reporting adjusted basis.

(v) *Average basis method adjustments.*—For a covered security for which basis may be determined by the average basis method, a broker must compute basis using the average basis method if a customer validly elects that method for the securities sold or, in the absence of any instruction from the customer, if the broker chooses that method as its default basis determination method. *See* § 1.1012-1(e).

(vi) *Regulated investment company and real estate investment trust adjustments.*—A broker must adjust the basis of a covered security issued by a regulated investment company or real estate investment trust for the effects of undistributed capital gains reported to or by the broker under section 852(b)(3)(D) or section 857(b)(3)(D).

(vii) *Examples.*—The following examples, in which all the securities are covered securities, illustrate the rules of this paragraph (d)(6):

*Example 1.* (i) On September 21, 2012, P purchases 100 shares of stock in an account with J, a broker. On December 14, 2012, P purchases 100 shares of stock with the same CUSIP number in the same account. On January 4, 2013, P sells the shares purchased on September 21, 2012, at a loss.

(ii) Because the sale of stock on January 4, 2013, and the purchase of stock on December 14, 2012, are of covered securities with the same CUSIP number, under paragraph (d)(6)(iii)(A) of this section, J must report the amount of loss disallowed by section 1091 in addition to the gross proceeds of the sale and the adjusted basis of the September 21, 2012, stock.

(iii) P later sells the stock acquired on December 14, 2012. When reporting the sale of the stock, under paragraph (d)(6)(iii)(A) of this section, J must increase the adjusted basis of the stock acquired on December 14, 2012, by the amount of loss disallowed on the January 4, 2013, sale.

*Example 2.* Assume the same facts as in *Example 1* except that the December 14, 2012, purchase occurs in another account P maintains with J. Because the December 14, 2012, purchase does not occur in the same account as the sale of the September 21, 2012, stock, under paragraph (d)(6)(iii)(B) of this section, J is not required to apply the wash sale rules in reporting the sale of stock acquired on September 21, 2012, or December 14, 2012. Under paragraphs (d)(2)(iii) and (d)(2)(iv)(B) of this section, J may choose to apply the wash sale rules as if the transactions occurred in the same account. The result is the same whether P keeps the stock purchased on December 14, 2012, in the other account or transfers the stock into the account from which P sells the stock sold on January 4, 2013.

*Example 3.* (i) K, a regulated investment company, offers two funds for sale, Fund D and Fund E. On April 22, 2012, Q purchases shares of Fund D and pays a separate load charge. By paying the load charge, Q acquires a reinvestment right in shares of Fund E. On April 23, 2012, at the request of Q, Fund D redeems the shares. Q uses the proceeds to purchase shares of Fund E in a separate account. As a result of the reinvestment right, Q pays no load charge in purchasing the Fund E shares.

(ii) Under paragraph (d)(6)(i) of this section, when reporting adjusted basis of the Fund D and Fund E shares at the time of their redemption, K is not required to adjust basis for any deferral of the load charge under section 852(f), because the transactions concerning Fund D and Fund E occur in separate accounts. Under paragraph (d)(2)(iv)(B) of this section, K may choose to apply the provisions of section 852(f).

*Example 4.* R, an employee of C, a corporation, participates in C's stock option plan. On April 2, 2014, C grants R a nonstatutory option under the plan to buy 100 shares of stock. The option becomes substantially vested on April 2, 2015. On October 2, 2015, R exercises the option and purchases 100 shares. On December 2, 2015, R sells the 100 shares. Under paragraph (d)(6)(ii)(A) of this section, C is required to determine adjusted basis from the amount R pays under the terms of the option. Under paragraph (d)(6)(ii)(A) of this section, C is not permitted to adjust basis for any amount R must include as wage income with respect to the October 2, 2015, stock purchase.

(7) *Long-term or short-term gain or loss.*—(i) *In general.*—In determining whether any gain or loss on the sale of a security is long-term or short-term within the meaning of section 1222 for purposes of this section, a broker must consider the information reported on a transfer statement (as described in § 1.6045A-1 and apply the relevant rules for property acquired from a decedent or by gift. A broker is not required to consider transactions, elections, or events occurring outside the account except for an organizational action taken by an issuer during the period the broker holds custody of the security (beginning with the date that the broker receives a transferred security) reported on an issuer statement (as described in § 1.6045B-1) furnished or deemed furnished to the broker.

(ii) *Adjustments for wash sales.*—(A) *In general.*—A broker must apply the wash sale rules under section 1091 if both the sale and purchase transactions are of covered securities with the same CUSIP number or other security identifier number that the Secretary may designate by publication in the **Federal Register** or in the Internal Revenue Bulletin (*see* § 601.601(d)(2) of this chapter).

(B) *Securities in different accounts.*—A broker is not required to apply paragraph (d)(7)(ii)(A) of this section if the securities are purchased and sold from different accounts, if the purchased security is transferred to another account before the wash sale, or if the securities are treated as held in separate accounts under § 1.1012-1(e). A security is not purchased in an account if it is purchased in another account and transferred into the account.

(C) *Effect of election under section 475(f)(1).*—A broker is not required to apply paragraph (d)(7)(ii)(A) of this section to securities in an account if a customer has in writing both informed the broker that the customer has made a valid and timely election under section 475(f)(1) and identified the account as solely containing securities subject to the election. For purposes of this paragraph (d)(7)(ii)(C), a writing may be in electronic format. If a customer subsequently informs a broker that the election no longer applies to the customer or the account, the broker must prospectively apply paragraph (d)(7)(ii)(A) of this section but is not required to apply paragraph (d)(7)(ii)(A) of this section for the period covered by the customer's prior instruction to the broker. A taxpayer that is not a trader in securities within the meaning of section 475(f)(1) does not become a trader in securities, or create an inference that it is a trader in securities, by notifying a broker that it has made a valid and timely election under section 475(f)(1).

(D) *Reporting at or near the time of sale.*—If a wash sale occurs after a broker has completed a return or statement reporting a sale of a covered security, the broker must redetermine whether gain or loss on the sale is long-term or short-term under this paragraph (d)(7)(ii) and, if the return or statement included information inconsistent with this redetermination, correct the return or statement by the applicable original due date set forth in this section for the return or statement.

(iii) *Constructive sale and mark-to-market adjustments.*—A broker is not required to apply section 1259 (regarding constructive sales), section 475 (regarding the mark-to-market method of accounting), or section 1296 (regarding the mark-to-market method of accounting for marketable stock in a passive foreign investment company) when determining whether any gain or loss on the sale of a security is long-term or short-term.

(iv) *Regulated investment company and real estate investment trust adjustments.*—A broker is not required to apply sections 852(b)(4)(A) and 857(b)(8) (regarding effect of distributed and undistributed capital gain dividends on a loss on sale of regulated investment company or real estate investment trust shares held six months or less) or section 852(b)(4)(B) (regarding loss disallowance on sale of regulated investment company shares held six months or less due to receipt of tax-exempt dividends) when determining whether any gain or loss on the sale of a security is long-term or short-term.

(v) *No adjustments for hedging transactions or offsetting positions.*—A broker is not required to apply section 1092 (regarding straddles), section 1233(b)(2) (regarding effect of short sale on holding period of substantially identical property), or § 1.1221-2(b) (regarding hedging transactions) when determining whether any gain or loss on the sale of a security is long-term or short-term.

(8) *Conversion into United States dollars of amounts paid or received in foreign currency.*—(i) *Conversion rules.*—(A) When a payment other than a payment of interest is made in a foreign currency, a broker must determine the U.S. dollar amount of the payment by converting the foreign currency into U.S. dollars on the date it receives, credits, or makes the payment, as applicable, at the spot rate (as defined in § 1.988-1(d)(1)) or pursuant to a reasonable spot rate convention. (For interest payments, see paragraph (n)(4)(v) of this section concerning a customer's spot rate election.) When reporting the sale of a security traded on an established securities market, however, a broker must

determine the U.S. dollar amounts at the spot rate or pursuant to a reasonable spot rate convention as of the settlement date of the purchase or sale, as applicable.

(B) A reasonable spot rate convention includes a month-end spot rate or a monthly average spot rate. A spot rate convention must be used consistently for all non-dollar amounts reported and from year to year. The convention may not be changed without the consent of the Commissioner or his or her delegate.

(ii) *Effect of identification under §1.988-5(a), (b), or (c) when the taxpayer effects a sale and a hedge through the same broker.*—In lieu of the amounts reportable under paragraph (d)(8)(i) of this section, the gross proceeds and adjusted basis must each be the integrated amount computed under §1.988-5(a), (b) or (c) if—

(A) A taxpayer effects through a broker a sale or exchange of nonfunctional currency (as defined in §1.988-1(c)) and hedges all or a part of the sale as provided in §1.988-5(a), (b) or (c) with the same broker; and

(B) The taxpayer complies with the requirements of §1.988-5(a), (b) or (c) and so notifies the broker prior to the end of the calendar year in which the sale occurs.

(iii) *Example.*—The following example illustrates the rules of this paragraph (d)(8):

*Example.* (i) Z, an individual, is a U.S. citizen. On July 4, 2012, Z purchases stock of C, SA, a French corporation traded on an established securities market, in an account with Q, a broker. Q uses a daily spot rate for converting euro and U.S. dollars. Z pays €1,200 for the stock. On the settlement date for the purchase, the spot rate is €1 = $1.30. On October 4, 2012, Z sells the stock for €1,000. On the settlement date for the sale, the spot rate is €1 = $1.35. On October 5, 2012, Z purchases additional shares of C, SA, that cause the €200 loss on the stock sold on October 4, 2012, to be disallowed under section 1091.

(ii) Under paragraph (d)(8)(i)(A) of this section, Q must determine adjusted basis by converting the €1,200 paid on behalf of Z into U.S. dollars using the €1 = $1.30 spot rate on the settlement date of the purchase. Q must convert the €1,000 gross proceeds into U.S. dollars using the €1 = $1.35 spot rate on the settlement date for the sale. Thus, Q must report adjusted basis equal to $1,560, gross proceeds equal to $1,350, and $210 in loss disallowed by section 1091.

(9) *Coordination with the reporting rules for widely held fixed investment trusts under §1.671-5.*—Information required to be reported under section 6045(a) for a sale of a security in a widely held fixed investment trust (WHFIT) (as defined under §1.671-5 and the sale of an interest in a WHFIT must be reported as provided by this section unless the information is also required to be reported under §1.671-5. To the extent that this section requires additional information under section 6045(g), those requirements are deemed to be met through compliance with the rules in §1.671-5.

(e) *Reporting of barter exchanges.*—(1) *Requirement of reporting.*—A barter exchange shall, except as otherwise provided, report in the manner prescribed in this section.

(2) *Exchanges required to be reported.*—(i) *In general.*—Except as provided in paragraphs (e)(2)(ii) and (g) of this section, a barter exchange must make a return of information for exchanges of personal property or services through the barter exchange during the calendar year among its members or clients or between these persons and the barter exchange. For this purpose, property or services are exchanged through a barter exchange if payment for property or services is made by means of a credit on the books of the barter exchange or scrip issued by the barter exchange or if the barter exchange arranges a direct exchange of property or services among its members or clients or exchanges property or services with a member or client.

(ii) *Exemption.*—A barter exchange through which there are fewer than 100 exchanges during the calendar year is not required to report for, or make a return of information with respect to exchanges during, such calendar year. The Commissioner may require multiple barter exchanges to be combined for purposes of the preceding sentence upon a determination that a material purpose for the formation or continuation of one or more of the barter exchanges to be combined was to receive one or more exemptions pursuant to this subparagraph.

(f) *Information required.*—(1) *In general.*—A person that is a barter exchange during a calendar year shall report on Form 1096 showing the information required thereon for such year.

(2) *Transactional reporting.*—(i) *In general.*—As to each exchange for which a barter exchange is required to make a return of information under this section, the barter exchange must show on Form 1099-B, "Proceeds From Broker and Barter Exchange Transactions,"

or any successor form the name, address, and taxpayer identification number of each member or client providing property or services in the exchange, the property or services provided, the amount received by the member or client for the property or services, the date on which the exchange occurred, and other information required by the form in the manner and number of copies required by the form.

(ii) *Exception for corporate member or client.*—As to each corporate member or client providing property or services in an exchange for which a return of information is required under this section, the barter exchange may report the name, address, and taxpayer identification number of the corporate member or client, the aggregate amount received by the corporate member or client during the reporting period for property or services provided by such corporate member or client in exchange for which a return of information is required, and such other information as may be required by Form 1099, in the form, manner, and number of copies required by Form 1099.

(iii) *Definition.*—For purposes of paragraph (f)(2)(ii) of this section, the term "corporate member or client" means a member or client of a barter exchange which is a corporation as defined in section 7701(a)(3) (including an insurance company). The term corporation includes a pool, syndicate, partnership, or unincorporated association composed exclusively of corporations. A barter exchange may treat a member or client as a corporation (and therefore as a corporate member or client) if such member or client provides an exemption certificate as described in §31.3406(h)-3(a) of this chapter or provided that—

(A) The name of the member or client contains the term "insurance company," "indemnity company," "reinsurance company," or "assurance company";

(B) The name of the member or client contains one of the following unambiguous expressions of corporate status: Incorporated, Inc., Corporation, Corp., or P.C., but not Company or Co.; or

(C) The member or client is known to the barter exchange to be a corporation through a corporate resolution or similar document on file with the barter exchange clearly indicating corporate status.

(3) *Exchange date.*—For purposes of this section an exchange is considered to occur with respect to a member or client of a barter exchange on the date cash, property, a credit, or scrip is actually or constructively received by the member or client as a result of the exchange. (See §1.451-2 for rules pertaining to constructive receipt.)

(4) *Amount received.*—The amount received by a member or client in an exchange includes cash received, the fair market value of any property or services received, and the fair market value of any credits to the account of the member or client on the books of the barter exchange or scrip issued to the member or client by the barter exchange, but does not include any amount received by the member or client in a subsequent exchange of credits or scrip. For purposes of this section, the fair market value of a credit or scrip is the value assigned to such credit or scrip by the issuing barter exchange for the purpose of exchanges unless the Commissioner requires the use of a different value that the Commissioner determines more accurately reflects fair market value.

(5) *Meaning of terms.*—For purposes of this paragraph (f)—

(i) A credit is an amount on the books of the barter exchange that is transferable from one member or client of the barter exchange to another such member or client, or to the barter exchange in payment for property or services;

(ii) Scrip is a token issued by the barter exchange that is transferable from one member or client of the barter exchange to another such member or client, or to the barter exchange, in payment for property or services; and

(iii) Property does not include a credit or scrip.

(6) *Reporting period.*—A barter exchange shall use the calendar year as the reporting period.

(g) *Exempt foreign persons.*—(1) *Brokers.*—No return of information is required to be made by a broker with respect to a customer who is considered to be an exempt foreign person under this paragraph (g)(1). A broker may treat a customer as an exempt foreign person under the circumstances described in paragraphs (g)(1)(i) through (iii) of this section.

(i) With respect to a sale effected at an office of a broker either inside or outside the United States, the broker may treat the customer as an exempt foreign person if the broker can, prior to the payment, reliably associate the payment with documentation upon which it can rely in order to treat the customer as a foreign beneficial owner in accordance with §1.1441-1(e)(1)(ii), as made to a foreign payee in accordance with §1.6049-5(d)(1), or presumed to be made to a foreign payee under §1.6049-5(d)(2) or (3). For purposes of this paragraph (g)(1)(i), the provisions in §1.6049-5(c) regarding rules applicable to documentation of foreign status shall apply with respect to a sale when the broker completes the acts necessary to effect the sale at an office outside the United States, as described in paragraph (g)(3)(iii)(A) of this section, and no office of the same broker within the United States negotiated the sale with the customer or received instructions with respect to the sale from the customer. The provisions in §1.6049-5(c) regarding the definitions of U.S. payor, U.S. middleman, non-U.S. payor, and non-U.S. middleman shall also apply for purposes of this paragraph (g)(1)(i). The provisions of §1.1441-1 shall apply by substituting the terms "broker" and "customer" for the terms "withholding agent" and "payee," respectively, and without regard for the fact that the provisions apply to amounts subject to withholding under chapter 3 of the Code. The provisions of §1.6049-5(d) shall apply by substituting the terms "broker" and "customer" for the terms "payor" and "payee," respectively. For purposes of this paragraph (g)(1)(i), a broker that is required to obtain, or chooses to obtain, a beneficial owner withholding certificate described in §1.1441-1(e)(2)(i) from an individual may rely on the withholding certificate only to the extent the certificate includes a certification that the beneficial owner has not been, and at the time the certificate is furnished, reasonably expects not to be present in the United States for a period aggregating 183 days or more during each calendar year to which the certificate pertains. The certification is not required if a broker receives documentary evidence under §1.6049-5(c)(1) or (4).

(ii) With respect to a redemption or retirement of stock or an obligation (the interest or original issue discount on which is described in §1.6049-5(b)(6), (7), (10), or (11) or the dividends on which are described in §1.6042-3(b)(1)(iv)) that is effected at an office of a broker outside the United States by the issuer (or its paying or transfer agent), the broker may treat the customer as an exempt foreign person if the broker is not also acting in its capacity as a custodian, nominee, or other agent of the payee.

(iii) With respect to a sale effected by a broker at an office of the broker either inside or outside the United States, the broker may treat the customer as an exempt foreign person for the period that those proceeds are assets blocked as described in §1.1441-2(e)(3). For purposes of this paragraph (g)(1)(iii) and section 3406, a sale is deemed to occur in accordance with paragraph (d)(4) of this section. The exemption in this paragraph (g)(1)(iii) shall terminate when payment of the proceeds is deemed to occur in accordance with the provisions of §1.1441-2(e)(3).

(2) *Barter exchange.*—No return of information is required by a barter exchange with respect to a client or a member that the barter exchange may treat as a foreign person pursuant to the procedures described in paragraph (g)(1) of this section.

(3) *Applicable rules.*—(i) *Joint owners.*—Amounts paid to joint owners for which a certificate or documentation is required as a condition for being exempt from reporting under paragraph (g)(1)(i) or (2) of this section are presumed made to U.S. payees who are not exempt recipients if, prior to payment, the broker or barter exchange cannot reliably associate the payment either with a Form W-9 furnished by one of the joint owners in the manner required in §§31.3406(d)-1 through 31.3406(d)-5 of this chapter, or with documentation described in paragraph (g)(1)(i) of this section furnished by each joint owner upon which it can rely to treat each joint owner as a foreign payee or foreign beneficial owner. For purposes of applying this paragraph (g)(3)(i), the grace period described in §1.6049-5(d)(2)(ii) shall apply only if each payee qualifies for such grace period.

(ii) *Special rules for determining who the customer is.*—For purposes of this paragraph (g), the determination of who the customer is shall be made on the basis of the provisions in §1.6049-5(d) by substituting in that section the terms *payor* and *payee* with the terms *broker* and *customer.*

(iii) *Place of effecting sale.*—(A) *Sale outside the United States.*—For purposes of this paragraph (g), a sale is considered to be effected by a broker at an office outside the United States if, in accordance with instructions directly transmitted to such office from outside the United States by the broker's customer, the office completes the acts necessary to effect the sale outside the United States. The acts necessary to effect the sale may be considered to have been completed outside the United States without regard to whether—

(1) Pursuant to instructions from an office of the broker outside the United States, an office of the same broker within the United States undertakes one or more steps of the sale in the United States; or

(2) The gross proceeds of the sale are paid by a draft drawn on a United States bank account or by a wire or other electronic transfer from a United States account.

(B) *Sale inside the United States.*—For purposes of this paragraph (g), a sale that is considered to be effected by a broker at an office outside the United States under paragraph (g)(3)(iii)(A) of this section shall nevertheless be considered to be effected by a broker at an office inside the United States if either—

(1) The customer has opened an account with a United States office of that broker;

(2) The customer has transmitted instructions concerning this and other sales to the foreign office of the broker from within the United States by mail, telephone, electronic transmission or otherwise (unless the transmissions from the United States have taken place in isolated and infrequent circumstances);

(3) The gross proceeds of the sale are paid to the customer by a transfer of funds into an account (other than an international account as defined in §1.6049-5(e)(4)) maintained by the customer in the United States or mailed to the customer at an address in the United States;

(4) The confirmation of the sale is mailed to a customer at an address in the United States; or

(5) An office of the same broker within the United States negotiates the sale with the customer or receives instructions with respect to the sale from the customer.

(iv) *Special rules where the customer is a foreign intermediary or certain U.S. branches.*—A foreign intermediary, as defined in §1.1441-1(c)(13), is an exempt foreign person, except when the broker has actual knowledge (within the meaning of §1.6049-5(c)(3)) that the person for whom the intermediary acts is a U.S. person that is not exempt from reporting under paragraph (c)(3) of this section or the broker is required to presume under §1.6049-5(d)(3) that the payee is a U.S. person that is not an exempt recipient. If a foreign intermediary, as described in §1.1441-1(c)(13), or a U.S. branch that is not treated as a U.S. person receives a payment from a payor or middleman, which payment the payor or middleman can reliably associate with a valid withholding certificate described in §1.1441-1(e)(3)(ii) or (iii) or §1.1441-1(e)(3)(v), respectively, furnished by such intermediary or branch, then the intermediary or branch is not required to report such payment when it, in turn, pays the amount, unless, and to the extent, the intermediary or branch knows that the payment is required to be reported under this section and was not so reported. For example, if a U.S. branch described in §1.1441-1(b)(2)(iv) fails to provide information regarding U.S. persons that are not exempt from reporting under paragraph (c)(3) of this section to the person from whom the U.S. branch receives the payment, the U.S. branch must report the payment on an information return. See, however, paragraph (c)(3)(ii) of this section for when reporting under section 6045 is coordinated with reporting under chapter 4 of the Code or an applicable IGA (as defined in §1.6049-4(f)(7)). The exception of this paragraph (g)(3)(iv) for amounts paid by a foreign intermediary shall not apply to a qualified intermediary that assumes reporting responsibility under chapter 61 of the Code except as provided under the agreement described in §1.1441-1(e)(5)(iii).

(4) *Examples.*—The application of the provisions of this paragraph (g) may be illustrated by the following examples:

*Example 1.* FC is a foreign corporation that is not a U.S. payor or U.S. middleman described in §1.6049-5(c)(5) that regularly issues and retires its own debt obligations. A is an individual whose residence address is inside the United States, who holds a bond issued by FC that is in registered form (within the meaning of section 163(f) and the regulations under that section). The bond is retired by FP, a foreign corporation that is a broker within the meaning of paragraph (a)(1) of this section and the designated paying agent of FC. FP mails the proceeds to A at A's U.S. address. The sale would be considered to be effected at an office outside the United States under paragraph (g)(3)(iii)(A) of this section except that the proceeds of the sale are mailed to a U.S. address. For that reason, the sale is considered to be effected at an office of the broker inside the United States under paragraph (g)(3)(iii)(B) of this section. Therefore, FC is a broker under paragraph (a)(1) of this section with respect to this transaction because, although it is not a U.S. payor or U.S. middleman, as described in §1.6049-5(c)(5), it is deemed to effect the sale in the United States. FP is a broker for the same reasons. However, under the multiple broker exception under paragraph (c)(3)(iii) of this section, FP, rather than FC, is required to report the payment because FP is responsible for paying the holder the proceeds from the retired obligations. Under paragraph (g)(1)(i) of this section, FP may not treat A as an exempt foreign person and must make an information return under section 6045 with respect to the retirement of the FC bond, unless FP obtains the certificate or documentation described in paragraph (g)(1)(i) of this section.

*Example 2.* The facts are the same as in *Example 1* except that FP mails the proceeds to A at an address outside the United States. Under paragraph (g)(3)(iii)(A) of this section, the sale is considered to be effected at an office of the broker outside the United States.

Therefore, under paragraph (a)(1) of this section, neither FC nor FP is a broker with respect to the retirement of the FC bond. Accordingly, neither is required to make an information return under section 6045.

*Example 3.* The facts are the same as in *Example 2* except that FP is also the agent of A. The result is the same as in *Example 2.* Neither FP nor FC are brokers under paragraph (a)(1) of this section with respect to the sale since the sale is effected outside the United States and neither of them are U.S. payors (within the meaning of §1.6049-5(c)(5)).

*Example 4.* The facts are the same as in *Example 1* except that the registered bond held by A was issued by DC, a domestic corporation that regularly issues and retires its own debt obligations. Also, FP mails the proceeds to A at an address outside the United States. Interest on the bond is not described in paragraph (g)(1)(ii) of this section. The sale is considered to be effected at an office outside the United States under paragraph (g)(3)(iii)(A) of this section. DC is a broker under paragraph (a)(1)(i)(B) of this section. DC is not required to report the payment under the multiple broker exception under paragraph (c)(3)(iii) of this section. FP is not required to make an information return under section 6045 because FP is not a U.S. payor described in §1.6049-5(c)(5) and the sale is effected outside the United States. Accordingly, FP is not a broker under paragraph (a)(1) of this section.

*Example 5.* The facts are the same as in *Example 4* except that FP is also the agent of A. DC is a broker under paragraph (a)(1) of this section. DC is not required to report under the multiple broker exception under paragraph (c)(3)(iii) of this section. FP is not required to make an information return under section 6045 because FP is not a U.S. payor described in §1.6049-5(c)(5) and the sale is effected outside the United States and therefore FP is not a broker under paragraph (a)(1) of this section.

*Example 6.* The facts are the same as in *Example 4* except that the bond is retired by DP, a broker within the meaning of paragraph (a)(1) of this section and the designated paying agent of DC. DP is a U.S. payor under §1.6049-5(c)(5). DC is not required to report under the multiple broker exception under paragraph (c)(3)(iii) of this section. DP is required to make an information return under section 6045 because it is the person responsible for paying the proceeds from the retired obligations unless DP obtains the certificate or documentary evidence described in paragraph (g)(1)(i) of this section.

*Example 7.* Customer A owns U.S. corporate bonds issued in registered form after July 18, 1984, and carrying a stated rate of interest. The bonds are held through an account with foreign bank, X, and are held in street name. X is a wholly-owned subsidiary of a U.S. company and is not a qualified intermediary within the meaning of §1.1441-1(e)(5)(ii). X has no documentation regarding A. A instructs X to sell the bonds. In order to effect the sale, X acts through its agent in the United States, Y. Y sells the bonds and remits the sales proceeds to X. X credits A's account in the foreign country. X does not provide documentation to Y and has no actual knowledge that A is a foreign person but it does appear that A is an entity (rather than an individual).

(i) *Y's obligations to withhold and report.* Y treats X as the customer, and not A, because Y cannot treat X as an intermediary because it has received no documentation from X. Y is not required to report the sales proceeds under the multiple broker exception under paragraph (c)(3)(iii) of this section, because X is an exempt recipient. Further, Y is not required to report the amount of accrued interest paid to X on Form 1042-S under §1.1461-1(c)(2)(ii) because accrued interest is not an amount subject to reporting under chapter 3 unless the withholding agent knows that the obligation is being sold with a primary purpose of avoiding tax.

(ii) *X's obligations to withhold and report.* Although X has effected, within the meaning of paragraph (a)(1) of this section, the sale of a security at an office outside the United States under paragraph (g)(3)(iii) of this section, X is treated as a broker, under paragraph (a)(1) of this section, because as a wholly-owned subsidiary of a U.S. corporation, X is a controlled foreign corporation and therefore is a U.S. payor. See §1.6049-5(c)(5). Under the presumptions described in §1.6049-5(d)(2) (as applied to amounts not subject to withholding under chapter 3), X must apply the presumption rules of §1.1441-1(b)(3)(i) through (iii), with respect to the sales proceeds, to treat A as a partnership that is a U.S. non-exempt recipient because the presumption of foreign status for offshore obligations under §1.1441-1(b)(3)(iii)(D) does not apply. See paragraph (g)(1)(i) of this section. Therefore, unless X is an FFI (as defined in §1.1471-1(b)(47)) that is excepted from reporting the sales proceeds under paragraph (c)(3)(ii) of this section, the payment of proceeds to A by X is reportable on a Form 1099 under paragraph (c)(2) of this section. X has no obligation to backup withhold on the payment based on the exemption under §31.3406(g)-1(e) of this chapter, unless X has actual knowledge that A is a U.S. person that is not an exempt recipient. X is also required to separately report the accrued interest (see para-

graph (d)(3) of this section) on Form 1099 under section 6049 because A is also presumed to be a U.S. person who is not an exempt recipient with respect to the payment because accrued interest is not an amount subject to withholding under chapter 3 and, therefore, the presumption of foreign status for offshore obligations under §1.1441-1(b)(3)(iii)(D) does not apply. See §1.6049-5(d)(2)(i).

*Example 8.* The facts are the same as in *Example 7,* except that X is a foreign corporation that is not a U.S. payor under §1.6049-5(c).

(i) *Y's obligations to withhold and report.* Y is not required to report the sales proceeds under the multiple broker exception under paragraph (c)(3)(iii) of this section, because X is the person responsible for paying the proceeds from the sale to A.

(ii) *X's obligations to withhold and report.* Although A is presumed to be a U.S. payee under the presumptions of §1.6049-5(d)(2), X is not considered to be a broker under paragraph (a)(1) of this section because it is a not a U.S. payor under §1.6049-5(c)(5). Therefore X is not required to report the sale under paragraph (c)(2) of this section.

(h) *Identity of customer.*—(1) *In general.*—For purposes of this section, a broker or barter exchange shall treat the person who appears on the books and records of the broker or barter exchange with respect to property or services as the principal with respect thereto.

(2) *Examples.*—The following examples illustrate the rule of this paragraph (h):

*Example 1.* The records of A, a broker, show an account in the name of "B". B is a nominee for C. All reporting with respect to such account shall treat B as the customer.

*Example 2.* J, an individual, places an order with H, a broker, to sell J's stock that is held by P, a broker/dealer, in an account for J with P designated as nominee for J, and to credit the gross proceeds from the sale to J's account with P. The account is in the name of P, so that H's customer is P.

(i) [Reserved.]

(j) *Time and place for filing; cross-reference to penalty.*—Forms 1096 and 1099 required under this section shall be filed after the last calendar day of the reporting period elected by the broker or barter exchange and on or before February 28 of the following calendar year with the appropriate Internal Revenue Service Center, the address of which is listed in the instructions for Form 1096. See paragraph (l) of this section for the requirement to file certain returns on magnetic media. For provisions relating to the penalty provided for the failure to file timely a correct information return under section 6045(a), see §301.6721-1 of this chapter. See §301.6724-1 of this chapter for the waiver of a penalty if the failure is due to reasonable cause and is not due to willful neglect.

(k) *Requirement and time for furnishing statement; cross reference to penalty.*—(1) *General requirements.*—A broker or barter exchange making a return of information under this section must furnish to the person whose identifying number is (or is required to be) shown on the return a written statement showing the information required by paragraph (c)(5), (d), or (f) of this section and containing a legend stating that the information is being reported to the Internal Revenue Service. If the return of information is not made on magnetic media, this requirement may be satisfied by furnishing to the person a copy of all Forms 1099 or any successor form for the person filed with the Internal Revenue Service Center. A statement is considered to be furnished to a person to whom a statement is required to be made under this paragraph (k) if it is mailed to the person at the last address of the person known to the broker or barter exchange.

(2) *Time for furnishing statements.*—A broker or barter exchange may furnish the statements required under this paragraph (k) yearly, quarterly, monthly, or on any other basis, without regard to the reporting period the broker or barter exchange elects; however, all statements required to be furnished under this paragraph (k) for a calendar year must be furnished on or before February 15 of the following calendar year.

(3) *Consolidated reporting.*—(i) The term *consolidated reporting statement* means a grouping of statements the same broker or barter exchange furnishes to the same customer or group of customers on the same date for the same reporting year that includes a statement required under this section. A consolidated reporting statement is limited to statements based on the same relationship of broker or barter exchange to customer as the statement required to be furnished under this section. For purposes of this paragraph (k)(3)(i), a broker may treat a shareholder of a broker as a customer of the broker and may treat a grouping of statements for a customer as including a statement required to be furnished under this section if the customer has an account with the broker for which a statement would be required to be furnished under this section if the customer purchased and sold stock in a corporation in the account during the year.

(ii) A consolidated reporting statement must be furnished on or before February 15 of the year following the calendar year reported. Any statement that otherwise must be furnished on or before January 31 must be furnished on or before February 15 if it is furnished in the consolidated reporting statement.

(iii) *Examples.*—The following examples illustrate the rules of this paragraph (k)(3):

*Example 1.* D has a taxable account with B, a broker, consisting solely of stock in a single corporation. In 2010, D receives reportable dividends from this stock and sells the stock. Under this section and § 1.6042-4, B must furnish a Form 1099-B, "Proceeds From Broker and Barter Exchange Transactions," and Form 1099-DIV, "Dividends and Distributions," to D in 2011 for the sale and the dividends. Under paragraph (k)(2) of this section, B is required to furnish the required statement under this section to D by February 15, 2011. B must furnish the statement reporting the dividends by the January 31, 2011, due date provided in § 1.6042-4. However, under paragraph (k)(3)(ii) of this section, B must furnish the statement reporting the dividends by February 15, 2011, if furnished in a consolidated reporting statement as defined in paragraph (k)(3)(i) of this section.

*Example 2.* Assume the same facts as in *Example 1* except that D has invested solely in a money market fund for which sales are excepted from the reporting required under this section. D therefore is not required to issue a statement under this section if D sells an interest in the money market fund. Under paragraph (k)(3)(i) of this section, B may treat a grouping of statements for D as including a required statement under this section because D has an account for which a statement would be required under this section if D purchased and sold stock in a corporation in the account during the year. Therefore, under paragraph (k)(3)(ii) of this section, B must furnish the statement reporting the dividends by February 15, 2011.

*Example 3.* E has a nontaxable IRA account with B, a broker. This account is the only account E holds with B. E sells stock in 2010 in this account. E also receives a cash distribution from the account in 2010. The cash distribution from the IRA is reportable on Form 1099-R, "Distributions From Pensions, Annuities, Retirement or Profit-Sharing Plans, IRAs, Insurance Contracts, etc.," under § 1.408-7. Because the account is not taxable, sales in the account are not subject to reporting under this section. Therefore, because no statement is required under this section, under paragraph (k)(3) of this section, B may not furnish any statements to E in a consolidated reporting statement. B must furnish the Form 1099-R by the date required under § 1.408-7.

*Example 4.* Assume the same facts as in *Example 3* except that E and F have a joint taxable account with B. Because sales in the joint taxable account are subject to reporting under this section, under paragraph (k)(3) of this section, B must furnish by February 15, 2011, all customer statements for 2010 that B otherwise must furnish jointly to E and F on or before January 31, 2011, if furnished on the same date in a consolidated reporting statement with the required statements under this section for any sales in the joint taxable account. However, B may not include any statement for E's IRA account in the consolidated reporting statement furnished jointly to E and F because the statements are not furnished to the same customer or group of customers.

(4) *Cross-reference to penalty.*—For provisions for failure to furnish timely a correct payee statement, see § 301.6724-1 of this chapter (Procedure and Administration Regulations). See § 301.6724-1 of this chapter for the waiver of a penalty if the failure is due to reasonable cause and is not due to willful neglect.

(l) *Use of magnetic media.*—For information returns filed after December 31, 1996, see § 301.6011-2 of this chapter for rules relating to filing information returns on magnetic media and for rules relating to waivers granted for undue hardship. A broker or barter exchange that fails to file a Form 1099 on magnetic media, when required, may be subject to a penalty under section 6721 for each such failure. See paragraph (j) of this section.

(m) *Additional rules for option transactions.*—(1) *In general.*—This paragraph (m) provides rules for a broker to determine and report the information required under this section for an option that is a covered security under paragraph (a)(15)(i)(E) of this section.

(2) *Scope.*—(i) *In general.*—Paragraph (m) of this section applies to the following types of options granted or acquired on or after January 1, 2014:

(A) An option on one or more specified securities (which includes an index substantially all the components of which are specified securities);

(B) An option on financial attributes of specified securities, such as interest rates or dividend yields; or

(C) A warrant or a stock right.

(ii) *Delayed effective date for certain options.*—(A) Notwithstanding paragraph (m)(2)(i) of this section, if an option, stock right, or warrant is issued as part of an investment unit described in § 1.1273-2(h), paragraph (m) of this section applies to the option, stock right, or warrant if it is acquired on or after January 1, 2016.

(B) Notwithstanding paragraph (m)(2)(i) of this section, if the property referenced by an option (that is, the property underlying the option) is a debt instrument that is issued by a non-U.S. person or that provides for one or more payments denominated in, or determined by reference to, a currency other than the U.S. dollar, paragraph (m) of this section applies to the option if it is granted or acquired on or after January 1, 2016.

(iii) *Compensatory option.*—Notwithstanding paragraphs (m)(2)(i) and (m)(2)(ii) of this section, paragraph (m) of this section does not apply to compensatory options.

(3) *Option subject to section 1256.*—If an option described in paragraph (m)(2) of this section is also described in section 1256(b), a broker must apply the rules described in paragraph (c)(5) of this section by treating the option as if it were a regulated futures contract and must report the information required under paragraph (c)(5) of this section. A broker is permitted, but not required, to report the amounts for options and the amounts for regulated futures contracts determined under paragraph (c)(5) of this section as a net amount for each reportable item.

(4) *Option not subject to section 1256.*—The following rules apply to an option that is described in paragraph (m)(2) of this section but is not also described in paragraph (m)(3) of this section:

(i) *Physical settlement.*—For purposes of paragraph (d) of this section, if a specified security (other than an option) is acquired or disposed of pursuant to the exercise of an option, the broker must adjust the basis of the acquired asset or the gross proceeds amount as appropriate to account for any payment related to the option, including the premium.

(ii) *Cash settlement.*—For purposes of paragraph (d) of this section, for an option that is settled for cash, a broker must reflect on Form 1099-B all payments made or received on the option. For a purchased option, a broker must report as basis the premium paid plus any costs (for example, commissions) related to the acquisition of the option and must report as proceeds the gross proceeds from settlement minus any costs related to the settlement of the option. For a written option, a broker must report as proceeds the premium received decreased by any amounts paid on the option and report $0 as the basis of the option.

(iii) *Rules for warrants and stock rights acquired in a section 305 distribution.*—For a right (including a warrant) to acquire stock received in the same account as the underlying security in a distribution that is described in section 305(a), a broker is permitted, but not required, to apply the rules described in sections 305 and 307 when reporting or accounting for the basis of the option and the underlying equity. If a stock right or warrant is acquired from the initial distributee, the buyer or transferee must treat it as an option covered by either paragraph (m)(4)(i) or (m)(4)(ii) of this section.

(iv) *Examples.*—The following examples illustrate the rules in this paragraph (m)(4):

*Example 1.* (i) On January 15, 2014, C, an individual who is neither a dealer nor a trader in securities, writes a 2-year exchange-traded option on 100 shares of Company X through Broker D. C receives a premium for the option of $100 and pays no commission. In C's hands, the option produces capital gain or loss and Company X stock is a capital asset. On December 16, 2014, C pays $110 to close out the option.

(ii) D is required to report information about the closing transaction because the option is a covered security as described in paragraph (a)(15)(i)(E) of this section and was part of a closing transaction described in paragraph (a)(8) of this section. Under paragraph (m)(4)(ii) of this section, D must report as gross proceeds on C's Form 1099-B -$10 (the $100 received as option premium minus the $110 C paid to close out the option) and report $0 in the basis box on the Form 1099-B. Under section 1234(b)(1) and paragraph (d)(2) of this section, D must also report the loss on the closing transaction as a short-term capital loss.

*Example 2.* (i) On January 15, 2014, E, an individual who is neither a dealer nor a trader in securities, buys a 2-year exchange-traded option on 100 shares of Company X through Broker F. E pays a premium of $100 for the option and pays no commission. In E's hands, both the option and Company X stock are capital assets. On December 16, 2014, E receives $110 to close out the option.

(ii) F is required to report information about the closing transaction because the option is a covered security as described in paragraph (a)(15)(i)(E) of this section and was part of a closing transaction described in paragraph (a)(8) of this section. Because the option is on the shares of a single company, it is an equity option described in section 1256(g)(6) and is not described in section 1256(b)(1)(C). Therefore, the rules of paragraph (m)(3) of this section do not apply, and F must report under paragraph (m)(4) of this section. Under paragraph (m)(4)(ii) of this section, F must report $110 as gross proceeds on the Form 1099-B for the gross proceeds E received and $100 in the basis box on the Form 1099-B to reflect the $100 option premium paid. Under section 1234(b)(1) and paragraph (d)(2) of this section, F must also report the gain on the closing transaction as a short-term capital gain.

(5) *Multiple options documented in a single contract.*—If more than one option described in paragraph (m)(2) of this section is documented in a single contract, a broker must separately report the required information for each option as that option is sold.

(6) *Determination of index status.*—Penalties will not be asserted under sections 6721 and 6722 if a broker in good faith determines that an index is, or is not, a narrow-based index described in section 1256(g)(6) and reports in a manner consistent with this determination.

(n) *Reporting for debt instrument transactions.*—(1) *In general.*—For purposes of this section, this paragraph (n) provides rules for a broker to determine and report information for a debt instrument that is a covered security under paragraph (a)(15)(i)(C) or (D) of this section. Neither a debt instrument subject to section 1272(a)(6) nor a short-term obligation described in section 1272(a)(2)(C) is subject to this paragraph (n) because neither is a specified security under paragraph (a)(14)(ii) of this section (a requirement for a debt instrument to be a covered security).

(2) *Debt instruments subject to January 1, 2014, reporting.*—(i) *In general.*—For purposes of paragraph (a)(15)(i)(C) of this section, except as provided in paragraph (n)(2)(ii) of this section, a debt instrument is described in this paragraph (n)(2)(i) if the debt instrument is one of the following:

(A) A debt instrument that provides for a single fixed payment schedule for which a yield and maturity can be determined for the instrument under §1.1272-1(b);

(B) A debt instrument that provides for alternate payment schedules for which a yield and maturity can be determined for the instrument under §1.1272-1(c); or

(C) A debt instrument for which the yield of the debt instrument can be determined under §1.1272-1(d).

(ii) *Exceptions.*—A debt instrument is not described in paragraph (n)(2)(i) of this section if the debt instrument is one of the following:

(A) A debt instrument that provides for more than one rate of stated interest (including a debt instrument that provides for stepped interest rates);

(B) A convertible debt instrument described in §1.1272-1(e);

(C) A stripped bond or stripped coupon subject to section 1286;

(D) A debt instrument that requires payment of either interest or principal in a currency other than the U.S. dollar;

(E) A debt instrument that, at one or more times in the future, entitles a holder to a tax credit;

(F) A debt instrument that provides for a payment-in-kind (PIK) feature (that is, under the terms of the debt instrument, a holder may receive one or more additional debt instruments of the issuer);

(G) A debt instrument issued by a non-U.S. issuer;

(H) A debt instrument for which the terms of the instrument are not reasonably available to the broker within 90 days of the date the debt instrument was acquired by the customer;

(I) A debt instrument that is issued as part of an investment unit described in §1.1273-2(h); or

(J) A debt instrument evidenced by a physical certificate unless such certificate is held (whether directly or through a nominee, agent, or subsidiary) by a securities depository or by a clearing organization described in §1.1471-1(b)(18).

(iii) *Remote or incidental.*—For purposes of paragraphs (n)(2)(i) and (n)(2)(ii) of this section, a remote or incidental contingency (as determined under §1.1275-2(h)) is ignored.

(iv) *Penalty rate.*—For purposes of paragraph (n)(2)(ii)(A) of this section, a debt instrument does not provide for more than one rate of stated interest merely because the instrument provides for a penalty interest rate or an adjustment to the stated interest rate in the event of a default or similar event.

(3) *Debt instruments subject to January 1, 2016, reporting.*—For purposes of paragraph (a)(15)(i)(D) of this section, a debt instrument is described in this paragraph (n)(3) if it is described in paragraph (n)(2)(ii) of this section or it otherwise is not described in paragraph (n)(2)(i) of this section. For example, this paragraph (n)(3) applies to variable rate debt instruments, inflation-indexed debt instruments, and contingent payment debt instruments because these instruments are not described in paragraph (n)(2)(i) of this section.

(4) *Holder elections.*—For purposes of this section, a broker is required to take into account an election described in this paragraph (n)(4), and the broker must take the election into account in accordance with the rules in paragraph (n)(5) of this section. A broker, however, may not take into account any other election. See paragraph (n)(11) of this section for the treatment of an election described in paragraph (n)(4)(iii) of this section (election to accrue market discount based on a constant yield) and an election described in paragraph (n)(4)(iv) of this section (election to treat all interest as OID).

(i) *Election to amortize bond premium.*—An election under section 171 and §1.171-4 to amortize bond premium on a taxable debt instrument (this election applies to all taxable debt instruments held by a taxpayer during the taxable year the election is effective and thereafter; this election may be revoked with the consent of the Commissioner).

(ii) *Election to currently include accrued market discount.*—An election under section 1278(b) to include market discount in income as it accrues (this election applies to all debt instruments acquired by a taxpayer during the taxable year the election is effective and thereafter; this election may be revoked with the consent of the Commissioner).

(iii) *Election to accrue market discount based on a constant yield.*—An election under section 1276(b)(2) to compute accruals of market discount using a constant yield method (this election is generally made on an instrument-byinstrument basis and must be made for the earliest taxable year for which the taxpayer is required to determine accrued market discount on the debt instrument; this election may not be revoked).

(iv) *Election to treat all interest as OID.*—An election under §1.1272-3 to treat all interest on a taxable debt instrument (adjusted for any acquisition premium or premium) as original issue discount (this election is generally made on an instrument-by-instrument basis and must be made for the taxable year the debt instrument is acquired by the taxpayer; this election may be revoked with the consent of the Commissioner). However, see paragraph (n)(11)(i)(A) of this section for a debt instrument acquired on or after January 1, 2014.

(v) *Election to translate interest income and expense at the spot rate.*—An election under §1.988-2(b)(2)(iii)(B) to translate interest income and expense at the spot rate on the last day of the interest accrual period or, in the case of a partial accrual period, the last day of the taxable year (this election applies to all taxable debt instruments held by a taxpayer during the taxable year the election is effective and thereafter; this election may be revoked with the consent of the Commissioner).

(5) *Broker assumptions and customer notice to brokers.*—(i) *Broker assumptions if the customer does not notify the broker.*—Except as provided in paragraph (n)(5)(ii)(A) of this section, a broker must report the information required under paragraph (d) of this section by assuming that a customer has made the election to amortize bond premium described in paragraph (n)(4)(i) of this section. In addition, except as provided in paragraph (n)(5)(ii)(B) of this section, a broker must report the information required under paragraph (d) of this section by assuming that a customer has not made an election described in paragraph (n)(4)(ii), (n)(4)(iii), (n)(4)(iv), or (n)(4)(v) of this section. However, see paragraph (n)(11) of this section for the treatment of an election described in paragraph (n)(4)(iii) of this section (election to accrue market discount based on a constant yield) and an election described in paragraph (n)(4)(iv) of this section (election to treat all interest as OID).

(ii) *Effect of customer notification of an election or revocation.*—(A) *Election to amortize bond premium.*—If a customer notifies a broker in writing that the customer does not want the broker to take into account the election to amortize bond premium, the broker must report the information required under paragraph (d) of this section without taking into account the election to amortize bond premium. The customer must provide this notification to the broker by the end of the calendar year for which the customer does not want to amortize bond premium. If for a subsequent calendar year, the customer wants the broker to take into account the election to amortize bond premium, the customer must notify the broker in writing by the end of the calendar year that the customer wants to amortize bond premium. If the customer provides such notification, the broker must report the information required under paragraph (d) of this section as if the customer made the election to amortize bond premium for that year.

(B) *Other debt elections.*—If a customer notifies a broker in writing that the customer has made or will make an election described in paragraph (n)(4)(ii), (iii), (iv), or (v) of this section, the broker must report the information required under paragraph (d) of this section by taking into account the election. A customer must notify the broker in writing of the election by the end of the calendar year in which a debt instrument subject to the election is acquired in, or transferred into, an account with the broker or, if later, by the end of the calendar year for which the election is effective. If a customer has revoked or will revoke an election described in paragraph (n)(4)(ii), (n)(4)(iv), or (n)(4)(v) of this section for a calendar year, the customer must notify the broker of the revocation in writing by the end of the calendar year for which the revocation is effective. If the customer provides such notification, the broker must report the information required under paragraph (d) of this section by taking into account the revocation.

(iii) *Electronic notification.*—For purposes of paragraph (n)(5)(ii) of this section, the written notification to the broker includes a writing in electronic format.

(6) *Reporting of accrued market discount.*—In addition to the information required to be reported under paragraph (d) of this section, if a debt instrument is subject to the market discount rules in sections 1276 through 1278, a broker also must report the information described in paragraph (n)(6)(i) or (n)(6)(ii) of this section, whichever is applicable. Such information must be shown in the manner and at the time required by Form 1099 and section 6045.

(i) *Sale.*—A broker must report the amount of market discount that has accrued on a debt instrument as of the date of the instrument's sale, as defined in paragraph (a)(9) of this section. See paragraphs (n)(5) and (n)(11)(i)(B) of this section to determine whether the amount reported should take into account a customer election under section 1276(b)(2). See paragraph (n)(8) of this section to determine the accrual period to be used to compute the accruals of market discount. This paragraph (n)(6)(i) does not apply if the customer notifies the broker under the rules in paragraph (n)(5) of this section that the customer elects under section 1278(b) to include market discount in income as it accrues.

(ii) *Current inclusion election.*—If a customer notifies a broker under the rules in paragraph (n)(5) of this section that the customer elects under section 1278(b) to include market discount in income as it accrues, the broker is required to report to the customer the amount of market discount that accrued on a debt instrument during a taxable year while held by the customer in the account. The broker also must adjust basis in accordance with section 1278(b)(4). If a customer notifies a broker under the rules in paragraph (n)(5) of this section that the customer is revoking its election under section 1278(b), the broker will not report the market discount accrued during the taxable year of the revocation and thereafter and will cease to adjust basis in accordance with section 1278(b)(4). See paragraph (n)(8) of this section to determine the accrual period to be used to compute the accruals of market discount. See paragraphs (n)(5) and (n)(11)(i)(B) of this section to determine whether the amount reported should take into account a customer election under section 1276(b)(2).

(7) *Adjusted basis.*—For purposes of this section, a broker must use the rules in paragraph (n) of this section to determine the adjusted basis of a debt instrument.

(i) *Original issue discount.*—If a debt instrument is subject to the original issue discount rules in sections 1271 through 1275, section 1286, or section 1288, a broker must increase a customer's basis in the debt instrument by the amount of original issue discount that accrued on the debt instrument while held by the customer in the account. See paragraph (n)(8) of this section to determine the accrual period to be used to compute the accruals of original issue discount.

(ii) *Amortizable bond premium.*—(A) *Taxable bond.*—A broker is required to adjust the customer's basis for any taxable bond acquired at a premium and held in the account in accordance with § 1.1016-5(b). If a customer, however, informs a broker under the rules in paragraph (n)(5)(ii)(A) of this section that the customer does not want to amortize bond premium, the broker must not adjust the customer's basis for any premium.

(B) *Tax-exempt bonds.*—A broker is required to adjust the customer's basis for any tax-exempt obligation acquired at a premium and held in the account in accordance with § 1.1016-5(b).

(iii) *Acquisition premium.*—If a debt instrument is acquired at an acquisition premium (as determined under § 1.1272-2(b)(3)), a broker must decrease the customer's basis in the debt instrument by the amount of acquisition premium that is taken into account each year to reduce the amount of the original issue discount that is otherwise includible in the customer's income for that year. See § 1.1272-2(b)(4) to determine the amount of the acquisition premium taken into account each year. However, if a broker took into account a customer election under § 1.1272-3 in 2014, the broker must decrease the customer's basis in the debt instrument by the amount of acquisition premium that is taken into account each year to reduce the amount of the original issue discount that is otherwise includible in the customer's income for that year in accordance with §§ 1.1272-2(b)(5) and 1.1272-3.

(iv) *Market discount.*—See paragraph (n)(6) of this section for rules to determine the adjusted basis of a debt instrument with market discount.

(v) *Principal and certain other payments.*—A broker must decrease the customer's basis in a debt instrument by the amount of any payment made to the customer during the period the debt instrument is held in the account, other than a payment of qualified stated interest as defined in § 1.1273-1(c).

(8) *Accrual period.*—For purposes of this section, a broker generally must use the same accrual period that is used to report any original issue discount or stated interest to a customer under section 6049 for a debt instrument. In any other situation, a broker must use a semi-annual accrual period or, if a debt instrument provides for scheduled payments of principal or interest at regular intervals of less than six months over the entire term of the debt instrument, a broker must use an accrual period equal in length to this shorter interval. For example, if a debt instrument provides for monthly payments of interest over the entire term of the debt instrument, the broker must use a monthly accrual period. The rules in § 1.1272-1(b)(4)(iii) apply for purposes of an initial short accrual period. In computing the length of an accrual period, any reasonable counting convention may be used (for example, 30 days per month/360 days per year, or actual days per month/365 days per year).

(9) *Premium on convertible bond.*—If a customer acquires a convertible bond (as defined in § 1.171-1(e)(1)(iii)(C)) at a premium (as determined under § 1.171-1(d)), then, solely for purposes of this section and § 1.6049-9, a broker must assume that the premium is attributable to the conversion feature. Based on this assumption, no portion of the premium is amortizable for purposes of this section and § 1.6049-9.

(10) *Effect of broker assumptions on customer.*—The rules in this paragraph (n) only apply for purposes of a broker's reporting obligation under section 6045. A customer is not bound by the assumptions that the broker uses to satisfy the broker's reporting obligations under section 6045. In addition, a notification to the broker under paragraph (n)(5) of this section does not constitute an effective election or revocation under the applicable rules for the election.

(11) *Additional rules for certain holder elections.*—(i) *In general.*—For purposes of this section, the rules in this paragraph (n)(11) apply notwithstanding any other rule in paragraph (n) of this section.

(A) *Election to treat all interest as OID.*—A broker must report the information required under paragraph (d) of this section without taking into account any election described in paragraph (n)(4)(iv) of this section (the election to treat all interest as OID in § 1.1272-3). As a result, for example, a broker must determine the amount of any acquisition premium taken into account each year for purposes of this section in accordance with § 1.1272-2(b)(4). This paragraph (n)(11)(i)(A) applies to a debt instrument acquired on or after January 1, 2015. A broker, however, may rely on this paragraph (n)(11)(i)(A) for a debt instrument acquired on or after January 1, 2014, and before January 1, 2015.

(B) *Election to accrue market discount based on a constant yield.*—A broker must report the information required under paragraph (d) of this section by assuming that a customer has made the election described in paragraph (n)(4)(iii) of this section (the election to accrue market discount based on a constant yield). However, if a customer notifies a broker in writing that the customer does not want the broker to take into account this election, the broker must report the information required under paragraph (d) of this section without taking into account this election. The customer must provide this notification to the broker by the end of the calendar year in which the customer acquired the debt instrument in an account with the broker. This paragraph (n)(11)(i)(B) applies to a debt instrument acquired on or after January 1, 2015. A broker, however, may rely on this paragraph (n)(11)(i)(B) to report accrued market discount for a debt instrument that is a covered security acquired on or after January 1, 2014, and before January 1, 2015, if the customer had not informed the broker that the customer had made a section 1278(b) election and there were no principal payments on the debt instrument during this period.

(ii) [Reserved].

(12) *Certain debt instruments treated as noncovered securities.*—(i) *In general.*—Notwithstanding paragraph (a)(15) of this section, a debt instrument is treated as a noncovered security for purposes of this section if the terms of the debt instrument are not reasonably available to the broker within 90 days of the date the debt instrument was acquired by the customer and the debt instrument is either—

(A) A debt instrument issued by a non-U.S. issuer; or

(B) A tax-exempt obligation issued before January 1, 2014.

(ii) *Effective/applicability date.*—Paragraph (n)(12)(i) of this section applies to a debt instrument described in paragraph (n)(12)(i)(A) or (B) of this section that is acquired on or after February 18, 2016. However, a broker may rely on paragraph (n)(12)(i) of this section for a debt instrument described in paragraph (n)(12)(i)(A) or (B) of this section acquired before February 18, 2016.

(o) *Additional reporting by stock transfer agents.*—[Reserved]

(p) *Electronic filing.*—Notwithstanding the time prescribed for filing in paragraph (j) of this section, Forms 1096 and 1099 required under this section for reporting periods ending during a calendar year shall, if filed electronically, be filed after the last calendar day of the reporting period elected by the broker or barter exchange and on or before March 31 of the following calendar year.

(q) *Effective/applicability date.*—Except as otherwise provided in paragraphs (m)(2)(ii), and (n)(12)(ii) of this section, this section applies on or after January 6, 2017. (For rules that apply after June 30, 2014, and before January 6, 2017, see this section as in effect and contained in 26 CFR part 1, as revised April 1, 2016). [Reg. § 1.6045-1.]

☐ [*T.D. 7873, 3-3-83. Amended by T.D. 7880, 3-22-83; T.D. 7932, 12-28-83; T.D. 7960, 5-23-84; T.D. 8445, 11-5-92; T.D. 8452, 12-11-92; T.D. 8683, 10-9-96; T.D. 8734, 10-6-97; T.D. 8772, 6-29-98; T.D. 8804, 12-30-98; T.D. 8856, 12-29-99; T.D. 8881, 5-15-2000 (corrected 4-5-2001); T.D. 8895, 8-17-2000; T.D. 9010, 7-25-2002; T.D. 9241, 1-23-2006; T.D. 9504, 10-12-2010; T.D. 9616, 4-17-2013, T.D. 9658, 2-28-2014, T.D. 9713, 3-12-2015, T.D. 9750, 2-17-2016 (corrected 4-26-2016), T.D. 9774, 7-7-2016 and T.D. 9808, 12-30-2016 (corrected 6-29-2017).]*

## [Reg. § 1.6045-2]

**§ 1.6045-2. Furnishing statement required with respect to certain substitute payments.**—(a) *Requirement of furnishing statements.*—(1) *In general.*—Any broker (as defined in paragraph (a)(4)(ii) of this section) that transfers securities (as defined in § 1.6045-1(a)(3)) of a customer (as defined in paragraph (a)(4)(iii) of this section) for use in a short sale and receives on behalf of the customer a substitute payment (as defined in paragraph (a)(4)(i)) shall, except as otherwise provided, furnish a statement to the customer identifying such payment as being a substitute payment.

(2) *Special rule for transfers for broker's own use.*—Any broker that borrows securities of a customer for use in a short sale entered into for the broker's own account shall be deemed to have transferred the stock to itself and received on behalf of the customer any substitute payment made with respect to the transferred securities, and shall be required to furnish a statement with respect to such payment in accordance with paragraph (a)(1) of this section.

(3) *Special rule for furnishing statements to individual customers with respect to payments in lieu of dividends.*—(i) *In general.*—Except as otherwise provided in paragraph (a)(3)(ii) of this section, for taxable years beginning before January 1, 2003, a broker that receives a substitute payment in lieu of a dividend on behalf of a customer who is an individual ("individual customer") need not furnish a statement to the customer.

(ii) *Reporting for certain dividends.*—Any broker that receives on behalf of an individual customer a substitute payment in lieu of—

(A) An exempt-interest dividend (as defined in paragraph (a)(4)(vii) of this section);

(B) A capital gain dividend (as defined in paragraph (a)(4)(vi) of this section);

(C) A distribution treated as a return of capital under section 301(c)(2) or (c)(3); or

(D) An FTC dividend (as defined in paragraph (a)(4)(viii) of this section) shall furnish a statement to the individual customer identifying the payment as being a substitute payment as prescribed by this section, provided that the broker has reason to know not later than the record date of the dividend payment that the payment is a substitute payment in lieu of an exempt-interest dividend, a capital gain dividend, a distribution treated as a return of capital, or an FTC dividend.

(4) *Meaning of terms.*—The following definitions apply for purposes of this section.

(i) The term "substitute payment" means a payment in lieu of—

(A) Tax-exempt interest, to the extent that interest has accrued on the obligation for the period during which the short sale is open;

(B) A dividend, the ex-dividend date for which occurs during the period after the transfer of stock for use in a short sale, and prior to the closing of the short sale; or

(C) Any other item specified in a rule-related notice published in the *Federal Register* (provided that such items shall be subject to the rules of this section only subsequent to the time of such publication).

For purposes of this section original issue discount accruing on an obligation (the interest upon which is exempt from tax under section 103) for the period during which the short sale is open shall be deemed a payment in lieu of tax-exempt interest.

(ii) The term "broker" means both a person described in § 1.6045-1(a)(1) and a person that, in the ordinary course of a trade or business during the calendar year, loans securities owned by others.

(iii) The term "customer" means, with respect to a transfer of securities for use in a short sale, the person that is the record owner of the securities so transferred.

(iv) The term "dividend" means a dividend (as defined in section 316) or a distribution that is treated as a return of capital under section 301(c)(2) or (c)(3).

(v) The term "tax-exempt interest" means interest to which the exception in section 6049(b)(2)(B) applies.

(vi) The term "capital gain dividend" means a capital gain dividend as defined in section 852(b)(3)(C) or section 857(b)(3)(C).

(vii) The term "exempt-interest dividend" means an exempt-interest dividend as defined in section 852(b)(5)(A).

(viii) The term "FTC dividend" means a dividend with respect to which the recipient is entitled to claim a foreign tax credit under section 901 (but not by virtue of taxes deemed paid under sections 902 or 960).

(5) *Examples.*—The following examples illustrate the definition of a substitute payment in lieu of tax-exempt interest found in paragraph (a)(4)(i)(A) of this section.

*Example (1).* On September 1, 1984, L, a broker, borrows 200 State Q Bonds (the interest upon which is exempt from tax under section 103) held in street name for customer R and transfers the bonds to W for use in a short sale. The bonds each have a face value of $100 and bear 12% stated annual interest paid semiannually on January 1 and July 1 of each year. The bonds were not issued with original issue discount. On November 1, 1984, W closes the short sale and returns State Q Bonds to L. On January 1, 1985, L receives a $1200 interest payment (6% × $100 × 200 bonds = $1200) from State Q with respect to R's bonds. Four hundred dollars (2 months the bonds were on loan/6 months in the interest period = $\frac{1}{3}$ × $1200 = $400) of the interest payment represents accrued interest on the obligations for the period during which the short sale was open, and is a substitute payment in lieu of tax-exempt interest within the meaning of paragraph (a)(4)(i)(A) of this section. L must furnish a statement under paragraph (a) of this section to R for calendar year 1985 with respect to the $400 substitute payment.

*Example (2).* Assume the same facts as in Example (1), except that W closes the short sale on February 1, 1985. On January 1, 1985, L receives a $1200 payment from W with respect to R's bonds. Eight hundred dollars (4 months the bonds were on loan prior to January 1, 1985/6 months in the interest period = $\frac{2}{3}$ × $1200 = $800) of the payment represents accrued interest on the obligation for the period during which the short sale was open and is a substitute payment in lieu of tax-exempt interest. On July 1, 1985, L receives another $1200 payment from State Q. Two hundred dollars (1 month the bonds were on loan after December 31, 1984/6 months in the interest period = 1/6 × $1200 = $200) of the payment represents accrued interest on the obligation for the period during which the short sale was open and is a substitute payment in lieu of the tax-exempt interest. Because both payments are received by L in 1985, L must furnish a statement under paragraph (a) of this section to R for that year with respect to both payments.

(b) *Exceptions.*—(1) *Minimal payments.*—No statement is required to be furnished under section 6045(d) or this section to any customer if the aggregate amount of the substitute payments received by a broker on behalf of the customer during a calendar year for which a statement must be furnished is less than $10.

(2) *Exempt recipients.*—(i) *In general.*—A statement shall not be required to be furnished with respect to substitute payments made to a broker on behalf of—

(A) An organization exempt from taxation under section 501(a);

(B) An individual retirement plan;

(C) The United States, a possession of the United States, or an instrumentality or a political subdivision or a wholly-owned agency of the foregoing;

(D) A State, the District of Columbia, or a political subdivision or a wholly-owned agency or instrumentality of either of the foregoing;

(E) A foreign government or a political subdivision thereof;

(F) An international organization, or

(G) A foreign central bank of issue, as defined in § 1.6049-4(c)(1)(ii)(H), or the Bank for International Settlements.

(ii) *Determination of whether a person is described in paragraph (b)(2)(i) of this section.*—The determination of whether a person is described in paragraph (b)(2)(i) of this section shall be made in the manner provided in § 1.6045-1(c)(3)(i)(B).

(3) *Exempt foreign persons.*—A statement shall not be required to be furnished with respect to substitute payments made to a broker on behalf of a person that is an exempt foreign person as described in § 1.6045-1(g).

(c) *Form of statement.*—A broker shall furnish the statement required by paragraph (a) of this section on Form 1099. The statement must show the aggregate dollar amount of all substitute payments received by the broker on behalf of a customer (for which the broker is required to furnish a statement) during a calendar year, and such other information as may be required by Form 1099. A statement shall be considered to be furnished to a customer if it is mailed to the customer at the last address of the customer known to the broker. An IRS truncated taxpayer identifying number (TTIN) may be used as the identifying number of the customer in lieu of the identifying number appearing on the information return filed with the Internal Revenue Service. For provisions relating to the use of TTINs, see § 301.6109-4 of this chapter (Procedure and Administration Regulations).

(d) *Time for furnishing statements.*—(1) *General requirements.*—A broker must furnish the statements required by paragraph (a) of this section for each calendar year. The statements must be furnished after April 30th of the calendar year but in no case before the final substitute payment for the calendar year is made, and on or before February 15 of the following calendar year.

(2) *Consolidated reporting.*—(i) The term *consolidated reporting statement* means a grouping of statements the same broker furnishes to the same customer or group of customers on the same date for the same reporting year that includes a statement required under this section. A consolidated reporting statement is limited to statements based on the same relationship of broker to customer as the statement required to be furnished under this section.

(ii) A consolidated reporting statement must be furnished on or before February 15 of the year following the calendar year reported. Any statement that otherwise must be furnished on or before January 31 must be furnished on or before February 15 if it is furnished in the consolidated reporting statement.

(e) *When substitute payment deemed received.*—A broker is deemed to have received a substitute payment on behalf of a customer when the amount is paid or deemed paid to the broker (or as it accrues in the case of original issue discount deemed a payment in lieu of tax-exempt interest).

(f) *Identification of customer and recordkeeping with respect to substitute payments.*—(1) *Payments in lieu of tax-exempt interest and exempt-interest dividends.*—A broker that receives substitute payments in lieu of tax-exempt interest, exempt-interest dividends, or other items (to the extent specified in a rule-related notice published pursuant to paragraph (a)(4)(i)(C) of this section) on behalf of a customer and is required to furnish a statement under paragraph (a) of this section must determine the identity of the customer whose security was transferred and on whose behalf the broker received such substitute payments by specific identification of the record owner of the security so transferred. A broker must keep adequate records of the determination so made.

(2) *Payments in lieu of dividends other than exempt-interest dividends.*—(i) *Requirements and methods.*—A broker that receives substitute payments in lieu of dividends other than exempt-interest dividends on behalf of a customer and is required to furnish a statement under paragraph (a) of this section must make a determination of the identity of the customer whose stock was transferred

and on whose behalf such broker receives substitute payments. Such determination must be made as of the record date with respect to the dividend distribution, and must be made in a consistent manner by the broker in accordance with any of the following methods:

(A) Specific identification of the record owner of the transferred stock;

(B) The method of allocation and selection specified in paragraph (f)(2)(ii) of this section; or

(C) Any other method, with the prior approval of the Commissioner.

A broker must keep adequate records of the determination so made.

(ii) *Method of allocation and selection.*—(A) *Allocation to individual and nonindividual pools.*—With respect to each substitute payment in lieu of a dividend received by a broker, the broker must allocate the transferred shares (*i.e.*, the shares giving rise to the substitute payment) among all shares of stock of the same class and issue as the transferred shares which were (1) borrowed by the broker, and (2) which the broker holds (or has transferred in a transaction described in paragraph (a)(1) of this section) and is authorized by its customers to transfer (including shares of stock of the same class and issue held for the broker's own account) ("loanable shares"). The broker may first allocate the transferred shares to any borrowed shares. Then to the extent that the number of transferred shares exceeds the number of borrowed shares (or if the broker does not allocate to the borrowed shares first), the broker must allocate the transferred shares between two pools, one consisting of the loanable shares of all individual customers (the "individual pool") and the other consisting of the loanable shares of all nonindividual customers (the "nonindividual pool"). The transferred shares must be allocated to the individual pool in the same proportion that the number of loanable shares held by individual customers bears to the total number of loanable shares available to the broker. Similarly, the transferred shares must be allocated to the nonindividual pool in the same proportion that the number of loanable shares held by nonindividual customers bears to the total number of loanable shares available to the broker.

(B) *Selection of deemed transferred shares within the nonindividual pool.*—The broker must select which shares within the nonindividual pool are deemed transferred for use in a short sale (the "deemed transferred shares"). Selection of deemed transferred shares may be made either by purely random lottery or on a first-in-first-out ("FIFO") basis.

(C) *Selection of deemed transferred shares within the individual pool.*—The broker must select which shares within the individual pool are deemed transferred shares (in the manner described in the preceding paragraph) only with respect to substitute payments as to which a statement is required to be furnished under paragraph (a)(2)(ii) of this section.

(3) *Examples.*—The following examples illustrate the identification of customer rules of paragraph (f)(2):

*Example (1).* A, a broker, holds X corporation common stock (of which there is only a single class) in street name for five customers: C, a corporation; D, a partnership; E, a corporation; F, an individual; and G, a corporation. C owns 100 shares of X stock, D owns 50 shares of X stock, E owns 100 shares of X stock, F owns 50 shares of X stock, and G owns 100 shares of X stock. A is authorized to loan all of the X stock of C, D, E, and F. G, however, has not authorized A to loan its X stocks. A transfers 150 shares of X stock to H for use in a short sale on July 1, 1985. A dividend of $2 per share is declared with respect to X stock on August 1, 1985, payable to the owners of record as of August 15, 1985 (the "record" date). A receives $2 per transferred share as a payment in lieu of a dividend with respect to X stock or a total of $300 on September 15, 1985. H closes the short sale and returns X stock to A on January 2, 1986. A's records specifically identify the owner of each loanable share of stock held in street name. From A's records it is determined that the shares transferred to H consisted of 100 shares owned by C, 25 shares owned by D, and 25 shares owned by F. The substitute payment in lieu of dividends with respect to X stock is therefore attributed to C, D and F based on the actual number of their shares that were transferred to H. Accordingly, C receives $200 (100 shares × $2 per share), and D and F each receive $50 (25 shares each × $2 per share). A must furnish statements identifying the payments as being in lieu of dividends to both C and D, unless they are exempt recipients as defined in paragraph (b)(2) of this section or exempt foreign persons as defined in paragraph (b)(3) of this section. Assuming that A has no reason to know on the record date of the payment that the dividend paid by X is of a type described in paragraph (a)(3)(ii)(A)-(D) of this section, A need not furnish F with a statement under section 6045(d) because F is an individual. (However, A may be required to furnish F with a statement in accordance with section 6042 and the regulations thereunder. See paragraph (h) of this section.) By recording the ownership of each share transferred to H, A has complied with the identification requirement of paragraph (f)(2) of this section.

*Example (2)*. Assume the same facts as in example (1), except that A's records do not specifically identify the record owner of each share of stock. Rather, all shares of X stock held in street name are pooled together. When A receives the $2 per share payment in lieu of a dividend, A determines the identity of the customers to which the payment relates by the method of allocation and selection prescribed in paragraph (f)(2)(ii) of this section. First, the transferred shares are allocated proportionately between the individual pool and the nonindividual pool. One-sixth of the transferred shares or 25 shares are allocated to the individual pool (50 loanable shares owned by individuals/300 total loanable shares = $1/6$; $1/6 \times 150$ transferred shares = 25 shares). Assuming A has no reason to know by the record date of the payment that the payment is in lieu of a dividend of a type described in paragraph (a)(3)(ii)(A)-(D) of this section, no selection of deemed transferred shares within the individual customer pool is required. (However, A may be required to furnish F with a statement under section 6042 and the regulations thereunder. See paragraph (h) of this section.) Five-sixths of the transferred shares or 125 shares are allocated to the nonindividual pool (250 loanable shares owned by nonindividuals/300 total loanable shares = $5/6$; $5/6 \times 150$ transferred shares = 125 shares). A must select which 125 shares within the nonindividual pool are deemed to have been transferred. Using a purely random lottery, A selects 100 shares identified as being owned by C, and 25 shares identified as being owned by D. Accordingly, A is deemed to have transferred 100 shares and 25 shares owned by C and D respectively, and received substitute payments in lieu of dividends of $200 (100 shares × $2 per share) and $50 (25 shares × $2 per share) on behalf of C and D respectively. A must furnish statements to both C and D identifying such payments as being in lieu of dividends unless they are exempt recipients as defined in paragraph (b)(2) of this section or exempt foreign persons as defined in paragraph (b)(3) of this section. A has complied with the identification requirement of paragraph (f)(2) of this section.

(g) *Reporting by brokers.*—(1) *Requirement of reporting.*—Any broker required to furnish a statement under paragraph (a) of this section shall report on Form 1096 showing such information as may be required by Form 1096, in the form, manner, and number of copies required by Form 1096. With respect to each customer for which a broker is required to furnish a statement, the broker shall make a return of information on Form 1099, in the form, manner and number of copies required by Form 1099.

(2) *Use of magnetic media.*—For information returns filed after December 31, 1996, see § 301.6011-2 of this chapter for rules relating to filing information returns on magnetic media and for rules relating to waivers granted for undue hardship. A broker or barter exchange that fails to file a Form 1099 on magnetic media, when required, may be subject to a penalty under section 6721 for each such failure. See paragraph (g)(4) of this section.

(3) *Time and place of filing.*—The returns required under this paragraph (g) for any calendar year shall be filed after September 30 of such year, but not before the final substitute payment for the year is received by the broker, and on or before February 28 (March 31 if filed electronically) of the following year with any of the Internal Revenue Service Centers, the addresses of which are listed in the instructions for Form 1096.

(4) *Cross-reference to penalties.*—For provisions relating to the penalty provided for failure to file timely a correct information return required under section 6045(d) and § 1.6045-2(g)(1), including a failure to file on magnetic media, see § 301.6721-1 of this chapter. For provisions relating to the penalty provided for failure to furnish timely a correct payee statement required under section 6045(d) and § 1.6045-2(a), see § 301.6722-1 of this chapter. See § 301.6724-1 of this chapter for the waiver of a penalty if the failure is due to reasonable cause and is not due to willful neglect.

(h) *Coordination with section 6042.*—In cases in which reporting is required by both sections 6042 and 6045(d) with respect to the same substitute payment in lieu of a dividend, the provisions of section 6045(d) control, and no report or statement under section 6042 need be made. If reporting is not required under section 6045(d) with respect to a substitute payment in lieu of a dividend, a report under section 6042 must be made if required in accordance with the rules of section 6042 and the regulations thereunder. Thus, if a broker receives a substitute payment in lieu of a dividend on behalf of an individual customer and the broker does not have reason to know by the record date of the payment that the payment is in lieu of a dividend of a type described in paragraph (a)(3)(ii)(A)-(D) of this section, the broker must report with respect to the substitute payment if required in accordance with section 6042 and the regulations thereunder.

(i) *Effective/applicability date.*—These regulations apply to substitute payments received by a broker after December 31, 1984. The amendments to paragraph (c) apply to payee statements due after December 31, 2014. For payee statements due before January 1, 2015, § 1.6045-2(c) (as contained in 26 CFR part 1, revised April 2013) shall apply. With regard to paragraph (g)(2) of this section, see section 6011(e) of the Internal Revenue Code for information returns required to be filed after December 31, 1989, and before January 1, 1997; and see paragraph (g)(2) of this section for information returns required to be filed after December 31, 1996. [Reg. § 1.6045-2.]

☐ [T.D. 8029, 6-4-85. *Amended by T.D. 8683*, 10-9-96; *T.D. 8734*, 10-6-97 (T.D. 8804 delayed the effective date of T.D. 8734 from January 1, 1999, to January 1, 2000; T.D. 8856 further delayed the effective date of T.D. 8734 until January 1, 2001); *T.D. 8772*, 6-29-98; *T.D. 8895*, 8-17-2000; *T.D. 9010*, 7-25-2002; *T.D. 9103*, 12-24-2003; *T.D. 9504*, 10-12-2010 *and T.D. 9675*, 7-14-2014.]

### [Reg. § 1.6045-3]

**§ 1.6045-3. Information reporting for an acquisition of control or a substantial change in capital structure.**—(a) *In general.*—Any broker (as defined in § 1.6045-1 (a)(1)) that holds shares on behalf of a customer in a corporation that the broker knows or has reason to know based on readily available information (including, for example, information from a clearing organization or from information published by the Internal Revenue Service (IRS)) has engaged in a transaction described in § 1.6043-4(c) (acquisition of control) or § 1.6043-4(d) (substantial change in capital structure) shall file a return of information with respect to the customer, unless the customer is an exempt recipient as defined in paragraph (b) of this section.

(b) *Exempt recipients.*—A broker is not required to file a return of information under this section with respect to the following customers:

(1) Any customer who receives only cash in exchange for its stock in the corporation, which must be reported by the broker pursuant to § 1.6045-1.

(2) Any customer who is an exempt recipient as defined in § 1.6043-4(b)(5) or § 1.6045-1(c)(3)(i).

(c) *Form, manner and time for making information returns.*—The return required by paragraph (a) of this section must be on Forms 1096, "Annual Summary and Transmittal of U.S. Information Returns," and 1099-B, "Proceeds from Broker and Barter Exchange Transactions," or on an acceptable substitute statement. Such forms must be filed on or before February 28 (March 31 if filed electronically) of the year following the calendar year in which the acquisition of control or the substantial change in capital structure occurs.

(d) *Contents of return.*—A separate Form 1099-B must be prepared for each customer. The Form 1099-B will request information with respect to the following and such other information as may be specified in the instructions:

(1) The name, address and taxpayer identification number (TIN) of the customer;

(2) The name of the corporation which engaged in the transaction described in § 1.6043-4(c) or (d);

(3) The number and class of shares in the corporation exchanged by the customer; and

(4) The aggregate amount of cash and the fair market value of any stock or other property provided to the customer in exchange for its stock.

(e) *Furnishing of forms to customers.*—(1) *General requirements.*—A broker must furnish Form 1099-B to the customer on or before February 15 of the year following the calendar year in which the customer receives stock, cash or other property. An IRS truncated taxpayer identifying number (TTIN) may be used as the identifying number of the customer. For provisions relating to the use of TTINs, see § 301.6109-4 of this chapter (Procedure and Administration Regulations).

(2) *Consolidated reporting.*—(i) The term *consolidated reporting statement* means a grouping of statements the same broker furnishes to the same customer or group of customers on the same date for the same reporting year that includes a statement required under this section. A consolidated reporting statement is limited to statements based on the same relationship of broker to customer as the statement required to be furnished under this section.

(ii) A consolidated reporting statement must be furnished on or before February 15 of the year following the calendar year reported. Any statement that otherwise must be furnished on or before January 31 must be furnished on or before February 15 if it is furnished in the consolidated reporting statement.

(f) *Single Form 1099.*—If a broker is required to file a Form 1099-B with respect to a customer under §§ 1.6045-3 and 1.6045-1(c) with respect to the same transaction, the broker may satisfy the requirements of both sections by filing and furnishing one Form 1099-B that contains all the relevant information, as provided in the instructions to Form 1099-B.

(g) *Effective/applicability date.*—This section applies with respect to any acquisition of control and any substantial change in capital

⫸➔ *Caution: Temporary Reg. §1.6045-3T, below, was removed by T.D. 9230, but it remains outstanding with respect to transactions not covered by Reg. §1.6045-3 while the IRS considers additional information reporting requirements under Code Secs. 6043(c), 6043A and 6045.*

### [Reg. §1.6045-3T]

**§1.6045-3T. Information reporting for an acquisition of control or a substantial change in capital structure (temporary).**—(a) *In general.*—Any broker (as defined in §1.6045-1(a)(1)) that holds shares on behalf of a customer in a corporation that the broker knows or has reason to know based on readily available information (including, for example, information from a clearing organization or from information published by the Internal Revenue Service (see §601.601(d)(2) of this chapter)) has engaged in a transaction described in §1.6043-4T(c) (acquisition of control) or §1.6043-4T(d) (substantial change in capital structure), shall file a return of information with respect to the customer, unless the customer is an exempt recipient as defined in paragraph (b) of this section.

(b) *Exempt recipients.*—A broker is not required to file a return of information under this section with respect to the following customers:

(1) Any customer who receives only cash in exchange for its stock in the corporation, which must be reported by the broker pursuant to §1.6045-1(a).

(2) Any customer who is an exempt recipient as defined in §1.6043-4T(b)(5) or §1.6045-1(c)(3)(i).

(c) *Form, manner and time for making information returns.*—The return required by paragraph (a) of this section must be on Forms 1096, "Annual Summary and Transmittal of U.S. Information Returns," and 1099-B, "Proceeds from Broker and Barter Exchange Transactions," or on an acceptable substitute statement. Such forms must be filed on or before February 28 (March 31 if filed electronically) of the year following the calendar year in which the acquisition of control or the substantial change in capital structure occurs.

(d) *Contents of return.*—A separate Form 1099-B must be prepared for each customer showing—

(1) The name, address and taxpayer identification number (TIN) of the customer;

(2) The name and address of the corporation which engaged in the transaction described in §1.6043-4T(c) or (d);

(3) The number and class of shares in the corporation exchanged by the customer;

(4) The aggregate amount of cash and the fair market value of any stock (other than stock described in 1.6043-4T(a)(1)(v)(C)) or other property provided to the customer in exchange for its stock; and

(5) Such other information as may be required by Form 1099-B.

(e) *Furnishing of forms to customers.*—The Form 1099-B prepared for each customer must be furnished to the customer on or before January 31 of the year following the calendar year in which the customer receives stock, cash or other property.

(f) *Single Form 1099.*—If a broker is required to file a Form 1099-B with respect to a customer under both this §1.6045-3T and §1.6045-1(b) with respect to the same transaction, the broker may satisfy the requirements of both sections by filing and furnishing one Form 1099-B that contains all the relevant information, as provided in the instructions to Form 1099-B.

(g) *Effective date.*—(1) This section applies with respect to any acquisition of control and any substantial change in capital structure occurring after December 31, 2001, if the reporting corporation or any shareholder is required to recognize gain (if any) as a result of the application of section 367(a) as a result of the transaction. However, paragraphs (a) through (f) of this section apply to acquisitions of control and substantial changes in capital structure occurring after December 31, 2002, if the reporting corporation or any shareholder is required to recognize gain (if any) as a result of the application of section 367(a) as a result of the transaction. For transactions prior to that date, see §1.6045-3T as published in 26 CFR Part 1 (revised as of April 1, 2003). This section expires on November 14, 2005.

(2) For any acquisition of control or any substantial change in capital structure occurring during the 2003 calendar year, a broker may elect to satisfy the requirements of this section by using Form 1099-CAP in lieu of Form 1099-B. [Temporary Reg. §1.6045-3T.]

structure occurring after December 5, 2005. The amendments to paragraph (e)(1) apply to payee statements due after December 31, 2014. For payee statements due before January 1, 2015, §1.6045-3(e)(1) (as contained in 26 CFR part 1, revised April 2013) shall apply. [Reg. §1.6045-3.]

☐ [T.D. 9230, 12-2-2005. *Amended by* T.D. 9504, 10-12-2010 *and* T.D. 9675, 7-14-2014.]

☐ [T.D. 9022, 11-13-2002 (corrected 2-5-2003). *Amended by* T.D. 9101, 12-29-2003 (corrected 2-13-2004). Removed by T.D. 9230, 12-2-2005.]

### [Reg. §1.6045-4]

**§1.6045-4. Information reporting on real estate transactions with dates of closing on or after January 1, 1991.**—(a) *Requirement of reporting.*—Except as otherwise provided in paragraphs (c) and (d) of this section, a real estate reporting person ("reporting person") must make an information return with respect to a real estate transaction and, under paragraph (m) of this section, must furnish a statement to the transferor. A reporting person may also report with respect to transactions otherwise excepted in paragraphs (c) and (d) of this section. However, if the reporting person so elects, the return must be filed and the statement furnished in accordance with the provisions of this section. For the definition of a real estate transaction for purposes of these reporting requirements, see paragraph (b) of this section. For rules for determining the reporting person with respect to a real estate transaction, see paragraph (e) of this section.

(b) *Definition of real estate transaction.*—(1) *In general.*—A transaction is a "real estate transaction" under this section if the transaction consists in whole or in part of the sale or exchange of "reportable real estate" (as defined in paragraph (b)(2) of this section) for money, indebtedness, property other than money, or services. The term "sale or exchange" shall include any transaction properly treated as a sale or exchange for Federal income tax purposes, whether or not the transaction is currently taxable. Thus, for example, a sale or exchange of a principal residence is a real estate transaction under this section even though the transferor is entitled to defer recognition under section 1034 (relating to rollover of gain on sale of principal residence), or the transferor is entitled to the special one-time exclusion of gain from the sale of a principal residence provided by section 121 to certain persons who have attained age 55.

(2) *Definition of reportable real estate.*—(i) Except as otherwise provided in paragraph (c)(2) of this section, the term "reportable real estate" means any present or future ownership interest in—

(A) Land (whether improved or unimproved), including air space;

(B) Any inherently permanent structure, including any residential, commercial or industrial building;

(C) Any condominium unit, including appurtenant fixtures and common elements (including land); or

(D) Any stock in a cooperative housing corporation (as defined in section 216).

(E) Any non-contingent interest in standing timber.

(ii) For purposes of this section, the term "ownership interest" includes fee simple interests, life estates, reversions, remainders, and perpetual easements. In addition, the term "ownership interest" includes any previously created rights to possession or use for all or a portion of any particular year (*i.e.*, a leasehold, easement, or "timeshare"), with a remaining term of at least 30 years, including any period for which such rights may be renewed at the option of the holder of the rights, as determined on the date of closing (as defined in paragraph (h)(2)(ii) of this section). Thus, for example, a pre-existing leasehold on a building with an original term of 99 years is an ownership interest in real estate for purposes of this section if it has a remaining term of 35 years as of the date of closing, but not if it has a remaining term of only 10 years as of the date of closing. However, the term "ownership interest" does not include an option to acquire otherwise reportable real estate. Further, the term "ownership interest" includes any contractual interest in a sale or exchange of standing timber for a lump-sum payment that is fixed and not contingent.

(c) *Exception for certain exempt transactions.*—(1) *Certain transfers.*—No return of information is required with respect to—

(i) A transaction that is not a sale or exchange (such as a gift (including a transaction treated as a gift under section 1041) or bequest, or a financing or refinancing that is not related to the acquisition of reportable real estate), even if the transaction involves reportable real estate, as defined in paragraph (b)(2) of this section;

(ii) A transfer in full or partial satisfaction of any indebtedness secured by the property so transferred including a foreclosure, a transfer in lieu of foreclosure or an abandonment; or

(iii) A transaction (a "de minimis transfer") in which it can be determined with certainty that the total consideration (in money, services and property), received or to be received in connection with the transaction is less than $600 in value (determined without regard to any allocation of gross proceeds among multiple transferors under paragraph (i)(5) of this section) as of the date of the closing (as defined in paragraph (h)(2)(ii) of this section), even if the transaction involves reportable real estate. Thus, for example, if a contract for sale of reportable real estate recites total consideration of "$1.00 plus other valuable consideration," the transfer is not a de minimis transfer unless the reporting person can determine that the "other valuable consideration" received or to be received is less than $599 in value as measured on the date of closing.

(2) *Certain property.*—Notwithstanding the provisions of paragraph (b)(2) of this section, no return of information is required with respect to a sale or exchange of an interest in any of the following property—provided the sale or exchange of such property is not related to the sale or exchange of reportable real estate—

(i) An interest in surface or subsurface natural resources (for example, water, ores, and other natural deposits) or crops, whether or not such natural resources or crops are severed from the land. For purposes of this section, the terms "natural resources" and "crops" do not include standing timber.

(ii) A burial plot or vault; or

(iii) A manufactured structure used as a dwelling that is manufactured and assembled at a location different from that where it is used, but only if such structure is not affixed, at the date of closing (as defined in paragraph (h)(2)(ii) of this section), to a foundation. Thus, a transfer of an unaffixed mobile home that is unrelated to the sale or exchange of reportable real estate is excepted from the reporting requirements of this section.

(d) *Exception for certain exempt transferors.*—(1) *General rule.*—No return of information is required with respect to a transferor that is a corporation under section 7701(a)(3) or section 7704(a) or is considered under paragraph (d)(2) of this section to be—

(i) A corporation;

(ii) A governmental unit; or

(iii) An exempt volume transferor.

In the case of a real estate transaction with respect to which there is one or more exempt transferor(s) and one or more non-exempt transferor(s), the reporting person is required to report with respect to any non-exempt transferor. The special rule for allocation of gross proceeds, as provided in paragraph (i)(5) of this section, applies to such a transaction.

(2) *Treatment as exempt transferor.*—Absent actual knowledge to the contrary, a reporting person may treat a transferor as—

(i) A corporation if—

(A) The name of the transferor contains an unambiguous expression of corporate status, such as Incorporated, Inc., Corporation, Corp., or P.C. (but not Company or Co.);

(B) The name of the transferor contains the term "insurance company," "reinsurance company," or "assurance company"; or

(C) The transfer or loan documents clearly indicate the corporate status of the transferor;

(ii) A governmental unit if the transferor is—

(A) The United States or a state, the District of Columbia, a possession of the United States, a political subdivision of any of the foregoing, or any wholly owned agency or instrumentality of any one or more of the foregoing; or

(B) A foreign government, a political subdivision thereof, an international organization, as defined in section 7701(a)(18), or any whollyowned agency or instrumentality of the foregoing; or

(iii) An exempt volume transferor if, and only if, the reporting person receives a certification of exempt status under paragraph (d)(3) of this section.

(3) *Certification of exempt status.*—(i) *In general.*—A certification of exempt status must contain—

(A) The name, address, and taxpayer identification number of the transferor (the address must be that of the permanent residence (in the case of an individual), that of the principal office (in the case of a corporation or partnership), or that of the permanent residence or principal office of any fiduciary (in the case of a trust or estate));

(B) Sufficient information to identify any otherwise reportable real estate not reported by virtue of the exempt status of the transferor; and

(C) A declaration that the transferor has sold or exchanged during either of the prior two calendar years, or previously sold or exchanged during the current calendar year, or, as of the date of closing (as defined in paragraph (h)(2)(ii) of this section); reasonably expects to sell or exchange during the current calendar year at least

25 separate items of reportable real estate (as defined in paragraph (b)(2) of this section) to at least 25 separate transferees, and that each such item, at the date of closing of the sale of such item was or will be held primarily for sale or resale to customers in the ordinary course of a trade or business. For example, the declaration may be worded as follows:

_____[INSERT NAME OF TRANSFEROR]

[check one or more]:

(1) _____has sold or exchanged during either of the prior two calendar years,

(2) _____previously sold or exchanged during the current calendar year,

(3) _____on the date of closing expects to sell or exchange during the current calendar year,

at least 25 separate items of reportable real estate to at least 25 separate transferees and each such item, at the date of closing of such item was or will be held primarily for sale or resale to customers in the ordinary course of a trade or business.

(ii) *Additional requirements.*—A certification of exempt status must be—

(A) Signed under penalties of perjury by the transferor or any person who is authorized to sign a declaration under penalties of perjury in behalf of the transferor as described in section 6061 and the regulations thereunder;

(B) Received by the reporting person no later than the time of closing; and

(C) Retained by the reporting person for four years following the close of the calendar year in which the date of closing (as determined under paragraph (h)(2)(ii) of this section) occurs.

(iii) *Reporting person may accent or disregard certification.*—A reporting person may solicit or merely accept a certification of exempt status. Moreover, notwithstanding a transferor's furnishing of such certification, a reporting person may disregard the certification and, instead, report with respect to the transaction. See paragraph (a) of this section for the requirement that such elective reporting must be in compliance with the provisions of this section.

(e) *Person required to report.*—(1) *In general.*—Although there may be other persons involved in a real estate transaction, only the reporting person is required to report with respect to any real estate transaction. Except as provided in a designation agreement under paragraph (e)(5) of this section, the reporting person with respect to a real estate transaction is—

(i) The person responsible for closing the transaction, as defined in paragraph (e)(3) of this section; or

(ii) If there is no person responsible for closing the transaction, the person determined to be the reporting person under paragraph (e)(4) of this section.

A person may be the reporting person with respect to a transaction whether or not such person performs or is licensed to perform real estate brokerage services for a commission or fee.

(2) *Employees, agents, and partners.*—For purposes of this paragraph (e), if an employee, agent, or partner (other than an employee, agent, or partner of the transferor or the transferee) acting within the scope of such person's employment, agency, or partnership participates in a real estate transaction—

(i) Such participation shall be attributed to such person's employer, principal, or partnership; and

(ii) Only the employer, principal, or partnership (and not such person) may be the reporting person with respect to such transaction as a result of such participation.

However, the participation of a person described in paragraph (e)(3)(i) of this section (*i.e.*, a person listed on the Uniform Settlement Statement as the settlement agent) acting as an agent of another is not attributed to the principal.

(3) *Person responsible for closing the transaction.*—(i) *Uniform Settlement Statement used.*—If a Uniform Settlement Statement prescribed under the Real Estate Settlement Procedures Act of 1974 (RESPA), 12 U.S.C. 2601 *et seq.* (a "Uniform Settlement Statement"), is used with respect to the real estate transaction and a person is listed as settlement agent on the statement, such person is the person responsible for closing the transaction. For purposes of this section, a Uniform Settlement Statement shall include any amendments or variations thereto, or substitutions therefor that may hereafter be prescribed under RESPA, provided that any such amended, varied, or substituted form requires disclosure of the parties to the transaction, the application of the proceeds of the transaction, and the identity of the settlement agent or other person responsible for preparing the form.

(ii) *Other closing statement used.*—If a Uniform Settlement Statement is not used, or if a Uniform Settlement Statement is used, but no person is listed as settlement agent, the person responsible for closing the transaction is the person who prepares a closing statement presented to the transferor and transferee at, or in connection with, the closing of the real estate transaction. For purposes of this section, a closing statement is any closing statement, settlement statement (including a Uniform Settlement Statement), or other written document that identifies the transferor and transferee, reasonably identifies the transferred real estate, and describes the manner in which the proceeds payable to the transferor are to be (or were) disbursed at, or in connection with, the closing.

(iii) *No closing statement used or multiple closing statements used.*—If no closing statement is used or multiple closing statements are used, the person responsible for closing the transaction is the first-listed of the persons that participate in the transaction as—

(A) The attorney for the transferee who is present at the occasion of the delivery of either the transferee's note or a significant portion of the cash proceeds to the transferor, or who prepares or reviews the preparation of the document(s) transferring legal or equitable ownership of the real estate.

(B) The attorney for the transferor who is present at the occasion of the delivery of either the transferee's note or a significant portion of the cash proceeds to the transferor, or who prepares or reviews the preparation of the document(s) transferring legal or equitable ownership of the real estate; or

(C) The disbursing title or escrow company that is most significant in terms of gross proceeds disbursed.

If more than one attorney would be the person responsible for closing the transaction under the preceding sentence, the person among such attorneys who is considered responsible for closing the transaction under this paragraph (e)(3)(iii) is the person whose involvement in the transaction is most significant.

(4) *Determination of the real estate reporting person in the absence of a person responsible for closing the transaction.*—If no person is responsible for closing the transaction (within the meaning of paragraph (e)(3) of this section), the reporting person with respect to the real estate transaction is the person first-listed below of the persons that participate in the transaction as—

(i) The mortgage lender (as defined in paragraph (e)(6)(i) of this section);

(ii) The transferor's broker (as defined in paragraph (e)(6)(ii) of this section);

(iii) The transferee's broker (as defined in paragraph (e)(6)(iii) of this section); or

(iv) The transferee (as defined in paragraph (e)(6)(iv) of this section).

(5) *Designation agreement.*—(i) *In general.*—If a written designation agreement executed at or prior to the time of closing designates one of the persons described in paragraph (e)(5)(ii) of this section as the reporting person with respect to the transaction and the designated person is a party to the agreement, the designated person is the reporting person with respect to the transaction. It is not necessary that all parties to the transaction (or that more than one party) be parties to the agreement.

(ii) *Persons eligible.*—A person may be designated as the reporting person under this paragraph (e)(5) only if the person is—

(A) The person responsible for closing the transaction (as defined in paragraph (e)(3) of this section);

(B) A person described in paragraph (e)(3)(iii)(A), (B) or (C) of this section (whether or not such person is responsible for closing the transaction); or

(C) The mortgage lender (as defined in paragraph (e)(6)(i) of this section).

(iii) *Form of designation agreement.*—A designation agreement may be in any form that is consistent with the requirements of this paragraph (e)(5), and may be included on a closing statement with respect to the transaction. The designation agreement must, however, include the name and address of the transferor and transferee and the address and any additional information necessary to identify the real estate transferred. The agreement must identify, by name and address, the person designated as the reporting person with respect to the transaction, and all other parties (if any) to the agreement. All parties to the agreement must date and sign the agreement and must retain the agreement for four years following the close of the calendar year in which the date of closing (as determined under paragraph (h)(2)(ii) of this section) occurs. Upon request by the Internal Revenue Service, or any person involved in the transaction who did not participate in the designation agreement, the agreement must be made available for inspection.

(6) *Meaning of terms.*—(i) *Mortgage lender.*—For purposes of this paragraph (e), the term "mortgage lender" means the person who lends new funds in connection with the transaction, but only if the repayment of such funds is secured in whole or in part by the real estate transferred. If new funds are advanced by more than one person, the mortgage lender is the person who advances the largest amount of new funds. If two or more persons advance equal amounts of new funds and no other person advances a greater amount of new funds, the mortgage lender among the persons advancing such equal amounts is the person with the security interest that is most senior in terms of priority. For purposes of this paragraph (e)(6)(i), any amounts advanced by the transferor are not treated as new funds.

(ii) *Transferor's broker.*—For purposes of this paragraph (e), the term "transferor's broker" means only the broker that contracts with the transferor and is compensated in connection with the transaction.

(iii) *Transferee's broker.*—For purposes of this paragraph (e), the term "transferee's broker" means only the broker that participates to a significant extent in the preparation of the transferee's offer to acquire the real estate or that presents such offer to the transferor. If more than one person is so described, the transferee's broker is the person whose participation in the preparation of the transferee's offer to acquire the real estate is most significant or, in the event there is no such person, the person whose participation in the presentation of the offer is most significant.

(iv) *Transferee.*—For purposes of this paragraph (e), the term "transferee" means the person who acquires the greatest interest in the real estate. If there is no such person, the transferee is the person listed first on the document(s) transferring legal or equitable ownership of the real estate.

(f) *Multiple transferors.*—(1) *General rule.*—In the case of multiple transferors, each of which transfers an interest in the same reportable real estate, the reporting person shall make a separate information return with respect to each transferor. Paragraph (i)(5) of this section provides rules for the determination of gross proceeds to be reported in the case of multiple transferors.

(2) *Rules for spouses.*—Transferors who are husband and wife at the time of closing and hold the reportable real estate as tenants in common, joint tenants, tenants by the entirety, or community property are treated as a single transferor for purposes of paragraphs (f)(1), (h)(1)(i), (i)(5) and (l)(1)(i) of this section, unless the reporting person receives, at or prior to the time of closing, an uncontested allocation of gross proceeds between them. In the case of a husband and wife treated as a single transferor, the reporting person may treat either as the transferor for purposes of paragraphs (h)(1)(i) and (l)(1) of this section, relating to reporting and soliciting taxpayer identification numbers.

(g) *Prescribed form.*—Except as otherwise provided in paragraph (k) of this section, the information return required by paragraph (a) of this section shall be made on Form 1099.

(h) *Information required.*—(1) *In general.*—The following information must be set forth on the Form 1099 required by this section:

(i) The name, address, and taxpayer identification number (TIN) of the transferor (see also paragraph (f)(2) of this section);

(ii) A general description of the real estate transferred (in accordance with paragraph (h)(2)(i) of this section);

(iii) The date of closing (as defined in paragraph (h)(2)(ii) of this section);

(iv) To the extent required by the Form 1099 and its instructions, the entire gross proceeds with respect to the transaction (as determined under the rules of paragraph (i) of this section), and, in the case of multiple transferors, the gross proceeds allocated to the transferor (as determined under paragraph (i)(5) of this section);

(v) To the extent required by the Form 1099 and its instructions, an indication that the transferor—

(A) Received (or will, or may, receive) property (other than cash and consideration treated as cash in computing gross proceeds) or services as part of the consideration for the transaction,

(B) May receive property (other than cash) or services in satisfaction of an obligation having a stated principal amount, or

(C) May receive, in connection with a contingent payment transaction, an amount of gross proceeds that cannot be determined with certainty using the method described in paragraph (i)(3)(iii) of this section and is therefore not included in gross proceeds under paragraphs (i)(3)(i) and (i)(3)(iii) of this section;

(vi) The real estate reporting person's name, address, and TIN;

(vii) [Reserved]; and

(viii) Any other information required by the Form 1099 or its instructions.

(2) *Meaning of terms.*—(i) *General description of the real estate transferred.*—A general description of the real estate transferred includes the complete address of the property. If the address would not

Reg. §1.6045-4(h)(2)(i)

sufficiently identify the property, a general description of the real estate also includes a legal description (*e.g.,* section, lot, and block) of the property.

(ii) *Date of closing.*—In the case of a real estate transaction with respect to which a Uniform Settlement Statement is used, the date of closing shall be the date (if any) properly described as the "Settlement Date" on such statement. In all other cases, the date of closing shall be the earlier of the date on which title is transferred or the date on which the economic burdens and benefits of ownership of the real estate shift from the transferor to the transferee.

(i) *Gross proceeds.*—(1) *In general.*—Except as otherwise provided in this paragraph (i), the term "gross proceeds" means the total cash received or to be received by or on behalf of the transferor in connection with the real estate transaction. For purposes of this paragraph (i), the following amounts are treated as cash received or to be received by or on behalf of the transferor in connection with the real estate transaction:

(i) The stated principal amount of any obligation to pay cash to or for the benefit of the transferor in the future (including any obligation having a stated principal amount that may be satisfied by the delivery of property (other than cash) or services);

(ii) The amount of any liability of the transferor assumed by the transferee as part of the consideration for the transfer or of any liability to which the real estate acquired is subject (whether or not the transferor is personally liable for the debt); and

(iii) In the case of a contingent payment transaction, as defined in paragraph (i)(3)(ii) of this section, the maximum determinable proceeds, as defined in paragraph (i)(3)(iii) of this section. Gross proceeds does not include the value of any property (other than cash and consideration treated as cash) or services received by, or on behalf of, the transferor in connection with the real estate transaction. See paragraph (h)(1)(v) of this section for the information that must be included on the Form 1099 required by this section in cases in which the transferor receives (or will, or may, receive) property (other than cash and consideration treated as cash) or services as part of the consideration for the transfer.

(2) *Treatment of sales commissions and similar expenses.*—In computing gross proceeds, the total cash received or to be received by or on behalf of the transferor shall not be reduced by expenses borne by the transferor (such as sales commissions, expenses of advertising the real estate, expenses of preparing the deed, and the cost of legal services in connection with the transfer).

(3) *Special rules for contingent payments.*—(i) *In general.*—If a real estate transaction is a contingent payment transaction, gross proceeds consist of the maximum determinable proceeds, if any.

(ii) *Contingent payment transaction.*—For purposes of this section, the term "contingent payment transaction" means a real estate transaction with respect to which the receipt, by or on behalf of the transferor, of cash or consideration treated as cash under paragraph (i)(1)(i) of this section is subject to a contingency.

(iii) *Maximum determinable proceeds.*—For purposes of this section, the term "maximum determinable proceeds" means the gross proceeds determined by assuming that all of the contingencies contemplated by the documents available at closing are met or otherwise resolved in a manner that will maximize the gross proceeds. If the maximum amount of gross proceeds cannot be determined with certainty using this method, the maximum determinable proceeds are the greatest amount that can be determined with certainty using this method. See paragraph (h)(1)(v)(C) of this section for the information that must be included on the Form 1099 required by this section in cases in which the maximum amount of gross proceeds cannot, by using the method described in this paragraph (i)(3)(iii), be determined with certainty.

(4) *Uniform Settlement Statement used.*—If a Uniform Settlement Statement is used with respect to a real estate transaction involving a transfer of reportable real estate solely for cash and consideration treated as cash in computing gross proceeds, the gross proceeds generally will be the same amount as the contract sales price properly shown on that statement.

(5) *Special rules for multiple transferors.*—(i) *General rules.*—In the case of multiple transferors (within the meaning of paragraph (f) of this section) each of which transfers an interest in the same reportable real estate, the reporting person must request the transferors to provide an allocation of the gross proceeds among the transferors. The request must be made at or before the time of closing. Neither the request nor the response is required to be in writing. The reporting person must make a reasonable effort to contact all transferors of whom the reporting person has actual knowledge. The reporting person may, however, rely on the unchallenged response of any

transferor and need not make additional efforts to contact other transferors after at least one complete allocation (whether or not contained in a single response) is received. Except as otherwise provided in this paragraph (i)(5), the reporting person shall report the gross proceeds in accordance with any allocation received at or before the time of closing. The reporting person may (but is not required to) report the gross proceeds in accordance with any allocation received after the time of closing and before the date (determined without regard to extensions) the Forms 1099 are required to be filed. The reporting person may not report the gross proceeds in accordance with any allocation received on or after the date (determined without regard to extensions) the Forms 1099 are required to be filed. If no gross proceeds are allocated to a transferor because no allocation or an incomplete allocation is received by the reporting person, the reporting person shall report the entire unallocated gross proceeds (if any) on the return of information made with respect to such transferor. If the reporting person receives conflicting allocations from the transferors, the reporting person shall report the entire gross proceeds on each return of information made with respect to the transaction.

(ii) *Rules for spouses.*—The reporting person need not request an allocation of gross proceeds if the only transferors are husband and wife at the time of closing. If there are other transferors, the reporting person need only make a reasonable effort to contact either the husband or wife in connection with the request for an allocation. See paragraph (f)(2) of this section for rules that treat a husband and wife as multiple transferors if an uncontested allocation of gross proceeds is received by the reporting person at or prior to the time of closing.

(6) *Multiple asset transactions.*—In the case of a real estate transaction reportable under this section that involves the transfer of reportable real estate and other assets, the amount attributable to both the real estate and other assets is treated as the gross proceeds with respect to that real estate transaction. No allocation of gross proceeds is made among the assets.

(j) *Time and place for filing.*—A reporting person shall file the information returns required by this section with respect to a real estate transaction after December 31 of the calendar year that includes the date of closing (as determined under paragraph (h)(2)(ii) of this section) and on or before February 28 (March 31 if filed electronically) of the following calendar year. The returns shall be filed with the appropriate Internal Revenue Service Center at the address listed in the Instructions to Form 1099.

(k) *Use of magnetic media and substitute forms.*—(1) *Magnetic media.*—(i) *General rule.*—A reporting person that is required to make a return of information under this section shall, except as otherwise provided in paragraph (k)(1)(ii) or (iii) of this section, submit the information required by this section on magnetic media (within the meaning of 26 CFR 301.6011-2). Returns on magnetic media shall be made in accordance with 26 CFR 301.6011-2 and applicable revenue procedures.

(ii) *Exception for low-volume filers.*—For rules allowing a reporting person to make the information returns required by this section on the prescribed paper Form 1099 if the reporting person is required by this section to file fewer than 250 returns during the calendar year, see section 6011(e) and guidance issued by the Internal Revenue Service thereunder.

(iii) *Undue hardship.*—The Commissioner may authorize a reporting person to file information returns on the prescribed paper Form 1099 instead of on magnetic media if undue hardship is shown either on Form 8508, Request for Waiver from Filing Information Returns on Magnetic Media, or on a written statement requesting a waiver for undue hardship filed with the Martinsburg Computing Center, Martinsburg, West Virginia in accordance with applicable revenue procedures.

(2) *Substitute forms.*—A reporting person that is described in paragraph (k)(1)(ii) of this section or that receives permission to file returns on the prescribed paper Form 1099 under paragraph (k)(1)(iii) of this section may prepare and use a form that contains provisions identical with those of Form 1099 if the reporting person complies with all applicable revenue procedures relating to substitute Form 1099, including any requirement relating to the use of machine-readable paper forms.

(l) *Requesting taxpayer identification numbers (TINS).*—(1) *Solicitation.*—(i) *General requirements.*—A reporting person who is required to make an information return with respect to a real estate transaction under this section must solicit a TIN from the transferor at or before the time of closing. The solicitation may be made in person or in a mailing that includes other items. Any person whose TIN is solicited under this paragraph (l) must furnish such TIN to the reporting person and certify that the TIN is correct. See paragraph (f)(2) of this section for rules that treat a husband and wife as a single transferor (and provide for the TIN solicitation of either) in the absence of an allocation of gross proceeds under paragraph (i)(5) of this section.

(ii) *Content of solicitation.*—The solicitation shall be made by providing to the person from whom the TIN is solicited a written statement that the person is required by law to furnish a correct TIN to the reporting person, and that the person may be subject to civil or criminal penalties for failing to furnish a correct TIN. For example, the solicitation may be worded as follows:

You are required by law to provide [insert name of reporting person] with your correct taxpayer identification number. If you do not provide [insert name of reporting person] with your correct taxpayer identification number, you may be subject to civil or criminal penalties imposed by law.

The solicitation shall contain space for the name, address, and TIN of the person from whom the TIN is solicited and for the person to certify under penalties of perjury that the TIN furnished is that person's correct TIN. The wording of the certification must be substantially similar to the following: "Under penalties of perjury, I certify that the number shown on this statement is my correct taxpayer identification number." The requirements of this paragraph (l)(1)(ii) may be met by providing to the transferor a copy of Form W-9. In the case of a real estate transaction for which a Uniform Settlement Statement is used, the requirements of this paragraph (l)(1)(ii) may be met by providing to the transferor a copy of such statement that is modified to conform to the requirements of this paragraph (l)(1)(ii).

(iii) *Retention requirement.*—The solicitation shall be retained by the reporting person for four years following the close of the calendar year that includes the date of closing (as determined under paragraph (h)(2)(ii) of this section). Such solicitation must be made available for inspection upon request by the Internal Revenue Service.

(2) *No TIN provided.*—A reporting person that does not receive the transferor's TIN will not be subject to any penalty cross-referenced in paragraph (n) of this section by reason of failure to report such TIN if the reporting person has complied with the requirements of paragraph (l)(1) of this section in good faith (determined with proper regard for a course of conduct and the overall results achieved for the year).

(m) *Furnishing statements to transferors.*—(1)(i) *Requirement of furnishing statements.*—A reporting person who is required to make a return of information under paragraph (a) of this section shall furnish to the transferor whose TIN is required to be shown on the return a written statement of the information required to be shown on such return. The written statement must bear either the legend shown on the recipient copy of Form 1099 or the following: "This is important tax information and is being furnished to the Internal Revenue Service. If you are required to file a return, a negligence penalty or other sanction may be imposed on you if this item is required to be reported and the IRS determines that it has not been reported."

(ii) This requirement may be satisfied by furnishing to the transferor a copy of a completed Form 1099 (or substitute Form 1099 that complies with current revenue procedures). An IRS truncated taxpayer identifying number (TTIN) may be used as the identifying number of the transferor in lieu of the identifying number appearing on the information return filed with the Internal Revenue Service. For provisions relating to the use of TTINs, see §301.6109-4 of this chapter (Procedure and Administration Regulations).

(iii) In the case of a real estate transaction for which a Uniform Settlement Statement is used, this requirement also may be satisfied by furnishing to the transferor a copy of a completed statement that is modified to comply with the requirements of this paragraph (m), and by designating on the Uniform Settlement Statement the items of information (such as gross proceeds or allocated gross proceeds) required to be set forth on the Form 1099. For purposes of this paragraph (m), a statement shall be considered furnished to a transferor if it is given to the transferor in person, either at the closing or thereafter, or is mailed to the transferor at the transferor's last known address.

(2) *Time for furnishing statement.*—The statement required under this paragraph (m) must be furnished to the transferor on or after the date of closing and on or before February 15 of the following calendar year.

(3) *Consolidated reporting.*—(i) The term *consolidated reporting statement* means a grouping of statements the same reporting person furnishes to the same transferor or group of transferors on the same date for the same reporting year that includes a statement required

under this section. A consolidated reporting statement is limited to statements based on the same relationship of reporting person to transferor as the statement required to be furnished under this section.

(ii) A consolidated reporting statement must be furnished on or before February 15 of the year following the calendar year reported. Any statement that otherwise must be furnished on or before January 31 must be furnished on or before February 15 if it is furnished in the consolidated reporting statement.

(n) *Cross-reference to penalties.*—See the following sections regarding penalties for failure to comply with the requirements of section 6045(e) and this section:

(1) Section 6721 for failure to file a correct information return;

(2) Section 6722 for failure to furnish a correct statement to the transferor;

(3) Section 6723 for failure to comply with other information reporting requirements (including the requirement to furnish a TIN);

(4) Section 6724 for definitions and rules relating to waiver and payment; and

(5) Section 7203 for willful failure to supply information (including a taxpayer identification number).

(o) *No separate charge.*—A reporting person may not separately charge any person involved in a real estate transaction for complying with any requirements of this section.

(p) *Backup withholding requirements.*—[Reserved.]

(q) *Federally-subsidized indebtedness.*—[Reserved.]

(r) *Examples.*—The following examples illustrate the application of this section:

*Example (1)—Sale or exchange.* (i) On June 1, 1991, A, an individual, buys a house from B, an individual, for $200,000. The entire $200,000 is financed by B under an "installment land contract," whereby A takes possession and assumes all significant economic benefits and burdens of ownership of the house, and B retains legal title to the property until A fully performs under the contract. On June 1, 1994, A refinances his purchase of the house with Z, a financial institution. The balance owed to B is repaid and B relinquishes title to the house. A retains possession and the benefits and burdens of ownership of the house.

(ii) For federal income tax purposes, the transaction occurring on June 1, 1991 is considered a sale of the house by B, notwithstanding his retention of legal title to the property. B's sale is subject to information reporting under this section. However, the transaction occurring on June 1, 1994 is not a sale or exchange for federal income tax purposes, and notwithstanding the change in legal title upon the deeding over of the property, that transaction is not subject to information reporting under this section.

*Example (2)—Sale or exchange.* On August 10, 1991, C, an individual, accepts an offer from Y, a corporation that acts on behalf of T (C's employer) to facilitate moves of T's transferred employees from one part of the country to another. Under the offer, C transfers his residence to Y for $250,000 by executing a deed to the property in blank and giving Y a power of attorney to dispose of the residence. C also immediately vacates the residence, whereupon Y begins paying all costs associated with the residence and is entitled to all income from the residence, including sales proceeds. On October 1, 1991, Y sells the residence to D and inserts C's name in the deed previously executed by C. Thus, neither Y nor T ever become record owners of the residence. C's transfer of the residence to Y on August 10, 1991 is a sale of reportable real estate and is subject to information reporting under this section; however, the sale on October 1, 1991 is not required to be reported because Y (the transferor in that sale) is a corporation. See paragraph (d) of this section.

*Example (3)—Definition of ownership interest.* E, an individual, owns a perpetual timeshare interest in a residential unit of real property at an oceanfront resort. For consideration, on November 15, 1991, E sells her rights in the property for the period January 1, 1992 through December 31, 1992 to F. The transfer of E's property interest is not the transfer of an ownership interest, as defined in paragraph (b)(2) of this section and therefore is not reportable real estate under paragraph (b)(2) of this section. Accordingly, the transfer is not a real estate transaction under section (b)(1) of this section, and no return of information is required with respect to E's property transfer.

*Example (4)—Gross proceeds (exchange).* (i) G, an individual, agrees to transfer Blackacre, which has a fair market value of $100,000, plus $10,000 cash to H, an individual, in exchange for Whiteacre, which has a fair market value of $120,000 and is encumbered by a $10,000 liability (which is assumed by G). No other liabilities are involved in the transaction.

(ii) With respect to the transfer of Blackacre by G to H, P must report gross proceeds of $ -0- (even though the exchange agreement may recite total exchange value of $120,000). See paragraph (i)(1) of this section. In addition (to the extent required by the Form 1099 and its instructions) P must indicate that G will receive property as part of the consideration for the transaction. See paragraph (h)(v)(A) of this section.

(iii) With respect to the transfer of Whiteacre by H to G, P must report gross proceeds of $20,000 (the amount received by H consisting of cash ($10,000) and consideration treated as cash ($10,000) under paragraph (i) of this section). No other amount is reported under paragraph (i)(1) of this section even though the exchange agreement may recite total exchange value of $120,000. In addition, to the extent required by the Form 1099 and its instructions, P must indicate that H will receive property as part of the consideration for the transaction. See paragraph (h)(v)(A) of this section.

*Example (5). Gross proceeds (deferred exchange).* [Reserved]

*Example (6). Gross proceeds (contingencies).* K, an individual, sells an unencumbered apartment building to L for $500,000, payable at closing, plus an amount equal to 2% of gross rents from the apartment building for each of the next 5 years, the contingent payments to be made annually with adequate stated interest. The agreement provides that the maximum amount K may receive (including the downpayment but excluding the interest) is $600,000. Under paragraph (i)(3)(ii) of this section the real estate transaction is a "contingent payment transaction." Under paragraph (i) (3)(iii) of this section, the maximum amount of gross proceeds determined by assuming all contingencies are satisfied is $600,000. Thus, $600,000 is the "maximum determinable proceeds" and is the amount reported.

*Example (7). Gross proceeds (contingencies).* The facts are the same as in example (6), except that the agreement does not provide for adequate stated interest. The result is the same as in example (6).

*Example (8). Gross proceeds (contingencies).* The facts are [the] same as in example (6), except that no maximum amount is stated in the agreement (or any other document available at closing). Under paragraph (i)(3)(iii) of this section, assuming all contingencies are satisfied, the maximum amount of gross proceeds cannot be determined with certainty. The greatest amount that can be determined with certainty at the time of the closing, assuming all contingencies are satisfied, is $500,000, the cash downpayment. Therefore, $500,000 is the "maximum determinable proceeds" under paragraph (i)(3)(iii) of this section and is the amount reported. In addition, to the extent required by the Form 1099 and its instructions, the reporting person must indicate that the gross proceeds cannot be determined with certainty. See paragraph (h)(1)(iv)(C) of this section.

*Example (9). Gross proceeds (contingencies).* The facts are the same as in example (8), except that the agreement provides that the minimum amount K will receive (including the downpayment) is $570,000. Thus, under paragraph (i)(3)(iii) of this section, assuming all contingencies are satisfied, the maximum amount of gross proceeds cannot be determined with certainty. The greatest amount that can be determined with certainty at the time of the closing, assuming all contingencies are satisfied, is $570,000, the minimum amount stated in the agreement. Therefore, $570,000 is the "maximum determinable proceeds" under paragraph (i)(3)(iii) of this section and is the amount reported. In addition, to the extent required by the Form 1099 and its instructions, the reporting person must indicate that the gross proceeds cannot be determined with certainty. See paragraph (h)(1)(iv)(C) of this section.

(s) *Effective/applicability date.*—This section applies for real estate transactions with dates of closing (as determined under paragraph (h)(2)(ii) of this section) that occur on or after January 1, 1991. The amendments to paragraphs (b)(2)(i)(E), (b)(2)(ii) and (c)(2)(i) of this section shall apply to sales or exchanges of standing timber for lump-sum payments completed after May 28, 2009. The amendments to paragraph (m)(1) apply to payee statements due after December 31, 2014. For payee statements due before January 1, 2015, §1.6045-4(m)(1) (as contained in 26 CFR part 1, revised April 2013) shall apply. [Reg. §1.6045-4.]

☐ [*T.D. 8323, 12-12-90. Amended by T.D. 8895, 8-17-2000; T.D. 9450, 5-27-2009; T.D. 9504, 10-12-2010 and T.D. 9675, 7-14-2014.*]

**[Reg. §1.6045-5]**

**§1.6045-5. Information reporting on payments to attorneys.**—(a) *Requirement of reporting.*—(1) *In general.*—Except as provided in paragraph (c) of this section, every payor engaged in a trade or business who, in the course of that trade or business, makes payments aggregating $600 or more during a calendar year to an attorney in connection with legal services (whether or not the services are performed for the payor) must file an information return for such payments. The information return must be filed on the form and in the manner required by the Commissioner. For the time and place for filing the form, see §1.6041-6. For definitions of the terms under this section, see paragraph (d) of this section. The requirements of this paragraph (a)(1) apply whether or not—

(i) A portion of a payment is kept by the attorney as compensation for legal services rendered; or

(ii) Other information returns are required with respect to some or all of a payment under other provisions of the Internal Revenue Code and the regulations thereunder.

(2) *Information required.*—The information return required under paragraph (a)(1) of this section must include the following information:

(i) The name, address, and taxpayer identifying number (TIN) (as defined in section 7701(a)) of the payor;

(ii) The name, address, and TIN of the payee attorney;

(iii) The amount of the payment or payments (as defined in paragraph (d)(5) of this section); and

(iv) Any other information required by the Commissioner in forms, instructions or publications.

(3) *Requirement to furnish statement.*—(i) *General requirements.*—A person required to file an information return under paragraph (a)(1) of this section must furnish to the attorney a written statement of the information required to be shown on the return. This requirement may be met by furnishing a copy of the return to the attorney. An IRS truncated taxpayer identifying number (TTIN) may be used as the identifying number of the attorney in lieu of the identifying number appearing on the information return filed with the Internal Revenue Service. For provisions relating to the use of TTINs, see §301.6109-4 of this chapter (Procedure and Administration Regulations). The written statement must be furnished to the attorney on or before February 15 of the year following the calendar year in which the payment was made.

(ii) *Consolidated reporting.*—(A) The term *consolidated reporting statement* means a grouping of statements the same payor furnishes to the same payee or group of payees on the same date for the same reporting year that includes a statement required under this section. A consolidated reporting statement is limited to statements based on the same relationship of payor to payee as the statement required to be furnished under this section.

(B) A consolidated reporting statement must be furnished on or before February 15 of the year following the calendar year reported. Any statement that otherwise must be furnished on or before January 31 must be furnished on or before February 15 if it is furnished in the consolidated reporting statement.

(b) *Special rules.*—(1) *Joint or multiple payees.*—(i) *Check delivered to one payee attorney.*—If more than one attorney is listed as a payee on a check, an information return must be filed under paragraph (a)(1) of this section with respect to the payee attorney to whom the check is delivered.

(ii) *Check delivered to payee nonattorney.*—If an attorney is listed as a payee on a check but the check is delivered to a nonattorney who is a payee on the check, an information return must be filed under paragraph (a)(1) of this section with respect to the payee attorney listed on the check. If more than one attorney is listed as a payee on a check but the check is delivered to a nonattorney who is a payee on the check, the information return must be filed with respect to the first-listed payee attorney on the check.

(iii) *Check delivered to nonpayee.*—If two or more attorneys are listed as payees on a check, but the check is delivered to a person who is not a payee on the check, an information return must be filed under paragraph (a)(1) of this section with respect to the first-listed payee attorney on the check.

(2) *Attorney required to report payments made to other attorneys.*—If an information return is required to be filed with respect to a payee attorney under paragraph (b)(1) of this section, the attorney with respect to whom the information return is required to be filed (tier-one attorney) must file an information return under this section for any payment that the tier-one attorney makes to other payee attorneys with respect to that check, regardless of whether the tier-one attorney is a payor under paragraph (d)(3) of this section.

(c) *Exceptions.*—Notwithstanding paragraphs (a) and (b) of this section, a return of information is not required under section 6045(f) with respect to the following payments:

(1) Payments of wages or other compensation paid to an attorney by the attorney's employer.

(2) Payments of compensation or profits paid or distributed to its partners by a partnership engaged in providing legal services.

(3) Payments of dividends or corporate earnings and profits paid to its shareholders by a corporation engaged in providing legal services.

(4) Payments made by a person to the extent that the person is required to report with respect to the same payee the payments or portions thereof under section 6041(a) and §1.6041-1(a) (or would be

required to so report the payments or portions thereof but for the dollar amount limitation contained in section 6041(a) and § 1.6041-1(a)).

(5) Payments made to a nonresident alien individual, foreign partnership, or foreign corporation that is not engaged in trade or business within the United States, and does not perform any labor or personal services in the United States, in the taxable year to which the payment relates. For how a payor determines whether a payment is subject to this exception, see § 1.6041-4(a)(1).

(6) Payments made to an attorney in the attorney's capacity as the person responsible for closing a transaction within the meaning of § 1.6045-4(e)(3) for the sale or exchange or financing of any present or future ownership interest in real estate described in § 1.6045-4(b)(2)(i) through (iv).

(7) Payments made to an attorney in the attorney's capacity as a trustee in bankruptcy under Title 11, United States Code.

(d) *Definitions.*—The following definitions apply for purposes of this section:

(1) *Attorney* means a person engaged in the practice of law, whether as a sole proprietorship, partnership, corporation, or joint venture.

(2) *Legal services* means all services related to, or in support of, the practice of law performed by, or under the supervision of, an attorney.

(3) *Payor* means a person who makes a payment if that person is an obligor on the payment, or the obligor's insurer or guarantor. For example, a payor includes—

(i) A person who pays a settlement amount to an attorney of a client who has asserted a tort, contract, violation of law, or workers' compensation claim against that person; and

(ii) The person's insurer if the insurer pays the settlement amount to the attorney.

(4) *Payments to an attorney* include payments by check or other method such as cash, wire or electronic transfer. Payment by check to an attorney means a check on which the attorney is named as a sole, joint, or alternative payee. The attorney is the payee on a check written to the attorney's client trust fund. However, the attorney is not a payee when the attorney's name is included on the payee line as "in care of," such as a check written to "client c/o attorney," or if the attorney's name is included on the check in any other manner that does not give the attorney the right to negotiate the check.

(5) *Amount of the payment* means the amount tendered (e.g., the amount of a check) plus the amount required to be withheld from the payment under section 3406(a)(1), because a condition for withholding exists with respect to the attorney for whom an information return is required to be filed under paragraph (a)(1) of this section.

(e) *Attorney to furnish TIN.*—A payor that is required to file an information return under this section must solicit a TIN from the attorney at or before the time the payor makes a payment to the attorney. The attorney must furnish the correct TIN to the payor, but is not required to certify the TIN. A payment for which a return of information is required under this section is subject to backup withholding under section 3406 and the regulations thereunder.

(f) *Examples.*—The following examples illustrate the provisions of this section. The examples assume that P is not a payor with respect to A, the attorney, under section 6041. See section 6041 and the regulations thereunder for rules regarding whether P is required under section 6041 to file information returns with respect to C. The examples are as follows:

*Example 1.* One check—joint payees—taxable to claimant. Employee C, who sues employer P for back wages, is represented by attorney A. P settles the suit for $300,000. The $300,000 represents taxable wages to C under existing legal principles. P writes a settlement check payable jointly to C and A in the amount of $200,000, net of income and FICA tax withholding with respect to C. P delivers the check to A. A retains $100,000 of the payment as compensation for legal services and disburses the remaining $100,000 to C. P must file an information return with respect to A for $200,000 under paragraph (a)(1) of this section. P also must file an information return with respect to C under sections 6041 and 6051, in the amount of $300,000. See §§ 1.6041-1(f) and 1.6041-2.

*Example 2.* One check—joint payees—excludable to claimant. C, who sues corporation P for damages on account of personal physical injuries, is represented by attorney A. P settles the suit for a $300,000 damage payment that is excludable from C's gross income under section 104(a)(2). P writes a $300,000 settlement check payable jointly to C and A and delivers the check to A. A retains $120,000 of the payment as compensation for legal services and remits the remaining $180,000 to C. P must file an information return with respect to A for $300,000 under paragraph (a)(1) of this section. P does not file an information return with respect to tax-free damages paid to C.

*Example 3.* Separate checks—taxable to claimant. C, an individual plaintiff in a suit for lost profits against corporation P, is represented by attorney A. P settles the suit for $300,000, all of which will be includible in C's gross income. A requests P to write two checks, one payable to A in the amount of $100,000 as compensation for legal services and the other payable to C in the amount of $200,000. P writes the checks in accordance with A's instructions and delivers both checks to A. P must file an information return with respect to A for $100,000 under paragraph (a)(1) of this section. Pursuant to § 1.6041-1(a) and (f), P must file an information return with respect to C for the $300,000.

*Example 4.* Check made payable to claimant, but delivered to nonpayee attorney. Corporation P is a defendant in a suit for damages in which C, the plaintiff, has been represented by attorney A throughout the proceeding. P settles the suit for $300,000. Pursuant to a request by A, P writes the $300,000 settlement check payable solely to C and delivers it to A at A's office. P is not required to file an information return under paragraph (a)(1) of this section with respect to A, because there is no payment to an attorney within the meaning of paragraph (d)(4) of this section.

*Example 5.* Multiple attorneys listed as payees. Corporation P, a defendant, settles a lost profits suit brought by C for $300,000 by issuing a check naming C's attorneys, Y, A, and Z, as payees in that order. Y, A, and Z do not belong to the same law firm. P delivers the payment to A's office. A deposits the check proceeds into a trust account and makes payments by separate checks to Y of $30,000 and to Z of $15,000, as compensation for legal services, pursuant to authorization from C to pay these amounts. A also makes a payment by check of $155,000 to C. A retains $100,000 as compensation for legal services. P must file an information return for $300,000 with respect to A under paragraphs (a)(1) and (b)(1)(i) of this section. A, in turn, must file information returns with respect to Y of $30,000 and to Z of $15,000 under paragraphs (a)(1) and (b)(2) of this section because A is not required to file information returns under section 6041 with respect to A's payments to Y and Z because A's role in making the payments to Y and Z is merely ministerial. See § 1.6041-1(e)(1), (e)(2) and (e)(5) *Example 7* for information reporting requirements with respect to A's payments to Y and Z. As described in *Example 3*, P must also file an information return with respect to C, pursuant to § 1.6041-1(a) and (f).

*Example 6.* Amount of the payment—attorney does not provide TIN. (i) Corporation P, a defendant, settles a suit brought by C for $300,000 of damages. P will pay the damages by a joint check to C and his attorney, A. A failed to furnish P with A's TIN. P is required to deduct and withhold 28 percent tax from the $300,000 under section 3406(a)(1)(A) and paragraph (e) of this section. P writes the check to C and A as joint payees, in the amount of $216,000. P also must file an information return with respect to A under paragraph (a)(1) of this section in the amount of $300,000, as prescribed in paragraph (d)(5) of this section. If the damages are reportable under section 6041 because they are not excludable from gross income under existing legal principles, and are not subject to any exception under section 6041, P must also file an information return with respect to C pursuant to § 1.6041-1(a) and (f) in the amount of $300,000.

(ii) Rather than paying by joint check to C and A, P will pay the damages by a joint check to C and F, A's law firm. F failed to furnish its TIN to P. P is required to deduct and withhold 28 percent tax from the $300,000 under section 3406(a)(1)(A) and paragraph (e) of this section. P writes the check to C and F as joint payees, in the amount of $216,000. P also must file an information return with respect to F under paragraph (a)(1) of this section in the amount of $300,000, as prescribed in paragraph (d)(5) of this section. If the damages are reportable under section 6041 because they are not excludable from gross income under existing legal principles, and are not subject to any exception under section 6041, P must also file an information return with respect to C pursuant to § 1.6041-1(a) and (f) in the amount of $300,000.

*Example 7.* Home mortgage lending transaction. (i) Individual P agrees to purchase a house that P will use solely as a residence. P obtains a loan from lender L to finance a portion of the cost of acquiring the house. L disburses loan proceeds of $300,000 to attorney A, who is the settlement agent, by a check naming A as the sole payee. A, in turn, writes checks from the loan proceeds and from other funds provided by P to the persons involved in the purchase of the house, including a check for $800 to attorney B, whom P hired to provide P with legal services relating to the closing.

(ii) P, not L, is the payor of the payment to A under paragraph (d)(3) of this section. P, however, is not required to file an information return with respect to A under paragraph (a)(1) of this section because the payment was not made in the course of P's trade or business. Even if P made the payment in the course of P's trade or business, P would not be required to file an information return under section 6045(f) with respect to A because P is excepted under paragraph (c)(6) of this section.

(iii) A is not required to file an information return under paragraph (a)(1) of this section with respect to the payment to B because A is not the payor as that term is defined under paragraph (d)(3) of this section. A is not required to file an information return under paragraph (b)(2) with respect to the payment to B because A was listed as sole payee on the check it received from P. See section 6041 and § 1.6041-1(e) for whether A or L must file information returns under that section. See section 6045(e) and § 1.6045-4 for whether A is required to file an information return under that section.

*Example 8.* Business mortgage lending transaction. The facts are the same as in *Example 7* except that P buys real property that P will use in a trade or business. P, not L, is the payor of the payment to A under paragraph (d)(3) of this section. P, however, is not required to file an information return under section 6045(f) with respect to A because P is excepted under paragraph (c)(6) of this section. A is not required to file an information return under paragraphs (a) or (b)(2) of this section with respect to the payment to B. See section 6041 and § 1.6041-1(e) to determine whether P or L must file an information return under that section with respect to the payment to A, and whether P or A must file a return with respect to the payment to B. See section 6045(e) for rules regarding whether A is required to file information returns under that section.

*Example 9.* Qualified settlement fund. Corporation P agrees to settle for $300,000 a class action lawsuit brought by attorney A on behalf of a claimant class. Pursuant to the settlement agreement and a preliminary order of approval by a court, A establishes a bank account in the name of Q Settlement Fund, which is a qualified settlement fund (QSF) under § 1.468B-1. A is also designated by the court as the administrator of the QSF. Corporation P transfers $300,000 by wire in Year 1 to A, who deposits the funds into the Q Settlement Fund. In Year 2, the court approves an award of attorney's fees of $105,000 for A. In Year 2, Q Settlement Fund delivers $105,000 to A. P is required to file an information return under paragraph (a) of this section with respect to A for Year 1 for the $300,000 payment it made to A. The Q Settlement Fund is required to file an information return under section 6041(a) and § 1.468B-2(1)(2) with respect to A for Year 2 for the $105,000 payment it made to A.

(g) *Cross reference to penalties.*—See the following sections regarding penalties for failure to comply with the requirements of section 6045(f) and this section:

(1) Section 6721 for failure to file a correct information return.

(2) Section 6722 for failure to furnish a correct payee statement.

(3) Section 6723 for failure to comply with other information reporting requirements (including the requirement to furnish a TIN).

(4) Section 7203 for willful failure to supply information (including a TIN).

(h) *Effective/applicability date.*—The rules in this section apply to payments made on or after January 1, 2007. The amendments to paragraph (a)(3)(i) apply to payee statements due after December 31, 2014. For payee statements due before January 1, 2015, § 1.6045-5(a)(3)(i) (as contained in 26 CFR part 1, revised April 2013) shall apply. [Reg. § 1.6045-5.]

☐ [*T.D.* 9270, 7-12-2006 (*corrected* 8-15-2006). *Amended by T.D.* 9504, 10-12-2010 *and T.D.* 9675, 7-14-2014.]

**[Reg. § 1.6045A-1]**

**§ 1.6045A-1 Statements of information required in connection with transfers of securities.**—(a) *Duty to furnish transfer statement.*—(1) *In general.*—(i) *Transfers between accounts.*—Except as provided in paragraphs (a)(1)(ii) through (v) of this section, every applicable person (transferor) (as described in paragraph (a)(4) of this section) that transfers custody of a specified security to a broker (as described in paragraph (a)(5) of this section) must furnish to the receiving broker a transfer statement that includes the information described in paragraph (b) of this section with respect to the transferred security. Except as provided in paragraphs (b)(1)(vii) and (b)(3) of this section (relating to noncovered securities and certain securities for which basis is determined under an average basis method), a transferor must furnish a separate statement for each security and, if transferring custody of the same security acquired on different dates or at different prices, for each acquisition.

(ii) *Cash on delivery accounts and multiple broker arrangements.*—(A) *Sales.*—A custodian or other transferor that transfers custody of a security to a broker solely to effect a sale must furnish a transfer statement only to the broker that effects the sale. However, no transfer statement is required if the transferor itself either effects the sale or is required to report the sale of the security under § 1.6045-1.

(B) *Purchases.*—A broker that effects a purchase but does not receive custody of the security must furnish a transfer statement to the broker receiving custody. However, no transfer statement is

required if the broker effects the purchase solely at the instruction of the broker receiving custody.

(iii) *Exempt recipients and exempt foreign payees.*—A transferor is not required to furnish a transfer statement for a security that, after the transfer, is held for a customer that is an exempt recipient under § 1.6045-1(c)(3)(i) or an exempt foreign person under § 1.6045-1(g)(1)(i).

(iv) *Securities lending transactions —transferor as principal.*—A transferor that lends or borrows securities as a principal is not required to furnish a transfer statement for a security that is transferred pursuant to such lending or borrowing arrangement (for example, when a customer opens or closes a short sale). This exception does not apply when a transferor transfers a security under a lending or borrowing arrangement of the customer. This exception also does not apply when a transferor transfers a previously borrowed security to another account of the same customer (for example, to satisfy an existing short sale obligation). *See* paragraph (b)(4) of this section.

(v) *Certain money market funds.*—A transferor of stock in a regulated investment company described in § 1.6045-1(c)(3)(vi) is not required to furnish a transfer statement.

(2) *Format of transfer statement.*—The transfer statement must be furnished in writing unless both the transferor and the receiving broker agree to a different format or method before the transfer. If a transfer occurs between accounts at the same or affiliated entities, a transfer statement is deemed to have been furnished and received if the required information, including any required adjustments, is incorporated into the records for the recipient account.

(3) *Time for furnishing statement.*—A transferor must furnish a transfer statement within fifteen days after the date of settlement for the transfer.

(4) *Applicable person effecting transfer.*—*Applicable person* means any transferor who is a person described in § 1.6045-1(a)(1), a person that acts as a custodian of securities in the ordinary course of a trade or business, an issuer of securities, a trustee or custodian of an individual retirement plan, or any agent of these persons. Applicable person does not include the beneficial owner of a security or any agent substituted for an undisclosed beneficial owner, any governmental unit or agency or instrumentality of a governmental unit holding escheated securities, or any organization that holds and transfers obligations among members of the organization as a service to its members.

(5) *Broker receiving custody.*—Solely for purposes of this section, *broker* means any person described in § 1.6045-1(a)(1), any person that acts as a custodian of securities in the ordinary course of a trade or business, any issuer of securities, and any agent of these persons. Broker does not include the beneficial owner of a security or any agent substituted for an undisclosed beneficial owner, any governmental unit or agency or instrumentality of a governmental unit holding escheated securities, or any organization that holds and transfers obligations among members of the organization as a service to its members.

(6) *Other terms.*—For purposes of this section, the terms sale, specified security, covered security, noncovered security, and customer have the same meaning as in § 1.6045-1(a)(9), (a)(14), (a)(15), (a)(16), and (h)(1).

(7) *Examples.*—The following examples illustrate the rules of this paragraph (a). Unless otherwise stated, in each example the customer is not treated as an exempt recipient under § 1.6045-1(c)(3)(i) or an exempt foreign person under § 1.6045-1(g)(1)(i). The examples are as follows:

*Example 1.* V, an entity treated as an exempt recipient under § 1.6045-1(c)(3)(i), owns a security in an account with E, a broker. On February 1, 2012, V instructs E to transfer custody of the security to an account V maintains with F, another broker. Because E may treat V as an exempt recipient under § 1.6045-1(c)(3)(i), under paragraph (a)(1)(iii) of this section, E is not required to furnish a transfer statement.

*Example 2.* W maintains an account with G, a custodial broker. On August 1, 2012, W instructs G to purchase a security. G places an order to purchase the security with H, a broker with which G has a clearing agreement. W does not maintain a direct account with H. H executes the purchase and has the security delivered to G. Under paragraph (a)(1)(ii)(B) of this section, H is not required to furnish a transfer statement because G received custody of the security and H purchased the security solely at the instruction of G.

*Example 3.* Assume the same facts as in *Example 2* except that W later instructs G to sell the security. G places an order with H to sell the security. H executes the sale. G delivers the security to settle the sale. G is required to report the sale of the security under § 1.6045-1.

Therefore, under paragraph (a)(1)(ii)(A) of this section, G is not required to furnish a transfer statement.

*Example 4.* (i) X maintains an account with J, an introducing broker. J contracts with K, a clearing broker, to allow K to execute trades on J's behalf under a clearing agreement. K uses L, a custodian of securities in the ordinary course of a trade or business, to hold custody of the securities of K's customers. K maintains a separate disclosed account for X as a clearing broker with custody at L. On May 1, 2012, X instructs J to purchase a security for X as the beneficial owner. J instructs K to purchase the security. K effects the purchase and has the security delivered to L.

(ii) K is a broker and therefore is an applicable person that is a transferor within the meaning of paragraph (a)(4) of this section. L acts as a custodian of securities in the ordinary course of a trade or business and therefore is a broker within the meaning of paragraph (a)(5) of this section. Because K effects the purchase of the security but does not receive custody of the security, under paragraphs (a)(1)(i) and (a)(1)(ii)(B) of this section, K must furnish a transfer statement to L.

*Example 5.* (i) Assume the same facts as in *Example 4* except that X later instructs J to sell the security. J instructs K to sell the security. K sells the security. L transfers custody of the security to settle X's sale in accordance with its custody arrangement with K by delivering the security to the purchasing broker. K deposits the sale proceeds in X's account with K. K is required to report the sale of the security under § 1.6045-1.

(ii) L acts as a custodian of securities in the ordinary course of a trade or business and therefore is an applicable person that is a transferor within the meaning of paragraph (a)(4) of this section. Because L transfers custody of the security to the purchaser's broker solely to effect the sale, under paragraphs (a)(1)(i) and (a)(1)(ii)(A) of this section, L must furnish a transfer statement to K.

(iii) If the terms of their custody arrangement so provide, K may furnish the transfer statement as L's agent and satisfy L's duty to furnish the transfer statement under paragraphs (a)(1)(i) and (a)(1)(ii)(A) of this section. Under paragraph (a)(2) of this section, K may satisfy this duty by maintaining the information required on the transfer statement, including all required adjustments, in its records for X's account.

*Example 6.* (i) Y, an investment advisor, wants to purchase shares of stock in C, a corporation, for several of Y's customers. Y establishes a delivery-on-payment account with M, a broker, and provides M a standing instruction to deliver stock purchased in the account to Y's account at N, a custodian of securities in the ordinary course of a trade or business. On November 1, 2012, Y enters into a cash-on-delivery transaction by instructing M to purchase shares of C stock. M executes the purchase and effects delivery of the C stock to N.

(ii) M is a broker and therefore is an applicable person that is a transferor within the meaning of paragraph (a)(4) of this section. N acts as a custodian of securities in the ordinary course of a trade or business and therefore is a broker within the meaning of paragraph (a)(5) of this section. Because M effects the purchase of the stock and N receives custody of the stock, under paragraphs (a)(1)(i) and (a)(1)(ii)(B) of this section, M must furnish a transfer statement to N.

*Example 7.* (i) Z owns shares of stock in C, a corporation, in an account with O, a broker. On February 1, 2013, Z instructs O to transfer the C stock to C so that ownership is held on the books of the issuer. C has an arrangement with D, a transfer agent, to keep records of ownership of the company's stock, how that stock is held, and how many shares each investor owns. O transfers the stock to D.

(ii) O is a broker and therefore is an applicable person that is a transferor within the meaning of paragraph (a)(4) of this section. D is an agent of C, the issuer of the stock, and therefore is a broker within the meaning of paragraph (a)(5) of this section. Because O transfers custody of the stock to D, under paragraph (a)(1)(i) of this section, O must furnish a transfer statement to D.

*Example 8.* Assume the same facts as in *Example 7* except that Z later instructs D to transfer the stock to an account Z maintains with P, another broker. D transfers the stock to P. D is an agent of C, the issuer of the stock, and therefore is an applicable person that is a transferor within the meaning of paragraph (a)(4) of this section. Because P is a broker and D transfers custody of the stock to P, under paragraph (a)(1)(i) of this section, D must furnish a transfer statement to P.

(b) *Information required.*—(1) *In general.*—For all specified securities, each transfer statement must include the information described in this paragraph (b)(1).

(i) *Statement date.*—The date the statement is furnished.

(ii) *Applicable person effecting transfer.*—The name, address, and telephone number of the applicable person furnishing the statement.

(iii) *Broker receiving custody.*—The name, address, and telephone number of the broker receiving custody of the security.

(iv) *Customers.*—The name and account number of the customer or customers for the account from which the security is transferred and, if different, the name and account number of the customer or customers for the account to which the security is transferred.

(v) *Security identifiers.*—The Committee on Uniform Security Identification Procedures (CUSIP) number of the security transferred (if applicable) or other security identifier number that the Secretary may designate by publication in the **Federal Register** or in the Internal Revenue Bulletin (*see* § 601.601(d)(2) of this chapter), quantity of shares, units, or amounts, and classification of the security (such as stock or debt).

(vi) *Transfer dates.*—The date the transfer was initiated and the settlement date of the transfer (if known when furnishing the statement).

(vii) *Adjusted basis and acquisition date.*—The total adjusted basis of the security, the original acquisition date of the security, and, if applicable, the holding period adjustment required by section 1091. The transferor must determine this information as provided under § § 1.6045-1(d), 1.6045-1(m), and 1.6045-1(n), including reporting the adjusted basis of the security in U.S. dollars. If the basis of the transferred security is determined using an average basis method (as described in § 1.1012-1(e)), the transferor may report any securities acquired more than five years before the transfer on a single statement on which the original acquisition date is reported as "VARI-OUS" if the other information reported on the statement applies to all of the securities.

(2) *Examples.*—The following examples illustrate the rules of paragraph (b)(1) of this section:

*Example 1.* (i) In a single account with P, a broker, Q purchases three lots of 100 shares of stock each in C, a corporation, at different prices on April 2, 2012, July 2, 2012, and October 2, 2012. Q instructs P to enroll the shares of the C stock in P's dividend reinvestment plan and to average the basis of the shares of the C stock. All of the C stock purchased by P has the same CUSIP number. On September 13, 2013, less than five years after the acquisition dates for all three lots, Q transfers all 300 shares of the C stock to an account with another broker.

(ii) Under paragraph (a)(1)(i) of this section, P must furnish three transfer statements. Under paragraph (b)(1) of this section, one statement must report the transfer of 100 shares with an original acquisition date of April 2, 2012, one statement must report the transfer of 100 shares with an original acquisition date of July 2, 2012, and one statement must report the transfer of 100 shares with an original acquisition date of October 2, 2012.

*Example 2.* Assume the same facts as in *Example 1* except that Q transfers the shares to the account with the other broker on September 13, 2017. For the 100 shares purchased on April 2, 2012, and the 100 shares purchased on July 2, 2012, under paragraph (b)(1)(vii) of this section, P may furnish a single transfer statement reporting the transfer of 200 shares with the original acquisition date as "VARI-OUS" instead of furnishing two separate transfer statements.

*Example 3.* (i) Assume the same facts as in *Example 1* except that, on June 15, 2012, Q sells the 100 shares purchased on April 2, 2012, at a loss.

(ii) Under paragraph (a)(1)(i) of this section, P must furnish two transfer statements. Under paragraph (b)(1)(vii) of this section and § 1.6045-1(d)(6)(iii) and (d)(7)(ii), P must determine the average basis for the 200 transferred shares and the date for computing whether any gain or loss with respect to the stock purchased on July 2, 2012, is long-term or short-term by applying the rules for broker reporting of wash sales to the stock purchased on July 2, 2012. Therefore, on both transfer statements, P must increase the average basis of the stock by the amount of loss disallowed under section 1091 on the sale of the 100 shares purchased on April 2, 2012. On the transfer statement reporting the transfer of the 100 shares purchased on July 2, 2012, P must adjust the holding period of the July 2, 2012, shares in accordance with section 1091.

*Example 4.* (i) R, an employee of C, a corporation, participates in C's employee stock purchase program that satisfies the requirements of section 423. D administers the plan. R purchases stock in the plan at a 15 percent discount to the fair market value of the stock determined on the date of purchase. R purchases stock through the plan during 2012 until R terminates employment on October 15, 2012. R later instructs D to transfer the plan shares to S, a broker.

(ii) D is the agent of C, the issuer of the securities, and therefore is an applicable person within the meaning of paragraph (a)(4) of this section. Because S is a broker and D transfers custody of the stock to S, under paragraph (a)(1)(i) of this section, D must furnish a transfer statement to S.

(iii) Under paragraph (b)(1)(vii) of this section and § 1.6045-1(d)(6)(ii)(A), D must report adjusted basis on the transfer statement based on the amount paid by R. Under paragraph (b)(1)(vii) of this section and §1.6045-1(d)(6)(ii)(A), D is permitted, but is not required, to increase the adjusted basis for the amount (if any) includible as wage income by R for R's purchases of the stock.

(3) *Additional information required for a transfer of a debt instrument.*—In addition to the information required in paragraph (b)(1) of this section, for a transfer of a debt instrument that is a covered security, the following additional information is required:

(i) A description of the payment terms used by the broker to compute any basis adjustments under §1.6045-1(n);

(ii) The issue price of the debt instrument;

(iii) The issue date of the debt instrument (if different from the original acquisition date of the debt instrument);

(iv) The adjusted issue price of the debt instrument as of the transfer date;

(v) The customer's initial basis in the debt instrument;

(vi) Any market discount that has accrued as of the transfer date (as determined under §1.6045-1(n));

(vii) Any bond premium that has been amortized as of the transfer date (as determined under §1.6045-1(n));

(viii) Any acquisition premium that has been amortized as of the transfer date (as determined under §1.6045-1(n));

(ix) Whether the transferring broker has computed any of the information described in this paragraph (b)(3) by taking into account one or more elections described in §1.6045-1(n), and, if so, which election or elections were taken into account by the transferring broker; and

(x) For a transfer that occurs on or after January 1, 2016, the last date on or before the transfer date that the transferor made an adjustment for a particular item (for example, the last date on or before the transfer date that bond premium was amortized). A broker, however, may rely on this paragraph (b)(3)(x) for a transfer of a covered security that occurs on or after June 30, 2015, and before January 1, 2016.

(4) *Additional information required for option transfers.*—In addition to the information required in paragraph (b)(1) of this section, for a transfer of an option that is a covered security, the following additional information is required:

(i) The date of grant or acquisition of the option;

(ii) The amount of premium paid or received;

(iii) Any other information required to fully describe the option, which may include a security identifier used by option exchanges, or details about the underlying asset, quantity covered, exercise type, strike price, and maturity date; and

(iv) For a transfer of an option described in §1.6045-1(m)(3) (section 1256 option) that occurs on or after January 1, 2016, the original basis of the option and the fair market value of the option as of the end of the prior calendar year.

(5) *Format of identification.*—An applicable person furnishing a transfer statement and a broker receiving the transfer statement may agree to combine the information in paragraphs (b)(1), (b)(3), and (b)(4) of this section in any format or to use a code in place of one or more required items. For example, a transferor and a receiving broker may agree to use a single code to represent the broker instead of the broker's name, address, and telephone number, or may use a security symbol or other identification number or scheme instead of the security identifier required by paragraphs (b)(1), (b)(3), and (b)(4) of this section. As another example, a transferor and a receiving broker may agree to use a security identifier for an exchange-traded option if that information would be sufficient to inform the receiving broker of the terms for that option.

(6) *Transfers of noncovered securities.*—The information described in paragraphs (b)(1)(vii), (b)(3), (b)(4), (b)(8), and (b)(9) of this section is not required for a transfer of a noncovered security if the transfer statement identifies the security as a noncovered security. A transferor that chooses to report nonrequired information is not subject to penalties under section 6722 for failure to report this information correctly if the transfer statement identifies the security as a noncovered security. A single transfer statement may report the transfer of multiple noncovered securities if the transfer statement clearly conveys, either specifically or generally, the information described in paragraph (b)(1)(v) of this section to identify each security. For purposes of this paragraph (b)(6), a transferor must treat a security for which a broker makes a single-account election described in §1.1012-1(e)(11)(i) as a covered security.

(7) *Transfers of borrowed securities.*—The transfer statement must indicate that a transferred security is borrowed if the transferor knows that the security is transferred pursuant to a lending or borrowing arrangement. The transfer statement must not report an adjusted basis If the transferor knows that the transferred security is lent or borrowed pursuant to a short sale. The receiving broker may

be subject to special transfer reporting rules upon receipt of a borrowed security if the security is used to satisfy an existing short sale obligation. *See* §1.6045-1(c)(3)(xi)(C).

(8) *Transfers pursuant to an inheritance.*—(i) *In general.*—A transfer statement for a transfer of a security from a decedent or decedent's estate must indicate that the security is inherited. The transfer statement must report the date of death as the original acquisition date and must report adjusted basis according to the instructions or valuations furnished by an authorized representative of the estate, including any required adjustments to basis for property acquired from a decedent. If a transferor has not received instructions or valuations from an authorized representative, the transferor must report basis as the fair market value of the security on the date of death. However, if the transferor neither knows nor can readily ascertain the fair market value of the security on the date of death at the time the transfer statement is prepared, the transfer statement must indicate that the transfer consists of an inherited security but may otherwise report the security as if it were a noncovered security. If the transferor cannot identify which securities in a joint account have been transferred from the decedent, the transferor must treat each security in the account as if it were a noncovered security but must not indicate that any security is an inherited security.

(ii) *Transfers of securities to satisfy a cash legacy.*—If a security is transferred from a decedent or a decedent's estate to satisfy a cash legacy, paragraphs (b)(1), (b)(3), and (b)(4) of this section apply and paragraph (b)(8)(i) of this section does not apply.

(iii) *Subsequent transfers of inherited securities.*—A transfer statement must indicate that the transfer consists of an inherited security if a prior transfer statement reported the security as inherited.

(9) *Gift or deemed gift transfers.*—(i) *In general.*—A transfer statement for a security transferred to a different owner (other than a transfer that the transferor knows is pursuant to a lending or borrowing arrangement or is from a decedent or decedent's estate) must indicate that the security is a gift and must report the date of the gift (if known when furnishing the statement) and the fair market value of the gift on that date (if known or readily ascertainable at the time the transfer statement is prepared). The transfer statement must report the adjusted basis and original acquisition date of the security in the hands of the donor. However, if the transfer is between persons for whom gift-related basis adjustments are inapplicable or between accounts that share at least one common customer, the transferor must apply paragraph (b)(1) of this section as if the security were not a gift or deemed gift.

(ii) *Subsequent transfers of gifts by the same customer.*—If a transferor transfers to a different account of the same customer a security that a prior transfer statement reported as a gifted security, the transferor must include on the transfer statement the information described in paragraph (b)(9)(i) of this section for the date of the gift to the customer. If the prior transfer statement did not report a date for the gift, the transferor must treat the settlement date for the prior transfer as the date of the gift.

(iii) *Examples.*—The following examples illustrate the rules of this paragraph (b)(9):

*Example 1.* X instructs S, a broker, to give to Y stock in a publicly traded company that X holds in an account with S. The stock is a covered security. On X's instruction, S transfers custody of the stock to T, Y's broker. The transfer settles on August 15, 2013. Under paragraph (b)(9)(i) of this section, S must provide a transfer statement to T that identifies the securities as gifted securities and indicates X's adjusted basis and original acquisition date. If S knows the settlement date, the transfer statement must also indicate that the date of the gift was August 15, 2013, and, because S can readily ascertain the fair market value of the stock on August 15, 2013, the fair market value of the stock on that date.

*Example 2.* Assume the same facts as in *Example 1* except that, one year later, Y transfers the stock to an account in his name with U, another broker. Under paragraph (b)(9)(ii) of this section, T must provide a transfer statement to U that identifies the securities as gifted securities and indicates X's adjusted basis and original acquisition date of the stock. The transfer statement must also indicate the date of the gift, August 15, 2013, and the fair market value of the stock on that date either by reporting the value that S reported to T or, because T can readily ascertain the fair market value of the stock on August 15, 2013, by determining the fair market value of the stock on that date.

(10) *Specific identification of securities.*—Except as provided in §1.1012-1(e)(7)(ii), a transfer statement must report a transfer of less than the entire position in an account of a security that was acquired on different dates or at different prices consistently with a customer's adequate and timely identification of the security to be transferred.

**Reg. §1.6045A-1(b)(3)**

*See* §1.1012-1(c). If the customer does not provide an adequate and timely identification for the transfer, a transferor must first report the transfer of any securities in the account for which the transferor does not know the acquisition or purchase date followed by the earliest securities purchased or acquired, whether covered securities or non-covered securities.

(11) *Information from other parties and other accounts.*—(i) *Transfer and issuer statements and transfers pursuant to an inheritance.*—When reporting a transfer of a covered security, a transferor must take into account all information, other than the classification of the security (such as stock), furnished on a transfer statement, all information furnished or deemed furnished on an issuer statement (as described in §1.6045B-1, and all instructions and valuations furnished by an authorized representative of the estate of a decedent, unless the statement or instructions are incomplete or the broker has actual knowledge that they are incorrect. A transferor may treat a customer as a minority shareholder when taking the information on an issuer statement into account unless the transferor knows that the customer is a majority shareholder and the issuer statement reports the action's effect on the basis of majority shareholders. Any failure to report correct information that arises solely from reliance on information furnished on a transfer statement or issuer statement or by an authorized representative of the estate is deemed to be due to reasonable cause for purposes of penalties under section 6722. *See* §301.6724-1(a)(1) of this chapter.

(ii) *Other information.*—A transferor is permitted, but not required, to take into account information about a covered security other than what is furnished on a transfer statement or issuer statement or by an authorized representative of the estate of a decedent, including any information the transferor has about securities held by the same customer in other accounts with the transferor. For purposes of penalties under section 6722, a transferor that takes into account information received from a customer or third party other than information furnished on a transfer statement or issuer statement or by an authorized representative of the estate of a decedent is deemed to have relied upon this information in good faith if the transferor neither knows nor has reason to know that the information is incorrect. *See* §301.6724-1(c)(6) of this chapter.

(12) *Failure to receive a complete transfer statement.*—(i) *In general.*—A receiving broker that has not received a complete transfer statement as required under paragraph (a)(3) of this section for the transfer must request a complete statement from the transferor unless, under paragraph (a) of this section, the transferor has no duty to furnish a transfer statement for the transfer. The receiving broker is only required to make this request once. If the receiving broker does not receive a complete transfer statement after requesting it, the receiving broker may treat the security as a noncovered security upon its subsequent sale or transfer. A transfer statement for a covered security is complete if, in the view of the receiving broker, it provides sufficient information to comply with §1.6045-1 when reporting the sale of the security. A transfer statement for a noncovered security is complete if it indicates that the security is a noncovered security.

(ii) *Transition rules for transfers of debt instruments, options, and securities futures contracts.*—If an option described in §1.6045-1(a)(14)(iii), a securities futures contract described in §1.6045-1(a)(14)(iv), or a debt instrument described in §1.6045-1(a)(15)(i)(C) is transferred in 2014 and no transfer statement is received, the receiving broker is not required to request a transfer statement from the transferor and may treat the security as a noncovered security. If a debt instrument described in §1.6045-1(a)(15)(i)(D) is transferred in 2016 and no transfer statement is received, the receiving broker is not required to request a transfer statement from the transferor and may treat the security as a noncovered security.

(c) *Reporting by other parties after a transfer.*—(1) *In general.*—A transferor that has furnished a transfer statement must furnish a corrected statement for a covered security within fifteen days of receiving a transfer statement, an issuer statement (as described in §1.6045B-1, or instructions or valuations from an authorized representative of an estate, that provides information under paragraph (b) of this section that was not reported on the initial transfer statement.

(2) *Exception.*—A transferor is not required to furnish a corrected transfer statement for a covered security under this paragraph (c) if the transferor receives the transfer statement or issuer statement or receives the instructions or valuations from an authorized representative of an estate more than eighteen months after the transferor furnished the transfer statement.

(d) *Effective/applicability dates.*—This section applies to:

(1) A transfer on or after January 1, 2011, of stock other than stock in a regulated investment company within the meaning of §1.1012-1(e)(5);

(2) A transfer on or after January 1, 2012, of stock in a regulated investment company;

(3) A transfer on or after January 1, 2015, of an option described in §1.6045-1(a)(14)(iii), a securities futures contract described in §1.6045-1(a)(14)(iv), or a debt instrument described in §1.6045-1(a)(15)(i)(C); and

(4) A transfer on or after January 1, 2017, of a debt instrument described in §1.6045-1(a)(15)(i)(D). [Reg. §1.6045A-1.]

☐ [*T.D.* 9504, 10-12-2010. *Amended by T.D.* 9616, 4-17-2013, *T.D.* 9713, 3-12-2015 *and T.D.* 9750, 2-17-2016 *(corrected* 4-26-2016).]

### [Reg. §1.6045B-1]

**§1.6045B-1 Returns relating to actions affecting basis of securities.**—(a) *In general.*—(1) *Information required.*—An issuer of a specified security (within the meaning of §1.6045-1(a)(14) that takes an organizational action that affects the basis of the security must file an issuer return setting forth the following information and any other information specified in the return form and instructions:

(i) *Reporting issuer.*—The name and taxpayer identification number of the reporting issuer.

(ii) *Security identifiers.*—The identifiers of each security involved in the organizational action including, as applicable, the Committee on Uniform Security Identification Procedures (CUSIP) number or other security identifier number that the Secretary may designate by publication in the **Federal Register** or in the Internal Revenue Bulletin (*see* §601.601(d)(2) of this chapter), classification of the security (such as stock), account number, serial number, and ticker symbol, as well as any descriptions about the class of security affected.

(iii) *Contact at reporting issuer.*—The name, address, e-mail address, and telephone number of a contact person at the issuer.

(iv) *Information about action.*—The type or nature of the organizational action including, as applicable, the date of the action or the date against which shareholders' ownership is measured for the action.

(v) *Effect of the action.*—The quantitative effect of the organizational action on the basis of the security in the hands of a U.S. taxpayer as an adjustment per share or as a percentage of old basis, including a description of the calculation, the applicable Internal Revenue Code section and subsection upon which the tax treatment is based, the data supporting the calculation such as the market values of securities and valuation dates, any other information necessary to implement the adjustment including the reportable taxable year, and whether any resulting loss may be recognized.

(2) *Time for filing the return.*—(i) *In general.*—An issuer must file an issuer return with the IRS pursuant to the prescribed form and instructions on or before the 45th day following the organizational action, or, if earlier, January 15 of the year following the calendar year of the organizational action. For purposes of this paragraph (a)(2), a redemption occurs on the last day a holder may redeem a security. The issuer may file the return before the organizational action if the quantitative effect on basis is determinable beforehand.

(ii) *Reasonable assumptions.*—To report the quantitative effect on basis by the due date in paragraph (a)(2)(i) of this section, an issuer may make reasonable assumptions about facts that cannot be determined before the due date. An issuer must file a corrected return within forty-five days of determining facts that result in a different quantitative effect on basis from what the issuer previously reported. However, for purposes of this paragraph (a)(2)(ii), an issuer must treat a payment that may be a dividend consistently with its treatment of the payment under section 6042(b)(3) and §1.6042-3(c).

(3) *Exception for public reporting.*—An issuer is not required to file a return with the IRS under this paragraph (a) if, by the due date described in paragraph (a)(2)(i) of this section, the issuer posts the return with the required information in a readily accessible format in an area of its primary public Web site dedicated to this purpose and keeps the return accessible for ten years to the public on its primary public Web site or the primary public Web site of any successor organization. An issuer may electronically sign a return that is publicly reported in accordance with this paragraph (a)(3). The electronic signature must identify the individual who attests to the declaration in the jurat.

(4) *Exception when holders are exempt recipients.*—No reporting is required under this paragraph (a) if the issuer reasonably determines

that all of the holders of the security are exempt recipients under paragraph (b)(5) of this section.

(5) *Exception for certain money market funds.*—No reporting is required under this paragraph (a) by a regulated investment company described in § 1.6045-1(c)(3)(vi).

(b) *Statements to nominees and certificate holders.*—(1) *In general.*— An issuer required to file an information return under this section must furnish a written statement with the same information to each holder of record of the security or to the holder's nominee. This issuer statement must indicate that the information is being reported to the IRS. An issuer may satisfy this requirement by furnishing a copy of the information return.

(2) *Time for furnishing statements.*—An issuer must furnish each issuer statement on or before January 15 of the year following the calendar year of the organizational action. For purposes of this paragraph (b)(2), a redemption occurs on the last day a holder may redeem a security. An issuer may furnish the statement before the organizational action if the quantitative effect on basis is determinable beforehand. An issuer must furnish a statement that corresponds to a corrected return described in paragraph (a)(2)(ii) of this section by the later of the due date described in this paragraph (b)(2) or forty-five days after determining the facts that result in a different quantitative effect on basis from what the issuer previously reported on the return.

(3) *Recipients of statements.*—An issuer must furnish a separate statement to each holder of record of the security as of the date of the organizational action and all subsequent holders of record up to the date the issuer furnishes the statement required under this section. If the issuer records the security on its books in the name of a nominee, the issuer must furnish the statement to the nominee in lieu of the holder. However, if the nominee is the issuer, an agent of the issuer, or a plan operated by the issuer, the issuer must furnish the statement to the holder.

(4) *Exception for public reporting.*—An issuer is deemed to furnish an issuer statement under this paragraph (b) to all holders and nominees if the issuer satisfies the public reporting requirements of paragraph (a)(3) of this section.

(5) *Exempt recipients.*—(i) *In general.*—An issuer is not required to furnish an issuer statement to a holder or its nominee if the holder is an exempt recipient under § 1.6045-1(c)(3)(i)(B), provided the issuer has actual knowledge that the holder is described in that section or has a properly completed exemption certificate from the holder asserting that the holder is an exempt recipient (as provided in § 31.3406(h)-3 of this chapter). An issuer may treat a holder as an exempt recipient based on the applicable indicators described in § 1.6049-4(c)(1)(ii)(A) through (M).

(ii) *Limitation for corporate holders.*—For an organizational action occurring on or after January 1, 2012, an issuer may treat a holder as an exempt recipient based on the indicator described in § 1.6049-4(c)(1)(ii)(A) only if one of the following applies:

(A) The name of the holder contains the term "insurance company," "indemnity company," "reinsurance company," or "assurance company."

(B) The name of the holder indicates that it is an entity listed as a per se corporation under § 301.7701-2(b)(8)(i) of this chapter.

(C) The issuer receives a properly completed exemption certificate (as provided in § 31.3406(h)-3 of this chapter) that asserts that the holder is not an S corporation as defined in section 1361(a).

(D) The issuer receives a withholding certificate described in § 1.1441-1(e)(2)(i) that includes a certification that the person whose name is on the certificate is a foreign corporation.

(iii) *Foreign holders.*—An issuer may treat a holder as an exempt recipient if the issuer, prior to the transaction, associates the holder with documentation upon which the issuer may rely in order to treat payments to the holder as made to a foreign beneficial owner in accordance with § 1.1441-1(e)(1)(ii) or as made to a foreign payee in accordance with § 1.6049-5(d)(1) or presumed to be made to a foreign payee under § 1.6049-5(d)(2) or (3). For purposes of this paragraph (b)(5)(iii), the provisions in § 1.6049-5(c) (regarding rules applicable to documentation of foreign status and definition of U.S. payor and non-U.S. payor) apply. Rules similar to the rules of § 1.1441-1 apply by substituting the terms "issuer" and "holder" in place of the terms "withholding agent" and "payee" and without regard to the limitation to amounts subject to withholding under chapter 3 of the Internal Revenue Code. Rules similar to the rules of § 1.6049-5(d) apply by substituting the terms "issuer" and "holder" in place of the terms "payor" and "payee."

(c) *Special rule for S corporations.*—An S corporation (as defined in section 1361(a)) is deemed to satisfy the requirements of paragraphs (a) and (b) of this section for any organizational action affecting the basis of its stock if the corporation reports the effect of the organizational action on a timely filed Schedule K-1 (Form 1120S), "Shareholder's Share of Income, Deductions, Credits, etc.," for each shareholder and timely furnishes copies of these schedules to all proper parties.

(d) *Special rule for certain regulated investment companies and real estate investment trusts.*—A regulated investment company (RIC) that reports undistributed capital gains to shareholders under section 852(b)(3)(D) or a real estate investment trust (REIT) that reports undistributed capital gains to shareholders under section 857(b)(3)(D) is deemed to have satisfied the requirements of paragraphs (a) and (b) of this section for undistributed capital gains affecting the basis of its stock if the RIC or REIT timely files and furnishes the information returns required under section 852(b)(3)(D) or section 857(b)(3)(D) to all proper parties for the organizational action.

(e) *Acquiring and successor entities.*—An acquiring or successor entity of an issuer that fails to satisfy the reporting obligations of paragraphs (a) or (b) of this section must satisfy these reporting obligations. If neither the issuer nor the acquiring or successor entity satisfies these reporting obligations, both parties are jointly and severally liable for any applicable penalties.

(f) *Penalties.*—An issuer may use an agent to satisfy the requirements of this section for the issuer. Nonetheless, the issuer remains liable for penalty for any failure to comply unless it is shown that the failure is due to reasonable cause and not willful neglect. *See* sections 6721 through 6724.

(g) *Examples.*—The following examples illustrate the rules of this section:

*Example 1.* (i) C, a corporation, distributes stock to shareholders on March 31, 2013.

(ii) Under paragraph (a)(2)(i) of this section, C must file an issuer return with the IRS on or before May 15, 2013 (45 days after the distribution date), reporting the quantitative effect of this distribution on the basis of C's stock. Under paragraph (b)(2) of this section, C must furnish issuer statements to its nominees and certificate holders on or before January 15, 2014.

(iii) Alternatively, under paragraphs (a)(3) and (b)(4) of this section, C may post by May 15, 2013, and maintain for ten years, the return with the required information in a readily accessible format in an area of its primary public Web site dedicated to this purpose.

*Example 2.* (i) D, a corporation, makes a cash distribution to shareholders on December 10, 2013.

(ii) Under paragraphs (a)(2)(i) and (b)(2) of this section, D is required to file an issuer return with the IRS and furnish issuer statements to its nominees and certificate holders on or before January 15, 2014.

(iii) On January 15, 2014, D is unsure whether the distribution will exceed its earnings and profits for the fiscal year. For purposes of section 6042(b)(3) and § 1.6042-3(c), D must treat the distribution as a dividend. Therefore, under paragraph (a)(2)(ii) of this section, D is not required to file an issuer return. If D later determines that dividend treatment was incorrect, D must file an issuer return reporting the correct quantitative effect on basis.

*Example 3.* E, a corporation, undertakes a stock split as of April 1, 2014. E furnishes issuer statements under paragraph (b) of this section on April 1, 2014, at which time the books and records of E show that 90 percent of its outstanding stock is owned by shareholders through a clearing organization as their nominee, 7 percent is owned by 5,000 individuals, and the remaining 3 percent is owned by a dividend reinvestment plan operated by E that has 1,000 members. Under paragraph (b)(3) of this section, E must furnish statements to the clearing organization, the 5,000 individuals, and the 1,000 members of the dividend reinvestment plan.

(h) *Rule for options.*—(1) *In general.*—For an option granted or acquired on or after January 1, 2014, if the original contract is replaced by a different number of option contracts, the following rules apply:

(i) If the option is an exchange-traded option, any clearinghouse or clearing facility that serves as a counterparty is treated as the issuer of the option for purposes of section 6045B.

(ii) If the option is not an exchange-traded option, the option writer is treated as the issuer of the option for purposes of section 6045B.

(2) *Examples.*—The following examples illustrate the rules of paragraph (h)(1) of this section:

*Example 1.* On January 15, 2014, F, an individual, purchases a one-year exchange-traded call option on 100 shares of Company X stock, with a strike price of $110. The call option is cleared through Clearinghouse G. Company X executes a 2-for-1 stock split as of April 1, 2014. Due to the stock split, the terms of F's option are altered, resulting in two option contracts, each on 100 shares of Company X stock with a strike price of $55. All other terms remain the same. Under paragraph (h)(1)(i) of this section, Clearinghouse G is required to prepare an issuer report for F.

*Example 2.* On January 31, 2014, J, an individual, purchases from K a non-exchange traded 7-month option on 100 shares of Company X stock, with a strike price of $110. Company X executes a 2-for-1 stock split as of April 1, 2014. Due to the stock split, the terms of J's option are altered, resulting in one option contract on 200 shares of Company X stock with a strike price of $55. All other terms of the option remain the same. Under paragraph (h)(1) of this section, because the number of option contracts did not change, K is not required to prepare an issuer report for J.

(i) [Reserved]

(j) *Effective/applicability dates.*—This section applies to—

(1) Organizational actions occurring on or after January 1, 2011, that affect the basis of specified securities within the meaning of §1.6045-1(a)(14)(i) other than stock in a regulated investment company within the meaning of §1.1012-1(e)(5);

(2) Organizational actions occurring on or after January 1, 2012, that affect the basis of stock in a regulated investment company;

(3) Organizational actions occurring on or after January 1, 2014, that affect the basis of debt instruments described in §1.6045-1(n)(2)(i) (not including the debt instruments described in §1.6045-1(n)(2)(ii));

(4) Organizational actions occurring on or after January 1, 2016, that affect the basis of debt instruments described in §1.6045-1(n)(3);

(5) Organizational actions occurring on or after January 1, 2014, that affect the basis of options described in §1.6045-1(a)(14)(iii); and

(6) Organizational actions occurring on or after January 1, 2014, that affect the basis of securities futures contracts described in §1.6045-1(a)(14)(iv). [Reg. §1.6045B-1.]

☐ *[T.D. 9504, 10-12-2010. Amended by T.D. 9616, 4-17-2013.]*

### [Reg. §1.6046-1]

**§1.6046-1. Returns as to organization or reorganization of foreign corporations and as to acquisitions of their stock.**—(a) *Officers or directors.*—(1) *When liability arises on January 1, 1963.*—Each United States citizen or resident who is on January 1, 1963, an officer or director of a foreign corporation shall make a return on Form 5471 (or subsequent form) showing the name, address, and identifying number of each United States person who, on January 1, 1963, owns 5 percent or more in value of the outstanding stock of such foreign corporation.

(2) *When liability arises after January 1, 1963.*—(i) *Requirement of return.*—Each United States citizen or resident who is at any time after January 1, 1963, an officer or director of a foreign corporation shall make a return on Form 5471 setting forth the information described in paragraph (a)(2)(ii) of this section with respect to each United States person who, during the time such citizen or resident is such an officer or director —

(a) Acquires (whether in one or more transactions) outstanding stock of such corporation which equals, or which when added to any such stock then owned by him equals, 10 percent or more of the total combined voting power of all classes of stock of the foreign corporation entitled to vote or the total value of the stock of the foreign corporation;

(b) Acquires (whether in one or more transactions) an additional 10 percent or more of the total combined voting power of all classes of stock of the foreign corporation entitled to vote or the total value of the stock of the foreign corporation; or

(c) Is not described in paragraph (a)(2)(i)(a) or (b) of this section, and who, at any time after January 1, 1987, is treated as a United States shareholder under section 953(c) with respect to such foreign corporation.

(ii) *Information required to be shown on return.*—The return required under subdivision (i) of this subparagraph shall contain the following information:

(a) Name, address, and identifying number of each shareholder with respect to whom the return is filed;

(b) A statement showing that the shareholder is either described in subdivision (i)(a) or (i)(b) of this subparagraph; and

(c) The date on which the shareholder became a person described in subdivision (i)(a) or (i)(b) of this subparagraph.

(3) *Application of rules.*—The provisions of this paragraph may be illustrated by the following examples:

*Example (1).* A, a United States citizen, is, on January 1, 1963, a director of M, a foreign corporation. X, on January 1, 1963, is a United States person owning 5 percent in value of the outstanding stock of M Corporation. A must file a return under the provisions of subparagraph (1) of this paragraph.

*Example 2.* (i) *Facts.* A, a United States citizen, is, on January 1, 2014, a director of M Corporation, a foreign corporation. X, on January 1, 2014, is a United States person owning 4% of the outstanding stock of M Corporation. On July 1, 2014, X acquires 4% of the outstanding stock of M Corporation and on September 1, 2014, he acquires an additional 4% of such stock.

(ii) *Results.* The July 1, 2014, transaction does not give rise to liability for A to file a return; however, A must file a return as a result of the September 1, 2014, transaction because X's holdings now exceed 10%.

*Example 3.* (i) *Facts.* The facts are the same as in *Example 2* and, on September 15, 2014, X acquires an additional 8% of the outstanding stock of M Corporation. (X's total holdings are now 20%.) On November 1, 2014, X acquires an additional 4% of the outstanding stock of M Corporation.

(ii) *Results.* The September 15, 2014, transaction does not give rise to liability to file a return since X has not acquired 10% of the outstanding stock of M Corporation since A last became liable to file a return. However, A must file a return as a result of the November 1, 2014, transaction because X has now acquired an additional 10% of the outstanding stock of M Corporation.

*Example 4.* (i) *Facts.* The facts are the same as in *Examples 2* and *3* and, in addition, B, a United States citizen, becomes an officer of M Corporation on September 10, 2014.

(ii) *Results.* B is not required to file a return either as a result of the facts set forth in *Example 2* or as a result of the September 15, 2014, transaction described in *Example 3.* However, B is required to file a return as a result of the November 1, 2014, transaction described in *Example 3* because X has acquired an additional 10% in value of the outstanding stock of M Corporation while B is an officer or director.

(b) *Returns required of United States persons when liability to file arises on January 1, 1963.*—Each United States person who, on January 1, 1963, owns 5 percent or more in value of the outstanding stock of a foreign corporation, shall make a return on Form 959 with respect to such foreign corporation setting forth the following information:

(1) The name, address, and identifying number of the shareholder (or shareholders) filing the return, and the internal revenue district in which such shareholder filed his most recent United States income tax return;

(2) The name, business address, and employer identification number, if any, of the foreign corporation, the name of the country under the laws of which it is incorporated, and the name of the country in which is located its principal place of business;

(3) The date of organization and, if any, of each reorganization of the foreign corporation if such reorganization occurred on or after January 1, 1960, while the shareholder owned 5 percent or more in value of the outstanding stock of such corporation;

(4) The name and address of the foreign corporation's statutory or resident agent in the country of incorporation;

(5) The name, address, and identifying number of any branch office or agent of the foreign corporation located in the United States;

(6) If the foreign corporation has filed a United States income tax return, or participated in the filing of a consolidated return, for any of its last three calendar or fiscal years immediately preceding January 1, 1963, state each year for which a return was filed (including, in the case of a consolidated return, the name of the corporation filing such return), the type of form used, the internal revenue office to which it was sent, and the amount of tax, if any, paid;

(7) The name and address of the person (or persons) having custody of the books of account and records of the foreign corporation, and the location of such books and records if different from such address;

(8) The names, addresses, and identifying numbers of all United States persons who are principal officers (for example, president, vice president, secretary, treasurer, and comptroller) or members of the board of directors of the foreign corporation as of January 1, 1963;

(9) A complete description of the principal business activities in which the foreign corporation is actually engaged and, if the foreign corporation is a member of a group constituting a chain of ownership with respect to each unit of which the shareholder owns 5 percent or more in value of the outstanding stock, a chart showing the foreign corporation's position in the chain of ownership and the percentages of ownership;

(10) The following information prepared in accordance with generally accepted accounting principles and in such detail as is customary for the corporation's accounting records:

(i) The corporation's profit and loss statement for the most recent complete annual accounting period; and

(ii) The corporation's balance sheet as of the end of the most recent complete annual accounting period;

(11) A statement showing as of January 1, 1963, the amount and type of any indebtedness of the foreign corporation—

(i) To any United States person owning 5 percent or more in value of its stock, or

(ii) To any other foreign corporation owning 5 percent or more in value of the outstanding stock of the foreign corporation with respect to which the return is filed provided that the shareholder filing the return owns 5 percent or more in value of the outstanding stock of such other foreign corporation, together with the name, address, and identifying number, if any, of each such shareholder or entity;

(12) A statement, as of January 1, 1963, showing the name, address, and identifying number, if any, of each person who is, on January 1, 1963, a subscriber to the stock of the foreign corporation, and the number of shares subscribed to by each;

(13) A statement showing the number of shares of each class of stock of the foreign corporation owned by each shareholder filing the return and—

(i) If such stock was acquired after December 31, 1953, the dates of acquisition, the amounts paid or value given therefor, the method of acquisition, i.e., by original issue, purchase on open market, direct purchase, gift, inheritance, etc., and from whom acquired; or

(ii) If such stock was acquired before January 1, 1954, a statement that such stock was acquired before such date, and the value at which such stock is carried on the books of such shareholder;

(14) A statement showing as of January 1, 1963, the name, address, and identifying number of each United States person who owns 5 percent or more in value of the outstanding stock of the foreign corporation, the classes of stock held, the number of shares of each class held, including the name, address, and identifying number, if any, of each actual owner if such person is different from the shareholder of record and a statement of the nature and amount of the interests of each such actual owner; and

(15) The total number of shares of each class of outstanding stock of the foreign corporation (or other data indicating the shareholder's percentage of ownership).

(c) *Returns required of United States persons when liability to file arises after January 1, 1963.*—(1) *United States persons required to file.*—A return on Form 5471, containing the information required by paragraph (c)(4) of this section, shall be made by each United States person when at any time after January 1, 1963:

(i) Such person acquires (whether in one or more transactions) outstanding stock of such foreign corporation which equals, or which when added to any such stock then owned by him equals, 10 percent or more of the total combined voting power of all classes of stock of the foreign corporation entitled to vote or the total value of the stock of the foreign corporation;

(ii) Such person, having already acquired the interest referred to in paragraph (b) of this section or in paragraph (c)(1)(i) of this section —

(a) Acquires (whether in one or more transactions) an additional 10 percent or more of the total combined voting power of all classes of stock of the foreign corporation entitled to vote or the total value of the stock of the foreign corporation;

(b) Owns 10 percent or more of the total combined voting power of all classes of stock of the foreign corporation entitled to vote or the total value of the stock of the foreign corporation when such foreign corporation is reorganized (as defined in paragraph (f)); or

(c) Disposes of sufficient stock in such foreign corporation to reduce his interest to less than 10 percent of the total combined voting power of all classes of stock of the foreign corporation entitled to vote or the total value of the stock of the foreign corporation; or

(iii) Such person is, at any time after January 1, 1987, treated as a United States shareholder under *section 953(c)* with respect to a foreign corporation.

(2) *Examples.*—The provisions of paragraph (c)(1) of this section may be illustrated by the following examples:

*Example 1.* (i) *Facts.* On January 15, 2014, A, a United States person, acquires 10% of the outstanding stock of M, a foreign corporation.

(ii) *Results.* A must file a return under the provisions of paragraph (c)(1) of this section.

*Example 2.* (i) *Facts.* On January 1, 2014, B, a United States person, owns 4% of the outstanding stock of M, a foreign corporation. On February 1, 2015, B acquires an additional 6% of the outstanding stock of M Corporation.

(ii) *Results.* B is not required to file a return for 2014 under the provisions of this section because he does not own 10% or more of the outstanding stock of M Corporation. B must file a return for 2015 under the provisions of paragraph (c)(1) of this section.

*Example 3.* (i) *Facts.* On January 1, 2014, C, a United States person, owns 12% of the outstanding stock of M Corporation, a foreign corporation. On February 1, 2014, C acquires an additional 4% of the outstanding stock of M Corporation in a transaction not involving a reorganization.

(ii) *Results.* C is not required to file a return under the provisions of paragraph (c)(1) of this section with respect to the acquisition of the additional 4% of M Corporation.

*Example 4.* (i) *Facts.* The facts are the same as in *Example 3* except that, in addition, on April 1, 2014, C acquires 4% of the outstanding stock of M Corporation in a transaction not involving a reorganization. (C's total holdings are now 20%.) On May 1, 2014, C acquires 2% of the outstanding stock of M Corporation.

(ii) *Results.* C is not required to file a return under the provisions of paragraph (c)(1) of this section as a result of the April 1, 2014, acquisition because he has not acquired 10% or more of the outstanding stock of M Corporation since he last became liable to file a return. C must file a return under the provisions of paragraph (c)(1) of this section as a result of the May 1, 2014, acquisition because C acquired 10% of the outstanding stock of M Corporation during 2014.

*Example 5.* (i) *Facts.* On June 1, 2014, D, a United States person, owns 24% of the outstanding stock of M Corporation, a foreign corporation. Also, on June 1, 2014, M Corporation is reorganized and, as a result of such reorganization, D owns only 12% of the outstanding stock of such foreign corporation.

(ii) *Results.* D must file a return under the provisions of paragraph (c)(1) of this section.

*Example 6.* (i) *Facts.* The facts are the same as in *Example 5* except that, in addition, on November 1, 2015, D donates 4% of the outstanding stock of M Corporation to a charity.

(ii) *Results.* Since D has disposed of sufficient stock to reduce his interest in M Corporation to less than 10% of the outstanding stock of such corporation, D must file a return under the provisions of paragraph (c)(1) of this section.

(3) *Shareholders who become United States persons.*—A return on Form 5471, containing the information required by paragraph (c)(4) of this section, shall be made by each person who at any time after January 1, 1963, becomes a United States person while owning 10 percent or more of the total combined voting power of all classes of stock of the foreign corporation entitled to vote or the total value of the stock of the foreign corporation.

(4) *Information required to be shown on return.*—(i) *In general.*—The return on Form 5471, required to be filed by persons described in paragraph (c)(1) or (3) of this section, shall set forth the same information as is required by the provisions of paragraph (b) of this section except that where such provisions require information with respect to January 1, 1963, such information shall be furnished with respect to the date on which liability arises to file the return required under this paragraph.

(ii) *Additional information.*—In addition to the information required under paragraph (c)(4)(i) of this section, the following information shall also be furnished in the return required under this paragraph:

(a) The date on or after January 1, 1963, if any, on which such shareholder (or shareholders) last filed a return under this section with respect to the corporation;

(b) If a return is filed by reason of becoming a United States person, the date the shareholder became a United States person;

(c) If a return is filed by reason of the disposition of stock, the date and method of such disposition and the person to whom such disposition was made; and

(d) If a return is filed by reason of the organization or reorganization of the foreign corporation on or after January 1, 1963, the following information with respect to such organization or reorganization:

(1) A statement showing a detailed list of the classes and kinds of assets transferred to the foreign corporation including a description of the assets (such as a list of patents, copyrights, stock, securities, etc.), the fair market value of each asset transferred (and, if such asset is transferred by a United States person, its adjusted basis), the date of transfer, the name, address, and identifying number, if any, of the owner immediately prior to the transfer, and the consideration paid by the foreign corporation for such transfer;

(2) A statement showing the assets transferred and the notes or securities issued by the foreign corporation, the name, address, and identifying number, if any, of each person to whom such transfer or issue was made, and the consideration paid to the foreign corporation for such transfer or issue; and

(3) An analysis of the changes in the corporation's surplus accounts occurring on or after January 1, 1963.

(iii) *Exclusion of information previously furnished.*—In any case where any identical item of information required to be filed under this paragraph by a shareholder with respect to a foreign corporation has previously been furnished by such shareholder in any return made in accordance with the provisions of this section, such shareholder may satisfy the requirements of this paragraph by filing Form 5471, identifying such item of information, the date furnished, and stating that it is unchanged.

(d) *Associations, etc.*—Returns are required to be filed in accordance with the provisions of this section with respect to any foreign association, foreign joint-stock company, or foreign insurance company, etc., which would be considered to be a corporation under §301.7701-2 of this chapter (Regulations on Procedure and Administration). Persons who would qualify by the nature of their functions and ownership in such associations, etc., as officers, directors, or shareholders thereof will be treated as such for purposes of this section without regard to their designations under local law.

(e) *Special provisions.*—(1) *Return jointly made.*—Any two or more persons required under paragraph (a) of this section to make a return with respect to one or more shareholders of the same corporation, or under paragraph (b) or (c) of this section to make a return with respect to the same corporation, may in lieu of making several returns, jointly make one return.

(2) *Separate return for each corporation.*—When returns are required with respect to more than one foreign corporation, a separate return must be made for each corporation.

(3) *Use of power of attorney by officers or directors.*—(i) *In general.*—Any two or more persons required under paragraph (a) of this section to make a return with respect to one or more shareholders of the same corporation may, by means of one or more duly executed powers of attorney, constitute one of their number as attorney in fact for the purpose of making such returns or for the purpose of making a joint return under subparagraph (1) of this paragraph.

(ii) *Nature of power of attorney.*—The power of attorney referred to in subdivision (i) of this subparagraph shall be limited to the making of returns required under paragraph (a) of this section and shall be limited to a single calendar year with respect to which such returns are required.

(iii) *Manner of execution of power of attorney.*—The use of technical language in the preparation of the power of attorney referred to in subdivision (i) of this subparagraph is not necessary. Such power of attorney shall be signed by the individual United States citizen or resident required to file a return or returns under paragraph (a) of this section. Such power of attorney must be acknowledged before a notary public or, in lieu thereof, witnessed by two disinterested persons. The notarial seal must be affixed unless such seal is not required under the laws of the state or country wherein such power of attorney is executed.

(iv) *Manner of execution of return under authority of power of attorney.*—A return made under authority of one or more powers of attorney referred to in subdivision (i) of this subparagraph shall be signed by the attorney in fact for each principal for which such attorney in fact is acting. A copy of such one or more powers of attorney shall be kept at a convenient and safe location accessible to internal revenue officers, and shall at all times be available for inspection by such officers.

(v) *Effect on penalties.*—The fact that a return is made under authority of a power of attorney referred to in subdivision (i) of this subparagraph shall not affect the principal's liability for penalties provided for failure to file a return required under paragraph (a) of this section or for filing a false or fraudulent return.

(4) *Persons excepted from filing returns.*—(i) *Return required of officer or director under paragraph (a)(1).*—Notwithstanding paragraph (a)(1) of this section, any United States citizen or resident required to make a return under such paragraph with respect to shareholders of a foreign corporation, need not make such return if, on January 1, 1963, three or fewer United States persons own 95 percent or more in value of the outstanding stock of such foreign corporation and file a return or returns with respect to such corporation under paragraph (b) of this section.

(ii) *Return required of officer or director under paragraph (a)(2).*—Notwithstanding paragraph (a)(2) of this section, any United States citizen or resident required to make a return under such paragraph with respect to a person acquiring stock of a foreign corporation in an acquisition described in subdivision (i)(a) or (b) of such paragraph need not make such return, if—

(a) As a result of such acquisition of stock of such foreign corporation, a United States person files a return as a shareholder under paragraph (c)(1) of this section, and

(b) Immediately after such acquisition of stock, three or fewer United States persons own 95 percent or more in value of the outstanding stock of such foreign corporation.

(iii) *Return required by reason of attribution rules.*—Notwithstanding paragraph (b) or (c) of this section, any person required to make a return under such paragraph with respect to a foreign corporation need not make such return, if—

(a) Such person does not directly own an interest in the foreign corporation,

(b) Such person is required to furnish the information solely by reason of attribution of stock ownership from a United States person under paragraph (i) of this section, and

(c) The person from whom the stock ownership is attributed furnishes all of the information required under paragraph (b) or (c) of this section of the person to whom such stock ownership is attributed.

(iv) *Return required of officer or director with respect to person described in subdivision (iii).*—Notwithstanding paragraph (a) of this section, any United States citizen or resident required to make a return under such paragraph with respect to a person exempted under subdivision (iii) of this subparagraph from making a return need not make a return with respect to such person.

(5) *Persons excepted from furnishing items of information.*—Any person required to furnish any item of information under paragraph (b) or (c) of this section with respect to a foreign corporation may, if such item of information is furnished by another person having an equal or greater stock interest (measured in terms of either the total combined voting power of all classes of stock of the foreign corporation entitled to vote or the total value of the stock of the foreign corporation) in such foreign corporation, satisfy such requirement by filing a statement with his return on Form 5471 indicating that such requirement has been satisfied and identifying the return in which such item of information was included. This paragraph (e)(5) does not apply to persons excepted from filing a return by reason of the provisions of paragraph (e)(4) of this section.

(f) *Meaning of terms.*—For purposes of this section—

(1) *Acquisition.*—Stock in a foreign corporation shall be considered acquired when a person has an unqualified right to receive such stock, even though such stock is not actually issued. For example, when under the law of a foreign country, all the necessary steps for incorporation are completed but stock in the corporation will not be issued within 30 days, every United States citizen or resident who is an officer or a director of such corporation, provided a United States person has an interest of 10 percent or more in such corporation, and every such United States person shall, within 90 days of the date of incorporation, file the returns required under section 6046 and this section. In the case of a reorganization, new stock may be acquired, depending on the type of reorganization, whether or not any stock certificates are surrendered or exchanged or the designation of such stock is altered.

(2) *Reorganization.*—With respect to a foreign corporation, the term "reorganization" shall mean not only a transaction described in section 368(a)(1) and the regulations thereunder but also any other transaction or series of transactions which has the same effect.

(3) *U.S. person.*—(i) *In general.*—For purposes of section 6046 and this section, the term *United States person* has the meaning assigned to it by section 7701(a)(30), except as provided in paragraphs (f)(3)(ii) and (iii) of this section.

(ii) *Special rule for individuals residing in certain possessions.*—(A) With respect to an individual who is a bona fide resident of Puerto Rico, the term United States person has the meaning assigned to it by §1.957-3 except that the rules of §1.937-2(g)(1) will apply.

(B) With respect to individuals who are bona fide residents of any section 931 possession, as defined in §1.931-1(c)(1), the term United States person has the meaning assigned to it by §1.957-3.

(iii) *Special rule for certain nonresident aliens.*—An individual for whom an election under section 6013(g) or (h) is in effect will, subject to the exceptions contained in paragraph (f)(3)(ii) of this section, be considered a United States person for purposes of section 6046 and this section.

(4) [Reserved].

(5) *Accounting period and taxable year.*—In the case of a specified foreign corporation (as defined in section 898), the taxable year of such corporation shall be treated as its annual accounting period.

(g) *Method of reporting.*—All amounts furnished in returns prescribed under this section shall be expressed in United States currency with a statement of the exchange rates used. All statements required to be submitted on or with returns under this section shall be rendered in the English language. For taxable years ending after December 31, 1994, with respect to returns filed after December 31, 1995, all amounts furnished under paragraph (c) of this section shall be expressed in United States dollars computed and translated in conformity with United States generally accepted accounting principles. Amounts furnished under paragraph (c)(3)(i) of this section shall also be furnished in the foreign corporation's functional currency as required on the form. Information described in paragraphs (b)(10) and (c)(3) of this section shall be submitted in such form or manner as the form shall prescribe. If an individual who is a United States person required to make a return with respect to a foreign corporation under section 6046 is entitled under a treaty to be treated as a nonresident of the United States, and if the individual claims this treaty benefit, and if there are no other United States persons that are required to furnish information under section 6046 with respect to the foreign corporation, then the individual may satisfy the requirements of paragraphs (b)(10), (11) and (12), (c)(3)(ii)(d), and (g) of this section by filing the audited foreign financial statements of the foreign corporation with the individual's return required under section 6046.

(h) *Actual ownership of stock.*—If any shareholder, referred to in this section, is not the actual owner of the stock of the foreign corporation, the information required under this section shall be furnished in the name of and by such actual owner. For example, in the case of stock held by a nominee, the information required under this section shall be furnished by the actual owner of such stock.

(i) *Constructive ownership of stock.*—(1) *In general.*—Stock owned directly or indirectly by or for a foreign corporation or a foreign partnership shall be considered as being owned proportionately by its shareholders or partners. Thus, any United States person who is a member of a nonresident foreign partnership which becomes a shareholder in a foreign corporation shall be considered to be a shareholder in such foreign corporation to the extent of his proportionate share in such partnership.

(2) *Members of family.*—An individual shall be considered as owning the stock owned directly or indirectly by or for his brothers and sisters (whether by the whole or half blood), his spouse, his ancestors, and his lineal descendants. However, when stock is treated as owned by an individual under the rule provided in this subparagraph, it shall not be treated as owned by him for the purpose of again applying such rule in order to make another the constructive owner of such stock. The provisions of this subparagraph may be illustrated by the following example:

*Example.* H, W, and HF are United States citizens. W, wife of H, owns 20 percent of the value of the outstanding stock of X, a foreign corporation. X Corporation owns 90 percent of the value of the outstanding stock of Y Corporation, a foreign corporation. Y Corporation becomes the owner of 50 percent of the value of the outstanding stock of each of two newly organized foreign corporations, M and N. In applying the "members of family" rule, H is considered to own 20 percent of the value of the outstanding stock of X Corporation, and 18 percent of the value of the outstanding stock of Y Corporation, and 9 percent of M Corporation and N Corporation. However, HF, the father of H, is not considered to own stock of X, Y, M, or N since his son, H, is not treated as the owner of such stock for purposes of again applying the "members of family" rule.

(j) *Time and place for filing return.*—(1) *Time for filing.*—Any return required by section 6046 and this section shall be filed on or before the 90th day after the date on which a United States citizen, resident, or person becomes liable to file such return under any provision of section 6046(a) and of paragraph (a), (b), or (c) of this section. With respect to returns filed after September 3, 1982, such return shall be filed on or before such later date (if any) as may be authorized by the return form. The Director of the Internal Revenue Service Center where the return is required to be filed is authorized to grant reasonable extensions of time for filing returns under section 6046 and this section in accordance with the applicable provisions of section 6081(a) and § 1.6081-1.

(2) *Place for filing.*—Returns required by section 6046 and this section shall be filed with the Internal Revenue Service Center designated in the instructions of the applicable form.

(k) *Penalties.*—(1) For criminal penalties for failure to file a return and filing a false or fraudulent return, see sections 7203, 7206, and 7207.

(2) For civil penalty for failure to file return, or failure to show information required on a return, under this section, see section 6679.

(l) *Effective/applicability date.*—(1) Paragraph (f)(3) of this section applies to taxable years ending after April 9, 2008.

(2) Paragraph (c)(1)(iii) of this section applies to taxable years ending on or after December 31, 2013.

(3) Paragraph (e)(5) of this section applies to returns filed on or after December 31, 2013. See paragraph (e)(5) of § 1.6046-1, as contained in 26 CFR part 1 revised as of April 1, 2012, for returns filed before December 31, 2013. [Reg. § 1.6046-1.]

☐ [*T.D. 6623,* 11-30-62. *Amended by T.D. 6997,* 1-17-69; *T.D. 7322,* 8-23-74; *T.D. 7925,* 12-12-83; *T.D. 8573,* 12-13-94; *T.D. 8733,* 10-6-97; *T.D. 9194,* 4-6-2005; *T.D. 9391,* 4-4-2008, *T.D. 9650,* 12-30-2013 (*corrected* 5-9-2014) *and T.D. 9806,* 12-27-2016.]

**[Reg. § 301.6046-1]**

**§ 301.6046-1. Returns as to organization or reorganization of foreign corporations and as to acquisitions of their stock.**—For provisions relating to requirement of returns as to organization or reorganization of foreign corporations and as to acquisitions of their stock, see § § 1.6046-1 to 1.6046-3, inclusive, of this chapter (Income Tax Regulations). [Reg. § 301.6046-1.]

☐ [*T.D. 6498,* 10-24-60. *Amended by T.D. 6700,* 1-6-64.]

**[Reg. § 1.6046A-1]**

**§ 1.6046A-1. Return requirement for United States persons who acquire or dispose of an interest in a foreign partnership, or whose proportional interest in a foreign partnership changes substantially.**—(a) *Return requirement.*—(1) *General rule.*—If a United States person has a reportable event (as defined in paragraph (b)(1) of this section) during the person's tax year, then, except as provided in paragraph (f) of this section, the United States person is required to complete and file Form 8865, "Return of U.S. Persons With Respect To Certain Foreign Partnerships," containing the information described in paragraph (c) of this section.

(2) *Separate return for each partnership.*—If a United States person has a reportable event with respect to an interest in more than one foreign partnership, the United States person must file a separate Form 8865 for each foreign partnership.

(b) *Definitions.*—(1) *Reportable event.*—There are three categories of reportable events under section 6046A: acquisitions, dispositions, and changes in proportional interests.

(i) *Acquisitions.*—A United States person that acquires a foreign partnership interest has a reportable event if—

(A) The person did not own a ten-percent or greater direct interest in the partnership and as a result of the acquisition the person owns a ten-percent or greater direct interest in the partnership. For purposes of this paragraph (b)(1)(i)(A), an acquisition includes an increase in a person's direct proportional interest; or

(B) Subject to paragraph (b)(2) of this section, compared to the person's direct interest when the person last had a reportable event, after the acquisition the person's direct interest has increased by at least a ten-percent interest.

(ii) *Dispositions.*—A United States person that disposes of a foreign partnership interest has a reportable event if—

(A) The person owned a ten-percent or greater direct interest in the partnership before the disposition and as a result of the disposition the person owns less than a ten-percent direct interest. For purposes of this paragraph (b)(1)(ii)(A), a disposition includes a decrease in a person's direct proportional interest; or

(B) Subject to paragraph (b)(2) of this section, compared to the person's direct interest when the person last had a reportable event, after the disposition the person's direct interest has decreased by at least a ten-percent interest.

(iii) *Changes in proportional interests not otherwise reportable as acquisitions or dispositions under paragraph (b)(1)(i)(A) or (b)(1)(ii)(A) of this section.*—A United States person has a reportable event if, subject to paragraph (b)(2) of this section, compared to the person's direct proportional interest the last time the person had a reportable event, the person's direct proportional interest has increased or decreased by at least the equivalent of a ten-percent interest.

(2) *Special rule for foreign partnership interests owned on December 31, 1999.*—If a United States person owned a ten-percent or greater direct interest in a foreign partnership on December 31, 1999, then to determine whether the person has a reportable event under paragraph (b)(1)(i)(B), (b)(1)(ii)(B), or (b)(1)(iii) of this section, the comparison should be made to the person's direct interest on December 31, 1999. Once the person has a reportable event after December 31, 1999, future comparisons should be made by reference to the last reportable event.

(3) *Change in a proportional interest.*—A partner's proportional interest in a foreign partnership may change for a number of reasons, for example, the change may be caused by changes in other partners' interests resulting from a partner withdrawing from the partnership. A proportional change may also occur by operation of the partnership agreement, for example, if the partnership agreement provides that a partner's interest in profits will change on a set date or when the partnership has earned a specified amount of profits and one of those events occurs.

(4) *Ten-percent interest.*—Under section 6046A(d) and this section, a *ten-percent interest* in a foreign partnership, as described in section 6038(e)(3)(C) and the regulations thereunder, means an interest equal to ten percent of the capital interest in such partnership, an interest equal to ten percent of the profits interest in such partnership, or an interest to which ten percent of the deductions or losses of such partnership are allocated.

(5) *United States person.*—*United States person* means a person described in section 7701(a)(30).

(6) *Foreign partnership.*—*Foreign partnership* means any partnership that is a foreign partnership under sections 7701(a)(2) and (5).

(7) *Examples.*—The rules of paragraph (a) of this section and this paragraph (b) are illustrated by the following examples:

*Example 1. Acquisition of an indirect interest. FP*, a foreign partnership, has two partners, *FC1* and *FC2*, both foreign corporations. *FC1* owns a 40% interest in *FP*, and *FC2* owns a 60% interest in *FP*. No United States person owns an interest in *FP*, either directly, or constructively under section 6038(e)(3)(C) and section 267(c). On January 1, 2001, *US*, a United States person and calendar year taxpayer, acquires by purchase 100% of *FC2*'s stock. *US* has acquired an indirect interest of 60% in *FP*. See sections 6038(e)(3)(C) and 267(c)(1). However, *US* is not required to report the January 1, 2001 indirect acquisition under section 6046A. *US* did not own a 10% or greater direct interest in *FP* before the acquisition, and *US* does not own a 10% or greater direct interest as a result of the acquisition. (*US* must, however, comply with the reporting requirements under section 6038 (controlled foreign corporation and controlled foreign partnership reporting) with respect to *FC2* and *FP*.)

*Example 2. Acquisition of direct interests.* (i) Assume the same facts as *Example 1*. In addition, on June 1, 2001, *US* purchases a 5% direct interest in *FP* from *FC1*. *US* did not own a 10% or greater direct interest in *FP* before the acquisition. After the acquisition, *US* does not own a direct interest of 10% or more. *US* owns a 10% or greater total interest (direct and indirect), but only a 5% direct interest. Therefore, *US* is not required to report the June 1, 2001, acquisition under section 6046A.

(ii) On September 1, 2001, *US* purchases a 7% direct interest in *FP* from *FC1*. The September 1, 2001 acquisition constitutes a reportable event under paragraph (b)(1)(i)(A) of this section. Before the September 1 acquisition, *US* did not own a 10% or greater direct interest in *FP*. After the September 1 acquisition, *US* owns a 12% direct interest, and therefore, as a result of the September 1 acquisition, *US* now owns a 10% or greater direct interest in *FP*. Consequently, *US* must report its September 1 acquisition under section 6046A on Form 8865 filed with *US*'s 2001 income tax return.

(iii) On December 1, 2001, *US* acquires an additional 4% direct interest in *FP* from *FC1*, so that *US*'s total direct interest has increased from 12% to 16%. This acquisition does not constitute a reportable event. Compared to *US*'s direct interest when *US* last had a reportable event (12% on September 1, 2001), after acquiring the 4% interest *US*'s direct interest has not increased by at least a 10% direct interest (i.e., its direct interest increased by only 4%). Therefore, *US* does not have to report the December 1, 2001, acquisition under section 6046A. On April 1, 2002, *FC2* distributes a 6% direct interest in *FP* to *US*. *US* now owns a 22% direct interest in *FP*. Compared to *US*'s direct interest when *US* last had a reportable event (12% on September 1, 2001), after the April 1 acquisition *US*'s direct interest has increased by at least a 10% interest (12% to 22%). *US* must report the April 1, 2002 acquisition on a Form 8865 attached to *US*'s 2002 income tax return.

*Example 3. Change in proportional interest resulting from withdrawal of a partner.* Assume the same facts as *Example 3*. In addition, on January 5, 2003, *FC2* withdraws entirely from *FP*. As a result, the direct interests of *US* and *FC1* in *FP* each increase by at least the equivalent of 10% interests. Compared to *US*'s direct interest the last time *US* had a reportable event (22% on April 1, 2002), *US*'s direct interest has increased by at least the equivalent of a ten percent interest. Therefore, *US* has had a reportable event pursuant to paragraph (b)(1)(iii) of this section, and *US* must report the change in its interest resulting from *FC2*'s withdrawal from the partnership on *US*'s Form 8865 filed with *US*'s 2003 tax year income tax return.

*Example 4. Change in proportional interest constituting an acquisition. FP* is a foreign partnership that has no United States persons as

direct or constructive partners. *US* is a United States person and a calendar year taxpayer. On January 1, 2001, *US* purchases an 8% direct interest in *FP*. *US* is not required to report this acquisition. *US* did not own a 10% or greater direct interest in *FP*, and *US* does not own a 10% or greater direct interest as a result of the acquisition. On March 1, 2001, *FC*, a foreign partner of *FP*, withdraws from *FP*, and as result, *US*'s direct interest in *FP* increases by a 7% interest. The increase in *US*'s direct interest is considered an acquisition of an interest under paragraph (b)(1)(i)(A) of this section. *US* did not own a 10% or greater direct interest in *FP* before *FC* withdrew, and as a result of the increase in *US*'s direct interest because of *FC*'s withdrawal from *FP*, *US* now owns a 10% or greater direct interest in *FP*. Therefore, *US* must report under section 6046A the increase in *US*'s direct interest resulting from the withdrawal of *FC* from *FP* on Form 8865 filed with *US*'s tax return for *US*'s 2001 tax year.

(c) *Content of return.*—The Form 8865 that must be filed under paragraph (a)(1) of this section must contain the following information in such form and manner and to the extent that Form 8865 and its instructions prescribe—

(1) The name, address, and taxpayer identification number of the United States person required to file the return;

(2) Information about other persons (foreign or domestic) whose interests in the foreign partnership the person reporting under section 6046A is considered to own under section 6038(e)(3)(C) and section 267(c);

(3) Information about all foreign entities that were disregarded as entities separate from their owners under "301.7701-2 and 301.7701-3 of this chapter that were owned by the foreign partnership during the partnership's tax year ending with or within the tax year of the person filing Form 8865 pursuant to section 6046A;

(4) For each reportable event, the date of the event, the type of event (acquisition, disposition, or change in proportional interest), and the United States person's direct percentage interest in the foreign partnership immediately before and immediately after the event;

(5) The fair market value of the interest acquired or disposed of;

(6) Information about partnerships (foreign and domestic) in which the foreign partnership owned a direct interest, or a constructive interest of ten percent or more under sections section 267(c)(1) and (5) and the regulations thereunder, during the partnership's tax year ending with or within the tax year of the person filing Form 8865 pursuant to section 6046A; and

(7) Any other information required to be submitted by Form 8865 and its instructions.

(d) *Time and manner for filing returns.*—The Form 8865 must be filed with the timely filed (including extensions) income tax return of the United States person for the tax year in which the reportable event occurs. If the United States person is not required to file an income tax return for its tax year in which the reportable event occurs, but is required to file an information return for that year (for example, Form 1065, "U.S. Partnership Return of Income," or Form 990, "Return of Organization Exempt from Income Tax"), the United States person should attach the Form 8865 to its information return filed for that tax year.

(e) *Duplicate returns.*—If required by the instructions to Form 8865, a duplicate Form 8865 (including attachments and schedules) must also be filed.

(f) *Persons excepted from filing return.*—(1) *Section 6038B overlap.*—If a United States person acquires an interest in a foreign partnership as a result of a section 721 contribution required to be reported under section 6038B, and the person properly reports the contribution under section 6038B, then the United States person is not required to report the acquisition of the partnership interest under section 6046A(a) should it constitute a reportable event under paragraph (b)(1) of this section. The acquisition will still constitute a reportable event for purposes of making future comparisons pursuant to paragraphs (b)(1)(i)(B), (b)(1)(ii)(B) and (b)(1)(iii) of this section. A person that fails to properly report the section 721 contribution under section 6038B and the regulations thereunder and that fails to properly report the acquisition of the partnership interest under section 6046A may be subject to the penalties applicable to a failure to comply with the requirements of section 6038B, as well as the penalties applicable for a failure to comply with the requirements of section 6046A. See paragraph (h) of this section for more information about the penalties for failure to comply with the requirements of section 6046A.

(2) *Trusts relating to state and local government employee retirement plans.*—The return requirement of section 6046A does not apply to trusts relating to state and local government employee retirement plans, unless the instructions to Form 8865 provide otherwise.

Reg. § 1.6046A-1(f)(2)

(3) *Reporting under this section not required of partnerships excluded from the application of subchapter K.*—The reporting requirements of this section will not apply to any United States person in respect of an eligible partnership as described in §1.761-2(a) in which that United States person is a partner, if such partnership has validly elected to be excluded from all of the provisions of subchapter K of chapter 1 of the Internal Revenue Code in the manner specified in §1.761-2(b)(2)(i), or is deemed to have elected to be excluded from all of the provisions of subchapter K of chapter 1 of the Internal Revenue Code in accordance with the provisions of §1.761-2(b)(2)(ii).

(4) *Exclusion for satellite organizations.*—The return requirement of section 6046A does not apply to the International Telecommunications Satellite Organization (or a successor organization) or the International Maritime Satellite Organization (or a successor organization).

(g) *Method of reporting.*—Except as otherwise provided on Form 8865, or the accompanying instructions, any amounts required to be reported under section 6046A and this section must be expressed in United States dollars, with a statement of the exchange rates used. All statements required on or with Form 8865 pursuant to this section must be in English.

(h) *Penalties for violating section 6046A.*—For penalties for violating section 6046A, see sections 6679 and 7203.

(i) *Statute of limitations.*—For exceptions to the limitations on assessment in the event of a failure to provide information under section 6046A, see section 6501(c)(8).

(j) *Effective date.*—This section applies to reportable events occurring after December 31, 1999. No reporting under section 6046A is required for reportable events occurring on or before December 31, 1999. [Reg. §1.6046A-1.]

☐ [T.D. 8851, 12-27-99.]

### [Reg. §1.6047-1]

**§1.6047-1. Information to be furnished with regard to employee retirement plan covering an owner-employee.**—(a) *Trustees and insurance companies.*—(1) *Requirement of return.*—(i) Every trustee of a trust described in section 401(a) and exempt from tax under section 501(a) which makes payments of amounts described in subparagraph (2) of this paragraph aggregating $10 or more during any calendar year to an individual (or his beneficiary) who was covered, within the meaning of paragraph (a)(2) of §1.401-10, as an owner-employee under the plan of which such trust is a part shall make a return on Forms 1096 and 1099 for such year showing the name and address of the person to whom paid, the aggregate amount of such payments, specifically identified as an amount to which this paragraph applies, and such other information as is required by the forms. A separate Form 1099 shall be filed with respect to each payee. The term "owner-employee" means an owner-employee as defined in section 401(c)(3) and paragraph (d) of §1.401-10. Any custodial account which satisfies the requirements of section 401(f) shall be treated as a qualified trust and the custodian of such a custodial account must comply with the requirements of this section as if he were the trustee.

(ii) Every issuer of a contract which is treated as an annuity contract under sections 401 through 404 purchased by a trust described in section 401(a) and exempt from tax under section 501(a) or under a plan described in section 403(a) which makes payments of amounts described in subparagraph (2) of this paragraph aggregating $10 or more during any calendar year to an individual (or his beneficiary) who was covered, within the meaning of paragraph (a)(2) of §1.401-10, as an owner-employee under the plan of which such trust is a part or under which such contract was purchased shall make a return on Forms 1096 and 1099 for such year showing the name and address of the person to whom paid, the aggregate amount of such payments, specifically identified as an amount to which this paragraph applies, and such other information as is required by the form. A separate Form 1099 shall be filed with respect to each payee.

(2) *Amounts subject to this section.*—The amounts subject to reporting under subparagraph (1) of this paragraph include all amounts distributed or made available to which section 402(a) (relating to employees' trusts) or section 403(a) (relating to employee annuity plans) applies, whether or not such amounts are includible in gross income and whether or not attributable to contributions made while the individual to whom they relate was an owner-employee. However, amounts subject to reporting do not include any amounts distributed or made available by the trustee of any trust or the issuer of any contract under any plan with respect to which he has not received the notification provided in either subparagraph (3) of this paragraph or paragraph (b) of this section. Amounts distributed or made available under the plan include, for example, amounts received by the individual as loans on contracts purchased under the

plan, and payments made to the individual by reason of the surrender of contracts purchased under the plan, whether or not prior to their maturity.

(3) *Notification by trustee.*—The trustee of any trust described in section 401(a) and exempt from tax under section 501(a) who receives notification from any owner-employee that contributions have been made to the trust on behalf of that owner-employee as an owner-employee shall notify in writing the issuer of any contract which is treated as an annuity contract under sections 401 through 404 purchased by the trust for the benefit of that owner-employee that such contributions have been made to such trust. Such notification shall be delivered to such issuer at the time such contract is purchased or within 90 days after the notification required by paragraph (b) of this section is received by the trustee, whichever is later. Only one such notification must be made with respect to any contract.

(4) *Record keeping.*—Any trustee, insurance company, or other person, which is referred to in subparagraph (1) of this paragraph and which is notified under section 6047(b) that contributions to the trust or under the plan have been made on behalf of an owner-employee shall maintain a record of such notification until all funds of the trust or under the plan on behalf of the owner-employee have been distributed.

(5) *Inclusion of other payments.*—The Form 1099 filed under this section by any person with respect to payments to another person during a calendar year may, at the election of the maker, include other payments made by him to such other person during such year which are required to be reported on Form 1099.

(6) *Time and place for filing.*—The return required under this section for any calendar year shall be filed after the close of that year and on or before February 28 (March 31 if filed electronically) of the following year with any of the Internal Revenue Service Centers, the addresses of which are listed in the instructions for Form 1096. For extensions of time for filing returns under this section, see §1.6081-1.

(b) *Notification by owner-employee.*—Any owner-employee on behalf of whom contributions are made to a trust described in section 401(a) and exempt under section 501(a) or under a plan described in section 403(a) shall notify in writing—

(1) The trustee of such a trust, or

(2) The issuer of any contract which is treated as an annuity contract under sections 401 through 404 under such plan,

that such contributions have been made to such trust or plan. Such notification shall be delivered to such trustee or such issuer during the first calendar year in which such contributions are made or on or before February 28 of the year following such year. Only one such notification must be made with respect to any contract or any trust.

(c) *Penalties.*—For civil penalty for failure to file a return required by this section, and for criminal penalty for furnishing fraudulent information under this section, see §§301.6652-3 and 301.7207-1, respectively.

(d) *Permission to submit information required by Form 1099 on magnetic tape.*—For rules relating to permission to submit the information required by Form 1099 on magnetic tape or other media, see §1.9101-1. [Reg. §1.6047-1.]

☐ [T.D. 6677, 9-16-63. Amended by T.D. 6883, 5-2-66; T.D. 7551, 7-3-78 and T.D. 8895, 8-17-2000.]

### [Reg. §301.6047-1]

**§301.6047-1. Information relating to certain trusts and annuity and bond purchase plans.**—For provisions relating to the requirement of returns of information regarding certain trusts and annuity and bond purchase plans, see §1.6047-1 of this chapter (Income Tax Regulations). [Reg. §301.6047-1.]

☐ [T.D. 6700, 1-6-64.]

### [Reg. §1.6047-2]

**§1.6047-2. Information relating to qualifying longevity annuity contracts.**—(a) *Requirement and form of report.*—(1) *In general.*—Any person issuing any contract that is intended to be a qualifying longevity annuity contract (QLAC), defined in A-17 of §1.401(a)(9)-6, shall make the report required by this section. This requirement applies only to contracts purchased or held under any plan, annuity, or account described in section 401(a), 403(a), 403(b), or 408 (other than a Roth IRA) or eligible governmental plan under section 457(b).

(2) *Annual report.*—The issuer shall make annual calendar-year reports on the applicable form prescribed by the Commissioner for this purpose concerning the status of the contract. The report shall identify that the contract is intended to be a QLAC and shall contain the following information—

(i) The name, address, and identifying number of the issuer of the contract, along with information on how to contact the issuer for more information about the contract;

(ii) The name, address, and identifying number of the individual in whose name the contract has been purchased;

(iii) If the contract was purchased under a plan, the name of the plan, the plan number, and the Employer Identification Number (EIN) of the plan sponsor;

(iv) If payments have not yet commenced, the annuity starting date on which the annuity is scheduled to commence, the amount of the periodic annuity payable on that date, and whether that date may be accelerated;

(v) For the calendar year, the amount of each premium paid for the contract and the date of the premium payment;

(vi) The total amount of all premiums paid for the contract through the end of the calendar year;

(vii) The fair market value of the QLAC as of the close of the calendar year; and

(viii) Such other information as the Commissioner may require.

(b) *Manner and time for filing.*—(1) *Timing.*—The report required by paragraph (a)(2) of this section shall be filed in accordance with the forms and instructions prescribed by the Commissioner. Such a report must be filed for each calendar year beginning with the year in which premiums for a contract are first paid and ending with the earlier of the year in which the individual in whose name the contract has been purchased attains age 85 (as adjusted pursuant to A-17(d)(2)(ii) of § 1.401(a)(9)-6) or dies.

(2) *Surviving spouse.*—If the individual dies and the sole beneficiary under the contract is the individual's spouse (in which case the spouse's annuity would not be required to commence until the individual would have commenced benefits under the contract had the individual survived), the report must continue to be filed for each calendar year until the calendar year in which the distributions to the spouse commence or in which the spouse dies, if earlier.

(c) *Issuer statements.*—Each issuer required to file the annual report required by paragraph (a)(2) of this section shall furnish to the individual in whose name the contract has been purchased a statement containing the information required to be included in the report, except that such statement shall be furnished to a surviving spouse to the extent that the report is required to be filed under paragraph (b)(2) of this section. A copy of the required form may be used to satisfy the statement requirement of this paragraph (c). If a copy of the required form is not used to satisfy the statement requirement of this paragraph (c), the statement shall contain the following language: "This information is being furnished to the Internal Revenue Service." The statement required by this paragraph (c) shall be furnished on or before January 31 following the calendar year for which the report required by paragraph (a)(2) of this section is required.

(d) *Penalty for failure to file report.*—Section 6652(e) prescribes a penalty for failure to file the report required by paragraph (a)(2) of this section.

(e) *Effective/applicability date.*—This section applies to contracts purchased on or after July 2, 2014. [Reg. § 1.6047–2.]

☐ [*T.D. 9673, 7-1-2014.*]

### [Reg. § 404.6048-1]

**§404.6048-1. [Reserved].**

☐ [*T.D. 7502, 8-18-77. Removed and reserved by T.D. 9849, 3-11-2019.*]

### [Reg. § 1.6049-1]

**§1.6049-1. Returns of information as to interest paid in calendar years before 1983 and original issue discount includible in gross income for calendar years before 1983.**—(a) *Requirement of reporting.*—(1) *In general.*—(i) Every person who makes payments of interest (as defined in § 1.6049-2) aggregating $10 or more to any other person during a calendar year before 1983 shall make an information return on Forms 1096 and 1099 for such calendar year showing the aggregate amount of such payments, the name and address of the person to whom paid, the total of such payments for all persons, and such other information as is required by the forms. In the case of interest paid during calendar years beginning with 1963 and continuing until such time as the Commissioner determines that it is feasible to aggregate payments on two or more accounts, insurance contracts, or investment certificates, and this subdivision is amended accordingly to provide for reporting on an aggregate basis, the requirement of this subdivision for the filing of Form 1099 will be met if a person making payments of interest to another person on two or more such accounts, insurance contracts, or investment certificates files a separate Form 1099 with respect to each such account, contract, or certificate on which $10 or more of interest is paid to such other person during the calendar year. In the case of evidences of indebtedness described in section 6049(b)(1)(A), separate Forms 1099 may be filed as provided in the preceding sentence with respect to holdings in different issues. Thus, if a bank pays to a person interest totaling $15 on one account and $20 on a second account, it may file separate Forms 1099 with respect to the payments of $15 and $20. If the interest on the second account totaled $5 instead of $20, no return would be required with respect to the $5.

(ii)(*a*) Every person which is a corporation that has outstanding any bond, debenture, note, or certificate or other evidence of indebtedness (referred to in this section and § 1.6049-2 as an obligation) in "registered form" (as defined in paragraph (d) of § 1.6049-2) issued after May 27, 1969 (other than an obligation issued by a corporation pursuant to a written commitment which was binding on May 27, 1969, and at all times thereafter) and on or before December 31, 1982, as to which there is during any calendar year before 1983 an amount of original issue discount (as defined in § 1.6049-2) aggregating $10 or more includible as interest in the gross income for such calendar year of any holder (determined, if semiannual record date reporting is being used under (*b*)(1) of this subdivision, by treating each holder as holding the obligation on every day it was outstanding during the calendar year), shall make an information return on Forms 1096 and 1099-OID for such calendar year showing the following:

(*1*) The name and address of each record holder for whom such aggregate amount of original issue discount is $10 or more and, for calendar years subsequent to 1972, the account, serial, or other identifying number of each obligation for which a return is being made.

(*2*) The aggregate amount of original issue discount includible by each such holder for the period during the calendar year for which the return is made (or, if the aggregation rules of (*b*)(2) of this subdivision are being used, that he held the obligations). If, however, the semiannual record date reporting rules are being used under (*b*)(1) of this subdivision, such aggregate amount shall be determined by treating each such record date holder as if he held each such obligation on every day it was outstanding during the calendar year. For purposes of this section, an obligation shall be considered to be outstanding from the date of original issue (as defined in paragraph (b)(3) of § 1.1232-3). In the case of a time deposit open account arrangement to which paragraph (e)(5) of § 1.1232-3A applies, for example, the amount to be shown under this subdivision (2) on the Forms 1096 and 1099-OID is the sum (computed under such paragraph (e)(5)) of the amounts separately computed for each deposit made pursuant to the arrangement.

(*3*) The issue price of the obligation (as defined in paragraph (b)(2) of § 1.1232-3).

(*4*) The stated redemption price of the obligation at maturity (as defined in paragraph (b)(1)(iii) of § 1.1232-3).

(*5*) The ratable monthly portion of original issue discount with respect to the obligation as defined in section 1232(a)(3)(A) (determined without regard to a reduction for a purchase allowance or whether the holder purchased at a premium).

(*6*) The name and address of the person filing the form.

(*7*) Such other information as is required by the form.

And

(*8*) The sum, for all such holders of the aggregate amounts of such original issue discount includible for such calendar year for each such holder.

(*b*) With respect to any obligation (other than an obligation to which paragraph (e) or (f) of § 1.1232-3A applies (relating respectively to deposits in banks and similar financial institutions and to face-amount certificates), the issuing corporation (or an agent acting on its behalf):

(*1*) Shall be permitted (until this subdivision (*1*) is amended) to prepare a Form 1099-OID only for each person who is a holder of record of the obligation on the semiannual record date (if any) used by the corporation (or agent) for the payment of stated interest or, if there is no such date, the semiannual record dates shall be considered to be June 30, and December 31.

(*2*) Shall be permitted to aggregate all original issue discount with respect to 2 or more obligations of the same issue for which the amounts specified in (*a*) (2), (*a*)(3), (*a*)(4), and (*a*)(5) of this subdivision are proportional and, therefore, may file one Form 1099-OID for all such obligations being aggregated, except that for calendar year 1971 this aggregation rule shall apply only where such specified amounts are identical. For an illustration of proportional aggregation, see example (4) in (*d*) of this subdivision.

(*c*) In any case in which any one holder of a particular obligation for the calendar year held such obligation on more than one record date, only one Form 1099-OID shall be filed for that year with respect to that holder and that obligation. This provision applies only in the case in which any corporation prepares Forms 1099-OID in accordance with the record date reporting rule of (*b*)(1) of this subdivision.

(*d*) The requirements of (*a*)(3), (*a*)(4) and (*a*)(5) of this subdivision shall not apply to a time deposit open account arrangement to which paragraph (e)(5) of § 1.1232-3A applies, or to a face-amount certificate to which paragraph (f) of § 1.1232-3A applies.

(*e*) The provisions of this subdivision (ii) may be illustrated by the following examples:

*Example (1).* On January 1, 1971, a corporation issued a 10-year bond in registered form which pays stated interest to the holder of record on June 30 and December 31. The bond has an issue price (as defined in paragraph (b)(2) of § 1.1232-3) of $7,600, a stated redemption price (as defined in paragraph (b)(1) of § 1.1232-3) at maturity of $10,000, and a ratable monthly portion of original issue discount (as defined in section 1232(a)(3)(A)) of $20. The corporation's books indicate that A was the holder of record on June 30, 1971, and B was the holder on December 31, 1971. Under (*b*)(1) of this subdivision, the corporation is permitted to file separate Forms 1099-OID for both A and B showing, on each form, all items required by (*a*) of this subdivision, including the total original issue discount of $240 for the entire calendar year (which includes original issue discount for all holders), the issue price of $7,600, the stated redemption price at maturity of $10,000, and the ratable monthly portion of original issue discount of $20.

*Example (2).* Assume the facts stated in Example (1), except that A is recorded on the books of the corporation as holding the bond on June 30 and December 31, 1971. The corporation shall complete and file only one Form 1099-OID for A.

*Example (3).* Assume the facts stated in Example (1), except that the books of the corporation show that A held 2 of the bonds at all times in 1971. The amounts of the items listed in (*a*)(2), (*a*)(3), (*a*)(4), and (*a*)(5) of this subdivision are identical for the 2 bonds. Under (*b*)(2) of this subdivision, the corporation is permitted to treat the 2 bonds as one for purposes of completing and filing a Form 1099-OID for 1971 and aggregate the amounts being reported.

*Example (4).* On January 1, 1972, a corporation issued to C 3 bonds in registered form of the same issue with stated redemption prices of $1,000, $5,000, and $10,000. The aggregate amounts of original issue discount for each year, the issue prices, the stated redemption prices, and the monthly portions of original issue discount are the same for each $1,000 of stated redemption price. Thus, all relevant amounts for any one bond are proportional to such amounts for any other bond. Therefore, so long as C holds the bonds the corporation shall be permitted to aggregate on one Form 1099-OID all original issue discount with respect to such obligations in accordance with (*b*)(2) of this subdivision.

*Example (5).* On June 1, 1971, a corporation issues a 10-year bond to D, for which the ratable monthly portion of original issue discount is $10. For 1971, the corporation uses the record date reporting system permitted by (*b*)(1) of this subdivision. The corporation's books show that E held the bond on June 30, 1971, and that F held the bond on December 31, 1971, the dates on which the corporation pays stated interest on the bond. The corporation shall file a Form 1099-OID for both E and F showing on each form the aggregate amount of original issue discount includible for 1971 of $70 since E and F are each treated as if each held the bond every day it was outstanding and it was outstanding 7 months in 1971. As to D, the corporation is not required to file a Form 1099-OID since D did not hold the bond on either of the 2 record dates.

(iii) Every person who during a calendar year before 1983 receives payments of interest as a nominee on behalf of another person aggregating $10 or more shall make an information return on Forms 1096 and 1087 for such calendar year showing the aggregate amount of such interest, the name and address of the person on whose behalf received, the total of such interest received on behalf of all persons, and such other information as is required by the forms.

(iv) Except with respect to an obligation to which paragraph (e) or (f) of § 1.1232-3A applies (relating respectively to deposits in banks and similar financial institutions and to face-amount certificates), every person who is a nominee on behalf of the actual owner of an obligation as to which there is original issue discount aggregating $10 or more includible in the gross income of such owner during a calendar year after 1970, regardless of whether he receives a Form 1099-OID with respect to such discount, shall make an information return on Forms 1096 and 1087-OID for such calendar year showing in the manner prescribed on such forms the same information for the actual owner as is required or permitted in subdivision (ii) of this subparagraph for the record holder.

(v) Notwithstanding the provisions of subdivisions (iii) and (iv) of this subparagraph, the filing of Form 1087 or Form 1087-OID is not required if—

(*a*) The record owner is required to file a fiduciary return on Form 1041 disclosing the name, address, and identifying number of the actual owner;

(*b*) The record owner is a nominee of a banking institution or trust company exercising trust powers, and such banking institution or trust company is required to file a fiduciary return on Form 1041 disclosing the name, address, and identifying number of the actual owner; or

(*c*) The record owner is a banking institution or trust company exercising trust powers, or a nominee thereof, and the actual owner is an organization exempt from taxation under section 501(a) for which such banking institution or trust company files an annual return,

but only if the name, address, and identifying number of the record owner are included on or with the Form 1041 fiduciary return filed for the estate or trust or the annual return filed for the tax exempt organization.

(vi) Every person carrying on the banking business who makes payments of interest to another person (whether or not aggregating $10 or more) during a calendar year with respect to a certificate of deposit issued in bearer form (other than such a certificate issued in an amount of $100,000 or more) shall make an information return on Forms 1096 and 1099-BCD for such calendar year. The preceding sentence applies whether such payments are made during the term of the certificate or at its redemption. The information return required by this subdivision for the calendar year shall show the following:

(*a*) The name, address, and taxpayer identification number of the person to whom the interest is paid;

(*b*) The aggregate amount of interest paid to such person during the calendar year with respect to the certificate of deposit;

(*c*) The name, address, and taxpayer identification number of the person to whom the certificate was originally issued;

(*d*) The portion of the interest with respect to the certificate reported under (*b*) that is attributable to the current calendar year; and

(*e*) Such other information as is required by the form.

The application of this subdivision (vi) may be illustrated by the following examples:

*Example (1).* On June 1, 1978, X Bank issues a $1,000 bearer certificate of deposit to A. The certificate of deposit is not redeemable until May 31, 1979, and no interest is to be paid on the instrument until its redemption. On September 1, 1978, A transfers the bearer certificate to B and on May 31, 1979, B presents the certificate to X for payment and receives the $1,000 principal amount plus all the accrued interest. Under paragraph (a)(1)(vi) of this section, X is not required to make an information return for 1978 with respect to the bearer certificate of deposit because no interest is actually paid to a holder of the certificate during 1978. X is required to file an information return for 1979 with respect to the certificate, identifying B as the payee of the entire amount of the interest and A as the original purchaser of the certificate. (For rules relating to statements to be made to recipients of interest payments, see § 1.6049-3.)

*Example (2).* On July 1, 1978, Y Bank issues a $5,000 bearer certificate of deposit to C. The certificate of deposit is not redeemable until June 30, 1981, and no interest is to be paid on the instrument until its redemption. C holds the certificate for the entire term and on June 30, 1981, presents it to Y for payment and receives the $5,000 principal amount plus the accrued interest. Under paragraph (a)(1)(vi) of this section, Y is not required to file an information return for calendar years 1978, 1979, or 1980 with respect to this bearer certificate of deposit because no interest is actually paid to C during those calendar years. Y is required to file an information return for 1981 with respect to the certificate identifying C as the payee of the entire amount of the interest and as the original purchaser. (Although Y is not required to file an information return for interest paid on the certificate until its redemption in 1981 C must report as income on his tax returns for 1978, 1979, 1980, and 1981 the ratable portion of such interest includible in income under section 1232.)

(2) *Definitions.*—(i) The term "person" when used in this section does not include the United States, a State, the District of Columbia, a foreign government, a political subdivision of a State or of a foreign government, or an international organization. Therefore interest paid by or to one of these entities need not be reported. Similarly, original issue discount in respect of an obligation issued by or to one of these entities need not be reported.

(ii) For purposes of this section, a person who receives interest shall be considered to have received it as a nominee if he is not the actual owner of such interest and if he was required under § 1.6109-1 to furnish his identifying number to the payer of the interest (or would have been so required if the total of such interest for the year had been $10 or more), and such number was (or would have been) required to be included on an information return filed by the payer with respect to the interest. However, a person shall not be considered to be a nominee as to any portion of an interest payment which is actually owned by another person whose name is also shown on the information return filed by the payer or nominee with respect to such interest payment. Thus, in the case of a savings account jointly owned by a husband and wife, the husband will not be considered as receiving any portion of the interest on that account as a nominee for his wife if his wife's name is included on the information return filed by the payer with respect to the interest.

(iii) For purposes of this section, in the case of a person who receives a Form 1099-OID, the determination of who is considered a nominee shall be made in a manner consistent with the principles of subdivision (ii) of this subparagraph.

(iv) For purposes of this section and §1.6049-3, the term "Form 1099-OID" means the appropriate Form 1099 for original issue discount prescribed for the calendar year.

(3) *Determination of person to whom interest is paid or for whom it is received.*—For purposes of applying the provisions of this section, the person whose identifying number is required to be included by the payer of interest on an information return with respect to such interest shall be considered the person to whom the interest is paid. In the case of interest received by a nominee on behalf of another person, the person whose identifying number is required to be included on an information return made by the nominee with respect to such interest shall be considered the person on whose behalf such interest is received by the nominee. Thus, in the case of interest made payable to a person other than the record owner of the obligation with respect to which the interest is paid, the record owner of the obligation shall be considered the person to whom the interest is paid for purposes of applying the reporting requirements of this section, since his identifying number is required to be included on the information return filed under such section by the payer of the interest. Similarly, if a stockbroker receives interest on a bond held in street name for the joint account of a husband and wife, the interest is considered as received on behalf of the husband since his identifying number should be shown on the information return filed by the nominee under this section. Thus, if the wife has a separate account with the same stockbroker, any interest received by the stockbroker for her separate account should not be aggregated with the interest received for the joint account for purposes of information reporting. For regulations relating to the use of identifying numbers, see §1.6109-1.

(4) *Determination of person by whom original issue discount is includible or for whom a Form 1099-OID showing original issue discount is received.*—For purposes of applying the provisions of this section, the determination of the person by whom original issue discount is includible or for whom a Form 1099-OID is received shall be made in a manner consistent with the principles of subparagraph (3) of this paragraph.

(5) *Inclusion of other payments.*—The Form 1099 filed by any person with respect to payments of interest to another person during a calendar year prior to 1972 may, at the election of the maker, include payments other than interest made by him to such other person during such year which are required to be reported on Form 1099. Similarly, the Form 1087 filed by a nominee with respect to payments of interest received by him on behalf of any other person during a calendar year prior to 1972 may include payments of dividends received by him on behalf of such person during such year which are required to be reported on Form 1087. However, except as provided in subparagraph (1)(ii)*(b)* of this paragraph, a separate Form 1087-OID or 1099-OID shall be filed for each obligation in respect of which original issue discount is required to be reported for any calendar year before 1983. In addition, any person required to report payments on both Forms 1087, 1087-OID, 1099, and 1099-OID, for any calendar year may use one Form 1096 to summarize and transmit such forms.

(b) *When payment deemed made.*—For purposes of section 6049, interest is deemed to have been paid when it is credited or set apart to a person without any substantial limitation or restriction as to the time or manner of payment or condition upon which payment is to be made, and is made available to him so that it may be drawn at any time, and its receipt brought within his own control and disposition.

(c) *Time and place for filing.*—(1) *Payment of interest.*—The returns required under this section for any calendar year for the payment of interest shall be filed after September 30 of such year, but not before the payer's final payment for the year, and on or before February 28 of the following year with any of the Internal Revenue Service Centers, the addresses of which are listed in the instructions for Form 1096. For extensions of time for filing returns under this section, see §1.6081-1.

(2) *Original issue discount.*—(i) The returns required under this section for any calendar year for original issue discount shall be filed after December 31 of such year and on or before February 28 of the following year with any of the Internal Revenue Service Centers, the addresses of which are listed in the instructions for Form 1096. For extensions of time for filing returns under this section, see §1.6081-1.

(ii) The time for filing returns for the calendar year 1971 required under this section for original issue discount in respect of obligations to which paragraph (e) of §1.1232-3A applies (relating to deposits in banks and other similar financial institutions) is extended to April 15, 1972.

(d) *Penalty.*—For penalty for failure to file the statements required by this section, see §301.6652-1 of this chapter (Regulations on Procedure and Administration).

(e) *Permission to submit information required by Form 1087 or 1099 on magnetic tape.*—For rules relating to permission to submit the information required by Form 1087 or 1099 on magnetic tape or other media, see §1.9101-1. [Reg. §1.6049-1.]

☐ [*T.D. 6628, 12-27-62. Amended by T.D. 6677, 9-16-63, T.D. 6879, 3-7-66, T.D. 6883, 5-2-66, T.D. 6891, 8-3-66, T.D. 7000, 1-17-69, T.D. 7154, 12-27-71, T.D. 7311, 3-29-74, T.D. 7584, 1-2-79, and T.D. 7881, 3-22-83.*]

### [Reg. §301.6049-1]

**§301.6049-1. Returns regarding payments of interest.**—For provisions relating to the requirement of returns regarding payments of interest, see §§1.6049-1 to 1.6049-3, inclusive, of this chapter (Income Tax Regulations). [Reg. §301.6049-1.]

☐ [*T.D. 6700, 1-6-64.*]

### [Reg. §1.6049-2]

**§1.6049-2. Interest and original issue discount subject to reporting in calendar years before 1983.**—(a) *Interest in general.*—Except as provided in paragraph (b) of this section, the term "interest" when used in this section and §§1.6049-1 and 1.6049-3 means:

(1) Interest on evidences of indebtedness issued by a corporation in "registered form" (as defined in paragraph (d) of this section). The phrase "evidences of indebtedness" includes bonds, debentures, notes, certificates and other similar instruments regardless of how denominated. An evidence of indebtedness is in registered form if it is registered as to both principal and interest (or, for purposes of reporting with respect to original issue discount, if it is registered as to principal) and if its transfer must be effected by the surrender of the old instrument and either the reissuance by the corporation of the old instrument to the new holder or the issuance by the corporation of a new instrument to the new holder.

(2) Interest on deposits (except deposits evidenced by negotiable time certificates of deposit issued in an amount of $100,000 or more) paid (or credited) by persons carrying on the banking business. In the case of a certificate of deposit issued in bearer form, the term "interest", as used in the preceding sentence and in paragraph (a)(1)(vi) of §1.6049-1, has the same meaning as in §1.61-7 (regardless of whether taxable to the payee in the year the information return is made).

(3) Amounts, whether or not designated as interest, paid (or credited) by mutual savings banks, savings and loan associations, building and loan associations, cooperative banks, homestead associations, credit unions, or similar organizations in respect of deposits, face amount certificates, investment certificates, or withdrawable or repurchasable shares. Thus, even though amounts paid or credited by such organizations with respect to deposits are designated as "dividends", such amounts are included in the definition of interest for purposes of section 6049.

(4) Interest on amounts held by insurance companies under agreements to pay interest thereon. This includes interest paid by insurance companies with respect to policy "dividend" accumulations (see sections 61 and 451 and the regulations thereunder for rules as to when such interest is considered paid), and interest paid with respect to the proceeds of insurance policies left with the insurer. The so-called "interest element" in the case of annuity or installment payments under life insurance or endowment contracts does not constitute interest for purposes of this section.

(5) Interest on deposits with stockbrokers, bondbrokers, and other persons engaged in the business of dealing in securities.

(b) *Exceptions.*—The term "interest" when used in section 6049 does not include—

(1) Interest on obligations described in section 103(a)(1) or (3), relating to certain governmental obligations.

(2) Any payment by—

  (i) A foreign corporation,

  (ii) A nonresident alien individual, or

(iii) A partnership composed in whole or in part of nonresident aliens,

if such corporation, individual, or partnership is not engaged in trade or business within the United States and does not have an office or place of business or a fiscal or paying agent in the United States.

(3) Any interest which is subject to withholding under section 1441 or 1442 (relating to withholding of tax on nonresident aliens and foreign corporations, respectively) by the person making the payment, or which would be so subject to withholding but for the provisions of a treaty, or for the fact that under section 861(a)(1) it is not from sources within the United States, or for the fact that withholding is not required by reason of paragraph (a) or (f) of § 1.1441-4.

(4) In the case of a nominee, any interest which he receives and with respect to which he is required to withhold under section 1441 or 1442 or would be so required to withhold but for the provisions of a treaty, or for the fact that under section 861(a)(1) it is not from sources within the United States, or for the fact that withholding is not required by reason of paragraph (a) or (f) of § 1.1441-4.

(5) Any amount on which the person making the payment is required to deduct and withhold a tax under section 1451 (relating to tax-free covenant bonds), or would be so required but for section 1451(d) (relating to benefit of personal exemptions).

(6) Any amount which is subject to reporting as original issue discount.

(c) *Original issue discount.*—(1) *In general.*—The term "original issue discount" when used in this section and §§ 1.6049-1 and 1.6049-3 means original issue discount subject to the ratable inclusion rules of paragraph (a) of § 1.1232-3A, determined without regard to any reduction by reason of a purchase allowance under paragraph (a)(2)(ii) of § 1.1232-3A or a purchase at a premium as defined in paragraph (d)(2) of § 1.1232-3.

(2) *Coordination with interest reporting.*—In the case of an obligation issued after May 27, 1969 (other than an obligation issued pursuant to a written commitment which was binding on May 27, 1969, and at all times thereafter) and on or before December 31, 1982, original issue discount which is not subject to the reporting requirements of paragraph (a)(1)(ii) of § 1.6049-1 is interest within the meaning of paragraph (a) of this section. Original issue discount which is subject to the reporting requirements of paragraph (a)(1)(ii) of § 1.6049-1 is not interest within the meaning of paragraph (a) of this section.

(3) *Exceptions.*—Reporting of original issue discount is not required in respect of an obligation which paragraph (b)(2) of this section except from interest reporting.

(d) *Definition of "in registered form."*.—For purposes of § 1.6049-1 and this section, an evidence of indebtedness is in registered form if it is registered as to both principal and interest (or, for purposes of reporting with respect to original issue discount, if it is registered as to principal) and if its transfer must be effected by the surrender of the old instrument and either the reissuance by the corporation of the old instrument to the new holder or the issuance by the corporation of a new instrument to the new holder. [Reg. § 1.6049-2.]

☐ [T.D. 6628, 12-27-62. *Amended by T.D.* 6908, 12-30-66, *T.D.* 6966, 8-7-68, *T.D.* 7154, 12-27-71, *T.D.* 7584, 1-2-79 *and T.D.* 7881, 3-22-83.]

### [Reg. § 1.6049-3]

**§ 1.6049-3. Statements to recipients of interest payments and holders of obligations to which there is attributed original issue discount in calendar years before 1983.**—(a) *Requirement.*—Every person filing (1) a Form 1099 or 1087 under section 6049(a)(1) and § 1.6049-1 with respect to payments of interest or (2) a Form 1099-OID or 1087-OID with respect to original issue discount includible in gross income, shall furnish to the person whose identifying number is (or should be) shown on the form a written statement showing the information required by paragraph (b) of this section. With respect to interest, no statement is required to be furnished under section 6049(c) and this section to any person if the aggregate of the payments to (or received on behalf of) such person shown on the form would be less than $10. With respect to original issue discount, no statement is required to be furnished under section 6049(c) and this section to any person if the aggregate amount of original issue discount on the statement to such person with respect to the obligation would be less than $10. References in this section to Form 1099 shall be construed to include Form 1099-BCD except that in applying paragraph (b)(2) of this section no information relating to the person to whom the certificate of deposit was originally issued shall be disclosed to another person to whom the payment of interest is made.

(b) *Form of statement.*—(1) *In general.*—The written statement required to be furnished to a person under paragraph (a) of this section shall show—

(i) With respect to payments of interest (as defined in § 1.6049-2) aggregating $10 or more to any person during a calendar year before 1983—

(a) The aggregate amount of payments shown on the Form 1099 or 1087 as having been made to (or received on behalf of) such person and a legend stating that such amount is being reported to the Internal Revenue Service, and

(b) The name and address of the person filing the form, and

(ii) With respect to original issue discount (as defined in § 1.6049-2) which would aggregate $10 or more on the statement to the holder during a calendar year after 1970 and prior to calendar year 1983—

(a) The aggregate amount of original issue discount includible by (or on behalf of) such person with respect to the obligation, as shown on Form 1099-OID or Form 1087-OID for such calendar year (determined by applying the rules of paragraph (a)(1)(ii) of § 1.6049-1 for purposes of completing either form),

(b) All other items shown on such Form 1099-OID or Form 1087-OID for such calendar year (so determined), and

(c) A legend stating that such amount and such items are being reported to the Internal Revenue Service.

(2) *Special rule.*—The requirements of this section for the furnishing of a statement to any person, including the legend requirement of this paragraph, may be met by the furnishing to such person of a copy of the Form 1099, 1099-OID, 1087, or 1087-OID filed pursuant to § 1.6049-1, or a reasonable facsimile thereof, in respect of such person. However, in the case of Form 1087-OID or 1099-OID, a copy of the instructions must also be sent to such person. A statement shall be considered to be furnished to a person within the meaning of this section if it is mailed to such person at his last known address.

(c) *Time for furnishing statements.*—(1) *In general.*—(i) *Payment of interest.*—Each statement required by this section to be furnished to any person for a calendar year for the payment of interest shall be furnished to such person after November 30 of the year and on or before January 31 of the following year, but no statement may be furnished before the final interest payment for the calendar year has been paid. However, the statement may be furnished at any time after April 30 if it is furnished with the final interest payment for the calendar year.

(ii) *Original issue discount.*—(a) Except as otherwise provided in this subdivision (ii), each statement required by this section to be furnished to any person for a calendar year for original issue discount shall be furnished to such person after December 31 of the year and on or before January 31 of the following year.

(b) The time for furnishing each statement required by this section to be furnished to any person for the calendar year 1971 for original issue discount in respect of obligations to which paragraph (e) of § 1.1232-3A applies (relating to deposits in banks and other similar financial institutions) is extended to March 15, 1972.

(c) The time for furnishing each statement required by this section to be furnished by a nominee to any person for the calendar year 1971 for original issue discount is extended to February 28, 1972.

(2) *Extensions of time.*—For good cause shown upon written application of the person required to furnish statements under this section, the district director may grant an extension of time not exceeding 30 days in which to furnish such statements. The application shall be addressed to the district director with whom the income tax returns of the applicant are filed and shall contain a full recital of the reasons for requesting the extension to aid the district director in determining the period of the extension, if any, which will be granted. Such a request in the form of a letter to the district director signed by the applicant will suffice as an application. The application shall be filed on or before the date prescribed in subparagraph (1) of this paragraph for furnishing the statements required by this section.

(3) *Last day for furnishing statement.*—For provisions relating to the time for performance of an act when the last day prescribed for performance falls on Saturday, Sunday, or a legal holiday, see § 301.7503-1 of this chapter (Regulations on Procedure and Administration).

(d) *Penalty.*—For provisions relating to the penalty provided for failure to furnish a statement under this section, see § 301.6678-1 of this chapter (Regulations on Procedure and Administration). [Reg. § 1.6049-3.]

☐ [T.D. 6628, 12-27-62. *Amended by T.D.* 6879, 3-7-66; *T.D.* 7154, 12-27-71; *T.D.* 7584, 1-2-79; *T.D.* 7624, 5-29-79 *and T.D.* 7881, 3-22-83.]

### [Reg. § 1.6049-4]

**§ 1.6049-4. Return of information as to interest paid and original issue discount includible in gross income after December 31, 1982.**—(a) *Requirement of reporting.*—(1) *In general.*—Except as provided in paragraph (c) of this section, an information return shall be made by a payor, as defined in paragraph (a)(2) of this section, of amounts of interest and original issue discount paid after December 31, 1982. Such return shall contain the information described in paragraph (b) of this section.

(2) *Payor.*—For payments made after December 31, 2002, a payor is a person described in paragraph (a)(2)(i) or (ii) of this section.

(i) Every person who makes a payment of the type and of the amount subject to reporting under this section (or under an applicable section under this chapter) to any other person during a calendar year.

(ii) Every person who collects on behalf of another person payments of the type and of the amount subject to reporting under this section (or under an applicable section under this chapter), or who otherwise acts as a middleman (as defined in paragraph (f)(4) of this section) with respect to such payment.

(b) *Information to be reported.*—(1) *Interest payments.*—Except as provided in paragraphs (b)(3) and (5) of this section, in the case of interest other than original issue discount treated as interest under §1.6049-5(f), an information return on Form 1099 shall be made for the calendar year showing the aggregate amount of the payments, the name, address, and taxpayer identification number of the person to whom paid, the amount of tax deducted and withheld under section 3406 from the payments, if any, and such other information as required by the forms. An information return is generally not required if the amount of interest paid to a person aggregates less than $10 or if the payment is made to a person who is an exempt recipient described in paragraph (c)(1)(ii) of this section, unless the payor backup withholds under section 3406 on such payment (because, for example, the payee (*i.e.*, exempt recipient) has failed to furnish a Form W-9 on request), in which case the payor must make a return under this section, unless the payor refunds the amount withheld pursuant to §31.6413(a)-3 (Employment Tax Regulations). For reporting interest paid to certain nonresident alien individuals, see §1.6049-8.

(2) *Original issue discount.*—Except as provided in paragraph (b)(3) and (b)(5) of this section, in the case of original issue discount, an information return on Forms 1096 and 1099 shall be made for each calendar year of any holder of an obligation as to which there is original issue discount includible in gross income aggregating $10 or more. For calendar years before 1992, semiannual record date reporting under §1.6049-1(a)(1)(ii)(*b*)(1) may be used, and if it is used, the original issue discount includible in gross income is determined by treating each holder as holding the obligation on every day it was outstanding during the calendar year. An information return shall be made, however, in any case in which an amount of tax is required to be deducted and withheld under section 3406. In such case, the amount required to be reported is the amount subject to withholding even if the amount of original issue discount includible in gross income is less than $10. With respect to an obligation described in §1.1232-3A(e) or (f) (relating respectively to deposits in banks and similar financial institutions and to face-amount certificates), §1.6049-1(a)(1)(ii)(*d*) and the last sentence of §1.6049-1(a)(1)(ii)(*a*)(2) shall apply. The information return shall show—

(i) The name, address, and taxpayer identification number of each record holder for whom an amount of original issue discount is includible in gross income;

(ii) The account, serial, or other identifying number of each obligation with respect to which a return is being made;

(iii) The aggregate amount of original issue discount includible in the gross income of each holder for the period during the calendar year for which the return is made (or, if the aggregation rules of §1.6049-1(a)(1)(ii)(*b*)(2) are being used, the aggregate amount or original issue discount for the period such holder held the obligations). For calendar years before 1992, semiannual record date reporting under §1.6049-1(a)(1)(ii)(*b*)(1) may be used, and if it is used, the original issue discount includible in gross income is determined by treating each holder as holding the obligation on every day it was outstanding during the calendar year. For purposes of this section, an obligation shall be considered to be outstanding from the date of original issue (as defined in §1.1232-3(b)(3));

(iv) The amount of tax withheld under section 3406, if any;

(v) The name and address of the person filing the return; and

(vi) Such other information as is required by the forms. Section 1.6049-1(a)(1)(ii)(*b*)(2) and, for calendar years before 1992, §1.6049-1(a)(1)(ii)(*b*)(1), and (*c*), apply for purposes of this paragraph.

(3) *Returns made by middleman.*—(i) *In general.*—Except as provided in paragraph (b)(5) of this section, every person acting as a middleman (as defined in paragraph (f)(4) of this section) shall make an information return for the calendar year. In the case of interest payments (other than original issue discount and other than interest described in §1.6049-8), the information return shall be made on

Form 1099 and shall show the aggregate amount of the interest, the name, address, and taxpayer identification number of the person on whose behalf received, the amount of tax withheld under section 3406, if any, and such other information as required by the forms. In the case of original issue discount, the information return shall show the information required to be shown for the person on whose behalf received, as described in paragraph (b)(2) of this section. See §1.6049-5(f) to determine whether a middleman is required to make an information return with respect to original issue discount. A middleman shall make an information return regardless of whether the middleman receives a Form 1099. A middleman shall not be required to make an information return if the payment of interest aggregates less than $10 or if the payment is made to an exempt recipient described in paragraph (c)(1)(ii) of this section, unless the payor backup withholds under section 3406 on such payment (because, for example, the payee has failed to furnish a Form W-9 on request), in which case the payor must make a return under this section, unless the payor refunds the amount withheld pursuant to §31.6413(a)-3 of this chapter (Employment Tax Regulations).

(ii) *Forwarding of interest coupons and original issue discount obligations.*—In the case of a middleman who, from within the United States, forwards an interest coupon or discount obligation on behalf of a payee for presentation, collection or payment outside the United States, the middleman shall make an information return on Form 1099 for the calendar year showing, in the case of an interest coupon, the information required under paragraph (b)(3)(i) of this section and, in the case of a discount obligation, information required under paragraph (b)(2) of this section. For purposes of this paragraph (b)(3)(ii), a middleman is considered to forward an interest coupon or discount obligation on behalf of a payee for presentation, collection or payment outside the United States if the middleman forwards the coupon or obligations outside the United States on or after the date when the payee is entitled to be paid or at an earlier date that is within 90 days of such date or if the middleman has actual knowledge that the coupon or obligation is being forwarded outside the United States for presentation, collection, or payment outside the United States. However, the transfer, although subject to information reporting under this section, is not subject to backup withholding under section 3406.

(iii) *Example.*—The following example illustrates the provisions of paragraph (b)(3)(ii) of this section:

*Example.* Individual F, who is entitled to payment on an interest coupon, instructs an office of Bank M in the United States to forward the coupon to Bank N for collection by Bank N outside the United States. Bank M in the United States forwards the interest coupon to Bank N outside the United States. Bank M is required to make an information return for the calendar year under paragraph (b)(3)(ii) of this section showing the aggregate amount of the interest coupon forwarded, the name, address of the permanent residence, and the taxpayer identification number, if any, of Individual F and such other information as the form requires.

(4) *Returns made with respect to payments on certificates of deposit issued in bearer form.*—Except as provided in paragraph (b)(5) of this section, every person carrying on the banking business who makes payments of interest to another person (whether or not aggregating $10 or more) during a calendar year with respect to a certificate of deposit issued in bearer form shall make an information return on Forms 1096 and 1099. The information return shall show the information required in §1.6049-1(a)(1)(vi)(*a*) through (*e*) inclusive and a statement as to amount of tax withheld under section 3406, if any.

(5) *Interest payments to certain nonresident alien individuals.*—(i) *General rule.*—In the case of interest aggregating $10 or more paid to a nonresident alien individual (as defined in section 7701(b)(1)(B)) that is reportable under §1.6049-8(a), the payor shall make an information return on Form 1042-S, "Foreign Person's U.S. Source Income Subject to Withholding," for the calendar year in which the interest is paid. The payor or middleman shall prepare and file Form 1042-S at the time and in the manner prescribed by section 1461 and the regulations under that section and by the form and its accompanying instructions. See §§1.1461-1(b) (rules regarding the preparation of a Form 1042) and §§1.6049-6(e)(4) (rules for furnishing a copy of the Form 1042-S to the recipient). To determine whether an information return is required for original issue discount, see §§1.6049-5(f) and §§1.6049-8(a).

(ii) *Effective/applicability date.*—Paragraph (b)(5)(i) of this section shall be applicable for payments made on or after January 1, 2013. (For interest paid to a Canadian nonresident alien individual on or before December 31, 2012, see paragraph (b)(5) of this section as in effect and contained in 26 CFR part 1 revised April 1, 2000.)

(c) *Information returns not required.*—(1) *Payment to exempt recipient.*—(i) *In general.*—No information return is required with respect to any payment made to an exempt recipient described in paragraph (c)(1)(ii) of this section, except to the extent otherwise provided in §1.6049-5(d)(3)(ii) and (iii). However, if the payor backup withholds under section 3406 on such payment (because, for example, the payee has failed to furnish a Form W-9 on request), then the payor is required to make a return under this section, unless the payor refunds the amount withheld in accordance with §31.6413(a)-3 of this chapter (Employment Tax Regulations).

(ii) *Exempt recipient defined.*—The term *exempt recipient* means any person described in paragraphs (c)(1)(ii)(A) through (Q) of this section. An exempt recipient is generally exempt from information reporting without filing a certificate claiming exempt status unless the provisions of this paragraph (c)(1)(ii) require a payee to file a certificate. A payor may, in any case, require a payee that is a U.S. person not otherwise required to file a certificate under this paragraph (c)(1)(ii) to file a certificate in order to qualify as an exempt recipient. See §31.3406(h)-3(a)(1)(iii) and (c)(2) of this chapter for the certificate that a payee that is a U.S. person must provide when a payor requires the certificate to treat the payee as an exempt recipient under this paragraph (c)(1)(ii). A payor may treat a payee as an exempt recipient based upon a properly completed form as described in §31.3406(h)-3(e)(2) of this chapter, its actual knowledge that the payee is a person described in this paragraph (c)(1)(ii), or the indicators described in this paragraph (c)(1)(ii).

(A) *Corporation.*—A corporation, as defined in section 7701(a)(3), whether domestic or foreign, is an exempt recipient. In addition, for purposes of this paragraph (c)(1), the term *corporation* includes a partnership all of whose members are corporations described in this paragraph (c)(1), but only if the partnership files with the payor a certificate stating that each member of the partnership meets one of the requirements of paragraphs (c)(1)(ii)(A)(*1*) through (*4*) of this section. Absent actual knowledge otherwise, a payor may treat a payee as a corporation (and, therefore, as an exempt recipient) if one of the requirements of paragraph (c)(1)(ii)(A)(*1*), (*2*), (*3*), or (*4*), of this section are met before a payment is made.

(*1*) The name of the payee contains an unambiguous expression of corporate status that is Incorporated, Inc., Corporation, Corp., P.C., (but not Company or Co.) or contains the term *insurance company*, *indemnity company*, *reinsurance company*, or *assurance company*, or its name indicates that it is an entity listed as a per se corporation under §301.7701-2(b)(8)(i) of this chapter.

(*2*) The payor has on file a corporate resolution or similar document clearly indicating corporate status. For this purpose, a similar document includes a copy of Form 8832, filed by the entity to elect classification as an association under §301.7701-3(b) of this chapter.

(*3*) The payor receives a Form W-9 which includes an EIN and a statement from the payee that it is a domestic corporation.

(*4*) The payor receives a withholding certificate described in §1.1441-1(e)(2)(i), that includes a certification that the person whose name is on the certificate is a foreign corporation.

(B) *Tax exempt organization.*—(1) *In general.*—Any organization that is exempt from taxation under section 501(a) is an exempt recipient. A custodial account under section 403(b)(7) shall be considered an exempt recipient under this paragraph. A payor may treat an organization as an exempt recipient under this paragraph (c)(1)(ii)(B) without requiring a certificate if the organization's name is listed in the compilation by the Commissioner of organizations for which a deduction for charitable contributions is allowed, if the name of the organization contains an unambiguous indication that it is a tax-exempt organization, or if the organization is known to the payor to be a tax-exempt organization.

(2) *Examples.*—The application of the provisions of this paragraph (c)(1)(ii)(B) may be illustrated by the following examples:

*Example 1.* The following persons maintain accounts at M Bank: N College, O University, and P Church. M may treat N, O, and P as exempt recipients even though such persons have not filed an exemption certificate with M because the names of the organizations contain an unambiguous indication that they are tax exempt organizations.

*Example 2.* Q is listed in the current edition of Internal Revenue Service Publication 78 as an organization for which deductions are permitted for charitable contributions under section 170(c). Such listing has not been revoked by an announcement published in the Internal Revenue Bulletin (see §601.601(d)(2) of this chapter). A payor may treat Q as an exempt recipient even though Q has not filed an exemption certificate with the payor.

*Example 3.* Employer R maintains a section 403(b)(7) custodial account with Regulated Investment Company S on behalf of R's employees. S may treat the account as an exempt recipient even though R or its employees have not filed an exemption certificate with S.

(C) *Individual retirement plan.*—An individual retirement plan as defined in section 7701(a)(37) is an exempt recipient. A payor may treat any such plan of which it is the trustee or custodian as an exempt recipient under this paragraph (c)(1) without requiring a certificate.

(D) *United States.*—The United States Government and any wholly-owned agency or instrumentality thereof are exempt recipients. A payor may treat a person as an exempt recipient under this paragraph (c)(1) without requiring a certificate if the name of such person reasonably indicates it is described in this paragraph (c)(1).

(E) *State.*—A State, the District of Columbia, a possession of the United States, a political subdivision of any of the foregoing, wholly-owned agency or instrumentality of any one or more of the foregoing, and a pool or partnership composed exclusively of any of the foregoing are exempt recipients. A payor may treat a person as an exempt recipient under this paragraph (c)(1) without requiring a certificate if the name of such person reasonably indicates it is described in this paragraph (c)(1) or if such person is known generally in the community to be a State, the District of Columbia, a possession of the United States or a political subdivision or a wholly-owned agency or instrumentality of any one or more of the foregoing (for example, an account held in the name of "Town of S" or "County of T" may be treated as held by an exempt recipient under this paragraph (c)(1)(ii)(E)).

(F) *Foreign government.*—A foreign government, a political subdivision of a foreign government, and any wholly-owned agency or instrumentality of either of the foregoing are exempt recipients. A payor may treat a foreign government or a political subdivisions thereof as an exempt recipient under this paragraph (c)(1) without requiring a certificate provided that its name reasonably indicates that it is a foreign government or provided that it is known to the payor to be a foreign government or a political subdivision thereof (for example, an account held in the name of the "Government of V" may be treated as held by a foreign government).

(G) *International organization.*—An international organization and any wholly owned agency or instrumentality thereof are exempt recipients. The term *international organization* shall have the meaning ascribed to it in section 7701(a)(18). A payor may treat a payee as an international organization without requiring a certificate if the payee is designated as an international organization by executive order (pursuant to 22 U.S.C. 288 through 288(f)).

(H) *Foreign central bank of issue.*—A foreign central bank of issue is an exempt recipient. A foreign central bank of issue is a bank which is by law or government sanction the principal authority, other than the government itself, issuing instruments intended to circulate as currency. See §1.895-1(b)(1). A payor may treat a person as a foreign central bank of issue (and, therefore, as an exempt recipient) without requiring a certificate provided that such person is known generally in the financial community as a foreign central bank of issue or if its name reasonably indicates that it is a foreign central bank of issue.

(I) *Securities or commodities dealer.*—A dealer in securities, commodities, or notional principal contracts, that is registered as such under the laws of the United States or a State or under the laws of a foreign country is an exempt recipient. A payor may treat a dealer as an exempt recipient under this paragraph (c)(1) without requiring a certificate if the person is known generally in the investment community to be a dealer meeting the requirements set forth in this paragraph (c)(1) (for example, a registered broker-dealer or a person listed as a member firm in the most recent publication of members of the National Association of Securities Dealers, Inc.).

(J) *Real estate investment trust.*—A real estate investment trust, as defined in section 856 and §1.856-1, is an exempt recipient. A payor may treat a person as a real estate investment trust (and, therefore, as an exempt recipient) without requiring a certificate if the person is known generally in the investment community as a real estate investment trust.

(K) *Entity registered under the Investment Company Act of 1940.*—An entity registered at all times during the taxable year under the Investment Company Act of 1940, as amended (15 U.S.C. 80a-1), (or during such portion of the taxable year that it is in existence), is an exempt recipient. An entity that is created during the taxable year will be treated as meeting the registration requirement of the preceding sentence provided that such entity is so registered at all times during the taxable year for which such entity is in existence. A payor may treat such an entity as an exempt recipient under this paragraph (c)(1) without requiring a certificate if the entity is known generally in the investment community to meet the requirements of the preceding sentence.

(L) *Common trust fund.*—A common trust fund, as defined in section 584(a), is an exempt recipient. A payor may treat the fund as an exempt recipient without requiring a certificate provided that its name reasonably indicates that it is a common trust fund or provided that it is known to the payor to be a common trust fund.

(M) *Financial institution.*—A financial institution such as a bank, mutual savings bank, savings and loan association, building and loan association, cooperative bank, homestead association, credit union, industrial loan association or bank, or other similar organization, whether organized in the United States or under the laws of a foreign country is an exempt recipient. A financial institution also includes a clearing organization defined in §1.163-5(c)(2)(i)(D)(*8*) and the Bank for International Settlements. A payor may treat any person described in the preceding sentence as an exempt recipient without requiring a certificate if the person's name (including a foreign name, such as "Banco" or "Banque") reasonably indicates the payee is a financial institution described in the preceding sentence. In the case of a foreign person, a payor may also treat a person on such list as the Internal Revenue Service may publish or approve (such as in the Thomson Bank Directory or a list approved by the Federal Reserve Board).

(N) *Trust.*—A trust which is exempt from tax under section 664(c) (i.e., a charitable remainder annuity trust or a charitable remainder unitrust) or is described in section 4947(a)(1) (relating to certain charitable trusts) is an exempt recipient. A payor which is a trustee of the trust may treat the trust as an exempt recipient without requiring a certificate.

(O) *Nominees or custodians.*—A nominee or custodian.

(P) *Brokers.*—A broker as defined in section 6045(c) and §1.6045-1(a)(1).

(Q) *Swap dealers.*—A dealer in notional principal contracts as defined in §1.446-3(c)(4)(iii).

(iii) *Exempt recipient no longer exempt.*—Any person who ceases to be an exempt recipient shall, no later than 10 days after such cessation, notify the payor in writing when it ceases to be an exempt recipient unless it reasonably appears that the person formerly qualifying as an exempt recipient will not thereafter receive a reportable payment from the payor. If a payor treats a person as an exempt recipient by requiring the exempt recipient to file a certificate claiming exempt status, that person shall revoke the certificate as provided in the preceding sentence. If the exempt recipient terminates its relationship with the payor prior to the time that the notice of change in status is otherwise required, the exempt recipient is not required to notify the payor. If, however, the person who formerly qualified as an exempt recipient later reinstates the relationship with the payor, the person must, prior to receiving a reportable payment from such relationship, notify the payor that it no longer qualifies as an exempt recipient in case the payor relies upon the previous treatment.

(2) *Payments by certain middlemen.*—An information return shall not be required if—

(i) The record owner is required to file a fiduciary return on Form 1041 disclosing the name, address, and taxpayer identification number of the actual owner, and furnishes Form K-1 to each actual owner containing the information required to be shown on the form, including amounts withheld under section 3406;

(ii) The record owner is a nominee of a banking institution or trust company exercising trust powers, and such banking institution or trust company is required to file a fiduciary return on Form 1041 disclosing the name, address, and identifying number of the actual owner, and furnishes Form K-1 to each actual owner containing the information required to be shown on the form, including amounts withheld under section 3406;

(iii) The record owner is a banking institution or trust company exercising trust powers, or a nominee thereof, and the actual owner is an organization exempt from taxation under section 501(a) for which such banking institution or trust company files an annual return, but only if the name, address, and taxpayer identification number of the record owner is included on or with the Form 1041 fiduciary return filed for the estate or trust or the annual return filed for the tax exempt organization.

(3) *Coordination with reporting rules for widely held fixed investment trusts under §1.671-5 of this chapter.*—See §1.671-5 for the reporting rules for widely held fixed investment trusts (as defined under that section).

(4) *Coordination of reporting with chapter 4 reporting or an applicable IGA.*—(i) *U.S. accounts reported by FFIs that are non-U.S. payors.*—An information return shall not be required with respect to an interest payment made by a participating FFI (including a reporting Model 2 FFI), or registered deemed-compliant FFI (including a reporting

Model 1 FFI), that is a non-U.S. payor (as defined in §1.6049-5(c)(5)) to an account holder of an account maintained by the FFI, when the payment is not subject to withholding under chapter 4 or to backup withholding under section 3406, and the conditions of paragraphs (c)(4)(i)(A), (B), or (C) of this section, as applicable, are met. See paragraph (c)(4)(iii) of this section for circumstances in which an FFI may allocate a payment described in this paragraph (c)(4)(i) to a chapter 4 withholding rate pool of U.S. payees.

(A) The FFI is a participating FFI (including a reporting Model 2 FFI) reporting the account holder of the U.S. account (as defined in §1.1471-1(b)(133)) pursuant to either §1.1471-4(d)(3) or (5) for the year in which the payment is made (including reporting of the account holder's TIN).

(B) The FFI is a registered deemed-compliant FFI (other than a reporting Model 1 FFI) reporting the account holder of the U.S. account pursuant to the conditions of its applicable deemed-compliant status under §1.1471-5(f)(1) for the year in which the payment is made (including reporting of the account holder's TIN).

(C) The FFI is a reporting Model 1 FFI reporting the account holder of the reportable U.S. account pursuant to an applicable Model 1 IGA for the year in which the payment is made (including reporting of the account holder's TIN).

(ii) *Other accounts reported by FFIs under chapter 4.*—An information return shall not be required under this section with respect to a payment that is not subject to withholding under chapter 3 (as defined in §1.1441-2(a)) or backup withholding under §31.3406(g)-1(e) and that is made to a recalcitrant account holder of a participating FFI or registered deemed-compliant FFI (or non-consenting U.S. account of a reporting Model 2 FFI), provided that the FFI reports such account holder in accordance with the classes of account holders described in §1.1471-4(d)(6) for the year in which the payment is made. See paragraph (c)(4)(iii) of this section for circumstances in which an FFI may allocate a payment described in this paragraph (c)(4)(ii) to a chapter 4 withholding rate pool of U.S. payees. In the case of a payment made by an FFI that is a reporting Model 1 FFI, an information return shall not be required with respect to a payment that is not subject to withholding under chapter 3 or backup withholding under §31.3406(g)-1(e) and that is made to an account holder of the FFI if the account—

(A) Has U.S. indicia for which appropriate documentation sufficient to treat the account as held by other than a specified U.S. person has not been provided pursuant to the due diligence requirements described in an applicable Model 1 IGA, and

(B) Is therefore treated as a U.S. reportable account that the FFI is required to report pursuant to the applicable Model 1 IGA.

(iii) *Coordination of reporting exceptions with reporting of chapter 4 withholding rate pools.*—For purposes of paragraphs (c)(4)(i) and (ii) of this section, a participating FFI (including a reporting Model 2 FFI) or registered deemed-compliant FFI (including a reporting Model 1 FFI) receiving a payment from another payor may provide a withholding statement to the payor allocating the payment to a chapter 4 withholding rate of pool of U.S. payees only if the payment is excepted from reporting under paragraph (c)(4)(i) of this section or if the payment is both excepted from reporting under paragraph (c)(4)(ii) of this section and not subject to withholding under chapter 4. See §1.6049-5(b)(14) (providing an exception from reporting under section 6049 to a payor that has been furnished a withholding statement from an participating FFI (including a reporting Model 2 FFI) or registered deemed-compliant FFI (including a reporting Model 1 FFI) and that allocates the payment to a chapter 4 withholding rate pool). Thus, for example, a U.S. payor that is a participating FFI may not allocate a payment to a chapter 4 withholding rate pool of U.S. payees on a withholding statement described in §1.6049-5(b)(14) when the payment is made to a U.S. account maintained by the FFI, regardless of whether the FFI reports the account in accordance with §1.1471-4(d)(3) because the U.S. payor is not excepted from reporting under this section pursuant to paragraph (c)(4)(i) of this section.

(iv) *Example.*—The application of the provisions of paragraphs (c)(4)(ii) and (iii) of this section may be illustrated by the following example:

*Example.* USP is a payor that makes an interest payment that is not a withholdable payment (as defined in paragraph (f)(15) of this section) to RM2, a U.S. payor and reporting Model 2 FFI. The payment is paid and received outside of the United States and is not an amount subject to withholding under chapter 3. RM2 receives the payment as an intermediary with respect to a preexisting account held by A. RM2 has account information with respect to A which includes U.S. indicia as described in §1.1441-7(b)(5) or (8). A does not provide consent for RM2 to report A's account. Under the presumption rules described in §1.6049-5(d)(2)(i), RM2 is required to treat A as a U.S. non-exempt recipient. Despite this presumption rule, and because backup withholding does not apply under §31.3406(g)-1(e), no information return shall be required with respect to the payment under paragraph (c)(4)(ii) of this section if A is reported by RM2 consistent with § 1.1471-4(d)(6) as a non-consenting account holder. Additionally, RM2 may include A in the chapter 4 withholding rate pool of U.S. payees on the withholding statement provided to USP consistent with the requirements of paragraph (c)(4)(iii) of this section.

(d) *Special rules.*—(1) *Aggregation of payments.*—For purposes of paragraph (b) of this section, until such time as the Commissioner determines that it is feasible to require aggregation of payments on two or more accounts, insurance contracts, or investment certificates, and, until this section is amended accordingly to provide for reporting on an aggregate basis, the requirement for filing Form 1099 under this section will be met if a person making payments of interest subject to reporting files a separate Form 1099 with respect to each account, insurance contract, or investment certificate. In the case of obligations described in section 6049(b)(1)(A), separate Forms 1099 may be filed as provided in the preceding sentence with respect to holdings in different issues.

(2) *Treatment of original issue discount.*—The amount of original issue discount subject to reporting under section 6049 shall be the amount of original issue discount includible in the gross income of any holder that is treated as paid under § 1.6049-5(f).

(3) *Conversion into United States dollars of amounts paid in foreign currency.*—(i) *Conversion rules.*—When a payment is made in foreign currency, the U.S. dollar amount of the payment shall be determined by converting such foreign currency into U.S. dollars on the date of payment at the spot rate (as defined in § 1.988-1(d)(1)) or pursuant to a reasonable spot rate convention. For example, a withholding agent may use a month-end spot rate or a monthly average spot rate. A spot rate convention must be used consistently with respect to all non-dollar amounts withheld and from year to year. Such convention cannot be changed without the consent of the Commissioner or the Commissioner's delegate.

(ii) *Special rule for § 1.988-5(a) transactions where the payor on both components of a qualified hedging transaction is the same person.*—(A) *In general.*—Interest or original issue discount on a qualified debt instrument that is part of a qualified hedging transaction under § 1.988-5(a) shall be computed for section 6049 reporting purposes under the rules described in § 1.988-5(a)(9)(ii) if—

(1) The payor on the qualified debt instrument and the counterparty to the § 1.988-5(a) hedge are the same person; and

(2) The payee complies with the requirements of § 1.988-5(a) and so notifies its payor prior to the date required for filing Form 1099 as required by this section.

(B) *Effective date.*—The provisions of this paragraph (d)(3)(ii) apply to transactions entered into after December 31, 2000.

(4) *Determination of person to whom interest or original issue discount is paid or for whom it is received.*—Section 1.6049-1(a)(3) and (4) shall apply with respect to payments of interest and original issue discount after December 31, 1982.

(5) *Payments by governmental units.*—In the case of payments made by any governmental unit or any agency or instrumentality thereof, the officer or employee having control of the payment of interest or original issue discount (or the person appropriately designated for purposes of this section) shall make the returns and statements required under section 6049.

(6) *When payment deemed made.*—(i) *In general.*—Except as provided in paragraph (d)(6)(ii) of this section, for purposes of section 6049, interest is deemed to have been paid when it is credited or set apart to a person without any substantial limitation or restriction as to the time or manner of payment or condition upon which payment is to be made, and is made available to him so that it may be drawn at any time, and its receipt brought within his own control and disposition.

(ii) *Instruments paid on presentment or demand.*—In the case of a payment made on an obligation described in paragraph (e)(2) of this section (relating to transactional reporting), interest is deemed to have been paid at the time the obligation is presented for payment. For example, interest represented by a coupon detached from a bond is considered paid for purposes of section 6049 when the coupon is presented for payment.

(7) *Magnetic media requirement.*—For rules relating to permission to submit the information required by Form 1099 on magnetic tape or other media, see § 1.9101-1. For the requirement to submit the information required by Form 1099 on magnetic media for payments after December 31, 1983, see section 6011(e) and § 301.6011-2 of this chapter (Regulations on Procedure and Administration).

(8) *Obligations that are not exempt from taxation.*—When an issuer of an obligation that is not exempt from taxation receives an envelope or "shell", signed by the payee, stating that interest on the obligation is exempt from taxation under section 103(a) (as described in § 1.6049-5(b)(2)), the issuer shall make an information return under section 6049. The information return shall show the name, address, and taxpayer identification number of the person who signed the statement claiming that interest on the obligation is exempt from taxation, the amount of interest paid, and such other information as is required by the form. An information return is required regardless of the amount of interest. The issuer shall also furnish a written statement to such person showing the information required by § 1.6049-6(b).

(9) *Savings bonds.*—(i) *In general.*—A person who makes payment on a United States savings bond when the bond is presented for payment shall report the difference between the amount to be paid and the amount paid for the bond. The amount subject to reporting shall not be reduced to take into account—

(A) Amounts previously included in the income of a holder as a result of an election under 454 to include annually the increase in the redemption price of the bond; or

(B) Amounts accrued prior to transfer of the bond where the bond has been reissued in the name of the person presenting the bond for payment. With respect to a savings bond that is reissued in another person's name, the amount subject to reporting when the bond is reissued is the amount of interest that has accrued. With respect to a savings bond that is exchanged in a tax-deferred transaction (as described in section 1037), the amount subject o reporting is the amount of cash paid to the holder at the time of the transaction.

(ii) *Examples.*—The application of the provisions of paragraph (d)(9)(i) of this section may be illustrated by the following examples:

*Example (1).* On June 10, 1943, A purchases a $50 Series E savings bond. The amount paid for the savings bond is $37.50. A elects under section 454 to include the increase in the redemption price of the bond annually in income. A presents the bond to Bank M to be cashed on July 1, 1983. The amount to be paid on the bond on that date is $204.96. Bank M is required to make an information return under section 6049 showing that it paid $167.46 (the difference between $204.96 and $37.50) of interest, without regard to A's election to include annually the increase in the redemption price of the bond.

*Example (2).* On December 1, 1970, B purchases a $500 Series E savings bond. The amount paid for the bond is $375. On August 1, 1984, the bond is reissued by the Bureau of Public Debt by deleting B's name and inserting the name of B's child. At the time of reissue, the redemption value of the bond is $1,015.80. The accrued interest is $640.80 (the difference between $1,015.80 and $375). The reissue is a taxable transaction, and B must include in income the accrued interest at the time of reissue. The Bureau of Public Debt is required to make an information return under section 6049 showing that it paid $640.80 of interest to B.

*Example (3).* Assume the same facts as in example (2) except that B exchanges the bond for a Series HH savings bond in the amount of $1,000 issued in B's name. The exchange is tax-deferred under section 1037. The Bureau of Public Debt stamps a legend on the bond stating that interest of $625 has been deferred. The amount of $15.80 is paid to B. The Bureau of the Public Debt must make an information return showing that it paid $15.80 of interest to B.

*Example (4).* Assume the same facts as in example (3) except that the exchange is not a tax-deferred exchange. The Bureau of the Public Debt must make an information return showing that it paid $640.80 of interest to B.

(e) *Transactional reporting.*—(1) *In general.*—An information return required to be made under paragraph (b) of this section may be made on a transaction-by-transaction basis, rather than on an annual aggregation basis, if payment described in paragraph (e)(2) of this section is made by a person described in paragraph (e)(3) of this section.

(2) *Payments subject to transactional reporting.*—An information return may be made on a transactional basis if payment is made on—

(i) A United States savings bond,

(ii) An interest coupon (but see § 1.6049-5(b) which provides that no information return is required to be made with respect to an interest coupon that is exempt from taxation),

(iii) A discount obligation having a maturity at issue of 1 year or less, including commercial paper and short-term government obligations defined in section 1232(a)(3), and

(iv) Any obligation similar to those described in subdivisions (i) through (iii). The information return with respect to payments on the types of obligations described in this paragraph shall be made on Form 1099-INT. A payor may include all interest paid in one transaction on one information return, irrespective of whether obligations of different issuers are paid as part of the transaction.

(3) *Persons subject to transactional reporting.*—A person may make a return on a transactional basis if the person is—

    (i) A middleman (as defined in paragraph (f)(4) of this section) who is required to make an information return under paragraph (b)(3) of this section with respect to any payment described in paragraph (e)(2) of this section, or

    (ii) A federal agency making payments on a United States savings bond.

    (4) *Transaction defined.*—For purposes of this paragraph (e), a transaction means a payment at one time on one or more obligations. For example, if an individual who is exempt from withholding under section 3406 presents at one time five Series EE bonds on each of which $3 of interest has accrued, $15 of interest will be paid as part of the transaction. Accordingly, an information return is required under § 1.6049-4(a)(2)(iii) because the interest paid in the transaction exceeds $10. If only three of the savings bonds were presented, however, no return would be required even if the remaining two bonds were redeemed the following day. See paragraph (a)(2)(i) of this section for the requirement that an information return be made if any amount of tax is withheld under section 3406.

    (5) *Information required.*—The information return for any transaction under paragraph (e) of this section shall show the following:

    (i) The name, address, and taxpayer identification number of the person to whom the interest is paid;

    (ii) The name and address of the person filing the form;

    (iii) The amount of interest paid;

    (iv) The amount of tax withheld under section 3406 if any; and

    (v) Such other information as is required by the form.

    (f) *Definitions.*—For purposes of section 6049, this section, and §§ 1.6049-5 and 1.6049-6—

    (1) *Person.*—The term "person" includes any governmental unit, international organization, and any agency or instrumentality thereof. Therefore, interest paid by one of these entities must be reported unless one of the exceptions under section 6049 applies.

    (2) *Natural person.*—The term "natural person" means any individual, but shall not include a partnership (whether or not composed entirely of individuals), a trust, or an estate.

    (3) *Obligation.*—The term *obligation* includes bonds, debentures, notes, certificates, and other evidences of indebtedness regardless of how denominated. For the definition of the term *offshore obligation*, see paragraph (f)(9) of this section.

    (4) *Middleman.*—(i) *In general.*—The term "middleman" means any person, including a financial institution as described in paragraph (c)(1)(ii)(M) of this section, a broker as defined in section 6045(c), or a nominee, who makes payment of interest for, or collects interest on behalf of, another person, or otherwise acts in a capacity as intermediary between a payor and a payee. For example, a person (other than an issuer of an obligation) who makes payment on an interest coupon of the obligation to another person is a middleman, irrespective of whether such person purchases the coupon for his own account, accepts the coupon as agent for the payee, or otherwise deals with the coupon. The term "middleman" also includes a trustee, including a corporate trustee of a trust where the trust is the payee. See § 1.6049-4(c)(2) providing that the trustee does not have to make an information return on Form 1099 to a beneficiary if the trustee is required to file Form 1041 and furnishes Form K-1 to the beneficiary showing the information required to be shown on the form, including amounts withheld under section 3406. A person shall be considered to be a middleman as to any portion of an interest payment made to such person which portion is actually owned by another person, whether or not the other person's name is also shown on the information return filed with respect to such interest payment, except that a husband or wife will not be considered as acting in the capacity of a middleman with respect to his or her spouse. A person who, from within the United States, forwards an interest coupon or discount obligation on behalf of a payee for presentation, collection or payment outside the United States is also a middleman for purposes of this section (but the transfer, although subject to information reporting under this section, does not make the payment subject to backup withholding under section 3406).

    (ii) *Example.*—The application of the provisions of paragraph (f)(4) of this section may be illustrated by the following example:

    *Example.* In January 1984, Broker B, a U.S. payor, purchases on behalf of its customer, Individual A, an obligation issued by partnership in a public offering on that date. Broker B holds the obligation for A throughout 1984. Broker B is required to make an information return showing the amount of original issue discount treated as paid to A under § 1.6049-5(f).

    (5) *Chapter 4 withholding rate pool.*—The term *chapter 4 withholding rate pool* has the meaning set forth in § 1.1471-1(b)(20). However, for determining the U.S. payees included in a chapter 4 withholding rate pool for purposes of section 6049, see paragraph (c)(4)(iii) of this section.

    (6) *Foreign financial institution (or FFI).*—The term *foreign financial institution* or *FFI* means an entity described in § 1.1471-1(b)(47),

    (7) *Intergovernmental agreement (or IGA).*—The term *intergovernmental agreement* or *IGA* has the meaning set forth in § 1.1471-1(b)(67) (*i.e.*, either a *Model 1 IGA* described in § 1.1471-1(b)(78) or a *Model 2 IGA* described in § 1.1471-1(b)(79)).

    (8) *Non-consenting U.S. accounts.*—The term *non-consenting U.S. accounts* has the meaning set forth in an applicable Model 2 IGA.

    (9) *Offshore obligation.*—The term offshore obligation means an offshore obligation defined in § 1.6049-5(c)(1). For the definition of the term *obligation*, see paragraph (f)(3) of this section.

    (10) *Participating FFI.*—The term *participating FFI* means an FFI that is described in § 1.1471-1(b)(91).

    (11) *Recalcitrant account holder.*—The term *recalcitrant account holder* has the same meaning set forth in § 1.1471-1(b)(110).

    (12) *Registered deemed-compliant FFI.*—The term *registered deemed-compliant FFI* means an FFI that is described in § 1.1471-1(b)(111).

    (13) *Reporting Model 1 FFI.*—The term *reporting Model 1 FFI* means an FFI that is described in § 1.1471-1(b)(114).

    (14) *Reporting Model 2 FFI.*—The term *reporting Model 2 FFI* means a participating FFI that is described in § 1.1471-1(b)(91).

    (15) *Withholdable payment.*—The term *withholdable payment* means a payment described in § 1.1471-1(b)(145).

    (16) *Paid and received outside the United States.*—(i) *In general.*—Except as otherwise provided in paragraphs (f)(16)(ii) and (iii) of this section, the term *paid and received outside the United States* means an amount that is paid by a payor or middleman outside the United States as described in § 1.6049-5(e).

    (ii) *Transfers to the United States.*—Without regard to the location of the account from which the amount is drawn, an amount that is described in paragraph (f)(16)(ii)(A) or (B) of this section and paid by transfer to an account maintained by the payee in the United States or by mail to a United States address (including an amount paid with respect to a bond or a discount obligation described in § 1.6049-5(e)(4)) is not considered to be paid and received outside the United States.

    (A) An amount is described in this paragraph (f)(16)(ii)(A) if it is paid by an issuer or the paying agent of the issuer with respect to an obligation that is—

    (1) Issued by a U.S. payor, as defined in § 1.6049-5(c)(5);

    (2) Registered under the Securities Act of 1933 (15 U.S.C. 77a); or

    (3) Listed on an exchange that is registered as a national securities exchange in the United States or included in an interdealer quotation system in the United States.

    (B) An amount is described in this paragraph (f)(16)(ii)(B) if it is paid by a U.S. middleman (as defined in § 1.6049-5(c)(5)) that, as a custodian, nominee, or other agent of a payee, collects the amount for or on behalf of the payee.

    (iii) *Deposits or accounts with banks and other financial institutions.*—In the case of an amount paid by a bank or other financial institution with respect to a deposit or an account that is considered paid at a branch or office outside the United States as described in § 1.6049-5(e)(2), the amount is not considered paid and received outside the United States if the institution has knowledge that the customer has transmitted instructions to an agent, branch, or office of the institution from inside the United States by mail, telephone, electronic transmission, or otherwise concerning the deposit or account (unless the transmission from the United States has taken place in isolated and infrequent circumstances).

    (iv) *Examples.*—The application of the provisions of paragraph (f)(16) of this section may be illustrated by the following examples:

    *Example 1.* FC is a foreign corporation that is not a U.S. payor or U.S. middleman, as defined in § 1.6049-5(c)(5). A holds FC coupon bonds that are not in registered form under section 163(f) and the regulations. FB, a foreign branch of DC, a domestic corporation, is the designated paying agent with respect to the bonds issued by FC. A does not have an account with FB. A presents a coupon to FB at its office outside the United States with instructions to transfer funds to a bank account maintained by A in the United States. FB transfers the funds in accordance with A's instructions. Even though the amount is credited to an account in the United States, the interest on the FC bonds is paid and received outside the United States under paragraph (f)(16)(ii) of this section and §1.6049-5(e)(3) because the coupon is presented for payment outside the United States; because FC is a foreign person that is not a U.S. payor or U.S. middleman, as defined in §1.6049-5(d)(1); because FB is not acting as A's agent; and because the obligation is not registered under the Securities Act of 1933 (15 U.S.C. 77a), listed on a securities exchange that is registered as a national securities exchange in the United States, or included in an interdealer quotation system.

*Example 2.* FC is a foreign corporation that is not a U.S. payor or U.S. middleman, as defined in §1.6049-5(d)(1). B, a United States citizen, holds a bond issued by FC in registered form under section 163(f) and the regulations thereunder and registered under the Securities Act of 1933 (15 U.S.C. 77a). The bond is not a foreign-targeted registered obligation as defined in §1.871-14(e)(2). DB, a United States branch of a foreign corporation engaged in the commercial banking business, is the registrar of the bonds issued by FC. DB supplies FC with a list of the holders of the FC bonds. Interest on the FC bonds is paid to B and other bondholders by checks prepared by FC at its principal office outside the United States, and B's check is mailed from there to his designated address in the United States. The bond is described in paragraph (f)(16)(ii)(A)(2) of this section. The interest on the FC bonds paid to B by FC is not paid and received outside the United States under paragraph (f)(16) of this section.

*Example 3.* The facts are the same as in *Example 2* except that the checks are prepared and mailed in the United States by DC, a U.S. corporation engaged in the commercial banking business that is the designated paying agent with respect to the bonds issued by FC, and B's check is mailed to his designated address outside the United States. For purposes of section 6049, the interest on the FC bonds paid by DC is not paid and received outside the United States under paragraph (f)(16)(i) of this section.

(g) *Time and place for filing a return for the payment of interest.*— (1) *Annual return.*—Except as provided in paragraph (g)(2) of this section, the returns required under this section for any calendar year for the payment of interest shall be filed after September 30 of such year, but not before the payor's final payment to the payee for the year, and on or before February 28 (March 31 if filed electronically) of the following year. Such returns shall be filed with the appropriate Internal Revenue Service Center, the address of which is listed in the instructions for Form 1096. For extensions of time for filing returns under this section, see §1.6081-1.

(2) *Transactional return.*—In the case of a return under paragraph (e) of this section, relating to returns on a transactional basis, such return shall be filed at any time but in no event later than February 28 (March 31 if filed electronically) of the year following the calendar year in which the interest was paid. The return shall be filed with the appropriate Internal Revenue Service Center, the address of which is listed in the instructions for Form 1096. For extensions of time for filing returns under this section, see §1.6081-1.

(3) *Cross-reference to penalty.*—For provisions relating to the penalty provided for failure to file timely a correct information return required under section 6049(a) and §1.6049-4(a)(1), see §301.6721-1 of this chapter (Procedure and Administration Regulations). See §301.6724-1 of this chapter for the waiver of a penalty if the failure is due to reasonable cause and is not due to willful neglect.

(h) *Effective/applicability dates.*—Except as otherwise provided in paragraphs (b)(5)(ii) and (d)(3)(ii)(B) of this section, this section applies to payments made on or after January 6, 2017. (For payments made after June 30, 2014, and before January 6, 2017, see this section as in effect and contained in 26 CFR part 1, as revised April 1, 2016.) [Reg. §1.6049-4.]

☐ [*T.D. 7881, 3-22-83. Amended by T.D. 8366, 9-27-91; T.D. 8664, 4-15-96; T.D. 8734, 10-6-97; T.D. 8804, 12-30-98; T.D. 8856, 12-29-99; T.D. 8881, 5-15-2000; T.D. 8895, 8-17-2000; T.D. 9010, 7-25-2002 T.D. 9241, 1-23-2006; T.D. 9584, 4-17-2012, T.D. 9658, 2-28-2014 and T.D. 9808, 12-30-2016.*]

### [Reg. §1.6049-5]

**§1.6049-5. Interest and original issue discount subject to reporting after December 31, 1982.**—(a) *Interest subject to reporting requirement.*—For purposes of §§1.6049-4, 1.6049-6 and this section, except as provided in paragraph (b) of this section, the term "interest" means—

(1) Interest on an obligation—

(i) In registered form (as defined in §5f.103-1(c)), or

(ii) Of a type offered to the public. Principles consistent with §5f.163-1 shall be applied to determine whether an obligation is of a type offered to the public.

(2) Interest on deposits with persons carrying on the banking business. Such term shall include deposits evidenced by time certificates of deposit issued in any amount whether negotiable or non-negotiable. The term "interest" includes payments to a mortgage escrow account and amounts paid with respect to repurchase agreements and banker's acceptances. Property which the payee receives from the payor as interest (or in lieu of a cash payment of interest) shall be interest for purposes of section 6049. The amount subject to reporting is the fair market value of such property.

(3) Amounts, whether or not designated as interest, paid or credited by mutual savings banks, savings and loan associations, building and loan associations, cooperative banks, homestead associations, credit unions, industrial loan associations or banks, or similar organizations, in respect of deposits, face amount certificates, investment certificates, or withdrawable or repurchasable shares. Thus, even though amounts paid or credited by such organizations with respect to deposits are designated as "dividends", such amounts are included in the definition of interest for purposes of section 6049. The term "interest" includes payments to a mortgage escrow account and amounts paid with respect to repurchase agreements. Property which the payee receives from the payor as interest (or in lieu of a cash payment of interest) is "interest" for purposes of section 6049. The fair market value of such property is the amount subject to reporting.

(4) Interest on amounts held by insurance companies under an agreement to pay interest thereon. Any increment in value of "advance premiums", "prepaid premiums", or "premium deposit funds" which is applied to the payment of premiums due on insurance policies, or made available for withdrawal by the policyholder, shall be considered interest subject to reporting. Interest that an insurance company pays pursuant to an agreement with the policyholder to a beneficiary because the payment due has been delayed is interest subject to reporting. Interest subject to reporting also includes interest paid by insurance companies with respect to policy "dividend" accumulations (see sections 61 and 451 and the regulations thereunder for rules as to when such interest is considered paid), and interest paid with respect to the proceeds of insurance policies left with the insurer. The so-called "interest element" in the case of annuity or installment payments under life insurance or endowment contracts does not constitute interest for purposes of section 6049.

(5) Interest on deposits with brokers as defined in section 6045(c) and the regulations thereunder. Any payment made in lieu of interest to a person whose obligation has been borrowed in connection with a short sale or other similar transaction is subject to reporting under section 6049. See §1.6045-2 for reporting requirements with respect to payments in lieu of tax-exempt interest.

(6) Interest paid on amounts held by investment companies as defined in section 3 of the Investment Company Act (15 U.S.C. section 80-a) and on amounts paid on pooled funds or trusts. The interest to be reported with respect to a widely held fixed investment trust, as defined in §1.671-5(b)(22), shall be the interest earned on the assets held by the trust. See §1.671-5 for the reporting rules for widely held fixed investment trusts (as defined under that section).

(b) *Interest excluded from reporting requirement.*—The term *interest* or *original issue discount* (OID) does not include—

(1) Interest on any obligation issued by a natural person as defined in §1.6049-4(f)(2), irrespective of whether such interest is collected on behalf of the holder of the obligation by a middleman.

(2) Interest on any obligation if such interest is exempt from taxation under section 103(a), relating to certain governmental obligations, or interest which is exempt from taxation under any other provision of law without regard to the identity of the holder. The holder of a tax exempt obligation that is not in registered form must provide written certification to the payor (other than the issuer of the obligation) that the obligation is exempt from taxation. A statement that interest coupons are tax exempt on the envelope or shell commonly used by financial institutions to process such coupons, signed by the payee, will be sufficient for this purpose if the envelope is properly completed (i.e., shows the name, address, and taxpayer identification number of the payee). A payor may rely on such written certification in treating such interest as tax exempt for purposes of section 6049. See §1.6049-4(d)(8) with respect to the requirement that the issuer of a taxable obligation shall make an information return if such issuer receives an envelope which improperly claims that the interest coupons contained therein are tax exempt.

(3) Interest on amounts held in escrow to guarantee performance on a contract or to provide security. However, interest on amounts held in escrow with a person described in paragraph (a)(2) or (3) of this section is interest subject to reporting under section 6049.

(4) Interest that a governmental unit pays with respect to tax refunds.

(5) Interest on deposits for security, such as deposits posted with a public utility company. However, interest on deposits posted

for security with a person described in paragraph (a)(2) or (3) of this section is interest subject to reporting under section 6049.

(6) Amounts from sources outside the United States (determined under the provisions of part I, subchapter N, chapter 1 of the Internal Revenue Code (Code) and the regulations under those provisions) paid by a non-U.S. payor or a non-U.S. middleman (as defined in paragraph (c)(5) of this section) and paid and received outside the United States. See § 1.6049-4(f)(16) for circumstances in which a payment is considered to be paid and received outside the United States.

(7) Portfolio interest, as defined in § 1.871-14(b)(1), paid with respect to obligations in bearer form described in section 871(h)(2)(A), as in effect prior to the amendment by section 502 of the Hiring Incentives to Restore Employment Act of 2010 (HIRE Act), Public Law 111-147, or section 881(c)(2)(A), as in effect prior to the amendment by section 502 of the HIRE Act, that were issued prior to March 19, 2012, or with respect to a foreign-targeted registered obligation described in § 1.871-14(e)(2) that was issued prior to January 1, 2016, and for which the documentation requirements described in § 1.871-14(e)(3) and (4) have been satisfied (other than by a U.S. middleman (as defined in paragraph (c)(5) of this section) that, as a custodian or nominee of the payee, collects the amount for, or on behalf of, the payee, regardless of whether the middleman is also acting as agent of the payor).

(8) Portfolio interest described in § 1.871-14(c)(1)(ii), paid with respect to obligations in registered form described in section 871(h)(2) or 881(c)(2) that is not described in paragraph (b)(7) of this section.

(9) Any amount paid by an international organization described in § 1.6049-4(c)(1)(ii)(G) (or its paying, transfer, or other agent that is not also a payee's agent) with respect to an obligation of which the international organization is the issuer.

(10)(i) Amounts paid and received outside the United States under § 1.6049-4(f)(16) (other than by a U.S. middleman (as defined in paragraph (c)(5) of this section) that are paid by a custodian or nominee or other agent of the payee, of amounts that that it receives for, or on behalf of, the payee, regardless of whether the middleman is also acting as agent of the payor) with respect to an obligation that: Has a face amount or principal amount of not less than $500,000 (as determined based on the spot rate on the date of issuance if in foreign currency); has a maturity (at issue) of 183 days or less; satisfies the requirements of sections 163(f)(2)(B)(i) and (ii)(I), as in effect prior to the amendment by section 502 of the HIRE Act, and the regulations thereunder (as if the obligation would otherwise be a registration-required obligation within the meaning of section 163(f)(2)(A)) (however, an original issue discount obligation with a maturity of 183 days or less from the date of issuance is not required to satisfy the certification requirement of § 1.163-5(c)(2)(i)(D)(3)) and is issued in accordance with the procedures of § 1.163-5(c)(2)(i)(D); and has on its face the following statement (or a similar statement having the same effect):

> By accepting this obligation, the holder represents and warrants that it is not a United States person (other than an exempt recipient described in section 6049(b)(4) of the Internal Revenue Code and regulations thereunder) and that it is not acting for or on behalf of a United States person (other than an exempt recipient described in section 6049(b)(4) of the Internal Revenue Code and the regulations thereunder).

(ii) If the obligation is in registered form, it must be registered in the name of an exempt recipient described in § 1.6049-4(c)(1)(ii). For purposes of this paragraph (b)(10), a middleman may treat an obligation as described in section 163(f)(2)(B)(i) and (f)(2)(B)(ii)(I), as in effect prior to the amendment by section 502 of the HIRE Act, and the regulations under that section if the obligation, or coupons detached therefrom, whichever is presented for payment, contains the statement described in this paragraph (b)(10). The exemption from reporting described in this paragraph (b)(10) shall not apply if the payor has actual knowledge that the payee is a U.S. person who is not an exempt recipient.

(11) Amounts paid with respect to an account or deposit with a U.S. or foreign branch of a domestic or foreign corporation or partnership that is paid with respect to an obligation described in either paragraph (b)(11)(i) or (ii) of this section, if the branch is engaged in the commercial banking business; and the interest or OID is paid and received outside the United States as defined in § 1.6049-4(f)(16) (other than by a U.S. middleman (as defined in paragraph (c)(5) of this section) that acts as a custodian, nominee, or other agent of the payee, and collects the amount for, or on behalf of, the payee, regardless of whether the middleman is also acting as agent of the payor). The exemption from reporting described in this paragraph (b)(11) shall not apply if the payor has actual knowledge that the payee is a U.S. person who is not an exempt recipient.

(i) An obligation is described in this paragraph (b)(11)(i) if it is not in registered form (within the meaning of section 163(f) and the regulations under that section), is described in section 163(f)(2)(B), as

in effect prior to the amendment by section 502 of the HIRE Act, and issued in accordance with the procedures of § 1.163-5(c)(2)(i)(C) or (D), and, in the case of a U.S. branch, is part of a larger single public offering of securities. For purposes of this paragraph (b)(11)(i), a middleman may treat an obligation as described in section 163(f)(2)(B), as in effect prior to the amendment by section 502 of the HIRE Act, if the obligation, and any detachable coupons, contains the statement described in section 163(f)(2)(B)(ii)(II), as in effect prior to the amendment by section 502 of the HIRE Act, and the regulations under that section.

(ii)(A) An obligation is described in this paragraph (b)(11)(ii) if it produces income described in section 871(i)(2)(A); has a face amount or principal amount of not less than $500,000 (as determined based on the spot rate on the date of issuance if in foreign currency); satisfies the requirements of sections 163(f)(2)(B)(i) and (ii)(I), as in effect prior to the amendment by section 502 of the HIRE Act, and the regulations thereunder (as if the obligation would otherwise be a registration-required obligation within the meaning of section 163(f)(2)(A)) and is issued in accordance with the procedures of § 1.163-5(c)(2)(i)(C) or (D) (however, an original issue discount obligation with a maturity of 183 days or less from the date of issuance is not required to satisfy the certification requirement of § 1.163-5(c)(2)(i)(D)(3)). For purposes of this paragraph (b)(11)(ii), a middleman may treat an obligation as described in sections 163(f)(2)(B)(i) and (ii), as in effect prior to the amendment by section 502 of the HIRE Act, and the regulations under that section if the obligation, or any detachable coupon, contains the statement described in paragraph (b)(11)(ii)(B) of this section.

(B) The obligation must have on its face, and on any detachable coupons, the following statement (or a similar statement having the same effect):

> By accepting this obligation, the holder represents and warrants that it is not a United States person (other than an exempt recipient described in section 6049(b)(4) and regulations under that section) and that it is not acting for or on behalf of a United States person (other than an exempt recipient described in section 6049(b)(4) and the regulations under that section).

(C) If the obligation is in registered form, it must be registered in the name of an exempt recipient described in § 1.6049-4(c)(1)(ii).

(12) Payments that a payor can, prior to payment, reliably associate with documentation upon which it may rely to treat the payment as made to a foreign beneficial owner in accordance with § 1.1441-1(e)(1)(ii) or as made to a foreign payee in accordance with paragraph (d)(1) of this section or presumed to be made to a foreign payee under paragraph (d)(2) or (3) of this section. However, such payments may be reportable under § 1.1461-1(b) and (c) or under § 1.1474-1(d)(2) (for a chapter 4 reportable amount (as described in § 1.1471-1(b)(18)). The provisions of § 1.1441-1 shall apply by substituting the term "payor" for the term "withholding agent" and without regard to the fact that the provisions apply only to amounts subject to withholding under chapter 3 of the Code. In the event of a conflict between the provisions of § 1.1441-1 and paragraph (d) of this section in determining the foreign status of the payee, the provisions of § 1.1441-1 shall govern for payments of amounts subject to withholding under chapter 3 of the Code and the provisions of paragraph (d) of this section shall govern in other cases. This paragraph (b)(12) does not apply to interest paid on or after January 1, 2013, to a nonresident alien individual to the extent provided in § 1.6049-8.

(13) Amounts for the period that the debt obligation with respect to which the interest arises represents an asset blocked as described in § 1.1441-2(e)(3). Payment of such amounts, including interest that is past due and OID on obligations that mature on or before the date that the assets are no longer blocked, is deemed to occur in accordance with the rules of § 1.1441-2(e)(3).

(14) Payments that a payor or middleman can, prior to payment, reliably associate with documentation upon which it may rely to treat as made to a foreign intermediary or flow-through entity in accordance with § 1.1441-1(b) if it obtains from the foreign intermediary or flow-through entity a withholding statement under § 1.1471-3(c)(3)(iii)(B)(2) (describing an FFI withholding statement), § 1.1471-3(c)(3)(iii)(B)(3) (describing a chapter 4 withholding statement), § 1.1441-1(e)(3)(iv) (describing a withholding statement provided by a non-qualified intermediary), § 1.1441-1(e)(5)(v) (describing a withholding statement provided by a qualified intermediary), or under § 1.1441-5 (describing a withholding statement provided by a foreign partnership, foreign simple trust, or foreign grantor trust), that allocates the payment (or portion of a payment) to a chapter 4 withholding rate pool or specific payees to which withholding applies under chapter 4. The provisions of each of the foregoing sections shall apply by substituting the term "payor" for

the term "withholding agent." A payor or middleman may rely on a withholding statement provided by a foreign intermediary or flow-through entity that identifies a chapter 4 withholding rate pool of U.S. payees (as described in §1.6049-4(c)(4)) or, with respect to a withholdable payment, a chapter 4 withholding rate pool of recalcitrant account holders (as described in §1.1471-4(d)(6)) provided that the payor or middleman identifies the foreign intermediary or flow-through entity that maintains the accounts (as described in §1.1471-5(b)(5)) included in the chapter 4 withholding rate pool as a participating FFI (including a reporting Model 2 FFI) or registered deemed-compliant FFI (including a reporting Model 1 FFI) by applying the rules in §1.1471-3(d)(4) or in §1.1471-3(e)(4)(vi)(B), as applicable, for identifying the payee of a payment (by substituting the term "payor" for the term "withholding agent"). See, however, §1.1441-1(e)(5)(v)(C)(2)(i) for when a qualified intermediary may provide a single pool of recalcitrant account holders (without the need to subdivide into the pools described in §1.1471-4(d)(6)). Additionally, when a foreign intermediary or flow through entity provides to a payor or middleman a withholding statement that allocates the payment (or portion of a payment) to a chapter 4 withholding rate pool of U.S. payees, the payor or middleman may also rely on the withholding statement if the payor or middleman identifies the intermediary or flow-through entity as a qualified intermediary (as defined in §1.1441-1(c)(15) by applying the rules described in §1.1441-1(b)(2)(vii)) that provides the certification described in §1.1441-1(e)(3)(ii)(D) with respect to U.S. payees that hold accounts with a foreign intermediary or flow-through entity other than the qualified intermediary providing the certification.

(15) If a foreign intermediary, as described in §1.1441-1(c)(13), or a U.S. branch that is not treated as a U.S. person receives a payment from a payor, which payment the payor can reliably associate with a valid withholding certificate described in §1.1441-1(e)(3)(ii) or (iii), or §1.1441-1(e)(3)(v), respectively, furnished by such intermediary or branch, then the intermediary or branch is not required to report such payment when it, in turn, pays the amount, unless, and to the extent, the intermediary or branch knows that the payment is required to be reported under this section and was not so reported. For example, if a U.S. branch described in §1.1441-1(b)(2)(iv) fails to provide information regarding U.S. persons that are not exempt from reporting under §1.6049-4(c)(1)(ii) to the person from whom the U.S. branch receives the payment, the amount paid by the U.S. branch to such person is interest or original issue discount. See, however, §1.6049-4(c)(4) for when reporting under section 6049 is coordinated with reporting under chapter 4 or an applicable IGA (as defined in §1.6049-4(f)(7)). The exception for payments described in this paragraph (b)(15) shall not apply to a qualified intermediary that assumes reporting responsibility under chapter 61 of the Code for the payment under the agreement described in §1.1441-1(e)(5)(iii).

(16) Amounts of interest as determined under the provisions of §1.446-3(g)(4) (dealing with interest in the case of a significant nonperiodic payment with respect to a notional principal contract). Such amounts are governed by the provisions of section 6041. See §1.6041-1(d)(5).

(c) *Applicable rules.*—(1) *Documentary evidence for offshore obligations and certain other obligations.*—(i) A payor may rely on documentary evidence described in §1.1471-3(c)(5)(i) instead of a beneficial owner withholding certificate described in §1.1441-1(e)(2)(i) in the case of an amount paid outside the United States (as described in paragraph (e) of this section) with respect to an offshore obligation, or, in the case of broker proceeds described in §1.6045-1(c)(2), to the extent provided in §1.6045-1(g)(1)(i). For purposes of this section, the term *offshore obligation* means—

(A) An account maintained at an office or branch of a bank or other financial institution located outside the United States; or

(B) An obligation as defined in §1.6049-4(f)(3) (other than an account described in paragraph (c)(1)(i)(A) of this section), contract, or other instrument with respect to which the payor is either engaged in business as a broker or dealer in securities or a financial institution (as defined in §1.1471-5(e)) that engages in significant activities at an office or branch located outside the United States. For purposes of the preceding sentence, an office or branch of such payor shall be considered to engage in significant activities with respect to an obligation when it participates materially and actively in negotiating the obligation under the principles described in §1.864-4(c)(5)(iii) (substituting the term "obligation" for the term "stock or security").

(ii) A payor may rely on documentary evidence if the payor has established procedures to obtain, review, and maintain documentary evidence sufficient to establish the identity of the payee and the status of that person as a foreign person; and the payor obtains, reviews, and maintains such documentary evidence in accordance with those procedures. A payor maintains the documents reviewed for purposes of this paragraph (c)(1) by retaining an original, certified copy, or photocopy (including a microfiche, electronic scan, or

similar means of electronic storage) of the documents reviewed for as long as it may be relevant to the determination of the payor's obligation to report under §1.6049-4 and this section and noting in its records the date on which the document was received and reviewed. Documentary evidence furnished for a payment of an amount subject to withholding under chapter 3 of the Code or that is a chapter 4 reportable amount under §1.1474-1(d)(2) must contain all of the information that is necessary to complete a Form 1042-S for that payment. See §§1.1471-3(c) and 1.1471-4(c) for additional documentation requirements to identify a payee or account holder for chapter 4 purposes that may apply in addition to the requirements under paragraph (c) of this section.

(iii) Even if an account or obligation (as defined in §1.6049-4(f)(3)) is not maintained outside the United States (maintained in the United States), a payor may rely on documentary evidence associated with a withholding certificate described in §1.1441-1(e)(3)(iii) with respect to the persons for whom an entity acting as an intermediary collects the payment. A payor may also rely on documentary evidence associated with a flow-through withholding certificate for payments treated as made to foreign partners of a nonwithholding foreign partnership, as defined in §1.1441-1(c)(28), the foreign beneficiaries of a foreign simple trust, as defined in §1.1441-1(c)(24), or foreign owners of a foreign grantor trust, as defined in §1.1441-1(c)(26), even though the partnership or trust account is an obligation maintained in the United States.

(iv) For accounts opened on or after July 1, 2014, and before January 1, 2015, and for obligations entered into on or after July 1, 2014, and before January 1, 2015, a payor may continue to apply the rules of §1.6049-5(c)(1) and (c)(4) as in effect and contained in 26 CFR part 1 revised April 1, 2013, rather than this paragraph (c)(1) and paragraph (c)(4) of this section. A payor that applies the rules of §1.6049-5(c)(1) and (c)(4) as in effect and contained in 26 CFR part 1 revised April 1, 2013, to an account or obligation must also apply §1.1441-6(c)(2) (to the extent applicable) and §1.6049-5(e) both as in effect and contained in 26 CFR part 1 revised April, 2013, with respect to the account or obligation.

(2) *Other applicable rules.*—The provisions of §1.1441-1(e)(4)(i) through (xii) (regarding who may sign a certificate, validity period of certificates and documentary evidence, retention of certificates, reliance rules, etc.) shall apply (by substituting the term "payor" for the term "withholding agent" and disregarding the fact that the provisions under §1.1441-1(e)(4) only apply to amounts subject to withholding under chapter 3 of the Code) to withholding certificates and documentary evidence furnished for purposes of this section. See §1.1441-1(b)(2)(vii) for provisions dealing with reliable association of a payment with documentation.

(3) *Standards of knowledge.*—A payor may not rely on a withholding certificate or documentary evidence described in paragraph (c)(1) or (4) of this section if it has actual knowledge or reason to know that any information or certification stated in the certificate or documentary evidence is unreliable. A payor has reason to know that information or certifications are unreliable only if the payor would have reason to know under the provisions of §1.1441-7(b)(2) and (3) that the information and certifications provided on the certificate or in the documentary evidence are unreliable or, in the case of a Form W-9 (or an acceptable substitute), it cannot reasonably rely on the documentation as set forth in §31.3406(h)-3(e) of this chapter (see the information and certification described in §31.3406(h)-3(e)(2)(i) through (iv) of this chapter that are required in order for a payor reasonably to rely on a Form W-9). The provisions of §1.1441-7(b)(2) and (3) shall apply for purposes of this paragraph (c)(3) irrespective of the type of income to which §1.1441-7(b)(2) is otherwise limited. The exemptions from reporting described in paragraphs (b)(10) and (11) of this section shall not apply if the payor has actual knowledge that the payee is a U.S. person who is not an exempt recipient.

(4) *Special documentation rules for certain payments.*—This paragraph (c)(4) modifies the provisions of paragraph (c)(1) of this section for payments of amounts that are not subject to withholding under chapter 3 of the Code, other than amounts described in paragraph (d)(3)(iii) of this section (dealing with U.S. short-term OID and U.S. source deposit interest described in section 871(i)(2)(A) or 881(d)(3)). Amounts are not subject to withholding under chapter 3 of the Code if they are not included in the definition of amounts subject to withholding under §1.1441-2(a) (*e.g.*, deposit interest with foreign branches of U.S. banks, foreign source income, or broker proceeds). A payor may rely upon documentation in lieu of documentary evidence (as described in paragraph (c)(1) of this section) or a written statement (as defined in §1.1471-1(b)(150)) or another statement to the extent permitted in paragraphs (c)(4)(i) through (iii) of this section, until the payor knows or has reason to know of a change in circumstance that makes the documentation unreliable or incorrect (as defined in §1.1441-1(e)) when the payor does not have customer information for the payee that includes any of the U.S. indicia de-

scribed in § 1.1471-3(c)(6)(ii)(C)(*1*). Further, a payor may maintain such documentation or documentary evidence as required in paragraph (c)(4)(iv) of this section.

(i) *Statement in lieu of documentary evidence with respect to accounts.*—If under the local laws, regulations, or practices of a country in which an account is maintained, it is not customary to obtain documentary evidence described in paragraph (c)(1) of this section with respect to the type of account, the payor may, instead of obtaining a beneficial owner withholding certificate described in § 1.1441-1(e)(2)(i) or documentary evidence described in paragraph (c)(1) of this section, establish a payee's foreign status based on the statement described in this paragraph (c)(4)(i) (or such substitute statement as the Internal Revenue Service may prescribe) made on an account opening form. However, see, also § 1.1471-4(c) or an applicable IGA for additional documentation requirements that may apply to a participating FFI (including a reporting Model 2 FFI) for determining the status of its account holders for chapter 4 purposes. The statement referred to in this paragraph (c)(4)(i) must appear near the signature line and must state, "By opening this account and signing below, the account owner represents and warrants that he/she/it is not a U.S. person for purposes of U.S. Federal income tax and that he/she/it is not acting for, or on behalf of, a U.S. person. A false statement or misrepresentation of tax status by a U.S. person could lead to penalties under U.S. law. If your tax status changes and you become a U.S. citizen or a resident, you must notify us within 30 days." Additionally, a payor may, instead of obtaining a beneficial owner withholding certificate described in § 1.1441-1(e)(2)(i) or § 1.1471-3(c)(3)(ii) or documentary evidence described in paragraph (c)(1) of this section, establish a payee's foreign status based on a written statement described in paragraph § 1.1471-1(b)(150) to the extent a payor uses such written statement to establish a payee's chapter 4 status and is permitted to use the written statement under § 1.1471-3(d) (by substituting the term "payor" for the term "withholding agent") without any other documentary evidence.

(ii) *Documentation under IGA.*—A payor that is a reporting Model 1 FFI or reporting Model 2 FFI may rely upon documentation or information establishing a payee's status that is permitted under an applicable IGA for determining whether the account of the payee is other than a U.S. account and regardless of whether such documentation or certification is described in paragraph (c)(1) of this section or § 1.1441-1(e)(2).

(iii) *Maintenance of documentation and written statement.*—A payor maintains documentation if it either maintains the documentary evidence as described in paragraph (c)(1) of this section or retains a record of the documentary evidence reviewed if the payor is not required to retain copies of the documentation pursuant to the payor's AML due diligence (as defined in § 1.1471-1(b)(4)). A payor retains a record of documentary evidence reviewed by noting in its records the type of documentation reviewed, the date the document was reviewed, the document's identification number (if any), and whether such documentation contained any U.S. indicia described in § 1.1441-7(b)(8). Any statement described in paragraph (c)(4)(i) of this section, must be retained in accordance with § 1.1471-3(c)(6)(iii).

(5) *U.S. payor, U.S. middleman, non-U.S. payor, and non-U.S. middleman.*—The terms *payor* and *middleman* have the meanings ascribed to them under § 1.6049-4(a). A *non-U.S. payor* or *non-U.S. middleman* means a payor or middleman other than a U.S. payor or U.S. middleman. The term *U.S. payor* or *U.S. middleman* means—

(i) *Definition.*—(A) A person described in section 7701(a)(30) (including a foreign branch or office of such person);

(B) The government of the United States or the government of any State or political subdivision thereof (or any agency or instrumentality of any of the foregoing);

(C) A controlled foreign corporation within the meaning of section 957, determined without applying section 318(a)(3)(A), (B), and (C) so as to consider a United States person as owning stock which is owned by a person who is not a United States person.

(D) A foreign partnership, if at any time during its tax year, one or more of its partners are U.S. persons (as defined in § 1.1441-1(c)(2)) who, in the aggregate hold more than 50 percent of the income or capital interest in the partnership or if, at any time during its tax year, it is engaged in the conduct of a trade or business in the United States;

(E) A foreign person 50 percent or more of the gross income of which, from all sources for the three-year period ending with the close of its taxable year preceding the collection or payment (or such part of such period as the person has been in existence), was effectively connected with the conduct of trade or business within the United States; or

(F) A U.S. branch or territory financial institution described in § 1.1441-1(b)(2)(iv) that is treated as a U.S. person.

(ii) *Reporting by U.S. payors in U.S. possessions.*—U.S. payors are not required to report on Form 1099 income that is from sources within a possession of the United States and that is exempt from taxation under section 931, 932, or 933, each of which sections exempts certain income from sources within a possession of the United States paid to a bona fide resident of that possession. For purposes of this paragraph (c)(5)(ii), a U.S. payor may treat the beneficial owner as a bona fide resident of the possession of the United States from which the income is sourced if, prior to payment of the income, the U.S. payor can reliably associate the payment with valid documentation that supports the claim of residence in the possession of the United States from which the income is sourced. This paragraph (c)(5)(ii) shall not apply if the U.S. payor has actual knowledge or reason to know that the documentation is unreliable or incorrect or that the income does not satisfy the requirements for exemption under section 931, 932, or 933. For the rules determining whether income is from sources within a possession of the United States, see section 937(b) and the regulations thereunder.

(6) *Examples.*—The following examples illustrate the provisions of paragraphs (b) and (c) of this section:

*Example 1.* FC is a foreign corporation that is not engaged in a trade or business in the United States during the current calendar year. D, an individual who is a resident and citizen of the United States, holds a registered obligation issued by FC in a public offering. Interest is paid on the obligation within the United States by DC, a U.S. corporation that is the designated paying agent of FC. D does not have an account with DC. Although interest paid on the obligation issued by FC is foreign source, the interest paid by DC to D is considered to be interest under paragraph (b)(6) of this section for purposes of information reporting under section 6049 because it is not paid and received outside the United States within the meaning of § 1.6049-4(f)(16).

*Example 2.* The facts are the same as in *Example 1* except that D is a nonresident alien individual who has furnished with a Form W-8 in accordance with the provisions of § 1.1441-1(e)(1)(ii). By reason of paragraph (b)(12) of this section, the payment of interest by DC to D is not considered to be a payment of interest for purposes of information reporting under section 6049. Therefore, DC is not required to make an information return under section 6049.

*Example 3.* The facts are the same as in *Example 2* except that the obligation of FC is held in a custodial account for D by FB, a foreign branch of a U.S. financial institution. By reason of paragraph (c)(5) of this section, FB is considered to be a U.S. middleman. Therefore, FB is required to make an information return unless FB may treat D as a beneficial owner that is a foreign person in accordance with the provisions of § 1.1441-1(e)(1)(ii).

*Example 4.* The facts are the same as in *Example 3* except that the FC obligation is held for D by NC, in a custodial account at NC's foreign branch. NC is a foreign corporation that is a non-U.S. middleman described in paragraph (c)(5) of this section. The payment by NC to D is paid and received outside of the United States under § 1.6049-4(f)(16) and therefore is not considered to be a payment of interest for purposes of section 6049 pursuant to paragraph (b)(6) of this section. Therefore, NC is not required to make an information return under section 6049 with respect to the payment.

(d) *Determination of status as U.S. or foreign payee and applicable presumptions in the absence of documentation.*—(1) *Identifying the payee.*—The provisions of § § 1.1441-1(b)(2), 1.1441-5(c)(1) and (e)(2) and (3) shall apply (by substituting the term "payor" for the term "withholding agent") to identify the payee (other than a payee included in a chapter 4 withholding rate pool described in paragraph (b)(14) of this section) for purposes of this section (and other sections of the regulations under this chapter to which this paragraph (d)(1) applies), except to the extent provided in this paragraph (d)(1) in the case of a payment of an amount that is not subject to withholding under chapter 3 of the Code and that is not a withholdable payment (as defined in § 1.6049-4(f)(15)). Amounts are not subject to withholding under chapter 3 of the Code if they are not included in the definition of amounts subject to withholding under § 1.1441-2(a) (*e.g.,* deposit interest with foreign branches of U.S. banks, foreign source income, or broker proceeds). The exceptions to the application of § 1.1441-1(b)(2) to amounts that are not subject to withholding under chapter 3 of the Code and that are not withholdable payments are as follows:

(i) The provisions of § 1.1441-1(b)(2)(ii), dealing with payments to a U.S. agent or intermediary of a foreign person, shall not apply. Thus, a payment to a U.S. agent or intermediary of a foreign person is treated as a payment to a U.S. payee.

(ii) Payments to U.S. branches or territory financial institution described in § 1.1441-1(b)(2)(iv) shall be treated as payments to a foreign payee, irrespective of the fact that the U.S. branch or territory financial institution is otherwise treated as a U.S. person for payments of amounts subject to withholding under chapter 3 and withholdable payments, and irrespective of the fact that the branch or territory financial institution is treated as a U.S. payor for purposes of paragraph (c)(5) of this section.

(2) *Presumptions of U.S. or foreign status in the absence of documentation.*—(i) *In general.*—Except as otherwise provided in this paragraph (d)(2)(i), for purposes of this section (and other sections of regulations under this chapter 61 to which this paragraph (d)(2) applies), the provisions of §1.1441-1(b)(3)(i) through (ix) and §1.1441-5(d) and (e)(6) shall apply (by substituting the term "payor" for the term "withholding agent") to determine the classification (*e.g.*, individual, corporation, partnership, trust), status (*i.e.*, a U.S. or a foreign person), and other relevant characteristics (*e.g.*, beneficial owner or intermediary) of a payee if a payment cannot be reliably associated with valid documentation under §1.1441-1(b)(2)(vii) irrespective of whether the payments are subject to withholding under chapter 3 of the Code or are withholdable payments. The provisions of §1.1441-1(b)(3)(iii)(D) and (vii)(B) (referencing presumption rules for payments with respect to offshore obligations) shall not apply to a payment of an amount not subject to withholding under chapter 3, unless it is an amount that is a withholdable payment made to a payee that is an entity. Thus, in the case of a withholdable payment made to an entity, the presumption rules of §1.1441-1(b)(3)(iii)(D) and (vii)(B) shall apply regardless of whether the payment is an amount subject to withholding under chapter 3. Additionally, in the case of an amount paid outside the United States with respect to an offshore obligation described in §1.1441-1(b)(3)(iii)(D) or (vii)(B) of an amount not subject to withholding under chapter 3 and that is treated as made to a payee that is an individual, the presumption rules of §1.1441-1(b)(3)(iii) shall not apply, and the payee shall be presumed a U.S. person only when the payee has any of the indicia of U.S. status that are described in §1.1441-7(b)(5) or (8). In a case in which a withholding agent makes a withholdable payment that cannot reliably be associated with documentation, see §1.1471-3(f)(4) and (5) for determining the status of the payee for chapter 4 purposes when the payment is treated as made to a foreign entity (by substituting the term "payor" for the term "withholding agent"). The rules of §1.1441-1(b)(2)(vii) shall apply for purposes of determining when a payment can reliably be associated with documentation, by substituting the term "payor" for the term "withholding agent." For this purpose, the information, documentary evidence, statement, or other documentation described in paragraph (c)(4) of this section can be treated as documentation with which a payment can be associated.

(ii) *Grace period in the case of indicia of a foreign payee.*—When the conditions of this paragraph (d)(2)(ii) are satisfied, the 30-day grace period provisions under section 3406(e) shall not apply and the provisions of this paragraph (d)(2)(ii) shall apply instead. A payor that, at any time during the grace period described in this paragraph (d)(2)(ii), credits an account with payments described in §1.1441-6(c)(2) (or credits an account with broker proceeds from securities described in §1.1441-6(c)(2)), that are reportable under section 6042, 6045, 6049, or 6050N may, instead of treating the account as owned by a U.S. person and applying backup withholding under section 3406, if applicable, choose to treat the account as owned by a foreign person (and apply the grace period described in §1.1441-1(b)(3)(iv)) if, at the beginning of the grace period, the address that the payor has in its records for the account holder is in a foreign country, the payor has been furnished the information contained in a withholding certificate described in §1.1441-1(e)(2), or the payor holds a withholding certificate that is no longer reliable other than because the validity period as described in §1.1441-1(e)(4)(ii)(A) has expired. In the case of a newly opened account, the grace period begins on the date that the payor first credits the account. In the case of an existing account for which the payor holds a Form W-8 or documentary evidence of foreign status, the payor may apply the provisions of the grace period described in §1.1441-1(b)(3)(iv), beginning on the date that the payor first credits the account after the existing documentation held with regard to the account can no longer be relied upon (other than because the validity period described in §1.1441-1(e)(4)(ii)(A) has expired). A new account shall be treated as an existing account for purposes of this paragraph (d)(2)(ii) if the account holder already holds an account at the branch location at which the new account is opened, or if the account is treated as a consolidated obligation as defined in §1.1471-(1)(b)(23) for purpose of chapter 4 to the extent the account does not receive any amounts subject to withholding under chapter 3. A new account shall also be treated as an existing account for purposes of this paragraph (d)(2)(ii) if an account is held at another branch location if the institution maintains an account information system described in §1.1441-1(e)(4)(ix). The grace period terminates on the earlier of the close of the 90th day from the date on which the grace period begins or the date that valid documentation is provided. The grace period also terminates when the remaining balance in the account (due to withdrawals or otherwise) is equal to or less than 28 percent (or other

statutory tax rate that is applicable to backup withholding) of the total amounts credited since the beginning of the grace period that would be subject to backup withholding if the provisions of this paragraph (d)(2)(ii) did not apply. At the end of the grace period, the payor shall treat the amounts credited to the account, or paid with respect to an account, during the grace period as paid to a U.S. or foreign payee depending upon whether documentation has been furnished and the nature of any such documentation furnished upon which the payor may rely to treat the account as owned by a U.S. or foreign payee. If the documentation has not been received on or before the date of expiration of the grace period, the payor may also apply the presumptions described in this paragraph (d) to amounts credited to the account after the date on which the grace period expires (until such time as the payor can reliably associate the documentation with amounts credited). See §31.6413(a)-3(a)(1)(iv) of this chapter for treating backup withheld amounts under section 3406 as erroneously withheld when the documentation establishing foreign status is furnished prior to the end of the calendar year in which backup withholding occurs. If the provisions of this paragraph (d)(2)(ii) apply, the provisions of §31.3406(d)-3 of this chapter shall not apply. For purposes of this paragraph (d)(2)(ii), an account holder's reinvestment of gross proceeds of a sale into other instruments constitutes a withdrawal and a non-qualified electronic transmission of information on a withholding certificate is a transmission that is not in accordance with the provisions of §1.1441-1(e)(4)(iv). See §1.1092(d)-1 for a definition of the term actively traded for purposes of this paragraph (d)(2)(ii).

(iii) *Joint owners.*—Amounts paid to accounts held jointly for which a certificate or documentation is required as a condition for being exempt from reporting under paragraph (b) of this section are presumed made to U.S. payees who are not exempt recipients if, prior to payment, the payor cannot reliably associate the payment either with a Form W-9 furnished by one of the joint owners in the manner required in §§31.3406(d)-1 through 31.3406(d)-5 of this chapter, or with documentation described in paragraph (b)(12) of this section furnished by each joint owner upon which it can rely to treat each joint owner as a foreign payee or foreign beneficial owner. In the case of an amount that is a withholdable payment made to a joint account, however, see §1.1471-3(f)(7) for when the payment is treated as made to a foreign payee that is a nonparticipating FFI (as defined in §1.1471-1(b)(82)). For purposes of applying this paragraph (d)(2)(iii), the grace period described in paragraph (d)(2)(ii) of this section shall apply only if each payee qualifies for such grace period.

(3) *Payments to foreign intermediaries or flow-through entities.*—(i) *Payments of amounts subject to withholding under chapter 3 of the Code or withholdable payments.*—In the case of payments of amounts that the payor may treat as made to a foreign intermediary or flow-through entity in accordance with §§1.1441-1(b)(3)(ii)(C) and (b)(3)(v)(A) and 1.1441-5(c) or (e) and that are subject to withholding under §1.1441-2(a), the provisions of §§1.1441-1(b)(2)(v) and 1.1441-5(c)(1), (e)(2), and (3) shall apply (by substituting the term "payor" for the term "withholding agent") to identify the payee. If a payment of an amount subject to withholding cannot be reliably associated with valid documentation from a payee in accordance with §1.1441-1(b)(2)(vii), the presumption rules of §§1.1441-1(b)(3)(v) and 1.1441-5(d) and (e)(6) shall apply to determine the payee's status for purposes of this section (and other sections of regulations under this chapter to which this paragraph (d)(3) applies). In the case of an amount that is a withholdable payment, see §1.1471-3(c)(3) for rules to identify the payee and see §1.1471-3(f)(5) for the presumption rule that shall apply to amounts treated as made to a foreign intermediary or flow-through entity (by substituting the term "payor" for the term "withholding agent"). For example, where a withholdable payment is made to an intermediary under §1.1471-3 that is treated as a nonparticipating FFI under §1.1471-3(f)(5), the nonparticipating FFI shall be treated as the payee under §1.1471-3(c)(3) and for purposes of this paragraph (d)(3)(i), therefore, no information return shall be required under this section.

(ii) *Payments of amounts not subject to withholding under chapter 3 of the Code and that are not withholdable payments.*—Except as provided in paragraph (d)(3)(iii) of this section, amounts that are not subject to withholding under chapter 3 of the Code and that are not withholdable payments that the payor may treat as paid to a foreign intermediary or flow-through entity shall be treated as made to an exempt recipient described in §1.6049-4(c) except to the extent that the payor has actual knowledge that any person for whom the intermediary or flow-through entity is collecting the payment is a U.S. person who is not an exempt recipient. In the case of such actual knowledge, the payor shall treat the payment that it knows is allocable to such U.S. person as a payment to a U.S. payee who is not an exempt recipient and has actual knowledge of the amount allocable to such a person.

(iii) *Special rule for payments of certain short-term original issue discount.*—(A) *General rule.*—A payment of U.S. source bank deposit interest not subject to chapter 4 withholding or U.S. source interest or original issue discount on the redemption of an obligation with a maturity from the date of issue of 183 days or less (short-term OID) described in section 871(g)(1)(B) or 881(e) that the payor may treat as paid to a foreign intermediary or flow-through entity in accordance with the provisions of §§1.1441-1(b)(3)(ii)(C), (b)(3)(v)(A), §1.1441-5(d) or (e) (by substituting the term "payor" for the term "withholding agent"), shall be treated as paid to an undocumented U.S. payee that is not an exempt recipient under paragraph §1.6049-4(c) unless the payor has documentation from the payees of the payment and the payment is allocated to foreign payees, as a group, and to each U.S. non-exempt recipient payee. See §1.1441-1(e)(3)(iv)(C)(2). However, a payor may rely on a withholding statement provided by an intermediary described in §1.1441-1(e)(3)(iv) (or similar withholding statement for a flow-through entity) that identifies a chapter 4 withholding rate pool of U.S. payees (as described in §1.6049-4(c)(4)(iii)) only if it identifies the foreign intermediary or flow-through entity as a participating FFI (including a reporting Model 2 FFI) or registered deemed-compliant FFI (including a reporting Model 1 FFI) under §1.1471-3(d)(4) (by substituting the term "payor" for the term "withholding agent"). See also §1.6049-4(c)(4)(iii) for when an FFI may provide a chapter 4 withholding rate pool of U.S. payees on a withholding statement.

(B) *Payee may be an intermediary.*—If a payment is made to a person described in §1.6049-4(c)(1)(ii) that has not provided an intermediary withholding certificate under §1.1441-1(e)(3)(i) but the payor knows or has reason to know that the payee may be an intermediary, the payor must apply the rules of paragraph (d)(3)(iii)(A) of this section. A payor has reason to know that such a person may be an intermediary if that person has provided documentation as an intermediary for another account with the same payor.

(iv) *Short-term deposits and repurchase transactions.*—The provisions of paragraph (d)(3)(ii) of this section and not paragraph (d)(3)(iii) of this section shall apply to deposits with banks and other financial institutions that remain on deposit for a period of two weeks or less, to amounts of original issue discount arising from a sale and repurchase transaction that is completed within a period of two weeks or less, or to amounts described in paragraphs (b)(7), (10) and (11) of this section (relating to certain obligations issued in bearer form).

(4) *Examples.*—The rules of paragraphs (d)(1) through (3) of this section are illustrated by the examples in this paragraph (d)(4). Unless otherwise specified in an example, the following facts apply: all FFIs, such as a nonqualified intermediary that is an FFI, are treated as participating FFIs; all payees have been identified with chapter 4 statuses that do not require withholding under chapter 4; and none of the payments are withholdable payments.

*Example 1.* (i) *Facts.* USP is a U.S. payor as defined in paragraph (c)(5) of this section. USP pays interest from sources within the United States that is a withholdable payment to an account maintained in the United States by X. The interest is not deposit interest described in sections 871(i)(2)(A) or 881(d). USP does not have a Form W-9, or withholding certificate from X as defined in §1.1441-1(c)(16). Moreover, USP cannot treat X as an exempt recipient, as defined in §1.6049-4(c)(1)(ii), without documentation and there is no indication that X is an individual, trust, or estate.

(ii) *Analysis.* The U.S. source interest is an amount subject to withholding as defined in §1.1441-2(a). Under paragraph (d)(1) of this section, USP must apply the provisions of §§1.1441-1(b)(2) and 1.1441-5(c) and (e) to determine the payee of the interest. Under §1.1441-1(b)(2)(i), X, the person to whom the payment is made, is considered to be the payee, unless X is determined to be a flow-through entity, in which case the rules of §1.1441-5 apply to determine the payee. Under paragraph (d)(2)(i) of this section, the rules of §1.1441-1(b)(3)(ii) apply to determine the classification of a payee as an individual, trust, estate, corporation, or partnership. Under §1.1441-1(b)(3)(ii)(B), X is presumed to be a partnership, since X does not appear to be an individual, trust or estate, and X cannot be presumed to be an exempt recipient in the absence of documentation. Paragraph (d)(2)(i) of this section requires USP to apply the provisions of §§1.1441-1(b)(3)(iii) and 1.1441-5(d) to determine whether X is presumed to be a U.S. or foreign partnership. Under §§1.1441-1(b)(3)(iii) and 1.1441-5(d)(2), X is presumed to be a U.S. partnership in absence of any indicia of foreign partnership status. The presumption of U.S. status applies even though the payment is a withholdable payment (see paragraph (d)(2) of this section and §1.1471-3(f)(2) cross referencing the presumption rules of §1.1441-1(b)(3)). The U.S. source interest paid to X is reportable under section 6049 on Form 1099 and the interest is subject to backup withholding under section 3406 because X has not provided its TIN

on a valid Form W-9. No withholding or reporting applies to the payment under chapter 3 or 4 of the Code.

*Example 2.* (i) *Facts.* The facts are the same as in *Example 1*, except that the interest paid by USP is from sources outside the United States.

(ii) *Analysis.* Interest from sources outside the United States is not an amount subject to withholding, as defined in §1.1441-2(a) or a withholdable payment. Under paragraph (d)(1) of this section, USP must apply the provisions of §§1.1441-1(b)(2) and 1.1441-5(c) and (e) to determine the payee. Under §1.1441-1(b)(2)(i), X, the person to whom the payment is made, is considered to be the payee, unless X is determined to be a flow-through entity, in which case the rules of §1.1441-5(c) or (e) apply to determine the payee. Under paragraph (d)(2)(i) of this section, the rules of §1.1441-1(b)(3)(ii) apply to determine the classification of a payee as an individual, trust, estate, corporation, or partnership. These rules apply irrespective of whether the payment is an amount subject to withholding. Under §1.1441-1(b)(3)(ii)(B), X is presumed to be a partnership, since X does not appear to be an individual, trust or estate, and X cannot be presumed to be an exempt recipient in the absence of documentation. Paragraph (d)(2)(i) of this section requires USP to apply the provisions of §§1.1441-1(b)(3)(iii) and 1.1441-5(d) to determine whether, X is presumed to be a U.S. or foreign partnership. Under §§1.1441-1(b)(3)(iii) and 1.1441-5(d)(2), X is presumed to be a U.S. partnership in absence of any indicia of foreign partnership status. The foreign source interest is a payment subject to reporting on Form 1099 under §1.6049-5(a). Further, because X is a non-exempt recipient that has failed to provide its TIN on a valid Form W-9, the foreign source interest is subject to backup withholding under section 3406.

*Example 3.* (i) *Facts.* USP is a U.S. payor as defined in paragraph (c)(5) of this section. USP makes a payment of U.S. source interest outside the United States to an offshore account of X. See paragraphs (c)(1) for a definition of offshore account and (e) for a payment outside the United States. USP does not have a withholding certificate from X as defined in §1.1441-1(c)(16) nor does it have documentary evidence as described in §1.1441-1(e)(1)(ii)(A)(2) and §1.6049-5(c)(1).

(ii) *Analysis.* The interest is an amount subject to withholding as defined in §1.1441-2(a). Under paragraph (d)(1) of this section, USP must apply the provisions of §1.1441-1(b)(2) and §1.1441-5(c) and (e) to determine the payee. Under §1.1441-1(b)(2)(i), X, the person to whom the payment is made, is considered to be the payee, unless X is determined to be a flow-through entity, in which case the rules of §1.1441-5(c) or (e) apply to determine the payee. Under paragraph (d)(2)(i) of this section, the rules of §1.1441-1(b)(3)(ii) apply to determine the classification of a payee as an individual, trust, estate, corporation, or partnership. Under §1.1441-1(b)(3)(ii)(B), X is presumed to be a partnership, since X does not appear to be an individual, trust or estate, and X cannot be presumed to be an exempt recipient in the absence of documentation. Paragraph (d)(2)(i) of this section requires USP to apply the provisions of §§1.1441-1(b)(3)(iii) and 1.1441-5(d) to determine whether, X is presumed to be a U.S. or foreign partnership. Under §§1.1441-1(b)(3)(iii)(D) and 1.1441-5(d)(2), X is presumed to be a foreign partnership. Therefore, under paragraph (d)(1) of this section and §1.1441-5(c)(1)(i)(E), the payees of the interest are presumed to be the partners of X. Under §1.1441-5(d)(3), the partners are presumed to be undocumented foreign persons. Therefore, USP must withhold 30% of the interest payment under §1.1441-1(b)(1) and report the payment on Form 1042-S in accordance with §1.1461-1(c).

*Example 4.* (i) *Facts.* The facts are the same as in *Example 3*, except that the interest is paid by F, a non-U.S. payor.

(ii) *Analysis.* The analysis and result are the same as in *Example 3.* F is a withholding agent under §1.1441-7 and its status as a non-U.S. payor under paragraph (c)(5) of this section is irrelevant.

*Example 5.* (i) *Facts.* USP is a U.S. payor as defined in paragraph (c)(5) of this section that is not an FFI. USP makes a payment outside the United States of interest from sources outside the United States with respect to an offshore obligation held by X. USP does not have a withholding certificate from X as defined in §1.1441-1(c)(16) nor does it have documentary evidence as described in §§1.1471-3(c)(5)(i) and 1.6049-5(c)(1). USP does not have actual knowledge of an employer identification number for X. X does not appear to be an individual, trust, or estate and cannot be treated as an exempt recipient, as defined in §1.6049-4(c)(1)(ii) in the absence of documentation.

(ii) *Analysis.* The interest is not an amount subject to withholding as defined in §1.1441-2(a) and is not a withholdable payment. Under paragraph (d)(1) of this section, USP must apply the rules of §§1.1441-1(b)(2) and 1.1441-5(c) and (e) to determine the payee of the interest. Under §1.1441-1(b)(2)(i), X, the person to whom the payment is made, is considered to be the payee, unless X is determined to be a flow-through entity, in which case the rules of §1.1441-5(c) or (e) apply to determine the payee. Under paragraph (d)(2)(i) of this section, §1.1441-1(b)(3)(ii) applies to determine X's classification as an individual, trust, estate, corporation or partnership. Under §1.1441-1(b)(3)(ii)(B), X is treated as a partnership, since it does not appear to be an individual, trust, or estate and cannot be treated as an exempt recipient without documentation. Paragraph (d)(2)(i) of this section requires USP to apply the provisions of §§1.1441-1(b)(3)(iii) and 1.1441-5(d) to determine whether, X is presumed to be a U.S. or foreign partnership. Paragraph (d)(2)(i) of this section also states that the presumptions of foreign status for payments made with respect to offshore obligations contained in §§1.1441-1(b)(3)(iii)(D) and 1.1441-5(d)(2) do not apply to amounts that are not subject to withholding and that are not withholdable payments described in paragraph (d)(2)(i). Therefore, under §§1.1441-1(b)(3)(iii) and 1.1441-5(d)(2), X is presumed to be a U.S. partnership because it does not have actual knowledge that X's employer identification number begins with the digits "98." Therefore, USP must treat X as a U.S. person that is not an exempt recipient and report the payment on Form 1099 under section 6049. Under §31.3406(g)-1(e) of this chapter, however, USP is not required to backup withhold on the payment unless it has actual knowledge that X is a U.S. person that is not an exempt recipient.

*Example 6.* (i) *Facts.* The facts are the same as in *Example 5*, except that the interest is paid by F, a non-U.S. payor, as defined under paragraph (c)(5) of this section.

(ii) *Analysis.* The analysis is the same as under *Example 5*. However, F is a non-U.S. payor paying foreign source interest outside the United States, and there is no indication that the amount is received in the United States under §1.6049-4(f)(16). Thus, paragraph (b)(6) of this section exempts the payment from reporting under section 6049.

*Example 7.* (i) *Facts.* USP, a U.S. payor as defined in paragraph (c)(5) of this section that is not an FFI, makes a payment of U.S. source interest that is a withholdable payment to NQI, a nonqualified intermediary as defined in §1.1441-1(c)(14), that is a certified deemed-compliant FFI under §1.1471-5(f)(2). The interest is paid inside the United States to an account of a bank or other financial institution maintained in the United States. NQI has provided USP with a nonqualified intermediary withholding certificate, as described in §1.1441-1(e)(3)(iii) that includes its chapter 4 status, but has not attached any documentation from the persons on whose behalf it acts or a withholding statement as described in §1.1441-1(e)(3)(iv).

(ii) *Analysis.* U.S. source interest is an amount subject to withholding under §1.1441-2(a). USP may treat the payment as made to a foreign intermediary under §1.1441-1(b)(3)(v)(A) because USP has received a nonqualified intermediary withholding certificate from NQI and may except NQI from withholding under chapter 4 of the Code given NQI's status for chapter 4 purposes as a deemed-compliant FFI. Under paragraph (d)(3)(i) of this section, USP must then apply §1.1471-3(c)(3) to treat the persons on whose behalf NQI is acting as the payees. Paragraph (d)(3)(i) of this section also requires USP to apply the presumption rules of §1.1441-1(b)(3)(v) if it cannot reliably associate the payment with valid documentation from a payee. See §1.1441-1(b)(2)(vii). As the payment is a withholdable payment, the interest is treated as paid to a nonparticipating FFI under §1.1471-3(f)(4). Therefore, the payment is not subject to reporting on Form 1099 under paragraph (b)(12) of this section. See §1.1471-2(a) for the withholding requirement with respect to the payment and §1.1474-1(d)(2) for the requirement to report the payment on Form 1042-S.

*Example 8.* (i) *Facts.* The facts are the same as in *Example 7*, except that the interest is paid outside the United States, as defined in paragraph (e) of this section to an offshore account, as defined in paragraph (c)(1) of this section and is not a withholdable payment.

(ii) *Analysis.* Under §1.1441-1(b)(3)(v)(B), the interest is treated as paid to an unknown foreign payee because it cannot be reliably associated with documentation under §1.1441-1(b)(2)(vii). Therefore, the payment is not subject to reporting on Form 1099 under paragraph (b)(12) of this section because the payment is presumed made to a foreign person. The payment is subject to withholding, however, under §1.1441-1(b) at a rate of 30% and is subject to reporting on Form 1042-S under §1.1461-1(c).

*Example 9.* (i) *Facts.* The facts are the same as in *Example 8*, except that the interest is paid by F, a non-U.S. payor, as defined in paragraph (c)(5) of this section.

(ii) *Analysis.* The analysis and results are the same as in *Example 8*.

*Example 10.* (i) *Facts.* USP, a U.S. payor as defined in paragraph (c)(5) of this section, makes a payment of foreign source interest (other than deposit interest) to NQI, a foreign corporation and a nonqualified intermediary as defined in §1.1441-1(c)(14). NQI has provided USP with a nonqualified intermediary withholding certificate, as described in §1.1441-1(e)(3)(iii), but has not attached any documentation from the persons on whose behalf it acts or a withholding statement as described in §1.1441-1(e)(3)(iv).

(ii) *Analysis.* Foreign source interest is not an amount subject to withholding under chapter 3 of the Code and is not a withholdable payment. See §§1.1441-2(a) and 1.1473-1(a). Under paragraph (d)(3)(ii) of this section, amounts that are not subject to withholding under chapter 3 of the Code and that are not withholdable payments described in paragraph (d)(2)(i) of this section that a payor may treat as paid to a foreign intermediary are treated as made to an exempt recipient described in §1.6049-4(c) absent actual knowledge that the payee is a U.S. person who is not an exempt recipient. Therefore, the foreign source interest is not subject to reporting on Form 1099.

*Example 11.* (i) *Facts.* USP is a U.S. payor as defined in paragraph (c)(5) of this section that is a bank. USP pays U.S. source original issue discount from the redemption of an obligation described in section 871(g)(1)(B) to NQI, a foreign corporation that is a nonqualified intermediary as defined in §1.1441-1(c)(14). The redemption proceeds are not paid outside of the United States as they are paid with respect to an account NQI has with a branch of a bank in the United States. See §1.6049-5(e)(2). NQI provides a nonqualified intermediary withholding certificate as described in §1.1441-1(e)(3)(iii) that includes a certification of its status as a registered deemed-compliant FFI but does not attach any payee documentation or a withholding statement described in §1.1441-1(e)(3)(iv).

(ii) *Analysis.* Under paragraph (d)(3)(ii)(A) of this section, USP must treat the payment as made to an undocumented U.S. payee that is not an exempt recipient and report the payment on Form 1099. Further, because the payment is made inside the United States, the exception to backup withholding with respect to offshore obligations contained in §31.3406(g)-1(e) of this chapter does not apply, and the payment is subject to backup withholding.

*Example 12.* (i) *Facts.* P, a payor, makes a payment to NQI of U.S. source interest on debt obligations issued prior to July 18, 1984, that mature 30 years from their issuance dates. Therefore, the interest does not qualify as portfolio interest under section 871(h) or 881(d). Additionally, the interest is not a withholdable payment under §1.1471-2(b) as the interest is a payment with respect to a grandfathered obligation for purposes of chapter 4 of the Code. NQI, a U.S. payor, is a nonqualified foreign intermediary, as defined in §1.1441-1(c)(14), and has furnished P a valid nonqualified intermediary withholding certificate described in §1.1441-1(e)(3)(iii) to which it has attached a valid Form W-9 for A, and two valid beneficial owner Forms W-8, one for B and one for C. A is not an exempt recipient under §1.6049-4(c). NQI furnishes a withholding statement, described in §1.1441-1(e)(3)(iv), in which it allocates 20% of the U.S. source interest to A, but does not allocate the remaining 80% of the interest between B and C. B's withholding certificate indicates that B is a foreign pension fund, exempt from U.S. tax under the U.S. income tax treaty with Country T. C's withholding certificate indicates that C is a foreign corporation not entitled to a reduced rate of withholding.

(ii) *Analysis.* As the interest is not a withholdable payment under paragraph (d)(3)(i) of this section, P applies the rules of §1.1441-1(b)(2)(v) to determine the payees of the interest even though NQI has not certified its status for purposes of chapter 4 of the Code. Under that section, the payees are the persons on whose behalf NQI acts—A, B and C. Because P can reliably associate 20% of the payment with valid documentation provided by A, P must treat 20% of the interest as paid to A, a U.S. person not exempt from reporting, and report the payment on Form 1099. P cannot reliably associate the remaining 80% of the payment with valid documentation under §1.1441-1(b)(2)(vii) and, therefore, under paragraph (d)(3)(i) of this section must apply the presumption rules of §1.1441-1(b)(3)(v). Under that section, the interest is presumed paid to an unknown foreign payee. Under paragraph (b)(12) of this section, P is not required to report the interest presumed paid to a foreign person on Form 1099. Under §1.1441-1(b), 80% of the interest is subject to 30% withholding, however, and the interest is reportable on Form 1042-S under §1.1461-1(c).

*Example 13.* (i) *Facts.* The facts are the same as in *Example 12*, except that P can reliably associate 30% of the payment of interest to B, but cannot reliably associate the remaining 70 percent with A or C.

(ii) *Analysis.* Under paragraph (d)(3)(i) of this section, P applies the rules of §1.1441-1(b)(2)(v) to determine the payees of the interest. Under that section, the payees are the persons on whose behalf NQI acts—A, B and C. Because P can reliably associate 30% of the payment with B, a foreign pensions fund exempt from withholding under an income tax treaty, P may treat that payment as paid to B and not subject to reporting on Form 1099 under paragraph (b)(12) of this section. P cannot reliably associate the remaining 70% of the payment with valid documentation under §1.1441-1(b)(2)(vii) and, therefore, under paragraph (d)(3)(i) of this section must apply the presumption rules of §1.1441-1(b)(3)(v). Under that section, the interest is presumed paid to an unknown foreign payee. Under paragraph (b)(12) of this section, P is not required to report the interest presumed paid to a foreign person on Form 1099. Under §1.1441-1(b),

80% of the interest is subject to 30% withholding, however, and the interest is reportable on Form 1042-S under §1.1461-1(c).

*Example 14.* (i) *Facts.* The facts are the same as in *Example 12,* except that P also makes a payment of foreign source interest to NQI.

(ii) *Analysis.* Under paragraph (d)(3)(ii), P may treat the foreign source interest as paid to an exempt recipient as defined in §1.6049-4(c) and not subject to reporting on Form 1099 even though some or all of the foreign source interest may in fact be owned by A, the U.S. person that is not exempt from reporting.

*Example 15.* (i) *Facts.* The facts are the same as in *Example 12,* except that NQI is a non-U.S. payor.

(ii) *Analysis.* The analysis is the same as under *Example 12* with respect to B and C. However, because NQI is a non-U.S. payor, it may under §1.6049-4(c)(4)(iii) allocate the portion of the payment to A to a chapter 4 withholding rate pool of U.S. payees on a withholding statement provided to P in lieu of furnishing the Form W-9 to P when NQI reports the payments in accordance with §1.6049-4(c)(4)(i). In such a case, provided that P obtains a certification form confirming NQI's status as a participating FFI, P is excepted from reporting the payment under paragraph (b)(14) of this section because P can reliably associate the payment with the documentation provided by NQI.

(e) *Determination of whether amounts are considered paid outside the United States.*—(1) *In general.*—For purposes of section 6049 and this section, an amount is considered to be paid by a payor or middleman outside the United States if the payor or middleman completes the acts necessary to effect payment outside the United States. See paragraphs (e)(2) through (5) of this section for further clarification of where amounts are considered paid. A payment shall not be considered to be made within the United States for purposes of section 6049 merely by reason of the fact that it is made on a draft drawn on a United States bank account or by a wire or other electronic transfer from a United States account.

(2) *Amounts paid with respect to deposits or accounts with banks and other financial institutions.*—Notwithstanding paragraph (e)(1) of this section, an amount paid by a bank or other financial institution with respect to a deposit or with respect to an account with the institution is considered paid at the branch or office at which the amount is credited unless the amount is collected by the financial institution as the agent of the payee. However, an amount will not be considered to be paid at the branch or office where the amount is considered to be credited unless the branch or office is a permanent place of business that is regularly maintained, occupied, and used to carry on a banking or similar financial business; the business is conducted by at least one employee of the branch or office who is regularly in attendance at such place of business during normal business hours; and the branch or office receives deposits and engages in one or more of the other activities described in §1.864-4(c)(5)(i).

(3) *Coupon bonds and discount obligations in bearer form.*—Notwithstanding paragraph (e)(1) of this section, an amount paid with respect to a bond with coupons attached (including a certificate of deposit with detachable interest coupons) or a discount obligation that is not in registered form (within the meaning of section 163(f) and the regulations thereunder) is considered to be paid where the coupon or the discount obligation is presented to the payor or its paying agent for payment.

(4) *Foreign-targeted registered obligations.*—Notwithstanding paragraph (e)(1) of this section, where the payor is the issuer or the issuer's agent, an amount is considered paid outside the United States with respect to a foreign-targeted registered obligation issued before January 1, 2016, as described in §1.871-14(e)(2), if either the amount is paid by transfer to an account maintained by the registered owner outside the United States, or by mail to an address of the registered owner outside the United States, or by credit to an international account. For purposes of this paragraph (e)(4), the term *international account* means the book-entry account of a financial institution (within the meaning of section 871(h)(4)(B)) or of an international financial organization with the Federal Reserve Bank of New York for which the Federal Reserve Bank of New York maintains records that specifically identify an international financial organization or a financial institution (within the meaning of section 871(h)(4)(B)) as either a non-United States person or a foreign branch of a United States person as registered owner. An international financial organization is a central bank or monetary authority of a foreign government or a public international organization of which the United States is a member to the extent that such central bank, authority, or organization holds obligations solely for its own account and is exempt from tax under section 892 or 895.

(5) *Examples.*—The application of the provisions of this paragraph (e) is illustrated by the following examples:

*Example 1.* FC is a foreign corporation that is not a U.S. payor or U.S. middleman, as defined in paragraph (c)(5) of this section. A holds FC coupon bonds that are not in registered form under section 163(f) and the regulations thereunder. FB, a foreign branch of DC, is the designated paying agent with respect to the bonds issued by FC. A does not have an account with FB. A presents a coupon from a FC bond for payment to FB at its office outside the United States. FB pays A with a check drawn against a bank account maintained in the United States. For purposes of section 6049, the place of payment of interest on the FC bond by FB to A is considered to be outside the United States under paragraph (e)(3) of this section.

*Example 2.* Individual C deposits funds in an account with FB, a foreign country X branch of DB, a U.S. corporation engaged in the commercial banking business. FB maintains an office and employees in foreign country X, accepts deposits, and conducts one or more of the other activities listed in §1.864-4(c)(5)(i). The terms of C's deposit provide that it will be payable with accrued interest. Under paragraph (e)(2) of this section, FB is considered to pay the interest on C's deposit outside the United States.

*Example 3.* DC, a U.S. corporation engaged in the commercial banking business, maintains FB, a branch in foreign country X. FB has an office and employees in foreign country X, accepts deposits, and engages in one or more of the other activities listed in §1.864-4(c)(5)(i). D, a United States citizen, purchases a certificate of deposit issued in 1980 by FB. The certificate of deposit has a maturity of 20 years and has detachable interest coupons payable at six-month intervals. D presents some of the coupons at the U.S. office of DC and receives payment in cash. Because the coupon is presented to DC for payment within the United States, DC is considered to have made the payment within the United States under paragraph (e)(3) of this section.

*Example 4.* FB is recognized by both foreign country X and by the Federal Reserve Bank as a foreign country X branch of DC, a U.S. corporation engaged in the commercial banking business. A local foreign country X bank serves as FB's resident agent in Country X. FB maintains no physical office or employees in foreign country X. All the records, accounts, and transactions of FB are handled at the United States office of DC. E deposits funds in an amount maintained with FB. Interest earned on the deposit is periodically credited to E's account with FB by employees of DC. For purposes of section 6049, the place of payment of the interest on E's deposit with FB is considered to be within the United States by reason of paragraphs (e)(1) and (e)(2) of this section.

*Example 5.* DC is a U.S. corporation. A holds bonds that were issued by DC in registered form under section 163(f), as in effect prior to the amendment by section 502 of the HIRE Act of 2010, and the regulations thereunder and that are foreign-targeted registered obligations as defined in §1.871-14(e)(2). DB, a commercial banking business, is the registrar of bonds issued by DC. Interest on the DC bonds is paid to A and other bondholders by check prepared by DB at its principal office inside the United States and mailed from there to A's address outside the United States. The check is drawn on a United States account maintained by DC with DB within the United States. The place of payment to A by DB of the interest on the DC bonds is considered to be outside the United States under paragraph (e)(4) of this section.

(f) *Original issue discount treated as payment of interest.*—In determining whether an obligation is one which was issued at a discount and the amount of discount which is includible in income of the holder, a payor (other than the issuer of the obligation) may rely on the Internal Revenue Service's publication of publicly traded original issue discount obligations. In the case of an obligation as to which there is during any calendar year an amount of original issue discount includible in the gross income of any holder (as determined under sections 1232 and 1232A and the regulations thereunder), the issuer of the obligation or a middleman (as defined in §1.6049-4(f)(4)) shall be treated as having paid to such holder during such calendar year an amount of interest equal to the amount of original issue discount so includible without regard to any reduction by reason of a purchase allowance under section 1232(a)(2)(C)(ii), 1232A(a)(6) or (b)(4) or a purchase at a premium under 1232A(c)(4)(A) or paragraph (d)(2) of §1.1232-3. Thus, the determination of the amount of original issue discount includible in the gross income of any holder with respect to any obligation shall be determined as if any holder of the obligation were the original holder. However, see §1.6049-9 for the reporting of premium for a debt instrument acquired on or after January 1, 2014. In the case of (1) an obligation to which section 1232A does not apply (for example, a short-term government obligation as defined in section 1232(a)(3)) and (2) and obligation issued on or before December 31, 1982, in bearer form, the amount of original issue discount includible in gross income shall be treated as if paid in the calendar year in which the date of maturity occurs or in which the date of redemption occurs if redemption occurs before maturity. The amount subject to reporting on an obligation issued in bearer form with a maturity at the date of issue of more than 1 year (a long term obligation) is the amount of original issue discount includible in the gross income of the holder during the calendar year of maturity or redemption if redemption occurs before maturity. The amount of original issue discount subject to reporting on a long term obligation shall not be reduced to reflect any purchase allowance. Discount on short term government obligations as defined in section 1232(a)(3), such as Treasury bills, and discount on other obligations with a maturity at the date of issue of not more than 1 year (a short term obligation), including commercial paper, when paid at maturity or redemption if redemption occurs before maturity, shall constitute a payment of interest for purposes of section 6049. In general, the amount subject to reporting on short term obligations is the difference between the stated redemption price at maturity and the original issue price. The procedure set forth in section 3455(b)(2)(B) and §31.3455(b)-1(b)(3) for establishing the price at which a holder purchased an obligation subsequent to the date of original issue shall apply for purposes of section 6049. Original issue discount on an obligation (including an obligation with a maturity of not more than six months from the date of original issue) held by a nonresident alien individual or foreign corporation is interest described in paragraph (b)(1)(vi)(A) or (B) of this section and, therefore is not interest subject to reporting under section 6049 unless it is described in §1.6049-8(a) (relating to deposit interest paid on or after January 1, 2013, to certain nonresident alien individuals).

(g) *Applicability dates.*—Except as otherwise provided in this paragraph (g), this section applies to payments made on or after January 6, 2017. For payments made after June 30, 2014, and before January 6, 2017, see this section as in effect and contained in 26 CFR part 1, as revised April 1, 2016. For payments made after December 31, 2000, and before July 1, 2014, see this section as in effect and contained in 26 CFR part 1, as revised April 1, 2013. Paragraph (c)(5)(i)(C) of this section applies to payments made on or after October 1, 2019. For payments made before October 1, 2019, a taxpayer may apply paragraph (c)(5)(i)(C) of this section for payments during the last taxable year of a foreign corporation beginning before January 1, 2018, and each subsequent taxable year of the foreign corporation, provided that the taxpayer and United States persons that are related (within the meaning of section 267 or 707) to the taxpayer consistently apply such paragraph with respect to all foreign corporations. For payments made before October 1, 2019, where the taxpayer does not apply the provisions of paragraph (c)(5)(i)(C) of this section, see paragraph (c)(5)(i)(C) of this section as in effect and contained in 26 CFR part 1, as revised April 1, 2020. [Reg. §1.6049-5.]

☐ [*T.D.* 7881, 3-22-83. *Amended by T.D.* 7987, 10-23-84; *T.D.* 8029, 6-4-85; *T.D.* 8664, 4-15-96; *T.D.* 8734, 10-6-97; *T.D.* 8804, 12-30-98; *T.D.* 8856, 12-29-99; *T.D.* 8881, 5-15-2000 (*corrected* 4-5-2001); *T.D.* 9241, 1-23-2006 *T.D.* 9253, 3-13-2006; *T.D.* 9584, 4-17-2012, *T.D.* 9658, 2-28-2014, *T.D.* 9713, 3-12-2015, *T.D.* 9808, 12-30-2016 (*corrected* 6-29-2017) *and T.D.* 9908, 9-21-2020.]

### [Reg. §1.6049-6]

**§1.6049-6. Statements to recipients of interest payments and holders of obligations for attributed original issue discount.**—(a) *Requirement of furnishing statement to recipient.*—Every person filing a Form 1099 under section 6049(a) and §1.6049-4(e) shall furnish to the person whose identifying number is required to be shown on the form a written statement showing the information required by paragraph (b) of this section. With respect to interest other than interest reported on a transactional basis under §1.6049-4(e), no statement is required to be furnished under section 6049(c) and this section if the aggregate of the payments for the calendar year is less than $10, unless such payment is subject to the tax imposed under section 3406. In the case of any payment that is subject to withholding under section 3406, a statement shall be furnished irrespective of the amount of the payment. With respect to payments which are reported on a transactional basis, no statement is required to be furnished under section 6049(c) and this section to a person if the payment of interest to (or received on behalf of) such person for the transaction is less than $10 unless the payment is subject to withholding under section 3406. Again, in the case of any payment that is subject to withholding under section 3406, a statement shall be furnished irrespective of the amount of the payment.

(b) *Form of statement.*—The written statement required to be furnished to a person under paragraph (a) of this section shall show the following information:

(1) With respect to payments of interest (other than original issue discount) to any person during a calendar year, the statement shall show—

(i) The aggregate amount of payments shown on Form 1099 as having been made to (or received on behalf of) such person;

(ii) The amount of tax withheld under section 3406, if any;

(iii) The name and address of the person filing the form; and

(iv) A legend stating that such amount is being reported to the Internal Revenue Service.

(2) With respect to original issue discount includible in the gross income of a holder of an obligation during a calendar year, the statement shall show—

(i) The aggregate amount of original issue discount includible in the gross income by (or on behalf of) such person for the calendar year with respect to the obligation (determined by applying the rules of paragraph (b)(2) of §1.6049-4);

(ii) The amount of tax withheld under section 3406, if any;

(iii) The account, serial, or other identifying number of each obligation with respect to which a return is being made;

(iv) All other items shown on Form 1099 for such calendar year, and

(v) A legend stating that such amount and such items are being reported to the Internal Revenue Service.

(3) With respect to both statements to persons receiving payments of interest and persons holding obligations, the statement shall include the name, address, and taxpayer identifying number of such person. An IRS truncated taxpayer identifying number (TTIN) may be used as the identifying number for the person. For provisions relating to the use of TTINs, see §301.6109-4 of this chapter (Procedure and Administration Regulations).

(c) *Time for furnishing statements.*—Each statement required by this section to be furnished to any person for a calendar year with respect to a payment of interest (other than interest where a middleman or a Federal agency makes a return on a transactional basis (as described in paragraph (e) of §1.6049-4)) shall be furnished to such person after April 30 of the year of payment and on or before January 31 of the following year, but no statement may be furnished before the final interest payment for the calendar year. If a middleman or a Federal agency makes a return on a transactional basis, the statement shall be furnished at, or any time subsequent to, the time of payment, but in no event later than January 31 of the year following the calendar year of payment. However, for a statement required to be furnished after December 31, 2008, the February 15 due date under section 6045 applies to the statement if the statement is furnished in a consolidated reporting statement under section 6045. See §§1.6045-1(k)(3), 1.6045-2(d)(2), 1.6045-3(e)(2), 1.6045-4(m)(3), and 1.6045-5(a)(3)(ii).

(d) *Special rule.*—The requirements of this section for the furnishing of a statement to any person, including the legend requirement of paragraph (b)(1)(iv) and (2)(v) of this section, may be met by the furnishing to such person a copy of the Form 1099 filed pursuant to §1.6049-4, or an acceptable substitute, in respect of such person. However, in the case of Form 1099 with respect to original issue discount on obligations subject to section 1232A, a copy of the instructions must also be sent to such person. A statement shall be considered to be furnished to a person within the meaning of this section if it is mailed to such person at his last known address.

(e) *Statements to recipients.*—(1) *Requirement.*—A person required to make an information return under section 6049(a) and §1.6049-4 must furnish a statement to each recipient whose identifying number is required to be shown on the related information return for interest or original issue discount paid or accrued.

(2) *Form, manner, and time for providing statements to recipients.*—The statement required by paragraph (e)(1) of this section must be either the official Form 1099 prescribed by the Internal Revenue Service for the respective calendar year or an acceptable substitute statement. The rules under §1.6042-4 (relating to statements with respect to dividends) apply comparably in determining the form of an acceptable substitute statement permitted by this paragraph (e). Those rules also apply for purposes of determining the manner of and time for providing the Form 1099 or its acceptable substitute to a recipient under paragraph (e)(1) of this section. However, with respect to original issue discount, the Form 1099 or acceptable substitute statement required by paragraph (e)(1) of this section must show the aggregate amount of original issue discount includible in the gross income by the recipient for the calendar year with respect to the obligation (determined by applying the rules of §1.6049-4(b)(2)), and the amount, serial number, or other identifying number of each obligation with respect to which a return is being made. With respect to interest or original issue discount, the Form 1099 or acceptable substitute statement required by paragraph (e)(1) of this section must be furnished to the recipient on or before January 31 of the year following the calendar year for which the return under section 6049(a)(1) was required to be made. However, for a statement required to be furnished after December 31, 2008, the February 15 due date under section 6045 applies to the statement if the statement is furnished in a consolidated reporting statement under section 6045. See §§1.6045-1(k)(3), 1.6045-2(d)(2), 1.6045-3(e)(2), 1.6045-4(m)(3), and 1.6045-5(a)(3)(ii).

(3) *Cross-reference to penalty.*—For provisions relating to the penalty provided for failure to furnish timely a correct payee statement required under section 6049(c) and §1.6049-6(a), see §301.6722-1 of this chapter (Procedure and Administration Regulations). See §301.6724-1 of this chapter for the waiver of a penalty if the failure is due to reasonable cause and is not due to willful neglect.

(4) *Special rule for amounts described in §1.6049-8(a).*—In the case of amounts described in §1.6049-8(a) (relating to payments of deposit interest to certain nonresident alien individuals) paid on or after January 1, 2013, any person who makes a Form 1042-S, "Foreign Person's U.S. Source Income Subject to Withholding," under section 6049(a) and §1.6049-4(b)(5) shall furnish a statement to the recipient either in person or by first class mail to the recipient's last known address. The statement shall include a copy of the Form 1042-S required to be prepared pursuant to §1.6049-4(b)(5) and a statement to the effect that the information on the form is being furnished to the United States Internal Revenue Service. A person required by this paragraph (e)(4) to furnish a recipient copy of Form 1042-S may furnish such copy electronically by complying with the requirements provided in §1.6050W-2(a)(2) through (5) applicable to statements required under section 6050W (substituting the phrase "Form 1042-S" for the phrases "statement required under section 6050W" or "statements required by section 6050W(f)" each place they appear).

(5) *Effective/applicability date.*—Paragraph (b)(3) applies to payee statements due after December 31, 2014. Paragraph (e)(4) of this section applies to payee statements reporting payments of deposit interest to nonresident alien individuals paid on or after January 2, 2020, but it may be applied to payments made on or after January 1, 2016. For payee statements reporting payments of deposit interest to nonresident alien individuals paid on or after January 1, 2013 and before January 2, 2020, see paragraph (e)(4) of this section as in effect and contained in 26 CFR part 1 revised April 1, 2019. For the substantially similar statement mailing requirements that apply with respect to forms required to be filed after October 22, 1986, and before January 1, 1996, see Rev. Proc. 84-70 (1984-2 C.B. 716)(or successor revenue procedures). See §601.601(d)(2) of this chapter. (For interest paid to a Canadian nonresident alien individual on or before December 31, 2012, see paragraph (e)(4) of this section as in effect and contained in 26 CFR part 1 revised April 1, 2000.) [Reg. §1.6049-6.]

☐ [*T.D. 7881, 3-22-83. Amended by T.D. 8637, 12-20-95; T.D. 8664, 4-15-96; T.D. 8734, 10-6-97 (T.D. 8804 delayed the effective date of T.D. 8734 from January 1, 1999, to January 1, 2000; T.D. 8856 further delayed the effective date of T.D. 8734 until January 1, 2001) T.D. 9504, 10-12-2010; T.D. 9584, 4-17-2012, T.D. 9675, 7-14-2014 and T.D. 9890, 12-27-2019.]*

[Reg. §1.6049-7]

**§1.6049-7. Returns of information with respect to REMIC regular interests and collateralized debt instruments.**—(a) *Definition of interest.*—(1) *In general.*—For purposes of section 6049(a), for taxable years beginning after December 31, 1986, the term "interest" includes:

(i) Interest actually paid with respect to a collateralized debt obligation (as defined in paragraph (d)(2) of this section),

(ii) Interest accrued with respect to a REMIC regular interest (as defined in section 860G(a)(1)), or

(iii) Original issue discount accrued with respect to a REMIC regular interest or a collateralized debt obligation.

(2) *Interest deemed paid.*—For purposes of this section and in determining who must make an information return under section 6049(a), interest as defined in paragraphs (a)(1)(ii) and (iii) of this section is deemed paid when includible in gross income under section 860B(b) or section 1272.

(b) *Information required to be reported to the Internal Revenue Service.*—(1) *Requirement of filing Form 8811 by REMICs and other issuers.*—(i) *In general.*—Except in the case of a REMIC all of whose regular interests are owned by one other REMIC, every REMIC and every issuer of a collateralized debt obligation (as defined in paragraph (d)(2) of this section) must make an information return on Form 8811, Information Return for Real Estate Mortgage Investment Conduits (REMICs) and Issuers of Collateralized Debt Obligations. Form 8811 must be filed in the time and manner prescribed in paragraph (b)(1)(iii) of this section. The submission of Form 8811 to the Internal Revenue Service does not satisfy the election requirement specified in §1.860D-1T(d) and does not require election of REMIC status.

(ii) *Information required to be reported.*—The following information must be reported to the Internal Revenue Service on Form 8811—

(A) The name, address, and employer identification number of the REMIC or the issuer of a collateralized debt obligation (as defined in paragraph (d)(2) of this section);

(B) The name, title, and either the address or the address and telephone number of the official or representative of the REMIC or the issuer of a collateralized debt obligation who will provide to any person specified in paragraph (e)(4) of this section the interest and original issue discount information specified in paragraph (e)(2) of this section;

(C) The startup day (as defined in section 860G(a)(9)) of the REMIC or the issue date (as defined in section 1275(a)(2)) of the collateralized debt obligation;

(D) The Committee on Uniform Security Identification Procedure (CUSIP) number, account number, serial number, or other identifying number or information, of each class of REMIC regular interest or collateralized debt obligation;

(E) The name, title, address, and telephone number of the official or representative of the REMIC or the issuer of a collateralized debt obligation whom the Internal Revenue Service may contact, and

(F) Any other information required by Form 8811.

(iii) *Time and manner of filing of information return.*—(A) *Manner of filing.*—Form 8811 must be filed with the Internal Revenue Service at the address specified on the form. The information specified in paragraph (b)(1)(ii) of this section must be provided on Form 8811 regardless of whether other information returns are filed by use of electronic media.

(B) *Time for filing.*—Form 8811 must be filed by each REMIC or issuer of a collateralized debt obligation on or before the later of July 31, 1989, or the 30th day after—

(1) the startup day (as defined in section 860G(a)(9)) in the case of a REMIC, or

(2) the issue date (as defined in section 1275(a)(2)) in the case of a collateralized debt obligation.

Further, each REMIC or issuer of a collateralized debt obligation must file a new Form 8811 on or before the 30th day after any change in the information previously provided on Form 8811.

(2) *Requirement of reporting by REMICs, issuers, and nominees.*—(i) *In general.*—Every person described in paragraph (b)(2)(ii) of this section who pays to another person $10 or more of interest (as defined in paragraph (a) of this section) during any calendar year must file an information return on Form 1099, unless the interest is paid to a person specified in paragraph (c) of this section.

(ii) *Person required to make reports.*—The persons required to make an information return under section 6049(a) and this section are—

(A) REMICs or issuers of collateralized debt obligations (as defined in paragraph (d)(2) of this section), and

(B) Any broker who holds as a nominee or middleman who holds as a nominee any REMIC regular interest or any collateralized debt obligation.

(iii) *Information to be reported.*—(A) *REMIC regular interests and collateralized debt obligations not issued with original issue discount.*—An information return on Form 1099 must be made for each holder of a REMIC regular interest or collateralized debt obligation not issued with original issue discount, but only if the holder has been paid interest (as defined in paragraph (a) of this section) of $10 or more for the calendar year. The information return must show—

(1) The name, address, and taxpayer identification number of the record holder,

(2) The CUSIP number, account number, serial number, or other identifying number or information, of each REMIC regular interest or collateralized debt obligation, with respect to which a return is being made,

(3) The aggregate amount of interest paid or deemed paid to the record holder for the period during the calendar year for which the return is made,

(4) The name, address, and taxpayer identification number of the person required to file this return, and

(5) Any other information required by the form.

(B) *REMIC regular interests and collateralized debt obligations issued with original issue discount.*—An information return on Form 1099 must be made for each holder of a REMIC regular interest or a collateralized debt obligation issued with original issue discount, but only if the holder has been paid interest (as defined in paragraph (a) of this section) of $10 or more for the calendar year. The information return must show—

(1) The name, address, and taxpayer identification number of the record holder,

(2) The CUSIP number, account number, serial number, or other identifying number or information, of each REMIC regular interest or collateralized debt obligation, with respect to which a return is being made,

(3) The aggregate amount of original issue discount deemed paid to the record holder for the period during the calendar year for which the return is made,

(4) The aggregate amount of interest, other than original issue discount, paid or deemed paid to the record holder for the period during the calendar year for which the return is made,

(5) The name, address, and taxpayer identification number of the person required to file this return, and

(6) Any other information required by the form.

(C) *Cross-reference.*—See § 1.67-3T(f)(3)(ii) for additional information required to be included on an information return on Form 1099 with respect to certain holders of regular interests in REMICs described in § 1.67-3T(a)(2)(ii).

(iv) *Time and place for filing a return with respect to amounts includible as interest.*—The returns required under this paragraph (b)(2) for any calendar year must be filed after September 30 of that year, but not before the payor's final payment to the payee for the year, and on or before February 28 (March 31 if filed electronically) of the following year. These returns must be filed with the appropriate Internal Revenue Service Center, the address of which is listed in the instructions for Form 1099. For extensions of time for filing returns under this section, see § 1.6081-1. For magnetic media filing requirements, see § 301.6011-2 of this chapter.

(c) *Information returns not required.*—An information return is not required under section 6049(a) and this section with respect to payments of interest on a REMIC regular interest or collateralized debt obligation, if the holder of the REMIC regular interest or the collateralized debt obligation is—

(1) An organization exempt from taxation under section 501(a) or an individual retirement plan;

(2) The United States or a State, the District of Columbia, a possession of the United States, or a political subdivision or a wholly-owned agency or instrumentality of any one or more of the foregoing;

(3) A foreign government, a political subdivision thereof, or an international organization;

(4) A foreign central bank of issue (as defined in § 1.895-1(b)(1)) or the Bank for International Settlements;

(5) A trust described in section 4947(a)(1) (relating to certain charitable trusts);

(6) For calendar quarters and calendar years after 1988, a broker (as defined in section 6045(c) and § 1.6045-1(a)(1));

(7) For calendar quarters and calendar years after 1988, a person who holds the REMIC regular interest or collateralized debt obligation as a middleman (as defined in § 1.6049-4(f)(4));

(8) For calendar quarters and calendar years after 1988, a corporation (as defined in section 7701(a)(3)), whether domestic or foreign;

(9) For calendar quarters and calendar years after 1988, a dealer in securities or commodities required to register as such under the laws of the United States or a State;

(10) For calendar quarters and calendar years after 1988, a real estate investment trust (as defined in section 856);

(11) For calendar quarters and calendar years after 1988, an entity registered at all times during the taxable year under the Investment Company Act of 1940;

(12) For calendar quarters and calendar years after 1988, a common trust fund (as defined in section 584(a));

(13) For calendar quarters and calendar years after 1988, a financial institution such as a mutual savings bank, savings and loan association, building and loan association, cooperative bank, homestead association, credit union, industrial loan association or bank, or other similar organization;

(14) For calendar quarters and calendar years after 1988, any trust which is exempt from tax under section 664(c) (*i.e.*, a charitable remainder annuity trust or a charitable remainder unitrust); and

(15) For calendar quarters and calendar years after 1988, a REMIC.

(d) *Special provisions and definitions.*—(1) *Incorporation of referenced rules.*—The special rules of § 1.6049-4(d) are incorporated in this section, as applicable, except that § 1.6049-4(d)(2) does not apply to any REMIC regular interest or any other debt instrument to which section 1272(a)(6) applies. Further, § 1.6049-5(c) does not apply to any REMIC regular interest or any other debt instrument to which section 1272(a)(6) applies.

(2) *Collateralized debt obligation.*—For purposes of this section, the term "collateralized debt obligation" means any debt instrument

(except a tax-exempt obligation) described in section 1272(a)(6)(C)(ii) that is issued after December 31, 1986.

(e) *Requirement of furnishing information to certain nominees, corporations, and other specified persons.*—(1) *In general.*—For calendar quarters and calendar years after 1988, each REMIC or issuer of a collateralized debt obligation (as defined in paragraph (d)(2) of this section) must provide the information specified in paragraph (e)(2) of this section in the time and manner prescribed in paragraph (e)(3) of this section to any persons specified in paragraph (e)(4) of this section who request the information.

(2) *Information required to be reported.*—For each class of REMIC regular interest or collateralized debt obligation and for each calendar quarter specified by the person requesting the information, the REMIC or issuer of a collateralized debt obligation must provide the following information—

(i) The name, address and Employer Identification Number of the REMIC or issuer of a collateralized debt obligation;

(ii) The CUSIP number, account number, serial number, or other identifying number or information, of each specified class of REMIC regular interest or collateralized debt obligation and, for calendar quarters and calendar years after 1991, whether the information being reported is with respect to a REMIC regular interest or a collateralized debt obligation;

(iii) Interest paid on a collateralized debt obligation in the specified class for each calendar quarter, and the aggregate amount for the calendar year if the request is made for the last quarter of the calendar year;

(iv) Interest accrued on a REMIC regular interest in the specified class for each accrual period any day of which is in the specified calendar quarter, and the aggregate amount for the calendar year if the request is made for the last quarter of the calendar year;

(v) Original issue discount accrued on a collateralized debt obligation or REMIC regular interest in the specified class for each accrual period any day of which is in that calendar quarter, and the aggregate amount for the calendar year if the request is made for the last quarter of the calendar year;

(vi) The daily portion of original issue discount per $1,000 of original principal amount (or for calendar quarters prior to 1992, per other specified unit) as determined under section 1272(a)(6) and the regulations thereunder for each accrual period any day of which is in the specified calendar quarter;

(vii) The length of the accrual period;

(viii) The adjusted issue price (as defined in section 1275(a)(4)(B)(ii)) of the REMIC regular interest or the collateralized debt obligation at the beginning of each accrual period any day of which is in the specified calendar quarter;

(ix) The information required by paragraph (f)(3) of this section;

(x) Information required to compute the accrual of market discount including, for calendar years after 1989, the information required by paragraphs (f)(2)(i)(G) or (f)(2)(ii)(K) of this section; and

(xi) For calendar quarters and calendar years after 1991, if the REMIC is a single class REMIC (as described in § 1.67-3T(a)(2)(ii)(B)), the information described in § 1.67-3T(f)(1) and (f)(3)(ii)(A) and (B).

(3) *Time and manner for providing information.*—(i) *Manner of providing information.*—The information specified in paragraph (e)(2) of this section may be provided as follows—

(A) By telephone;

(B) By written statement sent by first class mail to the address provided by the requesting party;

(C) By causing it to be printed in a publication generally read by and available to persons specified in paragraph (e)(4) and by notifying the requesting persons in writing or by telephone of the publication in which it will appear, the date of its appearance, and, if possible, the page upon which it appears; or

(D) By any other method agreed to by the parties.
If the information is published, then the publication should also specify the date and, if possible, the page on which corrections, if any, will be printed.

(ii) *Time for furnishing the information.*—Each REMIC or issuer of a collateralized debt obligation must furnish the information specified in paragraph (e)(2) of this section on or before the later of—

(A) The 30th day after the close of the calendar quarter for which the information was requested, or

(B) The day that is two weeks after the receipt of the request.

(4) *Persons entitled to request information.*—The following persons may request the information specified in paragraph (e)(2) of this section with respect to a specified class of REMIC regular interests or collateralized debt obligations from a REMIC or issuer of a collateral-

ized debt obligation in the manner prescribed in paragraph (e)(5) of this section—

(i) Any broker who holds on its own behalf or as a nominee any REMIC regular interest or collateralized debt obligation in the specified class,

(ii) Any middleman who is required to make an information return under section 6049(a) and paragraph (b)(2) of this section and who holds as a nominee any REMIC regular interest or collateralized debt obligation in the specified class,

(iii) Any corporation or non-calendar year taxpayer who holds a REMIC regular interest or collateralized debt obligation in the specified class directly, rather than through a nominee,

(iv) Any other person specified in paragraphs (c)(9) through (15) of this section who holds a REMIC regular interest or collateralized debt obligation in the specified class directly, rather than through a nominee, or

(v) A representative or agent for a person specified in paragraphs (e)(4)(i), (ii), (iii) or (iv) of this section.

(5) *Manner of requesting information from the REMIC.*—A requesting person specified in paragraph (e)(4) of this section should obtain Internal Revenue Service Publication 938, Real Estate Mortgage Investment Conduit (REMIC) and Collateralized Debt Obligation Reporting Information (or other guidance published by the Internal Revenue Service). This publication contains a directory of REMICs and issuers of collateralized debt obligations. The requesting person can locate the REMIC or issuer from whom information is needed and request the information from the official or representative of the REMIC or issuer in the manner specified in the publication. The publication will specify either an address or an address and telephone number. If the publication provides only an address, the request must be made in writing and mailed to the specified address. Further, the request must specify the calendar quarters (*e.g.*, all calendar quarters in 1989) and the classes of REMIC regular interests or collateralized debt obligations for which information is needed.

(f) *Requirement of furnishing statement to recipient.*—(1) *In general.*—Every person filing a Form 1099 under section 6049(a) and this section must furnish to the holder (the person whose identifying number is required to be shown on the form) a written statement showing the information required by paragraph (f)(2) of this section. The written statement provided by a REMIC must also contain the information specified in paragraph (f)(3) of this section.

(2) *Form of statement.*—(i) *REMIC regular interests and collateralized debt obligations not issued with original issue discount.*—For a REMIC regular interest or collateralized debt obligation issued without original issue discount, the written statement must specify for the calendar year the following information—

(A) The aggregate amount shown on Form 1099 to be included in income by that person for the calendar year;

(B) The name, address, and taxpayer identification number of the person required to furnish this statement;

(C) The name, address, and taxpayer identification number of the person who must include the amount of interest in gross income;

(D) A legend, including a statement that the amount is being reported to the Internal Revenue Service, that conforms to the legend on Form 1099, Copy B, For Recipient;

(E) The CUSIP number, account number, serial number, or other identifying number or information, of each REMIC regular interest or collateralized debt obligation, with respect to which a return is being made;

(F) All other items shown on Form 1099 for the calendar year; and

(G) Information necessary to compute accrual of market discount. For calendar years after 1989, this requirement is satisfied by furnishing to the holder for each accrual period during the year a fraction computed in the manner described in either paragraph (f)(2)(i)(G)(1) or (f)(2)(i)(G)(2) of this section. For calendar years after December 31, 1991, the REMIC or the issuer of the collateralized debt obligation must be consistent in the method used to compute this fraction.

(1) The numerator of the fraction equals the interest, other than original issue discount, allocable to the accrual period. The denominator of the fraction equals the interest, other than original issue discount, allocable to the accrual period plus the remaining interest, other than original issue discount, as of the end of that accrual period. The interest allocable to each accrual period and the remaining interest are calculated by taking into account events which have occurred before the close of the accrual period and the prepayment assumption, if any, determined as of the startup day (as defined in section 860G(a)(9)) of the REMIC or the issue date (as defined in section 1275(a)(2)) of the collateralized debt obligation that

would be made in computing original issue discount if the debt instrument had been issued with original issue discount.

(2) If the REMIC regular interest or the collateralized debt obligation has de minimis original issue discount (as defined in section 1273(a)(3) and any regulations thereunder), then, at the option of the REMIC or the issuer of the collateralized debt obligation, the fraction may be computed in the manner specified in paragraph (f)(2)(ii)(K) of this section taking into account the de minimis original issue discount.

(ii) *REMIC regular interests and collateralized debt obligations issued with original issue discount.*—For a REMIC regular interest or collateralized debt obligation issued with original issue discount, the written statement must specify for the calendar year the following information—

(A) The aggregate amount of original issue discount includible in the gross income of the holder for the calendar year with respect to the REMIC regular interest or the collateralized debt obligation;

(B) The aggregate amount of interest, other than original issue discount, includible in the gross income of the holder for the calendar year with respect to the REMIC regular interest or the collateralized debt obligation;

(C) The name, address, and taxpayer identification number of the person required to file this form;

(D) The name, address, and taxpayer identification number of the person who must include the amount of interest specified in paragraphs (f)(2)(ii)(A) and (B) of this section in gross income;

(E) For calendar years after 1987, the daily portion of original issue discount per $1,000 of original principal amount (or for calendar years prior to 1992, per other specified unit) as determined under section 1272(a)(6) and the regulations thereunder for each accrual period any day of which is in that calendar year;

(F) For calendar years after 1987, the length of the accrual period;

(G) All other items shown on Form 1099 for the calendar year;

(H) A legend, including a statement that the information required under paragraphs (f)(2)(ii)(A), (B), (C), (D) and (G) of this section is being reported to the Internal Revenue Service, that conforms to the legend on Form 1099, Copy B, For Recipient;

(I) For calendar years after 1987, the adjusted issue price (as defined in section 1275(a)(4)(B)(ii)) of the REMIC regular interest or the collateralized debt obligation at the beginning of each accrual period with respect to which interest income is required to be reported on Form 1099 for the calendar year;

(J) The CUSIP number, account number, serial number, or other identifying number or information, of each class of REMIC regular interest or collateralized debt obligation, with respect to which a return is being made; and

(K) Information necessary to compute accrual of market discount. For calendar years after 1989, this information includes:

(1) For each accrual period in the calendar year, a fraction, the numerator of which equals the original issue discount allocable to that accrual period, and the denominator of which equals the original issue discount allocable to that accrual period plus the remaining original issue discount as of the end of that accrual period, and

(2) [Reserved]

The original issue discount allocable to each accrual period and the remaining original issue discount are calculated by taking into account events which have occurred before the close of the accrual period and the prepayment assumption determined as of the startup day (as defined in section 860G(a)(9)) of the REMIC or the issue date (as defined in section 1275(a)(2)) of the collateralized debt obligation.

(3) *Information with respect to REMIC assets.*—(i) *95 percent asset test.*—For calendar years after 1988, the written statement provided by a REMIC must also contain the following information for each calendar quarter—

(A) The percentage of REMIC assets that are qualifying real property loans under section 593,

(B) The percentage of REMIC assets that are assets described in section 7701(a)(19), and

(C) The percentage of REMIC assets that are real estate assets defined in section 856(c)(6)(B),

computed by reference to the average adjusted basis (as defined in section 1011) of the REMIC assets during the calendar quarter (as described in § 1.860F-4(e)(1)(iii)). If for any calendar quarter the percentage of REMIC assets represented by a category is at least 95 percent, then the statement need only specify that the percentage for that category, for that calendar quarter, was at least 95 percent.

(ii) *Additional information required if the 95 percent test not met.*—If, for any calendar quarter after 1988, less than 95 percent of the assets of the REMIC are real estate assets defined in section 856(c)(6)(B), then, for that calendar quarter, the REMIC's written statement must also provide to any real estate investment trust (REIT) that holds a regular interest the following information—

(A) The percentage of REMIC assets described in section 856(c)(5)(A), computed by reference to the average adjusted basis of the REMIC assets during the calendar quarter (as described in § 1.860F-4(e)(1)(iii)),

(B) The percentage of REMIC gross income (other than gross income from prohibited transactions defined in section 860F(a)(2)) described in section 856(c)(3)(A) through (E), computed as of the close of the calendar quarter, and

(C) The percentage of REMIC gross income (other than gross income from prohibited transactions defined in section 860F(a)(2)) described in section 856(c)(3)(F), computed as of the close of the calendar quarter. For purposes of this paragraph (f)(3)(ii)(C), the term "foreclosure property" contained in section 856(c)(3)(F) shall have the meaning specified in section 860G(a)(8).

In determining whether a REIT satisfies the limitations of section 856(c)(2), all REMIC gross income is deemed to be derived from a source specified in section 856(c)(2).

(iii) *Calendar years 1988 and 1989.*—For calendar years 1988 and 1989, the percentage of assets required in paragraphs (f)(3)(i) and (ii) of this section may be computed by reference to the average fair market value of the assets of the REMIC during the calendar quarter (as described in § 1.860F-4(e)(1)(iii)), instead of by reference to the average adjusted basis of the assets of the REMIC during the calendar quarter.

(4) *Cross-reference.*—See § 1.67-3T(f)(2)(ii) for additional information that may be separately stated on the statement required by this paragraph (f) with respect to certain holders of regular interests in REMICs described in § 1.67-3T(a)(2)(ii).

(5) *Time for furnishing statements.*—(i) *For calendar quarters and calendar years after 1988.*—For calendar quarters and calendar years after 1988, each statement required under this paragraph (f) to be furnished to any person for a calendar year with respect to amounts includible as interest must be furnished to that person after April 30 of that year and on or before March 15 of the following year, but not before the final interest payment (if any) for the calendar year.

(ii) *For calendar quarters and calendar years prior to 1989.*—(A) *In general.*—For calendar quarters and calendar years prior to 1989, each statement required under this paragraph (f) to be furnished to any person for a calendar year with respect to amounts includible as interest must be furnished to that person after April 30 of that year and on or before January 31 of the following year, but not before the final interest payment (if any) for the calendar year.

(B) *Nominee reporting.*—For calendar quarters and calendar years prior to 1989, each statement required under this paragraph (f) to be furnished by a nominee must be furnished to the actual owner of a REMIC regular interest or a collateralized debt obligation to which section 1272(a)(6) applies on or before the later of—

(1) The 30th day after the nominee receives such information, or

(2) January 31 of the year following the calendar year to which the statement relates.

(6) *Special rules.*—(i) *Copy of Form 1099 permissible.*—The requirements of this paragraph (f) for the furnishing of a statement to any person, including the legend requirement of paragraphs (f)(2)(i)(D) and (f)(2)(ii)(H) of this section, may be met by furnishing to that person—

(A) A copy of the Form 1099 filed pursuant to paragraph (b)(2) of this section in respect of that person, plus a separate statement (mailed with the Form 1099) that contains the information described in paragraphs (f)(2)(i)(E) and (G), (f)(2)(ii)(E), (F), (I), and (K), (f)(3), and (f)(4) of this section, if applicable, or

(B) A substitute form that contains all the information required under this paragraph (f) and that complies with any current revenue procedure concerning the reproduction of paper substitutes of Forms 1099 and the furnishing of substitute statements to forms recipients. The inclusion on the substitute form of the information specified in this paragraph (f) that is not required by the official Forms 1099 will not cause the substitute form to fail to meet any requirements that limit the information that may be provided with a substitute form.

(ii) *Statement furnished by mail.*—A statement mailed to the last known address of any person shall be considered to be furnished to that person within the meaning of this section.

(7) *Requirement that nominees furnish information to corporations and certain other specified persons.*—(i) *In general.*—For calendar quarters and calendar years after 1988, every broker or middleman must provide in writing or by telephone the information specified in paragraph (e)(2) of this section to—

(A) A corporation,

(B) A non-calendar year taxpayer, or

(C) Any other person specified in paragraphs (c)(9) through (15) of this section

who requests the information and for whom the broker or middleman holds as a nominee a REMIC regular interest or a collateralized debt obligation. A corporation, non-calendar year taxpayer, or any other person specified in paragraphs (c)(9) through (15) of this section may request the information in writing or by telephone for any REMIC regular interest or collateralized debt obligation for calendar quarters any day of which the person held the interest or obligation.

(ii) *Time for furnishing information.*—The statement required in paragraph (f)(7)(i) of this section must be furnished on or before the later of—

(A) The 45th day after receipt of the request,

(B) The 45th day after the close of the calendar quarter for which the information was requested, or

(C) If the request is made for the last calendar quarter in a year, March 15 of the year following the calendar quarter for which the information was requested. [Reg. § 1.6049-7.]

☐ [*T.D. 8366, 9-27-91. Amended by T.D. 8431, 9-2-92; T.D. 8734, 10-6-97 (T.D. 8804 delayed the effective date of T.D. 8734 from January 1, 1999, to January 1, 2000; T.D. 8856 further delayed the effective date of T.D. 8734 until January 1, 2001; T.D. 8888, 6-15-2000 and T.D. 8895, 8-17-2000.]*

### [Reg. § 1.6049-8]

**§ 1.6049-8. Interest and original issue discount paid to certain nonresident aliens.**—(a) *Interest subject to reporting requirement.*—For purposes of §§ 1.6049-4, 1.6049-6, and this section, and except as provided in paragraph (b) of this section, the term *interest* means interest described in section 871(i)(2)(A) that relates to a deposit maintained at an office within the United States, and that is paid to a nonresident alien individual who is a resident of a country that is identified, in an applicable revenue procedure (see § 601.601(d)(2) of this chapter) as of December 31 prior to the calendar year in which the interest is paid, as a country with which the United States has in effect an income tax or other convention or bilateral agreement relating to the exchange of tax information within the meaning of section 6103(k)(4), under which the competent authority is the Secretary of the Treasury or his delegate and the United States agrees to provide, as well as receive, information. Notwithstanding the foregoing, for purposes of §§ 1.6049-4, 1.6049-6, and this section, for any year for which the information return under § 1.6049-4(b)(5) is required, a payor may elect to treat interest as including all interest described in section 871(i)(2)(A) that relates to a deposit maintained at an office within the United States and that is paid to any nonresident alien individual. A payor shall make this election by reporting all such interest. For purposes of the regulations under section 6049 (§§ 1.6049-1 through 1.6049-8), a nonresident alien individual is a person described in section 7701(b)(1)(B). A payor or middleman may rely upon the permanent residence address provided on a valid Form W-8BEN, "Beneficial Owners Certificate of Foreign Status for U.S. Tax Withholding", to determine the country in which a nonresident alien individual is resident unless such payor or middleman knows or has reason to know that such documentation of the country of residence is unreliable or incorrect. Amounts described in this paragraph (a) are not subject to backup withholding under section 3406 if the payor may treat the payee as a foreign beneficial owner or foreign payee under the rules of § 1.6049-5(b)(12). See § 31.3406(g)-1(d) of this chapter. However, if the payor or middleman does not have either a valid Form W-8BEN or valid Form W-9, "Request for Taxpayer Identification Number and Certification", the payor or middleman must report the payment as made to a U.S. nonexempt recipient if it must so treat the payee under the presumption rules of § 1.6049-5(d)(2) and § 1.1441-1(b)(3)(iii), and the payor must also backup withhold under section 3406. (For interest paid to a Canadian nonresident alien individual on or before December 31, 2012, see paragraph (a) of this section as in effect and contained in 26 CFR part 1 revised April 1, 2000).

(b) *Interest excluded from reporting requirement.*—The term *interest* does not include an amount that is paid by the issuer or its agent outside the United States with respect to an obligation that is described in paragraph (b)(1) or (2) of this section.

(1)(i) The obligation is not in registered form (within the meaning of section 163(f) and the regulations thereunder); is part of a larger single public offering of securities; and is described in section 163(f)(2)(B).

(ii) Unless it has actual knowledge to the contrary, a middleman may treat an obligation as if it is described in section 163(f)(2)(B) if the obligation or coupon therefrom, whichever is presented for payment, contains the statement described in section 163(f)(2)(B)(ii)(II) and the regulations thereunder.

(2)(i) The obligation has a face or principal amount of not less than $500,000, and satisfies the requirements described in paragraphs (b)(2)(i)(A), (B), and (C) of this section.

(A) The obligation satisfies the requirements of sections 163(f)(2)(B)(i) and (ii)(I) and the regulations thereunder (as if it were a registration-required obligation within the meaning of section 163(f)(2)(A)) and is issued in accordance with the procedures of §1.163-5(c)(2)(i)(D)).

(B) If the obligation is in registered form, it is registered in the name of an exempt recipient described in §1.6049-4(c)(1)(ii).

(C) The obligation has on its face and on any detachable coupons the following statement (or a similar statement having the same effect):"By accepting this obligation or coupon, the holder represents and warrants that it is not a United States person (other than an exempt recipient described in the regulations under section 6049(b)(4) of the Internal Revenue Code and the regulations thereunder) and that it is not acting for or on behalf of a United States person (other than an exempt recipient described in the regulations under section 6049(b)(4) of the Internal Revenue Code and the regulations thereunder)."

(ii) Unless the middleman has actual knowledge to the contrary, it may treat an obligation as satisfying the requirements of sections 163(f)(2)(B)(i) and (ii)(I) and the regulations thereunder if the obligation or a coupon therefrom, whichever is presented for payment, contains the statement in paragraph (b)(2)(i)(C) of this section. [Reg. §1.6049-8.]

☐ [*T.D. 8664, 4-15-96. Amended by T.D. 8734, 10-6-97 (T.D. 8804 delayed the effective date of T.D. 8734 from January 1, 1999, to January 1, 2000; T.D. 8856 further delayed the effective date of T.D. 8734 until January 1, 2001) and T.D. 9584, 4-17-2012.*]

### [Reg. §1.6049-9]

**§1.6049-9. Premium subject to reporting for a debt instrument acquired on or after January 1, 2014.**—(a) *General rule.*—Notwithstanding §1.6049-5(f), for a debt instrument acquired on or after January 1, 2014, if a broker (as defined in §1.6045-1(a)(1)) is required to file a statement for the debt instrument under §1.6049-6, the broker generally must report any bond premium (as defined in §1.171-1(d)) or acquisition premium (as defined in §1.1272-2(b)(3)) for the calendar year. This section, however, only applies to a debt instrument that is a covered security as defined in §1.6045-1(a)(15).

(b) *Reporting of bond premium amortization.*—Unless a broker has been notified in writing in accordance with §1.6045-1(n)(5) that a customer does not want to amortize bond premium under section 171, the broker must report the amount of any amortizable bond premium allocable to a stated interest payment made to the customer during the calendar year. See §§1.171-2 and 1.171-3 to determine the amount of amortizable bond premium allocable to a stated interest payment. Instead of reporting a gross amount for both stated interest and amortizable bond premium, a broker may report a net amount of stated interest that reflects the offset of the stated interest payment by the amount of amortizable bond premium allocable to the payment. In this case, the broker must not report the amortizable bond premium as a separate item. This paragraph (b) also applies to amortizable bond premium on a tax-exempt obligation, which is required to be amortized under section 171.

(c) *Reporting of acquisition premium amortization.*—A broker must report the amount of any acquisition premium amortization that reduces the amount of original issue discount includible in income by the customer during a calendar year. For a debt instrument acquired on or after January 1, 2015, a broker must use the rules in §1.1272-2(b)(4) to determine the amount of acquisition premium amortization. However, for a debt instrument acquired on or after January 1, 2014, and before January 1, 2015, if a customer timely notifies the broker in accordance with §1.6045-1(n)(5), a broker may use the rules in §1.1272-3 to determine the amount of acquisition premium amortization. Instead of reporting a gross amount for both original issue discount and acquisition premium amortization, a broker may report a net amount of original issue discount that reflects the offset of the original issue discount includible in income by the customer for the calendar year by the amount of acquisition premium allocable to the original issue discount. In this case, the broker must not report the acquisition premium amortization as a separate item. See §1.6049-10 for the reporting of acquisition premium on a tax-exempt obligation. [Reg. §1.6049-9.]

☐ [*T.D. 9713, 3-12-2015 (corrected 4-26-2016).*]

### [Reg. §1.6049-10]

**§1.6049-10. Reporting of original issue discount on a tax-exempt obligation.**—(a) *In general.*—For purposes of section 6049, a payor (as defined in §1.6049-4(a)(2)) of original issue discount (OID) on a tax-exempt obligation (as defined in section 1288(b)(2)) is required to report the daily portions of OID on the obligation as if the daily portions of OID that accrued during a calendar year were paid to the holder (or holders) of the obligation in the calendar year. The amount of the daily portions of OID that accrues during a calendar year is determined as if section 1272 and §1.1272-1 applied to a tax-exempt obligation. Notwithstanding any other rule in section 6049 and the regulations thereunder, a payor must determine whether a tax-exempt obligation was issued with OID and the amount of OID that accrues for each relevant period. As prescribed by section 1288(b)(1), OID on a tax-exempt obligation is determined without regard to the de minimis rules in section 1273(a)(3) and §1.1273-1(d).

(b) *Acquisition premium.*—A payor is required to report acquisition premium amortization on a tax-exempt obligation in accordance with the rules in §1.6049-9(c) as if section 1272 applied to a tax-exempt obligation. See paragraph (a) of this section to determine the amount of OID allocable to an accrual period.

(c) *Effective/applicability date.*—This section applies to a tax-exempt obligation that is a covered security (within the meaning of §1.6045-1(a)(15) and (n)(12)) acquired on or after January 1, 2017. For a taxable year beginning after December 31, 2016, a broker, however, may rely on this section to report OID and acquisition premium for a tax-exempt obligation that is a covered security acquired before January 1, 2017. [Reg. §1.6049-10]

☐ [*T.D. 9750, 2-17-2016.*]

### [Reg. §1.6049(d)-5T]

**§1.6049(d)-5T. Reporting by brokers of interest and original issue discount on and after January 1, 1986 (Temporary).**—For purposes of §1.6049-5(c), relating to original issue discount treated as interest subject to reporting, on and after January 1, 1986, a payor who is a broker or middleman holding as a nominee—

(a) A bank certificate of deposit (without regard to whether the broker or middleman sold the certificate of deposit to the owner), or

(b) Any other original issue discount debt instrument that is specified by the Commissioner,

must determine whether that obligation is one that was issued at a discount and the amount of discount that is includible in the income of the owner. However, before January 1, 1987, reporting is required only with respect to certificates of deposit (or any such other obligations) held by a broker or middleman as a nominee on or after June 1, 1986, that were sold by the broker or middleman (whether for the broker's account or as an agent of the issuer) to the owner. The preceding two sentences do not apply to certificates of deposit (or any such other obligations) held on or after January 1, 1986, but disposed of before June 1, 1986; reporting requirements with respect to such certificates of deposit (or any other such obligations) shall be determined under the provisions of §1.6049-5(c) as in effect immediately prior to publication of this §1.6049-5T. [Temporary Reg. §1.6049(d)-5T.]

☐ [*T.D. 8109, 12-12-86. Redesignated by T.D. 9658, 2-28-2014.*]

### [Reg. §1.6050A-1]

**§1.6050A-1. Reporting requirements of certain fishing boat operators.**—(a) *Requirement of reporting.*—The operator of a boat on which one or more individuals during a calendar year performs services described in §31.3121(b)(20)-1(a) shall make an information return on Form 1099-MISC for that calendar year. The return shall include the following information—

(1) The name and taxpayer identification number of each individual performing the services;

(2) The percentage of each individual's share of the catch of fish or other forms of aquatic life (hereinafter "fish");

(3) The percentage of the operator's share of the catch of fish;

(4) If the individual receives all or part of his share of the catch in kind, the type and weight of the share and, if it can be ascertained, the fair market value of his share;

(5) If the individual receives a share of the proceeds of the catch, the dollar amount received; and

(6) Any other information that is required by the form.

For purposes of this section, the term, "boat operator" means an employer (as defined in §31.3121(d)-2) of an employee whose services are excepted from employment by section 3121(b)(20) and §31.3121(b)(20)-1. The boat operator may make separate returns on Form 1099-MISC for each crew member for each voyage, or he may aggregate the information required by this paragraph for an individual for all or any part of a return period in which the type of catch (if required) and the percentage due the crew member remain the same.

(b) *Time and place for filing.*—Returns required to be made under this section on Form 1099-MISC shall be filed with the Internal Revenue Service Center, designated in the instructions for Form 1099-MISC, on or before February 28 (March 31 if filed electronically) of the year following the calendar year in which the relevant services were performed.

(c) *Requirement of and time for furnishing statements.*—(1) *Requirement of furnishing statement.*—Every person filing a Form 1099-MISC under this section shall furnish to the individual whose identifying number is (or should be) shown on the form a written statement showing the information required by paragraph (a) of this section. The requirement of the preceding sentence may be met by furnishing to the individual copy B of Form 1099-MISC or a reasonable facsimile of Form 1099-MISC that was filed pursuant to this section. An IRS truncated taxpayer identifying number (TTIN) may be used as the identifying number for the individual in lieu of the identifying number appearing on the information return filed with the Internal Revenue Service. For provisions relating to the use of TTINs, see § 301.6109-4 of this chapter (Procedure and Administration Regulations).

(2) *Time for furnishing statement.*—Each statement required by this paragraph to be furnished to any individual for a calendar year shall be furnished on or before January 31 of the year following the calendar year for which the return was made.

(d) *Cross-reference to penalties.*—For provisions relating to the penalty provided for failure to file timely a correct information return required under section 6050A(a) and § 1.6050A-1(a), see § 301.6721-1 of this chapter (Procedure and Administration Regulations). For provisions relating to the penalty provided for failure to furnish timely a correct payee statement required under section 6050A(b) and § 1.6050A-1(c), see § 301.6722-1 of this chapter. See § 301.6724-1 of this chapter for the waiver of a penalty if the failure is due to reasonable cause and is not due to willful neglect.

(e) *Effective/applicability date.*—The rules in this section apply to information returns and payee statements due after December 31, 2014. For rules applicable for information returns and payee statements due before January 1, 2015, § 1.6050A-1(c)(1) (as contained in 26 CFR part 1, revised April 2013) shall apply. [Reg. § 1.6050A-1.]

☐ [*T.D. 7716, 8-26-80. Amended by T.D. 8734,* 10-6-97 (T.D. 8804 delayed the effective date of T.D. 8734 from January 1, 1999, to January 1, 2000; T.D. 8856 further delayed the effective date of T.D. 8734 until January 1, 2001); *T.D. 8895,* 8-17-2000 *and T.D. 9675,* 7-14-2014.]

### [Reg. § 301.6050A-1]

**§ 301.6050A-1.  Information returns regarding services performed by certain crewmen on fishing boats.**—For provisions relating to the requirement of returns of information regarding services performed by certain crewmen on fishing boats, see § 1.6050A-1 of this chapter (Income Tax Regulations) and § 301.6652-1 of this chapter (Regulations on Procedure and Administration). [Reg. § 301.6050A-1.]

☐ [*T.D. 7716, 8-26-80.*]

### [Reg. § 1.6050B-1]

**§ 1.6050B-1.  Information returns by person making unemployment compensation payments.**—For taxable years beginning after December 31, 1978, every person who makes payments of unemployment compensation (as defined in section 85 (c)) aggregating $10 or more to any individual during any calendar year shall file a Form 1099UC in accordance with the instructions to such form. [Reg. § 1.6050B-1.]

☐ [*T.D. 7705, 7-8-80.*]

### [§ 1.6050D-1]

**§ 1.6050D-1.  Information returns relating to energy grants and financing.**—(a) *Requirement of reporting.*—Every person who administers a Federal, State, or local program a principal purpose of which is to provide subsidized energy financing (as defined in section 23(c)(10)(C) and the regulations thereunder) or grants for projects designed to conserve or produce energy shall make an information return for each calendar year beginning after December 31, 1983. However, the preceding sentence shall not apply if none of the financing and grants provided under such program during the calendar year relate either to expenditures described in section 23(c)(1) or (2), relating to the residential energy credit, made by a taxpayer before January 1, 1986, with respect to a dwelling unit or to section 38 property (as defined in section 48 and the regulations thereunder). That return shall be made on Form 6497 or, in the case

of taxable grants, on Form 1099-G. (The latter form is prescribed pursuant to section 6041 as well as section 6050D.) The return shall include the following information:

(1) The name, address, and taxpayer identification number of each taxpayer receiving financing or a grant made under such program during the calendar year with respect to either section 38 property or, in the case of financing or a grant for energy conservation expenditures or renewable energy source expenditures made by the taxpayer before January 1, 1986, a dwelling unit that is located in the United States;

(2) The aggregate amount of financing and grants received by the taxpayer under the program during the calendar year;

(3) In the case of returns for financing or nontaxable grants, the name of the program under which the financing or grants are made; and

(4) Any other information that is required by the form.

For purposes of this section, the term "person" means the officer or employee having control of the program, or the person appropriately designated for purposes of section 6050D and this section.

(b) *Time and place for filing.*—Returns required to be made under this section shall be filed with the Internal Revenue Service Center designated in the instructions for Form 6497 or 1099-G on or before the last day of February (March 31 if filed electronically) of the year following the calendar year for which the return is made. [Reg. § 1.6050D-1.]

☐ [*T.D. 8018, 3-28-85. Amended by T.D. 8146, 7-15-87 and T.D. 8895,* 8-17-2000.]

### [Reg. § 1.6050E-1]

**§ 1.6050E-1.  Reporting of State and local income tax refunds.**—(a) *Applicability.*—Section 6050E and this section apply to any refund officer who, with respect to an individual, makes payments of refunds of State or local income taxes or allows credits or offsets with respect to such taxes aggregating $10 or more for such individual in any calendar year.

(b) *Definitions.*—For purposes of this section—

(1) The term "refund officer" means the officer or employee of a State or local taxing jurisdiction having control of payments of refunds or the allowance of credits or offsets, or the person appropriately designated for purposes of this section.

(2) The term "State" shall include the District of Columbia but shall not include the Commonwealth of Puerto Rico or any possession of the United States.

(3) The term "individual" shall not include an estate or trust.

(4) The term "credit or offset" means an overpayment of tax which, in lieu of being refunded to the taxpayer, is:

(i) Applied against an existing liability of the taxpayer,

(ii) Available for application against a future liability of the taxpayer, or

(iii) Otherwise used or available for use for the taxpayer's benefit.

(c) *Requirement of reporting.*—Every refund officer described in paragraph (a) of this section shall make an information return in accordance with this section for each calendar year. An information return must be made even if the refund officer is not required to furnish a statement to the applicable taxpayer under paragraph (k)(2) of this section.

(d) *Prescribed Form.*—Except as otherwise provided in paragraph (i) of this section, the information return required by paragraph (c) of this section shall be made on Forms 1096 and 1099.

(e) *Refunds involving different taxable years.*—In the case of refunds paid or credits or offsets allowed during a calendar year with respect to two or more taxable years of an individual, a separate Form 1099 shall be filed with respect to each taxable year of the individual. Thus, if during calendar year 1983 a refund officer pays to an individual a refund of $15 with respect to that individual's taxable year ending in 1982 and $20 with respect to that individual's taxable year ending in 1981, a separate Form 1099 shall be filed for each of the two payments. If, instead, the refund with respect to the individual's taxable year ending in 1982 were $5 instead of $15, no return would be required for the payment of $5.

(f) *Information required.*—The information required to be reported on Forms 1096 and 1099 includes the aggregate amount of refunds, credits, and offsets made or allowed during the calendar year with respect to the taxable year of the individual covered by the return; the name, address, and taxpayer identification number of the individual with respect to whom such payment, credit, or offset was made or allowed; the taxable year covered by the return; and such other information as may be required by the forms. In addition, the nature of the tax is required to be indicated on the Form 1099 in any case where the refund, credit or offset is made or allowed with respect to a payment attributable to an income tax that applies exclusively to income from a trade or business and is not a tax of general application.

(g) *When credit or offset deemed allowed.*—For purposes of a return of information under this section, a credit or offset is deemed to be allowed when the liability to pay or credit such amount is admitted by the State or local taxing jurisdiction. Thus, if an amount with respect to a taxpayer's 1982 taxable year is credited in 1983 to reduce the liability of the taxpayer to make estimated tax payments in 1983, it is reportable as a credit allowed in 1983. It is not reportable in the taxable year that gives rise to the refund, credit or offset.

(h) *Time and place for filing.*—The returns required under this section for any calendar year shall be filed after September 30 of that calendar year, but not before the refund officer's final payment (or allowance of credit or offset) for the year, and on or before February 28 (March 31 if filed electronically) of the following year. Returns shall be filed with the appropriate Internal Revenue Service Center, the addresses of which are listed in the instructions for Forms 1099. For extensions of time for filing returns under this section, see § 1.6081-1.

(i) *Use of magnetic media and substitute forms.*—(1) *Magnetic media.*—A refund officer may be required to file the Forms 1099 required by this section on magnetic media or machine-readable paper forms. See section 6011(e) and applicable regulations and revenue procedures thereunder. If a refund officer is not required to file the Forms 1099 required by this section on magnetic media, the refund officer may request permission under applicable regulations and revenue procedures to submit the information required by this section on magnetic media.

(2) *Substitute forms.*—A refund officer may prepare and use a form which contains provisions identical with those of Form 1096 if the refund officer complies with all revenue procedures relating to substitute Form 1096 in effect at that time. In addition, if a refund officer is not required to file the Forms 1099 required by this section on magnetic media or machine-readable paper forms, the refund officer may prepare and use a form which contains provisions identical with those of Form 1099 if the refund officer complies with all revenue procedures relating to substitute Form 1099 in effect at that time.

(j) *Voluntary information exchange agreements.*—The requirements of reporting information to the Internal Revenue Service under this section may be satisfied for any calendar year by submission of the information required under paragraph (f) of this section in accordance with the terms of a voluntary information exchange agreement between the State and the United States in effect during such year.

(k) *Requirement of furnishing statements to recipients.*—(1) *In general.*—Except as provided in paragraph (k)(2) of this section, every refund officer required to make a return of information under this section shall furnish to the individual whose identifying number is required to be shown on the return a written statement showing the aggregate amount shown on the information return of refunds, credits and offsets made or allowed to such individual with respect to each taxable year of the individual, the name of the State or local taxing jurisdiction paying such refund or allowing such credits or offsets, the taxable year giving rise to the refund, credit or offset and a legend stating that such amount is being reported to the Internal Revenue Service. The requirement of this paragraph may be met by furnishing to the individual a copy of the Form 1099 filed with respect to that individual provided that the form bears a legend stating that such amount is being reported to the Internal Revenue Service. For purposes of this paragraph, a statement shall be considered to be furnished to an individual if it is mailed to the individual at the individual's last known address. An IRS truncated taxpayer identifying number (TTIN) may be used as the identifying number of the individual in lieu of the identifying number appearing on the information return filed with the Internal Revenue Service. For provisions relating to the use of TTINs, see § 301.6109-4 of this chapter (Procedure and Administration Regulations).

(2) *Exception for nonitemizers.*—A refund officer need not furnish a statement to an individual under paragraph (k)(1) of this section if the refund officer verifies that the individual did not claim itemized deductions for Federal income tax purposes for the taxable year giving rise to the refund, credit, or offset. This exception shall not apply, however, if the refund, credit, or offset is made or allowed with respect to a payment attributable to an income tax that applies exclusively to income from a trade or business and is not a tax of general application. For purposes of this paragraph (k)(2), verification shall be made solely from—

(i) The State or local income tax return, or

(ii) Information obtained through a voluntary information exchange agreement with the United States for the applicable taxable year.

(3) *Verification from the State or local income tax return.*—A refund officer shall verify from the State or local income tax return that an individual did not claim itemized deductions for Federal income tax purposes for the applicable taxable year only if—

(i)(A) An individual who itemized deductions for Federal income tax purposes either must attach a copy of Schedule A of the individual's Federal income tax return to the State or local income tax return or must transcribe information from Schedule A of the individual's Federal income tax return on the State or local income tax return;

(B) The information contained on or transcribed from the Schedule A is required for the purpose of computing liability for the State or local income tax; and

(C) The omission of a copy of the Schedule A, or of the information required to be transcribed from the Schedule A, is consistent with the taxpayer's computation of tax on the State or local income tax return; or

(ii) Individuals are required to transcribe information from their Federal income tax return (other than from Schedule A) on the State or local income tax return for the purpose of computing liability for the State or local income tax and the information can be used to determine conclusively whether the taxpayer itemized deductions for Federal income tax purposes.

(4) *Example.*—The provisions of paragraph (k)(3)(ii) of this section may be illustrated by the following example:

*Example.* State X asks for transcription of the following information on its 1983 income tax return from the taxpayer's 1983 Federal income tax return: Adjusted gross income; taxable income; and number of exemptions claimed. The amount of adjusted gross income and the number of exemptions claimed on the Federal income tax return are taken into account in computing the liability for income tax under the laws of State X. The amount of taxable income transcribed from the Federal return, however, does not enter into the computatin of liability for income tax under the laws of State X. Thus, this amount may not be taken into account by the refund officer of State X for purposes of verifying whether a taxpayer itemized deductions for Federal income tax purposes. Since the refund officer of State X will not be able to determine conclusively from the amount of adjusted gross income and the number of exemptions transcribed from the Federal return whether a taxpayer itemized deductions for Federal income tax purposes, the transcribed information does not meet the requirements of paragraph (k)(3)(ii) of this section.

(l) *Time for furnishing statements.*—(1) *General rule.*—The statement required under paragraph (k) of this section must be furnished after December 31 of the year in which the refund is paid or credit or offset is allowed, and on or before January 31 of the following year.

(2) *Extensions of time.*—For good cause shown upon written application of the refund officer, the service center director may grant an extension of time not exceeding 30 days in which to furnish statements under this paragraph. The application shall be addressed to the Service Center with which the Forms 1099 required under this section are required to be filed and shall contain a concise statement of the reasons for requesting the extension to aid the service center director in determining the period of the extension, if any, which will be granted. The application shall state at the top of the first page that it is made under this section and shall be signed by the refund officer. In general, the application shall be filed after September 30 of the year in which the refund is paid or credit or offset is allowed, and before January 15 of the following year.

(m) *Effective/applicability date.*—This section applies to payments of refunds and credits and offsets allowed after December 31, 1982. The amendments to paragraph (k)(1) apply to payee statements due after December 31, 2014. For payee statements due before January 1, 2015, § 1.6050E-5(k)(1) (as contained in 26 CFR part 1, revised April 2013) shall apply. [Reg. § 1.6050E-1.]

☐ [*T.D. 8052, 9-12-85. Amended by T.D. 8895, 8-17-2000 and T.D. 9675, 7-14-2014.*]

### [Reg. § 1.6050H-0]

**§ 1.6050H-0. Table of contents.**—This section lists the major captions that appear in § § 1.6050H-1 and 1.6050H-2.

*§ 1.6050H-1. Information reporting of mortgage interest received in a trade or business from an individual.*

    (a) Information reporting requirement.

        (1) Overview.

        (2) Reporting requirement.

        (3) Optional reporting.

(b) Qualified mortgage.

  (1) In general.

  (2) Mortgage.

   (i) In general.

   (ii) Transitional rule for certain obligations existing on December 31, 1984.

   (iii) Transitional rule for certain obligations existing on December 31, 1987.

  (3) Payor of record.

  (4) Lender of record.

(c) Interest recipient.

  (1) Trade or business requirement.

  (2) Interest received or collected on behalf of another person.

   (i) General rule.

   (ii) Exception.

  (3) Interest received in the form of points.

   (i) In general.

   (ii) If designation agreement is in effect.

  (4) Governmental unit.

  (5) Examples.

(d) Additional rules.

  (1) Reporting by foreign person.

  (2) Reporting with respect to nonresident alien individual.

   (i) In general.

   (ii) Nonresident alien individual status.

  (3) Reporting by cooperative housing corporations.

(e) Amount of interest received on mortgage for calendar year.

  (1) In general.

  (2) Calendar year.

   (i) In general.

   (ii) De minimis rule.

   (iii) Applicability to points.

  (3) Certain interest not received on mortgage.

   (i) Interest received from seller on payor of record's mortgage.

   (ii) Interest received from governmental unit.

  (4) Interest calculated under Rule of 78s method of accounting.

(f) Points treated as interest.

  (1) General rule.

  (2) Limitations.

  (3) Special rule.

   (i) Amounts paid directly by payor of record.

   (ii) Examples.

  (4) Construction loans.

   (i) In general.

   (ii) Limitation on refinancing of construction loans.

  (5) Amounts paid to mortgage brokers.

  (6) Effect on deduction of points.

(g) Effective date.

  (1) In general.

  (2) Points.

**§1.6050H-2. Time, form, and manner of reporting interest received on qualified mortgage.**

(a) Requirement to file return.

  (1) Form of return.

  (2) Information included on return.

  (3) Reimbursements of interest on a qualified mortgage.

  (4) Time and place for filing return.

  (5) Use of magnetic media.

(b) Requirement to furnish statement.

  (1) In general.

  (2) Information included on statement.

  (3) Statement furnished pursuant to Federal mortgage program.

  (4) Copy of Form 1098 to payor of record.

  (5) Furnishing statement with other information reports.

  (6) Time and place for furnishing statement.

(c) Notice requirement for use of Rule of 78s method of accounting.

  (1) In general.

  (2) Time and manner.

(d) Reporting under designation agreement.

  (1) In general.

  (2) Qualified person.

  (3) Designation agreement.

  (4) Penalties.

(e) Penalty provisions.

  (1) Returns and statements the due date for which (determined without regard for extensions) is after December 31, 1987, and before December 31, 1989.

   (i) Failure to file return or to furnish statement.

   (ii) Failure to furnish TIN.

   (iii) Failure to include correct information.

  (2) Returns and statements the due date for which (determined without regard for extensions) is after December 31, 1989.

   (i) Failure to file return or to furnish statement.

   (ii) Failure to furnish TIN.

   (iii) Failure to include correct information.

(f) Requirement to request and to obtain TIN.

  (1) In general.

  (2) Manner of requesting TIN.

(g) Effective date.

  (1) In general.

  (2) Points.

[Reg. §1.6050H-0.]

☐ [*T.D.* 8191, 4-11-88. *Amended by T.D.* 8571, 12-7-94.]

**[Reg §1.6050H-1]**

**§1.6050H-1. Information reporting of mortgage interest received in a trade or business from an individual.**—(a) *Information reporting requirement.*—(1) *Overview.*—The information reporting requirements of section 6050H, this section, and §1.6050H-2 apply to an interest recipient who receives at least $600 of interest on a qualified mortgage for a calendar year or who makes a reimbursement of interest described in §1.6050H-2(a)(2)(iv). Paragraph (b) of this section defines qualified mortgage. Paragraph (c) of this section defines interest recipient. Paragraph (d) of this section contains additional rules relating to the reporting requirement for foreign persons, cooperative housing corporations, and nonresident alien individuals. Paragraph (e) of this section contains rules for determining the amount of interest received on a mortgage for a calendar year. Paragraph (f) of this section provides rules for determining when prepaid interest in the form of points is taken into account as interest for purposes of section 6050H, and §1.6050H-2.

(2) *Reporting requirement.*—Except as otherwise provided in this section and §1.6050H-2, an interest recipient that either receives at least $600 of interest on a qualified mortgage for a calendar year or makes reimbursements of interest described in §1.6050H-2(a)(2)(iv) must, with respect to that interest—

  (i) File an information return with the Internal Revenue Service; and

  (ii) Furnish a statement to the payor of record on the mortgage.

(3) *Optional reporting.*—An interest recipient may, but is not required to, report its receipt of less than $600 of interest on a qualified mortgage for a calendar year. Similarly, an interest recipient also may report reimbursements of interest on a qualified mortgage even if the reimbursements are not required to be reported by §1.6050H-2(a)(2)(iv). An interest recipient that chooses, but is not required, to file a return as provided in this section and §1.6050H-2(a) or to furnish a statement as provided in this section and §1.6050H-2(b) is subject to the requirements of this section and §1.6050H-2.

(b) *Qualified mortgage.*—(1) *In general.*—A mortgage is a qualified mortgage if the payor of record on the mortgage is an individual, including an individual acting in a capacity as a sole proprietor of a business. A mortgage is not a qualified mortgage if the payor of record on the mortgage is not an individual (such as a trust, estate, partnership, association, company, or corporation), even though an individual is a co-borrower on the mortgage and all the trustees, beneficiaries, partners, members, or shareholders of the payor of record are individuals.

(2) *Mortgage.*—(i) *In general.*—Except as otherwise provided in paragraphs (b)(2)(ii) and (b)(2)(iii) of this section, an obligation is a mortgage if real property (regardless of where located) secures all or part of the obligation. An interest recipient must determine whether real property secures an obligation at the time the obligation is created or, if security is added or removed at a later time, at that later time. Real property includes a manufactured home as defined in section 25(e)(10). An obligation includes a line of credit or a credit card obligation. For purposes of this section and §1.6050H-2, a borrower incurs a line of credit or credit card obligation when the borrower first has the right to borrow against the line of credit or credit card, whether the borrower actually borrows an amount at that time. An obligation will not fail to be treated as a mortgage solely because, under an applicable State or local homestead law or other debtor protection law in effect on August 16, 1986, the security

interest is ineffective or the enforceability of the security interest is restricted.

(ii) *Transitional rule for certain obligations existing on December 31, 1984.*—(A) *In general.*—An obligation that existed on December 31, 1984, is not a mortgage if, at the time the payor of record incurred the obligation, the interest recipient reasonably classified the obligation as other than a mortgage, real property loan, real estate loan, or other similar type of obligation. A reasonable classification of an obligation must be consistent with industry practices and determined according to the purpose of the obligation, the property securing the obligation, and any other reasonable factor. For purposes of this paragraph (b)(2)(ii)(A), an obligation was not reasonably classified as other than a mortgage, real property loan, real estate loan, or other similar type of obligation if, at the time the payor of record incurred the obligation, more than one-half of the obligations in the particular class in which the obligation was classified were secured primarily by real property.

(B) *Examples.*—The following examples illustrate the rules of paragraph (b)(2)(ii)(A) of this section:

*Example (1).* B offers an unsecured line of credit and a line of credit secured by real property. B separately markets the two credit lines, and they are governed by different terms and conditions. For accounting purposes, B classifies the two types of loans as a single class. For purposes of paragraph (b)(2)(ii)(A) of this section, the two types of loans are different classes of obligations.

*Example (2).* B operates a program to make loans to small businesses. Depending on the amount of the loan and the credit history of the borrower, B may or may not require security for the loan. If B requires security, it may consist of real or personal property. For accounting purposes, B classifies all of the loans within this program as a single class. For purposes of paragraph (b)(2)(ii)(A) of this section, all of the loans within this program may be classified as belonging to a single class.

(iii) *Transitional rule for certain obligations existing on December 31, 1987.*—An obligation that was incurred after December 31, 1984, and that existed on December 31, 1987, is not a mortgage if the obligation is not primarily secured by real property.

(3) *Payor of record.*—A payor of record on a mortgage is the person carried on the books and records of the interest recipient as the principal borrower on the mortgage. If the books and records of the interest recipient do not indicate which borrower is the principal borrower, the interest recipient must designate a borrower as the principal borrower.

(4) *Lender of record.*—The lender of record is the person who, at the time the loan is made, is named as the lender on the loan documents and whose right to receive payment from the payor of record is secured by the payor of record's principal residence. An intention by the lender of record to sell or otherwise transfer the loan to a third party subsequent to the close of the transaction will not affect the determination of who is the lender of record.

(c) *Interest recipient.*—(1) *Trade or business requirement.*—Except as provided in paragraph (c)(4) of this section, an interest recipient is a person that is engaged in a trade or business (whether or not the trade or business of lending money) and that, in the course of the trade or business, either receives interest on a mortgage or makes a reimbursement of interest on a qualified mortgage described in §1.6050H-2(a)(3). For purposes of this paragraph (c)(1), if a person holds a mortgage which was originated or acquired in the course of a trade or business, the interest on the mortgage is considered to be received in the course of that trade or business. For example, if real estate developer A lends money to individual B to enable B to purchase a house in a subdivision owned and developed by A, and B gives a mortgage to A for the loan, A is an interest recipient for interest received on the mortgage. Alternatively, if C, a person engaged in the trade or business of being a physician, lends money to individual D to enable D to purchase C's home, and D gives a mortgage to C for the loan, C is not an interest recipient for interest received on the mortgage, because C will not receive the interest in the course of the trade or business of being a physician.

(2) *Interest received or collected on behalf of another person.*—(i) *General rule.*—Except as otherwise provided in paragraph (c)(2)(ii) or (3) of this section, a person that, in the course of its trade or business, receives or collects interest on a mortgage on behalf of another person (e.g., the lender of record) is the interest recipient (the initial recipient) for the mortgage. In this case, the reporting requirement of paragraph (a) of this section does not apply to the transfer of interest from the initial recipient to the person for which the initial recipient receives or collects the interest. For example, if financial institution A collects interest on behalf of financial institution B, A is the initial recipient for the mortgage and is subject to the reporting

requirements of section 6050H, and B is not required to report the interest received on the mortgage from A.

(ii) *Exception.*—(A) *Scope of exception.*—Paragraph (c)(2)(i) of this section does not apply for any period for which—

(1) An initial recipient does not possess the information needed to comply with the reporting requirement of paragraph (a) of this section; and

(2) The person for which the interest is received or collected would receive the interest in the course of its trade or business if the interest were paid directly to that person. For purposes of this paragraph (c)(2)(ii)(A)(2), if interest is received or collected on behalf of a person other than an individual, that person is presumed to receive interest in a trade or business.

(B) *Application of exception.*—If the exception provided by this paragraph (c)(2)(ii) applies, the person for which the interest is received or collected is the interest recipient with respect to interest received or collected on the mortgage during the period described in this paragraph (c)(2)(ii).

(3) *Interest received in the form of points.*—For purposes of this section and §1.6050H-2, in the case of prepaid interest received in the form of points (as defined in paragraph (f) of this section):

(i) *In general.*—Except as provided in paragraph (c)(3)(ii) of this section, only the lender of record or a qualified person (as defined in §1.6050H-2(d)(2)) is treated as receiving the points. The lender of record or qualified person is treated as receiving all points paid directly by the payor of record in connection with the purchase of the principal residence.

(ii) *If designation agreement is in effect.*—If a designation agreement is executed pursuant to §1.6050H-2(d) with respect to points, only the designated party under the agreement is treated as receiving points with respect to any mortgage to which the agreement applies. The designated party is treated as receiving all points with respect to any mortgage to which the agreement applies.

(4) *Governmental unit.*—A governmental unit or an agency or instrumentality of a governmental unit that receives interest on a mortgage is an interest recipient without regard to the requirement of paragraph (c)(1) of this section that the interest be received in the course of a trade or business. A governmental unit or an agency or instrumentality of a governmental unit that is an interest recipient must designate an officer or employee to satisfy the reporting requirements of paragraph (a) of this section.

(5) *Examples.*—The following examples illustrate the rules of paragraph (c) of this section:

*Example (1).* Financial institution F collects mortgage interest on behalf of financial institution G and deposits the amount collected into G's account held with F. F possesses the information needed to comply with the reporting requirement of paragraph (a) of this section. F is the interest recipient for the mortgage. G is not required to report.

*Example (2).* The facts are the same as in example (1), except that F does not possess the information needed to comply with the reporting requirement. G, the person for which F collects the interest, is the interest recipient for the mortgage. F is not required to report.

*Example (3).* S, an individual, sells real property to another individual, P, and takes back a mortgage from P to finance the sale. S does not receive the interest in the course of a trade or business. B, a bank, collects P's payments of principal and interest on behalf of S and deposits that amount into an account held at the bank in S's name. B does not possess the information needed to comply with the reporting requirement of paragraph (a) of this section. B is the interest recipient for P's mortgage without regard to paragraph (c)(2)(ii) of this section, because S would not receive the interest in the course of a trade or business. S is not required to report.

*Example (4).* X collects mortgage interest on behalf of Y, who would receive the interest in the course of a trade or business. X possesses the information needed to comply with the reporting requirement of paragraph (a) of this section. On July 1, 1988, Z assumes X's interest collection responsibilities. Z does not possess the information needed to comply with the reporting requirement of paragraph (a) of this section. X is the interest recipient for interest received from January 1, 1988, through June 30, 1988. Because Z does not possess the requisite information and Y would receive the interest in the course of a trade or business, Y is the interest recipient for interest received from July 1, 1988, through December 31, 1988.

*Example (5).* On December 1, Borrower obtains from Lender funds with which to purchase an existing structure to be used as Borrower's principal residence. In connection with the mortgage, Lender charges Borrower $300 as points. Borrower pays this amount to Lender at closing using unborrowed funds. In addition, Lender receives from Borrower with respect to the mortgage $300 as interest

Reg. §1.6050H-1(c)(5)

(as determined under paragraph (e) of this section) other than points. Because Lender has received at least $600 in interest, including points, with respect to Borrower's mortgage during the calendar year, Lender must report the payments in accordance with paragraph (a) of this section and §1.6050H-2. Under those sections, Lender must separately state on the information return and the statement to Borrower the $300 received as interest (other than points) and the $300 received as points.

(d) *Additional rules.*—(1) *Reporting by foreign person.*—An interest recipient that is not a United States person (as defined in section 7701(a)(30)) must report interest received on a qualified mortgage only if it receives the interest—

(i) At a location in the United States, or

(ii) At a location outside the United States if the interest recipient is—

(A) A controlled foreign corporation (within the meaning of section 957(a)), or

(B) A person, 50 percent or more of the gross income of which, from all sources for the three-year period ending with the close of the taxable year preceding the receipt of interest (or for such part of the period as the person was in existence), was effectively connected with the conduct of a trade or business within the United States.

(2) *Reporting with respect to nonresident alien individual.*—(i) *In general.*—The reporting requirement of paragraph (a) of this section does not apply if—

(A) The payor of record is a nonresident alien individual, and

(B) Real property located in the United States does not secure the mortgage.

(ii) *Nonresident alien individual status.*—For purposes of paragraph (d)(2)(i)(A) of this section, an interest recipient must apply the following documentary evidence rules to determine whether a payor of record is a nonresident alien individual:

(A) If interest is paid outside the United States, the interest recipient must satisfy the documentary evidence standard provided in §1.6049-5(c) with respect to the payor of record; and

(B) If interest is paid within the United States, the interest recipient must secure from the payor of record a Form W-8 or a substantially similar statement signed by the payor under penalty of perjury as described in §1.1441-1(e)(1).

For purposes of this paragraph (d)(2)(ii), the place of payment is the place where the payor of record completes the acts necessary to effect payment. An amount paid by transfer to an account maintained by an interest recipient in the United States or by mail to a United States address is considered to be paid within the United States.

(3) *Reporting by cooperative housing corporations.*—For purposes of this section and §1.6050H-2, an amount received by a cooperative housing corporation from an individual tenant-stockholder that represents the tenant-stockholder's proportionate share of interest described in section 216(a)(2) is interest received on a qualified mortgage in the course of the cooperative housing corporation's trade or business. A cooperative housing corporation is an interest recipient with respect to each tenant-stockholder's proportionate share of interest and must report $600 or more of interest received from an individual tenant-stockholder. The terms "cooperative housing corporation," "tenant-stockholder," and "tenant-stockholder's proportionate share" are defined in section 216 and the regulations thereunder.

(e) *Amount of interest received on mortgage for calendar year.*—(1) *In general.*—For purposes of this section and §1.6050H-2, interest includes mortgage prepayment penalties and late charges other than late charges for a specific mortgage service. Interest also includes prepaid interest in the form of points (as defined in paragraph (f) of this section). Whether an interest recipient receives $600 or more of interest on a mortgage for a calendar year is determined on a mortgage-by-mortgage basis. An interest recipient need not aggregate interest received on all of the mortgages of a payor of record held by the interest recipient to determine whether the $600 threshold is met. Therefore, an interest recipient need not report interest of less than $600 received on a mortgage, even though it receives a total of $600 or more of interest on all of the mortgages of the payor of record for a calendar year.

(2) *Calendar year.*—(i) *In general.*—Except as otherwise provided in paragraph (e)(2)(ii) or (iii) of this section, the calendar year for which interest is received is the later of the calendar year in which the interest is received or the calendar year in which the interest properly accrues.

(ii) *De minimis rule.*—An interest recipient may treat interest received during the current calendar year which properly accrues by January 15 of the subsequent calendar year as interest received for the current calendar year. For example, if an interest recipient receives a monthly interest payment on December 31, 1988, which includes interest accruing for the period December 5, 1988, to January 5, 1989, the interest recipient may treat the entire interest payment as received for 1988. If a portion of an interest payment received in a current calendar year accrues after January 15 of the subsequent calendar year, an interest recipient must report as interest received for the current calendar year only the portion that properly accrues by the end of the current calendar year. For example, if an interest recipient receives a monthly payment that includes interest accruing for the period December 20, 1988, through January 20, 1989, the interest recipient may not report as interest received for 1988 any interest accruing after December 31, 1988. The interest recipient must report the interest accruing after December 31, 1988, as received for calendar year 1989.

(iii) *Applicability to points.*—Paragraphs (e)(2)(i) and (ii) of this section do not apply to prepaid interest in the form of points (as defined in paragraph (f) of this section). Points (as defined in paragraph (f) of this section) must be reported in the calendar year in which they are received.

(3) *Certain interest not received on mortgage.*—(i) *Interest received from seller on payor of record's mortgage.*—Interest received from a seller or a person related to a seller within the meaning of section 267(b) or section 707(b)(1) on a payor of record's mortgage is not interest received on a mortgage. For example, interest is not received on a mortgage if a real estate developer deposits an amount in escrow with an interest recipient and advises it to draw on the account to pay interest on a payor of record's mortgage (e.g., a buy-down mortgage). Similarly, interest is not received on a mortgage if an interest recipient receives a lump sum from a real estate developer for interest on a payor of record's mortgage.

(ii) *Interest received from governmental unit.*—Interest received from a governmental unit or an agency or instrumentality of a governmental unit is not interest received on a mortgage. For example, interest is not received on a mortgage if received as a housing assistance payment from the Department of Housing and Urban Development on a mortgage insured under section 235 of the National Housing Act (12 U.S.C. 1701-1715z (1982 & Supp. 1983)). Except as otherwise provided in paragraph (e)(1) and (2) of this section, interest received on a mortgage is only the excess of interest received on the mortgage over interest received from a governmental unit or an agency or instrumentality of a governmental unit.

(4) *Interest calculated under Rule of 78s method of accounting.*—An interest recipient permitted by Revenue Procedure 83-40, 1983-1 C.B. 774, (or other revenue procedure) to use the Rule of 78s method of accounting to calculate interest earned on a transaction may report as interest received on a mortgage interest earned on the transaction as calculated under the Rule of 78s method of accounting only if the interest recipient satisifies the notice requirement of §1.6050H-2(c).

(f) *Points treated as interest.*—(1) *General rule.*—Subject to the limitations of paragraph (f)(2) of this section, an amount is deemed to be points paid in respect of indebtedness incurred in connection with the purchase of the payor of record's principal residence (points) for purposes of this section and §1.6050H-2 to the extent that the amount—

(i) Is clearly designated on the Uniform Settlement Statement prescribed under the Real Estate Settlement Procedures Act of 1974, 12 U.S.C. 2601 et seq., (e.g., the Form HUD-1) as points incurred in connection with the indebtedness, for example as *loan origination fees* (including amounts so designated on Veterans Affairs (VA) and Federal Housing Administration (FHA) loans), *loan discount, discount points, or points;*

(ii) Is computed as a percentage of the stated principal amount of the indebtedness incurred by the payor of record;

(iii) Conforms to an established practice of charging points in the area in which the loan is issued and does not exceed the amount generally charged in the area;

(iv) Is paid in connection with the acquisition by the payor of record of a residence that is the principal residence of the payor of record and that secures the loan. For this purpose, the lender of record may rely on a signed written statement of the payor of record that states whether the proceeds of the loan are for the purchase of the mortgagor's principal residence; and

(v) Is paid directly by the payor of record.

(2) *Limitations.*—An amount is not points for purposes of this section to the extent that the amount is—

(i) Paid in connection with indebtedness incurred for the improvement of a principal residence;

(ii) Paid in connection with indebtedness incurred to purchase or improve a residence that is not the payor of record's principal residence, such as a second home, vacation property, investment property, or trade or business property;

(iii) Paid in connection with a home equity loan or a line of credit, even though the loan is secured by the payor of record's principal residence;

(iv) Paid in connection with a refinancing loan (except as provided by paragraph (f)(4) of this section), including a loan incurred to refinance indebtedness owed by the borrower under the terms of a land contract, a contract for deed, or similar forms of seller financing;

(v) Paid in lieu of amounts that ordinarily are stated separately on the Form HUD-1, such as appraisal fees, inspection fees, title fees, attorney fees, and property taxes; or

(vi) Paid in connection with the acquisition of a principal residence, to the extent that the amount is allocable to indebtedness in excess of the aggregate amount that may be treated as acquisition indebtedness under section 163(h)(3)(B)(ii).

(3) *Special rule.*—(i) *Amounts paid directly by payor of record.*—For purposes of this section, an amount is considered *paid directly* by the payor of record if it is—

(A) Provided by the payor of record from funds that have not been borrowed from the lender of record for this purpose as part of the overall transaction. The amount provided may include amounts designated as down payments, escrow deposits, earnest money applied at the closing, and other funds actually paid over by the payor of record at or before the time of closing; or

(B) Paid as points (within the meaning of this paragraph (f)) on behalf of the payor of record by the seller. For this purpose, an amount paid as points to an interest recipient by the seller on behalf of the payor of record is treated as paid to the payor of record and then paid directly by the payor of record to the interest recipient.

(ii) *Examples.*—The provisions of this paragraph (f) are illustrated by the following examples:

*Example 1. Financed payment of points.* Buyer purchases a principal residence for $100,000. There is a total of $7,000 in closing costs (exclusive of down payment) charged in connection with the sale. Of this amount, $3,000 is charged as points (within the meaning of paragraph (f) of this section). At closing, Buyer makes a down payment of $20,000 and provides unborrowed funds in the amount of $4,000 for the payment of various closing costs other than points. Buyer finances payment of the points by increasing the principal amount of the loan by $3,000. Seller makes no payments on Buyer's behalf. Because Buyer has provided at closing funds that have not been borrowed from the lender of record for this purpose in an amount at least equal to the amount charged as points in the transaction, the lender of record (or a qualified person) must report $3,000 as points in accordance with this section and §1.6050H-2.

*Example 2. Seller-paid points.* Buyer purchases a principal residence for $100,000. There is a total of $7,000 in closing costs (exclusive of down payment) charged in connection with the sale. Of this amount, $3,000 is charged as points (within the meaning of this paragraph (f)). Seller agrees to pay all closing costs on behalf of Buyer, including the amount charged as points. Accordingly, the amount paid by Seller as points is treated as paid directly by Buyer, and the lender of record (or a qualified person) must report the $3,000 as points in accordance with this section and §1.6050H-2.

(4) *Construction loans.*—(i) *In general.*—An amount paid in connection with indebtedness incurred to construct a residence, or to refinance indebtedness incurred to construct a residence, is deemed to be points for purposes of this section to the extent the amount—

(A) Is clearly designated on the loan documents as points incurred in connection with the indebtedness, for example, as *loan origination fees, loan discount, discount points, or points*;

(B) Is computed as a percentage of the stated principal amount of the indebtedness incurred by the payor of record;

(C) Conforms to an established practice of charging points in the area in which the loan is issued and does not exceed the amount generally charged in the area;

(D) Is paid in connection with indebtedness incurred by the payor of record to construct (or to refinance construction of) a residence that is to be used, when completed, as the principal residence of the payor of record;

(E) Is paid directly by the payor of record; and

(F) Is not allocable to indebtedness in excess of the aggregate amount that may be treated as acquisition indebtedness under section 163(h)(3)(B)(ii).

(ii) *Limitation on refinancing of construction loans.*—Amounts paid in connection with refinancing indebtedness incurred to construct a residence are not treated as points to the extent they are allocable to indebtedness that exceeds the indebtedness incurred to construct the residence.

(5) *Amounts paid to mortgage brokers.*—Amounts received directly or indirectly by a mortgage broker are treated as points under this paragraph (f) to the same extent the amounts would be so treated if they were paid to and retained by the lender of record, and must be reported by the lender of record in accordance with this section and §1.6050H-2.

(6) *Effect on deduction of points.*—This section and §1.6050H-2 address only the information reporting requirements of section 6050H and do not affect a payor of record's deduction for any amount in accordance with applicable provisions of the Internal Revenue Code.

(g) *Effective date.*—(1) *In general.*—Except as provided in paragraph (g)(2) of this section, this section is effective for mortgage interest received after December 31, 1987.

(2) *Points.*—The reporting requirements of this section do not apply to prepaid interest received in the form of points before January 1, 1995. In addition, the inclusion of points in the determination of interest under paragraph (e)(1) of this section applies only to transactions occurring after December 31, 1994. [Reg. §1.6050H-1.]

☐ *T.D. 8191*, 4-11-88. *Amended by T.D. 8571*, 12-7-94, *T.D. 8734*, 10-6-97 (T.D. 8804 delayed the effective date of T.D. 8734 from January 1, 1999, to January 1, 2000; T.D. 8856 further delayed the effective date of T.D. 8734 until January 1, 2001) *and T.D. 9849*, 3-11-2019.]

## [Reg. §1.6050H-2]

**§1.6050H-2. Time, form, and manner of reporting interest received on qualified mortgage.**—(a) *Requirement to file return.*—(1) *Form of return.*—An interest recipient must file a return required by §1.6050H-1(a) on Form 1098 (with Form 1096 as the transmittal form). An interest recipient may use forms containing provisions substantially similar to those in Forms 1098 and 1096 if it complies with applicable revenue procedures relating to substitute Forms 1098 and 1096. An interest recipient must file a separate return for each qualified mortgage for which it receives $600 or more of interest for a calendar year.

(2) *Information included on return.*—An interest recipient must include on Form 1098:

(i) The name, address, and taxpayer identification number (TIN) (as defined in section 7701(a)(41)) of the payor of record;

(ii) The name, address, and TIN of the interest recipient;

(iii) The amount of interest (other than points) required to be reported with respect to the qualified mortgage for the calendar year;

(iv) With respect to reimbursements of interest on a qualified mortgage (as discussed in paragraph (a)(3) of this section) made to the payor of record in the calendar year—

(A) Reimbursements aggregating $600 or more; and

(B) Reimbursements aggregating less than $600, but only if $600 or more of interest on the qualified mortgage is received in the calendar year from the payor of record;

(v) The amount of points paid directly by the payor of record (within the meaning of §1.6050H-1(f)(3)) required to be reported with respect to the qualified mortgage for the calendar year; and

(vi) Any other information required by Form 1098 or its instructions.

Section 1.6050H-1(e) contains rules to determine the amount of interest received on a mortgage for a calendar year.

(3) *Reimbursements of interest on a qualified mortgage.*—For purposes of paragraph (a)(2)(iv) of this section, a reimbursement of interest on a qualified mortgage is a reimbursement of an amount received in a prior year that was required to be reported for that prior year under paragraph (a)(2)(iii) of this section by any interest recipient. Only the interest recipient that makes the reimbursement is required to report the reimbursement under this section. Form 1098 and the statement furnished to the payor of record under paragraph (b) of this section must not include any amount that constitutes interest on the reimbursement paid to the payor of record. Rules relating to the requirement to report interest on a reimbursement are, in the case of a person carrying on the banking business (or a middleman, as defined in §1.6049-4(f)(4), of a person carrying on the banking business), provided in section 6049 and the regulations thereunder, and, for other persons, provided in section 6041 and the regulations thereunder. Reimbursements of interest on a qualified mortgage (as described in this section) made in 1993 and subsequent calendar years must be reported on Form 1098 and statements furnished to payors of record. Reimbursements made prior to 1993 are not required to be reported.

(4) *Time and place for filing return.*—An interest recipient must file a return required by this paragraph (a) on or before February 28 (March 31 if filed electronically) of the year following the calendar year for which it receives the mortgage interest. If no interest is required to be reported for the calendar year, but a reimbursement of interest on a qualified mortgage is required to be reported for the calendar year, then a return required by this paragraph (a) must be filed on or before February 28 (March 31 if filed electronically) of the year following the calendar year in which the reimbursement was made. An interest recipient must file the return required by paragraph (a) of this section with the IRS office designated in the instructions for Form 1098.

(5) *Use of magnetic media.*—An interest recipient must file the return required by paragraph (a) of this section on magnetic media only if required by section 6011(e) and the regulations thereunder. An interest recipient not required by section 6011(e) to file returns on magnetic media may request permission to do so. Section 301.6011-2 contains rules relating to the use of magnetic media. A failure to file on magnetic media when required constitutes a failure to file an information return under section 6721.

(b) *Requirement to furnish statement.*—(1) *In general.*—An interest recipient that must file a return under paragraph (a) of this section must furnish a statement to the payor of record.

(2) *Information included on statement.*—An interest recipient must include on the statement that it must furnish to a payor of record:

(i) The information required under paragraph (a)(2) of this section;

(ii) A legend that—

(A) Identifies the statement as important tax information that is being furnished to the IRS; and

(B) Notifies the payor of record that if the payor of record is required to file a return, a negligence penalty or other sanction may be imposed on the payor of record if the IRS determines that an underpayment of tax results because the payor of record overstated a deduction for this mortgage interest (if any) or understated income from this mortgage interest reimbursement (if any) on the payor of record's return;

(iii) A legend stating that the payor of record may be unable to deduct the full amount of mortgage interest reported on the statement; that limitations based on the cost and value of the property securing the mortgage may apply; and that the payor of record may only deduct mortgage interest to the extent it was incurred, actually paid by the payor of record, and not reimbursed by another person; and

(iv) With respect to any information required to be reported under paragraph (a)(2)(iv) of this section, an instruction providing that the amount of the reimbursement is not to be deducted and that the amount must be included in the gross income of the payor of record if the reimbursed interest was deducted by the payor of record in a prior year so as to reduce income tax.

(3) *Statement furnished pursuant to Federal mortgage program.*—An interest recipient that furnishes a statement to a payor of record under a Federal mortgage program will satisfy the requirement of paragraph (b)(1) of this section if the statement contains all the information and legends required by paragraph (b)(2) of this section and is furnished by the time and at the place required by paragraph (b)(6) of this section.

(4) *Copy of Form 1098 to payor of record.*—An interest recipient will satisfy the requirement of paragraph (b)(1) of this section by furnishing to a payor of record a copy of Form 1098 (or a substitute statement that complies with applicable revenue procedures) containing all the information filed with the Internal Revenue Service and all the legends required by paragraph (b)(2) of this section by the time and at the place required by paragraph (b)(6) of this section.

(5) *Furnishing statement with other information reports.*—An interest recipient may transmit the statement required by paragraph (b)(1) of this section to the payor of record with other information, including other information returns, as permitted by applicable revenue procedures.

(6) *Time and place for furnishing statement.*—An interest recipient must furnish a statement required by paragraph (b)(1) of this section to a payor of record on or before January 31 of the year following the calendar year for which it receives the mortgage interest. If no mortgage interest is required to be reported for the calendar year, but a reimbursement of interest on a qualified mortgage is required to be reported for the calendar year, then the statement required by paragraph (b)(1) of this section must be furnished on or before January 31 of the year following the calendar year in which the reimbursement was made. The interest recipient will be considered to have furnished

the statement to the payor of record if it mails the statement to the payor of record's last known address.

(c) *Notice requirement for use of Rule of 78's method of accounting.*—(1) *In general.*—An interest recipient seeking to report interest received on a mortgage under the Rule of 78s method of accounting as permitted under §1.6050H-1(e)(4) must notify the payor of record that the Rule of 78s method of accounting was used to calculate interest received on the mortgage and that the payor of record may not deduct as interest the amount calculated under the Rule of 78s method of accounting unless the payor of record properly uses that method to determine interest deductions. The notice must state that the payor of record may use the Rule of 78s method of accounting to determine interest paid for Federal income tax purposes only for a self-amortizing consumer loan requiring level payments at regular intervals (at least annually) over no longer than a five-year period, with no balloon payment at the end of the loan term, and only when the loan agreement provides for use of the Rule of 78s method of accounting to determine interest earned. See Rev. Proc. 83-40, 1983-1 C.B. 774; Rev. Rul. 83-84, 1983-1 C.B. 97.

(2) *Time and manner.*—An interest recipient must provide notice required by paragraph (c)(1) of this section to a payor of record on or with the statement required by paragraph (b) of this section. An interest recipient may provide notice on a separate paper or on the statement required by paragraph (b) of this section.

(d) *Reporting under designation agreement.*—(1) *In general.*—An interest recipient that receives or collects interest (including points) on a mortgage may designate a qualified person to satisfy the reporting requirements of paragraphs (a), (b), and (c) of this section. If a designated qualified person reports as permitted under this paragraph (d), it will satisfy the requirement of paragraph (a)(2)(ii) of this section by including on Form 1098 (and Form 1096) the name, address, and TIN of the designated qualified person.

(2) *Qualified person.*—A qualified person is either—

(i) A trade or business with respect to which the interest recipient is under common control within the meaning of §1.414(c)-2; or

(ii) A person who is named as the designee by the lender of record or by a qualified person (under paragraph (d)(2) of this section) in a designation agreement entered into in accordance with paragraph (d)(3) of this section, and who either was involved in the original loan transaction or is a subsequent purchaser of the loan.

(3) *Designation agreement.*—An interest recipient that designates a qualified person to satisfy the reporting requirements described in paragraphs (a), (b), and (c) of this section must make that designation in a written designation agreement. The designation agreement must identify the mortgage(s) and calendar years for which the designated qualified person must report, and must be signed by both the designator and designee. A designee may report an amount as having been paid directly by the payor of record (for purposes of paragraph (a)(2)(v) of this section) only if the designation agreement contains the designator's representation that it did not lend such amount to the payor of record as part of the overall transaction. The designator must retain a copy of the designation agreement for four years following the close of the calendar year in which the loan is made. The designation agreement need not be filed with the Internal Revenue Service.

(4) *Penalties.*—A designated qualified person is subject to any applicable penalties provided in part II of subchapter B of chapter 68 of the Internal Revenue Code as if it were an interest recipient. A designator is relieved from liability for applicable penalties by designating a qualified person under the provisions of paragraph (d)(3) of this section. Paragraph (e) of this section describes applicable penalties.

(e) *Penalty provisions.*—(1) *Returns and statements the due date for which (determined without regard for extensions) is after December 31, 1987, and before December 31, 1989.*—For purposes of this paragraph (e)(1) only, all references to sections of the Internal Revenue Code refer to sections of the Internal Revenue Code of 1986, as amended on or before December 31, 1987.

(i) *Failure to file return or to furnish statement.*—The section 6721 penalty applies to an interest recipient that fails to file a return required by paragraph (a) of this section with respect to a payor of record. The section 6722 penalty applies to an interest recipient that fails to furnish a statement required by paragraph (b) of this section to a payor of record.

(ii) *Failure to furnish TIN.*—The section 6676 penalty may apply to an interest recipient that fails to furnish the TIN of a payor of record on a return required by paragraph (a) of this section. The section 6676 penalty may apply to an interest recipient that fails to request and to obtain the TIN of a payor of record under paragraph (f) of this section.

(iii) *Failure to include correct information.*—The section 6723 penalty may apply to an interest recipient that fails to include correct information on a return required by paragraph (a) of this section or on a statement required by paragraph (b) of this section to be furnished to a payor of record.

(2) *Returns and statements the due date for which (determined without regard for extensions) is after December 31, 1989.*—(i) *Failure to file return or to furnish statement.*—The section 6721 penalty applies to an interest recipient that fails to file a return required by paragraph (a) of this section with respect to a payor of record. The section 6722 penalty applies to an interest recipient that fails to furnish a statement required by paragraph (b) of this section to a payor of record.

(ii) *Failure to furnish TIN.*—The section 6721 penalty may apply to an interest recipient that fails to furnish the TIN of a payor of record on a return required by paragraph (a) of this section. The section 6721 penalty may apply to an interest recipient that fails to request and to obtain the TIN of a payor of record under paragraph (f) of this section.

(iii) *Failure to include correct information.*—The section 6721 penalty may apply to an interest recipient that fails to include correct information on a return required by paragraph (a) of this section. The section 6722 penalty may apply to an interest recipient that fails to include correct information on a statement required by paragraph (b) of this section to be furnished to a payor record.

(f) *Requirement to request and to obtain TIN.*—(1) *In general.*—For obligations incurred after December 31, 1987, an interest recipient must make all reasonable efforts to obtain the TIN of a payor of record when the payor of record incurs the obligation. For example, an interest recipient may require a borrower to furnish a TIN during the mortgage approval or application process. If an interest recipient does not maintain the TIN of a payor of record on a mortgage, whenever incurred, it must request the TIN at least annually and must process responses properly and promptly.

(2) *Manner of requesting TIN.*—An interest recipient need not separately mail a request for a TIN. An interest recipient may include a request in its regular mailing of payment coupon booklets or annual statements. If an interest recipient makes no mailing to a payor of record during the year in which the payor of record incurs the obligation, it must request the TIN in a separate mailing. No particular form is required to request a TIN. Nevertheless, an interest recipient must make the request on a separate paper and must clearly notify a payor of record that the Internal Revenue Service requires the payor of record to furnish a TIN in order to verify any mortgage interest deduction. An interest recipient must notify a payor of record that failure to furnish a TIN subjects the payor of record to a $50 penalty imposed by the Internal Revenue Service. A request for a TIN made on Form W-9 satisfies the requirement of this paragraph (f)(2).

(g) *Effective date.*—(1) *In general.*—Except as provided in paragraph (g)(2) of this section, this section is effective for mortgage interest received after December 31, 1987.

(2) *Points.*—The reporting requirement of this section does not apply to prepaid interest in the form of points received before January 1, 1995. [Reg. § 1.6050H-2.]

☐ [T.D. 8191, 4-11-88. *Amended by T.D. 8507, 12-28-93; T.D. 8571, 12-7-94, T.D. 8895, 8-17-2000 and T.D. 9849, 3-11-2019.*]

[Reg. § 1.6050H-3]

**§ 1.6050H-3. Information reporting of mortgage insurance premiums.**—(a) *Information reporting requirements.*—Any person who, in the course of a trade or business, receives premiums, including prepaid premiums, for mortgage insurance (as described in paragraph (b) of this section) from any individual aggregating $600 or more for any calendar year, must make an information return setting forth the total amount received from that individual during the calendar year.

(b) *Scope.*—Paragraph (a) of this section applies to mortgage insurance provided by the Federal Housing Administration, Department of Veterans Affairs, or the Rural Housing Service (or their successor organizations), or to private mortgage insurance (as defined by section 2 of the Homeowners Protection Act of 1998 (12 U.S.C. 4901) as in effect on December 20, 2006). The rule stated in paragraph (a) of this section applies to the receipt of all payments of mortgage insurance premiums, by cash or financing, without regard to source.

(c) *Aggregation.*—Whether a person receives $600 or more of mortgage insurance premiums is determined on a mortgage-by-mortgage basis. A recipient need not aggregate mortgage insurance premiums received on all of the mortgages of an individual to determine whether the $600 threshold is met. Therefore, a recipient need not report mortgage insurance premiums of less than $600 received on a mortgage, even though it receives a total of $600 or more of mortgage insurance premiums on all of the mortgages for an individual for a calendar year.

(d) *Time, form, and manner of reporting.*—Mortgage insurance premiums required to be reported under paragraph (a) of this section must be reported on the Form 1098 or successor form that is filed pursuant to § 1.6050H-2(a) with respect to the mortgage of the individual who paid the mortgage insurance premiums. For the requirements for furnishing statements with respect to Forms 1098 filed with the Internal Revenue Service, see § 1.6050H-2(b).

(e) *Cross reference.*—For rules concerning the allocation of certain prepaid qualified mortgage insurance premiums, see § 1.163-11 of this chapter.

(f) *Limitation on the reporting of mortgage insurance premiums.*—This section applies to mortgage insurance premiums described in paragraph (b) of this section that are paid or accrued on or after January 1, 2013, and during periods to which section 163(h)(3)(E) applies. This section does not apply to any amounts of mortgage insurance premiums that are allocable to any periods to which section 163(h)(3)(E) does not apply.

(g) *Effective/applicability date.*—This section applies to mortgage insurance premiums received on or after January 1, 2013. For regulations applicable before May 5, 2012, see § 1.6050H-3T as contained in 26 CFR part 1 (revised as of April 1, 2012). [Reg. § 1.6050H-3.]

☐ [T.D. 9642, 11-26-2013.]

[Reg. § 1.6050I-0]

**§ 1.6050I-0. Table of contents.**—This section lists the major captions that appear in § § 1.6050I-1 and 1.6050I-2.

(e) Time, manner, and form of reporting.
(1) Time of reporting.
(2) Form of reporting.
(3) Manner of reporting.
(i) Where to file.
(ii) Verification.
(iii) Retention of returns.
(f) Requirement of furnishing statements.
(1) In general.
(2) Form of statement.
(3) When statement is to be furnished.
(g) Cross-reference to penalty provisions.
(1) Failure to file correct information return.
(2) Failure to furnish correct statement.
(3) Criminal penalties.

*§1.6050I-2. Returns relating to cash in excess of $10,000 received as bail by court clerks.*
(a) Reporting requirement.
(b) Meaning of terms.
(c) Time, form, and manner of reporting.
(1) Time of reporting.
(i) In general.
(ii) Multiple payments.
(2) Form of reporting.
(3) Manner of reporting.
(i) Where to file.
(ii) Verification of identity.
(d) Requirement to furnish statements.
(1) Information to Federal prosecutors.
(i) In general.
(ii) Form of statement.
(2) Information to payors of bail.
(i) In general.
(ii) Form of statement.
(iii) Aggregate amount.
(e) Cross-reference to penalty provisions.
(f) Effective date.
[Reg. §1.6050I-0.]

☐ [*T.D. 8652, 12-29-95. Amended by T.D. 8974, 12-28-2001.*]

**[Reg. §1.6050I-1]**

**§1.6050I-1. Returns relating to cash in excess of $10,000 received in a trade or business.**—(a) *Reporting requirement.*—(1) *Reportable transaction.*—(i) *In general.*—Any person(as defined in section 7701(a)(1)) who, in the course of a trade or business in which such person is engaged, receives cash in excess of $10,000 in 1 transaction (or 2 or more related transactions) shall, except as otherwise provided, make a return of information with respect to the receipt of cash.

(ii) *Certain financial transactions.*—Section 6050I of title 26 of the United States Code requires persons to report information about financial transactions to the Internal Revenue Service, and section 5331 of title 31 of the United States Code requires persons to report similar information about certain transactions to the Financial Crimes Enforcement Network. This information shall be reported on the same form as prescribed by the Secretary.

(2) *Cash received for the account of another.*—Cash in excess of $10,000 received by a person for the account of another must be reported under this section. Thus, for example, a person who collects delinquent accounts receivable for an automobile dealer must report with respect to the receipt of cash in excess of $10,000 from the collection of a particular account even though the proceeds of the collection are credited to the account of the automobile dealer (*i.e.,* where the rights to the proceeds from the account are retained by the automobile dealer and the collection is made on a fee-for-service basis).

(3) *Cash received by agents.*—(i) *General rule.*—Except as provided in paragraph (a)(3)(ii) of this section, a person who in the course of a trade or business acts as an agent (or in some other similar capacity) and receives cash in excess of $10,000 from a principal must report the receipt of cash under this section.

(ii) *Exception.*—An agent who receives cash from a principal and uses all of the cash within 15 days in a cash transaction (the "second cash transaction") which is reportable under section 6050 I or section 5312 of Title 31 of the United States Code and the regulations thereunder (31 CFR Part 103), and who discloses the name, address, and taxpayer identification number of the principal to the recipient in the second cash transaction need not report the initial

receipt of cash under this section. An agent will be deemed to have met the disclosure requirements of this paragraph (a)(3)(ii) if the agent discloses only the name of the principal and the agent knows that the recipient has the principal's address and taxpayer identification number.

(iii) *Example.*—The following example illustrates the application of the rules in paragraphs (a)(3)(i) and (ii) of this section:
*Example.* B, the principal, gives D, an attorney, $75,000 in cash to purchase real property on behalf of B. Within 15 days D purchases real property for cash from E, a real estate developer, and discloses to E, B's name, address, and taxpayer identification number. Because the transaction qualifies for the exception provided in paragraph (a)(3)(ii) of this section, D need not report with respect to the initial receipt of cash under this section. The exception does not apply, however, if D pays E by means other than cash, or effects the purchase more than 15 days following receipt of the cash from B, or fails to disclose B's name, address, and taxpayer identification number (assuming D does not know that E already has B's address and taxpayer identification number), or purchases the property from a person whose sale of the property is not in the course of that person's trade or business. In any such case, D is required to report the receipt of cash from B under this section.

(b) *Multiple payments.*—The receipt of multiple cash deposits or cash installment payments (or other similar payments or prepayments) on or after January 1, 1990, relating to a single transaction (or two or more related transactions), is reported as set forth in paragraphs (b)(1) through (b)(3) of this section.

(1) *Initial payment in excess of $10,000.*—If the initial payment exceeds $10,000, the recipient must report the initial payment within 15 days of its receipt.

(2) *Initial payment of $10,000 or less.*—If the initial payment does not exceed $10,000, the recipient must aggregate the initial payment and subsequent payments made within one year of the initial payment until the aggregate amount exceeds $10,000, and report with respect to the aggregate amount within 15 days after receiving the payment that causes the aggregate amount to exceed $10,000.

(3) *Subsequent payments.*—In addition to any other required report, a report must be made each time that previously unreportable payments made within a 12-month period with respect to a single transaction (or two or more related transactions), individually or in the aggregate, exceed $10,000. The report must be made within 15 days after receiving the payment in excess of $10,000 or the payment that causes the aggregate amount received in the 12-month period to exceed $10,000. (If more than one report would otherwise be required for multiple cash payments within a 15-day period that relate to a single transaction (or two or more related transactions), the recipient may make a single combined report with respect to the payments. The combined report must be made no later than the date by which the first of the separate reports would otherwise be required to be made.) A report with respect to payments of $10,000 or less that are reportable under this paragraph (b)(3) and are received after December 31, 1989, but before July 10, 1990, is due July 24, 1990.

(4) *Example.*—The following example illustrates the application of the rules in paragraphs (b)(1) through (b)(3) of this section:
*Example.* On January 10, 1991, M receives an initial cash payment of $11,000 with respect to a transaction. M receives subsequent cash payments with respect to the same transaction of $4,000 on February 15, 1991, $6,000 on March 20, 1991, and $12,000 on May 15, 1991. M must make a report with respect to the payment received on January 10, 1991, by January 25, 1991. M must also make a report with respect to the payments totalling $22,000 received from February 15, 1991, through May 15, 1991. This report must be made by May 30, 1991, that is, within 15 days of the date that the subsequent payments, all of which were received within a 12-month period, exceeded $10,000.

(c) *Meaning of terms.*—The following definitions apply for purposes of this section—

(1) *Cash.*—(i) *Amounts received prior to February 3, 1992.*—For amounts received prior to February 3, 1992, the term "cash" means the coin and currency of the United States or of any other country, which circulate in and are customarily used and accepted as money in the country in which issued.

(ii) *Amounts received on or after February 3, 1992.*—For amounts received on or after February 3, 1992, the term "cash" means—

(A) The coin and currency of the United States or of any other country, which circulate in and are customarily used and accepted as money in the country in which issued; and

(B) A cashier's check (by whatever name called, including "treasurer's check" and "bank check"), bank draft, traveler's check, or money order having a face amount of not more than $10,000—

*(1)* Received in a designated reporting transaction as defined in paragraph (c)(1)(iii) of this section (except as provided in paragraphs (c)(1)(iv), (v), and (vi) of this section), or

*(2)* Received in any transaction in which the recipient knows that such instrument is being used in an attempt to avoid the reporting of the transaction under section 6050 I and this section.

(iii) *Designated reporting transaction.*—A designated reporting transaction is a retail sale (or the receipt of funds by a broker or other intermediary in connection with a retail sale) of—

(A) A consumer durable,

(B) A collectible, or

(C) A travel or entertainment activity.

(iv) *Exception for certain loans.*—A cashier's check, bank draft, traveler's check, or money order received in a designated reporting transaction is not treated as cash pursuant to paragraph (c)(1)(ii)(B)(1) of this section if the instrument constitutes the proceeds of a loan from a bank (as that term is defined in 31 CFR part 103). The recipient may rely on a copy of the loan document, a written statement from the bank, or similar documentation (such as a written lien instruction from the issuer of the instrument) to substantiate that the instrument constitutes loan proceeds.

(v) *Exception for certain installment sales.*—A cashier's check, bank draft, traveler's check, or money order received in a designated reporting transaction is not treated as cash pursuant to paragraph (c)(1)(ii)(B)(1) of this section if the instrument is received in payment on a promissory note or an installment sales contract (including a lease that is considered to be a sale for Federal income tax purposes). However, the preceding sentence applies only if—

(A) Promissory notes or installment sales contracts with the same or substantially similar terms are used in the ordinary course of the recipient's trade or business in connection with sales to ultimate consumers; and

(B) The total amount of payments with respect to the sale that are received on or before the 60th day after the date of the sale does not exceed 50 percent of the purchase price of the sale.

(vi) *Exception for certain down payment plans.*—A cashier's check, bank draft, traveler's check, or money order received in a designated reporting transaction is not treated as cash pursuant to paragraph (c)(1)(ii)(B)(1) of this section if the instrument is received pursuant to a payment plan requiring one or more down payments and the payment of the balance of the purchase price by a date no later than the date of the sale (in the case of an item of travel or entertainment, a date no later than the earliest date that any item of travel or entertainment pertaining to the same trip or event is furnished). However, the preceding sentence applies only if—

(A) The recipient uses payment plans with the same or substantially similar terms in the ordinary course of its trade or business in connection with sales to ultimate consumers; and

(B) The instrument is received more than 60 days prior to the date of the sale (in the case of an item of travel or entertainment, the date on which the final payment is due).

(vii) *Examples.*—The following examples illustrate the definition of "cash" set forth in paragraphs (c)(1)(ii) through (vi) of this section.

*Example 1.* D, an individual, purchases gold coins from M, a coin dealer, for $13,200. D tenders to M in payment United States currency in the amount of $6,200 and a cashier's check in the face amount of $7,000 which D had purchased. Because the sale is a designated reporting transaction, the cashier's check is treated as cash for purposes of section 6050 I and this section. Therefore, because M has received more than $10,000 in cash with respect to the transaction, M must make the report required by section 6050 I and this section.

*Example 2.* E, an individual, purchases an automobile from Q, an automobile dealer, for $11,500. E tenders to Q in payment United States currency in the amount of $2,000 and a cashier's check payable to E and Q in the amount of $9,500. The cashier's check constitutes the proceeds of a loan from the bank issuing the check. The origin of the proceeds is evident from provisions inserted by the bank on the check that instruct the dealer to cause a lien to be placed on the vehicle as security for the loan. The sale of the automobile is a designated reporting transaction. However, under paragraph (c)(1)(iv) of this section, because E has furnished Q documentary information establishing that the cashier's check constitutes the proceeds of a loan from the bank issuing the check, the cashier's check is not treated as cash pursuant to paragraph (c)(1)(ii)(B)(1) of this section.

*Example 3.* F, an individual, purchases an item of jewelry from S, a retail jeweler, for $12,000. F gives S traveler's checks totalling $2,400 and pays the balance with a personal check payable to S in the amount of $9,600. Because the sale is a designated reporting transac-

tion, the traveler's checks are treated as cash for purposes of section 6050 I and this section. However, because the personal check is not treated as cash for purposes of section 6050 I and this section, S has not received more than $10,000 in cash in the transaction and no report is required to be filed under section 6050 I and this section.

*Example 4.* G, an individual, purchases a boat from T, a boat dealer, for $16,500. G pays T with a cashier's check payable to T in the amount of $16,500. The cashier's check is not treated as cash because the face amount of the check is more than $10,000. Thus, no report is required to be made by T under section 6050 I and this section.

*Example 5.* H, an individual, arranges with W, a travel agent, for the chartering of a passenger aircraft to transport a group of individuals to a sports event in another city. H also arranges with W for hotel accommodations for the group and for admission tickets to the sports event. In payment, H tenders to W money orders which H had previously purchased. The total amount of the money orders, none of which individually exceeds $10,000 in face amount, exceeds $10,000. Because the transaction is a designated reporting transaction, the money orders are treated as cash for purposes of section 6050 I and this section. Therefore, because W has received more than $10,000 in cash with respect to the transaction, W must make the report required by section 6050 I and this section.

(2) *Consumer durable.*—The term "consumer durable" means an item of tangible personal property of a type that is suitable under ordinary usage for personal consumption or use, that can reasonably be expected to be useful for at least 1 year under ordinary usage, and that has a sales price of more than $10,000. Thus, for example, a $20,000 automobile is a consumer durable (whether or not it is sold for business use), but a $20,000 dump truck or a $20,000 factory machine is not.

(3) *Collectible.*—The term "collectible" means an item described in paragraphs (A) through (D) of section 408(m)(2) (determined without regard to section 408(m)(3)).

(4) *Travel or entertainment activity.*—The term "travel or entertainment activity" means an item of travel or entertainment (within the meaning of §1.274-2(b)(1)) pertaining to a single trip or event where the aggregate sales price of the item and all other items pertaining to the same trip or event that are sold in the same transaction (or related transactions) exceeds $10,000.

(5) *Retail sale.*—The term "retail sale" means any sale (whether for resale or for any other purpose) made in the course of a trade or business if that trade or business principally consists of making sales to ultimate consumers.

(6) *Trade or business.*—The term "trade or business" has the same meaning as under section 162 of the Internal Revenue Code of 1954.

(7) *Transaction.*—(i) The term "transaction" means the underlying event precipitating the payer's transfer of cash to the recipient. Transactions include (but are not limited to) a sale of goods or services; a sale of real property; a sale of intangible property; a rental of real or personal property; an exchange of cash for other cash; the establishment or maintenance of or contribution to a custodial, trust, or escrow arrangement; a payment of a preexisting debt; a conversion of cash to a negotiable instrument; a reimbursement for expenses paid; or the making or repayment of a loan. A transaction may not be divided into multiple transactions in order to avoid reporting under this section.

(ii) The term "related transactions" means any transaction conducted between a payer (or its agent) and a recipient of cash in a 24-hour period. Additionally, transactions conducted between a payer (or its agent) and a cash recipient during a period of more than 24 hours are related if the recipient knows or has reason to know that each transaction is one of a series of connected transactions.

(iii) The following examples illustrate the definition of paragraphs (c)(7)(i) and (ii).

*Example (1).* A person has a tacit agreement with a gold dealer to purchase $36,000 in gold bullion. The $36,000 purchase represents a single transaction under paragraph (c)(7)(i) of this section and the reporting requirements of this section cannot be avoided by recasting the single sales transaction into 4 separate $9,000 sales transactions.

*Example (2).* An attorney agrees to represent a client in a criminal case with the attorney's fee to be determined on an hourly basis. In the first month in which the attorney represents the client, the bill for the attorney's services comes to $8,000 which the client pays in cash. In the second month in which the attorney represents the client, the bill for the attorney's services comes to $4,000, which the client again pays in cash. The aggregate amount of cash paid ($12,000) relates to a single transaction as defined in paragraph (c)(7)(i) of this section, the sale of legal services relating to the criminal case, and the receipt of cash must be reported under this section.

*Example (3).* A person intends to contribute a total of $45,000 to a trust fund, and the trustee of the fund knows or has reason to know of that intention. The $45,000 contribution is a single transaction under paragraph (c)(7)(i) of this section and the reporting requirement of this section cannot be avoided by the grantor's making five separate $9,000 cash contributions to a single fund or by making five $9,000 cash contributions to five separate funds administered by a common trustee.

*Example (4).* K, an individual, attends a one day auction and purchases for cash two items, at a cost of $9,240 and $1,732.50 respectively (tax and buyer's premium included). Because the transactions are related transactions as defined in paragraph (c)(7)(ii) of this section, the auction house is required to report the aggregate amount of cash received from the related sales ($10,972.50), even though the auction house accounts separately on its books for each item sold and presents the purchaser with separate bills for each item purchased.

*Example (5).* F, a coin dealer, sells for cash $9,000 worth of gold coins to an individual on three successive days. Under paragraph (c)(7)(ii) of this section the three $9,000 transactions are related transactions aggregating $27,000 if F knows, or has reason to know, that each transaction is one of a series of connected transactions.

(8) *Recipient.*—(i) The term "recipient" means the person receiving the cash. Except as provided in paragraph (c)(8)(ii) of this section, each store, division, branch, department, headquarters, or office ("branch") (regardless of physical location) comprising a portion of a person's trade or business shall for purposes of this section be deemed a separate recipient.

(ii) A branch that receives cash payments will not be deemed a separate recipient if the branch (or a central unit linking such branch with other branches) would in the ordinary course of business have reason to know the identity of payers making cash payments to other branches of such person.

(iii) *Examples.*—The following examples illustrate the application of the rules in paragraphs (c)(8)(i) and (ii) of this section:

*Example (1).* N, an individual, purchases regulated futures contracts at a cost of $7,500 and $5,000, respectively, through two different branches of Commodities Broker X on the same day. N pays for each purchase with cash. Each branch of Commodities Broker X transmits the sales information regarding each of N's purchases to a central unit of Commodities Broker X (which settles the transactions against N's account). Under paragraph (c)(8)(ii) of this section the separate branches of Commodities Broker X are not deemed to be separate recipients; therefore, Commodities Broker X must report with respect to the two related regulated futures contracts sales in accordance with this section.

*Example (2).* P, a corporation, owns and operates a racetrack. P's racetrack contains 100 betting windows at which pari-mutuel wagers may be made. R, an individual, places cash wagers of $3,000 each at five separate betting windows. Assuming that in the ordinary course of business each betting window (or a central unit linking windows) does not have reason to know the identity of persons making wagers at other betting windows, each betting window would be deemed to be a separate cash recipient under paragraph (c)(8)(i) of this section. As no individual recipient received cash in excess of $10,000, no report need be made by P under this section.

(d) *Exceptions to the reporting requirements of section 6050I.*—(1) *Receipt of cash by certain financial institutions.*—A financial institution as defined in subparagraphs (A), (B), (C), (D), (E), (F), (G), (J), (K), (R), and (S) of section 5312(a)(2) of Title 31, United States Code is not required to report the receipt of cash exceeding $10,000 under section 6050 I.

(2) *Receipt of cash by certain casinos having gross annual gaming revenue in excess of $1,000,000.*—(i) *In general.*—If a casino receives cash in excess of $10,000 and is required to report the receipt of such cash directly to the Treasury Department under 31 CFR 103.22(a)(2) and 103.25 and is subject to the recordkeeping requirements of 31 CFR 103.36, then the casino is not required to make a return with respect to the receipt of such cash under section 6050 I and these regulations.

(ii) *Casinos exempt under 31 CFR 103.45(c).*—Under the authority of section 6050 I(c)(1)(A), the Secretary may exempt from the reporting requirements of section 6050 I casinos with gross annual gaming revenue in excess of $1,000,000 that are exempt under 31 CFR 103.45(c) from reporting certain cash transactions to the Treasury Department under 31 CFR 103.22(a)(2) and 103.25. The determination whether a casino which is granted an exemption under 31 CFR section 103.45(c) will be required to report under section 6050 I will be made on a case by case basis, concurrently with the granting of such an exemption.

(iii) *Reporting of cash received in a nongaming business.*—Nongaming businesses (such as shops, restaurants, entertainment, and hotels) at casino hotels and resorts are separate trades or businesses in which the receipt of cash in excess of $10,000 is reportable under section 6050 I and these regulations. Thus, a casino exempt under paragraph (d)(2)(i) or (ii) of this section must report with respect to cash in excess of $10,000 received in its nongaming businesses.

(iv) *Example.*—The following example illustrates the application of the rules in paragraphs (d)(2)(i) and (iii) of this section:

*Example.* A and B are casinos having gross annual gaming revenue in excess of $1,000,000. C is a casino with gross annual gaming revenue of less than $1,000,000. Casino A receives $15,000 in cash from a customer with respect to a gaming transaction which the casino reports to the Treasury Department under 31 CFR 103.22(a)(2) and 103.25. Casino B receives $15,000 in cash from a customer in payment for accommodations provided to that customer at Casino B's hotel. Casino C receives $15,000 in cash from a customer with respect to a gaming transaction. Casino A is not required to report the transaction under section 6050 I or these regulations because the exception for certain casinos provided in paragraph (d)(2)(i) ("the casino exception") applies. Casino B is required to report under section 6050 I and these regulations because the casino exception does not apply to the receipt of cash from a nongaming activity. Casino C is required to report under section 6050 I and these regulations because the casino exception does not apply to casinos having gross annual gaming revenue of $1,000,000 or less which do not have to report to the Treasury Department under 31 CFR 103.22(a)(2) and 103.25.

(3) *Receipt of cash not in the course of the recipient's trade or business.*—The receipt of cash in excess of $10,000 by a person other than in the course of the person's trade or business is not reportable under section 6050 I. Thus, for example, F, an individual in the trade or business of selling real estate, sells a motorboat for $12,000, the purchase price of which is paid in cash. F did not use the motorboat in any trade or business in which F was engaged. F is not required to report under section 6050 I or these regulations because the exception provided in this paragraph (d)(3) applies.

(4) *Receipt is made with respect to a foreign cash transaction.*—(i) *In general.*—Generally, there is no requirement to report with respect to a cash transaction if the entire transaction occurs outside the United States (the fifty states and the District of Columbia). An entire transaction consists of both the transaction as defined in paragraph (c)(7)(i) of this section and the receipt of cash by the recipient. If, however, any part of an entire transaction occurs in the Commonwealth of Puerto Rico or a possession or territory of the United States and the recipient of cash in that transaction is subject to the general jurisdiction of the Internal Revenue Service under Title 26 of the United States Code, the recipient is required to report the transaction under this section.

(ii) *Example.*—The following example illustrates the application of the rules in paragraph (d)(4)(i) of this section:

*Example.* W, an individual engaged in the trade or business of selling aircraft, reaches an agreement to sell an airplane to a U.S. citizen living in Mexico. The agreement, no portion of which is formulated in the United States, calls for a purchase price of $125,000 and requires delivery of and payment for the airplane to be made in Mexico. Upon delivery of the airplane in Mexico, W receives $125,000 in cash. W is not required to report under section 6050 I or these regulations because the exception provided in paragraph (d)(4)(i) of this section ("foreign transaction exception") applies. If, however, any part of the agreement to sell has been formulated in the United States, the foreign transaction exception would not apply and W would be required to report the receipt of cash under section 6050 I and these regulations.

(e) *Time, manner, and form of reporting.*—(1) *Time of reporting.*—The reports required by this section must be filed with the Internal Revenue Service by the 15th day after the date the cash is received. However, in the case of multiple payments relating to a single transaction (or two or more related transactions), see paragraph (b) of this section.

(2) *Form of reporting.*—A report required by paragraph (a) of this section must be made on Form 8300. A return of information made in compliance with this paragraph must contain the name, address, and taxpayer identification number of the person from whom the cash was received; the name, address, and taxpayer identification number of the person on whose behalf the transaction was conducted (if the recipient knows or has reason to know that the person from whom the cash was received conducted the transaction as an agent for another person); the amount of cash received; the date and nature of the transaction; and any other information required by Form 8300.

Form 8300 can be obtained from any Internal Revenue Service Forms Distribution Center.

(3) *Manner of reporting.*—(i) *Where to file.*—A person making a return of information under this section must file Form 8300 by mailing it to the address shown in the instructions to the form.

(ii) *Verification.*—A person making a return of information under this section must verify the identity of the person from whom the reportable cash is received. Verification of the identity of a person who purports to be an alien must be made by examination of such person's passport, alien identification card, or other official document evidencing nationality or residence. Verification of the identity of any other person may be made by examination of a document normally acceptable as a means of identification when cashing or accepting checks (for example, a driver's license or a credit card). In addition, a return will be considered incomplete if the person required to make a return knows (or has reason to know) that an agent is conducting the transaction for a principal, and the return does not identify both the principal and the agent.

(iii) *Retention of returns.*—A person required to make an information return under this section must keep a copy of each return filed for five years from the date of filing.

(f) *Requirement of furnishing statements.*—(1) *In general.*—Any person required to make an information return under this section must furnish a single, annual, written statement to each person whose name is set forth in a return ("identified person") filed with the Internal Revenue Service.

(2) *Form of statement.*—The statement required by the preceding paragraph need not follow any particular format, but it must contain the following information:

(i) The name and address of the person making the return;

(ii) The aggregate amount of reportable cash received by the person who made the information return required by this section during the calendar year in all cash transactions relating to the identified person; and

(iii) A legend stating that the information contained in the statement is being reported to the Internal Revenue Service.

(3) *When statement is to be furnished.*—Statements required under this paragraph (f) must be furnished to an identified person on or before January 31 of the year following the calendar year in which the cash is received. A statement shall be considered to be furnished to an identified person if it is mailed to the identified person at the identified person's last known address.

(g) *Cross-reference to penalty provisions.*—(1) *Failure to file correct information return.*—See section 6721 for civil penalties relating to the failure to file a correct return under section 6050 I(a) and paragraph (a) of this section.

(2) *Failure to furnish correct statement.*—See section 6722 for civil penalties relating to the failure to furnish a correct statement to identified persons under section 6050 I(e) and paragraph (f) of this section.

(3) *Criminal penalties.*—Any person who willfully fails to make a return or makes a false return under section 6050 I and this section may be subject to criminal prosecution. [Reg. §1.6050I-1.]

☐ [*T.D. 8098, 9-3-86. Amended by T.D. 8373, 11-14-91; T.D. 8479, 6-18-93 and T.D. 8974, 12-28-2001.*]

### [Reg. §1.6050I-2]

**§1.6050I-2. Returns relating to cash in excess of $10,000 received as bail by court clerks.**—(a) *Reporting requirement.*—Any clerk of a Federal or State court who receives more than $10,000 in cash as bail for any individual charged with a specified criminal offense must make a return of information with respect to that cash receipt. For purposes of this section, a clerk is the clerk's office or the office, department, division, branch, or unit of the court that is authorized to receive bail. If someone other than a clerk receives bail on behalf of a clerk, the clerk is treated as receiving the bail for purposes of this paragraph (a).

(b) *Meaning of terms.*—The following definitions apply for purposes of this section—

*Cash means*—

(1) The coin and currency of the United States, or of any other country, that circulate in and are customarily used and accepted as money in the country in which issued; and

(2) A cashier's check (by whatever name called, including treasurer's check and bank check), bank draft, traveler's check, or money order having a face amount of not more than $10,000.

*Specified criminal offense means*—

(1) A Federal criminal offense involving a controlled substance (as defined in section 802 of title 21 of the United States Code), provided the offense is described in Part D of Subchapter I or Subchapter II of title 21 of the United States Code;

(2) Racketeering (as defined in section 1951, 1952, or 1955 of title 18 of the United States Code);

(3) Money laundering (as defined in section 1956 or 1957 of title 18 of the United States Code); and

(4) Any State criminal offense substantially similar to an offense described in this paragraph (b).

(c) *Time, form, and manner of reporting.*—(1) Time of reporting

(i) In general.—The information return required by this section must be filed with the Internal Revenue Service by the 15th day after the date the cash bail is received.

(ii) *Multiple payments.*—If multiple payments are made to satisfy bail reportable under this section and the initial payment does not exceed $10,000, the initial payment and subsequent payments must be aggregated and the information return required by this section must be filed with the Internal Revenue Service by the 15th day after receipt of the payment that causes the aggregate amount to exceed $10,000. However, if payments are made to satisfy separate bail requirements, no aggregation is required. Thus, if in Month 1 a clerk receives $6,000 in bail for an individual charged with a specified criminal offense and later, in Month 2, receives $7,000 in bail for that same individual charged with another specified criminal offense, no aggregation is required.

(2) *Form of reporting.*—The return of information required by paragraph (a) of this section must be made on Form 8300 and must contain the following information—

(i) The name, address, and taxpayer identification number (TIN) of the individual charged with the specified criminal offense;

(ii) The name, address, and TIN of each person posting the bail (payor of bail), other than a person posting bail who is licensed as a bail bondsman in the jurisdiction in which the bail is received;

(iii) The amount of cash received;

(iv) The date the cash was received; and

(v) Any other information required by Form 8300 or its instructions.

(3) *Manner of reporting.*—(i) *Where to file.*—Returns required by this section must be filed with the Internal Revenue Service office designated in the instructions for Form 8300. A copy of the information return required to be filed under this section must be retained for five years from the date of filing.

(ii) *Verification of identity.*—A clerk required to make an information return under this section must, in accordance with §1.6050I-1(e)(3)(ii), verify the identity of each payor of bail listed in the return.

(d) *Requirement to furnish statements.*—(1) *Information to Federal prosecutors.*—(i) *In general.*—A clerk required to make an information return under this section must furnish a written statement to the United States Attorney for the jurisdiction in which the individual charged with the specified crime resides and the United States Attorney for the jurisdiction in which the specified criminal offense occurred (applicable United States Attorney(s)). The written statement must be filed with the applicable United States Attorney(s) by the 15th day after the date the cash bail is received.

(ii) *Form of statement.*—The written statement must include the information required by paragraph (c)(2) of this section. The requirement of this paragraph (d)(1)(ii) will be satisfied if the clerk provides to the applicable United States Attorney(s) a copy of the Form 8300 that is filed with the Internal Revenue Service pursuant to this section.

(2) *Information to payors of bail.*—(i) *In general.*—A clerk required to make an information return under this section must furnish a written statement to each payor of bail whose name is set forth in a return required by this section. A statement required under this paragraph (d)(2) must be furnished to a payor of bail on or before January 31 of the year following the calendar year in which the cash is received. A statement will be considered furnished to a payor of bail if it is mailed to the payor's last known address.

(ii) *Form of statement.*—The statement required by this paragraph (d)(2) need not follow any particular format, but must contain the following information—

(A) The name and address of the clerk's office making the return;

(B) The aggregate amount of reportable cash received during the calendar year by the clerk who made the information return required by this section in all cash transactions relating to the payor of bail; and

(C) A legend stating that the information contained in the statement has been reported to the Internal Revenue Service and the applicable United States Attorney(s).

(iii) *Aggregate amount.*—The requirement of furnishing the aggregate amount in paragraph (d)(2)(ii)(B) of this section will be satisfied if the clerk provides to the payor of bail either a single written statement listing the aggregate amount, or a copy of each Form 8300 relating to that payor of bail.

(e) *Cross-reference to penalty provisions.*—See sections 6721 through 6724 for penalties relating to the failure to comply with the provisions of this section.

(f) *Effective date.*—This section applies to cash received by court clerks on or after February 13, 1995. [Reg. §1.6050I-2.]

☐ [T.D. 8652, 12-29-95.]

### [Reg. §1.6050J-1T]

**§1.6050J-1T. Questions and answers concerning information returns relating to foreclosures and abandonments of security (Temporary).**—The following questions and answers relate to the requirement of reporting foreclosures and abandonments of security under section 6050J of the Internal Revenue Code of 1954, as added by section 148 of the Tax Reform Act of 1984 (98 Stat. 687).

*Requirement of reporting*

*In general*

Q-1. What does section 6050J provide with respect to the reporting of acquisitions and abandonments of property that secures indebtedness?

A-1. Section 6050J provides that an information return must be made by any person who, in connection with a trade or business conducted by the person (except as provided in A-13), lends money and, in full or partial satisfaction of the debt, acquires an interest in any property that is security for the debt, or has reason to know that the property has been abandoned. For purposes of these questions and answers, a person who lends money in connection with a trade or business is referred to as a "lender".

*Trade or business requirement*

Q-2. Must a person be in the trade or business of lending money in order to be subject to the reporting requirement of this section?

A-2. No. A person does not have to be in the trade or business of lending money to be subject to this reporting requirement. Thus, if L sells automobiles and lends money to B to enable B to purchase an automobile from L for use in B's trade or business, and that automobile is security for the loan, L would be subject to this reporting requirement. Similarly, if P promotes interests in an oil well, and lends money to I to enable I to invest in the oil well which is security for the loan, P would be subject to this reporting requirement.

Q-3. How does the reporting requirement apply in the case of pools, fixed investment trusts, or other similar arrangements through which undivided beneficial interests or participations in indebtedness are offered?

A-3. In these cases, the owners of the undivided beneficial interests or participations are not subject to this reporting requirement. Instead, the trustee, record owner, or person acting in a similar capacity is treated as the lender for purposes of this reporting requirement and is the party required to report. For purposes of both section 6050J and the applicable penalty provisions, only one return and one statement must be filed with respect to each loan or other evidence of indebtedness. For situations when more than one return or statement must be filed, see A-29, A-31, and A-41. The trustee, record owner, or person acting in a similar capacity, rather than the owners of beneficial interests or participations, is subject to the applicable penalty provisions (see A-43).

Q-4. How does the reporting requirement apply in the case of corporate, tax-exempt, or other bond issues?

A-4. In these cases, the owners or holders of a bond issue are not required to report. Instead, the trustee or person acting in a similar capacity is treated as the lender for purposes of this reporting requirement and is the party required to report. For purposes of both section 6050J and the applicable penalty provisions, only one return and one statement must be filed with respect to a bond issue. For situations when more than one return or statement must be filed, see A-29, A-31, and A-41. The trustee or person acting in a similar capacity, rather than the owners or holders of a bond issue, is subject to the applicable penalty provisions (see A-43).

*Property subject to reporting*

Q-5. Does the reporting requirement apply to all types of property securing indebtedness?

A-5. No. The reporting requirement does not apply to any loan made to an individual and secured by an interest in tangible personal property which is neither held for investment nor used in a trade or business. For rules governing when the reporting requirement applies to tangible personal property of a type ordinarily used for personal purposes, see A-8.

Q-6. Does the reporting requirement apply when property securing indebtedness is held both for personal use and for use in a trade or business?

A-6. Yes. The reporting requirement applies when property securing indebtedness is held both for personal use and for use in a trade or business. Similarly, the reporting requirement applies when the borrower holds such property both for personal use and for investment purposes.

Q-7. Does the reporting requirement apply to indebtedness secured by a personal residence?

A-7. Yes. A lender is subject to the reporting requirement if the property that is security for the loan is real property, including a personal residence, whether or not held for investment or used in a trade or business.

Q-8. In the case of a loan made to an individual and secured by personal property of a type that is ordinarily used for personal purposes, how does a lender know whether such property is used in a trade or business or held for investment purposes?

A-8. In the case of a loan made to an individual and secured by personal property of a type that is ordinarily used for personal purposes, such as an automobile, computer, or boat, the lender is subject to the reporting requirement if the lender knows that the property will be used in a trade or business held for investment purposes. For this purpose, a lender knows information if the information is included on the books and records of the lender or its agents pertaining to the loan, or is known by the lender or agent's officers, partners, principals or employees, but only if such information was acquired in the course of their ordinary business activities on behalf of the lender. For example, if a borrower indicates on the loan agreement or disclosure statement that the borrower intends to use the property securing the loan in the borrower's trade or business, the lender is subject to this reporting requirement. Similarly, the borrower notifies the lender that the borrower intends to convert the property from personal use to use in a trade or business, the lender is subject to the reporting requirement.

Q-9. If a lender maintains a system under which the lender classifies loans according to the use of property that secures the loan (such as use in a trade or business or personal use), may the lender rely on this system in determining whether the reporting requirement applies?

A-9. Yes. A lender may rely on the classification system to determine whether the reporting requirement applies, provided that the classification system is designed and reasonably maintained to ensure accuracy in identifying the use of property.

*Acquisition of an interest*

Q-10. For purposes of the reporting requirement, when is a lender treated as acquiring an interest in property that is security for indebtedness?

A-10. In general, an interest in property is acquired on the earlier of the date title is transferred to the lender or the date possession and the burdens and benefits of ownership are transferred to the lender. If State or other applicable law provides for an objection period within which the borrower and other appropriate parties may object to the lender's proposal to retain the property in satisfaction of the indebtedness, a lender is treated as acquiring an interest in the property on the date this objection period expires. If the lender purchases the property at a sale held to satisfy the indebtedness, such as at a foreclosure or execution sale, the lender is treated as acquiring an interest in the property on the later of the date of the sale or the date the borrower's right of redemption, if any, expires. See A-15 for rules governing reporting when a party other than the lender acquires property securing indebtedness at a foreclosure, execution or similar sale.

Q-11. If a lender takes possession of property that is security for a loan for a limited purpose, such as completing construction on or improvement to the property, is the lender treated as having acquired an interest in the property at that point?

A-11. No. The lender in these circumstances is not treated as acquiring an interest in the property. However, the lender must report if he later acquires an interest in the property in full or partial satisfaction of the indebtedness (see A-10 or A-15).

*Indirect Acquisition*

Q-12. If a lender acquires an interest in a partnership, trust, or other entity in full or partial satisfaction of a loan that is secured by the assets or property owned by the partnership, trust, or other entity, is the lender treated as acquiring an interest in the property securing the loan?

A-12. Yes. A lender in this case acquires an interest in the underlying assets or property and the reporting requirements of this section apply to the acquisition of that interest in a partnership, trust, or other entity.

*Treatment of governmental units*

Q-13. How does the reporting requirement apply to a governmental unit?

A-13. A governmental unit (or any agency or instrumentality thereof) which lends money secured by property is subject to the reporting requirement without regard to the requirement that the money be lent in connection with a trade or business. A governmental unit (or any agency or instrumentality thereof) subject to the reporting requirement must designate an officer or employee to make the return. The officer or employee appropriately designated must make the return in the form and manner prescribed by this section.

*Notification of sale under section 7425(b)*

Q-14. Does a return filed as required under this section constitute a notification of sale under section 7425(b)?

A-14. No. A return filed under this section is not considered a notification of sale under section 7425(b).

*Sale to third party*

Q-15. If a party other than the lender purchases property securing a loan at a foreclosure, execution, or similar sale, must the lender report under this section?

A-15. Yes. The lender must report if a party other than the lender purchases property securing the lender's loan at a foreclosure, execution, or similar sale. If the proceeds of that sale are applied to satisfy all or any portion of the lender's loan, the lender must treat the property as having been abandoned. The lender will be treated as having reason to know that the property has been abandoned as of the date of the sale (see A-19). If no proceeds of such a sale are made available to satisfy any portion of the lender's loan but the lender's security interest foreclosed upon is terminated, reduced, or otherwise impaired by reason of the sale, the lender will be treated as having reason to know that the property has been abandoned as of the date of the sale (see A-19).

*Treatment of foreign borrowers*

Q-16. How does the reporting requirement apply in the case of foreign borrowers where the property securing the loan is located outside the United States?

A-16. No reporting is required where both of the following requirements are met: (a) the property securing the loan is located outside the United States, and (b) at any time before the lender is required to report, the borrower furnishes the lender with a statement, signed upon penalty of perjury, that he is an exempt foreign person (unless an employee or other agent of the lender who is responsible for receiving or reviewing these statements has actual knowledge that the statement is incorrect). For purposes of this section, the borrower is an exempt foreign person if he:

(1) Is not a citizen of the United States, a resident of the United States, a person treated as a resident of the United States by reason of an election under section 6013(g) or (h) or a United States corporation or other United States entity;

(2) Is not subject to the provisions of section 877; and

(3) At the time the statement is furnished, is not, or reasonably expects not to be, engaged in a trade or business in the United States during the current year in connection with the loan or property securing the loan.

If, after providing the statement, the borrower ceases to be an exempt foreign person, he must so notify the lender in writing within 30 days of this change in status. If the lender is so notified, this exemption from the reporting requirement no longer applies.

*Abandonments*

Q-17. For purposes of this reporting requirement, when has an abandonment occurred?

A-17. An abandonment has occurred when the objective facts and circumstances indicate that the borrower intended to and has permanently discarded the property from use.

Q-18. Does the fact that a lender knows or has reason to know of an abandonment of property securing a loan mean that the borrower is entitled to an abandonment loss?

A-18. No. The definition of an abandonment of property securing a loan in A-17 applies only for purposes of this reporting requirement and is not intended to apply for other purposes, such as determining whether a borrower would be entitled to an abandonment loss.

Q-19. Under what circumstances will a lender be considered to have reason to know that property which is security for a loan has been abandoned?

A-19. Whether a lender has reason to know that property which is security for a loan has been abandoned is to be determined with reference to all the facts and circumstances concerning the status of the property. When the lender in the ordinary course of business becomes aware or should become aware of circumstances indicating that the property has been abandoned, the lender will be deemed to know all the information that would have been discovered through a reasonable inquiry. For example, if a borrower has failed (without adequate explanation) to make payments on the loan for a substantial period, the lender must make a reasonable inquiry to determine whether there has been an abandonment. If a reasonable inquiry would reveal objective facts and circumstances indicating that the borrower intended to and has permanently discarded the property from use, then the lender has reason to know that the property has been abandoned. If a lender knows or has reason to know that the property has been abandoned and reasonably expects to commence foreclosure, execution sale, or similar proceedings, see A-20.

Q-20. If a lender has reason to know that property that is security for a loan has been abandoned and reasonably expects to commence within three months foreclosure, execution sale, or similar proceedings, is reporting of the abandonment required?

A-20. In these circumstances, the lender need not report as of the date he knows or has reason to know that the property has been abandoned. Instead, the lender must report as of the date he acquires an interest in the property or a third party purchases the property at a foreclosure, execution or similar sale (see A-10 and A-15). In any other case, the lender must report as of the date the lender knows or has reason to know that the property has been abandoned (see A-18).

Q-21. If a lender has reason to know that property that is security for a loan has been abandoned and reasonably expects to commence within three months foreclosure, execution·sale or similar proceedings but in fact does not commence such proceedings within the three month period, must the lender report?

A-21. Yes. In these circumstances, the lender's obligation to report the abandonment arises at the close of the three month period. For example, if on December 31, 1985, a lender first has reason to know that property securing his loan has been abandoned and reasonably expects to commence foreclosure proceedings within three months, the lender is not required to report as of December 31, 1985 (see A-20). However, if the lender does not in fact commence foreclosure proceedings by March 31, 1986, the lender's obligation to report arises on this date. The lender must provide information on the abandonment under A-27 as of the date the lender first had reason to know of the abandonment (December 31, 1985). The lender must file the return required under this section with the Internal Revenue Service on or before February 28, 1987, and furnish a statement to the borrower on or before January 31, 1987 (see A-33 and A-40).

*Subsequent holder of a loan*

Q-22. To whom does the reporting requirement apply when a person lends money secured by property and subsequently transfers his interest in the indebtedness to another person?

A-22. The subsequent holder of a loan is treated as the lender for purposes of this reporting requirement and is the party required to report with respect to events occurring after the date he acquires the loan. This rule applies to all subsequent holders of a secured loan, including governmental units or any agencies or instrumentalities thereof. For example, if the Federal National Mortgage Association purchases real property loans from a lender, it would be subject to the reporting requirement.

*Multiple lenders*

Q-23. If more than one person lends money secured by the same property, and one lender forecloses upon or otherwise acquires an interest in the property, must the other lenders report under this section?

A-23. Yes. In these circumstances, other lenders must report if they know or have reason to know that the property securing their loans is foreclosed upon or otherwise acquired by another lender and the sale or other acquisition terminates, reduces, or otherwise impairs their security interests in the property (see A-15). For example, if there is a first and second mortgage on a building, and the second mortgagee knows or has reason to know that the first mortgagee has foreclosed upon the building, the second mortgagee is subject to the reporting requirement even if no part of the indebtedness owed to him is satisfied by the proceeds of the foreclosure sale. For a description of the reporting requirement applicable to the first mortgagee, see A-10 and A-15.

Q-24. If more than one person lends money secured by property, and one lender knows or has reason to know that the property has been abandoned, must each lender report under this section?

A-24. No. Each lender is required to report only when he knows or has reason to know that property has been abandoned (see A-19).

### Form and manner of return

*Form of return*

Q-25. What form shall be used to make a return required by section 6050J?

A-25. Except as provided in A-35, the return must be made on Forms 1096 and 1099. The person required to make the return, however, may prepare and use a form which contains provisions substantially similar with those of Forms 1096 and 1099 if the person complies with any revenue procedures relating to substitute Forms 1096 and 1099 in effect at that time.

*Information included on return*

Q-26. What information must be included on a return required by reason of an acquisition of an interest in property that is security for a loan?

A-26. The following information must be included on the return:

(a) The name and address of the borrower with respect to the secured indebtedness;

(b) The borrower's TIN, as defined in section 7701(a);

(c) A general description of the property in which an interest is acquired;

(d) Whether the borrower is personally liable for repayment of the indebtedness;

(e) The date on which the person acquired an interest in the property (see A-10 or A-15);

(f) The amount of the indebtedness outstanding at the time the interest in property is acquired;

(g) If the borrower is personally liable for repayment of the indebtedness, the fair market value of the property at the time the interest is acquired;

(h) The amount of the indebtedness satisfied by the acquisition; and

(i) Any other information as may be required by Forms 1096 and 1099.

Q-27. What information must be included on a return required because a person knows or has reason to know that property which is security for a loan has been abandoned?

A-27. The following information must be included on the return:

(a) The information required in A-26(a), (b), and (d);

(b) A general description of the property abandoned;

(c) The date on which the person first knows or has reason to know that the property has been abandoned;

(d) The amount of the indebtedness outstanding as of the date on which the person first knows or has reason to know that the property has been abandoned;

(e) If the borrower is personally liable for repayment of the indebtedness, the fair market value of the property at the time of abandonment; and

(f) Any other information as may be required by Forms 1096 and 1099.

*Partnership borrower*

Q-28. If a borrower is a partnership, must the TIN of each partner be reported?

A-28. No. If a borrower is a partnership, only the TIN of the partnership must be reported.

*Multiple borrowers*

Q-29. If there is more than one borrower on a single secured loan, must a person required to report under this section make a return with respect to each borrower on the loan?

A-29. Yes. Generally, a separate return must be made with respect to each borrower on a secured loan. However, only one report is required if the lender knows that the borrowers hold property as tenants by the entirety or that the property is held as community property.

*General description of property*

Q-30. What type of information constitutes a general description of the property?

A-30. A general description of the property consists of information that sufficiently identifies the property. In the case of real property, a general description consists of the property's address unless this information is not available or would not sufficiently identify the property, in which case a legal description (*i.e.*, section, lot, block) must be provided instead. A general description of personal property consists of the type, make and model (where applicable) of the property. For example, an automobile would be described as "Car— 1983 Pontiac Firebird." However, in the case of a single loan secured by more than one piece of personal property, a general description consists of the type or category of the pieces acquired or abandoned. For example, if the security for a single loan is six desks and seven typewriters, a general description of the property would be "Office Equipment."

*Multiple acquisitions and abandonments*

Q-31. Must each acquisition and abandonment that occurs in a taxable year be reported on a separate return?

A-31. Generally, each acquisition and abandonment required to be reported by a person for a taxable year must be reported on a separate return. However, in the case of a single loan secured by more than one piece of property, separate returns will not be required when a person acquires an interest in, or knows or has reason to know of the abandonment of, more than one piece of property that is security for the single loan in a taxable year. Instead, the person shall make one return for all of the acquisitions and one return for all

of the abandonments of property that are security for the loan for a taxable year.

*Fair market value*

Q-32. In the case of a foreclosure, execution, or similar sale, what is the fair market value of the property for purposes of the reporting requirement?

A-32. In general, in the absence of clear and convincing evidence to the contrary, the proceeds of the foreclosure, execution, or similar sale will be considered the fair market value of the property for purposes of this reporting requirement.

*Time for filing*

Q-33. When must a person file the return on returns required by section 6050J with the Internal Revenue Service?

A-33: The return or returns must be filed on or before February 28 (March 31 if filed electronically) of the year following the calendar year in which the acquisition of an interest in the property occurs or in which the lender knows or has reason to know of the abandonment of the property.

*Place for filing*

Q-34. Where must the return or returns be filed?

A-34. The return or returns must be filed with the appropriate Internal Revenue Service Center, the addresses of which are listed in the instructions for the Form 1099 series.

*Use of magnetic media*

Q-35. What rules apply with respect to the use of magnetic media?

A-35. Any return required under section 6050J must be filed on magnetic media to the extent required by section 6011(e). Any person not required by section 6011(e) to file returns under section 6050J on magnetic media may request permission to do so. See § 1.9101 for rules relating to permission to submit information on magnetic tape or other media. If a person required to file returns on magnetic media fails to do so, the penalty under section 6652 (failure to file an information return) applies.

*Requirement of furnishing statements to borrowers*

*In general*

Q-36. What statements must be furnished to borrowers?

A-36. Any person required to make an information return under section 6050J must furnish a statement to each borrower whose name is required to set forth in a return filed with the Internal Revenue Service. For the date when the statement must be furnished, see A-40.

Q-37. Is the statement considered to be furnished to the borrower if it is mailed to the borrower at the borrower's last known address?

A-37. Yes.

*Information included on statement*

Q-38. What information must be included on the statement?

A-38. The statement must include the following information:

(a) Except in the case where the return is made on behalf of a governmental unit (or any agency or instrumentality thereof), the name and address of the person required to make the information return;

(b) In the case where the return is made on behalf of a governmental unit or any agency or instrumentality thereof, the name and address of such unit, agency or instrumentality;

(c) The information required under A-26 or A-27, whichever is applicable; and

(d) A legend stating that the information is being reported to the Internal Revenue Service.

*Copy of Form 1099 to borrowers*

Q-39. May the requirement of furnishing a statement be met by furnishing a copy of the Form 1099 filed with respect to that borrower?

A-39. Yes. The requirement of furnishing a statement may be met by furnishing to the borrower a copy of the Form 1099 containing the same information filed with the Service with respect to that borrower, or a reasonable facsimile thereof, provided that the form or the reasonable facsimile bears a legend stating that the information is being reported to the Internal Revenue Service.

*Time of furnishing statement*

Q-40. When is a statement required to be furnished to the borrower?

A-40. A statement is required to be furnished to the borrower on or before January 31 of the year following the calendar year in which the acquisition or abandonment of property occurs.

*Multiple borrowers*

Q-41. If a person required to report under this section must make an information return with respect to more than one borrower on a single loan, of an interest in the property occurs or in which the lender knows or has reason to know of the abandonment of the property.

A-41. Yes. A separate statement must be furnished to each borrower with respect to which a separate return is required under section 6050J.

Reg. § 1.6050J-1T

*Extensions of time*

Q-42. Are there any circumstances under which an extension of time may be granted with respect to the requirement of furnishing statements to borrowers?

A-42. Yes. Upon written application of the person required to report, the service center director may, for good cause shown, grant that person an additional period (not to exceed 30 days) in which to furnish statements under section 6050J with respect to any calendar year. The application for an extension must be addressed to the director of the service center with which the returns must be filed. The application must contain a concise statement of the reasons for requesting the extension in order to aid the service center director in determining the period of extension, if any, to be granted. The application must state at the top of the first page that it is made under section 1.6050J-1T and must be signed by the person required to report under section 6050J. In general, the application should be filed not earlier than September 30 of the year in which the acquisition of an interest in the property occurs or in which the lender knows or has reason to know of the abandonment of the property, and not later than January 15 of the following year.

*Penalties*

Q-43. Are there penalties for failing to comply with the requirements of section 6050J and the regulations thereunder?

A-43. Yes. The penalty for failing to make any information return with respect to any borrower under section 6050J is provided in section 6652. The penalty for failing to furnish a statement to any borrower is provided in section 6678.

*Effective date*

Q-44. When is section 6050J effective?

A-44. Section 6050J is effective for acquisitions and abandonments of property after December 31, 1984. [Temporary Reg. § 1.6050J-1T.]

☐ [*T.D. 7971, 8-30-84. Amended by T.D. 8895, 8-17-2000.*]

### [Reg. § 1.6050K-1]

**§ 1.6050K-1. Returns relating to sales or exchanges of certain partnership interests.**—(a) *Partnership return required.*—(1) *In general.*—Except as otherwise provided in this paragraph (a), a partnership shall make a separate return on Form 8308 with respect to each section 751(a) exchange (as defined in paragraph (a)(4)(i) of this section) of an interest in such partnership which occurs after December 31, 1984. A partnership that is in doubt as to whether partnership property constitutes section 751 property to any extent or as to whether a transfer of a partnership interest constitutes a section 751(a) exchange may file Form 8308 in order to avoid the risk of incurring a penalty under section 6721. The penalty under section 6721 will generally apply, however, to partnerships that do not file Form 8308 where in fact a section 751(a) exchange occurred, except as provided in paragraphs (a)(2) and (e) of this section.

(2) *Return required under section 6045.*—No return shall be required under section 6050K(a) and paragraph (a)(1) of this section with respect to the sale or exchange of a partnership interest if a return is required to be filed under section 6045 with respect to such sale or exchange.

(3) *Single or composite documents.*—The Commissioner may authorize the use, at the option of the partnership, of a single document which includes all of the partnership's returns for a calendar year in the case of partnerships required under paragraph (a)(1) of this section to make 25 or more returns on Form 8308 for any calendar year. In addition, the Commissioner may authorize the use for this purpose, also at the option of such a partnership, of a composite document. These authorizations shall be subject to such conditions, limitations, and special rules governing the preparation, execution, filing, and correction thereof as the Commissioner may deem appropriate. Such composite document shall consist of a form prescribed by the Commissioner and an attachment or attachments of magnetic tape or other approved media. To the extent that the use of a single or composite document has been authorized by the Commissioner, references in this section to Form 8308 shall be deemed to refer also to returns included in a single or composite document under this paragraph (a)(3). Any single or composite document so authorized shall include the information required to be provided on Form 8308 under paragraph (b) of this section with respect to each section 751(a) exchange.

(4) *Definitions.*—For purposes of section 6050K of the Code and this section—

(i) *Section 751(a) exchange.*—The term "section 751(a) exchange" means any sale or exchange of a partnership interest (or portion thereof) in which any portion of any money or other property received by a transferor partner in exchange for all or a part of his or her interest in the partnership is attributable to section 751 property. The term does not include a distribution which is treated as a sale or

exchange between the distributee and the partnership under section 751(b) of the Code.

(ii) *Section 751 property.*—The term "section 751 property" means unrealized receivables, as defined in section 751(c) of the Code, and inventory items which have appreciated substantially in value ("substantially appreciated inventory items"), as defined in section 751(d) of the Code.

(iii) *Transferor and transferee.*—The term "transferor" means the beneficial owner of a partnership interest immediately before the transfer of that interest. The term "transferee" means the beneficial owner of a partnership interest immediately after the transfer of that interest. However, if a partnership does not know the identity of the beneficial owner of an interest in the partnership, the record holder of such interest shall be treated as the transferor or transferee (as the case may be) for purposes of paragraphs (b) and (c) of this section.

(b) *Contents of return.*—The return on Form 8308 shall include the following information:

(1) The names, addresses, and taxpayer identification numbers of the transferee and transferor in the exchange and of the partnership filing the return;

(2) The date of the exchange; and

(3) Such other information as may be required by Form 8308 or its instructions.

(c) *Statements to be furnished to transferor and transferee.*—(1) *In general.*—Every partnership required to file a return under paragraph (a) of this section must furnish to each person whose name is required to be set forth in such return a written statement on or before January 31 of the calendar year following the calendar year in which the section 751(a) exchange occurred to which the return under paragraph (a) relates (or, if later, 30 days after the partnership is notified of the exchange as defined in paragraph (e) of this section). The partnership shall use a copy of the completed Form 8308 as a statement unless the Form 8308 contains information with respect to more than one section 751(a) exchange (see paragraph (a)(3) of this section). If the partnership does not use a copy of Form 8308 as a statement, the statement shall include the information required to be shown on Form 8308 with respect to the section 751(a) exchange to which the person to whom the statement is furnished is a party. In addition, it shall state that—

(i) The information shown on the statement has been supplied to the Internal Revenue Service,

(ii) A transferor of a partnership interest in a sale or exchange described in section 751(a) of the Internal Revenue Code is required to treat a portion of any gain or loss resulting from the sale or exchange as ordinary income or loss, and

(iii) The transferor in a section 751(a) sale or exchange is required under paragraph (a)(3) of § 1.751-1 to attach a statement relating to the sale or exchange to his or her income tax return for the taxable year in which the sale or exchange occurred.

(2) *Information to be provided to transferors.*—The statement a partnership must provide to a transferor partner pursuant to paragraph (c)(1) of this section must also include the information necessary for the transferor to make the transferor's required statement under § 1.751-1(a)(3).

(3) *Transfers of partnership interests by foreign persons.*—For additional information required to be provided by the partnership if section 864(c)(8) applies to the transfer of a partnership interest by a foreign person, see § 1.864(c)(8)-2(b).

(d) *Requirement that transferor notify partnership.*—(1) *In general.*—The transferor of any partnership interest in a section 751(a) exchange shall notify the partnership of such exchange in writing within 30 days of the exchange (or, if earlier, January 15 of the calendar year following the calendar year in which the exchange occurred). The written notification from the transferor shall include the following information:

(i) The names and addresses of the transferor and transferee in the section 751(a) exchange;

(ii) The taxpayer identification numbers of the transferor and, if known, of the transferee; and

(iii) The date of the exchange.

Any transferor who notified a partnership under section 6050K(c)(1) prior to January 22, 1986 by a notification that does not meet the requirements of this paragraph (d) shall furnish such partnership with the written notification described in this paragraph (d) on or before February 21, 1986.

(2) *Return required under section 6045.*—No transferor shall be required to notify a partnership of the sale or exchange of a partnership interest under section 6050K(c)(1) or paragraph (d)(1) of this

section if a return is required to be filed under section 6045 with respect to such sale or exchange.

(3) *Transfers of partnership interests by foreign persons.*—For notifications required by foreign transferors of partnership interests, see § 1.864(c)(8)-2(a).

(e) *Partnership not required to make a return or furnish statements under this section until it has notice of the exchange.*—A partnership shall not be required to make a return or furnish statements under section 6050K and this section with respect to any section 751(a) exchange until it has been notified of the exchange. For purposes of section 6050K(c)(2) and this section, a partnership is notified of a section 751(a) exchange when either:

(1) The partnership receives the written notification from the transferor required under paragraph (d) of this section; or

(2) The partnership has knowledge that there has been a transfer of a partnership interest or any portion thereof, and, at the time of the transfer, the partnership had any section 751 property. However, no return or statements are required under section 6050K if the transfer was not a section 751(a) exchange (*e.g.,* a transfer which in its entirety constitutes a gift for federal income tax purposes). For purposes of this paragraph (e)(2), the partnership may rely on a written statement from the transferor that the transfer was not a section 751(a) exchange in the absence of knowledge to the contrary. For rules applicable where the partnership is in doubt as to whether partnership property constitutes section 751 property to any extent or as to whether a transfer of a partnership interest constitutes a section 751(a) exchange, see paragraph (a)(1) of this section.

(f) *Partnership return is to be attached to Form 1065.*—(1) *In general.*—Any partnership return on Form 8308 required under this section shall be filed as an attachment to the partnership's Form 1065 for its taxable year in which the calendar year in which the section 751(a) exchange occurred ends and shall be filed at the time (determined with regard to any extension of time for filing) and place prescribed for filing of the partnership's Form 1065 for that taxable year (see paragraph (e) of § 1.6031-1 for the time and place for filing Form 1065).

(2) *Notification after Form 1065 is filed.*—If a partnership is notified of an exchange (as defined in paragraph (e) of this section) after the partnership has filed Form 1065 for the taxable year with respect to which the exchange should have been reported, Form 8308 shall be filed with the service center or other Internal Revenue office with which the partnership's Form 1065 was filed, on or before the thirtieth day after the partnership is notified of the exchange.

(g) *Penalties.*—For penalties for failure of:

(1) Transferors to furnish the notification required by paragraph (d) of this section see section 6722(b);

(2) Partnerships to furnish any statement required under paragraph (c) of this section see section 6722(a); and

(3) Partnerships to file the return on Form 8308 as required by paragraph (a) of this section see section 6721.

(h) *Applicability date.*—Paragraphs (c)(2) and (3) of this section apply to returns filed on or after November 30, 2020. Paragraph (d)(3) of this section applies to transfers that occur on or after November 30, 2020. [Reg. § 1.6050K-1.]

☐ [*T.D. 8119, 12-31-86. Amended by T.D. 9926, 11-27-2020.*]

**[Reg. § 1.6050L-1]**

**§ 1.6050L-1. Information return by donees relating to certain dispositions of donated property.**—(a) *Information returns.*—(1) *Disposition of charitable deduction property.*—If a donee of any charitable deduction property (as defined in paragraph (e) of this section) sells, exchanges, consumes, or otherwise disposes of (with or without consideration) such property (or any portion thereof) within 2 years after the date of the donor's contribution of such property, the donee shall make an information return on the form prescribed by the Internal Revenue Service. For special rules with respect to successor donees, see paragraph (c) of this section.

(2) *Disposition of items appraised for $500 or less.*—(i) *In general.*—Paragraph (a)(1) of this section shall not apply with respect to an item of charitable deduction property disposed of by sale if the Form 8283 appraisal summary (as described in § 1.170A-13(c)(4) for contributions made on or before July 30, 2018 and § 1.170A-16(d)(3) for contributions made after July 30, 2018), or a successor form, signed by the donee with respect to the item contains, at the time of the donee's signature, a statement signed by the donor that the appraised value of the item does not exceed $500. In the case of a Form 8283 appraisal summary that describes more than one item, this exception shall apply only with respect to an item clearly identified as having an appraised value of $500 or less. For purposes of this paragraph

(a)(2)(i), items that form a set (such as, for example, a collection of books written by the same author, components of a stereo system, or a group of place settings of a pattern of silverware) are considered one item. In addition, all nonpublicly traded stock is considered one item as are all nonpublicly traded securities other than nonpublicly traded stock.

(ii) *Transitional rule.*—Paragraph (a)(2)(i) of this section is satisfied with respect to an appraisal summary submitted to the donee on or before January 31, 1986, if such donee obtained the required statement from the donor on or before March 31, 1986, on either an amended appraisal summary or an attachment to the original appraisal summary.

(3) *Consumption or distribution for exempt purpose.*—Paragraph (a)(1) of this section shall not apply with respect to an item of charitable deduction property consumed or distributed by a donee without consideration if the consumption or distribution is in furtherance of a purpose or function constituting a basis for such donee's exemption under section 501 of the Code. For example, no reporting is required with respect to medical supplies consumed or distributed by a tax-exempt relief organization in aiding disaster victims.

(b) *Information required to be provided on return.*—The information return required by paragraph (a)(1) of this section shall include the following:

(1) The name, address, and employer identification number of the donee making the information return;

(2) A description of the property (or portion disposed of) in sufficient detail to identify the charitable deduction property received by such donee;

(3) The name and taxpayer identification number of the donor (social security number if the donor is an individual or employer identification number if the donor is a corporation or partnership);

(4) The date of the contribution to such donee;

(5) Any amount received by such donee with respect to the disposition;

(6) The date of the disposition by such donee; and

(7) Such other information as may be specified by the form or its instructions.

(c) *Successor donees.*—(1) *In general.*—Section 6050L and this section shall apply to successor donees that receive charitable deduction property (as defined in paragraph (e) of this section) that was transferred by the original donee after July 5, 1988, (whether the successor donee received the property from the original donee or another successor donee). For definitions of the terms "donor," "donee," "original donee," and "successor donee," see § 1.170A-13(c)(7)(iv)-(vii).

(2) *Information required to be provided on return.*—With respect to charitable deduction property that is transferred to one or more successor donees to which this section applies, the information return required by paragraph (a)(1) of this section shall include, in addition to the information described in paragraph (b) of this section, the following:

(i) The name, address, and employer identification number of the immediately succeeding successor donee (if any) and the immediately preceding successor donee (if any);

(ii) The name, address, and employer identification number of the original donee if different from the information required by paragraph (b)(1) of this section;

(iii) The date of contribution to the original donee; and

(iv) Such other information as may be specified by the form or its instructions.

(3) *Information to be provided to transferor.*—Every successor donee to which this section applies that receives any charitable deduction property within the 2-year period described in paragraph (a)(1) of this section shall provide its name, address, and employer identification number to that preceding donee on or before the 15th day after the later of—

(i) The date of transfer to such successor donee, or

(ii) The date such successor donee receives a copy of the appraisal summary from the preceding donee.

(4) *Donees that transfer property to successor donees.*—In addition to complying with the requirements of paragraph (a)(1) of this section, every donee that transfers any charitable deduction property to a successor donee to which this section applies within the 2-year period described in paragraph (a)(1) of this section—

(i) Shall provide its name, address, and employer identification number and a copy of the Form 8283 appraisal summary (as described in § 1.170A-13(c)(4) for contributions made on or before July 30, 2018 and § 1.170A-16(d)(3) for contributions made after July

30, 2018) relating to the transferred property to the successor donee on or before the 15th day after the latest of—

    (A) The date of such transfer, or

    (B) The date the original donee signs the appraisal summary, or

    (C) In a case in which the transferring donee is a successor donee, the date such donee receives a copy of the appraisal summary from such donee's transferor, and

    (ii) Shall provide a copy of its information return required by paragraph (a)(1) of this section to the successor donee on or before the 15th day after the transferring donee files the information return pursuant to paragraph (e)(2) of this section.

    (5) *Donee.*—In the case of charitable deduction property that is transferred to a successor donee to which this section applies, the term "donee" as used in paragraph (a)(2) and (e) of this section means only the original donee.

    (d) *Special rules.*—(1) *Statement to be furnished to donors.*—Every donee making a return under section 6050L and this section with respect to the disposition of charitable deduction property shall furnish a copy of the return to the donor of the property.

    (2) *Retention of Form 8283 appraisal summary.*—Every donee shall retain the Form 8283 appraisal summary (as described in §1.170A-13(c)(4) for contributions made on or before July 30, 2018 and §1.170A-16(d)(3) for contributions made after July 30, 2018) in the donee's records for so long as it may be relevant in the administration of any internal revenue law.

    (e) *Charitable deduction property.*—For purposes of this section, the term charitable deduction property means any property (other than money and publicly traded securities to which §1.170A-13(c)(7)(xi)(B) does not apply) contributed after December 31, 1984, with respect to which the donee signs (or is presented with for signature in cases described in §1.170A-13(c)(4)(iv)(C)(2)) a Form 8283 appraisal summary (as described in §1.170A-13(c)(4) for contributions made on or before July 30, 2018 and §1.170A-16(d)(3) for contributions made after July 30, 2018). For purposes of this section, if such donee signs (or is presented with for signature in cases described in §1.170A-13(c)(4)(iv)(C)(2)) the appraisal summary after the date of contribution of the property, the property is deemed to be charitable deduction property from the date of contribution.

    (f) *Place and time for filing information returns.*—(1) *Place for filing.*—The donee information return required by section 6050L and this section shall be filed with the Internal Revenue Service center listed on the return form or its instructions.

    (2) *Time for filing.*—(i) *In general.*—Except as provided in paragraph (f)(2)(ii) of this section, the donee information return shall be filed on or before the 125th day after a donee sells, exchanges, consumes or otherwise disposes of the charitable deduction property. A donee information return filed pursuant to this paragraph (f)(2)(i) does not have to include the information required by paragraphs (b)(3), (4), (5), or (6), or (c)(2)(i)-(iii) of this section if such information is not available to the donee by the due date of the return.

    (ii) *Exception.*—Notwithstanding paragraph (f)(2)(i) of this section, in the case of a donee who, on the date of receipt of the transferred property, had no reason to believe that the substantiation requirements of §1.170A-13(c) or §1.170A-16(d) apply with respect to the property, the donee information return is not required to be filed until the 60th day after the date on which such donee has reason to believe that the substantiation requirements of §1.170A-13(c) or §1.170A-16(d) apply with respect to the property. A donee information return filed pursuant to this paragraph (f)(2)(ii) does not have to include the information required by paragraphs (b)(3), (4), (5), or (6), or (c)(2)(i)-(iii) of this section if such information is not available to the donee by the due date of the return.

    (g) *Penalties.*—For penalties for failure to comply with the requirements of this section, see sections 6676, 6721, and 6723.

    (h) *Effective/applicability dates.*—The first two sentences of paragraph (a)(2)(i), paragraphs (c)(4)(i) and (d)(2), and the first sentences of paragraphs (e) and (f)(2)(ii) apply to contributions made after July 30, 2018. [Reg. §1.6050L-1.]

    ☐ [*T.D.* 8199, 5-4-88. *Amended by T.D.* 9836, 7-27-2018.]

### [Reg. §1.6050L-2]

**§1.6050L-2. Information returns by donees relating to qualified intellectual property contributions.**—(a) *In general.*—Each donee organization described in section 170(c), except a private foundation (as defined in section 509(a)), other than a private foundation described in section 170(b)(1)(F), that receives or accrues net income during a taxable year from any qualified intellectual property contribution (as defined in section 170(m)(8)) must make an annual information return on the form prescribed by the IRS. The information return is required for any taxable year of the donee that includes any portion of the 10-year period beginning on the date of the contribution, but not for taxable years beginning after the expiration of the legal life of the qualified intellectual property.

    (b) *Information required to be provided on return.*—The information return required by section 6050L and paragraph (a) of this section shall include the following—

    (1) The name, address, taxable year, and employer identification number of the donee making the information return;

    (2) The name, address, and taxpayer identification number of the donor;

    (3) A description of the qualified intellectual property in sufficient detail to identify the qualified intellectual property received by such donee;

    (4) The date of the contribution to the donee;

    (5) The amount of net income of the donee for the taxable year that is properly allocable to the qualified intellectual property (determined without regard to paragraph (10)(B) of section 170(m) and with the modifications described in paragraphs (5) and (6) of such section); and

    (6) Such other information as may be specified by the form or its instructions.

    (c) *Special rule—statement to be furnished to donors.*—Every donee making an information return under section 6050L and this section with respect to a qualified intellectual property contribution shall furnish a copy of the information return to the donor of the property. The information return required by section 6050L and this section shall be furnished to the donor on or before the date the donee is required to file the return with the IRS.

    (d) *Place and time for filing information return.*—(1) *Place for filing.*—The information return required by section 6050L and this section shall be filed with the IRS location listed on the prescribed form or in its instructions.

    (2) *Time for filing.*—A donee is required to file the return required by section 6050L and this section on or before the last day of the first full month following the close of the donee's taxable year to which net income from the qualified intellectual property is properly allocable.

    (e) *Penalties.*—For penalties for failure to comply with the requirements of this section, see sections 6721 through 6724.

    (f) *Effective/applicability date.*—The rules of this section apply to qualified intellectual property contributions made after June 3, 2004. [Reg. §1.6050L-2.]

    ☐ [*T.D.* 9392, 4-4-2008.]

### [Reg. §1.6050M-1]

**§1.6050M-1. Information returns relating to persons receiving contracts from certain Federal executive agencies.**—(a) *General rule.*—Except as otherwise provided in paragraph (c) of this section, the head of every Federal executive agency or his or her delegate shall make an information return to the Internal Revenue Service reporting the following information with respect to each contract entered into by that Federal executive agency—

    (1) Name and address of the contractor;

    (2) Contractor's TIN and, if the contractor is a member of an affiliated group of corporations that files its Federal income tax returns on a consolidated basis, the name and TIN of the common parent of the affiliated group;

    (3) The date of the contract action;

    (4) The expected date of completion of the contract as determined under any reasonable method, such as the expected contract delivery date under the contract schedule;

    (5) The total amount obligated under the contract action;

    (6) Any other information required by Forms 8596 and 8596A and their instructions, or by any other administrative guidance issued by the Internal Revenue Service (such as a revenue procedure).

    See paragraph (e) of this section relating to the manner in which to report increases in amounts obligated under existing contracts. See paragraph (d)(5) of this section for special rules for agencies that submit contract information to the Federal Procurement Data Center. For provisions concerning the requesting and furnishing of identifying numbers, see section 6109 and the regulations thereunder.

    (b) *Definitions.*—The following definitions apply for purposes of this section—

    (1) *Federal executive agency.*—The term "Federal executive agency" means—

(i) Any executive agency (as defined in 5 U.S.C. 105) other than the General Accounting Office;

(ii) Any military department (as defined in 5 U.S.C. 102); and

(iii) The United States Postal Service and the Postal Rate Commission.

(2) *Contract.*—(i) *General rule.*—The term "contract" means an obligation of a Federal executive agency to make payment of money (or other property) to a person in return for the sale of property, the rendering of services, or other consideration. The term "contract" includes, for example, such an obligation arising from a written agreement executed by the agency and the contractor, an award or notice of award, a job order or task letter issued under a basic ordering agreement, a letter contract, an order that becomes effective only upon written acceptance or performance, or an action described in paragraph (e) of this section.

(ii) *Exceptions.*—For purposes of this section, the term "contract" does not include—

(A) A license granted by a Federal executive agency;

(B) An obligation of a contractor (other than a Federal executive agency) to a subcontractor;

(C) A debt instrument of the United States Government or a Federal agency, such as a Treasury note, Treasury bond, Treasury bill, savings bond, or similar instrument; or

(D) An obligation of a Federal executive agency to lend money, lease property to a lessee, or sell property.

(iii) *Special rule for certain contracts of the Small Business Administration.*—Any subcontract entered into by the Small Business Administration (SBA) under a prime contract between the SBA and a procuring Federal executive agency pursuant to section 8(a) of the Small Business Act (15 U.S.C. 637(a)) shall not be treated as a contract of the SBA but shall be treated as a contract of the procuring agency for purposes of this section.

(iv) *Certain schedule contracts.*—For purposes of this section, any of the following contracts entered into on behalf of one or more Federal executive agencies is not a "contract" to be reported by the General Services Administration or the Department of Veteran's Affairs at the time of execution:

(A) A Federal Supply Schedule Contract entered into by the General Services Administration,

(B) An Automated Data Processing Schedule Contract entered into by the General Services Administration, or

(C) A schedule contract entered into by the Department of Veteran's Affairs.

Instead, an order placed by a Federal executive agency, including the General Services Administration or the Department of Veteran's Affairs, under such a schedule contract is a "contract" for purposes of this section.

(v) *Blanket purchase agreements.*—For purposes of this section, the term "contract" does not include a blanket purchase agreement between one or more Federal executive agencies and one or more contractors. Instead, an order placed by a Federal executive agency under the terms of a blanket purchase agreement is a "contract" for purposes of this section.

(vi) *Contracts entered into using non-appropriated funds.*— [Reserved]

(3) *Contractor.*—The term "contractor" means any person who enters into a contract with a Federal executive agency.

(4) *Person and TIN.*—The terms "person" and "TIN" are defined in sections 7701 (a)(1) and (41), respectively.

(c) *Exceptions to information reporting requirement.*—(1) *General exceptions.*—The following do not need to be reported pursuant to this section:

(i) Any contract or contract action for which the amount obligated is $25,000 or less;

(ii) Any contract with a contractor who, in making the agreement, is acting in his or her capacity as an employee of a Federal executive agency (*e.g.*, any contract of employment under which the employee is paid wages subject to the withholding provisions contained in chapter 24 of subtitle C);

(iii) Any contract between a Federal executive agency and another Federal governmental unit (or any agency or instrumentality thereof);

(iv) Any contract with a foreign government (or any agency or instrumentality thereof);

(v) Any contract with a state or local governmental unit (or any agency or instrumentality thereof);

(vi) Any contract with a person who is not required to have a TIN (see, for example, § 301.6109-1(g));

(vii) Any contract the terms of which provide that all amounts payable under the contract by any Federal executive agency will be paid on or before the 120th day following the date of the contract action, and for which it is reasonable to expect that all amounts will be so paid.

(viii) Any contract under which all money (or other property) that will be received by the contractor after the 120th day after the date of the contract action will come from persons other than a Federal executive agency or an agent of such an agency (*e.g.*, a contract under which the contractor will collect amounts owed to a Federal executive agency by the agency's debtor and will remit to the agency the money collected less an amount that serves as the contractor's consideration under the contract).

(ix) Any contract for which the Commissioner determines that the information described in paragraph (a) of this section will not facilitate the collection of Federal tax liabilities because of the manner, method, or timing of payment by the agency under that contract.

(2) *Special rule for certain classified or confidential contracts.*—Contracts described in section 6050M(e)(3), relating to certain classified or confidential contracts, are to be reported only in accordance with section 6050M(e)(2).

(d) *Filing requirements.*—(1) *Frequency and time for filing.*—The information returns required by this section with respect to contracts of a Federal executive agency entered into on or after January 1, 1989, must be filed on a quarterly basis for the calendar quarters ending on the last day of March, June, September, and December. Except as provided in paragraph (d)(5) of this section, the returns for contracts entered into during a calendar quarter must be filed on or before the last day of the month following that quarter. Notwithstanding the preceding sentence, returns filed before May 7, 1990 will be considered timely filed.

(2) *Form of reporting.*—(i) *General rule concerning magnetic media.*—The information returns required by this section with respect to contracts of a Federal executive agency for each calendar quarter shall be made in one submission (or in multiple submissions if permitted by paragraph (d)(4) of this section). Except as provided in paragraph (d)(2)(ii) of this section, the required returns shall be made on magnetic media (within the meaning of § 301.6011-2(a)(1)) in accordance with any applicable revenue procedure or other guidance promulgated by the Internal Revenue Service for the filing of such returns under section 6050M.

(ii) *Magnetic media exception for low-volume filers.*—Any Federal executive agency that on any October 1 has a reasonable expectation of entering into, during the one year period beginning on that date, fewer than 250 contracts that are subject to the reporting requirements under this section may make the information returns required by this section for each quarter of that one year period on the prescribed paper Form 8596 in accordance with the instructions accompanying such form.

(3) *Place of filing.*—(i) *Returns on magnetic media.*—Information returns made under this section on magnetic media shall be filed with the Internal Revenue Service at the Martinsburg Computing Center, Martinsburg, West Virginia 25401-1359, in accordance with any applicable revenue procedure or other guidance promulgated by the Internal Revenue Service relating to the filing of returns under section 6050M.

(ii) *Form 8596.*—Information returns made on Form 8596 shall be filed with the Internal Revenue Service at the location specified in the instructions for that form.

(4) *Special rule concerning multiple returns.*—To the extent permitted in any revenue procedure or other guidance relating to the filing of information returns under this section, a Federal executive agency which files information returns under this section on magnetic media may make more than one magnetic media submission for any quarter, if each submission for that quarter contains all of the information required by paragraph (a) of this section with respect to contracts entered into by one or more departments, branches, bureaus, agencies, or other readily identifiable operating functions (such as a geographic region) of the Federal executive agency.

(5) *Special rules for agencies reporting to the Federal Procurement Data Center.*—(i) *Election to have the Director of the Federal Procurement Data Center make returns on behalf of agency.*—If, in complying with the requirements of the Federal Procurement Data System (FPDS) (as established under the authority of the Office of Federal Procurement Policy Act, as amended, 41 U.S.C. 401 *et. seq.*), a Federal executive agency is required to submit to the Federal Procurement Data Center (FPDC) all the information with respect to one or more contracts required to be reported by paragraph (a) of this section, that Federal executive agency may, in lieu of making returns directly to the

Internal Revenue Service with respect to those contracts, elect to have the Director of the FPDC (or his or her delegate) make the required returns with respect to all of those contracts on its behalf. In order to make this election for such contracts entered into during a calendar quarter, the head of a Federal executive agency (or his or her delegate) shall attach to its submission to the FPDC for that quarter a signed statement to the effect that:

(A) the Director of the FPDC (or his or her delegate) is authorized, in accordance with an election made under 26 CFR §1.6050M-1(d)(5), to make, on the agency's behalf, the required returns for such contracts for that quarter, and

(B) under the penalties of perjury, such official has examined the information to be submitted by the agency to the FPDC for making those returns and certifies that information to be, to the best of such official's knowledge and belief, a compilation of agency records maintained in the normal course of business for the purpose of providing the information necessary for making true, correct, and complete returns as required by section 6050M.

If the election is made, the Director of the FPDC (or his or her delegate) shall, on the electing agency's behalf, make the returns required by paragraph (a) of this section with respect to the contracts to which the election applies.

(ii) *Time, manner, and place of filing.*—The Director of the FPDC (or his or her delegate) must—

(A) make the required returns for a quarter on or before the earlier of (*1*) 45 days following the date that the contract information is required to be submitted to the FPDC, or (2) 90 days following the end of the calendar quarter for which the election is made, except that, if that calendar quarter ends September 30, 105 days following the end of that quarter, and

(B) comply with paragraph (d)(2)(i) and (3)(i) of this section, relating to form and place of filing. Notwithstanding the preceding sentence, returns made before May 7, 1990 will be considered timely filed.

(iii) *Contracts reported directly to the Internal Revenue Service.*— Even if the election is made, all information with respect to any particular contract required to be reported under paragraph (a) of this section must be reported directly to the Internal Revenue Service by the electing agency if the FPDS does not require that information to be submitted to the FPDC. An electing agency shall not, however, make direct returns to the Internal Revenue Service of contract information that is subject to the election.

(6) *Certification of return.*—(i) *Returns made directly with the Internal Revenue Service.*—Each return made under this section by a Federal executive agency directly with the Internal Revenue Service on magnetic media or on Forms 8596 and 8596-A shall be signed by the head of the Federal executive agency (or his or her delegate) under the penalties of perjury, certifying that such official has examined the return, that it is prepared pursuant to the requirements of section 6050M and that, to the best of such official's knowledge and belief, it is compiled from agency records maintained in the normal course of business for the purpose of making a true, correct, and complete return as required by section 6050M.

(ii) *Returns made by Director of FPDC on agency's behalf.*—Each return made under this section by the Director of the FPDC on behalf of a Federal executive agency shall be signed by the Director of the FPDC (or his or her delegate) under the penalties of perjury, certifying that such official has examined the return, that it is prepared pursuant to the requirements of section 6050M and that, to the best of such official's knowledge and belief, it is compiled from information submitted by the Federal executive agency to the FPDC pursuant to §1.6050M-1(d)(5)(i) for the purpose of making a true, correct, and complete return as required by section 6050M.

(e) *Special rules relating to increases in amount obligated.*—If, through the exercise of an option contained in a basic or initial contract or under any other rule of contract law, express or implied, the amount of money or other property obligated under the contract is increased by more than $25,000 in one contract action, then that action shall be treated as the entering into of a new contract with respect to which the information required by paragraph (a) of this section is to be reported to the Internal Revenue Service for the calendar quarter in which the increase occurs.

(f) *Effective date.*—(1) *Contracts required to be reported.*—Except as otherwise provided in this paragraph (f), this section applies to each Federal executive agency with respect to its contracts entered into on or after January 1, 1989 (including any increase in amount obligated on or after January 1, 1989, that is treated as a new contract under paragraph (e) of this section).

(2) *Contracts not required to be reported.*—A Federal executive agency is not required to report—

(i) any basic or initial contract entered into before January 1, 1989,

(ii) any increase contract action occurring before January 1, 1989, that is treated as a new contract under paragraph (e) of this section, or

(iii) any increase contract action that is treated as a new contract under paragraph (e) of this section if the basic or initial contract to which that contract action relates was entered into before January 1, 1989, and—

(A) the increase occurs before April 1, 1990, or

(B) the amount of the increase does not exceed $50,000.

(3) *Illustration.*—(i) If a Federal executive agency enters into an initial contract on December 1, 1988, and the amount of money obligated under the contract is increased by $55,000 on April 15, 1990, then (A) there is no reporting requirement with respect to the contract when entered into on December 1, 1988, and (B) the April 15, 1990, increase, which is treated as a new contract under paragraph (e) of this section, is subject to the reporting requirements of this section because it is considered to be a new contract entered into on April 15, 1990.

(ii) If the $55,000 increase had occurred before April 1, 1990, there would have been no reporting requirement with respect to that increase. [Reg. §1.6050M-1.]

☐ [*T.D. 8275, 12-5-89.*]

### [Reg. §301.6050M-1]

**§301.6050M-1. Information returns relating to persons receiving contracts from certain Federal executive agencies.**—For provisions relating to the requirements of returns of information relating to persons receiving contracts from certain Federal executive agencies, see §1.6050M-1 of this chapter (Income Tax Regulations). [Reg. §301.6050M-1.]

☐ [*T.D. 8275, 12-5-89.*]

### [Reg. §1.6050N-1]

**§1.6050N-1. Statements to recipients of royalties paid after December 31, 1986.**—(a) *Requirement.*—A person required to make an information return under section 6050N(a) must furnish a statement to each recipient whose name is required to be shown on the related information return for royalties paid.

(b) *Form, manner, and time for providing statements to recipients.*—The statement required by paragraph (a) of this section must be either the official Form 1099 prescribed by the Internal Revenue Service for the respective calendar year or an acceptable substitute statement. The rules under §1.6042-4 (relating to statements with respect to dividends) apply comparably in determining the form of the acceptable substitute statement permitted by this section. Those rules also apply for purposes of determining the manner of and time for providing the Form 1099 or its acceptable substitute statement to a recipient under this section. An IRS truncated taxpayer identifying number (TTIN) may be used as the identifying number of the recipient. For provisions relating to the use of TTINs, see §301.6109-4 of this chapter (Procedure and Administration Regulations).

(c) *Exempted foreign-related items.*—(1) *In general.*—No return shall be required under paragraph (a) of this section for payments of the items described in paragraphs (c)(1)(i) through (iv) of this section.

(i) Returns of information are not required for payments of royalties that a payor can, prior to payment, associate with documentation upon which it may rely to treat as made to a foreign beneficial owner in accordance with §1.1441-1(e)(1)(ii) or as made to a foreign payee in accordance with §1.6049-5(d)(1) or presumed to be made to a foreign payee under §1.6049-5(d)(2), (3), (4), or (5). However, such payments may be reportable under §1.1461-1(b) and (c). For purposes of this paragraph (c)(1)(i), the provisions in §1.6049-5(c) (regarding rules applicable to documentation of foreign status and definition of U.S. payor and non-U.S. payor) shall apply. See §1.1441-1(b)(3)(iii)(B) and (C) for special payee rules regarding scholarships, grants, pensions, annuities, etc. The provisions of §1.1441-1 shall apply by substituting the term *payor* for the term *withholding agent* and without regard to the fact that the provisions apply only to amounts subject to withholding under chapter 3 of the Internal Revenue Code.

(ii) Returns of information are not required for payments of royalties from sources outside the United States paid by a non-U.S. payor or non-U.S. middleman and that are paid and received outside the United States. For a definition of non-U.S. payor or non-U.S. middleman, see §1.6049-5(c)(5). For circumstances in which a payment is considered to be paid and received outside the United States, see §1.6049-4(f)(16).

(iii) Returns of information are not required for payments made by a foreign intermediary described in §1.1441-1(e)(3)(i) that it has received in its capacity as an intermediary and that are associated with a valid withholding certificate described in §1.1441-1(e)(3)(ii) or (iii) and payments made by a U.S. branch of a foreign bank or of a foreign insurance company described in §1.1441-1(b)(2)(iv) that are associated with a valid withholding certificate described in §1.1441-1(e)(3)(v), which certificate the intermediary or branch has furnished to the payor or middleman from whom it has received the payment, unless, and to the extent, the intermediary or branch knows that the payments are required to be reported and were not so reported.

(2) *Definitions.*—(i) *Payor.*—For purposes of this section, the term *payor* shall have the meaning ascribed to it under §1.6049-4(a).

(ii) *Joint owners.*—Amounts paid to joint owners for which a certificate or documentation is required as a condition for being exempt from reporting under this paragraph (c) of this section are presumed made to U.S. payees who are not exempt recipients if, prior to payment, the payor cannot reliably associate the payment either with a Form W-9 furnished by one of the joint owners in the manner required in §§31.3406(d)-1 through 31.3406(d)-5 of this chapter, or with documentation described in paragraph (c)(1)(i) of this section furnished by each joint owner upon which it can rely to treat each joint owner as a foreign payee or foreign beneficial owner. For purposes of applying this paragraph (c)(2)(ii), the grace period described in §1.6049-5(d)(2)(ii) shall apply only if each payee qualifies for such grace period.

(d) *Cross-reference to penalties.*—For provisions relating to the penalty provided for failure to file timely a correct information return required under section 6050N(a), see §301.6721-1 of this chapter (Procedure and Administration Regulations). For provisions relating to the penalty provided for failure to furnish timely a correct payee statement required under section 6050N(b) and §1.6050N-1(a), see §301.6722-1 of this chapter. See §301.6724-1 of this chapter for the waiver of a penalty if the failure is due to reasonable cause and is not due to willful neglect.

(e) *Effective/applicability date.*—This section applies to payee statements due after December 31, 2014, without regard to extensions. For payee statements due before January 1, 2015, §1.6050N-1 (as contained in 26 CFR part 1, revised April 2013) shall apply. [Reg. §1.6050N-1.]

☐ [*T.D. 8637, 12-20-95. Amended by T.D. 8734, 10-6-97; T.D. 8804, 12-30-98; T.D. 8856, 12-29-99, T.D. 9675, 7-14-2014 and T.D. 9808, 12-30-2016.*]

### [Reg. §1.6050N-2]

**§1.6050N-2. Coordination with reporting rules for widely held fixed investment trusts under §1.671-5.**—See §1.671-5 for the reporting rules for widely held fixed investment trusts (as defined under that section). [Reg. §1.6050N-2.]

☐ [*T.D. 9241, 1-23-2006.*]

### [Reg. §1.6050P-0]

**§1.6050P-0. Table of contents.**—This section lists the major captions that appear in §1.6050P-1 and §1.6050P-2.

[Reg. §1.6050P-0.]

☐ [*T.D. 8654, 1-3-96. Amended by T.D. 9160, 10-22-2004; T.D. 9430, 11-7-2008 and T.D. 9461, 9-16-2009.*]

### [Reg. §1.6050P-1]

**§1.6050P-1. Information reporting for discharges of indebtedness by certain entities.**—(a) *Reporting requirement.*—(1) *In general.*—Except as provided in paragraph (d) of this section, any applicable entity (as defined in section 6050P(c)(1)) that discharges an indebtedness of any person (within the meaning of section 7701(a)(1)) of at least $600 during a calendar year must file an information return on Form 1099-C with the Internal Revenue Service. Solely for purposes of the reporting requirements of section 6050P and this section, a discharge of indebtedness is deemed to have occurred, except as provided in paragraph (b)(3) of this section, if and only if there has occurred an identifiable event described in paragraph (b)(2) of this section, whether or not an actual discharge of indebtedness has occurred on or before the date on which the identifiable event has occurred. The return must include the following information—

(i) The name, address, and taxpayer identification number (TIN), as defined in section 7701(a)(41), of each person for which there was an identifiable event during the calendar year;

(ii) The date on which the identifiable event occurred, as described in paragraph (b) of this section;

(iii) The amount of indebtedness discharged, as described in paragraph (c) of this section;

(iv) An indication whether the identifiable event was a discharge of indebtedness in a bankruptcy, if known; and

(v) Any other information required by Form 1099-C or its instructions, or current revenue procedures.

(2) *No aggregation.*—For purposes of reporting under this section, multiple discharges of indebtedness of less than $600 are not required to be aggregated unless such separate discharges are pursuant to a plan to evade the reporting requirements of this section.

(3) *Amounts not includible in income.*—Except as otherwise provided in this section, discharged indebtedness must be reported regardless of whether the debtor is subject to tax on the discharged debt under sections 61 and 108 or otherwise by applicable law.

(4) *Time and place for reporting.*—(i) *In general.*—Except as provided in paragraph (a)(4)(ii) of this section, returns required by this section must be filed with the Internal Revenue Service office designated in the instructions for Form 1099-C on or before February 28 (March 31 if filed electronically) of the year following the calendar year in which the identifiable event occurs.

(ii) *Indebtedness discharged in bankruptcy.*—Indebtedness discharged in bankruptcy that is required to be reported under this section must be reported for the later of the calendar year in which the amount of discharged indebtedness first becomes ascertainable, or the calendar year in which the identifiable event occurs.

(b) *Date of discharge.*—(1) *In general.*—Solely for purposes of this section, except as provided in paragraph (b)(3) of this section, indebtedness is discharged on the date of the occurrence of an identifiable event specified in paragraph (b)(2) of this section.

(2) *Identifiable events.*—(i) *In general.*—An identifiable event is—

(A) A discharge of indebtedness under title 11 of the United States Code (bankruptcy);

(B) A cancellation or extinguishment of an indebtedness that renders a debt unenforceable in a receivership, foreclosure, or similar proceeding in a federal or State court, as described in section 368(a)(3)(A)(ii) (other than a discharge described in paragraph (b)(2)(i)(A) of this section);

(C) A cancellation or extinguishment of an indebtedness upon the expiration of the statute of limitations for collection of an indebtedness, subject to the limitations described in paragraph (b)(2)(ii) of this section, or upon the expiration of a statutory period for filing a claim or commencing a deficiency judgment proceeding;

(D) A cancellation or extinguishment of an indebtedness pursuant to an election of foreclosure remedies by a creditor that statutorily extinguishes or bars the creditor's right to pursue collection of the indebtedness;

(E) A cancellation or extinguishment of an indebtedness that renders a debt unenforceable pursuant to a probate or similar proceeding;

(F) A discharge of indebtedness pursuant to an agreement between an applicable entity and a debtor to discharge indebtedness at less than full consideration; or

(G) A discharge of indebtedness pursuant to a decision by the creditor, or the application of a defined policy of the creditor, to discontinue collection activity and discharge debt.

(ii) *Statute of limitations.*—In the case of an expiration of the statute of limitations for collection of an indebtedness, an identifiable event occurs under paragraph (b)(2)(i)(C) of this section only if, and at such time as, a debtor's affirmative statute of limitations defense is upheld in a final judgment or decision of a judicial proceeding, and the period for appealing the judgment or decision has expired.

(iii) *Decision to discontinue collection activity; creditor's defined policy.*—For purposes of the identifiable event described in paragraph (b)(2)(i)(G) of this section, a creditor's defined policy includes both a written policy of the creditor and the creditor's established business practice. Thus, for example, a creditor's established practice to discontinue collection activity and abandon debts upon expiration of a particular non-payment period is considered a defined policy for purposes of paragraph (b)(2)(i)(G) of this section.

(3) *Permitted reporting.*—If a discharge of indebtedness occurs before the date on which an identifiable event occurs, the discharge may, at the creditor's discretion, be reported under this section.

(c) *Indebtedness.*—For purposes of this section and §1.6050P-2, indebtedness means any amount owed to an applicable entity, including stated principal, fees, stated interest, penalties, administrative costs and fines. The amount of indebtedness discharged may represent all, or only a part, of the total amount owed to the applicable entity.

(d) *Exceptions from reporting requirement.*—(1) *Certain bankruptcy discharges.*—(i) *In general.*—Reporting is required under this section in the case of a discharge of indebtedness in bankruptcy only if the creditor knows from information included in the reporting entity's books and records pertaining to the indebtedness that the debt was incurred for business or investment purposes as defined in paragraph (d)(1)(ii) of this section.

(ii) *Business or investment debt.*—Indebtedness is considered incurred for business purposes if it is incurred in connection with the conduct of any trade or business other than the trade or business of performing services as an employee. Indebtedness is considered incurred for investment purposes if it is incurred to purchase property held for investment, as defined in section 163(d)(5).

(2) *Interest.*—The discharge of an amount of indebtedness that is interest is not required to be reported under this section.

(3) *Non-principal amounts in lending transactions.*—In the case of a lending transaction, the discharge of an amount other than stated principal is not required to be reported under this section. For this purpose, a lending transaction is any transaction in which a lender loans money to, or makes advances on behalf of, a borrower (including revolving credits and lines of credit).

(4) *Indebtedness of foreign debtors held by foreign branches of U.S. financial institutions.*—(i) *Reporting requirements.*—[Reserved]

(ii) *Definition.*—An indebtedness held by a foreign branch of a U.S. financial institution is described in this paragraph (d)(4) only if—

(A) The financial institution is engaged through a branch or office in the active conduct of a banking or similar business outside the United States;

(B) The branch or office is a permanent place of business that is regularly maintained, occupied, and used to carry on a banking or similar financial business;

(C) The business is conducted by at least one employee of the branch or office who is regularly in attendance at such place of business during normal working hours;

(D) The indebtedness is extended outside of the United States by the branch or office in connection with that trade or business; and

(E) The financial institution does not know or have reason to know that the debtor is a United States person.

(5) *Acquisition of indebtedness by related party.*—No reporting is required under this section in the case of a deemed discharge of indebtedness under section 108(e)(4) (relating to the acquisition of an indebtedness by a person related to the debtor), unless the disposition of the indebtedness by the creditor was made with a view to avoiding the reporting requirements of this section.

(6) *Releases.*—The release of a co-obligor is not required to be reported under this section if the remaining debtors remain liable for the full amount of any unpaid indebtedness.

(7) *Guarantors and sureties.*—Solely for purposes of the reporting requirements of this section, a guarantor is not a debtor. Thus, in the case of guaranteed indebtedness, reporting under this section is not required with respect to a guarantor, whether or not there has been a default and demand for payment made upon the guarantor.

(e) *Additional rules.*—(1) *Multiple debtors.*—(i) *In general.*—In the case of indebtedness of $10,000 or more incurred on or after January 1, 1995, that involves more than one debtor, a reporting entity is subject to the requirements of paragraph (a) of this section for each debtor discharged from such indebtedness. In the case of indebtedness incurred prior to January 1, 1995, and indebtedness of less than $10,000 incurred on or after January 1, 1995, involving multiple debtors, reporting under this section is required only with respect to the primary (or first-named) debtor. Additionally, only one return of information is required under this section if the reporting entity knows, or has reason to know, that co-obligors were husband and wife living at the same address when an indebtedness was incurred, and does not know or have reason to know that such circumstances have changed at the date of a discharge of the indebtedness. This paragraph (e)(1) applies to discharges of indebtedness after December 31, 1994.

(ii) *Amount to be reported.*—In the case of multiple debtors jointly and severally liable on an indebtedness, the amount of discharged indebtedness required to be reported under this section with respect to each debtor is the total amount of indebtedness discharged. For this purpose, multiple debtors are presumed to be jointly and severally liable on an indebtedness in the absence of clear and convincing evidence to the contrary.

(2) *Multiple creditors.*—(i) *In general.*—Except as otherwise provided in this paragraph (e)(2), if indebtedness is owned (or treated as owned for federal income tax purposes) by more than one creditor, each creditor that is an applicable entity must comply with the reporting requirements of this section with respect to any discharge of indebtedness of $600 or more allocable to such creditor. A creditor will be considered to have complied with the requirements of this section if a lead bank, fund administrator, or other designee of the creditor complies on its behalf in any reasonable manner, such as by filing a single return reporting the aggregate amount of indebtedness discharged, or by filing a return with respect to the portion of the discharged indebtedness allocable to the creditor. For purposes of this paragraph (e)(2)(i), any reasonable method may be used to determine the portion of discharged indebtedness allocable to each creditor.

(ii) *Partnerships.*—For purposes of paragraph (e)(2)(i) of this section, indebtedness owned by a partnership is treated as owned by the partners.

(iii) *Pass-through securitized indebtedness arrangement.*—(A) *Reporting requirements.*—[Reserved]

(B) *Definition.*—For purposes of this paragraph (e)(2)(iii), a pass-through securitized indebtedness arrangement is any arrangement whereby one or more debt obligations are pooled and held for twenty or more persons whose interests in the debt obligations are undivided co-ownership interests that are freely transferrable. Co-ownership interests that are actively traded personal property (as defined in § 1.1092(d)-1) are presumed to be freely transferrable and held by twenty or more persons.

(iv) *REMICs.*—[Reserved]

(v) *No double reporting.*—If multiple creditors are considered to hold interests in an indebtedness for purposes of this paragraph (e)(2) by virtue of holding ownership interests in an entity, and the entity is required to report a discharge of that indebtedness under paragraph (e)(5) of this section, then the multiple creditors are not required to report the discharge of indebtedness.

(3) *Coordination with reporting under section 6050J.*—If, in the same calendar year, a discharge of indebtedness reportable under section 6050P occurs in connection with a transaction also reportable under section 6050J (relating to foreclosures and abandonments of secured property), an applicable entity need not file both a Form 1099-A and a Form 1099-C with respect to the same debtor. The filing requirements of section 6050J will be satisfied with respect to a borrower if, in lieu of filing Form 1099-A, a Form 1099-C is filed in accordance with the instructions for the filing of that form. This paragraph (e)(3) applies to discharges of indebtedness after December 31, 1994.

(4) *Direct or indirect subsidiary.*—For purposes of section 6050P(c)(2)(C), the term direct or indirect subsidiary means a corporation in a chain of corporations beginning with an entity described in section 6050P(c)(2)(A), if at least 50 percent of the total combined voting power of all classes of stock entitled to vote, or at least 50 percent of the total value of all classes of stock, of such corporation is directly owned by the entity described in section 6050P(c)(2)(A), or by one or more other corporations in the chain.

(5) *Entity formed or availed of to hold indebtedness.*—Notwithstanding § 1.6050P-2(b)(3), if an entity (the transferee entity) is formed or availed of by an applicable entity (within the meaning of section 6050P(c)(1)) for the principal purpose of holding indebtedness acquired (including originated) by the applicable entity, then, for purposes of section 6050P(c)(2)(D), the transferee entity has a significant trade or business of lending money.

(6) *Use of magnetic media.*—Any return required under this section must be filed on magnetic media to the extent required by section 6011(e) and the regulations thereunder. A failure to file on magnetic media when required constitutes a failure to file an information return under section 6721. Any person not required by section 6011(e) to file returns on magnetic media may request permission to do so under applicable regulations and revenue procedures.

(7) *TIN solicitation requirement.*—(i) *In general.*—For purposes of reporting under this section, a reasonable effort must be made to obtain the correct name/taxpayer identification number (TIN) combination of a person whose indebtedness is discharged. A TIN obtained at the time an indebtedness is incurred satisfies the requirement of this section, unless the entity required to file knows that such TIN is incorrect. If the TIN is not obtained prior to the occurrence of an identifiable event, it must be requested of the debtor for purposes of satisfying the requirement of this paragraph (e)(7).

(ii) *Manner of soliciting TIN.*—Solicitations made in the manner described in § 301.6724-1(e)(1)(i) and (2) of this chapter will be deemed to have satisfied the reasonable effort requirement set forth in paragraph (e)(7)(i) of this section. A TIN solicitation made after the occurrence of an identifiable event must clearly notify the debtor that the Internal Revenue Service requires the debtor to furnish its TIN, and that failure to furnish such TIN may subject the debtor to a $50 penalty imposed by the Internal Revenue Service. A TIN provided under this section is not required to be certified under penalties of perjury.

(8) *Recordkeeping requirements.*—Any applicable entity required to file a return with the Internal Revenue Service under this section must also retain a copy of the return, or have the ability to reconstruct the data required to be included on the return under paragraph (a)(1) of this section, for at least four years from the date such return is required to be filed under paragraph (a)(4) of this section.

(9) *No multiple reporting.*—If discharged indebtedness is reported under this section, no further reporting under this section is required for the amount so reported, notwithstanding that a subsequent identifiable event occurs with respect to the same amount. Further, no additional reporting or Form 1099-C correction is required if a creditor receives a payment of all or a portion of a discharged indebtedness reported under this section for a prior calendar year.

(f) *Requirement to furnish statement.*—(1) *In general.*—Any applicable entity required to file a return under this section must furnish to each person whose name is shown on such return a written statement that includes the following information—

(i) The information required by paragraph (a)(1) of this section. An IRS truncated taxpayer identifying number (TTIN) may be used as the TIN of the person for whom there was an identifiable event in lieu of the identifying number appearing on the information return filed with the Internal Revenue Service. For provisions relating to the use of TTINs, see § 301.6109-4 of this chapter (Procedure and Administration Regulations);

(ii) The name, address, and TIN of the applicable entity required to file a return under paragraph (a) of this section;

(iii) A legend identifying the statement as important tax information that is being furnished to the Internal Revenue Service; and

(iv) Any other information required by Form 1099-C or its instructions, or current revenue procedures.

(2) *Furnishing copy of Form 1099-C.*—The requirement to provide a statement to the debtor will be satisfied if the applicable entity furnishes copy B of the Form 1099-C or a substitute statement that complies with the requirements of the current revenue procedure for substitute Forms 1099.

(3) *Time and place for furnishing statement.*—The statement required by this paragraph (f) must be furnished to the debtor on or before January 31 of the year following the calendar year in which the identifiable event occurs. The statement will be considered furnished to the debtor if it is mailed to the debtor's last known address.

(g) *Penalties.*—For penalties for failure to comply with the requirements of this section, see sections 6721 through 6724.

(h) *Applicability dates.*—This section applies to information returns required to be filed, and payee statements required to be furnished, after December 31, 2016. Section 1.6050P–1 (as contained in 26 CFR part 1, revised April 2016) applies to information returns required to be filed, and payee statements required to be furnished, on or before December 31, 2016. [Reg. § 1.6050P-1.]

☐ [*T.D.* 8654, 1-3-96. *Amended by T.D.* 8895, 8-17-2000; *T.D.* 9160, 10-22-2004; *T.D.* 9430, 11-7-2008; *T.D.* 9461, 9-16-2009, *T.D.* 9675, 7-14-2014 *and T.D.* 9793, 11-9-2016.]

**[Reg. § 1.6050P-2]**

**§ 1.6050P-2. Organization a significant trade or business of which is the lending of money.**—(a) *In general.*—For purposes of section 6050P(c)(2)(D), the lending of money is a significant trade or business of an organization in a calendar year if the organization lends money on a regular and continuing basis during the calendar year.

(b) *Safe harbors.*—(1) *Organizations not subject to section 6050P in the previous calendar year.*—For an organization that was not required to report under section 6050P in the previous calendar year, the lending of money is not treated as a significant trade or business for the calendar year in which the lending occurs if gross income from lending money (as described in paragraph (d) of this section) in the organization's most recent test year (as defined in paragraph (f) of this section) is both less than $5 million and less than 15 percent of the organization's gross income for that test year.

(2) *Organizations that were subject to section 6050P in the previous calendar year.*—For an organization that was required to report under section 6050P for the previous calendar year, the lending of money is not treated as a significant trade or business for the calendar year in which the lending occurs if gross income from lending money (as described in paragraph (d) of this section) in each of the organization's three most recent test years is both less than $3 million and less than 10 percent of the organization's gross income for that test year.

(3) *No test year.*—The lending of money is not treated as a significant trade or business for an organization for the calendar year in which the lending occurs if the organization does not have a test year for that calendar year.

(c) *Seller financing.*—If the principal trade or business of an organization is selling nonfinancial goods or providing nonfinancial services and if the organization extends credit to the purchasers of those goods or services to finance the purchases, then, for purposes of section 6050P(c)(2)(D), these extensions of credit are not a significant trade or business of lending money.

(d) *Gross income from lending of money.*—For purposes of this section, gross income from lending of money includes—

(1) Income from interest, including qualified stated interest, original issue discount, and market discount;

(2) Gains arising from the sale or other disposition of indebtedness;

(3) Penalties with respect to indebtedness (whether or not the penalty is interest for Federal tax purposes); and

(4) Fees with respect to indebtedness, including merchant discount or interchange (whether or not the fee is interest for Federal tax purposes).

(e) *Acquisition of an indebtedness from a person other than the debtor included in lending money.*—For purposes of this section, lending money includes acquiring an indebtedness not only from the debtor at origination but also from a prior holder of the indebtedness. Gross income arising from indebtedness is gross income from the lending of money without regard to who originated the indebtedness. If an organization acquires an indebtedness, the organization is required to report any cancellation of the indebtedness if the organization is engaged in a significant trade or business of lending money.

(f) *Test year.*—For any calendar year, a *test year* is a taxable year of the organization that ends before July 1 of the previous calendar year.

(g) *Predecessor organization.*—If an organization acquires substantially all of the property that was used in a trade or business of some other organization (the predecessor) (including when two or more corporations are parties to a merger agreement under which the surviving corporation becomes the owner of the assets and assumes the liabilities of the absorbed corporation(s)) or was used in a separate unit of the predecessor, then whether the organization at issue qualifies for one of the safe harbors in paragraph (b) of this section is determined by also taking into account the test years, reporting obligations, and gross income of the predecessor.

(h) *Examples.*—The rules of this section are illustrated by the following examples:

*Example 1.* (i) *Facts.* Finance Company A, a calendar year taxpayer, was formed in Year 1 as a non-bank subsidiary of Manufacturing Company and has no predecessor. A lends money to purchasers of Manufacturing Company's products on a regular and continuing basis to finance the purchase of those products. A's gross income from stated interest in Year 1 is $4.7 million. In Year 1, A's gross income from fees and penalties with respect to the indebtedness is $0.5 million, and A has no other gross income from lending money within the meaning of paragraph (d) of this section.

(ii) *Results.* Section 6050P does not require A to report discharges of indebtedness occurring in Years 1 or 2, because A has no test year for those years. Notwithstanding that A lends money in those years on a regular and continuing basis, under paragraph (b)(3) of this section, A does not have a significant trade or business of lending money in those years for purposes of section 6050P(c)(2)(D). However, for Year 3, A's test year is Year 1. A's gross income from lending in Year 1 is not less than $5 million for purposes of the applicable safe harbor of paragraph (b)(1) of this section. Because A lends money on a regular and continuing basis and does not meet the applicable safe harbor, section 6050P requires A to report discharges of indebtedness occurring in Year 3.

*Example 2.* (i) *Facts.* The facts are the same as in Example 1, except that A is a division of Manufacturing Company, rather than a separate subsidiary. Manufacturing Company's principal activity is the manufacture and sale of non-financial products, and, other than financing the purchase of those products, Manufacturing Company does not extend credit or otherwise lend money.

(ii) *Results.* Under paragraph (c) of this section, that financing activity is not a significant trade or business of lending money for purposes of section 6050P(c)(2)(D), and section 6050P does not require Manufacturing Company to report discharges of indebtedness.

*Example 3.* (i) *Facts.* Company B, a calendar year taxpayer, is formed in Year 1. B has no predecessor and a part of its activities consists of the lending of money. B packages and sells part of the indebtedness it originates and holds the remainder. B is engaged in these activities on a regular and continuing basis. For Year 1, the sum of B's gross income from sales of the indebtedness, plus other income described in paragraph (d) of this section, is only $4.8 million, but it is 16% of B's gross income in Year 1.

(ii) *Results.* Because B lends money on a regular and continuing basis and does not meet the applicable safe harbor of paragraph (b)(1) of this section, section 6050P requires B to report discharges of indebtedness occurring in Year 3. B is not required to report discharges of indebtedness in Years 1 and 2 because B has no test year for Years 1 and 2.

*Example 4.* (i) *Facts.* The facts are the same as in *Example 3.* In addition, in each of Years 2, 3, and 4, the sum of B's gross income from sales of the indebtedness, plus other income described in paragraph (d) of this section, is less than both $3 million and 10% of B's gross income.

(ii) *Results.* (A) Because B was required to report under section 6050P for Year 3, the applicable safe harbor for Year 4 is paragraph (b)(2) of this section, which is satisfied only if B's gross income from lending activities for each of the three most recent test years is less than both $3 million and 10% of B's gross income. For Year 4, even though B has only two test years, B's gross income in one of those test years, Year 1, causes B to fail to meet this safe harbor. Accordingly, B is required to report discharges of indebtedness under section 6050P in Year 4. For Year 5, B's three most recent test years are Years 1, 2, and 3. However, B's gross income from lending activities in Year 1 is not less than $3 million and 10% of B's gross income. Accordingly, section 6050P requires B to report discharges of indebtedness in Year 5.

(B) For Year 6, B satisfies the applicable safe harbor requirements of paragraph (b)(2) of this section for each of the three most recent test years (Years 2, 3, and 4). Therefore, section 6050P does not require B to report discharges of indebtedness in Year 6. Because B is not required to report for Year 6, the applicable safe harbor for Year 7 is the one contained in paragraph (b)(1) of this section, and thus the only relevant test year is Year 5.

*Example 5.* (i) *Facts.* (A) Company C, a calendar year taxpayer, was formed in Year 1 and, on a regular and continuing basis, enters into the following transactions with its clients, all of whom are unrelated parties to C. C does not have any other income.

(B) C's clients sell goods to customers, frequently accepting as payment accounts receivable that are due in 30 to 90 days. Under a contract with each client, C investigates the creditworthiness of the client's customers with respect to the prospective sales, and, for each customer, C determines whether, and to what extent, C is willing to assume the risk of loss on accounts receivable to be issued by the customer. C's decision whether to assume risk of loss may be based on an evaluation of the credit quality of particular customers or on the aggregate credit quality of all of the client's prospective customers. If C is unwilling to assume the risk, the client either may refuse to extend any credit to the customer or may accept the account receivable and bear the risk of loss.

(C) Pursuant to some contracts between C's clients and C, C's clients assign legal title to the accounts receivable to C when the accounts receivable are issued by the customers. For these accounts receivable, C agrees to undertake collections and to remit the amounts collected to the client, less a fee of 0.70 percent of the face value of the accounts receivable. Pursuant to other contracts between C's clients and C, C's clients retain legal title to the accounts receivable and retain the initial collection responsibility. For these accounts receivable, C's fee is reduced to 0.35 percent. Both groups of accounts receivable include accounts receivable for which C has assumed the risk of loss and accounts receivable for which C has not assumed the risk of loss.

(D) Based on all the facts and circumstances, C acquires ownership for Federal tax purposes of some, but not all, of the accounts receivable that it has agreed to collect and of some, but not all, of the accounts receivable for which the client has retained collection responsibility.

(E) In Year 1, C's total fee income with respect to accounts receivable of which it acquired tax ownership was $2 million. C's fee income in Year 1 from accounts receivable of which it did not acquire tax ownership was $700,000. C does not have any other income for Year 1.

(F) In Year 3, there were discharges of $950,000, representing $100,000 of customer defaults on those accounts receivable of which C was the owner for Federal tax purposes at the time of the identifiable event marking the discharge and $850,000 of customer defaults on the accounts receivable of which the clients, and not C, were the owner. Whenever C determined the uncollectibility of an account receivable for which it had not assumed the risk of loss, C reassigned title to the account receivable to the appropriate client. Each defaulting customer defaulted on an account receivable with an outstanding balance of at least $600.

(ii) *Results.* (A) For Year 3, C's test year is Year 1. Under paragraph (e) of this section, C's $2 million fee income from the accounts receivable of which it acquired tax ownership is "gross income from lending money" for purposes of paragraph (b) of this section, because C was the owner of the accounts for Federal tax purposes. Under paragraph (e) of this section, C's $700,000 fee income from the accounts receivable of which it did not acquire tax ownership is not "gross income from lending money" for purposes of paragraph (b) of this section, because C was not the owner of the accounts receivable for Federal tax purposes. In Year 1, therefore, C's gross income from lending money is less than $5 million but is not less than 15% of C's gross income. Because C lends money on a regular and continuing basis and does not meet the applicable safe harbor, section 6050P requires C to report discharges of indebtedness occurring in Year 3.

(B) In Year 3, section 6050P requires C to report the $100,000 of discharges of the accounts receivable of which C was the owner for Federal tax purposes at the time of the identifiable event marking the discharge. Unless an exception to reporting under paragraph (b) or (c) of this section applies, section 6050P requires C's clients to report the $850,000 of discharges of the accounts receivable of which C did not become the owner.

(i) *Effective date.*—This section applies to discharges of indebtedness occurring on or after January 1, 2005. [Reg. § 1.6050P-2.]

☐ [*T.D.* 9160, 10-22-2004.]

### [Reg. § 1.6050S-0]

**§ 1.6050S-0. Table of contents.**—This section lists captions contained in § § 1.6050S-1, 1.6050S-2T, 1.6050S-3, and 1.6050S-4T.

*§ 1.6050S-1 Information reporting for qualified tuition and related expenses.*
   (a) Information reporting requirement.
      (1) In general.
      (2) Exceptions.
         (i) No reporting by institutions or insurers for nonresident alien individuals.
         (ii) No reporting by institutions for noncredit courses.
            (A) In general.
            (B) Academic credit defined.
            (C) Example.
         (iii) No reporting by institutions for individuals whose qualified tuition and related expenses are waived or are paid with scholarships.
         (iv) No reporting by institutions for individuals whose qualified tuition and related expenses are covered by a formal billing arrangement.
            (A) In general.
            (B) Formal billing arrangement defined.
   (b) Requirement to file return.
      (1) In general.
      (2) Information reporting requirements for institutions that elect to report payments received for qualified tuition and related expenses.
         (i) In general.
         (ii) Information included on return.
         (iii) Reportable amount of payments received for qualified tuition and related expenses during calendar year determined.
         (iv) Separate reporting of reimbursements or refunds of payments of qualified tuition and related expenses that were reported for a prior calendar year.
         (v) Payments received for qualified tuition and related expenses determined.
         (vi) Reimbursements or refunds of payments for qualified tuition and related expenses determined.
         (vii) Examples.
      (3) Information reporting requirements for institutions that elect to report amounts billed for qualified tuition and related expenses.
         (i) In general.
         (ii) Information included on return.
         (iii) Reportable amounts billed for qualified tuition and related expenses during calendar year determined.
         (iv) Separate reporting of reductions made to amounts billed for qualified tuition and related expenses that were reported for a prior calendar year.

         (v) Examples.
      (4) Requirements for insurers.
         (i) In general.
         (ii) Information included on return.
      (5) Time and place for filing return.
         (i) In general.
         (ii) Return for nonresident alien individual.
         (iii) Extensions of time.
      (6) Use of magnetic media.
   (c) Requirement to furnish statement.
      (1) In general.
      (2) Time and manner for furnishing statement.
         (i) In general.
         (ii) Statement to nonresident alien individual.
         (iii) Extensions of time.
      (3) Copy of Form 1098-T.
   (d) Special rules.
      (1) Enrollment determined.
      (2) Payments of qualified tuition and related expenses received or collected by one or more persons.
         (i) In general.
         (ii) Exception.
      (3) Governmental units.
   (e) Penalty provisions.
      (1) Failure to file correct returns.
      (2) Failure to furnish correct information statements.
      (3) Waiver of penalties for failures to include a correct TIN.
         (i) In general.
         (ii) Acting in a responsible manner.
         (iii) Manner of soliciting TIN.
      (4) Failure to furnish TIN.
   (f) Effective date.

*§ 1.6050S-2T Electronic furnishing of information statements for qualified tuition and related expenses.*
   (a) Electronic furnishing of statements.
      (1) In general.
      (2) Consent.
         (i) In general.
         (ii) Change in hardware or software requirements.
         (iii) Example.
      (3) Required disclosures.
         (i) In general.
         (ii) Paper statement.
         (iii) Scope and duration of consent.
         (iv) Post-consent request for a paper statement.
         (v) Withdrawal of consent.
         (vi) Notice of termination.
         (vii) Updating information.
         (viii) Hardware and software requirements.
      (4) Format.
      (5) Posting.
      (6) Notice.
         (i) In general.
         (ii) Undeliverable electronic address.
         (iii) Corrected statements.
      (7) Retention.
   (b) Effective date.

*§ 1.6050S-3 Information reporting for payments of interest on qualified education loans.*
   (a) Information reporting requirement in general.
   (b) Definitions.
      (1) Interest.
      (2) Payor.
   (c) Requirement to file return.
      (1) Form of return.
      (2) Information included on return.
      (3) Time and place for filing return.
         (i) In general.
         (ii) Extensions of time.
      (4) Use of magnetic media.
   (d) Requirement to furnish statement.
      (1) In general.
      (2) Time and manner for furnishing statement.
         (i) In general.
         (ii) Extensions of time.
      (3) Copy of Form 1098-E.
   (e) Special rules.

(1) Transitional rule for reporting of loan origination fees and capitalized interest.

(2) Qualified education loan certification.

(3) Payments of interest received or collected by one or more persons.

(i) In general.

(ii) Exception.

(4) Reporting by foreign persons.

(5) Governmental units.

(f) Penalty provisions.

(1) Failure to file correct returns.

(2) Failure to furnish correct information statements.

(3) Waiver of penalties for failures to include a correct TIN.

(i) In general.

(ii) Acting in a responsible manner.

(iii) Manner of soliciting TIN.

(4) Failure to furnish TIN.

(g) Effective date.

*§ 1.6050S-4T Electronic furnishing of information statements for payments of interest on qualified education loans.*

(a) Electronic furnishing of statements.

(1) In general.

(2) Consent.

(i) In general.

(ii) Change in hardware or software requirements.

(iii) Example.

(3) Required disclosures.

(i) In general.

(ii) Paper statement.

(iii) Scope and duration of consent.

(iv) Post-consent request for a paper statement.

(v) Withdrawal of consent.

(vi) Notice of termination.

(vii) Updating information.

(viii) Hardware and software requirements.

(4) Format.

(5) Posting.

(6) Notice.

(i) In general.

(ii) Undeliverable electronic address.

(iii) Corrected statements.

(7) Retention.

(b) Effective date.

[Reg. § 1.6050S-0.]

☐ *[T.D. 8992, 4-26-2002. Amended by T.D. 9029, 12-18-2002.]*

### [Reg. § 1.6050S-1]

**§ 1.6050S-1. Information reporting for qualified tuition and related expenses.**—(a) *Information reporting requirement.*—(1) *In general.*—Except as provided in paragraph (a)(2) of this section, any eligible educational institution (as defined in section 25A(f)(2) and the regulations thereunder) (an institution) that enrolls (as determined under paragraph (d)(1) of this section) any individual for any academic period (as defined in the regulations under section 25A), and any person that is engaged in a trade or business of making payments under an insurance arrangement as reimbursements or refunds (or other similar amounts) of qualified tuition and related expenses (as defined in section 25A(f)(1) and the regulations thereunder) (an insurer) must—

(i) File an information return, as described in paragraph (b) of this section, with the Internal Revenue Service (IRS) with respect to each individual described in paragraph (b) of this section; and

(ii) Furnish a statement, as described in paragraph (c) of this section, to each individual described in paragraph (c) of this section.

(2) *Exceptions.*—(i) *No reporting by institution or insurer for nonresident alien individuals.*—The information reporting requirements of this section do not apply with respect to any individual who is a nonresident alien (as defined in section 7701(b) and § 301.7701(b)-3 of this chapter) during the calendar year, unless the individual requests the institution or insurer to report. If a nonresident alien individual requests an institution or insurer to report, the institution or insurer must comply with the requirements of this section for the calendar year with respect to which the request is made.

(ii) *No reporting by institutions for noncredit courses.*—(A) *In general.*—The information reporting requirements of this section do not apply with respect to any course for which no academic credit is offered by the institution.

(B) *Academic credit defined.*—*Academic credit* means credit offered by an institution for the completion of course work leading toward a post-secondary degree, certificate, or other recognized post-secondary educational credential.

(C) *Example.*—The following example illustrates the rules of this paragraph (a)(2)(ii):

*Example.* Student A, a medical doctor, takes a course at University X's medical school. Student A takes the course to fulfill State Y's licensing requirement that medical doctors attend continuing medical education courses each year. Student A is not enrolled in a degree program at University X and takes the medical course through University X's continuing professional education division. University X does not offer credit toward a post-secondary degree on an academic transcript for the completion of the course but gives Student A a certificate of attendance upon completion. Under this paragraph (a)(2)(ii), University X is not subject to the information reporting requirements of section 6050S and this section for the medical education course taken by Student A.

(iii) *No reporting by institutions for individuals whose qualified tuition and related expenses are waived or are paid with scholarships.*—The information reporting requirements of this section do not apply with respect to any individual whose qualified tuition and related expenses are waived in their entirety or are paid entirely with scholarships.

(iv) *No reporting by institutions for individuals whose qualified tuition and related expenses are covered by a formal billing arrangement.*—(A) *In general.*—The information reporting requirements of this section do not apply with respect to any individual whose qualified tuition and related expenses are covered by a formal billing arrangement as defined in paragraph (a)(2)(iv)(B) of this section.

(B) *Formal billing arrangement defined.*—A *formal billing arrangement* means—

(1) An arrangement in which the institution bills only an employer for education furnished by the institution to an individual who is the employer's employee and does not maintain a separate financial account for that individual;

(2) An arrangement in which the institution bills only a governmental entity for education furnished by the institution to an individual and does not maintain a separate financial account for that individual; or

(3) Any other similar arrangement in which the institution bills only an institutional third party for education furnished to an individual and does not maintain a separate financial account for that individual, but only if designated as a formal billing arrangement by the Commissioner in published guidance of general applicability or in guidance directed to participants in specific arrangements.

(b) *Requirement to file return.*—(1) *In general.*—Institutions may elect to report either the information described in paragraph (b)(2) of this section, or the information described in paragraph (b)(3) of this section. Once an institution elects to report under either paragraph (b)(2) or (3) of this section, the institution must use the same reporting method for all calendar years in which it is required to file returns, unless permission is granted to change reporting methods. Paragraph (b)(2) of this section requires institutions to report, among other information, the amount of payments received during the calendar year for qualified tuition and related expenses. Institutions must report separately adjustments made during the calendar year that relate to payments received for qualified tuition and related expenses that were reported for a prior calendar year. For purposes of paragraph (b)(2) of this section, an adjustment made to payments received means a reimbursement or refund. Paragraph (b)(3) requires institutions to report, among other information, the amounts billed during the calendar year for qualified tuition and related expenses. Institutions must report separately adjustments made during the calendar year that relate to amounts billed for qualified tuition and related expenses that were reported for a prior calendar year. For purposes of paragraph (b)(3) of this section, an adjustment made to amounts billed means a reduction in charges. Insurers must report the information described in paragraph (b)(4) of this section.

(2) *Information reporting requirements for institutions that elect to report payments received for qualified tuition and related expenses.*—(i) *In general.*—Except as provided in paragraph (a)(2) of this section, an institution reporting payments received for qualified tuition and related expenses must file an information return with the IRS on Form 1098-T, "Tuition Statement," with respect to each individual enrolled (as determined in paragraph (d)(1) of this section) for an academic period beginning during the calendar year or during a prior calendar year and for whom a transaction described in paragraphs (b)(2)(ii)(C), (E), (F) or (G) of this section is made during the calendar year. An institution may use a substitute Form 1098-T if the substitute form complies with applicable revenue procedures relating to substitute forms (see § 601.601(d)(2) of this chapter).

(ii) *Information included on return.*—An institution reporting payments received for qualified tuition and related expenses must include on Form 1098-T—

(A) The name, address, and taxpayer identification number (TIN) (as defined in section 7701(a)(41)) of the institution;

(B) The name, address, and TIN of the individual who is, or has been, enrolled by the institution;

(C) The amount of payments of qualified tuition and related expenses that the institution received from any source with respect to the individual during the calendar year;

(D) An indication by the institution whether any payments received for qualified tuition and related expenses reported for the calendar year relate to an academic period that begins during the first three months of the next calendar year;

(E) The amount of any scholarships or grants for the payment of the individual's costs of attendance that the institution administered and processed during the calendar year;

(F) The amount of any reimbursements or refunds of qualified tuition and related expenses made during the calendar year with respect to the individual that relate to payments of qualified tuition and related expenses that were reported by the institution for a prior calendar year;

(G) The amount of any reductions to the amount of scholarships or grants for the payment of the individual's costs of attendance that were reported by the institution with respect to the individual for a prior calendar year;

(H) A statement or other indication showing whether the individual was enrolled for at least half of the normal full-time work load for the course of study the individual is pursuing for at least one academic period that begins during the calendar year (see section 25A and the regulations thereunder);

(I) A statement or other indication showing whether the individual was enrolled in a program leading to a graduate-level degree, graduate-level certificate, or other recognized graduate-level educational credential; and

(J) Any other information required by Form 1098-T and its instructions.

(iii) *Reportable amount of payments received for qualified tuition and related expenses during calendar year determined.*—The amount of payments received for qualified tuition and related expenses with respect to an individual during the calendar year that is reportable on Form 1098-T is determined by netting the amount of payments received (as defined in paragraph (b)(2)(v) of this section) for qualified tuition and related expenses during the calendar year against any reimbursements or refunds (as defined in paragraph (b)(2)(vi) of this section) made during the calendar year that relate to payments received for qualified tuition and related expenses during the same calendar year.

(iv) *Separate reporting of reimbursements or refunds of payments of qualified tuition and related expenses that were reported for a prior calendar year.*—An institution must separately report on Form 1098-T any reimbursements or refunds (as defined in paragraph (b)(2)(vi) of this section) made during the current calendar year that relate to payments of qualified tuition and related expenses that were reported by the institution for a prior calendar year. Such reimbursements or refunds shall not be netted against the payments received for qualified tuition and related expenses during the current calendar year.

(v) *Payments received for qualified tuition and related expenses determined.*—For purposes of determining the amount of payments received for qualified tuition and related expenses during a calendar year, payments received with respect to an individual during the calendar year from any source (except for any scholarship or grant that, by its terms, must be applied to expenses other than qualified tuition and related expenses, such as room and board) are treated as payments of qualified tuition and related expenses up to the total amount billed by the institution for such expenses. For purposes of this section, a payment includes any positive account balance (such as any reimbursement or refund credited to an individual's account) that an institution applies toward current charges.

(vi) *Reimbursements or refunds of payments for qualified tuition and related expenses determined.*—For purposes of determining the amount of reimbursements or refunds made of payments received for qualified tuition and related expenses, any reimbursement or refund made with respect to an individual during a calendar year (except for any refund of a scholarship or grant that, by its terms, was required to be applied to expenses other than qualified tuition and related expenses, such as room and board) is treated as a reimbursement or refund of payments for qualified tuition and related expenses up to the amount of any reduction in charges for such expenses. For purposes of this section, a reimbursement or refund includes amounts that an institution credits to an individual's ac-

count, as well as amounts disbursed to, or on behalf of, the individual.

(vii) *Examples.*—The following examples illustrate the rules in this paragraph (b)(2):

*Example 1.* (i) In early August 2003, University X bills enrolled Student A $10,000 for qualified tuition and related expenses and $6,000 for room and board for the 2003 Fall semester. In late August 2003, Student A pays $11,000 to University X. In early September 2003, Student A drops to half-time enrollment for the 2003 Fall semester. In late September 2003, University X credits $5,000 to Student A's account, reflecting a $5,000 reduction in charges for qualified tuition and related expenses. In late September 2003, University X applies the $5,000 positive account balance toward current charges.

(ii) Under paragraph (b)(2)(v) of this section, the $11,000 payment is treated as a payment of qualified tuition and related expenses up to the $10,000 billed for qualified tuition and related expenses. Under paragraph (b)(2)(vi) of this section, the $5,000 credited to the student's account is treated as a reimbursement or refund of payments for qualified tuition and related expenses, because the current year charges for qualified tuition and related expenses were reduced by $5,000. Under paragraph (b)(2)(iii) of this section, University X is required to net the $10,000 payment received for qualified tuition and related expenses during 2003 against the $5,000 reimbursement or refund of payments received for qualified tuition and related expenses during 2003. Therefore, Institution X is required to report $5,000 of payments received for qualified tuition and related expenses during 2003.

*Example 2.* (i) The facts are the same as in *Example 1*, except that Student A pays the full $16,000 in late August 2003. In late September 2003, University X reduces the tuition charges by $5,000 and issues a $5,000 refund to Student A.

(ii) Under paragraph (b)(2)(v) of this section, the $16,000 payment is treated as a payment of qualified tuition and related expenses up to the $10,000 billed for qualified tuition and related expenses. Under paragraph (b)(2)(vi) of this section, the $5,000 refund is treated as reimbursement or refund of payments for qualified tuition and related expenses, because the current year charges for qualified tuition and related expenses were reduced by $5,000. Under paragraph (b)(2)(iii) of this section, University X is required to net the $10,000 payment received for qualified tuition and related expenses during 2003 against the $5,000 reimbursement or refund of payments received for qualified tuition and related expenses during 2003. Therefore, Institution X is required to report $5,000 of payments received for qualified tuition and related expenses during 2003.

*Example 3.* (i) The facts are the same as in *Example 1*, except that Student A is enrolled full-time, and, in early September 2003, Student A decides to live at home with her parents. In late September 2003, University X adjusts Student A's account to eliminate room and board charges and issues a $1,000 refund to Student A.

(ii) Under paragraph (b)(2)(v) of this section, the $11,000 payment is treated as a payment of qualified tuition and related expenses up to the $10,000 billed for qualified tuition and related expenses. Under paragraph (b)(2)(vi) of this section, the $1,000 refund is not treated as reimbursement or refund of payments for qualified tuition and related expenses, because there is no reduction in charges for qualified tuition and related expenses. Therefore, under paragraph (b)(2)(iii) of this section, University X is required to report $10,000 of payments received for qualified tuition and related expenses during 2003.

*Example 4.* (i) In early December 2003, College Y bills enrolled Student B $10,000 for qualified tuition and related expenses and $6,000 for room and board for the 2004 Spring semester. In late December 2003, Student B pays $16,000. In mid-January 2004, after the 2004 Spring semester classes begin, Student B drops to half-time enrollment. In mid-January 2004, College Y credits Student B's account with $5,000, reflecting a $5,000 reduction in charges for qualified tuition and related expenses, but does not issue a refund to Student B. In early August 2004, College Y bills Student B $10,000 for qualified tuition and related expenses and $6,000 for room and board for the 2004 Fall semester. In early September 2004, College Y applies the $5,000 positive account balance toward Student B's $16,000 bill for the 2004 Fall semester. In late September 2004, Student B pays $6,000 towards the charges.

(ii) In the reporting for calendar year 2003, under paragraph (b)(2)(v) of this section, the $16,000 payment in December 2003 is treated as a payment of qualified tuition and related expenses up to the $10,000 billed for qualified tuition and related expenses. Under paragraph (b)(2)(iii) of this section, College Y is required to report $10,000 of payments received for qualified tuition and related expenses during 2003. In addition, College Y is required to indicate that the payments reported for 2003 relate to an academic period that begins during the first three months of the next calendar year.

(iii) In the reporting for calendar year 2004, under paragraph (b)(2)(vi) of this section, the $5,000 credited to Student B's account is treated as a reimbursement or refund of qualified tuition and related expenses, because the charges for qualified tuition and related expenses were reduced by $5,000. Under paragraph (b)(2)(iv) of this section, the $5,000 reimbursement or refund of qualified tuition and related expenses must be separately reported on Form 1098-T because it relates to payments of qualified tuition and related expenses reported by College Y for 2003. Under paragraph (b)(2)(v) of this section, the $5,000 positive account balance that is applied toward charges for the 2004 Fall semester is treated as a payment. Therefore, College Y received total payments of $11,000 during 2004 (the $5,000 credit plus the $6,000 payment). Under paragraph (b)(2)(v) of this section, the $11,000 of total payments are treated as a payment of qualified tuition and related expenses up to the $10,000 billed for such expenses. Therefore, for 2004, College Y is required to report $10,000 of payments received for qualified tuition and related expenses during 2004 and a $5,000 refund of payments of qualified tuition and related expenses reported for 2003.

(3) *Information reporting requirements for institutions that elect to report amounts billed for qualified tuition and related expenses.*—(i) *In general.*—Except as provided in paragraph (a)(2) of this section, an institution reporting amounts billed for qualified tuition and related expenses must file an information return on Form 1098-T with respect to each individual enrolled (as determined in paragraph (d)(1) of this section) for an academic period beginning during the calendar year or during a prior calendar year and for whom a transaction described in paragraphs (b)(3)(ii)(C), (E), (F) or (G) of this section is made during the calendar year. An institution may use a substitute Form 1098-T if the substitute form complies with applicable revenue procedures relating to substitute forms (see § 601.601(d)(2) of this chapter).

(ii) *Information included on return.*—An institution reporting amounts billed for qualified tuition and related expenses must include on Form 1098-T—

(A) The name, address, and taxpayer identification number (TIN) (as defined in section 7701(a)(41)) of the institution;

(B) The name, address, and TIN of the individual who is, or has been, enrolled by the institution;

(C) The amount billed for qualified tuition and related expenses with respect to the individual during the calendar year;

(D) An indication by the institution whether any amounts billed for qualified tuition and related expenses reported for the calendar year relate to an academic period that begins during the first three months of the next calendar year;

(E) The amount of any scholarships or grants for the payment of the individual's costs of attendance that the institution administered and processed during the calendar year;

(F) The amount of any reductions in charges made during the calendar year with respect to the individual that relate to amounts billed for qualified tuition and related expenses that were reported by the institution for a prior calendar year;

(G) The amount of any reductions to the amount of scholarships or grants for the payment of the individual's costs of attendance that were reported by the institution with respect to the individual for a prior calendar year;

(H) A statement or other indication showing whether the individual was enrolled for at least half of the normal full-time work load for the course of study the individual is pursuing for at least one academic period that begins during the calendar year (see section 25A and the regulations thereunder);

(I) A statement or other indication showing whether the individual was enrolled in a program leading to a graduate-level degree, graduate-level certificate, or other recognized graduate-level educational credential; and

(J) Any other information required by Form 1098-T and its instructions.

(iii) *Reportable amounts billed for qualified tuition and related expenses during calendar year determined.*—The amount billed for qualified tuition and related expenses with respect to an individual during the calendar year that is reportable on Form 1098-T is determined by netting the amounts billed for qualified tuition and related expenses during the calendar year against any reductions in charges for qualified tuition and related expenses made during the calendar year that relate to amounts billed for qualified tuition and related expenses during the same calendar year.

(iv) *Separate reporting of reductions made to amounts billed for qualified tuition and related expenses that were reported for a prior calendar year.*—An institution must separately report on Form 1098-T any reductions in charges made during the current calendar year that relate to amounts billed for qualified tuition and related expenses that were reported by the institution for a prior calendar year. Such

reductions shall not be netted against amounts billed for qualified tuition and related expenses during the current calendar year.

(v) *Examples.*—The following examples illustrate the rules in this paragraph (b)(3):

*Example 1.* (i) In early August 2003, University X bills enrolled Student A $10,000 for qualified tuition and related expenses and $6,000 for room and board for the 2003 Fall semester. In late August 2003, Student A pays $11,000 to University X. In early September 2003, Student A drops to half-time enrollment for the 2003 Fall semester. In late September 2003, University X adjusts Student A's account and reduces the charges for qualified tuition and related expenses by $5,000 to reflect half-time enrollment. In late September 2003, University X applies the $5,000 account balance toward current charges.

(ii) Under paragraph (b)(3)(iii) of this section, University X is required to net the $10,000 amount of qualified tuition and related expenses billed during 2003 against the $5,000 reduction in charges for qualified tuition and related expenses during 2003. Therefore, Institution X is required to report $5,000 in amounts billed for qualified tuition and related expenses during 2003.

*Example 2.* (i) The facts are the same as in *Example 1*, except that, in addition, in early December 2003, College X bills Student A $10,000 for qualified tuition and related expenses and $6,000 for room and board for the 2004 Spring semester. In early January 2004, Student A pays $16,000. In mid-January 2004, after the 2004 Spring semester classes begin, Student A drops to half-time enrollment. In mid-January 2004, College X credits $5,000 to Student A's account, reflecting a $5,000 reduction in charges for qualified tuition and related expenses, but does not issue a refund check to Student A. In early August 2004, College X bills Student A $10,000 for qualified tuition and related expenses and $6,000 for room and board for the 2004 Fall semester. In early September 2004, College X applies the $5,000 positive account balance toward Student A's $16,000 bill for the 2004 Fall semester. In late September 2004, Student A pays $6,000 toward the charges.

(ii) In the reporting for calendar year 2003, under paragraph (b)(3)(iii) of this section, College X is required to report $15,000 amounts billed for qualified tuition and related expenses during 2003 ($5,000 for the 2003 Fall semester and $10,000 for the 2004 Spring semester). In addition, College X is required to indicate that some of the amounts billed for qualified tuition and related expenses reported for 2003 relate to an academic period that begins during the first three months of the next calendar year.

(iii) In the reporting for calendar year 2004, under paragraph (b)(3)(iv) of this section, the $5,000 reduction in charges for qualified tuition and related expenses must be separately reported on Form 1098-T because it relates to amounts billed for qualified tuition and related expenses that were reported by College X for 2003. Under paragraph (b)(3)(iii) of this section, College X is required to report $10,000 in amounts billed for qualified tuition and related expenses during 2004.

(4) *Requirements for insurers.*—(i) *In general.*—Except as otherwise provided in this section, an insurer must file an information return for each individual with respect to whom reimbursements or refunds of qualified tuition and related expenses are made during the calendar year on Form 1098-T. An insurer may use a substitute Form 1098-T if the substitute form complies with applicable revenue procedures relating to substitute forms (see § 601.601(d)(2) of this chapter).

(ii) *Information included on return.*—An insurer must include on Form 1098-T—

(A) The name, address, and taxpayer identification number (TIN) (as defined in section 7701(a)(41)) of the insurer;

(B) The name, address, and TIN of the individual with respect to whom reimbursements or refunds of qualified tuition and related expenses were made;

(C) The aggregate amount of reimbursements or refunds of qualified tuition and related expenses that the insurer made with respect to the individual during the calendar year; and

(D) Any other information required by Form 1098-T and its instructions.

(5) *Time and place for filing return.*—(i) *In general.*—Except as provided in paragraphs (b)(5)(ii) and (iii) of this section, Form 1098-T must be filed on or before February 28 (March 31 if filed electronically) of the year following the calendar year in which payments were received, or amounts were billed, for qualified tuition or related expenses, or reimbursements, refunds, or reductions of such amounts were made. An institution or insurer must file Form 1098-T with the IRS according to the instructions to Form 1098-T.

(ii) *Return for nonresident alien individual.*—In general, an institution or insurer is not required to file a return on behalf of a nonresident alien individual. However, if a nonresident alien individual requests an institution or insurer to report, the institution or insurer must file a return described in paragraph (b) of this section with the IRS on or before the date prescribed in paragraph (b)(5)(i) of this section, or on or before the thirtieth day after the request, whichever is later.

(iii) *Extensions of time.*—The IRS may grant an institution or insurer an extension of time to file returns required in this section upon a showing of good cause. See General Instructions for Forms 1099 series, 1098 series, 5498 series, and W-2G, "Certain Gambling Winnings," and applicable revenue procedures for rules relating to extensions of time to file (see § 601.601(d)(2) of this chapter).

(6) *Use of magnetic media.*—See section 6011(e) and § 301.6011-2 of this chapter for rules relating to the requirement to file Forms 1098-T on magnetic media.

(c) *Requirement to furnish statement.*—(1) *In general.*—An institution or insurer must furnish a statement to each individual for whom it is required to file a Form 1098-T. The statement must include—

(i) The information required under paragraph (b) of this section. An IRS truncated taxpayer identifying number (TTIN) may be used as the TIN of the individual in lieu of the identifying number appearing on the information return filed with the Internal Revenue Service. For provisions relating to the use of TTINs, see § 301.6109-4 of this chapter (Procedure and Administration Regulations);

(ii) A legend that identifies the statement as important tax information that is being furnished to the IRS;

(iii) Instructions that—

(A) State that the statement reports either total payments received by the institution for qualified tuition and related expenses during the calendar year, or total amounts billed by the institution for qualified tuition and related expenses during the calendar year, or the total reimbursements or refunds made by the insurer;

(B) State that, under section 25A and the regulations thereunder, the taxpayer may claim an education tax credit only with respect to qualified tuition and related expenses actually paid during the calendar year; and that the taxpayer may not be able to claim an education tax credit with respect to the entire amount of payments received, or amounts billed, for qualified tuition and related expenses reported for the calendar year;

(C) State that the amount of any scholarships or grants reported for the calendar year and other similar amounts not reported (because they are not administered and processed by the institution) may reduce the amount of any allowable education tax credit for the taxable year;

(D) State that the amount of any reimbursements or refunds of payments received, or reductions in charges, for qualified tuition and related expenses, or any reductions to the amount of scholarships or grants, reported by the institution with respect to the individual for a prior calendar year may affect the amount of any allowable education tax credit for the prior calendar year (and may result in an increase in tax liability for the year of the refund);

(E) State that the amount of any reimbursements or refunds of qualified tuition and related expenses reported by an insurer may reduce the amount of an allowable education tax credit for a taxable year (and may result in an increase in tax liability for the year of the refund);

(F) State that the taxpayer should refer to relevant IRS forms and publications, and should not refer to the institution or the insurer, for explanations relating to the eligibility requirements for, and calculation of, any allowable education tax credit; and

(G) Include the name, address, and phone number of the information contact of the institution or insurer that filed the Form 1098-T.

(2) *Time and manner for furnishing statement.*—(i) *In general.*—Except as provided in paragraphs (c)(2)(ii) and (iii) of this section, an institution or insurer must furnish the statement described in paragraph (c)(1) of this section to each individual for whom it is required to file a return, on or before January 31 of the year following the calendar year in which payments were received, or amounts were billed, for qualified tuition and related expenses, or reimbursements, refunds, or reductions of such amounts were made. If mailed, the statement must be sent to the individual's permanent address, or the individual's temporary address if the institution or insurer does not know the individual's permanent address. If furnished electronically, the statement must be furnished in accordance with the applicable regulations.

(ii) *Statement to nonresident alien individual.*—If an information return is filed for a nonresident alien individual, the institution or insurer must furnish a statement described in paragraph (c)(1) of this section to the individual in the manner prescribed in paragraph (c)(2)(i) of this section. The statement must be furnished on or before

the later of the date prescribed in paragraph (c)(2)(i) of this section or the thirtieth day after the nonresident alien's request to report.

(iii) *Extensions of time.*—The IRS may grant an institution or insurer an extension of time to furnish the statements required in this section upon a showing of good cause. See General Instructions for Forms 1099 series, 1098 series, 5498 series, and W-2G, "Certain Gambling Winnings," and applicable revenue procedures for rules relating to extensions of time to furnish statements (see § 601.601(d)(2) of this chapter).

(3) *Copy of Form 1098-T.*—An institution or insurer may satisfy the requirement of this paragraph (c) by furnishing either a copy of Form 1098-T and its instructions or another document that contains all of the information filed with the IRS and the information required by paragraph (c)(1) of this section if the document complies with applicable revenue procedures relating to substitute statements (see § 601.601(d)(2) of this chapter).

(d) *Special rules.*—(1) *Enrollment determined.*—An institution may determine its enrollment for each academic period under its own rules and policies for determining enrollment or as of any of the following dates—

(i) 30 days after the first day of the academic period;

(ii) A date during the academic period on which enrollment data must be collected for purposes of the Integrated Post Secondary Education Data System administered by the Department of Education; or

(iii) A date during the academic period on which the institution must report enrollment data to the State, the institution's governing body, or some other external governing body.

(2) *Payments of qualified tuition and related expenses received or collected by one or more persons.*—(i) *In general.*—Except as otherwise provided in paragraph (d)(2)(ii) of this section, if a person collects or receives payments of qualified tuition and related expenses on behalf of another person (e.g., an institution), the person collecting or receiving payments must satisfy the requirements of paragraphs (b) and (c) of this section. In this case, those requirements do not apply to the transfer of the payments to the institution.

(ii) *Exception.*—If the person collecting or receiving payments of qualified tuition and related expenses on behalf of another person (e.g., an institution) does not possess the information needed to comply with the requirements of paragraphs (b) and (c) of this section, the other person must satisfy those requirements.

(3) *Governmental units.*—An institution or insurer that is a governmental unit, or an agency or instrumentality of a governmental unit, is subject to the requirements of paragraphs (b) and (c) of this section and an appropriately designated officer or employee of the governmental entity must satisfy those requirements.

(e) *Penalty provisions.*—(1) *Failure to file correct returns.*—The section 6721 penalty may apply to an institution or insurer that fails to file information returns required by section 6050S and this section on or before the required filing date; that fails to include all of the required information on the return; or that includes incorrect information on the return. See section 6721, and the regulations thereunder, for rules relating to penalties for failure to file correct returns. See section 6724, and the regulations thereunder, for rules relating to waivers of penalties for certain failures due to reasonable cause.

(2) *Failure to furnish correct information statements.*—The section 6722 penalty may apply to an institution or insurer that fails to furnish statements required by section 6050S and this section on or before the prescribed date; that fails to include all the required information on the statement; or that includes incorrect information on the statement. See section 6722, and the regulations thereunder, for rules relating to penalties for failure to furnish correct statements. See section 6724, and the regulations thereunder, for rules relating to waivers of penalties for certain failures due to reasonable cause.

(3) *Waiver of penalties for failures to include a correct TIN.*—(i) *In general.*—In the case of a failure to include a correct TIN on Form 1098-T or a related information statement, penalties may be waived if the failure is due to reasonable cause. Reasonable cause may be established if the failure arose from events beyond the institution's or insurer's control, such as a failure of the individual to furnish a correct TIN. However, the institution or insurer must establish that it acted in a responsible manner both before and after the failure.

(ii) *Acting in a responsible manner.*—An institution or insurer must request the TIN of each individual for whom it is required to file a return if it does not already have a record of the individual's correct TIN. If the institution or insurer does not have a record of the individual's correct TIN, then it must solicit the TIN in the manner described in paragraph (e)(3)(iii) of this section on or before December 31 of each year during which it receives payments, or bills amounts, for qualified tuition and related expenses or makes reimbursements, refunds, or reductions of such amounts with respect to the individual. If an individual refuses to provide his or her TIN upon request, the institution or insurer must file the return and furnish the statement required by this section without the individual's TIN, but with all other required information. The specific solicitation requirements of paragraph (e)(3)(iii) of this section apply in lieu of the solicitation requirements of §301.6724-1(e) and (f) of this chapter for the purpose of determining whether an institution or insurer acted in a responsible manner in attempting to obtain a correct TIN. An institution or insurer that complies with the requirements of this paragraph (e)(3) will be considered to have acted in a responsible manner within the meaning of §301.6724-1(d) of this chapter with respect to any failure to include the correct TIN of an individual on a return or statement required by section 6050S and this section.

(iii) *Manner of soliciting TIN.*—An institution or insurer must request the individual's TIN in writing and must clearly notify the individual that the law requires the individual to furnish a TIN so that it may be included on an information return filed by the institution or insurer. A request for a TIN made on Form W-9S, "Request for Student's or Borrower's Taxpayer Identification Number and Certification," satisfies the requirements of this paragraph (e)(3)(iii). An institution or insurer may establish a system for individuals to submit Forms W-9S electronically as described in applicable forms and instructions. An institution or insurer may also develop a separate form to request the individual's TIN or incorporate the request into other forms customarily used by the institution or insurer, such as admission or enrollment forms or financial aid applications.

(4) *Failure to furnish TIN.*—The section 6723 penalty may apply to any individual who is required (but fails) to furnish his or her TIN to an institution or insurer. See section 6723, and the regulations thereunder, for rules relating to the penalty for failure to furnish a TIN.

(f) *Effective/applicability date.*—The rules in this section apply to information returns required to be filed, and information statements required to be furnished, after December 31, 2003. Paragraph (c)(1)(i) applies to payee statements due after December 31, 2014. For payee statements due before January 1, 2015, §1.6050S-1 (as contained in 26 CFR part 1, revised April 2013) shall apply. [Reg. §1.6050S-1.]

☐ [*T.D. 9029, 12-18-2002 (corrected 2-6-2003). Amended by T.D. 9675, 7-14-2014.*]

**[Reg. §1.6050S-2]**

**§1.6050S-2. Information reporting for payments and reimbursements or refunds of qualified tuition and related expenses.**— (a) *Electronic furnishing of statements.*—(1) *In general.*—A person required by section 6050S(d) to furnish a written statement regarding payments and reimbursements or refunds of qualified tuition and related expenses (furnisher) to the individual to whom it is required to be furnished (recipient) may furnish the statement in an electronic format in lieu of a paper format. A furnisher who meets the requirements of paragraphs (a)(2) through (6) of this section is treated as furnishing the required statement.

(2) *Consent.*—(i) *In general.*—The recipient must have affirmatively consented to receive the statement in an electronic format. The consent may be made electronically in any manner that reasonably demonstrates that the recipient can access the statement in the electronic format in which it will be furnished to the recipient. Alternatively, the consent may be made in a paper document if it is confirmed electronically.

(ii) *Withdrawal of consent.*—The consent requirement of this paragraph (a)(2) is not satisfied if the recipient withdraws the consent and the withdrawal takes effect before the statement is furnished. The furnisher may provide that a withdrawal of consent takes effect either on the date it is received by the furnisher or on a subsequent date. The furnisher may also provide that a request for a paper statement will be treated as a withdrawal of consent.

(iii) *Change in hardware or software requirements.*—If a change in the hardware or software required to access the statement creates a material risk that the recipient will not be able to access the statement, the furnisher must, prior to changing the hardware or software, provide the recipient with a notice. The notice must describe the revised hardware and software required to access the statement and inform the recipient that a new consent to receive the statement in the revised electronic format must be provided to the furnisher. After implementing the revised hardware and software, the furnisher must obtain from the recipient, in the manner described

in paragraph (a)(2)(i) of this section, a new consent or confirmation of consent to receive the statement electronically.

(iv) *Examples.*—The following examples illustrate the rules of this paragraph (a)(2):

*Example 1.* Furnisher F sends Recipient R a letter stating that R may consent to receive statements required by section 6050S(d) electronically on a website instead of in a paper format. The letter contains instructions explaining how to consent to receive the statements electronically by accessing the website, downloading the consent document, completing the consent document and emailing the completed consent back to F. The consent document posted on the website uses the same electronic format that F will use for the electronically furnished statements. R reads the instructions and submits the consent in the manner provided in the instructions. R has consented to receive the statements electronically in the manner described in paragraph (a)(2)(i) of this section.

*Example 2.* Furnisher F sends Recipient R an e-mail stating that R may consent to receive statements required by section 6050S(d) electronically instead of in a paper format. The e-mail contains an attachment instructing R how to consent to receive the statements electronically. The e-mail attachment uses the same electronic format that F will use for the electronically furnished statements. R opens the attachment, reads the instructions, and submits the consent in the manner provided in the instructions. R has consented to receive the statements electronically in the manner described in paragraph (a)(2)(i) of this section.

*Example 3.* Furnisher F posts a notice on its website stating that Recipient R may receive statements required by section 6050S(d) electronically instead of in a paper format. The website contains instructions on how R may access a secure webpage and consent to receive the statements electronically. By accessing the secure webpage and giving consent, R has consented to receive the statements electronically in the manner described in paragraph (a)(2)(i) of this section.

(3) *Required disclosures.*—(i) *In general.*—Prior to, or at the time of, a recipient's consent, the furnisher must provide to the recipient a clear and conspicuous disclosure statement containing each of the disclosures described in paragraphs (a)(3)(ii) through (viii) of this section.

(ii) *Paper statement.*—The recipient must be informed that the statement will be furnished on paper if the recipient does not consent to receive it electronically.

(iii) *Scope and duration of consent.*—The recipient must be informed of the scope and duration of the consent. For example, the recipient must be informed whether the consent applies to statements furnished every year after the consent is given until it is withdrawn in the manner described in paragraph (a)(3)(v)(A) of this section or only to the statement required to be furnished on or before the January 31 immediately following the date on which the consent is given.

(iv) *Post-consent request for a paper statement.*—The recipient must be informed of any procedure for obtaining a paper copy of the recipient's statement after giving the consent described in paragraph (a)(2)(i) of this section and whether a request for a paper statement will be treated as a withdrawal of consent.

(v) *Withdrawal of consent.*—The recipient must be informed that—

(A) The recipient may withdraw a consent by writing (electronically or on paper) to the person or department whose name, mailing address, telephone number, and e-mail address is provided in the disclosure statement;

(B) The furnisher will confirm the withdrawal and the date on which it takes effect in writing (either electronically or on paper); and

(C) A withdrawal of consent does not apply to a statement that was furnished electronically in the manner described in this paragraph (a) before the date on which the withdrawal of consent takes effect.

(vi) *Notice of termination.*—The recipient must be informed of the conditions under which a furnisher will cease furnishing statements electronically to the recipient.

(vii) *Updating information.*—The recipient must be informed of the procedures for updating the information needed by the furnisher to contact the recipient. The furnisher must inform the recipient of any change in the furnisher's contact information.

(viii) *Hardware and software requirements.*—The recipient must be provided with a description of the hardware and software required to access, print, and retain the statement, and the date when the statement will no longer be available on the website.

(4) *Format.*—The electronic version of the statement must contain all required information and comply with applicable revenue procedures relating to substitute statements to recipients.

(5) *Notice.*—(i) *In general.*—If the statement is furnished on a website, the furnisher must notify the recipient that the statement is posted on a website. The notice may be delivered by mail, electronic mail, or in person. The notice must provide instructions on how to access and print the statement. The notice must include the following statement in capital letters, "IMPORTANT TAX RETURN DOCUMENT AVAILABLE." If the notice is provided by electronic mail, the foregoing statement must be on the subject line of the electronic mail.

(ii) *Undeliverable electronic address.*—If an electronic notice described in paragraph (a)(5)(i) of this section is returned as undeliverable, and the correct electronic address cannot be obtained from the furnisher's records or from the recipient, then the furnisher must furnish the notice by mail or in person within 30 days after the electronic notice is returned.

(iii) *Corrected statements.*—If the furnisher has corrected a recipient's statement that was furnished electronically, the furnisher must furnish the corrected statement to the recipient electronically. If the recipient's statement was furnished through a website posting and the furnisher has corrected the statement, the furnisher must notify the recipient that it has posted the corrected statement on the website within 30 days of such posting in the manner described in paragraph (a)(5)(i) of this section. The corrected statement or the notice must be furnished by mail or in person if—

(A) An electronic notice of the website posting of an original statement was returned as undeliverable; and

(B) The recipient has not provided a new e-mail address.

(6) *Access Period.*—Statements furnished on a website must be retained on the website through October 15 of the year following the calendar year to which the statements relate (or the first business day after such October 15, if October 15 falls on a Saturday, Sunday, or legal holiday). The furnisher must maintain access to corrected statements that are posted on the website through October 15 of the year following the calendar year to which the statements relate (or the first business day after such October 15, if October 15 falls on a Saturday, Sunday, or legal holiday) or the date 90 days after the corrected statements are posted, whichever is later.

(b) *Paper statements after withdrawal of consent.*—If a recipient withdraws consent to receive a statement electronically and the withdrawal takes effect before the statement is furnished electronically, a paper statement must be furnished. A paper statement furnished after the statement due date under this paragraph (b) will be considered timely if furnished within 30 days after the date the withdrawal of consent is received by the furnisher.

(c) *Effective date.*—This section applies to statements required to be furnished after February 13, 2004. Paragraph (a)(6) of this section also applies to statements required to be furnished after December 31, 2003. [Reg. § 1.6050S-2.]

☐ [*T.D. 9114, 2-13-2004.*]

**[Reg. § 1.6050S-3]**

**§ 1.6050S-3. Information reporting for payments of interest on qualified education loans.**—(a) *Information reporting requirement in general.*—Except as otherwise provided in this section, any person engaged in a trade or business that, in the course of that trade or business, receives from any payor (as defined in paragraph (b)(2) of this section) interest payments that aggregate $600 or more for any calendar year on one or more qualified education loans (as defined in section 221(e)(1) and the regulations thereunder)(a payee) must—

(1) File an information return, as described in paragraph (c) of this section, with the Internal Revenue Service with respect to the payor; and

(2) Furnish a statement, as described in paragraph (d) of this section, to the payor.

(b) *Definitions.*—The following definitions apply for purposes of this section:

(1) *Interest.*—Interest includes stated interest, loan origination fees (other than fees for services), and capitalized interest as described in the regulations under section 221. See paragraph (e)(1) of this section for a special transitional rule relating to reporting of loan origination fees and capitalized interest.

(2) *Payor.*—Payor means the individual who is carried on the books and records of the payee as the borrower on a qualified education loan. If there are multiple borrowers, the principal borrower on the payee's books and records is treated as the payor for purposes of section 6050S and this section.

(c) *Requirement to file return.*—(1) *Form of return.*—A payee must file an information return for the payor on Form 1098-E, "Student Loan Interest Statement." A payee may use a substitute for Form 1098-E if the substitute form complies with the applicable revenue procedures relating to substitute forms.

(2) *Information included on return.*—A payee must include on Form 1098-E—

(i) The name, address, and taxpayer identification number (TIN)(as defined in section 7701(a)(41)) of the payee;

(ii) The name, address, and TIN of the payor;

(iii) The aggregate amount of interest payments received during the calendar year from the payor; and

(iv) Any other information required by Form 1098-E and its instructions.

(3) *Time and place for filing return.*—(i) *In general.*—Except as provided in paragraph (c)(3)(ii) of this section, the Form 1098-E must be filed on or before February 28 (March 31 if filed electronically) of the year following the calendar year in which interest payments were received. A payee must file Form 1098-E with the Internal Revenue Service according to the instructions to Form 1098-E.

(ii) *Extensions of time.*—The Internal Revenue Service may grant a payee an extension of time to file returns required in this section upon a showing of good cause. See the instructions to Form 1098-E and applicable revenue procedures for rules relating to extensions of time to file.

(4) *Use of magnetic media.*—See section 6011(e) and § 301.6011-2 of this chapter for rules relating to the requirement to file Forms 1098-E on magnetic media.

(d) *Requirement to furnish statement.*—(1) *In general.*—A payee must furnish a statement to each payor for whom it is required to file a Form 1098-E. The statement must include—

(i) The information required under paragraph (c)(2) of this section. An IRS truncated taxpayer identifying number (TTIN) may be used as the TIN of the payor in lieu of the identifying number appearing on the information return filed with the Internal Revenue Service. For provisions relating to the use of TTINs, see § 301.6109-4 of this chapter (Procedure and Administration Regulations).

(ii) A legend that identifies the statement as important tax information that is being furnished to the Internal Revenue Service;

(iii) Instructions that—

(A) State that, under section 221 and the regulations thereunder, the payor may not be able to deduct the full amount of interest reported on the statement;

(B) In the case of qualified education loans made before September 1, 2004, for which the payee does not report payments of interest other than stated interest, state that the payor may be able to deduct additional amounts (such as certain loan origination fees and capitalized interest) not reported on the statement;

(C) State that the payor should refer to relevant Internal Revenue Service forms and publications, and should not refer to the payee, for explanations relating to the eligibility requirements for, and calculation of, any allowable deduction for interest paid on a qualified education loan; and

(D) Include the name, address, and phone number of the office or department of the payee that is the information contact for the payee that filed the Form 1098-E.

(2) *Time and manner for furnishing statement.*—(i) *In general.*—Except as provided in paragraph (d)(2)(ii) of this section, a payee must furnish the statement described in paragraph (d)(1) of this section to the payor on or before January 31 of the year following the calendar year in which payments of interest on a qualified education loan were received. If mailed, the statement must be sent to the payor's last known address. If furnished electronically, the statement must be furnished in accordance with the applicable regulations.

(ii) *Extensions of time.*—The Internal Revenue Service may grant a payee an extension of time to furnish statements required in this section upon a showing of good cause. See the instructions to Form 1098-E and applicable revenue procedures for rules relating to extensions of time to furnish statements.

(3) *Copy of Form 1098-E.*—A payee may satisfy the requirement of this paragraph (d) by furnishing either a copy of Form 1098-E and its instructions or another document that contains all the information filed with the Internal Revenue Service and the information required by paragraph (d)(1) of this section if the document complies with applicable revenue procedures relating to substitute statements.

(e) *Special rules.*—(1) *Transitional rule for reporting of loan origination fees and capitalized interest.*—(i) *Loans made before September 1, 2004.*—For qualified education loans made before September 1, 2004, a payee is not required to report payments of loan origination fees or capitalized interest or to take such payments into account in determining the $600 amount for purposes of paragraph (a)(1) of this section.

(ii) *Loans made on or after September 1, 2004.*—For qualified education loans made on or after September 1, 2004, a payee is required to report payments of interest as described in §1.221-1(f). Under §1.221-1(f), interest includes loan origination fees that represent charges for the use or forbearance of money and capitalized interest. Under this paragraph (e)(1)(ii), a payee shall take such payments of interest into account in determining the $600 amount for purposes of paragraph (a)(1) of this section. For purposes of this section and section 6050S, interest (including capitalized interest and loan origination fees) is treated as received, and is reportable, in the year the interest is treated as paid under the allocation rules in §1.221-1(f)(3). See §1.221-1(f) for rules relating to capitalized interest, and §1.221-1(f)(2)(ii) for rules relating to loan origination fees, on qualified education loans.

(2) *Qualified education loan certification.*—If a loan is not subsidized, guaranteed, financed, or is not otherwise treated as a student loan under a program of the Federal, state, or local government or an eligible educational institution, a payee must request a certification from the payor that the loan will be used solely to pay for qualified higher education expenses. A payee may use Form W-9S, "Request for Student's or Borrower's Social Security Number and Certification," to obtain the certification. A payee may establish an electronic system for payors to submit Forms W-9S electronically as described in applicable forms and instructions. A payee may also develop a separate form to obtain the payor certification or may incorporate the certification into other forms customarily used by the payee, such as loan applications, provided the certification is clearly set forth. If the certification is not received, the loan is not a qualified education loan for purposes of section 6050S and this section.

(3) *Payments of interest received or collected by one or more persons.*—(i) *In general.*—Except as otherwise provided in paragraph (e)(3)(ii) of this section, if a person collects or receives payments of interest on a qualified education loan on behalf of another person (e.g., a lender), the person collecting or receiving the interest must satisfy the information reporting requirements of this section. In this case, the reporting requirements do not apply to the transfer of interest to the other person.

(ii) *Exception.*—If the person collecting or receiving payments of interest on a qualified education loan on behalf of another person (e.g., a lender) does not possess the information needed to comply with the information reporting requirements of this section, the other person must satisfy the information reporting requirements of this section.

(4) *Reporting by foreign persons.*—A payee that is not a United States person (as defined in section 7701(a)(30)) must report payments of interest it receives on a qualified education loan only if it receives the payment—

(i) At a location in the United States; or

(ii) At a location outside the United States if the payee is—

(A) A controlled foreign corporation (within the meaning of section 957(a)); or

(B) A person 50 percent or more of the gross income of which, from all sources for the three-year period ending with the close of the taxable year preceding the taxable year in which interest payments were received (or for such part of the period as the person was in existence), was effectively connected with the conduct of a trade or business within the United States.

(5) *Governmental units.*—A governmental unit, or an agency or instrumentality of a governmental unit, that receives from any payor interest payments that aggregate $600 or more for any calendar year on one or more qualified education loans is a payee, without regard to the requirement of paragraph (a) of this section that the interest be received in the course of a trade or business.

(f) *Penalty provisions.*—(1) *Failure to file correct returns.*—The section 6721 penalty may apply to a payee that fails to file information returns required by section 6050S and this section on or before the required filing date; that fails to include all of the required information on the return; or that includes incorrect information on the return. See section 6721, and the regulations thereunder, for rules relating to penalties for failure to file correct returns. See section 6724, and the regulations thereunder, for rules relating to waivers of penalties for certain failures due to reasonable cause.

(2) *Failure to furnish correct information statements.*—The section 6722 penalty may apply to a payee that fails to furnish statements required by section 6050S and this section on or before the prescribed date; that fails to include all the required information on the statement; or that includes incorrect information on the statement. See section 6722, and the regulations thereunder, for rules relating to penalties for failure to furnish correct statements. See section 6724, and the regulations thereunder, for rules relating to waivers of penalties for certain failures due to reasonable cause.

(3) *Waiver of penalties for failures to include a correct TIN.*—(i) *In general.*—In the case of a failure to include a correct TIN on Form 1098-E or a related information statement, penalties may be waived if the failure is due to reasonable cause. Reasonable cause may be established if the failure arose from events beyond the payee's control, such as a failure of the payor to furnish a correct TIN. However, the payee must establish that it acted in a responsible manner both before and after the failure.

(ii) *Acting in a responsible manner.*—A payee must request the TIN of each payor if it does not already have a record of the payor's correct TIN. If the payee does not have a record of the payor's correct TIN, then it must solicit the TIN in the manner described in paragraph (f)(3)(iii) of this section on or before December 31 of each year during which it receives payments of interest. If a payor refuses to provide his or her TIN upon request, the payee must file the return and furnish the statement required by this section without the payor's TIN, but with all other required information. The specific solicitation requirements of paragraph (f)(3)(iii) of this section apply in lieu of the solicitation requirements of §301.6724-1(e) and (f) of this chapter for the purpose of determining whether a payee acted in a responsible manner in attempting to obtain a correct TIN. A payee that complies with the requirements of this paragraph (f)(3) will be considered to have acted in a responsible manner within the meaning of §301.6724-1(d) of this chapter with respect to any failure to include the correct TIN of a payor on a return or statement required by section 6050S and this section.

(iii) *Manner of soliciting TIN.*—A payee must request the payor's TIN in writing and must clearly notify the payor that the law requires the payor to furnish a TIN so that it may be included on an information return filed by the payee. A request for a TIN made on Form W-9S, "Request for Student's or Borrower's Social Security Number and Certification," satisfies the requirements of this paragraph (f)(3)(iii). A payee may establish a system for payors to submit Forms W-9S electronically as described in applicable forms and instructions. A payee may also develop a separate form to request the payor's TIN or incorporate the request into other forms customarily used by the payee, such as loan applications.

(4) *Failure to furnish TIN.*—The section 6723 penalty may apply to any payor who is required (but fails) to furnish his or her TIN to a payee. See section 6723, and the regulations thereunder, for rules relating to the penalty for failure to furnish a TIN.

(g) *Effective/applicability date.*—The rules of this section apply to information returns required to be filed, and payee statements required to be furnished after December 31, 2014. For information returns required to be filed, and payee statements required to be furnished before January 1, 2015, §1.6050S-3 (as contained in 26 CFR part 1, revised April 2013) shall apply. [Reg. §1.6050S-3.]

☐ [*T.D.* 8992, 4-26-2002. *Amended by T.D.* 9125, 5-6-2004 *and T.D.* 9675, 7-14-2014.]

### [Reg. §1.6050S-4]

§1.6050S-4. **Information reporting for payments of interest on qualified education loans.**—(a) *Electronic furnishing of statements.*—(1) *In general.*—A person required by section 6050S(d) to furnish a written statement regarding payments of interest on qualified education loans (furnisher) to the individual to whom it is required to be furnished (recipient) may furnish the statement in an electronic format in lieu of a paper format. A furnisher who meets the requirements of paragraphs (a)(2) through (6) of this section is treated as furnishing the required statement.

(2) *Consent.*—(i) *In general.*—The recipient must have affirmatively consented to receive the statement in an electronic format. The consent may be made electronically in any manner that reasonably demonstrates that the recipient can access the statement in the electronic format in which it will be furnished to the recipient. Alternatively, the consent may be made in a paper document if it is confirmed electronically.

(ii) *Withdrawal of consent.*—The consent requirement of this paragraph (a)(2) is not satisfied if the recipient withdraws the consent and the withdrawal takes effect before the statement is furnished. The furnisher may provide that a withdrawal of consent takes effect either on the date it is received by the furnisher or on a subsequent date. The furnisher may also provide that a request for a paper statement will be treated as a withdrawal of consent.

(iii) *Change in hardware or software requirements.*—If a change in the hardware or software required to access the statement creates a material risk that the recipient will not be able to access the statement, the furnisher must, prior to changing the hardware or software, provide the recipient with a notice. The notice must describe the revised hardware and software required to access the statement and inform the recipient that a new consent to receive the statement in the revised electronic format must be provided to the furnisher. After implementing the revised hardware and software, the furnisher must obtain from the recipient, in the manner described in paragraph (a)(2)(i) of this section, a new consent or confirmation of consent to receive the statement electronically.

(iv) *Examples.*—The following examples illustrate the rules of this paragraph (a)(2):

*Example 1.* Furnisher F sends Recipient R a letter stating that R may consent to receive statements required by section 6050S(d) electronically on a website instead of in a paper format. The letter contains instructions explaining how to consent to receive the statements electronically by accessing the website, downloading the consent document, completing the consent document and e-mailing the completed consent back to F. The consent document posted on the website uses the same electronic format that F will use for the electronically furnished statements. R reads the instructions and submits the consent in the manner provided in the instructions. R has consented to receive the statements electronically in the manner described in paragraph (a)(2)(i) of this section.

*Example 2.* Furnisher F sends Recipient R an e-mail stating that R may consent to receive statements required by section 6050S(d) electronically instead of in a paper format. The e-mail contains an attachment instructing R how to consent to receive the statements electronically. The e-mail attachment uses the same electronic format that F will use for the electronically furnished statements. R opens the attachment, reads the instructions, and submits the consent in the manner provided in the instructions. R has consented to receive the statements electronically in the manner described in paragraph (a)(2)(i) of this section.

*Example 3.* Furnisher F posts a notice on its website stating that Recipient R may receive statements required by section 6050S(d) electronically instead of in a paper format. The website contains instructions on how R may access a secure webpage and consent to receive the statements electronically. By accessing the secure webpage and giving consent, R has consented to receive the statements electronically in the manner described in paragraph (a)(2)(i) of this section.

(3) *Required disclosures.*—(i) *In general.*—Prior to, or at the time of, a recipient's consent, the furnisher must provide to the recipient a clear and conspicuous disclosure statement containing each of the disclosures described in paragraphs (a)(3)(ii) through (viii) of this section.

(ii) *Paper statement.*—The recipient must be informed that the statement will be furnished on paper if the recipient does not consent to receive it electronically.

(iii) *Scope and duration of consent.*—The recipient must be informed of the scope and duration of the consent. For example, the recipient must be informed whether the consent applies to statements furnished every year after the consent is given until it is withdrawn in the manner described in paragraph (a)(3)(v)(A) of this section or only to the statement required to be furnished on or before the January 31 immediately following the date on which the consent is given.

(iv) *Post-consent request for a paper statement.*—The recipient must be informed of any procedure for obtaining a paper copy of the recipient's statement after giving the consent described in paragraph (a)(2)(i) of this section and whether a request for a paper statement will be treated as a withdrawal of consent.

(v) *Withdrawal of consent.*—The recipient must be informed that—

(A) The recipient may withdraw a consent by writing (electronically or on paper) to the person or department whose name, mailing address, telephone number, and e-mail address is provided in the disclosure statement;

(B) The furnisher will confirm the withdrawal and the date on which it takes effect in writing (either electronically or on paper); and

(C) A withdrawal of consent does not apply to a statement that was furnished electronically in the manner described in this paragraph (a) before the date on which the withdrawal of consent takes effect.

(vi) *Notice of termination.*—The recipient must be informed of the conditions under which a furnisher will cease furnishing statements electronically to the recipient.

(vii) *Updating information.*—The recipient must be informed of the procedures for updating the information needed by the furnisher to contact the recipient. The furnisher must inform the recipient of any change in the furnisher's contact information.

(viii) *Hardware and software requirements.*—The recipient must be provided with a description of the hardware and software required to access, print, and retain the statement, and the date when the statement will no longer be available on the website.

(4) *Format.*—The electronic version of the statement must contain all required information and comply with applicable revenue procedures relating to substitute statements to recipients.

(5) *Notice.*—(i) *In general.*—If the statement is furnished on a website, the furnisher must notify the recipient that the statement is posted on a website. The notice may be delivered by mail, electronic mail, or in person. The notice must provide instructions on how to access and print the statement. The notice must include the following statement in capital letters, "IMPORTANT TAX RETURN DOCUMENT AVAILABLE." If the notice is provided by electronic mail, the foregoing statement must be on the subject line of the electronic mail.

(ii) *Undeliverable electronic address.*—If an electronic notice described in paragraph (a)(5)(i) of this section is returned as undeliverable, and the correct electronic address cannot be obtained from the furnisher's records or from the recipient, then the furnisher must furnish the notice by mail or in person within 30 days after the electronic notice is returned.

(iii) *Corrected statements.*—If the furnisher has corrected a recipient's statement that was furnished electronically, the furnisher must furnish the corrected statement to the recipient electronically. If the recipient's statement was furnished though a website posting and the furnisher has corrected the statement, the furnisher must notify the recipient that it has posted the corrected statement on the website within 30 days of such posting in the manner described in paragraph (a)(5)(i) of this section. The corrected statement or the notice must be furnished by mail or in person if—

(A) An electronic notice of the website posting of an original statement or the corrected statement was returned as undeliverable; and

(B) The recipient has not provided a new e-mail address.

(6) *Access Period.*—Statements furnished on a website must be retained on the website through October 15 of the year following the calendar year to which the statements relate (or the first business day after such October 15, if October 15 falls on a Saturday, Sunday, or legal holiday). The furnisher must maintain access to corrected statements that are posted on the website through October 15 of the year following the calendar year to which the statements relate (or the first business day after such October 15, if October 15 falls on a Saturday, Sunday, or legal holiday) or the date 90 days after the corrected statements are posted, whichever is later.

(b) *Effective date.*—This section applies to statements required to be furnished after February 13, 2004. Paragraph (a)(6) of this section also applies to statements required to be furnished after December 31, 2003. [Reg. § 1.6050S-4.]

☐ [*T.D.* 9114, 2-13-2004.]

**[Reg. § 1.6050W-1]**

**§ 1.6050W-1. Information reporting for payments made in settlement of payment card and third party network transactions.**—(a) *In general.*—(1) *General rule.*—Every payment settlement entity, as defined in paragraph (a)(4) of this section, must file an information return for each calendar year with respect to payments made in settlement of reportable payment transactions, as defined in paragraph (a)(3) of this section, setting forth the following information:

(i) The name, address, and taxpayer identification number (TIN) of each participating payee, as defined in paragraph (a)(5) of this section, to whom one or more payments in settlement of reportable payment transactions are made.

(ii) With respect to each participating payee, the gross amount, as defined in paragraph (a)(6) of this section, of—

(A) The aggregate reportable payment transactions for the calendar year; and

(B) The aggregate reportable payment transactions for each month of the calendar year.

(iii) Any other information required by the form, instructions or current revenue procedures.

(2) *Payments in settlement of reportable payment transactions.*—A payment settlement entity, as defined in paragraph (a)(4) of this section (or an electronic payment facilitator, as defined in paragraph (d)(2) of this section), makes a payment in settlement of a reportable payment transaction if the payment settlement entity (or electronic payment facilitator) submits the instruction to transfer funds to the account of the participating payee for purposes of settling the reportable payment transaction.

(3) *Reportable payment transaction.*—The term *reportable payment transaction* means any payment card transaction (as defined in paragraph (b)(1) of this section) and any third party network transaction (as defined in paragraph (c)(1) of this section).

(4) *Payment settlement entity.*—(i) *Definition.*—The term *payment settlement entity* means a domestic or foreign entity that is—

(A) In the case of a payment card transaction, a merchant acquiring entity (as defined in paragraph (b)(2) of this section); and

(B) In the case of a third party network transaction, a third party settlement organization (as defined in paragraph (c)(2) of this section).

(ii) *Multiple payment settlement entities.*—If two or more persons qualify as payment settlement entities (as defined in paragraph (a)(4)(i) of this section) with respect to a reportable payment transaction, then only the payment settlement entity that in fact makes payment in settlement of the reportable payment transaction must file the information return required by paragraph (a)(1) of this section.

(5) *Participating payee.*—(i) *Definition.*—In general, the term *participating payee* means any person, including any governmental unit (and any agency or instrumentality thereof), who:

(A) In the case of a payment card transaction, accepts a payment card (as defined in paragraph (b)(3) of this section) as payment; and

(B) In the case of a third party network transaction, accepts payment from a third party settlement organization (as defined in paragraph (c)(2) of this section) in settlement of such transaction.

(ii) *Foreign payees.*—(A) *In general.*—For payments pursuant to contractual obligations entered into after December 31, 2010, a payment settlement entity that is a person described as a U.S. payor or U.S. middleman in § 1.6049-5(c)(5) is not required to make a return of information for payments to a participating payee with a foreign address as long as, prior to payment, the payment settlement entity has in its files documentation upon which the payment settlement entity may rely to treat the payment as made to a foreign person in accordance with § 1.1441-1(e)(1)(ii). For purposes of this paragraph (a)(5)(ii), the provisions of § 1.1441-1 shall apply by substituting the term payor for the term withholding agent and without regard to the limitation to amounts subject to withholding under chapter 3 of the Internal Revenue Code and the regulations under that chapter. Such a payment settlement entity need not make a return of information for payments made outside the United States (within the meaning of § 1.6049-5(e)) to an offshore account (as defined in § 1.6049-5(c)(1)) to a participating payee with only a foreign address if the name of the participating payee indicates that it is an entity listed as a per se corporation under § 301.7701-2(b)(8)(i) and the payment settlement entity does not know or have reason to know that the participating payee is a United States person. A payment settlement entity may apply the grace period rules of § 1.6049-5(d)(2)(ii) of the regulations for payments to a participating payee with only a foreign address, without regard to whether the amounts paid are described in § 1.1441-6(c)(2) or are reportable under section 6042, 6045, 6049, or 6050N. For payments pursuant to contractual obligations entered into before January 1, 2011, a payment settlement entity that is a person described as a U.S. payor or U.S. middleman in § 1.6049-5(c)(5) is not required to make a return of information for payments to a participating payee with a foreign address as long as the payment settlement entity neither knows nor has reason to know that the participating payee is a United States person. For this purpose, a renewal of such a contractual obligation will not result in a new contractual obligation unless there is a material modification to the contractual obligation.

(B) *Non-U.S. payor or middleman.*—A payment settlement entity that is not a person described as a U.S. payor or U.S middleman in § 1.6049-5(c)(5) is not required to make a return of information for a payment to a participating payee that does not have a United States address as long as the payment settlement entity neither knows nor has reason to know that the participating payee is a United States person. If the participating payee has any United States address, the payment settlement entity may treat the participating payee as a foreign person only if the payment settlement entity has in its files documentation upon which the payment settle-

ment entity may rely to treat the payment as made to a foreign person in accordance with § 1.1441-1(e)(1)(ii).

(C) *Foreign address; United States address.*—For purposes of this section, *foreign address* means any address that is not within the United States, as defined in section 7701(a)(9) of the Internal Revenue Code (the States and the District of Columbia). *United States address* means any address that is within the United States.

(6) *Gross amount.*—For purposes of this section, *gross amount* means the total dollar amount of aggregate reportable payment transactions for each participating payee without regard to any adjustments for credits, cash equivalents, discount amounts, fees, refunded amounts or any other amounts. The dollar amount of each transaction is determined on the date of the transaction.

(b) *Payment card transactions.*—(1) *Definition.*—The term *payment card transaction* means any transaction in which a payment card, or any account number or other indicia associated with a payment card, is accepted as payment.

(2) *Merchant acquiring entity.*—The term *merchant acquiring entity* means the bank or other organization that has the contractual obligation to make payment to participating payees (as defined in paragraph (a)(5)(i)(A) of this section) in settlement of payment card transactions.

(3) *Payment card.*—(i) The term *payment card* means any card, including any stored-value card as defined in paragraph (b)(4) of this section, issued pursuant to an agreement or arrangement that provides for—

(A) One or more issuers of such cards;

(B) A network of persons unrelated to each other, and to the issuer, who agree to accept such cards as payment; and

(C) Standards and mechanisms for settling the transactions between the merchant acquiring entities and the persons who agree to accept the cards as payment.

(ii) Persons who agree to accept such cards as payment as described in this paragraph (b)(3) are participating payees within the meaning of paragraph (a)(5)(i)(A) of this section.

(4) *Stored-value cards.*—The term *stored-value card* means any card with a prepaid value, including any gift card.

(5) *Transactions for which no return of information is required under section 6050W.*—(i) *Withdrawals and cash advances.*—The use of a "payment card" as defined in paragraph (b)(3) of this section by a cardholder to withdraw funds at an automated teller machine, or to obtain a cash advance or loan against the cardholder's account, is not a payment card transaction under paragraph (b)(1) of this section because the card is not being accepted as payment by a merchant or other payee.

(ii) *Convenience checks.*—The acceptance of a check issued in connection with a payment card account by a merchant or other payee is not a payment card transaction under paragraph (b)(1) of this section because the check is accepted and processed through the banking system in the same manner as a traditional check, not as a payment card.

(iii) *Payee related to issuer.*—No return of information is required under this section for any transaction in which a payment card within the meaning of paragraph (b)(3) is accepted as payment by a merchant or other payee who is related to the issuer of the payment card.

(c) *Third party network transactions.*—(1) *Definition.*—The term *third party network transaction* means any transaction that is settled through a third party payment network.

(2) *Third party settlement organization.*—The term *third party settlement organization* means the central organization that has the contractual obligation to make payments to participating payees (as defined in paragraph (a)(5)(i)(B) of this section) of third party network transactions. A central organization is a third party settlement organization if it provides a third party payment network (as defined in paragraph (c)(3)(i) of this section) that enables purchasers to transfer funds to providers of goods and services.

(3) *Third party payment network.*—(i) The term *third party payment network* means any agreement or arrangement that—

(A) Involves the establishment of accounts with a central organization by a substantial number of providers of goods or services who are unrelated to the organization and who have agreed to settle transactions for the provision of the goods or services to purchasers according to the terms of the agreement or arrangement;

(B) Provides standards and mechanisms for settling the transactions; and

(C) Guarantees payment to the persons providing goods or services in settlement of transactions with purchasers pursuant to the agreement or arrangement.

(ii) A third party payment network does not include any agreement or arrangement that provides for the issuance of payment cards.

(iii) Persons who are providers of goods and services as described in this paragraph (c)(3) are participating payees within the meaning of paragraph (a)(5)(i)(B) of this section.

(4) *Exception for de minimis payments.*—A third party settlement organization is required to report any information under paragraph (a)(1) of this section with respect to third party network transactions of any participating payee only if—

(i) The amount that would otherwise be reported under paragraph (a)(1)(ii) of this section with respect to such transactions exceeds $20,000; and

(ii) The aggregate number of such transactions exceeds 200.

(d) *Special rules.*—(1) *Aggregated payees.*—If a person receives payments from a payment settlement entity (as defined in paragraph (a)(4) of this section) on behalf of one or more participating payees and distributes such payments to one or more participating payees (as defined in paragraph (a)(5) of this section), the person is treated as:

(i) The participating payee with respect to the payment settlement entity; and

(ii) The payment settlement entity with respect to the participating payees to whom the person distributes payments.

(2) *Electronic payment facilitator.*—If a payment settlement entity (as defined in paragraph (a)(4) of this section) contracts with an electronic payment facilitator or other third party to make payments in settlement of reportable payment transactions on behalf of the payment settlement entity, the facilitator must file the annual information return under this section in lieu of the payment settlement entity. The facilitator need not have any agreement or arrangement with the participating payee. Also, the payment need not come from the facilitator's account. The facilitator need only submit instructions to transfer funds to the account of the participating payee in settlement of the reportable payment transaction. The facilitator is liable for any applicable penalties for failure to comply with the information reporting requirements of section 6050W.

(3) *Designations.*—The party with the obligation to file the annual information return under this section may designate by written agreement any other person to satisfy the requirements of this section. Thus, notwithstanding the rule in paragraph (d)(2) of this section imposing the obligation to file the annual information return on the electronic payment facilitator in lieu of the payment settlement entity, the payment settlement entity may file the information return by designation if the parties agree in writing. However, a designation does not relieve the party with the reporting obligation from liability for any reporting failures. The party with the obligation to file the annual information return under this section remains liable for any applicable penalties under sections 6721 and 6722 if the requirements of this section are not satisfied.

(4) *Conversion into United States dollars of amounts paid in foreign currency.*—When a payment is made or received in a foreign currency, the U.S. dollar amount shall be determined by converting such foreign currency into U.S. dollars on the date of the transaction at the spot rate (as defined in §1.988-1(d)(1)) or pursuant to a reasonable spot rate convention. For example, a payor may use a month-end spot rate or a monthly average spot rate. A spot rate convention must be used consistently with respect to all non-dollar amounts reported and from year to year. Such convention cannot be changed without the consent of the Commissioner or his or her delegate.

(5) *Unrelated persons.*—For purposes of this section, *unrelated* means any person who is not related to another person within the meaning of section 267(b) (providing a list of relationships), including the application of section 267(c) and (e)(3) (providing rules relating to constructive ownership), and section 707(b)(1) (relationships with partnerships).

(e) *Examples.*—The following examples illustrate the provisions of this section:

*Example 1. Merchant acquiring entity.* Customer A purchases goods from merchant B using a credit card issued by Bank X. B is one of a network of unrelated persons that has agreed to accept credit cards issued by X as payment under an agreement that provides standards and mechanisms for settling the transaction between a merchant acquiring bank and the persons who accept the cards. Bank Z is the merchant acquiring bank with the contractual obligation to make payment to B for goods provided to A in this transaction. As defined in paragraph (b)(2) of this section, Z is the merchant acquiring entity

that must file the annual information return required under paragraph (a)(1) of this section to report the payment made to settle the transaction for the sale of goods from B to A.

*Example 2. Third party settlement organization.* (i) Merchant B is one of a substantial number of persons selling goods or services over the Internet that have an account with X, an Internet payment service provider. None of these persons, including B, are related to X, and all have agreed to settle transactions for the sale of goods or services to customers according to the terms of their contracts with X. X has guaranteed payment to all of these persons, including B, for the sale of goods or services to customers. Customer A purchases goods from B. A pays X for the goods purchased from B. X, in turn, makes payment to B in settlement of the transaction for the sale of goods from B to A.

(ii) X's arrangement constitutes a third party payment network as defined in paragraph (c)(3) of this section because a substantial number of persons that are unrelated to X, including B, have established accounts with X, and X is contractually obligated to settle transactions for the provision of goods or services by these persons to purchasers. Thus, under paragraph (c)(2) of this section, X is a third party settlement organization and the transaction discussed in this *Example* is a third party network transaction under paragraph (c)(1) of this section. Therefore, X must file the annual information return required under paragraph (a)(1) of this section to report the payment made to B in settlement of the transaction with A provided that X's aggregate payments to B from third party network transactions exceed $20,000 and the aggregate number of X's transactions with B exceeds 200 (as provided in paragraph (c)(4) of this section).

*Example 3. Automated clearinghouse network.* A operates an automated clearinghouse ("ACH") network that merely processes electronic payments (such as wire transfers, electronic checks, and direct deposit payments) between buyers and sellers. There are no contractual agreements between A and the sellers for the purpose of permitting the sellers to use the ACH network. Thus, A is not a third party settlement organization under paragraph (c)(2) of this section, the ACH network is not a third party payment network under paragraph (c)(3) of this section, and the electronic payment transactions are not third party network transactions under paragraph (c)(1) of this section. A is not required to file the annual information return required under paragraph (a)(1) of this section.

*Example 4. ACH processor.* B provides a variety of ACH payment processing services to a large number of merchants, such as converting checks received in payment of bills into ACH transactions. B groups payment transactions into an ACH file and transmits the ACH file into the ACH network on behalf of merchants in order to initiate payment to merchants through the ACH network. B makes payments to the merchants after the ACH network verifies that the customers' accounts have sufficient funds. Because the ACH network is not a third party payment network under paragraph (c)(3) of this section, B cannot be a third party settlement organization with respect to the ACH network. Similarly, because the ACH itself is not a third party settlement organization under paragraph (c)(2) of this section, B cannot be an electronic payment facilitator because B is not acting on behalf of a payment settlement entity. However, B may itself be operating third party payment network under paragraph (c)(3) of this section if B has a separate agreement or arrangement that: involves the establishment of accounts with B by a substantial number of unrelated merchants who provide goods or services and have agreed to settle transactions for the provision of the goods or services pursuant to the agreement or arrangement; provides for standards and mechanisms for settling the transactions; and guarantees persons providing goods or services pursuant to such agreement or arrangement that these persons will be paid for providing such goods or services.

*Example 5. Gross amount.* On Day 1, Customer A uses a payment card to purchase $100 worth of goods from merchant B. Bank X, the merchant acquiring entity for B, is the party with the contractual obligation to make payment to B in settlement of the transaction. On Day 2, X, after deducting fees of $2, makes payment of $98 to settle the transaction for the sale of goods from B to A. Under paragraph (a)(6) of this section, X must report the amount of $100, the amount of the transaction on Day 1, without any reduction for fees or any other amount, as the gross amount of this reportable payment transaction on the annual information return filed under paragraph (a)(1) of this section.

*Example 6. Gift card.* (i) Customer A purchases a gift card from Merchant X that may be used only at X and its related network of stores. A purchases the gift card using cash. A gives the gift card to B. B uses the gift card to purchase goods at one of X's stores. The purchase of the gift card by A using cash is not a payment card transaction described in paragraph (b)(1) of this section and, thus, is not required to be reported in a return of information required under paragraph (a)(1) of this section. Under paragraph (b)(3) of this section, the gift card is not a payment card because the gift card is only accepted as payment by persons who are related to the issuer of the gift card and to each other. Therefore, the use of the gift card by B is not required to be reported in a return of information required under paragraph (a)(1) of this section.

(ii) The facts are the same as in paragraph (i), except that B adds value to the gift card using a credit card. The use of the credit card to add value to the gift card is a reportable payment transaction (as defined in paragraph (a)(3) of this section) and must be reported in a return of information under this section by the bank or other organization that has the contractual obligation to make payment to X in settlement of the transaction.

*Example 7. Private label card.* Bank B issues a card imprinted with Retailer C's logo to cardholder A. The "C-card" is accepted as payment only at C or at stores related (within the meaning of section 267(b), (c) and (e)(3) and, section 707(b)(1)) to C. A uses the card at C to purchase electronics equipment. Under paragraph (b)(3) of this section, the C-card is not a payment card because the card is accepted as payment only within a network of persons who are related to each other. Therefore, the use of the card by A at C is not required to be reported in a return of information required under paragraph (a)(1) of this section.

*Example 8. Quasi-private label card.* Bank B issues a card to cardholder A. The card, known as an "E-card," is issued by B pursuant to an agreement that provides that the E-card is accepted as payment only within a limited network of merchants that carry electronics equipment. The agreement provides for standards and mechanisms for settling the transactions between the merchants and the merchant acquiring entities. The merchants accepting the E-card as payment are not related (within the meaning of section 267(b), (c) and (e)(3) and section 707(b)(1)) to each other or to B. A uses the card to purchase electronics equipment at F Store, one of the stores within the network of merchants accepting the E-card. Under paragraph (b)(3) of this section, the E-card is a payment card because the card is issued pursuant to an agreement that provides for a network of persons unrelated to each other, and to the issuer, who agree to accept the card as payment. Therefore, the use of the E-card by A to purchase electronics equipment at F Store must be reported in a return of information required under paragraph (a)(1) of this section.

*Example 9. Campus card.* (i) University Y issues Student A a card that may be used on campus at various university-owned merchants and at various local merchants unrelated to Y. A uses the card in the university-owned cafeteria to purchase lunch. Under paragraph (b)(5)(iii) of this section, no return of information is required because the card is being accepted as payment by a person who is related to the issuer of the card.

(ii) The facts are the same as in paragraph (i), except that A uses the campus card to purchase lunch at a local restaurant, unrelated to Y, that has agreed to accept the campus card as payment. Under paragraph (b)(3) of this section, the campus card is a payment card in this transaction because the card is accepted as payment by a person that is unrelated to this issuer of the card pursuant to an agreement. Therefore, the use of the card by A in the local restaurant for the purchase of lunch must be reported in a return of information required under paragraph (a)(1) of this section by the bank or other organization that has the contractual obligation to make payment to the restaurant in settlement of the transaction.

*Example 10. Mall card.* Customer B purchases a card that is issued by shopping mall A. Pursuant to an agreement or arrangement, the card is accepted as payment by various merchants located within the mall, who are unrelated to the issuer of the card and to each other. B uses the card in the mall to purchase goods from merchant C. Under paragraph (b)(3) of this section, the mall card is a payment card because the card is accepted as payment by a network of persons who are unrelated to the issuer of the card and to the other merchants who have agreed to accept the card as payment. Therefore, the use of the mall card by B to purchase goods from merchant C is required to be reported in a return of information required under paragraph (a)(1) of this section.

*Example 11. Electronic benefit transactions card.* Government Agency A issues benefits electronically to recipients by loading these benefits onto a payment card. Pursuant to an agreement, a network of merchants unrelated to A, and to each other, has agreed to accept the benefits card as payment. A issues a card to B, who uses the card to purchase goods from Merchant C. The card issued by A is a payment card (as defined in paragraph (b)(3) of this section) because the card is accepted as payment by a network of persons that are unrelated to the issuer of the card, and to each other. The use of the card by B to purchase goods from C must be reported in a return of information required under paragraph (a)(1) of this section.

*Example 12. Prepaid telephone card.* A purchases a prepaid telephone card from Company X that may be used to make telephone calls using various long-distance providers unrelated to X that have agreed to accept the card as payment. A places a telephone call using the prepaid card as payment for the telephone call. Under paragraph (b)(3) of this section, the prepaid telephone card is a payment card

because the card is accepted as payment by a person that is unrelated to the issuer of the card pursuant to an agreement. Therefore, the use of the prepaid card to make payment for the telephone call must be reported in a return of information required under paragraph (a)(1) of this section by the bank or other organization that has the contractual obligation to make payment to the long distance provider in settlement of the transaction.

*Example 13. Transit card.* City Z accepts a transit card as payment for use of its mass transit system. The transit card is issued by B, an organization unrelated to Z. A network of persons, including Z, who are unrelated to each other and to B, have agreed to accept the transit card issued by B as payment for transit and for other goods and services. Transit rider X purchases a transit card and uses the card to pay for travel on Z's mass transit system. Under paragraph (b)(3) of this section, the transit card is a payment card because the card is accepted as payment by a person who is one of a network of persons that are unrelated to the issuer of the card, and to each other, and that have agreed to accept the card as payment. Therefore, the use of the transit card by X to pay for transit on Z's mass transit system is a payment card transaction described in paragraph (b)(1) of this section that must be reported in a return of information required under paragraph (a)(1) of this section by the bank or other organization that has the contractual obligation to make payment to Z. Z is the participating payee, described in paragraph (a)(5)(i)(A) of this section, of the payment card transaction.

*Example 14. Cash advance.* Bank A issues Cardholder B a credit card that is a payment card under paragraph (b)(3) of this section. B uses the card at a local bank to obtain a cash advance. Under paragraph (b)(5)(i) of this section, B's use of the payment card to obtain a cash advance is not a payment card transaction (as defined in paragraph (b)(1) of this section) because the card is not being accepted as payment by a merchant.

*Example 15. Withdrawals from automated teller machines.* Bank A issues Cardholder B a credit card that is a payment card under paragraph (b)(3) of this section. B uses the card at an automated teller machine to obtain cash. Under paragraph (b)(5)(i) of this section, B's use of the payment card to obtain cash is not a payment card transaction (as defined in paragraph (b)(1) of this section) because the card is not being accepted as payment by a merchant.

*Example 16. Convenience checks.* Bank A issues Cardholder B a credit card that is a payment card under paragraph (b)(3) of this section. A sends B paper checks imprinted with the account number associated with the credit card. B uses one of the checks to purchase goods from Merchant S. The check is accepted by S and processed through the bank system in the same manner as a traditional check. Under paragraph (b)(5)(ii) of this section, B's use of the convenience check to purchase goods is not a payment card transaction (as defined in paragraph (b)(1) of this section) because the check is accepted and processed as a traditional check, not as a payment card.

*Example 17. Healthcare network.* Health carrier A operates healthcare network Y. A collects premiums from covered persons pursuant to a plan agreement between A and the covered persons for the cost of membership in Y. Separately, A pays healthcare providers pursuant to provider agreements to compensate these providers for services rendered to covered persons who are members of Y. A is not a third party settlement organization under paragraph (c)(2) of this section because A does not operate a third party payment network that enables purchasers to transfer funds to providers of goods and services. Therefore, A is not required to file the annual information return required under paragraph (a)(1) of this section.

*Example 18. Third party accounts payable.* X is a "shared-service" organization that performs accounts payable services for numerous purchasers that are unrelated to X. A substantial number of providers of goods and services have established accounts with X and have agreed to accept payment from X in settlement of their transactions with purchasers. The provider agreement with X includes standards and mechanisms for settling the transactions and guarantees payment to the providers, and the arrangement enables purchasers to transfer funds to providers. Under paragraph (c)(3) of this section, X's accounts payable services constitute a third party payment network, of which X is the third party settlement organization (as defined in paragraph (c)(2) of this section). For each payee, X must file the annual information return required under paragraph (a)(1) of this section to report payments made by X in settlement of accounts payable to that payee if X's aggregate payments to that payee exceed $20,000 and the aggregate number of transactions with that payee exceeds 200 (as provided in paragraph (c)(4) of this section).

*Example 19. Toll collection network.* State A charges a toll to vehicles that travel its state highways. The tolling agency for A contracted with organization X to perform its toll collection. X provides an electronic toll collection system that allows the toll facility to record the passage of a vehicle with a transponder affixed to the vehicle. The customer account associated with the transponder is automatically debited for the amount of the toll. The customer funds a balance in the account, which is then depleted as the toll transactions occur. X periodically bills the customer to replenish the account. X then makes payment to A to settle the toll transactions that are recorded by the transponder. X also contracts with a substantial number of other entities unrelated to X that have established accounts with X and have agreed to accept payment using the electronic toll collection system provided by X. X guarantees payment to the entities for all toll transactions that are recorded by the transponders, and the arrangement enables customers to transfer funds to State A and other entities that charge tolls. Under paragraph (c)(3) of this section, X's electronic toll collection system constitutes a third party payment network, of which X is the third party settlement organization (as defined in paragraph (c)(2) of this section). For each payee, including A, X must file the annual information return required under paragraph (a)(1) of this section to report payments made by X in settlement of toll transactions if X's aggregate payments to that payee exceed $20,000 and the aggregate number of transactions with that payee exceeds 200 (as provided in paragraph (c)(4) of this section).

*Example 20. Hotel kiosk.* Under a "hotel kiosk" arrangement, Hotel B permits its customers to charge, to their room account, transactions for goods and services at a substantial number of sellers unrelated to B that operate on B's premises, or on the premises of hotels related to B, and that have established accounts in B's hotel kiosk system. Customers settle their room account with B when they check out, and B in turn settles the hotel kiosk transactions with the unrelated sellers. B guarantees payment to the sellers for these transactions and the arrangement enables customers to transfer funds to the sellers by means of one payment made to the hotel. Under paragraph (c)(3) of this section, B's hotel kiosk system constitutes a third party payment network, of which B is the third party settlement organization (as defined in paragraph (c)(2) of this section). For each payee, B must file the annual information return required under paragraph (a)(1) of this section to report payments made by B in settlement of the hotel kiosk transactions if B's aggregate payments to that payee exceed $20,000 and the aggregate number of transactions with that payee exceeds 200 (as provided in paragraph (c)(4) of this section).

*Example 21. Aggregated payee.* Corporation A, acting on behalf of A's independently-owned franchise stores, receives payment from Bank X for credit card sales effectuated at these franchise stores. X, the payment settlement entity (as defined in paragraph (a)(4)(i) of this section), is required under paragraph (d)(1)(i) of this section to report the gross amount of the reportable payment transactions distributed to A (notwithstanding the fact that A does not accept payment cards and would not otherwise be treated as a participating payee). In turn, under paragraph (d)(1)(ii) of this section, A is required to report the gross amount of the reportable payment transactions allocable to each franchise store. X has no reporting obligation under this section with respect to payments made by A to its franchise stores.

*Example 22. Electronic payment facilitator.* (i) Bank A is a merchant acquiring entity (as defined in paragraph (b)(2) of this section) with the contractual obligation to make payments to participating merchants to settle certain credit card transactions. A enters into a contract with Processor X. Pursuant to this contract, X prepares and submits instructions to move funds from A's account to the accounts of participating merchants to settle credit card transactions. X is making payment on A's behalf in settlement of payment card transactions pursuant to a contract between X and A. Therefore, under paragraph (d)(2) of this section, X is an electronic payment facilitator and must file the information return required under paragraph (a)(1) of this section with respect to credit card transactions settled by X. A has no reporting obligation with respect to payments made by X on A's behalf.

(ii) The facts are the same as in paragraph (i) except that A and X state in their contract that A will file the information return required under paragraph (a)(1) of this section. A may file the information return pursuant to this designation. However, X is liable for any applicable penalties under sections 6721 and 6722 if the reporting requirements of this section are not satisfied.

(iii) The facts are the same as in paragraph (i) except that X merely prepares the instructions to move the funds to the accounts of participating merchants, and the instructions are actually submitted by A. A, not X, is making payment in settlement of payment card transactions. Therefore, A retains the obligation to file the information return required under paragraph (a)(1) of this section with respect to credit card transactions settled by A.

(f) *Prescribed form.*—The return required by paragraph (a)(1) of this section must be made according to the forms and instructions published by the Internal Revenue Service.

(g) *Time and place for filing.*—Returns made under this section for any calendar year must be filed on or before February 28th (March 31st if filing electronically) of the following year at the Internal Revenue Service Center location designated in the instructions to the relevant form.

(h) *Time and place for furnishing statement.*—(1) *In general.*—Every payment settlement entity required to file a return under this section must also furnish to each participating payee a written statement with the same information (as described in paragraph (h)(2) of this section). The statement must be furnished to the payee on or before January 31st of the year following the calendar year in which the reportable payment is made. If the return of information is not made on magnetic media, this requirement may be satisfied by furnishing to such person a copy of all Forms 1099-K, "Merchant card and third-party payments," or any successor form with respect to such person filed with the Internal Revenue Service Center. The statement will be considered furnished to the payee if it is mailed to the payee's last known address. The payment settlement entity may furnish the statement electronically in accordance with the rules provided in § 1.6050W-2.

(2) *Information to be shown on statement furnished to payee.*—Each written statement furnished under paragraph (h)(1) of this section must include the following information—

(i) The name, address, and phone number (or email address if the statement is furnished electronically) of the information contact of the payment settlement entity.

(ii) With respect to the participating payee, the gross amount of—

(A) The aggregate reportable payment transactions for the calendar year; and

(B) The aggregate reportable payment transactions for each month of the calendar year.

(iii) Any other information required by the form, instructions, or current revenue procedures.

(i) *Cross-reference to penalties.*—For provisions relating to the penalty for failure to file timely a correct information return required under section 6050W, see section 6721 and the associated regulations. For provisions relating to the penalty for failure to furnish timely a correct payee statement required under section 6050W(f), see section 6722 and the associated regulations. See section 6724 and the associated regulations for the waiver of a penalty if failure is due to reasonable cause and is not due to willful neglect.

(j) *Effective/applicability date.*—The rules in this section apply to returns for calendar years beginning after December 31, 2010. [Reg. § 1.6050W-1.]

☐ [*T.D.* 9496, 8-13-2010.]

**[Reg. § 1.6050W-2]**

**§ 1.6050W-2. Electronic furnishing of information statements for payments made in settlement of payment card and third party network transactions.**—(a) *Electronic furnishing of statements.*—(1) *In general.*—A person required by section 6050W to furnish a written statement (furnisher) regarding payments made in settlement of payment card and third party network transactions to the person to whom it is required to be furnished (recipient) may furnish the statement in an electronic format in lieu of a paper format. A furnisher who meets the requirements of paragraphs (a)(2) through (a)(5) of this section is treated as furnishing the required statement.

(2) *Consent.*—(i) *In general.*—The recipient must have affirmatively consented to receive the statement required under section 6050W in an electronic format or, in the alternative, have previously consented to receive other federal tax statements in an electronic format from the furnisher. The consent may be made electronically in any manner that reasonably demonstrates that the recipient can access the statement in the electronic format in which it will be furnished to the recipient. Alternatively, the consent may be made in a paper document if it is confirmed electronically. Consents must be kept at all times available for inspection by the Internal Revenue Service. Recipients currently receiving electronic communications from the furnisher may elect to receive the statement required under section 6050W in a paper document in lieu of an electronic format. The election to receive a paper document may be made by notifying the furnisher electronically or in a paper document.

(ii) *Withdrawal of consent.*—The consent requirement of paragraph (a)(2)(i) of this section is not satisfied if the recipient withdraws the consent to receive electronic statements and the withdrawal takes effect before the statement is furnished. The furnisher may provide that a withdrawal of consent takes effect either on the date it is received by the furnisher or on a subsequent date. The furnisher may also provide that a request for a paper statement will be treated as a withdrawal of consent.

(iii) *Change in hardware or software requirements.*—If a change in the hardware or software required to access the statement creates a material risk that the recipient will not be able to access the statement, the furnisher must, prior to changing the hardware or software, provide notice to the recipient. The notice must describe the revised hardware and software required to access the statement and inform the recipient that a new consent to receive the statement in the revised electronic format must be provided to the furnisher. After implementing the revised hardware and software, the furnisher must obtain from the recipient, in the manner described in paragraph (a)(2)(i) of this section, a new consent or confirmation of consent to receive the statement electronically.

(iv) *Examples.*—The following examples illustrate the rules of this paragraph (a)(2):

*Example 1.* Recipient R has consented to receive the statements required under section 6041 in electronic format from Furnisher F. F has retained R's consent and keeps it available for inspection by the IRS. F may furnish to R the statement required under section 6050W in electronic format without securing an affirmative consent from R with respect to the statements required under section 6050W.

*Example 2.* Recipient R has not consented to receive any electronic federal income tax statements from Furnisher F. F may not furnish to R the statements required under section 6050W unless F first secures from R a consent to receive those statements in electronic format in accordance with the requirements of paragraphs (a)(2) through (a)(5) of this section.

*Example 3.* Furnisher F sends Recipient R a letter stating that R may consent to receive statements required by section 6050W(f) electronically on a website instead of in a paper format. The letter contains instructions explaining how to consent to receive the statements electronically by accessing the website, downloading the consent document, completing the consent document, and e-mailing the completed consent back to F. The consent document posted on the website uses the same electronic format that F uses to furnish statements electronically. R reads the instructions and submits the consent in the manner provided in the instructions. R has consented to receive the statements electronically in the manner described in paragraph (a)(2)(i) of this section.

*Example 4.* Furnisher F sends Recipient R an e-mail stating that R may consent to receive statements required by section 6050W(f) electronically instead of in a paper format. The e-mail contains an attachment instructing R how to consent to receive the statements electronically. The e-mail attachment uses the same electronic format that F uses to furnish statements electronically. R opens the attachment, reads the instructions, and submits the consent in the manner provided in the instructions. R has consented to receive the statements electronically in the manner described in paragraph (a)(2)(i) of this section.

*Example 5.* Furnisher F posts a notice on its website stating that Recipient R may receive statements required by section 6050W(f) electronically instead of in a paper format. The website contains instructions on how R may access a secure web page and consent to receive the statements electronically. By accessing the secure web page and giving consent, R has consented to receive the statements electronically in the manner described in paragraph (a)(2)(i) of this section.

(3) *Required disclosures.*—(i) *In general.*—Prior to, or at the time of, a recipient's consent, the furnisher must provide to the recipient a clear and conspicuous disclosure statement containing each of the disclosures described in paragraphs (a)(3)(ii) through (a)(3)(viii) of this section.

(ii) *Paper statement.*—The recipient must be informed that the statement will be furnished on paper if the recipient does not consent to receive it electronically.

(iii) *Scope and duration of consent.*—The recipient must be informed of the scope and duration of the consent. For example, the recipient must be informed whether the consent applies to statements furnished every year after the consent is given until it is withdrawn in the manner described in paragraph (a)(3)(v)(A) of this section or only to the statement required to be furnished on or before the January 31st immediately following the date on which the consent is given.

(iv) *Post-consent request for a paper statement.*—The recipient must be informed of any procedure for obtaining a paper copy of the recipient's statement after giving the consent described in paragraph (a)(2)(i) of this section and whether a request for a paper statement will be treated as a withdrawal of consent.

(v) *Withdrawal of consent.*—The recipient must be informed that—

(A) The recipient may withdraw a consent by writing (electronically or on paper) to the person or department whose name,

mailing address, telephone number, and e-mail address is provided in the disclosure statement;

(B) The furnisher will confirm the withdrawal and the date on which it takes effect in writing (either electronically or on paper); and

(C) A withdrawal of consent does not apply to a statement that was furnished electronically in the manner described in this paragraph (a) before the date on which the withdrawal of consent takes effect.

(vi) *Notice of termination.*—The recipient must be informed of the conditions under which a furnisher will cease furnishing statements electronically to the recipient.

(vii) *Updating information.*—The recipient must be informed of the procedures for updating the information needed by the furnisher to contact the recipient. The furnisher must inform the recipient of any change in the furnisher's contact information.

(viii) *Hardware and software requirements.*—The recipient must be provided with a description of the hardware and software required to access, print, and retain the statement, and the date when the statement will no longer be available on the website.

(4) *Format.*—The electronic version of the statement must contain all required information and comply with applicable revenue procedures relating to substitute statements to recipients.

(5) *Notice.*—(i) *In general.*—If the statement is furnished on a website, the furnisher must notify the recipient that the statement is posted on a website. The notice may be delivered by mail, electronic mail, or in person. The notice must provide instructions on how to access and print the statement. The notice must include the following statement in capital letters, "IMPORTANT TAX RETURN DOCUMENT AVAILABLE." If the notice is provided by electronic mail, the foregoing statement must be on the subject line of the electronic mail.

(ii) *Undeliverable electronic address.*—If an electronic notice described in paragraph (a)(5)(i) of this section is returned as undeliverable, and the correct electronic address cannot be obtained from the furnisher's records or from the recipient, then the furnisher must furnish the notice by mail or in person within 30 days after the electronic notice is returned.

(b) *Effective/applicability date.*—The rules in this section apply to returns for calendar years beginning after December 31, 2010. [Reg. § 1.6050W-2.]

☐ [*T.D. 9496, 8-13-2010.*]

### [Reg. § 1.6050X-1]

**1.6050X-1. Information reporting for fines, penalties, and other amounts by governments, governmental entities, and nongovernmental entities treated as governmental entities.**—(a) *Information reporting requirement.*—The appropriate official, as defined in paragraph (f)(1) of this section, of a government, as defined in paragraph (f)(2) of this section, a governmental entity, as defined in paragraph (f)(3) of this section, or nongovernmental entity treated as a governmental entity, as defined in paragraph (f)(4) of this section, that is a party to a suit or agreement to which section 6050X(a)(1) and (a)(2) applies, must—

(1) File an information return, as described in paragraph (b) of this section, if the aggregate amount the payor, as defined in paragraph (f)(5) of this section, is required to pay pursuant to all court orders (orders) and settlement agreements (agreements), relating to the violation of any law, or the investigation or inquiry into the potential violation of any law, equals or exceeds the threshold amount provided in paragraph (f)(6) of this section;

(2) Furnish a written statement as described in paragraph (c) of this section to each payor; and

(3) Request the payor's taxpayer identification number (TIN) if it is not already known, and notify the payor that the law requires the payor to furnish a TIN for inclusion on the information return and that the payor may be subject to a penalty for failure to furnish the TIN. See sections 6723, 6724(d)(3), and § 301.6723-1 of this chapter. The TIN may be requested in any manner, and the payor may provide the TIN in any manner, including orally, in writing, or electronically. If the TIN is furnished in writing, no particular form is required. Form W-9, Request for Taxpayer Identification Number and Certification, may be used, or the request may be incorporated into documents related to the order or agreement.

(b) *Requirement to file return.*—(1) *Content of information return.*—The information return must provide the following:

(i) The amount required to be paid to, or at the direction of, a government or governmental entity, pursuant to section 6050X(a)(1)(A), as a result of the orders and/or agreements;

(ii) The separate amounts required to be paid as restitution, remediation, or to come into compliance with a law, as described in section 6050X(a)(1)(B) and (C), as a result of the orders and/or agreements;

(iii) The payor's TIN; and

(iv) Any additional information required by the information return and the related instructions.

(2) *Form and manner of reporting.*—The appropriate official required to file an information return, under paragraph (a)(1) of this section, must file Form 1098-F, Fines, Penalties, and Other Amounts, or any successor form, as provided by the instructions, with Form 1096, Annual Summary and Transmittal of U.S. Information Returns.

(3) *Multiple orders and/or agreements.*—The appropriate official must file only one Form 1098-F for amounts required to be paid as a result of multiple orders and/or agreements with respect to the violation, investigation, or inquiry.

(4) *Time of reporting.*—Returns required to be made under paragraph (a) of this section must be filed with the Internal Revenue Service (IRS) on or before February 28 (March 31 if filed electronically) of the year following the calendar year in which the orders and/or agreements become binding under applicable law, determined without regard to whether all appeals have been exhausted or the time for filing an appeal has expired.

(c) *Requirement to furnish written statement.*—(1) *In general.*—The appropriate official must furnish a written statement to each payor for which it is required to file an information return under paragraphs (a)(1) and (b) of this section. The written statement must include:

(i) The information that was reported to the IRS relating to such payor; and

(ii) A legend that identifies the statement as important tax information that is being furnished to the IRS.

(2) *Copy of the Form 1098-F.*—The appropriate official may satisfy the requirement of this paragraph (c) by furnishing a copy of the Form 1098-F, or any successor form, filed regarding the payor, or another document that contains the information required by paragraph (c)(1) of this section if the document conforms to applicable revenue procedures or other guidance relating to substitute statements. See § 601.601 of this chapter.

(3) *Time for furnishing written statement.*—The appropriate official must furnish the written statement to the payor on or before January 31 of the year following the calendar year in which the order or agreement becomes binding under applicable law, determined without regard to whether all appeals have been exhausted or the time for filing an appeal has expired.

(d) *Rules for multiple payors.*—(1) *Multiple payors — individual liability.*—If, pursuant to an order or agreement, multiple individually liable payors are liable to pay, for the violation of any law, or the investigation or inquiry into the potential violation of any law, an amount that, in the aggregate, equals, or exceeds, the threshold amount under paragraph (f)(6) of this section, the appropriate official must file an information return under paragraphs (a)(1) and (b) of this section to report the amount required to be paid by each payor, even if a payor's payment liability is less than the threshold amount. The appropriate official must furnish a written statement, under paragraph (c) of this section, to each payor. If more than one person, as defined in section 7701(a)(1), is a party to an order or agreement, there is no information reporting requirement, or requirement to furnish a written statement, with respect to any person who does not have a payment obligation or obligation for costs to provide services or to provide property.

(2) *Multiple payors — joint and several liability.*—If, pursuant to an order or agreement, multiple payors are jointly and severally liable to pay, for the violation of any law, or the investigation or inquiry into the potential violation of any law, an amount that, in the aggregate, equals or exceeds the threshold amount under paragraph (f)(6) of this section, the appropriate official must file an information return, under paragraphs (a)(1) and (b) of this section for each of the jointly and severally liable payors. Each information return must report all amounts required to be paid by all of the payors pursuant to the order or agreement. The appropriate official must furnish a written statement, under paragraph (c) of this section, to each of the jointly and severally liable payors.

(e) *Payment amount not identified.*—If some or all of the payment amount is not identified, as described in § 1.162-21(b)(2)(iii), for paragraphs (a), (b), and (c) of this section, the appropriate official must file an information return, and furnish the written statement to the payor, as provided by the instructions to Form 1098-F, or any successor form, including instructions as to the amounts (if any) to

include on Form 1098-F, only if the government or governmental entity reasonably expects that the aggregate amount required to be paid or incurred pursuant to the order or agreement, relating to the violation of any law, or the investigation or inquiry into the potential violation of any law, will equal or exceed the threshold amount under paragraph (f)(6) of this section.

(f) *Definitions.*—The following definitions apply under this section:

(1) *Appropriate official.*—(i) *One government or governmental entity.*—If the government or governmental entity has not assigned one of its officers or employees to comply with the reporting requirements of paragraph (a), (b), and (c) of this section, the term *appropriate official* means the officer or employee of a government or governmental entity having control of the suit, investigation, or inquiry. If the government or governmental entity has assigned one of its officers or employees to comply with the reporting requirements of paragraph (a), (b), and (c) of this section, such officer or employee is the appropriate official.

(ii) *More than one government or governmental entity.*—(A) *In general.*—If more than one government or governmental entity is a party to an order or agreement, only the appropriate official of the government or governmental entity listed first on the most recently executed order or agreement is responsible for complying with all reporting requirements under paragraphs (a), (b), and (c) of this section, unless another appropriate official is appointed by agreement under paragraph (f)(1)(ii)(B) of this section.

(B) *By agreement.*—The governments or governmental entities that are parties to an order or agreement may agree to appoint one or more other appropriate officials to be responsible for complying with the information reporting requirements of paragraphs (a), (b), and (c) of this section.

(2) *Government.*—For purposes of this section, *government* means the government of the United States, a State, the District of Columbia, or a political subdivision (such as a local government unit) of any of the foregoing.

(3) *Governmental entity.*—For purposes of this section, *governmental entity* means—

(i) A corporation or other entity serving as an agency or instrumentality of a government (as defined in paragraph (f)(2) of this section), or

(ii) A nongovernmental entity treated as a governmental entity as described in paragraph (f)(4) of this section.

(4) *Nongovernmental entity treated as governmental entity.*—For purposes of this section, the definition of nongovernmental entity treated as a governmental entity as set forth in § 1.162-21(e)(3) applies but does not include a nongovernmental entity of a territory of the United States, including American Samoa, Guam, the Northern Mariana Islands, Puerto Rico, or the U.S. Virgin Islands, a foreign country, or an Indian tribe.

(5) *Payor.*—The payor is the person, as defined in section 7701(a)(1), which, pursuant to an order or agreement, has paid or incurred, or is liable to pay or incur, an amount to, or at the direction of, a government or governmental entity in relation to the violation or potential violation of any law. In general, the payor will be the person to which section 162(f) and § 1.162-21 of the regulations apply.

(6) *Threshold amount.*—The *threshold amount* is $50,000.

(g) *Applicability date.*—The rules of this section apply only to orders and agreements, pursuant to suits and agreements, which become binding under applicable law on or after January 1, 2022, determined without regard to whether all appeals have been exhausted or the time for filing an appeal has expired. [Reg. § 1.6050X-1.]

☐ [*T.D.* 9946, 1-14-2021.]

## [Reg. § 1.6050Y-1]

**§ 1.6050Y-1. Information reporting for reportable policy sales, transfers of life insurance contracts to foreign persons, and reportable death benefits.**—(a) *Definitions.*—The following definitions apply for purposes of this section and §§ 1.6050Y-2 through 1.6050Y-4:

(1) *Acquirer.*—The term *acquirer* means any person that acquires an interest in a life insurance contract (through a direct acquisition or indirect acquisition of the interest) in a reportable policy sale.

(2) *Buyer.*—The term *buyer* means, with respect to any interest in a life insurance contract that has been transferred in a reportable policy sale, the person that was the most recent acquirer of that interest in a reportable policy sale as of the date reportable death benefits are paid under the contract.

(3) *Direct·acquisition of an interest in a life insurance contract.*—The term *direct acquisition of an interest in a life insurance contract* has the meaning given to it in § 1.101-1(e)(3)(i).

(4) *Foreign person.*—The term *foreign person* means a person that is not a United States person, as defined in section 7701(a)(30).

(5) *Indirect acquisition of an interest in a life insurance contract.*—The term *indirect acquisition of an interest in a life insurance contract* has the meaning given to it in § 1.101-1(e)(3)(ii).

(6) *Interest in a life insurance contract.*—The term *interest in a life insurance contract* has the meaning given to it in § 1.101-1(e)(1).

(7) *Investment in the contract.*—(i) *Definition of investment in the contract.*—With respect to the original policyholder of a life insurance contract, the term *investment in the contract* on any date means that person's investment in the contract under section 72(e)(6) on that date. With respect to any other person, the term *investment in the contract* on any date means the *estimate of investment in the contract* on that date.

(ii) *Definition of estimate of investment in the contract.*—The term *estimate of investment in the contract* with respect to any person, other than the original policyholder, means, on any date, the aggregate amount of premiums paid for the contract by that person before that date, less the aggregate amount received under the contract by that person before that date to the extent such information is known to or can reasonably be estimated by the issuer or payor.

(8) *Issuer.*—(i) *In general.*—Except as provided in paragraph (a)(8)(ii) or (iii) of this section, the term *issuer* generally means, on any date, with respect to any interest in a life insurance contract, any person that bears any part of the risk with respect to the contract on that date and any person responsible on that date for administering the contract, including collecting premiums and paying death benefits. For instance, if a reinsurer reinsures on an indemnity basis all or a portion of the risks that the original issuer (and continuing contract administrator) of the contract might otherwise have incurred with respect to the contract, both the reinsurer and the original issuer of the contract are issuers of the contract for purposes of this paragraph (a)(8)(i). Any designee of an issuer of a contract is also considered an issuer of the contract for purposes of this paragraph (a)(8)(i).

(ii) *6050Y(a) issuer.*—For purposes of information reporting under section 6050Y(a) and § 1.6050Y-2, the 6050Y(a) issuer is the issuer that is responsible for administering the life insurance contract, including collecting premiums and paying death benefits under the contract, on the date of the reportable policy sale. In the case of the issuance of a life insurance contract to a policyholder in an exchange pursuant to section 1035, the 6050Y(a) issuer is the issuer that issues the new contract.

(iii) *6050Y(b) issuer.*—For purposes of information reporting under section 6050Y(b) and § 1.6050Y-3, a 6050Y(b) issuer is:

(A) Any person that receives an RPSS with respect to a life insurance contract or interest therein (or, in the case of a designee, receives notice that the issuer for whom it serves as designee received an RPSS), and is or was, on or before the date of receipt of the RPSS, an issuer with respect to the contract; or

(B) Any person that receives notice of a transfer to a foreign person of a life insurance contract, provided that the person is or was, on the date of transfer or on the date of receipt of the notice, an issuer with respect to the contract, and provided that the information is not received from the issuer responsible for administering the contract (or its designee), unless:

(1) That person (or, in the case of a designee, the issuer for whom it serves as designee) is not responsible for administering the contract, including collecting premiums and paying death benefits under the contract, on the date the notice of a transfer to a foreign person is received; and

(2) That person, or its designee, provides the issuer that is responsible on that date for administering the contract, including collecting premiums and paying death benefits under the contract, with such notice and with any available information necessary to accomplish reporting under section 6050Y(b) and § 1.6050Y-3.

(iv) *Designee.*—A person is treated as the designee of an issuer for purposes of this paragraph (a)(8) only if so designated in writing, including electronically. The designation must be signed and acknowledged, in writing or electronically, by the person named as designee, or that person's representative, and by the issuer making the designation, or its representative.

(9) *Life insurance contract.*—The term *life insurance contract* has the meaning given to it in section 7702(a). A life insurance contract may also be referred to as a life insurance policy.

(10) *Notice of a transfer to a foreign person.*—The term *notice of a transfer to a foreign person* means any notice of a transfer of title to, possession of, or legal ownership of a life insurance contract received by a 6050Y(b) issuer that includes foreign indicia, including information provided for nontax purposes such as a change of address notice for purposes of sending statements or for other purposes, and information relating to loans, premiums, or death benefits with respect to the contract, unless the 6050Y(b) issuer knows that no transfer of the contract has occurred or knows that the transferee is a United States person. For this purpose, a 6050Y(b) issuer may rely on a Form W-9, Request for Taxpayer Identification Number and Certification, or a valid substitute form that meets the requirements of § 1.1441-1(d)(2) (substituting "6050Y(b) issuer" for "withholding agent"), that indicates the transferee is a United States person. For instance, a change of address notice that changes the address to a foreign address or other updates to the information relating to the payment of premiums that includes foreign banking or other foreign financial institution information is notice of a transfer to a foreign person unless the 6050Y(b) issuer knows that no transfer has occurred or the transferee is a United States person.

(11) *Payor.*—The term *payor* means any person making a payment of reportable death benefits.

(12) *Reportable death benefits.*—The term *reportable death benefits* means amounts paid by reason of the death of the insured under a life insurance contract that are attributable to an interest in the contract that was transferred in a reportable policy sale.

(13) *Reportable death benefits payment recipient.*—The term *reportable death benefits payment recipient* means any person that receives reportable death benefits as a beneficiary under a life insurance contract or as the holder of an interest in a life insurance contract.

(14) *Reportable policy sale.*—The term *reportable policy sale* has the meaning given to it in § 1.101-1(c).

(15) *Reportable policy sale payment.*—The term *reportable policy sale payment* generally means the total amount of cash and the fair market value of any other consideration reducible to a money value transferred, or to be transferred, in a reportable policy sale, including any amount of a reportable policy sale payment recipient's debt assumed by the acquirer in a reportable policy sale. In the case of an indirect acquisition of an interest in a life insurance contract that is a reportable policy sale, the reportable policy sale payment is the total amount of cash and the fair market value of any other consideration reducible to a money value transferred, or to be transferred, for the ownership interest in the entity, including the amount of any debt assumed by the acquirer, that is appropriately allocable to the interest in the life insurance contract held by the entity.

(16) *Reportable policy sale payment recipient.*—(i) Except as provided in paragraph (a)(16)(ii) of this section, the term *reportable policy sale payment recipient* means any person that receives a reportable policy sale payment in a reportable policy sale. A broker or other intermediary that retains a portion of the cash or other consideration transferred in a reportable policy sale is also a reportable policy sale payment recipient.

(ii) A person other than the seller is not a reportable policy sale payment recipient with respect to a reportable policy sale if that person receives aggregate payments of less than $600 with respect to that reportable policy sale.

(17) *Reportable policy sale statement.*—The term *reportable policy sale statement (RPSS)* means a statement furnished by an acquirer to an issuer under section 6050Y(a)(2) and § 1.6050Y-2(d)(2)(i).

(18) *Seller.*—The term *seller* means any person that—

(i) Holds an interest in a life insurance contract and transfers that interest, or any part of that interest, to an acquirer in a reportable policy sale; or

(ii) Owns a life insurance contract and transfers title to, possession of, or legal ownership of that contract to a foreign person.

(19) *Transfer of an interest in a life insurance contract.*—The term *transfer of an interest in a life insurance contract* has the meaning given to it in § 1.101-1(e)(2).

(20) *United States person.*—The term *United States person* has the meaning given to it in section 7701(a)(30).

(b) *Applicability date.*—This section and § § 1.6050Y-2 through 1.6050Y-3 apply to reportable policy sales made after December 31, 2018. This section and § 1.6050Y-4 apply to reportable death benefits paid after December 31, 2018. This section and § 1.6050Y-3 apply to any notice of a transfer to a foreign person received after December 31, 2018. However, for reportable policy sales and payments of reportable death benefits occurring after December 31, 2018, and on or before December 31, 2019, and any notice of a transfer to a foreign person received after December 31, 2018, and on or before December 31, 2019, transition relief is provided as follows:

(1) Statements required to be furnished to issuers under section 6050Y(a)(2) and §1.6050Y-2(d)(2)(i) must be furnished by the later of the applicable deadline set forth in §1.6050Y-2(d)(2)(ii) or December 30, 2019.

(2) Statements required to be furnished to reportable policy sale payment recipients under section 6050Y(a)(2) and §1.6050Y-2(d)(1)(i) must be furnished by the later of the applicable deadline set forth in §1.6050Y-2(d)(1)(ii) or February 28, 2020.

(3) Statements required to be furnished to sellers under section 6050Y(b)(2) and §1.6050Y-3(d)(1) must be furnished by the later of the applicable deadline set forth in §1.6050Y-3(d)(2) or February 28, 2020.

(4) Statements required to be furnished to reportable death benefits payment recipients under section 6050Y(c)(2) and §1.6050Y-4(c)(1) must be furnished by the later of the applicable deadline set forth in §1.6050Y-4(c)(2) or February 28, 2020.

(5) Returns required to be filed under section 6050Y(a)(1) and §1.6050Y-2(a), section 6050Y(b)(1) and §1.6050Y-3(a), and section 6050Y(c)(1) and §1.6050Y-4 must be filed by the later of the applicable deadline set forth in §1.6050Y-2(c), §1.6050Y-3(c), and §1.6050Y-4(b) or February 28, 2020. [Reg. §1.6050Y-1.]

☐ [T.D. 9879, 10-25-2019 (corrected 12-12-2019).]

### [Reg. §1.6050Y-2]

**§1.6050Y-2. Information reporting by acquirers for reportable policy sale payments.**—(a) *Requirement of reporting.*—Except as provided in paragraph (f) of this section, every person that is an acquirer in a reportable policy sale during any calendar year must file a separate information return with the Internal Revenue Service (IRS) in the form and manner as required by the IRS for each reportable policy sale payment recipient, including any seller that is a reportable policy sale payment recipient. Each return must include the following information with respect to the seller or other reportable policy sale payment recipient to which the return relates:

(1) The name, address, and taxpayer identification number (TIN) of the acquirer;

(2) The name, address, and TIN of the seller or other reportable policy sale payment recipient to which the return relates;

(3) The date of the reportable policy sale;

(4) The name of the 6050Y(a) issuer of the life insurance contract acquired and the policy number of the life insurance contract;

(5) The aggregate amount of reportable policy sale payments made, or to be made, to the seller or other reportable policy sale payment recipient to which the return relates with respect to the reportable policy sale; and

(6) Any other information that is required by the form or its instructions.

(b) *Unified reporting.*—The information reporting requirement of paragraph (a) of this section applies to each acquirer in a series of prearranged transfers of an interest in a life insurance contract, as well as each acquirer in a simultaneous transfer of different interests in a single life insurance contract. In either case, an acquirer's reporting obligation is deemed satisfied if the information required by paragraph (a) of this section with respect to that acquirer is timely reported on behalf of that acquirer in a manner that is consistent with forms, instructions, and other IRS guidance by one or more other acquirers or by a third party information reporting contractor.

(c) *Time and place for filing.*—Returns required to be made under paragraph (a) of this section must be filed with the Internal Revenue Service Center designated on the prescribed form or in its instructions on or before February 28 (March 31 if filed electronically) of the year following the calendar year in which the reportable policy sale occurred. However, see §1.6050Y-1(b)(5) for transition rules.

(d) *Requirement of and time for furnishing statements.*—(1) *Statements to reportable policy sale payment recipients.*—(i) *Requirement of furnishing statement.*—Every person required to file an information return under paragraph (a) of this section with respect to a reportable policy sale payment recipient must furnish in the form and manner prescribed by the IRS to the reportable policy sale payment recipient whose name is set forth in that return a written statement showing the information required by paragraph (a) of this section with respect to the reportable policy sale payment recipient and the name, address, and phone number of the information contact of the person furnishing the written statement. The contact information of the person furnishing the written statement must provide direct access to a person that can answer questions about the statement. The statement is not required to include information with respect to any other reportable policy sale payment recipient in the reportable policy sale or information about reportable policy sale payments to any other reportable policy sale payment recipient.

(ii) *Time for furnishing statement.*—Each statement required by paragraph (d)(1)(i) of this section to be furnished to any reportable policy sale payment recipient must be furnished on or before February 15 of the year following the calendar year in which the reportable policy sale occurred. However, see §1.6050Y-1(b)(2) for transition rules.

(2) *Statements to 6050Y(a) issuers.*—(i) *Requirement of furnishing RPSS.*—(A) *In general.*—Except as provided in paragraph (d)(2)(i)(B) of this section, every person required to file a return under paragraph (a) of this section must furnish in the form and manner prescribed by the IRS to the 6050Y(a) issuer whose name is required to be set forth in the return an RPSS with respect to each reportable policy sale payment recipient that is also a seller. Each RPSS must show the information required by paragraph (a) of this section with respect to the seller named therein, except that the RPSS is not required to set forth the amount of any reportable policy sale payment. Each RPSS must also show the name, address, and phone number of the information contact of the person furnishing the RPSS. This contact information must provide direct access to a person that can answer questions about the RPSS.

(B) *Exception from reporting.*—An RPSS is not required to be furnished to the 6050Y(a) issuer by an acquirer acquiring an interest in a life insurance contract in an indirect acquisition.

(ii) *Time for furnishing RPSS.*—Except as provided in this paragraph (d)(2)(ii), each RPSS required by paragraph (d)(2)(i) of this section to be furnished to a 6050Y(a) issuer must be furnished by the later of 20 calendar days after the reportable policy sale, or 5 calendar days after the end of the applicable state law rescission period. However, if the later date is after January 15 of the year following the calendar year in which the reportable policy sale occurred, the RPSS must be furnished by January 15 of the year following the calendar year in which the reportable policy sale occurred. However, see §1.6050Y-1(b)(1) for transition rules.

(3) *Unified reporting.*—The information reporting requirements of paragraphs (d)(1)(i) and (d)(2)(i) of this section apply to each acquirer in a series of prearranged transfers of an interest in a life insurance contract, as well as each acquirer in a simultaneous transfer of different interests in a single life insurance contract, as described in paragraph (b) of this section. In either case, an acquirer's obligation to furnish statements is deemed satisfied if the information required by paragraphs (d)(1)(i) and (d)(2)(i) of this section with respect to that acquirer is timely reported on behalf of that acquirer consistent with forms, instructions, and other IRS guidance by one or more other acquirers or by a third party information reporting contractor.

(e) *Notice of rescission of a reportable policy sale.*—Any person that has filed a return required by section 6050Y(a)(1) and this section with respect to a reportable policy sale must file a corrected return within 15 calendar days of the receipt of notice of the rescission of the reportable policy sale. Any person that has furnished a written statement under section 6050Y(a)(2) and this section with respect to the reportable policy sale must furnish the recipient of that statement with a corrected statement within 15 calendar days of the receipt of notice of the rescission of the reportable policy sale.

(f) *Exceptions to requirement to file.*—(1) An acquirer that is a foreign person is not required to file an information return under paragraph (a) of this section with respect to a reportable policy sale unless—

(i) The life insurance contract (or interest therein) transferred in the sale is on the life of an insured who is a United States person at the time of the sale; or

(ii) The sale is subject to the laws of one or more States of the United States that pertain to acquisitions or sales of life insurance contracts (or interests therein).

(2) An acquirer is not required to file an information return under paragraph (a) of this section with respect to a reportable policy sale payment to a reportable policy sale payment recipient other than the seller if the reportable policy sale payment is reported by the acquirer under section 6041 or 6041A.

(3) An acquirer is not required to file an information return under paragraph (a) of this section with respect to the issuance of a life insurance contract in an exchange pursuant to section 1035. However, the acquirer is required to furnish the 6050Y(a) issuer with the statement required under paragraph (d)(2) of this section as if the acquirer were required to file an information return under paragraph (a) of this section.

(g) *Cross-reference to penalty provisions.*—(1) *Failure to file correct information return.*—For provisions relating to the penalty provided for failure to file timely a correct information return required under section 6050Y(a)(1) and this section, see section 6721 and §301.6721-1 of this chapter. See section 6724(a) and §301.6724-1 of this chapter for the waiver of a penalty if the failure is due to reasonable cause and is not due to willful neglect.

(2) *Failure to furnish correct statement.*—For provisions relating to the penalty provided for failure to furnish timely a correct statement to identified persons under section 6050Y(a)(2) and this section, see section 6722 and §301.6722-1 of this chapter. See section 6724(a) and §301.6724-1 of this chapter for the waiver of a penalty if the failure is due to reasonable cause and is not due to willful neglect. [Reg. §1.6050Y-2.]

☐ [*T.D.* 9879, 10-25-2019.]

### [Reg. §1.6050Y-3]

**§1.6050Y-3. Information reporting by 6050Y(b) issuers for reportable policy sales and transfers of life insurance contracts to foreign persons.**—(a) *Requirement of reporting.*—Except as provided in paragraph (f) of this section, each 6050Y(b) issuer that receives an RPSS or any notice of a transfer to a foreign person must file an information return with the Internal Revenue Service (IRS) with respect to each seller in the form and manner prescribed by the IRS. The return must include the following information with respect to the seller:

(1) The name, address, and taxpayer identification number (TIN) of the seller;

(2) The investment in the contract with respect to the seller;

(3) The amount the seller would have received if the seller had surrendered the life insurance contract on the date of the reportable policy sale or the transfer of the contract to a foreign person, or if the date of the transfer to a foreign person is not known to the 6050Y(b) issuer, the date the 6050Y(b) issuer received notice of the transfer; and

(4) Any other information that is required by the form or its instructions.

(b) *Unified reporting.*—Each 6050Y(b) issuer subject to the information reporting requirement of paragraph (a) of this section must satisfy that requirement, but a 6050Y(b) issuer's reporting obligation is deemed satisfied if the information required by paragraph (a) of this section with respect to that 6050Y(b) issuer is timely reported on behalf of that 6050Y(b) issuer in a manner that is consistent with forms, instructions, and other IRS guidance by one or more other 6050Y(b) issuers or by a third party information reporting contractor.

(c) *Time and place for filing.*—Except as provided in this paragraph (c), returns required to be made under paragraph (a) of this section must be filed with the Internal Revenue Service Center designated on the prescribed form or in its instructions on or before February 28 (March 31 if filed electronically) of the year following the calendar year in which the reportable policy sale or the transfer to a foreign person occurred. If the 6050Y(b) issuer does not receive notice of a transfer to a foreign person until after January 31 of the calendar year following the year in which the transfer occurred, returns required to be made under paragraph (a) of this section must be filed by the later of February 28 (March 31 if filed electronically) of the calendar year following the year in which the transfer occurred or thirty days after the date notice is received. However, see §1.6050Y-1(b)(5) for transition rules.

(d) *Requirement of and time for furnishing statements.*—(1) *Requirement of furnishing statement.*—Every 6050Y(b) issuer filing a return required by paragraph (a) of this section must furnish to each seller that is a reportable policy sale payment recipient or makes a transfer to a foreign person and whose name is required to be set forth in the return a written statement showing the information required by paragraph (a) of this section with respect to that seller and the name, address, and phone number of the information contact of the person filing the return. This contact information must provide direct access to a person that can answer questions about the statement.

(2) *Time for furnishing statement.*—Except as provided in this paragraph (d)(2), each statement required by paragraph (d)(1) of this section to be furnished to any seller must be furnished on or before February 15 of the year following the calendar year in which the reportable policy sale or transfer to a foreign person occurred. If a 6050Y(b) issuer does not receive notice of a transfer to a foreign person until after January 31 of the calendar year following the year in which the transfer occurred, each statement required to be made under paragraph (d) of this section must be furnished by the date thirty days after the date notice is received. However, see §1.6050Y-1(b)(3) for transition rules.

(3) *Unified reporting.*—Each 6050Y(b) issuer subject to the information reporting requirement of paragraph (d)(1) of this section must satisfy that requirement, but a 6050Y(b) issuer's reporting obligation is deemed satisfied if the information required by paragraph (d)(1) of this section with respect to that 6050Y(b) issuer is timely reported on behalf of that 6050Y(b) issuer consistent with forms, instructions, and other IRS guidance by one or more other 6050Y(b) issuers or by a third party information reporting contractor.

(e) *Notice of rescission of a reportable policy sale or transfer of an insurance contract to a foreign person.*—Any 6050Y(b) issuer that has filed a return required by section 6050Y(b)(1) and this section with respect to a reportable policy sale or transfer of an insurance contract to a foreign person must file a corrected return within 15 calendar days of the receipt of notice of the rescission of the reportable policy sale or transfer of the insurance contract to a foreign person. Any 6050Y(b) issuer that has furnished a written statement under section 6050Y(b)(2) and this section with respect to the reportable policy sale or transfer of the insurance contract to a foreign person must furnish the recipient of that statement with a corrected statement within 15 calendar days of the receipt of notice of the rescission of the reportable policy sale or transfer of the insurance contract to a foreign person.

(f) *Exceptions to requirement to file.*—A 6050Y(b) issuer is not required to file an information return under paragraph (a) of this section if paragraph (f)(1), (2), or (3) of this section applies.

(1) Except as provided in this paragraph (f)(1), the 6050Y(b) issuer obtains documentation upon which it may rely to treat a seller of a life insurance contract or interest therein as a foreign beneficial owner in accordance with §1.1441-1(e)(1)(ii), applying in such case the provisions of §1.1441-1 by substituting the term "6050Y(b) issuer" for the term "withholding agent" and without regard to the fact that that these provisions apply only to amounts subject to withholding under chapter 3 of subtitle A of the Internal Revenue Code. A 6050Y(b) issuer may also obtain from a seller that is a partnership or trust, in addition to documentation establishing the entity's foreign status, a written certification from the entity that no beneficial owner of any portion of the proceeds of the sale is a United States person. In such a case, the issuer may rely upon the written certification to treat the partnership or trust as a foreign beneficial owner for purposes of this paragraph (f)(1) provided that the seller does not have actual knowledge that a United States person is the beneficial owner of all or a portion of the proceeds of the sale. See §1.1441-1(c)(6)(ii) for the definition of beneficial owner that applies for purposes of this paragraph (f)(1). Additionally, for certifying its status as a foreign beneficial owner (as applicable) for purposes of this paragraph (f)(1), a seller that is required to report any of the income from the sale as effectively connected with the conduct of a trade or business in the United States under section 864(b) is required to provide to the 6050Y(b) issuer a Form W-8ECI, Certificate of Foreign Person's Claim that Income is Effectively Connected with the Conduct of a Trade or Business in the United States. If a 6050Y(b) issuer obtains a Form W-8ECI from a seller with respect to the sale or has reason to know that income from the sale is effectively connected with the conduct of a trade or business in the United States under section 864(b), the exception to reporting described in this paragraph (f)(1) does not apply.

(2) The 6050Y(b) issuer receives notice of a transfer to a foreign person, but does not receive an RPSS with respect to the transfer, provided that, at the time the notice is received—

(i) The 6050Y(b) issuer is not a United States person;

(ii) The life insurance contract (or interest therein) transferred is not on the life of a United States person; and

(iii) The 6050Y(b) issuer has not classified the seller as a United States person in its books and records.

(3) The RPSS received by the 6050Y(b) issuer is with respect to the 6050Y(b) issuer's issuance of a life insurance contract to a policyholder in an exchange pursuant to section 1035.

(g) *Cross-reference to penalty provisions.*—(1) *Failure to file correct information return.*—For provisions relating to the penalty provided for failure to file timely a correct information return required under section 6050Y(b)(1) and this section, see section 6721 and §301.6721-1 of this chapter. See section 6724(a) and §301.6724-1 of this chapter for the waiver of a penalty if the failure is due to reasonable cause and is not due to willful neglect.

(2) *Failure to furnish correct statement.*—For provisions relating to the penalty provided for failure to furnish timely a correct statement to identified persons under section 6050Y(b)(2) and this section, see section 6722 and §301.6722-1 of this chapter. See section 6724(a) and §301.6724-1 of this chapter for the waiver of a penalty if the failure is due to reasonable cause and is not due to willful neglect. [Reg. §1.6050Y-3.]

☐ [*T.D.* 9879, 10-25-2019.]

[Reg. §1.6050Y-4]

**§1.6050Y-4. Information reporting by payors for reportable death benefits.**—(a) *Requirement of reporting.*—Except as provided in paragraph (e) of this section, every person that is a payor of reportable death benefits during any calendar year must file a separate information return for such calendar year with the Internal Revenue Service (IRS) for each reportable death benefits payment recipient in the form and manner prescribed by the IRS. The return must include the following information with respect to the reportable death benefits payment recipient to which the return relates:

(1) The name, address, and taxpayer identification number (TIN) of the payor;

(2) The name, address, and TIN of the reportable death benefits payment recipient;

(3) The date of the payment;

(4) The gross amount of reportable death benefits paid to the reportable death benefits payment recipient during the taxable year;

(5) The payor's estimate of investment in the contract with respect to the buyer, limited to the payor's estimate of the buyer's investment in the contract with respect to the interest for which the reportable death benefits payment recipient was paid; and

(6) Any other information that is required by the form or its instructions.

(b) *Time and place for filing.*—Returns required to be made under this section must be filed with the Internal Revenue Service Center designated in the instructions for the form on or before February 28 (March 31 if filed electronically) of the year following the calendar year in which the payment of reportable death benefits was made. However, see § 1.6050Y-1(b)(5) for transition rules.

(c) *Requirement of and time for furnishing statements.*—(1) *Requirement of furnishing statement.*—Every person required to file an information return under paragraph (a) of this section must furnish to each reportable death benefits payment recipient whose name is required to be set forth in that return a written statement showing the information required by paragraph (a) of this section with respect to that reportable death benefits payment recipient and the name, address, and phone number of the information contact of the payor. This contact information must provide direct access to a person that can answer questions about the statement.

(2) *Time for furnishing statement.*—Each statement required by paragraph (c)(1) of this section to be furnished to any reportable death benefits payment recipient must be furnished on or before January 31 of the year following the calendar year in which the payment of reportable death benefits was made. However, see § 1.6050Y-1(b)(4) for transition rules.

(d) *Notice of rescission of a reportable policy sale.*—Any person that has filed a return required by section 6050Y(c) and this section with respect to a payment of reportable death benefits must file a corrected return within 15 calendar days of recovering any portion of the reportable death benefits payment from the reportable death benefits payment recipient as a result of the rescission of the reportable policy sale. Any person that has furnished a written statement under section 6050Y(c)(2) and this section with respect to a payment of reportable death benefits must furnish the recipient of that statement with a corrected statement within 15 calendar days of recovering any portion of the reportable death benefits payment from the reportable death benefits payment recipient as a result of the rescission of the reportable policy sale.

(e) *Exceptions to requirement to file.*—A payor is not required to file an information return under paragraph (a) of this section with respect to a payment of reportable death benefits if paragraph (e)(1), (2), or (3) of this section applies.

(1) Except as provided in this paragraph (e)(1), the payor obtains documentation in accordance with § 1.1441-1(e)(1)(ii) upon which it may rely to treat the reportable death benefits payment recipient as a foreign beneficial owner of the reportable death benefits, applying in such case the provisions of § 1.1441-1 by substituting the term "payor" for the term "withholding agent" and without regard to the fact that the provisions apply only to amounts subject to withholding under chapter 3 of subtitle A of the Internal Revenue Code. A payor may also obtain from a partnership or trust that is a reportable death benefits recipient, in addition to documentation establishing the entity's foreign status, a written certification from the entity that no beneficial owner of any portion of the reportable death benefits payment is a United States person. In such a case, a payor may rely upon the written certification to treat the partnership or trust as a foreign beneficial owner for purposes of this paragraph (e)(1) provided that the payor does not have actual knowledge that a United States person is the beneficial owner of all or a portion of the reportable death benefits payment. See § 1.1441-1(c)(6)(ii) for the

definition of beneficial owner that applies for purposes of this paragraph (e)(1). Other due diligence or reporting requirements may, however, apply to a payor that relies on the exception set forth in this paragraph (e)(1). See § 1.1441-5(c) and (e) (determination of payees of foreign partnerships and certain foreign trusts for amounts subject to withholding under § 1.1441-2(a)) and § 1.1461-1(b) and (c) (amounts subject to reporting for chapter 3 purposes).

(2) The buyer obtained the life insurance contract (or interest therein) under which reportable death benefits are paid in a reportable policy sale to which the exception to reporting described in § 1.6050Y-3(f)(2) applies.

(3) The payor never received, and has no knowledge of any issuer having received, an RPSS with respect to the interest in a life insurance contract with respect to which the reportable death benefits are paid.

(f) *Cross-reference to penalty provisions.*—(1) *Failure to file correct information return.*—For provisions relating to the penalty provided for failure to file timely a correct information return required under section 6050Y(c)(1) and this section, see section 6721 and § 301.6721-1 of this chapter. See section 6724(a) and § 301.6724-1 of this chapter for the waiver of a penalty if the failure is due to reasonable cause and is not due to willful neglect.

(2) *Failure to furnish correct statement.*—For provisions relating to the penalty provided for failure to furnish timely a correct statement to identified persons under section 6050Y(c)(2) and this section, see section 6722 and § 301.6722-1 of this chapter. See section 6724(a) and § 301.6724-1 of this chapter for the waiver of a penalty if the failure is due to reasonable cause and is not due to willful neglect. [Reg. § 1.6050Y-4.]

□ [*T.D.* 9879, 10-25-2019.]

[Reg. § 31.6051-1]

**§ 31.6051-1. Statement for employees.**—(a) *Requirement if wages are subject to withholding of income tax.*—(1) *General rule.*—(i) Every employer, as defined in section 3401(d), required to deduct and withhold from an employee a tax under section 3402, or who would have been required to deduct and withhold a tax under section 3402 (determined without regard to section 3402(n)) if the employee had claimed no more than one withholding exemption, shall furnish to each such employee, in respect of the remuneration paid by such employer to such employee during the calendar year, the tax return copy and the employee's copy of a statement on Form W-2. For example, if the wage bracket method of withholding provided in section 3402(c)(1) is used, a statement on Form W-2 must be furnished to each employee whose wages during any payroll period are equal to or in excess of the smallest wage from which tax must be withheld in the case of an employee claiming one exemption. If the percentage method is used, a statement on Form W-2 must be furnished to each employee whose wages during any payroll period, reduced by the amount of one withholding exemption, are equal to or in excess of the smallest amount of wages from which tax must be withheld. See section 3402(a) and (b) and the regulations thereunder. See paragraph (d) of this section for provisions relating to the time for furnishing the statement required by this subparagraph. See paragraph (f) of this section for an exception for employers filing composite returns from the requirement that statements for employees be on Form W-2. For the requirements relating to Form W-2 with respect to qualified State individual income taxes, see paragraph (d)(3)(ii) of § 301.6361-1 of this chapter (Regulations on Procedure and Administration). Each statement on Form W-2 shall show the following:

(A) The name, address, and identification number of the employer,

(B) The name, address, and social security number of the employee, which may be truncated to appear in the form of an IRS truncated taxpayer identification number (TTIN) on copies of Forms W-2 that are furnished to the employee (for provisions relating to the use of TTINs, see § 301.6109-4 of this chapter (Procedure and Administration Regulations)), if wages as defined in section 3121(a) have been paid or if the Form W-2 is required to be furnished to the employee,

(C) The total amount of wages as defined in section 3401(a),

(D) The total amount deducted and withheld as tax under section 3402,

(E) The total amount of wages as defined in section 3121(a),

(F) The total amount of employee tax under section 3101 deducted and withheld (increased by any adjustment in the calendar year for overcollection, or decreased by any adjustment in such year for undercollection, of such tax during any prior year) and the proportion thereof (expressed either as a dollar amount, as a percentage of the total amount of wages as defined in section 3121(a), or as a percentage of the total amount of employee tax under section 3101) withheld as tax under section 3101(b) for financing the cost of hospital insurance benefits,

(G) Such information relating to coverage the employee has earned under the Federal Insurance Contributions Act, as may be required by Form W-2 or its instructions, and

(H) The total amount paid to the employee under section 3507 (relating to advance payment of earned income credit).

(ii) Payments made in 1955 under a wage continuation plan shall be reported on Form W-2 to the extent, and in the manner, provided in paragraph (b)(8)(i) of §31.3401(a)-1 of Subpart E of the regulations in this part.

(iii) In the case of statements furnished by the employer for whom services are performed, with respect to wages paid after December 31, 1955, "the total amount of wages as defined in section 3401(a)", as used in section 6051(a)(3), shall include all payments made directly by such employer under a wage continuation plan which constitute wages in accordance with §31.3401(a)-1(b)(8)(ii)(a), without regard to whether tax has been withheld on such amounts.

(iv) Form W-2 is not required in respect of any wage continuation payment made to an employee by or on behalf of a person who is not the employer for whom the employee performs services but who is regarded as an employer under section 3401(d)(1). See paragraph (b)(8) of §31.3401(a)-1 of Subpart E of the regulations in this part.

(v) In the case of remuneration paid for service described in section 3121(m), relating to service in the uniformed services, performed after 1956, "wages as defined in section 3121(a)", as used in section 6051(a)(2) and (5), shall be determined in accordance with section 3121(i)(2) and section 3122.

(vi) In the case of remuneration in the form of tips received by an employee in the course of his employment, the amounts required to be shown by paragraphs (3) and (5) of section 6051(a) (see subdivision (i)(c) and (e) of this subparagraph) shall include only such tips as are reported by the employee to the employer in a written statement furnished to the employer pursuant to section 6053(a).

(2) *Statements for members of the Armed Forces of the United States.*—Section 6051(b) contains certain special provisions which are applicable in the case of members of the Armed Forces of the United States in active service. In such case, Form W-2 shall be furnished to each such member of the Armed Forces if any tax has been withheld under section 3402 during the calendar year from the remuneration of such member or if any of the remuneration paid during the calendar year for such active service is includible in the gross income of such member. Form W-2, in the case of such member, shall show, as "the total amount of wages as defined in section 3401(a)", as used in section 6051(a)(3), the amount of the remuneration paid during the calendar year which is not excluded under chapter 1 of the Internal Revenue Code of 1954 from the gross income of such member, whether or not such remuneration constitutes wages as defined in section 3401(a) and whether or not paid for such active service.

(3) *Undelivered statements for employees.*—The Internal Revenue Service copy and the employee's copy of each withholding statement for the calendar year which the employer is required to furnish to the employee and which after reasonable effort he is unable to deliver to the employee shall be retained by the employer for the 4-year period prescribed in paragraph (e)(2) of §31.6001-1.

(b) *Requirement if wages are not subject to withholding of income tax.*—(1) *General rule.*—If during the calendar year an employer pays to an employee wages subject to the employee tax imposed by section 3101, but not subject to income tax withholding under section 3402, the employer shall furnish to such employee the tax return copy and the employee's copy of a statement on Form W-2 for such calendar year. Such statement shall show the following:

(i) The name and address of the employer,

(ii) The name, address, and social security number of the employee, which may be truncated to appear in the form of a TTIN on copies of Forms W-2 that are furnished to the employee (for provisions relating to the use of TTINs, see §301.6109-4 of this chapter),

(iii) The total amount of wages as defined in section 3121(a),

(iv) The total amount of employee tax deducted and withheld from such wages (increased by any adjustment in such year for overcollection, or decreased by any adjustment in such year for undercollection, of employee tax during any prior year) and the proportion thereof (expressed either as a dollar amount, as a percentage of the total amount of wages as defined in section 3121(a), or as a percentage of the total amount of employee tax under section 3101) withheld as tax under section 3101(b) for financing the cost of hospital insurance benefits,

(v) Such information relating to coverage the employee has earned under the Federal Insurance Contributions Act, as may be required by Form W-2 or its instructions, and

(vi) The total amount paid to the employee under section 3507 (relating to advance payment of earned income credit).

See paragraph (d) of this section for provisions relating to the time for furnishing the statement required by this paragraph.

(2) *Uniformed services.*—In the case of remuneration paid for service described in section 3121(m), relating to service in the uniformed services, performed after 1956, "wages as defined in section 3121(a)", as used in section 6051(a)(5), shall be determined in accordance with section 3121(i)(2) and section 3122.

(c) *Correction of statements.*—(1) *Federal Insurance Contributions Act.*—If (i) the amount of employee tax under section 3101 deducted and withheld in the calendar year from the wages, as defined in section 3121(a), paid during such year was less or greater than the tax imposed by section 3101 on such wages by reason of the adjustment in such year of an overcollection or undercollection of the tax in any prior year, or (ii) regardless of the reason for the error or the method of its correction, the amount of wages as defined in section 3121(a), or tax under section 3101, entered on a statement furnished pursuant to this section to an employee for a prior year was incorrect, a corrected statement for such prior year reflecting the adjustment or the correct data shall be furnished to the employee. Such statement shall be marked "Corrected by Employer."

(2) *Income tax withholding.*—A corrected statement shall be furnished to the employee with respect to a prior calendar year (i) to show the correct amount of wages, as defined in section 3401(a), paid during the prior calendar year if the amount of such wages entered on a statement furnished to the employee for such prior year is incorrect, or (ii) to show the amount actually deducted and withheld as tax under section 3402 if such amount is less or greater than the amount entered as tax withheld on the statement furnished the employee for such prior year. Such statement shall be indicated as corrected.

(3) *Cross reference.*—For provisions relating to the disposition of the Internal Revenue Service copy of a corrected statement, see paragraph (b)(2) of §31.6011(a)-4 and paragraph (b) of §31.6051-2.

(d) *Time for furnishing statements.*—(1) *In general.*—(i) Each statement required by this section for a calendar year and each corrected statement required for the year shall be furnished to the employee on or before January 31 of the year succeeding such calendar year. If an employee's employment is terminated before the close of such calendar year, the employer, at his option, shall furnish the statement to the employee at any time after the termination but no later than January 31 of the year succeeding such calendar year. However, if an employee whose employment is terminated before the close of such calendar year requests the employer to furnish him the statement at an earlier time, and if there is no reasonable expectation on the part of both employer and employee of further employment during the calendar year, then the employer shall furnish the statement to the employee on or before the later of the 30th day after the day of the request or the 30th day after the day on which the last payment of wages is made. For provisions relating to the filing of the Internal Revenue Service copies of the statement, see §31.6051-2.

(ii) *Expedited furnishing.*—(A) *General rule.*—If an employer is required to make a final return under §31.6011(a)-6(a)(1) (relating to the final return for Federal Insurance Contributions Act taxes and income tax withholding from wages) on Form 941, or a variation thereof, the employer must furnish the statement required by this section on or before the date required for filing the final return. See §31.6071(a)-1(a)(1). However, if the final return under §31.6011(a)-6(a)(1) is a monthly return, as described in §31.6011(a)-5, the employer must furnish the statement required by this section on or before the last day of the month in which the final return is required to be filed. See §31.6071(a)-1(a)(2). Except as provided in paragraph (d)(2)(i) of this section, in no event may an employer furnish the statement required by this section later than January 31 of the year succeeding the calendar year to which it relates. The requirements set forth in this paragraph (d)(1)(ii) do not apply to employers with respect to employees whose wages are for domestic service in the private home of the employer. See §31.6011(a)-1(a)(3).

(B) *Requests by employees.*—An employer is not permitted to furnish a statement pursuant to the provisions of the third sentence of paragraph (d)(1)(i) of this section (relating to written requests by terminated employees for Form W-2) at a time later than that required by the provisions of paragraph (d)(1)(ii)(A) of this section.

(2) *Extensions of time.*—(i) *In general.*—(a) The Director, Martinsburg Computing Center, may grant an extension of time in which to

furnish to employees the statements required by this section. A request may be made by a letter to the Director, Martinsburg Computing Center. The request must contain:

*(1) The employer's name and address;*

*(2) The employer's taxpayer identification numbers;*

*(3) The type of return (i.e., Form W-2);.—and*

*(4) A concise statement of the reasons for requesting the* extension.

*(b)* The application must be mailed or delivered on or before the applicable due date prescribed in paragraph (d)(1) of this section for furnishing the statements required by this section.

*(c)* In any case in which an employer is unable, by reason of illness, absence, or other good cause, to sign a request for an extension, any person standing in close personal or business relationship to the employer may sign the request on his behalf, and shall be considered as a duly authorized agent for this purpose, provided the request sets forth a reason for a signature other than the employer's and the relationship existing between the employer and the signer. For provisions relating to extensions of time for filing the Social Security Administration copies of the statement, see § 31.6081(a)-1(a)(2).

*(ii) Automatic extension of time.*—The Commissioner may, in appropriate cases, publish procedures for automatic extensions of time to furnish Forms W-2 where the employer is required to furnish the Form W-2 on an expedited basis.

*(3) Cross references.*—For provisions relating to the penalties provided for the willful furnishing of a false or fraudulent statement, or for the willful failure to furnish a statement, see § 31.6674-1 and section 7204.

*(e) Reporting of reimbursements of or payments of expenses of moving from one residence to another residence after July 23, 1971.*—Every employer who after July 23, 1971, makes reimbursement to, or payment to (other than direct cash reimbursement), an employee for his expenses of moving from one residence to another residence which is includible in gross income under section 82 shall furnish to the best of his ability to such employee information sufficient to assist the employee in the computation of any deduction allowable under section 217 with respect to such reimbursement or payment. The information required under this paragraph may be furnished on Form 4782 provided by the Internal Revenue Service or may be furnished on forms provided by the employer so long as the employee receives the same information he would have received had he been furnished with a completed Form 4782. The information shall include the amount of the reimbursement or payment and whether the reimbursement or payment was made directly to a third party for the benefit of an employee or furnished in kind to the employee. In addition, information shall be furnished as to whether the reimbursement or payment represents an expense described in subparagraphs (A) through (E) of section 217(b)(1), and if so, the amount and nature of the expenses described in each such subparagraph. The information described in this paragraph shall be furnished at the same time or before the written statement required by section 6051(a) is furnished in respect of the calendar year for which the information provided under this paragraph is required. The information required under this paragraph shall be provided for the taxable year in which the payment or reimbursement is received by the employee. For determining the taxable year in which a payment or reimbursement is received, see section 82 and § 1.82-1.

*(f) Statements with respect to compensation, as defined in the Railroad Retirement Tax Act.*—(1) *Notification of possible credit or refund.*—With respect to compensation (as defined in section 3231(e)), every employer (as defined in section 3231(a)) who is required to deduct and withhold from an employee (as defined in section 3231(b)) a tax under section 3201, shall include on or with the statement required to be furnished to such employee under section 6051(a), a notice concerning the provisions of this title with respect to the allowance of a credit or refund of the tax on wages imposed by section 3101(b) and the tax on compensation imposed by section 3201 or 3211, which is treated as a tax on wages imposed by section 3101(b).

*(2) Information to be supplied to employees upon request.*—With respect to compensation (as defined in section 3231(e)), every employer (as defined in section 3231(a)) who is required to deduct and withhold tax under section 3201 from an employee (as defined in section 3231(b)) who has also received wages during such year subject to the tax imposed by section 3101(b), shall upon request of such employee furnish to him or her a written statement showing—

(i) The total amount of compensation with respect to which the tax imposed by section 3101(b) was deducted;

(ii) The total amount of employee tax under section 3201 deducted and withheld (increased by any adjustment in the calendar year for overcollection, or decreased by any adjustment in such year for undercollection, of such tax during any prior year); and

(iii) The proportion thereof (expressed either as a dollar amount, or a percentage of the total amount of compensation as defined in section 3231(e), or as a percentage of the total amount of employee tax under section 3201) withheld as tax under section 3201 for financing the cost of hospital insurance benefits.

*(g) Employers filing composite returns.*—Every employer who files a composite return pursuant to § 31.6011(a)-8 shall furnish to his employees the statements required under this section, except that in lieu of Form W-2 the statements may be in any form which is suitable for retention by the employee and which contains all information required to be shown on Form W-2.

*(h) Statements with respect to the refundable earned income credit.*—(1) *In general.*—In respect of remuneration paid in any calendar year beginning after December 31, 1986, for services performed after December 31, 1986, every employer shall furnish Notice 797 (You May Be Eligible for a Refund on Your Federal Income Tax Return Because of the Earned Income Credit (EIC)), or a written statement that contains an exact reproduction of the wording contained in Notice 797, to each employee with respect to whom the employer paid wages (within the meaning of section 3401(a)) during the calendar year and who did not have any income tax withheld by the employer during the calendar year. Notwithstanding the preceding sentence, no such statement need be furnished to an employee who claimed exemption from withholding pursuant to section 3402(n) for the calendar year.

*(2) Time for furnishing statement.*—The statement required by this paragraph (h) for a calendar year shall be furnished—

(i) In the case of an employee who is required to be furnished a Form W-2, Wage and Tax Statement, for the calendar year, within one week of (before or after) the date that the employee is furnished a timely Form W-2 for the calendar year (or, if a Form W-2 is not so furnished, on or before the date by which it is required to be furnished); and

(ii) In the case of an employee who is not required to be furnished a Form W-2 for the calendar year, on or before February 7 of the year succeeding the calendar year.

*(3) Manner of furnishing statement.*—If an employee is furnished a Form W-2 in a timely manner, the statement required by this paragraph (h) may be furnished with the employee's Form W-2. Any statement not so furnished shall be furnished by direct, personal delivery to the employee or by first class mail addressed to the employee at his or her current or last known address. For purposes of the preceding sentence, direct, personal delivery means hand delivery to the employee. Thus, for example, an employer does not meet the requirements of this paragraph (h) if the statement is sent through inter-office mail or is posted on a bulletin board.

*(i) Cross references.*—For provisions relating to the penalties provided for the willful furnishing of a false or fraudulent statement, or for the willful failure to furnish a statement, see § 31.6674-1 and section 7204. For additional provisions relating to the inclusion of identification numbers and account numbers in statements on Form W-2, see §§ 31.6109-1 and 31.6109-4. For the penalties applicable to information returns and payee statements, see sections 6721 through 6724 and the regulations in part 301 under sections 6721 through 6724.

*(j) Electronic furnishing of statements.*—(1) *In general.*—A person required by section 6051 to furnish a written statement on Form W-2 (furnisher) to the individual to whom it is required to be furnished (recipient) may furnish the Form W-2 in an electronic format in lieu of a paper format. A furnisher who meets the requirements of paragraphs (j)(2) through (6) of this section is treated as furnishing the Form W-2 in a timely manner.

*(2) Consent.*—(i) *In general.*—The recipient must have affirmatively consented to receive the Form W-2 in an electronic format. The consent may be made electronically in any manner that reasonably demonstrates that the recipient can access the Form W-2 in the electronic format in which it will be furnished to the recipient. Alternatively, the consent may be made in a paper document if it is confirmed electronically.

(ii) *Withdrawal of consent.*—The consent requirement of this paragraph (j)(2) is not satisfied if the recipient withdraws the consent and the withdrawal takes effect before the statement is furnished. The furnisher may provide that a withdrawal of consent takes effect either on the date it is received by the furnisher or on a subsequent date. The furnisher may also provide that a request for a paper statement will be treated as a withdrawal of consent.

(iii) *Change in hardware or software requirements.*—If a change in hardware or software required to access the Form W-2 creates a material risk that the recipient will not be able to access the Form W-2, the furnisher must, prior to changing the hardware or software, provide the recipient with a notice. The notice must describe the revised hardware and software required to access the Form W-2 and inform the recipient that a new consent to receive the Form W-2 in the revised electronic format must be provided to the furnisher. After implementing the revised hardware and software, the furnisher must obtain from the recipient, in the manner described in paragraph (j)(2)(i) of this section, a new consent or confirmation of consent to receive the Form W-2 electronically.

(iv) *Examples.*—The following examples illustrate the rules of this paragraph (j)(2):

*Example 1.* Furnisher F sends Recipient R a letter stating that R may consent to receive Form W-2 electronically on a website instead of in a paper format. The letter contains instructions explaining how to consent to receive Form W-2 electronically by accessing the website, downloading the consent document, completing the consent document and e-mailing the completed consent back to F. The consent document posted on the website uses the same electronic format that F will use for the electronically furnished Form W-2. R reads the instructions and submits the consent in the manner provided in the instructions. R has consented to receive the statements electronically in the manner described in paragraph (j)(2)(i) of this section.

*Example 2.* Furnisher F sends Recipient R an e-mail stating that R may consent to receive Form W-2 electronically instead of in a paper format. The e-mail contains an attachment instructing R how to consent to receive Form W-2 electronically. The e-mail attachment uses the same electronic format that F will use for the electronically furnished Form W-2. R opens the attachment, reads the instructions, and submits the consent in the manner provided in the instructions. R has consented to receive Form W-2 electronically in the manner described in paragraph (j)(2)(i) of this section.

*Example 3.* Furnisher F posts a notice on its website stating that Recipient R may receive Form W-2 electronically instead of in a paper format. The website contains instructions on how R may access a secure webpage and consent to receive the statements electronically. By accessing the secure webpage and giving consent, R has consented to receive Form W-2 electronically in the manner described in paragraph (j)(2)(i) of this section.

(3) *Required disclosures.*—(i) *In general.*—Prior to, or at the time of, a recipient's consent, the furnisher must provide to the recipient a clear and conspicuous disclosure statement containing each of the disclosures described in paragraphs (j)(3)(ii) through (viii) of this section.

(ii) *Paper statement.*—The recipient must be informed that the Form W-2 will be furnished on paper if the recipient does not consent to receive it electronically.

(iii) *Scope and duration of consent.*—The recipient must be informed of the scope and duration of the consent. For example, the recipient must be informed whether the consent applies to each Form W-2 required to be furnished after the consent is given until it is withdrawn in the manner described in paragraph (j)(3)(v)(A) of this section or only to the first Form W-2 required to be furnished following the date on which the consent is given.

(iv) *Post-consent request for a paper statement.*—The recipient must be informed of any procedure for obtaining a paper copy of the recipient's statement after giving the consent described in paragraph (j)(2)(i) of this section and whether a request for a paper statement will be treated as a withdrawal of consent.

(v) *Withdrawal of consent.*—The recipient must be informed that—

(A) The recipient may withdraw a consent by writing (electronically or on paper) to the person or department whose name, mailing address, telephone number, and e-mail address is provided in the disclosure statement;

(B) The furnisher will confirm the withdrawal and the date on which it takes effect in writing (either electronically or on paper); and

(C) A withdrawal of consent does not apply to a statement that was furnished electronically in the manner described in this paragraph (j) before the date on which the withdrawal of consent takes effect.

(vi) *Notice of termination.*—The recipient must be informed of the conditions under which a furnisher will cease furnishing statements electronically to the recipient (for example, termination of the recipient's employment with furnisher-employer).

(vii) *Updating information.*—The recipient must be informed of the procedures for updating the information needed by the furnisher to contact the recipient. The furnisher must inform the recipient of any change in the furnisher's contact information.

(viii) *Hardware and software requirements.*—The recipient must be provided with a description of the hardware and software required to access, print, and retain the Form W-2, and the date when the Form W-2 will no longer be available on the website. The recipient must be informed that the Form W-2 may be required to be printed and attached to a Federal, State, or local income tax return.

(4) *Format.*—The electronic version of the Form W-2 must contain all required information and comply with applicable revenue procedures relating to substitute statements to recipients.

(5) *Notice.*—(i) *In general.*—If the statement is furnished on a website, the furnisher must notify the recipient that the statement is posted on a website. The notice may be delivered by mail, electronic mail, or in person. The notice must provide instructions on how to access and print the statement. The notice must include the following statement in capital letters, "IMPORTANT TAX RETURN DOCUMENT AVAILABLE." If the notice is provided by electronic mail, the foregoing statement must be on the subject line of the electronic mail.

(ii) *Undeliverable electronic address.*—If an electronic notice described in paragraph (j)(5)(i) of this section is returned as undeliverable, and the correct electronic address cannot be obtained from the furnisher's records or from the recipient, then the furnisher must furnish the notice by mail or in person within 30 days after the electronic notice is returned.

(iii) *Corrected Form W-2.*—If the furnisher has corrected a recipient's Form W-2 that was furnished electronically, the furnisher must furnish the corrected Form W-2 to the recipient electronically. If the recipient's Form W-2 was furnished though a website posting and the furnisher has corrected the Form W-2, the furnisher must notify the recipient that it has posted the corrected Form W-2 on the website within 30 days of such posting in the manner described in paragraph (j)(5)(i) of this section. The corrected Form W-2 or the notice must be furnished by mail or in person if—

(A) An electronic notice of the website posting of an original Form W-2 or the corrected Form W-2 was returned as undeliverable; and

(B) The recipient has not provided a new e-mail address.

(6) *Access period.*—Forms W-2 furnished on a website must be retained on the website through October 15 of the year following the calendar year to which the Forms W-2 relate (or the first business day after October 15, if October 15 falls on a Saturday, Sunday, or legal holiday). The furnisher must maintain access to corrected Forms W-2 that are posted on the website through October 15 of the year following the calendar year to which the Forms W-2 relate (or the first business day after such October 15, if October 15 falls on a Saturday, Sunday, or legal holiday) or the date 90 days after the corrected forms are posted, whichever is later.

(7) *Paper statements after withdrawal of consent.*—If a recipient withdraws consent to receive a statement electronically and the withdrawal takes effect before the statement is furnished electronically, a paper statement must be furnished. A paper statement furnished after the statement due date under this paragraph (j)(7) will be considered timely if furnished within 30 days after the date the withdrawal of consent is received by the furnisher.

(k) *Applicability date.*—This section is applicable for statements required to be furnished under section 6051 after December 31, 2020. [Reg. § 31.6051-1.]

☐ [*T.D.* 6155, 12-29-55. *Amended by T.D.* 6472, 6-22-60; *T.D.* 6606, 8-24-62; *T.D.* 6983, 12-3-68; *T.D.* 7001, 1-17-69; *T.D.* 7048, 6-23-70; *T.D.* 7115, 5-20-71; *T.D.* 7195, 7-10-72; *T.D.* 7351, 4-16-75; *T.D.* 7374, 7-23-75; *T.D.* 7577, 12-19-78; *T.D.* 7580, 12-20-78; *T.D.* 7656, 11-28-79; *T.D.* 7683, 3-12-80; *T.D.* 8155, 9-9-87; *T.D.* 8222, 8-23-88; *T.D.* 8344, 4-12-91; *T.D.* 8636, 12-20-95; *T.D.* 9061, 6-10-2003, *T.D.* 9114, 2-13-2004 *and T.D.* 9861, 7-2-2019.]

### [Reg. § 301.6051-1]

§ 301.6051-1. Receipts for employees.—For provisions relating to statements for employees regarding remuneration paid during calendar year, see § 31.6051-1 of this chapter (Employment Tax Regulations). [Reg. § 301.6051-1.]

☐ [*T.D.* 6498, 10-24-60.]

Reg. § 301.6051-1

**[Reg. §31.6051-2]**

**§31.6051-2. Information returns on Form W-3 and Social Security Administration copies of Forms W-2.**—(a) *In general.*—Every employer who is required to make a return of tax under §31.6011(a)-1 (relating to returns under the Federal Insurance Contributions Act), §31.6011(a)-4 (relating to returns of income tax withheld from wages), or §31.6011(a)-5 (relating to monthly returns) for a calendar year or any period therein, shall file the Social Security Administration copy of each Form W-2 required under §31.6051-1 to be furnished by the employer with respect to wages paid during the calendar year. An employer may not truncate an employee's social security number to appear in the form of an IRS truncated taxpayer identification number (TTIN) on copies of Forms W-2 filed with the Social Security Administration. Each Form W-2 and the transmittal Form W-3 shall together constitute an information return to be filed with the Social Security Administration as indicated on the instructions to such forms. For the requirement to submit the information on Form W-2 on magnetic media, see section 6011(e) and §301.6011-2 of this chapter (Procedure and Administration Regulations).

(b) *Corrected returns.*—The Social Security Administration copies of corrected Forms W-2 (or magnetic tape or other approved media) for employees for the calendar year shall be submitted with Form W-3 (or Form 4804), on or before the date on which information returns for the period in which the correction is made would be due under paragraph (a)(3)(ii) of §31.6071(a)-1, to the Social Security Administration office with which Forms W-2 are required to be filed.

(c) *Cross references.*—For provisions relating to the time for filing the information returns required by this section and to extensions of the time for filing, see sections 6071 and 6081 and the regulations in this part under sections 6071 and 6081. For the penalties applicable to information returns and payee statements, see sections 6721 through 6724 and the regulations in part 301 under sections 6721 through 6724.

(d) *Applicability date.*—This section is applicable for statements required to be filed under section 6051 after July 3, 2019. [Reg. §31.6051-2.]

□ [*T.D.* 7351, 4-16-75. *Amended by T.D.* 7580, 12-28-78; *T.D.* 8155, 9-9-87; *T.D.* 8344, 4-12-91; *T.D.* 8636, 12-20-95, *T.D.* 9061, 6-10-2003 and *T.D.* 9861, 7-2-2019.]

**[Reg. §31.6051-3]**

**§31.6051-3. Statements required in case of sick pay paid by third parties.**—(a) *Statements required from payor.*—(1) Every payor of sick pay shall furnish to the employer of the payee of the sick pay a written statement. The written statement must contain the following information:

(i) The name and, if there is withholding from sick pay under section 3402(o) and the regulations in this part under section 3402(o), the social security account number of the payee (the payee's social security number may not be truncated to appear in the form of an IRS truncated taxpayer identification number (TTIN)),

(ii) The total amount of sick pay paid to the payee during the calendar year, and

(iii) The total amount (if any) deducted and withheld from sick pay under section 3402(o) and the regulations thereunder. The statement must be furnished to the employer on or before January 15 of the year following the calendar year in which any sick pay was paid.

(2) These reporting requirements are in lieu of the requirements of sections 6051(a) (relating to written statements for employees) and 6041 (relating to information returns). Statements required to be furnished by this paragraph shall be treated as statements required under section 6051 to be furnished to employees for purposes of sections 6674 (relating to fraudulent statement or failure to furnish statement to employee) and 7204 (relating to fraudulent statement or failure to make statement to employees).

(3) A multiemployer plan paying sick pay pursuant to a collectively bargained agreement may furnish the statement required to be furnished by this paragraph, which shall include the total amount of sick pay paid to the employee under the plan regardless of the identity or number of employers for whom the employee worked during the calendar year under the plan, to one of the following:

(i) The employer for whom the employee worked the most hours during the calendar year for which the statement is to be furnished,

(ii) The employer for whom the employee first worked during such year,

(iii) The employer for whom the employee last worked during such year,

(iv) The employer for whom the employee worked immediately preceding his absence for which sick pay was paid,

(v) The employer for whom the employee worked immediately following his absence for which sick pay was paid,

(vi) The employer designated through the operation of a specific clause of the collective bargaining agreement, or

(vii) The employer designated through the operation of a specific system of designation chosen by the payor.

(b) *Information required to be furnished by employer.*—Every employer of a payee of sick pay who receives a statement under paragraph (a) from a payor of sick pay shall furnish to each payee of sick pay a written statement, which must be furnished on Form W-2. The written statement must contain the following information:

(1) All of the information required to be furnished under paragraph (a) of this section, but the employer may truncate the payee's social security number to appear in the form of a TTIN on copies of Forms W-2 that are furnished to the payee (for provisions relating to the use of TTINs, see §301.6109-4 of this chapter (Procedure and Administration Regulations)).

(2) The name, the address, and the Employer Identification Number (EIN) of the employer,

(3) The words "sick pay", which shall be written in the box labelled "Employer's use", and

(4) If any portion of the sick pay is excludable from gross income under section 104(a)(3), the amount of the portion which is not so excludable and of the portion which is so excludable. Only sick pay payments includable in gross income shall be reported in the box labelled "Wages, tips, other compensation" on Form W-2. Any amount excludable from gross income under section 104(a)(3) shall be reported in the box labelled "Employer's use" on Form W-2 and any amount so reported shall be described as "Nontaxable". The information required to be furnished by this paragraph may be furnished either on the same Form W-2 that is required to be furnished under section 6051(a) or on a separate Form W-2. To the extent practicable, this statement should be furnished to the payee along with the statement (if any) required under section 6051(a) (relating to written statements for employees). The statement must be furnished to the payee on or before January 31 of the year following the calendar year in which any sick pay was paid. The employer shall file copy A of Form W-2 and Form W-3 with the Social Security Administration in accordance with section 6051(d) (relating to statements to constitute information returns) and the regulations thereunder.

(c) *Optional rule.*—The payor and the employer may at their option enter into an agency agreement valid under local law whereby the employer designates the payor to be the employer's agent for purposes of fulfilling the requirements of this section. This agreement must specify what portion, if any, of the sick pay is excludable from gross income under section 104(a)(3). If they enter into such an agreement, the payor shall not provide the statement required by paragraph (a) but shall instead furnish statements that meet all of the requirements of paragraph (b), except that the agreement must provide that the payor will furnish the statements with the payor's, rather than the employer's, name, address, and Employer Identification Number (EIN) if "Sick Pay Statement Furnished under an Agency Agreement with Your Employer" appears in the box labelled "Employer's Use" on Form W-2. Subparagraph (a)(2) remains applicable to statements furnished under this paragraph. In the case of sick pay paid under a multiemployer plan pursuant to a collectively bargained agreement, an amendment to either the multiemployer plan or the collectively bargained agreement designating the payor to be the employers' agent for purposes of fulfilling the requirements of this section shall be deemed an agency agreement that fulfills the requirements of the first sentence of this paragraph.

(d) *Definitions.*—For purposes of this section, the terms "payor", "payee", and "sick pay" shall have the same meaning as ascribed thereto in section 3402(o) and the regulations thereunder. For purposes of this section, the term "employer" shall have the same meaning as ascribed thereto in section 3401(d) and the regulations thereunder, except that the term "employer" shall not include the payor for purposes of this section.

(e) *Additional requirements.*—(1) Statements furnished to payees under this section must also comply with all requirements of section 6051(c) and (d) and the regulations thereunder.

(2) The provisions of §1.9101-1 (relating to permission to submit information required by certain returns and statements on magnetic tape) shall be applicable to the information required by this section to be furnished on Form W-2 if the employer properly complies with those provisions.

(3) The provisions of section 6109 (relating to identifying numbers) and the regulations in this part and part 301 under section 6109 shall be applicable to Form W-2 and to any payee of sick pay to whom a statement on Form W-2 is required by this section to be furnished. The employer must include the social security number of

the payee on all copies of Forms W-2. The employer may truncate the payee's social security number to appear in the form of a TTIN on copies of Forms W-2 that are furnished to the payee. For provisions relating to the use of TTINs, see § 301.6109-4 of this chapter.

(f) *Applicability date.*—This section is applicable for statements required to be furnished under section 6051 after December 31, 2020. [Reg. § 31.6051-3.]

☐ [*T.D. 7813, 3-15-82. Amended by T.D. 9861, 7-2-2019.*]

### [Reg. § 31.6051-4]

**§ 31.6051-4. Statement required in case of backup Withholding.**—(a) *Statements required from payor.*—Every payor of any reportable payment(as defined in section 3406(b)(1)) who is required to deduct and withhold tax under section 3406 must furnish to the payee a written statement containing the information required by paragraph(c) of this section.

(b) *Prescribed form.*—The prescribed form for the statement required by this section is Form 1099. In the case of any reportable interest or dividend payment as defined in section 3406(b)(2), the prescribed form is the Form 1099 required in § 1.6042-4 of this chapter (relating to payments of dividends), § 1.6044-5 of this chapter (relating to payments of patronage dividends), or § 1.6049-6(e) of this chapter (relating to payments of interest or original issue discount). Statements required to be furnished by this section will be treated as statements required by the respective sections with respect to any reportable payment, except that the statement required under this section must include the amount of tax withheld under section 3406. In no event will a statement be required under this section if a statement with the same information is required to be furnished to the recipient under another section.

(c) *Information required.*—Each statement on Form 1099 must show the following:

(1) The name, address, and taxpayer identification number of the person receiving any reportable payment;

(2) Except as provided in the prescribed form or instructions, the amount subject to reporting under section 6041, 6041A(a), 6042, 6044, 6045, 6049, 6050A, 6050N, or 6050W whether or not the amount of the reportable payment is less than the amount for which an information return is required or, if tax is withheld under section 3406, the amount of the payment withheld upon;

(3) The amount of tax deducted and withheld under section 3406;

(4) The name and address of the person filing the form;

(5) A legend stating that such amount is being reported to the Internal Revenue Service; and

(6) Such other information as is required by the form.

(d) *Time for furnishing statements.*—The statement must be furnished to the payee no later than January 31 of the year following the calendar year in which the payment was made. However, for a statement required to be furnished after December 31, 2008, the February 15 due date under section 6045 applies to the statement if the statement reports tax withheld from a payment reportable under section 6045 or is furnished in a consolidated reporting statement under section 6045. See § § 1.6045-1(k)(3), 1.6045-2(d)(2), 1.6045-3(e)(2), 1.6045-4(m)(3), and 1.6045-5(a)(3)(ii) of this chapter.

(e) *Aggregation.*—The payor or broker may combine the information required to be shown under this section with information required to be shown under another section even if they do not relate to the same type of reportable payment. [Reg. § 31.6051-4.]

☐ [*T.D. 8637, 12-20-95. Amended by T.D. 9496, 8-13-2010; T.D. 9504, 10-12-2010.*]

### [Reg. § 1.6052-1]

**§ 1.6052-1. Information returns regarding payment of wages in the form of group-term life insurance.**—(a) *Requirement of reporting.*—(1) *In general.*—Every employer, who during any calendar year provides any one of his employees remuneration for services in the form of group-term life insurance on the life of such employee any part of the cost of which is to be included in such employee's gross income as provided in section 79(a), shall make a separate return on Form W-2 with respect to each such employee for such year which includes the following information:

(i) Name, address, and identifying number of the employer;

(ii) Name, address, and social security number of the employee; and

(iii) Total amount includible in the employee's gross income by reason of the provisions of section 79(a), computed as if each employee reported his income on the basis of a calendar year (determined as if the employer making such return is the only employer paying the employee remuneration in the form of group-term life insurance on his life which is includible in his gross income under section 79(a)).

Returns on Form W-2 required to be filed pursuant to the provisions of this section shall be transmitted by Form W-3. In a case where, with respect to the same employee, an employer must make a return on Form W-2 under this section and also under § 31.6011(a)-4 or § 31.6011(a)-5 of this chapter (Employment Tax Regulations), or under § 1.6041-2 (relating to return of information as to payments to employees), such employer may make such returns on the same Form W-2 or on separate Forms W-2. In a case where an employer must file a Form W-3 under this section and also under § 31.6011(a)-4 or § 31.6011(a)-5 of this chapter (Employment Tax Regulations), the Form W-3 filed under such § 31.6011(a)-4 or § 31.6011(a)-5 shall also be used as the transmittal form for a return on Form W-2 made pursuant to the provisions of this section.

(2) *Definitions.*—Terms used in paragraph (a)(1) of this section and in section 79 and the regulations thereunder have the meaning ascribed to them in section 79 and the regulations thereunder.

(b) *Time and place for filing.*—(1) *Time for filing.*—(i) *General rule.*—In a case where an employer must file Forms W-3 and W-2 under this section and also under § 31.6011(a)-4 or § 31.6011(a)-5 of this chapter (Employment Tax Regulations), the time for filing such forms under this section shall be the same as the time (including extensions thereof) for filing such forms under § 31.6011(a)-4 or § 31.6011(a)-5.

(ii) *Exception.*—In a case where an employer is not required to file Forms W-3 and W-2 under § 31.6011(a)-4 or § 31.6011(a)-5 of this chapter, returns on Forms W-3 and W-2 required under paragraph (a) of this section for any calendar year shall be filed on or before February 28 (March 31 if filed electronically) of the following year.

(iii) *Cross reference.*—For extensions of time for filing returns, see section 6081 and the regulations thereunder.

(2) *Place for filing.*—The returns on Forms W-3 and W-2 required under paragraph (a) of this section shall be filed pursuant to the rules contained in § 31.6091-1 of this chapter (Employment Tax Regulations), relating to the place for filing certain returns.

(c) *Special rule for calendar years before 1972.*—For calendar years before 1972, the provisions of this section will be deemed to have been complied with if the returns for such years were filed in accordance with the provisions of this section in effect prior to [insert date on which final regulations under this section are published in the Federal Register] or with the instructions applicable to the appropriate forms.

(d) *Last day for filing return.*—For provisions relating to the time for performance of an act when the last day prescribed for performance falls on Saturday, Sunday, or a legal holiday, see § 301.7503-1 of this chapter (Regulations on Procedure and Administration).

(e) *Penalty.*—For provisions relating to the penalty provided for failure to file the information returns required by this section, see section 6652 and the regulations thereunder. [Reg. § 1.6052-1.]

☐ [*T.D. 6888, 7-5-66. Amended by T.D. 7284, 8-2-73, T.D. 7580, 12-20-78; T.D. 7623, 5-14-79 and T.D. 8895, 8-17-2000.*]

### [Reg. § 301.6052-1]

**§ 301.6052-1. Information returns and statements regarding payment of wages in the form of group-term life insurance.**—For provisions relating to information returns and statements required in connection with the payment of wages in the form of group-term life insurance, see § § 1.6052-1 and 1.6052-2 of this chapter (Income Tax Regulations). [Reg. § 301.6052-1.]

☐ [*T.D. 7275, 5-4-73.*]

### [Reg. § 1.6052-2]

**§ 1.6052-2. Statements to be furnished employees with respect to wages paid in the form of group-term life insurance.**—(a) *Requirement.*—Every employer filing a return under section 6052(a) and § 1.6052-1, with respect to group-term life insurance on the life of an employee, shall furnish to the employee whose name is set forth in such return the tax return copy and the employee's copy of Form W-2. Each copy of Form W-2 must show the information required to be shown on the Form W-2 filed under § 1.6052-1. An employer may truncate an employee's social security number to appear in the form of an IRS truncated taxpayer identification number (TTIN) on copies of Forms W-2 furnished to the employee. For provisions relating to the use of TTINs, see § 301.6109-4 of this chapter (Procedure and Administration Regulations). The rules in § 31.6051-1 of this chapter (Employment Taxes and Collection of Income Tax at Source Regulations) shall apply with respect to the means and time (including extensions thereof) for furnishing the employee's copy of Form W-2 required by this section to the employee and making corrections to such form.

(b) *Definitions.*—Terms used in this section and in section 79 and the regulations thereunder have the meaning ascribed to them in section 79 and the regulations thereunder.

(c) *Penalty.*—For provisions relating to the penalty provided for failure to furnish a statement under this section, see section 6722 and the regulations in part 301 under section 6722.

(d) *Applicability date.*—This section is applicable for statements required to be furnished under section 6052 after December 31, 2020. [Reg. § 1.6052-2.]

☐ [*T.D. 6888, 7-5-66. Amended by T.D. 7284, 8-2-73, T.D. 7580, 12-20-78, T.D. 7623, 5-14-79 and T.D. 9861, 7-2-2019.*]

### [Reg. § 31.6053-1]

**§ 31.6053-1. Report of tips by employee to employer.**—(a) *Requirement that tips be reported.*—(1) *In general.*—An employee who receives, in the course of employment by an employer, tips that constitute wages as defined in section 3121(a) or section 3401, or compensation as defined in section 3231(e), must furnish to the employer a statement, or statements, disclosing the total amount of the tips received by the employee in the course of employment by the employer. Tips received by an employee in a calendar month in the course of employment by an employer that are required to be reported to the employer must be reported on or before the 10th day of the following month. For example, tips received by an employee in January 2000 are required to be reported by the employee to the employer on or before February 10, 2000.

(2) *Cross references.*—For provisions relating to the treatment of tips as wages for purposes of the Federal Insurance Contributions Act (FICA) tax under sections 3101 and 3111, see sections 3102(c), 3121(a)(12), and 3121(q) and §§ 31.3102-3 and 31.3121(a)(12)-1. For provisions relating to the treatment of tips as wages for purposes of the tax under section 3402 (income tax withholding), see sections 3401(a)(16), 3401(f), and 3402(k) and §§ 31.3401(a)(16)-1, 31.3401(f)-1, and 31.3402(k)-1. For provisions relating to the treatment of tips as compensation for purposes of the Railroad Retirement Tax Act (RRTA) tax under sections 3201 and 3221, see section 3231(e) and § 31.3231(e)-1(a).

(b) *Statement for use in reporting tips.*—(1) *In general.*—The statement described in paragraph (a) of this section can be provided on paper or transmitted electronically. The statement must be signed by the employee and must disclose:

(i) The name, address, and social security number of the employee.

(ii) The name and address of the employer.

(iii) The period for which, and the date on which, the statement is furnished. If the statement is for a calendar month, the month and year should be specified. If the statement is for a period of less than 1 calendar month, the beginning and ending dates of the period must be included (for example, January 1 through January 8, 1998).

(iv) The total amount of tips received by the employee during the period covered by the statement which are required to be reported to the employer (see paragraph (a) of this section).

(2) *Form of statement.*—(i) *In general.*—No particular form is prescribed for use in furnishing the statement required by this section. The statement may be furnished on paper or transmitted electronically. An electronic system and all tip statements generated by that system must meet the requirements of paragraph (d) of this section. If the employer does not provide any other means for the employee to report tips, the employee may use Form 4070, "Employee's Report of Tips to Employer."

(ii) *Single-purpose forms.*—A statement may be furnished on an employer-provided form. The form may be on paper or in electronic form. An employer that provides a paper form must make blank copies of the form readily available to all tipped employees. Any form, whether paper or electronic, provided by an employer for use by its tipped employees solely to report tips must meet all the requirements of paragraph (b)(1) of this section.

(iii) *Regularly used forms.*—Instead of requiring that tips be reported as described in paragraph (b)(2)(ii) of this section on a special form used solely for tip reporting, an employer may prescribe regularly used forms for use by employees in reporting tips. A regularly used form may be on paper or in electronic form (such as a time card or report), must meet the requirements of paragraph (b)(1)(iii) and (iv) of this section, must contain identifying information that will ensure accurate identification of the employee by the employer, and is permitted to be used only if the employer furnishes the employee a statement suitable for retention showing the amount

of tips reported by the employee for the period. The employer statement may be furnished when the employee reports the tips, when wages are first paid following the reporting of tips by the employee, or within a short time after the wages are paid. The employer may meet this requirement, for example, through the use of a payroll check stub or other payroll document regularly furnished (if not less frequent than monthly) by the employer to the employee showing gross pay and deductions.

(c) *Period covered by, and due date of, tip statement.*—(1) *In general.*—A tip statement furnished by an employee to an employer may not cover a period greater than 1 calendar month. An employer may, however, require the submission of a statement in respect of a specified period of time, for example, on a weekly or biweekly basis, regular payroll period, etc. An employer may specify, subject to the limitation in paragraph (a) of this section, the time within which, or the date on which, the statement for a specified period of time should be submitted by the employee. For example, a statement covering a payroll period may be required to be submitted on the first (or second) day following the close of the payroll period. A statement submitted by an employee after the date specified by the employer for its submission nevertheless is a statement furnished pursuant to section 6053(a) and this section if it is submitted to the employer on or before the 10th day following the month in which the tips were received.

(2) *Termination of employment.*—If an employee's employment terminates, the employee must furnish a tip statement to the employer when the employee ceases to perform services for the employer. A statement submitted by an employee after the date on which the employee ceases to perform services for the employer is a statement furnished pursuant to section 6053(a) and this section if the statement is submitted to the employer on or before the earlier of the day on which the final wage payment is made by the employer to the employee or the 10th day following the month in which the tips were received.

(d) *Requirements for electronic systems.*—(1) *In general.*—The electronic system must ensure that the information received is the information transmitted by the employee and must document all occasions of access that result in the transmission of a tip statement. In addition, the design and operation of the electronic system, including access procedures, must make it reasonably certain that the person accessing the system and transmitting the statement is the employee identified in the statement transmitted.

(2) *Same information as on paper statement.*—The electronic tip statement must provide the employer with all the information required by paragraph (b)(1) of this section.

(3) *Signature.*—The electronic tip statement must be signed by the employee. The electronic signature must identify the employee transmitting the electronic tip statement and must authenticate and verify the transmission. For this purpose, the terms *authenticate* and *verify* have the same meanings as they do when applied to a written signature on a paper tip statement. Any form of electronic signature that satisfies the foregoing requirements is permissible.

(4) *Copies of electronic tip statements.*—Upon request by the Internal Revenue Service (IRS), the employer must supply the IRS with a hard copy of the electronic tip statement and a statement that, to the best of the employer's knowledge, the electronic tip statement was filed by the named employee. The hard copy of the electronic tip statement must provide the information required by paragraph (b)(1) of this section, but need not be a facsimile of Form 4070 or any employer-designed form.

(5) *Record retention.*—The record retention requirements applicable to automatic data processing systems also apply to electronic tip reporting systems.

(6) *Effective date.*—The provisions pertaining to electronic systems and electronic tip reports are applicable as of December 13, 2000. However, employers may apply these provisions to earlier periods. [Reg. § 31.6053-1.]

☐ [*T.D. 7001, 1-17-69. Amended by T.D. 8910, 12-12-2000.*]

### [Reg. § 31.6053-2]

**§ 31.6053-2. Employer statement of uncollected employee tax.**—(a) *Requirement that statement be furnished.*—If—

(1) The amount of the employee tax imposed by section 3101 in respect of tips reported by an employee to his employer pursuant to section 6053(a) (see § 31.6053-1) exceeds

(2) The amount of employee tax imposed by section 3101 in respect of such tips which can be collected by the employer from wages (exclusive of tips) of such employee or from funds furnished to the employer by the employee,

the employer shall furnish to the employee a statement showing the amount of the excess. For provisions relating to the collection of, and liability for, employee tax on tips, see § 31.3102-3.

(b) *Form of statement.*—Form W-2 is the form prescribed for use in furnishing the statement required by paragraph (a) of this section, except that if an employer files a composite return pursuant to §31.6011(a)-8 he may furnish to the employee, in lieu of Form W-2, a statement containing the required information in a form suitable for retention by the employee. A statement is required under this section in respect of an excess referred to in paragraph (a) of this section, even though the employer may not be required to furnish a statement to the employee under §31.6051. Provisions applicable to the furnishing of a statement under §31.6051 shall be applicable to statements under this section.

(c) *Excess to be shown on statement.*—If there is an excess in respect of the tips reported by an employee in two or more statements furnished pursuant to section 6053(a), only the total excess for the period covered by the employer statement shall be shown on such statement. [Reg. § 31.6053-2.]

☐ [*T.D. 7001, 1-17-69. Amended by T.D. 7351, 4-16-75.*]

### [Reg. § 31.6053-3]

**§31.6053-3. Reporting by certain large food or beverage establishments with respect to tips.**—(a) *Information return by an employer with respect to tips.*—(1) *In general.*—An employer shall file a separate information return for each calendar year (as defined in paragraph (j)(14) of this section) with respect to each large food or beverage establishment (as defined in paragraph (j)(7) of this section) in which such employer has employees. The information return shall contain the following:

    (i) The employer's name, address, and employer identification number;

    (ii) The establishment's name, address, and identification number (see paragraph (a)(5) of this section);

    (iii) The aggregate gross receipts (other than nonallocable receipts) of the establishment from the provision of food or beverages;

    (iv) The aggregate amount of charge receipts (other than nonallocable receipts) on which there were charged tips;

    (v) The aggregate amount of charged tips shown on such charge receipts;

    (vi) The aggregate amount of tips actually received by food or beverage employees of the establishment during the calendar year and reported to the employer under section 6053(a) (see paragraph (j)(15) of this section);

    (vii) The aggregate amount the employer is required to report under section 6051 and the regulations thereunder with respect to service charges of less than 10 percent;

    (viii) The name and social security number of each employee of the establishment during the calendar year to whom an allocation was made under section 6053(c)(3) and paragraph (d) of this section and the amount of such allocation.

(2) *Calendar year 1983 information return.*—In the case of the 1983 calendar year information return, the information required by paragraph (a)(1)(iii)-(viii) of this section shall be reported for the period beginning with the first payroll period ending on or after April 1, 1983, and ending with the end of the 1983 calendar year. See paragraph (c) of this section relating to information required for the first quarter of 1983.

(3) *Prescribed form.*—The return required by this paragraph shall be made on Form 8027 with the transmittal form being Form 8027T. The information required by paragraph (a)(1)(viii) of this section may be provided by attaching to Form 8027 photocopies of each employee's W-2 for whom an allocation was made. A copy of any written good faith agreements applicable to a given calendar year (see paragraph (e) of this section) shall be attached to Form 8027 for such calendar year.

(4) *Time and place for filing.*—The information return required by this paragraph (a) shall be filed on or before the last day of February (March 31 if filed electronically) of the year following the calendar year for which the return is made with the Internal Revenue Service Center specified by the Form 8027 or its instructions. See section 6652(a) relating to the penalty for failure to file this information return.

(5) *Large food or beverage establishment identification number.*—Each large food or beverage establishment shall have a unique identification number to be included on Form 8027 and any employer's application pursuant to paragraph (h) of this section. If an identification number is changed for any reason, for example if the establishment becomes a different "type" of establishment as described in paragraph (a)(5)(ii) of this section, or if the employer identification

number changes, the employer shall notify the Service by including both the old and new identification numbers on the Form 8027 filed for the year in which the identification number was changed. An establishment identification number shall be determined as follows:

    (i) The first nine digits shall be the employer's identification number (EIN).

    (ii) The next digit shall identify the type of large food or beverage establishment, with the categories as follows:

        (A) The number "1" signifies an establishment that serves evening meals only (with or without alcoholic beverages).

        (B) The number "2" signifies an establishment that serves evening meals and other meals (with or without alcoholic beverages).

        (C) The number "3" signifies an establishment that serves only meals other than evening meals (with or without alcoholic beverages).

        (D) The number "4" signifies an establishment that serves food, if at all, as only an incidental part of the business of serving alcoholic beverages.

    (iii) The last five digits are to differentiate between multiple establishments reporting under the same EIN number. For this purpose, the employer shall assign each establishment reporting under such employer's EIN number a unique five digit number. For example, each establishment could be assigned a unique number by beginning with "00001" and progressing in numerical sequence (*i.e.*, "00002", "00003", "00004", "00005") until each establishment has been assigned a number.

(6) *Definitions.*—See paragraph (j) of this section for definitions of various terms used in this section.

(b) *Employer statement to employees.*—(1) *In general.*—The employer shall furnish to each employee to whom an amount is allocated under section 6053(c)(3) and paragraph (d) of this section a written statement for each calendar year containing the following information:

    (i) The employer's name and address;

    (ii) The name of the employee;

    (iii) The aggregate amount allocated to the employee for the calendar year.

(2) *Prescribed form.*—The written statement required by this paragraph shall be made on Form W-2.

(3) *Time and manner for furnishing the statement.*—The written statement required by this paragraph shall be due at the same time and shall be furnished in the same manner as the statement required to be furnished under section 6051. See section 6678 relating to the penalty for failure to file this statement.

(4) *Employee's request for an early W-2.*—If an employee's employment is terminated prior to the end of a calendar year and the employee requests an early W-2 under section 6051 and §31.6051(d), a tip allocation under section 6053(c) is not required to be shown on such early W-2. However, the employer may include on such early W-2 the employee's actual tip allocation under section 6053(c), if known, or a good faith estimate of such allocation. A good faith estimate of an allocation shall be signified by placing the word "estimate" next to the allocation on the employee's copy of the early W-2. An amended W-2 must be furnished to each employee to whom an amount is allocated under section 6053(c), during January of the calendar year following the calendar year for which the statement is made, if there is no tip allocation on the early W-2 or if the estimated allocation is found to vary from the actual allocation by more than 5 percent of the amount of the actual allocation.

(5) *Employee reporting of tip income.*—Regardless of whether an employee receives an allocation under section 6053(c) and §31.6053-3, the employee is required to report as income on his or her Federal income tax return all tips received. For tips received before October 1, 1985, an employee must be able to substantiate the amount of reported tip income as provided in section 6001 and the regulations thereunder. For tips received on or after October 1, 1985, an employee must be able to substantiate the amount of reported tip income as provided in §31.6053-4. The Internal Revenue Service may determine that a tipped employee received a larger amount of tip income than is reflected by the employee's allocation.

(c) *First quarter report of 1983.*—(1) *In general.*—For the period beginning with the first day of calendar year 1983, and ending on the last day of the last payroll period ending before April 1, 1983, an employer must file an information return for each large food or beverage establishment that was a large food or beverage establishment on January 1, 1983, that contains the information required by paragraph (a)(1)(i)-(vii) of this section for such period.

(2) *Prescribed form.*—The information return required by this paragraph shall be made on Form 8027. The returns for the first

calendar quarter of 1983 and for calendar year 1983 may be incorporated onto a single Form 8027 but must separately set forth the required information for each of the two return periods.

(3) *Time and place for filing.*—The time and place for filing the information return required by this paragraph shall be the same as the calendar year 1983 information return. See paragraph (a)(4) of this section.

(d) *Allocation of excess of 8 percent of gross receipts over the aggregate amounts of reported tips.*—(1) *In general.*—An employer that operates a large food or beverage establishment shall allocate (as tips for purposes of the requirements of section 6053(c)) among tipped employees at such establishment performing services during any payroll period an amount equal to the excess of:

(i) Eight percent of the gross receipts (other than nonallocable receipts) of such establishment for the payroll period, over

(ii) The aggregate amount of tips reported by employees at such establishment to the employer under section 6053(a) for such period. For this purpose, if an employee reports under section 6053(a) on the basis of a period other than a payroll period such employee may specify what portion of his or her reported tips are attributable to a given payroll period when reporting tips to the employer under section 6053(a). In the absence of any specification by the employee, the employer shall allocate the amount of tips reported by an employee to a given payroll period either:

(A) By multiplying the aggregate amount of those reported tips by a fraction, the numerator of which is the gross receipts attributable to the tipped employee for the payroll period and the denominator of which is the gross receipts attributable by the employee for the entire tip reporting period; or

(B) By multiplying the aggregate amount of those reported tips by a fraction, the numerator of which is the hours worked by the employee during the payroll period and the denominator of which is the total hours worked by the employee during the entire tip reporting period.

With respect to each establishment, the employer shall choose the method described in either paragraph (d)(1)(ii)(A) or paragraph (d)(1)(ii)(B) of this section for a calendar year and apply such method consistently in making all allocations required by the preceding sentence. If an employee is employed in more than one of an employer's food or beverage operations, such employee may specify what portion of his or her reported tips are attributable to a given operation when reporting tips to the employer under section 6053(a). In the absence of any specification by the employee, the employer shall allocate the amount of tips reported by the employee to a given food or beverage operation in a manner similar to that provided above for allocation of tips among payroll periods. The employer shall choose the method described in either paragraph (d)(1)(ii)(A) or paragraph (d)(1)(ii)(B) of this section for a calendar year and apply such method consistently in making all allocations required by the preceding sentence.

(2) *Employer not liable to employees for allocations.*—An employer who makes allocations (as tips for purposes of the requirements of section 6053(c) and this section) among such employer's employees in accordance with paragraph (d) and either paragraph (e) or (f) of this section shall not be liable to any employee if any amount is improperly allocated. However, if an employee's total tip allocations for a calendar year as reported on Form W-2 varies from the correct allocation amount by more than 5 percent of the correct allocation amount, the employer shall adjust such employee's allocation. If such an adjustment of an employee's allocation is required, the employer shall also review all tips allocations made to other employees in the same establishment to assure that the error did not distort other allocated amounts by more than 5 percent. Any adjustments made for variances of more than 5 percent shall be reflected in amended W-2's issued to the affected employees. Tip allocations made under this section shall have no effect on the withholding responsibilities of the employer under subtitle C of the Code Withholding on tips is authorized only with respect to amounts of tips reported to employers by employees under section 6053(a).

(e) *Allocation pursuant to a good faith agreement.*—The amount determined under paragraph (d)(2) of this section for each payroll period must be allocated among tipped employees providing services during such payroll period either on the basis of a good faith agreement described in this paragraph, or, if there is no good faith agreement applicable with respect to the payroll period on the basis of the allocation method provided in paragraph (f) of this section. A good faith agreement is a written agreement consented to by the employer and at least two-thirds of the members of each occupational category of tipped employees (*e.g.,* waiters, busboys, maitre d's) employed in the large food or beverage establishment at the time the agreement is adopted which:

(1) Provides for the allocation of the amount described in paragraph (d)(1) among tipped employees in a manner that, in combination with the tips reported by such employees under section 6053(a), will reflect a good faith approximation of the actual distribution of tip income among such tipped employees;

(2) Is effective prospectively beginning with the first day of a payroll period that begins after the date of adoption, but in no event later than the first day of the succeeding calendar year. However, a good faith agreement may be effective for calendar year 1983 if adopted on or before December 31, 1983.

(3) Is adopted at a time when there are tipped employees employed by the employer in each occupational category of tipped employees (*e.g.,* waiters, busboys, maitre d's) which would be affected by the agreement; and

(4) May be revoked prospectively by a written instrument adopted by at least two-thirds of the tipped employees who are employed in the establishment in occupational categories affected by the agreement at the time of the revocation. A revocation of an agreement shall be effective only at the beginning of a payroll period.

(f) *Allocation method to be used in the absence of a good faith agreement.*—(1) In a case in which there is no good faith agreement in effect and the aggregate amount of tips reported pursuant to section 6053(a) with respect to a payroll period is less than 8 percent of the establishment's gross receipt's for the payroll period, the employer shall allocate the difference as tips for purposes of section 6053(c) as provided in this paragraph. No allocations shall be made to indirectly tipped employees. An allocation shall be made to each directly tipped employee performing services for the establishment who has a reporting shortfall (as determined under paragraph (f)(1)(v) of this section) for the payroll period. The amount of each allocation shall be determined in the following manner:

(i) Multiply the amount of the establishment's gross receipts for the payroll period by 8 percent (0.08).

(ii) Determine the aggregate amount of tips reported for the payroll period by indirectly tipped employees.

(iii) Subtract from the amount determined under paragraph (f)(1)(i) the aggregate amount of tips reported by indirectly tipped employees as determined under paragraph (f)(1)(ii). The excess is the directly tipped employees' aggregate share of 8 percent of the gross receipts of the establishment for the payroll period.

(iv) For each directly tipped employee, multiply the amount determined under paragraph (f)(1)(iii) by a fraction, the numerator of which is the amount of gross receipts of the establishment for the payroll period that is attributable to the employee and the denominator of which is the aggregate amount of gross receipts for the payroll period that is attributable to all directly tipped employees. The product is each directly tipped employee's share of 8 percent of the gross receipts of the establishment for the payroll period. The employer may determine the fraction described in the first sentence of this subparagraph by substituting for the numerator the number of hours worked by the directly tipped employee during the payroll period and by substituting for the denominator the number of hours worked by all directly tipped employees during the payroll period. For payroll periods beginning after December 31, 1986, the method of allocation described in the preceding sentence may be used only by an employer that employs less than the equivalent of 25 full-time employees (as defined in paragraph (j)(19) of this section) at the establishment during the payroll period.

(v) For each directly tipped employee, determine the excess, if any, of the amount determined under paragraph (f)(1)(iv) over the amount reported as tips by the employee for the payroll period pursuant to section 6053(a). Such excess, if any, is the employee's shortfall for the payroll period.

(vi) Subtract from the amount determined under paragraph (f)(1)(i) the aggregate amount of tips reported pursuant to section 6053(a) by all directly and indirectly tipped employees for the payroll period. The excess is the amount to be allocated as tips among directly tipped employees who had a shortfall for the payroll period as determined under paragraph (f)(1)(v).

(vii) For each directly tipped employee who had a shortfall for the payroll period, multiply the amount determined under paragraph (f)(1)(vi) by a fraction, the numerator of which is the amount of such employee's shortfall (determined under paragraph (f)(1)(v) and the denominator of which is the aggregate of all shortfalls for the payroll period for all directly tipped employees. The product is the employee's allocation for the payroll period.

(2) The provisions of this paragraph may be illustrated by the following examples:

*Example (1).* X is a large food or beverage establishment that has chosen to make tip allocations using its actual payroll period and gross receipts attributable to employees. X had gross receipts for a payroll period of $100,000 and tips reported for the payroll period of

$6,200. Directly tipped employees reported $5,700 while indirectly tipped employees reported $500.

| Directly tipped employees | Gross receipts for payroll period | Tips reported |
|---|---|---|
| A | $18,000 | $1,080 |
| B | 16,000 | 880 |
| C | 23,000 | 1,810 |
| D | 17,000 | 800 |
| E | 12,000 | 450 |

| Directly tipped employees | Gross receipts for payroll period | Tips reported |
|---|---|---|
| F | 14,000 | 680 |
| Total | $100,000 | $5,700 |

The allocation computations would be as follows:

(1) $100,000 (gross receipts) × 0.08 = $8,000.

(2) Tips reported by indirectly tipped employees = $500.

(3) $8,000 − $500 (indirect employees' tips) = $7,500.

(4)

| Directly tipped employees | Directly tipped share of 8% gross | | Gross receipts ratio | | Employee share of 8% gross |
|---|---|---|---|---|---|
| A | $7,500 | × | 18,000/100,000 | = | $1,350 |
| B | 7,500 | × | 16,000/100,000 | = | 1,200 |
| C | 7,500 | × | 23,000/100,000 | = | 1,725 |
| D | 7,500 | × | 17,000/100,000 | = | 1,275 |
| E | 7,500 | × | 12,000/100,000 | = | 900 |
| F | 7,500 | × | 14,000/100,000 | = | 1,050 |
| Total | | | | | $7,500 |

(5)

| Directly tipped employees | Employee share of 8% gross | | Tips reported | | Employee shortfall |
|---|---|---|---|---|---|
| A | $1,350 | − | $1,080 | = | $270 |
| B | 1,200 | − | 880 | = | 320 |
| C | 1,725 | − | 1,810 | = | . . . |
| D | 1,275 | − | 800 | = | 475 |
| E | 900 | − | 450 | = | 450 |
| F | 1,050 | − | 680 | = | 370 |
| Total shortfall | | | | | $1,885 |

Since employee C has no reporting shortfall there is no allocation to C.

(6) $8,000 − 6,200 (total tips reported) = $1,800 (amount allocable among shortfall employees).

(7)

| Shortfall employees | Allocable amount | | Shortfall ratio | | Amount of allocation |
|---|---|---|---|---|---|
| A | $1,800 | × | 270/1885 | = | $258 |
| B | 1,800 | × | 320/1885 | = | 306 |
| D | 1,800 | × | 475/1885 | = | 454 |
| E | 1,800 | × | 450/1885 | = | 430 |
| F | 1,800 | × | 370/1885 | = | 353 |

*Example (2).* Assume the same facts as in example (1) except that the employer uses employee hours worked to calculate tip allocations.

| Directly tipped employees | Hours worked in payroll period | Tips reported |
|---|---|---|
| A | 40 | $1,080 |
| B | 35 | 880 |
| C | 45 | 1,810 |
| D | 40 | 800 |

| Directly tipped employees | Hours worked in payroll period | Tips reported |
|---|---|---|
| E | 15 | 450 |
| F | 25 | 680 |
| Total | 200 | $5,700 |

The allocation computations would be as follows:

(1) $100,000 (gross receipts) × 0.08 = $8,000.

(2) Tips reported by indirectly tipped employees = $500.

(3) $8,000 − $500 (indirect employees' tips) = $7,500.

(4)

| Directly tipped employees | Directly tipped share of 8% gross | | Hours worked ratio | | Employee share of 8% gross |
|---|---|---|---|---|---|
| A | $7,500 | × | 40/200 | = | $1,500 |
| B | 7,500 | × | 35/200 | = | 1,313 |
| C | 7,500 | × | 45/200 | = | 1,688 |
| D | 7,500 | × | 40/200 | = | 1,500 |
| E | 7,500 | × | 15/200 | = | 563 |
| F | 7,500 | × | 25/200 | = | 938 |

(5)

| Directly tipped employees | Employee share of 8% gross | Tips reported | Employee shortfall |
|---|---|---|---|
| A | $1,500 | $1,080 | $420 |
| B | 1,313 | 880 | 433 |
| C | 1,688 | 1,810 | . . . |
| D | 1,500 | 800 | 700 |
| E | 563 | 450 | 113 |
| F | 938 | 680 | 258 |
| Total shortfall | | | $1,924 |

Since employee C has no reporting shortfall there is no allocation to C.

(6) $8,000 − 6,200 (total tips reported) = $1,800 (amount allocable among shortfall employees).

(7)

| Shortfall employees | Allocable amount | × | Shortfall ratio | = | Amount of allocation |
|---|---|---|---|---|---|
| A | $1,800 | | 420/1,924 | | $393 |
| B | 1,800 | | 433/1,924 | | 405 |
| D | 1,800 | | 700/1,924 | | 655 |

| Shortfall employees | Allocable amount | × | Shortfall ratio | = | Amount of allocation |
|---|---|---|---|---|---|
| E | 1,800 | | 113/1,924 | | 106 |
| F | 1,800 | | 258/1,924 | | 241 |

*Example (3).* X is a large food or beverage establishment that has chosen to make tip allocations using a calendar year period. X had gross receipts for a calendar year of $2,000,000 and tips reported for the calendar year of $176,000. The amount to be allocated as tips is equal to the excess of 8 percent of the gross receipts of the establishment for the calendar year over the aggregate amount of tips reported by the employees of the establishment to the employer under section 6053(a) for the calendar year. Because the reported tips for the year ($176,000) are in excess of 8 percent of the gross receipts ($2,000,000 × .08 = $160,000), no tip allocations are made to the employees of this establishment for the calendar year.

*Example (4).* X is a large food or beverage establishment that has chosen to make tip allocations using a calendar year period and gross receipts attributable to employees. X had gross receipts for a calendar year of $1,500,000 and tips reported for the calendar year of $110,000.

Directly tipped employees reported $94,000 while indirectly tipped employees reported $16,000.

| Directly tipped employees | Gross receipts for calendar year | Tips reported |
|---|---|---|
| A | $260,000 | $18,600 |
| B | 240,000 | 14,600 |
| C | 380,000 | 31,200 |
| D | 260,000 | 13,000 |
| E | 160,000 | 6,000 |
| F | 200,000 | 10,600 |
| Total | $1,500,000 | $94,000 |

The allocation computations are as follows:

(1) $1,500,000 (gross receipts) × 0.08 = $120,000.

(2) Tips reported by indirectly tipped employees = $16,000.

(3) $120,000 − 16,000 (indirect employees tips) = $104,000.

(4)

| Directly tipped employees | Directly tipped share of 8% gross | × | Gross receipts ratio | = | Employee share of 8% gross |
|---|---|---|---|---|---|
| A | $104,000 | | 260,000/1,500,000 | | $18,027 |
| B | 104,000 | | 240,000/1,500,000 | | 16,640 |
| C | 104,000 | | 380,000/1,500,000 | | 26,347 |
| D | 104,000 | | 260,000/1,500,000 | | 18,027 |
| E | 104,000 | | 160,000/1,500,000 | | 11,093 |
| F | 104,000 | | 200,000/1,500,000 | | 13,867 |

(5)

| Directly tipped employees | Employee share of 8% gross | − | Tips reported | = | Employee shortfall |
|---|---|---|---|---|---|
| A | $18,027 | | $18,600 | | . . . |
| B | 16,640 | | 14,600 | | $2,040 |
| C | 26,347 | | 31,200 | | . . . |
| D | 18,027 | | 13,000 | | 5,027 |
| E | 11,093 | | 6,000 | | 5,093 |
| F | 13,867 | | 10,600 | | 3,267 |
| Total shortfall | | | | | $15,427 |

Since employees A and C do not have a reporting shortfall there are no allocations to them.

(6) $120,000 − 110,000 (total tips reported) = $10,000 (amount allocable among shortfall employees).

(7)

| Shortfall employees | Allocable amount | × | Shortfall ratio | = | Amount of allocation |
|---|---|---|---|---|---|
| B | $10,000 | | 2,040/15,427 | | $1,322 |
| D | 10,000 | | 5,027/15,427 | | 3,259 |
| E | 10,000 | | 5,093/15,427 | | 3,301 |
| F | 10,000 | | 3,267/15,427 | | 2,118 |
| Total | | | | | $10,000 |

*Example (5).* Assume the same facts as in example (4) except that the employer has chosen the employee hours worked method of computing tip allocations, the calendar year gross receipts were $1,000,000, and the tips reported for the calendar year were $74,000. Directly tipped employees reported $70,000 while indirectly tipped employees reported $4,000.

| Directly tipped employees | Hours worked in the calendar year | Tips reported |
|---|---|---|
| A | 2,000 | $11,800 |
| B | 1,750 | 9,800 |
| C | 2,250 | 15,100 |
| D | 2,000 | 9,000 |
| E | 750 | 4,500 |
| F | 1,250 | 7,800 |
| G | 490 | 3,200 |
| H | 510 | 2,800 |
| I | 200 | 800 |
| J | 1,000 | 5,200 |
| Total | 12,200 | $70,000 |

The allocation computations would be as follows:

(1) $1,000,000 (gross receipts) × 0.08 = $80,000.

(2) Tips reported by indirectly tipped employees = $4,000.

(3) $80,000 − $4,000 (indirect employee tips) = $76,000.

(4)

| Directly tipped employees | Directly tipped share of 8% gross | × | Hours worked ratio | = | Employee share of 8% gross |
|---|---|---|---|---|---|
| A | $76,000 | | 2,000/12,200 | | $12,459 |
| B | 76,000 | | 1,750/12,200 | | 10,902 |
| C | 76,000 | | 2,250/12,200 | | 14,016 |
| D | 76,000 | | 2,000/12,200 | | 12,459 |
| E | 76,000 | | 750/12,200 | | 4,672 |
| F | 76,000 | | 1,250/12,200 | | 7,787 |
| G | 76,000 | | 490/12,200 | | 3,052 |
| H | 76,000 | | 510/12,200 | | 3,177 |
| I | 76,000 | | 200/12,200 | | 1,246 |
| J | 76,000 | | 1,000/12,200 | | 6,230 |
| Total | | | | | $76,000 |

(5)

| Directly tipped employees | Employee share of 8% gross | − | Tips reported | = | Employee shortfall |
|---|---|---|---|---|---|
| A | $12,459 | | $11,800 | | $659 |
| B | 10,902 | | 9,800 | | 1,102 |
| C | 14,016 | | 15,100 | | . . . |
| D | 12,459 | | 9,000 | | 3,459 |
| E | 4,672 | | 4,500 | | 172 |
| F | 7,787 | | 7,800 | | . . . |
| G | 3,052 | | 3,200 | | . . . |
| H | 3,177 | | 2,800 | | 377 |
| I | 1,246 | | 800 | | 446 |
| J | 6,230 | | 5,200 | | 1,030 |
| Total shortfall | | | | | $7,245 |

Since employees C, F, and G have no reporting shortfalls, there are no allocations made to them.

(6) $80,000 − 74,000 (total tips reported) = $6,000.

(7)

| Shortfall employees | Allocable amount | × | Shortfall ratio | = | Amount of allocation |
|---|---|---|---|---|---|
| A | $6,000 | | 659/7,245 | | $546 |
| B | 6,000 | | 1,102/7,245 | | 913 |
| D | 6,000 | | 3,459/7,245 | | 2,865 |
| E | 6,000 | | 172/7,245 | | 142 |
| H | 6,000 | | 377/7,245 | | 312 |
| I | 6,000 | | 446/7,245 | | 369 |
| J | 6,000 | | 1,030/7,245 | | 853 |
| Total | | | | | $6,000 |

(g) *Period of allocation.*—In applying paragraphs (d), (e), (f), and (h)(3) of this section an employer may substitute the calendar year or any period that results from a reasonable division of a calendar year for the term "payroll period" each place it appears in such paragraphs. If an employer makes such a substitution with respect to a large food or beverage establishment the substituted period shall be stated on Form 8027 for such large food or beverage establishment and shall be effective for such employer's large food or beverage establishment for the entire calendar year.

(h) *Lowering the percentage to be used.*—(1) *In general.*—On and after July 18, 1984, an employer or a majority of the employees (as defined in paragraph (h)(2)(iii) of this section) of an employer may petition the district director for the internal revenue district in which the employer's establishment is located to have the percentage of gross receipts that is used to determine the amount to be allocated under section 6053(c)(3)(A) and paragraph (d) of §31.6053-3 reduced from 8 percent to the percentage that the petitioning employer or employees believe to be the actual percentage of the amount of the establishment's gross receipts that reflects the amount of tips. The district director may thereafter reduce the percentage of gross receipts used to determine the amount to be so allocated to the percentage that the district director determines to be the proper estimate of the actual percentage of gross receipts constituting tips. The district director, however, may not reduce the percentage below 2 percent. For the rules in effect prior to July 18, 1984, see 26 CFR §31.6053-3(h) Rev. as of April 1, 1984).

(2) *Time and manner for petition to have percentage reduced.*—(i) *In general.*—The petition shall be in writing and shall include sufficient information to allow the district director to estimate with reasonable accuracy the actual tip rate of the establishment. For example, such information might include the charged tip rate, the type of establishment, menu prices, the location of the establishment, the amount of "self-service" required, the days and hours open for business, and whether the customer receives the check from or pays the server for the meal.

(ii) *Employer petitions.*—In the case of employer-originated petitions, the employer has the burden of supplying sufficient information to allow the district director to estimate with reasonable accuracy the actual tip rate of the establishment. The employer also shall attach to the petition copies of Form 8027 (if any) filed for the establishment for the 3 immediately preceding calendar years.

(iii) *Employee petitions.*—(A) In the case of employee-originated petitions, a majority of the employees of an establishment must consent to the petition. A majority for purposes of this paragraph is more than one-half of all the directly tipped employees (within the meaning of paragraph (j)(12) of this section) employed by the establishment at the time the petition is filed. In the case of a single petition for certain multi-establishment employers (see paragraph (h)(4) of this section), more than one-half of the aggregate directly tipped employees (at the time the petition is filed) of the establishments covered by the petition must consent. The petition filed with the district director must state the total number of directly tipped employees employed by the establishment (or establishments)

and the number of the directly tipped employees consenting to the petition.

(B) The petitioning employees have the burden of supplying sufficient information to allow the district director to estimate with reasonable accuracy the actual tip rate of the establishment to the extent they possess such information. If the employer possesses relevant information, the employer must provide such information to the district director upon the request of the petitioning employees or district director. Employees who file a petition under this paragraph must promptly notify their employer of the petition. Promptly upon receipt of such notification, their employer must submit to the district director copies of the Form 8027 (if any) filed for the establishment for the 3 immediately preceding calendar years. Any information supplied by the employer during the petitioning process constitutes return information (as defined in section 6103(b)(2)) which shall not be disclosed by the Internal Revenue Service (except as provided in section 6103) to any employees of the employer or to representatives of such employees.

(3) *Effective date for reduced percentage.*—The district director shall determine the term for which the reduced percentage is to be effective. At the end of such term, the reduced percentage shall cease to apply unless previously extended by the district director for the district in which the large food or beverage establishment is located. In no event shall the reduced percentage be applied to payroll periods before the date the petition described in paragraph (h)(2) of this section is filed unless the establishment is a new business (as described in paragraph (i) of §31.6053-3). In the case of a new business or a petition for reduction filed prior to September 30, 1983, the district director may allow the approved reduced percentage to be applied retroactively to the first day of the calendar year of the petition. Until such time as the employer is notified in writing by the district director of approval of a reduction, the employer must continue to use 8 percent of gross receipts for purposes of complying with section 6053(c) and this section.

(4) *Single petition for certain multi-establishment employers.*—An employer (including a single employer as defined in section 52(a) or (b)) or a majority of the employees of such employer may use a single petition for two or more of the employer's establishments if such establishments are essentially the same type of business, the petitioning employer or employees have made a good faith determination that the tip rates at such establishments are essentially the same, and the establishments are located in the same internal revenue region. Single petitions shall include the names and locations of the establishments for which a reduction is requested and the information required by paragraph (h)(2) of this section for a typical establishment. A single petition for multi-establishments located within an internal revenue region shall be filed with the district director for the internal revenue district in which the greatest number of the establishments included in the petition are located. If there is an equal number of establishments located in two or more internal revenue districts the employer or employees petitioning may choose the district to which the petition is sent.

(i) *Application of reporting requirements to new businesses.*—(1) *In general.*—A food or beverage operation is a new business if the employer of the operation did not operate any food or beverage operations during the preceding calendar year. An employer will not be considered to have operated a food or beverage operation during a calendar year if each food or beverage operation of the employer was operated for less than one calendar month during such year. In a calendar year in which a food or beverage operation is a new business, the determination of whether the operation is a large food or beverage establishment shall be made as provided in paragraph (i)(2) of this section and the employer shall comply with section 6053(c) and this section as provided in paragraph (i)(3) of this section.

(2) *Determination of status as a large food or beverage establishment.*—A food or beverage operation shall be considered a large food or beverage establishment during the calendar year in which it is a new business if the average number of hours worked per business day by all employees of the employer at the new business during each of any two consecutive calendar months of the calendar year, computed in the manner provided in the second sentence of paragraph (j)(9) of this section, is greater than 80 hours.

(3) *New business compliance under section 6053(c).*—A new business that is determined to be a large food or beverage establishment under paragraph (i)(2) of this section shall comply with section 6053(c) and this section beginning with the first payroll period that begins after the first period of two consecutive calendar months described in paragraph (i)(2) of this section.

(j) *Definitions.*—For purposes of section 6053(c) and this section:

(1) *Gross receipts.*—Gross receipts shall include all receipts (other than nonallocable receipts), from the provision of food or beverages by a large food or beverage establishment from cash sales, charge receipts (including charged tips only to the extent the cash sales amount has been reduced due to the employer paying cash to tipped employees for charged tips due them), charges to a hotel room (excluding tips charged to a hotel room only to the extent that the employer's accounting procedures allow such tips to be segregated out and excluding charges that are otherwise included in charge receipts), and the retail value of complimentary food or beverages (as defined in paragraph (j)(16) of this section) served to customers. Gross receipts shall not include state or local taxes. In the case of a trade or business that does not charge separately for the provision of food or beverages (*i.e.,* a trade or business that provides other goods or services along with food or beverages for a combined price, such as a "package deal" for food and lodging), the employer shall make a good faith estimate of the gross receipts attributable to the provision of the food or beverages that reflects the cost to the employer of providing the food or beverages plus a reasonable profit factor.

(2) *Gross receipts attributable to a directly tipped employee.*—Gross receipts attributable to a directly tipped employee are those gross receipts (as defined in paragraph (j)(1) of this section) from the provision of food or beverages to customers with respect to which the employee provided services. For example, if a directly tipped employee's name is on every check given to customers for whom the employee has provided services, the gross receipts attributable to such employee could be determined by aggregating the amounts of all checks bearing that employee's name (other than amounts from nonallocable receipts).

(3) *Nonallocable receipts.*—Nonallocable receipts are receipts which are attributable to carryout sales or to services with respect to which a service charge of 10 percent or more is added. Carryout sales are sales of food or beverages for consumption off the premises of the establishment. Room service is not a carryout sale. If an establishment's accounting system does not segregate receipts from carryout sales from the establishment's other receipts, receipts from carryout sales may be determined as an estimated percentage of total receipts. The applicable percentage shall be determined in good faith by the employer on the basis of generally accepted accounting practices, including but not limited to, surveys of carryout sales as a percentage of gross sales. An employer may rely upon estimates as to carryout sales which are established in good faith between the employer and state or local governments for purposes of state or local taxation.

(4) *Charge receipts.*—Charge receipts shall include credit card charges and charges under any other credit arrangement (e.g., house charges, city ledger, and charge arrangements to country club members. Charges to a hotel room may be excluded from charge receipts if such exclusion is consistent with the employer's normal accounting practices and the employer applies such exclusion consistently for a given large food or beverage establishment. Otherwise, charges to a hotel room shall be included in charge receipts.

(5) *Charged tips.*—A tip included on a charge receipt is a charged tip.

(6) *Food or beverage operation.*—A "food or beverage operation" is any business activity which provides food or beverages for consumption on the premises (other than "fast food" operations). If an employer conducts activities that provide food or beverages at more than one location, the activity at each separate location shall be considered to be a separate food or beverage operation. Each activity conducted within a single building shall be considered to be conducted at a separate location if the customers of the activity while being provided with food or beverages, occupy an area separate from that occupied by customers of other activities and the gross receipts of the activity are recorded separately from the gross receipts of other activities. For example, a gourmet restaurant, a coffee shop, and a cocktail lounge in a hotel would each be treated as a separate food or beverage operation if gross receipts from each activity are recorded separately. In addition, an employer may treat different activities conducted in the identical place at different times as separate food or beverage operations if the gross receipts of the activities at each time are recorded separately. For example, a restaurant may record the gross receipts from its cafeteria style lunch operation separately from the gross receipts of its full service food or beverage operations.

(7) *Large food or beverage establishment.*—A food or beverage operation is a "large food or beverage establishment" if:

(i) The employer at the food or beverage operation normally employed more than 10 employees on a typical business day during the preceding calendar year, and

(ii) The tipping of food or beverage employees of the food or beverage operation is customary. Generally, tipping would not be considered customary for a cafeteria style operation (as defined in paragraph (j)(18) of this section) or for a food or beverage operation where at least 95 percent of its total sales are nonallocable receipts, within the meaning of paragraph (j)(3) of this section, by reason of the addition of a service charge of 10 percent or more. Total sales shall include only gross receipts (as defined in paragraph (j)(1) of this section) and nonallocable receipts (other than carryout receipts) from the provision of food or beverages. In the case of an operation such as a restaurant that is cafeteria style operation at lunch and that has full service with tipping customary at dinner, the entire operation is generally a large food or beverage establishment if the employer meets the 10-employee test. However, if the gross receipts of the cafeteria style operation at lunch are recorded separately from the dinner operation gross receipts the employer may treat the dinner operation as a large food or beverage establishment and the lunch operation as a separate food or beverage operation that is not a large food or beverage establishment due to the fact that tipping is not considered customary for cafeteria style operations.

(8) *Employee.*—The term "employee" has the same meaning as in section 3401(c) and §31.3401(c)-1.

(9) *More than 10 employees on a typical business day.*—An employer shall be considered to have normally employed more than 10 employees on a typical business day during a calendar year if one-half of the sum of the average number of employee hours worked per business day during the calendar month in which the aggregate gross receipts from food or beverage operations were the greatest plus the average number of employee hours worked per business day during the calendar month in which the aggregate gross receipts from food or beverage operations were the least, is greater than 80 hours. The average number of employee hours worked per business day during a month shall be computed by dividing the total number of hours worked during the month by all employees of the employer who are employed in a food or beverage operation by the average of the number of days during the month that each food or beverage operation at which such employees worked was open for business. If an employer operates both a food or beverage operation and a nonfood or beverage operation, and one or more of his or her employees work for both operations, the employer may make a good faith estimate of the number of hours such employees worked for each operation in a given month. Similarly, in cases where one or more of an employer's employees work for more than one of such employer's food or beverage operations, a good faith estimate may be made of the number of hours such employees worked for each operation in a given month. For purposes of this subparagraph, employees who are employed in a food or beverage operation include all employees of the operation, not just food or beverage employees. The employees of an employer shall include all employees at all food or beverage operations who, along with the employees of such employer, would be treated as employees of a single employer under section 52(a) or (b) (as in effect on September 3, 1982) and the regulations thereunder. For example, if an employer at a food or beverage operation is a member of a controlled group of corporations, then all employees of all corporations which are members of such controlled group of corporations shall be treated as employed by each such employer for purposes of this paragraph. However, an individual who owns 50 percent or more in value of the

(10) *Food or beverage employee.*—A "food or beverage employee" is an employee who provides services in connection with the provision of food or beverages. Such employees include, but are not limited to, waiters, waitresses, busboys, bartenders, persons in charge of seating (such as a hostess, maitre d' or dining room captain), wine stewards, cooks, and kitchen help. Examples of employees who are not food or beverage employees include, but are not limited to, coat check persons, bellhops, and doormen.

(11) *Tipped employee.*—A "tipped employee" of a food or beverage operation is an employee who is a food or beverage employee that customarily receives tip income from employment at that operation. An employee who occasionally receives small amounts of tip income is not a tipped employee. Generally, an employee who receives less than $20 per month in tip income would not be considered as customarily receiving tip income.

(12) *Directly tipped employee.*—A "directly tipped employee" is any tipped employee who receives tips directly from customers, including an employee who after receiving tips directly from customers turns all the tips over to a tip pool. Examples of directly tipped employees are waiters, waitresses, and bartenders.

(13) *Indirectly tipped employee.*—An "indirectly tipped employee" is a tipped employee who does not normally receive tips directly from customers. Examples of indirectly tipped employees are busboys, service bartenders and cooks. An employee, such as a maitre d', who receives tips both directly from customers and indirectly through tip splitting or tip pooling shall be treated as a directly tipped employee.

(14) *Calendar year.*—The term "calendar year" shall mean either the period from January 1 through December 31 or the period that begins with the first day of the first payroll period ending on or after January 1 and ends with the last day of the last payroll period ending in December of the same year. With respect to any establishment, the employer shall choose one of these two descriptions and apply it consistently.

(15) *Tips reported for a specified period.*—Tips reported to an employer for a specified period under section 6053(a) are those tips actually received by an employee during such period without regard to the time when the tips are reported to the employer. Thus, if an employee reports to the employer in calendar year 1984 tips the employee actually received in calendar year 1983, the amount of tips actually received in calendar year 1983 must be included by the employer when making such information returns, statements and allocations required under section 6053(c) and this section for calendar year 1983.

(16) *Complimentary food or beverages.*—Food or beverages served to customers without charge are complimentary if:

(i) Tipping for the provision of such food or beverages is customary at the establishment, and

(ii) Such food or beverages are provided in connection with an activity that is engaged in for profit and whose receipts would not be included in gross receipts as defined in paragraph (j)(1) of this section but for this subparagraph and are not nonallocable receipts which are attributable to services with respect to which a service charge of 10 percent or more is added.

For example, the retail values of complimentary hors d'oeuvres served at a bar or a complimentary dessert served to a regular patron of a restaurant would not be included in gross receipts because the receipts of the bar or restaurant would be included in gross receipts as defined in paragraph (j)(1) of this section. The retail value of a complimentary fruit basket placed in a hotel room generally would not be included in gross receipts because tipping for the provision of such items is not customary. The retail value of complimentary drinks served to customers in a gambling casino would be included in gross receipts because tipping for the provision of such items is customary, the gambling casino is an activity engaged in for profit, and the gambling receipts of the casino would not be included in gross receipts as defined in paragraph (j)(1) of this section except for this subparagraph.

(17) *Fast food operation.*—An operation is a "fast food" operation only if its customers order, pick up, and pay for food or beverages at a counter, window, etc., and then carry the food or beverages to another location (either on or off the premises of such activities).

(18) *Cafeteria style operation.*—The term "cafeteria style" operation means a food or beverage operation which is primarily self-service and in which the total cost of food or beverages selected by a customer is paid prior to the customers' being seated or is stated on a check provided to the customer prior to the customers' being seated

and is paid by the customer to a cashier. Generally, operations are primarily self-service if food or beverages are ordered or selected by a customer at one location and carried by the customer from such location to the customer's seat. For example, cafeteria lines, buffets, and smorgasbords are primarily self-service. If, after a customer is seated, a food or beverage employee delivers items such as an item that required additional preparation after being selected by the customer, condiments, beverages, or refills at no additional cost to the customer, a food or beverage operation's status as primarily self-service would not be affected.

(19) *Less than the equivalent of 25 full-time employees.*—For purposes of paragraph (f)(1)(iv) of this section, an employer shall be considered to employ less than the equivalent of 25 full-time employees at an establishment during a payroll period (as defined in section 3401(b) and the regulations thereunder) if the average number of employee hours worked per business day during a payroll period is less than 200 hours. The average number of employee hours worked per business day during a payroll period shall be computed by dividing the total number of hours worked during the period by all employees of the employer who are employed in a food or beverage operation by the average of the number of days during the period that each food or beverage operation at which such employees worked was open for business. If an employer operates both a food or beverage operation and a nonfood or beverage operation, and one or more of his employees work for both operations, the employer may make a good faith estimate of the number of hours such employees worked for each operation in a given payroll period. Similarly, in cases where one or more of an employer's employees work for more than one of such employer's food or beverage operations, a good faith estimate may be made of the number of hours such employees worked for each operation in a given payroll period. If there is more than one payroll period for the establishment, the payroll period which is used for the greatest number of employees shall be the payroll period for purposes of this paragraph (j)(19). For purposes of this paragraph (j)(19), employees who are employed in a food or beverage operation include all employees of the operation, not just food or beverage employees. The employees of an employer shall include all employees at all food or beverage operations who, along with the employees of such employer, would be treated as employees of a single employer under section 52(a) or (b) (as in effect on September 3, 1982) and the regulations thereunder. For example, if an employer at a food or beverage operation is a member of a controlled group of corporations, then all employees of all corporations which are members of such controlled group of corporations shall be treated as employed by each such employer for purposes of this paragraph.

(k) *Permission to submit information on magnetic tape.*—For rules relating to permission to submit the information required by section 6053(c) and this section on magnetic tape of other media, see §31.6011(a)-8.

(l) *Recordkeeping requirements.*—An employer shall keep records sufficient to substantiate any information returns, employer statements to employees, applications, or tip allocations made pursuant to section 6053(c) and this section. The records required by this paragraph shall be retained for 3 years after the due date of the return or statement to which they pertain.

(m) *Food or beverage operations outside the United States.*—Employers at food or beverage operations outside the United States (as defined in section 7701(a)(9)) are not subject to the reporting requirements under section 6053(c) and this section.

(n) *Effective date.*—This section is effective for calendar year 1983 and thereafter. [Reg. §31.6053-3.]

☐ [*T.D.* 7906, 8-10-83. *Amended by T.D.* 8039, 7-18-85; *T.D.* 8141, 6-5-87 *and T.D.* 8895, 8-17-2000.]

### [Reg. §31.6053-4]

**§31.6053-4. Substantiation requirements for tipped employees.**—(a) *Substantiation of tip income.*—(1) *In general.*—An employee shall maintain sufficient evidence to establish the amount of tip income received by the employee during a taxable year. A daily record maintained by the employee (as described in paragraph (a)(2) of this section) shall constitute sufficient evidence. If the employee does not maintain a daily record, other evidence of the amount of tip income received during the year, such as documentary evidence (as described in paragraph (a)(3) of this section), shall constitute sufficient evidence, but only if such other evidence is as credible and as reliable as a daily record. The Commissioner may by revenue ruling, procedure or other guidance of general applicability provide for other methods of demonstrating evidence of tip income. However, notwithstanding any other provision of this paragraph (a)(1), a daily record or other evidence that is as credible and as reliable as a daily record may not be sufficient evidence if there are facts or circumstances which indicate that the employee received a larger amount of tip income. Moreover, oral statements of the employee, without corroboration, cannot constitute sufficient evidence.

(2) *Daily record.*—The daily record shall state the employee's name and address, the employer's name, and the establishment's name. The daily record shall show for each work day the amount of cash tips and charge tips received directly from customers or from other employees, and the amount of tips, if any, paid out to other employees through tip sharing, tip pooling or other arrangements and the names of such employees. The record shall also show the date that each entry is made. Form 4070A, *Employee's Daily Record of Tips*, may be used to maintain such daily record. In addition, an electronic system maintained by the employer that collects substantially similar information as Form 4070A may be used to maintain such daily record, provided the employee receives and maintains a paper copy of the daily record. The daily record of tips received by an employee shall be prepared and maintained in such manner that each entry is made on or near the date the tip income is received. A daily record made on or near the date the tip income is received has a high degree of credibility not present with respect to a record prepared subsequent thereto when generally there is a lack of accurate recall. An entry is made "near the date the tip income is received" if the required information with respect to tips received and paid out by the employee for the day is recorded at a time when the employee has full present knowledge of those receipts and payments.

(3) *Documentary evidence.*—Documentary evidence consists of copies of any documents that contain (i) amounts that were added to a check by customers as a tip and paid over to the employee or (ii) amounts that were paid by a customer for food or beverages with respect to which tips generally would be received by the employee. Examples of documentary evidence are copies of restaurant bills, credit card charges, or charges under any other arrangement (see §31.6053-3(j)(4)) containing amounts added by the customer as a tip.

(b) *Retention of records.*—Records maintained under this section shall be kept at all times available for inspection by authorized internal revenue officers or employees, and shall be retained so long as the contents thereof may become material in the administration of any internal revenue law.

(c) *Effective date.*—The substantiation requirements of this §31.6053-4 shall be effective for tips received on or after October 1, 1985. For the rules in effect prior to October 1, 1985, see section 6001 and the regulations thereunder. Substantiation considered sufficient as provided in this §31.6053-4 will also be considered sufficient for tips received before October 1, 1985. [Reg. §31.6053-4.]

☐ [T.D. 8141, 6-5-87. Amended by T.D. 8910, 12-12-2000.]

### [Reg. §1.6055-1]

**§1.6055-1. Information reporting for minimum essential coverage.**—(a) *Information reporting requirement.*—Every person that provides minimum essential coverage to an individual during a calendar year must file an information return and transmittal and furnish statements to responsible individuals on forms prescribed by the Internal Revenue Service.

(b) *Definitions.*—(1) *In general.*—The definitions in this paragraph (b) apply for purposes of this section.

(2) *Affordable Care Act.*—The term *Affordable Care Act* refers to the Patient Protection and Affordable Care Act, Public Law 111-148 (124 Stat. 119 (2010)), and the Health Care and Education Reconciliation Act of 2010, Public Law 111-152 (124 Stat. 1029 (2010)), and amendments to those acts.

(3) *ERISA.*—The term *ERISA* means the Employee Retirement Income Security Act of 1974, as amended (29 U.S.C. 1001 et seq.).

(4) *Exchange.*—*Exchange* has the same meaning as in 45 CFR 155.20.

(5) *Government employer.*—The term *government employer* means an employer that is a governmental unit or an agency or instrumentality of a governmental unit.

(6) *Governmental unit.*—The term *governmental unit* refers to the government of the United States, any State or political subdivision of a State, or any Indian tribal government (as defined in section 7701(a)(40)) or subdivision of an Indian tribal government (as defined in section 7871(d)).

(7) *Agency or instrumentality of a governmental unit.*—[Reserved]

(8) *Minimum essential coverage.*—Minimum essential coverage is defined in section 5000A(f) and regulations issued under that section.

(9) *Qualified health plan.*—The term *qualified health plan* has the same meaning as in section 1301(a) of the Affordable Care Act (42 U.S.C. 18021(a)).

(10) *Reporting entity.*—A *reporting entity* is any person that must report, under section 6055 and this section, minimum essential coverage provided to an individual.

(11) *Responsible individual.*—The term *responsible individual* includes a primary insured, employee, former employee, uniformed services sponsor, parent, or other related person named on an application who enrolls one or more individuals, including him or herself, in minimum essential coverage.

(12) *Taxpayer identification number.*—The term *taxpayer identification number* (TIN) has the same meaning as in section 7701(a)(41).

(c) *Persons required to report.*—(1) *In general.*—The following persons must file the information return and transmittal form required under paragraph (a) of this section to report minimum essential coverage—

(i) Health insurance issuers, or carriers (as used in 5 U.S.C. 8901), for all insured coverage, except as provided in paragraph (c)(3)(ii) of this section;

(ii) Plan sponsors of self-insured group health plan coverage;

(iii) The executive department or agency of a governmental unit that provides coverage under a government-sponsored program (within the meaning of section 5000A(f)(1)(A)); and

(iv) Any other person that provides minimum essential coverage to an individual.

(2) *Plan sponsors of self-insured group health plan coverage.*—(i) *In general.*—For purposes of this section, a plan sponsor of self-insured group health plan coverage is—

(A) The employer for a self-insured group health plan or arrangement established or maintained by a single employer (determined without application of section 414(b), (c), (m) or (o) in the case of an employer described in paragraph (f)(2)(i) of this section), including each participating employer with respect to a self-insured group health plan or arrangement established or maintained by more than one employer (and not including a multiemployer plan as defined in section 3(37) of ERISA or a Multiple Employer Welfare Arrangement as defined in section 3(40) of ERISA);

(B) The association, committee, joint board of trustees, or other similar group of representatives of the parties who establish or maintain the plan for a self-insured group health plan or arrangement that is a multiemployer plan (as defined in section 3(37) of ERISA).

(C) The employee organization for a self-insured group health plan or arrangement maintained solely by an employee organization;

(D) Each participating employer for a self-insured group health plan or arrangement maintained by a Multiple Employer Welfare Arrangement (as defined in section 3(40) of ERISA) with respect to the participating employer's own employees; and

(E) For a self-insured group health plan or arrangement for which a plan sponsor is not otherwise identified in paragraphs (c)(2)(i)(A) through (c)(2)(i)(D) of this section, the person designated by plan terms as the plan sponsor or plan administrator or, if no person is designated as the administrator and a plan sponsor cannot be identified, each entity that maintains the plan or arrangement.

(ii) *Government employers.*—Unless otherwise provided by statute or regulation, a government employer that maintains a self-insured group health plan or arrangement may enter into a written agreement with another governmental unit, or an agency or instrumentality of a governmental unit, that designates the other governmental unit, agency, or instrumentality as the person required to file the returns and to furnish the statements required by this section for some or all of the individuals receiving minimum essential coverage under that plan or arrangement. The designated governmental unit, agency, or instrumentality must be part of or related to the same governmental unit as the government employer (for example, a political subdivision of a State may designate the State or another political subdivision of the state) and agree to the designation. The government employer must make or revoke the designation before the earlier of the deadline for filing the returns or furnishing the statements required by this section and must retain a copy of the designation in its books and records. If the requirements of this paragraph (c)(2)(ii) are met, the designated governmental unit, agency, or instrumentality is the sponsor under paragraph (c)(2)(i) of this section. If no entity is designated, the government employer that maintains the self-insured group health plan or arrangement is the sponsor under paragraph (c)(2)(i) of this section.

(3) *Special rules for government-sponsored programs.*—(i) *Medicaid and Children's Health Insurance Program (CHIP) coverage.*—The State

agency that administers the Medicaid program under title XIX of the Social Security Act (42 U.S.C. 1396 and following sections) or the CHIP program under title XXI of the Social Security Act (42 U.S.C. 1396 and following sections) must file the returns and furnish the statements required by this section for those programs.

(ii) *Government-sponsored coverage provided through health insurance issuers.*—An executive department or agency of a governmental unit that provides coverage under a government-sponsored program through a health insurance issuer (such as Medicaid, CHIP, or Medicare, including Medicare Advantage) must file the returns and furnish the statements required by this section.

(iii) *Nonappropriated Fund Health Benefits Program.*—The Secretary of Defense may designate the Department of Defense components (as used in DoD Directive 5100.01, Functions of the Department of Defense and Its Major Components (December 21, 2010)) that must file the returns and furnish the statements required by this section for the Nonappropriated Fund Health Benefits Program.

(4) *Other arrangements recognized as minimum essential coverage.*—The Commissioner may designate in published guidance, see § 601.601(d) of this chapter, the reporting entity for arrangements the Secretary of Health and Human Services, in coordination with the Secretary of the Treasury, recognizes under section 5000A(f)(1)(E) as minimum essential coverage.

(d) *Reporting not required.*—(1) *Qualified health plans.*—A health insurance issuer is not required to file a return or furnish a report under this section for coverage in a qualified health plan in the individual market enrolled in through an Exchange.

(2) *Additional health benefits.*—No reporting is required under paragraph (a) of this section for minimum essential coverage that provides benefits in addition or as a supplement to a health plan or arrangement that constitutes minimum essential coverage if—

(i) The primary and supplemental coverages have the same plan sponsor; or

(ii) The coverage supplements government-sponsored coverage (as defined in section 5000A(f)(1)(A) and the regulations under that section) such as Medicare.

(3) *Individuals not enrolled in coverage.*—No reporting is required under this section for coverage offered to individuals who do not enroll.

(e) *Information required to be reported to the Internal Revenue Service.*—(1) *In general.*—All information returns required by this section must report the following information for the calendar year of coverage—

(i) The name, address, and employer identification number (EIN) of the reporting entity required to file the return;

(ii) The name, address, and TIN, or date of birth if a TIN is not available, of the responsible individual, except that reporting entities may but are not required to report the TIN of a responsible individual not enrolled in the coverage;

(iii) The name and TIN, or date of birth if a TIN is not available, of each individual who is covered under the policy or program;

(iv) For each covered individual, the months for which, for at least one day, the individual was enrolled in coverage and entitled to receive benefits; and

(v) Any other information specified in forms, instructions, or published guidance, see §§ 601.601(d) and 601.602 of this chapter.

(2) *Information relating to employer-provided coverage.*—In addition to the information described in paragraph (e)(1) of this section, information returns reporting minimum essential coverage provided to an individual that is coverage provided by a health insurance issuer through a group health plan must report—

(i) The name, address, and EIN of the employer sponsoring the plan;

(ii) Whether the coverage is a qualified health plan enrolled in through the Small Business Health Options Program (SHOP) and the SHOP's unique identifier; and

(iii) Other information specified in forms, instructions, and published guidance, see §§ 601.601(d) and 601.602 of this chapter.

(f) *Time and manner for filing return.*—(1) *In general.*—A reporting entity must file the return and transmittal form required under paragraph (a) of this section on or before February 28 (March 31 if filed electronically) of the year following the calendar year in which it provided minimum essential coverage to an individual. A reporting entity must file the return and transmittal form as specified in forms or instructions. For extensions of time for filing returns under this section see §§ 1.6081-1 and 1.6081-8. See § 301.6011-2 of this chapter for rules relating to electronic filing.

(2) *Form of return.*—(i) *Applicable large employer members.*—A reporting entity that is reporting under section 6055 as an applicable large employer member (as defined in § 54.4980H-1(a)(5) of this chapter) makes the return required under this paragraph (f) on Form 1094-C and Form 1095-C or other form designated by the Internal Revenue Service.

(ii) *Reporting entities not reporting as applicable large employer members.*—Entities reporting as health insurance issuers or carriers, sponsors of self-insured group health plans that are not reporting as applicable large employer members, sponsors of multiemployer plans, and providers of government-sponsored coverage, will report under section 6055 on Form 1094-B and Form 1095-B or other form designated by the Internal Revenue Service.

(iii) *Substitute forms.*—Reporting entities may make the return required under this paragraph (f) on a substitute form. A substitute form must comply with revenue procedures or other published guidance (see § 601.601(d)(2) of this chapter) that apply to substitute forms.

(g) *Statements to be furnished to responsible individuals.*—(1) *In general.*—Every person required to file a return under this section must furnish to the responsible individual identified on the return a written statement. For purposes of the penalty under section 6722, furnishing a statement to the responsible individual is treated as furnishing a statement to the payee. The statement must show—

(i) The phone number for a person designated as the reporting entity's contact person and policy number, if any; and

(ii) Information described in paragraph (e) of this section required to be shown on the section 6055 return for the responsible individual and each covered individual listed on the return.

(2) *Statements for individuals other than the responsible individual.*—A reporting entity is not required to provide a statement described in paragraph (g)(1) of this section to an individual who is not the responsible individual.

(3) *Form of the statement.*—A statement required under this paragraph (g) may be made either by furnishing to the responsible individual a copy of the return filed with the Internal Revenue Service or on a substitute statement. A substitute statement must include the information required to be shown on the return filed with the Internal Revenue Service and must comply with requirements in published guidance (see § 601.601(d)(2) of this chapter) relating to substitute statements. An Internal Revenue Service truncated taxpayer identification number may be used as the identification number for an individual in lieu of the identification number appearing on the corresponding information return filed with the Internal Revenue Service.

(4) *Time and manner for furnishing statements.*—(i) *Time for furnishing.*—(A) *In general.*—A reporting entity must furnish the statements required under this paragraph (g) on or before January 31 of the year following the calendar year in which minimum essential coverage is provided.

(B) *Extensions of time.*—(1) *In general.*—For good cause upon written application of the person required to furnish statements under this section, the Internal Revenue Service may grant an extension of time not exceeding 30 days in which to furnish these statements. The application must be addressed to the Internal Revenue Service, and must contain a full recital of the reasons for requesting the extension to aid the Internal Revenue Service in determining the period of the extension, if any, that will be granted. A request in the form of a letter to the Internal Revenue Service, signed by the applicant, suffices as an application. The application must be filed on or before the date prescribed in paragraph (g)(4)(i)(A) of this section.

(2) *Automatic extension of time.*—The Commissioner may, in appropriate cases, prescribe additional guidance or procedures, published in the Internal Revenue Bulletin (see § 601.601(d)(2) of this chapter), for automatic extensions of time to furnish to one or more individuals the statement required under section 6055.

(ii) *Manner of furnishing.*—If mailed, the statement must be sent to the responsible individual's last known permanent address or, if no permanent address is known, to the individual's temporary address. For purposes of this paragraph (g)(4), a reporting entity's first class mailing to the last known permanent address, or if no permanent address is known, the temporary address, discharges the requirement to furnish the statement. A reporting entity may furnish the statement electronically if the requirements of § 1.6055-2 are satisfied.

(h) *Penalties.*—(1) *In general.*—For provisions relating to the penalty for failure to file timely a correct information return required under section 6055, see section 6721 and the regulations under that section. For provisions relating to the penalty for failure to furnish timely a correct statement to responsible individuals required under section 6055, see section 6722 and the regulations under that section. See section 6724 and the regulations under that section for rules relating to the waiver of penalties if a failure to file timely or accurately is due to reasonable cause and is not due to willful neglect.

(2) *Application of section 6721 and 6722 penalties to section 6055 reporting.*—For purposes of section 6055 reporting, if the information reported on a return (including a transmittal) or a statement required by this section is incomplete or incorrect as a result of a change in circumstances (such as a retroactive change in coverage), a failure to timely file or furnish a corrected document is a failure to file or furnish a correct return or statement under sections 6721 and 6722.

(i) [Reserved.]

(j) *Effective/applicability date.*—This section applies for calendar years beginning after December 31, 2014. Reporting entities will not be subject to penalties under section 6721 or 6722 for failure to comply with the section 6055 reporting requirements for coverage in 2014 (for information returns filed and statements furnished in 2015). [Reg. § 1.6055-1.]

□ [T.D. 9660, 3-5-2014 (*corrected* 4-29-2014).]

**[Reg. § 1.6055-2]**

**§ 1.6055-2. Electronic furnishing of statements.**—(a) *Electronic furnishing of statements.*—(1) *In general.*—A person required by section 6055 to furnish a statement (furnisher) to a responsible individual (a recipient) may furnish the statement in an electronic format in lieu of a paper format. A furnisher who meets the requirements of paragraphs (a)(2) through (a)(6) of this section is treated as furnishing the statement in a timely manner.

(2) *Consent.*—(i) *In general.*—The recipient must have affirmatively consented to receive the statement in an electronic format. The consent may be made electronically in any manner that reasonably demonstrates that the recipient can access the statement in the electronic format in which it will be furnished. Alternatively, the consent may be made in a paper document that is confirmed electronically.

(ii) *Withdrawal of consent.*—The consent requirement of this paragraph (a)(2) is not satisfied if the recipient withdraws the consent and the withdrawal takes effect before the statement is furnished. The furnisher may provide that a withdrawal of consent takes effect either on the date the furnisher receives it or on another date no more than 60 days later. The furnisher also may provide that a recipient's request for a paper statement will be treated as a withdrawal of the recipient's consent.

(iii) *Change in hardware or software requirements.*—If a change in the hardware or software required to access the statement creates a material risk that the recipient will not be able to access a statement, a furnisher must, prior to changing the hardware or software, notify the recipient. The notice must describe the revised hardware and software required to access the statement and inform the recipient that a new consent to receive the statement in the revised electronic format must be provided to the furnisher. After implementing the revised hardware or software, the furnisher must obtain from the recipient, in the manner described in paragraph (a)(2)(ii) of this section, a new consent or confirmation of consent to receive the statement electronically.

(iv) *Examples.*—The following examples illustrate the rules of this paragraph (a)(2):

*Example 1.* Furnisher F sends Recipient R a letter stating that R may consent to receive the statement required under section 6055 electronically on a web site instead of in a paper format. The letter contains instructions explaining how to consent to receive the statement electronically by accessing the web site, downloading and completing the consent document, and e-mailing the completed consent back to F. The consent document posted on the web site uses the same electronic format that F will use for the electronically furnished statement. R reads the instructions and submits the consent in the manner provided in the instructions. R has consented to receive the statement required under section 6055 electronically in the manner described in paragraph (a)(2)(i) of this section.

*Example 2.* Furnisher F sends Recipient R an e-mail stating that R may consent to receive the statement required under section 6055 electronically instead of in a paper format. The e-mail contains an attachment instructing R how to consent to receive the statement electronically. The e-mail attachment uses the same electronic format that F will use for the electronically furnished statement. R opens the attachment, reads the instructions, and submits the consent in the manner provided in the instructions. R has consented to receive the

statement required under section 6055 electronically in the manner described in paragraph (a)(2)(i) of this section.

*Example 3.* Furnisher F posts a notice on its web site stating that Recipient R may receive the statement required under section 6055 electronically instead of in a paper format. The web site contains instructions on how R may access a secure web page and consent to receive the statement electronically. The consent via the secure web page uses the same electronic format that F will use for electronically furnishing the statement. R accesses the secure web page and follows the instructions for giving consent. R has consented to receive the statement required under section 6055 electronically in the manner described in paragraph (a)(2)(i) of this section.

(3) *Required disclosures.*—(i) *In general.*—Prior to, or at the time of, a recipient's consent, a furnisher must provide to the recipient a clear and conspicuous disclosure statement containing each of the disclosures described in this paragraph (a)(3).

(ii) *Paper statement.*—The furnisher must inform the recipient that the statement will be furnished on paper if the recipient does not consent to receive it electronically.

(iii) *Scope and duration of consent.*—The furnisher must inform the recipient of the scope and duration of the consent. For example, the recipient must be informed whether the consent applies to each statement required to be furnished after the consent is given until it is withdrawn or only to the first statement required to be furnished following the date of the consent.

(iv) *Post-consent request for a paper statement.*—The furnisher must inform the recipient of any procedure for obtaining a paper copy of the recipient's statement after giving the consent described in paragraph (a)(2)(i) of this section and whether a request for a paper statement will be treated as a withdrawal of consent.

(v) *Withdrawal of consent.*—The furnisher must inform the recipient that—

(A) The recipient may withdraw a consent by writing (electronically or on paper) to the person or department whose name, mailing address, telephone number, and e-mail address is provided in the disclosure statement;

(B) The furnisher will confirm the withdrawal and the date on which it takes effect in writing (either electronically or on paper); and

(C) A withdrawal of consent does not apply to a statement that was furnished electronically in the manner described in this paragraph (a) before the date on which the withdrawal of consent takes effect.

(vi) *Notice of termination.*—The furnisher must inform the recipient of the conditions under which the furnisher will cease furnishing statements electronically to the recipient (for example, termination of the recipient's employment with a furnisher who is the recipient's employer).

(vii) *Updating information.*—The furnisher must inform the recipient of the procedures for updating the information needed to contact the recipient. The furnisher must inform the recipient of any change in the furnisher's contact information.

(viii) *Hardware and software requirements.*—The furnisher must provide the recipient with a description of the hardware and software required to access, print, and retain the statement, and the date when the statement will no longer be available on the web site. The furnisher must advise the recipient that the statement may be required to be printed and attached to a Federal, State, or local income tax return.

(4) *Format.*—The electronic version of the statement must contain all required information and comply with applicable published guidance (see § 601.601(d) of this chapter) relating to substitute statements to recipients.

(5) *Notice.*—(i) *In general.*—If a statement is furnished on a web site, the furnisher must notify the recipient. The notice may be delivered by mail, electronic mail, or in person. The notice must provide instructions on how to access and print the statement and include the following statement in capital letters, "IMPORTANT TAX RETURN DOCUMENT AVAILABLE." If the notice is provided by electronic mail, this statement must be on the subject line of the electronic mail.

(ii) *Undeliverable electronic address.*—If an electronic notice described in paragraph (a)(5)(i) of this section is returned as undeliverable, and the furnisher cannot obtain the correct electronic address from the furnisher's records or from the recipient, the furnisher must furnish the notice by mail or in person within 30 days after the electronic notice is returned.

(iii) *Corrected statement.*—If the furnisher has corrected a recipient's statement and the original statement was furnished electronically, the furnisher must furnish a corrected statement to the recipient electronically. If the original statement was furnished through a web site posting, the furnisher must notify the recipient that it has posted the corrected statement on the web site in the manner described in paragraph (a)(5)(i) of this section within 30 days of the posting. The corrected statement or the notice must be furnished by mail or in person if—

(A) An electronic notice of the web site posting of an original statement or the corrected statement was returned as undeliverable; and

(B) The recipient has not provided a new e-mail address.

(6) *Access period.*—Statements furnished on a web site must be retained on the web site through October 15 of the year following the calendar year to which the statements relate (or the first business day after October 15, if October 15 falls on a Saturday, Sunday, or legal holiday). The furnisher must maintain access to corrected statements that are posted on the web site through October 15 of the year following the calendar year to which the statements relate (or the first business day after such October 15, if October 15 falls on a Saturday, Sunday, or legal holiday) or the date 90 days after the corrected forms are posted, whichever is later.

(7) *Paper statements after withdrawal of consent.*—A furnisher must furnish a paper statement if a recipient withdraws consent to receive a statement electronically and the withdrawal takes effect before the statement is furnished. A paper statement furnished after the statement due date under this paragraph (a)(7) is timely if furnished within 30 days after the date the furnisher receives the withdrawal of consent.

(b) *Effective/applicability date.*—This section applies for calendar years beginning after December 31, 2014. Reporting entities will not be subject to penalties under section 6722 with respect to the reporting requirements for 2014 (for statements furnished in 2015). [Reg. § 1.6055-2.]

☐ [*T.D. 9660, 3-5-2014.*]

### [Reg. § 301.6056-1]

**§ 301.6056-1. Rules relating to reporting by applicable large employers on health insurance coverage offered under employer-sponsored plans.**—(a) *In general.*—Section 6056 requires an applicable large employer subject to the requirements of section 4980H to report certain health insurance coverage information to the Internal Revenue Service, and to furnish certain related employee statements to its full-time employees. Paragraph (b) of this section contains definitions for purposes of this section. Paragraph (c) of this section prescribes general rules for filing the required information with the IRS and furnishing the required employee statements to employees. Paragraphs (d) and (e) of this section describe the information required to be reported on a section 6056 information return and the time and manner for filing. Paragraph (f) of this section provides information about the statement required to be furnished to a full-time employee. Paragraph (g) of this section prescribes the time and manner of furnishing the statement, including extensions of time to furnish, to a full-time employee. Paragraph (h) addresses corrections of returns. Paragraph (i) of this section describes the information return penalties applicable to section 6056 returns. Paragraph (j) of this section describes alternative reporting methods available to certain applicable large employers with certain employees. Paragraph (k) of this section describes certain special rules applicable to applicable large employers that are governmental units.

(b) *Definitions.*—(1) *In general.*—The definitions in this paragraph (b) apply for purposes of this section.

(2) *Applicable large employer.*—The term *applicable large employer* has the same meaning as in section 4980H(c)(2) and § 54.4980H-1(a)(4) of this chapter.

(3) *Applicable large employer member.*—The term *applicable large employer member* has the same meaning as in § 54.4980H-1(a)(5) of this chapter.

(4) *Dependent.*—The term *dependent* has the same meaning as in § 54.4980H-1(a)(11) of this chapter.

(5) *Eligible employer-sponsored plan.*—The term *eligible employer-sponsored plan* has the same meaning as in section 5000A(f)(2) and § 1.5000A-2(c)(1) of this chapter.

(6) *Full-time employee.*—The term *full-time employee* has the same meaning as in section 4980H and § 54.5980H-1(a)(21) [§ 54.4980H-1(a)(21)]of this chapter, as applied to the determination and calculation of liability under section 4980H(a) and (b) with respect to any individual employee, and not as applied to the determination of status as an applicable large employer, if different.

(7) *Governmental unit.*—The term *governmental unit* refers to the government of the United States, any State or political subdivision thereof, or any Indian tribal government (as defined in section 7701(a)(40)) or subdivision of an Indian tribal government (as defined in section 7871(d)).

(8) *Agency or instrumentality of a governmental unit.*—[Reserved]

(9) *Minimum essential coverage.*—The term *minimum essential coverage* has the same meaning as in section 5000A(f) and the regulations issued under that section.

(10) *Minimum value.*—The term *minimum value* has the same meaning as in section 36B and any applicable regulations.

(11) *Person.*—The term *person* has the same meaning as in section 7701(a)(1) and applicable regulations.

(c) *Content and timing of reporting by applicable large employer members.*—(1) *In general.*—Each applicable large employer member required to make a return and furnish a related statement to its full-time employees under section 6056 for a calendar year must make a return and furnish the related statement using such form(s) as may be prescribed by the Internal Revenue Service. An applicable large employer member will satisfy its reporting requirements under section 6056 if it files with the Internal Revenue Service a return for each full-time employee using Form 1095-C or another form the IRS designates, and a transmittal form using Form 1094-C or another form the IRS designates, as prescribed in this section and in the instructions to the forms. Each Form 1095-C and the transmittal Form 1094-C will together constitute an information return to be filed with the Internal Revenue Service.

(2) *Reporting facilitated by third parties.*—A separate section 6056 information return must be filed for each applicable large employer member. If more than one section 6056 information return is being filed for an applicable large employer member, there must be one authoritative section 6056 transmittal (Form 1094-C) reporting aggregate employer-level data for all full-time employees of the applicable large employer member, in accordance with forms and instructions. Additionally, there must be only one section 6056 employee statement (Form 1095-C) for each full-time employee with respect to that full-time employee's employment with the applicable large employer member, so that all required information for a particular full-time employee of the applicable large employer member is reflected on a single Form 1095-C.

(d) *Information required to be reported to the Internal Revenue Service.*—(1) *In general.*—Except as provided in paragraph (j) of this section (relating to alternative reporting methods for eligible applicable large employer members), every applicable large employer member must make a section 6056 information return with respect to each full-time employee. Each section 6056 information return must show—

(i) The name, address, and employer identification number of the applicable large employer member,

(ii) The name and telephone number of the applicable large employer member's contact person,

(iii) The calendar year for which the information is reported,

(iv) A certification as to whether the applicable large employer member offered to its full-time employees (and their dependents) the opportunity to enroll in minimum essential coverage under an eligible employer-sponsored plan, by calendar month,

(v) The months during the calendar year for which minimum essential coverage under the plan was available,

(vi) Each full-time employee's share of the lowest cost monthly premium (self-only) for coverage providing minimum value offered to that full-time employee under an eligible employer-sponsored plan, by calendar month;

(vii) The number of full-time employees for each month during the calendar year,

(viii) The name, address, and taxpayer identification number of each full-time employee during the calendar year and the months, if any, during which the employee was covered under the plan, and

(ix) Any other information specified in forms, instructions, or published guidance, see § § 601.601(d) and 601.602 of this chapter.

(2) *Form of the return.*—A return required under this paragraph (d) may be made on Forms 1094-C and 1095-C or other form(s) designated by the Internal Revenue Service, or a substitute form. A substitute form must include the information required to be reported on Forms 1094-C and 1095-C and must comply with applicable revenue procedures or other published guidance relating to substitute statements. See § 601.601(d)(2) of this chapter.

(e) *Time and manner for filing return.*—An applicable large employer member must file the return and transmittal form required under paragraph (d)(2) of this section on or before February 28 (March 31 if filed electronically) of the year succeeding the calendar year to which it relates in accordance with any applicable guidance and the instructions to the form. An applicable large employer member must file the return and transmittal form at the address specified on the return form or its instructions. For extensions of time for filing returns under this section, see §§ 1.6081-1 and 1.6081-8 of this chapter. See § 301.6011-2 for rules relating to electronic filing.

(f) *Statements required to be furnished to full-time employees.*—(1) *In general.*—Except as provided in paragraph (j) of this section, every applicable large employer member required to file a return under section 6056 must furnish to each of its full-time employees identified on the return a written statement showing—

(i) The name, address and employer identification number of the applicable large employer member, and

(ii) The information required to be shown on the section 6056 return with respect to the full-time employee.

(2) *Form of the statement.*—A statement required under this paragraph (f) may be made either by furnishing to the full-time employee a copy of Form 1095-C or another form the IRS designates as prescribed in this section and in the instructions to such forms, or a substitute statement. A substitute statement must include the information required to be shown on the return filed with the IRS and must comply with requirements in published guidance (see § 601.601(d)(2) of this chapter) relating to substitute statements. An IRS truncated taxpayer identification number may be used as the identifying number for an individual in lieu of the identifying number appearing on the corresponding information return filed with the IRS.

(g) *Time and manner for furnishing statements.*—(1) *Time for furnishing.*—(i) *In general.*—Each statement required by this section for a calendar year must be furnished to a full-time employee on or before January 31 of the year succeeding that calendar year in accordance with applicable Internal Revenue Service procedures and instructions

(ii) *Extensions of time.*—(A) *In general.*—For good cause upon written application of the person required to furnish statements under this section, the Internal Revenue Service may grant an extension of time not exceeding 30 days in which to furnish such statements. The application must be addressed to the Internal Revenue Service, and must contain a full recital of the reasons for requesting the extension to aid the Internal Revenue Service in determining the period of the extension, if any, that will be granted. A request in the form of a letter to the Internal Revenue Service, signed by the applicant, suffices as an application. The application must be filed on or before the date prescribed in paragraph (g)(1) of this section.

(B) *Automatic extension of time.*—The Commissioner may, in appropriate cases, prescribe additional guidance or procedures, published in the Internal Revenue Bulletin (see § 601.601(d)(2) of this chapter), for automatic extensions of time to furnish to one or more full-time employees the statement required under section 6056.

(2) *Manner of furnishing.*—If mailed, the statement must be sent to the full-time employee's last known permanent address or, if no permanent address is known, to the employee's temporary address. For purposes of this paragraph (g), an applicable large employer member's first class mailing to the last known permanent address, or if no permanent address is known, the temporary address, discharges the requirement to furnish the statement. An applicable large employer member may furnish the statement electronically in accordance with § 301.6056-2.

(h) *Correction of returns.*—See § 301.6056-1(i)(2).

(i) *Penalties.*—(1) *In general.*—For provisions relating to the penalty for failure to file timely a correct information return required under section 6056, see section 6721 and the regulations under that section. For provisions relating to the penalty for failure to furnish timely a correct statement to full-time employees required under section 6056, see section 6722 and the regulations under that section. See section 6724 and the regulations under that section for rules relating to the waiver of penalties if a failure to file timely or accurately is due to reasonable cause and is not due to willful neglect.

(2) *Application of section 6721 and 6722 penalties to section 6056 reporting.*—For purposes of section 6056 reporting, if the information reported on a return (including a transmittal) or a statement required by this section is incomplete or incorrect as a result of a change in circumstances (such as a retroactive change in coverage), a failure to timely file or furnish a corrected document is a failure to file or furnish a correct return or statement under sections 6721 and 6722.

(j) *Alternative reporting methods for eligible applicable large employer members.*—In lieu of the general reporting method described in paragraph (d) of this section, eligible applicable large employer members may use the following alternative reporting methods described in this paragraph (j).

(1) *Certification of qualifying offer.*—An applicable large employer member is an eligible applicable large employer member and is treated as meeting its reporting obligation under section 6056 if:

(i) The applicable large employer member certifies on the section 6056 transmittal form, in accordance with the form and the instructions to the form, that it made a qualifying offer. A qualifying offer is an offer to one or more of its full-time employees for all months during the year for which the employee was a full-time employee and which are not within a limited nonassessment period (as defined in § 54.4980H-1(a)(26) of this chapter), of minimum essential coverage providing minimum value at an employee cost for employee-only coverage not exceeding 9.5 percent of the mainland single federal poverty line, and that includes an offer of minimum essential coverage to the employees' spouses and dependents. For this purpose, the applicable federal poverty line is the federal poverty line as defined in § 54.4980H-1(a)(19) of this chapter, as calculated and applied to the 48 contiguous states and the District of Columbia;

(ii) The applicable large employer member provides on the Form 1095-C or other form as designated by the IRS, in accordance with the form and the instructions to the form, the information with respect to each full-time employee to whom a qualifying offer, as defined in paragraph (j)(1)(i) of this section, is made for all twelve months of the applicable calendar year;

(iii) The applicable large employer member provides a statement to each full-time employee to whom a qualifying offer (as defined in paragraph (j)(1)(i) of this section) was made for all twelve months of the applicable calendar year; in such form and manner as prescribed by the Secretary, or a copy of the Form 1095-C filed with the IRS with respect to that full-time employee; and

(D) The applicable large employer member files section 6056 returns and furnishes section 6056 employee statements with respect to all other full-time employees under the general reporting method described in paragraph (d) of this section, in accordance with forms and instructions.

(2) *Option to report without separate identification of full-time employees if certain conditions related to offers of coverage are satisfied (98 percent offers).*—An applicable large employer member that otherwise meets its reporting obligation under section 6056 is not required to identify on its section 6056 return whether a particular employee is a full-time employee for one or more calendar months of the reporting year or report the total number of its full-time employees for the reporting year, if it certifies that it offered minimum essential coverage providing minimum value that was affordable under section 4980H to at least 98 percent of the employees (and their dependents) with respect to whom it reports for purposes of section 6056 in accordance with paragraph (d) of this section (regardless of whether the employee is a full-time employee for purposes of section 4980H for a calendar month during the year).

(k) *Special rules for governmental units.*—(1) *Person appropriately designated.*—In the case of any applicable large employer member that is a governmental unit or any agency or instrumentality thereof, the person or persons appropriately designated under section 6056(e) for purposes of the filing and furnishing requirements of section 6056 must be part of or related to the same governmental unit as the applicable large employer member. The applicable large employer member must make (or revoke) the designation before the earlier of the deadline for filing the returns or furnishing the statements required by this section. A person that has been appropriately designated under section 6056(e) must file a separate section 6056 return and transmittal for each applicable large employer member for which the person is reporting. The person appropriately designated under section 6056(e) assumes responsibility for the section 6056 requirements on behalf of the applicable large employer member for which the person is designated. Notwithstanding the designation, a separate section 6056 information return must be filed for each applicable large employer member that is a governmental unit. If more than one section 6056 information return is being filed for an applicable large employer member, there must be one authoritative section 6056 transmittal (Form 1094-C) reporting aggregate employer-level data for all full-time employees of the applicable large employer member, in accordance with forms and instructions. In addition, notwithstanding the designation, there must be only one section 6056 employee statement (Form 1095-C) for each full-time employee with respect to that full-time employee's employment with the applicable large employer member, so that all required information for a particular full-time employee of the applicable large employer member is reflected on a single Form 1095-C.

(2) *Written designation.*—The designation under section 6056(e) must be made in writing, must be signed by both the applicable large employer member and the designated person, and must be effective under all applicable laws. The designation must set forth the name, address, and employer identification number of the designated person, and appoint such person as the person responsible for reporting under section 6056 on behalf of the applicable large employer member. The designation must contain information identifying the category of full-time employees (which may be full-time employees eligible for a specified health plan, or in a particular job category, as long as the specific employees covered by the designation can be identified) for which the designated person is responsible for reporting under section 6056 on behalf of the applicable large employer member. If the designated person is responsible for reporting under section 6056 for all full-time employees of an applicable large employer member, the designation must so indicate. The designation must contain language that the designated person agrees and certifies that it is the appropriately designated person under section 6056(e), and an acknowledgement that the designated person is responsible for reporting under section 6056 on behalf of the applicable large employer member and subject to the requirements of section 6056, including for purposes of information reporting requirements under sections 6721, 6722, and 6724. The designation must also set forth the name and employer identification number of the applicable large employer member, identifying the applicable large employer member as the person subject to the requirements of section 4980H. An equivalent applicable statutory or regulatory designation containing the language described in this paragraph (k)(2) will be treated as a written designation for purposes of section 6056(e) and this section. The designation will not be submitted to the IRS and should be maintained under the normal record-retention rules under section 6103.

(3) *Application to alternative reporting methods.*—A person designated under this paragraph (k) may use the alternative reporting method identified in paragraph (j)(1) of this section for the full-time employees for which it is reporting with respect to a particular governmental unit if that particular governmental unit meets the eligibility requirements with respect to those employees, but may use the alternative reporting method identified in paragraph (j)(2) of this section only if the governmental unit on whose behalf it is reporting would itself be eligible to use that alternative reporting method.

(l) *Additional guidance.*—The Commissioner may prescribe additional guidance of general applicability, published in the Internal Revenue Bulletin (see § 601.601(d)(2) of this chapter) to provide additional rules under section 6056, including rules permitting use of alternative optional methods to meet reporting requirements.

(m) *Effective/applicability date.*—This section applies for calendar years beginning after December 31, 2014. Reporting entities will not be subject to penalties under sections 6721 or 6722 for failure to comply with the section 6056 reporting requirements for 2014 (for information returns filed and for statements furnished to employees in 2015). [Reg. § 301.6056-1.]

☐ [*T.D.* 9661, 3-5-2014.]

**[Reg. § 301.6056-2]**

**§ 301.6056-2. Electronic furnishing of statements.**—(a) *Electronic furnishing of statements.*—(1) *In general.*—An applicable large employer member required by § 301.6056-1 to furnish a statement (furnisher) to a full-time employee (a recipient) as required by section 6056 may furnish the section 6056 employee statement (the statement) in an electronic format in lieu of a paper format, provided that the furnisher meets the requirements of paragraphs (a)(2) through (a)(6) of this section. An applicable large employer member who meets the requirements of paragraphs (a)(2) through (6) of this section is treated as furnishing the statement in a timely manner.

(2) *Consent.*—(i) *In general.*—The recipient must have affirmatively consented to receive the statement in an electronic format. The recipient may make the consent electronically in any manner that reasonably demonstrates that the recipient can access the statement in the electronic format in which it will be furnished to the recipient. Alternatively, the recipient may make the consent in a paper document if the recipient confirms the consent electronically.

(ii) *Withdrawal of consent.*—The consent requirement of this paragraph (a)(2) is not satisfied if the recipient withdraws the consent and the withdrawal takes effect before the statement is furnished. The furnisher may provide that a withdrawal of consent takes effect either on the date it is received by the furnisher or on a subsequent date. The furnisher may also provide that a recipient's request for a paper statement will be treated as a withdrawal of the recipient's consent.

(iii) *Change in hardware or software requirements.*—If a change in the hardware or software required to access the statement creates a material risk that the recipient will not be able to access the statement, the furnisher must, prior to changing the hardware or software, provide the recipient with a notice. The notice must describe the revised hardware and software required to access the statement and inform the recipient that a new consent to receive the statement in the revised electronic format must be provided to the furnisher. After implementing the revised hardware and software, the furnisher must obtain from the recipient, in the manner described in paragraph (a)(2)(i) of this section, a new consent or confirmation of consent to receive the statement electronically.

(iv) *Examples.*—The following examples illustrate the rules of this paragraph (a)(2):

*Example 1.* Furnisher F sends Recipient R a letter stating that R may consent to receive the statement required under section 6056 electronically on a web site instead of in a paper format. The letter contains instructions explaining how to consent to receive the statement electronically by accessing the web site, downloading the consent document, completing the consent document and e-mailing the completed consent back to F. The consent document posted on the web site uses the same electronic format that F will use for the electronically furnished statement. R reads the instructions and accesses the web site, downloads and completes the consent document, and emails the completed consent back to F. R has consented to receive the statement required under section 6056 electronically in the manner described in paragraph (a)(2)(i) of this section.

*Example 2.* Furnisher F sends Recipient R an e-mail stating that R may consent to receive the statement required under section 6056 electronically instead of in a paper format. The e-mail contains an attachment instructing R how to consent to receive the statement electronically. The e-mail attachment uses the same electronic format that F will use for the electronically furnished statement. R opens the attachment, reads the instructions, and submits the consent in the manner provided in the instructions. R has consented to receive the statement required under section 6056 electronically in the manner described in paragraph (a)(2)(i) of this section.

*Example 3.* Furnisher F posts a notice on its web site stating that Recipient R may receive the statement required under section 6056 electronically instead of in a paper format. The web site contains instructions on how R may access a secure web page and consent to receive the statement electronically. The consent via the secure web page uses the same electronic format that F will use for the electronically furnished statement. R accesses the web site and follows the instructions for giving consent. R has consented to receive section 6056 statements electronically in the manner described in paragraph (a)(2)(i) of this section.

(3) *Required disclosures.*—(i) *In general.*—Prior to, or at the time of, a recipient's consent, a furnisher must provide to the recipient a clear and conspicuous disclosure statement containing each of the disclosures described in paragraphs (a)(3)(ii) through (viii) of this section.

(ii) *Paper statement.*—The furnisher must inform the recipient that the statement will be furnished on paper if the recipient does not consent to receive it electronically.

(iii) *Scope and duration of consent.*—The furnisher must inform the recipient of the scope and duration of the consent. For example, the recipient must be informed whether the consent applies to each statement required to be furnished after the consent is given until it is withdrawn in the manner described in paragraph (a)(3)(v)(A) of this section or only to the first statement required to be furnished following the date of the consent.

(iv) *Post-consent request for a paper statement.*—The furnisher must inform the recipient of any procedure for obtaining a paper copy of the recipient's statement after giving the consent described in paragraph (a)(2)(i) of this section and whether a request for a paper statement will be treated as a withdrawal of consent.

(v) *Withdrawal of consent.*—The furnisher must inform the recipient that—

(A) The recipient may withdraw a consent by writing (electronically or on paper) to the person or department whose name, mailing address, telephone number, and email address is provided in the disclosure statement,

(B) The furnisher will confirm the withdrawal and the date on which it takes effect in writing (either electronically or on paper), and

(C) A withdrawal of consent does not apply to a statement that was furnished electronically in the manner described in this paragraph (a) before the date on which the withdrawal of consent takes effect.

(vi) *Notice of termination.*—The furnisher must inform the recipient of the conditions under which a furnisher will cease furnishing statements electronically to the recipient (for example, termination of the recipient's employment with furnisher-employer).

(vii) *Updating information.*—The furnisher must inform the recipient of the procedures for updating the information needed to contact the recipient. The furnisher must inform the recipient of any change in the furnisher's contact information.

(viii) *Hardware and software requirements.*—The furnisher must provide the recipient with a description of the hardware and software required to access, print, and retain the statement, and the date when the statement will no longer be available on the Web site. The furnisher must advise the recipient that the statement may be required to be printed and attached to a Federal, State, or local income tax return.

(4) *Format.*—The electronic version of the statement must contain all required information and comply with applicable revenue procedures relating to substitute statements to recipients.

(5) *Notice.*—(i) *In general.*—If the statement is furnished on a Web site, the furnisher must notify the recipient that the statement is posted on a Web site. The notice may be delivered by mail, electronic mail, or in person. The notice must provide instructions on how to access and print the statement. The notice must include the following statement in capital letters, "IMPORTANT TAX RETURN DOCUMENT AVAILABLE." If the notice is provided by electronic mail, the foregoing statement must be on the subject line of the electronic mail.

(ii) *Undeliverable electronic address.*—If an electronic notice described in paragraph (a)(5)(i) of this section is returned as undeliverable, and the correct electronic address cannot be obtained from the furnisher's records or from the recipient, then the furnisher must furnish the notice by mail or in person within 30 days after the electronic notice is returned.

(iii) *Corrected statement.*—If the furnisher has corrected a recipient's statement as directed in §301.6056-1(k) and the original statement was furnished electronically, the furnisher must furnish the corrected statement to the recipient electronically. If the original statement was furnished through a Web site posting and the furnisher has corrected the statement, the furnisher must notify the recipient that it has posted the corrected statement on the web site within 30 days of such posting in the manner described in paragraph (a)(5)(i) of this section. The corrected statement or the notice must be furnished by mail or in person if-

(A) An electronic notice of the web site posting of an original statement or the corrected statement was returned as undeliverable, and

(B) The recipient has not provided a new e-mail address.

(6) *Access period.*—Statements furnished on a web site must be retained on the web site through October 15 of the year following the calendar year to which the statements relate (or the first business day after October 15, if October 15 falls on a Saturday, Sunday, or legal holiday). The furnisher must maintain access to corrected statements that are posted on the web site through October 15 of the year following the calendar year to which the statements relate (or the first business day after such October 15, if October 15 falls on a Saturday, Sunday, or legal holiday) or the date 90 days after the corrected forms are posted, whichever is later.

(7) *Paper statements after withdrawal of consent.*—A furnisher must furnish a paper statement if a recipient withdraws consent to receive a statement electronically and the withdrawal takes effect before the statement is furnished. A paper statement furnished after the statement due date under this paragraph (a)(7) is timely if furnished within 30 days after the date the furnisher receives the withdrawal of consent.

(b) *Effective/applicability date.*—This section applies for calendar years beginning after December 31, 2014. Reporting entities will not be subject to penalties under section 6722 with respect to the reporting requirements for 2014 (for statements furnished in 2015). [Reg. §301.6056-2.]

☐ [*T.D.* 9661, 3-5-2014.]

**[Reg. §301.6057-1]**

**§301.6057-1. Employee retirement benefit plans; identification of participant with deferred vested retirement benefit.**—(a) *Annual registration statement.*—(1) *In general.*—Under section 6057(a), the plan administrator (within the meaning of section 414(g) of an employee retirement benefit plan must file with the Internal Revenue Service information relating to each plan participant who separates from service covered by the plan and is entitled to a deferred vested

retirement benefit under the plan, but is not paid this retirement benefit. Plans subject to this filing requirement are described in subparagraph(3) of this paragraph. Subparagraph (4) describes how the information is to be filed with the Internal Revenue Service. In the case of a plan to which only one employer contributes, the time for filing the information with respect to each separated participant is described in subparagraph(5). In the case of a plan to which more than one employer contributes the time for filing the information with respect to a participant is described in paragraph (b)(2). Paragraph (b) also provides other rules applicable only to plans to which more than one employer contributes.

(2) *Deferred vested retirement benefit.*—For purposes of this section, a plan participant's deferred retirement benefit is considered a vested benefit if it is vested under the terms of the plan at the close of the plan year described in paragraph (a)(5) or (b)(4) (whichever is applicable) for which information relating to any deferred vested retirement benefit of the participant must be filed. A participant's deferred retirement benefit need not be a nonforfeitable benefit within the meaning of section 411(a) for the filing requirements described in this section to apply. Accordingly, information relating to a participant's deferred vested retirement benefit must be filed as required by this section nonwithstanding that the benefit is subject to forfeiture by reason of an event or condition occurring subsequent to the close of the plan year described in paragraph (a)(5) or (b)(4) (whichever is applicable) for which information relating to any deferred vested retirement benefit of the participant must be filed.

(3) *Plans subject to filing requirement.*—The term "employee retirement benefit plan" means a plan to which the vesting standards of section 203 of part 2 of subtitle B of Title I of the Employee Retirement Income Security Act of 1974 (88 Stat. 854) apply for any day in the plan year. (For purposes of this section, "plan year" means the plan year as determined for purposes of the annual return required by section 6058(a). Accordingly, a plan need not be a qualified plan within the meaning of section 401(a) to be subject to these filing requirements. A plan to which more than one employer contributes must file the report of deferred vested retirement benefits described in this section, but see paragraph (b) for special rules applicable to such a plan. The filing requirements described in this section and §301.6057-2 (relating to notification of change in plan status) do not apply to a governmental or church plan described in section 414(d) or (e).

(4) *Filing requirements.*—Information relating to the deferred vested retirement benefit of a plan participant must be filed on Schedule SSA as an attachment to the Annual Return/Report of Employee Benefit Plan (Form 5500 series). Schedule SSA shall be filed on behalf of an employee retirement benefit plan for each plan year for which information relating to the deferred vested retirement benefit of a plan participant is filed under paragraph (a)(5) or (b)(2) of this section. There shall be filed on Schedule SSA the name and Social Security number of the participant, a description of the nature, form and amount of the deferred vested retirement benefit to which the participant is entitled, and such other information as is required by section 6057(a) or Schedule SSA and the accompanying instructions. The form of the benefit reported on Schedule SSA shall be the normal form of benefit under the plan, or, if the plan administrator (within the meaning of section 414(g)) considers it more appropriate, any other form of benefit.

(5) *Time for reporting deferred vested retirement benefit.*—(i) *In general.*—In the case of a plan to which only one employer contributes, information relating to the deferred vested retirement benefit of a plan participant must be filed no later than on the Schedule SSA filed for the plan year following the plan year within which the participant separates from service covered by the plan. Information relating to a separated participant may, at the option of the plan administrator, be reported earlier (that is, on the Schedule SSA filed for the plan year in which the participant separates from service covered by the plan). For purposes of this paragraph a participant is not considered to separate from service covered by the plan solely because the participant incurs a break in service under the plan. In addition, for purposes of this paragraph, in the case of a plan which uses the elapsed time method described in Department of Labor regulations for crediting service for benefit accrual purposes, a participant is considered to separate from service covered by the plan on the date the participant severs from service covered by the plan.

(ii) *Exception.*—Notwithstanding subdivision (i), no information relating to the deferred vested retirement benefit of a separated participant is required to be filed on Schedule SSA if, before the date such Schedule SSA is required to be filed (including any extension of time for filing granted pursuant to section 6081), the participant (A) is paid some or all of the deferred vested retirement benefit under the plan, (B) returns to service covered by the plan, or (C) forfeits all of the deferred vested retirement benefit under the plan.

(b) *Plans to which more than one employer contributes.*—(1) *Application.*—Section 6057 and this section apply to a plan to which more than one employer contributes with the modifications set forth in this paragraph. For purposes of section 6057 and this section, whether or not more than one employer contributes to a plan shall be determined by the number of employers who are required to contribute to the plan. Thus, for example, this paragraph applies to plans maintained by more than one employer which are collectively bargained as described in section 413(a), multiple-employer plans described in section 413(c) and the regulations thereunder, multiemployer plans described in section 414(f), and plans adopted by more than one employer of certain controlled and common control groups described in section 414(b) and (c).

(2) *Time for reporting deferred vested retirement benefit.*—(i) *In general.*—In the case of a plan to which more than one employer contributes, information relating to the deferred vested retirement benefit of a plan participant must be filed no later than on the Schedule SSA filed for the plan year within which the participant completes the second of two consecutive one-year breaks in service (as defined in the plan for vesting percentage purposes) in service computation periods (as defined in the plan for vesting percentage purposes) which begin after December 31, 1974. At the option of the plan administrator, information relating to a participant's deferred vested retirement benefit may be filed earlier (that is, on the Schedule SSA filed for the plan year in which the participant incurs the first one-year break in service or, in the case of a separated participant, on the Schedule SSA filed for the plan year in which the participant separates from service).

(ii) *Special rules.*—For purposes of this subparagraph (1)—

(A) For the definition of the term "one-year break in service" in the case of a plan which uses the elapsed time method described in Department of Labor Regulations for crediting service for vesting percentage purposes, see § 1.411(a)-6(c)(2).

(B) In the case of a plan which does not define the term "one-year break in service" for vesting percentage purposes, a plan participant shall be deemed to incur a one-year break in service under the plan in any plan year within which the participant does not complete more than 500 hours of service covered by the plan.

(iii) *Transitional rule.*—Notwithstanding subdivision (i), if the second consecutive one-year break in service described in subdivision (i) is incurred in a plan year beginning before January 1, 1978, information relating to the participant's deferred vested retirement benefit is not required to be filed earlier than on the Schedule SSA filed for the first plan year beginning after December 31, 1977.

(iv) *Exception.*—Notwithstanding subdivision (i) or (iii) of this subparagraph, no information relating to a participant's deferred vested retirement benefit is required to be filed on Schedule SSA if, before the date such Schedule SSA is required to be filed (including any extension of time for filing granted pursuant to section 6081), the participant (A) is paid some or all of the deferred vested retirement benefit under the plan, (B) accrues additional retirement benefits under the plan, or (C) forfeits all of the deferred vested retirement benefit under the plan.

(3) *Information relating to deferred vested retirement benefit.*—(i) *Incomplete records.*—Section 6057(a) and paragraph (a)(4) of this section require the filing on Schedule SSA of a description of the deferred vested retirement benefit to which the participant is entitled. If the plan administrator of a plan to which more than one employer contributes maintains records of a participant's service covered by the plan which are incomplete as of the close of the plan year with respect to which the plan administrator files information relating to the participant on Schedule SSA, the plan administrator may elect to file the information required by Schedule SSA based only upon these incomplete records. The plan administrator is not required, for purposes of completing Schedule SSA, to compile from sources other than such records a complete record of a participant's years of service covered by the plan. Similarly, if retirement benefits under the plan are determined by taking into account a participant's service with an employer which is not service covered by the plan, but the plan administrator maintains records only with respect to periods of service covered by the plan, the plan administrator may complete Schedule SSA taking into account only the participant's period of service covered by the plan.

(ii) *Inability to determine correct amount of participant's deferred vested retirement benefit.*—If the amount of a participant's deferred vested retirement benefit which is filed on Schedule SSA is computed on the basis of plan records maintained by the plan administrator which—

(A) Are incomplete with respect to the participant's service covered by the plan (as described in subdivision (i)), or

(B) Fail to account for the participant's service not covered by the plan which is relevant to a determination of the participant's deferred vested retirement benefit under the plan (as described in subdivision (i)),

then the plan administrator must indicate on Schedule SSA that the amount of the deferred vested retirement benefit shown therein may be other than that to which the participant is actually entitled because the amount is based upon incomplete records.

(iii) *Inability to determine whether participant vested in deferred retirement benefit.*—Where, as described in subdivision (i), information to be reported on Schedule SSA is to be based upon records which are incomplete with respect to a participant's service covered by the plan or which fail to take into account relevant service not covered by the plan, the plan administrator may be unable to determine whether or not the participant is vested in any deferred retirement benefit. If, in view of information provided either by the incomplete records or the plan participant, there is a significant likelihood that the plan participant is vested in a deferred retirement benefit under the plan, information relating to the participant must be filed on Schedule SSA with the notation that the participant may be entitled to a deferred vested retirement benefit under the plan, but information relating to the amount of the benefit may be omitted. This subdivision (iii) does not apply in a case in which it can be determined from plan records maintained by the plan administrator that the participant is vested in a deferred retirement benefit. Subdivision (ii), however, may apply in such a case.

(c) *Voluntary filing.*—(1) *In general.*—The plan administrator of an employee retirement benefit plan described in paragraph (a)(3) of this section, or any other employee retirement benefit plan (including a governmental or church plan), may at its option, file on Schedule SSA information relating to the deferred vested retirement benefit of any plan participant who separates at any time from service covered by the plan, including plan participants who separate from service in plan years beginning before 1976.

(2) *Deleting previously filed information.*—If, after information relating to the deferred vested retirement benefit of a plan participant is filed on Schedule SSA, the plan participant—

(i) Is paid some or all of the deferred vested retirement benefit under the plan, or

(ii) Forfeits all of the deferred vested retirement benefit under the plan, the plan administrator may, at its option, file on Schedule SSA (or such other form as may be provided for this purpose) the name and social security number of the participant with the notation that information previously filed relating to the participant's deferred vested retirement benefit should be deleted.

(d) *Filing incident to cessation of payment of benefits.*—(1) *In general.*—As described in this section, no information relating to the deferred vested retirement benefit of a plan participant is required to be filed on Schedule SSA if before the date such Schedule SSA is required to be filed, some of the deferred vested retirement benefit is paid to the participant, and information relating to a participant's deferred vested retirement benefit which was previously filed on Schedule SSA may be deleted if the participant is paid some of the deferred vested retirement benefit. If payment of the deferred vested retirement benefit ceases before all of the benefit to which the participant is entitled is paid to the participant, information relating to the deferred vested retirement benefit to which the participant remains entitled shall be filed on the Schedule SSA filed for the plan year following the last plan year within which a portion of the benefit is paid to the participant.

(2) *Exception.*—Notwithstanding subparagraph (1) of this paragraph, no information relating to the deferred vested retirement benefit to which the participant remains entitled is required to be filed on Schedule SSA if, before the date such Schedule SSA is required to be filed (including any extension of time for filing granted pursuant to section 6081), the participant (i) returns to service covered by the plan, (ii) accrues additional retirement benefits under the plan, or (iii) forfeits the benefit under the plan.

(e) *Individual statement to participant.*—The plan administrator of an employee retirement benefit plan defined in paragraph (a)(3) of this section must provide each participant with respect to whom information is required to be filed on Schedule SSA a statement describing the deferred vested retirement benefit to which the participant is entitled. The description provided the participant must include the information filed with respect to the participant on Schedule SSA. The statement is to be delivered to the participant or forwarded to the participant's last known address no later than the date on which any Schedule SSA reporting information with respect to the participant is required to be filed (including any extension of time for filing granted pursuant to section 6081).

(f) *Penalties.*—For amounts imposed in the case of failure to file the report of deferred vested retirement benefits required by section 6057(a) and paragraph (a) or (b) of this section, see section 6652(e)(1). For the penalty relating to a failure to provide the participant the individual statement of deferred vested retirement benefit required by section 6057(e) and paragraph (e) of this section, see section 6690.

(g) *Effective dates.*—(1) *Plans to which only one employer contributes.*—In the case of a plan to which only one employer contributes, this section is effective for plan years beginning after December 31, 1975, and with respect to a participant who separates from service covered by the plan in plan years beginning after that date.

(2) *Plans to which more than one employer contributes.*—In the case of a plan to which more than one employer contributes, this section is effective for plan years beginning after December 31, 1977, and with respect to a participant who completes two consecutive one-year breaks in service under the plan in service computation periods beginning after December 31, 1974. [Reg. § 301.6057-1.]

☐ [*T.D.* 7561, 8-24-78.]

### [Reg. § 301.6057-2]

**§ 301.6057-2. Employee retirement benefit plans; notification of change in plan status.**—(a) *Change in plan status.*—The plan administrator (within the meaning of section 414(g)) of an employee retirement benefit plan defined in § 301.6057-1(a)(3) (including a plan to which more than one employer contributes, as described in § 301.6057-1(b)(1)) must notify the Internal Revenue Service of the following changes in plan status—

(1) A change in the name of the plan,

(2) A change in the name or address of the plan administrator,

(3) The termination of the plan, or

(4) The merger or consolidation of the plan with another plan or the division of the plan into two or more plans.

(b) *Notification.*—A notification of a change in status described in paragraph (a) must be filed on the Annual Return/Report of Employee Benefit Plan (Form 5500 series) for the plan year in which the change in status occurred. The notification must be filed at the time and place and in the manner prescribed in the form and any accompanying instructions.

(c) *Penalty.*—For amounts imposed in the case of failure to file a notification of a change in plan status required by section 6057(b) and this section, see section 6652(e)(2).

(d) *Effective date.*—This section is effective for changes in plan status occurring within plan years beginning after December 31, 1975. [Reg. § 301.6057-2.]

☐ [*T.D.* 7561, 8-24-78.]

### [Reg. § 301.6057-3]

**§ 301.6057-3. Required use of magnetic media for filing requirements relating to deferred vested retirement benefit.**—(a) *Magnetic media filing requirements under section 6057.*—A registration statement required under section 6057(a) or a notification required under section 6057(b) with respect to an employee benefit plan must be filed on magnetic media if the filer is required by the Internal Revenue Code or regulations to file at least 250 returns during the calendar year that includes the first day of the plan year. Returns filed on magnetic media must be made in accordance with applicable revenue procedures, publications, forms, instructions, or other guidance on the IRS.gov Internet website. In prescribing revenue procedures, publications, forms, instructions, or other guidance on the IRS.gov Internet website, the Commissioner may direct the type of magnetic media filing. See § 601.601(d)(2)(ii)(*b*) of this chapter.

(b) *Economic hardship waiver.*—The Commissioner may waive the requirements of this section in cases of undue economic hardship. The principal factor in determining hardship will be the amount, if any, by which the cost of filing the registration statements or notifications on magnetic media in accordance with this section exceeds the cost of filing the registration statements or notifications on other media. A request for a waiver must be made in accordance with applicable published guidance, publications, forms, instructions, or other guidance on the IRS.gov Internet website. See § 601.601(d)(2)(ii)(*b*) of this chapter. The waiver will specify the type of filing (that is, a registration statement or notification under section 6057) and the period to which it applies. In addition, the waiver will be subject to such terms and conditions regarding the method of filing as may be prescribed by the Commissioner.

(c) *Failure to file.*—If a filer required to file a registration statement or other notification under section 6057 fails to file the statement or other notification on magnetic media when required to do so by this

section, the filer is deemed to have failed to file the statement or other notification. See section 6652(d) for the amount imposed for the failure to file a registration statement or other notification required under section 6057. In determining whether there is reasonable cause for the failure to file the registration statement or notification under section 6057, § 301.6652-3(b) and rules similar to the rules in § 301.6724-1(c)(3)(ii) (regarding undue economic hardship related to filing information returns on magnetic media) will apply.

(d) *Meaning of terms.*—The following definitions apply for purposes of this section.

(1) *Magnetic media.*—The term *magnetic media* means electronic filing, as well as other media specifically permitted under applicable regulations, revenue procedures, or publications, forms, instructions, or other guidance on the IRS.gov Internet website. See § 601.601(d)(2)(ii)(*b*) of this chapter.

(2) *Registration statement required under section 6057(a).*—The term *registration statement required under section 6057(a)* means a Form 8955-SSA (or its successor).

(3) *Notification required under section 6057(b).*—The term *notification required under section 6057(b)* means either a Form 8955-SSA (or its successor) or a return in the Form 5500 series (or its successor).

(4) *Determination of 250 returns.*—(i) *In general.*—For purposes of this section, a filer is required to file at least 250 returns if, during the calendar year that includes the first day of the plan year, the filer is required to file at least 250 returns of any type, including information returns (for example, Forms W-2 and Forms 1099), income tax returns, employment tax returns, and excise tax returns.

(ii) *Definition of filer.*—For purposes of this section, the term *filer* means the plan administrator within the meaning of section 414(g). If the plan administrator within the meaning of section 414(g) is the employer, the special rules in § 1.6058-2(d)(3)(iii) will apply.

(e) *Example.*—The following example illustrates the provisions of paragraph (d)(4) of this section:

*Example.* In 2015, P, the plan administrator of Plan B, is required to file 252 returns (including Forms 1099-R, "Distributions From Pensions, Annuities, Retirement or Profit-Sharing Plans, IRAs, Insurance Contracts, etc.;" Form 8955-SSA, "Annual Registration Statement Identifying Separated Participants with Deferred Vested Benefits;" Form 5500, "Annual Return/Report of Employee Benefit Plan;" and Form 945, "Annual Return of Withheld Federal Income Tax"). Plan B's plan year is the calendar year. Because P is required to file at least 250 returns during the 2015 calendar year, P must file the 2015 Form 8955-SSA for Plan B electronically.

(f) *Effective/applicability date.*—This section is applicable for registration statements and other notifications required to be filed under section 6057 for plan years that begin on or after January 1, 2014, but only for filings with a filing deadline (not taking into account extensions) on or after July 31, 2015. [Reg. § 301.6057-3.]

☐ [*T.D.* 9695, 9-26-2014.]

### [Reg. § 301.6058-1]

**§ 301.6058-1. Information required in connection with certain plans of deferred compensation.**—(a) *Reporting of information.*—(1) *Annual return.*—For each funded plan of deferred compensation an annual return must be filed with the Internal Revenue Service. The annual return of the plan is the appropriate Annual Return/Report of Employee Benefit Plan (Form 5500 series) as determined under these forms. The annual period for the annual return of the plan shall be either the plan year or the taxable year of the employer maintaining the plan as determined under these forms. These forms are hereinafter referred to as the "forms prescribed by section 6058(a)."

(2) *Plans subject to requirements.*—For purposes of this section, the term "funded plan of deferred compensation" means each pension, annuity, stock bonus, profit-sharing, or other funded plan of deferred compensation described in part 1 of subchapter D of chapter 1. Accordingly, the term includes qualified plans under sections 401(a), 403(a), and 405(a); individual retirement accounts and annuities described in sections 408(a) and 408(b); and custodial accounts under section 403(b)(7). The term also includes: funded plans of deferred compensation which are not qualified plans; funded governmental plans and church plans, whether or not qualified (See sections 414(d) and 414(e).); and plans maintained outside the United States primarily for nonresident aliens (as described in subsection (b)(4) of section 4 of Subtitle A of Title I of the Employee Retirement Income Security Act of 1974 (88 Stat. 840)). The term does not include annuity contracts described in section 403(b)(1) or individual retirement accounts (an individual participant or surviving beneficiary in

such account must file under paragraph (d)(2) of this section) and bonds described in sections 408(c) and 409.

(3) *Required information.*—The information required to be furnished on the forms prescribed by section 6058(a) shall include such information concerning the qualification of the plan, the financial condition of the trust, fund, or custodial or fiduciary account which is a part of the plan, and the operation of the plan as shall be required by the forms, applicable accompanying schedules and related instructions applicable to the annual period.

(4) *Time of filing.*—The forms prescribed by section 6058(a) shall be filed in the manner and at the time as required by the forms and related instructions applicable to the annual period.

(b) *Who must file.*—(1) *In general.*—The annual return required to be filed under section 6058(a) and paragraph (a) of this section for the annual period shall be filed by either the employer maintaining the plan or the plan administrator (as defined in section 414(g)) of the plan for that annual period. Whether the employer or plan administrator files shall be determined under the forms prescribed by section 6058(a) and related instructions applicable to the annual period. Nothing in these forms shall preclude an employer from filing the return on behalf of the plan administrator, or the plan administrator from filing on behalf of the employer.

(2) *Definition of employer.*—For purposes of subparagraph (1) of this paragraph, the term "employer" includes a sole proprietor and a partnership.

(c) *Other rules applicable to annual returns.*—(1) *Extensions of time for filing.*—For rules relating to the extension of time for filing, see section 6081 and the regulations thereunder and the instructions on the forms prescribed by section 6058(a).

(2) *Amended filing.*—Any form prescribed by this section may be filed as an amendment to a form previously filed under this section with respect to the same annual period pursuant to the instructions for such forms.

(3) *Additional information.*—In addition to the information otherwise required to be furnished by this section, the district director may require any further information that is considered necessary to determine allowable deductions under section 404, qualification under section 401, or the financial condition and operation of the plan.

(4) *Records.*—Records substantiating all data and information required by this section to be filed must be kept at all times available for inspection by internal revenue officers at the principal office or place of business of the employer or plan administrator.

(5) *Relief from filing.*—Notwithstanding paragraph (a) of this section, the Commissioner may, in his discretion, relieve an employer, or plan administrator, from reporting information on the forms prescribed by section 6058(a). This discretion includes the ability to relieve an employer, or plan administrator, from filing the applicable form.

(d) *Special rules for individual retirement arrangements.*—(1) *Application.*—This paragraph, in lieu of paragraph (a) of this section, applies to an individual retirement account described in section 408(a) and an individual retirement annuity described in section 408(b), including such accounts and annuities for which a deduction is allowable under section 220 (spousal individual retirement arrangements).

(2) *General rule.*—For each taxable year beginning after December 31, 1974, every individual who during such taxable year—

(i) Establishes or maintains an individual retirement account described in section 408(a) (including an individual who is a participant in an individual retirement account described in section 408(c)),

(ii) Purchases or maintains an individual retirement annuity described in section 408(b), or

(iii) Is a surviving beneficiary with respect to an account or annuity referred to in this subparagraph which is in existence during such taxable year, shall file Form 5329 (or any other form designated by the Commissioner for this purpose), as an attachment to or part of the Form 1040 filed by such individual for such taxable year, setting forth in full the information required by that form and the accompanying instructions.

(3) *Special information returns.*—If an individual described in subparagraph (2) of this paragraph is not required to file a Form 1040 for such taxable year, such individual shall file a Form 5329 (or any other designated form) with the Internal Revenue Service by the 15th day of the 4th month following the close of such individual's taxable year setting forth in full the information required by that form and the accompanying instructions.

(4) *Relief from filing.*—The Commissioner may, in his discretion, relieve an individual from filing the form prescribed by this paragraph.

(5) *Retirement bonds.*—An individual who purchases, holds, or maintains a retirement bond described in section 409 may be required to file a return under other provisions of the Code.

(e) *Actuarial statement in case of mergers, etc.*—For requirements with respect to the filing of actuarial statements in the case of a merger, consolidation, or transfer of assets or liabilities, see section 6058(b) and section 414(1) and the regulations thereunder.

(f) *Effective dates.*—(1) *Section 6058(a) requirements.*—The rules with respect to annual returns required under section 6058(a) (the rules in this section, other than paragraph (e) thereof) are effective for plan years beginning after September 2, 1974.

(2) *Section 6058(b) requirements.*—The requirements of section 6058(b) relating to mergers, etc., and paragraph (e) of this section are effective on September 2, 1974, with respect to events described in section 6058(b) occurring on or after such date. [Reg. § 301.6058-1.]

☐ [*T.D.* 7551, 7-3-78.]

### [Reg. § 301.6058-2]

**§ 301.6058-2. Required use of magnetic media for filing requirements relating to information required in connection with certain plans of deferred compensation.**—(a) *Magnetic media filing requirements under section 6058.*—A return required under section 6058 with respect to an employee benefit plan must be filed on magnetic media if the filer is required by the Internal Revenue Code or regulations to file at least 250 returns during the calendar year that includes the first day of the plan year. Returns filed on magnetic media must be made in accordance with applicable revenue procedures, publications, forms, instructions, or other guidance on the IRS.gov Internet website. In prescribing revenue procedures, publications, forms, and instructions, or other guidance on the IRS.gov Internet site, the Commissioner may direct the type of magnetic media filing. See § 601.601(d)(2)(ii)(*b*) of this chapter.

(b) *Economic hardship waiver.*—The Commissioner may waive the requirements of this section in cases of undue economic hardship. The principal factor in determining hardship will be the amount, if any, by which the cost of filing the return on magnetic media in accordance with this section exceeds the cost of filing the returns on other media. A request for a waiver must be made in accordance with applicable published guidance, publications, forms, instructions, or other guidance on the IRS.gov Internet website. See § 601.601(d)(2)(ii)(*b*) of this chapter. The waiver will specify the type of filing (that is, a return required under section 6058) and the period to which it applies. In addition, the waiver will be subject to such terms and conditions regarding the method of filing as may be prescribed by the Commissioner.

(c) *Failure to file.*—If a filer required to file a return under section 6058 fails to file the return on magnetic media when required to do so by this section, the filer is deemed to have failed to file the return. See section 6652(e) for the amount imposed for the failure to file a return required under section 6058. In determining whether there is reasonable cause for failure to file the return, § 301.6652-3(b) and rules similar to the rules in § 301.6724-1(c)(3)(ii) (regarding undue economic hardship related to filing information returns on magnetic media) will apply.

(d) *Meaning of terms.*—The following definitions apply for purposes of this section.

(1) *Magnetic media.*—The term *magnetic media* means electronic filing, as well as other media specifically permitted under applicable regulations, revenue procedures, or publications, forms, instructions, or other guidance on the IRS.gov Internet website. See § 601.601(d)(2)(ii)(*b*) of this chapter.

(2) *Return required under section 6058.*—The term *return required under section 6058* means a return in the Form 5500 series (or its successor).

(3) *Determination of 250 returns.*—(i) *In general.*—For purposes of this section, a filer is required to file at least 250 returns if, during the calendar year that includes the first day of the plan year, the filer is required to file at least 250 returns of any type, including information returns (for example, Forms W-2 and Forms 1099), income tax returns, employment tax returns, and excise tax returns.

(ii) *Definition of filer.*—For purposes of this section, the term *filer* means the employer or employers maintaining the plan and the plan administrator within the meaning of section 414(g).

(iii) *Special rules relating to determining 250 returns.*—For purposes of applying paragraph (d)(3)(ii) of this section, the aggregation rules of section 414(b), (c), (m), and (o) will apply to a filer that is or includes an employer. Thus, for example, a filer that is a member of a controlled group of corporations within the meaning of section 414(b) must file the Form 5500 series on magnetic media if the aggregate number of returns required to be filed by all members of the controlled group of corporations is at least 250.

(e) *Example.*—The following example illustrates the provisions of paragraph (d)(3) of this section:

*Example.* In 2016 Employer X (the plan sponsor of Plan A) and P (the plan administrator of Plan A) are required to file 267 returns. Employer X is required to file the following: one Form 1120, "U.S. Corporation Income Tax Return;" 195 Forms W-2, "Wage and Tax Statement;" 25 Forms 1099-DIV, "Dividends and Distributions;" one Form 940, "Employer's Annual Federal Unemployment (FUTA) Tax Return;" and four Forms 941, "Employer's Quarterly Federal Tax Return." P is required to file 40 Forms 1099-R, "Distributions From Pensions, Annuities, Retirement, Profit-Sharing Plans, IRAs, Insurance Contracts, etc." P and Employer X are jointly required to file one Form 5500 series return. Plan A's plan year is the calendar year. Because P and Employer X, in the aggregate, are required to file at least 250 returns during the calendar year, the 2016 Form 5500 for Plan A must be filed electronically.

(f) *Effective/applicability date.*—This section is applicable for returns required to be filed under section 6058 for plan years that begin on or after January 1, 2015, but only for filings with a filing deadline (not taking into account extensions) after December 31, 2015. [Reg. §301.6058-2.]

☐ [T.D. 9695, 9-26-2014.]

**[Reg. §301.6059-1]**

**§301.6059-1. Periodic report of actuary.**—(a) *In general.*—The actuarial report described in this section must be filed on behalf of a defined benefit plan to which the minimum funding standards of section 412 apply. The actuarial report must be filed by the plan administrator (within the meaning of section 414(g)) on Schedule B as an attachment to the annual Return/Report of Employee Benefit Plan (Form 5500 series). The instructions accompanying the Form 5500 series prescribe the place and date for filing Schedule B.

(b) *Plan years for which report required.*—In the case of a plan in existence on January 1, 1974, Schedule B must be filed for the first plan year beginning after December 31, 1975, for which the minimum funding standards apply to the plan, and for each plan year thereafter for which the Schedule must be filed under the instructions accompanying the Schedule and the Form 5500 series. In the case of a plan not in existence on January 1, 1974, Schedule B must be filed for the first plan year beginning after September 2, 1974, for which the minimum funding standards apply to the plan, and for each plan year thereafter for which the Schedule must be filed under the instructions accompanying the Schedule and the Form 5500 series. For rules relating to when a plan is considered to be in existence, see §1.410(a)-2(c). For purposes of this section, "plan year" means the plan year as determined for purposes of the minimum funding standards.

(c) *Contents of report.*—The actuarial report of a plan filed on Schedule B must contain—

(1) The date of the actuarial valuation applicable to the plan year for which the report is filed (see section 412(c)(9) for rules relating to the frequency with which an actuarial valuation of the plan is required to be made),

(2) A description of the funding method and actuarial assumptions used to determine costs under the plan,

(3) A certification of the contribution necessary to reduce the accumulated funding deficiency (as defined in section 412(a)) to zero,

(4) A statement by the enrolled actuary signing the report that to the best of the actuary's knowledge the report is complete and accurate,

(5) A statement by the enrolled actuary signing the report that in the actuary's opinion, the actuarial assumptions used are in the aggregate (i) reasonably related to the experience under the plan and to reasonable expectations, and (ii) represent the actuary's best estimate of anticipated experience under the plan,

(6) Such other information as may be necessary to fully and fairly disclose the actuarial position of the plan, and

(7) Such other information as may be required by Schedule B or the instructions accompanying the Schedule and the Form 5500 series.

(d) *Certification by enrolled actuary.*—The actuarial report filed on Schedule B must be signed by an enrolled actuary (within the meaning of section 7701(a)(35)) or there may be attached to the report a statement signed by the actuary that contains the statements described in paragraph (d)(1)(v) and paragraph (c)(4) and (5) of this section.

An actuarial report filed for a plan year ending after January 25, 1982, does not satisfy the requirements of this section if the actuary seeks to materially qualify such statements. For this purpose, the following are not considered to materially qualify a statement required by paragraph (c)(4) or (5) of this section:

(1) A statement that the report is based in part on information provided to the actuary by another person, that such information would customarily not be verified by the actuary, and that the actuary has no reason to doubt the substantial accuracy of the information (taking into account the facts and circumstances that are known or reasonably should be known to the actuary, including the contents of any other actuarial report prepared by the actuary for the plan),

(2) A statement that the report is based in part on information provided by another person, that the actuary believes such information is or may be inaccurate or incomplete, but that the inaccuracies or omissions are not material, the inaccuracies or omissions are not so numerous or flagrant as to suggest that there may be material inaccuracies, and that therefore the actuarial report is substantially accurate and complete and fairly discloses the actuarial position of the plan,

(3) A statement that the report reflects the requirement of a regulation or ruling, and that any statement regarding the actuarial position of the plan is made only in light of such requirement,

(4) A statement that the report reflects an interpretation of a statute, regulation or ruling, that the actuary has no reason to doubt the validity of that interpretation, and that any statement regarding the actuarial position of the plan is made only in light of such interpretation,

(5) A statement that in the opinion of the actuary the report fully reflects the requirements of an applicable statute, but does not conform to the requirements of a regulation or ruling promulgated under the statute that the actuary believes is contrary to the statute, or

(6) A statement reflecting the requirements of paragraph (c)(6) of this section.

A statement otherwise described in a subparagraph of this paragraph (d) shall not be considered to satisfy the requirements of such subparagraph unless the statement identifies, with particularity, that matter to which the statement relates and the facts and circumstances surrounding the statement. In addition, a statement otherwise described in subparagraph (5) of this paragraph (d) shall not be considered to satisfy the requirements of that subparagraph unless the statement indicates whether an accumulated funding deficiency or a contribution that is not wholly deductible may result if the actuary's belief is determined to be incorrect.

(e) *Relief from filing.*—Notwithstanding paragraph (a) of this section, the Commissioner may, in the Commissioner's discretion, relieve a plan administrator from filing Schedule B or from reporting information required by Schedule B or paragraph (c) of this section.

(f) *Penalty.*—For the penalty imposed in the case of a failure to file the actuarial report required by this section, see section 6692 and §301.6692-1. [Reg. §301.6059-1.]

☐ [T.D. 7798, 11-23-81.]

**[Reg. §301.6059-2]**

**§301.6059-2. Required use of magnetic media for filing requirements relating to periodic report of actuary.**—(a) *Magnetic media filing requirements under section 6059.*—An actuarial report required under section 6059 with respect to an employee benefit plan must be filed on magnetic media if the filer is required by the Internal Revenue Code or regulations to file at least 250 returns during the calendar year that includes the first day of the plan year. Actuarial reports filed on magnetic media must be made in accordance with applicable revenue procedures, publications, forms, instructions, or other guidance on the IRS.gov Internet website. In prescribing revenue procedures, publications, forms, instructions, or other guidance on the IRS.gov Internet website, the Commissioner may direct the type of magnetic media filing. See §601.601(d)(2)(ii)(*b*) of this chapter.

(b) *Economic hardship waiver.*—The Commissioner may waive the requirements of this section in cases of undue economic hardship. The principal factor in determining hardship will be the amount, if any, by which the cost of filing the reports on magnetic media in accordance with this section exceeds the cost of filing the reports on other media. A request for a waiver must be made in accordance with applicable published guidance, publications, forms, instructions, or other guidance on the IRS.gov Internet website. See §601.601(d)(2)(ii)(*b*) of this chapter. The waiver will specify the type of filing (that is, an actuarial report required under section 6059) and the period to which it applies. In addition, the waiver will be subject to such terms and conditions regarding the method of filing as may be prescribed by the Commissioner.

(c) *Failure to file.*—If a filer required to file an actuarial report under section 6059 fails to file the report on magnetic media when required to do so by this section, the filer is deemed to have failed to file the report. See section 6692 for the penalty for the failure to file an actuarial report. In determining whether there is reasonable cause for failure to file the report, § 301.6692-1(c) and rules similar to the rules in § 301.6724-1(c)(3)(ii) (regarding undue economic hardship related to filing information returns on magnetic media) will apply.

(d) *Meaning of terms.*—The following definitions apply for purposes of this section.

(1) *Magnetic media.*—The term *magnetic media* means electronic filing, as well as other media specifically permitted under applicable regulations, revenue procedures, or publications, forms, instructions, or other guidance on the IRS.gov Internet website. See § 601.601(d)(2)(ii)(*b*) of this chapter.

(2) *Actuarial report required under section 6059.*—(i) *Single employer plans.*—For a single employer plan, the term *actuarial report required under section 6059* means the Schedule SB, "Single-Employer Defined Benefit Plan Actuarial Information," of the Form 5500 series (or its successor).

(ii) *Multiemployer and certain money purchase plans.*—For multiemployer and certain money purchase plans, the term *actuarial report required under section 6059* means the Schedule MB, "Multiemployer Defined Benefit Plan and Certain Money Purchase Plan Actuarial Information," of the Form 5500 series (or its successor).

(3) *Determination of 250 returns.*—(i) *In general.*—For purposes of this section, a filer is required to file at least 250 returns if, during the calendar year that includes the first day of the plan year, the filer is required to file at least 250 returns of any type, including information returns (for example, Forms W-2 and Forms 1099), income tax returns, employment tax returns, and excise tax returns.

(ii) *Definition of filer.*—For purposes of this section, the term *filer* means the plan administrator within the meaning of section 414(g). If the plan administrator within the meaning of section 414(g) is the employer, the special rules in § 1.6058-2(d)(3)(iii) will apply.

(e) *Example.*—The following example illustrates the provisions of paragraph (d)(3) of this section:

*Example.* In 2016, P, the plan administrator of Plan B (a single employer defined benefit plan), is required to file 266 returns (including Forms 1099-R "Distributions From Pensions, Annuities, Retirement, Profit-Sharing Plans, IRAs, Insurance Contracts, etc." and one Form 5500 series). Plan B's plan year is the calendar year. Because P is required to file at least 250 returns during the calendar year, P must file the 2016 Schedule SB of the Form 5500 series return for Plan B electronically.

(f) *Effective/ applicability date.*—This section is applicable for actuarial reports required to be filed under section 6059 for plan years that begin on or after January 1, 2015, but only for filings with a filing deadline (not taking into account extensions) after December 31, 2015. [Reg. § 301.6059-2.]

☐ [*T.D. 9695, 9-26-2014.*]

### [Reg. § 1.6060-1]

**§ 1.6060-1. Reporting requirements for tax return preparers.—** (a) *In general.*—(1) Each person who employs one or more signing tax return preparers to prepare any return of tax or claim for refund of tax, other than for the person, at any time during a return period shall satisfy the requirements of section 6060 of the Internal Revenue Code by—

(i) Retaining a record of the name, taxpayer identification number, and principal place of work during the return period of each tax return preparer employed by the person at any time during that period; and

(ii) Making that record available for inspection upon request by the Commissioner.

(2) The record described in this paragraph (a) must be retained and kept available for inspection for the 3-year period following the close of the return period to which that record relates.

(3) The person may choose any form of documentation to be used under this section as a record of the signing tax return preparers employed during a return period. The record, however, must disclose on its face which individuals were employed as tax return preparers during that period.

(4) For the definition of the term "signing tax return preparer", see § 301.7701-15(b)(1) of this chapter. For the definition of the term "return period", see paragraph (b) of this section.

(5)(i) For purposes of this section, any individual who, in acting as a signing tax return preparer, is not employed by another tax return preparer shall be treated as his or her own employer. Thus, a sole proprietor shall retain and make available a record with respect to himself (or herself) as provided in this section.

(ii) A partnership shall, for purposes of this section, be treated as the employer of the partners of the partnership and shall retain and make available a record with respect to the partners and others employed by the partnership as provided in this section.

(b) *Return period defined.*—For purposes of this section, the term "return period" means the 12-month period beginning on July 1 of each year.

(c) *Penalty.*—For the civil penalty for failure to retain and make available a record of the tax return preparers employed during a return period as required under this section, or for failure to include an item in the record required to be retained and made available under this section, see § 1.6695-1(e).

(d) *Effective/applicability date.*—This section is applicable to returns and claims for refund filed after December 31, 2008. [Reg. § 1.6060-1.]

☐ [*T.D. 7519, 11-17-77. Amended by T.D. 7640, 8-22-79 and T.D. 9436, 12-15-2008.*]

### [Reg. § 20.6060-1]

**§ 20.6060-1. Reporting requirements for tax return preparers.—** (a) *In general.*—A person that employs one or more tax return preparers to prepare a return or claim for refund of estate tax under chapter 11 of subtitle B of the Internal Revenue Code, other than for the person, at any time during a return period, shall satisfy the recordkeeping and inspection requirements in the manner stated in § 1.6060-1 of this chapter.

(b) *Effective/applicability date.*—This section is applicable to returns and claims for refund filed after December 31, 2008. [Reg. § 20.6060-1.]

☐ [*T.D. 9436, 12-15-2008.*]

### [Reg. § 25.6060-1]

**§ 25.6060-1. Reporting requirements for tax return preparers.—** (a) *In general.*—A person that employs one or more tax return preparers to prepare a return or claim for refund of gift tax under chapter 12 of subtitle B of the Internal Revenue Code, other than for the person, at any time during a return period, shall satisfy the record keeping and inspection requirements in the manner stated in § 1.6060-1 of this chapter.

(b) *Effective/applicability date.*—This section is applicable to returns and claims for refund filed after December 31, 2008. [Reg. § 25.6060-1.]

☐ [*T.D. 9436, 12-15-2008.*]

### [Reg. § 26.6060-1]

**§ 26.6060-1. Reporting requirements for tax return preparers.—** (a) *In general.*—A person that employs one or more tax return preparers to prepare a return or claim for refund of generation-skipping transfer tax under chapter 13 of subtitle B of the Internal Revenue Code, other than for the person, at any time during a return period, shall satisfy the record keeping and inspection requirements in the manner stated in § 1.6060-1 of this chapter.

(b) *Effective/applicability date.*—This section is applicable to returns and claims for refund filed after December 31, 2008. [Reg. § 26.6060-1.]

☐ [*T.D. 9436, 12-15-2008.*]

### [Reg. § 31.6060-1]

**§ 31.6060-1. Reporting requirements for tax return preparers.—** (a) *In general.*—A person that employs one or more tax return preparers to prepare a return or claim for refund of employment tax under chapters 21 through 25 of subtitle C of the Internal Revenue Code, other than for the person, at any time during a return period, shall satisfy the record keeping and inspection requirements in the manner stated in § 1.6060-1 of this chapter.

(b) *Effective/applicability date.*—This section is applicable to returns and claims for refund filed after December 31, 2008. [Reg. § 31.6060-1.]

☐ [*T.D. 9436, 12-15-2008.*]

**[Reg. §40.6060-1]**

**§40.6060-1. Reporting requirements for tax return preparers.—**
(a) *In general.*—A person that employs one or more tax return preparers to prepare a return or claim for refund of any tax to which this part 40 applies other than for the person, at any time during a return period, shall satisfy the recordkeeping and inspection requirements in the manner stated in §1.6060-1 of this chapter.

(b) *Effective/applicability date.*—This section is applicable to returns and claims for refund filed after December 31, 2008. [Reg. §40.6060-1.]

☐ [*T.D.* 9436, 12-15-2008 (*corrected* 1-28-2009).]

**[Reg. §41.6060-1]**

**§41.6060-1. Reporting requirements for tax return preparers.—**
(a) *In general.*—A person that employs one or more tax return preparers to prepare a return or claim for refund of excise tax under section 4481, other than for the person, at any time during a return period, shall satisfy the record keeping and inspection requirements in the manner stated in §1.6060-1 of this chapter.

(b) *Effective/applicability date.*—This section is applicable for returns and claims for refund filed after December 31, 2008. [Reg. §41.6060-1.]

☐ [*T.D.* 9436, 12-15-2008.]

**[Reg. §44.6060-1]**

**§44.6060-1. Reporting requirements for tax return preparers.—**
(a) *In general.*—A person that employs one or more tax return preparers to prepare a return or claim for refund of tax on wagers under sections 4401 or 4411, other than for the person, at any time during a return period, shall satisfy the record keeping and inspection requirements in the manner stated in §1.6060-1 of this chapter.

(b) *Effective/applicability date.*—This section is applicable to returns and claims for refund filed after December 31, 2008. [Reg. §44.6060-1.]

☐ [*T.D.* 9436, 12-15-2008.]

**[Reg. §53.6060-1]**

**§53.6060-1. Reporting requirements for tax return preparers.—**
(a) *In general.*—A person that employs one or more tax return preparers to prepare a return or claim for refund of tax under Chapter 42 of the Internal Revenue Code, other than for the person, at any time during a return period, shall satisfy the record keeping and inspection requirements in the manner stated in §1.6060-1 of this chapter.

(b) *Effective/applicability date.*—This section is applicable to returns and claims for refund filed after December 31, 2008. [Reg. §53.6060-1.]

☐ [*T.D.* 9436, 12-15-2008.]

**[Reg. §54.6060-1]**

**§54.6060-1. Reporting requirements for tax return preparers.—**
(a) *In general.*—A person that employs one or more tax return preparers to prepare a return or claim for refund under Chapter 43 of subtitle D of the Internal Revenue Code, other than for the person, at any time during a return period, shall satisfy the record keeping and inspection requirements in the manner stated in §1.6060-1 of this chapter.

(b) *Effective/applicability date.*—This section is applicable to returns and claims for refund filed after December 31, 2008. [Reg. §54.6060-1.]

☐ [*T.D.* 9436, 12-15-2008.]

**[Reg. §55.6060-1]**

**§55.6060-1. Reporting requirements for tax return preparers.—**
(a) *In general.*—A person that employs one or more tax return preparers to prepare a return or claim for refund under chapter 44 of subtitle D of the Internal Revenue Code, other than for the person, at any time during a return period, shall satisfy the record keeping and inspection requirements in the manner stated in §1.6060-1 of this chapter.

(b) *Effective/applicability date.*—This section is applicable to returns and claims for refund filed after December 31, 2008. [Reg. §55.6060-1.]

☐ [*T.D.* 9436, 12-15-2008.]

**[Reg. §56.6060-1]**

**§56.6060-1. Reporting requirements for tax return preparers.—**
(a) *In general.*—A person that employs one or more tax return preparers to prepare a return or claim for refund of tax under chapter 41 of subtitle D of the Internal Revenue Code, other than for the person, at any time during a return period, shall satisfy the record keeping and inspection requirements in the manner stated in §1.6060-1 of this chapter.

(b) *Effective/applicability date.*—This section is applicable to returns and claims for refund filed after December 31, 2008. [Reg. §56.6060-1.]

☐ [*T.D.* 9436, 12-15-2008.]

**[Reg. §156.6060-1]**

**§156.6060-1. Reporting requirements for tax return preparers.—**
(a) *In general.*—A person that employs one or more tax return preparers to prepare a return or claim for refund under section 5881 of the Internal Revenue Code, other than for the person, at any time during a return period, shall satisfy the record keeping and inspection requirements in the manner stated in §1.6060-1 of this chapter.

(b) *Effective/applicability date.*—This section is applicable to returns and claims for refund filed after December 31, 2008. [Reg. §156.6060-1.]

☐ [*T.D.* 9436, 12-15-2008.]

**[Reg. §157.6060-1]**

**§157.6060-1. Reporting requirements for tax return preparers.—**
(a) *In general.*—A person that employs one or more tax return preparers to prepare a return or claim for refund for tax under section 5891 of the Internal Revenue Code, other than for the person, at any time during a return period, shall satisfy the record keeping and inspection requirements in the manner stated in §1.6060-1 of this chapter.

(b) *Effective/applicability date.*—This section is applicable to returns and claims for refund filed after December 31, 2008. [Reg. §157.6060-1.]

☐ [*T.D.* 9436, 12-15-2008.]

# Signing and Verifying of Returns and Other Documents

**[Reg. §1.6061-1]**

**§1.6061-1. Signing of returns and other documents by individuals.—**(a) *Requirement.*—Each individual (including a fiduciary) shall sign the income tax return required to be made by him, except that the return may be signed for the taxpayer by an agent who is duly authorized in accordance with paragraph (a)(5) or (b) of §1.6012-1 to make such return. Other returns, statements, or documents required under the provisions of subtitle A or F of the Code or of the regulations thereunder to be made by any person with respect to any tax imposed by subtitle A of the Code shall be signed in accordance with any regulations contained in this chapter, or any instructions, issued with respect to such returns, statements, or other documents.

(b) *Cross references.*—For provisions relating to the signing of returns, statements, or other documents required to be made by corporations and partnerships with respect to any tax imposed by subtitle A of the Code, see §§1.6062-1 and 1.6063-1, respectively. For provisions relating to the making of returns by agents, see paragraphs (a)(5) and (b) of §1.6012-1; and to the making of returns for minors and persons under a disability, see paragraph (a)(4) of §1.6012-1 and paragraph (b) of §1.6012-3. [Reg. §1.6061-1.]

☐ [*T.D.* 6364, 2-13-59. *Amended by T.D.* 7332, 12-20-74.]

**[Reg. §20.6061-1]**

**§20.6061-1. Signing of returns and other documents.—**Any return, statement, or other document required to be made under any provision of chapter 11 of subtitle F of the Code or regulations prescribed thereunder with respect to any tax imposed by chapter 11 of the Code shall be signed by the executor, administrator or other person required or duly authorized to sign in accordance with the regulations, forms or instructions prescribed with respect to such return, statement, or other document. See §20.2203 for definition of executor, administrator, etc. The person required or duly authorized to make the return may incur liability for the penalties provided for erroneous, false, or fraudulent returns. For criminal penalties see sections 7201, 7203, 7206, 7207, and 7269. [Reg. §20.6061-1.]

☐ *[T.D. 6600, 5-28-62.]*

### [Reg. §25.6061-1]

**§25.6061-1. Signing of returns and other documents.**—Any return, statement, or other document required to be made under any provision of chapter 12 or subtitle F of the Code or regulations prescribed thereunder with respect to any tax imposed by chapter 12 of the Code shall be signed by the donor or other person required or duly authorized to sign in accordance with the regulations, forms or instructions prescribed with respect to such return, statement, or other document. The person required or duly authorized to make the return may incur liability for the penalties provided for erroneous, false, or fraudulent returns. For criminal penalties see sections 7201, 7203, 7206, 7207, and 7269. [Reg. §25.6061-1.]

☐ *[T.D. 6600, 5-28-62.]*

### [Reg. §31.6061-1]

**§31.6061-1. Signing of returns.**—Each return required under the regulations in this subpart shall, if signature is called for by the form or instructions relating to the return, be signed by (a) the individual, if the person required to make the return is an individual; (b) the president, vice president, or other principal officer, if the person required to make the return is a corporation; (c) a responsible and duly authorized member or officer having knowledge of its affairs, if the person required to make the return is a partnership or other unincorporated organization; or (d) the fiduciary, if the person required to make the return is a trust or estate. The return may be signed for the taxpayer by an agent who is duly authorized in accordance with §31.6011(a)-7 to make such return. [Reg. §31.6061-1.]

☐ *[T.D. 6472, 6-22-60.]*

### [Reg. §53.6061-1]

**§53.6061-1. Signing of returns and other documents.**—Any return, statement, or other document required to be made with respect to a tax imposed by chapter 42 or the regulations thereunder shall be signed by the person required to file such return, statement or document, or by such other persons required or duly authorized to sign in accordance with the regulations, forms or instructions prescribed with respect to such return, statement or other document. The person required or duly authorized to make the return may incur liability for penalties provided for erroneous, false or fraudulent returns. For criminal penalties see sections 7201, 7203, 7206, and 7207. [Reg. §53.6061-1.]

☐ *[T.D. 7368, 7-15-75.]*

### [Reg. §54.6061-1]

**§54.6061-1. Signing of returns and other documents.**—Effective for any Form 8928 that is due on or after January 1, 2010, any return, statement, or other document required to be made with respect to a tax imposed by section 4980B, 4980D, 4980E, or 4980G of the Code or the regulations under section 4980B, 4980D, 4980E, or 4980G must be signed by the person required to file the return, statement, or other document, or by the persons required or duly authorized to sign in accordance with the regulations, forms, or instructions prescribed with respect to such return, statement, or document. An individual's signature on such return, statement, or other document shall be prima facie evidence that the individual is authorized to sign the return, statement, or other document. [Reg. §54.6061-1.]

☐ *[T.D. 9457, 9-4-2009.]*

### [Reg. §55.6061-1]

**§55.6061-1. Signing of returns and other documents.**—Any return required to be made by a real estate investment trust or a regulated investment company with respect to the tax imposed by chapter 44 shall be signed by a person authorized by section 6062 of the Code to sign the income tax return of the real estate investment trust or the regulated investment company. Any statement or other document required to be made with respect to the tax imposed by chapter 44 shall be signed by the person required or duly authorized to sign in accordance with the regulations, forms, or instructions prescribed with respect to such statement or document. An individual's signature on a return, statement, or other document made by or for the real estate investment trust or the regulated investment company shall be prima facie evidence that the individual is authorized to sign the return, statement, or other document. [Reg. §55.6061-1.]

☐ *[T.D. 7767, 2-3-81. Amended by T.D. 8180, 2-29-88.]*

### [Reg. §156.6061-1]

**§156.6061-1. Signing of returns and other documents.**—Any return, statement, or other document required to be made with respect to a tax imposed by chapter 54 (Greenmail) of the Code or the

regulations thereunder shall be signed by the person required to file the return, statement, or other document, or by the persons required or duly authorized to sign in accordance with the regulations, forms, or instructions prescribed with respect to such return, statement, or document. An individual's signature on such a return, statement, or other document shall be prima facie evidence that the individual is authorized to sign the return, statement, or other document. [Reg. §156.6061-1.]

☐ *[T.D. 8379, 12-17-91.]*

### [Reg. §157.6061-1]

**§157.6061-1. Signing of returns and other documents.**—Any return, statement, or other document required to be made with respect to a tax imposed by chapter 55 (Structured Settlement Factoring Transactions) of the Internal Revenue Code or the regulations under chapter 55 must be signed by the person required to file the return, statement, or other document, or by the persons required or duly authorized to sign in accordance with the regulations, forms, or instructions prescribed with respect to such return, statement, or document. An individual's signature on such return, statement, or other document shall be prima facie evidence that the individual is authorized to sign the return, statement, or other document. [Reg. §157.6061-1.]

☐ *[T.D. 9134, 7-7-2004.]*

### [Reg. §301.6061-1]

**§301.6061-1. Signing of returns and other documents.**—(a) *In general.*—For provisions concerning the signing of returns and other documents, see the regulations relating to the particular tax.

(b) *Method of signing.*—The Secretary may prescribe in forms, instructions, or other appropriate guidance the method of signing any return, statement, or other document required to be made under any provision of the internal revenue laws or regulations.

(c) *Effective dates.*—The rule in paragraph (a) is effective December 12, 1996. The rule in paragraph (b) is effective on July 21, 1995. [Reg. §301.6061-1.]

☐ *[T.D. 6498, 10-24-60. Amended by T.D. 8689, 12-11-96.]*

### [Reg. §1.6062-1]

**§1.6062-1. Signing of returns, statements, and other documents made by corporations.**—(a) *Returns.*—(1) *In general.*—Returns required to be made by corporations under the provisions of subtitle A or F of the Code, or the regulations thereunder, with respect to any tax imposed by subtitle A of the Code, shall be signed for the corporation by the president, vice-president, treasurer, assistant treasurer, chief accounting officer, or any other officer duly authorized to sign such returns. It is not necessary that the corporate seal be affixed to the return. Spaces provided on return forms for affixing the corporate seal are for the convenience of corporations required by charter, or by the law of the jurisdiction in which they are incorporated, to affix their corporate seals in the execution of instruments.

(2) *By fiduciaries.*—A return with respect to income required to be made for a corporation by a fiduciary, pursuant to the provisions of section 6012(b)(3), shall be signed by such fiduciary. See paragraph (b)(4) of §1.6012-3.

(3) *By agents.*—A return with respect to income required to be made by an agent for a foreign corporation shall be signed by such agent. See paragraph (g) of §1.6012-2.

(b) *Statements and other documents.*—Statements and other documents required to be made by or for corporations under the provisions of subtitle A or F of the Code, or the regulations thereunder, with respect to any tax imposed by subtitle A, shall be signed in accordance with the regulations contained in this chapter, or the forms and instructions, issued with respect to such statements or other documents.

(c) *Evidence of authority to sign.*—An individual's signature on a return, statement, or other document made by or for a corporation shall be prima facie evidence that such individual is authorized to sign such return, statement, or other document.

(d) *Related provisions.*—For the rules relating to the verification of returns, see §1.6065-1. [Reg. §1.6062-1.]

☐ *[T.D. 6364, 2-13-59. Amended by T.D. 6455, 3-1-60 and T.D. 7293, 11-27-73.]*

### [Reg. §301.6062-1]

**§301.6062-1. Signing of corporation returns.**—For provisions relating to the signing of corporation income tax returns, see §1.6062-1 of this chapter (Income Tax Regulations). [Reg. §301.6062-1.]

☐ [*T.D.* 6498, 10-24-60.]

### [Reg. §1.6063-1]

**§1.6063-1. Signing of returns, statements, and other documents made by partnerships.**—(a) *In general.*—Returns, statements, and other documents required to be made by partnerships under the provisions of subtitle A or F of the Code, or the regulations thereunder, with respect to any tax imposed by subtitle A of the Code shall be signed by any one of the partners. However, with respect to the signing of powers of attorney, see paragraph (a)(2) of §601.504 of this chapter (Statement of Procedural Rules).

(b) *Evidence of authority to sign.*—A partner's signature on a return, statement, or other document made by or for a partnership of which he is a member shall be prima facie evidence that such partner is authorized to sign such return, statement, or other document.

(c) *Certain partnership elections.*—(1) *In general.*—For rules regarding the authority of a partner to sign a partnership return filed solely for the purpose of making certain partnership-level elections, see §1.6031(a)-1(b)(5)(ii).

(2) *Effective date.*—Paragraph (c) of this section applies to taxable years of a partnership beginning after December 31, 1999. [Reg. §1.6063-1.]

☐ [*T.D.* 6498, 10-24-60. *Amended by T.D.* 8841, 11-10-99.]

### [Reg. §301.6063-1]

**§301.6063-1. Signing of partnership returns.**—For provisions relating to the signing of returns of partnership income, see §1.6063-1 of this chapter (Income Tax Regulations). [Reg. §301.6063-1.]

☐ [*T.D.* 6498, 10-24-60.]

### [Reg. §301.6064-1]

**§301.6064-1. Signature presumed authentic.**—An individual's name signed to a return, statement, or other document shall be prima facie evidence for all purposes that the return, statement, or other document was actually signed by him. [Reg. §301.6064-1.]

☐ [*T.D.* 6498, 10-24-60.]

### [Reg. §1.6065-1]

**§1.6065-1. Verification of returns.**—(a) *Persons signing returns.*—If a return, declaration, statement, or other document made under the provisions of subtitle A or F of the Code, or the regulation thereunder, with respect to any tax imposed by subtitle A of the Code is required by the regulations contained in this chapter, or the form and instructions, issued with respect to such return, declaration, statement, or other document, to contain or be verified by a written declaration that it is made under the penalties of perjury, such return, declaration, statement, or other document shall be so verified by the person signing it.

(b) *Persons preparing returns.*—(1) *In general.*—Except as provided in subparagraph (2) of this paragraph, if a return, declaration, statement, or other document is prepared for a taxpayer by another person for compensation or as an incident to the performance of other services for which such person receives compensation, and the return, declaration, statement, or other document requires that it shall contain or be verified by a written declaration that it is prepared under the penalties of perjury, the preparer must so verify the return, declaration, statement, or other document. A person who renders mere mechanical assistance in the preparation of a return, declaration, statement, or other document as, for example, a stenographer or typist, is not considered as preparing the return, declaration, statement, or other document.

(2) *Exception.*—The verification required by subparagraph (1) of this paragraph is not required on returns, declarations, statements, or other documents which are prepared—

(i) For an employee either by his employer or by an employee designated for such purpose by the employer, or

(ii) For an employer as a usual incident of the employment of one regularly or continuously employed by such employer. [Reg. §1.6065-1.]

☐ [*T.D.* 6364, 2-13-59.]

### [Reg. §20.6065-1]

**§20.6065-1. Verification of returns.**—(a) *Penalties of perjury.*—If a return, statement, or other document made under the provisions of chapter 11 or subtitle F of the Code or the regulations thereunder with respect to any tax imposed by chapter 11 of the Code, or the form and instructions issued with respect to such return, statement, or other document, requires that it shall contain or be verified by a written declaration that it is made under the penalties of perjury, it must be so verified by the person or persons required to sign such return, statement or other document. In addition, any other statement or document submitted under any provision of chapter 11 or subtitle F of the Code or regulations thereunder with respect to any tax imposed by chapter 11 of the Code may be required to contain or be verified by a written declaration that it is made under the penalties of perjury.

(b) *Oath.*—Any return, statement, or other document required to be submitted under chapter 11 or subtitle F of the Code or regulations prescribed thereunder with respect to any tax imposed by chapter 11 of the Code may be required to be verified by an oath. [Reg. §20.6065-1.]

☐ [*T.D.* 6600, 5-28-62.]

### [Reg. §25.6065-1]

**§25.6065-1. Verification of returns.**—(a) *Penalties of perjury.*—If a return, statement, or other document made under the provisions of chapter 12 or subtitle F of the Code or the regulations thereunder with respect to any tax imposed by chapter 12 of the Code, or the form and instructions issued with respect to such return, statement, or other document, requires that it shall contain or be verified by a written declaration that it is made under the penalties of perjury, it must be so verified by the person or persons required to sign such return, statement, or other document. In addition, any other statement or document submitted under any provision of chapter 12 or subtitle F of the Code or regulations thereunder with respect to any tax imposed by chapter 12 of the Code may be required to contain or be verified by a written declaration that it is made under the penalties of perjury.

(b) *Oath.*—Any return, statement, or other document required to be submitted under chapter 12 or subtitle F of the Code or regulations prescribed thereunder with respect to any tax imposed by chapter 12 of the Code may be required to be verified by an oath. [Reg. §25.6065-1.]

☐ [*T.D.* 6600, 5-28-62.]

### [Reg. §53.6065-1]

**§53.6065-1. Verification of returns.**—(a) *Penalties of perjury.*—If a return, statement, or other document made under the provisions of chapter 42 or subtitle F of the Code or the regulations thereunder with respect to any tax imposed by chapter 42 of the Code, or the form and instructions issued with respect to such return, statement, or other document, requires that it shall contain or be verified by a written declaration that it is made under the penalties of perjury, it must be so verified by the person or persons required to sign such return, statement, or other document. In addition, any other statement or document submitted under any provision of chapter 42 or subtitle F of the Code or regulations thereunder with respect to any tax imposed by chapter 42 of the Code may be required to contain or be verified by a written declaration that it is made under the penalties of perjury.

(b) *Oath.*—Any return, statement, or other document required to be submitted under chapter 42 or subtitle F of the Code or regulations prescribed thereunder with respect to any tax imposed by chapter 42 of the Code may be required to be verified by an oath. [Reg. §53.6065-1.]

☐ [*T.D.* 7368, 7-15-75.]

### [Reg. §55.6065-1]

**§55.6065-1. Verification of returns.**—If a return, statement, or other document made under the provisions of chapter 44 or subtitle F of the Code or the regulations thereunder with respect to any tax imposed by chapter 44 of the Code, or the form and instructions issued with respect to such return, statement, or other document, requires that it shall contain or be verified by a written declaration that it is made under the penalties of perjury, it must be so verified by the person or persons required to sign such return, statement, or other document. In addition, any other statement or document submitted under any provision of chapter 44 of subtitle F of the Code or regulations thereunder with respect to any tax imposed by chapter 44 of the Code may be required to contain or be verified by a written declaration that it is made under the penalties of perjury. [Reg. §55.6065-1.]

☐ [*T.D.* 7767, 2-3-81.]

### [Reg. §156.6065-1]

**§156.6065-1. Verification of returns.**—If a return, statement, or other document made under the provisions of chapter 54 (Greenmail) or of subtitle F of the Code, or the regulations thereunder with respect to any tax imposed by chapter 54, or the form and instructions issued with respect to such return, statement, or other document, requires that it shall contain or be verified by a written declaration that it is made under the penalties of perjury, it must be so verified by the person or persons required to sign such return, statement, or other document. In addition, any other statement or document submitted under any provision of chapter 54 or of subtitle F of the Code, or the regulations thereunder with respect to any tax imposed by chapter 54 may be required to contain or be verified by a written declaration that is made under the penalties of perjury. [Reg. § 156.6065-1.]

☐ [*T.D. 8379*, 12-17-91.]

### [Reg. § 157.6065-1]

**§ 157.6065-1. Verification of returns.**—If a return, statement, or other document made under the provisions of chapter 55 (Structured Settlement Factoring Transactions) or of subtitle F of the Internal Revenue Code, or the regulations under those provisions with respect to any tax imposed by chapter 55, or the form and instructions issued with respect to such return, statement, or other document, requires that it shall contain or be verified by a written declaration that it is made under the penalties of perjury, it must be so verified by the person or persons required to sign such return, statement, or other document. In addition, any other statement or document submitted under any provision of chapter 55 or subtitle F, or the regulations under those provisions, with respect to any tax imposed by chapter 55 may be required to contain or be verified by written declaration that it is made under the penalties of perjury. [Reg. § 157.6065-1.]

☐ [*T.D. 9134*, 7-7-2004.]

### [Reg. § 301.6065-1]

**§ 301.6065-1. Verification of returns.**—For provisions concerning the verification of returns and other documents, see the regulations relating to the particular tax. [Reg. § 301.6065-1.]

☐ [*T.D. 6498*, 10-24-60.]

### [Reg. § 31.6065(a)-1]

**§ 31.6065(a)-1. Verification of returns or other documents.**—If a return, statement, or other document made under the regulations in this part is required by the regulations contained in this part, or the form and instructions issued with respect to such return, statement, or other document, to contain or be verified by a written declaration that it is made under the penalties of perjury, such return, statement, or other document shall be so verified by the person signing it. [Reg. § 31.6065(a)-1.]

☐ [*T.D. 6472*, 6-22-60.]

### [Reg. § 1.6071-1]

**§ 1.6071-1. Time for filing returns and other documents.**—(a) *In general.*—Whenever a return, statement, or other document is required to be made under the provisions of subtitle A or F of the Code, or the regulations thereunder, with respect to any tax imposed by subtitle A of the Code, and the time for filing such return, statement, or other document is not provided for by the Code, it shall be filed at the time prescribed by the regulations contained in this chapter with respect to such return, statement, or other document.

(b) *Return for a short period.*—In the case of a return with respect to tax under subtitle A of the Code for a short period (as defined in section 443), the district director or director of the Internal Revenue Service Center may, upon a showing by the taxpayer of unusual circumstances, prescribe a time for filing the return for such period later than the time when such return would otherwise be due. However, the district director or director of the Internal Revenue Service Center may not extend the time when the return for a DISC (as defined in Section 992(a)(1)) must be filed, as specified in section 6072(b).

(c) *Time for filing certain information returns.*—(1) For provisions relating to the time for filing returns of partnership income, see paragraph (e)(2) of § 1.6031-1.

(2) For provisions relating to the time for filing information returns by banks with respect to common trust funds, see § 1.6032-1.

(3) For provisions relating to the time for filing information returns by certain organizations exempt from taxation under section 501(a), see paragraph (e) of § 1.6033-1.

(4) For provisions relating to the time for filing returns by trusts claiming charitable deductions under section 642(c), see paragraph (c) of § 1.6034-1.

(5) [Reserved].

(6) For provisions relating to the time for filing information returns with respect to certain stock option transactions, see paragraph (c) of § 1.6039-1.

(7) For provisions relating to the time for filing information returns by persons making certain payments, see § 1.6041-2(a)(3) and § 1.6041-6.

(8) For provisions relating to the time for filing information returns regarding payments of dividends, see § 1.6042-2(c).

(9) For provisions relating to the time for filing information returns by corporations with respect to contemplated dissolution or liquidations, see paragraph (a) of § 1.6043-1.

(10) For provisions relating to the time for filing information returns by corporations with respect to distributions in liquidation, see paragraph (a) of § 1.6043-2.

(11) For provisions relating to the time for filing information returns with respect to payments of patronage dividends, see § 1.6044-2(d).

(12) For provisions relating to the time for filing information returns with respect to formation or reorganization of foreign corporations, see § 1.6046-1.

(13) For provisions relating to the time for filing information returns regarding certain payments of interest, see § 1.6049-4(g).

(14) For provisions relating to the time for filing information returns with respect to payment of wages in the form of group-term life insurance, see paragraph (b) of § 1.6052-1.

(15) For provisions relating to the time for filing an annual information return on Form 1042-S, "Foreign Person's U.S. Source Income subject to Withholding," or Form 8805, "Foreign Partner's Information Statement of Section 1446 Withholding Tax," for any tax withheld under chapter 3 of the Internal Revenue Code (relating to withholding of tax on nonresident aliens and foreign corporations and tax-free covenant bonds), see § 1.1461-1(c) and § 1.1446-3(d).

(16) for provisions relating to the time for filing annual information returns on Form 1042S of the tax withheld under chapter 3 of the Code (relating to withholding of tax on nonresident aliens and foreign corporations and tax-free covenant bonds), see paragraph (c) of § 1.1461-2.

(d) *Effective/Applicability date.*—The references to Form 8805 and § 1.1446-3(d) in paragraph (c)(15) of this section shall apply to partnership taxable years beginning after April 29, 2008. [Reg. § 1.6071-1.]

☐ [*T.D. 6364*, 2-13-59. *Amended by T.D. 6628*, 12-27-62; *T.D. 6887*, 6-23-66; *T.D. 6908*, 12-30-66; *T.D. 7284*, 8-2-73; *T.D. 7533*, 2-14-78; *T.D. 8734*, 10-6-97 (T.D. 8804 delayed the effective date of T.D. 8734 from January 1, 1999, to January 1, 2000; T.D. 8856 further delayed the effective date of T.D. 8734 until January 1, 2001) *T.D. 9394*, 4-28-2008 *and T.D. 9849*, 3-11-2019.]

### [Reg. § 20.6071-1]

**§ 20.6071-1. Time for filing preliminary notice required by § 20.6036-1.**—In the case of the estate of a decedent dying before January 1, 1971, if a duly qualified executor or administrator of the estate of such a decedent who was a resident or a citizen of the United States qualifies within 2 months after a decedent's death, or if a duly qualified executor or administrator of the estate of such a decedent who was a nonresident not a citizen qualifies within the United States within 2 months after the decedent's death, the preliminary notice required by § 20.6036-1 must be filed within 2 months after his qualification. If no such executor or administrator qualifies within that period, the preliminary notice must be filed within 2 months of the decedent's death. [Reg. § 20.6071-1.]

☐ [*T.D. 7238*, 12-28-72.]

### [Reg. § 44.6071-1]

**§ 44.6071-1. Time for filing return.**—(a) *Return on Form 730.*—Each return required to be made on Form 730 pursuant to § 44.6011(a)-1 shall be filed on or before the last day of the first calendar month following the period for which it is made. For provisions relating to the time for filing a return when the prescribed due date falls on Saturday, Sunday, or a legal holiday, see the provisions of the Regulations on Procedure and Administration(Part 301 of this chapter) under section 7503.

(b) *Return on Form 11-C.*—(1) The first return required to be made on Form 11-C shall be filed to cover the period beginning with the first day of the calendar month in which a person engages (or expects to engage) in activities which make him liable for the special tax imposed by section 4411 and ending with the following June 30. Thereafter, each return required to be made on Form 11-C shall be filed on or before July 1 to cover a 1-year period (beginning July 1 and ending June 30 of the following calendar year) during which taxable activity continues.

(2) For additional provisions relating to the return on Form 11-C, see § 44.4412-1 and § § 44.4901 to 44.4905-3, inclusive. [Reg. § 44.6071-1.]

☐ [*T.D. 6370*, 4-4-59.]

**[Reg. § 53.6071-1]**

**§ 53.6071-1. Time for filing returns.**—(a) *General rule.*—Except as otherwise provided in this section, a return required by § 53.6011-1 shall be filed at the time the private foundation or trust described in section 4947(a)(2) is required to file its annual information or tax return under section 6033 or 6012 (as may be applicable).

(b) *Exception.*—The Form 4720 of a person whose taxable year ends on a date other than that on which the taxable year of the foundation or trust ends shall be filed on or before the 15th day of the fifth month following the close of such person's taxable year.

(c) *Form 5227.*—A Form 5227 required to be filed by paragraph (d) of § 53.6011-1 for a trust described in section 4947(a) shall be filed on or before the 15th day of the fourth month following the close of the trust's taxable year.

(d) *Taxes related to black lung benefit trusts.*—Forms 990-BL and 6069 shall be filed on or before the 15th day of the fifth month following the close of the filer's taxable year.

(e) *Taxes related to political expenditures of organizations described in section 501(c)(3) of the Internal Revenue Code.*—A Form 4720 required to be filed by § 53.6011-1(b) for an organization liable for tax imposed by section 4955(a) must be filed by the unextended due date for filing its annual information return under section 6033 or, if the organization is exempt from filing, the date the organization would be required to file an annual information return if it was not exempt from filing. The Form 4720 of a person whose taxable year ends on a date other than that on which the taxable year of the organization described in section 501(c)(3) ends must be filed on or before the 15th day of the fifth month following the close of the person's taxable year.

(f) *Taxes imposed on excess benefit transactions engaged in by organizations described in sections 501(c)(3) (except private foundations) and 501(c)(4).*—(1) *General rule.*—A Form 4720 required by § 53.6011-1(b) for a disqualified person or organization manager liable for tax imposed by section 4958(a) shall be filed by that person on or before the 15th day of the fifth month following the close of such person's taxable year.

(2) *Special rule for taxable years ending after September 13, 1995, and on or before July 30, 1996.*—A Form 4720 required by § 53.6011-1(b) for a disqualified person or organization manager liable for tax imposed by section 4958(a) on an excess benefit transaction occurring in such person's taxable year ending after September 13, 1995, and on or before July 30, 1996, is due on or before December 15, 1996.

(g) *Taxes imposed with respect to prohibited tax shelter transactions to which tax-exempt entities are parties.*—(1) *Returns by certain tax-exempt entities.*—A Form 4720, "Return of Certain Excise Taxes Under Chapters 41 and 42 of the Internal Revenue Code," required by § 53.6011-1(b) for a tax-exempt entity described in section 4965(c)(1), (c)(2) or (c)(3) that is a party to a prohibited tax shelter transaction and is liable for tax imposed by section 4965(a)(1) shall be filed on or before the due date (not including extensions) for filing the tax-exempt entity's annual information return under section 6033(a)(1). If the tax-exempt entity is not required to file an annual information return under section 6033(a)(1), the Form 4720 shall be filed on or before the 15th day of the fifth month after the end of the tax-exempt entity's taxable year or, if the entity has not established a taxable year for Federal income tax purposes, the entity's annual accounting period.

(2) *Returns by entity managers of tax-exempt entities described in section 4965(c)(1), (c)(2) or (c)(3).*—A Form 4720, required by § 53.6011-1(b) for an entity manager of a tax-exempt entity described in section 4965(c)(1), (c)(2) or (c)(3) who is liable for tax imposed by section 4965(a)(2) shall be filed on or before the 15th day of the fifth month following the close of the entity manager's taxable year during which the entity entered into the prohibited tax shelter transaction.

(3) *Transition rule.*—A Form 4720, for a section 4965 tax that was due on or before October 4, 2007, will be deemed to have been filed on the due date if it was filed by October 4, 2007, and if all section 4965 taxes required to be reported on that Form 4720 were paid by October 4, 2007.

(h) *Taxes on failures by charitable hospital organizations to satisfy the community health needs assessment requirements of section 501(r)(3).*—A hospital organization (as defined in § 1.501(r)-1(b)(18)) liable for tax imposed by section 4959 must file a Form 4720 as required by § 53.6011-1(b), on or before the 15th day of the fifth month after the end of the hospital organization's taxable year for which it failed to meet the requirements of section 501(r)(3).

(i) *Taxes under section 4960, 4966, 4967, or 4968.*—A person (including a governmental entity) required by § 53.6011-1(b) to file a return for a tax imposed by section 4960(a), 4966(a), 4967(a), or 4968(a) in a taxable year must file the Form 4720 on or before the 15th day of the fifth month after the end of the person's taxable year (or, if the person has not established a taxable year for Federal income tax purposes, the person's annual accounting period).

(j) *Effective/applicability date.*—(1) Paragraph (g) of this section applies on and after July 6, 2007.

(2) Paragraph (h) of this section applies on and after August 15, 2013.

(3) Paragraph (i) of this section applies on and after April 9, 2019. [Reg. § 53.6071-1.]

☐ [*T.D. 7368, 7-15-75. Amended by T.D. 7407, 3-3-76; T.D. 7838, 10-5-82; T.D. 8628, 12-4-95; T.D. 8736, 10-6-97; T.D. 9334, 7-5-2007; T.D. 9492, 7-2-2010 (corrected 8-3-2010); T.D. 9629, 8-14-2013, T.D. 9708, 12-29-2014 and T.D. 9855, 4-5-2019.*]

**[Reg. § 54.6071-1]**

**§ 54.6071-1. Time for filing returns.**—(a) *Returns under section 4980B.*—(1) *Due date for filing of return by employers or other persons responsible for benefits under a group health plan.*—If the person liable for the excise tax is an employer or other person responsible for providing or administering benefits under a group health plan (such as an insurer or a third party administrator), the return required by § 54.6011-2 must be filed on or before the due date for filing the person's income tax return and must reflect the portion of the noncompliance period for each failure under section 4980B that falls during the person's taxable year. An extension to file the person's income tax return does not extend the date for filing Form 8928.

(2) *Due date for filing of return by multiemployer plans.*—If the person liable for the excise tax is a multiemployer plan, the return required by § 54.6011-2 must be filed on or before the last day of the seventh month following the end of the plan's plan year. The filing of Form 8928 by a plan must reflect the portion of the noncompliance period for each failure under section 4980B that falls during the plan's plan year.

(b) *Returns under section 4980D.*—(1) *Due date for filing of return by employers.*—If the person liable for the excise tax is an employer, the return required by § 54.6011-2 must be filed on or before the due date for filing the employer's income tax return and must reflect the portion of the noncompliance period for each failure under chapter 100 that falls during the employer's taxable year. An extension to file the employer's income tax return does not extend the date for filing Form 8928.

(2) *Due date for filing of return by multiemployer plans or multiple employer health plans.*—If the person liable for the excise tax is a multiemployer plan or a specified multiple employer health plan, the return required by § 54.6011-2 must be filed on or before the last day of the seventh month following the end of the plan's plan year. The filing of Form 8928 by a plan must reflect the portion of the noncompliance period for each failure under chapter 100 that falls during the plan's plan year.

(c) *Returns under section 4980E.*—Any employer who is liable for the excise tax under section 4980E must report this tax by filing the return required by § 54.6011-2 on or before the 15th day of the fourth month following the calendar year in which the noncomparable contributions were made.

(d) *Returns under section 4980G.*—Any employer who is liable for the excise tax under section 4980E must report this tax by filing the return required by § 54.6011-2 on or before the 15th day of the fourth month following the calendar year in which the noncomparable contributions were made. See Q & A-4 of § 54.4980G-1 for the rules on computation of the excise tax under section 4980G.

(e) *Effective/applicability date.*—The rules in this section are effective for any Form 8928 that is due on or after January 1, 2010. [Reg. § 54.6071-1.]

☐ [*T.D. 9457, 9-4-2009.*]

**[Reg. § 55.6071-1]**

**§ 55.6071-1. Time for filing returns.**—(a) *Returns for calendar years beginning after December 31, 1986.*—A return required by § 55.6011-1 for any calendar year beginning after December 31, 1986, shall be filed on or before March 15 of the following calendar year. See § 55.6081-1 for rules relating to extensions of time for filing a return required by § 55.6011-1.

(b) *Returns for excise tax under section 4981 as in effect before amendment by the Tax Reform Act of 1986.*—A return required by § 55.6011-1 for any excise tax under section 4981, as in effect before amendment by the Tax Reform Act of 1986, shall be filed at the time (including any extension of time granted or allowed under section 6081) that the real estate investment trust is required to file its income tax return under section 6012 for the taxable year for which the tax under section 4981, as in effect before amendment by the Tax Reform Act of 1986, is imposed. [Reg. § 55.6071-1.]

☐ [*T.D. 7767, 2-3-81. Amended by T.D. 8180, 2-29-88.*]

### [Reg. § 156.6071-1]

**§ 156.6071-1. Time for filing returns relating to greenmail.—**
(a) *In general.*—Returns required by § 156.6011-1 (relating to liability for tax on greenmail under section 5881) shall be filed on or before the ninetieth day following receipt of any portion of the greenmail. Greenmail is considered to be received when gain or other income is realized, as determined according to the taxpayer's method of accounting, without regard to any provision of the Code providing for deferral of recognition.

(b) *Returns relating to greenmail received before the date these regulations become final.*—Returns required by § 156.6011-1 that relate to greenmail received on or before December 18, 1991, shall be filed on or before March 18, 1991. [Reg. § 156.6071-1.]

☐ [*T.D. 8379, 12-17-91.*]

### [Reg. § 157.6071-1]

**§ 157.6071-1. Time for filing returns.—**(a) *In general.*—Except as provided in paragraph (b) of this section, returns required by § 157.6011-1 (relating to returns of tax with respect to structured settlement factoring transactions) must be filed on or before the ninetieth day following the receipt of structured settlement payment rights in a structured settlement factoring transaction.

(b) *Returns relating to structured settlement payment rights received before February 19, 2003.*—Returns required by § 157.6011-1 that relate to structured settlement payment rights received on or before February 19, 2003, must be filed on or before May 20, 2003. [Reg. § 157.6071-1.]

☐ [*T.D. 9134, 7-7-2004.*]

### [Reg. § 301.6071-1]

**§ 301.6071-1. Time for filing returns and other documents.—**For provisions concerning the time for filing returns and other documents, see the regulations relating to the particular tax. [Reg. § 301.6071-1.]

☐ [*T.D. 6498, 10-24-60.*]

### [Reg. § 31.6071(a)-1]

**§ 31.6071(a)-1. Time for filing returns and other documents.—**
(a) *Federal Insurance Contributions Act and income tax withheld from wages and from nonpayroll payments.*—(1) *Quarterly or annual returns.*—Except as provided in paragraph (a)(4) of this section, each return required to be made under § 31.6011(a)-1, in respect of the taxes imposed by the Federal Insurance Contributions Act (26 U.S.C. 3101-3128), or required to be made under § 31.6011(a)-4, in respect of income tax withheld, shall be filed on or before the last day of the first calendar month following the period for which it is made. A return may be filed on or before the 10th day of the second calendar month following such period if timely deposits under section 6302(c) of the Code and the regulations have been made in full payment of such taxes due for the period.

(2) *Monthly tax returns.*—Each return in respect of the taxes imposed by the Federal Insurance Contributions Act or of income tax withheld which is required to be made under paragraph (a) of § 31.6011(a)-5 shall be filed on or before the fifteenth day of the first calendar month following the period for which it is made.

(3) *Information returns.*—(i) *General rule.*—Each information return in respect of wages as defined in the Federal Insurance Contributions Act or of income tax withheld from wages as required under § 31.6051-2 must be filed on or before January 31 of the year following the calendar year for which it is made, except that, if a tax return under § 31.6011(a)-5(a) is filed as a final return for a period ending prior to December 31, the information return must be filed on or before the last day of the first month following the period for which the tax return is filed.

(ii) *Expedited filing.*—If an employer who is required to make a return pursuant to § 31.6011(a)-1 or § 31.6011(a)-4 is required to make a final return on Form 941, or a variation thereof, under § 31.6011(a)-6(a)(1) (relating to the final return for Federal Insurance Contributions Act taxes and income tax withholding from wages), the return which is required to be made under § 31.6051-2 must be

filed on or before the last day of the first month following the period for which the final return is filed. The requirements set forth in this paragraph (a)(3)(ii) do not apply to employers with respect to employees whose wages are for domestic service in the private home of the employer. See § 31.6011(a)-1(a)(3).

(4) *Employee returns under Federal Insurance Contributions Act.*—A return of employee tax under section 3101 required under paragraph (d) of § 31.6011(a)-1 to be made by an individual for a calendar year on Form 1040 shall be filed on or before the due date of such individual's return of income (see § 1.6012-1 of this chapter (Income Tax Regulations)) for the calendar year, or, if the individual makes his return of income on a fiscal year basis, on or before the due date of his return of income for the fiscal year beginning in the calendar year for which a return of employee tax is required. A return of employee tax under section 3101 required under paragraph (d) of § 31.6011(a)-1 to be made for a calendar year—

(i) On Form 1040SS or Form 1040PR, or

(ii) On Form 1040 by an individual who is not required to make a return of income for the calendar year or for a fiscal year beginning in such calendar year,
shall be filed on or before the 15th day of the fourth month following the close of the calendar year.

(b) *Railroad Retirement Tax Act.*—Each return of the taxes imposed by the Railroad Retirement Tax Act required to be made under § 31.6011(a)-2 shall be filed on or before the last day of the second calendar month following the period for which it is made.

(c) *Federal Unemployment Tax Act.*—Each return of the tax imposed by the Federal Unemployment Tax Act required to be made under § 31.6011(a)-3 shall be filed on or before the last day of the first calendar month following the period for which it is made. However, a return may be filed on or before the 10th day of the second calendar month following such period if timely deposits under section 6302(c) of the Code and the regulations thereunder have been made in full payment of such taxes due for the period.

(d) *Last day for filing.*—For provisions relating to the time for filing a return when the prescribed due date falls on Saturday, Sunday, or a legal holiday, see the provisions of § 301.7503-1 of this chapter (Regulations on Procedure and Administration).

(e) *Late filing.*—For additions to the tax in case of failure to file a return within the prescribed time, see the provisions of § 301.6651-1 of this chapter (Regulations on Procedure and Administration).

(f) *Cross reference.*—For extensions of time for filing returns and other documents, see § 31.6081(a)-1.

(g) *Applicability date.*—This section applies to returns filed on or after January 30, 2020. Section 31.6071(a)-1T (as contained in 26 CFR part 31, revised April 2019) applies to returns filed before January 30, 2020. [Reg. § 31.6071(a)-1.]

☐ [*T.D. 6354, 1-13-59. Amended by T.D. 6893, 8-29-66; T.D. 6941, 12-15-67; T.D. 7001, 1-17-69; T.D. 7078, 12-5-70; T.D. 7351, 4-16-75; T.D. 7953, 5-8-84; T.D. 8504, 12-22-93; T.D. 8636, 12-20-95; T.D. 8895, 8-17-2000; T.D. 8952, 6-25-2001; T.D. 9239, 12-30-2005; T.D. 9507, 12-2-2010; T.D. 9524, 5-6-2011, T.D. 9566, 12-9-2011, T.D. 9586, 4-24-2012, T.D. 9821, 7-18-2017 and T.D. 9892, 1-29-2020.*]

### [Reg. § 40.6071(a)-1]

**§ 40.6071(a)-1. Time for filing returns.—**(a) *Quarterly returns.*—Each quarterly return required under § 40.6011(a)-1 (a)(2) must be filed by the last day of the first calendar month following the quarter for which it is made.

(b) *Monthly and semimonthly returns.*—(1) *Monthly returns.*—Each monthly return required under § 40.6011(a)-1(b) must be filed by the fifteenth day of the month following the month for which it is made.

(2) *Semimonthly returns.*—Each semimonthly return required under § 40.6011(a)-1(b) must be filed by the last day of the semimonthly period (as defined in § 40.0-1(c)) following the semimonthly period for which it is made.

(c) *Fees on health insurance policies and self-insured health plans.*—(1) *Specified health insurance policies.*—A return that reports liability for the fee imposed by section 4375 must be filed by July 31 of the calendar year immediately following the last day of the policy year. For issuers that determine the average number of lives covered under the policy for section 4375 using the member months method under § 46.4375-1(c)(2)(v) or the state form method under § 46.4375-1(c)(2)(vi), the return must be filed by July 31 of the immediately following calendar year. Thus, for example, a return that reports liability for the fee imposed by section 4375 for the year ending on December 31, 2012, must be filed by July 31, 2013.

(2) *Applicable self-insured health plans.*—A return that reports liability for the fee imposed by section 4376 for a plan year must be filed by July 31 of the calendar year immediately following the last day of the plan year. Thus, for example, a return that reports liability for the fee imposed by section 4376 for the plan year ending on January 31, 2013, must be filed by July 31, 2014.

(d) *Effective/Applicability date.*—Paragraphs (a) and (b) of this section apply to returns for calendar quarters beginning on or after October 1, 2001, and paragraph (c) of this section applies to returns that report liability imposed by section 4375 or 4376. [Reg. §40.6071(a)-1.]

☐ [*T.D. 8442, 10-21-92. Amended by T.D. 8963, 8-8-2001 and T.D. 9602, 12-5-2012.*]

### [Reg. §41.6071(a)-1]

**§41.6071(a)-1. Time for filing returns.**—(a) *In general.*—Except as provided in paragraph (b) of this section, a return described in §41.6011(a)-1 must be filed by the last day of the month following the month in which—

(1) A person becomes liable for tax under §41.4481-2(a)(1)(i)(A), (B), or (C);

(2) A person that is liable for tax under §41.4481-2(a)(1)(i)(D) is notified by the Commissioner that the tax has not been paid in full; or

(3) A transferee described in §41.4483-3(f) acquires the vehicle.

(b) *Certain transit-type buses.*—In the case of any bus of the transit type, the first taxable use of which in any taxable period occurs prior to the close of the test period (see paragraph (c) of §41.4483-2) with reference to which liability for the tax on the use of such transit-type bus for such taxable period is determined, the person in whose name the bus is registered at the time of such use shall, after such test period and on or before the last day of the following month make a return of such tax for such taxable period on the use of such transit-type bus.

(c) *Effect of sale during taxable period.*—A person that is liable for tax under §41.4481-2(a)(1)(i)(A), (B), (C), or (D) after taking into account the modification required under §41.4481-2(a)(2) is treated as liable for tax under the same provision of §41.4481-2(a)(1)(i) for purposes of this section.

(d) *Effective/applicability date.*—Paragraph (c) of this section applies on and after July 1, 2015. For rules applicable before that date, see 26 CFR 41.6071(a)-1 (revised as of April 1, 2014). [Reg. §41.6071(a)-1.]

☐ [*T.D. 6216, 12-6-56. Amended by T.D. 6743, 6-22-64; T.D. 8879, 3-30-2000; T.D. 9537, 7-15-2011 and T.D. 9698, 10-28-2014.*]

### [Reg. §1.6072-1]

**§1.6072-1. Time for filing returns of individuals, estates, and trusts.**—(a) *In general.*—(1) *Returns of income for individuals, estates and trusts.*—Except as provided in paragraphs (b) and (c) of this section, returns of income required under sections 6012, 6013, 6014, and 6017 of individuals, estates, domestic trusts, and foreign trusts having an office or place of business in the United States (including unrelated business tax returns of such trusts referred to in section 511(b)(2)) shall be filed on or before the fifteenth day of the fourth month following the close of the taxable year.

(2) *Return of trust, or portion of a trust, treated as owned by a decedent.*—(i) *In general.*—In the case of a return of a trust, or portion of a trust, that was treated as owned by a decedent under subpart E (section 671 and following), part I, subchapter J, chapter 1 of the Internal Revenue Code as of the date of the decedent's death that is filed in accordance with §1.671-4(a) for the fractional part of the year ending with the date of the decedent's death, the due date of such return shall be the fifteenth day of the fourth month following the close of the 12-month period which began with the first day of the decedent's taxable year.

(ii) *Effective date.*—This paragraph (a)(2) applies to taxable years ending on or after December 24, 2002.

(b) *Decedents.*—In the case of a final return of a decedent for a fractional part of a year, the due date of such return shall be the fifteenth day of the fourth month following the close of the 12-month period which began with the first day of such fractional part of the year.

(c) *Nonresident alien individuals and foreign trusts.*—The income tax return of a nonresident alien individual (other than one treated as a resident under section 6013(g) or (h)) and of a foreign trust which does not have an office or place of business in the United States (including unrelated business tax returns of such trusts referred to in section 511(b)(2)) shall be filed on or before the fifteenth day of the

sixth month following the close of the taxable year. However, a nonresident alien individual who for the taxable year has wages subject to withholding under chapter 24 of the Code shall file his income tax return on or before the fifteenth day of the fourth month following the close of the taxable year.

(d) *Last day for filing return.*—For provisions relating to the time for filing a return where the last day for filing falls on Saturday, Sunday, or a legal holiday, see section 7503 and §301.7503-1 of this chapter (Regulations on Procedure and Administration). [Reg. §1.6072-1.]

☐ [*T.D. 6364, 2-13-59. Amended by T.D. 7426, 8-6-76; T.D. 7670, 1-30-80 and T.D. 9032, 12-23-2002.*]

### [Reg. §301.6072-1]

**§301.6072-1. Time for filing income tax returns.**—For provisions relating to time for filing income tax returns, see §§1.6072-1 to 1.6072-4, inclusive, of this chapter (Income Tax Regulations). [Reg. §301.6072-1.]

☐ [*T.D. 6498, 10-24-60.*]

### [Reg. §1.6072-2]

**§1.6072-2. Time for filing returns of corporations.**—(a) *Domestic and certain foreign corporations.*—(1) *In general.*—(i) *C corporations.*—Except as provided in paragraph (a)(2) of this section, the income tax return required under section 6012 of a domestic C corporation (as defined in section 1361(a)(2)) or of a foreign C corporation having an office or place of business in the United States shall be filed on or before the fifteenth day of the fourth month following the close of the taxable year.

(ii) *S corporations.*—The income tax return required under sections 6012 and 6037 of an S corporation (as defined in section 1361(a)(1)) shall be filed on or before the fifteenth day of the third month following the close of the taxable year.

(2) *Exception.*—For taxable years beginning before January 1, 2026, the income tax return of a C corporation described in paragraph (a)(1)(i) of this section that has a taxable year that ends on June 30 shall be filed on or before the fifteenth day of the third month following the close of the taxable year. For purposes of this paragraph (a)(2), the return for a short period (within the meaning of section 443) that ends on any day in June shall be treated as the return for a taxable year that ends on June 30.

(b) *Foreign corporations not having an office or place of business in the United States.*—The income tax return of a foreign corporation which does not have an office or place of business in the United States shall be filed on or before the fifteenth day of the sixth month following the close of the taxable year.

(c) *Exempt organizations.*—For taxable years beginning after November 10, 1978, the income tax return required under section 6012 and §1.6012-2(e) of an organization exempt from taxation under section 501(a) (other than an employee's trust under section 401(a)) shall be filed on or before the fifteenth day of the fifth month following the close of the organization's taxable year.

(d) *Cooperative organizations.*—The income tax return of the following cooperative organizations shall be filed on or before the fifteenth day of the ninth month following the close of the taxable year:

(1) *Section 521 associations.*—A farmers', fruit growers', or like association, organized and operated in compliance with the requirements of section 521 and §1.521-1; and

(2) *Section 1381 corporations.*—For a taxable year beginning after December 31, 1962, a corporation described in section 1381(a)(2), which is under a valid enforceable written obligation to pay patronage dividends (as defined in section 1388(a) and §1.1388-1(a)) in an amount equal to at least 50 percent of its net earnings from business done with or for its patrons, or which paid patronage dividends in such an amount out of the net earnings from business done with or for patrons during the most recent taxable year for which it had such net *earnings. Net* earnings for purposes of this paragraph (d)(2) shall not be reduced by any taxes imposed by subtitle A of the Internal Revenue Code and shall not be reduced by dividends paid on capital stock or other proprietary interest.

(e) *DISC's and former DISC's.*—The return required under section 6011(c)(2) of a corporation which is a DISC (as defined in section 992(a)) shall be filed on or before the 15th day of the 9th month following the close of the taxable year. For the rule that a DISC may not have an extension of time in which to file such return, see §§1.6071-1(b), 1.6081-1(a), and 1.6081-3(e). The return required under §1.6011-2(b)(1) by a former DISC shall be filed at the time it is required to file its income tax return.

(f) *Cross references.*—For provisions relating to the time for filing a return where the last day for filing falls on Saturday, Sunday, or a legal holiday, see section 7503 and § 301.7503-1 of this chapter (Regulations on Procedure and Administration). For provisions relating to the fixing of a later time for filing in the case of a return for a short period, see paragraph (b) of § 1.6071-1. For provisions relating to time for filing consolidated returns and separate returns for short periods not included in consolidated returns, see §§ 1.1502-75 and 1.1502-76.

(g) *Applicability date.*—This section applies to returns filed on or after January 30, 2020. Section 1.6072-2T (as contained in 26 CFR part 1, revised April 2019) applies to returns before January 30, 2020. [Reg. § 1.6072-2.]

☐ [*T.D. 6364*, 2-13-59. *Amended by T.D. 6643*, 4-1-63; *T.D. 7244*, 12-29-72; *T.D. 7533*, 2-14-78, *T.D. 7896*, 5-26-83, *T.D. 9821*, 7-18-2017 *and T.D. 9892*, 1-29-2020.]

### [Reg. § 1.6072-3]

**§ 1.6072-3. Income tax due dates postponed in case of China Trade Act corporations.**—(a) With respect to a taxable year beginning after December 31, 1948, and ending before October 1, 1956, the income tax return of any corporation organized under the China Trade Act of 1922 (15 U.S.C.c. 4), as amended, shall not become due until December 31, 1956, provided that during any such taxable year conditions in China have been generally so unsettled as to militate against the normal commercial operations and corporate activities of such corporation. However, the postponement of the due date shall not apply to an income tax return for any such taxable year if—

(1) The books of account and business records are available so as to permit the filing of a proper return, and the corporation has otherwise been in a position to carry on its commercial operations and corporate activities and to make a proper distribution of its earnings or profits, if any, so as to permit the certification required by section 941(b); or

(2) All the commercial operations and corporate activities of such corporation have been carried on in Hong Kong, Macao, or Taiwan (Formosa).

(b) Notwithstanding the provisions of paragraph (a)(1) or (2) of this section, the postponed due date referred to in this section will apply if a corporation satisfies the Commissioner that special circumstances exist, related to the unsettled conditions in China, which warrant such postponement.

(c) The postponed due date provided for in this section is expressly subject to the power of the Commissioner to extend, as in other cases, the time for filing the income tax return. See section 6081 and the regulations thereunder. [Reg. § 1.6072-3.]

☐ [*T.D. 6364*, 2-13-59.]

### [Reg. § 1.6072-4]

**§ 1.6072-4. Time for filing other returns of income.**—(a) *Reports for recovery of excessive profits on Government contracts.*—For the time for filing annual reports by persons completing Government contracts, see 26 CFR (1939) 17.16 (Treasury Decision 4906, approved June 23, 1939), and 26 CFR (1939) 16.15 (Treasury Decision 4909, approved June 28, 1939), as made applicable to section 1471 of the Internal Revenue Code of 1954 by Treasury Decision 6091, approved August 16, 1954 (19 F.R. 5167, C.B. 1954-2, 47).

(b) [Reserved].
[Reg. § 1.6072-4.]

☐ [*T.D. 6364*, 2-13-59. *Amended by T.D. 6908*, 12-30-66 *and T.D. 9849*, 3-11-2019.]

### [Reg. § 20.6075-1]

**§ 20.6075-1. Returns; time for filing estate tax return.**—The estate tax return required by section 6018 must be filed on or before the due date. The due date is the date on or before which the return is required to be filed in accordance with the provisions of section 6075(a) or the last day of the period covered by an extension of time as provided in § 20.6081-1. The due date, for a decedent dying after December 31, 1970, is, unless an extension of time for filing has been obtained, the day of the ninth calendar month after the decedent's death numerically corresponding to the day of the calendar month on which death occurred. However, if there is no numerically corresponding day in the ninth month, the last day of the ninth month is the due date. For example, if the decedent dies on July 31, 2000, the estate tax return and tax payment must be made on or before April 30, 2001. When the due date falls on Saturday, Sunday, or a legal holiday, the due date for filing the return is the next succeeding day that is not Saturday, Sunday, or a legal holiday. For the definition of a legal holiday, see section 7503 and § 301.7503-1 of this chapter. As to additions to the tax in the case of failure to file the return or pay the tax within the prescribed time, see section 6651 and § 301.6651-1 of this chapter. For rules with respect to the right to elect to have the

property valued as of a date or dates subsequent to the decedent's death, see section 2032 and § 20.2032-1, and section 7502 and § 301.7502-1 of this chapter. This section applies to estates of decedents dying after August 16, 1954. [Reg. § 20.6075-1.]

☐ [*T.D. 7238*, 12-28-72. *Amended by T.D. 8957*, 7-24-2001.]

### [Reg. § 25.6075-1]

**§ 25.6075-1. Returns, time for filing gift tax returns for gifts made after December 31, 1981.**—(a) *In general.*—Except as provided in paragraphs (b)(1) and (2) of this section, a return required to be filed under section 6019 for gifts made after December 31, 1981, must be filed on or before the 15th day of April following the close of the calendar year in which the gift was made.

(b) *Special rules.*—(1) *Extensions.*—Except as provided in paragraph (b)(2) of this section, if a taxpayer files an income tax return on the calendar year basis and the taxpayer is granted an extension of time for filing the return of income tax imposed by Subtitle A of the Internal Revenue Code, then such taxpayer shall also be deemed to have been granted an extension of time for filing the gift tax return under section 6019 for such calendar year equal to the extension of time granted for filing the income tax return. See section 6081 and the regulations thereunder for rules relating to extension of time for filing returns.

(2) *Death of donor.*—Where a gift is made during the calendar year in which the donor dies, the time for filing the return made under section 6019 shall not be later than the time (including extensions) for filing the return made under section 6018 (relating to estate tax returns) with respect to such donor. In addition, should the time for filing the estate tax return fall later than the 15th day of April following the close of the calendar year, the time for filing the gift tax return shall be on or before the 15th day of April following the close of the calendar year, unless an extension (not extending beyond the time for filing the estate tax return) was granted for filing the gift tax return. If no estate tax return is required to be filed, the time for filing the gift tax return shall be on or before the 15th day of April following the close of the calendar year, unless an extension was granted for filing the gift tax return.

(c) Paragraphs (a) and (b) may be illustrated by the following examples.

*Example (1).* Donor makes a taxable gift on April 1, 1982, for which a return must be made under section 6019. Donor files the income tax return on the calendar year basis. The donor was granted a 4-month extension from April 15, 1983 to August 15, 1983, in which to file the 1982 income tax return. Under these circumstances, the donor is not required to file the gift tax return prior to August 15, 1983. See paragraph (b)(1) of this section.

*Example (2).* Donor makes a taxable gift on April 1, 1982, for which a return must be made under section 6019. The donor dies on May 1, 1982. Under these circumstances, since the due date for filing the estate tax return, February 1, 1983 (assuming an estate tax return under section 6018 was required to be filed), falls prior to the due date for the gift tax return (as specified in section 6075(b)(1)), the last day for filing the gift tax return is February 1, 1983. See paragraph (b)(2) of this section.

*Example (3).* The facts are the same as in example (2), except the donor dies on November 30, 1982. Although the estate tax return if [is] due on or before August 30, 1983, the last day for filing the gift tax return is April 15, 1983. See paragraph (b) of this section.

*Example (4).* The facts are the same as in example (3), except that the executor receives a 4-month extension for filing the decedent's income tax return. Under these circumstances, the last day for filing the gift tax return is August 15, 1983. See paragraphs (b)(1) and (2) of this section.

*Example (5).* The facts are the same as in example (3), except that the donor-decedent receives an extension of 6 months for filing the gift tax return. See section 6081 and § 25.6081-1. Since section 6075(b)(3) and § 25.6075-2(b) provide that the time for filing the gift tax return made under section 6019 shall not be later than the time (including extensions) for filing the estate tax return made under section 6018, the last day for filing the gift tax return is August 30, 1983.

(d) See section 7503 and § 301.7503-1 concerning the timely filing of a return that falls due on a Saturday, Sunday of [or] legal holiday. As to additions to the tax for failure to file the return within the prescribed time, see section 6651 and § 301.6651-1. [Reg. § 25.6075-1.]

☐ [*T.D. 7910*, 9-6-83.]

### [Reg. § 25.6075-2]

**§ 25.6075-2. Returns, time for filing gift tax returns for gifts made after December 31, 1976, and before January 1, 1982.**—(a) *Due date for filing quarterly gift tax returns.*—(1) Except as provided in paragraph (b) of this section, a return required to be filed under section

6019 for the first, second, or third calendar quarter of any calendar year must be filed on or before the 15th day of the second month following the close of the calendar quarter in which the taxable gift was made.

(2) If a return is required to be filed under section 6019 for the fourth calendar quarter, then—

(i) For gifts made after December 31, 1976 and before January 1, 1979, the return must be filed on or before February 15th following the close of the fourth calendar quarter, or

(ii) For gifts made after December 31, 1978, and before January 1, 1982, the return must be filed on or before April 15th following the close of the fourth calendar quarter.

(b) *Special rule.*—(1) If the total amount of taxable gifts (determined after the application of paragraph (c)(1) of this section, relating to split gifts) made by a person during a calendar quarter is $25,000 or less, the return required under section 6019 for that quarter must be filed on or before the date prescribed in paragraph (a)(1) of this section for filing the return for gifts made in the first subsequent calendar quarter (unless the first subsequent calendar quarter is the fourth calendar quarter in which case see paragraph (b)(2) of this section) in the calendar year in which the sum of—

(i) The taxable gifts made during such subsequent calendar quarter, plus

(ii) All other taxable gifts made in prior quarters of the calendar year for which no return has yet been required to be filed, exceeds $25,000.

The return must include transfers by gift (as required by section 6019 and the regulations under that section) made during such subsequent and prior quarters of the calendar year for which no return has yet been required to be filed and identify in which quarter such transfers were made. The return must meet all the requirements for a separate return as if a separate return had been made for each quarter in which a transfer by gift was made. This return will be treated as a separate return for each of the quarters identified on the return.

(2) If a return is not required to be filed under paragraph (b)(1) of this section, then—

(i) For gifts made after December 31, 1976 and before January 1, 1979, the return must be filed on or before February 15th following the close of the fourth calendar quarter, or

(ii) For gifts made after December 31, 1978, and before January 1, 1982, the return must be filed on or before April 15th following the close of the fourth calendar quarter.

The return must include all transfers by gift (as required under section 6019 and the regulations under that section) made during the calendar year for which no return has yet been required to be filed and identify in which quarter such transfers were made. The return must meet all the requirements for a separate return as if a separate return had been made for each quarter in which a transfer by gift was made. This return will be treated as a separate return for each of the quarters identified on the return.

(3) Under section 6075(b)(3), any extension of time granted a taxpayer for filing the return of income taxes imposed by subtitle A for any taxable year which is a calendar year shall be treated as an extension of time granted the taxpayer for filing any return under section 6019 which is due (under paragraphs (a)(2)(ii) and (b)(2)(ii) of this section) on or before April 15th following the close of the fourth calendar quarter. See also section 6081 and § 25.6081-1 for other rules relating to extensions of time for filing returns.

(4) See section 7503 and § 301.7503-1 for the due date of a return that falls on a Saturday, Sunday, or a legal holiday. As to additions to the tax for failure to file the return within the prescribed time, see section 6651 and § 301.6651-1.

(c) *Effect of section 2513.*—(1) In determining whether taxable gifts made during any calendar quarter exceed $25,000, and in determining whether taxable gifts made in the current calendar quarter and the preceding calendar quarters of the calendar year for which no return has yet been required to be filed exceed $25,000, the effect of section 2513 is not taken into account for any gifts made in the

current or previous quarters for which a return is now being filed unless an irrevocable consent was made by either spouse on a return that was required to be filed prior to the due date of the current return. See § 25.2513-3 for the rules relating to when a consent becomes irrevocable.

(2) Paragraph (c)(1) of this section may be illustrated by the following examples:

*Example (1).* During the first quarter of 1980 A made taxable gifts of $17,000 ($20,000—$3,000 annual exclusion under section 2503(b)) to D. During the second quarter A made another taxable gift of $10,000 to D. A's taxable gifts for the first two quarters are $27,000. Therefore, A is required to file a return for the first and second quarters on or before August 15, 1980. On that return A's wife, B, consented to the application of section 2513 (relating to split gifts) for the second quarter. Even though A split the second quarter gift with his wife, A's return is nevertheless required to be filed on or before August 15, 1980 because in determining whether taxable gifts exceed $25,000, the effect of section 2513 is only taken into account for the quarter in which an irrevocable consent was made on a return required to be filed before August 15, 1980.

*Example (2).* Assume the same facts as in Example (1). In addition, during the third quarter A made another taxable gift of $20,000 to D, and B made a taxable gift of $24,000 to D. B is required to file a return reporting the taxable gifts made during the second and third quarters on or before November 15, 1980 because B's total taxable gifts exceed $25,000 (second quarter gifts after taking section 2513 into account = 1/2 ($10,000) – $3,000 (annual exclusion under section 2503(b)) = $2,000 plus a $24,000 gift in the third quarter). Even if A and B had consented to the application of section 2513 for the third quarter, B's return would nevertheless be due on or before November 15, 1980, because an irrevocable consent was not made on a return that was required to be filed prior to November 15, 1980. However, the effect of section 2513 is taken into account for the second quarter because an irrevocable consent was made on a return that was required to be filed prior to November 15, 1980.

*Example (3).* During the first quarter of 1980 A made taxable gifts of $27,000 to F ($30,000 – $3,000 annual exclusion under section 2503(b)). A is required to file a return on or before May 15, 1980. A fails to file a return until August 1, 1980. On that return B, A's spouse, consented to the application of section 2513. The consent on that return is irrevocable under § 25.2513-3. During the second quarter B made taxable gifts of $14,000 to F. A and B made no other gifts during 1980. B has made total taxable gifts of $26,000 ($12,000 for the first quarter and $14,000 for the second quarter). Therefore, B is required to file a return on or before August 15, 1980. Even if A and B had consented to the application of section 2513 for the second quarter, B's return is nevertheless due on or before August 15, 1980. Assuming no other gifts were made during the year, A's return reporting the second quarter split gift would be due on or before April 15, 1981.

*Example (4).* During the first quarter of 1980 A made taxable gifts of $20,000 to G. B, A's spouse, files a gift tax return on June 15, 1980 reporting that gift and both A and B signify their consent to the application of section 2513 on that return. In determining whether either spouse has exceeded the $25,000 amount for the remainder of 1980, the effect of section 2513 will be taken into account for the transfer by gift made in the first quarter.

(d) *Nonresident not citizens of the United States.*—In the case of a donor who is a nonresident not a citizen of the United States, paragraphs (a) and (b) of this section shall be applied by substituting "$12,500" for "$25,000" each place it appears. For rules relating to whether certain residents of possessions are considered nonresidents not citizens of the United States, see section 2501(c) and § 25.2501-1(d).

(e) *Effective date.*—This section is effective for gifts made after December 31, 1976, and before January 1, 1982. [Reg. § 25.6075-2.]

☐ [*Amended by T.D. 7012, 5-14-69, T.D. 7238, 12-28-72 and T.D. 7757, 1-16-81. Redesignated and amended by T.D. 7910, 9-6-83.*]

# Extension of Time for Filing Returns

**[Reg. § 1.6081-1]**

**§ 1.6081-1. Extension of time for filing returns.**—(a) *In general.*— The Commissioner is authorized to grant a reasonable extension of time for filing any return, declaration, statement, or other document that relates to any tax imposed by subtitle A of the Internal Revenue Code (Code) and that is required under the provisions of subtitle A or F of the Code. However, other than in the case of taxpayers who are abroad or as specified in section 6081(b), such extensions of time shall not be granted for more than six months, and the extension of time for filing the return of a DISC (as defined in section 992(a)), as

specified in section 6072(b), shall not be granted. Except in the case of an extension of time pursuant to § 1.6081-5, an extension of time for filing an income tax return shall not operate to extend the time for the payment of the tax unless specified to the contrary in the extension. For rules relating to extensions of time for paying tax, see § 1.6161-1.

(b) *Application for extension of time.*—(1) *In general.*—Under other sections in this chapter, certain taxpayers may request an automatic extension of time to file certain returns. Except in undue hardship cases, no extension of time to file a return will be allowed under this section until an automatic extension of time to file the return has been allowed under the applicable section. No extension of time to file a return will be granted under this section for a period of time greater than that provided for by automatic extension. A taxpayer desiring an extension of the time for filing a return, statement, or other document shall submit an application for extension on or before the due date of such return, statement, or other document. If a form exists for the application for an extension, the taxpayer should use the form; however, taxpayers may apply for an extension in a letter that includes the information required by this paragraph. Except as provided in § 301.6091-1(b) of this chapter (relating to hand-carried documents), the taxpayer should make the application for extension to the Internal Revenue Service office where such return, statement, or other document is required to be filed. Except for requests for automatic extensions of time to file certain returns provided for elsewhere in this chapter, the application must be in writing, signed by the taxpayer or his duly authorized agent, and must clearly set forth—

(i) The particular tax return, information return, statement, or other document, including the taxable year or period thereof, for which the taxpayer requests an extension; and

(ii) An explanation of the reasons for requesting the extension to aid the internal revenue officer in determining whether to grant the request.

(2) *Taxpayer unable to sign.*—In any case in which a taxpayer is unable, by reason of illness, absence, or other good cause, to sign a request for an extension, any person standing in close personal or business relationship to the taxpayer may sign the request on his behalf, and shall be considered as a duly authorized agent for this purpose, provided the request sets forth the reasons for a signature other than the taxpayer's and the relationship existing between the taxpayer and the signer.

(c) *Applicability date.*—This section applies to requests for extension of time to file returns on or after January 30, 2020. Section 1.6081-1T (as contained in 26 CFR part 1, revised April 2019) applies to requests for extension of time to file returns before January 30, 2020. [Reg. § 1.6081-1.]

☐ [*T.D. 6364, 2-13-59. Amended by T.D. 6371, 4-6-59; T.D. 6436, 12-30-59; T.D. 6581, 12-5-61; T.D. 6950, 4-3-68; T.D. 7133, 7-21-71; T.D. 7160, 2-1-72; T.D. 7260, 2-9-73; T.D. 7533, 2-14-78; T.D. 7651, 10-25-79; T.D. 8241, 2-22-89; T.D. 9163, 12-6-2004, T.D. 9407, 6-30-2008, T.D. 9821, 7-18-2017 and T.D. 9892, 1-29-2020.*]

### [Reg. § 20.6081-1]

**§ 20.6081-1. Extension of time for filing the return.**— (a) *Procedures for requesting an extension of time for filing the return.*—A request for an extension of time to file the return required by section 6018 must be made by filing Form 4768, "Application for Extension of Time To File a Return and/or Pay U. S. Estate (and Generation-Skipping Transfer) Taxes." Form 4768 must be filed with the Internal Revenue Service office designated in the application's instructions (except as provided in § 301.6091-1(b) of this chapter for hand-carried documents). Form 4768 must include an estimate of the amounts of estate and generation-skipping transfer tax liabilities with respect to the estate.

(b) *Automatic extension.*—An estate will be allowed an automatic 6-month extension of time beyond the date prescribed in section 6075(a) to file Form 706, "United States Estate (and Generation-Skipping Transfer) Tax Return," if Form 4768 is filed on or before the due date for filing Form 706 and in accordance with the procedures under paragraph (a) of this section.

(c) *Extension for good cause shown.*—In its discretion, the Internal Revenue Service may, upon the showing of good and sufficient cause, grant an extension of time to file the return required by section 6018 in certain situations. Such an extension may be granted to an estate that did not request an automatic extension of time to file Form 706 prior to the due date under paragraph (b) of this section, to an estate or person that is required to file forms other than Form 706, or to an executor who is abroad and is requesting an additional extension of time to file Form 706 beyond the 6-month automatic extension. Unless the executor is abroad, the extension of time may not be for more than 6 months beyond the filing date prescribed in section 6075(a). To obtain such an extension, Form 4768 must be filed in accordance with the procedures under paragraph (a) of this section and must contain a detailed explanation of why it is impossible or impractical to file a reasonably complete return by the due date. Form 4768 should be filed sufficiently early to permit the Internal Revenue Service time to consider the matter and reply before what otherwise would be the due date of the return. Failure to file Form 4768 before that due date may indicate negligence and constitute sufficient cause for denial of the extension. If an estate did not request an automatic extension of time to file Form 706 under para-

graph (b) of this section, Form 4768 must also contain an explanation showing good cause for not requesting the automatic extension.

(d) *Filing the return.*—A return as complete as possible must be filed before the expiration of the extension period. The return thus filed will be the return required by section 6018(a), and any tax shown on the return will be the amount determined by the executor as the tax referred to in section 6161(a)(2), or the amount shown as the tax by the taxpayer upon the taxpayer's return referred to in section 6211(a)(1)(A). The return cannot be amended after the expiration of the extension period although supplemental information may subsequently be filed that may result in a finally determined tax different from the amount shown as the tax on the return.

(e) *Payment of the tax.*—An extension of time for filing a return does not operate to extend the time for payment of the tax. See § 20.6151-1 for the time for payment of the tax, and § § 20.6161-1 and 20.6163-1 for extensions of time for payment of the tax. If an extension of time to file a return is obtained, but no extension of time for payment of the tax is granted, interest will be due on the tax not paid by the due date and the estate will be subject to all applicable late payment penalties.

(f) *Effective date.*—This section applies to estates of decedents dying after August 16, 1954, except for paragraph (b) of this section which applies to estate tax returns due after July 25, 2001. [Reg. § 20.6081-1.]

☐ [*T.D. 6296, 6-23-58. Amended by T.D. 6711, 3-23-64; T.D. 7238, 12-28-72; T.D. 7710, 7-28-80 and T.D. 8957, 7-24-2001.*]

### [Reg. § 25.6081-1]

**§ 25.6081-1. Automatic extension of time for filing gift tax returns.**—(a) *In general.*—Under section 6075(b)(2), an automatic six-month extension of time granted to a donor to file the donor's return of income under § 1.6081-4 of this chapter shall be deemed also to be a six-month extension of time granted to file a return on Form 709, "United States Gift (and Generation-Skipping Transfer) Tax Return." If a donor does not obtain an extension of time to file the donor's return of income under § 1.6081-4 of this chapter, the donor will be allowed an automatic 6-month extension of time to file Form 709 after the date prescribed for filing if the donor files an application under this section in accordance with paragraph (b) of this section. In the case of an individual described in § 1.6081-5(a)(5) or (6) of this chapter, the automatic 6-month extension of time to file Form 709 will run concurrently with the extension of time to file granted pursuant to § 1.6081-5 of this chapter.

(b) *Requirements.*—To satisfy this paragraph (b), a donor must—

(1) Submit a complete application on Form 8892, "Payment of Gift/GST Tax and/or Application for Extension of Time To File Form 709," or in any other manner prescribed by the Commissioner;

(2) File the application on or before the later of—

(i) The date prescribed for filing the return; or

(ii) The expiration of any extension of time to file granted pursuant to § 1.6081-5 of this chapter; and

(3) File the application with the Internal Revenue Service office designated in the application's instructions.

(c) *No extension of time for the payment of tax.*—An automatic extension of time for filing a return granted under paragraph (a) of this section will not extend the time for payment of any tax due on such return.

(d) *Termination of automatic extension.*—The Commissioner may terminate an extension at any time by mailing to the donor a notice of termination at least 10 days prior to the termination date designated in such notice. The Commissioner must mail the notice of termination to the address shown on the Form 8892, or to the donor's last known address. For further guidance regarding the definition of last known address, see § 301.6212-2 of this chapter.

(e) *Penalties.*—See section 6651 for failure to file a gift tax return or failure to pay the amount shown as tax on the return.

(f) *Effective/applicability dates.*—This section is applicable for applications for an extension of time to file Form 709 filed after July 1, 2008. [Reg. § 25.6081-1.]

☐ [*T.D. 9407, 6-30-2008.*]

### [Reg. § 26.6081-1]

**§ 26.6081-1. Automatic extension of time for filing generation-skipping transfer tax returns.**—(a) *In general.*—A skip person distributee required to file a return on Form 706-GS(D), "Generation-Skipping Transfer Tax Return for Distributions," or a trustee required to file a return on Form 706-GS(T), "Generation-Skipping Transfer Tax Return for Terminations," will be allowed an automatic 6-month extension of time to file the return after the date prescribed for filing if the skip person distributee or trustee files an application under this section in accordance with paragraph (b) of this section.

(b) *Requirements.*—To satisfy this paragraph (b), a skip person distributee or trustee must—

(1) Submit a complete application on Form 7004, "Application for Automatic Extension of Time to File Certain Business Income Tax, Information, and Other Returns," or in any other manner prescribed by the Commissioner;

(2) File the application on or before the date prescribed for filing the return with the Internal Revenue Service office designated in the application's instructions; and

(3) Remit the amount of the properly estimated unpaid tax liability on or before the date prescribed for payment.

(c) *No extension of time for the payment of tax.*—An automatic extension of time for filing a return granted under paragraph (a) of this section will not extend the time for payment of any tax due on such return.

(d) *Termination of automatic extension.*—The Commissioner may terminate an automatic extension at any time by mailing to the skip person distributee or trustee a notice of termination at least 10 days prior to the termination date designated in such notice. The Commissioner must mail the notice of termination to the address shown on the Form 7004 or to the skip person distributee or trustee's last known address. For further guidance regarding the definition of last known address, see § 301.6212-2 of this chapter.

(e) *Penalties.*—See section 6651 for failure to file a generation-skipping transfer tax return or failure to pay the amount shown as tax on the return.

(f) *Effective/applicability dates.*—This section is applicable for applications for an automatic extension of time to file a generation-skipping transfer tax return filed after July 1, 2008. [Reg. § 26.6081-1.]

☐ [T.D. 9407, 6-30-2008.]

### [Reg. § 53.6081-1]

**§ 53.6081-1. Automatic extension of time for filing the return to report taxes due under section 4951 for self-dealing with a nuclear decommissioning fund.**—(a) *In general.*—A "disqualified person" for purposes of section 4951(e)(4) who engaged in self-dealing with a Nuclear Decommissioning Fund, and must report tax due under section 4951 on Form 1120-ND, "Return for Nuclear Decommissioning Funds and Certain Related Persons," will be allowed an automatic 6-month extension of time to file the return after the date prescribed for filing the return if the disqualified person files an application under this section in accordance with paragraph (b) of this section. For guidance on requesting an extension of time to file Form 1120-ND for purposes of reporting contributions received, income earned, administrative expenses of operating the fund, and the tax on modified gross income, see § 1.6081-3 of this chapter.

(b) *Requirements.*—To satisfy this paragraph (b), a disqualified person must—

(1) Submit a complete application on Form 7004, "Application for Automatic Extension of Time to File Certain Business Income Tax, Information, and Other Returns," or in any other manner prescribed by the Commissioner;

(2) File the application on or before the date prescribed for filing the return with the Internal Revenue Service office designated in the application's instructions; and

(3) Remit the amount of the properly estimated unpaid tax liability on or before the date prescribed for payment.

(c) *No extension of time for the payment of tax.*—An automatic extension of time for filing a return granted under paragraph (a) of this section will not extend the time for payment of any tax due on such return.

(d) *Termination of automatic extension.*—The Commissioner may terminate an automatic extension at any time by mailing to the disqualified person a notice of termination at least 10 days prior to the termination date designated in such notice. The Commissioner must mail the notice of termination to the address shown on the Form 7004 or to the disqualified person's last known address. For further guidance regarding the definition of last known address, see § 301.6212-2 of this chapter.

(e) *Penalties.*—See section 6651 for failure to file or failure to pay the amount shown as tax on the return.

(f) *Effective/applicability dates.*—This section is applicable for applications for an automatic extension of time to file a return to report

taxes due under section 4951 for self-dealing with a Nuclear Decommissioning Fund filed after July 1, 2008. [Reg. § 53.6081-1.]

☐ [T.D. 9407, 6-30-2008.]

### [Reg. § 54.6081-1]

**§ 54.6081-1. Automatic extension of time for filing returns for certain excise taxes under Chapter 43.**—(a) *In general.*—An employer, other person or health plan that is required to file a return on Form 8928, "Return of Certain Excise Taxes Under Chapter 43 of the Internal Revenue Code," will be allowed an automatic 6-month extension of time to file the return after the date prescribed for filing the return if the employer, other person or health plan files an application under this section in accordance with paragraph (b) of this section.

(b) *Requirements.*—To satisfy this paragraph (b), an employer, other person or health plan must—

(1) Submit a complete application on Form 7004, "Application for Automatic Extension of Time To File Certain Business Income Tax, Information, and Other Returns," or in any other manner prescribed by the Commissioner;

(2) File the application on or before the date prescribed for filing the return with the Internal Revenue Service office designated in the application's instructions; and

(3) Remit the amount of the properly estimated unpaid tax liability on or before the date prescribed for payment.

(c) *No extension of time for the payment of tax.*—An automatic extension of time for filing a return granted under paragraph (a) of this section will not extend the time for payment of any tax due on such return.

(d) *Termination of automatic extension.*—The Commissioner may terminate an automatic extension at any time by mailing to the employer, other person, or health plan a notice of termination at least 10 days prior to the termination date designated in such notice. The Commissioner must mail the notice of termination to the address shown on the Form 7004 or to the estate or trust's last known address. For further guidance regarding the definition of last known address, see § 301.6212-2 of this chapter.

(e) *Penalties.*—See section 6651 for failure to file a pension excise tax return or failure to pay the amount shown as tax on the return.

(f) *Effective/applicability date.*—This section is applicable for applications for an automatic extension of time to file a return due under chapter 43, filed on or after June 24, 2011. [Reg. § 54.6081-1.]

☐ [T.D. 9531, 6-23-2011.]

### [Reg. § 55.6081-1]

**§ 55.6081-1. Automatic extension of time for filing a return due under Chapter 44.**—(a) *In general.*—A Real Estate Investment Trust (REIT) required to file a return on Form 8612, "Return of Excise Tax on Undistributed Income of Real Estate Investment Trusts," or a Regulated Investment Company (RIC) required to file a return on Form 8613, "Return of Excise Tax on Undistributed Income of Regulated Investment Companies," will be allowed an automatic 6-month extension of time to file the return after the date prescribed for filing the return if the REIT or RIC files an application under this section in accordance with paragraph (b) of this section.

(b) *Requirements.*—To satisfy this paragraph (b), a REIT or RIC must—

(1) Submit a complete application on Form 7004, "Application for Automatic Extension of Time to File Certain Business Income Tax, Information, and Other Returns," or in any other manner prescribed by the Commissioner;

(2) File the application on or before the date prescribed for filing the return with the Internal Revenue Service office designated in the application's instructions; and

(3) Remit the amount of the properly estimated unpaid tax liability on or before the date prescribed for payment.

(c) *No extension of time for the payment of tax.*—An automatic extension of time for filing a return granted under paragraph (a) of this section will not extend the time for payment of any tax due on such return.

(d) *Termination of automatic extension.*—The Commissioner may terminate an automatic extension at any time by mailing to the REIT or RIC a notice of termination at least 10 days prior to the termination date designated in such notice. The Commissioner must mail the notice of termination to the address shown on the Form 7004 or to the REIT or RIC's last known address. For further guidance regarding the definition of last known address, see § 301.6212-2 of this chapter.

(e) *Penalties.*—See section 6651 for failure to file or failure to pay the amount shown as tax on the return.

(f) *Effective/applicable dates.*—This section is applicable for applications for an automatic extension of time to file a return due under chapter 44, filed after July 1, 2008. [Reg. § 55.6081-1.]

☐ [*T.D. 9407, 6-30-2008.*]

### [Reg. § 156.6081-1]

**§ 156.6081-1. Automatic extension of time for filing a return due under chapter 54.**—(a) *In general.*—A taxpayer required to file a return on Form 8725, "Excise Tax on Greenmail," will be allowed an automatic 6-month extension of time to file the return after the date prescribed for filing the return if the taxpayer files an application under this section in accordance with paragraph (b) of this section.

(b) *Requirements.*—To satisfy this paragraph (b), a taxpayer must—

(1) Submit a complete application on Form 7004, "Application for Automatic Extension of Time to File Certain Business Income Tax, Information, and Other Returns," or in any other manner prescribed by the Commissioner;

(2) File the application on or before the date prescribed for filing the return with the Internal Revenue Service office designated in the application's instructions; and

(3) Remit the amount of the properly estimated unpaid tax liability on or before the date prescribed for payment.

(c) *No extension of time for the payment of tax.*—An automatic extension of time for filing a return granted under paragraph (a) of this section will not extend the time for payment of any tax due on such return.

(d) *Termination of automatic extension.*—The Commissioner may terminate an automatic extension at any time by mailing to the taxpayer a notice of termination at least 10 days prior to the termination date designated in such notice. The Commissioner must mail the notice of termination to the address shown on the Form 7004 or to the taxpayer's last known address. For further guidance regarding the definition of last known address, see § 301.6212-2 of this chapter.

(e) *Penalties.*—See section 6651 for failure to file or failure to pay the amount shown as tax on the return.

(f) *Effective/applicable dates.*—This section is applicable for applications for an automatic extension of time to file a return due under chapter 54, filed after July 1, 2008. [Reg. § 156.6081-1.]

☐ [*T.D. 9407, 6-30-2008.*]

### [Reg. § 157.6081-1]

**§ 157.6081-1. Automatic extension of time for filing a return due under chapter 55.**—(a) *In general.*—A taxpayer required to file a return on Form 8876, "Excise Tax on Structured Settlement Factoring Transactions," will be allowed an automatic 6-month extension of time to file the return after the date prescribed for filing the return if the taxpayer files an application under this section in accordance with paragraph (b) of this section.

(b) *Requirements.*—To satisfy this paragraph (b), the taxpayer must—

(1) Submit a complete application on Form 7004, "Application for Automatic Extension of Time to File Certain Business Income Tax, Information, and Other Returns," or in any other manner prescribed by the Commissioner;

(2) File the application on or before the date prescribed for filing the return with the Internal Revenue Service office designated in the application's instructions; and

(3) Remit the amount of the properly estimated unpaid tax liability on or before the date prescribed for payment.

(c) *No extension of time for the payment of tax.*—An automatic extension of time for filing a return granted under paragraph (a) of this section will not extend the time for payment of any tax due on such return.

(d) *Termination of automatic extension.*—The Commissioner may terminate an automatic extension at any time by mailing to the taxpayer a notice of termination at least 10 days prior to the termination date designated in such notice. The Commissioner must mail the notice of termination to the address shown on the Form 7004 or to the taxpayer's last known address. For further guidance regarding the definition of last known address, see § 301.6212-2 of this chapter.

(e) *Penalties.*—See section 6651 for failure to file or failure to pay the amount shown as tax on the return.

(f) *Effective/applicability dates.*—This section is applicable for applications for an automatic extension of time to file a return due under chapter 55, filed after July 1, 2008. [Reg. § 157.6081-1.]

☐ [*T.D. 9407, 6-30-2008.*]

### [Reg. § 301.6081-1]

**§ 301.6081-1. Extension of time for filing returns.**—For provisions concerning extensions of time for filing returns or other documents, see the regulations relating to the particular tax. [Reg. § 301.6081-1.]

☐ [*T.D. 6498, 10-24-60.*]

### [Reg. § 1.6081-2]

**§ 1.6081-2. Automatic extension of time to file certain returns filed by partnerships.**—(a) *In general.*—A partnership required to file Form 1065, "U.S. Partnership Return of Income," or Form 8804, "Annual Return for Partnership Withholding Tax," for any taxable year will be allowed an automatic six-month extension of time to file the return after the date prescribed for filing the return if the partnership files an application under this section in accordance with paragraph (b) of this section. No additional extension will be allowed pursuant to § 1.6081-1(b) beyond the automatic six-month extension provided by this section. In the case of a partnership described in § 1.6081-5(a)(1), the automatic extension of time to file allowed under this section runs concurrently with an extension of time to file granted pursuant to § 1.6081-5.

(b) *Requirements.*—To satisfy this paragraph (b), the partnership must—

(1) Submit a complete application on Form 7004, "Application for Automatic Extension of Time to File Certain Business Income Tax, Information, and Other Returns," or in any other manner prescribed by the Commissioner;

(2) File the application on or before the later of—

(i) The date prescribed for filing the return of the partnership; or

(ii) The expiration of any extension of time to file granted under § 1.6081-5(a); and

(3) File the application with the Internal Revenue Service office designated in the application's instructions.

(c) *Payment of section 7519 amount.*—An automatic extension of time for filing a partnership return of income granted under paragraph (a) of this section does not extend the time for payment of any amount due under section 7519, relating to required payments for entities electing not to have a required taxable year.

(d) *Section 444 election.*—An automatic extension of time for filing a partnership return of income will run concurrently with any extension of time for filing a return allowed because of section 444, relating to the election of a taxable year other than a required taxable year.

(e) *Effect of extension on partner.*—An automatic extension of time for filing a partnership return of income under this section does not extend the time for filing a partner's income tax return or the time for the payment of any tax due on a partner's income tax return.

(f) *Termination of automatic extension.*—The Commissioner may terminate an automatic extension at any time by mailing to the partnership a notice of termination at least 10 days prior to the termination date designated in such notice. The Commissioner must mail the notice of termination to the address shown on the Form 7004 or to the partnership's last known address. For further guidance regarding the definition of last known address, *see* § 301.6212-2 of this chapter.

(g) *Penalties.*—*See* section 6698 for failure to file a partnership return.

(h) *Applicability date.*—This section applies to applications for an automatic extension of time to file the partnership returns listed in paragraph (a) of this section on or after January 30, 2020. Section 1.6081-2T (as contained in 26 CFR part 1, revised April 2019) applies to applications for an automatic extension of time to file before January 30, 2020. [Reg. § 1.6081-2.]

☐ [*T.D. 9531, 6-23-2011. Amended by T.D. 9821, 7-18-2017 and T.D. 9892, 1-29-2020.*]

### [Reg. § 301.6081-2]

**§ 301.6081-2. Automatic extension of time for filing an information return with respect to certain foreign trusts.**—(a) *In general.*—A trust required to file a return on Form 3520-A, "Annual Information Return of Foreign Trust with a U.S. Owner," will be allowed an automatic 6-month extension of time to file the return after the date prescribed for filing the return if the trust files an application under this section in accordance with paragraph (b) of this section.

(b) *Requirements.*—To satisfy this paragraph (b), a trust must—

(1) Submit a complete application on Form 7004, "Application for Automatic Extension of Time to File Certain Business Income Tax, Information, and Other Returns," or in any other manner prescribed by the Commissioner; and

(2) File the application on or before the date prescribed for filing the return with the Internal Revenue Service office designated in the application's instructions.

(c) *Termination of automatic extension.*—The Commissioner may terminate an automatic extension at any time by mailing to the trust a notice of termination at least 10 days prior to the termination date designated in such notice. The Commissioner must mail the notice of termination to the address shown on the Form 7004 or to the trust's last known address. For further guidance regarding the definition of last known address, see § 301.6212-2 of this chapter.

(d) *Penalties.*—See section 6677 for failure to file information returns with respect to certain foreign trusts.

(e) *Effective/applicability dates.*—This section is applicable for applications for an automatic extension of time to file an information return with respect to certain foreign trusts listed in paragraph (a) of this section filed after July 1, 2008. [Reg. § 301.6081-2.]

☐ [T.D. 9407, 6-30-2008.]

### [Reg. § 1.6081-3]

**§ 1.6081-3. Automatic extension of time for filing corporation income tax returns.**—(a) *In general.*—Except as provided in paragraphs (e) and (f) of this section, a corporation or an affiliated group of corporations filing a consolidated return will be allowed an automatic 6-month extension of time to file its income tax return after the date prescribed for filing the return if the following requirements are met.

(1) An application must be submitted on Form 7004, "Application for Automatic Extension of Time to File Certain Business Income Tax, Information, and Other Returns," or in any other manner prescribed by the Commissioner.

(2) The application must be filed on or before the date prescribed for the filing of the return of the corporation (or the consolidated return of the affiliated group of corporations) with the Internal Revenue Service office designated in the application's instructions.

(3) The corporation (or affiliated group of corporations filing a consolidated return) must remit the amount of the properly estimated unpaid tax liability on or before the date prescribed for payment.

(4) The application must include a statement listing the name and address of each member of the affiliated group if the affiliated group will file a consolidated return. Upon the timely filing of Form 7004, the 6-month extension of time to file shall be considered as granted to the affiliated group for the filing of its consolidated return or for the filing of each member's separate return.

(b) *No extension of time for the payment of tax.*—Any automatic extension of time for filing a corporation income tax return granted under paragraph (a) of this section shall not operate to extend the time for payment of any tax due on such return.

(c) *Termination of automatic extension.*—The Commissioner may terminate an automatic extension at any time by mailing a notice of termination to the corporation (parent corporation in the case of an affiliated group of corporations filing a consolidated return). The notice shall be mailed at least 10 days prior to the termination date designated in such notice. The notice of termination shall be sufficient for all purposes when mailed to the corporation at the address shown on Form 7004 or to the corporation's last known address. For further guidance regarding the definition of last known address, see § 301.6212-2 of this chapter.

(d) *No extension for DISCs.*—Paragraphs (a) through (c) of this section shall not apply to returns filed by a DISC pursuant to section 6011(c)(2).

(e) *Exception.*—In the case of any return for a taxable year of a C corporation that ends on June 30 and begins before January 1, 2026, the first sentence of paragraph (a) of this section shall be applied by substituting "7-month" for "6-month." For purposes of this paragraph (e), the return for a short period (within the meaning of section 443) that ends on any day in June shall be treated as the return for a taxable year that ends on June 30.

(f) *Cross reference.*—For provisions relating to extensions of time to file Form 1120-POL, "U.S. Income Tax Return for Certain Political Organizations," see § 1.6081-9.

(g) *Applicability date.*—This section applies to requests for extension of time to file corporation income tax returns on or after January

30, 2020. Section 1.6081-3T (as contained in 26 CFR part 1, revised April 2019) applies to applications for an automatic extension of time to file before January 30, 2020. [Reg. § 1.6081-3.]

☐ [T.D. 6364, 2-13-59. *Amended by* T.D. 6914, 3-7-67; T.D. 6950, 4-3-68; T.D. 7138, 8-10-71; T.D. 7260, 2-9-73; T.D. 7533, 2-14-78; T.D. 7567, 10-2-78; T.D. 7885, 4-13-83; T.D. 8939, 1-11-2001; T.D. 9163, 12-6-2004; T.D. 9229, 11-4-2005, T.D. 9407, 6-30-2008, T.D. 9821, 7-18-2017 *and* T.D. 9892, 1-29-2020.]

### [Reg. § 1.6081-4]

**§ 1.6081-4. Automatic extension of time for filing individual income tax return.**—(a) *In general.*—An individual who is required to file an individual income tax return will be allowed an automatic 6-month extension of time to file the return after the date prescribed for filing the return if the individual files an application under this section in accordance with paragraph (b) of this section. In the case of an individual described in § 1.6081-5(a)(5) or (6), the automatic 6-month extension will run concurrently with the extension of time to file granted pursuant to § 1.6081-5.

(b) *Requirements.*—To satisfy this paragraph (b), an individual must—

(1) Submit a complete application on Form 4868, "Application for Automatic Extension of Time To File U.S Individual Income Tax Return," or in any other manner prescribed by the Commissioner;

(2) File the application on or before the later of—

(i) The date prescribed for filing the return; or

(ii) The expiration of any extension of time to file granted pursuant to § 1.6081-5;

(3) File the application with the Internal Revenue Service office designated in the application's instructions; and

(4) Show the full amount properly estimated as tax for the taxable year.

(c) *No extension of time for the payment of tax.*—An automatic extension of time for filing a return granted under paragraph (a) of this section will not extend the time for payment of any tax due on such return.

(d) *Termination of automatic extension.*—The Commissioner may terminate an automatic extension at any time by mailing to the individual a notice of termination at least 10 days prior to the termination date designated in such notice. The Commissioner must mail the notice of termination to the address shown on the Form 4868 or to the individual's last known address. For further guidance regarding the definition of last known address, see § 301.6212-2 of this chapter.

(e) *Penalties.*—See section 6651 for failure to file an individual income tax return or failure to pay the amount shown as tax on the return. In particular, see § 301.6651-1(c)(3) of this chapter (relating to a presumption of reasonable cause in certain circumstances involving an automatic extension of time for filing an individual income tax return).

(f) *Effective/applicability dates.*—This section is applicable for applications for an automatic extension of time to file an individual income tax return filed after July 1, 2008. [Reg. § 1.6081-4.]

☐ [T.D. 9407, 6-30-2008.]

### [Reg. § 1.6081-5]

**§ 1.6081-5. Extensions of time in the case of certain partnerships, corporations and U.S. citizens and residents.**—(a) An extension of time for filing returns of income and for paying any tax shown on the return is hereby granted to and including the fifteenth day of the sixth month following the close of the taxable year in the case of—

(1) Partnerships, which are required under section 6072(b) to file returns on the fifteenth day of the third month following the close of the taxable year of the partnership, that keep their records and books of account outside the United States and Puerto Rico;

(2) Domestic corporations which transact their business and keep their records and books of account outside the United States and Puerto Rico;

(3) Foreign corporations which maintain an office or place of business within the United States;

(4) Domestic corporations whose principal income is from sources within the possessions of the United States;

(5) United States citizens or residents whose tax homes and abodes, in a real and substantial sense, are outside the United States and Puerto Rico; and

(6) United States citizens and residents in military or naval service on duty, including non-permanent or short term duty, outside the United States and Puerto Rico.

(b) In order to qualify for the extension under this section—

(1) A statement must be attached to the return showing that the person for whom the return is made is a person described in paragraph (a) of this section; or

(2) If a person described in paragraph (a) of this section requests additional time to file, the person must request the extension on or before the fifteenth day of the sixth month following the close of the taxable year and check the appropriate box on Form 4868, "Application for Automatic Extension of Time To File a U.S. Individual Income Tax Return," or Form 7004, "Application for Automatic Extension of Time to File Certain Business Income Tax, Information, and Other Returns," whichever is applicable, or in any other manner prescribed by the Commissioner.

(c) For purposes of paragraph (a)(5) of this section, whether a person is a United States resident will be determined in accordance with section 7701(b) of the Code. The term "tax home," as used in paragraph (a)(5), will have the same meaning which it has for purposes of section 162(a)(2) (relating to travel expenses away from home). If a person does not have a regular or principal place of business, that person's tax home will be considered to be his regular place of abode in a real and substantial sense.

(d) In order to qualify for the extension under paragraph (a)(6), the assigned tour of duty outside the United States and Puerto Rico must be for a period that includes the entire due date of the return.

(e) A person otherwise qualifying for the extension under paragraph (a)(5) or paragraph (a)(6) shall not be disqualified because he is physically present in the United States or Puerto Rico at any time, including the due date of the return.

(f) This section applies to returns filed on or after January 30, 2020. Section 1.6081-5T (as contained in 26 CFR part 1, revised April 2019) applies to applications for an automatic extension of time to file returns before January 30, 2020. [Reg. § 1.6081-5.]

☐ [T.D. 8312, 9-7-90. *Amended by T.D. 9163, 12-6-2004; T.D. 9229, 11-4-2005, T.D. 9407, 6-30-2008, T.D. 9821, 7-18-2017 and T.D. 9892, 1-29-2020.]*

### [Reg. § 1.6081-6]

**§ 1.6081-6. Automatic extension of time to file estate or trust income tax return.**—(a) *In general.*—(1) Except as provided in paragraph (a)(2) of this section, any estate, including but not limited to an estate defined in section 2031, or trust required to file an income tax return on Form 1041, "U.S. Income Tax Return for Estates and Trusts," will be allowed an automatic five and one-half month extension of time to file the return after the date prescribed for filing the return if the estate or trust files an application under this section in accordance with paragraph (b) of this section. No additional extension will be allowed pursuant to § 1.6081-1(b) beyond the automatic five and one-half month extension provided by this section.

(2) A bankruptcy estate that is created when an individual debtor files a petition under either chapter 7 or chapter 11 of Title 11 of the U.S. Code that is required to file an income tax return on Form 1041, "U.S. Income Tax Return for Estates and Trusts," and an estate or trust required to file an income tax return on Form 1041-N, "U.S. Income Tax Return for Electing Alaska Native Settlement," or Form 1041-QFT, "U.S. Income Tax Return for Qualified Funeral Trusts" for any taxable year will be allowed an automatic 6-month extension of time to file the return after the date prescribed for filing the return if the estate files an application under this section in accordance with paragraph (b) of this section.

(b) *Requirements.*—To satisfy this paragraph (b), an estate or trust must—

(1) Submit a complete application on Form 7004, "Application for Automatic Extension of Time to File Certain Business Income Tax, Information, and Other Returns," or in any other manner prescribed by the Commissioner;

(2) File the application on or before the date prescribed for filing the return with the Internal Revenue Service office designated in the application's instructions; and

(3) Show the amount properly estimated as tax for the estate or trust for the taxable year.

(c) *No extension of time for the payment of tax.*—An automatic extension of time for filing a return granted under paragraph (a) of this section will not extend the time for payment of any tax due on such return.

(d) *Effect of extension on beneficiary.*—An automatic extension of time to file an estate or trust income tax return under this section will not extend the time for filing the income tax return of a beneficiary of the estate or trust or the time for the payment of any tax due on the beneficiary's income tax return.

(e) *Termination of automatic extension.*—The Commissioner may terminate an automatic extension at any time by mailing to the estate or trust a notice of termination at least 10 days prior to the termination date designated in such notice. The Commissioner must mail the notice of termination to the address shown on the Form 7004 or to the estate or trust's last known address. For further guidance regarding the definition of last known address, see § 301.6212-2 of this chapter.

(f) *Penalties.*—*See* section 6651 for failure to file an estate or trust income tax return or failure to pay the amount shown as tax on the return.

(g) *Applicability date.*—This section applies to applications for an automatic extension of time to file an estate or trust income tax return on or after January 30, 2020. Section 1.6081-6T (as contained in 26 CFR part 1, revised April 2019) applies to applications for an automatic extension of time to file a return before January 30, 2020. [Reg. § 1.6081-6.]

☐ [T.D. 9531, 6-23-2011. *Amended by T.D. 9821, 7-18-2017 and T.D. 9892, 1-29-2020.]*

### [Reg. § 1.6081-7]

**§ 1.6081-7. Automatic extension of time to file Real Estate Mortgage Investment Conduit (REMIC) income tax return.**—(a) *In general.*—A Real Estate Mortgage Investment Conduit (REMIC) required to file an income tax return on Form 1066, "U.S. Real Estate Mortgage Investment Conduit Income Tax Return," or Form 8831, "Excise Tax on Excess Inclusions of REMIC Residual Interests," for any taxable year will be allowed an automatic 6-month extension of time to file the return after the date prescribed for filing the return if the REMIC files an application under this section in accordance with paragraph (b) of this section.

(b) *Requirements.*—To satisfy this paragraph (b), a REMIC must—

(1) Submit a complete application on Form 7004, "Application for Automatic Extension of Time to File Certain Business Income Tax, Information, and Other Returns," or in any other manner prescribed by the Commissioner;

(2) File the application on or before the date prescribed for filing the return with the Internal Revenue Service office designated in the application's instructions; and

(3) Show the full amount properly estimated as tax for the REMIC for the taxable year.

(c) *No extension of time for the payment of tax.*—An automatic extension of time for filing a return granted under paragraph (a) of this section will not extend the time for payment of any tax due on such return.

(d) *Effect of extension on residual or regular interest holders.*—An automatic extension of time to file a REMIC income tax return under this section will not extend the time for filing the income tax return of a residual or regular interest holder of the REMIC or the time for the payment of any tax due on the residual or regular interest holder's income tax return. An automatic extension will also not extend the time for payment of any excise tax on excess inclusions of REMIC residual interests.

(e) *Termination of automatic extension.*—The Commissioner may terminate an automatic extension at any time by mailing to the REMIC a notice of termination at least 10 days prior to the termination date designated in such notice. The Commissioner must mail the notice of termination to the address shown on the Form 7004 or to the REMIC's last known address. For further guidance regarding the definition of last known address, see § 301.6212-2 of this chapter.

(f) *Penalties.*—See sections 6698 and 6651 for failure to file a REMIC income tax return or failure to pay an amount shown as tax on the return.

(g) *Effective/applicability dates.*—This section applies to applications for an automatic extension of time to file REMIC income and excise tax returns listed in paragraph (a) of this section filed after July 1, 2008. [Reg. § 1.6081-7.]

☐ [T.D. 9407, 6-30-2008.]

>>>➔ *Caution: Reg. § 1.6081-8, below, as amended by T.D. 9838, applies to requests for extensions of time to file information returns required to be filed after December 31, 2018.*

### [Reg. § 1.6081-8]

**§ 1.6081-8. Extension of time to file certain information returns.**—(a) *Certain information returns eligible for an automatic extension of time to file.*—(1) *Automatic extension of time to file.*—A person required to file an information return (the filer) on the forms or form series listed in Table 1 will be allowed one automatic 30-day extension of time to file the information return beyond the due date for

⫸ *Caution: Reg. §1.6081-8, below, as amended by T.D. 9838, applies to requests for extensions of time to file information returns required to be filed after December 31, 2018.*

filing, if the filer or the person transmitting the information return for the filer (the transmitter) files an application in accordance with paragraph (c)(1) of this section.

*Table 1 to paragraph (a)(1)*

| Form or Form Series | Name of Form |
|---|---|
| Form W-2G | "Certain Gambling Winnings" |
| Form 1042-S | "Foreign Person's U.S. Source Income Subject to Withholding" |
| Form 1094-C | "Transmittal of Employer-Provided Health Insurance Offer and Coverage Information Returns" |
| Form 1095-B | "Health Coverage" |
| Form 1095-C | "Employer-Provided Health Insurance Offer and Coverage" |
| Form 3921 | "Exercise of an Incentive Stock Option Under Section 422(b)" |
| Form 3922 | "Transfer of Stock Acquired Through an Employee Stock Purchase Plan Under Section 423(c)" |
| Form 8027 | "Employer's Annual Information Return of Tip Income and Allocated Tips" |
| Form 1097 series | |
| Form 1098 series | |
| Form 1099 series (except forms reporting nonemployee compensation) | |
| Form 5498 series | |

(2) *Non-automatic extension of time to file.*—One additional 30-day extension of time to file an information return on a form listed in paragraph (a)(1) of this section may be allowed if the filer or transmitter submits a request for the additional extension of time to file before the expiration of the automatic 30-day extension of time to file. No extension of time to file will be granted under this paragraph (a)(2) unless the filer or transmitter has first obtained an automatic extension of time to file under paragraph (a)(1) of this section. To request the additional 30-day extension of time to file, the filer or transmitter must satisfy the requirements of paragraph (c)(2) of this section. No additional extension of time to file will be allowed for an information return on a form listed in paragraph (a)(1) of this section under §1.6081-1 beyond the extensions of time to file provided by paragraph (a)(1) of this section and this paragraph (a)(2).

(b) *The Form W-2 series (except Form W-2G) or forms reporting nonemployee compensation.*—Except as provided in paragraph (f) of this section, the filer or transmitter of an information return on the Form W-2 series (except Form W-2G) or a form reporting nonemployee compensation may only request one non-automatic 30-day extension of time to file the information return beyond the due date for filing it. To make such a request, the filer or transmitter must submit an application for an extension of time to file in accordance with paragraph (c)(2) of this section. No additional extension of time to file will be allowed for an information return on a form listed in this paragraph (b) under §1.6081-1 beyond the 30-day extension of time to file provided by this paragraph (b).

(c) *Requirements.*—(1) *Automatic extension of time to file.*—To satisfy this paragraph (c)(1), an application must—

(i) Be submitted on Form 8809, "Request for Extension of Time to File Information Returns," or in any other manner as may be prescribed by the Commissioner; and

(ii) Be filed with the Internal Revenue Service office designated in the application's instructions on or before the due date for filing the information return.

(2) *Non-automatic extension of time to file.*—To satisfy this paragraph (c)(2), a filer or transmitter must—

(i) Submit a complete application on Form 8809, or in any other manner prescribed by the Commissioner, indicating that at least one of the criteria set forth in the forms, instructions, or other guidance for granting an extension applies;

(ii) File the application with the Internal Revenue Service in accordance with forms, instructions, or other appropriate guidance on or before the due date for filing the information return (for purposes of paragraph (a)(2) of this section, determined with regard to the extension of time to file under paragraph (a)(1) of this section); and

(iii) Sign the application under penalties of perjury.

(d) *Penalties.*—See sections 6652, 6693, and 6721 through 6724 of the Code for failure to comply with information reporting requirements on information returns described in this section.

(e) *No effect on time to furnish statements.*—An extension of time to file an information return under this section does not extend the time for furnishing a statement to the person with respect to whom the information is required to be reported.

(f) *Form W-2 filed on expedited basis.*—This section does not apply to an information return on a form in the W–2 series if the procedures authorized in Rev. Proc. 96-57 (1996-2 CB 389) (or a successor revenue procedure) allow an automatic extension of time to file the information return. See §601.601(d)(2)(ii)(b) of this chapter.

(g) *Applicability date.*—This section applies to requests for extensions of time to file information returns required to be filed after December 31, 2018. Section 1.6081-8T (as contained in 26 CFR part 1, revised April 1, 2018) applies to extensions of time to file information returns required to be filed before January 1, 2019. [Reg. §1.6081-8.]

☐ [*T.D.* 9163, 12-6-2004. *Amended by T.D.* 9660, 3-5-2014, *T.D.* 9730, 8-12-2015 *and T.D.* 9838, 8-1-2018.]

⫸ *Caution: Temporary Reg. §1.6081-8T, below, was removed by T.D. 9838, but applies to extensions of time to file information returns required to be filed before January 1, 2019.*

**[Reg. §1.6081-8T]**

**§1.6081-8T. Extension of time to file certain information returns (temporary).**—(a) *Information returns on Form W-2G, 1042-S, 1094-C, 1095-B, 1095-C, 1097 series, 1098 series, 1099 series, 3921, 3922, 5498 series, or 8027*

(1) *Automatic extension of time to file.*—A person required to file an information return (the filer) on Form W-2G, 1042-S, 1094-C, 1095-B, 1095-C, 1097 series, 1098 series, 1099 series, 3921, 3922, 5498 series, or 8027 will be allowed one automatic 30-day extension of time to file the information return beyond the due date for filing it if the filer or the person transmitting the information return for the filer (the transmitter) files an application in accordance with paragraph (c)(1) of this section.

(2) *Non-automatic extension of time to file.*—One additional 30-day extension of time to file an information return on a form listed in paragraph (a)(1) of this section may be allowed if the filer or transmitter submits a request for the additional extension of time to file

before the expiration of the automatic 30-day extension of time to file. No extension of time to file will be granted under this paragraph (a)(2) unless the filer or transmitter has first obtained an automatic extension of time to file under paragraph (a)(1) of this section. To request the additional 30-day extension of time to file, the filer or transmitter must satisfy the requirements of paragraph (c)(2) of this section. No additional extension of time to file will be allowed for an information return on a form listed in paragraph (a)(1) of this section pursuant to §1.6081-1 beyond the extensions of time to file provided by paragraph (a)(1) of this section and this paragraph (a)(2).

(b) *Information returns on forms in the W-2 series (except Form W-2G).*—Except as provided in paragraph (f) of this section, the filer or transmitter of an information return on forms in the W-2 series (except Form W-2G) may only request one non-automatic 30-day extension of time to file the information return beyond the due date for filing it. To make such a request, the filer or transmitter must submit an application for an extension of time to file in accordance with paragraph (c)(2) of this section. No additional extension of time to file will be allowed for information returns on forms in the W-2

➤➤➤ *Caution: Temporary Reg. §1.6081-8T, below, was removed by T.D. 9838, but applies to extensions of time to file information returns required to be filed before January 1, 2019.*

series pursuant to § 1.6081-1 beyond the 30-day extension of time to file provided by this paragraph (b).

(c) *Requirements.*—(1) *Automatic extension of time to file.*—To satisfy this paragraph (c)(1), an application must—

(i) Be submitted on Form 8809, "Request for Extension of Time to File Information Returns," or in any other manner as may be prescribed by the Commissioner; and

(ii) Be filed with the Internal Revenue Service office designated in the application's instructions on or before the due date for filing the information return.

(2) *Non-automatic extension of time to file.*—To satisfy this paragraph (c)(2), a filer or transmitter must—

(i) Submit a complete application on Form 8809, or in any other manner prescribed by the Commissioner, including a detailed explanation of why additional time is needed;

(ii) File the application with the Internal Revenue Service in accordance with forms, instructions, or other appropriate guidance on or before the due date for filing the information return (for purposes of paragraph (a)(2) of this section, determined with regard to the extension of time to file under paragraph (a)(1) of this section); and

(iii) Sign the application under penalties of perjury.

(d) *Penalties.*—See sections 6652, 6693, and 6721 through 6724 for failure to comply with information reporting requirements on information returns described in this section.

(e) *No effect on time to furnish statements.*—An extension of time to file an information return under this section does not extend the time for furnishing a statement to the person with respect to whom the information is required to be reported.

(f) *Form W-2 filed on expedited basis.*—This section does not apply to an information return on a form in the W–2 series if the procedures authorized in Rev. Proc. 96-57 (1996-2 CB 389) (or a successor revenue procedure) allow an automatic extension of time to file the information return. See § 601.601(d)(2)(ii)(b) of this chapter.

(g) *Effective/applicability date.*—This section applies to requests for extensions of time to file information returns due after December 31, 2016.

(h) *Expiration date.*—The applicability of this section expires on August 10, 2018. [Temporary Reg. § 1.6081-8T.]

☐ [*T.D. 9730, 8-12-2015. Removed by T.D. 9838, 8-1-2018.*]

### [Reg. § 1.6081-9]

**§ 1.6081-9. Automatic extension of time to file exempt or political organization returns.**—(a) *In general.*—An entity required to file a return on a form in the Form 990 series (Form 990, "Return of Organization Exempt From Income Tax," Form 990-BL, "Information and Initial Excise Tax Return for Black Lung Benefit Trusts and Certain Related Persons," Form 990-EZ, "Short Form Return of Organization Exempt From Income Tax," Form 990-PF, "Return of Private Foundation," and Form 990-T, "Exempt Organization Business Tax Return"), Form 1041-A, "U.S. Information Return-Trust Accumulation of Charitable Amounts," Form 1120-POL, "U.S. Income Tax Return for Certain Political Organizations," Form 4720, "Return of Certain Excise Taxes Under Chapters 41 and 42 of the Internal Revenue Code," Form 5227, "Split-Interest Trust Information Return," Form 6069, "Return of Excise Tax on Excess Contributions to Black Lung Benefit Trust Under Section 4953 and Computation of Section 192 Deduction," and Form 8870, "Information Return for Transfers Associated With Certain Personal Benefit Contracts," will be allowed an automatic six-month extension of time to file the return after the date prescribed for filing if the entity files an application in accordance with paragraph (b) of this section.

(b) *Requirements.*—To satisfy this paragraph (b), an application for an automatic extension under this section must—

(1) Be submitted on Form 7004, "Application for Automatic Extension of Time to File Certain Business Income Tax, Information, and Other Returns" (in the case of an extension of time to file Form 1120-POL), Form 8868, "Application for Automatic Extension of Time to File an Exempt Organization Return" (in the case of an extension of time to file any other return listed in paragraph (a) of this section), or in any other manner as may be prescribed by the Commissioner;

(2) Be filed with the Internal Revenue Service office designated in the application's instructions on or before the date prescribed for filing the return;

(3) Show the full amount properly estimated as tentative tax for the entity for the taxable year; and

(4) Be accompanied by the full remittance of the amount properly estimated as tentative tax which is unpaid as of the date prescribed for the filing of the return.

(c) *Termination of automatic extension.*—The Commissioner may terminate an automatic extension at any time by mailing to the entity a notice of termination. The notice must be mailed at least 10 days prior to the termination date designated in such notice. The notice of termination must be mailed to the address shown on the application for extension or to the entity's last known address. For further guidance regarding the definition of last known address, see § 301.6212-2 of this chapter.

(d) *Penalties.*—See sections 6651 and 6652(c) for failure to file a return or failure to pay the amount shown as tax on the return.

(e) *Coordination with § 1.6081-1.*—No extension of time will be granted under § 1.6081-1 for filing a return listed in paragraph (a) of this section until an automatic extension has been allowed pursuant to this section.

(f) *Applicability date.*—This section applies to requests for extensions of time to file returns listed in paragraph (a) of this section on or after January 30, 2020. Sections 1.6081-3T and 1.6081-9T (as contained in 26 CFR part 1, revised April 2019) apply to requests for extensions before January 30, 2020. [Reg. § 1.6081-9.]

☐ [*T.D. 9163, 12-6-2004. Amended by T.D. 9821, 7-18-2017 and T.D. 9892, 1-29-2020.*]

### [Reg. § 1.6081-10]

**§ 1.6081-10. Automatic extension of time to file withholding tax return for U.S. source income of foreign persons.**—(a) *In general.*— A withholding agent or intermediary required to file a return on Form 1042, "Annual Withholding Tax Return for U.S. Source Income of Foreign Persons," for any taxable year will be allowed an automatic 6-month extension of time to file the return after the date prescribed for filing the return if the withholding agent or intermediary files an application under this section in accordance with paragraph (b) of this section.

(b) *Requirements.*—To satisfy this paragraph (b), a withholding agent or intermediary must—

(1) Submit a complete application on Form 7004, "Application for Automatic Extension of Time to File Certain Business Income Tax, Information, and Other Returns," or in any other manner prescribed by the Commissioner;

(2) File the application on or before the date prescribed for filing the return with the Internal Revenue Service office designated in the application's instructions; and

(3) Remit the amount of the properly estimated unpaid tax liability on or before the date prescribed for payment.

(c) *No extension of time for the payment of tax.*—An automatic extension of time for filing a return granted under paragraph (a) of this section will not extend the time for payment of any tax due on such return.

(d) *Termination of automatic extension.*—The Commissioner may terminate an automatic extension at any time by mailing to the withholding agent or intermediary a notice of termination at least 10 days prior to the termination date designated in such notice. The Commissioner must mail the notice of termination to the address shown on the Form 7004 or to the withholding agent or intermediary's last known address. For further guidance regarding the definition of last known address, see § 301.6212-2 of this chapter.

(e) *Penalties.*—See section 6651 for failure to file a return or failure to pay an amount shown as tax on the return.

(f) *Effective/applicability dates.*—This section is applicable for applications for an automatic extension of time to file the withholding tax return for U.S. source income of foreign persons return filed after July 1, 2008. [Reg. § 1.6081-10.]

☐ [*T.D. 9407, 6-30-2008.*]

### [Reg. § 1.6081-11]

**§ 1.6081-11. Automatic extension of time for filing certain employee plan returns.**—(a) *In general.*—An administrator or sponsor of an employee benefit plan required to file a return under the provisions of chapter 61 or the regulations under that chapter on Form 5500 (series), "Annual Return/Report of Employee Benefit Plan," will be allowed an automatic extension of time to file the return until the 15th day of the third month following the date prescribed for filing the return if the administrator or sponsor files an application under this section in accordance with paragraph (b) of this section.

(b) *Requirements.*—To satisfy this paragraph (b), an administrator or sponsor must—

(1) Submit a complete application on Form 5558, "Application for Extension of Time To File Certain Employee Plan Returns," or in any other manner as may be prescribed by the Commissioner; and

(2) File the application with the Internal Revenue Service office designated in the application's instructions on or before the date prescribed for filing the information return.

(c) *Termination of automatic extension.*—The Commissioner may terminate an automatic extension at any time by mailing to the administrator or sponsor a notice of termination at least 10 days prior to the termination date designated in such notice. The Commissioner must mail the notice of termination to the address shown on the Form 5558 or to the administrator or sponsor's last known address. For further guidance regarding the definition of last known address, see § 301.6212-2 of this chapter.

(d) *Penalties.*—See sections 6652, 6692, and the Employee Retirement Income Security Act of 1974 for penalties for failure to file a timely and complete Form 5500.

(e) *Effective/applicability dates.*—This section is applicable for applications for an automatic extension of time to file Forms 5500 for plan years ending after July 1, 2008. [Reg. § 1.6081-11.]

☐ [*T.D. 9407, 6-30-2008.*]

### [Reg. §31.6081(a)-1]

**§31.6081(a)-1. Extensions of time for filing returns and other documents.**—(a) *Federal Insurance Contributions Act; income tax withheld from wages; and Railroad Retirement Tax Act.*—(1) *In general.*—Except as otherwise provided in subparagraphs (2) and (3) of this paragraph, no extension of time for filing any return or other document required in respect of the Federal Insurance Contributions Act, income tax withheld from wages, or the Railroad Retirement Tax Act will be granted.

(2) *Information returns of employers on Forms W-2 and W-3.*—(i) *In general.*—The Commissioner may grant an extension of time in which to file the Social Security Administration copy of Forms W-2 and the accompanying transmittal form which constitutes an information return under § 31.6051-2(a). For further guidance regarding extensions of time to file the Social Security Administration copy of Forms W-2 and W-3, see § 1.6081-8 of this chapter.

(ii) *Automatic extension of time.*—The Commissioner may, in appropriate cases, publish procedures for automatic extensions of time to file Forms W-2 where the employer is required to file the Form W-2 on an expedited basis.

(b) *Federal Unemployment Tax Act.*—[Not reproduced herein.—CCH.]

(c) *Duly authorized agent.*—In any case in which an employer is unable, by reason of illness, absence, or other good cause, to sign a request for an extension, any person standing in close personal or business relationship to the employer may sign the request on his behalf, and shall be considered as a duly authorized agent for this purpose, provided the request sets forth the reasons for a signature other than the employer's and the relationship existing between the employer and the signer.

(d) *Effective date.*—Paragraph (a)(2)(i) of this section applies to requests for extensions of time to file the Social Security Administration copy of Forms W-2 and W-3 due after December 7, 2004. [Reg. § 31.6081(a)-1.]

☐ [*T.D. 6354, 1-13-59. Amended by T.D. 6950, 4-3-68; T.D. 7351, 4-16-75; T.D. 8636, 12-20-95; T.D. 9061, 6-10-2003 and T.D. 9163, 12-6-2004.*]

# Place for Filing Returns or Other Documents

### [Reg. § 1.6091-1]

**§ 1.6091-1. Place for filing returns or other documents.**—(a) *In general.*—Except as provided in § 1.6091-4, whenever a return, statement, or other document is required to be made under the provisions of subtitle A or F of the Code, or the regulations thereunder, with respect to any tax imposed by subtitle A of the Code, and the place for filing such return, statement, or other document is not provided for by the Code, it shall be filed at the place prescribed by the regulations contained in this chapter.

(b) *Place for filing certain information returns.*—(1) For the place for filing returns of partnership income, see paragraph (e)(1) of § 1.6031(a)-1.

(2) For the place for filing information returns by banks with respect to common trust funds, see § 1.6032-1.

(3) For the place for filing information returns by certain organizations exempt from taxation under section 501(a), see paragraph (e) of § 1.6033-1.

(4) For the place for filing information returns by trusts claiming charitable deductions under section 642(c), see paragraph (c) of § 1.6034-1.

(5) [Reserved].

(6) For the place for filing information returns relating to certain stock option transactions, see paragraph (c) of § 1.6039-1.

(7) For the place for filing returns of information reporting certain payments, see paragraph (a)(5) of § 1.6041-2 and § 1.6041-6.

(8) For the place for filing returns of information regarding payments of dividends, see paragraph (c) of § 1.6042-2 (relating to returns for calendar years after 1962).

(9) For the place for filing information returns by corporations relating to contemplated dissolution or liquidation, see paragraph (a) of § 1.6043-1.

(10) For the place for filing information returns by corporations relating to distributions in liquidation, see paragraph (a) of § 1.6043-2.

(11) For the place for filing returns of information regarding payments of patronage dividends, see paragraph (d) of § 1.6044-2.

(12) For the place for filing information returns relating to formation or reorganization of foreign corporations, see paragraph (j)(2) of § 1.6046-1.

(13) For the place for filing information returns regarding certain payments of interest, see paragraph (c) of § 1.6049-1.

(14) For the place for filing information returns with respect to payment of wages in the form of group-term life insurance, see paragraph (b) of § 1.6052-1.

(15) For the place for filing information returns on Forms 1042-S with respect to certain amounts paid to foreign persons, see instructions to the form.

(16) For the place for filing information returns on Form 5074 with respect to the allocation of individual income tax to Guam, see paragraph (b)(3) of § 1.935-1 and paragraph (d) of § 301.7654-1 of this chapter (Regulations on Procedure and Administration).

(17) For the place for filing information returns on Form 8805, "Foreign Partner's Information Statement of Section 1446 Withholding Tax," with respect to certain amounts paid on behalf of foreign partners, see the instructions to the form.

(c) *Effective/Applicability date.*—Paragraph (b)(17) of this section shall apply to partnership taxable years beginning after April 29, 2008. [Reg. § 1.6091-1.]

☐ [*T.D. 6364, 2-13-59. Amended by T.D. 6628, 12-27-62; T.D. 6887, 6-23-66; T.D. 6922, 6-16-67; T.D. 7284, 8-2-73; T.D. 7385, 10-28-75; T.D. 8734, 10-6-97 (T.D. 8804 delayed the effective date of T.D. 8734 from January 1, 1999, to January 1, 2000; T.D. 8856 further delayed the effective date of T.D. 8734 until January 1, 2001); T.D. 9156, 9-15-2004, T.D. 9394, 4-28-2008 and T.D. 9849, 3-11-2019.*]

### [Reg. § 20.6091-1]

**§ 20.6091-1. Place for filing returns or other documents.**—(a) *General rule.*—If the decedent was domiciled in the United States at the time of his death, the preliminary notice required by § 20.6036-1 in the case of the estate of a decedent dying before January 1, 1971, and the estate tax return required by § 20.6018-1 shall be filed with:

(1) The service center serving the location in which the decedent was domiciled at the time of his death, if the instructions applicable to the estate tax return provide that the return shall be filed with a service center, or

(2) Any person assigned the responsibility to receive returns in the local Internal Revenue Service office serving the location in which the decedent was domiciled at the time of his death, if paragraph (1) does not apply.

(b) *Non-U.S. domiciliaries.*—If the decedent was not domiciled in the United States at the time of his death, the preliminary notice required by § 20.6036-1 in the case of the estate of a decedent dying before January 1, 1971, and the estate tax return required by

§20.6018-1 shall be filed with the Internal Revenue Service Center, Philadelphia, Pennsylvania, or as designated on the return form or in the instructions issued with respect to such form. This paragraph applies whether or not the decedent was a citizen of the United States and whether or not the return is made by hand-carrying. [Reg. §20.6091-1.]

☐ [*T.D. 6600, 5-28-62; T.D. 7238, 12-28-72; T.D. 7302, 1-24-74; T.D. 7495, 6-29-77 and T.D. 9156, 9-15-2004.*]

### [Reg. §25.6091-1]

**§25.6091-1. Place for filing returns and other documents.**—(a) *In general.*—If the donor is a resident of the United States, the gift tax return required by section 6019 shall be filed with any person assigned the responsibility to receive returns in the local Internal Revenue Service office that serves the legal residence or principal place of business of the donor. If the donor is a nonresident (whether or not a citizen), and his principal place of business is served by a local Internal Revenue Service office, the gift tax return shall be filed with any person assigned the responsibility to receive returns in that office.

(b) *Returns filed with service centers.*—Notwithstanding paragraph (a) of this section, unless a return is filed by hand-carrying, whenever instructions applicable to gift tax returns provide that the returns be filed with a service center, the returns must be so filed in accordance with the instructions. Returns which are filed by hand carrying shall be filed with any person assigned the responsibility to receive hand-carried returns in the local Internal Revenue Service office in accordance with paragraph (a) of this section.

(c) *Returns of certain nonresidents.*—If the donor is a nonresident (whether or not a citizen), and he does not have a principal place of business in the United States, the gift tax return required by section 6019, whether or not such return is made by hand carrying, shall be filed with the Internal Revenue Service Center, Philadelphia, Pennsylvania, or as designated on the return form or in the instructions issued with respect to such form. [Reg. §25.6091-1.]

☐ [*Amended by T.D. 7012, 5-14-69; T.D. 7238, 12-28-72; T.D. 7302, 1-2-74; T.D. 7495, 6-29-77 and T.D. 9156, 9-15-2004.*]

### [Reg. §31.6091-1]

**§31.6091-1. Place for filing returns.**—(a) *Persons other than corporations.*—Except as provided in paragraph (c) of this section, the return of a person other than a corporation shall be filed with any person assigned the responsibility to receive returns in the local Internal Revenue Service office that serves the principal place of business or legal residence of such person.

(b) *Corporations.*—The return of a corporation shall be filed with any person assigned the responsibility to receive returns in the local Internal Revenue Service office that serves the principal place of business or principal office or agency of the corporation, except as provided in paragraph (c) of this section.

(c) *Returns of taxpayers outside the United States.*—The return of a person (other than a corporation) outside the United States having no legal residence or principal place of business in the United States, or the return of a corporation having no principal place of business or principal office or agency in the United States, shall be filed with the Internal Revenue Service, Philadelphia, Pennsylvania 19255, or as otherwise directed in the applicable forms and instructions.

(d) *Returns filed with internal revenue service centers or Social Security Administration offices.*—Notwithstanding paragraphs (a), (b), and (c) of this section, whenever instructions applicable to such returns provide that the returns shall be filed with an internal revenue service center or an office of the Social Security Administration, such returns shall be filed in accordance with such instructions.

(e) *Hand-carried returns.*—Except as provided in subparagraph (3) of this paragraph, and notwithstanding paragraphs (1) and (2) of section 6091 (b) and paragraph (d) of this section—

(1) *Persons other than corporations.*—Returns of persons other than corporations which are filed by hand carrying shall be filed with any person assigned the responsibility to receive hand-carried returns in the local Internal Revenue Service office as provided in paragraph (a) of this section.

(2) *Corporations.*—Returns of corporations which are filed by hand carrying shall be filed with any person assigned the responsibility to receive hand-carried returns in the local Internal Revenue Service office as provided in paragraph (b) of this section.

(3) *Exceptions.*—This paragraph shall not apply to returns of—

(i) Persons who have no legal residence, no principal place of business, nor principal office or agency served by a local Internal Revenue Service office,

(ii) Citizens of the United States whose principal place of abode for the period with respect to which the return is filed is outside the United States,

(iii) Persons who claim the benefits of section 911 (relating to earned income from sources without the United States), section 922 (relating to special deduction for Western Hemisphere trade corporations), section 931 (relating to income from sources within possessions of the United States), section 933 (relating to income from sources within Puerto Rico), or section 941 (relating to the special deduction for China Trade Act corporations), and

(iv) Nonresident alien persons and foreign corporations.

(f) *Permission to file in office other than required office.*—The Commissioner may permit the filing of any return required to be made under the regulations in this subpart in any local Internal Revenue Service office, notwithstanding the provisions of paragraphs (1), (2), and (4) of section 6091 (b) and paragraphs (a), (b), (c), (d) and (e) of this section.

(g) *Returns of officers and employees of the Internal Revenue Service.*—The Commissioner may require any officer or employee of the Internal Revenue Service to file any return required of him under the regulations in this subpart in any local Internal Revenue Service office selected by the Commissioner, notwithstanding the provisions of paragraphs (1), (2), and (4) of section 6091(b) and paragraphs (a), (b), (c), (d), and (e) of this section. [Reg. §31.6091-1.]

☐ [*T.D. 6472, 6-22-60. Amended by T.D. 6915, 3-28-67; T.D. 7495, 6-29-77; T.D. 7580, 12-20-78 and T.D. 9156, 9-15-2004.*]

### [Reg. §40.6091-1]

**§40.6091-1. Place for filing returns.**—(a) *Quarterly returns.*—Except as provided in paragraphs (b) and (c) of this section, returns must be filed in accordance with the instructions applicable to the form on which the return is made.

(b) *Hand-carried returns.*—(1) *Persons other than corporations.*—Returns of persons other than corporations that are filed by hand carrying must be filed with any person assigned the responsibility to receive hand-carried returns in the local Internal Revenue Service office that serves the principal place of business or legal residence of the person.

(2) *Corporations.*—Returns of corporations that are filed by hand carrying must be filed with any person assigned the responsibility to receive hand-carried returns in the local Internal Revenue Service office that serves the principal place of business or principal office or agency of the corporation.

(c) *Monthly and semimonthly returns.*—Monthly and semimonthly returns required under §40.6011(a)-1(b) must be filed in accordance with the forms and instructions, or other published guidance. [Reg. §40.6091-1.]

☐ [*T.D. 8442, 10-21-92. Amended by T.D. 8963, 8-8-2001; T.D. 9156, 9-15-2004 and T.D. 9602, 12-5-2012.*]

### [Reg. §41.6091-1]

**§41.6091-1. Place for filing returns.**—(a) *In general.*—Except as provided in paragraph (b) of this section, returns must be filed in accordance with the instructions applicable to the form on which the return is made.

(b) *Hand-carried returns.*—(1) *Persons other than corporations.*—Returns of persons other than corporations that are filed by hand carrying must be filed with any person assigned the responsibility to receive hand-carried returns in the local Internal Revenue Service office that serves the principal place of business or legal residence of the person.

(2) *Corporations.*—Returns of corporations that are filed by hand carrying must be filed with any person assigned the responsibility to receive hand-carried returns in the local Internal Revenue Service office that serves the principal place of business or principal office or agency of the corporation. [Reg. §41.6091-1.]

☐ [*T.D. 6216. Amended by T.D. 6743, 6-22-64; T.D. 8159, 9-3-87; T.D. 8879, 3-30-2000 and T.D. 9156, 9-15-2004.*]

### [Reg. §44.6091-1]

**§44.6091-1. Place for filing returns.**—(a) *In general.*—Except as provided in paragraph (b) of this section, a return on Form 730 or Form 11-C shall be filed with any person assigned the responsibility to receive returns in the local Internal Revenue Service office that serves the legal residence or principal place of business of the person making the return.

(b) *Returns of individuals outside the United States.*—The returns on Form 730 and Form 11-C individuals (whether citizens of the United States, citizens of possessions of the United States, or aliens) outside the United States having no legal residence or principal place of business in the United States shall be filed with the Internal Revenue Service Center, Cincinnati, Ohio 45999, or as otherwise directed in the applicable forms and instructions.

(c) *Returns filed with service centers.*—Notwithstanding paragraphs (a) and (b) of this section, whenever instructions applicable to returns filed on Form 730 or Form 11-C provide that the returns be filed with a service center, the returns shall be so filed in accordance with the instructions.

(d) *Hand-carried returns.*—Returns which are filed by hand carrying shall be filed with any person assigned the responsibility to receive hand-carried returns in the local Internal Revenue Service office as provided in paragraph (a) of this section. See § 301.6091-1(c) of this chapter (Regulations on Procedure and Administration) for provisions relating to the definition of hand carried. [Reg. § 44.6091-1.]

☐ [Subsections (a) and (b) adopted by T.D. 6370. Subsections (c) and (d) adopted by T.D. 7630. *Amended by T.D. 9156, 9-15-2004.*]

### [Reg. § 53.6091-1]

**§ 53.6091-1. Place for filing chapter 42 tax returns.**—Except as provided in § 53.6091-2 (relating to exceptional cases)—

(a) *Persons other than corporations.*—Chapter 42 tax returns of persons other than corporations shall be filed with any person assigned the responsibility to receive returns in the local Internal Revenue Service office that serves the legal residence or principal place of business of the person required to make the return.

(b) *Corporations.*—Chapter 42 tax returns of corporations shall be filed with any person assigned the responsibility to receive returns in the local Internal Revenue Service office that serves the principal place of business or principal office or agency of the corporation.

(c) *Returns filed with service centers.*—Notwithstanding paragraphs (a) and (b) of this section, unless a return is filed by hand carrying, whenever instructions applicable to chapter 42 tax returns provide that the returns be filed with a service center, the returns must be so filed in accordance with the instructions. Returns which are filed by hand carrying shall be filed with any person assigned the responsibility to receive hand-carried returns in the local Internal Revenue Service office in accordance with paragraph (a) or (b) of this section, whichever is applicable.

(d) *Returns of persons subject to a termination assessment.*—Notwithstanding paragraph (c) of this section, income tax returns of persons with respect to whom a chapter 42 tax assessment was made under section 6852(a) with respect to the taxable year must be filed with any person assigned the responsibility to receive returns in the local Internal Revenue Service office as provided in paragraphs (a) and (b) of this section. [Reg. § 53.6091-1.]

☐ [*T.D. 7368, 7-15-75. Amended by T.D. 7495, 6-29-77; T.D. 8628, 12-4-95 and T.D. 9156, 9-15-2004.*]

### [Reg. § 54.6091-1]

**§ 54.6091-1. Place for filing excise tax returns under section 4980B, 4980D, 4980E, or 4980G.**—Effective for any Form 8928 that is due on or after January 1, 2010, the return required by § 54.6011-2 must be filed at the place specified in the forms and instructions provided by the Internal Revenue Service. [Reg. § 54.6091-1.]

☐ [*T.D. 9457, 9-4-2009.*]

### [Reg. § 55.6091-1]

**§ 55.6091-1. Place for filing chapter 44 tax returns.**—Except as provided in § 55.6091-2 (relating to exceptional cases)—

(a) *In general.*—Chapter 44 tax returns shall be filed with any person assigned the responsibility to receive returns in the local Internal Revenue Service office serving the principal place of business or principal office or agency of the real estate investment trust or regulated investment company.

(b) *Returns filed with service centers or by hand carrying.*—Notwithstanding paragraph (a) of this section, unless a return is filed by hand carrying, whenever instructions applicable to chapter 44 tax returns provide that the returns be filed with a service center, the returns must be so filed in accordance with the instructions. Returns which are filed by hand carrying shall be filed with any person assigned the

responsibility to receive hand-carried returns in the local Internal Revenue Service office in accordance with paragraph (a) of this section. [Reg. § 55.6091-1.]

☐ [*T.D. 7767, 2-3-81. Amended by T.D. 8180, 2-29-88 and T.D. 9156, 9-15-2004.*]

### [Reg. § 156.6091-1]

**§ 156.6091-1. Place for filing chapter 54 (Greenmail) tax returns.**—Except as provided in § 156.6091-2 (relating to exceptional cases):

(a) *Individuals, estates, and trusts.*—In general, tax returns under chapter 54 of the Code of individuals, estates, and trusts shall be filed with any person assigned the responsibility to receive returns in the local Internal Revenue Service office that serves the legal residence or the principal place of business of the person required to make the return.

(b) *Corporations.*—In general, tax returns under chapter 54 of the Code of corporations shall be filed with any person assigned the responsibility to receive returns in the local Internal Revenue Service office that serves the principal place of business or the principal office or agency of the corporation.

(c) *Partnerships.*—In general, tax returns under chapter 54 of the Code of partnerships shall be filed with any person assigned the responsibility to receive returns in the local Internal Revenue Service office that serves the principal place of business or the principal office or agency of the partnership.

(d) *Returns of taxpayers outside the United States.*—The return of a person (other than a partnership or a corporation) outside the United States having no legal residence or principal place of business or agency in the United States, or the return of a partnership or a corporation having no principal place of business or principal office or agency in the United States, shall be filed with the Internal Revenue Service, Philadelphia, PA 19255, or as otherwise directed in the applicable forms and instructions.

(e) *Returns filed with service centers or by hand carrying.*—Notwithstanding paragraph (a), (b), (c), or (d) of this section, unless a return is filed by hand carrying, whenever instructions applicable to tax returns under chapter 54 of the Code provide that the returns be filed with a service center, the returns must be so filed in accordance with the instructions. Returns that are filed by hand carrying shall be filed with any person assigned the responsibility to receive hand-carried returns in the local Internal Revenue Service office in accordance with paragraphs (a), (b), (c), or (d) of this section. [Reg. § 156.6091-1.]

☐ [*T.D. 8379, 12-17-91. Amended by T.D. 9156, 9-15-2004.*]

### [Reg. § 157.6091-1]

**§ 157.6091-1. Place for filing returns.**—The return required by § 157.6011-1 (relating to returns of tax with respect to structured settlement factoring transactions) must be filed at the place specified in the forms and instructions provided by the Internal Revenue Service. [Reg. § 157.6091-1.]

☐ [*T.D. 9134, 7-7-2004.*]

### [Reg. § 301.6091-1]

**§ 301.6091-1. Place for filing returns of other documents.**—(a) *General rule.*—For provisions concerning the place for filing returns, including hand-carried returns, see the regulations relating to the particular tax. Except as provided in paragraph(b) of this section, for provisions concerning the place for filing documents other than returns, see the regulations relating to the particular tax.

(b) *Exception for hand-carried documents other than returns.*—Notwithstanding any other provisions of this chapter—

(1) *Persons other than corporations.*—If a document, other than a return, of a person (other than a corporation) is hand carried, and if the document is otherwise required to be filed with a service center, such document may be filed with any person assigned the responsibility to receive hand-carried returns in the local Internal Revenue Service office that serves the legal residence or principal place of business of such person, or, in the case of an estate, the local Internal Revenue Service office serving the domicile of the decedent at the time of his death. A document may also be filed by hand carrying such document to the appropriate service center, or, in the case of a document required to be filed with an office of the Alcohol and Tobacco Tax and Trade Bureau, by hand carrying as specified in regulations of the Alcohol and Tobacco Tax and Trade Bureau, see, 27 CFR chapter I, subchapter F.

(2) *Corporations.*—If a document, other than a return, of a corporation is hand carried, and if the document is otherwise required to

be filed with a service center, such document may be filed with any person assigned the responsibility to receive hand-carried returns in the local Internal Revenue Service office that serves the principal place of business or principal office or agency of the corporation. A document may also be filed by hand carrying such document to the appropriate service center, or, in the case of a document required to be filed with an office of the Alcohol and Tobacco Tax and Trade Bureau, by hand carrying as specified in regulations of the Alcohol and Tobacco Tax and Trade Bureau, see, 27 CFR chapter I, subchapter F.

(c) *Definition of hand carried.*—For purposes of this section and section 6091(b)(4) and the regulations issued thereunder, a return or document will be considered to be hand carried if it is brought to any person assigned the responsibility to receive hand-carried returns in the local Internal Revenue Service office by the person required to file the return or other document, or by his agent. Examples of persons who will be considered to be agents, for purposes of the preceding sentence, are: Members of the taxpayer's family, an employee of the taxpayer, the taxpayer's attorney, accountant, or tax advisor, and messengers employed by the taxpayer. A return or document will not be considered to be hand carried if it is sent to the Internal Revenue Service through the U.S. Mail. [Reg. § 301.6091-1.]

☐ [*T.D. 6498*, 10-24-60. *Amended by T.D. 6950*, 4-3-68; *T.D. 7008*, 2-28-69; *T.D. 7012*, 5-14-69; *T.D. 7188*, 6-28-72; *T.D. 7238*, 12-28-72; *T.D. 7495*, 6-29-77 *and T.D. 9156*, 9-15-2004.]

### [Reg. § 1.6091-2]

**§ 1.6091-2. Place for filing income tax returns.**—Except as provided in § 1.6091-3 (relating to certain international income tax returns) and § 1.6091-4 (relating to exceptional cases)—

(a) *Individuals, estates, and trusts.*—(1) Except as provided in paragraph (c) of this section, income tax returns of individuals, estates, and trusts shall be filed with any person assigned the responsibility to receive returns at the local Internal Revenue Service office that serves the legal residence or principal place of business of the person required to make the return.

(2) An individual employed on a salary or commission basis who is not also engaged in conducting a commercial or professional enterprise for profit on his own account does not have a "principal place of business" within the meaning of this section.

(b) *Corporations.*—Except as provided in paragraph (c) of this section, income tax returns of corporations shall be filed with any person assigned the responsibility to receive returns in the local Internal Revenue Service office that serves the principal place of business or principal office or agency of the corporation.

(c) *Returns filed with service centers.*—Notwithstanding paragraphs (a) and (b) of this section, whenever instructions applicable to income tax returns provide that the returns be filed with a service center, the returns must be so filed in accordance with the instructions.

(d) *Hand-carried returns.*—Notwithstanding paragraphs (1) and (2) of section 6091(b) and paragraph (c) of this section—

(1) *Persons other than corporations.*—Returns of persons other than corporations which are filed by hand carrying shall be filed with any person assigned the responsibility to receive hand-carried returns in the local Internal Revenue Service office as provided in paragraph (a) of this section.

(2) *Corporations.*—Returns of corporations which are filed by hand carrying shall be filed with any person assigned the responsibility to receive hand-carried returns in the local Internal Revenue Service office as provided in paragraph (b) of this section. See § 301.6091-1 of this chapter (Regulations on Procedure and Administration) for provisions relating to the definition of hand carried.

(e) *Amended returns.*—In the case of amended returns filed after April 14, 1968, except as provided in paragraph (d) of this section—

(1) *Persons other than corporations.*—Amended returns of persons other than corporations shall be filed with the service center serving the legal residence or principal place of business of the person required to make the return.

(2) *Corporations.*—Amended returns of corporations shall be filed with the service center serving the principal place of business or principal office or agency of the corporation.

(f) *Returns of persons subject to a termination assessment.*—Notwithstanding paragraph (c) of this section—

(1) *Persons other than corporations.*—Returns of persons other than corporations with respect to whom an assessment was made under section 6851(a) with respect to the taxable year shall be filed

with any person assigned the responsibility to receive returns in the local Internal Revenue Service office as provided in paragraph (a) of this section.

(2) *Corporations.*—Returns of corporations with respect to whom an assessment was made under section 6851(a) with respect to the taxable year shall be filed with any person assigned the responsibility to receive returns in the local Internal Revenue Service office as provided in paragraph (b) of this section.

(g) *Returns of persons subject to a termination assessment.*—Notwithstanding paragraph (c) of this section, income tax returns of persons with respect to whom an income tax assessment was made under section 6852(a) with respect to the taxable year must be filed with any person assigned the responsibility to receive returns in the local Internal Revenue Service office as provided in paragraphs (a) and (b) of this section. [Reg. § 1.6091-2.]

☐ [*T.D. 6364*, 2-13-59. *Amended by T.D. 6950*, 4-3-68; *T.D. 7012*, 5-14-69; *T.D. 7495*, 6-2-77; *T.D. 7575*, 12-15-78; *T.D. 8628*, 12-4-95 *and T.D. 9156*, 9-15-2004.]

### [Reg. § 20.6091-2]

**§ 20.6091-2. Exceptional cases.**—Notwithstanding the provisions of § 20.6091-1 the Commissioner may permit the filing of the preliminary notice required by § 20.6036-1 and the estate tax return required by § 20.6018-1 in any local Internal Revenue Service office. [Reg. § 20.6091-2.]

☐ [*T.D. 6600*, 5-28-62. *Amended by T.D. 9156*, 9-15-2004.]

### [Reg. § 25.6091-2]

**§ 25.6091-2. Exceptional cases.**—Notwithstanding the provisions of § 25.6091-1 the Commissioner may permit the filing of the gift tax return required by section 6019 in any local Internal Revenue Service office. [Reg. § 25.6091-2.]

☐ [*T.D. 6600*, 5-28-62. *Amended by T.D. 9156*, 9-15-2004.]

### [Reg. § 53.6091-2]

**§ 53.6091-2. Exceptional cases.**—Notwithstanding the provisions of § 53.6091-1, the Commissioner may permit the filing of any chapter 42 tax return in any local Internal Revenue Service office. [Reg. § 53.6091-2.]

☐ [*T.D. 7368*, 7-15-75. *Amended by T.D. 9156*, 9-15-2004.]

### [Reg. § 55.6091-2]

**§ 55.6091-2. Exceptional cases.**—Notwithstanding the provisions of § 55.6091-1, the Commissioner may permit the filing of any chapter 44 tax return in any local Internal Revenue Service office. [Reg. § 55.6091-2.]

☐ [*T.D. 7767*, 2-3-81. *Amended by T.D. 9156*, 9-15-2004.]

### [Reg. § 156.6091-2]

**§ 156.6091-2. Exceptional cases.**—Notwithstanding the provisions of § 156.6091-1, the Commissioner may permit the filing of any tax return under chapter 54 (Greenmail) of the Code in any local Internal Revenue Service office. [Reg. § 156.6091-2.]

☐ [*T.D. 8379*, 12-17-91. *Amended by T.D. 9156*, 9-15-2004.]

### [Reg. § 1.6091-3]

**§ 1.6091-3. Filing certain international income tax returns.**—The following income tax returns shall be filed as directed in the applicable forms and instructions:

(a) Income tax returns on which all, or a portion, of the tax is to be paid in foreign currency. See §§ 301.6316-1 to 301.6316-6 inclusive, and §§ 301.6316-8 and 301.6316-9 of this chapter (Regulations on Procedure and Administration).

(b) Income tax returns of an individual citizen of the United States whose principal place of abode for the period with respect to which the return is filed is outside the United States. A taxpayer's principal place of abode will be considered to be outside the United States if his legal residence is outside the United States or if his return bears a foreign address.

(c) Income tax returns of an individual citizen of a possession of the United States (whether or not a citizen of the United States) who has no legal residence or principal place of business in any internal revenue district in the United States.

(d) Except in the case of any departing alien return under section 6851 and § 1.6851-2, the income tax return of any nonresident alien (other than one treated as a resident under section (g) or (h)).

(e) The income tax return of an estate or trust the fiduciary of which is outside the United States and has no legal residence or principal place of business in any internal revenue district in the United States.

(f) Income tax returns of foreign corporations.

(g) The return by a withholding agent of the income tax required to be withheld at source under chapter 3 of the Code on nonresident aliens and foreign corporations and tax-free covenant bonds, as provided in § 1.1461-2.

(h) Income tax returns of persons who claim the benefits of section 911 (relating to earned income from sources without the United States).

(i) Income tax returns of corporations which claim the benefits of section 922 (relating to special deduction for Western Hemisphere trade corporations) except in the case of consolidated returns filed pursuant to the regulations under section 1502.

(j) Income tax returns of persons who claim the benefits of section 931 (relating to income from sources within possessions of the United States).

(k) Income tax returns of persons who claim the benefits of section 933 (relating to income from sources within Puerto Rico).

(l) Income tax returns of corporations which claim the benefits of section 941 (relating to the special deduction for China Trade Act corporations). [Reg. § 1.6091-3.]

☐ [*T.D. 6364, 2-13-59. Amended by T.D. 6872, 1-5-66; T.D. 6922, 6-16-67; T.D. 6950, 4-3-68; T.D. 7012, 5-14-69; T.D. 7670, 1-30-80 and T.D. 9156, 9-15-2004.*]

### [Reg. § 1.6091-4]

**§ 1.6091-4. Exceptional cases.**—(a) *Permission to file in office other than required office.*—(1) The Commissioner may permit the filing of any income tax return required to be made under the provisions of subtitle A or F of the Code, or the regulations in this part, in any Internal Revenue Service office, notwithstanding the provisions of paragraphs (1) and (2) of section 6091(b) and § § 1.6091-1 to 1.6091-3, inclusive.

(2) In cases where the Commissioner authorizes (for all purposes except venue) an internal revenue service center to receive returns, such returns pursuant to instructions issued with respect thereto, may be sent directly to that service center and are thereby filed there for all purposes except as a factor in determining venue. However, after initial processing all such returns shall be forwarded by the service center to the office with which such returns are, without regard to this subparagraph, required to be filed. For the sole purpose of determining venue, such returns are filed only with such office.

(3) Notwithstanding the provisions of other sections of this chapter or any rule issued under this chapter—

(i) In cases where, in accordance with subparagraph (2) of this paragraph, a return is filed with a service center, the authority of the members of the office with whom such return would, without regard to such subparagraph, be required to be filed shall remain the same as if the return had been so filed,

(ii) Unless a return or other document is a proper attachment to, or is, a return which the service center is expressly authorized to receive, such return or other document shall be filed as if all returns sent directly to the service centers, in accordance with subparagraph (2) of this paragraph, were filed in the office where such returns are, without regard to such subparagraph, required to be filed; and

(iii) Unless the performance of an act is directly related to the sending of a return directly to the service center, such act shall be performed as if all returns sent directly to the service centers, in accordance with subparagraph (2) of this paragraph, were filed in the office where such returns are, without regard to such subparagraph, required to be filed.

(4) The application of paragraphs (a)(2) and (3) of this section may be illustrated by the following example:

*Example.* The Commissioner has authorized the Internal Revenue Service Center, Philadelphia, Pennsylvania (for all purposes except venue), to receive Form 1120. Except for that authorization, A, a corporation with its principal place of business in Greensboro, North Carolina, is required to file its Form 1120 for Year X with the Internal Revenue Service Center, Atlanta, Georgia. In addition, A may file an election to defer development expenditures paid or incurred in Year X. Under § 1.616-2(e)(2) and applicable published guidance (in this case Notice 2003-19 (2003-1 C.B. 703)) that statement of election must be filed with the service center that serves A's principal place of business where A filed its income tax return. A may make that election on its income tax return or by filing it separately. Under paragraph (a)(2) of this section, A may send its Form 1120 to either the Internal Revenue Service Center, Philadelphia, Pennsylvania, or to the Internal Revenue Service Center, Atlanta, Georgia. If A files its statement of election separately from its income tax return for Year X, then the statement of election is not a proper attachment to A's income tax return and A should send the statement of election to the Internal Revenue Service Center, Atlanta, Georgia (with which A must, without regard to paragraph (a)(2) of this section, file its income tax return), no later than the time prescribed for filing Form 1120 for Year X (including extensions).

(b) *Returns of officers and employees of the Internal Revenue Service.*—The Commissioner may require any officer or employee of the Internal Revenue Service to file his income tax return in any Internal Revenue Service office selected by the Commissioner.

(c) *Residents of Guam.*—Income tax returns of an individual citizen of the United States who is a resident of Guam shall be filed with Guam, as provided in paragraph (b)(1) of § 1.935-1. [Reg. § 1.6091-4.]

☐ [*T.D. 6364, 2-13-59. Amended by T.D. 6793, 1-20-65; T.D. 7385, 10-28-75 and T.D. 9156, 9-15-2004.*]

## Presidential Election Campaign Fund

### [Reg. § 301.6096-1]

**§ 301.6096-1. Designation by individuals for taxable years beginning after December 31, 1972.**—(a) *In general.*—Every individual (other than a nonresident alien) whose income tax liability, as defined in paragraph (b) of this section, is one dollar or more may, at his option, designate that one dollar shall be paid over to the Presidential Election Campaign Fund, in accordance with the provisions of section 9006. In the case of a joint return of a husband and wife, each spouse may designate that one dollar be paid to the fund as provided in this paragraph only if the joint income tax liability of the husband and wife is two dollars or more.

(b) *Income tax liability.*—For purposes of paragraph (a) of this section, the income tax liability of an individual for any taxable year is the amount of the tax imposed by chapter 1 on such individual for the taxable year (as shown on his or her return) reduced by the sum of the credits (as shown on his or her return) allowable under sections 33, 37, 38, 40, 41, 42, 44, and 44A.

(c) *Manner and time of designation.*—(1) A designation under paragraph (a) of this section may be made with respect to any taxable year at the time of the filing of the return of the tax imposed by chapter 1 for such taxable year, and shall be made either on the first page of the return or on the page bearing the taxpayer's signature, in accordance with the instructions applicable thereto.

(2) With respect to any taxable year beginning after December 31, 1972, for which no designation was made under paragraph (c)(1) of this section, a designation may be made on the form furnished by the Internal Revenue Service for such purpose, filed within 20 and one half months after the due date for the original return for such taxable year. In the case of a joint return where neither spouse made a designation or where only one spouse made a designation, a designation may be made, as provided in this subparagraph, by the spouse or spouses who had not previously made a designation.

(3) A designation once made, whether by an original return or otherwise, may not be revoked.

(d) *Effective date.*—This section shall apply to taxable years beginning after December 31, 1972. [Reg. § 301.6096-1.]

☐ [*T.D. 7304, 2-1-74. Amended by T.D. 7391, 12-1-75 and T.D. 7643, 8-27-79.*]

## Miscellaneous Provisions

### [Reg. § 31.6101-1]

**§ 31.6101-1. Period covered by returns.**—The period covered by any return required under the regulations in this subpart shall be as provided in those provisions of the regulations under which the return is required to be made. See § 31.6011(a)-1, relating to returns of taxes under the Federal Insurance Contributions Act; § 31.6011(a)-2, relating to returns of taxes under the Railroad Retirement Tax Act; § 31.6011(a)-3, relating to returns of tax under the Federal Unemployment Tax Act; § 31.6011(a)-4, relating to returns of income tax withheld under section 3402; and § 31.6011(a)-5, relating to monthly returns of taxes under the Federal Insurance Contributions Act and of income tax withheld under section 3402. [Reg. § 31.6101-1.]

☐ [*T.D. 6472, 6-22-60.*]

### [Reg. § 40.6101-1]

**§ 40.6101-1. Period covered by returns.**—See § 40.6011(a)-1(a)(2) for the rules relating to the period covered by the return. [Reg. § 40.6101-1.]

☐ [*T.D. 8442, 10-21-92. Amended by T.D. 8963, 8-8-2001.*]

### [Reg. § 41.6101-1]

**§ 41.6101-1. Period covered by returns.**—Each return is for a taxable period as defined in section 4482. [Reg. § 41.6101-1.]

☐ [*T.D. 6216. Amended by T.D. 6743, 6-22-64 and T.D. 8879, 3-30-2000.*]

### [Reg. § 301.6101-1]

**§ 301.6101-1. Period covered by returns or other documents.**—For provisions concerning the period covered by returns or other documents, see the regulations relating to the particular tax. [Reg. § 301.6101-1.]

☐ [*T.D. 6498, 10-24-60.*]

### [Reg. § 1.6102-1]

**§ 1.6102-1. Computations on returns or other documents.**—For provisions with respect to the rounding off to whole-dollar amounts of money items on returns and accompanying schedules, see § 301.6102-1 of this chapter (Regulations on Procedure and Administration). [Reg. § 1.6102-1.]

☐ [*T.D. 6364, 2-13-59.*]

### [Reg. § 301.6102-1]

**§ 301.6102-1. Computations on returns or other documents.**—(a) *Amounts shown on forms.*—To the extent permitted by any internal revenue form or instructions prescribed for use with respect to any internal revenue return, declaration, statement, other document, or supporting schedules, any amount required to be reported on such form shall be entered at the nearest whole dollar amount. The extent to which, and the conditions under which, such whole dollar amounts shall be entered on any form will be set forth in the instructions issued with respect to such form. For the purpose of the computation to the nearest dollar, a fractional part of a dollar shall be disregarded unless it amounts to one-half dollar or more, in which case the amount (determined without regard to the fractional part of a dollar) shall be increased by $1. The following illustrates the application of this paragraph:

| Exact amount | To be reported as— |
|---|---|
| $18.49 | $18 |
| 18.50 | 19 |
| 18.51 | 19 |

(b) *Election not to use whole dollar amounts.*—(1) *Method of election.*—Where any internal revenue form, or the instructions issued with respect to such form, provide that whole dollar amounts shall be reported, any person making a return, declaration, statement, or other document on such form may elect not to use whole dollar amounts by reporting thereon all amounts in full, including cents.

(2) *Time of election.*—The election not to use whole dollar amounts must be made at the time of filing the return, declaration, statement, or other document. Such election may not be revoked after the time prescribed for filing such return, declaration, statement, or other document, including extensions of time granted for such filing. Such election may be made on any return, declaration, statement, or other document which is filed after the time prescribed for filing (including extensions of time), and such an election is irrevocable.

(3) *Effect of election.*—The taxpayer's election shall be binding only on the return, declaration, statement, or other document filed for a taxable year or period, and a new election may be made on the return, declaration, statement, or other document filed for a subsequent taxable year or period. An election by either a husband or a wife not to report whole dollar amounts on a separate income tax return shall be binding on any subsequent joint return filed under the provisions of section 6013(b).

(4) *Fractional part of a cent.*—For treatment of the fractional part of a cent in the payment of taxes, see section 6313 and § 301.6313-1.

(c) *Inapplicability to computation of amount.*—The provisions of paragraph (a) of this section apply only to amounts required to be reported on a return, declaration, statement, or other document. They do not apply to items which must be taken into account in making the computations necessary to determine such amounts. For example, each item of receipt must be taken into account at its exact amount, including cents, in computing the amount of total receipts required to be reported on an income tax return or supporting schedule. It is the amount of total receipts, so computed, which is to be reported at the nearest whole dollar on the return or supporting schedule.

(d) *Effect on accounting method.*—Section 6102 and this section have no effect on any authorized accounting method. [Reg. § 301.6102-1.]

☐ [*T.D. 6142, 9-2-55. Amended by T.D. 6498, 10-24-60.*]

### [Reg. § 301.6103(a)-1]

**§ 301.6103(a)-1. Disclosures after December 31, 1976 by officers and employees of Federal agencies of returns and return information (including taxpayer return information) disclosed to such officers and employees by the Internal Revenue Service before January 1, 1977 for a purpose not involving tax administration.**—(a) *General rule.*—Except as provided by paragraph (b) of this section, a return or return information (including taxpayer return information), as defined in section 6103(b)(1), (2), and (3) of the Internal Revenue Code, disclosed by the Internal Revenue Service before January 1, 1977, to an officer or employee of a Federal agency (as defined in section 6103(b)(9)) for a purpose not involving tax administration (as defined in section 6103(b)(4)) pursuant to the authority of section 6103 (or any order of the President under section 6103 or rules and regulations thereunder prescribed by the Secretary or his delegate and approved by the President) before amendment of such section by section 1202 of the Tax Reform Act of 1976 (Pub. L. 94-455, 90 Stat. 1667) may be disclosed by, or on behalf of, such officer, employee, or agency after December 31, 1976, for any purpose authorized by such section (or such order or rules and regulations) before such amendment.

(b) *Exception.*—Notwithstanding the provisions of paragraph (a) of this section, a return or return information (including taxpayer return information) disclosed before January 1, 1977, by the Service to an officer or employee of a Federal agency for a purpose unrelated to tax administration as described in paragraph (a) may, after December 31, 1976, be disclosed by, or on behalf of, such agency, officer, or employee in an administrative or judicial proceeding only if such proceeding is one described in section 6103(i)(4) of the Code and if the requirements of section 6103(i)(4) have first been met. [Reg. § 301.6103(a)-1.]

☐ [*T.D. 7723, 9-30-80.*]

### [Reg. § 301.6103(a)-2]

**§ 301.6103(a)-2. Disclosures after December 31, 1976 by attorneys of the Department of Justice and officers and employees of the Office of the Chief Counsel for the Internal Revenue Service of returns and return information (including taxpayer return information) disclosed to such attorneys, officers, and employees by the Service before January 1, 1977 for a purpose involving tax administration.**—(a) *General rule.*—Except as provided by paragraph (b) of this section and subject to the requirements of this paragraph, a return or return information (including taxpayer return information), as defined in section 6103(b)(1), (2), and (3) of the Internal Revenue Code disclosed by the Internal Revenue Service before January 1, 1977, to an attorney of the Department of Justice (including a United States attorney) or to an officer or employee of the Office of the Chief Counsel for the Service for a purpose involving tax administration(as defined in section 6103(b)(4)) pursuant to the authority of section 6103 (or any order of the President under section 6103 or rules and regulations thereunder prescribed by the Secretary or his delegate and approved by the President) before amendment of such section by section 1202 of the Tax Reform Act of 1976 (Pub. L. 94-455, 90 Stat. 1667) may be disclosed by, or on behalf of, such attorney, officer, or employee after December 31, 1976, for any purpose authorized by such section (or such order or rules and regulations) before such amendment.

(b) *Exception.*—Notwithstanding the provisions of paragraph (a) of this section, a return or return information (including taxpayer return information) disclosed before January 1, 1977, by the Service to an attorney of the Department of Justice or to an officer or employee of the Office of the Chief Counsel for the Service for a purpose related to tax administration as described in paragraph (a) may, after December 31, 1976, be disclosed by, or on behalf of, such attorney, officer, or employee in an administrative or judicial proceeding only if such proceeding is one described in section 6103(h)(4) of the Code and if the requirements of section 6103(h)(4) have first been met. [Reg. § 301.6103(a)-2.]

☐ [*T.D. 7723, 9-30-80.*]

### [Reg. § 301.6103(c)-1]

**§ 301.6103(c)-1. Disclosure of returns and return information to designee of taxpayer.**—(a) *Overview.*—Subject to such requirements and conditions as the Secretary may prescribe by regulation, section 6103(c) of the Internal Revenue Code authorizes the Internal Revenue

Service to disclose a taxpayer's return or return information to such person or persons as the taxpayer may designate in a request for or consent to such disclosure, or to any other person at the taxpayer's request to the extent necessary to comply with the taxpayer's request to such other person for information or assistance. This regulation contains the requirements that must be met before, and the conditions under which, the Internal Revenue Service may make such disclosures. Paragraph (b) of this section provides the requirements that are generally applicable to designate a third party to receive the taxpayer's returns and return information. Paragraph (c) of this section provides requirements under which the Internal Revenue Service may disclose information in connection with a taxpayer's written or nonwritten request for a third party to provide information or assistance with regard to a tax matter, for example, a Congressional inquiry. Paragraph (d) of this section provides the parameters for disclosure consents connected with electronic return filing programs and combined Federal-State filing. Finally, paragraph (e) of this section provides definitions and general rules related to requests for or consents to disclosure.

(b) *Disclosure of returns and return information to person or persons designated in a written request or consent.*—(1) *General requirements.*— Pursuant to section 6103(c) of the Internal Revenue Code, the Internal Revenue Service (or an agent or contractor of the Internal Revenue Service) may disclose a taxpayer's return or return information (in written or nonwritten form) to such person or persons as the taxpayer may designate in a request for or consent to such disclosure. A request for or consent to disclosure under this paragraph (b) must be in the form of a separate written document pertaining solely to the authorized disclosure. (For the meaning of separate written document, see paragraph (e)(1) of this section.) The separate written document must be signed (see paragraph (e)(2) of this section) and dated by the taxpayer who filed the return or to whom the return information relates. At the time it is signed and dated by the taxpayer, the written document must also indicate—

(i) The taxpayer's taxpayer identity information described in section 6103(b)(6);

(ii) The identity of the person or persons to whom the disclosure is to be made;

(iii) The type of return (or specified portion of the return) or return information (and the particular data) that is to be disclosed; and

(iv) The taxable year or years covered by the return or return information.

(2) *Requirement that request or consent be received within one hundred twenty days of when signed and dated.*—The disclosure of a return or return information authorized by a written request for or written consent to the disclosure shall not be made unless the request or consent is received by the Internal Revenue Service (or an agent or contractor of the Internal Revenue Service) within 120 days following the date upon which the request or consent was signed and dated by the taxpayer.

(c) *Disclosure of returns and return information to designee of taxpayer to comply with a taxpayer's request for information or assistance.*—If a taxpayer makes a written or nonwritten request, directly to another person or to the Internal Revenue Service, that such other person (for example, a member of Congress, friend, or relative of the taxpayer) provide information or assistance relating to the taxpayer's return or to a transaction or other contact between the taxpayer and the Internal Revenue Service, the Internal Revenue Service (or an agent or contractor of the Internal Revenue Service or a Federal government agency performing a Federal tax administration function) may disclose returns or return information (in written or nonwritten form) to such other person under the circumstances set forth in paragraphs (c) (1) through (3) of this section.

(1) *Written request for information or assistance.*—(i) The taxpayer's request for information or assistance may be in the form of a letter or other written document, which must be signed (see paragraph (e)(2) of this section) and dated by the taxpayer. The taxpayer must also indicate in the written request—

(A) The taxpayer's taxpayer identity information described in section 6103(b)(6);

(B) The identity of the person or persons to whom disclosure is to be made; and

(C) Sufficient facts underlying the request for information or assistance to enable the Internal Revenue Service to determine the nature and extent of the information or assistance requested and the returns or return information to be disclosed in order to comply with the taxpayer's request.

(ii) A person who receives a copy of a taxpayer's written request for information or assistance but who is not the addressee of the request, such as a member of Congress who is provided with a courtesy copy of a taxpayer's letter to another member of Congress

or to the Internal Revenue Service, cannot receive returns or return information under paragraph (c)(1) of this section.

(2) *Nonwritten request or consent.*—(i) A request for information or assistance may also be nonwritten. Disclosure of returns and return information to a designee pursuant to a taxpayer's nonwritten request will be made only after the Internal Revenue Service has—

(A) Obtained from the taxpayer sufficient facts underlying the request for information or assistance to enable the Internal Revenue Service to determine the nature and extent of the information or assistance requested and the return or return information to be disclosed in order to comply with the taxpayer's request;

(B) Confirmed the identity of the taxpayer and the designee; and

(C) Confirmed the date, the nature, and the extent of the information or assistance requested.

(ii) Examples of disclosures pursuant to nonwritten requests for information or assistance under this paragraph (c)(2) include, but are not limited to, disclosures to a friend, relative, or other person whom the taxpayer brings to an interview or meeting with Internal Revenue Service officials, and disclosures to a person whom the taxpayer wishes to involve in a telephone conversation with Internal Revenue Service officials.

(iii) As long as the requirements of this paragraph (c)(2) are met, the taxpayer does not need to be present, either in person or as part of a telephone conversation, for disclosures of returns and return information to be made to the other person.

(3) *Rules applicable to written and nonwritten requests for information or assistance.*—A return or return information will be disclosed to the taxpayer's designee as provided by this paragraph only to the extent considered necessary by the Internal Revenue Service to comply with the taxpayer's request or consent. Such disclosures shall not be made unless the request or consent is received by the Internal Revenue Service, its agent or contractor, or a Federal government agency performing a Federal tax administration function in connection with a request for advice or assistance relating to such function. This paragraph (c) does not apply to disclosures to a taxpayer's representative in connection with practice before the Internal Revenue Service (as defined in Treasury Department Circular No. 230, 31 CFR Part 10). For disclosures in these cases, see section 6103(e)(6) and §§ 601.501 through 601.508 of this chapter.

(d) *Acknowledgments of electronically filed returns and other documents; combined filing programs with State tax agencies.*—The requirements of paragraphs (b) and (c) of this section do not apply to this paragraph (d).

(1) *Acknowledgment of, and notices regarding, electronically filed returns and other documents.*—When a taxpayer files returns or other documents or information with the Internal Revenue Service electronically, the taxpayer may consent to the disclosure of return information to the transmitter or other third party, such as the taxpayer's financial institution, necessary to acknowledge that the electronic transmission was received and either accepted or rejected by the Internal Revenue Service, the reason for any rejection, and such other information as the Internal Revenue Service determines is necessary to the operation of the electronic filing program. The consent must inform the taxpayer of the return information that will be transmitted and to whom disclosure will be made.

(2) *Combined return filing programs with State tax agencies.*—(i) A taxpayer's participation in a combined return filing program between the Internal Revenue Service and a State agency, body, or commission (State agency) described in section 6103(d)(1) constitutes a consent to the disclosure by the Internal Revenue Service, to the State agency, of taxpayer identity information, signature, and items of common data contained on the return. For purposes of this paragraph, common data means information reflected on the Federal return required by State law to be attached to or included on the State return. Instructions accompanying the forms or published procedures involved in such program must indicate that by participating in the program, the taxpayer is consenting to the Internal Revenue Service's disclosure to the State agency of the taxpayer identity information, signature, and items of common data, and that such information will be treated by the State agency as if it had been directly filed with the State agency. Such instructions or procedures must also describe any verification that takes place before the taxpayer identity information, signature and common data is transmitted by the Internal Revenue Service to the State agency.

(ii) No disclosures may be made under this paragraph (d)(2) unless there are provisions of State law protecting the confidentiality of such items of common data.

(e) *Definitions and rules applicable to this section.*—(1) *Separate written document.*—(i) For the purposes of paragraph (b) of this section, *separate written document* means—

(A) Text appearing on one or more sheets of 8½-inch by 11-inch or larger paper, each of which pertains solely to the authorized disclosure, so long as such sheet or sheets, taken together, contain all the elements described in paragraph (b)(1) of this section;

(B) Text appearing on one or more computer screens, each of which pertains solely to the authorized disclosure, so long as such screen or, taken together, such screens—

(1) contain all the elements described in paragraph (b)(1) of this section,

(2) can be signed (see paragraph (e)(2) of this section) and dated by the taxpayer, and

(3) can be reproduced, if necessary; or

(C) A consent on the record in an administrative or judicial proceeding, or a transcript of such proceeding recording such consent, containing the information required under paragraph (b)(1) of this section.

(ii) A provision included in a taxpayer's application for a loan or other benefit authorizing the grantor of the loan or other benefit to obtain any financial information, including returns or return information, from any source as the grantor may request for purposes of verifying information supplied on the application, does not meet the requirements of paragraph (b)(1) of this section because the provision is not a separate written document relating solely to the disclosure of returns and return information. In addition, the provision does not contain the other information specified in paragraph (b)(1) of this section.

(2) *Method of signing.*—A request for or consent to disclosure may be signed by any method of signing the Secretary has prescribed pursuant to § 301.6061-1(b) in forms, instructions, or other appropriate guidance.

(3) *Permissible designees and public forums.*—Permissible designees under this section include individuals; trusts; estates; corporations; partnerships; Federal, State, local and foreign government agencies or subunits of such agencies; or the general public. When disclosures are to be made in a public forum, such as in a courtroom or congressional hearing, the request for or consent to disclosure must describe the circumstances surrounding the public disclosure, *e.g.,* congressional hearing, judicial proceeding, media, and the date or dates of the disclosure. When a designee is an individual, this section does not authorize disclosures to other individuals associated with such individual, such as employees of such individual or members of such individual's staff.

(4) *Authority to execute a request for or consent to disclosure.*—Any person who may obtain returns under section 6103(e)(1) through (5), except section 6103(e)(1)(D)(iii), may execute a request for or consent to disclose a return or return information to third parties. For taxpayers that are legal entities, such as corporations and municipal bond issuers, any officer of the entity with authority under applicable State law to legally bind the entity may execute a request for or consent to disclosure. A person described in section 6103(e)(6) (a taxpayer's representative or individual holding a power of attorney) may not execute a request for or consent to disclosure unless the designation of representation or power of attorney specifically delegates such authority. A designee pursuant to this section does not have authority to execute a request for or consent to disclosure permitting the Internal Revenue Service to disclose returns or return information to another person.

(5) *No disclosure of return information if impairment.*—A disclosure of return information shall not be made under this section if the Internal Revenue Service determines that the disclosure would seriously impair Federal tax administration (as defined in section 6103(b)(4) of the Internal Revenue Code).

(f) *Applicability date.*—This section is applicable on April 29, 2003, except that paragraph (b)(2) is applicable to section 6103(c) authorizations signed on or after October 19, 2009.

(g) *Effective date.*—This section is effective on April 29, 2003, except that paragraphs (b)(2) and (f) are effective on May 7, 2013. [Reg. § 301.6103(c)-1.]

☐ [*T.D. 9054, 4-28-2003. Amended by T.D. 9618, 5-6-2013.*]

### [Reg. § 301.6103(h)(2)-1]

**§ 301.6103(h)(2)-1. Disclosure of returns and return information (including taxpayer return information) to and by officers and employees of the Department of Justice for use in Federal grand jury proceeding, or in preparation for proceeding or investigation, involving tax administration.**—(a) *Disclosure of returns and return information (including taxpayer return information) to and by officers and employees of the Department of Justice.*—(1) Returns and return information (including taxpayer return information), as defined in section 6103(b)(1), (2), and (3) of the Internal Revenue Code, shall, to the

extent provided by section 6103(h)(2)(A), (B), and (C) and subject to the requirements of section 6103(h)(3), be open to inspection by or disclosure to officers and employees of the Department of Justice (including United States attorneys) personally and directly engaged in, and for their necessary use in, any Federal grand jury proceeding, or preparation for any proceeding (or for their necessary use in an investigation which may result in such a proceeding) before a Federal grand jury or any Federal or State court, in a matter involving tax administration (as defined in section 6103(b)(4)), including any such proceeding (or any such investigation) also involving the enforcement of a related Federal criminal statute which has been referred by the Secretary to the Department of Justice.

(2) Returns and return information (including taxpayer return information) inspected by or disclosed to officers and employees of the Department of Justice as provided in paragraph (a)(1) of this section may also be used by such officers and employees or disclosed by them to other officers and employees (including United States attorneys and supervisory personnel, such as Section Chiefs, Deputy Assistant Attorneys General, Assistant Attorneys General, the Deputy Attorney General, and the Attorney General), of the Department of Justice where necessary—

(i) In connection with any Federal grand jury proceeding, or preparation for any proceeding (or with an investigation which may result in such a proceeding), described in paragraph (a)(1), or

(ii) In connection with any Federal grand jury proceeding, or preparation for any proceeding (or with an investigation which may result in such a proceeding), described in paragraph (a)(1) which also involves enforcement of a specific Federal criminal statute other than one described in paragraph (a)(1) to which the United States is or may be a party, provided such matter involves or arises out of the particular facts and circumstances giving rise to the proceeding (or investigation) described in paragraph (a)(1) and further provided the tax portion of such proceeding (or investigation) has been duly authorized by or on behalf of the Assistant Attorney General for the Tax Division of the Department of Justice, pursuant to the request of the Secretary, as a proceeding (or investigation) described in paragraph (a)(1). If, in the course of a Federal grand jury proceeding, or preparation for a proceeding (or the conduct of an investigation which may result in such a proceeding), described in subdivision (ii) of this subparagraph, the tax administration portion thereof is terminated for any reason, any further use or disclosure of such returns or taxpayer return information in such Federal grand jury proceeding, or preparation or investigation, with respect to the remaining portion may be made only pursuant to, and upon the grant of, a court order as provided by section 6103(i)(1)(A), provided, however, that the returns and taxpayer return information may in any event be used for purposes of obtaining the necessary court order.

(b) *Disclosure of returns and return information (including taxpayer return information) by officers and employees of the Department of Justice.*—(1) Returns and return information (including taxpayer return information), as defined in section 6103(b)(1), (2), and (3) of the Code, inspected by or disclosed to officers and employees of the Department of Justice as provided by paragraph (a) of this section may be disclosed by such officers and employees to other persons, including, but not limited to, persons described in paragraph (b)(2), but only to the extent necessary in connection with a Federal grand jury proceeding, or the proper preparation for a proceeding (or in connection with an investigation which may result in such a proceeding), described in paragraph (a). Such disclosures may include, but are not limited to, disclosures—

(i) To properly accomplish any purpose or activity of the nature described in section 6103(k)(6) and the regulations thereunder which is essential to such Federal grand jury proceeding, or to such proper preparation (or to such investigation);

(ii) To properly interview, consult, depose, or interrogate or otherwise obtain relevant information from, the taxpayer to whom such return or return information relates (or such taxpayer's legal representative) or from any witness who may be called to give evidence in the proceeding; or

(iii) To properly conduct negotiations concerning, or obtain authorization for, settlement or disposition of the proceeding, in whole or in part, or stipulations of fact in connection with the proceeding.

Disclosure of a return or return information to a person other than the taxpayer to whom such return or return information relates or such taxpayer's legal representative to properly accomplish any purpose or activity described in this paragraph should be made, however, only if such purpose or activity cannot otherwise properly be accomplished without making such disclosure.

(2) Among those persons to whom returns and return information may be disclosed by officers and employees of the Department of Justice as provided by paragraph (a)(1) of this section are—

(i) Other officers and employees of the Department of Justice, such as personnel of an office, board, division, or bureau of such department (for example, the Federal Bureau of Investigation or the Drug Enforcement Administration), clerical personnel (for example secretaries, stenographers, docket and file room clerks, and mail room employees) and supervisory personnel (such as supervisory personnel of the Federal Bureau of Investigation or the Drug Enforcement Administration);

(ii) Officers and employees of another Federal agency (as defined in section 6103(b)(9)) working under the direction and control of any such officers and employees of the Department of Justice; and

(iii) Court reporters. [Reg. § 301.6103(h)(2)-1.]

☐ [*T.D. 7573, 11-28-78. Amended by T.D. 7723, 9-30-80.*]

### [Reg. § 301.6103(h)(4)-1]

**§301.6103(h)(4)-1. Disclosure of returns and return information in whistleblower administrative proceedings.**—(a) *In general.*—A whistleblower administrative proceeding (as described in § 301.7623-3) is an administrative proceeding pertaining to tax administration within the meaning of section 6103(h)(4).

(b) *Disclosures in whistleblower administrative proceedings.*—Pursuant to section 6103(h)(4) and paragraph (a) of this section, the Director, officers, and employees of the Whistleblower Office may disclose returns and return information (as defined by section 6103(b)) to a whistleblower (or the whistleblower's legal representative, if any) to the extent necessary to conduct a whistleblower administrative proceeding (as described in § 301.7623-3), including but not limited to—

(1) By communicating a preliminary award recommendation or preliminary denial letter to the whistleblower;

(2) By providing the whistleblower with an award report package;

(3) By conducting a meeting with the whistleblower to review documents supporting the preliminary award recommendation; and

(4) By sending an award decision letter, award determination letter, or award denial letter to the whistleblower.

(c) *Effective/applicability date.*—This rule is effective on August 12, 2014. This rule applies to information submitted on or after August 12, 2014, and to claims for award under sections 7623(a) and 7623(b) that are open as of August 12, 2014. [Reg. § 301.6103(h)(4)-1.]

☐ [*T.D. 9687, 8-7-2014.*]

### [Reg. § 301.6103(i)-1]

**§301.6103(i)-1. Disclosure of returns and return information (including taxpayer return information) to and by officers and employees of the Department of Justice or another Federal agency for use in Federal grand jury proceeding, or preparation for proceeding or investigation, involving enforcement of Federal criminal statute not involving tax administration.**—(a) *Disclosure of returns and return information (including taxpayer return information) to officers and employees of the Department of Justice or another Federal agency.*—Returns and return information (including taxpayer return information), as defined in section 6103(b)(1), (2), and (3) of the Internal Revenue Code, shall, to the extent provided by section 6103(i)(1), (2), and (3) and subject to the requirements of section 6103(i)(1) and (2), be open to inspection by or disclosure to officers and employees of the Department of Justice (including United States attorneys) or of another Federal agency (as defined in section 6103(b)(9)) personally and directly engaged in, and for their necessary use in, any Federal grand jury proceeding, or preparation for any administration or judicial proceeding (or their necessary use in an investigation which may result in such a proceeding), pertaining to enforcement of a specifically designated Federal criminal statute not involving or related to tax administration to which the United States or such agency is or may be a party.

(b) *Disclosure of returns and return information (including taxpayer return information) by officers and employees of the Department of Justice or another Federal agency.*—(1) Returns and return information (including taxpayer return information), as defined in section 6103(b)(1), (2), and (3) of the Code, disclosed to officers and employees of the Department of Justice or other Federal agency (as defined in section 6103(b)(9)) as provided by paragraph (a) of this section may be disclosed by such officers and employees to other persons, including, but not limited to, persons described in subparagraph (2) of this paragraph, but only to the extent necessary in connection with a Federal grand jury proceeding, or the proper preparation for a proceeding (or in connection with an investigation which may result in such a proceeding), described in paragraph (a). Such disclosures may include, but are not limited to, disclosures where necessary—

(i) To properly obtain the services of persons having special knowledge or technical skills (such as, but not limited to, handwriting analysis, photographic development, sound recording enhancement, or voice identification);

(ii) To properly interview, consult, depose, or interrogate or otherwise obtain relevant information from, the taxpayer to whom such return or return information relates (or such taxpayer's legal representative) or any witness who may be called to give evidence in the proceeding; or

(iii) To properly conduct negotiations concerning, or obtain authorization for, disposition of the proceeding, in whole or in part, or stipulations of fact in connection with the proceeding.

Disclosure of a return or return information to a person other than the taxpayer to whom such return or return information relates or such taxpayer's legal representative to properly accomplish any purpose or activity described in this subparagraph should be made, however, only if such purpose or activity cannot otherwise properly be accomplished without making such disclosures.

(2) Among those persons to whom returns and return information may be disclosed by officers and employees of the Department of Justice or other Federal agency as provided by subparagraph (1) of this paragraph are—

(i) Other officers and employees of the Department of Justice (including an office, board, division, or bureau of such department, such as the Federal Bureau of Investigation or the Drug Enforcement Administration) or other Federal agency described in subparagraph (1), such as clerical personnel (for example, secretaries, stenographers, docket and file room clerks, and mail room employees) and supervisory personnel (for example, in the case of the Department of Justice, Section Chiefs, Deputy Assistant Attorneys General, Assistant Attorneys General, the Deputy Attorney General, the Attorney General, and supervisory personnel of the Federal Bureau of Investigation or the Drug Enforcement Administration);

(ii) Officers and employees of another Federal agency (as defined in section 6103(b)(9)) working under the direction and control of such officers and employees of the Department of Justice or other Federal agency described in subparagraph (1); and

(iii) Court reporters. [Reg. § 301.6103(i)-1.]

☐ [*T.D. 7723, 9-30-80.*]

### [Reg. § 301.6103(j)(1)-1]

**§301.6103(j)(1)-1. Disclosures of return information reflected on returns to officers and employees of the Department of Commerce for certain statistical purposes and related activities.**—(a) *General rule.*—Pursuant to the provisions of section 6103(j)(1) of the Internal Revenue Code and subject to the requirements of paragraph (d) of this section, officers or employees of the Internal Revenue Service will disclose return information (as defined by section 6103(b)(2) but not including return information described in section 6103(o)(2)) reflected on returns to officers and employees of the Department of Commerce to the extent, and for such purposes as may be, provided by paragraphs (b) and (c) of this section. Further, in the case of any disclosure of return information reflected on returns so provided by paragraphs (b) and (c) of this section, the tax period or accounting period to which such information relates will also be disclosed. "Return information reflected on returns" includes, but is not limited to, information on returns, information derived from processing such returns, and information derived from the Social Security Administration and other sources for the purposes of establishing and maintaining taxpayer information relating to returns.

(b) *Disclosure of return information reflected on returns to officers and employees of the Bureau of the Census.*—(1) Officers or employees of the Internal Revenue Service will disclose the following return information reflected on returns of individual taxpayers to officers and employees of the Bureau of the Census for purposes of, but only to the extent necessary in, conducting and preparing, as authorized by chapter 5 of title 13, United States Code, intercensal estimates of population and income for all geographic areas included in the population estimates program and demographic statistics programs, censuses, and related program evaluation:

(i) Taxpayer identity information (as defined in section 6103(b)(6) of the Internal Revenue Code), validity code with respect to the taxpayer identifying number (as described in section 6109), and taxpayer identity information of spouse and dependents, if reported.

(ii) Location codes (including area/district office and campus/service center codes).

(iii) Marital status.

(iv) Number and classification of reported exemptions.

(v) Wage and salary income.

(vi) Dividend income.

(vii) Interest income.

(viii) Gross rent and royalty income.

(ix) Total of—

(A) Wages, salaries, tips, etc.;

(B) Interest income;

(C) Dividend income;

(D) Alimony received;

(E) Business income;

(F) Pensions and annuities;

(G) Income from rents, royalties, partnerships, estates, trusts, etc.;

(H) Farm income;

(I) Unemployment compensation; and

(J) Total Social Security benefits.

(x) Adjusted gross income.

(xi) Type of tax return filed.

(xii) Entity code.

(xiii) Code indicators for Form 1040, Form 1040 (Schedules A, C, D, E, F, and SE), and Form 8814.

(xiv) Posting cycle date relative to filing.

(xv) Social Security benefits.

(xvi) Earned Income (as defined in section 32(c)(2).

(xvii) Number of Earned Income Tax Credit-eligible qualifying children.

(xviii) Electronic Filing System Indicator.

(xix) Return Processing Indicator.

(xx) Paid Preparer Code.

(2) Officers or employees of the Internal Revenue Service will disclose to officers and employees of the Bureau of the Census for purposes of, but only to the extent necessary in, conducting, as authorized by chapter 5 of title 13, United States Code, demographic, economic, and agricultural statistics programs and censuses and related program evaluation—

(i) From the business master files of the Internal Revenue Service—the taxpayer name directory and entity records consisting of taxpayer identity information (as defined in section 6103(b)(6)) with respect to taxpayers engaged in a trade or business, the principal industrial activity code, the filing requirement code, the employment code, the physical location, the location codes (including area/district office and campus/service center codes), and monthly corrections of, and additions to, such entity records;

(ii) From Form SS-4—all information reflected on such form;

(iii) From an employment tax return—

(A) Taxpayer identifying number (as described in section 6109) of the employer;

(B) Total compensation reported;

(C) Master file tax account code (MFT);

(D) Taxable period covered by such return;

(E) Employer code;

(F) Document locator number;

(G) Record code;

(H) Total number of individuals employed in the taxable period covered by the return;

(I) Total taxable wages paid for purposes of chapter 21;

(J) Total taxable tip income reported for purposes of chapter 21;

(K) If a business has closed or stopped paying wages;

(L) Final date a business paid wages; and

(M) If a business is a seasonal employer and does not have to file a return for every quarter of the year;

(iv) From Form 1040 (Schedule SE)—

(A) Taxpayer identifying number of self-employed individual;

(B) Business activities subject to the tax imposed by chapter 21;

(C) Net earnings from farming;

(D) Net earnings from nonfarming activities;

(E) Total net earnings from self-employment; and

(F) Taxable self-employment income for purposes of chapter 2;

(v) Total Social Security taxable earnings; and

(vi) Quarters of Social Security coverage.

(3) Officers or employees of the Internal Revenue Service will disclose the following business-related return information reflected on returns of taxpayers to officers and employees of the Bureau of the Census for purposes of, but only to the extent necessary in, conducting and preparing, as authorized by chapter 5 of title 13, United States Code, demographic and economic statistics programs, censuses, and surveys. (The "returns of taxpayers" include, but are not limited to: Form 941; Form 990 series; Form 1040 series and Schedules C and SE; Form 1065 and all attending schedules and Form 8825; Form 1120 series and all attending schedules and Form 8825; Form 851; Form 1096; and other business returns, schedules and forms that the Internal Revenue Service may issue.):

(i) Taxpayer identity information (as defined in section 6103(b)(6)) including parent corporation, shareholder, partner, and employer identity information.

(ii) Gross income, profits, or receipts.

(iii) Returns and allowances.

(iv) Cost of labor, salaries, and wages.

(v) Total expenses or deductions, including totals of the following components thereof:

(A) Repairs (and maintenance) expense;

(B) Rents (or lease) expense;

(C) Taxes and licenses expense;

(D) Interest expense, including mortgage or other interest;

(E) Depreciation expense;

(F) Depletion expense;

(G) Advertising expense;

(H) Pension and profit-sharing plans (retirement plans) expense;

(I) Employee benefit programs expense;

(J) Utilities expense;

(K) Supplies expense;

(L) Contract labor expense; and

(M) Management (and investment advisory) fees.

(vi) Total assets.

(vii) Beginning-and end-of-year inventory.

(viii) Royalty income.

(ix) Interest income, including portfolio interest.

(x) Rental income, including gross rents.

(xi) Tax-exempt interest income.

(xii) Net gain from sales of business property.

(xiii) Other income.

(xiv) Total income.

(xv) Percentage of stock owned by each shareholder.

(xvi) Percentage of capital ownership of each partner.

(xvii) Principal industrial activity code, including the business description.

(xviii) Consolidated return indicator.

(xix) Wages, tips, and other compensation.

(xx) Social Security wages.

(xxi) Deferred wages.

(xxii) Social Security tip income.

(xxiii) Total Social Security taxable earnings.

(xxiv) Gross distributions from employer-sponsored and individual retirement plans from Form 1099-R.

(xxv) From Form 6765 (when filed with corporation income tax returns)—

(A) Indicator that total qualified research expenses is greater than zero, but less than $1 million; greater than or equal to $1 million, but less than $3 million; or, greater than or equal to $3 million;

(B) Cycle posted; and

(C) Research tax credit amount to be carried over to a business return, schedule, or form.

(xxvi) Total number of documents reported on Form 1096 transmitting Forms 1099-MISC.

(xxvii) Total amount reported on Form 1096 transmitting Forms 1099-MISC.

(xxviii) Type of REIT.

(xxix) From Form 1125-A— purchases.

(xxx) From Form 1040, Schedule C—

(A) Purchases less cost of items withdrawn for personal use; and

(B) Materials and supplies.

(xxxi) Electronic filing system indicator.

(xxxii) Posting cycle date relative to filing.

(xxxiii) Dividends, including ordinary or qualified.

(xxxiv) From Form 1120S, Schedule K-1—ordinary business income (loss).

(xxxv) From Form 1065, Schedule K-1—

(A) Publicly-traded partnership indicator;

(B) Partner's share of nonrecourse, qualified nonrecourse, and recourse liabilities; and

(C) Ordinary business income (loss).

(4) Officers or employees of the Internal Revenue Service will disclose return information reflected on returns of taxpayers contained in the exempt organization master files of the Internal Revenue Service to officers and employees of the Bureau of the Census for purposes of, but only to the extent necessary in, conducting and preparing, as authorized by chapter 5 of title 13, United States Code, economic censuses. This return information reflected on returns of taxpayers consists of taxpayer identity information (as defined in section 6103(b)(6)), activity codes, and filing requirement code, and monthly corrections of, and additions to, such information.

(5) Subject to the requirements of paragraph (d) of this section and § 301.6103(p)(2)(B)-1, officers or employees of the Social Security

Administration to whom the following return information reflected on returns has been disclosed as provided by section 6103(l)(1)(A) or (l)(5) may disclose such information to officers and employees of the Bureau of the Census for necessary purposes described in paragraph (b)(2) or (3) of this section:

(i) From Form SS-4—all information reflected on such form.

(ii) From Form 1040 (Schedule SE)—

(A) Taxpayer identifying number of self-employed individual;

(B) Business activities subject to the tax imposed by chapter 21;

(C) Net earnings from farming;

(D) Net earnings from nonfarming activities;

(E) Total net earnings from self-employment; and

(F) Taxable self-employment income for purposes of chapter 2.

(iii) From Form W-2, and related forms and schedules—

(A) Social Security number;

(B) Employer identification number;

(C) Wages, tips, and other compensation;

(D) Social Security wages; and

(E) Deferred wages.

(iv) Total Social Security taxable earnings.

(v) Quarters of Social Security coverage.

(6)(i) Officers or employees of the Internal Revenue Service will disclose the following return information (but not including return information described in section 6103(o)(2)) reflected on returns of corporations with respect to the tax imposed by chapter 1 to officers and employees of the Bureau of the Census for purposes of, but only to the extent necessary in, developing and preparing, as authorized by law, the Quarterly Financial Report:

(A) From the business master files of the Internal Revenue Service—

(1) Taxpayer identity information (as defined in section 6103(b)(6)), including parent corporation identity information;

(2) Document code;

(3) Location codes (including area/district office and campus/service center codes);

(4) Consolidated return and final return indicators;

(5) Principal industrial activity code;

(6) Partial year indicator;

(7) Annual accounting period;

(8) Gross receipts less returns and allowances; and

(9) Total assets.

(B) From Form SS-4—

(1) Month and year in which such form was executed;

(2) Taxpayer identity information; and

(3) Principal industrial activity, geographic, firm size, and reason for application codes.

(C) From Form 1120-REIT—

(1) Type of REIT; and

(2) Gross rents from real property;

(D) From Form 1120F—corporation's method of accounting.

(E) From Form 1096—total amount reported.

(ii) Subject to the requirements of paragraph (d) of this section and §301.6103(p)(2)(B)-1, officers or employees of the Social Security Administration to whom return information reflected on returns of corporations described in paragraph (b)(6)(i)(B) of this section has been disclosed as provided by section 6103(1)(1)(A) or (1)(5) may disclose such information to officers and employees of the Bureau of the Census for a purpose described in this paragraph (b)(6).

(iii) Return information reflected on employment tax returns disclosed pursuant to paragraphs (b)(2)(iii) (A), (B), (D), (I) and (J) of this section may be used by officers and employees of the Bureau of the Census for the purpose described in and subject to the limitations of this paragraph (b)(6).

(7) Officers or employees of the Internal Revenue Service will disclose the following return information reflected on Form 1098 "Mortgage Interest Statement" to officers and employees of the Bureau of the Census for purposes of, but only to the extent necessary in, conducting and preparing, as authorized by chapter 5 of title 13, United States Code, demographic statistics programs, censuses, and surveys—

(i) Payee/Payer/Employee Taxpayer Identification Number;

(ii) Payee/Payer/Employee Name (First, Middle, Last, Suffix);

(iii) Street Address;

(iv) City;

(v) State;

(vi) ZIP Code (9 digit);

(vii) Posting Cycle Week;

(viii) Posting Cycle Year; and

(ix) Document Code.

(c) *Disclosure of return information reflected on returns of corporations to officers and employees of the Bureau of Economic Analysis.*—(1) As authorized by law for purposes of, but only to the extent necessary in, conducting and preparing statistical analyses, the Internal Revenue Service will disclose to officers and employees of the Bureau of Economic Analysis all return information, regardless of format or medium and including edited information from the Statistics of Income sample, of designated classes or categories of corporations with respect to the tax imposed by chapter 1 of the Internal Revenue Code.

(2) [Reserved].

(3) The Internal Revenue Service will disclose the following return information reflected on returns filed by corporations to officers and employees of the Bureau of Economic Analysis:

(i) From the business master files of the Internal Revenue Service—

(A) Taxpayer identity information (as defined in section 6103(b)(6)) with respect to corporate taxpayers;

(B) Business or industry activity codes;

(C) Filing requirement code; and

(D) Physical location.

(ii) From Form SS-4, "Application for Employer Identification Number," filed by an entity identifying itself on the form as a corporation or a private services corporation—

(A) Taxpayer identity information (as defined in section 6103(b)(6), including legal, trade, and business name);

(B) Physical location;

(C) State or country of incorporation;

(D) Entity type (corporate only);

(E) Estimated highest number of employees expected in the next 12 months;

(F) Principal activity of the business;

(G) Principal line of merchandise;

(H) Posting cycle date relative to filing; and

(I) Document code.

(iii) From an employment tax return filed by a corporation—

(A) Taxpayer identity information (as defined in section 6103(b)(6));

(B) Total compensation reported;

(C) Taxable wages paid for purposes of Chapter 21 to each employee;

(D) Master file tax account code (MFT);

(E) Total number of individuals employed in the taxable period covered by the return;

(F) Posting cycle date relative to filing;

(G) Accounting period covered; and

(H) Document code.

(iv) From returns of corporate taxpayers, including Form 1120, "U.S. Corporation Income Tax Return," Form 851, "Affiliations Schedule," and other business returns, schedules and forms that the Internal Revenue Service may issue—

(A) Taxpayer identity information (as defined in section 6103(b)(6)), including that of a parent corporation, affiliate, or subsidiary; a shareholder; a foreign corporation of which one or more U.S. shareholders (as defined in section 951(b)) own at least 10% of the voting stock; a foreign trust; and a U.S. agent of a foreign trust;

(B) Gross sales and receipts;

(C) Gross income, including life insurance company gross income;

(D) Gross income from sources outside the U.S.;

(E) Gross rents from real property;

(F) Other Gross Rents;

(G) Total Gross Rents;

(H) Returns and allowances;

(I) Percentage of foreign ownership of corporations and trusts;

(J) Fact of ownership of foreign partnerships;

(K) Fact of ownership of foreign entity disregarded as a foreign entity;

(L) Country of the foreign owner;

(M) Gross value of the portion of the foreign trust owned by filer;

(N) Country of incorporation;

(O) Cost of labor, salaries, and wages;

(P) Total assets;

(Q) The quantity of certain forms attached that are returns of U.S. persons with respect to foreign disregarded entities, partnerships, and corporations.

(R) Posting cycle date relative to filing;

(S) Accounting period covered;

(T) Master file tax account code (MFT);

(U) Document code; and

(V) Principal industrial activity code.

(d) *Procedures and restrictions.*—Disclosure of return information reflected on returns by officers or employees of the Internal Revenue Service or the Social Security Administration as provided by paragraphs (b) and (c) of this section will be made only upon written request to the Commissioner of Internal Revenue by the Secretary of Commerce describing—

(1) The particular return information reflected on returns to be disclosed;

(2) The taxable period or date to which such return information reflected on returns relates; and

(3)(i) The particular purpose for which the return information reflected on returns is to be used, and designating by name and title the officers and employees of the Bureau of the Census or the Bureau of Economic Analysis to whom such disclosure is authorized.

(ii) No such officer or employee to whom return information reflected on returns is disclosed pursuant to the provisions of paragraph (b) or (c) of this section shall disclose such information to any person, other than the taxpayer to whom such return information reflected on returns relates or other officers or employees of such bureau whose duties or responsibilities require such disclosure for a purpose described in paragraph (b) or (c) of this section, except in a form which cannot be associated with, or otherwise identify, directly or indirectly, a particular taxpayer. If the Internal Revenue Service determines that the Bureau of the Census or the Bureau of Economic Analysis, or any officer or employee thereof, has failed to, or does not, satisfy the requirements of section 6103(p)(4) of the Internal Revenue Code or regulations or published procedures thereunder (see § 601.601(d)(2) of this chapter), the Internal Revenue Service may take such actions as are deemed necessary to ensure that such requirements are or will be satisfied, including suspension of disclosures of return information reflected on returns otherwise authorized by section 6103(j)(1) and paragraph (b) or (c) of this section, until the Internal Revenue Service determines that such requirements have been or will be satisfied.

(e) *Applicability date.*—Paragraphs (b)(2)(iii)(I), (b)(2)(iii)(K) through (b)(2)(iii)(M), (b)(3)(v), (b)(3)(xxv) through (b)(3)(xxxv), and (b)(6)(i)(C) through (b)(6)(i)(E) of this section apply to disclosure to the Bureau of the Census made on or after December 9, 2016. For rules that apply to disclosure to the Bureau of the Census before December 9, 2016, see 26 CFR 301.6103(j)(1)-1 (revised as of April 1, 2016). [Reg. § 301.6103(j)(1)-1.]

☐ [*T.D.* 7724, 10-2-80. *Amended by T.D.* 7824, 7-30-82; *T.D.* 8118, 1-29-86; *T.D.* 8296, 3-27-90; *T.D.* 8377, 12-13-91; *T.D.* 8811, 1-22-99; *T.D.* 8908, 11-29-2000; *T.D.* 9037, 1-17-2003; *T.D.* 9188, 3-10-2005; *T.D.* 9267, 7-6-2006; *T.D.* 9372, 12-26-2007; *T.D.* 9439, 12-24-2008; *T.D.* 9500, 8-25-2010, *T.D.* 9631, 8-26-2013, *T.D.* 9754, 2-24-2016 *and T.D.* 9856, 4-5-2019.]

### [Reg. § 301.6103(j)(5)-1]

**§ 301.6103(j)(5)-1. Disclosures of return information reflected on returns to officers and employees of the Department of Agriculture for conducting the census of agriculture.**—(a) *General rule.*—Pursuant to the provisions of section 6103(j)(5) of the Internal Revenue Code and subject to the requirements of paragraph (c) of this section, officers or employees of the Internal Revenue Service will disclose return information reflected on returns to officers and employees of the Department of Agriculture to the extent, and for such purposes, as may be provided by paragraph (b) of this section. "Return information reflected on returns" includes, but is not limited to, information on returns, information derived from processing such returns, and information derived from other sources for the purposes of establishing and maintaining taxpayer information relating to returns.

(b) *Disclosure of return information reflected on returns to officers and employees of the Department of Agriculture.*—(1) Officers or employees of the Internal Revenue Service will disclose the following return information reflected on returns described in this paragraph (b) for individuals, partnerships and corporations with agricultural activity, as determined generally by industry code classification or the filing of returns for such activity, to officers and employees of the Department of Agriculture for purposes of, but only to the extent necessary in, structuring, preparing, and conducting, as authorized by chapter 55 of title 7, United States Code, the census of agriculture.

(2) From Form 1040 "U.S. Individual Income Tax Return", Form 1041 "U.S. Income Tax Return for Estates and Trusts", Form 1065 "U.S. Return of Partnership Income" and Form 1065-B "U.S. Return of Income for Electing Large Partnerships" (Schedule F)—

(i) Taxpayer identity information (as defined in section 6103(b)(6) of the Internal Revenue Code);

(ii) Spouse's Social Security Number;

(iii) Annual accounting period;

(iv) Principal Business Activity (PBA) code;

(v) Taxable cooperative distributions;

(vi) Income from custom hire and machine work;

(vii) Gross income;

(viii) Master File Tax (MFT) code;

(ix) Document Locator Number (DLN);

(x) Cycle posted;

(xi) Final return indicator;

(xii) Part year return indicator; and

(xiii) Taxpayer telephone number.

(3) From Form 943, "Employer's Annual Tax Return for Agricultural Employees"—

(i) Taxpayer identity information;

(ii) Annual accounting period;

(iii) Total wages subject to Medicare taxes;

(iv) MFT code;

(v) DLN;

(vi) Cycle posted;

(vii) Final return indicator; and

(viii) Part year return indicator.

(4) From Form 1120 series, "U.S. Corporation Income Tax Return"—

(i) Taxpayer identity information;

(ii) Annual accounting period;

(iii) Gross receipts less returns and allowances;

(iv) PBA code;

(v) MFT Code;

(vi) DLN;

(vii) Cycle posted;

(viii) Final return indicator;

(ix) Part year return indicator; and

(x) Consolidated return indicator.

(5) From Form 1065 series, "U.S. Return of Partnership Income"—

(i) Taxpayer identity information;

(ii) Annual accounting period;

(iii) PBA code;

(iv) Gross receipts less returns and allowances;

(v) Net farm profit (loss);

(vi) MFT code;

(vii) DLN;

(viii) Cycle posted;

(ix) Final return indicator; and

(x) Part year return indicator.

(c) *Procedures and Restrictions.*—(1) Disclosure of return information reflected on returns by officers or employees of the Internal Revenue Service as provided by paragraph (b) of this section will be made only upon written request designating, by name and title, the officers and employees of the Department of Agriculture to whom such disclosure is authorized, to the Commissioner of Internal Revenue by the Secretary of Agriculture and describing—

(i) The particular return information reflected on returns for disclosure;

(ii) The taxable period or date to which such return information reflected on returns relates; and

(iii) The particular purpose for the requested return information reflected on returns.

(2)(i) No such officer or employee to whom the Internal Revenue Service discloses return information reflected on returns pursuant to the provisions of paragraph (b) of this section shall disclose such information to any person, other than the taxpayer to whom such return information reflected on returns relates or other officers or employees of the Department of Agriculture whose duties or responsibilities require such disclosure for a purpose described in paragraph (b)(1) of this section, except in a form that cannot be associated with, or otherwise identify, directly or indirectly, a particular taxpayer.

(ii) If the Internal Revenue Service determines that the Department of Agriculture, or any officer or employee thereof, has failed to, or does not, satisfy the requirements of section 6103(p)(4) of the Internal Revenue Code or regulations or published procedures, the Internal Revenue Service may take such actions as are deemed necessary to ensure that such requirements are or will be satisfied, including suspension of disclosures of return information reflected on returns otherwise authorized by section 6103(j)(5) and paragraph (b) of this section, until the Internal Revenue Service determines that such requirements have been or will be satisfied.

(d) *Effective date.*—This section is applicable on February 22, 2006.
[Reg. § 301.6103(j)(5)-1.]

☐ [T.D. 9245, 2-21-2006.]

### [Reg. § 301.6103(k)(6)-1]

**§ 301.6103(k)(6)-1. Disclosure of return information by certain officers and employees for investigative purposes.**—(a) *General rule.*—(1) Pursuant to the provisions of section 6103(k)(6) and subject to the conditions of this section, an internal revenue employee or an Office of Treasury Inspector General for Tax Administration (TIGTA) employee, in connection with official duties relating to any examination, administrative appeal, collection activity, administrative, civil or criminal investigation, enforcement activity, ruling, negotiated agreement, prefiling activity, or other proceeding or offense under the internal revenue laws or related statutes, or in preparation for any proceeding described in section 6103(h)(2) (or investigation which may result in such a proceeding), may disclose return information, of any taxpayer, to the extent necessary to obtain information relating to such official duties or to accomplish properly any activity connected with such official duties, including, but not limited to—

(i) Establishing or verifying the correctness or completeness of any return or return information;

(ii) Determining the responsibility for filing a return, for making a return if none has been made, or for performing such acts as may be required by law concerning such matters;

(iii) Establishing or verifying the liability (or possible liability) of any person, or the liability (or possible liability) at law or in equity of any transferee or fiduciary of any person, for any tax, penalty, interest, fine, forfeiture, or other imposition or offense under the internal revenue laws or related statutes or the amount thereof for collection;

(iv) Establishing or verifying misconduct (or possible misconduct) or other activity proscribed by the internal revenue laws or related statutes;

(v) Obtaining the services of persons having special knowledge or technical skills (such as, but not limited to, knowledge of particular facts and circumstances relevant to a correct determination of a liability described in paragraph (a)(1)(iii) of this section or skills relating to handwriting analysis, photographic development, sound recording enhancement, or voice identification) or having recognized expertise in matters involving the valuation of property if relevant to proper performance of official duties described in this paragraph;

(vi) Establishing or verifying the financial status or condition and location of the taxpayer against whom collection activity is or may be directed, to locate assets in which the taxpayer has an interest, to ascertain the amount of any liability described in paragraph (a)(1)(iii) of this section for collection, or otherwise to apply the provisions of the Internal Revenue Code relating to establishment of liens against such assets, or levy, seizure, or sale on or of the assets to satisfy any such liability;

(vii) Preparing for any proceeding described in section 6103(h)(2) or conducting an investigation which may result in such a proceeding; or

(viii) Obtaining, verifying, or establishing information concerned with making determinations regarding a taxpayer's liability under the Internal Revenue Code, including, but not limited to, the administrative appeals process and any ruling, negotiated agreement, or prefiling process.

(2) Disclosure of return information for the purpose of obtaining information to carry out properly the official duties described by this paragraph, or any activity connected with the official duties, is authorized only if the internal revenue or TIGTA employee reasonably believes, under the facts and circumstances, at the time of a disclosure, the information is not otherwise reasonably available, or if the activity connected with the official duties cannot occur properly without the disclosure.

(3) Internal revenue and TIGTA employees may identify themselves, their organizational affiliation (e.g., Internal Revenue Service (IRS), Criminal Investigation (CI) or TIGTA, Office of Investigations (OI)), and the nature of their investigation, when making an oral, written, or electronic contact with a third party witness. Permitted disclosures include, but are not limited to, the use and presentation of any identification media (such as a Federal agency badge, credential, or business card) or the use of an information document request, summons, or correspondence on Federal agency letterhead or which bears a return address or signature block that reveals affiliation with the Federal agency.

(4) This section does not address or affect the requirements under section 7602(c) (relating to contact of third parties).

(b) *Disclosure of return information in connection with certain personnel or claimant representative matters.*—In connection with official duties relating to any investigation concerned with enforcement of any provision of the Internal Revenue Code, including enforcement of any rule or directive prescribed by the Secretary or the Commissioner of Internal Revenue under any provision of the Internal Revenue Code, or the enforcement of any provision related to tax administration, that affects or may affect the personnel or employment rights or status, or civil or criminal liability, of any former, current, or prospective employee of the Treasury Department, Bureau of Alcohol, Tobacco, Firearms, and Explosives, United States Customs Service, United States Secret Service, or any successor agency, or the rights of any person who is, or may be, a party to an administrative action or proceeding pursuant to 31 U.S.C. 330 (relating to practice before the Treasury Department), an internal revenue, TIGTA, or other Federal officer or employee who is responsible for investigating such employees and persons and is properly in possession of relevant return information is authorized to disclose such return information to the extent necessary for the purpose of obtaining, verifying, or establishing other information which is or may be relevant and material to the investigation.

(c) *Definitions.*—The following definitions apply to this section—

(1) *Disclosure of return information to the extent necessary* means a disclosure of return information which an internal revenue or TIGTA employee, based on the facts and circumstances, at the time of the disclosure, reasonably believes is necessary to obtain information to perform properly the official duties described by this section, or to accomplish properly the activities connected with carrying out those official duties. The term *necessary* in this context does not mean essential or indispensable, but rather appropriate and helpful in obtaining the information sought. Nor does *necessary* in this context refer to the necessity of conducting an investigation or the appropriateness of the means or methods chosen to conduct the investigation. Section 6103(k)(6) does not limit or restrict internal revenue or TIGTA employees with respect to the decision to initiate or the conduct of an investigation. Disclosures under this paragraph (c)(1), however, may not be made indiscriminately or solely for the benefit of the recipient or as part of a negotiated quid pro quo arrangement. This paragraph (c)(1) is illustrated by the following examples:

*Example 1.* A revenue agent contacts a taxpayer's customer regarding the customer's purchases made from the taxpayer during the year under investigation. The revenue agent is able to obtain the purchase information only by disclosing the taxpayer's identity and the fact of the investigation. Depending on the facts and circumstances known to the revenue agent at the time of the disclosure, such as the way the customer maintains his records, it also may be necessary for the revenue agent to inform the customer of the date of the purchases and the types of merchandise involved for the customer to find the purchase information.

*Example 2.* A revenue agent contacts a third party witness to obtain copies of invoices of sales made to a taxpayer under examination. The third party witness provides copies of the sales invoices in question and then asks the revenue agent for the current address of the taxpayer because the taxpayer still owes money to the third party witness. The revenue agent may not disclose that current address because this disclosure would be only for the benefit of the third party witness and not necessary to obtain information for the examination.

*Example 3.* A revenue agent contacts a third party witness to obtain copies of invoices of sales made to a taxpayer under examination. The third party witness agrees to provide copies of the sales invoices in question only if the revenue agent provides him with the current address of the taxpayer because the taxpayer still owes money to the third party witness. The revenue agent may not disclose that current address because this disclosure would be a negotiated quid pro quo arrangement.

(2) *Disclosure of return information to accomplish properly an activity connected with official duties* means a disclosure of return information to carry out a function associated with official duties generally consistent with established practices and procedures. This paragraph (c)(2) is illustrated by the following example:

*Example.* A taxpayer failed to file an income tax return and pay the taxes owed. After the taxes were assessed and the taxpayer was notified of the balance due, a revenue officer filed a notice of federal tax lien and then served a notice of levy on the taxpayer's bank. The notices of lien and levy contained the taxpayer's name, social security number, amount of outstanding liability, and the tax period and type of tax involved. The taxpayer's assets were levied to satisfy the tax debt, but it was determined that, prior to the levy, the revenue officer failed to issue the taxpayer a notice of intent to levy, as required by section 6331, and a notice of right to hearing before the levy, as required by section 6330. The disclosure of the taxpayer's return information in the notice of levy is authorized by section 6103(k)(6) despite the revenue officer's failure to issue the notice of intent to levy or the notice of right to hearing. The ultimate validity of the underlying levy is irrelevant to the issue of whether the disclosure was authorized by section 6103(k)(6).

(3) *Information not otherwise reasonably available* means information that an internal revenue or TIGTA employee reasonably believes, under the facts and circumstances, at the time of a disclosure, cannot be obtained in a sufficiently accurate or probative form, or in a timely manner, and without impairing the proper performance of the official duties described by this section, without making the disclosure. This definition does not require or create the presumption or expectation that an internal revenue or TIGTA employee must seek information from a taxpayer or authorized representative prior to contacting a third party witness in an investigation. Neither the Internal Revenue Code, IRS procedures, nor these regulations require repeated contacting of an uncooperative taxpayer. Moreover, an internal revenue or TIGTA employee may make a disclosure to a third party witness to corroborate information provided by a taxpayer. This paragraph (c)(3) is illustrated by the following examples:

*Example 1.* A revenue agent is conducting an examination of a taxpayer. The taxpayer refuses to cooperate or provide any information to the revenue agent. Information relating to the taxpayer's examination would be information not otherwise reasonably available because of the taxpayer's refusal to cooperate and supply any information to the revenue agent. The revenue agent may seek information from a third party witness.

*Example 2.* A special agent is conducting a criminal investigation of a taxpayer. The special agent has acquired certain information from the taxpayer. Although the special agent has no specific reason to disbelieve the taxpayer's information, the special agent contacts several third party witnesses to confirm the information. The special agent may contact third party witnesses to verify the correctness of the information provided by the taxpayer because the IRS is not required to rely solely on information provided by a taxpayer, and a special agent may take appropriate steps, including disclosures to third party witnesses under section 6103(k)(6), to verify independently or corroborate information obtained from a taxpayer.

(4) *Internal revenue employee* means, for purposes of this section, an officer or employee of the IRS or Office of Chief Counsel for the IRS, or an officer or employee of a Federal agency responsible for administering and enforcing taxes under Chapters 32 (Part III of Subchapter D), 51, 52, or 53 of the Internal Revenue Code, or investigating tax refund check fraud under 18 U.S.C. 510.

(5) *TIGTA employee* means an officer or employee of the Office of Treasury Inspector General for Tax Administration.

(d) *Examples.*—The following examples illustrate the application of this section:

*Example 1.* A revenue agent is conducting an examination of a taxpayer. The taxpayer has been very cooperative and has supplied copies of invoices as requested. Some of the taxpayer's invoices show purchases that seem excessive in comparison to the size of the taxpayer's business. The revenue agent contacts the taxpayer's suppliers for the purpose of corroborating the invoices the taxpayer provided. In contacting the suppliers, the revenue agent discloses the taxpayer's name, the dates of purchase, and the type of merchandise at issue. These disclosures are permissible under section 6103(k)(6) because, under the facts and circumstances known to the revenue agent at the time of the disclosures, the disclosures were necessary to obtain information (corroboration of invoices) not otherwise reasonably available because suppliers would be the only source available for corroboration of this information.

*Example 2.* A revenue agent is conducting an examination of a taxpayer. The revenue agent asks the taxpayer for business records to document the deduction of the cost of goods sold shown on Schedule C of the taxpayer's return. The taxpayer will not provide the business records to the revenue agent, who contacts a third party witness for verification of the amount on the Schedule C. In the course of the contact, the revenue agent shows the Schedule C to the third party witness. This disclosure is not authorized under section 6103(k)(6). Section 6103(k)(6) permits disclosure only of return information, not the return (including schedules and attachments) itself. If necessary, a revenue agent may disclose return information extracted from a return when questioning a third party witness. Thus, the revenue agent could have extracted the amount of cost of goods sold from the Schedule C and disclosed that amount to the third party witness.

*Example 3.* A special agent is conducting a criminal investigation of a taxpayer, a doctor, for tax evasion. Notwithstanding the records provided by the taxpayer and the taxpayer's bank, the special agent decided to obtain information from the taxpayer's patients to verify amounts paid to the taxpayer for his services. Accordingly, the special agent sent letters to the taxpayer's patients to verify these amounts. In the letters, the agent disclosed that he was a special agent with IRS-CI and that he was conducting a criminal investigation of the taxpayer. Section 6103(k)(6) permits these disclosures (including the special agent disclosing his affiliation with CI and the nature of the investigation) to confirm the taxpayer's income. The decision whether to verify information already obtained is a matter of investigative judgment and is not limited by section 6103(k)(6).

*Example 4.* Corporation A requests a private letter ruling (PLR) as to the tax consequences of a planned transaction. Corporation A has represented that it is in compliance with laws administered by Agency B that may relate to the tax consequences of the proposed transaction. Further information is needed from Agency B relating to possible tax consequences. Under section 6103(k)(6), the IRS may disclose Corporation A's return information to Agency B to the extent necessary to obtain information from Agency B for the purpose of properly considering the tax consequences of the proposed transaction that is the subject of the PLR.

(e) *Effective date.*—This section is applicable on July 6, 2006. [Reg. § 301.6103(k)(6)-1.]

☐ [*T.D.* 9274, 7-6-2006 (*corrected* 10-16-2006).]

### [Reg. § 301.6103(k)(9)-1]

**§ 301.6103(k)(9)-1. Disclosure of returns and return information relating to payment of tax by credit card and debit card.**—Officers and employees of the Internal Revenue Service may disclose to card issuers, financial institutions, or other persons such return information as the Commissioner deems necessary in connection with processing credit card and debit card transactions to effectuate payment of tax as authorized by § 301.6311-2. Officers and employees of the Internal Revenue Service may disclose such return information to such persons as the Commissioner deems necessary in connection with billing or collection of the amounts charged or debited, including resolution of errors relating to the credit card or debit card account as described in § 301.6311-2(d). [Reg. § 301.6103(k)(9)-1.]

☐ [*T.D.* 8969, 12-13-2001.]

### [Reg. § 301.6103(l)-1]

**§ 301.6103(l)-1. Disclosure of returns and return information for purposes other than tax administration.**—(a) *Definition.*—For purposes of applying the provisions of section 6103(l) of the Internal Revenue Code, the term *agent* includes a contractor.

(b) *Effective date.*—This section is applicable January 6, 2004. [Reg. § 301.6103(l)-1.]

☐ [*T.D.* 9111, 12-31-2003.]

### [Reg. § 301.6103(l)(2)-1]

**§ 301.6103(l)(2)-1. Disclosure of returns and return information to Pension Benefit Guaranty Corporation for purposes of research and studies.**—(a) *General rule.*—Pursuant to the provisions of section 6103(l)(2) of the Internal Revenue Code and subject to the requirements of paragraph (b) of this section, officers and employees of the Internal Revenue Service may disclose returns and return information (as defined by section 6103(b)) to officers and employees of the Pension Benefit Guaranty Corporation for purposes of, but only to the extent necessary in, conducting research and studies authorized by title IV of the Employee Retirement Income Security Act of 1974.

(b) *Procedures and restrictions.*—Disclosure of returns or return information by officers or employees of the Service as provided by paragraph (a) of this section will be made only upon written request to the Commissioner of Internal Revenue by the Executive Director of the Pension Benefit Guaranty Corporation describing the returns or return information to be disclosed, the taxable period or date to which such returns or return information relates, and the purpose for which the returns or return information is needed in the administration of title IV of the Employee Retirement Income Security Act of 1974, and designating by title the officers and employees of such corporation to whom such disclosure is authorized. No such officer or employee to whom returns or return information is disclosed pursuant to the provisions of paragraph (a) shall disclose such returns or return information to any person, other than the taxpayer by whom the return was made or to whom the return information relates or other officers or employees of such corporation whose duties or responsibilities require such disclosure for a purpose described in paragraph (a), except in a form which cannot be associated with, or otherwise identify, directly or indirectly, a particular taxpayer. [Reg. § 301.6103(l)(2)-1.]

☐ [*T.D.* 7723, 9-30-80.]

### [Reg. § 301.6103(l)(2)-2]

**§ 301.6103(l)(2)-2. Disclosure of returns and return information to Department of Labor for purposes of research and studies.**—(a) *General rule.*—Pursuant to the provisions of section 6103(l)(2) of the Internal Revenue Code and subject to the requirements of paragraph (b) of this section, officers or employees of the Internal Revenue Service may disclose returns and return information (as defined by section 6103(b)) to officers and employees of the Department of Labor for purposes of, but only to the extent necessary in, conducting research and studies authorized by section 513 of the Employee Retirement Income Security Act of 1974.

(b) *Procedures and restrictions.*—Disclosure of returns or return information by officers or employees of the Service as provided by paragraph (a) of this section will be made only upon written request to the Commissioner of Internal Revenue by the Administrator of the Pension and Welfare Benefit Programs of the Department of Labor describing the returns or return information to be disclosed, the taxable period or date to which such returns or return information relates, and the purpose for which the returns or return information is needed in the administration of title I of the Employee Retirement Income Security Act of 1974, and designating by title the officers and employees of such department to whom such disclosure is authorized. No such officer or employee to whom returns or return information is disclosed pursuant to the provisions of paragraph (a) shall disclose such returns or return information to any person, other than the taxpayer by whom the return was made or to whom the return information relates or other officers or employees of such department whose duties or responsibilities require such disclosure for a purpose described in paragraph (a), except in a form which cannot be associated with, or otherwise identify, directly or indirectly, a particular taxpayer. [Reg. § 301.6103(l)(2)-2.]

☐ [*T.D.* 7723, 9-30-80.]

### [Reg. § 301.6103(l)(2)-3]

**§301.6103(l)(2)-3. Disclosure to Department of Labor and Pension Benefit Guaranty Corporation of certain returns and return information.**—(a) *Disclosures following general requests.*—Pursuant to the provisions of section 6103(l)(2) of the Internal Revenue Code and subject to the requirements of this paragraph, officers or employees of the Internal Revenue Service may disclose the following returns and return information(as defined by section 6103(b)) to officers and employees of the Department of Labor or the Pension Benefit Guaranty Corporation for purposes of, but only to the extent necessary in, the administration of title I or IV of the Employee Retirement Income Security Act of 1974 (hereinafter referred to in this section as the Act)—

(1) Notification of receipt by the Service of an application by a particular taxpayer for a determination of whether a pension, profit-sharing, or stock bonus plan, a trust which is a part of such plan, or an annuity or bond purchase plan meets the applicable requirements of part I of subchapter D of chapter 1 of the Code;

(2) Notification that a particular application described in subparagraph (1) of this paragraph alleges that certain employees may be excluded from participation by reason of section 410(b)(2)(A) and (B) for the purpose of obtaining the finding necessary for the application of such section;

(3) An application by a particular taxpayer for a determination of whether a pension, profit-sharing, or stock bonus plan, or an annuity or bond purchase plan, meets the applicable requirements of part I of subchapter D of chapter 1 of the Code with respect to a termination or proposed termination of the plan or to a partial termination or proposed partial termination of the plan, and any statement filed as provided by section 6058(b);

(4) Notification that the Service has determined that a plan or trust described in subparagraph (1) or (3) of this paragraph meets or does not meet the applicable requirements of part I of subchapter D of chapter 1 of the Code and has issued a determination letter to such effect to a particular taxpayer or that an application for such a determination has been withdrawn by the taxpayer;

(5) If the Department of Labor or the Pension Benefit Guaranty Corporation has commented on an application upon which a determination letter described in subparagraph (4) of this paragraph has been issued, a copy of the letter or document issued to the applicant;

(6) Notification to a particular taxpayer that the Service intends to disqualify a pension, profit-sharing, or stock bonus plan, a trust which is a part of such plan, or an annuity or bond purchase plan because such plan or trust does not meet the requirements of section 410(a) or 411 as of the date that such notification is issued;

(7) Notification required by section 3002(a) of the Act of the commencement of any proceeding to determine whether a particular pension, profit-sharing, or stock bonus plan, a trust which is a part of such plan, or an annuity or bond purchase plan meets the requirements of section 410(a) or 411;

(8) Prior to issuance of a notice of deficiency to a particular taxpayer under section 6212, notification that the Service has determined that a deficiency exists under section 6211 with respect to the tax imposed by section 4971(a) or (b) on such taxpayer, except that if the Service determines that the collection of such tax is in jeopardy within the meaning of section 6861(a), such notification may be disclosed after issuance of the notice of deficiency or jeopardy assessment;

(9) Notification of receipt by the Service of, and action taken with respect to, an application by or on behalf of a particular taxpayer for a waiver of the tax imposed by section 4971(b);

(10) Prior to issuance of a notice of deficiency to a particular taxpayer under section 6212, notification that a deficiency exists under section 6211 with respect to the tax imposed by section 4975(a) or (b) on such taxpayer, except that if the Service determines that the collection of such tax is in jeopardy within the meaning of section 6861(a), such notification may be disclosed after issuance of the notice of deficiency or jeopardy assessment;

(11) Notification that the Service has waived the tax imposed by section 4975(b) on a particular taxpayer;

(12) Notification of applicability of section 4975 to a particular pension, profit-sharing, or stock bonus plan, a trust which is a part of such plan, or an annuity or stock purchase plan engaged in prohibited transactions within the meaning of section 4975(c);

(13) Notification to a plan administrator that the Service has determined that a pension, profit-sharing, stock bonus, annuity, or stock purchase plan no longer meets the requirements of section 401(a) or 404(a)(2);

(14) Notification that the Service has determined that there has been a termination or partial termination of a particular pension, profit-sharing, stock bonus, annuity, or stock purchase plan within the meaning of section 411(d)(3);

(15) Notification of the occurrence of an event (other than an event described in subparagraph (13), (14), or (18) of this paragraph) which the Service has determined to indicate that a particular pension, profit-sharing, stock bonus, annuity, or stock purchase plan may not be sound under section 4043(c)(2) of the Act;

(16) Notification that the Service has received and responded to a request on behalf of a particular pension, profit-sharing, or stock bonus plan, a trust which is a part of such plan, or an annuity or stock purchase plan for an extension of time for filing an annual return by such plan or trust;

(17) Notification that the Service has received and responded to a request on behalf of a particular pension, profit-sharing, or stock bonus plan, a trust which is a part of such plan, or an annuity or stock purchase plan to change the annual accounting period of such plan or trust;

(18) Notification that the Service has determined that a particular plan does not meet the requirements of section 412 without regard to whether such plan is one described in section 4021(a)(2) of the Act;

(19) Notification of the results of an investigation by the Service requested by the Department of Labor or the Pension Benefit Guaranty Corporation, or both, with respect to whether the tax described in section 4971 should be imposed on any employer named in such request or whether the tax imposed by section 4975 should be paid by any person named in the request;

(20) Notification of receipt by the Service of an application by a particular taxpayer for exemption under section 4975(c)(2) or of initiation by the Service of an administrative proceeding for such exemption;

(21) Notification of receipt by the Service of, and action taken with respect to, an application by or on behalf of a particular taxpayer for a waiver or variance of the minimum funding standard under section 303 of the Act or section 412(d);

(22) Notification that the Service intends to undertake, is undertaking, or has completed an examination to determine whether—

(i) A particular pension, profit-sharing, or stock bonus plan, a trust which is a part of such plan, or an annuity or stock purchase plan meets the applicable requirements of part 1 of subchapter D of chapter 1 of the Code;

(ii) Any particular person is or may be liable for any tax imposed by section 4971 or 4975; or

(iii) A particular employee welfare benefit plan, as defined in section 3(1) of the Act, meets the applicable requirements of section 501(c) or 120,
together with any completed Department of Labor or Pension Benefit Guaranty Corporation form (and supplemental schedules) relating to such examination;

(23) Copies of initial pleadings indicating that the Service intends to intervene in a civil action under section 502(h) of the Act. Return information disclosed under this paragraph includes the taxpayer identity information (as defined in section 6103(b)(6)) of the plan or trust, the name and address of the sponsor and administrator of the plan or trustee of the trust, and the name and address of the person authorized to represent the plan or trust before the Service. Disclosure of returns or return information as provided by this paragraph will be made only following receipt by the Commissioner of Internal Revenue of an annual written request for such disclosure by the Administrator of Pension and Benefit Welfare Programs of the Department of Labor or the Executive Director of the Pension Benefit Guaranty Corporation describing the categories of returns or return information to be disclosed by the Service and the particular purpose

for which the returns or return information is needed in the administration of title I or IV of the Act, and designating by title the officers and employees of the Department of Labor or such corporation to whom such disclosure is authorized; and

(24) Notification of receipt by the Service of a request for technical advice as to whether a particular pension, profit-sharing, or stock bonus plan, a trust which is a part of such plan, or an annuity or bond purchase plan should be disqualified because of fiduciary actions subject to part 4 of subtitle B of title I of the Act which may violate the exclusive benefit rule of section 401(a);

(25) Notification of receipt by the National Office of the Service of a request by or on behalf of a particular taxpayer for a ruling, opinion, variance, or waiver under any provision of title I of the Act and a copy of any such ruling, opinion, variance or waiver;

(26) Notification that the Service proposes to take substantive action which would significantly impact on or substantially affect collectively bargained plans and a description of such proposed substantive action; and

(27) Notification of receipt by the Service of, and action taken with respect to, a request by a particular taxpayer for a ruling under section 412(c)(8), 412(e), or 412(f).

Disclosure of returns or return information as provided by this paragraph will be made only following receipt by the Commissioner of Internal Revenue or his delegate of an annual written request for such disclosure by the Secretary of Labor or his delegate or the Executive Director of the Pension Benefit Guaranty Corporation or his delegate describing the categories of returns or return information to be disclosed by the Service and the particular purpose for which the returns or return information is needed in the administration of title I or IV of the Act, and designating by title the officers and employees of the Department of Labor or such corporation to whom such disclosure is authorized.

(b) *Additional returns and return information subject to disclosure.*— (1) *Returns and return information relating to automatic notification.*— (i) Subject to the requirements of subparagraph (3)(i) of this paragraph, officers or employees of the Service may disclose to officers and employees of the Department of Labor or the Pension Benefit Guaranty Corporation for purposes of, but only to the extent necessary in, the administration of title I or IV of the Act additional returns and return information relating to any item described in paragraph (a) of this section.

(ii) Subject to the requirements of subparagraph (3)(ii) of this paragraph, in connection with the disclosure of any item as provided by paragraph (a) of this section, officers and employees of the Service may disclose to officers and employees of the Department of Labor or the Pension Benefit Guaranty Corporation such additional returns and return information relating to such item as the Service determines are or may be necessary in the administration of title I or IV of the Act.

(2) *Other returns and return information.*—Subject to the requirements of subparagraph (3)(i) of this paragraph, officers or employees of the Service may disclose to officers and employees of the Department of Labor or the Pension Benefit Guaranty Corporation returns and return information (other than returns and return information disclosed as provided by paragraph (a) of this section or § 301.6103(l)(2)-1 or § 301.6103(l)(2)-2 for purposes of, but only to the extent necessary in, administration of title I or IV of the Act.

(3) *Procedures.*—(i) Disclosure of returns or return information by officers or employees of the Service as provided by subparagraph (1)(i) or (2) of this paragraph will be made only following receipt by the Commissioner of Internal Revenue or his delegate of a written request for such disclosure by the Secretary of Labor or his delegate or the Executive Director of the Pension Benefit Guaranty Corporation or his delegate identifying the particular taxpayer by whom such return was made or to whom such return information relates, describing the particular returns or return information to be disclosed, stating the purpose for which the returns or return information is needed in the administration of title I or IV of the Act, and designating by title the officers and employees of such department or corporation to whom such disclosure is authorized.

(ii) Disclosure of returns or return information by officers or employees of the Service as provided by subparagraph (1)(ii) of this paragraph will be made only following receipt by the Commissioner of Internal Revenue or his delegate of an annual written request for such disclosure by the Secretary of Labor or his delegate or the Executive Director of the Pension Benefit Guaranty Corporation or his delegate stating the purpose for which the returns or return information is needed in the administration of title I or IV of the Act, and designating by title the officers and employees of such department or corporation to whom such disclosure is authorized.

(c) *Disclosure and use of returns and return information by officers and employees of Department of Labor, Pension Benefit Guaranty Corporation,* *and Department of Justice.*—(1) *Use by officers and employees of Department of Labor and Pension Benefit Guaranty Corporation.*—Returns and return information disclosed to officers and employees of the Department of Labor and the Pension Benefit Guaranty Corporation as provided by this section may be used by such officers and employees for purposes of, but only to the extent necessary in, administration of any provision of title I or IV of the Act, including any preparation for any administrative or judicial proceeding (or investigation which may result in such a proceeding) authorized by, or described in, title I or IV of the Act.

(2) *Disclosure by officers and employees of Department of Labor and Pension Benefit Guaranty Corporation to, and use by, other persons, including officers and employees of the Department of Justice.*—(i) Returns and return information disclosed to officers and employees of the Department of Labor or the Pension Benefit Guaranty Corporation as provided by this section may be disclosed by such officers and employees to officers and employees of the Department of Justice (including United States attorneys) personally and directly engaged in, and for their necessary use in, any Federal grand jury proceeding, or preparation for any civil or criminal judicial proceeding (or for their necessary use in an investigation which may result in such a proceeding), authorized by, or described in, title I or IV of the Act.

(ii) Returns and return information disclosed to officers and employees of the Department of Labor, the Pension Benefit Guaranty Corporation, and the Department of Justice as provided by this section may be disclosed by such officers and employees to other persons, including, but not limited to, persons described in subparagraph (2)(iii) of this paragraph, but only to the extent necessary in connection with administration of the provisions of title I or IV of the Act, including a Federal grand jury proceeding, and proper preparation for a proceeding (or investigation), described in subparagraph (1) or (2)(i). Such disclosures may include, but are not limited to, disclosures where necessary—

(A) To properly obtain the services of persons having special knowledge or technical skills;

(B) To properly interview, consult, depose, or interrogate or otherwise obtain relevant information from, the taxpayer to whom such return or return information relates (or the legal representative of such taxpayer) or any witness who may be called to give evidence in the proceeding; or

(C) To properly conduct negotiations concerning, or obtain authorization for, settlement or disposition of the proceeding, in whole or in part, or stipulations of fact in connection with the proceeding.

Disclosure of a return or return information to a person other than the taxpayer to whom such return or return information relates (or the legal representative of such taxpayer) to properly accomplish any purpose or activity described in this subparagraph should be made, however, only if such purpose or activity cannot otherwise properly be accomplished without making such disclosure.

(iii) Among those persons to whom returns and return information may be disclosed by officers and employees of the Department of Labor, the Pension Benefit Guaranty Corporation, and the Department of Justice as provided by subparagraph (2)(ii) of this paragraph are:

(A) Other officers and employees of the Department of Labor, the Pension Benefit Guaranty Corporation, and the Department of Justice;

(B) Officers and employees of another Federal agency (as defined in section 6103(b)(9)) working under the direction and control of such officers and employees of the Department of Labor, the Pension Benefit Guaranty Corporation, or the Department of Justice; and

(C) Court reporters.

Disclosure of returns or return information to other persons by officers and employees of the Department of Labor or the Pension Benefit Guaranty Corporation as provided by subparagraph (2)(ii) of this paragraph for purposes of conducting research, surveys, studies, and publications referred to in section 513(a), or authorized by title IV, of the Act shall be restricted, however, to disclosure to other officers and employees of such department or corporation to whom such disclosure is necessary in connection with such conduct or to the taxpayer by whom such return was made or to whom such return information relates if the return or return information can be associated with, or otherwise identify, directly or indirectly, a particular taxpayer.

(3) *Disclosure in judicial proceedings.*—A return or return information disclosed to officers and employees of the Department of Labor, the Pension Benefit Guaranty Corporation, or the Department of Justice as provided by this section may be entered into evidence by such officers or employees in a civil or criminal judicial proceeding authorized by, or described in, title I or IV of the Act, provide that, in

the case of a judicial proceeding described in section 6103(i)(4), the requirements of section 6103(i)(4) have first been met.

(d) *Disclosure of returns and return information in connection with certain consultations between Departments of the Treasury and Labor.*—Upon general written request to the Commissioner of Internal Revenue by the Secretary of Labor, officers and employees of the Service may disclose to officers and employees of the Department of Labor such returns and return information as may be necessary to properly carry out any consultation required by section 3002, 3003, or 3004 of the Act.

(e) *Return information open to public inspection under section 6104.*—Nothing in these regulations shall be construed to deny officers and employees of the Department of Labor and the Pension Benefit Guaranty Corporation the right to inspect return information available to the public under section 6104 of the Code. [Reg. §301.6103(l)(2)-3.]

☐ [T.D. 7723, 9-30-80. *Amended by T.D. 7757, 1-16-81 and T.D. 7911, 9-6-83.*]

### [Reg. §301.6103(l)(14)-1]

**§301.6103(l)(14)-1. Disclosure of return information to United States Customs Service.**—(a) *General rule.*—Pursuant to the provisions of section 6103(l)(14) of the Internal Revenue Code, officers and employees of the Internal Revenue Service may disclose to officers and employees of the United States Customs Service return information (as defined by section 6103(b)) with respect to taxes imposed by chapters 1 and 6 of the Internal Revenue Code solely for purposes of, and only to the extent necessary in—

(1) Ascertaining the correctness of any entry in audits as provided for in section 509 of the Tariff Act of 1930 or;

(2) Other actions to recover any loss of revenue, or to collect duties, taxes, and fees, determined to be due and owing pursuant to such audits.

(b) *Procedures.*—Disclosure of return information by officers or employees of the Internal Revenue Service as provided by paragraph (a) of this section will be made only following receipt by the Internal Revenue Service of a written request for the disclosure by the Commissioner of the U.S. Customs Service identifying—

(1) The particular items of return information to be disclosed;

(2) The particular taxpayer to whom the return information relates;

(3) The taxable period or date to which the return information relates;

(4) The particular purpose for which each item of return information is needed, including an explanation as to how the requested information is necessary to accomplish that purpose. In addition, the request must designate by title the officers and employees of the Customs Service to whom the disclosure is authorized and certify that the Customs Service has initiated or intends to initiate, under section 509 of the Tariff Act of 1930, an audit of each taxpayer for whom return information is requested or that the taxpayer has a transactional or ownership relationship with the subject of such an audit.

(c) *Return information subject to disclosure.*—Any return information requested must be necessary to a Customs determination of the correctness of any entry in audits conducted under section 509 of the Tariff Act of 1930. Taxpayers as to whom return information is requested must either be the subject of a Customs audit (or intended audit) or have a transactional or ownership relationship with the subject of a Customs audit. Requested information must relate to the declared value, classification or rate of duty applicable to entered merchandise. Requested information may also include any adjustment by the IRS to the items of return information described by this paragraph.

(d) *Return information not subject to disclosure.*—The following return information may not be requested or disclosed pursuant to section 6103(1)(14) of the Internal Revenue Code: any Advance Pricing Agreement or information submitted to or generated by the IRS as part of the negotiation process for an Advance Pricing Agreement, or any information to the extent its disclosure would be inconsistent with a tax treaty or executive agreement with respect to which the United States is a party.

(e) *Impairment of tax administration.*—Return information with respect to a taxpayer may not be disclosed pursuant to this section if the IRS determines that the disclosure would identify a confidential informant or seriously impair any civil or criminal tax investigation or proceeding.

(f) *Use by Customs Service.*—Return information disclosed under this section may be used by the U.S. Customs Service to the extent

necessary to ascertain or to document the correctness of any entry in audits as provided for in section 509 of the Tariff Act of 1930 and in any related administrative proceedings to recover any loss of revenue, or to collect duties, taxes or fees, determined to be due and owing pursuant to these audits. Uses may include, to the extent necessary, disclosure to the importer (or the legal representative of such importer) subject to the audit with respect to which the information was requested.

(g) *Disclosure to, and use by, the Department of Justice.*—Return information disclosed to officers and employees of the U.S. Customs Service as provided by this section may be disclosed by these officers and employees to officers and employees of the Department of Justice (including United States attorneys) personally and directly engaged in, and solely for their necessary use in, advocating or defending the correctness of Customs determinations with respect to any entry, in any civil judicial proceeding, or any preparations therefor (or for their necessary use in an investigation which may result in such a proceeding), to recover any loss of revenue, or to collect duties, taxes or fees, determined to be due and owing as a consequence of an audit provided for in section 509 of the Tariff Act of 1930.

(h) *Disclosure by officers and employees of the Department of Justice.*—Return information disclosed to officers and employees of the Department of Justice (including United States Attorneys) as provided by this section may be disclosed by these officers and employees to other persons as is necessary to properly accomplish the purposes or activities described in paragraph (g). Disclosure of return information to a person, other than the importer (or the legal representative of the importer) subject to the audit with respect to which the information was originally requested, to properly accomplish any purpose or activity described in paragraph (g) may be made, however, only if the purpose or activity cannot otherwise properly be accomplished without making the disclosure. Disclosures may include, but are not limited to, disclosures where necessary—

(1) To properly obtain the services of persons having special knowledge or technical skills;

(2) To properly interview, consult, depose, or interrogate or otherwise obtain relevant information from, the taxpayer (or the legal representative of the taxpayer) to whom the return information relates or any witness who may be called to give evidence in the proceeding; or

(3) To properly conduct negotiations concerning, or obtain authorization for, settlement or disposition of the proceeding, in whole or in part, or stipulations of fact in connection with the proceeding.

(i) *Use in criminal judicial proceedings.*—Return information disclosed pursuant to this section may not be used in any criminal judicial proceeding, or any preparations therefor (or in a criminal investigation which may result in such a proceeding), involving the enforcement of a criminal statute, without compliance with the requirements of section 6103(i)(1) or (2) as appropriate. However, the return information may in any event be used for purposes of complying with the requirements of section 6103(i).

(j) *Restrictions.*—Return information disclosed to officers and employees of the U.S. Customs Service or to the Department of Justice as provided by this section may not be used or disclosed for any purpose other than to ascertain, advocate or defend the correctness of, Customs determinations with respect to, any entry in the audits for which the information was requested or in certain actions resulting from the audits as described above. Return information disclosed to officers and employees of the U.S. Customs Service or to the Department of Justice as provided by this section may not be disclosed to any person, including any contractor of the U.S. Customs Service, except as provided by this section, or as otherwise provided by section 6103 of the Internal Revenue Code. [Reg. §301.6103(l)(14)-1.]

☐ [T.D. 8527, 3-8-94. *Amended by T.D. 8694, 12-16-96.*]

### [Reg. §301.6103(l)(21)-1]

**§301.6103(l)(21)-1. Disclosure of return information to the Department of Health and Human Services to carry out eligibility requirements for health insurance affordability programs.**—(a) *General rule.*—Pursuant to the provisions of section 6103(l)(21)(A) of the Internal Revenue Code, officers and employees of the Internal Revenue Service will disclose, upon written request, for each relevant taxpayer on a single application those items of return information that are described under section 6103(l)(21)(A) and paragraphs (a)(1) through (7) of this section, for the reference tax year, as applicable, to officers, employees, and contractors of the Department of Health and Human Services. Such information shall be provided solely for purposes of, and to the extent necessary in, establishing an individual's eligibility for participation in an Exchange established under the Patient Protection and Affordable Care Act, verifying the appropriate amount of any premium tax credit under section 36B or cost-sharing reduction under section 1402 of the Patient Protection and Affordable Care Act, or determining eligibility for the State programs described in section 6103(l)(21)(A).

(1) With respect to each relevant taxpayer for the reference tax year where the amount of social security benefits not included in gross income under section 86 of the Internal Revenue Code of that relevant taxpayer is unavailable:

(i) The aggregate amount of the following items of return information —

(A) Adjusted gross income, as defined by section 62 of the Internal Revenue Code;

(B) Any amount excluded from gross income under section 911 of the Internal Revenue Code; and

(C) Any amount of interest received or accrued by the taxpayer during the taxable year that is exempt from tax.

(ii) Information indicating that the amount of social security benefits not included in gross income under section 86 of the Internal Revenue Code is unavailable.

(2) Adjusted gross income, as defined by section 62 of the Internal Revenue Code, of a relevant taxpayer for the reference tax year, in circumstances where the modified adjusted gross income (MAGI), as defined by section 36B(d)(2)(B) of the Internal Revenue Code, of that relevant taxpayer is unavailable, as well as information indicating that the components of MAGI other than adjusted gross income must be taken into account to determine MAGI;

(3) The amount of social security benefits of the relevant taxpayer that is included in gross income under section 86 of the Internal Revenue Code for the reference tax year;

(4) Information indicating that certain return information of a relevant taxpayer is unavailable for the reference tax year because the relevant taxpayer jointly filed a U.S. Individual Income Tax Return for that year with a spouse who is not a relevant taxpayer listed on the same application;

(5) Information indicating that, although a return for an individual identified on the application as a relevant taxpayer for the reference tax year is available, return information is not being provided because of possible authentication issues with respect to the identity of the relevant taxpayer;

(6) Information indicating that a relevant taxpayer who is identified as a dependent for the tax year in which the premium tax credit under section 36B of the Internal Revenue Code would be claimed, did not have a filing requirement for the reference tax year based upon the U.S. Individual Income Tax Return the relevant taxpayer filed for the reference tax year; and

(7) Information indicating that a relevant taxpayer who received advance payments of the premium tax credit in the reference tax year did not file a tax return for the reference tax year reconciling the advance payments of the premium tax credit with any premium tax credit under section 36B of the Internal Revenue Code available for that year.

(b) *Relevant taxpayer defined.*—For purposes of paragraph (a) of this section, a relevant taxpayer is defined to be any individual listed, by name and social security number, on an application submitted pursuant to Title I, Subtitle E, of the Patient Protection and Affordable Care Act, whose income may bear upon a determination of any advance payment of any premium tax credit under section 36B of the Internal Revenue Code, cost-sharing reduction under section 1402 of the Patient Protection and Affordable Care Act, or eligibility for any program described in section 6103(l)(21)(A) of the Internal Revenue Code.

(c) *Reference tax year defined.*—For purposes of section 6103(l)(21)(A) of the Internal Revenue Code and this section, the reference tax year is the first calendar year or, where no return information is available in that year, the second calendar year, prior to the submission of an application pursuant to Title I, Subtitle E, of the Patient Protection and Affordable Care Act.

(d) *Effective/applicability date.*—This section applies to disclosures to the Department of Health and Human Services on or after August 14, 2013. [Reg. §301.6103(l)(21)-1.]

☐ [*T.D. 9628, 8-13-2013.*]

### [Reg. §301.6103(m)-1]

**§301.6103(m)-1. Disclosure of taxpayer identity information.**— (a) *Definition.*—For purposes of applying the provisions of section 6103(m) of the Internal Revenue Code, the term *agent* includes a contractor.

(b) *Effective date.*—This section is applicable January 6, 2004. [Reg. §301.6103(m)-1.]

☐ [*T.D. 9111, 12-31-2003.*]

### [Reg. §301.6103(n)-1]

**§301.6103(n)-1. Disclosure of returns and return information in connection with written contracts or agreements for the acquisition of property or services for tax administration purposes.**— (a) *General rule.*—(1) Pursuant to the provisions of section 6103(n) of the Internal Revenue Code and subject to the conditions of this section, officers and employees of the Treasury Department, a State tax agency, the Social Security Administration, or the Department of Justice, are authorized to disclose returns and return information (as defined in section 6103(b)) to any person (including, in the case of the Treasury Department, any person described in section 7513(a)), or to an officer or employee of the person, for purposes of tax administration (as defined in section 6103(b)(4)), to the extent necessary in connection with a written contract or agreement for the acquisition of—

(i) Equipment or other property; or

(ii) Services relating to the processing, storage, transmission, or reproduction of returns or return information, the programming, maintenance, repair, or testing of equipment or other property, or the providing of other services.

(2) Any person, or officer or employee of the person, who receives returns or return information under paragraph (a)(1) of this section, may—

(i) Further disclose the returns or return information to another officer or employee of the person whose duties or responsibilities require the returns or return information for a purpose described in this paragraph (a); or

(ii) Further disclose the returns or return information, when authorized in writing by the Internal Revenue Service (IRS), to the extent necessary to carry out the purposes described in this paragraph (a). Disclosures may include disclosures to an agent or subcontractor of the person, or officer or employee of the agent or subcontractor.

(3) An agent or subcontractor, or officer or employee of the agent or subcontractor, who receives returns or return information under paragraph (a)(2)(ii) of this section, may further disclose the returns or return information to another officer or employee of the agent or subcontractor whose duties or responsibilities require the returns or return information for a purpose described in this paragraph (a).

(4) Any person, or officer, employee, agent or subcontractor of the person, or officer or employee of the agent or subcontractor, who receives returns or return information under this paragraph (a), may, subject to the provisions of §301.6103(p)(2)(B)-1 (concerning disclosures by a Federal, State, or local agency, or its agents or contractors), further disclose the returns or return information for a purpose authorized by, and subject to all applicable conditions imposed, by section 6103.

(b) *Limitations.*—(1) Disclosure of returns or return information in connection with a written contract or agreement for the acquisition of property or services described in paragraph (a) of this section will be treated as necessary only if the performance of the contract or agreement cannot otherwise be reasonably, properly, or economically carried out without the disclosure.

(2) Disclosure of returns or return information in connection with a written contract or agreement for the acquisition of property or services described in paragraph (a) of this section shall be made only to the extent necessary to reasonably, properly, or economically perform the contract. For example, disclosure of returns or return information to employees of a contractor for purposes of programming, maintaining, repairing, or testing computer equipment used by the IRS or a State tax agency shall be made only if the services cannot be reasonably, properly, or economically performed without the disclosure. If it is determined that disclosure of returns or return information is necessary, and if the services can be reasonably, properly, or economically performed by disclosure of only parts or portions of a return or if deletion of taxpayer identity information (as defined in section 6103(b)(6)) reflected on a return would not seriously impair the ability of the employees to perform the services, then only the parts or portions of the return, or only the return with taxpayer identity information deleted, may be disclosed.

(c) *Penalties.*—Any person, or officer, employee, agent or subcontractor of the person, or officer or employee of the agent or subcontractor, who receives returns or return information under paragraph (a) of this section, is subject to the civil and criminal penalty provisions of sections 7431, 7213, and 7213A for the unauthorized inspection or disclosure of the returns or return information.

(d) *Notification requirements.*—Any person, or agent or subcontractor of the person, who receives returns or return information under paragraph (a) of this section shall provide written notice to his, her, or its officers and employees receiving the returns or return information that—

(1) Returns or return information disclosed to the officer or employee may be used only for a purpose and to the extent authorized by paragraph (a) of this section and that the officer or employee is subject to the civil and criminal penalty provisions of sections 7431, 7213, and 7213A for the unauthorized inspection or disclosure of the returns or return information;

(2) Further inspection of any returns or return information for a purpose or to an extent not authorized by paragraph (a) of this section constitutes a misdemeanor, punishable upon conviction by a fine of as much as $1,000, or imprisonment for as long as 1 year, or both, together with costs of prosecution;

(3) Further disclosure of any returns or return information for a purpose or to an extent not authorized by paragraph (a) of this section constitutes a felony, punishable upon conviction by a fine of as much as $5,000, or imprisonment for as long as 5 years, or both, together with the costs of prosecution;

(4) Further inspection or disclosure of returns or return information by any person who is not an officer or employee of the United States for a purpose or to an extent not authorized by paragraph (a) of this section may result also in an award of civil damages against that person in an amount not less than $1,000 for each act of unauthorized inspection or disclosure; or the sum of actual damages sustained by the plaintiff as a result of the unauthorized inspection or disclosure plus, in the case of a willful inspection or disclosure or an inspection or disclosure that is the result of gross negligence, punitive damages. In addition, costs and reasonable attorneys fees may be awarded; and

(5) A conviction for an offense referenced in paragraph (d)(2) or (3) of this section shall, in addition to any other punishment, result in dismissal from office or discharge from employment if the person convicted is an officer or employee of the United States.

(e) *Safeguards.*—(1) Any person, or agent or subcontractor of the person, who may receive returns or return information under paragraph (a) of this section, shall agree, before disclosure of any returns or return information to the person, agent, or subcontractor, to permit an inspection by the IRS of his, her, or its site or facilities.

(2) Any person, or officer, employee, agent or subcontractor of the person, or officer or employee of the agent or subcontractor, who receives returns or return information under paragraph (a) of this section, shall comply with all applicable conditions and requirements as the IRS may prescribe from time to time (prescribed requirements) for the purposes of protecting the confidentiality of returns and return information and preventing any disclosure or inspection of returns or return information in a manner not authorized by this section.

(3) The terms of any written contract or agreement for the acquisition of property or services as described in paragraph (a) of this section shall provide, or shall be amended to provide, that any person, or officer, employee, agent or subcontractor of the person, or officer or employee of the agent or subcontractor, who receives returns or return information under paragraph (a) of this section, shall comply with the prescribed requirements. Any contract or agreement shall be made available to the IRS before execution of the contract or agreement. For purposes of this paragraph (e)(3), a written contract or agreement shall include any contract or agreement between a person and an agent or subcontractor of the person to provide the property or services described in paragraph (a) of this section.

(4) If the IRS determines that any person, or officer, employee, agent or subcontractor of the person, or officer or employee of the agent or subcontractor, who receives returns or return information under paragraph (a) of this section, has failed to, or does not, satisfy the prescribed requirements, the IRS, consistent with the regulations under section 6103(p)(7), may take any actions it deems necessary to ensure that the prescribed requirements are or will be satisfied, including—

(i) Suspension of further disclosures of returns or return information by the IRS to the State tax agency, the Social Security Administration, or the Department of Justice, until the IRS determines that the conditions and requirements have been or will be satisfied;

(ii) Suspension of further disclosures by the Treasury Department otherwise authorized by paragraph (a) of this section; and

(iii) Suspension or termination of any duty or obligation arising under a contract or agreement with the Treasury Department.

(f) *Definitions.*—For purposes of this section—

(1) The term *Treasury Department* includes the IRS, the Office of the Chief Counsel for the IRS, and the Office of the Treasury Inspector General for Tax Administration.

(2) The term *State tax agency* means an agency, body, or commission described in section 6103(d); and

(3) The term *Department of Justice* includes offices of the United States Attorneys.

(g) *Effective date.*—This section is applicable on June 5, 2007. [Reg. § 1.6103(n)-1.]

☐ [*T.D.* 7723, 9-30-80. *Amended by T.D.* 8271, 11-2-89; *T.D.* 8695, 12-16-96; *T.D.* 9044, 3-11-2003 *and T.D.* 9327, 6-4-2007.]

[Reg. §301.6103(n)-2]

**§301.6103(n)-2. Disclosure of return information in connection with written contracts among the IRS, whistleblowers, and legal representatives of whistleblowers.**—(a) *General rule.*—(1) Pursuant to the provisions of sections 6103(n) and 7623 of the Internal Revenue Code and subject to the conditions of this section, an officer or employee of the Treasury Department is authorized to disclose return information (as defined in section 6103(b)(2)) to a whistleblower and, if applicable, the legal representative of the whistleblower, to the extent necessary in connection with a written contract among the Internal Revenue Service (IRS), the whistleblower and, if applicable, the legal representative of the whistleblower, for services relating to the detection of violations of the internal revenue laws or related statutes.

(2) The IRS shall have the discretion to determine whether to enter into a written contract pursuant to section 7623 with the whistleblower and, if applicable, the legal representative of the whistleblower, for services described in paragraph (a)(1) of this section.

(b) *Limitations.*—(1) Disclosure of return information in connection with a written contract for services described in paragraph (a)(1) of this section shall be made only to the extent the IRS deems it necessary in connection with the reasonable or proper performance of the contract. Disclosures may include, but are not limited to, disclosures to accomplish properly any purpose or activity of the nature described in section 6103(k)(6) and the regulations thereunder.

(2) If the IRS determines that the services of a whistleblower and, if applicable, the legal representative of the whistleblower, as described in paragraph (a)(1) of this section, can be performed reasonably or properly by disclosure of only parts or portions of return information, then only the parts or portions of the return information shall be disclosed.

(3) Upon written request by a whistleblower, or a legal representative of a whistleblower, with whom the IRS has entered into a written contract for services as described in paragraph (a)(1) of this section, the Director of the Whistleblower Office, or designee of the Director, may inform the whistleblower and, if applicable, the legal representative of the whistleblower, of the status of the whistleblower's claim for award under section 7623, including whether the claim is being evaluated for potential investigative action, or is pending due to an ongoing examination, appeal, collection action, or litigation. The information may be disclosed only if the IRS determines that the disclosure would not seriously impair Federal tax administration.

(4) Return information disclosed to a whistleblower and, if applicable, a legal representative of a whistleblower, under this section, shall not be further disclosed or otherwise used by the whistleblower or a legal representative of a whistleblower, except as expressly authorized in writing by the IRS.

(c) *Penalties.*—Any whistleblower, or legal representative of a whistleblower, who receives return information under this section, is subject to the civil and criminal penalty provisions of sections 7431, 7213, and 7213A for the unauthorized inspection or disclosure of the return information.

(d) *Safeguards.*—(1) Any whistleblower, or the legal representative of a whistleblower, who receives return information under this section, shall comply with all applicable conditions and requirements as the IRS may prescribe from time to time for the purposes of protecting the confidentiality of the return information and preventing any disclosure or inspection of the return information in a manner not authorized by this section (prescribed requirements).

(2) Any written contract for services as described in paragraph (a)(1) of this section shall provide that any whistleblower and, if applicable, the legal representative of a whistleblower, who has access to return information under this section, shall comply with the prescribed requirements.

(3) Any whistleblower, or the legal representative of a whistleblower, who may receive return information under this section, shall agree in writing, before any disclosure of return information is made, to permit an inspection of the whistleblower's or the legal representative's premises by the IRS relative to the maintenance of the return information disclosed under these regulations and, upon completion of services as described in the written contract with the IRS, to dispose of all return information by returning the return information, including any and all copies or notes made, to the IRS, or to the extent that it cannot be returned, by destroying the information in a manner consistent with prescribed requirements.

(4) If the IRS determines that any whistleblower, or the legal representative of a whistleblower, who has access to return information under this section, has failed to, or does not, satisfy the prescribed requirements, the IRS, using the procedures described in the regulations under section 6103(p)(7), may take any action it deems necessary to ensure that the prescribed requirements are or will be satisfied, including—

(i) Suspension of further disclosures of return information by the IRS to the whistleblower and, if applicable, the legal representative of the whistleblower, until the IRS determines that the conditions and requirements have been or will be satisfied; and

(ii) Suspension or termination of any duty or obligation arising under the contract with the IRS.

(e) *Definitions.*—For purposes of this section—

(1) The term *Treasury Department* includes the IRS and the Office of the Chief Counsel for the IRS.

(2) The term *whistleblower* means an individual who provides information to the IRS regarding violations of the tax laws or related statutes and submits a claim for an award under section 7623 with respect to the information.

(3) The term *legal representative* means any individual who is a member in good standing in the bar of the highest court of any state, possession, territory, commonwealth, or the District of Columbia, and who has a written power of attorney executed by the whistleblower.

(f) *Effective/applicability date.*—This section is applicable on March 15, 2011. [Reg. § 301.6103(n)-2.]

□ [*T.D.* 9516, 3-14-2011.]

## [Reg. § 301.6103(p)(2)(B)-1]

**§ 301.6103(p)(2)(B)-1. Disclosure of returns and return information by other agencies.**—(a) *General rule.*—Subject to the requirements of paragraphs (b), (c), and (d) of this section, returns or return information that have been obtained by a Federal, state or local agency, or its agents or contractors, in accordance with section 6103 (the first recipient) may be disclosed by the first recipient to another recipient authorized to receive such returns or return information under section 6103 (the second recipient).

(b) *Approval by Commissioner.*—A disclosure described in paragraph (a) of this section may be made if the Commissioner of Internal Revenue (the Commissioner) determines, after receiving a written request under this section, that such returns or return information are more readily available from the first recipient than from the Internal Revenue Service (IRS). The disclosure authorization by the Commissioner shall be directed to the head of the first recipient and may contain such conditions or restrictions as the Commissioner may prescribe. The disclosure authorization may be revoked by the Commissioner at any time.

(c) *Requirements and restrictions.*—The second recipient may receive only returns or return information as authorized by the provision of section 6103 applicable to such second recipient. Any returns or return information disclosed may be used by the second recipient only for a purpose authorized by and subject to any conditions imposed by section 6103 and the regulations thereunder, including, if applicable, safeguards imposed by section 6103(p)(4).

(d) *Records and reports of disclosure.*—The first recipient shall maintain to the satisfaction of the IRS a permanent system of standardized records regarding such disclosure authorization described in paragraph (a) of this section and any disclosure of returns and return information made pursuant to such authorization, and shall provide such information as prescribed by the Commissioner in order to enable the IRS to comply with its obligations under section 6103(p)(3) to keep accountings for disclosures and to make annual reports of disclosures to the Joint Committee on Taxation. The information required for reports to the Joint Committee on Taxation must be provided within 30 days after the close of each calendar year. The requirements of this paragraph do not apply to the disclosure of returns and return information as provided by paragraph (a) of this section which, had such disclosures been made directly by the IRS, would not have been subject to the recordkeeping requirements imposed by section 6103(p)(3)(A).

(e) *Effective date.*—This section is applicable on January 21, 2003. [Reg. § 301.6103(p)(2)(B)-1.]

□ [*T.D.* 9036, 1-17-2003.]

## [Reg. § 301.6103(p)(4)-1]

**§ 301.6103(p)(4)-1. Procedures relating to safeguards for returns or return information.**—For security guidelines and other safeguards for protecting returns and return information, see guidance pub-

lished by the Internal Revenue Service. For procedures for administrative review of a determination that an authorized recipient has failed to safeguard returns or return information, see § 301.6103(p)(7)-1. [Reg. § 301.6103(p)(4)-1.]

□ [*T.D.* 9445, 2-10-2009.]

## [Reg. § 301.6103(p)(7)-1]

**§ 301.6103(p)(7)-1. Procedures for administrative review of a determination that an authorized recipient has failed to safeguard returns or return information.**—(a) *In general.*—Notwithstanding any section of the Internal Revenue Code (Code), the Internal Revenue Service (IRS) may terminate or suspend disclosure of returns and return information to any authorized recipient specified in section (p)(4) of section 6103, if the IRS determines that:

(1) The authorized recipient has allowed an unauthorized inspection or disclosure of returns or return information and that the authorized recipient has not taken adequate corrective action to prevent the recurrence of an unauthorized inspection or disclosure; or

(2) The authorized recipient does not satisfactorily maintain the safeguards prescribed by section 6103(p)(4), and has made no adequate plan to improve its system to maintain the safeguards satisfactorily.

(b) *Notice of IRS's intention to terminate or suspend disclosure.*—Prior to terminating or suspending authorized disclosures, the IRS will notify the authorized recipient in writing of the IRS's preliminary determination and of the IRS's intention to discontinue disclosure of returns and return information to the authorized recipient. Upon so notifying the authorized recipient, the IRS, if it determines that tax administration otherwise would be seriously impaired, may suspend further disclosures of returns and return information to the authorized recipient pending a final determination by the Commissioner or a Deputy Commissioner described in paragraph (d)(2) of this section.

(c) *Authorized recipient's right to appeal.*—An authorized recipient shall have 30 days from the date of receipt of a notice described in paragraph (b) of this section to appeal the preliminary determination described in paragraph (b) of this section. The appeal shall be made directly to the Commissioner.

(d) *Procedures for administrative review.*—(1) To appeal a preliminary determination described in paragraph (b) of this section, the authorized recipient shall send a written request for a conference to: Commissioner of Internal Revenue (Attention: SE:S:CLD:GLD), 1111 Constitution Avenue, NW., Washington, DC 20224. The request must include a complete description of the authorized recipient's present system of safeguarding returns or return information received by the authorized recipient (and its authorized contractors or agents, if any). The request must state the reason or reasons the authorized recipient believes that such system or practice (including improvements, if any, to such system or practice expected to be made in the near future) is or will be adequate to safeguard returns or return information.

(2) Within 45 days of the receipt of the request made in accordance with the provisions of paragraph (d)(1) of this section, the Commissioner or Deputy Commissioner personally shall hold a conference with representatives of the authorized recipient, after which the Commissioner or Deputy Commissioner shall make a final determination with respect to the appeal.

(e) *Effective/applicability date.*—This section applies to all authorized recipients of returns and return information that are subject to the safeguard requirements set forth in section 6103(p)(4) on or after February 11, 2009. [Reg. § 301.6103(p)(7)-1.]

□ [*T.D.* 9445, 2-10-2009.]

## [Reg. § 301.6104(a)-1]

**§ 301.6104(a)-1. Public inspection of material relating to tax-exempt organizations.**—(a) *Applications for exemption from Federal income tax, applications for a group exemption letter, and supporting documents.*—If the Internal Revenue Service determines that an organization described in section 501(c) or section 501(d) is exempt from Federal income tax for any taxable year, the application upon which the determination is based, together with any supporting documents, shall be open to public inspection. Such applications and supporting documents shall be open for public inspection even after any revocation of the Internal Revenue Service's determination that the organization is exempt from Federal income tax. In the past, some applications were destroyed and therefore are not available for inspection. For purposes of determining the availability for public inspection, a claim for exemption from Federal income tax filed to reestablish exempt status after denial thereof under the provisions of section 503 or 504 (as in effect on December 31, 1969), or under the corresponding provisions of any prior revenue law, is considered an application for exemption from Federal income tax.

(b) *Notices of status filed by political organizations.*—If, in accordance with section 527(i), an organization notifies the Internal Revenue Service that it is a political organization as described in section 527, exempt from Federal income tax for any taxable year, the notice of status filed by the political organization shall be open to public inspection.

(c) *Letters or documents issued by the Internal Revenue Service with respect to an application for exemption from Federal income tax.*—If an application for exemption from Federal income tax is filed with the Internal Revenue Service after October 31, 1976, and is open to public inspection under paragraph (a) of this section, then any letter or document issued to the applicant by the Internal Revenue Service that relates to the application is also open to public inspection. For rules relating to when a letter or document is issued, see §301.6110-2(h). Letters or documents to which this paragraph (c) applies include, but are not limited to—

(1) Favorable rulings and determination letters, including group exemption letters, issued in response to applications for exemption from Federal income tax;

(2) Technical advice memoranda issued with respect to the approval, or subsequent approval, of an application for exemption from Federal income tax;

(3) Letters issued in response to an application for exemption from Federal income tax (including applications for a group exemption letter) that propose a finding that the applicant is not entitled to be exempt from Federal income tax, if the applicant is subsequently determined, on the basis of that application, to be exempt from Federal income tax; and

(4) Any letter or document issued by the Internal Revenue Service relating to an organization's status as an organization described in section 509(a), 4940(d)(2), 4942(j)(3), or 4943(f), including a determination letter that the organization is or is not a private foundation.

(d) *Requirement of exempt status.*—An application for exemption from Federal income tax (including applications for a group exemption letter), supporting documents, and letters or documents issued by the Internal Revenue Service that relate to the application shall not be open to public inspection before the organization is determined, on the basis of that application, to be exempt from Federal income tax for any taxable year. If an organization is determined to be exempt from Federal income tax for any taxable year, these materials shall not be withheld from public inspection on the basis that the organization is subsequently determined not to be exempt for any other taxable year.

(e) *Documents included in the term "application for exemption from Federal income tax".*—For purposes of this section—

(1) *Prescribed application form.*—If a form is prescribed for an organization's application for exemption from Federal income tax, the application includes the form and all documents and statements that the Internal Revenue Service requires to be filed with the form, any amendments or revisions to the original application, or any resubmitted applications where the original application was submitted in draft form or was withdrawn. An application includes an application for reinstatement of tax-exempt status after an organization's tax exempt status has been revoked pursuant to section 6033(j). An application submitted in draft form or an application submitted and later withdrawn is not considered an application.

(2) *No prescribed application form.*—If no form is prescribed for an organization's application for exemption from Federal income tax, the application includes the submission by letter requesting recognition of tax exemption and any statements or documents as prescribed by Revenue Procedure 2011-9, IRB 2011-2 (January 10, 2011), or any successor guidance describing procedures for application for exempt status pursuant to section 501 and section 521 of the Internal Revenue Code. See §601.601(d)(2)(ii)(*b*).

(3) *Application for a Group Exemption Letter.*—The application for a group exemption letter includes the letter submitted by or on behalf of subordinate organizations that seek exempt status pursuant to a group exemption letter and any statements or documents as prescribed by Revenue Procedure 80-27, 1980-1 CB 677 (June 20, 1980), and any successor guidance. See §601.601(d)(2)(ii)(*b*).

(4) *Notice of status filed under section 527(i).*—For purposes of this section, documents included in the term "notice of status filed under section 527(i)" include—

(i) Form 8871, "Political Organization Notice of Section 527 Status";

(ii) Form 8453-X, "Declaration of Electronic Filing of Notice of Section 527 Status"; and

(iii) Any other additional forms or documents that the Internal Revenue Service may prescribe.

(f) *Material open to public inspection under section 6110.*—Under section 6110, certain written determinations, including negative determinations issued to organizations that applied for an exemption from Federal income tax, issued by the Internal Revenue Service are made available for public inspection. Section 6110 does not apply, however, to material that is open to public inspection under section 6104. See sections 6104(a)(1) and 6110(l)(1).

(g) *Supporting documents defined.*—For purposes of this section, "supporting documents," with respect to an application for exemption from Federal income tax, means any statement or document not described in paragraph (e) of this section that is submitted by the organization or group in support of its application prior to a determination described in paragraph (a) of this section. Items submitted in connection with an application in draft form, or with an application submitted and later withdrawn, are not supporting documents. There are no supporting documents with respect to Notices of Status filed by political organizations.

(h) *Statement of exempt status.*—For efficient tax administration, the Internal Revenue Service may publish, in paper or electronic format, the names of organizations currently recognized as exempt from Federal income tax, including organizations recognized as exempt from Federal income tax under particular paragraphs of section 501(c) or section 501(d). In addition to having the opportunity to inspect material relating to an organization exempt from Federal income tax, a person may request a statement, or the Internal Revenue Service may disclose, in response to or in anticipation of a request, the following information—

(1) The subsection and paragraph of section 501 (or the corresponding provision of any prior revenue law) under which the organization or group has been determined, on the basis of an application open to public inspection, to qualify for exemption from Federal income tax; and

(2) Whether an organization or group is currently recognized as exempt from Federal income tax.

(i) *Publication of non-exempt status.*—(1) For publication of the notice of the revocation of a determination that an organization is described in section 501(c)(3), see section 7428(c).

(2) For publication of a list including any organization the tax exemption of which is revoked for failure to file required returns or notices for three consecutive years, see section 6033(j).

(3) For publication of notice of suspension of tax exemption of terrorist organizations, see section 501(p).

(j) *Withholding of certain information from public inspection.*—For rules relating to certain information contained in an application for exemption from Federal income tax and supporting documents that will be withheld from public inspection, see §301.6104(a)-5(a).

(k) *Procedures for inspection.*—For rules relating to procedures for public inspection of applications for exemption from Federal income tax and supporting documents, see §301.6104(a)-6.

(l) *Effective/applicability date.*—The rules of this section apply February 29, 2012. [Reg. §301.6104(a)-1.]

☐ [*T.D. 7845, 11-5-82. Amended by T.D. 9581, 2-28-2012.*]

**[Reg. §301.6104(a)-2]**

**§301.6104(a)-2. Public inspection of material relating to pension and other plans.**—(a) *Material open to inspection.*—Except as provided in §301.6104(a)-4 with respect to plans having fewer than 26 participants, an application for a determination letter which is filed with the Internal Revenue Service after September 2, 1974, together with supporting documents filed by the applicant in support of the application, will be open to public inspection under section 6104(a)(1)(B)(i) and (ii). An application for a determination letter and supporting documents will be open to public inspection whether or not the application is withdrawn by the applicant, and whether or not the Internal Revenue Service determines that the plan, account, or annuity to which the application relates is qualified or that any related trust or custodial account is exempt from tax.

(b) *Documents included in the term "application for a determination letter".*—(1) *Employees' plans and individual retirement plans.*—For purposes of this section, the term "application for a determination letter" includes the documents that an applicant files with respect to a request that the Internal Revenue Service determine the qualification of—

(i) A pension, profit-sharing, or stock bonus plan under section 401(a),

(ii) An annuity plan under section 403(a),

(iii) A bond purchase plan under section 405(a), or

(iv) An individual retirement account or annuity described in section 408(a), (b), or (c).

(2) *Tax exempt trusts or custodial accounts.*—The term "application for a determination letter" also includes the documents an applicant files with respect to a request that the Internal Revenue Service determine the exemption from tax under section 501(a) of an organization forming part of a plan or account described in subparagraph (1) of this paragraph, or a custodial account described in section 401(f).

(3) *Master, prototype and pattern plans.*—The term "application for a determination letter" also includes documents which an applicant files with respect to a request for approval of a master, prototype, pattern or other such plan or account.

(4) *Prescribed forms and application letters.*—With respect to an application for a determination letter described in this paragraph (b) for which an application form is prescribed, the application for a determination letter includes the form and all documents and statements required to be filed in connection with the form. With respect to an application for a determination letter for which no application form is prescribed, the application for a determination letter includes the application letter and all documents and statements the Internal Revenue Service requires to be submitted with the application letter.

(c) *Documents not constituting an "application for a determination letter".*—The following are not applications for a determination letter for purposes of this section:

(1) An incomplete application that is returned without action for proper completion,

(2) An application that is returned without action to the applicant for failure to notify all interested parties in accordance with the regulations under section 7476 (relating to declaratory judgments), and

(3) A request for a ruling as to whether a proposed transaction is a prohibited transaction under section 4975.

(d) *Supporting documents.*—"Supporting documents", as used with respect to an application for a determination letter which is open to public inspection under this section, means any statement or document submitted in support of the application which is not specifically required by the application form or the Internal Revenue Service. For example, a legal brief submitted in support of an application for a determination letter is a supporting document.

(e) *Applicant.*—For purposes of this section, § 301.6104(a)-3 (relating to Internal Revenue Service letters and documents open to public inspection) and § 301.6104(a)-5 (relating to the withholding of certain information from public inspection), an "applicant" includes, but is not limited to, an employer, plan administrator (as defined in section 414(g)), labor union, bank, or insurance company that files an application for a determination letter. [Reg. § 301.6104(a)-2.]

☐ [*T.D.* 7845, 11-5-82.]

### [Reg. § 301.6104(a)-3]

**§ 301.6104(a)-3. Public inspection of Internal Revenue Service letters and documents relating to pension and other plans.**—(a) *In general.*—Except as provided in § 301.6104(a)-4 with respect to plans having fewer than 26 participants, a letter or other document issued by the Internal Revenue Service after September 2, 1974, is open to public inspection under section 6104(a)(1)(B)(iv) and this section, if it is issued with respect to—

(1) The qualification of a pension, profit-sharing or stock bonus plan under section 401(a), an annuity plan under section 403(a), a bond purchase plan under section 405(a), or an individual retirement account or annuity described in section 408(a), (b) or (c),

(2) The exemption from tax under section 501(a) of an organization forming part of such a plan or account, or a custodial account described in section 401(f), or

(3) The approval of a master, prototype, pattern or other such plan or account.

(b) *Scope.*—Internal Revenue Service letters and documents open to public inspection under section 6104(a)(1)(B)(iv) and this section are not limited to those issued in response to an application for a determination letter described in § 301.6104(a)-2. They are, however, limited to those issued by the Internal Revenue Service to the person or organization which either did or could file an application for a determination letter for the plan, account or annuity to which the letter or document relates. If such a person or organization designates a representative having a power of attorney, however, then the letter or document will be open to inspection if issued to the representative. For rules relating to when a letter or document is

issued, see § 301.6110-2(h). Internal Revenue Service letters and documents are open to public inspection under section 6104(a)(1)(B)(iv) and this section whether or not the Internal Revenue Service determines that the plan, account or annuity to which the letter or document relates is qualified or that any related trust or custodial account is exempt from tax.

(c) *Letters and documents open to public inspection.*—Internal Revenue Service letters and documents open to public inspection under section 6104(a)(1)(B)(iv) and this section include, but are not limited to:

(1) Determination letters relating to the qualification of a plan, account or annuity described in paragraph (a)(1) of this section (see § 601.201(o)),

(2) Technical advice memoranda (see § 601.201(n)(9)) relating to the issuance of such determination letters,

(3) Technical advice memoranda relating to the continuing qualification of a plan, account or annuity previously determined to be qualified, or to the qualification of a plan, account or annuity for which no determination letter has been issued,

(4) Letters or documents revoking or modifying any prior favorable determination letter or denying the qualification of a plan, account or annuity for which no determination letter has been issued,

(5) Determination letters relating to the exemption from tax of a trust or custodial account described in paragraph (a)(2) of this section (see § 601.201(o)(2)(i)(*b*)), or

(6) Opinion letters relating to the acceptability of the form of any master, prototype or other such plan or account (see § 601.201(p) and (q)) or notification letters issued with respect to pattern plans.

(d) *Extent letter or document open to public inspection.*—A letter or document issued by the Internal Revenue Service is open to public inspection under section 6104(a)(1)(B)(iv) and this section only to the extent it relates directly to the qualification of a plan, account or annuity, the exemption from tax of a related organization or custodial account, or the approval of a master, prototype, pattern or other such plan. Any part of the letter or document which does not directly relate to such a qualification, exemption or approval is not open to public inspection. For example, a letter to an employer which concludes that an employees' plan is not qualified and the related trust is not tax exempt will be open to public inspection. However, that same letter may also assert an income tax deficiency because employer contributions to the trust are, therefore, not deductible. In such a case, that part of the letter relating to the tax deficiency will be deleted before the letter is opened to public inspection.

(e) *Letters or documents issued with respect to tax return examination.*—In the case of an examination of a taxpayer's return or consideration of a taxpayer's claim for credit or refund, no letter or document issued to the taxpayer before the preliminary or "30-day" letter described in § 601.105(d)(1) is issued to the taxpayer will be open to public inspection under section 6104(a)(1)(B)(iv) and this section. The "30-day" letter and any statutory notice of deficiency subsequently issued to the taxpayer under section 6212 will be open to public inspection to the extent provided in paragraph (d) of this section. If any letter or document other than a statutory notice of deficiency is issued to the taxpayer after the "30-day" letter is issued, such letter or document will be open to inspection to the extent provided in paragraph (d) of this section only if it finally resolves or otherwise disposes of a plan qualification or tax exemption issue raised in the "30-day" letter.

(f) *Letters or documents issued after September 2, 1974.*—Section 6104(a)(1)(B)(iv) and this section apply to letters or documents issued by the Internal Revenue Service after September 2, 1974, even though the relevant application for a determination letter or other initiating correspondence from the applicant was filed with the Internal Revenue Service before September 2, 1974. [Reg. § 301.6104(a)-3.]

☐ [*T.D.* 7845, 11-5-82.]

### [Reg. § 301.6104(a)-4]

**§ 301.6104(a)-4. Requirement for 26 or more plan participants.**—(a) *Inspection by plan participants.*—In the case of a plan, annuity or account described in § 301.6104(a)-2(b) and § 301.6104(a)-3(a) that has fewer than 26 participants, material described in §§ 301.6104(a)-2 and 301.6104(a)-3 as open to public inspection is only open to inspection by a plan participant or the participant's authorized representative. This limitation does not apply, however, with respect to documents which an applicant files with respect to a request for approval of a master, prototype, pattern or other such plan (see § 301.6104(a)-2(b)(3)) or to opinion, notification or other such letters issued by the Internal Revenue Service with respect to such plans (see § 301.6104(a)-3(a)(3)).

(b) *Determining number of plan participants.*—(1) *In general.*—For purposes of determining whether a plan has fewer than 26 participants, the number of plan participants will be the number indicated on the most recent annual return filed for the plan under section 6058. Where an annual return indicates the number of participants both at the beginning and end of the plan year, the number indicated on the return means the number at the end of the plan year. If no annual return has been filed for the plan, then the number of plan participants will be the number indicated on the most recent application for a determination letter filed for the plan. If, however, the number of plan participants is increased prior to final Internal Revenue Service action on the application, the number of plan participants will be that increased number.

(2) *Decreasing number of plan participants.*—If a plan having 26 or more participants, as indicated on an annual return or application for a determination letter, subsequently files an annual return indicating fewer than 26 plan participants, then material relating to the plan which is issued or received by the Internal Revenue Service after the date the annual return is filed will be open to inspection only by plan participants or their authorized representatives. Similarly, if a plan having 26 or more participants as indicated on an annual return or an application for a determination letter, subsequently files an application for a determination letter which indicates fewer than 26 plan participants, then that application and related material, as well as any other material relating to the plan which is received or issued by the Internal Revenue Service after the date of receipt of that application, will be open to inspection only by plan participants or their authorized representatives. In either case, material open to public inspection pursuant to the number of plan participants indicated on previous annual returns or applications for a determination letter will remain open to public inspection.

(3) *Increasing number of plan participants.*—If a plan having fewer than 26 plan participants, as indicated on an annual return or application for a determination letter, files a subsequent return or application indicating 26 or more plan participants, all the plan's prior applications and other material received or issued by the Internal Revenue Service after September 2, 1974, will be open to public inspection regardless of the number of plan participants indicated on any prior return or application.

(c) *Plan participant.*—Solely for purposes of determining who is a plan participant permitted to inspect material relating to a plan having fewer than 26 participants, the term "plan participant" includes, but is not limited to, former employees (such as certain retired and terminated employees) who have a nonforfeitable right to benefits under the plan. An individual who is merely a beneficiary of an employee or former employee is not a plan participant, unless the individual is a beneficiary of a deceased former employee and is receiving benefits or entitled to receive future benefits under the plan. The term "plan participant" also includes the administrator, executor, or trustee of the estate of a deceased plan participant if such administrator, executor, or trustee is receiving benefits or entitled to receive future benefits under the plan in his or her official capacity. That material may be available for inspection to an individual under this paragraph does not constitute a determination by the Internal Revenue Service that the individual is a plan participant for any purpose other than inspection under section 6104(a)(1)(B).

(d) *Authorized representative.*—"Authorized representative" means the representative of a plan participant designated by the participant in writing to inspect material described in §§ 301.6104(a)-2 and 301.6104(a)-3. The document designating the authorized representative must be signed by the plan participant and must specify that the representative is authorized to inspect the material. The document, or a copy, must be filed with the office of the Internal Revenue Service in which the authorized representative is to inspect the material. A copy which is reproduced by a photographic process need not be certified as a true and correct copy of the original. [Reg. § 301.6104(a)-4.]

□ [*T.D.* 7845, 11-5-82.]

**[Reg. § 301.6104(a)-5]**

**§301.6104(a)-5. Withholding of certain information from public inspection.**—(a) *Tax exempt organizations.*—(1) *Trade secrets, patents, processes, styles of work, or apparatus.*—An organization whose application for tax exemption is open to public inspection under section 6104(a)(1)(A) and §301.6104(a)-1 may in writing request the withholding of information contained in the application or supporting documents which relates to any trade secret, patent, process, style of work, or apparatus of the organization. The information will be withheld from the public inspection if the Commissioner determines that the disclosure of such information would adversely affect the organization. Requests for withholding information from public inspection should be filed with the office with which the organization files the documents containing the information. The request must clearly identify the material desired to be withheld (the document,

page, paragraph, and line) and must state why the information should not be open to public inspection. The organization will be notified of the Commissioner's determination as to whether the information will be withheld from public inspection. If the Commissioner determines that the information will be disclosed, the organization will be given 15 days after notification of the Commissioner's decision to contest that decision before the document is disclosed.

(2) *National defense material.*—The Internal Revenue Service will withhold from public inspection any information which is submitted by an organization whose application for tax exemption is open to inspection under section 6104(a)(1)(A) and §301.6104(a)-1, if the Commissioner determines that public disclosure would adversely affect the national defense.

(b) *Pension and other plans.*—(1) *Applicant's exclusion of certain information.*—Except as provided in subparagraph (2) of this paragraph, information that, in the opinion of the applicant, is of the type described in section 6104(a)(1)(C) or (D) should not be included in an application for a determination letter, supporting documents, or any other document open to inspection under section 6104(a)(1)(B). Accordingly, an applicant should not include in an application for a determination letter or supporting documents confidential compensation information as described in subparagraph (4) of this paragraph. Neither should an applicant include information relating to any trade secret, patent, process, style of work or apparatus, the disclosure of which would be adverse to the applicant.

(2) *Exception for separate document.*—The rule that an applicant should exclude from an application for a determination letter or other documents information of the type in section 6104(a)(1)(C) or (D) does not apply—

(i) In the case of the separate schedule to certain applications for a determination letter which is provided for the purpose of setting forth confidential compensation information (as described in subparagraph (4) of this paragraph) which must be submitted by the applicant,

(ii) If the applicant determines that it is impossible to provide the Internal Revenue Service with sufficient information to support an application for a determination letter without submitting what is believed to be information of the type described in section 6104(a)(1)(C) or (D), or

(iii) If the Internal Revenue Service requests that the applicant submit information of the type described in section 6104(a)(1)(C) and (D).

In a case described in subdivision (ii) or (iii) of this subparagraph, the applicant is to set forth the information in a document separate from the remainder of the application for a determination letter or other documents. The separate document is to state why the information is to be withheld from public inspection under section 6104(a)(1)(C) or (D). If the Internal Revenue Service has not requested the information, the separate document is to also state why it is impossible to provide the Internal Revenue Service sufficient information to support the application for a determination letter without including information which is to be withheld. The separate document should clearly identify the relevant portion of the application for a determination letter or other document (the document, page, paragraph, and line) to which the information set forth in the separate document relates. The Internal Revenue Service will withhold from public inspection (including inspection by a plan participant or authorized representative) information contained in the separate document if the Commissioner determines that the information is in fact information of the type described in section 6104(a)(1)(C) or (D), and, in the case of information relating to any trade secret, patent, process, style of work or apparatus, the Commissioner further determines that disclosure would be adverse to the applicant. If the Commissioner determines that the information will be disclosed, the organization will be given 15 days after notification of the Commissioner's decision to contest the decision before the document is disclosed.

(3) *National defense material.*—The Internal Revenue Service will withhold from public inspection (including inspection by a plan participant or authorized representative) any information which is included in an application for a determination letter or supporting documents if the Commissioner determines that public disclosure would adversely affect the national defense. The information will be withheld whether or not submitted on a separate document pursuant to subparagraph (2) of this paragraph.

(4) *Confidential compensation information.*—If an application for a determination letter, supporting document, or related letter or document referred to in section 6104(a)(1)(B) and §§ 301.6104(a)-2 and 301.6104(a)-3 contains information (including aggregate figures) from which an individual's compensation (including deferred compensation) may be ascertained, that information is not open to public inspection (including inspection by a plan participant or authorized

representative). Confidential compensation information includes the amount of benefit a specific plan participant may expect to receive at normal or early retirement age and the amount of the employer's contributions under the plan that may be allocated to a specific plan participant. However, so long as a plan has more than one participant, the amount of benefit provided under the plan to plan participants, in general, at normal or early retirement age, or the amount of the employer's contributions under the plan that are allocable to plan participants, in general, does not constitute confidential compensation information. Further, a description of the numbers of individuals covered and not covered by a plan, listed by compensation range, does not constitute confidential compensation information. [Reg. §301.6104(a)-5.]

☐ [*T.D. 7845, 11-5-82.*]

### [Reg. §301.6104(a)-6]

**§301.6104(a)-6. Procedural rules for inspection.**—(a) *Place of inspection; tax exempt organizations and pension and other plans.*—Material relating either to tax exempt organizations or to pension and other plans that is open to public inspection under section 6104(a)(1) and §301.6104(a)-1 through §301.6104(a)-3 will be made available for inspection at the Freedom of Information Reading Room, National Office, Internal Revenue Service, 1111 Constitution Avenue, N.W., Washington, D.C. 20224, and in the office of any district director of internal revenue.

(b) *Request for inspection.*—(1) *Tax exempt organizations and pension and other plans; public inspection.*—Material relating to either tax exempt organizations or pension and other plans that is open to public inspection under section 6104(a)(1) and §§301.6104(a)-1 through 301.6104(a)-3 will be available for inspection only upon request. If inspection at the National Office is desired, a request should be made in writing to the Commissioner of Internal Revenue, Attention: Freedom of Information Reading Room, 1111 Constitution Avenue, N.W., Washington, D.C. 20224. Requests for inspection in the office of a district director should be made in writing to the district director's office. The request must describe the material to be inspected in reasonably sufficient detail so that Internal Revenue Service personnel can locate the material. If a tax exempt organization has more than one application for tax exemption open to public inspection, or if a pension or other plan has more than one application for a determination letter open to public inspection, only the most recent application and related material will be made available for inspection unless the request states otherwise. Further, in the case of a pension or other plan, only Internal Revenue Service documents issued or delivered after the date of the filing of the most recent application for a determination letter will be made available for inspection, unless the request states otherwise.

(2) *Pension and other plans; inspection by plan participant or authorized representative.*—As described in §301.6104(a)-4, material relating to plans having fewer than 26 participants is only open to inspection by a plan participant or authorized representative. In the case of such a plan, the rules described in subparagraph (1) of this paragraph apply. The request for inspection must include satisfactory evidence that the person requesting inspection is a plan participant (see §301.6104(a)-4(c)) or an authorized representative of such a plan participant within the meaning of §301.6104(a)-4(d).

(c) *Time and extent of inspection.*—A person requesting inspection will be notified when the material will be made available for inspection. The material will be made available for inspection at times that will not interfere with its use by the Internal Revenue Service or exclude other persons from inspecting it. In addition, the Commissioner or district director may limit the number of applications for tax exemption, applications for a determination letter, supporting documents, or letters and documents issued by the Internal Revenue Service that will be made available to any person for inspection on a given date. Inspection will be allowed only in the presence of an Internal Revenue Service employee and only during regular business hours.

(d) *Copies.*—Notes may be taken of the material open for inspection. Copies may be made manually or, if a person provides the equipment, photographically at the place of inspection. Photographic copying is subject to reasonable supervision with regard to the facilities and equipment used. Any fees the Internal Revenue Service may charge for furnishing copies under this section shall be no more than under the fee schedule promulgated pursuant to section (a)(4)(A)(i) of the Freedom of Information Act, 5 U.S.C. 552, by the Commissioner from time to time. Copies will be certified upon request. [Reg. §301.6104(a)-6.]

☐ [*T.D. 7845, 11-5-82. Amended by T.D. 9070, 7-8-2003 and T.D. 9173, 1-4-2005.*]

### [Reg. §301.6104(b)-1]

**§301.6104(b)-1. Publicity of information on certain information returns.**—(a) *In general.*—The following information, together with the name and address of the organization or trust furnishing such information, shall be a matter of public record:

(1) Except as otherwise provided in section 6104 and the regulations thereunder, the information required by section 6033.

(2) The information furnished pursuant to section 6034 (relating to returns by certain trusts) on Form 1041-A.

(3) The information required to be furnished by section 6058.

(b) *Nondisclosure of certain information.*—(1) *Names and addresses of contributors.*—The names and addresses of contributors to an organization other than a private foundation shall not be made available for public inspection under section 6104(b).

(2) *Amounts of contributions.*—The amounts of contributions and bequests to an organization shall be available for public inspection unless the disclosure of such information can reasonably be expected to identify any contributor. Notwithstanding the preceding sentence, the amounts of contributions and bequests to a private foundation shall be available for public inspection.

(3) *Foreign organizations.*—The names, addresses, and amounts of contributions or bequests of persons who are not citizens of the United States to a foreign organization described in section 4948(b) shall not be made available for public inspection under section 6104(b).

(4) *Confidential business information.*—Confidential business information of contributors to any trust described in section 501(c)(21) (black lung trusts) shall not be available for public inspection under section 6104(b) provided:

(i) A request is filed with the office with which the trustee filed the documents in which the information to be withheld is contained,

(ii) Such request clearly specifies the information to be withheld and the reasons supporting the request for withholding, and

(iii) The Commissioner determines that such information is confidential business information.
Information such as the contributor's estimated total liability for black lung benefits, the contributor's coal pricing policies, or any background information necessary to establish estimated total liability or coal pricing policies are examples of confidential business information that shall not be disclosed to the public under this subparagraph.

(c) *Place of inspection.*—Information furnished on the public portion of returns (as described in paragraph (a) of this section) shall be made available for public inspection at the Freedom of Information Reading Room, Internal Revenue Service, 1111 Constitution Avenue, N.W., Washington, D.C. 20224, and at the office of any district director.

(d) *Procedure for public inspection.*—(1) *Requests for inspection.*—Information furnished on the public portion of returns (as described in paragraph (a) of this section) shall be available for public inspection only upon request. Requests for public inspection must be in writing to or at any of the offices mentioned in paragraph (c) of this section. Persons submitting requests for inspection must provide the name and address of the organization that filed the return, the type of return, and the year for which the organization filed.

(2) *Time and extent of inspection.*—A person requesting public inspection in the manner specified in subparagraph (1) of this paragraph shall be notified by the Internal Revenue Service when the material he desires to inspect will be made available for his inspection. Information on returns required by sections 6033, 6034, and 6058 will be made available for public inspection at such reasonable and proper times, and under such conditions, that will not interfere with their use by the Internal Revenue Service and will not exclude other persons from inspecting them. In addition, the Commissioner, Director of the Service Center, or district director may limit the number of returns to be made available to any person for inspection on a given date. Inspection will be allowed only in the presence of an internal revenue officer or employee and only during the regular hours of business of the Internal Revenue Service office.

(3) *Returns available.*—Returns filed before January 1, 1970, shall be available for public inspection only pursuant to the provisions of section 6104 in effect for such years. The information furnished on all returns filed after December 31, 1969, pursuant to the requirements of section 6033, 6034, or 6058, shall be available for public inspection in accordance with the provisions of section 6104.

(4) *Copies.*—Notes may be taken of material opened for inspection under this section. Copies may be made manually or, if a person

provides the equipment, photographically at the place of inspection, subject to reasonable supervision with regard to the facilities and equipment to be employed. Copies of the material opened for inspection will be furnished by the Internal Revenue Service to any person making request therefor. Request for such copies shall be made in the same manner as requests for inspection (see subparagraph (1) of this paragraph) to the office of the Internal Revenue Service in which such material is available for inspection as provided in paragraph (c) of this section. Copies may also be obtained by written request to the director of any service center. If made at the time of inspection, the request for copies need not be in writing. Any copies furnished will be certified upon request. Any fees the Internal Revenue Service may charge for furnishing copies under this section shall be no more than under the fee schedule promulgated pursuant to section (a)(4)(A)(i) of the Freedom of Information Act, 5 U.S.C. 552, by the Commissioner from time to time. [Reg. § 301.6104(b)-1.]

☐ [T.D. 6331, 10-31-58. *Amended by T.D.* 6565, 8-2-61; T.D. 6645, 4-1-63; T.D. 7122, 6-7-71; T.D. 7173, 3-16-72; T.D. 7290, 11-16-73; T.D. 7350, 4-3-75; T.D. 7785, 7-27-81. *Redesignated by T.D.* 7845, 11-5-82. *Amended by T.D.* 8019, 4-11-85; T.D. 9070, 7-8-2003 *and T.D.* 9173, 1-4-2005.]

### [Reg. § 301.6104(c)-1]

**§ 301.6104(c)-1. Disclosure of certain information to State officers.**—(a) *Notification of determinations.*—(1) *Automatic notification.*—Upon making a determination described in paragraph(c) of this section, the Internal Revenue Service will notify the Attorney General and the principal tax officer of each of the following States of such determination without application or request by such State officer—

(i) In the case of any organization described in section 501(c)(3), the State in which the principal office of the organization is located (as shown on the last-filed return required by section 6033, or on the application for exemption if no return has been filed), and the State in which the organization was incorporated, or if a trust, in which it was created, and

(ii) In the case of a private foundation, each State which the organization was required to list as an attachment to its last-filed return pursuant to § 1.6033-2(a)(2)(iv).

(2) *Applications for notification by other State officers.*—Other officers of States described in subparagraph (1) of this paragraph, and officers of States not described in such subparagraph, may request that they be notified (either generally or with respect to a particular organization or type of organization) of determinations described in paragraph (c) of this section. In such cases, these State officers must show that they are appropriate State officers within the meaning of section 6104(c)(2). The required showing may be made by presenting a letter from the Attorney General of the State setting forth (i) the functions and authority of the State officer under State law, and (ii) sufficient facts for the Internal Revenue Service to determine that such officer is an appropriate State officer within the meaning of section 6104(c)(2).

(3) *Manner of notification.*—A State officer who is entitled to be notified of a determination under this paragraph will be notified by sending him a copy of the communication from the Internal Revenue Service to the organization which informs such organization of the determination.

(b) *Inspection by State officers.*—(1) *In general.*—After a determination described in paragraph (c) of this section has been made, appropriate State officers within the meaning of section 6104(c)(2) may inspect the material described in subparagraph (3) of this paragraph. Such material may be inspected at an office of the Internal Revenue Service which will be designated upon receipt of a request for inspection; the location of such office will be determined with due consideration of the needs of the Internal Revenue Service and the needs of the State officer entitled to inspect.

(2) *State officers who may inspect material.*—Any State officer entitled to be notified of a determination without application (under paragraph (a)(1) of this section) may inspect the material described in subparagraph (3) of this paragraph upon demonstrating that he is so entitled. Any State officer who has in fact been notified by the Internal Revenue Service of a determination may inspect such material without further demonstration, unless it shall be determined by the Internal Revenue Service that such officer was not entitled to be so notified. Other State officers must demonstrate to the satisfaction of the Internal Revenue Service that they are entitled to be notified under paragraph (a)(2) of this section before they may inspect such material.

(3) *Material which may be inspected.*—(i) Except as provided in subdivision (ii) of this subparagraph, a State officer who is so entitled under subparagraphs (1) and (2) of this paragraph will be permitted to inspect and copy all returns, filed statements, records, reports, and other information relating to a determination described in paragraph (c) of this section which is relevant to a determination under State law, and which is in the hands of the Internal Revenue Service.

(ii) The following material will not be made available for inspection by State officers under section 6104(c) and this section—

(a) Interpretations by the Internal Revenue Service or other federal agency of federal laws (including the Internal Revenue Code of 1954 and its predecessors) which would not otherwise be made available to State officers under section 6103(d),

(b) Reports of informers, or any other material which would disclose the identity, or threaten the safety or anonymity, of an informer,

(c) Returns of persons (other than those exempt from taxation) which would not be available under section 6103(d) to the State officer requesting inspection, or

(d) Other material the disclosure of which the Commissioner has determined would prejudice the proper administration of the internal revenue laws.

(4) *Statement by State officer.*—Before any State officer will be permitted to inspect material described in this paragraph, he must submit a statement to the Internal Revenue Service that he intends to use such material solely in fulfilling his functions under State law relating to organizations of the type described in section 501(c)(3); material is made available to State officers under this section in reliance on such statements. For provisions relating to penalties for misuse of information which is made available under section 6104(c) and this section, see 18 U.S.C. 1001.

(c) *Determinations defined.*—For purposes of this section, a determination means a final determination by the Internal Revenue Service that—

(1) An organization is refused recognition as an organization described in section 501(c)(3), or has been operated in such a manner that it will not, or will no longer, be recognized as meeting the requirements for exemption under that section, or

(2) A deficiency of tax exists under section 507 or chapter 41 or 42.

For purposes of this paragraph, a determination by the Internal Revenue Service is not final until all administrative review with respect to such determination has been completed. For purposes of this section, a waiver of restrictions on assessment and collection of deficiency in tax is treated as a final determination that a deficiency of tax exists when such waiver has been finally accepted by the Internal Revenue Service. For example, a final determination that a deficiency of tax exists under section 507 or chapter 41 or 42 is made when the organization is sent a notice of deficiency with respect to such tax.

(d) *Effective date.*—The provisions of this section apply with respect to all determinations made after December 31, 1969. [Reg. § 301.6104(c)-1.]

☐ [T.D. 7122, 6-7-71. *Amended by T.D.* 7290, 11-16-73 *and T.D.* 7785, 7-27-81, *Redesignated by T.D.* 7845, 11-5-82.]

### [Reg. § 301.6104(d)-0]

**§ 301.6104(d)-0. Table of contents.**—This section lists the major captions contained in §§ 301.6104(d)-1 through 301.6104(d)-3 as follows:

(1) Time and place for providing copies in response to requests made in person.

    (i) In general.

    (ii) Unusual circumstances.

    (iii) Agents for providing copies.

(2) Request for copies in writing.

    (i) In general.

    (ii) Time and manner of fulfilling written requests.

      (A) In general.

      (B) Request for a copy of parts of document.

      (C) Agents for providing copies.

(3) Fees for copies.

    (i) In general.

    (ii) Form of payment.

      (A) Request made in person.

      (B) Request made in writing.

    (iii) Avoidance of unexpected fees.

    (iv) Responding to inquiries of fees charged.

(e) Documents to be provided by regional and district offices.

(f) Documents to be provided by local and subordinate organizations.

    (1) Applications for tax exemption.

    (2) Annual information returns.

    (3) Failure to comply.

(g) Failure to comply with public inspection or copying requirements.

(h) Effective date.

    (1) In general.

    (2) Private foundation annual information returns.

*§ 301.6104(d)-2 Making applications and returns widely available.*

    (a) In general.

    (b) Widely available.

    (1) In general.

    (2) Internet posting.

      (i) In general.

      (ii) Transition rule.

      (iii) Reliability and accuracy.

    (c) Discretion to prescribe other methods for making documents widely available.

    (d) Notice requirement.

    (e) Effective date.

*§ 301.6104(d)-3 Tax-exempt organization subject to harassment campaign.*

    (a) In general.

    (b) Harassment.

    (c) Special rule for multiple requests from a single individual or address.

    (d) Harassment determination procedure.

    (e) Effect of a harassment determination.

    (f) Examples.

    (g) Effective date.

[Reg. § 301.6104(d)-0.]

☐ [*T.D. 8818, 4-8-99. Redesignated and amended by T.D. 8861, 1-12-2000.*]

### [Reg. § 301.6104(d)-1]

**§ 301.6104(d)-1. Public inspection and distribution of applications for tax exemption and annual information returns of tax-exempt organizations.**—(a) *In general.*—Except as otherwise provided in this section, if a tax-exempt organization (as defined in paragraph (b)(1) of this section) filed an application for recognition of exemption under section 501, it shall make its application for tax exemption (as defined in paragraph(b)(3) of this section) available for public inspection without charge at its principal, regional and district offices during regular business hours. Except as otherwise provided in this section, a tax-exempt organization shall make its annual information returns (as defined in paragraph(b)(4) of this section) available for public inspection without charge in the same offices during regular business hours. Each annual information return shall be made available for a period of three years beginning on the date the return is required to be filed (determined with regard to any extension of time for filing) or is actually filed, whichever is later. In addition, except as provided in §§ 301.6104(d)-2 and 301.6104(d)-3, an organization shall provide a copy without charge, other than a reasonable fee for reproduction and actual postage costs, of all or any part of any application or return required to be made available for public inspection under this paragraph to any individual who makes a request for such copy in person or in writing. See paragraph (d)(3) of this section for rules relating to fees for copies.

(b) *Definitions.*—For purposes of applying the provisions of section 6104(d), this section and §§ 301.6104(d)-2 and 301.6104(d)-3, the following definitions apply:

(1) *Tax-exempt organization.*—The term *tax-exempt organization* means any organization that is described in section 501(c) or section 501(d) and is exempt from taxation under section 501(a). The term tax-exempt organization also includes any nonexempt charitable trust described in section 4947(a)(1) or nonexempt private foundation that is subject to the reporting requirements of section 6033 pursuant to section 6033(d).

(2) *Private foundation.*—The term *private foundation* means a private foundation as defined in section 509(a) or a nonexempt charitable trust described in section 4947(a)(1) or a nonexempt private foundation subject to the information reporting requirements of section 6033 pursuant to section 6033(d).

(3) *Application for tax exemption.*—(i) *In general.*—Except as described in paragraph (b)(3)(iii) of this section, the term *application for tax exemption* includes any prescribed application form (such as Form 1023 or Form 1024), all documents and statements the Internal Revenue Service requires an applicant to file with the form, any statement or other supporting document submitted by an organization in support of its application, and any letter or other document issued by the Internal Revenue Service concerning the application (such as a favorable determination letter or a list of questions from the Internal Revenue Service about the application). For example, a legal brief submitted in support of an application, or a response to questions from the Internal Revenue Service during the application process, is part of an application for tax exemption.

(ii) *No prescribed application form.*—If no form is prescribed for an organization's application for tax exemption, the application for tax exemption includes—

(A) The application letter and copy of the articles of incorporation, declaration of trust, or other similar instrument that sets forth the permitted powers or activities of the organization;

(B) The organization's bylaws or other code of regulations;

(C) The organization's latest financial statements showing assets, liabilities, receipts and disbursements;

(D) Statements describing the character of the organization, the purpose for which it was organized, and its actual activities;

(E) Statements showing the sources of the organization's income and receipts and their disposition; and

(F) Any other statements or documents the Internal Revenue Service required the organization to file with, or that the organization submitted in support of, the application letter.

(iii) *Exceptions.*—The term *application for tax exemption* does not include—

(A) Any application for tax exemption filed by an organization that the Internal Revenue Service has not yet recognized, on the basis of the application, as exempt from taxation under section 501 for any taxable year;

(B) Any application for tax exemption filed before July 15, 1987, unless the organization filing the application had a copy of the application on July 15, 1987;

(C) In the case of a tax-exempt organization other than a private foundation, the name and address of any contributor to the organization; or

(D) Any material, including the material listed in § 301.6104(a)-1(i) and information that the Secretary would be required to withhold from public inspection, that is not available for public inspection under section 6104.

(iv) *Local or subordinate organizations.*—For rules relating to applications for tax exemption of local or subordinate organizations, see paragraph (f)(1) of this section.

(4) *Annual information return.*—(i) *In general.*—Except as described in paragraph (b)(4)(ii) of this section, the term *annual information return* includes an exact copy of any return filed by a tax-exempt organization pursuant to section 6033. It also includes any amended return the organization files with the Internal Revenue Service after the date the original return is filed. Returns filed pursuant to section 6033 include Form 990, Return of Organization Exempt From Income Tax, Form 990-PF, Return of Private Foundation, or any other version of Form 990 (such as Forms 990-EZ or 990-BL, except Form 990-T) and Form 1065. Each copy of a return must include all information furnished to the Internal Revenue Service on the return, as well as all schedules, attachments and supporting documents. For example, in the case of a Form 990, the copy must include Schedule A of Form 990 (containing supplementary information on section 501(c)(3) organizations), and those parts of the return that show compensation paid to specific persons (currently, Part V of Form 990 and Parts I and II of Schedule A of Form 990).

(ii) *Exceptions.*—The term *annual information return* does not include Schedule A of Form 990-BL, Form 990-T, Exempt Organization Business Income Tax Return, Schedule K-1 of Form 1065 or Form 1120-POL, U.S. Income Tax Return For Certain Political Organizations. In the case of a tax-exempt organization other than a private foundation, the term *annual information return* does not include the name and address of any contributor to the organization.

(iii) *Returns more than 3 years old.*—The term *annual information return* does not include any return after the expiration of 3 years from the date the return is required to be filed (including any extension of time that has been granted for filing such return) or is actually filed, whichever is later. If an organization files an amended return, however, the amended return must be made available for a period of 3 years beginning on the date it is filed with the Internal Revenue Service.

(iv) *Local or subordinate organizations.*—For rules relating to annual information returns of local or subordinate organizations, see paragraph (f)(2) of this section.

(5) *Regional or district offices.*—(i) *In general.*—A regional or district office is any office of a tax-exempt organization, other than its principal office, that has paid employees, whether part-time or full-time, whose aggregate number of paid hours a week are normally at least 120.

(ii) *Site not considered a regional or district office.*—A site is not considered a regional or district office, however, if—

(A) The only services provided at the site further exempt purposes (such as day care, health care or scientific or medical research); and

(B) The site does not serve as an office for management staff, other than managers who are involved solely in managing the exempt function activities at the site.

(c) *Special rules relating to public inspection.*—(1) *Permissible conditions on public inspection.*—A tax-exempt organization may have an employee present in the room during an inspection. The organization, however, must allow the individual conducting the inspection to take notes freely during the inspection. If the individual provides photocopying equipment at the place of inspection, the organization must allow the individual to photocopy the document at no charge.

(2) *Organizations that do not maintain permanent offices.*—If a tax-exempt organization does not maintain a permanent office, the organization shall comply with the public inspection requirements of paragraph (a) of this section by making its application for tax exemption and its annual information returns, as applicable, available for inspection at a reasonable location of its choice. Such an organization shall permit public inspection within a reasonable amount of time after receiving a request for inspection (normally not more than 2 weeks) and at a reasonable time of day. At the organization's option, it may mail, within 2 weeks of receiving the request, a copy of its application for tax exemption and annual information returns to the requester in lieu of allowing an inspection. The organization may charge the requester for copying and actual postage costs only if the requester consents to the charge. An organization that has a permanent office, but has no office hours or very limited hours during certain times of the year, shall make its documents available during those periods when office hours are limited or not available as though it were an organization without a permanent office.

(d) *Special rules relating to copies.*—(1) *Time and place for providing copies in response to requests made in-person.*—(i) *In general.*—Except as provided in paragraph (d)(1)(iii) of this section, a tax-exempt organization shall provide copies of the documents it is required to provide under section 6104(d) in response to a request made in person at its principal, regional and district offices during regular business hours. Except as provided in paragraph (d)(1)(ii) of this section, an organization shall provide such copies to a requester on the day the request is made.

(ii) *Unusual circumstances.*—In the case of an in-person request, where unusual circumstances exist such that fulfilling the request on the same business day places an unreasonable burden on the tax-exempt organization, the organization must provide the copies no later than the next business day following the day that the unusual circumstances cease to exist or the fifth business day after the date of the request, whichever occurs first. Unusual circumstances include, but are not limited to, receipt of a volume of requests that exceeds the organization's daily capacity to make copies; requests received shortly before the end of regular business hours that require an extensive amount of copying; or requests received on a day when the organization's managerial staff capable of fulfilling the request is conducting special duties, such as student registration or

attending an off-site meeting or convention, rather than its regular administrative duties.

(iii) *Agents for providing copies.*—A principal, regional or district office of a tax-exempt organization subject to the requirements of this section may retain a local agent to process requests made in person for copies of its documents. A local agent must be located within reasonable proximity of the applicable office. A local agent that receives a request made in person for copies must provide the copies within the time limits and under the conditions that apply to the organization itself. For example, a local agent generally must provide a copy to a requester on the day the agent receives the request. When a principal, regional or district office of a tax-exempt organization using a local agent receives a request made in person for a copy, it must immediately provide the name, address and telephone number of the local agent to the requester. An organization that provides this information is not required to respond further to the requester. However, the penalty provisions of sections 6652(c)(1)(C), 6652(c)(1)(D), and 6685 continue to apply to the tax-exempt organization if the organization's local agent fails to provide the documents as required under section 6104(d).

(2) *Request for copies in writing.*—(i) *In general.*—A tax-exempt organization must honor a written request for a copy of documents (or the requested part) that the organization is required to provide under section 6104(d) if the request—

(A) Is addressed to, and delivered by mail, electronic mail, facsimile, or a private delivery service as defined in section 7502(f) to a principal, regional or district office of the organization; and

(B) Sets forth the address to which the copy of the documents should be sent.

(ii) *Time and manner of fulfilling written requests.*—(A) *In general.*—A tax-exempt organization receiving a written request for a copy shall mail the copy of the requested documents (or the requested parts of documents) within 30 days from the date it receives the request. However, if a tax-exempt organization requires payment in advance, it is only required to provide the copies within 30 days from the date it receives payment. For rules relating to payment, see paragraph (d)(3) of this section. In the absence of evidence to the contrary, a request or payment that is mailed shall be deemed received by an organization 7 days after the date of the postmark. A request that is transmitted to the organization by electronic mail or facsimile shall be deemed received the day the request is transmitted successfully. If an organization requiring payment in advance receives a written request without payment or with an insufficient payment, the organization must, within 7 days from the date it receives the request, notify the requester of its prepayment policy and the amount due. A copy is deemed provided on the date of the postmark or private delivery mark (or if sent by certified or registered mail, the date of registration or the date of the postmark on the sender's receipt). If an individual making a request consents, a tax-exempt organization may provide a copy of the requested document exclusively by electronic mail. In such case, the material is provided on the date the organization successfully transmits the electronic mail.

(B) *Request for a copy of parts of document.*—A tax-exempt organization must fulfill a request for a copy of the organization's entire application for tax exemption or annual information return or any specific part or schedule of its application or return. A request for a copy of less than the entire application or less than the entire return must specifically identify the requested part or schedule.

(C) *Agents for providing copies.*—A tax-exempt organization subject to the requirements of this section may retain an agent to process written requests for copies of its documents. The agent shall provide the copies within the time limits and under the conditions that apply to the organization itself. For example, if the organization received the request first (e.g., before the agent), the deadline for providing a copy in response to a request shall be determined by reference to when the organization received the request, not when the agent received the request. An organization that transfers a request for a copy to such an agent is not required to respond further to the request. If the organization's agent fails to provide the documents as required under section 6104(d), however, the penalty provisions of sections 6652(c)(1)(C), 6652(c)(1)(D), and 6685 continue to apply to the tax-exempt organization.

(3) *Fees for copies.*—(i) *In general.*—A tax-exempt organization may charge a reasonable fee for providing copies. A fee is reasonable only if it is no more than the total of the applicable per page copying charge prescribed by the fee schedule promulgated pursuant to section (a)(4)(A)(i) of the Freedom of Information Act, 5 U.S.C. 552, by the Commissioner from time to time, and the actual postage costs incurred by the organization to send the copies. The applicable per-page copying charge shall be determined without regard to any

applicable fee exclusion provided in the fee schedule for an initial or de minimis number of pages (e.g. the first 100 pages). Before the organization provides the documents, it may require that the individual requesting copies of the documents pay the fee. If the organization has provided an individual making a request with notice of the fee, and the individual does not pay the fee within 30 days, or if the individual pays the fee by check and the check does not clear upon deposit, the organization may disregard the request.

(ii) *Form of payment.*—(A) *Request made in person.*—If a tax-exempt organization charges a fee for copying (as permitted under paragraph (d)(3)(i) of this section), it shall accept payment by cash and money order for requests made in person. The organization may accept other forms of payment, such as credit cards and personal checks.

(B) *Request made in writing.*—If a tax-exempt organization charges a fee for copying and postage (as permitted under paragraph (d)(3)(i) of this section), it shall accept payment by certified check, money order, and either personal check or credit card for requests made in writing. The organization may accept other forms of payment.

(iii) *Avoidance of unexpected fees.*—Where a tax-exempt organization does not require prepayment and a requester does not enclose payment with a request, an organization must receive consent from a requester before providing copies for which the fee charged for copying and postage exceeds $20.

(iv) *Responding to inquiries of fees charged.*—In order to facilitate a requester's ability to receive copies promptly, a tax-exempt organization shall respond to any questions from potential requesters concerning its fees for copying and postage. For example, the organization shall inform the requester of its charge for copying and mailing its application for exemption and each annual information return, with and without attachments, so that a requester may include payment with the request for copies.

(e) *Documents to be provided by regional and district offices.*—Except as otherwise provided, a regional or district office of a tax-exempt organization must satisfy the same rules as the principal office with respect to allowing public inspection and providing copies of its application for tax exemption and annual information returns. A regional or district office is not required, however, to make its annual information return available for inspection or to provide copies until 30 days after the date the return is required to be filed (including any extension of time that is granted for filing such return) or is actually filed, whichever is later.

(f) *Documents to be provided by local and subordinate organizations.*—(1) *Applications for tax exemption.*—Except as otherwise provided, a tax-exempt organization that did not file its own application for tax exemption (because it is a local or subordinate organization covered by a group exemption letter referred to in §1.508-1 of this chapter) must, upon request, make available for public inspection, or provide copies of, the application submitted to the Internal Revenue Service by the central or parent organization to obtain the group exemption letter and those documents which were submitted by the central or parent organization to include the local or subordinate organization in the group exemption letter. However, if the central or parent organization submits to the Internal Revenue Service a list or directory of local or subordinate organizations covered by the group exemption letter, the local or subordinate organization is required to provide only the application for the group exemption ruling and the pages of the list or directory that specifically refer to it. The local or subordinate organization shall permit public inspection, or comply with a request for copies made in person, within a reasonable amount of time (normally not more than 2 weeks) after receiving a request made in person for public inspection or copies and at a reasonable time of day. In a case where the requester seeks inspection, the local or subordinate organization may mail a copy of the applicable documents to the requester within the same time period in lieu of allowing an inspection. In such a case, the organization may charge the requester for copying and actual postage costs only if the requester consents to the charge. If the local or subordinate organization receives a written request for a copy of its application for tax exemption, it must fulfill the request in the time and manner specified in paragraph (d)(2) of this section. The requester has the option of requesting from the central or parent organization, at its principal office, inspection or copies of the application for group exemption and the material submitted by the central or parent organization to include a local or subordinate organization in the group ruling. If the central or parent organization submits to the Internal Revenue Service a list or directory of local or subordinate organizations covered by the group exemption letter, it must make such list or directory available for public inspection, but it is required to provide copies only of those pages of the list or directory that refer to particular local

or subordinate organizations specified by the requester. The central or parent organization must fulfill such requests in the time and manner specified in paragraphs (c) and (d) of this section.

(2) *Annual information returns.*—A local or subordinate organization that does not file its own annual information return (because it is affiliated with a central or parent organization that files a group return pursuant to §1.6033-2(d) of this chapter) must, upon request, make available for public inspection, or provide copies of, the group returns filed by the central or parent organization. However, if the group return includes separate schedules with respect to each local or subordinate organization included in the group return, the local or subordinate organization receiving the request may omit any schedules relating only to other organizations included in the group return. The local or subordinate organization shall permit public inspection, or comply with a request for copies made in person, within a reasonable amount of time (normally not more than 2 weeks) after receiving a request made in person for public inspection or copies and at a reasonable time of day. In a case where the requester seeks inspection, the local or subordinate organization may mail a copy of the applicable documents to the requester within the same time period in lieu of allowing an inspection. In such a case, the organization may charge the requester for copying and actual postage costs only if the requester consents to the charge. If the local or subordinate organization receives a written request for a copy of its annual information return, it must fulfill the request by providing a copy of the group return in the time and manner specified in paragraph (d)(2) of this section. The requester has the option of requesting from the central or parent organization, at its principal office, inspection or copies of group returns filed by the central or parent organization. The central or parent organization must fulfill such requests in the time and manner specified in paragraphs (c) and (d) of this section.

(3) *Failure to comply.*—If an organization fails to comply with the requirements specified in this paragraph, the penalty provisions of sections 6652(c)(1)(C), 6652(c)(1)(D), and 6685 apply.

(g) *Failure to comply with public inspection or copying requirements.*—If a tax-exempt organization denies an individual's request for inspection or a copy of an application for tax exemption or an annual information return as required under this section, and the individual wants to alert the Internal Revenue Service to the possible need for enforcement action, the individual may provide a statement to the district director for the key district in which the applicable tax-exempt organization's principal office is located (or such other person as the Commissioner may designate) that describes the reason why the individual believes the denial was in violation of the requirements of section 6104(d).

(h) *Effective date.*—(1) *In general.*—For a tax-exempt organization, other than a private foundation, this section is applicable June 8, 1999. For a private foundation, this section is applicable (except as provided in paragraph (h)(2) of this section) beginning March 13, 2000.

(2) *Private foundation annual information returns.*—This section does not apply to any private foundation return the due date for which (determined with regard to any extension of time for filing) is before the applicable date for private foundations specified in paragraph (h)(1) of this section. [Reg. §301.6104(d)-1.]

☐ [*T.D.* 8818, 4-8-99. *Redesignated and amended by T.D.* 8861, 1-12-2000. *Amended by T.D. 9070, 7-8-2003 and T.D. 9173, 1-4-2005.*]

**[Reg. §301.6104(d)-2]**

**§301.6104(d)-2. Making applications and returns widely available.**—(a) *In general.*—A tax-exempt organization is not required to comply with a request for a copy of its application for tax exemption or an annual information return pursuant to §301.6104(d)-1(a) if the organization has made the requested document widely available in accordance with paragraph (b) of this section. An organization that makes its application for tax exemption and/or annual information return widely available must nevertheless make the document available for public inspection as required under §301.6104(d)-1(a), as applicable.

(b) *Widely available.*—(1) *In general.*—A tax-exempt organization makes its application for tax exemption and/or an annual information return widely available if the organization complies with the requirements specified in paragraph (b)(2) of this section, and if the organization satisfies the requirements of paragraph (d) of this section.

(2) *Internet posting.*—(i) *In general.*—A tax-exempt organization can make its application for tax exemption and/or an annual information return widely available by posting the document on a World Wide Web page that the tax-exempt organization establishes and

maintains or by having the document posted, as part of a database of similar documents of other tax-exempt organizations, on a World Wide Web page established and maintained by another entity. The document will be considered widely available only if—

(A) the World Wide Web page through which it is available clearly informs readers that the document is available and provides instructions for downloading it;

(B) the document is posted in a format that, when accessed, downloaded, viewed and printed in hard copy, exactly reproduces the image of the application for tax exemption or annual information return as it was originally filed with the Internal Revenue Service, except for any information permitted by statute to be withheld from public disclosure. (See section 6104(d)(3) and §301.6104(d)-3(b)(3) and (4)); and

(C) any individual with access to the Internet can access, download, view and print the document without special computer hardware or software required for that format (other than software that is readily available to members of the public without payment of any fee) and without payment of a fee to the tax-exempt organization or to another entity maintaining the World Wide Web page.

(ii) *Transition rule.*—A tax-exempt organization that posted its application for tax exemption or its annual information returns on a World Wide Web page on or before April 9, 1999 in a manner consistent with regulation project REG-246250-96 (1997 C.B. 627) (See §601.601(d)(2) of this chapter.) will be treated as satisfying the requirements of paragraphs (b)(2)(i)(B) & (C) of this section until June 8, 2000 provided that an individual can access, download, view and print the document without payment of a fee to the tax-exempt organization or to another entity maintaining the World Wide Web page.

(iii) *Reliability and accuracy.*—In order for the document to be widely available through an Internet posting, the entity maintaining the World Wide Web page must have procedures for ensuring the reliability and accuracy of the document that it posts on the page and must take reasonable precautions to prevent alteration, destruction or accidental loss of the document when posted on its page. In the event that a posted document is altered, destroyed or lost, the entity must correct or replace the document.

(c) *Discretion to prescribe other methods for making documents widely available.*—The Commissioner, from time to time, may prescribe additional methods, other than an Internet posting meeting the requirements of paragraph (b)(2) of this section, that a tax-exempt organization may use to make its documents widely available.

(d) *Notice requirement.*—If a tax-exempt organization has made its application for tax exemption and/or an annual information return widely available it must notify any individual requesting a copy where the documents are available (including the address on the World Wide Web, if applicable). If the request is made in person, the organization shall provide such notice to the individual immediately. If the request is made in writing, the notice shall be provided within 7 days of receiving the request.

(e) *Effective date.*—For a tax-exempt organization, other than a private foundation, this section is applicable June 8, 1999. For a private foundation, this section is applicable beginning March 13, 2000. [Reg. §301.6104(d)-2.]

☐ [*T.D.* 8818, 4-8-99. *Redesignated and amended by T.D.* 8861, 1-12-2000.]

### [Reg. §301.6104(d)-3]

**§301.6104(d)-3. Tax-exempt organization subject to harassment campaign.**—(a) *In general.*—If the district director for the key district in which the organization's principal office is located (or such other person as the Commissioner may designate) determines that the organization is the subject of a harassment campaign and compliance with the requests that are part of the harassment campaign would not be in the public interest, a tax-exempt organization is not required to fulfill a request for a copy (as otherwise required by §301.6104(d)-1(a)) that it reasonably believes is part of the campaign.

(b) *Harassment.*—A group of requests for an organization's application for tax exemption or annual information returns is indicative of a harassment campaign if the requests are part of a single coordinated effort to disrupt the operations of a tax-exempt organization, rather than to collect information about the organization. Whether a group of requests constitutes such a harassment campaign depends on the relevant facts and circumstances. Facts and circumstances that indicate the organization is the subject of a harassment campaign include: a sudden increase in the number of requests; an extraordinary number of requests made through form letters or similarly worded correspondence; evidence of a purpose to deter significantly the organization's employees or volunteers from pursuing the organ-

ization's exempt purpose; requests that contain language hostile to the organization; direct evidence of bad faith by organizers of the purported harassment campaign; evidence that the organization has already provided the requested documents to a member of the purported harassing group; and a demonstration by the tax-exempt organization that it routinely provides copies of its documents upon request.

(c) *Special rule for multiple requests from a single individual or address.*—A tax-exempt organization may disregard any request for copies of all or part of any document beyond the first two received within any 30-day-period or the first four received within any one-year-period from the same individual or the same address, regardless of whether the district director for the applicable key district (or such other person as the Commissioner may designate) has determined that the organization is subject to a harassment campaign.

(d) *Harassment determination procedure.*—A tax-exempt organization may apply for a determination that it is the subject of a harassment campaign and that compliance with requests that are part of the campaign would not be in the public interest by submitting a signed application to the district director for the key district where the organization's principal office is located (or such other person as the Commissioner may designate). The application shall consist of a written statement giving the organization's name, address, employer identification number, and the name, address and telephone number of the person to contact regarding the application. The application must describe in detail the facts and circumstances that the organization believes support a determination that the organization is subject to a harassment campaign. The organization may suspend compliance with respect to any request for a copy of its documents based on its reasonable belief that such request is part of a harassment campaign, provided that the organization files an application for a determination within 10 business days from the day the organization first suspends compliance with respect to a request that is part of the alleged campaign. In addition, the organization may suspend compliance with any request it reasonably believes to be part of the harassment campaign until it receives a response to its application for a harassment campaign determination.

(e) *Effect of a harassment determination.*—If the appropriate district director (or such other person as the Commissioner may designate) determines that a tax-exempt organization is the subject of a harassment campaign and it is not in the public interest to comply with requests that are part of the campaign, such organization is not required to comply with any request for copies that it reasonably believes is part of the campaign. This determination may be subject to other terms and conditions set forth by the district director (or such other person as the Commissioner may designate). A person (as defined in section 6652(c)(4)(C)) shall not be liable for any penalty under sections 6652(c)(1)(C), 6652(c)(1)(D) or 6685 for failing to timely provide a copy of documents in response to a request covered in a request for a harassment determination if the organization fulfills the request within 30 days of receiving a determination from the district director (or such other person as the Commissioner may designate) that the organization is not subject to a harassment campaign. Notwithstanding the preceding sentence, if the district director (or such other person as the Commissioner may designate) further determines that the organization did not have a reasonable basis for requesting a determination that it was subject to a harassment campaign or reasonable belief that a request was part of the campaign, the person (as defined in section 6652(c)(4)(C)) remains liable for any penalties that result from not providing the copies in a timely fashion.

(f) *Examples.*—The provisions of this section are illustrated by the following examples:

*Example 1.* V, a tax-exempt organization, receives an average of 25 requests per month for copies of its three most recent information returns. In the last week of May, V is mentioned in a national news magazine story that discusses information contained in V's 1996 information return. From June 1 through June 30, 1997 V receives 200 requests for a copy of its documents. Other than the sudden increase in the number of requests for copies, there is no other evidence to suggest that the requests are part of an organized campaign to disrupt V's operations. Although fulfilling the requests will place a burden on V, the facts and circumstances do not show that V is subject to a harassment campaign. Therefore, V must respond timely to each of the 200 requests it receives in June.

*Example 2.* Y is a tax-exempt organization that receives an average of 10 requests a month for copies of its annual information returns. From March 1, 1997 to March 31, 1997, Y receives 25 requests for copies of its documents. Fifteen of the requests come from individuals Y knows to be active members of the board of organization X. In the past X has opposed most of the positions and policies that Y advocates. None of the requesters have asked for copies of documents from Y during the past year. Y has no other information about the requesters. Although the facts and circumstances show that some of the individuals making requests are hostile to Y, they do not show that the individuals have organized a campaign that will place enough of a burden on Y to disrupt its activities. Therefore, Y must respond to each of the 25 requests it receives in March.

*Example 3.* The facts are the same as in *Example 2,* except that during March 1997, Y receives 100 requests. In addition to the fifteen requests from members of organization X's board, 75 of the requests are similarly worded form letters. Y discovers that several individuals associated with X have urged the X's members and supporters, via the Internet, to submit as many requests for a copy of Y's annual information returns as they can. The message circulated on the Internet provides a form letter that can be used to make the request. Both the appeal via the Internet and the requests for copies received by Y contain hostile language. During the same year but before the 100 requests were received, Y provided copies of its annual information returns to the headquarters of X. The facts and circumstances show that the 75 form letter requests are coordinated for the purpose of disrupting Y's operations, and not to collect information that has already been provided to an association representing the requesters' interests. Thus, the fact and circumstances show that Y is the subject of an organized harassment campaign. To confirm that it may disregard the 90 requests that constitute the harassment campaign, Y must apply to the applicable district director (or such other person as the Commissioner may designate) for a determination. Y may disregard the 90 requests while the application is pending and after the determination is received. However, it must respond within the applicable time limits to the 10 requests it received in March that were not part of the harassment campaign.

*Example 4.* The facts are the same as in *Example 3,* except that Y receives 5 additional requests from 5 different representatives of the news media who in the past have published articles about Y. Some of these articles were hostile to Y. Normally, the Internal Revenue Service will not consider a tax-exempt organization to have a reasonable belief that a request from a member of the news media is part of a harassment campaign absent additional facts that demonstrate that the organization could reasonably believe the particular requests from the news media to be part of a harassment campaign. Thus, absent such additional facts, Y must respond within the applicable time limits to the 5 requests that it received from representatives of the news media.

(g) *Effective date.*—For a tax-exempt organization, other than a private foundation, this section is applicable June 8, 1999. For a private foundation, this section is applicable beginning March 13, 2000. [Reg. § 301.6104(d)-3.]

☐ [*T.D. 8818, 4-8-99. Redesignated and amended by T.D. 8861, 1-12-2000.*]

### [Reg. § 1.6107-1]

**§ 1.6107-1. Tax return preparer must furnish copy of return or claim for refund to taxpayer and must retain a copy or record.**—(a) *Furnishing copy to taxpayer.*—(1) A person who is a signing tax return preparer of any return or claim for refund of tax under the Internal Revenue Code shall furnish a completed copy of the return or claim for refund to the taxpayer (or nontaxable entity) not later than the time the return or claim for refund is presented for the signature of the taxpayer (or nontaxable entity). The signing tax return preparer may, at its option, request a receipt or other evidence from the taxpayer (or nontaxable entity) sufficient to show satisfaction of the requirement of this paragraph (a).

(2) The tax return preparer must provide a complete copy of the return or claim for refund filed with the IRS to the taxpayer in any media, including electronic media, that is acceptable to both the taxpayer and the tax return preparer. In the case of an electronically filed return, a complete copy of a taxpayer's return or claim for refund consists of the electronic portion of the return or claim for refund, including all schedules, forms, pdf attachments, and jurats, that was filed with the IRS. The copy provided to the taxpayer must include all information submitted to the IRS to enable the taxpayer to determine what schedules, forms, electronic files, and other supporting materials have been filed with the return. The copy, however, need not contain the identification number of the paid tax return preparer. The electronic portion of the return or claim for refund may be contained on a replica of an official form or on an unofficial form. On an unofficial form, however, data entries must reference the line numbers or descriptions on an official form.

(3) For electronically filed Forms 1040EZ, "Income Tax Return for Single Filers and Joint Filers With No Dependents," and Form 1040A, "U.S. Individual Income Tax Return," filed for the 2009, 2010 and 2011 taxable years, the information may be provided on a replica of a Form 1040, "U.S. Individual Income Tax Return", that provides all of the information. For other electronically filed returns, the

information may be provided on a replica of an official form that provides all of the information.

(b) *Copy or record to be retained.*—(1) A person who is a signing tax return preparer of any return or claim for refund shall—

(i)(A) Retain a completed copy of the return or claim for refund; or

(B) Retain a record, by list, card file, or otherwise of the name, taxpayer identification number, and taxable year of the taxpayer (or nontaxable entity) for whom the return or claim for refund was prepared, and the type of return or claim for refund prepared;

(ii) Retain a record, by retention of a copy of the return or claim for refund, maintenance of a list, card file, or otherwise, for each return or claim for refund presented to the taxpayer (or nontaxable entity), of the name of the individual tax return preparer required to sign the return or claim for refund pursuant to § 1.6695-1(b); and

(iii) Make the copy or record of returns and claims for refund and record of the individuals required to sign available for inspection upon request by the Commissioner.

(2) The material described in this paragraph (b) shall be retained and kept available for inspection for the 3-year period following the close of the return period during which the return or claim for refund was presented for signature to the taxpayer (or nontaxable entity). In the case of a return that becomes due (with extensions, if any) during a return period following the return period during which the return was presented for signature, the material shall be retained and kept available for inspection for the 3-year period following the close of the later return period in which the return became due. For the definition of "return period," see section 6060(c). If the person subject to the record retention requirement of this paragraph (b) is a corporation or a partnership that is dissolved before completion of the 3-year period, then all persons who are responsible for the winding up of the affairs of the corporation or partnership under state law shall be subject, on behalf of the corporation or partnership, to these record retention requirements until completion of the 3-year period. If state law does not specify any person or persons as responsible for winding up, then, collectively, the directors or general partners shall be subject, on behalf of the corporation or partnership, to the record retention requirements of this paragraph (b). For purposes of the penalty imposed by section 6695(d), such designated persons shall be deemed to be the tax return preparer and will be jointly and severally liable for each failure.

(c) *Tax return preparer.*—For the definition of "signing tax return preparer," see § 301.7701-15(b)(1) of this chapter. For purposes of applying this section, a corporation, partnership or other organization that employs a signing tax return preparer to prepare for compensation (or in which a signing tax return preparer is compensated as a partner or member to prepare) a return of tax or claim for refund shall be treated as the sole signing tax return preparer.

(d) *Penalties.*—(1) For the civil penalty for failure to furnish a copy of the return or claim for refund to the taxpayers (or nontaxable entity) as required under paragraph (a) of this section, see section 6695(a) and § 1.6695-1(a).

(2) For the civil penalty for failure to retain a copy of the return or claim for refund, or to retain a record as required under paragraph (b) of this section, see section 6695(d) and § 1.6695-1(d).

(e) *Effective/applicability date.*—This section is applicable to returns and claims for refund filed after December 31, 2008. [Reg. § 1.6107-1.]

☐ [*T.D. 7519, 11-17-77. Amended by T.D. 7640, 8-22-79; T.D. 7948, 3-7-84 and T.D. 9436, 12-15-2008 (corrected 1-28-2009).*]

### [Reg. § 20.6107-1]

**§ 20.6107-1. Tax return preparer must furnish copy of return to taxpayer and must retain a copy or record.**—(a) *In general.*—A person who is a signing tax return preparer of any return or claim for refund of estate tax under chapter 11 of subtitle B of the Internal Revenue Code shall furnish a completed copy of the return or claim for refund to the taxpayer and retain a completed copy or record in the manner stated in § 1.6107-1 of this chapter.

(b) *Effective/applicability date.*—This section is applicable to returns and claims for refund filed after December 31, 2008. [Reg. § 20.6107-1.]

☐ [*T.D. 9436, 12-15-2008.*]

### [Reg. § 25.6107-1]

**§ 25.6107-1. Tax return preparer must furnish copy of return to taxpayer and must retain a copy or record.**—(a) *In general.*—A person who is a signing tax return preparer of any return or claim for refund of gift tax under chapter 12 of subtitle B of the Internal Revenue Code shall furnish a completed copy of the return or claim for refund to the taxpayer, and retain a completed copy or record in the manner stated in § 1.6107-1 of this chapter.

(b) *Effective/applicability date.*—This section is applicable to returns and claims for refund filed after December 31, 2008. [Reg. § 25.6107-1.]

☐ [*T.D.* 9436, 12-15-2008.]

### [Reg. § 26.6107-1]

**§ 26.6107-1. Tax return preparer must furnish copy of return to taxpayer and must retain a copy or record.**—(a) *In general.*—A person who is a signing tax return preparer of any return or claim for refund of generation-skipping transfer tax under chapter 13 of subtitle B of the Internal Revenue Code shall furnish a completed copy of the return or claim for refund to the taxpayer, and retain a completed copy or record in the manner stated in § 1.6107-1 of this chapter.

(b) *Effective/applicability date.*—This section is applicable to returns and claims for refund filed after December 31, 2008. [Reg. § 26.6107-1.]

☐ [*T.D.* 9436, 12-15-2008.]

### [Reg. § 31.6107-1]

**§ 31.6107-1. Tax return preparer must furnish copy of return to taxpayer and must retain a copy or record.**—(a) *In general.*—A person who is a signing tax return preparer of any return or claim for refund of employment tax under chapters 21 through 25 of subtitle C of the Internal Revenue Code shall furnish a completed copy of the return or claim for refund to the taxpayer and retain a completed copy or record in the manner stated in § 1.6107-1 of this chapter.

(b) *Effective/applicability date.*—This section is applicable to returns and claims for refund filed after December 31, 2008. [Reg. § 31.6107-1.]

☐ [*T.D.* 9436, 12-15-2008.]

### [Reg. § 40.6107-1]

**§ 40.6107-1. Tax return preparer must furnish copy of return to taxpayer and must retain a copy or record.**—(a) *In general.*—A person who is a signing tax return preparer of any return or claim for refund of any tax to which this part 40 applies shall furnish a completed copy of the return or claim for refund to the taxpayer and retain a completed copy or record in the manner stated in § 1.6107-1 of this chapter.

(b) *Effective/applicability date.*—This section is applicable for returns and claims for refund filed after December 31, 2008. [Reg. § 40.6107-1.]

☐ [*T.D.* 9436, 12-15-2008 (*corrected* 1-28-2009).]

### [Reg. § 41.6107-1]

**§ 41.6107-1. Tax return preparer must furnish copy of return to taxpayer and must retain a copy or record.**—(a) *In general.*—A person who is a signing tax return preparer of any return or claim for refund of excise tax under section 4481 shall furnish a completed copy of the return or claim for refund to the taxpayer and retain a completed copy or record in the manner stated in § 1.6107-1 of this chapter.

(b) *Effective/applicability date.*—This section is applicable for returns and claims for refund filed after December 31, 2008. [Reg. § 41.6107-1.]

☐ [*T.D.* 9436, 12-15-2008.]

### [Reg. § 44.6107-1]

**§ 44.6107-1. Tax return preparer must furnish copy of return to taxpayer and must retain a copy or record.**—(a) *In general.*—A person who is a signing tax return preparer of any return or claim for refund of tax on wagers under sections 4401 or 4411 shall furnish a completed copy of the return or claim for refund to the taxpayer, and retain a completed copy or record in the manner stated in § 1.6107-1 of this chapter.

(b) *Effective/applicability date.*—This section is applicable for returns and claims for refund filed after December 31, 2008. [Reg. § 44.6107-1.]

☐ [*T.D.* 9436, 12-15-2008.]

### [Reg. § 53.6107-1]

**§ 53.6107-1. Tax return preparer must furnish copy of return or claim for refund to taxpayer and must retain a copy or record.**—(a) *In general.*—A person who is a signing tax return preparer of any return or claim for refund of tax under Chapter 42 of the Internal Revenue Code shall furnish a completed copy of the return or claim

for refund to the taxpayer and retain a completed copy or record in the manner stated in § 1.6107-1 of this chapter.

(b) *Effective/applicability date.*—This section is applicable to returns and claims for refund filed after December 31, 2008. [Reg. § 53.6107-1.]

☐ [*T.D.* 9436, 12-15-2008.]

### [Reg. § 54.6107-1]

**§ 54.6107-1. Tax return preparer must furnish copy of return or claims for refund to taxpayer and must retain a copy or record.**—(a) *In general.*—A person who is a signing tax return preparer of any return or claim for refund of tax under chapter 43 of subtitle D of the Internal Revenue Code, shall furnish a completed copy of the return or claim for refund to the taxpayer, and retain a completed copy or record in the manner stated in § 1.6107-1 of this chapter.

(b) *Effective/applicability date.*—This section is applicable to returns and claims for refund filed after December 31, 2008. [Reg. § 54.6107-1.]

☐ [*T.D.* 9436, 12-15-2008.]

### [Reg. § 55.6107-1]

**§ 55.6107-1. Tax return preparer must furnish copy of return or claim for refund to taxpayer and must retain a copy or record.**—(a) *In general.*—A person who is a signing tax return preparer of any return or claim for refund of tax under Chapter 44 of subtitle D of the Internal Revenue Code shall furnish a completed copy of the return or claim for refund to the taxpayer, and retain a completed copy or record in the manner stated in § 1.6107-1 of this chapter.

(b) *Effective/applicability date.*—This section is applicable to returns and claims for refund filed after December 31, 2008. [Reg. § 55.6107-1.]

☐ [*T.D.* 9436, 12-15-2008.]

### [Reg. § 56.6107-1]

**§ 56.6107-1. Tax return preparer must furnish copy of return and claim for refund to taxpayer and must retain a copy or record.**—(a) *In general.*—A person who is a signing tax return preparer of any return or claim for refund of tax under Chapter 41 of subtitle D of the Internal Revenue Code shall furnish a completed copy of the return or claim for refund to the public charity and retain a completed copy or record in the manner stated in § 1.6107-1 of this chapter.

(b) *Effective/applicability date.*—This section is applicable to returns and claims for refund filed after December 31, 2008. [Reg. § 56.6107-1.]

☐ [*T.D.* 9436, 12-15-2008.]

### [Reg. § 156.6107-1]

**§ 156.6107-1. Tax return preparer must furnish copy of return and claim for refund to taxpayer and must retain a copy or record.**—(a) *In general.*—A person who is a signing tax return preparer of any return or claim for refund of tax under section 5881 of the Internal Revenue Code shall furnish a completed copy of the return or claim for refund to the taxpayer and retain a completed copy or record in the manner stated in § 1.6107-1 of this chapter.

(b) *Effective/applicability date.*—This section is applicable to returns and claims for refund filed after December 31, 2008. [Reg. § 156.6107-1.]

☐ [*T.D.* 9436, 12-15-2008.]

### [Reg. § 157.6107-1]

**§ 157.6107-1. Tax return preparer must furnish copy of return or claim for refund to taxpayer and must retain a copy or record.**—(a) *In general.*—A person who is a signing tax return preparer of any return or claim for refund of tax under section 5891 of the Internal Revenue Code shall furnish a completed copy of the return or claim for refund to the taxpayer and retain a completed copy or record in the manner stated in § 1.6107-1 of this chapter.

(b) *Effective/applicability date.*—This section is applicable to returns and claims for refund filed after December 31, 2008. [Reg. § 157.6107-1.]

☐ [*T.D.* 9436, 12-15-2008.]

### [Reg. § 1.6107-2]

**§ 1.6107-2. Form and manner of furnishing copy of return and retaining copy or record.**—(a) *In general.*—The Commissioner may prescribe the form and manner of satisfying the requirements imposed by section 6107(a) and (b) and § 1.6107-1(a) and (b) in forms, instructions, or other appropriate guidance (see § 601.601(d)(2) of this chapter).

(b) *Effective date.*—To the extent this section relates to section 6107(a) and § 1.6107-1(a), it applies to income tax returns and claims for refund presented to a taxpayer for signature after December 31, 2002. To the extent this section relates to section 6107(b) and § 1.6107-1(b), it applies after December 31, 2002, to returns and claims for refund for which the 3-year period described in section 6107(b) expires after December 31, 2002. [Reg. § 1.6107-2.]

☐ [*T.D.* 9119, 3-24-2004.]

### [Reg. § 301.6108-1]

**§ 301.6108-1. Publication of statistics of income.**—Pursuant to and in accordance with the provisions of section 6108, statistics reasonably available with respect to the operation of the income tax laws shall be prepared and published annually by the Commissioner. [Reg. § 301.6108-1.]

☐ [*T.D.* 6546, 1-18-61.]

### [Reg. § 1.6109-1]

**§ 1.6109-1. Identifying numbers.**—(a) *Information to be furnished after April 15, 1974.*—For provisions concerning the requesting and furnishing of identifying numbers with respect to returns, statements, and other documents which must be filed after April 15, 1974, see § 301.6109-1 of this chapter (Regulations on Procedure and Administration).

(b) *Information to be furnished before April 16, 1974.*—For provisions concerning the requesting and furnishing of identifying numbers with respect to returns, statements, and other documents which must be filed before April 16, 1974, see 26 CFR § 1.6109-1 (revised as of April 1, 1973). [Reg. § 1.6109-1.]

☐ [*T.D.* 6606, 8-24-62. *Amended by T.D.* 7012, 5-14-69 *and T.D.* 7306, 3-14-74.]

### [Reg. § 20.6109-1]

**§ 20.6109-1. Tax return preparers furnishing identifying numbers for returns or claims for refund.**—(a) *In general.*—Each estate tax return or claim for refund prepared by one or more signing tax return preparers must include the identifying number of the preparer required by § 1.6695-1(b) of this chapter to sign the return or claim for refund in the manner stated in § 1.6109-2 of this chapter.

(b) *Effective/applicability date.*—Paragraph (a) of this section is applicable to returns and claims for refund filed after December 31, 2008. [Reg. § 20.6109-1.]

☐ [*T.D.* 9436, 12-15-2008.]

### [Reg. § 25.6109-1]

**§ 25.6109-1. Tax return preparers furnishing identifying numbers for returns or claims for refund.**—(a) *In general.*—Each gift tax return or claim for refund prepared by one or more signing tax return preparers must include the identifying number of the preparer required by § 1.6695-1(b) of this chapter to sign the return or claim for refund in the manner stated in § 1.6109-2 of this chapter.

(b) *Effective/applicability date.*—Paragraph (a) of this section is applicable to returns and claims for refund filed after December 31, 2008. [Reg. § 25.6109-1.]

☐ [*T.D.* 9436, 12-15-2008.]

### [Reg. § 26.6109-1]

**§ 26.6109-1. Tax return preparers furnishing identifying numbers for returns or claims for refund.**—(a) *In general.*—Each generation-skipping transfer tax return or claim for refund prepared by one or more signing tax return preparers must include the identifying number of the preparer required by § 1.6695-1(b) of this chapter to sign the return or claim for refund in the manner stated in § 1.6109-2 of this chapter.

(b) *Effective/applicability date.*—Paragraph (a) of this section is applicable to returns and claims for refund filed after December 31, 2008. [Reg. § 26.6109-1.]

☐ [*T.D.* 9436, 12-15-2008.]

### [Reg. § 31.6109-1]

**§ 31.6109-1. Supplying of identifying numbers.**—(a) *In general.*—The returns, statements, and other documents required to be filed under this subchapter shall reflect such identifying numbers as are required by each return, statement, or document and its related instructions. See § 301.6109-1 of this chapter (Regulations on Procedure and Administration).

(b) *Effective date.*—The provisions of this section are effective for information which must be furnished after April 15, 1974. See 26 CFR § 31.6109-1 (revised as of April 1, 1973) for provisions with respect to information which must be furnished before April 16, 1974. [Reg. § 31.6109-1.]

☐ [*T.D.* 6606, 8-24-62. *Amended by T.D.* 7306, 3-14-74.]

### [Reg. § 40.6109-1]

**§ 40.6109-1. Tax return preparers furnishing identifying numbers for returns or claims for refund.**—(a) *In general.*—Each return or claim for refund of any tax to which this part 40 applies prepared by one or more signing tax return preparers must include the identifying number of the preparer required by § 1.6695-1(b) of this chapter to sign the return or claim for refund in the manner stated in § 1.6109-2 of this chapter.

(b) *Effective/applicability date.*—This section is applicable to returns and claims for refund filed after December 31, 2008. [Reg. § 40.6109-1.]

☐ [*T.D.* 9436, 12-15-2008 (*corrected* 1-28-2009).]

### [Reg. § 41.6109-1]

**§ 41.6109-1. Identifying numbers.**—Every person required under § 41.6011(a)-1 to make a return must provide the identifying number required by the instructions to the form on which the return is made. [Reg. § 41.6109-1.]

☐ [*T.D.* 6606, 8-24-62. *Amended by T.D.* 7012, 5-14-69 *and T.D.* 8879, 3-30-2000.]

### [Reg. § 44.6109-1]

**§ 44.6109-1. Tax return preparers furnishing identifying numbers for returns or claims for refund.**—(a) *In general.*—Each tax return or claim for refund of tax under sections 4401 or 4411 prepared by one or more signing tax return preparers must include the identifying number of the preparer required by § 1.6695-1(b) of this chapter to sign the return or claim for refund in the manner stated in § 1.6109-2 of this chapter.

(b) *Effective/applicability date.*—This section is applicable for returns and claims for refund filed after December 31, 2008. [Reg. § 44.6109-1.]

☐ [*T.D.* 9436, 12-15-2008.]

### [Reg. § 53.6109-1]

**§ 53.6109-1. Tax return preparers furnishing identifying numbers for returns or claims for refund filed.**—(a) *In general.*—Each tax return or claim for refund under Chapter 42 of the Internal Revenue Code prepared by one or more signing tax return preparers must include the identifying number of the preparer required by § 1.6695-1(b) of this chapter to sign the return or claim for refund in the manner stated in § 1.6109-2 of this chapter.

(b) *Effective/applicability date.*—Paragraph (a) of this section is applicable to returns and claims for refund filed after December 31, 2008. [Reg. § 53.6109-1.]

☐ [*T.D.* 9436, 12-15-2008.]

### [Reg. § 54.6109-1]

**§ 54.6109-1. Tax return preparers furnishing identifying numbers for returns or claims for refund filed.**—(a) *In general.*—Each tax return or claim for refund of tax under Chapter 43 of subtitle D prepared by one or more signing tax return preparers must include the identifying number of the preparer required by § 1.6695-1(b) of this chapter to sign the return or claim for refund in the manner stated in § 1.6109-2 of this chapter. [Reg. § 54.6109-1.]

(b) *Effective/applicability date.*—Paragraph (a) of this section is applicable to returns and claims for refund filed after December 31, 2008. [Reg. § 54.6109-1.]

☐ [*T.D.* 9436, 12-15-2008.]

### [Reg. § 55.6109-1]

**§ 55.6109-1. Tax return preparers furnishing identifying numbers for returns or claims for refund.**—(a) *In general.*—Each tax return or claim for refund of tax under chapter 44 of Subtitle D prepared by one or more signing tax return preparers must include the identifying number of the preparer required by § 1.6695-1(b) of this chapter to sign the return or claim for refund in the manner stated in § 1.6109-2 of this chapter.

(b) *Effective/applicability date.*—Paragraph (a) of this section is applicable to returns and claims for refund filed after December 31, 2008. [Reg. § 55.6109-1.]

☐ *[T.D. 9436, 12-15-2008.]*

### [Reg. § 56.6109-1]

**§ 56.6109-1. Tax return preparers furnishing identifying numbers for returns or claims for refund.**—(a) *In general.*—Each tax return or claim for refund for tax under chapter 41 of subtitle D prepared by one or more signing tax return preparers must include the identifying number of the preparer required by § 1.6695-1(b) of this chapter to sign the return or claim for refund in the manner stated in § 1.6109-2 of this chapter.

(b) *Effective/applicability date.*—Paragraph (a) of this section is applicable to returns and claims for refund filed after December 31, 2008. [Reg. § 56.6109-1.]

☐ *[T.D. 9436, 12-15-2008.]*

### [Reg. § 156.6109-1]

**§ 156.6109-1. Tax return preparers furnishing identifying numbers for returns or claims for refund.**—(a) *In general.*—Each tax return or claim for refund for tax under section 5881 of the Internal Revenue Code prepared by one or more signing tax return preparers must include the identifying number of the preparer required by § 1.6695-1(b) of this chapter to sign the return or claim for refund in the manner stated in § 1.6109-2 of this chapter.

(b) *Effective/applicability date.*—Paragraph (a) of this section is applicable to returns and claims for refund filed after December 31, 2008. [Reg. § 156.6109-1.]

☐ *[T.D. 9436, 12-15-2008.]*

### [Reg. § 157.6109-1]

**§ 157.6109-1. Tax return preparers furnishing identifying numbers for returns or claims for refund.**—(a) *In general.*—Each tax return or claim for refund for tax under section 5891 of the Internal Revenue Code prepared by one or more signing tax return preparers must include the identifying number of the preparer required by § 1.6695-1(b) of this chapter to sign the return or claim for refund in the manner stated in § 1.6109-2 of this chapter.

(b) *Effective/applicability date.*—Paragraph (a) of this section is applicable to returns and claims for refund filed after December 31, 2008. [Reg. § 157.6109-1.]

☐ *[T.D. 9436, 12-15-2008.]*

### [Reg. § 301.6109-1]

**§ 301.6109-1. Identifying numbers.**—(a) *In general.*—(1) *Taxpayer identifying numbers.*—(i) *Principal types.*—There are several types of taxpayer identifying numbers that include the following: social security numbers, Internal Revenue Service (IRS) individual taxpayer identification numbers, IRS adoption taxpayer identification numbers, and employer identification numbers. Social security numbers take the form 000-00-0000. IRS individual taxpayer identification numbers and IRS adoption taxpayer identification numbers also take the form 000-00-0000 but include a specific number or numbers designated by the IRS. Employer identification numbers take the form 00-0000000.

(ii) *Uses.*—Social security numbers, IRS individual taxpayer identification numbers, and IRS adoption taxpayer identification numbers are used to identify individual persons. Employer identification numbers are used to identify employers. For the definition of social security number and employer identification number, see §§ 301.7701-11 and 301.7701-12, respectively. For the definition of IRS individual taxpayer identification number, see paragraph (d)(3) of this section. For the definition of IRS adoption taxpayer identification number, see § 301.6109-3(a). Except as otherwise provided in applicable regulations under this chapter or on a return, statement, or other document, and related instructions, taxpayer identifying numbers must be used as follows:

(A) Except as otherwise provided in paragraph (a)(1)(ii)(B) and (D) of this section, and § 301.6109-3, an individual required to furnish a taxpayer identifying number must use a social security number.

(B) Except as otherwise provided in paragraph (a)(1)(ii)(D) of this section and § 301.6109-3, an individual required to furnish a taxpayer identifying number but who is not eligible to obtain a social security number must use an IRS individual taxpayer identification number.

(C) Any person other than an individual (such as corporations, partnerships, nonprofit associations, trusts, estates, and similar nonindividual persons) that is required to furnish a taxpayer identifying number must use an employer identification number.

(D) An individual, whether U.S. or foreign, who is an employer or who is engaged in a trade or business as a sole proprietor

should use an employer identification number as required by returns, statements, or other documents and their related instructions.

(2) *A trust that is treated as owned by one or more persons pursuant to sections 671 through 678.*—(i) *Obtaining a taxpayer identification number.*—(A) *General rule.*—Unless the exception in paragraph (a)(2)(i)(B) of this section applies, a trust that is treated as owned by one or more persons under sections 671 through 678 must obtain a taxpayer identification number as provided in paragraph (d)(2) of this section.

(B) *Exception for a trust all of which is treated as owned by one grantor or one other person and that reports under § 1.671-4(b)(2)(i)(A) of this chapter.*—A trust that is treated as owned by one grantor or one other person under sections 671 through 678 need not obtain a taxpayer identification number, provided the trust reports pursuant to § 1.671-4(b)(2)(i)(A) of this chapter. The trustee must obtain a taxpayer identification number as provided in paragraph (d)(2) of this section for the first taxable year that the trust is no longer owned by one grantor or one other person or for the first taxable year that the trust does not report pursuant to § 1.671-4(b)(2)(i)(A) of this chapter.

(ii) *Obligations of persons who make payments to certain trusts.*—Any payor that is required to file an information return with respect to payments of income or proceeds to a trust must show the name and taxpayer identification number that the trustee has furnished to the payor on the return. Regardless of whether the trustee furnishes to the payor the name and taxpayer identification number of the grantor or other person treated as an owner of the trust, or the name and taxpayer identification number of the trust, the payor must furnish a statement to recipients to the trustee of the trust, rather than to the grantor or other person treated as the owner of the trust. Under these circumstances, the payor satisfies the obligation to show the name and taxpayer identification number of the payee on the information return and to furnish a statement to recipients to the person whose taxpayer identification number is required to be shown on the form.

(3) *Obtaining a taxpayer identification number for a trust, or portion of a trust, following the death of the individual treated as the owner.*—(i) *In general.*—(A) *A trust all of which was treated as owned by a decedent.*—In general, a trust all of which is treated as owned by a decedent under subpart E (section 671 and following), part I, subchapter J, chapter 1 of the Internal Revenue Code as of the date of the decedent's death must obtain a new taxpayer identification number following the death of the decedent if the trust will continue after the death of the decedent.

(B) *Taxpayer identification number of trust with multiple owners.*—With respect to a portion of a trust treated as owned under subpart E (section 671 and following), part I, subchapter J, chapter 1 (subpart E) of the Internal Revenue Code by a decedent as of the date of the decedent's death, if, following the death of the decedent, the portion treated as owned by the decedent remains part of the original trust and the other portion (or portions) of the trust continues to be treated as owned under subpart E by a grantor(s) or other person(s), the trust reports under the taxpayer identification number assigned to the trust prior to the decedent's death and the portion of the trust treated as owned by the decedent prior to the decedent's death (assuming the decedent's portion of the trust is not treated as terminating upon the decedent's death) continues to report under the taxpayer identification number used for reporting by the other portion (or portions) of the trust. For example, if a trust, reporting under § 1.671-4(a) of this chapter, is treated as owned by three persons and one of them dies, the trust, including the portion of the trust no longer treated as owned by a grantor or other person, continues to report under the tax identification number assigned to the trust prior to the death of that person. See § 1.671-4(a) of this chapter regarding rules for filing the Form 1041, "U.S. Income Tax Return for Estates and Trusts," where only a portion of the trust is treated as owned by one or more persons under subpart E.

(ii) *Furnishing correct taxpayer identification number to payors following the death of the decedent.*—If the trust continues after the death of the decedent and is required to obtain a new taxpayer identification number under paragraph (a)(3)(i)(A) of this section, the trustee must furnish payors with a new Form W-9, "Request for Taxpayer Identification Number and Certification," or an acceptable substitute Form W-9, containing the new taxpayer identification number required under paragraph (a)(3)(i)(A) of this section, the name of the trust, and the address of the trustee.

(4) *Taxpayer identification number to be used by a trust upon termination of a section 645 election.*—(i) *If there is an executor.*—Upon the termination of the section 645 election period, if there is an executor, the trustee of the former electing trust may need to obtain a taxpayer identification number. If § 1.645-1(g) of this chapter regarding the

appointment of an executor after a section 645 election is made applies to the electing trust, the electing trust must obtain a new TIN upon termination of the election period. See the instructions to the Form 1041 for whether a new taxpayer identification number is required for other former electing trusts.

(ii) *If there is no executor.*—Upon termination of the section 645 election period, if there is no executor, the trustee of the former electing trust must obtain a new taxpayer identification number.

(iii) *Requirement to provide taxpayer identification number to payors.*—If the trustee is required to obtain a new taxpayer identification number for a former electing trust pursuant to this paragraph (a)(4), or pursuant to the instructions to the Form 1041, the trustee must furnish all payors of the trust with a completed Form W-9 or acceptable substitute Form W-9 signed under penalties of perjury by the trustee providing each payor with the name of the trust, the new taxpayer identification number, and the address of the trustee.

(5) *Persons treated as payors.*—For purposes of paragraphs (a)(2), (3), and (4) of this section, a *payor* is a person described in §§ 1.671-4(b)(4) of this chapter.

(6) *Effective date.*—Paragraphs (a)(3), (4), and (5) of this section apply to trusts of decedents dying on or after December 24, 2002.

(b) *Requirement to furnish one's own number.*—(1) *U.S. persons.*— Every U.S. person who makes under this title a return, statement, or other document must furnish its own taxpayer identifying number as required by the forms and the accompanying instructions. A U.S. person whose number must be included on a document filed by another person must give the taxpayer identifying number so required to the other person on request. For penalties for failure to supply taxpayer identifying numbers, see sections 6721 through 6724. For provisions dealing specifically with the duty of employees with respect to their social security numbers, see § 31.6011(b)-2(a) and (b) of this chapter (Employment Tax Regulations). For provisions dealing specifically with the duty of employers with respect to employer identification numbers, see § 31.6011(b)-1 of this chapter (Employment Tax Regulations).

(2) *Foreign persons.*—The provisions of paragraph (b)(1) of this section regarding the furnishing of one's own number shall apply to the following foreign persons—

(i) A foreign person that has income effectively connected with the conduct of a U.S. trade or business at any time during the taxable year;

(ii) A foreign person that has a U.S. office or place of business or a U.S. fiscal or paying agent at any time during the taxable year;

(iii) A nonresident alien treated as a resident under section 6013(g) or (h);

(iv) A foreign person that makes a return of tax (including income, estate, and gift tax returns), an amended return, or a refund claim under this title but excluding information returns, statements, or documents;

(v) A foreign person that makes an election under § 301.7701-3(c);

(vi) A foreign person that furnishes a withholding certificate described in § 1.1441-1(e)(2) or (3) of this chapter or § 1.1441-5(c)(2)(iv) or (3)(iii) of this chapter to the extent required under § 1.1441-1(e)(4)(vii) of this chapter;

(vii) A foreign person whose taxpayer identifying number is required to be furnished on any return, statement, or other document as required by the income tax regulations under section 897 or 1445. This paragraph (b)(2)(vii) applies as of November 3, 2003; and

(viii) A foreign person that furnishes a withholding certificate described in § 1.1446-1(c)(2) or (3) of this chapter or whose taxpayer identification number is required to be furnished on any return, statement, or other document as required by the income tax regulations under section 1446. This paragraph (b)(2)(viii) shall apply to partnership taxable years beginning after May 18, 2005, or such earlier time as the regulations under §§ 1.1446-1 through 1.1446-5 of this chapter apply by reason of an election under § 1.1446-7 of this chapter.

(c) *Requirement to furnish another's number.*—Every person required under this title to make a return, statement, or other document must furnish such taxpayer identifying numbers of other U.S. persons and foreign persons that are described in paragraph (b)(2)(i), (ii), (iii), (vi), (vii), or (viii) of this section as required by the forms and the accompanying instructions. The taxpayer identifying number of any person furnishing a withholding certificate referred to in paragraph (b)(2)(vi) or (viii) of this section shall also be furnished if it is actually known to the person making a return, statement, or other document described in this paragraph (c). If the person making the return, statement, or other document does not know the taxpayer identifying number of the other person, and such other person is one that is

described in paragraph (b)(2)(i), (ii), (iii), (vi), (vii), or (viii) of this section, such person must request the other person's number. The request should state that the identifying number is required to be furnished under authority of law. When the person making the return, statement, or other document does not know the number of the other person, and has complied with the request provision of this paragraph (c), such person must sign an affidavit on the transmittal document forwarding such returns, statements, or other documents to the Internal Revenue Service, so stating. A person required to file a taxpayer identifying number shall correct any errors in such filing when such person's attention has been drawn to them. References in this paragraph (c) to paragraph (b)(2)(viii) of this section shall apply to partnership taxable years beginning after May 18, 2005, or such earlier time as the regulations under §§ 1.1446-1 through 1.1446-5 of this chapter apply by reason of an election under § 1.1446-7 of this chapter.

(d) *Obtaining a taxpayer identifying number.*—(1) *Social security number.*—Any individual required to furnish a social security number pursuant to paragraph (b) of this section shall apply for one, if he has not done so previously, on Form SS-5, which may be obtained from any Social Security Administration or Internal Revenue Service office. He shall make such application far enough in advance of the first required use of such number to permit issuance of the number in time for compliance with such requirement. The form, together with any supplementary statement, shall be prepared and filed in accordance with the form, instructions, and regulations applicable thereto, and shall set forth fully and clearly the data therein called for. Individuals who are ineligible for or do not wish to participate in the benefits of the social security program shall nevertheless obtain a social security number if they are required to furnish such a number pursuant to paragraph (b) of this section.

(2) *Employer identification number.*—(i) *In general.*—Any person required to furnish an employer identification number must apply for one, if not done so previously, on Form SS-4. A Form SS-4 may be obtained from any office of the Internal Revenue Service, U.S. consular office abroad, or from an acceptance agent described in paragraph (d)(3)(iv) of this section. The person must make such application far enough in advance of the first required use of the employer identification number to permit issuance of the number in time for compliance with such requirement. The form, together with any supplementary statement, must be prepared and filed in accordance with the form, accompanying instructions, and relevant regulations, and must set forth fully and clearly the requested data.

(ii) *Updating of application information.*—(A) *Requirements.*— Persons issued employer identification numbers in accordance with the application process set forth in paragraph (d)(2)(i) of this section must provide to the Internal Revenue Service any updated application information in the manner and frequency required by forms, instructions, or other appropriate guidance.

(B) *Effective/applicability date.*—Paragraph (d)(2)(ii)(A) of this section applies to all persons possessing an employer identification number on or after January 1, 2014.

(iii) *Special rule for Section 708(b)(1)(B) terminations.*—A new partnership that is formed as a result of the termination of a partnership under section 708(b)(1)(B) will retain the employer identification number of the terminated partnership. This paragraph (d)(2)(iii) applies to terminations of partnerships under section 708(b)(1)(B) occurring on or after May 9, 1997; however, this paragraph (d)(2)(iii) may be applied to terminations occurring on or after May 9, 1996, provided that the partnership and its partners apply this paragraph (d)(2)(iii) to the termination in a consistent manner.

(3) *IRS individual taxpayer identification number.*—(i) *Definition.*— The term *IRS individual taxpayer identification number* means a taxpayer identifying number issued to an alien individual by the Internal Revenue Service, upon application, for use in connection with filing requirements under this title. The term *IRS individual taxpayer identification number* does not refer to a social security number or an account number for use in employment for wages. For purposes of this section, the term *alien individual* means an individual who is not a citizen or national of the United States.

(ii) *General rule for obtaining number.*—Any individual who is not eligible to obtain a social security number and is required to furnish a taxpayer identifying number must apply for an IRS individual taxpayer identification number on Form W-7, Application for IRS Individual Taxpayer Identification Number, or such other form as may be prescribed by the Internal Revenue Service. Form W-7 may be obtained from any office of the Internal Revenue Service, U.S. consular office abroad, or any acceptance agent described in paragraph (d)(3)(iv) of this section. The individual shall furnish the information required by the form and accompanying instructions, including the individual's name, address, foreign tax identification number (if any), and specific reason for obtaining an IRS individual taxpayer identification number. The individual must make such application far enough in advance of the first required use of the IRS individual taxpayer identification number to permit issuance of the number in time for compliance with such requirement. The application form, together with any supplementary statement and documentation, must be prepared and filed in accordance with the form, accompanying instructions, and relevant regulations, and must set forth fully and clearly the requested data.

(iii) *General rule for assigning number.*—Under procedures issued by the Internal Revenue Service, an IRS individual taxpayer identification number will be assigned to an individual upon the basis of information reported on Form W-7 (or/such other form as may be prescribed by the Internal Revenue Service) and any such accompanying documentation that may be required by the Internal Revenue Service. An applicant for an IRS individual taxpayer identification number must submit such documentary evidence as the Internal Revenue Service may prescribe in order to establish alien status and identity. Examples of acceptable documentary evidence for this purpose may include items such as an original (or a certified copy of the original) passport, driver's license, birth certificate, identity card, or immigration documentation.

(iv) *Acceptance agents.*—(A) *Agreements with acceptance agents.*—A person described in paragraph (d)(3)(iv)(B) of this section will be accepted by the Internal Revenue Service to act as an acceptance agent for purposes of the regulations under this section upon entering into an agreement with the Internal Revenue Service, under which the acceptance agent will be authorized to act on behalf of taxpayers seeking to obtain a taxpayer identifying number from the Internal Revenue Service. The agreement must contain such terms and conditions as are necessary to insure proper administration of the process by which the Internal Revenue Service issues taxpayer identifying numbers to foreign persons, including proof of their identity and foreign status. In particular, the agreement may contain—

(1) Procedures for providing Form SS-4 and Form W-7, or such other necessary form to applicants for obtaining a taxpayer identifying number;

(2) Procedures for providing assistance to applicants in completing the application form or completing it for them;

(3) Procedures for collecting, reviewing, and maintaining, in the normal course of business, a record of the required documentation for assignment of a taxpayer identifying number;

(4) Procedures for submitting the application form and required documentation to the Internal Revenue Service, or if permitted under the agreement, submitting the application form together with a certification that the acceptance agent has reviewed the required documentation and that it has no actual knowledge or reason to know that the documentation is not complete or accurate;

(5) Procedures for assisting taxpayers with notification procedures described in paragraph (g)(2) of this section in the event of change of foreign status;

(6) Procedures for making all documentation or other records furnished by persons applying for a taxpayer identifying number promptly available for review by the Internal Revenue Service, upon request; and

(7) Provisions that the agreement may be terminated in the event of a material failure to comply with the agreement, including failure to exercise due diligence under the agreement.

(B) *Persons who may be acceptance agents.*—An acceptance agent may include any financial institution as defined in section 265(b)(5) or §1.165-12(c)(1)(v) of this chapter, any college or university that is an educational organization as defined in §1.501(c)(3)-1(d)(3)(i) of this chapter, any federal agency as defined in section 6402(f) or any other person or categories of persons that may be authorized by regulations or Internal Revenue Service procedures. A person described in this paragraph (d)(3)(iv)(B) that seeks to qualify as an acceptance agent must have an employer identification number for use in any communication with the Internal Revenue Service. In addition, it must establish to the satisfaction of the Internal Revenue Service that it has adequate resources and procedures in place to comply with the terms of the agreement described in paragraph (d)(3)(iv)(A) of this section.

(4) *Coordination of taxpayer identifying numbers.*—(i) *Social security number.*—Any individual who is duly assigned a social security number or who is entitled to a social security number will not be issued an IRS individual taxpayer identification number. The individual can use the social security number for all tax purposes under this title, even though the individual is, or later becomes, a nonresident alien individual. Further, any individual who has an application pending with the Social Security Administration will be issued an

IRS individual taxpayer identification number only after the Social Security Administration has notified the individual that a social security number cannot be issued. Any alien individual duly issued an IRS individual taxpayer identification number who later becomes a U.S. citizen, or an alien lawfully permitted to enter the United States either for permanent residence or under authority of law permitting U.S. employment, will be required to obtain a social security number. Any individual who has an IRS individual taxpayer identification number and a social security number, due to the circumstances described in the preceding sentence, must notify the Internal Revenue Service of the acquisition of the social security number and must use the newly-issued social security number as the taxpayer identifying number on all future returns, statements, or other documents filed under this title.

(ii) *Employer identification number.*—Any individual with both a social security number (or an IRS individual taxpayer identification number) and an employer identification number may use the social security number (or the IRS individual taxpayer identification number) for individual taxes, and the employer identification number for business taxes as required by returns, statements, and other documents and their related instructions. Any alien individual duly assigned an IRS individual taxpayer identification number who also is required to obtain an employer identification number must furnish the previously-assigned IRS individual taxpayer identification number to the Internal Revenue Service on Form SS-4 at the time of application for the employer identification number. Similarly, where an alien individual has an employer identification number and is required to obtain an IRS individual taxpayer identification number, the Individual must furnish the previously-assigned employer identification number to the Internal Revenue Service on Form W-7, or such other form as may be prescribed by the Internal Revenue Service, at the time of application for the IRS individual taxpayer identification number.

(e) *Banks, and brokers and dealers in securities.*—For additional requirements relating to deposits, share accounts, and brokerage accounts, see 31 CFR 103.34 and 103.35.

(f) *Penalty.*—For penalties for failure to supply taxpayer identifying numbers, see sections 6721 through 6724.

(g) *Special rules for taxpayer identifying numbers issued to foreign persons.*—(1) *General rule.*—(i) *Social security number.*—A social security number is generally identified in the records and database of the Internal Revenue Service as a number belonging to a U.S. citizen or resident alien individual. A person may establish a different status for the number by providing proof of foreign status with the Internal Revenue Service under such procedures as the Internal Revenue Service shall prescribe, including the use of a form as the Internal Revenue Service may specify. Upon accepting an individual as a nonresident alien individual, the Internal Revenue Service will assign this status to the individuals social security number.

(ii) *Employer identification number.*—An employer identification number is generally identified in the records and database of the Internal Revenue Service as a number belonging to a U.S. person. However, the Internal Revenue Service may establish a separate class of employer identification numbers solely dedicated to foreign persons which will be identified as such in the records and database of the Internal Revenue Service. A person may establish a different status for the number either at the time of application or subsequently by providing proof of U.S. or foreign status with the Internal Revenue Service under such procedures as the Internal Revenue Service shall prescribe, including the use of a form as the Internal Revenue Service may specify. The Internal Revenue Service may require a person to apply for the type of employer identification number that reflects the status of that person as a U.S. or foreign person.

(iii) *IRS individual taxpayer identification number.*—An IRS individual taxpayer identification number is generally identified in the records and database of the Internal Revenue Service as a number belonging to a nonresident alien individual. If the Internal Revenue Service determines at the time of application or subsequently, that an individual is not a nonresident alien individual, the Internal Revenue Service may require that the individual apply for a social security number. If a social security number is not available, the Internal Revenue Service may accept that the individual use an IRS individual taxpayer identification number, which the Internal Revenue Service will identify as a number belonging to a U.S. resident alien.

(2) *Change of foreign status.*—Once a taxpayer identifying number is identified in the records and database of the Internal Revenue Service as a number belonging to a U.S. or foreign person, the status of the number is permanent until the circumstances of the taxpayer change. A taxpayer whose status changes (for example, a nonresident

alien individual with a social security number becomes a U.S. resident alien) must notify the Internal Revenue Service of the change of status under such procedures as the Internal Revenue Service shall prescribe, including the use of a form as the Internal Revenue Service may specify.

(3) *Waiver of prohibition to disclose taxpayer information when acceptance agent acts.*—As part of its request for an IRS individual taxpayer identification number or submission of proof of foreign status with respect to any taxpayer identifying number, where the foreign person acts through an acceptance agent, the foreign person will agree to waive the limitations in section 6103 regarding the disclosure of certain taxpayer information. However, the waiver will apply only for purposes of permitting the Internal Revenue Service and the acceptance agent to communicate with each other regarding matters related to the assignment of a taxpayer identifying number, including disclosure of any taxpayer identifying number previously issued to the foreign person, and change of foreign status. This paragraph (g)(3) applies to payments made after December 31, 2001.

(h) *Special rules for certain entities under § 301.7701-3.*—(1) *General rule.*—Any entity that has an employer identification number (EIN) will retain that EIN if its federal tax classification changes under § 301.7701-3.

(2) *Special rules for entities that are disregarded as entities separate from their owners.*—(i) *When an entity becomes disregarded as an entity separate from its owner.*—Except as otherwise provided in regulations or other guidance, a single owner entity that is disregarded as an entity separate from its owner under § 301.7701-3, must use its owner's taxpayer identifying number (TIN) for federal tax purposes.

(ii) *When an entity that was disregarded as an entity separate from its owner becomes recognized as a separate entity.*—If a single owner entity's classification changes so that it is recognized as a separate entity for federal tax purposes, and that entity had an EIN, then the entity must use that EIN and not the TIN of the single owner. If the entity did not already have its own EIN, then the entity must acquire an EIN and not use the TIN of the single owner.

(3) *Effective date.*—The rules of this paragraph (h) are applicable as of January 1, 1997.

(i) *Special rule for qualified subchapter S subsidiaries (Qsubs).*—(1) *General rule.*—Any entity that has an employer identification number (EIN) will retain that EIN if a QSub election is made for the entity under § 1.1361-3 or if a QSub election that was in effect for the entity terminates under § 1.1361-5.

(2) *EIN while QSub election in effect.*—Except as otherwise provided in regulations or other published guidance, a QSub must use the parent S corporation's EIN for Federal tax purposes.

(3) *EIN when QSub election terminates.*—If an entity's QSub election terminates, it may not use the EIN of the parent S corporation after the termination. If the entity had an EIN prior to becoming a QSub or obtained an EIN while it was a QSub in accordance with regulations or other published guidance, the entity must use that EIN. If the entity had no EIN, it must obtain an EIN upon termination of the QSub election.

(4) *Effective date.*—The rules of this paragraph (i) apply on January 20, 2000.

(j) *Effective date.*—(1) *General rule.*—Except as otherwise provided in this paragraph (j), the provisions of this section are generally effective for information that must be furnished after April 15, 1974. However, the provisions relating to IRS individual taxpayer identification numbers apply on and after May 29, 1996. An application for an IRS individual taxpayer identification number (Form W-7) may be filed at any time on or after July 1, 1996.

(2) *Special rules.*—(i) *Employer identification number of an estate.*—The requirement under paragraph (a)(1)(ii)(C) of this section that an estate obtain an employer identification number applies on and after January 1, 1984.

(ii) *Taxpayer identifying numbers of certain foreign persons.*—The requirement under paragraph (b)(2)(iv) of this section that certain foreign persons furnish a TIN on a return of tax is effective for tax returns filed after December 31, 1996.

(iii) Paragraphs (a)(1)(i), (a)(1)(ii) introductory text, (a)(1)(ii)(A), and (a)(1)(ii)(B) of this section apply to income tax returns due (without regard to extensions) on or after April 15, 1998. [Reg. § 301.6109-1.]

☐ [*T.D. 6606*, 8-24-62. *Amended by T.D. 7306*, 3-14-74; *T.D. 7670*, 1-30-80; *T.D. 7796*, 11-23-81; *T.D. 8633*, 12-20-95; *T.D. 8637*, 12-20-95; *T.D. 8671*, 5-23-96; *T.D. 8697*, 12-17-96; *T.D. 8717*, 5-8-97; *T.D. 8734*, 10-6-97 (*T.D. 8804* delayed the effective date of *T.D. 8734* from

January 1, 1999, to January 1, 2000; *T.D. 8856* further delayed the effective date of *T.D. 8734* until January 1, 2001); *T.D. 8739*, 11-21-97; *T.D. 8839*, 9-21-99; *T.D. 8844*, 11-26-99; *T.D. 8869*, 1-20-2000; *T.D. 8977*, 1-16-2002; *T.D. 9023*, 11-21-2002; *T.D. 9032*, 12-23-2002; *T.D. 9082*, 8-4-2003; *T.D. 9200*, 5-13-2005; *T.D. 9241*, 1-23-2006 *and T.D. 9617*, 5-3-2013.]

### [Reg. § 40.6109(a)-1]

**§ 40.6109(a)-1. Identifying numbers.**—Every person required under § 40.6011(a)-1 to make a return must provide the identifying number required by the instructions applicable to the form on which the return is made. [Reg. § 40.6109(a)-1.]

☐ [*T.D. 8442*, 10-21-92. *Amended by T.D. 8963*, 8-8-2001.]

### [Reg. § 1.6109-2]

**§ 1.6109-2. Tax return preparers furnishing identifying numbers for returns or claims for refund and related requirements.**—(a) *Furnishing identifying number.*—(1) Each filed return of tax or claim for refund of tax under the Internal Revenue Code prepared by one or more tax return preparers must include the identifying number of the tax return preparer required by § 1.6695-1(b) to sign the return or claim for refund. In addition, if there is an employment arrangement or association between the individual tax return preparer and another person (except to the extent the return prepared is for the person), the identifying number of the other person must also appear on the filed return or claim for refund. For the definition of the term "tax return preparer," see section 7701(a)(36) and § 301.7701-15 of this chapter.

(2)(i) For tax returns or claims for refund filed on or before December 31, 2010, the identifying number of an individual tax return preparer is that individual's social security number or such alternative number as may be prescribed by the Internal Revenue Service in forms, instructions, or other appropriate guidance.

(ii) For tax returns or claims for refund filed after December 31, 2010, the identifying number of a tax return preparer is the individual's preparer tax identification number or such other number prescribed by the Internal Revenue Service in forms, instructions, or other appropriate guidance.

(3) The identifying number of a person (whether an individual or entity) who employs or associates with an individual tax return preparer described in paragraph (a)(2) of this section to prepare the return or claim for refund (other than a return prepared for the person) is the person's employer identification number.

(b) and (c) [Reserved]. For further guidance, see § 1.6109-2A(b) and (c).

(d) Beginning after December 31, 2010, all tax return preparers must have a preparer tax identification number or other prescribed identifying number that was applied for and received at the time and in the manner, including the payment of a user fee, as may be prescribed by the Internal Revenue Service in forms, instructions, or other appropriate guidance. Except as provided in paragraph (h) of this section, beginning after December 31, 2010, to obtain a preparer tax identification number or other prescribed identifying number, a tax return preparer must be an attorney, certified public accountant, enrolled agent, or registered tax return preparer authorized to practice before the Internal Revenue Service under 31 U.S.C. 330 and the regulations thereunder.

(e) The Internal Revenue Service may designate an expiration date for any preparer tax identification number or other prescribed identifying number and may further prescribe the time and manner for renewing a preparer tax identification number or other prescribed identifying number, including the payment of a user fee, as set forth in forms, instructions, or other appropriate guidance. The Internal Revenue Service may provide that any identifying number issued by the Internal Revenue Service prior to the effective date of this regulation will expire on December 31, 2010, unless properly renewed as set forth in forms, instructions, or other appropriate guidance, including these regulations.

(f) As may be prescribed in forms, instructions, or other appropriate guidance, the IRS may conduct a Federal tax compliance check on a tax return preparer who applies for or renews a preparer tax identification number or other prescribed identifying number.

(g) Only for purposes of paragraphs (d), (e), and (f) of this section, the term *tax return preparer* means any individual who is compensated for preparing, or assisting in the preparation of, all or substantially all of a tax return or claim for refund of tax. Factors to consider in determining whether an individual is a tax return preparer under this paragraph (g) include, but are not limited to, the complexity of the work performed by the individual relative to the overall complexity of the tax return or claim for refund of tax; the amount of the items of income, deductions, or losses attributable to the work performed by the individual relative to the total amount of income, deductions, or losses required to be correctly reported on the tax return or claim for refund of tax; and the amount of tax or credit attributable to the work performed by the individual relative to the total tax liability required to be correctly reported on the tax return or claim for refund of tax. The preparation of a form, statement, or schedule, such as Schedule EIC (Form 1040), "Earned Income Credit," may constitute the preparation of all or substantially all of a tax return or claim for refund based on the application of the foregoing factors. A tax return preparer does not include an individual who is not otherwise a tax return preparer as that term is defined in § 301.7701-15(b)(2), or who is an individual described in § 301.7701-15(f). The provisions of this paragraph (g) are illustrated by the following examples:

*Example 1.* Employee A, an individual employed by Tax Return Preparer B, assists Tax Return Preparer B in answering telephone calls, making copies, inputting client tax information gathered by B into the data fields of tax preparation software on a computer, and using the computer to file electronic returns of tax prepared by B. Although Employee A must exercise judgment regarding which data fields in the tax preparation software to use, A does not exercise any discretion or independent judgment as to the clients' underlying tax positions. Employee A, therefore, merely provides clerical assistance or incidental services and is not a tax return preparer required to apply for a PTIN or other identifying number as the Internal Revenue Service may prescribe in forms, instructions, or other appropriate guidance.

*Example 2.* The facts are the same as in *Example 1*, except that Employee A also interviews B's clients and obtains from them information needed for the preparation of tax returns. Employee A determines the amount and character of entries on the returns and whether the information provided is sufficient for purposes of preparing the returns. For at least some of B's clients, A obtains information and makes determinations that constitute all or substantially all of the tax return. Employee A is a tax return preparer required to apply for a PTIN or other identifying number as the Internal Revenue Service may prescribe in forms, instructions, or other appropriate guidance. Employee A is a tax return preparer even if Employee A relies on tax preparation software to prepare the return.

*Example 3.* C is an employee of a firm that prepares tax returns and claims for refund of tax for compensation. C is responsible for preparing a Form 1040, "U.S. Individual Income Tax Return," for a client. C obtains the information necessary for the preparation of the tax return during a meeting with the client, and makes determinations with respect to the proper application of the tax laws to the information in order to determine the client's tax liability. C completes the tax return and sends the completed return to employee D, who reviews the return for accuracy before signing it. Both C and D are tax return preparers required to apply for a PTIN or other identifying number as the Internal Revenue Service may prescribe in forms, instructions, or other appropriate guidance.

*Example 4.* E is an employee at a firm which prepares tax returns and claims for refund of tax for compensation. The firm is engaged by a corporation to prepare its Federal income tax return on Form 1120, "U.S. Corporation Income Tax Return." Among the documentation that the corporation provides to E in connection with the preparation of the tax return is documentation relating to the corporation's potential eligibility to claim a recently enacted tax credit for the taxable year. In preparing the return, and specifically for purposes of the new tax credit, E (with the corporation's consent) obtains advice from F, a subject matter expert on this and similar credits. F advises E as to the corporation's entitlement to the credit and provides his calculation of the amount of the credit. Based on this advice from F, E prepares the corporation's Form 1120 claiming the tax credit in the amount recommended by F. The additional credit is one of many tax credits and deductions claimed on the tax return, and determining the credit amount does not constitute preparation of all or substantially all of the corporation's tax return under this paragraph (g). F will not be considered to have prepared all or substantially all of the corporation's tax return, and F is not a tax return preparer required to apply for a PTIN or other identifying number as the Internal Revenue Service may prescribe in forms, instructions, or other appropriate guidance. The analysis is the same whether or not the tax credit is a substantial portion of the return under § 301.7701-15 of this chapter (as opposed to substantially all of the return), and whether or not F is in the same firm with E. E is a tax return preparer required to apply for a PTIN or other identifying number as the Internal Revenue Service may prescribe in forms, instructions, or other appropriate guidance.

(h) The Internal Revenue Service, through forms, instructions, or other appropriate guidance, may prescribe exceptions to the requirements of this section, including the requirement that an individual be authorized to practice before the Internal Revenue Service before receiving a preparer tax identification number or other prescribed identifying number, as necessary in the interest of effective tax administration. The Internal Revenue Service, through other appropriate guidance, may also specify specific returns, schedules, and other forms that qualify as tax returns or claims for refund for purposes of these regulations.

(i) *Effective/applicability date.*—Paragraph (a)(1) of this section is applicable to tax returns and claims for refund filed after December 31, 2008. Paragraph (a)(2)(i) of this section is applicable to tax returns and claims for refund filed on or before December 31, 2010. Paragraph (a)(2)(ii) of this section is applicable to tax returns and claims for refund filed after December 31, 2010. Paragraph (d) of this section is applicable to tax return preparers after December 31, 2010. Paragraphs (e) through (h) of this section are effective after September 30, 2010. [Reg. § 1.6109-2.]

☐ [*T.D.* 9014, 8-12-2002. *Amended by T.D.* 9436, 12-15-2008 *and T.D.* 9501, 9-28-2010.]

### [Reg. § 1.6109-2A]

**§ 1.6109-2A. Furnishing identifying number of income tax return preparer.**—(a) *Furnishing identifying number.*—For returns or claims for refund filed prior to January 1, 2000, each return of tax under subtitle A of the Internal Revenue Code or claim for refund of tax under subtitle A of the Internal Revenue Code prepared by one or more income tax return preparers must bear the identifying number of the preparer required by § 1.6695-1(b) to sign the return or claim for refund. In addition, if there is a partnership or employment arrangement between two or more preparers, the identifying number of the partnership or the person who employs (or engages) one or more other persons to prepare for compensation the return or claim for refund shall also appear on the return or claim for refund. If the preparer is—

(1) An individual (not described in subparagraph (2) of this paragraph (a)) who is a citizen or resident of the United States, such preparer's social security account number shall be affixed; and

(2) A person (whether an individual, corporation, or partnership) who employs (or engages) one or more persons to prepare the return or claim for refund (other than for the person), or who is not a citizen or resident of the United States and also is not employed or engaged by another preparer, such preparer's employer identification number shall be affixed.

For the definition of the term "income tax return preparer" (or "preparer") see section 7701(a)(36) and § 301.7701-15.

(b) *Furnishing address.*—(1) Each return or claim for refund which is prepared by one or more income tax return preparers shall bear the street address, city, State, and postal ZIP code of that preparer's place of business where the preparation of the return or claim for refund was completed. However, if this place of business is not maintained on a year-round basis, the return or claim for refund shall bear the street address, city, State, and postal ZIP code of such preparer's principal office or business location which is maintained on a year-round basis, or, if none, that preparer's residence.

(2) For purposes of satisfying the requirement of the first sentence of paragraph (b)(1) of this section, an income tax return preparer may, on returns and claims for refund, disclose only the postal ZIP code of the described place of business as a satisfactory address, but only if the preparer first by written notice advises each affected Internal Revenue Service Center that he intends to follow this practice.

(c) *Penalty.*—For the civil penalty for failure to furnish an identifying number as required under paragraph (a) of this section, see section 6695(c) and § 1.6695-1(c).

(d) *Effective date.*—Paragraph (a) of this section and this paragraph (d) apply to returns or claims for refund filed prior to January 1, 2000. For returns or claims for refund filed after December 31, 1999, see § 1.6109-2(a). [Reg. § 1.6109-2A.]

☐ [*T.D.* 7519, 11-17-77. *Amended by T.D.* 8835, 8-11-99. *Redesignated and amended by T.D.* 9014, 8-12-2002.]

### [Reg. § 31.6109-2]

**§ 31.6109-2. Tax return preparers furnishing identifying numbers for returns or claims for refund.**—(a) *In general.*—Each employment tax return or claim for refund of employment tax under chapters 21 through 25 of subtitle C of the Internal Revenue Code prepared by one or more signing tax return preparers must include the identifying number of the preparer required by § 1.6695-1(b) of this chapter to sign the return or claim for refund in the manner stated in § 1.6109-2 of this chapter.

(b) *Effective/applicability date.*—Paragraph (a) of this section is applicable to returns and claims for refund filed after December 31, 2008. [Reg. § 31.6109-2.]

☐ [*T.D.* 9436, 12-15-2008.]

[Reg. §41.6109-2]

**§41.6109-2. Tax return preparers furnishing identifying numbers for returns or claims for refund filed after December 31, 2008.—**
(a) *In general.*—Each excise tax return or claim for refund under section 4481 prepared by one or more signing tax return preparers must include the identifying number of the preparer required by §1.6695-1(b) of this chapter to sign the return or claim for refund in the manner stated in §1.6109-2 of this chapter.

(b) *Effective/applicability date.*—This section is applicable for returns and claims for refund filed after December 31, 2008. [Reg. §41.6109-2.]

□ [*T.D. 9436, 12-15-2008.*]

[Reg. §301.6109-2]

**§301.6109-2. Authority of the Secretary of Agriculture to collect employer identification numbers for purposes of the Food Stamp Act of 1977.—**(a) *In general.*—The Secretary of Agriculture may require each applicant retail food store or wholesale food concern to furnish its employer identification number in connection with the administration of section 9 of the Food Stamp Act of 1977 (7 U.S.C. 2018) (relating to the determination of the qualifications of applicants under the Food Stamp Act).

(b) *Limited purpose.*—The Secretary of Agriculture may have access to the employer identification numbers obtained pursuant to paragraph (a) of this section, but only for the purpose of establishing and maintaining a list of the names and employer identification numbers of the stores and concerns for use in determining those applicants who have been previously sanctioned or convicted under section 12 or 15 of the Food Stamp Act of 1977 (7 U.S.C. 2021 or 2024). The Secretary of Agriculture may use this determination of sanctions and convictions in administering section 9 of the Food Stamp Act of 1977.

(c) *Sharing of information.*—(1) *Sharing permitted with certain United States agencies and instrumentalities.*—The Secretary of Agriculture may share the information contained in the list described in paragraph (b) of this section with any other agency or instrumentality of the United States that otherwise has access to employer identification numbers, but only to the extent the Secretary of Agriculture determines sharing such information will assist in verifying and matching that information against information maintained by the other agency or instrumentality.

(2) *Restrictions on the use of shared information.*—The information shared by the Secretary of Agriculture pursuant to this section may be used by any other agency or instrumentality of the United States only for the purpose of effective administration and enforcement of the Food Stamp Act of 1977 or for the purpose of investigation of violations of other Federal laws or enforcement of those laws.

(d) *Safeguards.*—(1) *Restrictions on access to employer identification numbers by individuals.*—(i) *Numbers maintained by the Secretary of Agriculture.*—The individuals who are permitted access to employer identification numbers obtained pursuant to paragraph (a) of this section and maintained by the Secretary of Agriculture are officers and employees of the United States whose duties or responsibilities require access to such employer identification numbers for the purpose of effective administration or enforcement of the Food Stamp Act of 1977 or for the purpose of sharing the information in accordance with paragraph (c) of this section.

(ii) *Numbers maintained by any other agency or instrumentality.*—The individuals who are permitted access to employer identification numbers obtained pursuant to paragraph (c) of this section and maintained by any agency or instrumentality of the United States other than the Department of Agriculture are officers and employees of the United States whose duties or responsibilities require access to such employer identification numbers for the purpose of effective administration and enforcement of the Food Stamp Act of 1977 or for the purpose of investigation of violations of other Federal laws or enforcement of those laws.

(2) *Other safeguards.*—The Secretary of Agriculture, and the head of any other agency or instrumentality referred to in paragraph (c) of this section, must provide for any additional safeguards that the Secretary of the Treasury determines to be necessary or appropriate to protect the confidentiality of the employer identification numbers. The Secretary of Agriculture, and the head of any other agency or instrumentality referred to in paragraph (c) of this section, may also provide for any additional safeguards to protect the confidentiality of employer identification numbers, provided these safeguards are consistent with safeguards determined by the Secretary of the Treasury to be necessary or appropriate.

(e) *Confidentiality and disclosure of employer identification numbers.*—Employer identification numbers obtained pursuant to paragraph (a) or (c) of this section are confidential. No officer or employee of the United States who has or had access to any such employer identification number may disclose that number in any manner to an individual not described in paragraph (d) of this section. For purposes of this paragraph (e), *officer or employee* includes a former officer or employee.

(f) *Sanctions.*—(1) *Unauthorized, willful disclosure of employer identification numbers.*—Sections 7213(a)(1), (2), and (3) apply with respect to the unauthorized, willful disclosure to any person of employer identification numbers that are maintained pursuant to this section by the Secretary of Agriculture, or any other agency or instrumentality with which information is shared pursuant to paragraph (c) of this section, in the same manner and to the same extent as sections 7213(a)(1), (2), and (3) apply with respect to unauthorized disclosures of returns and return information described in those sections.

(2) *Willful solicitation of employer identification numbers.*—Section 7213(a)(4) applies with respect to the willful offer of any item of material value in exchange for any employer identification number maintained pursuant to this section by the Secretary of Agriculture, or any other agency or instrumentality with which information is shared pursuant to paragraph (c) of this section, in the same manner and to the same extent as section 7213(a)(4) applies with respect to offers (in exchange for any return or return information) described in that section.

(g) *Delegation.*—All references in this section to the Secretary of Agriculture are references to the Secretary of Agriculture or his or her delegate.

(h) *Effective date.*—Except as provided in the following sentence, this section is effective on February 1, 1992. Any provisions relating to the sharing of information by the Secretary of Agriculture with any other agency or instrumentality of the United States are effective on August 15, 1994. [Reg. §301.6109-2.]

□ [*T.D. 8369, 9-30-91. Amended by T.D. 8621, 10-2-95.*]

[Reg. §301.6109-3]

**§301.6109-3. IRS adoption taxpayer identification numbers.—**
(a) *In general.*—(1) *Definition.*—An *IRS adoption taxpayer identification number*(ATIN) is a temporary taxpayer identifying number assigned by the Internal Revenue Service (IRS) to a child (other than an alien individual as defined in §301.6109-1(d)(3)(i)) who has been placed, by an authorized placement agency, in the household of a prospective adoptive parent for legal adoption. An ATIN is assigned to the child upon application for use in connection with filing requirements under the Internal Revenue Code and the regulations thereunder. When an adoption becomes final, the adoptive parent must apply for a social security number for the child. After the social security number is assigned, that number, rather than the ATIN, must be used as the child's taxpayer identification number on all returns, statements, or other documents required under the Internal Revenue Code and the regulations thereunder.

(2) *Expiration and extension.*—An ATIN automatically expires two years after the number is assigned. However, upon request, the IRS may grant an extension if the IRS determines the extension is warranted.

(b) *Definitions.*—For purposes of this section—

(1) *Authorized placement agency.*—has the same meaning as in §1.152-2(c) of this chapter;

(2) *Prospective adoptive child.*—or *child* means a child who has not been adopted, but who has been placed in the household of a prospective adoptive parent for legal adoption by an authorized placement agency; and

(3) *Prospective adoptive parent.*—or *parent* means an individual in whose household a prospective adoptive child is placed by an authorized placement agency for legal adoption.

(c) *General rule for obtaining a number.*—(1) *Who may apply.*—A prospective adoptive parent may apply for an ATIN for a child if—

(i) The prospective adoptive parent is eligible to claim a personal exemption under section 151 with respect to the child;

(ii) An authorized placement agency places the child with the prospective adoptive parent for legal adoption;

(iii) The Social Security Administration will not process an application for an SSN by the prospective adoptive parent on behalf of the child (for example, because the adoption is not final); and

(iv) The prospective adoptive parent has used all reasonable means to obtain the child's assigned social security number, if any, but has been unsuccessful in obtaining this number (for example, because the biological parent who obtained the number is not legally required to disclose the number to the prospective adoptive parent).

(2) *Procedure for obtaining an ATIN.*—If the requirements of paragraph (c)(1) of this section are satisfied, the prospective adoptive parent may apply for an ATIN for a child on Form W-7A, *Application for Taxpayer Identification Number for Pending Adoptions* (or such other form as may be prescribed by the IRS). An application for an ATIN should be made far enough in advance of the first intended use of the ATIN to permit issuance of the ATIN in time for such use. An application for an ATIN must include the information required by the form and accompanying instructions, including the name and address of each prospective adoptive parent and the child's name and date of birth. In addition, the application must include such documentary evidence as the IRS may prescribe to establish that a child was placed in the prospective adoptive parent's household by an authorized placement agency for legal adoption. Examples of acceptable documentary evidence establishing placement for legal adoption by an authorized placement agency may include—

(i) A copy of a placement agreement entered into between the prospective adoptive parent and an authorized placement agency;

(ii) An affidavit or letter signed by the adoption attorney or government official who placed the child for legal adoption pursuant to state law;

(iii) A document authorizing the release of a newborn child from a hospital to a prospective adoptive parent for adoption; and

(iv) A court document ordering or approving the placement of a child for adoption.

(d) *Effective date.*—The provisions of this section apply to income tax returns due (without regard to extension) on or after April 15, 1998. [Reg. § 301.6109-3.]

☐ [*T.D.* 8839, 9-21-99.]

### [Reg. § 301.6109-4]

**§ 301.6109-4. IRS truncated taxpayer identification numbers.**—(a) *In general—Definition.*—An IRS truncated taxpayer identification number (TTIN) is an individual's social security number (SSN), IRS individual taxpayer identification number (ITIN), IRS adoption taxpayer identification number (ATIN), or IRS employer identification number (EIN) in which the first five digits of the nine-digit number are replaced with Xs or asterisks. The TTIN takes the same format of the identifying number it replaces, for example XXX-XX-1234 when replacing an SSN, or XX-XXX1234 when replacing an EIN.

(b) *Use of a TTIN.*—(1) *In general.*—Except as provided in paragraph (b)(2) of this section, a TTIN may be used to identify any person on any statement or other document that the internal revenue laws require to be furnished to another person. Use of a TTIN is permissive and not mandatory. Use of a TTIN as permitted by this section will not result in application of any penalty for failure to include a correct taxpayer identifying number on any payee statement or other document. For example, the section 6722 penalty for failure to timely furnish a correct statement would not apply solely because the payor used a TTIN as permitted by this section.

(2) *TTIN not permitted.*—Use of a TTIN is not permitted in the following circumstances:

(i) A TTIN may not be used on a statement or other document if such use is prohibited by statute, regulation, other guidance published in the Internal Revenue Bulletin, form, or instructions.

(ii) A TTIN may not be used on a statement or document if a statute, regulation, other guidance published in the Internal Revenue Bulletin, form, or instructions, specifically requires use of an SSN, ITIN, ATIN, or EIN and does not specifically state that the taxpayer identifying number may be truncated. For example, a TTIN may not be used on a Form W-8ECI or Form W-8IMY because the forms and/or form instructions specifically prescribe use of an SSN, EIN, or ITIN for the U.S. taxpayer identification number.

(iii) A TTIN may not be used on any return, statement, or other document that is required to be filed with or furnished to the Internal Revenue Service or the Social Security Administration in the case of forms required to be filed with the Social Security Administration under the internal revenue laws.

(iv) A person may not truncate its own taxpayer identifying number on any statement or other document that it furnishes to another person. For example, an employer may not truncate its EIN on a Form W-2, Wage and Tax Statement, that the employer furnishes to an employee; and a person may not truncate its TIN on a Form W-9, Request for Taxpayer Identification Number and Certification.

(3) *Examples.*—The provisions of this paragraph (b) are illustrated by the following examples:

(i) *Example 1.* Pursuant to section 6051(d) and § 31.6051-2(a) of this chapter, Employer files the Social Security Administration copy of Employee's Form W-2, Wage and Tax Statement, with the Social Security Administration. Employer may not truncate any identifying number on the Social Security Administration copy. Pursuant to section 6051(a) and § 31.6051-1(a)(1)(i) of this chapter, Employer furnishes copies of Forms W-2 to Employee. There are no applicable statutes, regulations, other published guidance, forms, or instructions that prohibit use of a TTIN on Form W-2, and § 31.6051-1(a)(1)(i) specifically permits truncating employees' SSNs. Accordingly, Employer may truncate Employee's SSN to appear in the form of a TTIN on copies of Forms W-2 furnished to Employee. Employer may not truncate its own EIN on copies of Forms W-2 furnished to Employee.

(ii) *Example 2.* On April 5, year 1, Donor contributes a used car with a blue book value of $1,100 to Charitable Organization. On April 20, year 1, Charitable Organization sends Donor copies B and C of the Form 1098-C as a contemporaneous written acknowledgement of the $1,100 contribution as required by section 170(f)(12). In late-February, year 2, Charitable Organization prepares and files copy A of Form 1098-C with the IRS, reporting Donor's donation of a qualified vehicle in year 1. Charitable Organization may truncate Donor's SSN to appear in the form of a TTIN in the Donor's Identification Number box on copies B and C of the Form 1098-C because copies B and C of the Form 1098-C are documents required by the Internal Revenue Code and regulations to be furnished to another person; there are no applicable statutes, regulations, other published guidance, forms or instructions that prohibit the use of a TTIN on those copies; and there are no applicable statutes, regulations, other published guidance, forms, or instructions that specifically require use of an SSN or other identifying number on those copies. Charitable Organization may not truncate its own EIN on copies B and C of the Form 1098-C because a person cannot truncate its own taxpayer identifying number on any statement or other document the person furnishes to another person. Charitable Organization may not truncate any identifying number on copy A of the Form 1098-C because copy A is required to be filed with the IRS.

(c) *Applicability date.*—This section is applicable to returns, statements, and other documents required to be filed or furnished after December 31, 2020. [Reg. § 301.6109-4.]

☐ [*T.D.* 9675, 7-14-2014. *Amended by T.D.* 9861, 7-2-2019.]

### [Reg. § 301.6110-1]

**§ 301.6110-1. Public inspection of written determinations and background file documents.**—(a) *General rule.*—Except as provided in § 301.6110-3, relating to deletion of certain information, § 301.6110-5(b), relating to actions to restrain disclosure, paragraph (b)(2) of this section, relating to technical advice memoranda involving civil fraud and criminal investigations, and jeopardy and termination assessments, and paragraph (b)(3) of this section, relating to general written determinations relating to accounting or funding periods and methods, the text of any written determination (as defined in § 301.6110-2(a)) issued pursuant to a request postmarked or hand delivered after October 31, 1976, shall be open to public inspection in the places provided in paragraph (c)(1) of this section. The text of any written determination issued pursuant to a request postmarked or hand delivered before November 1, 1976, shall be open to public inspection pursuant to section 6110(h) and § 301.6110-6, when funds are appropriated by Congress for such purpose. The procedures and rules set forth in §§ 301.6110-1 through 301.6110-5 and § 301.6110-7 do not apply to written determinations issued pursuant to requests postmarked or hand delivered before November 1, 1976, unless § 301.6110-6 states otherwise. There shall also be open to public inspection in each place of public inspection an index to the written determinations subject to inspection at such place. Each such index shall be arranged by section of the Internal Revenue Code, related statute or tax treaty and by subject matter description within such section in such manner as the Commissioner may from time to time provide. The Commissioner shall not be required to make any written determination or background file document open to public inspection pursuant to section 6110 or refrain from disclosure of any such documents or any information therein, except as provided by section 6110 or with respect to a discovery order made in connection with a judicial proceeding. The provisions of section 6110 shall not apply to material that is open to public inspection under section 6104. See section 6110(l)(1).

(b) *Items that may be inspected only under certain circumstances.*—(1) *Background file documents.*—A background file document (as such term is defined in § 301.6110-2(g)) relating to a particular written determination issued pursuant to a request postmarked or hand delivered after October 31, 1976, shall not be subject to inspection until such written determination is open to public inspection or available for inspection pursuant to paragraph (b)(2) or (3) of this section, and then only if a written request pursuant to paragraph (c)(4) of this section is made for inspection of such background file document. Background file documents relating to written determinations issued pursuant to requests postmarked or hand delivered before November 1, 1976, shall be subject to inspection pursuant to section 6110(h) and §301.6110-6, when funds are appropriated by Congress for such purpose. The version of the background file document which is available for inspection shall be the version originally made available for inspection, as modified by any additional disclosure pursuant to section 6110(d)(3) and (f)(4).

(2) *Technical advice memoranda involving civil fraud and criminal investigations, jeopardy and termination assessments.*—Any technical advice memorandum (as such term is defined in §301.6110-2(f)) involving any matter that is the subject of a civil fraud or criminal investigation, a jeopardy assessment (as such term is defined in section 6861), or a termination assessment (as such term is defined in section 6851) shall not be subject to inspection until all actions relating to such investigation or assessment are completed and then only if a written request pursuant to paragraph (c)(4) of this section is made for inspection of such technical advice memorandum. A "civil fraud investigation" is any administrative step or judicial proceeding in which an issue for determination is whether the Commissioner should impose additional tax pursuant to section 6653(b). A "criminal investigation" is any administrative step or judicial proceeding in which an issue for determination is whether a taxpayer should be charged with or is guilty of criminal conduct. An action relating to a civil fraud or criminal investigation includes any such administrative step or judicial proceeding, the review of subsequent related activities and related returns of the taxpayer or related taxpayers, and any other administrative step or judicial procedure or proceeding or appellate process that is initiated as a consequence of the facts and circumstances disclosed by such investigation. An action relating to a jeopardy or termination assessment includes any administrative step or judicial proceeding that is initiated to determine whether to make such assessment, that is brought pursuant to section 7429 to determine the appropriateness or reasonableness of such assessment, or that is brought to resolve the legal consequences of the tax status or liability issue underlying the making of such assessment. Any action relating to a civil fraud or criminal investigation, a jeopardy assessment, or a termination assessment is not completed until all available administrative steps and judicial proceedings and remedies, including appeals, have been completed.

(3) *Written determinations with respect to adoption of or change in certain accounting or funding periods and methods.*—Any general written determination (as defined in §301.6110-2(c)) that relates solely to approval of any adoption of or change in:

(i) The funding method or plan year of a plan under section 412,

(ii) A taxpayer's annual accounting period under section 442,

(iii) A taxpayer's method of accounting under section 446(e), or

(iv) A partnership's or partner's taxable year under section 706

shall not be subject to inspection until such written determination would, but for this paragraph (b)(3), be open to public inspection pursuant to §301.6110-5(c) and then only if a written request pursuant to paragraph (c)(4) of this section is made for inspection of such written determination.

(c) *Procedure for public inspection.*—(1) *Place of public inspection.*—The text of any ruling (as such term is defined in §301.6110-2(d)) or technical advice memorandum that is open to public inspection pursuant to section 6110 shall be located in the National Office Reading Room. The text of any determination letter (as such term is defined in §301.6110-2(e)) that is open to public inspection pursuant to section 6110 shall be located in the Reading Room of the Regional Office in which is located the district office that issued such determination letter. Inspection of any written determination subject to inspection only upon written request shall be requested from the National Office Reading Room. Inspection of any background file document shall be requested only from the reading room in which the related written determination is either open to public inspection or subject to inspection upon written request. The locations and mailing addresses of the reading rooms are set forth in §601.702(b)(3)(ii) of this chapter.

(2) *Time and manner of public inspection.*—The inspection authorized by section 6110 will be allowed only in the place provided for such inspection in the presence of an Internal Revenue officer or employee and only during the regular hours of business of the Internal Revenue Service office in which the reading room is located. The public will not be allowed to remove any record from a reading room. A person who wishes to inspect reading room material without visiting a reading room may submit a written request pursuant to paragraph (c)(4) of this section for copies of any such material to the Internal Revenue Service reading room in which is located such material.

(3) *Copies.*—Notes may be taken of any material open to public inspection under section 6110, and copies may be made manually. Copies of any material open to public inspection or subject to inspection upon written request will be furnished by the Internal Revenue Service to any person making requests therefor pursuant to paragraph (c)(4) of this section. If made at the time of inspection, the request for copies need not be in writing, unless the material is not immediately available for copying. The Commissioner may prescribe fees pursuant to section 6110(j) for furnishing copies of material open or subject to inspection.

(4) *Requests.*—Any request for copies of written determinations, for inspection of general written determinations relating to accounting or funding periods and methods or technical advice memoranda involving civil fraud and criminal investigations, and jeopardy and termination assessments, for inspection or copies of background file documents, and for copies of the index shall be submitted to the reading room in which is located the requested material. If made in person, the request may be submitted to the Internal Revenue employee supervising the reading room. The request shall contain:

(i) Authorization for the Internal Revenue Service to charge the person making such request for making copies, searching for material, and making deletions therefrom;

(ii) The maximum amount of charges which the Internal Revenue Service may incur without further authorization from the person making such request;

(iii) With respect to requests for inspection and copies of background file documents, the file number of the written determination to which such background file document relates and a specific identification of the nature or type of the background file document requested;

(iv) With respect to requests for inspection of general written determinations relating to accounting or funding periods and methods, the day, week, or month of issuance of such written determination, and the applicable category as selected from a special summary listing of categories prepared by the Internal Revenue Service;

(v) With respect to requests for copies of written determinations, the file number of the written determination to be copied, which can be ascertained in the reading room or from the index;

(vi) With respect to requests for copies of portions of the index, the section of the Internal Revenue Code, related statute or tax treaty in which the person making such request is interested;

(vii) With respect to material which is to be mailed, the name, address, and telephone number of the person making such request and the address to which copies of the requested material should be sent; and

(viii) Such other information as the Internal Revenue Service may from time to time require in its operation of reading rooms.

(d) *Effective/applicability date.*—The rules of paragraph (a) apply February 29, 2012. [Reg. §301.6110-1.]

☐ [*T.D. 7524, 12-15-77. Amended by T.D. 9581, 2-28-2012.*]

### [Reg. §301.6110-2]

**§301.6110-2. Meanings of terms.**—(a) *Written determination.*—A "written determination" is a ruling, a determination letter, or a technical advice memorandum, as such terms are defined in paragraphs (d), (e), and (f) of this section, respectively. Notwithstanding paragraphs (d) through (f) of this section, a written determination does not include, for example, opinion letters (as defined in §601.201(a)(4) of this chapter), information letters (as defined in §601.201(a)(5) of this chapter), technical information responses, technical assistance memoranda, notices of deficiency, reports on claims for refund, Internal Revenue Service decisions to accept taxpayers' offers in compromise, earnings and profits determinations, or documents issued by the Internal Revenue Service in the course of tax administration that are not disclosed to the persons to whose tax returns or tax liability the documents relate.

(b) *Reference written determination.*—A "reference written determination" is any written determination that the Commissioner determines to have significant reference value. Any written determination that the Commissioner determines to be the basis for a published Revenue Ruling is a reference written determination until such Revenue Ruling is obsoleted, revoked, superseded or otherwise held to have no effect.

(c) *General written determination.*—A "general written determination" is any written determination that is not a reference written determination.

(d) *Ruling.*—A "ruling" is a written statement issued by the National Office to a taxpayer or to the taxpayer's authorized representative (as such term is defined in §601.201(e)(7) of this chapter) on behalf of the taxpayer, that interprets and applies tax laws to a specific set of facts. A ruling generally recites the relevant facts, sets forth the applicable provisions of law, and shows the application of the law to the facts.

(e) *Determination letter.*—A "determination letter" is a written statement issued by a district director in response to a written inquiry by an individual or an organization that applies principles and precedents previously announced by the National Office to the particular facts involved.

(f) *Technical advice memorandum.*—A "technical advice memorandum" is a written statement issued by the National Office to, and adopted by, a district director in connection with the examination of a taxpayer's return or consideration of a taxpayer's claim for refund or credit. A technical advice memorandum generally recites the relevant facts, sets forth the applicable law, and states a legal conclusion.

(g) *Background file document.*—(1) *General rule.*—A "background file document" is:

(i) The request for a written determination.

(ii) Any written material submitted in support of such request by the person by whom or on whose behalf the request for a written determination was made.

(iii) Any written communication, or memorandum of a meeting, telephone communication, or other contact, between employees of the Internal Revenue Service or Office of its Chief Counsel and persons outside the Internal Revenue Service in connection with such request or written determination which is received prior to the issuance (as such term is defined in paragraph (h) of this section) of the written determination, but not including communications described in paragraph (g)(2) of this section, and

(iv) Any subsequent communication between the National Office and a district director concerning the factual circumstances underlying the request for a technical advice memorandum, or concerning a request by the district director for reconsideration by the National Office of a proposed technical advice memorandum.

(2) *Limitations.*—Notwithstanding paragraph (g)(1) of this section, a "background file document" shall not include any:

(i) Communication between the Department of Justice and the Internal Revenue Service or the Office of its Chief Counsel relating to any pending civil or criminal case or investigation,

(ii) Communication between Internal Revenue Service employees and employees of the Office of its Chief Counsel,

(iii) Internal memorandum or attorney work product prepared by the Internal Revenue Service or Office of its Chief Counsel which relates to the development of the conclusion of the Internal Revenue Service in a written determination, including, with respect to a technical advice memorandum, the Transmittal Memorandum, as defined in §601.105(b)(5)(vi)(*c*) of this chapter,

(iv) Correspondence or any portion of correspondence between the Internal Revenue Service and any person relating solely to the making of or extent of deletions pursuant to section 6110(c), or a request pursuant to section 6110(g)(3) and (4) for postponement of the time at which a written determination is made open or subject to inspection,

(v) Material relating to (A) a request for a ruling or determination letter that is withdrawn prior to issuance thereof or that the Internal Revenue Service declines to answer, (B) a request for technical advice that the National Office declines to answer, or (C) the appeal of a taxpayer from the decision of a district director not to seek technical advice, or

(vi) Response to a request for technical advice which the district director declines to adopt, and the district director's request for reconsideration thereof.

(h) *Issuance.*—"Issuance" of a written determination occurs, with respect to rulings and determination letters, upon the mailing of the ruling or determination letter to the person to whom it pertains. Issuance of a technical advice memorandum occurs upon the adoption of the technical advice memorandum by the district director.

(i) *Person to whom written determination pertains.*—A "person to whom a written determination pertains" is the person by whom a ruling or determination letter is requested, but if requested by an authorized representative, the person on whose behalf the request is made. With respect to a technical advice memorandum, a "person to whom a written determination pertains" is the taxpayer whose return is being examined or whose claim for refund or credit is being considered.

(j) *Person to whom a background file document relates.*—A "person to whom a background file document relates" is the person to whom

the related written determination pertains, as such term is defined in paragraph (i) of this section.

(k) *Person who has a direct interest in maintaining confidentiality.*—A "person who has direct interest in maintaining the confidentiality of a written determination" is any person whose name and address is listed in the request for such written determination, as required by §601.201(e)(2) of this chapter. A "person who has a direct interest in maintaining the confidentiality of a background file document" is any person whose name and address is in such background file document, or who has a direct interest in maintaining the confidentiality of the written determination to which such background file document relates.

(l) *Successor in interest.*—A "successor in interest" to any person to whom a written determination pertains or background file document relates is any person who acquires the rights and assumes the liabilities of such person with respect to the transaction which was the subject matter of the written determination, provided that the successor in interest notifies the Commissioner with respect to the succession in interest. [Reg. §301.6110-2.]

☐ [T.D. 7524, 12-15-77.]

**[Reg. §301.6110-3]**

**§301.6110-3. Deletion of certain information in written determinations open to public inspection.**—(a) *Information subject to deletion.*—There shall be deleted from the text of any written determination open to public inspection or subject to inspection upon written request and background file document subject to inspection upon written request pursuant to section 6110 the following types of information:

(1) *Identifying details.*—(i) The names, addresses, and identifying numbers (including telephone, license, social security, employer identification, credit card, and selective service numbers) of any person, other than the identifying details of a person who makes a third-party communication described in §301.6110-4(a), and

(ii) Any other information that would permit a person generally knowledgeable with respect to the appropriate community to identify any person. The determination of whether information would permit identification of a particular person will be made in view of information available to the public at the time the written determination or background file document is made open or subject to inspection and in view of information that will subsequently become available, provided the Internal Revenue Service is made aware of such information and the potential that such information may identify any person. The "appropriate community" is that group of persons who would be able to associate a particular person with a category of transactions one of which is described in the written determination or background file document. The appropriate community may vary according to the nature of the transaction which is the subject of the written determination. For example, if a steel company proposes to enter a transaction involving the purchase and installation of blast furnaces, the "appropriate community" may include all steel producers and blast furnace manufacturers, but if the installation process is a unique process of which everyone in national industry is aware, the "appropriate community" might also include the national industrial community. On the other hand, if the steel company proposes to enter a transaction involving the purchase of land on which to construct a building to house the blast furnaces, the "appropriate community" may also include those residing or doing business within the geographical locale of the land to be purchased.

(2) *Information concerning national defense and foreign policy.*—Information specifically authorized under criteria established by an Executive order to be kept secret in the interest of national defense or foreign policy and which is in fact properly classified pursuant to such order.

(3) *Information exempted by other statutes and agency rules.*—Information specifically exempted from disclosure by any statute other than the Internal Revenue Code of 1954 and 5 U.S.C. 552 which is applicable to the Internal Revenue Service, and any information obtained by the Internal Revenue Service solely and directly from another Federal agency subject to a nondisclosure rule of such agency. Deletion of information shall not be made solely because the same information was submitted to another Federal agency subject to a nondisclosure rule applicable only to such agency.

(4) *Trade secrets and privileged or confidential commercial or financial information.*—(i) *Deletions to be made.*—Any—

(A) Trade secrets, and

(B) Commercial or financial information obtained from any person which, despite the fact that identifying details are deleted pursuant to paragraph (a)(1) of this section, nonetheless remains privileged or confidential.

(ii) *Trade secret.*—For purposes of paragraph (a)(4)(i)(A) of this section, a trade secret may consist of any formula, pattern, device or compilation of information that is used in one's business, and that gives one an opportunity to obtain an advantage over competitors who do not know or use it. It may be a formula for a chemical compound, a process of manufacturing, treating or preserving materials, a pattern for a machine or other device, or a list of customers. The subject of a trade secret must be secret, that is, it must not be of public knowledge or of a general knowledge in the trade or business. Novelty, in the patent law sense, is not required for a trade secret.

(iii) *Privileged or confidential.*—For purposes of paragraph (a)(4)(i)(B) of this section, information is privileged or confidential if from examination of the request and supporting documents relating to a written determination, and in consideration of the fact that identifying details are deleted pursuant to paragraph (a)(1) of this section, it is determined that disclosure of such information would cause substantial harm to the competitive position of any person. For example, while determining whether disclosure of certain information would cause substantial harm to X's competitive position, the Internal Revenue Service becomes aware that this information has previously been disclosed to the public. In this situation, the Internal Revenue Service will not agree with X's argument that disclosure of the information would cause substantial harm to X's competitive position. An example of information previously disclosed to the public is financial information contained in the published annual reports of widely held public corporations.

(5) *Information within the ambit of personal privacy.*—Information the disclosure of which would constitute a clearly unwarranted invasion of personal privacy, despite the fact that identifying details are deleted pursuant to paragraph (a)(1) of this section. Personal privacy information encompasses embarrassing or sensitive information that a reasonable person would not reveal to the public under ordinary circumstances. Matters of personal privacy include, but are not limited to, details not yet public of a pending divorce, medical treatment for physical or mental disease or injury, adoption of a child, the amount of a gift, and political preferences. A clearly unwarranted invasion of personal privacy exists if from analysis of information submitted in support of the request for a written determination it is determined that the public interest purpose for requiring disclosure is outweighed by the potential harm attributable to such invasion of personal privacy.

(6) *Information concerning agency regulation of financial institutions.*—Information contained in or related to reports prepared by, on behalf of, or for the use of an agency responsible for the regulation or supervision of financial institutions concerning examination, operation or condition of a financial institution, disclosure of which would damage the standing of such financial institution.

(7) *Information concerning wells.*—Geological or geophysical information and data, including maps, concerning wells.

(b) *Manner of deletions.*—Whenever information, which is not to be disclosed pursuant to section 6110(c), is deleted from the text of a written determination or background file document, substitutions therefore shall be made to the extent feasible if necessary for an understanding of the legal analysis developed in such written determination or to make the disclosed text of a background file document comprehensible. Wherever any material is deleted, an indication of such deletion, and of any substitution therefor, shall be made in such manner as the Commissioner deems appropriate.

(c) *Limitations on the making of deletions.*—Any portion of a written determination or background file document that has been deleted will be restored to the text thereof—

(1) If pursuant to section 6110(d)(3) or (f)(4)(A) a court orders disclosure of such portion, or

(2) If pursuant to §301.6110-5(d)(1) an agreement is reached to disclose information. [Reg. § 301.6110-3.]

☐ [*T.D. 7524, 12-15-77.*]

### [Reg. § 301.6110-4]

**§301.6110-4. Communications from third parties.**—(a) *General rule.*—Except as provided in paragraph (b) of this section, a record will be made of any communication, whether written, by telephone, at a meeting, or otherwise, received by the Internal Revenue Service or Office of its Chief Counsel prior to the issuance of a written determination from any person other than a person to whom the written determination pertains or the authorized respresentative of such person. This rule applies to any communication concerning such written determination, any communication concerning the request for such written determination, or any communication concerning other matters involving such written determination. A

notation that such communication has been made shall be placed on such written determination when it is made open to public inspection or available for inspection upon written request pursuant to §301.6110-5. The notation to be placed on a written determination shall consist of the date on which the communication was received and the category of the person making such communication, for example, Congressional, Department of Commerce, Treasury, trade association, White House, educational institution. Any person may request the Internal Revenue Service to disclose the name of any person about whom a notation has been made pursuant to this paragraph.

(b) *Limitations.*—The provisions of paragraph (a) of this section shall not apply to communications received by the Internal Revenue Service from employees of the Internal Revenue Service or Office of its Chief Counsel, from the Chief of Staff of the Joint Committee on Internal Revenue Taxation, from the Department of Justice with respect to any pending civil or criminal case or investigation, or from another government agency in response to a request made by the Internal Revenue Service to such agency for assistance involving the expertise of such agency.

(c) *Action to obtain disclosure of identity of person to whom written determination pertains.*—(1) *Creation of remedy.*—With respect to any written determination on which a notation has been placed pursuant to paragraph (a) of this section, any person may file a petition in the United States Tax Court or file a complaint in the United States District Court for the District of Columbia for an order requiring that the identity of any person to whom such written determination pertains be disclosed, but such petition or complaint must be filed within 36 months of the date such written determination is made open or subject to inspection.

(2) *Necessary disclosure.*—Whenever an action is brought pursuant to section 6110(d)(3), the court may order that the identity of any person to whom the written determination pertains be disclosed. Such disclosure may be ordered if the court determines that there is evidence in the record from which it could reasonably be concluded that an impropriety occurred or undue influence was exercised with respect to such written determination by or on behalf of the person to whom the written determination pertains. The court may, pursuant to section 6110(d)(3), also order the disclosure of any material deleted pursuant to section 6110(c) if such disclosure is in the public interest. The written determination or background file document with respect to which the disclosure was sought shall be revised to disclose the information which the court orders to be disclosed.

(3) *Required notice.*—If a proceeding is commenced pursuant to section 6110(d)(3) and paragraph (c)(1) of this section with respect to any written determination, the Secretary shall send notice of the commencement of such proceeding to any person whose identity is subject to being disclosed and to the person about whom a third-party communication notation has been made pursuant to section 6110(d)(1). Such notice shall be sent, by registered or certified mail, to the last known address of the persons described in this paragraph (c)(3) within 15 days after notice of the petition or complaint filed pursuant to section 6110(d)(3) is served on the Secretary. For further guidance regarding the definition of last known address, see §301.6212-2.

(4) *Intervention.*—Any person who is entitled to receive notice pursuant to paragraph (c)(3) of this section shall have the right to intervene in any action brought pursuant to section 6110(d)(3). If appropriate such person shall be permitted to intervene anonymously. [Reg. § 301.6110-4.]

☐ [*T.D. 7524, 12-15-77. Amended by T.D. 8939, 1-11-2001.*]

### [Reg. § 301.6110-5]

**§301.6110-5. Notice and time requirements; actions to restrain disclosure; actions to obtain additional disclosure.**—(a) *Notice.*—(1) *General rule.*—Before a written determination is made open to public inspection or subject to inspection upon written request, or before a background file document is subject to inspection upon written request, the person to whom the written determination pertains or background file document relates shall be notified by the Commissioner of intention to disclose such written determination or background file document. The notice with respect to a written determination, other than a written determination described in §301.6110-1(b)(2) or (3) shall be mailed when such written determination is issued. The notice with respect to any written determination relating to accounting or funding periods and methods, any technical advice memoranda involving civil fraud and criminal investigations, and jeopardy and termination assessments, and any background file document shall be mailed within a reasonable time after the receipt of the first written request for inspection thereof.

(2) *Contents of notice.*—The notice required by paragraph (a)(1) of this section shall—

(i) Include a copy of the text of the written determination or background file document, which the Commissioner proposes to make open to public inspection or subject to inspection pursuant to a written request, on which is indicated (A) the material that the Commissioner proposes to delete pursuant to section 6110(c), (B) any substitutions proposed to be made therefor, and (C) any third-party communication notations required to be placed pursuant to § 301.6110-4(a) on the face of the written determination,

(ii) State that the written determination or background file document is to be open to public inspection or subject to inspection pursuant to a written request pursuant to section 6110,

(iii) State that the recipient of the notice has the right to seek administrative remedies pursuant to paragraph (b)(1) of this section and to commence judicial proceedings pursuant to section 6110(f)(3) within indicated time periods, and

(iv) Prominently indicate the date on which the notice is mailed.

(b) *Actions to restrain disclosure.*—(1) *Administrative remedies.*—Any person to whom a written determination pertains or background file document relates, and any successor in interest, executor or authorized representative of such person may pursue the administrative remedies described in § 601.105(b)(5)(iii)(*i*) and (vi)(*f*) and § 601.201(e)(11) and (16) of this chapter. Any person who has a direct interest in maintaining the confidentiality of any written determination or background file document or portion thereof may pursue the administrative remedies described in § 601.105(b)(5)(vi)(*f*) and § 601.201(e)(16) of this chapter. No person about whom a third-party communication notation has been made pursuant to § 301.6110-4(a) may pursue any administrative remedy for the purpose of restraining disclosure of the identity of such person where such identity appears with respect to the making of such third-party communication.

(2) *Judicial remedy.*—Except as provided in paragraph (b)(3) of this section, any person permitted to resort to administrative remedies pursuant to paragraph (b)(1) of this section may, if such person proposes any deletion not made pursuant to § 301.6110-3 by the Commissioner, file a petition in the United States Tax Court pursuant to section 6110(f)(3) for a determination with respect to such proposed deletion. If appropriate, such petition may be filed anonymously. Any petition filed pursuant to section 6110(f)(3) must be filed within 60 days after the date on which the Commissioner mails the notice of intention to disclose required by section 6110(f)(1).

(3) *Limitations on right to bring judicial actions.*—No petition shall be filed pursuant to section 6110(f)(3) unless the administrative remedies provided by paragraph (b)(1) of this section have been exhausted. However, if the petitioner has responded within the prescribed time period to the notice pursuant to section 6110(f)(1) of intention to disclose, but has not received the final administrative conclusion of the Internal Revenue Service within 50 days after the date on which the Commissioner mails the notice of intention to disclose required by section 6110(f)(1), the petitioner may file a petition pursuant to section 6110(f)(3). No judicial action with respect to any written determination or background file document shall be commenced pursuant to section 6110(f)(3) by any person who has received a notice with respect to such written determination or background file document pursuant to paragraph (b)(4) of this section.

(4) *Required notice.*—If a proceeding is commenced pursuant to section 6110(f)(3) with respect to any written determination or background file document, the Secretary shall send notice of the commencement of such proceeding to any person to whom such written determination pertains or to whom such background file document relates. No notice is required to be sent to persons who have filed the petition that commenced the proceeding pursuant to section 6110(f)(3) with respect to such written determination or background file document. The notice shall be sent, by registered or certified mail, to the last known address of the persons described in this paragraph (b)(4) within 15 days after notice of the petition filed pursuant to section 6110(f)(3) is served on the Secretary. For further guidance regarding the definition of last known address, see § 301.6212-2.

(5) *Intervention.*—Any person who is entitled to receive notice pursuant to paragraph (b)(4) of this section shall have the right to intervene in any action brought pursuant to this section. If appropriate, such person shall be permitted to intervene anonymously.

(c) *Time at which open to public inspection.*—(1) *General rule.*—Except as otherwise provided in paragraph (c)(2) of this section, the text of any written determination or background file document open to public inspection or available for inspection upon written request pursuant to section 6110 shall be made open to or available for

inspection no earlier than 75 days and no later than 90 days after the date on which the Commissioner mails the notice required by paragraph (a)(1) of this section. However, if an action is brought pursuant to section 6110(f)(3) to restrain disclosure of any portion of such written determination or background file document the disputed portion of such written determination or background file document shall be made open to or available for inspection pursuant to paragraph (c)(2)(i) of this section.

(2) *Limitations.*—(i) *Court order.*—The portion of the text of any written determination or background file document that was subject to an action pursuant to section 6110(f)(3) to restrain disclosure in which the court determined that such disclosure should not be restrained shall be made open to or available for inspection within 30 days of the date that the court order becomes final. However, in no event shall such portion of the text of such written determination or background file document be made open to or available for inspection earlier than 75 days after the date on which the Commissioner mails the notice of intention to disclose required by section 6110(f)(1) and paragraph (a)(1) of this section. Such 30-day period may be extended for such time as the court finds necessary to allow the Commissioner to comply with its decision. Any portion of a written determination or background file document which a court orders open to public inspection or subject to inspection upon written request pursuant to section 6110(f)(4) or disclosed pursuant to section 6110(d)(3) shall be made open or subject to inspection or disclosed within such time as the court provides.

(ii) *Postponement based on incomplete status of underlying transaction.*—(A) *Initial period not to exceed 90 days.*—The time period set forth in paragraph (c)(1) of this section within which a written determination shall be made open to public inspection or available for inspection upon written request shall be extended, upon the written request of the person to whom such written determination pertains or the authorized representative of such person, until 15 days after the date on which the transaction set forth in the written determination is scheduled to be completed, but such day shall be no later than 180 days after the date on which the Commissioner mails the notice of intention to disclose.

(B) *Additional period.*—The time period determined pursuant to paragraph (c)(2)(ii)(A) of this section shall be further extended upon an additional written request, if the Commissioner determines from the information contained in such request that good cause exists to warrant such extension. This further extension shall be until 15 days after the date on which the transaction set forth in the written determination is expected to be completed, but such day shall be no later than 360 days after the date on which the Commissioner mails the notice of intention to disclose. The good cause required by this (B) exists if the person requesting the delay in inspection demonstrates to the satisfaction of the Commissioner that it is likely that the lack of such extension will cause interference with consummation of the pending transaction.

(C) *Written request for extension.*—The written request for extension of the time when a written determination is to be made open to public inspection or available for inspection upon written request shall set forth the date on which it is expected that the underlying transaction will be completed, and, with respect to the additional extension described in paragraph (c)(2)(ii)(B) of this section, set forth the reason for requesting such extension. A request for extension of time may not be submitted until the notice of intention to disclose is mailed and must be received by the Internal Revenue Service office which issued such written determination no later than—

(1) In the case of the initial extension, 60 days after the date on which the Commissioner mails the notice of intention to disclose, or

(2) In the case of the additional extension, 15 days before the day on which, for purposes of paragraph (c)(2)(ii)(A) of this section, the transaction set forth in the written determination was expected to have been completed.

(D) *Notice and determination of actual completion.*—If an extension of time for inspection has been granted, and the transaction is completed prior to the day on which it was expected to have been completed, the Internal Revenue Service office which issued such written determination shall be so notified by the person who requested such extension. In such event, the written determination shall be made open to public inspection or available for inspection upon written request on the earlier of (1) 30 days after the day on which the Commissioner is notified that the transaction is completed, or (2) the day on which the written determination was scheduled to be made open to public inspection or available for inspection upon written request pursuant to paragraph (c)(2)(ii) of this section. Similarly, if the Commissioner determines that the transaction was completed prior to the day on which it was expected to have been completed, even if the person requesting such extension has not so notified the Internal Revenue Service, the written determination shall be made open to public inspection or available for inspection upon written request on the earlier of (1) the day which is 30 days after the Commissioner ascertains that the transaction is completed sooner than has been expected, or (2) the day on which the written determination was scheduled to be made open to public inspection or available for inspection upon written request pursuant to paragraph (c)(2)(ii) of this section.

(d) *Actions to obtain additional disclosure.*—(1) *Administrative remedies.*—Under section 6110(f)(4) any person may seek to obtain additional disclosure of information contained in any written determination or background file document that has been made open or subject to inspection. A request for such additional disclosure shall be submitted to the Internal Revenue Service office which issued such written determination, or to which the request for inspection of such background file document has been submitted pursuant to §301.6110-1(c)(4), and must contain the file number of the written determination or a description of the background file document (including the file number of the related written determination), the deleted information which in the opinion of such person should be open or subject to inspection, and the basis for such opinion. If the Internal Revenue Service determines that the request constitutes a request for disclosure of the name, address, or the identifying numbers described in §301.6110-3(a)(1)(i) of any person, it shall within a reasonable time notify the person requesting such disclosure that disclosure will not be made. If the Internal Revenue Service determines that the request or any portion thereof constitutes a request for disclosure of information other than the name, address, or the identifying numbers described in §301.6110-3(a)(1)(i) of any person, it shall send a notice that such additional disclosure has been requested to any person to whom the written determination pertains or background file document relates, and to all persons who are identified by name and address in the written determination or background file document. Notice that such persons have been contacted shall be sent to the person requesting the additional disclosure. The notice that additional disclosure has been requested shall state that the Internal Revenue Service has determined that additional disclosure of information other than the name, address, or the identifying numbers described in §301.6110-3(a)(1)(i) of any person has been requested, inform the recipient of the notice that the person seeking the additional disclosure has the right under section 6110(f)(4) to bring a judicial action to attempt to compel such disclosure, and request the recipient of the notice to reply within 20 days by submitting a statement of whether or not the recipient of the notice agrees to the requested disclosure or portion thereof. If all persons to whom a notice is sent pursuant to this (1) agree to disclose the requested information or any portion thereof, the person seeking such disclosure will be so informed; the written determination or background file document shall be accordingly revised to disclose the information with respect to which an agreement to disclose has been reached. If any of the persons to whom a notice is sent pursuant to this (1) do not agree to the additional disclosure or do not respond to such notice, the Internal Revenue Service shall within a reasonable time so notify the person requesting such disclosure, and deny the request for additional disclosure.

(2) *Judicial remedy.*—Except as provided in paragraph (d)(3) of this section, any person who seeks to obtain additional disclosure of information contained in any written determination or background file document may file a petition pursuant to section 6110(f)(4) in the United States Tax Court or a complaint in the United States District Court for the District of Columbia for an order requiring that such information be made open or subject to inspection. Nothing in this paragraph shall prevent the Commissioner from disposing of written determinations and related background file documents pursuant to §301.6110-7(a).

(3) *Limitations on right to bring judicial action.*—(i) *Exhaustion of administrative remedies.*—No petition or complaint shall be filed pursuant to section 6110(f)(4) unless the administrative remedies provided by paragraph (d)(1) of this section have been exhausted. However, if the Internal Revenue Service does not approve or deny the request for additional disclosure within 180 days after the request is submitted, the person making the request may file a petition pursuant to section 6110(f)(4).

(ii) *Actions to obtain identity.*—No petition or complaint shall be filed pursuant to section 6110(f)(4) to obtain disclosure of the identity of any person to whom a written determination on which a third-party communication notation has been placed pursuant to §301.6110-4(a) pertains. Such actions shall be brought pursuant to section 6110(d)(3).

(4) *Required notice.*—If a proceeding is commenced pursuant to section 6110(f)(4) with respect to any written determination or background file document, the Secretary shall send notice of the commencement of such proceeding to any person to whom the written determination pertains or background file document relates, and to all persons who are identified by name and address in the written determination or background file document. The notice shall be sent, by registered or certified mail, to the last known address of the persons described in this paragraph (d)(4) within 15 days after notice of the petition or complaint filed pursuant to section 6110(f)(4) is served on the Secretary.

(5) *Intervention.*—Any person who is entitled to receive notice pursuant to paragraph (d)(4) of this section shall have the right to intervene in any action brought pursuant to this section. If appropriate, such person shall be permitted to intervene anonymously. [Reg. §301.6110-5.]

☐ [*T.D. 7524, 12-15-77. Amended by T.D. 8939, 1-11-2001.*]

**[Reg. §301.6110-6]**

**§301.6110-6. Written determinations issued in response to requests submitted before November 1, 1976.**—(a) *Inspection of written determinations and background file documents.*—(1) *General rule.*—Except as provided in this section, the text of any written determination issued in response to a request postmarked or hand delivered before November 1, 1976 and any related background file document shall be open or subject to inspection in accordance with the rules in §§301.6110-1 through 301.6110-5 and 301.6110-7. However, the rules in §301.6110-4 do not apply to inspection under this section. The rules in §301.6110-5(a), (b) and (c) also do not apply, except with respect to background file documents.

(2) *Exclusions.*—The following written determinations are not open or subject to inspection:

(i) Written determinations with respect to matters for which the determination of whether public inspection should occur is made under section 6104. Some of these matters are listed in §301.6110-1(a).

(ii) Written determinations issued before September 2, 1974, dealing with the qualification of a plan described in section 6104(a)(1)(B)(i) or the exemption from tax under section 501(a) of an organization forming part of such a plan.

(iii) General written determinations that related solely to accounting or funding periods and methods, as defined in §301.6110-1(b)(3).

(iv) Determination letters.

(v) Written determinations issued pursuant to requests submitted before November 1, 1976 with respect to the exempt status under section 501(a) of organizations described in section 501(c) or (d), the status of organizations as private foundations under section 509(a), or the status of organizations as operating foundations under section 4942(j)(3).

(3) *Items that may be inspected only under certain circumstances.*—(i) *Background file documents.*—A background file document relating to a particular written determination issued in response to a request submitted before November 1, 1976 shall not be subject to inspection until the related written determination is open to public inspection or available for inspection, and then only if a written request pursuant to §301.6110-1(c)(4) is made for inspection of the background file document. However, the following background file documents are not open or subject to inspection:

(A) Background file documents relating to general written determinations issued before July 5, 1967.

(B) Background file documents relating to written determinations described in paragraph (a)(2) of this section.

(ii) *General written determinations issued before July 5, 1967.*—General written determinations issued before July 5, 1967 shall not be subject to inspection until all other written determinations issued in response to requests postmarked or hand delivered before November 1, 1976 that are open to inspection under this section have been made open to public inspection, and then only if a written request pursuant to §301.6110-1(c)(4) is made for inspection of the written determination. In this regard, the request for inspection must also contain the section of the Internal Revenue Code in which the requester is interested and the dates of issuance of the written determinations.

(b) *Notice and time requirements, and actions to restrain disclosure.*—(1) *Notice.*—(i) *General rule.*—Before a written determination is made open to public inspection and before a particular written determination is subject to inspection in response to the first written request therefor, the Commissioner shall publish in the Federal Register a notice that the written determination is to be made open or subject to inspection. Notices with respect to written determinations, other than those described in paragraph (a)(3)(ii) of this section, shall be published at the earliest practicable time after this regulation is adopted as a Treasury decision. Notices with respect to written determinations subject to inspection upon written request shall be published within a reasonable time after the receipt of the first written request for inspection thereof, but no sooner than the day as of which all other written determinations open to public inspection under this section have been made open to public inspection. Notices with respect to background file documents shall be sent in accordance with the rules in § 301.6110-5(a) and will be mailed by the Internal Revenue Service to the most recent addresses of the persons to whom the background file document relates that are in the written determination file.

(ii) *Sequence of notices.*—Notices with respect to written determinations, other than general written determinations issued before July 5, 1967, shall be published in the following order. The first category is notices with respect to reference written determinations issued under the Internal Revenue Code of 1954. The second category is notices with respect to general written determinations issued after July 4, 1967. The third category is notices with respect to reference written determinations issued under the Internal Revenue Code of 1939 or corresponding provisions of prior law. Within a category, the Commissioner may publish notices individually or for groups of written determinations arranged according to the jurisdictions of the ruling branches in the Offices of the Assistant Commissioner (Technical) and the Assistant Commissioner (Employee Plans and Exempt Organizations), as the Commissioner may find reasonable. To the extent practicable, notices published individually shall be published in the reverse order of the issuance of the written determinations for which they are published, starting with the most recent written determination issued. To the extent practicable, each group shall consist of consecutively issued written determinations. Notices for groups shall be published, to the extent practicable, in the reverse order of the time period of issuance of the written determinations in each group, starting with the most recent time period.

(iii) *Contents of notice.*—The notice required by paragraph (b)(1)(i) of this section shall—

(A) Identify by subject matter description and dates of issuance the written determinations that the Commissioner proposes to make open or subject to inspection,

(B) State that the written determinations will be made open or subject to inspection pursuant to section 6110(h),

(C) State that the persons to whom the written determinations pertain have the right to seek administrative remedies under paragraph (b)(2)(ii) of this section and to commence judicial proceedings under section 6110(h)(4) within indicated time periods,

(D) State that there exist the possibilities that someone might request additional disclosure under section 6110(f)(4) and that someone might request inspection of a related background file document, and

(E) State that any notice that must be mailed by the Internal Revenue Service will be sent to the most recent address of the person to whom the notice must be sent that is in the relevant written determination file.

(2) *Actions to restrain disclosure.*—(i) *Information on written determinations described by notice.*—Any person may, within 15 days after the Commissioner publishes in the Federal Register a notice of intention to disclose a written determination under section 6110(h), request the Internal Revenue Service to provide certain information. This information includes whether any of the written determinations described by the notice is one that was issued to the person requesting this information. The Internal Revenue Service will also inform the person whether any of the written determinations described by the notice is one that was issued to a person with respect to whom the person requesting this information is a successor in interest, executor or authorized representative. However, in order to do so, the Internal Revenue Service must be given the name and taxpayer identifying number of this other person and documentation of the relationship between that person and the person requesting the information. If the person requesting this information is a person to whom a written determination described by the notice pertains, or a successor in interest, executor, or authorized representative of that person, the Internal Revenue Service will also provide the person with a copy of the written determination on which is indicated the material that the Commissioner proposes to delete under section 6110(c) and any substitution proposed to be made therefor.

(ii) *Administrative remedies.*—Any person to whom a written determination described by the notice in the Federal Register pertains, and any successor in interest, executor or authorized representative of that person may pursue the administrative remedies described in this paragraph (b)(2)(ii). If, after receiving the information described in paragraph (b)(2)(i) of this section, the person pursuing these administrative remedies desires to protest the disclosure of

certain information in the written determination, that person must within 35 days after the notice is published submit a written statement identifying those deletions not made by the Internal Revenue Service which the person believes should have been made. The person pursuing these administrative remedies must also submit a copy of the version of the written determination proposed to be open or subject to inspection on which that person indicates, by the use of brackets, the deletions which the person believes should have been made. The Internal Revenue Service shall, within 20 days after receipt of the response by the person pursuing these administrative remedies, mail to that person its final administrative conclusion with respect to the deletions to be made.

(iii) *Judicial remedy.*—Except as provided in paragraph (b)(2)(iv) of this section, any person permitted to resort to administrative remedies under paragraph (b)(2)(ii) of this section may, if that person proposed any deletion not made under section 6110(c) by the Commissioner, file a petition in the United States Tax Court under section 6110(h)(4) for a determination with respect to the proposed deletion. If appropriate, the petition may be filed anonymously. Any petition filed under section 6110(h)(4) must be filed within 75 days after the date on which the Commissioner publishes in the Federal Register the notice of intention to disclose required under section 6110(h)(4).

(iv) *Limitations on right to bring judicial actions.*—No petition shall be filed under section 6110(h)(4) unless the administrative remedies provided by paragraph (b)(2)(ii) of this section have been exhausted. However, under two circumstances the petition may be filed even though the administrative remedies have not been exhausted. The first circumstance is if the petitioner requests the information described in paragraph (b)(2)(i) of this section within 15 days after the notice of intention to disclose is published in the Federal Register, but does not receive it within 30 days after the notice is published. The other circumstance is if the petitioner submits the statement of deletions within 35 days after the notice is published, but does not receive the final administrative conclusion of the Internal Revenue Service within 65 days after the notice is published. No judicial action with respect to any written determination shall be commenced under section 6110(h)(4) by any person who has received a notice with respect to the written determination under paragraph (b)(2)(v) of this section.

(v) *Required notice.*—If a proceeding is commenced under section 6110(h)(4) with respect to any written determination, the Secretary shall send notice of the commencement of the proceeding to any person to whom the written determination pertains. No notice is required to be sent to persons who have filed the petition that commenced the proceeding under section 6110(h)(4) with respect to the written determination. The notice shall be sent, by registered or certified mail, to the last known address of the persons described in this paragraph (b)(2)(v) within 15 days after notice of the petition filed under section 6110(h)(4) is served on the Secretary. For further guidance regarding the definition of last known address, see § 301.6212-2.

(vi) *Intervention.*—Any person who is entitled to receive notice under paragraph (b)(2)(v) of this section has the right to intervene in any action brought under this paragraph (b)(2). If appropriate, this person shall be permitted to intervene anonymously.

(vii) *Background file documents.*—The following qualifications of the rules in § 301.6110-5(b) apply with respect to the restraint of disclosure of background file documents related to written determinations to which this section applies. First, the administrative remedies described in § § 601.105(b)(5)(iii) (*i*) and 601.201(e)(11) of this chapter do not apply. Second, the rule in those sections that the Internal Revenue Service will not consider the deletion of material not proposed for deletion prior to the issuance of the written determination does not apply.

(3) *Time at which open to public inspection.*—(i) *General rule.*—Except as otherwise provided in paragraph (b)(3)(ii) of this section, the text of any written determination open to public inspection or available for inspection upon written request under section 6110 shall be made open to or available for inspection no earlier than 90 days and no later than 120 days after the date on which the Commissioner publishes in the Federal Register the notice of intention to disclose required under section 6110(h)(4). However, if an action is brought under section 6110(h)(4) to restrain disclosure of any portion of a written determination, the disputed portion of that written determination shall be made open to or available for inspection under paragraph (b)(3)(ii) of this section.

(ii) *Limitation on account of court order.*—The portion of the text of any written determination that was subject to an action under section 6110(h)(4) to restrain disclosure in which the court determined that the disclosure should be restrained shall be made open to or available for inspection within 30 days of the date that the court order becomes final. However, in no event shall that portion of the text of that written determination be made open to or available for inspection earlier than 90 days after the date on which the Commissioner publishes in the Federal Register the notice of intention to disclose required by section 6110(h)(4) and paragraph (b)(1) of this section. This 30-day period may be extended for such time as the court finds necessary to allow the Commissioner to comply with its decision. Any portion of a written determination which a court orders open to public inspection or subject to inspection upon written request under section 6110(f)(4) shall be open or subject to inspection within such time as the court provides.

(iii) *Background file documents.*—The rules in § 301.6110-5(c)(2)(ii) do not apply with respect to the time at which background file documents related to written determinations to which this section applies are subject to inspection. [Reg. § 301.6110-6.]

☐ [*T.D. 7548, 5-12-78. Amended by T.D. 8939, 1-11-2001.*]

### [Reg. § 301.6110-7]

**§ 301.6110-7. Miscellaneous provisions.**—(a) *Disposition of written determinations and background file documents.*—(1) *Reference written determinations.*—The Internal Revenue Service shall not dispose of any reference written determinations or related background file documents. The Commissioner may reclassify reference written determinations as general written determinations if the classification as reference was erroneous or if the Commissioner determined that such written determination no longer has any significant reference value. Notwithstanding the preceding sentence, the Commissioner shall not classify as a general written determination any written determination which is determined to be the basis for a published Revenue Ruling unless such Revenue Ruling is obsolete, revoked, superseded or otherwise held to have no effect.

(2) *General written determinations.*—The Internal Revenue Service may dispose of general written determinations and any background file document relating to such written determination pursuant to its established records disposition procedures. Disposition of a written determination shall not occur earlier than 3 years after the date on which such written determination is made open to public inspection or available for inspection upon written request. Disposition of a background file document shall not occur earlier than 3 years after the date on which the related written determination is made open to public inspection or available for inspection upon written request.

(b) *Precedential status of written determinations open to public inspection.*—A written determination may not be used or cited as precedent, but the rule set forth in this paragraph shall not apply to change the precedential status, if any, of written determinations issued with respect to taxes imposed by subtitle D of the Internal Revenue Code of 1954.

(c) *Civil remedies.*—(1) *Liability for failure to make deletions or to conform to time limitations.*—(i) *Creation of remedy.*—An exclusive remedy against the Commissioner shall exist in the Court of Claims for—

(A) The person to whom the written determination pertains whenever the Commissioner fails to act in accordance with the time requirements of section 6110(g), and

(B) The person to whom the written determination pertains and any person identified in such written determination whenever the Commissioner fails to make deletions required by section 6110(c) if as a consequence of such failure there is disclosed the identity of such person or other information with respect to such person that is required to be deleted pursuant to section 6110(c).

(ii) *Limitations.*—The remedy provided in paragraph (c)(1)(i) of this section for failure to make deletions shall be available only if—

(A) The failure of the Commissioner to make the deletions required by section 6110(c) is intentional or willful.

(B) The Commissioner fails to make any deletion required by section 6110(c) which the Commissioner has agreed to make, or

(C) The Commissioner fails to make any deletion which a court has ordered to be made pursuant to section 6110(f)(3).

(iii) *Damages.*—In any suit brought pursuant to paragraph (c)(1)(i) of this section in which the court determines that an employee of the Internal Revenue Service intentionally or willfully failed to make a deletion required by section 6110(c), or intentionally or willfully failed to act in accordance with the time requirements of section 6110(g), the United States shall be liable, to the person described in paragraph (c)(1)(i) of this section who brought the action, in an amount equal to the sum of—

(A) Actual damages sustained by such person but in no case shall such person be entitled to receive less than the sum of $1,000,

(B) The costs of the action, and

(C) Reasonable attorney's fees as determined by the court.

(2) *Liability for making additional disclosure of information.*—The Commissioner shall not be liable for making any additional disclosure ordered pursuant to an action described in § 301.6110-5(d)(2) if the notice required by § 301.6110-5(d)(4) is sent.

(3) *Obligation to defend action for additional disclosure.*—The Commissioner shall not be required to defend any action brought to obtain additional disclosure pursuant to section 6110(f)(4) if the notice required by § 301.6110-5(d)(4) is sent.

(4) *Obligation to make deletions.*—The Commissioner shall be obligated to make only those deletions required by section 6110(c) which he has agreed to make, those which a court has ordered to be made pursuant to § 301.6110-5(b)(2) and those the omission of which would be intentional or willful.

(d) *Fees.*—(1) *General rule.*—(i) *Copies.*—The Commissioner may prescribe fees pursuant to § 601.702(f)(4) of this chapter for the costs of furnishing copies of material open to public inspection or subject to inspection upon written request pursuant to section 6110.

(ii) *Preparation of information available upon request.*—The Commissioner may prescribe fees pursuant to § 601.702(f) of this chapter for the costs of searching for and making deletions from any written determinations and background file documents that are subject to inspection only upon written request pursuant to § 301.6110-1(b).

(2) *Reduction or waiver of fees.*—(i) *Public interest.*—The Commissioner shall reduce or waive the fees described in paragraph (d)(1) of this section if the Commissioner determines that furnishing copies of, searching for, or making deletions from any written determination or background file document primarily benefits the general public, as described in § 601.702(f)(2)(ii)(B) of this chapter.

(ii) *Previous requests.*—The Commissioner may waive the fees described in paragraph (d)(1) of this section for searching for any written determination or background file document if the search for such written determination or background file document was made pursuant to a previous request for inspection thereof. The Commissioner shall waive the fees described in paragraph (d)(1) of this section for making deletions from any written determination or background file document if the making of such deletions from such written determination or background file document was made pursuant to a previous request to inspection thereof. Nothing in this (d)(2)(ii) shall prevent the Commissioner from prescribing fees for making additional deletions from such written determination or background file document pursuant to § 301.6110-5(b). [Reg. § 301.6110-7.]

☐ [*T.D. 7524, 12-15-77.*]

### [Reg. § 301.6111-1T]

**§ 301.6111-1T. Questions and answers relating to tax shelter registration (Temporary).**—The following questions and answers relate to the tax shelter registration requirements of section 6111 of the Internal Revenue Code of 1954, as added by section 14-1(a) of the Tax Reform Act of 1984 (Pub. L. 98-369, 98 Stat. 678).
*Table of Contents*

The following table of contents is provided as part of these temporary regulations to help the reader locate relevant provisions. The headings are to be used only as a matter of convenience and have no substantive effect.

*In general*

Q-1. What is tax shelter registration?

A-1. Tax shelter registration is a new provision of the Internal Revenue Code that affects organizers, sellers, investors and certain other persons associated with investments that are considered tax shelters. The new provision imposes the following three requirements. First, a tax shelter must be registered by the tax shelter organizer. (See A-4 of this section for the definition of a tax shelter. See A-25 through A-39 of this section for rules relating to tax shelter organizers. See A-26 of this section for rules regarding when the seller of an interest in a tax shelter is treated as the tax shelter organizer.) Registration is accomplished by filing a properly completed Form 8264 with the Internal Revenue Service. The Internal Revenue Service will assign a registration number to each tax shelter that is registered. Second, any person who sells or otherwise transfers an interest in a tax shelter must furnish the registration number of the tax shelter to the purchaser or transferee of the interest. (See A-51 through A-54 of this section for the time and manner in which the number must be furnished.) Third, any person who claims a deduction, loss, credit, or other tax benefit or reports any income from the tax shelter must report the registration number of the tax shelter on any return on which the deduction, loss, credit, benefit, or income is included. (See A-55 through A-57 of this section for rules relating to the reporting of tax shelter registration numbers.)

Q-2. Are penalties provided for failure to comply with the requirements of tax shelter registration?

A-2. Yes. Separate penalties are provided for failure to satisfy any of the requirements set forth in A-1 of this section. See A-1 of §301.6707-1T for the penalty for failure to register a tax shelter and A-8 of §301.6707-1T for the penalty for filing false or incomplete information with respect to the registration of a tax shelter. See A-12 of §301.6707-1T for the penalty for failure to furnish the tax shelter registration number to purchasers or transferees. See A-13 of §301.6707-1T for the penalty for failure to report the tax shelter registration number on a tax return on which a deduction, loss, credit, income, or other tax benefit is included. In addition, criminal penalties may be imposed for willful noncompliance with the requirements of tax shelter registration. See, for example, section 7203, relating to willful failure to supply information, and section 7206, relating to fraudulent and false statements.

Q-3. Does registration of a tax shelter with the Internal Revenue Service indicate that the Internal Revenue Service has reviewed, examined, or approved the tax shelter or the claimed tax benefits?

A-3. No. Moreover, any representation to prospective investors that states that a tax shelter is registered with the Internal Revenue Service (or that registration is being sought) must include a legend stating that registration does not indicate that the Internal Revenue Service has reviewed, examined or approved the tax shelter or any of the claimed tax benefits. (See A-50 of this section for the form and content of the legend.)

*Tax shelter defined*

Q-4. What investments are tax shelters that are required to be registered with the Internal Revenue Service?

A-4. A tax shelter is any investment that meets the following two requirements:

(I) The investment must be one with respect to which a person could reasonably infer, from the representations made or to be made in connection with any offer for sale of any interest in the investment, that the tax shelter ratio for any investor may be greater than 2 to 1 as of the close of any of the first 5 years ending after the date on which the investment is offered for sale.

(II) The investment must be (i) required to be registered under a federal or state law regulating securities, (ii) sold pursuant to an exemption from registration requiring the filing of a notice with a federal or state agency regulating the offering or sale of securities, or (iii) a substantial investment. An investment that satisfies these two requirements is considered a tax shelter for registration purposes regardless of whether it is marketed or customarily designated as a tax shelter. See A-5 of this section for the definition of tax shelter ratio. See A-17 and A-18 of this section for the definition of an investment required to be registered under a federal or state law regulating securities. See A-19 and A-20 of this section for the definition of an investment sold pursuant to an exemption from registration requiring the filing of a notice. See A-21 of this section for the definition of a substantial investment.

*Tax shelter ratio*

Q-5. What does the term "tax shelter ratio" mean?

A-5. The term "tax shelter ratio" means, with respect to any year, the ratio that the aggregate amount of deductions and 200 percent of the credits that are or will be represented as potentially allowable to an investor under subtitle A of the Internal Revenue Code for all periods up to (and including) the close of such year, bears to the investment base for such investor as of the close of such year.

*Deductions and credits represented as potentially allowable*

Q-6. What do the terms "amount of deductions" and "credits" mean?

A-6. The term "amount of deductions" means the amount of gross deductions and other similar tax benefits potentially allowable with respect to the investment. The gross deductions are not to be offset by any gross income to be derived or potentially derived from the investment. Thus, the term "amount of deductions" is not equivalent to the net loss, if any, attributable to the investment. The term "credits" means the gross amount of credits potentially allowable with respect to the investment without regard to any possible tax liability resulting from the investment or any potential recapture of the credits.

Q-7. What does the term "year" mean for purposes of determining the tax shelter ratio?

A-7. The term "year" means the taxable year of a tax shelter, or if the tax shelter has no taxable year, the calendar year.

Q-8. Under what circumstances is a deduction or credit considered to be represented as being potentially allowable to an investor?

A-8. A deduction or credit is considered to be represented as being potentially allowable to an investor if any statement is made (or will be made) in connection with the offering for sale of an interest in an investment indicating that a tax deduction or credit is available or may be used to reduce federal income tax or federal taxable income. Representations of tax benefits may be oral or written and include those made at the time of the initial offering for sale of interests in the investment, such as advertisements, written offering materials, prospectuses, or tax opinions, and those that are expected to be made subsequent to the initial offering. Representations are not confined solely to statements regarding actual dollar amounts of tax benefits, but also include general representations that tax benefits are available with respect to an investment. Thus, for example, an advertisement stating that "purchase of restaurant includes trade fixtures (5-year write-off and investment tax credit)" constitutes an explicit representation of tax benefits.

Q-9. If a deduction or credit is not explicitly represented as being potentially allowable to an investor may it be inferred as a represented tax benefit that is includible in the tax shelter ratio?

A-9. Yes. Although some explicit representation concerning tax benefits is necessary before an investment may be considered a tax shelter, once an explicit representation is made (or will be made) regarding any tax benefit, all deductions or credits typically associated with the investment will be inferred to have been represented as potentially allowable. Thus, the tax shelter ratio will be determined with reference to those tax benefits that are explicitly represented as being potentially allowable as well as all other tax benefits that are typically associated with the investment. The amount of each deduction or credit that is includible in the tax shelter ratio, if not specifically represented as to amount, should be reasonably estimated based on representations of economic value or economic projections, if any, or on any other information available to the tax shelter organizer. Reasonable estimates of deductions or credits may take into account past experience with similar investments. Reasonable estimates must assume use of the most accelerated allowable basis for cost recovery deductions.

As an example of the application of this A-9, assume that an advertisement explicitly states that a building is eligible for the investment tax credit for rehabilitation of a certified historic structure, but makes no mention of cost recovery deductions, amortization deductions for construction period interest and taxes, real estate taxes after construction, ongoing maintenance expenses, or other deductions or credits typically associated with a building. Reasonable estimates of all such deductions and credits must be included with the investment tax credit explicitly represented in determining the tax shelter ratio associated with any investor's acquisition of an interest in the building.

Q-10. Does the fact that representations are made (or to be made) indicating that a deduction may be offset by income from the investment or that a deduction or credit may be subject to recapture or may be disallowed on audit affect the computation of the tax shelter ratio?

A-10. No. Deductions and credits represented as being potentially allowable are taken into account in computing the tax shelter ratio regardless of whether any qualifying statements are made.

Q-11. Is interest to be paid by an investor with respect to a debt obligation incurred in connection with the acquisition of an interest in the tax shelter included in the aggregate amount of deductions?

A-11. If a deduction for such interest is explicitly represented (or will be represented) as being potentially allowable, the interest is includible in the aggregate amount of the deductions. In addition, any interest to be paid with respect to a debt obligation the proceeds of which reduce the investment base (see A-14 of this section), regardless of whether a deduction for such interest is explicitly represented as being allowable, will be considered a deduction typically associated with the investment (see A-9 of this section). Accordingly, such interest will be considered to be represented as being potentially allowable and must be taken into account in computing the tax shelter ratio. If interest to be paid with respect to a debt obligation the proceeds of which do not reduce the investment base (see A-14 of this section) is not explicitly represented as being potentially allowable, however, such interest will not be considered typically associated with the investment and will not be taken into account in computing the tax shelter ratio.

Q-12. If representations are made that part or all of an amount invested in a tax shelter will be deductible upon the occurrence of an unintended event, will the deduction be included in the aggregate amount of deductions?

A-12. No. Thus, for example, if representations are made that a person's investment in a tax shelter may give rise to a loss deduction if the investment becomes worthless, the amount of the loss deduction will not be included in the aggregate amount of deductions and will not be taken into account in computing the tax shelter ratio. Similarly, if representations are made that the costs of acquiring oil and gas lease interests may be deductible if the lease is proved worthless by abandonment, the amount of any loss deduction will not be included in the aggregate amount of deductions.

*Investment base*

Q-13. What does the term "investment base" mean?

A-13. The term "investment base" means, with respect to any year (as defined in A-7 of this section), the cumulative amount of money and the adjusted basis of other property (reduced by any liability to which such other property is subject) that is unconditionally required to be contributed or paid directly to the tax shelter on or before the close of such year by an investor.

Q-14. What amounts must be eliminated from the investment base?

A-14. The investment base must be reduced by the following amounts:

(1) Any amount borrowed by the investor, even if borrowed on a recourse basis, from any person who participated in the organization, sale, or management of the investment or who has an interest (other than an interest as a creditor) in the investment ("a participating person") or from any person who is related (as defined in section 168(e)(4)) to a participating person, unless the amount is unconditionally required to be repaid by the investor before the close of the year for which the determination is being made. An amount will be considered unconditionally required to be repaid by the investor only if any offering material in which the borrowed amount is described and any agreement to be entered into between a participating (or related) person and the investor provide that the amount must be repaid (without exception) by the end of the year for which the determination is being made. An amount that is to be repaid only from earnings of the investment is not an amount that is unconditionally required to be repaid and is thus excluded from the investment base. In addition, an amount is not unconditionally required to be repaid if the amount will be (or is expected to be) reloaned to the investor during the 5-year period ending after the date the investment is offered for sale.

(2) Any amount borrowed by the investor, even if borrowed on a recourse basis, from any person, if the loan is arranged by a participating (or related) person, unless the amount is unconditionally required to be repaid by the investor before the close of the year for which the determination is being made. Any borrowing that is represented (orally or in writing) as being available from a specific source will be treated as arranged by a participating (or related) person, if the participating (or related) person provides a list of investors, or information relating to the investment, to the lender or otherwise informs the lender about the investment. However, in the case of an amount borrowed on a recourse basis, the mere fact that a lender who is actively and regularly engaged in the business of lending money obtained information relating to the investment, from a participating (or related) person, solely in response to a lender's request made in connection with such borrowing or a prior loan to the investment, a participating (or related) person, or an investor, will not, by itself, result in a determination that the loans are arranged by a participating (or related) person. Financing may be treated as arranged by a participating (or related) person regardless of whether a commitment to provide the financing is made by the lender to the participating or related person.

For example, assume that a tax shelter organizer represents that the purchase of an interest in a tax shelter may be financed with the proceeds of a revolving loan, and the tax shelter organizer provides investors with the names of several banks or other lending institutions to which the tax shelter organizer has provided information about the investment. Assume further that the information was not provided in response to requests from such lending institutions made in connection with prior loans. The proceeds of the revolving loan will be excluded from the investment base because the loan is not unconditionally required to be repaid and it is treated as having been arranged by the tax shelter organizer.

(3) Any amount borrowed, directly or indirectly, from a lender located outside the United States ("foreign-connected financing"), of which a participating (or related) person knows or has reason to know.

(4) Any amounts to be held for the benefit of investors in cash, cash equivalents, or marketable securities. An amount is to be held in cash equivalents if the amount is to be held in a checking account, savings account, mutual fund, certificate of deposit, book entry government obligation, or any other similar account or arrangement. Marketable

securities are any securities that are part of an issue any portion of which is traded on an established securities market and any securities that are regularly quoted by brokers or dealers making a market.

(5) Any distributions (whether of cash or property) that will be made without regard to the income of the tax shelter, but only to the extent such distributions exceed the amount to be held as of the close of the year in cash, cash equivalents, or marketable securities.

*Tax shelter ratio—Miscellaneous*

Q-15. Does an investment satisfy the requirement in A-4(I) of this section ("the tax shelter ratio requirement") if it may be inferred from the representations made or to be made to investors that the tax shelter ratio for some, but not all, of the investors may be greater than 2 to 1 as of the close of any one of the first five years?

A-15. Yes. If the tax shelter ratio for any one investor may be greater than 2 to 1, the investment satisfies the tax shelter ratio requirement and is a tax shelter if it also meets the requirement in A-4 (II) of this section. Moreover, an investment will satisfy the tax shelter ratio requirement even if the tax shelter ratio for a single investor exceeds 2 to 1 as of the close of only one of the first five years.

For purposes of computing the tax shelter ratio for a year, all persons with interests in the investment are considered investors, except that general partners in a limited partnership will not be treated as investors in the partnership if the general partners' aggregate interest in each item of partnership income, gain, loss, deduction, and credit for such year is not expected to exceed 2 percent. In determining the general partners' interest in such items, limited partnership interests owned by general partners shall not be taken into account. For purposes other than the computation of the tax shelter ratio, however, all general partners will be treated as investors. Thus, for example, a general partner with a 1 percent interest in a limited partnership will be treated as an investor for the purpose of determining whether the partnership is a substantial investment.

Q-16. If a person could reasonably infer from the representations made or to be made about an investment that the tax shelter ratio for the investment may be greater than 2 to 1 under one arrangement for financing the purchase of an interest by an investor, but would be 2 to 1 or less under an alternative financing arrangement, does the investment satisfy the tax shelter ratio requirement of A-4(I) of this section?

A-16. Yes. An investment satisfies the tax shelter ratio requirement of A-4(I) of this section if a person could reasonably infer from the representations made or to be made that the tax shelter ratio for any person may be greater than 2 to 1 as of the close of any one of the first five years. The tax shelter ratio requirement is met if the tax shelter ratio may exceed 2 to 1 under any type of financing arrangement that is or will be represented as being available to investors.

*Investments subject to securities regulation*

Q-17. What is an investment that is required to be registered under a federal law regulating securities?

A-17. An investment required to be registered under a federal law regulating securities is any public offering of an investment that is required to be registered under the Securities Act of 1933 (1933 Act), the Investment Company Act of 1940, or any other federal law regulating securities. An investment is required to be registered under the 1933 Act, the Investment Company Act, or any other federal law regulating securities, if failure to register the investment would result in a violation of the applicable federal law, whether or not the investment has in fact been registered and, if proper notice has not been filed, whether or not the investment could have been sold pursuant to an exemption listed in A-19 of this section if such notice had been filed.

Q-18. What is an investment required to be registered under a state law regulating securities?

A-18. An investment required to be registered under a state law regulating securities is any investment required to be registered under a blue sky law or other similar state statute regulating securities. The term "state" includes the 50 states, the District of Columbia, and possessions of the United States.

Q-19. What is an investment sold pursuant to an exemption from registration requiring the filing of a notice with a federal agency regulating the offering or sale of securities?

A-19. An investment sold pursuant to an exemption from registration requiring the filing of a notice with such a federal agency is any investment that is sold pursuant to an exemption from registration requiring the filing or submission of a notice or other document with the Securities and Exchange Commission or any other federal agency regulating the offering or sale of securities, including the following exemptions (and applicable filing):

(1) Regulation A, as promulgated under section (3)(b) of the 1933 Act (Form 1(A)),

(2) Regulation B, as promulgated under section 3(b) of the 1933 Act (Schedules A through F),

(3) Regulation D, as promulgated under sections (3)(b) and 4(2) of the 1933 Act (Form D), and

(4) Any other statutory or regulatory exemption from registration requiring the filing or submission of a notice or other document.

Q-20. What is an investment sold pursuant to an exemption from registration requiring the filing of a notice with a state agency regulating the offering or sale of securities?

A-20. An investment sold pursuant to an exemption from registration requiring the filing of a notice with such a state agency is any investment sold pursuant to an exemption under a blue sky law or other similar state statutory or regulatory scheme that requires the filing or submission of a notice or other document with such a state agency. See A-18 of this section for the definition of state.

*Substantial investments*

Q-21. What is a substantial investment?

A-21. An investment is a substantial investment if the aggregate amount that may be offered for sale to all investors exceeds $250,000 and 5 or more investors are expected. The aggregate amount offered for sale is the aggregate amount to be received from the sale of interests in the investment and includes all cash, the fair market value of all property contributed, and the principal amount of all indebtedness received in exchange for interests in the investment, regardless of whether the proceeds of the indebtedness are included in the investment base under A-14 of this section.

For purposes of determining whether 5 or more investors are expected in an investment involving real property (and related personal property) that is used as a farm (as defined in section 2032A(e)(4)) for farming purposes (as defined in section 2032A(e)(5)), interests in the investment expected to be held by a husband and wife, their children and parents, and the spouses of their children (or any of them) will be treated as if the interests were to be held by one investor. Thus, for example, interests in a farm that are offered to two brothers and their wives would be treated as interests offered to one investor. Such an investment could be a substantial investment only if four or more persons who were not members of the family were expected to be investors in the farm.

Q-22. Will an investment be considered a substantial investment if the investment involves a number of parts each including fewer than 5 investors or an aggregate amount of $250,000 or less?

A-22. Yes, under the circumstances described in this A-22. For purposes of determining whether investments are parts of a substantial investment, similar investments offered by the same person or related persons (as defined in section 168(e)(4)) are aggregated together. Investments are considered similar if they involve similar principal business assets and similar plans or arrangements. Investments that include no business assets will be considered similar if they involve similar plans or arrangements.

Similar investments are aggregated solely for the purpose of determining whether investments involving fewer than 5 investors or an aggregate amount of $250,000 or less are substantial investments. For this purpose, similar investments are aggregated even though some, but not all, of the investments are (i) required to be registered under a federal or state law regulating securities or are sold pursuant to an exemption from securities registration requiring the filing of a notice with a federal or state agency regulating the offering or sale of securities (*i.e.*, required to be registered as tax shelters whether or not a substantial investment) or (ii) substantial investments without regard to aggregation.

Assume, for example, that a person develops similar arrangements involving 8 different partnerships, each investing in a separate but similar asset (such as a separate master recording or separate piece of similar real estate), each with a different general partner and each with 3 different limited partners. Assume further that the arrangements of all of the partnerships are similar. These partnerships involving similar arrangements and similar assets would be aggregated together. Thus, if each partner is expected to invest $11,000, there will be 32 investors (1 general partner plus 3 limited partners times 8 partnerships) and an aggregate investment of $352,000 (32 partners times $11,000). Accordingly, each partnership will constitute part of a substantial investment. If representations are made that $1,000 in tax credits and $3,000 in deductions are available to each limited partner in the first year and $10,000 of the cash invested was expected to be the proceeds of a loan arranged by the organizer, the tax shelter ratio as of the close of the first year (assuming there are no deductions or credits typically associated with such investment, as described in A-9 of this section) would be 5 to 1 ($5,000 in total tax benefits and $1,000 investment base). Accordingly, the organizer would be required to register the partnerships with the Internal Revenue Service.

Q-23. If an investment involving fewer than 5 investors or an aggregate amount of $250,000 or less is offered for sale and, at the time of the offering, it is not known (and there is no reason to know) that subsequent similar investments will be offered by the person who made the first offering (or a related person), will subsequent similar investments offered by that person (or a related person) be aggregated with the first investment for purposes of determining whether the investments constitute a substantial investment?

A-23. No. However, a tax shelter organizer will be presumed to have known of any similar investments (as defined in A-22 of this section) offered during the 12 months following the first offering of an investment.

*Exceptions from tax shelter registration*

Q-24. Are there any investments that will not be subject to tax shelter registration even if they satisfy the requirements of a tax shelter (as defined in A-4 of this section)?

A-24. Yes. The following investments are not subject to tax shelter registration:

(1) Sales of residences primarily to persons who are expected to use the residences as their principal place of residence,

(2) Sales or leases of tangible personal property (other than master sound recordings, motion picture or television films, videotapes, lithograph plates, or other property relating to a literary, musical, or artistic composition) by the manufacturer (or a member of an affiliated group, within the meaning of section 1502, including the manufacturer) of the property primarily to persons who are expected to use the property in their principal active trade or business (see, however, A-32 and A-46 of this section for the additional rules applicable to a purchaser of property described in this A-24 who organizes an investment involving the property),

(3) Any other investment as specified by the Secretary in a rule-related notice published in the Federal Register.

Q-24A. Under what other circumstances are particular sales or leases of tangible personal property to certain persons or the performance of particular services for certain persons exempt from tax shelter registration?

A-24A. A person who, in the ordinary course of a trade or business, sells or leases tangible personal property (other than collectibles (as defined in section 408(m)(2)), master sound recordings, motion picture or television films, videotapes, lithograph plates, or other property that includes or relates to a literary, musical or artistic composition) to a purchaser or lessee who is reasonably expected to use the property either for a personal use or in the purchaser's or lessee's principal active trade or business is not required for any purpose to treat such a purchaser or lessee as an investor in a tax shelter. Property may be reasonably expected to be used by a purchaser or lessee for personal use only if sold or leased to the purchaser or lessee in a quantity that is customary for such use. Similarly, a person who performs services for another person in connection with the principal active trade or business of the recipient of the services or for the recipient's personal use is not required to treat the recipient as an investor in a tax shelter. Persons who are not reasonably expected to use property or services either in their principal active trade or business or for personal use must be treated as tax shelter investors in the event the sales, leases, or performance of services otherwise constitute a tax shelter.

Assume, for example, that an organizer forms Z corporation to feed cattle and to provide services in connection with the cattle feeding operations. Z will agree to serve customers with a minimum of 200 head of cattle. The fee for the services is $20 per head. Feed for the cattle will cost $280 per head. Z represents that the service fee and the cost of the feed may be financed by $5,000 of cash and $55,000 of proceeds of a revolving recourse note that Z has arranged to be available. Z provides its services to 100 customers. Ninety-five of the customers are persons whose principal active trade or business is reasonably expected to be farming (as defined in section 464(e)(1)). Five of the customers are not reasonably expected to engage in farming as their principal active trade or business. Although all the individual investments involve similar principal business assets and similar plans or arrangements, only the 5 customers who are not reasonably expected to be in the principal active trade or business of farming will be treated as investors in a tax shelter and aggregated to determine whether a substantial investment exists. Thus, there will be 5 investors and an aggregate investment of $300,000. If representations are made that the service fee and the cost of the feed are tax deductible, the tax shelter ratio (assuming there are no deductions or credits typically associated with such an investment, as described in A-9 of this section) would be 12 to 1 ($60,000 in total tax benefits and $5,000 investment base) and the organizer would be required to register the five aggregated feeding arrangements as a tax shelter. The registration number of the tax shelter must be provided to the five customers treated as investors in the tax shelter, but would not be required to be furnished to the customers whose principal active trade or business is reasonably expected to be farming.

*Persons required to register a tax shelter.*

Q-25. Who has the legal obligation to register a tax shelter?

A-25. A tax shelter organizer is obligated to register the tax shelter.

Q-26. What is the definition of tax shelter organizer?

A-26. Several categories of persons may be tax shelter organizers. In general, the term tax shelter organizer means a person principally responsible for organizing a tax shelter. If a person principally responsible for organizing a tax shelter has not registered the tax shelter by the day on which interests in the shelter are first offered for sale, any other person who participated in the organization of the tax shelter will be treated as a tax shelter organizer. If neither a person principally responsible for organizing the tax shelter nor any other person who participated in the organization of tax shelter has registered the tax shelter by the day on which interests in the tax shelter are first offered for sale, then any person who participates in the management of the tax shelter at a time when the tax shelter is not registered will be treated as a tax shelter organizer. Finally, if a person participates in the sale of a tax shelter at a time when the person knows or has reason to know that a tax shelter has not been registered, that person will be treated as a tax shelter organizer. See A-38 of this section for rules relating to the execution of an agreement among persons who may be treated as tax shelter organizers to designate one person to register a tax shelter.

Q-27. Who is a person principally responsible for organizing a tax shelter?

A-27. A person principally responsible for organizing a tax shelter ("principal organizer") is any person who discovers, creates, investigates, or initiates the investment, devises the business or financial plans for the investment, or carries out those plans through negotiations or transactions with others.

Q-28. What constitutes participation in the organization of a tax shelter?

A-28. Participation in the organization of a tax shelter includes the performance of any act (directly or through an agent) related to the establishment of the tax shelter, including the following:

(1) Preparation of any document establishing the tax shelter (for example, articles of incorporation, a trust instrument, or a partnership agreement);

(2) Preparation of any document in connection with the registration (or exemption from registration) of the tax shelter with any federal, state, or local government body;

(3) Preparation of a prospectus, offering memorandum, financial statement, or other statement describing the tax shelter;

(4) Preparation of a tax or other legal opinion relating to the tax shelter;

(5) Preparation of an appraisal relating to the tax shelter;

(6) Negotiation or other participation on behalf of the tax shelter in the purchase of any property relating to the tax shelter.

Q-29. What constitutes participation in the management of a tax shelter?

A-29. Participation in the management of a tax shelter includes managing the assets of the tax shelter, directing the business activity of the tax shelter, or, depending on the form of the tax shelter, acting as a general partner who actively participates in the management of a partnership, a trustee of a trust, a director or an officer of a corporation (including a corporate general partner of a partnership), or performing activities similar to those performed by such a general partner, a trustee, a director, or an officer.

Q-30. Will the performance of any act described in A-27 through A-29 of this section constitute participation in the organization or management of a tax shelter if the person performing the act is unrelated to the tax shelter (or any principal organizer of the tax shelter) and does not participate in the entrepreneurial risks or benefits of the tax shelter?

A-30. No. The performance of an act described in A-27 through A-29 of this section will not constitute participation in the organization or management of a tax shelter unless the person performing the act is related to the tax shelter (or any principal organizer of the tax shelter) or the person participates in the entrepreneurial risks or benefits of the tax shelter. A person will be considered related to a tax shelter if the person is related to the tax shelter or a principal organizer of the tax shelter within the meaning of section 168(e)(4) or is employed by the tax shelter or a principal organizer of the tax shelter or has an interest (other than an interest as a creditor) in the tax shelter. A person will be considered a participant in the entrepreneurial risks or benefits of a tax shelter if the person's compensation for performing an act described in A-27 through A-29 of this section is contingent on any matter relating to the tax shelter (*e.g.*, the compensation is based in whole or in part upon (i) whether interests in the tax shelter are actually sold or (ii) the number or value of the units in the tax shelter that are sold), or if the person will receive an interest in the tax shelter as part or all of the person's compensation.

For example, assume that A forms Z partnership, a tax shelter for which registration is required. Z hires the X law firm, none of the partners of which is related to the tax shelter, to prepare the documents necessary to register the offering of Z securities with the Securities and Exchange Commission. X charges $100 an hour for its services in connection with the preparation of the necessary documents, and payment of the fee is not contingent. X will not be treated as a participant in the organization of the tax shelter. If, however, X were to charge a fee equal to 1 percent of the value of the units in the tax shelter that are sold, X would be considered a participant in the organization of the shelter.

As another example, assume that individual C is an attorney employed by W corporation, the corporate general partner and principal organizer of Z, and that C prepares the documents necessary to register the tax shelter with the Securities and Exchange Commission. C will be treated as having participated in the organization of the tax shelter regardless of the way in which C's compensation is structured, because C, as an employee, is related to the principal organizer of the tax shelter.

Q-31. What constitutes participation in the sale of a tax shelter?

A-31. Participation in the sale of a tax shelter includes any marketing activities (directly or through an agent) with respect to an investment, including the following:

(1) Direct contact with a prospective purchaser of an interest, or with a representative or agent of a prospective purchaser, but only if the contact relates to the possible purchase of an interest in the tax shelter;

(2) Solicitation of investors using the mail, telephone, or other means, or by placing an advertisement for the tax shelter in a newspaper, magazine, or other publication or medium;

(3) Instructing or advising salespersons regarding the tax shelter or sales presentations.

Q-32. May persons be treated as tax shelter organizers if such persons do not make any representations of tax benefits to investors?

A-32. Yes. If a person described in A-26 of this section knows or has reason to know that representations of tax benefits have been made, that person may be treated as a tax shelter organizer. For example, a participant in the sale of a tax shelter may know or have reason to know that representations of tax benefits have been made by the principal organizer or others who participate in the organization of the tax shelter. In addition, a person who acquires property from a manufacturer in a transaction exempt from tax shelter registration under A-24 of this section and who organizes an investment involving the property may know or have reason to know of any representation of tax benefits made by the manufacturer.

Q-33. If a person performs support services such as typing, photocopying, or printing for a tax shelter (or a tax shelter organizer) or performs other ministerial functions for the tax shelter (or a tax shelter organizer), may the person be considered to have participated in the organization, management, or sale of the tax shelter?

A-33. No. Merely performing support services or ministerial functions will not be considered participation in the organization, management, or sale of a tax shelter.

*Circumstances under which tax shelter organizers are required to register a tax shelter*

Q-34. When is a principal organizer or a person who participates in the organization of a tax shelter required to register a tax shelter?

A-34. A principal organizer or a person who participates in the organization of a tax shelter (*i.e.*, a person who could be treated as a tax shelter organizer within the meaning of A-26 of this section) is required to register the tax shelter by the day on which the first offering for sale of interests in the tax shelter occurs, unless the person has signed a designation agreement pursuant to A-38 of this section. If a group of persons who could be treated as tax shelter organizers has signed a designation agreement pursuant to A-38 of this section, the designated organizer is required to register the tax shelter by the day on which the first offering for sale of interests in the tax shelter occurs. See A-39 of this section for additional rules applicable to tax shelter organizers (other than a designated organizer) who have signed a designation agreement.

Q-35. When is a person who participates in the management of a tax shelter ("manager") required to register a tax shelter?

A-35. A manager who has not signed a designation agreement pursuant to A-38 of this section must register the tax shelter if the manager participates in the management of the tax shelter on or after the first offering for sale of interests in the tax shelter at a time when the tax shelter has not been properly registered (*i.e.*, the manager is treated as a tax shelter organizer within the meaning of A-26 of this section). Such a manager must register the tax shelter by the day on which the first offering for sale of interests in the tax shelter occurs, or by the day on which the manager's participation in the management of the tax shelter commences, whichever is later. See A-39 of this section for rules applicable to a manager who has signed a designation agreement.

Q-36. When is a person who participates in the sale of a tax shelter ("seller") required to register the tax shelter?

A-36. A seller who has not signed a designation agreement pursuant to A-38 of this section must register the tax shelter if the seller participates in the sale of the tax shelter at a time when the seller

knows or has reason to know that the tax shelter has not been properly registered (*i.e.*, the seller is treated as a tax shelter organizer within the meaning of A-26 of this section). A seller who has not signed a designation agreement will be deemed to have reason to know that the tax shelter has not been properly registered if the seller does not receive a copy of the Internal Revenue Service tax shelter registration notice containing the registration number within the 30-day period after the seller first offers interests in the tax shelter for sale. A seller must register the tax shelter as soon as practicable after the seller first knows or has reason to know that the tax shelter has not been properly registered. See A-39 of this section for rules applicable to a seller who has signed a designation agreement.

Q-37. When is a person who acts in more than one capacity with respect to a tax shelter required to register the shelter?

A-37. A person who acts in more than one capacity with respect to a tax shelter (*i.e.*, as two or more of the following: principal organizer, participant in the organization, manager, or seller) must register the tax shelter by the earliest day on which a tax shelter organizer acting in any of the person's several capacities would be required to register the tax shelter.

Q-38. May a group of persons who could be treated as tax shelter organizers under A-26 of this section designate one person to register the tax shelter?

A-38. Yes. A group of persons who could be treated as tax shelter organizers under A-26 of this section may enter into a written agreement designating one person as the tax shelter organizer responsible for registering the tax shelter ("designated organizer"). The designated organizer should ordinarily be a person principally responsible for organizing the tax shelter, but may be any person who participates in the organization of the tax shelter. Although persons who participate only in the sale or management of a tax shelter may sign a designation agreement, they may not be the designated organizer. In addition, the designated organizer may not be a person who is resident in a country other than the United States. Any person who signs a designation agreement, other than the designated organizer, will not be liable for failing to register the tax shelter and will not be subject to a penalty, even if the designated organizer fails to register the tax shelter, unless the person fails to register the tax shelter when such registration is required under A-39 of this section. See A-7 of §301.6707-1T for additional rules relating to the reasonable cause exception applicable to persons who sign a designation agreement.

Q-39. Is a tax shelter organizer who has signed a designation agreement and who is not the designated organizer required to register the tax shelter under any circumstances?

A-39. Yes. If a tax shelter organizer who has signed a designation agreement pursuant to A-38 of this section knows or has reason to know on or after the day on which the first offering for sale of interests in a tax shelter occurs that the designated organizer failed to register the tax shelter, such tax shelter organizer must register the tax shelter as soon as practicable after he first knows or has reason to know of the failure. A tax shelter organizer who has signed a designation agreement is deemed to have reason to know that the designated organizer has failed to register the tax shelter if the tax shelter organizer does not receive a copy of the Internal Revenue Service registration notice containing the registration number from the designated organizer within the 60-day period after the day on which the first offering for sale of interests in the tax shelter occurs (or the person signs the designation agreement, if later). See A-41 of this section for the requirement that the designated organizer provide a copy of the registration notice and number to persons who have signed the designation agreement.

*Registration—General Rules*

Q-40. By what date must a tax shelter be registered?

A-40. A tax shelter must be registered not later than the day on which the first offering for sale of an interest in the tax shelter occurs.

Q-41. Is a tax shelter organizer (including a designated organizer) who registers a tax shelter responsible for performing any act with respect to tax shelter registration other than registering the tax shelter?

A-41. Yes. A tax shelter organizer (including a designated organizer) who registers a tax shelter must provide a copy of the Internal Revenue Service registration notice, containing the registration number within 7 days after the notice is received from the Internal Revenue Service to the principal organizer (if a different person) and to any persons who the tax shelter organizer knows or has reason to know are participating in the sale of interests in the tax shelter (if such persons begin to participate after the registration number is received, they must be provided the notice within 7 days after they commence their participation). In addition, a designated organizer must provide a copy of the notice within 7 days after it is received to all persons who have signed the designation agreement.

Q-42. What is the sale of an interest in a tax shelter?

A-42. The sale of an interest in a tax shelter includes the sale of property, or any interest in property, the entry into a leasing arrangement, a consulting, management or other agreement for the performance of services, or the sale or entry into any other plan, investment, or arrangement.

Q-43. What does the term "offering for sale" mean?

A-43. The term "offering for sale" means making any representation, whether oral or written, relating to participation in a tax shelter as an investor. The term includes any advertisement relating to the tax shelter and any mail, telephonic, or other contact with prospective investors. A representation relating to participation in a tax shelter will be considered an offering for sale of an interest in the tax shelter even though there is included in the representation an explicit statement that the representation does not constitute an offer to sell or a solicitation of an offer to buy an interest in the tax shelter. In determining whether an offering for sale of an interest has occurred, federal and state laws regulating securities are not controlling.

Q-44. After a tax shelter has been registered, must it be registered again each year that it continues to be offered for sale?

A-44. No. Registration is effective for the year in which first accomplished and all subsequent years.

Q-45. If the facts relating to a tax shelter change after the tax shelter has been registered, must the tax shelter be registered again or must an amended application for registration be filed by the tax shelter organizer?

A-45. No. The tax shelter organizer, however, is permitted to file an amended application if a material change in facts occurs after the initial registration. A material change in facts is—

(1) A change in the identifying information relating to the tax shelter or tax shelter organizer,

(2) The acquisition or construction of a principal asset not reported on the initial application for registration,

(3) A change in the method of financing a minimum investment unit, or

(4) A change in the principal business activity.

In addition, a change in any tax shelter ratio reported on the initial application for registration that increases or decreases the reciprocal of the tax shelter ratio (*i.e.*, the fraction in which the amount of the applicable investment base is the numerator and the amount of the applicable deductions and credits is the denominator) by 50 percent or more is a material change in facts. For example, if the tax shelter ratio increases from 2 to 1 to 4 to 1, the reciprocal of the tax shelter ratio decreases from $1/2$ to $1/4$, a 50-percent decrease. Similarly, if the tax shelter ratio decreases from 6 to 1 to 4 to 1, the reciprocal of the tax shelter ratio increases from $1/6$ to $1/4$, a 50-percent increase. In either case, there is a material change in facts and an amended application could be filed.

Q-45A. What information should be included on an amended application for registration?

A-45A. The tax shelter organizer must include the identifying information requested on Form 8264, Application for Registration of a Tax Shelter, and the tax shelter registration number that has been assigned to the tax shelter. In addition, the tax shelter organizer should include any other information requested on Form 8264 (1) that has changed since the tax shelter was registered, or (2) that the tax shelter organizer did not know at the time the tax shelter was registered but has learned of since the registration.

For example, assume that A organizes partnership L, a blind pool that will invest in real estate. Before the real estate is identified or acquired, interests in L will be offered to the public in an offering that must be registered with the Securities and Exchange Commission. Although A does not know what real estate L will acquire and therefore is unable to calculate the tax shelter ratio with certainty, A concludes (based on representations made or to be made) that the tax shelter ratio will exceed 2 to 1 as to some of the investors. Accordingly, A registers L as a tax shelter. A attaches a statement to the application for registration, explaining that L is a blind pool organized to invest in real estate, but that L has not yet acquired any real estate. In addition, A attaches a statement explaining that although the tax shelter ratio is expected to exceed 2 to 1, A cannot compute the tax shelter ratio with certainty because L has not yet acquired any real estate. Several months after L is registered, L acquires a shopping center. A may file an amended application for registration. In addition to reporting the identifying information and the tax shelter registration number on the amended application, A should report the shopping center as the principal asset and the recomputed tax shelter ratio.

As another example, assume that C organizes a limited partnership that is a tax shelter. On the application for registration, C reports that the tax shelter ratio is 2.2 to 1. After the partnership has been registered, C finds that the partnership is unable to attract sufficient investors. To make investing in the partnership more attractive, C decides to offer financing for the purchase of interests in the partnership. As a result of the change in financing, the tax shelter ratio will be 5 to 1. Because there is a change in financing and a change in the

tax shelter ratio that decreases the reciprocal of the tax shelter ratio by 50 percent or more, C may file an amended application for registration. In addition to reporting the identifying information and the tax shelter registration number on the amended application, C should report the recomputed tax shelter ratio and information relating to the change in financing.

Q-46. If assets constituting a tax shelter are sold ("original sale") and, subsequently, either the assets or interests in the assets are offered for sale by the purchaser ("resale"), must the purchaser file a new application for registration if the resale is an offering or sale of interests in a tax shelter?

A-46. If the resale constitutes a tax shelter, the purchaser must file a new application for registration, unless the tax shelter organizer with respect to the original sale is also the tax shelter organizer with respect to the resale and the facts pertaining to the resale were reflected in the application for registration filed with respect to the original sale. For example, assume that A intends to sell a building with an estimated fair market value of $2.5 million to a group of 5 investors (*i.e.*, a substantial investment, as defined in A-21 of this section). A also intends to make representations of tax benefits attributable to an investment in the building. Based on these representations and the investment base, the tax shelter ratio attributable to an investment in the building may be greater than 2 to 1. A therefore files an application for registration relating to the building with the Internal Revenue Service. The Internal Revenue Service issues a registration number for the investment, and A furnishes the registration number to each of the 5 investors in accordance with A-53 of this section. In an unrelated transaction, the 5 investors decide to syndicate the building and to offer interests in the syndicate to approximately 500 investors. In connection with this offer, the investors expect to make representations concerning tax benefits with respect to the syndication. If based on these representations and the investment base, the tax shelter ratio may be greater than 2 to 1 for an investor in the syndicate, the 5 investors must file an application for registration for the syndicate before interests in the syndicate may be offered for sale. The investors in the syndicate must be furnished with the new registration number and not the registration number issued with respect to A. On the other hand, if the original sale and the syndication were part of A's plan to sell interests in the building, A is a tax shelter organizer with respect to the syndication. If the facts pertaining to the syndication were reflected on A's application for registration with respect to the original sale, a second application for registration would not be required with respect to the syndication. However, the investors in the syndicate would have to be furnished with the tax shelter registration number issued to A.

Q-47. When is a tax shelter considered registered?

A-47. A tax shelter is considered registered when a properly completed Form 8264, Application for Registration of a Tax Shelter, is filed with the appropriate Internal Revenue Service Center. See A-7 of §301.6111-2T for rules relating to the information required to be included on the form, and A-8 of §301.6707-1T for rules relating to the penalty for filing incomplete information.

Q-48. Must a person registering a tax shelter that is a substantial investment only by reason of an aggregation of multiple investments under A-22 of this section complete a separate Form 8264 for each investment constituting part of the substantial investment?

A-48. A separate Form 8264 must be completed for each investment that differs from the other investments in a substantial investment with respect to any of the following:

(1) Principal asset,

(2) Accounting methods,

(3) Federal or state agencies with which the investment is registered or with which an exemption notice is filed,

(4) Methods of financing the purchase of an interest in the investment,

(5) Tax shelter ratio.

Such aggregated investments, however, are part of a single tax shelter.

Q-49. Do the rules of section 7502 of the Internal Revenue Code, regarding timely mailing, apply to the filing of registration forms?

A-49. Yes.

Q-50. After a tax shelter has been registered, may representations that the investment has been registered with the Internal Revenue Service be made to potential investors?

A-50. Investors may be informed that the investment has been registered with the Internal Revenue Service. Investors also must be informed, however, that registration does not imply that the Internal Revenue Service has reviewed, examined, or approved the investment or the claimed tax benefits. The disclaimer must be substantially in the form provided below:

Issuance of a registration number does not indicate that this investment or the claimed tax benefits have been reviewed, examined, or approved by the Internal Revenue Service.

**Reg. §301.6111-1T**

See A-53 of this section for rules relating to the legend that must be included on any statement on which the tax shelter registration number is furnished to investors.

*Furnishing tax shelter registration numbers*

Q-51. Who must furnish investors in a tax shelter with the registration number of the tax shelter?

A-51. Any person who sells (or otherwise transfers) an interest in a tax shelter is required to furnish the registration number assigned to that tax shelter to each person who purchases (or otherwise acquires) an interest in that tax shelter from the seller or transferor. For example, X, a tax shelter organizer, sells an interest in a tax shelter to A. One year later A sells A's interest in the shelter to B. X must furnish the tax shelter registration number to A, and A must furnish the number to B. If B sells or otherwise transfers the interest (by gift, for example), B must furnish the number to the purchaser or transferee of B's interest in the tax shelter.

Q-52. When must the registration number be furnished to purchasers of interests in the tax shelter?

A-52. The person who sells (or otherwise transfers) an interest in a tax shelter must furnish the registration number to the purchaser (or transferee) at the time of sale (or transfer) of the interest (or, if later, within 20 days after the seller or transferor receives the registration number). If the registration number is not furnished at the time of the sale (or other transfer), the seller (or transferor) must furnish the statement described in A-54 to the purchaser (or transferee) at the time of the sale (or other transfer). If interests in a tax shelter were sold before September 1, 1984, all investors who acquired their interests in the tax shelter before September 1, 1984, must be furnished with the registration number of the tax shelter by December 31, 1984. The registration number will be considered furnished to the investor if it is mailed to the investor at the last address of the investor known to the person required to furnish the number.

Q-53. How is a seller or transferor of an interest in a tax shelter required to furnish the registration number to investors?

A-53. The person who sells (or otherwise transfers) an interest in a tax shelter must furnish the registration number of the tax shelter to the purchaser (or transferee) on a written statement. The written statement shall show the name, registration number, and taxpayer identification number of the tax shelter, and include a prominent legend in bold and conspicuous type stating that the registration number must be included on any return on which the investor claims any deduction, loss, credit, or other tax benefit, or reports any income, by reason of the tax shelter. The statement must also include a prominent legend in bold and conspicuous type stating that the issuance of the registration number does not indicate that the Internal Revenue Service has reviewed, examined, or approved the investment or the claimed tax benefits. The statement shall be substantially in the form provided below:

You have acquired an interest in [name and address of tax shelter]whose taxpayer identification number is [if any]. The Internal Revenue Service has issued [name of tax shelter] the following tax shelter registration number: [Number]

You must report this registration number to the Internal Revenue Service, if you claim any deduction, loss, credit, or other tax benefit or report any income by reason of your investment in [name of tax shelter].

You must report the registration number (as well as the name, and taxpayer identification number of [name of tax shelter]) on Form 8271.

Form 8271 must be attached to the return on which you claim the deduction, loss, credit, or other tax benefit or report any income.

Issuance of a registration number does not indicate that this investment or the claimed tax benefits have been reviewed, examined, or approved by the Internal Revenue Service.

This statement may be modified as necessary if the tax shelter is not a separate entity (*e.g.*, certain Schedule F or Schedule C activities) or has no name or taxpayer identification number.

Q-54. If a registration number has not been received by a seller (or transferor) from the person who registered the tax shelter by the time interests in the tax shelter are sold (or otherwise transferred), must the seller (or transferor) of the interests furnish the purchaser (or transferee) with any information regarding the registration?

A-54. Yes. At the time of the sale (or other transfer) the seller (or other transferor) must furnish the purchaser (or transferee) with a written statement in substantially the form prescribed in A-53 of this section, except that the second sentence of the form prescribed in A-53 shall be replaced by a statement in the form provided below:

On behalf of [name of tax shelter], [name of tax shelter organizer who has applied for registration] has applied to the Internal Revenue Service for a tax shelter registration number. The number will be furnished to you when it is received.

*Including the registration number on tax returns*

Q-55. Is an investor required to report the registration number of a tax shelter in which the investor has acquired an interest to the Internal Revenue Service?

A-55. Yes. Any person claiming any deduction, loss, credit, or other tax benefit by reason of a tax shelter must report the registration number of the tax shelter on Form 8271, Investor Reporting of Tax Shelter Registration Number, which must be attached to the return on which any deduction, loss, credit, or other tax benefit attributable to the tax shelter is claimed. For purposes of determining whether the tax shelter registration number must be reported by an investor, income attributable to an investment, such as a partner's distributive share of income, constitutes a deduction or tax benefit that is claimed, because gross deductions and other tax benefits are included in the net income reported by the investor. Thus, the registration number also must be reported on any return on which an investor reports any income attributable to a tax shelter.

Q-56. What should the investor do if the investor has received a notice that a registration number for the tax shelter has been applied for, but the investor has not received the registration number by the time the investor files a return on which a deduction, loss, credit, other tax benefit, or income attributable to the tax shelter is included?

A-56. The investor must attach to the return a Form 8271 with the words "Applied For" written in the space for the registration number and must include on the Form 8271 the name and taxpayer identification number (if any) of the tax shelter and the name of the person who has applied for registration of the tax shelter.

Q-57. Does the requirement to include the tax shelter registration number on a return apply to applications for tentative refund (Form 1045 and Form 1139) and amended returns (Form 1040X, Form 1120X)?

A-57. Yes. A completed Form 8271 must be attached to any such return on which any deduction, loss, credit, other tax benefit, or income relating to a tax shelter is included.

*Projected income investments*

Q-57A. Are the registration requirements suspended with respect to any tax shelters?

A-57A. Yes. If a tax shelter is a projected income investment, it is not required to be registered before the first offering for sale of an interest in the tax shelter occurs, but is subject only to the registration requirements set forth in A-57H through A-57J of this section. A tax shelter is a projected income investment if—

(a) The tax shelter is not expected to reduce the cumulative tax liability of any investor for any year during the 5-year period described in A-4(I) of this section; and

(b) The assets of the tax shelter do not include or relate to any property described in A-57E of this section.

Q-57B. Under what circumstances does a tax shelter satisfy the requirement of paragraph (a) of A-57A of this section?

A-57B. A tax shelter is not expected to reduce the cumulative tax liability of an investor for any year during the 5-year period described in A-4(I) of this section only if—

(a) A written financial projection or other written representation that is provided to investors before the sale of interests in the investment states (or leads a reasonable investor to believe) that the investment will not reduce the cumulative tax liability of any investor with respect to any year (within the meaning of A-7 of this section) in such 5-year period; and

(b) No written or oral projections or representations, other than those related to circumstances that are highly unlikely to occur, state (or lead a reasonable investor to believe) that the investment may reduce the cumulative tax liability of any investor with respect to any such year.

Thus, a tax shelter for which there are multiple written or oral financial projections or other representations is not a projected income investment if any such projection or representation that relates to circumstances that are not highly unlikely to occur states (or leads a reasonable investor to believe) that the investment may reduce the cumulative tax liability of any investor. See A-57D and A-57F of this section for rules relating to financial projections or other representations that are not made in good faith, that are not based on reasonable economic and business assumptions, or that relate to circumstances that are highly unlikely.

Q-57C. When does an investment reduce the cumulative tax liability of an investor?

A-57C. (a) An investment reduces the cumulative tax liability of an investor with respect to a year during the 5-year period described in A-4(I) of this section if, as of the close of such year, (i) cumulative projected deductions for the investor exceed cumulative projected income for the investor, or (ii) cumulative projected credits for the investor exceed cumulative projected tax liability (without regard to credits) for the investor.

(b) The cumulative projected deductions for an investor as of the close of a year are the gross deductions of the investor with respect to the investment, for all periods up to (and including) the end of such year, that are included in the financial projection or upon which the representation is based. The deductions with respect to an investment include all deductions explicitly represented as being allowable and all deductions typically associated (within the meaning of A-9 of this section) with the investment. Therefore, interest to be paid by the investor that is taken into account in determining the tax shelter ratio of the investment (see A-11 of this section) is treated as a deduction with respect to the investment.

(c) The cumulative projected income for an investor as of the close of a year is the gross income of the investor with respect to the investment, for all periods up to (and including) the end of such year, that is included in the financial projection or upon which the representation is based. For this purpose, income attributable to cash, cash equivalents, or marketable securities (within the meaning of A-14(4) of this section) may not be treated as income from the investment.

(d) The cumulative projected credits for an investor as of the close of a year are the gross credits of the investor with respect to the investment, for all periods up to (and including) the close of such year, that are included in the financial projection or upon which the representation is based. The credits with respect to an investment include all credits explicitly represented as being allowable and all credits typically associated (within the meaning of A-9 of this section) with the investment.

(e) The cumulative projected tax liability (without regard to credits) for an investor as of the close of a year is 50 percent of the excess of cumulative projected income for the investor over cumulative projected deductions for the investor with respect to the investment as of the close of such year.

(f) The following examples illustrate the application of the principles of this A-57C:

*Example (1).* The promotional material with respect to a tax shelter includes a written financial projection indicating that the expected income of the investment in each of its first 5 years is $800,000. In subsequent oral discussions, investors are advised that, in certain circumstances that are not highly unlikely, the income expected from the investment may be as little as $500,000 per year. The subsequent oral discussions are taken into account in determining whether any projections or representations state or lead a reasonable investor to believe that the investment may reduce the cumulative tax liability of any investor. Thus, if the written financial projections indicate that the gross deductions attributable to the investment in each of its first 5 years are expected to be $600,000 and the subsequent oral discussions do not indicate that the amount of those deductions will change under the circumstances in which the income expected may be as little as $500,000, the subsequent oral discussions taken together with the written financial projections state (or lead a reasonable investor to believe) that the cumulative tax liability of an investor may be reduced (*i.e.,* the subsequent oral discussions (taken together with the projections) state or lead a reasonable investor to believe that cumulative projected deductions may exceed cumulative projected income under circumstances that are not highly unlikely). Accordingly, under paragraph (b) of A-57B of this section, the tax shelter would not qualify as a projected income investment.

*Example (2).* The written promotional material with respect to a tax shelter states that certain deductions are allowable to an investor (without specifying their amount), but there is no written statement relating to the amount of income expected from the investment. Because there is no written financial projection or other written representation that states or leads a reasonable investor to believe that the investment will not reduce the investor's cumulative tax liability (*i.e.,* the cumulative projected deductions, although not specified in the projections, may exceed the cumulative projected income (0)), the requirement of paragraph (a) of A-57B of this section would not be satisfied. The result in this example would be the same if there were only oral representations that the income to be derived from the investment would exceed the deductions with respect to the investment, because there would be no written statement as required by paragraph (a) of A-57B of this section. The tax shelter in this case would qualify as a projected income investment, however, if the written promotional material contains good-faith representations based on reasonable economic and business assumptions that state or lead reasonable investors to believe that the cumulative projected income from the investment will exceed the cumulative projected deductions allowable with respect to the investment for each year in the 5-year period, even though the amounts of income and deductions are not specified.

*Example (3).* The written promotional material with respect to a tax shelter includes a good-faith financial projection for the first 5 years of the investment. Based on reasonable economic and business assumptions, the projection indicates that the expected net income of the investment in each of its first 4 years is $100,000 ($500,000 of gross income and $400,000 of gross deductions), but as a result of the

anticipated acquisition of new business assets a loss of $20,000 is expected in the fifth year of the investment ($500,000 of gross income and $520,000 of gross deductions). The projection also indicates that a credit of $50,000 is expected in the fifth year of the investment. Such a written financial projection would be considered to state that the investment will not reduce the cumulative tax liability of any investor with respect to any year in the 5-year period described in A-4(I) of this section. Although a loss and a credit are projected in the fifth year of the investment, as of the close of such year, cumulative projected income ($2,500,000) exceeds cumulative projected deductions ($2,120,000), and cumulative projected tax liability (without regard to credits) ($380,000 × 50 percent = $190,000) exceeds cumulative projected credits ($50,000). Assuming no contrary oral or written projections or representations are made, the tax shelter would thus be a projected income investment.

*Example (4).* The written promotional material with respect to a tax shelter states that an investor will be entitled to a "1.5 to 1 write-off" in the year of investment. This statement is a representation that the investment will reduce the cumulative tax liability of an investor with respect to the first year of the investment and, accordingly, the investment is not a projected income investment. The result in this example would be the same if any "write-off" were represented, even if the write-off were less than 1.5 to 1.

Q-57D. Are all financial projections and representations relating to the cumulative tax liability of an investor taken into account for purposes of A-57B of this section?

A-57D. (a) No. A financial projection or other representation relating to the cumulative tax liability of an investor is not taken into account for purposes of A-57B of this section unless it is made in good faith and is based on reasonable economic and business assumptions. In addition, a financial projection or other representation is not taken into account if it relates to circumstances that are highly unlikely. Moreover, a general statement or disclaimer indicating that projected income is not guaranteed or otherwise assured, standing alone, is not a projection or representation for purposes of paragraph (b) of A-57B of this section.

(b) The following example illustrates the application of the principles of this A-57D:

*Example.* The written promotional material with respect to a tax shelter contains a representation stating that the investment is projected to produce net income for all investors in each of its first five years and there are no credits potentially allowable with respect to the investment. This statement is based on reasonable economic and business assumptions. Such a written representation, if made in good faith, would be considered under paragraph (a) of A-57B of this section to state that the investment will not reduce the cumulative tax liability of any investor with respect to any year in the 5-year period described in A-4(I) of this section. In addition, no oral or written statements or representations are communicated to investors that would indicate under paragraph (b) of A-57B of this section that the investment might reduce the cumulative tax liability of any investor with respect to any year in the 5-year period.

Assume the tax shelter organizer has knowledge of certain other facts that lead the tax shelter organizer to believe that it is more likely than not that the investment will produce a net loss in the first year. The representation projecting net income is thus contrary to the tax shelter organizer's belief that it is more likely than not that the investment will produce a net loss in the first year. Therefore, the representation is not made in good faith. Since representations not made in good faith are ignored under A-57D, the tax shelter would not be a projected income investment. If, on the other hand, the tax shelter organizer did not know of the other facts so that the tax shelter organizer did not believe that the investment would produce a net loss in the first year, the representation projecting income is made in good faith. In that case, the tax shelter would be a projected income investment.

Q-57E. What assets may not be held by a projected income investment?

A-57E. A tax shelter is not a projected income investment if more than an incidental amount of its assets include or relate to any interest in a collectible (as defined in section 408(m)(2)), a master sound recording, motion picture or television film, videotape, lithograph plate, copyright, or a literary, musical, or artistic composition.

Q-57F. What are the consequences if financial projections or other representations are not made in good faith or are not based on reasonable economic and business assumptions?

A-57F. If a tax shelter is not a projected income investment because the financial projections or other representations are not made in good faith or are not based on reasonable economic and business assumptions, it must be registered not later than the day on which the first offering for sale of an interest in the tax shelter occurs. If the tax shelter is not registered timely, the tax shelter organizer may be subject to a penalty. (See A-1 of § 301.6707-1T.)

Q-57G. When does a tax shelter cease to be a projected income investment?

A-57G. A tax shelter ceases to be a projected income investment on the last day of the first year (as defined in A-7 of this section) in the 5-year period described in A-4(I) of this section for which, for any investor, (i) the gross deductions allocable to the investor for that year and prior years exceed the gross income allocable to the investor for such years, or (ii) the credits allocable to the investor for that year and prior years exceed 50 percent of the amount by which gross income allocable to the investor exceeds gross deductions allocable to the investor for such years. For purposes of determining when a tax shelter ceases to be a projected income investment, the tax shelter organizer is not required to take into account interest that may be incurred by an investor with respect to debt described in A-14(2) or (3) of this section, but is required to take into account interest incurred by an investor with respect to debt described in A-14(1) of this section. In addition, the tax shelter organizer may not take into account income attributable to cash, cash equivalents, or marketable securities (within the meaning of A-14(4) of this section).

Q-57H. How does the requirement to register apply with respect to a tax shelter that is a projected income investment?

A-57H. In the case of a tax shelter that is a projected income investment, registration is not required unless the tax shelter ceases to be a projected income investment under A-57G of this section. If the tax shelter ceases to be a projected income investment, the tax shelter organizer must register the tax shelter in accordance with the rules set forth in A-1 through A-39 and A-41 through A-50 of this section. The tax shelter must be registered—

(a) Within 30 days after the date on which the tax shelter ceases to be a projected income investment, and

(b) Before the date on which the tax shelter or a tax shelter organizer sends the investor any schedule of profit or loss, or income, deduction, or credit that may be used in preparing the investor's income tax return for the taxable year that includes the date on which the tax shelter ceases to be a projected income investment. If a tax shelter organizer fails to register timely as required by this A-57H, the tax shelter organizer may be subject to a penalty. (See A-1 of § 301.6707-1T.) For example, assume that C is the principal organizer and general partner of a limited partnership. Interests in the partnership will be offered for sale in a public offering required to be registered with the Securities and Exchange Commission. C knows that the tax shelter ratio (as defined in A-5 of this section) for the limited partners will be 5 to 1. Although C knows the partnership is a tax shelter, C does not register the partnership by the day on which the first offering for sale of an interest occurs because C believes the partnership is a projected income investment. In the second year of the partnership, the gross deductions allocable to each of the limited partners for the first two years of the partnership exceed the gross income allocable to the limited partners in such years. Thus, the partnership ceases to be a projected income investment under A-57G of this section. Assuming further that C continues as the general partner and knowingly fails to register the partnership as a tax shelter within the time prescribed in this A-57H, C will be subject to a penalty of 1 percent of the aggregate amount invested in the partnership. Because there is an intentional disregard of the registration requirements, the $10,000 limitation will not apply.

Q-57I. How does the requirement to furnish registration numbers (A-51 through A-54 of this section) apply in the case of a tax shelter that is a projected income investment?

A-57I. In the case of a tax shelter that is a projected income investment, a person who sells or transfers an interest in the tax shelter is not required to furnish a registration number under A-51 of this section or a notice under A-54 of this section unless the tax shelter ceases to be a projected income investment. If the tax shelter ceases to be a projected income investment, the tax shelter organizer who registers the tax shelter is required to furnish the registration number to all persons who the tax shelter organizer knows or has reason to know are participating in the sale of interests in the tax shelter and to all persons who the tax shelter organizer knows or has reason to know have acquired interests in the tax shelter. A person who sold (or otherwise transferred) an interest in the tax shelter before the date on which the tax shelter ceased to be a projected income investment is required to furnish the registration number to the purchaser or transferee as provided in A-51 of this section only if the seller or transferor knows or has reason to know that the tax shelter has ceased to be a projected income investment and that the tax shelter organizer who registered the tax shelter has not provided a registration number to such purchaser or transferee. In the case of persons who acquired interests in the tax shelter before the date on which the tax shelter ceased to be a projected income investment, the registration number must be provided not later than the date described in paragraph (b) of A-57H of this section or, if the tax shelter does not provide any schedule described in paragraph (b) of A-57H of this section, within 60 days after the date on which the tax shelter

ceases to be a projected income investment. Thus, for example, if a tax shelter that ceases to be a projected income investment is a partnership, the tax shelter organizer would be required to provide the registration number to each partner not later than the date the Schedule K-1 for the year in which the tax shelter ceases to be a projected income investment is provided to each partner.

The registration number must be provided in accordance with A-51 and A-52 of this section and must be accompanied by a statement explaining that the tax shelter has ceased to be a projected income investment and instructing the recipient to furnish the registration number to any persons to whom the recipient has sold or otherwise transferred interests in the tax shelter. A tax shelter organizer who fails to provide the registration number as provided in this A-57I may be subject to penalties. (See A-12 of § 301.6707-1T.)

Q-57J. How does the requirement to include the registration number on tax returns (A-55 through A-57 of this section) apply in the case of a tax shelter that is a projected income investment?

A-57J. In the case of a tax shelter that is a projected income investment, an investor is not required to report a registration number on the investor's tax return unless the tax shelter ceases to be a projected income investment. If the tax shelter ceases to be a projected income investment, the requirements of A-55 through A-57 apply with respect to returns for taxable years ending on or after the date on which the tax shelter ceases to be a projected income investment.

*Effective dates*

Q-58. On what date does the requirement to register a tax shelter become effective?

A-58. In general, a tax shelter must be registered if any interest in the tax shelter (other than an interest previously sold to an investor) is sold on or after September 1, 1984 (whether or not interests in the tax shelter were sold or offered for sale before September 1, 1984). The tax shelter must be registered with the Internal Revenue Service not later than the first day after August 31, 1984 on which an interest in the tax shelter is offered for sale.

Q-59. By what date must the tax shelter registration number be furnished to investors who acquired interests before September 1, 1984 in a tax shelter that is required to be registered.

A-59. All investors who acquired their interests in a tax shelter before September 1, 1984 must be supplied with the tax shelter registration number by December 31, 1984. See A-52 of this section for the date by which registration numbers must be furnished to investors who acquire their interests on or after September 1, 1984.

Q-60. What interests will be taken into account in determining whether an investment in which interests were sold before September 1, 1984, is a substantial investment?

A-60. The determination of whether an investment is a substantial investment will be made by taking into account only the interests that are offered for sale on or after September 1, 1984. An investment will be considered a substantial investment if there are expected to be 5 or more investors on or after September 1, 1984, and the aggregate amount offered for sale on or after September 1, 1984 is expected to exceed $250,000. Amounts received from the sale of interests before September 1, 1984, however, are taken into account in computing the amount of the penalty for failure to register. [Temporary Reg. § 301.6111-1T.]

☐ [*T.D.* 7964, 8-13-84 (*corrected* 12-1-2008). *Amended by T.D.* 7990, 10-26-84 *and T.D.* 8078, 3-3-86.]

## [Reg. § 301.6111-2]

§ 301.6111-2. Confidential corporate tax shelters.—(a) *In general.*—(1) Under section 6111(d) and this section, a confidential corporate tax shelter is treated as a tax shelter subject to the requirements of sections 6111(a) and (b).

(2) A confidential corporate tax shelter is any transaction—

(i) A significant purpose of the structure of which is the avoidance or evasion of Federal income tax, as described in paragraph (b) of this section, for a direct or indirect corporate participant;

(ii) That is offered to any potential participant under conditions of confidentiality, as described in paragraph (c) of this section; and

(iii) For which the tax shelter promoters may receive fees in excess of $100,000 in the aggregate, as described in paragraph (d) of this section.

(3) For purposes of this section, references to the term *transaction* include all of the factual elements relevant to the expected tax treatment of any investment, entity, plan, or arrangement, and include any series of steps carried out as part of a plan. For purposes of this section, the term *substantially similar* includes any transaction that is expected to obtain the same or similar types of tax consequences and that is either factually similar or based on the same or similar tax strategy. Receipt of an opinion regarding the tax consequences of the transaction is not relevant to the determination of whether the trans-

action is the same as or substantially similar to another transaction. Further, the term *substantially similar* must be broadly construed in favor of registration. For examples, see § 1.6011-4(c)(4) of this chapter.

(4) A transaction described in paragraph (b) of this section is for a direct or an indirect corporate participant if it is expected to provide Federal income tax benefits to any corporation (U.S. or foreign) whether or not that corporation participates directly in the transaction.

(b) *Transactions structured for avoidance or evasion of Federal income tax.*—(1) *In general.*—The avoidance or evasion of Federal income tax will be considered a significant purpose of the structure of a transaction if the transaction is described in paragraph (b)(2) or (3) of this section. However, a transaction described in paragraph (b)(3) of this section need not be registered if the transaction is described in paragraph (b)(4) of this section. For purposes of this section, Federal income tax benefits include deductions, exclusions from gross income, nonrecognition of gain, tax credits, adjustments (or the absence of adjustments) to the basis of property, status as an entity exempt from Federal income taxation, and any other tax consequences that may reduce a taxpayer's Federal income tax liability by affecting the amount, timing, character, or source of any item of income, gain, expense, loss, or credit.

(2) *Listed transactions.*—A transaction is described in this paragraph (b)(2) if the transaction is the same as or substantially similar to one of the types of transactions that the Internal Revenue Service (IRS) has determined to be a tax avoidance transaction and identified by notice, regulation, or other form of published guidance as a listed transaction. If a transaction becomes a listed transaction after the date on which registration would otherwise be required under this section, and if the transaction otherwise satisfies the confidentiality and fee requirements of paragraphs (a)(2)(ii) and (iii) of this section, registration shall in all events be required with respect to any interests in the transaction that are offered for sale after the transaction becomes a listed transaction. However, because a transaction identified as a listed transaction is generally considered to have been structured for a significant tax avoidance purpose, such a transaction ordinarily will have been subject to registration under this section before becoming a listed transaction if the transaction previously satisfied the confidentiality and fee requirements of paragraphs (a)(2)(ii) and (iii) of this section.

(3) *Other tax-structured transactions.*—A transaction is described in this paragraph (b)(3) if it has been structured to produce Federal income tax benefits that constitute an important part of the intended results of the transaction and the tax shelter promoter (or other person who would be responsible for registration under this section) reasonably expects the transaction to be presented in the same or substantially similar form to more than one potential participant, unless the promoter reasonably determines that—

(i) The potential participant is expected to participate in the transaction in the ordinary course of its business in a form consistent with customary commercial practice (a transaction involving the acquisition, disposition, or restructuring of a business, including the acquisition, disposition, or other change in the ownership or control of an entity that is engaged in a business, or a transaction involving a recapitalization or an acquisition of capital for use in the taxpayer's business, shall be considered a transaction carried out in the ordinary course of a taxpayer's business); and

(ii) There is a generally accepted understanding that the expected Federal income tax benefits from the transaction (taking into account any combination of intended tax consequences) are properly allowable under the Internal Revenue Code for substantially similar transactions. There is no minimum period of time for which such a generally accepted understanding must exist. In general, however, a tax shelter promoter (or other person who would be responsible for registration under this section) cannot reasonably determine whether the intended tax treatment of a transaction has become generally accepted unless information relating to the tax treatment and tax structure of such transactions has been in the public domain (e.g., rulings, published articles, etc.) and widely known for a sufficient period of time (ordinarily a period of years) to provide knowledgeable tax practitioners and the IRS reasonable opportunity to evaluate the intended tax treatment. The mere fact that one or more knowledgeable tax practitioners have provided an opinion or advice to the effect that the intended tax treatment of the transaction should or will be sustained, if challenged by the IRS, is not sufficient to satisfy the requirements of this paragraph (b)(3)(ii).

(4) *Excepted transactions.*—The avoidance or evasion of Federal income tax will not be considered a significant purpose of the structure of a transaction if the transaction is described in either paragraph (b)(4)(i), (ii), or (iii) of this section.

(i) In the case of a transaction other than a transaction described in paragraph (b)(2) of this section, the tax shelter promoter

(or other person who would be responsible for registration under this section) reasonably determines that there is no reasonable basis under Federal tax law for denial of any significant portion of the expected Federal income tax benefits from the transaction. This paragraph (b)(4)(i) applies only if the tax shelter promoter (or other person who would be responsible for registration under this section) reasonably determines that there is no basis that would meet the standard applicable to taxpayers under § 1.6662-3(b)(3) of this chapter under which the IRS could disallow any significant portion of the expected Federal income tax benefits of the transaction. Thus, the reasonable basis standard is not satisfied by an IRS position that would be merely arguable or that would constitute merely a colorable claim. However, the determination of whether the IRS would or would not have a reasonable basis for such a position must take into account the entirety of the transaction and any combination of tax consequences that are expected to result from any component steps of the transaction, must not be based on any unreasonable or unrealistic factual assumptions, and must take into account all relevant aspects of Federal tax law, including the statute and legislative history, treaties, administrative guidance, and judicial decisions that establish principles of general application in the tax law (e.g., *Gregory v. Helvering*, 293 U.S. 465 (1935)). The determination of whether the IRS would or would not have such a reasonable basis is qualitative in nature and does not depend on any percentage or other quantitative assessment of the likelihood that the taxpayer would ultimately prevail if a significant portion of the expected tax benefits were disallowed by the IRS.

(ii) The IRS makes a determination by published guidance that the transaction is not subject to the registration requirements of this section.

(iii) The IRS makes a determination by individual ruling under paragraph (b)(5) of this section that a specific transaction is not subject to the registration requirements of this section for the taxpayer requesting the ruling.

(5) *Requests for ruling.*—If a tax shelter promoter (or other person who would be responsible for registration under this section) is uncertain whether a transaction is properly classified as a confidential corporate tax shelter or is otherwise uncertain whether registration is required under this section, that person may, on or before the date that registration would otherwise be required under this section, submit a request to the IRS for a ruling as to whether the transaction is subject to the registration requirements of this section. If the request fully discloses all relevant facts relating to the transaction, that person's potential obligation to register the transaction will be suspended during the period that the ruling request is pending and, if the IRS subsequently concludes that the transaction is a confidential corporate tax shelter subject to registration under this section, until the sixtieth day after the issuance of the ruling (or, if the request is withdrawn, sixty days from the date that the request is withdrawn). In the alternative, that person may register the transaction in accordance with the requirements of this section and append a statement to the Form 8264, "Application for Registration of a Tax Shelter," which states that the person is uncertain whether the transaction is required to be registered as a confidential corporate tax shelter, and that the Form 8264 is being filed on a protective basis.

(6) *Example.*—The following example illustrates the application of paragraphs (b)(1) through (4) of this section. Assume, for purposes of the example, that the transaction is not the same as or substantially similar to any of the types of transactions that the IRS has identified as listed transactions under section 6111 and, thus, is not described in paragraph (b)(2) of this section. The example is as follows:

*Example.* (i) *Facts.* Y has designed a combination of financial instruments to be issued as a package by corporations. The financial instruments are expected to be treated as equity for financial accounting purposes and as debt giving rise to allowable interest deductions for Federal income tax purposes. Y reasonably expects to present this method of raising capital to more than one potential corporate participant. Assume that, because of the unusual nature of the combination of financial instruments, Y cannot conclude either that the transaction represented by the financial instruments is in customary commercial form or that there is a generally accepted understanding that interest deductions are available to issuers of substantially similar combinations of financial instruments. Further, assume that Y cannot reasonably determine that the IRS would have no reasonable basis to deny the deductions.

(ii) *Analysis.* The transaction represented by this combination of financial instruments is a transaction described in paragraph (b)(3) of this section. However, if Y is uncertain whether this transaction is described in paragraph (b)(3) of this section, or is otherwise uncertain whether registration is required, Y may apply for a ruling under paragraph (b)(5) of this section, and Y will not be required to register the transaction while the ruling is pending or for sixty days thereafter.

(c) *Conditions of confidentiality.*—(1) *In general.*—All the facts and circumstances relating to the transaction will be considered when determining whether an offer is made under conditions of confidentiality as described in section 6111(d)(2), including prior conduct of the parties. Pursuant to section 6111(d)(2)(A), if an offeree's disclosure of the tax treatment or tax structure of the transaction is limited in any manner by an express or implied understanding or agreement with or for the benefit of any tax shelter promoter, an offer is considered made under conditions of confidentiality, whether or not such understanding or agreement is legally binding. The tax treatment of a transaction is the purported or claimed Federal income tax treatment of the transaction. The tax structure of a transaction is any fact that may be relevant to understanding the purported or claimed Federal income tax treatment of the transaction. Pursuant to section 6111(d)(2)(B), an offer will also be considered made under conditions of confidentiality in the absence of any such understanding or agreement if any tax shelter promoter knows or has reason to know that the offeree's use or disclosure of information relating to the tax treatment or tax structure of the transaction is limited for the benefit of any person other than the offeree in any other manner, such as where the transaction is claimed to be proprietary or exclusive to the tax shelter promoter or any party other than the offeree.

(2) *Exceptions.*—(i) *Securities law.*—An offer is not considered made under conditions of confidentiality if disclosure of the tax treatment or tax structure of the transaction is subject to restrictions reasonably necessary to comply with securities laws and such disclosure is not otherwise limited.

(ii) *Mergers and acquisitions.*—In the case of a proposed taxable or tax-free acquisition of historic assets of a corporation (other than an investment company, as defined in section 351(e), that is not publicly traded) that constitute an active trade or business the acquirer intends to continue, or a proposed taxable or tax-free acquisition of more than 50 percent of the stock of a corporation (other than an investment company, as defined in section 351(e), that is not publicly traded) that owns historic assets used in an active trade or business the acquirer intends to continue, the transaction is not considered offered under conditions of confidentiality under paragraph (c)(1) of this section if the offeree is permitted to disclose the tax treatment and tax structure of the transaction no later than the earlier of the date of the public announcement of discussions relating to the transaction, the date of the public announcement of the transaction, or the date of the execution of an agreement (with or without conditions) to enter into the transaction. However, this exception is not available where the offeree's ability to consult any tax advisor (including a tax advisor independent from all other entities involved in the transaction) regarding the tax treatment or tax structure of the transaction is limited in any way.

(3) *Presumption.*—Unless facts and circumstances indicate otherwise, an offer is not considered made under conditions of confidentiality if the tax shelter promoter provides express written authorization to each offeree permitting the offeree (and each employee, representative, or other agent of such offeree) to disclose to any and all persons, without limitation of any kind, the tax treatment and tax structure of the transaction, and all materials of any kind (including opinions or other tax analyses) that are provided to the offeree related to such tax treatment and tax structure. Except as provided in paragraph (c)(2) of this section, this presumption is available only in cases in which each written authorization permits the offeree to disclose the tax treatment and tax structure of the transaction immediately upon commencement of discussions with the tax shelter promoter providing the authorization and each written authorization is given no later than 30 days from the day the tax shelter promoter commenced discussions with the offeree. A transaction that is exclusive or proprietary to any party other than the offeree will not be considered offered under conditions of confidentiality if written authorization to disclose is provided to the offeree in accordance with this paragraph (c)(3) and the transaction is not otherwise confidential.

(d) *Determination of fees.*—All the facts and circumstances relating to the transaction will be considered when determining the amount of fees, in the aggregate, that the tax shelter promoters may receive. For purposes of this paragraph (d), all consideration that tax shelter promoters may receive is taken into account, including contingent fees, fees in the form of equity interests, and fees the promoters may receive for other transactions as consideration for promoting the tax shelter. For example, if a tax shelter promoter may receive a fee for arranging a transaction that is a confidential corporate tax shelter and a separate fee for another transaction that is not a confidential corporate tax shelter, part or all of the fee paid with respect to the other transaction may be treated as a fee paid with respect to the confidential corporate tax shelter if the facts and circumstances indi-

cate that the fee paid for the other transaction is in consideration for the confidential corporate tax shelter. For purposes of determining whether the tax shelter promoters may receive fees in excess of $100,000, the fees from all substantially similar transactions are considered part of the same tax shelter and must be aggregated.

(e) *Registration.*—(1) *Time for registering.*—(i) *In general.*—A tax shelter must be registered not later than the day on which the first offering for sale of interests in the shelter occurs. An offer to participate in a confidential corporate tax shelter shall be treated as an offer for sale. If interests in a confidential corporate tax shelter were first offered for sale on or before February 28, 2000, the first offer for sale of interests in the shelter that occurs after February 28, 2000 shall be considered the first offer for sale under this section.

(ii) *Special rule.*—If a transaction becomes a confidential corporate tax shelter (e.g., because of a change in the law or factual circumstances, or because the transaction becomes a listed transaction) subsequent to the first offering for sale after February 28, 2000, and the transaction was not previously required to be registered as a confidential corporate tax shelter under this section, the transaction must be registered under this section if interests are offered for sale after the transaction becomes a confidential corporate tax shelter. The transaction must be registered by the next offering for sale of interests in the shelter. If, subsequent to the first offering for sale, a transaction becomes a confidential corporate tax shelter because the transaction becomes a listed transaction on or after February 28, 2003, and the transaction was not previously required to be registered as a confidential corporate tax shelter under this section, the transaction must be registered under this section within 60 days after the transaction becomes a listed transaction/confidential corporate tax shelter if any interests were offered for sale within the previous six years.

(2) *Procedures for registering.*—To register a confidential corporate tax shelter, the person responsible for registering the tax shelter must file Form 8264, "Application for Registration of a Tax Shelter." (Form 8264 is also used to register tax shelters defined in section 6111(c).) Similar to the treatment provided under Q&A-22 and Q&A-48 of §301.6111-1T, transactions involving similar business assets and similar plans or arrangements that are offered to corporate taxpayers by the same person or related persons are aggregated and considered part of a single tax shelter. However, in contrast with the requirement of Q&A-48 of §301.6111-1T, the tax shelter promoter may file a single Form 8264 with respect to any such aggregated tax shelter, provided an amended Form 8264 is filed to reflect any material changes and to include any additional or revised written materials presented in connection with an offer to participate in the shelter. Furthermore, all transactions that are part of the same tax shelter and that are to be carried out by the same corporate participant (or one or more other members of the same affiliated group within the meaning of section 1504) must be registered on the same Form 8264.

(f) *Definition of tax shelter promoter.*—For purposes of section 6111(d)(2) and this section, the term *tax shelter promoter* includes a tax shelter organizer and any other person who participates in the organization, management or sale of a tax shelter (as those persons are described in section 6111(e)(1) and §301.6111-1T (Q&A-26 through Q&A-33) or any person related (within the meaning of section 267 or 707) to such tax shelter organizer or such other person.

(g) *Person required to register.*—(1) *Tax shelter promoters.*—The rules in section 6111(a) and (e) and §301.6111-1T (Q&A-34 through Q&A-39) determine who is required to register a confidential corporate tax shelter. A promoter of a confidential corporate tax shelter must register the tax shelter only if it is a person required to register under the rules in section 6111(a) and (e) and §301.6111-1T (Q&A-34 through Q&A-39).

(2) *Persons who discuss the transaction; all promoters are foreign persons.*—(i) *In general.*—If all of the tax shelter promoters of a confidential corporate tax shelter are foreign persons, any person who discusses participation in the transaction must register the shelter under this section within 90 days after beginning such discussions.

(ii) *Exceptions.*—Registration by a person discussing participation in a transaction is not required if either—

(A) The person does not participate, directly or indirectly, in the shelter and notifies the tax shelter promoter in writing, within 90 days of beginning such discussions, that the person will not participate; or

(B) Within 90 days after beginning such discussions, the person obtains and reasonably relies on both—

(1) A written statement from one of the tax shelter promoters that such promoter has registered the tax shelter under this section; and

(2) A copy of the registration.

(iii) *Determination of foreign status.*—For purposes of this paragraph (g)(2), a person must presume that all tax shelter promoters are foreign persons unless the person either—

(A) Discusses participation in the tax shelter with a promoter that is a United States person; or

(B) Obtains and reasonably relies on a written statement from one of the promoters that at least one of the promoters is a United States person.

(iv) *Discussion.*—Discussing participation in a transaction includes discussing such participation with any person that conveys the tax shelter promoter's proposal. For purposes of this paragraph (g)(2), any person that participates directly or indirectly in a transaction will be treated as having discussed participation in the transaction not later than the date of the agreement to participate. Thus, a tax shelter participant will be treated as having discussed participation in the transaction even if all discussions were conducted by an intermediary and the agreement to participate was made indirectly through another person acting on the participant's behalf (for example, through an intermediary empowered to commit the participant to participate in the shelter).

(v) *Special rule for controlled entities.*—A person (first person) will be treated as participating indirectly in a confidential corporate tax shelter if a foreign person controlled by the first person participates in the shelter, and a significant purpose of the shelter is the avoidance or evasion of the first person's Federal income tax. For purposes of this paragraph (g)(2)(v), control of a foreign corporation or partnership will be determined under the rules of section 6038(e)(2) and (3), except that such section shall be applied by substituting "10" for "50" each place it appears and "at least" for "more than" each place it appears. In addition, section 6038(e)(2) shall be applied for these purposes without regard to the constructive ownership rules of section 318 and by treating stock as owned if it is owned directly or indirectly. Section 6038(e)(3) shall be applied for these purposes without regard to the last sentence of section 6038(e)(3)(B). Any beneficiary with a 10 percent or more interest in a foreign trust or estate shall be treated as controlling that trust or estate for purposes of this paragraph (g)(2)(v).

(vi) *Other rules.*—(A) For purposes of the registration requirements under section 6111(d)(3), it is presumed that the tax shelter promoters will receive fees in excess of $100,000 in the aggregate unless the person responsible for registering the tax shelter can show otherwise.

(B) Any person treated as a tax shelter promoter under section 6111(d) solely by reason of being related (within the meaning of section 267 or 707) to a foreign promoter will be treated as a foreign promoter for purposes of this paragraph (g)(2).

(h) *Effective dates.*—This section applies to confidential corporate tax shelters in which any interests are offered for sale after February 28, 2000. If an interest is sold after February 28, 2000, it is treated as offered for sale after February 28, 2000, unless the sale was pursuant to a written binding contract entered into on or before February 28, 2000. However, paragraphs (a) through (g) of this section apply to confidential corporate tax shelters in which any interests are offered for sale on or after February 28, 2003, and to transactions described in paragraph (e)(1)(ii) of this section. The rules that apply to confidential corporate tax shelters in which any interests are offered for sale after February 28, 2000, and before February 28, 2003, are contained in § 301.6111-2T in effect prior to February 28, 2003 (see 26 CFR part 301 revised as of April 1, 2002, 2002-28 I.R.B 91, and 2002-45 I.R.B. 823 (see § 601.601(d)(2) of this chapter)). [Reg. § 301.6111-2.]

☐ [*T.D.* 9046, 2-28-2003.]

**[Reg. § 301.6111-3]**

**§ 301.6111-3. Disclosure of reportable transactions.**—(a) *In general.*—Each material advisor, as defined in paragraph (b) of this section, with respect to any reportable transaction, as defined in § 1.6011-4(b) of this chapter, must file a return as described in paragraph (d) of this section by the date described in paragraph (e) of this section.

(b) *Material advisor.*—(1) *In general.*—A person is a material advisor with respect to a transaction if the person provides any material aid, assistance, or advice with respect to organizing, managing, promoting, selling, implementing, insuring, or carrying out any reportable transaction, and directly or indirectly derives gross income in excess of the threshold amount as defined in paragraph (b)(3) of this section for the material aid, assistance, or advice. The term transaction includes all of the factual elements relevant to the expected tax treatment of any investment, entity, plan or arrangement, and includes any series of steps carried out as part of a plan.

(2) *Material aid, assistance, or advice.*—(i) *In general.*—Except as provided in paragraph (b)(5) of this section, a person provides material aid, assistance, or advice with respect to organizing, managing, promoting, selling, implementing, insuring, or carrying out any transaction if the person makes or provides a tax statement to or for the benefit of—

(A) A taxpayer who either is required to disclose the transaction under §§ 1.6011-4, 20.6011-4, 25.6011-4, 26.6011-4, 31.6011-4, 53.6011-4, 54.6011-4, or 56.6011-4 of this chapter because the transaction is a listed transaction or a transaction of interest, or would have been required to disclose the transaction under §§ 1.6011-4, 20.6011-4, 25.6011-4, 26.6011-4, 31.6011-4, 53.6011-4, 54.6011-4, or 56.6011-4 of this chapter if the transaction had become a listed transaction or a transaction of interest within the period of limitations in § 1.6011-4(e) of this chapter;

(B) A taxpayer who the potential material advisor knows is or reasonably expects to be required to disclose the transaction under § 1.6011-4 of this chapter because the transaction is or is reasonably expected to become a transaction described in § 1.6011-4(b)(3) through (5) or (7) of this chapter;

(C) A material advisor who is required to disclose the transaction under this section because it is a listed transaction or a transaction of interest; or

(D) A material advisor who the potential material advisor knows is or reasonably expects to be required to disclose the transaction under this section because the transaction is or is reasonably expected to become a transaction described in § 1.6011-4(b)(3) through (5) or (7) of this chapter.

(ii) *Tax statement.*—(A) *In general.*—A tax statement is any statement (including another person's statement), oral or written, that relates to a tax aspect of a transaction that causes the transaction to be a reportable transaction as defined in § 1.6011-4(b)(2) through (7) of this chapter. A tax statement under this section includes tax result protection that insures some or all of the tax benefits of a reportable transaction.

(B) *Confidential transactions.*—A statement relates to a tax aspect of a transaction that causes it to be a confidential transaction if the statement concerns a tax benefit related to the transaction and either the taxpayer's disclosure of the tax treatment or tax structure of the transaction is limited in the manner described in § 1.6011-4(b)(3) of this chapter by or for the benefit of the person making the statement, or the person making the statement knows the taxpayer's disclosure of the tax structure or tax aspects of the transaction is limited in the manner described in § 1.6011-4(b)(3) of this chapter.

(C) *Transactions with contractual protection.*—A statement relates to a tax aspect of a transaction that causes it to be a transaction with contractual protection if the statement concerns a tax benefit related to the transaction and either—

(1) The taxpayer has the right to a full or partial refund of fees paid to the person making the statement or the fees are contingent in the manner described in § 1.6011-4(b)(4) of this chapter; or

(2) The person making the statement knows or has reason to know that the taxpayer has the right to a full or partial refund of fees (described in § 1.6011-4(b)(4)(ii) of this chapter) paid to another if all or part of the intended tax consequences from the transaction are not sustained or that fees (as described in § 1.6011-4(b)(4)(ii) of this chapter) paid by the taxpayer to another are contingent on the taxpayer's realization of tax benefits from the transaction in the manner described in § 1.6011-4(b)(4) of this chapter.

(D) *Loss transactions.*—A statement relates to a tax aspect of a transaction that causes it to be a loss transaction if the statement concerns an item that gives rise to a loss described in § 1.6011-4(b)(5) of this chapter.

(E) *[Reserved].*

(iii) *Special rules.*—(A) *Capacity as an employee.*—A material advisor generally does not include a person who makes a tax statement solely in the person's capacity as an employee, shareholder, partner or agent of another person. Any tax statement made by that person will be attributed to that person's employer, corporation, partnership or principal. However, a person shall be treated as a material advisor if that person forms or avails of an entity with the purpose of avoiding the rules of section 6111 or 6112 or the penalties under section 6707 or 6708.

(B) *Post-filing advice.*—A person will not be considered to be a material advisor with respect to a transaction if that person does not make or provide a tax statement regarding the transaction until after the first tax return reflecting tax benefit(s) of the transaction is filed with the IRS. However, this exception does not apply to a person who makes a tax statement with respect to the transaction if it is expected that the taxpayer will file a supplemental or amended return reflecting additional tax benefits from the transaction.

(C) *Publicly filed statements.*—A tax statement with respect to a transaction that includes only information about the transaction contained in publicly available documents filed with the Securities and Exchange Commission no later than the close of the transaction will not be considered a tax statement to or for the benefit of a person described in paragraph (b)(2) of this section.

(3) *Gross income derived for material aid, assistance, or advice.*—(i) *Threshold amount.*—(A) *In general.*—The threshold amount of gross income is $50,000 in the case of a reportable transaction substantially all of the tax benefits from which are provided to natural persons (looking through any partnerships, S corporations, or trusts). For all other transactions, the threshold amount is $250,000.

(B) *Listed transactions and transactions of interest.*—For listed transactions described in § § 1.6011-4, 20.6011-4, 25.6011-4, 26.6011-4, 31.6011-4, 53.6011-4, 54.6011-4, or 56.6011-4 of this chapter, the threshold amounts in paragraph (b)(3)(i)(A) of this section are reduced from $50,000 to $10,000 and from $250,000 to $25,000. For transactions of interest described in § § 1.6011-4, 20.6011-4, 25.6011-4, 26.6011-4, 31.6011-4, 53.6011-4, 54.6011-4, or 56.6011-4 of this chapter, the threshold amounts in paragraph (b)(3)(i)(A) of this section may be reduced as identified in the published guidance describing the transaction.

(C) *[Reserved].*

(D) *Substantially all of the tax benefits.*—For purposes of this section, the determination of whether substantially all of the tax benefits from a reportable transaction are provided to natural persons is made based on all the facts and circumstances. Generally, unless the facts and circumstances prove otherwise, if 70 percent or more of the tax benefits from a reportable transaction are provided to natural persons (looking through any partnerships, S corporations, or trusts) then substantially all of the tax benefits will be considered to be provided to natural persons.

(ii) *Gross income derived directly or indirectly for the material aid, assistance, or advice.*—In determining the amount of gross income a person derives directly or indirectly for material aid, assistance, or advice, all fees for a tax strategy or for services for advice (whether or not tax advice) or for the implementation of a reportable transaction are taken into account. Fees include consideration in whatever form paid, whether in cash or in kind, for services to analyze the transaction (whether or not related to the tax consequences of the transaction), for services to implement the transaction, for services to document the transaction, and for services to prepare tax returns to the extent return preparation fees are unreasonable in light of all of the facts and circumstances. A fee does not include amounts paid to a person, including an advisor, in that person's capacity as a party to the transaction. For example, a fee does not include reasonable charges for the use of capital or the sale or use of property. The IRS will scrutinize carefully all of the facts and circumstances in determining whether consideration received in connection with a reportable transaction constitutes gross income derived directly or indirectly for aid, assistance, or advice. For purposes of this section, the threshold amount must be met independently for each transaction that is a reportable transaction and aggregation of fees among transactions is not required.

(4) *Date a person becomes a material advisor.*—(i) *In general.*—A person will be treated as becoming a material advisor when all of the following events have occurred (in no particular order)—
(A) The person provides material aid, assistance or advice as described in paragraph (b)(2) of this section;
(B) The person directly or indirectly derives gross income in excess of the threshold amount as described in paragraph (b)(3) of this section; and
(C) The transaction is entered into by the taxpayer to whom or for whose benefit the person provided the tax statement, or in the case of a tax statement provided to another material advisor, when the transaction is entered into by a taxpayer to whom or for whose benefit that material advisor provided a tax statement.

(ii) *Determining if the taxpayer entered into the transaction.*—Material advisors, including those who cease providing services before the time the transaction is entered into, must make reasonable and good faith efforts to determine whether the event described in paragraph (b)(4)(i)(C) of this section has occurred.

(iii) *Listed transactions and transactions of interest.*—If a transaction that was not a reportable transaction is identified as a listed transaction or a transaction of interest in published guidance after the occurrence of the events described in paragraph (b)(4)(i) of this section, the person will be treated as becoming a material advisor on the date the transaction is identified as a listed transaction or a transaction of interest.

(5) *Other persons designated as material advisors.*—Published guidance may identify other types or classes of persons as material advisors.

(c) *Definitions.*—For purposes of this section, the following definitions apply:

(1) *Reportable transaction.*—The term *reportable transaction* is defined in § 1.6011-4(b)(1) of this chapter.

(2) *Listed transaction.*—The term *listed transaction* is defined in § 1.6011-4(b)(2) of this chapter. See also § § 20.6011-4(a), 25.6011-4(a), 26.6011-4, 31.6011-4(a), 53.6011-4(a), 54.6011-4(a), or 56.6011-4(a) of this chapter.

(3) *Derive.*—The term *derive* means receive or expect to receive.

(4) *Person.*—The term *person* means any person described in section 7701(a)(1), including an affiliated group of corporations that join in the filing of a consolidated return under section 1501.

(5) *Substantially similar.*—The term *substantially similar* is defined in § 1.6011-4(c)(4) of this chapter.

(6) *Tax.*—The term *tax* means Federal tax.

(7) *Tax benefit.*—A tax benefit includes deductions, exclusions from gross income, nonrecognition of gain, tax credits, adjustments (or the absence of adjustments) to the basis of property, status as an entity exempt from Federal income taxation, and any other tax consequences that may reduce a taxpayer's Federal tax liability by affecting the amount, timing, character, or source of any item of income, gain, expense, loss, or credit.

(8) *Tax return.*—The term *tax return* means a Federal tax return and a Federal information return.

(9) *Tax structure.*—The tax structure of a transaction is any fact that may be relevant to understanding the purported or claimed Federal tax treatment of the transaction.

(10) *Tax treatment.*—The tax treatment of a transaction is the purported or claimed Federal tax treatment of the transaction.

(11) *Taxpayer.*—The term *taxpayer* is defined in § 1.6011-4(c)(1) of this chapter.

(12) *Tax result protection.*—The term *tax result protection* includes insurance company and other third party products commonly described as tax result insurance.

(13) *Transaction of interest.*—The term *transaction of interest* is defined in § 1.6011-4(b)(6) of this chapter. See also § § 20.6011-4(a), 25.6011-4(a), 26.6011-4, 31.6011-4(a), 53.6011-4(a), 54.6011-4(a), or 56.6011-4(a) of this chapter.

(d) *Form and content of material advisor's disclosure statement.*—(1) *In general.*—A material advisor required to file a disclosure statement under this section must file a completed Form 8918, "Material Advisor Disclosure Statement" (or successor form) in accordance with this paragraph (d) and the instructions to the form. To be considered complete, the information provided on the form must describe the expected tax treatment and all potential tax benefits expected to result from the transaction, describe any tax result protection with respect to the transaction, and identify and describe the transaction in sufficient detail for the IRS to be able to understand the tax structure of the reportable transaction and the identity of any material advisor(s) whom the material advisor knows or has reason to know acted as a material advisor as defined in paragraph (b) of this section with respect to the transaction. An incomplete form containing a statement that information will be provided upon request is not considered a complete disclosure statement. A material advisor may file a single form for substantially similar transactions. An amended form must be filed if information previously provided is no longer accurate, if additional information that was not disclosed becomes available, or if there are material changes to the transaction. A material advisor is not required to file an additional form for each additional taxpayer that enters into the same or substantially similar transaction. If the form is not completed in accordance with the provisions in this paragraph (d) and the instructions to the form, the material advisor will not be considered to have complied with the disclosure requirements of this section.

(2) *Reportable transaction number.*—The IRS will issue to a material advisor a reportable transaction number with respect to the disclosed reportable transaction. Receipt of a reportable transaction number does not indicate that the disclosure statement is complete, nor does it indicate that the transaction has been reviewed, ex-

amined, or approved by the IRS. Material advisors must provide the reportable transaction number to all taxpayers and material advisors for whom the material advisor acts as a material advisor as defined in paragraph (b) of this section. The reportable transaction number must be provided at the time the transaction is entered into, or, if the transaction is entered into prior to the material advisor receiving the reportable transaction number, within 60 calendar days from the date the reportable transaction number is mailed to the material advisor.

(e) *Time of providing disclosure.*—The material advisor's disclosure statement for a reportable transaction must be filed with the Office of Tax Shelter Analysis (OTSA) by the last day of the month that follows the end of the calendar quarter in which the advisor became a material advisor with respect to the reportable transaction or in which the circumstances necessitating an amended disclosure statement occur. The disclosure statement must be sent to OTSA at the address provided in the instructions for Form 8918 (or a successor form).

(f) *Designation agreements.*—If more than one material advisor is required to disclose a reportable transaction under this section, the material advisors may designate by written agreement a single material advisor to disclose the transaction. The transaction must be disclosed by the last day of the month following the end of the calendar quarter that includes the earliest date on which a material advisor who is a party to the agreement became a material advisor with respect to the transaction as described in paragraph (b)(4) of this section. The designation of one material advisor to disclose the transaction does not relieve the other material advisors of their obligation to disclose the transaction to the IRS in accordance with this section, if the designated material advisor fails to disclose the transaction to the IRS in a timely manner.

(g) *Protective disclosures.*—If a potential material advisor is uncertain whether a transaction must be disclosed under this section, the advisor may disclose the transaction in accordance with the requirements of this section and comply with all the provisions of this section, and indicate on the disclosure statement that the disclosure statement is being filed on a protective basis. The IRS will not treat disclosure statements filed on a protective basis any differently than other disclosure statements filed under this section. For a protective disclosure to be effective, the advisor must comply with the regulations under this section and § 301.6112-1 by providing to the IRS all information requested by the IRS under these sections.

(h) *Rulings.*—If a potential material advisor requests a ruling as to whether a specific transaction is a reportable transaction on or before the date that disclosure would otherwise be required under this section, the Commissioner in his discretion may determine that the submission satisfies the disclosure rules under this section for that transaction if the request fully discloses all relevant facts relating to the transaction which would otherwise be required to be disclosed under this section. The potential obligation of the person to disclose the transaction under this section (or to maintain or furnish the list under § 301.6112-1) will not be suspended during the period that the ruling request is pending.

(i) *Effective/applicability date.*—(1) *In general.*—This section applies to transactions with respect to which a material advisor makes a tax statement on or after August 3, 2007. However, this section applies to transactions of interest entered into on or after November 2, 2006, with respect to which a material advisor makes a tax statement under this section on or after November 2, 2006. Paragraphs (b)(2)(i)(A), (b)(3)(i)(B), (c)(2), and (c)(13) of this section apply to transactions with respect to which a material advisor makes a tax statement under this section after November 14, 2011. Paragraph (h) of this section applies to ruling requests received on or after November 2, 2006. Otherwise, the rules that apply on or before November 14, 2011 are contained in this section in effect prior to November 14, 2011 (see 26 CFR part 301 revised as of April 1, 2011).

(2) *[Reserved].*

[Reg. § 301.6111-3.]

☐ [*T.D. 9351, 7-31-2007. Amended by T.D. 9556, 11-10-2011.*]

### [Reg. § 301.6112-1]

**§ 301.6112-1. Material advisors of reportable transactions must keep lists of advisees, etc.**—(a) *In general.*—Each material advisor, as defined in § 301.6111-3(b), with respect to any reportable transaction, as defined in § 1.6011-4(b) of this chapter, shall prepare and maintain a list in accordance with paragraph (b) of this section and shall furnish such list to the Internal Revenue Service (IRS) in accordance with paragraph (e) of this section.

(b) *Preparation and maintenance of lists.*—(1) *In general.*—A separate list must be prepared and maintained for each reportable transaction.

However, one list must be maintained for substantially similar transactions. A material advisor will have 30 calendar days from the date the list maintenance requirement first arises (see § 301.6111-3(b)(4) and paragraph (a) of this section) with respect to a reportable transaction to prepare the list that must be maintained under this section with respect to that transaction. The Commissioner in his discretion also may provide in published guidance designating a transaction as a reportable transaction a list preparation time period greater than 30 calendar days. If a list is requested under this section during the list preparation time period, the request for the list will be treated as having been made on the day after the list preparation time period ends. A list must be maintained in a form that enables the IRS to determine without undue delay or difficulty the information required in paragraph (b)(3) of this section. The Commissioner in his discretion may provide in published guidance a form or method for maintaining or furnishing the list.

(2) *Persons required to be included on lists.*—A material advisor is required to maintain a list identifying each person with respect to whom the advisor acted as a material advisor with respect to the reportable transaction. However, a material advisor is not required to identify a person on the list if the person entered into a listed transaction or a transaction of interest more than 6 years before the transaction was identified in published guidance as a listed transaction or a transaction of interest.

(3) *Contents.*—Each list must include the three components described in paragraph (b)(3)(i), (ii), and (iii) of this section.

(i) *Statement.*—An itemized statement containing the following information—

(A) The name of each reportable transaction, the citation to the published guidance number identifying the transaction if the transaction is a listed transaction or a transaction of interest, and the reportable transaction number obtained under section 6111;

(B) The name, address, and TIN of each person required to be included on the list;

(C) The date on which each person required to be included on the list entered into each reportable transaction, if known by the material advisor;

(D) The amount invested in each reportable transaction by each person required to be included on the list, if known by the material advisor;

(E) A summary or schedule of the tax treatment that each person is intended or expected to derive from participation in each reportable transaction; and

(F) The name of each other material advisor to the transaction, if known by the material advisor.

(ii) *Description of the transaction.*—A detailed description of each reportable transaction that describes both the tax structure of the transaction and the purported tax treatment of the transaction.

(iii) *Documents.*—The following documents—

(A) A copy of any designation agreement (as described in paragraph (f) of this section) to which the material advisor is a party; and

(B) Copies of any additional written materials, including tax analyses or opinions, relating to each reportable transaction that are material to an understanding of the purported tax treatment or tax structure of the transaction that have been shown or provided to any person who acquired or may acquire an interest in the transactions, or to their representatives, tax advisors, or agents, by the material advisor or any related party or agent of the material advisor. However, a material advisor is not required to retain earlier drafts of a document provided the material advisor retains a copy of the final document (or, if there is no final document, the most recent draft of the document) and the final document (or most recent draft) contains all the information in the earlier drafts of such document that is material to an understanding of the purported tax treatment or the tax structure of the transaction.

(c) *Definitions.*—For purposes of this section, the following terms are defined as:

(1) *Material advisor.*—The term *material advisor* is defined in § 301.6111-3(b).

(2) *Reportable transaction.*—The term *reportable transaction* is defined in § 1.6011-4(b)(1) of this chapter.

(3) *Listed transaction.*—The term *listed transaction* is defined in § 1.6011-4(b)(2) of this chapter. See also §§ 20.6011-4(a), 25.6011-4(a), 26.6011-4, 31.6011-4(a), 53.6011-4(a), 54.6011-4(a), or 56.6011-4(a) of this chapter.

(4) *Substantially similar.*—The term *substantially similar* is defined in § 1.6011-4(c)(4) of this chapter.

(5) *Person.*—The term *person* is defined in §301.6111-3(c)(4).

(6) *Related party.*—A person is a related party with respect to another person if such person bears a relationship to such other person described in section 267(b) or 707(b).

(7) *Tax.*—The term *tax* is defined in §301.6111-3(c)(6).

(8) *Tax benefit.*—The term *tax benefit* is defined in §301.6111-3(c)(7).

(9) *Tax return.*—The term *tax return* is defined in §301.6111-3(c)(8).

(10) *Tax structure.*—The term *tax structure* is defined in §301.6111-3(c)(9).

(11) *Tax treatment.*—The term *tax treatment* is defined in §301.6111-3(c)(10).

(12) *Transaction of interest.*—The term *transaction of interest* is defined in §1.6011-4(b)(6) of this chapter. See also §§20.6011-4(a), 25.6011-4(a), 26.6011-4, 31.6011-4(a), 53.6011-4(a), 54.6011-4(a), or 56.6011-4(a) of this chapter.

(d) *Retention of lists.*—Each material advisor must maintain each component of the list described in paragraph (b)(3) of this section in a readily accessible form for seven years following the earlier of the date on which the material advisor last made a tax statement relating to the transaction, or the date the transaction was last entered into, if known. If the material advisor required to prepare, maintain, and furnish the list is a corporation, partnership, or other entity (entity) that has dissolved or liquidated before completion of the seven-year period, the person responsible under state law for winding up the affairs of the entity must prepare, maintain and furnish each component of the list on behalf of the entity, unless the entity submits the list to the Office of Tax Shelter Analysis (OTSA) within 60 days after the dissolution or liquidation. If state law does not specify any person as responsible for winding up the affairs, then each of the directors of the corporation, the general partners of the partnership, or the trustees, owners, or members of the entity are responsible for preparing, maintaining and furnishing each component of the list on behalf of the entity, unless the entity submits the list to the OTSA within 60 days after the dissolution or liquidation. The responsible person must also provide notice to OTSA of such dissolution or liquidation within 60 days after the dissolution or liquidation. The list and the notice provided to OTSA must be sent to: Internal Revenue Service, OTSA Mail Stop 4915, 1973 North Rulon White Blvd., Ogden, Utah 84404, or to such other address as provided by the Commissioner.

(e) *Furnishing of lists.*—(1) *In general.*—Each material advisor responsible for maintaining a list must, upon written request by the IRS, make each component of the list described in paragraph (b)(3) of this section available to the IRS. Each component of the list must be furnished to the IRS in a form that enables the IRS to determine without undue delay or difficulty the information required in paragraph (b)(3) of this section. If any component of the list is not in a form that enables the IRS to determine without undue delay or difficulty the information required in paragraph (b)(3) of this section, the material advisor will not be considered to have complied with the list maintenance provisions in section 6112 and this section. A material advisor must make the list or each component of the list available to the IRS within the period prescribed in section 6708 or published guidance relating to section 6708.

(2) *Claims of privilege.*—Each material advisor who is required to maintain a list with respect to a reportable transaction, must still maintain the list pursuant to the requirements of this section even if a person asserts a claim of privilege with respect to the information specified in paragraph (b)(3)(iii)(B) of this section.

(f) *Designation agreements.*—If more than one material advisor is required to maintain a list of persons for a reportable transaction, in accordance with paragraph (b) of this section, the material advisors may designate by written agreement a single material advisor (the designated material advisor) to maintain the list or a portion of the list. A designation agreement does not relieve material advisors from their obligation to maintain a list in accordance with paragraph (b) of this section or to furnish their list to the IRS in accordance with paragraph (e)(1) of this section, but a designation agreement may allow one material advisor to maintain a list on behalf of the other material advisors who are a party to the designation agreement. A material advisor is not relieved from the requirement of this section because a material advisor is unable to obtain the list from any designated material advisor, any designated material advisor did not maintain a list, or the list maintained by any designated material advisor is not complete. The existence of a designation agreement

does not affect the ability of the IRS to request a list from any party to the designation agreement. The IRS may request a list from any party to the designation agreement, and the party receiving the request must furnish their list to the IRS in accordance with paragraph (e)(1) of this section, regardless of whether their list was maintained by another party pursuant to the terms of a designation agreement.

(g) *Effective/applicability date.*—In general, this section applies to transactions with respect to which a material advisor makes a tax statement under §301.6111-3 on or after August 3, 2007. However, this section applies to transactions of interest entered into on or after November 2, 2006, with respect to which a material advisor makes a tax statement under §301.6111-3 on or after November 2, 2006. Paragraphs (b)(1), (c)(3), (c)(12), and (f) of this section apply to transactions with respect to which a material advisor makes a tax statement under §301.6111-3 after November 14, 2011. Otherwise, the rules that apply on or before November 14, 2011 are contained in this section in effect prior to November 14, 2011 (see 26 CFR part 301 revised as of April 1, 2011). [Reg. §301.6112-1.]

☐ [T.D. 9046, 2-28-2003. *Amended by* T.D. 9108, 12-29-2003 T.D. 9295, 11-1-2006; T.D. 9352, 7-31-2007 *and* T.D. 9556, 11-10-2011.]

## [Reg. §301.6114-1]

**§301.6114-1. Treaty-based return positions.**—(a) *Reporting requirement.*—(1) *General rule.*—(i) Except as provided in paragraph (c) of this section, if a taxpayer takes a return position that any treaty of the United States (including, but not limited to, an income tax treaty, estate and gift tax treaty, or friendship, commerce and navigation treaty) overrules or modifies any provision of the Internal Revenue Code and thereby effects (or potentially effects) a reduction of any tax incurred at any time, the taxpayer shall disclose such return position on a statement (in the form required in paragraph (d) of this section) attached to such return.

(ii) If a return of tax would not otherwise be required to be filed, a return must nevertheless be filed for purposes of making the disclosure required by this section. For this purpose, such return need include only the taxpayer's name, address, taxpayer identifying number, and be signed under penalties of perjury (as well as the subject disclosure). Also, the taxpayer's taxable year shall be deemed to be the calendar year (unless the taxpayer has previously established, or timely chooses for this purpose to establish, a different taxable year). In the case of a disclosable return position relating solely to income subject to withholding (as defined in §1.1441-2(a) of this chapter), however, the statement required to be filed in paragraph (d) of this section must instead be filed at times and in accordance with procedures published by the Internal Revenue Service.

(2) *Application.*—(i) A taxpayer is considered to adopt a return position when the taxpayer determines its tax liability with respect to a particular item of income, deduction or credit. A taxpayer may be considered to adopt a return position whether or not a return is actually filed. To determine whether a return position is a "treaty-based return position" so that reporting is required under this paragraph (a), the taxpayer must compare:

(A) The tax liability (including credits, carrybacks, carry-overs, and other tax consequences or attributes for the current year as well as for any other affected tax years) to be reported on a return of the taxpayer, and

(B) The tax liability (including such credits, carrybacks, carryovers, and other tax consequences or attributes) that would be reported if the relevant treaty provision did not exist.

If there is a difference (or potential difference) in these two amounts, the position taken on a return is a treaty-based return position that must be reported.

(ii) In the event a taxpayer's return position is based on a conclusion that a treaty provision is consistent with a Code provision, but the effect of the treaty provision is to alter the scope of the Code provision from the scope that it would have in the absence of the treaty, then the return position is a treaty-based return position that must be reported.

(iii) A return position is a treaty-based return position unless the taxpayer's conclusion that no reporting is required under paragraphs (a)(2)(i) and (ii) of this section has a substantial probability of successful defense if challenged.

(3) *Examples.*—The application of section 6114 and paragraph (a)(2) of this section may be illustrated by the following examples:

*Example (1).* X, a Country A corporation, claims the benefit of a provision of the income tax treaty between the United States and Country A that modifies a provision of the Code. This position does not result in a change of X's U.S. tax liability for the current tax year but does give rise to, or increases, a net operating loss which may be carried back (or forward) such that X's tax liability in the carryback (or forward) year may be affected by the position taken by X in the current year. X must disclose this treaty-based return position with its tax return for the current tax year.

*Example (2)*. Z, a domestic corporation, is engaged in a trade or business in Country B. Country B imposes a tax on the income from certain of Z's petroleum activities at a rate significantly greater than the rate applicable to income from other activities. Z claims a foreign tax credit for this tax on its tax return. The tax imposed on Z is specifically listed as a creditable tax in the income tax treaty between the United States and Country B; however, there is no specific authority that such tax would otherwise be a creditable tax for U.S. purposes under sections 901 or 903 of the Code. Therefore, in the absence of the treaty, the creditability of this petroleum tax would lack a substantial probability of successful defense if challenged, and Z must disclose this treaty-based return position (see also paragraph (b)(7) of this section).

(b) *Reporting specifically required*.—Reporting is required under this section except as expressly waived under paragraph (c) of this section. The following list is not a list of all positions for which reporting is required under this section but is a list of particular positions for which reporting is specifically required. These positions are as follows:

(1) That a nondiscrimination provision of a treaty precludes the application of any otherwise applicable Code provision, other than with respect to the making of or the effect of an election under section 897(i);

(2) That a treaty reduces or modifies the taxation of gain or loss from the disposition of a United States real property interest;

(3) That a treaty exempts a foreign corporation from (or reduces the amount of tax with respect to) the branch profits tax (section 884(a)) or the tax on excess interest (section 884(f)(1)(B));

(4) That, notwithstanding paragraph (c)(1)(i) of this section,

(i) A treaty exempts from tax, or reduces the rate of tax on, interest or dividends paid by a foreign corporation that are from sources within the United States by reason of section 861(a)(2)(B) or section 884(f)(1)(A); or

(ii) A treaty exempts from tax, or reduces the rate of tax on, fixed or determinable annual or periodical income subject to withholding under section 1441 or 1442 that a foreign person receives from a U.S. person, but only if described in paragraphs (b)(4)(ii)(A) and (B) of this section, or in paragraph (b)(4)(ii)(C) or (D) of this section as follows:

(A) The payment is not properly reported to the Service on a Form 1042S; and

(B) The foreign person is any of the following:

*(1)* A controlled foreign corporation (as defined in section 957) in which the U.S. person is a U.S. shareholder within the meaning of section 951(b);

*(2)* A foreign corporation that is controlled within the meaning of section 6038 by the U.S. person;

*(3)* A foreign shareholder of the U.S. person that, in the case of tax years beginning on or before July 10, 1989, is controlled within the meaning of section 6038A by the foreign shareholder, or, in the case of tax years beginning after July 10, 1989, is 25-percent owned within the meaning of section 6038A by the foreign shareholder; or

*(4)* With respect to payments made after October 10, 1990, a foreign related party, as defined in section 6038A(c)(2)(B), to the U.S. person; or

(C) For payments made after December 31, 2000, with respect to a treaty that contains a limitation on benefits article, that—

*(1)* The treaty exempts from tax, or reduces the rate of tax on income subject to withholding (as defined in § 1.1441-2(a) of this chapter) that is received by a foreign person (other than a State, including a political subdivision or local authority) that is the beneficial owner of the income and the beneficial owner is related to the person obligated to pay the income within the meaning of sections 267(b) and 707(b), and the income exceeds $500,000; and

*(2)* A foreign person (other than an individual or a State, including a political subdivision or local authority) meets the requirements of the limitation on benefits article of the treaty; or

(D) For payments made after December 31, 2000, with respect to a treaty that imposes any other conditions for the entitlement of treaty benefits, for example as a part of the interest, dividends, or royalty article, that such conditions are met;

(5) That, notwithstanding paragraph (c)(1)(i) of this section, under a treaty—

(i) Income that is effectively connected with a U.S. trade or business of a foreign corporation or a nonresident alien is not attributable to a permanent establishment or a fixed base of operations in the United States and, thus, is not subject to taxation on a net basis, or that

(ii) Expenses are allowable in determining net business income so attributable, notwithstanding an inconsistent provision of the Code;

(6) Except as provided in paragraph (c)(1)(iv) of this section, that a treaty alters the source of any item of income or deduction;

(7) That a treaty grants a credit for a specific foreign tax for which a foreign tax credit would not be allowed by the Code; or

(8) For returns relating to taxable years for which the due date for filing returns (without extensions) is after December 15, 1997, that residency of an individual is determined under a treaty and apart from the Internal Revenue Code.

(c) *Reporting requirement waived*.—(1) Pursuant to the authority contained in section 6114(b), reporting is waived under this section with respect to any of the following return positions taken by the taxpayer:

(i) For amounts received on or after January 1, 2001, reporting under paragraph (b)(4)(ii) is waived, unless reporting is specifically required under paragraphs (b)(4)(ii)(A) and (B) of this section, paragraph (b)(4)(ii)(C) of this section, or paragraph (b)(4)(ii)(D) of this section;

(ii) Notwithstanding paragraph (b)(4) or (5) of this section, that a treaty has reduced the rate of withholding tax otherwise applicable to a particular type of fixed or determinable annual or periodical income subject to withholding under section 1441 or 1442, such as dividends, interest, rents, or royalties to the extent such income is beneficially owned by an individual or a State (including a political subdivision or local authority);

(iii) For returns relating to taxable years for which the due date for filing returns (without extensions) is on or before December 15, 1997, that residency of an individual is determined under a treaty and apart from the Internal Revenue Code.

(iv) That a treaty reduces or modifies the taxation of income derived from dependent personal services, pensions, annuities, social security and other public pensions, or income derived by artistes, athletes, students, trainees or teachers;

(v) That income of an individual is resourced (for purposes of applying the foreign tax credit limitation) under a treaty provision relating to elimination of double taxation;

(vi) That a nondiscrimination provision of a treaty allows the making of an election under section 897(i);

(vii) That a Social Security Totalization Agreement or a Diplomatic or Consular Agreement reduces or modifies the taxation of income derived by the taxpayer; or

(viii) That a treaty exempts the taxpayer from the excise tax imposed by section 4371, but only if:

(A) The person claiming such treaty-based return position is an insured, as defined in section 4372(d) (without the limitation therein referring to section 4371(1)), or a U.S. or foreign broker of insurance risks,

(B) Reporting under this section that would otherwise be required to be made by foreign insurers or reinsurers on a Form 720 on a quarterly basis is made on an annual basis on a Form 720 by a date no later than the date on which the return is due for the first quarter after the end of the calendar year, or

(C) A closing agreement relating to entitlement to the exemption from the excise tax has been entered into with the Service by the foreign insurance company that is the beneficial recipient of the premium that is subject to the excise tax.

(ix) Notwithstanding paragraph (b)(1) of this section, that a nondiscrimination provision of a qualified income tax treaty, as defined in Treas. Reg. § 1.5000C-1(c)(13), exempts a payment from tax under section 5000C, but only if the foreign person claiming such relief has provided a Section 5000C Certificate (such as Form W-14, "Certificate of Foreign Contracting Party Receiving Federal Procurement Payments") to the acquiring agency in accordance with section 5000C and the regulations thereunder.

(2) Reporting is waived for an individual if payments or income items otherwise reportable under this section (other than by reason of paragraph (b)(8) of this section), received by the individual during the course of the taxable year do not exceed $10,000 in the aggregate or, in the case of payments or income items reportable only by reason of paragraph (b)(8) of this section, do not exceed $100,000 in the aggregate.

(3) Reporting with respect to payments or income items the treatment of which is mandated by the terms of a closing agreement with the Internal Revenue Service, and that would otherwise be subject to the reporting requirements of this section, is also waived.

(4) If a partnership, trust, or estate that has the taxpayer as a partner or beneficiary discloses on its information return a position for which reporting is otherwise required by the taxpayer, the taxpayer (partner or beneficiary) is then excused from disclosing that position on a return.

(5) This section does not apply to a withholding agent with respect to the performance of its withholding functions.

(6)(i) For taxable years ending after December 31, 2004, except as provided in paragraph (c)(6)(ii) of this section, reporting under paragraph (b)(4)(ii) of this section is waived for amounts received by a related party, within the meaning of section 6038A(c)(2), from a withholding agent that is a reporting corporation, within the meaning of section 6038A(a), and that are properly reported on Form 1042-S.

(ii) Paragraph (c)(6)(i) of this section does not apply to any amounts for which reporting is specifically required under the instructions to Form 8833.

(7)(i) For taxable years ending after December 31, 2004, except as provided in paragraph (c)(7)(iv) of this section, reporting under paragraph (b)(4)(ii) of this section is waived for amounts properly reported on Form 1042-S (on either a specific payee or pooled basis) by a withholding agent described in paragraph (c)(7)(ii) of this section if the beneficial owner is described in paragraph (c)(7)(iii) of this section.

(ii) A withholding agent described in this paragraph (c)(7)(ii) is a U.S. financial institution, as defined in §1.1441-1(c)(5) of this chapter, a qualified intermediary, as defined in §1.1441-1(e)(5)(ii) of this chapter, a withholding foreign partnership, as defined §1.1441-5(c)(2)(i) of this chapter, or a withholding foreign trust, as defined in §1.1441-5(e)(5)(v) of this chapter.

(iii) A beneficial owner described in this paragraph (c)(7)(iii) of this section is a direct account holder of a U.S. financial institution or qualified intermediary, a direct partner of a withholding foreign partnership, or a direct beneficiary or owner of a simple or grantor trust that is a withholding foreign trust. A beneficial owner described in this paragraph (c)(7)(iii) also includes an account holder to which a qualified intermediary has applied section 4A.01 or 4A.02 of the qualified intermediary agreement, contained in Revenue Procedure 2000-12 (2000-1 C.B. 387), (as amended by Revenue Procedure 2003-64, (2003-2 C.B. 306); Revenue Procedure 2004-21 (2004-1 C.B. 702); Revenue Procedure 2005-77 (2005-51 I.R.B. 1176) (see §601.601(b)(2) of this chapter) a partner to which a withholding foreign partnership has applied section 10.01 or 10.02 of the withholding foreign partnership agreement, and a beneficiary or owner to which a withholding foreign trust has applied section 10.01 or 10.02 of the withholding foreign trust agreement, contained in Revenue Procedure 2003-64, (2003-2 C.B. 306), (as amended by Revenue Procedure 2004-21 (2004-1 C.B. 702); Revenue Procedure 2005-77 (2005-51 I.R.B. 1176); (see §601.601(b)(2) of this chapter).

(iv) Paragraph (c)(7)(i) of this section does not apply to any amounts for which reporting is specifically required under the instructions to Form 8833.

(8)(i) For taxable years ending after December 31, 2004, except as provided in paragraph (c)(8)(ii) of this section, reporting under paragraph (b)(4)(ii) of this section is waived for taxpayers that are not individuals or States and that receive amounts of income that have been properly reported on Form 1042-S, that do not exceed $500,000 in the aggregate for the taxable year and that are not received through an account with an intermediary, as defined in §1.1441-1(c)(13), or with respect to interest in a flow-through entity, as defined in §1.1441-1(c)(23),

(ii) The exception contained in paragraph (c)(8)(i) of this section does not apply to any amounts for which reporting is specifically required under the instructions to Form 8833.

(d) *Information to be reported.*—(1) *Returns due after December 15, 1997.*—When reporting is required under this section for a return relating to a taxable year for which the due date (without extensions) is after December 15, 1997, the taxpayer must furnish, in accordance with paragraph (a) of this section, as an attachment to the return, a fully completed Form 8833 (Treaty-Based Return Position Disclosure Under Section 6114 or 7701(b)) or appropriate successor form.

(2) *Earlier returns.*—For returns relating to taxable years for which the due date for filing returns (without extensions) is on or before December 15, 1997, the taxpayer must furnish information in accordance with paragraph (d) of this section in effect prior to December 15, 1997 (see §301.6114-1(d) as contained in 26 CFR part 301, revised April 1, 1997).

(3) *In general.*—(i) *Permanent establishment.*—For purposes of determining the nature and amount (or reasonable estimate thereof) of gross receipts, if a taxpayer takes a position that it does not have a permanent establishment or a fixed base in the United States and properly discloses that position, it need not separately report its payment of actual or deemed dividends or interest exempt from tax by reason of a treaty (or any liability for tax imposed by reason of section 884).

(ii) *Single income item.*—For purposes of the statement of facts relied upon to support each separate Treaty-Based Return Position

taken, a taxpayer may treat payments or income items of the same type (e.g., interest items) received from the same ultimate payor (e.g., the obligor on a note) as a single separate payment or income item.

(iii) *Foreign source effectively connected income.*—If a taxpayer takes the return position that, under the treaty, income that would be income effectively connected with a U.S. trade or business is not subject to U.S. taxation because it is income treated as derived from sources outside the United States, the taxpayer may treat payments or income items of the same type (e.g., interest items) as a single separate payment or income item.

(iv) *Sales or services income.*—Income from separate sales or services, whether or not made or preformed by an agent (independent or dependent), to different U.S. customers on behalf of a foreign corporation not having a permanent establishment in the United States may be treated as a single payment or income item.

(v) *Foreign insurers or reinsurers.*—For purposes of reporting by foreign insurers or reinsurers, as described in paragraph (c)(1)(vii)(B) of this section, such reporting must separately set forth premiums paid with respect to casualty insurance and indemnity bonds (subject to section 4371(1)); life insurance, sickness and accident policies, and annuity contracts (subject to section 4371(2)); and reinsurance (subject to section 4371(3)). All premiums paid with respect to each of these three categories may be treated as a single payment or income item within that category. For reports first due before May 1, 1991, the report may disclose, for each of the three categories, the total amount of premiums derived by the foreign insurer or reinsurer in U.S. dollars (even if a portion of these premiums relate to risks that are not U.S. situs). Reasonable estimates of the amounts required to be disclosed will satisfy these reporting requirements.

(e) *Effective/applicability date.*—(1) *In general.*—This section is effective for taxable years of the taxpayer for which the due date for filing returns (without extensions) occurs after December 31, 1988. However, if—

(i) A taxpayer has filed a return for such a taxable year, without complying with the reporting requirement of this section, before November 13, 1989, or

(ii) A taxpayer is not otherwise than by paragraph (a) of this section required to file a return for a taxable year before November 13, 1989, such taxpayer must file (apart from any earlier filed return) the statement required by paragraph (d) of this section before June 12, 1990, by mailing the required statement to the Internal Revenue Service, P.O. Box 21086, Philadelphia, PA 19114. Any such statement filed apart from a return must be dated, signed and sworn to by the taxpayer under the penalties of perjury. In addition, with respect to any return due (without extensions) on or before March 10, 1990, the reporting required by paragraph (a) of this section must be made no later than June 12, 1990. If a taxpayer files or has filed a return on or before November 13, 1989, that provides substantially the same information required by paragraph (d) of this section, no additional submission will be required. Foreign insurers and reinsurers subject to reporting described in paragraph (c)(7)(ii) of this section must so report for calendar years 1988 and 1989 no later than August 15, 1990.

(2) *Section 5000C.*—Paragraph (c)(1)(ix) of this section applies to payments made on and after November 16, 2016 pursuant to contracts entered into on and after January 2, 2011. However, a taxpayer that receives payments exempt from tax under section 5000C by reason of a qualified income tax treaty before November 16, 2016 is not required to disclose this position on Form 8833, provided it has properly relied on Notice 2015-35, I.R.B. 2016-14, 533, in claiming the exemption.

(f) *Cross reference.*—For the provisions concerning penalties for failure to disclose a treaty-based return position, see section 6712 and §301.6712-1. [Reg. §301.6114-1.]

☐ [*T.D. 8292, 3-13-90. Amended by T.D. 8305, 7-11-90; T.D. 8733, 10-6-97; T.D. 8734, 10-6-97; T.D. 8804, 12-30-98; T.D. 8856, 12-29-99, T.D. 9253, 3-13-2006 and T.D. 9782, 8-17-2016.*]

**[Reg. §1.6115-1]**

**§1.6115-1. Disclosure requirements for quid pro quo contributions.**—(a) *Good faith estimate defined.*—(1) *In general.*—A good faith estimate of the value of goods or services provided by an organization described in section 170(c) in consideration for a taxpayer's payment to that organization is an estimate of the fair market value, within the meaning of §1.170A-1(c)(2), of the goods or services. The organization may use any reasonable methodology in making a good faith estimate, provided it applies the methodology in good faith. If the organization fails to apply the methodology in good faith, the organization will be treated as not having met the requirements of section 6115. See section 6714 for the penalties that apply for failure to meet the requirements of section 6115.

(2) *Good faith estimate for goods or services that are not commercially available.*—A good faith estimate of the value of goods or services that are not generally available in a commercial transaction may be determined by reference to the fair market value of similar or comparable goods or services. Goods or services may be similar or comparable even though they do not have the unique qualities of the goods or services that are being valued.

(3) *Examples.*—The following examples illustrate the rules of this paragraph (a).

*Example 1. Facility not available on a commercial basis.* Museum M, an organization described in section 170(c), is located in Community N. In return for a payment of $50,000 or more, M allows a donor to hold a private event in a room located in M. Private events other than those held by such donors are not permitted to be held in M. In Community N, there are four hotels, O, P, Q, and R, that have ballrooms with the same capacity as the room in M. Of these hotels, only O and P have ballrooms that offer amenities and atmosphere that are similar to the amenities and atmosphere of the room in M (although O and P lack the unique collection of art that is displayed in the room in M). Because the capacity, amenities, and atmosphere of ballrooms in O and P are comparable to the capacity, amenities, and atmosphere of the room in M, a good faith estimate of the benefits received from M may be determined by reference to the cost of renting either the ballroom in O or the ballroom in P. The cost of renting the ballroom in O is $2500 and, therefore, a good faith estimate of the fair market value of the right to host a private event in the room at M is $2500. In this example, the ballrooms in O and P are considered similar and comparable facilities to the room in M for valuation purposes, notwithstanding the fact that the room in M displays a unique collection of art.

*Example 2. Services available on a commercial basis.* Charity S is an organization described in section 170(c). S offers to provide a one-hour tennis lesson with Tennis Professional T in return for the first payment of $500 or more that it receives. T provides one-hour tennis lessons on a commercial basis for $100. Taxpayer pays $500 to S and in return receives the tennis lesson with T. A good faith estimate of the fair market value of the lesson provided in exchange for Taxpayer's payment is $100.

*Example 3. Celebrity presence.* Charity U is an organization described in section 170(c). In return for the first payment of $1000 or more that it receives, U will provide a dinner for two followed by an evening tour of Museum V conducted by Artist W, whose most recent works are on display at V. W does not provide tours of V on a commercial basis. Typically, tours of V are free to the public. Taxpayer pays $1000 to U and in return receives a dinner valued at $100 and an evening tour of V conducted by W. Because tours of V are typically free to the public, a good faith estimate of the value of the evening tour conducted by W is $0. In this example, the fact that Taxpayer's tour of V is conducted by W rather than V's regular tour guides does not render the tours dissimilar or incomparable for valuation purposes.

(b) *Certain goods or services disregarded.*—For purposes of section 6115, an organization described in section 170(c) may disregard goods or services described in § 1.170A-13(f)(8)(i).

(c) *Value of the right to purchase tickets to college or university athletic events.*—For purposes of section 6115, the right to purchase tickets for seating at an athletic event in exchange for a payment described in section 170(l) is treated as having a value equal to twenty percent of such payment.

(d) *Goods or services provided to employees or partners of donors.*—(1) *Certain goods or services disregarded.*—For purposes of section 6115, goods or services provided by an organization described in section 170(c) to employees of a donor or to partners of a partnership that is a donor in return for a payment to the donee organization may be disregarded to the extent that the goods or services provided to each employee or partner are the same as those described in § 1.170A-13(f)(8)(i).

(2) *Description permitted in lieu of good faith estimate for other goods or services.*—The written disclosure statement required by section 6115 may include a description of goods or services, in lieu of a good faith estimate of their value, if the donor is—

(i) An employer and, in return for the donor's quid pro quo contribution, an organization described in section 170(c) provides the donor's employees with goods or services other than those described in paragraph (d)(1) of this section; or

(ii) A partnership and, in return for its quid pro quo contribution, the organization provides partners in the partnership with goods or services other than those described in paragraph (d)(1) of this section.

(e) *Effective date.*—This section applies to contributions made on or after December 16, 1996. However, taxpayers may rely on the rules of this section for contributions made on or after January 1, 1994. [Reg. § 1.6115-1.]

☐ [*T.D.* 8690, 12-13-96.]

**[The next page is 66,801.]**

# Time and Place for Paying Tax

# PLACE AND DUE DATE FOR PAYMENT OF TAX

See p. 20,601 for regulations not amended to reflect law changes

## [Reg. §1.6151-1]

**§1.6151-1. Time and place for paying tax shown on returns.—** (a) *In general.*—Except as provided in section 6152 and paragraph (b) of this section, the tax shown on any income tax return shall, without assessment or notice and demand, be paid to the internal revenue officer with whom the return is filed at the time fixed for filing the return (determined without regard to any extension of time for filing the return). For provisions relating to the time for filing income tax returns, see section 6072 and §§1.6072-1 to 1.6072-4, inclusive. For provisions relating to the place for filing income tax returns, see section 6091 and §§1.6091-1 to 1.6091-4, inclusive.

(b) *Returns on which tax is not shown.*—If a taxpayer files a return and, in accordance with section 6014 and the regulations thereunder, elects not to show the tax on the return, the amount of tax determined to be due shall be paid within 30 days after the date of mailing to the taxpayer a notice stating the amount payable and making demand upon the taxpayer therefor. However, if the notice is mailed to the taxpayer more than 30 days before the due date of the return, payment of the tax shall not be required prior to such due date.

(c) *Date fixed for payment of tax.*—In any case in which a tax imposed by subtitle A of the Code is required to be paid on or before a certain date, or within a certain period, any reference in subtitle A or F of the Code to the date fixed for payment of such tax shall be deemed a reference to the last day fixed for such payment (determined without regard to any extension of time for paying the tax).

(d) *Use of Government depositaries.*—(1) For provisions relating to the use of authorized financial institutions in depositing income and estimated income taxes of certain corporations, see §1.6302-1.

(2) For provisions relating to the use of such financial institutions for the deposit of taxes required to be withheld under chapter 3 of the Code on nonresident aliens and foreign corporations and tax-free covenant bonds, see §1.6302-2. With respect to section 1446, the previous sentence shall apply only to a publicly traded partnership described in §1.1446-4.

(e) *Effective/Applicability date.*—Paragraph (d)(2) of this section shall apply to publicly traded partnerships described in §1.1446-4 for partnership taxable years beginning after April 29, 2008. [Reg. §1.6151-1.]

☐ [*T.D. 6364, 2-13-59. Amended by T.D. 6914, 3-7-67; T.D. 6922, 6-16-67; T.D. 6950, 4-3-68; T.D. 7102, 3-23-71; T.D. 7953, 5-8-84; T.D. 8952, 6-25-2001 and T.D. 9394, 4-28-2008 (corrected 4-1-2009).*]

## [Reg. §20.6151-1]

**§20.6151-1. Time and place for paying tax shown on the return.—**(a) *General rule.*—The tax shown on the estate tax return is to be paid at the time and place fixed for filing the return (determined without regard to any extension of time for filing the return). For provisions relating to the time and place for filing the return, see §§20.6075-1 and 20.6091-1. For the duty of the executor to pay the tax, see §20.2002-1.

(b) *Extension of time for paying.*—(1) *In general.*—For general provisions relating to extension of time for paying the tax, see §20.6161-1.

(2) *Reversionary or remainder interests.*—For provisions relating to extension of time for payment of estate tax on the value of a reversionary or remainder interest in property, see §20.6163-1.

(c) *Payment with obligations of the United States.*—Treasury bonds of certain issues which were owned by the decedent at the time of his death or which were treated as part of his gross estate under the rules contained in §306.28 of Treasury Department Circular No. 300, Revised (31 CFR Part 306), may be redeemed at par plus accrued interest for the purpose of payment of the estate tax, as provided in said section. Whether bonds of particular issues may be redeemed for this purpose will depend on the terms of the offering circulars cited on the face of the bonds. A current list of eligible issues may be obtained from any Federal reserve bank or branch, or from the Bureau of Public Debt, Washington, D.C. See section 6312 and §§301.6312-1 and 301.6312-2 of this chapter (Regulations on Procedure and Administration) for provisions relating to the payment of taxes with United States Treasury obligations.

(d) *Receipt for payment.*—For provisions relating to duplicate receipts for payment of the tax, see §20.6314-1. [Reg. §20.6151-1.]

☐ [*T.D. 6296, 6-23-58.*]

## [Reg. §25.6151-1]

**§25.6151-1. Time and place for paying tax shown on return.—** The tax shown on the gift tax return is to be paid by the donor at the time and place fixed for filing the return (determined without regard to any extension of time for filing the return), unless the time for paying the tax is extended in accordance with the provisions of section 6161. However, for provisions relating to certain cases in which the time for paying the gift tax is postponed by reason of an individual serving in, or in support of, the Armed Forces of the United States in a combat zone, see section 7508. For provisions relating to the time and place for filing the return, see §§25.6075-1 and 25.6091-1. [Reg. §25.6151-1.]

☐ [*T.D. 6334, 11-14-58.*]

## [Reg. §31.6151-1]

**§31.6151-1. Time for paying tax.**—(a) *In general.*—The tax required to be reported on each tax return required under this subpart is due and payable to the internal revenue officer with whom the return is filed at the time prescribed in §31.6071(a)-1 for filing such return. See the applicable sections in Part 301 of this chapter (Regulations on Procedure and Administration), for provisions relating to interest on underpayments, additions to tax, and penalties.

(b) *Cross references.*—For provisions relating to the use of authorized financial institutions in depositing the taxes, see §§31.6302(c)-1, 31.6302(c)-2, and 31.6302(c)-3. For rules relating to the payment of taxes in nonconvertible foreign currency, see §301.6316-7 of this chapter (Regulations on Procedure and Administration). [Reg. §31.6151-1.]

☐ [*T.D. 6354, 1-13-59. Amended by T.D. 6872, 1-5-66; T.D. 6915, 3-28-67; T.D. 7037, 4-27-70; T.D. 7953, 5-8-84 and T.D. 8952, 6-25-2001.*]

## [Reg. §40.6151(a)-1]

**§40.6151(a)-1. Time and place for paying tax shown on return.—** Except as provided by statute, the tax must be paid at the time prescribed in §40.6071(a)-1 for filing the return, and at the place prescribed in §40.6091-1 for filing the return. [Reg. §40.6151(a)-1.]

☐ [*T.D. 8442, 10-21-92. Amended by T.D. 8963, 8-8-2001.*]

## [Reg. §41.6151(a)-1]

**§41.6151(a)-1. Time and place for paying tax.**—(a) *In general.*— The tax must be paid at the time prescribed in §41.6071(a)-1 for filing the return and at the place prescribed in §41.6091-1 for filing the return.

(b) *Effective/applicability date.*—This section applies on and after July 1, 2015. For rules applicable before that date, see 26 CFR 41.6151(a)-1 and 41.6151(a)-1T (revised as of April 1, 2014). [Reg. §41.6151(a)-1.]

☐ [*T.D. 6216. Amended by T.D. 6743, 6-22-64; T.D. 8879, 3-30-2000; T.D. 9537, 7-15-2011 and T.D. 9698, 10-28-2014.*]

## [Reg. §44.6151-1]

**§44.6151-1. Time and place for paying taxes.**—The taxes imposed by sections 4401 and 4411 shall, without assessment or notice and demand, be paid to the internal revenue officer with whom the returns are required to be filed at the time fixed for filing the returns. For provisions relating to the time for filing returns, see §§44.6071 and 44.6071-1. For provisions relating to the place for filing returns, see §§44.6091 and 44.6091-1. [Reg. §44.6151-1.]

☐ [*T.D. 6370.*]

## [Reg. §53.6151-1]

**§53.6151-1. Time and place for paying tax shown on returns.—** The chapter 42 tax shown on any return shall, without assessment or notice and demand, be paid to the internal revenue officer with whom the return is filed at the time and place for filing such return (determined without regard to any extension of time for filing the return). For provisions relating to the time and place for filing such return, see §§53.6071-1 and 53.6091-1. For provisions relating to the extension of time for paying the tax, see §53.6161-1. [Reg. §53.6151-1.]

☐ [*T.D. 7368, 7-15-75.*]

### [Reg. §54.6151-1]

**§54.6151-1. Time and place for paying of tax shown on returns.**—Effective for any Form 8928 that is due on or after January 1, 2010, the tax shown on any return which is imposed under section 4980B, 4980D, 4980E or 4980G shall, without assessment or notice and demand, be paid to the internal revenue officer with whom the return is filed at the time and place for filing such return (determined without regard to any extension of time for fling the return). For provisions relating to the time and place for fling such return, see §§54.6071-1 and 54.6091-1. [Reg. §54.6151-1.]

☐ [*T.D. 9457*, 9-4-2009.]

### [Reg. §55.6151-1]

**§55.6151-1. Time and place for paying of tax shown on returns.**—The tax shown on any return which is imposed by Chapter 44 shall, without notice or assessment and demand, be paid to the internal revenue officer with whom the return is filed at the time and place for filing such return (determined without regard to any extension of time for filing the return). For provisions relating to the time and place for filing such return, see §§55.6071-1 and 55.6091-1. For provisions relating to the extension of time for paying the tax, see §55.6161-1. [Reg. §55.6151-1.]

☐ [*T.D. 8180*, 2-28-88.]

### [Reg. §156.6151-1]

**§156.6151-1. Time and place for paying of tax shown on returns.**—The tax under chapter 54 (Greenmail) of the Code shown on any return shall, without notice of assessment and demand, be paid to the internal revenue officer with whom the return is filed at the time and place for filing such return (determined without regard to any extension of time for filing the return). For provisions relating to the time and place for filing such return, see §§156.6071-1 and 156.6091-1. For provisions relating to the extension of time for paying the tax, see §156.6161-1. [Reg. §156.6151-1.]

☐ [*T.D. 8379*, 12-17-91.]

### [Reg. §157.6151-1]

**§157.6151-1. Time and place for paying of tax shown on returns.**—The tax under chapter 55 (Structured Settlement Factoring Transactions) of the Internal Revenue Code shown on any return must, without assessment or notice and demand, be paid at the time and place specified in the forms and instructions provided by the Internal Revenue Service. For provisions relating to the time and place for filing such return, see §157.6071-1 and §157.6091-1. For provisions relating to the extension of time for paying the tax, see §157.6161-1. [Reg. §157.6151-1.]

☐ [*T.D. 9134*, 7-7-2004.]

### [Reg. §301.6151-1]

**§301.6151-1. Time and place for paying tax shown on returns.**—For provisions concerning the time and place for paying tax shown on returns with respect to a particular tax, see regulations relating to such tax. [Reg. §301.6151-1.]

☐ [*T.D. 6498*, 10-24-60.]

→ *Caution: Former Code Sec. 6153 was repealed and reenacted in part in Code Sec. 6654.*

→ *Caution: Former Code Sec. 6154 was repealed and reenacted in part in Code Sec. 6655.*

### [Reg. §301.6155-1]

**§301.6155-1. Payment on notice and demand.**—Upon receipt of notice and demand from the district director (including the Director of International Operations) or the director of the regional service center, there shall be paid at the place and time stated in such notice and amount of any tax (including any interest, additional amounts, additions to the tax, and assessable penalties) stated in such notice and demand. [Reg. §301.6155-1.]

☐ [*T.D. 6498*, 10-24-60. *Amended by T.D. 6585*, 12-27-61.]

### [Reg. §6.3]

**§6.3. Election by a qualified bank holding corporation to pay in installments the tax attributable to sales under the Bank Holding Company Act (Temporary).**—[Reg. §6.3 was redesignated as Reg. §301.9100-11T by T.D. 8435, 9-18-92.—CCH.]

### [Reg. §300.0]

**§300.0. User fees; in general.**—(a) *In general.*—The regulations in this part 300 are designated the User Fee Regulations and provide rules relating to user fees under 31 U.S.C. 9701.

(b) *Applicability.*—User fees are imposed on the following services:

(1) Entering into an installment agreement.

(2) Restructuring or reinstating an installment agreement.

(3) Processing an offer to compromise.

(4) Taking the special enrollment examination to become an enrolled agent.

(5) Enrolling an enrolled agent.

(6) Renewing the enrollment of an enrolled agent.

(7) Enrolling an enrolled actuary.

(8) Renewing the enrollment of an enrolled actuary.

(9) Taking the special enrollment examination to become an enrolled retirement plan agent.

(10) Renewing the enrollment of an enrolled retirement plan agent.

(11) Taking the registered tax return preparer competency examination.

(12) Applying for a preparer tax identification number. [Reg. § 300.0.]

☐ [*T.D. 8589*, 2-10-95. *Amended by T.D. 9086*, 8-14-2003; *T.D. 9288*, 10-3-2006; *T.D. 9306*, 12-27-2006; *T.D. 9370*, 12-18-2007; *T.D. 9503*, 9-28-2010; *T.D. 9523*, 4-14-2011, *T.D. 9559*, 11-22-2011 and *T.D. 9858*, 5-10-2019.]

### [Reg. §300.1]

**§300.1. Installment agreement fee.**—(a) *Applicability.*—This section applies to installment agreements under section 6159 of the Internal Revenue Code.

(b) *Fee.*—The fee for entering into an installment agreement before January 1, 2017, is $120. The fee for entering into an installment agreement on or after January 1, 2017, is $225. A reduced fee applies in the following situations:

(1) For installment agreements entered into before January 1, 2017, the fee is $52 when the taxpayer pays by way of a direct debit from the taxpayer's bank account. The fee is $107 when the taxpayer pays by way of a direct debit from the taxpayer's bank account for installment agreements entered into on or after January 1, 2017;

(2) For online payment agreements entered into before January 1, 2017, the fee is $120, except that the fee is $52 when the taxpayer pays by way of a direct debit from the taxpayer's bank account. The fee is $149 for entering into online payment agreements on or after January 1, 2017, except that the fee is $31 when the taxpayer pays by way of a direct debit from the taxpayer's bank account; and

(3) Notwithstanding the type of installment agreement and method of payment, the fee is $43 if the taxpayer is a low-income taxpayer, that is, an individual who falls at or below 250 percent of the dollar criteria established by the poverty guidelines updated annually in the **Federal Register** by the U.S. Department of Health and Human Services under authority of section 673(2) of the Omnibus Budget Reconciliation Act of 1981 (95 Stat. 357, 511), or such other measure that is adopted by the Secretary, except that the fee is $31 when the taxpayer pays by way of a direct debit from the taxpayer's bank account with respect to online payment agreements entered into on or after January 1, 2017;

(c) *Person liable for fee.*—The person liable for the installment agreement fee is the taxpayer entering into an installment agreement.

(d) *Applicability date.*—This section is applicable beginning January 1, 2017. [Reg. §300.1.]

☐ [*T.D. 8589*, 2-10-95. *Amended by T.D. 9306*, 12-27-2006; *T.D. 9503*, 9-28-2010, *T.D. 9647*, 11-29-2013 *and T.D. 9798*, 11-29-2016.]

### [Reg. §300.2]

**§300.2. Restructuring or reinstatement of installment agreement fee.**—(a) *Applicability.*—This section applies to installment agreements under section 6159 of the Internal Revenue Code that are in default. An installment agreement is deemed to be in default when a taxpayer fails to meet any of the conditions of the installment agreement.

(b) *Fee.*—The fee for restructuring or reinstating an installment agreement before January 1, 2017, is $50. The fee for restructuring or reinstating an installment agreement on or after January 1, 2017, is $89. If the taxpayer is a low-income taxpayer, that is, an individual who falls at or below 250 percent of the dollar criteria established by the poverty guidelines updated annually in the **Federal Register** by the U.S. Department of Health and Human Services under authority of section 673(2) of the Omnibus Budget Reconciliation Act of 1981

(95 Stat. 357, 511), or such other measure that is adopted by the Secretary, then the fee for restructuring or reinstating an installment agreement on or after January 1, 2017 is $43.

(c) *Person liable for fee.*—The person liable for the restructuring or reinstatement fee is the taxpayer that has an installment agreement restructured or reinstated.

(d) *Applicability date.*—This section is applicable beginning January 1, 2017. [Reg. § 300.2.]

☐ [*T.D.* 8589, 2-10-95. *Amended by T.D.* 9306, 12-27-2006; *T.D.* 9503, 9-28-2010, *T.D.* 9647, 11-29-2013 *and T.D.* 9798, 11-29-2016.]

## [Reg. § 300.3]

**§ 300.3. Offer to compromise fee.**—(a) *Applicability.*—This section applies to the processing of offers to compromise tax liabilities pursuant to § 301.7122-1 of this chapter. Except as provided in this section, this fee applies to all offers to compromise accepted for processing.

(b) *Fee.*—(1) The fee for processing an offer to compromise submitted before April 27, 2020, is $186. The fee for processing an offer to compromise submitted on or after April 27, 2020, is $205. No fee will be charged if an offer is—

(i) Based solely on doubt as to liability as defined in § 301.7122-1(b)(1) of this chapter;

(ii) Made by a low-income taxpayer, that is, an individual whose income falls at or below the dollar criteria established by the poverty guidelines updated annually in the **Federal Register** by the U.S. Department of Health and Human Services under authority of section 673(2) of the Omnibus Budget Reconciliation Act of 1981 (95 Stat. 357, 511) or such other measure that is adopted by the Secretary; or

(iii) Made by a low-income taxpayer, as described in section 7122(c)(3) of the Internal Revenue Code, and submitted after July 1, 2019.

(2) The fee will be applied against the amount of the offer, unless the taxpayer requests that it be refunded, if the offer is—

(i) Accepted to promote effective tax administration pursuant to § 301.7122-1(b)(3) of this chapter; or

(ii) Accepted based on doubt as to collectibility and a determination that collection of an amount greater than the amount offered would create economic hardship within the meaning of § 301.6343-1 of this chapter.

(3) Except as otherwise provided in this paragraph (b), the fee will not be refunded to the taxpayer if the offer is accepted, rejected, withdrawn, or returned as nonprocessable after acceptance for processing.

(4) No additional fee will be charged if a taxpayer resubmits an offer the Secretary determines to have been rejected in error or returned in error after acceptance for processing.

(c) *Person liable for the fee.*—The person liable for the processing fee is the taxpayer whose tax liabilities are the subject of the offer.

(d) *Applicability date.*—This section is applicable beginning April 27, 2020. [Reg. § 300.3.]

☐ [*T.D.* 9086, 8-14-2003. *Amended by T.D.* 9503, 9-28-2010, *T.D.* 9647, 11-29-2013 *and T.D.* 9894, 3-12-2020.]

## [Reg. § 300.4]

**§ 300.4. Enrolled agent special enrollment examination fee.**—(a) *Applicability.*—This section applies to the special enrollment examination to become an enrolled agent pursuant to 31 CFR 10.4(a).

(b) *Fee.*—The fee for taking the enrolled agent special enrollment examination is $81 per part, which is the cost to the government for overseeing the development and administration of the examination and does not include any fees charged by the administrator of the examination.

(c) *Person liable for the fee.*—The person liable for the special enrollment examination fee is the applicant taking the examination.

(d) *Applicability date.*—This section applies to registrations that occur on or after March 1, 2018, for the enrolled agent special enrollment examination. Section 300.4 (as contained in 26 CFR part 300, revised April 2017) applies to registrations that occur before March 1, 2018. [Reg. § 300.4.]

☐ [*T.D.* 9288, 10-3-2006. *Amended by T.D.* 9503, 9-28-2010, *T.D.* 9523, 4-14-2011 *and T.D.* 9820, 7-18-2017.]

## [Reg. § 300.5]

**§ 300.5. Enrollment of enrolled agent fee.**—(a) *Applicability.*—This section applies to the initial enrollment of enrolled agents with

the IRS Office of Professional Responsibility pursuant to 31 CFR 10.5(b).

(b) *Fee.*—The fee for initially enrolling as an enrolled agent with the IRS is $67.

(c) *Person liable for the fee.*—The person liable for the enrollment fee is the applicant filing for enrollment as an enrolled agent with the IRS Office of Professional Responsibility.

(d) *Applicability date.*—This section applies beginning June 12, 2019. [Reg. § 300.5.]

☐ [*T.D.* 9288, 10-3-2006. *Amended by T.D.* 9503, 9-28-2010, *T.D.* 9523, 4-14-2011 *and T.D.* 9858, 5-10-2019.]

## [Reg. § 300.6]

**§ 300.6. Renewal of enrollment of enrolled agent fee.**—(a) *Applicability.*—This section applies to the renewal of enrollment of enrolled agents with the IRS Office of Professional Responsibility pursuant to 31 CFR 10.6(d)(6).

(b) *Fee.*—The fee for renewal of enrollment as an enrolled agent with the IRS is $67.

(c) *Person liable for the fee.*—The person liable for the renewal of enrollment fee is the person renewing their enrollment as an enrolled agent with the IRS Office of. Professional Responsibility.

(d) *Applicability date.*—This section applies beginning June 12, 2019. [Reg. § 300.6.]

☐ [*T.D.* 9288, 10-3-2006. *Amended by T.D.* 9503, 9-28-2010, *T.D.* 9523, 4-14-2011 *and T.D.* 9858, 5-10-2019.]

## [Reg. § 300.7]

**§ 300.7. Enrollment of enrolled actuary fee.**—(a) *Applicability.*—This section applies to the initial enrollment of enrolled actuaries with the Joint Board for the Enrollment of Actuaries pursuant to 20 CFR Part 901.

(b) *Fee.*—The fee for initially enrolling as an enrolled actuary with the Joint Board for the Enrollment of Actuaries is $250.00.

(c) *Person liable for the fee.*—The person liable for the enrollment fee is the applicant filing for enrollment as an enrolled actuary with the Joint Board for the Enrollment of Actuaries.

(d) *Effective/applicability date.*—This section is applicable beginning January 22, 2008. [Reg. § 300.7.]

☐ [*T.D.* 9370, 12-18-2007. *Amended by T.D.* 9503, 9-28-2010.]

## [Reg. § 300.8]

**§ 300.8. Renewal of enrollment of enrolled actuary fee.**—(a) *Applicability.*—This section applies to the renewal of enrollment of enrolled actuaries with the Joint Board for the Enrollment of Actuaries pursuant to 20 CFR Part 901.

(b) *Fee.*—The fee for renewal of enrollment as an enrolled actuary with the Joint Board for the Enrollment of Actuaries is $250.00.

(c) *Person liable for the fee.*—The person liable for the renewal of enrollment fee is the person renewing their enrollment as an enrolled actuary with the Joint Board for the Enrollment of Actuaries.

(d) *Effective/applicability date.*—This section is applicable beginning January 22, 2008. [Reg. § 300.8.]

☐ [*T.D.* 9370, 12-18-2007. *Amended by T.D.* 9503, 9-28-2010.]

## [Reg. § 300.9]

**§ 300.9. Enrolled retirement plan agent special enrollment examination fee.**—(a) *Applicability.*—This section applies to the special enrollment examination to become an enrolled retirement plan agent pursuant to 31 CFR 10.4(b).

(b) *Fee.*—The fee for taking the enrolled retirement plan agent special enrollment examination is $11 per part, which is the cost to the government for overseeing the examination and does not include any fees charged by the administrator of the examination.

(c) *Person liable for the fee.*—The person liable for the enrolled retirement plan agent special enrollment examination fee is the applicant taking the examination.

(d) *Effective/applicability date.*—This section is applicable beginning April 19, 2011. [Reg. § 300.9.]

☐ [*T.D.* 9523, 4-14-2011.]

### [Reg. §300.10]

**§300.10. Renewal of enrollment of enrolled retirement plan agent fee.**—(a) *Applicability.*—This section applies to the renewal of enrollment of enrolled retirement plan agents with the IRS pursuant to 31 CFR 10.5(b).

(b) *Fee.*—The fee for renewal of enrollment as an enrolled retirement plan agent with the IRS is $67.

(c) *Person liable for the fee.*—The person liable for the renewal of enrollment fee is the person renewing enrollment as an enrolled retirement plan agent with the IRS.

(d) *Applicability date.*—This section applies beginning June 12, 2019. [Reg. §300.10.]

☐ [*T.D.* 9523, 4-14-2011. *Redesignated and amended by T.D.* 9858, 5-10-2019.]

### [Reg. §300.11]

**§300.11. Registered tax return preparer competency examination fee.**—(a) *Applicability.*—This section applies to the competency examination to become a registered tax return preparer pursuant to 31 CFR 10.4(c).

(b) *Fee.*—The fee for taking the registered tax return preparer competency examination is $27, which is the government cost for overseeing the examination and does not include any fees charged by the administrator of the examination.

(c) *Person liable for the fee.*—The person liable for the competency examination fee is the applicant taking the examination.

(d) *Effective/applicability date.*—This section is applicable beginning November 25, 2011. [Reg. §300.11.]

☐ [*T.D.* 9559, 11-22-2011. *Redesignated by T.D.* 9858, 5-10-2019.]

### [Reg. §300.12]

**§300.12. Fee for obtaining a preparer tax identification number.**—(a) *Applicability.*—This section applies to the application for and renewal of a preparer tax identification number pursuant to 26 CFR 1.6109-2(d).

(b) *Fee.*—The fee to apply for or renew a preparer tax identification number is $21 per year and is in addition to the fee charged by the contractor.

(c) *Person liable for the fee.*—The individual liable for the application or renewal fee is the individual applying for and renewing a preparer tax identification number from the IRS.

(d) *Applicability date.*—This section applies to applications for or renewal of a preparer tax identification number filed on or after August 17, 2020. [Reg. §300.12.]

☐ [*T.D.* 9503, 9-28-2010. *Redesignated by T.D.* 9523, 4-14-2011. *Amended by T.D.* 9559, 11-22-2011, *T.D.* 9742, 10-29-2015 and *T.D.* 9781, 8-9-2016. *Redesignated by T.D.* 9858, 5-10-2019. *Amended by T.D.* 9903, 7-15-2020.]

### [Reg. §301.6159-0]

**§301.6159-0. Table of contents.**—(a) Authority.
(b) Procedures for submission and consideration of proposed installment agreements.
(c) Acceptance, form, and terms of installment agreements.
(d) Rejection of a proposed installment agreement.
(e) Modification or termination of installment agreements by the Internal Revenue Service.
(f) Effect of installment agreement or pending installment agreement on collection activity.
(g) Suspension of the statute of limitations on collection.
(h) Annual statement.
(i) Biennial review of partial payment installment agreements.
(j) Cross reference.
(k) Effective/applicability date. [Reg. §301.6159-0.]

☐ [*T.D.* 9473, 11-24-2009.]

### [Reg. §301.6159-1]

**§301.6159-1. Agreements for payment of tax liability in installments.**—(a) *Authority.*—The Commissioner may enter into a written agreement with a taxpayer that allows the taxpayer to make scheduled periodic payments of any tax liability if the Commissioner determines that such agreement will facilitate full or partial collection of the tax liability.

(b) *Procedures for submission and consideration of proposed installment agreements.*—(1) *In general.*—A proposed installment agreement must be submitted according to the procedures, and in the form and manner, prescribed by the Commissioner.

(2) *When a proposed installment agreement becomes pending.*—A proposed installment agreement becomes pending when it is accepted for processing. The Internal Revenue Service (IRS) may not accept a proposed installment agreement for processing following reference of a case involving the liability that is the subject of the proposed installment agreement to the Department of Justice for prosecution or defense. The proposed installment agreement remains pending until the IRS accepts the proposal, the IRS notifies the taxpayer that the proposal has been rejected, or the proposal is withdrawn by the taxpayer. If a proposed installment agreement that has been accepted for processing does not contain sufficient information to permit the IRS to evaluate whether the proposal should be accepted, the IRS will request the taxpayer to provide the needed additional information. If the taxpayer does not submit the additional information that the IRS has requested within a reasonable time period after such a request, the IRS may reject the proposed installment agreement.

(3) *Revised proposals of installment agreements submitted following rejection.*—If, following the rejection of a proposed installment agreement, the IRS determines that the taxpayer made a good faith revision of the proposal and submitted the revision within 30 days of the date of rejection, the provisions of this section shall apply to that revised proposal. If, however, the IRS determines that a revision was not made in good faith, the provisions of this section do not apply to the revision and the appeal period in paragraph (d)(3) of this section continues to run from the date of the original rejection.

(c) *Acceptance, form, and terms of installment agreements.*—(1) *Acceptance of an installment agreement.*—(i) *In general.*—A proposed installment agreement has not been accepted until the IRS notifies the taxpayer or the taxpayer's representative of the acceptance. Except as provided in paragraph (c)(1)(iii) of this section, the Commissioner has the discretion to accept or reject any proposed installment agreement.

(ii) *Acceptance does not reduce liabilities.*—The acceptance of an installment agreement by the IRS does not reduce the amount of taxes, interest, or penalties owed. (However, penalties may continue to accrue at a reduced rate pursuant to section 6651(h).)

(iii) *Guaranteed installment agreements.*—In the case of a liability of an individual for income tax, the Commissioner shall accept a proposed installment agreement if, as of the date the individual proposes the installment agreement—

(A) The aggregate amount of the liability (not including interest, penalties, additions to tax, and additional amounts) does not exceed $10,000;

(B) The taxpayer (and, if the liability relates to a joint return, the taxpayer's spouse) has not, during any of the preceding five taxable years—

(1) Failed to file any income tax return;

(2) Failed to pay any required income tax; or

(3) Entered into an installment agreement for the payment of any income tax;

(C) The Commissioner determines that the taxpayer is financially unable to pay the liability in full when due (and the taxpayer submits any information the Commissioner requires to make that determination);

(D) The installment agreement requires full payment of the liability within three years; and

(E) The taxpayer agrees to comply with the provisions of the Internal Revenue Code for the period the agreement is in effect.

(2) *Form of installment agreements.*—An installment agreement must be in writing. A written installment agreement may take the form of a document signed by the taxpayer and the Commissioner or a written confirmation of an agreement entered into by the taxpayer and the Commissioner that is mailed or personally delivered to the taxpayer.

(3) *Terms of installment agreements.*—(i) Except as otherwise provided in this section, an installment agreement is effective from the date the IRS notifies the taxpayer or the taxpayer's representative of its acceptance until the date the agreement ends by its terms or until it is superseded by a new installment agreement.

(ii) By its terms, an installment agreement may end upon the expiration of the period of limitations on collection in section 6502 and §301.6502-1, or at some prior date.

(iii) As a condition to entering into an installment agreement with a taxpayer, the Commissioner may require that—

(A) The taxpayer agree to a reasonable extension of the period of limitations on collection; and

**Place and Due Date for Payment of Tax**
See p. 20,601 for regulations not amended to reflect law changes
**66,805**

(B) The agreement contain terms that protect the interests of the Government.

(iv) Except as otherwise provided in an installment agreement, all payments made under the installment agreement will be applied in the best interests of the Government.

(v) While an installment agreement is in effect, the Commissioner may request, and the taxpayer must provide, a financial condition update at any time.

(vi) At any time after entering into an installment agreement, the Commissioner and the taxpayer may agree to modify or terminate an installment agreement or may agree to a new installment agreement that supersedes the existing agreement.

(d) *Rejection of a proposed installment agreement.*—(1) *When a proposed installment agreement becomes rejected.*—A proposed installment agreement has not been rejected until the IRS notifies the taxpayer or the taxpayer's representative of the rejection, the reason(s) for rejection, and the right to an appeal.

(2) *Independent administrative review.*—The IRS may not notify a taxpayer or taxpayer's representative of the rejection of an installment agreement until an independent administrative review of the proposed rejection is completed.

(3) *Appeal of rejection of a proposed installment agreement.*—The taxpayer may administratively appeal a rejection of a proposed installment agreement to the IRS Office of Appeals (Appeals) if, within the 30-day period commencing the day after the taxpayer is notified of the rejection, the taxpayer requests an appeal in the manner provided by the Commissioner.

(e) *Modification or termination of installment agreements by the Internal Revenue Service.*—(1) *Inadequate information or jeopardy.*—The Commissioner may terminate an installment agreement if the Commissioner determines that—

(i) Information which was provided to the IRS by the taxpayer or the taxpayer's representative in connection with either the granting of the installment agreement or a request for a financial update was inaccurate or incomplete in any material respect; or

(ii) Collection of any liability to which the installment agreement applies is in jeopardy.

(2) *Change in financial condition, failure to timely pay an installment or another Federal tax liability, or failure to provide requested financial information.*—The Commissioner may modify or terminate an installment agreement if—

(i) The Commissioner determines that the financial condition of a taxpayer that is party to the agreement has significantly changed; or

(ii) A taxpayer that is party to the installment agreement fails to—

(A) Timely pay an installment in accordance with the terms of the installment agreement;

(B) Pay any other Federal tax liability when the liability becomes due; or

(C) Provide a financial condition update requested by the Commissioner.

(3) *Request by taxpayer.*—Upon request by a taxpayer that is a party to the installment agreement, the Commissioner may terminate or modify the terms of an installment agreement if the Commissioner determines that the financial condition of the taxpayer has significantly changed. The taxpayer's request will not suspend the statute of limitations under section 6502 for collection of any liability. While the Commissioner is considering the request, the taxpayer shall comply with the terms of the existing installment agreement.

(4) *Notice.*—Unless the Commissioner determines that collection of the tax is in jeopardy, the Commissioner will notify the taxpayer in writing at least 30 days prior to modifying or terminating an installment agreement pursuant to paragraph (e)(1) or (2) of this section. The notice provided pursuant to this section must briefly describe the reason for the intended modification or termination. Upon receiving notice, the taxpayer may provide information showing that the reason for the proposed modification or termination is incorrect.

(5) *Appeal of modification or termination of an installment agreement.*—The taxpayer may administratively appeal the modification or termination of an installment agreement to Appeals if, following issuance of the notice required by paragraph (e)(4) of this section and prior to the expiration of the 30-day period commencing the day after the modification or termination is to take effect, the taxpayer requests an appeal in the manner provided by the Commissioner.

(f) *Effect of installment agreement or pending installment agreement on collection activity.*—(1) *In general.*—No levy may be made to collect a tax liability that is the subject of an installment agreement during the period that a proposed installment agreement is pending with the IRS, for 30 days immediately following the rejection of a proposed installment agreement, during the period that an installment agreement is in effect, and for 30 days immediately following the termination of an installment agreement. If, prior to the expiration of the 30-day period following the rejection or termination of an installment agreement, the taxpayer appeals the rejection or termination decision, no levy may be made while the rejection or termination is being considered by Appeals. This section will not prohibit levy to collect the liability of any person other than the person or persons named in the installment agreement.

(2) *Exceptions.*—Paragraph (f)(1) of this section shall not prohibit levy if the taxpayer files a written notice with the IRS that waives the restriction on levy imposed by this section, the IRS determines that the proposed installment agreement was submitted solely to delay collection, or the IRS determines that collection of the tax to which the installment agreement or proposed installment agreement relates is in jeopardy.

(3) *Other actions by the IRS while levy is prohibited.*—(i) *In general.*—The IRS may take actions other than levy to protect the interests of the Government with regard to the liability identified in an installment agreement or proposed installment agreement. Those actions include, for example—

(A) Crediting an overpayment against the liability pursuant to section 6402;

(B) Filing or refiling notices of Federal tax lien; and

(C) Taking action to collect from any person who is not named in the installment agreement or proposed installment agreement but who is liable for the tax to which the installment agreement relates.

(ii) *Proceedings in court.*—Except as otherwise provided in this paragraph (f)(3)(ii), the IRS will not refer a case to the Department of Justice for the commencement of a proceeding in court, against a person named in an installment agreement or proposed installment agreement, if levy to collect the liability is prohibited by paragraph (f)(1) of this section. Without regard to whether a person is named in an installment agreement or proposed installment agreement, however, the IRS may authorize the Department of Justice to file a counterclaim or third-party complaint in a refund action or to join that person in any other proceeding in which liability for the tax that is the subject of the installment agreement or proposed installment agreement may be established or disputed, including a suit against the United States under 28 U.S.C. 2410. In addition, the United States may file a claim in any bankruptcy proceeding or insolvency action brought by or against such person. If a person named in an installment agreement is joined in a proceeding, the United States obtains a judgment against that person, and the case is referred back to the IRS for collection, collection will continue to occur pursuant to the terms of the installment agreement. Notwithstanding the installment agreement, any claim or suit permitted will be for the full amount of the liabilities owed.

(g) *Suspension of the statute of limitations on collection.*—The statute of limitations under section 6502 for collection of any liability shall be suspended during the period that a proposed installment agreement relating to that liability is pending with the IRS, for 30 days immediately following the rejection of a proposed installment agreement, and for 30 days immediately following the termination of an installment agreement. If, within the 30 days following the rejection or termination of an installment agreement, the taxpayer files an appeal with Appeals, the statute of limitations for collection shall be suspended while the rejection or termination is being considered by Appeals. The statute of limitations for collection shall continue to run if an exception under paragraph (f)(2) of this section applies and levy is not prohibited with respect to the taxpayer.

(h) *Annual statement.*—The Commissioner shall provide each taxpayer who is party to an installment agreement under this section with an annual statement setting forth the initial balance owed at the beginning of the year, the payments made during the year, and the remaining balance as of the end of the year.

(i) *Biennial review of partial payment installment agreements.*—The Commissioner shall perform a review of the taxpayer's financial condition in the case of a partial payment installment agreement at least once every two years. The purpose of this review is to determine whether the taxpayer's financial condition has significantly changed so as to warrant an increase in the value of the payments being made or termination of the agreement.

(j) *Cross reference.*—Pursuant to section 6601(b)(1), the last day prescribed for payment is determined without regard to any installment agreement, including for purposes of computing penalties and interest provided by the Internal Revenue Code. For special rules regarding the computation of the failure to pay penalty while certain installment agreements are in effect, see section 6651(h) and §301.6651-1(a)(4).

(k) *Effective/applicability date.*—This section is applicable on November 25, 2009. [Reg. §301.6159-1.]

☐ [*T.D. 8583, 12-22-94. Amended by T.D. 9473, 11-24-2009.*]

**[Reg. §1.6161-1]**

**§1.6161-1. Extension of time for paying tax or deficiency.**—(a) *In general.*—(1) *Tax shown or required to be shown on return.*—A reasonable extension of the time for payment of the amount of any tax imposed by subtitle A of the Code and shown or required to be shown on any return, or for payment of the amount of any installment of such tax, may be granted by the district directors (including the Director of International Operations) at the request of the taxpayer. The period of such extension shall not be in excess of six months from the date fixed for payment of such tax or installment, except that if the taxpayer is abroad the period of the extension may be in excess of six months.

(2) *Deficiency.*—The time for payment of any amount determined as a deficiency in respect of tax imposed by chapter 1 of the Code, or for the payment of any part thereof, may, at the request of the taxpayer, be extended by the internal revenue officer to whom the tax is required to be paid for a period not to exceed 18 months from the date fixed for payment of the deficiency, as shown on the notice and demand, and, in exceptional cases, for a further period not in excess of 12 months. No extension of the time for payment of a deficiency shall be granted if the deficiency is due to negligence, to intentional disregard of rules and regulations, or to fraud with intent to evade tax.

(b) *Undue hardship required for extension.*—An extension of the time for payment shall be granted only upon a satisfactory showing that payment on the due date of the amount with respect to which the extension is desired will result in an undue hardship. The extension will not be granted upon a general statement of hardship. The term "undue hardship" means more than an inconvenience to the taxpayer. It must appear that substantial financial loss, for example, loss due to the sale of property at a sacrifice price, will result to the taxpayer from making payment on the due date of the amount with respect to which the extension is desired. If a market exists, the sale of property at the current market price is not ordinarily considered as resulting in an undue hardship.

(c) *Application for extension.*—An application for an extension of the time for payment of the tax shown or required to be shown on any return, or for the payment of any installment thereof, or for the payment of any amount determined as a deficiency shall be made on Form 1127 and shall be accompanied by evidence showing the undue hardship that would result to the taxpayer if the extension were refused. Such application shall also be accompanied by a statement of the assets and liabilities of the taxpayer and an itemized statement showing all receipts and disbursements for each of the three months immediately preceding the due date of the amount to which the application relates. The application, with supporting documents, must be filed on or before the date prescribed for payment of the amount with respect to which the extension is desired. If the tax is required to be paid to the Director of International Operations, such application must be filed with him, otherwise, the application must be filed with the applicable district director referred to in paragraph (a) or (b) of §1.6091-2, regardless of whether the return is to be filed with, or tax is to be paid to, such district director. The application will be examined, and within 30 days, if possible, will be denied, granted, or tentatively granted subject to certain conditions of which the taxpayer will be notified. If an additional extension is desired, the request therefor must be made on or before the expiration of the period for which the prior extension is granted.

(d) *Payment pursuant to extension.*—If an extension of time for payment is granted, the amount the time for payment of which is so extended shall be paid on or before the expiration of the period of the extension without the necessity of notice and demand. The granting of an extension of the time for payment of the tax or deficiency does not relieve the taxpayer from liability for the payment of interest thereon during the period of the extension. See section 6601 and §301.6601-1 of this chapter (Regulations on Procedure and Administration). Further, the granting of an extension of the time for payment of one installment of the tax does not extend the time for payment of subsequent installments.

(e) *Cross reference.*—For extensions of time for payment of estimated tax, see §§1.6073-4 and 1.6074-3. [Reg. §1.6161-1.]

☐ [*T.D. 6364, 2-13-59. Amended by T.D. 6950, 4-3-68, T.D. 7133, 7-21-71, and T.D. 7260, 2-9-73.*]

**[Reg. §20.6161-1]**

**§20.6161-1. Extension of time for paying tax shown on the return.**—(a) *Basis for granting an extension of time.*—(1) *Reasonable cause.*—With respect to the estate of a decedent dying after December 31, 1970, an extension of time beyond the due date to pay any part of the tax shown on the estate tax return may be granted for a reasonable period of time, not to exceed 12 months, by the district director or the director of a service center, at the request of the executor, if an examination of all the facts and circumstances discloses that such request is based upon reasonable cause. (See paragraph (b) of this section for rules relating to application for extension.) The following examples illustrate cases involving reasonable cause for granting an extension of time pursuant to this paragraph:

*Example (1).* An estate includes sufficient liquid assets to pay the estate tax when otherwise due. The liquid assets, however, are located in several jurisdictions and are not immediately subject to the control of the executor. Consequently, such assets cannot readily be marshalled by the executor, even with the exercise of due diligence.

*Example (2).* An estate is comprised in substantial part of assets consisting of rights to receive payments in the future (i.e., annuities, copyright royalties, contingent fees, or accounts receivable). These assets provide insufficient present cash with which to pay the estate tax when otherwise due and the estate cannot borrow against these assets except upon terms which would inflict loss upon the estate.

*Example (3).* An estate includes a claim to substantial assets which cannot be collected without litigation. Consequently, the size of the gross estate is unascertainable as of the time the tax is otherwise due.

*Example (4).* An estate does not have sufficient funds (without borrowing at a rate of interest higher than that generally available) with which to pay the entire estate tax when otherwise due, to provide a reasonable allowance during the remaining period of administration of the estate for the decedent's widow and dependent children, and to satisfy claims against the estate that are due and payable. Furthermore, the executor has made a reasonable effort to convert assets in his possession (other than an interest in a closely held business to which §6166 applies) into cash.

(2) *Undue hardship.*—(i) *General rule.*—In any case where the district director finds that payment on the due date of any part of the tax shown on the return, or payment of any part of an installment under section 6166 (including any part of a deficiency prorated to an installment the date for payment of which had not arrived) on the date fixed for payment thereof, would impose undue hardship upon the estate, he may extend the time for payment for a period or periods not to exceed one year for any one period and for all periods not to exceed 10 years from the date prescribed in section 6151(a) for payment of the tax. See paragraph (a) of §20.6151-1. In addition, if the district director finds that payment upon notice and demand of any part of a deficiency prorated under the provisions of section 6166 to installments the date for payment of which had arrived would impose undue hardship upon the estate, he may extend the time for payment for a similar period or periods.

(ii) *Definition of "undue hardship".*—The extension provided under this subparagraph on the basis of undue hardship to the estate will not be granted upon a general statement of hardship or merely upon a showing of reasonable cause. The term "undue hardship" means more than an inconvenience to the estate. A sale of property at a price equal to its current fair market value, where a market exists, is not ordinarily considered as resulting in an undue hardship to the estate. The following examples illustrate cases in which an extension of time will be granted based on undue hardship pursuant to this paragraph:

*Example (1).* A farm (or other closely held business) comprises a significant portion of an estate, but the percentage requirements of section 6166(a) (relating to an extension where the estate includes a closely held business) are not satisfied and, therefore, that section does not apply. Sufficient funds for the payment of the estate tax when otherwise due are not readily available. The farm (or closely held business) could be sold to unrelated persons at a price equal to its fair market value, but the executor seeks an extension of time to facilitate the raising of funds from other sources for the payment of the estate tax.

*Example (2).* The assets in the gross estate which must be liquidated to pay the estate tax can only be sold at a sacrifice price or in a depressed market if the tax is to be paid when otherwise due.

(b) *Application for extension.*—An application containing a request for an extension of time for paying the tax shown on the return shall be in writing, shall state the period of the extension requested, and shall include a declaration that it is made under penalties of perjury. If the application is based upon reasonable cause (see paragraph (a)(1) of this section), a statement of such reasonable cause shall be included in the application. If the application is based upon undue hardship to the estate (see paragraph (a)(2) of this section), the application shall include a statement explaining in detail the undue hardship to the estate that would result if the requested extension were refused. At the option of the executor, an application for an extension of time based upon undue hardship may contain an alternative request for an extension based upon reasonable cause if the application for an extension based upon undue hardship is denied. However, an application for an extension of time based solely upon reasonable cause will be treated as such even though an examination of all the facts and circumstances discloses that an application for an extension of time based upon undue hardship might have been granted had such an application therefor been made. If the application is based solely on reasonable cause, it shall be filed with the internal revenue officer with whom the estate tax return is required to be filed under the provisions of § 20.6091-1(a). If the application is based on undue hardship (including an application in which the executor makes an alternative request for an extension based on reasonable cause), it shall be filed with the appropriate district director referred to in paragraph (a)(2) of § 20.6091-1 whether or not the return is to be filed with, or the tax is to be paid to, such district director. An application for an extension of time relating to the estate of a decedent who was not domiciled in the United States at the time of death shall be filed with the Director of International Operations, Internal Revenue Service, Washington, D. C. 20225. When received, the application will be examined, and, if possible, within 30 days will be denied, granted, or tentatively granted subject to certain conditions of which the executor will be notified. An application for an extension of time for payment of the tax, or of an installment under section 6166 (including any part of a deficiency prorated to an installment the date for payment of which had not arrived), will not be considered unless the extension is applied for on or before the date fixed for payment of the tax or installment. Similarly, an application for such extension of time for payment of any part of a deficiency prorated under the provisions of section 6166 to installments the date for payment of which had arrived, will not be considered unless the extension is applied for on or before the date prescribed for payment of the deficiency as shown by the notice and demand from the district director. If the executor desires to obtain an additional extension of time for payment of any part of the tax shown on the return, or any part of an installment under section 6166 (including any part of a deficiency prorated to installment), it must be applied for on or before the date of the expiration of the previous extension. The granting of the extension of time for paying the tax is discretionary with the appropriate internal revenue officer and his authority will be exercised under such conditions as he may deem advisable. However, if a request for an extension of time for payment of estate tax under this section is denied by a district director or a director of a service center, a written appeal may be made, by registered or certified mail or hand delivery, to the regional commissioner with authority over such district director or service center director within 10 days after the denial is mailed to the executor. The provisions of sections 7502 (relating to timely mailing treated as timely filing) and 7503 (relating to time for performance of acts where the last day falls on Saturday, Sunday, or a legal holiday) apply in the case of appeals filed under this paragraph. When received, the appeal will be examined, and if possible, within 30 days will be denied, granted, or tentatively granted subject to certain conditions of which the executor will be notified. If in the mistaken belief that an estate satisfies the requirements of section 6166 the executor, within the time prescribed in paragraph (e) of § 20.6166-1, files a notification of election to pay estate tax in installments, the notification of election to pay tax in installments will be treated as a timely filed application for an extension, under section 6161, of time for payment of the tax if the executor so requests, in writing, within a reasonable time after being notified by the district director that the estate does not satisfy the requirements of section 6166. A request that the election under section 6166 be treated as a timely filed application for an extension under section 6161 must contain, or be supported by the same information required by this paragraph with respect to an application for such an extension.

(c) *Special rules.*—(1) *Payment pursuant to extension.*—The amount of the tax for which an extension is granted, with the additions thereto, shall be paid on or before the expiration of the period of extension without the necessity of notice and demand from the district director.

(2) *Interest.*—The granting of an extension of the time for payment of the tax will not relieve the estate from liability for the payment of interest thereon during the period of the extension. See section 6601.

(3) *Duty to file timely return.*—The granting of an extension of time for paying the tax will not relieve the executor from the duty of filing the return on or before the date provided for in § 20.6075-1.

(4) *Credit for taxes.*—An extension of time to pay the tax may extend the period within which State and foreign death taxes allowed as a credit under sections 2011 and 2014 are required to be paid and the credit therefor claimed. See paragraph (c) of § § 20.2011-1 and 20.2014-6.

(d) *Cross references.*—For provisions requiring the furnishing of security for the payment of the tax for which an extension is granted, see paragraph (a) of § 20.6165-1. For provisions relating to extensions of time for payment of tax on the value of a reversionary or remainder interest in property, see § 20.6163-1. [Reg. § 20.6161-1.]

☐ [*Amended by T.D. 6711, 3-23-64, T.D. 7238, 12-28-72 and T.D. 7384, 10-21-75.*]

### [Reg. § 25.6161-1]

**§ 25.6161-1. Extension of time for paying tax or deficiency.**—(a) *In general.*—(1) *Tax shown on return.*—A reasonable extension of time to pay the amount of tax shown on the return may be granted by the district director at the request of the donor. The period of such extension shall not be in excess of six months from the date fixed for the payment of the tax, except that if the taxpayer is abroad the period of extension may be in excess of six months.

(2) *Deficiency.*—The time for payment of any amount determined as a deficiency in respect of tax imposed by chapter 12 of the Code, or for payment of any part thereof may be extended by the district director at the request of the donor for a period not to exceed 18 months from the date fixed for the payment of the deficiency, as shown on the notice and demand from the district director, and, in exceptional cases, for a further period not in excess of 12 months. No extension of time for the payment of a deficiency shall be granted if the deficiency is due to negligence, to intentional disregard of rules and regulations, or to fraud with intent to evade tax.

(3) *Extension of time for filing distinguished.*—The granting of an extension of time for filing a return does not operate to extend the time for the payment of the tax or any part thereof, unless so specified in the extension.

(b) *Undue hardship required for extension.*—An extension of the time for payment shall be granted only upon a satisfactory showing that payment on the due date of the amount with respect to which the extension is desired will result in an undue hardship. The extension will not be granted upon a general statement of hardship. The term "undue hardship" means more than an inconvenience to the taxpayer. It must appear that substantial financial loss, for example, loss due to the sale of property at a sacrifice price, will result to the donor from making payment on the due date of the amount with respect to which the extension is desired. If a market exists, the sale of the property at the current market price is not ordinarily considered as resulting in an undue hardship.

(c) *Application for extension.*—An application for an extension of the time for payment of the tax shown on the return, or for the payment of any amount determined as a deficiency, shall be in writing and shall be accompanied by evidence showing the undue hardship that would result to the donor if the extension were refused. The application shall also be accompanied by a statement of the assets and liabilities of the donor and an itemized statement showing all receipts and disbursements for each of the three months immediately preceding the due date of the amount to which the application relates. The application, with supporting documents, must be filed with the applicable district director referred to in paragraph (a) of § 25.6091-1 regardless of whether the return is to be filed with, or the tax is to be paid to, such district director on or before the date prescribed for payment of the amount with respect to which the extension is desired. The application will be examined by the district director, and within 30 days, if possible, will be denied, granted, or tentatively granted subject to certain conditions of which the donor will be notified. If an additional extension is desired, the request therefor must be made to the district director on or before the expiration of the period for which the prior extension is granted.

(d) *Payment pursuant to extension.*—If an extension of time for payment is granted, the amount the time for payment of which is so extended shall be paid on or before the expiration of the period of the extension without the necessity of notice and demand from the district director. The granting of an extension of the time for payment of the tax or deficiency does not relieve the donor from liability for the payment of interest thereon during the period of the extension. See section 6601 and § 301.6601-1 of this chapter (Regulations on Procedure and Administration). [Reg. § 25.6161-1.]

☐ [*T.D. 6334, 11-14-58. Amended by T.D. 7012, 5-14-69.*]

**[Reg. § 53.6161-1]**

**§ 53.6161-1. Extension of time for paying tax or deficiency.—** (a) *In general.*—(1) *Tax shown or required to be shown on return.*—A reasonable extension of the time for payment of the amount of any tax imposed by chapter 42 and shown or required to be shown on any return, may be granted by the district directors and directors of the service centers at the request of the taxpayer. The period of such extension shall not be in excess of 6 months from the date fixed for payment of such tax, except that if the taxpayer is abroad the period of the extension may be in excess of 6 months.

(2) *Deficiency.*—The time for payment of any amount determined as a deficiency in respect of tax imposed by chapter 42 may, at the request of the taxpayer, be extended by the internal revenue officer to whom the tax is required to be paid for a period not to exceed 18 months from the date fixed for payment of the deficiency, as shown on the notice and demand, and, in exceptional cases for a further period not in excess of 12 months. No extension of the time for payment of a deficiency shall be granted if the deficiency is due to negligence, to intentional disregard of rules and regulations, or to fraud with intent to evade tax.

(3) *Extension of time for filing distinguished.*—The granting of an extension of time for filing a return does not operate to extend the time for the payment of the tax or any part thereof unless so specified in the extension.

(b) *Undue hardship required for extension.*—An extension of the time for payment shall be granted only upon a satisfactory showing that payment on the due date of the amount with respect to which the extension is desired will result in an undue hardship. The extension will not be granted upon a general statement of hardship. The term "undue hardship" means more than an inconvenience to the taxpayer. It must appear that substantial financial loss, for example, loss due to the sale of property at a sacrifice price, will result to the taxpayer from making payment on the due date of the amount with respect to which the extension is desired. If a market exists, the sale of the property at the current market price is not ordinarily considered as resulting in an undue hardship.

(c) *Application for extension.*—An application for an extension of the time for payment of the tax shown or required to be shown on any return, or for the payment of any amount determined as a deficiency shall be made on Form 1127 and shall be accompanied by evidence showing the undue hardship that would result to the taxpayer if the extension were refused. Such application shall also be accompanied by a statement of the assets and liabilities of the taxpayer and an itemized statement showing all receipts and disbursements for each of the three months immediately preceding the due date of the amount to which the application relates. The application, with supporting documents, must be filed on or before the date prescribed for payment of the amount with respect to which the extension is desired with the internal revenue officer to whom the tax is to be paid. The application will be examined, and within 30 days, if possible, will be denied, granted, or tentatively granted subject to certain conditions of which the taxpayer will be notified. If an additional extension is desired, the request therefor must be made on or before the expiration of the period for which the prior extension is granted.

(d) *Payment pursuant to extension.*—If an extension of time for payment is granted, the amount the time for payment of which is so extended shall be paid on or before the expiration of the period of the extension without the necessity of notice and demand. The granting of an extension of the time for payment of the tax or deficiency does not relieve the taxpayer from liability for the payment of interest thereon during the period of the extension. See section 6601 and § 301.6601-1 of this chapter (Regulations on Procedure and Administration). [Reg. § 53.6161-1.]

☐ *[T.D. 7368, 7-15-75.]*

**[Reg. § 55.6161-1]**

**§ 55.6161-1. Extension of time for paying tax or deficiency.—** (a) *In general.*—(1) *Tax shown or required to be shown on return.*—A reasonable extension of the time for payment of the amount of any tax imposed by chapter 44 and shown or required to be shown on any return, may be granted by the district directors at the request of the taxpayer. The period of such extension shall not be in excess of 6 months from the date fixed for payment of such tax.

(2) *Deficiency.*—The time for payment of any amount determined as a deficiency in respect of tax imposed by Chapter 44 may, at the request of the taxpayer, be extended by the internal revenue officer to whom the tax is required to be paid. The extension may be for a period not to exceed 18 months from the date fixed for payment

of the deficiency, as shown on the notice and demand. In exceptional cases, a further extension for a period not in excess of 12 months may be granted. No extension of time for payment of a deficiency shall be granted if the deficiency is due to negligence, to intentional disregard of rules and regulations, or to fraud with intent to evade tax.

(3) *Extension of time for filing distinguished.*—The granting of an extension of time for filing a return does not operate to extend the time for the payment of the tax or any part thereof unless so specified in the extension.

(b) *Certain rules relating to extension of time for paying income tax to apply.*—The provisions of § 1.6161–1 (b), and (c), and (d) of this chapter (relating to a requirement for undue hardship, the application for extension, and payment pursuant to an extension) shall apply to extensions of time for payment of the tax imposed by Chapter 44. [Reg. § 55.6161-1.]

☐ *[T.D. 7767, 2-3-81.]*

**[Reg. § 156.6161-1]**

**§ 156.6161-1. Extension of time for paying tax or deficiency.—** (a) *In general.*—(1) *Tax shown or required to be shown on return.*—A reasonable extension of the time for payment of the amount of any tax imposed by chapter 54 (Greenmail) of the Code and shown or required to be shown on any return may be granted by the appropriate district director at the request of the taxpayer. The period of such extension shall not exceed 6 months from the date fixed for payment of such tax.

(2) *Deficiency.*—The time for payment of any amount determined as a deficiency in respect of tax imposed by chapter 54 of the Code may, at the request of the taxpayer, be extended by the internal revenue officer to whom the tax is required to be paid. The extension may be for a period not to exceed 18 months from the date fixed for payment of the deficiency, as shown on the notice and demand. In exceptional cases, a further extension for a period not in excess of 12 months may be granted. No extension of time for payment of a deficiency shall be granted if the deficiency is due to negligence, to intentional disregard of rules and regulations, or to fraud with intent to evade tax.

(3) *Extension of time for filing distinguished.*—The granting of an extension of time for filing a return does not operate to extend the time for the payment of the tax or any part thereof unless so specified in the extension.

(b) *Certain rules relating to extensions of time for paying income tax to apply.*—The provisions of § 1.6161-1(b), (c), and (d) of this chapter (relating to a requirement for undue hardship, to the application for extension, and to payment pursuant to an extension) shall apply to extensions of time for payment of the tax imposed by chapter 54 of the Code. [Reg. § 156.6161-1.]

☐ *[T.D. 8379, 12-17-91.]*

**[Reg. § 157.6161-1]**

**§ 157.6161-1. Extension of time for paying tax.—**(a) *In general.*—(1) *Tax shown or required to be shown on return.*—The Internal Revenue Service may, at the request of the taxpayer, grant a reasonable extension of time for payment of the amount of any tax imposed by chapter 55 (Structured Settlement Factoring Transactions) of the Internal Revenue Code and shown or required to be shown on any return. The period of such extension shall not exceed 6 months from the date fixed for payment of such tax, except that in the case of a taxpayer that is abroad, such extension may exceed 6 months.

(2) *Extension of time for filing distinguished.*—The granting of an extension of time for filing a return does not extend the time for the payment of the tax or any part thereof unless so specified in the extension.

(b) *Certain rules relating to extension of time for paying income tax to apply.*—The provisions of § 1.6161-1(b), (c), and (d) of this chapter (relating to a requirement for undue hardship, to the application for extension, and to payment pursuant to an extension) shall apply to extensions of time for payment of the tax imposed by chapter 55 of the Code. [Reg. § 157.6161-1.]

☐ *[T.D. 9134, 7-7-2004.]*

**[Reg. § 301.6161-1]**

**§ 301.6161-1. Extension of time for paying tax.—**For provisions concerning the extension of time for paying a particular tax or for paying an amount determined as a deficiency, see the regulations relating to such tax. [Reg. § 301.6161-1.]

☐ *[T.D. 6498, 10-24-60.]*

### [Reg. §31.6161(a)(1)-1]

**§31.6161(a)(1)-1. Extensions of time for paying tax.**—No extension of time will be granted for payment of any of the taxes to which the regulations in this part have application. [Reg. §31.6161(a)(1)-1.]

☐ [*T.D. 6472, 6-22-60.*]

### [Reg. §20.6161-2]

**§20.6161-2. Extension of time for paying deficiency in tax.**—(a) In any case in which the district director finds that payment, on the date prescribed therefor, of any part of a deficiency would impose undue hardship upon the estate, he may extend the time for payment for a period or periods not to exceed one year for any one period and for all periods not to exceed four years from the date prescribed for payment thereof. However, see §20.6161-1 for extensions of time for payment of the part of a deficiency which is prorated to installments under the provisions of section 6166.

(b) The extension will not be granted upon a general statement of hardship. The term "undue hardship" means more than an inconvenience to the estate. It must appear that a substantial financial loss, for example, due to the sale of property at a sacrifice price, will result to the estate from making payment of the deficiency at the date prescribed therefor. If a market exists, a sale of property at the current market price is not ordinarily considered as resulting in an undue hardship. No extension will be granted if the deficiency is due to negligence or intentional disregard of rules and regulations or to fraud with intent to evade the tax.

(c) An application for such an extension must be in writing and must contain, or be supported by, information in a written statement declaring that it is made under penalties of perjury showing the undue hardship that would result to the estate if the extension were refused. The application, with the supporting information, must be filed with the district director. When received, it will be examined, and, if possible, within thirty days will be denied, granted, or tentatively granted subject to certain conditions of which the executor will be notified. The district director will not consider an application for such an extension unless it is applied for on or before the date prescribed for payment of the deficiency, as shown by the notice and demand from the district director. If the executor desires to obtain an additional extension, it must be applied for on or before the date of the expiration of the previous extension. The granting of the extension of time for paying the deficiency is discretionary with the district director.

(d) The amount of the deficiency for which an extension is granted, with the additions thereto, shall be paid on or before the expiration of the period of extension without the necessity of notice and demand from the district director.

(e) The granting of an extension of time for paying the deficiency will not operate to prevent the running of interest. See section 6601. An extension of time to pay the deficiency may extend the period within which State and foreign death taxes allowed as a credit under sections 2011 and 2014 are required to be paid and the credit therefor claimed. See paragraph (c) of §20.2011-1 and §20.2014-6.

(f) For provisions requiring the furnishing of security for the payment of the deficiency for which an extension is granted, see §20.6165-1. [Reg. §20.6161-2.]

☐ [*T.D. 6296, 6-23-58. Amended by T.D. 6522, 12-28-60.*]

### [Reg. §20.6163-1]

**§20.6163-1. Extension of time for payment of estate tax on value of reversionary or remainder interest in property.**—(a)(1) In case there is included in the gross estate a reversionary or remainder interest in property, the payment of the part of the tax attributable to that interest may, at the election of the executor, be postponed until six months after the termination of the precedent interest or interests in the property. The provisions of this section are limited to cases in which the reversionary or remainder interest is included in the decedent's gross estate as such and do not extend to cases in which the decedent creates future interests by his own testamentary act.

(2) If the district director finds that the payment of the tax at the expiration of the period of postponement described in subparagraph (1) of this paragraph would result in undue hardship to the estate, he may—

(i) After September 2, 1958, and before February 27, 1964, extend the time for payment for a reasonable period or periods not to exceed in all 2 years from the expiration of the period of postponement, but only if the precedent interest or interests in the property terminated after March 2, 1958, or

(ii) After February 26, 1964, extend the time for payment for a reasonable period or periods not to exceed in all 3 years from the expiration of the period of postponement, but only if the time for payment of the tax, including any extensions thereof, did not expire before February 26, 1964.

See paragraph (a)(2)(ii) of §20.6161-1 for the meaning of the term "undue hardship". An example of undue hardship is a case where, by reason of the time required to settle the complex issues involved in a trust, the decedent's heirs or beneficiaries cannot reasonably expect to receive the decedent's remainder interest in the trust before the expiration of the period of postponement. The extension will be granted only in the manner provided in paragraph (b) of §20.6161-1, and the amount of the tax for which the extension is granted, with the additions thereto, shall be paid on or before the expiration of the period of extension without the necessity of notice and demand from the district director.

(b) Notice of the exercise of the election to postpone the payment of the tax attributable to a reversionary or remainder interest should be filed with the district director before the date prescribed for payment of the tax. The notice of election may be made in the form of a letter addressed to the district director. There shall be filed with the notice of election a certified copy of the will or other instrument under which the reversionary or remainder interest was created, or a copy verified by the executor if the instrument is not filed of record. The district director may require the submission of such additional proof as he deems necessary to disclose the complete facts. If the duration of the precedent interest is dependent upon the life of any person, the notice of election must show the date of birth of that person.

(c) If the decedent's gross estate consists of both a reversionary or remainder interest in property and other property, the tax attributable to the reversionary or remainder interest, within the meaning of this section, is an amount which bears the same ratio to the total tax as the value of the reversionary or remainder interest (reduced as provided in the following sentence) bears to the entire gross estate (reduced as provided in the last sentence of this paragraph). In applying this ratio, the value of the reversionary or remainder interest is reduced by (1) the amount of claims, mortgages, and indebtedness which is a lien upon such interest; (2) losses in respect of such interest during the settlement of the estate which are deductible under the provisions of section 2054 or section 2106(a)(1); (3) any amount deductible in respect of such interest under section 2055 or 2106(a)(2) for charitable, etc., transfers; and (4) the portion of the marital deduction allowed under the provisions of section 2056 on account of bequests, etc., of such interests to the decedent's surviving spouse. Likewise, in applying the ratio, the value of the gross estate is reduced by such deductions having similar relationship to the items comprising the gross estate.

(d) For provisions requiring the payment of interest during the period of the extension occurring before July 1, 1975, see section 6601(b) prior to its amendment by section 7(d)(1) of the Act of Jan. 3, 1975 (Pub. L. 93-625, 88 Stat. 2115). For provisions requiring the furnishing of security for the payment of the tax for which the extension is granted, see paragraph (b) of §20.6165-1. For provisions concerning the time within which credit for State and foreign death taxes on such a reversionary or remainder interest may be taken, see section 2015 and the regulations thereunder. [Reg. §20.6163-1.]

☐ [*T.D. 6296, 6-23-58. Amended by T.D. 6526, 1-18-61, T.D. 6716, 3-25-64, T.D. 6736, 5-27-64, T.D. 7238, 12-28-72, and T.D. 7384, 10-21-75.*]

### [Reg. §1.6164-1]

**§1.6164-1. Extensions of time for payment of taxes by corporations expecting carrybacks.**—(a) *In general.*—If a corporation in any taxable year files a statement with respect to an expected net operating loss carryback from such taxable year, such corporation may extend the time for the payment of all or part of any tax imposed by subtitle A of the Code for the taxable year immediately preceding such taxable year to the extent and subject to the limitations provided in section 6164. A corporation may extend the time for payment with respect to only such taxes as meet the following requirements:

(1) The tax must be one imposed by subtitle A of the Code;

(2) The tax must be for the taxable year immediately preceding the taxable year of the expected net operating loss;

(3) The tax must be shown on the return or must be assessed within the taxable year of the expected net operating loss; and

(4) The tax must not have been paid or required to have been paid prior to the filing of the statement.

(b) *Statement for purpose of extending time for payment.*—(1) The time for payment of the tax is automatically extended upon the filing of a statement on Form 1138 by the corporation with the district director for the district where the tax is payable. The statement on Form 1138 must be filled out in accordance with the instructions accompanying the form, and all information required by the form and the instructions must be furnished by the taxpayer. The district director, upon request, will furnish a receipt for any statement filed. Such receipt will show the date the statement was filed.

(2) The period of extension is that provided in section 6164(d) and §1.6164-5 unless sooner terminated by action of either the district director or the corporation. [Reg. §1.6164-1.]

☐ [*T.D.* 6364, 2-13-59.]

### [Reg. §301.6164-1]

**§301.6164-1. Extension of time for payment of taxes by corporations expecting carrybacks.**—For provisions relating to the extension of time for payment of taxes by corporations expecting carrybacks, see §§1.6164-1 to 1.6164-9, inclusive, of this chapter (Income Tax Regulations). [Reg. §301.6164-1.]

☐ [*T.D.* 6498, 10-24-60.]

### [Reg. §1.6164-2]

**§1.6164-2. Amount of tax the time for payment of which may be extended.**—(a) *Total amount to which extension may relate.*—The total amount of tax the time for payment of which may be extended under section 6164 may not exceed the amount of the reduction of the taxes previously determined attributable to the expected carryback.

(b) *Amount of tax to which extension may relate.*—(1) The taxpayer shall specify on Form 1138 the kind of tax and the amount thereof the time for payment of which is to be extended. The amount of tax to which an extension may relate shall not exceed the amount of such tax shown on the return as filed, increased by any amount assessed as a deficiency (or as interest or addition to the tax) prior to the date of filing the statement and decreased by any amount paid or required to be paid prior to such date. In determining the amount of tax required to be paid prior to the date of filing the statement, only the following amounts shall be taken into consideration:

(i) The amount of the tax shown on the return as filed; and

(ii) Any amount assessed as a deficiency (or as interest or addition to the tax) if the tenth day after notice and demand for its payment occurs prior to the date of the filing of the statement.

(2) Delinquent installments are to be considered amounts required to be paid prior to the date of filing the statement. In the case of any authorized extension of time under sections 6161 and 6162, the amount of tax the time for payment of which is so extended is not to be considered required to be paid prior to the end of such extension. Similarly, any amount assessed as a deficiency (or as interest or addition to the tax) is not to be considered required to be paid prior to the date of the filing of the statement unless the tenth day after notice and demand for its payment falls prior to the date of the filing of the statement.

(3) The taxpayer may choose to extend the time for payment of all of one or more taxes, or it may choose to extend the time for payment of portions of several taxes. The taxes chosen by the taxpayer need not be those taxes which are affected by the carryback. [Reg. §1.6164-2.]

☐ [*T.D.* 6364, 2-13-59.]

### [Reg. §1.6164-3]

**§1.6164-3. Computation of the amount of reduction of the tax previously determined.**—(a) *Tax previously determined.*—The taxpayer is to determine the amount of the reduction, attributable to the expected carryback, in the aggregate of the taxes previously determined for taxable years prior to the taxable year of the expected net operating loss. The tax previously determined is to be ascertained in accordance with the method prescribed in section 1314(a). Thus, the tax previously determined will be the tax shown on the return as filed, increased by any amounts assessed (or collected without assessment) as deficiencies prior to the date of the filing of the statement, and decreased by any amounts abated, credited, refunded, or otherwise repaid prior to such date. Any items as to which the Internal Revenue Service and the taxpayer are in disagreement at the time of the filing of the statement shall be taken into account in ascertaining the tax previously determined only if, and to the extent that, they were reported in the return, or were reflected in any amounts assessed (or collected without assessment) as deficiencies, or in any amounts abated, credited, refunded, or otherwise repaid, prior to the date of the filing of the statement. The tax previously determined will reflect the foreign tax credit and the credit for tax withheld at source provided in section 32.

(b) *Reduction attributable to the expected carryback.*—The reduction, attributable to the expected carryback or related adjustments, in any tax previously determined is to be ascertained by applying the expected carryback as if it were a determined net operating loss carryback, in accordance with the provisions of section 172 and the regulations thereunder. Items must be taken into account only to the extent that such items were included in the return, or were reflected in amounts assessed (or collected without assessment) as deficiencies, or in amounts abated, credited, refunded, or otherwise repaid, prior to the date of the filing of the statement. Thus, for example, if

the taxpayer claims a deduction for depreciation of $10,000 in its return and the Internal Revenue Service asserts that only $4,000 is properly deductible, no change is to be made in the $10,000 depreciation deduction as shown by the taxpayer on his return unless a deficiency has been assessed, or an amount collected without assessment, prior to the date of filing of the statement as a result of a change in the depreciation deduction, or unless such change in the depreciation deduction was reflected in an amount abated, credited, refunded, or otherwise repaid prior to such date. [Reg. §1.6164-3.]

☐ [*T.D.* 6364, 2-13-59. *Amended by T.D.* 6862, 11-17-65.]

### [Reg. §1.6164-4]

**§1.6164-4. Payment of remainder of tax where extension relates to only part of the tax.**—(a) *Time for payment.*—If an extension of time relates to only part of the tax, the time for payment of the remainder of the tax shall be considered to be the dates on which payments would have been required if such remainder had been the tax and the taxpayer had elected to pay the tax in installments as provided in section 6152(a).

(b) *Example.*—The provisions of this section may be illustrated by the following example:

*Example.* Corporation X, which keeps its books and makes its tax returns on the calendar year basis, filed its income tax return for 1956 on March 15, 1957. The corporation showed a tax of $1,000 on its return and paid 50 percent of such tax, or $500 on March 15, 1957. On June 3, 1957, corporation X, pursuant to the provisions of section 6164, extended the time for payment of $400 of such tax. The remainder of the tax the time for payment of which was not so extended, i.e., $600, is to be considered the tax for purposes of determining when it is to be paid. The remainder is considered to be due on the dates on which payment would have been required if such remainder had been the tax. Since the taxable year ended on December 31, 1956, the tax is payable in two equal installments of $300 each on March 15, 1957, and June 17, 1957. The taxpayer, having paid $500 on March 15, 1957, will have $100 to pay on June 17, 1957. [Reg. §1.6164-4.]

☐ [*T.D.* 6364, 2-13-59.]

### [Reg. §1.6164-5]

**§1.6164-5. Period of extension.**—If the time for the payment of any tax has been extended pursuant to section 6164, such extension shall expire:

(a) On the last day of the month in which falls the last date prescribed by law (including any extension of time granted the taxpayer) for the filing of the return for the taxable year of the expected net operating loss; or

(b) If an application for a tentative carryback adjustment provided in section 6411 with respect to such loss is filed before the expiration of the period specified in paragraph (a) of this section, on the date on which notice is mailed by registered mail prior to September 3, 1958, and by either registered or certified mail on and after September 3, 1958, to the taxpayer that such application is allowed or disallowed in whole or in part. [Reg. §1.6164-5.]

☐ [*T.D.* 6364, 2-13-59.]

### [Reg. §1.6164-6]

**§1.6164-6. Revised statements.**—(a) *Requirements and effect.*—A corporation may file more than one statement under section 6164 with respect to any one taxable year. Each statement is to be considered a new statement and not an amendment of any prior statement. Each such new statement is to be in lieu of the last statement previously filed with respect to the taxable year. The new statement may extend the time for payment of a greater or lesser amount of tax than was extended under the prior statement or may charge the kind of tax the time for payment of which is to be extended. The extension may not relate to any amount of tax which was paid or required to be paid prior to the date of filing the new statement. Any amount of tax the time for payment of which was extended under a prior statement, however, may continue to be extended under the new statement. If the amount the time for payment of which is extended under the new statement is less than the amount so extended under the last statement previously filed, the extension of time shall be terminated on the date the new statement is filed as to the difference between the two amounts. See §1.6164-8 for the dates on which such difference must be paid. If a corporation pays any amount of tax, the time for payment of which was extended, prior to the date the extension would otherwise terminate, the extension with respect to such amount shall be deemed terminated, without regard to whether a new statement is filed, on the date such amount is paid. The corporation shall indicate on each new statement filed that it has already filed one or more prior statements with respect to the taxable year. The corporation shall likewise indicate the date each prior statement was filed and the amount of each tax the time for payment of which was extended under each prior statement.

(b) *Example.*—The provisions of this section may be illustrated by the following example:

*Example.* Corporation Y, which keeps its books and makes its tax returns on the calendar year basis, filed its income tax return for 1956 on March 15, 1957, showing a tax of $100,000. At the same time it filed a statement under section 6164 in which it stated that it expected to have a net operating loss of $75,000 in 1957 and that the reduction in the tax previously determined for 1955 (the second taxable year preceding the year of the expected net operating loss) attributable to the expected net operating loss carryback resulting from such expected loss, would be $39,000. The corporation accordingly extended the time for payment of $39,000 of its income tax for 1956, and paid $30,500 (50 percent of the excess of $100,000 over $39,000) of such tax on March 15, 1957 (see section 6164(c) and §1.6164-4). As a result of its operations during the next several months, the corporation filed a second statement on June 3, 1957, in which it stated that its expected net operating loss for 1957 would amount to $150,000 and that the corresponding reduction in the tax for 1955 would amount to $78,000. Corporation Y under the new statement may extend the time for payment of $30,500, the installment due on June 17, 1957, and the time for payment of the $39,000 extended under the first statement filed on March 15, 1957, may continue to be extended under the second statement. The $30,500 which was paid on March 15, 1957, will not be affected by the second statement filed on June 3, 1957. [Reg. §1.6164-6.]

☐ [*T.D.* 6364, 2-13-59.]

### [Reg. §1.6164-7]

**§1.6164-7. Termination by district director.**—(a) *After an examination of the statement filed by the corporation is made.*—The district director is authorized to make such examination of the statements filed as he deems necessary and practicable. If, upon such examination as he may make, the district director believes that, as of the time he makes the examination, all or any part of the statement is in a material respect erroneous or unreasonable, he will terminate the extension as to any part of the amount to which such extension relates which he deems should be terminated.

(b) *Jeopardy.*—If the district director believes that the collection of any amount to which an extension under section 6164 relates is in jeopardy, he will immediately terminate the extension. In the case of such a termination, notice and demand shall be made by the district director for payment of such amount, and there may be no further extension of time under section 6164 with respect to such amount. [Reg. §1.6164-7.]

☐ [*T.D.* 6364, 2-13-59.]

### [Reg. §1.6164-8]

**§1.6164-8. Payments on termination.**—(a) *In general.*—If an extension of time under section 6164 is terminated with respect to any amount either (1) by the filing of a new statement by the taxpayer under section 6164(e) extending the time for payment of a lesser amount than was extended in a prior statement, or (2) by action of the district director under section 6164(f) after making an examination of the statement filed by the corporation, no further extension of time may be made under section 6164 with respect to such amount. The time for payment of such amount shall be the dates on which payments would have been required if there had been no extension with respect to such amount and the taxpayer had elected under section 6152(a) to pay the tax in installments.

(b) *Example.*—The provisions of this section may be illustrated by the following example:

*Example.* Corporation Z, which keeps its books and makes its tax returns on the calendar year basis, filed its income tax return for 1956 on March 15, 1957, showing a tax of $100,000. At the same time it filed a statement under section 6164 extending the time for payment of the entire $100,000 on the basis of an expected net operating loss carryback from 1957. On April 10, 1957, the corporation filed a new statement indicating that the reduction, attributable to the carryback from 1957, in its income tax for 1956, would only be $80,000, and thus terminated the above extension of $20,000. The time for payment of such $20,000 may not be extended again, and such $20,000 is payable as if it were the tax for 1956 and corporation Z had elected to pay such tax in installments. That is, $10,000 is payable on March 15, 1957, and $10,000 payable on June 17, 1957. Inasmuch as the March 15 date had already passed when the corporation Z terminated the extension with respect to the $20,000, $10,000 is payable immediately upon such termination, and the other installment of $10,000 is payable on June 17, 1957. This example would also apply if the extension of time for payment of the $20,000 were terminated instead by the district director on April 10, 1957. [Reg. §1.6164-8.]

☐ [*T.D.* 6364, 2-13-59.]

### [Reg. §1.6164-9]

**§1.6164-9. Cross references.**—For provisions with respect to interest due on amounts the payment of which is extended under section 6164, see section 6601 and paragraph (e) of §301.6601-1 of this chapter (Regulations on Procedure and Administration). For extensions of time under section 6164 in the case of corporations making or required to make consolidated returns, see §1.1502-77(a). [Reg. §1.6164-9.]

☐ [*T.D.* 6364, 2-13-59. *Amended by T.D.* 7244, 12-29-72.]

### [Reg. §1.6165-1]

**§1.6165-1. Bonds where time to pay the tax or deficiency has been extended.**—The district director, including the Director of International Operations, may, as a condition to the granting of an extension of time within which to pay any tax or any deficiency therein, require the taxpayer to furnish a bond in an amount not exceeding double the amount of the tax with respect to which the extension is granted. Such bond shall be furnished in accordance with the provisions contained in section 7101 and the regulations in Part 30 of this Chapter (Regulations on Procedure and Administration). [Reg. §1.6165-1.]

☐ [*T.D.* 6455, 3-1-60.]

### [Reg. §20.6165-1]

**§20.6165-1. Bonds where time to pay tax or deficiency has been extended.**—(a) *Extensions under sections 6161 and 6163(b) of time to pay tax or deficiency.*—If an extension of time for payment of tax or deficiency is granted under section 6161 or 6163(b), the district director may, if he deems it necessary, require the executor to furnish a bond for the payment of the amount in respect of which the extension is granted in accordance with the terms of the extension. However, such bond shall not exceed double the amount with respect to which the extension is granted. For other provisions relating to bonds required where extensions of time to pay estate taxes or deficiencies are granted under sections 6161 and 6163(b), see the regulations under section 7101 contained in Part 301 of this chapter (Regulations on Procedure and Administration).

(b) *Extensions under section 6163 of time to pay estate tax attributable to reversionary or remainder interests.*—As a prerequisite to the postponement of the payment of the tax attributable to a reversionary or remainder interest as provided in §20.6163-1, a bond equal to double the amount of the tax and interest for the estimated duration of the precedent interest must be furnished conditioned upon the payment of the tax and interest accrued thereon within six months after the termination of the precedent interest. If after the acceptance of a bond it is determined that the amount of the tax attributable to the reversionary or remainder interest was understated in the bond, a new bond or a supplemental bond may be required, or the tax, to the extent of the understatement, may be collected. The bond must be conditioned upon the principal or surety promptly notifying the district director when the precedent interest terminates and upon the principal or surety notifying the district director during the month of September of each year as to the continuance of the precedent interest, if the duration of the precedent interest is dependent upon the life or lives of any person or persons, or is otherwise indefinite. For other provisions relating to bonds where an extension of time has been granted for paying the tax, see the regulations under section 7101 contained in Part 301 of this chapter (Regulations on Procedure and Administration). [Reg. §20.6165-1.]

☐ [*T.D.* 6296, 6-23-58. *Amended by T.D.* 6526, 1-18-61, *T.D.* 6600, 5-28-62.]

### [Reg. §25.6165-1]

**§25.6165-1. Bonds where time to pay tax or deficiency has been extended.**—If an extension of time for payment of tax or deficiency is granted under section 6161, the district director may, if he deems it necessary, require a bond for the payment of the amount in respect of which the extension is granted in accordance with the terms of the extension. However, such bond shall not exceed double the amount with respect to which the extension is granted. For provisions relating to form of bonds, see the regulations under section 7101 contained in Part 301 of this chapter (Regulations on Procedure and Administration). [Reg. §25.6165-1.]

☐ [*T.D.* 6334, 11-14-58. *Amended by T.D.* 6600, 5-28-62.]

### [Reg. §53.6165-1]

**§53.6165-1. Bonds where time to pay tax or deficiency has been extended.**—If an extension of time for payment of tax or deficiency is granted under section 6161, the district director or the director of the service center may, if he deems it necessary, require a bond for the payment of the amount in respect of which the extension is granted in accordance with the terms of the extension. However, such bond shall not exceed double the amount with respect to which the extension is granted. For provisions relating to form of bonds, see the regulations under section 7101 contained in Part 301 of this chapter (Regulations on Procedure and Administration). [Reg. §53.6165-1.]

☐ [T.D. 7368, 7-15-75.]

### [Reg. §55.6165-1]

**§55.6165-1. Bonds where time to pay tax or deficiency has been extended.**—If an extension of time for payment of tax or deficiency is granted under section 6161, the district director or the director of the service center may, if he deems it necessary, require a bond for the payment of the amount in respect of which the extension is granted in accordance with the terms of the extension. However, the bond shall not exceed double the amount with respect to which the extension is granted. For provisions relating to form of bonds, see the regulations under section 7101 contained in Part 301 of this chapter (Regulations on Procedure and Administration). [Reg. §55.6165-1.]

☐ [T.D. 7767, 2-3-81.]

### [Reg. §156.6165-1]

**§156.6165-1. Bonds where time to pay tax or deficiency has been extended.**—If an extension of time for payment is granted under section 6161 of the Code, the district director or the director of the service center may, if he deems it necessary, require a bond for the payment of the amount in respect to which the extension is granted in accordance with the terms of the extension. However, the bond shall not exceed double the amount with respect to which the extension is granted. For provisions relating to form of bonds, see the regulations under section 7101 of the Code contained in Part 301 of title 26 (Regulations on Procedure and Administration). [Reg. §156.6165-1.]

☐ [T.D. 8379, 12-17-91.]

### [Reg. §157.6165-1]

**§157.6165-1. Bonds where time to pay tax has been extended.**—If an extension of time for payment is granted under section 6161, the Internal Revenue Service may, if it deems necessary, require a bond for the payment, in accordance with the terms of the extension, of the amount with respect to which the extension is granted. However, the bond shall not exceed double the amount with respect to which the extension is granted. For provisions relating to the form of bonds, see the regulations under section 7101 contained in part 301 (Regulations on Procedure and Administration) of this chapter. [Reg. §157.6165-1.]

☐ [T.D. 9134, 7-7-2004.]

### [Reg. §301.6165-1]

**§301.6165-1. Bonds where time to pay the tax or deficiency has been extended.**—For provisions concerning bonds where time to pay a tax or deficiency has been extended, see the regulations relating to the particular tax. [Reg. §301.6165-1.]

☐ [T.D. 6498, 10-24-60.]

### [Reg. §20.6166-1]

**§20.6166-1. Election of alternate extension of time for payment of estate tax where estate consists largely of interest in closely held business.**—(a) *In general.*—Section 6166 allows an executor to elect to extend payment of part or all of the portion of the estate tax which is attributable to a closely held business interest (as defined in section 6166(b)(1)). If it is made at the time the estate tax return is filed, the election is applicable both to the tax originally determined to be due and to certain deficiencies. If no election is made when the estate tax return is filed, up to the full amount of certain later deficiencies (but not any tax originally determined to be due) may be paid in installments.

(b) *Time and manner of election.*—The election provided under section 6166(a) is made by attaching to a timely filed estate tax return a notice of election containing the following information:

(1) The decedent's name and taxpayer identification number as they appear on the estate tax return;

(2) The amount of tax which is to be paid in installments;

(3) The date selected for payment of the first installment;

(4) The number of annual installments, including the first installment, in which the tax is to be paid;

(5) The properties shown on the estate tax return which constitute the closely held business interest (identified by schedule and item number); and

(6) The facts which formed the basis for the executor's conclusion that the estate qualifies for payment of the estate tax in installments. In the absence of a statement in the notice of election as to the

amount of tax to be paid in installments, the date selected for payment of the first installment, or the number of installments, the election is presumed to be for the maximum amount so payable and for payment thereof in 10 equal installments, the first of which is due on the date which is 5 years after the date prescribed in section 6151(a) for payment of estate tax.

(c) *Treatment of certain deficiencies.*—(1) *No election before assessment of deficiency.*—Where a deficiency is assessed and no election, including a protective election, has been made under section 6166(a) to pay any tax in installments, the executor may elect under section 6166(h) to pay the portion of the deficiency attributable to the closely held business interest in installments. However, this is true only if the estate qualifies under section 6166 based upon values as finally determined (or agreed to following examination of a return). Such an election is exercised by filing a notice of election with the Internal Revenue Service office where the estate tax return was filed. The notice of election must be filed within 60 days after issuance of notice and demand for payment of the deficiency, and it must contain the same information as is required under paragraph (b) of this section. The notice of election is to be accompanied by payment of the amount of tax and interest, the date for payment of which has arrived as determined under paragraphs (e) and (f) of this section, plus any amount of unpaid tax and interest which is not attributable to the closely held business interest and which is not eligible for further extension (or currently extended) under another section (other than section 6166A).

(2) *Election made with estate tax return.*—If the executor makes an election under section 6166(a) (other than a protective election) at the time the estate tax return is filed and a deficiency is later assessed, the portion of the deficiency which is attributable to the closely held business interest (but not any accrued interest thereon) will be prorated to the installments payable pursuant to the original section 6166(a) election. Any part of the deficiency prorated to an installment, the date for payment of which has arrived, is due upon notice and demand. Interest for any such period, including the deferral period, is payable upon notice and demand.

(3) *Portion of deficiency attributable to closely held business interest.*—Only that portion of any deficiency which is attributable to a closely held business interest may be paid in installments under section 6166. The amount of any deficiency which is so attributable is the difference between the amount of tax which the executor has previously elected to pay in installments under section 6166 and the maximum amount of tax which the executor could have elected to pay in installments on the basis of a return which reflects the adjustments that resulted in the deficiency.

(d) *Protective election.*—A protective election may be made to defer payment of any portion of tax remaining unpaid at the time values are finally determined (or agreed to following examination of a return) and any deficiencies attributable to the closely held business interest (within the meaning of paragraph (c)(3) of this section). Extension of tax payments pursuant to this election is contingent upon final values meeting the requirements of section 6166. A protective election does not, however, extend the time for payment of any amount of tax. Rules for such extensions are contained in sections 6161, 6163, and 6166A. A protective election is made by filing a notice of election with a timely filed estate tax return stating that the election is being made. Within 60 days after values are finally determined (or agreed to following examination of a return), a final notice of election which sets forth the information required under paragraph (b) of this section must be filed with the Internal Revenue Service office where the original estate tax return was filed. That notice of final election is to be accompanied by payment of any amount of previously unpaid tax and interest, the date for payment of which has arrived as determined under paragraphs (e) and (f) of this section, plus any amount of unpaid tax and interest which is not attributable to the closely held business interest and which is not eligible for further extension (or currently extended) under another section (other than section 6166A).

(e) *Special rules.*—(1) *Effect of deficiencies and protective elections upon payment.*—Upon election to extend the time for payment of a deficiency or upon final determination of values following a protective election, the executor must prorate the tax or deficiency attributable to the closely held business interest among all installments. All amounts attributed to installments which would have been due had the election been made at the time the tax was due to be paid under section 6151(a) and all accrued interest must be paid at the time the election is made.

(2) *Determination of date for payment of first installment.*—The executor may defer payment of tax (but not interest) for any period up to 5 years from the date determined under section 6151(a) for payment of the estate tax. The date chosen for payment of the first

**Place and Due Date for Payment of Tax**
See p. 20,601 for regulations not amended to reflect law changes
**66,813**

installment of tax is not required to be on an annual anniversary of the original due date of the tax; however, it must be the date within any month which corresponds to the day of the month determined under section 6151(a).

(f) *Rule for computing interest.*—Section 6601(j) provides a special 4 percent interest rate for the amount of tax (including deficiencies) which is to be paid in installments under section 6166. This special interest rate applies only to that amount of tax which is to be paid in installments and which does not exceed the limitation of section 6601(j)(2). Where payment of a greater amount of tax than is subject to section 6601(j)(2) is extended under section 6166, each installment is deemed to be comprised of both tax subject to the 4 percent interest rate and tax subject to the rate otherwise prescribed by section 6621. The percentage of any installment subject to the special 4 percent rate is equal to the percentage of the total tax payable in installments which is subject to the 4 percent rate. Where an election is made under the provisions of paragraphs (b) or (c)(1) of this section, the 4 percent rate applies from the date on which the estate tax was originally due to be paid. If only a protective election is made, section 6601(j) applies to the amount which is to be paid in installments, limited to the amount of any deficiency, from the due date for payment of estate tax. After the date upon which the section 6166 election is made final, section 6601(j) applies to the entire amount to be paid in installments.

(g) *Relation of section 6166 and 6166A.*—No election may be made under section 6166 if an election under section 6166A applies with respect to an estate. For example, no election can be made under section 6166(h) where an executor has made an election under section 6166A. If an election is timely made under either section 6166 or section 6166A, however, a protective election can be made under the other section at the same time. If the executor then files a timely notice of final election under the section protectively elected and pays any amounts determined to be due currently following final determination of (or agreement as to) estate tax values, the original election under the other provision will be deemed never to have applied to the estate.

(h) *Special rule for estates for which elections under section 6166 are made on or before August 30, 1980.*—An election to extend payment of estate tax under section 6166 that is made on or before August 30, 1980 may be revoked. To revoke an election, the executor must file a notice of revocation with the Internal Revenue Service office where the original estate tax return was filed on or before January 31, 1981 (or if earlier, the date on which the period of limitation on assessment expires). This notice of revocation must contain the decedent's name, date of death, and taxpayer identification number, and is to be accompanied by remittance of any additional amount of estate tax and interest determined to be due.

(i) *Examples.*—The provisions of this section may be illustrated by the following examples:

*Example (1)*—(i). Based upon values shown on decedent A's timely filed estate tax return, 60 percent of the value of A's adjusted gross estate consisted of a farm which was a closely held business within the meaning of section 6166. A's executor, B, made a protective election under section 6166 when he filed A's estate tax return. B also applied for an extension of time under section 6161 to pay $15,000 of the $30,000 of estate tax shown due on the return. The requested extension was granted and was renewed at the end of 1 year. Eighteen months after the return was filed and after examination of A's estate tax return, the value of the farm was found to constitute 67 percent of the adjusted gross estate. B entered into an agreement consenting to the values as established on examination and to a deficiency of $5,000. B then filed a final notice of election under section 6166, choosing a 5-year deferral followed by 10 annual installment payments and thereby terminated his extension under section 6161 because that amount of tax was then included under the section 6166 election. B could have extended payment of 67 percent of the total estate tax, or $23,450. $23,450 is eligible for installment payments under section 6166 and the section 6166 election is considered to be for that amount. B is considered to have prepaid $3,450 of tax since only $20,000 of tax remained unpaid. The $3,450 is attributed to the first installment of $2,345 and to $1,105 of the second installment which would have been payable under the section 6166 election.

(ii) Had B been granted an extension of time under section 6161 to pay $20,000 of tax, $25,000 would remain unpaid when the final section 6166 election is made. Payment of the full $23,450 (67 percent) of tax which is attributable to the closely held business interest is included under the section 6166 election. The balance of unpaid tax ($1,550) is due upon expiration of the estate's section 6161 extension.

(iii) Assume the facts under example (1)(i). B must pay all unpaid accrued interest with his notice of final election. Since only 18 months have passed, no installments of tax are due. Interest on the $5,000 deficiency is computed at 4 percent per annum for the entire 18 months, and interest for 12 months of that period is currently due to be paid. Interest for the remaining 6 months is due at the next succeeding date for payment of interest. Interest on the $15,000 of tax extended under section 6161 is computed at the rate determined under section 6621 until the date of the final section 6166 election and is due upon termination of the section 6161 extension. After that date, the interest on the $15,000 will also accrue at 4 percent per annum.

*Example (2)*. Assume the facts as in example (1), except B initially made an election under section 6166A and made no protective election under section 6166. Following final determination of values, B is not permitted to make any election under section 6166; however, had B protectively elected section 6166 at the time he made the section 6166A election, he could have terminated the section 6166A election and finally elected under section 6166. In such a case, the full $23,450 of tax attributable to the farm would have been eligible for extension under section 6166. The 4 percent interest rate would apply to the $5,000 deficiency from the original due date of the tax, and, as with the extension under section 6161, it would apply to the amounts extended under section 6166A only from the date on which the election under section 6166 was finalized.

*Example (3)*. C died in 1977. His estate owes Federal estate taxes of $750,000, $500,000 of which is attributable to a closely held business interest. Payment of the $500,000 was extended under section 6166. A 5-year deferral followed by 10 annual installment payments was chosen by C's executor. Under paragraph (f) of this section, only 63.16 percent of each installment will be subject to the special 4 percent interest rate and the remainder will be subject to the rate determined under section 6621. The same rule applies in computing interest for the 5 years during which payment of tax is deferred. (This is so because the 4 percent interest rate applies only to a maximum of $345,800 of tax less the $30,000 of credit allowable under section 2010(a) rather than to the entire $500,000 extended amount.) [Reg. §20.6166-1.]

☐ [*T.D. 7710, 7-28-80.*]

### [Reg. §20.6166A-1]

**§20.6166A-1. Extension of time for payment of estate tax where estate consists largely of interest in closely held business.**—(a) *In general.*—Section 6166 provides that where the value of an interest in a closely held business, which is included in the gross estate of a decedent who was a citizen or resident of the United States at the time of his death, exceeds either (1) 35 percent of the value of the gross estate, or (2) 50 percent of the taxable estate, the executor may elect to pay part or all of the Federal estate tax in installments. The election to pay the tax in installments applies to deficiencies in tax as well as to the tax shown on the return, unless the deficiency is due to negligence, to intentional disregard of rules and regulations, or to fraud with intent to evade tax. Except as otherwise provided in section 6166(i) and §20.6166-4, the provisions of section 6166 and this section apply only if the due date of the return is after September 2, 1958. See §20.6166-4 for special rules applicable where the decedent died after August 16, 1954, and the due date of the return was on or before September 2, 1958. See also §20.6075-1 for the due date of the return, and §20.6166-2 for definition of the term "interest in a closely held business." Since the election must be made on or before the due date of the return, the provisions of section 6166 will not apply to a deficiency in a case where, for whatever reason, no election was made to pay in installments the tax shown on the return. However, see paragraph (e)(3) of this section concerning a protective election. The general administrative provisions of subtitle F of the Code are applicable in connection with an election by the executor to pay the estate tax in installments in the same manner in which they are applied in a case where an extension of time under section 6161 is granted for payment of the tax. See paragraph(a) of §20.6165-1 for provisions requiring the furnishing of security for the payment of the tax in cases where an extension is granted under section 6161.

(b) *Limitation on amount of tax payable in installments.*—The amount of estate tax which the executor may elect to pay in installments is limited to an amount A, which bears the same ratio to B (the gross Federal estate tax, reduced by the credits authorized by sections 2011 through 2014 and any death tax convention) as C (the value of the interest in a closely held business which is included in the gross estate) bears to D (the value of the gross estate). Stated algebraically, the limitation (A) equals

$$\frac{\text{value of interest in a closely held business which is included in the gross estate (C)}}{\text{value of gross estate (D)}} \times \frac{\text{gross Federal estate tax, reduced by the credits authorized by sections 2011 through 2014 and any death tax convention (B).}}{}$$

Reg. §20.6166A-1(b)

The executor may elect to pay in installments an amount less than the amount computed under the limitation in this paragraph. For example, if the total estate tax payable is $100,000 and the amount computed under the limitation in this paragraph is $60,000, the executor may elect to pay in installments some lesser sum such as $30,000, in which event the executor must pay $73,000 to the district director on or before the date prescribed by section 6151(a) for payment of the tax. Of such payment, $70,000 represents tax which the executor either could not elect to pay in installments or did not choose to so elect, and $3,000 represents a payment of the first installment of the tax which the executor elected to pay in installments.

(c) *Number of installments and dates for payment.*—The executor may elect to pay part or all of the tax (determined after application of the limitation contained in paragraph (b) of this section) in two or more, but not exceeding 10, equal annual installments. The first installment shall be paid on or before the date prescribed by section 6151(a) for payment of the tax (see paragraph (a) of §20.6151-1), and each succeeding installment shall be paid on or before the date which is one year after the date prescribed for the payment of the preceding installment. See §20.6166-3 for the circumstances under which the privilege of paying the tax in installments will terminate.

(d) *Deficiencies.*—The amount of a deficiency which may be paid in installments shall not exceed the difference between the amount of tax which the executor elected to pay in installments and the maximum amount of tax (determined under paragraph (b) of this section) which the executor could have elected to pay in installments on the basis of a return which reflects the adjustments which resulted in the deficiency. This amount is then prorated to the installments in which the executor elected to pay the tax. The part of the deficiency prorated to installments not yet due shall be paid at the same time as, and as a part of, such installments. The part of the deficiency prorated to installments already paid or due shall be paid upon notice and demand from the district director. At the time the executor receives such notice and demand he may, of course, prepay the portions of the deficiency which have been prorated to installments not yet due. See paragraph (h) of this section.

(e) *Notice of election.*—(1) *Filing of notice.*—The notice of election to pay the estate tax in installments shall be filed with the district director on or before the due date of the return. However, if the due date of the return is after September 2, 1958, but before November 3, 1958, the election will be considered as timely made if the notice is filed with the district director on or before November 3, 1958. See §20.6075-1 for the due date of the return.

(2) *Form of notice.*—The notice of election to pay the estate tax in installments may be in the form of a letter addressed to the district director. The executor shall state in the notice the amount of tax which he elects to pay in installments, and the total number of installments (including the installment due 9 months (15 months, in the case of a decedent dying before January 1, 1971) after the date of the decedent's death) in which he elects to pay the tax. The properties in the gross estate which constitute the decedent's interest in a closely held business should be listed in the notice, and identified by the schedule and item number at which they appear on the estate tax return. The notice should set forth the facts which formed the basis for the executor's conclusion that the estate qualifies for the payment of the estate tax in installments.

(3) *Protective election.*—In a case where the estate does not qualify under section 6166(a) on the basis of the values as returned, or where the return shows no tax as due, an election may be made, contingent upon the values as finally determined meeting the percentage requirements set forth in section 6166(a), to pay in installments any portion of the estate tax, including a deficiency, which may be unpaid at the time of such final determination and which does not exceed the limitation provided in section 6166(b). The protective election must be made on or before the due date of the return and should state that it is a protective election. In the absence of a statement in the protective election as to the amount of tax to be paid in installments and the number of installments, the election will be presumed to be made for the maximum amount so payable and for the payment thereof in 10 equal annual installments, the first of which would have been due on the date prescribed in section 6151(a) for payment of the tax. The unpaid portion of the tax which may be paid in installments is prorated to the installments which would have been due if the provisions of section 6166(a) had applied to the tax, if any, shown on the return. The part of the unpaid portion of the tax so prorated to installments the date for payment of which would not have arrived before the deficiency is assessed shall be paid at the time such installments would have been due. The part of the unpaid portion of the tax so prorated to any installment the date for payment of which would have arrived before the deficiency is assessed shall be paid upon receipt of notice and demand from the district director. At the time the executor receives such notice and demand he may, of course, prepay the unpaid portions of the tax which have been

prorated to installments not yet due. See paragraph (h) of this section.

(f) *Time for paying interest.*—Under the provisions of section 6601, interest at the annual rate referred to in the regulations under section 6621 shall be paid on the unpaid balance of the estate tax which the executor has elected to pay in installments, and on the unpaid balance of any deficiency prorated to the installments. Interest on such unpaid balance of estate tax shall be paid annually at the same time as, and as a part of, each installment of the tax. Accordingly, interest is computed on the entire unpaid balance for the period from the preceding installment date to the current installment date, and is paid with the current installment. In making such a computation, proper adjustment shall be made for any advance payments made during the period, whether the advance payments are voluntary or are brought about by the operation of section 6166(h)(2). In computing the annual interest payment, the portion of any deficiency which is prorated to installments the date for payment of which has not arrived shall be added to the unpaid balance at the beginning of the annual period during which the assessment of the deficiency occurs. Interest on such portion of the deficiency for the period from the original due date of the tax to the date fixed for the payment of the last installment preceding the date of assessment of a deficiency shall be paid upon notice and demand from the district director. Any extension of time under section 6161(a)(2) (on account of undue hardship to the estate) for payment of an installment will not extend the time for payment of the interest which is due on the installment date.

(g) *Extensions of time for payment in hardship cases.*—The provisions of section 6161, under which extensions of time may be granted for payment of estate tax in cases involving undue hardship, apply to both the portion of the tax which may be paid in installments under section 6166 and the portion of the tax which is not so payable. Therefore, in a case involving undue hardship, the executor may elect under section 6166 to pay in installments the portion of the tax which is attributable to the interest in the closely held business and, in addition, may file an application under section 6161 for an extension of time to pay both the portion of the tax which is not attributable to the interest in the closely held business and such of the installments as are payable within the period of the requested extension. If an executor files a notice of election to pay the tax in installments and thereafter it is determined that the estate does not qualify for the privilege of paying the tax in installments, the executor is not deprived of the right to request an extension under section 6161 of time for payment of the tax to which the purported election applied. See §20.6161-1 for the circumstances under which a timely filed election to pay the tax in installments will be treated as a timely filed application for an extension of time to pay the tax on account of undue hardship to the estate.

(h) *Prepayments.*—Voluntary prepayment may be made at any time of all, or of any part, of the unpaid portion of the tax (including deficiencies) payable in installments. Voluntary prepayments shall be applied in payment of such installments, installment, or part of an installment as the person making the prepayment shall designate. For purposes of this paragraph, a payment described in paragraph (d)(2) of §20.6166-3 of tax in an amount not less than the amount of money or other property distributed in a section 303 redemption is considered to be a voluntary prepayment to the extent paid before the date prescribed for payment of the first installment after the redemption or, if paid on the date prescribed for payment of such installment, to the extent it exceeds the amount due on the installment. See paragraph (b)(3) of §20.6166-3 for the application to be made of the prepayment required by section 6166(h)(2). [Reg. §20.6166A-1.]

☐ [*T.D. 6522, 12-28-60. Amended by T.D. 7238, 12-28-72 and T.D. 7384, 10-21-75. Redesignated by T.D. 7710, 7-28-80.*]

### [Reg. §20.6166A-2]

**§20.6166A-2. Definition of an interest in a closely held business.**—(a) *In general.*—For purposes of §§20.6166-1, 20.6166-3, and 20.6166-4, the term "interest in a closely held business" means

(1) An interest as a proprietor in a trade or business carried on as a proprietorship.

(2) An interest as a partner in a partnership carrying on a trade or business if 20 percent or more of the total capital interest in the partnership is included in determining the decedent's gross estate or if the partnership had 10 or less partners.

(3) Stock in a corporation carrying on a trade or business if 20 percent or more in value of the voting stock of the corporation is included in determining the decedent's gross estate or if the corporation had 10 or less shareholders.

(b) *Number of partners or shareholders.*—The number of partners of the partnership or shareholders of the corporation is determined as of the time immediately before the decedent's death. Where an

Place and Due Date for Payment of Tax
See p. 20,601 for regulations not amended to reflect law changes
**66,815**

interest in a partnership, or stock in a corporation, is the community property of husband and wife, both the husband and the wife are counted as partners or shareholders in arriving at the number of partners or shareholders. Similarly, if stock is held by co-owners, tenants in common, tenants by the entirety, or joint tenants, each co-owner, tenant in common, tenant by the entirety, or joint tenant is counted as a shareholder.

(c) *Carrying on a trade or business.*—(1) In order for the interest in a partnership or the stock of a corporation to qualify as an interest in a closely held business it is necessary that the partnership or the corporation be engaged in carrying on a trade or business at the time of the decedent's death. However, it is not necessary that all the assets of the partnership or the corporation be utilized in the carrying on of the trade or business.

(2) In the case of a trade or business carried on as a proprietorship, the interest in the closely held business includes only those assets of the decedent which were actually utilized by him in the trade or business. Thus, if a building was used by the decedent in part as a personal residence and in part for the carrying on of a mercantile business, the part of the building used as a residence does not form any part of the interest in the closely held business. Whether an asset will be considered as used in the trade or business will depend on the facts and circumstances of the particular case. For example, if a bank account was held by the decedent in his individual name (as distinguished from the trade or business name) and it can be clearly shown that the amount on deposit represents working capital of the business as well as nonbusiness funds (e.g., receipts from investments, such as dividends and interest), then that part of the amount on deposit which represents working capital of the business will constitute a part of the interest in the closely held business. On the other hand, if a bank account is held by the decedent in the trade or business name and it can be shown that the amount represents nonbusiness funds as well as working capital, then only that part of the amount on deposit which represents working capital of the business will constitute a part of the interest in the closely held business. In a case where an interest in a partnership or stock of a corporation qualifies as an interest in a closely held business, the decedent's entire interest in the partnership, or the decedent's entire holding of stock in the corporation, constitutes an interest in a closely held business even though a portion of the partnership or corporate assets is used for a purpose other than the carrying on of a trade or business.

(d) *Interests in two or more closely held businesses.*—For purposes of paragraphs (a) and (b) of §20.6166-1 and paragraphs (d) and (e) of §20.6166-3, interests in two or more closely held businesses shall be treated as an interest in a single closely held business if more than 50 percent of the total value of each such business is included in determining the value of the decedent's gross estate. For the purpose of the 50 percent requirement set forth in the preceding sentence, an interest in a closely held business which represents the surviving spouse's interest in community property shall be considered as having been included in determining the value of the decedent's gross estate. [Reg. §20.6166A-2.]

□ [*T.D. 6522, 12-28-60. Redesignated by T.D. 7710, 7-28-80.*]

### [Reg. §20.6166A-3]

**§20.6166A-3. Acceleration of payment.**—(a) *In general.*—Under the circumstances described in this section all or a part of the tax which the executor has elected to pay in installments shall be paid before the dates fixed for payment of the installments. Upon an estate's having undistributed net income described in paragraph (b) of this section for any taxable year after its fourth taxable year, the executor shall pay an amount equal to such undistributed net income in liquidation of the unpaid portion of the tax payable in installments. Upon the happening of any of the events described in paragraphs (c), (d), and (e) of this section, any unpaid portion of the tax payable in installments shall be paid upon notice and demand from the district director.

(b) *Undistributed net income of estate.*—(1) If an estate has undistributed net income for any taxable year after its fourth taxable year, the executor shall pay an amount equal to such undistributed net income in liquidation of the unpaid portion of the tax payable in installments. The amount shall be paid to the district director on or before the time prescribed for the filing of the estate's income tax return for such taxable year. For this purpose extensions of time granted for the filing of the income tax return are taken into consideration in determining the time prescribed for filing the return and making such payment. In determining the number of taxable years, a short taxable year is counted as if it were a full taxable year.

(2) The term "undistributed net income" of the estate for any taxable year for purposes of this section is the amount by which the distributable net income of the estate, as defined in section 643, exceeds the sum of—

(i) The amount for such year specified in section 661(a)(1) and (2),

(ii) The amount of the Federal income tax imposed on the estate for such taxable year under chapter 1 of the Code, and

(iii) The amount of the Federal estate tax, including interest thereon, paid for the estate during such taxable year (other than any amount paid by reason of the application of this acceleration rule).

(3) The payment described in subparagraph (1) of this paragraph shall be applied against the total unpaid portion of the tax which the executor elected to pay in installments, and shall be divided equally among the installments due after the date of such payment. The application of this subparagraph may be illustrated by the following example:

*Example.* The decedent died on January 1, 1959. The executor elects under section 6166 to pay tax in the amount of $100,000 in 10 installments of $10,000. The first installment is due on April 1, 1960. The estate files its income tax returns on a calendar year basis. For its fifth taxable year (calendar year 1963) it has undistributed net income of $6,000. If the prepayment of $6,000 required by section 6166(h)(2)(A), and due on or before April 15, 1964, is paid before the fifth installment (due April 1, 1964), the $6,000 is apportioned equally among installments 5 through 10, leaving $9,000 as the amount due on each of such installments. However, if the prepayment of $6,000 is paid after the fifth installment, it is apportioned equally among installments 6 through 10, leaving $8,800 as the amount due on each of such installments.

(c) *Failure to pay installment on or before due date.*—If any installment of tax is not paid on or before the date fixed for its payment (including any extension of time for the payment thereof), the whole of the unpaid portion of the tax which is payable in installments becomes due and shall be paid upon notice and demand from the district director. See paragraph (c) of §20.6166-1 for the dates fixed for the payment of installments. See also §20.6161-1 for the circumstances under which an extension of time for the payment of an installment will be granted.

(d) *Withdrawal of funds from business.*—(1) In any case where money or other property is withdrawn from the trade or business and the aggregate withdrawals of money or other property equal or exceed 50 percent of the value of the trade or business, the privilege of paying the tax in installments terminates and the whole of the unpaid portion of the tax which is payable in installments becomes due and shall be paid upon notice and demand from the district director. The withdrawals of money or other property from the trade or business must be in connection with the interest therein included in the gross estate, and must equal or exceed 50 percent of the value of the entire trade or business (and not just 50 percent of the value of the interest therein included in the gross estate). The withdrawal must be a withdrawal of money or other property which constitutes "included property" within the meaning of that term as used in paragraph (d) of §20.2032-1. The provisions of this section do not apply to the withdrawal of money or other property which constitutes "excluded property" within the meaning of that term as used in such paragraph (d).

(2) If a distribution in redemption of stock is (by reason of the provisions of section 303 or so much of section 304 as relates to section 303) treated for income tax purposes as a distribution in full payment in exchange for the stock so redeemed, the amount of such distribution is not counted as a withdrawal of money or other property made with respect to the decedent's interest in the trade or business for purposes of determining whether the withdrawals of money or other property made with respect to the decedent's interest in the trade or business for purposes of determining whether the withdrawals of money or other property made with respect to the decedent's interest in the trade or business equal or exceed 50 percent of the value of the trade or business. However, in the case described in the preceding sentence the value of the trade or business for purposes of applying the rule set forth in subparagraph (1) of this paragraph is the value thereof reduced by the proportionate part thereof which such distribution represents. The proportionate part of the value of the trade or business which the distribution represents is determined at the time of the distribution, but the reduction in the value of the trade or business represented by it relates back to the time of the decedent's death, or the alternate valuation date if an election is made under section 2032, for purposes of determining whether other withdrawals with respect to the decedent's interest in the trade or business constitute withdrawals equaling or exceeding 50 percent of the value of the trade or business. See example (3) of paragraph (e)(6) of this section for illustration of this principle. The rule stated in the first sentence of this subparagraph does not apply unless after the redemption, but on or before the date prescribed for payment of the first installment which becomes due after the redemption, there is paid an amount of estate tax not less than the amount of money or other property distributed. Where there are a series of section 303 redemptions, each redemption is treated sepa-

rately and the failure of one redemption to qualify under the rule stated in the first sentence of this subparagraph does not necessarily mean that another redemption will not qualify.

(3) The application of this paragraph may be illustrated by the following examples, in each of which the executor elected to pay the estate tax in installments:

*Example (1).* A, who died on July 1, 1957, owned an 80 percent interest in a partnership which qualified as an interest in a closely held business. B owned the other 20 percent interest in the partnership. On the date of A's death the value of the business was $200,000 and the value of A's interest therein was included in his gross estate at $160,000. On October 1, 1958, when the value of the business was

$$\frac{\$80,000 \text{ (withdrawal)}}{\$200,000 \text{ (value of trade or business at time of withdrawal)}}$$

Immediately following the October withdrawal the remaining portion of the business represents 60 percent of the value of the trade or business in existence at the time of A's death (100 percent less 40 percent withdrawn). The executor is considered as having with-

$$\frac{\$20,000 \text{ (withdrawal)}}{\$160,000 \text{ (value of trade or business at time of withdrawal)}}$$

B's withdrawal—

$$\frac{\$10,000 \text{ (withdrawal)}}{\$160,000 \text{ (value of trade or business at time of withdrawal)}}$$

Immediately following the December withdrawal the then remaining portion of the business represented 48.75 percent of the value of the trade or business in existence at the time of A's death (100 percent less 40 percent withdrawn by executor in October, 7.5 percent withdrawn by executor in December, and 3.75 percent withdrawn by B in December). It should be noted that while at this point the total withdrawals by the executor and B from the trade or business exceed 50 percent of the value thereof, the aggregate of the withdrawals by

$$\frac{\$15,000 \text{ (withdrawal)}}{\$150,000 \text{ (value of trade or business at time of withdrawal)}}$$

As of February 1, 1959, the total withdrawals from the trade or business made with respect to A's interest therein was 52.375 percent of the value of the trade or business.

*Example (2).* The decedent's 40 percent interest in the XYZ partnership constituted an interest in a closely held business. Since the decedent's interest in the closely held business amounted to less than 50 percent of the value of the business, money or other property equaling or exceeding 50 percent of the value of the business could not be withdrawn from the decedent's interest in the business. Therefore, withdrawals of money or other property from this trade or business never would accelerate the payment of the tax under the provisions of this paragraph.

*Example (3).* The decedent died on September 1, 1957. He owned 100 shares of B Corporation (the total number of shares outstanding at the time of his death) and a 75 percent interest in a partnership of which C was the other partner. The B Corporation stock and the interest in the partnership together make up the interest in the closely held business which was included in the decedent's gross estate. The B Corporation stock was included in the gross estate at a value of $400,000 and the interest in the partnership was included at a value of $300,000. On November 1, 1957, at which time the value of the corporation's assets had not changed, in a section 303 redemption the executor surrendered 26 shares of B Corporation stock for $104,000. On December 1, 1957, at which time the value of the partnership's assets had not changed, the partners withdrew 90 percent of the assets of the partnership, with the executor receiving $270,000 and C receiving $90,000. The estate tax amounts to $240,000, of which the executor elected under section 6166 to pay $140,000 in 10 installments of $14,000 each. On December 1, 1958, the due date for paying the estate tax which was not payable in installments and for paying the first installment under section 6166, the executor paid estate tax of $114,000, of which $100,000 represented the tax not payable in installments and $14,000 represented the first installment. Inasmuch as after the section 303 distribution and on or before the due date of the first installment (December 1, 1958) after the section 303 distribution the executor paid as estate tax an amount not less than the amount of the distribution, the section 303 distribution does not constitute a

the same as at A's death, the executor withdrew $80,000 from the business. On December 1, 1958, when the value of the remaining portion of the business was $160,000, the executor withdrew $20,000 from the business and B withdrew $10,000. On February 1, 1959, when the value of the then remaining portion of the business was $150,000 the executor withdrew $15,000. The withdrawals of money or other property from the trade or business with respect to the interest therein included in the gross estate are considered as not having equaled or exceeded 50 percent of the value of the trade or business until February 1, 1959. The executor is considered as having withdrawn 40 percent of the value of the trade or business on October 1, 1958, computed as follows:

$$\times \quad 100 \text{ percent} = 40 \text{ percent}$$

drawn 7.5 percent of the value of the trade or business on December 1, 1958, and B as having withdrawn 3.75 percent of the value thereof at that time, computed as follows:
Executor's withdrawal—

$$\times \quad 60 \text{ percent} = 7.5 \text{ percent}$$

$$\times \quad 60 \text{ percent} = 3.75 \text{ percent}$$

the executor were less than 50 percent of the value of the trade or business. Also it should be noted that while the total withdrawals by the executor exceeded 50 percent of the value of A's interest in the trade or business, they did not exceed 50 percent of the value of the entire trade or business. The executor is considered as having withdrawn 4.875 percent of the value of the trade or business on February 1, 1959, computed as follows:

$$\times \quad 48.75 \text{ percent} = 4.875 \text{ percent}$$

withdrawal of money or other property from the business for purposes of section 6166(h)(1). Therefore, the value of the trade or business is reduced by the amount of the section 303 distribution. Accordingly, the value of the entire trade or business is $696,000, of which $400,000 represents the value of the partnership and $296,000 represents the value of the B Corporation stock. Since the executor is considered as having withdrawn only $270,000 (the withdrawal from the partnership) from the trade or business, the withdrawal of money or other property from the trade or business made with respect to the decedent's interest therein was 270,000/696,000 of the value of the entire trade or business, or less than 50 percent thereof.

(e) *Disposition of interest in business.*—(1) In any case where in the aggregate 50 percent or more of the decedent's interest in a closely held business has been distributed, sold, exchanged, or otherwise disposed of, the privilege of paying the tax in installments terminates and the whole of the unpaid portion of the tax which is payable in installments becomes due and shall be paid upon notice and demand from the district director. A transfer by the executor of an interest in a closely held business to a beneficiary or trustee named in the decedent's will or to an heir who is entitled to receive it under the applicable intestacy law does not constitute a distribution thereof for purposes of determining whether 50 percent or more of an interest in a closely held business has been distributed, sold, exchanged, or otherwise disposed of. However, a subsequent transfer of the interest by the beneficiary, trustee, or heir will constitute a distribution, sale, exchange, or other disposition thereof for such purposes. The disposition must be a disposition of an interest which constitutes "included property" within the meaning of that term as used in paragraph (d) of §20.2032-1. The provisions of this section do not apply to the disposition of an interest which constitutes "excluded property" within the meaning of that term as used in such paragraph (d).

(2) The phrase "distributed, sold, exchanged, or otherwise disposed of" comprehends all possible ways by which an interest in a closely held business ceases to form a part of the gross estate. The term includes the surrender of a stock certificate for corporate assets

in complete or partial liquidation of a corporation pursuant to section 331. The term also includes the surrender of stock for stock pursuant to a transaction described in subparagraphs (A), (B), or (C) of section 368(a)(1). In general the term does not, however, extend to transactions which are mere changes in form. It does not include a transfer of assets to a corporation in exchange for its stock in a transaction with respect to which no gain or loss would be recognizable for income tax purposes under section 351. It does not include an exchange of stock in a corporation for stock in the same corporation or another corporation pursuant to a plan of reorganization described in subparagraphs (D), (E), or (F) of section 368(a)(1), nor to an exchange to which section 355 (or so much of section 356 as relates to section 355) applies. However, any stock received in an exchange to which the two preceding sentences apply shall for purposes of this paragraph be treated as an interest in a closely held business.

(3) An interest in a closely held business may be "distributed" by either a trustee who received it from the executor, or a trustee of an interest which is included in the gross estate under sections 2035 through 2038, or section 2041. See subparagraph (1) of this paragraph relative to the distribution of an interest by the executor to the person entitled to receive it under the decedent's will or an intestacy law.

(4) An interest in a closely held business may be "sold, exchanged, or otherwise disposed of" by (i) the executor; (ii) a trustee or other donee to whom the decedent in his lifetime transferred the interest included in his gross estate under sections 2035 through 2038, or section 2041; (iii) a beneficiary, trustee, or heir entitled to receive the property from the executor under the decedent's will or under the applicable law of descent and distribution, or to whom title to the interest passed directly under local law; (iv) a surviving joint tenant or tenant by the entirety; or (v) any other person.

(5) If a distribution in redemption of stock is (by reason of the provisions of section 303 or so much of section 304 as relates to section 303) treated for income tax purposes as a distribution in full payment in exchange for the stock redeemed, the stock so redeemed is not counted as distributed, sold, exchanged, or otherwise disposed of for purposes of determining whether 50 percent or more of the decedent's interest in a closely held business has been distributed, sold, exchanged, or otherwise disposed of. However, in the case described in the preceding sentence the interest in the closely held business for purposes of applying the rule set forth in subparagraph (1) of this paragraph is such interest reduced by the proportionate part thereof which the redeemed stock represents. The proportionate

$$\frac{1,000 \text{ (shares sold)}}{8,000 \text{ (shares owned)}} \times \$400,000 \quad \text{(value of shares owned, as included in gross estate)}$$

Taken together the two sales represented a sale of 50 percent (350,000/700,000) of the interest in the closely held business. Therefore, as of February 1, 1959 (the date of the sale of 1,000 shares of E Corporation), 50 percent or more in value of the interest in the closely held business is considered as distributed, sold, exchanged, or otherwise disposed of.

*Example (2).* The decedent died on September 1, 1958. The interest owned by him in a closely held business consisted of 100 shares of the M Corporation. On February 1, 1959, in a section 303 redemption, 20 shares were redeemed for cash and an amount equivalent to the proceeds was paid on the Federal estate tax before the date of the next installment. On July 1, 1959, the executor sold 40 of the remaining shares of the stock. The section 303 redemption is not considered to be a distribution, sale, exchange, or other disposition of the portion of the interest represented by the 20 shares redeemed. As a result of the section 303 redemption the remaining 80 shares represent the decedent's entire interest in the closely held business for purposes of determining whether in the aggregate 50 percent or more of the interest in the closely held business has been distributed, sold, exchanged, or otherwise disposed of. The sale on July 1, 1959, of the 40 shares represents a sale of 50 percent of the interest in the closely held business.

*Example (3).* The facts are the same as in example (2) except that the 40 shares were sold on December 1, 1958 (before the section 303 redemption was made) instead of on July 1, 1959 (after the section 303 redemption was made). The sale of the 40 shares in December represents, as of that date, a sale of 40 percent of the interest in the closely held business. However, the section 303 redemption of 20 shares does not count as a distribution, sale, exchange, or other disposition of the interest, but it does reduce the interest to 80 shares (100 shares less 20 shares redeemed) for purposes of determining whether other distributions, sales, exchanges, and dispositions in the aggregate equal or exceed 50 percent of the interest in the closely held business. Since the reduction of the interest to 80 shares relates back to the time of the decedent's death, or the alternate valuation date if an election is made under section 2032, the sale of the 40 shares, as recomputed represents a sale of 50 percent of the interest.

part of the interest which the redeemed stock represents is determined at the time of the redemption, but the reduction in the interest represented by it relates back to the time of the decedent's death, or the alternate valuation date if an election is made under section 2032, for purposes of determining whether other distributions, sales, exchanges, and dispositions of the decedent's interest in the closely held business equal or exceed in the aggregate 50 percent of such interest. See example (3) of subparagraph (6) of this paragraph for illustration of this principle. The rule stated in the first sentence of this subparagraph does not apply unless after the redemption, but on or before the date prescribed for payment of the first installment which becomes due after the redemption, there is paid an amount of estate tax not less than the amount of money or other property distributed. Where there are a series of section 303 redemptions, each redemption is treated separately and the failure of one redemption to qualify under the rule stated in the first sentence of this subparagraph does not necessarily mean that another redemption will not qualify.

(6) The application of this paragraph may be illustrated by the following examples, in each of which the executor elected to pay the tax in installments:

*Example (1).* The decedent died on October 1, 1957. He owned 8,000 of the 12,000 shares of D Corporation outstanding at the time of his death and 3,000 of the 5,000 shares of E Corporation outstanding at that time. The D Corporation stock was included in the gross estate at $50 per share, or a total of $400,000. The E Corporation stock was included in the gross estate at $100 per share, or a total of $300,000. On November 1, 1958, the executor sold the 3,000 shares of E Corporation and on February 1, 1959, he sold 1,000 shares of D Corporation. Since the decedent's shares of D Corporation and E Corporation together constituted the interest in a closely held business, the value of such interest was $700,000 ($400,000 plus $300,000) and the D Corporation stock represented 400,000/700,000 thereof and the E Corporation stock represented 300,000/700,000 thereof. While the sale of 3,000 shares of E Corporation on November 1, 1958, was a sale of the decedent's entire interest in E Corporation and a sale of more than 50 percent of the outstanding stock of E Corporation, nevertheless it constituted a sale of only 300,000/700,000 of the interest in the closely held business. The sale of 1,000 shares of D Corporation stock on February 1, 1959, represented a sale of 50,000/700,000 of the interest in the closely held business. The numerator of $50,000 is determined as follows:

However, since the sale of the 40 shares did not represent a sale of 50 percent of the interest until the section 303 distribution was made, February 1, 1959 (the date of the section 303 distribution) is considered the date on which 50 percent of the interest was distributed, sold, exchanged, or otherwise disposed of.

(f) *Information to be furnished by executor.*—(1) If the executor acquires knowledge of the happening of any transaction described in paragraph (d) or (e) of this section which, in his opinion, standing alone or when taken together with other transactions of which he has knowledge, would result in

(i) Aggregate withdrawals of money or other property from the trade or business equal to or exceeding 50 percent of the value of the entire trade or business, or

(ii) Aggregate distributions, sales, exchanges, and other dispositions equal to or exceeding 50 percent of the interest in the closely held business which was included in the gross estate,

the executor shall so notify the district director, in writing, within 30 days of acquiring such knowledge.

(2) On the date fixed for payment of each installment of tax (determined without regard to any extension of time for the payment thereof), other than the final installment, the executor shall furnish the district director, in writing, with either

(i) A complete disclosure of all transactions described in paragraphs (d) and (e) of this section of which he has knowledge and which have not previously been made known by him to the district director, or

(ii) A statement that to the best knowledge of the executor all transactions described in paragraphs (d) and (e) of this section which have occurred have not produced a result described in subparagraph (1)(i) or (ii) of this paragraph.

(3) The district director may require the submission of such additional information as is deemed necessary to establish the estate's right to continue payment of the tax in installments. [Reg. §20.6166A-3.]

☐ [*T.D. 6522, 12-28-60. Redesignated by T.D. 7710, 7-28-80.*]

**Reg. § 20.6166A-3(f)(3)**

[Reg. §20.6166A-4]

**§20.6166A-4. Special rules applicable where due date of return was before September 3, 1958.**—(a) *In general.*—Section 206(f) of the Small Business Tax Revision Act of 1958 (72 Stat. 1685) provides that section 6166(i) of the Code shall apply in cases where the decedent died after August 16, 1954, but only if the date for filing the estate tax return (including extensions thereof) expired before September 3, 1958. Therefore, the privilege of paying the estate tax in installments as described in §§20.6166-1 through 20.6166-3 is available also in cases where the due date of the return is before September 3, 1958, but under somewhat different circumstances. These differences are explained in paragraphs (b) through (e) of this section. Therefore, except as otherwise provided in paragraphs (b) through (e) of this section, the regulations contained in §§20.6166-1 through 20.6166-3 apply also in cases where the due date of the return is before September 3, 1958. See §20.6075-1 for the due date of the return. The value of the gross estate as determined for purposes of a deficiency in tax assessed after September 2, 1958, and the value at which the interest in the closely held business, to which the election applies, is included in such value of the gross estate are used in ascertaining whether an estate coming within the purview of section 6166(i) and this section satisfies the percentage requirements as to qualification set forth in section 6166(a).

(b) *Tax to which election applies.*—In a case where the due date of the return was before September 3, 1958, an election to pay estate tax in installments does not apply to the tax shown on the return nor to a deficiency in tax assessed before that date. It does apply to a deficiency in tax assessed after September 2, 1958, unless the deficiency is due to negligence, to intentional disregard of rules and regulations, or to fraud with intent to evade tax. The amount of the deficiency which may be paid in installments shall not exceed that proportion of the total tax (including the deficiency) which is determined by apply-

ing thereto the ratio set forth in paragraph (b) of §20.6166-1. See paragraph (c) of this section for the method of prorating the deficiency to the installments.

(c) *Proration of deficiency to installments.*—The deficiency in tax which may be paid in installments is prorated to the installments which would have been due if the provisions of section 6166(a) had applied to the tax shown on the return and if an election had been timely made at the time the estate tax return was filed. The part of the deficiency so prorated to any installment the date for payment of which would have arrived before the election is made shall be paid at the time the election is made. The portion of the deficiency so prorated to installments the date for payment of which would not have arrived before the election is made shall be paid at the time such installments would have been due if such an election had been made.

(d) *Notice of election.*—The notice of election to pay the deficiency in installments shall be filed with the district director not later than 60 days after issuance of notice and demand by the district director for payment of the deficiency. The number of installments in which the executor elects to pay the deficiency includes those installments the dates for payment of which would have arrived within the meaning of paragraph (c) of this section. See paragraph (c)(2) of §20.6166-1 for further information relative to the notice of election.

(e) *Undistributed income of estate.*—In any case where the due date of the estate tax return was before September 3, 1958, the provisions of paragraph (b) of §20.6166-3 (providing for acceleration of payment of estate tax by amount of estate's undistribtuted net income for any taxable year after its fourth taxable year) shall not apply with respect to the estate's undistributed net income for any taxable year ending before January 1, 1960. [Reg. §20.6166A-4.]

☐ [*T.D. 6522, 12-28-60. Redesignated by T.D. 7710, 7-28-80.*]

# Assessment

# IN GENERAL

See p. 20,601 for regulations not amended to reflect law changes

[Reg. §301.6201-1]

**§301.6201-1. Assessment authority.**—(a) *In general.*—The district director is authorized and required to make all inquiries necessary to the determination and assessment of all taxes imposed by the Internal Revenue Code of 1954 or any prior internal revenue law. The district director is further authorized and required, and the director of the regional service center is authorized, to make the determinations and the assessments of such taxes. However, certain inquiries and determinations are, by direction of the Commissioner, made by other officials, such as assistant regional commissioners. The term "taxes" includes interest, additional amounts, additions to the taxes, and assessable penalties. The authority of the district director and the director of the regional service center to make assessments includes the following:

(1) *Taxes shown on return.*—The district director or the director of the regional service center shall assess all taxes determined by the taxpayer or by the district director or the director of the regional service center and disclosed on a return or list.

(2) *Unpaid taxes payable by stamp.*—(i) If without the use of the proper stamp:

*(a)* Any article upon which a tax is required to be paid by means of a stamp is sold or removed for sale or use by the manufacturer thereof, or

*(b)* Any transaction or act upon which a tax is required to be paid by means of a stamp occurs;

the district director, upon such information as he can obtain, must estimate the amount of the tax which has not been paid and the district director or the director of the regional service center must make assessment therefor upon the person the district director determines to be liable for the tax. However, the district director or the director of the regional service center may not assess any tax which is payable by stamp unless the taxpayer fails to pay such tax at the time and in the manner provided by law or regulations.

(ii) If a taxpayer gives a check or money order as a payment for stamps but the check or money order is not paid upon presentment, then the district director or the director of the regional service center shall assess the amount of the check or money order against the taxpayer as if it were a tax due at the time the check or money order was received by the district director.

(3) *Erroneous income tax prepayment credits.*—If the amount of income tax withheld or the amount of estimated income tax paid is overstated by a taxpayer on a return or on a claim for refund, the amount so overstated which is allowed against the tax shown on the return or which is allowed as a credit or refund shall be assessed by the district director or the director of the regional service center in the same manner as in the case of a mathematical error on the return. See section 6213(b)(1), relating to exceptions to restrictions on assessment.

(b) *Estimated income tax.*—Neither the district director nor the director of the regional service center shall assess any amount of estimated income tax required to be paid under section 6153 or 6154 which is unpaid.

(c) *Compensation of child.*—Any income tax assessed against a child, to the extent of the amount attributable to income included in the gross income of the child solely by reason of section 73(a) or the corresponding provision of prior law, if not paid by the child, shall, for the purposes of the income tax imposed by chapter 1 (or the corresponding provisions of prior law), be considered as having also been properly assessed against the parent. In any case in which the earnings of the child are included in the gross income of the child solely by reason of section 73(a) or the corresponding provision of prior law, the parent's liability is an amount equal to the amount by which the tax assessed against the child (and not paid by him) has been increased by reason of the inclusion of such earnings in the gross income of the child. Thus, if for the calendar year 1954 the child has income of $1,000 from investments and of $3,000 for services rendered, and the latter amount is includible in the gross income of the child under section 73(a) and the child has no wife or dependents, the tax liability determined under section 3 is $625. If the child had only the investment income of $1,000, his tax liability would be $62. If the tax of $625 is assessed against the child, the difference between $625 and $62, or $563, is the amount of such tax which is considered to have been properly assessed against the parent, if not paid by the child. [Reg. §301.6201-1.]

☐ [*T.D. 6119, 12-31-54. Amended by T.D. 6498, 10-24-60 and T.D. 6885, 12-27-61.*]

[Reg. §301.6203-1]

**§301.6203-1. Method of assessment.**—The district director and the director of the regional service center shall appoint one or more assessment officers. The district director shall also appoint assessment officers in a Service Center servicing his district. The assessment shall be made by an assessment officer signing the summary record of assessment. The summary record, through supporting records, shall provide identification of the taxpayer, the character of the liability assessed, the taxable period, if applicable, and the amount of the assessment. The amount of the assessment shall, in the case of tax shown on a return by the taxpayer, be the amount so shown, and in all other cases the amount of the assessment shall be the amount shown on the supporting list or record. The date of the assessment is the date the summary record is signed by an assessment officer. If the taxpayer requests a copy of the record of assessment, he shall be furnished a copy of the pertinent parts of the assessment which set forth the name of the taxpayer, the date of assessment, the character of the liability assessed, the taxable period, if applicable, and the amounts assessed. [Reg. § 301.6203-1.]

☐ [*T.D. 6119, 12-31-54. Amended by T.D. 6585, 12-27-61 and T.D. 7838, 10-5-82.*]

### [Reg. § 301.6204-1]

**§ 301.6204-1. Supplemental assessments.**—If any assessment is incomplete or incorrect in any material respect, the district director or the director of the regional service center, subject to the restrictions with respect to the assessment of deficiencies in income, estate, gift, chapter 41, 42, 43, and 44 taxes, and subject to the applicable period of limitation, may make a supplemental assessment for the purpose of correcting or completing the original assessment. [Reg. § 301.6204-1.]

☐ [*T.D. 6119, 12-31-54. Amended by T.D. 6585, 12-27-61 and T.D. 7838, 10-5-82.*]

### [Reg. § 31.6205-1]

**§ 31.6205-1. Adjustments of underpayments.**—(a) *In general.*— (1) An employer who has underreported and underpaid employee Federal Insurance Contributions Act (FICA) tax under section 3101 or employer FICA tax under section 3111, employee Railroad Retirement Tax Act (RRTA) tax under section 3201 or employer RRTA tax under section 3221, or income tax required under section 3402 to be withheld, with respect to any payment of wages or compensation, shall correct such error as provided in this section. Such correction may constitute an interest-free adjustment as provided in paragraph (b) or (c) of this section.

(2) No correction will be eligible for interest-free adjustment treatment if the failure to report relates to an issue that was raised in an examination of a prior return period or if the employer knowingly underreported its employment tax liability.

(3) Every correction under this section of an underpayment of tax with respect to a payment of wages or compensation shall be made on the form prescribed by the IRS that corresponds to the return being corrected. The form, filed in accordance with this section and the instructions, will constitute an adjusted return for the return period being corrected.

(4) Every adjusted return on which an underpayment is corrected pursuant to this section shall designate the return period in which the error was ascertained and the return period being corrected, explain in detail the grounds and facts relied upon to support the correction, and set forth such other information as may be required by the regulations in this section and by the instructions relating to the adjusted return.

(5) For purposes of this section, an error is ascertained when the employer has sufficient knowledge of the error to be able to correct it.

(6) No correction will be eligible for interest-free adjustment treatment pursuant to this section after the earlier of the following:

(i) Receipt from the IRS of notice and demand for payment thereof based upon an assessment.

(ii) Receipt from the IRS of a Notice of Determination of Worker Classification (Notice of Determination) in connection with such underpayment. Prior to receipt of a Notice of Determination, the taxpayer may, in lieu of making a payment, make a cash bond deposit that would have the effect of stopping the accrual of any interest, but would not deprive the taxpayer of its right to receive a Notice of Determination and to petition the Tax Court under section 7436.

(7) Subject to the exceptions specified in paragraphs (a)(2) and (a)(6) of this section, Form 2504, "Agreement and Collection of Additional Tax and Acceptance of Overassessment (Excise or Employment Tax)," Form 2504-WC, "Agreement to Assessment and Collection of Additional Tax and Acceptance of Overassessment in Worker Classification Cases (Employment Tax)," and such other forms as may be prescribed by the IRS, constitute adjusted returns for purposes of this section.

(8) For provisions related to furnishing employee statements and corrected employee statements reporting wages and withheld taxes, see sections 6041 and 6051 and § § 1.6041-2 and 31.6051-1. For provisions relating to filing information returns and corrected information returns reporting wages and withheld taxes, see sections 6041 and 6051 and § § 1.6041-2 and 31.6051-2.

(9) For the period of limitations upon assessment and collection of taxes, see § 301.6501(a)-1.

(b) *Federal Insurance Contributions Act and Railroad Retirement Tax Act.*—(1) *Undercollection ascertained before return is filed.*—If an employer collects less than the correct amount of employee FICA or RRTA tax from an employee with respect to a payment of wages or compensation, and if the employer ascertains the error before filing the return on which the employee tax with respect to such wages or compensation is required to be reported, the employer shall nevertheless report on the return and pay to the IRS the correct amount of employee tax. If the employer does not report the correct amount of tax in these circumstances, the employer may not later correct the error through an interest-free adjustment.

(2) *Error ascertained after return is filed.*—(i) If an employer files a return on which FICA tax or RRTA tax is required to be reported, and reports on the return less than the correct amount of employee or employer FICA or RRTA tax with respect to a payment of wages or compensation, and if the employer ascertains the error after filing the return, the employer shall correct the error through an interest-free adjustment as provided in this section, except as provided in paragraph (b)(4) of this section for Additional Medicare Tax. The employer shall adjust the underpayment of tax by reporting the additional amount due on an adjusted return for the return period in which the wages or compensation was paid, accompanied by a detailed explanation of the amount being reported on the adjusted return and any other information as may be required by this section and by the instructions relating to the adjusted return. The reporting of the underpayment on an adjusted return constitutes an adjustment within the meaning of this section only if the adjusted return is filed within the period of limitations for assessment for the return period being corrected, and by the due date for filing the return for the return period in which the error is ascertained. For purposes of the preceding sentence, the due date for filing the adjusted return is determined by reference to the return being corrected, without regard to the employer's current filing requirements. For example, an employer with a current annual filing requirement who is correcting an error on a previously filed quarterly return must file the adjusted return by the due date for filing a quarterly return for the quarter in which the error is ascertained. The amount of the underpayment adjusted in accordance with this section must be paid to the IRS by the time the adjusted return is filed. If an adjustment is reported pursuant to this section, but the amount of the adjustment is not paid when due, interest accrues from that date (see section 6601).

(ii) If an employer files a return reporting FICA tax for a return period although the employer was required to file a return reporting RRTA tax, and if the employer ascertains the error after filing the return, the employer shall correct the error through an interest-free adjustment as provided in this section. However, if the employer also reported less than the correct amount of Additional Medicare Tax, the employer shall correct the underwithheld and underpaid Additional Medicare Tax in accordance with paragraph (b)(4) of this section. The employer shall adjust the underpayment of RRTA tax by reporting the correct amount of RRTA tax on an original return for reporting RRTA tax for the return period for which the incorrect return was filed, accompanied by an adjusted return corresponding to the incorrect return that was filed to correct the erroneously reported and paid FICA tax. The adjusted return must include a detailed explanation of the amounts being reported on the original return and the adjusted return and any other information as may be required by the regulations in this section and by the instructions relating to the adjusted return. The reporting of the correct amounts for the period constitutes an adjustment within the meaning of this section only if the returns are filed by the due date of the return for reporting the RRTA tax for the return period in which the error is ascertained. Pursuant to § 31.3503-1, the amount of erroneously paid FICA tax will be credited against the underpaid RRTA tax. Any remaining underpayment of RRTA tax adjusted in accordance with this section must be paid to the IRS by the time the returns are filed in accordance with this paragraph. If an adjustment is reported pursuant to this section, but the amount of the remaining underpayment is not paid when due, interest accrues from that date (see section 6601).

(iii) If an employer files a return reporting RRTA tax for a return period although the employer was required to file a return reporting FICA tax, and if the employer ascertains the error after filing the return, the employer shall correct the error through an interest-free adjustment as provided in this section. However, if the employer also reported less than the correct amount of Additional Medicare Tax, the employer shall correct the underwithheld and underpaid Additional Medicare Tax in accordance with paragraph (b)(4) of this section. The employer shall adjust the underpayment of FICA tax by reporting the correct amount of FICA tax on an original return for reporting FICA tax for the return period for which the incorrect return was filed (or an adjusted return for reporting the FICA tax if an original return was already filed for such return period to report the income tax required to be withheld under section 3402), accompanied by an adjusted return corresponding to the incorrect return that was filed to correct the erroneously reported and paid RRTA tax. The adjusted return(s) must include a detailed explanation of the amount being reported on the original return and/or the adjusted return(s) and any other information as may be required by the regulations in this section and by the instructions relating to the form. The reporting of the correct amounts for the period constitutes an adjustment within the meaning of this section only if the returns are filed by the due date of the return for reporting the FICA tax for the return period in which the error is ascertained. Pursuant to § 31.3503-1, the amount of erroneously paid RRTA tax will be credited against the underpaid FICA tax. Any remaining underpayment of FICA tax adjusted in accordance with this section must be paid to the IRS by the time the returns are filed in accordance with this paragraph (b)(2)(iii). If an adjustment is reported pursuant to this section, but the amount of the remaining underpayment is not paid when due, interest accrues from that date (see section 6601).

(3) *Return not filed because of failure to treat individual as employee.*—If an employer fails to file a return for a return period solely because the employer failed to treat any individuals properly as employees for the return period (and, therefore, failed to withhold and pay any employer or employee FICA or RRTA tax with respect to wages or compensation paid to the employees) and if the employer ascertains the error after the due date of the return, the employer shall correct the error through an interest-free adjustment as provided in this section. The employer shall report the amount due by filing an original return required to be filed to report the tax for the return period for which the employer failed to file a return, accompanied by an adjusted return as provided in the instructions to the adjusted return. The adjusted return must include a detailed explanation of the amount being reported on the original return and adjusted return and any other information as may be required by this section and by the instructions relating to the adjusted return. The reporting of the correct amount of tax for the return period constitutes an adjustment within the meaning of this section only if the original and adjusted returns are filed by the due date of the return for reporting such tax for the return period in which the error is ascertained. For purposes of the preceding sentence, the due date for filing the adjusted return is determined by reference to the return being corrected, without regard to the employer's current filing requirements. For example, an employer with a current annual filing requirement who is correcting an error on a previously filed quarterly return must file the adjusted return by the due date for filing a quarterly return for the quarter in which the error is ascertained. However, an adjustment of Additional Medicare Tax required to be withheld under section 3101(b)(2) or section 3201(a) may only be reported pursuant to this section if the error is ascertained within the same calendar year that the wages or compensation were paid to the employee, or if section 3509 applies to determine the amount of the underpayment, or if the adjustment is reported on a Form 2504 or Form 2504-WC. See paragraph (b)(4) of this section. The amount of the underpayment adjusted in accordance with this section must be paid to the IRS by the time the returns are filed in accordance with this paragraph. If an adjustment is reported pursuant to this section, but the amount of the adjustment is not paid when due, interest accrues from that date (see section 6601).

(4) *Additional Medicare Tax.*—If an employer files a return on which FICA tax or RRTA tax is required to be reported, and reports on the return less than the correct amount of Additional Medicare Tax required to be withheld with respect to a payment of wages or compensation, and if the employer ascertains the error after filing the return, the employer shall correct the error through an interest-free adjustment as provided in this section. An adjustment of Additional Medicare Tax may only be reported pursuant to this paragraph (b)(4) if the error is ascertained within the same calendar year that the wages or compensation were paid to the employee, unless the underpayment is attributable to an administrative error (that is, an error involving the inaccurate reporting of the amount actually withheld), section 3509 applies to determine the amount of the underpayment, or the adjustment is reported on a Form 2504 or Form 2504-WC. The employer shall adjust the underpayment of Additional Medicare Tax by reporting the additional amount due on an adjusted return for the return period in which the wages or compensation were paid, accompanied by a detailed explanation of the amount being reported on the adjusted return and any other information as may be required by this section and by the instructions relating to the adjusted return. The reporting of the underpayment on an adjusted return constitutes an adjustment within the meaning of this section only if the adjusted

return is filed within the period of limitations for assessment for the return period being corrected, and by the due date for filing the return for the return period in which the error is ascertained. For purposes of the preceding sentence, the due date for filing the adjusted return is determined by reference to the return being corrected, without regard to the employer's current filing requirements. For example, an employer with a current annual filing requirement who is correcting an error on a previously filed quarterly return must file the adjusted return by the due date for filing a quarterly return for the quarter in which the error is ascertained. The amount of the underpayment adjusted in accordance with this section must be paid to the IRS by the time the adjusted return is filed. If an adjustment is reported pursuant to this section, but the amount of the adjustment is not paid when due, interest accrues from that date (see section 6601).

(c) *Income tax required to be withheld from wages.*—(1) *Undercollection ascertained before return is filed.*—If an employer collects less than the correct amount of income tax required to be withheld from wages under section 3402, and if the employer ascertains the error before filing the return on which the withheld tax is required to be reported, the employer shall nevertheless report on the return and pay to the IRS the correct amount of tax required to be withheld. If the employer does not report the correct amount of tax in these circumstances, the employer may not correct the error through an interest-free adjustment.

(2) *Error ascertained after return is filed.*—If an employer files a return on which income tax required to be withheld from wages is required to be reported and reports on the return less than the correct amount of income tax required to be withheld, and if the employer ascertains the error after filing the return, the employer shall correct the error through an interest-free adjustment as provided in this section. The employer shall adjust the underpayment of tax by reporting the additional amount due on an adjusted return for the return period in which the wages were paid, accompanied by a detailed explanation of the amount being reported on the adjusted return and any other information as may be required by this section and by the instructions relating to the adjusted return. The reporting of the underpayment on an adjusted return constitutes an adjustment within the meaning of this section only if the adjusted return is filed by the due date for filing the return for the return period in which the error is ascertained. For purposes of the preceding sentence, the due date for filing the adjusted return is determined by reference to the return being corrected, without regard to the employer's current filing requirements. For example, an employer with a current annual filing requirement who is correcting an error on a previously filed quarterly return must file the adjusted return by the due date for filing a quarterly return for the quarter in which the error is ascertained. However, an adjustment may only be reported pursuant to this section if the error is ascertained within the same calendar year that the wages to the employee were paid, unless the underpayment is attributable to an administrative error (that is, an error involving the inaccurate reporting of the amount actually withheld), section 3509 applies to determine the amount of the underpayment, or the adjustment is reported on a Form 2504 or Form 2504-WC. The amount of the underpayment adjusted in accordance with this section must be paid to the IRS by the time the adjusted return is filed. If an adjustment is reported pursuant to this section, but the amount of the adjustment is not paid when due, interest accrues from that date (see section 6601).

(3) *Return not filed because of failure to treat individual as employee.*—If an employer fails to file a return for a return period solely because the employer failed to treat any individuals properly as employees for the return period (and, therefore, failed to withhold and pay any income tax required to be withheld from wages), the employer shall correct the error through an interest-free adjustment as provided in this section. The employer shall report the amount due by filing an original return for the return period for which the employer failed to file a return, accompanied by an adjusted return as provided in the instructions to the adjusted return. The adjusted return must include a detailed explanation of the amount being reported on the original and adjusted returns and any other information as may be required by this section and by the instructions relating to the adjusted return. The reporting of the correct amount of tax for the return period constitutes an adjustment within the meaning of this section only if the original and adjusted returns are filed by the due date of the return for reporting such tax for the return period in which the error is ascertained. For purposes of the preceding sentence, the due date for filing the adjusted return is determined by reference to the return being corrected, without regard to the employer's current filing requirements. For example, an employer with a current annual filing requirement who is correcting an error on a previously filed quarterly return must file the adjusted return by the due date for filing a quarterly return for the quarter in which the error is ascertained. However, an adjustment may only be reported

pursuant to this section if the error is ascertained within the same calendar year that the wages to the employee were paid, or if section 3509 applies to determine the amount of the underpayment, or if the adjustment is reported on a Form 2504 or Form 2504-WC. The amount of the underpayment adjusted in accordance with this section must be paid to the IRS by the time the returns are filed in accordance with this paragraph. If an adjustment is reported pursuant to this section, but the amount of the adjustment is not paid when due, interest accrues from that date (see section 6601).

(d) *Deductions from employee.*—(1) *Federal Insurance Contributions Tax Act and Railroad Retirement Tax Act.*—If an employer collects less than the correct amount of employee FICA or RRTA tax from an employee with respect to a payment of wages or compensation, the employer must collect the amount of the undercollection by deducting the amount from remuneration of the employee, if any, paid after the employer ascertains the error. If an employer collects less than the correct amount of Additional Medicare Tax required to be withheld under section 3101(b)(2) or section 3201(a), the employer must collect the amount of the undercollection on or before the last day of the calendar year by deducting the amount from remuneration of the employee, if any, paid after the employer ascertains the error. Such deductions may be made even though the remuneration, for any reason, does not constitute wages or compensation. The correct amount of employee tax must be reported and paid, as provided in paragraph (b) of this section, whether or not the undercollection is corrected by a deduction made as prescribed in this paragraph (d)(1), and even if the deduction is made after the return on which the employee tax must be reported is due. If such a deduction is not made, the obligation of the employee to the employer with respect to the undercollection is a matter for settlement between the employee and the employer. If an employer makes an erroneous collection of employee tax from two or more of its employees, a separate settlement must be made with respect to each employee. An overcollection of employee tax from one employee may not be used to offset an undercollection of such tax from another employee. For provisions relating to the employer's liability for the tax, whether or not it collects the tax from the employee, see §§ 31.3102-1(d), 31.3102-4(c), and 31.3202-1. This paragraph (d)(1) does not apply if section 3509 applies to determine the employer's liability.

(2) *Income tax required to be withheld from wages.*—If an employer collects less than the correct amount of income tax required to be withheld from wages during a calendar year, the employer must collect the amount of the undercollection on or before the last day of the year by deducting the amount from remuneration of the employee, if any, paid after the employer ascertains the error. Such deductions may be made even though the remuneration, for any reason, does not constitute wages. The correct amount of of income tax must be reported and paid, as provided in paragraph (c) of this section, whether or not the undercollection is corrected by a deduction made as prescribed in this paragraph (d)(2), and even if the deduction is made after the return on which the tax must be reported is due. If such a deduction is not made, the obligation of the employee to the employer with respect to the undercollection is a matter for settlement between the employee and the employer within the calendar year. If an employer makes an erroneous collection of income tax from two or more of its employees, a separate settlement must be made with respect to each employee. An overcollection of income tax from one employee may not be used to offset an undercollection of such tax from another employee. For provisions relating to the employer's liability for the tax, whether or not it collects the tax from the employee, see § 31.3403-1. For provisions relating to the employer's liability for an underpayment of tax unless the employer can show that the income tax against which the tax under section 3402 may be credited has been paid, see § 31.3402(d)-1. This paragraph (d)(2) does not apply if section 3509 applies to determine the employer's liability.

(e) *Effective/applicability date.*—Paragraphs (b) and (d) of this section apply to adjusted returns filed on or after November 29, 2013. [Reg. § 31.6205-1.]

☐ [*T.D.* 6472, 6-22-60. *Amended by T.D.* 7783, 7-22-81; *T.D.* 8959, 7-31-2001; *T.D.* 9405, 6-30-2008 *and T.D.* 9645, 11-26-2013.]

**[Reg. § 301.6205-1]**

**§ 301.6205-1. Special rules applicable to certain employment taxes.**—For regulations under section 6205, see Reg. § 31.6205-1 of this chapter (Employment Tax Regulations). [Reg. § 301.6205-1.]

☐ [*T.D.* 6119, 12-31-54. *Amended by T.D.* 6498, 10-24-60.]

# DEFICIENCY PROCEDURES

**[Reg. § 301.6211-1]**

**§ 301.6211-1. Deficiency defined.**—(a) In the case of the income tax imposed by subtitle A of the Code, the estate tax imposed by chapter 11, subtitle B, of the Code, the gift tax imposed by chapter 12, subtitle B, of the Code, and any excise tax imposed by chapter 41, 42, 43, or 44 of the Code, the term "deficiency" means the excess of the tax (income, estate, gift, or excise tax as the case may be) over the sum of the amount shown as such tax by the taxpayer upon his return and the amounts previously assessed (or collected without assessment) as a deficiency; but such sum shall first be reduced by the amount of rebates made. If no return is made, or if the return (except a return of income tax pursuant to sec. 6014) does not show any tax, for the purpose of the definition "the amount shown as the tax by the taxpayer upon his return" shall be considered as zero. Accordingly, in any such case, if no deficiencies with respect to the tax have been assessed, or collected without assessment, and no rebates with respect to the tax have been made, the deficiency is the amount of the income tax imposed by subtitle A, the estate tax imposed by chapter 11, the gift tax imposed by chapter 12, or any excise tax imposed by chapter 41, 42, 43, or 44. Any amount shown as additional tax on an "amended return," so-called (other than amounts of additional tax which such return clearly indicates the taxpayer is protesting rather than admitting) filed after the due date of the return, shall be treated as an amount shown by the taxpayer "upon his return" for purposes of computing the amount of a deficiency.

(b) For purposes of the definition, the income tax imposed by subtitle A and the income tax shown on the return shall both be determined without regard to the credit provided in section 31 for income tax withheld at the source and without regard to so much of the credit provided in section 32 for income taxes withheld at the source as exceeds 2 percent of the interest on tax-free covenant bonds described in section 1451. Payments on account of estimated income tax, like other payments of tax by the taxpayer, shall likewise be disregarded in the determination of a deficiency. Any credit resulting from the collection of amounts assessed under section 6851 or 6852 as the result of a termination assessment shall not be taken into account in determining a deficiency.

(c) The computation by the Internal Revenue Service, pursuant to section 6014, of the income tax imposed by subtitle A shall be considered as having been made by the taxpayer and the tax so computed shall be considered as the tax shown by the taxpayer upon his return.

(d) If so much of the credit claimed on the return for income taxes withheld at the source as exceeds 2 percent of the interest on tax-free covenant bonds is greater than the amount of such credit allowable, the unpaid portion of the tax attributable to such difference will be collected not as a deficiency but as an underpayment of the tax shown on the return.

(e) This section may be illustrated by the following examples:

*Example (1).* The amount of income tax shown by the taxpayer upon his return for the calendar year 1954 was $1,600. The taxpayer had no amounts previously assessed (or collected without assessment) as a deficiency. He claimed a credit in the amount of $2,050 for tax withheld at source on wages under section 3402, and a refund of $450 (not a rebate under section 6211) was made to him as an overpayment of tax for the taxable year. It is later determined that the correct tax for the taxable year is $1,850. A deficiency of $250 is determined as follows:

| | |
|---|---:|
| Tax imposed by subtitle A | $1,850 |
| Tax shown on return .......... $1,600 | |
| Tax previously assessed (or collected without assessment) as a deficiency .......... None | |
| Total .......... $1,600 | |
| Amount of rebates made .......... None | |
| Balance | $1,600 |
| Deficiency | 250 |

*Example (2).* The taxpayer made a return for the calendar year 1954 showing a tax of $1,250 before any credits for tax withheld at the source. He claimed a credit in the amount of $800 for tax withheld at source on wages under section 3402 and $60 for tax paid at source under section 1451 upon interest on bonds containing a tax-free covenant. The taxpayer had no amounts previously assessed (or collected without assessment) as a deficiency. The district director determines that the 2 percent tax paid at the source on tax-free covenant bonds is $40 instead of $60 as claimed by the taxpayer and that the tax imposed by subtitle A is $1,360 (total tax $1,400 less $40 paid at source on tax-free covenant bonds). A deficiency in the amount of $170 is determined as follows:

| | |
|---|---:|
| Tax imposed by subtitle A ($1,400 minus $40) . . . . . . . . | $1,360 |
| Tax shown on return ($1,250 minus $60) . . . . . . . . . | $1,190 |
| Tax previously assessed (or collected without assessment) as a deficiency . . . . . . . . . . . . . . . . . . . . . . . . . . | None |
| Total . . . . . . . . . . . . . . . . . . . . . . . . . . . . . . . . . . | $1,190 |
| Amount of rebates made . . . . . . . . . . . . . . . . . . . . | None |
| Balance . . . . . . . . . . . . . . . . . . . . . . . . . . . . . . . . . | $1,190 |
| Deficiency . . . . . . . . . . . . . . . . . . . . . . . . . . . . . . . | 170 |

(f) As used in section 6211, the term "rebate" means so much of an abatement, credit, refund, or other repayment as is made on the ground that the income tax imposed by subtitle A, the estate tax imposed by chapter 11, the gift tax imposed by chapter 12, or the excise tax imposed by chapter 41, 42, 43, or 44, is less than the excess of (1) the amount shown as the tax by the taxpayer upon the return increased by the amount previously assessed (or collected without assessment) as a deficiency over (2) the amount of rebates previously made. For example, assume that the amount of income tax shown by the taxpayer upon his return for the taxable year is $600 and the amount claimed as a credit under section 31 for income tax withheld at the source is $900. If the district director determines that the tax imposed by subtitle A is $600 and makes a refund of $300, no part of such refund constitutes a "rebate" since the refund is not made on the ground that the tax imposed by subtitle A is less than the tax shown on the return. If, however, the district director determines that the tax imposed by subtitle A is $500 and refunds $400, the amount of $100 of such refund would constitute a rebate since it is made on the ground that the tax imposed by subtitle A ($500) is less than the tax shown on the return ($600). The amount of such rebate ($100) would be taken into account in arriving at the amount of any deficiency subsequently determined. [Reg. § 301.6211-1.]

☐ [*T.D. 6119, 12-31-54. Amended by T.D. 6498, 10-24-60; T.D. 7102, 3-23-71; T.D. 7498, 7-12-77; T.D. 7575, 12-15-78; T.D. 7838, 10-5-82 and T.D. 8628, 12-4-95.*]

### [Reg. § 301.6212-1]

**§ 301.6212-1. Notice of deficiency.**—(a) *General rule.*—If a district director or director of a service center (or regional director of appeals), determines that there is a deficiency in respect of income, estate, or gift tax imposed by subtitle A or B, or excise tax imposed by chapter 41, 42, 43, or 44, of the Code, such official is authorized to notify the taxpayer of the deficiency by either registered or certified mail.

(b) *Address for notice of deficiency.*—(1) *Income, gift, and chapter 41, 42, 43, and 44 taxes.*—Unless the district director for the district in which the return in question was filed has been notified under the provisions of section 6903 as to the existence of a fiduciary relationship, notice of a deficiency in respect of income tax, gift tax, or tax imposed by chapter 41, 42, 43, or 44 shall be sufficient if mailed to the taxpayer at his last known address, even though such taxpayer is deceased, or is under a legal disability, or, in the case of a corporation, has terminated its existence.

(2) *Joint income tax returns.*—If a joint income tax return has been filed by husband and wife, the district director (or assistant regional commissioner, appellate) may, unless the district director for the district in which such joint return was filed has been notified by either spouse that a separate residence has been established, send either a joint or separate notice of deficiency to the taxpayers at their last known address. If, however, the proper district director has been so notified, a separate notice of deficiency, that is, a duplicate original of the joint notice, must be sent by registered mail prior to September 3, 1958, and by either registered or certified mail on and after September 3, 1958, to each spouse at his or her last known address. The notice of separate residences should be addressed to the district director for the district in which the joint return was filed.

(3) *Estate tax.*—In the absence of notice, under the provisions of section 6903 as to the existence of a fiduciary relationship, to the district director for the district in which the estate tax return was filed, notice of a deficiency in respect of the estate tax imposed by chapter 11 of subtitle B shall be sufficient if addressed in the name of the decedent or other person subject to liability and mailed to his last known address.

(c) *Further deficiency letters restricted.*—If the district director or director of a service center (or regional director of appeals) mails to the taxpayer notice of a deficiency, and the taxpayer files a petition with the Tax Court within the prescribed period, no additional deficiency may be determined with respect to income tax for the same taxable year, gift tax for the same "calendar period" (as defined in § 25.2502-1(c)(1)), estate tax with respect to the taxable estate of the same decedent, chapter 41, 43, or 44 tax of the taxpayer for the same taxable year, section 4940 tax for the same taxable year, or chapter 42

tax of the taxpayer (other than under section 4940) with respect to the same act (or failure to act) to which such petition relates. This restriction shall not apply in the case of fraud, assertion of deficiencies with respect to any qualified tax (as defined in paragraph (b) of § 301.6361-4) in respect of which no deficiency was asserted for the taxable year in the notice, assertion of deficiencies with respect to the Federal tax when deficiencies with respect to only a qualified tax (and not the Federal tax) were asserted for the taxable year in the notice, assertion of greater deficiencies before the Tax Court as provided in section 6214(a), mathematical errors as provided in section 6213(b)(1), termination assessments in section 6851 or 6852, or jeopardy assessments as provided in section 6961(c). Solely for purposes of applying the restriction of section 6212(c), a notice of deficiency with respect to second tier tax under chapter 43 shall be deemed to be a notice of deficiency for the taxable year in which the taxable event occurs. See § 53.4963-1(e)(7)(iii) or (iv) for the date on which the taxable event occurs. [Reg. § 301.6212-1.]

☐ [*T.D. 6119, 12-31-54. Amended by T.D. 6425, 11-10-59; T.D. 6498, 10-24-60; T.D. 7238, 12-28-72; T.D. 7577, 12-19-78; T.D. 7838, 10-5-82; T.D. 7910, 9-6-83; T.D. 8084, 5-1-86 and T.D. 8628, 12-4-95.*]

### [Reg. § 301.6212-2]

**§ 301.6212-2. Definition of last known address.**—(a) *General rule.*—Except as provided in paragraph (b)(2) of this section, a taxpayer's last known address is the address that appears on the taxpayer's most recently filed and properly processed Federal tax return, unless the Internal Revenue Service (IRS) is given clear and concise notification of a different address. Further information on what constitutes clear and concise notification of a different address and a properly processed Federal tax return can be found in Rev. Proc. 90-18 (1990-1 C.B. 491) or in procedures subsequently prescribed by the Commissioner.

(b) *Address obtained from third party.*—(1) *In general.*—Except as provided in paragraph (b)(2) of this section, change of address information that a taxpayer provides to a third party, such as a payor or another government agency, is not clear and concise notification of a different address for purposes of determining a last known address under this section.

(2) *Exception for address obtained from the United States Postal Service.*—(i) *Updating taxpayer addresses.*—The IRS will update taxpayer addresses maintained in IRS records by referring to data accumulated and maintained in the United States Postal Service (USPS) National Change of Address database that retains change of address information for thirty-six months (NCOA database). Except as provided in paragraph (b)(2)(ii) of this section, if the taxpayer's name and last known address in IRS records match the taxpayer's name and old mailing address contained in the NCOA database, the new address in the NCOA database is the taxpayer's last known address, unless the IRS is given clear and concise notification of a different address.

(ii) *Duration of address obtained from NCOA database.*—The address obtained from the NCOA database under paragraph (b)(2)(i) of this section is the taxpayer's last known address until one of the following events occurs—

(A) The taxpayer files and the IRS properly processes a Federal tax return with an address different from the address obtained from the NCOA database; or

(B) The taxpayer provides the Internal Revenue Service with clear and concise notification of a change of address, as defined in procedures prescribed by the Commissioner, that is different from the address obtained from the NCOA database.

(3) *Examples.*—The following examples illustrate the rules of paragraph (b)(2) of this section:

*Example 1.* (i) A is an unmarried taxpayer. The address on A's 1999 Form 1040, U.S. Individual Income Tax Return, filed on April 14, 2000, and 2000 Form 1040 filed on April 13, 2001, is 1234 Anyplace Street, Anytown, USA 43210. On May 15, 2001, A informs the USPS of a new permanent address (9876 Newplace Street, Newtown, USA 12345) using the USPS Form 3575, "Official Mail Forwarding Change of Address Form." The change of address is included in the weekly update of the USPS NCOA database. On May 29, 2001, A's address maintained in IRS records is changed to 9876 Newplace Street, Newtown, USA 12345.

(ii) In June 2001 the IRS determines a deficiency for A's 1999 tax year and prepares to issue a notice of deficiency. The IRS obtains A's address for the notice of deficiency from IRS records. On June 15, 2001, the Internal Revenue Service mails the notice of deficiency to A at 9876 Newplace Street, Newtown, USA 12345. For purposes of section 6212(b), the notice of deficiency mailed on June 15, 2001, is mailed to A's last known address.

*Example 2.* (i) The facts are the same as in *Example 1*, except that instead of determining a deficiency for A's 1999 tax year in June 2001, the IRS determines a deficiency for A's 1999 tax year in May 2001.

(ii) On May 21, 2001, the IRS prepares a notice of deficiency for A and obtains A's address from IRS records. Because A did not inform the USPS of the change of address in sufficient time for the IRS to process and post the new address in Internal Revenue Service's records by May 21, 2001, the notice of deficiency is mailed to 1234 Anyplace Street, Anytown, USA 43210. For purposes of section 6212(b), the notice of deficiency mailed on May 21, 2001, is mailed to A's last known address.

*Example 3.* (i) C and D are married taxpayers. The address on C and D's 2000 Form 1040, U.S. Individual Income Tax Return, filed on April 13, 2001, and 2001 Form 1040 filed on April 15, 2002, is 2468 Spring Street, Little City, USA 97531. On August 15, 2002, D informs the USPS of a new permanent address (8642 Peachtree Street, Big City, USA 13579) using the USPS Form 3575, "Official Mail Forwarding Change of Address Form." The change of address is included in the weekly update of the USPS NCOA database. On August 29, 2002, D's address maintained in IRS records is changed to 8642 Peachtree Street, Big City, USA 13579.

(ii) In October 2002 the IRS determines a deficiency for C and D's 2000 tax year and prepares to issue a notice of deficiency. The Internal Revenue Service obtains C's address and D's address for the notice of deficiency from IRS records. On October 15, 2002, the IRS mails a copy of the notice of deficiency to C at 2468 Spring Street, Little City, USA 97531, and to D at 8642 Peachtree Street, Big City, USA 13579. For purposes of section 6212(b), the notices of deficiency mailed on October 15, 2002, are mailed to C and D's respective last known addresses.

(c) *Last known address for all notices, statements, and documents.*—The rules in paragraphs (a) and (b) of this section apply for purposes of determining whether all notices, statements, or other documents are mailed to a taxpayer's last known address whenever the term *last known address* is used in the Internal Revenue Code or the regulations thereunder.

(d) *Effective Date.*—(1) *In general.*—Except as provided in paragraph (d)(2) of this section, this section is effective on January 29, 2001.

(2) *Individual moves in the case of joint filers.*—In the case of taxpayers who file joint returns under section 6013, if the NCOA database contains change of address information for only one spouse, paragraphs (b)(2) and (3) of this section will not apply to notices, statements, and other documents mailed before the processing of the taxpayers' 2000 joint return. [Reg. § 301.6212-2.]

☐ [*T.D.* 8939, 1-11-2001.]

### [Reg. § 301.6213-1]

§ 301.6213-1. Restrictions applicable to deficiencies; petition to Tax Court.—(a) *Time for filing petition and restrictions on assessment.*—(1) *Time for filing petition.*—Within 90 days after notice of the deficiency is mailed (or within 150 days after mailing in the case of such notice addressed to a person outside the States of the Union and the District of Columbia), as provided in section 6212, a petition may be filed with the Tax Court of the United States for a redetermination of the deficiency. In determining such 90-day or 150-day period, Saturday, Sunday, or a legal holiday in the District of Columbia is not counted as the 90th or 150th day. In determining the time for filing a petition with the Tax Court in the case of a notice of deficiency mailed to a resident of Alaska prior to 12:01 p.m., e.s.t., January 3, 1959, and in the case of a notice of deficiency mailed to a resident of Hawaii prior to 4:00 p.m. e.d.s.t., August 21, 1959, the term "States of the Union" does not include Alaska or Hawaii, respectively, and the 150-day period applies. In determining the time within which a petition to the Tax Court may be filed in the case of a notice of deficiency mailed to a resident of Alaska after 12:01 p.m., e.s.t., January 3, 1959, and in the case of a notice of deficiency mailed to a resident of Hawaii after 4:00 p.m., e.d.s.t., August 21, 1959, the term "States of the Union" includes Alaska and Hawaii, respectively, and the 90-day period applies.

(2) *Restrictions on assessment.*—Except as otherwise provided by this section, by sections 6851, 6852, and 6861(a) (relating to termination and jeopardy assessments), by section 6871(a) (relating to immediate assessment of claims for income, estate, and gift taxes in bankruptcy and receivership cases), or by section 7485 (in case taxpayer petitions for a review of a Tax Court decision without filing bond), no assessment of a deficiency in respect to a tax imposed by subtitle A or B or chapter 41, 42, 43, or 44 of the Code and no levy or proceeding in court for its collection shall be made until notice of deficiency has been mailed to the taxpayer, nor until the expiration of the 90-day or 150-day period within which a petition may be filed with the Tax Court, nor, if a petition has been filed with the Tax

Court, until the decision of the Tax Court has become final. As to the date on which a decision of the Tax Court becomes final, see section 7481. Notwithstanding the provisions of section 7421(a), the making of an assessment or the beginning of a proceeding or levy which is forbidden by this paragraph may be enjoined by a proceeding in the proper court. In any case where the running of the time prescribed for filing a petition in the Tax Court with respect to a tax imposed by chapter 42 or 43 is suspended under section 6213(e), no assessment of a deficiency in respect of such tax shall be made until expiration of the entire period for filing the petition.

(b) *Exceptions to restrictions on assessment of deficiencies.*—(1) *Mathematical errors.*—If a taxpayer is notified of an additional amount of tax due on account of a mathematical error appearing upon the return, such notice is not deemed a notice of deficiency, and the taxpayer has no right to file a petition with the Tax Court upon the basis of such notice, nor is the assessment of such additional amount prohibited by section 6213(a).

(2) *Tentative carryback adjustments.*—(i) If the district director or the director of the regional service center determines that any amount applied, credited, or refunded under section 6411(b) with respect to an application for a tentative carryback adjustment is in excess of the overassessment properly attributable to the carryback upon which such application was based, the district director or the director of the regional service center may assess the amount of the excess as a deficiency as if such deficiency were due to a mathematical error appearing on the return. That is, the district director or the director of the regional service center may assess an amount equal to the excess, and such amount may be collected, without regard to the restrictions on assessment and collection imposed by section 6213(a). Thus, the district director or the director of the regional service center may assess such amount without regard to whether the taxpayer has been mailed a prior notice of deficiency. Either before or after assessing such an amount, the district director or the director of the regional service center will notify the taxpayer that such assessment has been or will be made. Such notice will not constitute a notice of deficiency, and the taxpayer may not file a petition with the Tax Court of the United States based on such notice. However, the taxpayer within the applicable period of limitation, may file a regular claim for credit or refund based on the carryback, if he has not already filed such a claim, and may maintain a suit based on such claim if it is disallowed or if it is not acted upon by the Internal Revenue Service within 6 months from the date the claim was filed.

(ii) The method provided in subdivision (i) of this subparagraph to recover any amount applied, credited, or refunded in respect of an application for a tentative carryback adjustment which should not have been so applied, credited, or refunded is not an exclusive method. Two other methods are available to recover such amount: (*a*) By way of a deficiency notice under section 6212; or (*b*) by a suit to recover an erroneous refund under section 7405. Any one or more of the three available methods may be used to recover any amount which was improperly applied, credited, or refunded in respect of an application for a tentative carryback adjustment.

(3) *Assessment of amount paid.*—Any payment made after the mailing of a notice of deficiency which is made by the taxpayer as a payment with respect to the proposed deficiency may be assessed without regard to the restrictions on assessment and collection imposed by section 6213(a) even though the taxpayer has not filed a waiver of restrictions on assessment as provided in section 6213(d). A payment of all or part of the deficiency asserted in the notice together with the assessment of the amount so paid will not affect the jurisdiction of the Tax Court. If any payment is made before the mailing of a notice of deficiency, the district director or the director of the regional service center is not prohibited by section 6213(a) from assessing such amount, and such amount may be assessed if such action is deemed to be proper. If such amount is assessed, the assessment is taken into account in determining whether or not there is a deficiency for which a notice of deficiency must be issued. Thus, if such a payment satisfies the taxpayer's tax liability, no notice of deficiency will be mailed and the Tax Court will have no jurisdiction over the matter. In any case in which there is a controversy as to the correct amount of the tax liability, the assessment of any amount pursuant to the provisions of section 6213(b)(3) shall in no way be considered to be the acceptance of an offer by the taxpayer to settle such controversy.

(4) *Jeopardy.*—If the district director believes that the assessment or collection of a deficiency will be jeopardized by delay, such deficiency shall be assessed immediately, as provided in section 6861(a).

(c) *Failure to file petition.*—If no petition is filed with the Tax Court within the period prescribed in section 6213(a), the district director or the director of the regional service center shall assess the amount determined as the deficiency and of which the taxpayer was notified by registered or certified mail and the taxpayer shall pay the same upon notice and demand therefor. In such case the district director will not be precluded from determining a further deficiency and notifying the taxpayer thereof by registered or certified mail. If a petition is filed with the Tax Court the taxpayer should notify the district director who issued the notice of deficiency that the petition has been filed in order to prevent an assessment of the amount determined to be the deficiency.

(d) *Waiver of restrictions.*—The taxpayer may at any time by a signed notice in writing filed with the district director waive the restrictions on the assessment and collection of the whole or any part of the deficiency. The notice must in all cases be filed with the district director or other authorized official under whose jurisdiction the audit or other consideration of the return in question is being conducted. The filing of such notice with the Tax Court does not constitute filing with the district director within the meaning of the Internal Revenue Code. After such waiver has been acted upon by the district director and the assessment has been made in accordance with its terms, the waiver cannot be withdrawn.

(e) *Suspension of filing period for certain chapter 42 and chapter 43 taxes.*—The period prescribed by section 6213(a) for filing a petition in the Tax Court with respect to the taxes imposed by section 4941, 4942, 4943, 4944, 4945, 4951, 4952, 4955, 4958, 4971, or 4975, shall be suspended for any other period which the Commissioner has allowed for making correction under §53.4963-1(e)(3). Where the time for filing a petition with the Tax Court has been suspended under the authority of this paragraph (e), the extension shall not be reduced as a result of the correction being made prior to expiration of the period allowed for making correction. [Reg. §301.6213-1.]

□ [*T.D.* 6119, 12-31-54. *Amended by T.D.* 6425, 11-10-59; *T.D.* 6498, 10-24-60; *T.D.* 6585, 12-27-61; *T.D.* 7838, 10-5-82; *T.D.* 8084, 5-1-86; *T.D.* 8628, 12-4-95 *and T.D.* 8920, 1-9-2001.]

**[Reg. §301.6215-1]**

**§301.6215-1. Assessment of deficiency found by Tax Court.**— Where a petition has been filed with the Tax Court, the entire amount redetermined as the deficiency by the decision of the Tax Court which has become final shall be assessed by the district director or the director of the regional service center and the unpaid portion of the amount so assessed shall be paid by the taxpayer upon notice and demand therefor. [Reg. §301.6215-1.]

□ [*T.D.* 6119, 12-13-54. *Amended by T.D.* 6585, 12-27-61.]

# TAX TREATMENT OF PARTNERSHIP ITEMS

**[Reg. §301.6221-1]**

**§301.6221-1. Tax treatment determined at partnership level.**— (a) *In general.*—A partner's treatment of partnership items on the partner's return may not be changed except as provided in sections 6222 through 6231 and the regulations thereunder. Thus, for example, if a partner treats an item on the partner's return consistently with the treatment of the item on the partnership return, the IRS generally cannot adjust the treatment of that item on the partner's return except through a partnership-level proceeding. Similarly, the taxpayer may not put partnership items in issue in a proceeding relating to nonpartnership items. For example, the taxpayer may not offset a potential increase in taxable income based on changes to nonpartnership items by a potential decrease based on partnership items.

(b) *Restrictions inapplicable after items become nonpartnership items.*— Section 6221 and paragraph (a) of this section cease to apply to items arising from a partnership with respect to a partner when those items cease to be partnership items with respect to that partner under section 6231(b).

(c) *Penalties determined at partnership level.*—Any penalty, addition to tax, or additional amount that relates to an adjustment to a partnership item shall be determined at the partnership level. Partner-level defenses to such items can only be asserted through refund actions following assessment and payment. Assessment of any penalty, addition to tax, or additional amount that relates to an adjustment to a partnership item shall be made based on partnership-level determinations. Partnership-level determinations include all the legal and factual determinations that underlie the determination of any penalty, addition to tax, or additional amount, other than partner-level defenses specified in paragraph (d) of this section.

(d) *Partner-level defenses.*—Partner-level defenses to any penalty, addition to tax, or additional amount that relates to an adjustment to a partnership item may not be asserted in the partnership-level proceeding, but may be asserted through separate refund actions following assessment and payment. See section 6230(c)(4). Partner-level defenses are limited to those that are personal to the partner or are dependent upon the partner's separate return and cannot be determined at the partnership level. Examples of these determinations are whether any applicable threshold underpayment of tax has been met with respect to the partner or whether the partner has met the criteria of section 6664(b) (penalties applicable only where return is filed), or section 6664(c)(1) (reasonable cause exception) subject to partnership-level determinations as to the applicability of section 6664(c)(2).

(e) *Cross-references.*—See §§301.6231(c)-1 and 301.6231(c)-2 for special rules relating to certain applications and claims for refund based on losses, deductions, or credits from abusive tax shelter partnerships.

(f) *Effective date.*—This section is applicable to partnership taxable years beginning on or after October 4, 2001. For years beginning prior to October 4, 2001, see §301.6221-1T contained in 26 CFR part 1, revised April 1, 2001. [Reg. §301.6221-1.]

□ [*T.D.* 8965, 10-3-2001.]

**[Reg. §301.6221(a)-1]**

**§301.6221(a)-1. Determination at partnership level.**—(a) *In general.*—Except as otherwise provided under subchapter C of chapter 63 of the Internal Revenue Code (subchapter C of chapter 63) and the regulations in this part, any adjustment to a partnership-related item (as defined in §301.6241-1(a)(6)(ii)) is determined, any tax imposed by chapter 1 of the Internal Revenue Code (Code) attributable thereto is assessed and collected, and the applicability of any penalty, addition to tax, or additional amount that relates to an adjustment to any partnership-related item is determined at the partnership level under subchapter C of chapter 63.

(b) *Legal and factual determinations at the partnership level.*—Except as otherwise provided under subchapter C of chapter 63, any legal or factual determinations underlying any adjustment or determination made in accordance with paragraph (a) of this section are also determined at the partnership level under subchapter C of chapter 63. For instance, determinations under this paragraph (b) include any determinations necessary to calculate the imputed underpayment or any modification of the imputed underpayment under section 6225 and the period of limitations on making adjustments under subchapter C of chapter 63.

(c) *Applicability date.*—(1) *In general.*—Except as provided in paragraph (c)(2) of this section, this section applies to partnership taxable years beginning after December 31, 2017, and ending after August 12, 2018.

(2) *Election under §301.9100-22 in effect.*—This section applies to any partnership taxable year beginning after November 2, 2015, and before January 1, 2018, for which a valid election under §301.9100-22 is in effect. [Reg. §301.6221(a)-1.]

□ [T.D. 9844, 2-21-2019.]

**[Reg. §301.6221(b)-1]**

**§301.6221(b)-1. Election out for certain partnerships with 100 or fewer partners.**—(a) *In general.*—The provisions of subchapter C of chapter 63 of the Internal Revenue Code (subchapter C of chapter 63) do not apply for any partnership taxable year for which an eligible partnership under paragraph (b) of this section makes a valid election in accordance with paragraph (c) of this section. For rules regarding deficiency procedures, see subchapter B of chapter 63 of the Internal Revenue Code and §§301.6211-1 through 301.6215-1.

(b) *Eligible partnership.*—(1) *In general.*—Only an eligible partnership may make an election under this section. A partnership is an eligible partnership for purposes of this section if—

(i) The partnership has 100 or fewer partners as determined in accordance with paragraph (b)(2) of this section, and

(ii) Each statement the partnership is required to furnish under section 6031(b) for the partnership taxable year is furnished to a partner that was an eligible partner (as defined in paragraph (b)(3) of this section) for the partnership's entire taxable year.

(2) *100 or fewer partners.*—(i) *In general.*—Except as provided in paragraph (b)(2)(ii) of this section, a partnership has 100 or fewer partners if the partnership is required to furnish 100 or fewer statements under section 6031(b) for the taxable year.

(ii) *Special rule for S corporations.*—For purposes of this paragraph (b)(2), a partnership with a partner that is an S corporation (as defined in section 1361(a)(1)) must take into account each statement required to be furnished by the S corporation to its shareholders under section 6037(b) for the taxable year of the S corporation ending with or within the partnership's taxable year.

(iii) *Examples.*—The following examples illustrate the provisions of this paragraph (b)(2). For purposes of these examples, each partnership is required to file a return under section 6031(a):

*Example 1.* During its 2020 partnership taxable year, Partnership has four partners each owning an interest in Partnership. Two of the partners are Spouse 1 and Spouse 2 who are married to each other during all of 2020. Spouse 1 and Spouse 2 each own a separate interest in Partnership. The two other partners are unmarried individuals. Under section 6031(b), Partnership is required to furnish a separate statement (that is, Schedule K-1 (Form 1065), *Partner's Share of Income, Deductions, Credits, etc.*) to each individual partner, including separate statements to Spouse 1 and Spouse 2. Therefore, for purposes of this paragraph (b)(2), Partnership has four partners during its 2020 taxable year.

*Example 2.* The facts are the same as in *Example 1* of this paragraph (b)(2)(iii), except Spouse 2 does not separately own an interest in Partnership during 2020 and Spouse 1 and Spouse 2 live in a community property state, State A. Spouse 1 acquired the partnership interest in such a manner that by operation of State A law, Spouse 2 has a community property interest in Spouse 1's partnership interest. Because Spouse 2's community property interest in Spouse 1's partnership interest is not taken into account for purposes of determining the number of statements Partnership is required to furnish under section 6031(b), Partnership is required to furnish a statement to Spouse 1, but not to Spouse 2. Therefore, for purposes of this paragraph (b)(2), Partnership has three partners during its 2020 taxable year.

*Example 3.* At the beginning of 2020, Partnership, which has a taxable year ending December 31, 2020, has three partners - individuals A, B, and C. Each individual owns an interest in Partnership. On June 30, 2020, Individual A dies, and A's interest in Partnership becomes an asset of A's estate. A's estate owns the interest for the remainder of 2020. On September 1, 2020, B sells his interest in Partnership to Individual D, who holds the interest for the remainder of the year. Under section 6031(b), Partnership is required to furnish five statements for its 2020 taxable year – one each to Individual A, the estate of Individual A, Individual B, Individual C, and Individual D. Therefore, for purposes of this paragraph (b)(2), Partnership has five partners during its 2020 taxable year.

*Example 4.* During its 2020 taxable year, Partnership has 51 partners - 50 partners who are individuals and S, an S corporation. S and Partnership are both calendar year taxpayers. S has 50 shareholders during the 2020 taxable year. Under section 6031(b), Partnership is required to furnish 51 statements for the 2020 taxable year – one to S and one to each of Partnership's 50 partners who are individuals. Under section 6037(b), S is required to furnish a statement (that is, Schedule K-1 (Form 1120-S), *Shareholder's Share of Income, Deductions, Credits, etc.*) to each of its 50 shareholders. Under paragraph (b)(2)(ii) of this section, the number of statements required to be furnished by S under section 6037(b), which is 50, is taken into account to determine whether partnership has 100 or fewer partners. Accordingly, for purposes of this paragraph (b)(2), Partnership has a total of 101 partners (51 statements furnished by Partnership to its partners plus 50 statements furnished by S to its shareholders) and is therefore not an eligible partnership under paragraph (b)(1) of this section. Because Partnership is not an eligible partnership, it cannot make the election under paragraph (a) of this section.

*Example 5.* During its 2020 taxable year, Partnership has two partners, A, an individual, and E, an estate of a deceased partner. E has 10 beneficiaries. Under section 6031(b), Partnership is required to furnish two statements, one to A and one to E. Any statements that E may be required to furnish to its beneficiaries are not taken into account for purposes of this paragraph (b)(2). Therefore, for purposes of this paragraph (b)(2), Partnership has two partners.

(3) *Eligible Partners.*—(i) *In general.*—For purposes of paragraph (b)(1)(ii) of this section, the term *eligible partner* means a partner that is an individual, a C corporation (as defined by section 1361(a)(2)), an eligible foreign entity described in paragraph (b)(3)(iii) of this section, an S corporation, or an estate of a deceased partner. An S corporation is an eligible partner regardless of whether one or more shareholders of the S corporation are not an eligible partner.

(ii) *Partners that are not eligible partners.*—A partner is not an eligible partner under paragraph (b)(3)(i) of this section if the partner is —

(A) A partnership,

(B) A trust,

(C) A foreign entity that is not an eligible foreign entity described in paragraph (b)(3)(iii) of this section,

(D) A disregarded entity described in § 301.7701-2(c)(2)(i),

(E) An estate of an individual other than a deceased partner, or

(F) Any person that holds an interest in the partnership on behalf of another person.

(iii) *Eligible foreign entity.*—For purposes of this paragraph (b)(3), a foreign entity is an eligible partner if the foreign entity would be treated as a C corporation if it were a domestic entity. For purposes of the preceding sentence, a foreign entity would be treated as a C corporation if it were a domestic entity if the entity is classified as a per se corporation under § 301.7701-2(b)(1), (3), (4), (5), (6), (7), or (8), is classified by default as an association taxable as a corporation under § 301.7701-3(b)(2)(i)(B), or is classified as an association taxable as a corporation in accordance with an election under § 301.7701-3(c).

(iv) *Examples.*—The following examples illustrate the rules of this paragraph (b)(3). For purposes of these examples, each partnership is required to file a return under section 6031(a):

*Example 1.* During the 2020 taxable year, Partnership has four equal partners. Two partners are individuals. One partner is a C corporation. The fourth partner, D, is a partnership. Because D is a partnership, D is not an eligible partner under paragraph (b)(3)(i) of this section. Accordingly, Partnership is not an eligible partnership under paragraph (b)(1) of this section and, therefore, cannot make the election under paragraph (a) of this section for its 2020 taxable year.

*Example 2.* During its 2020 taxable year, Partnership has four equal partners. Two partners are individuals. One partner is a C corporation. The fourth partner, S, is an S corporation. S has ten shareholders. One of S's shareholders is a disregarded entity, and one is a qualified small business trust. S is an eligible partner under paragraph (b)(3)(i) of this section even though S's shareholders would not be considered eligible partners if those shareholders held direct interests in Partnership. See paragraph (b)(3)(i) of this section. Accordingly, Partnership meets the requirements under this paragraph (b)(3) for its 2020 taxable year.

*Example 3.* During its 2020 taxable year, Partnership has two equal partners, A, an individual, and C, a disregarded entity, wholly owned by B, an individual. C is not an eligible partner under paragraph (b)(3)(i) of this section. Accordingly, Partnership is not an eligible partnership under paragraph (b)(1) of this section and, therefore, is ineligible to make the election under paragraph (a) of this section for its 2020 taxable year.

(c) *Election.*—(1) *In general.*—An election under this section must be made on the eligible partnership's timely filed return, including extensions, for the taxable year to which the election applies and include all information required by the Internal Revenue Service (IRS) in forms, instructions, or other guidance. An election is not valid unless the partnership discloses to the IRS all of the information required under paragraph (c)(2) of this section and, in the case of a partner that is an S corporation, the shareholders of such S corporation. An election once made may not be revoked without the consent of the IRS.

(2) *Disclosure of partner information to the IRS.*—A partnership making an election under this section must disclose to the IRS information about each person that was a partner at any time during the taxable year of the partnership to which the election applies, including each partner's name and correct U.S. taxpayer identification number (TIN) (or alternative form of identification required by forms, instructions, or other guidance), each partner's Federal tax classification, an affirmative statement that the partner is an eligible partner under paragraph (b)(3)(i) of this section, and any other information required by the IRS in forms, instructions, or other guidance. If a partner is an S corporation, the partnership must also disclose to the IRS information about each shareholder of the S corporation that was a shareholder at any time during the taxable year of the S corporation ending with or within the partnership's taxable year, including each shareholder's name and correct TIN (or alternative form of identification as prescribed by forms, instructions, or other guidance), each shareholder's Federal tax classification, and any other information required by the IRS in forms, instructions, or other guidance.

(3) *Partner notification.*—A partnership that makes an election under this section must notify each of its partners of the election within 30 days of making the election in the form and manner determined by the partnership.

(d) *Election made by a partnership that is a partner.*—(1) *In general.*— The fact that a partnership has made an election under this section does not affect whether the provisions of subchapter C of chapter 63 apply to any other partnership, including a partnership in which the partnership making the election is a partner. Accordingly, the provi-

**Reg. § 301.6221(b)-1(d)(1)**

sions of subchapter C of chapter 63 that apply to partners in a partnership that has not made an election under this section apply, to the extent provided in the regulations under subchapter C of chapter 63, to partners (that are themselves partnerships that have made an election under this section) in their capacity as partners in the other partnership.

(2) *Examples.*—The following examples illustrate the rules of paragraph (d)(1) of this section. For purposes of these examples, each partnership is required to file a return under section 6031(a):

*Example 1.* During its 2020 taxable year, Partnership, a calendar year taxpayer, has two partners. One partner, A, is also a calendar year partnership. A files a valid election under this section with its timely filed partnership return for its 2020 taxable year. Partnership does not file an election under this section. Notwithstanding A's valid election under this section, with respect to A's interest in Partnership, A is subject to the rules applicable to partners in a partnership subject to the rules under subchapter C of chapter 63, including the consistency requirements of section 6222 and the regulations thereunder.

*Example 2.* The facts are the same as *Example 1* of this paragraph (d)(2). The IRS mails to Partnership a notice of final partnership adjustment under section 6231 with respect to Partnership's 2020 taxable year. Partnership timely elects the alternative to payment of imputed underpayment under section 6226 and the regulations thereunder. Partnership must provide A with a statement under section 6226 reflecting A's share of the adjustments for Partnership's 2020 taxable year. A is subject to the rules applicable to partners in a partnership subject to the rules under subchapter C of chapter 63 with respect to A's interest in Partnership.

(e) *Effect of an election.*—(1) *In general.*—An election made under this section is an action taken under subchapter C of chapter 63 by the partnership for purposes of section 6223. Accordingly, the partnership and all partners are bound by an election of the partnership under this section unless the IRS determines that the election is invalid. See § 301.6223-2 for the binding nature of actions taken by a partnership under subchapter C of chapter 63.

(2) *IRS determination that election is invalid.*—If the IRS determines that an election under this section for a partnership taxable year is invalid, the IRS will notify the partnership in writing and the provisions of subchapter C of chapter 63 will apply to that partnership taxable year.

(f) *Applicability date.*—These regulations are applicable to partnership taxable years beginning after December 31, 2017. [Reg. § 301.6221(b)-1.]

□ [T.D. 9829, 12-29-2017.]

[Reg. § 301.6222-1]

**§ 301.6222-1. Partner's return must be consistent with partnership return.**—(a) *Consistent treatment of partnership-related items.*—(1) *In general.*—The treatment of partnership-related items (as defined in § 301.6241-1(a)(6)(ii)) on a partner's return must be consistent with the treatment of such items on the partnership return in all respects, including the amount, timing, and characterization of such items. A partner has not satisfied the requirement of this paragraph (a) if the treatment of the partnership-related item on the partner's return is consistent with how such item was treated on a schedule or other information furnished to the partner by the partnership but inconsistent with the treatment of the item on the partnership return actually filed. For rules relating to the election to be treated as having reported the inconsistency where the partner treats a partnership-related item consistently with an incorrect schedule or other information furnished by the partnership, see paragraph (d) of this section. For purposes of this section, the term *partner's return* includes any return, statement, schedule, or list, and any amendment or supplement thereto, filed by the partner with respect to any tax imposed by the Internal Revenue Code (Code).

(2) *Partner that is a partnership with an election in effect under section 6221(b).*—The rules of this section apply to all partners, including a partnership-partner (as defined in § 301.6241-1(a)(7)) that has an election in effect under section 6221(b) for any taxable year. Accordingly, unless the requirements of paragraph (c) of this section are satisfied, a partnership-partner must treat partnership-related items of a partnership in which it is a partner consistent with the treatment of such items on the partnership return filed by the partnership in which it is a partner.

(3) *Partnership does not file a return.*—A partner's treatment of a partnership-related item attributable to a partnership that does not file a return is per se inconsistent.

(4) *Treatment of items on a partnership return.*—For purposes of this section, the treatment of a partnership-related item on a partnership return includes—

(i) The treatment of such item on the partnership's return of partnership income filed with the Internal Revenue Service (IRS) under section 6031, and any amendment or supplement thereto, including an administrative adjustment request (AAR) filed pursuant to section 6227; and

(ii) The treatment of such item on any statement, schedule or list, and any amendment or supplement thereto, filed by the partnership with the IRS, including any statements filed pursuant to section 6226.

(5) *Examples.*—The following examples illustrate the rules of this paragraph (a). For purposes of these examples, each partnership is subject to the provisions of subchapter C of chapter 63 of the Code (subchapter C of chapter 63), and each partnership and its partners are calendar year taxpayers, unless otherwise stated.

(i) *Example 1.* A is a partner in Partnership during 2018 and 2019. In December 2018, Partnership receives an advance payment for services to be performed in 2019 and reports this amount as income on its partnership return for 2018. A includes its distributive share of income from the advance payment on A's income tax return for 2019 and not on A's income tax return for 2018. A has not satisfied the requirements of paragraph (a) of this section because A's treatment of the income attributable to Partnership is inconsistent with the treatment of that item by Partnership on its partnership return.

(ii) *Example 2.* B is a partner in Partnership during 2018. Partnership incurred start-up costs before it was actively engaged in its business. Partnership capitalized these costs on its 2018 partnership return. B deducted his distributive share of the start-up costs on B's 2018 income tax return. B has not satisfied the requirements of paragraph (a) of this section because B's treatment of the start-up costs is inconsistent with the treatment of that item by Partnership on its partnership return.

(iii) *Example 3.* C is a partner in Partnership during 2018. Partnership reports a loss of $100,000 on its partnership return for 2018. On the 2018 Schedule K-1 attached to the partnership return, Partnership reports $5,000 as C's distributive share of that loss. On the 2018 Schedule K-1 furnished to C, however, Partnership reports $15,000 as C's distributive share of the loss. C reports the $15,000 loss on C's 2018 income tax return. C has not satisfied the requirements of paragraph (a) of this section because C reported C's distributive share of the loss in a manner that is inconsistent with how C's distributive share of the loss was reported on the 2018 partnership return actually filed. See, however, paragraph (d) of this section for the election to be treated as having reported the inconsistency where the partner treats an item consistently with an incorrect schedule.

(iv) *Example 4.* D was a partner in Partnership during 2018. Partnership reports a loss of $100,000 on its partnership return for 2018. In 2020, Partnership files an AAR under section 6227 reporting that the amount of the loss on its 2018 partnership return is $90,000, rather than $100,000 as originally reported. Pursuant to section 6227, Partnership elects to have its partners take the adjustment into account, and furnishes D a statement showing D's share of the reduced loss for 2018. D fails to take his share of the reduced loss for 2018 into account in accordance with section 6227. D has not satisfied the requirements of paragraph (a) of this section because D has not taken into account his share of the loss in a manner consistent with how Partnership treated such items on the partnership return actually filed.

(v) *Example 5.* E was a partner in Partnership during 2018. In 2021, Partnership receives a notice of final partnership adjustment (FPA) in an administrative proceeding under subchapter C of chapter 63 with respect to Partnership's 2018 taxable year. The FPA reflects an imputed underpayment. Partnership properly elects the application of section 6226 with respect to the imputed underpayment and files with the IRS and furnishes to E a statement of E's share of adjustments with respect to Partnership's 2018 taxable year. E fails to take his share of the adjustments into account in accordance with section 6226. E has not satisfied the requirements of paragraph (a) of this section because E has not taken into account his share of adjustments with respect to Partnership's 2018 taxable year in a manner consistent with how Partnership treated such items on the section 6226 statement filed with the IRS.

(vi) *Example 6.* F was a partner in Partnership during 2018. F has a valid election under section 6221(b) in effect with respect to F's 2018 partnership taxable year. Notwithstanding F's election under section 6221(b) for its 2018 taxable year, F is subject to section 6222 for taxable year 2018. F must treat, on its 2018 partnership return, any items attributable to F's interest in Partnership in a manner that is consistent with the treatment of those items on the 2018 partnership return actually filed by Partnership.

(vii) *Example 7.* G was a partner in Partnership during 2018. G's taxable year ends on the same day as Partnership's 2018 taxable year.

Partnership did not file a partnership return for its 2018 taxable year. G files an income tax return for its 2018 taxable year and reports G's share of a loss attributable to G's interest in Partnership. Because Partnership failed to file a partnership return, G's treatment of such loss is per se inconsistent pursuant to paragraph (a)(3) of this section.

(b) *Effect of inconsistent treatment.*—(1) *Determination of underpayment of tax resulting from inconsistent treatment.*—If a partner fails to satisfy the requirements of paragraph (a) of this section, unless the partner provides notice in accordance with paragraph (c) of this section, the IRS may adjust the inconsistently reported partnership-related item on the partner's return to make it consistent with the treatment of such item on the partnership return (or where no partnership return was filed, remove any treatment of such items from the partner's return) and determine any underpayment of tax that results from that adjustment. For purposes of this section, except as provided in paragraph (b)(3) of this section, the underpayment of tax is the amount by which the correct tax, as determined by making the partner's return consistent with the partnership return, exceeds the tax shown on the partner's return.

(2) *Assessment and collection of tax.*—The IRS may assess and collect any underpayment of tax resulting from an adjustment described in paragraph (b)(1) of this section in the same manner as if the underpayment of tax were on account of a mathematical or clerical error appearing on the partner's return, except that the procedures under section 6213(b)(2) for requesting abatement of an assessment do not apply.

(3) *Effect when partner is a partnership.*—For the effect of a failure to satisfy the requirements of paragraph (a) of this section where the partner is itself a partnership (a partnership-partner), see section 6232(d)(1)(B) and § 301.6232-1(d).

(4) *Examples.*—The following examples illustrate the rules of this paragraph (b). For purposes of these examples, each partnership is subject to the provisions of subchapter C of chapter 63, and each partnership and its partners are calendar year taxpayers, unless otherwise stated.

(i) *Example 1.* H, an individual, is a partner in Partnership. On its partnership return for taxable year 2018, Partnership reports $100,000 in ordinary income. On the Schedule K-1 attached to the partnership return, as well as on the Schedule K-1 furnished to H, Partnership reports $15,000 as H's distributive share of the $100,000 in ordinary income. H reports only $5,000 of the $15,000 of ordinary income on his 2018 income tax return. The IRS may determine the amount of tax that results from adjusting the ordinary income attributable to H's interest in Partnership reported on H's 2018 income tax return from $5,000 to $15,000 and assess that resulting underpayment in tax as if it were on account of a mathematical or clerical error appearing on H's return. H may not request an abatement of that assessment under section 6213(b).

(ii) *Example 2.* J was a partner in Partnership during 2018. In 2021, Partnership receives an FPA in an administrative proceeding under subchapter C of chapter 63 with respect to Partnership's 2018 taxable year. The FPA reflects an imputed underpayment. Partnership properly elects the application of section 6226 with respect to the imputed underpayment and files with the IRS and furnishes to J a statement of J's share of adjustments with respect to Partnership's 2018 taxable year. J fails to report one adjustment reflected on the statement, J's share of a decrease in the amount of losses for 2018, on J's return as required by section 6226. The IRS may determine the amount of tax that results from adjusting the decrease in the amount of losses on J's return to be consistent with the amount included on the section 6226 statement filed with the IRS and may assess the resulting underpayment in tax as if it were on account of a mathematical or clerical error appearing on J's return. J may not request an abatement of that assessment under section 6213(b).

(c) *Notification to the IRS when items attributable to a partnership are treated inconsistently.*—(1) *In general.*—Paragraphs (a) and (b) of this section (regarding the consistent treatment of partnership-related items and the effect of inconsistent treatment) do not apply to partnership-related items identified as inconsistent (or that may be inconsistent) in a statement that the partner provides to the IRS according to the forms, instructions, and other guidance prescribed by the IRS. Instead, the procedures in paragraph (c)(3) of this section apply. A statement does not identify an inconsistency for purposes of this paragraph (c) unless it is attached to the partner's return on which the partnership-related item is treated inconsistently.

(2) *Coordination with section 6223.*—Paragraph (c)(1) of this section is not applicable to a partnership-related item the treatment of which is binding on the partner because of actions taken by the partnership under subchapter C of chapter 63 or because of a final decision in a proceeding with respect to the partnership under subchapter C of chapter 63. For instance, the provisions of paragraph

(c)(1) of this section do not apply with respect to the partner's treatment of a partnership-related item reflected on a statement described in § 301.6226-2 filed by the partnership with the IRS. See § 301.6226-1(e) (regarding the binding nature of statements described in § 301.6226-2). Any underpayment resulting from the inconsistent treatment of an item described in this paragraph (c)(2) may be assessed and collected in accordance with paragraph (b)(2) of this section.

(3) *Partner protected only to extent of notification.*—A partner who reports the inconsistent treatment of a partnership-related item is not subject to paragraphs (a) and (b) of this section only with respect to those items identified in the statement described in paragraph (c)(1) of this section. Thus, if a partner notifying the IRS with respect to one partnership-related item does not report the inconsistent treatment of another partnership-related item, the IRS may determine the amount of tax that results from adjusting the unidentified, inconsistently reported item on the partner's return to make it consistent with the treatment of such item on the partnership return and assess the resulting underpayment of tax in accordance with paragraph (b)(2) of this section.

(4) *Adjustment after notification.*—(i) *In general.*—If a partner notifies the IRS of the inconsistent treatment of a partnership-related item in accordance with paragraph (c)(1) of this section and the IRS disagrees with the inconsistent treatment, the IRS may adjust the identified, inconsistently reported item in a proceeding with respect to the partner. Nothing in this paragraph (c)(4)(i) precludes the IRS from also conducting a proceeding with respect to the partnership. If the IRS conducts a proceeding with respect to the partnership regarding the identified, inconsistently reported item, each partner of the partnership, including any partner that notified the IRS of inconsistent treatment in accordance with paragraph (c)(1) of this section, is bound by actions taken by the partnership and by any final decision in the proceeding with respect to the partnership. See paragraph (c)(2) of this section.

(ii) *Adjustments in partner proceeding.*—In a proceeding with respect to a partner described in paragraph (c)(4)(i) of this section, the IRS may adjust any identified, inconsistently reported partnership-related item to make the item consistent with the treatment of that item on the partnership return or determine that the correct treatment of such item differs from the treatment on the partnership return and instead adjust the item to reflect the correct treatment, notwithstanding the treatment of that item on the partnership return. The IRS may also adjust any item on the partner's return, including items that are not partnership-related items. Any final decision with respect to an inconsistent position in a proceeding to which the partnership is not a party is not binding on the partnership.

(5) *Limitation on treating partnership-related items inconsistently after notice of administrative proceeding.*—After a notice of administrative proceeding with respect to a partnership taxable year has been mailed by the IRS under section 6231, a partner may not notify the IRS the partner is treating a partnership-related item on the partner's return inconsistently with how such item was treated on the partnership return for such taxable year, except as provided in § 301.6225-2.

(6) *Examples.*—The following examples illustrate the rules of this paragraph (c). For purposes of these examples, each partnership is subject to the provisions of subchapter C of chapter 63, and each partnership and partner is a calendar year taxpayer, unless otherwise stated.

(i) *Example 1.* K is a partner in Partnership during 2018. K treats a deduction and a capital gain attributable to Partnership on K's 2018 income tax return in a manner that is inconsistent with the treatment of those items by Partnership on its 2018 partnership return. K reports the inconsistent treatment of the deduction in accordance with paragraph (c)(1) of this section, but not the inconsistent treatment of the gain. Because K did not notify the IRS of the inconsistent treatment of the gain in accordance with paragraph (c)(1) of this section, the IRS may determine the amount of tax that results from adjusting the gain reported on K's 2018 income tax return in order to make the treatment of that gain consistent with how the gain was treated on Partnership's partnership return. Pursuant to paragraph (c)(3) of this section, the IRS may assess and collect the underpayment of tax resulting from the adjustment to the gain as if it were on account of a mathematical or clerical error appearing on K's return.

(ii) *Example 2.* L is a partner in Partnership during 2018. On its 2018 partnership return, Partnership treats partner L's distributive share of ordinary loss attributable to Partnership as $8,000. L, however, claims an ordinary loss of $9,000 as attributable to Partnership on its 2018 income tax return and notifies the IRS of the inconsistent treatment in accordance with paragraph (c)(1) of this section. As a result of the notice of inconsistent treatment, the IRS conducts a separate proceeding under subchapter B of chapter 63 of the Internal

Revenue Code with respect to L's 2018 income tax return, a proceeding to which Partnership is not a party. During the proceeding, the IRS determines that the proper amount of L's distributive share of the ordinary loss from Partnership is $3,000. During the same proceeding, the IRS also determines that L overstated a charitable contribution deduction in the amount of $2,500 on its 2018 income tax return. The determination of the adjustment of L's share of ordinary loss is not binding on Partnership. The charitable contribution deduction is not attributable to Partnership or to another partnership subject to the provisions of subchapter C of chapter 63. The IRS may determine the amount of tax that results from adjusting the $9,000 ordinary loss deduction to $3,000 and from adjusting the charitable contribution deduction. Pursuant to paragraph (c)(4)(ii) of this section, the IRS is not limited to only adjusting the ordinary loss of $9,000, as originally reported on L's partner return, to $8,000, as originally reported by Partnership on its partnership return, nor is the IRS prohibited from adjusting the charitable contribution deduction in the proceeding with respect to L.

(d) *Partner receiving incorrect information.*—(1) *In general.*—A partner is treated as having complied with section 6222(c)(1)(B) and paragraph (c)(1) of this section with respect to a partnership-related item if the partner–

(i) Demonstrates that the treatment of such item on the partner's return is consistent with the treatment of that item on the statement, schedule, or other form prescribed by the IRS and furnished to the partner by the partnership; and

(ii) The partner makes an election in accordance with paragraph (d)(2) of this section.

(2) *Time and manner of making election.*—(i) *In general.*—An election under paragraph (d) of this section must be filed in writing with the IRS office set forth in the notice that notified the partner of the inconsistency no later than 60 days after the date of such notice.

(ii) *Contents of election.*—The election described in paragraph (d)(2)(i) of this section must be–

(A) Clearly identified as an election under section 6222(c)(2)(B);

(B) Signed by the partner making the election;

(C) Accompanied by a copy of the statement, schedule, or other form furnished to the partner by the partnership and a copy of the IRS notice that notified the partner of the inconsistency; and

(D) Include any other information required in forms, instructions, or other guidance prescribed by the IRS.

(iii) *Treatment of partnership-related item is unclear.*—Generally, the requirement described in paragraph (d)(2)(ii)(C) of this section will be satisfied by attaching a copy of the statement, schedule, or other form furnished to the partner by the partnership to the election (in addition to a copy of the IRS notice that notified the partner of the inconsistency). However, if it is not clear from the statement, schedule, or other form furnished by the partnership that the partner's treatment of the partnership-related item on the partner's return is consistent, the election must also include an explanation of how the treatment of such item on the statement, schedule, or other form furnished by the partnership is consistent with the treatment of the item on the partner's return, including with respect to the characterization, timing, and amount of such item.

(3) *Example.*—M is a partner in Partnership for 2018. Partnership is subject to subchapter C of chapter 63, and both Partnership and M are calendar year taxpayers. On its 2018 partnership return, Partnership reports that M's distributive share of ordinary income attributable to Partnership is $1,000. Partnership furnishes to M a Schedule K-1 for 2018 showing $500 as M's distributive share of ordinary income. M reports $500 of ordinary income attributable to Partnership on its 2018 income tax return consistent with the Schedule K-1 furnished to M. The IRS notifies M that M's treatment of the ordinary income attributable to Partnership on its 2018 income tax return is inconsistent with how Partnership treated the ordinary income allocated to M on its 2018 partnership return. Within 60 days of receiving the notice from the IRS of the inconsistency, M files an election with the IRS in accordance with paragraph (d)(2) of this section. Because M made a valid election under section 6222(c)(2)(B) and paragraph (d)(1) of this section, M is treated as having notified the IRS of the inconsistency with respect to the ordinary income attributable to Partnership under paragraph (c)(1) of this section.

(e) *Applicability date.*—(1) *In general.*—Except as provided in paragraph (e)(2) of this section, this section applies to partnership taxable years beginning after December 31, 2017, and ending after August 12, 2018.

(2) *Election under § 301.9100-22 in effect.*—This section applies to any partnership taxable year beginning after November 2, 2015, and before January 1, 2018, for which a valid election under § 301.9100-22 is in effect. [Reg. § 301.6222-1.]

☐ [T.D. 9844, 2-21-2019.]

### [Reg. § 301.6222(a)-1]

**§ 301.6222(a)-1. Consistent treatment of partnership items.**—(a) *In general.*—The treatment of a partnership item on the partner's return must be consistent with the treatment of that item by the partnership on the partnership return in all respects including the amount, timing, and characterization of the item.

(b) *Treatment must be consistent with partnership return.*—The treatment of a partnership item on the partner's return must be consistent with the treatment of that item on the partnership return. Thus, a partner who treats an item consistently with a schedule or other information furnished to the partner by the partnership has not satisfied the requirement of paragraph (a) of this section if the treatment of that item is inconsistent with the treatment of the item on the partnership return actually filed. For rules relating to the election to be treated as having reported the inconsistency where the partner treats an item consistently with an incorrect schedule, see § 301.6222(b)-3.

(c) *Examples.*—The following examples illustrate the principles of this section:

*Example 1.* B is a partner of Partnership P. Both B and P use the calendar year as the taxable year. In December 2001, P receives an advance payment for services to be performed in 2002 and reports this amount as income for calendar year 2001. However, B reports B's distributive share of this amount on B's income tax return for 2002 and not on B's return for 2001. B's treatment of this partnership item is inconsistent with the treatment of the item by P.

*Example 2.* Partnership P incurred certain start-up costs before P was actively engaged in its business. P capitalized these costs. C, a partner in P, deducted C's proportionate share of these start-up costs. C's treatment of the partnership expenditure is inconsistent with the treatment of that item by P.

*Example 3.* D is a partner in partnership P. P reports a loss of $100,000 on its return, $5,000 of which it reports on the Schedule K-1 attached to its return as D's distributive share. However, P reports $15,000 as D's distributive share of P's loss on the Schedule K-1 furnished to D. D reports the $15,000 loss on D's income tax return. D has not satisfied the consistent reporting requirement. See, however, § 301.6222(b)-3 for an election to be treated as having reported the inconsistency.

(d) *Effective date.*—This section is applicable to partnership taxable years beginning on or after October 4, 2001. For years beginning prior to October 4, 2001, see § 301.6222(a)-1T contained in 26 CFR part 1, revised April 1, 2001. [Reg. § 301.6222(a)-1.]

☐ [T.D. 8965, 10-3-2001.]

### [Reg. § 301.6222(a)-2]

**§ 301.6222(a)-2. Application of consistent reporting and notification rules to indirect partners.**—(a) *In general.*—The consistent reporting requirement of § 301.6222(a)-1 is generally applied with respect to the *source partnership.* For purposes of this section, the term source partnership means the partnership (within the meaning of section 6231(a)(1)) from which the partnership item originates.

(b) *Indirect partner files consistently with source partnership.*—An indirect partner who treats an item from a source partnership in a manner consistent with the treatment of that item on the source partnership's return satisfies the consistency requirement of section 6222(a) regardless of whether the indirect partner treats that item in a manner consistent with the treatment of that item by the pass-thru partner through which the indirect partner holds the interest in the source partnership. Under these circumstances, therefore, the Internal Revenue Service shall not send to the indirect partner the notice described in section 6231(b)(1)(A).

(c) *Indirect partner files inconsistently with source partnership.*—(1) *Indirect partner notifies the Internal Revenue Service of inconsistency.*—An indirect partner who—

(i) Treats an item from a source partnership in a manner inconsistent with the treatment of that item on the source partnership's return; and

(ii) Files a statement identifying the inconsistency with the source partnership in accordance with § 301.6222(b)-1, shall not be subject to a computational adjustment to conform the treatment of that item to the treatment of that item on the return of the source partnership.

(2) *Indirect partner does not notify the Internal Revenue Service of inconsistency.*—Except as provided in paragraph (c)(3) of this section, an indirect partner who—

(i) Treats an item from a source partnership in a manner inconsistent with the treatment of that item on the source partnership's return; and

(ii) Fails to file a statement identifying the inconsistency with the source partnership in accordance with §301.6222(b)-1, is subject to a computational adjustment to conform the treatment of that item to the treatment of that item on the return of the source partnership.

(3) *Indirect partner files consistently with a pass-thru partner that notifies the Internal Revenue Service of the inconsistency.*—If an indirect partner treats an item from a source partnership in a manner consistent with the treatment of that item by a pass-thru partner through which the indirect partner holds the interest in the source partnership and that pass-thru partner—

(i) Treats that item in a manner inconsistent with the treatment of that item on the source partnership's return; and

(ii) Files a statement identifying the inconsistency with the source partnership in accordance with §301.6222(b)-1, the indirect partner is not subject to a computational adjustment to conform to the treatment of that item on the return of the source partnership.

(d) *Examples.*—The following examples illustrate the principles of this section:

*Example 1.* One of the partners in Partnership A is Partnership B, which has four equal partners C, D, E, and F. Both A and B are partnerships within the meaning of section 6231(a)(1). On its return, A reports $100,000 as B's distributive share of A's ordinary income. B, however, reports only $80,000 as its distributive share of the income and does not notify the Internal Revenue Service of this inconsistent treatment with respect to A. C reports $20,000 as its distributive share of the item. Although C reports the item consistently with B, C is subject to a computational adjustment to conform the treatment of that item on C's return to the treatment of that item on A's return.

*Example 2.* Assume the same facts as in *Example 1*, except that B notified the Internal Revenue Service of its inconsistent treatment with respect to source partnership A. C is not subject to a computational adjustment.

*Example 3.* Assume the same facts as in *Example 1*. D reports only $15,000 as D's distributive share of the income and does not report the inconsistency. F reports only $9,000 as its distributive share of the item but reports this inconsistency with respect to source partnership A. D is subject to a computational adjustment to conform the treatment of that item on D's return to the treatment of that item on A's return. F is not subject to a computational adjustment.

*Example 4.* Assume the same facts as in *Example 3*, except that F reported the inconsistency with respect to B and did not report the inconsistency with respect to source partnership A. F is subject to a computational adjustment to conform the treatment of that item on F's return to the treatment of that item on A's return.

*Example 5.* Assume the same facts as in *Example 1*. E reports $25,000 as its distributive share of the item. Regardless of whether E reports the inconsistency between its treatment of the item and that by B, E is neither subject to a computational adjustment to conform E's treatment of that item to that of B nor subject to the notice described in section 6231(b)(1)(A) with respect to any such notification of inconsistent treatment.

(e) *Effective date.*—This section is applicable to partnership taxable years beginning on or after October 4, 2001. For years beginning prior to October 4, 2001, see §301.6222(a)-2T contained in 26 CFR part 1, revised April 1, 2001. [Reg. §301.6222(a)-2.]

☐ [*T.D.* 8965, 10-3-2001.]

### [Reg. §301.6222(b)-1]

**§301.6222(b)-1. Notification to the Internal Revenue Service when partnership items are treated inconsistently.**—(a) *In general.*—The statement identifying an inconsistency described in section 6222(b)(1)(B) shall be filed by filing the form prescribed for that purpose in accordance with the instructions accompanying that form.

(b) *Effective date.*—This section is applicable to partnership taxable years beginning on or after October 4, 2001. For years beginning prior to October 4, 2001, see §301.6222(b)-1T contained in 26 CFR part 1, revised April 1, 2001. [Reg. §301.6222(b)-1.]

☐ [*T.D.* 8965, 10-3-2001.]

### [Reg. §301.6222(b)-2]

**§301.6222(b)-2. Effect of notification of inconsistent treatment.**—(a) *In general.*—Generally, if a partner treats a partnership item on the partner's return in a manner inconsistent with the treatment of that item on the partnership return, the Internal Revenue Service may make a computational adjustment to conform the treatment of

the item by the partner with the treatment of that item on the partnership return. Any additional tax resulting from that computational adjustment may be assessed without either the commencement of a partnership proceeding or notification to the partner that all partnership items arising from that partnership will be treated as nonpartnership items. However, if a partner notifies the Internal Revenue Service of the inconsistent treatment of a partnership item in the manner prescribed in §301.6222(b)-1, the Internal Revenue Service generally may not make an adjustment with respect to that partnership item unless the Internal Revenue Service—

(1) Conducts a partnership-level proceeding; or

(2) Notifies the partner under section 6231(b)(1)(A) that all partnership items arising from that partnership will be treated as nonpartnership items. See, however, §§301.6231(c)-1 and 301.6231(c)-2 for special rules relating to certain applications and claims for refund based on losses, deductions, or credits from abusive tax shelter partnerships.

(b) *Partner protected only to extent of notification.*—(1) A partner who reports the inconsistent treatment of partnership items on the partner's return is protected from computational adjustments under section 6222(c) only with respect to those partnership items the inconsistent treatment of which is reported. Thus, if a partner notifying the Internal Revenue Service with respect to one item fails to report the inconsistent treatment of another item, the partner is subject to a computational adjustment with respect to that other item.

(2) The following example illustrates the principles of this paragraph (b):

*Example.* Partner A of Partnership P treats a deduction and a capital gain arising from P on A's return in a manner that is inconsistent with the treatment of those items by P. A reports the inconsistent treatment of the deduction but not of the gain. A is subject to a computational adjustment under section 6222(c) with respect to the gain.

(c) *Adjustments in a separate proceeding not limited to conforming adjustments.*—(1) If the Internal Revenue Service conducts a separate proceeding with a partner whose partnership items are treated as nonpartnership items under section 6231(b), the Internal Revenue Service is not limited to making adjustments that merely conform the partner's return to the partnership return.

(2) *Example.*—The following example illustrates the principles of this paragraph (c):

*Example.* Partnership P allocates to E, one of its partners, a loss of $8,000. E, however, claims a loss of $9,000 and reports the inconsistent treatment. The Internal Revenue Service notifies E that it will treat all of E's partnership items arising from P as nonpartnership items. As a result of a separate proceeding with E, the Internal Revenue Service may issue a deficiency notice which could include reducing the loss to $3,000.

(d) *Effective date.*—This section is applicable to partnership taxable years beginning on or after October 4, 2001. For years beginning prior to October 4, 2001, see §301.6222(b)-2T contained in 26 CFR part 1, revised April 1, 2001. [Reg. §301.6222(b)-2.]

☐ [*T.D.* 8965, 10-3-2001.]

### [Reg. §301.6222(b)-3]

**§301.6222(b)-3. Partner receiving incorrect schedule.**—(a) *In general.*—A partner shall be treated as having complied with section 6222(b)(1)(B) and §301.6222(b)-1 with respect to a partnership item if the partner—

(1) Demonstrates that the treatment of the partnership item on the partner's return is consistent with the treatment of that item on the schedule prescribed by the Internal Revenue Service and furnished to the partner by the partnership showing the partner's share of income, credits, deductions, etc.; and

(2) Elects in accordance with the rules prescribed in paragraph (b) of this section to have this section apply with respect to that item.

(b) *Election provisions.*—(1) *Time and manner of making election.*—The election described in paragraph (a) of this section shall be made by filing a statement with the Internal Revenue Service office issuing the notice of computational adjustment within 30 days after the notice is mailed to the partner.

(2) *Contents of statement.*—The statement described in paragraph (b)(1) of this section shall be—

(i) Clearly identified as an election under section 6222(b)(2);

(ii) Signed by the partner making the election; and

(iii) Accompanied by copies of the schedule furnished to the partner by the partnership and of the notice of computational adjustment. The partner need not enclose a copy of the notice of computational adjustment, however, if the partner clearly identifies the notice of computational adjustment. Generally, the requirement described in paragraph (a)(1) of this section will be satisfied by attaching to the statement a copy of the schedule furnished to the partner by the partnership. However, if it is not clear from the information contained on the schedule that the treatment of the partnership item on the schedule is consistent with the partner's treatment of such item on the partner's return the statement shall also include an explanation of how the treatment of such item on the schedule is consistent with the treatment on the partner's return with respect to the characterization, timing, and amount of such item.

(c) *Effective date.*—This section is applicable to partnership taxable years beginning on or after October 4, 2001. For years beginning prior to October 4, 2001, see § 301.6222(b)-3T contained in 26 CFR part 1, revised April 1, 2001. [Reg. § 301.6222(b)-3.]

☐ [*T.D. 8965, 10-3-2001.*]

### [Reg. § 301.6223-1]

**§ 301.6223-1. Partnership representative.**—(a) *Each partnership must have a partnership representative.*—A partnership subject to subchapter C of chapter 63 of the Internal Revenue Code (subchapter C of chapter 63) for a partnership taxable year must designate a partnership representative for the partnership taxable year in accordance with this section. There may be only one designated partnership representative for a partnership taxable year at any time. The designation of a partnership representative for a partnership taxable year under this section remains in effect until the date on which the designation of the partnership representative is terminated by valid resignation (as described in paragraph (d) of this section), valid revocation (as described in paragraph (e) of this section), or a determination by the Internal Revenue Service (IRS) that the designation is not in effect (as described in paragraph (f) of this section). A designation of a partnership representative for a partnership taxable year under paragraphs (e) or (f) of this section supersedes all prior designations of a partnership representative for that year. If required by forms, instructions, and other guidance prescribed by the IRS, a partnership representative must update the partnership representative's contact information when such information changes. Only a person designated as a partnership representative in accordance with this section will be recognized as the partnership representative under section 6223. A power of attorney (including a Form 2848, Power of Attorney) may not be used to designate a partnership representative. See § 301.6223-2(a), (b), and (c) with regard to the binding effect of actions taken by the partnership representative. See § 301.6223-2(d) with regard to the sole authority of the partnership representative to act on behalf of the partnership. See paragraph (f) of this section for rules regarding designation of a partnership representative by the IRS.

(b) *Eligibility to serve as a partnership representative.*—(1) *In general.*—Any person (as defined in section 7701(a)(1)) that meets the requirements of paragraphs (b)(2) and (3) of this section, as applicable, is eligible to serve as a partnership representative, including a wholly owned entity disregarded as separate from its owner for federal tax purposes. A person designated under this section as partnership representative is deemed to be eligible to serve as the partnership representative unless and until the IRS determines that the person is ineligible. A partnership can designate itself as its own partnership representative provided it meets the requirements of paragraphs (b)(2) and (3) of this section.

(2) *Substantial presence in the United States.*—A person must have substantial presence in the United States to be the partnership representative. A person has substantial presence in the United States for the purposes of this section if—

(i) The person makes themselves available to meet in person with the IRS in the United States at a reasonable time and place as determined by the IRS in accordance with § 301.7605-1; and

(ii) The person has a United States taxpayer identification number, a street address that is in the United States and a telephone number with a United States area code.

(3) *Eligibility of an entity to be a partnership representative.*—(i) *In general.*—A person who is not an individual may be a partnership representative only if an individual who meets the requirements of paragraph (b)(2) of this section is appointed by the partnership as the sole individual through whom the partnership representative will act for all purposes under subchapter C of chapter 63. A partnership representative meeting the requirements of this paragraph (b)(3) is an *entity partnership representative,* and the individual through whom such entity partnership representative acts is the *designated individual.* Designated individual status automatically terminates on the date that the designation of the entity partnership representative for which the designated individual was appointed is no longer in effect in accordance with paragraph (d), (e), or (f) of this section.

(ii) *Appointment of a designated individual.*—A designated individual must be appointed by the partnership at the time of the designation of the entity partnership representative in the manner prescribed by the IRS in forms, instructions, and other guidance. Accordingly, if the entity partnership representative is designated on the partnership return for the taxable year in accordance with paragraph (c)(2) of this section, the designated individual must be appointed by the partnership at that time. Similarly, if the entity partnership representative is designated under paragraph (e) of this section (regarding revocation and subsequent designation after revocation of a partnership representative), the designated individual must be appointed at that time. If the partnership fails to appoint a designated individual at the time and in the manner set forth in this paragraph (b)(3)(ii), the IRS may determine that the entity partnership representative designation is not in effect under paragraph (f) of this section.

(4) *Examples.*—The following examples illustrate the rules of this paragraph (b).

*Example 1.* Partnership designates PR as its partnership representative for its 2018 tax year on its timely filed 2018 partnership return. The IRS initiates an administrative proceeding with respect to Partnership's 2018 tax year. PR has a United States taxpayer identification number, a United States street address, and a phone number with a United States area code. The IRS contacts PR and requests an in-person meeting with respect to the administrative proceeding. PR works with the IRS and agrees to meet. PR has substantial presence in the United States because she meets all the requirements under paragraph (b)(2) of this section.

*Example 2.* The facts are the same as in *Example 1* of this paragraph (b)(4), except that PR is an entity and Partnership appointed DI, a designated individual to act on behalf of PR for its 2018 tax year on its timely filed 2018 partnership return. DI has a United States taxpayer identification number and a phone number with a United States area code. However, the address provided for DI is not a United States address. Accordingly, PR is not an eligible partnership representative because PR is an entity and DI does not satisfy the requirements of paragraph (b)(3)(i) of this section. Although DI does not have substantial presence in the United States under paragraph (b)(2) of this section and therefore PR is not an eligible partnership representative, until there is a resignation or revocation under paragraph (d) or (e) of this section or until the IRS determines the partnership representative designation is no longer in effect under paragraph (f) of this section, the designation of PR as the partnership representative remains in effect in accordance with paragraph (a) of this section, and Partnership and all its partners are bound by the actions of PR as the partnership representative.

*Example 3.* The facts are the same as in *Example 1* of this paragraph (b)(4), except PR works in a foreign country and spends the majority of her time there. Unless PR otherwise fails to meet one of the requirements under paragraph (b)(2) of this section, PR has substantial presence in the United States. However, even if PR fails to meet one of the requirements under paragraph (b)(2) of this section, until there is a resignation or revocation under paragraph (d) or (e) of this section and the IRS determines the partnership representative designation is no longer in effect under paragraph (f) of this section, the designation of PR as the partnership representative remains in effect in accordance with paragraph (a) of this section, and Partnership and all its partners are bound by the actions of PR as the partnership representative.

(c) *Designation of partnership representative by the partnership.*—(1) *In general.*—The partnership must designate a partnership representative separately for each taxable year. The designation of a partnership representative for one taxable year is effective only for the taxable year for which it is made.

(2) *Designation.*—Except in the case of a designation of a partnership representative (and the appointment of the designated individual, if applicable) after an event described in paragraph (d) of this section (regarding resignation), paragraph (e) of this section (regarding revocation by the partnership), or paragraph (f) of this section (regarding designation made by the IRS), or except as prescribed in forms, instructions, and other guidance, designation of a partnership representative (and the appointment of the designated individual, if applicable) must be made on the partnership return for the partnership taxable year to which the designation relates and must include all of the information required by forms, instructions, and other guidance, including information about the designated individual if paragraph (b)(3) of this section applies. The designation of the partnership representative (and the appointment of the designated individual, if applicable) is effective on the date that the partnership return is filed.

(3) *Example.*—The following example illustrates the rules of this paragraph (c).

*Example.* Partnership properly designates PR1 as its partnership representative for taxable year 2018 on its 2018 partnership return. Partnership designates PR2 as its partnership representative for taxable year 2021 on its 2021 partnership return. In 2022, the IRS mails Partnership a notice of administrative proceeding under section 6231(a)(1) with respect to Partnership's 2018 taxable year. PR1 is the partnership representative for the 2018 partnership taxable year, notwithstanding the designation of PR2 as partnership representative for the 2021 partnership taxable year.

(d) *Resignations.*—(1) *In general.*—A partnership representative or designated individual may resign as partnership representative or designated individual, as applicable, for a partnership taxable year for any reason by notifying the IRS in writing of the resignation in accordance with forms, instructions, and other guidance prescribed by the IRS. A resigning partnership representative may not designate a successor partnership representative. A resigning designated individual may not designate a successor designated individual or partnership representative. No later than 30 days after the IRS receives a written notification of resignation, the IRS will send written confirmation of receipt of the written notification to the partnership and the resigning partnership representative (to the attention of the designated individual if appropriate). A failure by the IRS to send any notification under this paragraph (d) does not invalidate a valid resignation made pursuant to this paragraph (d). A failure by the partnership representative (or designated individual, if the designated individual is the person resigning) to satisfy the requirements of this paragraph (d) is treated as if there were no resignation, and the partnership representative designation (and designated individual appointment, if applicable) remains in effect until the designation (or appointment) is terminated by valid resignation (as described in this paragraph (d)), valid revocation by the partnership (as described in paragraph (e) of this section), or a determination by the IRS that the designation is not in effect (as described in paragraph (f) of this section). See §301.6223-2 for binding nature of actions taken by the partnership representative or designated individual on behalf of a partnership representative, if applicable, prior to resignation.

(2) *Time for resignation.*—A partnership representative or designated individual may submit the written notification of resignation described in paragraph (d)(1) of this section to the IRS only after the IRS issues a notice of administrative proceeding (NAP) under section 6231(a)(1) for the partnership taxable year for which the partnership representative designation is in effect or at such other time as prescribed by the IRS in forms, instructions, or other guidance. If the IRS withdraws the NAP pursuant to §301.6231-1(f), any valid resignation by the partnership representative or designated individual under this paragraph (d) prior to the withdrawal of the NAP remains in effect.

(3) *Effective date of resignation.*—A valid resignation is immediately effective upon the IRS's receipt of the written notification described in paragraph (d)(1) of this section. As of the effective date of the resignation—

(i) The resigning partnership representative (and designated individual, if applicable) may not take any action on behalf of the partnership with respect to the partnership taxable year affected by the resignation;

(ii) The partnership representative designation is no longer in effect with respect to the partnership taxable year affected by the resignation;

(iii) In the case of a resigning entity partnership representative, the appointment of the designated individual is no longer in effect with respect to the partnership taxable year affected by the resignation; and

(iv) In the case of a resigning designated individual, the designation of the entity partnership representative is no longer in effect with respect to the partnership taxable year affected by the resignation.

(e) *Revocations.*—(1) *In general.*—A partnership may revoke a designation of a partnership representative or appointment of a designated individual for a partnership taxable year for any reason by notifying the IRS in writing of the revocation in accordance with forms, instructions, and other guidance prescribed by the IRS. The partnership may make such revocation regardless of when and how the designation or appointment was made, except as provided in paragraph (e)(6) of this section (regarding designation by the IRS). The revocation must include the designation of a successor partnership representative (and the appointment of a designated individual, if applicable). In the case of a revocation of only the designated individual appointment, the partnership must designate a successor designated individual. No later than 30 days after the IRS receives a written notification of revocation submitted at the time described in paragraph (e)(2)(i) of this section, the IRS will send written confirmation of receipt of the written notification to the partnership, the

revoked partnership representative or, in the case of a revocation of only the appointment of a designated individual, to the revoked designated individual, and to the newly designated partnership representative. In the case of a revocation of an entity partnership representative, the notification will be sent to the entity partnership representative, to the attention of the designated individual. A failure by the IRS to send any notification under this paragraph (e) does not invalidate a valid revocation made pursuant to this paragraph (e). A failure by the partnership to satisfy the requirements of this paragraph (e), including failure to designate a successor, is treated as if no revocation has occurred and the partnership representative designation (and designated individual appointment, if applicable) remains in effect until the designation (or appointment) is terminated either by valid resignation (as described in paragraph (d) of this section), valid revocation by the partnership (as described in this paragraph (e)), or determination by the IRS that the designation is not in effect (as described in paragraph (f) of this section). See §301.6223-2 for binding nature of actions taken by the partnership representative or designated individual on behalf of a partnership representative, if applicable, prior to revocation.

(2) *Time for revocation.*—(i) *Revocation during an administrative proceeding.*—Except as provided in paragraph (e)(2)(ii) of this section or in forms, instructions, or other guidance prescribed by the IRS, a partnership may revoke a designation of a partnership representative or appointment of a designated individual only after the IRS issues a notice of selection for examination or a NAP under section 6231(a)(1) for the partnership taxable year for which the designation or appointment is in effect. If the IRS withdraws the NAP pursuant to §301.6231-1(f), any valid revocation of a partnership representative designation or designated individual appointment under this paragraph (e) prior to the withdrawal of the NAP remains in effect.

(ii) *Revocation with an AAR.*—The partnership may revoke a designation of a partnership representative or appointment of a designated individual for the taxable year prior to receiving a notice of selection for examination or a NAP by filing a valid administrative adjustment request (AAR) in accordance with section 6227 for a partnership taxable year. A partnership may not use the form prescribed by the IRS for filing an AAR solely for the purpose of revoking a designation of a partnership representative or appointment of a designated individual. See §301.6227-1 for the rules regarding the time and manner of filing an AAR.

(3) *Effective date of revocation.*—Except as described in paragraph (e)(6)(ii) of this section (regarding the effective date of a revocation of a partnership representative designated by the IRS under paragraph (f)(5) of this section), a valid revocation is immediately effective upon the IRS's receipt of the written notification described in paragraph (e)(1) of this section. A revocation of a partnership representative designation and a designation of a new partnership representative (and appointment of a new designated individual, if applicable) is effective on the date the partnership files a valid AAR. Similarly, a revocation of a designated individual appointment and appointment of a new designated individual is effective on the date the partnership files a valid AAR. As of the effective date of the revocation—

(i) The revoked partnership representative (and designated individual, if applicable) may not take any action on behalf of the partnership with respect to the partnership taxable year affected by the revocation;

(ii) The designation of the revoked partnership representative is no longer in effect, and the successor partnership representative designation (and designated individual appointment, if applicable) is in effect with respect to the partnership taxable year affected by the revocation;

(iii) In the case of a revoked entity partnership representative, the appointment of the designated individual is no longer in effect with respect to the partnership taxable year affected by the revocation; and

(iv) In the case of a revoked designated individual where the designation of the entity partnership representative has not been revoked, the revoked designated individual may not take any action on behalf of the partnership with respect to the partnership taxable year affected by the revocation, the appointment of the revoked designated individual is no longer in effect, and the appointment of the successor designated individual is in effect.

(4) *Partners who may sign revocation.*—A revocation under this paragraph (e) must be signed by a person who was a partner at any time during the partnership taxable year to which the revocation relates or as provided in forms, instructions, and other guidance prescribed by the IRS.

(5) *Form of the revocation.*—The written notification of revocation described in paragraph (e)(1) of this section must include the items described in this paragraph (e)(5). A notification of revocation de-

scribed in paragraph (e)(1) of this section that does not include each of the following items is not a valid revocation:

(i) A certification under penalties of perjury that the person signing the notification is a partner described in paragraph (e)(4) of this section authorized by the partnership to revoke the designation of the partnership representative (or appointment of the designated individual, if applicable).

(ii) A statement that the person signing the notification is revoking the designation of the partnership representative (or appointment of the designated individual, if applicable);

(iii) A designation of a successor partnership representative (and appointment of a designated individual, if applicable) in accordance with this section and forms, instructions, and other guidance prescribed by the IRS; and

(iv) In the case of a revocation of an appointment of a designated individual, appointment of a successor designated individual in accordance with this section and forms, instructions, and other guidance prescribed by the IRS.

(6) *Partnership representative designated by the IRS.*—(i) *In general.*—If a partnership representative is designated (and a designated individual is appointed, if applicable) by the IRS pursuant to paragraph (f)(5) of this section, the partnership may only revoke that designation (or the appointment of the designated individual, if applicable) with the permission of the IRS, which the IRS will not unreasonably withhold.

(ii) *Effective date of revocation.*—The effective date of any revocation submitted in accordance with paragraph (e)(6)(i) of this section is the date on which the IRS sends notification that the revocation is valid.

(7) *Multiple revocations.*—(i) *In general.*—The IRS may determine that a designation is not in effect under paragraph (f) of this section if:

(A) The IRS receives a revocation of a designation of a partnership representative or appointment of a designated individual, and

(B) Within the 90-day period prior to the date the revocation described in paragraph (e)(7)(i)(A) of this section was received, the IRS received another revocation for the same partnership taxable year.

(ii) *Time limitation.*—The IRS may not determine that a designation is not in effect in accordance with paragraph (e)(7)(i) of this section later than 90 days after the IRS's receipt of the revocation described in paragraph (e)(7)(i)(A) of this section.

(8) *Examples.*—The following examples illustrate the rules of this paragraph (e).

*Example 1.* Partnership properly designates PR, an individual, as partnership representative for its 2018 taxable year on its timely filed 2018 partnership return. In 2020, Partnership mails written notification to the IRS to revoke designation of PR as its partnership representative for Partnership's 2018 taxable year. The revocation is not made in connection with an AAR for Partnership's 2018 taxable year, and the IRS has not mailed Partnership a notice of selection for examination or a NAP under section 6231(a)(1) with respect to Partnership's 2018 taxable year. Because the revocation was not made when permitted under paragraph (e)(2) of this section, the revocation is not effective and B remains the partnership representative for Partnership's 2018 taxable year unless and until B's status as partnership representative is properly revoked under paragraph (e) of this section or terminated in accordance with paragraph (d) (regarding resignation) or (f) (regarding IRS designation) of this section.

*Example 2.* During an administrative proceeding with respect to Partnership's 2018 taxable year, Partnership provides the IRS with written notification to revoke its designation of PR, an individual, as its partnership representative for the 2018 taxable year. The written notification does not include a designation of a new partnership representative for Partnership's 2018 taxable year. Because the revocation does not include a designation of a new partnership representative as required under paragraph (e)(1) of this section, the revocation is not effective and PR remains the partnership representative for Partnership's 2018 taxable year unless and until B's status as partnership representative is properly revoked under paragraph (e) of this section or terminated in accordance with paragraph (d) (regarding resignation) or (f) (regarding IRS designation) of this section.

(f) *Designation of the partnership representative by the IRS.*—(1) *In general.*—If the IRS determines that a designation of a partnership representative is not in effect for a partnership taxable year in accordance with paragraph (f)(2) of this section, the IRS will notify the partnership that a partnership representative designation is not in effect. The IRS will also notify the most recent partnership represen-

tative for the partnership taxable year, except as described in paragraph (f)(2)(iii) of this section. In the case of an entity partnership representative, the notification will be sent to the entity partnership representative, to the attention of the designated individual. The determination that a designation is not in effect is effective on the date the IRS mails the notification. Except as described in paragraph (f)(4) of this section, the partnership may designate, in accordance with paragraph (f)(3) of this section, a successor partnership representative (and designated individual, if applicable) eligible under paragraph (b) of this section within 30 days of the date the IRS mails the notification. In the case of a resignation of a partnership representative, this notification may include the written confirmation of receipt described in paragraph (d)(1) of this section. See paragraph (f)(2)(iv) of this section. If the partnership does not designate a successor within 30 days from the date of IRS notification, the IRS will designate a partnership representative in accordance with paragraph (f)(5) of this section. A partnership representative designation made in accordance with paragraphs (c), (e), or (f) of this section remains in effect until the IRS determines the designation is not in effect. See §301.6223-2 for binding nature of actions taken by the partnership representative or designated individual on behalf of a partnership representative, if applicable, prior to a determination by the IRS that the designation is not in effect.

(2) *IRS determination that partnership representative designation not in effect.*—The IRS may, but is not required to, determine that a partnership representative designation is not in effect. The IRS is not obligated to search for or otherwise seek out information related to the circumstances in which the IRS may determine a partnership representative designation is not in effect, and the fact that the IRS is aware of any such circumstances does not obligate the IRS to determine that a partnership representative designation is not in effect. The IRS may determine that the partnership representative designation is not in effect if the IRS determines that—

(i) The partnership representative or the designated individual does not have substantial presence as described in paragraph (b)(2) of this section;

(ii) The partnership failed to appoint a designated individual as described in paragraph (b)(3) of this section, as applicable;

(iii) The partnership failed to make a valid designation as described in paragraph (c) of this section;

(iv) The partnership representative or designated individual resigns as described in paragraph (d) of this section;

(v) The partnership has made multiple revocations as described in paragraph (e)(7) of this section; or

(vi) The partnership representative designation is no longer in effect as described in other published guidance.

(3) *Designation by the partnership during the 30-day period.*—Designation of a partnership representative (and appointment of a designated individual, if applicable) by the partnership during the 30-day period described in paragraph (f)(1) of this section must be made in accordance with forms, instructions, and other guidance prescribed by the IRS. If the partnership fails to provide all information required by forms, instructions, and other guidance, the partnership will have failed to make a designation (and appointment, if applicable). If the partnership does not fully comply with the requirement of this paragraph (f)(3) within the 30-day period described in paragraph (f)(1) of this section, the IRS will designate a partnership representative (and appoint a designated individual, if applicable).

(4) *No opportunity for designation by the partnership in the case of multiple revocations.*—In the event that the IRS determines a partnership representative designation is not in effect due to multiple revocations as described in paragraph (e)(7) of this section, the partnership will not be given an opportunity to designate the successor partnership representative prior to the designation by the IRS as described in paragraph (f)(5) of this section. However, see paragraph (e)(6) of this section regarding revocation of a partnership representative designated by the IRS.

(5) *Designation by the IRS.*—(i) *In general.*—The IRS designates a partnership representative under this paragraph (f)(5) by notifying the partnership of the name, address, and telephone number of the new partnership representative. If the IRS designates an entity partnership representative, the IRS will also appoint a designated individual to act on behalf of the entity partnership representative. The designation of a partnership representative (and appointment of a designated individual, if applicable) by the IRS is effective on the date on which the IRS mails the notification of the designation (and appointment, if applicable) to the partnership. The IRS will also mail a copy of the notification of the designation (and appointment, if applicable) to the new partnership representative (through the new designated individual, if applicable) that has been designated (and appointed, if applicable) by the IRS under this section.

(ii) *Factors considered when partnership representative designated by the IRS.*—The IRS will ordinarily consider one or more of the factors set forth in this paragraph (f)(5)(ii) when determining whom to designate as partnership representative. No single factor is determinative, and other than as described in paragraph (f)(5)(iii) of this section, the IRS may exercise its discretion to designate a person as partnership representative even if none of the factors are applicable to such person. The factors are not requirements for eligibility to be designated by the IRS as partnership representative; the only requirements for eligibility are described under paragraph (b) of this section. The IRS is not obligated to search for or otherwise seek out information related to the factors, and the fact that the IRS is aware of any information related to such factors does not obligate the IRS to designate a particular person. Although the IRS may designate any person to be the partnership representative, a principal consideration in determining whom to designate as a partnership representative is whether there is a reviewed year partner that is eligible to serve as the partnership representative in accordance with paragraph (b)(1) of this section or whether there is a partner at the time the partnership representative designation is made that is eligible to serve as the partnership representative. Other factors that will ordinarily be considered by the IRS in determining whom to designate as a partnership representative include, but are not limited to:

(A) The views of the partners having a majority interest in the partnership regarding the designation;

(B) The general knowledge of the person in tax matters and the administrative operation of the partnership;

(C) The person's access to the books and records of the partnership;

(D) Whether the person is a United States person (within the meaning of section 7701(a)(30)); and

(E) The profits interest of the partner in the case of a partner.

(iii) *IRS employees.*—The IRS will not designate a current employee, agent, or contractor of the IRS as the partnership representative unless that employee, agent, or contractor was a reviewed year partner or is currently a partner in the partnership.

(6) *Examples.*—The following examples illustrate the rules of this paragraph (f).

*Example 1.* The IRS determines that Partnership has designated a partnership representative that does not have substantial presence in the United States as defined in paragraph (b)(2) of this section. The IRS may, but is not required to, determine that the designation is not in effect and designate a new partnership representative after following the procedures in this paragraph (f).

*Example 2.* Partnership designates as its partnership representative a corporation but fails to appoint a designated individual to act on behalf of the corporation as required under paragraph (b)(3) of this section. The IRS may, but is not required to, determine that the partnership representative designation is not in effect and may designate a new partnership representative after following the procedures in this paragraph (f).

*Example 3.* The partnership representative resigns pursuant to paragraph (d) of this section. The IRS mails Partnership a notification informing Partnership that no designation is in effect and that the IRS plans to designate a new partnership representative. Partnership fails to respond within 30 days of the date the IRS mails the notification. The IRS must designate a partnership representative pursuant to this paragraph (f).

*Example 4.* Partnership designated on its partnership return a partnership representative, PR1. After Partnership received a NAP, Partnership submits to the IRS the form described in paragraph (e)(4) of this section requesting the revocation of PR1's designation as partnership representative and designating PR2 as the partnership representative. Sixty days later, Partnership signs and submits a form described in paragraph (e)(4) of this section requesting the revocation of PR2's designation as partnership representative and designating PR3 as the partnership representative. The IRS accepts the revocation of PR2 and designation of PR3 as valid and effective upon receipt pursuant to paragraph (e)(3) of this section. However, because PR2's revocation was within 90 days of PR1's revocation, the IRS may determine within 90 days of IRS's receipt of PR2's revocation, pursuant to paragraphs (e)(7) and (f)(2) of this section, that there is no designation in effect due to multiple revocations. The IRS may then designate a new partnership representative pursuant to this paragraph (f) without allowing Partnership an opportunity to designate a partnership representative within the 30-day period described in paragraph (f)(1) of this section.

(g) *Reliance on forms required by this section.*—The IRS may rely on any form or other document filed or submitted under this section as evidence of the designation, resignation, or revocation on such form

and as evidence of the date on which such form was filed or submitted relating to a designation, resignation, or revocation.

(h) *Applicability date.*—(1) *In general.*—Except as provided in paragraph (h)(2) of this section, this section applies to partnership taxable years beginning after December 31, 2017.

(2) *Election under § 301.9100-22 in effect.*—This section applies to any partnership taxable years beginning after November 2, 2015 and before January 1, 2018 for which a valid election under § 301.9100-22 is in effect. [Reg. § 301.6223-1.]

☐ [T.D. 9839, 8-6-2018 *(corrected 9-3-2019).*]

**[Reg. § 301.6223-2]**

**§ 301.6223-2. Binding effect of actions of the partnership and partnership representative.**—(a) *Binding nature of actions by partnership and final decision in a partnership proceeding.*—The actions of the partnership and the partnership representative taken under subchapter C of chapter 63 of the Internal Revenue Code (subchapter C of chapter 63) and any final decision in a proceeding brought under subchapter C of chapter 63 with respect to the partnership bind the partnership, all partners of the partnership (including partnership-partners as defined in § 301.6241-1(a)(7) that have a valid election under section 6221(b) in effect for any taxable year that ends with or within the taxable year of the partnership), and any other person whose tax liability is determined in whole or in part by taking into account directly or indirectly adjustments determined under subchapter C of chapter 63 (for example, indirect partners as defined in § 301.6241-1(a)(4)). For instance, a settlement agreement entered into by the partnership representative on behalf of the partnership, a notice of final partnership adjustment (FPA) with respect to the partnership that is not contested by the partnership, or the final decision of a court with respect to the partnership if the FPA is contested, binds all persons described in the preceding sentence.

(b) *Actions by the partnership representative before termination of designation.*—A termination of the designation of a partnership representative because of a resignation under § 301.6223-1(d) or a revocation under § 301.6223-1(e), or as a result of a determination by the Internal Revenue Service (IRS) under § 301.6223-1(f) that the designation is not in effect, does not affect the validity of any action taken by that partnership representative during the period prior to such termination. For example, if a partnership representative properly designated under § 301.6223-1 consented to an extension of the period of limitations on making adjustments under section 6235(b) in accordance with § 301.6235-1(d), that extension remains valid even after termination of the designation of that partnership representative.

(c) *Actions by the partnership representative upon withdrawal of notice of administrative proceeding.*—If the IRS issues a notice of administrative proceeding (NAP) under section 6231(a)(1) and subsequently withdraws such NAP pursuant to § 301.6231-1(f), any actions taken by a partnership representative (or successor partnership representative after a change to the partnership representative that occurred after the issuance of the NAP and before the NAP was withdrawn) are binding as described in paragraph (a) of this section even though the NAP has been withdrawn and has no effect for purposes of subchapter C of chapter 63.

(d) *Partnership representative has the sole authority to act on behalf of the partnership.*—(1) *In general.*—The partnership representative has the sole authority to act on behalf of the partnership for all purposes under subchapter C of chapter 63. In the case of an entity partnership representative, the designated individual has the sole authority to act on behalf of the partnership representative and the partnership. Except for a partner that is the partnership representative or the designated individual, no partner, or any other person, may participate in an administrative proceeding without the permission of the IRS. The failure of the partnership representative to follow any state law, partnership agreement, or other document or agreement has no effect on the authority of the partnership representative or the designated individual as described in section 6223, § 301.6223-1, and this section. Nothing in this section affects, or otherwise restricts, the ability of a partnership representative to authorize a person to represent the partnership representative, in the partnership representative's capacity as the partnership representative, before the IRS under a valid power of attorney in a proceeding involving the partnership under subchapter C of chapter 63.

(2) *Designation provides authority to bind the partnership.*—(i) *Partnership representative.*—A partnership representative, by virtue of being designated under section 6223 and § 301.6223-1, has the authority to bind the partnership for all purposes under subchapter C of chapter 63.

(ii) *Designated individual.*—A partnership that is required to appoint a designated individual described under § 301.6223-1(b)(3)(i) acts through such designated individual. By virtue of being appointed as part of the designation of the partnership representative under §301.6223-1, the designated individual has the sole authority to bind the partnership representative and therefore the partnership, its partners, and any other person as described in paragraph (a) of this section for all purposes under subchapter C of chapter 63 so long as the partnership representative designation and designated individual appointment are in effect.

(e) *Examples.*—The following examples illustrate the rules of this section.

*Example 1.* Partnership designates a partnership representative, PR, on its timely filed partnership return for 2020. PR is a partner in Partnership. The partnership agreement for Partnership includes a clause that requires PR to consult with an identified management group of partners in Partnership before taking any action with respect to an administrative proceeding before the IRS. The IRS initiates an administrative proceeding with respect to Partnership's 2020 taxable year. During the course of the administrative proceeding, PR consents to an extension of the period of limitations on making adjustments under section 6235(b) allowing additional time for the IRS to mail an FPA. PR failed to consult with the management group of partners prior to agreeing to this extension of time. PR's consent provided to the IRS to extend the time period is valid and binding on Partnership because, pursuant to section 6223, PR, as the designated partnership representative, has authority to bind Partnership and all its partners.

*Example 2.* Partnership designates a partnership representative, PR, on its timely filed partnership return for 2020. PR is not a partner in Partnership. During an administrative proceeding with respect to Partnership's 2020 taxable year, PR agrees to certain partnership adjustments and within 45 days after the issuance of the FPA elects the alternative to payment of the imputed underpayment under section 6226. Certain partners in Partnership challenge the actions taken by PR during the administrative proceeding and the validity of the section 6226 statements furnished to those partners, alleging that PR was never authorized to act on behalf of Partnership under state law or the partnership agreement. Because PR was designated by Partnership as the partnership representative under section 6223 and this section, PR was authorized to act on behalf of Partnership for all purposes under subchapter C of chapter 63, and the IRS may rely on that designation as conclusive evidence of PR's authority to act on behalf of Partnership.

*Example 3.* Partnership designates an entity partnership representative, EPR, and appoints an individual, A, as the designated individual on its timely filed partnership return for 2020. EPR is a C corporation. A is unaffiliated with EPR and is not an officer, director, or employee of EPR. During an administrative proceeding with respect to Partnership's 2020 taxable year, A, acting for EPR, agrees to an extension of the period of limitations on making adjustments under section 6235(b) from March 15, 2024 to December 31, 2024. The IRS mails an FPA with respect to the 2020 partnership taxable year on December 13, 2024, before expiration of the extended period of limitations on making adjustments as agreed to by EPR, but after the expiration of the unextended period of limitations on making adjustments. Partnership challenges the FPA as untimely, alleging that A was not authorized under state law to act on behalf of EPR and thus the extension agreement was invalid. Because A was appointed by the partnership as the designated individual to act on behalf of EPR, A was authorized to act on behalf of EPR for all purposes under subchapter C of chapter 63, and the IRS may rely on that appointment as conclusive evidence of A's authority to act on behalf of EPR and Partnership.

*Example 4.* The partnership representative, PR, consents to an extension of the period of limitations on making adjustments under section 6235(b) and §301.6235-1(d) for Partnership for the partnership taxable year. After signing the consent, PR resigns as partnership representative in accordance with §301.6223-1(d). The consent to extend the period of limitations on making adjustments under section 6235(b) remains valid even after PR resigns.

*Example 5.* Partnership designates a partnership representative who does not make themselves available to meet with the IRS in person in the United States as required by §301.6223-1(b). Although the partnership representative does not have substantial presence in the United States within the meaning of §301.6223-1(b)(2), until a termination occurs under §301.6223-1(d) or (e) or the IRS determines the partnership representative designation is no longer in effect under §301.6223-1(f), the partnership representative designation remains in effect, and Partnership and all its partners are bound by the actions of the partnership representative.

*Example 6.* Partnership designates PR1 as the partnership representative on its timely filed partnership return for 2020. On September 1, 2022, the IRS sends a NAP for the 2020 taxable year to Partnership and PR, and Partnership revokes PR1's designation and designates

PR2 as the partnership representative in accordance with §301.6223-1(e). On November 1, 2023, PR2 consents to an extension of the period of limitations on making adjustments under section 6235(b) and §301.6235(d) for Partnership's 2020 taxable year. On December 1, 2023, the IRS then withdraws the NAP. PR2 remains the partnership representative, and the consent to extend the period of limitations on making adjustments under section 6235(b) remains valid even after the NAP is withdrawn.

(f) *Applicability date.*—(1) *In general.*—Except as provided in paragraph (f)(2) of this section, this section applies to partnership taxable years beginning after December 31, 2017.

(2) *Election under §301.9100-22 in effect.*—This section applies to any partnership taxable years beginning after November 2, 2015 and before January 1, 2018 for which a valid election under §301.9100-22 is in effect. [Reg. §301.6223-2.]

☐ [*T.D.* 9839, 8-6-2018.]

### [Reg. §301.6223(a)-1]

**§301.6223(a)-1. Notice sent to tax matters partner.**—(a) *In general.*—For purposes of subchapter C of chapter 63 of the Internal Revenue Code, a notice is treated as mailed to the tax matters partner on the earlier of—

(1) The date on which the notice is mailed to "THE TAX MATTERS PARTNER" at the address of the partnership (as provided on the partnership return, except as updated under §301.6223(c)-1); or

(2) The date on which the notice is mailed to the person who is the tax matters partner at the address of that person (as provided on the partner's return, except as updated under §301.6223(c)-1) or the partnership. See §301.6223(c)-1 for rules relating to the information used by the Internal Revenue Service in providing notices, etc.

(b) *Example.*—The provisions of this section may be illustrated by the following example:

*Example.* Partnership P designates B as its tax matters partner in accordance with §301.6231(a)(7)-1(b). On December 1 a notice of the beginning of an administrative proceeding is mailed to "THE TAX MATTERS PARTNER" at the address of P. On January 10, a copy of the notice is mailed to B at B's address. December 1 is treated as the date that the notice was mailed to the tax matters partner.

(c) *Effective date.*—This section is applicable to partnership taxable years beginning on or after October 4, 2001. For years beginning prior to October 4, 2001, see §301.6223(a)-2T contained in 26 CFR part 1, revised April 1, 2001. [Reg. §301.6223(a)-1.]

☐ [*T.D.* 8965, 10-3-2001.]

### [Reg. §301.6223(a)-2]

**§301.6223(a)-2. Withdrawal of notice of the beginning of an administrative proceeding.**—(a) *In general.*—If the Internal Revenue Service, within 45 days after the day on which the notice specified in section 6223(a)(1) is mailed to the tax matters partner, decides not to propose any adjustments to the partnership return as filed, the Internal Revenue Service may withdraw the notice specified in section 6223(a)(1) by mailing a letter to that effect to the tax matters partner within that 45-day period. Even if the Internal Revenue Service does not withdraw the notice specified in section 6223(a)(1), the Internal Revenue Service is not required to issue a notice of final partnership administrative adjustment. If the Internal Revenue Service withdraws the notice specified in section 6223(a)(1), neither the Internal Revenue Service nor the tax matters partner is required to furnish any notice with respect to that proceeding to any other partner. Except as provided in paragraph (b) of this section, a notice specified in section 6223(a)(1) which has been withdrawn shall be treated for purposes of subchapter C of chapter 63 of the Internal Revenue Code as if that notice had never been mailed to the tax matters partner.

(b) *Internal Revenue Service may not reissue notice except under certain circumstances.*—If the notice specified in section 6223(a)(1) was mailed to the tax matters partner with respect to a partnership taxable year and that notice was later withdrawn as provided in paragraph (a) of this section, the Internal Revenue Service shall not mail a second notice specified in section 6223(a)(1) with respect to that taxable year unless—

(1) There is evidence of fraud, malfeasance, collusion, concealment, or misrepresentation of a material fact;

(2) The prior proceeding involved the misapplication or erroneous interpretation of an established Internal Revenue Service position existing at the time of the previous examination, or the failure to make an adjustment based on such a position; or

(3) Other circumstances exist which indicate that failure to reissue the notice would be a serious administrative omission.

(c) *Effective date.*—This section is applicable to partnership taxable years beginning on or after October 4, 2001. For years beginning prior to October 4, 2001, see §301.6223(a)-2T contained in 26 CFR part 1, revised April 1, 2001. [Reg. §301.6223(a)-2.]

□ [*T.D.* 8965, 10-3-2001.]

### [Reg. §301.6223(b)-1]

**§301.6223(b)-1. Notice group.**—(a) *In general.*—If a group of partners having in the aggregate a 5 percent or more interest in the profits of a partnership requests and designates one of their members to receive the notices described in section 6223(a)(1) and (2), the member so designated shall be treated as a partner to whom section 6223(a) applies. Thus, the designated representative is entitled to receive any notice described in section 6223(a) that is mailed to the tax matters partner 30 days or more after the day on which the Internal Revenue Service receives the request from the group.

(b) *Request for notice.*—(1) *In general.*—The Internal Revenue Service shall mail to the member of the notice group designated to receive such notice any notice described in section 6223(a) that is mailed to the tax matters partner 30 days or more after the day on which the Internal Revenue Service receives the request for notice from the group if such request for notice is made in accordance with the rules prescribed in this paragraph (b).

(2) *Content of request.*—The request for notice from a notice group shall—

(i) Identify the partnership by name, address, and taxpayer identification number;

(ii) Specify the taxable year or years for which the notice group is formed;

(iii) Designate the member of the group to receive the notices;

(iv) Set out the name, address, taxpayer identification number, and profits interest of each member of the group; and

(v) Be signed by all partners comprising the notice group.

(3) *Place for filing.*—The request for notice from a notice group generally must be filed with the service center where the partnership return is filed. However, if the notice group representative knows that the notice described in section 6223(a)(1) (beginning of an administrative proceeding) has already been mailed to the tax matters partner, the statement should be filed with the Internal Revenue Service office that mailed that notice.

(4) *Copy to be sent to the tax matters partner.*—A copy of the request for notice from a notice group shall be provided to the tax matters partner by the notice group representative within 30 days after the request is filed with the Internal Revenue Service.

(5) *Years covered by request.*—A request for notice by a notice group may relate only to partnership taxable years that have ended before the request is filed. A request, however, may relate to more than one partnership taxable year if the 5 percent or more profits interest requirement of section 6223(b)(2) is satisfied for each year to which the request relates.

(c) *Composition of notice group.*—(1) *In general.*—A notice group shall be comprised only of persons who were partners at some time during the partnership taxable year for which the group is formed. If a notice group is formed for more than one taxable year, each member of the group must have been a partner at some time during at least one of the taxable years for which the group is formed. A notice group may include a partner entitled to separate notice. See section 6231(d) and §301.6231(d)-1 for rules relating to determining the interest of a partner in the profits of a partnership for a partnership taxable year for purposes of section 6223(b). See paragraph (c)(6) of this section for rules relating to indirect and pass-thru partners.

(2) *Partner may be a member of only one group.*—A partner cannot be a member of more than one notice group with respect to the same partnership for the same partnership taxable year. See paragraph (c)(6) of this section for rules relating to indirect and pass-thru partners.

(3) *Partner may join group after formation.*—A partner may join a notice group at any time after the formation of that group by filing with the Internal Revenue Service office where the notice group filed its request a statement that it is joining the notice group. The statement shall identify the partner joining the notice group, the partnership, and the members of the notice group by name, address, and taxpayer identification number and shall be signed by the joining partner. A copy of the statement shall be provided by the joining partner to both the tax matters partner and the notice group representative within 30 days after the request is filed with the Internal Revenue Service. The partner shall become a member of the notice group for each partnership taxable year for which the group was formed and for which the partner was a partner at any time during such partnership taxable year.

(4) *Date on which a partner becomes a member of notice group.*—A partner shall become a member of a notice group on the 30th day after the day on which the Internal Revenue Service receives—

(i) A request for notice from a notice group that identifies that partner as a member of that notice group; or

(ii) A statement filed in accordance with paragraph (c)(3) of this section that states that the partner is joining the notice group.

(5) *No withdrawal from notice group.*—A partner who has signed a notice group request filed with the Internal Revenue Service remains a member of that notice group until the group terminates. A partner cannot withdraw from the notice group.

(6) *Indirect and pass-thru partners.*—(i) *Pass-thru partners and unidentified indirect partners.*—A pass-thru partner may become a member of a notice group as provided in this section. For purposes of applying the aggregate interest requirement specified in paragraph (a) of this section to a pass-thru partner, the partnership interest held by the pass-thru partner shall not include any interest held through the pass-thru partner by an indirect partner that has been identified as provided in section 6223(c)(3) and §301.6223(c)-1 before the date on which the pass-thru partner becomes a member of the notice group.

(ii) *Indirect partners identified before the pass-thru partner joins a notice group.*—An indirect partner may become a member of a notice group with respect to a partnership taxable year only if—

(A) The indirect partner held an interest in the partnership (either directly or through one or more pass-thru partners) at some time during that taxable year; and

(B) The indirect partner was identified as provided in section 6223(c)(3) and §301.6223(c)-1 on or before the date on which the pass-thru partner became a member of a notice group.

(d) *Termination of notice group.*—Unless the original request for notice from the notice group or a subsequent statement filed by the representative (in accordance with paragraphs (b)(3) and (4) of this section) designates a successor to the designated group representative, the group terminates if the representative dies (or, in the case of an entity, if the entity is dissolved), resigns, or is adjudicated incompetent.

(e) *Notice group is not a 5-percent group.*—The forming of a notice group under this section does not constitute the forming of a 5-percent group for purposes of litigation. A notice group is formed solely for the purpose of receiving notices. A 5-percent group is formed solely for the purpose of filing a petition for judicial review or appealing a judicial determination. See §301.6226(b)-1. Thus, a member of a notice group may choose not to join a 5-percent group formed by other members of the notice group.

(f) *Effective date.*—This section is applicable to partnership taxable years beginning on or after October 4, 2001. For years beginning prior to October 4, 2001, see §301.6223(b)-1T contained in 26 CFR part 1, revised April 1, 2001. [Reg. §301.6223(b)-1.]

□ [*T.D.* 8965, 10-3-2001.]

### [Reg. §301.6223(c)-1]

**§301.6223(c)-1. Additional information regarding partners furnished to the Internal Revenue Service.**—(a) *In general.*—In addition to the names, addresses, and profits interests as shown on the partnership return, the Internal Revenue Service will use additional information as provided in this section for purposes of administering subchapter C of chapter 63 of the Internal Revenue Code.

(b) *Procedure for furnishing additional information.*—(1) *In general.*—Any person may furnish additional information at any time by filing a written statement with the Internal Revenue Service. However, the information contained in the statement will be considered for purposes of determining whether a partner is entitled to a notice described in section 6223(a) only if the Internal Revenue Service receives the statement at least 30 days before the date on which the Internal Revenue Service mails the notice to the tax matters partner. Similarly, information contained in the statement generally will not be taken into account for other purposes by the Internal Revenue Service until 30 days after the statement is received.

(2) *Where statement must be filed.*—A statement furnished under this section generally must be filed with the service center where the partnership return is filed. However, if the person filing the statement knows that the notice described in section 6223(a)(1) (beginning of an administrative proceeding) has already been mailed to the tax matters partner, the statement should be filed with the Internal Revenue Service office that mailed such notice.

(3) *Contents of statement.*—The statement shall—

(i) Identify the partnership, each partner for whom information is supplied, and the person supplying the information by name, address, and taxpayer identification number;

(ii) Explain that the statement is furnished to correct or supplement earlier information with respect to the partners in the partnership;

(iii) Specify the taxable year to which the information relates;

(iv) Set out the corrected or additional information; and

(v) Be signed by the person supplying the information.

(c) *No incorporation by reference to previously furnished documents.*—Incorporation by reference of information contained in another document previously furnished to the Internal Revenue Service will not be given effect for purposes of section 6223(c) or 6229(e). For example, reference to a return filed by a pass-thru partner which contains identifying information with respect to the indirect partners of that pass-thru partner is not sufficient to identify the indirect partners unless a copy of the document referred to is attached to the statement. Furthermore, reference to a prior general notification to the Internal Revenue Service that a partner who would otherwise be the tax matters partner is a debtor in a bankruptcy proceeding or has had a receiver appointed for the partner in a receivership proceeding is not sufficient unless a copy of the notification document referred to is attached to the statement.

(d) *Information supplied by a person other than the tax matters partner.*—The Internal Revenue Service may require appropriate verification in the case of information furnished by a person other than the tax matters partner. The 30-day period referred to in paragraph (b)(1) of this section shall not begin until that verification is supplied.

(e) *Power of attorney.*—(1) *In general.*—This paragraph (e) applies to powers of attorney with respect to proceedings under subchapter C of chapter 63 of the Internal Revenue Code (chapter 63C) that begin on or after January 2, 2002.

(2) *Specifically for purposes of subchapter C of chapter 63 of the Internal Revenue Code.*—A power of attorney specifically for purposes of subchapter C of chapter 63 of the Internal Revenue Code shall be furnished in accordance with paragraph (b)(2) of this section.

(3) *Existing power of attorney.*—A power of attorney granted to another person by a partner for other tax purposes shall not be given effect for purposes of subchapter C of chapter 63 unless the partner specifically requests that the power be given such effect in a statement furnished to the Internal Revenue Service in accordance with paragraph (b) of this section.

(f) *Internal Revenue Service may use other information.*—In addition to the information on the partnership return and that supplied on statements filed under this section, the Internal Revenue Service may use other information in its possession (for example, a change in address reflected on a partner's return) in administering subchapter C of chapter 63 of the Internal Revenue Code. However, the Internal Revenue Service is not obligated to search its records for information not expressly furnished under this section.

(g) *Effective date.*—Except as provided in paragraph (e)(1) of this section, this section is applicable to partnership taxable years beginning on or after October 4, 2001. For years beginning prior to October 4, 2001, see § 301.6223(c)-1T contained in 26 CFR part 1, revised April 1, 2001. [Reg. § 301.6223(c)-1.]

☐ [T.D. 8965, 10-3-2001.]

### [Reg. § 301.6223(e)-1]

**§ 301.6223(e)-1. Effect of Internal Revenue Service's failure to provide notice.**—(a) *Notice group.*—Section 6223(e)(1)(B)(ii) applies with respect to a notice group only if the request for notice described in § 301.6223(b)-1 is received by the Internal Revenue Service at least 30 days before the notice is mailed to the tax matters partner.

(b) *Indirect partners.*—(1) *In general.*—For purposes of section 6223(e), the Internal Revenue Service's failure to provide notice to a pass-thru partner entitled to notice under section 6223(b) is deemed a failure to provide notice to indirect partners holding an interest in the partnership through the pass-thru partner. However, this rule does not apply if the indirect partner—

(i) Receives notice from the Internal Revenue Service;

(ii) Is identified as provided in section 6223(c)(3) and § 301.6223(c)-1 at least 30 days before the notice is mailed to the tax matters partner; or

(iii) Is a member of a notice group entitled to notice under paragraph (a) of this section.

(2) *Examples.*—The provisions of paragraph (b)(1) of this section may be illustrated by the following examples:

*Example 1.* Partnership ABC has as one of its partners, A, a partnership with three partners, X, Y, and Z. ABC does not have more than 100 partners, and partnership A is entitled to notice under section 6223(a). In addition, Z was identified as provided in section 6223(c)(3) and § 301.6223(c)-1 on May 1, 2002. The Internal Revenue Service mailed a notice to the tax matters partner of ABC on July 1, 2002, but failed to provide notice to partnership A. Notwithstanding the Internal Revenue Service's notice to the tax matters partner, the Internal Revenue Service is deemed to have failed to provide notice to X and Y. The Internal Revenue Service's failure to provide notice to A, however, has no effect on Z; whether notice was provided to Z is determined independently.

*Example 2.* Assume the same facts as in *Example 1*, except that the Internal Revenue Service provided notice to partnership A but did not provide separate notice to Z. Notwithstanding the Internal Revenue Service's notice to partnership A, the Internal Revenue Service is deemed to have failed to provide notice to Z.

*Example 3.* Assume the same facts as in *Example 1*, except that partnership ABC has more than 100 partners and partnership A is entitled to notice under section 6223(b) because it had at least a 1 percent profits interest in partnership ABC. In addition, X became a member of a notice group on June 1, 2002, and the Internal Revenue Service mailed a notice to the designated member of that notice group. The Internal Revenue Service also mailed a separate notice to Z. The Internal Revenue Service's failure to provide notice to partnership A only affects Y, who is deemed not to have been provided notice by the Internal Revenue Service.

(c) *Effective date.*—This section is applicable to partnership taxable years beginning on or after October 4, 2001. For years beginning prior to October 4, 2001, see § 301.6223(e)-1T contained in 26 CFR part 1, revised April 1, 2001. [Reg. § 301.6223(e)-1.]

☐ [T.D. 8965, 10-3-2001.]

### [Reg. § 301.6223(e)-2]

**§ 301.6223(e)-2. Elections if Internal Revenue Service fails to provide timely notice.**—(a) *In general.*—This section applies in any case in which the Internal Revenue Service fails to timely mail any notice described in section 6223(a) of the Internal Revenue Code to a partner entitled to such notice within the period specified in section 6223(d). The failure to issue any notice within the period specified in section 6223(d) does not invalidate the notice of the beginning of an administrative proceeding or final partnership administrative adjustment (FPAA). An untimely FPAA enables the recipient of the untimely notice to make the elections described in paragraphs (b), (c), and (d) of this section. The period within which to make the elections described in paragraphs (b), (c), and (d) of this section commences with the mailing of an FPAA to the partner. In the absence of an election, paragraphs (b) and (c) of this section provide for the treatment of a partner's partnership items.

(b) *Proceeding finished.*—If at the time the Internal Revenue Service mails the partner an FPAA—

(1) The period within which a petition for review of the FPAA under section 6226 may be filed has expired and no petition has been filed; or

(2) The decision of a court in an action begun by such a petition has become final, the partner may elect in accordance with paragraph (d) of this section to have that adjustment, that decision, or a settlement agreement described in section 6224(c)(2) with respect to the partnership taxable year to which the adjustment relates apply to that partner. If the partner does not make an election in accordance with paragraph (d) of this section, the partnership items of the partner for the partnership taxable year to which the proceeding relates shall be treated as having become nonpartnership items as of the day on which the Internal Revenue Service mails the partner the FPAA.

(c) *Proceeding still going on.*—If at the time the Internal Revenue Service mails the partner an FPAA, paragraphs (b)(1) and (2) of this section do not apply, the partner shall be a party to the proceeding unless the partner elects, in accordance with paragraph (d) of this section, to have—

(1) A settlement agreement described in section 6224(c)(2) with respect to the partnership taxable year to which the proceeding relates apply to the partner; or

(2) The partnership items of the partner for the partnership taxable year to which the proceeding relates treated as having become nonpartnership items as of the day on which the Internal Revenue Service mails the partner the FPAA.

(d) *Election.*—(1) *In general.*—The election described in paragraph (b) or (c) of this section shall be made in the manner prescribed in this paragraph (d). The election shall apply to all partnership items for the partnership taxable year to which the election relates.

(2) *Time and manner of making election.*—The election shall be made by filing a statement with the Internal Revenue Service office mailing the FPAA within 45 days after the date on which the FPAA was mailed to the partner making the election.

(3) *Contents of statement.*—The statement shall—

(i) Be clearly identified as an election under section 6223(e)(2) or (3);

(ii) Specify the election being made (that is, application of final partnership administrative adjustment, court decision, consistent settlement agreement, or nonpartnership item treatment);

(iii) Identify the partner making the election and the partnership by name, address, and taxpayer identification number;

(iv) Specify the partnership taxable year to which the election relates; and

(v) Be signed by the partner making the election.

(e) *Effective date.*—This section is applicable to partnership taxable years beginning on or after October 4, 2001. For years beginning prior to October 4, 2001, see §301.6223(e)-2T contained in 26 CFR part 1, revised April 1, 2001. [Reg. §301.6223(e)-2.]

□ [*T.D.* 8965, 10-3-2001.]

### [Reg. §301.6223(f)-1]

**§301.6223(f)-1. Duplicate copy of final partnership administrative adjustment.**—(a) *In general.*—Section 6223(f) does not prohibit the Internal Revenue Service from issuing a duplicate copy of the notice of final partnership administrative adjustment (for example, in the event the original notice is lost).

(b) *Effective date.*—This section is applicable to partnership taxable years beginning on or after October 4, 2001. For years beginning prior to October 4, 2001, see §301.6223(f)-1T contained in 26 CFR part 1, revised April 1, 2001. [Reg. §301.6223(f)-1.]

□ [*T.D.* 8965, 10-3-2001.]

### [Reg. §301.6223(g)-1]

**§301.6223(g)-1. Responsibilities of the tax matters partner.**—(a) *Notices described in section 6223(a).*—(1) *Notice of beginning of proceeding.*—Except as otherwise provided in §301.6223(a)-2, the tax matters partner shall, within 75 days after the Internal Revenue Service mails the notice specified in section 6223(a)(1), forward a copy of that notice to each partner not entitled to notice from the Internal Revenue Service under section 6223. See §301.6230(e)-1 for information to be furnished to the Internal Revenue Service.

(2) *Notice of final partnership administrative adjustment.*—The tax matters partner shall, within 60 days after the Internal Revenue Service mails the notice specified in section 6223(a)(2), forward a copy of that notice to each partner not entitled to notice from the Internal Revenue Service under section 6223.

(3) *Requirement inapplicable in certain cases.*—The tax matters partner is not required to send notice to a partner if—

(i) Before the expiration of the applicable 75-day or 60-day period the partnership items of that partner have become nonpartnership items (for example, by settlement);

(ii) That partner is an indirect partner and has not been identified to the tax matters partner at least 30 days before the tax matters partner is required to send such notice;

(iii) That partner is treated as a partner solely by virtue of §301.6231(a)(2)-1;

(iv) That partner was a member of a notice group as of the date on which the notice was mailed to the tax matters partner (see §301.6223(b)-1(c)(4) for the date on which a partner becomes a member of a notice group);

(v) The notice has already been provided to that partner by another person; or

(vi) The notice is withdrawn by the Internal Revenue Service under §301.6223(a)-2.

(b) *Other notices or information.*—(1) *In general.*—The tax matters partner shall furnish to the partners specified in paragraph (b)(2) of this section information with respect to the following—

(i) Closing conference with the examining agent;

(ii) Proposed adjustments, rights of appeal, and requirements for filing of a protest;

(iii) Time and place of any Appeals conference;

(iv) Acceptance by the Internal Revenue Service of any settlement offer;

(v) Consent to the extension of the period of limitations with respect to all partners;

(vi) Filing of a request for administrative adjustment (including a request for substituted return treatment under §301.6227(c)-1) on behalf of the partnership;

(vii) Filing by the tax matters partner or any other partner of any petition for judicial review under sections 6226 or 6228(a);

(viii) Filing of any appeal with respect to any judicial determination provided for in sections 6226 or 6228(a); and

(ix) Final judicial redetermination.

(2) *Partners to be notified.*—The tax matters partner shall provide information with respect to any action or other matter specified in paragraph (b)(1) of this section to all notice group representatives and all other partners except partners—

(i) Whose partnership items become nonpartnership items before the expiration of the period specified in paragraph (b)(3) of this section for furnishing that information;

(ii) Who are indirect partners and who are not identified to the tax matters partner at least 30 days before the tax matters partner is required to provide the information;

(iii) Who are treated as partners solely by virtue of §301.6231(a)(2)-1;

(iv) Who are members of a notice group as of the date on which the tax matters partner takes that action or receives information with respect to that matter (see §301.6223(b)-1(c)(4) for the date on which a partner becomes a member of a notice group); or

(v) Who have already received information with respect to the action or matter from any other person.

(3) *Time for furnishing information.*—The tax matters partner shall furnish information with respect to an action or other matter described in paragraph (b)(1) of this section within 30 days of taking the action or receiving information with respect to that matter.

(c) *Effective date.*—This section is applicable to partnership taxable years beginning on or after October 4, 2001. For years beginning prior to October 4, 2001, see §301.6223(g)-1T contained in 26 CFR part 1, revised April 1, 2001. [Reg. §301.6223(g)-1.]

□ [*T.D.* 8965, 10-3-2001.]

### [Reg. §301.6223(h)-1]

**§301.6223(h)-1. Responsibilities of pass-thru partner.**—(a) *In general.*—The pass-thru partner shall, within 30 days of receiving notice or any other information regarding a partnership proceeding from the Internal Revenue Service, the tax matters partner, or another pass-thru partner, forward a copy of that notice or information to the person or persons holding an interest through the pass-thru partner in the profits or losses of the partnership for the partnership taxable year to which the notice or information relates. In the case of a pass-thru partner that is a partnership within the meaning of section 6231(a)(1), the tax matters partner of such partnership shall forward copies of the notice or information to the partners of such partnership.

(b) *Effective date.*—This section is applicable to partnership taxable years beginning on or after October 4, 2001. For years beginning prior to October 4, 2001, see §301.6223(h)-1T contained in 26 CFR part 1, revised April 1, 2001. [Reg. §301.6223(h)-1.]

□ [*T.D.* 8965, 10-3-2001.]

### [Reg. §301.6224(a)-1]

**§301.6224(a)-1. Participation in administrative proceedings.**—(a) *In general.*—Every partner in the partnership, including an indirect partner, has the right to participate in any phase of administrative proceedings. However, except as provided in section 6223 and the regulations thereunder, neither the Internal Revenue Service nor the tax matters partner is required to provide notice of any proceeding to the partners. Consequently, a partner who wishes, for example, to be present during a preliminary discussion between an examining agent and the tax matters partner should make special arrangements with the tax matters partner to obtain information as to the time and place of the discussion. The Internal Revenue Service and the tax matters partner will determine the time and place for all administrative proceedings. Arrangements will generally not be changed merely for the convenience of another partner.

(b) *Effective date.*—This section is applicable to partnership taxable years beginning on or after October 4, 2001. For years beginning prior to October 4, 2001, see §301.6224(a)-1T contained in 26 CFR part 1, revised April 1, 2001. [Reg. §301.6224(a)-1.]

□ [*T.D.* 8965, 10-3-2001.]

### [Reg. §301.6224(b)-1]

**§301.6224(b)-1. Partner may waive rights.**—(a) *In general.*—A partner may at any time waive any right that the partner has or any restriction on action by the Internal Revenue Service under subchapter C of chapter 63 of the Internal Revenue Code.

(b) *Form and manner of making waiver.*—The waiver described in paragraph (a) of this section shall be made by a written statement. If the Internal Revenue Service furnishes a form to be used for this purpose, the partner may make the waiver by completing the form in accordance with the form's instructions. If such a form is not furnished, the statement shall—

(1) Be clearly identified as a waiver under section 6224(b);

(2) Identify the partner and the partnership by name, address, and taxpayer identification number;

(3) Specify the right or restriction being waived and the taxable year(s) to which the waiver applies;

(4) Be signed by the partner making the waiver; and

(5) Be filed with the service center where the partnership return is filed. However, if the person filing the statement knows that the notice described in section 6223(a)(1) (beginning of an administrative proceeding) has already been mailed to the tax matters partner, the statement shall be filed with the Internal Revenue Service office that mailed such notice.

(c) *Effective date.*—This section is applicable to partnership taxable years beginning on or after October 4, 2001. For years beginning prior to October 4, 2001, see § 301.6224(b)-1T contained in 26 CFR part 1, revised April 1, 2001. [Reg. § 301.6224(b)-1.]

☐ [*T.D.* 8965, 10-3-2001.]

### [Reg. § 301.6224(c)-1]

**§ 301.6224(c)-1. Tax matters partner may bind nonnotice partners.**—(a) *In general.*—In the absence of a showing of fraud, malfeasance, or misrepresentation of fact, if the tax matters partner enters into a settlement agreement with the Internal Revenue Service with respect to partnership items, including partnership-level determinations relating to any penalty, addition to tax, or additional amounts that relate to adjustments to partnership items, and expressly states that the agreement shall be binding on the other partners, then that agreement shall be binding on all partners except those who—

(1) Are, as of the day on which the agreement is entered into, either notice partners or members of a notice group (see § 301.6223(b)-1(c)(4) for the date on which a partner becomes a member of a notice group); or

(2) Have, at least 30 days before the day on which the agreement is entered into, filed with the Internal Revenue Service the statement described in paragraph (c) of this section.

(b) *Indirect partners.*—(1) *In general.*—If, under paragraph (a) of this section, a pass-thru partner is not bound by an agreement entered into by the tax matters partner, all indirect partners holding an interest in the partnership through that pass-thru partner shall not be bound by that agreement. If, however, the pass-thru partner is bound by an agreement entered into by the tax matters partner, paragraph (a) of this section shall be applied separately to each indirect partner holding an interest in the partnership through the pass-thru partner to determine whether the indirect partner is also bound by the agreement.

(2) *Example.*—The following example illustrates the principles of this section:

*Example.* Partnership P has over 100 partners. Partnership J is a partner in partnership P with a profits interest of less than 1 percent. Partnership J has three partners, A, B, and C. A is a member of a notice group with respect to partnership P, but B and C are not. On July 1, 2002, B filed the statement described in paragraph (c) of this section not to be bound by any settlement agreement entered into by the tax matters partner of partnership P. On August 1, 2002, the tax matters partner of partnership P enters into a settlement agreement with the Internal Revenue Service and states that the agreement is binding on other partners as provided in section 6224(c)(3). Because partnership J is bound by the settlement agreement, paragraph (a) of this section is applied separately to each of the indirect partners to determine whether they are bound. A is not bound by the agreement because A was a member of a notice group on the day the agreement was entered into and B is not bound because B filed the statement not to be bound at least 30 days before the agreement was entered into. C is bound by the settlement agreement.

(c) *Statement not to be bound.*—(1) *Contents of statement.*—The statement referred to in paragraph (a)(2) of this section shall—

(i) Be clearly identified as a statement to deny settlement authority to the tax matters partner under section 6224(c)(3)(B);

(ii) Identify the partner and partnership by name, address, and taxpayer identification number;

(iii) Specify the taxable year or years to which the statement applies; and

(iv) Be signed by the partner filing the statement.

(2) *Place where statement is to be filed.*—The statement described in paragraph (c)(1) of this section generally shall be filed with the Internal Revenue Service service center where the partnership return is filed. However, if the partner knows that the notice described in section 6223(a)(1) (beginning of an administrative proceeding) has already been mailed to the tax matters partner, the statement shall be filed with the Internal Revenue Service office that mailed that notice.

(3) *Consolidated statements.*—The statement described in paragraph (c)(1) of this section may be filed with respect to more than one partner if the requirements of that paragraph (c)(1) (including signatures) are satisfied with respect to each partner.

(d) *Effective date.*—This section is applicable to partnership taxable years beginning on or after October 4, 2001. For years beginning prior to October 4, 2001, see § 301.6224(c)-1T contained in 26 CFR part 1, revised April 1, 2001. [Reg. § 301.6224(c)-1.]

☐ [*T.D.* 8965, 10-3-2001.]

### [Reg. § 301.6224(c)-2]

**§ 301.6224(c)-2. Pass-thru partner binds indirect partners.**—(a) *Pass-thru partner binds unidentified indirect partners.*—(1) *In general.*—If a pass-thru partner enters into a settlement agreement with the Internal Revenue Service with respect to partnership items, that agreement binds all indirect partners holding an interest in that partnership through the pass-thru partner except those indirect partners who have been identified as provided in section 6223(c)(3) and § 301.6223(c)-1 at least 30 days before the date on which the agreement is entered into. A settlement with respect to partnership items includes partnership-level determinations relating to any penalty, addition to tax, and additional amounts that relate to adjustments to partnership items. However, if, in addition to the interest in the partnership held through the pass-thru partner entering into a settlement agreement, an indirect partner holds a separate interest in that partnership, either directly or indirectly through a different pass-thru partner, then the indirect partner shall not be bound by that settlement agreement with respect to the interests held directly or indirectly through a pass-thru partner other than the pass-thru partner entering into the settlement agreement.

(2) *Example.*—The provisions of paragraph (a)(1) of this section may be illustrated by the following example:

*Example.* Partnership J is a partner in partnership P. C is a partner in J but has not been identified as provided in section 6223(c)(3) and § 301,6223(c)-1. The only interest that C holds in P is through J. The tax matters partner of J enters into a settlement agreement with the Internal Revenue Service with respect to partnership items arising from P. C is bound by the settlement agreement entered into by the tax matters partner of J.

(b) *Person in pass-thru partner authorized to enter into settlement agreement that binds indirect partners.*—In the case of a pass-thru partner that is—

(1) A partnership within the meaning of section 6231(a)(1), the tax matters partner of that partnership;

(2) A partnership other than a partnership described in paragraph (b)(1) of this section, any general partner of that partnership;

(3) An S corporation, any officer of that S corporation; or

(4) A trust, estate, or nominee, any person authorized in writing to act on behalf of that trust, estate, or nominee, may enter into a settlement agreement with the Internal Revenue Service on behalf of its respective entity that would bind the unidentified indirect partners that hold a partnership interest through the pass-thru partner.

(c) *Effective date.*—This section is applicable to partnership taxable years beginning on or after October 4, 2001. For years beginning prior to October 4, 2001, see § 301.6224(c)-2T contained in 26 CFR part 1, revised April 1, 2001. [Reg. § 301.6224(c)-2.]

☐ [*T.D.* 8965, 10-3-2001.]

### [Reg. § 301.6224(c)-3]

**§ 301.6224(c)-3. Consistent settlements.**—(a) *In general.*—If the Internal Revenue Service enters into a settlement agreement with any partner with respect to partnership items, whether comprehensive or partial, the Internal Revenue Service shall offer to any other partner who so requests in accordance with paragraph (c) of this section, settlement terms consistent with those contained in the settlement agreement entered into.

(b) *Requirements for consistent settlement terms.*—(1) *In general.*—Consistent settlement terms are those based on the same determinations with respect to partnership items. However, consistent settlement terms also may include partnership-level determinations of any penalty, addition to tax, or additional amount that relates to partnership items. Settlements with respect to partnership items shall be self-contained; thus, a concession by one party with respect to a partnership item may not be based upon a concession by another party with respect to any item that is not a partnership item other than a partnership-level determination of any penalty, addition to tax, or additional amount that relates to an adjustment to a partnership item. Consistent agreements must be identical to the original settlement (that is, the settlement upon which the offered settlement terms are based). A consistent agreement must mirror the original settlement and may not be limited to selected items from the original settlement. Once a partner has settled a partnership item, or a partnership-level determination of any penalty, addition to tax, or additional amount that relates to an adjustment to a partnership item, that partner may not subsequently request settlement terms consistent with a settlement that contains the previously settled item. The requirement for consistent settlement terms applies only if—

(i) The items were partnership items (or a partnership-level determination of any related penalty, addition to tax, or additional amount) for the partner entering into the original settlement immediately before the original settlement; and

(ii) The items are partnership items (or a partnership-level determination of any related penalty, addition to tax, or additional amount) for the partner requesting the consistent settlement at the time the partner files the request.

(2) *Effect of consistent agreement.*—Consistent settlement terms are reflected in a consistent agreement. A consistent agreement is not a settlement agreement that gives rise to further consistent settlement rights because it is required to be given without volitional agreement of the Secretary. Therefore, a consistent agreement required to be offered to a requesting taxpayer is not a settlement agreement under section 6224(c)(2) or paragraph (c)(3) of this section which starts a new period for requesting consistent settlement terms. For all other purposes of the Internal Revenue Code, however, (e.g., binding effect under section 6224(c)(1) and conversion to nonpartnership items under section 6231(b)(1)(C)), a consistent agreement is treated as a settlement agreement.

(c) *Time and manner of requesting consistent settlements.*—(1) *In general.*—A partner desiring settlement terms consistent with the terms of any settlement agreement entered into between any other partner and the Internal Revenue Service shall submit a written statement to the Internal Revenue Service office that entered into the settlement.

(2) *Contents of statement.*—Except as otherwise provided in instructions to the taxpayer from the Internal Revenue Service, the written statement described in paragraph (c)(1) of this section shall—

(i) Identify the statement as a request for consistent settlement terms under section 6224(c)(2);

(ii) Contain the name, address, and taxpayer identification number of the partnership and of the partner requesting the settlement offer (and, in the case of an indirect partner, of the pass-thru partner through which the indirect partner holds an interest);

(iii) Identify the earlier agreement to which the request refers; and

(iv) Be signed by the partner making the request.

(3) *Time for filing request.*—The statement shall be filed not later than the later of—

(i) The 150th day after the day on which the notice of final partnership administrative adjustment is mailed to the tax matters partner; or

(ii) The 60th day after the day on which the settlement agreement was entered into.

(d) *Examples.*—The following examples illustrate the principles of this section:

*Example 1.* The Internal Revenue Service seeks to disallow a $100,000 loss reported by Partnership P $20,000 of which was allocated to partner X, and $10,000 of which was allocated to partner Y. The Internal Revenue Service agrees to a settlement with X in which the Internal Revenue Service allows $12,000 of the loss, accepts the treatment of all other partnership items on the partnership return, and imposes a penalty for negligence related to the $8,000 loss disallowance. Partner Y requests settlement terms consistent with the settlement made between X and the Internal Revenue Service. The items are partnership items (or a related penalty) for X immediately before X enters into the settlement agreement and are partnership items (or a related penalty) for Y at the time of the request. The Internal Revenue Service must offer Y settlement terms allowing a $6,000 loss, a negligence penalty on the $4,000 disallowance, and otherwise reflecting the treatment of partnership items on the partnership return.

*Example 2.* F files inconsistently with Partnership P and reports the inconsistency. The Internal Revenue Service notifies F that it will treat all partnership items arising from P as nonpartnership items

with respect to F. Later, the Internal Revenue Service enters into a settlement with F on these items. The Internal Revenue Service is not required to offer the other partners of P settlement terms consistent with the settlement reached between F and the Internal Revenue Service because the items arising from P are not partnership items with respect to F.

*Example 3.* G, a partner in Partnership P, filed suit under section 6228(b) after the Internal Revenue Service failed to allow an administrative adjustment request with respect to a partnership item arising from P for a taxable year. Under section 6231(b)(1)(B), the partnership items of G for the partnership taxable year became nonpartnership items as of the date G filed suit. After G filed suit, another partner and the Internal Revenue Service entered into a settlement agreement with respect to items arising from P in that year. G is not entitled to consistent settlement terms because, at the time of the settlement, the items arising from P are no longer partnership items with respect to G.

(e) *Effective date.*—This section is applicable to partnership taxable years beginning on or after October 4, 2001. For years beginning prior to October 4, 2001, see § 301.6224(c)-3T contained in 26 CFR part 1, revised April 1, 2001. [Reg. § 301.6224(c)-3.]

☐ [*T.D.* 8965, 10-3-2001.]

### [Reg. § 301.6225-1]

**§ 301.6225-1. Partnership adjustment by the Internal Revenue Service.**—(a) *Imputed underpayment based on partnership adjustments.*—(1) *In general.*—In the case of any partnership adjustments (as defined in § 301.6241-1(a)(6)) by the Internal Revenue Service (IRS), if the adjustments result in an imputed underpayment (as determined in accordance with paragraph (b) of this section), the partnership must pay an amount equal to such imputed underpayment in accordance with paragraph (a)(2) of this section. If the adjustments do not result in an imputed underpayment (as described in paragraph (f) of this section), such adjustments must be taken into account by the partnership in the adjustment year (as defined in § 301.6241-1(a)(1)) in accordance with § 301.6225-3. Partnership adjustments may result in more than one imputed underpayment pursuant to paragraph (g) of this section. Each imputed underpayment determined under this section is based solely on partnership adjustments with respect to a single taxable year.

(2) *Partnership pays the imputed underpayment.*—An imputed underpayment (determined in accordance with paragraph (b) of this section and included in a notice of final partnership adjustment (FPA) under section 6231(a)(3)) must be paid by the partnership in the same manner as if the imputed underpayment were a tax imposed for the adjustment year in accordance with § 301.6232-1. The FPA will include the amount of any imputed underpayment, as modified under § 301.6225-2 if applicable, unless the partnership waives its right to such FPA under section 6232(d)(2). See § 301.6232-1(d)(2). For the alternative to payment of the imputed underpayment by the partnership, see § 301.6226-1. If a partnership pays an imputed underpayment, the partnership's expenditure for the imputed underpayment is taken into account by the partnership in accordance with § 301.6241-4. For interest and penalties with respect to an imputed underpayment, see section 6233.

(3) *Imputed underpayment set forth in notice of proposed partnership adjustment.*—An imputed underpayment set forth in a notice of proposed partnership adjustment (NOPPA) under section 6231(a)(2) is determined in accordance with paragraph (b) of this section without regard to any modification under § 301.6225-2. Modifications under § 301.6225-2, if allowed by the IRS, may change the amount of an imputed underpayment set forth in the NOPPA and determined in accordance with paragraph (b) of this section. Only the partnership adjustments set forth in a NOPPA are taken into account for purposes of determining an imputed underpayment under this section and for any modification under § 301.6225-2.

(b) *Determination of an imputed underpayment.*—(1) *In general.*—In the case of any partnership adjustment by the IRS, an imputed underpayment is determined by—

(i) Grouping the partnership adjustments in accordance with paragraph (c) of this section and, if appropriate, subgrouping such adjustments in accordance with paragraph (d) of this section;

(ii) Netting the adjustments in accordance with paragraph (e) of this section;

(iii) Calculating the total netted partnership adjustment in accordance with paragraph (b)(2) of this section;

(iv) Multiplying the total netted partnership adjustment by the highest rate of Federal income tax in effect for the reviewed year under section 1 or 11; and

(v) Increasing or decreasing the product that results under paragraph (b)(1)(iv) of this section by–

(A) Any amounts treated as net positive adjustments (as defined in paragraph (e)(4)(i) of this section) under paragraph (e)(3)(ii) of this section; and

(B) Except as provided in paragraph (e)(3)(ii) of this section, any amounts treated as net negative adjustments (as defined in paragraph (e)(4)(ii) of this section) under paragraph (e)(3)(ii) of this section.

(2) *Calculation of the total netted partnership adjustment.*—For purposes of determining an imputed underpayment under paragraph (b)(1) of this section, the *total netted partnership adjustment* is the sum of all net positive adjustments in the reallocation grouping described in paragraph (c)(2) of this section and the residual grouping described in paragraph (c)(5) of this section.

(3) *Adjustments to items for which tax has been collected under chapters 3 and 4 of the Internal Revenue Code.*—A partnership adjustment is disregarded for purposes of calculating the imputed underpayment under paragraph (b) of this section to the extent that the IRS has collected the tax required to be withheld under chapter 3 or chapter 4 (as defined in § 301.6241-6(b)(2)(ii) and (iii)) that is attributable to the partnership adjustment. See § 301.6241-6(b)(3) for rules that apply when a partnership pays an imputed underpayment that includes a partnership adjustment to an amount subject to withholding (as defined in § 301.6241-6(b)(2)(i)) under chapter 3 or chapter 4 for which such tax has not yet been collected.

(4) *Treatment of adjustment as zero for purposes of calculating the imputed underpayment.*—If the effect of one partnership adjustment is reflected in one or more other partnership adjustments, the IRS may treat the one adjustment as zero solely for purposes of calculating the imputed underpayment.

(c) *Grouping of partnership adjustments.*—(1) *In general.*—To determine an imputed underpayment under paragraph (b) of this section, partnership adjustments are placed into one of four groupings. These groupings are the reallocation grouping described in paragraph (c)(2) of this section, the credit grouping described in paragraph (c)(3) of this section, the creditable expenditure grouping described in paragraph (c)(4) of this section, and the residual grouping described in paragraph (c)(5) of this section. Adjustments in groupings may be placed in subgroupings, as appropriate, in accordance with paragraph (d) of this section. The IRS may, in its discretion, group adjustments in a manner other than the manner described in this paragraph (c) when such grouping would appropriately reflect the facts and circumstances. For requests to modify the groupings, see § 301.6225-2(d)(6).

(2) *Reallocation grouping.*—(i) *In general.*—Any adjustment that allocates or reallocates a partnership-related item to and from a particular partner or partners is a *reallocation adjustment*. Except in the case of an adjustment to a credit (as described in paragraph (c)(3) of this section) or to a creditable expenditure (as described in paragraph (c)(4) of this section), reallocation adjustments are placed in the reallocation grouping. Adjustments that reallocate a credit to and from a particular partner or partners are placed in the credit grouping (see paragraph (c)(3) of this section), and adjustments that reallocate a creditable expenditure to and from a particular partner or partners are placed in the creditable expenditure grouping (see paragraph (c)(4) of this section).

(ii) *Each reallocation adjustment results in at least two separate adjustments.*—Each reallocation adjustment generally results in at least two separate adjustments. One adjustment reverses the effect of the improper allocation of a partnership-related item, and the other adjustment effectuates the proper allocation of the partnership-related item. Generally, a reallocation adjustment results in one positive adjustment (as defined in paragraph (d)(2)(iii) of this section) and one negative adjustment (as defined in paragraph (d)(2)(ii) of this section).

(3) *Credit grouping.*—Each adjustment to a partnership-related item that is reported or could be reported by a partnership as a credit on the partnership's return, including a reallocation adjustment, is placed in the credit grouping.

(4) *Creditable expenditure grouping.*—(i) *In general.*—Each adjustment to a creditable expenditure, including a reallocation adjustment to a creditable expenditure, is placed in the creditable expenditure grouping.

(ii) *Adjustment to a creditable expenditure.*—(A) *In general.*—For purposes of this section, an adjustment to a partnership-related item is treated as an adjustment to a creditable expenditure if any person could take the item that is adjusted (or item as adjusted if the item was not originally reported by the partnership) as a credit. See § 1.704-1(b)(4)(ii) of this chapter. For instance, if the adjustment is a reduction of qualified research expenses, the adjustment is to a

creditable expenditure for purposes of this section because any person allocated the qualified research expenses by the partnership could claim a credit with respect to their allocable portion of such expenses under section 41, rather than a deduction under section 174.

(B) *Creditable foreign tax expenditures.*—The creditable expenditure grouping includes each adjustment to a creditable foreign tax expenditure (CFTE) as defined in § 1.704-1(b)(4)(viii)(*b*) of this chapter, including any reallocation adjustment to a CFTE.

(5) *Residual grouping.*—(i) *In general.*—Any adjustment to a partnership-related item not described in paragraph (c)(2), (3), or (4) of this section is placed in the residual grouping.

(ii) *Adjustments to partnership-related items that are not allocated under section 704(b).*—The residual grouping includes any adjustment to a partnership-related item that derives from an item that would not have been required to be allocated by the partnership to a reviewed year partner under section 704(b).

(6) *Recharacterization adjustments.*—(i) *Recharacterization adjustment defined.*—An adjustment that changes the character of a partnership-related item is a recharacterization adjustment. For instance, an adjustment that changes a loss from ordinary to capital or from active to passive is a recharacterization adjustment.

(ii) *Grouping recharacterization adjustments.*—A recharacterization adjustment is placed in the appropriate grouping as described in paragraphs (c)(2) through (5) of this section.

(iii) *Recharacterization adjustments result in two partnership adjustments.*—In general, a recharacterization adjustment results in at least two separate adjustments in the appropriate grouping under paragraph (c)(6)(ii) of this section. One adjustment reverses the improper characterization of the partnership-related item, and the other adjustment effectuates the proper characterization of the partnership-related item. A recharacterization adjustment results in two adjustments regardless of whether the amount of the partnership-related item is being adjusted. Generally, recharacterization adjustments result in one positive adjustment and one negative adjustment.

(d) *Subgroupings.*—(1) *In general.*—If all partnership adjustments are positive adjustments, this paragraph (d) does not apply. If any partnership adjustment within any grouping described in paragraph (c) of this section is a negative adjustment, the adjustments within that grouping are subgrouped in accordance with this paragraph (d). The IRS may, in its discretion, subgroup adjustments in a manner other than the manner described in this paragraph (d) when such subgrouping would appropriately reflect the facts and circumstances. For requests to modify the subgroupings, see § 301.6225-2(d)(6).

(2) *Definition of negative adjustments and positive adjustments.*—(i) *In general.*—For purposes of this section, partnership adjustments made by the IRS are treated as follows:

(A) An increase in an item of gain is treated as an increase in an item of income;

(B) A decrease in an item of gain is treated as a decrease in an item of income;

(C) An increase in an item of loss or deduction is treated as a decrease in an item of income; and

(D) A decrease in an item of loss or deduction is treated as an increase in an item of income.

(ii) *Negative adjustment.*—A *negative adjustment* is any adjustment that is a decrease in an item of income, a partnership adjustment treated under paragraph (d)(2)(i) of this section as a decrease in an item of income, or an increase in an item of credit.

(iii) *Positive adjustment.*—(A) *In general.*—A *positive adjustment* is any adjustment that is not a negative adjustment as defined in paragraph (d)(2)(ii) of this section.

(B) *Treatment of adjustments that cannot be allocated under section 704(b).*—For purposes of determining an imputed underpayment under this section, an adjustment described in paragraph (c)(5)(ii) of this section that could result in an increase in income or decrease in a loss, deduction, or credit for any person without regard to any particular person's specific circumstances is treated, to the extent appropriate, either as a positive adjustment to income or to a credit.

(3) *Subgrouping rules.*—(i) *In general.*—Except as otherwise provided in this paragraph (d)(3), an adjustment is subgrouped according to how the adjustment would be required to be taken into account separately under section 702(a) or any other provision of the Code, regulations, forms, instructions, or other guidance prescribed by the IRS applicable to the adjusted partnership-related item. A negative adjustment must be placed in the same subgrouping as another adjustment if the negative adjustment and the other adjust-

ment would have been properly netted at the partnership level and such netted amount would have been required to be allocated to the partners of the partnership as a single partnership-related item for purposes of section 702(a), other provision of the Code, regulations, forms, instructions, or other guidance prescribed by the IRS. For purposes of creating subgroupings under this section, if any adjustment could be subject to any preference, limitation, or restriction under the Code (or not allowed, in whole or in part, against ordinary income) if taken into account by any person, the adjustment is placed in a separate subgrouping from all other adjustments within the grouping.

(ii) *Subgrouping reallocation adjustments.*—(A) *Reallocation adjustments in the reallocation grouping.*—Each positive adjustment and each negative adjustment resulting from a reallocation adjustment as described in paragraph (c)(2)(ii) of this section is placed in its own separate subgrouping within the reallocation grouping. For instance, if the reallocation adjustment reallocates a deduction from one partner to another partner, the decrease in the deduction (positive adjustment) allocated to the first partner is placed in a subgrouping within the reallocation grouping separate from the increase in the deduction (negative adjustment) allocated to the second partner. Notwithstanding the requirement that reallocation adjustments be placed into separate subgroupings, if a particular partner or group of partners has two or more reallocation adjustments allocable to such partner or group, such adjustments may be subgrouped in accordance with paragraph (d)(3)(i) of this section and netted in accordance with paragraph (e) of this section.

(B) *Reallocation adjustments in the credit grouping.*—In the case of a reallocation adjustment to a credit, which is placed in the credit grouping pursuant to paragraph (c)(3) of this section, the decrease in credits allocable to one partner or group of partners is treated as a positive adjustment, and the increase in credits allocable to another partner or group of partners is treated as a negative adjustment. Each positive adjustment and each negative adjustment resulting from a reallocation adjustment to credits is placed in its own separate subgrouping within the credit grouping.

(iii) *Subgroupings within the creditable expenditure grouping.*—(A) *In general.*—Each adjustment in the creditable expenditure grouping described in paragraph (c)(4) of this section is subgrouped in accordance with paragraphs (d)(3)(i) and (iii) of this section. For rules related to creditable expenditures other than CFTEs, see paragraph (d)(3)(iii)(C) of this section.

(B) *Subgroupings for adjustments to CFTEs.*—Each adjustment to a CFTE is subgrouped based on the separate category of income to which the CFTE relates in accordance with section 904(d) and the regulations in part 1 of this chapter, and to account for any different allocation of the CFTE between partners. Two or more adjustments to CFTEs are included within the same subgrouping only if each adjustment relates to CFTEs in the same separate category, and each adjusted partnership-related item would be allocated to the partners in the same ratio had those items been properly reflected on the partnership return for the reviewed year.

(C) [Reserved]

(iv) *Subgrouping recharacterization adjustments.*—Each positive adjustment and each negative adjustment resulting from a recharacterization adjustment as described in paragraph (c)(6) of this section is placed in its own separate subgrouping within the residual grouping. If a particular partner or group of partners has two or more recharacterization adjustments allocable to such partner or group, such adjustments may be subgrouped in accordance with paragraph (d)(3)(i) of this section and netted in accordance with paragraph (e) of this section.

(e) *Netting adjustments within each grouping or subgrouping.*—(1) *In general.*—All adjustments within a subgrouping determined in accordance with paragraph (d) of this section are netted in accordance with this paragraph (e) to determine whether there is a net positive adjustment (as defined in paragraph (e)(4)(i) of this section) or net negative adjustment (as defined in paragraph (e)(4)(ii) of this section) for that subgrouping. If paragraph (d) of this section does not apply because a grouping only includes positive adjustments, all adjustments in that grouping are netted in accordance with this paragraph (e). For purposes of this paragraph (e), netting means summing all adjustments together within each grouping or subgrouping, as appropriate.

(2) *Limitations on netting adjustments.*—Positive adjustments and negative adjustments may only be netted against each other if they are in the same grouping in accordance with paragraph (c) of this section. If a negative adjustment is in a subgrouping in accordance with paragraph (d) of this section, the negative adjustment may only net with a positive adjustment also in that same subgrouping in

accordance with paragraph (d) of this section. An adjustment in one grouping or subgrouping may not be netted against an adjustment in any other grouping or subgrouping. Adjustments from one taxable year may not be netted against adjustments from another taxable year.

(3) *Results of netting adjustments within groupings or subgroupings.*—(i) *Groupings other than the credit and creditable expenditure groupings.*—Except as described in paragraphs (e)(3)(ii) and (iii) of this section, each net positive adjustment (as defined in paragraph (e)(4)(i) of this section) with respect to a particular grouping or subgrouping that results after netting the adjustments in accordance with this paragraph (e) is included in the calculation of the total netted partnership adjustment under paragraph (b)(2) of this section. Each net negative adjustment (as defined in paragraph (e)(4)(ii) of this section) with respect to a grouping or subgrouping that results after netting the adjustments in accordance with this paragraph (e) is excluded from the calculation of the total netted partnership adjustment under paragraph (b)(2) of this section. Adjustments underlying a net negative adjustment described in the preceding sentence are adjustments that do not result in an imputed underpayment (as described in paragraph (f) of this section).

(ii) *Credit grouping.*—Any net positive adjustment or net negative adjustment in the credit grouping (including any such adjustment with respect to a subgrouping within the credit grouping) is excluded from the calculation of the total netted partnership adjustment. A net positive adjustment described in this paragraph (e)(3)(ii) is taken into account under paragraph (b)(1)(v) of this section. A net negative adjustment described in this paragraph (e)(3)(ii), including a negative adjustment to a credit resulting from a reallocation adjustment that was placed in a separate subgrouping pursuant to paragraph (d)(3)(ii)(B) of this section, is treated as an adjustment that does not result in an imputed underpayment in accordance with paragraph (f)(1)(i) of this section, unless the IRS determines that such net negative adjustment should be taken into account under paragraph (b)(1)(v) of this section.

(iii) *Treatment of creditable expenditures.*—(A) *Creditable foreign tax expenditures.*—A net decrease to a CFTE in any CFTE subgrouping (as described in paragraph (d)(3)(iii) of this section) is treated as a net positive adjustment described in paragraph (e)(3)(ii) of this section and is excluded from the calculation of the total netted partnership adjustment under paragraph (b)(2) of this section. A net increase to a CFTE in any CFTE subgrouping is treated as a net negative adjustment described in paragraph (e)(3)(i) of this section. For rules related to creditable expenditures other than CFTEs, see paragraph (e)(3)(iii)(B) of this section.

(B) [Reserved]

(4) *Net positive adjustment and net negative adjustment defined.*—(i) *Net positive adjustment.*—A *net positive adjustment* means an amount that is greater than zero which results from netting adjustments within a grouping or subgrouping in accordance with this paragraph (e). A net positive adjustment includes a positive adjustment that was not netted with any other adjustment. A net positive adjustment includes a net decrease in an item of credit.

(ii) *Net negative adjustment.*—A *net negative adjustment* means any amount which results from netting adjustments within a grouping or subgrouping in accordance with this paragraph (e) that is not a net positive adjustment (as defined in paragraph (e)(4)(i) of this section). A net negative adjustment includes a negative adjustment that was not netted with any other adjustment.

(f) *Partnership adjustments that do not result in an imputed underpayment.*—(1) *In general.*—Except as otherwise provided in paragraph (e) of this section, a partnership adjustment does not result in an imputed underpayment if–

(i) After grouping, subgrouping, and netting the adjustments as described in paragraphs (c), (d), and (e) of this section, the result of netting with respect to any grouping or subgrouping that includes a particular partnership adjustment is a net negative adjustment (as described in paragraph (e)(4)(ii) of this section); or

(ii) The calculation under paragraph (b)(1) of this section results in an amount that is zero or less than zero.

(2) *Treatment of an adjustment that does not result in an imputed underpayment.*—Any adjustment that does not result in an imputed underpayment (as described in paragraph (f)(1) of this section) is taken into account by the partnership in the adjustment year in accordance with §301.6225-3. If the partnership makes an election pursuant to section 6226 with respect to an imputed underpayment, the adjustments that do not result in that imputed underpayment that are associated with that imputed underpayment (as described in paragraph (g)(2)(iii)(B) of this section) are taken into account by the reviewed year partners in accordance with §301.6226-3.

(g) *Multiple imputed underpayments in a single administrative proceeding.*—(1) *In general.*—The IRS, in its discretion, may determine that partnership adjustments for the same partnership taxable year result in more than one imputed underpayment. The determination of whether there is more than one imputed underpayment for any partnership taxable year, and if so, which partnership adjustments are taken into account to calculate any particular imputed underpayment is based on the facts and circumstances and nature of the partnership adjustments. See § 301.6225-2(d)(6) for modification of the number and composition of imputed underpayments.

(2) *Types of imputed underpayments.*—(i) *In general.*—There are two types of imputed underpayments: a general imputed underpayment (described in paragraph (g)(2)(ii) of this section) and a specific imputed underpayment (described in paragraph (g)(2)(iii) of this section). Each type of imputed underpayment is separately calculated in accordance with this section.

(ii) *General imputed underpayment.*—The general imputed underpayment is calculated based on all adjustments (other than adjustments that do not result in an imputed underpayment under paragraph (f) of this section) that are not taken into account to determine a specific imputed underpayment under paragraph (g)(2)(iii) of this section. There is only one general imputed underpayment in any administrative proceeding. If there is one imputed underpayment in an administrative proceeding, it is a general imputed underpayment and may take into account adjustments described in paragraph (g)(2)(iii) of this section, if any, and all adjustments that do not result in that general imputed underpayment (as described in paragraph (f) of this section) are associated with that general imputed underpayment.

(iii) *Specific imputed underpayment.*—(A) *In general.*—The IRS may, in its discretion, designate a specific imputed underpayment with respect to adjustments to a partnership-related item or items that were allocated to one partner or a group of partners that had the same or similar characteristics or that participated in the same or similar transaction or on such other basis as the IRS determines properly reflects the facts and circumstances. The IRS may designate more than one specific imputed underpayment with respect to any partnership taxable year. For instance, in a single partnership taxable year there may be a specific imputed underpayment with respect to adjustments related to a transaction affecting some, but not all, partners of the partnership (such as adjustments that are specially allocated to certain partners) and a second specific imputed underpayment with respect to adjustments resulting from a reallocation of a distributive share of income from one partner to another partner. The IRS may, in its discretion, determine that partnership adjustments that could be taken into account to calculate one or more specific imputed underpayments under this paragraph (g)(2)(iii)(A) for a partnership taxable year are more appropriately taken into account in determining the general imputed underpayment for such taxable year. For instance, the IRS may determine that it is more appropriate to calculate only the general imputed underpayment if, when calculating the specific imputed underpayment requested by the partnership, there is an increase in the number of the partnership adjustments that after grouping and netting result in net negative adjustments and are disregarded in calculating the specific imputed underpayment.

(B) *Adjustments that do not result in an imputed underpayment associated with a specific imputed underpayment.*—If the IRS designates a specific imputed underpayment, the IRS will designate which adjustments that do not result in an imputed underpayment, if any, are appropriate to associate with that specific imputed underpayment. If the adjustments underlying that specific imputed underpayment are reallocation adjustments or recharacterization adjustments, the net negative adjustment that resulted from the reallocation or recharacterization is associated with the specific imputed underpayment. Any adjustments that do not result in an imputed underpayment that are not associated with a specific imputed underpayment under this paragraph (g)(2)(iii)(B) are associated with the general imputed underpayment.

(h) *Examples.*—The following examples illustrate the rules of this section. For purposes of these examples, unless otherwise stated, each partnership is subject to the provisions of subchapter C of chapter 63 of the Code, each partnership and its partners are calendar year taxpayers, all partners are U.S. persons, the highest rate of income tax in effect for all taxpayers is 40 percent for all relevant periods, and no partnership requests modification under § 301.6225-2.

(1) *Example 1.* Partnership reports on its 2019 partnership return $100 of ordinary income and an ordinary deduction of -$70. The IRS initiates an administrative proceeding with respect to Partnership's 2019 taxable year and determines that ordinary income was $105 instead of $100 ($5 adjustment) and that the ordinary deduction was -

$80 instead of -$70 (-$10 adjustment). Pursuant to paragraph (c) of this section, the adjustments are both in the residual grouping. The -$10 adjustment to the ordinary deduction would not have been netted at the partnership level with the $5 adjustment to ordinary income and would not have been required to be allocated to the partners of the partnership as a single partnership-related item for purposes of section 702(a), other provision of the Code, regulations, forms, instructions, or other guidance prescribed by the IRS. Because the -$10 adjustment to the ordinary deduction would result in a decrease in the imputed underpayment if netted with the $5 adjustment to ordinary income and because it might be limited if taken into account by any person, the -$10 adjustment must be placed in a separate subgrouping from the $5 adjustment to ordinary income. See paragraph (d)(3)(i) of this section. The total netted partnership adjustment is $5, which results in an imputed underpayment of $2. The -$10 adjustment to the ordinary deduction is a net negative amount and is an adjustment that does not result in an imputed underpayment which is taken into account by Partnership in the adjustment year in accordance with § 301.6225-3.

(2) *Example 2.* The facts are the same as *Example 1* in paragraph (h)(1) of this section, except that the -$10 adjustment to the ordinary deduction would have been netted at the partnership level with the $5 adjustment to ordinary income and would have been required to be allocated to the partners of the partnership as a single partnership-related item for purposes of section 702(a), other provision of the Code, regulations, forms, instructions, or other guidance prescribed by the IRS. Therefore, the $5 adjustment and the -$10 adjustment must be placed in the same subgrouping within the residual grouping. The $5 adjustment and the -$10 adjustments are then netted in accordance with paragraph (e) of this section. Such netting results in a net negative adjustment (as defined under paragraph (e)(4)(ii) of this section) of -$5. Pursuant to paragraph (f) of this section, the -$5 net negative adjustment is an adjustment that does not result in an imputed underpayment. Because the only net adjustment is an adjustment that does not result in an imputed underpayment, there is no imputed underpayment.

(3) *Example 3.* Partnership reports on its 2019 partnership return ordinary income of $300, long-term capital gain of $125, long-term capital loss of -$75, a depreciation deduction of -$100, and a tax credit that can be claimed by the partnership of $5. In an administrative proceeding with respect to Partnership's 2019 taxable year, the IRS determines that ordinary income is $500 ($200 adjustment), long-term capital gain is $200 ($75 adjustment), long-term capital loss is -$25 ($50 adjustment), the depreciation deduction is -$70 ($30 adjustment), and the tax credit is $3 ($2 adjustment). Pursuant to paragraph (c) of this section, the adjustment to the tax credit is in the credit grouping under paragraph (c)(3) of this section. The remaining adjustments are part of the residual grouping under paragraph (c)(5) of this section. Pursuant to paragraph (d)(2) of this section, all of the adjustments in the residual grouping are positive adjustments. Because there are no negative adjustments, there are no subgroupings within the residual grouping. Under paragraph (b)(2) of this section, the adjustments in the residual grouping are summed for a total netted partnership adjustment of $355. Under paragraph (b)(1)(iv) of this section, the total netted partnership adjustment is multiplied by 40 percent (highest tax rate in effect), which results in $142. Under paragraph (b)(1)(v) of this section, the $142 is increased by the $2 credit adjustment, resulting in an imputed underpayment of $144.

(4) *Example 4.* Partnership reported on its 2019 partnership return long-term capital gain of $125. In an administrative proceeding with respect to Partnership's 2019 taxable year, the IRS determines the long-term capital gain should have been reported as ordinary income of $125. There are no other adjustments for the 2019 taxable year. This recharacterization adjustment results in two adjustments in the residual grouping pursuant to paragraph (c)(6) of this section: an increase in ordinary income of $125 ($125 adjustment) as well as a decrease of long-term capital gain of $125 (-$125 adjustment). The decrease in long-term capital gain is a negative adjustment under paragraph (d)(2)(ii) of this section and the increase in ordinary income is a positive adjustment under paragraph (d)(2)(iii) of this section. Under paragraph (d)(3)(i) of this section, the adjustment to long-term capital gain is placed in a subgrouping separate from the adjustment to ordinary income because the reduction of long-term capital gain is required to be taken into account separately pursuant to section 702(a). The $125 decrease in long-term capital gain is a net negative adjustment in the long-term capital subgrouping and, as a result, is an adjustment that does not result in an imputed underpayment under paragraph (f) of this section and is taken into account in accordance with § 301.6225-3. The $125 increase in ordinary income results in a net positive adjustment under paragraph (e)(4)(i) of this section. Because the ordinary subgrouping is the only subgrouping resulting in a net positive adjustment, $125 is the total netted partnership adjustment under paragraph (b)(2) of this section. Under paragraph (b)(1)(iv) of this section, $125 is multiplied by 40 percent resulting in an imputed underpayment of $50.

(5) *Example 5.* Partnership reported a $100 deduction for certain expenses on its 2019 partnership return and an additional $100 deduction with respect to the same type of expenses on its 2020 partnership return. The IRS initiates an administrative proceeding with respect to Partnership's 2019 and 2020 taxable years and determines that Partnership reported a portion of the expenses as a deduction in 2019 that should have been taken into account in 2020. Therefore, for taxable year 2019, the IRS determines that Partnership should have reported a deduction of $75 with respect to the expenses ($25 adjustment in the 2019 residual grouping). For 2020, the IRS determines that Partnership should have reported a deduction of $125 with respect to these expenses (-$25 adjustment in the 2020 residual grouping). There are no other adjustments for the 2019 and 2020 partnership taxable years. Pursuant to paragraph (e)(2) of this section, the adjustments for 2019 and 2020 are not netted with each other. The 2019 adjustment of $25 is the only adjustment for that year and a net positive adjustment under paragraph (e)(4)(i) of this section, and therefore the total netted partnership adjustment for 2019 is $25 pursuant to paragraph (b)(2) of this section. The $25 total netted partnership adjustment is multiplied by 40 percent resulting in an imputed underpayment of $10 for Partnership's 2019 taxable year. The $25 increase in the deduction for 2020, a net negative adjustment under paragraph (e)(4)(ii) of this section, is an adjustment that does not result in an imputed underpayment for that year. Therefore, there is no imputed underpayment for 2020.

(6) *Example 6.* On its partnership return for the 2020 taxable year, Partnership reported ordinary income of $100 and a capital gain of $50. Partnership had four equal partners during the 2020 tax year, all of whom were individuals. On its partnership return for the 2020 tax year, the capital gain was allocated to partner E and the ordinary income was allocated to all partners based on their interests in Partnership. In an administrative proceeding with respect to Partnership's 2020 taxable year, the IRS determines that for 2020 the capital gain allocated to E should have been $75 instead of $50 and that Partnership should have recognized an additional $10 in ordinary income. In the NOPPA mailed by the IRS, the IRS may determine pursuant to paragraph (g) of this section that there is a general imputed underpayment with respect to the increase in ordinary income and a specific imputed underpayment with respect to the increase in capital gain specially allocated to E.

(7) *Example 7.* On its partnership return for the 2020 taxable year, Partnership reported a recourse liability of $100. During an administrative proceeding with respect to Partnership's 2020 taxable year, the IRS determines that the $100 recourse liability should have been reported as a $100 nonrecourse liability. Under paragraph (d)(2)(iii)(B) of this section, the adjustment to the character of the liability is an adjustment to an item that cannot be allocated under section 704(b). The adjustment therefore is treated as a $100 increase in income because such recharacterization of a liability could result in up to $100 in taxable income if taken into account by any person. The $100 increase in income is a positive adjustment in the residual grouping under paragraph (c)(5)(ii) of this section. There are no other adjustments for the 2020 partnership taxable year. The $100 positive adjustment is treated as a net positive adjustment under paragraph (e)(4)(i) of this section, and the total netted partnership adjustment under paragraph (b)(2) of this section is $100. Pursuant to paragraph (b)(1) of this section, the total netted partnership adjustment is multiplied by 40 percent for an imputed underpayment of $40.

(8) *Example 8.* Partnership reports on its 2019 partnership return $400 of CFTEs in the general category under section 904(d). The IRS initiates an administrative proceeding with respect to Partnership's 2019 taxable year and determines that the amount of CFTEs was $300 instead of $400 (-$100 adjustment to CFTEs). No other adjustments are made for the 2019 taxable year. The -$100 adjustment to CFTEs is placed in the creditable expenditure grouping described in paragraph (c)(4) of this section. Pursuant to paragraph (e)(3)(iii) of this section, the decrease to CFTEs in the creditable expenditure grouping is treated as a positive adjustment to (decrease in) credits in the credit grouping under paragraph (c)(3) of this section. Because no other adjustments have been made, the $100 decrease in credits produces an imputed underpayment of $100 under paragraph (b)(1) of this section.

(9) *Example 9.* Partnership reports on its 2019 partnership return $400 of CFTEs in the passive category under section 904(d). The IRS initiates an administrative proceeding with respect to Partnership's 2019 taxable year and determines that the CFTEs reported by Partnership were general category instead of passive category CFTEs. No other adjustments are made. Under the rules in paragraph (c)(6) of this section, an adjustment to the category of a CFTE is treated as two separate adjustments: an increase to general category CFTEs of $400 and a decrease to passive category CFTEs of $400. Both adjustments are included in the creditable expenditure grouping under paragraph (c)(4) of this section, but they are included in separate subgroupings. Therefore, the two amounts do not net. Instead, the $400 increase to CFTEs in the general category subgrouping is treated as a net nega-

tive adjustment under paragraph (e)(3)(iii)(A) of this section and is an adjustment that does not result in an imputed underpayment under paragraph (f) of this section. The decrease to CFTEs in the passive category subgrouping of the creditable expenditure grouping results in a decrease in CFTEs. Therefore, pursuant to paragraph (e)(3)(iii)(A) of this section, it is treated as a positive adjustment to (decrease in) credits in the credit grouping under paragraph (c)(3) of this section, which results in an imputed underpayment of $400 under paragraph (b)(1) of this section.

(10) *Example 10.* Partnership has two partners, A and B. Under the partnership agreement, $100 of the CFTE is specially allocated to A for the 2019 taxable year. The IRS initiates an administrative proceeding with respect to Partnership's 2019 taxable year and determines that $100 of CFTE should be reallocated from A to B. Because the adjustment reallocates a creditable expenditure, paragraph (c)(4) of this section provides that it is included in the creditable expenditure grouping rather than the reallocation grouping. The partnership adjustment is a -$100 adjustment to general category CFTE allocable to A and an increase of $100 to general category CFTE allocable to B. Pursuant to paragraph (d)(3)(iii) of this section, the -$100 adjustment to general category CFTE and the increase of $100 to general category CFTE are included in separate subgroupings in the creditable expenditure grouping. The $100 increase in general category CFTEs, B-allocation subgrouping, is a net negative adjustment, which does not result in an imputed underpayment and is therefore taken into account by the partnership in the adjustment year in accordance with § 301.6225-3. The net decrease to CFTEs in the general-category, A-allocation subgrouping, is treated as a positive adjustment to (decrease in) credits in the credit grouping under paragraph (c)(3) of this section, resulting in an imputed underpayment of $100 under paragraph (b)(1) of this section.

(11) *Example 11.* Partnership has two partners, A and B. Partnership owns two entities, DE1 and DE2, that are disregarded as separate from their owner for Federal income tax purposes and are operating in and paying taxes to foreign jurisdictions. The partnership agreement provides that all items from DE1 and DE2 are allocable to A and B in the following manner. Items related to DE1: to A 75 percent and to B 25 percent. Items related to DE2: to A 25 percent and to B 75 percent. On Partnership's 2018 return, Partnership reports CFTEs in the general category of $300, $100 with respect to DE1 and $200 with respect to DE2. Partnership allocates the $300 of CFTEs $125 and $175 to A and B respectively. During an administrative proceeding with respect to Partnership's 2018 taxable year, the IRS determines that Partnership understated the amount of creditable foreign tax paid by DE2 by $40 and overstated the amount of creditable foreign tax paid by DE1 by $80. No other adjustments are made. Because the two adjustments each relate to CFTEs that are subject to different allocations, the two adjustments are in different subgroupings under paragraph (d)(3)(iii)(B) of this section. The adjustment reducing the CFTEs related to DE1 results in a decrease in CFTEs within that subgrouping and under paragraph (e)(3)(iii)(A) of this section is treated as a decrease in credits in the credit grouping under paragraph (c)(3) of this section and results in an imputed underpayment of $80 under paragraph (b)(1) of this section. The increase of $40 of general category CFTE related to the DE2 subgrouping results in an increase in CFTEs within that subgrouping and is treated as a net negative adjustment, which does not result in an imputed underpayment and is taken into account in the adjustment year in accordance with § 301.6225-3.

(12) *Example 12.* Partnership has two partners, A and B. For the 2019 taxable year, Partnership allocated $70 of long term capital loss to B as well as $30 of ordinary income. In an administrative proceeding with respect to Partnership's 2019 taxable year, the IRS determines that the $30 of ordinary income and the $70 of long term capital loss should be reallocated from B to A. The partnership adjustments are a decrease of $30 of ordinary income (-$30 adjustment) allocated to B and a corresponding increase of $30 of ordinary income ($30 adjustment) allocated to A, as well as a decrease of $70 of long term capital loss ($70 adjustment) allocated to B and a corresponding increase of $70 of long term capital loss (-$70 adjustment) allocated to A. See paragraph (c)(2)(ii) of this section. Pursuant to paragraph (d)(3)(ii)(A) of this section, for purposes of determining the imputed underpayment, each positive adjustment and each negative adjustment allocated to A and B is placed in its own separate subgrouping. However, notwithstanding the general requirement that reallocation adjustments be subgrouped separately, the reallocation adjustments allocated to A and B may be subgrouped in accordance with paragraph (d)(3)(i) of this section because there are two reallocation adjustments allocated to each of A and B, respectively. Pursuant to paragraph (d)(3)(i) of this section, because the partnership adjustment allocated to A would not have been netted at the partnership level and would not have been allocated to A as a single partnership-related item for purposes of section 702(a), other provisions of the Code, regulations, forms, instructions, or other guidance prescribed by the IRS, the positive adjustment and the negative

adjustment allocated to A remain in separate subgroupings. For the same reasons with respect to the adjustments allocated to B, the positive adjustment and the negative adjustment allocated to B also remain in separate subgroupings. As a result, the reallocation grouping would have four subgroupings, one for each adjustment: the decrease in ordinary income allocated to B (-$30 adjustment), the increase in ordinary income allocated to A ($30 adjustment), the decrease in long term capital loss allocated to B ($70 adjustment), and the increase long term capital loss allocated to A (-$70 adjustment). Pursuant to paragraph (e) of this section, no netting may occur between subgroupings. Accordingly, the ordinary income allocated to A ($30 adjustment) and the long term capital loss allocated to B ($70 adjustment) are both net positive adjustments. These net positive adjustments are added together to determine the total netted partnership adjustment of $100. The total netted partnership adjustment is multiplied by 40 percent, which results in an imputed underpayment of $40. The ordinary income allocated to B (-$30 adjustment) and the long term capital loss allocated to A (-$70 adjustment) are net negative adjustments treated as adjustments that do not result in an imputed underpayment taken into account by the partnership pursuant to § 301.6225-3.

(i) *Applicability date.*—(1) *In general.*—Except as provided in paragraph (i)(2) of this section, this section applies to partnership taxable years beginning after December 31, 2017, and ending after August 12, 2018.

(2) *Election under § 301.9100-22 in effect.*—This section applies to any partnership taxable year beginning after November 2, 2015 and before January 1, 2018, for which a valid election under § 301.9100-22T is in effect. [Reg. § 301.6225-1.]

☐ [T.D. 9844, 2-21-2019.]

[Reg. § 301.6225-2]

**§ 301.6225-2. Modification of imputed underpayment.—** (a) *Partnership may request modification of an imputed underpayment.*— A partnership that has received a notice of proposed partnership adjustment (NOPPA) under section 6231(a)(2) from the Internal Revenue Service (IRS) may request modification of a proposed imputed underpayment set forth in the NOPPA in accordance with this section and any forms, instructions, and other guidance prescribed by the IRS. The effect of modification on a proposed imputed underpayment is described in paragraph (b) of this section. Unless otherwise described in paragraph (d) of this section, a partnership may request any type of modification of an imputed underpayment described in paragraph (d) of this section in the time and manner described in paragraph (c) of this section. A partnership may request modification with respect to a partnership adjustment (as defined in § 301.6241-1(a)(6)) that does not result in an imputed underpayment (as described in § 301.6225-1(f)(1)(ii)) as described in paragraph (e) of this section. Only the partnership representative may request modification under this section. See section 6223 and § 301.6223-2 for rules regarding the binding authority of the partnership representative. For purposes of this section, the term *relevant partner* means any person for whom modification is requested by the partnership that is–

(1) A reviewed year partner (as defined in § 301.6241-1(a)(9)), including any pass-through partner (as defined in § 301.6241-1(a)(5)), except for any reviewed year partner that is a wholly-owned entity disregarded as separate from its owner for Federal income tax purposes; or

(2) An indirect partner (as defined in § 301.6241-1(a)(4)) except for any indirect partner that is a wholly-owned entity disregarded as separate from its owner for Federal income tax purposes.

(b) *Effect of modification.*—(1) *In general.*—A modification of an imputed underpayment under this section that is approved by the IRS may result in an increase or decrease in the amount of an imputed underpayment set forth in the NOPPA. A modification under this section has no effect on the amount of any partnership adjustment determined under subchapter C of chapter 63 of the Internal Revenue Code (subchapter C of chapter 63). See paragraph (e) of this section for the effect of modification on adjustments that do not result in an imputed underpayment. A modification may increase or decrease an imputed underpayment by affecting the extent to which adjustments factor into the determination of the imputed underpayment (as described in paragraph (b)(2) of this section), the tax rate that is applied in calculating the imputed underpayment (as described in paragraph (b)(3) of this section), and the number and composition of imputed underpayments, including the placement of adjustments in groupings and subgroupings (if applicable) (as described in paragraph (b)(4) of this section), as well as to the extent of other modifications allowed under rules provided in forms, instructions, or other guidance prescribed by the IRS (as described in paragraph (b)(5) of this section). If a partnership requests more than one modification under

this section, modifications are taken into account in the following order:

(i) Modifications that affect the extent to which an adjustment factors into the determination of the imputed underpayment under paragraph (b)(2) of this section;

(ii) Modification of the number and composition of imputed underpayments under paragraph (b)(4) of this section;

(iii) Modifications that affect the tax rate under paragraph (b)(3) of this section.

(2) *Modifications that affect partnership adjustments for purposes of determining the imputed underpayment.*—If the IRS approves modification with respect to a partnership adjustment, such partnership adjustment is excluded from the determination of the imputed underpayment as determined under § 301.6225-1(b). This paragraph (b)(2) applies to modifications under–

(i) Paragraph (d)(2) of this section (amended returns and the alternative procedure to filing amended returns);

(ii) Paragraph (d)(3) of this section (tax-exempt status);

(iii) Paragraph (d)(5) of this section (specified passive activity losses);

(iv) Paragraph (d)(7) of this section (qualified investment entities);

(v) Paragraph (d)(8) of this section (closing agreements), if applicable;

(vi) Paragraph (d)(9) of this section (tax treaty modifications), if applicable; and

(vii) Paragraph (d)(10) of this section (other modifications), if applicable.

(3) *Modifications that affect the tax rate.*—(i) *In general.*—If the IRS approves a modification with respect to the tax rate applied to a partnership adjustment, such modification results in a reduction in tax rate applied to the total netted partnership adjustment with respect to the partnership adjustments in accordance with this paragraph (b)(3). A modification of the tax rate does not affect how the partnership adjustment factors into the calculation of the total netted partnership adjustment. This paragraph (b)(3) applies to modifications under–

(A) Paragraph (d)(4) of this section (rate modification);

(B) Paragraph (d)(8) of this section (closing agreements), if applicable;

(C) Paragraph (d)(9) of this section (tax treaty modifications), if applicable; and

(D) Paragraph (d)(10) of this section (other modifications), if applicable.

(ii) *Determination of the imputed underpayment in the case of rate modification.*—Except as described in paragraph (b)(3)(iv) of this section, in the case of an approved modification described under paragraph (b)(3)(i) of this section, the imputed underpayment is the sum of the total netted partnership adjustment consisting of the net positive adjustments not subject to rate reduction under paragraph (b)(3)(i) of this section (taking into account any approved modifications under paragraph (b)(2) of the section), plus the *rate-modified netted partnership adjustment* determined under paragraph (b)(3)(iii) of this section, reduced or increased by any adjustments to credits (taking into account any modifications under paragraph (b)(4) of this section). The total netted partnership adjustment not subject to rate reduction under paragraph (b)(3)(i) of this section (taking into account any approved modifications under paragraph (b)(2) of the section) is determined by multiplying the partnership adjustments included in the total netted partnership adjustment that are not subject to rate modification under paragraph (b)(3)(i) of this section (including any partnership adjustment that remains after applying paragraph (b)(3)(iii) of this section) by the highest tax rate (as described in § 301.6225-1(b)(1)(iv)).

(iii) *Calculation of rate-modified netted partnership adjustment in the case of a rate modification.*—The *rate-modified netted partnership adjustment* is determined as follows–

(A) Determine each relevant partner's distributive share of the partnership adjustments subject to an approved modification under paragraph (b)(3)(i) of this section based on how each adjustment subject to rate modification was allocated in the NOPPA, or if the appropriate allocation was not addressed in the NOPPA, how the adjustment would be properly allocated under subchapter K of chapter 1 of the Internal Revenue Code (subchapter K) to such relevant partner in the reviewed year (as defined in § 301.6241-1(a)(8)).

(B) Multiply each partnership adjustment determined under paragraph (b)(3)(iii)(A) of this section by the tax rate applicable to such adjustment based on the approved modification described under paragraph (b)(3)(i) of this section.

(C) Add all of the amounts calculated under paragraph (b)(3)(iii)(B) of this section with respect to each partnership adjustment subject to an approved modification described under paragraph (b)(3)(i) of this section.

(iv) *Rate modification in the case of special allocations.*—If an imputed underpayment results from adjustments to more than one partnership-related item and any relevant partner for whom modification described under paragraph (b)(3)(i) of this section is approved has a distributive share of such items that is not the same with respect to all such items, the imputed underpayment as modified based on the modification types described under paragraph (b)(3)(i) of this section is determined as described in paragraphs (b)(3)(ii) and (iii) of this section except that each relevant partner's distributive share is determined based on the amount of net gain or loss to the partner that would have resulted if the partnership had sold all of its assets at their fair market value as of the close of the reviewed year appropriately adjusted to reflect any approved modification under paragraphs (d)(2), (3), and (5) through (10) of this section with respect to any relevant partner. Notwithstanding the preceding sentence, the partnership may request that the IRS apply the rule in paragraph (b)(3)(iii)(A) of this section when determining each relevant partner's distributive share for purposes of this paragraph (b)(3)(iv). Upon request by the IRS, the partnership may be required to provide the relevant partners' capital account calculation through the end of the reviewed year, a calculation of asset liquidation gain or loss, and any other information necessary to determine whether rate modification is appropriate, consistent with the rules of paragraph (c)(2) of this section. Any calculation by the partnership that is necessary to comply with the rules in this paragraph (b)(3)(iv) is not considered a revaluation for purposes of section 704.

(4) *Modification of the number and composition of imputed underpayments.*—Once approved by the IRS, a modification under paragraph (d)(6) of this section affects the manner in which adjustments are placed into groupings and subgroupings (as described in §301.6225-1(c) and (d)) or whether the IRS designates one or more specific imputed underpayments (as described in §301.6225-1(g)). If the IRS approves a request for modification under this paragraph (b)(4), the imputed underpayment and any specific imputed underpayment affected by or resulting from the modification is determined according to the rules of §301.6225-1 subject to any other modifications approved by the IRS under this section.

(5) *Other modifications.*—The effect of other modifications described in paragraph (d)(10) of this section, including the order that such modification will be taken into account for purposes of paragraph (b)(1) of this section, may be set forth in forms, instructions, or other guidance prescribed by the IRS.

(c) *Time, form, and manner for requesting modification.*—(1) *In general.*—In addition to the requirements described in paragraph (d) of this section, a request for modification under this section must be submitted in accordance with, and include the information required by, the forms, instructions, and other guidance prescribed by the IRS. The partnership representative must submit any request for modification and all relevant information (including information required under paragraphs (c)(2) and (d) of this section) to the IRS within the time described in paragraph (c)(3) of this section. The IRS will notify the partnership representative in writing of the approval or denial, in whole or in part, of any request for modification. A request for modification, including a request by the IRS for information related to a request for modification, and the determination by the IRS to approve or not approve all or a portion of a request for modification, is part of the administrative proceeding with respect to the partnership under subchapter C of chapter 63 and does not constitute an examination, inspection, or other administrative proceeding with respect to any other person for purposes of section 7605(b).

(2) *Partnership must substantiate facts supporting a request for modification.*—(i) *In general.*—A partnership requesting modification under this section must substantiate the facts supporting such a request to the satisfaction of the IRS. The documents and other information necessary to substantiate a particular request for modification are based on the facts and circumstances of each request, as well as the type of modification requested under paragraph (d) of this section, and may include tax returns, partnership operating documents, certifications in the form and manner required with respect to the particular modification, and any other information necessary to support the requested modification. The IRS may, in forms, instructions, or other guidance, set forth procedures with respect to information and documents supporting the modification, including procedures to require particular documents or other information to substantiate a particular type of modification, the manner for submitting documents and other information to the IRS, and recordkeeping requirements. Pursuant to section 6241(10), the IRS may require the partnership to file or submit anything required to be filed or submitted under this section to be filed or submitted elec-

tronically. The IRS will deny a request for modification if a partnership fails to provide information the IRS determines is necessary to substantiate a request for modification, or if the IRS determines there is a failure by any person to make any required payment, within the time restrictions described in paragraph (c) of this section.

(ii) *Information to be furnished for any modification request.*—In the case of any modification request, the partnership representative must furnish to the IRS such information as is required by forms, instructions, and other guidance prescribed by the IRS or that is otherwise requested by the IRS related to the requested modification. Such information may include a detailed description of the partnership's structure, allocations, ownership, and ownership changes, its relevant partners for each taxable year relevant to the request for modification, as well as the partnership agreement as defined in §1.704-1(b)(2)(ii)(*h*) of this chapter for each taxable year relevant to the modification request. In the case of any modification request with respect to a relevant partner that is an indirect partner, the partnership representative must provide to the IRS any information that the IRS may require relevant to any pass-through partner or wholly-owned entity disregarded as separate from its owner for Federal income tax purposes through which the relevant partner holds its interest in the partnership. For instance, if the partnership requests modification with respect to an amended return filed by a relevant partner pursuant to paragraph (d)(2) of this section, the partnership representative may be required to provide to the IRS information that would have been required to have been filed by pass-through partners through which the relevant partner holds its interest in the partnership as if those pass-through partners had also filed their own amended returns.

(3) *Time for submitting modification request and information.*—(i) *Modification request.*—Unless the IRS grants an extension of time, all information required under this section with respect to a request for modification must be submitted to the IRS in the form and manner prescribed by the IRS on or before 270 days after the date the NOPPA is mailed.

(ii) *Extension of the 270-day period.*—The IRS may, in its discretion, grant a request for extension of the 270-day period described in paragraph (c)(3)(i) of this section provided the partnership submits such request to the IRS, in the form and manner prescribed by forms, instructions, or other guidance prescribed by the IRS before expiration of such period, as extended by any prior extension granted under this paragraph (c)(3)(ii).

(iii) *Expiration of the 270-day period by agreement.*—The 270-day period described in paragraph (c)(3)(i) of this section (including any extensions under paragraph (c)(3)(ii) of this section) expires as of the date the partnership and the IRS agree, in the form and manner prescribed by form, instructions, or other guidance prescribed by the IRS to waive the 270-day period after the mailing of the NOPPA and before the IRS may issue a notice of final partnership adjustment. See section 6231(b)(2)(A); §301.6231-1(b)(2).

(4) *Approval of modification by the IRS.*—Notification of approval will be provided to the partnership only after receipt of all relevant information (including any supplemental information required by the IRS) and all necessary payments with respect to the particular modification requested before expiration of the 270-day period in paragraph (c)(3)(i) of this section plus any extension granted by the IRS under paragraph (c)(3)(ii) of this section.

(d) *Types of modification.*—(1) *In general.*—Except as otherwise described in this section, a partnership may request one type of modification or more than one type of modification described in paragraph (d) of this section.

(2) *Amended returns by partners.*—(i) *In general.*—A partnership may request a modification of an imputed underpayment based on an amended return filed by a relevant partner provided all of the partnership adjustments properly allocable to such relevant partner are taken into account and any amount due is paid in accordance with paragraph (d)(2) of this section. Only adjustments to partnership-related items or adjustments to a relevant partner's tax attributes affected by adjustments to partnership-related items may be taken into account on an amended return under paragraph (d)(2) of this section. A partnership may request a modification for purposes of paragraph (d)(2) of this section by submitting a modification request based on the alternative procedure to filing amended returns as described in paragraph (d)(2)(x) of this section. The partnership may not request an additional modification of any imputed underpayment for a partnership taxable year under this section with respect to any relevant partner that files an amended return (or utilizes the alternative procedure to filing amended returns) under paragraph (d)(2) of this section or with respect to any partnership adjustment allocated to such relevant partner.

(ii) *Requirements for approval of a modification request based on amended return.*—Except as otherwise provided under the alternative procedure described in paragraph (d)(2)(x) of this section, an amended return modification request under paragraph (d)(2) of this section will not be approved unless the provisions of this paragraph (d)(2)(ii) are satisfied. The partnership may satisfy the requirements of paragraph (d)(2) of this section by demonstrating in accordance with forms, instructions, and other guidance provided by the IRS that a relevant partner has previously taken into account the partnership adjustments described in paragraph (d)(2)(i) of this section, made any required adjustments to tax attributes resulting from the partnership adjustments for the years described in paragraph (d)(2)(ii)(B) of this section, and made all required payments under paragraph (d)(2)(ii)(A) of this section.

(A) *Full payment required.*—An amended return modification request under paragraph (d)(2) of this section will not be approved unless the relevant partner filing the amended return has paid all tax, penalties, additions to tax, additional amounts, and interest due as a result of taking into account all partnership adjustments in the first affected year (as defined in §301.6226-3(b)(2)) and all modification years (as described in paragraph (d)(2)(ii)(B) of this section) at the time such return is filed with the IRS. Except for a pass-through partner calculating its payment amount pursuant to paragraph (d)(2)(vi) of this section, for purposes of this paragraph (d)(2)(ii)(A), the term *tax* means tax imposed by chapter 1 of the Internal Revenue Code (chapter 1).

(B) *Amended returns for all relevant taxable years must be filed.*—Modification under paragraph (d)(2) of this section will not be approved by the IRS unless a relevant partner files an amended return for the first affected year and any modification year. A *modification year* is any taxable year with respect to which any tax attribute (as defined in §301.6241-1(a)(10)) of the relevant partner is affected by reason of taking into account the relevant partner's distributive share of all partnership adjustments in the first affected year. A modification year may be a taxable year before or after the first affected year, depending on the effect on the relevant partner's tax attributes of taking into account the relevant partner's distributive share of the partnership adjustments in the first affected year.

(C) *Amended returns for partnership adjustments that reallocate distributive shares.*—Except as described in this paragraph (d)(2)(ii)(C), in the case of partnership adjustments that reallocate the distributive shares of any partnership-related item from one partner to another, a modification under paragraph (d)(2) of this section will be approved only if all partners affected by such adjustments file amended returns in accordance with paragraph (d)(2) of this section. The IRS may determine that the requirements of this paragraph (d)(2)(ii)(C) are satisfied even if not all relevant partners affected by such adjustments file amended returns provided any relevant partners affected by the reallocation not filing amended returns take into account their distributive share of the adjustments through other modifications approved by the IRS (including the alternative procedure to filing amended returns under paragraph (d)(2)(x) of this section) or if a pass-through partner takes into account the relevant adjustments in accordance with paragraph (d)(2)(vi) of this section. For instance, in the case of adjustments that reallocate a loss from one partner to another, the IRS may determine that the requirements of this paragraph (d)(2)(ii)(C) have been satisfied if one affected relevant partner files an amended return taking into account the adjustments and the other affected relevant partner signs a closing agreement with the IRS taking into account the adjustments. Similarly, in the case of adjustment that reallocate income from one partner to another, the IRS may determine that the requirements of this paragraph (d)(2)(ii)(C) have been satisfied to the extent an affected relevant partner meets the requirements of paragraph (d)(3) of this section (regarding tax-exempt partners) and through such modification fully takes into account all adjustments reallocated to the affected relevant partner.

(iii) *Form and manner for filing amended returns.*—A relevant partner must file all amended returns required for modification under paragraph (d)(2) of this section with the IRS in accordance with forms, instructions, and other guidance prescribed by the IRS. Except as otherwise provided under the alternative procedure described in paragraph (d)(2)(x) of this section, the IRS will not approve modification under paragraph (d)(2) of this section unless prior to the expiration of the 270-day period described in paragraph (c)(3) of this section, the partnership representative provides to the IRS, in the form and manner prescribed by the IRS, an affidavit from each relevant partner signed under penalties of perjury by such partner stating that all of the amended returns required to be filed under paragraph (d)(2) of this section has been filed (including the date on which such amended returns were filed) and that the full amount of

tax, penalties, additions to tax, additional amounts, and interest was paid (including the date on which such amounts were paid).

(iv) *Period of limitations.*—Generally, the period of limitations under sections 6501 and 6511 do not apply to an amended return filed under paragraph (d)(2) of this section provided the amended return otherwise meets the requirements of paragraph (d)(2) of this section.

(v) *Amended returns in the case of adjustments allocated through certain pass-through partners.*—A request for modification related to an amended return of a relevant partner that is an indirect partner holding its interest in the partnership (directly or indirectly) through a pass-through partner that could be subject to tax imposed by chapter 1 (chapter 1 tax) on the partnership adjustments that are properly allocated to such pass-through partner will not be approved unless the partnership—

(A) Establishes that the pass-through partner is not subject to chapter 1 tax on the adjustments that are properly allocated to such pass-through partner; or

(B) Requests modification with respect to the adjustments resulting in chapter 1 tax for the pass-through partner, including full payment of such chapter 1 tax for the first affected year and all modification years under paragraph (d)(2) of this section or in accordance with forms, instructions, or other guidance prescribed by the IRS.

(vi) *Amended returns in the case of pass-through partners.*—(A) *Pass-through partners may file amended returns.*—A relevant partner that is a pass-through partner, including a partnership-partner (as defined in §301.6241-1(a)(7)) that has a valid election under section 6221(b) in effect for a partnership taxable year, may, in accordance with forms, instructions, and other guidance provided by the IRS and solely for purposes of modification under paragraph (d)(2) of this section, take into account its share of the partnership adjustments and determine and pay an amount calculated in the same manner as the amount computed under §301.6226-3(e)(4)(iii) subject to paragraph (d)(2)(vi)(B) of this section.

(B) *Modifications with respect to upper-tier partners of the pass-through partner.*—In accordance with forms, instructions, and other guidance provided by the IRS, for purposes of determining and calculating the amount a pass-through partner must pay under paragraph (d)(2)(vi)(A) of this section, the pass-through partner may take into account modifications with respect to its direct and indirect partners to the extent that such modifications are requested by the partnership requesting modification and approved by the IRS under this section.

(vii) *Limitations on amended returns.*—(A) *In general.*—A relevant partner may not file an amended return or claim for refund that takes into account partnership adjustments except as described in paragraph (d)(2) of this section.

(B) *Further amended returns restricted.*—Except as described in paragraph (d)(2)(vii)(C) of this section, if a relevant partner files an amended return under paragraph (d)(2) of this section, or satisfies paragraph (d)(2) of this section by following the alternative procedure under paragraph (d)(2)(x) of this section (the alternative procedure), such partner may not file a subsequent amended return or claim for refund to change the treatment of partnership adjustments taken into account through amended return or the alternative procedure.

(C) *Subsequent returns in the case of changes to partnership adjustments or denial of modification.*—Notwithstanding paragraph (d)(2)(vii)(B) of this section, a relevant partner that has previously filed an amended return under paragraph (d)(2) of this section, or satisfied the requirements of paragraph (d)(2) of this section through the alternative procedure, to take partnership adjustments into account may, in accordance with forms, instructions, and other guidance prescribed by the IRS, file a subsequent return or claim for refund if a determination is made by a court or by the IRS that results in a change to the partnership adjustments taken into account in modification under paragraph (d)(2) of this section or a denial of modification by the IRS under paragraph (c)(2)(i) of this section with respect to a modification request under paragraph (d)(2) of this section. Such determinations include a court decision that changes the partnership adjustments for which modification was requested or a settlement between the IRS and the partnership pursuant to which the partnership is not liable for all or a portion of the imputed underpayment for which modification was requested. Any amended return or claim for refund filed under this paragraph (d)(2)(vii) is subject to the period of limitations under section 6511.

(viii) *Penalties.*—The applicability of any penalties, additions to tax, or additional amounts that relate to an adjustment to a partnership-related item is determined at the partnership level in accordance with section 6221(a). However, the amount of penalties, additions to tax, and additional amounts a relevant partner must pay under paragraph (d)(2)(ii)(A) of this section for the first affected year and for any modification year is based on the underpayment or understatement of tax, if any, reflected on the amended return filed by the relevant partner under paragraph (d)(2) of this section. For instance, if after taking into account the adjustments, the return of the relevant partner for the first affected year or any modification year reflects an underpayment or an understatement that falls below the applicable threshold for the imposition of a penalty under section 6662(d), no penalty would be due from that relevant partner for such year. Unless forms, instructions or other guidance provided by the IRS allow for an alternative procedure for raising a partner-level defense (as described in §301.6226-3(d)(3)), a relevant partner may raise a partner-level defense by first paying the penalty, addition to tax, or additional amount with the amended return filed under paragraph (d)(2) of this section and then filing a claim for refund in accordance with forms, instructions, and other guidance.

(ix) *Effect on tax attributes binding.*—Any adjustments to the tax attributes of any relevant partner which are affected by modification under paragraph (d)(2) of this section are binding on the relevant partner with respect to the first affected year and all modification years (as defined in paragraph (d)(2)(ii)(B) of this section). A failure to adjust any tax attribute in accordance with this paragraph (d)(2)(ix) is a failure to treat a partnership-related item in a manner which is consistent with the treatment of such item on the partnership return within the meaning of section 6222. The provisions of section 6222(c) and §301.6222-1(c) (regarding notification of inconsistent treatment) do not apply with respect to tax attributes under this paragraph (d)(2)(ix).

(x) *Alternative procedure to filing amended returns.*—(A) *In general.*—A partnership may satisfy the requirements of paragraph (d)(2) of this section by submitting on behalf of a relevant partner, in accordance with forms, instructions, and other guidance provided by the IRS, all information and payment of any tax, penalties, additions to tax, additional amounts, and interest that would be required to be provided if the relevant partner were filing an amended return under paragraph (d)(2) of this section, except as otherwise provided in relevant forms, instructions, and other guidance provided by the IRS. A relevant partner for which the partnership seeks modification under paragraph (d)(2)(x) of this section must agree to take into account, in accordance with forms, instructions, and other guidance provided by the IRS, adjustments to any tax attributes of such relevant partner. A modification request submitted in accordance with the alternative procedure under paragraph (d)(2)(x) of this section is not a claim for refund with respect to any person.

(B) *Modifications with respect to reallocation adjustments.*—A submission made in accordance with paragraph (d)(2)(x) of this section with respect to any relevant partner is treated as if such relevant partner filed an amended return for purposes of paragraph (d)(2)(ii)(C) of this section (regarding the requirement that all relevant partners affected by a reallocation must file an amended return to be eligible to for the modification under paragraph (d)(2) of this section) provided the submission is with respect to the first affected year and all modification years of such relevant partner as required under paragraph (d)(2) of this section.

(3) *Tax-exempt partners.*—(i) *In general.*—A partnership may request modification of an imputed underpayment with respect to partnership adjustments that the partnership demonstrates to the satisfaction of the IRS are allocable to a relevant partner that would not owe tax by reason of its status as a tax-exempt entity (as defined in paragraph (d)(3)(ii) of this section) in the reviewed year (tax-exempt partner).

(ii) *Definition of tax-exempt entity.*—For purposes of paragraph (d)(3) of this section, the term *tax-exempt entity* means a person or entity defined in section 168(h)(2)(A), (C), or (D).

(iii) *Modification limited to portion of partnership adjustments for which tax-exempt partner not subject to tax.*—Only the portion of the partnership adjustments properly allocated to a tax-exempt partner with respect to which the partner would not be subject to tax for the reviewed year (tax-exempt portion) may form the basis of a modification of the imputed underpayment under paragraph (d)(3) of this section. A modification under paragraph (d)(3) of this section will not be approved by the IRS unless the partnership provides documentation in accordance with paragraph (c)(2) of this section to support the tax-exempt partner's status and the tax-exempt portion of the partnership adjustment allocable to the tax-exempt partner.

(4) *Modification based on a rate of tax lower than the highest applicable tax rate.*—A partnership may request modification based on a

lower rate of tax for the reviewed year with respect to adjustments that are attributable to a relevant partner that is a C corporation and adjustments with respect to capital gains or qualified dividends that are attributable to a relevant partner who is an individual. In no event may the lower rate determined under the preceding sentence be less than the highest rate in effect for the reviewed year with respect to the type of income and taxpayer. For instance, with respect to adjustments that are attributable to a C corporation, the highest rate in effect for the reviewed year with respect to all C corporations would apply to that adjustment, regardless of the rate that would apply to the C corporation based on the amount of that C corporation's taxable income. For purposes of this paragraph (d)(4), an S corporation is treated as an individual.

(5) *Certain passive losses of publicly traded partnerships.*—(i) *In general.*—In the case of a publicly traded partnership (as defined in section 469(k)(2)) requesting modification under this section, an imputed underpayment is determined without regard to any adjustment that the partnership demonstrates would be reduced by a specified passive activity loss (as defined in paragraph (d)(5)(ii) of this section) which is allocable to a specified partner (as defined in paragraph (d)(5)(iii) of this section) or qualified relevant partner (as defined in paragraph (d)(5)(iv) of this section).

(ii) *Specified passive activity loss.*—A specified passive activity loss carryover amount for any specified partner or qualified relevant partner of a publicly traded partnership is the lesser of the section 469(k) passive activity loss of that partner which is separately determined with respect to such partnership–

(A) At the end of the first affected year (affected year loss); or

(B) At the end of–

(1) The specified partner's taxable year in which or with which the adjustment year (as defined in §301.6241-1(a)(1)) of the partnership ends, reduced to the extent any such partner has utilized any portion of its affected year loss to offset income or gain relating to the ownership or disposition of its interest in such publicly traded partnership during either the adjustment year or any other year; or

(2) If the adjustment year has not yet been determined, the most recent year for which the publicly traded partnership has filed a return under section 6031, reduced to the extent any such partner has utilized any portion of its affected year loss to offset income or gain relating to the ownership or disposition of its interest in such publicly traded partnership during any year.

(iii) *Specified partner.*—A specified partner is a person that for each taxable year beginning with the first affected year through the person's taxable year in which or with which the partnership adjustment year ends satisfies the following three requirements–

(A) The person is a partner of the publicly traded partnership requesting modification under this section;

(B) The person is an individual, estate, trust, closely held C corporation, or personal service corporation; and

(C) The person has a specified passive activity loss with respect to the publicly traded partnership.

(iv) *Qualified relevant partner.*—A *qualified relevant partner* is a relevant partner that meets the three requirements to be a specified partner (as described in paragraphs (d)(5)(iii)(A), (B), and (C) of this section) for each year beginning with the first affected year through the year described in paragraph (d)(5)(ii)(B)(2) of this section. Notwithstanding the preceding sentence, an indirect partner of the publicly traded partnership requesting modification under this section may also be a qualified relevant partner under this paragraph (d)(5)(iv) if that indirect partner meets the requirements of paragraph (d)(5)(iii)(B) and (C) of this section for each year beginning with the first affected year through the year described in paragraph (d)(5)(ii)(B)(2) of this section.

(v) *Partner notification requirement to reduce passive losses.*—If the IRS approves a modification request under paragraph (d)(5) of this section, the partnership must report, in accordance with forms, instructions, or other guidance prescribed by the IRS, to each specified partner the amount of that specified partner's reduction of its suspended passive activity loss carryovers at the end of the adjustment year to take into account the amount of any passive activity losses applied in connection with such modification request. In the case of a qualified relevant partner, the partnership must report, in accordance with forms, instructions, or other guidance prescribed by the IRS, to each qualified relevant partner the amount of that qualified relevant partner's reduction of its suspended passive activity loss carryovers at the end of the taxable year for which the partnership's next return is due to be filed under section 6031 to be taken into account by the qualified relevant partner on the partner's return for the year that includes the end of the partnership's taxable year for which the partnership's next return is due to be filed under section

6031. In the case of an indirect partner that is a qualified relevant partner, the IRS may prescribe additional guidance through forms, instructions, or other guidance to require reporting under this paragraph (d)(5)(v). The reduction in suspended passive activity loss carryovers as reported to a specified partner or qualified relevant partner under this paragraph (d)(5)(v) is a determination of the partnership under subchapter C of chapter 63 and is binding on the specified partners and qualified relevant partners under section 6223.

(6) *Modification of the number and composition of imputed underpayments.*—(i) *In general.*—A partnership may request modification of the number or composition of any imputed underpayment included in the NOPPA by requesting that the IRS include one or more partnership adjustments in a particular grouping or subgrouping (as described in § 301.6225-1(c) and (d)) or specific imputed underpayments (as described in § 301.6225-1(g)) different from the grouping, subgrouping, or imputed underpayment set forth in the NOPPA. For example, a partnership may request under paragraph (d)(6) of this section that one or more partnership adjustments taken into account to determine a general imputed underpayment set forth in the NOPPA be taken into account to determine a specific imputed underpayment.

(ii) *Request for particular treatment regarding limitations or restrictions.*—A modification request under paragraph (d)(6) of this section includes a request that one or more partnership adjustments be treated as if no limitations or restrictions under § 301.6225-1(d) apply and as a result such adjustments may be subgrouped with other adjustments.

(7) *Partnerships with partners that are "qualified investment entities" described in section 860.*—(i) *In general.*—A partnership may request a modification of an imputed underpayment based on the partnership adjustments allocated to a relevant partner where the modification is based on deficiency dividends distributed as described in section 860(f) by a relevant partner that is a qualified investment entity (QIE) under section 860(b) (which includes both a regulated investment company (RIC) and a real estate investment trust (REIT)). Modification under paragraph (d)(7) of this section is available only to the extent that the deficiency dividends take into account adjustments described in § 301.6225-1 that are also adjustments within the meaning of section 860(d)(1) or (d)(2) (whichever applies).

(ii) *Documentation of deficiency dividend.*—The partnership must provide documentation in accordance with paragraph (c) of this section of the "determination" described in section 860(e). Under section 860(e)(2), § 1.860-2(b)(1)(i) of this chapter, and paragraph (d)(8) of this section, a closing agreement entered into by the QIE partner pursuant to section 7121 and paragraph (d)(8) of this section is a determination described in section 860(e), and the date of the determination is the date in which the closing agreement is approved by the IRS. In addition, under section 860(e)(4), a determination also includes a Form 8927, *Determination Under Section 860(e)(4) by a Qualified Investment Entity,* properly completed and filed by the RIC or REIT pursuant to section 860(e)(4). To establish the date of the determination under section 860(e)(4) and the amount of deficiency dividends actually paid, the partnership must provide a copy of Form 976, *Claim for Deficiency Dividends Deductions by a Personal Holding Company, Regulated Investment Company, or Real Estate Investment Trust,* properly completed by or on behalf of the QIE pursuant to section 860(g), together with a copy of each of the required attachments for Form 976.

(8) *Closing agreements.*—A partnership may request modification based on a closing agreement entered into by the IRS and the partnership or any relevant partner, or both if appropriate, pursuant to section 7121. If modification under this paragraph (d)(8) is approved by the IRS, any partnership adjustment that is taken into account under such closing agreement and for which any required payment under the closing agreement is made will not be taken into account in determining the imputed underpayment under § 301.6225-1. Any required payment under the closing agreement may include amounts of tax, including tax under chapters other than chapter 1, interest, penalties, additions to tax and additional amounts. Generally, the IRS will not approve any additional modification under this section with respect to a relevant partner to which a modification under this paragraph (d)(8) has been approved.

(9) *Tax treaty modifications.*—A partnership may request a modification under this paragraph (d)(9) with respect to a relevant partner's distributive share of an adjustment to a partnership-related item if, in the reviewed year, the relevant partner was a foreign person who qualified under an income tax treaty with the United States for a reduction or exemption from tax with respect to such partnership-related item. A partnership requesting modification under this section may also request a treaty modification under this paragraph (d)(9) regardless of the treaty status of its partners if, in

the reviewed year, the partnership itself was an entity eligible for such treaty benefits.

(10) *Other modifications.*—A partnership may request a modification not otherwise described in paragraph (d) of this section, and the IRS will determine whether such modification is accurate and appropriate in accordance with paragraph (c)(4) of this section. Additional types of modifications and the documentation necessary to substantiate such modifications may be set forth in forms, instructions, or other guidance prescribed by the IRS.

(e) *Modification of adjustments that do not result in an imputed underpayment.*—A partnership may request modification of adjustments that do not result in an imputed underpayment (as described in § 301.6225-1(f)(1)(ii)) using modifications described in paragraph (d)(2) of this section (amended returns and the alternative procedure to filing amended returns), paragraph (d)(6) of this section (number and composition of the imputed underpayment), paragraph (d)(8) of this section (closing agreements), or, if applicable, paragraph (d)(10) of this section (other modifications).

(f) *Examples.*—The following examples illustrate the rules of this section. For purposes of these examples, each partnership is subject to the provisions of subchapter C of chapter 63, each partnership and its relevant partners are calendar year taxpayers, all relevant partners are U.S. persons (unless otherwise stated), the highest rate of income tax in effect for all taxpayers is 40 percent for all relevant periods, and no partnership requests modification under this section except as provided in the example.

(1) *Example 1.* Partnership has two partners during its 2019 partnership taxable year: P and S. P is a partnership, and S is an S corporation. P has four partners during its 2019 partnership taxable year: A, C, T and DE. A is an individual, C is a C corporation, T is a trust, and DE is a wholly-owned entity disregarded as separate from its owner for Federal income tax purposes. The owner of DE is B, an individual. T has two beneficiaries during its 2019 taxable year: F and G, both individuals. S has 3 shareholders during its 2019 taxable year: H, J, and K, all individuals. For purposes of this section, if Partnership requests modification with respect to A, B, C, F, G, H, J, and K, those persons are all relevant partners (as defined in paragraph (a) of this section). P, S, and DE are not relevant partners (as defined in paragraph (a) of this section) because DE is a wholly-owned entity disregarded as separate from its owner for Federal income tax purposes and modification was not requested with respect to P and S.

(2) *Example 2.* The IRS initiates an administrative proceeding with respect to Partnership's 2019 taxable year. The IRS mails a NOPPA to Partnership for the 2019 partnership taxable year proposing a single partnership adjustment increasing ordinary income by $100, resulting in a $40 imputed underpayment ($100 multiplied by the 40 percent tax rate). Partner A, an individual, held a 20 percent interest in Partnership during 2019. Partnership timely requests modification under paragraph (d)(2) of this section based on A's filing an amended return for the 2019 taxable year taking into account $20 of the partnership adjustment and paying the tax and interest due attributable to A's share of the increased income and the tax rate applicable to A for the 2019 tax year. No tax attribute in any other taxable year of A is affected by A's taking into account A's share of the partnership adjustment for 2019. In accordance with paragraph (d)(2)(iii) of this section, Partnership's partnership representative provides the IRS with documentation demonstrating that A filed the 2019 return and paid all tax and interest due. The IRS approves the modification and, in accordance with paragraph (b)(2) of this section, the $20 increase in ordinary income allocable to A is not included in the calculation of the total netted partnership adjustment (determined in accordance with § 301.6225-1). Partnership's total netted partnership adjustment is reduced to $80 ($100 adjustment less $20 taken into account by A), and the imputed underpayment is reduced to $32 (total netted partnership adjustment of $80 after modification multiplied by 40 percent).

(3) *Example 3.* The IRS initiates an administrative proceeding with respect to Partnership's 2019 taxable year. Partnership has two equal partners during its entire 2019 taxable year: an individual, A, and a partnership-partner, B. During all of 2019, B has two equal partners: a tax-exempt entity, C, and an individual, D. The IRS mails a NOPPA to Partnership for its 2019 taxable year proposing a single partnership adjustment increasing Partnership's ordinary income by $100, resulting in a $40 imputed underpayment ($100 total netted partnership adjustment multiplied by 40 percent). Partnership timely requests modification under paragraph (d)(3) of this section with respect to B's partner, C, a tax-exempt entity. In accordance with paragraph (d)(3)(iii) of this section, Partnership's partnership representative provides the IRS with documentation substantiating to the IRS's satisfaction that C held a 25 percent indirect interest in Partnership through its interest in B during the 2019 taxable year, that C was a tax-exempt entity defined in paragraph (d)(3)(ii) of this section during the 2019 taxable year, and that C was not subject to tax with

respect to its entire allocable share of the partnership adjustment allocated to B (which is $25 (50 percent x 50 percent x $100)). The IRS approves the modification and, in accordance with paragraph (b)(2) of this section, the $25 increase in ordinary income allocated to C, through B, is not included in the calculation of the total netted partnership adjustment (determined in accordance with § 301.6225-1). Partnership's total netted partnership adjustment is reduced to $75 ($100 adjustment less C's share of the adjustment, $25), and the imputed underpayment is reduced to $30 (total netted partnership adjustment of $75, after modification, multiplied by 40 percent).

(4) *Example 4.* The facts are the same as in *Example 3* in paragraph (f)(3) of this section, except $10 of the $25 of the adjustment allocated to C is unrelated business taxable income (UBTI) as defined in section 512 because it is debt-financed income within the meaning of section 514 (no section 512 UBTI modifications apply) with respect to which C would be subject to tax if taken into account by C. As a result, the modification under paragraph (d)(3) of this section with respect to C relates only to $15 of the $25 of ordinary income allocated to C that is not UBTI. Therefore, only a modification of $15 ($25 less $10) of the total $100 partnership adjustment may be approved by the IRS under paragraph (d)(3) of this section and, in accordance with paragraph (b)(2) of this section, excluded when determining the imputed underpayment for Partnership's 2019 taxable year. The total netted partnership adjustment (determined in accordance with § 301.6225-1) is reduced to $85 ($100 less $15), and the imputed underpayment is reduced to $34 (total netted partnership adjustment of $85, after modification, multiplied by 40 percent).

(5) *Example 5.* The facts are the same as in *Example 3* in paragraph (f)(3) of this section, except that Partnership also timely requests modification under paragraph (d)(2) of this section with respect to an amended return filed by B, and, in accordance with (d)(2)(iii) of this section, Partnership's partnership representative provides the IRS with documentation demonstrating that B filed the 2019 return and paid all tax and interest due. B reports 50 percent of the partnership adjustments ($50) on its amended return, and B calculates an amount under paragraph (d)(2)(vi)(A) of this section and § 301.6226-3(e)(4)(iii) that, pursuant to paragraph (d)(2)(vi)(B) of this section, takes into account the modification under paragraph (d)(3) of this section approved by the IRS with respect to B's partner C, a tax-exempt entity. B makes a payment pursuant to paragraph (d)(2)(ii)(A) of this section, and the IRS approves the requested modification. Partnership's total netted partnership adjustment is reduced by $50 (the amount taken into account by B). Partnership's total netted partnership adjustment (determined in accordance with § 301.6225-1) is $50, and the imputed underpayment, after modification, is $20.

(6) *Example 6.* The facts are the same as in *Example 3* in paragraph (f)(3) of this section, except that in addition to the modification with respect to tax-exempt entity C, which reduced the imputed underpayment by excluding from the determination of the imputed underpayment $25 of the $100 partnership adjustment reflected in the NOPPA, Partnership timely requests modification under paragraph (d)(2) of this section with respect to an amended return filed by individual D, and, in accordance with paragraph (d)(2)(iii) of this section, Partnership's partnership representative provides the IRS with documentation demonstrating that D filed the 2019 return and paid all tax and interest due. D's amended return for D's 2019 taxable year takes into account D's share of the partnership adjustment (50 percent of B's 50 percent interest in Partnership, or $25) and D paid the tax and interest due as a result of taking into account D's share of the partnership adjustment in accordance with paragraph (d)(2) of this section. No tax attribute in any other taxable year of D is affected by D taking into account D's share of the partnership adjustment for 2019. The IRS approves the modification and the $25 increase in ordinary income allocable to D is not included in the calculation of the total netted partnership adjustment (determined in accordance with § 301.6225-1). As a result, Partnership's total netted partnership adjustment is $50 ($100, less $25 allocable to C, less $25 taken into account by D), and the imputed underpayment, after modification, is $20.

(7) *Example 7.* The IRS initiates an administrative proceeding with respect to Partnership's 2019 taxable year. All of Partnership's partners during its 2019 taxable year are individuals. The IRS mails a NOPPA to Partnership for the 2019 taxable year proposing three partnership adjustments. The first partnership adjustment is an increase to ordinary income of $75 for 2019. The second partnership adjustment is an increase in the depreciation deduction allowed for 2019 of $25, which under § 301.6225-1(d)(2)(i) is treated as a $25 decrease in income. The third adjustment is an increase in long-term capital gain of $10 for 2019. Under the partnership agreement in effect for Partnership's 2019 taxable year, the long-term capital gain and the increase in depreciation would be specially allocated to B and the increase in ordinary income would be specially allocated to

A. In accordance with § 301.6225-1(c) and (d), the three adjustments are placed into three separate subgroupings within the residual grouping because the partnership adjustments would not have been netted at the partnership level and would not have been required to be allocated to the partners of the partnership as a single, net partnership-related item for purposes of section 702(a), other provisions of the Code, regulations, forms, instructions, or other guidance prescribed by the IRS. Accordingly, the total netted partnership adjustment is $85 ($75 net positive adjustment to ordinary income plus $10 net positive adjustment to long term capital gain), and the imputed underpayment is $34 ($85 multiplied by 40 percent). The net negative adjustment to depreciation is an adjustment that does not result in an imputed underpayment subject to treatment under § 301.6225-3. Partnership requests a modification under paragraph (d)(6) of this section to determine a specific imputed underpayment with respect to the $75 adjustment to ordinary income allocated to A. The specific imputed underpayment is with respect to $75 of the increase in income specially allocated to A and the general imputed underpayment is with respect to $10 of the increase in capital gain and the $25 increase in depreciation deduction specially allocated to B. If the modification is approved by the IRS, the specific imputed underpayment would consist of the $75 increase in ordinary income, and thus the total netted partnership adjustment for the specific imputed underpayment would be $75. The specific imputed underpayment is thus $30 ($75 multiplied by 40 percent). The general imputed underpayment would consist of two adjustments: the long term capital gain adjustment and the depreciation adjustment. The long term capital gain adjustment and the depreciation adjustment would be placed in different subgroupings under § 301.6225-1(d) because they are treated separately under section 702. Accordingly, the long term capital gain adjustment and the depreciation adjustment are not netted, and the long term capital gain adjustment would be a net positive adjustment while the depreciation adjustment would be a net negative adjustment. The long term capital gain net positive adjustment would be the only net positive adjustment, resulting in a total netted partnership adjustment of $10. The general imputed underpayment is $4 ($10 multiplied by 40 percent), and the net negative adjustment to depreciation of $25 would be an adjustment that does not result in an imputed underpayment under § 301.6225-1(f) associated with the general imputed underpayment.

(8) *Example 8.* Partnership has two reviewed year partners, C1 and C2, both of which are C corporations. The IRS mails to Partnership a NOPPA with two adjustments, both based on rental real estate activity. The first adjustment is an increase of rental real estate income of $100 attributable to Property A. The second adjustment is an increase of rental real estate loss of $30 attributable to Property B. The Partnership did not treat the leasing arrangement with respect to Property A and Property B as an appropriate economic unit for purposes of section 469. If the $100 increase in income attributable to Property A and the $30 increase in loss attributable to Property B were included in the same subgrouping and netted, then taking the $30 increase in loss into account would result in a decrease in the amount of the imputed underpayment. Also, the $30 increased loss might be limited or restricted if taken into account by any person under the passive activity rules under section 469. For instance, under section 469, rental activities of the two properties could be treated as two activities, which could limit a partner's ability to claim the loss. In addition to the potential limitations under section 469, there are other potential limitations that might apply if the $30 loss were taken into account by any person. Therefore, in accordance with § 301.6225-1(d), the two adjustments are placed in separate subgroupings within the residual grouping, the total netted partnership adjustment is $100, the imputed underpayment is $40 ($100 x 40 percent), and the $30 increase in loss is an adjustment that does not result in an imputed underpayment under § 301.6225-1(f). Partnership requests modification under paragraph (d)(6) of this section, substantiating to the satisfaction of the IRS that C1 and C2 are publicly traded C corporations, and therefore, the passive activity loss limitations under section 469 of the Code do not apply. Partnership also substantiates to the satisfaction of the IRS that no other limitation or restriction applies that would prevent the grouping of the $100 with the $30 loss. The IRS approves Partnership's modification request and places the $100 of income and the $30 loss into the subgrouping in the residual grouping under the rules described in § 301.6225-1(c)(5). Under § 301.6225-1(e), because the two adjustments are in one subgrouping, they are netted together, resulting in a total netted partnership adjustment of $70 ($100 plus -$30) and an imputed underpayment of $28 ($70 x 40 percent). After modification, none of the adjustments is an adjustment that does not result in an imputed underpayment under § 301.6225-1(f) because the $30 loss is now netted with the $100 of income in a net positive adjustment for the residual grouping.

(g) *Applicability date.*—(1) *In general.*—Except as provided in paragraph (g)(2) of this section, this section applies to partnership taxable years beginning after December 31, 2017, and ending after August 12, 2018.

(2) *Election under § 301.9100-22 in effect.*—This section applies to any partnership taxable year beginning after November 2, 2015, and before January 1, 2018, for which a valid election under § 301.9100-22 is in effect. [Reg. § 301.6225-2.]

☐ [T.D. 9844, 2-21-2019.]

### [Reg. § 301.6225-3]

**§ 301.6225-3. Treatment of partnership adjustments that do not result in an imputed underpayment.**—(a) *In general.*—Partnership adjustments (as defined in § 301.6241-1(a)(6)) that do not result in an imputed underpayment (as described in § 301.6225-1(f)) are taken into account by a partnership in the adjustment year (as defined in § 301.6241-1(a)(1)) in accordance with paragraph (b) of this section.

(b) *Treatment of adjustments by the partnership.*—(1) *In general.*—Except as described in paragraphs (b)(2) through (7) of this section, a partnership adjustment that does not result in an imputed underpayment is taken into account as a reduction in non-separately stated income or as an increase in non-separately stated loss for the adjustment year depending on whether the adjustment is to a partnership-related item that is an item of income or loss.

(2) *Separately stated items.*—In the case of a partnership adjustment to partnership-related item that is required to be separately stated under section 702, the adjustment is taken into account by the partnership in the adjustment year as a reduction in such separately stated item or as an increase in such separately stated item depending on whether the adjustment is a reduction or an increase to the separately stated item.

(3) *Credits.*—In the case of an adjustment to a partnership-related item that is reported or could be reported by a partnership as a credit on the partnership's return for the reviewed year (as defined in § 301.6241-1(a)(8)), the adjustment is taken into account by the partnership in the adjustment year as a separately stated item.

(4) *Reallocation adjustments.*—A partnership adjustment that reallocates a partnership-related item to or from a particular partner or partners that also does not result in an imputed underpayment pursuant to § 301.6225-1(f) is taken into account by the partnership in the adjustment year as a separately stated item or a non-separately stated item, as required by section 702. Except as provided in forms, instructions, and other guidance prescribed by the Internal Revenue Service (IRS), the portion of an adjustment allocated under this paragraph (b)(4) is allocated to adjustment year partners (as defined in § 301.6241-1(a)(2)) who are also reviewed year partners (as defined in § 301.6241-1(a)(9)) with respect to whom the amount was reallocated.

(5) *Adjustments taken into account by partners as part of the modification process.*—If, as part of modification under § 301.6225-2, a relevant partner (as defined in § 301.6225-2(a)) takes into account a partnership adjustment that does not result in an imputed underpayment, and the IRS approves the modification, such partnership adjustment is not taken into account by the partnership in the adjustment year in accordance with § 301.6225-1(a).

(6) *Effect of election under section 6226.*—If a partnership makes a valid election under § 301.6226-1 with respect to an imputed underpayment, a partnership adjustment that does not result in an imputed underpayment and that is associated with such imputed underpayment as described in § 301.6225-1(g) is taken into account by the reviewed year partners in accordance with § 301.6226-3 and is not taken into account under this section.

(7) *Adjustments taken into account previously by partners.*—If, prior to the mailing of a notice of administrative proceeding by the IRS or the filing of an administrative adjustment request by the partnership, a partner has previously taken into account an adjustment that does not result in an imputed underpayment that would have been taken into account under this section, such partnership adjustment is not taken into account by such partner.

(c) *Treatment of adjustment year partners.*—The rules under subchapter K of chapter 1 of the Internal Revenue Code with respect to the treatment of partners apply in the case of adjustments taken into account by the partnership under this section.

(d) *Examples.*—The following examples illustrate the rules of this section. For purposes of these examples, unless otherwise provided, each partnership is subject to the provisions of subchapter C of chapter 63 of the Internal Revenue Code, each partnership and its relevant partners are calendar year taxpayers, all relevant partners are U.S. persons (unless otherwise stated), the highest rate of income

tax in effect for all taxpayers is 40 percent for all relevant periods, and no partnership requests modification.

(1) *Example 1.* For all of Partnership's 2019, 2020, and 2021 partnership taxable years, Partnership has two equal partners, A and B. The IRS initiates an administrative proceeding with respect to Partnership's 2019 partnership taxable year. The IRS mails a notice of proposed partnership adjustment (NOPPA) to Partnership for the 2019 partnership taxable year proposing a recharacterization adjustment, changing a $100 ordinary loss to a $100 long term capital loss. Under § 301.6225-1, this recharacterization adjustment results in two adjustments: a $100 increase to ordinary income (positive adjustment) and a -$100 decrease in long term capital gain (negative adjustment). Under § 301.6225-1(b), the $100 positive adjustment is the total netted partnership adjustment, which is multiplied by the highest rate of 40 percent, resulting in a $40 imputed underpayment. Under § 301.6225-1(f), the -$100 negative adjustment is an adjustment that does not result in an imputed underpayment and is taken into account in accordance with this section. On March 1, 2021, the IRS mails a notice of final partnership adjustment (FPA), and because Partnership does not file a petition for readjustment with respect to the FPA, the adjustments are finally determined in 2021, and the adjustment year is determined to be 2021 pursuant to § 301.6241-1(a)(1). Pursuant to paragraph (a) of this section, Partnership takes into account the -$100 adjustment that does not result in an imputed underpayment on its 2021 partnership return. In addition to the -$100 adjustment to partnership's 2019 taxable year taken into account under this section, Partnership has an additional $300 in long term capital gain reportable in its 2021 taxable year. The -$100 negative adjustment and the $300 long term capital gain are Partnership's only long term capital gains and losses for its 2021 taxable year. Because the -$100 net negative adjustment is an adjustment to long term capital gain, which is a separately stated item under section 702(a)(2), the -$100 negative adjustment must be taken into account in accordance with paragraph (b)(2) of this section. Partnership includes both the -$100 negative adjustment and the $300 in long term capital gain as separately stated items on its 2021 tax return.

(2) *Example 2.* The facts are the same as in *Example 1* in paragraph (d)(1) of this section, except that the IRS proposes a reallocation adjustment instead of a recharacterization adjustment. The IRS determines that the -$100 ordinary loss that the Partnership allocated equally to A and B should instead all be allocated all to A. The IRS mails a NOPPA for the 2019 partnership taxable year proposing a reallocation adjustment resulting in a $50 increase in ordinary loss allocated to A (negative adjustment) and a $50 decrease in ordinary loss allocated to B (positive adjustment). Because the adjustments are the result of a reallocation, they are placed in separate subgroupings pursuant to § 301.6225-1(d). Because the adjustments are in different subgroupings, the adjustments are not netted under § 301.6225-1(e), resulting in a net negative adjustment of -$50 allocated to A and a net positive adjustment of $50 to B. Pursuant to § 301.6225-1(b), the total netted partnership adjustment includes the $50 net positive adjustment, and the imputed underpayment is $20 ($50 total netted partnership adjustment x 40 percent). Pursuant to § 301.6225-1(f), the -$50 net negative adjustment is an adjustment that does not result in an imputed underpayment and is taken into account in accordance with this section. On March 1, 2021, the IRS mails an FPA, and because Partnership does not file a petition for readjustment with respect to the FPA, the adjustments are finally determined in 2021, and the adjustment year is determined to be 2021 pursuant to § 301.6241-1(a)(1). Pursuant to paragraph (a) of this section, Partnership takes into account the -$50 adjustment that does not result in an imputed underpayment on its 2021 partnership return. In addition to the -$50 net negative adjustment to partnership's 2019 taxable year taken into account under this section, Partnership also has an additional $300 in ordinary income reportable in its 2021 taxable year unrelated to the administrative proceeding with respect to Partnership's 2019 partnership taxable year. Because the -$50 net negative adjustment is due to a reallocation, the adjustment must be taken into account under paragraph (b)(4) of this section. Because the net negative adjustment was determined to have been entirely allocable to A, and because A was a reviewed year partner and is also an adjustment year partner, the net negative adjustment is taken into account by Partnership by allocating the entire adjustment to A on its 2021 tax return. The -$50 negative adjustment does not reduce the $300 in ordinary income.

(e) *Applicability date.*—(1) *In general.*—Except as provided in paragraph (e)(2) of this section, this section applies to partnership taxable years beginning after December 31, 2017, and ending after August 12, 2018.

(2) *Election under § 301.9100-22 in effect.*—This section applies to any partnership taxable year beginning after November 2, 2015, and

before January 1, 2018, for which a valid election under §301.9100-22 is in effect. [Reg. §301.6225-3.]

☐ [T.D. 9844, 2-21-2019.]

### [Reg. §301.6226-1]

**§301.6226-1. Election for an alternative to the payment of the imputed underpayment.**—(a) *In general.*—A partnership may elect under this section an alternative to the payment by the partnership of an imputed underpayment determined under section 6225. In addition, a partnership making a valid election under paragraph (c) of this section is no longer liable for the imputed underpayment (as defined in §301.6241-1(a)(3)) to which the election applies. If a notice of final partnership adjustment (FPA) mailed under section 6231 includes more than one imputed underpayment (as described in §301.6225-1(g)), a partnership may make an election under this section with respect to one or more imputed underpayments included in the FPA.

(b) *Effect of election.*—(1) *Reviewed year partners.*—If a partnership makes a valid election under this section with respect to any imputed underpayment, the reviewed year partners (as defined in §301.6241-1(a)(9)) must take into account their share of the partnership adjustments (as defined in §301.6241-1(a)(6)) that are associated with that imputed underpayment and are liable for any tax, penalties, additions to tax, additional amounts, and interest as described in §301.6226-3. See §301.6226-2(f) regarding the determination of each reviewed year partner's share of the partnership adjustments, including the effect of any modification approved by the Internal Revenue Service (IRS) under §301.6225-2.

(2) *Partnership.*—A partnership making a valid election under this section is not liable for the imputed underpayment to which the election applies (and no assessment of tax, levy, or proceeding in any court for the collection of such imputed underpayment may be made against such partnership). Any adjustments that do not result in an imputed underpayment described in §301.6225-1(f) that are associated with an imputed underpayment (as described in §301.6225-1(g)) for which an election under this section is made are not taken into account by the partnership in the adjustment year (as defined in §301.6241-1(a)(1)) and instead each reviewed year partners. share of the adjustments determined in accordance with §301.6226-2(f) must be included on the statement described in §301.6226-2.

(c) *Time, form, and manner for making the election.*—(1) *In general.*—An election under this section is valid only if all of the provisions of this section and §301.6226-2 (regarding statements filed with the IRS and furnished to reviewed year partners) are satisfied. An election under this section is valid until the IRS determines that the election is invalid. An election under this section may only be revoked with the consent of the IRS.

(2) *Time for making the election.*—An election under this section must be filed within 45 days of the date the FPA is mailed by the IRS. The time for filing such an election may not be extended.

(3) *Form and manner of the election.*—(i) *In general.*—An election under this section must be signed by the partnership representative and filed in accordance with forms, instructions, and other guidance prescribed by the IRS and include the information specified in paragraph (c)(3)(ii) of this section.

(ii) *Contents of the election.*—An election under this section must include the following correct information—

(A) The name, address, and taxpayer identification number (TIN) of the partnership;

(B) The taxable year to which the election relates;

(C) A copy of the FPA to which the election relates;

(D) In the case of an FPA that includes more than one imputed underpayment, identification of the imputed underpayment to which the election applies;

(E) The name and TIN (or alternative form of identification as prescribed by forms, instructions, or other guidance) of each reviewed year partner of the partnership;

(F) The current or last address of each reviewed year partner that is known to the partnership; and

(G) Any other information prescribed by the IRS in forms, instructions, and other guidance.

(d) *Determining an election is invalid.*—The IRS may determine an election to be invalid without first notifying the partnership or providing the partnership an opportunity to correct any failure to satisfy all of the provisions of this section and §301.6226-2. If an election under this section is determined by the IRS to be invalid, the IRS will notify the partnership and the partnership representative within 30 days of the determination that the election is invalid and the reason for the determination that the election is invalid. If the IRS makes a determination that an election under this section is invalid, section 6225 applies with respect to the imputed underpayment as if the election was never made, the IRS may assess the imputed underpayment against the partnership (without regard to the limitations under section 6232(b)), and the partnership must pay the imputed underpayment under section 6225 and any penalties and interest under section 6233. The IRS may not determine that an election is invalid based on errors timely corrected by the partnership in accordance with §301.6226-2(d).

(e) *Binding nature of statements.*—The election under this section, which includes filing and furnishing statements described in §301.6226-2, are actions of the partnership under section 6223 and, unless determined otherwise by the IRS, the partner's share of the adjustments and the applicability of any penalties, additions to tax, and additional amounts as set forth in the statement are binding on the partner pursuant to section 6223. Accordingly, a partner may not treat any partnership-related items (as defined in §301.6241-1(a)(6)(ii)) reflected on a statement described in §301.6226-2 on the partner's return inconsistently with how those items are treated on the statement that is filed with the IRS. See §301.6222-1(c)(2) (regarding partnership-related items the treatment of which a partner is bound to under section 6223).

(f) *Coordination with section 6234 regarding judicial review.*—Nothing in this section affects the rules regarding judicial review of a partnership adjustment. Accordingly, a partnership that makes an election under this section is not precluded from filing a petition under section 6234(a). See §301.6226-2(b)(3)(iii).

(g) *Applicability date.*—(1) *In general.*—Except as provided in paragraph (g)(2) of this section, this section applies to partnership taxable years beginning after December 31, 2017, and ending after August 12, 2018.

(2) *Election under §301.9100-22 in effect.*—This section applies to any partnership taxable year beginning after November 2, 2015, and before January 1, 2018, for which a valid election under §301.9100-22 is in effect. [Reg. §301.6226-1.]

☐ [T.D. 9844, 2-21-2019.]

### [Reg. §301.6226-2]

**§301.6226-2. Statements furnished to partners and filed with the IRS.**—(a) *In general.*—A partnership that makes an election under §301.6226-1 must furnish to each reviewed year partner (as defined in §301.6241-1(a)(9)) and file with the Internal Revenue Service (IRS) a statement that includes the items required by paragraphs (e) and (f) of this section with respect to each reviewed year partner's share of partnership adjustments (as defined in §301.6241-1(a)(6)) associated with the imputed underpayment for which an election under §301.6226-1 is made. The statements furnished to the reviewed year partners under this section are in addition to, and must be filed and furnished separate from, any other statements required to be filed with the IRS and furnished to partners, including any statements under section 6031(b). A separate statement under this section must be furnished to each reviewed year partner with respect to each reviewed year (as defined in §301.6241-1(a)(8)) subject to an election under §301.6226-1. A failure to furnish a correct statement in accordance with this section is subject to penalty under section 6722. See section 6724(d)(2).

(b) *Time and manner for furnishing the statements to partners.*—(1) *In general.*—The statements described in paragraph (a) of this section must be furnished to the reviewed year partners no later than 60 days after the date all of the partnership adjustments to which the statement relates are finally determined. The partnership adjustments are finally determined upon the later of:

(i) The expiration of the time to file a petition under section 6234; or

(ii) If a petition under section 6234 is filed, the date when the court's decision becomes final.

(2) *Address used for reviewed year partners.*—The partnership must furnish the statements described in paragraph (a) of this section to each reviewed year partner in accordance with the forms, instructions, and other guidance prescribed by the IRS. If the partnership mails the statement, it must mail the statement to the current or last address of the reviewed year partner that is known to the partnership. If a statement is returned to the partnership as undeliverable, the partnership must undertake reasonable diligence to identify a correct address for the reviewed year partner to which the statement relates and, if a correct address is identified, mail the statement to the reviewed year partner at the correct address.

(3) *Examples.*—The following examples illustrate the rules of this paragraph (b).

(i) *Example 1.* During Partnership's 2020 taxable year, A, an individual, was a partner in Partnership and had an address at 123 Main St. On February 1, 2021, A sells his interest in Partnership and informs Partnership that A moved to 456 Broad St. On March 15, 2021, Partnership mails A's statement under section 6031(b) for the 2020 taxable year to 456 Broad St. On June 1, 2023, A moves again but does not inform Partnership of A's new address. In 2023, the IRS initiates an administrative proceeding with respect to Partnership's 2020 taxable year and mails a notice of final partnership adjustment (FPA) to Partnership for that year that includes a single imputed underpayment. Partnership makes a timely election under section 6226 in accordance with § 301.6226-1 with respect to the imputed underpayment and on May 31, 2024, timely mails a statement described in paragraph (a) of this section to A at 456 Broad St. Although the statement was mailed to the last address for A that was known to Partnership, it is returned to Partnership as undeliverable because unknown to Partnership, A had moved. After undertaking reasonable diligence to obtain the correct address of A, Partnership is unable to ascertain the correct address. Therefore, pursuant to paragraph (b)(2) of this section, Partnership properly furnished the statement to A when it mailed the statement to 456 Broad St.

(ii) *Example 2.* The facts are the same as in *Example 1* in paragraph (b)(3)(i) of this section, except that A lives at 789 Forest Ave during all of 2024 and reasonable diligence would have revealed that 789 Forest Ave is the correct address for A, but Partnership did not undertake such diligence. Because the statement was returned as undeliverable and Partnership did not undertake reasonable diligence to obtain the correct address for A, Partnership failed to properly furnish the statement with respect to A pursuant to paragraph (b)(2) of this section.

(iii) *Example 3.* Partnership is a calendar year taxpayer. The IRS initiates an administrative proceeding with respect to Partnership's 2020 taxable year. On January 1, 2024, the IRS mails an FPA with respect to the 2020 taxable year to Partnership that includes a single imputed underpayment. Partnership makes a timely election under section 6226 in accordance with § 301.6226-1 with respect to the imputed underpayment. Partnership timely files a petition for readjustment under section 6234 with the Tax Court. The IRS prevails, and the Tax Court sustains all of the adjustments in the FPA with respect to the 2020 taxable year. The time to appeal the Tax Court decision expires, and the Tax Court decision becomes final on April 10, 2025. Under paragraph (b)(1)(ii) of this section, the adjustments in the FPA are finally determined on April 10, 2025, and Partnership must furnish the statements described in paragraph (a) of this section to its reviewed year partners and electronically file the statements with the IRS no later than June 9, 2025. See paragraph (c) of this section for the rules regarding filing the statements with the IRS.

(c) *Time and manner for filing the statements with the IRS.*—No later than 60 days after the date the partnership adjustments are finally determined (as described in paragraph (b)(1) of this section), the partnership must electronically file with the IRS the statements that the partnership furnishes to each reviewed year partner under this section, along with a transmittal that includes a summary of the statements filed and such other information required in forms, instructions, and other guidance prescribed by the IRS.

(d) *Correction of statements.*—(1) *In general.*—A partnership corrects an error in a statement furnished under paragraph (b) of this section or filed under paragraph (c) of this section by filing the corrected statement with the IRS in the manner prescribed in paragraph (c) of this section and furnishing a copy of the corrected statement to the reviewed year partner to whom the statement relates in accordance with the forms, instructions, and other guidance prescribed by the IRS.

(2) *Error discovered by partnership.*—(i) *Discovery within 60 days of statement due date.*—If a partnership discovers an error in a statement within 60 days of the due date for furnishing the statements to partners and filing the statements with the IRS (as described in paragraphs (b) and (c) of this section and § 301.6226-3(e)(3)(ii)), the partnership must correct the error in accordance with paragraph (d)(1) of this section and does not have to seek consent of the IRS prior to doing so.

(ii) *Error discovered more than 60 days after statement due date.*—If a partnership discovers an error more than 60 days after the due date for furnishing the statements to partners and filing the statements with the IRS (as described in paragraphs (b) and (c) of this section and § 301.6226-3(e)(3)(ii)), the partnership may only correct the error after receiving consent of the IRS in accordance with the forms, instructions, and other guidance prescribed by the IRS. The partnership may not furnish corrected statements unless it receives consent of the IRS to make the correction.

(3) *Error discovered by the IRS.*—If the IRS discovers an error in the statements furnished or filed under paragraphs (b) and (c) of this section and § 301.6226-3(e)(3) or the IRS cannot determine whether the statements furnished or filed by the partnership are correct because of a failure by the partnership to comply with any requirement under this section or § 301.6226-3(e), the IRS may require the partnership to correct such errors in accordance with paragraph (d)(1) of this section or to provide additional information as necessary. Failure by the partnership to correct an error or to provide information when required by the IRS may be treated by the IRS as a failure to properly furnish correct statements to partners and file the correct statements with the IRS as described in paragraphs (b) and (c) of this section or in § 301.6226-3(e)(3). Whether the IRS requires the partnership to correct any errors discovered by the IRS or provide additional information is discretionary on the part of the IRS and the IRS is under no obligation to require the partnership to provide additional information or to correct any errors discovered or brought to the IRS's attention at any time.

(4) *Adjustments in the corrected statements taken into account by the reviewed year partners.*—The adjustments included on a corrected statement are taken into account by a reviewed year partner in accordance with § 301.6226-3 for the reporting year (as defined in § 301.6226-3(a)).

(e) *Content of the statements.*—Each statement described in paragraph (a) of this section must include the following correct information:

(1) The name and TIN (or alternative form of identification as prescribed by forms, instructions, or other guidance) of the reviewed year partner to whom the statement is being furnished;

(2) The current or last address of the reviewed year partner that is known to the partnership;

(3) The reviewed year partner's share of items as originally reported for the reviewed year to the partner on statements furnished to the partner under section 6031(b) and, if applicable, section 6227;

(4) The reviewed year partner's share of partnership adjustments determined under paragraph (f)(1) of this section;

(5) Modifications approved by the IRS with respect to the reviewed year partner (or with respect to any indirect partner (as defined in § 301.6241-1(a)(4)) that holds its interest in the partnership through its interest in the reviewed year partner);

(6) The applicability of any penalty, addition to tax, or additional amount determined at the partnership level that relates to any adjustments allocable to the reviewed year partner and the adjustments to which the penalty, addition to tax, or additional amount relates, the section of the Internal Revenue Code (Code) under which each penalty, addition to tax, or additional amount is imposed, and the applicable rate of each penalty, addition to tax, or additional amount determined at the partnership level;

(7) The date the statement is furnished to the reviewed year partner;

(8) The partnership taxable year to which the adjustments relate; and

(9) Any other information required by forms, instructions, and other guidance prescribed by the IRS.

(f) *Determination of each partner's share of adjustments.*—(1) *Adjustments and other amounts.*—(i) *In general.*—Except as described in paragraph (f)(1)(ii) or (iii) or (f)(2) of this section, the adjustments set forth in the statement described in paragraph (a) of this section are reported to the reviewed year partner in the same manner as each adjusted partnership-related item was originally allocated to the reviewed year partner on the partnership return for the reviewed year.

(ii) *Adjusted partnership-related item not reported on the partnership's return for the reviewed year.*—Except as described in paragraph (f)(1)(iii) of this section, if the adjusted partnership-related item was not reported on the partnership return for the reviewed year, each reviewed year partner's share of the adjustments must be determined in accordance with how such partnership-related items would have been allocated under rules that apply with respect to partnership allocations, including under the partnership agreement.

(iii) *Adjustments that specifically allocate items.*—If an adjustment involves an allocation of a partnership-related item to a specific partner or in a specific manner, including a reallocation of such an item, the reviewed year partner's share of the adjustment set forth in the statement is determined in accordance with the adjustment as finally determined (as described in paragraph (b)(1) of this section).

(2) *Treatment of modifications disregarded.*—Any modifications approved by the IRS with respect to the reviewed year partner (or with respect to any indirect partner that holds its interest in the partnership through its interest in the reviewed year partner) under

§ 301.6225-2 are disregarded for purposes of determining each partner's share of the adjustments under paragraph (f)(1) of this section.

(g) *Coordination with other provisions under subtitle A of the Code.*—(1) *Statements furnished to qualified investment entities described in section 860.*—If a reviewed year partner is a qualified investment entity within the meaning of section 860(b) and the partner receives a statement described in paragraph (a) of this section, the partner may be able to avail itself of the deficiency dividend procedure described in § 301.6226–3(b)(4).

(2) *Liability for tax under section 7704(g)(3).*—An election under this section has no effect on a partnership's liability for any tax under section 7704(g)(3) (regarding the exception for electing 1987 partnerships from the general rule that certain publicly traded partnerships are treated as corporations).

(3) *Adjustments subject to chapters 3 and 4 of the Internal Revenue Code.*—A partnership that makes an election under § 301.6226-1 with respect to an imputed underpayment must pay the amount of tax required to be withheld under chapter 3 or chapter 4, if any, in accordance with § 301.6241-6(b)(4).

(h) *Applicability date.*—(1) *In general.*—Except as provided in paragraph (h)(2) of this section, this section applies to partnership taxable years beginning after December 31, 2017, and ending after August 12, 2018.

(2) *Election under § 301.9100-22 in effect.*—This section applies to any partnership taxable year beginning after November 2, 2015, and before January 1, 2018, for which a valid election under § 301.9100-22 is in effect. [Reg. § 301.6226-2.]

☐ [T.D. 9844, 2-21-2019.]

### [Reg. § 301.6226-3]

**§ 301.6226-3. Adjustments taken into account by partners.**—(a) *Effect of taking adjustments into account on tax imposed by chapter 1.*—Except as otherwise provided in this section, the tax imposed by chapter 1 of the Internal Revenue Code (chapter 1 tax) for each reviewed year partner (as defined in § 301.6241-1(a)(9)) for the taxable year that includes the date a statement was furnished in accordance with § 301.6226-2 (the reporting year) is increased by the additional reporting year tax, or if the additional reporting year tax is less than zero, decreased by such amount. The additional reporting year tax is the aggregate of the correction amounts (determined in accordance with paragraph (b) of this section). In addition to being liable for the additional reporting year tax, a reviewed year partner must also calculate and pay for the reporting year any penalties, additions to tax, and additional amounts (as determined under paragraph (d) of this section). Finally, a reviewed year partner must also calculate and pay for the reporting year any interest (as determined under paragraph (c) of this section).

(b) *Determining the aggregate of the correction amounts.*—(1) *In general.*—For purposes of paragraph (a) of this section, the aggregate of the correction amounts is the sum of the correction amounts described in paragraphs (b)(2) and (3) of this section. A correction amount under paragraph (b)(2) or (3) of this section may be less than zero, and any correction amount that is less than zero may reduce any other correction amount with the result that the aggregate of the correction amounts under this paragraph (b)(1) may also be less than zero. However, nothing in this section entitles any partner to a refund of chapter 1 tax to which such partner is not entitled. See paragraphs (c) and (d) of this section requiring a separate determination of interest and penalties, additions to tax, and additional amounts on the correction amount for each applicable taxable year (as defined in paragraph (c)(1) of this section) without regard to the correction amount for any other applicable taxable year.

(2) *Correction amount for the first affected year.*—(i) *In general.*—The correction amount for the taxable year of the partner that includes the end of the reviewed year (the first affected year) is the amount by which the reviewed year partner's chapter 1 tax would increase or decrease for the first affected year if the partner's taxable income for such year was recomputed by taking into account the reviewed year partner's share of the partnership adjustments (as defined in § 301.6241-1(a)(6)) reflected on the statement described in § 301.6226-2 with respect to the partner.

(ii) *Calculation of the correction amount for the first affected year.*—The correction amount is the amount of chapter 1 tax that would have been imposed for the first affected year if the items as adjusted in the statement described in § 301.6226-2 had been reported as such on the return for the first affected year less the sum of:

(A) The amount of chapter 1 tax shown by the partner on the return for the first affected year (which includes amounts shown on an amended return for such year, including an amended return filed under section 6225(c)(2) by the reviewed year partner); plus

(B) Amounts not included in paragraph (b)(2)(ii)(A) of this section but previously assessed or collected (including the amounts defined in § 1.6664-2(d) of this chapter and any amounts paid by the partner in accordance with § 301.6225-2); less

(C) The amount of rebates made (as defined in § 1.6664-2(e) of this chapter).

(iii) *Formulaic expression of the correction amount for the first affected year.*—The correction amount also may be expressed as–
*Correction amount* = A – (B + C –D)
Where:

A = the amount of chapter 1 tax that would have been imposed had the items as adjusted been properly reported on the return for the first affected year;

B = the amount shown as chapter 1 tax on the return for the first affected year (taking into account amended returns);

C = amounts previously assessed or collected; and

D = the amount of rebates made.

(3) *Correction amount for the intervening years.*—(i) *In general.*—The correction amount for all taxable years after the first affected year and before the reporting year (the intervening years) is the aggregate of the correction amounts determined for each intervening year. Determining the correction amount for each intervening year is a year-by-year determination. The correction amount for each intervening year is the amount by which the reviewed year partner's chapter 1 tax for such year would increase or decrease if the partner's taxable income for such year was recomputed by taking into account any adjustments to tax attributes (as defined in § 301.6241-1(a)(10)) of the partner under paragraph (b)(3) of this section.

(ii) *Calculation of the correction amount for the intervening years.*—The correction amount for each intervening year is the amount of chapter 1 tax that would have been imposed for the intervening year if any tax attribute of the partner for the intervening year had been adjusted after taking into account the reviewed year partner's share of the adjustments for the first affected year as described in paragraph (b)(2) of this section (and if any tax attribute of the partner for the intervening year had been adjusted, after taking into account any adjustments to tax attributes of the partner in any prior intervening year(s)) exceeds less the sum of–

(A) The amount of chapter 1 tax shown by the partner on the return for the intervening year (which includes amounts shown on an amended return for such year, including an amended return filed under section 6225(c)(2) by a reviewed year partner); plus

(B) Amounts not included in paragraph (b)(3)(ii)(A) of this section but previously or collected (including the amounts defined in § 1.6664-2(d) of this chapter and any amounts paid by the partner in accordance with § 301.6225-2); less

(C) The amount of rebates made (as defined in § 1.6664-2(e) of this chapter).

(iii) *Formulaic expression of the correction amount for the intervening years.*—The correction amount also may be expressed as–
*Correction amount* = A – (B + C –D)
Where:

A = the amount of chapter 1 tax that would have been imposed for the intervening year;

B = the amount shown as chapter 1 tax on the return for the intervening year (taking into account amended returns);

C = amounts previously assessed or collected; and

D = the amount of rebates made.

(4) *Coordination of sections 860 and 6226.*—If a qualified investment entity (QIE) within the meaning of section 860(b) receives a statement described in § 301.6226-2(a) and correctly makes a determination within the meaning of section 860(e)(4) that one or more of the adjustments reflected in the statement is an adjustment within the meaning of section 860(d) with respect to that QIE for a taxable year, the QIE may distribute deficiency dividends within the meaning of section 860(f) for that taxable year and avail itself of the deficiency dividend procedures set forth in section 860. If the QIE utilizes the deficiency dividend procedures with respect to adjustments in a statement described in § 301.6226-2(a), the QIE may claim a deduction for deficiency dividends against the adjustments furnished to the QIE in the statement in calculating any correction amounts under paragraphs (b)(2) and (3) of this section, and interest on such correction amounts under paragraph (c) of this section, to the extent that the QIE makes deficiency dividend distributions under section 860(f) and complies with all requirements of section 860 and the regulations under part 1 of this chapter.

(c) *Interest.*—(1) *Interest on the correction amounts.*—Interest on the correction amounts determined under paragraph (b) of this section is the aggregate of all interest calculated for each applicable taxable year in which there was a correction amount greater than zero at the rate set forth in paragraph (c)(3) of this section. For each applicable taxable year, interest on the correction amount is calculated from the due date (without extension) of the reviewed year partner's return for such applicable taxable year until the amount is paid. For purposes of this paragraph (c)(1), the term *applicable taxable year* means the reviewed year partner's taxable year affected by taking into account adjustments as described in paragraph (b) of this section (for instance, the first affected year and any intervening year in which there is a correction amount greater than zero). For purposes of calculating interest under this paragraph (c), a correction amount under paragraph (b)(2) or (3) of this section for an applicable taxable year that is less than zero does not reduce the correction amount for any other applicable taxable year.

(2) *Interest on penalties.*—Interest on any penalties, additions to tax, or additional amounts determined under paragraph (d) of this section is calculated at the rate set forth in paragraph (c)(3) of this section from the due date (including any extension) of the reviewed year partner's return for the applicable taxable year until the amount is paid.

(3) *Rate of interest.*—For purposes of paragraph (c) of this section, interest is calculated using the underpayment rate under section 6621(a)(2) by substituting "5 percentage points" for "3 percentage points" in section 6621(a)(2)(B).

(d) *Penalties.*—(1) *Applicability determined at the partnership level.*—In the case of a partnership that makes an election under section 6226, the applicability of any penalty, addition to tax, and additional amount that relates to an adjustment to any partnership-related item is determined at the partnership level in accordance with section 6221(a). The partnership's reviewed year partners are liable for such penalties, additions to tax, and additional amounts as determined under paragraph (d)(2) of this section.

(2) *Amount calculated at partner level.*—A reviewed year partner calculates the amount of any penalty, addition to tax, or additional amount relating to the partnership adjustments taken into account under paragraph (b)(1) of this section as if the correction amount were an underpayment or understatement of the reviewed year partner for the first affected year or intervening year, as applicable. The calculation of any penalty, addition to tax, or additional amount is based on the characteristics of, and facts and circumstances applicable to, the reviewed year partner for the first affected year or intervening year, as applicable after taking into account the partnership adjustments reflected on the statement. If after taking into account the partnership adjustments in accordance with this section, the reviewed year partner does not have an underpayment, or has an understatement that falls below the applicable threshold for the imposition of a penalty, no penalty is due from that reviewed year partner under this paragraph (d)(2). For penalties in the case of a pass-through partner that makes a payment under paragraph (e)(4) of this section, see paragraph (e)(4)(iv) of this section.

(3) *Partner-level defenses to penalties.*—A reviewed year partner (including a pass-through partner (as defined in §301.6241-1(a)(5))) claiming that a penalty, addition to tax, or additional amount that relates to a partnership adjustment reflected on a statement described in §301.6226-2 (or paragraph (e)(3) of this section) is not due because of a partner-level defense must first pay the penalty and file a claim for refund for the reporting year. Partner-level defenses are limited to those that are personal to the reviewed year partner (for example, a reasonable cause and good faith defense under section 6664(c) that is based on the facts and circumstances applicable to the partner).

(e) *Pass-through partners.*—(1) *In general.*—Except as provided in paragraph (e)(6) of this section, if a pass-through partner is furnished a statement described in §301.6226-2 (including a statement described in paragraph (e)(3) of this section) with respect to adjustments of a partnership that made an election under §301.6226-1 (audited partnership), the pass-through partner must file with the IRS a partnership adjustment tracking report in accordance with forms, instructions, or other guidance prescribed by the IRS on or before the due date described in paragraph (e)(3)(ii) of this section, and file and furnish statements in accordance with paragraph (e)(3) of this section. The pass-through partner must comply with paragraph (e) of this section with respect to each statement furnished to the pass-through partner.

(2) *Failure to file and furnish required documents.*—(i) *Failure to timely file and furnish statements.*—If any pass-through partner fails to timely file and furnish correct statements in accordance with paragraph (e)(3) of this section, the pass-through partner must compute and pay an imputed underpayment, as well as any penalties, additions to tax, additional amounts, and interest with respect to the

adjustments reflected on the statement furnished to the pass-through partner in accordance with paragraph (e)(4) of this section. The IRS may assess such imputed underpayment against such pass-through partner without regard to the limitations under section 6232(b). See §301.6232-1(c)(2). A failure to furnish statements in accordance with paragraph (e)(3) of this section is treated as a failure to timely pay an imputed underpayment required under paragraph (e)(4)(i) of this section, unless the pass-through partner computes and pays an imputed underpayment in accordance with paragraph (e)(4) of this section. See section 6651(i).

(ii) *Failures relating to partnership adjustment tracking report.*—Failure to timely file the partnership adjustment tracking report as required in paragraph (e)(1) of this section, or filing such report without showing the information required under paragraph (e)(1) of this section, is subject to the penalty imposed by section 6698.

(3) *Furnishing statements to partners.*—(i) *In general.*—A pass-through partner described in paragraph (e)(1) of this section must furnish a statement that includes the items required by paragraph (e)(3)(iii) of this section to each partner that held an interest in the pass-through partner at any time during the taxable year of the pass-through partner to which the adjustments in the statement furnished to the pass-through partner relate (affected partner). The statements described in this paragraph (e)(3) must be filed with the IRS by the due date prescribed in paragraph (e)(3)(ii) of this section. Except as otherwise provided in paragraphs (e)(3)(ii), (iii), and (v) of this section, the rules applicable to statements described in §301.6226-2 are applicable to statements described in this paragraph (e)(3).

(ii) *Time for filing and furnishing the statements.*—In accordance with forms, instructions, and other guidance prescribed by the IRS, the pass-through partner must file with the IRS and furnish to its affected partners the statements described in paragraph (e)(3) of this section no later than the extended due date for the return for the adjustment year (as defined in §301.6241-1(a)(1)) of the audited partnership. For purposes of this section, the extended due date is the extended due date under section 6081 regardless of whether the audited partnership is required to file a return for the adjustment year or timely files a request for an extension under section 6081.

(iii) *Contents of statements.*—Each statement described in paragraph (e)(3) of this section must include the following correct information–

(A) The name and taxpayer identification number (TIN) of the audited partnership;

(B) The adjustment year of the audited partnership;

(C) The extended due date for the return for the adjustment year of the audited partnership (as described in paragraph (e)(3)(ii) of this section);

(D) The date on which the audited partnership furnished its statements required under §301.6226-2(b);

(E) The name and TIN of the partnership that furnished the statement to the pass-through partner if different from the audited partnership;

(F) The name and TIN of the pass-through partner;

(G) The pass-through partner's taxable year to which the adjustments reflected on the statements described in paragraph (e)(3) of this section relates;

(H) The name and TIN (or alternative form of identification as prescribed by forms, instructions, or other guidance) of the affected partner to whom the statement is being furnished;

(I) The current or last address of the affected partner that is known to the pass-through partner;

(J) The affected partner's share of items as originally reported to such partner under section 6031(b) and, if applicable, section 6227, for the taxable year to which the adjustments reflected on the statement furnished to the pass-through partner relate;

(K) The affected partner's share of partnership adjustments determined under §301.6226-2(f)(1) as if the affected partner were the reviewed year partner and the pass-through partner were the partnership;

(L) Modifications approved by the IRS with respect to the affected partner that holds its interest in the audited partnership through the pass-through partner;

(M) The applicability of any penalties, additions to tax, or additional amounts determined at the audited partnership level that relate to any adjustments allocable to the affected partner and the adjustments allocated to the affected partner to which such penalties, additions to tax, or additional amounts relate, the section of the Internal Revenue Code under which each penalty, addition to tax, or additional amount is imposed, and the applicable rate of each penalty, addition to tax, or additional amount; and

(N) Any other information required by forms, instructions, and other guidance prescribed by the IRS.

(iv) *Affected partner must take into account the adjustments.*—A statement furnished to an affected partner in accordance with paragraph (e)(3) of this section is treated as if it were a statement described in §301.6226-2. An affected partner that is a pass-through partner must take into account the adjustments reflected on such a statement in accordance with this paragraph (e). An affected partner that is not a pass-through partner must take into account the adjustments reflected on such a statement in accordance with this section by treating references to "reviewed year partner" as "affected partner". For purposes of this paragraph (e)(3)(iv), an affected partner that is not a pass-through partner takes into account the adjustments in accordance with this section by determining its reporting year based on the date upon which the audited partnership furnished its statements to its reviewed year partners (as described in paragraph (a) of this section). No addition to tax under section 6651 related to any additional reporting year tax will be imposed if an affected partner that is not a pass-through partner reports and pays the additional reporting year tax within 30 days of the extended due date for the return for the adjustment year of the audited partnership (as described in paragraph (e)(3)(ii) of this section).

(v) *Adjustments subject to chapters 3 and 4 of the Internal Revenue Code.*—If a pass-through partner furnishes statements to its affected partners in accordance with paragraph (e)(3) of this section, the pass-through partner must comply with the requirements of §301.6241-6(b)(4), and an affected partner must comply with the requirements of paragraph (f) of this section. For purposes of applying both §301.6241-6(b)(4) and paragraph (f) of this section, as appropriate, references to the "partnership" should be replaced with references to the "pass-through partner"; references to the "reviewed year partner" should be replaced with references to the "affected partner"; references to the statement required under paragraph (a) of this section and its due date should be replaced with references to the statement required under paragraph (e)(3) of this section and its due date described in paragraph (e)(3)(ii) of this section; references to the "reporting year" should be read in accordance with paragraph (e)(3)(iv) of this section; and references to the partnership return should be read as references to the return for the adjustment year of the audited partnership as described in paragraph (e)(3)(ii) of this section.

(4) *Pass-through partner pays an imputed underpayment.*—(i) *In general.*—If a pass-through partner described in paragraph (e)(1) of this section does not furnish statements in accordance with paragraph (e)(3) of this section, the pass-through partner must compute and pay an imputed underpayment determined under paragraph (e)(4)(iii) of this section. The pass-through partner must also pay any penalties, additions to tax, additional amounts, and interest as determined under paragraph (e)(4)(iv) of this section. A failure to timely pay an imputed underpayment required under this paragraph (e)(4) is subject to penalty under section 6651(i).

(ii) *Time of payment.*—A pass-through partner must file a partnership adjustment tracking report and compute and pay the imputed underpayment and any penalties, additions to tax, additional amounts, and interest, as described in paragraph (e)(4)(i) of this section, in accordance with forms, instructions, and other guidance no later than the extended due date for the return for the adjustment year of the audited partnership.

(iii) *Computation of the imputed underpayment.*—The imputed underpayment under paragraph (e)(4)(i) of this section is computed in the same manner as an imputed underpayment under section 6225 and §301.6225-1, except that adjustments reflected on the statement furnished to the pass-through partner under §301.6226-2 are treated as partnership adjustments (as defined in §301.6241-1(a)(6)) for the first affected year. Any modification approved by the IRS under §301.6225-2 with respect to the pass-through partner (including any modifications with respect to a relevant partner (as defined in §301.6225-2(a)) that holds its interest in the audited partnership through its interest in the pass-through partner) reflected on the statement furnished to the pass-through partner under §301.6226-2 (or paragraph (e)(3) of this section) is taken into account in calculating the imputed underpayment under this paragraph (e)(4)(iii). Any modification that was not approved by the IRS under §301.6225-2 may not be taken into account in calculating the imputed underpayment under this paragraph (e)(4)(iii).

(iv) *Penalties and interest.*—(A) *Penalties.*—A pass-through partner must compute and pay any applicable penalties, additions to tax, and additional amounts on the imputed underpayment calculated under paragraph (e)(4)(iii) of this section as if such amount were an imputed underpayment for the pass-through partner's first affected year. See §301.6233(a)-1(c).

(B) *Interest.*—A pass-through partner must pay interest on the imputed underpayment calculated under paragraph (e)(4)(iii) of

this section in accordance with paragraph (c) of this section as if such imputed underpayment were a correction amount for the first affected year.

(v) *Adjustments that do not result in an imputed underpayment.*—Adjustments taken into account under paragraph (e)(4) of this section that do not result in an imputed underpayment (as defined in §301.6225-1(f)) are taken into account by the pass-through partner in accordance with §301.6225-3 in the taxable year of the pass-through partner that includes the date the imputed underpayment required under paragraph (e)(4)(i) of this section is paid. If, after making the computation described in paragraph (e)(4)(iii) of this section, no imputed underpayment exists and therefore no payment is required under paragraph (e)(4)(i) of this section, the adjustments that did not result in an imputed underpayment are taken into account by the pass-through partner in accordance with §301.6225-3 in the taxable year of the pass-through partner that includes the date the statement described in §301.6226-2 (or paragraph (e)(3) of this section) is furnished to the pass-through partner.

(vi) *Coordination with chapters 3 and 4.*—If a pass-through partner pays an imputed underpayment described in paragraph (e)(4)(i) of this section, §301.6241-6(b)(3) applies to the pass-through partner by substituting "pass-through partner" for "partnership" where §301.6241-6(b)(3) refers to the partnership that pays the imputed underpayment.

(5) *Treatment of pass-through partners that are not partnerships.*—(i) *S corporations.*—For purposes of this paragraph (e), an S corporation is treated as a partnership and its shareholders are treated as partners.

(ii) *Trusts and estates.*—Except as provided in paragraph (g) of this section, for purposes of paragraph (e) of this section, a trust and its beneficiaries, and an estate and its beneficiaries are treated in the same manner as a partnership and its partners.

(6) *Pass-through partners subject to chapter 1 tax.*—A pass-through partner that is subject to tax under chapter 1 of the Code on the adjustments (or a portion of the adjustments) reflected on the statement furnished to such partner under §301.6226-2 (or paragraph (e)(3) of this section) takes the adjustments into account under this paragraph (e)(6) when the pass-through partner calculates and pays the additional reporting year tax as determined under paragraph (b) of this section and furnishes statements to its partners in accordance with paragraph (e)(3) of this section. Notwithstanding the prior sentence, a pass-through partner is only required to include on a statement under paragraph (e)(3) of this section the adjustments that would be required to be included on statements furnished to owners or beneficiaries under sections 6037 and 6034A, as applicable, if the pass-through partner had correctly reported the items for the year to which the adjustments relate. If the pass-through partner fails to comply with the requirements of this paragraph (e)(6), the pass-through partner must compute and pay an imputed underpayment, as well as any penalties, additions to tax, additional amounts, and interest with respect to the adjustments reflected on the statement furnished to such partner in accordance with paragraph (e)(4) of this section.

(f) *Partners subject to withholding under chapters 3 and 4.*—A reviewed year partner that is subject to withholding under §301.6241-6(b)(4) must file an income tax return for the reporting year to report its additional reporting year tax and its share of any penalties, additions to tax, additional amounts, and interest (notwithstanding any filing exception in §1.6012-1(b)(2)(i) or §1.6012-2(g)(2)(i) of this chapter). The amount of tax paid by a partnership under §301.6241-6(b)(4) is allowed as a credit under section 33 to the reviewed year partner to the extent that the tax is allocable to the reviewed year partner (within the meaning of §1.1446-3(d)(2) of this chapter) or is actually withheld from the reviewed year partner (within the meaning of §1.1464-1(a) or §1.1474-3 of this chapter). The credit is allowed against the reviewed year partner's income tax liability for its reporting year. The reviewed year partner must substantiate the credit by attaching the applicable Form 1042-S, Foreign Person's U.S. Source Income Subject to Withholding, or Form 8805, Foreign Partner's Information Statement of Section 1446 Withholding Tax, to its income tax return for the reporting year, as well as satisfying any other requirements prescribed by the IRS in forms and instructions.

(g) *Treatment of disregarded entities and wholly-owned grantor trusts.*—In the case of a reviewed year partner that is a wholly-owned entity disregarded as separate from its owner for Federal income tax purposes in the reviewed year or a trust that is wholly owned by only one person in the reviewed year, whether the grantor or another person, and where the trust reports the owner's information to payors under §1.671-4(b)(2)(i)(A) of this chapter and that is furnished a statement described in §301.6226-2 (or paragraph (e)(3) of this section), the owner of the disregarded entity or wholly-owned grantor trust must take into account the adjustments reflected on that statement in accordance with this section as if the owner were the reviewed year partner.

(h) *Examples*.—The following examples illustrate the rules of this section. For purposes of these examples, unless otherwise stated, each partnership is subject to subchapter C of chapter 63 of the Code, each partnership and partner has a calendar year taxable year, no modifications are requested by any partnership under §301.6225-2, no penalties, additions to tax, or additional amounts are determined at the partnership level, all persons are U.S. persons, the highest rate of income tax in effect for is 40 percent for all relevant periods, the highest rate of income tax in effect for corporations is 20 percent for all relevant periods, and the highest rate of tax for individuals for capital gains is 15 percent for all relevant periods.

(1) *Example 1.* On its partnership return for the 2020 tax year, Partnership reported ordinary income of $1,000 and charitable contributions of $400. On June 1, 2023, the IRS mails a notice of final partnership adjustment (FPA) to Partnership for Partnership's 2020 year disallowing the charitable contribution in its entirety and determining that a 20 percent accuracy-related penalty under section 6662(b) applies to the disallowance of the charitable contribution, and setting forth a single imputed underpayment with respect to such adjustments. Partnership makes a timely election under section 6226 in accordance with §301.6226-1 with respect to the imputed underpayment in the FPA for Partnership's 2020 year and files a timely petition in the Tax Court challenging the partnership adjustments. The Tax Court determines that Partnership is not entitled to any of the claimed $400 in charitable contributions and upholds the applicability of the penalty. The decision regarding Partnership's 2020 tax year becomes final on December 15, 2025. Pursuant to §301.6226-2(b), the partnership adjustments are finally determined on December 15, 2025. On February 2, 2026, Partnership files the statements described under §301.6226-2 with the IRS and furnishes to partner A, an individual who was a partner in Partnership during 2020, a statement described in §301.6226-2. A had a 25 percent interest in Partnership during all of 2020 and was allocated 25 percent of all items from Partnership for that year. The statement shows A's share of ordinary income reported on Partnership's return for the reviewed year of $250 and A's share of the charitable contribution reported on Partnership's return for the reviewed year of $100. The statement also shows an adjustment to A's share of the charitable contribution, a reduction of $100 resulting in $0 charitable contribution allocated to A from Partnership for 2020. In addition, the statement reports that a 20 percent accuracy-related penalty under section 6662(b) applies. A must pay the additional reporting year tax as determined in accordance with paragraph (b) of this section, in addition to A's penalties and interest. A computes his additional reporting year tax as follows. First, A determines the correction amount for the first affected year (the 2020 taxable year) by taking into account A's share of the partnership adjustment (-$100 reduction in charitable contribution) for the 2020 taxable year. A determines the amount by which his chapter 1 tax for 2020 would have increased or decreased if the $100 adjustment to the charitable contribution from Partnership were taken into account for that year. There is no adjustment to tax attributes in A's intervening years as a result of the adjustment to the charitable contribution for 2020. Therefore, A's aggregate of the correction amounts is the correction amount for 2020, A's first affected year. In addition to the aggregate of the correction amounts being added to the chapter 1 tax that A owes for 2026, the reporting year, A must calculate a 20 percent accuracy-related penalty on A's underpayment attributable to the $100 adjustment to the charitable contribution, as well as interest on the correction amount for the first affected year and the penalty determined in accordance with paragraph (c) of this section. Interest on the correction amount for the first affected tax year runs from April 15, 2021, the due date of A's 2020 return (the first affected tax year) until A pays this amount. In addition, interest runs on the penalty from April 15, 2021, the due date of A's 2020 return for the first affected year until A pays this amount. On his 2026 income tax return, A must report the additional reporting year tax determined in accordance with paragraph (b) of this section, which is the correction amount for 2020, plus the accuracy-related penalty determined in accordance with paragraph (d) of this section, and interest determined in accordance with paragraph (c) of this section on the correction amount for 2020 and the penalty.

(2) *Example 2.* On its partnership return for the 2020 tax year, Partnership reported an ordinary loss of $500. On June 1, 2023, the IRS mails an FPA to Partnership for the 2020 taxable year determining that $300 of the $500 in ordinary loss should be recharacterized as a long-term capital loss. Partnership has no long-term capital gain for its 2020 tax year. The FPA for Partnership's 2020 tax year reflects an adjustment of an increase in ordinary income of $300 (as a result of

the disallowance of the recharacterization of $300 from ordinary loss to long-term capital loss) and an imputed underpayment related to that adjustment, as well as an adjustment of an additional $300 in long-term capital loss for 2020 which does not result in an imputed underpayment under §301.6225-1(f). Partnership makes a timely election under section 6226 in accordance with §301.6226-1 with respect to the imputed underpayment in the FPA and does not file a petition for readjustment under section 6234. Accordingly, under §301.6226-1(b)(2) and §301.6225-3(b)(6), the adjustment year partners (as defined in §301.6241-1(a)(2)) do not take into account the $300 long-term capital loss that does not result in an imputed underpayment. Rather, the $300 long-term capital loss is taken into account by the reviewed year partners. The time to file a petition expires on August 30, 2023. Pursuant to §301.6226-2(b), the partnership adjustments become finally determined on August 31, 2023. On September 30, 2023, Partnership files with the IRS statements described in §301.6226-2 and furnishes statements to all of its reviewed year partners in accordance with §301.6226-2. One partner of Partnership in 2020, B (an individual), had a 25 percent interest in Partnership during all of 2020 and was allocated 25 percent of all items from Partnership for that year. The statement filed with the IRS and furnished to B shows B's allocable share of the ordinary loss reported on Partnership's return for the 2020 taxable year as $125. The statement also shows an adjustment to B's allocable share of the ordinary loss in the amount of -$75, resulting in a corrected ordinary loss allocated to B of $50 for taxable year 2020 ($125 originally allocated to B less $75 which is B's share of the adjustment to the ordinary loss). In addition, the statement shows an increase to B's share of long-term capital loss in the amount of $75 (B's share of the adjustment that did not result in the imputed underpayment with respect to Partnership). B must pay the additional reporting year tax as determined in accordance with paragraph (b) of this section. B computes his additional reporting year tax as follows. First, B determines the correction amount for the first affected year (the 2020 taxable year) by taking into account B's share of the partnership adjustments (a $75 reduction in ordinary loss and an increase of $75 in long-term capital loss) for the 2020 taxable year. B determines the amount by which his chapter 1 tax for 2020 would have increased or decreased if the $75 adjustment to ordinary loss and the $75 adjustment to long-term capital loss from Partnership were taken into account for that year. Second, B determines if there is any increase or decrease in chapter 1 tax for any intervening year as a result of the adjustment to the ordinary and capital losses for 2020. B's aggregate of the correction amounts is the correction amount for 2020, B's first affected year plus any correction amounts for any intervening years. B is also liable for any interest on the correction amount for the first affected year and for any intervening year as determined in accordance with paragraph (c) of this section.

(3) *Example 3.* On its partnership return for the 2020 tax year, Partnership, a domestic partnership, reported U.S. source dividend income of $2,000. On June 1, 2023, the IRS mails an FPA to Partnership for Partnership's 2020 year increasing the amount of U.S. source dividend income to $4,000 and determining that a 20 percent accuracy-related penalty under section 6662(b) applies to the increase in U.S. source dividend income. Partnership makes a timely election under section 6226 in accordance with §301.6226-1 with respect to the imputed underpayment in the FPA for Partnership's 2020 year and does not file a petition for readjustment under section 6234. The time to file a petition expires on August 30, 2023. Pursuant to §301.6226-2(b), the partnership adjustments become finally determined on August 31, 2023. On September 30, 2023, Partnership files the statements described under §301.6226-2 with the IRS and furnishes to partner C, a nonresident alien individual who was a partner in Partnership during 2020 (and remains a partner in Partnership in 2023), a statement described in §301.6226-2. C had a 50 percent interest in Partnership during all of 2020 and was allocated 50 percent of all items from Partnership for that year. The statement shows C's share of U.S. source dividend income reported on Partnership's return for the reviewed year of $1,000 and an adjustment to U.S. source dividend income of $1,000. In addition, the statement reports that a 20 percent accuracy-related penalty under section 6662(b) applies. Under §301.6241-6(b)(4)(i), because the additional $1,000 in U.S. source dividend income allocated to C is an amount subject to withholding (as defined in §301.6241-6(b)(2)), Partnership must pay the amount of tax required to be withheld on the adjustment. See §§1.1441-1(b)(1) and 1.1441-5(b)(2)(i)(A) of this chapter. Under §301.6241-6(b)(4)(ii), Partnership may reduce the amount of withholding tax it must pay because it has valid documentation from 2020 that establishes that C was entitled to a reduced rate of withholding in 2020 on U.S. source dividend income of 10 percent pursuant to a treaty. Partnership withholds $100 of tax from C's distributive share, remits the tax to the IRS, and files the necessary return and information returns required by §1.1461-1 of this chapter. On his 2023 return, C must report the additional reporting year tax determined in accordance with paragraph (b) of this section, the

accuracy-related penalty determined in accordance with paragraph (d) of this section, and interest determined in accordance with paragraph (c) of this section on the correction amount for the first affected year, the correction amount for any intervening year, and the penalty. Under paragraph (f) of this section, C may claim the $100 withholding tax paid by Partnership pursuant to § 301.6241-6(b)(4)(i) as a credit under section 33 against C's income tax liability on his 2023 return.

(4) *Example 4*. On its partnership return for the 2020 tax year, Partnership reported ordinary income of $100 and a long-term capital gain of $40. Partnership had four equal partners during the 2020 tax year: E, F, G, and H, all of whom were individuals. On its partnership return for the 2020 tax year, the entire long-term capital gain was allocated to partner E and the ordinary income was allocated to all partners based on their equal (25 percent) interest in Partnership. The IRS initiates an administrative proceeding with respect to Partnership's 2020 taxable year and determines that the long-term capital gain should have been allocated equally to all four partners and that Partnership should have recognized an additional $10 in ordinary income. On June 1, 2023, the IRS mails an FPA to Partnership reflecting the reallocation of the $40 long-term capital gain so that F, G, and H each have $10 increase in long-term capital gain and E has a $30 reduction in long-term capital gain for 2020. In addition, the FPA reflects the partnership adjustment increasing ordinary income by $10. The FPA reflects a general imputed underpayment with respect to the increase in ordinary income and a specific imputed underpayment with respect to the increase in long-term capital gain allocated to F, G, and H. In addition, the FPA reflects a $30 partnership adjustment that does not result in an imputed underpayment, that is, the reduction of $30 in long-term capital gain with respect to E that is associated with the specific imputed underpayment in accordance with § 301.6225-1(g)(2)(iii)(B). Partnership makes a timely election under section 6226 in accordance with § 301.6226-1 with respect to the specific imputed underpayment relating to the reallocation of long-term capital gain. Partnership does not file a petition for readjustment under section 6234. The time to file a petition expires on August 30, 2023. Pursuant to § 301.6226-2(b), the partnership adjustments become finally determined on August 31, 2023. Partnership timely pays the general imputed underpayment that resulted from the partnership adjustment to ordinary income. On September 30, 2023, Partnership files with the IRS statements described in § 301.6226-2 and furnishes statements to its partners reflecting their share of the partnership adjustments as finally determined in the FPA that relate to the specific imputed underpayment, that is, the reallocation of long-term capital gain. The statements for F, G, and H each reflect a partnership adjustment of an additional $10 of long-term capital gain for 2020. The statement for E reflects a partnership adjustment of a reduction of $30 of long-term capital gain for 2020. Because E, F, G, and H are all individuals, all partners must report the additional reporting year tax as determined in accordance with paragraph (b) of this section in the partners. reporting year, which is 2023. They compute their additional reporting year tax as follows. First, they determine the correction amount for the first affected year (the 2020 taxable year) by taking into account their share of the partnership adjustments for the 2020 taxable year. They each determine the amount by which their chapter 1 tax for 2020 would have increased or decreased if the adjustment to long-term capital gain from Partnership were taken into account for that year. Second, they determine if there is any increase or decrease in chapter 1 tax for any intervening year as a result of the adjustment to the long-term capital gain for 2020. Their aggregate of the correction amounts is the sum of the correction amount for 2020, their first affected year and any correction amounts for any intervening years. They are also liable for any interest on the correction amount for the first affected year and for any intervening year as determined in accordance with paragraph (c) of this section.

(5) *Example 5*. On its partnership return for the 2020 taxable year, Partnership reported a long-term capital loss of $500. During an administrative proceeding with respect to Partnership's 2020 taxable year, the IRS mails a notice of proposed partnership adjustment (NOPPA) in which it proposes to disallow $200 of the reported $500 long-term capital loss, the only adjustment. Accordingly, the imputed underpayment reflected in the NOPPA is $80 ($200 x 40 percent). F, a C corporation partner with a 50 percent interest in Partnership, received 50 percent of all long-term capital losses for 2020. As part of the modification process described in § 301.6225-2(d)(2), F files an amended return for 2020 taking into account F's share of the partnership adjustment ($100 reduction in long-term capital loss) and pays the tax owed for 2020, including interest. Also as part of the modification process, F also files amended returns for 2021 and 2022 and pays additional tax (and interest) for these years because the reduction in long-term capital loss for 2020 affected the tax due from F for 2021 and 2022. See § 301.6225-2(d)(2). The reduction of the long-term capital loss in 2020 did not affect any other taxable year of F. This is the only modifica-

tion requested. The IRS approves the modification with respect to F and on June 1, 2023, mails an FPA to Partnership for Partnership's 2020 year reflecting the partnership adjustment reducing the long-term capital loss in the amount of $200. The FPA also reflects the modification to the imputed underpayment based on the amended returns filed by F taking into account F's share of the reduction in the long-term capital loss. Therefore, the imputed underpayment in the FPA is $40 ($100 x 40 percent). Partnership makes a timely election under section 6226 in accordance with § 301.6226-1 with respect to the imputed underpayment in the FPA for Partnership's 2020 year and files a timely petition in the Tax Court challenging the partnership adjustments. The Tax Court upholds the determinations in the FPA and the decision regarding Partnership's 2020 tax year becomes final on December 15, 2025. Pursuant to § 301.6226-2(b), the partnership adjustments are finally determined on December 15, 2025. On February 1, 2026, Partnership files the statements described under § 301.6226-2 with the IRS and furnishes to its partners statements reflecting their shares of the partnership adjustment. The statement issued to F reflects F's share of the partnership adjustment for Partnership's 2020 taxable year as finally determined by the Tax Court. The statement shows F's share of the long-term capital loss adjustment for the reviewed year of $100, as well as the $100 long-term capital loss taken into account by F as part of the amended return modification. Accordingly, in accordance with paragraph (b) of this section, when F computes its correction amounts for the first affected year (the 2020 taxable year) and the intervening years (the 2021 through 2026 taxable years), F computes any increase or decrease in chapter 1 tax for those years using the returns for the 2020, 2021, and 2022 taxable years as amended during the modification process and taking into account any chapter 1 tax paid with those amended returns. F also takes into account the interest paid with F's amended returns when determining the interest under paragraph (c) of this section that must be paid in the reporting year.

(6) *Example 6*. Partnership has two equal partners for the 2020 tax year: M (an individual) and J (a partnership). For the 2020 tax year, J has two equal partners — K and L — both individuals. On June 1, 2023, the IRS mails an FPA to Partnership for Partnership's 2020 year increasing Partnership's ordinary income by $500,000 and asserting an imputed underpayment of $200,000. Partnership makes a timely election under section 6226 in accordance with § 301.6226-1 with respect to the imputed underpayment in the FPA for Partnership's 2020 year and does not file a petition for readjustment under section 6234. The time to file a petition expires on August 30, 2023. Pursuant to § 301.6226-2(b), the partnership adjustments become finally determined on August 31, 2023. Therefore, Partnership's adjustment year is 2023, the due date of the adjustment year return is March 15, 2024 and the extended due date for the adjustment year return is September 16, 2024. On October 12, 2023, Partnership timely files with the IRS statements described in § 301.6226-2 and timely furnishes statements to its partners reflecting their share of the partnership adjustments as finally determined in the FPA. The statements to M and J each reflect a partnership adjustment of $250,000 of ordinary income. M takes her share of the adjustments reflected on the statements furnished by Partnership into account on M's return for the 2023 tax year in accordance with paragraph (b) of this section. On April 1, 2024, J files the adjustment tracking report and files and furnishes statements to K and L reflecting each partner's share of the adjustments reflected on the statements Partnership furnished to J. K and L must take their share of adjustments reflected on the statements furnished by J into account on their returns for the 2023 tax year in accordance with paragraph (b) of this section by treating themselves as reviewed year partners for purposes of paragraph (b).

(7) *Example 7*. On its partnership return for the 2020 tax year, Partnership reported that it placed Asset, which had a depreciable basis of $210,000, into service in 2020 and depreciated Asset over 5 years, using the straight-line method. Accordingly, Partnership claimed depreciation of $42,000 in each year related to Asset. Partnership has two equal partners for the 2020 tax year: M (a partnership) and N (an S corporation). For the 2020 tax year, N has one shareholder, O, who is an individual. On June 1, 2023, the IRS mails an FPA to Partnership for Partnership's 2020 year. In the FPA, the IRS determines that Asset should have been depreciated over 7 years instead of 5 years and adjusts the depreciation for the 2020 tax year to $30,000 instead of $42,000 resulting in a $12,000 adjustment. This adjustment results in an imputed underpayment of $4,800 ($12,000 x 40 percent). Partnership makes a timely election under section 6226 in accordance with § 301.6226-1 with respect to the imputed underpayment in the FPA for Partnership's 2020 year and does not file a petition for readjustment under section 6234. The time to file a petition expires on August 30, 2023. Pursuant to § 301.6226-2(b), the partnership adjustments become finally determined on August 31, 2023. On October 12, 2023, Partnership timely files with the IRS statements described in § 301.6226-2 and furnishes statements to its partners reflecting their share of the partnership adjustments as finally determined in the FPA. The statements to M and N reflect a

partnership adjustment of $6,000 of ordinary income for the 2020 tax year. On February 1, 2024, N takes the adjustments into account under paragraph (e)(3) of this section by filing a partnership adjustment tracking report and furnishing a statement to O reflecting her share of the adjustments reported to N on the statement it received from Partnership. M does not furnish statements and instead chooses to calculate and pay an imputed underpayment under paragraph (e)(4) of this section equal to $1,200 ($6,000 x 40 percent) on the adjustments reflected on the statement it received from Partnership plus interest on the amount calculated in accordance with paragraph (e)(4)(iv)(B) of this section. On her 2023 return, O properly takes the adjustments into account under this section. Therefore, O reports and pays the additional reporting year tax determined in accordance with paragraph (b) of this section, which is the correction amount for 2020 plus any correction amounts for 2021 and 2022 (if the adjustments in 2020 resulted in any changes to the tax attributes of O in those years), and pays interest determined in accordance with paragraph (c) of this section on the correction amounts for each of those years.

(8) *Example 8.* On its partnership return for the 2020 tax year, Partnership reported $1,000 of ordinary loss. Partnership has two equal partners for the 2020 tax year: P and Q, both S corporations. For the 2020 tax year, P had one shareholder, R, an individual. For the 2020 tax year, Q had two shareholders, S and T, both individuals. On June 1, 2023, the IRS mails an FPA to Partnership for Partnership's 2020 year determining $500 of the $1,000 of ordinary loss should be recharacterized as $500 of long-term capital loss and $500 of the ordinary loss should be disallowed. The FPA asserts an imputed underpayment of $400 ($1,000 x 40 percent) with respect to the $1,000 reduction to ordinary loss and reflecting an adjustment that does not result in an imputed underpayment of a $500 capital loss. Partnership makes a timely election under section 6226 in accordance with §301.6226-1 with respect to the imputed underpayment in the FPA for Partnership's 2020 year and does not file a petition for readjustment under section 6234. The time to file a petition expires on August 30, 2023. Pursuant to §301.6226-2(b), the partnership adjustments become finally determined on August 31, 2023. On October 12, 2023, Partnership timely files with the IRS statements described in §301.6226-2 and furnishes statements to its partners reflecting their share of the partnership adjustments as finally determined in the FPA. The statements to P and Q each reflect a partnership adjustment of $500 increase in ordinary income and a $250 increase in capital loss in accordance with §301.6225-3(b)(6). P takes the adjustments into account under paragraph (e)(3) of this section by timely filing a partnership adjustment tracking report and furnishing a statement to R. Q timely filed a partnership adjustment tracking report, but chooses not to furnish statements and instead must calculate and pay an imputed underpayment under paragraph (e)(4) of this section as well as interest on the imputed underpayment determined under paragraph (e)(4)(iv)(B) of this section. After applying the rules set forth in §301.6225-1, Q calculates the imputed underpayment that it is required to pay of $200 ($500 adjustment to ordinary income x 40 percent). Q also has one adjustment that does not result in an imputed underpayment – the $250 increase to capital loss. Pursuant to paragraph (e)(1) of this section, Q files the partnership adjustment tracking report and pay the amounts due under paragraph (e)(4) of this section by September 15, 2024, the extended due date of Partnership's return for the adjustment year, 2023. Pursuant to paragraph (e)(4)(v) of this section, on its 2024 return, the year in which Q made its payment of the imputed underpayment, Q reports and allocates the $250 capital loss to its shareholders for its 2024 taxable year as a capital loss as provided in §301.6225-3.

(9) *Example 9.* On its partnership return for the 2020 tax year, Partnership reported a $1,000 long-term capital gain on the sale of Stock. Partnership has two equal partners for the 2020 tax year: U (an individual) and V (a partnership). For the 2020 tax year, V has two equal partners: W (an individual) and X (a partnership). For the 2020 tax year, X has two equal partners: Y and Z, both of which are C corporations. On June 1, 2023, the IRS mails a NOPPA to Partnership for Partnership's 2020 year proposing a $500 increase in the long-term capital gain from the sale of Stock and an imputed underpayment of $200 ($500 x 40 percent). On July 17, 2023, Partnership timely submits a request to modify the rate used in calculating the imputed underpayment under §301.6225-2(d)(4). Partnership submits sufficient information demonstrating that $375 of the $500 adjustment is allocable to individuals (50 percent of the $500 adjustment allocable to U and 25 percent of the $500 adjustment allocable to W) and the remaining $125 is allocable to C corporations (the indirect partners Y and Z). The IRS approves the modification and the imputed underpayment is reduced to $81.25 (($375 x 15 percent) + ($125 x 20 percent)). See §301.6225-2(b)(3). No other modifications are requested. On February 28, 2024, the IRS mails an FPA to Partnership for Partnership's 2020 year determining a $500 increase in the long-term capital gain on the sale of Stock and asserting an imputed underpayment of $81.25 after taking into account the approved modifications. Partnership makes a timely election under section 6226 in

accordance with §301.6226-1 with respect to the imputed underpayment in the FPA for Partnership's 2020 year and does not file a petition for readjustment under section 6234. The time to file a petition expires on May 28, 2024. Pursuant to §301.6226-2(b), the partnership adjustments become finally determined on May 29, 2024. On July 26, 2024, Partnership timely files with the IRS statements described in §301.6226-2 and furnishes statements to its partners reflecting their share of the partnership adjustments as finally determined in the FPA. The statements to U and V each reflect a partnership adjustment of a $250 increase in long-term capital gain. V timely files the adjustment tracking report but fails to furnish statements and therefore must calculate and pay an imputed underpayment under paragraph (e)(4) of this section as well as interest on the imputed underpayment determined under paragraph (e)(4)(iv)(B) of this section. On February 3, 2025, V pays an imputed underpayment of $43.75 (($125 x 20 percent for the adjustments allocable to X) + ($125 x 15 percent for the adjustments allocable to W)) which takes into account the rate modifications approved by the IRS with respect to Y and Z. V must also pay any interest on the amount as determined in accordance with paragraph (e)(4)(iv)(B) of this section. V must file the adjustment tracking report and pay the amounts due under paragraph (e)(4) of this section no later than September 15, 2025, the extended due date of Partnership's return for the 2024 year, which is the adjustment year.

(i) *Applicability date.*—(1) *In general.*—Except as provided in paragraph (i)(2) of this section, this section applies to partnership taxable years beginning after December 31, 2017, and ending after August 12, 2018.

(2) *Election under §301.9100-22 in effect.*—This section applies to any partnership taxable year beginning after November 2, 2015, and before January 1, 2018, for which a valid election under §301.9100-22 is in effect. [Reg. §301.6226-3.]

☐ [T.D. 9844, 2-21-2019.]

### [Reg. §301.6226(a)-1]

**§301.6226(a)-1. Principal place of business of partnership.**— (a) *In general.*—The principal place of a partnership's business for purposes of determining the appropriate district court in which a petition for a readjustment of partnership items may be filed is its principal place of business as of the date the petition is filed.

(b) *Example.*—The provisions of paragraph (a) of this section may be illustrated by the following example:

*Example.* The principal place of Partnership A's business on the day that the notice of the final partnership administrative adjustment was mailed to A's tax matters partner was Cincinnati, Ohio. However, by the day on which a petition seeking judicial review of that adjustment was filed, A had moved its principal place of business to Louisville, Kentucky. For purposes of section 6226(a)(2), A's principal place of business is Louisville.

(c) *Effective date.*—This section is applicable to partnership taxable years beginning on or after October 4, 2001. For years beginning prior to October 4, 2001, see §301.6226(a)-1T contained in 26 CFR part 1, revised April 1, 2001. [Reg. §301.6226(a)-1.]

☐ [T.D. 8965, 10-3-2001.]

### [Reg. §301.6226(b)-1]

**§301.6226(b)-1. 5-percent group.**—(a) *In general.*—All members of a 5-percent group shall join in filing any petition for judicial review. The designation of a partner as a representative of a notice group does not authorize that partner to file a petition for a readjustment of partnership items on behalf of the notice group.

(b) *Effective date.*—This section is applicable to partnership taxable years beginning on or after October 4, 2001. For years beginning prior to October 4, 2001, see §301.6226(b)-1T contained in 26 CFR part 1, revised April 1, 2001. [Reg. §301.6226(b)-1.]

☐ [T.D. 8965, 10-3-2001.]

### [Reg. §301.6226(e)-1]

**§301.6226(e)-1. Jurisdictional requirement for bringing an action in District Court or United States Court of Federal Claims.**— (a) *Amount to be deposited.*—(1) *In general.*—The jurisdictional amount that the filing partner (or, in the case of a petition filed by a 5-percent group, each member of the group, or, for civil actions beginning on or after April 2, 2002, in the case of a petition filed by a pass-thru partner, each indirect partner holding an interest through the pass-thru partner) shall deposit is the amount by which the tax liability of the partner would be increased if the treatment of the partnership items on the partner's return were made consistent with the treatment of partnership items on the partnership return, as adjusted by the notice of final partnership administrative adjustment.

The partner is not required to pay other outstanding liabilities in order to deposit a jurisdictional amount.

(2) *Example.*—The provisions of paragraph (a)(1) of this section may be illustrated by the following example:

*Example.* A files a petition for readjustment of partnership items in the United States Court of Federal Claims. A's tax liability would be increased by $4,000 if partnership items on A's return were conformed to the partnership return, as adjusted by the notice of final partnership administrative adjustment. A has an unpaid liability of $10,000 attributable to nonpartnership items. A is required to deposit $4,000 in order to satisfy the jurisdictional requirement.

(b) *Deposit taken into account in computing interest.*—The amount deposited is treated as a payment of tax for purposes of chapter 67 of the Internal Revenue Code (relating to interest).

(c) *Deposit generally not treated as payment of tax.*—Except as provided in paragraph (b) of this section, an amount deposited under section 6226(e) shall not be treated as a payment of tax. Thus, the Internal Revenue Service may proceed against the depositor for a deficiency based on nonpartnership items without regard to this deposit.

(d) *Amount deposited may be applied against assessment.*—If the restriction on assessment provided under section 6225(a) lapses with respect to a deficiency attributable to partnership items for a partnership taxable year while an amount is on deposit under section 6226(e) in connection with a petition relating to those items, the Internal Revenue Service may apply the amount deposited against any such deficiency that is assessed.

(e) *Effective date.*—Except as otherwise provided in paragraph (a)(1) of this section, this section is applicable to civil actions beginning on or after October 4, 2001. For civil actions beginning prior to October 4, 2001, see § 301.6226(e)-1T contained in 26 CFR part 1, revised April 1, 2001. [Reg. § 301.6226(e)-1.]

☐ [*T.D.* 8965, 10-3-2001.]

### [Reg. § 301.6226(f)-1]

**§ 301.6226(f)-1. Scope of judicial review.**—(a) *In general.*—A court reviewing a notice of final partnership administrative adjustment has jurisdiction to determine all partnership items for the taxable year to which the notice relates and the proper allocation of such items among the partners. Thus, the review is not limited to the items adjusted in the notice. In addition, the court has jurisdiction in the partnership-level proceeding to determine any penalty, addition to tax, or additional amount that relates to an adjustment to a partnership item. However, the court does not have jurisdiction in the partnership-level proceeding to consider any partner-level defenses to any penalty, addition to tax, or additional amount that relates to an adjustment to a partnership item. See section 6230(c)(4) and § 301.6221-1(c) and (d).

(b) *Example.*—The provisions of paragraph (a) of this section may be illustrated by the following example:

*Example.* The Internal Revenue Service issues a notice of final partnership administrative adjustment with respect to Partnership ABC in which the only item adjusted is depreciation. A petition for judicial review of that notice is filed. During the judicial proceeding, a partner of ABC, in accordance with the applicable court rules, raises an issue relating to the treatment of intangible drilling costs. The court reviewing the notice has jurisdiction to determine the intangible drilling cost issue in addition to the depreciation issue.

(c) *Effective date.*—This section is applicable to partnership taxable years beginning on or after October 4, 2001. For years beginning prior to October 4, 2001, see § 301.6226(f)-1T contained in 26 CFR part 1, revised April 1, 2001. [Reg. § 301.6226(f)-1.]

☐ [*T.D.* 8965, 10-3-2001.]

### [Reg. § 301.6227-1]

**§ 301.6227-1. Administrative adjustment request by partnership.**—(a) *In general.*—A partnership may file a request for an administrative adjustment with respect to any partnership-related item (as defined in § 301.6241-1(a)(6)(ii)) for any partnership taxable year. When filing an administrative adjustment request (AAR), the partnership must determine whether the adjustments requested in the AAR result in an imputed underpayment in accordance with § 301.6227-2(a) for the reviewed year (as defined in § 301.6241-1(a)(8)). If the adjustments requested in the AAR result in an imputed underpayment, the partnership must take the adjustments into account under the rules described in § 301.6227-2(b) unless the partnership makes an election under § 301.6227-2(c), in which case each reviewed year partner (as defined in § 301.6241-1(a)(9)) must take the adjustments into account in accordance with

§ 301.6227-3. If the adjustments requested in the AAR are adjustments described in § 301.6225-1(f)(1) that do not result in an imputed underpayment (as determined under § 301.6227-2(a)), such adjustments must be taken into account by the reviewed year partners in accordance with § 301.6227-3. A partner may not make a request for an administrative adjustment of a partnership-related item except in accordance with § 301.6222-1 or if the partner is doing so on behalf of the partnership in the partner's capacity as the partnership representative designated under section 6223. In addition, a partnership may not file an AAR solely for the purpose of changing the designation of a partnership representative or changing the appointment of a designated individual. See § 301.6223-1 (regarding designation of the partnership representative). When the partnership changes the designation of the partnership representative (or appointment of the designated individual) in conjunction with the filing of an AAR in accordance with § 301.6223-1(e), the change in designation (or appointment) is treated as occurring prior to the filing of the AAR. For rules regarding a notice of change to the amount of creditable foreign tax expenditures see paragraph (g) of this section.

(b) *Time for filing an AAR.*—An AAR may only be filed by a partnership with respect to a partnership taxable year after a partnership return for that taxable year has been filed with the Internal Revenue Service (IRS). A partnership may not file an AAR with respect to a partnership taxable year more than three years after the later of the date the partnership return for such partnership taxable year was filed or the last day for filing such partnership return (determined without regard to extensions). Except as provided in § 301.6231-1(f), an AAR (including a request filed by a partner in accordance with § 301.6222-1) may not be filed for a partnership taxable year after a notice of administrative proceeding with respect to such taxable year has been mailed by the IRS under section 6231.

(c) *Form and manner for filing an AAR.*—(1) *In general.*—An AAR by a partnership, including any required statements, forms, and schedules as described in this section, must be filed with the IRS in accordance with the forms, instructions, and other guidance prescribed by the IRS, and must be signed under penalties of perjury by the partnership representative (as described in § § 301.6223-1 and 301.6223-2).

(2) *Contents of AAR filed with the IRS.*—A partnership must include the information described in this paragraph (c)(2) when filing an AAR with the IRS. In the case of a failure by the partnership to provide the information described in this paragraph (c)(2), the IRS may, but is not required to, invalidate an AAR or readjust any items that were adjusted on the AAR. An AAR filed with the IRS must include—

(i) The adjustments requested;

(ii) If a reviewed year partner is required to take into account the adjustments requested under § 301.6227-3, statements described in paragraph (e) of this section, including any transmittal with respect to such statements required by forms, instructions, and other guidance prescribed by the IRS; and

(iii) Other information prescribed by the IRS in forms, instructions, or other guidance.

(d) *Copy of statement furnished to reviewed year partners in certain cases.*—If a reviewed year partner is required to take into account adjustments requested in an AAR under § 301.6227-3, the partnership must furnish a copy of the statement described in paragraph (e) of this section to the reviewed year partner to whom the statement relates in accordance with the forms, instructions and other guidance prescribed by the IRS. If the partnership mails the statement, it must mail the statement to the current or last address of the reviewed year partner that is known to the partnership. The statement must be furnished to the reviewed year partner on the date the AAR is filed with the IRS.

(e) *Statements.*—(1) *Contents.*—Each statement described in this paragraph (e) must include the following correct information:

(i) The name and TIN of the reviewed year partner to whom the statement is being furnished;

(ii) The current or last address of the partner that is known to the partnership;

(iii) The reviewed year partner's share of items as originally reported on statements furnished to the partner under section 6031(b) and, if applicable, section 6227;

(iv) The reviewed year partner's share of the adjustments as described under paragraph (e)(2) of this section;

(v) The date the statement is furnished to the partner;

(vi) The partnership taxable year to which the adjustments relate; and

(vii) Any other information required by forms, instructions, and other guidance prescribed by the IRS.

(2) *Determination of each partner's share of adjustments.*—(i) *In general.*—Except as provided in paragraphs (e)(2)(ii) and (iii) of this section, each reviewed year partner's share of the adjustments requested in the AAR is determined in the same manner as each adjusted partnership-related item was originally allocated to the reviewed year partner on the partnership return for the reviewed year. If the partnership pays an imputed underpayment under § 301.6227-2(b) with respect to the adjustments requested in the AAR, the reviewed year partner's share of the adjustments requested in the AAR only includes any adjustments that did not result in the imputed underpayment, as determined under § 301.6227-2(a).

(ii) *Adjusted partnership-related item not reported on the partnership's return for the reviewed year.*—Except as provided in paragraph (e)(2)(iii) of this section, if the adjusted partnership-related item was not reported on the partnership return for the reviewed year, each reviewed year partner's share of the adjustments must be determined in accordance with how such items would have been allocated under rules that apply with respect to partnership allocations, including under the partnership agreement.

(iii) *Allocation adjustments.*—If an adjustment involves allocation of a partnership-related item to a specific partner or in a specific manner, including a reallocation of an item, the reviewed year partner's share of the adjustment requested in the AAR is determined in accordance with the AAR.

(f) *Administrative proceeding for a taxable year for which an AAR is filed.*—Within the period described in section 6235, the IRS may initiate an administrative proceeding with respect to the partnership for any partnership taxable year regardless of whether the partnership filed an AAR with respect to such taxable year and may adjust any partnership-related item, including any partnership-related item adjusted in an AAR filed by the partnership. The amount of an imputed underpayment determined by the partnership under § 301.6227-2(a)(1), including any modifications determined by the partnership under § 301.6227-2(a)(2), may be re-determined by the IRS.

(g) *Notice requirement and partnership adjustments required as a result of a foreign tax redetermination.*—For special rules applicable when an adjustment to a partnership related item (as defined in section 6241(2)) is required as part of a redetermination of U.S. tax liability under section 905(c) and § 1.905-3(b) of this chapter as a result of a foreign tax redetermination (as defined in § 1.905-3(a) of this chapter), see § 1.905-4(b)(2)(ii) of this chapter.

(h) *Applicability date.*—(1) *In general.*—Except as provided in paragraph (h)(2) of this section, this section applies to partnership taxable years beginning after December 31, 2017, and ending after August 12, 2018.

(2) *Election under § 301.9100-22 in effect.*—This section applies to any partnership taxable year beginning after November 2, 2015, and before January 1, 2018, for which a valid election under § 301.9100-22 is in effect. [Reg. § 301.6227-1.]

☐ [T.D. 9844, 2-21-2019 *Amended by T.D.* 9922, 11-2-2020.]

### [Reg. § 301.6227-2]

**§ 301.6227-2. Determining and accounting for adjustments requested in an administrative adjustment request by the partnership.**—(a) *Determining whether adjustments result in an imputed underpayment.*—(1) *Determination of an imputed underpayment.*—The determination of whether adjustments requested in an administrative adjustment request (AAR) result in an imputed underpayment in the reviewed year (as defined in § 301.6241-1(a)(8)) and the determination of the amount of any imputed underpayment is made in accordance with the rules under § 301.6225-1.

(2) *Modification of imputed underpayment for purposes of this section.*—A partnership may apply modifications to the amount of an imputed underpayment determined under paragraph (a)(1) of this section using only the provisions under § 301.6225-2(d)(3) (regarding tax-exempt partners), § 301.6225-2(d)(4) (regarding modification of applicable tax rate), § 301.6225-2(d)(5) (regarding specified passive activity losses), § 301.6225-2(d)(6)(ii) (regarding limitations or restrictions in the grouping of adjustments), § 301.6225-2(d)(7) (regarding certain qualified investment entities), § 301.6225-2(d)(9) (regarding tax treaty modifications), or as provided in forms, instructions, or other guidance prescribed by the IRS with respect to AARs. The partnership may not modify an imputed underpayment resulting from adjustments requested in an AAR except as described in this paragraph (a)(2). When applying modifications to the amount of an imputed underpayment under this paragraph (a)(2):

(i) The partnership is not required to seek the approval from the Internal Revenue Service (IRS) prior to applying modifications to

the amount of any imputed underpayment under paragraph (a)(1) of this section reported on the AAR; and

(ii) As part of the AAR filed with the IRS in accordance with forms, instructions, and other guidance prescribed by the IRS, the partnership must –

(A) Notify the IRS of any modification;

(B) Describe the effect of the modification on the imputed underpayment;

(C) Provide an explanation of the basis for such modification; and

(D) Provide documentation to support the partnership's eligibility for the modification.

(b) *Adjustments resulting in an imputed underpayment taken into account by the partnership.*—(1) *In general.*—Except in the case of a valid election under paragraph (c) of this section, a partnership must pay any imputed underpayment (as determined under paragraph (a) of this section) resulting from the adjustments requested in an AAR on the date the partnership files the AAR. For the rules applicable to the partnership's expenditure for an imputed underpayment, as well as any penalties and interest paid by the partnership with respect to an imputed underpayment, see § 301.6241-4.

(2) *Penalties and interest.*—The IRS may impose a penalty, addition to tax, and additional amount with respect to any imputed underpayment determined under this section in accordance with section 6233(a)(3) (penalties determined from the reviewed year). In addition, the IRS may impose a penalty, addition to tax, and additional amount with respect to a failure to pay any imputed underpayment on the date an AAR is filed in accordance with section 6233(b)(3) (penalties with respect to the adjustment year return). Interest on an imputed underpayment is determined under chapter 67 of the Internal Revenue Code for the period beginning on the date after the due date of the partnership return for the reviewed year (as defined in § 301.6241-1(a)(8)) (determined without regard to extension) and ending on the date the AAR is filed. See § 301.6233(a)-1(b). In the case of any failure to pay an imputed underpayment on the date the AAR is filed, interest is determined in accordance with section 6233(b)(2) and § 301.6233(b)-1(c).

(3) *Coordination with chapters 3 and 4 of the Internal Revenue Code.*—(i) *Coordination when partnership pays an imputed underpayment.*—If a partnership pays an imputed underpayment resulting from adjustments requested in an AAR under paragraph (b)(1) of this section, the rules in § 301.6241-6(b)(3) apply to treat the partnership as having paid the amount required to be withheld under chapter 3 or chapter 4 (as defined in § 301.6241-6(b)(2)).

(ii) *Coordination when partnership elects to have adjustments taken into account by reviewed year partners.*—If a partnership elects under paragraph (c) of this section to have its reviewed year partners take into account adjustments requested in an AAR, the rules in § 301.6226-2(g)(3) apply to the partnership, and the rules in § 301.6226-3(f) apply to the reviewed year partners that take into account the adjustments pursuant to § 301.6227-3.

(c) *Election to have adjustments resulting in an imputed underpayment taken into account by reviewed year partners.*—In lieu of paying an imputed underpayment under paragraph (b) of this section, the partnership may elect to have each reviewed year partner (as defined in § 301.6241-1(a)(9)) take into account the adjustments requested in the AAR that are associated with such imputed underpayment in accordance with § 301.6227-3. A partnership makes an election under this paragraph (c) at the time the AAR is filed in accordance with the forms, instructions, and other guidance prescribed by the IRS. If the partnership makes a valid election in accordance with this paragraph (c), the partnership is not liable for, nor required to pay, the imputed underpayment to which the election relates. Rather, each reviewed year partner must take into account their share of the adjustments requested in the AAR that are associated with such imputed underpayment in accordance with § 301.6227-3. If an election is made under this paragraph (c) with respect to an imputed underpayment, modifications applied under paragraph (a)(2) of this section to such imputed underpayment are disregarded and all adjustments requested in the AAR that are associated with such imputed underpayment must be taken into account by each reviewed year partner in accordance with § 301.6227-3.

(d) *Adjustments not resulting in an imputed underpayment.*—If any adjustments requested in an AAR are adjustments that do not result in an imputed underpayment (as determined under paragraph (a) of this section), the partnership must furnish statements to each reviewed year partner and file such statements with the IRS in accordance with § 301.6227-1. Each reviewed year partner must take into account its share of the adjustments that do not result in an imputed underpayment requested in the AAR in accordance with § 301.6227-3.

(e) *Applicability date.*—(1) *In general.*—Except as provided in paragraph (e)(2) of this section, this section applies to partnership taxable years beginning after December 31, 2017, and ending after August 12, 2018.

(2) *Election under § 301.9100-22 in effect.*—This section applies to any partnership taxable year beginning after November 2, 2015, and before January 1, 2018, for which a valid election under § 301.9100-22 is in effect. [Reg. § 301.6227-2.]

☐ [T.D. 9844, 2-21-2019.]

### [Reg. § 301.6227-3]

**§ 301.6227-3. Adjustments requested in an administrative adjustment request taken into account by reviewed year partners.**—(a) *In general.*—Each reviewed year partner (as defined in § 301.6241-1(a)(9)) is required to take into account its share of adjustments requested in an administrative adjustment request (AAR) that either do not result in an imputed underpayment (as described in § 301.6225-1(f)(1)) or are associated with an imputed underpayment for which the partnership makes an election under § 301.6227-2(c). Each reviewed year partner receiving a statement furnished in accordance with § 301.6227-1(d) must take into account adjustments reflected in the statement in the reviewed year partner's taxable year that includes the date the statement is furnished (reporting year) in accordance with paragraph (b) of this section.

(b) *Adjustments taken into account by the reviewed year partner in the reporting year.*—(1) *In general.*—Except as provided in paragraph (c) of this section, a reviewed year partner that is furnished a statement described in paragraph (a) of this section must treat the statement as if it were issued under section 6226(a)(2) and, on or before the due date for the reporting year must report and pay the additional reporting year tax (as defined in § 301.6226-3(a)), if any, determined after taking into account that partner's share of the adjustments requested in the AAR in accordance with § 301.6226-3. A reviewed year partner may, in accordance with § 301.6226-3(a), reduce chapter 1 tax for the reporting year where the additional reporting year tax is less than zero. For purposes of paragraph (b) of this section, the rule under § 301.6226-3(c)(3) (regarding the increased rate of interest) does not apply. Nothing in this section entitles any partner to a refund of tax imposed by chapter 1 of the Internal Revenue Code (chapter 1 tax) to which such partner is not entitled. For instance, a partnership-partner (as defined in § 301.6241-1(a)(7)) may not claim a refund with respect to its share of any adjustment.

(2) *Examples.*—The following examples illustrate the rules of paragraph (b) of this section.

(i) *Example 1.* In 2022, partner A, an individual, received a statement described in paragraph (a) of this section from Partnership with respect to Partnership's 2020 taxable year. Both A and Partnership are calendar year taxpayers and A is not claiming any refundable tax credit in 2020. The only adjustment shown on the statement is an increase in ordinary loss. Taking into account the adjustment, A determines that his additional reporting year tax for 2022 (the reporting year) is -$100 (that is, a reduction of $100.) A's chapter 1 tax for 2022 (without regard to any additional reporting year tax) is $150. Applying the rules in paragraph (b)(1) of this section, A's chapter 1 tax for 2022 is reduced to $50 ($150 chapter 1 tax without regard to the additional reporting year tax plus -$100 additional reporting year tax).

(ii) *Example 2.* The facts are the same as in *Example 1* in paragraph (b)(2)(i) of this section, except A's chapter 1 tax for 2022 (without regard to any additional reporting year tax) is $75. Applying the rules in paragraph (b)(1) of this section, A's chapter 1 tax for 2022 is reduced by the -$100 of additional reporting year tax. Accordingly, A's chapter 1 tax for 2022 is -$25 ($75 chapter 1 tax without regard to any additional reporting year tax plus -$100 of additional reporting year tax), A owes no chapter 1 tax for 2022, and A may make a claim for refund with respect to any overpayment.

(c) *Reviewed year partners that are pass-through partners.*—(1) *In general.*—Except as provided in paragraph (c) of this section, if a statement described in paragraph (a) of this section (including a statement described in this paragraph (c)(1)) is furnished to a reviewed year partner that is a pass-through partner (as defined in § 301.6241-1(a)(5)), the pass-through partner must take into account the adjustments reflected on that statement in accordance with § 301.6226-3(e) by treating the partnership that filed the AAR as the partnership that made an election under § 301.6226-1. A pass-through partner that furnishes statements in accordance with § 301.6226-3(e)(3) must provide the information described in paragraph (c)(3) of this section in lieu of the information described in § 301.6226-3(e)(3)(iii) on the statements the pass-through partner furnishes to its partners. A pass-through partner that computes and pays an imputed underpayment in accordance with

§ 301.6226-3(e)(4)(iii) may not apply any modifications to the amount of imputed underpayment. For purposes of this paragraph (c)(1), the statement furnished to the pass-through partner by the partnership filing the AAR is treated as if it were a statement issued under section 6226(a)(2) and described in § 301.6226-2.

(2) *Adjustments that do not result in an imputed underpayment.*—If adjustments on a statement received by the pass-through partner under paragraph (a) or (c)(1) of this section do not result in an imputed underpayment for the pass-through partner (as described in § 301.6225-1(f)(1)), the pass-through partner must take the adjustments that do not result in an imputed underpayment into account in accordance with § 301.6226-3(e)(3). The pass-through partner must take such adjustments into account under this paragraph (c)(2) even in situations where the pass-through partner pays an imputed underpayment in accordance with § 301.6226-3(e)(4)(iii). The pass-through partner must provide the information described in paragraph (c)(3) of this section in lieu of the information described in § 301.6226-3(e)(3)(iii) on the statements the pass-through partner furnishes to its affected partners (as defined in § 301.6226-3(e)(3)(i)).

(3) *Contents of statements.*—Each statement described in paragraph (c)(1) or (2) of this section must include the following correct information –

(i) The name and taxpayer identification number (TIN) of the partnership that filed the AAR with respect to the adjustments reflected on the statements described in paragraph (c)(1) of this section;

(ii) The adjustment year (as defined in § 301.6241-1(a)(1)) of the partnership described in paragraph (c)(3)(i) of this section;

(iii) The extended due date for the return for the adjustment year of the partnership described in paragraph (c)(3)(i) of this section (as described in § 301.6226-3(e)(3)(ii));

(iv) The date on which the partnership described in paragraph (c)(3)(i) of this section furnished its statements required under § 301.6227-1(d);

(v) The name and TIN of the partnership that furnished the statement to the pass-through partner if different from the partnership described in paragraph (c)(3)(i) of this section;

(vi) The name and TIN of the pass-through partner;

(vii) The pass-through partner's taxable year to which the adjustments set forth in the statement described in paragraph (c)(1) of this section relate;

(viii) The name and TIN of the affected partner to whom the statement is being furnished;

(ix) The current or last address of the affected partner that is known to the pass-through partner;

(x) The affected partner's share of items as originally reported to such partner under section 6031(b) and, if applicable, section 6227, for the taxable year to which the adjustments reflected on the statement furnished to the pass-through partner relate;

(xi) The affected partner's share of partnership adjustments determined under § 301.6227-1(e)(2) as if the affected partner were the reviewed year partner and the partnership were the pass-through partner;

(xii) Any other information required by forms, instructions, and other guidance prescribed by the IRS.

(4) *Affected partners must take into account the adjustments.*—A statement furnished to an affected partner in accordance with paragraph (c)(1) or (2) of this section is to be treated by the affected partner as if it were a statement described in paragraph (a) of this section. The affected partner must take into account its share of the adjustments reflected on such a statement in accordance with this section by treating references to "reviewed year partner" as "affected partner." When taking into account the adjustments as described in § 301.6226-3(e)(3)(iv), the rules under § 301.6226-3(c)(3) (regarding the increased rate of interest) do not apply.

(d) *Applicability date.*—(1) *In general.*—Except as provided in paragraph (d)(2) of this section, this section applies to partnership taxable years beginning after December 31, 2017, and ending after August 12, 2018.

(2) *Election under § 301.9100-22 in effect.*—This section applies to any partnership taxable year beginning after November 2, 2015, and before January 1, 2018, for which a valid election under § 301.9100-22 is in effect. [Reg. § 301.6227-3.]

☐ [T.D. 9844, 2-21-2019.]

### [Reg. § 301.6227(c)-1]

**§ 301.6227(c)-1. Administrative adjustment request by the tax matters partner on behalf of the partnership.**—(a) *In general.*—A request for an administrative adjustment filed by the tax matters partner on behalf of the partnership shall be filed on the form prescribed by the Internal Revenue Service for that purpose in accordance with that form's instructions. Except as otherwise provided in that form's instructions, the request shall be—

(1) Filed with the service center where the original partnership return was filed (but, if the notice described in section 6223(a)(1) (beginning of an administrative proceeding) has already been mailed to the tax matters partner, the statement should be filed with the Internal Revenue Service office that mailed such notice);

(2) Signed by the tax matters partner; and

(3) Accompanied by revised schedules showing the effects of the proposed changes on each partner and an explanation of the changes.

(b) *Denied request for treatment as a substituted return remains administrative adjustment request.*—An administrative adjustment request filed by the tax matters partner on behalf of the partnership for which substituted return treatment is requested but not granted remains an administrative adjustment request. Thus, for example, the tax matters partner may file suit under section 6228(a) if the Internal Revenue Service fails to take timely action on the request.

(c) *Effective date.*—This section is applicable to partnership taxable years beginning on or after October 4, 2001. For years beginning prior to October 4, 2001, see § 301.6227(b)-1T contained in 26 CFR part 1, revised April 1, 2001. [Reg. § 301.6227(c)-1.]

☐ [*T.D.* 8965, 10-3-2001.]

### [Reg. § 301.6227(d)-1]

**§ 301.6227(d)-1. Administrative adjustment request filed on behalf of a partner.**—(a) *In general.*—A request for an administrative adjustment on behalf of a partner shall be filed on the form prescribed by the Internal Revenue Service for that purpose in accordance with that form's instructions. Except as otherwise provided in that form's instructions, the request shall—

(1) Be filed in duplicate, the original copy filed with the partner's amended income tax return (on which the partner computes the amount by which the partner's tax liability should be adjusted if the request is granted) and the other copy filed with the service center where the partnership return is filed (but, if the notice described in section 6223(a)(1) (beginning of an administrative proceeding) has already been mailed to the tax matters partner, the statement should be filed with the Internal Revenue Service office that mailed such notice);

(2) Identify the partner and the partnership by name, address, and taxpayer identification number;

(3) Specify the partnership taxable year to which the administrative adjustment request applies;

(4) Relate only to partnership items; and

(5) Relate only to one partnership and one partnership taxable year.

(b) *Effective date.*—This section is applicable to partnership taxable years beginning on or after October 4, 2001. For years beginning prior to October 4, 2001, see § 301.6227(c)-1T contained in 26 CFR part 1, revised April 1, 2001. [Reg. § 301.6227(d)-1.]

☐ [*T.D.* 8965, 10-3-2001.]

### [Reg. § 301.6229(b)-1]

**§ 301.6229(b)-1. Extension by agreement.**—(a) *In general.*—Any partnership may authorize any person to extend the period described in section 6229(a) with respect to all partners by filing a statement to that effect with the service center where the partnership return is filed (but, if the notice described in section 6223(a)(1) (beginning of an administrative proceeding) has already been mailed to the tax matters partner, the statement should be filed with the Internal Revenue Service office that mailed such notice). The statement shall—

(1) Provide that it is an authorization for a person other than the tax matters partner to extend the assessment period with respect to all partners;

(2) Identify the partnership and the person being authorized by name, address, and taxpayer identification number;

(3) Specify the partnership taxable year or years for which the authorization is effective; and

(4) Be signed by all persons who were general partners (or, in the case of an LLC, member-managers, as those terms are defined in § 301.623(a)(7)-2(b)) at any time during the year or years for which the authorization is effective.

(b) *Effective date.*—This section is applicable to partnership taxable years beginning on or after October 4, 2001. For years beginning prior to October 4, 2001, see § 301.6229(b)-1T contained in 26 CFR part 1, revised April 1, 2001. [Reg. § 301.6229(b)-1.]

☐ [*T.D.* 8965, 10-3-2001.]

### [Reg. § 301.6229(b)-2]

**§ 301.6229(b)-2. Special rule with respect to debtors in Title 11 cases.**—(a) *In general.*—Notwithstanding any other law or rule of law, if an agreement is entered into under section 6229(b)(1)(B), and the agreement is signed by a person who would be the tax matters partner but for the fact that, at the time that the agreement is executed, the person is a debtor in a bankruptcy proceeding under Title 11 of the United States Code, such agreement shall be binding on all partners in the partnership unless the Internal Revenue Service has been notified of the bankruptcy proceeding in accordance with paragraph (b) of this section.

(b) *Procedures for notifying the Internal Revenue Service of a partner's bankruptcy proceeding.*—(1) The Internal Revenue Service shall be notified of the bankruptcy proceeding of the tax matters partner in accordance with the procedures set forth in § 301.6223(c)-1.

(2) In addition to the information specified in § 301.6223(c)-1, notification that a person is (or was) a debtor in a bankruptcy proceeding shall include the date the bankruptcy proceeding was filed, the name and address of the court in which the bankruptcy proceeding exists (or took place), the caption of the bankruptcy proceeding (including the docket number or other identification number used by the court), and the status of the proceeding as of the date of notification.

(c) *Effective date.*—This section is applicable to partnership taxable years beginning on or after October 4, 2001. For years beginning prior to October 4, 2001, see § 301.6229(b)-2T contained in 26 CFR part 1, revised April 1, 2001. [Reg. § 301.6229(b)-2.]

☐ [*T.D.* 8965, 10-3-2001.]

### [Reg. § 301.6229(c)(2)-1]

**§ 301.6229(c)(2)-1. Substantial omission of income.**—(a) *Partnership return.*—(1) *General rule.*—(i) If any partnership omits from the gross income stated in its return an amount properly includible therein and that amount is described in clause (i) of section 6501(e)(1)(A), subsection (a) of section 6229 shall be applied by substituting "6 years" for "3 years."

(ii) For purposes of paragraph (a)(1)(i) of this section, the term *gross income*, as it relates to a trade or business, means the total of the amounts received or accrued from the sale of goods or services, to the extent required to be shown on the return, without reduction for the cost of those goods or services.

(iii) For purposes of paragraph (a)(1)(i) of this section, the term *gross income*, as it relates to any income other than from the sale of goods or services in a trade or business, has the same meaning as provided under section 61(a), and includes the total of the amounts received or accrued, to the extent required to be shown on the return. In the case of amounts received or accrued that relate to the disposition of property, and except as provided in paragraph (a)(1)(ii) of this section, gross income means the excess of the amount realized from the disposition of the property over the unrecovered cost or other basis of the property. Consequently, except as provided in paragraph (a)(1)(ii) of this section, an understated amount of gross income resulting from an overstatement of unrecovered cost or other basis constitutes an omission from gross income for purposes of section 6229(c)(2).

(iv) An amount shall not be considered as omitted from gross income if information sufficient to apprise the Commissioner of the nature and amount of the item is disclosed in the return, including any schedule or statement attached to the return.

(b) *Effective/applicability date.*—This section applies to taxable years with respect to which the period for assessing tax was open on or after September 24, 2009. [Reg. § 301.6229(c)(2)-1.]

☐ [*T.D.* 9511, 12-14-2010.]

### [Reg. § 301.6229(e)-1]

**§ 301.6229(e)-1. Information with respect to unidentified partner.**—(a) *In general.*—A partner who is not properly identified on the partnership return (including an indirect partner) remains an unidentified partner for purposes of section 6229(e) until identifying information is furnished as provided in § 301.6223(c)-1.

(b) *Effective date.*—This section is applicable to partnership taxable years beginning on or after October 4, 2001. For years beginning prior to October 4, 2001, see § 301.6229(e)-1T contained in 26 CFR part 1, revised April 1, 2001. [Reg. § 301.6229(e)-1.]

☐ [*T.D.* 8965, 10-3-2001.]

### [Reg. § 301.6229(f)-1]

**§ 301.6229(f)-1. Special rule for partial settlement agreements.**—(a) *In general.*—If a partner enters into a settlement agreement with the Internal Revenue Service with respect to the treatment of some of the partnership items or partnership-level determinations of any penalty, addition to tax, or additional amount in dispute for a partnership taxable year, but one or more other partnership items or determinations remain in dispute, the period of limitations for assessing any tax attributable to the settled items shall be determined as if such agreement had not been entered into.

(b) *Other items remaining in dispute.*—Pursuant to section 6226(c), a partner is a party to a partnership-level judicial proceeding with respect to partnership items and partnership-level determinations of penalties, additions to tax or additional amounts. When a partner settles partnership items, the settled partnership items convert to nonpartnership items under section 6231(b)(1)(C) and will not be subject to any future or pending partnership-level proceeding pursuant to section 6226(d)(1). The remaining unsettled partnership items, as well as any unsettled penalty, addition to tax, or additional amount that relates to an adjustment to a partnership item (regardless of whether the partnership item to which it relates has been settled), however, will remain subject to determination under partnership-level administrative and judicial procedures. Consequently, any remaining unsettled items, including any unsettled penalty, addition to tax, or additional amount that relates to an adjustment to a partnership item, will be deemed to remain in dispute. Thus, the period for assessing any tax attributable to the settled items will be governed by the period for assessing any tax attributable to the remaining unsettled items.

(c) *Effective date.*—This section is applicable to partnership taxable years beginning on or after October 4, 2001. For years beginning prior to October 4, 2001, see §301.6229(f)-1T contained in 26 CFR part 1, revised April 1, 2001. [Reg. §301.6229(f)-1.]

☐ [T.D. 8965, 10-3-2001.]

### [Reg. §301.6230(b)-1]

**§301.6230(b)-1. Request that correction not be made.**—(a) *In general.*—The request that a correction not be made under section 6230(b)(2) shall be in writing and shall—

(1) State that it is a request that a correction not be made under section 6230(b);

(2) Identify the partnership and the partner filing the request by name, address, and taxpayer identification number;

(3) Be signed by the partner filing the request; and

(4) Be filed with the Internal Revenue Service office that provided the notice of the correction of the error.

(b) *Effective date.*—This section is applicable to partnership taxable years beginning on or after October 4, 2001. For years beginning prior to October 4, 2001, see §301.6230(b)-1T contained in 26 CFR part 1, revised April 1, 2001. [Reg. §301.6230(b)-1.]

☐ [T.D. 8965, 10-3-2001.]

### [Reg. §301.6230(c)-1]

**§301.6230(c)-1. Claim arising out of erroneous computation, etc.**—(a) *In general.*—A claim for refund under section 6230(c) shall state the grounds for the claim and shall be filed with the service center where the partner's return is filed.

(b) *Effective date.*—This section is applicable to partnership taxable years beginning on or after October 4, 2001. For years beginning prior to October 4, 2001, see §301.6230(c)-1T contained in 26 CFR part 1, revised April 1, 2001. [Reg. §301.6230(c)-1.]

☐ [T.D. 8965, 10-3-2001.]

### [Reg. §301.6230(e)-1]

**§301.6230(e)-1. Tax matters partner required to furnish names.**—(a) *In general.*—If a notice of the beginning of an administrative proceeding is mailed to the tax matters partner with respect to any partnership taxable year, the tax matters partner shall furnish to the Internal Revenue Service office that issued the notice the name, address, profits interest, and taxpayer identification number of each person who was a partner in the partnership at any time during that taxable year if that information was not provided on the partnership return filed for that year.

(b) *Revised or additional information.*—If the tax matters partner discovers that any information furnished to the Internal Revenue Service on the partnership return or under paragraph (a) of this section was incorrect or incomplete, the tax matters partner shall furnish revised or additional information to the Internal Revenue Service within 15 days of discovering that the information furnished to the Internal Revenue Service was incorrect or incomplete.

(c) *Information required with respect to indirect partners.*—The requirements of this section for identifying information apply with respect to indirect partners to the extent that the tax matters partner has such information.

(d) *Effective date.*—This section is applicable to partnership taxable years beginning on or after October 4, 2001. For years beginning prior to October 4, 2001, see §301.6230(e)-1T contained in 26 CFR part 1, revised April 1, 2001. [Reg. §301.6230(e)-1.]

☐ [T.D. 8965, 10-3-2001.]

### [Reg. §301.6231-1]

**§301.6231-1. Notice of proceedings and adjustments.**—(a) *Notices to which this section applies.*—In the case of any administrative proceeding under subchapter C of chapter 63 of the Internal Revenue Code (subchapter C of chapter 63), including an administrative proceeding with respect to an administrative adjustment request (AAR) filed by a partnership under section 6227, the following notices must be mailed to the partnership and the partnership representative (as described in section 6223 and §301.6223-1)—

(1) Notice of any administrative proceeding initiated at the partnership level with respect to an adjustment of any partnership-related item (as defined in §301.6241-1(a)(6)(ii)) for any partnership taxable year under subchapter C of chapter 63 (notice of administrative proceeding (NAP));

(2) Notice of any proposed partnership adjustment resulting from an administrative proceeding under subchapter C of chapter 63 (notice of proposed partnership adjustment (NOPPA)); and

(3) Notice of any final partnership adjustment resulting from an administrative proceeding under subchapter C of chapter 63 (notice of final partnership adjustment (FPA)).

(b) *Time for mailing notices.*—(1) *Notice of proposed partnership adjustment.*—A NOPPA is timely if it is mailed before the expiration of the period for making adjustments under section 6235(a)(1) (including any extensions under section 6235(b) and any special rules under section 6235(c)).

(2) *Notice of final partnership adjustment.*—An FPA may not be mailed earlier than 270 days after the date on which the NOPPA is mailed unless the partnership agrees, in writing, with the Internal Revenue Service (IRS) to waive the 270-day period. See §301.6225-2(c)(3)(iii) for the effect of a waiver under this paragraph (b)(2) on the 270-period for requesting a modification under section 6225(c). See §301.6232-1(d)(2) for the rules regarding a waiver of the limitations on assessment under §301.6232-1(c).

(c) *Last known address.*—A notice described in paragraph (a) of this section is sufficient if mailed to the last known address of the partnership representative and the partnership (even if the partnership or partnership representative has terminated its existence).

(d) *Notice mailed to partnership representative.*—(1) *In general.*—A notice described in paragraph (a) of this section will be treated as mailed to the partnership representative if the notice is mailed to the partnership representative that is reflected in the IRS records as of the date the letter is mailed.

(2) *No partnership representative in effect.*—In any case in which no partnership representative designation is in effect in accordance with §301.6223-1(f), a notice described in paragraph (a) of this section mailed to "PARTNERSHIP REPRESENTATIVE" at the last known address of the partnership satisfies the requirements of this section.

(e) *Restrictions on additional FPAs after petition filed.*—The IRS may mail more than one FPA to any partnership for any partnership taxable year. However, except in the case of fraud, malfeasance, or misrepresentation of a material fact, the IRS may not mail an FPA to a partnership with respect to a partnership taxable year after the partnership has filed a timely petition for readjustment under section 6234 with respect to an FPA issued with respect to such partnership taxable year.

(f) *Withdrawal of NAP or NOPPA.*—The IRS may, without consent of the partnership, withdraw any NAP or NOPPA. Except as described in §301.6223-1(d)(2) and (e)(2), if the IRS withdraws a NAP or NOPPA under this paragraph (f), the NAP or NOPPA is treated as if it were never issued, and the withdrawn NAP or NOPPA has no effect for purposes of subchapter C of chapter 63. For instance, if the IRS withdraws a NAP with respect to a partnership taxable year, the limitation under §301.6222-1(c)(5) regarding inconsistent treatment, and the prohibition under section 6227(c) on filing an AAR, after the mailing of a NAP no longer applies with respect to such taxable year.

(g) *Rescission of FPA.*—The IRS may, with the consent of the partnership, rescind any FPA. An FPA that is rescinded is not an FPA for purposes of subchapter C of chapter 63, and the partnership cannot bring a proceeding under section 6234 with respect to such FPA.

(h) *Applicability date.*—(1) *In general.*—Except as provided in paragraph (h)(2) of this section, this section applies to partnership taxable years beginning after December 31, 2017, and ending after August 12, 2018.

(2) *Election under § 301.9100-22 in effect.*—This section applies to any partnership taxable year beginning after November 2, 2015, and before January 1, 2018, for which a valid election under § 301.9100-22 is in effect. [Reg. § 301.6231-1.]

☐ [T.D. 9844, 2-21-2019.]

### [Reg. § 301.6231(a)(1)-1]

**§ 301.6231(a)(1)-1. Exception for small partnerships.**—(a) *In general.*—For purposes of the exception for small partnerships under section 623 1(a)(1)(B), the rules contained in this section shall apply.

(1) *10 or fewer.*—The 10 or fewer limitation described in section 6231(a)(1)(B)(i) is applied to the number of natural persons, C corporations, and estates of deceased partners that were partners at any one time during the partnership taxable year. Thus, for example, a partnership that at no time during the taxable year had more than 10 partners may be treated as a small partnership even if, because of transfers of interests in the partnership, 11 or more natural persons, C corporations, or estates of deceased partners owned interests in the partnership for some portion of the taxable year. See section 1361(a)(2) for the definition of a C corporation. For purposes of section 6231(a)(1)(B) and this section, a husband and wife (and their estates) are treated as one person.

(2) *Pass-thru partner.*—The exception provided in section 6231(a)(1)(B) does not apply to a partnership for a taxable year if any partner in the partnership during that taxable year is a pass-thru partner as defined in section 6231(a)(9). For purposes of this paragraph (a)(2), an estate shall not be treated as a pass-thru partner.

(3) *Determination made annually.*—The determination of whether a partnership meets the requirements for the exception for small partnerships under section 6231(a)(1)(B) and this paragraph (a) shall be made with respect to each partnership taxable year. Thus, a partnership that does not qualify as a small partnership in one taxable year may qualify as a small partnership in another taxable year if the requirements for the exception under section 6231(a)(1)(B) and this paragraph (a) are met with respect to that other taxable year.

(b) *Election to have subchapter C of chapter 63 apply.*—(1) *In general.*—Any partnership that meets the requirements set forth in section 6231(a)(1)(B) and paragraph (a) of this section (relating to the exception for small partnerships) may elect under paragraph (b)(2) of this section to have the provisions of subchapter C of chapter 63 of the Internal Revenue Code apply with respect to that partnership.

(2) *Method of election.*—A partnership shall make the election described in paragraph (b)(1) of this section by attaching a statement to the partnership return for the first taxable year for which the election is to be effective. The statement shall be identified as an election under section 6231(a)(1)(B)(ii), shall be signed by all persons who were partners of that partnership at any time during the partnership taxable year to which the return relates, and shall be filed at the time (determined with regard to any extension of time for filing) and place prescribed for filing the partnership return. However, for any partnership taxable year for which the due date of the return (determined without regard to extensions) is before January 2, 2002, the partnership may file the statement described in the preceding sentence on or before the date which is one year before the date specified in section 6229(a) for the expiration of the period of limitations with respect to that partnership (determined with regard to extensions of that period under section 6229(b)).

(3) *Years covered by election.*—The election shall be effective for the partnership taxable year to which the return relates and all subsequent partnership taxable years unless revoked with the consent of the Commissioner.

(c) *Effective date.*—This section is applicable to partnership taxable years beginning on or after October 4, 2001. For years beginning prior to October 4, 2001, see § 301.6231(a)(1)-1T contained in 26 CFR part 1, revised April 1, 2001. [Reg. § 301.6231(a)(1)-1.]

☐ [T.D. 8965, 10-3-2001.]

### [Reg. § 301.6231(a)(2)-1]

**§ 301.6231(a)(2)-1. Persons whose tax liability is determined indirectly by partnership items.**—(a) *Spouse filing joint return with individual holding a separate interest.*—(1) *In general.*—Except as otherwise provided in this paragraph (a), a spouse who files a joint return with an individual holding a separate interest in the partnership shall be treated as a partner for purposes of subchapter C of chapter 63 of the

Internal Revenue Code. Thus, the spouse who files a joint return with a partner will be permitted to participate in administrative and judicial proceedings.

(2) *Counting rules.*—A spouse who files a joint return with an individual holding a separate interest in the partnership shall not be counted as a partner for purposes of applying section 6223(b) (relating to special rules for partnerships with more than 100 partners) and section 6231(a)(1)(B) (relating to the exception for small partnerships).

(3) *Notice rules.*—(i) *In general.*—Except as provided in paragraph (a)(3)(ii) of this section, for purposes of subchapter C of chapter 63 of the Internal Revenue Code, a spouse who files a joint return with an individual holding a separate interest in the partnership shall be treated as receiving any notice received by the individual holding the separate interest.

(ii) *Spouse identified on partnership return or by statement.*—Paragraph (a)(3)(i) of this section shall not apply to a spouse who files a joint return with an individual holding a separate interest in the partnership if that spouse—

(A) Is identified on the partnership return; or

(B) Is identified as a partner entitled to notice as provided in § 301.6223(c)-1(b).

(4) *Conversion of partnership items*

(i) Individual holding a separate interest. A spouse who files a joint return with an individual holding a separate interest in the partnership shall cease to be treated as a partner in the partnership under paragraph (a)(1) of this section upon the conversion of the partnership items of the individual holding the separate interest in the partnership to nonpartnership items pursuant to section 6231(b). If each spouse holds a separate interest in the partnership, the previous sentence shall be applied separately with respect to each partnership interest.

(ii) *Spouse who files a joint return with an individual holding a separate interest in the partnership.*—A spouse who files a joint return with an individual holding a separate interest in the partnership shall cease to be treated as a partner in the partnership under paragraph (a)(1) of this section upon the occurrence of an event that would convert the partnership items of the spouse to nonpartnership items if the spouse were the owner of a separate interest.

(iii) *Examples.*—The following examples illustrate the application of paragraph (a)(4) of this section:

*Example 1.* Husband owns a separate interest in ABC partnership and files a joint return with Wife. Husband files for bankruptcy. Pursuant to § 301.6231(c)-7, upon filing for bankruptcy, the partnership items of the debtor convert to nonpartnership items. Thus, Husband's partnership items converted to nonpartnership items upon the filing of Husband's bankruptcy petition. Pursuant to paragraph (a)(4)(i) of this section, Wife is no longer treated as a partner of ABC partnership as of the date the partnership items of Husband converted to nonpartnership items.

*Example 2.* Wife owns a separate interest in XYZ partnership and files a joint return with Husband. Husband files for bankruptcy. Because the filing of the bankruptcy petition by Husband is an event that would convert Husband's partnership items to nonpartnership items if Husband were the owner of a separate interest, Husband shall no longer be treated as a partner as of the filing of the bankruptcy petition. Pursuant to paragraph (a)(4)(ii) of this section, the partnership items of Wife are not affected by Husband's bankruptcy.

(5) *Cross-reference.*—See § 301.6231(a)(12)-1 for special rules relating to spouses holding a joint interest in a partnership.

(b) *Shareholder of C corporation.*—A shareholder of a C corporation (as defined in section 1361(a)(2)) is not a partner in a partnership merely because the C corporation is a partner in that partnership.

(c) *Effective date.*—This section is applicable to partnership taxable years beginning on or after October 4, 2001. For years beginning prior to October 4, 2001, see § 301.6231(a)(2)-1T contained in 26 CFR part 1, revised April 1, 2001. [Reg. § 301.6231(a)(2)-1.]

☐ [T.D. 8965, 10-3-2001.]

### [Reg. § 301.6231(a)(3)-1]

**§ 301.6231(a)(3)-1. Partnership items.**—(a) *In general.*—For purposes of subtitle F of the Internal Revenue Code of 1954, the following items which are required to be taken into account for the taxable year of a partnership under subtitle A of the Code are more appropriately determined at the partnership level than at the partner level and, therefore, are partnership items:

(1) The partnership aggregate and each partner's share of each of the following:

(i) Items of income, gain, loss, deduction, or credit of the partnership;

(ii) Expenditures by the partnership not deductible in computing its taxable income (for example, charitable contributions);

(iii) Items of the partnership which may be tax preference items under section 57(a) for any partner;

(iv) Income of the partnership exempt from tax;

(v) Partnership liabilities (including determinations with respect to the amount of the liabilities, whether the liabilities are nonrecourse, and changes from the preceding taxable year); and

(vi) Other amounts determinable at the partnership level with respect to partnership assets, investments, transactions and operations necessary to enable the partnership or the partners to determine—

(A) The investment credit determined under section 46(a);

(B) Recapture under section 47 of the investment credit;

(C) Amounts at risk in any activity to which section 465 applies;

(D) The depletion allowance under section 613A with respect to oil and gas wells; and

(E) The application of section 751(a) and (b);

(2) Guaranteed payments;

(3) Optional adjustments to the basis of partnership property pursuant to an election under section 754 (including necessary preliminary determinations, such as the determination of a transferee partner's basis in a partnership interest); and

(4) Items relating to the following transactions, to the extent that a determination of such items can be made from determinations that the partnership is required to make with respect to an amount, the character of an amount, or the percentage interest of a partner in the partnership, for purposes of the partnership books and records or for purposes of furnishing information to a partner:

(i) Contributions to the partnership;

(ii) Distributions from the partnership; and

(iii) Transactions to which section 707(a) applies (including the application of section 707(b)).

(b) *Factors that affect the determination of partnership items.*—The term "partnership item" includes the accounting practices and the legal and factual determinations that underlie the determination of the amount, timing, and characterization of items of income, credit, gain, loss, deduction, etc. Examples of these determinations are: The partnership's method of accounting, taxable year, and inventory method; whether an election was made by the partnership; whether partnership property is a capital asset, section 1231 property, or inventory; whether an item is currently deductible or must be capitalized; whether partnership activities have been engaged in with the intent to make a profit for purposes of section 183; and whether the partnership qualifies for the research and development credit under section 30.

(c) *Illustrations.*—(1) *In general.*—This paragraph (c) illustrates the provisions of paragraph (a)(4) of this section. The determinations illustrated in this paragraph (c) that the partnership is required to make are not exhaustive; there may be additional determinations that the partnership is required to make which relate to a transaction listed in paragraph (a)(4) of this section. The critical element is that the partnership needs to make a determination with respect to a matter for the purposes stated; failure by the partnership actually to make a determination (for example, because it does not maintain proper books and records) does not prevent an item from being a partnership item.

(2) *Contributions.*—For purposes of its books and records, or for purposes of furnishing information to a partner, the partnership needs to determine:

(i) The character of the amount received from a partner (for example, whether it is a contribution, a loan, or a repayment of a loan);

(ii) The amount of money contributed by a partner;

(iii) The applicability of the investment company rules of section 721(b) with respect to a contribution; and

(iv) The basis to the partnership of contributed property (including necessary preliminary determinations, such as the partner's basis in the contributed property).

To the extent that a determination of an item relating to a contribution can be made from these and similar determinations that the partnership is required to make, therefore, that item is a partnership item. To the extent that the determination requires other information, however, that item is not a partnership item. For example, it may be necessary to determine whether contribution of the property causes recapture by the contributing partner of the investment credit under section 47 in certain circumstances in which that determination is irrelevant to the partnership.

(3) *Distributions.*—For purposes of its books and records, or for purposes of furnishing information to a partner, the partnership needs to determine:

(i) The character of the amount transferred to a partner (for example, whether it is a distribution, a loan, or a repayment of a loan);

(ii) The amount of money distributed to a partner;

(iii) The adjusted basis to the partnership of distributed property; and

(iv) The character of partnership property (for example, whether an item is inventory or a capital asset).

To the extent that a determination of an item relating to a distribution can be made from these and similar determinations that the partnership is required to make, therefore, that item is a partnership item. To the extent that that determination requires other information, however, that item is not a partnership item. Such other information would include those factors used in determining the partner's basis for the partnership interest that are not themselves partnership items, such as the amount that the partner paid to acquire the partnership interest from a transferor partner if that transfer was not covered by an election under section 754.

(4) *Transactions to which section 707(a) applies.*—For purposes of its books and records, the partnership needs to determine:

(i) The amount transferred from the partnership to a partner or from a partner to the partnership in any transaction to which section 707(a) applies;

(ii) The character of such an amount (for example, whether or not it is a loan; in the case of amounts paid over time for the purchase of an asset, what portion is interest); and

(iii) The percentage of the capital interests and profits interests in the partnership owned by each partner.

To the extent that a determination of an item relating to a transaction to which section 707(a) applies can be made from these and similar determinations that the partnership is required to make, therefore, that item is a partnership item. To the extent that that determination requires other information, however, that item is not a partnership item. An example of such other information is the cost to the partner of goods sold to the partnership.

(d) *Effective date.*—This section shall apply with respect to partnership taxable years beginning after September 3, 1982. This section shall also apply with respect to any partnership taxable year ending after September 3, 1982, if with respect to that year there is an agreement entered into pursuant to section 407(a)(3) of the Tax Equity and Fiscal Responsibility Act of 1982. [Reg. § 301.6231(a)(3)-1.]

☐ [*T.D.* 8082, 4-15-86.]

### [Reg. § 301.6231(a)(5)-1]

**§ 301.6231(a)(5)-1. Definition of affected item.**—(a) *In general.*—The term *affected item* means any item to the extent such item is affected by a partnership item. It includes items unrelated to the items reflected on the partnership return (for example, an item, such as the threshold for the medical expense deduction under section 213, that varies if there is a change in an individual partner's adjusted gross income).

(b) *Basis in a partner's partnership interest.*—The basis of a partner's partnership interest is an affected item to the extent it is not a partnership item.

(c) *At-risk limitation.*—The application of the at-risk limitation under section 465 to a partner with respect to a loss incurred by a partnership is an affected item to the extent it is not a partnership item.

(d) *Passive losses.*—The application of the passive loss rules under section 469 to a partner with respect to a loss incurred by a partnership is an affected item to the extent it is not a partnership item.

(e) *Penalty, addition to tax, or additional amount.*—(1) *In general.*—The term *affected item* includes any penalty, addition to tax, or additional amount provided by subchapter A of chapter 68 of the Internal Revenue Code of 1986 to the extent provided in this paragraph (e).

(2) *Penalty, addition to tax, or additional amount without floor.*—If a penalty, addition to tax, or additional amount that does not contain a floor (that is, a threshold amount of underpayment or understatement necessary before the imposition of the penalty, addition to tax, or additional amount) is imposed on a partner as the result of an adjustment to a partnership item, the term *affected item* shall include the penalty, addition to tax, or additional amount computed with reference to the portion of the underpayment that is attributable to the partnership item adjustment(s) to which the penalty, addition to tax, or additional amount applies.

(3) *Penalty, addition to tax, or additional amount containing floor.*—(i) *Floor exceeded prior to adjustment.*—If a partner would have been subject to a penalty, addition to tax, or additional amount that contains a floor in the absence of an adjustment to a partnership item (that is, the partner's understatement or underpayment exceeded the floor even without an adjustment to a partnership item) the term *affected item* shall include only the portion of the penalty, addition to tax, or additional amount computed with reference to the partnership item (or affected item) adjustments.

(ii) *Floor not exceeded prior to adjustment.*—In the case of a penalty, addition to tax, or additional amount that contains a floor, if the taxpayer's understatement or underpayment does not exceed the floor prior to an adjustment to a partnership item but does so after such adjustment, the term *affected item* shall include the penalty, addition to tax, or additional amount computed with reference to the entire underpayment or understatement to which the penalty, addition to tax, or additional amount applies.

(4) *Examples.*—The provisions of this paragraph (e) may be illustrated by the following examples:

*Example 1.* A, a partner of P, had an aggregate underpayment of $1,000 of which $100 is attributable to an adjustment to partnership items. A is negligent in reporting the partnership items. The accuracy-related penalty under section 6662 for negligence computed with reference to the $100 underpayment attributable to the partnership item adjustments is an affected item.

*Example 2.* B, a partner of P, understated B's income tax liability attributable to nonpartnership items by $6,000. An adjustment to a partnership item resulting from a partnership proceeding increased B's income tax by an additional $2,000. Prior to the adjustment, B would have been subject to the accuracy-related penalty under section 6662 for a substantial understatement of income tax with respect to the $6,000 understatement attributable to nonpartnership items. The portion of the accuracy-related penalty under section 6662 computed with reference to the $2,000 understatement attributable to partnership items to which the accuracy-related penalty applies is an affected item. The portion of the accuracy-related penalty under section 6662 computed with reference to the $6,000 pre-existing understatement is not an affected item.

*Example 3.* C, a partner in partnership P, understated C's income tax liability attributable to nonpartnership items by $4,000. As a result of an adjustment to partnership items, that understatement is increased to $10,000. Prior to the adjustment, C would not have been subject to the accuracy-related penalty under section 6662 for a substantial understatement of income tax. The accuracy-related penalty under section 6662 computed with reference to the entire $10,000 understatement to which the accuracy-related penalty applies is an affected item.

(f) *Effective date.*—This section is applicable to partnership taxable years beginning on or after October 4, 2001. For years beginning prior to October 4, 2001, see §301.6231(a)(5)-1T contained in 26 CFR part 1, revised April 1, 2001. [Reg. §301.6231(a)(5)-1.]

□ [*T.D. 8965, 10-3-2001.*]

### [Reg. §301.6231(a)(6)-1]

**§301.6231(a)(6)-1. Computational adjustments.**—(a) *Changes in a partner's tax liability.*—(1) *In general.*—A change in the tax liability of a partner to properly reflect the treatment of a partnership item under subchapter C of chapter 63 of the Internal Revenue Code is made through a computational adjustment. A computational adjustment includes a change in tax liability that reflects a change in an affected item where that change is necessary to properly reflect the treatment of a partnership item, or any penalty, addition to tax, or additional amount that relates to an adjustment to a partnership item. However, if a change in a partner's tax liability cannot be made without making one or more partner-level determinations, that portion of the change in tax liability attributable to the partner-level determinations shall be made under the deficiency procedures(as described in subchapter B of chapter 63 of the Internal Revenue Code), except for any penalty, addition to tax, or additional amount that relates to an adjustment to a partnership item.

(2) *Affected items that do not require partner-level determinations.*—Changes in a partner's tax liability with respect to affected items that do not require partner-level determinations (such as the threshold amount of medical deductions under section 213 that changes as the result of determinations made at the partnership level) are computational adjustments that are directly assessed. When making computational adjustments, the Internal Revenue Service may assume that amounts the partner reported on the partner's individual return include all amounts reported to the partner by the partnership (on the Schedule K-1s attached to the partnership's original return), absent contrary notice to the Internal Revenue Service (for example, a "Notice of Inconsistent Treatment" pursuant to §301.6222(a)-2(c)).

Such an assumption by the Internal Revenue Service does not constitute a partner-level determination. Moreover, substituting redetermined partnership items for the partner's previously reported partnership items (including partnership items included in carryover amounts) does not constitute a partner-level determination where the Internal Revenue Service otherwise accepts, for the sole purpose of determining the computational adjustment, all nonpartnership items (including, for example, nonpartnership item components of carryover amounts) as reported.

(3) *Affected items that require partner-level determinations.*—Changes in a partner's tax liability with respect to affected items that require partner-level determinations (such as a partner's at-risk amount to the extent it depends upon the source from which the partner obtained the funds that the partner contributed to the partnership) are computational adjustments that are subject to the deficiency procedures. Notwithstanding the preceding sentence, any penalty, addition to tax, or additional amount that relates to an adjustment to a partnership item is not subject to the deficiency procedures, but rather may be directly assessed as part of the computational adjustment that is made following the partnership proceeding, based on determinations in that proceeding, regardless of whether any partner-level determinations may be required.

(b) *Interest.*—A computational adjustment includes any interest due with respect to any underpayment or overpayment of tax attributable to adjustments to reflect properly the treatment of partnership items.

(c) *Effective date.*—This section is applicable to partnership taxable years beginning on or after October 4, 2001. For years beginning prior to October 4, 2001, see §301.6231(a)(6)-1T contained in 26 CFR part 1, revised April 1, 2001. [Reg. §301.6231(a)(6)-1.]

□ [*T.D. 8965, 10-3-2001.*]

### [Reg. §301.6231(a)(7)-1]

**§301.6231(a)(7)-1. Designation or selection of tax matters partner.**—(a) *In general.*—A partnership may designate a partner as its tax matters partner for a specific taxable year only as provided in this section. Similarly, the designation of a partner as the tax matters partner for a specific taxable year may be terminated only as provided in this section. If a partnership does not designate a general partner as the tax matters partner for a specific taxable year, or if the designation is terminated without the partnership designating another general partner as the tax matters partner, the tax matters partner is the partner determined under this section.

(b) *Person who may be designated tax matters partner.*—(1) *General requirement.*—A person may be designated as the tax matters partner of a partnership for a taxable year only if that person—

(i) Was a general partner in the partnership at some time during the taxable year for which the designation is made; or

(ii) Is a general partner in the partnership as of the time the designation is made.

(2) *Limitation on designation of tax matters partner who is not a United States person.*—If any United States person would be eligible under paragraph (a) of this section to be designated as the tax matters partner of a partnership for a taxable year, no person who is not a United States person may be designated as the tax matters partner of the partnership for that year without the consent of the Commissioner. For the definition of *United States person*, see section 7701(a)(30).

(c) *Designation of tax matters partner at time partnership return is filed.*—The partnership may designate a tax matters partner for a partnership taxable year on the partnership return for that taxable year in accordance with the instructions for that form.

(d) *Certification by current tax matters partner of selection of successor.*—If a partner properly designated as the tax matters partner of a partnership for a partnership taxable year under this section certifies that another partner has been selected as the tax matters partner of the partnership for that taxable year, that other partner is thereby designated as the tax matters partner for that year. The current tax matters partner shall make the certification by filing with the service center with which the partnership return is filed a statement that—

(1) Identifies the partnership, the partner filing the statement, and the successor tax matters partner by name, address, and taxpayer identification number;

(2) Specifies the partnership taxable year to which the designation relates;

(3) Declares that the partner filing the statement has been properly designated as the tax matters partner of the partnership for the partnership taxable year and that that designation is in effect immediately before the filing of the statement;

(4) Certifies that the other named partner has been selected as the tax matters partner of the partnership for that taxable year in accordance with the partnership's procedure for making that selection; and

(5) Is signed by the partner filing the statement.

(e) *Designation by general partners with majority interest.*—The partnership may designate a tax matters partner for a partnership taxable year at any time after the filing of a partnership return for that taxable year by filing a statement with the service center with which the partnership return was filed. The statement shall—

(1) Identify the partnership and the designated partner by name, address, and taxpayer identification number;

(2) Specify the partnership taxable year to which the designation relates;

(3) Declare that it is a designation of a tax matters partner for the taxable year specified; and

(4) Be signed by persons who were general partners at the close of the year and were shown on the return for that year to hold more than 50 percent of the aggregate interest in partnership profits held by all general partners as of the close of that taxable year. For purposes of this paragraph (e)(4), all limited partnership interests held by general partners shall be included in determining the aggregate interest in partnership profits held by such general partners.

(f) *Designation by partners with majority interest under certain circumstances.*—(1) *In general.*—A tax matters partner may be designated for a partnership taxable year under this paragraph (f) only if, at the time the designation is made, each partner who was a general partner at the close of such partnership taxable year is described in one or more of paragraphs (f)(1)(i) through (iv) of this section as follows:

(i) The general partner is dead, or, if the general partner is an entity, has been liquidated or dissolved;

(ii) The general partner has been adjudicated by a court of competent jurisdiction to be no longer capable of managing his or her person or estate;

(iii) The general partner's partnership items have become nonpartnership items under section 6231(b); or

(iv) The general partner is no longer a partner in the partnership.

(2) *Method of making designation.*—A tax matters partner for a partnership taxable year may be designated under this paragraph (f) at any time after the filing of the partnership return for such taxable year by filing a written statement with the service center with which the partnership return was filed. The statement shall—

(i) Identify the partnership and the designated tax matters partner by name, address, and taxpayer identification number;

(ii) Specify the partnership taxable year to which the designation relates;

(iii) Declare that it is a designation of a tax matters partner for the partnership taxable year specified; and

(iv) Be signed by persons who were partners at the close of such taxable year and were shown on the return for that year to hold more than 50 percent of the aggregate interest in partnership profits held by all partners as of the close of such taxable year.

(g) *Designation of alternate tax matters partner.*—If an individual is designated as the tax matters partner of a partnership under paragraph (c), (d), (e), or (f) of this section, the document by which that individual is designated may also designate an alternate tax matters partner who will become tax matters partner upon the occurrence of one or more of the events described in paragraph (l)(1)(i) or (ii) of this section. The person designated as the alternate tax matters partner becomes the tax matters partner as of the time the designation of the tax matters partner is terminated under paragraph (l)(1)(i) or (ii) of this section. The designation of a person as the alternate tax matters partner shall have no effect in any other case.

(h) *Prior designations superseded.*—A designation of a tax matters partner for a partnership taxable year under paragraphs (d), (e), or (f) of this section shall supersede all prior designations of a tax matters partner for that year, including a prior designation of an alternate tax matters partner under paragraph (g) of this section.

(i) *Resignation of designated tax matters partner.*—A person designated as the tax matters partner of a partnership under this section may resign at any time by a written statement to that effect. The statement shall specify the partnership taxable year to which the resignation relates and shall identify the partnership and the tax matters partner by name, address, and taxpayer identification number. The statement shall also be signed by the resigning tax matters partner and shall be filed with the service center with which the partnership return was filed.

(j) *Revocation of designation.*—The partnership may revoke the designation of the tax matters partner for a partnership taxable year at any time after the filing of a partnership return for that taxable year by filing a statement with the service center with which the partnership return was filed. The statement shall—

(1) Identify by name, address, and taxpayer identification number the partnership and the general partner whose designation as tax matters partner is being revoked;

(2) Specify the partnership taxable year to which the revocation relates;

(3) Declare that it is a revocation of a designation of the tax matters partner for the taxable year specified; and

(4) Be signed by the persons described in paragraph (e)(4) of this section, or, if at the time that the revocation is made, each partner who was a general partner at the close of the partnership taxable year to which the revocation relates is described in one or more of paragraphs (f)(1)(i) through (iv) of this section, by the persons described in paragraph (f)(2)(iv) of this section.

(k) *When designation, etc., becomes effective.*—(1) *In general.*—Except as otherwise provided in paragraph (k)(2) of this section, a designation, resignation, or revocation provided for in this section becomes effective on the day that the statement required by the applicable paragraph of this section is filed.

(2) *Notice of proceeding mailed.*—If a notice of beginning of an administrative proceeding with respect to a partnership taxable year is mailed before the date on which a statement of designation, resignation, or revocation provided for in this section with respect to that taxable year is filed, the Service is not required to give effect to such designation, resignation, or revocation until 30 days after the statement is filed.

(l) *Termination of designation.*—(1) *In general.*—A designation of a tax matters partner for a taxable year under this section shall remain in effect until—

(i) The death of the designated tax matters partner;

(ii) An adjudication by a court of competent jurisdiction that the individual designated as the tax matters partner is no longer capable of managing the individual's person or estate;

(iii) The liquidation or dissolution of the tax matters partner, if the tax matters partner is an entity;

(iv) The partnership items of the tax matters partner become nonpartnership items under section 6231(c) (relating to special enforcement areas); or

(v) The day on which—

(A) The resignation of the tax matters partner under paragraph (i) of this section;

(B) A subsequent designation under paragraph (d), (e), or (f) of this section; or

(C) A revocation of the designation under paragraph (j) of this section becomes effective.

(2) *Actions by the tax matters partner before termination of designation.*—The termination of the designation of a partner as the tax matters partner under paragraph (l)(1) of this section does not affect the validity of any action taken by that partner as tax matters partner before the designation is terminated. For example, if that tax matters partner had previously consented to an extension of the period for assessments under section 6229(b)(1)(B), that extension remains valid even after termination of the designation.

(m) *Tax matters partner where no partnership designation made.*—(1) *In general.*—The tax matters partner for a partnership taxable year shall be determined under this paragraph (m) if—

(i) The partnership has not designated a tax matters partner under this section for that taxable year; or

(ii) The partnership has designated a tax matters partner under this section for that taxable year, that designation has been terminated under paragraph (l)(1) of this section, and the partnership has not made a subsequent designation under this section for that taxable year.

(2) *General partner having the largest profits interest is the tax matters partner.*—The tax matters partner for any partnership taxable year to which this paragraph (m) applies is the general partner having the largest profits interest in the partnership at the close of that taxable year (or where there is more than one such partner, the one of such partners whose name would appear first in an alphabetical listing). For purposes of this paragraph (m)(2), all limited partnership interests held by a general partner shall be included in determining that general partner's profits interest in the partnership. For purposes of this paragraph (m)(2), the general partner with the largest profits interest is determined based on the year-end profits interests reported on the Schedules K-1 filed with the partnership

income tax return for the taxable year for which the determination is being made.

(3) *Termination of designation.*—A designation of a tax matters partner for a partnership taxable year under this paragraph (m) shall remain in effect until the earlier of the occurrence of one or more of the events described in paragraphs (l)(1)(i) through (iv) of this section or the day on which a designation under paragraph (d), (e), or (f) of this section becomes effective. If a designation of a tax matters partner for a partnership taxable year is terminated under this paragraph (m)(3) and the partnership has not subsequently designated a tax matters partner for that taxable year under paragraph (d), (e), or (f) of this section, the tax matters partner for that taxable year shall be determined under paragraph (m)(2) of this section, and, for purposes of applying paragraph (m)(2) of this section, the general partner whose designation was so terminated shall be treated as having no profits interest in the partnership for that taxable year.

(n) *Selection of tax matters partner by Commissioner when impracticable to apply the largest-profits-interest rule.*—If the partnership has not designated a tax matters partner under this section for the taxable year and it is impracticable (as determined under paragraph (o) of this section) to apply the largest-profits-interest rule of paragraph (m)(2) of this section, the Commissioner will select a tax matters partner as described in paragraph (p) of this section.

(o) *Impracticability of largest-profits-interest rule.*—It is impracticable to apply the largest-profits-interest rule of paragraph (m)(2) of this section if, on the date the rule is applied, any one of the following three conditions is met:

(1) *General partner with the largest profits interest is not apparent.*— The general partner with the largest profits interest is not apparent from the Schedules K-1 and is not otherwise readily determinable.

(2) *Each general partner is deemed to have no profits interest in the partnership.*—Each general partner is deemed to have no profits interest in the partnership under paragraph (m)(3) of this section (concerning termination of a designation under the largest-profits-interest rule) because of the occurrence of one or more of the events described in paragraphs (l)(1)(i) through (iv) of this section (involving death, adjudication of incompetency, liquidation, and conversion of partnership items to nonpartnership items).

(3) *General partner with the largest profits interest is disqualified.*— The general partner with the largest profits interest determined under paragraph (m)(2) of this section—

(i) Has been notified of suspension from practice before the Internal Revenue Service;

(ii) Is incarcerated;

(iii) Is residing outside the United States, its possessions, or territories; or

(iv) Cannot be located or cannot perform the functions of a tax matters partner for any reason, except that lack of cooperation with the Internal Revenue Service by the general partner with the largest profits interest is not a basis for finding that the partner cannot perform the functions of a tax matters partner.

(p) *Commissioner's selection of the tax matters partner.*—(1) *When the general partner with the largest profits interest is not apparent.*—If it is impracticable under paragraph (o)(1) of this section to apply the largest-profits-interest rule of paragraph (m)(2) of this section, the Commissioner will select (in accordance with the notification procedures set forth in paragraph (r) of this section) as the tax matters partner any person who was a general partner at any time during the taxable year under examination.

(2) *When each general partner is deemed to have no profits interest in the partnership.*—If it is impracticable under paragraph (o)(2) of this section to apply the largest-profits-interest rule of paragraph (m)(2) of this section, the Commissioner will select a partner (including a general or limited partner) as the tax matters partner in accordance with the criteria set forth in paragraph (q) of this section. The Commissioner will notify, within 30 days of the selection, the partner selected, the partnership, and all partners required to receive notice under section 6223(a) of the selection of the tax matters partner, effective as of the date specified in the notice.

(3) *When the general partner with the largest profits interest is disqualified.*—(i) *In general.*—Except as otherwise provided in paragraph (p)(3)(ii) of this section, if it is impracticable under paragraph (o)(3) of this section to apply the largest-profits-interest rule of paragraph (m)(2) of this section, the Commissioner will treat each general partner who fits the criteria contained in paragraph (o)(3) of this section as having no profits interest in the partnership for the taxable year and will select (in accordance with the notification procedures set forth in paragraph (r) of this section) a tax matters partner from

the remaining persons who were general partners at any time during the taxable year.

(ii) *Partner selected if no general partner may be selected.*—If all general partners during the taxable year either are treated as having no profits interest in the partnership for the taxable year under paragraph (m)(3) of this section (concerning termination of a designation under the largest-profits-interest rule) or are described in paragraph (o)(3) of this section (general partner with the largest profits interest is disqualified), the Commissioner will select a partner (including a general or limited partner) as the tax matters partner in accordance with the criteria set forth in paragraph (q) of this section. The Commissioner will notify both the partner selected and the partnership of the selection, effective as of the date specified in the notice.

(q) *Criteria for selecting a partner as tax matters partner.*—(1) *In general.*—The Commissioner will select a partner as the tax matters partner under paragraph (p)(2) or (3)(ii) of this section only if the partner was a partner in the partnership at the close of the taxable year under examination.

(2) *Criteria to be considered.*—The Commissioner may consider the following criteria in selecting a partner as the tax matters partner:

(i) The general knowledge of the partner in tax matters and the administrative operation of the partnership.

(ii) The partner's access to the books and records of the partnership.

(iii) The profits interest held by the partner.

(iv) The views of the partners having a majority interest in the partnership regarding the selection.

(v) Whether the partner is a partner of the partnership at the time the tax-matters-partner selection is made.

(vi) Whether the partner is a United States person (within the meaning of section 7701(a)(30)).

(3) *Limited restriction on subsequent designation of a tax matters partner by the partnership.*—For purposes of paragraphs (p)(2) and (3)(ii) of this section, the partnership cannot designate a partner who is not a general partner to serve as tax matters partner in lieu of a partner selected by the Commissioner.

(r) *Notification of partnership.*—(1) *In general.*—If the Commissioner selects a tax matters partner under the provisions of paragraph (p)(1) or (p)(3)(i) of this section, the Commissioner will notify, within 30 days of the selection, the partner selected, the partnership, and all partners required to receive notice under section 6223(a) of the selection of the tax matters partner, effective as of the date specified in the notice.

(2) *Limited opportunity for partnership to designate the tax matters partner.*—(i) Before the Commissioner selects a tax matters partner under paragraphs (p)(1) and (3)(i) of this section, the Commissioner will notify the partnership by mail that, after 30 days from the date of the notice, the Commissioner will make a determination that it is impracticable to apply the largest-profits-interest rule of paragraph (m)(2) of this section and will select the tax matters partner unless a prior designation is made by the partnership. This delay in making the determination will permit the partnership to designate a tax matters partner under paragraph (e) of this section (designation by general partners with a majority interest) or paragraph (f) of this section (designation by partners with a majority interest under certain circumstances), thereby avoiding a selection made by the Commissioner.

(ii) During the 30-day period and prior to a tax-matters-partner designation by the partnership, the Commissioner will communicate with the partnership by sending all correspondence or notices to "The Tax Matters Partner" in care of the partnership at the partnership's address.

(iii) Any subsequent designation of a tax matters partner by the partnership after the 30-day period will become effective as provided under paragraph (k)(2) of this section (concerning designations made after a notice of beginning of administrative proceeding is mailed).

(s) *Effective date.*—This section applies to all designations, selections, and terminations of a tax matters partner occurring on or after December 23, 1996, except for paragraphs (p)(2) and (r)(1), that are applicable on or after October 4, 2001. [Reg. § 301.6231(a)(7)-1.]

☐ [*T.D. 8698, 12-20-96. Amended by T.D. 8808, 1-25-99 and T.D. 8965, 10-3-2001.*]

**[Reg. § 301.6231(a)(7)-2]**

**§ 301.6231(a)(7)-2. Designation or selection of tax matters partner for a limited liability company (LLC).**—(a) *In general.*—Solely for purposes of applying section 6231(a)(7) and § 301.6231(a)(7)-1 to an

LLC, only a member-manager of an LLC is treated as a general partner, and a member of an LLC who is not a member-manager is treated as a partner other than a general partner.

(b) *Definitions.*—(1) *LLC.*—Solely for purposes of this section, *LLC* means an organization—

(i) Formed under a law that allows the limitation of the liability of all members for the organization's debts and other obligations within the meaning of § 301.7701-3(b)(2)(ii); and

(ii) Classified as a partnership for Federal tax purposes.

(2) *Member.*—Solely for purposes of this section, *member* means any person who owns an interest in an LLC.

(3) *Member-manager.*—Solely for purposes of this section, *member-manager* means a member of an LLC who, alone or together with others, is vested with the continuing exclusive authority to make the management decisions necessary to conduct the business for which the organization was formed. Generally, an LLC statute may permit the LLC to choose management by one or more managers (whether or not members) or by all of the members. If there are no elected or designated member-managers (as so defined in this paragraph (b)(3)) of the LLC, each member will be treated as a member-manager for purposes of this section.

(c) *Effective date.*—This section applies to all designations, selections, and terminations of a tax matters partner of an LLC occurring on or after December 23, 1996. Any other reasonable designation or selection of a tax matters partner of an LLC is binding for periods prior to December 23, 1996. [Reg. § 301.6231(a)(7)-2.]

☐ [*T.D.* 8698, 12-20-96.]

### [Reg. § 301.6231(a)(12)-1]

**§ 301.6231(a)(12)-1. Special rules relating to spouses.**—(a) *Spouses holding a joint interest.*—(1) *In general.*—Except as otherwise provided in this section, spouses holding a joint interest in a partnership shall be treated as separate partners for purposes of subchapter C of chapter 63 of the Internal Revenue Code. Thus, both spouses may participate in administrative and judicial proceedings. The term *joint interest* includes tenancies in common, joint tenancies, tenancies by the entirety, and community property.

(2) *Identification of joint interest.*—For purposes of this section, an interest shall be treated as a joint interest in a partnership only if both spouses are identified on the partnership return or are identified as partners entitled to notice as provided in § 301.6223(c)-1(b).

(3) *Failure to identify both spouses as partners.*—If both spouses are not identified as set forth in paragraph (a)(2) of this section, then the partnership interest shall be treated as separately owned by the identified spouse.

(4) *Example.*—The following example illustrates the application of paragraph (a)(3) of this section:

*Example.* Wife owns an interest in ABC Partnership and is identified on the Schedule K-1 of the partnership return. Wife and Husband live in a community property state. The partnership return of ABC partnership does not identify Husband, and Husband is not identified as a partner entitled to notice as provided in § 301.6223(c)-1(b). Pursuant to paragraph (a)(3) of this section, the partnership interest of Wife shall be treated as separately owned by Wife.

(b) *Notice and counting rules.*—(1) *In general.*—Except as provided in paragraph (b)(2) of this section, for purposes of applying section 6223 (relating to notice to partners of proceedings) and section 6231(a)(1)(B) (relating to the exception for small partnerships), spouses holding a joint interest in a partnership shall be treated as one partner. Except as provided in paragraph (b)(2) of this section, the Internal Revenue Service or the tax matters partner may send any required notice to either spouse.

(2) *Identified spouse entitled to notice.*—For purposes of applying section 6223 (relating to notice to partners of proceeding) for a partnership taxable year, an individual who holds a joint interest in a partnership with a spouse who is entitled to notice under section 6223 shall be entitled to receive separate notice under section 6223 if such individual—

(i) Is identified as a partner on the partnership return for that taxable year; or

(ii) Is identified as a partner entitled to notice as provided in § 301.6223(c)-1(b).

(c) *Conversion of partnership items.*—(1) *In general.*—If spouses holding a joint interest in a partnership are treated as separate partners under this section, then section 6231(b) (relating to the conversion of partnership items) shall be applied separately to each spouse.

(2) *Example.*—The following example illustrates the application of paragraph (c) of this section:

*Example.* Husband and Wife own a joint interest in XYZ Partnership. The partnership return identifies both spouses on the Schedule K-1. Under this section, each spouse is treated as a separate partner. If Wife enters into a settlement agreement, Wife's partnership items convert to nonpartnership items pursuant to section 6231(b)(1)(C). Accordingly, Wife no longer has the right to participate in the partnership proceeding subsequent to entering into the settlement agreement. Pursuant to paragraph (c) of this section, however, the partnership items of Husband are not affected by the conversion of the partnership items of Wife, and Husband continues to have the right to participate in the partnership proceeding. This result is the same regardless of whether the partnership items are reported on a joint return or on separate returns.

(d) *Cross-reference.*—See § 301.6231(a)(2)-1(a) for special rules relating to spouses who file joint returns with individuals holding a separate interest in a partnership.

(e) *Effective date.*—This section is applicable to partnership taxable years beginning on or after October 4, 2001. For years beginning prior to October 4, 2001, see § 301.6231(a)(12)-1T contained in 26 CFR part 1, revised April 1, 2001. [Reg. § 301.6231(a)(12)-1.]

☐ [*T.D.* 8965, 10-3-2001.]

### [Reg. § 301.6231(c)-1]

**§ 301.6231(c)-1. Special rules for certain applications for tentative carryback and refund adjustments based on partnership losses, deductions, or credits.**—(a) *Application subject to this section.*—This section applies in the case of an application under section 6411 (relating to tentative carryback and refund adjustments) based on losses, deductions, or credits of a partnership if the Commissioner, or the Commissioner's delegate, determines, after review of the available relevant information, that it is highly likely that a person described in section 6700(a)(1) made, with respect to the partnership—

(1) A gross valuation overstatement; or

(2) A false or fraudulent statement with respect to the tax benefits to be secured by reason of holding an interest in the partnership that would be subject to a penalty under section 6700 (relating to penalty for promoting abusive tax shelters, etc.). This section applies only with respect to an application based upon the original reporting on the partner's income tax return of partnership losses, deductions, or credits. Thus, this section does not apply to a request for administrative adjustment under section 6227 through which a partner seeks to change the partner's reporting of partnership items on the partner's income tax return (or on an earlier request for administrative adjustment).

(b) *Determination of special enforcement area.*—In the case of an application under section 6411 described in paragraph (a) of this section, precluding an assessment under section 6225 that would be permitted under section 6213(b)(3) (relating to assessments arising out of tentative carryback or refund adjustments) with respect to any amount applied, credited, or refunded as a result of the application may encourage the proliferation of abusive tax shelter partnerships and make the eventual collection of taxes due more difficult. Consequently, the Secretary hereby determines that such applications present special enforcement considerations within the meaning of section 6231(c)(1)(E).

(c) *Assessment permitted under section 6213(b)(3).*—Notwithstanding section 6225 (relating to restrictions on assessment with respect to partnership items), an assessment that would be permitted under section 6213(b)(3) with respect to any amount applied, credited, or refunded as a result of an application described in paragraph (a) of this section may be made before there is a final partnership-level determination with respect to the losses, deductions, or credits on which the application is based. As provided in section 6213(b)(1), the Internal Revenue Service shall mail notice of any such assessment to the partner filing the application. The notice shall also inform the partner of the partner's limited right to elect to treat items as nonpartnership items as provided in paragraph (d) of this section.

(d) *Limited right to elect to treat items as nonpartnership items.*—(1) *In general.*—A partner to whom the Internal Revenue Service mails a notice of suspension of action on a refund claim under paragraph (c) of this section may elect in accordance with this paragraph (d) to have all partnership items for the partnership taxable year in which the losses, deductions, or credits at issue arose treated as nonpartnership items.

(2) *Time and place of making election.*—The election shall be made by filing a statement with the Internal Revenue Service office that

mailed the notice of suspension. The statement may be filed at any time—

(i) After the date which is one year after the date on which the partnership return was filed for the partnership taxable year in which the items at issue arose; and

(ii) Before the date on which the Internal Revenue Service mails to the tax matters partner the notice of final partnership administrative adjustment for the partnership taxable year in which the items at issue arose. For purposes of this paragraph (d)(2), a partnership return filed before the last day prescribed by law for its filing (determined without regard to extensions) shall be treated as filed on the last day.

(3) *Contents of the statement.*—The statement shall—

(i) Be clearly identified as an election to have partnership items treated as nonpartnership items because of notification of an assessment under section 6213(b)(3);

(ii) Identify the partnership by name, address, and taxpayer identification number;

(iii) Identify the partner making the election by name, address, and taxpayer identification number;

(iv) Specify the partnership taxable year to which the election applies; and

(v) Be signed by the partner making the election.

(e) *Effective date.*—This section is applicable to partnership taxable years beginning on or after October 4, 2001. For years beginning prior to October 4, 2001, see § 301.6231(c)-1T contained in 26 CFR part 1, revised April 1, 2001. [Reg. § 301.6231(c)-1.]

☐ [*T.D.* 8965, 10-3-2001.]

### [Reg. § 301.6231(c)-2]

**§ 301.6231(c)-2. Special rules for certain refund claims based on losses, deductions, or credits from abusive tax shelter partnerships.**—(a) *Claims subject to this section.*—This section applies in the case of a claim for credit or refund based on losses, deductions or credits of a partnership if the Commissioner, or the Commissioner's delegate, determines, after review of available relevant information, that it is highly likely that a person described in section 6700(a)(1) made, with respect to the partnership—

(1) A gross valuation overstatement; or

(2) A false or fraudulent statement with respect to the tax benefits to be secured by reason of holding an interest in the partnership that would be subject to a penalty under section 6700 (relating to penalty for promoting abusive tax shelters, etc.). This section applies only with respect to a claim that is based upon the partner's original reporting on the partner's income tax return of partnership losses, deductions, or credits. Thus, this section does not apply to a request for administrative adjustment under section 6227 through which a partner seeks to change the partner's reporting of partnership items on the partner's income tax return (or on an earlier request for administrative adjustment). For purposes of this section, any income tax return requesting a credit or refund shall be treated as a claim for a credit or refund.

(b) *Determination of special enforcement area.*—Granting a claim for credit or refund described in paragraph (a) of this section may encourage the proliferation of abusive tax shelter partnerships and make the eventual collection of taxes more difficult. Consequently, the Secretary hereby determines that such claims present special enforcement considerations within the meaning of section 6231(c)(1)(E).

(c) *Action on refund claims suspended.*—In the case of a claim described in paragraph (a) of this section, the Internal Revenue Service may mail to the partner filing the claim a notice stating that no action will be taken on the partner's claim until the completion of the partnership-level proceedings. The notice shall also inform the partner of the partner's limited right to elect to treat items as nonpartnership items as provided in paragraph (d) of this section.

(d) *Limited right to elect to treat items as nonpartnership items.*—(1) *In general.*—A partner to whom the Internal Revenue Service mails a notice of suspension under paragraph (c) of this section may elect in accordance with this paragraph (d) to have all partnership items for the partnership taxable year in which the losses, deductions, or credits at issue arose treated as nonpartnership items.

(2) *Time and place of making election.*—The election shall be made by filing a statement with the Internal Revenue Service office that mailed the notice of suspension. The statement may be filed at any time—

(i) After the date which is one year after the date on which the partnership return was filed for the partnership taxable year in which the items at issue arose; and

(ii) Before the date on which the Internal Revenue Service mails to the tax matters partner the notice of final partnership administrative adjustment for the partnership taxable year in which the items at issue arose. For purposes of this paragraph (d)(2), a partnership return filed before the last day prescribed by law for its filing (determined without regard to extensions) shall be treated as filed on the last day.

(3) *Contents of the statement.*—The statement shall—

(i) Be clearly identified as an election to have partnership items treated as nonpartnership items because of notification of suspension of action on a refund claim;

(ii) Identify the partnership by name, address, and taxpayer identification number;

(iii) Identify the partner making the election by name, address, and taxpayer identification number;

(iv) Specify the partnership taxable year to which the election applies; and

(v) Be signed by the partner making the election.

(e) *Effective date.*—This section applies with respect to any claim described in paragraph (a) of this section that is filed on or after October 4, 2001. For claims filed prior to October 4, 2001, see § 301.6231(c)-2T contained in 26 CFR part 1, revised April 1, 2001. [Reg. § 301.6231(c)-2.]

☐ [*T.D.* 8965, 10-3-2001.]

### [Reg. § 301.6231(c)-3]

**§ 301.6231(c)-3. Limitation on applicability of §§ 301.6231(c)-4 through 301.6231(c)-8.**—(a) *In general.*—A provision of §§ 301.6231(c)-4 through 301.6231(c)-8 shall not apply with respect to partnership items arising in a partnership taxable year if, as of the date on which those items would otherwise begin to be treated as nonpartnership items under that provision—

(1) A notice of final partnership administrative adjustment with respect to those items has been mailed to the tax matters partner; and

(2) Either—

(i) The period during which an action with respect to that final partnership administrative adjustment may be brought under section 6226 has expired and no such action has been brought; or

(ii) The decision of the court in an action brought under section 6226 with respect to that final partnership administrative adjustment has become final.

(b) *Effective date.*—This section is applicable to partnership taxable years beginning on or after October 4, 2001. For years beginning prior to October 4, 2001, see § 301.6231(c)-3T contained in 26 CFR part 1, revised April 1, 2001. [Reg. § 301.6231(c)-3.]

☐ [*T.D.* 8965, 10-3-2001.]

### [Reg. § 301.6231(c)-4]

**§ 301.6231(c)-4. Termination and jeopardy assessment.**—(a) *In general.*—The treatment of items as partnership items with respect to a partner against whom an assessment of income tax under section 6851 (termination assessment) or section 6861 (jeopardy assessment) is made will interfere with the effective and efficient enforcement of the internal revenue laws. Accordingly, partnership items of such a partner arising in any partnership taxable year ending with or within the partner's taxable year for which an assessment of income tax under section 6851 or 6861 is made shall be treated as nonpartnership items as of the moment before such assessment is made.

(b) *Effective date.*—This section is applicable to partnership taxable years beginning on or after October 4, 2001. For years beginning prior to October 4, 2001, see § 301.6231(c)-4T contained in 26 CFR part 1, revised April 1, 2001. [Reg. § 301.6231(c)-4.]

☐ [*T.D.* 8965, 10-3-2001.]

### [Reg. § 301.6231(c)-5]

**§ 301.6231(c)-5. Criminal investigations.**—(a) *In general.*—The treatment of items as partnership items with respect to a partner under criminal investigation for violation of the internal revenue laws relating to income tax will interfere with the effective and efficient enforcement of the internal revenue laws. Accordingly, partnership items of such a partner arising in any partnership taxable year ending on or before the last day of the latest taxable year of the partner to which the criminal investigation relates shall be treated as nonpartnership items as of the date on which the partner is notified that the partner is the subject of a criminal investigation and written notification is sent by the Internal Revenue Service that the partner's partnership items shall be treated as nonpartnership items. The partnership items of a partner who is notified that the partner is the subject of a criminal investigation shall not be treated as nonpartnership items under this section unless and until such partner is sent written notification from the Internal Revenue Service of such treatment.

(b) *Effective date.*—This section is applicable to partnership taxable years beginning on or after October 4, 2001. For years beginning prior to October 4, 2001, see § 301.6231(c)-5T contained in 26 CFR part 1, revised April 1, 2001. [Reg. § 301.6231(c)-5.]

☐ [*T.D.* 8965, 10-3-2001.]

### [Reg. § 301.6231(c)-6]

**§ 301.6231(c)-6. Indirect method of proof of income.**—(a) *In general.*—The treatment of items as partnership items with respect to a partner whose taxable income is determined by use of an indirect method of proof of income will interfere with the effective and efficient enforcement of the internal revenue laws. Accordingly, partnership items of such a partner arising in any partnership taxable year ending on or before the last day of the taxable year of the partner for which a deficiency notice based upon an indirect method of proof of income is mailed to the partner shall be treated as nonpartnership items as of the date on which that deficiency notice is mailed to the partner.

(b) *Effective date.*—This section is applicable to partnership taxable years beginning on or after October 4, 2001. For years beginning prior to October 4, 2001, see § 301.6231(c)-6T contained in 26 CFR part 1, revised April 1, 2001. [Reg. § 301.6231(c)-6.]

☐ [*T.D.* 8965, 10-3-2001.]

### [Reg. § 301.6231(c)-7]

**§ 301.6231(c)-7. Bankruptcy and receivership.**—(a) *Bankruptcy.*—The treatment of items as partnership items with respect to a partner named as a debtor in a bankruptcy proceeding will interfere with the effective and efficient enforcement of the internal revenue laws. Accordingly, partnership items of such a partner arising in any partnership taxable year ending on or before the last day of the latest taxable year of the partner with respect to which the United States could file a claim for income tax due in the bankruptcy proceeding shall be treated as nonpartnership items as of the date the petition naming the partner as debtor is filed in bankruptcy.

(b) *Receivership.*—The treatment of items as partnership items with respect to a partner for whom a receiver has been appointed in any receivership proceeding before any court of the United States or of any State or the District of Columbia will interfere with the effective and efficient enforcement of the internal revenue laws. Accordingly, partnership items of such a partner arising in any partnership taxable year ending on or before the last day of the latest taxable year of the partner with respect to which the United States could file a claim for income tax due in the receivership proceeding shall be treated as nonpartnership items as of the date a receiver is appointed in any receivership proceeding before any court of the United States or of any State or the District of Columbia.

(c) *Effective date.*—This section is applicable to partnership taxable years beginning on or after October 4, 2001. For years beginning prior to October 4, 2001, see § 301.6231(c)-7T contained in 26 CFR part 1, revised April 1, 2001. [Reg. § 301.6231(c)-7.]

☐ [*T.D.* 8965, 10-3-2001.]

### [Reg. § 301.6231(c)-8]

**§ 301.6231(c)-8. Prompt assessment.**—(a) *In general.*—The treatment of items as partnership items with respect to a partner on whose behalf a request for a prompt assessment of tax under section 6501(d) is filed will interfere with the effective and efficient enforcement of the internal revenue laws. Accordingly, partnership items of such a partner arising in any partnership taxable year ending with or within any taxable year of the partner with respect to which a request for a prompt assessment of tax is filed shall be treated as nonpartnership items as of the date that the request is filed.

(b) *Effective date.*—This section is applicable to partnership taxable years beginning on or after October 4, 2001. For years beginning prior to October 4, 2001, see § 301.6231(c)-8T contained in 26 CFR part 1, revised April 1, 2001. [Reg. § 301.6231(c)-8.]

☐ [*T.D.* 8965, 10-3-2001.]

### [Reg. § 301.6231(d)-1]

**§ 301.6231(d)-1. Time for determining profits interest of partners for purposes of sections 6223(b) and 6231(a)(11).**—(a) *Partner owns interest at close of year.*—For purposes of section 6223(b) (relating to special rules for partnerships with more than 100 partners) and section 6231(a)(11) (relating to 5-percent groups), except as otherwise provided in this section, the profits interest held by a partner, directly or indirectly through one or more pass-thru partners, in a partner-

ship (the source partnership) to which subchapter C of chapter 63 of the Internal Revenue Code applies shall be determined at the close of the source partnership's taxable year.

(b) *Partner does not own interest at close of year.*—If the entire direct and indirect interest of a partner in a source partnership is terminated by virtue of a disposition by such partner of such interest (or by virtue of the disposition of an interest held by one or more pass-thru partners through which the partner holds an interest), then the profits interest of such partner in the source partnership shall be measured as of the moment before the disposition causing such termination. The preceding sentence shall not apply with respect to a termination if subsequent to such termination and before the close of the source partnership's taxable year the partner acquires a direct or indirect interest in the source partnership.

(c) *Disposition of last remaining portion of interest is disposition of entire interest.*—If a partner (or a pass-thru partner through which a partner holds an interest) makes several partial dispositions of an interest in a source partnership during a taxable year of the source partnership, paragraph (b) of this section will apply with respect to the disposition which causes a termination of the partner's entire direct and indirect interest in the source partnership.

(d) *No profits interest in certain cases.*—If—

(1) The interest of a partner in a partnership is entirely disposed of before the close of the taxable year of the partnership; and

(2) No items of the partnership for that taxable year are required to be taken into account by the partner, then that partner has no profits interest in the partnership for that taxable year.

(e) *Examples.*—The provisions of this section may be illustrated by the following examples. Assume in all examples that there have been no reacquisitions prior to the close of the source partnership's taxable year. The examples are as follows:

*Example 1.* B holds an interest in partnership P through T, a pass-thru partner. P uses a fiscal year ending June 30 as P's taxable year; B and T use the calendar year as the taxable year. As of the close of P's taxable year ending June 30, 2002, T holds an interest in P and B holds an interest in P through T. The profits interest held by B in P through T for that year is determined as of June 30, 2002.

*Example 2.* Assume the same facts as in *Example 1*, except that B sold the entire interest that B held in P through T on November 5, 2001. The profits interest held by B in P through T for P's taxable year ending June 30, 2002, is determined as of the moment before the sale on November 5, 2001.

*Example 3.* C holds an interest in partnership P through T, a pass-thru partner. C, P, and T all use the calendar year as the taxable year. T disposes of T's interest in P on June 5, 2002. The profits interest held by C in P through T for 2002 is determined as of the moment before the disposition on June 5, 2002.

*Example 4.* Assume the same facts as in *Example 3*, except that C sold C's entire interest in T (and, therefore, C's entire interest that C held in P through T) on March 15, 2002. The profits interest held by C in P through T for 2002 is determined as of the moment before the sale on March 15, 2002.

*Example 5.* On January 1, 2002, D held a 2 percent profits interest in partnership P. Both D and P use the calendar year as the taxable year. On August 1, 2002, D transfers three-fourths of D's profits interest in P to E. On September 1, 2002, D sells D's remaining .5 percent profits interest in P to F. For purposes of sections 6223(b) and 6231(a)(11), D had a .5 percent profits interest in P for 2002.

*Example 6.* Assume the same facts as in *Example 5*, except that on January 1, 2002, D also held a 1 percent profits interest in partnership P through T, a pass-thru partner which also uses the calendar year as the taxable year. In addition to the sale to E on August 1, 2002, D sold a portion of D's interest in T on December 1, 2002, such that after the sale, D held a .2 percent profits interest in P through T. D made no other transfers of interests in either P or T. For purposes of sections 6223(b) and 6231(a)(11), D had a .7 percent profits interest in P for 2002.

(f) *Effective date.*—This section is applicable to partnership taxable years beginning on or after October 4, 2001. For years beginning prior to October 4, 2001, see § 301.6231(d)-1T contained in 26 CFR part 1, revised April 1, 2001. [Reg. § 301.6231(d)-1.]

☐ [*T.D.* 8965, 10-3-2001.]

### [Reg. § 301.6231(e)-1]

**§ 301.6231(e)-1. Effect of a determination with respect to a nonpartnership item on the determination of a partnership item.**—(a) *In general.*—The determination of an item after it has become a nonpartnership item with respect to a partner is not controlling in the determination of that item with respect to other partners. Thus, for example, the determination by a court in a separate proceeding relating to a partner that a certain partnership expenditure was deductible does not bind either the Internal Revenue Service or the other partners in a later partnership or other proceeding.

(b) *Effective date.*—This section is applicable to partnership taxable years beginning on or after October 4, 2001. For years beginning prior to October 4, 2001, see § 301.6231(e)-1T contained in 26 CFR part 1, revised April 1, 2001. [Reg. § 301.6231(e)-1.]

☐ [*T.D.* 8965, 10-3-2001.]

### [Reg. § 301.6231(e)-2]

**§ 301.6231(e)-2. Judicial decision not a bar to certain adjustments.**—(a) *In general.*—A court decision with respect to a partner's income tax liability attributable to nonpartnership items shall not be a bar to further proceedings with respect to that partner's income tax liability if that partner's partnership items become nonpartnership items after the appropriate time to include such nonpartnership items in the earlier court proceeding has passed. Thus, the Internal Revenue Service could issue a later deficiency notice for the same taxable year with respect to that partner or that partner could bring a refund suit with respect to those items that have become nonpartnership items.

(b) *Effective date.*—This section is applicable to partnership taxable years beginning on or after October 4, 2001. For years beginning prior to October 4, 2001, see § 301.6231(e)-2T contained in 26 CFR part 1, revised April 1, 2001. [Reg. § 301.6231(e)-2.]

☐ [*T.D.* 8965, 10-3-2001.]

### [Reg. § 301.6231(f)-1]

**§ 301.6231(f)-1. Disallowance of losses and credits in certain cases.**—(a) *Application of section.*—This section applies if—

(1) A partnership, whether domestic or foreign, that is required to file a return under section 6031 for a taxable year fails to file the return within the time prescribed; and

(2) At any time after the close of that taxable year, either—

(i) The tax matters partner of that partnership resides outside the United States; or

(ii) The books and records of that partnership are maintained outside the United States.

(b) *Computational adjustment permitted if return is not filed after mailing of notice.*—Except as otherwise provided in paragraph (c) of this section, if—

(1) This section applies with respect to a partnership for a partnership taxable year;

(2) The Internal Revenue Service mails notice to a partner that the losses and credits arising from that partnership for that year will be disallowed to that partner unless the partnership files a return for that year within 60 days after the date on which the notice is mailed; and

(3) The partnership fails to file a return for that year within that 60-day period, the Internal Revenue Service may, without conducting a partnership-level proceeding, mail a notice of computational adjustment to that partner to reflect the disallowance of any loss (including a capital loss) or credit arising from that partnership for that year.

(c) *Restriction on notices under paragraph (b) of this section.*—Neither the notice referred to in paragraph (b)(2) of this section nor the notice of computational adjustment referred to in paragraph (b) of this section may be mailed on a day on which—

(1) The tax matters partner of the partnership resides within the United States; and

(2) The books and records of the partnership are maintained within the United States. Thus, if this section applies with respect to a partnership for a taxable year solely because the tax matters partner of that partnership resided outside the United States for a period after the close of that taxable year and the tax matters partner later takes up residence within the United States, no notice may be mailed under paragraph (b) of this section while the tax matters partner resides within the United States.

(d) *No disallowance in certain circumstances.*—If the person to whom the notice referred to in paragraph (b)(2) of this section is mailed establishes to the satisfaction of the Internal Revenue Service—

(1) That the losses and credits arising from the partnership for the year are proper; and

(2) That the partner has made a good faith effort to have the partnership file the required return; the Internal Revenue Service may allow the losses and credits in whole or in part.

(e) *Effective date.*—This section is applicable to partnership taxable years beginning on or after October 4, 2001. For years beginning

prior to October 4, 2001, see § 301.6231(f)-1T contained in 26 CFR part 1, revised April 1, 2001. [Reg. § 301.6231(f)-1.]

☐ [*T.D.* 8965, 10-3-2001.]

### [Reg. § 301.6232-1]

**§ 301.6232-1. Assessment, collection, and payment of imputed underpayment.**—(a) *In general.*—An imputed underpayment determined under subchapter C of chapter 63 of the Internal Revenue Code (Code) is assessed and collected in the same manner as if the imputed underpayment were a tax imposed by subtitle A of the Code for the adjustment year (as defined in § 301.6241-1(a)(1)) except that the deficiency procedures under subchapter B of chapter 63 of the Code do not apply to an assessment of an imputed underpayment. Accordingly, no notice under section 6212 is required for, and the restrictions under section 6213 do not apply to, the assessment of any imputed underpayment. See paragraph (c) of this section for limitations on assessment and paragraph (d) of this section for exceptions to restrictions on adjustments.

(b) *Payment of the imputed underpayment.*—Upon receipt of notice and demand from the Internal Revenue Service (IRS), an imputed underpayment must be paid by the partnership at the place and time stated in the notice. In the case of an adjustment requested in an administrative adjustment request (AAR) under section 6227(b)(1) that is taken into account by the partnership under § 301.6227-2(b), payment of the imputed underpayment is due on the date the AAR is filed. The IRS may assess the amount of the imputed underpayment reflected on the AAR on the date the AAR is filed. For interest with respect to an imputed underpayment, see § 301.6233(a)-1(b).

(c) *Limitation on assessment.*—(1) *In general.*—Except as otherwise provided by this section or subtitle F of the Code (except for subchapter B of chapter 63), no assessment of an imputed underpayment may be made (and no levy or proceeding in any court for the collection of an imputed underpayment may be made, begun, or prosecuted) before—

(i) The close of the 90th day after the day on which a notice of a final partnership adjustment (FPA) under section 6231(a)(3) was mailed; and

(ii) If a petition for readjustment is filed under section 6234 with respect to such FPA, the decision of the court has become final.

(2) *Specified similar amount.*—The limitations under paragraph (c)(1) of this section do not apply in the case of a specified similar amount as defined in section 6232(f)(2).

(d) *Exceptions to restrictions on adjustments and assessments.*—(1) *Adjustments treated as mathematical or clerical errors.*—(i) *In general.*—A notice to a partnership that, on account of a mathematical or clerical error appearing on the partnership return or as a result of a failure by a partnership-partner (as defined in § 301.6241-1(a)(7)) to comply with section 6222(a), the IRS has adjusted or will adjust partnership-related items (as defined in § 301.6241-1(a)(6)(ii)) to correct the error or to make the items consistent under section 6222(a) and has assessed or will assess any imputed underpayment (determined in accordance with § 301.6225-1) resulting from the adjustment is not considered an FPA under section 6231(a)(3). A petition for readjustment under section 6234 may not be filed with respect to such notice. The limitations under section 6232(b) and paragraph (c) of this section do not apply to an assessment under this paragraph (d)(1)(i). For the definition of mathematical or clerical error generally, see section 6213(g)(2). For application of mathematical or clerical error in the case of inconsistent treatment by a partner that fails to give notice, see § 301.6222-1(b).

(ii) *Request for abatement.*—(A) *In general.*—Except as provided in paragraph (d)(1)(ii)(B) of this section, a partnership that is mailed a notice described in paragraph (d)(1)(i) of this section may file with the IRS, within 60 days after the date of such notice, a request for abatement of any assessment of an imputed underpayment specified in such notice. Upon receipt of the request, the IRS must abate the assessment. Any subsequent assessment of an imputed underpayment with respect to which abatement was made is subject to the provisions of subchapter C of chapter 63 of the Code, including the limitations under paragraph (c) of this section.

(B) *Adjustments with respect to inconsistent treatment by a partnership-partner.*—If an adjustment that is the subject of a notice described in paragraph (d)(1)(i) of this section is due to the failure of a partnership-partner to comply with section 6222(a), paragraph (d)(1)(ii)(A) of this section does not apply, and abatement of any assessment specified in such notice is not available. However, prior to assessment, a partnership-partner that has failed to comply with section 6222(a) may correct the inconsistency by filing an administrative adjustment request in accordance with section 6227 or filing an amended partnership return and furnishing amended statements, as appropriate.

(iii) *Partnerships that have an election under section 6221(b) in effect.*—In the case of a partnership-partner that has an election under section 6221(b) in effect for the reviewed year (as defined in §301.6241-1(a)(8)), any tax resulting from an adjustment due to the partnership-partner's failure to comply with section 6222(a) may be assessed with respect to the reviewed year partners (as defined in §301.6241-1(a)(9)) of the partnership-partner (or indirect partners of the partnership-partner, as defined in §301.6241-1(a)(4)). Such tax may be assessed in the same manner as if the tax were on account of a mathematical or clerical error appearing on the reviewed year partner's or indirect partner's return, except that the procedures under section 6213(b)(2) for requesting an abatement of such assessment do not apply.

(2) *Partnership may waive limitations.*—A partnership may at any time by a signed notice in writing filed with the IRS waive the limitations under paragraph (c) of this section (whether or not an FPA under section 6231(a)(3) has been mailed by the IRS at the time of the waiver).

(e) *Limit on amount of imputed underpayment where no proceeding is begun.*—If no proceeding under section 6234 is begun with respect to an FPA under section 6231(a)(3) before the close of the 90th day after the day on which such FPA was mailed, the amount for which the partnership is liable under section 6225 with respect to such FPA cannot exceed the amount determined in such FPA.

(f) *Applicability date.*—(1) *In general.*—Except as provided in paragraph (f)(2) of this section, this section applies to partnership taxable years beginning after December 31, 2017, and ending after August 12, 2018.

(2) *Election under §301.9100-22 in effect.*—This section applies to any partnership taxable year beginning after November 2, 2015, and before January 1, 2018, for which a valid election under §301.9100-22 is in effect. [Reg. §301.6232-1.]

☐ [T.D. 9844, 2-21-2019.]

**[Reg. §301.6233-1]**

**§301.6233-1. Extension to entities filing partnership returns.**— (a) *Entities filing a partnership return.*—Except as provided in paragraph (c)(1) of this section, the provisions of subchapter C of chapter 63 of the Internal Revenue Code (subchapter C) and the regulations thereunder shall apply with respect to any taxable year of an entity for which such entity files a partnership return as well as to such entity's items for that taxable year and to any person holding an interest in such entity at any time during that taxable year. Any final partnership administrative adjustment or judicial determination resulting from a proceeding under subchapter C with respect to such taxable year may include a determination that the entity is not a partnership for such taxable year as well as determinations with respect to all items of the entity that would be partnership items, as defined in section 6231(a)(3) and the regulations thereunder, if such entity had been a partnership in such taxable year (including, for example, any amounts taxable to an entity determined to be an association taxable as a corporation). For example, a final determination under subchapter C that an entity that filed a partnership return is an association taxable as a corporation will serve as a basis for a computational adjustment reflecting the disallowance of any loss or credit claimed by a purported partner with respect to thai entity.

(b) *Partnership return filed but no entity found to exist.*—Paragraph (a) of this section shall apply where a partnership return is filed for a taxable year but it is determined that there is no entity for such taxable year. For purposes of applying paragraph (a) of this section, the partnership return shall be treated as if it were filed by an entity. However, any final partnership administrative adjustment or judicial determination resulting from a proceeding under subchapter C with respect to such taxable year may also include a determination that there is no entity for such taxable year.

(c) *Exceptions.*—Paragraph (a) of this section shall not apply to—

(1) Entities for any taxable year in which such entity would be excepted from the provisions of subchapter C of the Internal Revenue Code under section 6231(a)(1)(B) and the regulations thereunder (relating to the exception for small partnerships) if such entity were a partnership for such taxable year; and

(2) Entities for any taxable year for which a partnership return was filed for the sole purpose of making the election described in section 761(a).

(d) *Effective dates.*—This section is applicable to partnership taxable years beginning on or after October 4, 2001. For years beginning

prior to October 4, 2001, see §301.6233-1T contained in 26 CFR part 1, revised April 1, 2001. [Reg. §301.6233-1.]

☐ [T.D. 8965, 10-3-2001.]

**[Reg. §301.6233(a)-1]**

**§301.6233(a)-1. Interest and penalties determined from reviewed year.**—(a) *Interest and penalties with respect to the reviewed year.*— Except to the extent provided in section 6226(c), in the case of a partnership adjustment (as defined in §301.6241-1(a)(6)) for a reviewed year (as defined in §301.6241-1(a)(8)), a partnership is liable for–

(1) Interest computed in accordance with paragraph (b) of this section; and

(2) Any penalty, addition to tax, or additional amount as provided under paragraph (c) of this section.

(b) *Computation of interest with respect to partnership adjustments for the reviewed year.*—(1) *Interest on an imputed underpayment.*—The interest imposed on an imputed underpayment resulting from partnership adjustments for the reviewed year is the interest that would be imposed under chapter 67 of the Internal Revenue Code (Code) if the imputed underpayment were treated as an underpayment of tax for the reviewed year. The interest imposed on an imputed underpayment under paragraph (b) of this section begins on the day after the due date of the partnership return (without regard to extension) for the reviewed year and ends on the earlier of–

(i) The date prescribed for payment (as described in §301.6232-1(b));

(ii) The due date of the partnership return (without regard to extension) for the adjustment year (as defined in §301.6241-1(a)(1)); or

(iii) The date the imputed underpayment is fully paid.

(2) *Interest on penalties with respect to the reviewed year.*—The interest imposed on any penalties, additions to tax, and additional amounts determined under paragraph (c) of this section is the interest that would be imposed under chapter 67 of the Code treating the partnership return for the reviewed year as the return of tax with respect to which such penalty, addition to tax, or additional amount is imposed.

(c) *Penalties with respect to partnership adjustments for the reviewed year.*—(1) *In general.*—In accordance with section 6221(a), the applicability of any penalties, additions to tax, and additional amounts that relate to an adjustment to any partnership-related item for the reviewed year is determined at the partnership level as if the partnership had been an individual subject to tax imposed by chapter 1 of the Code for the reviewed year, and the imputed underpayment were an actual underpayment of tax or understatement for such year. Nothing in this paragraph (c)(1) affects the application of any penalty, addition to tax, or additional amount that may apply to the partnership or to any reviewed year partner (as defined in §301.6241-1(a)(9)) or to any indirect partner (as defined in §301.6241-1(a)(4)) that is unrelated to an adjustment to a partnership-related item under subchapter C of chapter 63 of the Code. Except as provided in §301.6225-2(d), a partner-level defense (as described in §301.6226-3(d)(3)) may not be raised in a proceeding of the partnership.

(2) *Determination of the amount of accuracy-related penalty and fraud penalty.*—(i) *In general.*—The amount of any penalty under part II of subchapter A of chapter 68 of the Code (accuracy-related or fraud penalties) that relates to any partnership adjustment for the reviewed year is determined in accordance with this paragraph (c)(2). If in determining the imputed underpayment under §301.6225-1 (or §301.6225-2 in the case of modification), any grouping or subgrouping contains a negative adjustment (as defined in §301.6225-1(d)(2)(ii)) and at least one positive adjustment (as defined in §301.6225-1(d)(2)(iii)) that is subject to penalty, first apply the rules for allocating negative adjustments in paragraph (c)(2)(iii) of this section. Then, apply the rules in paragraph (c)(2)(ii) of this section to calculate penalty amounts. If there are no negative adjustments, do not apply the rules in paragraph (c)(2)(iii) of this section and instead apply only the rules in paragraph (c)(2)(ii) of this section. For all purposes under paragraph (c)(2) of this section, adjustments that do not result in the imputed underpayment (as described in §301.6225-1(f)) and adjustments excluded from the determination of the imputed underpayment under §301.6225-2(b)(2) are disregarded.

(ii) *Calculating the portion of an imputed underpayment subject to penalty and penalty amounts.*—To determine the portion of an imputed underpayment subject to a penalty and the amount of a particular penalty, apply the following steps to all adjustments subject to penalty remaining after application of negative adjustments (as described in paragraph (c)(2)(iii) of this section) and to all adjustments subject to penalty contained in groupings or subgroupings that do not contain a negative adjustment.

(A) For purposes of applying this paragraph (c)(2)(ii)(A), disregard adjustments to credits or adjustments treated as adjustments to credits. Total all adjustments to which a particular penalty was imposed and to which the highest rate of tax in effect for the reviewed year under section 1 or 11 was applied when calculating the imputed underpayment. See § 301.6225-1(b)(1)(iv).

(B) Multiply the total in paragraph (c)(2)(ii)(A) of this section by the highest rate of tax in effect for the reviewed year under section 1 or 11.

(C) If the imputed underpayment was modified in accordance with § 301.6225-2(b)(3), repeat the steps in paragraphs (c)(2)(ii)(A) and (B) of this section for every tax rate applied in calculating the imputed underpayment by substituting the applicable tax rate determined under § 301.6225-2(b)(3) for the highest rate of tax in effect for the reviewed year under section 1 or 11.

(D) Total all amounts determined after completing the steps in paragraphs (c)(2)(ii)(A) through (C) of this section.

(E) Adjust the amount calculated in paragraph (c)(2)(ii)(D) of this section by:

(1) Increasing by the net adjustments subject to the penalty in the credit grouping (as described in paragraph (c)(2)(iii)(C)(1) of this section) after application of paragraph (c)(2)(iii)(A) of this section; or

(2) Decreasing in accordance with the rules in paragraph (c)(2)(iii)(C)(2) of this section by the amount of negative adjustments in the credit grouping if, after application of paragraph (c)(2)(iii)(A) of this section, only negative adjustments in the credit grouping remain.

(3) The result after completing the calculation in paragraphs (c)(2)(ii)(E)(1) and (2) of this section is the portion of the imputed underpayment to which the particular penalty was imposed.

(F) Multiply the total calculated in paragraph (c)(2)(ii)(E) of this section by the penalty rate applicable to the particular penalty. This is the total penalty amount for adjustments to which the particular penalty was imposed.

(iii) *Allocating negative adjustments.*—(A) *In general.*—Negative adjustments offset positive adjustments within the same grouping or, if the negative adjustment is in a subgrouping, within that same subgrouping. For purposes of applying this paragraph (c)(2)(iii), all adjustments to credits and adjustments treated as adjustments to credits are treated as grouped in the credit grouping without regard to whether the adjustments were subgrouped for purposes of § 301.6225-1 (or § 301.6225-2 in the case of modification). Adjustments that do not result in the imputed underpayment are disregarded as provided in paragraph (c)(2) of this section. Negative adjustments are allocated in accordance with the following rules:

(1) Negative adjustments are first applied to offset positive adjustments to which no penalties have been imposed.

(2) Any amount of negative adjustments remaining after application of paragraph (c)(2)(iii)(A)(1) of this section are applied to offset adjustments to which a penalty has been imposed at the lowest penalty rate.

(3) Any amount of negative adjustments remaining after application of paragraph (c)(2)(iii)(A)(2) of this section are applied to offset adjustments to which a penalty has been imposed at the next highest rate in ascending order of rate until no amount of negative adjustments remain or no positive adjustments to which a penalty has been imposed remain.

(B) *Allocation of negative adjustment within a penalty rate.*—The Internal Revenue Service (IRS) may provide additional guidance regarding the ordering or allocation of negative adjustments for purposes of paragraph (c)(2)(iii)(A) of this section where more than one penalty is imposed at the same penalty rate.

(C) *Adjustments remaining after allocation of negative adjustments.*—(1) *In general.*—For purposes of paragraph (c)(2)(ii) of this section, any positive adjustment to which a penalty has been imposed that has not been fully offset by a negative adjustment after application of paragraph (c)(2)(iii)(A) of this section is a *net adjustment subject to penalty* remaining after allocation of negative adjustments.

(2) *Additional rules regarding allocation of negative credit amounts.*—If, after application of paragraph (c)(2)(iii)(A) of this section, an amount of negative adjustments remain in the credit grouping, the amount of remaining negative adjustments may reduce the portion of the imputed underpayment that is subject to a penalty, but not below zero, in accordance with the following rules:

(i) The amount of remaining negative adjustments in the credit grouping are first applied to the portion of the imputed

underpayment to which no penalty has been imposed, as calculated in accordance with paragraph (c)(2)(iii)(C)(3) of this section.

(ii) Any amount of negative adjustment in the credit grouping remaining after application of paragraph (c)(2)(iii)(C)(2)(i) of this section is applied to the portion of the imputed underpayment to which a penalty has been imposed at the lowest penalty rate as calculated in accordance with paragraph (c)(2)(ii) of this section.

(iii) Any amount of negative adjustments in the credit grouping remaining after application of paragraph (c)(2)(iii)(C)(1)(ii) of this section is applied to the portion of the imputed underpayment to which a penalty has been imposed at the next highest rate in ascending order of rate in accordance with paragraph (c)(2)(iii) of this section until no negative amount remains.

(3) *Calculating the portion of the imputed underpayment to which no penalty was imposed before the application of negative adjustments to credits.*—To determine the portion of the imputed underpayment that is not subject to penalty for purposes of paragraph (c)(2)(iii)(C)(2)(i) of this section, apply the rules in paragraphs (c)(2)(ii)(A) through (E) of this section but substitute adjustment to which no penalty was imposed for adjustments to which a particular penalty was imposed.

(iv) *Special rules.*—(A) *Fraud penalties under section 6663.*—If any portion of an imputed underpayment is determined by the IRS to be attributable to fraud, the entire imputed underpayment is treated as attributable to fraud. This paragraph (c)(2)(iv)(A) does not apply to any portion of the imputed underpayment the partnership establishes by a preponderance of the evidence is not attributable to fraud.

(B) *Substantial understatement penalty under section 6662(d).*—(1) *In general.*—For purposes of application of the penalty under section 6662(d) (substantial understatement of income tax), the imputed underpayment is treated as an understatement under section 6662(d)(2). To determine whether an imputed underpayment treated as an understatement under this paragraph (c)(2)(iv)(B)(1) is a substantial understatement under section 6662(d)(1), the rules of section 6662(d)(1)(A) apply by treating the amount described in paragraph (c)(2)(iv)(B)(2) of this section as the tax required to be shown on the return for the taxable year under section 6662(d)(1)(A)(i).

(2) *Amount of tax required to be shown on the return.*—The amount described in this paragraph (c)(2)(iv)(B)(2) is the tax that would result by treating the net income or loss of the partnership for the reviewed year, reflecting any partnership adjustments as finally determined, as taxable income described in section 1(c) (determined without regard to section 1(h)).

(C) *Reportable transaction understatement under section 6662A.*—For purposes of application of the penalty under section 6662A (reportable transaction understatement penalty), the portion of an imputed underpayment attributable to an item described under section 6662A(b)(2) is treated as a reportable transaction understatement under section 6662A(b).

(D) *Reasonable cause and good faith.*—For purposes of determining whether a partnership satisfies the reasonable cause and good faith exception under section 6664(c) or (d) with respect to a penalty under section 6662, section 6662A, or section 6663, the partnership is treated as the taxpayer. See § 1.6664-4 of this chapter. Accordingly, the facts and circumstances taken into account to determine whether the partnership has established reasonable cause and good faith are the facts and circumstances applicable to the partnership.

(v) *Examples.*—The following examples illustrate the rules of paragraph (c) of this section. For purposes of these examples, each partnership has a calendar taxable year, and the highest tax rate in effect for all taxpayers is 40 percent for all relevant periods.

(A) *Example 1.* In an administrative proceeding with respect to Partnership's 2018 partnership return, the IRS makes a positive adjustment to ordinary income of $100. The $100 adjustment is due to negligence or disregard of rules or regulations under section 6662(c), and a 20-percent accuracy-related penalty applies under section 6662(a). The IRS also makes a positive adjustment to long-term capital gain of $300, but no penalty applies with respect to that adjustment. These are the only adjustments. The portion of the imputed underpayment to which the 20-percent penalty applies is $40 ($100 x 40 percent), and the penalty is $8 ($40 x 20 percent).

(B) *Example 2.* The facts are the same as in *Example 1* in paragraph (c)(2)(v)(A) of this section, except that the IRS makes a positive adjustment to credits of $10. The adjustment to credits is due to negligence or disregard of rules or regulations under section 6662(c), and a 20-percent accuracy-related penalty applies under section 6662(a). The portion of the imputed underpayment to which the 20-percent accuracy-related penalty applies is $50 (($100 x 40 percent) + $10), and the penalty is $10 ($50 x 20 percent).

(C) *Example 3.* The facts are the same as in *Example 2* in paragraph (c)(2)(v)(B) of this section, except that there is also a negative adjustment to ordinary income of $50 that was subgrouped under §301.6225-1 with the $100 positive adjustment to ordinary. Because the $50 negative adjustment to ordinary income was subgrouped under §301.6225-1 with the $100 positive adjustment to ordinary income, in determining the portion of the imputed underpayment subject to penalty, the $50 negative adjustment is applied to offset part of the $100 positive adjustment to ordinary income ($100-$50=$50). Accordingly, the portion of the imputed underpayment to which the 20-percent accuracy-related penalty applies is $30 (($50 x 40 percent) + $10), and the penalty is $6 ($30 x 20 percent).

(D) *Example 4.* The facts are the same as in *Example 3* in paragraph (c)(2)(v)(C) of this section, except that the $300 adjustment to long-term capital gain is due to a gross valuation misstatement. A 40-percent accuracy-related penalty under section 6662(a) and (h) applies to the portion of the imputed underpayment attributable to the gross valuation misstatement. The portion of the imputed underpayment to which the 20 percent accuracy-related penalty applies remains $30, and the 20-percent accuracy-related penalty remains $6. The portion of the imputed underpayment to which the 40-percent gross valuation misstatement penalty applies is $120 ($300 x 40 percent), and the gross valuation misstatement penalty is $48 ($120 x 40 percent). The total accuracy-related penalty under section 6662(a) is $54.

(E) *Example 5.* Partnership has four equal partners during its 2019 taxable year: two partners are partnerships, A and B; one partner is a tax-exempt entity, C; and the fourth partner is an individual, D. In an administrative proceeding with respect to Partnership's 2019 taxable year, the IRS timely mails a notice of proposed partnership adjustment (NOPPA) to Partnership for its 2019 taxable year proposing a single partnership positive adjustment to Partnership's ordinary income by $400,000. The $400,000 positive adjustment is due to negligence or disregard of rules or regulations under section 6662(c). A 20-percent accuracy-related penalty under section 6662(a) and (c) applies to the portion of the imputed underpayment attributable to the negligence or disregard of the rules or regulations. In the NOPPA, the IRS determines an imputed underpayment of $160,000 ($400,000 x 40 percent) and that the 20-percent penalty applies to the entire imputed underpayment. The penalty is $32,000 ($160,000 x 20 percent). Partnership requests modification under §301.6225-2(d)(3) (regarding tax-exempt partners) with respect to the amount of additional income allocated to C, and the IRS approves the modification request. As a result, Partnership's total netted partnership adjustment under §301.6225-1(b)(2) is $300,000 ($400,000 less $100,000 allocable to C). The imputed underpayment is $120,000 (($300,000) x 40 percent), and the penalty is $24,000 ($120,000 x 20 percent).

(F) *Example 6.* The facts are the same as in *Example 5* in paragraph (c)(2)(v)(E) of this section, except in addition to the modification with respect to C's tax-exempt status, Partnership requests a modification under §301.6225-2(d)(2) (regarding amended returns) with respect to the $100,000 of additional income allocated to D. In accordance with the rules under §301.6225-2(d)(2), D files an amended return for D's 2019 taxable year taking into account $100,000 of additional ordinary income. In addition, in accordance with §301.6225-2(d)(2)(viii), D takes into account on D's return the 20-percent accuracy-related penalty for negligence or disregard of rules or regulations that relates to the ordinary income adjustment. D's tax attributes for other taxable years are not affected. The IRS approves the modification request. As a result, Partnership's total netted partnership adjustment under §301.6225-1(b)(2) is $200,000 ($400,000 less $100,000 allocable to C and $100,000 taken into account by D). The imputed underpayment, after modification, is $80,000 ($200,000 x 40 percent), and the penalty is $16,000 ($80,000 x 20 percent).

(d) *Applicability date.*—(1) *In general.*—Except as provided in paragraph (d)(2) of this section, this section applies to partnership taxable years beginning after December 31, 2017, and ending after August 12, 2018.

(2) *Election under §301.9100-22 in effect.*—This section applies to any partnership taxable year beginning after November 2, 2015, and before January 1, 2018, for which a valid election under §301.9100-22 is in effect. [Reg. §301.6233(a)-1.]

☐ [T.D. 9844, 2-21-2019.]

#### [Reg. §301.6233(b)-1]

**§301.6233(b)-1. Interest and penalties with respect to the adjustment year return.**—(a) *Interest and penalties with respect to failure to pay imputed underpayment on the date prescribed.*—In the case of any failure to pay an imputed underpayment on the date prescribed for

such payment (as described in §301.6232-1(b)), a partnership is liable for—

(1) Interest as determined under paragraph (c) of this section; and

(2) Any penalty, addition to tax, or additional amount as determined under paragraph (d) of this section.

(b) *Imputed underpayments to which this section applies.*—This section applies to the portion of an imputed underpayment determined by the Internal Revenue Service (IRS) under section 6225(a)(1), or an imputed underpayment resulting from adjustments requested by a partnership in an administrative adjustment request under section 6227, that is not paid by the date prescribed for payment under §301.6232-1(b).

(c) *Interest.*—Interest determined under this paragraph (c) is the interest that would be imposed under chapter 67 of the Internal Revenue Code (Code) by treating any unpaid amount of the imputed underpayment as an underpayment of tax imposed for the adjustment year (as defined in §301.6241-1(a)(1)). The interest under this paragraph (c) begins on the date prescribed for payment (as described in §301.6232-1(b)) and ends on the date payment of the imputed underpayment is made.

(d) *Penalties.*—If a partnership fails to pay an imputed underpayment by the date prescribed for payment (as described in §301.6232-1(b)), section 6651(a)(2) applies to such failure, and any unpaid amount of the imputed underpayment is treated as if it were an underpayment of tax for purposes of part II of subchapter A of chapter 68 of the Code. For purposes of this section, the penalty under 6651(a)(2) is applied by treating the unpaid amount of the imputed underpayment as the unpaid amount shown as tax on a return required under subchapter A of chapter 61 of the Code.

(e) *Applicability date.*—(1) *In general.*—Except as provided in paragraph (e)(2) of this section, this section applies to partnership taxable years beginning after December 31, 2017, and ending after August 12, 2018.

(2) *Election under §301.9100-22 in effect.*—This section applies to any partnership taxable year beginning after November 2, 2015, and before January 1, 2018, for which a valid election under §301.9100-22 is in effect. [Reg. §301.6233(b)-1.]

☐ [T.D. 9844, 2-21-2019.]

#### [Reg. §301.6234-1]

**§301.6234-1. Judicial review of partnership adjustment.**—(a) *In general.*—Within 90 days after the date on which a notice of a final partnership adjustment (FPA) under section 6231(a)(3) with respect to any partnership taxable year is mailed, a partnership may file a petition for a readjustment of any partnership adjustment (as defined in §301.6241-1(a)(6)) reflected in the FPA for such taxable year (without regard to whether an election under section 6226 has been made with respect to any imputed underpayment (as defined in §301.6241-1(a)(3)) reflected in such FPA) with—

(1) The Tax Court;

(2) The district court of the United States for the district in which the partnership's principal place of business is located; or

(3) The Court of Federal Claims.

(b) *Jurisdictional requirement for bringing action in district court or Court of Federal Claims.*—A petition for readjustment under this section with respect to any partnership adjustment may be filed in a district court of the United States or the Court of Federal Claims only if the partnership filing the petition deposits with the Internal Revenue Service (IRS), on or before the date the petition is filed, the amount of (as of the date of the filing of the petition) any imputed underpayment (as shown on the FPA) and any penalties, additions to tax, and additional amounts with respect to such imputed underpayment. If there is more than one imputed underpayment reflected in the FPA, the partnership must deposit the amount of each imputed underpayment to which the petition for readjustment relates and the amount of any penalties, additions to tax, and additional amounts with respect to each such imputed underpayment.

(c) *Treatment of deposit as payment of tax.* Any amount deposited in accordance with paragraph (b) of this section, while deposited, will not be treated as a payment of tax for purposes of the Internal Revenue Code (Code). Notwithstanding the preceding sentence, an amount deposited in accordance with paragraph (b) of this section will be treated as a payment of tax for purposes of chapter 67 of the Code (relating to interest). Interest will be allowed and paid in accordance with section 6611.

(d) *Effect of decision dismissing action.*—If an action brought under this section is dismissed other than by reason of a rescission of the FPA under section 6231(d) and §301.6231-1(g), the decision of the court dismissing the action is considered as its decision that the FPA is correct.

(e) *Amount deposited may be applied against assessment.*—If the limitations on assessment under section 6232(b) and § 301.6232-1(c) no longer apply with respect to an imputed underpayment for which a deposit under paragraph (b) of this section was made, the IRS may apply the amount deposited against any such imputed underpayment that is assessed. In the case of a deposit made under this section that is in an amount in excess of the amount assessed against the partnership (excess deposit), a partnership may obtain a return of the excess deposit by making a request in writing in accordance with forms, instructions, or other guidance prescribed by the IRS.

(f) *Applicability date.*—(1) *In general.*—Except as provided in paragraph (f)(2) of this section, this section applies to partnership taxable years beginning after December 31, 2017, and ending after August 12, 2018.

(2) *Election under § 301.9100-22 in effect.*—This section applies to any partnership taxable year beginning after November 2, 2015, and before January 1, 2018, for which a valid election under § 301.9100-22 is in effect. [Reg. § 301.6234-1.]

☐ [T.D. 9844, 2-21-2019.]

### [Reg. § 301.6235-1]

**§ 301.6235-1. Period of limitations on making adjustments.**—(a) *In general.*—Except as provided in section 6235(c), section 905(c), or paragraph (d) of this section (regarding extensions), no partnership adjustment (as defined in § 301.6241-1(a)(6)) for any partnership taxable year may be made after the later of the date that is—

(1) 3 years after the latest of—

(i) The date on which the partnership return for such taxable year was filed;

(ii) The return due date (as defined in section 6241(3)) for the taxable year; or

(iii) The date on which the partnership filed an administrative adjustment request with respect to such taxable year under section 6227;

(2) The date described in paragraph (b) of this section with respect to a request for modification; or

(3) The date described in paragraph (c) of this section with respect to a notice of proposed partnership adjustment.

(b) *Modification requested under section 6225(c).*—(1) *In general.*—For purposes of paragraph (a)(2) of this section, in the case of any request for modification of any imputed underpayment under section 6225(c), the date by which the Internal Revenue Service (IRS) may make a partnership adjustment is the date that is 270 days (plus the number of days of an extension of the period for requesting modification (as described in § 301.6225-2(c)(3)(i)) agreed to by the IRS under section 6225(c)(7) and § 301.6225-2(c)(3)(ii)) after the date on which everything required to be submitted to the IRS pursuant to section 6225(c) is so submitted.

(2) *Date on which everything is required to be submitted.*—(i) *In general.*—For purposes of paragraph (b)(1) of this section, the date on which everything required to be submitted to the IRS pursuant to section 6225(c) is so submitted is the earlier of—

(A) The date the period for requesting modification ends (including extensions) as described in § 301.6225-2(c)(3)(i) and (ii); or

(B) The date the period for requesting modification expires as a result of a waiver of the prohibition on mailing a notice of final partnership adjustment (FPA) under § 301.6231-1(b)(2). See § 301.6225-2(c)(3)(iii).

(ii) *Incomplete submission has no effect.*—A determination by the IRS that the information submitted as part of a request for modification is incomplete has no effect on the applicability of paragraph (b)(2) of this section.

(c) *Notice of proposed partnership adjustment.*—For purposes of paragraph (a)(3) of this section, the date by which the IRS may make a partnership adjustment is the date that is 330 days (plus the number of days of an extension of the modification period (as described in § 301.6225-2(c)(3)(i) agreed to by the IRS under section 6225(c)(7) and § 301.6225-2(c)(3)(ii)) after the date the last notice of proposed partnership adjustment (NOPPA) under section 6231(a)(2) is mailed, regardless of whether modification is requested by the partnership under section 6225(c).

(d) *Extension by agreement.*—The periods described in paragraphs (a), (b), and (c) of this section (including any extension of those periods pursuant to this paragraph (d)) may be extended by an agreement, in writing, entered into by the partnership and the IRS before the expiration of such period.

(e) *Examples.*—The following examples illustrate the rules of this section. For purposes of these examples, each partnership has a calendar taxable year.

(1) *Example 1.* Partnership timely files its partnership return for the 2020 taxable year on March 1, 2021. On September 1, 2023, Partnership files an administrative adjustment request (AAR) under section 6227 with respect to its 2020 taxable year. As of September 1, 2023, the IRS has not initiated an administrative proceeding under subchapter C of chapter 63 of the Internal Revenue Code with respect to Partnership's 2020 taxable year. Therefore, as of September 1, 2023, under paragraph (a)(1) of this section, the period for making partnership adjustments with respect to Partnership's 2020 taxable year expires on September 1, 2026.

(2) *Example 2.* Partnership timely files its partnership return for the 2020 taxable year on the due date, March 15, 2021. On February 1, 2023, the IRS mails to Partnership and the partnership representative of Partnership (PR) a notice of administrative proceeding under section 6231(a)(1) with respect to Partnership's 2020 taxable year. Assuming no AAR has been filed with respect to Partnership's 2020 taxable year and the IRS has not yet mailed a NOPPA under section 6231(a)(2) with respect to Partnership's 2020 taxable year, the period for making partnership adjustments for Partnership's 2020 taxable year expires on the date determined under paragraph (a)(1) of this section, March 15, 2024.

(3) *Example 3.* The facts are the same as in *Example 2* in paragraph (e)(2) of this section, except that on June 1, 2023, pursuant to paragraph (d) of this section, PR signs an agreement extending the period for making partnership adjustments under section 6235(a) for Partnership's 2020 taxable year to December 31, 2025. In addition, on June 2, 2025, the IRS mails to Partnership and PR a timely NOPPA under section 6231(a)(2). Pursuant to § 301.6225-2(c)(3)(i), the period for requesting modification expires on February 27, 2026 (270 days after June 2, 2025, the date the NOPPA is mailed), but PR does not submit a request for modification on or before this date. Under paragraph (c) of this section, the date for purposes of paragraph (a)(3) of this section is April 28, 2026, the date that is 330 days from the mailing of the NOPPA. Because April 28, 2026 is later than the date under paragraph (a)(1) of this section (December 31, 2025, as extended under paragraph (d) of this section), and because no modification was requested, paragraph (a)(2) of this section is not applicable, April 28, 2026 is the date on which the period for making partnership adjustments expires under section 6235.

(4) *Example 4.* The facts are the same as in *Example 3* in paragraph (e)(3) of this section, except that PR notifies the IRS that Partnership will be requesting modification. On January 5, 2026, PR and the IRS agree to extend the period for requesting modification pursuant to section 6225(c)(7) and § 301.6225-2(c)(3)(ii) for 45 days—from February 27, 2026 to April 13, 2026. PR submits the request for modification to the IRS on April 13, 2026. Therefore, the date determined under paragraph (b) of this section is February 22, 2027, which is 270 days after the date everything required to be submitted was so submitted pursuant to paragraph (b)(2) of this section plus the additional 45-day extension of the period for requesting modification agreed to by PR and the IRS. Because February 22, 2027 is later than the date under paragraph (a)(1) of this section (December 31, 2025, as extended under paragraph (d) of this section) and the date under paragraph (a)(3) of this section (June 12, 2026, which is 330 days from the date the NOPPA was mailed plus the 45-day extension under section 6225(c)(7)), February 22, 2027 is the date on which the period for making partnership adjustments expires under section 6235.

(5) *Example 5.* The facts are the same as in *Example 4* in paragraph (e)(4) of this section, except that PR does not request an extension of the period for requesting modification. On February 1, 2026, PR submits a request for modification and PR, and the IRS agree in writing to waive the prohibition on mailing an FPA pursuant to § 301.6231-1(b)(2). Pursuant to § 301.6225-2(c)(3)(iii), the period for requesting modification expires as of February 1, 2026, rather than February 27, 2026. Accordingly, under paragraph (b)(2) of this section, the date on which everything required to be submitted pursuant to section 6225(c) is so submitted is February 1, 2026, and the 270-day period described in paragraph (b)(1) of this section begins to run on that date. Therefore, the date for purposes of paragraph (a)(2) of this section is October 29, 2026, which is 270 days after February 1, 2026, the date on which everything required to be submitted under section 6225(c) is so submitted. Because October 29, 2026 is later than the date under paragraph (a)(1) of this section (December 31, 2025, as extended under paragraph (d) of this section) and the date under paragraph (a)(3) of this section (April 28, 2026), October 29, 2026 is the date on which the period for making partnership adjustments expires under section 6235.

(6) *Example 6.* The facts are the same as in *Example 5* in paragraph (e)(5) of this section, except PR completes its submission of information to support a request for modification on July 1, 2025, but does not execute a waiver pursuant to § 301.6231-1(b)(2). Therefore, pursuant to paragraph (b)(2) of this section, February 27, 2026, the date the

period requesting modification expires, is the date on which everything required to be submitted pursuant to section 6225(c) is so submitted. As a result, the 270-day period described in paragraph (b)(1) of this section expires on November 24, 2026. Because November 24, 2026 is later than the date under paragraph (a)(1) of this section (December 31, 2025, as extended under paragraph (d) of this section) and the date under paragraph (a)(3) of this section (April 28, 2026), November 24, 2026 is the date on which the period for making partnership adjustments expires under section 6235.

(f) *Applicability date.*—(1) *In general.*—Except as provided in paragraph (f)(2) of this section, this section applies to partnership taxable years beginning after December 31, 2017, and ending after August 12, 2018.

(2) *Election under § 301.9100-22 in effect.*—This section applies to any partnership taxable year beginning after November 2, 2015, and before January 1, 2018, for which a valid election under § 301.9100-22 is in effect. [Reg. § 301.6235-1.]

☐ [T.D. 9844, 2-21-2019.]

# TAX TREATMENT OF SUBCHAPTER S ITEMS

## [Reg. § 301.6241-1]

**§ 301.6241-1. Definitions.**—(a) *Definitions.*—For purposes of subchapter C of chapter 63 of the Internal Revenue Code (Code) and the regulations in this part under sections 6221 through 6241 of the Code—

(1) *Adjustment year.*—The term *adjustment year* means the partnership taxable year in which—

(i) In the case of an adjustment pursuant to the decision of a court in a proceeding brought under section 6234, such decision becomes final;

(ii) In the case of an administrative adjustment request (AAR) under section 6227, such AAR is filed; or

(iii) In any other case, a notice of final partnership adjustment is mailed under section 6231 or, if the partnership waives the restrictions under section 6232(b) (regarding limitations on assessment), the waiver is executed by the IRS.

(2) *Adjustment year partner.*—The term *adjustment year partner* means any person who held an interest in a partnership at any time during the adjustment year.

(3) *Imputed underpayment.*—Except as otherwise provided in this paragraph (a)(3), the term *imputed underpayment* means the amount determined in accordance with section 6225 of the Code, § 301.6225-1, and, if applicable, § 301.6225-2. In the case of an election under section 6226, the term *imputed underpayment* means the amount determined in accordance with § 301.6226-3(e)(4). In the case of an administrative adjustment request, the term *imputed underpayment* means the amount determined in accordance with § 301.6227-2 or § 301.6227-3(c).

(4) *Indirect partner.*—The term *indirect partner* means any person who has an interest in a partnership through their interest in one or more pass-through partners (as defined in paragraph (a)(5) of this section) or through a wholly-owned entity disregarded as separate from its owner for Federal income tax purposes.

(5) *Pass-through partner.*—The term *pass-through partner* means a pass-through entity that holds an interest in a partnership. A pass-through entity is a partnership required to file a return under section 6031(a), an S corporation, a trust (other than a wholly-owned trust disregarded as separate from its owner for Federal income tax purposes), and a decedent's estate. For purposes of this paragraph (a)(5), a pass-through entity is not a wholly-owned entity disregarded as separate from its owner for Federal income tax purposes.

(6) *Partnership adjustment.*—(i) *In general.*—The term *partnership adjustment* means any adjustment to a partnership-related item and includes any portion of an adjustment to a partnership-related item.

(ii) *Partnership-related item.*—The term *partnership-related item* means—

(A) Any item or amount with respect to the partnership (as defined in paragraph (a)(6)(iii) of this section) which is relevant in determining the tax liability of any person under chapter 1 of the Code (chapter 1) (as defined in paragraph (a)(6)(iv) of this section);

(B) Any partner's distributive share of any such item or amount; and

(C) Any imputed underpayment determined under subchapter C of chapter 63 of the Code (subchapter C of chapter 63).

(iii) *Item or amount with respect to the partnership.*—For purposes of paragraph (a)(6)(ii) of this section, an item or amount is with respect to the partnership if the item or amount is shown or reflected, or required to be shown or reflected, on a return of the partnership under section 6031 or the forms and instructions prescribed by the Internal Revenue Service (IRS) for the partnership's taxable year or is required to be maintained in the partnership's books or records. Items or amounts relating to any transaction with, liability of, or basis in the partnership are with respect to the partnership only if those items or amounts are described in the preceding sentence. An

item or amount shown or required to be shown on a return of a person other than the partnership (or in that person's books and records) that results after application of the Code to a partnership-related item based upon the person's specific facts and circumstances, including an incorrect application of the Code or taking into account erroneous facts and circumstances of the partner, is not an item or amount with respect to the partnership. For instance, a deduction shown on the return of a partner that results after applying a limitation under the Code (such as section 170(b)) at the partner level to a partnership-related item based on the partner's facts and circumstances is not an item or amount with respect to the partnership, even though the corresponding expense on the return of the partnership is an item or amount with respect to the partnership. Likewise, an amount on the return of a partner that is after either an incorrect application of a limitation under the Code or based on facts and circumstances of the partner that are erroneous, or both (such as an incorrect application of section 170(b)) at the partner level to a partnership-related item is not an item or amount with respect to the partnership. Similarly, a partner's adjusted basis is not with respect to the partnership because it is an item or amount shown in the partner's books or records that results after application of the Code to partnership-related items taking into account the facts and circumstances specific to that partner.

(iv) *Relevant in determining the tax liability of any person under chapter 1.*—For purposes of this section, an item or amount with respect to the partnership is relevant in determining the tax liability of any person under chapter 1 without regard to the application of subchapter C of chapter 63 and without regard to whether such item or amount, or an adjustment to such item or amount, has an effect on the tax liability of any particular person under chapter 1.

(v) *Examples of partnership-related items.*—The term partnership-related item includes—

(A) The character, timing, source, and amount of the partnership's income, gain, loss, deductions, and credits;

(B) The character, timing, and source of the partnership's activities;

(C) The character, timing, source, value, and amount of any contributions to, and distributions from, the partnership;

(D) The partnership's basis in its assets, the character and type of the assets, and the value (or revaluation such as under § 1.704-1(b)(2)(iv)(f) or (s) of this chapter) of the assets;

(E) The amount and character of partnership liabilities and any changes to those liabilities from the preceding tax year;

(F) The category, timing, and amount of the partnership's creditable expenditures;

(G) Any item or amount resulting from a partnership termination;

(H) Any item or amount of the partnership resulting from an election under section 754;

(I) Partnership allocations and any special allocations; and

(J) The identity of a person as a partner in the partnership.

(vi) *Examples.*—The following examples illustrate the provisions of this section. For purposes of these examples, Partnership is subject to the provisions of subchapter C of chapter 63 and all taxpayers are calendar year taxpayers.

(A) *Example 1.* Partnership enters into a transaction with A to purchase widgets for $100 in taxable year 2020. Partnership pays A $100 for the widgets. Any deduction or expense of the Partnership for the purchase of the widgets is an item or amount with respect to Partnership because it is shown on Partnership's return and is relevant to determining the liability of any person under chapter 1 pursuant to paragraphs (a)(6)(iii) and (iv) of this section. Therefore, the deduction or expense is a partnership-related item. However, the income to A resulting from the transaction with Partnership is not an item or amount with respect to Partnership under paragraph (a)(6)(iii) of this section because although the amount of income relates to a transaction with Partnership and Partnership is required to show a deduction or expense related to the payment to A, the amount of income to A is not shown or required to be shown on Partnership's return. It is only required to be shown of the return of A, a person other than Partnership and requires determinations about A's reporting of the item. Accordingly, the amount of income shown, or required to be shown, by A on his return is not a partnership-related item.

(B) *Example 2.* B loans Partnership $100 in Partnership's 2020 taxable year. Partnership makes an interest payment to B in 2020 of $5. Partnership's liability relating to the loan by B to Partnership and the $5 of interest expense paid by the Partnership are items or amounts that are with respect to Partnership because they were shown on Partnership's return and are relevant in determining the liability of any person under chapter 1 pursuant to paragraphs (a)(6)(iii) and (iv) of this section. However, the treatment of the loan by B and the amount of interest income received by B are not items or amounts with respect to Partnership under paragraph (a)(6)(iii) of this section because although they relate to a transaction with or liability of Partnership and Partnership's treatment of the loan is shown on Partnership's return, B's treatment of the loan and the amount of interest income to B are shown, or required to be shown, on the return of B, a person other than Partnership and require determinations about B's reporting of the items. Accordingly, the loan as treated by B and the amount of interest income to B is not a partnership-related item.

(C) *Example 3.* On its partnership return for the 2020 tax year, Partnership reported $200 of non-cash charitable contributions related to its contribution of merchandise. Partnership has two equal partners for the 2020 tax year: C and D, both individuals. Partnership correctly reports $100 in non-cash charitable contributions to both C and D for the 2020 taxable year. On her return for the 2020 taxable year, C erroneously deducts the entire $100 of non-cash charitable contributions, even though C's deduction for charitable contributions would be limited by section 170(b)(1)(A) to $50 because of C's income. The $100 of non-cash charitable contribution reported by Partnership to C is a partnership-related item. However, the amount of the deduction taken by C on her return for 2020 and the amount of that deduction allowed after application of the limitation contained in section 170(b)(1)(A) to the $100 in non-cash charitable contributions reported by Partnership to C is not a partnership-related item under paragraph (a)(6)(ii) of this section because it is not with respect to the partnership.

(D) *Example 4.* The facts are the same as in *Example 3* in paragraph (a)(6)(vi)(C) of this section. On his return for the 2020 taxable year, D also deducts the entire $100 in charitable contributions but treats the charitable contributions as if they were cash contributions, instead of non-cash contributions. D does not file a notice of inconsistent treatment under section 6222. If D had treated the $100 in charitable contributions as non-cash contributions, D's deduction for the charitable contributions from Partnership would have be limited by section 170(b)(1)(A) due to D's income. D's deduction of the $100 in charitable contributions is an item or amount shown on D's return, derives from the charitable contributions reported by the partnership, and is subject to the application of the limitation under section 170(b)(1)(A). Therefore, D's deduction is not an item or amount with respect to the partnership. The charitable contribution reported by the partnership and its character are items or amounts with respect to the partnership pursuant to paragraph (a)(6)(iii) of this section. An adjustment to the character of the contributions is a partnership adjustment. Because D's treatment of the charitable contributions is inconsistent with the treatment of that item by Partnership on its partnership return, the IRS may make that partnership adjustment in a proceeding with respect to D and determine and assess any underpayment that results from conforming D's treatment to the treatment of the contributions by Partnership and applying the limit in section 170(b)(1)(A). See § 301.6222-1(b).

(7) *Partnership-partner.*—The term *partnership-partner* means a partnership that holds an interest in another partnership.

(8) *Reviewed year.*—The term *reviewed year* means the partnership taxable year to which a partnership adjustment relates.

(9) *Reviewed year partner.*—The term *reviewed year partner* means any person who held an interest in a partnership at any time during the reviewed year.

(10) *Tax attribute.*—A tax attribute is anything that can affect the amount or timing of a partnership-related item (as defined in paragraph (a)(6)(ii) of this section) or that can affect the amount of tax due in any taxable year. Examples of tax attributes include, but are not limited to, basis and holding period, as well as the character of items of income, gain, loss, deduction, or credit and carryovers and carrybacks of such items.

(b) *Applicability date.*—(1) *In general.*—Except as provided in paragraph (b)(2) of this section, this section applies to partnership taxable

years beginning after December 31, 2017, and ending after August 12, 2018.

(2) *Election under § 301.9100-22 in effect.*—This section applies to any partnership taxable year beginning after November 2, 2015, and before January 1, 2018, for which a valid election under § 301.9100-22 is in effect. [Reg. § 301.6241-1.]

☐ [T.D. 9844, 2-21-2019.]

### [Reg. § 301.6241-2]

**§ 301.6241-2. Bankruptcy of the partnership.**—(a) *Coordination between Title 11 and proceedings under subchapter C of chapter 63.*—(1) *In general.*—If a partnership is a debtor in a case under Title 11 of the United States Code (Title 11 case), the running of any period of limitations under section 6235 with respect to the time for making a partnership adjustment (as defined in § 301.6241-1(a)(6)) and under sections 6501 and 6502 with respect to the assessment or collection of any imputed underpayment (as defined in § 301.6241-1(a)(3)) determined under subchapter C of chapter 63 of the Internal Revenue Code (subchapter C of chapter 63) is suspended during the period the Internal Revenue Service (IRS) is prohibited by reason of the Title 11 case from making the adjustment, assessment, or collection until–

(i) 60 days after the suspension ends, for adjustments or assessments; and

(ii) 6 months after the suspension ends, for collection.

(2) *Interaction with section 6232(b).*—The filing of a proof of claim or request for payment (or the taking of any other action) in a Title 11 case is not be treated as an action prohibited by section 6232(b) (regarding limitations on assessment).

(3) *Suspension of the time for judicial review.*—In a Title 11 case, the running of the period specified in section 6234 (regarding judicial review of partnership adjustments) is suspended during the period during which the partnership is prohibited by reason of the Title 11 case from filing a petition under section 6234, and for 60 days thereafter.

(4) *Actions not prohibited.*—The filing of a petition under Title 11 does not prohibit the following actions:

(i) An administrative proceeding with respect to a partnership under subchapter C of chapter 63;

(ii) The mailing of any notice with respect to a proceeding with respect to a partnership under subchapter C of chapter 63, including:

(A) A notice of administrative proceeding;

(B) A notice of proposed partnership adjustment; and

(C) A notice of final partnership adjustment;

(iii) A demand for tax returns;

(iv) The assessment of any tax, including the assessment of any imputed underpayment with respect to a partnership; and

(v) The issuance of notice and demand for payment of an assessment under subchapter C of chapter 63 (but see section 362(b)(9)(D) of Title 11 of the United States Code regarding the timing of when a tax lien takes effect by reason of such assessment).

(b) *Applicability date.*—(1) *In general.*—Except as provided in paragraph (b)(2) of this section, this section applies to partnership taxable years beginning after December 31, 2017, and ending after August 12, 2018.

(2) *Election under § 301.9100-22 in effect.*—This section applies to any partnership taxable year beginning after November 2, 2015, and before January 1, 2018, for which a valid election under § 301.9100-22 is in effect. [Reg. § 301.6241-2.]

☐ [T.D. 9844, 2-21-2019.]

### [Reg. § 301.6241-3]

**§ 301.6241-3. Treatment where a partnership ceases to exist.**—(a) *Former partners take adjustments into account.*—(1) *In general.*—If the Internal Revenue Service (IRS) determines that any partnership (including a partnership-partner as defined in § 301.6241-1(a)(7)) ceases to exist (as defined in paragraph (b) of this section) before any partnership adjustment (as defined in § 301.6241-1(a)(6)) under subchapter C of chapter 63 of the Internal Revenue Code (subchapter C of chapter 63) takes effect (as described in paragraph (c) of this section), the partnership adjustment is taken into account by the former partners (as described in paragraph (d) of this section) of the partnership in accordance with paragraph (e) of this section.

(2) *Partnership no longer liable for any unpaid amounts resulting from a partnership adjustment.*—A partnership that ceases to exist is no longer liable for any unpaid amounts resulting from a partnership adjustment required to be taken into account by a former partner under this section.

(3) *Application of this section to partnership-partners.*—This section applies to a partnership-partner and its former partners, regardless of whether the partnership-partner has an election under section 6221(b) in effect for any relevant partnership taxable year.

(b) *Cease to exist defined.*—(1) *In general.*—If a partnership ceases to exist, the IRS will notify the partnership and the former partners (as defined in paragraph (d) of this section), in writing, within 30 days of such determination using the last known address of the partnership and the former partners. A failure by the IRS to send a notification under this paragraph (b)(1) to a former partner of the partnership does not invalidate the determination by the IRS that the partnership ceases to exist. If an audited partnership (as defined in § 301.6226-3(e)(1)) ceases to exist, the IRS will also notify the partnership representative for the reviewed year. For purposes of this section, a partnership ceases to exist if the IRS makes a determination that a partnership ceases to exist because:

(i) The partnership terminates within the meaning of section 708(b)(1); or

(ii) The partnership does not have the ability to pay, in full, any amount due under the provisions of subchapter C of chapter 63 for which the partnership is or becomes liable. For purposes of this section, a partnership does not have the ability to pay if the IRS determines that the amount due with respect to the partnership is not collectible based on the information the IRS has at the time of such determination.

(2) *Exceptions.*—For purposes of this section, the IRS will not determine that a partnership ceases to exist solely because the partnership has –

(i) A valid election under section 6226 in effect with respect to any imputed underpayment (as defined in § 301.6241-1(a)(3));

(ii) Received a statement under section 6226(a)(2) (or § 301.6226-3(e)) and has furnished statements to its partners in accordance with § 301.6226-3(e)(3); or

(iii) Not paid any amount required to be paid under subchapter C of chapter 63.

(3) *Year in which a partnership ceases to exist.*—If a partnership terminates under section 708(b)(1), the partnership ceases to exist on the last day of the partnership's final taxable year. If a partnership does not have the ability to pay, the partnership ceases to exist on the date that the IRS makes a determination under paragraph (b)(1) of this section that the partnership ceases to exist.

(4) *Limitation on IRS determination that partnership ceases to exist.*—In no event may the IRS determine that a partnership ceases to exist with respect to a partnership adjustment after the expiration of the period of limitations on collection applicable to the assessment made against the partnership for the amount due resulting from such adjustment.

(c) *Partnership adjustment takes effect.*—(1) *Full payment of amounts resulting from a partnership adjustment.*—For purposes of this section, a partnership adjustment under subchapter C of chapter 63 takes effect when there is full payment of amounts resulting from a partnership adjustment. For purposes of this section, *full payment of amounts resulting from a partnership adjustment* means all amounts due under subchapter C of chapter 63 resulting from the partnership adjustment are fully paid by the partnership.

(2) *Partial payment of amount due by the partnership.*—If a partnership pays part, but not all, of any amount due resulting from a partnership adjustment before the partnership ceases to exist, the former partners (as defined in paragraph (d) of this section) of the partnership that has ceased to exist are not required to take into account any partnership adjustment to the extent amounts have been paid by the partnership with respect to such adjustment. The notification that the IRS has determined that the partnership has ceased to exist will include information regarding the portion of the partnership adjustments with respect to which appropriate amounts have not already been paid by the partnership and therefore must be taken into account by the former partners (described in paragraph (d) of this section) in accordance with paragraph (e) of this section.

(d) *Former partners.*—(1) *Adjustment year partners.*—(i) *In general.*—Except as described in paragraphs (d)(1)(ii) and (d)(2) of this section, the term *former partners* means, for a partnership that has ceased to exist, the partners of the partnership during the adjustment year (as defined in § 301.6241-1(a)(1)) that corresponds to the reviewed year for which the adjustments were made.

(ii) *Partnership-partner ceases to exist.*—If the adjustment year partner is a partnership-partner that the IRS has determined ceased to exist, the partners of such partnership-partner during the partnership-partner's taxable year that includes the end of the adjustment year of the partnership that is subject to a proceeding under subchapter C of chapter 63 are the former partners for purposes of this section. If the partnership-partner ceased to exist before the partnership-partner's taxable year that includes the end of the adjustment year of the partnership that is subject to a proceeding under subchapter C of chapter 63, the former partners for purposes of this section are the partners of such partnership-partner during the last partnership taxable year for which the a partnership return of the partnership-partner under section 6031 is filed.

(2) *No adjustment year partners.*—If there are no adjustment year partners of a partnership that ceases to exist, the term *former partners* means the partners of the partnership during the last taxable year for which a partnership return under section 6031 was filed with respect to such partnership. For instance, if a partnership terminates under section 708(b)(1) before the adjustment year and files a final partnership return for the partnership taxable year of such partnership, the former partners for purposes of this section are the partners of the partnership during the partnership taxable year for which a final partnership return is filed.

(e) *Taking adjustments into account.*—(1) *In general.*—For purposes of paragraph (a) of this section, a former partner of a partnership that ceases to exist takes a partnership adjustment into account as if the partnership had made an election under section 6226 (regarding the alternative to payment of the imputed underpayment). A former partner must take into account the former partner's share of a partnership adjustment as set forth in the statement described in paragraph (e)(2) of this section in accordance with § 301.6226-3.

(2) *Statements furnished to former partners.*—If a partnership is notified by the IRS that the partnership has ceased to exist as described in paragraph (b)(1) of this section, the partnership must furnish to each former partner a statement reflecting such former partner's share of the partnership adjustment required to be taken into account under this section and file a copy of such statement with the IRS in accordance with the rules under § 301.6226-2, except that –

(i) The adjustments are taken into account by the applicable former partner (as described in paragraph (d) of this section), rather than the reviewed year partners (as defined in § 301.6241-1(a)(9)); and

(ii) The partnership must furnish statements to the former partners and file the statements with the IRS no later than 30 days after the date of the notification to the partnership that the IRS has determined that the partnership has ceased to exist.

(3) *Authority to issue statements.*—If any statements required by paragraph (e) of this section are not timely furnished to a former partner and filed with the IRS in accordance with paragraph (e)(2)(ii) of this section, the IRS may notify the former partner in writing of such partner's share of the partnership adjustments based on the information reasonably available to the IRS at the time such notification is provided. For purposes of paragraph (e) of this section, a notification to a former partner under this paragraph (e)(3) is treated the same as a statement required to be furnished and filed under paragraph (e)(2) of this section.

(f) *Examples.*—The following examples illustrate the provisions of this section. For purposes of the examples, all partnerships and partners are calendar year taxpayers and each partnership is subject to the provisions of subchapter C of chapter 63 of the Code (unless otherwise stated).

(1) *Example 1.* The IRS initiates a proceeding under subchapter C of chapter 63 with respect to the 2020 partnership taxable year of Partnership. During 2023, in accordance with section 6235(b), Partnership extends the period of limitations on adjustments under section 6235(a) until December 31, 2025. On February 1, 2025, the IRS mails Partnership a notice of final partnership adjustment (FPA) that determines partnership adjustments that result in a single imputed underpayment. Partnership does not timely file a petition under section 6234 and does not make a valid election under section 6226. On June 2, 2025, the IRS mails Partnership notice and demand for payment of the amount due resulting from the adjustments determined in the FPA. Partnership fails to make a payment. On September 1, 2029, the IRS determines Partnership ceases to exist for purposes of this section because the Partnership does not have the ability to pay under paragraph (b)(1)(ii) of this section. Under § 301.6241-1(a)(1), the adjustment year is 2025 and A and B, both individuals, are the only adjustment year partners of Partnership during 2025. Accordingly, under paragraph (d)(1) of this section, A and B are former partners. Therefore, A and B are required to take their share of the partnership adjustments determined in the FPA into account under paragraph (e) of this section.

(2) *Example 2.* The IRS initiates a proceeding under subchapter C of chapter 63 with respect to the 2020 partnership taxable year of P, a partnership. G, a partnership that has an election under section 6221(b) in effect for the 2020 taxable year, is a partner of P during

2020 and for every year thereafter. On February 3, 2025, the IRS mails P an FPA that determines partnership adjustments that result in a single imputed underpayment. P does not timely file a petition under section 6234 and does not make a timely election under section 6226. On May 6, 2025, the IRS mails P notice and demand for payment of the amount due resulting from the adjustments determined in the FPA. P does not make a payment. On September 1, 2025, the IRS determines P ceases to exist for purposes of this section because P does not have the ability to pay under paragraph (b)(1)(ii) of this section. G terminated under section 708(b)(1) on December 31, 2024. On September 1, 2025, the IRS determines that G ceased to exist in 2024 for purposes of this section in accordance with paragraph (b)(1)(i) of this section. J and K, individuals, were the only partners of G during 2024. Therefore, under paragraph (d)(1)(ii) of this section, J and K, the partners of G during G's 2024 partnership taxable year, are the former partners of G for purposes of this section. Therefore, J and K are required to take into account their share of the adjustments contained in the statement furnished by P to G in accordance with paragraph (e) of this section.

(g) *Applicability date.*—(1) *In general.*—Except as provided in paragraph (g)(2) of this section, this section applies to partnership taxable years beginning after December 31, 2017, and ending after August 12, 2018.

(2) *Election under § 301.9100-22 in effect.*—This section applies to any partnership taxable year beginning after November 2, 2015, and before January 1, 2018, for which a valid election under § 301.9100-22 is in effect. [Reg. § 301.6241-3.]

☐ [T.D. 9844, 2-21-2019.]

**[Reg. § 301.6241-4]**

**§ 301.6241-4. Payments nondeductible.**—(a) *Payments nondeductible.*—No deduction is allowed under subtitle A of the Internal Revenue Code (Code) for any payment required to be made by a partnership under subchapter C of chapter 63 of the Code (subchapter C of chapter 63). Payment by a partnership of any amount required to be paid under subchapter C of chapter 63, including any imputed underpayment (as defined in § 301.6241-1(a)(3)), or interest, penalties, additions to tax, or additional amounts with respect to an imputed underpayment, is treated as an expenditure described in section 705(a)(2)(B).

(b) *Applicability date.*—(1) *In general.*—Except as provided in paragraph (b)(2) of this section, this section applies to partnership taxable years beginning after December 31, 2017, and ending after August 12, 2018.

(2) *Election under § 301.9100-22 in effect.*—This section applies to any partnership taxable year beginning after November 2, 2015, and before January 1, 2018, for which a valid election under § 301.9100-22 is in effect. [Reg. § 301.6241-4.]

☐ [T.D. 9844, 2-21-2019.]

**[Reg. § 301.6241-5]**

**§ 301.6241-5. Extension to entities filing partnership returns.**—(a) *Entities filing a partnership return.*—Except as described in paragraph (c) of this section, an entity that files a partnership return for any taxable year is subject to the provisions of subchapter C of chapter 63 of the Internal Revenue Code (subchapter C of chapter 63) with respect to such taxable year even if it is determined that the entity filing the partnership return was not a partnership for such taxable year. Accordingly, any partnership-related item (as defined in § 301.6241-1(a)(6)(ii)) and any person holding an interest in the entity, either directly or indirectly, at any time during that taxable year are subject to the provisions of subchapter C of chapter 63 for such taxable year.

(b) *Partnership return filed but no entity found to exist.*—Paragraph (a) of this section also applies where a partnership return is filed for a taxable year, but the IRS determines that no entity existed at all for such taxable year. For purposes of applying paragraph (a) of this section, the partnership return is treated as if it were filed by an entity.

(c) *Exceptions.*—Paragraph (a) of this section does not apply to –

(1) Any taxable year for which an election under section 6221(b) is in effect, treating the return as if it were filed by a partnership for the taxable year to which the election relates; and

(2) Any taxable year for which a valid section 761(a) election is made (regarding election out of subchapter K of chapter 1 of the Internal Revenue Code for certain unincorporated organizations).

(d) *Applicability date.*—(1) *In general.*—Except as provided in paragraph (d)(2) of this section, this section applies to partnership taxable

years beginning after December 31, 2017, and ending after August 12, 2018.

(2) *Election under § 301.9100-22 in effect.*—This section applies to any partnership taxable year beginning after November 2, 2015, and before January 1, 2018, for which a valid election under § 301.9100-22 is in effect. [Reg. § 301.6241-5.]

☐ [T.D. 9844, 2-21-2019.]

**[Reg. § 301.6241-6]**

**§ 301.6241-6. Coordination with other chapters of the Internal Revenue Code.**—(a) *Coordination with other chapters.*—(1) *In general.*—Subchapter C of chapter 63 of the Internal Revenue Code (subchapter C of chapter 63) only applies to tax imposed by chapter 1 of the Internal Revenue Code (Code) and not to any tax imposed (including any amount required to be deducted or withheld) under any chapter of the Code other than chapter 1 of the Code (chapter 1), including chapter 2, 2A, 3, or 4 of the Code. Accordingly, for purposes of determining taxes imposed under chapters of the Code other than chapter 1, the Internal Revenue Service (IRS) may make an adjustment to any partnership-related item (as defined in § 301.6241-1(a)(6)(ii)) in a proceeding that is not under subchapter C of chapter 63. To the extent an adjustment or determination is made under subchapter C of chapter 63 for purposes of chapter 1 and is relevant in determining tax imposed under a chapter of the Code other than chapter 1, such adjustment or determination must be taken into account for purposes of determining such tax.

(2) *Examples.*—The following examples illustrate the rules of paragraph (a) of this section as applied to cases in which a partnership has a withholding obligation under chapter 3 or chapter 4 with respect to income that the partnership earns. For purposes of these examples, each partnership is subject to the provisions of subchapter C of chapter 63 of the Code, and the partnership and its partners are calendar year taxpayers.

(i) *Example 1.* Partnership, a partnership created or organized in the United States, has two equal partners, A and B. A is a nonresident alien who is a resident of Country A, and B is a U.S. citizen. In 2018, Partnership earned $200 of U.S. source royalty income. Partnership was required to withhold 30 percent of the gross amount of the royalty income allocable to A unless Partnership had documentation that it could rely on to establish that A was entitled to a reduced rate of withholding. See §§ 1.1441-1(b)(1) and 1.1441-5(b)(2)(i)(A) of this chapter. Partnership withheld $15 from the $100 of royalty income allocable to A based on its incorrect belief that A is entitled to a reduced rate of withholding under the U.S.-Country A Income Tax Treaty. In 2020, the IRS determines in an examination of Partnership's Form 1042, Annual Withholding Tax Return for U.S. Source Income of Foreign Persons, that Partnership should have withheld $30 instead of $15 on the $100 of royalty income allocable to A because Partnership failed to obtain documentation from A establishing a valid treaty claim for a reduced rate of withholding. The tax imposed on Partnership for its failure to withhold on that income, however, is not a tax imposed by chapter 1. Rather, it is a tax imposed by chapter 3, which is not a partnership-related item under § 301.6241-1(a)(6)(ii). Therefore, in accordance with section 6221(a), the adjustment to increase Partnership's withholding tax liability by $15 is not determined under subchapter C of chapter 63, and instead must be determined as part of the Form 1042 examination.

(ii) *Example 2.* Partnership, a partnership created or organized in the United States, has two equal partners, A and B. A is a nonresident alien who is a resident of Country A, and B is a U.S. citizen. In 2018, Partnership earned $100 of U.S. source dividend income. Partnership was required to report the dividend income on its 2018 Form 1065, U.S. Return of Partnership Income, and withhold 30 percent of the gross amount of the dividend income allocable to A unless Partnership had documentation that it could rely on to establish that A was entitled to a reduced rate of withholding. See §§ 1.1441-1(b)(1) and 1.1441-5(b)(2)(i)(A) of this chapter. In 2020, in an examination of Partnership's Form 1042, the IRS determines that Partnership earned but failed to report the $100 of U.S. source dividend income in 2018. The adjustment to increase Partnership's dividend income by $100 is an adjustment to a partnership-related item. The tax imposed on Partnership for its failure to withhold on that income, however, is not a tax imposed by chapter 1; rather, it is a tax imposed by chapter 3. Pursuant to § 301.6221(a)-1(a), only chapter 1 tax attributable to adjustments to partnership-related items is assessed under subchapter C of chapter 63. Therefore, because the tax imposed with respect to the adjustment is a chapter 3 tax, under paragraph (a)(1) of this section, the IRS may determine, assess, and collect chapter 3 tax attributable to an adjustment to a partnership-related item without conducting a proceeding under subchapter C of chapter 63. Accordingly, the IRS may determine the chapter 3 tax in the examination of Partnership's Form 1042 by adjusting Partnership's withholding tax liability by an additional $15 for failing to withhold on the $50 of dividend income allocable to A. However, the IRS must initiate an administrative proceeding under subchapter C of chapter 63 to make any adjustments for purposes of chapter 1 attributable to the income. If the IRS subsequently initiates an administrative proceeding under subchapter C of chapter 63 and makes an adjustment to the same item of income, the portion of the dividend income allocable to A will be disregarded in the calculation of the total netted partnership adjustment to the extent that the chapter 3 tax has been collected with respect to such income. See § 301.6225-1(b)(3).

(b) *Coordination with chapters 3 and 4.*—(1) *In general.*—In the case of any tax imposed under chapter 3 or chapter 4 that is determined with respect to a partnership adjustment determined under subchapter C of chapter 63 for purposes of chapter 1, such tax is determined with respect to the reviewed year (as defined in § 301.6241-1(a)(8)) and is imposed (or required to be deducted and withheld) with respect to the adjustment year (as defined in § 301.6241-1(a)(1)).

(2) *Definitions.*—The following definitions apply for purposes of this paragraph (b) and the regulations under subchapter C of chapter 63.

(i) *Amount subject to withholding.*—The term *amount subject to withholding* means an amount subject to withholding (as defined in § 1.1441-2(a) of this chapter), a withholdable payment (as defined in § 1.1473-1(a) of this chapter), or the allocable share of effectively connected taxable income (as computed under § 1.1446-2(b) of this chapter).

(ii) *Chapter 3.*—The term *chapter 3* means sections 1441 through 1464 of the Code, but does not include section 1443(b) of the Code.

(iii) *Chapter 4.*—The term *chapter 4* means sections 1471 through 1474 of the Code.

(3) *Partnership pays an imputed underpayment.*—If a partnership pays an imputed underpayment (as determined under § 301.6225-1(b)) and the total netted partnership adjustment (as calculated under § 301.6225-1(b)(2)) includes a partnership adjustment to an amount subject to withholding, the partnership is treated as having paid (at the time that the imputed underpayment is paid) the amount required to be withheld with respect to that partnership adjustment under chapter 3 or chapter 4 for purposes of applying § § 1.1463-1 and 1.1474-4 of this chapter. See § 301.6225-1(b)(3) for the coordination rule that applies for calculating an imputed underpayment when an adjustment is made to an amount subject to withholding for which tax has been collected under chapter 3 or chapter 4.

(4) *Partnership makes an election under section 6226 with respect to an imputed underpayment.*—(i) *In general.*—A partnership that makes an election under § 301.6226-1 with respect to an imputed underpayment must pay the amount of tax required to be withheld under chapter 3 or chapter 4 on the amount of any adjustment set forth in the statement described in § 301.6226-2(a) to the extent that it is an adjustment to an amount subject to withholding, and the IRS has not already collected tax attributable to the adjustment under chapter 3 or chapter 4. The partnership must pay the amount due under this paragraph (b)(4)(i) on or before the due date of the partnership return for the adjustment year (without regard to extension), and must make the payment in the manner prescribed by the IRS in forms, instructions, and other guidance. For the rules governing partners subject to the taxes imposed by chapters 3 and 4 when the partner receives a statement under § 301.6226-2, see § 301.6226-3(f). See § 301.6226-3(e)(3)(v) for the application of the rules of this paragraph (b)(4) to pass-through partners (as defined in § 301.6241-1(a)(5)).

(ii) *Reduced rate of tax.*—A partnership may reduce the amount of tax it is required to pay under paragraph (b)(4)(i) of this section to the extent that it can associate valid documentation from a reviewed year partner pursuant to the regulations under chapter 3 or chapter 4 (other than pursuant to § 1.1446-6 of this chapter) with the portion of the adjustment that would have been subject to a reduced rate of tax in the reviewed year. For this purpose, the partnership may rely on documentation that the partnership possesses that is valid with respect to the reviewed year (determined without regard to the expiration after the reviewed year of any validity period prescribed in § 1.1441-1(e)(4)(ii), § 1.1446-1(c)(2)(iv)(A), or § 1.1471-3(c)(6)(ii) of this chapter), or new documentation that the partnership obtains from the reviewed year partner that includes a signed affidavit stating that the information and representations associated with the documentation are accurate with respect to the reviewed year.

(iii) *Reporting requirements.*—A partnership required to pay tax under paragraph (b)(4)(i) of this section must file the appropriate return and issue information returns as required by regulations under chapter 3 or chapter 4. For return and information return requirements, see § § 1.1446-3(d)(1)(iii); 1.1461-1(b), (c); and 1.1474-1(c), (d) of this chapter. The partnership must file the return and issue information returns for the year that includes the date on which the partnership pays the tax required to be withheld under paragraph (b)(4)(i) of this section. The partnership must report the information on the return and information returns in the manner prescribed by the IRS in forms, instructions, and other guidance.

(iv) *Partners subject to withholding.*—A reviewed year partner that is subject to withholding under paragraph (b)(4)(i) of this section must follow the rules under § 301.6226-3(f).

(c) *Applicability date.*—(1) *In general.*—Except as provided in paragraph (c)(2) of this section, this section applies to partnership taxable years beginning after December 31, 2017, and ending after August 12, 2018.

(2) *Election under § 301.9100-22 in effect.*—This section applies to any partnership taxable year beginning after November 2, 2015, and before January 1, 2018, for which a valid election under § 301.9100-22 is in effect. [Reg. § 301.6241-6.]

☐ [T.D. 9844, 2-21-2019.]

# Collection

# GENERAL PROVISIONS

See p. 20,601 for regulations not amended to reflect law changes

### [Reg. § 301.6301-1]

**§ 301.6301-1. Collection authority.**—The taxes imposed by the internal revenue laes shall be collected by district directors of internal revenue. See, however, section 6304, relating to the collection of certain taxes under the provisions of the Tariff Act of 1930. [Reg. § 301.6301-1.]

☐ [T.D. 6119, 12-31-54. *Amended by T.D. 6498, 10-24-60.*]

### [Reg. § 31.6302-0]

**§ 31.6302-0. Table of contents.**—This section lists the table of contents for § § 31.6302-1 through 31.6302-4.

(2) Shortfall defined.

(3) Shortfall make-up date.

　(i) Monthly rule.

　(ii) Semi-Weekly and One-Day rule.

(4) De minimis rule.

　(i) De minimis deposit rules for quarterly and annual return periods beginning on or after January 1, 2001.

　(ii) De minimis deposit rule for quarterly return periods beginning on or after January 1, 2010

　(iii) De minimis deposit rule for employers who file Form 944.

(5) Examples.

(g) Agricultural employers—Special rules.

(1) In general.

(2) Monthly depositor.

(3) Semi-weekly depositor.

(4) Lookback period.

　(i) In general.

　(ii) Adjustments and Claims for Refund.

(5) Example.

(h) Time and manner of deposit—deposits required to be made by electronic funds transfer.

(1) In general.

(2) Applicability of requirement.

　(i) Deposits for return periods beginning before January 1, 2000.

　(ii) Deposits for return periods beginning after December 31, 1999, and made before January 1, 2011.

　(iii) Deposits made after December 31, 2010.

　(iv) Voluntary deposits.

(3) Taxes required to be deposited by electronic funds transfer.

(4) Definitions.

　(i) Electronic funds transfer.

　(ii) Taxpayer.

(5) Exemptions.

(6) Separation of deposits.

(7) Payment of balance due.

(8) Time deemed deposited.

(9) Time deemed paid.

(i) Time and manner of deposit.

(1) General rules.

(2) Payment of balance due.

(3) Time deemed paid.

(4) Procurement of FTD coupons.

(5) Time deemed deposited.

(6) Time deemed paid.

(j) Voluntary payments by electronic funds transfer.

(k) Special rules.

(1) Notice exception.

(2) Wages paid in nonconvertible foreign currency.

(l) [Reserved].

(m) Cross references.

(1) Failure to deposit penalty.

(2) Saturday, Sunday, or legal holiday.

(n) Effective/applicability dates.

(o) Effective/Applicability date.

*§31.6302-2. Deposit rules for taxes under the Railroad Retirement Tax Act (R.R.T.A.).*

(a) General rule.

(b) Separate application of deposit rules.

(c) Modification of Monthly rule determination.

(1) General rule.

(2) Exception.

(d) Effective/applicability date.

*§31.6302-3. Federal tax deposit rules for amounts withheld under the backup withholding requirements of Section 3406 for payments made after December 31, 1992.*

(a) General Rule.

(b) Treatment of backup withholding amounts separately.

(c) Example.

*§31.6302-4. Deposit rules for withheld income taxes attributable to nonpayroll taxes.*

[Reg. §31.6302-0.]

☐ [*T.D. 8436, 9-22-92. Amended by T.D. 9239, 12-30-2005; T.D. 9405, 6-30-2008; T.D. 9440, 12-24-2008; T.D. 9507, 12-2-2010 and T.D. 9566, 12-9-2011.*]

**Reg. §1.6302-1**

**[Reg. §1.6302-1]**

**§1.6302-1. Deposit rules for corporation income and estimated income taxes and certain taxes of tax-exempt organizations.—**
(a) *Requirement.*—A corporation, any organization subject to the tax imposed by section 511, and any private foundation subject to the tax imposed by section 4940, shall deposit all payments of tax imposed by chapter 1 of the Internal Revenue Code (or treated as so imposed by section 6154(h)), including any payments of estimated tax, on or before the date otherwise prescribed for paying such tax. This paragraph (a) does not apply to a foreign corporation or entity that has no office or place of business in the United States.

(b) *Deposits by electronic funds transfer.*—For the requirement to deposit corporation income and estimated income taxes and certain taxes of tax-exempt organizations by electronic funds transfer, see §31.6302-1(h) of this chapter. A taxpayer not required to deposit by electronic funds transfer pursuant to §31.6302-1(h) of this chapter remains subject to the rules of paragraph (b)(1) of this section.

(c) *Failure to deposit.*—For provisions relating to the penalty for failure to make a deposit within the prescribed time, see section 6656.

(d) *Effective/applicability date.*—This section applies to deposits and payments made after December 31, 2010. [Reg. §1.6302-1.]

☐ [*T.D. 6914, 3-7-67. Amended by T.D. 6941, 12-15-67; T.D. 7293, 11-27-73; T.D. 7953, 5-8-84; T.D. 8157, 9-4-87; T.D. 8723, 7-11-97; T.D. 8947, 6-14-2001; T.D. 8952, 6-25-2001; T.D. 9239, 12-30-2005 and T.D. 9507, 12-2-2010.*]

**[Reg. §20.6302-1]**

**§20.6302-1. Voluntary payments of estate taxes by electronic funds transfer.**—Any person may voluntarily remit by electronic funds transfer any payment of tax to which this part 20 applies. Such payment must be made in accordance with procedures prescribed by the Commissioner. [Reg. §20.6302-1.]

☐ [*T.D. 8828, 7-12-99.*]

**[Reg. §25.6302-1]**

**§25.6302-1. Voluntary payments of gift taxes by electronic funds transfer.**—Any person may voluntarily remit by electronic funds transfer any payment of tax to which this part 25 applies. Such payment must be made in accordance with procedures prescribed by the Commissioner. [Reg. §25.6302-1.]

☐ [*T.D. 8828, 7-12-99.*]

**[Reg. §31.6302-1]**

**§31.6302-1. Deposit rules for taxes under the Federal Insurance Contributions Act (FICA) and withheld income taxes.—**
(a) *Introduction.*—With respect to employment taxes attributable to payments made after December 31, 1992, an employer is either a monthly depositor or a semi-weekly depositor based on an annual determination. An employer must generally deposit employment taxes under one of two rules: the Monthly rule in paragraph (c)(1) of this section, or the Semi-Weekly rule in paragraph (c)(2) of this section. Various exceptions and safe harbors are provided. Paragraph (f) of this section provides certain safe harbors for employers who inadvertently fail to deposit the full amount of taxes. Paragraph (c)(3) of this section provides an overriding exception to the Monthly and Semi-Weekly rules where an employer has accumulated $100,000 or more of employment taxes. Paragraph (e) of this section provides the definition of employment taxes.

(b) *Determination of status.*—(1) *In general.*—The determination of whether an employer is a monthly or semi-weekly depositor for a calendar year is based on an annual determination and generally depends upon the aggregate amount of employment taxes reported by the employer for the lookback period as defined in paragraph (b)(4) of this section.

(2) *Monthly depositor.*—(i) *In general.*—An employer is a monthly depositor for the entire calendar year if the aggregate amount of employment taxes reported for the lookback period is $50,000 or less.

(ii) *Special rule.*—An employer ceases to be a monthly depositor on the first day after the employer is subject to the One-Day ($100,000) rule in paragraph (c)(3) of this section. At that time, the employer immediately becomes a semi-weekly depositor for the remainder of the calendar year and for the following calendar year.

(3) *Semi-weekly depositor.*—An employer is a semi-weekly depositor for the entire calendar year if the aggregate amount of employment taxes reported for the lookback period exceeds $50,000.

(4) *Lookback period.*—(i) *In general.*—For employers who file Form 941, "Employer's QUARTERLY Federal Tax Return," (or any

related Spanishlanguage returns or returns for U.S. possessions) the lookback period for each calendar year is the twelve month period ended the preceding June 30. For example, the lookback period for calendar year 2006 is the period July 1, 2004, to June 30, 2005. The lookback period for employers who file Form 944, "Employer's AN-NUAL Federal Tax Return," or filed Form 944 (or any related Spanish-language returns or returns for U.S. possessions) for either of the two previous calendar years, is the second calendar year preceding the current calendar year. For example, the lookback period for calendar year 2006 is calendar year 2004. In determining status as either a monthly or semi-weekly depositor, an employer should determine the aggregate amount of employment tax liabilities reported on its return(s) (Forms 941 or Form 944) for the lookback period. The amount of employment tax liabilities reported for the lookback period is the amount the employer reported on either Forms 941 or Form 944 even if the employer is required to file the other form for the current calendar year. New employers shall be treated as having employment tax liabilities of zero for any part of the lookback period before the date the employer started or acquired its business.

(ii) *Adjustments and claims for refund.*—The employment tax liability reported on the original return for the return period is the amount taken into account in determining whether the aggregate amount of employment taxes reported for the lookback period exceeds $50,000. Any amounts reported on adjusted returns or claims for refund pursuant to sections 6205, 6402, 6413, and 6414 filed after the due date of the original return are not taken into account when determining the aggregate amount of employment taxes reported for the lookback period. Prior period adjustments reported on Forms 941 or Form 944 for 2008 and earlier years are taken into account in determining the employment tax liability for the return period in which the adjustments are reported.

(c) *Deposit rules.*—(1) *Monthly rule.*—An employer that is a monthly depositor must deposit employment taxes accumulated with respect to payments made during a calendar month by electronic funds transfer by the 15th day of the following month. If the 15th day of the following month is a Saturday, Sunday, or legal holiday in the District of Columbia under section 7503, taxes will be treated as timely deposited if deposited on the next succeeding day which is not a Saturday, Sunday, or legal holiday.

(2) *Semi-Weekly rule.*—(i) *In general.*—An employer that is a semi-weekly depositor for a calendar year must deposit employment taxes by electronic funds transfer by the dates set forth below:

| Payment dates/semi-weekly periods | Deposit date |
| --- | --- |
| (A) Wednesday, Thursday and/or Friday | On or before the following Wednesday. |
| (B) Saturday, Sunday, Monday and/or Tuesday | On or before the following Friday. |

(ii) *Semi-weekly period spanning two return periods.*—If the return period ends during a semi-weekly period in which an employer has two or more payment dates, two deposit obligations may exist. For example, if one quarterly return period ends on Thursday and a new quarterly return period begins on Friday, employment taxes from payments on Wednesday and Thursday are subject to one deposit obligation, and employment taxes from payments on Friday are subject to a separate deposit obligation. Two separate federal tax deposits are required.

(iii) *Special rule for computing days.*—Semi-weekly depositors have at least three business days following the close of the semi-weekly period by which to deposit employment taxes accumulated during the semi-weekly period. Business days include every calendar day other than Saturdays, Sundays, or legal holidays in the District of Columbia under section 7503. If any of the three weekdays following the close of a semi-weekly period is a legal holiday, the employer has an additional day for each day that is a legal holiday by which to make the required deposit. For example, if the Monday following the close of a Wednesday to Friday semi-weekly period is Memorial Day, a legal holiday, the required deposit for the semi-weekly period is not due until the following Thursday rather than the following Wednesday.

(3) *Exception—One-Day rule.*—Notwithstanding paragraphs (c)(1) and (c)(2) of this section, if on any day within a deposit period (monthly or semi-weekly) an employer has accumulated $100,000 or more of employment taxes, those taxes must be deposited by electronic funds transfer in time to satisfy the tax obligation by the close of the next day. If the next day is a Saturday, Sunday, or legal holiday in the District of Columbia under section 7503, the taxes will be treated as timely deposited if deposited on the next succeeding day which is not a Saturday, Sunday, or legal holiday. For purposes of determining whether the $100,000 threshold is met—

(i) A monthly depositor takes into account only those employment taxes accumulated in the calendar month in which the day occurs; and

(ii) A semi-weekly depositor takes into account only those employment taxes accumulated in the Wednesday-Friday or Saturday-Tuesday semi-weekly period in which the day occurs.

(4) *Deposits required only on business days.*—No taxes are required to be deposited under this section on any day that is a Saturday, Sunday, or legal holiday. Deposits are required only on business days. Business days include every calendar day other than Saturdays, Sundays, or legal holidays. For purposes of this paragraph (c), legal holidays shall have the same meaning provided in section 7503. Pursuant to section 7503, the term *legal holiday* means a legal holiday in the District of Columbia. For purposes of this paragraph (c), the term "legal holiday" does not include other Statewide legal holidays.

(5) *Exception to the monthly and semi-weekly deposit rules for employers in the Employers' Annual Federal Tax Program (Form 944).*—Generally, an employer who files Form 944 for a taxable year may remit its accumulated employment taxes with its timely filed return for that taxable year and is not required to deposit under either the monthly or semi-weekly rules set forth in paragraphs (c)(1) and (c)(2) of this section during that taxable year. An employer who files Form

944 whose actual employment tax liability exceeds the eligibility threshold, as set forth in §§ 31.6011(a)-1(a)(5) and 31.6011(a)-4(a)(4), will not qualify for this exception and should follow the deposit rules set forth in this section.

(6) *Extension of time to deposit for employers in the Employers' Annual Federal Tax Program (Form 944) during the preceding year.*—An employer who filed Form 944 for the preceding year but will file Forms 941 instead for the current year will be deemed to have timely deposited its current year's January deposit obligation(s) under paragraphs (c)(1) through (c)(4) of this section if the employer deposits the amount of such deposit obligation(s) by March 15 of that year.

(7) *Exception to the monthly and semi-weekly deposit rules for employers making interest-free adjustments.*—An employer filing an adjusted return under § 31.6205-1 to report taxes that were accumulated in a prior return period shall pay the amount of the adjustment by the time it files the adjusted return, and the amount timely paid will be deemed to have been timely deposited by the employer. The payment may be made by a check or money order with the adjusted return, by electronic funds transfer, or by other methods of payment as provided by the instructions relating to the adjusted return.

(d) *Examples.*—The provisions of paragraphs (a), (b) and (c) of this section are illustrated by the following examples:

*Example 1. Monthly depositor.* (i) *Determination of status.* For calendar year 2011, Employer A determines its depositor status using the lookback period July 1, 2009 to June 30, 2010. For the four calendar quarters within this period, A reported aggregate employment tax liabilities of $42,000 on its quarterly Forms 941. Because the aggregate amount did not exceed $50,000, A is a monthly depositor for the entire calendar year 2011.

(ii) *Monthly rule.* During December 2011, A (a monthly depositor) accumulates $3,500 in employment taxes. A has a $3,500 deposit obligation that must be satisfied by the 15th day of the following month. Since January 15, 2012, is a Sunday, and January 16, 2012, Dr. Martin Luther King, Jr.'s Birthday, is a legal holiday, A's deposit obligation will be satisfied if the deposit is made by electronic funds transfer by the next business day, January 17, 2012.

*Example 2. Semi-weekly depositor.* (i) *Determination of status.* For the calendar year 2011, Employer B determines its depositor status using the lookback period July 1, 2009 to June 30, 2010. For the four calendar quarters within this period, B reported aggregate employment tax liabilities of $88,000 on its quarterly Forms 941. Because that amount exceeds $50,000, B is a semi-weekly depositor for the entire calendar year 2011.

(ii) *Semi-weekly rule.* On Friday, January 7, 2011, B (a semi-weekly depositor) has a pay day on which it accumulates $4,000 in employment taxes. B has a $4,000 deposit obligation that must be satisfied by the following Wednesday, January 12, 2011.

(iii) *Deposit made within three business days.* On Friday, January 14, 2011, B (a semi-weekly depositor) has a pay day on which it accumulates $4,200 in employment taxes. Generally, B would have a required deposit obligation of employment taxes that must be satisfied by the following Wednesday, January 19, 2011. Because Monday, January 17, 2011, is Dr. Martin Luther King, Jr.'s Birthday, a legal holiday, B has an additional day to make the required deposit. B has a $4,200 deposit obligation that must be satisfied by the following Thursday, January 20, 2011.

*Example 3. One-Day rule.* On Monday, January 10, 2011, Employer C accumulates $110,000 in employment taxes with respect to wages paid on that date. C has a deposit obligation of $110,000 that must be satisfied by the next business day. If C was not subject to the semi-weekly rule on January 10, 2011, C becomes subject to that rule as of January 11, 2011. See paragraph (b)(2)(ii) of this section.

*Example 4. One-Day rule in combination with subsequent deposit obligation.* Employer D is subject to the semiweekly rule for calendar year 2011. On Monday, January 10, 2011, D accumulates $115,000 in employment taxes. D has a deposit obligation that must be satisfied by the next business day. On Tuesday, January 11, D accumulates an additional $30,000 in employment taxes. Although D has a $115,000 deposit obligation incurred earlier in the semiweekly period, D has an additional and separate deposit obligation of $30,000 on Tuesday that must be satisfied by the following Friday.

*Example 5. Legal Holidays.* Employer E conducts business in State X. Wednesday, August 31, 2011, is a statewide legal holiday in State X which is not a legal holiday in the District of Columbia. On Friday, August 26, 2011, E (a semi-weekly depositor) has a pay day on which it accumulates $4,000 in employment taxes. E has a $4,000 deposit obligation that must be satisfied on or before the following Wednesday, August 31, 2011, notwithstanding that the day is a statewide legal holiday in State X.

*Example 6. Extension of time to deposit for employers who filed Form 944 for the preceding year satisfied.* F (a monthly depositor) was notified to file Form 944 to report its employment tax liabilities for the 2006 calendar year. F filed Form 944 on January 31, 2007, reporting a total employment tax liability for 2006 of $3,000. Because F's annual employment tax liability for the 2006 taxable year exceeded $1,000 (the applicable eligibility threshold for that taxable year), the IRS notified F to file Forms 941 for calendar year 2007 and thereafter. Based on F's liability during the lookback period (calendar year 2005, pursuant to paragraph (b)(4)(i) of this section), F is a monthly depositor for 2007. F accumulates $1,000 in employment taxes during January 2007. Because F is a monthly depositor, F's January deposit obligation is due February 15, 2007. F does not deposit these accumulated employment taxes on February 15, 2007. F accumulates $1,500 in employment taxes during February 2007. F's February deposit is due March 15, 2007. F deposits the $2,500 of employment taxes accumulated during January and February on March 15, 2007. Pursuant to paragraph (c)(6) of this section, F will be deemed to have timely deposited the employment taxes due for January 2007, and, thus, the IRS will not impose a failure-to-deposit penalty under section 6656 for that month.

(e) *Employment taxes defined.*—(1) For purposes of this section, the term "employment taxes" means—

(i) The employee portion of the tax withheld under section 3102;

(ii) The employer tax under section 3111;

(iii) The income tax withheld under sections 3402 and 3405, except income tax withheld with respect to payments made after December 31, 1993, on the following—

(A) Certain gambling winnings under section 3402(q);

(B) Retirement pay for services in the Armed Forces of the United States under section 3402;

(C) Certain annuities described in section 3402(o)(1)(B); and

(D) Pensions, annuities, IRAs, and certain other deferred income under section 3405; and

(iv) The income tax withheld under section 3406, relating to backup withholding with respect to reportable payments made before January 1, 1994.

(2) The term *employment taxes* does not include taxes with respect to wages for domestic service in a private home of the employer, unless the employer is otherwise required to file a Form 941 or Form 944 under § 31.6011(a)-4 or § 31.6011(a)-5. In the case of employers paying advance earned income credit amounts for periods ending before January 1, 2011, the amount of taxes required to be deposited shall be reduced by advance amounts paid to employees. Also, see § 31.6302-3 concerning a taxpayer's option with respect to payments made before January 1, 1994, to treat backup withholding amounts under section 3406 separately.

(f) *Save harbor/De minimis rules.*—(1) *Single deposit safe harbor.*—An employer will be considered to have satisfied its deposit obligation imposed by this section if—

(i) The amount of any shortfall does not exceed the greater of $100 or 2 percent of the amount of employment taxes required to be deposited; and

(ii) The employer deposits the shortfall on or before the shortfall make-up date.

(2) *Shortfall defined.*—For purposes of this paragraph (f), the term "shortfall" means the excess of the amount of employment taxes required to be deposited for the period over the amount deposited for the period. For this purpose, a period is either a monthly, semi-weekly or daily period.

(3) *Shortfall make-up date.*—(i) *Monthly rule.*—A shortfall with respect to a deposit required under the Monthly rule must be deposited or remitted no later than the due date for the quarterly return, in accordance with the applicable form and instructions.

(ii) *Semi-Weekly rule and One-Day rule.*—A shortfall with respect to a deposit required under the Semi-Weekly rule or the One-Day rule must be deposited on or before the first Wednesday or Friday (whichever is earlier), falling on or after the 15th day of the month following the month in which the deposit was required to be made, or, if earlier, the return due date for the return period.

(4) *De minimis rule.*—(i) *De minimis deposit rules for quarterly and annual return periods beginning on or after January 1, 2001.*—If the total amount of accumulated employment taxes for the return period is de minimis and the amount is fully deposited or remitted with a timely filed return for the return period, the amount deposited or remitted will be deemed to have been timely deposited. The total amount of accumulated employment taxes is de minimis if it is less than $2,500 for the return period or if it is de minimis pursuant to paragraph (f)(4)(ii) of this section.

(ii) *De minimis deposit rule for quarterly return periods beginning on or after January 1, 2010.*—For purposes of paragraph (f)(4)(i) of this section, if the total amount of accumulated employment taxes for the immediately preceding quarter was less than $2,500, unless § 31.6302-1(c)(3) applies to require a deposit at the close of the next day, then the employer will be deemed to have timely deposited the employer's employment taxes for the current quarter if the employer complies with the time and method payment requirements contained in paragraph (f)(4)(i) of this section.

(iii) *De minimis deposit rule for employers who file Form 944.*—An employer who files Form 944 whose employment tax liability for the year equals or exceeds $2,500 but whose employment tax liability for a quarter of the year is de minimis pursuant to paragraph (f)(4)(i) of this section will be deemed to have timely deposited the employment taxes due for that quarter if the employer fully deposits the employment taxes accumulated during the quarter by the last day of the month following the close of that quarter. Employment taxes accumulated during the fourth quarter can be either deposited by January 31 or remitted with a timely filed return for the return period.

(5) *Examples.*—The provisions of this paragraph (f) may be illustrated by the following examples:

*Example 1. Safe-harbor rule satisfied.* On Monday, January 4, 1993, J (a semi-weekly depositor), pays wages and accumulates employment taxes. As required under this section, J makes a deposit on or before the following Friday, January 8, 1993, in the amount of $4,000. Subsequently, J determines that it was actually required to deposit $4,090 by Friday. J has a shortfall of $90. The $90 shortfall does not exceed the greater of $100 or 2% of the amount required to be deposited (2% of $4,090 = $81.80). Therefore, J satisfies the safe harbor of paragraph (f)(1) of this section as long as the $90 shortfall is deposited by the first deposit date (Wednesday or Friday) on or after the 15th day of the next month (in this case Wednesday, February 17, 1993).

*Example 2. Safe-harbor rule not satisfied.* The facts are the same as in *Example 1* except that on Friday, January 8, 1993, J makes a deposit of $25,000, and later determines that it was actually required to deposit $26,000. Since the $1,000 shortfall ($26,000 less $25,000) exceeds $520 (the greater of $100 or 2% of the amount required to be deposited (2% of $26,000 = $520)), the safe harbor of paragraph (f)(1) of this section is not satisfied, and absent reasonable cause, J will be subject to a failure-to-deposit penalty under section 6656.

*Example 3. De minimis deposit rule for employers who file Form 944 satisfied.* K (a monthly depositor) was notified to file Form 944 to report its employment tax liabilities for the 2006 calendar year. In the first quarter of 2006, K accumulates employment taxes in the amount of $1,000. On April 28, 2006, K deposits the $1,000 of employment taxes accumulated in the first quarter. K accumulates another $1,000 of employment taxes during the second quarter of 2006. On July 31, 2006, K deposits the $1,000 of employment taxes accumulated in the second quarter. K's business grows and accumulates $1,500 in employment taxes during the third quarter of 2006. On October 31, 2006, K deposits the $1,500 of employment taxes accumulated in the third quarter. K accumulates another $2,000 in employment taxes during the fourth quarter. K files Form 944 on January 31, 2007, reporting a total employment tax liability for 2006 of $5,500 and submits a check for the remaining $2,000 of employment taxes with the return. K will be deemed to have timely deposited the employment taxes due for all of 2006 because K complied with the de minimis deposit rule provided in paragraph (f)(4)(iii) of this section. Therefore, the IRS will not impose a failure-to-deposit penalty under section 6656 for any month of the year. Under this de minimis deposit rule, because K was required to file Form 944 for calendar year 2006, if K's employment tax liability for a quarter is de minimis, then K may deposit that quarter's liability by the last day of the month following the close of the quarter. This de minimis rule allows K to have the benefit of the same quarterly de minimis amount K would have received if K filed Form 941 each quarter instead of Form 944 annually. Thus, because K's employment tax liability for each quarter was de minimis, K could deposit quarterly.

(g) *Agricultural employers—special rules.*—(1) *In general.*—An agricultural employer reports wages paid to farm workers annually on Form 943 (Employer's Annual Tax Return for Agricultural Employees) and reports wages paid to nonfarm workers quarterly on Form 941 or annually on Form 944. Accordingly, an agricultural employer must treat employment taxes reportable on Form 943 ("Form 943 taxes") separately from employment taxes reportable on Form 941 or Form 944 ("Form 941 or Form 944 taxes"). Form 943 taxes and Form 941 or Form 944 taxes are not combined for purposes of determining whether a deposit of either is due, whether the One-Day rule of paragraph (c)(3) of this section applies, or whether any safe harbor is applicable. In addition, Form 943 taxes and Form 941 or Form 944 taxes must be deposited separately. (See paragraph (b) of this section for rules for determining an agricultural employer's deposit status for Form 941 taxes). Whether an agricultural employer is a monthly or semi-weekly depositor of Form 943 taxes is determined according to the rules of this paragraph (g).

(2) *Monthly depositor.*—An agricultural employer is a monthly depositor of Form 943 taxes for a calendar year if the amount of Form 943 taxes accumulated in the lookback period (as defined in paragraph (g)(4) of this section) is $50,000 or less. An agricultural employer ceases to be a monthly depositor of Form 943 taxes on the first day after the employer is subject to the One-Day rule in paragraph (c)(3) of this section. At that time, the agricultural employer immediately becomes a semi-weekly depositor of Form 943 taxes for the remainder of the calendar year and the succeeding calendar year.

(3) *Semi-weekly depositor.*—An agricultural employer is a semi-weekly depositor of Form 943 taxes for a calendar year if the amount of Form 943 taxes accumulated in the lookback period (as defined in paragraph (g)(4) of this section) exceeds $50,000.

(4) *Lookback period.*—(i) *In general.*—For purposes of this paragraph (g), the lookback period for Form 943 taxes is the second calendar year preceding the current calendar year. For example, the lookback period for calendar year 1993 is calendar year 1991. New employers shall be treated as having employment tax liabilities of zero for any lookback period before the date the employer started or acquired its business.

(ii) *Adjustments and Claims for Refund.*—The employment tax liability reported on the original return for the return period is the amount taken into account in determining whether the amount of Form 943 taxes accumulated in the lookback period exceeds $50,000. Any amounts reported on adjusted returns or claims for refund pursuant to sections 6205, 6402, 6413 and 6414 filed after the due date

of the original return are not taken into account when determining the amount of Form 943 taxes accumulated in the lookback period. However, prior period adjustments reported on Form 943 for 2008 and earlier years are taken into account in determining the employment tax liability for the return period in which the adjustments are reported.

(5) The following example illustrates the provisions of this section.

*Example. A*, an agricultural employer, employs both farm workers and nonfarm workers (employees in its administrative offices). *A*'s depositor status for calendar year 1993 for Form 941 taxes will be based upon its employment tax liabilities reported on Forms 941 for the third and fourth quarters of 1991 and the first and second quarters of 1992 (the period July 1 to June 30). *A*'s depositor status for Form 943 taxes will be based upon its employment tax liability reported on its annual Form 943 for calendar year 1991.

(h) *Time and manner of deposit—deposits required to be made by electronic funds transfer.*—(1) *In general.*—Section 6302(h) requires the Secretary to prescribe such regulations as may be necessary for the development and implementation of an electronic funds transfer system to be used for the collection of the depository taxes as described in paragraph (h)(3) of this section. Section 6302(h)(2) provides a phase-in schedule that sets forth escalating minimum percentages of those depository taxes to be deposited by electronic funds transfer. This paragraph (h) prescribes the rules necessary for implementing an electronic funds transfer system for collection of depository taxes and for effecting an orderly and expeditious phase-in of that system.

(2) *Applicability of requirement.*—(i) *Deposits for return periods beginning before January 1, 2000.*—(A) Taxpayers whose aggregate deposits of the taxes imposed by Chapters 21 (Federal Insurance Contributions Act), 22 (Railroad Retirement Tax Act), and 24 (Collection of Income Tax at Source on Wages) of the Internal Revenue Code during a 12-month determination period exceed the applicable threshold amount are required to deposit all depository taxes described in paragraph (h)(3) of this section by electronic funds transfer (as defined in paragraph (h)(4) of this section) unless exempted under paragraph (h)(5) of this section. If the applicable effective date is January 1, 1995, or January 1, 1996, the requirement to deposit by electronic funds transfer applies to all deposits required to be made on or after the applicable effective date. If the applicable effective date is July 1, 1997, the requirement to deposit by electronic funds transfer applies to all deposits required to be made on or after July 1, 1997 with respect to deposit obligations incurred for return periods beginning on or after January 1, 1997. If the applicable effective date is January 1, 1998, or thereafter, the requirement to deposit by electronic funds transfer applies to all deposits required to be made with respect to deposit obligations incurred for return periods beginning on or after the applicable effective date. In general, each applicable effective date has one 12-month determination period. However, for the applicable effective date January 1, 1996, there are two determination periods. If the applicable threshold amount is exceeded in either of those determination periods, the taxpayer becomes subject to the requirement to deposit by electronic funds transfer, effective January 1, 1996. The threshold amounts, determination periods and applicable effective dates for purposes of this paragraph (h)(2)(i)(A) are as follows:

| Threshold Amount | Determination Period | Applicable Effective Date |
|---|---|---|
| $78 million | 1–1–93 to 12–31–93 | January 1, 1995 |
| $47 million | 1–1–93 to 12–31–93 | January 1, 1996 |
| $47 million | 1–1–94 to 12–31–94 | January 1, 1996 |
| $50 thousand | 1–1–95 to 12–31–95 | July 1, 1997 |
| $50 thousand | 1–1–96 to 12–31–96 | January 1, 1998 |
| $50 thousand | 1–1–97 to 12–31–97 | January 1, 1999 |

(B) Unless exempted under paragraph (h)(5) of this section, a taxpayer that does not deposit any of the taxes imposed by chapters 21, 22, and 24 during the applicable determination periods set forth in paragraph (h)(2)(i)(A) of this section, but that does make deposits of other depository taxes (as described in paragraph (h)(3) of this section), is nevertheless subject to the requirement to deposit by electronic funds transfer if the taxpayer's aggregate deposits of all depository taxes exceed the threshold amount set forth in this para-

graph (h)(2)(i)(B) during an applicable 12-month determination period. This requirement to deposit by electronic funds transfer applies to all depository taxes due with respect to deposit obligations incurred for return periods beginning on or after the applicable effective date. The threshold amount, determination periods, and applicable effective dates for purposes of this paragraph (h)(2)(i)(B) are as follows:

| Threshold Amount | Determination Period | Applicable Effective Date |
|---|---|---|
| $50 thousand | 1–1–95 to 12–31–95 | January 1, 1998 |
| $50 thousand | 1–1–96 to 12–31–96 | January 1, 1998 |
| $50 thousand | 1–1–97 to 12–31–97 | January 1, 1999 |

(C) This paragraph (h)(2)(i) applies only to deposits required to be made for return periods beginning before January 1, 2000. Thus, a taxpayer, including a taxpayer that is required under this paragraph (h)(2)(i) to make deposits by electronic funds transfer

beginning in 1999 or an earlier year, is not required to use electronic funds transfer to make deposits for return periods beginning after December 31, 1999, unless deposits by electronic funds transfer are required under paragraph (h)(2)(ii) of this section.

(ii) *Deposits for return periods beginning after December 31, 1999, and made before January 1, 2011.*—Unless exempted under paragraph (h)(5) of this section, for deposits for return periods beginning after December 31, 1999, and made before January 1, 2011, a taxpayer that deposits more than $200,000 of taxes described in paragraph (h)(3) of this section during a calendar year beginning after December 31, 1997, must use electronic funds transfer (as defined in paragraph (h)(4) of this section) to make all deposits of those taxes that are required to be made for return periods beginning after December 31 of the following year and must continue to deposit by electronic funds transfer in all succeeding years. As an example, a taxpayer that exceeds the $200,000 deposit threshold during calendar year 1998 is required to make deposits for return periods beginning in or after calendar year 2000 by electronic funds transfer.

(iii) *Deposits made after December 31, 2010.*—Unless exempted under paragraph (h)(5) of this section, a taxpayer that has a required tax deposit obligation described in paragraph (h)(3) of this section must use electronic funds transfer (as defined in paragraph (h)(4) of this section) to make all deposits of those taxes made after December 31, 2010.

(iv) *Voluntary deposits.*—A taxpayer that is authorized to make payment of taxes with a return under regulations may voluntarily make a deposit by electronic funds transfer.

(3) *Taxes required to be deposited by electronic funds transfer.*—The requirement to deposit by electronic funds transfer under paragraph (h)(2) of this section applies to all the taxes required to be deposited under §§ 1.6302-1, 1.6302-2, and 1.6302-3 of this chapter; §§ 31.6302-1, 31.6302-2, 31.6302-3, 31.6302-4, and 31.6302(c)-3; and § 40.6302(c)-1 of this chapter.

(4) *Definitions.*—(i) *Electronic funds transfer.*—An *electronic funds transfer* is any transfer of depository taxes made in accordance with Revenue Procedure 97-33, (1997-30 I.R.B.), (see § 601.601(d)(2) of this chapter), or in accordance with procedures subsequently prescribed by the Commissioner.

(ii) *Taxpayer.*—For purposes of this section, a *taxpayer* is any person required to deposit federal taxes, including not only individuals, but also any trust, estate, partnership, association, company or corporation.

(5) *Exemptions.*—If any categories of taxpayers are to be exempted from the requirement to deposit by electronic funds transfer, the Commissioner will identify those taxpayers by guidance published in the Internal Revenue Bulletin. (See § 601.601(d)(2)(ii)(*b*) of this chapter.)

(6) *Separation of deposits.*—A deposit for one return period must be made separately from a deposit for another return period.

(7) *Payment of balance due.*—If the aggregate amount of taxes reportable on the applicable tax return for the return period exceeds the total amount deposited by the taxpayer with regard to the return period, then the balance due must be remitted in accordance with the applicable form and instructions.

(8) *Time deemed deposited.*—A deposit of taxes by electronic funds transfer will be deemed made when the amount is withdrawn from the taxpayer's account, provided the U.S. Government is the payee and the amount is not returned or reversed.

(9) *Time deemed paid.*—In general, an amount deposited under this paragraph (h) will be considered to be a payment of tax on the last day prescribed for filing the applicable return for the return period (determined without regard to any extension of time for filing the return) or, if later, at the time deemed deposited under paragraph (h)(8) of this section. In the case of the taxes imposed by chapters 21 and 24 of the Internal Revenue Code, solely for purposes of section 6511 and the regulations thereunder (relating to the period of limitation on credit or refund), if an amount is deposited prior to April 15th of the calendar year immediately succeeding the calendar year that includes the period for which the amount was deposited, the amount will be considered paid on April 15th.

(i) *Time and manner of remittance with a return.*—(1) *General rules.*—A remittance required to be made by this section that is authorized to be made with a return under regulations and is made with a return must be made separately from a remittance required by any other section. Further, a remittance for a deposit period in one return period must be made separately from a remittance for a deposit period in another return period.

(2) *Payment of balance due.*—If the aggregate amount of taxes reportable on the return for the return period exceeds the total amount deposited by the employer with regard to the return period

pursuant to this section, the balance due must be remitted in accordance with the applicable form and instructions.

(3) *Time deemed paid.*—In general, amounts remitted with a return under this section will be considered as paid on the date payment is received by the Internal Revenue Service at the place prescribed for filing by regulations or forms and instructions (or if section 7502(a) applies, by the date the payment is treated as received under section 7502(a)), or on the last day prescribed for filing the return (determined without regard to any extension of time for filing the return), whichever is later. In the case of the taxes imposed by chapter 21 and 24 of the Internal Revenue Code, solely for purposes of section 6511 and the regulations thereunder (relating to the period of limitation on credit or refund), if an amount is remitted with a return under this section prior to April 15th of the calendar year immediately succeeding the calendar year that contains the period for which the amount was remitted, the amount will be considered paid on April 15th of the succeeding calendar year.

(j) *Voluntary payments by electronic funds transfer.*—Any person may voluntarily remit by electronic funds transfer any payment of tax imposed by subtitle C of the Internal Revenue Code. Such payment must be made in accordance with procedures prescribed by the Commissioner.

(k) *Special rules.*—(1) *Notice exception.*—The provisions of this section are not applicable with respect to employment taxes for any month in which the employer receives notice that a return is required under § 31.6011(a)-5 (or for any subsequent month for which such a return is required), if those taxes are also required to be deposited under the separate accounting procedures provided in § 301.7512-1 of the Regulations on Procedure and Administration (which procedures are applicable if notification is given by the Commissioner of failure to comply with certain employment tax requirements). In cases in which a monthly return is required under § 31.6011(a)-5 but the taxes are not required to be deposited under the separate accounting procedures provided in § 301.7512-1, the provisions of this section shall apply except those provisions shall not authorize the deferral of any deposit to a date after the date on which the return is required to be filed.

(2) *Wages paid in nonconvertible foreign currency.*—The provisions of this section are not applicable with respect to wages paid in nonconvertible foreign currency pursuant to § 301.6316-7.

(l) [Reserved].

(m) *Cross references.*—(1) *Failure to deposit penalty.*—For provisions relating to the penalty for failure to make a deposit within the prescribed time, see section 6656.

(2) *Saturday, Sunday, or legal holiday.*—For provisions relating to the time for performance of acts where the last day falls on Saturday, Sunday, or a legal holiday, see the provisions of § 301.7503-1.

(n) *Effective/applicability dates.*—Sections 31.6302-1 through 31.6302-3 apply with respect to the deposit of employment taxes attributable to payments made after December 31, 1992. To the extent that the provisions of §§ 31.6302-1 through 31.6302-3 are inconsistent with the provisions of §§ 31.6302(c)-1 and 31.6302(c)-2, a taxpayer will be considered to be in compliance with §§ 31.6302-1 through 31.6302-3 if the taxpayer makes timely deposits during 1993 in accordance with §§ 31.6302(c)-1 and 31.6302(c)-2. Paragraphs (b)(4), (c)(5), (c)(6), (d) *Example 6*, (e)(2), (f)(4)(i), (f)(4)(iii), (f)(5) *Example 3*, and (g)(1) of this section apply to taxable years beginning on or after December 30, 2008. Paragraph (f)(4)(ii) of this section applies to taxable years beginning on or after January 1, 2010. The rules of paragraphs (e)(2) and (g)(1) of this section that apply to taxable years beginning before December 30, 2008, are contained in § 31.6302-1 as in effect prior to December 30, 2008. The rules of paragraphs (b)(4), (c)(5), (c)(6), (d) *Example 6*, (f)(4)(i), (f)(4)(iii), and (f)(5) *Example 3* of this section that apply to taxable years beginning on or after January 1, 2006, and before December 30, 2008, are contained in § 31.6302-1T as in effect prior to December 30, 2008. The rules of paragraphs (b)(4) and (f)(4) of this section that apply to taxable years beginning before January 1, 2006, are contained in § 31.6302-1 as in effect prior to January 1, 2006. The rules of paragraph (g) of this section eliminating use of Federal tax deposit coupons apply to deposits and payments made after December 31, 2010.

(o) *Effective/applicability date.*—Paragraphs (c), (d) *Examples 1 through 5*, (h)(2)(ii), (h)(2)(iii), (h)(2)(iv), (i)(1) and (i)(3) of this section apply to deposits and payments made after December 31, 2010. [Reg. § 31.6302-1.]

☐ [*T.D. 8436, 9-22-92 (corrected 10-27-92 and 2-9-94). Amended by T.D. 8504, 12-22-93; T.D. 8723, 7-11-97; T.D. 8771, 6-15-98; T.D. 8822, 6-16-99; T.D. 8828, 7-12-99; T.D. 8909, 12-5-2000; T.D. 8946, 5-22-2001; T.D. 8947, 6-14-2001; T.D. 8952, 6-25-2001; T.D. 9239, 12-30-2005; T.D.*

9405, 6-30-2008; *T.D. 9440,* 12-24-2008 *T.D. 9507,* 12-2-2010; *T.D. 9524,* 5-6-2011; *T.D. 9566,* 12-9-2011 *and T.D. 9586,* 4-24-2012.]

### [Reg. §51.6302-1]

**§51.6302-1. Method of paying the branded prescription drug fee.**—(a) *Fee to be paid by electronic funds transfer.*—Under the authority of section 6302(a), the fee imposed on branded prescription drug sales by section 9008 and §51.5 must be paid by electronic funds transfer as defined in §31.6302-1(h)(4)(i) of this title, as if the fee were a depository tax. For the time for paying the fee, see §51.8.

(b) *Effective/applicability date.*—This section applies on and after July 28, 2014. [Reg. §51.6302-1.]

☐ *[T.D. 9684, 7-24-2014.]*

### [Reg. §57.6302-1]

**§57.6302-1. Method of paying the health insurance providers fee.**—(a) *Fee to be paid by electronic funds transfer.*—Under the authority of section 6302(a), the fee imposed on covered entities engaged in the business of providing health insurance for United States health risks under section 9010 and §57.4 must be paid by electronic funds transfer as defined in §31.6302-1(h)(4)(i) of this chapter, as if the fee were a depository tax. For the time for paying the fee, see §57.7.

(b) *Effective/Applicability date.*—This section applies with respect to any fee that is due on or after September 30, 2014. [Reg. §57.6302-1.]

☐ *[T.D. 9643, 11-26-2013.]*

### [Reg. §301.6302-1]

**§301.6302-1. Manner or time of collection of taxes.**—(a) *Employment and excise taxes.*—For provisions relating to the manner or time of collection of certain employment and excise taxes and deposits in connection with the payment thereof, see the regulations relating to the particular tax.

(b) *Income taxes.*—(1) For provisions relating to the deposits of income and estimated income taxes of certain corporations, see §1.6302-1 of this chapter (Income Tax Regulations).

(2) For provisions relating to the deposits of tax required to be withheld under chapter 3 of the Code on nonresident aliens and foreign corporations and tax-free covenant bonds, see §1.6302-2 of this chapter.

(c) *Effective/applicability date.*—This section applies to deposits and payments made after December 31, 2010. [Reg. §301.6302-1.]

☐ [T.D. 6498, 10-24-60. *Amended by T.D. 6922,* 6-16-67; *T.D. 8952,* 6-25-2001 *and T.D. 9507,* 12-2-2010.]

### [Reg. §1.6302-2]

**§1.6302-2. Deposit rules for tax withheld on nonresident aliens and foreign corporations.**—(a) *Time for making deposits.*—(1) *Deposits.*—(i) *Monthly deposits.*—Except as provided in paragraphs (a)(1)(ii) and (iv) of this section, every withholding agent that, pursuant to chapter 3 of the Internal Revenue Code, has accumulated at the close of any calendar month an aggregate amount of undeposited taxes of $200 or more shall deposit such aggregate amount by the 15th day of the following month. However, the preceding sentence shall not apply if the withholding agent has made a deposit of taxes pursuant to paragraph (a)(1)(ii) of this section to a quarter-monthly period that occurred during such month. If the 15th day of the following month is a Saturday, Sunday, or legal holiday in the District of Columbia under section 7503, taxes will be treated as timely deposited if deposited on the next succeeding day which is not a Saturday, Sunday, or legal holiday. With respect to section 1446(a), this section applies only to a publicly traded partnership or nominee described in §1.1446-4 and, with respect to section 1446(f), only to a publicly traded partnership or broker described in §1.1446(f)-4.

(ii) *Quarter-monthly deposits.*—If at the close of any quarter-monthly period within a calendar month, the aggregate amount of undeposited taxes required to be withheld pursuant to chapter 3 of the Internal Revenue Code is $2,000 or more, the withholding agent shall deposit such aggregate amount within 3 business days after the close of such quarter-monthly period. Business days include every calendar day other than Saturdays, Sundays, or legal holidays in the District of Columbia under section 7503. If any of the three weekdays following the close of a quarter-monthly period is a legal holiday under section 7503, the withholding agent has an additional day for each day that is a legal holiday by which to make the required deposit. For example, if the Monday following the close of a quarter-monthly period is New Year's Day, a legal holiday, the required deposit for the quarter-monthly period is not due until the following Thursday rather than the following Wednesday.

(iii) *Excess deposits.*—The excess (if any) of a deposit over the actual taxes for a monthly or quarter-monthly deposit period shall be applied in order of time to each of the withholding agent's succeeding deposits with respect to the same calendar year, until exhausted, to the extent that the amount by which the taxes for a subsequent deposit period exceed the deposit for such subsequent deposit period.

(iv) *Annual deposits.*—If at the close of December of each calendar year, the aggregate amount of undeposited taxes required to be withheld pursuant to chapter 3 of the Internal Revenue Code is less than $200, the withholding agent may deposit such aggregate amount by March 15 of the following calendar year. If such aggregate amount is not so deposited, it shall be remitted in accordance with paragraph (a)(1) of §1.1461-1.

(2) *Cross reference.*—For rules relating to the adjustment of deposits, see §§1.1461-2(b) and 1.6414-1. For rules requiring payment of any undeposited tax, see §1.1461-1.

(b) *Manner of payment.*—(1) *Payments not required by electronic funds transfer.*—A payment that is not required to be deposited by this section shall be made separately from a payment required by any other section. The payment may be submitted with the filed return. The timeliness of the payment will be determined by the date payment is received by the Internal Revenue Service at the place prescribed for filing by regulations or forms and instructions, or if section 7502(a) applies, by the date the payment is treated as received under section 7502(a), or on the last day prescribed for filing the return (determined without regard to any extension of time for filing the return), whichever is later. Each withholding agent making payments under this section shall report on the return, for the period to which such payments are made, information regarding such payments according to the instructions that apply to such return.

(2) *Voluntary deposits.*—An amount of tax which is not required to be deposited may nevertheless be deposited if the withholding agent so desires.

(3) *Separation of deposits.*—A deposit required by paragraph (a) of this section for any period occurring in one calendar year shall be made separately from any deposit for any period occurring in another calendar year. In addition, a deposit required to be made by paragraph (a) of this section shall be made separately from a deposit required by any other section.

(4) *Multiple remittances.*—A withholding agent may make one, or more than one, remittance of the amount required to be deposited if each remittance is accompanied by the applicable deposit form.

(5) *Time deemed paid.*—In general, amounts deposited under this section shall be considered as paid on the last day prescribed for filing the return (Form 1042) in respect of such tax (determined without regard to any extension of time for filing such return), or at the time deposited, whichever is later. For purposes of section 6511 and the regulations thereunder, relating to period of limitation on credit or refund, if an amount is so deposited prior to April 15th of a calendar year immediately succeeding the calendar year in which occurs the period for which such amount was so deposited, such amount shall be considered as paid on such April 15th.

(c) *Deposits by electronic funds transfer.*—For the requirement to deposit taxes withheld on nonresident aliens and foreign corporations by electronic funds transfer, see §31.6302-1(h) of this chapter. A taxpayer not required to deposit by electronic funds transfer pursuant to §31.6302-1(h) of this chapter remains subject to the rules of paragraph (b) of this section.

(d) *Penalties for failure to make deposits.*—For provisions relating to the penalty for failure to make a deposit within the prescribed time, see section 6656.

(e) *Saturday, Sunday, or legal holidays.*—For provisions relating to the time for performance of acts where the last day falls on Saturday, Sunday, or a legal holiday, see §301.7503-1 of this chapter (Procedure and Administration Regulations).

(f) *Employer identification number.*—For the definition of the term "employer identification number," see §301.7701-12 of this chapter (Procedure and Administration Regulations). For provisions relating to the penalty for failure to include the employer identification number in a return, statement, or other document, see §301.6676-1 of such chapter.

(g) *Applicability dates.*—Except as otherwise provided, this section shall apply to tax required to be withheld under chapter 3 of the Internal Revenue Code after 1966. In the last sentence of paragraph (a)(1)(i) of this section, the reference to §1.1446-4 shall apply to partnership taxable years beginning after April 29, 2008, and the reference to § 1.1446(f)-4 shall apply to tax required to be withheld on or after January 1, 2022. Paragraph (b)(1) of this section applies to deposits and payments made after December 31, 2010. [Reg. § 1.6302-2.]

☐ [*T.D.* 6922, 6-16-67. *Amended by T.D.* 6941, 12-15-67; *T.D.* 6957, 6-3-68; *T.D.* 7243, 1-2-73; *T.D.* 7953, 5-8-84; *T.D.* 8723, 7-11-97; *T.D.* 8947, 6-14-2001; *T.D.* 8952, 6-25-2001; *T.D.* 9239, 12-30-2005; *T.D.* 9394, 4-28-2008, *T.D.* 9507, 12-2-2010 *and T.D.* 9926, 11-27-2020.]

### [Reg. § 31.6302-2]

**§ 31.6302-2. Deposit rules for taxes under the Railroad Retirement Tax Act (RRTA).**—(a) *General rule.*—Except as otherwise provided in this section, the rules of § 31.6302-1 determine the time and manner of making deposits of employee tax withheld under section 3202 and employer tax imposed under sections 3221(a) and (b) attributable to payments made after December 31, 1992. Railroad retirement taxes described in section 3221(c) arising during the month must be deposited on or before the first date after the 15th day of the following month on which taxes are otherwise required to be deposited under § 31.6302-1.

(b) *Separate application of deposit rules.*—A person who accumulates tax under sections 3202 or 3221 shall not take that tax into account for purposes of determining when taxes described in paragraph (e) of § 31.6302-1 must otherwise be deposited.

(c) *Modification of Monthly rule determination.*—(1) *General rule.*—Except as otherwise provided in this section, any person is allowed to use the Monthly rule of § 31.6302-1(c)(1) for an entire calendar year unless the amount of R.R.T.A. taxes required to be deposited under this section during the lookback period was more than $50,000. The lookback period is defined as the calendar year preceding the calendar year just ended. Thus, for purposes of determining if an R.R.T.A. employer qualifies to use the Monthly rule for calendar year 1993, a lookback must be made to calendar year 1991. New employers shall be treated as having employment tax liabilities of zero for any calendar year during which the employer did not exist.

(2) *Exception.*—An employer shall immediately cease to be allowed to use the Monthly rule after any day on which that employer is subject to the One-Day rule set forth in § 31.6302-1(c)(3). Such employer immediately becomes subject to the Semi-Weekly rule of § 31.6302-1(c)(2) for the remainder of the calendar year and the following calendar year.

(d) *Effective/applicability date.*—This section applies to deposits and payments made after December 31, 2010. [Reg. § 31.6302-2.]

☐ [*T.D.* 8436, 9-22-92. *Amended by T.D.* 9507, 12-2-2010.]

### [Reg. § 1.6302-3]

**§ 1.6302-3. Deposit rules for estimated taxes of certain trusts.**—(a) *Requirement.*—A bank or other financial institution described in paragraph (b) of this section shall deposit all payments of estimated tax under section 6654(l) with respect to trusts for which such institution acts as a fiduciary by the date otherwise prescribed for paying such tax in the manner set forth in published guidance, publications, forms and instructions.

(b) *Banks and financial institutions subject to this requirement.*—The requirement of paragraph (a) of this section applies to banks and other financial institutions described in sections 581 and 591 that have been designated as authorized Federal tax depositaries described in section 6302(c) and that act as fiduciaries for at least 200 trusts to which section 6654(l) applies that during the calendar year are required to make installment payments of estimated tax with respect to such trusts. For purposes of this section, a fiduciary is the person responsible for filing the tax returns and paying the taxes with respect to a trust.

(c) *Cross-references.*—For the requirement to deposit estimated tax payments of taxable trusts by electronic funds transfer, see § 31.6302-1(h) of this chapter.

(d) *Effective/applicability date.*—This section applies to deposits and payments made after December 31, 2010. [Reg. § 1.6302-3.]

☐ [*T.D.* 8192, 4-8-88. *Amended by T.D.* 8723, 7-11-97; *T.D.* 8952, 6-25-2001 *and T.D.* 9507, 12-2-2010.]

### [Reg. § 31.6302-3]

**§ 31.6302-3. Federal tax deposit rules for amounts withheld under the backup withholding requirements of section 3406 for payments made after December 31, 1992.**—(a) *General rule.*—The rules of § 31.6302-1 shall apply to determine the time and manner of making deposits of amounts withheld under the backup withholding requirements of section 3406.

(b) *Treatment of backup withholding amounts separately.*—A taxpayer that withholds income tax under section 3406 with respect to reportable payments made after December 31, 1992, and before January 1, 1994, may, in accordance with the instructions provided with Form 941, deposit such tax under the rules of § 31.6302-1 without taking into account the other taxes described in paragraph (e) of § 31.6302-1 for purposes of determining when tax withheld under section 3406 must be deposited. A taxpayer that treats backup withholding amounts separately with respect to reportable payments made after December 31, 1992, and before January 1, 1994, shall not take tax withheld under section 3406 into account for purposes of determining when the other taxes described in paragraph (e) of § 31.6302-1 must otherwise be deposited under that section. See § 31.6302-4 for rules regarding the deposit of income tax withheld under section 3406 with respect to reportable payments made after December 31, 1993.

(c) *Example.*—The following example illustrates the provisions of this section.

*Example.* For the last two calendar quarters of 1991 and the first two calendar quarters of 1992, Bank *A* reports employment taxes with respect to wages paid totalling in excess of $50,000. For the same four quarters, pursuant to section 3406, *A* withholds income tax with respect to dividend payments in an amount aggregating less than $50,000. For deposit and reporting purposes, *A* treated the backup withholding amounts separately from the employment taxes with respect to wages paid. Accordingly, for calendar year 1993, if *A* chooses to treat the items separately, *A* must use the Semi-Weekly rule of § 31.6302-1(c)(2) to deposit taxes with respect to wages paid but may use the Monthly rule of § 31.6302-1(c)(1) for the deposit of backup withholding amounts. If *A* chooses not to treat the items separately, the Semi-Weekly rule would apply to the combined amount of both the taxes with respect to wages paid and the backup withholding amounts. [Reg. § 31.6302-3.]

☐ [*T.D.* 8436, 9-22-92. *Amended by T.D.* 8504, 12-22-93.]

### [Reg. § 1.6302-4]

**§ 1.6302-4. Voluntary payments by electronic funds transfer.**—(a) *Electronic funds transfer.*—Any person may voluntarily remit by electronic funds transfer any payment of tax imposed by subtitle A of the Internal Revenue Code, including any payment of estimated tax. Such payment must be made in the manner set forth in published guidance, publications, forms and instructions.

(b) *Effective/applicability date.*—This section applies to deposits and payments made after December 31, 2010. [Reg. § 1.6302-4.]

☐ [*T.D.* 8723, 7-11-97. *Amended by T.D.* 8828, 7-12-99 *and T.D.* 9507, 12-2-2010.]

### [Reg. § 31.6302-4]

**§ 31.6302-4. Deposit rules for withheld income taxes attributable to nonpayroll payments.**—(a) *General rule.*—With respect to nonpayroll withheld taxes attributable to nonpayroll payments made after December 31, 1993, a taxpayer is either a monthly or a semi-weekly depositor based on an annual determination. Except as provided in this section, the rules of § 31.6302-1 shall apply to determine the time and manner of making deposits of nonpayroll withheld taxes as though they were employment taxes. Paragraph (b) of this section defines nonpayroll withheld taxes. Paragraph (c) of this section provides rules for determining whether a taxpayer is a monthly or a semi-weekly depositor.

(b) *Nonpayroll withheld taxes defined.*—For purposes of this section, effective with respect to payments made after December 31, 1993, *nonpayroll withheld taxes* means—

(1) Amounts withheld under section 3402(q), relating to withholding on certain gambling winnings;

(2) Amounts withheld under section 3402 with respect to amounts paid as retirement pay for service in the Armed Forces of the United States;

(3) Amounts withheld under section 3402(o)(1)(B), relating to certain annuities;

(4) Annuities withheld under section 3405, relating to withholding on pensions, annuities, IRAs, and certain other deferred income; and

(5) Amounts withheld under section 3406, relating to backup withholding with respect to reportable payments.

(c) *Determination of deposit status.*—(1) *Rules for calendar years 1994 and 1995.*—On January 1, 1994, a taxpayer's depositor status for nonpayroll withheld taxes is the same as the taxpayer's status on January 1, 1994, for taxes reported on Form 941 under § 31.6302-1. A taxpayer generally retains that depositor status for nonpayroll withheld taxes for all of calendar years 1994 and 1995. However, a taxpayer that under this paragraph (c) is a monthly depositor for

1994 and 1995 will immediately lose that status and become a semi-weekly depositor of nonpayroll withheld taxes if the One-Day rule of §31.6302-1(c)(3) is triggered with respect to nonpayroll withheld taxes. See paragraph (d) of this section for a special rule regarding the application of the One-Day rule of §31.6302-1(c)(3) to nonpayroll withheld taxes.

(2) *Rules for calendar years after 1995.*—(i) *In general.*—For calendar years after 1995, the determination of whether a taxpayer is a monthly or a semi-weekly depositor for a calendar year is based on an annual determination and generally depends on the aggregate amount of nonpayroll withheld taxes reported by the taxpayer for the lookback period as defined in paragraph (c)(2)(iv) of this section.

(ii) *Monthly depositor.*—A taxpayer is a monthly depositor of nonpayroll withheld taxes for a calendar year if the amount of nonpayroll withheld taxes accumulated in the lookback period (as defined in paragraph (c)(2)(iv) of this section) is $50,000 or less. A taxpayer ceases to be a monthly depositor of nonpayroll withheld taxes on the first day after the taxpayer is subject to the One-Day rule in §31.6302-1(c)(3) with respect to nonpayroll withheld taxes. At that time, the taxpayer immediately becomes a semi-weekly depositor of nonpayroll withheld taxes for the remainder of the calendar year and the succeeding calendar year. See paragraph (d) of this section for a special rule regarding the application of the One-Day rule of §31.6302-1(c)(3) to nonpayroll withheld taxes.

(iii) *Semi-weekly depositor.*—A taxpayer is a semi-weekly depositor of nonpayroll withheld taxes for a calendar year if the amount of nonpayroll withheld taxes accumulated in the lookback period (as defined in paragraph (c)(2)(iv) of this section) exceeds $50,000.

(iv) *Lookback period.*—For purposes of this section, the lookback period for nonpayroll withheld taxes is the second calendar year preceding the current calendar year. For example, the lookback period for calendar year 1996 is calendar year 1994. A new taxpayer is treated as having nonpayroll withheld taxes of zero for any calendar year in which the taxpayer did not exist.

(d) *Special rules.*—A taxpayer must treat nonpayroll withheld taxes, which are reported on Form 945, "Annual Return of Withheld Federal Income Tax," separately from taxes reportable on Form 941, "Employer's QUARTERLY Federal Tax Return" (or any other return, for example, Form 943, "Employer's Annual Federal Tax Return for Agricultural Employees"). Taxes reported on Form 945 and taxes reported on Form 941 are not combined for purposes of determining whether a deposit of either is due, whether the One-Day rule of §31.6302-1(c)(3) applies, or whether any safe harbor is applicable. In addition, taxes reported on Form 945 and taxes reported on Form 941 must be deposited separately. (See paragraph (b) of §31.6302-1 for rules for determining an employer's deposit status for taxes reported on Form 941.) Taxes reported on Form 945 for one calendar year must be deposited separately from taxes reported on Form 945 for another calendar year.

(e) *Effective/applicability date.*—Section 31.6302-4(d) applies to deposits and payments made after December 31, 2010. [Reg. §31.6302-4.]

☐ [*T.D.* 8504, 12-22-93. *Amended by T.D.* 9507, 12-2-2010; *T.D.* 9524, 5-6-2011 *and T.D.* 9586, 4-24-2012.]

### [Reg. §40.6302(a)-1]

**§40.6302(a)-1. Voluntary payments of excise taxes by electronic funds transfer.**—Any person may voluntarily remit by electronic funds transfer any payment of tax to which this part 40 applies. Such payment must be made in accordance with procedures prescribed by the Commissioner. [Reg. §40.6302(a)-1.]

☐ [*T.D.* 8828, 7-12-99.]

### [Reg. §31.6302(b)-1]

**§31.6302(b)-1. Method of collection.**—For provisions relating to collection by means of returns of the taxes imposed by chapter 21 (Federal Insurance Contributions Act), see §§31.6011(a)-1 and 31.6011(a)-5. [Reg. §31.6302(b)-1.]

☐ [*T.D.* 6516, 12-20-60.]

### [Reg. §31.6302(c)-1]

**§31.6302(c)-1. Use of Government depositaries in connection with taxes under Federal Insurance Contributions Act and income tax withheld for amounts attributable to payments made before January 1, 1993.**—(a) *Requirement for calendar months beginning after December 31, 1980, but before January 1, 1993.*—(1) *In general.*—(i) In the case of a calendar month which begins after December 31, 1980, but before April 1, 1991—

(a) Except as provided in paragraph (b) of this section and hereinafter in this subdivision (i), if at the close of any calendar month the aggregate amount of undeposited taxes (as defined in paragraph (a)(1)(iii) of this section) is $500 or more, the employer shall deposit the undeposited taxes in a Federal Reserve bank or authorized financial institution (see subparagraph (3)(iii) of this paragraph) within 15 calendar days after the close of such calendar month.

However, this (a) of subdivision (i) shall not apply if the employer was required to make a deposit of taxes pursuant to (b) of this subdivision (i) with respect to an eighth-monthly period which occurred during the calendar month.

(b) Except as provided in paragraph (b) of this section and except in the case of first-time 3-banking-day depositors, if at the close of any eighth-monthly period the aggregate amount of undeposited taxes is $3,000 or more, the employer shall deposit the undeposited taxes in a Federal Reserve bank or authorized financial institution within 3 banking days after the close of such eighth-monthly period. For purposes of determining the amount of undeposited taxes at the close of an eighth-monthly period, undeposited taxes with respect to wages paid during a prior eighth-monthly period shall not be taken into account if the employer has made a deposit with respect to such prior eighth-monthly period. An employer will be considered to have complied with the requirements of this subdivision (i)(b) for a deposit with respect to the close of an eighth-monthly period if—

(1) His deposit is not less than 95 percent (90 percent before January 1, 1982) of the aggregate amount of the taxes with respect to wages paid during the period for which the deposit is made, and

(2) If such eighth-monthly period occurs in a month other than the last month of a period for which a return is required to be filed (hereinafter in this subparagraph referred to as a return period), he deposits any underpayment with his first deposit which is otherwise required by this subdivision (i)(b) to be made after the 15th day of the following month. For purposes of this subdivision (i)(b), a "first-time 3-banking-day depositor" is an employer who establishes to the satisfaction of the Commissioner that he was not required (but for this exception) to make a deposit pursuant to this subdivision (i)(b) (or pursuant to subdivision (ii)(b) of this subparagraph) with respect to each period in any preceding month of the current calendar quarter and with respect to each period in the 4 calendar quarters preceding the current calendar quarter. An employer may in no event qualify as a "first-time 3-banking-day depositor" with respect to any eighth-monthly period if the undeposited taxes at the close of that period are $10,000 or more.

The excess (if any) of a deposit over the actual taxes for a deposit period shall be applied in order of time to each of the employer's succeeding deposits with respect to the same return period, until exhausted, to the extent that the amount by which the taxes for a subsequent deposit period exceed the deposit for such subsequent deposit period. For purposes of this subdivision (i), "eight-monthly period" means the first 3 days of a calendar month, the 4th day through the 7th day of a calendar month, the 8th day through the 11th day of a calendar month, the 12th day through the 15th day of a calendar month, the 16th day through the 19th day of a calendar month, the 20th day through the 22nd day of a calendar month, the 23rd day through the 25th day of a calendar month, or the portion of a calendar month following the 25th day of such month.

(c) The periods within which taxes must be deposited under this section are determined, in the case of employers paying advance earned income credit amounts, by reference to the amount of taxes required to be deposited after reduction for advance amounts paid to employees.

(ii) In the case of a calendar month which begins after March 31, 1991, but before January 1, 1993—

(a) Except as provided in §31.6302(c)-1(a)(1)(ii)(b) or (c), or §31.6302(c)-1(b), if with respect to any calendar month the aggregate amount of taxes (as defined in §31.6302(c)-1(a)(1)(iii)) accumulated with respect to wages paid is $500 or more, but less than $3,000, then the employer shall deposit that aggregate amount in a Federal Reserve bank or authorized financial institution within 15 calendar days after the close of that calendar month. Taxes accumulated with respect to wages paid in a prior calendar month within the same return period shall not be taken into account in determining the aggregate amount of taxes accumulated if a deposit was required to be made under this section with respect to such tax amounts. Deposits made during the calendar month of taxes with respect to wages paid during that month do not reduce the aggregate amount of taxes accumulated for purposes of determining the deposit requirement (if any) for that month. However, this paragraph (a)(1)(ii)(a) shall not apply if the employer was required to make a deposit of taxes pursuant to paragraph (a)(1)(ii)(b) of this section with respect to an eighth-month period which occurred during the calendar month.

*Example 1:* Employer *A*'s aggregate amount of taxes accumulated with respect to wages paid in April 1991 is $800. Since that amount is in excess of $500, but less than $3,000, *A* must deposit the $800 in a Federal Reserve bank or authorized financial institution by May 15, 1991.

*Example 2:* Employer *B*'s aggregate amount of taxes accumulated with respect to wages paid in April 1991 is $400. Since that amount is less than $500, *B* has no deposit obligation for the month of April. In May 1991 *B*'s aggregate amount of taxes accumulated with respect to wages paid during the month is $450. Since the $400 in taxes in April was not required to be deposited, that amount is taken into account in determining if a deposit is required for May. The aggregate amount of taxes accumulated with respect to wages paid for the two months is in excess of $500, thus requiring a deposit. Since June 15, 1991, is a Saturday, *B* must deposit the $850 in a Federal Reserve bank or authorized financial institution by Monday, June 17, 1991, pursuant to section 7503 of the Code.

*Example 3:* The facts are the same as in *Example 2* except that *B* deposits the $400 in taxes from April on May 15, 1991. Because the $400 was not required to be deposited, that amount is taken into account in determining if a deposit obligation exists for May. Since the aggregate amount of taxes accumulated with respect to wages paid for the two months, $850, is in excess of $500, a deposit in the aggregate amount of $850 is required by Monday, June 17, 1991. Since $400 was previously deposited, *B* must deposit an additional $450 by June 17, 1991.

*Example 4:* On Friday, April 5, 1991, a payroll date, Employer *C* accumulates $450 in taxes with respect to wages paid on that date. Although not required to do so, *C* deposits the $450 in an authorized depository. On Friday, April 19, 1991, *C* accumulates an additional $450 in taxes with respect to wages paid. The aggregate amount of taxes accumulated with respect to wages paid during the calendar month is $900. *C* has a deposit obligation of $900 for the calendar month and must deposit an additional $450 in an authorized depository by May 15, 1991.

(b) Except as provided in §31.6302(c)-1(a)(1)(ii)(*c*) or §31.6302(c)-1(b), and except in the case of first-time 3-banking-day depositors (as defined in §31.6302(c)-1(a)(1)(i)(*b*)(2)), if with respect to any eighth-monthly period (as defined in §31.6302(c)-1(a)(1)(i)(*b*)) the aggregate amount of taxes accumulated with respect to wages paid is $3,000 or more, but less than $100,000, the employer shall deposit that aggregate amount in a Federal Reserve bank or authorized financial institution within 3 banking days after the close of that eighth-monthly period. Taxes accumulated with respect to wages paid during a prior eighth-monthly period shall not be taken into account if a deposit was required to be made under this section with respect to such tax amounts. Deposits made during the eighth-monthly period of taxes with respect to wages paid during that eighth-monthly period do not reduce the aggregate amount of taxes accumulated for purposes of determining the deposit requirement (if any) for that eighth-monthly period. Solely for purposes of the examples in this paragraph (a)(1)(ii)(*b*) and paragraphs (a)(1)(ii)(*c*), (*d*), and (*f*) of this section, "banking days" are assumed to include all calendar days except Saturdays, Sundays, and Federal holidays.

*Example 1:* For the eighth-monthly period April 1-3, 1991, Employer *D*'s aggregate amount of taxes accumulated with respect to wages paid is $3,500. Since that amount is in excess of $3,000, but less than $100,000, *D* has a deposit obligation of $3,500 that must be satisfied by April 8, 1991, the third banking day after the close of the eighth-monthly period.

*Example 2:* For the eighth-monthly period April 1-3, 1991, Employer *E*'s aggregate amount of taxes accumulated with respect to wages paid is $3,500. *E* has a deposit obligation of $3,500 that must be satisfied by April 8, 1991, three banking days after the close of the April 1-3 eighth-monthly period. For the eighth-monthly period April 4-7, 1991, *E*'s aggregate amount of taxes accumulated with respect to wages paid is $2,800. Since *E* was required to make a deposit for the April 1-3 eighth-monthly period, that $3,500 amount is not taken into account in determining any obligations that arise in subsequent eighth-monthly periods. *E* does not have an eighth-monthly deposit obligation with respect to the April 4-7 eighth-monthly period.

*Example 3:* For the eighth-monthly period April 1-3, 1991, Employer *F*'s aggregate amount of taxes accumulated with respect to wages paid is $2,800. Since that amount is less than $3,000, no deposit is required with respect to that eighth-monthly period. For the eighth-monthly period April 4-7, 1991, *F*'s aggregate amount of taxes accumulated with respect to wages paid is $2,500. Since *F* was not required to deposit the $2,800 in taxes from the April 1-3 eighth-monthly period, that amount is taken into account in determining *F*'s deposit obligation for the April 4-7 eighth-monthly period. The aggregate amount of taxes accumulated for the two eighth-monthly periods is $5,300. *F* has a deposit obligation of $5,300 that must be satisfied by April 10, 1991, three banking days after the close of the April 4-7 eighth-monthly period.

*Example 4:* The facts are the same as in *Example 3* except that *F* deposits the $2,800 from the April 1-3 eighth-monthly period on April 4, 1991. Because the $2,800 was not required to be deposited, that amount is taken into account in determining *F*'s deposit obligation for the April 4-7 eighth-monthly period. The aggregate amount of taxes accumulated for the two eighth-monthly periods is $5,300. Since that amount is in excess of $3,000, a deposit obligation exists after the close of the April 4-7 eighth-monthly period. As $2,800 of that amount was previously deposited, *F* has a deposit obligation of $2,500 that must be satisfied by April 10, 1991, three banking days after the close of the April 4-7 eighth-monthly period.

*Example 5:* On Friday, April 12, 1991, the beginning of an eighth-monthly period (April 12-15), *G* accumulates $3,500 in taxes with respect to wages paid and deposits the $3,500 in an authorized depository on that date although a deposit of the $3,500 was not required to be made on that date. On Monday, April 15, 1991, the end of the April 12-15 eighth-monthly period, *G* accumulates an additional $2,000 in taxes with respect to wages paid. The aggregate amount of taxes accumulated with respect to wages paid during the April 12-15 eighth-monthly period is $5,500. *G* has a deposit obligation for the eighth-monthly period of $5,500. Since $3,500 of that amount was previously deposited, *G* has a remaining deposit obligation of $2,000 that must be satisfied by Thursday, April 18, 1991, three banking days after the close of the eighth-monthly period.

(c) If on any day within an eighth-monthly period the aggregate amount of taxes accumulated with respect to wages paid is $100,000 or more, the employer shall deposit that aggregate amount in a Federal Reserve bank or authorized financial institution on the first banking day after that day. Taxes accumulated with respect to wages paid prior to that day shall not be taken into account if a deposit was required under this section with respect to such tax amounts. Taxes deposited on any given day with respect to wages paid on that day do not reduce the aggregate amount of taxes accumulated on that day for purposes of determining the deposit requirement (if any) for that day.

*Example 1:* On Thursday, April 4, 1991, the beginning of the April 4-7 eighth-monthly period, Employer *H* accumulates $55,000 in taxes with respect to wages paid on that date. On Saturday, April 6, 1991, *H* accumulates an additional $50,000 in taxes with respect to wages paid. *H* has a deposit obligation of $105,000 that must be satisfied by Monday, April 8, the next banking day after Saturday, April 6.

*Example 2:* On Friday, April 12, 1991, the beginning of the April 12-15 eighth-monthly period, *J* accumulates $60,000 in taxes with respect to wages paid and deposits the $60,000 in an authorized depository on that date although a deposit of the $60,000 was not required to be made on that date. On Monday, April 15, 1991, the last day in the April 12-15 eighth-monthly period, *J* accumulates an additional $50,000 in taxes with respect to wages paid. On Monday, April 15, the aggregate amount of taxes accumulated with respect to wages paid during the eighth-monthly period to date totals $110,000. *J* has a $110,000 deposit obligation that must be satisfied by the next banking day after the $100,000 threshold is reached. Since $60,000 of the $110,000 was already deposited, *J* has a remaining deposit obligation of $50,000 that must be satisfied by Tuesday, April 16, 1991, the next banking day following April 15th.

*Example 3:* On Monday, April 1, 1991, Employer *K* accumulates $105,000 in taxes with respect to wages paid on that date. On that same day, *K* deposits in an authorized depository $10,000 of the $105,000 accumulated. *K* has a $105,000 deposit obligation that must be satisfied by the next banking day, April 2, 1991. The $10,000 deposited on April 1 cannot be used to reduce the aggregate amount of accumulated taxes with respect to that date. *K* has a remaining deposit obligation of $95,000 that must be satisfied by April 2, 1991.

(d) If, with respect to any eighth-monthly period, an employer incurs an obligation to deposit in accordance with §31.6302(c)-1(a)(1)(ii)(*c*), and later, within the same eighth-monthly period, accumulates with respect to wages paid taxes of $3,000 or more, but less than $100,000, an additional deposit is required in accordance with §31.6302(c)-1(a)(1)(ii)(*b*). However, if the amount of taxes is $100,000 or more, an additional deposit is required in accordance with §31.6302(c)-1(a)(1)(ii)(*c*).

*Example:* On Tuesday, April 2, 1991, Employer *L* accumulates $110,000 in aggregate taxes with respect to wages paid. In accordance with paragraph (a)(1)(ii)(*c*) of this section, *L* has a $110,000 deposit obligation that must be satisfied by Wednesday, April 3, 1991, the next banking day following April 2. On Wednesday, April 3, 1991, *L* accumulates an additional $10,000 in taxes with respect to wages paid that date. In accordance with paragraph (a)(1)(ii)(*b*), *L* now has an additional deposit obligation of $10,000 that must be satisfied by Monday, April 8, 1991, the 3rd banking day following the close of the April 1-3 eighth-monthly period. The obligation to deposit the $10,000 is separate and distinct from the obligation to deposit the $110,000.

(e) An employer will be considered to have satisfied the deposit obligation imposed by paragraphs (a)(1)(ii)(b), (c) and (d) of this section if—

(1) The deposit that is made is not less than 95 percent of the aggregate amount of taxes accumulated with respect to wages paid during the period for which the deposit is made, and

(2) If the eighth-monthly period (or, in the case of a deposit required under paragraph (a)(1)(ii)(c) of this section, the day on which the obligation arose) is in a month other than the last month of the return period, the employer deposits any remaining amount due with the first deposit otherwise required to be made after the fifteenth day of the following month. In the case of the last month of the return period, see § 31.6302(c)-1(a)(1)(iv).

(f) Any excess of a deposit over the actual taxes required to be deposited to date (overdeposit) during the return period shall be applied in order of time to each of the employer's succeeding deposit obligations within the same return period. In the determination of the aggregate amount of taxes accumulated with respect to wages paid in succeeding deposit periods, the overdeposit does not reduce the aggregate amount accumulated although the overdeposit is credited to the depositor's account.

Example: Employer M's deposit obligation for the eighth-monthly period April 1-3, 1991, is $3,200. On April 8, 1991, three banking days after the close of the eighth-monthly period, M deposits $4,000 in an authorized depository, $800 in excess of the amount required to be deposited. During the eighth-monthly period April 4-7, 1991, M accumulates $3,750 in taxes with respect to wages paid during such period. Although the $800 overdeposit for the April 1-3 eighth-monthly period is credited to M's account, it may not be used to determine whether a deposit obligation exists for the April 4-7 eighth-monthly period. The two deposit obligations are separate and distinct. Since the amount of taxes accumulated with respect to the April 4-7 eighth-monthly period is an amount greater than $3,000, a deposit is required under paragraph (a)(1)(ii)(b) of this section within three banking days after the close of the period. M has a remaining deposit obligation of $2,950 ($3,750 accumulated less $800 overdeposit) that must be satisfied by April 10, 1991, three banking days after the close of the period.

(g) The periods within which taxes must be deposited under this section are determined, in the case of employers paying advance earned income credit amounts, by reference to the amount of taxes required to be deposited after reduction for advance amounts paid to employees.

(h) For purposes of this paragraph (a)(1)(ii), the term "wages paid" includes all amounts included in wages, e.g., under section 3121(v) of the Code, regardless of whether they have actually been paid.

(iii) As used in subdivisions (i) and (ii) of this subparagraph, the term "taxes" means—

(a) The employee tax withheld under section 3102,

(b) The employer tax under section 3111, and

(c) The income tax withheld under section 3402, including amounts withheld with respect to qualified State individual income taxes, exclusive of taxes with respect to wages for domestic service in a private home of the employer or, if paid before April 1, 1971, wages for agricultural labor. In addition, with respect to wages paid after December 31, 1970, and before April 1, 1971, for agricultural labor, any taxes described in subparagraph (2)(ii) of this paragraph which are not required under such subparagraph to be deposited, and any income tax (including qualified State individual income tax) withheld under section 3402 with respect to such wages, shall be deemed to be "taxes" on and after April 1, 1971. For the requirements relating to the deposit and payment of withheld tax with respect to qualified State individual income taxes, see paragraph (d)(3)(iii) of § 301.6361-1 of this chapter (Regulations on Procedure and Administration).

(iv) If the aggregate amount of taxes reportable on a return (other than a return on Form 942) for a return period exceeds the total amount deposited by the employer pursuant to subdivision (i) or (ii) of this subparagraph for such return period (a) by $500 or more in the case of a return period which ends after December 31, 1980, or (b) by more than $200 in the case of a return period which ends after December 31, 1970, and before January 1, 1981, the employer shall, on or before the last day of the first calendar month following the return period, deposit with a Federal Reserve bank or authorized financial institution an amount equal to the amount by which the taxes reportable on the return exceed the total deposits (if any) made pursuant to subdivision (i) or (ii) of this subparagraph for such period. As used in this subdivision, the term "taxes" shall have the meaning assigned to such term in subdivision (iii) of this subparagraph, except that the term shall include the taxes referred to in (a), (b), and (c) of such subdivision (iii) of this subparagraph with respect to any wages for domestic service in a private home of the employer which the employer elects to report on a quarterly return other than a quarterly return made on Form 942.

(v) If the aggregate amount of taxes reportable on Form CT-1, the return relating to an employer's railroad retirement tax payments, for a return period exceeds the total amount deposited by the employer pursuant to paragraph (a)(1)(i) of this section for such return period by $100 or more, the employer shall, on or before the last day of the second calendar month following the return period, deposit with a Federal Reserve bank or authorized financial institution an amount equal to the amount by which the taxes reportable on Form CT-1 exceed the total deposits (if any) of such taxes made pursuant to subdivision (i) of this subparagraph for such period.

(2) Depositary forms.—(i) In general.—A deposit required to be made by this section shall be made separately from a deposit required by any other section. An employer may make one, or more than one, remittance of the amount required to be deposited. However, a deposit for a period in one calendar quarter shall be made separately from any deposit for a period in another calendar quarter. An amount of tax which is not required to be deposited may nevertheless be deposited if the employer so desires.

(ii) Deposits.—Each remittance of amounts required to be deposited under paragraph (a)(1) of this section shall be accompanied by a Federal Tax Deposit form. Such form shall be prepared in accordance with the instructions applicable thereto. The remittance, together with the Federal Tax Deposit form, shall be forwarded to a financial institution authorized as a depositary for Federal taxes in accordance with 31 CFR Part 214 or, at the election of the employer, to a Federal Reserve bank. For procedures governing the deposit of Federal taxes at a Federal Reserve bank, see 31 CFR Part 214.7. The timeliness of the deposit will be determined by the date stamped on the Federal Tax Deposit form by the Federal Reserve bank or the authorized financial institution or, if section 7502(e) applies, by the date the deposit is treated as received under section 7502(e). Each employer making deposits under this section shall report on the return, for the period with respect to which such deposits are made, information regarding such deposits according to the instructions that apply to such return and pay at that time (or deposit by the due date of such return) the balance, if any, of the taxes due for such period.

(iii) Time deemed paid.—In general, amounts deposited under subdivision (ii) of this subparagraph shall be considered as paid on the last day prescribed for filing the return in respect of such tax (determined without regard to any extension of time for filing such return), or at the time deposited, whichever is later. For purposes of section 6511 and the regulations thereunder, relating to period of limitation on credit or refund, if an amount is so deposited prior to April 15th of a calendar year immediately succeeding the calendar year which contains the period for which such amount was so deposited, such amount shall be considered as paid on such April 15th.

(3) Procurement of prescribed form.—Copies of the Federal Tax Deposit form will so far as possible be furnished employers. An employer will not be excused from making a deposit, however, by the fact that no form has been furnished to it. An employer not supplied with the Federal Tax Deposit form should make application therefor in ample time to make the required deposits within the time prescribed. The employer may secure the form or additional forms by application therefor; such application shall supply the employer's name, identification number, address, and the taxable period to which the deposits will relate.

(b) Exceptions.—(1) Monthly returns.—The provisions of this section are not applicable with respect to taxes for the month in which the employer receives notice that returns are required under § 31.6011(a)-5 (or for any subsequent month for which such a return is required), if those taxes are also required to be deposited under the separate accounting procedures provided in § 301.7512-1 of this chapter (Regulations on Procedure and Administration) (which procedures are applicable if notification is given of failure to comply with certain employment tax requirements). In cases in which a monthly return is required under § 31.6011(a)-5 but the taxes are not required to be deposited under the separate accounting procedures provided in § 301.7512-1, the provisions of this section shall apply except that paragraph (a)(1)(iv) shall not authorize the deferral of any deposit to a date after the date on which the return is required to be filed.

(2) Wages paid in nonconvertible foreign currency.—The provisions of this section are not applicable with respect to taxes paid in nonconvertible foreign currency pursuant to § 301.6316-7 of this chapter (Regulations on Procedure and Administration). [Reg. § 31.6302(c)-1.]

☐ [T.D. 6354, 1-13-59. Amended by T.D. 6872, 1-5-66; T.D. 6884, 5-16-66; T.D. 6903, 12-19-66; T.D. 6915, 3-28-67; T.D. 6941, 12-15-67; T.D. 6957, 6-3-68; T.D. 7078, 12-4-70; T.D. 7096, 3-17-71; T.D. 7574, 11-30-78; T.D. 7577, 12-19-78; T.D. 7701, 6-9-80; T.D. 7766, 1-28-81;

T.D. 7931, 12-23-83; T.D. 7953, 5-8-84; T.D. 8341, 3-27-91; T.D. 8436, 9-22-92 and T.D. 9239, 12-30-2005.]

### [Reg. § 40.6302(c)-1]

**§ 40.6302(c)-1. Deposits.—(a)** *In general.*—(1) *Semimonthly deposits required.*—Except as provided by statute or by paragraph (e) of this section, each person required under § 40.6011(a)-1(a)(2) to file a quarterly return must make a deposit of tax for each semimonthly period (as defined in § 40.0-1(c)) in which tax liability is incurred.

(2) *Treatment of taxes imposed by chapter 33.*—For purposes of this part 40, tax imposed by chapter 33 (relating to communications and air transportation) is treated as a tax liability incurred during the semimonthly period—

(i) In which that tax is collected; or

(ii) In the case of the alternative method, in which that tax is considered as collected.

(3) *Definition of net tax liability.*—Net tax liability means the tax liability for the specified period plus or minus any adjustments allowable in accordance with the instructions applicable to the form on which the return is made.

(4) *Computation of net tax liability for a semimonthly period.*—The net tax liability for a semimonthly period may be computed by—

(i) Determining the net tax liability incurred during the semimonthly period; or

(ii) Dividing by two the net tax liability incurred during the calendar month that includes that semimonthly period, provided that this method of computation is used for all semimonthly periods in the calendar quarter.

**(b)** *Amount of deposit.*—(1) *In general.*—The deposit of tax for each semimonthly period must be not less than 95 percent of the amount of net tax liability incurred during the semimonthly period.

(2) *Safe harbor rules.*—(i) *Applicability.*—The safe harbor rules of this paragraph (b)(2) are applied separately to taxes deposited under the alternative method provided in § 40.6302(c)-3 (alternative method taxes) and to the other taxes for which deposits are required under this section (regular method taxes).

(ii) *Regular method taxes.*—Any person that made a return of tax reporting regular method taxes for the second preceding calendar quarter (the look-back quarter) is considered to have complied with the requirement of this part 40 for deposit of regular method taxes for the current calendar quarter if—

(A) The deposit of regular method taxes for each semimonthly period in the current calendar quarter is not less than 1/6 of the net tax liability for regular method taxes reported for the look-back quarter;

(B) Each deposit is made on time;

(C) The amount of any underpayment of regular method taxes is paid by the due date of the return; and

(D) The person's liability does not include any regular method tax that was not imposed at all times during the look-back quarter or a tax on a chemical not subject to tax at all times during the look-back quarter.

(iii) *Alternative method taxes.*—Any person that made a return of tax reporting alternative method taxes for the look-back quarter is considered to have complied with the requirement of this part 40 for deposit of alternative method taxes for the current calendar quarter if—

(A) The deposit of alternative method taxes for each semimonthly period in the current calendar quarter is not less than 1/6 of the net tax liability for alternative method taxes reported for the look-back quarter;

(B) Each deposit is made on time;

(C) The amount of any underpayment of alternative method taxes is paid by the due date of the return; and

(D) The person's liability does not include any alternative method tax that was not imposed at all times during the look-back quarter and the month preceding the look-back quarter.

(iv) *Modification for tax rate increase.*—The safe harbor rules of this paragraph (b)(2) do not apply to regular method taxes or alternative method taxes for the first and second calendar quarters beginning on or after the effective date of an increase in the rate of any tax to which this part 40 applies unless the deposit of those taxes for each semimonthly period in the calendar quarter is not less than 1/6 of the tax liability the person would have had with respect to those taxes for the look-back quarter if the increased rate of tax had been in effect for the look-back quarter.

(v) *Failure to comply with deposit requirements.*—If a person fails to make deposits as required under this part 40, the IRS may with-

draw the person's right to use the safe harbor rules of this paragraph (b)(2).

**(c)** *Time to deposit.*—(1) *In general.*—The deposit of tax for any semimonthly period must be made by the 14th day of the following semimonthly period unless such day is a Saturday, Sunday, or legal holiday in the District of Columbia in which case the immediately preceding day which is not a Saturday, Sunday, or legal holiday in the District of Columbia is treated as the 14th day. Thus, generally, the deposit of tax for the first semimonthly period in a month is due by the 29th day of that month and the deposit of tax for the second semimonthly period in a month is due by the 14th day of the following month.

(2) *Exceptions.*—See § 40.6302(c)-2 for the special rules for September. See § 40.6302(c)-3 for the special rules for deposits under the alternative method.

**(d)** *Deposits required by electronic funds transfer.*—All deposits required by this part must be made by *electronic funds transfer*, as that term is defined in § 31.6302-1(h)(4) of this chapter.

**(e)** *Exceptions.*—(1) *Taxes excluded.*—No deposit is required in the case of the taxes imposed by—

(i) Section 4042 (relating to fuel used on inland waterways);

(ii) Section 4161 (relating to sport fishing equipment and bows and arrow components);

(iii) Section 4682(h) (relating to floor stocks tax on ozone-depleting chemicals);

(iv) Sections 4375 and 4376 (relating to fees on health insurance policies and self-insured health plans); and

(v) Section 5000B (relating to indoor tanning services).

(2) *One-time filings.*—No deposit is required in the case of any taxes reportable on a one-time filing (as defined in § 40.6011(a)-2(b)).

(3) *De minimis exception.*—For any calendar quarter, no deposit is required if the net tax liability for the quarter does not exceed $2,500.

**(f)** *Effective/applicability date.*—This section applies to deposits and payments made after March 31, 2013. For rules that apply before that date, see 26 CFR part 40 (revised as of April 1, 2013). [Reg. § 40.6302(c)-1.]

☐ [T.D. 8442, 10-21-92. Amended by T.D. 8609, 8-4-95; T.D. 8685, 11-8-96; T.D. 8723, 7-11-97; T.D. 8887, 6-7-2000; T.D. 8952, 6-25-2001; T.D. 8963, 8-8-2001; T.D. 9486, 6-11-2010; T.D. 9507, 12-2-2010; T.D. 9602, 12-5-2012 and T.D. 9621, 6-10-2013.]

### [Reg. § 46.6302(c)-1]

**§ 46.6302(c)-1. Use of Government depositaries.—(a)** *Requirements.*—(1) *In general.*—(i) Except as provided in subdivision (ii) of this subparagraph, if for any calendar month, other than the last month of a calendar quarter, any person required to file a quarterly excise tax return on Form 720 has a total liability of more than $100 for all excise taxes reportable on such form, the amount of such liability for taxes (to which this part relates) shall be deposited by him with a Federal Reserve bank on or before the last day of the month following such month.

(ii) This subdivision shall apply to excise taxes (to which this part relates) which are reportable on Form 720 by any person for February and March 1967, or for a calendar quarter thereafter, if such person's total liability for all excise taxes reportable on such form for any calendar month in the preceding calendar quarter exceeded $2,000. In any case to which this subdivision applies, the excise tax for a semimonthly period (as defined in paragraph (b)(1) of this section) shall be deposited by such person in a Federal Reserve Bank on or before the depositary receipt date (as defined in paragraph (b)(2) of this section). A person will be considered to have complied with the requirements of this subdivision for a semimonthly period if—

(a)(1) His deposit for such semimonthly period is not less than 90 percent of the total amount of the excise taxes (to which this part and Part 48 relate) reportable by him on Form 720 for such period, and (2) if such period occurs in a month other than the last month in a calendar quarter, he deposits any underpayment for such month by the first day of the second month following such month; or

(b)(1) His deposit for each semimonthly period in the month is not less than 45 percent of the total amount of the excise taxes (to which this part and Part 48 relate) reportable by him on Form 720 for the month, and (2) if such month is other than the last month in a calendar quarter, he deposits any underpayment for such month by the first day of the second month following such month; or

(c)(1) His deposit for each semimonthly period in the month is not less than 50 percent of the total amount of the excise taxes (to which this part and Part 118 relate) reportable by him on

Form 720 for the preceding calendar month, and (2) if such month is other than the last month in a calendar quarter, he deposits any underpayment for such month by the first day of the second month following such month.

Accordingly, a person who makes his deposits in accordance with the provisions of (b) or (c) of this subdivision will not find it necessary to keep his books and records on a semimonthly basis. However, (b) and (c) of this subdivision shall not apply to any such person who normally incurs in the first semimonthly period in each month more than 75 percent of his total excise tax liability (to which this part and Part 48 relate) for the month.

(iii) The provisions of this section shall not apply with respect to taxes for the month or the semimonthly period in which the taxpayer receives notice from the district director that returns are required under paragraph (b) of § 46.6011(a)-1, or for any subsequent month or semimonthly period for which such a return is required.

(2) *Special requirement.*—The provisions of this subparagraph shall apply to every person (whether or not required by subparagraph (1) of this paragraph to make a deposit of taxes) required to file a quarterly excise tax return on Form 720 for a calendar quarter which begins after March 31, 1968, who has a total liability for all excise taxes (to which this part and Part 48 of this chapter relate) reportable on such form which exceeds by more than $100 the total amount of taxes deposited by him pursuant to subparagraph (1) of this paragraph for such quarter. Such person shall, on or before the last day of the month following the calendar quarter for which the return is required to be filed, deposit with a Federal Reserve bank or authorized financial institution the full amount by which his liability for all excise taxes reportable on such form for that calendar quarter exceeds the amount of excise taxes previously deposited by him for that calendar quarter.

(b) *Definitions.*—For purposes of this part—

(1) *Semimonthly period.*—A "semimonthly period" means the first 15 days of a calendar month or the portion of a calendar month following the 15th day of such month.

(2) *Depositary receipt date.*—With respect to the first semimonthly period of a month, the "depositary receipt date" is the first day of the month following such month. With respect to the second semimonthly period of a month, the "depositary receipt date" is the 15th day of the month following such month.

(c) *Depositary forms.*—(1) *In general.*—A person required to make deposits by paragraph (a) of this section may make one, or more than one, remittance of the amount required to be deposited. An amount of such tax which is not required to be deposited may nevertheless be deposited if the person liable for the tax so desires.

(2) *Deposits.*—Each remittance of amounts required to be deposited shall be accompanied by a Federal Tax Deposit form which shall be prepared in accordance with the instructions applicable thereto. The remittance, together with a Federal Tax Deposit form, shall be forwarded to a financial institution authorized as a depositary for Federal taxes in accordance with 31 CFR Part 214 or, at the election of the person making the remittance, to a Federal Reserve bank. For procedures covering the deposit of Federal taxes at a Federal Reserve bank, see 31 CFR part 214.7. The timeliness of the deposit is determined by the date stamped on the Federal Tax Deposit form by the Federal Reserve bank or the authorized financial institution or, if section 7502(e) applies, by the date the deposit is treated as received under section 7502(e). Each person making deposits under this section shall report on the return, for the period with respect to which such deposits are made, information regarding such deposits according to the instructions that apply to such return and pay at that time (or deposit by the due date of such return) the balance, if any, of the taxes due for such period.

(3) *Time deemed paid.*—Amounts deposited under subparagraph (2) of this paragraph shall be considered as paid on the last day prescribed for filing the return in respect of such tax (determined without regard to any extension of time for filing such return), or at the time deposited, whichever is later.

(d) *Procurement of prescribed form.*—Copies of the Federal Tax Deposit form will so far as possible be furnished persons required to deposit. Such a person will not be excused from making a deposit, however, by the fact that no form has been furnished to it. A person not supplied with the proper form should make application therefor in ample time to make the required deposits within the time prescribed. The person may secure the Federal Tax Deposit form or additional forms by applying therefor and supplying its name, identification number, address, and the taxable period to which the deposits will relate. Copies of the Federal Tax Deposit form may be

secured by application therefor to the district director or director of a service center. [Reg. § 46.6302(c)-1.]

☐ [T.D. 6498. *Amended by* T.D. 6910, 1-27-67; T.D. 6915, 3-28-67; T.D. 6941, 12-15-67; T.D. 6957, 6-3-68 *and* T.D. 7953, 5-9-84.]

[Reg. § 49.6302(c)-1]

**§ 49.6302(c)-1. Use of Government depositaries.**—(a) *Requirement.*—(1) *In general.*—(i) If for any calendar month, other than the last month of a calendar quarter, any person required to file a quarterly excise tax return on Form 720 has a total liability of more than $100 for all excise taxes collected (see subdivision (iii) of this subparagraph for amounts which are considered as collected) during such month and reportable on such form, the amount of such total liability shall be deposited by him with a Federal Reserve bank on or before the last day of the month following such month.

(ii) This subdivision shall apply to excise taxes (to which this part relates) which are collected (see subdivision (iii) of this subparagraph for amounts which are considered as collected), by any person required to pay over such taxes, if such person's total liability for all excise taxes reportable on Form 720 for any calendar month in the preceding calendar quarter exceeded $2,000. A person shall deposit the excise taxes to which this subdivision applies in a Federal Reserve bank within 3 banking days after the close of the semimonthly period (as defined in paragraph (b) of this section) during which such taxes were collected. A person will be considered to have complied with the requirements of this subdivision for a semimonthly period if—

(a)(1) His deposit for such semimonthly period is not less than 90 percent of the total amount of the excise taxes (to which this part relates) collected by him during such period, and (2) if such period occurs in a month other than the last month in a calendar quarter, he deposits any underpayment for such month by the last day of the following month; or

(b)(1) His deposit for each semimonthly period in the month is not less than 45 percent of the total amount of the excise taxes (to which this part relates) collected by him during the month, and (2) if such month is other than the last month in a calendar quarter, he deposits any underpayment for such month by the last day of the following month; or

(c)(1) His deposit for each semimonthly period in the month is not less than 50 percent of the total amount of the excise taxes (to which this part relates) collected by him during the preceding calendar month, and (2) if such month is other than the last month in a calendar quarter, he deposits any underpayment for such month by the last day of the following month.

Accordingly, a person who makes his deposits in accordance with the provisions of (b) or (c) of this subdivision will not find it necessary to keep his books and records on a semimonthly basis. However, (b) and (c) of this subdivision shall not apply to any such person who normally collects in the first semimonthly period in each month more than 75 percent of his total excise taxes (to which this part relates) collected during the month.

(iii) For purposes of applying this subparagraph to a person who computes amounts of tax required to be paid over on the basis of amounts billed (in the case of the tax imposed by section 4251) or tickets sold (in the case of the tax imposed by section 4261), the tax so computed for a monthly period ended after March 31, 1967, shall be considered as collected during the succeeding monthly period and the tax so computed for a semimonthly period shall be considered as collected during the second succeeding semimonthly period. A person must notify the Commissioner before changing from one method of computing the tax to another, so that proper adjustments may be made in order to properly reflect the person's excise tax liability.

(iv) The provisions of this section shall not apply with respect to taxes for the month or the semimonthly period in which the person receives notice from the district director that returns are required under paragraph (b) of § 49.6011(a)-1, or for any subsequent month or semimonthly period for which such a return is required.

(v) See paragraph (e) of this section for special rule in case of continuation of certain excise tax rates.

(2) *Special requirement.*—The provisions of this subparagraph shall apply to every person (whether or not required by subparagraph (1) of this paragraph to make a deposit of taxes) required to file a quarterly excise tax return on Form 720 for a calendar quarter which begins after March 31, 1968, who has a total liability for all excise taxes (to which this part relates) reportable on such form which exceeds by more than $100 the total amount of taxes deposited by him pursuant to subparagraph (1) of this paragraph for such quarter. Such person shall, on or before the last day of the second month following the calendar quarter for which the return is required to be filed, deposit with a Federal Reserve bank or authorized financial institution the full amount by which liability for all excise taxes reportable on such form for that calendar quarter exceeds the

amount of excise taxes previously deposited by him for that calendar quarter.

(b) *Definition of semimonthly period.*—A "semimonthly period" means the first 15 days of a calendar month or the portion of a calendar month following the 15th day of such month.

(c) *Depositary forms.*—(1) *In general.*—A person required to make deposits by paragraph (a) of this section may make one, or more than one, remittance of the amount required to be deposited. An amount of such tax which is not required to be deposited may nevertheless be deposited if the person liable for the tax so desires.

(2) *Deposits.*—Each remittance of amounts required to be deposited shall be accompanied by a Federal Tax Deposit form which shall be prepared in accordance with the instructions applicable thereto. The remittance, together with a Federal Tax Deposit form, shall be forwarded to a financial institution authorized as a depositary for Federal taxes in accordance with 31 CFR Part 214 or, at the election of the person making the remittance, to a Federal Reserve bank. For procedures governing the deposit of Federal taxes at a Federal Reserve bank, see 31 CFR Part 214.7. The timeliness of the deposit is determined by the date stamped on the Federal Tax Deposit form by the Federal Reserve bank or the authorized financial institution or, if section 7502(e) applies, by the date the deposit is treated as received under section 7502(e). Each person making deposits under this section shall report on the return, for the period with respect to which such deposits are made, information regarding such deposits according to the instructions that apply to such return and pay at that time (or deposit by the due date of such return) the balance, if any, of the taxes due for such period.

(3) *Times deemed paid.*—Amounts deposited under subparagraph (2) of this paragraph shall be considered as paid on the last day prescribed for filing the return in respect of such tax (determined without regard to any extension of time for filing such return), or at the time deposited, whichever is later.

(4) *Procurement of prescribed form.*—Copies of the Federal Tax Deposit form will so far as possible be furnished persons required to deposit. Such a person will not be excused from making a deposit, however, by the fact that no form has been furnished to it. A person not supplied with the form should make application therefor in ample time to make the required deposits within the time prescribed. The person may secure the form or additional forms by applying therefor and supplying its name, identification number, address, and the taxable period to which the deposits will relate. Copies of the Federal Tax Deposit form may be secured by application therefor to the district director or director of a service center.

(d) *Special rule in case of certain continuation of tax rates.*—(1) *Application of paragraph.*—This paragraph shall apply to amounts, due under section 4251 with respect to amounts paid pursuant to bills first rendered after April 30, 1968, and collected (see paragraph (a)(1)(iii) of this section for amounts considered as collected) during any monthly or semimonthly period ending before the date of enactment of legislation, enacted subsequent to April 30, 1968, which increases the rate of tax applicable under section 4251 to such amounts.

(2) *Amount to be deposited under this paragraph.*—The amount to be deposited under this paragraph is an amount equal to the difference between—

(i) The amount required to be deposited, with respect to amounts paid pursuant to bills first rendered during the period described in subparagraph (1) of this paragraph, determined by reference to a sale of tax of one percent, and

(ii) The amount required to be deposited, with respect to amounts paid pursuant to bills first rendered during such period, determined by reference to a rate of tax of 10 percent.

(3) *Time for making deposits.*—The amount described in subparagraph (2) of this paragraph shall be deposited on or before the later of—

(i) The third banking day following the enactment of the legislation described in subparagraph (1) of this paragraph,

(ii) July 3, 1968, or

(iii) The date prescribed by paragraph (a) of this section. [Reg. § 49.6302(c)-1.]

☐ [*T.D. 6910, 1-27-67. Amended by T.D. 6915, 3-28-67; T.D. 6941, 12-15-67; T.D. 6957, 6-3-68; T.D. 6959, 6-18-68 and T.D. 7953, 5-9-84.*]

### [Reg. § 31.6302(c)-2]

**§ 31.6302(c)-2. Use of Government depositaries in connection with employee and employer taxes under Railroad Retirement Tax Act for amounts attributable to payments made before January 1, 1993.**—(a) *Requirement.*—(1) *In general: after 1983 and before April 1,*

1991.—In the case of a calendar month which begins after December 31, 1983, and before April 1, 1991, if, at a time prescribed under § 31.6302(c)-1(a)(1) (i) or (v) for the deposit of undeposited taxes, the aggregate amount of undeposited employee tax withheld after December 31, 1983, and before April 1, 1991, under section 3202 and employer tax imposed after December 31, 1983, and before April 1, 1991, under section 3221(a) and (b) equals an amount required to be deposited under § 31.6302(c)-1(a)(1) (i) or (v) the employer shall deposit the undeposited railroad retirement taxes described in sections 3202 and 3221 at such time in the manner prescribed in § 31.6302(c)-1(a)(1) (i) or (v) (except that undeposited railroad retirement taxes described in section 3221 (c) shall in no case be required to be deposited earlier than the first day on which a deposit is otherwise required by § 31.6302(c)-1(a)(1)(i) to be made after the 15th day of the month following the month in which the section 3221 (c) tax arises).

Notwithstanding the preceding sentence, and notwithstanding subdivision (v) of § 31.6302 (c)-1 (a) (1), if, for the calendar year prior to the calendar year preceding the current calendar year, the aggregate amount of taxes imposed under sections 3202 and 3221 with respect to an employer equalled or exceeded $1 million, such employer shall deposit his undeposited railroad retirement taxes required to be deposited for the current calendar year in accordance with Revenue Procedure 83-90, 1983-52 I.R.B. 18, (relating to transfers by wire to the Treasury).

(2) *In general: After March 31, 1991 and before January 1, 1993.*—In the case of a calendar month which begins after March 31, 1991, if, at a time prescribed under § 31.6302(c)-1(a)(1)(ii) or (v) for the deposit of accumulated taxes, the aggregate amount of accumulated employee tax withheld after March 31, 1991, under section 3202 and employer tax imposed after March 31, 1991, under section 3221(a) and (b) equals an amount required to be deposited under § 31.6302(c)-1(a)(1)(ii) or (v), the employer shall deposit the accumulated railroad retirement taxes described in sections 3202 and 3221 at the time and in the manner prescribed in § 31.6302(c)-1(a)(1)(ii) or (v) (except that accumulated railroad retirement taxes described in section 3221(c) shall in no case be required to be deposited earlier than the first day on which a deposit is otherwise required by § 31.6302(c)-1(a)(1)(ii) to be made after the 15th day of the month following the month in which the section 3221(c) tax arises). Notwithstanding the preceding sentence, and notwithstanding § 31.6302(c)-1(a)(1)(v), if, for the calendar year prior to the calendar year preceding the current calendar year, the aggregate amount of taxes imposed under sections 3202 and 3221 with respect to an employer equalled or exceeded $1 million, such employer shall deposit the aggregate amount of railroad retirement taxes required to be deposited for the current calendar year in accordance with Revenue Procedure 83-90, 1983-2 C.B. 615 (relating to transfers by wire to the Treasury).

(3) *Special requirement.*—If an employer files a return on Form CT-1 for a return period beginning before January 1, 1984, and the taxes shown thereon exceed by more than $100 the total amount deposited by him pursuant to paragraph (a)(1) of this section for such return period the employer shall, on or before the last day of the second calendar month following the period for which the return is filed, deposit with a Federal Reserve bank or authorized financial institution an amount equal to the amount by which the taxes shown on the return exceed the total deposits (if any) made pursuant to paragraph (a)(1) of this section for such return period.

(b) *Depositary forms.*—(1) *In general.*—A deposit required to be made by this section shall be made separately from a deposit required by any other section. An employer may make one, or more than one remittance of the amount required to be deposited. An amount of tax which is not required to be deposited may nevertheless be deposited if the employer so desires. If the aggregate amount of the taxes deposited is in excess of the taxes shown on the return, a credit or refund may be obtained; and in the event the excess is applied as a credit against such taxes for a subsequent return period, the employer shall reduce the amount of one or more of the deposits otherwise required for such subsequent return period by the amount of such credit.

(2) *Deposits.*—Each remittance of amounts required to be deposited shall be accompanied by a Federal Tax Deposit form which shall be prepared in accordance with the instructions applicable thereto. Except as provided in paragraph (a)(1) or (a)(2) of this section, the remittance, together with the form, shall be forwarded to a financial institution authorized as a depositary for Federal taxes in accordance with 31 CFR part 214 or, at the election of the employer, to a Federal Reserve bank. For procedures governing the deposit of Federal taxes at a Federal Reserve bank, see 31 CFR part 214.7. The timeliness of the deposit will be determined by the date stamped on the Federal Tax Deposit form by the Federal Reserve bank or the authorized

financial institution or, if section 7502(e) applies, by the date the deposit is treated as received under section 7502(e). Each employer making deposits under this section shall report on the return, for the period with respect to which such deposits are made, information regarding such deposits according to the instructions that apply to such return and pay at that time (or deposit by the due date of such return) the balance, if any, of the taxes due for such period.

(3) *Time deemed paid.*—In general, amounts deposited under subparagraph (2) of this paragraph shall be considered as paid on the last day prescribed for filing the return in respect of such tax (determined without regard to any extension of time for filing such return), or at the time deposited, whichever is later. For purposes of section 6511 and the regulations thereunder, relating to period of limitation on credit or refund, if an amount is so deposited prior to April 15th of a calendar year immediately succeeding the calendar year in which occurs the period for which such amount was so deposited, such amount shall be considered as paid on such April 15th.

(c) *Procurement of prescribed form.*—Copies of the Federal Tax Deposit form will so far as possible be furnished employers. An employer will not be excused from making a deposit, however, by the fact that no form has been furnished to it. An employer not supplied with the form should make application therefor in ample time to make the required deposits within the time prescribed. The employer may secure the form or additional forms by applying therefor and supplying its name, identification number, address, and the taxable period to which the deposits will relate. Copies of the Federal Tax Deposit form may be secured by application therefor. [Reg. § 31.6302(c)-2.]

☐ [*T.D. 6516, 12-20-60. Amended by T.D. 6941, 12-16-67; T.D. 6957, 6-3-68; T.D. 7419, 5-12-76; T.D. 7931, 12-23-83; T.D. 7953, 5-8-84; T.D. 8341, 3-27-91; T.D. 8436, 9-22-92 and T.D. 9239, 12-30-2005.*]

### [Reg. § 40.6302(c)-2]

**§ 40.6302(c)-2. Special rules for September.**—(a) *In general.*— (1) *Separate deposits required for the second semimonthly period.*—In the case of deposits of taxes not deposited under the alternative method (regular method taxes) for the second semimonthly period in September, separate deposits are required for the period September 16th through 26th and for the period September 27th through 30th.

(2) *Amount of deposit.*—(i) *In general.*—The deposits of regular method taxes for the period September 16th through 26th and the period September 27th through 30th must be not less than 95 percent of the net tax liability for regular method taxes incurred during the respective periods. The net tax liability for regular method taxes incurred during these periods may be computed by—

(A) Determining the amount of net tax liability for regular method taxes reasonably expected to be incurred during the second semimonthly period in September;

(B) Treating 11/15 of the amount determined under paragraph (a)(2)(i)(A) of this section as the net tax liability for regular method taxes incurred during the period September 16th through 26th; and

(C) Treating the remainder of the amount determined under paragraph (a)(2)(i)(A) of this section (adjusted to reflect the amount of net tax liability for regular method taxes actually incurred through the end of September) as the net tax liability for regular method taxes incurred during the period September 27th through 30th.

(ii) *Safe harbor rules.*—The safe harbor rules in § 40.6302(c)-1(b)(2) do not apply for the third calendar quarter unless—

(A) The deposit of taxes for the period September 16th through 26th is not less than 11/90 of the net tax liability for regular method taxes reported for the look-back quarter; and

(B) The total deposit of taxes for the second semimonthly period in September is not less than 1/6 of the net tax liability for regular method taxes reported for the look-back quarter.

(3) *Time to deposit.*—(i) The deposit required for the period beginning September 16th must be made by September 29th unless—

(A) September 29th is a Saturday, in which case the deposit must be made by September 28th; or

(B) September 29th is a Sunday, in which case the deposit must be made by September 30th.

(ii) The deposit required for the period ending September 30th must be made at the time prescribed in § 40.6302(c)-1(c).

(b) *Persons not required to use electronic funds transfer.*—The rules of this section are applied with the following modifications in the case of a person not required to deposit taxes by electronic funds transfer.

(1) *Periods.*—The deposit periods for the separate deposits required under paragraph (a) of this section are September 16th through 25th and September 26th through 30th.

(2) *Amount of deposit.*—In computing the amount of deposit required under paragraph (a)(2)(i)(B) of this section, the applicable fraction is 10/15. In computing the amount of deposit required under paragraph (a)(2)(ii)(A) of this section, the applicable fraction is 10/90.

(3) *Time to deposit.*—In the case of the deposit required under paragraph (a) of this section for the period beginning September 16th, the deposit must be made by September 28th unless—

(i) September 28th is a Saturday, in which case the deposit must be made by September 27th; or

(ii) September 28th is a Sunday, in which case the deposit must be made by September 29th.

(c) *Effective date.*—This section is applicable with respect to deposits that relate to calendar quarters beginning on or after October 1, 2001, except that paragraph (b) of this section does not apply after December 31, 2010. [Reg. § 40.6302(c)-2.]

☐ [*T.D. 8442, 10-21-92. Amended by T.D. 8685, 11-8-96; T.D. 8887, 6-7-2000; T.D. 8963, 8-8-2001 and T.D. 9507, 12-2-2010.*]

### [Reg. § 31.6302(c)-3]

**§ 31.6302(c)-3. Deposit rules for taxes under the Federal Unemployment Tax Act.**—(a) *Requirement.*—(1) *In general.*—Except as provided in paragraph (a)(2) of this section, every person that, by reason of the provisions of section 6157, computes the tax imposed by section 3301 on a quarterly or other time period basis shall—

(i) If the person is described in section (a)(1) of section 6157, deposit the amount of such tax by the last day of the first calendar month following the close of each of the first three calendar quarters in the calendar year; or

(ii) If the person is other than a person described in section (a)(1) of section 6157, deposit the amount of such tax by the last day of the first calendar month following the close of—

(a) The period beginning with the first day of the calendar year and ending with the last day of the calendar quarter (excluding the last calendar quarter) in which such person becomes an employer (as defined in section 3306(a)), and

(b) The third calendar quarter of such year, if the period specified in (a) of this subdivision includes only the first two calendar quarters of the calendar year.

(2) *Special rule where accumulated amount does not exceed $500.*— The provisions of paragraph (a)(1) of this section shall not apply with respect to any period described therein if the amount of the tax imposed by section 3301 for such period (as computed under section 6157) plus amounts not deposited for prior periods does not exceed $500 ($100 in the case of periods ending on or before December 31, 2004). Thus, an employer shall not be required to make a deposit for a period unless his tax for such period plus tax not deposited for prior periods exceeds $500.

(b) *Manner of deposit.*—(1) *In general.*—A deposit required to be made by an employer under this section shall be made separately from a deposit required by any other section. An employer may make one, or more than one, remittance of the amount required to be deposited. An employer that is not required to deposit an amount of tax by this section may nevertheless voluntarily make that deposit. For the requirement to deposit tax under the Federal Unemployment Tax Act by electronic funds transfer, see § 31.6302-1(h).

(2) *Time deemed paid.*—For the time an amount deposited by electronic funds transfer is deemed paid, see § 31.6302-1(h)(9). For the time an amount remitted with a return is deemed paid, see § 31.6302-1(i)(3).

(c) *Effective/applicability date.*—This section applies to deposits and payments made after December 31, 2010. [Reg. § 31.6302(c)-3.]

☐ [*T.D. 7037, 4-27-70. Amended by T.D. 7062, 9-23-70; T.D. 7953, 5-8-84; T.D. 8723, 7-11-97; T.D. 8952, 6-25-2001; T.D. 9162, 11-30-2004; T.D. 9239, 12-30-2005 and T.D. 9507, 12-2-2010.*]

### [Reg. § 40.6302(c)-3]

**§ 40.6302(c)-3. Deposits under chapter 33.**—(a) *Overview.*—This section sets forth an alternative method for computing the amount of deposits of taxes imposed by chapter 33, and provides rules relating to the time for making a deposit and the amount of tax to be reported on the return of tax for each quarter by persons using the alternative method. The safe harbor rules for computing deposits of tax using the alternative method and the general rules relating to deposits are set forth in § 40.6302(c)-1 and apply unless inconsistent with the rules set forth below.

(b) *Alternative method for computing deposits.*—(1) *In general.*—(i) *Alternative method.*—Any person required to collect and pay over any tax imposed by chapter 33 may compute the amount of that tax to be deposited on the basis of amounts considered as collected (the "alternative method") instead of on the basis of actual collections of tax.

(ii) *Using more than one method to compute deposits.*—A person may compute deposits of tax imposed by one or more sections of chapter 33 using the alternative method provided by this section and compute deposits of taxes imposed by other sections of chapter 33 on the basis of amounts actually collected using the rule of § 40.6302(c)-1(c)(1). For purposes of this paragraph (b)(1)(ii), the taxes imposed by section 4261(a) and (b) are treated as taxes imposed by the same section.

(2) *Applicability.*—(i) *In general.*—A person may use the alternative method with respect to a tax only if the person—

(A) Separately accounts for the tax in accordance with paragraph (b)(2)(ii) of this section; and

(B) Makes a return of the tax on the basis of the amount of the tax that is considered as collected.

(ii) *Separate account.*—The account required under paragraph (b)(2)(i)(A) of this section (the separate account)—

(A) Must reflect for each month all items of tax that are included in amounts billed or tickets sold to customers during the month;

(B) May not reflect an item of adjustment for any month during a quarter if the adjustment results from a refusal to pay or inability to collect the tax and the uncollected tax has not been reported under § 49.4291-1 of this chapter on or before the due date of the return for that quarter; and

(C) Must reflect for each month items of adjustment (including bad debts and errors) relating to the tax for prior months within the period of limitations on credits or refunds.

(iii) *Change of method.*—The method of computing deposits of tax imposed by a section of chapter 33 (as described in paragraph (b)(1)(ii) of this section) may be changed only at the beginning of a calendar quarter. Before a person changes the method used to compute the amount of tax to be deposited and reported for a calendar quarter, the person must notify the Commissioner so that proper adjustments may be made in order to properly reflect that person's collections of excise tax.

(3) *Period during which tax is considered as collected.*—For purposes of this section, the tax included in amounts billed or tickets sold during a semimonthly period (as defined in § 40.0-1(c)) is considered as collected during the first seven days of the second following semimonthly period. Thus, the tax included in amounts billed or tickets sold during the first semimonthly period of a calendar month is considered as collected during the period of the 1st day through the 7th day of the following month; the tax included in amounts billed or tickets sold during the second semimonthly period of a calendar month is considered as collected during the period of the 16th day through the 22nd day of the following month.

(4) *When amounts are billed.*—For purposes of this section, an amount is billed on the earlier of the date the amount is received or the date a bill for the amount is rendered.

(c) *Time to deposit.*—Under the alternative method, the deposit of tax for any semimonthly period must be made by the third business day after the seventh day of that semimonthly period. For purposes of this paragraph (c), a "business day" is any calendar day other than a Saturday, Sunday, or legal holiday. The term *legal holiday* means a legal holiday in the District of Columbia as defined in section 7503. Thus, for example, the deposit for the semimonthly period beginning on January 1, 2011 (relating to amounts billed between December 1st and December 15, 2010) is due by January 12, 2011, three business days after January 7, the seventh day of the semimonthly period. The deposit for the semimonthly period beginning on October 1, 2011 (relating to amounts billed between September 1st and September 15, 2011), is due by October 13, 2011, due to the October 10, 2011, Columbus Day holiday.

(d) *Computation of net amount of tax that is considered as collected during a semimonthly period.*—The net amount of tax that is considered as collected during the semimonthly period must be either the net amount of tax reflected in the separate account for the corresponding semimonthly period of the preceding month or one-half the net amount of tax reflected in the separate account for the preceding month.

(e) *Reporting of tax.*—If a tax is deposited under the alternative method for a calendar quarter, the return of tax for the quarter must report the net amount of the tax that is considered as collected during the quarter and not the amount of the tax that is actually collected during the quarter. The amount to be reported for each month is the net amount of tax reflected in the separate account for the preceding month. For example, amounts billed in December, January, and February are considered as collected during January, February, and March, and are reported as the collections of tax for January, February, and March (the first calendar quarter). Thus, the net amount of tax reflected in the separate accounts for December, January, and February is the amount reported as collections for the first quarter.

(f) *Special rules for September.*—(1) *Deposits required.*—In the case of alternative method taxes charged (that is, included in amounts billed or tickets sold) during the first semimonthly period in September, separate deposits are required for the taxes charged during the period September 1st-11th and the period September 12th-15th.

(2) *Time to deposit.*—(i) *In general.*—The deposit required for alternative method taxes charged during the period beginning September 1st must be made by September 29. The deposit required for alternative method taxes charged during the period ending September 15th must be made at the time prescribed in paragraph (c) of this section for making deposits for the first semimonthly period in October.

(ii) *Due date on Saturday or Sunday.*—A deposit that would otherwise be due on September 29 must be made by September 28 if September 29 is a Saturday and by September 30 if September 29 is a Sunday.

(3) *Amount of deposit.*—The deposits of alternative method taxes required for the period September 1st-11th and the period September 12th-15th must be not less than the amount of alternative method taxes charged during the respective periods. The amount of alternative method taxes charged during these periods may be computed by—

(i) Determining the net amount of alternative method taxes reflected in the separate account for the first semimonthly period in September (or one-half of the net amount of alternative method taxes reasonably expected to be reflected in the separate account for the month of September);

(ii) Treating $^{11}/_{15}$ of that amount as the amount of taxes charged during the period September 1st-11th; and

(iii) Treating the remainder of the amount determined under paragraph (f)(3)(i) of this section (adjusted, if that amount is based on reasonable expectations, to reflect actual taxes charged through the end of September) as the amount charged during the period September 12th-15th.

(4) *Safe harbor rule based on look-back quarter liability.*—The safe harbor rule of § 40.6302(c)-1(b)(2) does not apply for the fourth calendar quarter unless—

(i) The deposit for alternative method taxes charged during the period September 1st-11th is not less than $^{11}/_{90}$ of the net tax liability reported for alternative method taxes for the look-back quarter; and

(ii) The total deposit for alternative method taxes charged during the first semimonthly period in September is not less than $^1/_6$ of the net tax liability reported for alternative method taxes for the look-back quarter.

(5) *Persons not required to use electronic funds transfer.*—In the case of a person that is not required to deposit excise taxes by electronic funds transfer (a non-EFT depositor), the rules of this paragraph (f) apply with the following modifications:

(i) The taxes for which separate deposits must be made are the taxes charged during the periods September 1st-10th and September 11th-15th.

(ii) The deposit required for taxes charged during the period beginning September 1st must be made by September 28. A deposit that would otherwise be due on September 28 must be made by September 27 if September 28 is a Saturday and by September 29 if September 28 is a Sunday.

(iii) The generally applicable fractions and percentage are modified to reflect the different deposit periods in accordance with the following table:

| Generally applicable fractions and percentage | Modifications for non-EFT depositors |
|---|---|
| $^{15}/_{11}$ | $^{15}/_{10}$ |
| $^{90}/_{11}$ | $^{90}/_{10}$ |
| 69.67 percent | 63.33 percent |

(g) *Effective date.*—This section is applicable with respect to deposits and returns that relate to taxes that are considered as collected in calendar quarters beginning on or after October 1, 2001, except that paragraph (b)(2)(ii)(B) of this section is applicable October 1, 2004, and except that paragraph (f)(5) of this section does not apply after December 31, 2010. [Reg. § 40.6302(c)-3.]

☐ [*T.D. 8442, 10-21-92. Amended by T.D. 8685, 11-8-96 (technical amendments, 3-30-98); T.D. 8963, 8-8-2001; T.D. 9051, 4-1-2003; T.D. 9149, 8-9-2004; T.D. 9221, 8-24-2005 and T.D. 9507, 12-2-2010 (corrected 1-5-2011).*]

### [Reg. §31.6302(c)-4]

§31.6302(c)-4. Cross references.—(a) *Failure to deposit.*—For provisions relating to the penalty for failure to make a deposit within the prescribed time, see section 6656.

# PAYMENT OF FEDERAL TAXES AND THE TREASURY TAX AND LOAN PROGRAM—31 CFR, Part 203

## Subpart A—General Information

### [Reg. §203.1]

§203.1. Scope.—The regulations in this part govern the processing of Federal tax payments by financial institutions and the Federal Reserve Banks (FRB) using electronic payment or paper methods; the designation of Treasury Tax and Loan (TT&L) depositaries; and the operation of the Department of the Treasury's (Treasury) investment program. [Reg. §203.1.]

☐ [*Final Rule, 2-2-98.*]

### [Reg. §203.2]

§203.2. Definitions.—As used in this part:

(a) *Advice of credit.*—means the Treasury form used in the Federal Tax Deposit system that is supplied to depositaries to summarize and report Federal tax deposits. The current form is Treasury Form 2284. Advice of credit information also may be delivered electronically.

(b) *Automated Clearing House (ACH) credit entry.*—means a transaction originated by a financial institution in accordance with applicable ACH formats and applicable laws, regulations, and procedural instructions.

(c) *Automated Clearing House (ACH) debit entry.*—means a transaction originated by a Treasury Financial Agent (TFA), in accordance with applicable ACH formats and applicable laws, regulations, and instructions.

(d) *Business day.*—means any day on which the FRB of the district is open.

(e) *Direct Access transaction.*—means same-day Federal tax payment information transmitted by a financial institution directly to the Electronic Tax Application at an FRB using the Fedline Taxpayer Deposit Application.

(f) *Direct investment.*—means placement of Treasury funds with a depositary and a corresponding increase in a depositary's note balance.

(g) *Direct investment.*—means placement of Treasury funds with a depositary and a corresponding increase in a depositary's main note balance.

(h) *Electronic Tax Application (ETA).*—means a sub-system of EFTPS that receives, processes, and transmits same-day Federal tax payment information for taxpayers. ETA activity is comprised of Fedwire value transfers, Fedwire non-value transactions, and Direct Access transactions.

(i) *Electronic Tax Application (ETA) reference number.*—means the unique number assigned to each ETA transaction by an FRB.

(j) *Federal funds rate.*—means the Federal funds rate published weekly by the Board of Governors of the Federal Reserve System.

(k) *Federal Reserve account.*—means an account with reserve or clearing balances held by a financial institution at an FRB.

(l) *Federal Reserve Bank of the district.*—means the FRB that services the geographical area in which the financial institution is located, or such other FRB that may be designated in an FRB operating circular.

(m) *Federal Tax Deposit (FTD).*—means a tax deposit or payment made using an FTD coupon.

(n) *Federal Tax Deposit coupon (FTD coupon).*—means a paper form supplied to a taxpayer by the Treasury for use in the FTD system to accompany deposits of Federal taxes. The current paper form is Form 8109.

(b) *Saturday, Sunday, or legal holiday.*—For provisions relating to the time for performance of acts where the last day falls on Saturday, Sunday, or a legal holiday, see the provisions of the Regulations on Procedure and Administration (Part 301 of this chapter) under section 7503. [Reg. §31.6302(c)-4.]

☐ [*T.D. 6354, 1-13-59. Amended by T.D. 7037, 4-27-70 and T.D. 8947, 6-14-2001.*]

(o) *Federal Tax Deposit system (FTD system).*—means the paper-based system through which taxpayers remit Federal tax payments by presenting an FTD coupon and payment to a depositary or an FRB. The depositary prepares an advice of credit summarizing all FTDs.

(p) *Federal taxes.*—means those Federal taxes or other payments specified by the Secretary of the Treasury as eligible for payment through the procedures prescribed in this part.

(q) *Fedwire.*—means the funds transfer system owned and operated by the FRBs.

(r) *Fedwire non-value transaction.*—means the same-day Federal tax payment information transmitted by a financial institution to an FRB using a Fedwire type 1090 message to authorize a payment.

(s) *Fedwire value transfer.*—means a Federal tax payment made by a financial institution using a Fedwire type 1000 message.

(t) *Financial institution.*—means any bank, savings bank, savings and loan association, credit union, or similar institution.

(u) *Fiscal Agent.*—means the Federal Reserve acting as agent for the Treasury.

(v) *Input Message Accountability Data (IMAD).*—means a unique number assigned to each Fedwire transaction by the financial institution sending the transaction to an FRB.

(w) *Main note balance.*—means an open-ended interest-bearing note balance maintained at the FRB of the district.

(x) *Note option.*—means that program available to a TT & L depositary under which Treasury invests in obligations of the depositary. The amount of such investments will be evidenced by interest-bearing note balances maintained at the FRB of the district.

(y) *Procedural instructions.*—means the procedures contained in the Treasury Financial Manual, Volume IV (IV TFM), other Treasury instructions issued through the TFAs, and FRB operating circulars issued consistent with this part.

(z) *Recognized insurance coverage.*—means the insurance provided by the Federal Deposit Insurance Corporation, the National Credit Union Administration, and by insurance organizations specifically qualified by the Secretary.

(aa) *Remittance option.*—means that program available to a depositary that processes FTD payments, under which the amount of deposits credited by the depositary to the TT&L account will be withdrawn by the FRB for deposit to the Treasury General Account on the day that the FRB receives the advices of credit supporting such deposits.

(bb) *Same-day payment.*—means the following ETA payment options:
(1) Direct Access transaction;
(2) Fedwire non-value transaction; and
(3) Fedwire value transfer.

(cc) *Secretary.*—means the Secretary of the Treasury, or the Secretary's delegate.

(dd) *Special direct investment.*—means the placement of Treasury funds with a depositary and a corresponding increase in a depositary's main note balance, where the investment specifically is identified as a "special direct investment" and may be secured by collateral retained in the possession of the depositary pursuant to the terms of §203.24(c)(2)(i).

(ee) *Tax due date.*—means the day on which a tax payment is due to Treasury, as determined by statute and Internal Revenue Service (IRS) regulations.

(ff) *Term investment option.*—means the program available to financial institutions that offers the ability to borrow excess Treasury operating funds for a predetermined period of time.

(gg) *Term note balance.*—means an interest-bearing note balance maintained at the FRB of the district for a predetermined period of time.

(hh) *Transaction trace number.*—means an identifying number assigned by the taxpayer's financial institution to each ACH credit transaction.

(ii) *Treasury Financial Agent (TFA).*—means a financial institution designated as an agent of Treasury for processing EFTPS enrollments, receiving EFTPS tax payment information, and originating ACH debit entries on behalf of Treasury as authorized by the taxpayer.

(jj) *Treasury General Account (TGA).*—means an account maintained in the name of the United States Treasury at an FRB.

(kk) *Treasury Tax and Loan (TT&L) account.*—means the Treasury account maintained by a depositary in which funds are credited by the depositary after receiving and collateralizing FTDs.

(ll) *Treasury Tax and Loan depositary (depositary).*—means a financial institution designated as a depositary by the FRB of the district for the purpose of maintaining a TT&L account and/or note balance.

(mm) *Treasury Tax and Loan (TT&L) Program.*—means the program for collecting Federal taxes and investing the Government's excess operating funds.

(nn) *Treasury Tax and Loan (TT & L) rate of interest.*—means the interest charged on the main note balance. The TT & L rate of interest is the rate prescribed by the Secretary taking into consideration prevailing market interest rates. The rate and any rate changes will be announced through a *TT & L Special Notice to Depositaries* and will be published in the Federal Register and on a web site maintained by Treasury's Financial Management Service at http://www.fms.treas.gov. [Reg. §203.2.]

☐ [*Final Rule,* 2-2-98. *Amended by Final Rule,* 3-14-2002.]

**[Reg. §203.3]**

**§203.3. Financial institution eligibility for designation as a Treasury Tax and Loan depositary.**—(a) To be designated as a TT&L depositary, a financial institution shall be insured as a national banking association, state bank, savings bank, savings and loan, building and loan, homestead association, Federal home loan bank, credit union, trust company, or a U.S. branch of a foreign banking corporation, the establishment of which has been approved by the Comptroller of the Currency.

(b) A financial institution shall possess the authority to pledge collateral to secure TT&L account balances and/or a note balance.

(c) In order to be designated as a TT & L depositary for the purposes of processing tax deposits in the FTD system, a financial institution shall possess under its charter either general or specific authority permitting the maintenance of the TT & L account, the balance of which is payable on demand without previous notice of intended withdrawal. In addition, note option depositaries shall possess either general or specific authority permitting the maintenance of a note balance. In the case of note option depositaries maintaining main note balances, the authority shall permit the maintenance of a main note balance which is payable on demand without previous notice of intended withdrawal. [Reg. §203.3.]

☐ [*Final Rule,* 2-2-98. *Amended by Final Rule,* 3-14-2002.]

**[Reg. §203.4]**

**§203.4. Designation of financial institutions as Treasury Tax and Loan depositaries.**—(a) *Parties to the agreement.*—To be designated as a TT&L depositary, a financial institution shall enter into a depositary agreement with Treasury's fiscal agent, the FRB. By entering into this agreement, the financial institution agrees to be bound by this part, and procedural instructions issued pursuant to this part.

(b)(1) *Application procedures.*—An eligible financial institution seeking designation as a depositary and, thereby, the authority to maintain a TT&L account and/or a note balance shall file with the FRB, Financial Management Service Form 458, "Financial Institution Agreement and Application for Designation as a TT&L Depositary," and Financial Management Service Form 459, "Resolution Authorizing the Financial Institution Agreement and Application for Designation as a TT&L Depositary," certified by its board of directors. Financial Management Service Forms 458 and 459 are available upon request from the FRB of the district.

(2) Depositaries processing tax payments in the FTD system are required to elect either the remittance or the note option.

(c) *Designation.*—Each financial institution satisfying the eligibility requirements and the application procedures will receive from the FRB notification of its specific designation as a TT&L depositary. A financial institution is not authorized to maintain a TT&L account or note balance until it has been designated as a TT&L depositary by the FRB. [Reg. §203.4.]

☐ [*Final Rule,* 2-2-98.]

**[Reg. §203.5]**

**§203.5. Obligations of the depositary.**—A depositary shall:

(a) Administer a note balance, if not participating in the FTD System.

(b) Administer a TT&L account and, if applicable, a note balance, if participating in the FTD System.

(c) Comply with the requirements of Section 202 of Executive Order 11246, entitled "Equal Employment Opportunity" (3 CFR, 1964-1965 Comp. p. 339) as amended by Executive Orders 11375 and 12086 (3 CFR, 1966-1970 Comp., p. 684; 3 CFR, 1978 Comp. p. 230), and the regulations issued thereunder at 41 CFR Chapter 60.

(d) Comply with the requirements of Section 503 of the Rehabilitation Act of 1973, as amended, and the regulations issued thereunder at 41 CFR part 60-741, requiring Federal contractors to take affirmative action to employ and advance in employment qualified individuals with disabilities.

(e) Comply with the requirements of Section 503 of the Vietnam Era Veterans' Readjustment Assistance Act of 1972, as amended, 38 U.S.C. 4212, Executive Order 11701 (3 CFR 1971-1975 Comp. p. 752), and the regulations issued thereunder at 41 CFR parts 60-250 and 61-250, requiring Federal contractors to take affirmative action to employ and advance in employment qualified special disabled veterans and Vietnam-era veterans. [Reg. §203.5.]

☐ [*Final Rule,* 2-2-98.]

**[Reg. §203.6]**

**§203.6. Compensation for services.**—Except as provided in the procedural instructions, Treasury will not compensate financial institutions for servicing and maintaining the TT&L account, or for processing tax payments through the EFTPS or the FTD system. [Reg. §203.6.]

☐ [*Final Rule,* 2-2-98.]

**[Reg. §203.7]**

**§203.7. Termination of agreement or change of election or option.**—(a) *Termination by Treasury.*—The Secretary may terminate the agreement of a depositary at any time upon notice to that effect to that depositary, effective on the date set forth in the notice.

(b) *Termination or change of election or option by the depositary.*—A depositary may terminate its depositary agreement, or change its option or election, consistent with this part and the procedural instructions, by submitting notice to that effect in writing to the FRB effective at a prospective date set forth in the notice. [Reg. §203.7.]

☐ [*Final Rule,* 2-2-98.]

**[Reg. §203.8]**

**§203.8. Application of part and procedural instructions.**—The terms of this part and procedural instructions issued pursuant to this part shall be binding on financial institutions that process tax payments and/or maintain a note balance under this part. By accepting or originating Federal tax payments, the financial institution agrees to be bound by this part and by procedural instructions issued pursuant to this part. [Reg. §203.8.]

☐ [*Final Rule,* 2-2-98.]

## Subpart B—Electronic Federal Tax Payments

**[Reg. §203.9]**

**§203.9. Scope of the subpart.**—This subpart prescribes the rules by which financial institutions shall process Federal tax payment transactions electronically. A financial institution does not need to be designated as a TT&L depositary in order to process electronic Federal tax payments. In addition, a financial institution that does process electronic Federal tax payments under this subpart does not thereby become a Federal Government depositary and shall not advertise itself as one because of that fact. [Reg. §203.9.]

☐ [*Final Rule,* 2-2-98.]

**[Reg. §203.10]**

**§203.10. Enrollment.**—(a) *General.*—Taxpayers shall complete an enrollment process with the TFA prior to making their first electronic Federal tax payment.

(b) *Enrollment forms.*—The TFA shall provide financial institutions and taxpayers with enrollment forms upon request. The taxpayer is responsible for completing the enrollment form, obtaining the verifications required on the form, and returning the enrollment form to the TFA.

(c) *Verification.*—If the taxpayer elects the ACH debit entry method of paying taxes, an authorized representative of the financial institution shall verify the accuracy of the financial institution routing number, taxpayer account number, and taxpayer account type at the request of the taxpayer. [Reg. § 203.10.]

☐ [*Final Rule,* 2-2-98.]

### [Reg. § 203.11]

**§ 203.11. Electronic payment methods.**—(a) *General.*—Electronic payment methods for Federal tax payments available under this subpart include ACH debit entries, ACH credit entries, and same-day payments. Any financial institution that is capable of originating and/or receiving transactions for these payment methods, by itself or through a correspondent financial institution, may do so on behalf of a taxpayer.

(b) *Conditions to making an electronic payment.*—Nothing contained in this part shall affect the authority of financial institutions to enter into contracts with their customers regarding the terms and conditions for processing payments, provided that such terms and conditions are not inconsistent with this subpart and applicable law governing the particular transaction type.

(c) *Payment of interest for time value of funds held.*—Treasury will not pay interest on any payments erroneously paid to Treasury and subsequently refunded to the financial institution. [Reg. § 203.11.]

☐ [*Final Rule,* 2-2-98.]

### [Reg. § 203.12]

**§ 203.12. Future-day reporting and payment mechanisms.**—(a) *General.*—A financial institution may receive an ACH debit entry, originated by the TFA at the direction of the taxpayer; or, a financial institution may originate an ACH credit entry, at the direction of the taxpayer. Taxpayers will be credited for the actual amount received by Treasury.

(b) *ACH debit.*—A financial institution receiving an ACH debit entry originated by the TFA shall, as applicable:

(1) Timely verify the account number and account type contained in an ACH prenotification entry;

(2) Timely and properly return a prenotification entry that contains an invalid account number or account type, or otherwise is erroneous or unprocessable;

(3) Timely and accurately notify the TFA of incorrect information on entries received, using a Notification of Change entry; and

(4) Timely and accurately return an entry not posted, including but not limited to, a return or a contested dishonored return for acceptable return reasons, as set forth in the procedural instructions.

(c) *ACH credit.*—A financial institution originating an ACH credit entry at the direction of a taxpayer shall:

(1) At the request of the taxpayer, originate either an ACH prenotification containing the taxpayer's identification number or a zero dollar ACH entry with the appropriate addenda record. Additional format information is contained in the procedural instructions;

(2) Format the ACH credit entry in the ACH format approved by Treasury for Federal tax payments;

(3) Originate an ACH credit entry by the appropriate deadline, as specified by the FRB or Treasury, whichever is earlier, in order to meet the tax due date specified by the taxpayer; and

(4) Provide the taxpayer, upon request, a transaction trace number, or some other method to trace the tax payment.

(d) *ACH credit reversals.*—Reversals may be initiated for a duplicate or erroneous file or entry. No advance approval from, or notification to, the IRS is required when originating an ACH credit reversal. Documentation of reversals shall be made available as set forth in the procedural instructions. [Reg. § 203.12.]

☐ [*Final Rule,* 2-2-98.]

### [Reg. § 203.13]

**§ 203.13. Same-day reporting and payment mechanisms.**—(a) *General.*—A financial institution or its authorized correspondent may initiate same-day reporting and payment transactions on behalf of taxpayers. A same-day payment must be received by the FRB of the district by the deadline established by the Treasury in the procedural instructions. Taxpayers will be credited for the actual amount received by Treasury.

(b) *Fedwire value transfer.*—To initiate a Fedwire value tax payment, the financial institution shall be a Fedwire participant and shall comply with the FRB's Fedwire format for tax payments. The taxpayer's financial institution shall provide the taxpayer, upon request, the IMAD and the ETA reference numbers for a Fedwire value transfer. The financial institution may obtain the ETA reference number for Fedwire value transfers from its FRB by supplying the related IMAD number. Fedwire value transfers settle immediately to the TGA and thus are not credited to a depositary's main note balance.

(c) *Fedwire non-value transaction.*—By initiating a Fedwire non-value transaction, a financial institution authorizes the FRB of the district to debit its Federal Reserve account or, for a TT&L depositary, to debit the Federal Reserve account of the depositary or its designated correspondent financial institution, for the amount of the tax payment specified in the transaction. To initiate a Fedwire non-value transaction, the financial institution shall be a Fedwire participant and shall comply with the FRB's Fedwire format for tax payments. The taxpayer's financial institution shall provide the taxpayer, upon request, the IMAD and ETA reference numbers for the Fedwire non-value transaction. The financial institution may obtain the ETA reference number for Fedwire non-value transactions from its FRB by supplying the related IMAD number.

(1) For a note option depositary using a Fedwire non-value transaction, the tax payment amount will be credited to the depositary's main note balance on the day of the transaction.

(2) For a remittance option depositary using a Fedwire non-value transaction, the tax payment amount will be debited from the Federal Reserve account of the depositary or the depositary's designated correspondent and credited to the TGA on the day of the transaction.

(3) For a non-TT&L depositary financial institution using a Fedwire non-value transaction, the tax payment amount will be debited from the financial institution's Federal Reserve account and credited to the TGA on the day of the transaction.

(d) *Direct Access Transaction.*—By initiating a Direct Access transaction, a financial institution authorizes the FRB of the district to debit its Federal Reserve account or, for a TT&L depositary, to debit the Federal Reserve account of the depositary or its designated correspondent financial institution for the amount of the tax payment specified in the transaction. The taxpayer's financial institution shall provide the taxpayer, upon request, the ETA reference number for the Direct Access transaction.

(1) For a note option depositary using a Direct Access transaction, the tax payment amount will be credited to the depositary's main note balance on the day of the transaction.

(2) For a remittance option depositary or a non-TT&L depositary financial institution using a Direct Access transaction, the tax payment amount will be debited from the Federal Reserve account of the financial institution or its designated correspondent financial institution, and credited to the TGA on the day of the transaction.

(e) *Cancellations and reversals.*—In addition to cancellations due to insufficient funds in the financial institution's Federal Reserve account, the FRB may reverse a same-day transaction:

(1) If the transaction:

(i) Is originated by a financial institution after the deadline established by the Treasury in the procedural instructions;

(ii) Has an unenrolled taxpayer identification number; or

(iii) Does not meet the edit and format requirements set forth in the procedural instructions; or,

(2) At the direction of the IRS, for the following reasons:

(i) Incorrect taxpayer name;

(ii) Overpayment; or

(iii) Unidentified payment; or,

(3) At the request of the financial institution that sent the same-day transaction, if the request is made prior to the deadline established by Treasury in the procedural instructions on the day the payment was made.

(f) Other than as stated in paragraph (e) of this section, Treasury is not obligated to reverse all or any part of a payment. [Reg. § 203.13.]

☐ [*Final Rule,* 2-2-98. *Amended by Final Rule,* 3-14-2002.]

### [Reg. § 203.14]

**§ 203.14. Electronic Federal Tax Payment System interest assessments.**—(a) *Circumstances subject to interest assessments.*—Treasury may assess interest on a financial institution in instances where a taxpayer that failed to meet a tax due date proves to the IRS that the delivery of tax payment instructions to the financial institution was timely and that the taxpayer satisfied the conditions imposed by the financial institution pursuant to § 203.11(b). Treasury also may assess interest where a financial institution failed to respond to an ACH prenotification entry on an ACH debit as required in § 203.12(b) or failed to originate an ACH prenotification or zero dollar entry on an ACH credit as described in §203.12(c) which then resulted in a late payment.

(b) *Calculation of interest assessment.*—Any interest assessed under this section will be at the TT&L rate. The interest will be assessed from the day the taxpayer specified that its payment should settle to the Treasury until the receipt of the payment by Treasury, subject to the following limitations: for ACH debit transactions, interest will be limited to no more than seven calendar days; for ACH credit and same-day transactions, interest will be limited to no more than 45 calendar days. The limitation of liability in this paragraph does not apply to any interest assessment in which there is an indication of fraud, the presentation of a false claim, or misrepresentation or embezzlement on the part of the financial institution or any employee or agent of the financial institution.

(c) *Authorization to assess interest.*—A financial institution that processes Federal tax payments made by electronic payment methods under this subpart is deemed to authorize the FRB to debit its Federal Reserve account or the account of its designated correspondent financial institution for any interest assessed under this section. Upon the direction of Treasury, the FRB shall debit the Federal Reserve account of the financial institution or the account of its designated correspondent financial institution for the amount of the assessed interest.

(d)(1) *Circumstances not subject to the assessment of interest.*—Treasury will not assess interest on a taxpayer's financial institution if a taxpayer fails to meet a tax due date because the taxpayer has not satisfied conditions imposed by the financial institution pursuant to §203-11(b) and the financial institution has not contributed to the delay. The burden is on the financial institution to establish, pursuant to the procedures in §203.16, that the taxpayer has not satisfied the conditions and that the financial institution has not contributed to the delay.

(2) Treasury will not assess interest on a financial institution if the delay causing the interest assessment is due to the FRB or the TFA and the financial institution did not contribute to the delay. The burden is on the financial institution to establish, pursuant to the procedures in §203.16, that it did not cause or contribute to the delay. [Reg. §203.14.]

☐ [*Final Rule*, 2-2-98.]

**[Reg. §203.15]**

**§203.15. Prohibited debits through the Automated Clearing House.**—(a) *General.*—The Treasury has instituted operational safeguards to scrutinize all entries that remove funds from the TGA. In the event funds are removed from the TGA without authority, this section sets forth the liability of financial institutions originating such entries. Accordingly, a financial institution shall not originate an ACH transaction to debit the TGA without the prior written permission of Treasury. Unauthorized entries under this section do not include reversal entries of previously initiated ACH credits authorized in §203.12(d).

(b) *Liability.*—A financial institution that originates an unauthorized ACH entry that debits the TGA shall be liable to Treasury for the amount of the transaction and shall be liable for interest charges as specified in paragraph (d) of this section.

(c) *Authorization to recover principal and assess interest charge.*—By initiating unauthorized debits to the TGA through the ACH, a financial institution is deemed to authorize the FRB to debit its Federal Reserve account or the account of its designated correspondent financial institution for any principal and, if applicable, an interest charge assessed by Treasury under this section.

(d) *Interest charge calculation.*—The interest charge shall be at a rate equal to the Federal funds rate plus two percent. The interest charge shall be assessed for each calendar day from the day the TGA was debited to the day the TGA is recredited with the full amount of principal due. [Reg. §203.15.]

☐ [*Final Rule*, 2-2-98.]

**[Reg. §203.16]**

**§203.16. Appeal and dispute resolution.**—(a) *Contest.*—A financial institution may contest any interest assessed under §203.14, any principal or interest assessed under §203.15, or any late fees assessed under §203.20. The financial institution shall submit information supporting its position and the relief sought. The information must be received, in writing, by the Treasury officer or fiscal agent identified in the procedural instructions, no later than 90 calendar days after the date the FRB debits the reserve account of the financial institution under §§203.14, 203.15, or 203.20. The Treasury officer or

fiscal agent will: uphold the assessment, or reverse the assessment, or modify the assessment, or mandate other action.

(b) *Appeal.*—The financial institution may appeal the decision to Treasury as set forth in the procedural instructions. No further administrative review of the Treasury's decision is available under this Part.

(c) *Recoveries.*—In the event of an over or under recovery of either interest, principal, or late fees, Treasury will instruct the FRB to credit or debit the Federal Reserve account of the financial institution or its designated correspondent financial institution, as appropriate. [Reg. §203.16.]

☐ [*Final Rule*, 2-2-98.]

## Subpart C—Federal Tax Deposits

**[Reg. §203.17]**

**§203.17. Scope of the subpart.**—This subpart applies to all depositaries that accept FTD coupons and governs the acceptance and processing of those coupons. [Reg. §203.17.]

☐ [*Final Rule*, 2-2-98.]

**[Reg. §203.18]**

**§203.18. Tax deposits using Federal Tax Deposit coupons.**—(a) *FTD coupons.*—A depositary that accepts FTD coupons, through any of its offices that accept demand and/or savings deposits, shall:

(1) Accept from a taxpayer, cash, a postal money order drawn to the order of the depositary, or a check or draft drawn on and to the order of the depositary, covering an amount to be deposited as Federal taxes when accompanied by an FTD coupon on which the amount of the deposit has been properly entered in the space provided. A depositary may accept, at its discretion, a check drawn on another financial institution, but it does so at its option and absorbs for its own account any float and other costs involved.

(2) Issue a counter receipt when requested to do so by a taxpayer that makes an FTD deposit over the counter.

(3) Place a stamp impression on the face of each FTD coupon in the space provided. The stamp shall reflect the date on which the tax deposit was received and the name and location of the depositary. The timeliness of the tax payment will be determined by reference to the date stamped by the depositary on the FTD coupon.

(4) Credit, on the date of receipt, all FTD deposits to the TT&L account and administer that account pursuant to the provisions of this part.

(5) Forward, each day, to the IRS Center servicing the geographical area in which the depositary is located, the FTD coupons for all FTD deposits received that day. The FTD coupons shall be accompanied by an advice of credit reflecting the total amount of all FTD coupons.

(6) Establish an adequate record of all FTD deposits prior to transmittal to the IRS Center so that the depositary will be able to identify deposits in the event tax deposit coupons are lost in shipment. For tracking purposes, a record shall be made of each FTD deposit showing, at a minimum, the date of deposit, the taxpayer identification number, and the amount of the deposit. The depositary's copy of the advice of credit may be used to provide the necessary information if individual deposits are listed separately, showing date, taxpayer identification number, and amount.

(7) Deliver its advices of credit to the FRB by the cutoff hour designated by the FRB for receipt of advices.

(8) Not accept compensation from taxpayers for accepting FTDs and handling them as required by this section.

(b) *FTD deposits with Federal Reserve Banks.*—An FRB shall:

(1) Accept an FTD directly from a taxpayer when such tax deposit is:

(i) Mailed or delivered by a taxpayer; and

(ii) Provided in the form of cash or a check or postal money order payable to the order of that FRB; and,

(iii) Accompanied by an FTD coupon on which the amount of the tax deposit has been properly entered in the space provided.

(2) Issue a counter receipt, when requested to do so by a taxpayer that makes an FTD over the counter; and,

(3) Place, in the space provided on the face of each FTD coupon accepted directly from a taxpayer, a stamp impression reflecting the name of the FRB and the date on which the tax deposit will be credited to the TGA. Timeliness of the Federal tax payment will be determined by this date. However, if a deposit is mailed to an FRB, it shall be subject to the "Timely mailing treated as timely filing and paying" clause of the Internal Revenue Code, 26 U.S.C. §7502; and,

(4) Credit the TGA with the amount of the tax payment;

(i) On the date the payment is received, if payment is made in cash; or,

(ii) On the date the proceeds of the tax payment are collected, if payment is made by postal money order or check. [Reg. §203.18.]

☐ [*Final Rule*, 2-2-98.]

### [Reg. §203.19]

**§203.19. Note option.**—(a) *Late delivery of advices of credit.*—If an advice of credit does not arrive at the FRB before the designated cutoff hour for receipt of such advices, the FRB will post the funds to the main note balance as of the next business day after the date on the advice of credit. This is the date on which funds will begin to earn interest for Treasury.

(b) *Transfer of funds from TT & L account to the main note balance.*—For a depositary selecting the note option, funds equivalent to the amount of deposits credited by a depositary to the TT & L account shall be withdrawn by the depositary and credited to the main note balance on the business day following the receipt of the tax payment. [Reg. §203.19.]

☐ [*Final Rule*, 2-2-98. *Amended by Final Rule*, 3-14-2002.]

### [Reg. §203.20]

**§203.20. Remittance option.**—(a) *FTD late fee.*—If an advice of credit does not arrive at the FRB before the designated cutoff hour for receipt of such advices, an FTD late fee in the form of interest at the TT&L rate will be assessed for each day's delay in receipt of such advice. Upon the direction of Treasury, the FRB shall debit the Federal Reserve account of the financial institution or the account of its designated correspondent financial institution for the amount of the late fee.

(b) *Withdrawals.*—For a depositary selecting the Remittance Option, the amount of deposits credited by a depositary to the TT&L account will be withdrawn upon receipt by the FRB of the advices of credit. The FRB will charge the depositary's Federal Reserve account or the account of the depositary's designated correspondent financial institution. [Reg. §203.20.]

☐ [*Final Rule*, 2-2-98.]

## Subpart D—Investment Program and Collateral Security Requirements for Treasury Tax and Loan Depositaries

### [Reg. §203.21]

**§203.21. Scope of the subpart.**—This subpart provides rules for TT & L depositaries on crediting main note balances under the various payment methods; debiting main note balances; maintaining term note balances; and pledging collateral security. [Reg. §203.21.]

☐ [*Final Rule*, 2-2-98. *Amended by Final Rule*, 3-14-2002.]

### [Reg. §203.22]

**§203.22. Sources of balances.**—Depositaries electing to participate in the investment program can receive Treasury's investments in obligations of the depositary from the following sources:

(a) FTDs that have been credited to the TT&L account pursuant to subpart C of this part;

(b) EFTPS ACH credit and debit transactions, Fedwire non-value transactions, and Direct Access transactions pursuant to subpart B of this part;

(c) Direct investments and special direct investments pursuant to subpart D of this part; and

(d) Other excess Treasury operating funds. [Reg. §203.22.]

☐ [*Final Rule*, 2-2-98. *Amended by Final Rule*, 3-14-2002.]

### [Reg. §203.23]

**§203.23. Note balance.**—(a) *Additions.*—Treasury will invest funds in obligations of depositaries selecting the note option. Such obligations shall be in the form of open-ended, interest-bearing notes; and additions and reductions will be reflected on the books of the FRB of the district.

(1) *FTD system.*—A depositary processing tax deposits using the FTD system and electing the note option shall debit the TT & L account and credit its main note balance as stated in §203.19(b).

(2) *EFTPS.*—(i) *ACH debit and ACH credit.*—A note option depositary processing EFTPS ACH debit entries and/or ACH credit entries shall credit its main note balance for the value of the transactions on the date that an exchange of funds is reflected on the books of the Federal Reserve Bank of the district. Financial institutions may

refer to the procedural instructions for information on how to ascertain the amount of the credit to the main note balance.

(ii) *Fedwire non-value and Direct Access.*—A note option depositary processing Fedwire non-value and/or Direct Access transactions pursuant to subpart B of this part shall credit its main note balance and debit its customer's account for the value of the transactions on the date ETA receives and processes the transactions.

(b) *Other additions.*—Other funds from Treasury may be offered from time to time to certain note option depositaries through direct investments, special direct investments, or other investment programs.

(c) *Main note balance withdrawals.*—The amount of the main note balance shall be payable on demand without prior notice. Calls for payment on the note will be by direction of the Secretary through the FRBs. On behalf of Treasury, the FRB shall charge the reserve account of the depositary or the depositary's designated correspondent on the day specified in the call for payment.

(d) *Interest.*—A main note balance shall bear interest at the TT & L rate. Such interest is payable by a charge to the Federal Reserve account of the depositary or its designated correspondent in the manner prescribed in the procedural instructions.

(e) *Maximum balance.*—(1) *Note option depositaries.*—A depositary selecting the note option shall establish a maximum for its main note balance by providing notice to that effect in writing to the FRB of the district. The maximum balance is the amount of funds for which a main note option depositary is willing to provide collateral in accordance with §203.24(c)(1). The depositary shall provide the advance notice required in the procedural instructions before reducing the established maximum balance unless it is a reduction resulting from a collateral re-evaluation as determined by the depositary's FRB. That portion of any advice of credit or EFTPS tax payment, which, when posted at the FRB, would cause the main note balance to exceed the maximum balance amount specified by the depositary, will be withdrawn by the FRB that day.

(2) *Direct investment depositaries.*—A main note option depositary that participates in direct investment shall set a maximum for its main note balance for direct investment purposes which is higher than its peak balance normally generated by the depositary's advices of credit and EFTPS tax payment inflow. The direct investment note option depositary shall provide the advance notice required in the procedural instructions before reducing the established maximum balance.

(3) *Special direct investment depositaries.*—Special direct investments, when credited to the main note balance, shall not be considered in setting the amount of the maximum balance or in determining the amounts to be withdrawn where a depositary's maximum balance is exceeded.

(f) *Term investment option.*—Treasury may, from time to time, invest excess operating funds in obligations of depositaries selecting the term investment option. Such obligations shall be in the form of interest-bearing notes payable upon a predetermined period of time not to exceed 90 days. Such notes shall bear interest at a rate prescribed by the Secretary by auction or otherwise taking into consideration prevailing market interest rates. [Reg. §203.23.]

☐ [*Final Rule*, 2-2-98. *Amended by Final Rule*, 3-14-2002.]

### [Reg. §203.24]

**§203.24. Collateral security requirements.**—Financial institutions that process EFTPS tax payments, but are not TT&L depositaries, have no collateral requirements under this part. Financial institutions that are note option depositaries or remittance option depositaries have collateral security requirements, as follows:

(a) *Note option—main note balance.*—(1) *FTD deposits and EFTPS tax payments.*—A depositary shall pledge collateral security in accordance with the requirements of paragraphs (d)(1), (e), and (f) of this section in an amount that is sufficient to cover the pre-established maximum balance for the main note balance, and, if applicable, the closing balance in the TT & L account which exceeds recognized insurance coverage. Depositaries shall pledge collateral for the full amount of the maximum balance at the time the maximum balance is established. If the depositary maintains a TT & L account, the depositary shall pledge collateral security before crediting deposits to the TT & L account.

(2) *Direct investments.*—A note option depositary that participates in direct investment is not required to pledge collateral continuously in the amount of the pre-established maximum balance. However, each note option depositary participating in direct investment shall pledge, no later than the day the direct investment is

placed, the additional collateral in accordance with paragraphs (d)(1), (e), and (f) of this section to cover the total main note balance including those funds received through direct investment. If a direct investment depositary has a history of frequent collateral deficiencies, it shall fully collateralize its maximum balance at all times.

(3) *Special direct investments.*—Before special direct investments are credited to a depositary's main note balance, the note option depositary shall pledge collateral security, in accordance with the requirements of paragraphs (d)(2) and (f) of this section, to cover 100 percent of the amount of the special direct investments to be received.

(b) *Note option—term note balance.*—Each note option depositary participating in the term investment program shall pledge, prior to the time the term investment is placed, collateral in accordance with paragraphs (d)(1), (e), and (f) of this section sufficient to cover the total term note balance.

(c) *Remittance option.*—Prior to crediting FTD deposits to the TT&L account, a remittance option depositary shall pledge collateral security in accordance with the requirements of paragraph (c)(1), (d), and (e) of this section in an amount which is sufficient to cover the balance in the TT&L account at the close of business each day, less recognized insurance coverage.

(d) *Deposits of securities.*—(1) Collateral security required under paragraphs (a)(1), (2), (b), and (c) of this section shall be deposited with the FRB of the district, or, where appropriate, with a custodian or custodians within the United States designated by the FRB, under terms and conditions prescribed by the FRB.

(2)(i) Collateral security required under paragraph (a)(3) of this section shall be pledged under a written security agreement on a form provided by the FRB of the district. The collateral security pledged to satisfy the requirements of paragraph (a)(3) of this section may remain in the pledging depositary's possession and the fact that it has been pledged shall be evidenced by advices of custody to be incorporated by reference in the written security agreement. The written security agreement and all advices of custody covering collateral security pledged under that agreement shall be provided by the depositary to the FRB of the district. Collateral security pledged under the agreement shall not be substituted for or released without the advance approval of the FRB of the district, and any collateral security subject to the security agreement shall remain so subject until an approved substitution is made. No substitution or release shall be approved until an advice of custody containing the description required by the written security agreement is received by the FRB of the district.

(ii) Treasury's security interest in collateral security pledged by a depositary in accordance with paragraph (c)(2)(i) of this section to secure special direct investments is perfected without Treasury taking possession of the collateral security for a period not to exceed 21 calendar days from the day of the depositary's receipt of the special direct investment.

(e) *Acceptable securities.*—Types and valuations of acceptable collateral security are addressed in 31 CFR Part 380. For a current list of acceptable classes of securities and instruments described in 31 CFR Part 380 and their valuations, see the Bureau of the Public Debt's web site at www.publicdebt.treas.gov.

(f) *Assignment of securities.*—A TT&L depositary that pledges acceptable securities which are not negotiable without its endorsement or assignment may furnish, in lieu of placing its unqualified endorsement on each security, an appropriate resolution and irrevocable power of attorney authorizing the FRB to assign the securities. The resolution and power of attorney shall conform to such terms and conditions as the FRB shall prescribe.

(g) *Effecting payments of principal and interest on securities pledged as collateral.*—(1) *General.*—If the depositary fails to pay, when due, the whole or any part of the funds received by it for credit to the TT&L account, and/or if applicable, its note balance; or otherwise violates or fails to perform any of the terms of this part, or fails to pay when due amounts owed to the United States or the United States Treasury; or if the depositary is closed for business by regulatory action or by proper corporate action, or in the event that a receiver, conservator, liquidator or any other officer is appointed; then the Treasury, without notice or demand, may sell, or otherwise collect the proceeds of all or part of the collateral, including additions and substitutions; and apply the proceeds, to satisfy any claims of the United States against the depositary. All principal and interest payments on any security pledged to protect the note balance (if applicable) and/or the TT&L account (if applicable), due as of the date of the insolvency or closure, or thereafter becoming due, shall be held separate and apart from any other assets and shall constitute a part of the pledged security available to satisfy any claim of the United States.

(2) *Payment procedures.*—(i) Subject to the waiver in paragraph (f)(2)(iii) of this section, each depositary (including, with respect to such depositary, an assignee for the benefit of creditors, a trustee in bankruptcy, or a receiver in equity) shall immediately remit each payment of principal and/or interest received by it with respect to collateral pledged pursuant to this section to the FRB of the district, as fiscal agent of the United States, and in any event shall so remit no later than 10 days after receipt of such a payment.

(ii) Subject to the waiver in paragraph (f)(2)(iii) of this section, each obligor on a security pledged by a depositary pursuant to this section, upon notification that the Treasury is entitled to any payment associated with that pledged security, shall make each payment of principal and/or interest due with respect to such security directly to the FRB of the district, as fiscal agent of the United States.

(iii) The requirements of paragraphs (f)(2)(i) and (ii) of this section are hereby waived for only so long as a pledging depositary avoids both termination from the program under § 203.7; and also, those circumstances identified in paragraph (f)(1) which may lead to the collection of the proceeds of collateral or the waiver is otherwise terminated by Treasury. [Reg. § 203.24.]

☐ [*Final Rule*, 2-2-98. *Amended by Final Rule*, 9-12-2000 *and Final Rule*, 3-14-2002.]

### [Reg. § 301.6303-1]

**§ 301.6303-1. Notice and demand for tax.**—(a) *General rule.*—Where it is not otherwise provided by the Code, the district director or the director of the regional service center shall, after the making of an assessment of a tax pursuant to section 6203, give notice to each person liable for the unpaid tax, stating the amount and demanding payment thereof. Such notice shall be given as soon as possible and within 60 days. However, the failure to give notice within 60 days does not invalidate the notice. Such notice shall be left at the dwelling or usual place of business of such person, or shall be sent by mail to such person's last known address. For further guidance regarding the definition of last known address, see § 301.6212-2.

(b) *Assessment prior to last date for payment.*—If any tax is assessed prior to the last date prescribed for payment of such tax, demand that such tax be paid will not be made before such last date, except where it is believed collection would be jeopardized by delay. [Reg. § 301.6303-1.]

☐ [*T.D.* 6119, 12-31-54. *Amended by T.D.* 6585, 12-27-61 *and T.D.* 8939, 1-11-2001.]

### [Reg. § 301.6305-1]

**§ 301.6305-1. Assessment and collection of certain liability.**—(a) *Scope.*—Section 6305(a) requires the Secretary of the Treasury or his delegate to assess and collect amounts which have been certified by the Secretary of Health and Human Services as the amount of a delinquency determined under a court order, or an order of an administrative process established under State law, for support and maintenance of a child or of a child and the parent with whom the child is living. These amounts, referred to as "child and spousal support", are to be collected in the same manner and with the same powers exercised by the Secretary of the Treasury or his delegate in the collection of an employment tax which would be jeopardized by delay. However, where the assessment is the first assessment against an individual for a delinquency described in this paragraph for a particular individual or individuals, the collection is to be stayed for a period of 60 days following notice and demand. In addition, no interest or penalties (with the exception of the penalties imposed by sections 6332(c)(2) and 6657) shall be assessed or collected on the amounts, paragraphs (4), (6) and (8) of section 6334(a) (relating to property exempt from levy) shall not apply; and, there shall be exempt from levy so much of the salary, wages, or other income of the individual which is subject to garnishment pursuant to a judgment entered by a court for the support of his or her minor children. Section 6305(b) provides that sole jurisdiction for any action brought to restrain or review assessment and collection of the certified amounts shall be in a State court or a State administrative agency.

(b) *Assessment and collection.*—(1) *General rule.*—Upon receipt of a certification or recertification from the Secretary of Health and Human Services or his delegate under section 452(b) of Title IV of the Social Security Act as amended (relating to collection of child and spousal support obligations with respect to an individual), the district director or his delegate shall assess and collect the certified amount (or recertified amount). Except as provided in paragraph (c) of this section, the amount so certified shall be assessed and collected in the same manner, with the same powers, and subject to the same limitations as if the amount were an employment tax the collection of which would be jeopardized by delay. However, the provisions of subtitle F with respect to assessment and collection of taxes shall not apply with respect to assessment and collection of a certified amount where such provisions are clearly inappropriate to, and incompatible with, the collection of certified amounts generally. For example, section 6861(g) which allows the Secretary or his delegate to abate a jeopardy assessment if he finds a jeopardy does not exist will not apply.

(2) *Method of assessment.*—An assessment officer appointed by the district director pursuant to §301.6203-1 to make assessments of tax shall also make assessments of certified amounts. The assessment of a certified amount shall be made by the assessment officer signing the summary record of assessment. The date of assessment is the date the summary record is signed by the assessment officer. The summary record, through supporting records as necessary, shall provide—

(i) The assessed amount;

(ii) The name, social security number, and last known address of the individual owing the assessed amount. For further guidance regarding the definition of last known address, see §301.6212-2;

(iii) A designation of the assessed amount as a certified amount, together with the date on which the amount was certified and the name, position, and governmental address of the officer of the Department of Health and Human Services who certified the amount;

(iv) The period to which the child and spousal support obligation represented by the certified amount relates;

(v) The State in which was entered the court or administrative order giving rise to the child and spousal support obligation represented by the certified amount;

(vi) The name of the person or persons to whom the child and spousal support obligation represented by the certified amount is owed; and

(vii) The name of the child or children or the parent of the child or children for whose benefit the child and spousal support obligation exists.

Upon request, the individual assessed shall be furnished a copy of pertinent parts of this assessment which set forth the information listed in subdivision (i) through (vii) of this paragraph (b)(2).

(3) *Supplemental assessments and abatements.*—If any assessment is incomplete or incorrect in any material respect, the district director or his delegate may make a supplemental assessment or abatement but only for the purpose of completing or correcting the original assessment. A supplemental assessment will not be used as a substitute for an additional assessment against an individual.

(4) *Method of collection.*—(i) The district director or his delegate shall make notice and demand for immediate payment of certified amounts. Upon failure or refusal to pay such amounts, collection by levy shall be lawful without regard to the 10-day waiting period provided in section 6331(a). However, in the case of certain first assessments, paragraph (c)(4) of this section provides a rule for a stay of collection for 60 days. For purposes of collection, refunds of any internal revenue tax owed to the individual may be offset against a certified amount.

(ii) The district director or his delegate shall make diligent and reasonable efforts to collect certified amounts as if such amounts were taxes. He shall have no authority to compromise a proceeding by collection of only part of a certified amount in satisfaction of the full certified amount owing. However, he may arrange for payment of a certified amount by installments where advisable.

(iii) The district director or his delegate may offset the amount of any overpayment of any internal revenue tax (as described in section 301.6401-1) to be refunded to the person making the overpayment by the amount of any past-due support (as defined in the regulations under section 6402) owed by the person making the overpayment. The amounts offset under section 6402(c) may be amounts of child and spousal support certified (or recertified) for collection under section 6305 and this section or they may be amounts of past-due support of which the Secretary of the Treasury has been notified under section 6402(c) and the regulations under that section.

(5) *Credits or refunds.*—In the case of any overpayment of a certified amount, the Secretary of the Treasury or his delegate, within the period of limitations for credit or refund of employment taxes, may credit the amount of the overpayment against any liability in respect of an internal revenue tax on the part of the individual who made the overpayment and shall refund any balance to the individual. However, the full amount of any overpayment collected by levy upon property described in paragraph (c)(2) (i), (ii), or (iii) of this section shall be refunded to the individual. For purposes of applying this subparagraph, the rules of §301.6402-2 apply where appropriate.

(6) *Disposition of certified amounts collected.*—Any certified amount collected shall be deposited in the general fund of the United

States, and the officer of the Department of Health and Human Services who certified the amount shall be promptly notified of its collection. There shall be established in the Treasury, pursuant to section 452 of Title IV of the Social Security Act as amended, a revolving fund which shall be available to the Secretary of Health and Human Services or his delegate, without fiscal year limitation, for distribution to the States in accordance with the provisions of section 457 of the Act. Section 452(c)(2) of the Act appropriates to this revolving fund out of any monies not otherwise appropriated, amounts equal to the certified amounts collected under this paragraph reduced by the amounts credited or refunded as overpayments of the certified amounts so collected. The certified amounts deposited shall be transferred at least quarterly from the general fund of the Treasury to the revolving fund on the basis of estimates made by the Secretary of the Treasury or his delegate. Proper adjustments shall be made in the amounts subsequently transferred to the extent prior estimates were in excess of or less than the amounts required to be transferred. See, however, paragraph (c)(1) of this section for the special rule requiring retention in the general fund of certain penalties which may be collected.

(c) *Additional limitations and conditions.*—(1) *Interest and penalties.*—No interest, penalties or additional amounts, other than normal and reasonable collection costs, may be assessed or collected in addition to the certified amount, other than the penalty imposed by section 6332(c)(2) for failure to surrender property subject to levy and the penalty imposed by section 6657 for the tender of bad checks. Any such penalties and collection costs, if collected, will not be treated as part of the certified amount and will be retained by the United States as a part of its general fund. No interest shall be allowed or paid on any overpayment of a certified amount.

(2) *Property not exempt from levy.*—In addition to property not exempt from levy under section 6334(c) and the regulations thereunder, the following property shall not be exempt from a levy to collect a certified amount:

(i) Unemployment benefits described in section 6334(a)(4);

(ii) Certain annuities and pension payments described in section 6334(a)(6); or

(iii) Salary, wages, or other income described in section 6334(a)(8).

(3) *Property exempt from levy.*—In addition to property exempt from levy under section 6334(a) and the regulations thereunder, other than property described in paragraph (c)(2)(i), (ii), or (iii) of this section, there shall be exempt from levy to collect a certified amount so much of the salary, wages, or other income of an individual as is withheld therefrom in garnishment pursuant to judgment entered by a court of competent jurisdiction for the support of minor children of the individual.

(4) *First assessment.*—In the case of a first assessment against an individual for a certified amount in whole or part for the benefit of a particular child or children or the child or children and their parent, the collection of the certified amount shall be stayed for the period of 60 days immediately following notice and demand as described in section 6303. However, no other stay of the collection of a certified amount may be granted. Thus, the provisions of section 6863(a), relating to bonds to stay collection of jeopardy assessments, shall not apply to the collection of certified amounts.

(5) *Priority of liens.*—A lien for a certified amount shall be valid as against a lien for taxes imposed by section 6321 only if the date of assessment of the certified amount precedes the date of assessment of the taxes. However, no amount collected by levy upon property described in paragraph (c)(2)(i), (ii), or (iii) of this section may be applied other than in whole or partial satisfaction of certified amounts. In the case of two liens for certified amounts, the lien for the certified amount which is first assessed shall be valid as against the lien for the certified amount which is later assessed.

(6) *Statute of limitations on collections.*—The periods of limitation on collection of taxes after assessment prescribed by section 6502 shall apply to the collection of certified (or recertified) amounts. Such periods of limitation with respect to a certified amount shall terminate upon recertification of the amount, and the period of limitation prescribed by section 6502 shall then apply and commence to run with respect to the recertified amount.

(d) *Review of assessments and collections.*—(1) *Federal courts.*—No court of the United States established under article I or article III of the Constitution has jurisdiction of any legal or equitable action to restrain or review the assessment or collection of certified amounts by the district director or his delegate. See, however, paragraph (d)(3) of this section for the rule that the prohibition of this paragraph (d)(1) does not preclude courts established for the District of Columbia from exercising jurisdiction over certain actions.

Reg. §301.6305-1(d)(1)

(2) *Secretary of the Treasury.*—Neither the Secretary of the Treasury nor his delegate may subject to review the assessment or collection of certified amounts in any legal, equitable, or administrative proceeding.

(3) *State courts.*—This paragraph (d) does not preclude a State court or appropriate State agency, as the case may be, from exercising jurisdiction over a legal, equitable, or administrative action against the State by an individual to determine his liability for any certified amount assessed against him and collected, or to recover any such certified amount collected, under section 6305 and this section. For purposes of the preceding sentence, the term "State" includes the District of Columbia.

(e) *Internal Revenue regional service centers.*—For purposes of this section, the terms "district director or his delegate" and "district director" include the director of the Internal Revenue service center or his delegate, as the case may be. [Reg. § 301.6305-1.]

☐ *T.D. 7576, 12-20-78. Amended by T.D. 7808, 2-3-82 and T.D. 8939, 1-11-2001.]*

# RECEIPT OF PAYMENT

## [Reg. § 301.6311-1]

**§ 301.6311-1. Payment by check or money order.**—(a) *Authority to receive.*—(1) *In general.*—(i) District directors, Service Center directors, and Compliance Center directors (director) may accept checks or drafts drawn on any financial institution incorporated under the laws of the United States or under the laws of any State, the District of Columbia, or any possession of the United States, or money orders in payment for internal revenue taxes, provided the checks, drafts, or money orders are collectible in United States currency at par, and subject to the further provisions contained in this section. The director may accept the checks, drafts, or money orders in payment for internal revenue stamps to the extent and under the conditions prescribed in paragraph (a)(2) of this section. A check or money order in payment for internal revenue taxes or internal revenue stamps should be made payable to the United States Treasury. A check or money order is payable at par only if the full amount thereof is payable without any deduction for exchange or other charges. As used in this section, the term "money order" means: (*a*) United States postal, bank, express, or telegraph money order; (*b*) money order issued by a domestic building and loan association (as defined in section 7701(a)(19)) or by a similar association incorporated under the laws of a possession of the United States; (*c*) a money order issued by such other organization as the Commissioner may designate; and (*d*) a money order described in subdivision (ii) of this paragraph in cases therein described. However, the director may refuse to accept any personal check whenever he or she has good reason to believe that such check will not be honored upon presentment.

(ii) An American citizen residing in a country with which the United States maintains direct exchange of money orders on a domestic basis may pay his tax by postal money order of such country. For a list of such countries, see section 171.27 of the Postal Manual of the United States.

(iii) If one check or money order is remitted to cover two or more persons' taxes, the remittance should be accompanied by a letter of transmittal clearly identifying—

(*a*) Each person whose tax is to be paid by the remittance;

(*b*) The amount of the payment on account of each such person; and

(*c*) The kind of tax paid.

(2) *Payment for internal revenue stamps.*—The director may accept checks, drafts, and money orders described in paragraph (a)(1) of this section in payment for internal revenue stamps. However, the director may refuse to accept any personal check whenever he or she has good reason to believe that such check will not be honored upon presentment.

(b) *Checks or money orders not paid.*—(1) *Ultimate liability.*—The person who tenders any check (whether certified or uncertified, cashier's, treasurer's, or other form of check or draft) or money order in payment for taxes or stamps is not released from his or her liability until the check, draft, or money order is paid; and, if the check, draft, or money order is not duly paid, the person shall also be liable for all legal penalties and additions, to the same extent as if such check, draft, or money order had not been tendered.

(2) *Liability of financial institutions and others.*—If any certified, treasurer's, or cashier's check, or other guaranteed draft, or money order is not duly paid, the United States shall have a lien for the amount of such check or draft upon all assets of the financial institution on which drawn, or for the amount of such money order upon the assets of the issuer thereof. The unpaid amount shall be paid out of such assets in preference to any other claims against such financial institution or issuer except the necessary costs and expenses of administration and the reimbursement of the United States for the amount expended in the redemption of the circulating notes of such financial institution. In addition, the Government has the right to exact payment from the person required to make the payment.

(c) *Payment in nonconvertible foreign currency.*—For rules relating to payment of income taxes and taxes under the Federal Insurance Contributions Act in nonconvertible foreign currency, see section 6316 and the regulations thereunder.

(d) *Financial institution.*—For purposes of section 6311 and this section, *financial institution* includes but is not limited to—

(1) A bank or trust company (as defined in section 581);

(2) A domestic building and loan association (as defined in section 7701(a)(19));

(3) A mutual savings bank (including but not limited to a mutual savings bank as defined in section 591(b));

(4) A credit union (including both state and federal credit unions, and including but not limited to a credit union as defined in section 501(c)(14)); and,

(5) A regulated investment company (as defined in section 851(a)). [Reg. § 301.6311-1.]

☐ *[T.D. 6119, 12-31-54. Amended by T.D. 6498, 10-24-60; T.D. 6872, 1-5-66; T.D. 6890, 7-18-66; T.D. 7188, 6-28-72; T.D. 8595, 4-27-95 and T.D. 8969, 12-13-2001.]*

## [Reg. § 301.6311-2]

**§ 301.6311-2. Payment by credit card and debit card.**—(a) *Authority to receive.*—(1) *Payments by credit card and debit card.*—Internal revenue taxes may be paid by credit card or debit card as authorized by this section. Payment of taxes by credit card or debit card is voluntary on the part of the taxpayer. Only credit cards or debit cards approved by the Commissioner may be used for this purpose, only the types of tax liabilities specified by the Commissioner may be paid by credit card or debit card, and all such payments must be made in the manner and in accordance with the forms, instructions and procedures prescribed by the Commissioner. All references in this section to *tax* also include interest, penalties, additional amounts, and additions to tax.

(2) *Payments by electronic funds transfer other than payments by credit card and debit card.*—Provisions relating to payments by electronic funds transfer other than payments by credit card and debit card are contained in section 6302 and the Treasury Regulations promulgated pursuant to section 6302.

(3) *Definitions.*—(i) *Credit card.*—means any credit card as defined in section 103(k) of the Truth in Lending Act (15 U.S.C. 1602(k)), including any credit card, charge card, or other credit device issued for the purpose of obtaining money, property, labor, or services on credit.

(ii) *Debit card.*—means any accepted card or other means of access as defined in section 903(1) of the Electronic Fund Transfer Act (15 U.S.C. 1693a(1)), including any debit card or similar device or means of access to an account issued for the purpose of initiating electronic fund transfers to obtain money, property, labor, or services.

(b) *When payment is deemed made.*—A payment of tax by credit card or debit card shall be deemed made when the issuer of the credit card or debit card properly authorizes the transaction, provided that the payment is actually received by the United States in the ordinary course of business and is not returned pursuant to paragraph (d)(3) of this section.

(c) *Payment not made.*—(1) *Continuing liability of taxpayer.*—A taxpayer who tenders payment of taxes by credit card or debit card is not relieved of liability for such taxes until the payment is actually received by the United States and is not required to be returned pursuant to paragraph (d)(3) of this section. This continuing liability of the taxpayer is in addition to, and not in lieu of, any liability of the issuer of the credit card or debit card or financial institution pursuant to paragraph (c)(2) of this section.

(2) *Liability of financial institutions.*—If a taxpayer has tendered a payment of internal revenue taxes by credit card or debit card, the

credit card or debit card transaction has been guaranteed expressly by a financial institution, and the United States is not duly paid, then the United States shall have a lien for the guaranteed amount of the transaction upon all the assets of the institution making such guarantee. The unpaid amount shall be paid out of such assets in preference to any other claims whatsoever against such guaranteeing institution, except the necessary costs and expenses of administration and the reimbursement of the United States for the amount expended in the redemption of the circulating notes of such institution.

(d) *Resolution of errors relating to the credit card or debit card account.*—(1) *In general.*—Payments of taxes by credit card or debit card shall be subject to the applicable error resolution procedures of section 161 of the Truth in Lending Act (15 U.S.C. 1666), section 908 of the Electronic Fund Transfer Act (15 U.S.C. 1693f), or any similar provisions of state or local law, for the purpose of resolving errors relating to the credit card or debit card account, but not for the purpose of resolving any claims, disputes or adjustments relating to the underlying tax liability.

(2) *Matters covered by error resolution procedures.*—(i) The error resolution procedures of paragraph (d)(1) of this section apply to the following types of errors—

(A) An incorrect amount posted to the taxpayer's account as a result of a computational error, numerical transposition, or similar mistake;

(B) An amount posted to the wrong taxpayer's account;

(C) A transaction posted to the taxpayer's account without the taxpayer's authorization; and

(D) Other similar types of errors that would be subject to resolution under section 161 of the Truth in Lending Act (15 U.S.C. 1666), section 908 of the Electronic Fund Transfer Act (15 U.S.C. 1693f), or similar provisions of state or local law.

(ii) An error described in paragraph (d)(2)(i) of this section may be resolved only through the procedures referred to in paragraph (d)(1) of this section and cannot be a basis for any claim or defense in any administrative or court proceeding involving the Commissioner or the United States.

(3) *Return of funds pursuant to error resolution procedures.*—Notwithstanding section 6402, if a taxpayer is entitled to a return of funds pursuant to the error resolution procedures of paragraph (d)(1) of this section, the Commissioner may, in the Commissioner's sole discretion, effect such return by arranging for a credit to the taxpayer's account with the issuer of the credit card or debit card or any other financial institution or person that participated in the transaction in which the error occurred.

(4) *Matters not subject to error resolution procedures.*—The error resolution procedures of paragraph (d)(1) of this section do not apply to any error, question, or dispute concerning the amount of tax owed by any person for any year. For example, these error resolution procedures do not apply to determine a taxpayer's entitlement to a refund of tax for any year for any reason, nor may they be used to pay a refund. All such matters shall be resolved through administrative and judicial procedures established pursuant to the Internal Revenue Code and the rules and regulations thereunder.

(5) *Section 170 of the Truth in Lending Act not applicable.*—Payments of taxes by credit card or debit card are not subject to section 170 of the Truth in Lending Act (15 U.S.C. 1666i) or to any similar provision of state or local law.

(e) *Fees or charges.*—The Internal Revenue Service may not impose any fee or charge on persons making payment of taxes by credit card or debit card. This section does not prohibit the imposition of fees or charges by issuers of credit cards or debit cards or by any other financial institution or person participating in the credit card or debit card transaction. The Internal Revenue Service may not receive any part of any fees that may be charged.

(f) *Authority to enter into contracts.*—The Commissioner may enter into contracts related to receiving payments of tax by credit card or debit card if such contracts are cost beneficial to the Government. The determination of whether the contract is cost beneficial shall be based on an analysis appropriate for the contract at issue and at a level of detail appropriate to the size of the Government's investment or interest. The Commissioner may not pay any fee or charge or provide any other monetary consideration under such contracts for such payments.

(g) *Use and disclosure of information relating to payment of taxes by credit card and debit card.*—Any information or data obtained directly or indirectly by any person other than the taxpayer in connection with payment of taxes by a credit card or debit card shall be treated as confidential, whether such information is received from the Inter-

nal Revenue Service or from any other person (including the taxpayer).

(1) No person other than the taxpayer shall use or disclose such information except as follows—

(i) Card issuers, financial institutions, or other persons participating in the credit card or debit card transaction may use or disclose such information for the purpose and in direct furtherance of servicing cardholder accounts, including the resolution of errors in accordance with paragraph (d) of this section. This authority includes the following—

(A) Processing the credit card or debit card transaction, in all of its stages through and including the crediting of the amount charged on account of tax to the United States Treasury;

(B) Billing the taxpayer for the amount charged or debited with respect to payment of the tax liability;

(C) Collecting the amount charged or debited with respect to payment of the tax liability;

(D) Returning funds to the taxpayer in accordance with paragraph (d)(3) of this section;

(E) Sending receipts or confirmation of a transaction to the taxpayer, including secured electronic transmissions and facsimiles; and

(F) Providing information necessary to make a payment to state or local government agencies, as explicitly authorized by the taxpayer (e.g., name, address, taxpayer identification number).

(ii) Card issuers, financial institutions or other persons participating in the credit card or debit card transaction may use and disclose such information for the purpose and in direct furtherance of any of the following activities—

(A) Assessment of statistical risk and profitability;

(B) Transfer of receivables or accounts or any interest therein;

(C) Audit of account information;

(D) Compliance with federal, state, or local law; and

(E) Cooperation in properly authorized civil, criminal, or regulatory investigations by federal, state, or local authorities.

(2) Notwithstanding the provisions of paragraph (g)(1) of this section, use or disclosure of information relating to credit card and debit card transactions for purposes related to any of the following is not authorized—

(i) Sale of such information (or transfer of such information for consideration) separate from a sale of the underlying account or receivable (or transfer of the underlying account or receivable for consideration);

(ii) Marketing for any purpose, such as, marketing tax-related products or services, or marketing any product or service that targets those who have used a credit card or debit card to pay taxes; and

(iii) Furnishing such information to any credit reporting agency or credit bureau, except with respect to the aggregate amount of a cardholder's account, with the amount attributable to payment of taxes not separately identified.

(3) Use and disclosure of information other than as authorized by this paragraph (g) may result in civil liability under sections 7431(a)(2) and (h).

(h) *Effective date.*—This section applies to payments of taxes made on and after December 14, 2001. [Reg. § 301.6311-2.]

☐ [*T.D.* 8969, 12-13-2001 (*corrected* 1-10-2002).]

### [Reg. § 301.6313-1]

§ 301.6313-1. **Fractional parts of a cent.**—In the payment of any tax not payable by stamp, a fractional part of a cent shall be disregarded unless it amounts to one-half cent or more, in which case it shall be increased to one cent. Fractional parts of a cent shall not be disregarded in the computation of taxes. [Reg. § 301.6313-1.]

☐ [*T.D.* 6119, 12-31-54.]

### [Reg. § 20.6314-1]

§ 20.6314-1. **Duplicate receipts for payments of estate taxes.**—The internal revenue officer with whom the estate tax return is filed will, upon request, give to the person paying the tax duplicate receipts, either of which will be sufficient evidence of such payment and entitle the executor to be credited with the amount by any court having jurisdiction to audit or settle his accounts. [Reg. § 20.6314-1.]

☐ [*T.D.* 6296, 6-23-58. *Amended by T.D.* 7238, 12-28-72.]

### [Reg. § 301.6314-1]

§ 301.6314-1. **Receipt for taxes.**—(a) *In general.*—The district director or the director of a service center shall, upon request, issue a receipt for each tax payment made (other than a payment for stamps sold and delivered). In addition, the district director or the director of a service center shall issue a receipt for each payment of one dollar or more made in cash, whether or not requested. In the case of payments made by check, the cancelled check is usually a sufficient receipt. No receipt shall be issued in lieu of a stamp representing a tax, whether the payment is in cash or otherwise.

(b) *Duplicate receipt for payment of estate taxes.*—Upon request, the district director or the director of a service center will issue duplicate receipts to the person paying the estate tax, either of which will be sufficient evidence of such payment and entitle the executor to be credited with the amount by any court having jurisdiction to audit or settle his accounts. For definition of the term "executor", see section 2203. [Reg. § 301.6314-1.]

☐ [T.D. 6119, 12-31-54. *Amended by T.D. 7214, 10-30-72.*]

### [Reg. § 301.6315-1]

**§ 301.6315-1. Payments of estimated income tax.**—The payment of any installment of the estimate income tax (see sections 6015 and 6016) shall be considered payment on account of the income tax for the taxable year for which the estimate is made. The aggregate amount of the payments of estimated tax should be entered upon the income tax return for such taxable year as payments to be applied against the tax shown on such return. [Reg. § 301.6315-1.]

☐ [T.D. 6119, 12-31-54.]

### [Reg. § 301.6316-1]

**§ 301.6316-1. Payment of income tax in foreign currency.**—Subject to the provisions of §§ 301.6316-3 to 301.6316-5, inclusive, that portion of the income tax which is attributable to amounts received by a citizen of the United States in nonconvertible foreign currency may be paid in such currency—

(a) For any taxable year beginning on or after January 1, 1955, and before January 1, 1964, if such amounts—

(1) Are disbursed from funds made available to a foundation or commission established in a foreign country pursuant to an agreement made under the authority of section 32(b) of the Surplus Property Act of 1944, as amended (50 U.S.C. App. 1641(b)(2)), or reestablished under the authority of the Mutual Educational and Cultural Exchange Act of 1961, as amended (22 U.S.C. 2451);

(2) Constitute either a grant made for authorized purposes of the agreement or compensation for personal services performed in the employ of the foundation or commission;

(3) Are at least 75 percent of the entire amount of the grant or compensation; and

(4) Are treated as income from sources without the United States under the provisions of sections 861 to 864, inclusive, and §§ 1.861-1 to 1.864, inclusive, of this chapter (Income Tax Regulations); and

(b) For any taxable year beginning on or after January 1, 1964, if such amounts—

(1) Are disbursed from funds made available either to a foundation or commission, established pursuant to an agreement made under the authority of section 32(b) of the Surplus Property Act of 1944, as amended, or to a foundation or commission established or continued pursuant to an agreement made under the authority of the Mutual Educational and Cultural Exchange Act of 1961, as amended; or are paid from grants made to such citizen, or to a foundation or an educational or other institution, under the authority of the Mutual Educational and Cultural Exchange Act of 1961, as amended, or section 104(h), (j), (k), (o), or (p) of the Agricultural Trade Development and Assistance Act of 1954, as amended (7 U.S.C. 1704(h), (j), (k), (o), (p));

(2) Constitute either a grant made for a purpose authorized under any such agreement or law, or compensation for personal services performed in the employ of any organization engaged in administering any program or activity pursuant to any such agreement or law;

(3) Are at least 70 percent of the entire amount of the grant or compensation; and

(4) Are treated as income from sources without the United States under the provisions of sections 861 to 864, inclusive, and §§ 1.861-1 to 1.864, inclusive, of this chapter (Income Tax Regulations). [Reg. § 301.6316-1.]

☐ [T.D. 6191, 7-18-56. *Amended by T.D. 6498, 10-24-60 and T.D. 6872, 1-5-66.*]

### [Reg. § 301.6316-2]

**§ 301.6316-2. Definitions.**—For purposes of §§ 301.6316-1 to 301.6316-9, inclusive:

(a) The term "tax", as used in §§ 301.6316-1, 301.6316-3, 301.6316-4, 301.6316-5, and 301.6316-6 means the income tax imposed for the taxable year by chapter 1 of the Internal Revenue Code of 1954, and as used in § 301.6316-7 means the Federal Insurance Contributions Act taxes imposed by chapter 21 of the Code (or by the

corresponding provisions of the Internal Revenue Code of 1939). The term "tax", as used in §§ 301.6316-8 and 301.6316-9 shall relate to either of such taxes, whichever is appropriate.

(b) The term "nonconvertible foreign currency" means currency of the government of a foreign country which, owing to (1) monetary, exchange, or other restrictions imposed by the foreign country, (2) an agreement entered into with the United States of America, or (3) the terms and conditions of the United States Government grant, is not convertible into United States dollars or into other money which is convertible into United States dollars. The term shall not, however, include currency which, notwithstanding such restrictions, agreement, terms, or conditions, is in fact converted into United States dollars or into property which is readily disposable for United States dollars.

(c) If the taxpayer computes taxable income under the accrual method, then the term "received" shall be construed to mean "accrued". [Reg. § 301.6316-2.]

☐ [T.D. 6191, 7-18-56. *Amended by T.D. 6498, 10-24-60 and T.D. 6872, 1-5-66.*]

### [Reg. § 301.6316-3]

**§ 301.6316-3. Allocation of tax attributable to foreign currency.**—(a) *Adjusted gross income ratio.*—The portion of the tax which is attributable to amounts received in nonconvertible foreign currency shall, for purposes of applying § 301.6316-1 to the currency of each foreign country, be the amount by which:

(1) The amount which bears the same ratio to the entire tax for the taxable year as (i) the taxpayer's adjusted gross income received in that currency bears to (ii) the adjusted gross income determined under section 62 by taking into account the entire gross income and all deductions allowable under that section without distinction as to amounts received in foreign currency, exceeds

(2) The total of the allowable credits against tax, and payments on account of tax, which are properly allocable to the amount of that currency included in gross income.

(b) *Example.*—(1) For the calendar year 1955 Mr. Jones and his wife filed a joint return on which the adjusted gross income is as follows, after amounts received in foreign currency had been properly translated into United States dollars for tax computation purposes:

| | |
|---|---:|
| Fulbright grant received by Mr. Jones in nonconvertible foreign currency | $8,000 |
| Dividends received by Mr. Jones entitled to dividends-received credit | 500 |
| Compensation for personal services of Mrs. Jones | 3,000 |
| Net profit from business carried on by Mrs. Jones | 2,500 |
| Total adjusted gross income | $14,000 |

(2) The following amounts are allowable as properly deductible from adjusted gross income, no determination being made as to whether or not any part of them is properly allocable to the Fulbright grant:

| | |
|---|---:|
| Deduction for personal exemptions | $3,000 |
| Charitable contributions | 500 |
| Interest expense | 400 |
| Taxes | 300 |
| Total allowable deductions | $4,200 |

(3) For the taxable year the following amounts are allowable as credits against the tax, or as payments on account of the tax:

| | | |
|---|---:|---:|
| Foreign tax credit for foreign taxes paid on Fulbright grant | | $300.00 |
| Dividends-received credit | | 20.00 |
| Credit for income tax withheld upon compensation of Mrs. Jones | | 304.80 |
| Payments of estimated tax (see § 301.6316-6(b)(2) for determination of amounts): | | |
|    United States dollars | $426.32 | |
|    Foreign currency | 893.88 | 1,320.20 |
|     Total allowable credits and payments | | $1,945.00 |

(4) The portion of the tax which is attributable to amounts received in nonconvertible foreign currency is $33.49, determined as follows:

| | |
|---|---:|
| Adjusted gross income | $14,000.00 |
| Less: Allowable deductions | 4,200.00 |
| Taxable income | 9,800.00 |
| Tax computed under section 2 | 2,148.00 |
| Ratio of adjusted gross income received in nonconvertible foreign currency to entire adjusted gross income ($8,000 ÷ $14,000) (percent) | 57.14 |
| Portion of tax attributable to nonconvertible foreign currency ($2,148 × 57.14) (percent) | $1,227.37 |

| Less: Credit for foreign taxes paid on Fulbright grant . . . . . . . . . | $300.00 | |
| Payment in foreign currency of estimated tax . . . . . . . . | 893.88 | $1,193.88 |

| Portion of tax attributable to amounts received in nonconvertible foreign currency . . . . . . . . . . . . | | $33.49 |

[Reg. § 301.6316-3.]

☐ [T.D. 6191, 7-18-56.]

### [Reg. § 301.6316-4]

**§ 301.6316-4. Return requirements.**—(a) *Place for filing.*—A return of income which includes amounts received in foreign currency on which the tax is paid in accordance with § 301.6316-1 shall be filed with the Director of International Operations, Internal Revenue Service, Washington, D.C. 20225. For the time for filing income tax returns, see sections 6072 and 6081 and § § 1.6072-1, 1.6081-1, and 1.6081-2 of this chapter(Income Tax Regulations).

(b) *Statements required.*—(1) A statement, prepared by the taxpayer, and certified by the foundation, commission, or other person having control of the payments made to the taxpayer in nonconvertible foreign currency, shall be attached to the return showing that for the taxable year involved the taxpayer is entitled to pay tax in foreign currency in accordance with section 6316 and the regulations thereunder. This statement shall disclose the total amount of grants or compensation received by the taxpayer during the taxable year under the authority of section 32(b) of the Surplus Property Act of 1944, as amended (50 U.S.C. App. 1641(b)(2)), or of the Mutual Educational and Cultural Exchange Act of 1961, as amended (22 U.S.C. 2451), or section 104(h), (j), (k), (o), or (p) of the Agricultural Trade Development and Assistance Act of 1954, as amended (7 U.S.C. 1704(h), (j), (k), (o), (p)), and the amount thereof paid in nonconvertible foreign currency. It shall also state that with respect to the grant or compensation the applicable percentage requirement of § 301.6316-1 is satisfied.

(2) The taxpayer shall also attach to the return a detailed statement showing (i) the computation, in the manner prescribed by § 301.6316-3, of the portion of the tax attributable to amounts received in nonconvertible foreign currency and (ii) the rates of exchange used in determining the tax liability in United States dollars. See paragraph (c) of § 301.6316-5. [Reg. § 301.6316-4.]

☐ [T.D. 6191, 7-18-56. *Amended by T.D. 6498, 10-24-60 and T.D. 6872,* 1-5-66.]

### [Reg. § 301.6316-5]

**§ 301.6316-5. Manner of paying tax by foreign currency.**—(a) *Time and place to pay.*—The unpaid tax required to be shown on a return filed in accordance with § 301.6316-4, whether payable in whole or in part in foreign currency, is due and payable to the Director of International Operations, Internal Revenue Service, Washington, D.C. 20225, at the time the return is filed. However, see paragraph (d) of this section with respect to the depositing of the foreign currency with the disbursing officer of the Department of State.

(b) *Certified statement.*—Every taxpayer who desires to pay tax in foreign currency under the provisions of § 301.6316-1 shall first obtain the certified statement referred to in paragraph (b)(1) of § 301.6316-4.

(c) *Determination of the tax.*—In determining the tax payable for the taxable year in United States dollars, the taxpayer, with respect to amounts described in paragraph (a) of § 301.6316-1, or amounts described in paragraph (b) of § 301.6316-1 received before November 1, 1965, shall use the rates of exchange which most clearly reflect the correct tax liability in dollars, whether it be the official rate, the open market rate, or any other appropriate rate. With respect to amounts described in paragraph (b) of § 301.6316-1 received on or after November 1, 1965, the taxpayer shall use the official rate of exchange in determining the tax payable for the taxable year in United States dollars. After determining the correct tax liability in United States dollars the taxpayer shall then ascertain, in accordance with the principles of § 301.6316-3, the portion of the tax which is attributable to amounts received in nonconvertible foreign currency.

(d) *Deposit of foreign currency with disbursing officer.*—(1) After the portion of the tax which is attributable to amounts received in nonconvertible foreign currency is determined in United States dollars, the amount so determined shall be deposited in the same nonconvertible foreign currency with the disbursing officer of the Department of State for the foreign country where the fund is located from which the payments in nonconvertible foreign currency are made to the taxpayer. The amount of foreign currency to be deposited shall be that amount which, when converted at the rate of exchange used on the date of deposit by that disbursing officer for

the acquisition of such currency for his official disbursements, equals the portion of the tax so determined in United States dollars.

(2) The disbursing officer may rely upon the taxpayer for the determination of the amount of tax payable in foreign currency but may not accept any such currency for deposit until the taxpayer has presented for inspection the certified statement referred to in paragraph (b)(1) of § 301.6316-4. Upon acceptance of foreign currency for deposit the disbursing officer shall give the taxpayer a receipt in duplicate showing the name and address of the depositor, the date of deposit, the amount of foreign currency deposited, and its equivalent in United States dollars on the date of deposit.

(3) Every taxpayer making a deposit of foreign currency in accordance with this paragraph shall attach to the return required to be filed in accordance with § 301.6316-4, in part or full payment of the taxes shown thereon, the original of the receipt given by the disbursing officer and shall pay to the Director of International Operations in United States dollars the balance, if any, of the tax shown to be due. Tender of such receipt to the Director of International Operations shall be considered as payment of tax in an amount equal to the United States dollars represented by the receipt.

(4) A taxpayer shall make the deposit required by this paragraph in ample time to permit him to attach the receipt to his return for filing within the time prescribed by section 6072 or 6081 and the regulations thereunder. [Reg. § 301.6316-5.]

☐ [T.D. 6191, 7-18-56. *Amended by T.D. 6498, 10-24-60 and T.D. 6872,* 1-5-66.]

### [Reg. § 301.6316-6]

**§ 301.6316-6. Declarations of estimated tax.**—(a) *Filing of declaration.*—A declaration of estimated tax in respect of amounts on which the tax is to be paid in foreign currency under the provisions of § 301.6316-1 shall be filed with the Director of International Operations, Internal Revenue Service, Washington, D.C. 20225, and shall have attached thereto the statements required by paragraph (b)(1) and (2)(i) of § 301.6316-4 in respect of the tax return except that the statement certified by the foundation, commission, or other person having control of the payments to the taxpayer in nonconvertible foreign currency may be based upon amounts expected to be received by the taxpayer during the taxable year if they are not in fact known at the time of certification. A copy of this certified statement shall be retained by the taxpayer for the purpose of exhibiting it to the disbursing officer when making installment deposits of foreign currency under the provisions of paragraph (c) of this section. For the time for filing declarations of estimated tax, see sections 6073 and 6081 and § § 1.6073-1 to 1.6073-4, inclusive, and § § 1.6081-1 and 1.6081-2 of this chapter (Income Tax Regulations).

(b) *Determination of estimated tax.*—(1) *Allocation of tax attributable to foreign currency.*—In determining the amount of estimated tax for purposes of this section, all items of income, deduction, and credit, whether or not attributable to amounts received in nonconvertible foreign currency, shall be taken into account. The portion of the estimated tax which is attributable to amounts to be received during the taxable year in nonconvertible foreign currency shall be determined consistently with the manner prescribed by § 301.6316-3.

(2) *Example.*—(i) For the calendar year 1955 Mr. Jones and his wife filed a joint declaration of estimated tax in the determination of which the adjusted gross income was estimated to be as follows, after amounts received in foreign currency had been properly translated into United States dollars for tax computation purposes:

| | |
| --- | --- |
| Fulbright grant to be received by Mr. Jones in nonconvertible foreign currency . . . . . . . . . . . . . . . . . . . | $8,000 |
| Dividends to be received by Mr. Jones entitled to dividends-received credit . . . . . . . . . . . . . . . . . . . | 375 |
| Compensation to be received by Mrs. Jones for personal services . . . . . . . . . . . . . . . . . . . | 3,000 |
| Net profit to be derived from business carried on by Mrs. Jones . . . . . . . . . . . . . . . . . . . | 1,625 |
| Total estimated adjusted gross income . . . . . . . . . . . . | $13,000 |

(ii) The following amounts were determined to be allowable as properly deductible from estimated adjusted gross income, no determination being made as to whether or not any part of them was properly allocable to the Fulbright grant:

| | |
| --- | --- |
| Deduction for personal exemptions . . . . . . . . . . . . . . | $3,000 |
| Charitable contributions . . . . . . . . . . . . . . . . . . . | 300 |
| Interest expense . . . . . . . . . . . . . . . . . . . | 400 |
| Taxes . . . . . . . . . . . . . . . . . . . | 300 |
| Total allowable deductions . . . . . . . . . . . . . . . . . . | $4,000 |

(iii) The following estimated amounts were determined to be allowable as credits against the tax for the taxable year:

| | |
| --- | --- |
| Foreign tax credit for foreign taxes to be paid on Fulbright grant . . . . . . . . . . . . . . . . . . . | $300.00 |
| Credit for income tax expected to be withheld upon compensation of Mrs. Jones . . . . . . . . . . . . . . . . . . . | 304.80 |

| | |
|---|---:|
| Dividends-received credit . . . . . . . . . . . . . . . . . . . . . . | 15.00 |
| Total allowable estimated credits . . . . . . . . . . . . . | $619.80 |

(iv) The portion of the estimated tax which is attributable to amounts to be received during the taxable year in nonconvertible foreign currency is $893.88, determined as follows:

| | |
|---|---:|
| Estimated adjusted gross income . . . . . . . . . . . . . . . . . | $13,000.00 |
| Less: Allowable deductions . . . . . . . . . . . . . . . . | 4,000.00 |
| Estimated taxable income . . . . . . . . . . . . . . . . . . . . . | 9,000.00 |
| Tax computed under section 2 . . . . . . . . . . . . . . . . . . | 1,940.00 |
| Ratio of estimated adjusted gross income to be received in nonconvertible foreign currency to entire estimated adjusted gross income ($8,000 ÷ $13,000) (percent) . . . . . . . . . . . . . | 61.54 |
| Portion of above tax attributable to nonconvertible foreign currency ($1,940 × 61.54) (percent) . . . . . . . . . . . . . . | 1,193.88 |
| Less: Credit for foreign taxes expected to be paid on Fulbright grant . . . . . . . . . . . . . . . . . . . . . . . . . . . | 300.00 |
| Portion of estimated tax which is attributable to amounts to be received during the taxable year in nonconvertible foreign currency . . . . . . . . . . . . . . . . . . . . | $893.88 |

(v) The portion of the estimated tax which is payable in United States dollars is $426.32, determined as follows:

| | |
|---|---:|
| Tax computed under section 2 . . . . . . . . . . . . . . . . . | $1,940.00 |
| Less: Total allowable estimated credits . . . . . . . . . . . . | 619.80 |
| Total estimated tax . . . . . . . . . . . . . . . . . . . . . . . | $1,320.20 |
| Less: Portion of estimated tax payable in foreign currency . . | 893.88 |
| Portion of estimated tax payable in United States dollars | $426.32 |

(c) *Payment of estimated tax.*—(1) The provisions of § 301.6316-5 relating to the certified statement, determination of the tax, and the depositing of the foreign currency shall apply for purposes of this section. The full amount of estimated tax payable in foreign currency, as determined under paragraph (b) of this section, may be deposited before the date prescribed for the payment thereof.

(2) Every taxpayer making a deposit of foreign currency in accordance with this paragraph shall tender to the Director of International Operations, Internal Revenue Service, Washington, D.C. 20225, the original of the receipt from the disbursing officer as payment, to the extent of the amount represented thereby in United States dollars, of the estimated tax. For the dates prescribed for the payment of estimated tax, see sections 6153 and 6161 and §§ 1.6153-1 to 1.6153-4, inclusive, and § 1.6161-1 of this chapter (Income Tax Regulations). A taxpayer should make the deposit required by this paragraph in ample time to permit him to tender such receipt by the date prescribed for payment of the estimated tax.

(d) *Credit on return for the taxable year.*—The receipt given by the disbursing officer of the Department of State and tendered in payment of estimated tax under this section shall, for purposes of paragraph (a)(2) of § 301.6316-3, be considered as payment on account of the tax for the taxable year. The amount so considered to be paid shall be the amount in United States dollars represented by the receipt. [Reg. § 301.6316-6.]

☐ [*T.D. 6191, 7-18-56. Amended by T.D. 6498, 10-24-60 and T.D. 6872, 1-5-66.*]

### [Reg. § 301.6316-7]

§ 301.6316-7. Payment of Federal Insurance Contributions Act taxes in foreign currency.—(a) *In general.*—The taxes imposed on employees and employers by sections 3101 and 3111, respectively, of chapter 21 of the Code (Federal Insurance Contributions Act) or the corresponding sections of the Internal Revenue Code of 1939 may, with respect to wages (as defined in section 3121(a) of chapter 21 of the Code or the corresponding section of the Internal Revenue Code of 1939) paid in nonconvertible foreign currency(as defined in paragraph (b) of § 301.6316-2) for services performed on or after January 1, 1951, be paid in that currency if all such wages—

(1) Are paid from funds made available to a foundation or commission established in a foreign country pursuant to an agreement made under the authority of section 32(b) of the Surplus Property Act of 1944, as amended (50 U.S.C. App. 1641(b)(2)), or established or continued pursuant to an agreement made under authority of the Mutual Educational and Cultural Exchange Act of 1961, as amended (22 U.S.C. 2451); and

(2) Are paid to a United States citizen for services performed in the employ of such foundation or commission.

(b) *Return requirements.*—(1) *Statements required.*—(i) A return on which payment of Federal Insurance Contributions Act taxes is made in accordance with this section shall have attached thereto a statement, certified by the foundation or commission filing the return, stating that the foundation or commission is an organization estab-

lished pursuant to an agreement made under authority of section 32(b) of the Surplus Property Act of 1944, as amended, or established or continued pursuant to an agreement made under authority of the Mutual Educational and Cultural Exchange Act of 1961, as amended.

(ii) The taxpayer shall also attach to the return a statement showing the rates of exchange used in determining in United States dollars the wages reported on the return and the taxes due with respect thereto. See paragraph (c)(1) of this section.

(2) *Cross references.*—For the place for filing returns of the Federal Insurance Contributions Act taxes, see § 31.6091-1(c) of this chapter (Employment Tax Regulations). For the time for filing returns of the Federal Insurance Contributions Act taxes, see § 31.6071(a)-1 of this chapter (Employment Tax Regulations).

(c) *Payment of tax.*—(1) *Determination of the tax.*—In determining in United States dollars the wages required to be reported on the return and the taxes due with respect thereto, the taxpayer shall use the rate of exchange which most clearly reflects the correct equivalent in dollars, whether it be the official rate, the open market rate, or any other appropriate rate.

(2) *Deposit of foreign currency with disbursing officer.*—(i) After determination is made in United States dollars of the Federal Insurance Contributions Act taxes with respect to wages paid in nonconvertible foreign currency, the amount so determined shall be deposited in the same nonconvertible foreign currency with the disbursing officer of the Department of State for the foreign country where the fund is located from which such wages were paid. The amount of the foreign currency to be deposited shall be that amount which, when converted at the rate of exchange used on the date of deposit by the disbursing officer for the acquisition of such currency for his official disbursement, equals the taxes determined in United States dollars.

(ii) The disbursing officer may rely upon the taxpayer for the determination of the amount of tax payable in foreign currency but may not accept any such currency for deposit until the taxpayer has presented for inspection the certified statement referred to in paragraph (b)(1) of this section. Upon acceptance of foreign currency for deposit the disbursing officer shall give the taxpayer a receipt in duplicate showing the name and address of the depositor, the date of the deposit, the amount of foreign currency deposited and its equivalent in United States dollars on the date of deposit, and the kind of tax for which the deposit is made.

(iii) Every taxpayer making a deposit of foreign currency in accordance with this paragraph shall attach to the return required to be filed in accordance with paragraph (b) of this section the original of the receipt given by the disbursing officer. Tender of such receipt to the Director of International Operations shall be considered as payment of tax in an amount equal to the United States dollars represented by the receipt.

(iv) A taxpayer shall make the deposit required by this paragraph in ample time to permit it to attach the receipt to its return for filing within the time prescribed by § 31.6071(a)-1 of this chapter (Employment Tax Regulations). [Reg. § 301.6316-7.]

☐ [*T.D. 6872, 1-5-66.*]

### [Reg. § 301.6316-8]

§ 301.6316-8. Refunds and credits in foreign currency.—(a) *Refunds.*—The refund of any overpayment of tax which has been paid under section 6316 in foreign currency may, in the discretion of the Commissioner, be made in the same foreign currency by which the tax was paid. The amount of any such refund made in foreign currency shall be the amount of the overpayment in United States dollars converted, on the date of the refund check, at the rate of exchange then used for his official disbursements by the disbursing officer of the Department of State in the country where the foreign currency was originally deposited.

(b) *Credits.*—Unless otherwise in the best interest of the Internal Revenue Service, no credit of any overpayment of tax which has been paid under section 6316 in foreign currency shall be allowed against any outstanding liability of the person making the overpayment except in respect of that portion of the liability which, in accordance with § 301.6316-1 or § 301.6316-7, would otherwise be permitted to be paid in the same foreign currency. [Reg. § 301.6316-8.]

☐ [*T.D. 6191, 7-18-56. Amended by T.D. 6872, 1-5-66.*]

### [Reg. § 301.6316-9]

§ 301.6316-9. Interest, additions to tax, etc.—Any reference in §§ 301.6316-1 to 301.6316-8, inclusive, to "tax" shall be deemed also to refer to the interest, additions to the tax, additional amounts, and penalties attributable to the tax. [Reg. § 301.6316-9.]

☐ [*T.D. 6191, 7-18-56. Amended by T.D. 6872, 1-5-66.*]

# LIEN FOR TAXES

## [Reg. §301.6320-1]

**§301.6320-1. Notice and opportunity for hearing upon filing of notice of federal tax lien.**—(a) *Notification.*—(1) *In general.*—For a notice of Federal tax lien (NFTL) filed on or after January 19, 1999, the Commissioner, or his or her delegate (the Commissioner), will prescribe procedures to notify the person described in section 6321 of the filing of a NFTL not more than five business days after the date of any such filing. The Collection Due Process Hearing Notice (CDP Notice) and other notices given under section 6320 must be given in person, left at the dwelling or usual place of business of such person, or sent by certified or registered mail to such person's last known address, not more than five business days after the day the NFTL was filed. For further guidance regarding the definition of last known address, see §301.6212-2.

(2) *Questions and answers.*—The questions and answers illustrate the provisions of this paragraph (a) as follows:

Q-A1. Who is the person entitled to notice under section 6320?

A-A1. Under section 6320(a)(1), notification of the filing of a NFTL on or after January 19, 1999, is required to be given only to the person described in section 6321 who is named on the NFTL that is filed. The person described in section 6321 is the person liable to pay the tax due after notice and demand who refuses or neglects to pay the tax due (hereinafter, referred to as the taxpayer).

Q-A2. When will the Internal Revenue Service (IRS) provide the notice required under section 6320?

A-A2. The IRS will provide this notice within five business days after the filing of the NFTL.

Q-A3. Will the IRS give notification to the taxpayer for each tax period listed in a NFTL filed on or after January 19, 1999?

A-A3. Yes. A NFTL can be filed for more than one tax period. The notification of the filing of a NFTL will specify each unpaid tax and tax period listed in the NFTL.

Q-A4. Will the IRS give notification to the taxpayer of any filing of a NFTL for the same tax period or periods at another place of filing?

A-A4. Yes. The IRS will notify a taxpayer when a NFTL is filed on or after January 19, 1999, for a tax period or periods at any recording office.

Q-A5. Will the IRS give notification to the taxpayer if a NFTL is filed on or after January 19, 1999, for a tax period or periods for which a NFTL was filed in another recording office prior to that date?

A-A5. Yes. The IRS will notify a taxpayer when each NFTL is filed on or after January 19, 1999, for a tax period or periods at any recording office.

Q-A6. Will the IRS give notification to the taxpayer when a NFTL is refiled on or after January 19, 1999?

A-A6. No. Section 6320(a)(1) does not require the IRS to notify the taxpayer of the refiling of a NFTL. A taxpayer may, however, seek reconsideration by the IRS office that is collecting the tax or refiling the NFTL, an administrative hearing before the IRS Office of Appeals (Appeals), or assistance from the National Taxpayer Advocate.

Q-A7. Will the IRS give notification to a known nominee of, or a person holding property of, the taxpayer of the filing of the NFTL?

A-A7. No. Such person is not the person described in section 6321 and, therefore, is not entitled to notice, but such persons have other remedies. See A-B5 of paragraph (b)(2) of this section.

Q-A8. Will the IRS give notification to the taxpayer when a subsequent NFTL is filed for the same period or periods?

A-A8. Yes. If the IRS files an additional NFTL with respect to the same tax period or periods for which an original NFTL was filed, the IRS will notify the taxpayer when the subsequent NFTL is filed. Not all such notices will, however, give rise to a right to a CDP hearing (see paragraph (b) of this section).

Q-A9. How will notification under section 6320 be accomplished?

A-A9. The IRS will notify the taxpayer by letter. Included with this letter will be the additional information the IRS is required to provide taxpayers as well as, when appropriate, a Form 12153, Request for a Due Process Hearing. The IRS may effect delivery of the letter (and accompanying materials) in one of three ways: by delivering the notice personally to the taxpayer; by leaving the notice at the taxpayer's dwelling or usual place of business; or by mailing the notice to the taxpayer at his last known address by certified or registered mail.

Q-A10. What must a CDP Notice given under section 6320 include?

A-A10. These notices must include, in simple and nontechnical terms:

(i) The amount of the unpaid tax.

(ii) A statement concerning the taxpayer's right to request a CDP hearing during the 30-day period that commences the day after the end of the five business day period within which the IRS is required to provide the taxpayer with notice of the filing of the NFTL.

(iii) The administrative appeals available to the taxpayer with respect to the NFTL and the procedures relating to such appeals.

(iv) The statutory provisions and the procedures relating to the release of liens on property.

Q-A11. What are the consequences if the taxpayer does not receive or accept a CDP Notice that is properly left at the taxpayer's dwelling or usual place of business, or sent by certified or registered mail to the taxpayer's last known address?

A-A11. A CDP Notice properly sent by certified or registered mail to the taxpayer's last known address or left at the taxpayer's dwelling or usual place of business is sufficient to start the 30-day period, commencing the day after the end of the five business day notification period, within which the taxpayer may request a CDP hearing. Actual receipt is not a prerequisite to the validity of the CDP Notice.

Q-A12. What if the taxpayer does not receive the CDP Notice because the IRS did not send that notice by certified or registered mail to the taxpayer's last known address, or failed to leave it at the dwelling or usual place of business of the taxpayer, and the taxpayer fails to request a CDP hearing with Appeals within the 30-day period commencing the day after the end of the five business day notification period?

A-A12. A NFTL becomes effective upon filing. The validity and priority of a NFTL is not conditioned on notification to the taxpayer pursuant to section 6320. Therefore, the failure to notify the taxpayer concerning the filing of a NFTL does not affect the validity or priority of the NFTL. When the IRS determines that it failed properly to provide a taxpayer with a CDP Notice, it will promptly provide the taxpayer with a substitute CDP Notice and provide the taxpayer with an opportunity to request a CDP hearing. Substitute CDP Notices are discussed in Q & A-B3 of paragraph (b)(2) and Q & A-C8 of paragraph (c)(2) of this section.

(3) *Examples.*—The following examples illustrate the principles of this paragraph (a):

*Example 1.* H and W are jointly and severally liable with respect to a jointly filed income tax return for 1996. IRS files a NFTL with respect to H and W in County X on January 26, 1999. This is the first NFTL filed on or after January 19, 1999, for their 1996 liability. H and W will each be notified of the filing of the NFTL.

*Example 2.* Employment taxes for 1997 are assessed against ABC Corporation. A NFTL is filed against ABC Corporation for the 1997 liability in County X on June 5, 1998. A NFTL is filed against ABC Corporation for the 1997 liability in County Y on June 17, 1999. The IRS will notify the ABC Corporation with respect to the filing of the NFTL in County Y.

*Example 3.* Federal income tax liability for 1997 is assessed against individual D. D buys an asset and puts it in individual E's name. A NFTL is filed against D in County X on June 5, 1999, for D's federal income tax liability for 1997. On June 17, 1999, a NFTL for the same tax liability is filed in County Y against E, as nominee of D. The IRS will notify D of the filing of the NFTL in both County X and County Y. The IRS will not notify E of the NFTL filed in County X. The IRS is not required to notify E of the NFTL filed in County Y. Although E is named on the NFTL filed in County Y, E is not the person described in section 6321 (the taxpayer) who is named on the NFTL.

(b) *Entitlement to a CDP hearing.*—(1) *In general.*—A taxpayer is entitled to one CDP hearing with respect to the first filing of a NFTL (on or after January 19, 1999) for a given tax period or periods with respect to the unpaid tax shown on the NFTL if the taxpayer timely requests such a hearing. The taxpayer must request such a hearing during the 30-day period that commences the day after the end of the five business day period within which the IRS is required to provide the taxpayer with notice of the filing of the NFTL.

(2) *Questions and answers.*—The questions and answers illustrate the provisions of this paragraph (b) as follows:

Q-B1. Is a taxpayer entitled to a CDP hearing with respect to the filing of a NFTL for a type of tax and tax periods previously subject to a CDP Notice with respect to a NFTL filed in a different location on or after January 19, 1999?

A-B1. No. Although the taxpayer will receive notice of each filing of a NFTL, under section 6320(b)(2), the taxpayer is entitled to only one CDP hearing under section 6320 for the type of tax and tax periods with respect to the first filing of a NFTL that occurs on or after January 19, 1999, with respect to that unpaid tax. Accordingly, if the taxpayer does not timely request a CDP hearing with respect to the first filing of a NFTL on or after January 19, 1999, for a given tax period or periods with respect to an unpaid tax, the taxpayer foregoes the right to a CDP hearing with Appeals and judicial review of the Appeals determination with respect to the NFTL. Under such circumstances, the taxpayer may request an equivalent hearing as described in paragraph (i) of this section.

Q-B2. Is the taxpayer entitled to a CDP hearing when a NFTL for an unpaid tax is filed on or after January 19, 1999, in one recording office and a NFTL was previously filed for the same unpaid tax in another recording office prior to that date?

A-B2. Yes. Under section 6320(b)(2), the taxpayer is entitled to a CDP hearing under section 6320 for each tax period with respect to the first filing of a NFTL on or after January 19, 1999, with respect to an unpaid tax, whether or not a NFTL was filed prior to January 19, 1999, for the same unpaid tax and tax period or periods.

Q-B3. When the IRS provides the taxpayer with a substitute CDP Notice and the taxpayer timely requests a CDP hearing, is the taxpayer entitled to a CDP hearing before Appeals?

A-B3. Yes. Unless the taxpayer provides the IRS a written withdrawal of the request that Appeals conduct a CDP hearing, the taxpayer is entitled to a CDP hearing before Appeals. Following the hearing, Appeals will issue a Notice of Determination, and the taxpayer is entitled to seek judicial review of that Notice of Determination.

Q-B4. If the IRS sends a second CDP Notice under section 6320 (other than a substitute CDP Notice) for a tax period and with respect to an unpaid tax for which a section 6320 CDP Notice was previously sent, is the taxpayer entitled to a section 6320 CDP hearing based on the second CDP Notice?

A-B4. No. The taxpayer is entitled to a CDP hearing under section 6320 for each tax period only with respect to the first filing of a NFTL on or after January 19, 1999, with respect to an unpaid tax.

Q-B5. Is a nominee of, or a person holding property of, the taxpayer entitled to a CDP hearing or an equivalent hearing?

A-B5. No. Such person is not the person described in section 6321 and is, therefore, not entitled to a CDP hearing or an equivalent hearing (as discussed in paragraph (i) of this section). Such person, however, may seek reconsideration by the IRS office collecting the tax or filing the NFTL, an administrative hearing before Appeals under its Collection Appeals Program, or assistance from the National Taxpayer Advocate. However, any such administrative hearing would not be a CDP hearing under section 6320 and any determination or decision resulting from the hearing would not be subject to judicial review under section 6320. Such person also may avail himself of the administrative procedure included in section 6325(b)(4) or of any other procedures to which he is entitled.

(3) *Examples.*—The following examples illustrate the principles of this paragraph (b):

*Example 1.* H and W are jointly and severally liable with respect to a jointly filed income tax return for 1996. The IRS files a NFTL with respect to H and W in County X on January 26, 1999. This is the first NFTL filed on or after January 19, 1999, for their 1996 liability. H and W are each entitled to a CDP hearing with respect to the NFTL filed in County X. On June 17, 1999, a NFTL for the same tax liability is filed against H and W in County Y. The IRS will give H and W notification of the NFTL filed in County Y. H and W, however, are not entitled to a CDP hearing or an equivalent hearing with respect to the NFTL filed in County Y.

*Example 2.* Federal income tax liability for 1997 is assessed against individual D. D buys an asset and puts it in individual E's name. A NFTL is filed against E, as nominee of D in County X on June 5, 1999, for D's federal income tax liability for 1997. The IRS will give D a CDP Notice with respect to the NFTL filed in County X. The IRS will not notify E of the NFTL filed in County X. The IRS is not required to notify E of the filing of the NFTL in County X. Although E is named on the NFTL filed in County X, E is not the person described in section 6321 (the taxpayer) who is named on the NFTL.

(c) *Requesting a CDP hearing.*—(1) *In general.*—When a taxpayer is entitled to a CDP hearing under section 6320, the CDP hearing must be requested during the 30-day period that commences the day after the end of the five business day period within which the IRS is required to provide the taxpayer with a CDP Notice with respect to the filing of the NFTL.

(2) *Questions and answers.*—The questions and answers illustrate the provisions of this paragraph (c) as follows:

Q-C1. What must a taxpayer do to obtain a CDP hearing?

A-C1. (i) The taxpayer must make a request in writing for a CDP hearing. The request for a CDP hearing shall include the information

and signature specified in A-C1(ii) of this paragraph (c)(2). See A-D7 and A-D8 of paragraph (d)(2).

(ii) The written request for a CDP hearing must be dated and must include the following:

(A) The taxpayer's name, address, daytime telephone number (if any), and taxpayer identification number (e.g., SSN, ITIN or EIN).

(B) The type of tax involved.

(C) The tax period at issue.

(D) A statement that the taxpayer requests a hearing with Appeals concerning the filing of the NFTL.

(E) The reason or reasons why the taxpayer disagrees with the filing of the NFTL.

(F) The signature of the taxpayer or the taxpayer's authorized representative.

(iii) If the IRS receives a timely written request for CDP hearing that does not satisfy the requirements set forth in A-C1(ii) of this paragraph (c)(2), the IRS will make a reasonable attempt to contact the taxpayer and request that the taxpayer comply with the unsatisfied requirements. The taxpayer must perfect any timely written request for a CDP hearing that does not satisfy the requirements set forth in A-C1(ii) of this paragraph (c)(2) within a reasonable period of time after a request from the IRS.

(iv) Taxpayers are encouraged to use Form 12153, "Request for a Collection Due Process Hearing," in requesting a CDP hearing so that the request can be readily identified and forwarded to Appeals. Taxpayers may obtain a copy of Form 12153 by contacting the IRS office that issued the CDP Notice, by downloading a copy from the IRS Internet site, *www.irs.gov/pub/irs-pdf/f12153.pdf*, or by calling, toll-free, 1-800-829-3676.

(v) The taxpayer must affirm any timely written request for a CDP hearing which is signed or alleged to have been signed on the taxpayer's behalf by the taxpayer's spouse or other unauthorized representative by filing, within a reasonable period of time after a request from the IRS, a signed, written affirmation that the request was originally submitted on the taxpayer's behalf. If the affirmation is filed within a reasonable period of time after a request, the timely CDP hearing request will be considered timely with respect to the non-signing taxpayer. If the affirmation is not filed within a reasonable period of time after a request, the CDP hearing request will be denied with respect to the non-signing taxpayer.

Q-C2. Must the request for the CDP hearing be in writing?

A-C2. Yes. There are several reasons why the request for a CDP hearing must be in writing. The filing of a timely request for a CDP hearing is the first step in what may result in a court proceeding. A written request will provide proof that the CDP hearing was requested and thus permit the court to verify that it has jurisdiction over any subsequent appeal of the Notice of Determination issued by Appeals. In addition, the receipt of the written request will establish the date on which the periods of limitation under section 6502 (relating to collection after assessment), section 6531 (relating to criminal prosecutions), and section 6532 (relating to suits) are suspended as a result of the CDP hearing and any judicial appeal. Moreover, because the IRS anticipates that taxpayers will contact the IRS office that issued the CDP Notice for further information or assistance in filling out Form 12153, or to attempt to resolve their liabilities prior to going through the CDP hearing process, the requirement of a written request should help prevent any misunderstanding as to whether a CDP hearing has been requested. If the information requested on Form 12153 is furnished by the taxpayer, the written request also will help to establish the issues for which the taxpayer seeks a determination by Appeals.

Q-C3. When must a taxpayer request a CDP hearing with respect to a CDP Notice issued under section 6320?

A-C3. A taxpayer must submit a written request for a CDP hearing within the 30-day period that commences the day after the end of the five business day period following the filing of the NFTL. Any request filed during the five business day period (before the beginning of the 30-day period) will be deemed to be filed on the first day of the 30-day period. The period for submitting a written request for a CDP hearing with respect to a CDP Notice issued under section 6320 is slightly different from the period for submitting a written request for a CDP hearing with respect to a CDP Notice issued under section 6330. For a CDP Notice issued under section 6330, the taxpayer must submit a written request for a CDP hearing within the 30-day period commencing the day after the date of the CDP Notice.

Q-C4. How will the timeliness of a taxpayer's written request for a CDP hearing be determined?

A-C4. The rules and regulations under section 7502 and section 7503 will apply to determine the timeliness of the taxpayer's request for a CDP hearing, if properly transmitted and addressed as provided in A-C6 of this paragraph (c)(2).

Q-C5. Is the 30-day period within which a taxpayer must make a request for a CDP hearing extended because the taxpayer resides outside the United States?

A-C5. No. Section 6320 does not make provision for such a circumstance. Accordingly, all taxpayers who want a CDP hearing under section 6320 must request such a hearing within the 30-day period that commences the day after the end of the five business day notification period.

Q-C6. Where must the written request for a CDP hearing be sent?

A-C6. The written request for a CDP hearing must be sent, or hand delivered (if permitted), to the IRS office and address as directed on the CDP Notice. If the address of that office does not appear on the CDP Notice, the taxpayer should obtain the address of the office to which the written request should be sent or hand delivered by calling, toll-free, 1-800-829-1040 and providing the taxpayer's identification number (e.g., SSN, ITIN or EIN).

Q-C7. What will happen if the taxpayer does not request a CDP hearing in writing within the 30-day period that commences the day after the end of the five business day notification period?

A-C7. If the taxpayer does not request a CDP hearing in writing within the 30-day period that commences on the day after the end of the five-business-day notification period, the taxpayer foregoes the right to a CDP hearing under section 6320 with respect to the unpaid tax and tax periods shown on the CDP Notice. A written request submitted within the 30-day period that does not satisfy the requirements set forth in A-C1(ii)(A), (B), (C), (D) or (F) of this paragraph (c)(2) is considered timely if the request is perfected within a reasonable period of time pursuant to A-C1(iii) of this paragraph (c)(2). If the request for CDP hearing is untimely, either because the request was not submitted within the 30-day period or not perfected within the reasonable period provided, the taxpayer will be notified of the untimeliness of the request and offered an equivalent hearing. In such cases, the taxpayer may obtain an equivalent hearing without submitting an additional request. See paragraph (i) of this section.

Q-C8. When must a taxpayer request a CDP hearing with respect to a substitute CDP Notice?

A-C8. A CDP hearing with respect to a substitute CDP Notice must be requested in writing by the taxpayer prior to the end of the 30-day period commencing the day after the date of the substitute CDP Notice.

Q-C9. Can taxpayers attempt to resolve the matter of the NFTL with an officer or employee of the IRS office collecting the tax or filing the NFTL either before or after requesting a CDP hearing?

A-C9. Yes. Taxpayers are encouraged to discuss their concerns with the IRS office collecting the tax or filing the NFTL, either before or after they request a CDP hearing. If such a discussion occurs before a request is made for a CDP hearing, the matter may be resolved without the need for Appeals consideration. However, these discussions do not suspend the running of the 30-day period, commencing the day after the end of the five business day notification period, within which the taxpayer is required to request a CDP hearing, nor do they extend that 30-day period. If discussions occur after the request for a CDP hearing is filed and the taxpayer resolves the matter with the IRS office collecting the tax or filing the NFTL, the taxpayer may withdraw in writing the request that a CDP hearing be conducted by Appeals. The taxpayer can also waive in writing some or all of the requirements regarding the contents of the Notice of Determination.

(3) *Examples.*—The following examples illustrate the principles of this paragraph (c):

*Example 1.* A NFTL for a 1997 income tax liability assessed against individual A is filed in County X on June 17, 1999. The IRS mails a CDP Notice to individual A's last known address on June 18, 1999. Individual A has until July 26, 1999, a Monday, to request a CDP hearing. The five business day period within which the IRS is required to notify individual A of the filing of the NFTL in County X expires on June 24, 1999. The 30-day period within which individual A may request a CDP hearing begins on June 25, 1999. Because the 30-day period expires on July 24, 1999, a Saturday, individual A's written request for a CDP hearing will be considered timely if it is properly transmitted and addressed to the IRS in accordance with section 7502 and the regulations thereunder no later than July 26, 1999.

*Example 2.* Same facts as in *Example 1*, except that individual A is on vacation, outside the United States, or otherwise does not receive or read the CDP Notice until July 19, 1999. As in *Example 1*, individual A has until July 26, 1999, to request a CDP hearing. If individual A does not request a CDP hearing, individual A may request an equivalent hearing as to the NFTL at a later time. The taxpayer

should make a request for an equivalent hearing at the earliest possible time.

*Example 3.* Same facts as in *Example 2*, except that individual A does not receive or read the CDP Notice until after July 26, 1999, and does not request a hearing by July 26, 1999. Individual A is not entitled to a CDP hearing. Individual A may request an equivalent hearing as to the NFTL at a later time. The taxpayer should make a request for an equivalent hearing at the earliest possible time.

*Example 4.* Same facts as in *Example 1*, except the IRS determines that the CDP Notice mailed on June 18, 1999, was not mailed to individual A's last known address. As soon as practicable after making this determination, the IRS will mail a substitute CDP Notice to individual A at individual A's last known address, hand deliver the substitute CDP Notice to individual A, or leave the substitute CDP Notice at individual A's dwelling or usual place of business. Individual A will have 30 days commencing on the day after the date of the substitute CDP Notice within which to request a CDP hearing.

(d) *Conduct of CDP hearing.*—(1) *In general.*—If a taxpayer requests a CDP hearing under section 6320(a)(3)(B) (and does not withdraw that request), the CDP hearing will be held with Appeals. The taxpayer is entitled under section 6320 to a CDP hearing for the unpaid tax and tax periods set forth in a NFTL only with respect to the first filing of a NFTL on or after January 19, 1999. To the extent practicable, the CDP hearing requested under section 6320 will be held in conjunction with any CDP hearing the taxpayer requests under section 6330. A CDP hearing will be conducted by an employee or officer of Appeals who, prior to the first CDP hearing under section 6320 or section 6330, has had no involvement with respect to the unpaid tax for the tax periods to be covered by the hearing, unless the taxpayer waives this requirement.

(2) *Questions and answers.*—The questions and answers illustrate the provisions of this paragraph (d) as follows:

Q-D1. Under what circumstances can a taxpayer receive more than one CDP hearing under section 6320 with respect to a tax period?

A-D1. The taxpayer may receive more than one CDP hearing under section 6320 with respect to a tax period where the tax involved is a different type of tax (for example, an employment tax liability, where the original CDP hearing for the tax period involved an income tax liability), or where the same type of tax for the same period is involved, but where the amount of the unpaid tax has changed as a result of an additional assessment of tax (not including interest or penalties) for that period or an additional accuracy-related or filing-delinquency penalty has been assessed. The taxpayer is not entitled to another CDP hearing under section 6320 if the additional assessment represents accruals of interest, accruals of penalties, or both.

Q-D2. Will a CDP hearing with respect to one tax period be combined with a CDP hearing with respect to another tax period?

A-D2. To the extent practicable, a CDP hearing with respect to one tax period shown on the NFTL will be combined with any and all other CDP hearings which the taxpayer has requested.

Q-D3. Will a CDP hearing under section 6320 be combined with a CDP hearing under section 6330?

A-D3. To the extent practicable, a CDP hearing under section 6320 will be held in conjunction with a CDP hearing under section 6330.

Q-D4. What is considered to be prior involvement by an employee or officer of Appeals with respect to the unpaid tax and tax period involved in the hearing?

A-D4. Prior involvement by an Appeals officer or employee includes participation or involvement in a matter (other than a CDP hearing held under either section 6320 or section 6330) that the taxpayer may have had with respect to the tax and tax period shown on the CDP Notice. Prior involvement exists only when the taxpayer, the tax and the tax period at issue in the CDP hearing also were at issue in the prior non-CDP matter, and the Appeals officer or employee actually participated in the prior matter.

Q-D5. How can a taxpayer waive the requirement that the officer or employee of Appeals have no prior involvement with respect to the tax and tax periods involved in the CDP hearing?

A-D5. The taxpayer must sign a written waiver.

Q-D6. How are CDP hearings conducted?

A-D6. The formal hearing procedures required under the Administrative Procedure Act, 5 U.S.C. 551 *et seq.*, do not apply to CDP hearings. CDP hearings are much like Collection Appeal Program (CAP) hearings in that they are informal in nature and do not require the Appeals officer or employee and the taxpayer, or the taxpayer's representative, to hold a face-to-face meeting. A CDP hearing may, but is not required to, consist of a face-to-face meeting, one or more written or oral communications between an Appeals officer or employee and the taxpayer or the taxpayer's representative, or some combination thereof. A transcript or recording of any face-to-face meeting or conversation between an Appeals officer or employee and the taxpayer or the taxpayer's representative is not required. The taxpayer or the taxpayer's representative does not have the right to subpoena and examine witnesses at a CDP hearing.

Q-D7. If a taxpayer wants a face-to-face CDP hearing, where will it be held?

A-D7. Except as provided in A-D8 of this paragraph (d)(2), a taxpayer who presents in the CDP hearing request relevant, non-frivolous reasons for disagreement with the NFTL filing will ordinarily be offered an opportunity for a face-to-face conference at the Appeals office closest to taxpayer's residence. A business taxpayer will ordinarily be offered an opportunity for a face-to-face conference at the Appeals office closest to the taxpayer's principal place of business. If that is not satisfactory to the taxpayer, the taxpayer will be given an opportunity for a hearing by telephone or by correspondence. In all cases, the Appeals officer or employee will review the case file, as described in A-F4 of paragraph (f)(2). If no face-to-face or telephonic conference is held, or other oral communication takes place, review of the documents in the case file, as described in A-F4 of paragraph (f)(2), will constitute the CDP hearing for purposes of section 6320(b).

Q-D8. In what circumstances will a face-to-face CDP conference not be granted?

A-D8. A taxpayer is not entitled to a face-to-face CDP conference at a location other than as provided in A-D7 of this paragraph (d)(2) and this A-D8. If all Appeals officers or employees at the location provided for in A-D7 of this paragraph (d)(2) have had prior involvement with the taxpayer as provided in A-D4 of this paragraph (d)(2), the taxpayer will not be offered a face-to-face conference at that location, unless the taxpayer elects to waive the requirement of section 6320(b)(3). The taxpayer will be offered a face-to-face conference at another Appeals office if Appeals would have offered the taxpayer a face-to-face conference at the location provided in A-D7 of this paragraph (d)(2), but for the disqualification of all Appeals officers or employees at that location. A face-to-face CDP conference concerning a taxpayer's underlying liability will not be granted if the request for a hearing or other taxpayer communication indicates that the taxpayer wishes only to raise irrelevant or frivolous issues concerning that liability. A face-to-face CDP conference concerning a collection alternative, such as an installment agreement or an offer to compromise liability, will not be granted unless other taxpayers would be eligible for the alternative in similar circumstances. For example, because the IRS does not consider offers to compromise from taxpayers who have not filed required returns or have not made certain required deposits of tax, as set forth in Form 656, "Offer in Compromise," no face-to-face conference will be granted to a taxpayer who wishes to make an offer to compromise but has not fulfilled those obligations. Appeals in its discretion, however, may grant a face-to-face conference if Appeals determines that a face-to-face conference is appropriate to explain to the taxpayer the requirements for becoming eligible for a collection alternative. In all cases, a taxpayer will be given an opportunity to demonstrate eligibility for a collection alternative and to become eligible for a collection alternative, in order to obtain a face-to-face conference. For purposes of determining whether a face-to-face conference will be granted, the determination of a taxpayer's eligibility for a collection alternative is made without regard to the taxpayer's ability to pay the unpaid tax. A face-to-face conference need not be granted if the taxpayer does not provide the required information set forth in A-C1(ii)(E) of paragraph (c)(2). See also A-C1(iii) of paragraph (c)(2).

(3) *Examples.*—The following examples illustrate the principles of this paragraph (d):

*Example 1.* Individual A timely requests a CDP hearing concerning a NFTL filed with respect to the 1998 income tax liability assessed against individual A. Appeals employee B previously conducted a CDP hearing regarding a proposed levy for individual A's 1998 income tax liability. Because employee B's only prior involvement with individual A's 1998 income tax liability was in connection with a section 6330 CDP hearing, employee B may conduct the CDP hearing under section 6320 involving the NFTL filed for the 1998 income tax liability.

*Example 2.* Individual C timely requests a CDP hearing concerning a NFTL filed with respect to the 1998 income tax liability assessed against individual C. Appeals employee D previously conducted a Collection Appeals Program (CAP) hearing regarding a NFTL filed with respect to individual C's 1998 income tax liability. Because employee D(s prior involvement with individual C's 1998 income tax liability was in connection with a non-CDP hearing, employee D may not conduct the CDP hearing under section 6320 unless individual C waives the requirement that the hearing will be conducted by an Appeals officer or employee who has had no prior involvement with respect to individual C's 1998 income tax liability.

*Example 3.* Same facts as in *Example 2,* except that the prior CAP hearing only involved individual C's 1997 income tax liability and

employment tax liabilities for 1998 reported on Form 941, "Employer's Quarterly Federal Tax Return." Employee D would not be considered to have prior involvement because the prior CAP hearing in which she participated did not involve individual C's 1998 income tax liability.

*Example 4.* Appeals employee F is assigned to a CDP hearing concerning a NFTL filed with respect to a trust fund recovery penalty (TFRP) assessed pursuant to section 6672 against individual E. Appeals employee F participated in a prior CAP hearing involving individual E's 1999 income tax liability, and participated in a CAP hearing involving the employment taxes of business entity X, which incurred the employment tax liability to which the TFRP assessed against individual E relates. Appeals employee F would not be considered to have prior involvement because the prior CAP hearings in which he participated did not directly involve the TFRP assessed against individual E.

*Example 5.* Appeals employee G is assigned to a CDP hearing concerning a NFTL filed with respect to a TFRP assessed pursuant to section 6672 against individual H. In preparing for the CDP hearing, Appeals employee G reviews the Appeals case file concerning the prior CAP hearing involving the TFRP assessed pursuant to section 6672 against individual H. Appeals employee G is not deemed to have participated in the previous CAP hearing involving the TFRP assessed against individual H by such review.

(e) *Matters considered at CDP hearing.*—(1) *In general.*—Appeals will determine the timeliness of any request for a CDP hearing that is made by a taxpayer. Appeals has the authority to determine the validity, sufficiency, and timeliness of any CDP Notice given by the IRS and of any request for a CDP hearing that is made by a taxpayer. Prior to issuance of a determination, Appeals is required to obtain verification from the IRS office collecting the tax that the requirements of any applicable law or administrative procedure with respect to the filing of the NFTL have been met. The taxpayer may raise any relevant issue relating to the unpaid tax at the hearing, including appropriate spousal defenses, challenges to the appropriateness of the NFTL filing, and offers of collection alternatives. The taxpayer also may raise challenges to the existence or amount of the underlying liability, including a liability reported on a self-filed return, for any tax period specified on the CDP Notice if the taxpayer did not receive a statutory notice of deficiency for that tax liability or did not otherwise have an opportunity to dispute the tax liability. Finally, the taxpayer may not raise an issue that was raised and considered at a previous CDP hearing under section 6330 or in any other previous administrative or judicial proceeding if the taxpayer participated meaningfully in such hearing or proceeding. Taxpayers will be expected to provide all relevant information requested by Appeals, including financial statements, for its consideration of the facts and issues involved in the hearing.

(2) *Spousal defenses.*—A taxpayer may raise any appropriate spousal defenses at a CDP hearing unless the Commissioner has already made a final determination as to spousal defenses in a statutory notice of deficiency or final determination letter. To claim a spousal defense under section 66 or section 6015, the taxpayer must do so in writing according to rules prescribed by the Commissioner or the Secretary. Spousal defenses raised under sections 66 and 6015 in a CDP hearing are governed in all respects by the provisions of sections 66 and section 6015 and the regulations and procedures thereunder.

(3) *Questions and answers.*—The questions and answers illustrate the provisions of this paragraph (e) as follows:

Q-E1. What factors will Appeals consider in making its determination?

A-E1. Appeals will consider the following matters in making its determination:

(i) Whether the IRS met the requirements of any applicable law or administrative procedure.

(ii) Any issues appropriately raised by the taxpayer relating to the unpaid tax.

(iii) Any appropriate spousal defenses raised by the taxpayer.

(iv) Any challenges made by the taxpayer to the appropriateness of the NFTL filing.

(v) Any offers by the taxpayer for collection alternatives.

(vi) Whether the continued existence of the filed NFTL represents a balance between the need for the efficient collection of taxes and the legitimate concern of the taxpayer that any collection action be no more intrusive than necessary.

Q-E2. When is a taxpayer entitled to challenge the existence or amount of the tax liability specified in the CDP Notice?

A-E2. A taxpayer is entitled to challenge the existence or amount of the underlying liability for any tax period specified on the CDP Notice if the taxpayer did not receive a statutory notice of deficiency for such liability or did not otherwise have an opportunity to dispute such liability. Receipt of a statutory notice of deficiency for this purpose means receipt in time to petition the Tax Court for a redetermination of the deficiency determined in the notice of deficiency. An opportunity to dispute the underlying liability includes a prior opportunity for a conference with Appeals that was offered either before or after the assessment of the liability. An opportunity for a conference with Appeals prior to the assessment of a tax subject to deficiency procedures is not a prior opportunity for this purpose.

Q-E3. Are spousal defenses subject to the limitations imposed under section 6330(c)(2)(B) on a taxpayer's right to challenge the tax liability specified in the CDP Notice at a CDP hearing?

A-E3. The limitations imposed under section 6330(c)(2)(B) do not apply to spousal defenses. When a taxpayer asserts a spousal defense, the taxpayer is not disputing the amount or existence of the liability itself, but asserting a defense to the liability which may or may not be disputed. A spousal defense raised under section 66 or section 6015 is governed by section 66 or section 6015 and the regulations and procedures thereunder. Any limitation under those sections, regulations, and procedures therefore will apply.

Q-E4. May a taxpayer raise a spousal defense at a CDP hearing under section 66 or section 6015 if that defense was raised and considered administratively and the Commissioner has issued a statutory notice of deficiency or final determination letter addressing the spousal defense?

A-E4. No. A taxpayer is precluded from raising a spousal defense at a CDP hearing when the Commissioner has made a final determination under section 66 or section 6015 in a final determination letter or statutory notice of deficiency. However, a taxpayer may raise spousal defenses in a CDP hearing when the taxpayer has previously raised spousal defenses, but the Commissioner has not yet made a final determination regarding this issue.

Q-E5. May a taxpayer raise at a CDP hearing a spousal defense under section 66 or section 6015 if that defense was raised and considered in a prior judicial proceeding that has become final?

A-E5. No. A taxpayer is precluded by the doctrine of res judicata and by the specific limitations under section 66 or section 6015 from raising a spousal defense in a CDP hearing under these circumstances.

Q-E6. What collection alternatives are available to the taxpayer?

A-E6. Collection alternatives include, for example, a proposal to withdraw the NFTL in circumstances that will facilitate the collection of the tax liability, subordination of the NFTL, discharge of the NFTL from specific property, an installment agreement, an offer to compromise, the posting of a bond, or the substitution of other assets. A collection alternative is not available unless the alternative would be available to other taxpayers in similar circumstances. See A-D8 of paragraph (d)(2).

Q-E7. What issues may a taxpayer raise in a CDP hearing under section 6320 if the taxpayer previously received a notice under section 6330 with respect to the same tax and tax period and did not request a CDP hearing with respect to that notice?

A-E7. The taxpayer may raise appropriate spousal defenses, challenges to the appropriateness of the NFTL filing, and offers of collection alternatives. The existence or amount of the underlying liability for any tax period specified in the CDP Notice may be challenged only if the taxpayer did not have a prior opportunity to dispute the tax liability. If the taxpayer previously received a CDP Notice under section 6330 with respect to the same tax and tax period and did not request a CDP hearing with respect to that earlier CDP Notice, the taxpayer had a prior opportunity to dispute the existence or amount of the underlying tax liability.

Q-E8. How will Appeals issue its determination?

A-E8. (i) Taxpayers will be sent a dated Notice of Determination by certified or registered mail. The Notice of Determination will set forth Appeals' findings and decisions. It will state whether the IRS met the requirements of any applicable law or administrative procedure; it will resolve any issues appropriately raised by the taxpayer relating to the unpaid tax; it will include a decision on any appropriate spousal defenses raised by the taxpayer; it will include a decision on any challenges made by the taxpayer to the appropriateness of the NFTL filing; it will respond to any offers by the taxpayer for collection alternatives; and it will address whether the continued existence of the filed NFTL represents a balance between the need for the efficient collection of taxes and the legitimate concern of the taxpayer that any collection action be no more intrusive than necessary. The Notice of Determination will also set forth any agreements that Appeals reached with the taxpayer, any relief given the taxpayer, and any actions the taxpayer or the IRS are required to take. Lastly, the Notice of Determination will advise the taxpayer of the taxpayer's right to seek judicial review within 30 days of the date of the Notice of Determination.

(ii) Because taxpayers are encouraged to discuss their concerns with the IRS office collecting the tax or filing the NFTL, certain matters that might have been raised at a CDP hearing may be resolved without the need for Appeals consideration. Unless, as a result of these discussions, the taxpayer agrees in writing to withdraw the request that Appeals conduct a CDP hearing, Appeals will still issue a Notice of Determination. The taxpayer can, however, waive in writing Appeals' consideration of some or all of the matters it would otherwise consider in making its determination.

Q-E9. Is there a period of time within which Appeals must conduct a CDP hearing or issue a Notice of Determination?

A-E9. No. Appeals will, however, attempt to conduct a CDP hearing and issue a Notice of Determination as expeditiously as possible under the circumstances.

Q-E10. Why is the Notice of Determination and its date important?

A-E10. The Notice of Determination will set forth Appeals' findings and decisions with respect to the matters set forth in A-E1 of this paragraph (e)(3). The 30-day period within which the taxpayer is permitted to seek judicial review of Appeals' determination commences the day after the date of the Notice of Determination.

Q-E11. If an Appeals officer considers the merits of a taxpayer's liability in a CDP hearing when the taxpayer had previously received a statutory notice of deficiency or otherwise had an opportunity to dispute the liability prior to the NFTL, will the Appeals officer's determination regarding those liability issues be considered part of the Notice of Determination?

A-E11. No. An Appeals officer may consider the existence and amount of the underlying tax liability as a part of the CDP hearing only if the taxpayer did not receive a statutory notice of deficiency for the tax liability in question or otherwise have a prior opportunity to dispute the tax liability. Similarly, an Appeals officer may not consider any other issue if the issue was raised and considered at a previous hearing under section 6330 or in any other previous administrative or judicial proceeding in which the person seeking to raise the issue meaningfully participated. In the Appeals officer's sole discretion, however, the Appeals officer may consider the existence or amount of the underlying tax liability, or such other precluded issues, at the same time as the CDP hearing. Any determination, however, made by the Appeals officer with respect to such a precluded issue shall not be treated as part of the Notice of Determination issued by the Appeals officer and will not be subject to any judicial review. Because any decisions made by the Appeals officer on such precluded issues are not properly a part of the CDP hearing, such decisions are not required to appear in the Notice of Determination issued following the hearing. Even if a decision concerning such precluded issues is referred to in the Notice of Determination, it is not reviewable by the Tax Court because the precluded issue is not properly part of the CDP hearing.

(4) *Examples.*—The following examples illustrate the principles of this paragraph (e):

*Example 1.* The IRS sends a statutory notice of deficiency to the taxpayer at his last known address asserting a deficiency for the tax year 1995. The taxpayer receives the notice of deficiency in time to petition the Tax Court for a redetermination of the asserted deficiency. The taxpayer does not timely file a petition with the Tax Court. The taxpayer is precluded from challenging the existence or amount of the tax liability in a subsequent CDP hearing.

*Example 2.* Same facts as in *Example 1*, except the taxpayer does not receive the notice of deficiency in time to petition the Tax Court and did not have another prior opportunity to dispute the tax liability. The taxpayer is not precluded from challenging the existence or amount of the tax liability in a subsequent CDP hearing.

*Example 3.* The IRS properly assesses a trust fund recovery penalty against the taxpayer. The IRS offers the taxpayer the opportunity for a conference with Appeals at which the taxpayer would have the opportunity to dispute the assessed liability. The taxpayer declines the opportunity to participate in such a conference. The taxpayer is precluded from challenging the existence or amount of the tax liability in a subsequent CDP hearing.

(f) *Judicial review of Notice of Determination.*—(1) *In general.*—Unless the taxpayer provides the IRS a written withdrawal of the request that Appeals conduct a CDP hearing, Appeals is required to issue a Notice of Determination in all cases where a taxpayer has timely requested a CDP hearing. The taxpayer may appeal such determinations made by Appeals within the 30-day period commencing the day after the date of the Notice of Determination to the Tax Court.

(2) *Questions and answers.*—The questions and answers illustrate the provisions of this paragraph (f) as follows:

Q-F1. What must a taxpayer do to obtain judicial review of a Notice of Determination?

A-F1. Subject to the jurisdictional limitations described in A-F2 of this paragraph (f)(2), the taxpayer must, within the 30-day period commencing the day after the date of the Notice of Determination, appeal the determination by Appeals to the Tax Court.

Q-F2. With respect to the relief available to the taxpayer under section 6015, what is the time frame within which a taxpayer may seek Tax Court review of Appeals' determination following a CDP hearing?

A-F2. If the taxpayer seeks Tax Court review not only of Appeals' denial of relief under section 6015, but also of relief requested with respect to other issues raised in the CDP hearing, the taxpayer should request Tax Court review within the 30-day period commencing the day after the date of the Notice of Determination. If the taxpayer only seeks Tax Court review of Appeals' denial of relief under section 6015, then the taxpayer should request Tax Court review, as provided by section 6015(e), within 90 days of Appeals' determination. If a request for Tax Court review is filed after the 30-day period for seeking judicial review under section 6320, then only the taxpayer's section 6015 claims may be reviewable by the Tax Court.

Q-F3. What issue or issues may the taxpayer raise before the Tax Court if the taxpayer disagrees with the Notice of Determination?

A-F3. In seeking Tax Court review of a Notice of Determination, the taxpayer can only ask the court to consider an issue, including a challenge to the underlying tax liability, that was properly raised in the taxpayer's CDP hearing. An issue is not properly raised if the taxpayer fails to request consideration of the issue by Appeals, or if consideration is requested but the taxpayer fails to present to Appeals any evidence with respect to that issue after being given a reasonable opportunity to present such evidence.

Q-F4. What is the administrative record for purposes of Tax Court review?

A-F4. The case file, including the taxpayer's request for hearing, any other written communications and information from the taxpayer or the taxpayer's authorized representative submitted in connection with the CDP hearing, notes made by an Appeals officer or employee of any oral communications with the taxpayer or the taxpayer's authorized representative, memoranda created by the Appeals officer or employee in connection with the CDP hearing, and any other documents or materials relied upon by the Appeals officer or employee in making the determination under section 6330(c)(3), will constitute the record in the Tax Court review of the Notice of Determination issued by Appeals.

(g) *Effect of request for CDP hearing and judicial review on periods of limitation and collection activity.*—(1) *In general.*—The periods of limitation under section 6502 (relating to collection after assessment), section 6531 (relating to criminal prosecutions), and section 6532 (relating to suits) are suspended until the date the IRS receives the taxpayer's written withdrawal of the request for a CDP hearing by Appeals or the determination resulting from the CDP hearing becomes final by expiration of the time for seeking judicial review or the exhaustion of any rights to appeals following judicial review. In no event shall any of these periods of limitation expire before the 90th day after the date on which the IRS receives the taxpayer's written withdrawal of the request that Appeals conduct a CDP hearing or the determination with respect to such hearing becomes final upon either the expiration of the time for seeking judicial review or upon exhaustion of any rights to appeals following judicial review.

(2) *Questions and answers.*—The questions and answers illustrate the provisions of this paragraph (g) as follows:

Q-G1. For what period of time will the periods of limitation under sections 6502, 6531, and 6532 remain suspended if the taxpayer timely requests a CDP hearing concerning the filing of a NFTL?

A-G1. The suspension period commences on the date the IRS receives the taxpayer's written request for a CDP hearing. The suspension period continues until the IRS receives a written withdrawal by the taxpayer of the request for a CDP hearing or the Notice of Determination resulting from the CDP hearing becomes final. In no event shall any of these periods of limitation expire before the 90th day after the day on which the IRS receives the taxpayer's written withdrawal of the request that Appeals conduct a CDP hearing or there is a final determination with respect to such hearing. The periods of limitation that are suspended under section 6320 are those which apply to the taxes and the tax period or periods to which the CDP Notice relates.

Q-G2. For what period of time will the periods of limitation under sections 6502, 6531, and 6532 be suspended if the taxpayer does not request a CDP hearing concerning the filing of a NFTL, or the taxpayer requests a CDP hearing, but his request is not timely?

A-G2. Under either of these circumstances, section 6320 does not provide for a suspension of the periods of limitation.

Q-G3. What, if any, enforcement actions can the IRS take during the suspension period?

A-G3. Section 6330(e), made applicable to section 6320 CDP hearings by section 6320(c), provides for the suspension of the peri-

ods of limitation discussed in paragraph (g)(1) of these regulations. Section 6330(e) also provides that levy actions that are the subject of the requested CDP hearing under that section shall be suspended during the same period. Levy actions, however, are not the subject of a CDP hearing under section 6320. The IRS may levy for tax periods and taxes covered by the CDP Notice under section 6320 and for other taxes and periods if the CDP requirements under section 6330 for those taxes and periods have been satisfied. The IRS also may file NFTLs for tax periods or taxes not covered by the CDP Notice, may file a NFTL for the same tax and tax period stated on the CDP Notice at another recording office, and may take other non-levy collection actions such as initiating judicial proceedings to collect the tax shown on the CDP Notice or offsetting overpayments from other periods, or of other taxes, against the tax shown on the CDP Notice. Moreover, the provisions in section 6330 do not apply when the IRS levies for the tax and tax period shown on the CDP Notice to collect a state tax refund due the taxpayer, or determines that collection of the tax is in jeopardy. Finally, section 6330 does not prohibit the IRS from accepting any voluntary payments made for the tax and tax period stated on the CDP Notice.

(3) *Examples.*—The following examples illustrate the principles of this paragraph (g):

*Example 1.* The period of limitation under section 6502 with respect to the taxpayer's tax period listed in the NFTL will expire on August 1, 1999. The IRS sent a CDP Notice to the taxpayer on April 30, 1999. The taxpayer timely requested a CDP hearing. The IRS received this request on May 15, 1999. Appeals sends the taxpayer its determination on June 15, 1999. The taxpayer timely seeks judicial review of that determination. The period of limitation under section 6502 would be suspended from May 15, 1999, until the determination resulting from that hearing becomes final by expiration of the time for seeking review or reconsideration before the Tax Court, plus 90 days.

*Example 2.* Same facts as in *Example 1*, except the taxpayer does not seek judicial review of Appeals' determination. Because the taxpayer requested the CDP hearing when fewer than 90 days remained on the period of limitation, the period of limitation will be extended to October 13, 1999 (90 days from July 15, 1999).

(h) *Retained jurisdiction of Appeals.*—(1) *In general.*—The Appeals office that makes a determination under section 6320 retains jurisdiction over that determination, including any subsequent administrative hearings that may be requested by the taxpayer regarding the NFTL and any collection actions taken or proposed with respect to Appeals' determination. Once a taxpayer has exhausted his other remedies, Appeals' retained jurisdiction permits it to consider whether a change in the taxpayer's circumstances affects its original determination. Where a taxpayer alleges a change in circumstances that affects Appeals' original determination, Appeals may consider whether changed circumstances warrant a change in its earlier determination.

(2) *Questions and answers.*—The questions and answers illustrate the provisions of this paragraph (h) as follows:

Q-H1. Are the periods of limitation suspended during the course of any subsequent Appeals consideration of the matters raised by a taxpayer when the taxpayer invokes the retained jurisdiction of Appeals under section 6330(d)(2)(A) or (d)(2)(B)?

A-H1. No. Under section 6320(b)(2), a taxpayer is entitled to only one CDP hearing under section 6320 with respect to the tax and tax period or periods specified in the CDP Notice. Any subsequent consideration by Appeals pursuant to its retained jurisdiction is not a continuation of the original CDP hearing and does not suspend the periods of limitation.

Q-H2. Is a decision of Appeals resulting from a retained jurisdiction hearing appealable to the Tax Court?

A-H2. No. As discussed in A-H1, a taxpayer is entitled to only one CDP hearing under section 6320 with respect to the tax and tax period or periods specified in the CDP Notice. Only determinations resulting from CDP hearings are appealable to the Tax Court.

(i) *Equivalent hearing.*—(1) *In general.*—A taxpayer who fails to make a timely request for a CDP hearing is not entitled to a CDP hearing. Such a taxpayer may nevertheless request an administrative hearing with Appeals, which is referred to herein as an "equivalent hearing." The equivalent hearing will be held by Appeals and generally will follow Appeals' procedures for a CDP hearing. Appeals will not, however, issue a Notice of Determination. Under such circumstances, Appeals will issue a Decision Letter.

(2) *Questions and answers.*—The questions and answers illustrate the provisions of this paragraph (i) as follows:

Q-I1. What must a taxpayer do to obtain an equivalent hearing?

A-I1. (i) A request for an equivalent hearing must be made in writing. A written request in any form that requests an equivalent hearing will be acceptable if it includes the information and signature required in A-I1(ii) of this paragraph (i)(2).

(ii) The request must be dated and must include the following:

(A) The taxpayer's name, address, daytime telephone number (if any), and taxpayer identification number (e.g., SSN, ITIN or EIN).

(B) The type of tax involved.

(C) The tax period at issue.

(D) A statement that the taxpayer is requesting an equivalent hearing with Appeals concerning the filing of the NFTL.

(E) The reason or reasons why the taxpayer disagrees with the filing of the NFTL.

(F) The signature of the taxpayer or the taxpayer's authorized representative.

(iii) The taxpayer must perfect any timely written request for an equivalent hearing that does not satisfy the requirements set forth in A-I1(ii) of this paragraph (i)(2) within a reasonable period of time after a request from the IRS. If the requirements are not satisfied within a reasonable period of time, the taxpayer's equivalent hearing request will be denied.

(iv) The taxpayer must affirm any timely written request for an equivalent hearing that is signed or alleged to have been signed on the taxpayer's behalf by the taxpayer's spouse or other unauthorized representative, and that otherwise meets the requirements set forth in A-I1(ii) of this paragraph (i)(2), by filing, within a reasonable period of time after a request from the IRS, a signed written affirmation that the request was originally submitted on the taxpayer's behalf. If the affirmation is filed within a reasonable period of time after a request, the timely equivalent hearing request will be considered timely with respect to the non-signing taxpayer. If the affirmation is not filed within a reasonable period of time, the equivalent hearing request will be denied with respect to the non-signing taxpayer.

Q-I2. What issues will Appeals consider at an equivalent hearing?

A-I2. In an equivalent hearing, Appeals will consider the same issues that it would have considered at a CDP hearing on the same matter.

Q-I3. Are the periods of limitation under sections 6502, 6531, and 6532 suspended if the taxpayer does not timely request a CDP hearing and is subsequently given an equivalent hearing?

A-I3. No. The suspension period provided for in section 6330(e) relates only to hearings requested within the 30-day period that commences on the day after the end of the five business day period following the filing of the NFTL, that is, CDP hearings.

Q-I4. Will collection action, including the filing of additional NFTLs, be suspended if a taxpayer requests and receives an equivalent hearing?

A-I4. Collection action is not required to be suspended. Accordingly, the decision to take collection action during the pendency of an equivalent hearing will be determined on a case-by-case basis. Appeals may request the IRS office with responsibility for collecting the taxes to suspend all or some collection action or to take other appropriate action if it determines that such action is appropriate or necessary under the circumstances.

Q-I5. What will the Decision Letter state?

A-I5. The Decision Letter will generally contain the same information as a Notice of Determination.

Q-I6. Will a taxpayer be able to obtain Tax Court review of a decision made by Appeals with respect to an equivalent hearing?

A-I6. Section 6320 does not authorize a taxpayer to appeal the decision of Appeals with respect to an equivalent hearing. A taxpayer may under certain circumstances be able to seek Tax Court review of Appeals' denial of relief under section 6015. Such review must be sought within 90 days of the issuance of Appeals' determination on those issues, as provided by section 6015(e).

Q-I7. When must a taxpayer request an equivalent hearing with respect to a CDP Notice issued under section 6320?

A-I7. A taxpayer must submit a written request for an equivalent hearing within the one-year period commencing the day after the end of the five-business-day period following the filing of the NFTL. This period is slightly different from the period for submitting a written request for an equivalent hearing with respect to a CDP Notice issued under section 6330. For a CDP Notice issued under section 6330, a taxpayer must submit a written request for an equivalent hearing within the one-year period commencing the day after the date of the CDP Notice issued under section 6330.

Q-I8. How will the timeliness of a taxpayer's written request for an equivalent hearing be determined?

A-I8. The rules and regulations under section 7502 and section 7503 will apply to determine the timeliness of the taxpayer's request for an equivalent hearing, if properly transmitted and addressed as provided in A-I10 of this paragraph (i)(2).

Q-I9. Is the one-year period within which a taxpayer must make a request for an equivalent hearing extended because the taxpayer resides outside the United States?

A-I9. No. All taxpayers who want an equivalent hearing concerning the filing of the NFTL must request the hearing within the one-year period commencing the day after the end of the five-business-day period following the filing of the NFTL.

Q-I10. Where must the written request for an equivalent hearing be sent?

A-I10. The written request for an equivalent hearing must be sent, or hand delivered (if permitted), to the IRS office and address as directed on the CDP Notice. If the address of the issuing office does not appear on the CDP Notice, the taxpayer should obtain the address of the office to which the written request should be sent or hand delivered by calling, toll-free, 1-800-829-1040 and providing the taxpayer's identification number (e.g., SSN, ITIN or EIN).

Q-I11. What will happen if the taxpayer does not request an equivalent hearing in writing within the one-year period commencing the day after the end of the five-business-day period following the filing of the NFTL?

A-I11. If the taxpayer does not request an equivalent hearing with Appeals within the one-year period commencing the day after the end of the five-business-day period following the filing of the NFTL, the taxpayer foregoes the right to an equivalent hearing with respect to the unpaid tax and tax periods shown on the CDP Notice. A written request submitted within the one-year period that does not satisfy the requirements set forth in A-I1(ii) of this paragraph (i)(2) is considered timely if the request is perfected within a reasonable period of time pursuant to A-I1(iii) of this paragraph (i)(2). If a request for equivalent hearing is untimely, either because the request was not submitted within the one-year period or not perfected within the reasonable period provided, the equivalent hearing request will be denied. The taxpayer, however, may seek reconsideration by the IRS office collecting the tax, assistance from the National Taxpayer Advocate, or an administrative hearing before Appeals under its Collection Appeals Program or any successor program.

(j) *Effective date.*—This section is applicable on or after November 16, 2006 with respect to requests made for CDP hearings or equivalent hearings on or after November 16, 2006. [Reg. §301.6320-1.]

☐ [*T.D. 8979, 1-17-2002. Amended by T.D. 9290, 10-16-2006.*]

### [Reg. §20.6321-1]

**§20.6321-1. Lien for taxes.**—For regulations concerning the lien for taxes, see §301.6321-1 of this chapter (Regulations on Procedure and Administration). [Reg. §20.6321-1.]

☐ [*T.D. 6296, 6-23-58.*]

### [Reg. §25.6321-1]

**§25.6321-1. Lien for taxes.**—For regulations concerning the lien for taxes, see §301.6321-1 of this chapter (Regulations on Procedure and Administration). [Reg. §25.6321-1.]

☐ [*T.D. 6334, 10-14-58.*]

### [Reg. §301.6321-1]

**§301.6321-1. Lien for taxes.**—If any person liable to pay any tax neglects or refuses to pay the same after demand, the amount (including any interest, additional amount, addition to tax, or assessable penalty, together with any costs that may accrue in addition thereto) shall be a lien in favor of the United States upon all property and rights to property, whether real or personal, tangible or intangible, belonging to such person. For purposes of section 6321 and this section, the term "any tax" shall include a State individual income tax which is a "qualified tax", as defined in paragraph(b) of §301.6361-4. The lien attaches to all property and rights to property belonging to such person at any time during the period of the lien, including any property or rights to property acquired by such person after the lien arises. Solely for purposes of sections 6321 and 6331, any interest in restricted land held in trust by the United States for an individual noncompetent Indian (and not for a tribe) shall not be deemed to be property, or a right to property, belonging to such Indian. For the method of allocating amounts collected pursuant to a lien between the Federal Government and a State or States imposing a qualified tax with respect to which the lien attached, see paragraph (f) of §301.6361-1. For the special lien for estate and gift taxes, see section 6324 and §301.6324-1. [Reg. §301.6321-1.]

☐ [*T.D. 6119, 12-31-54. Amended by T.D. 7139, 8-11-71 and T.D. 7577,* 12-19-78.]

### [Reg. §20.6323-1]

**§20.6323-1. Validity and priority against certain persons.**—For regulations concerning the validity of the lien imposed by section

6321 against certain persons, see §§ 301.6323(a)-1 through 301.6323(i)-1 of this chapter (Regulations on Procedure and Administration). [Reg. § 20.6323-1.]

☐ [*T.D. 6296, 6-23-58. Amended by T.D. 7429, 8-20-76.*]

### [Reg. § 25.6323-1]

**§ 25.6323-1. Validity and priority against certain persons.**—For regulations concerning the validity of the lien imposed by section 6321 against certain persons, see §§ 301.6323(a)-1 through 301.6323(i)-1 of this chapter (Regulations on Procedure and Administration). [Reg. § 25.6323-1.]

☐ [*T.D. 6334, 10-14-58. Amended by T.D. 7429, 8-20-76.*]

### [Reg. § 301.6323(a)-1]

**§ 301.6323(a)-1. Purchasers, holders of security interests, mechanic's lienors, and judgment lien creditors.**—(a) *Invalidity of lien without notice.*—The lien imposed by section 6321 is not valid against any purchaser (as defined in paragraph (f) of § 301.6323(h)-1), holder of a security interest (as defined in paragraph (a) of § 301.6323(h)-1), mechanic's lienor (as defined in paragraph (b) of § 301.6323(h)-1), or judgment lien creditor (as defined in paragraph (g) of § 301.6323(h)-1 until a notice of lien is filed in accordance with § 301.6323(f)-1. Except as provided by section 6323, if a person becomes a purchaser, holder of a security interest, mechanic's lienor, or judgment lien creditor after a notice of lien is filed in accordance with § 301.6323(f)-1, the interest acquired by such person is subject to the lien imposed by section 6321.

(b) *Cross references.*—For provisions relating to the protection afforded a security interest arising after tax lien filing, which interest is covered by a commercial transactions financing agreement, real property construction or improvement financing agreement, or an obligatory disbursement agreement, see §§ 301.6323(c)-1, 301.6323(c)-2, and 301.6323(c)-3, respectively. For provisions relating to the protection afforded to a security interest coming into existence by virtue of disbursements made before the 46th day after the date of tax lien filing, see § 301.6323(d)-1. For provisions relating to priority afforded to interest and certain other expenses with respect to a lien or security interest having priority over the lien imposed by section 6321, see § 301.6323(e)-1. For provisions relating to certain other interests arising after tax lien filing, see § 301.6323(b)-1. [Reg. § 301.6323(a)-1.]

☐ [*T. D. 7429, 8-20-76.*]

### [Reg. § 301.6323(b)-1]

**§ 301.6323(b)-1. Protection for certain interests even though notice filed.**—(a) *Securities.*—(1) *In general.*—Even though a notice of a lien imposed by section 6321 is filed in accordance with § 301.6323(f)-1, the lien is not valid with respect to a security (as defined in paragraph (d) of § 301.6323(h)-1) against—

(i) A purchaser (as defined in paragraph (f) of § 301.6323(h)-1) of the security who at the time of purchase did not have actual notice or knowledge (as defined in paragraph (a) of § 301.6323(i)-1) of the existence of the lien;

(ii) A holder of a security interest (as defined in paragraph (a) of § 301.6323(h)-1) in the security who did not have actual notice or knowledge (as defined in paragraph (a) of § 301.6323(i)-1) of the existence of the lien at the time the security interest came into existence or at the time such security interest was acquired from a previous holder for a consideration in money or money's worth; or

(iii) A transferee of an interest protected under subdivision (i) or (ii) of this subparagraph to the same extent the lien is invalid against his transferor.

For purposes of subdivision (iii) of this subparagraph, no person can improve his position with respect to the lien by reacquiring the interest from an intervening purchaser or holder of a security interest against whom the lien is invalid.

(2) *Examples.*—The application of this paragraph may be illustrated by the following examples:

*Example (1).* On May 1, 1969, in accordance with § 301.6323(f)-1, a notice of lien is filed with respect to A's delinquent tax liability. On May 20, 1969, A sells 100 shares of common stock in X corporation to B, who, on the date of the sale, does not have actual notice or knowledge of the existence of the lien. Because B purchased the stock without actual notice or knowledge of the lien, under subdivision (i) of subparagraph (1) of this paragraph, the stock purchased by B is not subject to the lien.

*Example (2).* Assume the same facts as in example (1) except that on May 30, 1969, B sells the 100 shares of common stock in X corporation to C who on May 5, 1969, had actual notice of the existence of the tax lien against A. Because the X stock when purchased by B was not subject to the lien, under subdivision (iii) of

subparagraph (1) of this paragraph, the stock purchased by C is not subject to the lien. C succeeds to B's rights, even though C had actual notice of the lien before B's purchase.

*Example (3).* On June 1, 1970, in accordance with § 301.6323(f)-1, a notice of lien is filed with respect to D's delinquent tax liability. D owns 20 $1,000 bonds issued by the Y company. On June 10, 1970, D obtains a loan from M bank for $5,000 using the Y company bonds as collateral. At the time the loan is made M bank does not have actual notice or knowledge of the existence of the tax lien. Because M bank did not have actual notice or knowledge of the lien when the security interest came into existence, under subdivision (ii) of subparagraph (1) of this paragraph, the tax lien is not valid against M bank to the extent of its security interest.

*Example (4).* Assume the same facts as in example (3) except that on June 19, 1970, M bank assigns the chose in action and its security interest to N, who had actual notice or knowledge of the existence of the lien on June 1, 1970. Because the security interest was not subject to the lien to the extent of M bank's security interest, the security interest held by N is to the same extent entitled to priority over the tax lien because N succeeds to M bank's rights. See subdivision (iii) of subparagraph (1) of this paragraph.

*Example (5).* On July 1, 1970, in accordance with § 301.6323(f)-1, a notice of lien is filed with respect to E's delinquent tax liability. E owns ten $1,000 bonds issued by the Y company. On July 5, 1970, E borrows $4,000 from F and delivers the bonds to F as collateral for the loan. At the time the loan is made, F has actual knowledge of the existence of the tax lien and, therefore, holds the security interest subject to the lien on the bonds. On July 10, 1970, F sells the security interest to G for $4,000 and delivers the Y company bonds pledged as collateral. G does not have actual notice or knowledge of the existence of the lien on July 10, 1970. Because G did not have actual notice or knowledge of the lien at the time he purchased the security interest, under subdivision (ii) of subparagraph (1) of this paragraph, the tax lien is not valid against G to the extent of his security interest.

*Example (6).* Assume the same facts as in example (5) except that, instead of purchasing the security interest from F on July 10, 1970, G lends $4,000 to F and takes a security interest in F's security interest in the bonds on that date. Because G became the holder of a security interest in a security interest after notice of lien was filed and does not directly have a security interest in a security, the security interest held by G is not entitled to a priority over the tax lien under the provisions of subparagraph (1) of this paragraph.

(b) *Motor vehicles.*—(1) *In general.*—Even though a notice of a lien imposed by section 6321 is filed in accordance with § 301.6323(f)-1, the lien is not valid against a purchaser (as defined in paragraph (f) of § 301.6323(h)-1) of a motor vehicle (as defined in paragraph (c) of § 301.6323(h)-1) if—

(i) At the time of the purchase, the purchaser did not have actual notice or knowledge (as defined in paragraph (a) of § 301.6323(i)-1) of the existence of the lien, and

(ii) Before the purchaser obtains such notice or knowledge, he has acquired actual possession of the motor vehicle and has not thereafter relinquished actual possession to the seller or his agent.

(2) *Examples.*—The application of this paragraph may be illustrated by the following examples:

*Example (1).* A, a delinquent taxpayer against whom a notice of tax lien has been filed in accordance with § 301.6323(f)-1, sells his automobile (which qualifies as a motor vehicle under paragraph (c) of § 301.6323(h)-1) to B, an automobile dealer. B takes actual possession of the automobile and does not thereafter relinquish actual possession to the seller or his agent. Subsequent to his purchase, B learns of the existence of the tax lien against A. Even though notice of lien was filed before the purchase, the lien is not valid against B, because B did not know of the existence of the lien before the purchase and before acquiring actual possession of the vehicle.

*Example (2).* C is a wholesaler of used automobiles. A notice of lien has been filed with respect to C's delinquent tax liability in accordance with § 301.6323(f)-1. Subsequent to such filing, D, a used automobile dealer, purchases and takes actual possession of 20 automobiles (which qualify as motor vehicles under the provisions of paragraph (c) of § 301.6323(h)-1) from C at an auction and places them on his lot for sale. C does not reacquire possession of any of the automobiles. At the time of his purchase, D does not have actual notice or knowledge of the existence of the lien against C. Even though notice of lien was filed before D's purchase, the lien was not valid against D because D did not know of the existence of the lien before the purchase and before acquiring actual possession of the vehicles.

(3) *Cross reference.*—For provisions relating to additional circumstances in which the lien imposed by section 6321 may not be valid against the purchaser of tangible personal property (including a motor vehicle) purchased at retail, see paragraph (c) of this section.

(c) *Personal property purchased at retail.*—(1) *In general.*—Even though a notice of a lien imposed by section 6321 is filed in accordance with § 301.6323(f)-1, the lien is not valid against a purchaser (as defined in paragraph (f) of § 301.6323(h)-1) of tangible personal property purchased at a retail sale (as defined in subparagraph (2) of this paragraph) unless at the time of purchase the purchaser intends the purchase to (or knows that the purchase will) hinder, evade, or defeat the collection of any tax imposed by the Internal Revenue Code of 1954.

(2) *Definition of retail sale.*—For purposes of this paragraph, the term "retail sale" means a sale, made in the ordinary course of the seller's trade or business, of tangible personal property of which the seller is the owner. Such term includes a sale in customary retail quantities by a seller who is going out of business, but does not include a bulk sale or an auction sale in which goods are offered in quantities substantially greater than are customary in the ordinary course of the seller's trade or business or an auction sale of goods the owner of which is not in the business of selling such goods.

(3) *Example.*—The application of this paragraph may be illustrated by the following example:

*Example.* A purchases a refrigerator from the M company, a retail appliance dealer. Prior to such purchase, a notice of lien was filed with respect to M's delinquent tax liability in accordance with § 301.6323(f)-1. At the time of the purchase A knows of the existence of the lien. However, A does not intend the purchase to hinder, evade, or defeat the collection of any internal revenue tax, and A does not have any reason to believe that the purchase will affect the collection of any internal revenue tax. Even though notice of lien was filed before the purchase, the lien is not valid against A because A in good faith purchased the refrigerator at retail in the ordinary course of the M company's business.

(d) *Personal property purchased in casual sale.*—(1) *In general.*—Even though a notice of a lien imposed by section 6321 is filed in accordance with § 301.6323(f)-1, the lien is not valid against a purchaser (as defined in § 301.6323(h)-1(f)) of household goods, personal effects, or other tangible personal property of a type described in § 301.6334-1 (which includes wearing apparel; school books; fuel, provisions, furniture, arms for personal use, livestock, and poultry (whether or not the seller is the head of a family); and books and tools of a trade, business, or profession (whether or not the trade, business, or profession of the seller)), purchased, other than for resale, in a casual sale for less than $1,380, effective for 2010 and adjusted each year based on the rate of inflation (excluding interest and expenses described in § 301.6323(e)-1).

(2) *Limitation.*—This paragraph applies only if the purchaser does not have actual notice or knowledge (as defined in paragraph (a) of § 301.6323(i)-1)—

    (i) Of the existence of the tax lien, or

    (ii) That the sale is one of a series of sales.

For purposes of subdivision (ii) of this subparagraph, a sale is one of a series of sales if the seller plans to dispose of, in separate transactions, substantially all of his household goods, personal effects, and other tangible personal property described in § 301.6334-1.

(3) *Examples.*—The application of this paragraph may be illustrated by the following examples:

*Example (1).* A, an attorney's widow, sells a set of law books for $200 to B, for B's own use. Prior to the sale a notice of lien was filed with respect to A's delinquent tax liability in accordance with § 301.6323(f)-1. B has no actual notice or knowledge of the tax lien. In addition, B does not know that the sale is one of a series of sales. Because the sale is a casual sale for less than $1,380 and involves books of a profession (tangible personal property of a type described in § 301.6334-1, irrespective of the fact that A has never engaged in the legal profession), the tax lien is not valid against B even though a notice of lien was filed prior to the time of B's purchase.

*Example (2).* Assume the same facts as in example (1) except that B purchases the books for resale in his second-hand bookstore. Because B purchased the books for resale, he purchased the books subject to the lien.

*Example (3).* In an advertisement appearing in a local newspaper, G indicates that he is offering for sale a lawn mower, a used television set, a desk, a refrigerator, and certain used dining room furniture. In response to the advertisement, H purchases the dining room furniture for $200. H does not receive any information which would impart notice of a lien, or that the sale is one of a series of sales, beyond the information contained in the advertisement. Prior to the sale a notice of lien was filed with respect to G's delinquent tax liability in accordance with § 301.6323(f)-1. Because H had no actual notice or knowledge that substantially all of G's household goods were being sold or that the sale is one of a series of sales, and because the sale is a casual sale for less than $1,380, H does not purchase the dining room furniture subject to the lien. The household goods are of a type described in § 301.6334-1(a)(2) irrespective of whether G is the head of a family or whether all such household goods offered for sale exceed $8,250 in value.

(e) *Personal property subject to possessory liens.*—Even though a notice of a lien imposed by section 6321 is filed in accordance with § 301.6323(f)-1, the lien is not valid against a holder of a lien on tangible personal property which under local law secures the reasonable price of the repair or improvement of the property if the property is, and has been, continuously in the possession of the holder of the lien from the time the possessory lien arose. For example, if local law gives an automobile repairman the right to retain possession of an automobile he has repaired as security for payment of the repair bill and the repairman retains continuous possession of the automobile until his lien is satisfied, a tax lien filed in accordance with § 301.6323(f)(1) which has attached to the automobile will not be valid to the extent of the reasonable price of the repairs. It is immaterial that the notice of tax lien was filed before the repairman undertook his work or that he knew of the lien before undertaking the work.

(f) *Real property tax and special assessment liens.*—(1) *In general.*—Even though a notice of a lien imposed by section 6321 is filed in accordance with § 301.6323(f)-1, the lien is not valid against the holder of another lien upon the real property (regardless of when such other lien arises), if such other lien is entitled under local law to priority over security interests in real property which are prior in time and if such other lien on real property secures payment of—

    (i) A tax of general application levied by any taxing authority based upon the value of the property;

    (ii) A special assessment imposed directly upon the property by any taxing authority, if the assessment is imposed for the purpose of defraying the cost of any public improvement; or

    (iii) Charges for utilities or public services furnished to the property by the United States, a State or political subdivision thereof, or an instrumentality of any one or more of the foregoing.

(2) *Examples.*—The application of this paragraph may be illustrated by the following examples:

*Example (1).* A owns Blackacre in the city of M. A notice of lien affecting Blackacre is filed in accordance with § 301.6323(f)-1. Subsequent to the filing of the notice of lien, the city of M acquires a lien against Blackacre to secure payment of real estate taxes. Such taxes are levied against all property in the city in proportion to the value of the property. Under local law, the holder of a lien for real property taxes is entitled to priority over a security interest in real property even though the security interest is prior in time. Because the real property tax lien held by the city of M secures payment of a tax of general application and is entitled to priority over security interests which are prior in time, the lien held by the city of M is entitled to priority over the Federal tax lien with respect to Blackacre.

*Example (2).* B owns Whiteacre in N county. A notice of lien affecting Whiteacre is filed in accordance with § 301.6323(f)-1. Subsequent to the filing of the notice of lien, N county constructs a sidewalk, paves the street, and installs water and sewer lines adjacent to Whiteacre. In order to defray the cost of these improvements, N county imposes upon Whiteacre a special assessment which under local law results in a lien upon Whiteacre that is entitled to priority over security interests that are prior in time. Because the special assessment lien is (i) entitled under local law to priority over security interests which are prior in time, and (ii) imposed directly upon real property to defray the cost of a public improvement, the special assessment lien has priority over the Federal tax lien with respect to Whiteacre.

*Example (3).* C owns Greenacre in town O. A notice of lien affecting Greenacre is filed in accordance with § 301.6323(f)-1. Town O furnishes water and electricity to Greenacre and periodically collects a fee for these services. Subsequent to the filing of the notice of lien, town O supplies water and electricity to Greenacre, and C fails to pay the charges for these services. Under local law, town O acquires a lien to secure charges for the services, and this lien has priority over security interests which are prior in time. Because the lien of town O (i) is for services furnished to the real property and (ii) has priority over earlier security interests, town O's lien has priority over the Federal tax lien with respect to Greenacre.

(g) *Residential property subject to a mechanic's lien for certain repairs and improvements.*—(1) *In general.*—Even though a notice of a lien imposed by section 6321 is filed in accordance with § 301.6323(f)-1, the lien is not valid against a mechanic's lienor (as defined in § 301.6323(h)-1(b)) who holds a lien for the repair or improvement of a personal residence if—

    (i) The residence is occupied by the owner and contains no more than four dwelling units, and

(ii) The contract price on the prime contract with the owner for the repair or improvement (excluding interest and expenses described in §301.6323(e)-1) is not more than $6,890, effective for 2010 and adjusted each year based on the rate of inflation.

(iii) For purposes of paragraph (g)(1)(ii) of this section, the amounts of subcontracts under the prime contract with the owner are not to be taken into consideration for purposes of computing the $6,890 prime contract price. It is immaterial that the notice of tax lien was filed before the contractor undertakes his work or that he knew of the lien before undertaking his work.

(2) *Examples.*—The application of this paragraph may be illustrated by the following examples:

*Example (1).* A owns a building containing four apartments, one of which he occupies as his personal residence. A notice of lien which affects the building is filed in accordance with §301.6323(f)-1. Thereafter, A enters into a contract with B in the amount of $800, which includes labor and materials, to repair the roof of the building. B purchases roofing shingles from C for $300. B completes the work and A fails to pay B the agreed amount. In turn, B fails to pay C for the shingles. Under local law, B and C acquire mechanic's liens on A's building. Because the contract price on the prime contract with A is not more than $6,890 and under local law B and C acquire mechanic's liens on A's building, the liens of B and C have priority over the Federal tax lien.

*Example (2).* Assume the same facts as in *Example 1*, except that the amount of the prime contract between A and B is $7,100. Because the amount of the prime contract with the owner, A, is in excess of $6,890, the tax lien has priority over the entire amount of each of the mechanic's liens of B and C, even though the amount of the contract between B and C is $300.

*Example (3).* Assume the same facts as in *Example 1*, except that A and B do not agree in advance upon the amount due under the prime contract but agree that B will perform the work for the cost of materials and labor plus 10 percent of such cost. When the work is completed, it is determined that the total amount due is $850. Because the prime contract price is not more than $6,890 and under local law B and C acquire mechanic's liens on A's residence, the liens of B and C have priority over the Federal tax lien.

(h) *Attorney's liens.*—(1) *In general.*—Even though notice of a lien imposed by section 6321 is filed in accordance with §301.6323(f)-1, the lien is not valid against an attorney who, under local law, holds a lien upon, or a contract enforceable against, a judgment or other amount in settlement of a claim or of a cause of action. The priority afforded an attorney's lien under this paragraph shall not exceed the amount of the attorney's reasonable compensation for obtaining the judgment or procuring the settlement. For purposes of this paragraph, reasonable compensation means the amount customarily allowed under local law for an attorney's services for litigating or settling a similar case or administrative claim. However, reasonable compensation shall be determined on the basis of the facts and circumstances of each individual case. It is immaterial that the notice of tax lien is filed before the attorney undertakes his work or that the attorney knows of the tax lien before undertaking his work. This paragraph does not apply to an attorney's lien which may arise from the defense of a claim or cause of action against a taxpayer except to the extent such lien is held upon a judgment or other amount arising from the adjudication or settlement of a counterclaim in favor of the taxpayer. In the case of suits against the taxpayer, see §301.6325-1(d)(2) for rules relating to the subordination of the tax lien to facilitate tax collection.

(2) *Claim or cause of action against the United States.*—Paragraph (h)(1) of this section does not apply to an attorney's lien with respect to—

(i) Any judgment or other fund resulting from the successful litigation or settlement of an administrative claim or cause of action against the United States to the extent that the United States, under any legal or equitable right, offsets its liability under the judgment or settlement against any liability of the taxpayer to the United States, or

(ii) Any amount credited against any liability of the taxpayer in accordance with section 6402.

(3) *Examples.*—The provisions of this paragraph may be illustrated by the following examples:

*Example (1).* A notice of lien is filed against A in accordance with §301.6323(f)-1. Subsequently, A is struck by an automobile and retains B, an attorney to institute suit on A's behalf against the operator of the automobile. B knows of the tax lien before he begins his work. Under local law, B is entitled to a lien upon any recovery in order to secure payment of his fee. A is awarded damages of $10,000. B charges a fee of $3,000 which is the fee customarily allowed under local law in similar cases and which is found to be reasonable under the circumstances of this particular case. Because, under local law, B

holds a lien for the amount of his reasonable compensation for obtaining the judgment, B's lien has priority over the Federal tax lien.

*Example (2).* Assume the same facts as in example (1), except that before suit is instituted A and the owner of the automobile settle out of court for $7,500. B charges a reasonable and customary fee of $1,800 for procuring the settlement and under local law holds a lien upon the settlement in order to secure payment of the fee. Because, under local law, B holds a lien for the amount of his reasonable compensation for obtaining the settlement, B has priority over the Federal tax lien.

*Example (3).* In accordance with §301.6323(f)-1, a notice of lien in the amount of $8,000 is filed against C, a contractor. Subsequently C retains D, an attorney, to initiate legal proceedings to recover the amount allegedly due him for construction work he has performed for the United States. C and D enter into an agreement which provides that D will receive a reasonable and customary fee of $2,500 as compensation for his services. Under local law, the agreement will give rise to a lien which is enforceable by D against any amount recovered in the suit. C is successful in the suit and is awarded $10,000. D claims $2,500 of the proceeds as his fee. The United States, however, exercises its right to set-off and applies $8,000 of the $10,000 award to satisfy C's tax liability. Because the $10,000 award resulted from the successful litigation of a cause of action against the United States, B's contract for attorney's fees is not enforceable against the amount recovered to the extent the United States offsets its liability under the judgment against C's tax liability. It is immaterial that D had no notice or knowledge of the tax lien at the time he began work on the case.

(i) *Certain insurance contracts.*—(1) *In general.*—Even though a notice of a lien imposed by section 6321 is filed in accordance with §301.6323(f)-1, the lien is not valid with respect to a life insurance, endowment, or annuity contract, against an organization which is the insurer under the contract, at any time—

(i) Before the insuring organization has actual notice or knowledge (as defined in paragraph (a) of §301.6323(i)-1) of the existence of the tax lien,

(ii) After the insuring organization has actual notice or knowledge of the tax lien (as defined in paragraph (a) of §301.6323(i)-1), with respect to advances (including contractual interest thereon as provided in paragraph (a) of §301.6323(e)-1) required to be made automatically to maintain the contract in force under an agreement entered into before the insuring organization had such actual notice or knowledge, or

(iii) After the satisfaction of a levy pursuant to section 6332(b), unless and until the Internal Revenue Service delivers to the insuring organization a notice (for example, another notice of levy, a letter, etc.) executed after the date of such satisfaction, that the lien exists. Delivery of the notice described in subdivision (iii) of this subparagraph may be made by any means, including regular mail, and delivery of the notice shall be effective only from the time of actual receipt of the notification by the insuring organization. The provisions of this paragraph are applicable to matured as well as unmatured insurance contracts.

(2) *Examples.*—The provisions of this paragraph may be illustrated by the following examples:

*Example (1).* On May 1, 1964, the X insurance company issues a life insurance policy to A. On June 1, 1970, a tax assessment is made against A, and on June 2, 1970, a notice of lien with respect to the assessment is filed in accordance with §301.6323(f)-1. On July 1, 1970, without actual notice or knowledge of the tax lien, the X company makes a "policy loan" to A. Under subparagraph (1)(i) of this paragraph, the loan, including interest (in accordance with the provisions of paragraph (a) of §301.6323(e)-1), will have priority over the tax lien because X company did not have actual notice or knowledge of the tax lien at the time the policy loan was made.

*Example (2).* On May 1, 1964, B enters into a life insurance contract with the Y insurance company. Under one of the provisions of the contract, in the event a premium is not paid, Y is to advance out of the cash loan value of the policy the amount of an unpaid premium in order to maintain the contract in force. The contract also provides for interest on any advances so made. On June 1, 1971, a tax assessment is made against B, and on June 2, 1971, in accordance with section 6323(f)-1, a notice of lien is filed. On July 1, 1971, B fails to pay the premium due on that date, and Y makes an automatic premium loan to keep the policy in force. At the time the automatic premium loan is made, Y had actual knowledge of the tax lien. Under subparagraph (1)(ii) of this paragraph, the lien is not valid against Y with respect to the advance (and the contractual interest thereon), because the advance was required to be made automatically under an agreement entered into before Y had actual notice or knowledge of the tax lien.

*Example (3).* On May 1, 1964, C enters into a life insurance contract with the Z insurance company. On January 4, 1971, an assessment is made against C for $5,000 unpaid income taxes, and on January 11, 1971, in accordance with §301.6323(f)-1, a notice of lien is filed. On January 29, 1971, a notice of levy with respect to C's delinquent tax is served on Z company. The amount which C could have had advanced to him from Z company under the contract on the 90th day after service of the notice of levy on Z company is $2,000. The Z company pays $2,000 pursuant to the notice of levy, thereby satisfying the levy upon the contract in accordance with section 6332(b). On February 1, 1973, Z company advances $500 to C, which is the increment in policy loan value since satisfaction of the levy of January 29, 1971. On February 5, 1973, a new notice of levy for the unpaid balance of the delinquent taxes, executed after the first levy was satisfied, is served upon Z company. Because the new notification was not received by Z company until after the policy loan was made, under paragraph (1)(iii) of this paragraph, the tax lien is not valid against Z company with respect to the policy loan (including interest thereon in accordance with paragraph (a) of §301.6323(e)-1).

*Example (4).* On June 1, 1973, a tax assessment is made against D and on June 2, 1973, in accordance with §301.6323(f)-1, a notice of lien with respect to the assessment is filed. On July 2, 1973, D executes an assignment of his rights, as the insured, under an insurance contract to M bank as security for a loan. M bank holds its security interest subject to the lien because it is not an insurer entitled to protection under section 6323(b)(9) and did not become a holder of the security interest prior to the filing of the notice of lien for purposes of section 6323(a). It is immaterial that a notice of levy had not been served upon the insurer before the assignment to M bank was made.

(j) *Effective/applicability date.*—(1) *In general.*—This section applies to any notice of Federal tax lien filed on or after April 4, 2011. [Reg. §301.6323(b)-1.]

☐ [*T.D. 7429, 8-20-76. Amended by T.D. 9520, 4-1-2011.*]

**[Reg. §301.6323(c)-1]**

**§301.6323(c)-1. Protection for commercial transactions financing agreements.**—(a) *In general.*—Even though a notice of a lien imposed by section 6321 is filed in accordance with §301.6323(f)-1, the lien is not valid with respect to a security interest which:

(1) Comes into existence after the tax lien filing,

(2) Is in qualified property covered by the terms of a commercial transactions financing agreement entered into before the tax lien filing, and

(3) Is protected under local law against a judgment lien arising, as of the time of the tax lien filing, out of an unsecured obligation.

See paragraphs (a) and (e) of §301.6323(h)-1 for definitions of the terms "security interest" and "tax lien filing," respectively. For purposes of this section, a judgment lien is a lien held by a judgment lien creditor as defined in paragraph (g) of §301.6323(h)-1.

(b) *Commercial transactions financing agreement.*—For purposes of this section, the term "commercial transactions financing agreement" means a written agreement entered into by a person in the course of his trade or business—

(1) To make loans to the taxpayer (whether or not at the option of the person agreeing to make such loans) to be secured by commercial financing security acquired by the taxpayer in the ordinary course of his trade or business, or

(2) To purchase commercial financing security, other than inventory, acquired by the taxpayer in the ordinary course of his trade or business.

Such an agreement qualifies as a commercial transactions financing agreement only with respect to loans or purchases made under the agreement before (i) the 46th day after the date of tax lien filing or, (ii) the time when the lender or purchaser has actual notice or knowledge (as defined in paragraph (a) of §301.6323(i)-1) of the tax lien filing, if earlier. For purposes of this paragraph, a loan or purchase is considered to have been made in the course of the lender's or purchaser's trade or business if such person is in the business of financing commercial transactions (such as a bank or commercial factor) or if the agreement is incidental to the conduct of such person's trade or business. For example, if a manufacturer finances the accounts receivable of one of his customers, he is considered to engage in such financing in the course of his trade or business. The extent of the priority of the lender or purchaser over the tax lien is the amount of his disbursements made before the 46th day after the date the notice of tax lien is filed, or made before the day (before such 46th day) on which the lender or purchaser has actual notice or knowledge of the filing of the notice of the tax lien.

(c) *Commercial financing security.*—(1) *In general.*—The term "commercial financing security" means—

(i) Paper of a kind ordinarily arising in commercial transactions,

(ii) Accounts receivable (as defined in subparagraph (2) of this paragraph),

(iii) Mortgages on real property, and

(iv) Inventory.

For purposes of this subparagraph, the term "paper of a kind ordinarily arising in commercial transactions" in general includes any written document customarily used in commercial transactions. For example, such written documents include paper giving contract rights (as defined in subparagraph (2) of this paragraph), chattel paper, documents of title to personal property, and negotiable instruments or securities. The term "commercial financing security" does not include general intangibles such as patents or copyrights. A mortgage on real estate (including a deed of trust, contract for sale, and similar instrument) may be commercial financing security if the taxpayer has an interest in the mortgage as a mortgagee or assignee. The term "commercial financing security" does not include a mortgage where the taxpayer is the mortgagor of realty owned by him. For purposes of this subparagraph, the term "inventory" includes raw materials and goods in process as well as property held by the taxpayer primarily for sale to customers in the ordinary course of his trade or business.

(2) *Definitions.*—For purposes of §§301.6323(d)-1, 301.6323(h)-1 and this section—

(i) A contract right is any right to payment under a contract not yet earned by performance and not evidenced by an instrument or chattel paper, and

(ii) An account receivable is any right to payment for goods sold or leased or for services rendered which is not evidenced by an instrument or chattel paper.

(d) *Qualified property.*—For purposes of paragraph (a) of this section, qualified property consists solely of commercial financing security acquired by the taxpayer-debtor before the 46th day after the date of tax lien filing. Commercial financing security acquired before such day may be qualified property even though it is acquired by the taxpayer after the lender received actual notice or knowledge of the filing of the notice of the tax lien. For example, although the receipt of actual notice or knowledge of the filing of the tax lien has the effect of ending the period within which protected disbursements may be made to the taxpayer, property which is acquired by the taxpayer after the lender receives actual notice or knowledge of such filing and before such 46th day, which otherwise qualifies as a commercial financing security, becomes commercial financing security to which the priority of the lender extends for loans made before he received the actual notice or knowledge. An account receivable (as defined in paragraph (c)(2)(ii) of this section) is acquired by a taxpayer at the time, and to the extent, a right to payment is earned by performance. Chattel paper, documents of title, negotiable instruments, securities, and mortgages on real estate are acquired by a taxpayer when he obtains rights in the paper or mortgage. Inventory is acquired by the taxpayer when title passes to him. A contract right (as defined in paragraph (c)(2)(i) of this section) is acquired by a taxpayer when the contract is made. Identifiable proceeds, which arise from the collection or disposition of qualified property by the taxpayer, are considered to be acquired at the time such qualified property is acquired if the secured party has a continuously perfected security interest in the proceeds under local law. The term "proceeds" includes whatever is received when collateral is sold, exchanged, or collected. For purposes of this paragraph, the term "identifiable proceeds" does not include money, checks and the like which have been commingled with other cash proceeds. Property acquired by the taxpayer after the 45th day following tax lien filing, by the expenditure of proceeds, is not qualified property.

(e) *Purchaser treated as acquiring security interest.*—A person who purchases commercial financing security, other than inventory, pursuant to a commercial transactions financing agreement is treated, for purposes of this section, as having acquired a security interest in the commercial financing security. In the case of a bona fide purchase at a discount, a purchaser of commercial financing security who satisfies the requirements of this section has priority over the tax lien to the full extent of the security.

(f) *Examples.*—The provisions of this section may be illustrated by the following examples:

*Example (1).* (i) On June 1, 1970, a tax is assessed against M, a tool manufacturer, with respect to his delinquent tax liability. On June 15, 1970, M enters into a written financing agreement with X, a bank. The agreement provides that, in consideration of such sums as X may advance to M, X is to have a security interest in all of M's presently owned and subsequently acquired commercial paper, accounts receivable, and inventory (including inventory in the manufacturing stages and raw materials). On July 6, 1970, notice of the tax lien is filed in accordance with §301.6323(f)-1. On August 3, 1970, without actual notice or knowledge of the tax lien filing, X advances $10,000 to M. On August 5, 1970, M acquires additional inventory through the purchase of raw materials. On August 20, 1970, M has accounts receivable, arising from the sale of tools, amounting to $5,000. Under local law X's security interest arising by reason of the $10,000 advance on August 3, 1970, has priority, with respect to the raw materials and accounts receivable, over a judgment lien against M arising July 6, 1970 (the date of the tax lien filing) out of an unsecured obligation.

(ii) Because the $10,000 advance was made before the 46th day after the tax lien filing, and the accounts receivable in the amount of $5,000 and the raw materials were acquired by M before such 46th day, X's $10,000 security interest in the accounts receivable and the inventory has priority over the tax lien. The priority of X's security interest also extends to the proceeds, received on or after the 46th day after the tax lien filing, from the liquidation of the accounts receivable and inventory held by M on August 20, 1970, if X has a continuously perfected security interest in identifiable proceeds under local law. However, the priority of X's security interest will not extend to other property acquired with such proceeds.

*Example (2).* Assume the same facts as in example (1) except that on July 15, 1970, X has actual knowledge of the tax lien filing. Because an agreement does not qualify as a commercial transactions financing agreement when a disbursement is made after tax lien filing with actual knowledge of the filing, X's security interest will not have priority over the tax lien with respect to the $10,000 advance made on August 3, 1970.

*Example (3).* Assume the same facts as in example (1) except that, instead of additional inventory, on August 5, 1970, M acquires an account receivable as the result of the sale of machinery which M no longer needs in his business. Even though the account receivable was acquired by taxpayer M before the 46th day after tax lien filing, the tax lien will have priority over X's security interest arising in the account receivable pursuant to the earlier written agreement because the account receivable was not acquired by the taxpayer in the ordinary course of his trade or business.

*Example (4).* Pursuant to a written agreement with the N Manufacturing Company entered into on January 4, 1971, Y, a commercial factor, purchases the accounts receivable arising out of N's regular sales to its customers. On November 1, 1971, in accordance with §301.6323(f)-1, a notice of lien is filed with respect to N's delinquent tax liability. On December 6, 1971, Y, without actual notice or knowledge of the tax lien filing, purchases all of the accounts receivable resulting from N's November 1971 sales. Y has taken appropriate steps under local law so that the December 6, 1971, purchase is protected against a judgment lien arising November 1, 1971 (the date of tax lien filing) out of an unsecured obligation. Because the purchaser of commercial financing security, other than inventory, is treated as having acquired a security interest in commercial financing security, and because Y otherwise meets the requirements of this section, the tax lien is not valid with respect to Y's December 6, 1971, purchase of N's accounts receivable. [Reg. §301.6323(c)-1.]

☐ [*T.D. 7429,* 8-20-76.]

### [Reg. §301.6323(c)-2]

**§301.6323(c)-2. Protection for real property construction or improvement financing agreements.**—(a) *In general.*—Even though a notice of a lien imposed by section 6321 is filed in accordance with §301.6323(f)-1, the lien is not valid with respect to a security interest which:

(1) Comes into existence after the tax lien filing,

(2) Is in qualified property covered by the terms of real property construction or improvement financing agreement entered into before the tax lien filing, and

(3) Is protected under local law against a judgment lien arising, as of the time of tax lien filing, out of an unsecured obligation.

For purposes of this section, it is immaterial that the holder of the security interest had actual notice or knowledge of the lien at the time disbursements are made pursuant to such an agreement. See paragraphs (a) and (e) of §301.6323(h)-1 for general definitions of the terms "security interest" and "tax lien filing." For purposes of this section, a judgment lien is a lien held by a judgment lien creditor as defined in paragraph (g) of §301.6323(h)-1.

(b) *Real property construction or improvement financing agreement.*— For purposes of this section, the term "real property construction or improvement financing agreement" means any written agreement to make cash disbursements (whether or not at the option of the party agreeing to make such disbursements):

(1) To finance the construction, improvement, or demolition of real property if the agreement provides for a security interest in the real property with respect to which the construction, improvement, or demolition has been or is to be made;

(2) To finance a contract to construct or improve, or demolish real property if the agreement provides for a security interest in the proceeds of the contract; or

(3) To finance the raising or harvesting of a farm crop or the raising of livestock or other animals if the agreement provides for a security interest in any property subject to the lien imposed by section 6321 at the time of tax lien filing, in the crop raised or harvested, or in the livestock or other animals raised.

For purposes of subparagraphs (1) and (2) of this paragraph, construction or improvement may include demolition. For purposes of any agreement described in subparagraph (3) of this paragraph, the furnishing of goods and services is treated as the disbursement of cash.

(c) *Qualified property.*—For purposes of this section, the term "qualified property" includes only—

(1) In the case of an agreement described in paragraph (b)(1) of this section, the real property with respect to which the construction or improvement has been or is to be made;

(2) In the case of an agreement described in paragraph (b)(2) of this section, the proceeds of the contract to construct or improve real property; or

(3) In the case of an agreement described in paragraph (b)(3) of this section, property subject to the lien imposed by section 6321 at the time of tax lien filing, the farm crop raised or harvested, or the livestock or other animals raised.

(d) *Examples.*— The provisions of this paragraph may be illustrated by the following examples:

*Example (1).* A, in order to finance the construction of a dwelling on a lot owned by him, mortgages the property to B. The mortgage, executed January 4, 2006, includes an agreement that B will make cash disbursements to A as the construction progresses. On February 1, 2006, in accordance with §301.6323(f)-1-1, a notice of lien is filed and recorded in the public index with respect to A's delinquent tax liability. A continues the construction, and B makes cash disbursements on June 15, 2006, and December 15, 2006. Under local law B's security interest arising by virtue of the disbursements is protected against a judgment lien arising February 1, 2006 (the date of tax lien filing) out of an unsecured obligation. Because B is the holder of a security interest coming into existence by reason of cash disbursements made pursuant to a written agreement, entered into before tax lien filing, to make cash disbursements to finance the construction of real property, and because B's security interest is protected, under local law, against a judgment lien arising as of the time of tax lien filing out of an unsecured obligation, B's security interest has priority over the tax lien.

*Example (2).* (i) C is awarded a contract for the demolition of several buildings. On March 3, 2004, C enters into a written agreement with D which provides that D will make cash disbursements to finance the demolition and also provides that repayment of the disbursements is secured by any sums due C under the contract. On April 1, 2004, in accordance with §301.6323(f)-1, a notice of lien is filed with respect to C's delinquent tax liability. With actual notice of the tax lien, D makes cash disbursements to C on August 13, September 13, and October 13, 2004. Under local law D's security interest in the proceeds of the contract with respect to the disbursements is entitled to priority over a judgment lien arising on April 1, 2004 (the date of tax lien filing) out of an unsecured obligation.

(ii) Because D's security interest arose by reason of disbursements made pursuant to a written agreement, entered into before tax lien filing, to make cash disbursements to finance a contract to demolish real property, and because D's security interest is valid under local law against a judgment lien arising as of the time of tax lien filed out of an unsecured obligation, the tax lien is not valid with respect to D's security interest in the proceeds of the demolition contract.

*Example (3).* Assume the same facts as in *Example 2* and, in addition, assume that, as further security for the cash disbursements, the March 3, 2004, agreement also provides for a security interest in all of C's demolition equipment. Because the protection of the security interest arising from the disbursements made after tax lien filing under the agreement is limited under section 6323(c)(3) to the proceeds of the demolition contract and because, under the circumstances, the security interest in the equipment is not otherwise protected under section 6323, the tax lien will have priority over D's security interest in the equipment.

*Example (4).* (i) On January 3, 2006, F and G enter into a written agreement, whereby F agrees to provide G with cash disbursements, seed, fertilizer, and insecticides as needed by G, in order to finance the raising and harvesting of a crop on a farm owned by G. Under the terms of the agreement F is to have a security interest in the crop, the farm, and all other property then owned or thereafter acquired by G. In accordance with §301.6323(f)-1, on January 10, 2006, a notice of lien is filed and recorded in the public index with respect to G's delinquent tax liability. On March 3, 2006, with actual notice of the tax lien, F makes a cash disbursement of $5,000 to G and furnishes him seed, fertilizer, and insecticides having a value of $10,000. Under local law F's security interest, coming into existence by reason of the cash disbursement and the furnishing of goods, has priority over a judgment lien arising January 10, 2006 (the date of tax lien filing and recording in the public index) out of an unsecured obligation.

(ii) Because F's security interest arose by reason of a disbursement (including the furnishing of goods) made under a written agreement which was entered into before tax lien filing and which constitutes an agreement to finance the raising or harvesting of a farm crop, and because F's security interest is valid under local law against a judgment lien arising as of the time of tax lien filing out of an unsecured obligation, the tax lien is not valid with respect to F's security interest in the crop even though a notice of lien was filed before the security interest arose. Furthermore, because the farm is property subject to the tax lien at the time of tax lien filing, F's security interest with respect to the farm also has priority over the tax lien.

*Example (5).* Assume the same facts as in *Example 4* and in addition that on October 2, 2006, G acquires several tractors to which F's security interest attaches under the terms of the agreement. Because the tractors are not property subject to the tax lien at the time of tax lien filing, the tax lien has priority over F's security interest in the tractors.

(e) *Effective/applicability date.*—This section applies with respect to any notice of Federal tax lien filed on or after April 4, 2011. [Reg. § 301.6323(c)-2.]

☐ *[T.D. 7429, 8-20-76. Amended by T.D. 9520, 4-1-2011.]*

### [Reg. § 301.6323(c)-3]

**§ 301.6323(c)-3. Protection for obligatory disbursement agreements.**—(a) *In general.*—Even though a notice of a lien imposed by section 6321 is filed in accordance with § 301.6323(f)-1, the lien is not valid with respect to a security interest which:

(1) Comes into existence after the tax lien filing,

(2) Is in qualified property covered by the terms of an obligatory disbursement agreement entered into before the tax lien filing, and

(3) Is protected under local law against a judgment lien arising, as of the time of tax lien filling, out of an unsecured obligation.

See paragraphs (a) and (e) of § 301.6323(h)-1 for definitions of the terms "security interest" and "tax lien filing." For purposes of this section, a judgment lien is a lien held by a judgment lien creditor as defined in paragraph (g) of § 301.6323(h)-1.

(b) *Obligatory disbursement agreement.*—For purposes of this section the term "obligatory disbursement agreement" means a written agreement, entered into by a person in the course of his trade or business, to make disbursements. An agreement is treated as an obligatory disbursement agreement only with respect to disbursements which are required to be made by reason of the intervention of the rights of a person other than the taxpayer. The obligation to pay must be conditioned upon an event beyond the control of the obligor. For example, the provisions of this section are applicable where an issuing bank obligates itself to honor drafts or other demands for payment on a letter of credit and a bank, in good faith, relies upon that letter of credit in making advances. The provisions of this section are also applicable, for example, where a bonding company obligates itself to make payments to indemnify against loss or liability and, under the terms of the bond, makes a payment with respect to a loss. The priority described in this section is not applicable, for example, in the case of an accommodation endorsement by an endorser who assumes his obligation other than in the course of his trade or business.

(c) *Qualified property.*—Except as provided under paragraph (d) of this section, the term "qualified property," for purposes of this section, means property subject to the lien imposed by section 6321 at the time of tax lien filing and, to the extent that the acquisition is directly traceable to the obligatory disbursement, property acquired by the taxpayer after tax lien filing.

(d) *Special rule for surety agreements.*—Where the obligatory disbursement agreement is an agreement insuring the performance of a contract of the taxpayer and another person, the term "qualified property" shall be treated as also including—

(1) The proceeds of the contract the performance of which was insured, and

(2) If the contract the performance of which was insured is a contract to construct or improve real property, to produce goods, or to furnish services, any tangible personal property used by the taxpayer in the performance of the insured contract.

For example, a surety company which holds a security interest, arising from cash disbursements made after tax lien filing under a payment or performance bond on a real estate construction project, has priority over the tax lien with respect to the proceeds of the construction contract and, in addition, with respect to any tangible personal property used by the taxpayer in the construction project if its security interest in the tangible personal property is protected under local law against a judgment lien arising, as of the time the tax lien was filed, out of an unsecured obligation.

(e) *Examples.*—This section may be illustrated by the following examples:

*Example (1).* (i) On January 2, 1969, H, an appliance dealer, in order to finance the acquisition from O of a large inventory of appliances, enters into a written agreement with Z, a bank. Under the terms of the agreement, in return for a security interest in all of H's inventory, presently owned and subsequently acquired, Z issues an irrevocable letter of credit to allow H to make the purchase. On December 31, 1968 and January 10, 1969, in accordance with § 301.6323(f)-1, separate notices of lien are filed with respect to H's delinquent tax liabilities. On March 31, 1969, Z honors the letter of credit. Under local law, Z's security interest in both existing and after-acquired inventory is protected against a judgment lien arising on or after January 10, 1969, out of an unsecured obligation. Under local law, Z's security interest in the inventory purchased under the letter of credit qualifies as a purchase money security interest and is valid against persons acquiring security interests in or liens upon such inventory at any time.

(ii) Because Z's security interest in H's inventory did not arise under a written agreement entered into before the filing of notice of the first tax lien on December 31, 1968, that lien is superior to Z's security interest except to the extent of Z's purchase money security interest. Because Z's interest qualifies as a purchase money security interest with respect to the inventory purchased under the letter of credit, the tax liens attach under section 6321 only to the equity acquired by H, and the rights of Z in the inventory so purchased are superior even to the lien filed on December 31, 1968, without regard to this section.

(iii) Because Z's security interest arose by reason of disbursements made under a written agreement which was entered into before the filing of notice of the second tax lien on January 10, 1969, and which constitutes an agreement to make disbursements required to be made by reason of the intervention of the rights of O, a person other than the taxpayer, and because Z's security interest is valid under local law against a judgment lien arising as of the time of such tax lien filing on January 10, 1969, out of an unsecured obligation, the second tax lien is, under this section, not valid with respect to Z's security interest in inventory owned by H on January 10, 1969, as well as any after-acquired inventory directly traceable to Z's disbursements (apart from such greater protection as Z enjoys, with respect to the latter, under its purchase money security interest). No protection against the second tax lien is provided under this section with respect to a security interest in any other inventory acquired by H after January 10, 1969, because such other inventory is neither subject to the tax lien at the time of tax lien filing nor directly traceable to Z's disbursements.

*Example (2).* On June 1, 1971, K is awarded a contract to construct an office building. At the same time, S, a surety company, agrees in writing to insure the performance of the contract. The agreement provides that in the event S must complete the job as the result of a default by K, S will be entitled to the proceeds of the contract. In addition, the agreement provides that S is to have a security interest in all property belonging to K. On December 1, 1971, prior to the completion of the building, K defaults. On the same date, under § 301.6323(f)-1, a notice of lien is filed with repect to K's delinquent tax liability. S completes the building on June 1, 1972. Under local law S's security interest in the proceeds of the contract and S's security interest in the property of K are entitled to priority over a judgment lien arising December 1, 1971 (the date of tax lien filing) out of an unsecured obligation. Because, for purposes of an obligatory disbursement agreement which is a surety agreement, the security interest may be in the proceeds of the insured contract, S's security interest in the proceeds of the contract has priority over the tax lien even though a notice of lien was filed before S's security interest arose. Furthermore, because the insured contract was a contract to construct real property, S's security interest in any of K's tangible personal property used in the performance of the contract also has priority over the tax lien.

*Example (3).* (i) On February 2, 1970, L enters into an agreement with M, a contractor, to construct an apartment building on land owned by L. Under a separate agreement, N bank agrees to furnish funds on a short-term basis to L for the payment of amounts due to M during the course of construction. Simultaneously, X, a financial institution, makes a binding commitment to N bank and L to provide long-term financing for the project after its completion. Under its commitment, X is obligated to pay off the balance of the construction loan held by N bank upon the execution by L of a new promissory note secured by a mortgage deed of trust upon the improved property. On September 4, 1970, in accordance with § 301.6323(f)-1, notice of lien is properly filed with respect to L's delinquent tax liability. On September 8, 1970, X obtains actual notice of the tax lien filing. On September 14, 1970, the documents creating X's security interest are executed and recorded, N bank's lien for its construction loan is released, and X makes the required disbursements to N bank. Under local law, X's security interest is protected against a judgment lien arising on September 4, 1970 (the time of tax lien filing) out of an unsecured obligation.

(ii) Because X's security interest arose by reason of a disbursement made under a written agreement entered into before tax lien filing, which constitutes an agreement to make disbursements required to be made by reason of the intervention of the rights of N bank, a person other than the taxpayer, and because X's security interest is valid under local law against a judgment lien arising as of the time of the tax lien filing out of an unsecured obligation, the tax lien is not valid with respect to X's security interest to the extent of the disbursement to N bank. The obligatory disbursement is protected under section 6323(c)(4) even if X is not subrogated to N bank's rights or X's agreement is not itself a real property construction financing agreement. [Reg. § 301.6323(c)-3].

☐ [T.D. 7429, 8-20-76.]

### [Reg. § 301.6323(d)-1]

**§ 301.6323(d)-1. 45-day period for making disbursements.**—(a) *In general.*—Even though a notice of a lien imposed by section 6321 is filed in accordance with § 301.6323(f)-1, the lien is not valid with respect to a security interest which comes into existence, after tax lien filing, by reason of disbursements made before the 46th day after the date of tax lien filing, or if earlier, before the person making the disbursements has actual notice or knowledge of the tax lien filing, but only if the security interest is—

(1) In property which is subject, at the time of tax lien filing, to the lien imposed by section 6321 and which is covered by the terms of a written agreement entered into before tax lien filing, and

(2) Protected under local law against a judgment lien arising, as of the time of tax lien filing, out of an unsecured obligation.

For purposes of subparagraph (1) of this paragraph, a contract right (as defined in paragraph (c)(2)(i) of § 301.6323(c)-1) is subject, at the time of tax lien filing, to the lien imposed by section 6321 if the contract has been made by such time. An account receivable (as defined in paragraph (c)(2)(ii) of § 301.6323(c)-1) is subject, at the time of tax lien filing, to the lien imposed by section 6321 if, and to the extent, a right to payment has been earned by performance at such time. For purposes of subparagraph (2) of this paragraph, a judgment lien is a lien held by a judgment lien creditor as defined in paragraph (g) of § 301.6323(h)-1. For purposes of this section, it is immaterial that the written agreement provides that the disbursements are to be made at the option of the person making the disbursements. See paragraphs (a) and (e) of § 301.6323(h)-1 for definitions of the terms "security interest" and "tax lien filing," respectively. See paragraph (a) of § 301.6323(i)-1 for certain circumstances under which a person is deemed to have actual notice or knowledge of a fact.

(b) *Examples.*—The application of this section may be illustrated by the following examples:

*Example (1).* On December 1, 1967, an assessment is made against A with respect to his delinquent tax liability. On January 2, 1968, A enters into a written agreement with B whereby B agrees to lend A $10,000 in return for a security interest in certain property owned by A. On January 10, 1968, in accordance with § 301.6323(f)-1 notice of the tax lien affecting the property is filed. On February 1, 1968, B, without actual notice or knowledge of the tax lien filing, disburses the loan to A. Under local law, the security interest arising by reason of the disbursement is entitled to priority over a judgment lien arising January 10, 1968 (the date of tax lien filing) out of an unsecured obligation. Because the disbursement was made before the 46th day after tax lien filing, because the disbursement was made pursuant to a written agreement entered into before tax lien filing, and because the resulting security interest is protected under local law against a judgment lien arising as of the date of tax lien filing out of an unsecured obligation, B's $10,000 security interest has priority over the tax lien.

*Example (2).* Assume the same facts as in example (1) except that when B disburses the $10,000 to A on February 10, 1968, B has actual knowledge of the tax lien filing. Because the disbursement was made with actual knowledge of tax lien filing, B's security interest does not have priority over the tax lien even though the disbursement was made before the 46th day after the tax lien filing. Furthermore, B is not protected under § 301.6323(a)-1(a) as a holder of a security interest because he had not parted with money or money's worth prior to the time the notice of tax lien was filed (Jan. 10, 1968) even though he had made a firm commitment to A before that time. [Reg. § 301.6323(d)-1.]

☐ [T.D. 7429, 8-20-76.]

### [Reg. § 301.6323(e)-1]

**§ 301.6323(e)-1. Priority of interest and expenses.**—(a) *In general.*—If the lien imposed by section 6321 is not valid as against another lien or security interest, the priority of the other lien or security interest also extends to each of the following items to the extent that under local law the item has the same priority as the lien or security interest to which it relates:

(1) Any interest or carrying charges (including finance, service, and similar charges) upon the obligation secured,

(2) The reasonable charges and expenses of an indenture trustee (including, for example, the trustee under a deed of trust) or agent holding the security interest for the benefit of the holder of the security interest,

(3) The reasonable expenses, including reasonable compensation for attorneys, actually incurred in collecting or enforcing the obligation secured,

(4) The reasonable costs of insuring, preserving, or repairing the property to which the lien or security interest relates,

(5) The reasonable costs of insuring payment of the obligation secured (including amounts paid by the holder of the security interest for mortgage insurance, such as that issued by the Federal Housing Administration), and

(6) Amounts paid to satisfy any lien on the property to which the lien or security interest relates, but only if the lien so satisfied is entitled to priority over the lien imposed by section 6321.

(b) *Collection expenses.*—The reasonable expenses described in paragraph (a)(3) of this section include expenditures incurred by the protected holder of the lien or security interest to establish the priority of his interest or to collect, by foreclosure or otherwise, the amount due him from the property subject to his lien. Accordingly, the amount of the encumbrance which is protected is increased by the amounts so expended by the holder of the security interest.

(c) *Costs of insuring, preserving, etc.*—The reasonable costs of insuring, preserving, or repairing described in paragraph (a)(4) of this section include expenditures by the holder of a security interest for fire and casualty insurance on the property subject to the security interest and amounts paid by the holder of the lien or security interest to repair the property. Such reasonable costs also include the amounts paid by the holder of the lien or security interest in a leasehold to the lessor of the leasehold to preserve the leasehold subject to the lien or security interest. Accordingly, the amount of the lien or security interest which is protected is increased by the amounts so expended by the holder of the lien or security interest.

(d) *Satisfaction of liens.*—The amounts described in paragraph (a)(6) of this section include expenditures incurred by the protected holder of a lien or security interest to discharge a statutory lien for State sales taxes on the property subject to his lien or security interest if both his lien or security interest and the sales tax lien have priority over a Federal tax lien. Accordingly, the amount of the lien or security interest is increased by the amounts so expended by the holder of the lien or security interest even though under local law the holder of the lien or security interest is not subrogated to the rights of the holder of the State sales tax lien. However, if the holder of the lien or security interest is subrogated, within the meaning of paragraph (b) of § 301.6323(i)-1, to the rights of the holder of the sales tax lien, he will also be entitled to any additional protection afforded by section 6323(i)(2). [Reg. § 301.6323(e)-1.]

☐ [T.D. 7429, 8-20-76.]

### [Reg. § 301.6323(f)-1]

**§ 301.6323(f)-1. Place for filing notice; form.**—(a) *Place for filing.*—The notice of lien referred to in § 301.6323(a)-1 shall be filed as follows:

(1) *Under State laws.*—(i) *Real property.*—In the case of real property, notice shall be filed in one office within the State (or the county or other governmental subdivision), as designated by the laws of the State, in which the property subject to the lien is deemed situated under the provisions of paragraph (b)(1) of this section.

(ii) *Personal property.*—In the case of personal property, whether tangible or intangible, the notice shall be filed in one office within the State (or the county or other governmental subdivision), as designated by the laws of the State, in which the property subject to the lien is deemed situated under the provisions of paragraph (b)(2) of this section.

(2) *With the clerk of the U.S. district court.*—Whenever a State has not by law designated one office which meets the requirements of subparagraph (1)(i) or (1)(ii) of this paragraph, the notice shall be filed in the office of the clerk of the U.S. district court for the judicial district in which the property subject to the lien is deemed situated

under the provisions of paragraph (b) of this section. For example, a State has not by law designated one office meeting the requirements of subparagraph (1)(i) of this paragraph if more than one office is designated within the State, county, or other governmental subdivision for filing notices with respect to all real property located in such State, county, or other governmental subdivision. A State has not by law designated one office meeting the requirements of subparagraph (1)(ii) of this paragraph if more than one office is designated in the State, county, or other governmental subdivision for filing notices with respect to all of the personal property of a particular taxpayer. A state law that conforms to or reenacts a federal law establishing a national filing system does not constitute a designation by state law of an office for filing liens against personal property. Thus, if state law provides that a notice of lien affecting personal property must be filed in the office of the county clerk for the county in which the taxpayer resides and also adopts a federal law that requires a notice of lien to be filed in another location in order to attach to a specific type of property, the state is considered to have designated only one office for the filing of the notice of lien, and to protect its lien the Internal Revenue Service need only file its notice in the office of the county clerk for the county in which the taxpayer resides.

(3) *With the Recorder of Deeds of the District of Columbia.*—If the property subject to the lien imposed by section 6321 is deemed situated, under the provisions of paragraph (b) of this section, in the District of Columbia, the notice shall be filed in the office of the Recorder of Deeds of the District of Columbia.

(b) *Situs of property subject to lien.*—For purposes of paragraph (a) of this section, property is deemed situated as follows:

(1) *Real property.*—Real property is deemed situated at its physical location.

(2) *Personal property.*—Personal property, whether tangible or intangible, is deemed situated at the residence of the taxpayer at the time the notice of lien is filed.

For purposes of subparagraph (2) of this paragraph the residence of a corporation or partnership is deemed to be the place at which the principal executive office of the business is located, and the residence of a taxpayer whose residence is not within the United States is deemed to be in the District of Columbia.

(c) *National filing system.*—The filing of federal tax liens is to be governed solely by the Internal Revenue Code and is not subject to any other federal law that may establish a national system for filing liens and encumbrances against a particular type of personal property. Thus, for example, the Service is not subject to the requirements established by the Federal Aviation Agency for filing liens against civil aircraft in Oklahoma City, Oklahoma.

(d) *Form.*—(1) *In general.*—The notice referred to in § 301.6323 (a)-1 shall be filed on Form 668, "Notice of Federal Tax Lien under Internal Revenue Laws". Such notice is valid notwithstanding any other provision of law regarding the form or content of a notice of lien. For example, omission from the notice of lien of a description of the property subject to the lien does not affect the validity thereof even though State law may require that the notice contain a description of the property subject to the lien.

(2) *Form 668 defined.*—The term *Form 668* means either a paper form or a form transmitted electronically, including a form transmitted by facsimile (fax) or electronic mail (e-mail). A Form 668 must identify the taxpayer, the tax liability giving rise to the lien, and the date the assessment arose regardless of the method used to file the notice of Federal tax lien.

(e) *Examples.*—The provisions of this section may be illustrated by the following examples:

*Example (1).* The law of State X provides that notices of Federal tax lien affecting personal property are to be filed in the Office of the Recorder of Deeds of the county where the taxpayer resides. The laws of State X also provide that notices of lien affecting real property are to be filed with the recorder of deeds of the county where the real property is located. On June 1, 1970, in accordance with § 301.6323(f)-1, a notice of lien is filed in county M with respect to the delinquent tax liability of A. At the time the notice is filed, A is a resident of county M and owns real property in that county. One year later A moves to county N and one year after that A moves to county O. Because the situs of personal property is deemed to be at the residence of the taxpayer at the time the notice of lien is filed, the notice continues to be effectively filed with respect to A's personal property even though A no longer resides in county M. Furthermore, because the situs of real property is deemed to be at its physical location, the notice of lien also continues to be effectively filed with respect to A's real property.

*Example (2).* B is a resident of Canada but owns personal property in the United States. On January 4, 1971, in accordance with § 301.6323(f)-1, a notice of lien is filed with the Office of the Recorder of Deeds of the District of Columbia. On January 2, 1973, B changes his residence to State Y in the United States. Because the residence of a taxpayer who is not a resident of the United States is deemed to be in the District of Columbia and the situs of personal property is deemed to be at the residence of the taxpayer at the time of filing, the lien continues to be effectively filed with respect to the personal property of B located in the United States even though B has returned to the United States and taken up residence in State Y and even though B has at no time been in the District of Columbia.

*Example (3).* The law of State Z in effect before July 1, 1967, provides that notices of lien affecting real property are to be filed in the office of the recorder of deeds of the county in which the real property is located, but that if the real property is registered under the Torrens system of title registration the notice is to be filed with the registrar of titles rather than the recorder of deeds. The law of State Z in effect after June 30, 1967, provides that all notices of lien affecting real property are to be filed with the recorder of deeds of the county in which the real property is located. Accordingly, where the Torrens system is adopted by a county in State Z, there were before July 1, 1967, two offices designated for filing notices of Federal tax lien affecting real property in the county because one office was designated for Torrens real property and another office was designated for non-Torrens real property. Because State Z had not designated one office within the State, county, or other governmental subdivision for filing notices before July 1, 1967, with respect to all real property located in the State, county, or governmental subdivision, before July 1, 1967, the place for filing notices of lien under this section, affecting property located in counties adopting the Torrens system, was with the clerk of the U.S. district court for the judicial district in which the real property is located. However, after June 30, 1967, the place for filing notices of lien under this section, affecting both Torrens and non-Torrens real property in counties adopting the Torrens system is with the recorder of deeds for each such county. Notices of lien filed under this section with the clerk of the U.S. district court before July 1, 1967, remain validly filed whether or not refiled with the recorder of deeds after the change in State law or upon refiling during the required refiling period.

*Example (4).* The law of State W provides that notices of lien affecting personal property of corporations and partnerships are to be filed in the office of the Secretary of State. Notices of lien affecting personal property of any other person are to be filed in the office of the clerk of court for the county where the person resides. Because the State law designates only one filing office within State W with respect to personal property of any particular taxpayer, notices of lien filed under this section, affecting personal property, shall be filed in the office designated under State law.

*Example 5.* The law of State F provides that notices of lien affecting personal property are to be filed with the clerk of the circuit court in the county in which the personal property is located. State F has conformed state law to federal law to provide that all instruments affecting title to an interest in any civil aircraft of the United States must be recorded in the Office of the Federal Aviation Administrator (FAA) in Oklahoma City, Oklahoma. On July 1, 1990, a tax lien arises against ABC airline, which owns aircraft situated in State F. The Internal Revenue Service files a Notice of Federal Tax Lien with the clerk of the circuit court in the county in which the aircraft is located but does not file the notice with the FAA in Oklahoma City, Oklahoma. Because the FAA system adopted by State F does not constitute a second place of filing pursuant to section 6323(f), the federal tax lien is validly filed.

*Example 6.* Assume the same facts as *Example 5* except that State F did not reenact or conform state law to the FAA requirements. The result is the same because the filing of federal tax liens is governed solely by the Internal Revenue Code, and is not subject to any other national filing system.

(f) *Effective/applicability date.* This section applies with respect to any notice of Federal tax lien filed on or after April 4, 2011. [Reg. § 301.6323(f)-1.]

☐ [*T.D. 7429, 8-20-76. Amended by T.D. 8234, 11-23-88; T.D. 8557, 7-26-94; and T.D. 9520, 4-1-2011.*]

**[Reg. § 301.6323(g)-1]**

**§ 301.6323(g)-1. Refiling of notice of tax lien.**—(a) *In general.*—(1) *Requirement to refile.*—In order to continue the effect of a notice of lien, the notice must be refiled in the place described in paragraph (b) of this section during the required refiling period (described in paragraph (c) of this section). If two or more notices of lien are filed with respect to a particular tax assessment, and each notice of lien contains a certificate of release that releases the lien when the required refiling period ends, the failure to comply with the provisions of paragraphs (b)(1)(i) and (c) of this section in respect to one of the notices of lien releases the lien and renders ineffective the refiling of any other notice of lien.

(2) *Effect of refiling.*—A timely refiled notice of lien is effective as of the date on which the notice of lien to which it relates was effective.

(3) *Effect of failure to refile.*—If the Internal Revenue Service fails to refile a notice of lien in the manner described in paragraphs (b) and (c) of this section, the notice is not effective, after the expiration of the required refiling period, as against any person described in section 6323(a) ,without regard to when the interest of the person in the property subject to the lien was acquired. If a notice of lien contains a certificate of release that provides that the lien is released at the end of the required refiling period unless the notice of lien is refiled, and the notice of lien is not refiled, then the lien is extinguished and the notice of lien is ineffective.

(i) However, neither the failure to refile before the expiration of the refiling period, nor the release of the lien, shall alter or impair any right of the United States to property or its proceeds that is the subject of a levy or judicial proceeding commenced prior to the end of the refiling period or the release of the lien, except to the extent that a person acquires an interest in the property for adequate consideration after the commencement of the proceeding and does not have notice of, and is not bound by, the outcome of the proceeding.

(ii) If a suit or levy referred to in the preceding sentence is dismissed or released and the property is subject to the lien at such time, a notice of lien with respect to the property is not effective after the suit or levy is dismissed or released unless refiled during the required refiling period.

(4) *Filing of new notice.*—If a notice of lien is not refiled, and the notice of lien contains a certificate of release that automatically releases the lien when the required refiling period ends, the lien is released as of that date and is no longer in existence. The Internal Revenue Service must revoke the release before it can file a new notice of lien. This new filing must meet the requirements of section 6323(f) and § 301.6323(f)-1 and is effective from the date on which such filing is made.

(b) *Place for refiling notice of lien.*—(1) *In general.*—A notice of lien refiled during the required refiling period (described in paragraph (c) of this section) shall be effective only—

(i) If the notice of lien is refiled in the office in which the prior notice of lien (including a refiled notice) was filed under the provisions of section 6323; and

(ii) In any case in which 90 days or more prior to the date the refiling of the notice of lien under subdivision (i) is completed, the Internal Revenue Service receives written information (in the manner described in subparagraph (2) of this paragraph) concerning a change in the taxpayer's residence, if a notice of such lien is also filed in accordance with section 6323(f)(1)(A)(ii) in the State in which such new residence is located (or, if such new residence is located without the United States, in the District of Columbia).
A notice of lien is considered as refiled in the office in which the prior notice or refiled notice was filed under the provisions of section 6323 if it is refiled in the office which, pursuant to a change in the applicable local law, assumed the functions of the office in which the prior notice or refiled notice was filed. If on or before the 90th day referred to in subdivision (ii) more than one written notice is received concerning a change in the taxpayer's residence, a notice of lien is required by this subdivision to be filed only with respect to the residence shown on the written notice received on the most recent date. Subdivision (ii) is applicable regardless of whether the taxpayer resides at the new residence on the date the refiling of notice of lien under subdivision (i) of this subparagraph is completed.

(2) *Notice of change of taxpayer's residence.*—(i) *In general.*—Except as provided in subdivision (ii) or (iii) of this subparagraph, for purposes of this section, a notice of change of a taxpayer's residence will be effective only if it (A) is received, in writing, from the taxpayer or his representative by the district director or the service center director having jurisdiction where the original notice of lien was filed, (B) relates to an unpaid tax liability of the taxpayer, and (C) states the taxpayer's name and the address of his new residence. Although it is not necessary that a written notice contain the taxpayer's identifying number authorized by section 6109, it is preferable that it include such number. For purposes of this subdivision, a notice of change of a taxpayer's residence shown on a return or an amended return (including a return of the same tax) will not be effective to notify the Internal Revenue Service.

(ii) *Notice received before August 23, 1976.*—For purposes of this section, a notice of a change of a taxpayer's residence will also be effective if it (A) is received, in writing, by any office of the Internal Revenue Service before August 23, 1976, from the taxpayer or his

representative, (B) relates to an unpaid tax liability of the taxpayer, and (C) states the taxpayer's name and the address of his new residence.

(iii) *By return or amended return.*—For purposes of this section, in the case of a notice of lien which relates to an assessment of tax made after December 31, 1966, a notice of change of a taxpayer's residence will also be effective if it is contained in a return or amended return of the same type of tax filed with the Internal Revenue Service by the taxpayer or his representative which on its face indicates that there is a change in the taxpayer's address and correctly states the taxpayer's name, the address of his new residence, and his identifying number required by section 6109.

(iv) *Other rules applicable.*—Except as provided in subdivisions (i), (ii), and (iii) of this subparagraph, no communication (either written or oral) to the Internal Revenue Service will be considered effective as notice of a change of a taxpayer's residence under this section, whether or not the Service has actual notice or knowledge of the taxpayer's new residence. For the purpose of determining the date on which a notice of change of a taxpayer's residence is received under this section, the notice shall be treated as received on the date it is actually received by the Internal Revenue Service without reference to the provisions of section 7502.

(3) *Examples.*—The following examples illustrate the provisions of this section:

*Example 1.* A, a delinquent taxpayer, is a resident of State M and owns real property in State N. In accordance with § 301.6323(f)-1, notices of lien are filed in States M and N. The notices of lien contain certificates of release that release the lien at the end of the required refiling period. In order to continue the effect of the notice of lien filed in either M or N, the Internal Revenue Service must refile, during the required refiling period, the notice of lien with the appropriate office in M as well as with the appropriate office in N.

*Example (2).* B, a delinquent taxpayer, is a resident of State M. In accordance with § 301.6323(f)-1, notice of lien is properly filed in that State. One year before the beginning of the required refiling period, B establishes his residence in State N, and B immediately notifies the Internal Revenue Service of his change in residence in accordance with the provisions of paragraph (b)(2) of this section. In order to continue the effect of the notice of lien filed in M, the Internal Revenue Service must refile, during the required refiling period, notices of lien with (i) the appropriate office in M, and (ii) the appropriate office in N, because B properly notified the Internal Revenue Service of his change in residence to N more than 89 days prior to the date refiling of the notice of lien in M is completed. Even if the Internal Revenue Service had acquired actual notice or knowledge of B's change in residence by other means, if B had not properly notified the Internal Revenue Service of his change in residence, the effect of the notice of lien in State M could have been continued without any refiling in State N.

*Example (3).* C, a delinquent taxpayer, is a resident of State O. In accordance with § 301.6323(f)-1, notice of lien is properly filed in that State. Four years before the required refiling period, C establishes his residence in State P, and C immediately notifies the Internal Revenue Service of his change in residence in accordance with the provisions of paragraph (b)(2) of this section. Three years before the required refiling period, C establishes his residence in State R, and again C immediately notifies the Internal Revenue Service of his change in residence in accordance with the provisions of paragraph (2) of this section. In order to continue the effect of the notice of lien filed in O, the Internal Revenue Service must refile, during the required refiling period, notices of lien with (i) the appropriate office in O, and (ii) the appropriate office in R. Refiling in R is required because the notice received by the Service of C's change in residence to R was the most recent notice received more than 89 days prior to the date refiling in O is completed. The notice of lien is not required to be filed in P, even though C properly notified the Internal Revenue Service of his change in residence to P, because such notice is not the most recent one received.

*Example (4).* Assume the same facts as in example (3), except that C does not notify the Internal Revenue Service of his change in residence to R in accordance with the provisions of paragraph (b)(2) of this section. In order to continue the effect of the notice of lien filed in O, the Internal Revenue Service must refile, during the required refiling period, the notice of lien with (i) the appropriate office in O, and (ii) the appropriate office in P. Refiling in P is required because C properly notified the Internal Revenue Service of his change in residence to P, even though C is not a resident of P on the date refiling of the notice of lien in O is completed. The Internal Revenue Service is not required to file a notice of lien in R because C did not properly notify the Service of his change in residence to R.

*Example 5.* D, a delinquent taxpayer, is a resident of State M and owns real property in States N and O. In accordance with § 301.6323(f)-1, the Internal Revenue Service files notices of lien in M,

N, and O States. Nine years and 6 months after the date of the assessment shown on the notice of lien, D establishes his residence in P, and at that time the Internal Revenue Service receives from D a notification of his change in residence in accordance with the provisions of paragraph (b)(2) of this section. On a date which is 9 years and 7 months after the date of the assessment shown on the notice of lien, the Internal Revenue Service properly refiles notices of lien in M, N, and O which refilings are sufficient to continue the effect of each of the notices of lien. The Internal Revenue Service is not required to file a notice of lien in P because D did not notify the Internal Revenue Service of his change of residence to P more than 89 days prior to the date each of the refilings in M, N, and O was completed.

*Example (6).* Assume the same facts as in example (5) except that the refiling of the notice of lien in O occurs 100 days after D notifies the Internal Revenue Service of his change in residence to P in accordance with the provisions of paragraph (b)(2) of this section. In order to continue the effect of the notice of lien filed in O, in addition to refiling the notice of lien in O, the Internal Revenue Service must also refile, during the required refiling period, a notice of lien in P because D properly notified the Internal Revenue Service of his change of residence to P more than 89 days prior to the date the refiling in O was completed. However, the Internal Revenue Service is not required to refile the notice of lien in P to maintain the effect of the notices of lien in M and N because D did not notify the Internal Revenue Service of his change in residence to P more than 89 days prior to the date the refilings in M and N were completed.

*Example (7).* E, a delinquent taxpayer, is a resident of State T. Because T has not designated one office in the case of personal property for filing notices of lien in accordance with the provisions of section 6323(f)(1)(A)(ii), the Internal Revenue Service properly files a notice of lien with the clerk of the appropriate United States district court. However, solely as a matter of convenience for those who may have occasion to search for notices of lien, and not as a matter of legal effectiveness, the Internal Revenue Service also files notice of lien with the recorder of deeds of the county in T where E resides. In addition, the Internal Revenue Service sends a copy of the notice of lien to the X life insurance company to give the company actual notice of the notice of lien. In order to continue the effect of the notice of lien, the Internal Revenue Service must refile the notice of lien with the clerk of the appropriate United States district court during the required refiling period. In order to continue the effect of the notice of the lien, it is not necessary to refile the notice of lien with the recorder of deeds of the county where E resides, because the refiling of the notice of lien with the recorder of deeds does not constitute a proper filing for the purposes of section 6323(f). In addition, to continue the effect of the notice of lien under this section it is not necessary to send a copy of the notice of lien to the X life insurance company, because the sending of a notice of lien to an insurance company does not constitute a proper filing for the purposes of section 6323(f).

(c) *Required refiling period.*—(1) *In general.*—For the purpose of this section, except as provided in paragraph (c)(2) of this section, the term *required refiling period* means—

(i) The 1-year period ending 30 days after the expiration of 10 years after the date of the assessment of the tax; and

(ii) The 1-year period ending with the expiration of 10 years after the close of the preceding required refiling period for such notice of lien.

(2) *Examples.*—The following examples illustrate the provisions of this paragraph:

*Example 1.* On March 10, 1998, an assessment of tax is made against B, a delinquent taxpayer, and a lien for the amount of the assessment arises on that date. On July 10, 1998, in accordance with §301.6323(f)-1, a notice of lien is filed. The notice of lien filed on July 10, 1998, is effective through April 9, 2008. The first required refiling period for the notice of lien begins on April 10, 2007, and ends on April 9, 2008. A refiling of the notice of lien during that period will extend the effectiveness of the notice of lien filed on July 10, 1998, through April 9, 2018. The second required refiling period for the notice of lien begins on April 10, 2017, and ends on April 9, 2018.

*Example 2.* Assume the same facts as in *Example 1,* except that the Internal Revenue Service fails to refile a notice of lien during the first required refiling period (April 10, 2007, through April 9, 2008). A notice of lien is filed on June 9, 2009, in accordance with §301.6323(f)-1. This notice is ineffective if the original notice contained a certificate of release, as the certificate of release would have had the effect of extinguishing the lien as of April 10, 2008. The Internal Revenue Service could revoke the release and file a new notice of lien, which would be effective as of the date it was filed.

(d) *Effective/applicability date.*—This section applies with respect to any notice of Federal tax lien filed on or after April 4, 2011. [Reg. §301.6323(g)-1.]

☐ [*T.D.* 7429, 8-20-76. *Amended by T.D.* 9520, 4-1-2011.]

### [Reg. §301.6323(h)-0]

**§301.6323(h)-0. Scope of definitions.**—Except as otherwise provided by §301.6323(h)-1, the definitions provided by §301.6323(h)-1 apply for purposes of §§301.6323(a)-1 through 301.6324-1. [Reg. §301.6323(h)-0.]

☐ [*T.D.* 7429, 8-20-76.]

### [Reg. §301.6323(h)-1]

**§301.6323(h)-1. Definitions.**—(a) *Security interest.*—(1) *In general.*—The term "security interest" means any interest in property acquired by contract for the purpose of securing payment or performance of an obligation or indemnifying against loss or liability. A security interest exists at any time—

(i) If, at such time, the property is in existence and the interest has become protected under local law against a subsequent judgment lien (as provided in subparagraph (2) of this paragraph) arising out of an unsecured obligation; and

(ii) To the extent that, at such time, the holder has parted with money or money's worth (as defined in subparagraph (3) of this paragraph).

For purposes of this subparagraph, a contract right (as defined in paragraph (c)(2)(i) of §301.6323(c)-1) is in existence when the contract is made. An account receivable (as defined in paragraph (c)(2)(ii) of §301.6323(c)-1) is in existence when, and to the extent, a right to payment is earned by performance.

A security interest must be in existence, within the meaning of this paragraph, at the time as of which its priority against a tax lien is determined. For example, to be afforded priority under the provisions of paragraph (a) of §301.6323(a)-1 a security interest must be in existence within the meaning of this paragraph before a notice of lien is filed.

(2) *Protection against a subsequent judgment lien.*—(i) For purposes of this paragraph, a security interest is deemed to be protected against a subsequent judgment lien on—

(A) The date on which all actions required under local law to establish the priority of a security interest against a judgment lien have been taken, or

(B) If later, the date on which all required actions are deemed effective under local law, to establish the priority of the security interest against a judgment lien.

For purposes of this subdivision, the dates described in (A) and (B) of this subdivision (i) shall be determined without regard to any rule or principle of local law which permits the relation back of any requisite action to a date earlier than the date on which the action is actually performed. For purposes of this paragraph, a judgment lien is a lien held by a judgment lien creditor as defined in paragraph (g) of this section.

(ii) The following example illustrates the application of paragraph (a)(2):

*Example.* (i) Under the law of State X, a security interest in certificated securities, negotiable documents, or instruments may be perfected, and hence protected against a judgment lien, by filing or by the secured party taking possession of the collateral. However, a security interest in such intangible personal property is considered to be temporarily perfected for a period of 20 days from the time the security interest attaches, to the extent that it arises for new value given under an authenticated security agreement. Under the law of X, a security interest attaches to such collateral when there is an agreement between the creditor and debtor that the interest attaches, the debtor has rights in the property, and consideration is given by the creditor. Under the law of X, in the case of temporary perfection, the security interest in such property is protected during the 20-day period against a judgment lien arising, after the security interest attaches, out of an unsecured obligation. Upon expiration of the 20-day period, the holder of the security interest must perfect its security interest under local law.

(ii) Because the security interest is perfected during the 20-day period against a subsequent judgment lien arising out of an unsecured obligation, and because filing or the taking of possession before the conclusion of the period of temporary perfection is not considered, for purposes of paragraph (a)(2)(i) of this section, to be a requisite action which relates back to the beginning of such period, the requirements of this paragraph are satisfied. Because filing or taking possession is a condition precedent to continued perfection, filing or taking possession of the collateral is a requisite action to establish such priority after expiration of the period of temporary perfection. If there is a lapse of perfection for failure to file or take possession, the determination of when the security interest exists (for purposes of protection against the tax lien) is made without regard to the period of temporary perfection.

(3) *Money or money's worth.*—For purposes of this paragraph, the term *money or money's worth* includes money, a security (as defined in paragraph (d) of this section), tangible or intangible property, services, and other consideration reducible to a money value. Money or money's worth also includes any consideration which otherwise would constitute money or money's worth under the preceding sentence which was parted with before the security interest would otherwise exist if, under local law, past consideration is sufficient to support an agreement giving rise to a security interest, and provided that the grant of the security interest is not a fraudulent transfer under local law or 28 U.S.C. § 3304(a)(2). A firm commitment to part with money, a security, tangible or intangible property, services, or other consideration reducible to a money value does not, in itself, constitute a consideration in money or money's worth. A relinquishing or promised relinquishment of dower, curtesy, or of a statutory estate created in lieu of dower or curtesy, or of other marital rights is not a consideration in money or money's worth. Nor is love and affection, promise of marriage, or any other consideration not reducible to a money value a consideration in money or money's worth.

(4) *Holder of a security interest.*—For purposes of this paragraph, the holder of a security interest is the person in whose favor there is a security interest. For provisions relating to the treatment of a purchaser of commercial financing security as a holder of a security interest, see § 301.6323(c)-1(e).

(b) *Mechanic's lienor.*—(1) *In general.*—The term "mechanic's lienor" means any person who under local law has a lien on real property (or on the proceeds of a contract relating to real property) for services, labor, or materials furnished in connection with the construction or improvement (including demolition) of the property. A mechanic's lienor is treated as having a lien on the later of—

(i) The date on which the mechanic's lien first becomes valid under local law against subsequent purchasers of the real property without actual notice, or

(ii) The date on which the mechanic's lienor begins to furnish the services, labor, or materials.

(2) *Examples.*—The provisions of this paragraph may be illustrated by the following example:

*Example (1).* On February 1, 1968, A lets a contract for the construction of an office building on property owned by him. On March 1, 1968, in accordance with § 301.6323(f)-1, a notice of lien for delinquent Federal taxes owed by A is filed. On April 1, 1968, B, a lumber dealer, delivers lumber to A's property. On May 1, 1968, B records a mechanic's lien against the property to secure payment of the price of the lumber. Under local law, B's mechanic's lien is valid against subsequent purchasers of real property without notice from February 1, 1968, which is the date the construction contract was entered into. Because the date on which B's mechanic's lien is valid under local law against subsequent purchasers is February 1, and the date on which B begins to furnish the materials is April 1, the date on which B becomes a mechanic's lienor within the meaning of this paragraph is April 1, the later of these two dates. Under paragraph (a) of § 301.6323(a)-1, B's mechanic's lien will not have priority over the Federal tax lien, even though under local law the mechanic's lien relates back to the date of the contract.

(c) *Motor vehicle.*—(1) The term "motor vehicle" means a self-propelled vehicle which is registered for highway use under the laws of any State, the District of Columbia, or a foreign country.

(2) A motor vehicle is "registered for highway use" at the time of a sale if immediately prior to the sale it is so registered under the laws of any State, the District of Columbia, or a foreign country. Where immediately prior to the sale of a motor vehicle by a dealer, the dealer is permitted under local law to operate it under a dealer's tag, license, or permit issued to him, the motor vehicle is considered to be registered for highway use in the name of the dealer at the time of the sale.

(d) *Security.*—The term "security" means any bond, debenture, note, or certificate or other evidence of indebtedness, issued by a corporation or a government or political subdivision thereof, with interest coupons or in registered form, share of stock, voting trust certificate, or any certificate of interest or participation in, certificate of deposit or receipt for, temporary or interim certificate for, or warrant or right to subscribe to or purchase, any of the foregoing; negotiable instrument; or money.

(e) *Tax lien filing.*—The term "tax lien filing" means the filing of notice of the lien imposed by section 6321 in accordance with § 301.6323(f)-1.

(f) *Purchaser.*—(1) *In general.*—The term "purchaser" means a person who, for adequate and full consideration in money or money's worth (as defined in subparagraph (3) of this paragraph), acquires an interest (other than a lien or security interest) in property which is valid under local law against subsequent purchasers without actual notice.

(2) *Interest in property.*—For purposes of this paragraph, each of the following interests is treated as an interest in property, if it is not a lien or security interest:

(i) A lease of property,

(ii) A written executory contract to purchase or lease property,

(iii) An option to purchase or lease property and any interest therein, or

(iv) An option to renew or extend a lease of property.

(3) *Adequate and full consideration in money or money's worth.*—For purposes of this paragraph, the term "adequate and full consideration in money or money's worth" means a consideration in money or money's worth having a reasonable relationship to the true value of the interest in property acquired. See paragraph (a)(3) of this section for definition of the term "money or money's worth." Adequate and full consideration in money or money's worth may include the consideration in a bona fide bargain purchase. The term also includes the consideration in a transaction in which the purchaser has not completed performance of his obligation, such as the consideration in an installment purchase contract, even though the purchaser has not completed the installment payments.

(4) *Examples.*—The provisions of this paragraph may be illustrated by the following examples:

*Example (1).* A enters into a contract for the purchase of a house and lot from B. Under the terms of the contract A makes a down payment and is to pay the balance of the purchase price in 120 monthly installments. After payment of the last installment, A is to receive a deed to the property. A enters into possession, which under local law protects his interest in the property against subsequent purchasers without actual notice. After A has paid five monthly installments, a notice of lien for Federal taxes is filed against B in accordance with § 301.6323(f)-1. Because the contract is an executory contract to purchase property and is valid under local law against subsequent purchasers without actual notice, A qualifies as a purchaser under this paragraph.

*Example (2).* C owns a residence which he leases to his son-in-law, D, for a period of 5 years commencing January 1, 1968. The lease provides for payment of $100 a year, although the fair rental value of the residence is $2,500 a year. The lease is recorded on December 31, 1967. On March 1, 1968, a notice of tax lien for unpaid Federal taxes of C is filed in accordance with § 301.6323(f)-1. Under local law, D's interest is protected against subsequent purchasers without actual notice. However, because the rental paid by D has no reasonable relationship to the value of the interest in property acquired, D does not qualify as a purchaser under this paragraph.

(g) *Judgment lien creditor.*—The term "judgment lien creditor" means a person who has obtained a valid judgment, in a court of record and of competent jurisdiction, for the recovery of specifically designated property or for a certain sum of money. In the case of a judgment for the recovery of a certain sum of money, a judgment lien creditor is a person who has perfected a lien under the judgment on the property involved. A judgment lien is not perfected until the identity of the lienor, the property subject to the lien, and the amount of the lien are established. Accordingly, a judgment lien does not include an attachment or garnishment lien until the lien has ripened into judgment, even though under local law the lien of the judgment relates back to an earlier date. If recording or docketing is necessary under local law before a judgment becomes effective against third parties acquiring liens on real property, a judgment lien under such local law is not perfected with respect to real property until the time of such recordation or docketing. If under local law levy or seizure is necessary before a judgment lien becomes effective against third parties acquiring liens on personal property, then a judgment lien under such local law is not perfected until levy or seizure of the personal property involved. The term "judgment" does not include the determination of a quasi-judicial body or of an individual acting in a quasi-judicial capacity such as the action of State taxing authorities.

(h) *Effective/applicability date.*—This section applies with respect to any notice of Federal tax lien filed on or after April 4, 2011. [Reg. § 301.6323(h)-1.]

☐ [*T.D.* 7429, 8-20-76. *Amended by T.D.* 9520, 4-1-2011.]

## [Reg. § 301.6323(i)-1]

§ 301.6323(i)-1. **Special rules.**—(a) *Actual notice or knowledge.*—For purposes of subchapter C (section 6321 and following), chapter 64 of the Code, an organization is deemed, in any transaction, to have actual notice or knowledge of any fact from the time the fact is brought to the attention of the individual conducting the transaction, and in any event from the time the fact would have been brought to the individual's attention if the organization had exercised due diligence. An organization exercises due diligence if it maintains reasonable routines for communicating significant information to the person conducting the transaction and there is reasonable compliance with the routines. Due diligence does not require an individual acting for the organization to communicate information unless such communication is part of his regular duties or unless he has reason to know of the transaction and that the transaction would be materially affected by the information.

(b) *Subrogation.*—(1) *In general.*—Where, under local law, one person is subrogated to the rights of another with respect to a lien or interest, such person shall be subrogated to such rights for purposes of any lien imposed by section 6321 or 6324. Thus, if a tax lien imposed by section 6321 or 6324 is not valid with respect to a particular interest as against the holder of that interest, then the tax lien also is not valid with respect to that interest as against any person who, under local law, is a successor in interest to the holder of that interest.

(2) *Example.*—The application of this paragraph may be illustrated by the following example:

*Example.* On February 1, 1968, an assessment is made and a tax lien arises with respect to A's delinquent tax liability. On February 25, 1968, in accordance with § 301.6323(f)-1, a notice of lien is properly filed. On March 1, 1968, A negotiates a loan from B, the security for which is a second mortgage on property owned by A. The first mortgage on the property is held by C and has priority over the tax lien. Upon default by A, C begins proceedings to foreclose upon the first mortgage. On September 1, 1968, B pays the amount of principal and interest in default to C in order to protect the second mortgage against the pending foreclosure of C's senior mortgage. Under local law, B is subrogated to C's rights to the extent of the payment to C. Therefore, the tax lien is invalid against B to the extent he became subrogated to C's rights even though the tax lien is valid against B's second mortgage on the property.

(c) *Disclosure of amount of outstanding lien.*—If a notice of lien has been filed (see § 301.6323(f)-1), the amount of the outstanding obligation secured by the lien is authorized to be disclosed as a matter of public record on Form 668 "Notice of Federal Tax Lien Under Internal Revenue Laws." The amount of the outstanding obligation secured by the lien remaining unpaid at the time of an inquiry is authorized to be disclosed to any person who has a proper interest in determining this amount. Any person who has a right in the property or intends to obtain a right in the property by purchase or otherwise will, upon presentation by him of satisfactory evidence, be considered to have a proper interest. Any person desiring this information may make his request to the office of the Internal Revenue Service named on the notice of lien with respect to which the request is made. The request should clearly describe the property subject to the lien, identify the applicable lien, and give the reasons for requesting the information. [Reg. § 301.6323(i)-1.]

☐ [*T.D.* 7429, 8-20-76.]

### [Reg. § 301.6323(j)-1]

**§ 301.6323(j)-1. Withdrawal of notice of federal tax lien in certain circumstances.**—(a) *In general.*—The Commissioner or his delegate (Commissioner) may withdraw a notice of federal tax lien filed under this section, if the Commissioner determines that any of the conditions in paragraph(b) of this section exist. A notice of federal tax lien is withdrawn by the filing by the Commissioner of a notice of withdrawal in the office in which the notice of federal tax lien is filed. If a notice of withdrawal is filed, chapter 64 of subtitle F, relating to collection, will be applied as if the withdrawn notice had never been filed. A copy of the notice of withdrawal will be provided to the taxpayer. Upon written request by a taxpayer with respect to whom a notice of federal tax lien has been or will be withdrawn, the Commissioner will promptly make reasonable efforts to notify any credit reporting agency and any financial institution or creditor identified by the taxpayer of the withdrawal of such notice. The withdrawal of a notice of federal tax lien will not affect the underlying federal tax lien.

(b) *Conditions authorizing withdrawal.*—The Commissioner may authorize the withdrawal of a notice of federal tax lien upon determining that one of the following conditions exists:

(1) *Premature or not in accordance with administrative procedures.*—The filing of the notice of federal tax lien was premature or otherwise not in accordance with the administrative procedures of the Secretary.

(2) *Installment agreement.*—The taxpayer has entered into an agreement under section 6159 to satisfy the liability for which the lien

was imposed by means of installment payments. Entry into an installment agreement may not, however, be the basis for withdrawal of a notice of lien if the installment agreement specifically provides that a notice of federal tax lien will not be withdrawn.

(3) *Facilitate collection.*—The withdrawal of the notice of federal tax lien will facilitate the collection of the tax liability for which the lien was imposed.

(4) *Best interests of the United States and the taxpayer.*—(i) *In general.*—The taxpayer or the National Taxpayer Advocate (or his delegate) has consented to the withdrawal of the notice of federal tax lien, and withdrawal of the notice would be in the best interest of the taxpayer, as determined by the taxpayer or the National Taxpayer Advocate (or his delegate), and in the best interest of the United States, as determined by the Commissioner.

(ii) *Best interest of the taxpayer.*—When a taxpayer requests the withdrawal of notice of federal tax lien based on the best interests of the United States and the taxpayer, the National Taxpayer Advocate (or his delegate) generally will determine whether the withdrawal of the notice of federal tax lien is in the best interest of the taxpayer. If, however, a taxpayer requests the Commissioner to withdraw a notice and has not specifically requested the National Taxpayer Advocate (or his delegate) to determine the taxpayer's best interest, a finding by the Commissioner that the withdrawal of notice is in the best interest of the taxpayer will be sufficient to support withdrawal. If the Commissioner decides independently of a request by the taxpayer to withdraw a notice of federal tax lien, the taxpayer or the National Taxpayer Advocate (or his delegate) must consent to the withdrawal.

(5) *Examples.*—The following examples illustrate the provisions of this paragraph (b):

*Example 1.* A owes $1,000 in Federal income taxes. The IRS files a notice of federal tax lien to secure A's tax liability. However, the IRS failed to follow procedure provided by the Internal Revenue Manual (but not required by statute) with regard to managerial approval prior to the filing of a notice of federal tax lien. The Commissioner may withdraw the notice of federal tax lien because the filing of the notice was not in accordance with the Secretary's administrative procedures.

*Example 2.* A owes $1,000 in federal income taxes. A enters into an agreement to pay the outstanding federal income tax liability in installments. The agreement provides that a notice of federal tax lien may be filed if the taxpayer defaults. A timely pays the installments each month and has not defaulted in any way. Eleven months after entering into the installment agreement, the Internal Revenue Service files a notice of federal tax lien. Noting that there has been no default, the taxpayer asks the Internal Revenue Service to withdraw the notice of federal tax lien. In this situation, the Commissioner may withdraw the notice of federal tax lien because the taxpayer has entered into an installment agreement.

*Example 3.* A is an employee of X Corporation. A notice of federal tax lien has been filed to secure an outstanding tax liability against A. A, who has no assets and no other secured creditors, has agreed to pay the balance of tax due through payroll deductions at a rate higher than the Internal Revenue Service could obtain through a wage levy in order to get the notice of federal tax lien withdrawn. X Corporation has agreed to allow A to enter into a payroll deduction agreement. In this situation, the Commissioner may withdraw the notice of federal tax lien to facilitate collection.

*Example 4.* A is owner of a farm machinery dealership against whom a notice of federal tax lien has been filed to secure an outstanding tax liability. A currently is paying the tax liability by an installment agreement. X Corporation has agreed to provide A with 100 tractors to increase A's inventory if the notice of federal tax lien is withdrawn. A asks the Internal Revenue Service to withdraw the notice of federal tax lien. The Commissioner determines that the larger inventory would enable A to generate additional tractor sales. Increased sales would enable A to increase the amount of installment payments and, consequently, reduce the amount of time needed to satisfy the liability. A, who has no other assets or secured creditors, has agreed to modify the installment agreement. The Commissioner may withdraw the notice of federal tax lien because the withdrawal is in the best interest of the taxpayer and the United States.

(c) *Determinations by the Commissioner.*—The Commissioner must determine whether any of the conditions authorizing the withdrawal of a notice of federal tax lien exist if a taxpayer submits a request for withdrawal in accordance with paragraph (d) of this section. The Commissioner may also make this determination independent of a request from the taxpayer based on information received from a source other than the taxpayer. If the Commissioner determines that conditions authorizing the withdrawal are not present, the Commissioner may not authorize the withdrawal. If the Commissioner determines conditions for withdrawal are present, the Commissioner may (but is not required to) authorize the withdrawal.

(d) *Procedures for request for withdrawal.*—(1) *Manner.*—A request for the withdrawal of a notice of federal tax lien must be made in writing in accordance with procedures prescribed by the Commissioner.

(2) *Form.*—The written request will include the following information and documents—

(i) Name, current address, and taxpayer identification number of the person requesting the withdrawal of notice of federal tax lien;

(ii) A copy of the notice of federal tax lien affecting the taxpayer's property, if available;

(iii) The grounds upon which the withdrawal of notice of federal tax lien is being requested;

(iv) A list of the names and addresses of any credit reporting agency and any financial institution or creditor that the taxpayer wishes the Commissioner to notify of the withdrawal of notice of federal tax lien; and

(v) A request to disclose the withdrawal of notice of federal tax lien to the persons listed in paragraph (d)(2)(iv) of this section.

(e) *Supplemental list of credit agencies, financial institutions, and creditors.*—(1) *In general.*—If the Commissioner grants a withdrawal of notice of federal tax lien, the taxpayer may supplement the list in paragraph (d)(2)(iv) of this section. If no list was provided in the request to withdraw the notice of federal tax lien, the list in paragraph (d)(2)(iv) of this section and the request for notification in paragraph (d)(2)(v) of this section may be submitted after the notice is withdrawn.

(2) *Manner.*—A request to supplement the list of any credit agencies and any financial institutions or creditors that the taxpayer wishes the Commissioner to notify of the withdrawal of notice of federal tax lien must be made in writing in accordance with procedures prescribed by the Commissioner.

(3) *Form.*—The request must include the following information and documents—

(i) Name, current address, and taxpayer identification number of the person requesting the notification of any credit agency or any financial institution or creditor of the withdrawal of notice of federal tax lien;

(ii) A copy of the notice of withdrawal, if available;

(iii) A supplemental list, identified as such, of the names and addresses of any credit reporting agency and any financial institution or creditor that the taxpayer wishes the Commissioner to notify of the withdrawal of notice of federal tax lien; and

(iv) A request to disclose the withdrawal of notice of federal tax lien to the persons listed in paragraph (e)(3)(iii) of this section.

(f) *Effective date.*—This section applies on or after June 22, 2001, with respect to a withdrawal of any notice of federal tax lien. [Reg. § 301.6323(j)-1.]

☐ [*T.D.* 8951, 6-21-2001.]

**[Reg. § 20.6324-1]**

**§ 20.6324-1. Special lien for estate tax.**—For regulations concerning the special lien for the estate tax, see § 301.6324-1 of this chapter (Regulations on Procedure and Administration). [Reg. § 20.6324-1.]

☐ [*T.D.* 6296, 6-23-58.]

**[Reg. § 25.6324-1]**

**§ 25.6324-1. Special lien for gift tax.**—For regulations concerning the special lien for the gift tax, see § 301.6324-1 of this chapter (Regulations on Procedure and Administration). [Reg. § 25.6324-1.]

☐ [*T.D.* 6334, 10-14-58.]

**[Reg. § 301.6324-1]**

**§ 301.6324-1. Special liens for estate and gift taxes; personal liability of transferees and others.**—(a) *Estate tax.*—(1) The lien imposed by section 6324(a) attaches at the date of the decedent's death to every part of the gross estate, whether or not the property comes into the possession of the duly qualified executor or administrator. The lien attaches to the extent of the tax shown to be due by the return and of any deficiency in tax found to be due upon review and audit. If the estate tax is not paid when due, then the spouse, transferee, trustee (except the trustee of an employee's trust which meets the requirements of section 401(a)), surviving tenant, person in possession of the property by reason of the exercise, nonexercise, or release of a power of appointment, or beneficiary, who receives, or has on the date of the decedent's death, property included in the gross estate under sections 2034 to 2042, inclusive, shall be personally liable for the tax to the extent of the value, at the time of the decedent's death, of the property.

(2) Unless the tax is paid in full or becomes unenforceable by reason of lapse of time, and except as otherwise provided in paragraph (c) of this section, the lien upon the entire property constituting the gross estate continues for a period of 10 years after the decedent's death, except that the lien shall be divested with respect to—

(i) The portion of the gross estate used for the payment of charges against the estate and expenses of its administration allowed by any court having jurisdiction thereof;

(ii) Property included in the gross estate under sections 2034 to 2042, inclusive, which is transferred by (or transferred by the transferee of) the spouse, transferee, trustee, surviving tenant, person in possession of the property by reason of the exercise, nonexercise, or release of a power of appointment, or beneficiary to a purchaser or holder of a security interest. In such case a like lien attaches to all the property of the spouse, transferee, trustee, surviving tenant, person in possession, beneficiary, or transferee of any such person, except the part which is transferred to a purchaser or a holder of a security interest. See section 6323(h)(1) and (6) and the regulations thereunder, respectively, for the definitions of "security interest" and "purchaser";

(iii) The portion of the gross estate (or any interest therein) which has been transferred to a purchaser or holder of a security interest if payment is made of the full amount of tax determined by the district director pursuant to a request of the fiduciary (executor, in the case of the estate of a decedent dying before January 1, 1971) for discharge from personal liability as authorized by section 2204 (relating to discharge of fiduciary from personal liability) but there is substituted a like lien upon the consideration received from the purchaser or holder of a security interest; and

(iv) Property as to which the district director has issued a certificate releasing a lien under section 6325(a) and the regulations thereunder.

(b) *Lien for gift tax.*—Except as provided in paragraph (c) of this section, a lien attaches upon all gifts made during the period for which the return was filed (see § 25.6019-1 of this chapter) for the amount of tax imposed upon the gifts made during such period. The lien extends for a period of 10 years from the time the gifts are made, unless the tax is sooner paid in full or becomes unenforceable by reason of lapse of time. If the tax is not paid when due, the donee of any gift becomes personally liable for the tax to the extent of the value of his gift. Any part of the property comprised in the gift transferred by the donee (or by a transferee of the donee) to a purchaser or holder of a security interest is divested of the lien, but a like lien, to the extent of the value of the gift, attaches to all the property (including after-acquired property) of the donee (or the transferee) except any part transferred to a purchaser or holder of a security interest. See section 6323(h)(1) and (6) and the regulations thereunder, respectively, for the definitions of "security interest" and "purchaser."

(c) *Exceptions.*—(1) A lien described in either paragraph (a) or paragraph (b) of this section is not valid against a mechanic's lienor (as defined in section 6323(h)(2) and the regulations thereunder) and, subject to the conditions set forth under section 6323(b) (relating to protection for certain interests even though notice filed), is not valid with respect to any lien or interest described in section 6323(b) and the regulations thereunder.

(2) If a lien described in either paragraph (a) or paragraph (b) of this section is not valid against a lien or security interest (as defined in section 6323(h)(1) and the regulations thereunder), the priority of the lien or security interest extends to any item described in section 6323(e) (relating to priority of interest and expenses) to the extent that, under local law, the item has the same priority as the lien or security interest to which it relates.

(d) *Application of lien imposed by section 6321.*—The general lien under section 6321 and the special lien under subsection (a) or (b) of section 6324 for the estate or gift tax are not exclusive of each other, but are cumulative. Each lien will arise when the conditions precedent to the creation of such lien are met and will continue in accordance with the provisions applicable to the particular lien. Thus, the special lien may exist without the general lien being in force, or the general lien may exist without the special lien being in force, or the general lien and the special lien may exist simultaneously, depending upon the facts and pertinent statutory provisions applicable to the respective liens. [Reg. § 301.6324-1.]

☐ [*T.D.* 6119, 12-31-54. *Amended by T.D.* 6498, 10-24-60 *and T.D.* 7238, 12-28-72.]

**[Reg. § 20.6324A-1]**

**§ 20.6324A-1. Special lien for estate tax deferred under section 6166 or 6166A.**—(a) *In general.*—If the executor of an estate of a decedent dying after December 31, 1976, makes an election under section 6166 or 6166A (as in effect prior to its repeal by the Economic Recovery Tax Act of 1981) to defer the payment of estate tax, the executor may make an election under section 6324A. An election under section 6324A will cause a lien in favor of the United States to attach to the estate's section 6166 lien property, as defined in paragraph (b)(1) of this section. This lien is in lieu of the bonds required by sections 2204 and 6165 and in lieu of any lien under section 6324 on the same property with respect to the same estate. The value of the property which the district director may require under section 6324A as section 6166 lien property may not exceed the sum of the deferred amount (as defined in paragraph (e)(1) of this section) and the required interest amount (as defined in paragraph (e)(2) of this section). The unpaid portion of the deferred amount (plus any unpaid interest, additional amount, addition to tax, assessable penalty, and cost attributable to the deferred amount) shall be a lien in favor of the United States on the section 6166 lien property. See § 301.6324A-1 of this chapter (Regulations on Procedure and Administration) for provisions relating to the election of and agreement to the special lien for estate tax deferred under section 6166 or 6166A (as in effect prior to its repeal by the Economic Recovery Tax Act of 1981).

(b) *Section 6166 lien property.*—(1) *In general.*—Section 6166 lien property consists of those interests in real and personal property designated in the agreement referred to in section 6324A(c) (see paragraph (b) of § 301.6324A-1 of this chapter). An interest in property may be designated as section 6166 lien property only to the extent such interest can be expected to survive the deferral period (as defined in paragraph (e)(3) of this section). Property designated, however, need not be property included in the decedent's estate.

(2) *Maximum value of required property.*—The fair market value of the property required by the district director to be designated as section 6166 lien property with respect to any estate shall not be greater than the sum of the deferred amount and the required interest amount, as these terms are defined in paragraphs (e)(1) and (2) of this section. However, the parties to the agreement referred to in section 6324A(c) may voluntarily designate property having a fair market value in excess of that sum. The fair market value of the section 6166 lien property shall be determined as of the date prescribed in section 6151(a) (without regard to any extension) for payment of the estate tax. Such value must take into account any encumbrance on the property (such as a mortgage or a lien under section 6324B).

(3) *Additional lien property may be required.*—If, at any time, the unpaid portion of the deferred amount and the required interest amount exceeds the fair market value of the section 6166 lien property, the district director may require the addition of property to the agreement in an amount up to such excess. When additional property is required, the district director shall make notice and demand upon the agent designated in the agreement setting forth the amount of additional property required. Property having the required value (or other security equal to the required value) must be added to the agreement within 90 days after notice and demand from the district director. Failure to comply with the demand within the 90-day period shall be treated as an act accelerating payment of installments under section 6166(g) or 6166A(h) (as in effect prior to its repeal by the Economic Recovery Tax Act of 1981).

(4) *Partial substitution of bond.*—See paragraph (c) of § 301.6324A-1 of this chapter for rules relating to the partial substitution of a bond for the lien where the value of property designated as section 6166 lien property is less than the amount of unpaid estate tax plus interest.

(c) *Special rules.*—(1) *Period of lien.*—The lien under section 6324A arises at the earlier of the date—

(i) The executor is discharged from liability under section 2204; or

(ii) Notice of lien is filed in accordance with § 301.6323(f)-1 of this chapter.

The section 6324A lien continues until the liability for the deferred amount is satisfied or becomes unenforceable by reason of lapse of time. The provisions of § 301.6325-1(c), relating to release of lien or discharge of property, shall apply to this paragraph (c)(1).

(2) *Requirement that lien be filed.*—The lien imposed by section 6324A is not valid against a purchaser (as defined in paragraph (f) of § 301.6323(h)-1), holder of a security interest (as defined in paragraph (a) of § 301.6323(h)-1), mechanic's lienor (as defined in paragraph (b) of § 301.6323(h)-1), or judgment lien creditor (as defined in paragraph

(g) of § 301.6323(h)-1) until notice of the lien is filed. Once filed, the notice of lien remains effective without being refiled.

(3) *Priorities.*—Although a notice of lien under section 6324A has been properly filed, that lien is not valid—

(i) To the extent provided in section 6323(b)(6), relating to real property tax and special assessment liens, regardless of whether such liens came into existence before or after the filing of the notice of Federal tax lien;

(ii) In the case of any real property subject to a lien for repair or improvement, as against a mechanic's lienor, whether or not such lien came into existence before or after the notice of tax lien was filed; and

(iii) As against any security interest set forth in section 6323(c)(3), relating to real property construction or improvement financing agreements, regardless whether such security interest came into existence before or after the filing of the notice of tax lien. However, paragraphs (c)(3)(ii) and (iii) of this section shall not apply to any security interest that came into existence after the date of filing of notice (in a manner similar to a notice filed under section 6323(f)) that payment of the deferred amount has been accelerated under section 6166(g) or 6166A(h) (as in effect prior to its repeal by the Economic Recovery Tax Act of 1981).

(d) *Release or discharge of lien.*—For rules relating to release of the lien imposed by section 6324A or discharge of the section 6166 lien property, see section 6325 and § 301.6325-1 of this chapter.

(e) *Definitions.*—For purposes of section 6324A of this section—

(1) *Deferred amount.*—The deferred amount is the aggregate amount of estate tax deferred under section 6166 or 6166A (as in effect prior to its repeal by the Economic Recovery Tax Act of 1981) determined as of the date prescribed by section 6151(a) for payment of the estate tax.

(2) *Required interest amount.*—The required interest amount is the aggregate amount of interest payable over the first four years of the deferral period. For purposes of computing the required interest amount, the interest rate prescribed by section 6621 in effect on the date prescribed by section 6151(a) for payment of the estate tax shall be used for computing the interest for the first four years of the deferral period. The 4-percent interest rate prescribed by section 6601(j) shall apply to the extent provided in that section. For purposes of computing interest during deferral periods beginning after December 31, 1982, interest shall be compounded daily.

(3) *Deferral period.*—The deferral period is the period for which the payment of tax is deferred pursuant to the election under section 6166 or 6166A (as in effect prior to its repeal by the Economic Recovery Tax Act of 1981).

(4) *Application of definitions.*—In the case of a deficiency, a separate deferred amount, required interest amount, and deferral period shall be determined as of the due date of the first installment after the deficiency is prorated to installments under section 6166 or 6166A (as in effect prior to its repeal by the Economic Recovery Tax Act of 1981). [Reg. § 20.6324A-1.]

☐ [*T.D. 7710, 7-28-80. Amended by T.D. 7941, 2-6-84.*]

**[Reg. § 301.6324A-1]**

**§ 301.6324A-1. Election of and agreement to special lien for estate tax deferred under section 6166 or 6166A.**—(a) *Election of lien.*—If payment of a portion of the estate tax is deferred under section 6166 or 6166A (as in effect prior to its repeal by [the] Economic Recovery Tax Act of 1981), an executor of a decedent's estate who seeks to be discharged from personal liability may elect a lien in favor of the United States in lieu of the bonds required by sections 2204 and 6165. This election is made by applying to the Internal Revenue Service office where the estate tax return is filed at any time prior to payment of the full amount of estate tax and interest due. The application is to be a notice of election requesting the special lien provided by section 6324A and is to be accompanied by the agreement described in paragraph (b)(1) of this section.

(b) *Agreement to lien.*—(1) *In general.*—A lien under this section will not arise unless all parties having any interest in all property designated in the notice of election as property to which the lien is to attach sign an agreement in which they consent to the creation of the lien. (Property so designated need not be property included in the decedent's estate.) The agreement is to be attached to the notice in which the lien under section 6324A is elected. It must be in a form that is binding on all parties having any interest on the property and must contain the following:

(i) The decedent's name and taxpayer identification number as they appear on the estate tax return;

(ii) The amount of the lien;

(iii) The fair market value of the property to be subject to the lien as of the date of the decedent's death and the date of the election under this section;

(iv) The amount, as of the date of the decedent's death and the date of the election, of all encumbrances on the property, including mortgages and any lien under section 6324B;

(v) A clear description of the property which is to be subject to the lien, and in the case of property other than land, a statement of its estimated remaining useful life; and

(vi) Designation of an agent (including the agent's address) for the beneficiaries of the estate and the consenting parties to the lien for all dealings with the Internal Revenue Service on matters arising under section 6166 or 6166A (as in effect prior to its repeal by [the] Economic Recovery Tax Act of 1981), or under section 6324A.

(2) *Persons having an interest in designated property.*—An interest in property is any interest which as of the date of the election can be asserted under applicable local law so as to affect the disposition of any property designated in the agreement required under this section. Any person in being at the date of the election who has any such interest in the property, whether present or future, or vested or contingent, must enter into the agreement. Included among such persons are owners of remainder and executory interests, the holders of general or special powers of appointment, beneficiaries of a gift over in default of exercise of any such power, co-tenants, joint tenants, and holders of other undivided interests when the decedent held a joint or undivided interest in the property, and trustees of trusts holding any interest in the property. An heir who has the power under local law to caveat (challenge) a will and thereby affect disposition of the property is not, however, considered to be a person with an interest in property under section 6324A solely by reason of that right. Likewise, creditors of an estate are not such persons solely by reason of their status as creditors.

(3) *Consent on behalf of interested party.*—If any person required to enter into the agreement provided for by this paragraph either desires that an agent act for him or her or cannot legally bind himself or herself due to infancy or other incompetency, a representative authorized under local law to bind the interested party in an agreement of this nature is permitted to sign the agreement on his or her behalf.

(4) *Duties of agent designated in agreement.*—The Internal Revenue Service will contact the agent designated in the agreement under paragraph (b)(1) on all matters relating to continued qualification of the estate under section 6166 or 6166A (as in effect prior to its repeal by [the] Economic Recovery Tax Act of 1981) and on all matters relating to the special lien arising under section 6324A. It is the duty of the agent as attorney-in-fact for the parties with interests in the property subject to the lien under section 6324A to furnish the Service with any requested information and to notify the Service of any event giving rise to acceleration of the deferred amount of tax.

(c) *Partial substitution of bond for lien.*—If the amount of unpaid estate tax plus interest exceeds the value (determined for purposes of section 6324A(b)(2)) of property listed in the agreement under paragraph (b) of this section, the Internal Revenue Service may condition the release from personal liability upon the executor's submitting an agreement listing additional property or furnishing an acceptable bond in the amount of such excess.

(d) *Relation of sections 6324A and 2204.*—The lien under section 6324A is deemed to be a bond under section 2204 for purposes of determining an executor's release from personal liability. If an election has been made under section 6324A, the executor may not substitute a bond pursuant to section 2204 in lieu of that lien. If a bond has been supplied under section 2204, however, the executor may, by filing a proper notice of election and agreement, substitute a lien under section 6324A for any part or all of such bond.

(e) *Relation of sections 6324A and 6324.*—If there is a lien under this section on any property with respect to an estate, that lien is in lieu of the lien provided by section 6324 on such property with respect to the same estate.

(f) *Section 6324A lien to be in lieu of bond under section 6165.*—The lien under section 6324A is in lieu of any bond otherwise required under section 6165 with respect to tax to be paid in installments under section 6166 or section 6166A (as in effect prior to its repeal by [the] Economic Recovery Tax Act of 1981).

(g) *Special rule for estates for which elections under section 6324A are made on or before August 30, 1980.*—If a lien is elected under section 6324A on or before August 30, 1980, the original election may be revoked. To revoke an election, the executor must file a notice of revocation containing the decedent's name, date of death, and taxpayer identification number with the Internal Revenue Service office

where the original estate tax return for the decedent was filed. The notice must be filed on or before January 31, 1981 (or if earlier, the date on which the period of limitation for assessment expires). [Reg. §301.6324A-1.]

☐ [*T.D. 7710, 7-28-80. Amended by T.D. 7941, 2-6-84.*]

**[Reg. §20.6324B-1]**

**§20.6324B-1. Special lien for additional estate tax attributable to farm, etc., valuation.**—(a) *General rule.*—In the case of an estate of a decedent dying after December 31, 1976, which includes any interest in qualified real property, if the executor elects to value part or all of such property pursuant to section 2032A, a lien arises in favor of the United States on the property to which the election applies. The lien is in the amount equal to the adjusted tax difference attributable to such interest (as defined by section 2032A(c)(2)(B)). The term "qualified real property" means qualified real property as defined in section 2032A(b), qualified replacement property within the meaning of section 2032A(h)(3)(B), and qualified exchange property within the meaning of section 2032A(i)(3). The rules set forth in the regulations under section 2032A shall apply in determining whether this section is applicable to otherwise qualified real property held by a partnership, corporation or trust.

(b) *Period of lien.*—The lien shall arise at the time the executor files an election under section 2032A. It shall remain in effect until one of the following occurs:

(1) The liability for the additional estate tax under section 2032A(c) with respect to such interest has been satisfied; or

(2) Such liability has become unenforceable by reason of lapse of time; or

(3) The district director is satisfied that no further liability for additional estate tax with respect to such interest may arise under section 2032A(c), i.e., the required time period has elapsed since the decedent's death without the occurrence of an event described in section 2032A(c)(1), or the qualified heir (as defined in section 2032A(e)(1)) has died.

For procedures regarding the release or subordination of liens or discharge of property from liens, see §301.6325-1 of this chapter (Regulations on Procedure and Administration).

(c) *Substitution of security for lien.*—The district director may, upon written application of the qualified heir (as defined in section 2032A(e)(1)) acquiring any interest in qualified real property to which a lien imposed by section 6324B attaches, issue a certificate of discharge of any or all property subject to such lien, after receiving a bond or other security in an amount or value determined by the district director as sufficient security for the maximum potential liability for additional estate tax with respect to such interest. Any bond shall be in the form and with the security prescribed in §301.7101-1 of this chapter.

(d) *Special rules.*—The rules set forth in section 6324A(d)(1), (3), and (4), and the regulations thereunder, shall apply with respect to a lien imposed by section 6324B as if it were a lien imposed by section 6324A. [Reg. §20.6324B-1.]

☐ [*T.D. 7847, 11-9-82.*]

**[Reg. §20.6325-1]**

**§20.6325-1. Release of lien or partial discharge of property; transfer certificates in nonresident estates.**—(a) A transfer certificate is a certificate permitting the transfer of property of a nonresident decedent without liability. Except as provided in paragraph (b) of this section, no domestic corporation or its transfer agent should transfer stock registered in the name of a nonresident decedent (regardless of citizenship) except such shares which have been submitted for transfer by a duly qualified executor or administrator who has been appointed and is acting in the United States, without first requiring a transfer certificate covering all of the decedent's stock of the corporation and showing that the transfer may be made without liability. Corporations, transfer agents of domestic corporations, transfer agents of foreign corporations (except as to shares held in the name of a nonresident decedent not a citizen of the United States), banks, trust companies, or other custodians in actual or constructive possession of property, of such a decedent can insure avoidance of liability for taxes and penalties only by demanding and receiving transfer certificates before transfer of property of nonresident decedents.

(b)(1) Subject to the provisions of paragraph (b)(2) of this section—

(i) In the case of a nonresident not a citizen of the United States dying on or after January 1, 1977, a transfer certificate is not required with respect to the transfer of any property of the decedent if the value on the date of death of that part of the decedent's gross estate situated in the United States did not exceed the lesser of $60,000 or $60,000 reduced by the adjustments, if any, required by section 6018(a)(4) for certain taxable gifts made by the decedent and for the aggregate amount of certain specific exemptions.

(ii) In the case of a nonresident not a citizen of the United States dying on or after November 14, 1966, a transfer certificate is not required with respect to the transfer before June 24, 1981, of any property of the decedent if the value on the date of death of that part of the decedent's gross estate situated in the United States did not exceed $30,000.

(2)(i) If the transfer of the estate is subject to the tax imposed by section 2107(a) (relating to expatriation to avoid tax), any amounts which are includible in the decedent's gross estate under section 2107(b) must be added to the date of death value of the decedent's gross estate situated in the United States to determine the value on the date of death of the decedent's gross estate for purposes of paragraph (b)(1) of this section.

(ii) If the transfer of the estate is subject to tax pursuant to a Presidential proclamation made under section 2108(a) (relating to Presidential proclamations of the application of pre-1967 estate tax provisions), a transfer certificate is not required with respect to the transfer of any property of the decedent if the value on the date of death of that part of the decedent's gross estate situated in the United States did not exceed $2,000.

(3) A corporation, transfer agent, bank, trust company, or other custodian will not incur liability for a transfer of the decedent's property without a transfer certificate if the corporation or other person, having no information to the contrary, first receives from the executor or other responsible person, who may be reasonably regarded as in possession of the pertinent facts, a statement of the facts relating to the estate showing that the sum of the value on the date of the decedent's death of that part of his gross estate situated in the United States, and, if applicable, any amounts includible in his gross estate under section 2107(b), is such an amount that, pursuant to the provisions of paragraph (b)(1) or (b)(2) of this section, a transfer certificate is not required.

(4) For the determination of the gross estate situated in the United States, see §§ 20.2103-1 and 20.2104-1.

(c) A transfer certificate will be issued by the service center director or the district director when he is satisfied that the tax imposed upon the estate, if any, has been fully discharged or provided for. The tax will be considered fully discharged for purposes of the issuance of a transfer certificate only when investigation has been completed and payment of the tax, including any deficiency finally determined, has been made. If the tax liability has not been fully discharged, transfer certificates may be issued permitting the transfer of particular items of property without liability upon the filing with the district director of such security as he may require. No transfer certificate is required in an estate of a resident decedent. Further, in the case of an estate of a nonresident decedent (regardless of citizenship) a transfer certificate is not required with respect to property which is being administered by an executor or administrator appointed, qualified, and acting within the United States. For additional regulations under section 6325, see § 301.6325-1 of this chapter (Regulations on Procedure and Administration). [Reg. § 20.6325-1.]

☐ [T.D. 6296, 6-23-58. Amended by T.D. 7296, 12-11-73, T.D. 7302, 1-2-74 and T.D. 7825, 8-12-82.]

[Reg. § 301.6325-1]

§ 301.6325-1. Release of lien or discharge of property.—
(a) Release of lien.—(1) Liability satisfied or unenforceable.—The appropriate official shall issue a certificate of release for a filed notice of Federal tax lien, no later than 30 days after the date on which he finds that the entire tax liability listed in such notice of Federal tax lien either has been fully satisfied (as defined in paragraph (a)(4) of this section) or has become legally unenforceable. In all cases, the liability for the payment of the tax continues until satisfaction of the tax in full or until the expiration of the statutory period for collection, including such extension of the period for collection as is agreed to.

(2) Bond accepted.—The appropriate official shall issue a certificate of release of any tax lien if he is furnished and accepts a bond that is conditioned upon the payment of the amount assessed (together with all interest in respect thereof), within the time agreed upon in the bond, but not later than 6 months before the expiration of the statutory period for collection, including any agreed upon extensions. For provisions relating to bonds, see sections 7101 and 7102 and §§ 301.7101-1 and 301.7102-1.

(3) Certificate of release for a lien which has become legally unenforceable.—The appropriate official shall have the authority to file a notice of Federal tax lien which also contains a certificate of release pertaining to those liens which become legally unenforceable. Such release will become effective as a release as of a date prescribed in the document containing the notice of Federal tax lien and certificate of release.

(4) Satisfaction of tax liability.—For purposes of paragraph (a)(1) of this section, satisfaction of the tax liability occurs when—

(i) The appropriate official determines that the entire tax liability listed in a notice of Federal tax lien has been fully satisfied. Such determination will be made as soon as practicable after tender of payment; or

(ii) The taxpayer provides the appropriate official with proof of full payment (as defined in paragraph (a)(5) of this section) with respect to the entire tax liability listed in a notice of Federal tax lien together with the information and documents set forth in paragraph (a)(7) of this section. See paragraph (a)(6) of this section if more than one tax liability is listed in a notice of Federal tax lien.

(5) Proof of full payment.—As used in paragraph (a)(4)(ii) of this section, the term proof of full payment means—

(i) An internal revenue cashier's receipt reflecting full payment of the tax liability in question;

(ii) A canceled check in an amount sufficient to satisfy the tax liability for which the release is being sought;

(iii) A record, made in accordance with procedures prescribed by the Commissioner, of proper payment of the tax liability by credit or debit card or by electronic funds transfer; or

(iv) Any other manner of proof acceptable to the appropriate official.

(6) Notice of a Federal tax lien which lists multiple liabilities.—When a notice of Federal tax lien lists multiple tax liabilities, the appropriate official shall issue a certificate of release when all of the tax liabilities listed in the notice of Federal tax lien have been fully satisfied or have become legally unenforceable. In addition, if the taxpayer requests that a certificate of release be issued with respect to one or more tax liabilities listed in the notice of Federal tax lien and such liability has been fully satisfied or has become legally unenforceable, the appropriate official shall issue a certificate of release. For example, if a notice of Federal tax lien lists two separate liabilities and one of the liabilities is satisfied, the taxpayer may request the issuance of a certificate of release with respect to the satisfied tax liability and the appropriate official shall issue a release.

(7) Taxpayer requests.—A request for a certificate of release with respect to a notice of Federal tax lien shall be submitted in writing to the appropriate official. The request shall contain the information required in the appropriate IRS Publication.

(b) Discharge of specific property from the lien.—(1) Property double the amount of the liability.—(i) The appropriate official may, in his discretion, issue a certificate of discharge of any part of the property subject to a Federal tax lien imposed under chapter 64 of the Internal Revenue Code if he determines that the fair market value of that part of the property remaining subject to the Federal tax lien is at least double the sum of the amount of the unsatisfied liability secured by the Federal tax lien and of the amount of all other liens upon the property which have priority over the Federal tax lien. In general, fair market value is that amount which one ready and willing but not compelled to buy would pay to another ready and willing but not compelled to sell the property.

(ii) The following example illustrates a case in which a certificate of discharge may not be given under this subparagraph:

Example. The Federal tax liability secured by a lien is $1,000. The fair market value of all property which after the discharge will continue to be subject to the Federal tax lien is $10,000. There is a prior mortgage on the property of $5,000, including interest, and the property is subject to a prior lien of $100 for real estate taxes. Accordingly, the taxpayer's equity in the property over and above the amount of the mortgage and real estate taxes is $4,900, or nearly five times the amount required to pay the assessed tax on which the Federal tax lien is based. Nevertheless, a discharge under this subparagraph is not permissible. In the illustration, the sum of the amount of the Federal tax liability ($1,000) and of the amount of the prior mortgage and the lien for real estate taxes ($5,000 + $100 = $5,100) is $6,100. Double the sum is $12,200, but the fair market value of the remaining property is only $10,000. Hence, a discharge of the property is not permissible under this subparagraph, since the Code requires that the fair market value of the remaining property be at least double the sum of two amounts, one amount being the outstanding Federal tax liability and the other amount being all prior liens upon such property. In order that the discharge may be issued, it would be necessary that the remaining property be worth not less than $12,200.

(2) Part payment; interest of United States valueless.—(i) Part payment.—The appropriate official may, in his discretion, issue a certificate of discharge of any part of the property subject to a Federal tax lien imposed under chapter 64 of the Internal Revenue Code if there is paid over to him in partial satisfaction of the liability secured by the Federal tax lien an amount determined by him to be not less than

the value of the interest of the United States in the property to be so discharged. In determining the amount to be paid, the appropriate official will take into consideration all the facts and circumstances of the case, including the expenses to which the government has been put in the matter. In no case shall the amount to be paid be less than the value of the interest of the United States in the property with respect to which the certificate of discharge is to be issued.

(ii) *Interest of the United States valueless.*—The appropriate official may, in his discretion, issue a certificate of discharge of any part of the property subject to the Federal tax lien if he determines that the interest of the United States in the property to be so discharged has no value.

(3) *Discharge of property by substitution of proceeds of sale.*—The appropriate official may, in his discretion, issue a certificate of discharge of any part of the property subject to a Federal tax lien imposed under chapter 64 of the Internal Revenue Code if such part of the property is sold and, pursuant to a written agreement with the appropriate official, the proceeds of the sale are held, as a fund subject to the Federal tax liens and claims of the United States, in the same manner and with the same priority as the Federal tax liens or claims had with respect to the discharged property. This paragraph does not apply unless the sale divests the taxpayer of all right, title, and interest in the property sought to be discharged. Any reasonable and necessary expenses incurred in connection with the sale of the property and the administration of the sale proceeds shall be paid by the applicant or from the proceeds of the sale before satisfaction of any Federal tax liens or claims of the United States.

(4) *Right of substitution of value.*—(i) *Issuance of certificate of discharge to property owner who is not the taxpayer.*—If an owner of property subject to a Federal tax lien imposed under chapter 64 of the Internal Revenue Code submits an application for a certificate of discharge pursuant to paragraph (b)(5) of this section, the appropriate official shall issue a certificate of discharge of such property after the owner either deposits with the appropriate official an amount equal to the value of the interest of the United States in the property, as determined by the appropriate official pursuant to paragraph (b)(6) of this section, or furnishes an acceptable bond in a like amount. This paragraph does not apply if the person seeking the discharge is the person whose unsatisfied liability gave rise to the Federal tax lien. Thus, if the property is owned by both the taxpayer and another person, the other person may obtain a certificate of discharge of the property under this paragraph, but the taxpayer may not.

(ii) *Refund of deposit and release of bond.*—The appropriate official may, in his discretion, determine that either the entire unsatisfied tax liability listed on the notice of Federal tax lien can be satisfied from a source other than the property sought to be discharged, or the value of the interest of the United States is less than the prior determination of such value. The appropriate official shall refund the amount deposited with interest at the overpayment rate determined under section 6621 or release the bond furnished to the extent that he makes this determination.

(iii) *Refund request.*—If a property owner desires an administrative refund of his deposit or release of the bond, the owner shall file a request in writing with the appropriate official. The request shall contain such information as the appropriate IRS Publication may require. The request must be filed within 120 days after the date the certificate of discharge is issued. A refund request made under this paragraph neither is required nor is effective to extend the period for filing an action in court under section 7426(a)(4).

(iv) *Internal Revenue Service's use of deposit if court action not filed.*—If no action is filed under section 7426(a)(4) for refund of the deposit or release of the bond within the 120-day period specified therein, the appropriate official shall, within 60 days after the expiration of the 120-day period, apply the amount deposited or collect on such bond to the extent necessary to satisfy the liability listed on the notice of Federal tax lien, and shall refund, with interest at the overpayment rate determined under section 6621, any portion of the amount deposited that is not used to satisfy the liability. If the appropriate official has not completed the application of the deposit to the unsatisfied liability before the end of the 60-day period, the deposit will be deemed to have been applied to the unsatisfied liability as of the 60th day.

(5) *Application for certificate of discharge.*—Any person desiring a certificate of discharge under this paragraph (b) shall submit an application in writing to the appropriate official. The application shall contain the information required by the appropriate IRS Publication. For purposes of this paragraph (b), any application for certificate of discharge made by a property owner who is not the taxpayer, and any amount submitted pursuant to the application, will be

treated as an application for discharge and a deposit under section 6325(b)(4) unless the owner of the property submits a statement, in writing, that the application is being submitted under another paragraph of section 6325 and not under section 6325(b)(4), and the owner in writing waives the rights afforded under paragraph (b)(4), including the right to seek judicial review.

(6) *Valuation of interest of United States.*—For purposes of paragraphs (b)(2) and (b)(4) of this section, in determining the value of the interest of the United States in the property, or any part thereof, with respect to which the certificate of discharge is to be issued, the appropriate official shall give consideration to the value of the property and the amount of all liens and encumbrances thereon having priority over the Federal tax lien. In determining the value of the property, the appropriate official may, in his discretion, give consideration to the forced sale value of the property in appropriate cases.

(c) *Estate or gift tax liability fully satisfied or provided for.*—(1) *Certificate of discharge.*—If the appropriate official determines that the tax liability for estate or gift tax has been fully satisfied, he may issue a certificate of discharge of any or all property from the lien imposed thereon. If the appropriate official determines that the tax liability for estate or gift tax has been adequately provided for, he may issue a certificate discharging particular items of property from the lien. If a lien has arisen under section 6324B (relating to special lien for additional estate tax attributable to farm, etc., valuation) and the appropriate official determines that the liability for additional estate tax has been fully secured in accordance with § 20.6324B-1(c) of this chapter, the appropriate official may issue a certificate of discharge of the real property from the section 6324B lien. The issuance of such a certificate is a matter resting within the discretion of the appropriate official, and a certificate will be issued only in case there is actual need therefor. The primary purpose of such discharge is not to evidence payment or satisfaction of the tax, but to permit the transfer of property free from the lien in case it is necessary to clear title. The tax will be considered fully satisfied only when investigation has been completed and payment of the tax, including any deficiency determined, has been made.

(2) *Application for certificate of discharge.*—An application for a certificate of discharge of property from the lien for estate or gift tax should be filed with the appropriate official responsible for the collection of the tax. It should be made in writing under penalties of perjury and should explain the circumstances that require the discharge, and should fully describe the particular items for which the discharge is desired. Where realty is involved each parcel sought to be discharged from the lien should be described on a separate page and each such description submitted in duplicate. In the case of an estate tax lien, the application should show the applicant's relationship to the estate, such as executor, heir, devisee, legatee, beneficiary, transferee, or purchaser. If the estate or gift tax return has not been filed, a statement under penalties of perjury may be required showing (i) the value of the property to be discharged, (ii) the basis for such valuation, (iii) in the case of the estate tax, the approximate value of the gross estate and the approximate value of the total real property included in the gross estate, (iv) in the case of the gift tax, the total amount of gifts made during the calendar year and the prior calendar years subsequent to the enactment of the Revenue Act of 1932 and the approximate value of all real estate subject to the gift tax lien, and (v) if the property is to be sold or otherwise transferred, the name and address of the purchaser or transferee and the consideration, if any, paid or to be paid by him.

(d) *Subordination of lien.*—(1) *By payment of the amount subordinated.*—The appropriate official may, in his discretion, issue a certificate of subordination of a lien imposed under chapter 64 of the Internal Revenue Code upon any part of the property subject to the lien if there is paid over to the appropriate official an amount equal to the amount of the lien or interest to which the certificate subordinates the lien of the United States. For this purpose, the tax lien may be subordinated to another lien or interest on a dollar-for-dollar basis. For example, if a notice of a Federal tax lien is filed and a delinquent taxpayer secures a mortgage loan on a part of the property subject to the tax lien and pays over the proceeds of the loan to the appropriate official after an application for a certificate of subordination is approved, the appropriate official will issue a certificate of subordination. This certificate will have the effect of subordinating the tax lien to the mortgage.

(2) *To facilitate tax collection.*—(i) *In general.*—The appropriate official may, in his discretion, issue a certificate of subordination of a lien imposed under chapter 64 of the Internal Revenue Code upon any part of the property subject to the lien if the appropriate official believes that the subordination of the lien will ultimately result in an increase in the amount realized by the United States from the prop-

erty subject to the lien and will facilitate the ultimate collection of the tax liability.

(ii) *Examples.*—The provisions of this subparagraph may be illustrated by the following examples:

*Example (1).* A, a farmer, needs money in order to harvest his crop. A Federal tax lien, notice of which has been filed, is outstanding with respect to A's property. B, a lending institution, is willing to make the necessary loan if the loan is secured by a first mortgage on the farm which is prior to the Federal tax lien. Upon examination, the appropriate official believes that ultimately the amount realizable from A's property will be increased and the collection of the tax liability will be facilitated by the availability of cash when the crop is harvested and sold. In this case, the appropriate official may, in his discretion, subordinate the tax lien on the farm to the mortgage securing the crop harvesting loan.

*Example (2).* C owns a commercial building which is deteriorating and in unsalable condition. Because of outstanding Federal tax liens, notices of which have been filed, C is unable to finance the repair and rehabilitation of the building. D, a contractor, is willing to do the work if his mechanic's lien on the property is superior to the Federal tax liens. Upon examination, the appropriate official believes that ultimately the amount realizable from C's property will be increased and the collection of the tax liability will be facilitated by arresting deterioration of the property and restoring it to salable condition. In this case, the appropriate official may, in his discretion, subordinate the tax lien on the building to the mechanic's lien.

*Example (3).* E, a manufacturer of electronic equipment, obtains financing from F, a lending institution, pursuant to a security agreement, with respect to which a financing statement was duly filed under the Uniform Commercial Code on June 1, 1970. On April 15, 1971, F gains actual notice or knowledge that notice of a Federal tax lien had been filed against E on March 31, 1971, and F refuses to make further advances unless its security interest is assured of priority over the Federal tax lien. Upon examination, the appropriate official believes that ultimately the amount realizable from E's property will be increased and the collection of the tax liability will be facilitated if the work in process can be completed and the equipment sold. In this case, the appropriate official may, in his discretion, subordinate the tax lien to F's security interest for the further advances required to complete the work.

*Example (4).* Suit is brought against G by H, who claims ownership of property the legal title to which is held by G. A Federal tax lien against G, notice of which has previously been filed, will be enforceable against the property if G's title is confirmed. Because section 6323(b)(8) is inapplicable, J, an attorney, is unwilling to defend the case for G unless he is granted a contractual lien on the property, superior to the Federal tax lien. Upon examination, the appropriate official believes that the successful defense of the case by G will increase the amount ultimately realizable from G's property and will facilitate collection of the tax liability. In this case, the appropriate official may, in his discretion, subordinate the tax lien to J's contractual lien on the disputed property to secure J's reasonable fees and expenses.

(3) *Subordination of section 6324B lien.*—The appropriate official may issue a certificate of subordination with respect to a lien imposed by section 6324B if the appropriate official determines that the interests of the United States will be adequately secured after such subordination. For example, *A*, a qualified heir of qualified real property, needs to borrow money for farming purposes. If the current fair market value of the real property is $150,000, the amount of the claim to which the special lien is to be subordinated is $40,000, the potential liability for additional tax (as defined in section 2032A(c)) is less than $55,000, and there are no other facts to indicate that the interest of the United States will not be adequately secured, the appropriate official may issue a certificate of subordination. The result would be the same if the loan were for bona fide purposes other than farming.

(4) *Application for certificate of subordination.*—Any person desiring a certificate of subordination under this paragraph shall submit an application therefor in writing to the appropriate official responsible for the collection of the tax. The application shall contain such information as the appropriate official may require.

(e) *Nonattachment of lien.*—If the appropriate official determines that, because of confusion of names or otherwise, any person (other than the person against whom the tax was assessed) is or may be injured by the appearance that a notice of lien filed in accordance with § 301.6323(f)-1 refers to such person, the appropriate official may issue a certificate of nonattachment. Such certificate shall state that the lien, notice of which has been filed, does not attach to the property of such person. Any person desiring a certificate of nonattachment under this paragraph shall submit an application therefor in writing to the appropriate official responsible for the collection of

the tax. The application shall contain such information as the appropriate official may require.

(f) *Effect of certificate.*—(1) *Conclusiveness.*—Except as provided in subparagraphs (2) and (3) of this paragraph, if a certificate is issued under section 6325 by the appropriate official and the certificate is filed in the same office as the notice of lien to which it relates (if the notice of lien has been filed), the certificate shall have the following effect—

(i) In the case of a certificate of release issued under paragraph (a) of this section, the certificate shall be conclusive that the tax lien referred to in the certificate is extinguished;

(ii) In the case of a certificate of discharge issued under paragraph (b) or (c) of this section, the certificate shall be conclusive that the property covered by the certificate is discharged from the tax lien;

(iii) In the case of a certificate of subordination issued under paragraph (d) of this section, the certificate shall be conclusive that the lien or interest to which the Federal tax lien is subordinated is superior to the tax lien; and

(iv) In the case of a certificate of nonattachment issued under paragraph (e), the certificate shall be conclusive that the lien of the United States does not attach to the property of the person referred to in the certificate.

(2) *Revocation of certificate of release or nonattachment.*—(i) *In general.*—If the appropriate official determines that either—

(a) A certificate of release or a certificate of nonattachment of the general tax lien imposed by section 6321 was issued erroneously or improvidently, or

(b) A certificate of release of such lien was issued in connection with a compromise agreement under section 7122 which has been breached,

and if the period of limitation on collection after assessment of the tax liability has not expired, the appropriate official may revoke the certificate and reinstate the tax lien. The provisions of this subparagraph do not apply in the case of the lien imposed by section 6324 relating to estate and gift taxes.

(ii) *Method of revocation and reinstatement.*—The revocation and reinstatement described in subdivision (i) of this subparagraph is accomplished by—

(a) Mailing notice of the revocation to the taxpayer at his last known address (see § 301.6212-2 for further guidance regarding the definition of last known address); and

(b) Filing notice of the revocation of the certificate in the same office in which the notice of lien to which it relates was filed (if the notice of lien has been filed).

(iii) *Effect of reinstatement.*—(a) *Effective date.*—A tax lien reinstated in accordance with the provisions of this subparagraph is effective on and after the date the notice of revocation is mailed to the taxpayer in accordance with the provisions of subdivision (ii)(a) of this subparagraph, but the reinstated lien is not effective before the filing of notice of revocation, in accordance with the provisions of subdivision (ii)(b) of this subparagraph, if the filing is required by reason of the fact that a notice of the lien had been filed.

(b) *Treatment of reinstated lien.*—As of the effective date of reinstatement, a reinstated lien has the same force and effect as a general tax lien imposed by section 6321 which arises upon assessment of a tax liability. The reinstated lien continues in existence until the expiration of the period of limitation on collection after assessment of the tax liability to which it relates. The reinstatement of the lien does not retroactively reinstate a previously filed notice of lien. The reinstated lien is not valid against any holder of a lien or interest described in § 301.6323(a)-1 until notice of the reinstated lien has been filed in accordance with the provisions of § 301.6323(f)-1 subsequent to or concurrent with the time the reinstated lien became effective.

(iv) *Example.*—The provisions of this subparagraph may be illustrated by the following example:

*Example.* On March 1, 1967, an assessment of an unpaid Federal tax liability is made against A. On March 1, 1968, notice of the Federal tax lien, which arose at the time of assessment, is filed. On April 1, 1968, A executes a bona fide mortgage on property belonging to him to B. On May 1, 1968, a certificate of release of the tax lien is erroneously issued and is filed by A in the same office in which the notice of lien was filed. On June 3, 1968, the lien is reinstated in accordance with the provisions of this subparagraph. On July 1, 1968, A executes a bona fide mortgage on property belonging to him to C. On August 1, 1968, a notice of the lien which was reinstated is properly filed in accordance with the provisions of § 301.6323(f)-1. The mortgages of both B and C will have priority over the rights of the United States with respect to the tax liability in question. Because a reinstated lien continues in existence only until the expiration of the period of limitation on collection after assessment of the tax liability to which the lien relates, in the absence of any extension or suspension of the period of limitation on collection after assessment, the reinstated lien will become unenforceable by reason of lapse of time after February 28, 1973.

(3) *Certificates void under certain conditions.*—Notwithstanding any other provisions of subtitle F of the Internal Revenue Code, any lien for Federal taxes attaches to any property with respect to which a certificate of discharge has been issued if the person liable for the tax reacquires the property after the certificate has been issued. Thus, if property subject to a Federal tax lien is discharged therefrom and is later reacquired by the delinquent taxpayer at a time when the lien is still in existence, the tax lien attaches to the reacquired property and is enforceable against it as in the case of after-acquired property generally.

(g) *Filing of certificates and notices.*—If a certificate or notice described in this section may not be filed in the office designated by State law in which the notice of lien imposed by section 6321 (to which the certificate or notice relates) is filed, the certificate or notice is effective if filed in the office of the clerk of the United States district court for the judicial district in which the State office where the notice of lien is filed is situated.

(h) As used in this section, the term *appropriate official* means either the official or office identified in the relevant IRS Publication or, if such official or office is not so identified, the Secretary or his delegate.

(i) *Effective/applicability date.*—This section applies to any release of lien or discharge of property that is requested after January 31, 2008. [Reg. § 301.6325-1.]

☐ [*T.D. 6119, 12-31-54. Amended by T.D. 6425, 11-10-59; T.D. 6498, 10-24-60; T.D. 6700, 1-6-64; T.D. 7429, 8-20-76; T.D. 7847, 11-9-82; T.D. 8939, 1-11-2001 and T.D. 9378, 1-30-2008 (corrected 2-21-2008).*]

### [Reg. § 301.6326-1]

**§ 301.6326-1. Administrative appeal of the erroneous filing of notice of federal tax lien.**—(a) *In general.*—Any person may appeal to the district director of the district in which a notice of federal tax lien was filed on the property or rights to property of such person for a release of lien alleging an error in the filing of notice of lien. Such appeal may be used only for the purpose of correcting the erroneous filing of a notice of lien, not to challenge the underlying deficiency that led to the impositon of a lien. If the district director determines that the Internal Revenue Service has erroneously filed the notice of any federal tax lien, the district director shall expeditiously, and, to the extent practicable, within 14 days after such determination, issue a certificate of release of lien. The certificate of release of such lien shall include a statement that the filing of notice of lien was erroneous.

(b) *Appeal alleging an error in the filing of notice of lien.*—For purposes of paragraph (a) of this section, an appeal of the filing of notice of federal tax lien must be based on any one of the following allegations:

(1) The tax liability that gave rise to the lien, plus any interest and additions to tax associated with said liability, was satisfied prior to the filing of notice of lien;

(2) The tax liability that gave rise to the lien was assessed in violation of the deficiency procedures set forth in section 6213 of the Internal Revenue Code;

(3) The tax liability that gave rise to the lien was assessed in violation of Title 11 of the United States Code (the Bankrupty Code); or

(4) The statutory period for collection of the tax liability that gave rise to the lien expired prior to the filing of notice of federal tax lien.

(c) *Notice of federal tax lien that lists multiple liabilities.*—When a notice of federal tax lien lists multiple liabilities, a person may appeal the filing of notice of lien with respect to one or more of the liabilities listed in the notice, if the notice was erroneously filed with respect to such liabilities. If a notice of federal tax lien was erroneously filed with respect to one or more liabilities listed in the notice, the district director shall issue a certificate of release with respect to such liabilities. For example, if a notice of federal tax lien lists tax liabilities for years 1980, 1981 and 1982, and the entire liabilities for 1981 and 1982 were paid prior to the filing of notice of lien, the taxpayer may appeal the filing of notice of lien with respect to the 1981 and 1982 liabilities and the district director must issue a certificate of release with respect to the 1981 and 1982 liabilities.

(d) *Procedures for appeal.*—(1) *Manner.*—An appeal of the filing of notice of federal tax lien shall be made in writing to the district director (marked for the attention of the Chief, Special Procedures Function) of the district in which the notice of federal tax lien was filed.

(2) *Form.*—The appeal shall include the following information and documents:

(i) Name, current address, and taxpayer identification number of the person appealing the filing of notice of federal tax lien;

(ii) A copy of the notice of federal tax lien affecting the property, if available; and

(iii) The grounds upon which the filing of notice of federal tax lien is being appealed.

(A) If the ground upon which the filing of notice is being appealed is that the tax liability in question was satisfied prior to the filing, proof of full payment as defined in paragraph (e) of this section must be provided.

(B) If the ground upon which the filing of notice is being appealed is that the tax liability that gave rise to lien was assessed in violation of the deficiency procedures set forth in section 6213 of the Internal Revenue Code, the appealing party must explain how the assessment was erroneous.

(C) If the ground upon which the filing of notice is being appealed is that the tax liability that gave rise to the lien was assessed in violation of Title 11 of the United States Code (the Bankruptcy Code), the appealing party must provide the following:

(1) The identity of the court and the district in which the bankruptcy petition was filed; and

(2) The docket number and the date of filing of the bankruptcy petition.

(3) *Time.*—An administrative appeal of the erroneous filing of notice of federal tax lien shall be made within 1 year after the taxpayer becomes aware of the erroneously filed tax lien.

(e) *Proof of full payment.*—As used in paragraph (d)(2)(iii) of this section, the term "proof of full payment" means:

(1) An internal revenue cashier's receipt reflecting full payment of the tax liability in question prior to the date the federal tax lien at issue was filed;

(2) A canceled check to the Internal Revenue Service in an amount which was sufficient to satisfy the tax liability for which release is being sought; or

(3) Any other manner of proof acceptable to the district director.

(f) *Exclusive remedy.*—The appeal established by section 6326 of the Internal Revenue Code and by this section shall be the exclusive administrative remedy with respect to the erroneous filing of a notice of federal tax lien.

(g) *Effective date.*—The provisions of this section are effective July 7, 1989. [Reg. § 301.6326-1.]

☐ [*T.D. 8250, 5-5-89. Amended by T.D. 8347, 4-30-91.*]

# SEIZURE OF PROPERTY FOR COLLECTION OF TAXES

### [Reg. § 301.6330-1]

**§ 301.6330-1. Notice and opportunity for hearing prior to levy.**—(a) *Notification.*—(1) *In general.*—Except as specified in paragraph (a)(2) of this section, the Commissioner, or his or her delegate(the Commissioner), will prescribe procedures to provide persons upon whose property or rights to property the IRS intends to levy (hereinafter referred to as the taxpayer) on or after January 19, 1999, notice of that intention and to give them the right to, and the opportunity for, a pre-levy Collection Due Process (CDP) hearing with the Internal Revenue Service (IRS) Office of Appeals (Appeals). This pre-levy Collection Due Process Hearing Notice (CDP Notice) must be given in person, left at the dwelling or usual place of business of the taxpayer, or sent by certified or registered mail, return receipt re-

quested, to the taxpayer's last known address. For further guidance regarding the definition of last known address, see § 301.6212-2.

(2) *Exceptions.*—(i) *state tax refunds.*—Section 6330(f) does not require the Commissioner to provide the taxpayer with notification of the taxpayer's right to a CDP hearing prior to issuing a levy to collect state tax refunds owing to the taxpayer. However, the Commissioner will prescribe procedures to give the taxpayer notice of the right to, and the opportunity for, a CDP hearing with Appeals with respect to any such levy issued on or after January 19, 1999, within a reasonable time after the levy has occurred. The notification required to be given following a levy on a state tax refund is referred to as a post-levy CDP Notice.

(ii) *Jeopardy.*—Section 6330(f) does not require the Commissioner to provide the taxpayer with notification of the taxpayer's right to a CDP hearing prior to a levy when there has been a determination that collection of the tax is in jeopardy. However, the Commissioner will prescribe procedures to provide notice of the right to, and the opportunity for, a CDP hearing with Appeals to the taxpayer with respect to any such levy issued on or after January 19, 1999, within a reasonable time after the levy has occurred. The notification required to be given following a jeopardy levy also is referred to as post-levy CDP Notice.

(3) *Questions and answers.*—The questions and answers illustrate the provisions of this paragraph (a) as follows:

Q-A1. Who is the person to be notified under section 6330?

A-A1. Under section 6330(a)(1), a pre-levy or post-levy CDP Notice is required to be given only to the person whose property or right to property is intended to be levied upon, or, in the case of a levy made on a state tax refund or a jeopardy levy, the person whose property or right to property was levied upon. The person described in section 6330(a)(1) is the same person described in section 6331(a)— i.e., the person liable to pay the tax due after notice and demand who refuses or neglects to pay (referred to here as the taxpayer). A pre-levy or post-levy CDP Notice therefore will be given only to the taxpayer.

Q-A2. Will the IRS give notification to a known nominee of, a person holding property of, or a person who holds property subject to a lien with respect to, the taxpayer of the IRS' intention to issue a levy?

A-A2. No. Such a person is not the person described in section 6331(a)(1), but such persons have other remedies. See A-B5 of paragraph (b)(2) of this section.

Q-A3. Will the IRS give notification for each tax and tax period it intends to include or has included in a levy issued on or after January 19, 1999?

A-A3. Yes. The notification of an intent to levy or of the issuance of a jeopardy or state tax refund levy will specify each tax and tax period that will be or was included in the levy.

Q-A4. Will the IRS give notification to a taxpayer with respect to levies for a tax and tax period issued on or after January 19, 1999, even though the IRS had issued a levy prior to January 19, 1999, with respect to the same tax and tax period?

A-A4. Yes. The IRS will provide appropriate pre-levy or post-levy notification to a taxpayer regarding the first levy it intends to issue or has issued on or after January 19, 1999, with respect to a tax and tax period, even though it had issued a levy with respect to that same tax and tax period prior to January 19, 1999.

Q-A5. When will the IRS provide this notice?

A-A5. Beginning on January 19, 1999, the IRS will give a pre-levy CDP Notice to the taxpayer of the IRS' intent to levy on property or rights to property, other than in state tax refund and jeopardy levy situations, at least 30 days prior to the first such levy with respect to a tax and tax period. If the taxpayer has not received a pre-levy CDP Notice and the IRS levies on a state tax refund or issues a jeopardy levy on or after January 19, 1999, the IRS will provide a post-levy CDP Notice to the taxpayer within a reasonable time after that levy.

Q-A6. What must a pre-levy CDP Notice include?

A-A6. Pursuant to section 6330(a)(3), a pre-levy CDP Notice must include, in simple and nontechnical terms:

(i) The amount of the unpaid tax.

(ii) Notification of the right to request a CDP hearing.

(iii) A statement that the IRS intends to levy.

(iv) The taxpayer's rights with respect to the levy action, including a brief statement that sets forth—

(A) The statutory provisions relating to the levy and sale of property;

(B) The procedures applicable to the levy and sale of property;

(C) The administrative appeals available to the taxpayer with respect to the levy and sale and the procedures relating to those appeals;

(D) The alternatives available to taxpayers that could prevent levy on the property (including installment agreements); and

(E) The statutory provisions and the procedures relating to the redemption of property and the release of liens on property.

Q-A7. What must a post-levy CDP Notice include?

A-A7. A post-levy CDP Notice must include, in simple and nontechnical terms:

(i) The amount of the unpaid tax.

(ii) Notification of the right to request a CDP hearing.

(iii) A statement that the IRS has levied upon the taxpayer's state tax refund or has made a jeopardy levy on property or rights to property of the taxpayer, as appropriate.

(iv) The taxpayer's rights with respect to the levy action, including a brief statement that sets forth—

(A) The statutory provisions relating to the levy and sale of property;

(B) The procedures applicable to the levy and sale of property;

(C) The administrative appeals available to the taxpayer with respect to the levy and sale and the procedures relating to those appeals;

(D) The alternatives available to taxpayers that could prevent any further levies on the taxpayer's property (including installment agreements); and

(E) The statutory provisions and the procedures relating to the redemption of property and the release of liens on property.

Q-A8. How will this pre-levy or post-levy notification under section 6330 be accomplished?

A-A8. The IRS will notify the taxpayer by means of a pre-levy CDP Notice or a post-levy CDP Notice, as appropriate. The additional information the IRS is required to provide, together with Form 12153, Request for a Collection Due Process Hearing, will be included with the CDP Notice.

(i) The IRS may effect delivery of a pre-levy CDP Notice (and accompanying materials) in one of three ways:

(A) By delivering the notice personally to the taxpayer.

(B) By leaving the notice at the taxpayer's dwelling or usual place of business.

(C) By mailing the notice to the taxpayer at the taxpayer's last known address by certified or registered mail, return receipt requested.

(ii) The IRS may effect delivery of a post-levy CDP Notice (and accompanying materials) in one of three ways:

(A) By delivering the notice personally to the taxpayer.

(B) By leaving the notice at the taxpayer's dwelling or usual place of business.

(C) By mailing the notice to the taxpayer at the taxpayer's last known address by certified or registered mail.

Q-A9. What are the consequences if the taxpayer does not receive or accept the notification which was properly left at the taxpayer's dwelling or usual place of business, or properly sent by certified or registered mail, return receipt requested, to the taxpayer's last known address?

A-A9. Notification properly sent to the taxpayer's last known address or left at the taxpayer's dwelling or usual place of business is sufficient to start the 30-day period within which the taxpayer may request a CDP hearing. See paragraph (c) of this section for when a request for a CDP hearing must be filed. Actual receipt is not a prerequisite to the validity of the CDP Notice.

Q-A10. What if the taxpayer does not receive the CDP Notice because the IRS did not send that notice by certified or registered mail to the taxpayer's last known address, or failed to leave it at the dwelling or usual place of business of the taxpayer, and the taxpayer fails to request a CDP hearing with Appeals within the 30-day period commencing the day after the date of the CDP Notice?

A-A10. When the IRS determines that it failed properly to provide a taxpayer with a CDP Notice, it will promptly provide the taxpayer with a substitute CDP Notice and provide the taxpayer with an opportunity to request a CDP hearing. Substitute CDP Notices are discussed in Q&A-B3 of paragraph (b) (2) and Q&A-C8 of paragraph (c) (2) of this section.

(4) *Examples.*—The following examples illustrate the principles of this paragraph (a):

*Example 1.* Prior to January 19, 1999, the IRS issues a continuous levy on a taxpayer's wages and a levy on that taxpayer's fixed right to future payments. The IRS is not required to release either levy on or after January 19, 1999, until the requirements of section 6343(a)(1) are met. The taxpayer is not entitled to a CDP Notice or a CDP hearing under section 6330 with respect to either levy because both levy actions were initiated prior to January 19, 1999.

*Example 2.* The same facts as in *Example 1*, except the IRS intends to levy upon a taxpayer's bank account on or after January 19, 1999. The taxpayer is entitled to a pre-levy CDP Notice with respect to this proposed new levy.

(b) *Entitlement to a CDP hearing.*—(1) *In general.*—A taxpayer is entitled to one CDP hearing with respect to the unpaid tax and tax periods covered by the pre-levy or post-levy CDP Notice provided to the taxpayer. The taxpayer must request the CDP hearing within the 30-day period commencing on the day after the date of the CDP Notice.

(2) *Questions and answers.*—The questions and answers illustrate the provisions of this paragraph (b) as follows:

Q-B1. Is the taxpayer entitled to a CDP hearing where a levy for state tax refunds is issued on or after January 19, 1999, even though the IRS had previously issued other levies prior to January 19, 1999, seeking to collect the taxes owed for the same period?

A-B1. Yes. The taxpayer is entitled to a CDP hearing under section 6330 for the type of tax and tax periods set forth in the state tax refund levy issued on or after January 19, 1999.

Q-B2. Is the taxpayer entitled to a CDP hearing when the IRS, more than 30 days after issuance of a CDP Notice under section 6330 with respect to the unpaid tax and periods, provides subsequent notice to that taxpayer that the IRS intends to levy on property or rights to property of the taxpayer for the same tax and tax periods shown on the CDP Notice?

A-B2. No. Under section 6330, only the first pre-levy or post-levy CDP Notice with respect to the unpaid tax and tax periods entitles the taxpayer to request a CDP hearing. If the taxpayer does not timely request a CDP hearing with Appeals following that first notification, the taxpayer foregoes the right to a CDP hearing with Appeals and judicial review of Appeals' determination with respect to levies relating to that tax and tax period. The IRS generally provides additional notices or reminders (reminder notifications) to the taxpayer of its intent to levy when no collection action has occurred within 180 days of a proposed levy. Under such circumstances, a taxpayer may request an equivalent hearing as described in paragraph (i) of this section.

Q-B3. When the IRS provides a taxpayer with a substitute CDP Notice and the taxpayer timely requests a CDP hearing, is the taxpayer entitled to a CDP Hearing before Appeals?

A-B3. Yes. Unless the taxpayer provides the IRS a written withdrawal of the request that Appeals conduct a CDP hearing, the taxpayer is entitled to a CDP hearing before Appeals. Following the hearing, Appeals will issue a Notice of Determination, and the taxpayer is entitled to seek judicial review of that Notice of Determination.

Q-B4. If the IRS sends a second CDP Notice under section 6330 (other than a substitute CDP Notice) for a tax period and with respect to an unpaid tax for which a CDP Notice under section 6330 was previously sent, is the taxpayer entitled to a section 6330 CDP hearing based on the second CDP Notice?

A-B4. No. The taxpayer is entitled to only one CDP hearing under section 6330 with respect to the tax and tax period. The taxpayer must request the CDP hearing within 30 days of the date of the first CDP Notice provided for that tax and tax period.

Q-B5. Will the IRS give pre-levy or post-levy CDP Notices to known nominees of, persons holding property of, or persons holding property subject to a lien with respect to the taxpayer?

A-B5. No. Such person is not the person described in section 6331(a) and is, therefore, not entitled to a CDP hearing or an equivalent hearing (as discussed in paragraph (i) of this section). Such person, however, may seek reconsideration by the IRS office collecting the tax, assistance from the National Taxpayer Advocate, or an administrative hearing before Appeals under its Collection Appeals Program. However, any such administrative hearing would not be a CDP hearing under section 6330 and any determination or decision resulting from the hearing would not be subject to judicial review.

(3) *Example.*—The following example illustrates the principles of this paragraph (b):

*Example.* Federal income tax liability for 1997 is assessed against individual D. D buys an asset and puts it in individual E's name. The IRS gives D a CDP Notice of intent to levy with respect to the 1997 tax liability. The IRS will not notify E of its intent to levy. The IRS is not required to notify E of its intent to levy although E holds property of individual D. E is not the taxpayer.

(c) *Requesting a CDP hearing.*—(1) *In general.*—When a taxpayer is entitled to a CDP hearing under section 6330, the CDP hearing must be requested during the 30-day period that commences the day after the date of the CDP Notice.

(2) *Questions and answers.*—The questions and answers illustrate the provisions of this paragraph (c) as follows:

Q-C1. What must a taxpayer do to obtain a CDP hearing?

A-C1. (i) The taxpayer must make a request in writing for a CDP hearing. The request for a CDP hearing shall include the information and signature specified in A-C1(ii) of this paragraph (c)(2). See A-D7 and A-D8 of paragraph (d)(2).

(ii) The written request for a CDP hearing must be dated and must include the following:

(A) The taxpayer's name, address, daytime telephone number (if any), and taxpayer identification number (e.g., SSN, ITIN or EIN).

(B) The type of tax involved.

(C) The tax period at issue.

(D) A statement that the taxpayer requests a hearing with Appeals concerning the proposed levy.

(E) The reason or reasons why the taxpayer disagrees with the proposed levy.

(F) The signature of the taxpayer or the taxpayer's authorized representative.

(iii) If the IRS receives a timely written request for CDP hearing that does not satisfy the requirements set forth in A-C1(ii) of this paragraph (c)(2), the IRS will make a reasonable attempt to contact the taxpayer and request that the taxpayer comply with the unsatisfied requirements. The taxpayer must perfect any timely written request for a CDP hearing that does not satisfy the requirements set forth in A-C1(ii) of this paragraph (c)(2) within a reasonable period of time after a request from the IRS.

(iv) Taxpayers are encouraged to use Form 12153, "Request for a Collection Due Process Hearing," in requesting a CDP hearing so that the request can be readily identified and forwarded to Appeals. Taxpayers may obtain a copy of Form 12153 by contacting the IRS office that issued the CDP Notice, by downloading a copy from the IRS Internet site, *www.irs.gov/pub/irs-pdf/f12153.pdf*, or by calling, toll-free, 1-800-829-3676.

(v) The taxpayer must affirm any timely written request for a CDP hearing which is signed or alleged to have been signed on the taxpayer's behalf by the taxpayer's spouse or other unauthorized representative by filing, within a reasonable period of time after a request from the IRS, a signed, written affirmation that the request was originally submitted on the taxpayer's behalf. If the affirmation is filed within a reasonable period of time after a request, the timely CDP hearing request will be considered timely with respect to the non-signing taxpayer. If the affirmation is not filed within a reasonable period of time after a request, the CDP hearing request will be denied with respect to the non-signing taxpayer.

Q-C2. Must the request for the CDP hearing be in writing?

A-C2. Yes. There are several reasons why the request for a CDP hearing must be in writing. The filing of a timely request for a CDP hearing is the first step in what may result in a court proceeding. A written request will provide proof that the CDP hearing was requested and thus permit the court to verify that it has jurisdiction over any subsequent appeal of the Notice of Determination issued by Appeals. In addition, the receipt of the written request will establish the date on which the periods of limitation under section 6502 (relating to collection after assessment), section 6531 (relating to criminal prosecutions), and section 6532 (relating to suits) are suspended as a result of the CDP hearing and any judicial appeal. Moreover, because the IRS anticipates that taxpayers will contact the IRS office that issued the CDP Notice for further information or assistance in filling out Form 12153, or to attempt to resolve their liabilities prior to going through the CDP hearing process, the requirement of a written request should help prevent any misunderstanding as to whether a CDP hearing has been requested. If the information requested on Form 12153 is furnished by the taxpayer, the written request also will help to establish the issues for which the taxpayer seeks a determination by Appeals.

Q-C3. When must a taxpayer request a CDP hearing with respect to a CDP Notice issued under section 6330?

A-C3. A taxpayer must submit a written request for a CDP hearing within the 30-day period commencing the day after the date of the CDP Notice issued under section 6330. This period is slightly different from the period for submitting a written request for a CDP hearing with respect to a CDP Notice issued under section 6320. For a CDP Notice issued under section 6320, a taxpayer must submit a written request for a CDP hearing within the 30-day period commencing the day after the end of the five business day period following the filing of the notice of federal tax lien (NFTL).

Q-C4. How will the timeliness of a taxpayer's written request for a CDP hearing be determined?

A-C4. The rules and regulations under section 7502 and section 7503 will apply to determine the timeliness of the taxpayer's request for a CDP hearing, if properly transmitted and addressed as provided in A-C6 of this paragraph (c)(2).

Q-C5. Is the 30-day period within which a taxpayer must make a request for a CDP hearing extended because the taxpayer resides outside the United States?

A-C5. No. Section 6330 does not make provision for such a circumstance. Accordingly, all taxpayers who want a CDP hearing under section 6330 must request such a hearing within the 30-day period commencing the day after the date of the CDP Notice.

Q-C6. Where must the written request for a CDP hearing be sent?

A-C6. The written request for a CDP hearing must be sent, or hand delivered (if permitted), to the IRS office and address as directed on the CDP Notice. If the address of that office does not appear on the CDP Notice, the taxpayer should obtain the address of the office to which the written request should be sent or hand delivered by calling, toll-free, 1-800-829-1040 and providing the taxpayer's identification number (e.g., SSN, ITIN or EIN).

**Reg. §301.6330-1(b)(3)**

Q-C7. What will happen if the taxpayer does not request a CDP hearing in writing within the 30-day period commencing on the day after the date of the CDP Notice issued under section 6330?

A-C7. If the taxpayer does not request a CDP hearing in writing within the 30-day period that commences on the day after the date of the CDP Notice, the taxpayer foregoes the right to a CDP hearing under section 6330 with respect to the unpaid tax and tax periods shown on the CDP Notice. A written request submitted within the 30-day period that does not satisfy the requirements set forth in A-C1(ii)(A), (B), (C), (D) or (F) of this paragraph (c)(2) is considered timely if the request is perfected within a reasonable period of time pursuant to A-C1(iii) of this paragraph (c)(2). If the request for CDP hearing is untimely, either because the request was not submitted within the 30-day period or not perfected within the reasonable period provided, the taxpayer will be notified of the untimeliness of the request and offered an equivalent hearing. In such cases, the taxpayer may obtain an equivalent hearing without submitting an additional request. See paragraph (i) of this section.

Q-C8. When must a taxpayer request a CDP hearing with respect to a substitute CDP Notice?

A-C8. A CDP hearing with respect to a substitute CDP Notice must be requested in writing by the taxpayer prior to the end of the 30-day period commencing the day after the date of the substitute CDP Notice.

Q-C9. Can taxpayers attempt to resolve the matter of the proposed levy with an officer or employee of the IRS office collecting the tax liability stated on the CDP Notice either before or after requesting a CDP hearing?

A-C9. Yes. Taxpayers are encouraged to discuss their concerns with the IRS office collecting the tax, either before or after they request a CDP hearing. If such a discussion occurs before a request is made for a CDP hearing, the matter may be resolved without the need for Appeals consideration. However, these discussions do not suspend the running of the 30-day period within which the taxpayer is required to request a CDP hearing, nor do they extend that 30-day period. If discussions occur after the request for a CDP hearing is filed and the taxpayer resolves the matter with the IRS office collecting the tax, the taxpayer may withdraw in writing the request that a CDP hearing be conducted by Appeals. The taxpayer can also waive in writing some or all of the requirements regarding the contents of the Notice of Determination.

(3) *Examples.*—The following examples illustrate the principles of this paragraph (c):

*Example 1.* The IRS mails a CDP Notice of intent to levy to individual A's last known address on June 24, 1999. Individual A has until July 26, 1999, a Monday, to request a CDP hearing. The 30-day period within which individual A may request a CDP hearing begins on June 25, 1999. Because the 30-day period expires on July 24, 1999, a Saturday, individual A's written request for a CDP hearing will be considered timely if it is properly transmitted and addressed to the IRS in accordance with section 7502 and the regulations thereunder no later than July 26, 1999.

*Example 2.* Same facts as in *Example 1*, except that individual A is on vacation, outside the United States, or otherwise does not receive or read the CDP Notice until July 19, 1999. As in *Example 1*, individual A has until July 26, 1999, to request a CDP hearing. If individual A does not request a CDP hearing, individual A may request an equivalent hearing as to the levy at a later time. The taxpayer should make a request for an equivalent hearing at the earliest possible time.

*Example 3.* Same facts as in *Example 2*, except that individual A does not receive or read the CDP Notice until after July 26, 1999, and does not request a hearing by July 26, 1999. Individual A is not entitled to a CDP hearing. Individual A may request an equivalent hearing as to the levy at a later time. The taxpayer should make a request for an equivalent hearing at the earliest possible time.

*Example 4.* Same facts as in *Example 1*, except the IRS determines that the CDP Notice mailed on June 24, 1999, was not mailed to individual A's last known address. As soon as practicable after making this determination, the IRS will mail a substitute CDP Notice to individual A at individual A's last known address, hand deliver the substitute CDP Notice to individual A, or leave the substitute CDP Notice at individual A's dwelling or usual place of business. Individual A will have 30 days commencing on the day after the date of the substitute CDP Notice within which to request a CDP hearing.

(d) *Conduct of CDP hearing.*—(1) *In general.*—If a taxpayer requests a CDP hearing under section 6330(a)(3)(B) (and does not withdraw that request), the CDP hearing will be held with Appeals. The taxpayer is entitled to only one CDP hearing under section 6330 with respect to the unpaid tax and tax periods shown on the CDP Notice. To the extent practicable, the CDP hearing requested under section 6330 will be held in conjunction with any CDP hearing the taxpayer requests under section 6320. A CDP hearing will be conducted by an employee or officer of Appeals who, prior to the first CDP hearing under section 6320 or section 6330, has had no involvement with respect to the tax for the tax periods to be covered by the hearing, unless the taxpayer waives this requirement.

(2) *Questions and answers.*—The questions and answers illustrate the provisions of this paragraph (d) as follows:

Q-D1. Under what circumstances can a taxpayer receive more than one pre-levy CDP hearing under section 6330 with respect to a tax period?

A-D1. The taxpayer may receive more than one CDP pre-levy hearing under section 6330 with respect to a tax period where the tax involved is a different type of tax (for example, an employment tax liability, where the original CDP hearing for the tax period involved an income tax liability), or where the same type of tax for the same period is involved, but where the amount of the unpaid tax has changed as a result of an additional assessment of tax (not including interest or penalties) for that period or an additional accuracy-related or filing-delinquency penalty has been assessed. The taxpayer is not entitled to another CDP hearing under section 6330 if the additional assessment represents accruals of interest, accruals of penalties, or both.

Q-D2. Will a CDP hearing with respect to one tax period be combined with a CDP hearing with respect to another tax period?

A-D2. To the extent practicable, a CDP hearing with respect to one tax period shown on a CDP Notice will be combined with any and all other CDP hearings which the taxpayer has requested.

Q-D3. Will a CDP hearing under section 6330 be combined with a CDP hearing under section 6320?

A-D3. To the extent it is practicable, a CDP hearing under section 6330 will be held in conjunction with a CDP hearing under section 6320.

Q-D4. What is considered to be prior involvement by an employee or officer of Appeals with respect to the tax and tax period or periods involved in the hearing?

A-D4. Prior involvement by an Appeals officer or employee includes participation or involvement in a matter (other than a CDP hearing held under either section 6320 or section 6330) that the taxpayer may have had with respect to the tax and tax period shown on the CDP Notice. Prior involvement exists only when the taxpayer, the tax and the tax period at issue in the CDP hearing also were at issue in the prior non-CDP matter, and the Appeals officer or employee actually participated in the prior matter.

Q-D5. How can a taxpayer waive the requirement that the officer or employee of Appeals have no prior involvement with respect to the tax and tax period or periods involved in the CDP hearing?

A-D5. The taxpayer must sign a written waiver.

Q-D6. How are CDP hearings conducted?

A-D6. The formal hearing procedures required under the Administrative Procedure Act, 5 U.S.C. 551 *et seq.*, do not apply to CDP hearings. CDP hearings are much like Collection Appeal Program (CAP) hearings in that they are informal in nature and do not require the Appeals officer or employee and the taxpayer, or the taxpayer's representative, to hold a face-to-face meeting. A CDP hearing may, but is not required to, consist of a face-to-face meeting, one or more written or oral communications between an Appeals officer or employee and the taxpayer or the taxpayer's representative, or some combination thereof. A transcript or recording of any face-to-face meeting or conversation between an Appeals officer or employee and the taxpayer or the taxpayer's representative is not required. The taxpayer or the taxpayer's representative does not have the right to subpoena and examine witnesses at a CDP hearing.

Q-D7. If a taxpayer wants a face-to-face CDP hearing, where will it be held?

A-D7. Except as provided in A-D8 of this paragraph (d)(2), a taxpayer who presents in the CDP hearing request relevant, non-frivolous reasons for disagreement with the proposed levy will ordinarily be offered an opportunity for a face-to-face conference at the Appeals office closest to taxpayer's residence. A business taxpayer will ordinarily be offered an opportunity for a face-to-face conference at the Appeals office closest to the taxpayer's principal place of business. If that is not satisfactory to the taxpayer, the taxpayer will be given an opportunity for a hearing by telephone or by correspondence. In all cases, the Appeals officer or employee will review the case file, as described in A-F4 of paragraph (f)(2). If no face-to-face or telephonic conference is held, or other oral communication takes place, review of the documents in the case file, as described in A-F4 of paragraph (f)(2), will constitute the CDP hearing for purposes of section 6330(b).

Q-D8. In what circumstances will a face-to-face CDP conference not be granted?

A-D8. A taxpayer is not entitled to a face-to-face CDP conference at a location other than as provided in A-D7 of this paragraph (d)(2) and this A-D8. If all Appeals officers or employees at the location provided for in A-D7 of this paragraph (d)(2) have had prior involvement with the taxpayer as provided in A-D4 of this paragraph (d)(2), the taxpayer will not be offered a face-to-face conference at that location, unless the taxpayer elects to waive the requirement of section 6330(b)(3). The taxpayer will be offered a face-to-face conference at another Appeals office if Appeals would have offered the taxpayer a face-to-face conference at the location provided in A-D7 of this paragraph (d)(2), but for the disqualification of all Appeals officers or employees at that location. A face-to-face CDP conference concerning a taxpayer's underlying liability will not be granted if the request for a hearing or other taxpayer communication indicates that the taxpayer wishes only to raise irrelevant or frivolous issues concerning that liability. A face-to-face CDP conference concerning a collection alternative, such as an installment agreement or an offer to compromise liability, will not be granted unless other taxpayers would be eligible for the alternative in similar circumstances. For example, because the IRS does not consider offers to compromise from taxpayers who have not filed required returns or have not made certain required deposits of tax, as set forth in Form 656, "Offer in Compromise," no face-to-face conference will be granted to a taxpayer who wishes to make an offer to compromise but has not fulfilled those obligations. Appeals in its discretion, however, may grant a face-to-face conference if Appeals determines that a face-to-face conference is appropriate to explain to the taxpayer the requirements for becoming eligible for a collection alternative. In all cases, a taxpayer will be given an opportunity to demonstrate eligibility for a collection alternative and to become eligible for a collection alternative, in order to obtain a face-to-face conference. For purposes of determining whether a face-to-face conference will be granted, the determination of a taxpayer's eligibility for a collection alternative is made without regard to the taxpayer's ability to pay the unpaid tax. A face-to-face conference need not be granted if the taxpayer does not provide the required information set forth in A-C1(ii)(E) of paragraph (c)(2). See also A-C1(iii) of paragraph (c)(2).

(3) *Examples.*—The following examples illustrate the principles of this paragraph (d):

*Example 1.* Individual A timely requests a CDP hearing concerning a proposed levy for the 1998 income tax liability assessed against individual A. Appeals employee B previously conducted a CDP hearing regarding a NFTL filed with respect to individual A's 1998 income tax liability. Because employee B's only prior involvement with individual A's 1998 income tax liability was in connection with a section 6320 CDP hearing, employee B may conduct the CDP hearing under section 6330 involving the proposed levy for the 1998 income tax liability.

*Example 2.* Individual C timely requests a CDP hearing concerning a proposed levy for the 1998 income tax liability assessed against individual C. Appeals employee D previously conducted a Collection Appeals Program (CAP) hearing regarding a NFTL filed with respect to individual C's 1998 income tax liability. Because employee D's prior involvement with individual C's 1998 income tax liability was in connection with a non-CDP hearing, employee D may not conduct the CDP hearing under section 6330 unless individual C waives the requirement that the hearing will be conducted by an Appeals officer or employee who has had no prior involvement with respect to individual C's 1998 income tax liability.

*Example 3.* Same facts as in *Example 2*, except that the prior CAP hearing only involved individual C's 1997 income tax liability and employment tax liabilities for 1998 reported on Form 941, "Employer's Quarterly Federal Tax Return." Employee D would not be considered to have prior involvement because the prior CAP hearing in which she participated did not involve individual C's 1998 income tax liability.

*Example 4.* Appeals employee F is assigned to a CDP hearing concerning a proposed levy for a trust fund recovery penalty (TFRP) assessed pursuant to section 6672 against individual E. Appeals employee F participated in a prior CAP hearing involving individual E's 1999 income tax liability, and participated in a CAP hearing involving the employment taxes of business entity X, which incurred the employment tax liability to which the TFRP assessed against individual E relates. Appeals employee F would not be considered to have prior involvement because the prior CAP hearings in which he participated did not directly involve the TFRP assessed against individual E.

*Example 5.* Appeals employee G is assigned to a CDP hearing concerning a proposed levy for a TFRP assessed pursuant to section 6672 against individual H. In preparing for the CDP hearing, Appeals employee G reviews the Appeals case file concerning the prior CAP hearing involving the TFRP assessed pursuant to section 6672 against individual H. Appeals employee G is not deemed to have participated in the previous CAP hearing involving the TFRP assessed against individual H by such review.

(e) *Matters considered at CDP hearing.*—(1) *In general.*—Appeals will determine the timeliness of any request for a CDP hearing that is made by a taxpayer. Appeals has the authority to determine the validity, sufficiency, and timeliness of any CDP Notice given by the IRS and of any request for a CDP hearing that is made by a taxpayer. Prior to issuance of a determination, Appeals is required to obtain verification from the IRS office collecting the tax that the requirements of any applicable law or administrative procedure with respect to the proposed levy have been met. The taxpayer may raise any relevant issue relating to the unpaid tax at the hearing, including appropriate spousal defenses, challenges to the appropriateness of the proposed levy, and offers of collection alternatives. The taxpayer also may raise challenges to the existence or amount of the underlying liability, including a liability reported on a self-filed return, for any tax period specified on the CDP Notice if the taxpayer did not receive a statutory notice of deficiency for that tax liability or did not otherwise have an opportunity to dispute the tax liability. Finally, the taxpayer may not raise an issue that was raised and considered at a previous CDP hearing under section 6320 or in any other previous administrative or judicial proceeding if the taxpayer participated meaningfully in such hearing or proceeding. Taxpayers will be expected to provide all relevant information requested by Appeals, including financial statements, for its consideration of the facts and issues involved in the hearing.

(2) *Spousal defenses.*—A taxpayer may raise any appropriate spousal defenses at a CDP hearing unless the Commissioner has already made a final determination as to spousal defenses in a statutory notice of deficiency or final determination letter. To claim a spousal defense under section 66 or section 6015, the taxpayer must do so in writing according to rules prescribed by the Commissioner or the Secretary. Spousal defenses raised under sections 66 and 6015 in a CDP hearing are governed in all respects by the provisions of sections 66 and section 6015 and the regulations and procedures thereunder.

(3) *Questions and answers.*—The questions and answers illustrate the provisions of this paragraph (e) as follows:

Q-E1. What factors will Appeals consider in making its determination?

A-E1. Appeals will consider the following matters in making its determination:

(i) Whether the IRS met the requirements of any applicable law or administrative procedure.

(ii) Any issues appropriately raised by the taxpayer relating to the unpaid tax.

(iii) Any appropriate spousal defenses raised by the taxpayer.

(iv) Any challenges made by the taxpayer to the appropriateness of the proposed collection action.

(v) Any offers by the taxpayer for collection alternatives.

(vi) Whether the proposed collection action balances the need for the efficient collection of taxes and the legitimate concern of the taxpayer that any collection action be no more intrusive than necessary.

Q-E2. When is a taxpayer entitled to challenge the existence or amount of the tax liability specified in the CDP Notice?

A-E2. A taxpayer is entitled to challenge the existence or amount of the underlying liability for any tax period specified on the CDP Notice if the taxpayer did not receive a statutory notice of deficiency for such liability or did not otherwise have an opportunity to dispute such liability. Receipt of a statutory notice of deficiency for this purpose means receipt in time to petition the Tax Court for a redetermination of the deficiency determined in the notice of deficiency. An opportunity to dispute the underlying liability includes a prior opportunity for a conference with Appeals that was offered either before or after the assessment of the liability. An opportunity for a conference with Appeals prior to the assessment of a tax subject to deficiency procedures is not a prior opportunity for this purpose.

Q-E3. Are spousal defenses subject to the limitations imposed under section 6330(c)(2)(B) on a taxpayer's right to challenge the tax liability specified in the CDP Notice at a CDP hearing?

A-E3. The limitations imposed under section 6330(c)(2)(B) do not apply to spousal defenses. When a taxpayer asserts a spousal defense, the taxpayer is not disputing the amount or existence of the liability itself, but asserting a defense to the liability which may or may not be disputed. A spousal defense raised under section 66 or section 6015 is governed by section 66 or section 6015 and the regulations and procedures thereunder. Any limitation under those sections, regulations, and procedures therefore will apply.

Q-E4. May a taxpayer raise at a CDP hearing a spousal defense under section 66 or section 6015 if that defense was raised and considered administratively and the Commissioner has issued a statutory notice of deficiency or final determination letter addressing the spousal defense?

A-E4. No. A taxpayer is precluded from raising a spousal defense at a CDP hearing when the Commissioner has made a final determination (under section 66 or section 6015) as to spousal defenses in a final determination letter or statutory notice of deficiency. However, a taxpayer may raise spousal defenses in a CDP hearing when the taxpayer has previously raised spousal defenses, but the Commissioner has not yet made a final determination regarding this issue.

Q-E5. May a taxpayer raise at a CDP hearing a spousal defense under section 66 or section 6015 if that defense was raised and considered in a prior judicial proceeding that has become final?

A-E5. No. A taxpayer is precluded by the doctrine of res judicata and by the specific limitations under section 66 or section 6015 from raising a spousal defense in a CDP hearing under these circumstances.

Q-E6. What collection alternatives are available to the taxpayer?

A-E6. Collection alternatives include, for example, a proposal to withhold the proposed levy or future collection action in circumstances that will facilitate the collection of the tax liability, an installment agreement, an offer to compromise, the posting of a bond, or the substitution of other assets. A collection alternative is not available unless the alternative would be available to other taxpayers in similar circumstances. See A-D8 of paragraph (d)(2).

Q-E7. What issues may a taxpayer raise in a CDP hearing under section 6330 if the taxpayer previously received a notice under section 6320 with respect to the same tax and tax period and did not request a CDP hearing with respect to that notice?

A-E7. The taxpayer may raise appropriate spousal defenses, challenges to the appropriateness of the proposed collection action, and offers of collection alternatives. The existence or amount of the underlying liability for any tax period specified in the CDP Notice may be challenged only if the taxpayer did not have a prior opportunity to dispute the tax liability. If the taxpayer previously received a CDP Notice under section 6320 with respect to the same tax and tax period and did not request a CDP hearing with respect to that earlier CDP Notice, the taxpayer had a prior opportunity to dispute the existence or amount of the underlying tax liability.

Q-E8. How will Appeals issue its determination?

A-E8. (i) Taxpayers will be sent a dated Notice of Determination by certified or registered mail. The Notice of Determination will set forth Appeals' findings and decisions. It will state whether the IRS met the requirements of any applicable law or administrative procedure; it will resolve any issues appropriately raised by the taxpayer relating to the unpaid tax; it will include a decision on any appropriate spousal defenses raised by the taxpayer; it will include a decision on any challenges made by the taxpayer to the appropriateness of the collection action; it will respond to any offers by the taxpayer for collection alternatives; and it will address whether the proposed collection action represents a balance between the need for the efficient collection of taxes and the legitimate concern of the taxpayer that any collection action be no more intrusive than necessary. The Notice of Determination will also set forth any agreements that Appeals reached with the taxpayer, any relief given the taxpayer, and any actions the taxpayer or the IRS are required to take. Lastly, the Notice of Determination will advise the taxpayer of the taxpayer's right to seek judicial review within 30 days of the date of the Notice of Determination.

(ii) Because taxpayers are encouraged to discuss their concerns with the IRS office collecting the tax, certain matters that might have been raised at a CDP hearing may be resolved without the need for Appeals consideration. Unless, as a result of these discussions, the taxpayer agrees in writing to withdraw the request that Appeals conduct a CDP hearing, Appeals will still issue a Notice of Determination, but the taxpayer can waive in writing Appeals' consideration of some or all of the matters it would otherwise consider in making its determination.

Q-E9. Is there a period of time within which Appeals must conduct a CDP hearing or issue a Notice of Determination?

A-E9. No. Appeals will, however, attempt to conduct a CDP hearing and issue a Notice of Determination as expeditiously as possible under the circumstances.

Q-E10. Why is the Notice of Determination and its date important?

A-E10. The Notice of Determination will set forth Appeals' findings and decisions with respect to the matters set forth in A-E1 of this paragraph (e)(3). The 30-day period within which the taxpayer is permitted to seek judicial review of Appeals' determination commences the day after the date of the Notice of Determination.

Q-E11. If an Appeals officer considers the merits of a taxpayer's liability in a CDP hearing when the taxpayer had previously received a statutory notice of deficiency or otherwise had an opportunity to dispute the liability prior to the issuance of a notice of intention to levy, will the Appeals officer's determination regarding those liability issues be considered part of the Notice of Determination?

A-E11. No. An Appeals officer may consider the existence and amount of the underlying tax liability as a part of the CDP hearing only if the taxpayer did not receive a statutory notice of deficiency for the tax liability in question or otherwise have a prior opportunity to dispute the tax liability. Similarly, an Appeals officer may not consider any other issue if the issue was raised and considered at a previous hearing under section 6320 or in any other previous administrative or judicial proceeding in which the person seeking to raise the issue meaningfully participated. In the Appeals officer's sole discretion, however, the Appeals officer may consider the existence or amount of the underlying tax liability, or such other precluded issues, at the same time as the CDP hearing. Any determination, however, made by the Appeals officer with respect to such a precluded issue shall not be treated as part of the Notice of Determination issued by the Appeals officer and will not be subject to any judicial review. Because any decisions made by the Appeals officer on such precluded issues are not properly a part of the CDP hearing, such decisions are not required to appear in the Notice of Determination issued following the hearing. Even if a decision concerning such precluded issues is referred to in the Notice of Determination, it is not reviewable by the Tax Court because the precluded issue is not properly part of the CDP hearing.

(4) *Examples.*—The following examples illustrate the principles of this paragraph (e):

*Example 1.* The IRS sends a statutory notice of deficiency to the taxpayer at his last known address asserting a deficiency for the tax year 1995. The taxpayer receives the notice of deficiency in time to petition the Tax Court for a redetermination of the asserted deficiency. The taxpayer does not timely file a petition with the Tax Court. The taxpayer is precluded from challenging the existence or amount of the tax liability in a subsequent CDP hearing.

*Example 2.* Same facts as in *Example 1*, except the taxpayer does not receive the notice of deficiency in time to petition the Tax Court and did not have another prior opportunity to dispute the tax liability. The taxpayer is not precluded from challenging the existence or amount of the tax liability in a subsequent CDP hearing.

*Example 3.* The IRS properly assesses a trust fund recovery penalty against the taxpayer. The IRS offers the taxpayer the opportunity for a conference with Appeals at which the taxpayer would have the opportunity to dispute the assessed liability. The taxpayer declines the opportunity to participate in such a conference. The taxpayer is precluded from challenging the existence or amount of the tax liability in a subsequent CDP hearing.

(f) *Judicial review of Notice of Determination.*—(1) *In general.*—Unless the taxpayer provides the IRS a written withdrawal of the request that Appeals conduct a CDP hearing, Appeals is required to issue a Notice of Determination in all cases where a taxpayer has timely requested a CDP hearing. The taxpayer may appeal such determinations made by Appeals within the 30-day period commencing the day after the date of the Notice of Determination to the Tax Court.

(2) *Questions and answers.*—The questions and answers illustrate the provisions of this paragraph (f) as follows:

Q-F1. What must a taxpayer do to obtain judicial review of a Notice of Determination?

A-F1. Subject to the jurisdictional limitations described in A-F2 of this paragraph (f)(2), the taxpayer must, within the 30-day period commencing the day after the date of the Notice of Determination, appeal the determination by Appeals to the Tax Court.

Q-F2. With respect to the relief available to the taxpayer under section 6015, what is the time frame within which a taxpayer may seek Tax Court review of Appeals' determination following a CDP hearing?

A-F2. If the taxpayer seeks Tax Court review not only of Appeals' denial of relief under section 6015, but also of relief with respect to other issues raised in the CDP hearing, the taxpayer should request Tax Court review within the 30-day period commencing the day after the date of the Notice of Determination. If the taxpayer only seeks Tax Court review of Appeals' denial of relief under section 6015, the taxpayer should request review by the Tax Court, as provided by section 6015(e), within 90 days of Appeals' determination. If a request for Tax Court review is filed after the 30-day period for seeking judicial review under section 6330, then only the taxpayer's section 6015 claims may be reviewable by the Tax Court.

Q-F3. What issue or issues may the taxpayer raise before the Tax Court if the taxpayer disagrees with the Notice of Determination?

A-F3. In seeking Tax Court review of a Notice of Determination, the taxpayer can only ask the court to consider an issue, including a challenge to the underlying tax liability, that was properly raised in the taxpayer's CDP hearing. An issue is not properly raised if the taxpayer fails to request consideration of the issue by Appeals, or if consideration is requested but the taxpayer fails to present to Appeals any evidence with respect to that issue after being given a reasonable opportunity to present such evidence.

Q-F4. What is the administrative record for purposes of Tax Court review?

A-F4. The case file, including the taxpayer's request for hearing, any other written communications and information from the taxpayer or the taxpayer's authorized representative submitted in connection with the CDP hearing, notes made by an Appeals officer or employee of any oral communications with the taxpayer or the taxpayer's authorized representative, memoranda created by the Appeals officer or employee in connection with the CDP hearing, and any other documents or materials relied upon by the Appeals officer or employee in making the determination under section 6330(c)(3), will constitute the record in the Tax Court review of the Notice of Determination issued by Appeals.

(g) *Effect of request for CDP hearing and judicial review on periods of limitation and collection activity.*—(1) *In general.*—The periods of limitation under section 6502 (relating to collection after assessment), section 6531 (relating to criminal prosecutions), and section 6532 (relating to suits) are suspended until the date the IRS receives the taxpayer's written withdrawal of the request for a CDP hearing by Appeals or the determination resulting from the CDP hearing becomes final by expiration of the time for seeking judicial review or the exhaustion of any rights to appeals following judicial review. In no event shall any of these periods of limitation expire before the 90th day after the date on which the IRS receives the taxpayer's written withdrawal of the request that Appeals conduct a CDP hearing or the Notice of Determination with respect to such hearing becomes final upon either the expiration of the time for seeking judicial review or upon exhaustion of any rights to appeals following judicial review.

(2) *Questions and answers.*—The questions and answers illustrate the provisions of this paragraph (g) as follows:

Q-G1. For what period of time will the periods of limitation under section 6502, section 6531, and section 6532 remain suspended if the taxpayer timely requests a CDP hearing concerning a pre-levy or post-levy CDP Notice?

A-G1. The suspension period commences on the date the IRS receives the taxpayer's written request for a CDP hearing. The suspension period continues until the IRS receives a written withdrawal by the taxpayer of the request for a CDP hearing or the Notice of Determination resulting from the CDP hearing becomes final upon either the expiration of the time for seeking judicial review or upon exhaustion of any rights to appeals following judicial review. In no event shall any of these periods of limitation expire before the 90th day after the day on which there is a final determination with respect to such hearing. The periods of limitation that are suspended under section 6330 are those which apply to the taxes and the tax period or periods to which the CDP Notice relates.

Q-G2. For what period of time will the periods of limitation under section 6502, section 6531, and section 6532 be suspended if the taxpayer does not request a CDP hearing concerning the CDP Notice, or the taxpayer requests a CDP hearing, but his request is not timely?

A-G2. Under either of these circumstances, section 6330 does not provide for a suspension of the periods of limitation.

Q-G3. What, if any, enforcement actions can the IRS take during the suspension period?

A-G3. Section 6330(e) provides for the suspension of the periods of limitation discussed in paragraph (g)(1) of these regulations. Section 6330(e) also provides that levy actions that are the subject of the requested CDP hearing under that section shall be suspended during the same period. The IRS, however, may levy for other taxes and periods not covered by the CDP Notice if the CDP requirements under section 6330 for those taxes and periods have been satisfied. The IRS also may file NFTLs for tax periods and taxes, whether or not covered by the CDP Notice issued under section 6330, and may take other non-levy collection actions such as initiating judicial proceedings to collect the tax shown on the CDP Notice or offsetting overpayments from other periods, or of other taxes, against the tax shown on the CDP Notice. Moreover, the provisions in section 6330 do not apply when the IRS levies for the tax and tax period shown on the CDP Notice to collect a state tax refund due the taxpayer, or determines that collection of the tax is in jeopardy. Finally, section 6330 does not prohibit the IRS from accepting any voluntary payments made for the tax and tax period stated on the CDP Notice.

(3) *Examples.*—The following examples illustrate the principles of this paragraph (g):

*Example 1.* The period of limitation under section 6502 with respect to the taxpayer's tax period listed in the CDP Notice will expire on August 1, 1999. The IRS sent a CDP Notice to the taxpayer on April 30, 1999. The taxpayer timely requested a CDP hearing. The IRS received this request on May 15, 1999. Appeals sends the taxpayer its determination on June 15, 1999. The taxpayer timely seeks judicial review of that determination. The period of limitation under

section 6502 would be suspended from May 15, 1999, until the determination resulting from that hearing becomes final by expiration of the time for seeking review or reconsideration before the Tax Court, plus 90 days.

*Example 2.* Same facts as in *Example 1*, except the taxpayer does not seek judicial review of Appeals' determination. Because the taxpayer requested the CDP hearing when fewer than 90 days remained on the period of limitation, the period of limitation will be extended to October 13, 1999 (90 days from July 15, 1999).

(h) *Retained jurisdiction of Appeals.*—(1) *In general.*—The Appeals office that makes a determination under section 6330 retains jurisdiction over that determination, including any subsequent administrative hearings that may be requested by the taxpayer regarding levies and any collection actions taken or proposed with respect to Appeals' determination. Once a taxpayer has exhausted his other remedies, Appeals' retained jurisdiction permits it to consider whether a change in the taxpayer's circumstances affects its original determination. Where a taxpayer alleges a change in circumstances that affects Appeals' original determination, Appeals may consider whether changed circumstances warrant a change in its earlier determination.

(2) *Questions and answers.*—The questions and answers illustrate the provisions of this paragraph (h) as follows:

Q-H1. Are the periods of limitation suspended during the course of any subsequent Appeals consideration of the matters raised by a taxpayer when the taxpayer invokes the retained jurisdiction of Appeals under section 6330(d)(2)(A) or (B)?

A-H1. No. Under section 6330(b)(2), a taxpayer is entitled to only one CDP hearing under section 6330 with respect to the tax and tax periods specified in the CDP Notice. Any subsequent consideration by Appeals pursuant to its retained jurisdiction is not a continuation of the original CDP hearing and does not suspend the periods of limitation.

Q-H2. Is a decision of Appeals resulting from a retained jurisdiction hearing appealable to the Tax Court?

A-H2. No. As discussed in A-H1, a taxpayer is entitled to only one CDP hearing under section 6330 with respect to the tax and tax period or periods specified in the CDP Notice. Only determinations resulting from CDP hearings are appealable to the Tax Court.

(i) *Equivalent hearing.*—(1) *In general.*—A taxpayer who fails to make a timely request for a CDP hearing is not entitled to a CDP hearing. Such a taxpayer may nevertheless request an administrative hearing with Appeals, which is referred to herein as an "equivalent hearing." The equivalent hearing will be held by Appeals and generally will follow Appeals procedures for a CDP hearing. Appeals will not, however, issue a Notice of Determination. Under such circumstances, Appeals will issue a Decision Letter.

(2) *Questions and answers.*—The questions and answers illustrate the provisions of this paragraph (i) as follows:

Q-I1. What must a taxpayer do to obtain an equivalent hearing?

A-I1. (i) A request for an equivalent hearing must be made in writing. A written request in any form that requests an equivalent hearing will be acceptable if it includes the information and signature required in A-I1(ii) of this paragraph (i)(2).

(ii) The request must be dated and must include the following:

(A) The taxpayer's name, address, daytime telephone number (if any), and taxpayer identification number (e.g., SSN, ITIN or EIN).

(B) The type of tax involved.

(C) The tax period at issue.

(D) A statement that the taxpayer is requesting an equivalent hearing with Appeals concerning the levy.

(E) The reason or reasons why the taxpayer disagrees with the proposed levy.

(F) The signature of the taxpayer or the taxpayer's authorized representative.

(iii) The taxpayer must perfect any timely written request for an equivalent hearing that does not satisfy the requirements set forth in A-I1(ii) of this paragraph (i)(2) within a reasonable period of time after a request from the IRS. If the requirements are not satisfied within a reasonable period of time, the taxpayer's equivalent hearing request will be denied.

(iv) The taxpayer must affirm any timely written request for an equivalent hearing that is signed or alleged to have been signed on the taxpayer's behalf by the taxpayer's spouse or other unauthorized representative, and that otherwise meets the requirements set forth in A-I1(ii) of this paragraph (i)(2), by filing, within a reasonable period of time after a request from the IRS, a signed written affirmation that the request was originally submitted on the taxpayer's behalf. If the affirmation is filed within a reasonable period of time after a request, the timely equivalent hearing request will be considered timely with respect to the non-signing taxpayer. If the affirmation is not filed

### Seizure of Property For Collection of Taxes
See p. 20,601 for regulations not amended to reflect law changes
**66,941**

within a reasonable period of time, the equivalent hearing request will be denied with respect to the non-signing taxpayer.

Q-I2. What issues will Appeals consider at an equivalent hearing?

A-I2. In an equivalent hearing, Appeals will consider the same issues that it would have considered at a CDP hearing on the same matter.

Q-I3. Are the periods of limitation under sections 6502, 6531, and 6532 suspended if the taxpayer does not timely request a CDP hearing and is subsequently given an equivalent hearing?

A-I3. No. The suspension period provided for in section 6330(e) relates only to hearings requested within the 30-day period that commences the day following the date of the pre-levy or post-levy CDP Notice, that is, CDP hearings.

Q-I4. Will collection action be suspended if a taxpayer requests and receives an equivalent hearing?

A-I4. Collection action is not required to be suspended. Accordingly, the decision to take collection action during the pendency of an equivalent hearing will be determined on a case-by-case basis. Appeals may request the IRS office with responsibility for collecting the taxes to suspend all or some collection action or to take other appropriate action if it determines that such action is appropriate or necessary under the circumstances.

Q-I5. What will the Decision Letter state?

A-I5. The Decision Letter will generally contain the same information as a Notice of Determination.

Q-I6. Will a taxpayer be able to obtain Tax Court review of a decision made by Appeals with respect to an equivalent hearing?

A-I6. Section 6330 does not authorize a taxpayer to appeal the decision of Appeals with respect to an equivalent hearing. A taxpayer may under certain circumstances be able to seek Tax Court review of Appeals' denial of relief under section 6015. Such review must be sought within 90 days of the issuance of Appeals' determination on those issues, as provided by section 6015(e).

Q-I7. When must a taxpayer request an equivalent hearing with respect to a CDP Notice issued under section 6330?

A-I7. A taxpayer must submit a written request for an equivalent hearing within the one-year period commencing the day after the date of the CDP Notice issued under section 6330. This period is slightly different from the period for submitting a written request for an equivalent hearing with respect to a CDP Notice issued under section 6320. For a CDP Notice issued under section 6320, a taxpayer must submit a written request for an equivalent hearing within the one-year period commencing the day after the end of the five-business-day period following the filing of the NFTL.

Q-I8. How will the timeliness of a taxpayer's written request for an equivalent hearing be determined?

A-I8. The rules and regulations under section 7502 and section 7503 will apply to determine the timeliness of the taxpayer's request for an equivalent hearing, if properly transmitted and addressed as provided in A-I10 of this paragraph (i)(2).

Q-I9. Is the one-year period within which a taxpayer must make a request for an equivalent hearing extended because the taxpayer resides outside the United States?

A-I9. No. All taxpayers who want an equivalent hearing must request the hearing within the one-year period commencing the day after the date of the CDP Notice issued under section 6330.

Q-I10. Where must the written request for an equivalent hearing be sent?

A-I10. The written request for an equivalent hearing must be sent, or hand delivered (if permitted), to the IRS office and address as directed on the CDP Notice. If the address of the issuing office does not appear on the CDP Notice, the taxpayer should obtain the address of the office to which the written request should be sent or hand delivered by calling, toll-free, 1-800-829-1040 and providing the taxpayer's identification number (e.g., SSN, ITIN or EIN).

Q-I11. What will happen if the taxpayer does not request an equivalent hearing in writing within the one-year period commencing the day after the date of the CDP Notice issued under section 6330?

A-I11. If the taxpayer does not request an equivalent hearing with Appeals within the one-year period commencing the day after the date of the CDP Notice issued under section 6330, the taxpayer foregoes the right to an equivalent hearing with respect to the unpaid tax and tax periods shown on the CDP Notice. A written request submitted within the one-year period that does not satisfy the requirements set forth in A-I1(ii) of this paragraph (i)(2) is considered timely if the request is perfected within a reasonable period of time pursuant to A-I1(iii) of this paragraph (i)(2). If a request for equivalent hearing is untimely, either because the request was not submitted within the one-year period or not perfected within the reasonable period provided, the equivalent hearing request will be denied. The taxpayer, however, may seek reconsideration by the IRS

office collecting the tax, assistance from the National Taxpayer Advocate, or an administrative hearing before Appeals under its Collection Appeals Program or any successor program.

(j) *Effective date.*—This section is applicable on or after November 16, 2006 with respect to requests made for CDP hearings or equivalent hearings on or after November 16, 2006. [Reg. § 301.6330-1.]

☐ [T.D. 8980, 1-17-2002. *Amended by* T.D. 9291, 10-16-2006.]

### [Reg. § 301.6331-1]

**§ 301.6331-1. Levy and distraint.**—(a) *Authority to levy.*—(1) *In general.*—If any person liable to pay any tax neglects or refuses to pay the tax within 10 days after notice and demand, the district director to whom the assessment is charged (or, upon his request, any other district director) may proceed to collect the tax by levy. The district director may levy upon any property, or rights to property, whether real or personal, tangible or intangible, belonging to the taxpayer. The district director may also levy upon property with respect to which there is a lien provided by section 6321 or 6324 for the payment of the tax. For exemption of certain property from levy, see section 6334 and the regulations thereunder. As used in section 6331 and this section, the term "tax" includes any interest, additional amount, addition to tax, or assessable penalty, together with costs and expenses. Property subject to a Federal tax lien which has been sold or otherwise transferred by the taxpayer may be seized while in the hands of the transferee or any subsequent transferee. However, see provisions under sections 6323 and 6324(a)(2) and (b) for protection of certain transferees against a Federal tax lien. Levy may be made by serving a notice of levy on any person in possession of, or obligated with respect to, property or rights to property subject to levy, including receivables, bank accounts, evidences of debt, securities, and salaries, wages, commissions, or other compensation. A levy on a bank reaches any interest that accrues on the taxpayer's balance under the terms of the bank's agreement with the depositor during the 21-day holding period provided for in section 6332(c). Except as provided in § 301.6331-1(b)(1) with regard to a levy on salary or wages, a levy extends only to property possessed and obligations which exist at the time of the levy. Obligations exist when the liability of the obligor is fixed and determinable although the right to receive payment thereof may be deferred until a later date. For example, if on the first day of the month a delinquent taxpayer sold personal property subject to an agreement that the buyer remit the purchase price on the last day of the month, a levy made on the buyer on the 10th day of the month would reach the amount due on the sale, although the buyer need not satisfy the levy by paying over the amount to the district director until the last day of the month. Similarly, a levy only reaches property in the possession of the person levied upon at the time the levy is made together with interest that accrues during the 21-day holding period provided for in section 6332(c). For example, a levy made on a bank with respect to the account of a delinquent taxpayer is satisfied if the bank surrenders the amount of the taxpayer's balance at the time the levy is made. The levy has no effect upon any subsequent deposit made in the bank by the taxpayer. Subsequent deposits may be reached only by a subsequent levy on the bank.

(2) *Jeopardy cases.*—If the district director finds that the collection of any tax is in jeopardy, he or she may make notice and demand for immediate payment of such tax and, upon failure or refusal to pay such tax, collection thereof by levy shall be lawful without regard to the 10-day period provided in section 6331(a), the 30-day period provided in section 6331(d), or the limitation on levy provided in section 6331(g)(1).

(3) *Bankruptcy or receivership cases.*—During a bankruptcy proceeding or a receivership proceeding in either a Federal or a State court, the assets of the taxpayer are in general under the control of the court in which such proceeding is pending. Taxes cannot be collected by levy upon assets in the custody of a court, whether or not such custody is incident to a bankruptcy or receivership proceeding, except where the proceeding has progressed to such a point that the levy would not interfere with the work of the court or where the court grants permission to levy. Any assets which under applicable provisions of law are not under the control of the court may be levied upon, for example, property exempt from court custody under State law or the bankrupt's earnings and property acquired after the date of bankruptcy. However, levy upon such property is not mandatory and the Government may rely upon payment of taxes in the proceeding.

(4) *Certain types of compensation.*—(i) *Federal employees.*—Levy may be made upon the salary or wages of any officer or employee (including members of the Armed Forces), or elected or appointed official, of the United States, the District of Columbia, or any agency or instrumentality of either, by serving a notice of levy on the

employer of the delinquent taxpayer. As used in this subdivision, the term "employer" means (a) the officer or employee of the United States, the District of Columbia, or of the agency or instrumentality of the United States or the District of Columbia, who has control of the payment of the wages, or (b) any other officer or employee designated by the head of the branch, department, agency, or instrumentality of the United States or of the District of Columbia as the party upon whom service of the notice of levy may be made. If the head of such branch, department, agency, or instrumentality designates an officer or employee other than one who has control of the payment of the wages, as the party upon whom service of the notice of levy may be made, such head shall promptly notify the Commissioner of the name and address of each officer or employee so designated and the scope or extent of his authority as such designee.

(ii) *State and municipal employees.*—Salaries, wages, or other compensation of any officer, employee, or elected or appointed official of a State or Territory, or of any agency, instrumentality, or political subdivision thereof, are also subject to levy to enforce collection of any Federal tax.

(iii) *Seamen.*—Notwithstanding the provisions of section 12 of the Seamen's Act of 1915 (38 Stat. 1169; 46 U.S.C. 601), wages of seamen, apprentice seamen, or fishermen employed on fishing vessels are subject to levy. See section 6334(c).

(5) *Noncompetent Indians.*—Solely for purposes of sections 6321 and 6331, any interest in restricted land held in trust by the United States for an individual noncompetent Indian (and not for a tribe) shall not be deemed to be property, or a right to property, belonging to such Indian.

(b) *Continuing levies and successive seizures.*—(1) *Continuing effect of levy on salary and wages.*—A levy on salary or wages has continuous effect from the time the levy originally is made until the levy is released pursuant to section 6343. For this purpose, the term *salary or wages* includes compensation for services paid in the form of fees, commissions, bonuses, and similar items. The levy attaches to both salary or wages earned but not yet paid at the time of the levy, advances on salary or wages made subsequent to the date of the levy, and salary or wages earned and becoming payable subsequent to the date of the levy, until the levy is released pursuant to section 6343. In general, salaries or wages that are the subject of a continuing levy and are not exempt from levy under section 6334(a)(8) or (9), are to be paid to the district director, the service center director, or the compliance center director (director) on the same date the payor would otherwise pay over the money to the taxpayer. For example, if an individual normally is paid on the Wednesday following the close of each work week, a levy made upon his or her employer on any Monday would apply to both wages due for the prior work week and wages for succeeding work weeks as such wages become payable. In such a case, the levy would be satisfied if, on the first Wednesday after the levy and on each Wednesday thereafter until the employer receives a notice of release from levy described in section 6343, the employer pays over to the director wages that would otherwise be paid to the employee on such Wednesday (less any exempt amount pursuant to section 6334).

(2) *Successive seizures.*—Whenever any property or rights to property upon which a levy has been made are not sufficient to satisfy the claim of the United States for which the levy is made, the district director may thereafter, and as often as may be necessary, proceed to levy in like manner upon any other property or rights to property subject to levy of the person against whom such claim exists or on which there is a lien imposed by section 6321 or 6324 (or the corresponding provision of prior law) for the payment of such claim until the amount due from such person, together with all costs and expenses, is fully paid.

(c) *Service of notice of levy by mail.*—A notice of levy may be served by mailing the notice to the person upon whom the service of a notice of levy is authorized under paragraph (a)(1) of this section. In such a case the date and time the notice is delivered to the person to be served is the date and time the levy is made. If the notice is sent by certified mail, return receipt requested, the date of delivery on the receipt is treated as the date the levy is made. If, after receipt of a notice of levy, an officer or other person authorized to act on behalf of the person served signs and notes the date and time of receipt on the notice of levy, the date and time so noted will be presumed to be, in the absence of proof to the contrary, the date and time of delivery. Any person may, upon written notice to the district director having audit jurisdiction over such person, have all notices of levy by mail sent to one designated office. After such a notice is received by the district director, notices of levy by mail will be sent to the designated office until a written notice withdrawing the request or a written notice designating a different office is received by the district director.

(d) *Effective date.*—These regulations are effective December 10, 1992. [Reg. §301.6331-1.]

☐ [*T.D.* 6119, 12-31-54. *Amended by T.D.* 6498, 10-24-60; *T.D.* 7139, 8-11-71; *T.D.* 7180, 4-12-72; *T.D.* 7253, 2-23-73; *T.D.* 7620, 5-11-79; *T.D.* 7874, 3-8-83 *and T.D.* 8558, 7-29-94.]

### [Reg. §301.6331-2]

**§301.6331-2. Procedures and restrictions on levies.**—(a) *Notice of intent to levy.*—(1) *In general.*—Levy may be made upon the salary, wages, or other property of a taxpayer for any unpaid tax no less than 30 days after the district director, the service center director, or the compliance center director (director) has notified the taxpayer in writing of the intent to levy. The notice must be given in person, be left at the dwelling or usual place of business of the taxpayer, or be sent by registered or certified mail to the taxpayer's last known address. For further guidance regarding the definition of last known address, see §301.6212-2. The notice of intent to levy is separate from, but may be given at the same time as, the notice and demand described in §301.6331-1.

(2) *Content of Notice.*—The notice of intent to levy is to contain a brief statement in nontechnical terms including the following information—

(i) The Internal Revenue Code provisions and the procedures relating to levy and sale of property;

(ii) The administrative appeals available with respect to the levy and sale of property and the procedures relating to such appeals;

(iii) The alternatives available that could prevent levy on the property (including the use of an installment agreement under section 6159); and

(iv) The Internal Revenue Code provisions and the procedures relating to redemption of property and release of liens on property.

(b) *Uneconomical levy.*—(1) *In general.*—No levy may be made on property if the director estimates that the anticipated expenses with respect to the levy and sale will exceed the fair market value of the property. The estimate is to be made on an aggregate basis for all of the items that are anticipated to be seized pursuant to the levy. Generally, no levy should be made on individual items of insignificant monetary value. For the definition of fair market value, see §301.6325-1(b)(1)(i). See §301.6341-1 concerning the expenses of levy and sale.

(2) *Time of estimate.*—The estimate, which may be formal or informal, is to be made at the time of the seizure or within a reasonable period of time prior to a seizure. The estimate may be based on earlier estimates of fair market value and anticipated expenses of the same or similar property.

(3) *Examples.*—The following examples illustrate the application of this paragraph (b):

*Example 1.* A director anticipates that the taxpayer has only one item of property that can be seized and sold. This item is estimated to have a fair market value of $250.00. The director also estimates that the costs of seizure and sale will total $300.00 if this item is seized. The director is prohibited from levying on this one item of the taxpayer's property because the costs of seizure and sale are estimated to exceed the property's fair market value.

*Example 2.* The facts are the same as in *Example 1* except that the director anticipates that the taxpayer has 10 items of property that can be seized and sold. Each of those items is estimated to have a fair market value of $250.00. The director also estimates that the costs of seizure and sale will total $300.00 regardless of how many of those items are seized. The director is prohibited from levying on only one item of the taxpayer's property because the costs of seizure and sale are estimated to exceed the fair market value of the single item of property. The director, however, would not be prohibited from levying on two or more items of the taxpayer's property because the aggregate fair market value of the seized property would exceed the estimated costs of seizure and sale.

*Example 3.* The taxpayer has three items of property, A, B, and C. The director anticipates that the value of items A, B, and C depends on their being sold as a unit. The director estimates that due to high anticipated costs of storing or maintaining item B prior to the sale, the aggregate fair market value of items A, B, and C will not exceed the anticipated expenses of seizure and sale if all three items are seized. Accordingly, the director is prohibited from levying on items A, B, and C.

*Example 4.* The facts are the same as in *Example 3* except that the director does not anticipate that the value of items A, B, and C depends on those items being sold as a unit. If the director estimates that the aggregate fair market value of items A and C exceeds the aggregate anticipated costs of the seizure and sale of those two items,

items A and C can be seized and sold. The director is prohibited from levying on item B because the high cost of storing or maintaining item B is estimated to exceed the fair market value of item B.

(c) *Restriction on levy on date of appearance.*—Except for continuing levies on salaries or wages described in §301.6331-1(b)(1), no levy may be made on any property of a person on the day that person, or an officer or employee of that person, is required to appear in response to a summons served for the purpose of collecting any underpayment of tax from that person. For purposes of this paragraph (c), the date on which an appearance is required is the date fixed by an officer or employee of the Internal Revenue Service pursuant to section 7605 or the date (if any) fixed as the result of a judicial proceeding instituted under sections 7604 and 7402(b) seeking the enforcement of the summons.

(d) *Jeopardy.*—Paragraphs (a) and (c) of this section do not apply to a levy if the director finds, for purposes of §301.6331-1(a)(2), that the collection of tax is in jeopardy.

(e) *Effective date.*—These regulations are effective December 10, 1992. [Reg. §301.6331-2.]

☐ [*T.D. 7620, 5-11-79. Amended by T.D. 8558, 7-29-94 and T.D. 8939, 1-11-2001.*]

### [Reg. §301.6331-3]

**§301.6331-3. Restrictions on levy while offers to compromise are pending.**—*Cross-reference.* For provisions relating to the making of levies while an offer to compromise is pending, see §301.7122-1.

☐ [*T.D. 9027, 12-17-2002.*]

### [Reg. §301.6331-4]

**§301.6331-4. Restrictions on levy while installment agreements are pending or in effect.**—(a) *Prohibition on levy.*—(1) *In general.*—No levy may be made to collect a tax liability that is the subject of an installment agreement during the period that a proposed installment agreement is pending with the Internal Revenue Service (IRS), for 30 days immediately following the rejection of a proposed installment agreement, during the period that an installment agreement is in effect, and for 30 days immediately following the termination of an installment agreement. If, within the 30 days following the rejection or termination of an installment agreement, the taxpayer files an appeal with the IRS Office of Appeals, no levy may be made while the rejection or termination is being considered by Appeals. This section will not prohibit levy to collect the liability of any person other than the person or persons named in the installment agreement.

(2) *When a proposed installment agreement becomes pending.*—A proposed installment agreement becomes pending when it is accepted for processing. The IRS may not accept a proposed installment agreement for processing following reference of a case involving the liability that is the subject of the proposed installment agreement to the Department of Justice for prosecution or defense. The proposed installment agreement remains pending until the IRS accepts the proposal, the IRS notifies the taxpayer that the proposal has been rejected, or the proposal is withdrawn by the taxpayer. If a proposed installment agreement that has been accepted for processing does not contain sufficient information to permit the IRS to evaluate whether the proposal should be accepted, the IRS will request the taxpayer to provide the needed additional information. If the taxpayer does not submit the additional information that the IRS has requested within a reasonable time period after such a request, the IRS may reject the proposed installment agreement.

(3) *Revised proposals of installment agreements submitted following rejection.*—If, following the rejection of a proposed installment agreement, the taxpayer makes a good faith revision of the proposal and submits the revision within 30 days of the date of rejection, the provisions of this section shall apply to that revised proposal.

(4) *Exceptions.*—Paragraph (a)(1) of this section shall not prohibit levy if the taxpayer files a written notice with the IRS that waives the restriction on levy imposed by this section, the IRS determines that the proposed installment agreement was submitted solely to delay collection, or the IRS determines that collection of the tax to which the installment agreement or proposed installment agreement relates is in jeopardy.

(b) *Other actions by the IRS while levy is prohibited.*—(1) *In general.*—The IRS may take actions other than levy to protect the interests of the Government with regard to the liability identified in an installment agreement or proposed installment agreement. Those actions include, for example—

(i) Crediting an overpayment against the liability pursuant to section 6402;

(ii) Filing or refiling notices of Federal tax lien; and

(iii) Taking action to collect from any person who is not named in the installment agreement or proposed installment agreement but who is liable for the tax to which the installment agreement relates.

(2) *Proceedings in court.*—Except as otherwise provided in this paragraph (b)(2), the IRS will not refer a case to the Department of Justice for the commencement of a proceeding in court, against a person named in an installment agreement or proposed installment agreement, if levy to collect the liability is prohibited by paragraph (a)(1) of this section. Without regard to whether a person is named in an installment agreement or proposed installment agreement, however, the IRS may authorize the Department of Justice to file a counterclaim or third-party complaint in a refund action or to join that person in any other proceeding in which liability for the tax that is the subject of the installment agreement or proposed installment agreement may be established or disputed, including a suit against the United States under 28 U.S.C. 2410. In addition, the United States may file a claim in any bankruptcy proceeding or insolvency action brought by or against such person. If a person named in an installment agreement is joined in a proceeding, the United States obtains a judgment against that person, and the case is referred back to the IRS for collection, collection will continue to occur pursuant to the terms of the installment agreement.

(c) *Statute of limitations.*—(1) *Suspension of the statute of limitations on collection.*—The statute of limitations under section 6502 for collection of any liability shall be suspended during the period that a proposed installment agreement relating to that liability is pending with the IRS, for 30 days immediately following the rejection of a proposed installment agreement, and for 30 days immediately following the termination of an installment agreement. If, within the 30 days following the rejection or termination of an installment agreement, the taxpayer files an appeal with the IRS Office of Appeals, the statute of limitations for collection shall be suspended while the rejection or termination is being considered by Appeals. The statute of limitations for collection shall continue to run if an exception under paragraph (a)(4) of this section applies and levy is not prohibited with respect to the taxpayer.

(2) *Waivers of the statute of limitations on collection.*—The IRS may continue to request, to the extent permissible under section 6502 and §301.6159-1, that the taxpayer agree to a reasonable extension of the statute of limitations for collection.

(d) *Cross-reference.*—For provisions relating to the making of levies while an installment agreement is pending or in effect, see §301.6159-1.

(e) *Effective /applicability date.*—Paragraphs (a), (b), and (c) are applicable beginning December 18, 2002. Paragraph (d) is applicable beginning November 25, 2009. [Reg. §301.6331-4.]

☐ [*T.D. 9027, 12-17-2002. Amended by T.D. 9473, 11-24-2009.*]

### [Reg. §301.6332-1]

**§301.6332-1. Surrender of property subject to levy.**—(a) *Requirement.*—(1) *In general.*—Except as otherwise provided in §301.6332-2, relating to levy in the case of life insurance and endowment contracts, and in §301.6332-3, relating to property held by banks, any person in possession of (or obligated with respect to) property or rights to property subject to levy and upon which a levy has been made shall, upon demand of the district director, surrender the property or rights (or discharge the obligation) to the district director, except that part of the property or rights (or obligation) which, at the time of the demand, is actually or constructively under the jurisdiction of a court because of an attachment or execution under any judicial process.

(2) *Levy on bank deposits held in offices outside the United States.*—Notwithstanding subparagraph (1) of this paragraph, if a levy has been made upon property or rights to property subject to levy which a bank engaged in the banking business in the United States or a possession of the United States is in possession of (or obligated with respect to), the Commissioner shall not enforce the levy with respect to any deposits held in an office of the bank outside the United States or a possession of the United States, unless the notice of levy specifies that the district director intends to reach such deposits. The notice of levy shall not specify that the district director intends to reach such deposits unless the district director believes—

(i) That the taxpayer is within the jurisdiction of a United States court at the time the levy is made and that the bank is in possession of (or obligated with respect to) deposits of the taxpayer in an office of the bank outside the United States or a possession of the United States; or

(ii) That the taxpayer is not within the jurisdiction of a United States court at the time the levy is made, that the bank is in possession of (or obligated with respect to) deposits of the taxpayer in an office outside the United States or a possession of the United States, and that such deposits consist, in whole or in part, of funds transferred from the United States or a possession of the United States in order to hinder or delay the collection of a tax imposed by the Code. For purposes of this subparagraph, the term "possession of the United States" includes Guam, the Midway Islands, the Panama Canal Zone, the Commonwealth of Puerto Rico, American Samoa, the Virgin Islands, and Wake Island.

(b) *Enforcement of levy.*—(1) *Extent of personal liability.*—Any person who, upon demand of the district director, fails or refuses to surrender any property or right to property subject to levy is liable in his own person and estate in a sum equal to the value of the property or rights not so surrendered, together with costs and interest. The liability, however, may not exceed the amount of the taxes for the collection of which the levy was made. Interest is to be computed at the annual rate referred to in regulations under section 6621 from the date of the levy, or, in the case of a continuing levy on salary or wages (see section 6331(d)(3)), from the date the person would otherwise have been obligated to pay over the wages or salary to the taxpayer. Any amount recovered, other than costs, will be credited against the tax liability for the collection of which the levy was made.

(2) *Penalty for violation.*—In addition to the personal liability described in subparagraph (1) of this paragraph, any person who is required to surrender property or rights to property and who fails or refuses to surrender them without reasonable cause is liable for a penalty equal to 50 percent of the amount recoverable under section 6332(d)(1). No part of the penalty described in this subparagraph shall be credited against the tax liability for the collection of which the levy was made. The penalty described in this subparagraph is not applicable in cases where bona fide dispute exists concerning the amount of the property to be surrendered pursuant to a levy or concerning the legal effectiveness of the levy. However, if a court in a later enforcement suit sustains the levy, then reasonable cause would usually not exist to refuse to honor a later levy made under similar circumstances.

(c) *Effect of honoring levy.*—(1) *In general.*—Any person in possession of, or obligated with respect to, property or rights to property subject to levy and upon which a levy has been made who, upon demand by the district director, surrenders the property or rights to property, or discharges the obligation, to the district director, or who pays a liability described in paragraph (b)(1) of this section, is discharged from any obligation or liability to the delinquent taxpayer and any other person with respect to the property or rights to property arising from the surrender or payment.

(2) *Exception for certain incorrectly surrendered property.*—Any person who surrenders to the Internal Revenue Service property or rights to property not properly subject to levy in which the delinquent taxpayer has no apparent interest is not relieved of liability to a third party who has an interest in the property. However, if the delinquent taxpayer has an apparent interest in property or rights to property, a person who makes a good faith determination that such property or rights to property in his or her possession has been levied upon by the Internal Revenue Service and who surrenders the property to the United States in response to the levy is relieved of liability to a third party who has an interest in the property or rights to property, even if it is subsequently determined that the property was not properly subject to levy.

(3) *Remedy.*—In situations described in paragraphs (c)(1) and (c)(2) of this section, taxpayers and third parties who have an interest in property surrendered in response to a levy may secure from the Internal Revenue Service the administrative relief provided for in section 6343(b) or may bring suit to recover the property under section 7426.

(4) *Examples.*—The provisions of this paragraph (c) may be illustrated by the following examples:

*Example 1.* M Bank is served with a notice of levy for an unpaid tax liability due from A in the amount of $2,000. M Bank holds $2,000 in a checking account in the names of A or B or C. Although all of the deposits into the account were made by B and C, A has an unrestricted right to withdraw the funds from the account. M Bank surrenders the entire account to the district director at the end of the holding period provided in section 6332(c). Under paragraph (c)(1) of this section, M Bank is not liable to B or C for any amount, even if B or C prove that the funds in the account did not belong to A, because A's unrestricted right to withdraw the funds is an interest which is subject to levy. B or C may, however, seek the return of the funds from the United States as provided in sections 6343(b) and 7426 of the Internal Revenue Code.

*Example 2.* A is indebted to B for $400. Unbeknownst to A, B has assigned his right to receive payment to C. A is served with a notice of levy for an unpaid tax liability due from B for $400. A, acting with no knowledge of the assignment to C, surrenders $400 to the district director. A is discharged from his obligation to pay B, the taxpayer. Under paragraph (c)(2) of this section, because B had an apparent interest in the funds that A owed to B, and because A determined in good faith that those funds had been levied upon, A is also discharged from any liability to C, even though the money is not properly subject to levy. C may, however, seek return of the payment from the United States as provided in sections 6343(b) and 7426 of the Internal Revenue Code.

*Example 3.* M Bank is served with a notice of levy for an unpaid tax liability due from "John H. Smith, Sr." in the amount of $5,000. M Bank fails to read the notice of levy carefully. When searching its records, M Bank finds the name of "John H. Smith, Jr." and looks no further. M Bank surrenders $5,000 from John H. Smith, Jr.'s checking account to the district director. M Bank is not discharged from liability under section 6332(e) of the Internal Revenue Code because the delinquent taxpayer (John H. Smith, Sr.) had no apparent interest in the account of John H. Smith, Jr. (Generally, John H. Smith Jr. may seek return of the payment from the United States as provided in sections 6343 and 7426 of the Internal Revenue Code.)

*Example 4.* M Bank is served with a notice of levy for an unpaid tax liability due from "Robert A. Jones" in the amount of $5,000. M Bank searches its records and identifies four separate accounts of $1,000 each in the name of "Robert A. Jones." All four accounts list different addresses and social security identification numbers. M Bank surrenders all four accounts totalling $4,000 in response to the levy. M Bank could not in good faith have determined that all four accounts were levied upon. Therefore, M Bank is not discharged from liability to any person other than the taxpayer whose account was levied upon.

(5) *Effective date.*—Paragraph (c) of this section is effective [January 11, 1993]. However, persons surrendering property to the Internal Revenue Service may rely on the regulations with respect to levies issued after November 10, 1988.

(d) *Person defined.*—The term "person," as used in section 6332(a) and this section, includes an officer or employee of a corporation or a member or employee of a partnership, who is under a duty to surrender the property or rights to property or to discharge the obligation. In the case of a levy upon the salary or wages of an officer, employee, or elected or appointed official of the United States, the District of Columbia, or any agency or instrumentality of either, the term "person" includes the officer or employee of the United States, of the District of Columbia, or of such agency or instrumentality who is under a duty to discharge the obligation. As to the officer or employee who is under such duty, see paragraph (a)(4)(i) of § 301.6331-1. [Reg. § 301.6332-1.]

☐ [*T.D.* 6119, 12-31-54. *Amended by T.D.* 6498, 10-24-60; *T.D.* 6746, 7-20-64; *T.D.* 7180, 4-12-72; *T.D.* 7384, 10-21-75; *T.D.* 7620, 5-11-79; *T.D.* 8466, 12-31-92 *and T.D.* 8467, 1-11-93.]

**[Reg. § 301.6332-2]**

**§ 301.6332-2. Surrender of property subject to levy in the case of life insurance and endowment contracts.**—(a) *In general.*—This section provides special rules relating to the surrender of property subject to levy in the case of life insurance and endowment contracts. The provisions of § 301.6332-1 which relate generally to the surrender of property subject to levy apply, to the extent not inconsistent with the special rules set forth in this section, to a levy in the case of life insurance and endowment contracts.

(b) *Effect of service of notice of levy.*—(1) *In general.*—(i) A notice of levy served by a district director on an insuring organization with respect to a life insurance or endowment contract issued by the organization shall constitute—

(A) A demand by the district director for the payment of the cash loan value of the contract adjusted in accordance with paragraph (c) of this section, and

(B) The exercise of the right of the person against whom the tax is assessed to the advance of such cash loan value.

(ii) It is unnecessary for the district director to surrender the contract document to the insuring organization upon which the levy is made. However, the notice of levy will include a certification by the district director that a copy of the notice of levy has been mailed to the person against whom the tax is assessed at his last known address. For further guidance regarding the definition of last known address, see § 301.6212-2. At the time of service of the notice of levy, the levy is effective with respect to the cash loan value of the insurance contract, subject to the condition that if the levy is not satisfied or released before the 90th day after the date of service, the levy can be satisfied only by payment of the amount described in paragraph (c) of this section. Other than satisfaction or release of the levy, no event during the 90-day period subsequent to the date of service of the notice of levy shall release the cash loan value from the effect of the levy. For example, the termination of the policy by the taxpayer or by the death of the insured during such 90-day period shall not release the levy. For the rules relating to the time when the insuring organization is to pay over the required amount, see paragraph (c) of this section.

(2) *Notification of amount subject to levy.*—(i) *Full payment before the 90th day.*—In the event that the unpaid liability to which the levy relates is satisfied at any time during the 90-day period subsequent to the date of service of the notice of levy, the district director will promptly give the insuring organization written notification that the levy is released.

(ii) *Notification after the 90th day.*—In the event that notification is not given under subdivision (i) of this subparagraph, the district director will, promptly following the 90th day after service of the notice of levy, give the insuring organization written notification of the current status of all accounts listed on the notice of levy, and of the total payments received since service of the notice of levy. This notification will be given to the insuring organization whether or not there has been any change in the status of the accounts.

(c) *Satisfaction of levy.*—(1) *In general.*—The levy described in paragraph (b) of this section with respect to a life insurance or endowment contract shall be deemed to be satisfied if the insuring organization pays over to the district director the amount which the person against whom the tax is assessed could have had advanced to him by the organization on the 90th day after service of the notice of levy on the organization. However, this amount is increased by the amount of any advance (including contractual interest thereon), generally called a policy loan, made to the person on or after the date the organization has actual notice or knowledge, within the meaning of section 6323 (i)(1), of the existence of the tax lien with respect to which the levy is made. The insuring organization may, nevertheless, make an advance (including contractual interest thereon), generally called an automatic premium loan, made automatically to maintain the contract in force under an agreement entered into before the organization has such actual notice or knowledge. In any event, the amount paid to the district director by the insuring organization is not to exceed the amount of the unpaid liability shown on the notification described in paragraph (b)(2) of this section. The amount, determined in accordance with the provisions of this section, subject to the levy shall be paid to the district director by the insuring organization promptly after receipt of the notification described in paragraph (b)(2). The satisfaction of a levy with respect to a life insurance or endowment contract will not discharge the contract from the tax lien. However, see section 6323(b)(9)(C) and the regulations thereunder concerning the liability of an insurance company after satisfaction of a levy with respect to a life insurance or endowment contract. If the person against whom the tax is assessed so directs, the insuring organization, on a date before the 90th day after service of the notice of levy, may satisfy the levy by paying over an amount computed in accordance with the provisions of this subparagraph substituting such date for the 90th day. In the event of termination of the policy by the taxpayer or by the death of the insured on a date before the 90th day after service of the notice of levy, the amount to be paid over to the district director by the insuring organization in satisfaction of the levy shall be an amount computed in accordance with the provisions of this subparagraph substituting the date of termination of the policy or the date of death for the 90th day.

(2) *Examples.*—The provisions of this section may be illustrated by the following examples:

*Example (1).* On March 5, 1968, a notice of levy for an unpaid income tax assessment due from A in the amount of $3,000 is served on the X Insurance Company with respect to A's life insurance policy. On March 5, 1968, the cash loan value of the policy is $1,500. On April 9, 1968, A does not pay a premium due on the policy in the amount of $200. Under an automatic premium advance provision contained in the policy originally issued in 1960, X advances the premium out of the cash value of the policy. As of June 3, 1968 (the 90th day after service of the notice of levy), pursuant to the provisions of the policy, the amount of accrued charges upon the automatic premium advance in the amount of $200 for the period April 9, 1968, through June 3, 1968, is $2. On June 5, 1968, the district director gives written notification to X indicating that A's unpaid tax assessment is $2,500. Under this section, X is required to pay to the district director, promptly after receipt of the June 5, 1968, notification, the sum of $1,298 ($1,500 less $200 less $2), which is the amount A could have had advanced to him by X on June 3, 1968.

*Example (2).* Assume the same facts as in example (1) except that on May 10, 1968, A requests and X grants an advance in the amount

of $1,000. X has actual notice of the existence of the lien by reason of the service of the notice of levy on March 5, 1968. This advance is not required to be made automatically under the policy and reduces the amount of the cash value of the policy. For the use of the $1,000 advance during the period May 10, 1968, through June 3, 1968, X charges A the sum of $3. Under this section, X is required to pay to the district director, promptly after receipt of the June 5, 1968, notification, the sum of $1,298. This $1,298 amount is composed of the $295 amount ($1,500 less $200 less $2 less $1,000 less $3) A could have had advanced to him by X on June 3, 1968, plus the $1,000 advance plus the charges in the amount of $3 with respect thereto.

*Example (3).* Assume the same facts as in example (1) except that the insurance contract does not contain an automatic premium advance provision. The contract does provide that, upon default in the payment of premiums, the policy shall automatically be converted to paid-up term insurance with no cash or loan value. A fails to make the premium payment of $200 due on April 9, 1968. After expiration of a grace period to make the premium payment, the X Insurance Company applies the cash loan value of $1,500 to effect the conversion. Since the service of the notice of levy constitutes the exercise of A's right to receive the cash loan value and the amount applied to effect the conversion is not an automatic advance to A to maintain the policy in force, the conversion of the policy is not an event which will release the cash loan value from the effect of the levy. Therefore, X Insurance Company is required to pay to the district director, promptly after receipt of the June 5, 1968 notification, the sum of $1,500.

(d) *Other enforcement proceedings.*—The satisfaction of the levy described in paragraph (b) of this section by an insuring organization shall be without prejudice to any civil action for the enforcement of any Federal tax lien with respect to a life insurance or endowment contract. Thus, this levy procedure is not the exclusive means of subjecting the life insurance and endowment contracts of the person against whom a tax is assessed to the collection of his unpaid assessment. The United States may choose to foreclose the tax lien in any case where it is appropriate, as, for example, to reach the cash surrender value (as distinguished from cash loan value) of a life insurance or endowment contract.

(e) *Cross references.*—(1) For provisions relating to priority of certain advances with respect to a life insurance or endowment contract after satisfaction of a levy pursuant to section 6332(b), see section 6323(b)(9) and the regulations thereunder.

(2) For provisions relating to the issuance of a certificate of discharge of a life insurance or endowment contract subject to a tax lien, see section 6325(b) and the regulations thereunder. [Reg. §301.6332-2.]

☐ [*T.D. 7180, 4-12-72. Amended by T.D. 8939, 1-11-2001.*]

### [Reg. §301.6332-3]

**§301.6332-3. The 21-day holding period applicable to property held by banks.**—(a) *In general.*—This section provides special rules relating to the surrender, after 21 days, of deposits subject to levy which are held by banks. The provisions of §301.6332-1 which relate generally to the surrender of property subject to levy apply, to the extent not inconsistent with the special rules set forth in this section, to a levy on property held by banks.

(b) *Definition of bank.*—For purposes of this section, the term "bank" means—

(1) A bank or trust company or domestic building and loan association incorporated and doing business under the laws of the United States (including laws relating to the District of Columbia) or of any State, a substantial part of the business of which consists of receiving deposits and making loans and discounts, or of exercising fiduciary powers similar to those permitted to national banks under authority of the Comptroller of the Currency, and which is subject by law to supervision and examination by State or Federal authority having supervision over banking institutions;

(2) Any credit union the member accounts of which are insured in accordance with the provisions of title II of the Federal Credit Union Act, 12 U.S.C. 1781 et seq.; and

(3) A corporation which, under the laws of the State of its incorporation, is subject to supervision and examination by the Commissioner of Banking or other officer of such State in charge of the administration of the banking laws of such State.

(c) *21-day holding period.*—(1) *In general.*—When a levy is made on deposits held by a bank, the bank shall surrender such deposits (not otherwise subject to an attachment or execution under judicial process) only after 21 calendar days after the date the levy is made. The district director may request an extension of the 21-day holding period pursuant to paragraph (d)(2) of this section. During the prescribed holding period, or any extension thereof, the levy shall be released only upon notification to the bank by the district director of a decision by the Internal Revenue Service to release the levy. If the bank does not receive such notification from the district director within the prescribed holding period, or any extension thereof, the bank must surrender the deposits, including any interest thereon as determined in accordance with paragraph (c)(2) of this section (up to the amount of the levy), on the first business day after the holding period, or any extension thereof, expires. See § 301.6331-1(c) to determine when a levy served by mail is made.

(2) *Payment of interest on deposits.*—When a bank surrenders levied deposits at the end of the 21-day holding period (or at the end of any longer period that has been requested by the district director), the bank must include any interest that has accrued on the deposits prior to and during the holding period, and any extension thereof, under the terms of the bank's agreement with its depositor, but the bank must not surrender an amount greater than the amount of the levy. If the deposits are held in a non-interest bearing account at the time the levy is made, the bank need not include any interest on the deposits at the end of the holding period, or any extension thereof, under this paragraph. Interest that accrues on deposits and is surrendered to the district director at the end of the holding period, or any extension thereof, is treated as a payment to the bank's customer.

(3) *Transactions affecting accounts.*—A levy on deposits held by a bank applies to those funds on deposit at the time the levy is made, up to the amount of the levy, and is effective as of the time the levy is made. No withdrawals may be made on levied upon deposits during the 21-day holding period, or any extension thereof.

(4) *Waiver of 21-day holding period.*—A depositor may waive the 21-day holding period by notifying the bank of the depositor's intention to do so. Where more than one depositor is listed as the owner of a levied account, all depositors listed as owners of the account must agree to a waiver of the 21-day holding period. If the 21-day holding period is waived, the bank must include with the surrendered deposits a notification to the district director of the waiver.

(5) *Examples.*—The provisions of this paragraph (c) may be illustrated by the following examples:

*Example 1.* On April 2, 1992, a notice of levy for an unpaid income tax assessment due from A in the amount of $10,000 is served on X Bank with respect to A's savings account. At the time the notice of levy is served, X Bank holds $5,000 in A's interest-bearing savings account. On April 24, 1992, (the first business day after the 21-day holding period) X Bank must surrender $5,000 plus any interest that accrued on the account under the terms of A's contract with X Bank up through April 23, 1992 (the last day of the holding period).

*Example 2.* The facts are the same as in *Example* 1 except that on April 3, 1992, A deposits an additional $5,000 into the account. On April 24, 1992, X Bank must still surrender only $5,000 plus the interest which accrued thereon until the end of the holding period, because the notice of levy served on April 2, 1992, attached only to those funds on deposit at the time the notice was served and not to any subsequent deposits.

*Example 3.* The facts are the same as in *Example* 1 except that at the time the notice of levy is served on X Bank, A's savings account contains $50,000. On April 24, 1992, X Bank must surrender $10,000, which is the amount of the levy. The levy will not apply to any interest that accrues on the deposit during the 21-day holding period, because the entire amount of the levy is satisfied by the deposits existing at the time the levy is served.

*Example 4.* The facts are the same as in *Example* 1 except that the amount of the levy is $5,002. Under the terms of A's contract with the bank, the account will earn more than $2 of interest during the 21-day holding period. On April 24, 1992, X Bank must surrender $5,002 to the district director. The remaining interest which accrued during the 21-day holding period is not subject to the levy.

*Example 5.* On September 3, 1992, A opens a $5,000 six-month certificate of deposit account with X Bank. Under the terms of the account, the depositor must forfeit up to 30 days of interest on the account in the event of early withdrawal. On January 4, 1993, a notice of levy for an unpaid income tax assessment due from A in the amount of $10,000 is served with respect to A's certificate of deposit account. On January 26, 1993, the bank must surrender $5,000 plus the interest which accrued on the account through January 25, 1993, minus the penalty of 30 days of interest as provided in the deposit agreement.

*Example 6.* Same facts as in *Example 5* except that the notice of levy is served on X Bank on February 15, 1993. The certificate matures on March 2, 1993. On March 8, X Bank must surrender $5,000 plus the interest that accrued on the certificate without any reduction for penalties.

(d) *Notification to the district director of errors with respect to levied upon bank accounts.*—(1) *In general.*—If a depositor believes that there

is an error with respect to the levied upon account which the depositor wishes to have corrected, the depositor shall notify the district director to whom the assessment is charged by telephone to the telephone number listed on the face of the notice of levy in order to enable the district director to conduct an expeditious review of the alleged error. The district director may require any supporting documentation necessary to the review of the alleged error. The notification by telephone provided for in this section does not constitute or substitute for the filing by a third party of a written request under § 301.6343-1(b)(2) for the return of property wrongfully levied upon.

(2) *Disputes regarding the merits of the underlying assessment.*— This section does not constitute an additional procedure for an appeal regarding the merits of an underlying assessment. However, if in the judgment of the district director a genuine dispute regarding the merits of an underlying assessment appears to exist, the district director may request an extension of the 21-day holding period.

(3) *Notification of errors from sources other than the depositor.*—The district director may take action to release the levy on the bank account based on information obtained from a source other than the depositor, including the bank in which the account is maintained.

(e) *Effective date.*—These provisions are effective with respect to levies issued on or after January 4, 1993. [Reg. § 301.6332-3.]

☐ [T.D. 8466, 12-31-92.]

**[Reg. § 301.6333-1]**

**§ 301.6333-1. Production of books.**—If a levy has been made or is about to be made on any property or rights to property, any person, having custody or control of any books or records containing evidence or statements relating to the property or rights to property subject to levy, shall, upon demand of the internal revenue officer who has made or is about to make the levy, exhibit such books or records to such officer. [Reg. § 301.6333-1.

☐ [T.D. 6119, 12-31-54.]

**[Reg. § 301.6334-1]**

**§ 301.6334-1. Property exempt from levy.**—(a) *Enumeration.*—In addition to exemptions allowed as a matter of Internal Revenue Service policy, there shall be exempt from levy—

(1) *Wearing apparel and school books.*—Such items of wearing apparel and such school books as are necessary for the taxpayer or for members of his family. Expensive items of wearing apparel, such as furs, which are luxuries and are not necessary for the taxpayer or for members of his family, are not exempt from levy.

(2) *Fuel, provisions, furniture, and personal effects.*—So much of the fuel, provisions, furniture, and personal effects in the taxpayer's household, and of the arms for personal use, livestock, and poultry of the taxpayer, that does not exceed $6,250 in value.

(3) *Books and tools of a trade, business or profession.*—So many of the books and tools necessary for the trade, business, or profession of an individual taxpayer as do not exceed in the aggregate $3,125 in value.

(4) *Unemployment benefits.*—Any amount payable to an individual with respect to his unemployment (including any portion thereof payable with respect to dependents) under an unemployment compensation law of the United States, of any State, or of the District of Columbia or of the Commonwealth of Puerto Rico.

(5) *Undelivered mail.*—Mail, addressed to any person, which has not been delivered to the addressee.

(6) *Certain annuity and pension payments.*—Annuity or pension payments under the Railroad Retirement Act (45 U.S.C. ch. 9), benefits under the Railroad Unemployment Insurance Act (45 U.S.C. ch. 11), special pension payments received by a person whose name has been entered on the Army, Navy, Air Force, and Coast Guard Medal of Honor roll (38 U.S.C. 562), and annuities based on retired or retainer pay under chapter 73 of title 10 of the United States Code.

(7) *Workmen's compensation.*—Any amount payable to an individual as workmen's compensation (including any portion thereof payable with respect to dependents) under a workmen's compensation law of the United States, any State, the District of Columbia, or the Commonwealth of Puerto Rico.

(8) *Judgments for support of minor children.*—If the taxpayer is required under any type of order or decree (including an interlocutory decree or a decree of support pendente lite) of a court of competent jurisdiction, entered prior to the date of levy, to contribute to the support of that taxpayer's minor children, so much of that taxpayer's salary, wages, or other income as is necessary to comply with such order or decree. The taxpayer must establish the amount

necessary to comply with the order or decree. The Service is not required to release a levy until such time as it is established that the amount to be released from levy actually will be applied in satisfaction of the support obligation. The Service may make arrangements with a delinquent taxpayer to establish a specific amount of such taxpayer's salary, wage, or other income for each pay period that shall be exempt from levy, for purposes of complying with a support obligation. If the taxpayer has more than one source of income sufficient to satisfy the support obligation imposed by the order or decree, the amount exempt from levy, at the discretion of the Service, may be allocated entirely to one salary, wage or source of other income or be apportioned between the several salaries, wages, or other sources of income.

(9) *Minimum exemption for wages, salary, and other income.*— Amounts payable to or received by the taxpayer as wages or salary for personal services, or as other income, to the extent provided in §301.6334-2 through §301.6334-4.

(10) *Certain service-connected disability payments.*—Any amount payable to an individual as a service-connected (within the meaning of section 101(16) of title 38, United States Code (U.S.C.)) disability benefit under—

(i) Subchapters II (wartime disability compensation), III (wartime death compensation), IV (peacetime disability compensation), V (peacetime death compensation), or VI (general compensation provisions) of chapter 11 of title 38, U.S.C.; or

(ii) Chapters 13 (dependency and indemnity compensation for service commenced deaths), 21 (specially adapted housing for disabled veterans), 23 (burial benefits), 31 (vocational rehabilitation), 32 (post-Vietnam era veterans' educational assistance), 34 (veterans' educational assistance), 35 (survivors' and dependents' educational assistance), 37 (home, condominium, and mobile home loans), or 39 (automobiles and adaptive equipment for certain disabled veterans and members of the armed forces) of title 38, U.S.C.

(11) *Certain public assistance payments.*—Any amount payable to an individual as a recipient of public assistance under—

(i) Title IV or title XVI (relating to supplemental security income for the aged, blind, and disabled) of the Social Security Act, (42 U.S.C. 301 et seq.); or

(ii) State or local government public assistance or public welfare programs for which eligibility is determined by a needs or income test.

(12) *Assistance under Job Training Partnership Act.*—Any amount payable to a participant under the Job Training Partnership Act (29 U.S.C. 1501 et seq.) from funds appropriated pursuant to such Act.

(13) *Residences exempt in small deficiency cases and principal residences and certain business assets exempt in absence of certain approval or jeopardy.*—(i) *Residences in small deficiency cases.* If the amount of the levy does not exceed $5,000, any real property used as a residence of the taxpayer or any real property of the taxpayer (other than real property which is rented) used by any other individual as a residence.

(ii) *Principal residences and certain business assets.* Except to the extent provided in section 6334(e), the principal residence (within the meaning of section 121) of the taxpayer and tangible personal property or real property (other than real property which is rented) used in the trade or business of an individual taxpayer.

(b) *Appraisal.*—The internal revenue officer seizing property of the type described in section 6334(a) shall appraise and set aside to the owner the amount of such property declared to be exempt. If the taxpayer objects at the time of the seizure to the valuation fixed by the officer making the seizure, such officer shall summon three disinterested individuals who shall make the valuation.

(c) *Other property.*—No other property or rights to property are exempt from levy except the property specifically exempted by section 6334(a). No provision of a State law may exempt property or rights to property from levy for the collection of any Federal tax. Thus, property exempt from execution under State personal or homestead exemption laws is, nevertheless, subject to levy by the United States for collection of its taxes.

(d) *Levy allowed on principal residence.*—The Service will seek approval, in writing, by a judge or magistrate of a district court of the United States prior to levy of property that is owned by the taxpayer and used as the principal residence of the taxpayer, the taxpayer's spouse, the taxpayer's former spouse, or the taxpayer's minor child.

(1) *Nature of judicial proceeding.*—The Government will initiate a proceeding for judicial approval of levy on a principal residence by filing a petition with the appropriate United States District Court demonstrating that the underlying liability has not been satisfied, the requirements of any applicable law or administrative procedure relevant to the levy have been met, and no reasonable alternative for collection of the taxpayer's debt exists. The petition will ask the court to issue to the taxpayer an order to show cause why the principal residence property should not be levied and will also ask the court to issue a notice of hearing.

(2) The taxpayer will be granted a hearing to rebut the Government's prima facie case if the taxpayer files an objection within the time period required by the court raising a genuine issue of material fact demonstrating that the underlying tax liability has been satisfied, that the taxpayer has other assets from which the liability can be satisfied, or that the Service did not follow the applicable laws or procedures pertaining to the levy. The taxpayer is not permitted to challenge the merits underlying the tax liability in the proceeding. Unless the taxpayer files a timely and appropriate objection, the court would be expected to enter an order approving the levy of the principal residence property.

(3) *Notice letter to be issued to certain family members.*—If the property to be levied is owned by the taxpayer but is used as the principal residence of the taxpayer's spouse, the taxpayer's former spouse, or the taxpayer's minor child, the Government will send a letter to each such person providing notice of the commencement of the proceeding. The letter will be addressed in the name of the taxpayer's spouse or exspouse, individually or on behalf of any minor children. If it is unclear who is living in the principal residence property and/or what such person's relationship is to the taxpayer, a letter will be addressed to "Occupant". The purpose of the letter is to provide notice to the family members that the property may be levied. The family members may not be joined as parties to the judicial proceeding because the levy attaches only to the taxpayer's legal interest in the subject property and the family members have no legal standing to contest the proposed levy.

(e) *Levy allowed on certain business assets.*—The property described in section 6334(a)(13)(B)(ii) shall not be exempt from levy if—

(1) An Area Director of the Service personally approves (in writing) the levy of such property; or

(2) The Secretary finds that the collection of tax is in jeopardy. An Area Director may not approve a levy under paragraph (e)(1) unless the Area Director determines that the taxpayer's other assets subject to collection are insufficient to pay the amount due, together with expenses of the proceeding. When other assets of an individual taxpayer include permits issued by a State and required under State law for the harvest of fish or wildlife in the taxpayer's trade or business, the taxpayer's other assets also include future income that may be derived by such taxpayer from the commercial sale of fish or wildlife under such permit.

(f) *Levy allowed on certain specified payments.*—Any payment described in section 6331(h)(2)(B) or (C) shall not be exempt from levy if the Secretary approves the levy thereon under section 6331(h).

(g) *Inflation adjustment.*—For any calendar year beginning after 1999, each dollar amount referred to in paragraphs (a)(2) and (3) of this section will be increased by an amount equal to the dollar amount multiplied by the cost-of-living adjustment determined under section 1(f)(3) for the calendar year (using the language "calendar year 1998" instead of "calendar year 1992" in section 1(f)(3)(B)). If any dollar amount as adjusted is not a multiple of $10, the dollar amount will be rounded to the nearest multiple of $10 (rounding up if the amount is a multiple of $5).

(h) *Effective date.*—This section is generally effective with respect to levies made on or after July 1, 1989. However, any reasonable attempt by a taxpayer to comply with the statutory amendments addressed by the regulations in this section prior to February 21, 1995, will be considered as meeting the requirements of the regulations in this section. In addition, paragraph (a)(11)(i) of this section is applicable with respect to levies issued after December 31, 1996. Paragraphs (a)(2), (a)(3), (a)(8), (a)(13), (d), (e), (f), (g) and (h) of this section apply as of March 7, 2005. [Reg. §301.6334-1.]

☐ [T.D. 6119, 12-31-54. *Amended by* T.D. 6292, 4-18-58; T.D. 6425, 11-10-59; T.D. 6498, 10-24-60; T.D. 6870, 12-30-65; T.D. 7180, 4-12-72; T.D. 7182, 4-20-72; T.D 7620, 5-11-79; T.D. 8568, 10-20-94; T.D. 8725, 7-21-97 and T.D. 9189, 3-4-2005.]

**[Reg. §301.6334-2]**

**§301.6334-2. Wages, salary and other income.**—(a) *In general.*— Under section 6334(a)(9) and (d) certain amounts payable to or received by a taxpayer as wages, salary, or other income are exempt from levy. This section describes the income of a taxpayer that is eligible for the exemption from levy (paragraph (b) of this section) and how exempt amounts are to be paid to the taxpayer(paragraph (c) of this section). Section 301.6334-3 describes that sum that will be exempt from levy for each of the taxpayer's pay periods. Pay periods are described in §301.6334-3. For the amounts exempt from levy, see §301.6334-3.

(b) *Eligible taxpayer income.*—Only wages, salary, or other income payable to the taxpayer after the levy is made on the payor may be exempt from levy under section 6334(a)(9). No amount of wages, salary, or other income that is paid to the taxpayer before levy is made on the payor will be so exempt from levy under section 6334(a)(9). The provisions of this paragraph (b) may be illustrated by the following example:

*Example.* Delinquent taxpayer A, an individual, is employed by the M Corporation and is paid wages on Friday of each week. Accordingly, A is paid wages on Friday, February 16, 1990. On Saturday, February 17, A deposits these wages into his personal checking account at Bank N. On Tuesday, February 20, a notice of levy is served on the M Corporation and also on Bank N. Amounts payable to A as wages on Friday, February 23, 1990, and any payday thereafter may be exempt from levy under section 6334(a)(9). No amount of wages A deposited in his account at Bank N on February 17, 1990, is exempt from levy under section 6334(a)(9).

(c) *Payment of exempt amounts to taxpayer.*—(1) *From wages, salary, or income from other sources where levy on all sources not made.*—In the case of a taxpayer who has more than one source of wages, salary, or other income, the district director may elect to levy on only one or more sources while leaving other sources of income free from levy. If the wages, salary, or other income that the district director leaves free from levy equal or exceed the amount to which the taxpayer is entitled as an exemption from levy under section 6334(a)(9), computed in accordance with §301.6334-3 (and are not otherwise exempt), the district director may treat no amount of the taxpayer's wages, salary, or other income on which the district director elects to levy as exempt from levy. In such a case, the district director must notify the employer or other person upon whom the levy is served that no amount of the taxpayer's wages, salary, or other income is exempt from levy. The employer or other person upon whom the levy is served may rely on such notification in paying over amounts pursuant to the levy. In the absence of such notification from the district director, however, the employer or other person upon whom the levy is served must determine the amount exempt from levy pursuant to §301.6334-3 as if that employer or other person upon whom the levy is served is the only source of wages, salary, or other income. Amounts not exempt from levy are to be paid to the district director in accordance with the terms of the levy. The provisions of this paragraph (c)(1) may be illustrated by the following example:

*Example.* Delinquent taxpayer C is an employee of O Corporation and is paid wages totalling $450 on Friday of each week. C also performs services for P Corporation and is paid a salary of $250 on Friday of each week. On Tuesday, February 20, 1990, a levy is served on O Corporation with respect to the wages payable to C. A levy is not served on P Corporation. C's filing status is single and C is entitled to 1 personal exemption. Under §301.6334-3, C is entitled to an exemption from levy under 6334(a)(9) totalling $101.92 for each weekly pay period. However, because levy has not been made on C's salary paid by the P Corporation ($250 per week) and that salary exceeds the weekly amount ($101.92) to which C is entitled as exempt from levy, the district director may treat no amount of C's wages paid by the O Corporation as exempt from levy. If the district director requires such treatment, the district director must notify O Corporation that no amount of C's wages is exempt from levy and O Corporation may rely on such notification; in the absence of such notification O Corporation must treat $101.92 as exempt from levy.

(2) *Where sources not levied upon are less than exempt amount.*—If the taxpayer's income upon which the district director does not levy is less than the amount to which the taxpayer is entitled as exempt from levy, then an additional amount, determined to be exempt from levy pursuant to §301.6334-3, may be paid to the taxpayer from the sources of wages, salary, or other income upon which levy has been made. In such a case, the district director must designate those wages, salary, or other income from which the exempt amount is to be paid to the taxpayer, and must notify the employer or other person upon whom the levy is served of the amount of the taxpayer's wages, salary, or other income that is exempt from levy. The employer or other person may rely on such notification in paying over amounts pursuant to the levy. In the absence of such notification from the district director, the employer or other person upon whom the levy is served must determine the amount exempt from levy pursuant to §301.6334-3 as if that employer or other person upon whom the levy is served is the only source of wages, salary, or other income. Amounts not exempt from levy are to be paid to the district director in accordance with the terms of the levy. The provisions of this paragraph (c)(2) may be illustrated by the following example:

*Example.* Delinquent taxpayer C is an employee of O Corporation and is paid wages totalling $50 on Friday of each week. C also performs services for P Corporation and is paid a salary of $75 on

Friday of each week. On Tuesday, February 20, 1990, a levy is served on P Corporation with respect to the wages and salary of C. C's filing status is single and C is entitled to 1 personal exemption. Under §301.6334-3, C is entitled to an exemption from levy under section 6334(a)(9) totalling $101.92 for each weekly pay period. The district director may notify P Corporation that only $51.92 of C's wages is exempt from levy and P Corporation may rely on such notification; in the absence of such notification, P Corporation must treat the entire $75 salary as exempt from levy.

(d) *Effective date.*—These provisions are effective with respect to levies made on or after July 1, 1989. However, any reasonable attempt by a taxpayer to comply with the statutory amendments addressed by these regulations prior to February 21, 1995 will be considered as meeting the requirements of these regulations. [Reg. §301.6334-2.]

☐ [*T.D. 7620, 5-11-79. Amended by T.D. 8568, 10-20-94.*]

**[Reg. §301.6334-3]**

§301.6334-3. **Determination of exempt amount.**—(a) *Individuals paid on weekly basis.*—In the case of any individual who is paid or receives all of his or her wages, salary, and other income on a weekly basis, the amount of wages, salary, and other income payable to or received by him or her during any week that is exempt from levy under section 6334(a)(9) is the exempt amount.

(b) *Term defined.*—The term *exempt amount* means an amount equal to—

(1) The sum of—

(i) The standard deduction (including additional standard deductions on account of age or blindness); and

(ii) The aggregate amount of the deductions for personal exemptions allowed the taxpayer under section 151 in the taxable year in which such levy occurs;

(2) Divided by 52.

(c) *Written and properly verified statement.*—Unless the taxpayer submits to the employer for forwarding to the district director a written and properly verified statement (as described in §301.6334-4) specifying the facts necessary to determine the proper amount under paragraphs (b)(1)(i) and (ii) of this section, paragraphs (b)(1)(i) and (ii) of this section must be applied as if the taxpayer were a married individual filing a separate return with only 1 personal exemption.

(d) *Individuals paid on basis other than weekly.*—(1) *In general.*—In the case of an individual who is paid or receives wages, salary, and other income other than on a weekly basis, the amount payable to that individual during any applicable pay period that is exempt from levy under section 6334(a)(9) is the amount that as nearly as possible will result in the same total exemption from levy for such individual over that period of time other than weekly as that to which the individual would have been entitled under paragraph (b) of this section if, during such period of time, the individual were paid or received such wages, salary, and other income on a regular weekly basis.

(2) *Specific pay periods other than weekly.*—In the case of wages, salary, or other income paid to an individual on the basis of an established calendar period regularly used by the employer or other person levied upon for payroll or payment purposes, the exempt amount of wages, salary, and other income payable to or received by an individual during an applicable pay period other than weekly equals—

(i) The sum of—

(A) The standard deduction (including additional standard deductions on account of age or blindness); and

(B) The aggregate amount of the deductions for personal exemptions allowed the taxpayer under section 151 in the taxable year in which such levy occurs;

(ii) Divided by—

(A) 260 in the case of a daily pay period;

(B) 26 in the case of a bi-weekly pay period;

(C) 24 in the case of a semi-monthly pay period; and

(D) 12 in the case of a monthly pay period.

(3) *Nonspecific pay periods.*—In the case of wages, salary, or other income paid to an individual on a one-time or a recurrent but irregular basis and which is not paid on the basis of an established calendar period regularly used by the employer or other person levied upon for payroll or payment purposes, the exempt amount of wages, salary, and other income payable to or received by an individual equals the exempt amount defined in paragraph (b) of this section multiplied by the number (but not more than 52) of full weeks (consisting of seven calendar days) to which such payment is attributable. The provisions of this paragraph (d)(3) may be illustrated by the following example:

*Example.* Taxpayer A's exempt amount per week (as determined under paragraph (b) of this section) is $100. Taxpayer A is hired by Corporation X to perform a specific task for Corporation X at a flat fee of $1,500 which is to be paid at the completion of the task. Taxpayer A completes the task in 10 weeks. The total exempt amount is $1,000 and $500 is subject to levy.

(e) *Levies continuing into following years.*—The exempt amount is computed on the basis of the standard deduction (including additional standard deductions on account of age or blindness) for the taxpayer's filing status and the amount of the deduction for a personal exemption in effect in the taxable year in which the original notice of levy is served. Unless the taxpayer submits a new verified statement in accordance with §301.6334-4, the exempt amount remains the same for pay periods following the pay period in which the notice of levy is served even if there is a change in the taxpayer's factual situation or a change by operation of law (such as by indexing or otherwise) to the standard deduction or personal exemption amounts.

(f) *Effective date.*—These provisions are effective with respect to levies made on or after July 1, 1989. However, any reasonable attempt by a taxpayer to comply with the statutory amendments addressed by these regulations prior to February 21, 1995 will be considered as meeting the requirements of these regulations. [Reg. §301.6334-3.]

☐ [*T.D.* 7620, 5-11-79. *Amended by T.D.* 8568, 10-20-94.]

### [Reg. §301.6334-4]

**§301.6334-4. Verified statements.**—(a) *In general.*—For purposes of §§301.6334-2 and 301.6334-3, the amount of wages, salary, or other income that is exempt from levy must be determined on the basis of a written and properly verified statement submitted by the taxpayer to his or her employer for submission to the district director specifying the facts necessary to determine the standard deduction and the aggregate amount of the deductions for personal exemptions allowed the taxpayer under section 151 in the taxable year in which the levy is served. In the absence of submission of such statement, the amount that is exempt from levy must be determined as if the taxpayer were a married individual filing a separate return with only 1 personal exemption.

(b) *Content of statement.*—The statement in paragraph (a) of this section must be a written statement signed under penalty of perjury, and dated, containing the following information—

(1) The filing status of the taxpayer as either:

(i) Single;

(ii) Married filing a joint return;

(iii) Married filing a separate return;

(iv) Head of household; or

(v) Qualifying widow or widower with dependent child;

(2) The name, relationship, and Social Security Number of each individual whom the taxpayer can claim as a personal exemption on the taxpayer's income tax return; and

(3) Any additional standard deductions that the taxpayer can claim on account of age (65 or older) or blindness on the taxpayer's income tax return.

(c) *Submission of verified statement.*—(1) *Obligation of employer.*—An employer upon whom a notice of levy for wages, salary, or other income of a taxpayer is served must promptly notify the taxpayer of the fact that a notice of levy has been served. Unless otherwise indicated on the face of the notice of levy, the employer must request the taxpayer to provide the employer with a written statement signed under penalty of perjury, and dated, containing the information set forth in paragraph (b) of this section, and this statement must be submitted by the employer to the district director. The employer must submit this statement to the district director at the time the employer first responds to the notice of levy.

(2) *Submission by taxpayer.*—The taxpayer must provide the employer upon whom the notice of levy has been served with a verified statement complying with paragraph (b) of this section. Unless the taxpayer provides a verified statement, the amount that is exempt from levy must be determined as if the taxpayer were a married individual filing a separate return with only 1 personal exemption.

(3) *Additional statements.*—A taxpayer may submit a verified statement to his or her employer at any time. Except as otherwise provided in paragraph (d) of this section, such verified statement will be effective for any payment of wages, salary, or other income made after the date of submission and will replace any previously submitted verified statement. The employer must provide the district director with the statement on the next occasion on which the employer responds to the notice of levy.

(d) *Effect of verified statement.*—(1) A verified statement submitted by an employee is effective upon receipt by the employer, and the employer is required to compute the exempt amount on the basis of the information contained in the verified statement unless notified to the contrary by the Internal Revenue Service.

(2) The Internal Revenue Service may find that a verified statement submitted by an employee contains a materially incorrect statement, or it may determine, after written request to the employee for verification of information contained in the verified statement, that it lacks sufficient information to determine whether the verified statement is correct. If the Internal Revenue Service so finds or determines, and notifies the employer in writing that the verified statement is defective, upon receipt of such notice the employer shall consider the verified statement to be defective for purposes of computing the exempt amount.

(3) If the Internal Revenue Service notifies the employer that the verified statement is defective, the Internal Revenue Service will, based upon its finding, advise the employer that the employer is to compute the exempt amount as if no verified statement had been submitted by the employee or will describe upon what basis the exempt amount is to be computed. The Internal Revenue Service will also specify which Internal Revenue Service office to contact for further information.

(4) In addition to any notice furnished to the employer for the employer's use, the Internal Revenue Service will provide the employer with a copy for the employee of each notice it furnishes the employer.

(5) The employer must promptly furnish the employee with a copy of any Internal Revenue Service notice with respect to a verified statement submitted by the employee.

(6) Once paragraph (d)(3) of this section applies, the employer must continue to compute the exempt amount on the basis of the written notice from the Internal Revenue Service until the Internal Revenue Service by written notice advises the employer to compute the exempt amount on the basis of a new verified statement (as described in paragraph (d)(7) of this section) and revokes its earlier written notice.

(7) Once paragraph (d)(3) of this section applies, the employee may submit a new verified statement together with a written explanation of any circumstances of the employee which have changed since the Internal Revenue Service's earlier written notice, or any other circumstances or reasons as justification or support for the claims made by the employee on the new verified statement. The employee may submit the new verified statement and written explanation either—

(i) To the Internal Revenue Service office specified in the notice furnished to the employer under paragraph (d)(3) of this section; or

(ii) To the employer, who must forward the new verified statement and written explanation to the Internal Revenue Service office specified in the notice earlier furnished to the employer on the next occasion on which the employer responds to the notice of levy.

(e) *Effective date.*—These provisions are effective with respect to levies made on or after July 1, 1989. However, any reasonable attempt by a taxpayer to comply with the statutory amendments addressed by these regulations prior to February 21, 1995 will be considered as meeting the requirements of these regulations. [Reg. §301.6334-4.]

☐ [*T.D.* 7620, 5-11-79. *Amended by T.D.* 8568, 10-20-94.]

### [Reg. §301.6335-1]

**§301.6335-1. Sale of seized property.**—(a) *Notice of seizure.*—As soon as practicable after seizure of property, the internal revenue officer seizing the property shall give notice in writing to the owner of the property (or, in the case of personal property, to the possessor thereof). The written notice shall be delivered to the owner (or to the possessor, in the case of personal property) or left at his usual place of abode or business if he has such within the internal revenue district where the seizure is made. If the owner cannot be readily located, or has no dwelling or place of business within such district, the notice may be mailed to his last known address. Such notice shall specify the sum demanded and shall contain, in the case of personal property, a list sufficient to identify the property seized and, in the case of real property, a description with reasonable certainty of the property seized.

(b) *Notice of sale.*—(1) As soon as practicable after seizure of the property, the district director shall give notice of sale in writing to the owner. Such notice shall be delivered to the owner or left at his usual place of abode or business if located within the internal revenue district where the seizure is made. If the owner cannot be readily located, or has no dwelling or place of business within such district, the notice may be mailed to his last known address. For further guidance regarding the definition of last known address, see §301.6212-2. The notice shall specify the property to be sold, and the time, place, manner, and conditions of the sale thereof, and shall expressly state that only the right, title, and interest of the delinquent taxpayer in and to such property is to be offered for sale. The notice shall also be published in some newspaper published in the county wherein the seizure is made or in a newspaper generally circulated in that county. For example, if a newspaper of general circulation in a county but not published in that county will reach more potential bidders for the property to be sold than a newspaper published within the county, or if there is a newspaper of general circulation within the county but no newspaper published within the county, the district director may cause public notice of the sale to be given in the newspaper of general circulation within the county. If there is no newspaper published or generally circulated in the county, the notice shall be posted at the post office nearest the place where the seizure is made, and in not less than two other public places.

(2) The district director may use other methods of giving notice of sale and of advertising seized property in addition to those referred to in subparagraph (1) when he believes that the nature of the property to be sold is such that a wider or more specialized advertising coverage will enhance the possibility of obtaining a higher price for the property.

(3) Whenever levy is made without regard to the 10-day period provided in section 6331(a) (relating to cases in which collection is in jeopardy), a public notice of sale of the property seized shall not be made within such 10-day period unless section 6336 (relating to perishable goods) is applicable.

(c) *Time, place, manner, and conditions of sale.*—The time, place, manner, and conditions of the sale of property seized by levy shall be as follows:

(1) *Time and place of sale.*—The time of sale shall not be less than 10 days nor more than 40 days from the time of giving public notice under section 6335(b) (see paragraph (b) of this section). The place of sale shall be within the county in which the property is seized, except that if it appears to the district director under whose supervision the seizure was made that substantially higher bids may be obtained for the property if the sale is held at a place outside such county, he may order that the sale be held in such other place. The sale shall be held at the time and place stated in the notice of sale.

(2) *Adjournment of sale.*—When it appears to the district director that an adjournment of the sale will best serve the interest of the United States or that of the taxpayer, the district director may adjourn, or cause the internal revenue officer conducting the sale to adjourn, the sale from time to time, but the date of the sale shall not be later than one month after the date fixed in the original notice of sale.

(3) *Determinations relating to minimum price.*—(i) *Minimum price.*—Before the sale of property seized by levy, the district director shall determine a minimum price, taking into account the expenses of levy and sale, for which the property shall be sold. The internal revenue officer conducting the sale may either announce the minimum price before the sale begins, or defer announcement of the minimum price until after the receipt of the highest bid, in which case, if the highest bid is greater than the minimum price, no announcement of the minimum price shall be made.

(ii) *Purchase by the United States.*—Before the sale of property seized by levy, the district director shall determine whether the purchase of property by the United States at the minimum price would be in the best interest of the United States. In determining whether the purchase of property would be in the best interest of the United States, the district director may consider all relevant facts and circumstances including for example—

(a) Marketability of the property;

(b) Cost of maintaining the property;

(c) Cost of repairing or restoring the property;

(d) Cost of transporting the property;

(e) Cost of safeguarding the property;

(f) Cost of potential toxic waste cleanup; and

(g) Other factors pertinent to the type of property.

(iii) *Effective date.*—This paragraph (c)(3) applies to determinations relating to minimum price made on or after December 17, 1996.

(4) *Disposition of property at sale.*—(i) *Sale to highest bidder at or above minimum price.*—If one or more persons offer to buy the property for at least the amount of the minimum price, the property shall be sold to the highest bidder.

(ii) *Property deemed sold to United States at minimum price.*—If no one offers at least the amount of the minimum price for the property and the Secretary has determined that it would be in the best interest of the United States to purchase the property for the minimum price, the property shall be declared to be sold to the United States for the minimum price.

(iii) *Release to owner.*—If the property is not declared to be sold under paragraph (c)(4)(i) or (ii) of this section, the property shall be released to the owner of the property and the expense of the levy and sale shall be added to the amount of tax for the collection of which the United States made the levy. Any property released under this paragraph (c)(4)(iii) shall remain subject to any lien imposed by subchapter C of chapter 64 of subtitle F of the Internal Revenue Code.

(iv) *Effective date.*—This paragraph (c)(4) applies to dispositions of property at sale made on or after December 17, 1996.

(5) *Offering of property.*—(i) *Sale of indivisible property.*—If any property levied upon is not divisible, so as to enable the district director by sale of a part thereof to raise the whole amount of the tax and expenses of levy and sale, the whole of such property shall be sold. For application of surplus proceeds of sale, see section 6342(b).

(ii) *Separately, in groups, or in the aggregate.*—The seized property may be offered for sale—

(a) As separate items, or

(b) As groups of items, or

(c) In the aggregate, or

(d) Both as separate items (or in groups) and in the aggregate. In such cases, the property shall be sold under the method which produces the highest aggregate amount.

The district director shall select whichever of the foregoing methods of offering the property for sale as, in his opinion, is most feasible under all the facts and circumstances of the case, except that if the property to be sold includes both real and personal property, only the personal property may be grouped for the purpose of offering such property for sale. However, real and personal property may be offered for sale in the aggregate, provided the real property, as separate items, and the personal property as a group, or as groups, or as separate items, are first offered separately.

(iii) *Condition of title and of property.*—Only the right, title, and interest of the delinquent taxpayer in and to the property seized shall be offered for sale, and such interest shall be offered subject to any prior outstanding mortgages, encumbrances, or other liens in favor of third parties which are valid as against the delinquent taxpayer and are superior to the lien of the United States. All seized property shall be offered for sale "as is" and "where is" and without recourse against the United States. No guaranty or warranty, express or implied, shall be made by the internal revenue officer offering the property for sale, as to the validity of the title, quality, quantity, weight, size, or condition of any of the property, or its fitness for any use or purpose. No claim shall be considered for allowance or adjustment or for rescission of the sale based upon failure of the property to conform with any representation, express or implied.

(iv) *Terms of payment.*—The property shall be offered for sale upon whichever of the following terms is fixed by the district director in the public notice of sale:

(a) Payment in full upon acceptance of the highest bid, without regard to the amount of such bid, or

(b) If the aggregate price of all property purchased by a successful bidder at the sale is more than $200, an initial payment of $200 or 20 percent of the purchase price, whichever is the greater, and payment of the balance (including all costs incurred for the protection or preservation of the property subsequent to the sale and prior to final payment) within a specified period, not to exceed one month from the date of the sale.

(6) *Method of sale.*—The district director shall sell the property either—

(i) At public auction, at which open competitive bids shall be received, or

(ii) At public sale under sealed bids. The following rules, in addition to the other rules provided in this paragraph, shall be applicable to public sale under sealed bids:

(a) *Invitation to bidders.*—Bids shall be solicited through a public notice of sale.

(b) *Form for use by bidders.*—A bid shall be submitted on a form which will be furnished by the district director upon request. The form shall be completed in accordance with the instructions thereon.

(c) *Remittance with bid.*—If the total bid is $200 or less, the full amount of the bid shall be submitted therewith. If the total bid is more than $200, 20 percent of such bid or $200, whichever is greater, shall be submitted therewith. (In the case of alternative bids submit-

**Seizure of Property For Collection of Taxes**
See p. 20,601 for regulations not amended to reflect law changes
**66,951**

ted by the same bidder for items of property offered separately, or in groups, or in the aggregate, the bidder shall remit the full amount of the highest alternative bid submitted, if that bid is $200 or less. If the highest alternative bid submitted is more than $200, the bidder shall remit 20 percent of the highest alternative bid or $200, whichever is greater.) Such remittance shall be by a certified, cashier's, or treasurer's check drawn on any bank or trust company incorporated under the laws of the United States or under the laws of any State, Territory, or possession of the United States, or by a United States postal, bank, express, or telegraph money order.

*(d) Time for receiving and opening bids.*—Each bid shall be submitted in a securely sealed envelope. The bidder shall indicate in the upper left hand corner of the envelope his name and address and the time and place of sale as announced in the public notice of sale. A bid will not be considered unless it is received by the internal revenue officer conducting the sale prior to the opening of the bids. The bids will be opened at the time and place stated in the notice of sale, or at the time fixed in the announcement of the adjournment of the sale.

*(e) Consideration of bids.*—The public notice of sale shall specify whether the property is to be sold separately, by groups, or in the aggregate or by a combination of these methods, as provided in subparagraph (4)(ii) of this paragraph. If the notice specifies an alternative method, bidders may submit bids under one or more of the alternatives. In case of error in the extension of prices in any bid, the unit price will govern. The internal revenue officer conducting the sale shall have the right to waive any technical defects in a bid. In the event two or more highest bids are equal in amount, the internal revenue officer conducting the sale shall determine the successful bidder by drawing lots. After the opening, examination, and consideration of all bids, the internal revenue officer conducting the sale shall announce the amount of the highest bid or bids and the name of the successful bidder or bidders. Any remittance submitted in connection with an unsuccessful bid shall be returned at the conclusion of the sale.

*(f) Withdrawal of bids.*—A bid may be withdrawn on written or telegraphic request received from the bidder prior to the time fixed for opening the bids. A technical defect in a bid confers no right on the bidder for the withdrawal of his bid after it has been opened.

(7) *Payment of bid price.*—All payments for property sold under this section shall be made by cash or by a certified, cashier's, or treasurer's check drawn on any bank or trust company incorporated under the laws of the United States or under the laws of any State, Territory, or possession of the United States, or by a United States postal, bank, express, or telegraph money order. If payment in full is required upon acceptance of the highest bid, the payment shall be made at such time. If deferred payment is permitted, the initial payment shall be made upon acceptance of the bid, and the balance shall be paid on or before the date fixed for payment thereof. Any remittance submitted with a successful sealed bid shall be applied toward the purchase price.

(8) *Delivery and removal of personal property.*—Responsibility of the United States for the protection or preservation of seized personal property shall cease immediately upon acceptance of the highest bid. The risk of loss is on the purchaser of personal property upon acceptance of his bid. Possession of any personal property shall not be delivered to the purchaser until the purchase price has been paid in full. If payment of part of the purchase price for personal property is deferred, the United States will retain possession of such property as security for the payment of the balance of the purchase price and, as agent for the purchaser, will cause the property to be cared for until the purchase price has been paid in full or the sale is declared null and void for failure to make full payment of the purchase price. In such case, all charges and expenses incurred in caring for the property after the acceptance of the bid shall be borne by the purchaser.

(9) *Default in payment.*—If payment in full is required upon acceptance of the bid and is not then and there paid, the internal revenue officer conducting the sale shall forthwith proceed again to sell the property in the manner provided in section 6335(e) and the regulations thereunder. If the conditions of the sale permit part of the payment to be deferred, and if such part is not paid within the prescribed period, suit may be instituted against the purchaser for the purchase price or such part thereof as has not been paid, together with interest at the rate of 6 percent per annum from the date of the sale; or, in the discretion of the district director, the sale may be declared by the district director to be null and void for failure to make full payment of the purchase price and the property may again be advertised and sold as provided in subsections (b), (c), and (e) of section 6335 and the regulations thereunder. In the event of such readvertisement and sale, any new purchaser shall receive such

property or rights to property free and clear of any claim or right of the former defaulting purchaser, of any nature whatsoever, and the amount paid upon the bid price by such defaulting purchaser shall be forfeited to the United States.

(10) *Stay of sale of seized property pending Tax Court decision.*—For restrictions on sale of seized property pending Tax Court decision, see section 6863(b)(3) and the regulations thereunder.

*(d) Right to request the sale of seized property.*—(1) *In general.*—The owner of any property seized by levy may request that the district director sell such property within 60 days after such request, or within any longer period specified by the owner. The district director must comply with such a request unless the district director determines that compliance with the request is not in the best interests of the Internal Revenue Service and notifies the owner of such determination within the 60 day period, or any longer period specified by the owner.

(2) *Procedures to request the sale of seized property.*—(i) *Manner.*—A request for the sale of seized property shall be made in writing to the group manager of the revenue officer whose signature is on Levy Form 668-B. If the owner does not know the group manager's name or address, the owner may send the request to the revenue officer, marked for the attention of his or her group manager.

(ii) *Form.*—The request for sale of seized property within 60 days, or such longer period specified by the owner, shall include:

(A) The name, current address, current home and work telephone numbers and any convenient times to be contacted, and taxpayer identification number of the owner making the request;

(B) A description of the seized property that is the subject of the request;

(C) A copy of the notice of seizure, if available;

(D) The period within which the owner is requesting that the property be sold; and

(E) The signature of the owner or duly authorized representative. For purposes of these regulations, a duly authorized representative is any attorney, certified public accountant, enrolled actuary, or any other person permitted to represent the owner before the Internal Revenue Service who is not disbarred or suspended from practice before the Internal Revenue Service and who has a written power of attorney executed by the owner.

(3) *Notification to owner.*—The group manager shall respond in writing to a request for sale of seized property as soon as practicable after receipt of such request and in no event later than 60 days after receipt of the request, or, if later, the date specified by the owner for the sale. [Reg. §301.6335-1.]

☐ [*T.D. 6119, 12-31-54. Amended by T.D. 6498, 10-24-60; T.D. 7180, 4-12-72; T.D. 8398, 3-2-92; T.D. 8691, 12-16-96 and T.D. 8939, 1-11-2001.*]

## [Reg. §301.6336-1]

**§301.6336-1. Sale of perishable goods.**—(a) *Appraisal of certain seized property.*—If the district director determines that any property seized by levy is liable to perish or become greatly reduced in price or value by keeping, or that such property cannot be kept without great expense, he shall appraise the value of such property and return it to the owner if the owner complies with the conditions prescribed in paragraph (b) of this section or, if the owner does not comply with such conditions, dispose of the property in accordance with paragraph (c) of this section.

(b) *Return to owner.*—If the owner of the property can be readily found, the district director shall give him written notice of his determination of the appraised value of the property. However, if the district director determines that the circumstances require immediate action, he may give the owner an oral notice of his determination of the appraised value of the property, which notice shall be confirmed in writing prior to sale. The property shall be returned to the owner if, within the time specified in the notice, the owner—

(1) Pays to the district director an amount equal to the appraised value, or

(2) Gives an acceptable bond as prescribed by section 7101 and the regulations thereunder. Such bond shall be in an amount not less than the appraised value of the property and shall be conditioned upon the payment of such amount at such time as the district director determines to be appropriate in the circumstances.

(c) *Immediate sale.*—If the owner does not pay the amount of the appraised value of the seized property within the time specified in the notice, or furnish bond as provided in paragraph (b) within such time, the district director shall as soon as practicable make public sale of the property in accordance with the following terms and conditions—

(1) *Notice of sale.*—If the owner can readily be found, a notice shall be given to him. A notice of sale also shall be posted in two public places in the county in which the property is to be sold. The notice shall specify the time and place of sale, the property to be sold, and the manner and conditions of sale. The district director may give such other notice and in such other manner as he deems advisable under the circumstances.

(2) *Sale.*—The property shall be sold at public auction to the highest bidder.

(3) *Terms.*—The purchase price shall be paid in full upon acceptance of the highest bid. The payment shall be made in cash, or by a certified, cashier's, or treasurer's check drawn on any bank or trust company incorporated under the laws of the United States or under the laws of any State, Territory, or possession of the United States, or by a United States postal, bank express, or telegraph money order. [Reg. § 301.6336-1.]

☐ [*T.D.* 6119, 12-31-54. *Amended by T.D.* 6498, 10-24-60.]

### [Reg. § 301.6337-1]

§ 301.6337-1. Redemption of property.—(a) *Before sale.*—Any person whose property has been levied upon shall have the right to pay the amount due, together with costs and expenses of the proceeding, if any, to the district director at any time prior to the sale of the property. Upon such payment the district director shall restore such property to the owner and all further proceedings in connection with the levy on such property shall cease from the time of such payment.

(b) *Redemption of real estate after sale.*—(1) *Period.*—The owner of any real estate sold as provided in section 6335, his heirs, executors, or administrators, or any person having any interest therein, or a lien thereon, or any person in their behalf, shall be permitted to redeem the property sold, or any particular tract of such property, at any time within 120 days after the sale thereof.

(2) *Price.*—Such property or tract of property may be redeemed upon payment to the purchaser, or in case he cannot be found in the county in which the property to be redeemed is situated, then to the district director for the internal revenue district in which the property is situated, for the use of the purchaser, his heirs, or assigns, the annum. In case real and personal property (or several tracts of real property) are purchased in the aggregate, the redemption price of the real property (or of each of the several tracts) shall be determined on the basis of the ratio, as of the time of sale, of the value of the real property (or tract) to the value of the total property purchased. For this purpose the minimum price or the highest bid price, whichever is higher, offered for the property separately or in groups shall be treated as the value.

(c) *Record.*—When any real property is redeemed, the district director shall cause entry of the fact to be made upon the record of sale kept in accordance with section 6340, and such entry shall be evidence of such redemption. The party who redeems the property shall notify the district director of the internal revenue district in which the property is situated of the date of such redemption and of the transfer of the certificate of sale, the amount of the redemption price, and the name of the party to whom such redemption price was paid. [Reg. § 301.6337-1.]

☐ [*T.D.* 6119, 12-31-54. *Amended by T.D.* 7180, 4-12-72.]

### [Reg. § 301.6338-1]

§ 301.6338-1. Certificate of sale; deed of real property.—(a) *Certificate of sale.*—In the case of property sold as provided in section 6335 (relating to sale of seized property), the district director shall give to the purchaser a certificate of sale upon payment in full of the purchase price. A certificate of sale of real property shall set forth the real property purchased, for whose taxes the same was sold, the name of the purchaser, and the price paid therefor.

(b) *Deed to real property.*—In the case of any real property sold as provided in section 6335 and not redeemed in the manner and within the time prescribed in section 6337, the district director shall execute (in accordance with the laws of the State in which the real property is situated pertaining to sales of real property under execution) to the purchaser of such real property at the sale or his assigns, upon surrender of the certificate of sale, a deed of the real property so purchased, reciting the facts set forth in the certificate.

(c) *Deed to real property purchased by the United States.*—If real property is declared purchased by the United States at a sale pursuant to section 6335, the district director shall at the proper time execute a deed therefor and shall, without delay, cause the deed to be duly recorded in the proper registry of deeds. [Reg. § 301.6338-1.]

☐ [*T.D.* 6119, 12-31-54. *Amended by T.D.* 6425, 11-10-59 *and T.D.* 7180, 4-12-72.]

### [Reg. § 301.6339-1]

§ 301.6339-1. Legal effect of certificate of sale of personal property and deed of real property.—(a) *Certificate of sale of property other than real property.*—In all cases of sale pursuant to section 6335 of property (other than real property), the certificate of such sale—

(1) *As evidence.*—Shall be prima facie evidence of the right of the officer to make such sale, and conclusive evidence of the regularity of his proceedings in making the sale; and

(2) *As conveyance.*—Shall transfer to the purchaser all right, title, and interest of the party delinquent in and to the property sold; and

(3) *As authority for transfer of corporate stock.*—If such property consists of corporate stocks, shall be notice, when received, to any corporation, company, or association of such transfer, and shall be authority to such corporation, company, or association to record the transfer on its books and records in the same manner as if the stocks were transferred or assigned by the party holding the stock certificate, in lieu of any original or prior certificate, which shall be void, whether canceled or not; and

(4) *As receipts.*—If the subject of sale is securities or other evidences of debt, shall be a good and valid receipt to the person holding the certificate of sale as against any person holding or claiming to hold possession of such securities or other evidences of debt; and

(5) *As authority for transfer of title to motor vehicle.*—If such property consists of a motor vehicle, shall be notice, when received, to any public official charged with the registration of title to motor vehicles, of such transfer and shall be authority to such official to record the transfer on his books and records in the same manner as if the certificate of title to such motor vehicle were transferred or assigned by the party holding the certificate of title, in lieu of any original or prior certificate, which shall be null and void, whether canceled or not.

(b) *Deed to real property.*—In the case of the sale of real property pursuant to section 6335—

(1) *Deed as evidence.*—The deed of sale given pursuant to section 6338 shall be prima facie evidence of the facts therein stated; and

(2) *Deed as conveyance of title.*—If the proceedings of the district director as set forth have been substantially in accordance with the provisions of law, such deed shall be considered and operate as a conveyance of all the right, title, and interest the party delinquent had in and to the real property thus sold at the time the lien of the United States attached thereto.

(c) *Effect of junior encumbrances.*—A certificate of sale of personal property given or a deed to real property executed pursuant to section 6338 discharges the property from all liens, encumbrances, and titles over which the lien of the United States, with respect to which the levy was made, has priority. For example, a mortgage on real property executed after a notice of a federal tax lien has been filed is extinguished when the district director executes a deed to the real property to a purchaser thereof at a sale pursuant to section 6335 following the seizure of the property by the United States. The proceeds of such a sale are distributed in accordance with priority of the liens, encumbrances, or titles. See section 6342(b) and the regulations thereunder for provisions relating to the distribution of surplus proceeds. See section 7426(a)(2) and the regulations thereunder for judicial procedures with respect to surplus proceeds. [Reg. § 301.6339-1.]

☐ [*T.D.* 6119, 12-31-54. *Amended by T.D.* 7180, 4-12-72.]

### [Reg. § 301.6340-1]

§ 301.6340-1. Records of sale.—(a) *Requirement.*—Each district director shall keep a record of all sales under section 6335 of real property situated within his district and of redemptions of such property. The records shall set forth (1) the tax for which any such sale was made, the dates of seizure and sale, the name of the party assessed and all proceedings in making such sale, the amount of expenses, the names of the purchasers, the date of the deed, and, in the case of redemption of the property, (2) the date of such redemption and of the transfer of the certificate of sale, the amount of the redemption price, and the name of the party to whom such redemption price was paid.

(b) *Copy as evidence.*—A copy of such record, or any part thereof, certified by the district director shall be evidence in any court of the truth of the facts therein stated. [Reg. § 301.6340-1.]

☐ [*T.D.* 6119, 12-31-54.]

## [Reg. §301.6341-1]

**§301.6341-1. Expense of levy and sale.**—The district director shall determine the expenses to be allowed in all cases of levy and sale. Such expenses shall include the expenses of protection and preservation of the property during the period subsequent to the levy, as well as the actual expenses incurred in connection with the sale thereof. In case real and personal property (or several tracts of real property) are sold in the aggregate, the district director shall properly apportion the expenses to the real property (or to each tract). [Reg. §301.6341-1.]

☐ [*T.D. 6119, 12-31-54.*]

## [Reg. §301.6342-1]

**§301.6342-1. Application of proceeds of levy.**—(a) *Collection of liability.*—Any money realized by proceedings under subchapter D, chapter 64, of the Code or by sale of property redeemed by the United States (if the interest of the United States in the property was a lien arising under the provisions of the Internal Revenue Code) is applied in the manner specified in subparagraphs (1), (2), and (3) of this paragraph. Money realized by proceedings under subchapter D, chapter 64, of the Code includes money realized by seizure, by sale of seized property, or by surrender under section 6332 (except money realized by the imposition of a 50% penalty pursuant to section 6332(c)(2)).

(1) *Expense of levy and sale.*—First, against the expenses of the proceedings or sale, including expenses allowable under section 6341 and amounts paid by the United States to redeem property.

(2) *Specific tax liability on seized property.*—If the property seized and sold is subject to a tax imposed by any internal revenue law which has not been paid, the amount remaining after applying subparagraph (1) shall then be applied against such tax liability (and, if such tax was not previously assessed, it shall then be assessed).

(3) *Liability of delinquent taxpayer.*—The amount, if any, remaining after applying subparagraphs (1) and (2) of this paragraph shall then be applied against the liability in respect of which the levy was made or the sale of redeemed property was conducted.

(b) *Surplus proceeds.*—Any surplus proceeds remaining after the application of paragraph (a) of this section shall, upon application and satisfactory proof in support thereof, be credited or refunded by the district director to the person or persons legally entitled thereto. The delinquent taxpayer is the person entitled to the surplus proceeds unless another person establishes a superior claim thereto. [Reg. §301.6342-1.]

☐ [*T.D. 6119, 12-31-54. Amended by T.D. 6498, 10-24-60 and T.D. 7180, 4-12-72.*]

## [Reg. §301.6343-1]

**§301.6343-1. Requirement to release levy and notice of release.**—(a) *In general.*—A district director, service center director, or compliance center director (*director*) must promptly release a levy upon all, or part of, property or rights to property levied upon and must promptly notify the person upon whom the levy was made of such a release, if the director determines that any of the conditions in paragraph (b) of this section (conditions requiring release) exist. The director must make a determination whether any of the conditions requiring release exist if a taxpayer submits a request for release of levy in accordance with paragraph (c) or (d) of this section; however, the director may make this determination based upon information received from a source other than the taxpayer. The director may require any supporting documentation as is reasonably necessary to determine whether a condition requiring release exists.

(b) *Conditions requiring release.*—The director must release the levy upon all or a part of the property or rights to property levied upon if he or she determines that one of the following conditions exists—

(1) *Liability satisfied or unenforceable.*—(i) *General rule.*—The liability for which the levy was made is satisfied or the period of limitations provided in section 6502 (and any period during which the period of limitations is suspended as provided by law) has lapsed. A levy is considered made on the date on which the notice of seizure provided in section 6335(a) is given. A levy that is made within the period of limitations provided in section 6502 does not become unenforceable simply because the person who receives the levy does not surrender the subject property within the period of limitations. In this case, the liability remains enforceable to the extent of the value of the levied upon property. However, a levy made outside the period of limitations (normally ten years without suspensions) must be released unless—

(A) The taxpayer agreed in writing to extend the period of limitations as provided in section 6502(a)(2) and §301.6502-1; or

(B) A proceeding in court to collect the liability has begun within the period of limitations.

(ii) *Special situations.*—A continuing levy on salary or wages made under section 6331(e) must be released at the end of the period of limitations in section 6502. However, a levy on a fixed and determinable right to payment which right includes payments to be made after the period of limitations expires does not become unenforceable upon the expiration of the period of limitations and will not be released under this condition unless the liability is satisfied.

(2) *Release will facilitate collection.*—The release of the levy will facilitate collection of the liability. A director has the discretion to release the levy in all situations, including those where the proceeds from the sale will not fully satisfy the tax liabilities of the taxpayer, under terms and conditions as he or she determines are warranted.

(i) *Example.*—The following example illustrates the provisions of this paragraph (b)(2):

*Example.* A and B each own machines which, when used together, produce widgets. A owes delinquent federal taxes. A notice of federal tax lien is properly filed against all property or rights to property belonging to A. A's machine is seized to satisfy A's delinquent tax liability. The fair market value of A's property is greater than the expenses of seizure and sale, but less than the amount of A's tax liability. A and B find a buyer who wants to buy both machines together. The buyer will only buy the machines together. A's property has a greater value as part of the package than it does by itself. The larger value, as shown in the sale contract, is enough to pay A's tax liability in full. In this situation a release of the levy will facilitate collection because the sale of both machines can be completed and A's liability will be paid in full at the settlement.

(ii) *Compliance with other conditions.*—The director may find that collection will be facilitated by the taxpayer's compliance with conditions other than immediate payment, such as:

(A) The delinquent taxpayer delivers a satisfactory arrangement, which is accepted by the director, for placing property in escrow to secure the payment of the liability (including the expenses of the levy) which is the basis of the levy.

(B) The delinquent taxpayer delivers an acceptable bond to the director conditioned upon the payment of the liability (including the expenses of levy) which is the basis of the levy. This bond shall be in the form provided in section 7101 and §301.7101-1.

(C) There is paid to the director an amount determined by the director to be equal to the interest of the United States in the seized property or the part of the seized property to be released.

(D) The delinquent taxpayer executes an agreement to extend the statute of limitations in accordance with section 6502(a)(2) and §301.6502-1.

(iii) *Expenses of sale exceed the government's interest.*—If the director determines that the value of the United States' interest in the seized property does not exceed the expenses of sale of the property, a release of the levy will be deemed to facilitate collection of the liability even though the fair market value of property which has been seized exceeds the expenses of seizure and sale.

(3) *Installment agreement.*—The taxpayer has entered into an agreement under section 6159 to satisfy the liability by means of installment payments, unless the agreement provides otherwise. However, the director is not required to release the levy under this condition if a release of the levy will jeopardize the secured creditor status of the United States, e.g., where there is an intervening judgment lien creditor and a notice of tax lien has not been filed.

(4) *Economic hardship.*—(i) *General rule.*—The levy is creating an economic hardship due to the financial condition of an individual taxpayer. This condition applies if satisfaction of the levy in whole or in part will cause an individual taxpayer to be unable to pay his or her reasonable basic living expenses. The determination of a reasonable amount for basic living expenses will be made by the director and will vary according to the unique circumstances of the individual taxpayer. Unique circumstances, however, do not include the maintenance of an affluent or luxurious standard of living.

(ii) *Information from taxpayer.*—In determining a reasonable amount for basic living expenses the director will consider any information provided by the taxpayer including—

(A) The taxpayer's age, employment status and history, ability to earn, number of dependents, and status as a dependent of someone else;

(B) The amount reasonably necessary for food, clothing, housing (including utilities, home-owner insurance, home-owner dues, and the like), medical expenses (including health insurance), transportation, current tax payments (including federal, state, and local), alimony, child support, or other court-ordered payments, and expenses necessary to the taxpayer's production of income (such as dues for a trade union or professional organization, or child care payments which allow the taxpayer to be gainfully employed);

    (C) The cost of living in the geographic area in which the taxpayer resides;

    (D) The amount of property exempt from levy which is available to pay the taxpayer's expenses;

    (E) Any extraordinary circumstances such as special education expenses, a medical catastrophe, or natural disaster; and

    (F) Any other factor that the taxpayer claims bears on economic hardship and brings to the attention of the director.

    (iii) *Good faith requirement.*—In addition, in order to obtain a release of a levy under this subparagraph, the taxpayer must act in good faith. Examples of failure to act in good faith include, but are not limited to, falsifying financial information, inflating actual expenses or costs, or failing to make full disclosure of assets.

    (5) *Fair market value exceeds liability.*—The fair market value of the property exceeds the liability for which the levy was made and release of the levy on a part of the property can be made without hindering the collection of the liability. The following example illustrates the provisions of this paragraph (b)(5):

    *Example.* The Internal Revenue Service levies upon ten widgets which belong to the taxpayer to satisfy the taxpayer's outstanding tax liabilities. Subsequent to the levy, the taxpayer establishes that market conditions have increased the aggregate fair market value of widgets so that the value of seven widgets equals the aggregate anticipated expenses of sale and seizure and the tax liabilities for which the levy was made. The director must release three widgets from the levy and return them to the taxpayer.

    (c) *Request for release of levy.*—(1) *Information to be submitted by taxpayer.*—A taxpayer who wishes to obtain a release of a levy must submit a request for release in writing or by telephone to the district director for the Internal Revenue district in which the levy was made. The taxpayer making the request must provide the following information—

    (i) The name, address, and taxpayer identification number of the taxpayer;

    (ii) A description of the property levied upon;

    (iii) The type of tax and the period for which the tax is due;

    (iv) The date of the levy and the originating Internal Revenue district, if known; and

    (v) A statement of the grounds upon which the request for release of the levy is based.

    (2) *Time for submission.*—Except in extraordinary circumstances, a request for release of a levy must be made more than five days prior to a scheduled sale of the property to which the levy relates.

    (3) *Determination by director.*—(i) *When required.*—The director must promptly make a determination concerning release prior to sale in all cases where a request for release of a levy is made except those where the request for release is made five or fewer days prior to a scheduled sale of the property to which the levy relates.

    (ii) *Time for making required determination.*—The determination will be made, generally, within 30 days of a request for release made 30 or more days prior to a scheduled sale of the property to which the levy relates. If a request for release is made less than 30 days prior to the scheduled sale but more than 5 days before the scheduled sale, a determination must be made prior to the scheduled sale. If necessary the director may postpone the scheduled sale in order to make this determination.

    (iii) *Discretionary determination.*—The director has the discretion, but is not required, to make a determination concerning release prior to sale in cases where a request for release of a levy is made five or fewer days prior to a scheduled sale of the property to which the levy relates.

    (4) *Notification to taxpayer of determination.*—The director must promptly notify the taxpayer if the levy is released. If the director determines that none of the conditions requiring release of the levy exist, the director must promptly notify the taxpayer of the decision not to release the levy and the reason why the levy is not being released.

    (d) *Expedited determination with respect to certain business property.*—(1) *General procedure.*—(i) *Submission by taxpayer.*—If a levy is made on essential business property as is described in paragraph (d)(2) of this section, the taxpayer may obtain an expedited determination of whether any of the conditions requiring release of the levy exist. In order to obtain an expedited determination, the taxpayer must submit, within the time frame specified in paragraph (c)(2) of this section, the information required in paragraph (c)(1) of this section

and include with the information an explanation of why the property levied upon qualifies for an expedited determination of whether a condition requiring release of the levy exists.

    (ii) *Time for making required determination.*—The director must make such a determination by the later of 10 business days from the time the director receives the request for release, or 10 business days from the time the director receives any necessary supporting documentation, if 10 or more business days remain before a scheduled sale of the property to which the levy relates. An expedited determination concerning release must be made prior to sale in all cases where a request for release of a levy is made within the time frame specified in paragraph (c)(2) of this section. If necessary the director may postpone the scheduled sale in order to make this determination.

    (iii) *Discretionary determination.*—The director has the discretion, but is not required, to make an expedited determination concerning release in cases where the taxpayer does not submit, within the time frame specified in paragraph (c)(2) of this section, the information required in paragraph (c)(1) of this section and include with the information an explanation of why the property levied upon qualifies for an expedited determination of whether a condition requiring release of the levy exists.

    (2) *Essential business property defined.*—For purposes of this section, *essential business property* means tangible personal property used in carrying on the trade or business of the taxpayer which when levied upon prevents the taxpayer from continuing to carry on the trade or business.

    (3) *Seizure of perishable goods.*—The provisions of this paragraph do not apply in the case of a seizure of perishable goods. Those seizures are governed by the provisions of section 6336 and §301.6336-1.

    (e) *Effect of a release of levy.*—If property has not yet been surrendered to the director in response to a levy, a release of the levy under section 6343(a) will relieve the possessor of any obligation to surrender the property. Otherwise, a release of a levy under section 6343(a) will cause the property to be returned to the custody of the person or persons legally entitled thereto. The release of a levy on any property under this section does not prevent any subsequent levy on the property. Section 301.6343-2, dealing with return of wrongfully levied upon property, is subject to section 6402 which prohibits the Internal Revenue Service from refunding a payment of money that has been deposited in the Treasury and credited to the taxpayer's liability unless there is an overpayment.

    (f) *Effective date.*—This section is effective as of December 30, 1994. [Reg. §301.6343-1.]

    ☐ [*T.D. 6119,* 12-31-54. *Amended by T.D. 6425,* 11-10-59; *T.D. 6498,* 10-24-60; *T.D. 7180,* 4-12-72 *and T.D. 8587,* 12-30-94.]

**[Reg. §301.6343-2]**

    **§301.6343-2. Return of wrongfully levied upon property.**— (a) *Return of property.*—(1) *General rule.*—If the Internal Revenue Service (IRS) determines that property has been wrongfully levied upon, the IRS may return—

    (i) The specific property levied upon;

    (ii) An amount of money equal to the amount of money levied upon; or

    (iii) An amount of money equal to the amount of money received by the United States from a sale of the property.

    (2) *Time of return.*—If the United States is in possession of specific property, the property may be returned at any time. An amount equal to the amount of money levied upon or received from a sale of the property may be returned at any time before the expiration of 9 months from the date of the levy. When a request described in paragraph (b) of this section is filed for the return of property before the expiration of 9 months from the date of levy, an amount of money may be returned after a reasonable period of time subsequent to the expiration of the 9-month period if necessary for the investigation and processing of such request.

    (3) *Specific property.*—In general the specific property levied upon will be returned whenever possible. For this purpose, money that is specifically identifiable, as in the case of a coin collection which may be worth substantially more than its face value, is treated as specific property.

    (4) *Purchase by United States.*—For purposes of paragraph (a)(1)(iii) of this section, if property is declared purchased by the United States at a sale pursuant to section 6335(e), the United States is treated as having received an amount of money equal to the

minimum price determined by the IRS before the sale or, if larger, the amount received by the United States from the resale of the property.

(b) *Request for return of property.*—A written request for the return of property wrongfully levied upon must be given to the IRS official, office and address specified in IRS Publication 4528, "Making an Administrative Wrongful Levy Claim Under Internal Revenue Code (IRC) Section 6343(b)," or any successor publication. The relevant IRS publications may be downloaded from the IRS internet site at *www.irs.gov*. Under this section, a request for the return of property wrongfully levied upon is not effective if it is given to an office other than the office listed in the relevant publication. The written request must contain the following information—

(1) The name and address of the person submitting the request;

(2) A detailed description of the property levied upon;

(3) A description of the claimant's basis for claiming an interest in the property levied upon; and

(4) The name and address of the taxpayer, the originating IRS office, and the date of the levy as shown on the notice of levy form, or levy form, or, in lieu thereof, a statement of the reasons why such information cannot be furnished.

(c) *Inadequate request.*—A request for the return of property wrongfully levied upon will not be considered adequate unless it is a written request containing the information required by paragraph (b) of this section. However, unless a notification is mailed by the IRS to the claimant within 30 days of receipt of the request to inform the claimant of the inadequacies, any written request will be considered adequate. If the IRS timely notifies the claimant of the inadequacies of his request, the claimant has 30 days from the receipt of the notification of inadequacy to supply in writing any omitted information. Where the omitted information is so supplied within the 30-day period, the request will be considered to be adequate from the time the original request was made for purposes of determining the applicable period of limitation upon suit under section 6532(c).

(d) *Payment of interest.*—Interest is paid at the overpayment rate established under section 6621—

(1) In the case of money returned under paragraph (a)(1)(ii) of this section, from the date the IRS received the money to a date (to be determined by the director) preceding the date of return by not more than 30 days; or

(2) In the case of money returned under paragraph (a)(1)(iii) of this section, from the date of the sale of the property to a date (to be determined by the IRS) preceding the date of return by not more than 30 days.

(e) *Effective/applicability date.*—These regulations are effective on July 8, 2008. [Reg. § 301.6343-2.]

☐ *T.D. 8587, 12-30-94. Amended by T.D. 9344, 7-19-2007 and T.D. 9410, 7-7-2008.*]

### [Reg. § 301.6343-3]

**§ 301.6343-3. Return of property in certain cases.**—(a) *In general.*—If money has been levied upon and applied toward the taxpayer's liability, or property has been levied upon and sold, and the receipts have been applied toward the taxpayer's liability, or property has been levied upon and purchased by the United States and the United States still possesses the property, and the Commissioner determines that any of the conditions in paragraph (c) of this section exist, the Commissioner may return—

(1) An amount of money equal to the amount of money levied upon;

(2) An amount of money equal to the amount of money received by the United States from a sale of the property; or

(3) The specific property levied upon and purchased by the United States.

(b) *Return of levied upon property in possession of the Internal Revenue Service (IRS) pending sale under section 6335.*—Other than as provided in § 301.6343-1(b) or in paragraph (d) of this section, the Commissioner, in his or her discretion, may return levied upon property that is in the possession of the United States pending sale under section 6335.

(c) *Conditions authorizing the return of property.*—The Commissioner may return property upon determining that one of the following conditions exist:

(1) *Premature or not in accordance with administrative procedures.*—The levy was premature or otherwise not in accordance with the administrative procedures of the Secretary.

(2) *Installment agreement.*—Subsequent to the levy, the taxpayer enters into an agreement under section 6159 to satisfy the liability for which the levy was made by means of installment payments. If,

however, the agreement specifically provides that already levied upon property will not be returned under section 6343(d), the Commissioner may not grant a request for return of property under this paragraph (c)(2).

(3) *Facilitate collection.*—The return of property will facilitate the collection of the tax liability for which the levy was made.

(4) *Best interests of the United States and the taxpayer.*—(i) *In general.*—The taxpayer or the National Taxpayer Advocate (or his or her delegate) has consented to the return of property, and the return of property would be in the best interest of the taxpayer, as determined by the National Taxpayer Advocate (or his or her delegate), and in the best interest of the United States, as determined by the Commissioner.

(ii) *Best interest of the taxpayer.*—The National Taxpayer Advocate (or his or her delegate) generally will determine whether the return of property is in the best interest of the taxpayer. If, however, a taxpayer requests the Commissioner to return property and has not specifically requested the National Taxpayer Advocate (or his or her delegate) to determine the taxpayer's best interest, a finding by the Commissioner that the return of property is in the best interest of the taxpayer will be sufficient to support the return of property. Only the National Taxpayer Advocate (or his or her delegate) may determine that a return of property is not in the best interest of the taxpayer.

(5) *Examples.*—The following examples illustrate the provisions of this paragraph (c):

*Example 1.* A owes $1,000 in Federal income taxes. The IRS levies on a broker with respect to a money market account belonging to the taxpayer and receives payment from the broker which it applies to the taxpayer's outstanding liability. However, the IRS failed to follow procedure provided by the Internal Revenue Manual (but not required by statute) with regard to managerial approval prior to the making of the levy. The Commissioner may return an amount of money equal to the amount of money the IRS levied upon and applied toward the taxpayer's tax liability.

*Example 2.* B owes $1,000 in Federal income taxes. The IRS levies on a bank with respect to a savings account belonging to the taxpayer and receives funds from the bank, which it applies to the taxpayer's liability. Subsequent to the levy, B enters into an installment agreement, under which B will pay timely installments to satisfy the entire liability. The installment agreement does not by its terms preclude the return of levied upon property. The revenue officer verifies that B is financially capable of paying the entire liability, including accruals, in the agreed-upon installment payments. The Commissioner may return an amount of money equal to the amount of money levied upon and applied toward the taxpayer's liability.

*Example 3.* C owns a house that is deteriorating and in unsalable condition. C is in the process of renovating the house for sale when the IRS levies upon C's bank account for the payment of a $20,000 outstanding Federal tax liability and receives funds in the amount of $3,000, which it applies toward C's liability. A notice of federal tax lien is the only lien encumbrancing the house. C requests that an amount of money equal to the amount seized from the bank account be returned so that C can complete the renovations on the house. Without the funds, C will be unable to complete the renovations and sell the house. Upon examination, the Commissioner determines that the IRS will be able to collect the entire tax liability if C's house is restored to salable condition. If the National Taxpayer Advocate, or the Commissioner in lieu of the National Taxpayer Advocate, determines that the return of the seized money is in the taxpayer's best interest, the Commissioner may return an amount of money equal to the amount seized from the bank account, in the best interest of the taxpayer and the United States.

(d) *Best interests of the United States and the taxpayer to release levy and return of property where levy made in violation of law.*—(1) *In general.*—If the IRS makes a levy in violation of the law, it is in the best interests of the United States and the taxpayer to release the levy and the IRS will return to the taxpayer any property obtained pursuant to the levy. For example, the IRS will release the levy and return the taxpayer's property if the levy was made—

(i) Without giving the requisite thirty-day notice of the right to a hearing under section 6330;

(ii) During the pendency of a proceeding for refund of divisible tax in violation of section 6331(i);

(iii) Before investigation of the status of levied upon property in violation of section 6331(j);

(iv) During the pendency of an offer-in-compromise in violation of section 6331(k)(1); or

(v) During the period an offer to enter into an installment agreement is pending (or for 30 days following the rejection of an offer, or, if the rejection is timely appealed, during the period that the appeal is pending) or during the period an installment agreement is in effect (or during the 30 days following a termination or, if a timely appeal of termination is filed, during the period the appeal is pending) in violation of section 6331(k)(2).

(2) *Property may not be credited to outstanding liability without the taxpayer's permission.*—When the release of a levy and the return of property are required under this paragraph (d), the property or the proceeds from the sale of the property received by the IRS pursuant to the levy must be returned to the taxpayer unless the taxpayer requests otherwise. The property or proceeds of sale may not be credited to any outstanding tax liability of the taxpayer, including the one with respect to which the IRS made the levy, without the written permission of the taxpayer.

(e) *Time of return.*—Levied upon property in possession of the IRS (other than money) may be returned under paragraphs (c) and (d) of this section at any time. An amount of money equal to the amount of money levied upon or received from a sale of property may be returned at any time before the expiration of 9 months from the date of the levy. When a request for the return of money filed in accordance with paragraph (h) of this section is filed before the expiration of the 9-month period, or a determination to return an amount of money is made before the expiration of the 9-month period, the money may be returned within a reasonable period of time after the expiration of the 9-month period if additional time is necessary for investigation or processing.

(f) *Purchase by the United States.*—For purposes of paragraph (a)(2) of this section, if property is declared purchased by the United States at a sale pursuant to section 6335(e)(1)(C), the United States will be treated as having received an amount of money equal to the minimum price determined by the Commissioner before the sale.

(g) *Determinations by the Commissioner.*—The Commissioner must determine whether any of the conditions authorizing the return of property exists if a taxpayer submits a request for the return of property in accordance with paragraph (h) of this section. The Commissioner also may make this determination independently. If the Commissioner determines that conditions authorizing the return of property are not present, the Commissioner may not authorize the return of property. If the Commissioner determines that conditions authorizing the return of property are present, the Commissioner may (but is not required to, unless the reason for the return of property is that the levy was made in violation of law and is governed by paragraph (d) of this section) authorize the return of property. If the Commissioner decides independently to return property under paragraph (c)(4) of this section based on the best interests of the taxpayer and the United States, the taxpayer or the National Taxpayer Advocate (or his or her delegate) must consent to the return of property.

(h) *Procedures for request for the return of property.*—(1) *Manner.*—A request for the return of property must be made in writing to the address on the levy form.

(2) *Form.*—The written request must include the following information—

(i) The name, current address, and taxpayer identification number of the person requesting the return of money (or property purchased by the United States);

(ii) A description of the property levied upon;

(iii) The date of the levy; and

(iv) A statement of the grounds upon which the return of money is being requested (or property purchased by the United States).

(i) *No interest.*—No interest will be paid on any money returned under this section.

(j) *Administrative collection upon default.*—If the Commissioner returns property under this section, and the taxpayer fails to pay the previously assessed liability for which the levy was made on the returned property, the Commissioner may administratively collect the liability. Collection may include levying again on the returned property as long as statutory and administrative requirements are followed.

(k) *Effective date.*—This section is applicable on July 14, 2005. [Reg. §301.6343-3.]

□ T.D. 9213, 7-13-2005.]

# COLLECTION OF STATE INDIVIDUAL INCOME TAXES

### [Reg. §1.6361-1]

§1.6361-1. Collection and administration of qualified State individual income taxes.—Except as otherwise provided in §§301.6361-1 to 301.6365-2, inclusive, of this chapter (Regulations on Procedure and Administration), the provisions of this part under subtitle F of the Internal Revenue Code of 1954 relating to the collection and administration of the taxes imposed by chapter 1 of such Code on the incomes of individuals (or relating to civil or criminal sanctions with respect to such collection and administration) shall apply to the collection and administration of qualified State individual income taxes (as defined in section 6362 of such Code and the regulations thereunder) as if such taxes were imposed by chapter 1. [Reg. §1.6361-1.]

□ [T.D. 7577, 12-19-78.]

### [Reg. §31.6361-1]

§31.6361-1. Collection and administration of qualified State individual income taxes.—Except as otherwise provided in §§301.6361-1 to 301.6365-2, inclusive, of this chapter (Regulations on Procedure and Administration), the provisions of this part under subtitle F or chapter 24 of the Internal Revenue Code of 1954 relating to the collection and administration of the taxes imposed by chapter 1 of such Code on the incomes of individuals (or relating to civil or criminal sanctions with respect to such collection and administration) shall apply to the collection and administration of qualified State individual income taxes (as defined in section 6362 of such Code and the regulations thereunder) as if such taxes were imposed by chapter 1 or chapter 24. [Reg. §31.6361-1.]

□ [T.D. 7577, 12-19-78.]

### [Reg. §301.6361-1]

§301.6361-1. Collection and administration of qualified taxes.—(a) *In general.*—In the case of any State which has in effect a State agreement (as defined in paragraph (a) of §301.6361-4), the Commissioner of Internal Revenue shall collect and administer each qualified tax (as defined in paragraph (b) of §301.6361-4) of such State. No fee or other charge shall be imposed upon any State for the collection or administration of any qualified tax of such State or any other State. In any such case of collection and administration of qualified taxes, the provisions of subtitle F (relating to procedure and administration),

subtitle G (relating to the Joint Committee on Taxation), and chapter 24 (relating to the collection of income tax at source on wages), and the provisions of regulations thereunder, insofar as such provisions relate to the collection and administration of the taxes imposed on the income of individuals by chapter 1 (and the civil and criminal sanctions provided by subtitle F, or by title 18 of the United States Code (relating to crimes and criminal procedure), with respect to such collection and administration) shall apply to the collection and administration of qualified taxes as if such taxes were imposed by chapter 1, except to the extent that the application of such provisions (and sanctions) are modified by regulations issued under subchapter E (as defined in paragraph (d) of §301.6361-4). Any extension of time which is granted for the making of a payment, or for the filing of any return, which relates to any Federal tax imposed by subtitle A (or by subtitle C with respect to filing a return) shall constitute automatically an extension of the same amount of time for the making of the corresponding payment or for the filing of the corresponding return relating to any qualified tax.

(b) *Returns of qualified taxes.*—Every individual, estate, or trust which has liability for one or more qualified taxes for a taxable year—

(1) Shall file a Federal income tax return at the time prescribed pursuant to section 6072(a) (whether or not such return is required by section 6012), and shall file therewith on the prescribed form a return under penalties of perjury for each tax which is—

(i) A qualified resident tax imposed by a State of which the taxpayer was a resident, as defined in §301.6362-6, for any part of the taxable year;

(ii) A qualified nonresident tax imposed by a State within which was located the source or sources from which the taxpayer derived, while not a resident of such State and while not exempt from liability for the tax by reason of a reciprocal agreement between such State and the State of which he is a resident, 25 percent or more of his aggregate wage and other business income, as defined in paragraph (c) of §301.6362-5, for the taxable year; or

(iii) A qualified resident or nonresident tax with respect to which any amount was currently collected from the taxpayer's income (including collection by withholding on wages or by payment of estimated income tax), as provided in paragraph (f) of §301.6362-6, for any part of the taxable year; and

(2) Shall declare (in addition to the declaration required with respect to the return of the Federal income tax and in the place and manner prescribed by form or instructions thereto) under penalties of perjury that, to the best of the knowledge and belief of the taxpayer (or, in the case of an estate or trust, of the fiduciary who executes the Federal income tax return), he has no liability for any qualified tax for the taxable year other than any such liabilities returned with the Federal income tax return (pursuant to subparagraph (1) of this paragraph). Such declaration shall constitute a return indicating no liability with respect to each qualified tax other than any such tax for which liability is so returned. A Federal income tax return form which is filed but which does not contain such declaration shall constitute a Federal income tax return only if the taxpayer in fact has no liability for any qualified State tax for the taxable year.

(c) *Credits.*—(1) *Credit for tax of another State or political subdivision.*—(i) *In general.*—A credit allowable under a qualified tax law against the tax imposed by such law for a taxpayer's tax liability to another State or a political subdivision of another State shall be allowed if the requirements of subdivision (ii) of this subparagraph are met, and if the credit meets the requirements of paragraph (c) of § 301.6362-4. Such credit shall be allowed without regard to whether the tax imposed by the other State or subdivision thereof is a qualified tax, and without regard to whether such tax has been paid.

(ii) *Substantiation of tax liability for which a credit is allowed.*—If the liability which gives rise to a credit of the type described in subdivision (i) of this subparagraph is with respect to a qualified tax, then the fact of such liability shall be substantiated by filing the return on which such liability is reported. If such liability is not with respect to a qualified tax, then the Commissioner may require a taxpayer who claims entitlement to such a credit to complete a form to be submitted with his return of the qualified tax against which the credit is claimed. On such form the taxpayer shall identify each of the other States (the liabilities to which were not substantiated as provided in the first sentence of this subdivision) or political subdivisions to which the taxpayer reported a liability for a tax giving rise to the credit, furnish the name or description of each such tax, state the amount of the liability so reported with respect to each such tax and the beginning and ending dates of the taxable period for which such liability was reported, and provide such other information as is requested in the form or in the instructions thereto. In addition, the taxpayer shall agree on such form to notify the Commissioner in the event that the amount of any tax liability (or portion thereof) which is claimed as giving rise to a credit of the type described in subdivision (i) of this subparagraph is changed or adjusted, whether as a result of an amended return filed by the taxpayer, a determination by the jurisdiction imposing the tax, or in any other manner.

(2) *Credit or withheld qualified tax.*—An individual from whose wages an amount is withheld on account of a qualified tax shall receive a credit for such amount against his aggregate liability for all such qualified taxes and the Federal income tax for the taxable year, whether or not such tax has been paid over to the Federal Government by the employer. The credit shall operate in the manner provided by section 31(a) of the Code and the regulations thereunder with respect to Federal income tax withholding.

(d) *Collection of qualified taxes at source on wages.*—(1) *In general.*—Except as otherwise provided in subparagraph (2) of this paragraph, every employer making payment of wages to an employee described in such subparagraph shall deduct and withhold upon such wages the amount prescribed with respect to the qualified tax designated in such subparagraph. The amounts prescribed for withholding with respect to each such qualified tax shall be published in Circular E (Employer's Tax Guide) or other appropriate Internal Revenue Service publications. See paragraph (f)(1) of § 301.6362-7 with respect to civil and criminal penalties to which an employer shall be subject with respect to his responsibilities relating to qualified taxes.

(2) *Specific withholding requirements.*—An employer shall deduct and withhold upon an employee's wages the amount prescribed with respect to a qualified tax with respect to which such employee is subject to the current collection provisions pursuant to paragraph (f) of § 301.6362-6, unless:

(i) In the case of a qualified resident tax, the employee's services giving rise to the wages are performed in another State, and such other State or a political subdivision thereof imposes a nonresident tax on such employee with respect to which the withholding amount exceeds the prescribed withholding amount with respect to such qualified resident tax, and the State imposing such qualified resident tax grants a credit against it for such nonresident tax.

(ii) In the case of a qualified nonresident tax, either:

(A) Residents of the State in which the employee resides are exempt from liability for the qualified nonresident tax imposed by the State from sources within which his wage income is derived, by reason of an interstate compact or agreement to which the two States are parties, or

(B) The State in which the employee resides imposes a qualified resident tax on such employee with respect to which the prescribed withholding amounts exceed the prescribed withholding amounts with respect to the qualified nonresident tax imposed by the State from sources within which his wage income is derived, and the State in which he resides grants a credit against its qualified resident tax for such qualified nonresident tax.

If the nonresident tax described in subdivision (i) of this subparagraph is a qualified nonresident tax imposed by a State, then the reference in such subdivision to the State in which the services are performed shall be construed as a reference to the State from sources within which the wage income is derived, within the meaning of paragraph (d)(1) of § 301.6362-5.

(3) *Forms, procedures, and returns relating to withholding with respect to qualified taxes.*—(i) *Forms W-4 and W-4P.*—Forms W-4 (Employee's Withholding Allowance Certificate) and W-4P (Annuitant's Request for Income Tax Withholding) shall include information as to the State in which the employee resides, and shall be used for purposes of withholding with respect to both Federal and qualified taxes. An employee shall show on his Form W-4 the State in which he resides for purposes of this paragraph, and shall file a new Form W-4 within 10 days after he changes his State of residence. An employee who fails to meet either of the requirements set forth in the preceding sentence, with the intent to evade the withholding tax imposed with respect to a qualified tax, shall be subject to the penalty provided in section 7205 of the Code. An employer shall be responsible for determining the State within which are located the sources from which the employee's wage income is derived for purposes of this paragraph; and, if the employee does not file a Form W-4, the employer shall assume for such purposes that the employee resides in that State. When an employer and an employee enter into a voluntary withholding agreement pursuant to § 31.3402(p)-1, the employer shall withhold the amount prescribed with respect to the qualified resident tax imposed by the State in which the employee resides, as indicated on Form W-4. Similarly, if an annuitant requests withholding with respect to his annuity payments pursuant to section 3402(o)(1)(B) of the Code, the payer shall withhold the whole dollar amount specified by the annuitant with respect to a qualified resident tax, provided that the combined withholding with respect to Federal and qualified taxes on each annuity payment shall be a whole dollar amount not less than $5, and that the net amount of any annuity payment received by the payee shall not be reduced to less than $10.

(ii) *Forms W-2 and W-2P.*—Forms W-2 (Wage and Tax Statement) and W-2P (the corresponding form for annuities) shall show:

(A) The total amount withheld with respect to the Federal income tax;

(B) The total amount withheld with respect to qualified taxes;

(C) The name of each State imposing a qualified tax in which the employee (or annuitant) resided during the taxable year, as shown on Form W-4 (or W-4P);

(D) The name of each State imposing a qualified nonresident tax within which were located sources from which the employee's wage income was derived during a period of the taxable year in which he was not shown as a resident of such State on Form W-4, and the amount of the employee's wage income so derived; and

(E) The name of each State or locality that imposes an income tax which is not a qualified tax and with respect to which the employer withheld on the employee's wage income for the taxable year, and the amount of wage income with respect to which the employer so withheld.

(iii) *Requirements relating to deposit and payment of withheld tax.*—Rules relating to the deposit and remittance of withheld Federal income and FICA taxes, including those prescribed in section 6302 of the Code and the regulations thereunder, shall apply also to amounts withheld with respect to qualified taxes. Thus, an employer's liability with respect to the deposit and payment of withheld taxes shall be for the combined amount of withholding with respect to Federal and qualified taxes. The Federal Tax Deposit form shall separately indicate:

(A) The combined total amount of Federal income, FICA, and qualified taxes withheld;

(B) The combined total amount of qualified taxes withheld; and

(C) The total amount of qualified taxes withheld with respect to each electing State.

Data indicating the total amount of tax deposits processed by the Internal Revenue Service with respect to the qualified taxes of an electing State will be available to that State upon request on as frequent as a weekly basis. These data will be available no later than 10 working days after the end of the calendar week in which the deposits were processed by the Service.

(iv) *Employment tax returns.*—Forms 941 (Employer's Quarterly Federal Tax Return), 941-E (Quarterly Return of Withheld Income Tax), 941-M (Employer's Monthly Federal Tax Return), 942 (Employer's Quarterly Tax Return for Household Employees), and 943 (Employer's Annual Tax Return for Agricultural Employees) shall indicate the total amount withheld with respect to each qualified tax, as directed by such forms or their instructions.

(e) *Criminal penalties.*—A criminal offense committed with respect to a qualified tax shall be treated as a separate offense from a similar offense committed with respect to the Federal tax. Thus, for example, if a taxpayer willfully attempts to evade both the Federal tax and a qualified tax by failing to report a portion of his income, he shall be considered as having committed two criminal offenses, each subject to a separate penalty under section 7201. See also § 301.6362-7(f) with respect to criminal penalties.

(f) *Allocation of amounts collected with respect to tax and criminal fines.*—(1) *In general.*—The aggregate amount that has been collected from a taxpayer (including amounts collected by withholding) in respect of liability for both one or more qualified taxes and the Federal income tax for a taxable year shall be allocated among the Federal Government and the States imposing qualified taxes for which the taxpayer is liable in the proportion which the taxpayer's liability for each such tax bears to his aggregate liability for such year to all of such taxing jurisdictions with respect to such taxes. A reallocation shall be made either when an amount is collected from the taxpayer or his employer or is credited or refunded to the taxpayer, subsequent to the making of the initial allocation, or when a determination is made by the Commissioner that an error was made with respect to a previous allocation. However, any such allocation or reallocation shall not affect the amount of a taxpayer's or employer's liability to either jurisdiction, or the amount of the assessment and collection which may be made with respect to a taxpayer or employer. Accordingly, such allocations and reallocations shall not be taken into consideration for purposes of the application of statutes of limitation or provisions relating to interest, additions to tax, penalties, and criminal sanctions. See example (4) in subparagraph (4) of this paragraph. In addition, any such allocation or reallocation shall not affect the amount of the deduction to which a taxpayer is entitled under section 164 for a year in which he made payment (including payments made by withholding) of an amount which was designated as being in respect of his liability for a qualified tax. However, to the extent that an amount which was paid by a taxpayer and designated as being in respect of his liability for a qualified tax is allocated or reallocated in such a manner as to apply it toward the taxpayer's liability for the Federal income tax, such allocation or reallocation shall be treated as a refund to the taxpayer of an amount paid in respect of a State income tax, and shall be included in the gross income of the taxpayer to the extent appropriate under section 111 and the regulations thereunder in the year in which the allocation or reallocation is made. See section 451 and the regulations thereunder. Similarly, to the extent that an amount which was paid by a taxpayer and designated as being in respect of his Federal income tax liability is allocated or reallocated in such a manner as to apply it toward his liability for a qualified tax, such allocation or reallocation shall be treated as a payment made by the taxpayer in respect of a State income tax, and shall be deductible under section 164 in the year in which the allocation or reallocation is made. The Internal Revenue Service shall notify the taxpayer in writing of any allocation or reallocation of tax liabilities in a proportion other than that of the respective tax liabilities shown on the taxpayer's returns.

(2) *Amounts of collections and liabilities.*—For purposes of this paragraph the aggregate amount that has been collected from a taxpayer or his employer in respect of tax liability shall include the amounts of interest provided in chapter 67, and additions to tax and assessable penalties provided in chapter 68, which are collected with respect to such tax; but shall not include criminal fines provided in chapter 75, or in title 18 of the United States Code, which are collected with respect to offenses relating to such tax. (See subparagraph (3) of this paragraph with respect to the treatment of such criminal fines.) However, for purposes of this paragraph, the amount of the taxpayer's liability for each tax shall exclude his liability for such interest, additions to tax, and assessable penalties with respect to such tax, and his liability for criminal fines imposed with respect to offenses relating to such tax. For purposes of this paragraph, the amount of the taxpayer's liability for each tax shall be computed by taking credits into account, except that there shall be no reduction for any amounts paid on account of such liability, whether by means of withholding, estimated tax payment, or otherwise.

(3) *Special rules relating to criminal fines.*—(i) Except as otherwise provided in subdivision (ii) of this subparagraph, when a criminal charge is brought against a taxpayer with respect to a taxable year pursuant to chapter 75, or to title 18 of the United States Code, or to a corresponding provision of a qualified tax law, alleging that an offense was committed against the United States with respect to the Federal income tax or against a State with respect to a qualified tax, and an amount of money is collected by the Federal Government as a fine as a result of such charge, then the Federal Government shall remit an amount to each State, if any, which is an affected jurisdiction. The amount remitted to each such State shall bear the same proportion to the total amount collected as a fine as the taxpayer's liability with respect to the qualified taxes of that State bears to the aggregate of the taxpayer's income tax liabilities to all affected jurisdictions for the taxable year, as determined under subparagraphs (1) and (2) of this paragraph. For purposes of this subparagraph, an affected jurisdiction is (A) a jurisdiction with respect to the tax of which a criminal charge described in the preceding sentence was brought for the taxable year, or (B) a jurisdiction with respect to the Federal income tax or the qualified tax of which the acts or omissions alleged in such a criminal charge would constitute the basis for the bringing of a criminal charge for the same taxable year. However, in no case shall the amount received by an affected State, or the amount of the excess of the amount received by the Federal Government over the amount of its remissions to the States, with respect to a fine exceed the maximum fine prescribed by statute for the offense against that jurisdiction with respect to which a criminal charge was brought, or with respect to which the bringing of a criminal charge could have been supported on the basis of the acts or omissions alleged in a criminal charge brought. For purposes of this subparagraph, the amount collected as a fine as a result of a criminal charge shall include amounts paid in settlement of an actual or potential liability for a fine, amounts paid pursuant to a conviction and amounts paid pursuant to a plea of guilty or *nolo contendere*.

(ii) If a criminal charge described in the first sentence of subdivision (i) of this subparagraph is actually brought with respect to the income tax of every affected jurisdiction with respect to the taxable year, and if a Court adjudicates on the merits the taxpayer's liability for a fine to each such jurisdiction, and includes in its decree a direction of the amount, if any, to be paid as a fine to each such jurisdiction, then that decree shall govern the allocation of the amount of money collected by the Federal Government as a fine with respect to the taxable year.

(4) *Examples.*—The application of this paragraph may be illustrated by the following examples:

*Example (1).* The total combined amount of State X qualified tax and Federal income tax collected from A, a resident of State X, for the taxable year is $5,100. The amounts of A's liabilities for such taxes for that year are $800 to State X and $4,000 to the Federal Government. Since A's tax liability to State X is one-sixth of the combined tax liability ($4,800), one-sixth ($50) of the amount to be refunded to A ($300) is chargeable against State X's account, and five-sixths ($250) is chargeable against the Federal Government's account.

*Example (2).* Assume the same facts as in example (1) except that the total amount collected from A is $4,500. Since A's liabilities for the State X tax and the Federal tax are one-sixth and five-sixths, respectively, of the combined tax liability, the Federal Government shall pay over to State X one-sixth ($750) of the amount actually collected from A, and the Federal Government shall retain five-sixths ($3,750).

*Example (3).* The total amount of State X qualified tax, State Y qualified tax, and Federal income tax collected from B, a resident of State X who is employed in State Y, for the taxable year is $5,500. The amounts of B's liabilities for such taxes for that year are: $250 for the State X tax (after allowance of a credit for State Y's qualified tax), $750 for the State Y tax, and $4,000 for the Federal tax. Since B's liability for the State X tax ($250) is 5 percent of the combined tax liability ($5,000), his liability for the State Y tax ($750) is 15 percent of such combined liability, and his liability for the Federal tax ($4,000) is 80 percent of such combined liability, the total amount to be refunded to B ($500) shall be chargeable in the following manner: 5 percent ($25) against State X's account, 15 percent ($75) against State Y's account, and 80 percent ($400) against the Federal Government's account.

*Example (4).* C is liable for $2,000 in Federal income tax and $500 in State X qualified tax (a resident tax) for the taxable year. However, on his Federal income tax return for such year, C erroneously described himself as a resident of State Y (which does not have a qualified tax), and he filed with such return his declaration to the effect that he had no qualified tax liability for the year. Accordingly, C paid only $2,000 for his Federal tax liability, and such amount was retained in the account of the Federal Government. Subsequently, C's error is discovered. The amount collected by the Federal Government from C for such year must be allocated between the Federal Government and State X in proportion to C's tax liability to both. Accordingly, the Federal Government must pay over to State X the amount of $400 (which is $^1/_5$ ($500/$2,500) of the $2,000 collected). If the Federal Government collects from C the additional $500 owed, it will retain $400 of such amount and pay the remaining $100 to State X. Similarly, if the Federal Government collects from C any interest, or any additions to tax or assessable penalties under chapter 68, $^4/_5$ of the amount of such collections shall be retained by the Federal Government, and $^1/_5$ of such amount shall be paid over to State X. However, notwithstanding the allocation of the funds between the taxing jurisdictions, C's liability for the $500 retains its character as a liability for State X tax. Therefore, any interest, additions to tax, or assessable penalties imposed with respect to the State X tax shall be imposed with respect to C's full $500 liability for such tax, notwithstanding the fact that amounts collected with respect to such items shall be allocated $^4/_5$ to the Federal Government.

*Example (5).* A criminal charge is brought against D pursuant to chapter 75, alleging that he willfully evaded the payment of Federal income tax by failing to report interest income derived from obligations of the United States. D enters a plea of *non contendere* to the charge and pays $2,500 as a fine to the Federal Government. The act alleged in the criminal charge would not support the bringing of a criminal charge under a State law corresponding to chapter 75, or to title 18 of the United States Code, with respect to the qualified tax of any State; accordingly, the United States is the only affected jurisdiction, and no remittances shall be made to any State with respect to the amount collected by the Federal Government as a fine.

*Example (6).* A criminal charge is brought against E pursuant to chapter 75, alleging that he willfully attempted to evade the assessment of liability for both Federal income tax and the qualified tax of State X by filing false and fraudulent income tax returns. E's case is settled upon the condition that he pay a fine in the amount of $5,000. As determined pursuant to subparagraph (2) of this paragraph, E's liabilities for the taxable year are in the amounts of $7,200 to the Federal Government and $800 to State X. Accordingly, after the Federal Government collects the fine, $500 ($5,000 × $800/$8,000) is remitted to State X.

*Example (7).* Assume the same facts as in example (6), except that E is tried and convicted on both charges, and pursuant to court decree he pays to the United States a fine of $6,000 with respect to each charge, or a total of $12,000. Because a criminal charge was brought with respect to each affected jurisdiction, and the allocation of the total amount paid as a fine was specifically imposed by a court decree, the direction of the Court shall govern the allocation. Accordingly, after the Federal Government collects the fine it pays over $6,000 to the account of State X. [Reg. § 301.6361-1.]

☐ [*T.D.* 7577, 12-19-78.]

### [Reg. § 301.6361-2]

**§ 301.6361-2. Judicial and administrative proceedings; Federal representation of State interests.**—(a) *Civil proceedings.*—(1) *General rule.*—Any person shall have the same right to bring or contest a civil action, and to obtain a review thereof, with respect to a qualified tax (including the current collection thereof) in the same court or courts which would be available to him, and pursuant to the same requirements and procedures to which he would be subject, under chapter 76 (relating to judicial proceedings), and under title 28 of the United States Code (relating to the judiciary and judicial procedure), if the tax were imposed by section 1 or chapter 24 of the Internal Revenue Code. For purposes of this section, the term "person" includes the Federal Government. Except as provided in subparagraph (2) of this paragraph, to the extent that the preceding sentence provides judicial procedures (including review procedures) with respect to any matter, such procedures shall replace civil judicial procedures under State law.

(2) *Exception.*—The right or power of the courts of any State to pass on matters involving the constitution of such State is unaffected by any provision of this paragraph; however, the jurisdiction of a State court in such matters shall not extend beyond the issue of constitutionality. Thus, if in a case involving the validity of a qualified tax statute under the State constitution, the State court holds such statute constitutional, such court shall not proceed to decide the amount of the tax liability.

(b) *Criminal proceedings.*—Only the Federal Government shall have the right to bring a criminal action with respect to a qualified tax (including the current collection thereof). Such an action shall be brought in the same court or courts which would be available to the Federal Government, and pursuant to the same requirements and procedures to which the Federal Government would be subject, if the tax were imposed by section 1 or chapter 24 of the Internal Revenue Code.

(c) *Administrative proceedings.*—Any person shall have the same rights in administrative proceedings of the Internal Revenue Service with respect to a qualified tax (including the current collection thereof) which would be available to him, and shall be subject to the same administrative requirements and procedures to which he would be subject, if the tax were imposed by section 1 or chapter 24 of the Internal Revenue Code.

(d) *United States representation of State interests.*—(1) *General rule.*—Except as provided in subparagraphs (2) and (3) of this paragraph, the Federal Government shall appear on behalf of any State the qualified tax of which it collects (or did collect for the year in issue), and shall represent such State's interests in any administrative or judicial proceeding, either civil or criminal in nature, which relates to the administration and collection of such qualified tax, in the same manner as it represents the interests of the United States in corresponding proceedings involving Federal income tax matters.

(2) *Exceptions.*—The Federal Government shall not so represent a State's interests either—

(i) In proceedings in a State court involving the constitution of such State, to the extent of such constitutional issue, or

(ii) In proceedings in any court involving the relationship between the United States and the State, to the extent of the issue pertaining to such relationship, if either:

(A) The proceeding is one which is initiated by the United States against the State, or by the State against the United States, and no individual (except in his official capacity as a governmental official) is an original party to the proceeding, or

(B) The proceeding is not one described in (A), but the State elects to represent its own interests to the extent permissible under this subdivision.

(3) *Finality of Federal administrative determinations.*—State and local government officials and employees may not review Federal administrative determinations concerning tax liabilities of, refunds owed to, or criminal prosecutions of, individuals with respect to qualified taxes. See, however, § 301.6363-3 relating to State administration of a qualified tax with respect to transition years. If requested by an electing State, the Commissioner or his delegate may, under terms and conditions set forth in an agreement with such State, permit such State to carry on operations supplementary to the Federal administration of the State's qualified tax (including supplemental audits or examinations of tax returns by State audit personnel), but all administrative determinations shall be made by the Federal Government without review by the State. An agreement which permits supplemental audits or examinations of tax returns by State audit personnel shall provide that the audits and examinations shall be conducted under the supervision and control of the Commissioner or his delegate, who shall have the authority to determine which returns shall be audited and when the audits shall occur. Also, such agreements shall provide that the results of any such supplemental audit shall be referred to the Commissioner or his delegate for final administrative determination. The Commissioner or his delegate shall, to the extent permitted by law, allow an electing State reasonable access to tax returns and other appropriate records and information relating to its qualified tax for the purpose of conducting any such supplemental operations. In addition, the Secretary or his delegate shall permit an electing State to inspect the workpapers which are compiled in the course of verification by the Treasury Department of the correctness of the accounting by which the amounts of the actual net collections attributable to the electing State's qualified taxes are determined. [Reg. § 301.6361-2.]

☐ [*T.D.* 7577, 12-19-78.]

### [Reg. § 301.6361-3]

**§ 301.6361-3. Transfers to States.**—(a) *Periodic transfers.*—In general, amounts collected by the Federal Government which are allocable to qualified taxes (including criminal fines which are required to be paid to a State, as determined under paragraph (f)(3) of § 301.6361-1) shall be promptly transferred to each State imposing such a tax. Transfers of such amounts, based on percentages of estimated Federal collections, shall be made not less frequently than every third business day unless the State agrees to accept transfers at less frequent intervals.

(b) *Determination of amounts of transfers.*—The amounts allocable to the qualified taxes of each State for purposes of periodic transfer shall be determined as a percentage of the estimated aggregate net individual income tax collections made by the Federal Government. For purposes of this paragraph, the "aggregate net individual income tax collections" shall include amounts collected on account of the Federal individual income tax and all qualified taxes by all means (including withholding, tax returns, and declarations of estimated tax), and shall be reduced to the extent of any liability to taxpayers for credits or refunds by reason of overpayments of such taxes. The percentage of the estimated amount of such collections which is allocated to each State shall be based on an estimate which is to be made by the Office of Tax Analysis prior to the beginning of each calendar year as to what portion of the estimated aggregate net individual income tax collections for the forthcoming year will be attributable to the qualified taxes of that State. Each State will be notified prior to the beginning of each calendar year of the amount which it is estimated that the State will receive by application of that percentage for the year. However, the Office of Tax Analysis shall, from time to time throughout the calendar year, revise the percentage estimates when such a revision is, in the opinion of that office necessary to conform such estimates to the actual receipts. When such a revision is made, the payments to the State will be adjusted accordingly.

(c) *Adjustment of difference between actual collections and periodic transfers.*—At least once annually the Secretary or his delegate shall determine the difference between the aggregate amount of the actual net collections made (taking into account credits, refunds, and amounts received by withholding with respect to which a tax return is not filed) which is attributable to each State's qualified taxes during the preceding year and the aggregate amount actually transferred to such State based on estimates during such year. The amount of such difference, as so determined, shall be a charge against, or an addition to, the amounts otherwise determined to be payable to the State.

(d) *Recipient of transferred funds.*—All funds transferred pursuant to section 6361(c) and paragraph (a) of this section shall be transferred by the Federal Government to the State official designated by the Governor to receive such funds in the State agreement pursuant to paragraph (d)(5) of §301.6363-1, unless the Governor notifies the Secretary or his delegate in writing of the designation of a different State official to receive the funds. [Reg. §301.6361-3.]

☐ [*T.D.* 7577, 12-19-78.]

### [Reg. §301.6361-4]

**§301.6361-4. Definitions.**—For purposes of the regulations in this part under subchapter E of chapter 64 of the Internal Revenue Code of 1954, relating to collection and administration of State individual income taxes—

(a) *State agreement.*—The term "State agreement" means an agreement between a State and the Federal Government which was entered into pursuant to section 6363 and the regulations thereunder, and which provides for the Federal collection and administration of the qualified tax or taxes of that State.

(b) *Qualified tax.*—The term "qualified tax" means a tax which is a "qualified State individual income tax," as defined in section 6362 (including subsection (f)(1) thereof, which requires that a State agreement be in effect) and the regulations thereunder.

(c) *Chapters and subtitles.*—References in regulations in this part under subchapter E to chapters and subtitles are to chapters and subtitles of the Internal Revenue Code of 1954, unless otherwise indicated.

(d) *Subchapter E.*—The term "subchapter E" means subchapter E of chapter 64 of the Internal Revenue Code of 1954, relating to collection and administration of State individual income taxes, as amended from time to time. [Reg. §301.6361-4.]

☐ [*T.D.* 7577, 12-19-78.]

### [Reg. §301.6361-5]

**§301.6361-5. Effective date of section 6361.**—Section 6361 shall take effect on the first January 1 which is more than 1 year after the first date on which at least one State has filed a notice of election with the Secretary or his delegate to enter into a State agreement. For purposes of this section, a notice of election shall be deemed to have been filed by a State only if there is no defect in either the State's notice of election or the State's tax law of which the Secretary notified the Governor pursuant to paragraph (c) of §301.6363-1, and which has not been retroactively cured under the provisions of such paragraph. [Reg. §301.6361-5.]

☐ [*T.D.* 7577, 12-19-78.]

### [Reg. §301.6362-1]

**§301.6362-1. Types of qualified tax.**—(a) *In general.*—A qualified tax may be either a "qualified resident tax" within the meaning of paragraph (b) of this section, or a "qualified nonresident tax" within the meaning of paragraph (c) of this section.

(b) *Qualified resident tax.*—A tax imposed by a State on the income of individuals, estates, and trusts which are residents of such State within the meaning of section 6362(e) and §301.6362-6 shall be a "qualified resident tax" if it is either:

(1) A tax based on Federal taxable income which meets the requirements of section 6362(b), (e), and (f), and of §§301.6362-2, 301.6362-6, and 301.6362-7; or

(2) A tax which is a percentage of the Federal tax and which meets the requirements of section 6362(c), (e), and (f), and of §§301.6362-3, 301.6362-6, and 301.6362-7.

(c) *Qualified nonresident tax.*—A tax imposed by a State on the wage and other business income of individuals who are not residents of such State within the meaning of section 6362(e)(1) and paragraph (b) of §301.6362-6 shall be a "qualified nonresident tax" if it meets the requirements of section 6362(d), (e), and (f), and of §§301.6362-5, 301.6362-6, and 301.6362-7. [Reg. §301.6362-1.]

☐ [*T.D.* 7577, 12-19-78.]

### [Reg. §301.6362-2]

**§301.6362-2. Qualified resident tax based on taxable income.**—(a) *In general.*—A tax meets the requirements of section 6362(b) and this section only if it is imposed on the amount of the taxable income, as defined in section 63, of the individual, estate, or trust, adjusted—

(1) By subtracting an amount equal to the amount of the taxpayer's interest on obligations of the United States which was included in his gross income for the taxable year;

(2) By adding an amount equal to the amount of the taxpayer's net State income tax deduction, as defined in paragraph (a) of §301.6362-4, for the taxable year;

(3) By adding an amount equal to the amount of the taxpayer's net tax-exempt income, as defined in paragraph (b) of §301.6362-4, for the taxable year; and

(4) If a credit is allowed against the tax in accordance with paragraph (b)(3) of this section for sales tax imposed by the State or a political subdivision thereof, by adding an amount equal to the amount of the taxpayer's deduction under section 164(a)(4) for such sales tax.

The tax may provide for either a single rate or multiple rates which vary with the amount of taxable income, as adjusted.

(b) *Permitted adjustments.*—A tax which otherwise meets the requirements of paragraph (a) of this section shall not be deemed to fail to meet such requirements solely because it provides for one or more of the following adjustments:

(1) A credit meeting the requirements of paragraph (c) of §301.6362-4 is allowed against the tax for taxpayer's income tax liability to another State or a political subdivision thereof.

(2) A tax is imposed on the amount taxed under section 56 (relating to the minimum tax for tax preferences).

(3) A credit is allowed against the tax for all or a portion of any general sales tax imposed by the State or a political subdivision thereof with respect to sales either to the taxpayer or to one or more of his dependents.

(c) *Method of making mandatory adjustments.*—The mandatory adjustments provided in paragraph (a) of this section shall be made directly to taxable income. Except as provided in paragraph (c)(2) of §301.6362-4, no account shall be taken of any reduction or increase in the Federal adjusted gross income which would result from the exclusion from, or inclusion in, gross income of the items which are the subject of the adjustments. Thus, for example, when for purposes of the calculation the taxpayer's Federal taxable income is adjusted to reflect the exclusion from gross income of interest on obligations of the United States, no change shall be made in the amount of the taxpayer's deduction for medical expenses, or in the amount of his charitable contribution base, even though such amounts would ordinarily depend upon the amount of adjusted gross income. [Reg. §301.6362-2.]

☐ [*T.D.* 7577, 12-19-78.]

### [Reg. §301.6362-3]

**§301.6362-3. Qualified resident tax which is a percentage of Federal tax.**—(a) *In general.*—A tax meets the requirements of section 6362(c) and this section only if:

(1) The tax is imposed as a single specified percentage of the excess of the taxes imposed by chapter 1 over the sum of the credits allowable under part IV of subchapter A of chapter 1 (other than the credits allowable under sections 31 and 39), and

(2) The amount of the tax is decreased by the amount of the decrease in such liability which would result from excluding from the taxpayer's gross income an amount equal to the amount of interest on obligations of the United States which was included in his gross income for the taxable year.

*(b) Permitted adjustments.*—A tax which otherwise meets the requirements of paragraph (a) of this section shall not be deemed to fail to meet such requirements solely because it provides for one or more of the following three adjustments:

(1) The amount of a taxpayer's liability for tax is increased by the amount of the increase in such liability which would result from including in such taxpayer's gross income all of the following:

(i) An amount equal to the amount of his net State income tax deduction, as defined in paragraph (a) of §301.6362-4, for the taxable year,

(ii) An amount equal to the amount of his net tax-exempt income, as defined in paragraph (b) of §301.6362-4, for the taxable year, and

(iii) If a credit is allowed against the tax under paragraph (b)(3) of this section for sales tax imposed by the State or a political subdivision thereof, an amount equal to the amount of his deduction under section 164(a)(4) for such sales tax.

(2) A credit meeting the requirements of paragraph (c) of §301.6362-4 is allowed against the tax for the income tax of another State or a political subdivision thereof.

(3) A credit is allowed against the tax for all or a portion of any general sales tax imposed by the State or a political subdivision thereof with respect to sales either to the taxpayer or to one or more of his dependents.

*(c) Method of making adjustments.*—Except as specifically provided in paragraphs (a)(2) and (b)(1) of this section and in paragraphs (c)(2) of §301.6362-4, no account shall be taken of any reduction or increase in the Federal adjusted gross income which would result from the exclusion from, or inclusion in, gross income of the items which are the subject of the adjustments provided in those paragraphs. Thus, for example, when for purposes of the calculation the taxpayer's Federal income tax liability is adjusted to reflect the exclusion from gross income of interest on obligations of the United States, no change shall be made in the amount of the taxpayer's deduction for medical expenses, or in the amount of his charitable contribution base, even though such amounts would ordinarily depend upon the amount of adjusted gross income. Also, when calculating the adjusted Federal tax liability to which the rate of the State tax is to be applied, no adjustment shall be made in the amount of any credit against Federal tax to which a taxpayer is entitled. [Reg. §301.6362-3.]

☐ [*T.D. 7577*, 12-19-78.]

**[Reg. §301.6362-4]**

**§301.6362-4. Rules for adjustments relating to qualified resident taxes.**—*(a) Net State income tax deduction.*—For purposes of section 6362(b)(1)(B) and (c)(3)(B), and §§301.6362-2 and 301.6362-3, the "net State income tax deduction" shall be the excess (if any) of (1) the amount deducted from income under section 164(a)(3) as taxes paid to a State or to a political subdivision thereof, over (2) the amounts included in income as recoveries of prior income taxes which were paid to a State or to a political subdivision thereof and which had been deducted under section 164(a)(3).

*(b) Net tax-exempt income.*—For purposes of section 6362(b)(1)(C) and (c)(3)(A) and §§301.6362-2 and 301.6362-3, the "net tax-exempt income" shall be the excess (if any) of:

(1) The sum of (i) the interest on obligations described in section 103(a)(1) other than obligations of the State imposing the tax and the political subdivisions thereof, and (ii) the interest on obligations described in such section of such State and the political subdivisions thereof which under the law of the State is subject to the tax; over

(2) The sum of (i) the amount of deductions allocable to the interest described in subparagraph (1)(i) or (ii) of this paragraph which is disallowed pursuant to section 265 and the regulations thereunder, and (ii) the amount of the adjustment to basis allocable to such obligations which is required to be made for the taxable year under section 1016(a)(5) or (6).

For purposes of subparagraph (1)(ii) of this paragraph, a State may, at its option, subject to the tax the interest from all, none, or some of its section 103(a)(1) obligations and those of its political subdivisions. For example, a State may subject to tax all of such obligations other than those which it or its political subdivisions issued prior to a specified date, which may be the date that subchapter E became applicable to the State.

*(c) Credits for taxes of other jurisdictions.*—*(1) In general.*—A State tax law that provides for a credit, pursuant to section 6362(b)(2)(B) or (C) or section 6362(c)(4), and paragraph (b)(1) of §301.6362-2 or paragraph (b)(2) of §301.6362-3, for income tax of another State or a political subdivision thereof shall provide that, in the case of each taxpayer, the amount of the credit shall equal the amount of his liability with respect to such other jurisdiction's tax for the taxable year which runs concurrently with, or which ends in, the taxable year

used by the taxpayer for purposes of the State tax which provides for the credit. Such a credit may be allowed with respect to every income tax (whether or not qualified) imposed on the taxpayer by another State or a political subdivision thereof, or only with respect to certain of such taxes. However, for purposes of this paragraph, the amount which is treated as being the amount of the taxpayer's liability with respect to any such tax imposed by another jurisdiction shall not exceed the amount of liability for such tax which is both—

(A) Reported to the taxing authorities responsible for collecting such other jurisdiction's tax, and

(B) Substantiated pursuant to the requirements of paragraph (c)(1)(ii) of §301.6361-1.

*(2) Limitation.*—The amount of any credit allowed for the taxable year pursuant to this paragraph shall not exceed the product of the amount of the resident tax against which the credit is allowed, as computed without subtracting any such credit, multiplied by a fraction the numerator of which is the amount of income subject to tax by both the State imposing the resident tax against which the credit is allowed and the other jurisdiction whose tax is being credited, and the denominator of which is the amount of income subject to tax by the State imposing the resident tax against which the credit is allowed. For purposes of the preceding sentence, "income subject to tax" means the amount of the taxpayer's adjusted gross income which is taken into account for purposes of computing tax liability; in the case of a qualified resident tax, an appropriate modification shall be made to take into account any adjustments which are made pursuant to paragraph (a)(1) and (3) of §301.6362-2, or pursuant to paragraph (a)(2) or (b)(1)(ii) of §301.6362-3.

*(3) Examples.*—The application of this paragraph may be illustrated by the following examples:

*Example (1).* (i) A, a calendar-year, cash-basis taxpayer, is a resident of State X throughout the taxable year. For such year, his adjusted gross income for Federal income tax purposes consists of $24,000, consisting of $3,000 derived from employment in State X, $5,000 derived from employment in State Y, $15,000 derived from employment in State Z, and $1,000 in interest income from United States savings bonds. In addition, he received net tax-exempt income in the amount of $2,000. For the taxable year, he incurs liabilities of $200 for the State Y nonresident income tax, and $1,400 for the State Z nonresident income tax. State X, which has in effect a State agreement for the taxable year, imposes a resident tax against which credits are allowed for the nonresident taxes imposed by States Y and Z. Without taking any such credits into account, however, the amount of A's liability for such resident tax would be $1,500. A properly reports his nonresident income tax liabilities to States Y and Z at the same time that he files his return with respect to the State X tax, and he substantiates on such return his liabilities to States Y and Z.

(ii) The amount of A's income subject to tax in State X is $25,000 (his adjusted gross income of $24,000, minus the United States savings bond income of $1,000, plus the net tax-exempt income of $2,000). The amount of the credit allowable against the State X resident tax for the amount of A's liability with respect to the State Y nonresident tax is calculated as follows: The maximum amount of credit is the actual amount of his liability to Y, or $200. Under subparagraph (2) of this paragraph, the amount of the credit is limited to $300 ($1,500 × $5,000/$25,000). Thus, such limit has no effect, and the full $200 is allowable as a credit against A's liability for the resident tax of State X. The amount of the credit allowable against the State X resident tax for the amount of A's liability with respect to the State Z nonresident tax is calculated as follows: The maximum amount of the credit is the actual amount of his liability to Z, or $1,400. Under subparagraph (2) of this paragraph, the amount of the credit is limited to $900 ($1,500 × $15,000/$25,000). Thus, such limit has the effect of reducing to $900 the amount of the credit allowable for tax of State Z against A's liability for the resident tax of State X.

*Example (2).* (i) (B), a calendar-year, cash-basis taxpayer, is a resident of State X employed in State Y through March 14, 1977. On March 15, 1977, B becomes a resident of State Z and remains a resident of such State through the remainder of 1977. For 1977, the amount of B's adjusted gross income for Federal income tax purposes is $20,000, consisting of $6,000 derived from employment in State Y which B held during the period of his residence in State X, $12,000 derived from employment in State Z which B held during the period of his residence in State Z, and $2,000 in interest income from various bank accounts. During 1977, B has no interest income from United States obligations, and no tax-exempt income. For 1977, B incurs a liability of $200 to State Y on account of its nonresident income tax imposed with respect to his $6,000 of income derived from sources within that State. State Z, which has in effect a State agreement for 1977, imposes a resident income tax on B which, if B had been a resident of State Z for all 1977, would amount to $1,200 prior to the allowance of any credits under this paragraph. However, by reason of paragraph (e)(1) of § 301.6362-6, B's liability for the resident tax of State Z, before taking into account credits allowed under this paragraph, is reduced to $960 ($1,200 × 292/365, or ⁴/₅). Furthermore, State Z allows a credit for the nonresident tax imposed by State Y.

(ii) The amount of the credit allowable against the State Z resident tax for the amount of B's liability with respect to the State Y nonresident tax is calculated as follows: The maximum amount of the credit is the amount of his actual liability to State Y, or $200. Under subparagraph (2) of this paragraph, the amount of the credit is limited to $288 ($960 × $6,000/$20,000). Thus, such limit has no effect, and the full $200 is allowable as a credit for tax of State Y against B's liability for the resident tax of State Z. [Reg. § 301.6362-4.]

☐ [*T.D.* 7577, 12-19-78.]

### [Reg. § 301.6362-5]

**§ 301.6362-5. Qualified nonresident tax.**—(a) *In general.*—A tax meets the requirements of section 6362(d) and this section only if:

(1) The tax is imposed by a State which simultaneously imposes a resident tax meeting the requirements of section 6362(b) and § 301.6362-2 or of section 6362(c) and § 301.6362-3;

(2) The tax is required to be computed in accordance with either the method prescribed in paragraph (b) of this section or another method of which the Secretary or his delegate approves upon submission by the State of the laws pertaining to the tax;

(3) The tax is imposed only on the wage and other business income derived from sources within such State (as defined in paragraph (d) of this section), of all individuals each of whom derives 25 percent or more of his aggregate wage and other business income for the taxable year from sources within such State while he is neither (i) a resident of such State within the meaning of section 6362(e) and § 301.6362-6, nor (ii) exempt from liability for the tax by reason of a reciprocal agreement between such State and the State of which he is a resident within the meaning of those provisions;

(4) The amount of the tax imposed with respect to any individual does not exceed the amount of tax for which such individual would be liable under the qualified resident tax imposed by such State if he were a resident of the State for the period during which he earned wage or other business income from sources within the State, and if his taxable income for such period were an amount equal to the sum of the zero bracket amount (within the meaning of section 63(d) and determined as if he had been a resident of the State for such period) and the excess of:

(i) The amount of his wage and other business income derived from sources within the State, over

(ii) That portion of the sum of the zero bracket amount and the nonbusiness deductions (*i.e.*, all deductions from adjusted gross income allowable in computing taxable income) taken into account for purposes of the State's qualified resident tax which bears the same ratio to such sum as the amount described in subdivision (i) of this subparagraph bears to his total adjusted gross income for the year; and

(5) For purposes of the tax, wage or other business income is considered as being the income of the individual whose income it is for purposes of section 61.

(b) *Approved method of computing liability for qualified nonresident tax.*—A tax satisfies the requirement of paragraph (a)(2) of this section if the amount of the tax is computed either as a percentage of the excess of the amount described in paragraph (a)(4)(i) of this section over the amount described in paragraph (a)(4)(ii) of this section, or by application of progressive rates to such excess.

(c) *Definition of wage and other business income.*—For purposes of section 6362(d) and this section, the term "wage and other business income" means the following types of income:

(1) Wages, as defined in section 3401(a) and the regulations thereunder, but for these purposes:

(i) The amount of wages shall exclude amounts which are treated as wages under section 3402(o) or (p) (relating to supplemental unemployment compensation benefits, annuity payments, and voluntary withholding agreements), and amounts which are treated as disability payments to the extent that they are excluded from gross income for Federal income tax purposes, pursuant to section 105(d), and

(ii) The amount of wages shall be reduced by those expenses which are directly related to the earning of such wages and with respect to which deductions are properly claimed from gross income in computing adjusted gross income;

(2) Net earnings from self-employment, as defined in section 1402(a); and

(3) The distributive share of income of any trade or business carried on by a trust, estate, or electing small business corporation (as defined in section 1371(a) and the regulations thereunder), to the extent that such share:

(i) Is includible in the gross income of the taxpayer for the taxable year, and

(ii) Would constitute net earnings from self-employment if the trade or business were carried on by a partnership.

For purposes of this subparagraph, "distributive share" includes the income of a trust or estate which is taxable to the taxpayer as a beneficiary under applicable Federal income tax rules, and the undistributed taxable income of an electing small business corporation which is taxable to the taxpayer as a shareholder under section 1373.

(d) *Income derived from sources within a State.*—(1) *Income attributable primarily to services.*—Except as otherwise provided by Federal statute (see paragraphs (h), (i), and (j) of § 301.6362-7), wage income and other business income (net earnings from self-employment or distributive shares) which is attributable more to services performed by the taxpayer than to a capital investment of the taxpayer shall be considered to have been derived from sources within a State only if the services of the taxpayer which give rise to the income are performed in such State. If for a taxable year only a portion of the taxpayer's services giving rise to the income from one employment, trade, or business is performed within a State, then it shall be presumed that the amount of income from such employment, trade, or business which is derived from sources within that State equals that portion of the total income derived from such employment, trade, or business for the year which the amount of time spent by the taxpayer for such year performing services with respect to that employment, trade, or business in that State bears to the aggregate amount of time spent by the taxpayer for such year performing all of such services. However, the presumption stated in the preceding sentence may be rebutted in the event that the taxpayer proves, by use of detailed records, that the correct allocation of his income is otherwise.

(2) *Income attributable primarily to investment.*—Except as otherwise provided by Federal statute (see paragraph (j) of § 301.6362-7), business income (net earnings from self-employment or distributive shares) which is attributable more to a capital investment of the taxpayer than to services performed by the taxpayer shall be considered to have been derived from sources within the State, if any, in which the significant activities of the trade or business are conducted. If for the taxable year only a portion of the significant activities conducted with respect to one trade or business is conducted within a certain State, then the portion of the taxpayer's total income for the year from such trade or business which is considered to be derived from sources within that State shall be computed as follows:

(i) *Allocation by records.*—The portion of the taxpayer's total income from the trade or business which is considered to be derived from sources within the State shall be the portion which is allocable to such sources according to the records of the taxpayer or of the partnership, trust, estate, or electing small business corporation from which his income is derived, provided that the taxpayer establishes to the satisfaction of the district director, when requested to do so, that those records fairly and equitably reflect the income which is allocable to sources within the State. An allocation made pursuant to this subdivision shall be based on the location of the significant activities of the trade or business, and not on the location at which the taxpayer's personal services are performed.

(ii) *Allocation by formula.*—If the taxpayer (or the trade or business) does not keep records meeting the requirements of subdivision (i) of this subparagraph, or if the taxpayer fails to meet the burden of proof set forth therein, then the amount of the taxpayer's income from the trade or business which is considered to be derived from sources within the State shall be determined by multiplying the total of his income (as defined in paragraphs (c)(2) and (3) of this section) from the trade or business for the taxable year by the percentage which is the average of these three percentages:

(A) *Property percentage.*—The percentage computed by dividing the average of the value, at the beginning and end of the taxable year, of real and tangible personal property connected with the taxpayer's trade or business and located within the State, by the average of the value, at the beginning and end of the taxable year, of all such property located both within and without the State. For this purpose, real property shall include real property rented to the taxpayer in connection with the trade or business, or rented to the trade or business.

(B) *Payroll percentage.*—The percentage computed by dividing the total wages, salaries, and other compensation for personal services which is paid or incurred during the taxable year to employees in connection with the taxpayer's trade or business, and which would be treated as derived by such employees from sources within the State pursuant to subparagraph (1) of this paragraph, by the total of all such wages, salaries, and other compensation for personal services which is so paid or incurred without regard to whether such payments would be treated as derived by the employees from sources within the State. For purposes of this subdivision (ii), no amount paid as deferred compensation pursuant to a retirement plan to a former employee shall be taken into consideration.

(C) *Gross income percentage.*—The percentage computed by dividing the gross sales or charges for services performed by or through an agency located within the State by the total of all gross sales or charges for services performed both within and without the State. The sales or charges to be allocated to the State shall include all sales which are negotiated, and charges which are for services performed, by an employee, agent, agency, or independent contractor chiefly situated at, or working principally out of an office located within, the State.

(3) *Income attributable to real estate investment.*—Notwithstanding subparagraph (2) of this paragraph, income and deductions from the rental of real property, and gain and loss from the sale, exchange, or other disposition of real property, shall not be subject to allocation under subparagraph (2), but shall be considered as entirely derived from sources located within the State in which such property is located.

(4) *Treatment of losses.*—A loss attributable to the taxpayer's employment, or to his conduct of, participation in, or investment in a trade or business, shall be allocated in the same manner as the income attributable to such employment or trade or business would be allocated pursuant to this paragraph.

(5) *Examples.*—The application of this paragraph may be illustrated by the following examples:

*Example (1).* A, an employee who earns $10,000 in wage income attributable to services, and who has no other wage or other business income, spends 60 percent of his working time performing services for his employer in State X, 30 percent in State Y, and 10 percent in State Z. In the absence of the requisite proof to the contrary, A's wage income is considered to have been derived 60 percent from sources located within State X, 30 percent within State Y, and 10 percent within State Z. Assuming that A is a nonresident with respect to all three States, and that they all impose qualified nonresident taxes, then the qualified nonresident tax of State X is imposed in $6,000, the qualified nonresident tax of State Y is imposed on $3,000, and the qualified nonresident tax of State Z is not imposed on any of the income because A did not derive at least 25 percent of his wage and other business income from sources located within State Z.

*Example (2).* B, who earns no wage income but who has a total of $10,000 of other business income for the taxable year, all of which is net income from self-employment attributable primarily to services, spends 45 percent of his working time performing services in State X, 30 percent in State Y, and 25 percent in State Z. However, the rates that B is able to charge for his services and the business expenses which he incurs vary in the different States, and he is able to prove by detailed records that his net income from self-employment was in fact derived 50 percent from sources located within State X, 35 percent from sources within State Y, and 15 percent from sources located within State Z. Assuming that B is a nonresident with respect to all three States, and that they all impose qualified nonresident taxes, then the qualified nonresident tax of State X is imposed on $5,000, the qualified nonresident tax of State Y is imposed on $3,500, and the qualified nonresident tax of State Z is not imposed on any of the income because B did not derive at least 25 percent of his wage and other business income from sources located within State Z.

*Example (3).* C is a partner in a profitable business concern, in which he has a substantial capital investment. His net earnings from self-employment attributable to his partnership interest are $75,000 for the taxable year. The fair market value of the services which C performs for the partnership during the taxable year is $30,000. C's income is therefore attributable primarily to his capital investment. The partnership business is carried on partially within and partially without State X. Neither C nor the partnership maintains records from which the portion of C's $75,000 income which is considered to be derived from sources within State X can be satisfactorily proven. As determined under subparagraph (2) of this paragraph, the partnership's "property percentage" in State X is 70, its "payroll percentage" therein is 60, and its "gross income percentage" therein is 56. The amount of C's partnership income considered to be derived from sources within State X is $46,500 ($75,000 × 62 percent). This result would obtain even if C's services for the partnership are performed entirely within State X.

*Example (4).* Assume the same facts as in (3), except that the records of the partnership of which C is a member indicate that the net profits of the partnership are derived 40 percent from business activities conducted in State X, and 60 percent from business activities conducted in State Y. C is requested to prove that those records fairly and equitably reflect the income which is allocable to sources within State X. The documentary evidence which he adduces in support of the allocation made by the records shows how such allocation results from a careful step-by-step tracing of the profitability of each phase and aspect of the partnership's operations, and shows the State in which each such phase and aspect of the operations is conducted. C's proof is satisfactory to show that the percentage allocation, and the amount of his partnership income considered to be derived from sources within State X is $30,000, or $75,000 multiplied by 40 percent. This result would obtain even if B's services for the partnership are performed entirely within State X. [Reg. § 301.6362-5.]

☐ [*T.D. 7577, 12-19-78.*]

**[Reg. § 301.6362-6]**

**§ 301.6362-6. Requirements relating to residence.**—(a) *In general.*—A tax imposed by a State meets the requirements of section 6362(e) and this section if in effect it provides that:

(1) The State of residence of an individual, estate, or trust is determined according to paragraph (1), (2), or (3), respectively, of section 6362(e), and according to paragraph (b), (c), or (d), respectively, of this section.

(2) The liability for a resident tax imposed by such State upon an individual or trust which changes residence to another State in the taxable year is determined according to section 6362(e)(4) and paragraph (e) of this section.

(3) The rules relating to current collection of tax apply as provided in section 6362(e)(5) and paragraph (f) of this section.

(b) *Residence of an individual.*—(1) *In general.*—Except as otherwise provided in subparagraph (5) of this paragraph, an individual is treated as a resident of a State with respect to a taxable year only if:

(i) His principal place of residence (as defined in subparagraph (2) of this paragraph) is within such State for a period of at least 135 consecutive days, at least 30 days of which are in such taxable year; or

(ii) In the case of a citizen or resident of the United States who is not a resident of any State (determined as provided in subdivision (i) of this subparagraph) with respect to such taxable year, his domicile (as defined in subparagraph (3) of this paragraph) is in such State for at least 30 days during such taxable year.

With respect to an individual who is a resident (determined as provided in subdivision (i) of this subparagraph) of more than one State during a taxable year, see paragraph (e) of this section.

(2) *Principal place of residence.*—(i) *Definition.*—For purposes of subparagraph (1)(i) of this paragraph and paragraph (d)(4) of this section, the term "principal place of residence" shall mean the place which is an individual's primary home. An individual's temporary absence from his primary home shall not effect a change with respect thereto. On the other hand, if an individual moves to another State, other than as a mere transient or sojourner, he shall be treated as having changed the location of his primary home.

(ii) *Examples.*—The application of this subparagraph may be illustrated by the following examples:

*Example (1).* A has a city home and a country home. He resides in the city home for 7 months of the year and uses the address of that home as his legal residence for purposes of driver's license, automobile registration, and voter registration. He resides in the country home 5 months of the year. His city home is considered his principal place of residence.

*Example (2).* During the taxable year, B, a construction worker, is employed at several different locations in different States. The duration of each job on which he is employed ranges from a few weeks to several months, and he knows when he accepts a job what its approximate duration will be. He owns a house in State X which he uses as his legal residence for purposes of driver's license, automobile registration, and voter registration. In addition, his family lives there during the entire year, and B lives there during periods between jobs. However, the duration of the jobs and the distance between the job-sites and his house require him to live in the localities of the respective job-sites during the period of his employment, although occasionally he returns to his house in State X on weekends. B's house in State X is his principal place of residence during all of the taxable year.

*Example (3).* C, a dependent of his parents who are residents of State X, is a full-time student in a 4-year degree program at a college in State Y. During the 9-month academic year, C lives on the college campus, but he returns to his parents' home in State X for the summer recess. C gives the State Y as his residence for purposes of his driver's license and voter registration, but lists the address of his parents' home in State X as his "permanent address" on the records of the college which he attends. Although C's domicile remains at his parents' home in State X, his presence in State Y cannot be regarded as that of a mere transient or sojourner; accordingly, C's principal place of residence is in State Y for that portion of the taxable year during which he attends college.

*Example (4).* D loses his job in State X, where he lived and worked for many years. After a series of unsuccessful attempts to find other employment in State X, he accepts a job in State Y. D gives up his apartment in State X and moves to State Y upon commencing his new job; however, he intends to continue to explore available employment opportunities in State X so that he may return there as soon as an opportunity to do so arises. D changes his principal place of residence when he moves to State Y.

(3) *Domicile defined.*—For purposes of subparagraph (1)(ii) of this paragraph and paragraph (d)(4) of this section, the term "domicile" shall mean an individual's fixed or permanent home. An individual acquires a domicile in a place by living there; even for a brief period of time, with no definite present intention of later removing therefrom. Residence without the requisite intention to remain indefinitely will not suffice to change domicile, nor will intention to change domicile effect such a change until accompanied by actual removal. A domicile, once acquired, is maintained until a new domicile is acquired.

(4) *Period of residence.*—(i) *General rule.*—An individual who becomes a resident of a State pursuant to subparagraph (1) of this paragraph, or who is at the beginning of a taxable year a resident of a State pursuant to such provision, shall be treated as continuing to be a resident of such State through the end of the taxable year, unless, prior thereto, such individual becomes a resident, under the principles of subparagraph (1), of another State or a possession or foreign country. In the event that the individual becomes a resident of such another jurisdiction prior to the end of the taxable year, his residence in such State shall be treated as ending on the day prior to the day on which he becomes a resident of such other jurisdiction pursuant to subparagraph (1).

(ii) *Examples.*—The application of this subparagraph may be illustrated by the following examples:

*Example (1).* A, a calendar-year taxpayer, has his principal place of residence in State X from the beginning of 1976 through August 1, 1976, when he gives up permanently such principal place of residence. He spends the remainder of 1976 traveling outside of the United States, but does not become a resident of any other country. A is considered to be a resident of State X for the entire year 1976.

*Example (2).* Assume the same facts as in example (1), except that A ceases his traveling and establishes his principal place of residence in State Y on November 15, 1976. Assume, also, that A maintains that principal place of residence for more than 135 consecutive days. Under these circumstances, for his taxable year 1976, A is considered to be a resident of State X from January 1 through November 14, and a resident of State Y from November 15 through December 31.

(5) *Special rules.*—(i) No provision of subchapter E or the regulations thereunder shall be construed to require or authorize the treatment of a Senator, Representative, Delegate, or Resident Commissioner as a resident of a State other than the State which he represents in Congress.

(ii) For special rules relating to members of the Armed Forces, see paragraph (h) of §301.6362-7.

(6) *Examples.*—The application of this paragraph may be illustrated by the following examples:

*Example (1).* A, a calendar-year taxpayer, maintains his principal place of residence in State X from December 1, 1976, through April 15, 1977. Assuming that A was not a resident of any other jurisdiction at any time during 1976, A is treated as a resident of State X for the entire year 1976. Such result would obtain even if A was absent from State X on vacation for some portion of December 1976. Moreover, such result would obtain even if it is assumed that A was a domiciliary of State Y from January 1, 1976, through April 15, 1977, because an individual's domicile does not determine his residence so long as residence in one State for the taxable year can be determined from the general rule stated in the first sentence of paragraph (b)(1) of this section.

*Example (2).* Assume the same facts as in example (1) (including the fact of A's domicile in State Y), except that A maintained his principal place of residence in State Z from September 15, 1975, through January 31, 1976, inclusive. With respect to the year 1976, A is treated as a resident of State Z from January 1 through November 30, and as a resident of State X from December 1 through December 31. A's liability for the qualified taxes of the respective States for 1976 shall be determined pursuant to the provisions in paragraph (e) of this section.

(c) *Residence of an estate.*—An estate of an individual is treated as a resident of the last State of which such individual was a resident, as

determined under the rules of paragraph (b) of this section, prior to his death. However, the estate of an individual who was not a resident of any State (as determined without regard to the 30-day requirement in paragraph (b)(1) of this section) immediately prior to his death, and who was not a resident of any State at any time during the 3-year period ending on the date of his death, is not treated as a resident of any State. For purposes of determining the decedent's last State of residence, the rules of paragraph (b) shall be applied irrespective of whether subchapter E was in effect at the time the period of 135 consecutive days of residence began, or whether the decedent's last State of residence is a State electing to enter into an agreement pursuant to subchapter E. The determination of the State of residence of an estate pursuant to this paragraph shall not be governed by any determination under State law as to which State is treated as the residence or domicile of the decedent for purposes other than its individual income tax (such as liability for State inheritance tax or jurisdiction of probate proceedings).

(d) *Residence of a trust.*—(1) *In general.*—(i) The State of residence of a trust shall be determined by reference to the circumstances of the individual who, by either an inter-vivos transfer or a testamentary transfer, is deemed to be the "principal contributor" to the trust under the provisions of subdivision (ii) of this subparagraph.

(ii) If only one individual has ever contributed assets to the trust, including the assets which were transferred to the trust at its inception, then such individual is the principal contributor to the trust. However, if on any day subsequent to the initial creation of the trust, such trust receives assets having a value greater than the aggregate value of all assets theretofore contributed to it, then the trust shall be deemed (for the limited purpose of determining the State of residence) to have been "created" anew, and the individual who on the day of such creation contributed more (in value) than any other individual contributed on that day shall become the principal contributor to the trust. When a trust is created anew, all references in this paragraph to the creation of the trust shall be construed as referring to the most recent creation. For purposes of this paragraph, the value of any asset shall be its fair market value on the day that it was contributed to the trust; any subsequent appreciation or depreciation in the value of the asset shall be disregarded.

(2) *Testamentary trust.*—A trust with respect to which a deceased individual is the principal contributor by reason of property passing on his death is treated as a resident of the last State of which such individual was a resident, as determined under the rules of paragraph (b) of this section, before his death. However, if such deceased individual was not a resident of any State (as determined without regard to the 30-day requirement in paragraph (b)(1) of this section) immediately prior to his death, and was not a resident of any State at any time during the 3-year period ending on the date of his death, then a testamentary trust of which he is the principal contributor by reason of property passing on his death is not treated as a resident of any State. All property passing on the transferor's death is treated for this purpose as a contribution made to the trust on the date of death, regardless of when the property is actually paid over to the trust.

(3) *Nontestamentary trust.*—A trust which is not a trust described in subparagraph (2) of this paragraph is treated as a resident of the State in which the principal contributor to the trust, during the 3-year period ending on the date of the creation of the trust, had his principal place of residence for an aggregate number of days longer than the aggregate number of days he had his principal place of residence in any other State. However, if the principal contributor to such a trust was not a resident of any State at any time during such 3-year period, then the trust is not treated as a resident of any State.

(4) *Special rules.*—If the application of the provisions of the foregoing subparagraphs of this paragraph results in a determination of more than one State of residence for a trust, or does not provide a rule by which the residence or nonresidence of the trust can be determined, then the determination of the State of residence of such trust shall be made according to the rules of the applicable subdivision of this subparagraph.

(i) If, at the time of creation of the trust, 50 percent or more in value of the trust corpus consists of real property, then the trust shall be treated as a resident of the State in which more of the real property (in value) which was in the trust at such time was located than any other State.

(ii) If, at the time of creation of the trust, less than 50 percent in value of the trust corpus consists of real property, then the trust shall be treated as a resident of the State in which, at such time, the trustee, if an individual, had his principal place of residence, or, if a corporation, had its principal place of business. If there were two or more trustees, then the foregoing sentence shall be applied by reference to the principal places of residence, or of business, of the majority of trustees who had authority to make investment and other management decisions for the trust.

(iii) If, after application of the provisions of subdivisions (i) and (ii) of this subparagraph, the State of residence of the trust still cannot be ascertained, then the Commissioner of Internal Revenue shall determine the State of residence of such trust for purposes of qualified taxes. Such determination shall be made by reference to the number of significant contacts each State had with the trust at the time of its creation. Significant contacts shall include the principal place of residence of the principal contributor or contributors to the trust, the principal place of residence or business of the trustee (or trustees), the situs of the assets of which the trust corpus was composed, and the location from which management decisions emanated with respect to the business and investment interests of the trusts.

(5) *Examples.*—The application of this paragraph may be illustrated by the following examples:

*Example (1).* A created a trust in 1950 by transferring to it certain stock in a corporation. At the time of such transfer, the stock had a fair market value of $1,000. A at all relevant times had his principal place of residence in State X, and accordingly the trust is treated as a resident of such State for qualified tax purposes. As of January 1, 1977, the stock originally contributed by A, which was at all times the only property in the trust, has a fair market value of $3,000. On such date, B, who has had his principal place of residence in State Y for more than 3 years, contributes to the trust property having a fair market value of $1,200. For purposes of determining the identity of the principal contributor to the trust and the State of residence of the trust, the stock contributed by A in 1950 continues to be valued for such purposes at $1,000. Thus, the trust is treated as being created anew on January 1, 1977, with B as the principal contributor, and with State Y as its State of residence.

*Example (2).* C has his principal place of residence in State X continuously for many years, until August 1, 1978, when he establishes his principal place of residence in State Y. The change of residence is intended to be permanent, and C has no further contact with State X after such change. On January 1, 1980, C creates a nontestamentary trust. During the 3-year period ending on such date C had his principal place of residence in State X for 576 days, and in State Y for 519 days. Therefore, the trust is treated as a resident of State X.

(e) *Liability for tax on change of residence during taxable year.*—(1) *In general.*—If, under the principles contained in paragraph (b) or (d) of this section, an individual or trust becomes a resident, or ceases to be a resident, of a State, and is also a resident of another jurisdiction outside of such State during the same taxable year, the liability of such individual or trust for the resident tax of such State shall be determined by multiplying the amount which would be his or its liability for tax (computed after allowing the nonrefundable credits (i.e., credits not corresponding to the credits referred to in section 6401(b) available against the tax)) if he or it had been a resident of such State for the entire taxable year by a fraction, the numerator of which is the number of days he or it was a resident of such State during the taxable year, and the denominator of which is the total number of days in the taxable year. The preceding sentence shall not apply by reason of the fact that an individual is born or dies during the taxable year, or by reason of the fact that a trust comes into existence or ceases to exist during the taxable year.

(2) *Residence determined by domicile.*—When an individual is treated as a resident of a State by reason of being domiciled in such State, pursuant to paragraph (b)(1)(ii) of this section, then the numerator of the fraction provided in subparagraph (1) of this paragraph shall be the number of days the individual was domiciled in the State during the taxable year.

(3) *Example.*—The application of this paragraph may be illustrated by the following example:

*Example.* A, a calendar-year taxpayer, is a resident of State X continuously for many years prior to March 15, 1977. On such date, A retires and establishes a new principal place of residence in State Y. A earns $6,000 in 1977 prior to March 15, but receives no taxable income for the remainder of such year. If A had been a resident of State X for the entire taxable year 1977, his liability with respect to the qualified tax of such State (computed after allowing the nonrefundable credits available against the tax) would be $600. If he had been a resident of State Y for the entire taxable year 1977, his liability with respect to the qualified tax on that State (computed similarly) would be $400. Pursuant to the provisions in paragraph (e) of this section, A's liabilities for State qualified taxes for 1977 are as follows:

$$\text{Liability for State } X \text{ tax} = \$600 \times \frac{73}{\frac{365}{292}} = \$120$$

$$\text{Liability for State } Y \text{ tax} = \$400 \times \frac{}{365} = \$320.$$

(f) *Current collection of tax.*—The State tax laws shall contain provisions for methods of current collection with respect to individuals which correspond to the provisions of the Internal Revenue Code of 1954 with respect to such current collection, including chapter 24 (relating to the collection of income tax at source on wages) and sections 6015, 6073, 6153, and other provisions of the Code relating to declarations (and amendments thereto) and payments of estimated income tax. Except as otherwise provided by Federal statute (see paragraphs (h), (i), and (j) of § 301.6362-7), in applying such provisions of the State tax laws:

(1) In the case of a resident tax, an individual shall be subject to the current collection provisions if either—

(i) He is a resident of the State within the meaning of paragraph (b) of this section, or

(ii) He has his principal place of residence (as defined in paragraph (b)(2) of this section) within the State,

and it is reasonable to expect him to have it within the State for 30 days or more during the taxable year.

(2) In the case of a nonresident tax, an individual shall be subject to the current collection provisions if he does not meet either description relating to an individual in subparagraph (1) of this paragraph, if he is not exempt from liability for the tax by reason of a reciprocal agreement between the State of which he is a resident and the State imposing the tax, and if it is reasonable to expect him to receive wage or other business income derived from sources within the State imposing the tax (as defined in paragraph (d) of § 301.6362-5) for services performed on 30 days or more of the taxable year.

For additional rules relating to withholding see paragraph (d) of § 301.6361-1. [Reg. § 301.6362-6.]

☐ [T.D. 7577, 12-19-78.]

### [Reg. § 301.6362-7]

**§ 301.6362-7. Additional requirements.**—A State tax meets the additional requirements of section 6362(f) and this section only if:

(a) *State agreement must be in effect for period concerned.*—A State agreement, as defined in paragraph (a) of § 301.6361-4, is in effect with respect to such tax for the taxable period in question.

(b) *State laws contain certain provisions.*—Under the laws of such State, the provisions of subchapter E and the regulations thereunder, as in effect from time to time, are applicable for the entire period for which the State agreement is in effect. Any change made by the State in such tax (other than an adjustment in the State law which is made solely in order to comply with a change in the Federal law or regulations) shall not apply to taxable years beginning in any calendar year for which the State agreement is in effect unless the change is enacted before November 1 of such year.

(c) *State individual income tax laws can be only of certain kinds.*—Such State does not impose any tax on the income of individuals other than (1) a qualified resident tax, and (2) either or both a qualified nonresident tax and a separate tax on income which is not wage and other business income as defined in paragraph (c) of § 301.6362-5 and which is received or accrued by individuals who are domiciled in the State, but who are not residents of the State (as defined in paragraph (b) of § 301.6362-6). For purposes of this paragraph, a tax imposed on the amount taxed under section 56 (as permitted under § 301.6362-2(b)(2)) shall be treated as an adjustment to and a part of the qualified resident tax. Also, tax laws which were in effect prior to the effective date of a State agreement and which are not repealed, but which are made inapplicable for the period during which the State agreement is in effect, shall be disregarded.

(d) *Taxable years must coincide.*—The taxable years of all individuals, estates, and trusts under such tax are required to coincide with their taxable years used for purposes of the taxes imposed by chapter 1. Accordingly, when subchapter E begins to apply to a State, a taxpayer whose taxable year for purposes of the Federal income tax is different from his taxable year for purposes of the State income tax which precedes the qualified tax may have one short taxable year for purposes of such State income tax, so that thereafter his taxable years for purposes of the qualified tax will coincide with the Federal taxable year.

(e) *Married individuals.*—Individuals who are married within the meaning of section 143 of the Code are prohibited from filing (1) a joint return for purposes of such State tax if they file separate Federal income tax returns, or (2) separate returns for purposes of such State tax if they file a joint Federal income tax return.

(f) *Penalties; no double jeopardy.*—Under the laws of such State:

(1) Civil and criminal sanctions identical to those provided by subtitle F, and by title 18 of the United States Code (relating to crimes and criminal procedures), with respect to the taxes imposed on the income of individuals by chapter 1 and on the wages of individuals by chapter 24, apply to individuals and their employers who are subject to such State tax (and the collection and administration thereof, including the corresponding withholding tax imposed to implement the current collection of such State tax) as if such tax were imposed by chapter 1 (or chapter 24, in the case of the withholding tax), except to the extent that the application of such sanctions is modified by regulations issued under subchapter E; and

(2) No other sanctions or penalties apply with respect to any act or omission to act in respect of such State tax.
See also paragraph (e) of §301.6361-1 with respect to criminal penalties.

(g) *Partnerships, trusts, subchapter S corporations, and other conduit entities.*—Under the laws of such State, the State tax treatment of—

(1) Partnerships and partners,

(2) Trusts and their beneficiaries,

(3) Estates and their beneficiaries,

(4) Electing small business corporations (within the meaning of section 1371(a)) and their shareholders, and

(5) Any other entity and the individuals having beneficial interests therein (such as a cooperative corporation and its shareholders), to the extent that such entity is treated as a conduit for purposes of the taxes imposed by chapter 1,
corresponds to the tax treatment provided therefor with respect to the taxes imposed by chapter 1. For example, a subchapter S corporation shall not be subject to the State's corporate income tax on amounts which are includible in shareholders' incomes which are subject to that State's individual income tax, except to the extent that the subchapter S corporation is subject to tax under Federal law. Similarly, a partnership shall not be subject to the State's unincorporated business income tax on amounts which are includible in partners' incomes which are subject to that State's individual income tax. However, the laws of the State which set forth the provisions of such State individual income tax shall authorize the Commissioner of Internal Revenue to require that the conduit entities described in this paragraph (or some of them) supply information to the Federal Government with respect to the source of income, the State of residence, or the amount of income of a particular type, of an individual, estate, or trust holding a beneficial interest in such conduit entity.

(h) *Members of armed forces.*—The relief provided to any member of the Armed Forces by section 514 of the Soldiers' and Sailors' Civil Relief Act (50 U.S.C. App. sec. 574) is in no way diminished. Accordingly, for purposes of such State tax, an individual shall not be considered to have become a resident of a State solely because of his absence from his original State of residence under military order. Moreover, compensation for military service shall not be considered as income derived from a source within a State of which the individual earning such compensation is not a resident, within the meaning of paragraph (d) of §301.6362-5. The preceding sentence shall not apply to nonmilitary compensation. Thus, for example, if an individual who is serving in State X as a member of the Armed Forces, and who is regarded as a resident of State Y under the Soldiers' and Sailors' Civil Relief Act, earns nonmilitary income in State X from a part-time job, such nonmilitary income may be subject to a qualified nonresident tax imposed by State X.

(i) *Withholding on compensation of employees of railroads, motor carriers, airlines, and water carriers.*—There is no contravention of the provisions of section 26, 226A, or 324 of the Interstate Commerce Act, or of section 1112 of the Federal Aviation Act of 1958, with respect to the withholding of compensation to which such sections apply for purposes of the nonresident tax.

(j) *Income derived from interstate commerce.*—There is no contravention of the provisions of the Act of September 14, 1959 (73 Stat. 555), with respect to the taxation of income derived from interstate commerce to which such statute applies. [Reg. §301.6362-7.]

☐ [T.D. 7577, 12-19-78.]

**[Reg. §301.6363-1]**

**§301.6363-1. State agreements.**—(a) *Notice of election.*—If a State elects to enter into a State agreement it shall file notice of such election with the Secretary or his delegate. The notice of election shall include the following:

(1) *Statement by the Governor.*—A written statement by the Governor of the electing State:

(i) Requesting that the Secretary enter into a State agreement, and

(ii) Binding the Governor and his successors in office to notify the Secretary or his delegate immediately of the enactment, between the time of the filing of the notice of election and the time of the execution of the State agreement, of any law of that State which meets the description given in any of the subdivisions of subparagraph (2) of this paragraph, whether or not such law is intended to be administered by the United States pursuant to subchapter E.

(2) *Copy of State laws.*—Certified copies of all laws of that State described in any of the following subdivisions of this subparagraph, and a specification of laws described in subdivision (i) of this subparagraph as "subchapter E laws", of laws described in subdivision (ii) as "other tax laws", of laws described in subdivision (iii) as "non-tax laws", and of laws described in subdivision (iv) as "interstate cooperation laws":

(i) All of the State individual income tax laws (including laws relating to the collection or administration of such taxes or to the prosecution of alleged civil or criminal violations with respect to such taxes) which the State would expect the United States to administer pursuant to subchapter E if the State agreement is executed as requested. In order to have a valid notice, the State must have a tax which would meet the requirements for qualification specified in section 6362 and the regulations thereunder if a State agreement were in effect with respect thereto, with no conditions attached to the effectiveness of such tax other than the execution of a State agreement. Such tax must be effective no later than the January 1 specified in the State's notice of election as the date as of which subchapter E is desired to become applicable to the electing State, except that such effective date shall be deferred to the date provided in the State agreement for the beginning of applicability of subchapter E to the State, if the latter date is different from the date specified in the notice of election.

(ii) All of the State income tax laws applicable to individuals (including laws relating to the collection or administration of such taxes or to the prosecution of alleged civil or criminal violations with respect to such taxes) which the State would not expect the United States to administer but which may be in effect simultaneously (for any period of time) with the State agreement.

(iii) All of the State laws other than individual income tax laws which provide for the making of any payments by the State based on one or more criteria which the State may desire to verify by reference to information contained in returns of qualified taxes.

(iv) All of the State laws which may be in effect simultaneously (for any period of time) with the State agreement and which provide for cooperation or reciprocal agreement between the electing State and another State with respect to income taxes applicable to individuals.

(3) *Approval by legislature or authorization by constitutional amendment.*—A certified copy of an Act or Resolution of the legislature of the electing State in which the legislature affirmatively expresses its approval of the State's entry into a State agreement, or a certified copy of an amendment to the constitution of such State by which the voters of the State affirmatively authorize such entry.

(4) *Opinion by State Attorney General or judgment of highest court.*—A written statement by the State Attorney General to the effect that, in his opinion, no provision of the State's Constitution would be violated by the State law's incorporation by reference of the Federal individual income tax laws and regulations, as amended from time to time, by the Federal prosecution and trial of individuals who are alleged to have committed crimes with respect to the State's qualified tax (when it goes into effect as such), or by any other provision relating to such tax, considered as of the time it is being collected and administered by the Federal Government pursuant to subchapter E. However, if such a statement is not included in the notice of election, a judgment of the highest court of the State to the same effect may be submitted in its place.

(5) *Effective date.*—A written specification of the January as of which subchapter E is desired to become applicable to the electing State.

(b) *Rules relating to time for filing notice of election.*—An electing State must file its notice of election more than 6 months prior to the January 1 as of which the notice specifies that the provisions of subchapter E are desired to become applicable to such State. Thus, for example, if the date specified in the notice is January 1, 1979, the notice must be filed no later than June 30, 1978. However, because under the provisions of section 204(b) of the Federal-State Tax Collection Act of 1972 (86 Stat. 945), as amended by section 2116(a) of the Tax Reform Act of 1976 (90 Stat. 1910), the provisions of subchapter E will initially take effect on the first January 1 which is more than 1 year after the first date on which at least one State has filed a notice of its election (see §301.6361-5), the notice of an election which causes subchapter E to initially take effect must be filed with the Secretary or his delegate more than 1 year prior to the January 1 as of which such notice specifies that the provisions of subchapter E are desired to become applicable to such State. Thus, for example, if such an initially electing State desires to elect subchapter E as of January 1, 1979, its notice must be filed no later than December 31, 1977. For purposes of this section, if the notice of election is sent by either registered or certified mail to the Secretary of the Treasury, Washington, D.C. 20220, then it shall be deemed to be filed on the date of mailing; otherwise, the notice of election shall be deemed to be filed when it is received by the Secretary or his delegate.

(c) *Procedures relating to defects in notice or tax laws.*—If a State has filed a notice of election, then the Secretary shall, within 90 days after the notice is filed, notify the Governor of such State in writing of any defect in the notice of election which prevents it from being valid, and of any defect in the State's tax laws which causes the tax submitted to fail to meet the requirements for qualification specified in section 6362 and the regulations thereunder, other than the fact that no State agreement is in effect with respect thereto. Any such defect of which the Secretary does not notify the Governor within such 90-day period is waived. The Secretary or his delegate may, in his discretion, permit any of such defects of which the Governor is timely notified to be cured retroactively to the date of the filing of the notice of election, by amendment of the notice or the State law. Judicial review of the Secretary's determination that the notice of election or the tax laws, or both, contain defects, may be obtained as set forth in section 6363(d) and § 301.6363-4.

(d) *Execution and contents of State agreement.*—If the Secretary does not timely notify the Governor of a defect in the notice of election or in the State's tax laws, as provided in paragraph (c) of this section, or if, as provided in such paragraph, all such defects have been cured retroactively, then the Secretary shall enter into a State agreement. The agreement shall include the following elements:

(1) *Effective date.*—The agreement shall specify the January 1 as of which subchapter E will commence to be applicable to the State. Such date shall be the same as that specified in the notice of election pursuant to paragraph (a)(5) of this section, unless the parties agree to a different January 1, except that in no event shall a State agreement executed after November 1 specify the next January 1.

(2) *Obligation of Governor to notify the United States of changes in pertinent State laws.*—The agreement shall require the Governor of the State, and his successors in office, to notify the Secretary or his delegate within 30 days of the enactment of any law of the State, after the execution of the agreement, of a type described in paragraph (a)(2) of this section.

(3) *Obligation of Governor to furnish to the United States information needed to administer State tax laws.*—The agreement shall require the Governor and his successors to furnish to the Secretary or his delegate any information needed by the Federal Government to administer the State tax laws. Such information shall include, for example, a list (which shall be maintained on a current basis) of those obligations of the State or its political subdivisions described in section 103(a)(1) from which the interest is not subject to the qualified taxes of the State.

(4) *Identification of State official to act as liaison with Federal Government.*—The agreement shall include a designation by the Governor of the State official or officials with whom the Secretary or his delegate should coordinate in connection with any questions or problems which may arise during the period for which the State agreement is effective, including those which may result from changes or contemplated changes in pertinent State laws.

(5) *Identification of State official to receive transferred funds.*—The agreement shall include a designation by the Governor of the State official who shall initially receive the funds on behalf of the State when they are transferred pursuant to section 6361(c) and § 301.6361-3.

(6) *Other obligations.*—If the Secretary and the Governor both so agree, the agreement shall provide for additional obligations.

(e) *State agreement superseding certain other agreements.*—For the period of its effectiveness, a State agreement shall supersede an otherwise effective agreement entered into by the State and the Secretary for the withholding of State income taxes from the compensation of Federal employees pursuant to 5 U.S.C. 5517 (or pursuant to 5 U.S.C. 5516, in the case of the District of Columbia). [Reg. § 301.6363-1.]

☐ [*T.D. 7577,* 12-19-78.]

[Reg. § 301.6363-2]

**§ 301.6363-2. Withdrawal from State agreements.**—(a) *By notification.*—If a State which has entered into a State agreement desires to withdraw from the agreement, its Governor shall file a notice of withdrawal with the Secretary or his delegate. A notice of withdrawal shall include the following documents:

(1) *Request by the Governor.*—A request by the Governor of the State that the State agreement cease to be effective with respect to taxable years beginning on or after a specified January 1, except as provided in paragraph (b)(2) of § 301.6365-2 with respect to withholding in the case of fiscal-year taxpayers.

(2) *Legislative approval of withdrawal.*—A certified copy of an act or Resolution of the legislature of the State in which the legislature affirmatively expresses its approval of the State's withdrawal from the State agreement.

(3) *Identification of State official.*—A written identification of the State official or officials with whom the Secretary or his delegate should coordinate in connection with the State's withdrawal from the State agreement.

(b) *By change in State law.*—If any law of a State which has entered into a State agreement is enacted pertaining to individual income taxes (including the collection or administration of such taxes, and the prosecution of alleged civil or criminal violations with respect to such taxes), and if the Secretary or his delegate determines that as a result of such law the State no longer has a qualified tax, then such change in the State law shall be treated as a notification of withdrawal from the agreement. The Secretary shall notify the Governor in writing when a change is to be so treated. Such notification shall have the same effect as if, on the effective date of the disqualifying change in the law, the Governor had filed with the Secretary or his delegate a valid and sufficient notice of withdrawal requesting that the State agreement cease to be effective with respect to taxable years beginning on or after the first January 1 which is more than 6 months thereafter, subject to the exception with respect to withholding in the case of fiscal-year taxpayers. However, the cessation of effectiveness may be deferred to a subsequent January 1 if the Governor so requests and if the Secretary or his delegate in his discretion determines that the date of cessation provided in the preceding sentence would subject the State or its taxpayers to undue hardship. In addition, the Governor may request the Secretary or his delegate to permit the State's early withdrawal from the agreement, pursuant to paragraph (c)(2) of this section. Until the date of cessation of effectiveness of the State agreement, the change in State law which was treated as a notification of withdrawal, and any other such subsequent change that would be similarly treated, shall not be given effect for purposes of the Federal collection and administration of the State taxes. Similarly, such changes shall not be given effect for such purposes during the period of litigation if the State seeks judicial review of the action of the Secretary or his delegate pursuant to section 6363(d) or § 301.6363-4, even if such changes are ultimately found by the court not to disqualify the State's qualified tax. However, a change in State law which would be treated as a notice of withdrawal in the absence of this sentence shall not be so treated if, prior to the last November 1 preceding the January 1 on which the cessation of effectiveness of the State agreement is to occur, either such change in State law is retroactively repealed, or the State law is retroactively modified and the Secretary or his delegate determines that with such modification the State has a qualified tax.

(c) *Rules relating to time of withdrawal.*—(1) *General rule.*—Except as provided in subparagraph (2) of this paragraph, a notice of withdrawal shall not be valid unless the January 1 specified therein is not earlier than the first January 1 which is more than 6 months subsequent to the date on which the notice is received by the Secretary of his delegate. Thus, for example, if the notice specifies January 1, 1980, for withdrawal, the notice must be received no later than June 30, 1979.

(2) *Early withdrawal.*—The Secretary or his delegate may, in his discretion and upon written request by a Governor of a State who has filed a notice of withdrawal, waive the 6-months requirement of section 6363(b)(1) and subparagraph (1) of this paragraph if the Secretary determines that:

(i) The State will suffer a hardship if required to meet such requirement, and

(ii) The early withdrawal requested by the Governor would be practicable from the standpoint of orderly collection of the qualified tax and administration of the State law by the Federal Government. [Reg. § 301.6363-2.]

☐ [*T.D. 7577,* 12-19-78.]

### [Reg. § 301.6363-3]

**§ 301.6363-3. Transition years.**—The State may by law provide for the transition to or from a qualified tax to the extent necessary to prevent double taxation or other unintended hardships, or to prevent unintended benefits, under State law. Generally, such provisions shall be administered by the State; but, if requested to do so by the Governor of the State, the Secretary or his delegate may, in his discretion, agree to administer such provisions either solely or jointly with the State. [Reg. § 301.6363-3.]

☐ [T.D. 7577, 12-19-78.]

### [Reg. § 301.6363-4]

**§ 301.6363-4. Judicial review.**—(a) *General rule.*—If the Secretary or his delegate determines pursuant to paragraph (c) of § 301.6363-1 that a State did not file a valid notice of election or does not have a tax which would meet the requirements for qualification specified in section 6362 and the regulations thereunder if a State agreement were in effect with respect thereto, or if he determines pursuant to paragraph (b) of § 301.6363-2 that a participating State has enacted a law as a result of which the State no longer has a qualified tax, such State may, within 60 days after its Governor has received notification of such determination, file a petition for the review of such determination with either the United States Court of Appeals for the circuit in which the State is located or the United States Court of Appeals for the District of Columbia. If a State files such a petition, the clerk of the court shall forthwith transmit a copy of the petition to the Secretary or his delegate, who in turn shall thereupon file in the court the record of proceedings on which the determination adverse to the States was based, as provided in section 2112 of title 28, United States Code.

(b) *Court of Appeals' jurisdiction.*—The Court of Appeals may affirm or set aside, in whole or in part, the action of the Secretary or his delegate; and (subject to the rules delaying the effectiveness of the change in State law provided in paragraph (b) of § 301.6363-2) the court may issue such other orders as may be appropriate with respect to taxable years which include any part of the period of litigation.

(c) *Review of Court of Appeals' judgment.*—The judgment of the Court of Appeals shall be subject to review by the Supreme Court of the United States upon certiorari or certification sought by either party as provided in section 1254 of title 28, United States Code.

(d) *Effect of final judgment.*—If a final judgment, rendered with respect to litigation involving a State's petition to review a determination of the Secretary or his delegate to the effect that the State's individual income tax laws included in its notice of election would not meet the requirements for qualification specified in section 6362 and the regulations thereunder if a State agreement were in effect with respect thereto, includes a determination that the State's tax would in fact meet such requirements, then the provisions of subchapter E shall apply to the State with respect to taxable years beginning on or after the first January 1 which is more than 6 months after the date of such final judgment. If a final judgment, rendered with respect to litigation involving a State's petition to review a determination of the Secretary or his delegate to the effect that the State's previously-qualified tax ceases to qualify because of a change in the State's law, includes a determination that the State's tax does in fact cease to qualify, then the provisions of subchapter E (other than section 6363) shall cease to apply to the State with respect to taxable years beginning on or after the first January 1 which is more than 6 months after the date of such final judgment. See paragraph (b) of § 301.6365-2 for special rules with respect to withholding in the case of fiscal-year taxpayers.

(e) *Expeditious treatment of judicial proceedings.*—Under section 6363(d)(4), any judicial proceedings to which a State and the United States are parties, and which are brought pursuant to section 6363, are entitled to receive a preference, and to be heard and determined as expeditiously as possible, upon request of the Secretary or the State. [Reg. § 301.6363-4.]

☐ [T.D. 7577, 12-19-78.]

### [Reg. § 301.6365-1]

**§ 301.6365-1. Definitions.**—(a) *State.*—For purposes of subchapter E and the regulations thereunder, the term "State" shall include the District of Columbia, but shall not include the Commonwealth of Puerto Rico or any possession of the United States.

(b) *Governor.*—For purposes of subchapter E and the regulations thereunder, the term "Governor" shall include the Mayor of the District of Columbia. [Reg. § 301.6365-1.]

☐ [T.D. 7577, 12-19-78.]

### [Reg. § 301.6365-2]

**§ 301.6365-2. Commencement and cessation of applicability of subchapter E to individual taxpayers.**—(a) *General rule.*—Except for purposes of chapter 24 (relating to the collection of income tax at source on wages), whenever subchapter E begins or ceases to apply to any State (i.e., a State agreement begins or ceases to be effective) as of any January 1, such commencement or cessation of applicability shall apply to taxable years of individuals beginning on or after such date. For example, if subchapter E begins to apply to a particular State on January 1, 1980, it would become applicable for calendar year 1980 for calendar-year taxpayers in that State; but if a taxpayer in the State is using a fiscal year running from July 1 to June 30, the subchapter would begin to apply (except for purposes of chapter 24) to that taxpayer on July 1, 1980, for his taxable year ending June 30, 1981. Similarly, if the subchapter ceases to apply to such State on January 1, 1982, it would cease to apply to calendar-year taxpayers after the end of calendar year 1981; but it would cease to apply (except for purposes of chapter 24) to fiscal-year taxpayers at the end of their fiscal years which are in progress on January 1, 1982. The cessation of applicability of subchapter E to a State does not affect rights, duties, and liabilities with respect to any taxable year for which subchapter E does apply with respect to any taxpayer (or his employer).

(b) *Special rules pertaining to withholding.*—(1) *Subchapter E beginning to apply.*—The Federal withholding system provided in chapter 24 shall go into effect for State individual income tax purposes with respect to wages paid on or after January 1 as of which subchapter E begins to apply to a State. If an employee is subject to a qualified tax imposed by the State, such with holding system shall apply to his wages paid on or after that January 1, without regard to whether he is a calendar-year or fiscal-year taxpayer. See § 301.6363-3 with respect to transition-year rules.

(2) *Subchapter E ceasing to apply.*—The Federal withholding system provided in chapter 24 shall cease to be effective for State tax purposes with respect to wages paid on or after the January 1 as of which subchapter E ceases to apply to the State, although fiscal-year taxpayers of that State continue to be subject to the other provisions of subchapter E for the remainder of their fiscal years then in progress. See § 301.6363-3 with respect to transition-year rules. [Reg. § 301.6365-2.]

☐ [T.D. 7577, 12-19-78.]

## Abatements, Credits and Refunds

## PROCEDURE IN GENERAL

See p. 20,601 for regulations not amended to reflect law changes

### [Reg. § 301.6401-1]

**§ 301.6401-1. Amounts treated as overpayments.**—(a) The term "overpayment" includes:

(1) Any payment of any internal revenue tax which is assessed or collected after the expiration of the period of limitation applicable thereto.

(2) Any amount allowable for a taxable year as credits under sections 31 (relating to tax withheld on wages), 39 (relating to certain uses of gasoline, special fuels, and lubricating oil), 43 (relating to earned income credit), and 667(b) (relating to taxes paid by certain trusts) which exceeds the tax imposed by subtitle A of the Code (reduced by the credits allowable under subpart A of part IV of subchapter A of chapter 1 of the Code, other than the credits allowable under sections 31, 39 and 43) for such year.

(b) An amount paid as tax shall not be considered not to constitute an overpayment solely by reason of the fact that there was no tax liability in respect of which such amount was paid. [Reg. § 301.6401-1.]

☐ [T.D. 6119, 12-31-54. *Amended by* T.D. 6498, 10-24-60; T.D. 7204, 8-24-72 *and* T.D. 7537, 3-31-78.]

### [Reg. § 301.6402-1]

**§ 301.6402-1. Authority to make credits or refunds.**—The Commissioner, within the applicable period of limitations, may credit any overpayment of tax, including interest thereon, against any outstanding liability for any tax (or for any interest, additional amount, addition to the tax, or assessable penalty) owed by the person making the overpayment and the balance, if any, shall be refunded, subject to section 6402(c) and (d) and the regulations thereunder, to that person by the Commissioner. [Reg. § 301.6402-1.]

□ [T.D. 6119, 12-31-54. Amended by T.D. 7808, 2-3-82 and T.D. 8053, 9-27-85.]

### [Reg. § 301.6402-2]

**§ 301.6402-2. Claims for credit or refund.**—(a) *Requirement that claim be filed.*—(1) Credits or refunds of overpayments may not be allowed or made after the expiration of the statutory period of limitation properly applicable unless, before the expiration of such period, a claim therefor has been filed by the taxpayer. Furthermore, under section 7422, a civil action for refund may not be instituted unless a claim has been filed within the properly applicable period of limitation.

(2) Except as provided in paragraph (b) of § 301.6091-1 (relating to hand-carried documents), if a taxpayer is required to file a claim for credit or refund using a particular form, then the claim, together with appropriate supporting evidence, shall be filed in a manner consistent with such form, form instructions, publications, or other guidance found on the IRS.gov website. If a taxpayer is filing a claim in response to an IRS notice or correspondence, then the claim must be filed in accordance with the specific instructions contained in the notice or correspondence regarding the manner of filing. Any other claim not described in the preceding sentences generally must be filed with the service center at which the taxpayer currently would be required to file a tax return for the type of tax to which the claim relates or via the appropriate electronic portal. For rules relating to interest in the case of credits or refunds, see section 6611. For rules treating timely mailing as timely filing, see section 7502. For rules relating to the time for filing a claim when the last day falls on Saturday, Sunday, or a legal holiday, see section 7503.

(b) *Grounds set forth in claim.*—(1) No refund or credit will be allowed after the expiration of the statutory period of limitation applicable to the filing of a claim therefor except upon one or more of the grounds set forth in a claim filed before the expiration of such period. The claim must set forth in detail each ground upon which a credit or refund is claimed and facts sufficient to apprise the Commissioner of the exact basis thereof. The statement of the grounds and facts must be verified by a written declaration that it is made under the penalties of perjury. A claim which does not comply with this paragraph will not be considered for any purpose as a claim for refund or credit.

(2) The IRS does not have the authority to refund on equitable grounds penalties or other amounts legally collected.

(c) *Form for filing claim.*—If a particular form is prescribed on which the claim must be made, then the claim must be made on the form so prescribed. For special rules applicable to refunds of income taxes, see § 301.6402-3. For provisions relating to credits and refunds of taxes other than income tax, see the regulations relating to the particular tax. All claims by taxpayers for the refund of taxes, interest, penalties, and additions to tax that are not otherwise provided for must be made on Form 843, "Claim for Refund and Request for Abatement."

(d) *Separate claims for separate taxable periods.*—In the case of income and gift taxes, income tax withheld, taxes under the Federal Insurance Contributions Act, taxes under the Railroad Retirement Tax Act, and taxes under the Federal Unemployment Tax Act, a separate claim must be made for each return for each taxable period.

(e) *Proof of representative capacity.*—If a return is filed by an individual and, after his death, a refund claim is filed by his legal representative, certified copies of the letters testamentary, letters of administration, or other similar evidence must be annexed to the claim, to show the authority of the legal representative to file the claim. If an executor, administrator, guardian, trustee, receiver, or other fiduciary files a return and thereafter a refund claim is filed by the same fiduciary, documentary evidence to establish the legal authority of the fiduciary need not accompany the claim, provided a statement is made in the claim showing that the return was filed by the fiduciary and that the latter is still acting. In such cases, if a refund is to be paid, letters testamentary, letters of administration, or other evidence may be required, but should be submitted only upon the receipt of a specific request therefor. If a claim is filed by a fiduciary other than the one by whom the return was filed, the necessary documentary evidence should accompany the claim. A claim may be executed by an agent of the person assessed, but in such case a power of attorney must accompany the claim.

(f) *Mailing of refund check.*—(1) Checks in payment of claims allowed will be drawn in the names of the persons entitled to the money and, except as provided in subparagraph (2) of this paragraph, the checks may be sent direct to the claimant or to such person in care of an attorney or agent who has filed a power of attorney specifically authorizing him to receive such checks.

(2) Checks in payment of claims which have either been reduced to judgment or settled in the course or as a result of litigation will be drawn in the name of the person or persons entitled to the money and will be sent to the Assistant Attorney General, Tax Division, Department of Justice, for delivery to the taxpayer or the counsel of record in the court proceeding.

(3) For restrictions on the assignment of claims, see sections 3477 of the Revised Statutes (31 U.S.C. 203).

(g) *Misdirected direct deposit refund.*—(1) *Definition.*—The term *misdirected direct deposit refund* includes any refund of an overpayment of tax that is disbursed as a direct deposit but is not deposited into the account designated on the claim for refund to receive the direct deposit refund.

(2) *Procedures for reporting a misdirected direct deposit refund.*—(i) *In general.*—A taxpayer or a taxpayer's authorized representative may report to the IRS that the taxpayer never received a direct deposit refund and request a replacement refund. The report must include the name of the taxpayer who requested the refund, the taxpayer identification number of the taxpayer, the taxpayer's mailing address, the type of return to which the refund is related, the account number and routing number that the taxpayer requested the refund be directly deposited into, and any other information necessary to locate the misdirected direct deposit refund.

(ii) *How to report a misdirected direct deposit refund.*—A reporting described in paragraph (g)(2)(i) of this section may be made in the following ways:

(A) By calling the IRS;

(B) On the form prescribed by the IRS and in accordance with the applicable publications, instructions, or other appropriate guidance;

(C) By contacting the Office of the Taxpayer Advocate by telephone, by mail, facsimile, or in person; or

(D) By submitting the appropriate form in person at a Taxpayer Assistance Center.

(3) *Procedures for coordination with financial institutions.*—(i) *Identification of the account that received the misdirected direct deposit refund.*—If the IRS receives a report described in paragraph (g)(2)(ii) of this section, the IRS will confirm that the overpayment was issued as a direct deposit. The IRS will confirm that the overpayment was not credited or offset pursuant to the law in effect immediately prior to the direct deposit being disbursed. If the direct deposit described in the report was issued, the IRS will initiate a refund trace to request the assistance of the Department of the Treasury's Bureau of the Fiscal Service. In accordance with its own procedures, the Bureau of the Fiscal Service coordinates with the financial institution that holds directly or indirectly the deposit account into which the refund was made, requesting from the financial institution such information as is necessary to identify whether the financial institution received the refund; whether the financial institution returned, or will return, the refund to the IRS, or if no funds are available for return; whether a deposit was made into the account designated on the claim for refund; and the identity of the deposit account owner to whom the deposit was disbursed.

(ii) *Coordination to recover the amounts transferred.*—Recovery of the misdirected direct deposit refund from a financial institution shall follow the procedures established by the Bureau of the Fiscal Service. The Bureau of the Fiscal Service shall request the return of the misdirected direct deposit refund from the financial institution that received it. The IRS may contact the financial institution directly to recover the misdirected direct deposit refund.

(4) *Issuance of replacement refund.*—When the IRS has determined that a misdirected direct deposit refund has occurred, the IRS will issue a replacement refund in the full amount of the refund that was misdirected. The replacement refund may be issued as a direct deposit or as a paper check sent to the taxpayer's last known address.

(5) *Applicability of this paragraph (g) to missing refunds.*—The provisions of paragraphs (g)(2) through (g)(3)(i) of this section should be used for any refund that was disbursed as a direct deposit and that the taxpayer reports as missing. For example, although a refund that was deposited into an incorrect bank account because the taxpayer transposed two digits in their bank account number is not considered to be a misdirected direct deposit refund, the provisions of paragraphs (g)(2) through (g)(3)(i) of this section should be used. If the application of these procedures results in an amount recovered by

the IRS, the recovered amount will be refunded or credited as allowed by law.

(h) *Applicability dates.*—Paragraphs (a)(2), (b)(2), (c), and (d) of this section apply to claims for credit or refund filed on or after July 24, 2015. Paragraphs (a)(1), (b)(1), (e), and (f) of this section apply to claims for credit or refund filed before, on or after July 24, 2015. Paragraph (g) of this section applies to reports described in paragraph (g)(2)(ii) of this section made after December 22, 2020. [Reg. §301.6402-2.]

☐ [*T.D.* 6119, 12-31-54. *Amended by T.D.* 6292, 4-18-58; *T.D.* 6498, 10-24-60; *T.D.* 6585, 12-27-61; *T.D.* 6950, 4-3-68; *T.D.* 7008, 2-28-69; *T.D.* 7188, 6-28-72; *T.D.* 7410, 3-15-76, *T.D.* 7484, 4-29-77, *T.D.* 9727, 7-23-2015 *and T.D.* 9940, 12-18-2020.]

### [Reg. §301.6402-3]

**§301.6402-3. Special rules applicable to income tax.**—(a) The following rules apply to a claim for credit or refund of income tax:—

(1) In general, in the case of an overpayment of income taxes, a claim for credit or refund of such overpayment shall be made on the appropriate income tax return.

(2) In the case of an overpayment of income taxes for a taxable year of an individual for which a Form 1040 or 1040A has been filed, a claim for refund shall be made on Form 1040X ("Amended U.S. Individual Income Tax Return").

(3) In the case of an overpayment of income taxes for a taxable year of a corporation for which a Form 1120 has been filed, a claim for refund shall be made on Form 1120X ("Amended U.S. Corporation Income Tax Return").

(4) In the case of an overpayment of income taxes for a taxable year for which a form other than Form 1040, 1040A, or 1120 was filed (such as Form 1041 (U.S. Fiduciary Income Tax Return) or Form 990T (Exempt Organization Business Income Tax Return)), a claim for credit or refund shall be made on the appropriate amended income tax return.

(5) A properly executed individual, fiduciary, or corporation original income tax return or an amended return (on 1040X or 1120X if applicable) shall constitute a claim for refund or credit within the meaning of section 6402 and section 6511 for the amount of the overpayment disclosed by such return (or amended return). For purposes of section 6511, such claim shall be considered as filed on the date on which such return (or amended return) is considered as filed, except that if the requirements of §301.7502-1, relating to timely mailing treated as timely filing are met, the claim shall be considered to be filed on the date of the postmark stamped on the cover in which the return (or amended return) was mailed. A return or amended return shall constitute a claim for refund or credit if it contains a statement setting forth the amount determined as an overpayment and advising whether such amount shall be refunded to the taxpayer or shall be applied as a credit against the taxpayer's estimated income tax for the taxable year immediately succeeding the taxable year for which such return (or amended return) is filed. If the taxpayer indicates on its return (or amended return) that all or part of the overpayment shown by its return (or amended return) is to be applied to its estimated income tax for its succeeding taxable year, such indication shall constitute an election to so apply such overpayment, and no interest shall be allowed on such portion of the overpayment credited and such amount shall be applied as a payment on account of the estimated income tax for such year or the installments thereof.

(6) Notwithstanding paragraph (a)(5) of this section, the Internal Revenue Service, within the applicable period of limitations, may credit any overpayment of individual, fiduciary, or corporation income tax, including interest thereon, against—

(i) First, any outstanding liability for any tax (or for any interest, additional amount, additions to the tax, or assessable penalty) owed by the taxpayer making the overpayment;

(ii) Second, in the case of an individual taxpayer, amounts of past-due support assigned to a State under section 402(a)(26) or 471(a)(17) of the Social Security Act under procedures set forth in the regulations under section 6402(c);

(iii) Third, past-due and legally enforceable debt under procedures set forth in the regulations under section 6402(d); and

(iv) Fourth, qualifying amounts of past-due support not assigned to a State under procedures set forth in the regulations under section 6402(c).

Only the balance, if any, of the overpayment remaining after credits described in this paragraph (a)(6) shall be treated in the manner so elected.

(b) [Reserved]

(c) If the taxpayer is not required to show the tax on the form (see section 6014 and the accompanying regulations), the IRS will treat a properly filed income tax return as a claim for refund and such return will constitute a claim for refund within the meaning of

section 6402 and section 6511 for the amount of the overpayment shown by the computation of the tax made by the IRS on the basis of the return. For purposes of the limitations period of section 6511, such claim will be treated as filed on the date the return is treated as filed.

(d) In any case in which a taxpayer elects to have an overpayment refunded to him he may not thereafter change his election to have the overpayment applied as a payment on account of his estimated income tax.

(e) In the case of a nonresident alien individual or foreign corporation, the appropriate income tax return on which the claim for refund or credit is made must contain the tax identification number of the taxpayer required pursuant to section 6109 and the entire amount of income of the taxpayer subject to tax, even if the tax liability for that income was fully satisfied at source through withholding under chapters 3 or 4 of the Internal Revenue Code (Code). Also, if the overpayment of tax resulted from the withholding of tax at source under chapter 3 or 4 of the Code, a copy of the Form 1042-S, "Foreign Person's U.S. Source Income subject to Withholding," Form 8805, "Foreign Partner's Information Statement of Section 1446 Withholding Tax," or other statement (required under §1.1446-3(d)(2) of this chapter) required to be provided to the beneficial owner or partner pursuant to §1.1461-1(c)(1)(i), §1.1474-1(d)(1)(i), or §1.1446-3(d) of this chapter must be attached to the return. For purposes of claiming a refund, the Form 8805 or other statement must include the taxpayer identification number of the beneficial owner or partner even if not otherwise required. No claim for refund or credit under chapter 65 of the Code may be made by the taxpayer for any amount that the payor has repaid to the taxpayer pursuant to reimbursement or set-off procedures (described in §1.1461-2(a)(2), (3) or §1.1474-2(a)(3), (4) of this chapter). In addition, no claim for refund or credit may be made by a taxpayer for any amount that has been repaid to a qualified intermediary (as described in §1.1441-1(e)(5)(ii)) or a participating FFI (as described in §1.1471-1(b)(91)) pursuant to a collective refund filed by such entity on behalf of the taxpayer. See §1.1441-1(e)(5)(iii) (describing a qualified intermediary agreement) and §1.1471-4(h) (describing a collective refund). Upon request, a taxpayer must also submit such documentation as the IRS, may require establishing that the taxpayer is the beneficial owner of the income for which a claim for refund or credit is being made and verifying the grounds and facts set forth in taxpayer's claim as required by §301.6402-2(b)(1). See §1.1474-5 for additional requirements that may apply in the case of a refund of tax withheld under chapter 4.

(f) *Effective/applicability date.*—(1) Except as provided in paragraph (f)(2) of this section, this section applies on or after January 6, 2017. (For payments made after June 30, 2014, and before January 6, 2017, see this section as in effect and contained in 26 CFR part 1, revised April 1, 2016.)

(2) References in paragraph (e) of this section to Form 8805 or other statements required under §1.1446-3(d)(2) shall apply to partnership taxable years beginning after April 29, 2008. References in paragraph (e) of this section to amounts withheld under chapter 4 of the Code and claims made with respect to amounts withheld under chapter 4 of the Code shall apply to withholdable payments made after June 30, 2014. [Reg. §301.6402-3.]

☐ [*T.D.* 6119, 12-31-54. *Amended by T.D.* 6292, 4-18-58; *T.D.* 6425, 11-10-59; *T.D.* 6498, 10-24-60; *T.D.* 6585, 12-27-61; *T.D.* 7057, 9-2-70; *T.D.* 7102, 3-23-71; *T.D.* 7234, 12-20-72; *T.D.* 7269, 4-12-73; *T.D.* 7293, 11-27-73; *T.D.* 7298, 12-21-73; *T.D.* 7410, 3-15-76; *T.D.* 7808, 2-3-82; *T.D.* 8053, 9-27-85; *T.D.* 8734, 10-6-97 (T.D. 8804 delayed the effective date of T.D. 8734 from January 1, 1999, to January 1, 2000; T.D. 8856 further delayed the effective date of T.D. 8734 until January 1, 2001); *T.D.* 9394, 4-28-2008, *T.D.* 9658, 2-28-2014, *T.D.* 9727, 7-23-2015 *and T.D.* 9808, 12-30-2016.]

### [Reg. §301.6402-4]

**§301.6402-4. Payments in excess of amounts shown on return.**—(a) If the IRS determines that the payments by the taxpayer that are made within the period prescribed for payment and before the filing of the return exceed the amount of tax shown on the return (for example, excessive estimated income tax payments or excessive withholding), the IRS may credit or refund such overpayment without awaiting examination of the completed return and without awaiting the filing of a claim for refund. The provisions of §§301.6402-2 and 301.6402-3 are applicable to such overpayment, and taxpayers should submit claims for refund (if the income tax return is not itself a claim for refund, as provided in §301.6402-3) to protect themselves in the event the IRS fails to make such determination and credit or refund. The provisions of section 6405 (relating to reports of refunds in excess of the statutorily prescribed threshold referral amount to the Joint Committee on Taxation) do not apply to the overpayments described in this section.

(b) *Effective/applicability date.*—The rules of this section apply to payments made on or after July 24, 2015. [Reg. §301.6402-4.]

☐ [*T.D.* 6119, 12-31-54. *Amended by T.D.* 6585, 12-27-61 *and T.D.* 9727, 7-23-2015.]

### [Reg. §301.6402-5]

**§301.6402-5. Offset of past-due support against overpayments.—**
(a) *Introduction.*—(1) *Scope.*—Section 6402(c) requires the Secretary of the Treasury or his delegate to reduce the amount of any overpayment to be refunded to a person making an overpayment by the amount of past-due support owed by that person of which the Secretary has been notified in accordance with section 464 of the Social Security Act. Past-due support shall be collected by offset under section 6402(c) and this section in the same manner as if it were a liability for tax imposed by the Internal Revenue Code of 1954 (except that a liability for tax shall be given priority with respect to offset arising under section 6402(a)). Collection by offset under section 6402(c) of this section is a collection procedure separate from the collection procedures provided by section 6305 and §301.6305-1, relating to assessment and collection of certain child and spousal support liabilities. The sole collection procedure provided by section 6402(c) and this section is that of offset against overpayment. Section 6305 and §301.6305-1, by contrast, provide for other collection procedures in addition to collection by offset against overpayment. Sections 6305 and 6402(c) have differing procedural requirements and may be used separately or in conjunction with each other.

(2) *General rule.*—An amount of past-due support qualifies for offset under this section if it satisfies the requirements of paragraph (b) of this section. A State shall submit to the Department of Health and Human Services a notification of liability for qualifying past-due support containing the information described in paragraph (c) of this section. A qualifying amount of past-due support owed by a taxpayer who has made an overpayment shall be collected in accordance with the procedures set forth in paragraph (d) of this section. Under paragraph (d), the balance of any overpayment remaining after crediting of the overpayment under section 6402(a) to any liability for an internal revenue tax on the part of the taxpayer shall be offset by the amount of past-due support of which the Internal Revenue Service has been notified. The amount of the overpayment not subject to offset for any liability for an internal revenue tax or for past-due support shall be promptly refunded to the taxpayer. Paragraph (e) of this section requires that the Internal Revenue Service notify the taxpayer of the amount of the offset and of the State to which it has been paid. Under procedures set forth in paragraph (f) of this section, amounts collected by offset shall be transferred to a special account maintained by the Bureau of Government Financial Operations for distribution to the States. The Internal Revenue Service shall make monthly collection reports to the Secretary of Health and Human Services or his delegate. The States shall reimburse the Secretary of the Treasury for the full cost of the refund offset under paragraph (g) of this section.

(b) *Past-due support.*—(1) *Definition.*—For purposes of this section, the term "past-due support" means the amount of a delinquent obligation, which amount was determined under a court order, or an order pursuant to an administrative process established under State law, for support and maintenance of a child or of a child and the parent with whom the child is living.

(2) *Past-due support qualifying for offset.*—Past-due support qualifies for offset under section 6402(c) and this section if—

(i) There has been an assignment of the support obligation to a State pursuant to section 402(a)(26) of the Social Security Act (relating to aid and service to needy families with children) and that State has made reasonable efforts to collect the amount of the obligation;

(ii) The amount of past-due support is not less than $150.00;

(iii) The past-due support has been delinquent for three months or longer; and

(iv) A notification of liability for past-due support has been received by the Secretary of the Treasury as prescribed by paragraph (c) of this section.

(c) *Notification of liability for past-due support.*—(1) *Form.*—A State shall, by October 1 of each year, submit a notification (or notifications) of liability for past-due support on magnetic tape to the Special Collection Activities Unit, Office of Child Support Enforcement, Department of Health and Human Services, 6110 Executive Boulevard, Suite 900, Rockville, Maryland 20852, Attention: Tax Refund Offset—Tape Processing.

(2) *Content.*—The notification of liability for past-due support shall contain with respect to each taxpayer—

(i) The name of the taxpayer who owes the past-due support;

(ii) The social security number of that taxpayer;

(iii) The amount of past-due support owed; and

(iv) The alphabetical designation of the State submitting the notification of liability for past-due support.

The Secretary of Health and Human Services may also require such other information from the State submitting the notification as is necessary for his orderly consolidation of data for transmittal to the Internal Revenue Service.

(3) *Transmittal of notification to Internal Revenue Service.*—The Secretary of Health and Human Services shall, by December 1 of each year, consolidate and transmit to the Internal Revenue Service on magnetic tape the data contained in the notifications of liability for past-due support submitted by the participating States.

(4) *Correction of notification.*—If, after submitting a notification of liability for past-due support, a State determines that an error has been made with respect to the information contained in the notification, or if a State receives a payment or credits a payment to the account of a taxpayer named in this notification, the State shall promptly notify the Office of Child Support Enforcement of the Department of Health and Human Services of these corrections in accordance with any time limitations specified by the Office of Child Support Enforcement. That Office shall promptly transmit these corrections to the Internal Revenue Service and the Internal Revenue Service shall make the appropriate correction of the notification of liability for past-due support. However, in no case shall a State notify the Office of Child Support Enforcement under this paragraph (c)(4) of an increased amount of past-due support owed by a taxpayer named in its notification of liability for past-due support. The correction of notification described in this paragraph (c)(4) is to be submitted only for the purpose of completing or correcting the information contained in the notification of liability for past-due support.

(d) *Collection.*—(1) *Priority of offset for outstanding tax liability.*—Under section 6402(a) and §301.6402-1, the Commissioner may credit any overpayment of tax against any outstanding liability for any tax owed by the person making the overpayment. Only the balance remaining after such crediting is available for offset under section 6402(c) of this section. Thus, if a taxpayer making an overpayment has both an outstanding tax liability and a liability for past-due support subject to this section, then the entire amount of the overpayment shall be credited first against the outstanding tax liability under section 6402(a) and §301.6402-1 and only the remainder, if any, of the overpayment will be offset by the amount of past-due support. However, an overpayment shall be offset by an amount of past-due support under section 6402(c) before any crediting of the overpayment to any future liability for an internal revenue tax. Thus, for example, if no outstanding tax liability is owed and the amount of an overpayment is equal to or less than the amount of past-due support, the Internal Revenue Service shall offset the overpayment by the amount of past-due support before crediting the overpayment against the taxpayer's estimated income tax for the succeeding taxable year under section 6402(b).

(2) *Amounts subject to offset.*—The balance of any overpayment remaining after a crediting of the overpayment under section 6402(a) to any outstanding liability for tax on the part of the taxpayer shall be offset by the amount of past-due support of which the Internal Revenue Service has been notified under this section.

(3) *Amounts not subject to offset.*—The amount of an overpayment not subject to offset for any liability for tax or for past-due support shall be promptly refunded to the taxpayer.

(e) *Notice of offset.*—The Internal Revenue Service shall notify the taxpayer in writing of the amount and date of the offset for past-due support and of the State to which this amount of past-due support has been paid.

(f) *Disposition of amounts collected.*—Amounts collected under this section shall be transferred to a special account maintained by the Bureau of Government Financial Operations. The Internal Revenue Service shall advise the Secretary of Health and Human Services or his delegate on a monthly basis of the names and social security numbers of the taxpayers from whom the amounts of past-due support were collected, of the amounts collected from each taxpayer, and of the State on whose behalf each collection was made. After authorization by the Division of Finance of the Social Security Administration, the Bureau of Government Financial Operations of the Department of the Treasury shall pay to the participating States amounts equal to the amounts collected under this section.

(g) *Fee.*—A refund offset fee in the amount of $17.00 per offset for taxable year 1981, or such greater or smaller amount as the Secretary of the Treasury and the Secretary of Health and Human Services have agreed to be sufficient to reimburse the Internal Revenue Service for the full cost of the offset procedure, shall be billed and collected from the participating States by the Secretary of Health and Human Services or his delegate and deposited in the United States Treasury and credited to the appropriation accounts of the Internal Revenue Service which bore all or part of the costs involved in making the collection.

(h) *Effective dates.*—This section applies to refunds payable on or before January 1, 1999. For the rules applicable after January 1, 1999, see 31 CFR part 285. [Reg. § 301.6402-5.]

☐ [*T.D. 7895, 5-19-83. Amended by T.D. 8837, 9-3-99.*]

### [Reg. § 301.6402-6]

**§ 301.6402-6. Offset of past-due, legally enforceable debt against overpayment.**—(a) *General rule.*—(1) A Federal agency (as defined in section 6402(f)) that has entered into an agreement with the Internal Revenue Service with regard to its participation in the tax refund offset program and that is owed a past-due, legally enforceable debt may refer the past-due, legally enforceable debt to the Internal Revenue Service to be collected by Federal tax refund offset. The Service shall, after making appropriate credits as provided by § 301.6402-3(a)(6)(i) and (ii), reduce the amount of any overpayment payable to a taxpayer by the amount of any past-due, legally enforceable debt owed to the agency and properly referred to the Service. This section does not apply to any debt subject to section 464 of the Social Security Act (past-due support).

(2)(i) This section applies to OASDI overpayments provided the requirements of 31 U.S.C. 3720A(f)(1) and (2) are met with respect to such overpayments.

(ii) For purposes of this section, "OASDI overpayment" means any overpayment of benefits made to an individual under title II of the Social Security Act.

(b) *Eligible Federal agencies.*—(1) A Federal agency is eligible to participate in the tax refund offset program if the agency—

(i) Has promulgated temporary or final regulations under 31 U.S.C. 3720A, governing the operation of the Federal tax refund offset program in the agency;

(ii) Has promulgated temporary or final regulations under 31 U.S.C. 3716, governing the operation of the administrative offset program in the agency; and

(iii) Has promulgated temporary or final regulations under 5 U.S.C. 5514(a), governing the operation of the salary offset program in the agency (unless the agency has certified that, relying on the most current information reasonably available, it will not refer to the Service any names of present or former Federal employees or other persons whose debts are subject to offset under the provisions of 5 U.S.C. 5514(a)(1)).

(2) An agency prohibited by Federal law from meeting any of the requirements of paragraph (b)(1) or (c) of this section shall notify the Service in writing of the specific legal impediment to meeting these requirements. This notification shall be made prior to entering into an agreement with the Service to participate in the tax refund offset program. The Service will determine in writing whether the agency is prohibited by Federal law from meeting any of the requirements of paragraph (b)(1) or (c) of this section. The Service will waive in writing any requirement that it determines the agency is prohibited by Federal law from meeting.

(c) *Past-due, legally enforceable debt eligible for refund offset.*—For purposes of this section, a Federal agency may refer a past-due, legally enforceable debt to the Service for offset if—

(1) Except in the case of a judgment debt or any debts specifically exempt from this requirement (for example, debts referred by the Department of Education that were pending on or after April 9, 1991, and referred to the Service for offset before November 15, 1992), the debt is referred for offset within ten years after the agency's right of action accrues;

(2) The debt cannot be currently collected pursuant to the salary offset provisions of 5 U.S.C. 5514(a)(1);

(3) The debt is ineligible for administrative offset under 31 U.S.C. 3716(a) by reason of 31 U.S.C. 3716(c)(2), or cannot be currently collected by administrative offset under 31 U.S.C. 3716(a) by the referring agency against amounts payable to the taxpayer by the referring agency;

(4) The agency has notified, or has made a reasonable attempt to notify, the taxpayer that the debt is past-due, and unless repaid within 60 days thereafter, will be referred to the Service for offset against an overpayment of tax;

(5) The agency has given the taxpayer at least 60 days to present evidence that all or part of the debt is not past-due or legally enforceable, has considered any evidence presented by the taxpayer, and has determined that the debt is past-due and legally enforceable;

(6) The debt has been disclosed by the agency to a consumer reporting agency as authorized by 31 U.S.C. 3711(f), unless the consumer reporting agency would be prohibited from reporting infor-

mation concerning the debt by reason of 15 U.S.C. 1681c, or unless the amount of the debt does not exceed $100;

(7) The debt is at least $25; and

(8) In the case of an OASDI overpayment—

(i) The individual is not currently entitled to monthly insurance benefits under title II of the Social Security Act;

(ii) The notice describes conditions under which the Department of Health and Human Services is required to waive recovery of the overpayment, as provided under section 204(b) of the Social Security Act; and

(iii) If the taxpayer files for a waiver under section 204(b) of the Social Security Act within the 60-day notice period, the agency has considered the taxpayer's request.

(d) *Pre-offset notice and consideration of evidence.*—(1) For purposes of paragraph (c)(4) of this section, an agency has made a reasonable attempt to notify the taxpayer if the agency uses the most recent address information obtained from the Service pursuant to section 6103(m)(2), (4), or (5) of the Code, unless the agency receives clear and concise notification from the taxpayer that notices from the agency are to be sent to an address different from the address obtained from the Service. Clear and concise notification means that the taxpayer has provided the agency with written notification including the taxpayer's name and identifying number (as defined in section 6109), the taxpayer's new address, and the taxpayer's intent to have agency notices sent to the new address.

(2) For purposes of paragraph (c)(5) of this section, if the evidence presented by the taxpayer is considered by an agent of the agency, or other entities or persons acting on the agency's behalf, the taxpayer must be accorded at least 30 days from the date the agent or other entity or person determines that all or part of the debt is past-due and legally enforceable to request review by an officer or employee of the agency of any unresolved dispute. The agency must then notify the taxpayer of its decision.

(e) *Referral of past-due, legally enforceable debt.*—A Federal agency must refer a past-due, legally enforceable debt to the Service in the time and manner prescribed by the Service. The referral must contain—

(1) The name and identifying number (as defined in section 6109) of the taxpayer who is responsible for the debt;

(2) The amount of such past-due and legally enforceable debt;

(3) The date on which the debt became past-due;

(4) The designation of the Federal agency or subagency referring the debt; and

(5) In the case of an OASDI overpayment, a certification by the Secretary of Health and Human Services designating whether the amount payable to the agency is to be deposited in either the Federal Old-Age and Survivors Insurance Trust Fund or the Federal Disability Insurance Trust Fund, but not both.

(f) *Correction of referral.*—If, after referring a past-due, legally enforceable debt to the Service as provided by paragraph (e) of this section, an agency determines that an error has been made with respect to the information transmitted to the Service, or if an agency receives a payment or credits a payment to the account of a taxpayer referred to the Service for offset, the agency shall promptly notify the Service. The Service shall make the appropriate correction of its records. However, this paragraph (f) does not permit an agency to increase the amount of a past-due, legally enforceable debt or refer additional debtors to the Service for offset after an agency makes its original referral of debts for tax refund offset. The agency may refer additional debts to the Service for refund offset in subsequent tax refund offset years.

(g) *Priorities for offset.*—(1) An overpayment shall be reduced first by the amount of an outstanding liability for any tax under section 6402(a); second, by the amount of any past-due support assigned to a State under section 402(a)(26) or section 471(a)(17) of the Social Security Act which is to be offset under section 6402(c) and the regulations thereunder; third, by the amount of any past-due, legally enforceable debt owed to a Federal agency under section 6402(d) and this section; and fourth, by the amount of any qualifying past-due support not assigned to a State which is to be offset under section 6402(c) and the regulations thereunder.

(2) If a taxpayer owes more than one past-due, legally enforceable debt to a Federal agency or agencies, the overpayment shall be credited against the debts in the order in which the debts accrued. A debt shall be considered to have accrued at the time at which the agency determines that the debt became past due.

(3) Reduction of the overpayment pursuant to section 6402(a), (c), and (d) shall occur prior to crediting the overpayment to any future liability for an internal revenue tax. Any amount remaining after offset under section 6402(a), (c), and (d) shall be refunded to the taxpayer, or applied to estimated tax, if elected by the taxpayer.

(h) *Post-offset notice to the taxpayer and the agency.*—(1) The Service shall notify the taxpayer in writing of the amount and date of the offset for a past-due, legally enforceable debt and of the Federal agency to which this amount has been paid or credited. For joint returns, see paragraph (i) of this section.

(2) The Service shall advise each agency of the names, mailing addresses, and identifying numbers of the taxpayers from whom amounts of past-due, legally enforceable debt were collected and of the amounts collected from each taxpayer. If the refund from which an amount of past-due, legally enforceable debt is to be withheld is based upon a joint return, the Service shall notify the agency and furnish the names and addresses of each taxpayer filing the joint return.

(i) *Offset made with regard to refund based upon joint return.*—(1) In the case of an offset from a refund based on a joint return, the Service shall issue a notice in writing to any person who may have filed a joint return with the taxpayer, including the amount and date of any offset and the steps which the non-debtor spouse may take in order to secure his or her proper share of the refund (unless the non-debtor spouse has already taken these steps prior to offset).

(2) If the person filing the joint return with the taxpayer owing the past-due, legally enforceable debt takes appropriate action to secure his or her proper share of a refund from which an offset was made, the Service shall pay the person his or her share of the refund and shall deduct that amount from amounts payable to the agency.

(j) *Disposition of amounts collected.*—Amounts collected under this section shall be transferred to a special account maintained by the Financial Management Service (FMS) for each Federal agency. If an erroneous payment is made to any agency, the Service shall deduct the amount of such payment from amounts payable to the agency.

(k) *Fees.*—The agency shall enter into a separate agreement with the Service and FMS to reimburse the Service and FMS for the full cost of administering the tax refund offset program. The fees shall be deducted from amounts collected prior to disposition. The fees shall be deposited in the United States Treasury and credited to the appropriation accounts which bore all or part of the costs involved in administering the refund offset procedures.

(l) *Review of offset of refunds.*—Any reduction of a taxpayer's refund made pursuant to section 6402(c) or (d) shall not be subject to review by any court of the United States or by the Service in an administrative proceeding. No action brought against the United States to recover the amount of this reduction shall be considered to be a suit for refund of tax. Any legal, equitable, or administrative action by any person seeking to recover the amount of the reduction of the overpayment must be taken against the Federal agency to which the amount of the reduction was paid. Any action which is otherwise available with respect to recoveries of overpayments of benefits under section 204 of the Social Security Act must be taken against the Secretary of Health and Human Services.

(m) *Access to and use of confidential tax information.*—Access to and use of confidential tax information in connection with the tax refund offset program are restricted by section 6103 of the Code. However, section 6103(l)(10) permits Federal officers and employees of agencies participating in the tax refund offset program to have access to and use of confidential tax information. Agencies receiving such information are subject to the safeguard, recordkeeping, and reporting requirements of section 6103(p)(4) and the regulations thereunder. The agency shall inform its officers and employees who access or use confidential tax information of the restrictions and penalties under the Internal Revenue Code for misuse of confidential tax information.

(n) *Effective dates.*—This section applies to refunds payable under section 6402 after April 15, 1992, and on or before January 1, 1998. For the rules applicable after January 1, 1998, see 31 CFR part 285. [Reg. § 301.6402-6.]

☐ [*T.D.* 8413, 4-14-92. *Amended by T.D.* 8837, 9-3-99.]

>>>→ *Caution: AUTHORITY: The provisions of 31 CFR Part 285 are issued under the Debt Collection Improvement Act of 1996 (P.L. 104-134), 110 Stat. 1321-358 et seq., codified at 31 U.S.C. 3720A.*

### [Reg. § 285.1]

§ 285.1. Collection of past-due support by administrative offset.—(a) *Definitions.*—For purposes of this section:

*Administrative offset* means withholding funds payable by the United States (including funds payable by the United States on behalf of a State government) to, or held by the United States for, a person to satisfy a debt.

*Debt* as used in this section is synonymous with the term past-due support.

*Disbursing official* includes an official who has authority to disburse public money pursuant to 31 U.S.C. 3321 or another Federal law.

*Fiscal Service* means the Bureau of the Fiscal Service, a bureau of the Department of the Treasury. Fiscal Service is the designee of the Secretary of the Treasury for all matters concerning this section, unless otherwise specified.

*HHS* means the Department of Health and Human Services, Office of Child Support Enforcement.

*Past-due support* means the amount of support determined under a court order, or an order of an administrative procedure established under State law, for support and maintenance of a child, or of a child and the parent with whom the child is living, which has not been paid. The term child as used in this definition is not limited to minor children.

*Past-due support being enforced by the State* means there has been an assignment of the support rights to the State, or the State making the request for offset is providing services to individuals pursuant to 42 U.S.C. 654(5) (section 454(5) of the Social Security Act), or the State is enforcing support pursuant to a cooperative agreement with or by an Indian tribal government.

*State* means the several States of the United States. The term State also includes the District of Columbia, American Samoa, Guam, the United States Virgin Islands, the Commonwealth of the Northern Mariana Islands, and the Commonwealth of Puerto Rico.

*Secretary* means the Secretary of the Treasury.

(b) *General rule.*—Fiscal Service may enter into a reciprocal agreement with a State for the collection of past-due support being enforced by the State by administrative offset from certain Federal payments. Upon notification of past-due support either directly from a State which has entered into such an agreement or from HHS, disbursing officials of Fiscal Service or any other disbursing official of the United States shall offset Federal payments which are subject to offset under this section, to collect past-due support. The amount offset, minus the offset fee, shall be forwarded to the State to be distributed in accordance with applicable laws and procedures.

(c) *Agreements.*—Fiscal Service may enter into reciprocal agreements with States for disbursing officials of Fiscal Service and any other Federal disbursing official to offset certain Federal payments to collect past-due support being enforced by the State. The agreement shall contain any requirements which Fiscal Service considers appropriate to facilitate the offset and prevent duplicative efforts and shall require States to prescribe procedures governing the collection of past-due support by Federal administrative offset. For purposes of this section, reciprocal means of mutual benefit. An agreement between Fiscal Service and a State to collect past-due support by offsetting Federal payments will be considered of mutual benefit and it is not required that States conduct administrative offsets to collect debts owed to the Federal Government. States which have entered into an agreement with Fiscal Service pursuant to this section may thereafter request, in the manner prescribed herein, that an offset be performed. Such requests shall be made by the appropriate State disbursing official which, for purposes of this section, means an appropriate official of the State agency which administers or supervises the administration of the State plan under Title IV-D of the Social Security Act.

(d) *Notification to Fiscal Service of past-due support.*—(1) States notifying Fiscal Service of past-due support must do so in the manner and format prescribed by Fiscal Service. States notifying HHS of past-due support must do so in the manner and format prescribed by HHS. HHS shall notify Fiscal Service of all past-due support referred to HHS by States for collection by administrative offset provided that the requirements of paragraphs (d)(3) and (h) of this section have been met.

(2) When a State has knowledge that past-due support is being enforced by more than one State, the State notifying Fiscal Service or HHS of the past-due support must inform any other State involved in enforcing the past-due support when it refers the debt for offset and when it receives the offset amount.

(3) The notification of past-due support must be accompanied by a certification that the debt is past-due, legally enforceable, and that the State has complied with all the requirements as set forth in paragraph (h) of this section and with any requirements imposed by State law or procedure. For debts so certified, the Secretary may waive sections 552a (o) and (p) of Title 5, United States Code, where applicable, in accordance with the Secretary's authority under 31 U.S.C. 3716(f).

(4) Fiscal Service may reject a notification of past-due support which does not comply with the requirements of this section. The State will be notified of the rejection along with the reason for the rejection.

»»→ *Caution: AUTHORITY: The provisions of 31 CFR Part 285 are issued under the Debt Collection Improvement Act of 1996 (P.L. 104-134), 110 Stat. 1321-358 et seq., codified at 31 U.S.C. 3720A.*

(e) *Minimum amount of past-due support.*—Fiscal Service will reject a notification of past-due support where the past-due support owed is less than $25.00. This amount may be adjusted from time to time by Fiscal Service to ensure that the cost of collection does not exceed the debt.

(f) *Limitations.*—Debts properly submitted to Fiscal Service for administrative offset will remain subject to collection by administrative offset until withdrawn by the State provided the debt remains past-due and legally enforceable.

(g) *Notification of changes in status of debt.*—The State notifying Fiscal Service or HHS of past-due support shall, in the manner and in the time frames provided by Fiscal Service or HHS, notify Fiscal Service or HHS of deletions or decreases in the amount of a debt referred for collection by administrative offset. The State may notify Fiscal Service or HHS of any increases in the amount of a debt referred for collection by administrative offset provided the State has complied with the requirements of paragraph (h) of this section with regard to those amounts.

(h) *Advance notification of intent to collect by administrative offset.*—(1) The State, or Fiscal Service or HHS on behalf of the State, if the State requests and Fiscal Service or HHS agrees, shall send a written notification, at least 30 days in advance of referral of the debt for offset, to the individual owing past-due support, informing the individual that the State intends to refer the debt for collection by administrative offset against Federal payments. The notice must also inform the individual of:

(i) The nature and amount of the debt; and

(ii) The right to an administrative review by the State referring the debt or, upon the request of the individual, by the State with the order upon which the referral was based, of the determination of the State with respect to the debt and of the procedures and time frames established by the State for such reviews.

(2) Prior to referring a debt to Fiscal Service for collection by administrative offset, States must provide individuals with a reasonable opportunity to exercise the rights enumerated in paragraph (h)(1) of this section in accordance with procedures prescribed by the State.

(i) *Payments subject to offset.*—Federal payments subject to offset under this section include all Federal payments except:

(1) Payments due to an individual under

(i) Title IV of the Higher Education Act of 1965;

(ii) The Social Security Act;

(iii) Part B of the Black Lung Benefits Act;

(iv) Any law administered by the Railroad Retirement Board;

(2) Payments which the Secretary determines are exempt from offset in accordance with paragraph (k) of this section;

(3) Payments from which collection of past-due support by administrative offset is expressly prohibited by law;

(4) Payments made under the Internal Revenue Code of 1986 (except that tax refund payments are subject to offset under separate authority); and

(5) Payments made under the tariff laws of the United States.

(j) *Special provisions applicable to Federal salary payments.*—(1) Unless a lower maximum offset limitation is provided by applicable State law, the maximum part of a Federal salary payment per pay period subject to offset to collect past-due support shall not exceed those amounts set forth at section 1673(b)(2) (A) and (B) of Title 15, United States Code, as follows:

(i) Fifty (50%) percent of the debtor's aggregate disposable earnings for any pay period, where the debtor asserts by affidavit, or by other acceptable evidence, that he/she is supporting a spouse and/or dependent child, other than the former spouse and/or child for whom support is being collected, except that an additional five (5%) percent will apply if it appears that such earnings are to enforce past-due support for a period which is twelve (12) weeks or more prior to the pay period to which the offset applies. A debtor shall be considered to be supporting a spouse and/or dependent child only if the debtor provides over half of the spouse's and/or dependent child's support.

(ii) Sixty (60%) percent of the debtor's aggregate disposable earnings for any pay period where the debtor fails to assert by affidavit or establish by other acceptable evidence that he/she is supporting a spouse and/or dependent child, other than a former spouse and/or child for whom support is being collected, except that an additional five (5%) percent will apply if it appears that such earnings are to enforce past-due support for a period which is twelve (12) weeks or more prior to the pay period to which the offset applies.

(2) The maximum allowable offset amount shall be reduced by the amount of any deductions in pay resulting from a garnishment order for support. Nothing in this rule is intended to alter rules applicable to processing garnishment orders for child support and/or alimony.

(3) Federal salary payments subject to offset for the collection of past-due support include current basic pay, special pay, incentive pay, retainer pay, overtime, or in the case of an employee not entitled to basic pay, other authorized pay. Aggregate disposable earnings for purposes of determining the maximum amounts which may be offset under paragraph (j) (1) of this section is Federal salary pay remaining after the deduction of:

(i) Any amount required by law to be withheld;

(ii) Amounts properly withheld for Federal, State or local income tax purposes;

(iii) Amounts deducted as health insurance premiums;

(iv) Amounts deducted as normal retirement contributions, not including amounts deducted for supplementary coverage; and

(v) Amounts deducted as normal life insurance premiums not including amounts deducted for supplementary coverage.

(4) At least 30 days in advance of offset, the disbursing official shall send written notice to the debtor of the maximum offset limitations described in paragraph (j)(1) of this section. The notice shall include a request that the debtor submit supporting affidavits or other documentation necessary to determine the applicable offset percentage limitation. The notice shall also inform the debtor of the percentage that will be deducted if he/she fails to submit the requested documentation.

(5) At the time the past-due support debt is submitted for offset, the State shall advise Fiscal Service or HHS if the maximum amount of a Federal salary payment that may be offset is less than the amount described under this paragraph.

(k) *Payments exempt from administrative offset to collect past-due support being enforced by a State.*—The Secretary will exempt from administrative offset under this part payments made under means-tested programs when requested by the head of the Federal agency which administers the program. For purposes of this section, means-tested programs are programs for which eligibility is based on a determination that income and/or assets of the beneficiary are inadequate to provide the beneficiary with an adequate standard of living without program assistance. The Secretary may exempt from administrative offset under this section any other class or type of payment upon the written request of the head of the agency which authorizes the payments. In determining whether or not to grant such exemptions, the Secretary shall give due consideration to whether administrative offset would tend to interfere substantially with or defeat the purposes of the payment agency's program.

(l) *Fees.*—A fee which Fiscal Service has determined to be sufficient to reimburse Fiscal Service for the full cost of the offset procedure, shall be deducted from each offset amount. Fiscal Service will notify the States, annually and in advance, of the amount of the fee to be charged for each offset.

(m) *Offsetting payments.*—(1) *Conducting the offset.*—Disbursing officials of the Department of the Treasury, the Department of Defense, the United States Postal Service, or any other Government corporation, any disbursing official of the United States designated by the Secretary, or any disbursing official of an executive department or agency that disburses Federal payments shall offset payments subject to offset under this section to satisfy, in whole or part, a debt owed by the payee. Disbursing officials shall compare payment certification records with records of debts submitted to Fiscal Service for collection by administrative offset. A match will occur when the taxpayer identifying number and name control of a payment record are the same as the taxpayer identifying number and name control of a debt record. The taxpayer identifying number for an individual is the individual's social security number. When a match occurs and all other requirements for offset have been met, the disbursing official shall offset the payment to satisfy, in whole or part, the debt. Any amounts not offset shall be paid to the payee. The amount that can be offset from a single payment is the lesser of the amount of the debt (including interest, penalties, and administrative costs); the amount of the payment; or the amount of the payment available for offset if a statute or regulation prohibits offset of the entire amount. Debts remain subject to collection by offset until paid in full.

(2) *Disposition of amounts collected.*—Fiscal Service will transmit amounts collected for debts, less fees charged under paragraph (l) of this section, to HHS or to the appropriate State. If Fiscal Service learns that an erroneous offset payment has been made to HHS or any State, Fiscal Service will notify HHS or the appropriate State that

**»»→ Caution: AUTHORITY: The provisions of 31 CFR Part 285 are issued under the Debt Collection Improvement Act of 1996 (P.L. 104-134), 110 Stat. 1321-358 et seq., codified at 31 U.S.C. 3720A.**

an erroneous offset payment has been made. Fiscal Service may deduct the amount of the erroneous offset payment from amounts payable to HHS or the State, as the case may be. Alternatively, upon Fiscal Service' request, the State shall return promptly to the affected payee or Fiscal Service an amount equal to the amount of the erroneous payment (unless the State previously has paid such amounts, or any portion of such amounts, to the affected payee). HHS and States shall notify Fiscal Service any time HHS or a State returns an erroneous offset payment to an affected payee. Fiscal Service and HHS, or the appropriate State, will adjust their debtor records accordingly.

(n) *Administrative offset priorities.*—(1) A levy pursuant to the Internal Revenue Code of 1986 shall take precedence over deductions under this section.

(2) Offsets will be applied first to past-due support being enforced by the State before any other offsets under this part.

(o) *Notification of offset.*—(1) Disbursing officials of Fiscal Service or any other disbursing official which conducts an offset will notify the payee in writing of the occurrence of the offset to satisfy past-due support. The notice shall inform the payee of the type and amount of the payment that was offset; the identity of the State which requested the offset; and a contact point within the State that will handle concerns regarding the offset. Disbursing officials shall not be liable for failure to provide this notice.

(2) Disbursing officials of Fiscal Service or any other disbursing official which conducts an offset under this section will share with HHS, upon request by the Secretary of HHS, information contained in payment certification records of persons who are delinquent in child support obligations that would assist in the collection of such debts. When no offset is conducted, disbursing officials of Fiscal Service or any other disbursing official, will provide such information to HHS to the extent such information is available from offset activities conducted by Fiscal Service and other disbursing officials.

(p) *Liability of disbursing officials and payment agencies.*—Neither the disbursing official nor the agency authorizing the payment shall be liable for the amount of the administrative offset on the basis that the underlying obligation, represented by the payment before the administrative offset was taken, was not satisfied. Disbursing officials will notify the agency authorizing the payment that the offset has occurred so that the agency authorizing the payment may direct any inquiries concerning the offset to the appropriate State. [Reg. § 285.1.]

☐ [*Final Rule, 8-27-98. Amended by Final Rule 6-10-2009.*]

### [Reg. § 285.2]

**§ 285.2. Offset of tax refund payments to collect past-due, legally enforceable nontax debt.**—(a) *Definitions.*—For purposes of this section:

*Creditor agency* means a Federal agency owed a claim that seeks to collect that claim through tax refund offset.

*Debt* or *claim* refers to an amount of money, funds, or property which has been determined by an agency official to be due the United States from any person, organization, or entity, except another Federal agency. For the purposes of this section, the terms "claim" and "debt" are synonymous and interchangeable and includes debt administered by a third party acting as an agent for the Federal Government.

*Debtor* means a person who owes a debt or claim. The term "person" includes any individual, organization or entity, except another Federal agency.

*Fiscal Service* means the Bureau of the Fiscal Service, a bureau of the Department of the Treasury.

*IRS* means the Internal Revenue Service, a bureau of the Department of the Treasury.

*Tax refund offset* means withholding or reducing a tax refund payment by an amount necessary to satisfy a debt owed by the payee(s) of a tax refund payment.

*Tax refund payment* means any overpayment of Federal taxes to be refunded to the person making the overpayment after the IRS makes the appropriate credits as provided in 26 U.S.C. 6402(a) and 26 CFR 6402-3(a)(6)(i) for any liabilities for any tax on the part of the person who made the overpayment.

(b) *General rule.*—(1) A Federal agency (as defined in 26 U.S.C. 6402(g)) that is owed by a person a past-due, legally enforceable nontax debt shall notify Fiscal Service of the amount of such debt for collection by tax refund offset. However, any agency subject to section 9 of the Act of May 18, 1933 (16 U.S.C. 831h) owed such a debt may, but is not required to, notify Fiscal Service of the amount of such debt for collection by tax refund offset.

(2) Fiscal Service will compare tax refund payment records, as certified by the IRS, with records of debts submitted to Fiscal Service. A match will occur when the taxpayer identifying number (as that term is used in 26 U.S.C. 6109) and name (or derivation of the name, known as a "name control") of a payment certification record are the same as the taxpayer identifying number and name control of a debtor record. When a match occurs and all other requirements for tax refund offset have been met, Fiscal Service will reduce the amount of any tax refund payment payable to a debtor by the amount of any past-due, legally enforceable debt owed by the debtor. Any amounts not offset will be paid to the payee(s) listed in the payment certification record.

(3) This section does not apply to any debt or claim arising under the Internal Revenue Code.

(4)(i) This section applies to Federal Old Age, Survivors and Disability Insurance (OASDI) overpayments provided the requirements of 31 U.S.C. 3720A(f)(1) and (2) are met with respect to such overpayments.

(ii) For purposes of this section, *OASDI overpayment* means any overpayment of benefits made to an individual under title II of the Social Security Act (42 U.S.C. 401 *et seq.*).

(5) A creditor agency is not precluded from using debt collection procedures, such as wage garnishment, to collect debts that have been submitted to Fiscal Service for purposes of offset under this part. Such debt collection procedures may be used separately or in conjunction with offset collection procedures.

(c) *Regulations.*—Prior to submitting debts to Fiscal Service for collection by tax refund offset, Federal agencies shall promulgate temporary or final regulations under 31 U.S.C. 3716 and 31 U.S.C. 3720A, governing the agencies' authority to collect debts by administrative offset, in general, and offset of tax refund payments, in particular.

(d) *Agency certification and referral of debt.*—(1) *Past-due, legally enforceable debt eligible for tax refund offset.*—For purposes of this section, when a Federal agency refers a past-due, legally enforceable debt to Fiscal Service for tax refund offset, the agency will certify to Fiscal Service that:

(i) The debt is past-due and legally enforceable in the amount submitted to Fiscal Service and that the agency will ensure that collections are properly credited to the debt;

(ii) The creditor agency has made reasonable efforts to obtain payment of the debt in that the agency has:

(A) Submitted the debt to Fiscal Service for collection by administrative offset and complied with the provisions of 31 U.S.C. 3716(a) and related regulations, to the extent that collection of the debt by administrative offset is not prohibited by statute;

(B) Notified, or has made a reasonable attempt to notify, the debtor that the debt is past-due, and unless repaid within 60 days after the date of the notice, will be referred to Fiscal Service for tax refund offset;

(C) Given the debtor at least 60 days to present evidence that all or part of the debt is not past-due or legally enforceable, considered any evidence presented by the debtor, and determined that the debt is past-due and legally enforceable; and

(D) Provided the debtor with an opportunity to make a written agreement to repay the amount of the debt;

(iii) The debt is at least $25; and

(iv) In the case of an OASDI overpayment—

(A) The individual is not currently entitled to monthly insurance benefits under title II of the Social Security Act (42 U.S.C. 401 *et seq.*);

(B) The notice describes conditions under which the Commissioner of Social Security is required to waive recovery of the overpayment, as provided under 42 U.S.C. 404(b); and

(C) If the debtor files a request for a waiver under 42 U.S.C. 404(b) within the 60-day notice period, the agency has considered the debtor's request.

(2) *Pre-offset notice and consideration of evidence for past-due, legally enforceable debt.*—(i) For purposes of paragraph (d)(1)(iii)(B) of this section, a creditor agency has made a reasonable attempt to notify the debtor if the agency uses the current address information contained in the agency's records related to the debt. Agencies may, but are not required to, obtain address information from the IRS pursuant to 26 U.S.C. 6103(m)(2), (4), or (5).

(ii) For purposes of paragraph (d)(1)(iii)(C) of this section, if the evidence presented by the debtor is considered by an agent of the creditor agency, or other entities or persons acting on the agency's behalf, the debtor must be accorded at least 30 days from the date the agent or other entity or person determines that all or part of the debt

⫸→ *Caution: AUTHORITY: The provisions of 31 CFR Part 285 are issued under the Debt Collection Improvement Act of 1996 (P.L. 104-134), 110 Stat. 1321-358 et seq., codified at 31 U.S.C. 3720A.*

is past-due and legally enforceable to request review by an officer or employee of the agency of any unresolved dispute. The agency must then notify the debtor of its decision.

(3) *Referral of past-due, legally enforceable debt.*—A Federal agency will submit past-due, legally enforceable debt information for tax refund offset to Fiscal Service in the time and manner prescribed by Fiscal Service. For each debt, the creditor agency will include the following information:

(i) The name and taxpayer identifying number (as defined in 26 U.S.C. 6109) of the debtor who is responsible for the debt;

(ii) The amount of such past-due and legally enforceable debt;

(iii) The date on which the debt became past-due;

(iv) The designation of the Federal agency or subagency referring the debt; and

(v) In the case of an OASDI overpayment, a certification by the Commissioner of Social Security designating whether the amount payable to the agency is to be deposited in either the Federal Old-Age and Survivors Insurance Trust Fund or the Federal Disability Insurance Trust Fund, but not both.

(4) *Correcting and updating referral.*—If, after referring a past-due, legally enforceable debt to Fiscal Service as provided in paragraph (d)(3) of this section, a creditor agency determines that an error has been made with respect to the information transmitted to Fiscal Service, or if an agency receives a payment or credits a payment to the account of a debtor referred to Fiscal Service for offset, or if the debt amount is otherwise incorrect, the agency shall promptly notify Fiscal Service and make the appropriate correction of the agency's records. Creditor agencies will provide certification as required under paragraph (d)(1) of this section for any increases to amounts owed.

(5) Fiscal Service may reject a certification which does not comply with the requirements of paragraph (d)(1) of this section. Upon notification of the rejection and the reason for the rejection, a creditor agency may resubmit the debt with a corrected certification.

(6)(i) Creditor agencies may submit debts to Fiscal Service for collection by tax refund offset irrespective of the amount of time the debt has been outstanding. Accordingly, all nontax debts, including debts that were delinquent for ten years or longer prior to December 28, 2009 may be collected by tax refund offset.

(ii) For debts outstanding more than ten years on or before December 28, 2009, creditor agencies must certify to Fiscal Service that the notice of intent to offset described in paragraph (d)(1)(ii)(B) of this section was sent to the debtor after the debt became ten years delinquent. This requirement will apply even in a case where notice was also sent prior to the debt becoming ten years delinquent, but does not apply to any debt that could be collected by offset without regard to any time limitation prior to December 28, 2009.

(e) *Post-offset notice to the debtor, the creditor agency, and the IRS.*—(1)(i) Fiscal Service will notify the payee(s) to whom the tax refund payment is due, in writing of:

(A) The amount and date of the offset to satisfy a past-due, legally enforceable nontax debt;

(B) The creditor agency to which this amount has been paid or credited; and

(C) A contact point within the creditor agency that will handle concerns or questions regarding the offset.

(ii) The notice in paragraph (e)(1)(i) of this section will also advise any non-debtor spouse who may have filed a joint tax return with the debtor of the steps which a non-debtor spouse may take in order to secure his or her proper share of the tax refund. See paragraph (f) of this section.

(2) Fiscal Service will advise each creditor agency of the names, mailing addresses, and identifying numbers of the debtors from whom amounts of past-due, legally enforceable debt were collected and of the amounts collected from each debtor for that agency. Fiscal Service will not advise the creditor agency of the source of payment from which such amounts were collected. If a payment from which an amount of past-due, legally enforceable debt is to be withheld is payable to two individual payees, Fiscal Service will notify the creditor agency and furnish the name and address of each payee to whom the payment was payable.

(3) At least weekly, Fiscal Service will notify the IRS of the names and taxpayer identifying numbers of the debtors from whom amounts of past-due, legally enforceable debt were collected and the amounts collected from each debtor.

(f) *Offset made with regard to a tax refund payment based upon joint return.*—If the person filing a joint return with a debtor owing the past-due, legally enforceable debt takes appropriate action to secure

his or her proper share of a tax refund from which an offset was made, the IRS will pay the person his or her share of the refund and request that Fiscal Service deduct that amount from amounts payable to the creditor agency. Fiscal Service and the creditor agency will adjust their debtor records accordingly.

(g) *Disposition of amounts collected.*—Fiscal Service will transmit amounts collected for past-due, legally enforceable debts, less fees charged under paragraph (h) of this section, to the creditor agency's account. If an erroneous payment is made to any agency, Fiscal Service will notify the creditor agency that an erroneous payment has been made. The agency shall pay promptly to Fiscal Service an amount equal to the amount of the erroneous payment (without regard to whether any other amounts payable to such agency have been paid).

(h) *Fees.*—The creditor agency will reimburse Fiscal Service and the IRS for the full cost of administering the tax refund offset program. Fiscal Service will deduct the fees from amounts collected prior to disposition and transmit a portion of the fees deducted to reimburse the IRS for its share of the cost of administering the tax refund offset program. To the extent allowed by law, creditor agencies may add the offset fees to the debt.

(i) *Review of tax refund offsets.*—Any reduction of a taxpayer's refund made pursuant to 26 U.S.C. 6402(d) shall not be subject to review by any court of the United States or by the Secretary of the Treasury, Fiscal Service or IRS in an administrative proceeding. No action brought against the United States to recover the amount of this reduction shall be considered to be a suit for refund of tax. Any legal, equitable, or administrative action by any person seeking to recover the amount of the reduction of the overpayment must be taken against the Federal creditor agency to which the amount of the reduction was paid. Any action which is otherwise available with respect to recoveries of overpayments of benefits under 42 U.S.C. 404 must be taken against the Commissioner of Social Security.

(j) *Access to and use of confidential tax information.*—Access to and use of confidential tax information in connection with the tax refund offset program are restricted by 26 U.S.C. 6103. Generally, agencies will not receive confidential tax information from Fiscal Service. To the extent such information is received, agencies are subject to the safeguard, recordkeeping, and reporting requirements of 26 U.S.C. 6103(p)(4) and the regulations thereunder. The agency shall inform its officers and employees who access or use confidential tax information of the restrictions and penalties under the Internal Revenue Code for misuse of confidential tax information.

(k) *Effective date.*—This section applies to tax refund payments payable under 26 U.S.C. 6402 after January 1, 1998. [Reg. § 285.2.]

☐ [*Final Rule*, 8-27-98. *Amended by Final Rules* on 6-10-2009, 10-28-2009 and 1-4-2010.]

### [Reg. § 285.3]

**§ 285.3. Offset of tax refund payments to collect past-due support.**—(a) *Definitions.*—For purposes of this section:

*Debt* as used in this section is synonymous with the term past-due support unless otherwise indicated.

*Debtor* as used in this section means a person who owes past-due support.

*Fiscal Service* means the Bureau of the Fiscal Service, a bureau of the Department of the Treasury.

*HHS* means the Department of Health and Human Services, Office of Child Support Enforcement.

*IRS* means the Internal Revenue Service, a bureau of the Department of the Treasury.

*Past-due support* means the amount of support, determined under a court order, or an order of an administrative process established under State law, for support and maintenance of a child, or of a child and the parent with whom the child is living, which has not been paid, as defined in 42 U.S.C. 664(c).

*State* means the several States of the United States. The term "State" also includes the District of Columbia, American Samoa, Guam, the United States Virgin Islands, the Commonwealth of the Northern Mariana Islands, and the Commonwealth of Puerto Rico.

*Tax refund offset* means withholding or reducing a tax refund payment by an amount necessary to satisfy a debt owed by the payee(s) of a tax refund payment.

*Tax refund payment* means any overpayment of Federal taxes to be refunded to the person making the overpayment after the IRS makes the appropriate credits as provided in 26 U.S.C. 6402(a) and 26 CFR 6402-3(a)(6)(i) for any liabilities for any Federal tax on the part of the person who made the overpayment.

⋙➤ *Caution: AUTHORITY: The provisions of 31 CFR Part 285 are issued under the Debt Collection Improvement Act of 1996 (P.L. 104-134), 110 Stat. 1321-358 et seq., codified at 31 U.S.C. 3720A.*

(b) *General rule.*—(1) Past-due support will be collected by tax refund offset upon notification to Fiscal Service in accordance with 26 U.S.C. 6402(c), 42 U.S.C. 664 and this section. Collection by offset under 26 U.S.C. 6402(c) is a collection procedure separate from the collection procedures provided by 26 U.S.C. 6305 and 26 CFR 301.6305-1, relating to the assessment and collection of certain child and spousal support liabilities. Tax refund offset may be used separately or in conjunction with the collection procedures provided in 26 U.S.C. 6305, as well as other collection procedures.

(2) Fiscal Service will compare tax refund payment records, as certified by the IRS, with records of debts submitted to Fiscal Service. A match will occur when the taxpayer identifying number (as that term is used in 26 U.S.C. 6109) and name of a payment certification record are the same as the taxpayer identifying number and name of a delinquent debtor record. When a match occurs and all other requirements for tax refund offset have been met, Fiscal Service will reduce the amount of any tax refund payment payable to a debtor by the amount of any past-due support debt owed by the debtor. Any amounts not offset will be paid to the payee(s) listed in the payment certification record.

(c) *Notification of past-due support.*—(1) *Past-due support eligible for tax refund offset.*—Past-due support qualifies for tax refund offset if:

(i)(A) There has been an assignment of the support obligation to a State and the amount of past-due support is not less than $25.00, or such higher amount as HHS rules may allow, whichever is greater; or

(B) A State agency is providing support collection services under 42 U.S.C. 654(4) and the amount of the past-due support is not less than $500.00; and

(ii) A notification of liability for past-due support has been received by Fiscal Service as prescribed by paragraphs (c)(2) or (c)(3) of this section.

(2) *Notification of liability for past-due support and transmission of information to Fiscal Service by HHS.*—States notifying HHS of past-due support shall do so in the manner and format prescribed by HHS. The notification of liability shall be accompanied by a certification that the State has complied with the requirements contained in paragraph (c)(4) of this section and with any requirements applicable to the offset of Federal tax refunds to collect past-due support imposed by State law or procedures. HHS shall consolidate and transmit to Fiscal Service the information contained in the notifications of liability for past-due support submitted by the States provided that the State has certified that the requirements of paragraph (c)(4) of this section have been met.

(3) *Notification of liability for past-due support transmitted directly to Fiscal Service by States.*—States must notify HHS of past-due support in accordance with the provisions of paragraph (c)(2) of this section unless HHS rules authorize notification to Fiscal Service directly. If authorized by HHS rules, States may notify Fiscal Service directly of past-due support. States notifying Fiscal Service directly of past-due support shall do so in the manner and format prescribed by Fiscal Service. The notification of liability shall be accompanied by a certification that the State has complied with the requirements contained in paragraph (c) (4) of this section and with any requirements applicable to the offset of Federal tax refunds to collect past-due support imposed by State law or procedures. Fiscal Service may reject a notification of past-due support which does not comply with the requirements of this section. Upon notification of the rejection and the reason for rejection, the State may resubmit a corrected notification.

(4) *Advance notification to debtor of intent to collect by tax refund offset.*—The State, or HHS if the State requests and HHS agrees, is required to provide a written notification to the debtor, pursuant to the provisions of 42 U.S.C. 664(a)(3) and 45 CFR 303.72(e), informing the debtor that the State intends to refer the debt for collection by tax refund offset. The notice also shall:

(i) Instruct the debtor of the steps which may be taken to contest the State's determination that past-due support is owed or the amount of the past-due support;

(ii) Advise any non-debtor who may file a joint tax return with the debtor of the steps which a non-debtor spouse may take in order to secure his or her proper share of the tax refund; and

(iii) In cases when a debt is being enforced by more than one State, advise the debtor of his or her opportunities to request a review with the State enforcing collection or the State issuing the support order as prescribed by the provisions of 45 CFR 303.72(g).

(5) *Correcting and updating notification.*—The State shall, in the manner and in the time frames provided by Fiscal Service or HHS, notify Fiscal Service or HHS of any deletion or net decrease in the amount of past-due support referred to Fiscal Service, or HHS as the case may be, for collection by tax refund offset. The State may notify Fiscal Service or HHS of any increases in the amount of the debt referred to Fiscal Service for collection by tax refund offset provided that the State has complied with the requirements of paragraph (c)(4) of this section with regard to those debts.

(6) *Collection of past-due support enforced by multiple States.*— When a State has knowledge that the debt is being enforced by more than one State, the State notifying Fiscal Service, or HHS as the case may be, of the debt shall inform any such other State involved in enforcing the debt when it receives the offset amount.

(d) *Priorities for offset.*—(1) As provided in 26 U.S.C. 6402, a tax refund payment shall be reduced in the following order of priority:

(i) First, by the amount of any past-due support which is to be offset under 26 U.S.C. 6402(c) and 42 U.S.C. 464;

(ii) Second, by the amount of any past-due, legally enforceable debt owed to a Federal agency which is to be offset under 26 U.S.C. 6402(d), 31 U.S.C. 3720A and § 285.2 of this part; and

(iii) Third, by the amount of any past-due, legally enforceable debt owed to States (other than past-due support) which is to be offset under 26 U.S.C. 6402(e) or 26 U.S.C. 6402(f).

(2) Reduction of the tax refund payment pursuant to 26 U.S.C. 6402(a), (c), (d), and (e) shall occur prior to crediting the overpayment to any future liability for an internal revenue tax. Any amount remaining after tax refund offset under 26 U.S.C. 6402(a), (c), (d), and (e) shall be refunded to the taxpayer, or applied to estimated tax, if elected by the taxpayer pursuant to IRS regulations.

(e) *Post-offset notice.*—(1)(i) Fiscal Service shall notify the debtor in writing of:

(A) The amount and date of the offset to satisfy past-due support;

(B) The State to which this amount has been paid or credited; and

(C) A contact point within the State that will handle concerns or questions regarding the offset.

(ii) The notice in paragraph (e)(1)(i) of this section also will advise any non-debtor who may have filed a joint tax return with the debtor of the steps which a non-debtor spouse may take in order to secure his or her proper share of the tax refund. See paragraph (f) of this section.

(2) Fiscal Service will advise HHS of the names, mailing addresses, and identifying numbers of the debtors from whom amounts of past-due support were collected, of the amounts collected from each debtor through tax refund offset, the names of any non-debtor spouses who may have filed a joint return with the debtor, and of the State on whose behalf each collection was made. Alternatively, Fiscal Service will provide such information to each State that refers debts directly to Fiscal Service. Fiscal Service will inform HHS and each State that the payment source is a tax refund payment.

(3) At least weekly, Fiscal Service will notify the IRS of the names and taxpayer identifying numbers of the debtors from whom amounts owed for past-due support were collected from tax refund offsets and the amounts collected from each debtor.

(4) At such time and in such manner as Fiscal Service and HHS agree, but no less than annually, Fiscal Service will advise HHS of the States which have furnished notices of past-due support, the number of cases in each State with respect to which such notices have been furnished, the amount of past-due support sought to be collected by each State, and the amount of such tax refund offset collections actually made in the case of each State. As Fiscal Service and HHS may agree, Fiscal Service may provide additional offset-related information about States which have furnished notices of past-due support.

(f) *Offset made with regard to a tax refund payment based upon joint return.*—If the person filing a joint return with a debtor owing the past-due support takes appropriate action to secure his or her proper share of a tax refund from which an offset was made, the IRS will pay the person his or her share of the refund and request that Fiscal Service deduct that amount from amounts payable to HHS or the State, as the case may be. Fiscal Service and HHS, or the appropriate State, will adjust their debtor records accordingly.

(g) *Disposition of amounts collected.*—Fiscal Service will transmit amounts collected for debts, less fees charged under paragraph (i) of this section, to HHS or to the appropriate State. If IRS notifies Fiscal Service that a tax refund payment that was offset was erroneous or otherwise not due to the taxpayer, Fiscal Service will notify HHS or the appropriate State that the tax refund payment was not eligible for offset. Subject to paragraph (h) of this section, Fiscal Service may

⫸→ *Caution: AUTHORITY: The provisions of 31 CFR Part 285 are issued under the Debt Collection Improvement Act of 1996 (P.L. 104-134), 110 Stat. 1321-358 et seq., codified at 31 U.S.C. 3720A.*

deduct the amount of the erroneous offset funds from amounts payable to HHS or the State, as the case may be; or, upon Fiscal Service's request, the State shall return promptly to the affected taxpayer or Fiscal Service an amount equal to the amount of the erroneous funds (unless the State previously has forwarded such amounts, or any portion of such amounts, to the affected taxpayer). HHS and States shall notify Fiscal Service any time HHS or a State returns an erroneous offset payment to an affected taxpayer. Fiscal Service and HHS, or the appropriate State, will adjust their debtor records accordingly.

(h) *Time limitation.*—If IRS notifies Fiscal Service on or after January 1, 2016, that a tax refund payment that was offset was erroneous or otherwise not due to the taxpayer, Fiscal Service shall not deduct the amount of the erroneous offset funds from amounts due to HHS or the State, or otherwise demand return of the offset funds from the State pursuant to paragraph (g) of this section, if the date of IRS's notification to Fiscal Service in paragraph (g) is more than six months after the date the tax refund was offset (*i.e.*, the tax refund payment date); and the State has already forwarded the funds as required or authorized by 42 U.S.C. 657. This paragraph does not apply to paragraph (f) of this section.

(i) *Fees.*—The State will pay a fee to Fiscal Service for the full cost of administering the tax refund offset program. The fee (not to exceed $25 per case submitted) will be established annually in such amount as Fiscal Service and HHS agree to be sufficient to reimburse Fiscal Service for the full cost of the offset procedure. Fiscal Service will deduct the fees from amounts collected prior to disposition and transmit a portion of the fees deducted to reimburse the IRS for its share of the cost of administering the tax refund offset program. Fees will be charged only for actual tax refund offsets completed.

(j) *Review of tax refund offsets.*—In accordance with 26 U.S.C. 6402(f), any reduction of a taxpayer's refund made pursuant to 26 U.S.C. 6402(c), (d), or (e) shall not be subject to review by any court of the United States or by the Secretary of the Treasury, Fiscal Service or IRS in an administrative proceeding. No action brought against the United States to recover the amount of this reduction shall be considered to be a suit for refund of tax.

(k) *Access to and use of confidential tax information.*—Access to and use of confidential tax information in connection with the tax refund offset program is permitted to the extent necessary in establishing appropriate agency records, locating any person with respect to whom a reduction under 26 U.S.C. 6402(c) is sought for purposes of collecting the debt, and in the defense of any litigation or administrative procedure ensuing from a reduction made under section 6402(c).

(l) *Effective date.*—This section applies to tax refund payments payable under 26 U.S.C. 6402 after January 1, 1999. [Reg. § 285.3]

☐ [*Final Rule*, 12-29-98. *Amended by Final Rules* on 10-19-2007, 6-10-2009 and 12-30-2015.]

**[Reg. § 285.8]**

**§ 285.8. Offset of tax refund payments to collect state income tax obligations.**—(a) *Definitions.*—For purposes of this section:

*Debt* means past-due, legally enforceable State income tax obligation or unemployment compensation debt unless otherwise indicated.

*Debtor* means a person who owes a debt.

*Fiscal Service* means the Bureau of the Fiscal Service, a bureau of the Department of the Treasury.

*IRS* means the Internal Revenue Service, a bureau of the Department of the Treasury.

*Past-due, legally enforceable State income tax obligation* means a debt which resulted from:

(1) A judgment rendered by a court of competent jurisdiction which has determined an amount of State income tax to be due,

(2) A determination after an administrative hearing which has determined an amount of state income tax to be due and which is no longer subject to judicial review, or

(3) A State income tax assessment (including self-assessments) which has become final in accordance with State law but not collected and which has not been delinquent for more than 10 years.

*State* means the several States of the United States. The term "State" also includes the District of Columbia, American Samoa, Guam, the United States Virgin Islands, the Commonwealth of the Northern Mariana Islands, and the Commonwealth of Puerto Rico.

*State income tax obligation* means State income tax obligations as determined under State law. For purposes of this section, State income tax obligation includes any local income tax administered by the chief tax administration agency of the State.

*Tax refund offset* means withholding or reducing a tax refund overpayment by an amount necessary to satisfy a debt owed by the payee(s).

*Tax refund payment* means any overpayment of Federal taxes to be refunded to the person making the overpayment after the IRS makes the appropriate credits as provided in 26 U.S.C. 6402(a) and 26 CFR 6402-3(a)(6)(i) for any liabilities for any Federal tax on the part of the person who made the overpayment.

*Unemployment compensation debt* has the same meaning as the term "covered unemployment debt" as defined in 26 U.S.C. 6402(f)(4), and means—

(1) A past-due debt for erroneous payment of unemployment compensation due to fraud or the person's failure to report earnings which has become final under the law of a State certified by the Secretary of Labor pursuant to 26 U.S.C. 3304 and which remains uncollected;

(2) Contributions due to the unemployment fund of a State for which the State has determined the person to be liable and which remain uncollected; and

(3) Any penalties and interest assessed on such debt.

(b) *General rule.*—(1) Fiscal Service will offset tax refunds to collect debt under this section in accordance with 26 U.S.C. 6402(e) and (f) and this section.

(2) Fiscal Service will compare tax refund payment records, as certified by the IRS, with records of debts submitted to Fiscal Service. A match will occur when the taxpayer identifying number (as that term is used in 26 U.S.C. 6109) and name on a payment certification record are the same as the taxpayer identifying number and name (or derivative of the name) on a delinquent debt record. When a match occurs and all other requirements for tax refund offset have been met, Fiscal Service will reduce the amount of any tax refund payment payable to a debtor by the amount of any past-due, legally enforceable State income tax obligation or unemployment compensation debt owed by the debtor. Any amounts not offset will be paid to the payee(s) listed in the payment certification record.

(3) Fiscal Service will only offset a tax refund payment for a State income tax obligation if the address shown on the Federal tax return for the taxable year of the overpayment is an address within the State seeking the offset.

(c) *Notification of past-due, legally enforceable State income tax obligations or unemployment compensation debts.*—(1) *Notification.*—States shall notify Fiscal Service of debts in the manner and format prescribed by Fiscal Service. The notification of liability must be accompanied by a certification that the debt is past due and legally enforceable and that the State has complied with the requirements contained in paragraph (c)(3) of this section and with all Federal or State requirements applicable to the collection of debts under this section. With respect to State income tax obligations only, the certification must specifically state that none of the debts submitted for collection by offset are debts owed by an individual who has claimed immunity from State taxation by reason of being an enrolled member of an Indian tribe who lives on a reservation and derives all of his or her income from that reservation unless such claim has been adjudicated de novo on its merits in accordance with paragraph (c)(3). Fiscal Service may reject a notification that does not comply with the requirements of this section. Upon notification of the rejection and the reason for rejection, the State may resubmit a corrected notification.

(2) Minimum amount of past-due, legally enforceable State income tax obligations that may be submitted. Fiscal Service only will accept notification of past-due, legally enforceable State income tax obligations of $25 or more or such higher amounts as determined by Fiscal Service. States will be notified annually of any changes in the minimum debt amount.

(3)(i) *Advance notification to the debtor of the State's intent to collect by Federal tax refund offset.*—The State is required to provide a written notification to the debtor informing the debtor that the State intends to refer the debt for collection by tax refund offset. The notice must give the debtor at least 60 days to present evidence, in accordance with procedures established by the State, that all or part of the debt is not past due or not legally enforceable, or, in the case of a covered unemployment compensation debt, the debt is not due to fraud or the debtor's failure to report earnings. In the case of a State income tax obligation, the notice must be sent certified mail, return receipt requested.

(ii) *Determination.*—The State must, in accordance with procedures established by the State, consider any evidence presented by a debtor in response to the notice described in paragraph (c)(3)(i) of this section and determine whether an amount of such debt is past

>>>→ *Caution:  AUTHORITY: The provisions of 31 CFR Part 285 are issued under the Debt Collection Improvement Act of 1996 (P.L. 104-134), 110 Stat. 1321-358 et seq., codified at 31 U.S.C. 3720A.*

due and legally enforceable and, in the case of a covered unemployment compensation debt, the debt is due to fraud or the debtor's failure to report earnings. With respect to State income tax obligations only, where the debtor claims that he or she is immune from State taxation by reason of being an enrolled member of an Indian tribe who lives on a reservation and derives all of his or her income from that reservation, State procedures shall include de novo review on the merits, unless such claims have been previously adjudicated by a court of competent jurisdiction. States shall, upon request from the Secretary of the Treasury, make such procedures available to the Secretary of the Treasury for review.

(iii) *Reasonable efforts.*—Prior to submitting a debt to Fiscal Service for collection by tax refund offset the State must make reasonable efforts to collect the debt. Reasonable efforts include making written demand on the debtor for payment and complying with any other prerequisites to offset established by the State.

(4) *Correcting and updating notification.*—The State shall, in the manner and in the time frames provided by Fiscal Service, notify Fiscal Service of any deletion or decrease in the amount of past-due, legally enforceable State income tax obligation or unemployment compensation debt referred to Fiscal Service for collection by tax refund offset. The State may notify Fiscal Service of any increases in the amount of the debt referred to Fiscal Service for collection by tax refund offset provided that the State has complied with the requirements of paragraph (c)(3) of this section with regard to those debts.

(d) *Priorities for offset.*—(1) As provided in 26 U.S.C. 6402, a tax refund payment shall be reduced first by the amount of any past-due support being enforced under section 464 of the Social Security Act which is to be offset under 26 U.S.C. 6402(c); second by the amount of any past-due, legally enforceable debt owed to a Federal agency which is to be offset under 26 U.S.C. 6402(d); and third by any past-due, legally enforceable debt owed to a State (other than past-due support) which is to be offset under 26 U.S.C. 6402(e) or 26 U.S.C. 6402(f).

(2) Reduction of the tax refund payment pursuant to 26 U.S.C. 6402(a), (c), (d), (e) and (f) shall occur prior to crediting the overpayment to any future liability for an internal revenue tax. Any amount remaining after tax refund offset under 26 U.S.C. 6402(a), (c), (d), (e) and (f) shall be refunded to the taxpayer, or applied to estimated tax, if elected by the taxpayer pursuant to IRS regulations.

(3) If Fiscal Service receives notice from a State of more than one debt subject to this section that is owed by a debtor to the State, any overpayment by the debtor shall be applied against such debts in the order in which such debts accrued.

(e) *Post-offset notice.*—(1) When an offset occurs, Fiscal Service shall notify the debtor in writing of:

(i) The amount and date of the offset and that the purpose of the offset was to satisfy a past-due, legally enforceable State income tax obligation or unemployment compensation debt;

(ii) The State to which this amount has been paid or credited; and

(iii) A contact point within the State that will handle concerns or questions regarding the offset.

(2) The notice in paragraph (e)(1) of this section also will advise any non-debtor spouse who may have filed a joint return with the debtor of the steps which the non-debtor spouse may take in order to secure his or her proper share of the tax refund. See paragraph (f) of this section.

(3) Fiscal Service will advise States of the names, mailing addresses, and taxpayer identifying numbers of the debtors from whom amounts of State income tax obligations or unemployment compensation debts were collected, and of the amounts collected from each debtor through tax refund offset.

(4) At least weekly, Fiscal Service will notify the IRS of the names and taxpayer identifying numbers of the debtors from whom amounts owed for past-due, legally enforceable State income tax obligations or unemployment compensation debts were collected from tax refund offsets and the amounts collected from each debtor.

(f) *Offset made with regard to a tax refund payment based upon joint return.*—If the person filing a joint return with a debtor owing the past-due, legally enforceable State income tax obligation or unemployment compensation debt takes appropriate action to secure his or her proper share of a tax refund from which an offset was made, the IRS will pay the person his or her share of the refund and request that Fiscal Service deduct that amount from future amounts payable to the State or that Fiscal Service otherwise obtain the funds back from the State. Fiscal Service, or the appropriate State, will adjust their debtor records accordingly.

(g) *Disposition of amounts collected.*—Fiscal Service will transmit amounts collected for debts, less fees charged under paragraph (h) of this section, to the appropriate State. If Fiscal Service learns that an erroneous offset payment is made to any State, Fiscal Service will notify the appropriate State that an erroneous offset payment has been made. Fiscal Service may deduct the amount of the erroneous offset payment from future amounts payable to the State. Alternatively, upon Fiscal Service' request, the State shall return promptly to the affected taxpayer or Fiscal Service an amount equal to the amount of the erroneous payment (unless the State previously has paid such amounts, or any portion of such amounts, to the affected taxpayer). States shall notify Fiscal Service any time a State returns an erroneous offset payment to an affected taxpayer. Fiscal Service, or the appropriate State, will adjust their debtor records accordingly.

(h) *Fees.*—The State will pay a fee to Fiscal Service to cover the full cost of offsets taken. The fee will be established annually in such amount as Fiscal Service determines to be sufficient to reimburse Fiscal Service for the full cost of the offset procedure. Fiscal Service will deduct the fees from amounts collected prior to disposition and transmit a portion of the fees deducted to reimburse the IRS for its share of the cost of administering the tax refund offset program for purposes of collecting past-due, legally enforceable State income tax obligations or unemployment compensation debts reported to Fiscal Service by the States. Fees will be charged only for actual tax refund offsets completed.

(i) *Review of tax refund offsets.*—In accordance with 26 U.S.C. 6402(g), any reduction of a taxpayer's refund made pursuant to 26 U.S.C. 6402(e) or (f) shall not be subject to review by any court of the United States or by the Secretary of the Treasury, Fiscal Service or IRS in an administrative proceeding. No action brought against the United States to recover the amount of this reduction shall be considered to be a suit for refund of tax. This subsection does not preclude any legal, equitable, or administrative action against the State to which the amount of such reduction was paid.

(j) *Access to and use of confidential tax information.*—Access to and use of confidential tax information in connection with the tax refund offset program is permitted to the extent necessary in establishing appropriate agency records, locating any person with respect to whom a reduction under 26 U.S.C. 6402(e) or (f) is sought for purposes of collecting the debt, and in the defense of any litigation or administrative procedure ensuing from a reduction made under section 6402(e) or (f). [Reg. § 285.8.]

☐ [*Interim Rule,* 12-17-99. *Final Rule,* 1-25-2005. *Amended by Final Rules* on 6-10-2009 and 1-28-2011.]

### [Reg. § 301.6402-7]

**§ 301.6402-7. Claims for refunds and applications for tentative carryback adjustments involving consolidated groups that include insolvent financial institutions.**—(a) *In general.*—(1) *Overview.*—Section 6402(i) authorizes the Secretary to issue regulations providing for the payment of a refund directly to the statutory or court-appointed fiduciary of an insolvent corporation that was a subsidiary in a consolidated group, to the extent the Secretary determines that the refund is attributable to losses or credits of the insolvent corporation. This section provides rules for the payment of refunds and tentative carryback adjustments to the fiduciary of an insolvent financial institution that was a subsidiary in a consolidated group.

(2) *Notice.*—This section provides notice to the common parent of a consolidated group of which an insolvent financial institution is or was a member that—

(i) The fiduciary for the institution may, in addition to the common parent, act as agent for the group in certain matters relating to the tax liability of the group in the year in which a loss arose and for the year to which a claim for refund or application for tentative carryback adjustment relates; and

(ii) The Internal Revenue Service may deal directly with the common parent or the fiduciary (or both) as agent for the group to the extent provided in this section.

(b) *Definitions.*—For purposes of this section, the following terms have the meanings set forth below:

(1) *Carryback year group.*—A carryback year group is a consolidated group of which a corporation that is or becomes an insolvent financial institution is a member during a consolidated carryback year.

(2) *Consolidated carryback year.*—A consolidated carryback year is a consolidated return year to which a loss arising in a loss year is carried back.

(3) *Fiduciary.*—A fiduciary is—

(i) The Federal Deposit Insurance Corporation;

(ii) The Resolution Trust Corporation; or

(iii) Any other entity established by federal law, or a federal agency, that is identified by the Commissioner in a revenue ruling or revenue procedure as a fiduciary for purposes of this section;

in its capacity as an authorized receiver or conservator of an insolvent financial institution.

(4) *Insolvent Financial Institution.*—An insolvent financial institution (an institution) is a bank or domestic building and loan association for which the fiduciary is authorized to act as a receiver or conservator—

(i) On the ground that the institution is insolvent within the meaning of 12 U.S.C. 191, 12 U.S.C. 1821(c)(5)(A), 12 U.S.C. 1464(d)(2)(A)(i), or 12 U.S.C. 1464(d)(2)(C)(i) or any applicable state law (or any successor statute which adopts a substantially similar standard); or

(ii) On grounds other than insolvency, provided that the institution is insolvent within the meaning of paragraph (b)(4)(i) of this section at any time after commencement of the conservatorship or receivership.

A reference to an institution under these regulations includes, as the context requires, a reference to predecessors and successors of the institution.

(5) *Loss year.*—A loss year is a taxable year for which any member or former member of the carryback year group claims a loss that may be carried back.

(6) *Loss year group.*—A loss year group is a consolidated group of which a corporation that is or becomes an insolvent financial institution is a member during a loss year.

(7) *Procedure effective date.*—The procedure effective date is the day on which the Internal Revenue Service has processed the notice described in paragraph (d)(1) of this section to the extent necessary for all Internal Revenue Service Centers to have access to information indicating that—

(i) Appropriate notice to the Internal Revenue Service has been filed; and

(ii) Payments with respect to losses of an institution are to be paid in accordance with the procedures set forth in this section.

(8) *Definitions in §1.1502-1.*—Unless otherwise provided, the definitions contained in §1.1502-1 of this chapter apply in this section.

(c) *Deemed agency status of fiduciary.*—(1) *In general.*—Notwithstanding the general treatment of a common parent as the agent of a group under §§1.1502-77 and 1.1502-78 of this chapter, if the fiduciary satisfies the notice requirements of paragraph (d)(1) of this section, the fiduciary may also be deemed to be an agent under §§1.1502-77 and 1.1502-78 of this chapter—

(i) Of the loss year group (if any) for purposes of filing a consolidated return for the loss year;

(ii) Of the carryback year group for purposes of filing a claim for refund or an application for a tentative carryback adjustment for the consolidated carryback year under paragraph (e) of this section and receiving payments of any refund or tentative carryback adjustment under paragraph (g) of this section; and

(iii) Of the carryback year group, the loss year group or any other group of which the institution is a member for any matter pertaining to the determination of the refund or tentative carryback adjustment, but only to the extent provided in paragraph (c)(2) of this section.

(2) *Limitation.*—The fiduciary may act as an agent for matters described in paragraph (c)(1)(iii) of this section only to the extent—

(i) Authorized by the district director, in his/her sole discretion, after receiving a written request from the fiduciary; or

(ii) Requested by the Internal Revenue Service under paragraph (f)(3) of this section.

(d) *Notice requirements.*—(1) *Notice to the Internal Revenue Service.*—To satisfy the notice requirement of this paragraph (d)(1), the fiduciary must file Form 56-F, Notice Concerning Fiduciary Relationship of Financial Institution, with the Internal Revenue Service Center indicated on the form. However, in its sole discretion, the Internal Revenue Service may treat notice to it in any other manner as satisfying the notice requirement under this paragraph (d)(1).

(2) *Notice to the common parent.*—(i) *Form 56-F.*—The fiduciary must send a copy of the Form 56-F filed with the Internal Revenue Service Center or any other notice provided to the Service under paragraph (d)(1) of this section to the common parent of the loss year group (if any) and the common parent of all carryback year groups (if different from the loss year group).

(ii) *Claim for refund and loss year return.*—If a claim for refund is filed by the fiduciary in accordance with paragraph (e)(1) of this section, the fiduciary must provide a copy of the claim for refund to the common parent of the carryback year group. If a loss year return is filed by the fiduciary in accordance with paragraph (e)(3) of this section, the fiduciary must provide a copy of the loss year return to the common parent of the loss year group (if any).

(iii) *Additional information.*—The fiduciary must provide to the affected common parent a copy of the request for agency status referred to in paragraphs (c)(2)(i) and (ii) of this section, and a copy of any additional information submitted to the Internal Revenue Service as agent under paragraph (c)(1)(iii) of this section.

(e) *Filing requirements of the fiduciary.*—(1) *Claim for refund by the fiduciary.*—If the fiduciary accepts a claim for refund filed by the common parent, the fiduciary may claim a refund under this section by filing a copy of the common parent's claim for refund. If no claim for refund is filed by the common parent for the consolidated carryback year or the fiduciary does not accept a claim for refund filed by the common parent, the fiduciary may claim a refund under this section by filing its own claim for refund under section 6402, based on all information pertaining to the institution and all information pertaining to other members of the carryback year group and the loss year group to which the fiduciary has reasonable access. Any claim for refund filed by the fiduciary under this paragraph (e)(1) must contain the title "Claim for refund under section 6402(i) of the Code" at the top of the first page of the claim, and the following must be attached to the claim:

(i) The name and employer identification number of the institution that was a member of the carryback year group;

(ii) The name of the fiduciary;

(iii) A schedule demonstrating that the amount of the refund claimed by the fiduciary is determined in accordance with paragraph (g) of this section;

(iv) A representation that the institution is an insolvent financial institution as defined in paragraph (b)(4) of this section;

(v) A representation that the fiduciary has satisfied the requirements set forth in paragraphs (d)(2)(i) and (ii) of this section; and

(vi) A statement executed by an authorized representative of the fiduciary and any paid preparer utilized by the fiduciary that provides "Under penalties of perjury, I declare that I have examined the items listed in section 301.6402-7T(e)(1)(i) through (v), including accompanying schedules and statements, and to the best of my knowledge and belief, they are true, correct, and complete. Declaration of preparer (other than fiduciary) is based on all information of which the preparer has any knowledge."

(2) *Application for tentative carryback adjustment pursuant to section 6411.*—Notwithstanding section 6411 and §1.1502-78 of this chapter, an application for a tentative carryback adjustment must be signed by both the common parent of the carryback year group and the fiduciary if the payment with respect to the tentative carryback adjustment is not made before the procedure effective date (whether or not the application was filed before the procedure effective date). Any application for a tentative carryback adjustment filed under this paragraph (e)(2) must contain the title "Application for tentative carryback adjustment under section 6402(i) of the Code" at the top of the first page of the application. In addition, the following must be attached to the application:

(i) The name and employer identification number of the institution that was a member of the carryback year group;

(ii) The name of the fiduciary;

(iii) A schedule demonstrating that the amount claimed by the fiduciary is determined in accordance with paragraph (g) of this section;

(iv) A representation that the institution is an insolvent financial institution as defined in paragraph (b)(4) of this section; and

(v) A representation that the fiduciary has satisfied the requirements set forth in paragraph (d)(2)(i) of this section.

(3) *Loss year return by the fiduciary.*—If the institution is a member of a loss year group, and either the common parent does not file a loss year return or the fiduciary does not accept the loss year return filed by the common parent, the fiduciary may file a loss year return with respect to the loss year group. A loss year return can only be filed by the fiduciary in conjunction with the filing of a claim for refund under paragraph (e)(1). The return must be based on all information pertaining to the institution and all information pertaining to other members to which the fiduciary has reasonable access. Any return filed by the fiduciary under this paragraph (e)(3) must contain the title "Loss year return under section 6402(i) of the Code"

at the top of the first page of the return, and the following must be attached to the return:

(i) The name and employer identification number of the institution that is a member of the loss year group;

(ii) The name of the fiduciary;

(iii) A representation that the institution is an insolvent financial institution as defined in paragraph (b)(4) of this section; and

(iv) A representation that the fiduciary has satisfied the requirements set forth in paragraphs (d)(2)(i) and (ii) of this section.

(4) *Additional information.*—If the fiduciary files additional information under paragraph (c)(1)(iii) of this section, the fiduciary must attach a representation that it has satisfied the requirements set forth in paragraph (d)(2)(iii) of this section.

(5) *Election to waive carryback.*—Any election filed after December 30, 1991 by the common parent of a loss year group under section 172(b)(3) to relinquish the entire carryback period with respect to a consolidated net operating loss arising in a loss year is not effective with respect to the portion of the consolidated net operating loss attributable to a subsidiary that is an institution. Instead, the fiduciary may make the election under section 172(b)(3) with respect to the portion attributable to the institution after the notice described in paragraph (d)(1) of this section is filed. For purposes of this paragraph section is filed. For purposes of this paragraph (e)(5), the portion attributable to an institution is determined under the principles of paragraph (g)(2)(ii) of this section.

(f) *Processing and reconciliation of information by the Internal Revenue Service.*—(1) *Loss year return if the insolvent financial institution is a member of a loss year group.*—The Internal Revenue Service may, in its sole discretion, adjust a loss year return filed by the common parent of a loss year group to take into account information filed by the fiduciary in accordance with paragraph (e) of this section, or accept or adjust a loss year return for the loss year group filed by the fiduciary. Nothing in this section relieves the common parent of a loss year group of its duty to file a consolidated return taking into account an institution's items of income, gain, loss, deduction, and credit for any taxable year, or obligates the Internal Revenue Service to accept a return filed by the fiduciary as the return of the loss year group.

(2) *Claim for refund with respect to consolidated carryback year.*—The Internal Revenue Service may, in its sole discretion, adjust a claim for refund filed by the common parent of a carryback year group to take into account information filed by the fiduciary in accordance with paragraph (e) of this section, or accept or adjust a claim for refund for the carryback year group filed by the fiduciary. Nothing in this section obligates the Internal Revenue Service to pay a claim for refund, or to accept a claim for refund, filed by the fiduciary as a claim for refund for the carryback year group.

(3) *Additional information.*—In determining the amount of any refund that may be paid to the fiduciary under paragraph (g) of this section, the Internal Revenue Service may, in its sole discretion, take into account any information that the Internal Revenue Service deems relevant and may require the fiduciary to file any additional information the Internal Revenue Service deems appropriate.

(g) *Payment of a refund or a tentative carryback adjustment to fiduciary.*—(1) *In general.*—If a claim for refund or an application for a tentative carryback adjustment is filed for the consolidated carryback year in accordance with paragraph (e) of this section, the Internal Revenue Service may, in its sole discretion, pay to the fiduciary all or any portion of the refund or tentative carryback adjustment that the Internal Revenue Service determines under this section to be attributable to the net operating losses of the institution. Nothing in this section obligates the Internal Revenue Service to pay to the fiduciary all or any portion of a claim for refund or application for tentative carryback adjustment.

(2) *Portion of refund or tentative carryback adjustment attributable to the net operating loss of an insolvent financial institution.*—(i) *In general.*—The portion of a refund or tentative carryback adjustment attributable to a net operating loss of an institution that is carried to a consolidated carryback year is determined based on the absorption, as described in paragraph (g)(2)(iii) of this section, of the institution's net operating loss carried to the consolidated carryback year.

(ii) *Member's net operating loss.*—If the loss year is a consolidated return year, references in this section to the net operating loss of a member of the loss year group is a reference to the portion of the loss year group's consolidated net operating loss attributable to the member. The consolidated net operating loss for a taxable year that is attributable to a member is determined by a fraction, the numerator of which is the separate net operating loss of the member for the year of the loss and the denominator of which is the sum of the separate

net operating losses for that year of all members having such losses. For this purpose, the separate net operating loss of a member is determined by computing the consolidated net operating loss by taking into account only the member's items of income, gain, deduction, and loss, including the member's losses and deductions actually absorbed by the group in the taxable year (whether or not absorbed by the member).

(iii) *Absorption of net operating losses.*—The absorption of net operating losses generally is determined under applicable principles of the Code and regulations, including the principles of section 172 and § 1.1502-21(b) or 1.1502-21A(b) (as appropriate) of this chapter. Notwithstanding any contrary rule or principle of the Code or regulations, if an institution and another member of the carryback year group have net operating losses that arise in taxable years ending on the same date and are carried to the same consolidated carryback year, the carryback year group's consolidated taxable income for that year is treated as offset first by the loss attributable to the institution to the extent thereof.

(3) *Examples.*—For purposes of the examples in this section, all groups file consolidated returns, all corporations have calendar taxable years, the facts set forth the only corporate activity, the fiduciary has met the notice and filing requirements of this section, and the common parent has filed a return for the loss year and a claim for refund. The principles of this paragraph (g) are illustrated by the following examples.

*Example 1. Absorption of net operating losses.*

(a) P owns all the stock of S1, an insolvent financial institution, and S2, a corporation that is not a financial institution. For Year 1, P, S1, and S2 each have $50 of income, and the P group's consolidated taxable income is $150. On May 31 of Year 2, S1 becomes insolvent and is placed in receivership under the supervision of a fiduciary. For Year 2, the P group has a consolidated net operating loss of $200, of which $100 is attributable to S1 and $100 is attributable to S2.

(b) Under paragraph (g)(2)(iii) of this section, the $150 of consolidated taxable income for Year 1 is offset first by the $100 portion of the consolidated net operating loss for Year 2 attributable to S1. The remaining $50 is treated as offset by $50 of the $100 of consolidated net operating loss attributable to S2. Thus, the refund attributable to $100 of the loss may be payable to the fiduciary and the refund attributable to $50 of the loss may be payable to P. The remaining $50 consolidated net operating loss, available to be carried forward, is entirely attributable to S2.

*Example 2. Separate return net operating loss.* The facts are the same as in *Example 1,* except that S1 left the P group at the end of Year 1 and its $100 of loss in Year 2 is incurred in a separate return limitation year. Under paragraph (g)(2)(iii) of this section, the generally applicable absorption principles of section 172 and § 1.1502-21 of this chapter apply. Although S1 and S2 are carrying back losses to Year 1 from taxable years ending on the same date (Year 2), S1's loss is subject to a $50 limitation under § 1.1502-21(c) of this chapter and only $50 of S1's loss is absorbed before S2's net operating loss. Therefore, the refund attributable to $50 of the net operating loss of S1 may be payable to the fiduciary, and the refund attributable to $100 of the net operating loss of S2 may be payable to P. The remaining $50 net operating loss of S1 is available to be carried forward.

(4) *Refund or tentative carryback adjustment allocation agreement.*—The determination of the portion of any refund or tentative carryback adjustment payable to the fiduciary under this paragraph (g) shall be made without regard to—

(i) Any agreement among the members of the consolidated group; or

(ii) Whether the fiduciary is otherwise entitled to any portion of the refund or tentative carryback adjustment under applicable law.

(h) *Credits, net capital losses, and subgroups.*—(1) *Credits and net capital losses.*—(i) *In general.*—The principles of this section also apply to credits and net capital losses, with appropriate adjustments to reflect differences between the rules applicable to net operating losses and those applicable to credits and net capital losses.

(ii) *Example.*—The principles of this paragraph (h)(1) are illustrated by the following example.

*Example. Net capital loss.* (a) P owns all the stock of S1, an insolvent financial institution, and S2, a corporation that is not a financial institution. For Year 1, P, S1, and S2 each have $50 of capital gain, and the P group's consolidated capital gain net income is $150. On May 31 of Year 2, S1 becomes insolvent and is placed in receivership under the supervision of a fiduciary. For Year 2, the P group has a consolidated net operating loss of $100 that is attributable to S1, and a consolidated net capital loss of $100 that is attributable to S2.

(b) Under paragraphs (g)(2)(iii) and (h)(1) of this section, the generally applicable absorption principles of sections 172 and 1212 and §§ 1.1502-21(b) and 1.1502-22(b) of this chapter apply. Consequently, S2's capital loss is absorbed before S1's net operating loss. Therefore, the $150 of consolidated capital gain net income is offset first by S2's $100 capital loss and the remaining $50 by S1's net operating loss. The refund attributable to $50 of the net operating loss may be payable to the fiduciary, and the refund attributable to the $100 of capital loss may be payable to P. The remaining $50 consolidated net operating loss available to be carried forward is entirely attributable to S1.

(2) *Insolvent financial institution subgroup.*—(i) *In general.*—The principles of this section apply to all members included in an insolvent financial institution subgroup with appropriate adjustments to reflect differences resulting from the application to more than one corporation in a group. Unless otherwise determined by the Internal Revenue Service in its sole discretion, an insolvent financial institution subgroup is composed of an insolvent financial institution and those other members of a loss year group that, at any time during the conservatorship or receivership of the institution, bear the same relationship to the institution that the members of a group bear to their common parent under section 1504(a)(1).

(ii) *Examples.*—The principles of this paragraph (h)(2) are illustrated by the following examples.

*Example 1. Loss of other subgroup members.* (a) S1 is a financial institution, and P, S2, and S3 are not financial institutions. P owns all the stock of S1, S1 owns all the stock of S2, and the stock of S3 is owned 20 percent by S2 and 80 percent by P. For Year 1, P, S1, and S2 each have $100 of income, S3 has no income or loss, and the P group's consolidated taxable income is $300. On May 31 of Year 2, S1 becomes insolvent and is placed in receivership under the supervision of a fiduciary. For Year 2, the P group has a consolidated net operating loss of $300, of which $200 is attributable to S1 and $100 is attributable to S2.

(b) S1 and S2 compose a subgroup because S2 bears the same relationship to S1 that the member of a group bears to its common parent under section 1504(a). S3 is not included in the subgroup because it is not connected to S1 through 80 percent stock ownership as described in section 1504(a).

(c) Because S1 and S2 are members of a subgroup, a claim for refund under paragraph (e) of this section must be based on the aggregate consolidated net operating loss of both S1 and S2. Under paragraph (e)(5) of this section, P may not elect under section 172(b)(3) to relinquish the entire carryback period with respect to the $300 of consolidated net operating loss arising in Year 2 that is attributable to S1 and S2. Any refund payable under paragraph (g)(1) of this section with respect to the $300 loss of S1 and S2 may be paid by the Internal Revenue Service directly to the fiduciary.

*Example 2. Income of other subgroup members.* (a) The facts are the same as in *Example 1*, except that S2 has $100 of income in Year 2 rather than $100 of loss. Any refund payable under paragraph (g) of this section with respect to the loss of S1 in Year 2 must take into account the income of S2, and therefore the refund will be based on a $100 loss of the subgroup.

(b) Although P and S3 are not members included in the subgroup, the loss year return and the claim for refund filed by the fiduciary under paragraph (e) of this section must be completed based on all information to which the fiduciary has reasonable access. Under paragraph (e)(3) of this section, P does not file a loss year return that is accepted by S1, and S1 has reasonable access to information indicating that P and S3 have income in Year 2, S1 must take that income into account in filing the P group's return for Year 2 and reduce the amount of S1's loss that may be carried to Year 1 accordingly. However, if P or S3 has a loss in Year 2, any refund attributable to that loss will not be paid to the fiduciary.

(i) [Reserved]

(j) *Determination of ownership.*—This section determines the party to whom a refund or tentative carryback adjustment will be paid but is not determinative of ownership of any such amount among current or former members of a consolidated group (including the institution).

(k) *Liability of the Government.*—Any refund or tentative carryback adjustment paid to the fiduciary discharges any liability of the Government to the same extent as payment to the common parent under § 1.1502-77 or § 1.1502-78 of this chapter. Furthermore, any refund or tentative carryback adjustment paid to the fiduciary is considered a payment to all members of the carryback year group. Any determination made by the Internal Revenue Service under this section to pay a refund or tentative carryback adjustment to a fiduciary or the common parent may not be challenged by the common parent, any member of the group, or the fiduciary.

(l) *Effective dates.*—This section applies to refunds and tentative carryback adjustments paid after December 30, 1991. [Reg. § 301.6402-7.]

☐ [*T.D.* 8387, 12-30-91. *Redesignated and amended by T.D.* 8446, 11-5-92. *Amended by T.D.* 8677, 6-26-96 *and T.D.* 8823, 6-25-99.]

### [Reg. § 31.6402(a)-1]

**§ 31.6402(a)-1. Credit or refunds.**—(a) *In general.*—For regulations under section 6402 of special application to credits or refunds of employment taxes, see §§ 31.6402(a)-2, 31.6402(a)-3, and 31.6414-1. For regulations under section 6402 of general application to credits or refunds, see §§ 301.6402-1 and 301.6402-2. For provisions relating to adjustments without interest of overpayments of taxes under the Federal Insurance Contributions Act or the Railroad Retirement Tax Act or income tax withholding, see §§ 31.6413(a)-1 and 31.6413(a)-2.

(b) *Period of limitation.*—For the period of limitation upon credit or refund of taxes imposed by the Internal Revenue Code of 1954, see § 301.6511(a)-1 of this chapter (Regulations on Procedure and Administration). For the period of limitation upon credit or refund of any tax imposed by the Internal Revenue Code of 1939, see the regulations applicable with respect to such tax. [Reg. § 31.6402(a)-1.]

☐ [*T.D.* 6472, 6-22-60. *Amended by T.D.* 9405, 6-30-2008.]

### [Reg. § 31.6402(a)-2]

**§ 31.6402(a)-2. Credit or refund of tax under Federal Insurance Contributions Act or Railroad Retirement Tax Act.**—(a) *Claim by person who paid tax to IRS.*—(1) *In general.*—(i) Except as provided in paragraph (a)(1)(iii) of this section, any person may file a claim for credit or refund for an overpayment (except to the extent that the overpayment must be credited pursuant to § 31.3503-1) if the person paid to the Internal Revenue Service (IRS) more than the correct amount of employee Federal Insurance Contributions Act (FICA) tax under section 3101 or employer FICA tax under section 3111, employee Railroad Retirement Tax Act (RRTA) tax under section 3201, employee representative RRTA tax under section 3211, or employer RRTA tax under section 3221, or interest, addition to the tax, additional amount, or penalty with respect to any such tax.

(ii) Except as provided in paragraph (a)(1)(iii) of this section, the claim for credit or refund must be made in the manner and subject to the conditions stated in this section. The claim for credit or refund must be filed on the form prescribed by the IRS and must designate the return period to which the claim relates, explain in detail the grounds and facts relied upon to support the claim, and set forth such other information as may be required by this section and by the instructions relating to the form used to make such claim. No refund or credit pursuant to this section for employer tax will be allowed unless the employer has first repaid or reimbursed its employee or has secured the employee's consent to the allowance of the claim for refund and includes a claim for the refund of such employee tax. However, this requirement does not apply to the extent that the taxes were not withheld from the employee or, after the employer makes reasonable efforts to repay or reimburse the employee or secure the employee's consent, the employer cannot locate the employee or the employee will not provide consent. No refund or credit of employee FICA or RRTA tax overcollected in an earlier year will be allowed if the employee has claimed a refund or credit of the amount of the overcollection which has not been rejected or if the employee has taken the amount of such tax into account in claiming a credit against or refund of the employee's income tax, including instances in which the employee has included an overcollection of employee FICA or RRTA tax in computing a special refund (see § 31.6413(c)-1).

(iii) *Additional Medicare Tax.*—No refund or credit to the employer will be allowed for the amount of any overpayment of Additional Medicare Tax imposed under section 3101(b)(2) or section 3201(a) (as calculated under section 3101(b)(2)), which the employer deducted or withheld from an employee.

(iv) For adjustments without interest of overpayments of FICA or RRTA taxes, including Additional Medicare Tax, see § 31.6413(a)-2.

(v) For corrections of FICA and RRTA tax paid under the wrong chapter, see § 31.6205-1(b)(2)(ii) and (b)(2)(iii) and § 31.3503-1.

(vi) For provisions related to furnishing employee statements and corrected employee statements reporting wages and withheld taxes, see sections 6041 and 6051 and §§ 1.6041-2 and 31.6051-1. For provisions relating to filing information returns and corrected information returns reporting wages and withheld taxes, see sections 6041 and 6051 and §§ 1.6041-2 and 31.6051-2.

(vii) For the period of limitations on credit or refund of taxes, see § 301.6511(a)-1.

(2) *Statements supporting employer's claims for employee tax.*— (i) Every employer who files a claim for refund or credit of employee FICA tax under section 3101 or employee RRTA tax under section 3201 collected from an employee must certify as part of the claim process that the employer has repaid or reimbursed the tax to its employee or has secured the employee's written consent to allowance of the filing of the claim for refund except to the extent that the taxes were not withheld from the employee. The employer must retain as part of its records the written receipt of the employee showing the date and amount of the repayment, evidence of reimbursement, or the written consent of the employee, whichever is used in support of the claim.

(ii) Every employer who files a claim for refund or credit of employee FICA tax under section 3101 or employee RRTA tax under section 3201 collected from an employee in a calendar year prior to the year in which the credit or refund is claimed, also must certify as part of the claim process that the employer has obtained the employee's written statement that the employee has not claimed refund or credit of the amount of the overcollection, or if so, such claim has been rejected, and that the employee will not claim refund or credit of the amount. The employer must retain the employee's written statement as part of the employer's records.

(b) *Claim by employee.*—(1) *In general.*—Except as provided in (b)(3) of this section, if more than the correct amount of employee tax under section 3101 or section 3201 is collected by an employer from an employee and paid to the IRS, the employee may file a claim for refund of the overpayment if—

(i) The employee does not receive repayment or reimbursement in any manner from the employer and does not authorize the employer to file a claim and receive refund or credit,

(ii) The overcollection cannot be corrected under § 31.3503-1, and

(iii) In the case of overpaid employee social security tax due to having received wages or compensation from multiple employers, the employee has not taken the overcollection into account in claiming a credit against, or refund of, his or her income tax, or if so, such claim has been rejected. See § 31.6413(c)-1.

(2) *Statements supporting employee's claim.*—(i) Except as provided in (b)(3) of this section, each employee who makes a claim under paragraph (b)(1) of this section shall submit with such claim a statement setting forth (a) the extent, if any, to which the employer has repaid or reimbursed the employee in any manner for the overcollection, and (b) the amount, if any, of credit or refund of such overpayment claimed by the employer or authorized by the employee to be claimed by the employer. The employee shall obtain such statement, if possible, from the employer, who should include in such statement the fact that it is made in support of a claim against the United States to be filed by the employee for refund of employee tax paid by such employer to the IRS. If the employer's statement is not submitted with the claim, the employee shall make the statement to the best of his or her knowledge and belief, and shall include therein an explanation of his or her inability to obtain the statement from the employer.

(ii) Except as provided in paragraph (b)(3) of this section, each individual who makes a claim under paragraph (b)(1) of this section also shall submit with such claim a statement setting forth whether the individual has taken the amount of the overcollection into account in claiming a credit against, or refund of, his or her income tax, and the amount, if any, so claimed (see § 31.6413(c)-1.)

(3) *Additional Medicare Tax.*—(i) If more than the correct amount of Additional Medicare Tax under section 3101(b)(2) or section 3201(a) (as calculated under section 3101(b)(2)), is collected by an employer from an employee and paid to the IRS, the employee may file a claim for refund of the overpayment and receive a refund or credit if the overcollection cannot be corrected under § 31.3503-1 and if the employee has not received repayment or reimbursement from the employer in the context of an interest-free adjustment. The claim for refund shall be made on Form 1040, "U.S. Individual Income Tax Return," by taking the overcollection into account in claiming a credit against, or refund of, tax. The form to be used by residents of the U.S. Virgin Islands, Guam, American Samoa, or the Northern Mariana Islands is Form 1040-SS, "U.S. Self-Employment Tax Return (Including Additional Child Tax Credit for Bona Fide Residents of Puerto Rico)." The form to be used by residents of Puerto Rico is either Form 1040-SS or Form 1040-PR, "Planilla para la Declaración de la Contribución Federal sobre el Trabajo por Cuenta Propia (Incluyendo el Crédito Tributario Adicional por Hijos para Residentes Bona Fide de Puerto Rico)." The employee may not authorize the employer to claim the credit or refund for the employee. See § 31.6402(a)-2(a)(1)(iii).

(ii) In the case of an overpayment of Additional Medicare Tax under section 3101(b)(2) or section 3201(a) for a taxable year of an individual for which a Form 1040 (or other applicable return in the Form 1040 series) has been filed, a claim for refund shall be made by the individual on Form 1040X, "Amended U.S. Individual Income Tax Return."

(c) *Effective/applicability date.*—This section applies to claims for refund filed on or after November 29, 2013. [Reg. § 31.6402(a)-2.]

☐ [*T.D. 6472, 6-22-60. Amended by T.D. 9405, 6-30-2008 and T.D. 9645, 11-26-2013.*]

### [Reg. § 31.6402(a)-3]

**§ 31.6402(a)-3. Refund of Federal unemployment tax.**—Any person who pays to the district director more than the correct amount of—

(a) Tax under section 3301 of the Federal Unemployment Tax Act or a corresponding provision of prior law, or

(b) Interest, addition to the tax, additional amount, or penalty with respect to such tax,

may file a claim for refund of the overpayment, in the manner and subject to the conditions stated in § 301.6402-2 of this chapter (Regulations on Procedure and Administration) [¶ 11,260.85]. See § 31.6413(d) and the corresponding section of prior law for provisions which bar the allowance or payment of interest on the amount of any refund based on credit allowable for contributions paid under the unemployment compensation law of a State. [Reg. § 31.6402(a)-3.]

☐ [*T.D. 6472, 6-22-60.*]

### [Reg. § 301.6403-1]

**§ 301.6403-1. Overpayment of installment.**—If any installment of tax is overpaid, the overpayment shall first be applied against any outstanding installments of such tax. If the overpayment exceeds the correct amount of tax due, the overpayment shall be credited or refunded as provided in section 6402 and § § 301.6402-1 to 301.6402-4, inclusive. [Reg. § 301.6403-1.]

☐ [*T.D. 6119, 12-31-54. Amended by T.D. 6498, 10-24-60.*]

### [Reg. § 31.6404(a)-1]

**§ 31.6404(a)-1. Abatements.**—For regulations under section 6404 of general application to the abatement of taxes, see § 301.6404-1 of this chapter (Regulations on Procedure and Administration). Every claim filed by an employer for abatement of employee tax under section 3101 or section 3201, or a corresponding provision of prior law, shall be made in the manner and subject to the conditions stated in paragraphs (a)(2) and (c) of § 31.6402(a)-2, as if the claim for abatement were a claim for refund. [Reg. § 31.6404(a)-1.]

☐ [*T.D. 6472, 6-22-60.*]

### [Reg. § 301.6404-0]

**§ 301.6404-0. Table of contents.**—This section lists the paragraphs contained in § § 301.6404-1 through 301.6404-4.

§ 301.6404-4. Suspension of interest and certain penalties when the Internal Revenue Service does not timely contact the taxpayer.

(a) Suspension.

(1) In general.

(2) Treatment of amended returns and other documents.

(i) Amended returns filed on or after December 21, 2005, that show an increase in tax liability.

(ii) Amended returns that show a decrease in tax liability.

(iii) Amended returns and other documents as notice.

(iv) Joint return after filing separate return.

(3) Separate application.

(4) Duration of suspension period.

(5) Certain notices provided on or after November 26, 2007.

(i) Eighteen-month period has closed.

(ii) All other cases.

(6) Examples.

(7) Notice of liability and the basis for the liability.

(i) In general.

(ii) Tax attributable to TEFRA partnership items.

(iii) Examples.

(8) Providing notice.

(i) In general.

(ii) Providing notice in TEFRA partnership proceedings.

(b) Exceptions.

(1) Failure to file tax return or to pay tax.

(2) Fraud.

(3) Tax shown on return.

(4) Gross misstatement.

(i) Description.

(ii) Effect of gross misstatement.

(5) Listed transactions and undisclosed reportable transactions.

(i) In general.

(ii) Special rule for certain listed or undisclosed reportable transactions.

(A) Participant in a settlement initiative.

(1) Participant in a settlement initiative who as of January 23, 2006, had not reached agreement with the IRS.

(2) Participant in a settlement initiative who, as of January 23, 2006, had reached agreement with the IRS.

(B) Taxpayer acting in good faith.

(1) In general.

(2) Presumption.

(3) Examples.

(C) Closed transactions.

(c) Special rules.

(1) Tentative carryback and refund adjustments.

(2) Election under section 183(e).

(i) In general.

(ii) Example.

(d) Effective/applicability date.

[Reg. § 301.6404-0.]

☐ [*T.D. 8254, 5-12-89. Redesignated and amended by T.D. 8299, 4-16-90. Amended by T.D. 9488, 6-15-2010 and T.D. 9545, 8-19-2011.*]

**[Reg. § 301.6404-1]**

§ 301.6404-1. Abatements.—(a) The district director or the director of the regional service center may abate any assessment, or unpaid portion thereof, if the assessment is in excess of the correct tax liability, if the assessment is made subsequent to the expiration of the period of limitations applicable thereto, or if the assessment has been erroneously or illegally made.

(b) No claim for abatement may be filed with respect to income, estate, or gift tax.

(c) Except in case of income, estate, or gift tax, if more than the correct amount of tax, interest, additional amount, addition to the tax, or assessable penalty is assessed but not paid to the district director, the person against whom the assessment is made may file a claim for abatement of such overassessment. Each claim for abatement under this section shall be made on Form 843. In the case of a claim filed prior to April 15, 1968, the claim shall be filed in the office of the internal revenue officer by whom the tax was assessed or with the assistant regional commissioner (alcohol, tobacco, and firearms) where the regulations respecting the particular tax to which the claim relates specifically require the claim to be filed with that officer. Except as provided in paragraph (b) of § 301.6091-1 (relating to hand-carried documents), in the case of a claim filed after April 14, 1968, the claim shall be filed (1) with the Director of International Operations if the tax was assessed by him, or (2) with the assistant regional commissioner (alcohol, tobacco, and firearms) where the regulations respecting the particular tax to which the claim relates specifically

require the claim to be filed with that officer; otherwise, the claim shall be filed with the service center serving the internal revenue district in which the tax was assessed. Form 843 shall be made in accordance with the instructions relating to such form.

(d) The Commissioner may issue uniform instructions to district directors authorizing them, to the extent permitted in such instructions, to abate amounts the collection of which is not warranted because of the administration and collection costs. [Reg. § 301.6404-1.]

☐ [*T.D. 6119, 12-31-54. Amended by T.D. 6585, 12-27-61; T.D. 6950, 4-3-68; T.D. 7008, 2-28-69 and T.D. 7188, 6-28-72.*]

**[Reg. § 301.6404-2]**

§ 301.6404-2. Abatement of interest.—(a) *In general.*—(1) Section 6404(e)(1) provides that the Commissioner may (in the Commissioner's discretion) abate the assessment of all or any part of interest on any—

(i) Deficiency (as defined in section 6211(a), relating to income, estate, gift, generation-skipping, and certain excise taxes) attributable in whole or in part to any unreasonable error or delay by an officer or employee of the Internal Revenue Service (IRS) (acting in an official capacity) in performing a ministerial or managerial act; or

(ii) Payment of any tax described in section 6212(a) (relating to income, estate, gift, generation-skipping, and certain excise taxes) to the extent that any unreasonable error or delay in payment is attributable to an officer or employee of the IRS (acting in an official capacity) being erroneous or dilatory in performing a ministerial or managerial act.

(2) An error or delay in performing a ministerial or managerial act will be taken into account only if no significant aspect of the error or delay is attributable to the taxpayer involved or to a person related to the taxpayer within the meaning of section 267(b) or section 707(b)(1). Moreover, an error or delay in performing a ministerial or managerial act will be taken into account only if it occurs after the IRS has contacted the taxpayer in writing with respect to the deficiency or payment. For purposes of this paragraph (a)(2), no significant aspect of the error or delay is attributable to the taxpayer merely because the taxpayer consents to extend the period of limitations.

(b) *Definitions.*—(1) *Managerial act.*—means an administrative act that occurs during the processing of a taxpayer's case involving the temporary or permanent loss of records or the exercise of judgment or discretion relating to management of personnel. A decision concerning the proper application of federal tax law (or other federal or state law) is not a managerial act. Further, a general administrative decision, such as the IRS's decision on how to organize the processing of tax returns or its delay in implementing an improved computer system, is not a managerial act for which interest can be abated under paragraph (a) of this section.

(2) *Ministerial act.*—means a procedural or mechanical act that does not involve the exercise of judgment or discretion, and that occurs during the processing of a taxpayer's case after all prerequisites to the act, such as conferences and review by supervisors, have taken place. A decision concerning the proper application of federal tax law (or other federal or state law) is not a ministerial act.

(c) *Examples.*—The following examples illustrate the provisions of paragraphs (b)(1) and (2) of this section. Unless otherwise stated, for purposes of the examples, no significant aspect of any error or delay is attributable to the taxpayer, and the IRS has contacted the taxpayer in writing with respect to the deficiency or payment. The examples are as follows:

*Example 1.* A taxpayer moves from one state to another before the IRS selects the taxpayer's income tax return for examination. A letter explaining that the return has been selected for examination is sent to the taxpayer's old address and then forwarded to the new address. The taxpayer timely responds, asking that the audit be transferred to the IRS's district office that is nearest the new address. The group manager timely approves the request. After the request for transfer has been approved, the transfer of the case is a ministerial act. The Commissioner may (in the Commissioner's discretion) abate interest attributable to any unreasonable delay in transferring the case.

*Example 2.* An examination of a taxpayer's income tax return reveals a deficiency with respect to which a notice of deficiency will be issued. The taxpayer and the IRS identify all agreed and unagreed issues, the notice is prepared and reviewed (including review by District Counsel, if necessary), and any other relevant prerequisites are completed. The issuance of the notice of deficiency is a ministerial act. The Commissioner may (in the Commissioner's discretion) abate interest attributable to any unreasonable delay in issuing the notice.

*Example 3.* A revenue agent is sent to a training course for an extended period of time, and the agent's supervisor decides not to reassign the agent's cases. During the training course, no work is done on the cases assigned to the agent. The decision to send the revenue agent to the training course and the decision not to reassign the agent's cases are not ministerial acts; however, both decisions are managerial acts. The Commissioner may (in the Commissioner's discretion) abate interest attributable to any unreasonable delay resulting from these decisions.

*Example 4.* A taxpayer appears for an office audit and submits all necessary documentation and information. The auditor tells the taxpayer that the taxpayer will receive a copy of the audit report. However, before the report is prepared, the auditor is permanently reassigned to another group. An extended period of time passes before the auditor's cases are reassigned. The decision to reassign the auditor and the decision not to reassign the auditor's cases are not ministerial acts; however, they are managerial acts. The Commissioner may (in the Commissioner's discretion) abate interest attributable to any unreasonable delay resulting from these decisions.

*Example 5.* A taxpayer is notified that the IRS intends to audit the taxpayer's income tax return. The agent assigned to the case is granted sick leave for an extended period of time, and the taxpayer's case is not reassigned. The decision to grant sick leave and the decision not to reassign the taxpayer's case to another agent are not ministerial acts; however, they are managerial acts. The Commissioner may (in the Commissioner's discretion) abate interest attributable to any unreasonable delay caused by these decisions.

*Example 6.* A revenue agent has completed an examination of the income tax return of a taxpayer. There are issues that are not agreed upon between the taxpayer and the IRS. Before the notice of deficiency is prepared and reviewed, a clerical employee misplaces the taxpayer's case file. The act of misplacing the case file is a managerial act. The Commissioner may (in the Commissioner's discretion) abate interest attributable to any unreasonable delay resulting from the file being misplaced.

*Example 7.* A taxpayer invests in a tax shelter and reports a loss from the tax shelter on the taxpayer's income tax return. IRS personnel conduct an extensive examination of the tax shelter, and the processing of the taxpayer's case is delayed because of that examination. The decision to delay the processing of the taxpayer's case until the completion of the examination of the tax shelter is a decision on how to organize the processing of tax returns. This is a general administrative decision. Consequently, interest attributable to a delay caused by this decision cannot be abated under paragraph (a) of this section.

*Example 8.* A taxpayer claims a loss on the taxpayer's income tax return and is notified that the IRS intends to examine the return. However, a decision is made not to commence the examination of the taxpayer's return until the processing of another return, for which the statute of limitations is about to expire, is completed. The decision on how to prioritize the processing of returns based on the expiration of the statute of limitations is a general administrative decision. Consequently, interest attributable to a delay caused by this decision cannot be abated under paragraph (a) of this section.

*Example 9.* During the examination of an income tax return, there is disagreement between the taxpayer and the revenue agent regarding certain itemized deductions claimed by the taxpayer on the return. To resolve the issue, advice is requested in a timely manner from the Office of Chief Counsel on a substantive issue of federal tax law. The decision to request advice is a decision concerning the proper application of federal tax law; it is neither a ministerial nor a managerial act. Consequently, interest attributable to a delay resulting from the decision to request advice cannot be abated under paragraph (a) of this section.

*Example 10.* The facts are the same as in *Example 9* except the attorney who is assigned to respond to the request for advice is granted leave for an extended period of time. The case is not reassigned during the attorney's absence. The decision to grant leave and the decision not to reassign the taxpayer's case to another attorney are not ministerial acts; however, they are managerial acts. The Commissioner may (in the Commissioner's discretion) abate interest attributable to any unreasonable delay caused by these decisions.

*Example 11.* A taxpayer contacts an IRS employee and requests information with respect to the amount due to satisfy the taxpayer's income tax liability for a particular taxable year. Because the employee fails to access the most recent data, the employee gives the taxpayer an incorrect amount due. As a result, the taxpayer pays less than the amount required to satisfy the tax liability. Accessing the most recent data is a ministerial act. The Commissioner may (in the Commissioner's discretion) abate interest attributable to any unreasonable error or delay arising from giving the taxpayer an incorrect amount due to satisfy the taxpayer's income tax liability.

*Example 12.* A taxpayer contacts an IRS employee and requests information with respect to the amount due to satisfy the taxpayer's income tax liability for a particular taxable year. To determine the current amount due, the employee must interpret complex provisions of federal tax law involving net operating loss carrybacks and foreign tax credits. Because the employee incorrectly interprets these provisions, the employee gives the taxpayer an incorrect amount due. As a result, the taxpayer pays less than the amount required to satisfy the tax liability. Interpreting complex provisions of federal tax law is neither a ministerial nor a managerial act. Consequently, interest attributable to an error or delay arising from giving the taxpayer an incorrect amount due to satisfy the taxpayer's income tax liability in this situation cannot be abated under paragraph (a) of this section.

*Example 13.* A taxpayer moves from one state to another after the IRS has undertaken an examination of the taxpayer's income tax return. The taxpayer asks that the audit be transferred to the IRS's district office that is nearest the new address. The group manager approves the request, and the case is transferred. Thereafter, the taxpayer moves to yet another state, and once again asks that the audit be transferred to the IRS's district office that is nearest that new address. The group manager approves the request, and the case is again transferred. The agent then assigned to the case is granted sick leave for an extended period of time, and the taxpayer's case is not reassigned. The taxpayer's repeated moves result in a delay in the completion of the examination. Under paragraph (a)(2) of this section, interest attributable to this delay cannot be abated because a significant aspect of this delay is attributable to the taxpayer. However, as in *Example 5*, the Commissioner may (in the Commissioner's discretion) abate interest attributable to any unreasonable delay caused by the managerial decisions to grant sick leave and not to reassign the taxpayer's case to another agent.

(d) *Effective dates.*—(1) *In general.*—Except as provided in paragraph (d)(2) of this section, the provisions of this section apply to interest accruing with respect to deficiencies or payments of any tax described in section 6212(a) for taxable years beginning after July 30, 1996.

(2) *Special rules.*—(i) *Estate tax.*—The provisions of this section apply to interest accruing with respect to deficiencies or payments of—

(A) Estate tax imposed under section 2001 on estates of decedents dying after July 30, 1996;

(B) The additional estate tax imposed under sections 2032A(c) and 2056A(b)(1)(B) in the case of taxable events occurring after July 30, 1996; and

(C) The additional estate tax imposed under section 2056A(b)(1)(A) in the case of taxable events occurring after December 31, 1996.

(ii) *Gift tax.*—The provisions of this section apply to interest accruing with respect to deficiencies or payments of gift tax imposed under chapter 12 on gifts made after December 31, 1996.

(iii) *Generation-skipping transfer tax.*—The provisions of this section apply to interest accruing with respect to deficiencies or payments of generation-skipping transfer tax imposed under chapter 13—

(A) On direct skips occurring at death, if the transferor dies after July 30, 1996; and

(B) On inter vivos direct skips, and all taxable terminations and taxable distributions occurring after December 31, 1996. [Reg. §301.6404-2.]

☐ [*T.D.* 8789, 12-17-98.]

**[Reg. §301.6404-3]**

**§301.6404-3. Abatement of penalty or addition to tax attributable to erroneous written advice of the Internal Revenue Service.**— (a) *General rule.*—Any portion of any penalty or addition to tax that is attributable to erroneous advice furnished to the taxpayer in writing by an officer or employee of the Internal Revenue Service (Service), acting in his or her official capacity, shall be abated, provided the requirements of paragraph(b) of this section are met.

(b) *Requirements.*—(1) *In general.*—Paragraph (a) of this section shall apply only if—

(i) The written advice was reasonably relied upon by the taxpayer;

(ii) The advice was issued in response to a specific written request for advice by the taxpayer; and

(iii) The taxpayer requesting advice provided adequate and accurate information.

(2) *Advice was reasonably relied upon.*—(i) *In general.*—The written advice from the Service must have been reasonably relied upon by the taxpayer in order for any penalty to be abated under paragraph (a) of this section.

(ii) *Advice relating to a tax return.*—In the case of written advice from the Service that relates to an item included on a federal tax return of a taxpayer, if such advice is received by the taxpayer subsequent to the date on which the taxpayer filed such return, the taxpayer shall not be considered to have reasonably relied upon such written advice for purposes of this section, except as provided in paragraph (b)(2)(iii) of this section.

(iii) *Amended returns.*—If a taxpayer files an amended federal tax return that conforms with written advice received by the taxpayer from the Service, the taxpayer will be considered to have reasonably relied upon the advice for purposes of the position set forth in the amended return.

(iv) *Advice not related to a tax return.*—In the case of written advice that does not relate to an item included on a federal tax return (for example, the payment of estimated taxes), if such written advice is received by the taxpayer subsequent to the act or omission of the taxpayer that is the basis for the penalty or addition of tax, then the taxpayer shall not be considered to have reasonably relied upon such written advice for purposes of this section.

(v) *Period of reliance.*—If the written advice received by the taxpayer relates to a continuing action or series of actions, the taxpayer may rely on that advice until the taxpayer is put on notice that the advice is no longer consistent with Service position and, thus, no longer valid. For purposes of this section, the taxpayer will be put on notice that written advice is no longer valid if the taxpayer receives correspondence from the Service stating that the advice no longer represents Service position. Further, any of the following events, occurring subsequent to the issuance of the advice, that set forth a position that is inconsistent with the written advice received from the Service shall be deemed to put the taxpayer on notice that the advice is no longer valid—

(A) Enactment of legislation or ratification of a tax treaty;

(B) A decision of the United States Supreme Court;

(C) The issuance of temporary or final regulations; or

(D) The issuance of a revenue ruling, a revenue procedure, or other statement published in the Internal Revenue Bulletin.

(3) *Advice was in response to written request.*—No abatement under paragraph (a) of this section shall be allowed unless the penalty or addition to tax is attributable to advice issued in response to a specific written request for advice by the taxpayer. For purposes of the preceding sentence, a written request from a representative of the taxpayer shall be considered a written request by the taxpayer only if—

(i) The taxpayer's representative is an attorney, a certified public accountant, an enrolled agent, an enrolled actuary, or any other person permitted to represent the taxpayer before the Service and who is not disbarred or suspended from practice before the Service; and

(ii) The written request for advice either is accompanied by a power of attorney that is signed by the taxpayer and that authorizes the representative to represent the taxpayer for purposes of the request, or such a power of attorney is currently on file with the Service.

(4) *Taxpayer's information must be adequate and accurate.*—No abatement under paragraph (a) of this section shall be allowed with respect to any portion of any penalty or addition to tax that resulted because the taxpayer requesting the advice did not provide the Service with adequate and accurate information. The Service has no obligation to verify or correct the taxpayer's submitted information.

(c) *Definitions.*—(1) *Advice.*—For purposes of section 6404(f) and the regulations thereunder, a written response issued to a taxpayer by an officer or employee of the Service shall constitute "advice" if, and only if, the response applies the tax laws to the specific facts submitted in writing by the taxpayer and provides a conclusion regarding the tax treatment to be accorded the taxpayer upon the application of the tax law to those facts.

(2) *Penalty and addition to tax.*—For purposes of section 6404(f) and the regulations thereunder, the terms "penalty" and "addition to tax" refer to any liability of a particular taxpayer imposed under Subtitle F, Chapter 68, Subchapter A and Subchapter B of the Internal Revenue Code, and the liabilities imposed by sections 6038(b), 6038(c), 6038A(d), 6038B(b), 6039E(c), and 6332(d)(2). In addition, the terms "penalty" and "addition to tax" shall include any liability resulting from the application of other provisions of the Code where the Commissioner of Internal Revenue has designated by regulation, revenue ruling, or other guidance published in the Internal Revenue Bulletin that such provision shall be considered a penalty or addition to tax for purposes of section 6404(f). The terms "penalty" and "addition to tax" shall also include interest imposed with respect to any penalty or addition to tax.

(d) *Procedures for abatement.*—Taxpayers entitled to an abatement of a penalty or addition to tax pursuant to section 6404(f) and this section should complete and file Form 843. If the erroneous advice received relates to an item on a federal tax return, taxpayers should submit Form 843 to the Internal Revenue Service Center where the return was filed. If the advice does not relate to an item on a federal tax return, the taxpayer should submit Form 843 to the Service Center where the taxpayer's return was filed for the taxable year in which the taxpayer relied on the erroneous advice. At the top of Form 843 taxpayers should write, "Abatement of penalty or addition to tax pursuant to section 6404(f)." Further, taxpayers must state on Form 843 whether the penalty or addition to tax has been paid. Taxpayers must submit, with Form 843, copies of the following—

(1) The taxpayer's written request for advice;

(2) The erroneous written advice furnished by the Service to the taxpayer and relied on by the taxpayer; and

(3) The report (if any) of tax adjustments that identifies the penalty or addition to tax and the item relating to the erroneous written advice.

(e) *Period for requesting abatement.*—An abatement of any penalty or addition to tax pursuant to section 6404(f) and this section shall be allowed only if the request for abatement described in paragraph (d) of this section is submitted within the period allowed for collection of such penalty or addition to tax, or, if the penalty or addition to tax has been paid, the period allowed for claiming a credit or refund of such penalty or addition to tax.

(f) *Examples.*—The following examples illustrate the application of section 6404(f) of the Code and the regulations thereunder:

*Example 1.* In February 1989, an individual submitted a written request for advice to an Internal Revenue Service Center and included adequate and accurate information to consider the request. The question posed by the taxpayer concerned whether a certain amount was includible in income on the taxpayer's 1989 federal income tax return. An employee of the Service Center issued the taxpayer a written response that concluded that based on the specific facts submitted by the taxpayer, the amount was not includible in income on the taxpayer's 1989 return. Since the response provided a conclusion regarding the tax treatment accorded the taxpayer on the basis of the facts submitted, the response constitutes "advice" for purposes of section 6404(f). The taxpayer filed his 1989 return and, relying on the Service's advice, did not include the item in income. Upon examination, it was determined that the item should have been included in income on the taxpayer's 1989 return. Because the taxpayer reasonably relied upon erroneous written advice from the Service, any penalty or addition to tax attributable to the erroneous advice will be abated by the Service. However, the erroneous advice will not affect the amount of any taxes and interest owed by the taxpayer (except to the extent interest relates to a penalty or addition to tax attributable to the erroneous advice) due to the fact that the item was not included in income.

*Example 2.* In March 1989, an individual submitted a written request to the National Office of the Internal Revenue Service regarding whether a certain activity constitutes a passive activity within the meaning of section 469 of the Code. The request did not meet the procedural requirements set forth by the National Office for consideration of the submission as a private letter ruling request and, thus, was not treated as such by the Service. The Service furnished the taxpayer with a written response that transmitted various published provisions of section 469 and the regulations thereunder relevant to the determination of whether an activity is passive within the meaning of those provisions. The Service also included a Publication regarding the tax treatment of passive activities. However, the Service's response contained no opinion or determination regarding whether the taxpayer's described activity was or was not passive under section 469. The Service's response is not advice within the meaning of section 6404(f), and cannot be relied upon for purposes of an abatement of a portion of a penalty or addition to tax under that section.

*Example 3.* On April 1, 1989, an individual submitted a written request for advice to an Internal Revenue Service Center. The advice related to an item included on a federal tax return. The individual filed a federal income tax return with the appropriate Service Center on April 15, 1989. Subsequently, on May 1, 1989, the individual received advice from the Service Center concerning the written request made on April 1. Because the individual filed his tax return prior to the date on which written advice from the Service was received, the individual did not rely on the Service's written advice for purposes of section 6404(f). If, however, the individual amends his tax return to conform with the written advice received from the Service, the individual will be considered to have reasonably relied upon the Service's advice.

*Example 4.* Individual A, on May 1, 1989, received advice from the Service that concluded that interest paid by the taxpayer with respect to a specific loan was interest paid or accrued in connection with a trade or business, within the meaning of section 163(h)(2)(A) of the Code. The advice relates to a continuing action. Therefore, provided the facts submitted by the taxpayer to obtain the advice remain adequate and accurate (that is, the circumstances relating to the indebtedness do not change), Individual A may rely on the Service's advice for subsequent taxable years until the individual is put on notice that the advice no longer represents Service position and, thus, is no longer valid.

*Example 5.* An individual, on June 1, 1989, received advice from the Service that concluded that no gain or loss would be recognized with respect to a transfer of property to his spouse under section 1041. The advice does not relate to a continuing action. Therefore, the taxpayer may not rely on the advice of the Service for transfers other than the transfer discussed in the taxpayer's written request for advice.

(g) *Effective date.*—Section 6404(f) shall apply with respect to advice requested on or after January 1, 1989. [Reg. § 301.6404-3.]

☐ [*T.D. 8254, 5-12-89. Redesignated and amended by T.D. 8299, 4-16-90.*]

### [Reg. § 301.6404-4]

**§ 301.6404-4. Suspension of interest and certain penalties when the Internal Revenue Service does not timely contact the taxpayer.**—(a) *Suspension.*—(1) *In general.*—Except as provided in paragraph (b) of this section, if an individual taxpayer files a return of tax imposed by subtitle A on or before the due date for the return (including extensions) and the Internal Revenue Service does not timely provide the taxpayer with a notice specifically stating the amount of any increased liability and the basis for that liability, then the IRS must suspend the imposition of any interest, penalty, addition to tax, or additional amount, with respect to any failure relating to the return that is computed by reference to the period of time the failure continues to exist and that is properly allocable to the suspension period. The notice described in this paragraph (a) is timely if provided before the close of the 18- month period (36-month period in the case of notices provided after November 25, 2007, subject to the provisions of paragraph (a)(5)) beginning on the later of the date on which the return is filed or the due date of the return without regard to extensions.

(2) *Treatment of amended returns and other documents.*— (i) *Amended returns filed on or after December 21, 2005, that show an increase in tax liability.*—If a taxpayer, on or after December 21, 2005, provides to the IRS an amended return or one or more other signed written documents showing an increase in tax liability, the date on which the return was filed will, for purposes of this paragraph (a), be the date on which the last of the documents was provided. Documents described in this paragraph (a)(2)(i) are provided on the date that they are received by the IRS.

(ii) *Amended returns that show a decrease in tax liability.*—If a taxpayer provides to the IRS an amended return or other signed written document that shows a decrease in tax liability, any interest, penalty, addition to tax, or additional amount will not be suspended if the IRS at any time proposes to adjust the changed item or items on the amended return or other signed written document.

(iii) *Amended returns and other documents as notice.*—(A) As to the items reported, an amended return or one or more other signed written documents showing that the taxpayer owes an additional amount of tax for the taxable year serves as the notice described in paragraph (a)(1) of this section with respect to the items reported on the amended return.

(B) *Example.*—An individual taxpayer timely files a Federal income tax return for taxable year 2008 on April 15, 2009. On January 19, 2010, the taxpayer mails to the IRS an amended return reporting an additional item of income and an increased tax liability for taxable year 2008. The IRS receives the amended return on January 21, 2010. The amended return will be treated for purposes of this paragraph (a) as filed on January 21, 2010, the date the IRS received it. Pursuant to paragraph (a)(2)(iii) of this section, the amended return serves as the notice described in paragraph (a)(1) of this section with respect to the item reported on the amended return. Accordingly, because the filing of the amended return and the provision of notice occur simultaneously, no suspension of any interest, penalty, addition to tax or additional amount will occur under this paragraph (a) with respect to the item reported on the amended return.

(iv) *Joint return after filing separate return.*—A joint return filed under section 6013(b) is subject to the rules for amended returns described in this paragraph (a)(2). The IRS will not suspend any interest, penalty, addition to tax, or additional amount on a joint return filed under section 6013(b) after the filing of a separate return

unless each spouse's separate return, if required to be filed, was timely.

(3) *Separate application.*—This paragraph (a) shall be applied separately with respect to each item or adjustment.

(4) *Duration of suspension period.*—The suspension period described in paragraph (a)(1) of this section begins the day after the close of the 18-month period (36-month period, in the case of notices provided after November 25, 2007, subject to the provisions of paragraph (a)(5)) beginning on the later of the date on which the return is filed or the due date of the return without regard to extensions. The suspension period ends 21 days after the earlier of the date on which the IRS mails the required notice to the taxpayer's last known address, the date on which the required notice is hand-delivered to the taxpayer, or the date on which the IRS receives an amended return or other signed written document showing an increased tax liability.

(5) *Certain notices provided on or after November 26, 2007.*—If the IRS provides the notice described in paragraph (a)(1) of this section to a taxpayer on or after November 26, 2007, and the notice relates to an individual Federal income tax return that was timely filed before that date, the following rules will apply:

(i) *Eighteen-month period has closed.*—If, as of November 25, 2007, the 18-month period described in paragraph (a)(1) of this section has closed and the IRS has not provided the taxpayer with the notice described in that paragraph (a)(1), the suspension described in paragraph (a)(1) of this section will begin on the day after the close of the 18-month period. The suspension will end on the date that is 21 days after the notice is provided.

(ii) *All other cases.*—In all other cases, the suspension described in paragraph (a)(1) of this section will begin on the day after the close of the 36-month period described in that paragraph (a)(1) and end on the date that is 21 days after the notice described in paragraph (a)(1) of this section is provided.

(6) *Examples.*—The following examples, which assume that no exceptions in section 6404(g)(2) to the general rule of suspension apply, illustrate the rules of this paragraph (a).

*Example 1.* An individual taxpayer timely files a Federal income tax return for taxable year 2005 on April 17, 2006. On December 11, 2007, the taxpayer mails to the IRS an amended return reporting an additional item of income and an increased tax liability for taxable year 2005. The IRS receives the amended return on December 13, 2007. On January 16, 2008, the IRS provides the taxpayer with a notice stating that the taxpayer has an additional tax liability based on the disallowance of a deduction the taxpayer claimed on his original return and did not change on his amended return. The date the amended return was received substitutes for the date that the original return was filed with respect to the additional item of tax liability reported on the amended return. Thus, the IRS will not suspend any interest, penalty, addition to tax, or additional amount with respect to the additional item of income and the increased tax liability reported on the amended return. The suspension period for the additional tax liability based on the IRS's disallowance of the deduction begins on October 17, 2007, so the IRS will suspend any interest, penalty, addition to tax, and additional amount with respect to the disallowed deduction and additional tax liability from that date through February 6, 2008, which is 21 days after the IRS provided notice of the additional tax liability and the basis for that liability. The suspension period in this example begins 18 months after filing the return (not 36 months) because, as of November 25, 2007, the 18-month period beginning on the date the return was filed had closed without the IRS giving notice of the additional liability. Thus, under the rules in paragraph (a)(5) of this section, the suspension period begins 18 months from the April 17, 2006 return filing date.

*Example 2.* An individual taxpayer files a Federal income tax return for taxable year 2008 on April 15, 2009. The taxpayer consents to extend the time within which the IRS may assess any tax due on the return until June 30, 2013. On December 20, 2012, the IRS provides a notice to the taxpayer specifically stating the taxpayer's liability and the basis for the liability. The suspension period for the liability identified by the IRS begins on April 15, 2012, so the IRS will suspend any interest, penalty, addition to tax, and additional amount with respect to that liability from that date through January 10, 2013, which is 21 days after the IRS provided notice of the additional tax liability and the basis for that liability.

(7) *Notice of liability and the basis for the liability.*—(i) *In general.*— Notice to the taxpayer must be in writing and specifically state the amount of the liability and the basis for the liability. The notice must provide the taxpayer with sufficient information to identify which items of income, deduction, loss, or credit the IRS has adjusted or proposes to adjust, and the reason for that adjustment. Notice of the

reason for the adjustment does not require a detailed explanation or a citation to any Internal Revenue Code section or other legal authority. The IRS need not incorporate all of the information necessary to satisfy the notice requirement within a single document or provide all of the information at the same time. Documents that may contain information sufficient to constitute notice, either alone or in conjunction with other documents, include, but are not limited to, statutory notices of deficiency; examination reports (for example, Form 4549, *Income Tax Examination Changes* or Form 886-A, *Explanation of Items*); Form 870, *Waiver of Restriction on Assessments and Collection of Deficiency in Tax and Acceptance of Overassessment*; notices of proposed deficiency that allow the taxpayer an opportunity for review in the Office of Appeals (30-day letters); notices pursuant to section 6213(b) (mathematical or clerical errors); and notice and demand for payment of a jeopardy assessment under section 6861.

(ii) *Tax attributable to TEFRA partnership items.*—Notice to the partner or the tax matters partner (TMP) of a partnership subject to the unified audit and litigation procedures of subchapter C of chapter 63 of subtitle F of the Internal Revenue Code (TEFRA partnership procedures) that provides specific information about the basis for the adjustments to partnership items is sufficient notice if a partner could reasonably compute the specific tax attributable to the partnership item based on the proposed adjustments as applied to the partner's individual tax situation. Documents provided by the IRS during a TEFRA partnership proceeding that may contain information sufficient to satisfy the notice requirements include, but are not limited to, a Notice of Final Partnership Administrative Adjustment (FPAA); examination reports (for example, Form 4605-A or Form 886-A); or a letter that allows the partners an opportunity for review in the Office of Appeals (60-day letter).

(iii) *Examples.*—The following examples illustrate the rules of this paragraph (a)(7).

*Example 1.* During an audit of Taxpayer A's 2005 taxable year return, the IRS questions a charitable deduction claimed on the return. The IRS provides A with a 30-day letter that proposes to disallow the charitable contribution deduction resulting in a deficiency of $1,000 and informs A that A may file a written protest of the proposed disallowance with the Office of Appeals within 30 days. The letter includes as an attachment a copy of the revenue agent's report that states, "It has not been established that the amount shown on your return as a charitable contribution was paid during the tax year. Therefore, this deduction is not allowable." The information in the 30-day letter and attachment provides A with notice of the specific amount of the liability and the basis for that liability as described in this paragraph (a)(7).

*Example 2.* Taxpayer B is a partner in partnership P, a TEFRA partnership for taxable year 2005. B claims a distributive share of partnership income on B's Federal income tax return for 2005 timely filed on April 17, 2006. On October 1, 2007, during the course of a partnership audit of P for taxable year 2005, the IRS provides P's TMP with a 60-day letter proposing to adjust P's income by $10,000. The IRS previously had provided the TMP with a copy of the examination report explaining that the adjustment was based on $10,000 of unreported net income. On October 31, 2007, P's TMP informs B of the proposed adjustment as required by § 301.6223(g)-1(b). By accounting for B's distributive share of the $10,000 of unreported income from P with B's other income tax items, B can determine B's tax attributable to the $10,000 partnership adjustment. The information in the 60-day letter and the examination report allows B to compute the specific amount of the liability attributable to the adjustment to the partnership item and the basis for that adjustment and therefore satisfies the notice requirement of paragraph (a). Because the IRS provided that notice to the TMP, B's agent under the TEFRA partnership provisions, within 18 months of the April 17, 2006 filing date of B's return, any interest, penalty, addition to tax, or additional amount with respect to B's tax liability attributable to B's distributive share of the $10,000 of unreported partnership income will not be suspended under section 6404(g).

(8) *Providing notice.*—(i) *In general.*—The IRS may provide notice by mail or in person to the taxpayer or the taxpayer's representative. If the IRS mails the notice, it must be sent to the taxpayer's last known address under rules similar to section 6212(b), except that certified or registered mail is not required. Notice is considered provided as of the date of mailing or delivery in person.

(ii) *Providing notice in TEFRA partnership proceedings.*—In the case of TEFRA partnership proceedings, the IRS must provide notice of final partnership administrative adjustments (FPAA) by mail to those partners specified in section 6223. Within 60 days of an FPAA being mailed, the TMP is required to forward notice of the FPAA to those partners not entitled to direct notice from the IRS under section 6223. Certain partners with small interests in partnerships with more than 100 partners may form a Notice Group and designate a partner

to receive the FPAA on their behalf. The IRS may provide other information after the beginning of the partnership administrative proceeding to the TMP who, in turn, must provide that information to the partners specified in § 301.6223(g)-1 within 30 days of receipt. Pass-thru partners who receive notices and other information from the IRS or the TMP must forward that notice or information within 30 days to those holding an interest through the pass-thru partner. Information provided by the IRS to the TMP is deemed to be notice for purposes of this section to those partners specified in § 301.6223(g)-1 as of the date the IRS provides that notice to the TMP. A similar rule applies to notice provided to the designated partner of a Notice Group, and to notice provided to a pass-thru partner. In the foregoing situations, the TMP, designated partner, and pass-thru partner are agents for direct and indirect partners. Consequently, notice to these agents is deemed to be notice to the partners for whom they act.

(b) *Exceptions.*—(1) *Failure to file tax return or to pay tax.*—Paragraph (a) of this section does not apply to any penalty imposed by section 6651.

(2) *Fraud.*—Paragraph (a) of this section does not apply to any interest, penalty, addition to tax, or additional amount for a year involving a false or fraudulent return. If a taxpayer files a fraudulent return for a particular year, paragraph (a) of this section may apply to any other tax year of the taxpayer that does not involve fraud. Fraud affecting a particular item on a return precludes paragraph (a) of this section from applying to any other items on that return.

(3) *Tax shown on return.*—Paragraph (a) of this section does not apply to any interest, penalty, addition to tax, or additional amount with respect to any tax liability shown on a return.

(4) *Gross misstatement.*—(i) *Description.*—Paragraph (a) of this section does not apply to any interest, penalty, addition to tax, or additional amount with respect to a gross misstatement. A *gross misstatement* for purposes of this paragraph (b) means:

(A) a substantial omission of income as described in section 6501(e)(1) or section 6229(c)(2);

(B) a gross valuation misstatement within the meaning of section 6662(h)(2)(A) and (B); or

(C) a misstatement to which the penalty under section 6702(a) applies.

(ii) *Effect of gross misstatement.*—If a gross misstatement occurs, then paragraph (a) of this section does not apply to any interest, penalty, addition to tax, or additional amount with respect to any items of income omitted from the return and with respect to overstated deductions, even though one or more of the omitted items would not constitute a substantial omission, gross valuation misstatement, or misstatement to which section 6702(a) applies.

(5) *Listed transactions and undisclosed reportable transactions.*—(i) *In general.*—The general rule of suspension under section 6404(g)(1) does not apply to any interest, penalty, addition to tax, or additional amount with respect to any listed transaction as defined in section 6707A(c) or any undisclosed reportable transaction. For purposes of this section, an *undisclosed reportable transaction* is a reportable transaction described in the regulations under section 6011 that is not adequately disclosed under those regulations and that is not a listed transaction. The date that the IRS provides notice to the taxpayer specifically stating the taxpayer's liability regarding a listed transaction or an undisclosed reportable transaction and the basis for that liability is the controlling date for determining whether the transaction is a listed transaction or an undisclosed reportable transaction for purposes of the suspension rules under section 6404(g).

(ii) *Special rule for certain listed or undisclosed reportable transactions.*—With respect to interest relating to listed transactions and undisclosed reportable transactions accruing on or before October 3, 2004, the exception to the general rule of interest suspension will not apply to a taxpayer who is a participant in a settlement initiative with respect to that transaction, to any transaction in which the taxpayer has acted reasonably and in good faith, or to a closed transaction. For purposes of this special rule, a "participant in a settlement initiative," a "taxpayer acting in good faith," and a "closed transaction" have the following meanings:

(A) *Participant in a settlement initiative.*—(1) *Participant in a settlement initiative who, as of January 23, 2006, had not reached agreement with the IRS.*—A *participant in a settlement initiative* includes a taxpayer who, as of January 23, 2006, was participating in a settlement initiative described in Internal Revenue Service Announcement 2005-80, 2005-2 C.B. 967. See § 601.601(d)(2)(ii)(b) of this chapter. A taxpayer participates in the initiative by complying with Section 5 of the Announcement. A taxpayer is not a participant in a settlement initiative if, after January 23, 2006, the taxpayer withdraws from or terminates participation in the initiative, or the IRS determines that a settlement agreement will not be reached under the initiative within a reasonable period of time.

*(2) Participant in a settlement initiative who, as of January 23, 2006, had reached agreement with the IRS.*—A *participant in a settlement initiative* is a taxpayer who, as of January 23, 2006, had entered into a settlement agreement under Announcement 2005-80 or any other prior or contemporaneous settlement initiative either offered through published guidance or, if the initiative was not formally published, direct contact with taxpayers known to have participated in a tax shelter promotion.

(B) *Taxpayer acting in good faith .*—(1) *In general.*—The IRS may suspend interest relating to a listed transaction or an undisclosed reportable transaction accruing on or before October 3, 2004, if the taxpayer has acted reasonably and in good faith. The IRS's determination of whether a taxpayer has acted reasonably and in good faith will take into account all the facts and circumstances surrounding the transaction. The facts and circumstances include, but are not limited to, whether the taxpayer disclosed the transaction and the taxpayer's course of conduct after being identified as participating in the transaction, including the taxpayer's response to opportunities afforded to the taxpayer to settle the transaction, and whether the taxpayer engaged in unreasonable delay at any stage of the matter.

*(2) Presumption.*—If a taxpayer and the IRS promptly enter into a settlement agreement with respect to a transaction on terms proposed by the IRS or, in the event of atypical facts and circumstances, on terms more favorable to the taxpayer, and the taxpayer has complied with the terms of that agreement without unreasonable delay, the taxpayer will be presumed to have acted reasonably and in good faith except in rare and unusual circumstances. Rare and unusual circumstances must involve specific actions involving harm to tax administration. Even if a taxpayer does not qualify for the presumption described in this paragraph (b)(5)(iii)(B)(2), the taxpayer may still be granted interest suspension under the general facts and circumstances test set forth in paragraph (b)(5)(iii)(B)(1) of this section.

*(3) Examples.*—The following examples illustrate the rules the IRS uses in determining whether a taxpayer has acted reasonably and in good faith.

*Example 1.* The taxpayer participated in a listed transaction. The IRS, in a letter sent directly to the taxpayer in July 2005, proposed a settlement of the transaction. The taxpayer informed the IRS of his interest in the settlement within the prescribed time period. The revenue agent assigned to the taxpayer's case was not able to calculate the taxpayer's liability under the settlement or tender a closing agreement to the taxpayer until March 2006. The taxpayer promptly executed the closing agreement and returned it to the IRS with a proposal for arrangements to pay the agreed-upon liability. The IRS agreed with the proposed arrangements for full payment. For purposes of the application of section 6404(g)(2)(E), the taxpayer has acted reasonably and in good faith. Interest accruing on or before October 3, 2004, relating to the transaction in which the taxpayer participated will be suspended.

*Example 2.* The facts are the same as in *Example 1*, except that the letter was sent by the IRS in February 2006, and the closing agreement was tendered to the taxpayer in April 2006. For purposes of the application of section 6404(g)(2)(E), the taxpayer has acted reasonably and in good faith. Interest accruing on or before October 3, 2004, relating to the transaction in which the taxpayer participated will be suspended.

*Example 3.* The taxpayer participated in a listed transaction. In response to an offer of settlement extended by the IRS in August 2005, the taxpayer informed the IRS of her interest in entering into a closing agreement on the terms proposed by the IRS. The revenue agent assigned to the transaction calculated the taxpayer's liability under the settlement and tendered a closing agreement to the taxpayer in November 2005. The taxpayer executed the closing agreement but failed to make any arrangement for payment of the agreed-upon liability stated in the closing agreement. Taking into account all the facts and circumstances surrounding the transaction, the taxpayer did not act reasonably and in good faith. Interest accruing on or before October 3, 2004, relating to the transaction in which the taxpayer participated will not be suspended.

*Example 4.* The taxpayer participated in a listed transaction. In a letter sent by the IRS directly to the taxpayer in July 2005, the IRS extended an offer of settlement. The July 2005 letter informed the taxpayer that, absent atypical facts and circumstances, the taxpayer should not expect resolution of the tax issues on more favorable terms than proposed in the letter. The taxpayer declined the proposed settlement terms of the letter and proceeded to Appeals to present what the taxpayer claimed were atypical facts and circum-

stances. The administrative file did not contain sufficient information bearing on atypical facts and circumstances, and the taxpayer failed to provide additional information when requested by Appeals to explain how the transaction originally proposed to the taxpayer differed in structure or types of tax benefits claimed, from the transaction as implemented by the taxpayer. Appeals determined that the taxpayer's facts and circumstances were not significantly different from those of other taxpayers who participated in that listed transaction and thus, were not atypical. In September 2006, the taxpayer and Appeals entered into a closing agreement on terms consistent with those originally proposed in the July 2005 letter. The taxpayer has complied with the terms of that closing agreement. For purposes of the application of section 6404(g)(2)(E), this taxpayer is not presumed to have acted reasonably and in good faith; instead, the IRS will apply the general rule to determine whether to suspend interest accruing on or before October 3, 2004, relating to the transaction in which the taxpayer participated.

*Example 5.* The facts are the same as in *Example 4*, except that Appeals agrees that atypical facts were present that warrant additional concessions by the government. A settlement is reached on terms more favorable to the taxpayer than those proposed in the July 2005 letter. For purposes of the application of section 6404(g)(2)(E), this taxpayer is presumed to have acted reasonably and in good faith, and absent evidence of rare or unusual circumstances harmful to tax administration, is eligible for suspension of interest accruing on or before October 3, 2004, relating to the transaction in which the taxpayer participated.

(C) *Closed transactions.*—A transaction is considered closed for purposes of this clause if, as of December 14, 2005, the assessment of all federal income taxes for the taxable year in which the tax liability to which the interest relates is prevented by the operation of any law or rule of law, or a closing agreement under section 7121 has been entered into with respect to the tax liability arising in connection with the transaction.

(c) *Special rules.*—(1) *Tentative carryback and refund adjustments.*—If an amount applied, credited or refunded under section 6411 exceeds the overassessment properly attributable to a tentative carryback or refund adjustment, any interest, penalty, addition to tax, or additional amount with respect to the excess will not be suspended.

(2) *Election under section 183(e).*—(i) *In general.*—If a taxpayer elects under section 183(e) to defer the determination of whether the presumption that an activity is engaged in for profit applies, the 18-month (or 36-month) notification period described in paragraph (a)(1) of this section will be tolled for the period to which the election applies. If the 18-month (or 36-month) notification period has passed as of the date the section 183(e) election is made, the suspension period described in paragraph (a)(4) of this section will be tolled for the period to which the election applies and will resume the day after the tolling period ends. Tolling will begin on the date the election is made and end on the later of the date the return for the last taxable year to which the election applies is filed or is due without regard to extensions.

(ii) *Example.*—In taxable year 2007, taxpayer begins training and showing horses. On January 4, 2011, the taxpayer elects under section 183(e) to defer the determination of whether the horse-related activity will be presumed (under section 183(d)) to be engaged in for profit. Accordingly, under section 183(e)(1), a determination of whether the section 183(d) presumption applies will not occur before the close of the 2013 taxable year. Assume that in 2014, the IRS is considering issuing a notice of deficiency for taxable year 2009 regarding tax deductions claimed for the horse-related activity. Pursuant to paragraph (c)(2)(i) of this section, the 36-month notification period under paragraph (a)(1) of this section will be tolled with respect to taxable year 2009 for the period to which the section 183(e) election applies. This tolling of the notification period begins on January 4, 2011 (the date the taxpayer made the section 183(e) election) and ends on the later of April 15, 2014, or the date the taxpayer's return for taxable year 2013 is filed.

(d) *Effective/Applicability date.*—Paragraph (b)(5) of these regulations applies to interest relating to listed transactions and undisclosed reportable transactions accruing before, on, or after October 3, 2004. Paragraphs (a), (b)(1) through (b)(4), and (c) are effective on August 22, 2011. [Reg. § 301.6404-4.]

☐ [*T.D. 9488, 6-15-2010. Amended by T.D. 9545, 8-19-2011.*]

### [Reg. § 301.6405-1]

**§301.6405-1. Reports of refunds and credits.**—Section 6405 requires that a report be made to the Joint Committee on Taxation of proposed refunds or credits in excess of $100,000 of any income tax (including any qualified State individual income tax collected by the Federal Government), war profits tax, excess profits tax, estate tax, or gift tax. An exception is provided under which refunds and credits made after July 1, 1972, and attributable to an election under section 165(h) to deduct a disaster loss for the taxable year in which the disaster occurred, may be made prior to the submission of such report to the Joint Committee on Taxation. [Reg. §301.6405-1.]

☐ [*T.D. 6119, 12-31-54. Amended by T.D. 7224, 12-5-72 and T.D. 7577, 12-19-78.*]

# RULES OF SPECIAL APPLICATION

**[Reg. §1.6411-1]**

**§1.6411-1. Tentative carryback adjustments.**—(a) *In general.*— Any taxpayer who has a net operating loss under section 172, a net capital loss under section 1211(a) which is a carryback under section 1212, or an unused investment credit under section 46, may file an application under section 6411 for a tentative carryback adjustment of the taxes for taxable years prior to the taxable year of the net operating or capital loss or the unused credit, whichever is applicable, which are affected by the net operating loss carryback, the capital loss carryback, or the unused investment credit carryback, resulting from such loss or unused credit. The regulations under section 6411 shall apply with respect to investment credit carrybacks for taxable years ending after December 31, 1961, but only with respect to applications for tentative carryback adjustments for investment credit carrybacks filed after November 2, 1966. The right to file an application for a tentative carryback adjustment is not limited to corporations, but is available to any taxpayer otherwise entitled to carry back a loss or unused credit. A corporation may file an application for a tentative carryback adjustment even though it has not extended the time for payment of tax under section 6164. In determining any decrease in tax under §§1.6411-1 through 1.6411-4, the decrease in tax is determined net of any increase in the tax imposed by section 56 (relating to the minimum tax for tax preferences).

(b) *Contents of application.*—(1) The application for a tentative carryback adjustment shall be filed, in the case of a corporation, on Form 1139, and in the case of taxpayers other than corporations, on Form 1045. The application shall be filled out in accordance with the instructions accompanying the form, and all information required by the form and the instructions must be furnished by the taxpayer.

(2) An application for a tentative carryback adjustment does not constitute a claim for credit or refund. If such application is disallowed by the district director or director of a service center in whole or in part, no suit may be maintained in any court for the recovery of any tax based on such application. The filing of an application for a tentative carryback adjustment will not constitute the filing of a claim for credit or refund within the meaning of section 6511 for purposes of determining whether a claim for credit or refund was filed prior to the expiration of the applicable period of limitation. The taxpayer, however, may file a claim for credit or refund under section 6402 at any time prior to the expiration of the applicable period of limitation, and may maintain a suit based on such claim if it is disallowed or if the district director or director of a service center does not act on the claim within six months from the date it is filed. Such claim may be filed before, simultaneously with, or after the filing of the application for a tentative carryback adjustment. A claim for credit or refund under section 6402 filed after the filing of an application for a tentative carryback adjustment is not to be considered an amendment of such application. Such claim, however, in proper cases may constitute an amendment to a prior claim filed under section 6402.

(c) *Time and place for filing application.*—Except as otherwise provided in this paragraph the application for a tentative carryback adjustment shall be filed on or after the date of the filing of the return for the taxable year of the net operating loss, net capital loss, or unused investment credit and shall be filed within a period of twelve months from the end of such taxable year. With respect to any portion of an investment credit carryback from a taxable year attributable to a net operating loss carryback or a capital loss carryback from a subsequent taxable year, the twelve-month period shall be measured from the end of such subsequent taxable year. In the case of an application for a tentative carryback adjustment attributable to the carryback of an unused investment credit, the twelve-month period for filing shall not expire before the close of December 31, 1966. Any application filed prior to the date on which the return for the taxable year of the loss or unused credit is filed shall be considered to have been filed on the date such return is filed. In the case of an application filed before April 15, 1968, the application shall be filed with the internal revenue officer to whom the tax was paid or by whom the assessment was made. Except as provided in paragraph (b) of §301.6091-1 (relating to hand-carried documents), in the case of an application filed after April 14, 1968, if the tax was paid to the

**[Reg. §301.6407-1]**

**§301.6407-1. Date of allowance of refund or credit.**—The date on which the district director or the director of the regional service center, or an authorized certifying officer designated by either of them, first certifies the allowance of an overassessment in respect of any internal revenue tax shall be considered as the date of allowance of refund or credit in respect of such tax. [Reg. §301.6407-1.]

☐ [*T.D. 6119, 12-31-54. Amended by T.D. 6585, 12-27-61.*]

Director of International Operations, the application shall be filed with him; otherwise the application shall be filed with the internal revenue office with which the return was filed. [Reg. §1.6411-1.]

☐ [*T.D. 6364, 2-13-59. Amended by T.D. 6862, 11-17-65, T.D. 6950, 4-3-68, T.D. 7301, 1-3-74, T.D. 7564, 9-11-78 and T.D. 8107, 12-1-86.*]

**[Reg. §5.6411-1]**

**§5.6411-1. Tentative refund under claim of right adjustment (Temporary).**—(a) *Effective date.*—This section applies to applications for tentative refunds filed after November 5, 1978, under section 6411(d).

(b) *In general.*—Section 6411(d) allows taxpayers to apply for a tentative refund of amounts treated under section 1341(b)(1) as an overpayment of tax under a claim of right adjustment. This section contains rules for filing an application for this tentative refund. The computation of amounts treated as an overpayment must be made in accordance with section 1341 and the regulations under that section.

(c) *Method of applying for tentative refund.*—(1) *In general.*—For a corporation, the application is made by filing Form 1139. For taxpayers other than corporations, the application is made by filing Form 1045. The application must be made by filing those forms even if the taxpayer is not applying for a tentative carryback adjustment under section 6411(a). If the taxpayer files the form to apply for the section 6411(d) tentative refund only, it may disregard those lines on the form used to compute the section 6411(a) carryback adjustment. If the taxpayer has a carryback of a net operating loss, credit, or capital loss for the taxable year (determined without the deduction described in section 1341(a)(2)) and applies for both the section 6411(a) tentative carryback adjustment and the section 6411(d) tentative refund, an ordering rule applies. The taxpayer must take into account any adjustments made in applying for the tentative carryback adjustment under section 6411(a) before determining the amount of the overpayment for which an application under section 6411(d) is being made. The taxpayer must attach to the form a separate schedule containing the information required under paragraph (d) of this section.

(2) *Applications made before.*—February 7, 1980. Applications made before February 7, 1980 that are made under penalties of perjury will be considered meeting the requirements of this section if made by filing a separate statement whether or not it is attached to Form 1139 or 1045. This application, however, must contain the information required under paragraph (d) of this section (other than paragraph (d)(2)).

(d) *Information required.*—(1) *In general.*—The application must contain (i) the taxpayer's name, address, and identification number and (ii) the information set forth in paragraph (d)(2) and (3) of this section, determined in accordance with section 1341 and the regulations under that section. For example, the decrease in tax under paragraph (d)(3)(iii) of this section is determined under §1.1341-1(d)(4).

(2) *Computation under section 1341(a)(4).*—The application must contain the following information related to the computation under section 1341(a)(4):

(i) The amount of income restored by the taxpayer to another during the taxable year and the amount of the corresponding deduction described in section 1341(a)(2);

(ii) The tax for the taxable year computed with the deduction described in section 1341(a)(2); and

(iii) The tax for each prior taxable year (determined before adjustment under section 1341) to which any net operating loss described in section 1341(b)(4)(A) may be carried and the decrease in tax for each of those years that results from the carryback of that loss.

(3) *Computation under section 1341(a)(5).*—The application must contain the following information related to the computation under section 1341(a)(5):

(i) The tax for the taxable year without the deduction described in section 1341(a)(2);

(ii) The tax for each prior taxable year (determined before adjustment under section 1341) for which a decrease in tax is computed under section 1341(a)(5)(B);

(iii) The decrease in tax for each prior taxable year computed under section 1341(a)(5)(B), including any decrease resulting from a net operating loss or capital loss described in section 1341(b)(4)(B); and

(iv) The amount treated as an overpayment of tax under section 1341(b)(1).

(e) *Time and place for filing.*—The application must be filed no earlier than the date of filing the return for the taxable year of restoration and no later than the date 12 months from the last day of that taxable year. The application must be filed with the Internal Revenue Service Center (or other office) where the taxpayer filed its return for the taxable year of restoration.

(f) *Not a claim for credit or refund.*—An application for tentative refund under section 6411(d) is not a claim for credit or refund. The principles of paragraph (b)(2) of §1.6411-1 apply in determining the effect of an application for a tentative refund. For example, the filing of an application for tentative refund under section 6411(d) is not a claim for credit or refund in determining whether a claim for credit or refund was timely filed. [Temporary Reg. §5.6411-1.]

☐ [*T.D. 7672, 2-6-80.*]

### [Reg. §301.6411-1]

**§301.6411-1. Tentative carryback adjustments.**—For regulations under this section 6411, see §§1.6411-1 to 1.6411-4, inclusive, of this chapter (Income Tax Regulations). [Reg. §301.6411-1.]

☐ [*T.D. 6119, 12-31-54. Amended by T.D. 6498, 10-24-60.*]

### [Reg. §1.6411-2]

**§1.6411-2. Computation of tentative carryback adjustment.**— (a) *Tax previously determined.*—The taxpayer is to determine the amount of decrease, attributable to the carryback, in tax previously determined for each taxable year before the taxable year of the net operating loss, net capital loss, or unused investment credit. The tax previously determined is to be ascertained in accordance with the method prescribed in section 1314(a). Thus, the tax previously determined will be the tax shown on the return as filed, increased by any amounts assessed (or collected without assessment) as deficiencies before the date of the filing of the application for a tentative carryback adjustment, and decreased by any amounts abated, credited, refunded, or otherwise repaid prior to that date. Any items as to which the Commissioner and the taxpayer are in disagreement at the time of the filing of the application shall, for purposes of §1.6411-2, be taken into account in ascertaining the tax previously determined only if, and to the extent that, they were reported on the return, or were reflected in any amounts assessed (or collected without assessment) as deficiencies, or in any amounts abated, credited, refunded, or otherwise repaid, before the date of filing the application. The tax previously determined, therefore, will reflect the foreign tax credit and the credit for tax withheld at source provided in section 33.

(b) *Decrease attributable to carryback.*—After ascertaining the tax previously determined in the manner described in paragraph (a) of this section, the taxpayer shall determine the decrease in tax previously determined attributable to the carryback and any related adjustments on the basis of the items of tax taken into account in computing the tax previously determined. In determining any decrease attributable to the carryback or any related adjustment, items shall be taken into account under this subsection only to the extent that they were reported on the return, or were reflected in amounts assessed (or collected without assessment) as deficiencies, or in amounts abated, credited, refunded, or otherwise repaid, before the date of filing the application for a tentative carryback adjustment. If the Commissioner and the taxpayer are in disagreement as to the proper treatment of any item, it shall be assumed, for purposes of determining the decrease in the tax previously determined, that the item was reported correctly by the taxpayer unless, and to the extent that, the disagreement has resulted in the assessment of a deficiency (or the collection of an amount without an assessment), or the allowing or making of an abatement, credit, refund, or other repayment, before the date of filing the application. Thus, if the taxpayer claimed a deduction on its return of $50,000 for salaries paid its officers but the Commissioner proposes that the deduction should not exceed $20,000, and the Commissioner and the taxpayer have not agreed on the amount properly deductible before the date the application for a tentative carryback adjustment is filed, $50,000 shall be considered as the amount properly deductible for purposes of determining the decrease in tax previously determined in respect of the application for a tentative carryback adjustment. In determining the decrease in tax previously determined, any items that are affected by the carryback must be adjusted to reflect the carryback. Thus, unless

otherwise provided, any deduction limited, for example, by adjusted gross income, such as the deduction for medical, dental, etc., expenses, is to be recomputed on the basis of the adjusted gross income as affected by the carryback. See §1.6411-3(d) for rules on the application of the decrease in tax to any tax liability.

(c) *Effective/applicability date.*—These regulations apply with respect to applications for tentative refund filed on or after August 27, 2007. [Reg. §1.6411-2.]

☐ [*T.D. 6364, 2-13-59. Amended by T.D. 7301, 1-3-74; T.D. 9355, 8–24–2007 and T.D. 9499, 8-23-2010.*]

### [Reg. §1.6411-3]

**§1.6411-3. Allowance of adjustments.**—(a) *Time prescribed.*—The Commissioner shall act upon any application for a tentative carryback adjustment filed under section 6411(a) within a period of 90 days from whichever of the following two dates is the later:

(1) The date the application is filed; or

(2) The last day of the month in which falls the last date prescribed by law (including any extension of time granted the taxpayer) for filing the return for the taxable year of the net operating loss, net capital loss, or unused investment credit from which the carryback results.

(b) *Examination.*—Within the 90-day period described in paragraph (a) of this section, the Commissioner shall make, to the extent deemed practicable within this period, an examination of the application to discover omissions and errors of computation. The Commissioner shall determine within this period the decrease in tax previously determined, affected by the carryback or any related adjustments, upon the basis of the application and examination. The decrease shall be determined in the same manner as that provided in section 1314(a) for the determination by the taxpayer of the decrease in taxes previously determined, which must be set forth in the application for a tentative carryback adjustment. The Commissioner, may correct any errors of computation or omissions discovered upon examination of the application. In determining the decrease in tax previously determined which is affected by the carryback or any related adjustment, the Commissioner may correct any mathematical error appearing on the application and may correct any modification required by the law and incorrectly made by the taxpayer in computing the net operating loss, net capital loss, or unused investment credit, the resulting carrybacks, or the net operating loss deduction, capital loss deduction, or investment credit allowable. If the required modification has not been made by the taxpayer and the Commissioner has the necessary information to make the modification within the 90-day period, the Commissioner may, in the Commissioner's discretion, make the modification. In determining the decrease, the Commissioner will not, for example, change the amount claimed on the return as a deduction for depreciation because the Commissioner believes that the taxpayer has claimed an excessive amount; and the Commissioner will not include in gross income any amount not so included by the taxpayer, even though the Commissioner believes that the amount is subject to tax and properly should be included in gross income.

(c) *Disallowance in whole or in part.*—If the Commissioner finds that an application for a tentative carryback adjustment contains material omissions or errors of computation, the Commissioner may disallow the application in whole or in part without further action. If the Commissioner deems that any error of computation can be corrected within the 90-day period, the Commissioner may do so and allow the application in whole or in part. The Commissioner's determination as to whether the Commissioner can correct any error of computation within the 90-day period shall be conclusive. The Commissioner's action in disallowing, in whole or in part, any application for a tentative carryback adjustment shall be final and may not be challenged in any proceeding. The taxpayer may, however, file a claim for credit or refund under section 6402, and may maintain a suit based on the claim if the claim is disallowed or if the Commissioner does not act upon the claim within 6 months from the date it is filed.

(d) *Application of decrease.*—(1) Each decrease determined by the Commissioner in any previously determined tax that is affected by the carryback or any related adjustments shall first be applied against any unpaid amount of the tax with respect to which such decrease was determined. The unpaid amount of tax may include one or more of the following:

(i) An amount with respect to which the taxpayer is delinquent;

(ii) An amount the time for payment of which has been extended under section 6164 and which is due and payable on or after the date of the allowance of the decrease.

(iii) An amount (not including an amount the time for payment of which has been extended under section 6164) which is due and payable on or after the date of the allowance of the decrease, including any assessed liabilities, unassessed liabilities determined in a statutory notice of deficiency, unassessed liabilities identified in a proof of claim filed in a bankruptcy proceeding, and other unassessed liabilities in rare and unusual circumstances.

(2) If the unpaid amount of tax includes more than one unpaid amount, the Commissioner may determine against which amount or amounts, and in what proportion, the decrease is to be applied. In general, however, the decrease will be applied against any amounts described in paragraphs (d)(1)(i) through (iii) of this section in the order named. If there are several amounts of the type described in paragraph (d)(1)(iii) of this section, any amount of the decrease that is to be applied against the amount will be applied by assuming that the tax previously determined minus the amount of the decrease to be so applied is "the tax" and that the taxpayer had elected to pay the tax in installments. The unpaid amount of tax against which a decrease may be applied under paragraph (d)(1) of this section may not include any amount of tax for any taxable year other than the year of the decrease. After making the application, the Commissioner will credit any remainder of the decrease against any unsatisfied amount of any tax for the taxable year immediately preceding the taxable year of the net operating loss, capital loss, or unused investment credit, the time for payment of which has been extended under section 6164.

(3) Any remainder of the decrease after the application and credits may, within the 90-day period, in the discretion of the Commissioner, be credited against any tax liability or installment thereof then due from the taxpayer (including assessed liabilities, unassessed liabilities determined in a statutory notice of deficiency, unassessed liabilities identified in a proof of claim filed in a bankruptcy proceeding, and other unassessed liabilities in rare and unusual circumstances), and, if not so credited, shall be refunded to the taxpayer within the 90-day period.

(e) *Effective/applicability date.*—These regulations apply with respect to applications for tentative refund filed on or after August 27, 2007. [Reg. §1.6411-3.]

☐ [*T.D.* 6364, 2-13-59. *Amended by T.D.* 6950, 4-3-68; *T.D.* 7301, 1-3-74; *T.D.* 9355, 8-24-2007 *and T.D.* 9499, 8-23-2010.]

### [Reg. §1.6411-4]

**§1.6411-4. Consolidated groups.**—For further rules applicable to consolidated groups, see §1.1502-78. For further rules applicable to consolidated groups that include insolvent financial institutions, see §301.6402-7 of this chapter. [Reg. §1.6411-4.]

☐ [*T.D.* 6364, 2-13-59. *Amended by T.D.* 7244, 12-29-72; *T.D.* 8387, 12-30-91 *and T.D.* 8446, 11-5-92.]

### [Reg. §48.6412-1]

**§48.6412-1. Floor stocks credit or refund.**—(a) *In general.*—This section sets forth the procedures to be followed in claiming the credit or refund authorized by section 6412 for manufacturers excise taxes paid in respect of certain articles held by dealers as floor stocks on October 1, 1988. See §48.6412-2 for definitions of the following terms when used in this section: "floor stocks", "inventory date", "dealer", "held by a dealer", "old rate", "new rate", "dealer request limitation date", "claim limitation date", and "tax paid". See §48.6412-3 for determining the amount of tax paid on articles that are held as floor stocks. The manufacturers excise taxes for which credit or refund may be claimed under this section are those imposed by section 4071, relating to tires of the type used on highway vehicles; and section 4081, relating to gasoline. For definition of the term "highway vehicle", see §48.4061(a)-1(d).

(b) *Computation of the amount of floor stocks credit or refund.*—The amount of floor stocks credit or refund which may be claimed by the manufacturer under section 6412(a)(1) may not exceed an amount equal to the difference between the tax paid by the manufacturer on the sale of the article and the amount of tax made applicable to the article on the inventory date. No interest is allowable with respect to any amount of tax credited or refunded under section 6412 and this section. In applying the floor stocks credit or refund provisions, the date on which the manufacturer paid the tax with respect to the article held as floor stocks is not relevant. Thus, the period of limitations provided in section 6511 with respect to claims for credit or refund does not apply; however, see paragraph (f) of this section. For definition of the term "manufacturer", see §48.0-2(a)(4).

(c) *Limitation.*—Except as provided in §48.6412-3, no credit or refund is allowable under this section for an amount paid as tax which may be credited or refunded under any provisions of law other than section 6412(a)(1), or which was allowable as a credit or refund under section 6412 with respect to an earlier inventory date.

(d) *Relationship between credits or refunds for floor stocks and credits or refunds for price readjustments.*—The amount which may be credited or refunded for floor stocks and for price readjustments on an article may not in the aggregate exceed the tax paid in respect of the article. A credit or refund computed on the basis of the old tax rate will be allowed with respect to a price readjustment of an article on which a floor stock credit or refund was allowed, but only if the amount of the floor stock credit or refund otherwise allowable was reduced by taking into account such price readjustment, as determined under §48.6412-3(e). The manufacturer must keep readily available for inspection sufficient records to enable examining officers of the Internal Revenue Service to ascertain the correctness of any claim for credit or refund for a price readjustment of an article on which a floor stock refund was claimed.

(e) *Participation of dealers.*—(1) *Request by dealer.*—On or before the dealer request limitation date, a dealer may submit to a manufacturer a request with respect to a credit or refund allowable under this section for tax paid by the manufacturer with respect to articles held by the dealer as floor stocks. This request may be submitted directly to the manufacturer, or it may be submitted to him indirectly through another dealer in the distribution chain if the request is received by the manufacturer or an authorized agent of the manufacturer on or before the dealer request limitation date.

(2) *Requirements for claim by manufacturer.*—No amount of credit or refund under this section may be claimed by a manufacturer with respect to articles held by a dealer as floor stocks unless—

(i) The claim for the amount is based upon a request submitted by the dealer to the claimant on or before the dealer request limitation date;

(ii) The amount is paid by the claimant to the dealer, or the dealer's written consent to allowance of the credit or refund has been received by the claimant, on or before the claim limitation date; and

(iii) The request by the dealer is supported by an inventory statement, made under the penalties of perjury and signed by the dealer or by the dealer's authorized representative, setting forth the following information:

(A) The name and address of the dealer and of the applicable manufacturer (if the name and address of the applicable manufacturer is unknown to the dealer, these items may be added by any person in the chain of distribution);

(B) The identification number, if any, of the article, such as a serial, stock, model, type, or class number, or some other suitable means of identification;

(C) A brief description of the article, such as its common name or designation; and

(D) The quantity of articles held by the dealer as floor stocks on the inventory date.

(3) *Actual manufacturer unknown.*—If a dealer addresses a request to the person, who from markings on the article the dealer presumes to be the manufacturer, the request may be treated as made to the actual manufacturer if the actual manufacturer accepts the dealer's request.

(4) *Payment to dealer by claimant.*—Payment may be made directly to the dealer or to the dealer's authorized agent or representative by the claimant or by the claimant's authorized agent or representative. If a claimant pays a dealer through the claimant's agent or representative, the evidence must show that the dealer actually received the payment. If a dealer authorizes the claimant to pay the dealer through the dealer's agent or representative, evidence showing receipt of the payment by the agent or representative will be accepted as proof of actual payment to the dealer. Payment shall be made, at the manufacturer's option, in cash, by check, or by credit to the dealer's account as maintained by the claimant. The amount of the payment which may be made by crediting the dealer's account may not exceed the undisputed debit balance due at the time the credit is made. However, payment may be made in merchandise at the dealer's option with the concurrence of the manufacturer.

(5) *Date of performance.*—The date on which any act described in this paragraph (e) is performed by an agent or representative on behalf of a claimant or dealer is deemed to be the date on which the act is performed by the principal.

(6) *Record of inventories.*—For provisions relating to the record of a dealer's inventories to be kept by the claimant, see paragraph (g) of this section.

(7) *Sample written consent.*—No particular form is prescribed or required for the written consent of the dealer described in paragraph (e)(2)(ii) of this section. However, the following is an example of an acceptable consent statement by a dealer:

## Consent Statement of Dealer

(For use by dealer in requesting manufacturer, producer, or importer to obtain credit under section 6412 of the Internal Revenue Code of 1954 with respect to floor stocks.)

I hereby consent to the allowance to the manufacturer, producer, or importer of the floor stocks credit or refund of the excise tax imposed by the Internal Revenue Code of 1954 with respect to the articles in my inventory on_____

*(Name)*

By_____

*(Signature of Officer)*

_____

*(Title)*

_____

*(Date)*

(f) *Procedure for claiming credit or refund.*—(1) *In general.*—Each claim for credit or refund under this section shall be filed on or before the applicable claim limitation date, in the manner and subject to the conditions stated in this section and in § 301.6402-2 of this chapter (Regulations on Procedure and Administration). Either credit or refund, or a combination thereof, may be claimed, but the amount which may be claimed as a credit on a return shall not exceed the total tax liability shown on the return, reduced by the amount of any deposits made under § 48.6302(c)-1 with respect to the return and by any amount of credit claimed on the return pursuant to any provision of law other than section 6412. If the total amount which may be claimed exceeds the amount that may be claimed as credit on a return, the excess amount may be claimed on or before the applicable claim limitation date either as a refund or as a credit on a subsequent return. If credit is claimed the amount of the credit shall be entered as a credit on a timely filed return of tax. The statement described in paragraph (f)(2) of this section must show the amount and date of each previous and concurrent claim for credit or refund under this section and indicate whether any future claims are expected to be filed.

(2) *Supporting evidence to be submitted by the manufacturer.*—No credit or refund shall be allowed under this section unless there is submitted, in support of the claim for credit or refund, a statement signed by the person making the claim, that describes in general terms the articles covered by the claim, sets forth the method of computing the amount claimed (including a description of any procedures used pursuant to § 48.6412-3), and states that—

(i) The claimant paid to the district director or the director of the internal revenue service center the tax for which credit or refund is claimed;

(ii) The total amount claimed represents payments requested by dealers before the dealer request limitation date;

(iii) The total amount claimed either was paid by the claimant to the dealers, or the claimant received the written consent of the dealers to the allowance of the amount claimed;

(iv) The claimant has in his possession, and available for inspection by internal revenue officers, the evidence with respect to inventories required by paragraph (g)(2) of this section, and any written consents referred to in paragraph (f)(2)(iii) of this section; and

(v) No other claim for credit or refund under this section has been or will be made by the claimant with respect to any amount covered by the claim.

(g) *Evidence to be retained in the manufacturer's records.*—Every person filing a claim for credit or refund pursuant to this section shall support the claim by keeping as part of the claimant's records—

(1) The dealer's inventory statements required by paragraph (e)(2)(iii) of this section, to the extent that the articles are covered by the claim;

(2) Records, in respect of the articles held by each dealer, showing—

(i) The name and address of the dealer.

(ii) The quantities of each article held by the dealer as floor stocks by taxable category, for example, by model or type number.

(iii) The amount of tax considered to be paid by the manufacturer with respect to each article held by the dealer, as determined under § 48.6412-3,

(iv) The amount of tax, if any, which the claimant would pay on the sale of each article held by the dealer if the tax were computed at the new rate,

(v) The total amount of reimbursement due the dealer.

(vi) The date on which the claimant received from the dealer the request described in paragraph (e)(1) of this section, but only if payment was not made to the dealer before the dealer request limitation date, and

(vii) The date and amount of each payment to a dealer, or the date of receipt by the claimant from the dealer of a written consent, as set forth in paragraph (e)(2)(ii) of this section; and

(3) Any such written consent received from a dealer.

(h) *Special rules where the presumed manufacturer is the agent of the actual manufacturer.*—For purposes of this section, if a manufacturer sells articles tax-paid to a second manufacturer for resale by the second manufacturer under its own brand name, the second manufacturer may perform any acts and keep any records which are a prerequisite to the first manufacturer's filing a claim for floor stocks credit or refund with respect to the articles. If such a procedure is followed, the claim filed by the first manufacturer shall include a statement indicating the name and address of the second manufacturer and the amount of its claim which relates to articles sold to the second manufacturer.

(i) *Effect on other claims for credit or refund.*—If a claim for credit or refund is made pursuant to section 6416 and the regulations thereunder, relating in part to returned sales, sales for export or for exempt use, sales to States, etc., with respect to a tax imposed by section 4071 or section 4081, and if the claim is made with respect to articles sold by the claimant before the date on which the tax is reduced in rate or terminated, the claim shall be based on the new rate of tax unless the claimant can establish that the tax was imposed at the old rate and that no refund or credit under this section was allowed with respect to the articles. See, however, paragraph (d) of this section.

(j) *Other applicable provisions.*—All provisions of law, including penalties, applicable in respect of the taxes imposed by sections 4071 and 4081 shall, insofar as applicable and not inconsistent with section 6412, apply in respect to the credits and refunds provided for in section 6412 to the same extent as if the credits or refunds constituted overpayments of the taxes. For provisions under which timely mailing is treated as timely filing, and for provisions applicable to the time for performance of acts when the last day falls on Saturday, Sunday, or a legal holiday, see §§ 301.7502-1 and 301.7503-1, respectively, of this chapter (Regulations on Procedure and Administration). [Reg. § 48.6412-1.]

☐ [*T.D.* 8043, 8-8-85.]

### [Reg. § 48.6412-2]

**§ 48.6412-2. Definitions for purposes of floor stocks credit or refund.**—For purposes of section 6412 and the regulations thereunder—

(a) *Floor stocks.*—The term "floor stocks" means any article subject to the tax imposed by section 4071 or section 4081 which—

(1) Is sold by the manufacturer (otherwise than in a tax-free sale) before October 1, 1988,

(2) Is held by a dealer at the first moment on October 1, 1988, and has not been used, and

(3) Is intended for sale.

However, the term "floor stocks" does not include gasoline in retail stocks held at the place where intended to be sold at retail, nor with respect to gasoline held for sale by a producer or importer of gasoline.

(b) *Inventory date.*—The term "inventory date" means the first moment on the date on which an article is treated as floor stocks within the meaning of paragraph (a) of this section.

(c) *Dealer.*—The term "dealer" includes a wholesaler, jobber, distributor, or retailer.

(d) *Held by a dealer.*—(1) *In general.*—(i) An article is considered as "held by a dealer" if title to the article has passed to the dealer (whether or not delivery to the dealer has been made), and if, for purposes of consumption, title to or possession of the article has not at any time been transferred to any person other than a dealer.

(ii) Floor samples, demonstrators, and articles undergoing repair (whether or not on the dealer's premises) that are carried in stock to be sold as new articles, and articles purchased tax-paid by a manufacturer or a sales subsidiary and held by the person on the inventory date for resale as such, will be considered as unused and held by a dealer, if title to or possession of the article has not at any time been transferred to any person for purposes of consumption.

(iii) Articles sold by a dealer to a consumer before the inventory date and thereafter repossessed by the dealer, and articles purchased tax-paid by a manufacturer for use in further manufacture within the meaning of section 4221(d)(6), will not be considered as held by a dealer.

(iv) The determination as to the time title or possession passes for purposes of consumption shall be made under applicable local law.

(2) *Examples.*—The application of this paragraph (d) may be illustrated by the following examples:

*Example (1).* If, under local law, title to an article sold by a dealer under a conditional sales contract is in the dealer on the inventory date, but the consumer has physical possession of the article on that date, the article is not considered as held by the dealer.

*Example (2).* If, under local law, title to an article is in the consumer on the inventory date because the article is specifically identified with a contract, but on that date the dealer still has physical possession of the article, for example, in his will-call department, the article is not considered as held by the dealer on that date because title to the article has passed to the consumer for purposes of consumption.

*Example (3).* If, under local law, title to an article is in the consumer on the inventory date because the dealer transferred the article to a common carrier for delivery to the consumer, the article in transit is not considered as held by the dealer on that date because title has passed to the consumer for purposes of consumption, even though neither the dealer nor the consumer has physical possession of the article.

*Example (4).* If, under local law, title to an article is in the dealer on the inventory date and does not pass to the consumer until delivery by a common carrier, the article in transit shall be considered as held by the dealer on that date because neither the title nor possession has passed to the consumer for purposes of consumption.

*Example (5).* If an article has been mortgaged or otherwise hypothecated by a dealer as security for a loan and, under local law, title to the article is in the creditor on the inventory date, and physical possession is in the dealer, the article shall be considered as held by the dealer on that date because neither title nor possession has passed to the consumer for purposes of consumption.

(e) *Old rate.*—The term "old rate" means the rate of tax in effect with respect to the sale of an article before the date designated in paragraph (a) or (b) of this section on which the tax is reduced in rate or is terminated.

(f) *New rate.*—The term "new rate" means the rate of tax, if any, in effect with respect to the sale of an article on the date designated in paragraph (a) or (b) of this section on which the tax is reduced in rate or is terminated.

(g) *Dealer request limitation date.*—The term "dealer request limitation date" is the date prescribed by section 6412(a)(1) before which the request on which the manufacturer's claim is based must be submitted to the manufacturer by the dealer who held the floor stocks on the inventory date. In the case of an article held by a dealer on October 1, 1988, the dealer request limitation date is January 1, 1989.

(h) *Claim limitation date.*—The term "claim limitation date" means the last date prescribed by section 6412(a)(1) on which refund or credit with respect to floor stocks may be claimed by a manufacturer. In the case of an article held by a dealer on October 1, 1988, the claim limitation date is March 31, 1989.

(i) *Tax paid.*—A tax is considered paid if it was paid or was offset by an allowable credit on the return on which it was reported. [Reg. §48.6412-2.]

☐ [*T.D.* 8043, 8-8-85.]

**[Reg. §48.6412-3]**

**§48.6412-3. Amount of tax paid on each article.**—(a) *General rule.*—For purposes of making the claim for credit or refund under §48.6412-1 in respect of floor stocks held by a dealer, the tax paid on each article must be separately computed. If desired, the procedures set forth in paragraphs (b) through (g) of this section may be used in making the computation. The procedure used in determining the tax paid on an article must also be used in determining the amount of tax, if any, made applicable to the article on the effective date of reduction or repeal of the tax involved. Prior approval of the Internal Revenue Service for the method of computation need not be obtained and should not be requested.

(b) *Selling price.*—In determining the price of an article on which the tax paid is to be computed, the average of the gross selling prices of identical articles sold during a representative period may be used. For example, truck chassis of the same model that are sold by the manufacturer with the same equipment and accessories are identical articles whose selling prices may be computed on the basis of an average.

(c) *Transportation charges.*—In determining the price of an article on which the tax paid is to be computed, the average of the exclusions authorized by section 4216(a) for transportation, delivery, insurance,

installation, etc., for a reasonable category of articles during a representative period may be used.

(d) *Credits for tax paid on inner tubes.*—The average of the credits authorized by section 6416(c) for tax paid on tires or inner tubes may be averaged for a reasonable category of articles during a representative period. The credits shall be subtracted from the gross excise tax to arrive at the net excise tax paid.

(e) *Price readjustments.*—(1) In determining the price on which the tax paid is to be computed, there must be taken into account any price readjustments with respect to which the manufacturer has filed a claim for credit or refund under section 6416(b). Other price readjustments which have been, or are reasonably expected to be, made with respect to the article may, at the option of the manufacturer, be taken into account in computing the price of the article.

(2) Price readjustments which cannot be attributed to specific articles as of the inventory date (as, for example, a price readjustment of a flat dollar amount which is made to dealers who meet a sales quota) may be taken into account on the basis of an average of the adjustments which is computed for a reasonable category of articles over a representative period.

(3) Price readjustments related to specific items (as, for example, an automatic rebate of a specific percentage of the price of each unit sold to a dealer) may not be averaged, and in such a case only the actual price readjustment attributable to a particular article may be taken into account in computing the tax on that article.

(4) If, because of the facts in a case, a price readjustment can be attributed to specific articles for purposes of consumer refunds but cannot be attributed to specific articles for purposes of floor stocks credits or refunds, the price adjustment may be averaged for purposes of both consumer refunds and floor stocks credits and refunds.

(f) *Representative period.*—A period will be considered a representative period if—

(1) It covers (i) at least four consecutive calendar quarters, the last of which ends with a period of six calendar months immediately preceding the effective date of the tax reduction or repeal involved or (ii) any other period of time which the taxpayer can demonstrate constitutes a representative period for the particular category, and

(2) The number of articles in the category involved sold by the manufacturer during the period either (i) equals or exceeds the number of articles in the category to which the average amount is to be applied or (ii) can be demonstrated by the taxpayer to be a representative quantity.

(g) *Reasonable category.*—Examples of a reasonable category of articles are articles that are identified by a common stock or class number or which are of the same model, class, or line. For the purpose of averaging exclusions, another example of a reasonable category of articles is a grouping of articles that are shipped in the same container. If a manufacturer sells articles bearing his own trademark and also sells articles as private brands, separate computations of the two brands must be made under this section. [Reg. §48.6412-3.]

☐ [*T.D.* 8043, 8-8-85.]

**[Reg. §301.6413-1]**

**§301.6413-1. Special rules applicable to certain employment taxes.**—For regulations under section 6413, see §§31.6413(a)-1 to 31.6413(c)-1, inclusive, of this chapter (Employment Tax Regulations). [Reg. §301.6413-1.]

☐ [*T.D.* 6498, 10-24-60.]

**[Reg. §31.6413(a)-1]**

**§31.6413(a)-1. Repayment or reimbursement by employer of tax erroneously collected from employee.**—(a) *Federal Insurance Contributions Act and Railroad Retirement Tax Act.*—(1) *Overcollection ascertained before return is filed.*—(i) If an employer during any return period collects from an employee more than the correct amount of employee Federal Insurance Contributions Act (FICA) tax under section 3101 or employee Railroad Retirement Tax Act (RRTA) tax under section 3201, and if the employer ascertains the error before filing the return on which the employee tax is required to be reported, repays or reimburses the amount of the overcollection to the employee before filing the return for such return period, and obtains and keeps as part of its records the written receipt of the employee showing the date and amount of the repayment or evidence of reimbursement, the employer shall not report on any return or pay to the IRS the amount of the overcollection.

(ii) Any overcollection not repaid or reimbursed to the employee as provided in paragraph (a)(1)(i) of this section shall be reported and paid to the IRS on the return for reporting such tax for the return period in which the overcollection is made. However, the reporting and payment of the overcollection may subsequently be treated as an overpayment error ascertained after the return is filed for purposes of paragraph (a)(2) of this section.

(iii) For purposes of this paragraph (a)(1), an error is ascertained when the employer has sufficient knowledge of the error to be able to correct it.

(2) *Error ascertained after return is filed.*—(i) Except as provided in paragraph (a)(2)(ii) of this section, if an employer files a return for a return period on which FICA tax or RRTA tax is reported, collects from an employee and pays to the IRS more than the correct amount of the employee FICA or RRTA tax, and if the employer ascertains the error after filing the return and within the applicable period of limitations on credit or refund, the employer shall repay or reimburse the employee in the amount of the overcollection prior to the expiration of such limitations period. However, this paragraph (a)(2) does not apply to the extent that, after reasonable efforts, the employer cannot locate the employee, or the employee does not provide the employer with the written statement required by §31.6413(a)-1(a)(2)(iv). This paragraph (a)(2) has no application in any case in which an overcollection is made the subject of a claim by the employer for refund or credit under the procedure provided in §31.6402(a)-2.

(ii) If an employer files a return for a return period on which Additional Medicare Tax under section 3101(b)(2) or section 3201(a) is reported, collects from an employee and pays to the IRS more than the correct amount of Additional Medicare Tax required to be withheld from wages or compensation, and if the employer ascertains the error after filing the return but before the end of the calendar year in which the wages or compensation were paid, the employer shall repay or reimburse the employee in the amount of the overcollection prior to the end of the calendar year. However, this paragraph does not apply to the extent that, after reasonable efforts, the employer cannot locate the employee.

(iii) If the employer repays the amount of the overcollection to an employee, the employer shall obtain and keep as part of its records the written receipt of the employee, showing the date and amount of the repayment.

(iv) If the employer reimburses the amount of the overcollection to an employee, the employer shall keep as part of its records evidence of reimbursement. However, for purposes of overcollected Additional Medicare Tax under section 3101(b)(2) or section 3201(a), the employer shall reimburse the employee by applying the amount of the overcollection against the employee FICA or RRTA tax which attaches to wages or compensation paid by the employer to the employee in the calendar year in which the overcollection is made. The employer shall reimburse the employee by applying the amount of the overcollection against the employee FICA or RRTA tax which attaches to wages or compensation paid by the employer to the employee prior to the expiration of the applicable period of limitations on credit or refund. If the amount of the overcollection exceeds the amount so applied against such employee tax, the excess amount shall be repaid to the employee as required by this section.

(v) If, in any calendar year, an employer repays or reimburses an employee in the amount of an overcollection of employee FICA or RRTA tax that was collected from the employee in a prior calendar year, the employer shall obtain from the employee and keep as part of its records a written statement that the employee has not claimed refund or credit of the amount of the overcollection, or if so, such claim has been rejected, and that the employee will not claim refund or credit of such amount. For this purpose, a claim for refund or credit by the employee includes instances in which the employee has included an overcollection of employee FICA or RRTA tax in computing a special refund (see §31.6413(c)-1). This paragraph (a)(2)(v) does not apply for purposes of overcollected Additional Medicare Tax under section 3101(b)(2) or section 3201(a) which must be repaid or reimbursed to the employee in the calendar year in which the overcollection is made.

(vi) For purposes of this paragraph (a)(2), an error is ascertained when the employer has sufficient knowledge of the error to be able to correct it.

(vii) For the period of limitations on credit or refund of taxes, see §301.6511(a)-1.

(viii) For corrections of FICA and RRTA tax paid under the wrong chapter, see §31.6205-1(b)(2)(ii) and (iii) and §31.3503-1.

(b) *Income tax withheld from wages.*—(1) *Overcollection ascertained before return is filed.*—(i) If an employer during any return period collects from an employee more than the correct amount of tax required to be withheld from wages under section 3402, and if the employer ascertains the error before filing the return on which such tax is required to be reported, repays or reimburses the amount of the overcollection to the employee before filing the return for such return period and before the end of the calendar year in which the overcollection was made, and obtains and keeps as part of its records the written receipt of the employee showing the date and amount of the

repayment or evidence of reimbursement, the employer shall not report on any return or pay to the IRS the amount of the overcollection.

(ii) Any overcollection not repaid or reimbursed to the employee as provided in paragraph (b)(1)(i) of this section shall be reported and paid to the IRS on the return for reporting such tax for the return period in which the overcollection is made. However, the reporting and payment of the overcollection may subsequently be treated as an overpayment error ascertained after the return is filed for purposes of paragraph (b)(2) of this section.

(iii) For purposes of this paragraph (b)(1), an error is ascertained when the employer has sufficient knowledge of the error to be able to correct it.

(2) *Error ascertained after return is filed.*—(i) If an employer files a return for a return period on which tax required to be withheld from wages is reported, collects from an employee and pays to the IRS more than the correct amount of the tax required to be withheld from wages, and if the employer ascertains the error after filing the return but before the end of the calendar year in which the wages were paid, the employer shall repay or reimburse the employee in the amount of the overcollection prior to the end of the calendar year. However, this paragraph does not apply to the extent that, after reasonable efforts, the employer cannot locate the employee.

(ii) If the employer repays the amount of the overcollection to an employee, the employer shall obtain and keep as part of its records the written receipt of the employee, showing the date and amount of the repayment.

(iii) If the employer reimburses the amount of the overcollection to an employee, the employer shall keep as part of its records evidence of reimbursement. The employer shall reimburse the employee by applying the amount of the overcollection against the tax under section 3402, which otherwise would be required to be withheld from wages paid by the employer to the employee in the calendar year in which the overcollection is made. If the amount of the overcollection exceeds the amount so applied against such tax, the excess amount shall be repaid to the employee as required by this section.

(iv) For purposes of this paragraph (b)(2), an error is ascertained when the employer has sufficient knowledge of the error to be able to correct it.

(c) *Effective/applicability date.*—Paragraph (a) of this section applies to adjusted returns filed on or after November 29, 2013. [Reg. §31.6413(a)-1.]

☐ [*T.D.* 6472, 6-22-60. *Amended by T.D.* 9405, 6-30-2008 *and T.D.* 9645, 11-26-2013.]

## [Reg. §31.6413(a)-2]

**§31.6413(a)-2. Adjustments of overpayments.**—(a) *In general.*—(1) An employer who has overcollected or overpaid employee Federal Insurance Contributions Act (FICA) tax under section 3101 or employer FICA tax under section 3111, employee Railroad Retirement Tax (RRTA) tax under section 3201 or employer RRTA tax under section 3221, or income tax required under section 3402 to be withheld, and has repaid or reimbursed the amount of the overcollection of such tax to the employee, shall correct such error as provided in this section. However, this section only applies to overcollected or overpaid Additional Medicare Tax under section 3101(b)(2) or section 3201(a) if the employer has repaid or reimbursed the amount of the overcollection of such tax to the employee in the year in which the overcollection was made. Such correction may constitute an interest-free adjustment as provided in paragraph (b) or (c) of this section.

(2) Every correction under this section of an overpayment of tax shall be made on the form prescribed by the IRS that corresponds to the return being corrected. The form, filed in accordance with this section and the instructions, will constitute an adjusted return for the return period being corrected.

(3) Every adjusted return on which an overpayment is corrected pursuant to this section shall certify that the employer has repaid or reimbursed its employee, except where taxes were not withheld from the employee or where, after reasonable efforts, the employer cannot locate the employee. Every adjusted return shall designate the return period in which the error was ascertained and the return period being corrected, explain in detail the grounds and facts relied upon to support the correction, and set forth such other information as may be required by this section and §31.6413(a)-1 and by the instructions relating to the adjusted return. Every adjusted return, filed by an employer, for overpayment of employee FICA tax under section 3101 or employee RRTA tax under section 3201 collected from an employee in a calendar year prior to the year in which the adjusted return is filed, must also certify that the employer has obtained the employee's written statement that the employee has not claimed refund or credit of the amount of the overcollection, or if so, such

claim has been rejected, and that the employee will not claim refund or credit of the amount.

(4) For purposes of this section, an error is ascertained when the employer has sufficient knowledge of the error to be able to correct it.

(5) For provisions related to furnishing employee statements and corrected employee statements reporting wages and withheld taxes, see sections 6041 and 6051 and §§ 1.6041-2 and 31.6051-1. For provisions relating to filing information returns and corrected information returns reporting wages and withheld taxes, see sections 6041 and 6051 and §§ 1.6041-2 and 31.6051-2.

(b) *Federal Insurance Contributions Act and Railroad Retirement Tax Act.*—(1) *Overcollection ascertained before return is filed.*—If an employer collects more than the correct amount of employee FICA or RRTA tax from an employee, and if the employer ascertains the error before filing the return on which the employee tax with respect to such wages or compensation is required to be reported, and repays or reimburses the employee under § 31.6413(a)-1(a)(1), the employer shall not report on any return or pay to the IRS the amount of the overcollection. If the employer does not repay or reimburse the amount of the overcollection under § 31.6413(a)-1(a)(1) before filing the return, the employer must report the amount of the overcollection on the return. However, the payment of the overcollection may subsequently be treated as an overpayment error ascertained after the return is filed for purposes of paragraph (b)(2) of this section.

(2) *Error ascertained after return is filed.*—(i) *Employee tax.*—If an employer files a return for a return period on which FICA tax or RRTA tax is required to be reported and reports on the return more than the correct amount of employee FICA or RRTA tax, and if the employer ascertains the error after filing the return, and repays or reimburses the employee the amount of the overcollection of employee tax, as provided in § 31.6413(a)-1(a)(2), the employer may correct the error through an interest-free adjustment as provided in this section. The employer shall adjust the overpayment of tax by reporting the overpayment on an adjusted return for the return period in which the wages or compensation was paid, accompanied by a detailed explanation of the amount being reported on the adjusted return as required by paragraph (a)(3) of this section. However, for purposes of Additional Medicare Tax under section 3101(b)(2) or section 3201(a), if the amount of the overcollection is not repaid or reimbursed to the employee under § 31.6413(a)-1(a)(2)(ii), there is no overpayment to be adjusted under this section and the employer may only adjust an overpayment of such tax attributable to an administrative error, that is, an error involving the inaccurate reporting of the amount withheld, pursuant to this section. Except as provided in paragraph (d) of this section, the reporting of the overpayment on an adjusted return constitutes an adjustment within the meaning of this section only if the adjusted return is filed before the expiration of the period of limitations on credit or refund. The employer shall take the adjusted amount as a credit towards payment of employment tax liabilities for the return period in which the adjusted return is filed unless the IRS notifies the employer that the adjustment is not permitted under paragraph (d) of this section.

(ii) *Employer tax.*—If an employer files a return for a return period on which FICA or RRTA tax is required to be reported and reports on the return more than the correct amount of employer FICA or RRTA tax, and if the employer ascertains the error after filing the return, the employer may correct the error through an interest-free adjustment as provided in this section. The employer must first repay or reimburse the employee the amount of any overcollection of employee tax, if any, as required by § 31.6413(a)-1(a)(2), before making the adjustment for the employer tax. The employer shall adjust the overpayment of tax by reporting the overpayment on an adjusted return for the return period in which the wages or compensation was paid, accompanied by a detailed explanation of the amount being reported on the adjusted return as required by paragraph (a)(3) of this section. Except as provided in paragraph (d) of this section, the reporting of the overpayment on an adjusted return constitutes an adjustment within the meaning of this section only if the adjusted return is filed before the expiration of the period of limitations on credit or refund. The employer shall take the adjusted amount as a credit towards payment of employment tax liabilities for the return period in which the adjusted return is filed unless the IRS notifies the employer that the adjustment is not permitted under paragraph (d) of this section.

(c) *Income tax withheld from wages.*—(1) *Overcollection ascertained before return is filed.*—If an employer collects more than the correct amount of income tax required to be withheld from wages, and if the employer ascertains the error before filing the return on which the tax is required to be reported, and repays or reimburses the employee under § 31.6413(a)-1(b)(1), the employer shall not report on any return or pay to the IRS the amount of the overcollection. If the

employer does not repay or reimburse the amount of the overcollection under § 31.6413(a)-1(b)(1) before filing the return, the employer must report the amount of the overcollection on the return. However, the reporting and payment of the overcollection may subsequently be treated as an overpayment error ascertained after the return is filed for purposes of paragraph (c)(2) of this section.

(2) *Error ascertained after return is filed.*—If an employer files a return for a return period on which income tax required to be withheld from wages is required to be reported and reports on the return more than the correct amount of income tax required to be withheld, and if the employer ascertains the error after filing the return, and repays or reimburses the employee in the amount of the overcollection as provided in § 31.6413(a)-1(b)(2), the employer may correct the error through an interest-free adjustment as provided in this section. The employer shall adjust the overpayment of tax by reporting the overpayment on an adjusted return for the return period in which the wages were paid, accompanied by a detailed explanation of the amount being reported on the adjusted return as required in paragraph (a)(3) of this section. Except as provided in paragraph (d) of this section, the reporting of the overpayment on an adjusted return constitutes an adjustment within the meaning of this section. If the amount of the overcollection is not repaid or reimbursed to the employee under § 31.6413(a)-1(b)(2), there is no overpayment to be adjusted under this section. However, the employer may adjust an overpayment of tax attributable to an administrative error, that is, an error involving the inaccurate reporting of the amount withheld, pursuant to this section. The employer shall take the adjusted amount as a credit towards payment of employment tax liabilities for the return period in which the adjusted return is filed unless the IRS notifies the employer that the adjustment is not permitted under paragraph (d) of this section.

(d) *Adjustments not permitted.*—(1) *In general.*—If an adjustment cannot be made, a claim for refund or credit may be filed in accordance with § 31.6402(a)-2 or § 31.6414-1.

(2) *90-day exception.*—No adjustment in respect of an overpayment may be made if the overpayment relates to a return period for which the period of limitations on credit or refund of such overpayment will expire within 90 days of filing the adjusted return.

(3) *No adjustment after claim for refund filed.*—No adjustment in respect of an overpayment may be made after the filing of a claim for credit or refund of such overpayment under § 31.6402(a)-2.

(4) *No adjustment after IRS notification.*—No adjustment may be made upon notification by the IRS that the adjustment is not permitted.

(e) *Effective/applicability date.*—Paragraphs (a) and (b) of this section apply to adjusted returns filed on or after November 29, 2013. [Reg. § 31.6413(a)-2.]

☐ [*T.D.* 6472, 6-22-60. *Amended by T.D.* 9405, 6-30-2008 *and T.D.* 9645, 11-26-2013 (*corrected* 1-28-2014).]

**[Reg. § 31.6413(a)-3]**

**§ 31.6413(a)-3. Repayment by payor of tax erroneously collected from payee.**—(a) *In general.*—(1) *Erroneous withholding under section 3406 of the Internal Revenue Code.*—If a payor or broker withholds under section 3406 from a payee in error or withholds more than the proper amount of the tax under section 3406, the payor or broker may refund the amount erroneously withheld as provided in section 6413 and this section. A payor or broker will be considered to have withheld erroneously under section 3406 only if the amount is withheld because of an error by the payor or broker (e.g., an error in flagging or identifying an account that is subject to withholding under section 3406). The payor or broker may, in its discretion, treat the amount withheld as an amount erroneously withheld and refund it to the payee if—

(i) The payor or broker requires a payee described in § 3l.3406(g)-1(a) or described in a provision of the Internal Revenue Code requiring the reporting of a payment subject to withholding under section 3406 to certify that it is an exempt recipient, the payee fails to make the required certification, and the payor or broker subsequently withholds under section 3406 from a payment to the payee;

(ii) The payor or broker does not require the payee to certify concerning its exempt status and the payor or broker withholds under section 3406;

(iii) The payor or broker withholds under section 3406 from a payee after the payee provides a taxpayer identification number or required certification (including the documentation described in § 1.1441-1(e)(1)(ii), 1.6045-1(g)(3), or 1.6049-5(c) of this chapter) to the payor, but before the payor or broker treats the number or required certification as having been received under § 31.3406(e)-1(b); or

(iv) The amount is withheld because a payor imposed backup withholding on a payment made to a person because the payee failed to furnish the documentation described in § 1.1441-1(e)(1)(ii) of this chapter and the payee subsequently furnishes, completes, or corrects the documentation. The documentation must be furnished, completed, or corrected prior to the end of the calendar year in which the payment is made and prior to the time the payor furnishes a Form 1099 to the payee with respect to the payment for which the withholding erroneously occurred.

(2) For purposes of paragraph (a)(1) of this section (other than erroneous withholding occurring under the circumstances described in paragraph (a)(1)(iv) of this section), if a payor or broker withholds because the payor or broker has not received a taxpayer identifying number or required certification and the payee subsequently provides a taxpayer identifying number or a required certification to the payor, the payor or broker may not refund the amount to the payee.

(b) *Refunding amounts erroneously withheld.*—(1) *Time and manner.*— If a payor or broker withholds under section 3406 from a payee in error (including withholding more than the correct amount, as described in paragraph (a) of this section), the payor or broker may refund the amount erroneously withheld to the payee if the refund is made prior to the end of the calendar year and prior to the time the payor or broker furnishes a Form 1099 to the payee with respect to the payment for which the erroneous withholding occurred. If the amount of the erroneous withholding is refunded to the payee, the payor or broker must—

(i) Keep as part of its records a receipt showing the date and amount of refund and must provide a copy of the receipt to the payee (a canceled check or an entry in a statement is sufficient, provided that the check or statement contains a specific notation that it is a refund of tax erroneously withheld);

(ii) Not report on a Form 1099 as tax withheld any amount which the payor or broker has refunded to a payee; and

(iii) Not deposit the amount erroneously withheld if the payor or broker has not deposited the amount of the tax prior to the time that the refund is made to the payee.

(2) *Adjustment after the deposit of the tax.*—(i) *In general.*—Except as provided in paragraph (b)(2)(ii) of this section, if the amount erroneously withheld has been deposited prior to the time that the refund is made to the payee, the payor or broker may adjust any subsequent deposit of the tax collected under chapter 24 of the Internal Revenue Code that the payor or broker is required to make in the amount of the tax that has been refunded to the payee.

(ii) *Erroneous withholding from a payee that is a foreign person.*— Where a payor withholds in error from a payee that is a nonresident alien or foreign person, as described in paragraph (a)(1)(iv) of this section, the payor may refund some or all of the amount subject to backup withholding under section 3406. A refund may be paid in accordance with the requirements of this paragraph (b)(2)(ii) where the documentation is furnished, completed, or corrected prior to the end of the calendar year in which the payment is made and prior to the time the payor furnishes a Form 1099 to the payee with respect to the payment for which the withholding erroneously occurred. The amount of the refund will be the amount erroneously withheld less the amount of tax required to be withheld, if any, under chapter 3 of the Internal Revenue Code and the regulations under that chapter. With respect to the amount of the payment to the foreign person and the amount of tax required to be withheld under chapter 3 of the Internal Revenue Code (and the regulations thereunder), returns must be made in accordance with the requirements of § 1.1461-1(b) and (c) of this chapter. [Reg. § 31.6413(a)-3.]

☐ [*T.D. 8637, 12-20-95. Amended by T.D. 8734, 10-6-97 (T.D. 8804 delayed the effective date of T.D. 8734 from January 1, 1999, to January 1, 2000; T.D. 8856 further delayed the effective date of T.D. 8734 until January 1, 2001).*]

### [Reg. § 31.6413(b)-1]

**§ 31.6413(b)-1. Overpayments of certain employment taxes.**—For provisions relating to the adjustment of overpayments of tax imposed by section 3101, 3111, 3201, 3221, or 3402, see § 31.6413(a)-2. For provisions relating to refunds of tax imposed by section 3101, 3111, 3201, or 3221, see § § 31.6402(a)-1 and 31.6402(a)-2. For provisions relating to refunds of tax imposed by section 3402, see § § 31.6402(a)-1 and 31.6414-1. [Reg. § 31.6413(b)-1.]

☐ [*T.D. 6472, 6-22-60.*]

### [Reg. § 31.6413(c)-1]

**§ 31.6413(c)-1. Special refunds.**—(a) *Who may make claims.*—(1) *In general.*—(i) If an employee receives wages, as defined in section 3121(a), from two or more employers in any calendar year:

(a) After 1954 and before 1959 in excess of $4,200,

(b) After 1958 and before 1966 in excess of $4,800,

(c) After 1965 and before 1968 in excess of $6,600, or

(d) After 1967 in excess of $7,800,

(e) After 1971 and before 1973 in excess of $9,000,

(f) After 1972 and before 1974 in excess of $10,800,

(g) After 1973 and before 1975 in excess of $13,200, or

(h) After 1974 in excess of the contribution and benefit base (as determined under section 230 of the Social Security Act) which is effective with respect to such year,

the employee shall be entitled to a special refund of the amount, if any, by which the employee tax imposed by section 3101 with respect to such wages and deducted therefrom (whether or not paid) exceeds the employee tax with respect to the amount specified in (a) through (h) of this subdivision for the calendar year in question. Employee tax imposed by section 3101 with respect to tips reported by an employee to his employer and collected by the employer from funds turned over by the employee to the employer (see section 3102(c)) shall be treated, for purposes of this paragraph, as employee tax deducted from wages received by the employee. If the employee is required to file an income tax return for such calendar year (or for his last taxable year beginning in such calendar year) he may obtain the benefit of the special refund only by claiming credit as provided in § 1.31-2 of this chapter (Income Tax Regulations).

(ii) The application of this subparagraph may be illustrated by the following examples:

*Example (1).* Employee A in the calendar year 1968 receives taxable wages in the amount of $5,000 from each of his employers, B, C, and D, for services performed during such year (or at any time after 1936), or a total of $15,000. Employee tax (computed at 4.4 percent, the aggregate employee tax rate in effect in 1968) is deducted from A's wages in the amount of $220 by B and $220 by C, or a total of $440. Employer D pays employee tax in the amount of $220 without deducting such tax from A's wages. The employee tax with respect to the first $7,800 of such wages is $343.20. A is entitled to a special refund of $96.80 ($440 minus $343.20). The $5,000 of wages received from employer D and the $220 of employee tax paid with respect thereto have no bearing in computing A's special refund since such tax was not deducted from his wages.

*Example (2).* Employee E in the calendar year 1968 performs services for employers F and G, for which E is entitled to wages of $7,800 from each employer, or a total of $15,600. On account of such services, E in 1967 received an advance payment of $1,800 of wages from F; and in 1968, receives wages in the amount of $6,000 from F and $7,800 from G. Employee tax was deducted as follows: In 1967, $79.20 ($1,800 × 4.4%, the aggregate employee tax rate in effect in 1967) by employer F; and in 1968, $264.00 ($6,000 × 4.4%, the aggregate employee tax rate in effect in 1968) by employer F, and $343.20 ($7,800 × 4.4%) by employer G. Thus, E in the calendar year 1968 received $13,800 in wages from which $607.20 of employee tax was deducted. The amount of employee tax with respect to the first $7,800 of such wages received in 1968 is $343.20. E is entitled to a special refund of $264.00 ($607.20 minus $343.20). The $1,800 advance of wages received in 1967 from F, and the $79.20 of employee tax with respect thereto, have no bearing in computing E's special refund for 1968, because the wages were not received in 1968. Such amounts could not form the basis for a special refund unless E during 1967 received from F and at least one more employer wages totaling more than $6,000.

(2) *Federal employees.*—For purposes of special refunds of employee tax, each head of a Federal agency or of a wholly-owned instrumentality of the United States who makes a return pursuant to section 3122 (and each agent designated by a head of a Federal agency or instrumentality who makes a return pursuant to such section) is considered a separate employer. For such purposes, the term "wages" includes the amount which each such head (or agent) determines to constitute wages paid an employee, but not in excess of the amount specified in subparagraph (1)(i)(a) through (h) of this paragraph for the calendar year in question. For example, if wages received by an employee during calendar year 1974 are reportable by two or more agents of one or more Federal agencies and the amount of such wages is in excess of $13,200 the employee shall be entitled to a special refund of the amount, if any, by which the employee tax imposed with respect to such wages and deducted therefrom exceeds the employee tax with respect to the first $13,200 of such wages. Moreover, if an employee receives wages during any calendar year from an agency or wholly-owned instrumentality of the United States and from one or more other employers, either private or governmental, the total amount of such wages shall be taken into account for purposes of the special refund provisions.

(3) *State employees.*—For purposes of special refunds of employee tax, the term "wages" includes such remuneration for services covered by an agreement made pursuant to section 218 of the Social Security Act, relating to voluntary agreements for coverage of em-

ployees of State and local governments, as would be wages if such services constituted employment (see §31.3121(a)-1 of Subpart B of the regulations in this part, relating to wages); the term "employer" includes a State or any political subdivision thereof, or any instrumentality of any one or more of the foregoing; and the term "tax" or "tax imposed by section 3101" includes an amount equivalent to the em ployee tax which would be imposed by section 3101 if such services constituted employment. The provisions of subparagraph (1) of this paragraph are applicable whether or not any amount deducted from an employee's remuneration as a result of an agreement made pursuant to section 218 of the Social Security Act has been paid pursuant to such agreement. Thus, the special refund provisions are applicable to amounts equivalent to employee tax deducted from employees' remuneration by States, political subdivisions, or instrumentalities by reason of agreements made under section 218 of the Social Security Act. Moreover, if during any calendar year an employee receives remuneration for services covered by such an agreement and during the same calendar year receives wages from one or more other employers, either private or governmental, the total amount of such remuneration and wages shall be taken into account for purposes of the special refund provisions.

(4) *Employees of certain foreign corporations.*—For purposes of special refunds of employee tax, the term "wages" includes such remuneration for services covered by an agreement made pursuant to section 3121(l), relating to agreements for coverage of employees of certain foreign corporations, as would be wages if such services constituted employment (see §31.3121(a)-1 of Subpart B of the regulations in this part, relating to wages); the term "employer" includes any domestic corporation which has entered into an agreement pursuant to section 3121(l); and the term "tax" or "tax imposed by section 3101" includes, in the case of services covered by an agreement entered into pursuant to section 3121(l), an amount equivalent to the employee tax which would be imposed by section 3101 if such services constituted employment. The provisions of subparagraph (1) of this paragraph are applicable whether or not any amount deducted from the employee's remuneration by reason of such agreement has been paid to the district director. Thus, the special refund provisions are applicable to amounts equivalent to employee tax deducted from employees' remuneration by reason of agreements made under section 3121(l). A domestic corporation which enters into an agreement pursuant to section 3121(l) shall, for purposes of this paragraph, be considered an employer in its capacity as a party to such agreement separate and distinct from its identity as an employer employing individuals on its own account (see section 3121(l)(9)). If during any calendar year an employee receives remuneration for services covered by such an agreement and during the same calendar year receives wages for services in employment, the total amount of such remuneration and wages shall be taken into account for purposes of the special refund provisions. For provisions relating to agreements entered into under section 3121(l), see the regulations in Part 36 of this chapter (Regulations on Contract Coverage of Employees of Foreign Subsidiaries).

(5) *Governmental employees in American Samoa.*—For purposes of special refunds of employee tax, the Governor of American Samoa and each agent designated by him who makes a return pursuant to section 3125(b) (see §31.3125) is considered a separate employer. For such purposes, the term "wages" includes the amount which the Governor (or any agent) determines to constitute wages paid an employee, but not in excess of the amount specified in subparagraph (1)(i) (*a*) through (*h*) of this paragraph for the calendar year in question. For example, if wages received by an employee during calendar year 1974 are reportable by two or more agents pursuant to section 3125(b) and the total amount of such wages is in excess of $13,200, the employee shall be entitled to a special refund of the amount, if any, by which the employee tax imposed with respect to such wages and deducted therefrom exceeds the employee tax with respect to the first $13,200 of such wages. Moreover, if an employee receives wages during any calendar year from the Government of American Samoa, from a political subdivision thereof, or from any wholly-owned instrumentality of such government or political subdivision and from one or more other employers, either private or governmental, the total amount of such wages shall be taken into account for purposes of the special refund provisions.

(6) *Governmental employees in the District of Columbia.*—For purposes of special refunds of employee tax, the Commissioner of the District of Columbia (or, prior to the transfer of functions pursuant to Reorganization Plan No. 3 of 1967 (81 Stat. 948), the Commissioners of the District of Columbia) and each agent designated by him who makes a return pursuant to section 3125(c) (see §31.3125) is considered a separate employer. For such purposes, the term "wages" includes the amount which the Commissioner (or any agent) determines to constitute wages paid an employee, but not in excess of the amount specified in subparagraph (1)(i) (*a*) through (*h*) of this para-

graph for the calendar year in question. For example, if wages received by an employee during calendar year 1974 are reportable by two or more agents pursuant to section 3125(c) and the total amount of such wages is in excess of $13,200 the employee shall be entitled to a special refund of the amount, if any, by which the employee tax imposed with respect to such wages and deducted therefrom exceeds the employee tax with respect to the first $13,200 of such wages. Moreover, if an employee receives wages during any calendar year from the Government of the District of Columbia or from a wholly-owned instrumentality thereof and from one or more other employers, either private or governmental, the total amount of such wages shall be taken into account for purposes of the special refund provisions.

(b) *Claims for special refund.*—(1) *In general.*—An employee who is entitled to a special refund under section 6413(c) may claim such refund under the provisions of this section only if the employee is not entitled to claim the amount thereof as a credit against income tax as provided in §1.31-2 of this chapter (Income Tax Regulations). Each claim under this section shall be made with respect to wages received within one calendar year (regardless of the year or years after 1936 during which the services were performed for which such wages are received), and shall be filed after the close of such year.

(2) *Form of claim.*—Each claim for special refund under this section shall be made on Form 843, in accordance with the regulations in this subpart and the instructions relating to such form. In the case of a claim filed prior to April 15, 1968, the claim shall be filed with the district director for the internal revenue district in which the employee resides or, if the employee does not reside in any internal revenue district, with the District Director, Baltimore, Md. 21202. Except as provided in paragraph (b) of §301.6091-1 (relating to hand-carried documents), in the case of a claim filed after April 14, 1968, the claim shall be filed with the service center serving such internal revenue district. However, in the case of an employee who does not reside in any internal revenue district and who is outside the United States, the claim shall be filed with the Director of International Operations, U.S. Internal Revenue Service, Washington, D.C. 20225, unless the employee resides in Puerto Rico or the Virgin Islands, in which case the claim shall be filed with the Director of International Operations, U.S. Internal Revenue Service, Hato Rey, Puerto Rico 00917. The claim shall include the employee's account number and the following information with respect to each employer from whom he received wages during the calendar year: (i) The name and address of such employer, (ii) the amount of wages received during the calendar year to which the claim relates, and (iii) the amount of employee tax collected by the employer from the employee with respect to such wages. Other information may be required but should be submitted only upon request.

(3) *Period of limitation.*—For the period of limitation upon special refund of employee tax imposed by section 3101, see §301.6511(a)-1 of this chapter (Regulations on Procedure and Administration).

(c) *Special refunds with respect to compensation as defined in the Railroad Retirement Tax Act.*—(1) *In general.*—In the case of any individual who, during any calendar year after 1967, receives wages (as defined by section 3121(a)) from one or more employers and also receives compensation (as defined by section 3231(e)) which is subject to the tax imposed on employees by section 3201 or the tax imposed on employee representatives by section 3211 such compensation shall, solely for purposes of applying section 6413(c)(1) and this section with respect to the hospital insurance tax imposed by section 3101(b), be treated as wages (as defined by section 3121(a)) received from an employer with respect to which the hospital insurance tax imposed by section 3101(b) was deducted. For purposes of this section, compensation received shall be determined under the principles provided in chapter 22 of the Code and the regulations thereunder (see section 3231(e) and §31.3231(e)-1). Therefore, compensation paid for time lost shall be deemed earned and received for purposes of this section in the month in which such time is lost, and compensation which is earned during the period for which a return of taxes under chapter 22 is required to be made and which is payable during the calendar month following such period shall be deemed to have been received for purposes of this section during such period only. Further, compensation is deemed to have been earned and received when an employee or employee representative performs services for which he is paid, or for which there is a present or future obligation to pay, regardless of the time at which payment is made or deemed to be made.

(2) *Example.*—The application of this paragraph may be illustrated by the following example.

*Example.* Employee A rendered services to X during 1973 for which he was paid compensation at the monthly rate of $650 which was taxable under the Railroad Retirement Tax Act. A was paid $550 by X in January 1973 which was earned and deemed received in

December 1972 and $650 in January of 1974 which was earned and deemed received in December of 1973. A also earned and received wages in 1973 from employer Y, which were subject to the employee tax under the Federal Insurance Contributions Act, in the amount of $6,000. A paid hospital insurance tax on $13,800 ($7,800 compensation from X including $650 earned and deemed received in December 1973 but paid in January 1974 and not including $550 paid in January 1973 but earned and deemed received in December 1972, $6,000 compensation from Y) received or deemed received or earned in 1973. For purposes of the hospital insurance tax imposed by section 3101(b), these amounts are all wages received from an employer in 1973. Therefore, A is entitled to a special refund for 1973 under section 6413(c) and this section of $30 (1.0% × $13,800—1.0% × $10,800). [Reg. §31.6413(c)-1.]

□ [T.D. 6472, 6-22-60. Amended by T.D. 6950, 4-3-68; T.D. 6983, 12-3-68 and T.D. 7374, 7-23-75 (corrected 9-24-2004).]

### [Reg. §1.6414-1]

**§1.6414-1. Credit or refund of tax withheld on nonresident aliens and foreign corporations.**—(a) *In general.*—Any withholding agent who for the calendar year pays more than the correct amount of—

(1) Tax required to be withheld under chapter 3 of the Code, or

(2) Interest, addition to the tax, additional amount, or penalty with respect to such tax,

may file a claim for credit or refund of the overpayment in the manner and subject to the conditions stated in the Procedure and Administration Regulations (Part 301 of this chapter) under section 6402, or may claim credit for the overpayment as provided in paragraph (b) of this section. With respect to the payment of withholding tax under section 1446, this section shall only apply to a publicly traded partnership described in §1.1446-4. See §1.1446-3(d)(2)(iv) for rules regarding refunds to a withholding agent under section 1446.

(b) *Claim for credit on Form 1042.*—The withholding agent may claim credit of an overpayment described in paragraph (a) of this section for any calendar year by showing the amount of overpayment on the return on Form 1042 for such calendar year, which shall constitute a claim for credit under this paragraph. The claim for credit shall be evidenced by a statement on the return setting forth the amount determined as an overpayment and showing such other information as may be required by the instructions relating to the return. The amount claimed as a credit may be applied, to the extent it has not been applied under §1.1461-2(b), by the withholding agent to reduce the amount of a payment or deposit of tax required by §1.1461-1 or §1.6302-2(a) for any payment period occurring in the calendar year following the calendar year of overwithholding. The amount so claimed as a credit shall also be entered on the annual return on Form 1042 for the calendar year following the calendar year of overwithholding and shall be applied as a payment on account of the tax shown on such form. If the withholding agent files a claim for credit or refund of the overpayment on Form 843 in accordance with §301.6402-2 of this chapter (Procedure and Administration Regulations), or a claim for refund of the overpayment on Form 1042 in accordance with §301.6402-3 of such chapter, he may not claim credit for the overpayment under this paragraph.

(c) *Overpayment of amounts actually withheld.*—No credit or refund to the withholding agent shall be allowed for the amount of any overpayment of tax which, after taking into account paragraph (b) of §1.1464-1, the withholding agent has actually withheld from an item of income under chapter 3 of the Code.

(d) *Effective/Applicability date.*—The last two sentences of paragraph (a) of this section shall apply to partnership taxable years beginning after April 29, 2008. [Reg. §1.6414-1.]

□ [T.D. 6922, 6-16-67. Amended by T.D. 9394, 4-28-2008.]

### [Reg. §31.6414-1]

**§31.6414-1. Credit or refund of income tax withheld from wages.**—

⫸→ *Caution: Reg. §31.6414-1(a), below, prior to amendment by T.D. 9405, is applicable to any error ascertained before January 1, 2008.*

(a) *In general.*—Any employer who pays to the district director more than the correct amount of—

(1) Tax under section 3402 or a corresponding provision of prior law, or

(2) Interest, addition to the tax, additional amount, or penalty with respect to such tax,

may file a claim for refund of the overpayment or may claim credit for such overpayment, in the manner and subject to the conditions stated in this section and §301.6402-2 of this chapter (Regulations on

Procedure and Administration). If credit is claimed pursuant to this section, the amount thereof shall be claimed by entering such amount as a deduction on a return of tax under section 3402 filed by the employer. If credit is taken pursuant to this section, a claim on Form 843 is not required, but the return on which the credit is claimed shall have attached as a part thereof a statement, which shall constitute the claim for credit, setting forth in detail the grounds and facts relied upon in support of the credit, and showing such other information as is required by the regulations in this subpart and by the instructions relating to the return. No refund or credit to the employer shall be allowed under this section for the amount of any overpayment of tax which the employer deducted or withheld from an employee.

⫸→ *Caution: Reg. §31.6414-1(a), below, as amended by T.D. 9405, is applicable to any error ascertained on or after January 1, 2008.*

(a) *In general.*—(1) Any employer who pays to the IRS more than the correct amount of income tax required to be withheld from wages under section 3402 or interest, addition to the tax, additional amount, or penalty with respect to such tax, may file a claim for refund of the overpayment in the manner and subject to the conditions stated in this section on the form prescribed by the IRS. The claim for refund must designate the return period to which the claim relates, explain in detail the grounds and facts relied upon to support the claim, and set forth such other information as may be required by the regulations in this section and by the instructions relating to the form used to make such claim. No refund to the employer will be allowed under this section for the amount of any overpayment of tax which the employer deducted or withheld from an employee.

(2) For provisions related to furnishing employee statements and corrected employee statements reporting wages and withheld taxes, see sections 6041 and 6051 and §§1.6041-2 and 31.6051-1. For provisions relating to filing information returns and corrected information returns reporting wages and withheld taxes, see sections 6041 and 6051 and §§1.6041-2 and 31.6051-2.

(3) For interest-free adjustments of overpayments of income tax withheld from wages, see §31.6413(a)-2.

(b) *Period of limitation.*—For the period of limitation upon credit or refund of taxes imposed by the Internal Revenue Code of 1954, see §301.6511(a)-1 of this chapter (Regulations on Procedure and Administration). For the period of limitation upon credit or refund of any tax imposed by the Internal Revenue Code of 1939, see the regulations applicable with respect to such tax. [Reg. §31.6414-1.]

□ [T.D. 6472, 6-22-60. Amended by T.D. 9405, 6-30-2008.]

### [Reg. §301.6414-1]

**§301.6414-1. Income tax withheld.**—For regulations under section 6414, see §31.6414-1 of this chapter (Employment Tax Regulations). [Reg. §301.6414-1.]

□ [T.D. 6119, 12-31-54. Amended by T.D. 6498, 10-24-60 and T.D. 6922, 6-16-67.]

### [Reg. §48.6416(a)-1]

**§48.6416(a)-1. Claims for credit or refund of overpayments of taxes on special fuels and manufacturers taxes.**—Any claims for credit or refund of an overpayment of a tax imposed by chapter 31 or chapter 32 shall be made in accordance with the applicable provisions of this subpart and the applicable provisions of §301.6402-2 of this chapter (Regulations on Procedure and Administration). A claim on Form 843 is not required in the case of a claim for credit, but the amount of the credit shall be claimed by entering that amount as a credit on a return of tax under this subpart filed by the person making the claim. In this regard, see §48.6416(f)-1. [Reg. §48.6416(a)-1.]

□ [T.D. 6650. Amended by T.D. 8043, 8-8-85.]

### [Reg. §48.6416(a)-2]

**§48.6416(a)-2. Credit or refund of tax on special fuels.**—(a) *Overpayments not described in section 6416(b)(2).*—(1) *Claims included.*—This paragraph applies only to claims for credit or refund of an overpayment of tax imposed by section 4041(a)(1)(A) (relating to tax on the sale of diesel fuel), section 4041(a)(2)(A) (relating to tax on the sale of special motor fuels), section 4041(c)(1)(A) (relating to tax on the sale of fuel for use in noncommercial aviation), or section 4041(c)(2)(A) (relating to the tax on sale of gasoline for use in noncommmercial aviation). It does not apply, however, to a claim for credit or refund of any overpayment described in paragraph (b) of this section which arises by reason of the application of section 6416(b)(2).

(2) *Supporting evidence required.*—No credit or refund of any overpayment to which this paragraph (a) applies shall be allowed unless the person who paid the tax submits with the claim a written consent of the ultimate purchaser to the allowance of the credit or

refund, or submits with the claim a statement, supported by sufficient available evidence, asserting that—

    (i) The person has neither included the tax in the price of the fuel with respect to which it was imposed nor collected the amount of the tax from a vendee, and identifying the nature of the evidence available to establish these facts, or

    (ii) The person has repaid the amount of the tax to the ultimate purchaser of the fuel.

    (3) *Ultimate purchaser.*—The term "ultimate purchaser", as used in paragraph (a)(2) of this section, means the vendee to whom the fuel was sold tax-paid by the person claiming credit or refund.

    (b) *Overpayments determined under section 6416(b)(2).*—(1) *Claims included.*—This paragraph applies only to claims for credit or refund of amounts paid as tax under section 4041(a)(1)(A) (relating to tax on the sale of diesel fuel) or section 4041(a)(2)(A) (relating to tax on the sale of special motor fuels) that are determined to be overpayments by reason of section 6416(b)(2) (relating to tax payments in respect of certain uses, sales, or resales of a taxable article).

    (2) *Supporting evidence required.*—No credit or refund of an overpayment to which this paragraph (b) applies shall be allowed unless the person who paid the tax submits with the claim a statement, supported by sufficient available evidence, asserting that—

    (i) The person has neither included the tax in the price of the fuel with respect to which it was imposed nor collected the amount of the tax from a vendee, and identifying the nature of the evidence available to establish these facts, or

    (ii) The person has repaid, or agreed to repay, the amount of the tax to the ultimate vendor of the fuel, or

    (iii) The person has secured, and will submit upon request of the Service, the written consent of the ultimate vendor to the allowance of the credit or refund.

    (3) *Ultimate vendor.*—The term "ultimate vendor", as used in paragraph (b)(2) of this section, means the seller making the sale which gives rise to the overpayment or which last precedes the exportation or use which gives rise to the overpayment.

    (c) *Nonapplication to tax on use of special fuels.*—This section shall not have any effect on overpayments of tax under section 4041(a)(1)(B) (relating to tax on the use of diesel fuel), section 4041(a)(2)(B) (relating to tax on the use of special motor fuels), section 4041(c)(1)(B) (relating to tax on the use of fuel other than gasoline in noncommercial aviation), section 4041(c)(2)(B) (relating to tax on the use of gasoline in noncommercial aviation), or section 4042 (relating to tax on fuel used in commercial transportation on inland waterways). [Reg. § 48.6416(a)-2.]

☐ [T.D. 8043, 8-8-85.]

**[Reg. § 48.6416(a)-3]**

**§ 48.6416(a)-3. Credit or refund of manufacturers tax under chapter 32.**—(a) *Overpayments not described in section 6416(b)(3)(C) or (4) (prior to April 1, 1983) and section 6416(b)(2).*—(1) *Claims included.*—This paragraph applies only to claims for credit or refund of an overpayment of manufacturers tax imposed by chapter 32. It does not apply, however, to a claim for credit or refund on any overpayment described in paragraph (b) of this section which arises by reason of the application of section 6416(b)(2), (3)(C), or (4).

    (2) *Supporting evidence required.*—No credit or refund of any overpayment to which this paragraph (a) applies shall be allowed unless the person who paid the tax submits with the claim a written consent of the ultimate purchaser to the allowance of the credit or refund, or submits with the claim a statement, supported by sufficient available evidence, asserting that—

    (i) The person has neither included the tax in the price of the article with respect to which it was imposed nor collected the amount of the tax from a vendee, and identifying the nature of the evidence available to establish these facts, or

    (ii) The person has repaid the amount of the tax to the ultimate purchaser of the article.

    (3) *Ultimate purchaser.*—(1) *General rule.*—The term "ultimate purchaser", as used in paragraph (a)(2) of this section, means the person who purchased the article for consumption, or for use in the manufacture of other articles and not for resale in the form in which purchased.

    (ii) *Special rule under section 6416(a)(3).*—(A) *Conditions to be met.*—If tax under chapter 32 is paid in respect of an article and the Commissioner determines that the article is not subject to tax under chapter 32, the term "ultimate purchaser", as used in paragraph (a)(2) of this section, includes any wholesaler, jobber, distributor, or retailer who, on the 15th day after the date of the determination,

holds for sale any such article with respect to which tax has been paid, if the claim for credit or refund of the overpayment in respect of the articles held for sale by the wholesaler, jobber, distributor, or retailer is filed on or before the date on which the person who paid the tax is required to file a return for the period ending with the first calendar quarter which begins more than 60 days after the date of the determination by the Commissioner.

    (B) *Supporting statement.*—A claim for credit or refund of an overpayment of tax in respect of an article as to which a wholesaler, jobber, distributor, or retailer is the ultimate purchaser, as provided in this paragraph (a)(3)(ii), must be supported by a statement that the person filing the claim has a statement, by each wholesaler, jobber, distributor, or retailer whose articles are covered by the claim, showing total inventory, by model number and quantity, of all such articles purchased tax-paid and held for sale as of 12:01 a.m. of the 15th day after the date of the determination by the Commissioner that the article is not subject to tax under chapter 32.

    (C) *Inventory requirement.*—The inventory shall not include any such article title to which, or possession of which, has previously been transferred to any person for purposes of consumption unless the entire purchase price was repaid to the person or credited to the person's account and the sale was rescinded or any such article purchased by the wholesaler, jobber, distributor, or retailer as a component part of, or on or in connection with, another article. An article in transit at the first moment of the 15th day after the date of the determination is regarded as being held by the person to whom it was shipped, except that if title to the article does not pass until delivered to the person the article is deemed to be held by the shipper.

    (b) *Overpayments described in section 6416(b)(3)(C) or (4) (prior to April 1, 1983) and section 6416(b)(2).*—(1) *Claims included.*—This paragraph applies only to claims for credit or refund of amounts paid as tax under chapter 32 that are determined to be overpayments by reason of section 6416(b)(2) (relating to tax payments in respect of certain uses, sales, or resales of a taxable article), section 6416(b)(3)(C) (relating to tax-paid tires or inner tubes used for further manufacture), or section 6416(b)(4) (relating to tires or inner tubes used by the manufacturer on another manufactured article).

    (2) *Supporting evidence required.*—No credit or refund of an overpayment to which this paragraph (b) applies shall be allowed unless the person who paid the tax submits with the claim a statement, supported by sufficient available evidence, asserting that—

    (i) The person neither included the tax in the price of the article with respect to which it was imposed nor collected the amount of the tax from a vendee, and identifying the nature of the evidence available to establish these facts, or

    (ii) The person repaid, or agreed to repay, the amount of the tax to the ultimate vendor of the article, or

    (iii) The person has secured, and will submit upon request of the Service, the written consent of the ultimate vendor to the allowance of the credit or refund.

    (3) *Ultimate vendor.*—(i) *General rule.*—The term "ultimate vendor", as used in paragraph (b)(2) of this section, means the seller making the sale which gives rise to the overpayment or which last precedes the exportation or use which has given rise to the overpayment.

    (ii) *Special rule under section 6416(a)(3)(B) prior to revision by the Highway Revenue Act of 1982.*—In the case of an overpayment determined under section 6416(b)(2)(F), (3)(C), or (4) in respect of tires or inner tubes, where the taxable article is used as a component part of, or sold on or in connection with or with the sale of, a second article which is exported, sold to a nonprofit educational organization for its exclusive use, sold to a State or local government for the exclusive use of a State or local government or used or sold for use as supplies for vessels or aircraft, the term "ultimate vendor", as used in paragraph (b)(2) of this section, means the ultimate vendor of the second article.

    (c) *Overpayments not included.*—This section does not apply to any overpayment determined under section 6416(b)(1) (relating to price readjustments), section 6416(b)(3)(A) (relating to certain cases in which refund or credit is allowable to the manufacturer who uses, in the further manufacture of a second article, a taxable article purchased by the manufacturer tax-paid), section 6416(b)(3)(B) prior to April 1, 1983 (relating to parts or accessories taxable under section 4061(b) and used by a subsequent manufacturer or producer as material or a component part of any other article manufactured or produced by him), section 6416(b)(4) after March 31, 1983 (relating to tires), section 6416(b)(5) (relating to the return to the seller of certain installment accounts which the seller had previously sold) or section 6416(b)(6) (relating to truck chassis, bodies, and semi-trailers used for further manufacture). In this regard, see §§ 48.6416(b)(1)-1, 48.6416(b)(3)-1, and 48.6416(b)(5)-1. [Reg. § 48.6416(a)-3.]

☐ [*T.D. 8043, 8-8-85. Amended by T.D. 8748, 12-31-97 (corrected 3-30-98).*]

### [Reg. § 48.6416(b)(1)-1]

**§48.6416(b)(1)-1. Price readjustments causing overpayments of manufacturers tax.**—In the case of any payment of tax under chapter 32 that is determined to be an overpayment by reason of a price readjustment within the meaning of section 6416(b)(1) and § 48.6416(b)(1)-2 or § 48.6416(b)(1)-3, the person who paid the tax may file a claim for refund of the overpayment or may claim credit for the overpayment on any return of tax under this subpart which the person subsequently files. Price readjustments may not be anticipated. However, if the readjustment has actually been made before the return is filed for the period in which the sale was made, the tax to be reported in respect of the sale may, at the election of the taxpayer, be based either (a) on the price as so readjusted or (b) on the original sale price and a credit or refund claimed in respect of the price readjustment. A price readjustment will be deemed to have been made at the time when the amount of the readjustment has been refunded to the vendor or the vendor has been informed that the vendor's account has been credited with the amount. No interest shall be paid on any credit or refund allowed under this section. For provisions relating to the evidence required in support of a claim for credit or refund, see § 301.6402-2 of this chapter (Regulations on Procedure and Administration), § 48.6416(a)-3(a)(2), and § 48.6416(b)(1)-4. For provisions authorizing the taking of a credit in lieu of filing a claim for refund, see section 6416(d) and § 48.6416(f)-1. [Reg. § 48.6416(b)(1)-1.]

☐ [*T.D. 8043, 8-8-85.*]

### [Reg. § 48.6416(b)(1)-2]

**§48.6416(b)(1)-2. Determination of price readjustments.**—(a) *In general.*—(1) *Rules of usual application.*—(i) *Amount treated as overpayment.*—If the tax imposed by chapter 32 has been paid and thereafter the price of the article on which the tax was based is readjusted, that part of the tax which is proportionate to the part of the price which is repaid or credited to the purchaser is considered to be an overpayment. A readjustment of price to the purchaser may occur by reason of—

(A) The return of the article,

(B) The repossession of the article,

(C) The return or repossession of the covering or container of the article, or

(D) A bona fide discount, rebate, or allowance against the price at which the article was sold.

(ii) *Requirements of price readjustment.*—A price readjustment will not be deemed to have been made unless the person who paid the tax either—

(A) Repays part or all of the purchase price in cash to the vendee,

(B) Credits the vendee's account for part or all of the purchase price, or

(C) Directly or indirectly reimburses a third party for part or all of the purchase price for the direct benefit of the vendee. In addition, to be deemed a price readjustment, the payment or credit must be contractually or economically related to the taxable sale that the payment or credit purports to adjust. Thus, commissions or bonuses paid to a manufacturer's own agents or salesperson for selling the manufacturer's taxable products are not price readjustments for purposes of this section, since those commissions or bonuses are not paid or credited either to the manufacturer's vendee or to a third party for the vendee's benefit. On the other hand, a bonus paid by the manufacturer to a dealer's salesperson for negotiating the sale of a taxable article previously sold to the dealer by the manufacturer is considered to be a readjustment of the price on the original sale of the taxable article, regardless of whether the payment to the salesperson is made directly by the manufacturer or to the salesperson through the dealer. In such a case, the payment is related to the sale of a taxable article and is made for the benefit of the dealer because it is made to the dealer's salesperson to encourage the sale of a product owned by the dealer. Similarly, payments or credits made by a manufacturer to a vendee as reimbursement of interest expense incurred by the vendee in connection with a so-called "free flooring" arrangement for the purchase of taxable articles is a price readjustment, regardless of whether the payment or credit is made directly to the vendee or to the vendee's creditor on behalf of the vendee.

(iii) *Limitation on credit or refund.*—The credit or refund allowable by reason of a price readjustment in respect of the sale of a taxable article may not exceed an amount which bears the same ratio to the total tax originally due and payable on the article as the amount of the tax-included readjustment bears to the original tax-included sale price of the article.

*Example.* A manufacturer sells a taxable article for $100 plus $10 excise tax, and reports and pays tax liability accordingly. Thereafter, the manufacturer credits the customer's account for $11 (tax included) in readjustment of the original sale price. The overpayment of tax is $1, determined as follows:

$$\frac{\text{Tax-included readjustment}}{\text{Tax-included sale price}} \times \frac{\text{Original}}{\text{tax due}} = \frac{\text{Tax}}{\text{overpayment.}}$$

$$\frac{\$11}{\$110} \times \$10 = \$1 \text{ tax overpaid.}$$

(2) *Rules of special application.*—(i) *Constructive sale price.*—If, in the case of a taxable sale, the tax imposed by chapter 32 is based on a constructive sale price determined under any paragraph of section 4216(b) and the regulations thereunder, as determined without reference to section 4218, then any price readjustment made with respect to the sale may be taken into account under this section only to the extent that the price readjustment reduces the actual sale price of the article below the constructive sale price.

*Example.* (A) A manufacturer sells a taxable article at retail for $110 tax included. Under section 4216(b)(1) the constructive sale price (tax included) of the article is determined to be $93. Thereafter, the manufacturer grants an allowance of $10 to the purchaser, which reduces the actual selling price (tax included) to $100. Since the readjustment price still exceeds the amounts of the constructive sale price, this readjustment is not recognized as a price readjustment under this section.

(B) Subsequently, the manufacturer extends to the purchaser an additional price allowance of $10, thereby reducing the actual sale price to $90. Since the actual sale price is now $3 less than the constructive sale price of $93, the manufacturer has overpaid by the amount of tax attributable to the $3. Assuming the tax rate involved is 10 percent, and the prices involved are tax-included, the overpayment of tax would be $0.27, determined as follows:

$$\frac{\text{percentage tax rate}}{\text{100 plus percentage tax rate}} \times \frac{\text{tax-included}}{\text{readjustment}} = \text{tax overpayment}$$

$$\frac{10}{110} \times \$3 = \$0.27).$$

(ii) *Price determined under section 4223(b)(2).*—If a manufacturer (within the meaning of section 4223(a)) to whom an article is sold or resold free of tax in accordance with the provisions of section 4221(a)(1) for use in further manufacture diverts the article to a taxable use or sells it in a taxable sale, and pursuant to the provisions of section 4223(b)(2) computes the tax liability in respect of the use or sale on the price for which the article was sold to the manufacturer or on the price at which the article was sold by the actual manufacturer, a reduction of the price on which the tax was based does not result in an overpayment within the meaning of section 6416(b)(1) or this section. Moreover, if a manufacturer purchases an article tax free and computes the tax in respect of a subsequent sale of the article pursuant to the provisions of section 4223(b)(2), an overpayment does not arise by reason of readjustment of the price for which the article was sold by the manufacturer except where the readjustment results from the return or repossession of the article by the manufacturer, and all of the purchase price is refunded by the manufacturer. See, however, paragraph (b)(4) of this section as to repurchased articles.

(b) *Return of an article.*—(1) *Price, readjustment.*—If a taxable article is returned to the manufacturer who paid the tax imposed by chapter 32 on the sale of the article, a price readjustment giving rise to an overpayment results—

(i) If the article is returned before use, and all of the purchase price is repaid to the vendee of credited to the vendee's account, or

(ii) If the article is returned under an express or implied warranty as to quality or service, and all or a part of the purchase price is repaid to the vendee or credited to the vendee's account, or

(iii) If title is still in the seller, as, for example, in the case of certain installment sales contracts, and all or a part of the purchase price is repaid to the vendee or credited to the vendee's account.

(2) *Return of purchase price.*—For purposes of paragraph (b)(1) of this section, if all of the purchase price of an article has been returned to the vendee, except for an amount retained by the manufacturer pursuant to contract as reimbursement of expense incurred in connection with the sale (such as a handling or restocking charge), all of the purchase price is considered to have been returned to the vendee.

**Reg. § 48.6416(b)(1)-2(b)(2)**

(3) *Taxability of subsequent sale or use.*—If, under any of the conditions described in paragraph (b)(1) of this section, an article is returned to the manufacturer who paid the tax and all of the purchase price is returned to the vendee, the sale is considered to have been rescinded. Any subsequent sale or use of the article by the manufacturer will be considered to be an original sale or use of the article by the manufacturer which is subject to tax under chapter 32 unless otherwise exempt. If under any such condition an article is returned to the manufacturer who paid the tax and only part of the purchase price is returned to the vendee, a subsequent sale of the article by the manufacturer will be subject to tax to the extent that the sale price exceeds the adjusted sale price of the first taxable sale.

(4) *Treatment of other transactions as repurchases.*—Except as provided in paragraph (b)(1) of this section, a price readjustment will not result when a taxable article is returned to the manufacturer who paid the tax on the sale of the article, even though all or a part of the purchase price is repaid to the vendee or credited to the vendee's account, since such a transaction will be considered to be a repurchase of the article by the manufacturer.

(c) *Repossession of an article.*—If a taxable article is repossessed by the manufacturer who paid the tax imposed by chapter 32 on the sale of the article, and all or a part of the purchase price is repaid to the vendee or credited to the vendee's account, a price readjustment giving rise to an overpayment will result. However, if the manufacturer later resells the repossessed article for a price in excess of the original adjusted sale price, the manufacturer will be liable for tax under chapter 32 to the extent that the resale price exceeds the original adjusted sale price.

(d) *Return or repossession of covering or container.*—If the covering or container of a taxable article is returned to, or repossessed by the manufacturer who paid the tax imposed by chapter 32 on the sale of the article, and all or a portion of the purchase price is repaid to the vendee or credited to the vendee's account by reason of the return or repossession of the covering or container, a price adjustment giving rise to an overpayment will result. If a taxable article is considered to have been repurchased, as provided in paragraph (b)(4) of this section, and the covering or container accompanies the taxable article as part of the transaction, the covering or container will also be considered to have been repurchased.

(e) *Bona fide discounts, rebates, or allowances.*—(1) *In general.*—Except as provided in §48.6416(b)(1)-3 (relating to readjustments in respect of local advertising), the basic consideration in determining, for purposes of this section, whether a bona fide discount, rebate, or allowance has been made is whether the price actually paid by, or charged against, the purchaser has in fact been reduced by subsequent transactions between the parties. Generally, the price will be considered to have been readjusted by reason of a bona fide discount, rebate, or allowance, only if the manufacturer who made the taxable sale repays a part of the purchase price in cash to the vendee, or credits the vendee's account, or directly or indirectly reimburses a third party for part or all of the purchase price for the direct benefit of the vendee, in consideration of factors which, if taken into account at the time of the original transaction, would have resulted at that time in a lower sale price. For example, a price readjustment will be considered to have been made when a bona fide discount, rebate, or allowance is given in consideration of such factors as prompt payment, quantity buying over a specified period, the vendee's inventory of an article when new models are introduced, or a general price reduction affecting articles held in stock by the vendee as of a certain date. On the other hand, repayments made to the vendee do not effectuate price readjustments if given in consideration of circumstances under which the vendee has incurred, or is required to incur, an expense which, if treated as a separate item in the original transaction, would have been includible in the price of the article for purposes of computing the tax.

*Examples.* The provisions of paragraph (e)(1) of this section may be illustrated by the following examples:

*Example (1).* B, a manufacturer of fishing rods, bills its distributors in a specific amount per fishing rods purchased by them. Thereafter, B issues to each distributor a credit memorandum in the amount of X dollars for each demonstration by the distributor of the fishing rods at a sporting goods exhibition. The credit which B allows the distributor for demonstration of B's product does not effect a readjustment of price.

*Example (2).* C, a manufacturer of automobiles, bills its dealers in a specified amount per automobile purchased by them. Thereafter, C remits to the dealer X dollars of the original sale price for each automobile sold by the dealer in the last month of the model year. An additional amount of Y dollars is paid to the dealer upon a showing by the dealer that the dealer has paid Y dollars to the salesperson who made the sale. In this case, the X dollars paid to the dealer by C

constitutes a bona fide discount, rebate, or allowance since payment of such amount is in the nature of a price reduction by reason of the dealer's inventory when new models are introduced. In addition, the Y dollars paid to the dealer in reimbursement for the amount paid by the dealer to the salesperson who made the sale, also constitutes a bona fide discount, rebate, or allowance.

(2) *Inability to collect price.*—A charge-off of an amount outstanding in an open account, due to inability to collect, is not a bona fide discount, rebate, or allowance and does not, in and of itself, give rise to a price readjustment within the meaning of this section.

(3) *Loss or damage in transit.*—If title to an article has passed to the vendee, the subsequent loss, damage, or destruction of the article while in the possession of a carrier for delivery to the vendee does not, in and of itself, affect the price at which the article was sold. However, if the article was sold under a contract providing that if the article was lost, damaged, or destroyed in transit, title would revert to the vendor and the vendor would reimburse the vendee in full for the sale price, then the original sale is considered to have been rescinded. The vendor is entitled to credit or refund of the tax paid upon reimbursement of the full tax-included sale price to the vendee. [Reg. §48.6416(b)(1)-2.]

☐ [T.D. 8043, 8-8-85.]

### [Reg. §48.6416(b)(1)-3]

§48.6416(b)(1)-3. **Readjustment for local advertising charges.**—(a) *In general.*—If a manufacturer has paid the tax imposed by chapter 32 on the price of any article sold by the manufacturer and thereafter has repaid a portion of the price to the purchaser or any subsequent vendee in reimbursement of expenses for local advertising of the article or any other article sold by the manufacturer which is taxable at the same rate under the same section of chapter 32, the reimbursement will be considered a price readjustment constituting an overpayment which the manufacturer may claim as a credit or refund. The amount of the reimbursement may not, however, exceed the limitation provided by section 4216(e)(2) and §48.4216(e)-2, determined as of the close of the calendar quarter in which the reimbursement is made or as of the close of any subsequent calendar quarter of the same calendar year in which it is made. The term "local advertisement", as used in this section, has the same meaning as prescribed by section 4216(e)(4) and includes generally, advertising which is broadcast over a radio station or television station, or appears in a newspaper or magazine, or is displayed by means of an outdoor advertising sign or poster.

(b) *Local advertising charges excluded from taxable price in one year but repaid in following year.*—(1) *Determination of price readjustments for year in which charge is repaid.*—If the tax imposed by chapter 32 was paid with respect to local advertising charges that were excluded in computing the taxable price of an article sold in any calendar year but are not repaid to the manufacturer's purchaser or any subsequent vendee before May 1 of the following calendar year, the subsequent repayment of those charges by the manufacturer in reimbursement of expenses for local advertising will be considered a price readjustment constituting an overpayment which the manufacturer may claim as a credit or refund. The amount of the reimbursement may not, however, exceed the limitation provided by section 4216(e)(2) and §48.4216(e)-(2), determined as of the close of the calendar quarter in which the reimbursement is made or as of the close of any subsequent calendar quarter of the same calendar year in which it is made.

(2) *Redetermination of price readjustments for year in which charge was made.*—If the tax imposed by chapter 32 was paid with respect to local advertising charges that were excluded in computing the taxable price of an article sold in any calendar year but are not repaid to the manufacturer's purchaser or any subsequent vendor before May 1 of the following calendar year, the manufacturer may make a redetermination, in respect of the calendar year in which the charge was made, of the price readjustments constituting an overpayment which the manufacturer may claim as a credit or refund. This redetermination may be made by excluding the local advertising charges made in the calendar year that became taxable as of May 1 of the following calendar year. [Reg. §48.6416(b)(1)-3.]

☐ [T.D. 8043, 8-8-85.]

### [Reg. §48.6416(b)(1)-4]

§48.6416(b)(1)-4. **Supporting evidence required in case of price readjustments.**—No credit or refund of an overpayment arising by reason of a price readjustment described in §48.6416(b)(1)-2 or §48.6416(b)(1)-3 shall be allowed unless the manufacturer who paid the tax submits a statement, supported by sufficient available evidence—

(a) Describing the circumstances which gave rise to the price readjustment,

(b) Identifying the article in respect of which the price readjustment was allowed,

(c) Showing the price at which the article was sold, the amount of tax paid in respect of the article, and the date on which the tax was paid,

(d) Giving the name and address of the purchaser to whom the article was sold, and

(e) Showing the amount repaid to the purchaser or credited to the purchaser's account. [Reg. § 48.6416(b)(1)-4.]

☐ [*T.D. 8043, 8-8-85.*]

### [Reg. § 48.6416(b)(2)-1]

**§ 48.6416(b)(2)-1. Certain exportations, uses, sales, or resales causing overpayments of tax.**—In the case of any payment of tax under section 4041(a)(1) or (a)(2) or under chapter 32 (diesel fuel and special fuels tax) (manufacturers tax) that is determined to be an overpayment by reason of certain exportations, uses, sales, or resales described in section 6416(b)(2) and § 48.6416(b)(2)-2, the person who paid the tax may file a claim for refund of the overpayment or, in the case of overpayments under chapter 32, may claim credit for the overpayment on any return of tax under this subpart which the person subsequently files. However, under the circumstances described in section 6416(c) and § 48,6416(e)-1, the overpayments under chapter 32 may be refunded to an exporter or shipper. No interest shall be paid on any credit or refund allowed under this section. For provisions relating to the evidence required in support of a claim for credit or refund under this section, see § 301.6402-2 of this chapter (Regulations on Procedure and Administration) and § § 48.6416(b)(2)-3 and 48.6416(b)(2)-4. For provisions authorizing the taking of a credit in lieu of filing a claim for refund, see section 6416(d) and § 48.6416(f)-1. [Reg. § 48.6416(b)(2)-1.]

☐ [*T.D. 8043, 8-8-85. Amended by T.D. 8879, 3-30-2000.*]

### [Reg. § 48.6416(b)(2)-2]

**§ 48.6416(b)(2)-2. Exportations, uses, sales, and resales included.**—(a) *In general.*—The tax paid under chapter 32 (or under section 4041(a) or (d) in respect of sales or under section 4051) with respect to any article is considered to be an overpayment in the case of any exportation, use, sale, or resale described in this section. This section applies only in those cases in which the exportation, use, sale, or resale (or any combination thereof) referred to in this section occurs before any other use. In addition, the following restrictions must be taken into account in applying the regulations under section 6416(b)(2):

(1) Sections 6416(b)(2)(C) and (D) do not apply to any tax paid under section 4064 (gas guzzler tax).

(2) Sections 6416(b)(2)(B), (C), and (D) do not apply to any tax paid under section 4131 (vaccine tax) and section 6416(b)(2)(A) applies only to the extent prescribed in paragraph (b)(2) of this section.

(3) Section 6416(b)(2) does not apply to any tax paid under section 4041(a)(1) or 4081 on diesel fuel or kerosene, section 4091 (aviation fuel tax), or section 4121 (coal tax).

(4) Beginning on January 1, 2013, sections 6416(b)(2)(B), (C), (D), and (E) do not apply to any tax paid under section 4191 (medical device tax).

(b) *Exportation of tax-paid articles.*—(1) *In general.*—Subject to the limitations of section 6416(b)(2) and paragraph (b)(2) of this section, tax paid under chapter 31 or 32 on the sale of any article will be considered to be an overpayment under section 6416(b)(2)(A) if the article is exported by any person. Except in the case of articles subject to the tax imposed by section 4061(a) prior to April 1, 1983, it is immaterial for purposes of this paragraph (b), whether the person who made the taxable sale had knowledge at the time of the sale that the article or fuel was being purchased for export to a foreign country or shipment to a possession of the United States. See § 48.6416(e)-1 for the circumstances under which a claim for refund by reason of the exportation of an article may be claimed by the exporter or shipper, rather than by the person who paid the tax. For definition of the term "possession of the United States", see § 48.0-2(a)(11).

(2) *Rule for exportation of vaccines.*—Paragraph (b)(1) of this section applies to tax paid under section 4131 on the sale of a vaccine, but only if the sale by the manufacturer occurs after August 10, 1993, and, in the case of vaccine sold to the United States or any of its agencies or instrumentalities, the condition of § 48.4221-3(e)(2) is satisfied.

(c) *Supplies for vessels or aircraft.*—A payment of tax under chapter 32 on the sale of any article, or under section 4041(a)(1) or (a)(2) on the sale of diesel fuel or special motor fuel, will be considered to be an overpayment under section 6416(b)(2)(B) if the article or fuel is used by any person, or is sold by any person for use by the purchaser, as supplies for vessels or aircraft.

The term "supplies for vessels or aircraft", as used in this paragraph, has the same meaning as when used in sections 4041(g), 4221(a)(3), 4221(d)(3), and 4221(e)(1), and the regulations thereunder.

(d) *Use by State or local government.*—A payment of tax under chapter 32 on the sale of any article, or under section 4041(a)(1) or (a)(2) on the sale of diesel fuel or special motor fuel, will be considered to be an overpayment under section 6416(b)(2)(C) if the article of fuel is sold by any person to a State, any political subdivision thereof, or the District of Columbia for the exclusive use of a State, any political subdivision thereof, or the District of Columbia. For provisions relating to tax-free sales to a State, any political subdivision thereof, or the District of Columbia, see section 4221(a)(4) and the regulations thereunder.

(e) *Use by nonprofit educational organization.*—A payment of tax under chapter 32 on the sale of any article, or under section 4041(a)(1) or (a)(2) on the sale of diesel fuel or special motor fuel, will be considered to be an overpayment under section 6416(b)(2)(D) if the article or fuel is sold by any person to a nonprofit educational organization for its exclusive use. The term "nonprofit educational organization", as used in this paragraph (e), has the same meaning as when used in section 4221(a)(5) or (d)(5), whichever applies, and the regulations thereunder.

(f) *Tax-paid tires or inner tubes resold for use in further manufacture.*— A payment of tax under section 4071 on the sale of a tire or, prior to January 1, 1984, on the sale of an inner tube will be considered to be an overpayment under section 6416(b)(2)(E) if—

(1) The tire or inner tube is, after the original sale of the article by the manufacturer, resold by any person to another manufacturer;

(2) The other manufacturer sells the tire or inner tube on or in connection with, or with the sale of, any other article manufactured or produced by the other manufacturer, and

(3) That other article is by any person either—

(i) Exported to a foreign country or to a possession of the United States,

(ii) Sold to a State, any political subdivision thereof, or the District of Columbia for the exclusive use of a State, any political subdivision thereof, or the District of Columbia,

(iii) Sold to a nonprofit educational organization for its exclusive use, or

(iv) Used or sold for use as supplies for vessels or aircraft. The overpayment described in this paragraph (f) is to be distinguished from the overpayment described in section 6416(b)(3)(C) prior to amendment by the Highway Revenue Act of 1982 and section 6416(b)(3) as amended by the Highway Revenue Act of 1982, and § 48.6416(b)(3)-2(d) in that the overpayment here described arises from a "resale" for the use described in this paragraph, while the section 6416(b)(3)(C) overpayment arises from the "use" of tires or inner tubes in the manufacture of other articles by a subsequent manufacturer who purchases tax-paid tires or tubes and disposes of finished articles on the basis of one of the exemptions set forth in section 6416(B)[b](3)(C). A manufacturer claiming a credit or refund under this paragraph (f) must have substantially the same information available in support of the claim as is required under § 48.4221-7(c)(2) in support of exempt sales of tires or inner tubes under the provisions of section 4221(e)(2), except that none of the parties involved need be registered under section 4222. [Reg. § 48.6416(b)(2)-2.]

☐ [*T.D. 8043, 8-8-85. Amended by T.D. 8561, 8-19-94; T.D. 8659, 3-13-96 T.D. 8879, 3-30-2000 and T.D. 9604, 12-5-2012.*]

### [Reg. § 48.6416(b)(2)-3]

**§ 48.6416(b)(2)-3. Supporting evidence required in case of manufacturers tax involving exportations, uses, sales, or resales.**— (a) *Evidence to be submitted by claimant.*—No claim for credit or refund of an overpayment, within the meaning of section 6416(b)(2) and § 48.6416(b)(2)-2, of tax under chapter 32 shall be allowed unless the person who paid the tax submits with the claim the evidence required by paragraph (b)(2) of § 48.6416(a)-3 and a statement, supported by sufficient available evidence—

(1) Showing the amount claimed in respect of each category of exportations, uses, sales, or resales on which the claim is based and which give rise to a right of credit or refund under section 6416(b)(2) and § 48.6416(b)(2)-1,

(2) Identifying the article, both as to nature and quantity, in respect of which credit or refund is claimed,

(3) Showing the amount of tax paid in respect of the article or articles and the dates of payment, and

(4) In the case of an overpayment determined under section 6416(b)(2)(A) and paragraph (b) of § 48.6416(b)(2)-2 in respect of an article which was taxable prior to April 1, 1983, under section 4061(a), indicating that, pursuant to section 6416(g), the person claiming a credit or refund possessed at the time that person shipped the

article or at the time title to the article passed to the vendee, whichever is earlier, evidence that the article was to be exported to a foreign country or shipped to a possession of the United States, or

(5) In the case of any overpayment other than an overpayment determined under section 6416(b)(2)(E) and paragraph (f) of § 48.6416(b)(2)-2, indicating that the person claiming a credit or refund possesses evidence (as set forth in paragraph (b)(1) of this section) that the article has been exported, or has been used, sold, or resold in a manner or for a purpose which gives rise to an overpayment within the meaning of section 6416(b)(2) and § 48.6416(b)(2)-2, or

(6) In the case of an overpayment determined under section 6416(b)(2)(E) and paragraph (f) of § 48.6416(b)(2)-2, relating to a tax-paid tire or inner tube sold on or in connection with, or with the sale of, a second article that has been manufactured, indicating that the person claiming a credit or refund possesses (i) evidence (as set forth in paragraph (b)(2) of this section) that the second article has been exported, or has been used or sold as provided in § 48.6416(b)(2)-2(f), and (ii) a statement, executed and signed by the ultimate purchaser of the tire or inner tube, that the ultimate purchaser purchased the tire or inner tube from a person other than the person who paid the tax on the sale of the tire or inner tube.

(b) *Evidence required to be in possession of claimant.*—(1) *Evidence required under paragraph (a)(5).*—(i) *In general.*—The evidence required to be retained by the person who paid the tax, as provided in paragraph (a)(5) of this section must, in the case of an article exported, consist of proof of exportation in the form prescribed in the regulations under section 4221 or must, in the case of other articles sold tax-paid by that person, consist of a certificate, executed and signed by the ultimate purchaser of the article, in the form prescribed in paragraph (b)(1)(ii) of this section. However, if the article to which the claim relates has passed through a chain of sales from the person who paid the tax to the ultimate purchaser, the evidence required to be retained by the person who paid the tax may consist of a certificate, executed and signed by the ultimate vendor of the article, in the form provided in paragraph (b)(1)(iii) of this section, rather than the proof of exportation itself or the certificate of the ultimate purchaser.

(ii) *Certificate of ultimate purchaser.*

(A) The certificate executed and signed by the ultimate purchaser of the article to which the claim relates must identify the article, both as to nature and quantity; show the address of the ultimate purchaser of the article, and the name and address of the ultimate vendor of the article; and describe the use actually made of the article in sufficient detail to establish that credit or refund is due, except that the use to be made of the article must be described in lieu of actual use if the claim is made by reason of the sale or resale of an article for a specified use which gives rise to the overpayment.

(B) If the certificate sets forth the use to be made of any article, rather than its actual use, it must show that the ultimate purchaser has agreed to notify the claimant if the article is not in fact used as specified in the certificate.

(C) The certificate must also contain a statement that the ultimate purchaser understands that the ultimate purchaser and any other party may, for fraudulent use of the certificate, be subject under section 7201 to a fine of not more than $10,000, or imprisonment for not more than 5 years, or both, together with the costs of prosecution.

(D) A purchase order will be acceptable in lieu of a separate certificate of the ultimate purchaser if it contains all the information required by this paragraph (b)(1)(ii).

(iii) *Certificate of ultimate vendor.*—Any certificate executed and signed by an ultimate vendor as evidence to be retained by the person who paid the tax, as provided in paragraph (a)(5) of this section, may be executed with respect to any one or more overpayments by the person which arose under section 6416(b)(2) and §§ 48.6416(b)(2)-2 by reason of exportations, uses, sales or resales, occurring within any period of not more than 12 consecutive calendar quarters, the beginning and ending dates of which are specified in the certificate.

The certificate must be in substantially the following form:

### Statement of Ultimate Vendor

(For use in claiming credit or refund of overpayment determined under section 6416(b)(2) (other than section 6416(b)(2)(E) of the Internal Revenue Code.)
The undersigned or the . . . . . . . . . . . . . . . (Name of ultimate vendor if other than undersigned) of which the undersigned is . . . . . . . . . . . . . . . (Title), is the ultimate vendor of the article specified below or on the reverse side hereof.
The article was purchased by the ultimate vendor tax-paid and was thereafter exported, used, sold, or resold (as indicated below or on the reverse side hereof).

The ultimate vendor possesses . . . . . . . . . . . . . . . . . . . . . . . . . . . (Proof of exportation in respect of the article, or a certificate as to use executed by the ultimate purchaser of the article)
The . . . . . . . . . . . . . . . . (Proof of exportation or certificate) (1) is retained by the ultimate vendor, (2) will, upon request, be forwarded to . . . . . . . . . . . . . . . . . . (Name or person who paid the tax) at any time within 3 years from the date of this statement for use by that person to establish that credit or refund is due in respect of the article, and (3) will otherwise be held by the ultimate vendor for the required 3-year period.
According to the best knowledge and belief of the undersigned, no statement in respect of the . . . . . . . . . . . . . . . (Proof of exportation or certificate) has previously been executed, and the undersigned understands that the fraudulent use of this statement may, under section 7201, subject the undersigned or any other party making such fraudulent use to a fine of not more than $10,000, or imprisonment for not more than 5 years, or both, together with the costs of prosecution.
. . . . . . . . . . . . . . . . . . . . . . . (Signature)
. . . . . . . . . . . . . . . . . . . . . . . (Address)
. . . . . . . . . . . . . . . . . . . . . . . (Date)

| Vendor's invoice | Articles | Date of resale | Quantity | Exported or use made or to be made (specify) |
|---|---|---|---|---|
| | | | | |

(2) *Evidence required under paragraph (a)(6).*—(i) *In general.*—The evidence required to be retained by the person who paid the tax, as provided in paragraph (a)(6) of this section, must, in the case of an exportation of the second article, consist of proof of exportation of the second article in the form prescribed in the regulations under section 4221 or must, in other cases, consist of a certificate, executed and signed by the ultimate purchaser of the second article, in the form prescribed in paragraph (b)(2)(ii) of this section. However, the evidence required to be retained by the person who paid the tax may consist of a certificate, executed and signed by the ultimate vendor of the second article, in the form provided in paragraph (b)(2)(iii) of this section, rather than the proof of exportation itself or the certificate of the ultimate purchaser.

(ii) *Certificate of ultimate purchaser.*—The certificate of the ultimate purchaser of the second article must contain the same information as that required in paragraph (b)(1)(ii) of this section, except that the information must be furnished in respect of the second article, rather than the article to which the claims relates.

(iii) *Certificate of ultimate vendor.*—Any certificate executed and signed by an ultimate vendor as evidence to be retained by the person who paid the tax, as provided in paragraph (a)(6) of this section, may be executed with respect to any one of more overpayments by that person which arose under section 6416(b)(2)(E) and § 48.6416(b)(2)-2(f) by reason of exportations, uses, sales, or resales of a second article occurring within any period of not more than 12 consecutive calendar quarters, the beginning and ending dates of which are specified in the certificate. The certificate must be in substantially the following form:

### STATEMENT OF ULTIMATE VENDOR

(For use in claiming credit or refund of overpayment determined under section 6416(b)(2)(E) Internal Revenue Code, involving tires or inner tubes sold on or with another article)
The undersigned or the . . . . . . . . . . . . . . . . (Name of ultimate vendor of second article if other than undersigned) of which the undersigned is . . . . . . . . . . . . . . . . (Title), is the ultimate vendor of an article, specified below or on the reverse side hereof, on which or with which a tax-paid tire or inner tube was sold.
The ultimate vendor possesses . . . . . . . . . . . . . . . . . . . . . . . . . . . . . . . (Proof of exportation in respect of the article on which or with which the tire or inner tube was sold, or a certificate as to use of the article executed by the ultimate purchaser of the article)
The . . . . . . . . . . . . . . . . (Proof of exportation or certificate) (1) is retained by the ultimate vendor, (2) will, upon request, be forwarded to . . . . . . . . . . . . . . . . . . . (Name of person who paid the tax on the tire or inner tube) at any time within 3 years from the date of this statement for use in establishing that credit or refund is due in respect of the tire or inner tube, and (3) will otherwise be held by the ultimate vendor for the required 3-year period.
According to the best knowledge and belief of the undersigned, no statement in respect of the . . . . . . . . . . . . . . . (Proof of exportation or certificate) has previously been executed, and the undersigned understands that the fraudulent use of this statement may, under section 7201, subject the undersigned or any other party making such fraudulent use to a fine of not more than $10,000, or imprisonment for not more than 5 years, or both, together with the costs of prosecution.
. . . . . . . . . . . . . . . . . . . . . . . (Signature)
. . . . . . . . . . . . . . . . . . . . . . . (Address)
. . . . . . . . . . . . . . . . . . . . . . . (Date)

| Tires or inner tubes (specify and state quantity) | Vendor's invoice on second article | Second article (specify and state quantity) | Date of sale of second article | Exported or use made of or to be made (specify in respect of second article) |
|---|---|---|---|---|

(3) *Repayment or consent of ultimate vendor.*—If the person claiming credit or refund of an overpayment to which this section applies has repaid, or agreed to repay, the amount of the overpayment to the ultimate vendor or if the ultimate vendor consents to the allowance of the credit or refund, a statement to that effect, signed by the ultimate vendor, must be shown on, or made a part of, the evidence required under this section to be retained by the person claiming the credit or refund. In this regard, see § 48.6416(a)-3(b)(2). [Reg. § 48.6416(b)(2)-3.]

☐ [*T.D. 8043, 8-8-85.*]

### [Reg. § 48.6416(b)(2)-4]

**§ 48.6416(b)(2)-4. Supporting evidence required in case of special fuels tax involving exportations, uses, sales, or resales of special fuels.**—(a) *Evidence to be submitted by claimant.*—No claim for credit or refund of an overpayment, within the meaning of section 6416(b)(2) and § 48.6416(b)(2)-2 of tax under section 4041(a)(1) or (a)(2) shall be allowed unless the person who paid the tax submits with the claim the evidence required by paragraph (b)(2) of § 48.6416(a)-2 and a statement, supported by sufficient available evidence—

(1) Showing the amount claimed in respect of each category of exportations, uses, sales, or resales on which the claim is based and which give rise to right of credit or refund under section 6416(b)(2) and § 48.6416(b)(2)-1,

(2) Identifying the fuel, both as to nature and quantity, in respect of which credit or refund is claimed,

(3) Showing the amount of tax paid in respect of the fuel and the dates of payment, and

(4) Indicating that the fuel has been exported, or has been used, sold, or resold in a manner or for a purpose which gives rise to an overpayment within the meaning of section 6416(b)(2) and § 48.6416(b)(2)-2.

(b) *Evidence required to be in possession of claimant.*—(1) The evidence required to be retained by the person who paid the tax, as provided in paragraph (a)(4) of this section, must, in the case of fuel exported, consist of proof of exportation or must, in the case of other fuel sold tax-paid by that person, consist of a certificate, executed and signed by the person who purchased the fuel in a resale or for the use which gave rise to the overpayment.

(2) The certificate must identify the fuel, both as to nature and quantity, in respect of which credit or refund is claimed; show the address of the purchaser; show the name and address of the person from whom the fuel was purchased and the date or dates on which the fuel was purchased; and show that the fuel was resold and the date of the resale.

(3) If the claim is not based on resale of the fuel, the certificate must describe the use actually made of the fuel in sufficient detail to establish that credit or refund is due. However, the use to be made of the fuel must be described in lieu of actual use if the claim is made by reason of the sale of the fuel for a specified use which gives rise to an overpayment under § 48.6416(b)(2)-2.

(4) If the certificate sets forth the use to be made of the fuel, rather than its actual use, it must show that the purchaser has agreed to notify the claimant if the fuel is not in fact used as specified in the certificate.

(5) The certificate must also contain a statement that the purchaser has not previously executed a certificate in respect of the fuel and understands that any party may, for fraudulent use of the certificate, be subject under section 7201 to a fine of not more than $10,000, or imprisonment for not more than 5 years, or both, together with the costs of prosecution. [Reg. § 48.6416(b)(2)-4.]

☐ [*T.D. 8043, 8-8-85.*]

### [Reg. § 48.6416(b)(3)-1]

**§ 48.6416(b)(3)-1. Tax-paid articles used for further manufacture and causing overpayments of tax.**—In the case of any payment of tax under chapter 32 that is determined to be an overpayment under section 6416(b)(3) and § 48.6416(b)(3)-2 by reason of the sale of an article(other than coal taxable under section 4121), directly or indirectly, by the manufacturer of the article to a subsequent manufacturer who uses the article in further manufacture of a second article or who sells the article with, or as a part of, the second article manufactured or produced by the subsequent manufacturer, the subsequent manufacturer may file claim for refund of the overpayment or may claim credit for the overpayment on any return of tax under this subpart subsequently filed. No interest shall be paid on any credit or refund allowed under this section. For provisions relating to the evidence required in support of a claim for credit or refund, see § 301.6402-2 of this chapter (Regulations on Procedure and Administration) and § § 48.6416(a)-3 and 48.6416(b)(3)-3. For provisions authorizing the taking of a credit in lieu of filing a claim for refund, see section 6416(d) and § 48.6416(f)-1. [Reg. § 48.6416(b)(3)-1.]

☐ [*T.D. 8043, 8-8-85.*]

### [Reg. § 48.6416(b)(3)-2]

**§ 48.6416(b)(3)-2. Further manufacture included.**—(a) *In general.*—The payment of tax imposed by chapter 32 on the sale of any article (other than coal taxable under section 4121) by a manufacturer of the article will be considered to be an overpayment by reason of any use in further manufacture, or sale as part of a second manufactured article, described in any one of paragraphs (b) through (f) of this section. This section applies in those cases where the exportation, use, or sale (or any combination of those activities) referred to in any one or more of those paragraphs occurs before any other use. For provisions relating to overpayments arising by reason of resales of tax-paid articles for use in further manufacture as provided in this section, see section 6416(b)(2)(E) and paragraph (f) of § 48.6416(b)(2)-2.

(b) *Use of tax-paid articles in further manufacture described in section 6416(b)(3)(A).*—A payment of tax under chapter 32 on the sale of any article (other than coal taxable under section 4121), directly or indirectly, by the manufacturer of the article to a subsequent manufacturer will be considered to be an overpayment under section 6416(b)(3)(A) if the article is used by the subsequent manufacturer as material in the manufacture or production of, or as a component part of, a second article manufactured or produced by the subsequent manufacturer which is—

(1) Taxable under chapter 32, or

(2) An automobile bus chassis or an automobile bus body.

For this purpose it is immaterial whether the second article is sold or otherwise disposed of, or if sold, whether the sale is a taxable sale. Any article to which this paragraph (b) applies which would have been used in the manufacture or production of a second article, except for the fact that it was broken or rendered useless in the process of manufacturing or producing the second article, will be considered to have been used as a component part of the second article. This paragraph (b) does not apply to articles sold and used as provided in any of paragraphs (c) through (f) of this section.

(c) *Use of truck, bus, etc., parts or accessories.*—A payment of tax under section 4061(b) on the sale prior to January 7, 1983, of any truck, bus, etc., part or accessory, directly or indirectly, by the manufacturer of the article to a subsequent manufacturer will be considered to be an overpayment under section 6416(b)(3)(B) if the part or accessory is used by the subsequent manufacturer as material in the manufacture or production of or as a component part of, a second article manufactured or produced by the subsequent manufacturer. For this purpose it is immaterial whether the second article is or is not taxable under chapter 32. Any article to which this paragraph (c) applies which would have been used in the manufacture or production of a second article, except for the fact that it was broken or rendered useless in the process of manufacturing or producing the second article, will be considered to have been used as a component part of the second article.

(d) *Tax-paid tires or inner tubes used in further manufacture.*—(1) A payment of tax under section 4071 on the sale prior to January 1, 1984, of a tire or inner tube, directly or indirectly, by the manufacturer of the article to a subsequent manufacturer will be considered to be an overpayment under section 6416(b)(3)(C) if the subsequent manufacturer sells the tire or inner tube on or in connection with, or with the sale of, any other article manufactured or produced by the subsequent manufacturer and if the other article is—

(i) An automobile bus chassis or automobile bus body, or

(ii) By any person (A) exported to a foreign country or to a possession of the United States, (B) sold to a State, any political subdivision thereof, or the District of Columbia for the exclusive use of a State, any political subdivision thereof, or the District of Columbia, (C) sold to a nonprofit educational organization for its exclusive use, or (D) used or sold for use as supplies to vessels or aircraft.

For tax-paid tires used in further manufacture after December 31, 1983, see section 6416 (b)(3)(A) and the regulations thereunder.

(2) The overpayment in this paragraph (d) is to be distinguished from that overpayment described in section 6416(b)(2)(E) and § 48.6416(b)(2)-2(f) in that this overpayment arises from the "use"

described in this paragraph, whereas the overpayment under section 6416(b)(2)(E) arises from the "resale" of tax-paid tires or inner tubes by any person to a subsequent manufacturer who disposes of the articles on or in connection with, or with the sale of, a second article manufactured or produced by the subsequent manufacturer which is disposed of on the basis of one of the exemptions set forth in section 6416(b)(3)(C).

(3) If the second article is exported or shipped as provided in this paragraph (d), it is immaterial whether the subsequent manufacturer sold the article with the knowledge that it would be exported or shipped.

(4) An overpayment arises under paragraph (d)(1) of this section only if the tire or inner tube constitutes a part of, or is associated with, the second article at the time the second article is exported, shipped, sold, used, or sold for use, as prescribed in this paragraph.

(5) For definition of certain terms used in this paragraph, see section 4221 and the regulations thereunder.

(6) For provisions relating to overpayments arising by reason of tires or inner tubes sold tax-paid by the manufacturer of the same, on or in connection with, or with the sale of, any article manufactured or produced by that manufacturer and exported, sold, or used or sold for use, as provided in this paragraph (d), see section 6416(b)(4).

(7) For provisions relating to credit allowable in respect of tires and inner tubes sold on or in connection with, or with the sale of, another article taxable under chapter 32, prior to January 1, 1984, see section 6416(c) and §48.6416(c)-1.

(8) If a second article referred to in paragraph (d)(1) of this section is sold for a use described in that paragraph and is not so used, this paragraph (d) is in all respects inapplicable.

(e) *Use of bicycle tires or tubes in further manufacture.*—A payment of tax under section 4071 on the sale, prior to January 1, 1984, of a bicycle or tricycle tire or inner tube, directly or indirectly, by the manufacturer of the same to a subsequent manufacturer will be considered to be an overpayment under section 6416(b)(3)(E) if the tire or tube is used by the subsequent manufacturer as material in the manufacture or production of, or as a component part of, a bicycle or tricycle manufactured or produced by the subsequent manufacturer which is not a rebuilt or reconditioned bicycle or tricycle. For definition of the term "bicycle tire", see section 4221(e)(4)(B) and the regulations thereunder.

(f) *Use of gasoline in further manufacture.*—A payment of tax under section 4081 on the sale of gasoline, directly or indirectly, by the manufacturer of the same to a subsequent manufacturer will be considered an overpayment under section 6416(b)(3)(B) if the gasoline is used for nonfuel purposes by the subsequent manufacturer as a material in the manufacture or production of any other article manufactured or produced by the subsequent manufacturer. For this purpose it is immaterial whether the other article is or is not taxable under chapter 32. For provisions relating to the use of gasoline for nonfuel purposes, see section 4221 and the regulations thereunder. [Reg. §48.6416(b)(3)-2.]

☐ [*T.D.* 8043, 8-8-85. *Amended by T.D.* 8748, 12-31-97 (*corrected* 3-30-98).]

### [Reg. §48.6416(b)(3)-3]

**§48.6416(b)(3)-3. Supporting evidence required in case of tax-paid articles used for further manufacture.**—(a) *Evidence to be submitted by claimant.*—No claim for credit or refund of an overpayment, within the meaning of section 6416(b)(3) and §48.6416(b)(3)-2 shall be allowed unless the subsequent manufacturer submits with the claim the evidence required by §48.6416(a)-3, *and* a statement, supported by sufficient available evidence—

(1) Showing the amount claimed in respect of each category of exportations, uses, or sales on which the claim is based and which give rise to a right of credit or refund under section 6416(b)(3) and §48.6416(b)(3)-1,

(2) Showing the name and address of the manufacturer, producer, or importer of the article in respect of which credit or refund is claimed,

(3) Identifying the article, both as to nature and quantity, in respect of which credit or refund is claimed,

(4) Showing the amount of tax paid in respect of the article by the manufacturer or producer of the article and the date of payment,

(5) Indicating that the article was used by the claimant as material in the manufacture or production of, or as a component part of, a second article manufactured or produced by the manufacturer or was sold on or in connection with, or with the sale of, a second article manufactured or produced by the manufacturer,

(6) Identifying the second article, both as to nature and quantity, and

(7) In the case of an overpayment determined under section 6416(b)(3)(C) as it existed prior to January 1, 1984, and paragraph

(d)(1) of §48.6416(b)(3)-2 in respect of a tire or inner tube taxable under section 4071, indicating that the manufacturer has evidence available (as set forth in paragraph (b) of this section) that the second article is an automobile bus chassis or automobile bus body, or has been exported, used, or sold as provided in section 6416(b)(3)(C)(ii) and §48.6416(b)(3)-2(d)(1)(ii).

(b) *Evidence required to be in possession of claimant.*—(1) *In general.*—The evidence required to be retained by the person claiming credit or refund, as provided in paragraph (a)(7) of this section, must, in the case of an exportation of the second article, consist of proof of exportation of the second article in the form prescribed in the regulations under section 4221, or must, in other cases (except when the second article is an automobile bus chassis or automobile bus body), consist of a certificate, executed and signed by the ultimate purchaser of the second article, in the form prescribed in paragraph (b)(2) of this section. However, if the second article has passed through a chain of sales from the manufacturer of the second article to the ultimate purchaser of the second article, the evidence may consist of a certificate, executed and signed by the ultimate vendor of the second article, in the form provided in paragraph (b)(3) of this section, rather than the proof of exportation itself of the second article or the certificate of the ultimate purchaser of the second article.

(2) *Certificate of ultimate purchaser of second article.*—The certificate executed and signed by the ultimate purchaser of the second article must contain the same information as that required in paragraph (b)(1)(ii) of §48.6416(b)(2)-3, except that the information must be furnished in respect of the second article, rather than the article to which the claim relates.

(3) *Certificate of ultimate vendor of second article.*—Any certificate executed and signed by an ultimate vendor as evidence to be retained by the person claiming credit or refund must be executed in the same form and manner as that provided in paragraph (b)(2)(iii) and §48.6416(b)(2)-3.

(4) *Repayment or consent of ultimate vendor.*—If the person claiming credit or refund of an overpayment to which this section applies has repaid, or agreed to repay, the amount of the overpayment to the ultimate vendor or if the ultimate vendor consents to the allowance of the credit or refund, a statement to that effect, signed by the ultimate vendor, must be shown on, or made a part of, the evidence required to be retained by the person claiming the credit or refund. In this regard, see §48.6416(a)-3(b)(2). [Reg. §48.6416(b)(3)-3.]

☐ [*T.D.* 8043, 8-8-85.]

### [Reg. §48.6416(b)(5)-1]

**§48.6416(b)(5)-1. Return of installment accounts causing overpayments of tax.**—(a) *In general.*—In the case of any payment of tax under section 4216(d)(1) in respect of the sale of any installment account that is determined to be an overpayment under section 6416(b)(5) and paragraph(b) of this section upon return of the installment account, the person who paid the tax may file a claim for refund of the overpayment or may claim credit for the overpayment on any return of tax under this subpart which that person subsequently files. No interest shall be paid on any credit or refund allowed under this section. For provisions relating to the evidence required in support of a claim for credit or refund under this section, see §301.6402-2 of this chapter (Regulations on Procedure and Administration) and paragraph(c) of this section. For provisions authorizing the taking of a credit in lieu of filing a claim for refund, see section 6416(d) and §48.6416(f)-1.

(b) *Overpayment of tax allocable to repaid consideration.*—The payment of tax imposed by section 4216(d)(1) on the sale of an installment account by the manufacturer will be considered to be an overpayment under section 6416(b)(5) to the extent of the tax allocable to any consideration repaid or credited to the purchaser of the installment account upon the return of the account to the manufacturer pursuant to the agreement under which the account originally was sold, if the readjustment of the consideration occurs pursuant to the provisions of the agreement. The tax allocable to the repaid or credited consideration is the amount which bears the same ratio to the total tax paid under section 4216(d)(1) with respect to the installment account as the amount of consideration repaid or credited to the purchaser bears to the total consideration for which the account was sold. This paragraph (b) does not apply where an installment account is originally sold pursuant to the order of, or subject to the approval of, a court of competent jurisdiction in a bankruptcy or insolvency proceeding.

(c) *Evidence to be submitted by claimant.*—No claim for credit of refund of an overpayment, within the meaning of section 6416(b)(5) and paragraph (b) of this section, of tax under section 4216(d)(1) shall be allowed unless the person who paid the tax submits with the claim a statement supported by sufficient available evidence, indicating—

(1) The name and address of the person to whom the installment account was sold,

(2) The amount of tax due under section 4216(d)(1) by reason of the sale of the installment account, the amount of the tax paid under section 4216(d)(1) with respect to the sale, and the date of payment,

(3) The amount for which the installment account was sold,

(4) The amount which was repaid or credited to the purchaser of the account by reason of the return of the account to the person claiming the credit or refund, and

(5)(i) The fact that the amount repaid or credited to the purchaser of the account was so repaid or credited pursuant to the agreement under which the account was sold, and

(ii) The fact that the account was returned to the manufacturer pursuant to that agreement. [Reg. § 48.6416(b)(5)-1.]

☐ [*T.D.* 8043, 8-8-85.]

### [Reg. § 48.6416(c)-1]

**§ 48.6416(c)-1. Credit for tax paid on tires or, prior to January 1, 1984, inner tubes.**—(a) *Allowance of credit against tax on sale of taxable article.*—If tax has been paid under section 4071 on the sale, or under section 4218 on the use, of a tire or inner tube, and the manufacturer of another article taxable under chapter 32 sells the tire or inner tube on or in connection with the sale of that other article, a credit in respect of the tire or inner tube is allowable under section 6416(c) against the tax imposed on the sale of that other article. The amount of the credit is to be determined as provided in paragraph (b) or (c) of this section.

(b) *Tires or tubes purchased by manufacturer of the other article.*—If the manufacturer of the other article purchased the tire or inner tube tax-paid, the amount of the credit shall be determined by applying to the purchase price of the tire or inner tube the percentage rate of tax applicable to the sale of the other article. For this purpose, the purchase price shall be determined by including any tax passed on to the manufacturer and, in the case of a tire, by excluding any part of the price attributable to the metal rim or rim base. For example, if the selling price of an automobile truck is $24,000, tax equivalent to 10 percent of the price (*i.e.,* $2,400) is imposed under section 4601(a) on the sale (before April 1, 1983) of the automobile truck. If the tires or inner tubes sold on or in connection with the automobile truck are purchased by the manufacturer of the automobile truck for $1,500 (computed as provided in this paragraph) a credit of $150 (10 percent of $1,500) is allowable against the tax imposed on the sale of the automobile truck.

(c) *Tires or tubes manufactured by manufacturer or other articles.*—If the manufacturer of the other article is also the manufacturer of the tire or inner tube and incurs tax liability under section 4218 on the use by that manufacturer of the tire or inner tube, the amount of the credit shall be determined by applying to the fair market price of the tire or inner tube, the percentage rate of tax applicable to the sale of the other article. For this purpose, the fair market price of the tire or inner tube shall be the price at which the same or similar tires or inner tubes are sold by manufacturers of tires or inner tubes in the ordinary course of trade, as determined by the Commissioner, and by excluding, in the case of a tire, any part of the price attributable to the metal rim or rim base. The determination of the Commissioner shall be made in the same manner as determinations made under section 4218.

(d) *Other applicable rules.*—(1) For purposes of this section, the term "manufacturer" includes the original manufacturer of the other article and any succeeding purchaser of the article who further manufactures the article so as to become liable as a manufacturer of an article taxable under chapter 32. Therefore, the credit provided by section 6416(c) and this section is available both to the original manufacturer of the other article and also to every succeeding purchaser of that article who sells that article on or in connection with, or with the sale of, another article taxable under chapter 32.

(2) No interest shall be paid on any credit allowed under this section.

(3) If credit is not claimed under this section against the tax applicable to the sale of the other article, the manufacturer of the other article may claim refund of an amount equivalent to the credit or may claim credit on any return of tax under this subpart subsequently filed. [Reg. § 48.6416(c)-1.]

☐ [*T.D.* 6650. *Amended by T.D.* 8043, 8-8-85.]

### [Reg. § 48.6416(e)-1]

**§ 48.6416(e)-1. Refund to exporter or shipper.**—(a) *In general.*—Any payment of tax imposed by section 4041, 4051 or chapter 32 that

is determined to be an overpayment within the meaning of section 6416(b)(2)(A) or (E), section 6416(b)(3)(C) (prior to January 7, 1983), or section 6416(b)(4) and the regulations thereunder, by reason of the exportation of any article may be refunded to the exporter or shipper of the article pursuant to section 6416(c) of this section, if—

(1) The exporter or shipper files a claim for refund of the overpayment, and

(2) The person who paid the tax waives the right to claim credit or refund of the tax.

No interest shall be paid on any refund allowed under this section. For provisions relating to the evidence required in support of a claim under this paragraph (a), see § 301.6402 of this chapter (Regulations on Procedure and Administration) and paragraph (b) of this section.

(b) *Supporting evidence required.*—No claim for refund of any overpayment of tax to which this section applies shall be allowed unless the exporter or shipper submits with that claim proof of exportation in the form prescribed by the regulations under section 4221, and a statement, signed by the person who paid the tax, showing—

(1) That the person who paid the tax waives the right to claim credit or refund of the tax,

(2) In the case of an overpayment determined under section 6416(b)(2)(A) and paragraph (b) of § 48.6416(b)(2)-2 in respect of a truck, bus, tractor, etc., taxable under section 4061(a), that, pursuant to section 6416(g), the person who paid the tax possessed at the time that person shipped the article or at the time title to the article passed to that person's vendee, whichever is earlier, evidence that the article was to be exported to a foreign country or shipped to a possession of the United States,

(3) The amount of tax paid on the sale of the article and the date of payment, and

(4) The internal revenue service office to which the tax was paid. [Reg. § 48.6416(e)-1.]

☐ [*T.D.* 6650. *Amended by T.D.* 8043, 8-8-85.]

### [Reg. § 48.6416(f)-1]

**§ 48.6416(f)-1. Credit on returns.**—Any person entitled to claim refund of any overpayment of tax imposed by section 4041, 4042, 4051 or chapter 32 may, in lieu of claiming refund of the overpayment, claim credit for the overpayment on any return of tax under this subpart subsequently filed. Any such credit claimed on a return must be supported by the evidence prescribed in the applicable regulations in this subpart and § 301.6402 of this chapter (Regulations on Procedure and Administration). [Reg. § 48.6416(f)-1.]

☐ [*T.D.* 6650. *Amended by T.D.* 8043, 8-8-85.]

### [Reg. § 48.6416(h)-1]

**§ 48.6416(h)-1. Accounting procedures for like articles.**—(a) *Identification of manufacturer.*—In applying section 6416 and the regulations thereunder, a person who has purchased like articles from various manufacturers may determine the particular manufacturer from whom that person purchased any one of those articles by a first-in-first-out (FIFO) method, by a last-in-first-out (LIFO) method, or by any other consistent method been approved by the district director. For the first year for which a person makes a determination under this section, the person may adopt any one of the following methods without securing prior approval by the district director.

(1) FIFO method.

(2) LIFO method.

(3) Any method by which the actual manufacturer of the article is in fact identified.

Any other method of determining the manufacturer of a particular article must be approved by the district director before its adoption. After any method for identifying the manufacturer has been properly adopted, it may not be changed without first securing the consent of the district director.

(b) *Determining amount of tax paid.*—In applying section 6416 and the regulations thereunder, if the identity of the manufacturer of any article has been determined by a person pursuant to a method prescribed in paragraph (a) of this section, that manufacturer of the article must determine the tax paid under chapter 32 with respect to that article consistently with the method used in identifying the manufacturer. [Reg. § 48.6416(h)-1.]

☐ [*T.D.* 6650. *Amended by T.D.* 8043, 8-8-85.]

### [Reg. § 44.6419-1]

**§ 44.6419-1. Credit or refund generally.**—(a) *Overpayment of wagering tax; in general.*—If a person overpays the tax imposed under section 4401, he may either file a claim for refund on Form 843 or take credit for such overpayment against the tax due on a subsequent monthly return. A complete statement of the facts involving the overpayment shall be attached either to the claim or to the return on which the credit is claimed. Every claim for refund shall be supported by evidence showing the name and address of the taxpayer, the date of payment of the tax, and the amount of such tax. A credit taken on a return shall be supported by evidence of the same character.

(b) *Statement supporting credit or refund.*—No credit or refund shall be allowed whether in pursuance of a court decision or otherwise unless the taxpayer files a statement explaining satisfactorily the reason for claiming the credit or refund and establishing (1) that he has not collected (whether as a separate charge or otherwise) the amount of the tax from the person who placed the wager on which the tax was imposed, or (2) that he has either repaid the amount of the tax to the person who placed the wager or has secured the written consent of such person to the allowance of the credit or refund. In the latter case, the written consent of the person who placed the wager shall accompany the statement filed with the credit or refund claim. The statement supporting the credit or refund claim shall also show whether any previous claim for credit or refund covering the amount involved, or any part thereof, has been filed. If the overpayment of tax relates to a laid-off wager accepted by the taxpayer, no credit or refund shall be allowed or made unless the taxpayer complies with the provisions of the first sentence of this paragraph, not only as to the person who placed the laid-off wager, but also with respect to the person who placed the original wager.

(c) *Limitation on credit or refund.*—No claim for credit or refund of tax shall be allowed unless presented within the period of limitations prescribed in section 6511. (For regulations under section 6511, see the Regulations on Procedure and Administration (Part 301 of this Chapter).) [Reg. §44.6419-1.]

☐ [T.D. 6370.]

## [Reg. §44.6419-2]

**§44.6419-2. Credit or refund on wagers laid off by taxpayer.—**
(a) *Laid-off wagers; in general.*—If a taxpayer accepts a wager and lays off all or a part thereof with another person who is liable for tax under section 4401 with respect to such laid-off wager, a credit may be allowed to such taxpayer in the amount of the tax due with respect to the amount of the wager so laid off, provided there is attached to the return for the month during which the wager was accepted and laid off by him the certificate prescribed in paragraph (d) of this section.

(b) *Claim for refund.*—If a taxpayer has paid the tax with respect to a wager laid off by him, he may file a claim for refund of such tax on Form 843 or take a credit for the tax paid by him against the tax shown to be due on any subsequent monthly return. If a refund is claimed, Form 843 shall be completed in accordance with the instructions thereon and, in addition, there shall be attached to such form a statement setting forth the reason for claiming the refund, the month in which such tax was paid, the date of payment, and whether any previous claim for refund covering the amount involved or any part thereof has been filed. There shall also be attached to the Form 843 the certificate prescribed below. In the case of a credit, the statement and certificate shall be attached to the monthly return on which the credit is claimed.

(c) *Credit or refund not allowed.*—No credit or refund will be allowed under this section if the wager is laid off with a person or organization not liable for tax under section 4401 with respect to such laid-off wager. No interest shall be allowed on any amount of tax credited or refunded under this section.

(d) *Certificate required.*—The certificate prescribed for use in support of a credit or refund with respect to a laid-off wager shall be in the following form:

## CERTIFICATE

(In support of credit or refund with respect to laid-off wagers under section 6419(b) of the Internal Revenue Code.)
I hereby certify that I, or the . . . . . . . . . . . . . . . (Corporation, partnership, or syndicate) of which I am an officer or member, doing business at . . . . . . . . . . . . . . . (Address), registered with the District Director of Internal Revenue at . . . . . . . . . . . . , under Registration No. . . . . . . . . as a person accepting wagers within the meaning of section 4401 of the Internal Revenue Code, accepted laid-off wagers, in the amounts and on the dates indicated below, from . . . . . . . . . . . . . (Name), . . . . . . . . . . . . . . . (Address), during the month of . . . . . . . . . . , 19 . . . .

| DATE | AMOUNT OF LAID-OFF WAGER | SUBJECT OF LAID-OFF WAGER (Identify horse and track, particular contest, or contestant, etc.) |
|------|--------------------------|-----------------------------------------------------------------------------------------------|
| . . . . . . . . . . . | . . . . . . . . . . . | . . . . . . . . . . . . . . . . . . . . . . . |
| . . . . . . . . . . . | . . . . . . . . . . . | . . . . . . . . . . . . . . . . . . . . . . . |
| . . . . . . . . . . . | . . . . . . . . . . . | . . . . . . . . . . . . . . . . . . . . . . . |

(Attach supplemental sheets for additional entries, if necessary.)

The undersigned further certifies that he, or the corporation, partnership, or syndicate of which he is a member, will make return of and account for the tax, under section 4401 of the Internal Revenue Code, with respect to the laid-off wagers so accepted.

It is understood by the undersigned that this certificate is given for the purpose of enabling the person from whom the laid-off wagers were accepted to claim credit with respect to the tax due on such laid-off wagers or to claim credit or refund of the tax, if any, paid on such laid-off wagers.

It is further understood that the fraudulent use of this certificate will subject the undersigned and all guilty parties to a fine of not more than $10,000 or to imprisonment for not more than five years, or both, together with costs of prosecution.

(Signed) . . . . . . . . . . . . (Date) . . . . . . . . .

(Title) . . . . . . . . . . . . . . . . . . . . . . . . . . . . .

(Owner, President, Partner, Member, etc.)

[Reg. §44.6419-2.]

☐ [T.D. 6370.]

## [Reg. §48.6420-1]

**§48.6420-1. Credits or payments to ultimate purchaser of gasoline used on a farm.—**(a) *In general.*—If gasoline is used on a farm for farming purposes after June 30, 1965, a credit (under the circumstances described in paragraph (b) of this section) or a payment (under the circumstances described in paragraph (c) of this section) in respect of the gasoline shall be allowed or made to the ultimate purchaser of the gasoline in an amount determined by multiplying (1) the number of gallons of gasoline so used by (2) the rate of tax on gasoline under section 4081 that applied on the date the gasoline was purchased by the ultimate purchaser. No interest shall be paid on any payment, allowed under paragraph (c) of this section. However, interest may be paid on any overpayment (as defined by section 6401) arising from a credit allowed under paragraph (b) of this section. See section 34(a), relating to credit for certain uses of gasoline and special fuels (and lubricating oil used prior to January 7, 1983). See §48.6420-2 for the time within which a claim for credit or

payment must be made. See section 4081 and the regulations thereunder for the rates of tax on gasoline. See §48.6420-2 for meaning of the terms "Used on a farm for farming purposes," "farm," "gasoline," "ultimate purchaser," and "taxable year."

(b) *Allowance of income tax credit in lieu of payment.*—With respect to persons subject to income tax, repayment of the tax paid under section 4081 on gasoline used on a farm for farming purposes may be obtained only by claiming a credit for the amount of this tax against the income tax imposed by subtitle A of the Code. The amount of the credit shall be an amount equal to the payment which would be made under section 6420 with respect to gasoline used during the taxable year on a farm for farming purposes if section 6420(g)(1) and paragraph (c) of this section did not apply. See section 34(a)(1).

(c) *Allowance of payment.*—Payments in respect of gasoline upon which tax was paid under section 4081 that is used on a farm for farming purposes shall be made only to—

(1) The United States or agency or instrumentality thereof, a State, a political subdivision of a State, or an agency or instrumentality of one or more States or political subdivisions of a State, or the District of Columbia, or

(2) An organization which is exempt from tax under section 501(a) and is not required to make a return of the income tax imposed under subtitle A for its taxable year.

(d) *Use of gasoline.*—(1) The credit or payment described in paragraph (a) of this section is allowable only in respect of gasoline used on a farm in the United States for farming purposes. The credit or payment is not allowable with respect to gasoline used for nonfarming purposes, or gasoline used off a farm, regardless of the nature of the use. If a vehicle or other equipment is used both on a farm and off the farm, or if it is used on a farm both for farming and non-farming purposes, the credit or payment is allowable only with respect to that portion of the gasoline which was "used on a farm for farming purposes" as defined in paragraph (a) of §48.6420-4. In determining if this requirement is met, neither the type of equipment or vehicle used nor its registration for highway use is material. However, the actual use of the equipment or vehicle and the place where it is used are material. For example, if a truck used on a farm for farming purposes is also used on the highways, gasoline used in connection with operating the truck on the highways is not taken into account in computing the credit or payment.

(2) For purposes of determining the allowable credit or payment in respect of gasoline used on a farm for farming purposes, gasoline on hand shall be considered used in the order in which it was purchased. Thus, if the owner, tenant, or operator of a farm has on hand gasoline acquired in two purchases made at different times and subject to different rates of tax, in determining credit or payment for gasoline used on a farm for farming purposes, it will be assumed that the gasoline purchased first was the first gasoline used, and the rate applicable to that purchase will apply in determining the credit or payment, until all that gasoline is accounted for. [Reg. §48.6420-1.]

☐ [*T.D.* 8043, 8-8-85.]

**[Reg. §48.6420-2]**

**§48.6420-2. Time for filing claim for credit or payment.**—(a) *In general.*—A claim for credit or payment described in §48.6420-1 with respect to gasoline used after June 30, 1965, on a farm for farming purposes, shall cover only gasoline used during the taxable year on a farm for farming purposes. Therefore, gasoline on hand at the end of a taxable year as, for example, in fuel supply tanks of farm machinery or in storage tanks or drums, must be excluded from a claim filed for that taxable year (but may be included in a claim filed for a later taxable year if used during that later year on a farm for farming purposes). Gasoline used during a taxable year may be covered by a claim filed for that taxable year although the gasoline was not paid for at the time the claim is filed. For purposes of applying this section, a governmental unit or exempt organization described in §48.6420-1(c) is considered to have as its taxable year, the calendar year or fiscal year on the basis of which it regularly keeps its books; see paragraph (h) of this section.

(b) *Time for filing.*—(1) A claim for credit with respect to gasoline used on a farm for farming purposes shall not be allowed unless it is filed no later than the time prescribed by section 6511 and the regulations thereunder for filing a claim for credit or refund of income tax for the particular taxable year.

(2) A claim for payment of a governmental unit or exempt organization described in §48.6420-1(c) must be filed no later than 3 years following the close of its taxable year. (See paragraph (h) of this section.)

(3) See §301.7502-1 of this chapter (Regulations on Procedure and Administration) for provisions treating timely mailing as timely filing and §301.7502-1 of this chapter for time for performance of an act where the last day falls on Saturday, Sunday, or a legal holiday.

(c) *Limit of one claim per taxable year.*—Not more than one claim may be filed under section 6420 by any person with respect to gasoline used during the same taxable year.

(d) *Form and content of claim.*—(1) *Claim for credit.*—(i) The claim for credit with respect to gasoline used on a farm for farming purposes must be made by attaching a Form 4136 to the income tax return of an individual or a corporation. Form 4136 must be executed in accordance with the instructions prescribed for the preparation of the form. A partnership may not file Form 4136. When a partnership files Form 1065, U.S. Partnership Return of Income, it must include a statement showing how many gallons of gasoline are allocated to each partner and use made of the gasoline.

(ii) If an individual dies during the taxable year, the claim for credit may be made only for that portion of the individual's taxable year ending with the date of death. If a sole proprietorship, a partnership or corporation is terminated or liquidated during the taxable year, the claim for credit may be made only for the portion of its year ending with the date of the termination or liquidation.

(2) *Claim for payment.*—The claim for payment with respect to gasoline used on a farm for farming purposes by a governmental unit or exempt organization described in §48.6420-1(c) must be made on Form 843 in accordance with the instructions prescribed for the preparation of the form. The claim by such a unit or organization must be filed with the service center for the internal revenue region in which the principal place of business or principal office of the claimant is located. [Reg. §48.6420-2.]

☐ [*T.D.* 8043, 8-8-85.]

**[Reg. §48.6420-3]**

**§48.6420-3. Exempt sales; other payments or refunds available.**—(a) *Exempt sales.*—Credits or payments are allowable only for gasoline that was sold by the producer or importer in a transaction that was subject to tax under section 4081. No credit or payment shall be allowed or made under §48.6420-1 with respect to gasoline which was exempt from the tax imposed by section 4081. For example, a State or local government may not file a claim with respect to any gasoline which it purchased tax free from the producer, even though the State or local government used the gasoline on a farm for farming purposes. Similarly, payment may not be made with respect to gasoline purchased by a State tax free for its exclusive use, as provided in section 4221, which is used on a State prison farm for farming purposes.

(b) *Other payments or refunds available.*—Any amount which, without regard to the second sentence of section 6420(d) and this paragraph (b), would be allowable as a credit or payable to any person under §48.6420-1 with respect to any gasoline is reduced by any other amount which is allowable as a credit or payable under section 6420, or is refundable under any other provision of the Code, to any person with respect to the same gasoline. Thus, a person who is the ultimate purchaser of gasoline may not file a claim for credit or payment with respect to that gasoline if another person is entitled to claim a payment, credit, or refund with respect to the same gasoline. For example, a State or local government may not file a claim for payment if it has executed, or intends to execute, a written consent to enable the producer to claim a credit or refund for the tax that was paid. See, for example, §§48.6416(a)-3(b)(2), 48.6416(b)(2)-2(d), and 48.6416(b)(2)-3(b)(1). [Reg. §48.6420-3.]

☐ [*T.D.* 8043, 8-8-85.]

**[Reg. §48.6420-4]**

**§48.6420-4. Meaning of terms.**—For purposes of the regulations under section 6420, unless otherwise expressly indicated—

(a) *Used on a farm for farming purposes.*—The term "used on a farm for farming purposes" applies only to gasoline which is used (1) in carrying on a trade or business of farming, (2) on a farm in the United States, and (3) for farming purposes. Gasoline used in an aircraft will qualify if its use otherwise satisfies these requirements. For the meaning of the term "trade or business of farming," see paragraph (b) of this section. For the definition of the term "farm," see paragraph (c) of this section. For the definition of the term "farming purposes," see paragraphs (d) through (g) of this section. The term "United States" has the meaning assigned to it by section 7701(a)(9).

(b) *Trade or business of farming.*—A person will be considered to be engaged in the trade or business of farming if the person cultivates, operates, or manages a farm for gain or profit, either as an owner or a tenant. A person engaged in forestry or the growing of timber is not thereby engaged in the trade or business of farming. A person who operates a garden plot, orchard, or farm for the primary purpose of growing produce for the person's own use is not considered to be engaged in the trade or business of farming. Generally, the operation of a farm does not constitute the carrying on of a trade or business if the farm is occupied by a person primarily for residential purposes or is used primarily for pleasure, such as for the entertainment of guests or as a hobby.

(c) *Farm.*—The term "farm" is used in its ordinary and accepted sense, and generally means land used for the production of crops, fruits, or other agricultural products or for the sustenance of livestock or poultry. The term "livestock" includes cattle, hogs, horses, mules, donkeys, sheep, goats, and captive fur-bearing animals. The term "poultry" includes chickens, turkeys, geese, ducks, and pigeons. Thus, a farm includes livestock, dairy, poultry, fish, fruit, fur-bearing animals, and truck farms, plantations, ranches, nurseries, ranges, orchards, feed yards for fattening cattle, and greenhouses and other similar structures used primarily for the raising of agricultural or horticultural commodities. Greenhouses and other similar structures that are used primarily for purposes other than the raising of agricultural or horticultural commodities do not constitute farms, as, for example, structures that are used primarily for the display, storage, fabrication, or sale of wreaths, corsages, and bouquets. A fish farm is an area where fish are grown or raised, as opposed to merely caught or harvested.

(d) *Gasoline used in cultivating, raising, or harvesting.*—Gasoline is used for "farming purposes" when it is used on a farm by the owner, tenant, or operator of the farm in connection with cultivating the soil, raising or harvesting any agricultural or horticultural commodity, or raising, shearing, feeding, caring for, training, or managing livestock, poultry, bees, or wildlife. Examples of operations which are considered to be operations for "farming purposes" within the meaning of this paragraph include plowing, seeding, fertilizing, weed killing, corn or cotton picking, threshing, combining, baling, silo filling, and chopping silage.

(e) *Gasoline used in handling, packing, or storing.*—(1) Gasoline is used for "farming purposes" when it is used by the owner, tenant, or operator of the farm in handling, drying, packing, grading, or storing any agricultural or horticultural commodity in its unmanufactured state, but only if the owner, tenant, or operator produced more than one-half of the commodity which was so treated during the taxable year for which claim for credit or payment is filed.

(2) Gasoline used in connection with canning, freezing, packaging, or processing operations will not be considered to be used for farming purposes, even though these operations are performed on a farm. Thus, for example, although gasoline used on a farm in connection with the production or harvesting of maple sap or oleoresin from a living tree is considered to be used for farming purposes under paragraph (d) of this section, gasoline used in the processing of maple sap into maple syrup or maple sugar or used in the processing of oleoresin into gum spirits of turpentine or gum resin is not used for farming purposes, even though these processing operations are conducted on a farm.

(3) Gasoline used in connection with processing operations which change a commodity from its raw or natural state, or operations performed with respect to a commodity after its character has been changed from its raw or natural state by a processing operation, will not be considered to be used for farming purposes. For example, gasoline used for the extraction of juices from fruits or vegetables is used in a processing operation which changes the character of the fruits or vegetables from their raw or natural state and will not be considered to be used for "farming purposes."

(4) The term "commodity," as used in this paragraph (e), refers to a single agricultural or horticultural product. For example, all apples are treated as a single commodity while apples and peaches are treated as two separate commodities. Operations with respect to each commodity are to be considered separately in applying the "one-half" production test described in paragraph (e)(1) of this section.

(f) *Gasoline used in planting, cultivating, or caring for trees.*—Gasoline is used "for farming purposes" when it is used by the owner, tenant, or operator of the farm in connection with the planting, cultivating, caring for, or cutting of trees that is incidental to the farming operations of the farm on which it is performed or incidental to the farming operations of the owner, tenant, or operator of the farm, or in connection with the preparation (other than milling) of trees for market that is incidental to these farming operations. These operations include the felling of trees and cutting them into logs or firewood but do not include sawing logs into lumber, chipping, or other milling operations. Operations of the prescribed character will be considered incidental to farming operations only if they are of a minor nature in comparison with the total farming operations involved. Therefore, a tree farmer or timber grower may not claim credit or payment under §48.6420-1 with respect to gasoline used in connection with the trade or business of tree farming or timber growing.

(g) *Gasoline used in the maintenance of a farm or farm equipment.*—Gasoline is used "for farming purposes" when it is used by the owner, tenant, or operator of a farm in connection with the operation, management, conservation, improvement, or maintenance of the farm and its tools and equipment. The activities included are those which contribute in any way to the conduct of the farm as such, as distinguished from any other enterprise in which the owner, tenant, or operator may be engaged. Examples of included operations are clearing land, repairing fences and farm buildings, building terraces or irrigation ditches, cleaning tools or farm machinery, and painting farm buildings. Since the gasoline must be used by the owner, tenant, or operator of the farm to which the operations relate, gasoline used by an organization which contracts with a farmer to renovate his farm properties is not used for farming purposes. Gasoline used in a gasoline powered lawn mower for maintaining a lawn is not used for farming purposes.

(h) *Taxable year.*—The "taxable year" of a governmental unit or tax-exempt organization described in §48.6420-1(c) is the calendar or fiscal year on the basis of which it regularly keeps its books. The "taxable year" of persons subject to income tax shall have the meaning as it has under section 7701 (a)(23).

(i) *Gasoline.*—The term "gasoline" has the same meaning given to this term by section 4082(b) and the regulations thereunder.

(j) *Ultimate purchaser.*—The term "ultimate purchaser" includes only a person who is an owner, tenant, or operator of a farm. A person who is an owner, tenant, or operator of a farm is an ultimate purchaser of gasoline only with respect to such gasoline as is purchased by the person and used for farming purposes on a farm of which the person is the owner, tenant, or operator. Thus the owner of a farm who purchases gasoline which is used on the farm by its owner, tenant, or operator for farming purposes is generally the ultimate purchaser of the gasoline. If, however, the cost of gasoline supplied by an owner, tenant, or operator of a farm, is by agreement or other arrangement borne by a second person who is an owner, or operator of the farm, the second person who bore the cost of the gasoline is considered to be the ultimate purchaser of the gasoline.

(k) *Certain farming use by persons other than the owner, tenant or operator.*—(1) *In general.*—Except as provided in paragraph (1) of this section, the owner, tenant, or operator of a farm on which gasoline is used by any other person for the purposes described in section 6420(c)(3)(A) and paragraph (d) of this section (relating to gasoline used in cultivating, raising, or harvesting) will be treated, for the purposes of §48.6420-1(a), as the ultimate purchaser who used the gasoline on the farm for farming purposes.

(2) *Example.*—The rule of paragraph (k)(1) of this section may be illustrated by the following example.

*Example.* Farmer A hired custom operator B to cultivate the soil on A's farm. B used 200 gallons of gasoline which B had purchased in performing the work on A's farm. In addition, A hired Farmer C to do some plowing on A's farm, using C's own tractor and 50 gallons of gasoline which C had purchased. A is deemed to be the ultimate purchaser and user of the gasoline used on A's farm by B and C, and A is entitled to take a credit in respect of the gasoline. Accordingly, no credit in respect to the gasoline may be taken by either B or C.

(l) *Aerial applicators treated as ultimate purchasers.*—(1) *General rule.*—Section 6420(c)(3)(A) provides that only the owner, tenant, or operator of a farm is entitled to be treated as a user and ultimate purchaser. Section 6420(c)(4) provides that, under section 6420(c)(3)(A), an aerial applicator or other applicator is entitled to be treated as the user and ultimate purchaser of gasoline used by it on a farm for the purposes described in section 6420(c)(3)(A), but only if the owner, tenant, or operator who is otherwise entitled to treatment as the user and ultimate purchaser waives the right to credit or payment. See paragraph (1)(2) of this section.

(2) *Form and manner of waiver.*—To waive the right to be treated as user and ultimate purchaser of gasoline which is used on a farm by an aerial applicator or other applicator, the owner, tenant, or operator of a farm who is otherwise entitled to treatment as user and ultimate purchaser must execute an irrevocable written agreement (as here described) no later than the date on which the aerial applicator or other applicator claiming the credit or payment files its return for the taxable year in which the gasoline is used. The agreement must identify the period for which the owner, tenant, or operator waives the right to credit or payment. The effective period of the waiver cannot extend beyond the last day of the taxable year of the owner, tenant, or operator of the farm on which the gasoline was used. If the owner, tenant, or operator's taxable year extends beyond the taxable year of the applicator, the applicator can only claim a credit or payment for periods included in the applicator's taxable year. Periods after the last day of the applicator's taxable year which are included under the agreement must be claimed on the applicator's return for the next succeeding taxable year. The waiver may be in the form shown under paragraph (1)(6) of this section or in any other form that meets the requirements of this paragraph and clearly states that the owner, tenant, or operator of the farm knowingly waives the right to receive the credit or payment.

(3) *Agreement included on aerial applicator's invoice.*—The agreement waiving a right to receive a credit or payment under section 6420 may be a separate document or may appear on the invoice for aerial application services or other unrelated document from the aerial applicator to the owner, tenant, or operator of the farm. If the waiver agreement appears on an invoice or other unrelated document, however, it must be printed in a section of the invoice or other document clearly set off from all other material contained in the invoice or other document, and it must be printed in type sufficiently large to put the owner, tenant, or operator of the farm on notice that

the person has waived the right to receive a credit or payment under section 6420. Additionally, if the waiver agreement appears as part of any invoice or other unrelated document, it must be executed separately from any other item included in the invoice or other document which requires the owner, tenant, or operator's signature.

(4) *Copies of agreement waiving right to credit or payment.*—No copies of any agreement waiving a right to credits or payments under section 6420 are to be submitted to the Internal Revenue Service unless a request is made by the Service to the taxpayer for the waivers. Aerial applicators must, however, retain copies of all waivers, and a copy of each waiver must be supplied by the aerial applicator to the owner, tenant, or operator of the farm who waives the right to receive a credit or payment. See regulations § 48.6420-6 for general requirements for records to be kept.

(5) *Waiver on behalf of owner, tenant, or operator of farm.*—An agent of the owner, tenant, or operator of a farm who is expressly authorized to act on behalf of and to bind the owner, tenant, or operator may waive that person's rights to a credit or payment under section 6420 by signing the waiver on the person's behalf.

(6) *Sample form of agreement.*—While no specific form is required for an effective waiver, an acceptable form waiving the right to receive a credit or payment under section 6420 follows:

I hereby waive my right as owner/tenant/operator of a farm located at .... (address) .... to receive credit or payment from the United States for gasoline used by .... (aerial applicator) .... on the farm in connection with cultivating the soil, or the raising or harvesting of any agricultural or horticultural commodity. This waiver applies to gasoline used during the period ...., both dates inclusive. I understand that by signing this waiver, I give up my right to claim any credit or payment for gasoline by the aerial applicator during the period indicated, and I acknowledge that I have not previously claimed any credit for that gasoline.

.............

(Signature of Owner/Tenant/Operator)
[Reg. § 48.6420-4.]

☐ [*T.D.* 8043, 8-8-85. *Amended by T.D.* 8152, 8-27-87.]

**[Reg. § 48.6420-5]**

**§ 48.6420-5. Applicable laws.**—(a) *Penalties, excessive claims, etc.*—All provisions of law, including penalties, applicable in respect of the tax imposed by section 4081 shall, to the extent applicable and consistent with section 6420, apply in respect of the payments provided for in section 6420 to the same extent as if these payments were refunds of overpayments of the tax imposed on the sale of gasoline under section 4081. For special rules applicable to the assessment and collection of amounts constituting excessive payments under section 6420, see section 6206 and the regulations thereunder. For the civil penalty assessable in the case of excessive claims under section 6420, see section 6675 and the regulations thereunder. For the treatment as an overpayment of an amount allowable as an excessive credit under section 39 with respect to amounts payable under section 6420, see section 6401(b).

(b) *Examination of books and witnesses.*—For the purpose of ascertaining (1) the correctness of any claim made under section 6420 or (2) the correctness of any credit or payment made in respect of the claim, the Commissioner shall have the same authority granted by paragraphs (1), (2), and (3) of section 7602, relating to examination of books and witnesses, as if the person claiming credit or payment under section 6420 were the person liable for tax.

(c) *Fractional part of a dollar.*—Section 6420(e)(3) provides that section 7504, relating to fractional parts of a dollar, shall not apply with respect to the allowance of any amount as a credit or payment under section 6420. Accordingly, credits or payments authorized by section 6420 shall be made in the exact amount to which the claimant is entitled and shall not be rounded to the nearest whole dollar amount. [Reg. § 48.6420-5.]

☐ [*T.D.* 8043, 8-8-85.]

**[Reg. § 48.6420-6]**

**§ 48.6420-6. Records to be kept in substantiation of credits or payments.**—(a) *In general.*—Every person making a claim for credit or payment under section 6420 must keep records sufficient to enable the district director to determine whether the person is entitled to credit or payment under section 6420 and, if so, the amount of the credit or payment. No particular form is prescribed for keeping the records, but the records must include a copy of the income tax return or claim and a copy of any statement or document submitted with the return or claim. The records must also show with respect to the taxable year covered by the claim—

(1) The number of gallons of gasoline purchased and the dates of purchase,

(2) The name and address of each vendor from whom gasoline was purchased and the total number of gallons purchased from each,

(3) The number of gallons of gasoline purchased by the claimant and used during the taxable year for farming purposes on a farm of which the claimant is the owner, tenant, or operator,

(4) The number of gallons of gasoline used during the taxable year for the purposes described in section 6420(c)(3)(A) and § 48.6420-4(d) (relating to cultivating, raising, or harvesting) by a person other than the owner, tenant, or operator on a farm of which the claimant is the owner, tenant, or operator, and

(5) Other information as necessary to establish the correctness of the claim.

(b) *Acceptable records.*—(1) Evidence of purchases of gasoline, and the purposes for which it was used, to substantiate claims may include paid duplicate sales invoices or tickets from the gasoline dealer or other vendor, and detailed records of all fuel used which show the amount consumed on a farm for farming purposes and the amount used for other purposes.

(2) Records maintained for Federal or State income tax purposes, or to support claims for refund of a State tax on gasoline, may be used to the extent that they contain the information necessary to substantiate the accuracy of the claim for credit under section 6420. However, the records must show separately the number of gallons of gasoline used on a farm for farming purposes.

(3) If trucks or other vehicles are used both on and off the farm, an allocation of gasoline used in the vehicle will be required to show separately the number of gallons of gasoline used on a farm for farming purposes in respect of which the claim is made.

(4) If the owner, tenant, or operator is entitled under section 6420(c)(4)(A) to claim credit or payment in respect of gasoline used on the person's farm by another person other than an owner, tenant, or operator of the farm for a purpose described in section 6420(c)(3)(A) and § 48.6420-4(d), the claimant must have records showing (i) the name and address of the person who performed the farming operation, (ii) a description of the type of work (such as plowing, threshing, combining, etc.) and the type of equipment used, (iii) the date or dates on which the work was done, and (iv) the number of gallons of gasoline so used on the claimant's farm.

(c) *Place and period for keeping records.*—(1) All records required by this section must be kept by the claimant at a convenient and safe location within the United States which is accessible to internal revenue officers and shall during normal business hours be available for inspection by internal revenue officers. If the claimant has a principal place of business in the United States, the records must be kept at that place of business.

(2) Records required to substantiate a claim under section 6420 must be maintained for a period of at least 3 years from the last date prescribed for the filing of the claim for credit or payment. [Reg. § 48.6420-6.]

☐ [*T.D.* 8043, 8-8-85.]

**[Reg. § 48.6420(a)-2]**

**§ 48.6420(a)-2. Gasoline includible in claim.**—Payment may be claimed under section 6420 only in respect of gasoline used on a farm in the United States for farming purposes. No payment is allowable under section 6420 with respect to gasoline used for nonfarming purposes, or gasoline used off a farm, regardless of the nature of such use. If a vehicle or other equipment is used both on a farm and off the farm, or if it is used on a farm both for farming and nonfarming purposes, payment is allowable only with respect to that portion of the gasoline which was "used on a farm for farming purposes" as defined in paragraph (a) of § 48.6420(c)-1. The type of equipment or vehicle and whether or not it is registered for highway use is immaterial. However, the actual use of the equipment or vehicle and place where it is used are material. For example, if a truck used on a farm for farming purposes is also used on the highways (even though in connection with operating the farm), the gasoline used in operating the truck on the highways is not to be taken into account in computing the payment for which a claim is filed, since such gasoline was used off the farm. [Reg. § 48.6420(a)-2.]

☐ [*T.D.* 6433, 12-22-59.]

**[Reg. § 48.6421-0]**

**§ 48.6421-0. Off-highway business use.**—For purposes of the regulations under section 6421, after March 31, 1983, the term "off-highway business use" is used in lieu of the term "qualified business use" and has the same meaning as "qualified business use" under § 48.6421-4(b). [Reg. § 48.6421-0.]

☐ [*T.D.* 8043, 8-8-85.]

[Reg. §48.6421-1]

**§48.6421-1. Credits or payments to ultimate purchaser of gasoline used for certain nonhighway purposes.**—(a) *In general.*—(1) If gasoline is used in a qualified business use or as fuel in an aircraft (other than aircraft in noncommercial aviation), a credit (under the circumstances described in paragraph (b) of this section) or a payment (under the circumstances described in paragraph (c) of this section) in respect of the gasoline shall be allowed or made to the ultimate purchaser of the gasoline. For gasoline used in a qualified business use prior to April 1, 1983, the credit or payment under this section shall be an amount equal to 1 cent for each gallon of gasoline so used on which the tax was paid at the rate of 3 cents a gallon and 2 cents for each gallon of gasoline so used on which the tax was paid at the rate of 4 cents a gallon. For gasoline used in an off-highway business use after March 31, 1983, the credit or payment under this section shall be an amount equal to the amount determined by multiplying the number of gallons so used by the rate at which tax was imposed on such gasoline under section 4081. For gasoline used as a fuel in an aircraft (other than aircraft in noncommercial aviation) the credit or payment under this section shall be an amount equal to the amount determined by multiplying the number of gallons so used by the rate at which tax was imposed on the gasoline under section 4081. No interest shall be paid on any payment allowed under paragraph (c) of this section. However, interest may be paid on any overpayment (as defined by section 6401) arising from a credit allowed under paragraph (b) of this section. See section 34(a), relating to credit for certain uses of gasoline and special fuels (and lubricating oil used prior to January 7, 1983). See §48.6421-3 for the time within which a claim for credit or payment must be made under this section. See §48.6421-4 for the meaning of the terms "gasoline," "qualified business use," "noncommercial aviation," and "taxable year."

(2) For purposes of determining the allowable credit or payment in respect of gasoline used in a qualified business use or as fuel in an aircraft (other than aircraft in noncommercial aviation), gasoline on hand shall be considered used in the order in which it was purchased. Thus, if the ultimate purchaser has on hand gasoline acquired in two purchases made at different times and subject to different rates of tax, in determining credit or payment for the gasoline used in a qualified business use or as fuel in an aircraft (other than aircraft in noncommercial aviation), it will be assumed that the gasoline first purchased was the first gasoline used, and the rate applicable to that purchase will apply in determining the credit or payment, until all that gasoline is accounted for.

(b) *Allowance of income tax credit in lieu of payment.*—Except as provided in paragraph (c) of this section, repayment under this section of the tax paid under section 4081 on gasoline used in a qualified business use or as a fuel in an aircraft (other than aircraft in noncommercial aviation) by a person subject to income tax may be obtained only by claiming a credit for the amount of this tax against the tax imposed by subtitle A of the Code. The amount of the credit shall be an amount equal to the payment which would be made under section 6421 with respect to gasoline used during the taxable year in a qualified business use or as a fuel in an aircraft (other than aircraft in noncommercial aviation) if section 6421(i) and paragraph (c) of this section did not apply. See section 34(a)(2).

(c) *Allowance of payment.*—Payments in respect of gasoline upon which tax was paid under section 4081 that is used in a qualified business use or as a fuel in an aircraft (other than aircraft in noncommercial aviation) shall be made only to—

(1) The United States or any agency or instrumentality thereof, a State, a political subdivision of a State, or an agency or instrumentality of one or more State political subdivisions of a State, or the District of Columbia,

(2) An organization which is exempt from tax under section 501(a) and is not required to make a return of the income tax imposed under subtitle A for its taxable year, or

(3) A person described in section 6421(c)(2) to whom $1,000 or more is payable (without regard to paragraph (b) of this section) under this section with respect to gasoline used during any of the first three quarters of the person's taxable year.

(d) *Dual use of gasoline.*—(1) No credit or payment may be claimed in respect of gasoline used in a highway vehicle used in a trade or business or for the production of income solely by reason of the fact that the propulsion motor in the vehicle is also used for a purpose other than the propulsion of the vehicle. Thus, if the propulsion motor of a highway vehicle (used in a trade or business or for the production of income) also operates special equipment, such as a mixing unit on a concrete mixer truck or a pump for discharging fuel from a tank truck, by means of a power takeoff or power transfer, no credit or payment may be claimed in respect of the gasoline used to operate the special equipment, even though the special equipment is mounted on the highway vehicle.

(2) If a highway vehicle is equipped with a separate motor to operate the special equipment used in a trade or business or for the production of income, such as a refrigeration unit, pump, generator, or mixing unit, credit or payment may be claimed in respect of the gasoline used in the separate motor.

(3) If gasoline used in a separate motor is drawn from the same tank as the one which supplies gasoline for the propulsion of the highway vehicle, the determination as to the quantity of gasoline used in the separate motor operating the special equipment must be based on operating experience and supported by records.

(4) Devices to measure the number of miles the highway vehicle has traveled, such as hubometers, may be used in making a preliminary determination of the number of gallons of gasoline used to propel the vehicle. In order to make a final determination of the number of gallons of gasoline used to propel the vehicle, there must be added to this preliminary determination the number of gallons of gasoline consumed while idling or warming up the motor preparatory to propelling the vehicle.

(e) *Gasoline lost or destroyed.*—Gasoline lost or destroyed through spillage, fire, or other casualty is not considered to have been "used" in a qualified business use or as fuel in an aircraft (other than aircraft in noncommercial aviation) and, accordingly, credit or payment in respect of the gasoline may not be claimed.

(f) *Supporting evidence required.*—Each claim under this section for credit or payment must include a statement showing—

(1) The total number of gallons of gasoline purchased and used during the period covered by the claim in a qualified business use multiplied by the rate of payment allowable in respect of the gasoline. (For the rate of payment allowable, see paragraph (a)(1) of this section.)

(2) The total number of gallons of gasoline purchased and used during the period covered by the claim for use as fuel in an aircraft (other than aircraft in noncommercial aviation) multiplied by the rate of payment allowable in respect of the gasoline.

(3) The purpose or purposes for which the gasoline was used, determined by reference to general categories, and the amount used for each purpose; and

(4) If a claim on Form 843 is being filed, the internal revenue district or service center with which the claimant last filed an income tax return (if any). [Reg. §48.6421-1.]

☐ [T.D. 8043, 8-8-85.]

[Reg. §48.6421-2]

**§48.6421-2. Credits or payments to ultimate purchasers of gasoline used in intercity, local, or school buses.**—(a) *In general.*—If gasoline is used in an intercity or local bus while engaged in furnishing (for compensation) passenger land transportation available to the general public or in a school bus engaged in the transportation of students or employees of schools, a credit (under the circumstances described in paragraph (b) of this section) or a payment (under the circumstances described in paragraph (c) of this section) in respect to the gasoline shall be allowed or made to the ultimate purchaser of the gasoline. The credit or payment under this section shall be an amount equal to the product of the number of gallons of gasoline so used multiplied by the rate at which tax was imposed on the gasoline by section 4081. No interest shall be paid on any payment allowed under paragraph (c) of this section. However, interest may be paid on an overpayment (as defined by section 6401) arising from a credit allowed under paragraph (b) of this section. See section 34(a) relating to credit for certain uses of gasoline and special fuels, (and lubricating oil used prior to January 7, 1983). See §48.6421-3 for the time within which a claim for credit or payment must be made under this section. See §48.6421-4 for the meaning of "gasoline."

(b) *Allowance of income tax credit.*—Except as provided in paragraph (c) of this section, repayment under this section of the tax paid under section 4081 of gasoline used while engaged in furnishing (for compensation) passenger land transportation available to the general public or in school bus transportation operations by a person subject to income tax may be obtained only by claiming a credit for the amount of this tax against the tax imposed by subtitle A of the Code. The amount of the credit shall be an amount equal to the payment which would be made under section 6421 with respect to gasoline used during the taxable year for this passenger land transportation or school bus operations if section 6421(i) and paragraph (c) of this section did not apply. See section 34(a)(2).

(c) *Allowance of payment.*—Payments in respect of gasoline upon which tax was paid under section 4081 that is used while engaged in furnishing (for compensation) passenger land transportation available to the general public or in school bus transportation operations shall be made only to—

(1) The United States or any agency or instrumentality thereof, a State, or political subdivision of a State, or an agency or instrumentality of one or more States or political subdivisions of a State, or the District of Columbia,

(2) An organization which is exempt from tax under section 501(a) and is not required to make a return of the income tax imposed under subtitle A for its taxable year, or

(3) A person described in section 6421(c)(2) to whom $1,000 or more is payable (without regard to paragraph (b) of this section) under this section with respect to gasoline used during any of the first three quarters of the person's taxable year.

(d) *Supporting evidence required.*—Each claim under this section for credit or payment must include a statement showing—

(1) The total number of gallons of gasoline purchased and used during the period covered by the claim for each intercity or local bus while engaged in furnishing (for compensation) passenger land transportation available to the general public multiplied by the rate at which tax was imposed on the gasoline by section 4081.

(2) The total number of gallons of gasoline purchased and used in each bus while engaged in school bus transportation operations multiplied by the rate at which tax was imposed on the gasoline by section 4081, and

(3) If a claim on Form 843 is being filed, the internal revenue district or service center with which the claimant last filed an income tax return (if any). [Reg. § 48.6421-2.]

☐ [*T.D. 8043, 8-8-85. Amended by T.D. 8879, 3-30-2000.*]

### [Reg. § 48.6421-3]

**§ 48.6421-3. Time for filing claim for credit or payment.**—(a) *In general.*—A claim for credit or payment described in § 48.6421-1 with respect to gasoline used in a qualified business use or as a fuel in an aircraft (other than aircraft in noncommercial aviation) or in § 48.6421-2 with respect to gasoline used either in an intercity or local bus while engaged in furnishing (for compensation) passenger land transportation available to the general public or in school bus transportation operations, shall cover only gasoline used during the taxable year, or when paragraph (b)(2) of this section applies, gasoline used during the calendar quarter. Therefore, gasoline on hand at the end of a taxable year, or, if applicable, a calendar quarter, such as gasoline in fuel supply tanks of vehicles or in storage tanks or drums, must be excluded from a claim filed for the taxable year or calendar quarter, as the case may be. However, this gasoline may be included in a claim filed for a later taxable year or a later calendar quarter if it is used during that later year or quarter in a qualified business use, as fuel in an aircraft (other than aircraft in noncommercial aviation), or in intercity, local, or school buses. Gasoline used during the taxable year or calendar quarter may be covered by the claim for that period although the gasoline was not paid for at the time the claim is filed. For purposes of applying this section, a governmental unit or exempt organization described in § 48.6421-1(c) or § 48.6421-2(c) is considered to have as its taxable year, the calendar year or fiscal year on the basis of which it regularly keeps its books; see § 48.6421-4(g).

(b) *Time for filing.*—(1) *Annual claims.*—(i) A claim under this section for credit or payment with respect to gasoline shall not be allowed unless it is filed no later than the time prescribed by section 6511 and the regulations thereunder for filing a claim for credit or refund of income tax for the particular taxable year.

(ii) A claim for payment of a governmental unit or exempt organization described in § 48.6421-1(c) or § 48.6421-2(c) must be filed no later than 3 years following the close of its taxable year (see § 48.6421-4).

(2) *Quarterly claims.*—A claim for payment of $1,000 or more in respect of gasoline used during any of the first three quarters of the taxable year, filed either under § 48.6421-1(c)(3) in respect of gasoline used in a qualified business use or as a fuel in an aircraft (other than aircraft used in noncommercial aviation) or under § 48.6421-2(c)(3) in respect of gasoline used while engaged in furnishing (for compensation) passenger land transportation available to the general public or in school bus operations, shall not be allowed unless the claim is filed on or before the last day of the first calendar quarter for which the claim is filed. No quarterly claim may be filed for the last calendar quarter of the taxable year. Amounts for which payment is disallowed under this paragraph (b)(2) merely because the claim was not filed on time may be included in an annual claim filed under paragraph (b)(1) of this section, but other amounts for which a claim for payment has been filed under this paragraph (b)(2) may not be included in an annual claim filed under paragraph (b)(1) of this section.

(3) *Other applicable rules.*—See § 301.7502-1 of this chapter (Regulations on Procedure and Administration) for provisions treating timely mailing as timely filing and § 301.7503-1 of this chapter for time for performance of an act where the last day falls on Saturday, Sunday, or a legal holiday.

(c) *Limit on claims per taxable year.*—Not more than one claim may be filed under § 48.6421-1 or § 48.6421-2 by any person with respect to gasoline used during any taxable year, except to the extent that quarterly claims may be filed under paragraph (b)(2) of this section with respect to any calendar quarter (other than the last calendar quarter) of the taxable year.

(d) *Form and content of claim.*—(1) *Claim for credit.*—The claim for credit to which this section applies must be made by attaching a Form 4136 to the income tax return of an individual or a corporation. Form 4136 must be executed in accordance with the instructions prescribed for the preparation of the form. A partnership may not file Form 4136. When a partnership files Form 1065, U.S. Partnership Return of Income, it must include a statement showing how many gallons are allocated to each partner and the use made of the gasoline.

(2) *Claim for payment.*—The claim for payment to which this section applies must be made on Form 8849 (or on such other form as the Commissioner may designate) in aaccordance with the instructions prescribed for the preparation of the form. Each form must designate the taxable year, or calendar quarter, for which it is filed.

(3) *Death or termination.*—(i) If an individual dies, or if a sole proprietorship, partnership, or corporation is terminated or liquidated, during the taxable year, the claim for credit or payment may be filed in respect of gasoline used during the short taxable year in the same manner as is provided for gasoline used in a full taxable year. Those months which constitute a quarter of a full taxable year will constitute the same quarter of the short taxable year. For example, if a corporation using the calendar year is liquidated on September 30, 1982, and is entitled to $900 under § 48.6421-1 in respect of gasoline used in a qualified business use for the calendar quarters ending June 30 and September 30, it may file a claim for payment in respect of the gasoline used during the calendar quarters ending June 30, and September 30, 1981, and take a credit of $900 on its income tax return for the short taxable year in respect of the gasoline used during the calendar quarter ending March 31, 1982.

(ii) A claim for payment on behalf of a decedent may be filed by the decedent's executor, administrator, or any other person charged with responsibility for the decedent's affairs. Such a claim must be accompanied by copies of the letters testamentary, letters of administration, or, in the case of a claim filed by other than the executor or administrator, the information called for in Form 1310 (Statement of Person Claiming Refund Due a Deceased Taxpayer). The claim may cover only gasoline in respect of which the decedent would have been entitled to claim payment. For example, if an individual dies on July 15, 1982, prior to claiming payment under § 48.6421-1 or $1,000 or more applicable to gasoline purchased and used in a qualified business use during the calendar quarter ending June 30, 1982, the decedent's executor or other legal representative may file a claim for payment covering that calendar quarter, and take the credit provided by section 39(a)(2) against the decedent's income tax on the income tax return for the short taxable year in respect of gasoline purchased by the decedent and so used during the period from July 1, 1982, to July 15, 1982, the date of death.

(e) *Restrictions on claims for credit or payment.*—Credits or payments are allowable only in respect of gasoline that was sold by the producer or importer in a transaction that was subject to tax under section 4081. For example, a State or local government may not file a claim with respect to any gasoline which it purchased tax free from the producer, even though the State or local government used the gasoline as a fuel for the purposes described in paragraph (a) of this section. Similarly, a governmental unit or tax-exempt organization that is the ultimate purchaser of gasoline may not file a claim for payment if it is known that another person is entitled to claim credit, payment, or refund with respect to the same gasoline. For example, a State or local government may not file a claim for payment if it has executed, or intends to execute, a written consent, or other documentation, to enable the producer to claim credit or refund for the tax that was paid. See, for example, § § 48.6416(a)-3 and 48.6416(b)(2)-3(b)(1). [Reg. § 48.6421-3.]

☐ [*T.D. 8043, 8-8-85. Amended by T.D. 8659, 3-13-96 and T.D. 8748, 12-31-97.*]

### [Reg. § 48.6421-4]

**§ 48.6421-4. Meaning of terms.**—For purposes of the regulations under section 6421, unless otherwise expressly indicated—

(a) *Gasoline.*—The term "gasoline" has the same meaning given to such term by section 4082(b) and regulations thereunder.

(b) *Qualified business use.*—(1) The term "qualified business use" means any use by a person in a trade or business of the person or in an activity of the person described in section 212 (relating to production of income) otherwise than as a fuel in a highway vehicle—

(i) That at the time of the use is registered, or is required to be registered, for highway use under the laws of any state, the District of Columbia, or a foreign country, or

(ii) That, in the case of a highway vehicle owned by the United States, is used on the highway.

The term "qualified business use" does not include any use in a motorboat, other than a vessel used in the fisheries or whaling business. See paragraph (c) of this section for the definition of "highway vehicle." See paragraph (d) of this section for the definition of "highway."

(2) Any highway vehicle operated under a dealer's tag, license, or permit will be considered to be registered. A highway vehicle is not considered to be "registered" solely because there has been issued a special permit for operation of the vehicle at particular times and under specified conditions. However, a highway vehicle that is required to be registered and that is also issued a special permit for operation of the vehicle under specified conditions, such as carrying an oversize load, is still considered to be "registered."

(3) Nonbusiness, off-highway use of gasoline by such vehicles and equipment as minibikes, snowmobiles, power lawn mowers, chain saws, and other yard equipment does not qualify as gasoline used in a qualified business use.

(4) Examples of gasoline used in a qualified business use include (i) gasoline used (in a trade or business or for the production of income) in stationary engines to operate pumps, generators, compressors, and power saws; (ii) gasoline used (in a trade or business or for the production of income) for cleaning purposes; (iii) gasoline used (in a trade or business or for the production of income) in forklift trucks, bulldozers, and earthmovers; and (iv) gasoline used by a nonhighway vehicle in connection with the trade or business of construction, mining or logging.

(5) *Illustration.*—The application of this paragraph (b) may be illustrated by the following example.

*Example.* M Corporation, a logging company, files its income tax return on the basis of the calendar year. During 1982, the company used 20,000 gallons of gasoline in its logging business. Of this amount, 12,000 gallons were used as fuel in registered highway vehicles which were operated both on the public highways and on the company's private roads. Of the remaining 8,000 gallons, 6,000 were used in nonhighway vehicles, such as tractors and bulldozers, and 2,000 gallons were used in highway vehicles, such as heavy trucks which, at the time of use, were neither registered nor required to be registered under state law for highway use by reason of being operated entirely on the company's property. As the ultimate purchaser, M may take a credit on its income tax return for 1982 under this section in respect of the 6,000 gallons used in the nonhighway vehicles and the 2,000 gallons used in the unregistered highway vehicles. However, no credit may be allowed with respect to the 12,000 gallons used in the registered highway vehicles even though a portion of this gasoline was used in operating the vehicles on the company's own property.

(c) *Highway vehicle.*—The term "highway vehicle" has the same meaning assigned to this term under §48.4061(a)-1(d).

(d) *Highway.*—The term "highway" includes any road, whether a Federal highway, State highway, city street, or otherwise, in the United States which is not a private roadway.

(e) *Noncommercial aviation.*—The term "non-commercial aviation" has the same meaning given to such term by section 4041(c)(4).

(f) *Calendar quarter.*—The term "calendar quarter" means a period of three calendar months ending on March 31, June 30, and September 30, or December 31.

(g) *Taxable year.*—The "taxable year" of a governmental unit or tax-exempt organization described in §48.6421-1(c) or §48.6421-2(c) is the calendar or fiscal year on the basis of which it regularly keeps its books. The "taxable year" of persons subject to income tax shall have the meaning it has under section 7701(a)(23). [Reg. §48.6421-4.]

☐ [*T.D.* 8043, 8-8-85.]

### [Reg. §48.6421-5]

**§48.6421-5. Exempt sales; other payments or refunds available.**—(a) *Exempt sales.*—No credit or payment shall be allowed or made under §48.6421-1 or §48.6421-2 with respect to gasoline which was exempt from the tax imposed by section 4081. For example, credit or payment may not be allowed or made with respect to gasoline purchased tax free for use as supplies for certain vessels and airplanes, or with respect to gasoline purchased by a State tax free for its exclusive use, as provided in section 4221.

(b) *Other payments or refunds available.*—Any amount which, without regard to the second sentence of section 6421(e)(1) and this paragraph (b), would be allowable as a credit or payable to any person under §48.6421-1 or §48.6421-2 is reduced by any other amount which is allowable as a credit or payable under section 6421, or is refundable under any other provision of the Code, to any person with respect to the same gasoline.

(c) *Gasoline used on farms.*—Payments with respect to gasoline used on a farm for farming purposes shall be claimed under section 6420 and §48.6420-1, and no claim in respect of that gasoline may be made under section 6421 and the regulations thereunder. [Reg. §48.6421-5.]

☐ [*T.D.* 8043, 8-8-85.]

### [Reg. §48.6421-6]

**§48.6421-6. Applicable laws.**—(a) *Penalties, excessive claims, etc.*—All provisions of law, including penalties, applicable in respect of the tax imposed by section 4081 shall, to the extent applicable and consistent with section 6421, apply in respect of the payments provided for in section 6421 to the same extent as if these payments were refunds of overpayments of the tax imposed on the sale of gasoline by section 4081. For special rules applicable to the assessment and collection of amounts constituting excessive payments under section 6421, see section 6206 and the regulations thereunder. For the civil penalty assessable in the case of excessive claims under section 6421, see section 6675 and the regulations thereunder. For the treatment as an overpayment of an amount allowable as an excessive credit under section 34 (section 39 of the Internal Revenue Code of 1954 prior to its revision by the Tax Reform Act of 1984) with respect to amounts payable under section 6421, see section 6401(b).

(b) *Examination of books and witnesses.*—For the purpose of ascertaining (1) the correctness of any claim made under section 6421 or (2) the correctness of any credit or payment made in respect of the claim, the Commissioner shall have the same authority granted by paragraphs (1), (2), and (3) of section 7602, relating to examination of books and witnesses, as if the person claiming credits or payment under section 6421 were the person liable for tax. [Reg. §48.6421-6.]

☐ [*T.D.* 8043, 8-8-85.]

### [Reg. §48.6421-7]

**§48.6421-7. Records to be kept in substantiation of credits or payments.**—(a) *In general.*—Every person making a claim for credit or payment under section 6421 must keep records sufficient to enable the district director to determine whether the person is entitled to credit or payment under section 6421 and, if so, the amount of the credit or payment under section 6421. No particular form is prescribed for keeping the records, but the records must include a copy of any statement or document submitted with the return or claim. The records must also show with respect to the period covered by the claim—

(1) The number of gallons of gasoline purchased and the dates of purchase,

(2) The name and address of each vendor from whom gasoline was purchased and the total number of gallons purchased from each,

(3) The number of gallons of gasoline purchased by the claimant and used during the period covered by the claim for nonhighway purposes or in intercity, local or school buses,

(4) Other information as necessary to establish the correctness of the claim.

(b) *Acceptable records.*—(1) Evidence of purchases of gasoline, and the purposes for which it was used, to substantiate claims may include paid duplicate sales invoices or tickets from the gasoline dealer or other vendor, and detailed records of all fuel used which show the amount used for the prescribed purpose and the amount used for other purposes.

(2) Records maintained for Federal or State income tax purposes, or to support claims for refund of a State tax on gasoline, may be used to the extent that they contain the information necessary to substantiate the accuracy of the claim for credit under section 6421. However, the records must show separately the number of gallons of gasoline used for nonhighway purposes or in intercity, local, or school buses during the period covered by the claim.

(c) *Place and period for keeping records.*—(1) All records required by this section must be kept by the claimant at a convenient and safe location within the United States which is accessible to internal revenue officers and shall during normal business hours be available for inspection by internal revenue officers. If the claimant has a principal place of business in the United States, the records must be kept at that place of business.

(2) Records required to substantiate a claim under section 6421 must be maintained for a period of at least 3 years from the last date prescribed for the filing of the claim for credit or payment. [Reg. § 48.6421-7.]

☐ [*T.D.* 8043, 8-8-85.]

### [Reg. § 1.6425-1]

**§ 1.6425-1. Adjustment of overpayment of estimated income tax by corporation.**—(a) *In general.*—Any corporation which has made an overpayment of estimated income tax for a taxable year beginning after December 31, 1967, may file an application for an adjustment of such overpayment. The right to file an application for an adjustment of overpayment of estimated income tax is limited to corporations.

(b) *Contents of application.*—(1) The application for an adjustment of overpayment of estimated income tax shall be filed on Form 4466. The application shall be filled out in accordance with the instructions accompanying the form, and all information required by the form and instructions must be furnished by the corporation. The application shall be verified in the manner prescribed by section 6065 as in the case of a return of the corporation.

(2) An application for an adjustment of overpayment of estimated income tax does not constitute a claim for credit or refund. If such application is disallowed by the district director, or director of a service center, in whole or in part, no suit may be maintained in any court for the recovery of any tax based on such application. The filing of an application for an adjustment of overpayment of estimated income tax will not constitute the filing of a claim for credit or refund within the meaning of section 6511 for the purpose of determining whether a claim for refund was filed prior to the expiration of the applicable period of limitation. The corporation, however, may file a claim for credit or refund under section 6402 at any time prior to the expiration of the applicable period of limitation and may maintain a suit based on such claim if it is disallowed or if the district director, or director of a service center, does not act on the claim within six months from the date it is filed. Such claim may be filed before, simultaneously with, or after the filing of the application for the adjustment of overpayment of estimated tax. A claim for credit or refund under section 6402 filed after the filing of an application for an adjustment of overpayment of estimated income tax is not to be considered an amendment of such application. Such claim, however, in proper cases, may constitute an amendment to a prior claim filed under section 6402.

(c) *Time and place for filing application.*—(1) The application for an adjustment of overpayment of estimated income tax shall be filed after the last day of the taxable year and on or before the fifteenth day of the third month thereafter, or before the date on which the corporation first files its income tax return for such taxable year (whether or not it subsequently amends the return), whichever is earlier.

(2) Except as provided in paragraph (b)(2) of § 301.6091-1 (relating to hand-carried documents), the application on Form 4466 shall be filed with the internal revenue officer designated in instructions applicable to such form. [Reg. § 1.6425-1.]

☐ [*T.D.* 7059, 9-16-70.]

### [Reg. § 301.6425-1]

**§ 301.6425-1. Adjustment of overpayment of estimated income tax by corporation.**—For regulations under section 6425, see §§ 1.6425-1 to 1.6425-3, inclusive, of this chapter (Income Tax Regulations). [Reg. § 301.6425-1.]

☐ [*T.D.* 7059, 9-16-70.]

### [Reg. § 1.6425-2]

**§ 1.6425-2. Computation of adjustment of overpayment of estimated tax.**—(a) Income tax liability defined. For purposes of § 1.6425-1, this section, §§ 1.6425-3 and 1.6655-7, relating to excessive adjustment, the term income tax liability means the excess of—

(1) The sum of—

(i) The tax imposed by section 11 or 1201(a), or subchapter L of chapter 1 of the Internal Revenue Code, whichever is applicable; plus

(ii) The tax imposed by section 55; over

(2) The credits against tax provided by part IV of subchapter A of chapter 1 of the Internal Revenue Code.

(b) *Computation of adjustment.*—The amount of an adjustment under section 6425 is an amount equal to the excess of the estimated income tax paid by the corporation during the taxable year over the

amount which, at the time of filing Form 4466, the corporation estimates as its income tax liability for the taxable year.

(c) *Effective/applicability date.*—Paragraph (a) of this section is applicable to applications for adjustments of overpayments of estimated income tax that are filed in taxable years beginning after September 6, 2007. [Reg. § 1.6425-2.]

☐ [*T.D.* 7059, 9-16-70. *Amended by T.D.* 9347, 8-6-2007.]

### [Reg. § 1.6425-3]

**§ 1.6425-3. Allowance of adjustments.**—(a) *Limitation.*—No application under section 6425 shall be allowed unless the amount of the adjustment is (1) at least 10 percent of the amount which, at the time of filing Form 4466 the corporation estimates as its income tax liability for the taxable year, *and* (2) at least $500.

(b) *Time prescribed.*—The Internal Revenue Service shall act upon an application for an adjustment of overpayment of estimated income tax within a period of 45 days from the date on which such application is filed.

(c) *Examination.*—Within the 45-day period described in paragraph (b) of this section, the Internal Revenue Service shall make, to the extent it deems practicable in such period, a limited examination of the application to discover omissions and errors therein. The Service shall verify the calculation of the adjustment, which calculation must be set forth by the corporation in the application for such adjustment, in the manner provided in section 6425(c)(2) for the determination by the corporation of such adjustment. The Service, however, may correct any material error or omission that is discovered upon examination of the application. In determining the adjustment, the Service may correct any mathematical error appearing on the application, and it may likewise make any modification required by the law to correct the corporation's computation of the adjustment. If the required modification has not been made by the corporation and the Service has available the necessary information to make such modification within the 45-day period, it may make such modification. The examination of the application and the allowance of the adjustment shall not prejudice any right of the Service to claim later that the adjustment was improper.

(d) *Disallowance in whole or in part.*—If the Internal Revenue Service finds that an application for an adjustment of overpayment of estimated tax contains material omissions or errors, the Service may disallow such application in whole or in part without further action. If, however, the Service deems that any omission or error can be corrected by it within the 45-day period, it may do so and allow the application in whole or in part. In the case of a disallowance or modification, the Service shall notify the corporation of such action. The Service's determination as to whether it can correct any omission or error shall be conclusive. Similarly, its action in disallowing, in whole or in part, any application for an adjustment of overpayment of estimated income tax shall be final and may not be challenged in any proceeding. The corporation in such case, however, may file a claim for credit or refund under section 6402, and may maintain a suit based on such claim if it is disallowed or if the Service does not act upon the claim within six months from the date it is filed.

(e) *Application of adjustment.*—If the Internal Revenue Service allows the adjustment, it may first credit the amount of the adjustment against any liability in respect of an internal revenue tax on the part of the corporation which is due and payable on the date of the allowance of the adjustment before making payment of the balance to the corporation. In such a case, the Service shall notify the corporation of the credit, and refund the balance of the adjustment.

(f) *Effect of adjustment.*—(1) For purposes of all sections of the Internal Revenue Code except section 6655, relating to additions to tax for failure to pay estimated income tax, any adjustment under section 6425 is to be treated as a reduction of prior estimated tax payments as of the date the credit is allowed or the refund is paid. For the purpose of sections 6655(a) through (g), (i), and (j), credit or refund of an adjustment is to be treated as if not made in determining whether there has been any underpayment of estimated income tax and, if there is an underpayment, the period during which the underpayment existed. However, an excessive adjustment under section 6425 is taken into account in applying the addition to tax under section 6655(h).

(2) For the effect of an excessive adjustment under section 6425, see § 1.6655-7.

(3) Effective/applicability date: This paragraph (f) is applicable to applications for adjustments of overpayments of estimated income tax that are filed in taxable years beginning after September 6, 2007. [Reg. § 1.6425-3.]

☐ [*T.D.* 7059, 9-16-70. *Amended by T.D.* 9347, 8-6-2007.]

[Reg. §48.6427-0]

**§48.6427-0. Off-highway business use.**—For purposes of the regulations under section 6427, after March 31, 1983, the term "off-highway business use" is used in lieu of the term "qualified business use" and has the same meaning as "qualified business use" under §48.6421-1(b). [Reg. §48.6427-0.]

☐ [T.D. 8043, 8-8-85.]

[Reg. §48.6427-1]

**§48.6427-1. Credit or payments to purchaser of special fuels resold or used for nontaxable, farming, or other purposes.**—(a) *Amount of repayment.*—(1) *Nontaxable or other uses.*—(i) If tax has been paid under section 4041(a)(1) on the sale of diesel fuel for use as a fuel in a diesel-powered highway vehicle or under section 4041(a)(2) on the sale of special motor fuel for use as a fuel in a motor vehicle or a motorboat and the fuel is used by the purchaser for a nontaxable purpose or for a purpose taxable at a lower rate than the purposes for which sold, a credit (under the circumstances described in paragraph (b) of this section) or a payment (under the circumstances described in paragraph (c) of this section) in respect of the fuel shall be allowed or made to the purchaser of the fuel in an amount equal to—

(A) The amount of the tax imposed on the sale of the fuel to the purchaser if the purchaser resells the fuel, or

(B) If the purchaser uses the fuel, the amount of tax imposed on the sale of the fuel to the purchaser, less the amount of tax, if any, that would have been imposed on the purchaser's use of the fuel if no tax had been imposed on the sale of the fuel to the purchaser.

(ii) For purposes of paragraph (a)(1)(i) of this section, and for the regulations under section 6427 applying such paragraph, tax imposed on the sale of fuel will be treated as an overpayment by the purchaser if the person resells the fuel or uses it for a nontaxable purpose or for a purpose taxable at a lower rate than that for which sold to the purchaser. Thus, for example, special motor fuel which was sold tax paid to the purchaser for use otherwise than in a qualified business use in a motor vehicle will qualify for the payment under section 6427 if the purchaser uses it as a fuel in a qualified business use.

(2) *Used for farming purposes.*—(i) If tax has been paid under section 4041(a)(1) on the sale of diesel fuel for use as a fuel in a diesel-powered highway vehicle, or under section 4041(a)(2) on the sale of special motor fuel for use as a fuel in a motor vehicle or a motor boat and the fuel is used on a farm for farming purposes, a credit (under the circumstances described in paragraph (b) of this section) or a payment (under the circumstances described in paragraph (c)(1) or (2) of this section) in respect of the fuel shall be allowed or made to the purchaser of the fuel in an amount equal to the amount of tax that was imposed under section 4041 on the sale of the fuel. The provisions of section 6420(c)(1), (2), and (3) and §48.6420-4 shall apply under this paragraph (a)(2) in determining whether the fuel is used on a farm for farming purposes.

(ii) The term "purchaser," as used in paragraph (a)(2)(i) of this section, includes only a person who is an owner, tenant, or operator of a farm. A person who is owner, tenant, or operator of a farm is a purchaser of fuel only with respect to such fuel as is purchased by the person and used for farming purposes on a farm of which the person is the owner, tenant, or operator. Thus, the owner of a farm who purchases fuel which is used on the farm by its owner, tenant, or operator for farming purposes is generally the purchaser of the fuel. If, however, the cost of fuel supplied by an owner, tenant, or operator of a farm, is by agreement or other arrangement borne by a second person who is an owner, tenant, or operator of the farm, the second person who bore the cost of the fuel is considered to be the purchaser of the fuel.

(iii) Except as provided in paragraph (a)(2)(iv) of this section, if fuel is used on a farm by any person other than the owner, tenant, or operator for the purposes described in section 6420(c)(3)(A) and §48.6420-4(d) (relating to gasoline used in cultivating, raising, or harvesting), the owner, tenant, or operator (as the case may be) will be treated for the purposes of §48.6427-1(a)(2)(i) as the purchaser who used the fuel on the farm for farming purposes.

(iv) Section 6427(c) provides that an aerial applicator or other applicator is entitled to be treated as the user and ultimate purchaser of fuel that the applicator uses on a farm for the purposes described in section 6420(c)(3)(A), but only if the owner, tenant, or operator of the farm who is otherwise entitled to be treated as the ultimate purchaser waives the right to credit or payment. The rules contained in section 6420 and the regulations under the section regarding waivers by owners, tenants, and operators of farms of their rights to payments under section 6420 for gasoline used by aerial applicators on a farm for farming purposes apply to waivers under this section.

(3) *Definitions, uses, and other rules.*—(i) No interest shall be paid on any payment allowed under paragraph (c) of this section. However, interest may be paid on any overpayment (as defined by section 6401) arising from a credit. See section 34(a), relating to credit for certain uses of gasoline and special fuels. See section 39(a) of the Internal Revenue Code of 1954 prior to its revision by the Highways Revenue Act of 1982, relating to credit for certain uses of lubricating oil. See section 6611, relating to interest on overpayments.

(ii) See §48.6427-3 for the time within which a claim for credit or payment must be made under this section.

(iii) See §48.6420-4 for the meaning of the terms "used on a farm for farming purposes" and "farm." The term "gasoline" has the same meaning given to this term by section 4082(b) and the regulations thereunder. For the meaning of the terms "diesel fuel," "special motor fuel," "motor vehicle," "highway vehicle," and "registered" see section 4041 and the regulations thereunder. The term "fuel" means diesel fuel, special motor fuel, or gasoline, as the context requires. Where appropriate, the term "use" includes a resale. See §48.6421-4 for the meaning of "calendar quarter" and "taxable year".

(iv) For purposes of determining the allowable credit or payment in respect of fuel used for nontaxable purposes, on a farm for farming purposes, or for purposes taxable at a lower rate, fuel on hand shall be considered used in the order in which it was purchased. Thus, if the purchaser made purchases at different times and subject to different rates of tax, then in determining credit or payment for fuel used for a described purpose, it will be assumed that the fuel first purchased was the first fuel used, and the rate applicable to that purchase will appy in determining the credit of payment, until all of that fuel is accounted for.

(v) Fuel lost or destroyed through spillage, fire, or other casualty is not considered to have been "used" within the meaning of this section, and, accordingly, no credit or payment of the tax paid on the sale of the fuel may be made under this section.

(b) *Allowance of income tax credit in lieu of payment.*—Except as provided in paragraph (c) of this section, repayment under this section of the tax paid under section 4041 on fuel used by a person subject to income tax may be obtained only by claiming a credit for the amount of this tax against the tax imposed by subtitle A of the Code. The amount of the credit shall be an amount equal to the payment which would be made under section 6427 with respect to fuel used during the taxable year for nontaxable purposes on a farm for farming purposes, or for purposes taxable at a lower rate, if section 6427(i) and paragraph (c) of this section did not apply. See section 34(a)(3).

(c) *Allowance of payment.*—Payments in respect of fuel upon which tax was paid under section 4041 that is used for nontaxable purposes, on a farm for farming purposes, or for purposes taxable at a lower rate, shall be made only to—

(1) The United States or any agency or instrumentality thereof, a State, a political subdivision of a State, or an agency or instrumentality of one or more States or political subdivisions of a State, or the District of Columbia,

(2) An organization which is exempt from tax under section 501(a) and is not required to make a return of the income tax imposed under subtitle A for its taxable year, or

(3) In the case of fuel used for nontaxable purposes to which section 6427(a) applies, to a person described in section 6427(g)(2) to whom $1,000 or more is payable (without regard to paragraph (b) of this section) under this section with respect to fuel used during any of the first three quarters of his taxable year.

(d) *Dual use of fuel.*—The principles set forth in §48.4041-7, relating to dual use of fuel, for determining whether liability is incurred under section 4041 at the time of sale of the fuel, are equally applicable in determining whether a credit or payment is to be allowed under this section. Thus, if diesel fuel or special motor fuel used in a separate motor is drawn from the same tank as the one which supplies fuel for the propulsion of the vehicle, a reasonable determination of the quantity of the fuel used in the separate motor will be acceptable for purposes of computing the payment or credit under this section. The determination must be based, however, on the operating experience of the person using the fuel, and a statement, signed by the person, evidencing the operating experience must be maintained as a part of the records of the person claiming the payment or credit.

(e) *Supporting evidence required.*—Each claim under this section for credit or payment must include a statement showing—

(1) The total number of gallons of fuel purchased and used for nontaxable or farming purposes during the period covered by the claim, multiplied by the rate of payment allowable under this section with respect to such fuel;

(2) The purpose or purposes for which the fuel was used, determined by reference to general categories, and the amount used for each of the purposes; and

(3) If a claim on Form 843 is being filed, the internal revenue district or service center with which the claimant last filed an income tax return, (if any).

(f) *Illustrations.*—The application of this section may be illustrated by the following example:

*Example.* Special motor fuel was sold for use as fuel in a highway vehicle that was registered for highway use. Tax was imposed on the sale at the rate of 9 cents a gallon under section 4041(a)(2). The special motor fuel was eventually used by the purchaser in a qualified business use. The credit or payment of tax is to be computed as follows:

|  | Cents per gallon |
|---|---|
| Rate at which tax was paid . . . . . . . . . . . . . . . . . . . . . . . | 9 |
| Less: Rate at which tax would have been imposed on a qualified business use under sec. 4041(b). . . . . . . . . . . . . . . . . . | 0 |
| Net credit or payment under sec. 6427(a) . . . . . . . . . . . . . | 9 |

[Reg. § 48.6427-1.]

☐ [T.D. 8043, 8-8-85.]

### [Reg. § 48.6427-2]

**§ 48.6427-2. Credits or payments to purchaser of diesel or special motor fuels used in intercity, local, or school buses.**—(a) *In general.*—(1) If tax has been paid under section 4041(a)(1) on the sale of diesel fuel for use as a fuel in a diesel-powered highway vehicle or under section 4041(a)(2) on the sale of special motor fuel for use as a fuel in a motor vehicle or a motorboat and the fuel is used by the purchaser in an intercity or local bus while engaged in furnishing (for compensation) passenger land transportation available to the general public or in a school bus in the transportation of students and employees of schools, a credit (under the circumstances described in paragraph (b) of this section) or a payment (under the circumstances described in paragraph (c) of this section) in respect of the fuel so used shall be allowed or made to the purchaser of the fuel. The credit or payment under this section shall be an amount equal to the product of the number of gallons of fuel so used multiplied by the rate at which tax was imposed on the fuel by section 4041(a)(1) or section 4041(a)(2), reduced as limited by section 6427(b)(2). No interest shall be paid on any payment allowed under paragraph (c) of this section. However, interest may be paid on any overpayment (as defined by section 6401) arising from a credit. See section 34(a), relating to credit for certain uses of gasoline and special fuels, (and lubricating oil prior to January 7, 1983). See section 6611, relating to interest on overpayments. See § 48.6427-3 for the time within which a claim for credit or payment must be made under this section.

(2) The terms "diesel fuel" and "special motor fuel" have the same meaning as in section 4041 and the regulations thereunder. The term "fuel" means diesel fuel and special motor fuel. See § 48.6421-4 for the meaning of "calendar quarter" and "taxable year."

(b) *Allowance of income tax credit.*—Except as provided in paragraph (c) of this section, repayment under this section of the tax paid under section 4041(a)(1) or section 4041(a)(2) on diesel or special motor fuel used while engaged in furnishing (for compensation) passenger land transportation available to the general public or in school bus transportation operations by a person subject to income tax may be obtained only by claiming a credit for the amount of this tax against the tax imposed by subtitle A of the Code. The amount of the credit shall be an amount equal to the payment which would be made under section 6427 with respect to fuel used during the taxable year for passenger land transportation or school bus operations if section 6427(i) and paragraph (c) of this section did not apply. See section 34(a)(3).

(c) *Allowance of payment.*—Payments in respect of diesel or special motor fuel upon which tax was paid under section 4041(a)(1) or section 4041(a)(2) that is used while engaged in furnishing (for compensation) passenger land transportation available to the general public or in school bus transportation operations shall be made only to—

(1) The United States or any agency or instrumentality thereof, a State, a political subdivision of a State, or an agency or instrumentality of one or more States or political subdivisions of a State, or the District of Columbia.

(2) An organization which is exempt from tax under section 501(a) and is not required to make a return of the income tax imposed under subtitle A for its taxable year, or

(3) A person described in section 6427(g)(2) to whom $1,000 or more is payable (without regard to paragraph (b) of this section) under this section with respect to fuel used during any of the first three quarters of the person's taxable year.

(d) *Supporting evidence required.*—Each claim under this section for credit or payment must include a statement showing—

(1) The total number of gallons of fuel purchased and used in each intercity or local bus while engaged in furnishing (for compensation) passenger land transportation available to the general public multiplied by the rate at which tax was imposed on the fuel by section 4041(a)(1) or section 4041(a)(2). See, however, section 6427(b)(2) with respect to the limitation on the amount of credit for buses other than qualified local buses.

(2) The total number of gallons of fuel purchased and used in each bus while engaged in school bus transportation operations multiplied by the rate at which tax was imposed on the fuel by subsection (a)(1) or (a)(2) of section 4041. See, however, section 6427(b)(2) with respect to the limitation on the amount of credit for buses other than qualified local buses.

(3) If a claim on Form 843 is being filed, the internal revenue district or service center with which the purchaser last filed an income tax return (if any). [Reg. § 48.6427-2.]

☐ [T.D. 8043, 8-8-85.]

### [Reg. § 48.6427-3]

**§ 48.6427-3. Time for filing claim for credit or payment.**—(a) *In general.*—A claim for credit or payment described in § 48.6427-1 with respect to fuel used for nontaxable, farming, or other purposes taxable at a lower rate or in § 48.6427-2 with respect to fuel used either in an intercity or local bus while engaged in furnishing (for compensation) passenger land transportation available to the general public or in school bus transportation operations shall cover only fuel used during the taxable year, or when paragraph (b)(2) of this section applies, used during the calendar quarter. Therefore, fuel on hand at the end of a taxable year, or, if applicable, a calendar quarter, such as fuel in supply tanks of vehicles or in storage tanks or drums, must be excluded from a claim filed for the taxable year or calendar quarter, as the case may be. However, this fuel may be included in a claim filed for a later taxable year or a later calendar quarter if it is used during that later year or quarter for nontaxable or farming purposes, or in an intercity or local bus while engaged in furnishing (for compensation) passenger land transportation available to the general public or in school bus transportation operations. Fuel used during the taxable year or calendar quarter may be covered by the claim for that period although the fuel has not been paid for at the time the claim is filed. The purposes of applying this section, a governmental unit or exempt organization described in § 48.6427-1(c) or § 48.6427-2(c) is considered to have as its taxable year the calendar year or fiscal year on the basis of which it regularly keeps its books; see § 48.6421-4.

(b) *Time for filing.*—(1) *Annual claims.*—(i) A claim under this section for credit or payment with respect to fuel used during a taxable year shall not be allowed unless it is filed no later than the time prescribed by section 6511 and the regulations thereunder for filing a claim for credit or refund of income tax for the particular taxable year.

(ii) A claim for payment of a governmental unit or exempt organization described in § 48.6427-1(c) or unit or exempt organization described in § 48.6427-2(c), must be filed no later than 3 years following the close of its taxable year. See § 48.6421-4.

(2) *Quarterly claims.*—A claim for payment of $1,000 or more in respect to fuel used during any of the first three quarters of the taxable year, filed either under § 48.6427-1(c)(3) in respect of fuel used for nontaxable purposes or for purposes taxable at a lower rate, or under § 48.6427-2(c)(3) in respect of fuel used while engaged in furnishing (for compensation) passenger land transportation available to the general public or in school bus transportation operations, shall not be allowed unless the claim is filed on or before the last day of the first calendar quarter following the calendar quarter for which the claim is filed. No quarterly claim may be filed for the last calendar quarter of the taxable year. Amount for which payment is disallowed under this paragraph (b)(2) merely because the claim was not filed on time may be included in an annual claim filed under paragraph (b)(1) of this section, but other amounts for which a claim for payment has been filed under this paragraph (b)(2) may not be included in an annual claim filed under paragraph (b)(1) of this section.

(3) *Other applicable rules.*—See § 301.7502-1 of this chapter (Regulations on Procedure and Administration) for provisions treating timely mailing as timely filing and § 301.7503-1 of this chapter for time for performance of an act where the last day falls on Saturday, Sunday, or a legal holiday.

(c) *Limit on claims per taxable year.*—Not more than one claim may be filed under § 48.6427-1 or § 48.6427-2 by any person with respect to fuel used during any taxable year, except to the extent that quarterly claims may be filed under paragraph (b)(2) of this section with respect to any calendar quarter (other than the last calendar quarter) of the taxable year.

(d) *Form and content of claim.*—(1) *Claim for credit.*—The claim for credit to which this section applies must be made by attaching a Form 4136, to the income tax return of an individual or a corporation. Form 4136 must be executed in accordance with the instructions prescribed for the preparation of the form. A partnership may not file Form 4136. When a partnership files Form 1065, U.S. Partnership Return of Income, it must include a statement showing how many gallons of fuel are allocated to each partner and the use made of the fuel.

(2) *Claim for payment.*—The claim for payment to which this section applies must be made on Form 8849 (or on such other form as the Commissioner may designate) in accordance with the instructions prescribed for the preparation of the form. Each form must designate the taxable year, or calendar quarter, for which it is filed.

(3) *Death or termination.*—(i) If an individual dies, or if a sole proprietorship, partnership, or corporation is terminated or liquidated, during the taxable year, the claim for credit or payment may be filed in respect of fuel used during the short taxable year in the same manner as is provided for fuel used in a full taxable year. Those months which constitute a quarter of a full taxable year will constitute the same quarter of the short taxable year. For example, if a corporation using the calendar year is liquidated on September 30, 1982, and is entitled to $900 under §48.6427-1 in respect of fuel used for nontaxable purposes for the calendar quarter ending March 31 and is also entitled to payments of $1,500 for each of the calendar quarters ending June 30 and September 30, it may file a claim for payment in respect of the fuel used for nontaxable purposes during the calendar quarters ending June 30, and September 30, 1982, and take a credit of $900 on its income tax return for the short taxable year in respect of the fuel used during the calendar quarter ending March 31, 1982.

(ii) A claim for payment on behalf of a decedent may be filed by the decedent's executor, administrator, or any other person charged with responsibility for the decedent's affairs. Such a claim must be accompanied by copies of the letters testamentary, letters of administration, or, in the case of a claim filed by other than the executor or administrator, the information called for in Form 1310 (Statement of Person Claiming Refund Due a Deceased Taxpayer). The claim may cover only fuel in respect of which the decedent would have been entitled to claim payments. For example, if an individual dies on July 15, 1982, prior to claiming payment under §48.6427-1 of $1,000 or more applicable to fuel purchased and used for nontaxable purposes during the calendar quarter ending June 30, 1982, the decedent's executor or other legal representative may file a claim for payment covering that calendar quarter, and take the credit provided by section 39(a)(3) against the decedent's income tax on the income tax return for the short taxable year in respect of fuel purchased by the decedent and so used during the period from July 1, 1982, to July 15, 1982, the date of death.

(e) *Restrictions on claims for credit or payment.*—Credits or payments are allowable only in respect of fuel that was sold by the producer or importer in a transaction that was subject to tax under section 4041. For example, a State or local government may not file a claim with respect to any fuel which it purchased tax free from the producer, even though the State or local government used the fuel for the purposes described in paragraph (a) of this section. Similarly, a State or local government may not file a claim with respect to the use of fuel if it is known that another person is entitled to claim a payment, credit, or refund with respect to the same fuel. For example, a State or local government may not file a claim in respect of tax-paid fuel that has been resold by the purchaser to the State or local government. [Reg. §48.6427-3.]

☐ [*T.D.* 8043, 8-8-85. *Amended by T.D.* 8659, 3-13-96 *and T.D.* 8748, 12-31-97.]

**[Reg. §48.6427-4]**

**§48.6427-4. Applicable laws.**—(a) *Penalties, excessive claims, etc.*—All provisions of law, including penalties, applicable in respect of the tax imposed by section 4041 shall, to the extent applicable and consistent with section 6427, apply in respect of the payments provided for in section 6427 to the same extent as if these payments constituted refunds of overpayments of the tax imposed on the sale of fuels by section 4041. For special rules applicable to the assessment and collection of amounts constituting excessive payments under section 6427, see section 6206 and the regulations thereunder. For the civil penalty assessable in the case of excessive claims under section 6427, see section 6675 and the regulations thereunder. For the treatment as an overpayment of an amount allowable as an excessive

credit under section 34 with respect to amounts payable under section 6427, see section 6401(b).

(b) *Examination of books and witnesses.*—For the purpose of ascertaining (1) the correctness of any claim made under section 6427 or (2) the correctness of any credit or payment made in respect of the claim, the Commissioner shall have the same authority granted by paragraphs (1), (2), and (3) of section 7602, relating to examination of books and witnesses, as if the person claiming credit or payment under section 6427 were the person liable for tax. [Reg. §48.6427-4.]

☐ [*T.D.* 8043, 8-8-85.]

**[Reg. §48.6427-5]**

**§48.6427-5. Records to be kept in substantiation of credits or payments.**—(a) *In general.*—Every person making a claim for credit or payment under section 6427 must keep records sufficient to enable the district director to determine whether the person is entitled to credit or payment under such section and, if so, the amount of the credit or payment. No particular form is prescribed for keeping the records, but the records must include a copy of the income tax return or claim and a copy of any statement or document submitted with the return or claim. The records must also show with respect to the period covered by the claim—

(1) The number of gallons of fuel purchased and the dates of purchase,

(2) The name and address of each vendor from whom fuel was purchased and the total number of gallons purchased from each,

(3) The number of gallons of fuel purchased by the claimant and used during the period covered by the claim for nontaxable purposes, farming purposes, for other purposes taxable at a lower rate, in local, intercity, or school buses, and

(4) Other information as necessary to establish the correctness of the claim.

(b) *Acceptable records.*—(1) Evidence of purchases of fuel, and the purposes for which it was used, to substantiate claims may include paid duplicate sales invoices or tickets from the fuel dealer or other vendor, and detailed records of all fuel used which show the amount used the prescribed purpose and the amount used for other purposes.

(2) Records maintained for Federal or State income tax purposes, or to support claims for refund of a State tax on fuel, may be used to the extent that they contain the information necessary to substantiate the accuracy of the claim for credit under section 6427. However, the records must show separately the number of gallons of fuel used for nontaxable purposes, farming purposes, other purposes, taxable at a lower rate, or in intercity, local, or school buses during the period covered by the claim.

(c) *Place and period for keeping records.*—(1) All records required by this section must be kept by the claimant at a convenient and safe location within the United States which is accessible to internal revenue officers and shall during normal business hours be available for inspection by internal revenue officers. If the claimant has a principal place of business in the United States, the records must be kept at that place of business.

(2) Records required to substantiate a claim under section 6427 must be maintained for a period of at least 3 years from the last date prescribed for the filing of the claim for credit or payment. [Reg. §48.6427-5.]

☐ [*T.D.* 8043, 8-8-85.]

**[Reg. §48.6427-6]**

**§48.6427-6. Limitation on credit or refund of tax paid on fuel used in intercity, local or school buses after July 31, 1984.**—(a) *Limitation on amount of credit or refund.*—(1) *In general.*—In the case of fuel sold or used after July 31, 1984, on which tax was imposed under section 4041(a), the amount of credit or refund under section 6427(b)(1) shall not exceed 12 cents per gallon except where fuel is used in a bus while such bus is being operated as a "qualified local bus" in which case the credit or refund shall be the full amount of tax paid under section 4041(a) on such fuel.

(2) *Qualified local bus.*—A bus is considered to be operated as a "qualified local bus" if such bus—

(i) Is engaged in furnishing (for compensation) intracity passenger land transportation that is available to the general public and is scheduled and along regular routes,

(ii) Has a seating capacity of at least 20 adults (not including the driver), and

(iii) Is under contract with (or is receiving more than a nominal subsidy from) any State or local government (as defined in section 4221(d)(4)) to furnish such transportation.

A company that operates qualified local buses is eligible for a full refund or credit only with respect to fuel used while such buses are operating as qualified local buses. For example, a company that operates its buses along subsidized intracity routes and also on intercity or unsubsidized intracity routes may obtain a full refund or credit only with respect to fuel used while operating the subsidized intracity routes.

(b) *Meaning of terms.*—(1) *Contract with a State or local government.*—A bus is under contract with a State or local government only if the contract imposes a bona fide obligation on the operator of the bus to furnish the transportation to which the contract relates.

(2) *More than a nominal subsidy.*—A subsidy is more than nominal if the subsidy is reasonably expected to exceed an amount equal to 3 cents multiplied by the number of gallons of fuel used while operating on subsidized routes.

(3) *Intracity passenger land transportation.*—The term "intracity passenger land transportation" means the land transportation of passengers to and from points located within the same metropolitan area. The term includes transportation along routes that cross State, city or county boundaries provided such routes remain within the metropolitan area. [Reg. § 48.6427-6.]

☐ [T.D. 8027, 5-23-85.]

### [Reg. § 48.6427-8]

**§ 48.6427-8. Diesel fuel and kerosene; claims by ultimate purchasers.**—(a) *Overview.*—This section provides rules under which ultimate purchasers of taxed diesel fuel and kerosene may claim the income tax credits or payments allowed by section 6427(l). Generally, these claims relate to diesel fuel and kerosene used in nontaxable uses. Claims relating to diesel fuel and kerosene sold for use on a farm for farming purposes and by a State are made by registered ultimate vendors under § 48.6427-9; claims relating to kerosene sold from a blocked pump are made by registered ultimate vendors (blocked pump) under § 48.6427-10; and claims relating to kerosene sold during certain periods of extreme cold for blending with diesel fuel to be used for heating purposes are made by registered ultimate vendors (blending) under § 48.6427-11.

(b) *Conditions to allowance of credit or payment.*—(1) *In general.*—Except as provided in section 6427(l)(5), a claim for an income tax credit or payment with respect to diesel fuel or kerosene is allowed under section 6427(l) only if—

(i) Tax was imposed by section 4081 on the diesel fuel or kerosene to which the claim relates;

(ii) The claimant produced or bought the diesel fuel or kerosene and did not sell it in the United States;

(iii) The claimant has filed a timely claim for a credit or payment that contains the information required under paragraph (d) of this section;

(iv) The diesel fuel or kerosene was not bought under a certificate described in § 48.6427-9(e)(2) (relating to Certificate of Farming Use or State Use);

(v) The diesel fuel or kerosene was not used on a farm for farming purposes (as defined in § 48.6420-4) or by a State;

(vi) With respect to kerosene, the kerosene was not sold from a blocked pump or sold for blending with diesel fuel under the conditions described in § 48.6427-11; and

(vii) The diesel fuel or kerosene was either—

(A) Used in a use described in § 48.4082-4(c)(3) through (c)(8);

(B) Exported;

(C) Used other than as a fuel in a propulsion engine of a diesel-powered highway vehicle; or

(D) Used as a fuel in the propulsion engine of a diesel-powered bus if the bus was engaged in a use described in section 6427(b)(1) (after the application of section 6427(b)(3)).

(2) *Examples.*—The following examples illustrate this paragraph (b).

*Example 1.* (i) In September 2000, F bought 250 gallons of undyed diesel fuel. In October 2000, F used 200 gallons of the fuel in a farm tractor. This use qualifies as use on a farm for farming purposes (as defined in § 48.6420-4). The farm tractor is not a diesel-powered highway vehicle (as defined in § 48.4081-1(b)). F used the remaining 50 gallons to heat F's residence. F filed a complete and timely claim for a credit relating to the 250 gallons.

(ii) A credit or payment is not allowable to F with respect to the 200 gallons of diesel fuel used in the farm tractor. Even though this fuel was used other than as a fuel in a propulsion engine of a diesel-powered highway vehicle (thus meeting the condition in paragraph (b)(1)(vii)(C) of this section), the condition in paragraph (b)(1)(v) of this section is not satisfied because the fuel was used on a farm for farming purposes.

(iii) A credit is allowable to F with respect to the 50 gallons F used for heating purposes because the conditions in paragraph (b)(1) of this section have been met. F used this fuel other than as a fuel in a propulsion engine of a diesel-powered highway vehicle and the use of the fuel for residential heating is not use on a farm for farming purposes.

*Example 2.* (i) In September 2000, W, a wholesale distributor, sold 3,500 gallons of diesel fuel on which tax has been imposed to C, a construction company located in the United States. W's selling price to C did not include an amount equal to the federal excise tax on the fuel. C used the fuel other than as a fuel in a propulsion engine of a diesel-powered highway vehicle. Both W and C file a complete and timely claim for a credit relating to the fuel.

(ii) Because W resold the fuel in the United States, the condition of paragraph (b)(1)(ii) of this section is not met. Thus, W is not allowed a credit or payment with respect to the fuel.

(iii) C is eligible for a credit or payment with respect to the fuel because the conditions to allowance in paragraph (b)(1) of this section have been met. The conditions to allowance do not include a requirement that C buy the fuel at a price that includes the amount of the tax.

(c) *Form of claim.*—Each claim for an income tax credit under this section must be made on Form 4136 (or on such other form as the Commissioner may designate) in accordance with the instructions for that form. Each claim for a payment under this section must be made on Form 8849 (or on such other form as the Commissioner may designate) in accordance with the instructions for that form.

(d) *Content of claim.*—Each claim for a credit or payment under this section must contain the following information with respect to all the diesel fuel or kerosene covered by the claim:

(1) The total number of gallons.

(2) A statement by the claimant that—

(i) The diesel fuel or kerosene did not contain visible evidence of dye; or

(ii) In the case of diesel fuel or kerosene that contains visible evidence of dye, explains the circumstances under which tax was imposed on that fuel.

(3) The use made of the diesel fuel or kerosene covered by the claim described by reference to specific categories listed in paragraph (b)(1)(vii) of this section (such as use in a qualified local bus or the exclusive use of a nonprofit educational organization).

(4) If the diesel fuel or kerosene covered by the claim was exported, a declaration that the claimant has proof of exportation (as described in § 48.4221-3(d)(1)).

(5) A declaration that the claimant has in its possession the name and address of the person(s) that sold the diesel fuel or kerosene to the claimant and the date(s) of the purchase(s).

(e) *Time and place for filing claim.*—For rules relating to the time for filing a claim under section 6427, see section 6427(i). A claim under this section is not filed unless it contains all the information required by paragraph (d) of this section and is filed at the place required by the form.

(f) *Effective date.*—This section is applicable with respect to diesel fuel after December 31, 1993, except for paragraph (b)(1)(iv) of this section, which is applicable to diesel fuel bought by ultimate purchasers after June 30, 1994. This section is applicable with respect to kerosene after June 30, 1998. [Reg. § 48.6427-8.]

☐ [T.D. 8659, 3-13-96. *Amended by* T.D. 8879, 3-30-2000 *and* T.D. 9051, 4-1-2003.]

### [Reg. § 48.6427-9]

**§ 48.6427-9. Diesel fuel and kerosene; claims by registered ultimate vendors (farming and State use).**—(a) *Overview.*—This section provides rules under which certain registered ultimate vendors of taxed diesel fuel and kerosene may claim the income tax credits or payments allowed by section 6427(l)(5)(A). These claims relate to diesel fuel and kerosene sold for use on a farm for farming purposes and by a State. Claims relating to diesel fuel and kerosene used for other nontaxable purposes are made by ultimate purchasers under § 48.6427-8; claims relating to kerosene sold from a blocked pump are made by registered ultimate vendors (blocked pump) under § 48.6427-10; and claims relating to kerosene sold during certain periods of extreme cold for blending with diesel fuel to be used for heating purposes are made by registered ultimate vendors (blending) under § 48.6427-11.

(b) *Definitions.*—(1) An *ultimate vendor*, as used in this section, is a person that sells undyed diesel fuel or undyed kerosene to—

(i) The owner, tenant, or operator of a farm for use by such person on a farm for farming purposes (as defined in § 48.6420-4);

(ii) A person other than the owner, tenant, or operator of a farm for use by such person for any of the purposes described in § 48.6420-4(d) (relating to cultivating, raising, or harvesting); or

(iii) Any State for its exclusive use.

(2) A *registered ultimate vendor* is an ultimate vendor that is registered under section 4101 as an ultimate vendor.

(c) *Conditions to allowance of credit or payment.*—A claim for an income tax credit or payment with respect to diesel fuel or kerosene is allowed by section 6427(l)(5)(A) only if—

(1) Tax was imposed by section 4081 on the diesel fuel or kerosene to which the claim relates;

(2) The claimant sold the diesel fuel or kerosene to—

(i) The owner, tenant, or operator of a farm for use by such person on a farm for farming purposes (as defined in § 48.6420-4);

(ii) A person other than the owner, tenant, or operator of a farm for use by such person for any of the purposes described in § 48.6420-4(d) (relating to cultivating, raising, or harvesting); or

(iii) Any State for its exclusive use;

(3) The claimant is a registered ultimate vendor; and

(4) The claimant has filed a timely claim for a credit or payment that contains the information required under paragraph (e) of this section.

(d) *Form of claim.*—Each claim for an income tax credit under this section must be made on Form 4136 (or on such other form as the Commissioner may designate) in accordance with the instructions for that form. Each claim for a payment under this section must be made on Form 8849 (or on such other form as the Commissioner may designate) in accordance with the instructions for that form.

(e) *Content of claim.*—(1) *In general.*—Each claim for credit or payment under this section must contain the following information with respect to all the diesel fuel or kerosene covered by the claim:

(i) The total number of gallons.

(ii) A statement by the claimant that—

(A) The diesel fuel or kerosene did not contain visible evidence of dye; or

(B) In the case of diesel fuel or kerosene that contains visible evidence of dye, explains the circumstances under which tax was imposed on that fuel.

(iii) The claimant's registration number.

(iv) The name and taxpayer identification number of each person that bought diesel fuel or kerosene from the claimant in a transaction described in paragraph (c)(2) of this section and the number of gallons that the claimant sold to that person.

(v) A statement that the claimant—

(A) Has not included the amount of the tax in its sales price of the diesel fuel or kerosene and has not collected the amount of tax from its buyer;

(B) Has repaid the amount of the tax to the ultimate purchaser of the fuel; or

(C) Has obtained the written consent of its buyer to the allowance of the claim.

(vi) A statement that the claimant has in its possession an unexpired certificate described in paragraph (e)(2) of this section and the claimant has no reason to believe any information in the certificate is false.

(2) *Certificate.*—(i) *In general.*—The certificate to be provided to the ultimate vendor consists of a statement that is signed under penalties of perjury by a person with authority to bind the buyer, is in substantially the same form as the model certificate provided in paragraph (e)(2)(ii) of this section, and contains all information necessary to complete such model certificate. A new certificate must be given if any information in the current certificate changes. The certificate may be included as part of any business records normally used to document a sale. The certificate expires on the earlier of the following dates:

(A) The date one year after the effective date of the certificate.

(B) The date a new certificate is provided to the seller.

(ii) *Model certificate.*

CERTIFICATE OF FARMING USE OR STATE USE

(To support vendor's claim for a credit or payment under section 6427 of the Internal Revenue Code.)

_____

Name, address, and employer identification number of vendor

The undersigned buyer ("Buyer") hereby certifies the following under penalties of perjury:

Buyer will use the diesel fuel or kerosene to which this certificate relates—(check one)

___ On a farm for farming purposes (as defined in § 48.6420-4(c) of the Manufacturers and Retailers Excise Tax Regulations) and Buyer is the owner, tenant, or operator of the farm on which the fuel will be used;

___ On a farm (as defined in § 48.6420-4(c)) for any of the purposes described in paragraph (d) of that section (relating to cultivating, raising, or harvesting) and Buyer is a person that is not the owner, tenant, or operator of the farm on which the fuel will be used; or

___ For the exclusive use of a State or local government, or the District of Columbia.

This certificate applies to the following (complete as applicable):

If this is a single purchase certificate, check here ___ and enter:
1. Invoice or delivery ticket number _____
2. ___ (number of gallons)

If this is a certificate covering all purchases under a specified account or order number, check here ___ and enter:
1. Effective date _____
2. Expiration date _____
(period not to exceed 1 year after the effective date)
3. Buyer account or order number _____

Buyer will provide a new certificate to the vendor if any information in this certificate changes.

If Buyer uses the diesel fuel or kerosene to which this certificate relates for a purpose other than stated in the certificate Buyer will be liable for tax.

Buyer understands that the fraudulent use of this certificate may subject Buyer and all parties making such fraudulent use of this certificate to a fine or imprisonment, or both, together with the costs of prosecution.

_____

Printed or typed name of person signing

_____

Title of person signing

_____

Name of Buyer

_____

Employer identification number

_____

Address of Buyer

_____

Signature and date signed

(f) *Time and place for filing claim.*—For rules relating to the time for filing a claim under section 6427, see section 6427(i). A claim under this section is not filed unless it contains all the information required by paragraph (e) of this section and is filed at the place required by the form.

(g) *Effective date.*—This section is applicable with respect to diesel fuel after December 31, 1993, and with respect to kerosene after June 30, 1998. [Reg. § 48.6427-9.]

☐ [*T.D. 8659, 3-13-96. Amended by T.D. 8879, 3-30-2000.*]

**[Reg. § 48.6427-10]**

**§ 48.6427-10. Kerosene; claims by registered ultimate vendors (blocked pumps).**—(a) *Overview.*—This section provides rules under which certain registered ultimate vendors of taxed kerosene may claim the income tax credits or payments allowed by section 6427(l)(5)(B)(i). These claims relate to kerosene sold from a blocked pump. Claims relating to kerosene sold for use on a farm for farming purposes and by a State are made by registered ultimate vendors under § 48.6427-9; claims relating to kerosene sold during certain periods of extreme cold for blending with diesel fuel to be used for heating purposes are made by registered ultimate vendors (blending) under § 48.6427-11; and claims relating to kerosene used for nontaxable purposes are made by ultimate purchasers under § 48.6427-8.

(b) *Definitions.*—The following definitions apply to this section:

(1) A *blocked pump* is a fuel pump that—

(i) Is used to dispense undyed kerosene that is sold at retail for use by the buyer in any nontaxable use;

(ii) Is at a fixed location;

(iii) Is identified with a legible and conspicuous notice stating *"UNDYED UNTAXED KEROSENE, NONTAXABLE USE ONLY"*; and

(iv)(A) Cannot reasonably be used to dispense fuel directly into the fuel supply tank of a diesel-powered highway vehicle or diesel-powered train (because, for example, of its distance from a road surface or train track or the length of its delivery hose); or

(B) Is locked by the vendor after each sale and unlocked by the vendor only in response to a request by a buyer for undyed kerosene for use other than as a fuel in a diesel-powered highway vehicle or diesel-powered train.

(2) A *registered ultimate vendor (blocked pump)* is a person that is registered under section 4101 as an ultimate vendor (blocked pump).

(3) An *ultimate vendor (blocked pump)* is a person that sells undyed kerosene from a blocked pump.

(c) *Conditions to allowance of credit or payment.*—A claim for an income tax credit or payment with respect to undyed kerosene is allowed by section 6427(l)(5)(B)(i) only if—

(1) Tax was imposed by section 4081 on the kerosene to which the claim relates;

(2) The claimant sold the kerosene from a blocked pump for its buyer's use other than as a fuel in a diesel-powered highway vehicle or diesel-powered train and the claimant has no reason to believe that the kerosene will not be so used;

(3) The claimant is a registered ultimate vendor (blocked pump);

(4) With respect to each sale of more than five gallons of kerosene from a blocked pump that does not meet the conditions of paragraph (b)(1)(iv)(A) of this section, the claimant has in its possession the date of the sale, name and address of the buyer, and the number of gallons sold to the buyer; and

(5) The claimant has filed a timely claim for a credit or payment that contains the information required under paragraph (e) of this section.

(d) *Form of claim.*—Each claim for an income tax credit under this section must be made on Form 4136 (or such other form as the Commissioner may designate) in accordance with the instructions for that form. Each claim for a payment under this section must be made on Form 8849 (or such other form as the Commissioner may designate) in accordance with the instructions for that form.

(e) *Content of claim.*—Each claim for a credit or payment under this section must contain the following information with respect to all of the kerosene covered by the claim:

(1) The claimant's ultimate vendor (blocked pump) registration number.

(2) The total number of gallons.

(3) A statement by the claimant that—

(i) The kerosene did not contain visible evidence of dye; or

(ii) In the case of kerosene that contains visible evidence of dye, explains the circumstances under which tax was imposed on that kerosene.

(4) With respect to each sale of more than five gallons of kerosene from a blocked pump that does not meet the conditions of paragraph (b)(1)(iv)(A) of this section, a statement by the claimant that it has in its possession the date of the sale, name and address of the buyer, and the number of gallons sold to the buyer.

(5) A statement by the claimant that it—

(i) Has not included the amount of the tax in its sales price of the kerosene and has not collected the amount of the tax from its buyer;

(ii) Has repaid the amount of the tax to its buyer; or

(iii) Has obtained the written consent of its buyer to the allowance of the claim.

(f) *Time and place for filing claim.*—For rules relating to the time for filing a claim under section 6427, see section 6427(i). A claim under this section is not filed unless it contains all the information required by paragraph (e) of this section and is filed at the place required by the form.

(g) *Cross reference.*—For a rule prohibiting a registered ultimate vendor (blocked pump) from delivering kerosene from a blocked pump into the fuel supply tank of a diesel-powered highway vehicle or diesel-powered train, see § 48.4101-1(h)(2)(iv).

(h) *Effective date.*—This section is applicable after March 30, 2000. [Reg. § 48.6427-10.]

☐ [*T.D.* 8879, 3-30-2000.]

### [Reg. § 48.6427-11]

**§ 48.6427-11. Kerosene; claims by registered ultimate vendors (blending).**—(a) *Overview.*—This section provides rules under which certain registered ultimate vendors of taxed kerosene may claim the income tax credits or payments allowed by section 6427(l)(5)(B)(ii). These claims relate to kerosene sold during certain periods of extreme cold for blending with diesel fuel to be used for heating purposes. Claims relating to kerosene sold for use on a farm for farming purposes and by a State are made by registered ultimate vendors under § 48.6427-9; claims relating to kerosene sold from a blocked pump for nontaxable uses are made by registered ultimate

vendors (blocked pump) under § 48.6427-10; and other claims relating to kerosene used for nontaxable purposes are made by ultimate purchasers under § 48.6427-8.

(b) *Definitions.*—The following definitions apply to this section:

(1) A *declaration of extreme cold* is a declaration by the Commissioner that a specific geographic area (such as a state or a county within a state) is affected by extremely or unseasonably cold weather conditions. A declaration will be in effect during the period determined by the Commissioner.

(2) A *cold weather blend* is a blend of kerosene and diesel fuel that is produced in an area described in a declaration of extreme cold and that is sold for use or used for heating purposes.

(3) A *registered ultimate vendor (blending)* is a taxable fuel registrant, a registered ultimate vendor, or a registered ultimate vendor (blocked pump).

(c) *Conditions to allowance of credit or payment.*—A claim for an income tax credit or payment with respect to kerosene is allowed by section 6427(l)(5)(B)(ii) only if—

(1) Tax was imposed by section 4081 on the kerosene to which the claim relates;

(2) The claimant sold the kerosene in an area described in a declaration of extreme cold for the production of a cold weather blend;

(3) The claimant is a registered ultimate vendor (blending); and

(4) The claimant has filed a timely claim for an income tax credit or payment that contains the information required under paragraph (e) of this section.

(d) *Form of claim.*—Each claim for an income tax credit under this section must be made on Form 4136 (or such other form as the Commissioner may designate) in accordance with the instructions for that form. Each claim for a payment under this section must be made on Form 8849 (or such other form as the Commissioner may designate) in accordance with the instructions for that form.

(e) *Content of claim.*—(1) *In general.*—Each claim for credit or payment under this section must contain the following information with respect to all of the kerosene covered by the claim:

(i) The claimant's registration number.

(ii) The total number of gallons.

(iii) A statement by the claimant that—

(A) The kerosene did not contain visible evidence of dye; or

(B) In the case of kerosene that contains visible evidence of dye, explains the circumstances under which tax was imposed on that kerosene.

(iv) A statement by the claimant that it—

(A) Has not included the amount of the tax in its sales price of the kerosene and has not collected the amount of the tax from its buyer;

(B) Has repaid the amount of the tax to its buyer; or

(C) Has obtained the written consent of its buyer to the allowance of the claim.

(v) A statement that the claimant has in its possession an unexpired certificate described in paragraph (e)(2) of this section and the claimant has no reason to believe any information in the certificate is false.

(2) *Certificate.*—(i) *In general.*—The certificate described in this paragraph (e) is a statement by a buyer that is signed under penalties of perjury by a person with authority to bind the buyer, is in substantially the same form as the model certificate provided in paragraph (e)(2)(iii) of this section, and contains all information necessary to complete the model certificate. A certificate must be given for each purchase of kerosene. The certificate may be included as part of any business records normally used to document a sale.

(ii) *Withdrawal of the right to provide a certificate.*—The Internal Revenue Service may withdraw the right of a buyer of kerosene to provide a certificate under this section if the buyer uses the kerosene to which a certificate relates other than for producing a cold weather blend. The Internal Revenue Service may notify any seller to whom the buyer has provided a certificate that the buyer's right to provide a certificate has been withdrawn.

(iii) *Model certificate.*

---

**CERTIFICATE OF BUYER FOR PRODUCTION OF A COLD WEATHER BLEND**

(To support vendor's claim for a credit or payment under section 6427 of the Internal Revenue Code.)

_____ (Buyer) certifies the following under penalties of perjury:

Name of Buyer

The kerosene to which this certificate applies will be used by Buyer to produce a blend of kerosene and diesel fuel in an area described in a declaration of extreme cold and the blend will be sold for use or used for heating purposes.

This certificate applies to ____ percent of Buyer's purchases from _____ (name, address, and employer identification number of seller) on invoice or delivery ticket number _____.

If Buyer violates the terms of this certificate, the Internal Revenue Service may withdraw Buyer's right to provide a certificate.

Buyer has not been notified by the Internal Revenue Service that its right to provide a certificate has been withdrawn.

Buyer understands that the fraudulent use of this certificate may subject Buyer and all parties making such fraudulent use of this certificate to a fine or imprisonment, or both, together with the costs of prosecution.

_Printed or typed name of person signing_

_Title of person signing_

_Employer identification number_

_Address of Buyer_

_Signature and date signed_

(f) _Time and place for filing claim._—For rules relating to the time for filing a claim under section 6427, see section 6427(i). A claim under this section is not filed unless it contains all the information required by paragraph (e) of this section and is filed at the place required by the form.

(g) _Effective date._—This section is applicable after March 30, 2000. [Reg. § 48.6427-11.]

☐ [_T.D._ 8879, 3-30-2000 (_corrected_ 5-5-2000).]

# Limitations

# LIMITATIONS ON ASSESSMENT AND COLLECTION

See p. 20,601 for regulations not amended to reflect law changes

### [Reg. § 301.6501(a)-1]

**§ 301.6501(a)-1. Period of limitations upon assessment and collection.**—(a) The amount of any tax imposed by the Internal Revenue Code (other than a tax collected by means of stamps) shall be assessed within 3 years after the return was filed. For rules applicable in cases where the return is filed prior to the due date thereof, see section 6501(b). In the case of taxes payable by stamp, assessment shall be made at any time after the tax became due and before the expiration of 3 years after the date on which any part of the tax was paid. For exceptions and additional rules, see subsections (b) to (g) of section 6501, and for cross references to other provisions relating to limitations on assessment and collection, see sections 6501(h) and 6504.

(b) No proceeding in court without assessment for the collection of any tax shall be begun after the expiration of the applicable period for the assessment of such tax. [Reg. § 301.6501(a)-1.]

☐ [_T.D._ 6172, 5-2-56. _Amended by T.D._ 6425, 11-10-59 _and T.D._ 6498, 10-24-60.]

### [Reg. § 301.6501(b)-1]

**§ 301.6501(b)-1. Time return deemed filed for purposes of determining limitations.**—(a) _Early return._—Any return, other than a return of tax referred to in paragraph (b) of this section, filed before the last day prescribed by law or regulations for the filing thereof (determined without regard to any extension of time for filing) shall be considered as filed on such last day.

(b) _Returns of social security tax and of income tax withholding._—If a return on or after November 13, 1966, of tax imposed by chapter 3 of the Code (relating to withholding of tax on nonresident aliens and foreign corporations and tax-free covenant bonds), or if a return of tax imposed by chapter 21 of the Code (relating to the Federal Insurance Contributions Act) or by chapter 24 of the Code (relating to collection of income tax at source on wages), for any period ending with or within a calendar year is filed before April 15 of the succeeding calendar year, such return shall be deemed filed on April 15 of such succeeding calendar year. For example, if quarterly returns of the tax imposed by chapter 24 of the Code are filed for the four quarters of 1955 on April 30, July 31, and October 31, 1955, and on January 31, 1956, the period of limitation for assessment with respect to the tax required to be reported on such return is measured from April 15, 1956. However, if any of such returns is filed after April 15, 1956, the period of limitation for assessment of the tax required to be reported on that return is measured from the date it is in fact filed.

(c) _Returns executed by district directors or other internal revenue officers._—The execution of a return by a district director or other authorized internal revenue officer or employee under the authority

of section 6020(b) shall not start the running of the statutory period of limitations on assessment and collection. [Reg. § 301.6501(b)-1.]

☐ [_T.D._ 6172, 5-2-56. _Amended by T.D._ 6498, 10-24-60 _and T.D._ 6922, 6-16-67.]

### [Reg. § 301.6501(c)-1]

**§ 301.6501(c)-1. Exceptions to general period of limitations on assessment and collection.**—(a) _False return._—In the case of a false or fraudulent return with intent to evade any tax, the tax may be assessed, or a proceeding in court for the collection of such tax may be begun without assessment, at any time after such false or fraudulent return is filed.

(b) _Willful attempt to evade tax._—In the case of a willful attempt in any manner to defeat or evade any tax imposed by the Code (other than a tax imposed by subtitle A or B, relating to income, estate, or gift taxes), the tax may be assessed, or a proceeding in court for the collection of such tax may be begun without assessment, at any time.

(c) _No return._—In the case of a failure to file a return, the tax may be assessed, or a proceeding in court for the collection of such tax may be begun without assesment, at any time after the date prescribed for filing the return. For special rules relating to filing a return for chapter 42 and similar taxes, see § § 301.6501(n)-1, 301.6501(n)-2, and 301.6501(n)-3.

(d) _Extension by agreement._—The time prescribed by section 6501 for the assessment of any tax (other than the estate tax imposed by chapter 11 of the Code) may, prior to the expiration of such time, be extended for any period of time agreed upon in writing by the taxpayer and the district director or an assistant regional commissioner. The extension shall become effective when the agreement has been executed by both parties. The period agreed upon may be extended by subsequent agreements in writing made before the expiration of the period previously agreed upon.

(e) _Gifts subject to chapter 14 of the Internal Revenue Code not adequately disclosed on the return._—(1) _In general._—If any transfer of property subject to the special valuation rules of section 2701 or section 2702, or if the occurrence of any taxable event described in section § 25.2701-4 of this chapter, is not adequately shown on a return of tax imposed by chapter 12 of subtitle B of the Internal Revenue Code (without regard to section 2503(b)), any tax imposed by chapter 12 of subtitle B of the Code on the transfer or resulting from the taxable event may be assessed, or a proceeding in court for the collection of the appropriate tax may be begun without assessment, at any time.

(2) _Adequately shown._—A transfer of property valued under the rules of section 2701 or section 2702 or any taxable event described in § 25.2701-4 of this chapter will be considered adequately shown on a

return of tax imposed by chapter 12 of subtitle B of the Internal Revenue Code only if, with respect to the entire transaction or series of transactions (including any transaction that affected the transferred interest) of which the transfer (or taxable event) was a part, the return provides:

(i) A description of the transactions, including a description of transferred and retained interests and the method (or methods) used to value each;

(ii) The identity of, and relationship between, the transferor, transferee, all other persons participating in the transactions, and all parties related to the transferor holding an equity interest in any entity involved in the transaction; and

(iii) A detailed description (including all actuarial factors and discount rates used) of the method used to determine the amount of the gift arising from the transfer (or taxable event), including, in the case of an equity interest that is not actively traded, the financial and other data used in determining value. Financial data should generally include balance sheets and statements of net earnings, operating results, and dividends paid for each of the 5 years immediately before the valuation date.

(3) *Effective date.*—The provisions of this paragraph (e) are effective as of January 28, 1992. In determining whether a transfer or taxable event is adequately shown on a gift tax return filed prior to that date, taxpayers may rely on any reasonable interpretation of the statutory provisions. For these purposes, the provisions of the proposed regulations and the final regulations are considered a reasonable interpretation of the statutory provisions.

(f) *Gifts made after December 31, 1996, not adequately disclosed on the return.*—(1) *In general.*—If a transfer of property, other than a transfer described in paragraph (e) of this section, is not adequately disclosed on a gift tax return (Form 709, "United States Gift (and Generation-Skipping Transfer) Tax Return"), or in a statement attached to the return, filed for the calendar period in which the transfer occurs, then any gift tax imposed by chapter 12 of subtitle B of the Internal Revenue Code on the transfer may be assessed, or a proceeding in court for the collection of the appropriate tax may be begun without assessment, at any time.

(2) *Adequate disclosure of transfers of property reported as gifts.*—A transfer will be adequately disclosed on the return only if it is reported in a manner adequate to apprise the Internal Revenue Service of the nature of the gift and the basis for the value so reported. Transfers reported on the gift tax return as transfers of property by gift will be considered adequately disclosed under this paragraph (f)(2) if the return (or a statement attached to the return) provides the following information—

(i) A description of the transferred property and any consideration received by the transferor;

(ii) The identity of, and relationship between, the transferor and each transferee;

(iii) If the property is transferred in trust, the trust's tax identification number and a brief description of the terms of the trust, or in lieu of a brief description of the trust terms, a copy of the trust instrument;

(iv) Except as provided in § 301.6501-1(f)(3), a detailed description of the method used to determine the fair market value of property transferred, including any financial data (for example, balance sheets, etc. with explanations of any adjustments) that were utilized in determining the value of the interest, any restrictions on the transferred property that were considered in determining the fair market value of the property, and a description of any discounts, such as discounts for blockage, minority or fractional interests, and lack of marketability, claimed in valuing the property. In the case of a transfer of an interest that is actively traded on an established exchange, such as the New York Stock Exchange, the American Stock Exchange, the NASDAQ National Market, or a regional exchange in which quotations are published on a daily basis, including recognized foreign exchanges, recitation of the exchange where the interest is listed, the CUSIP number of the security, and the mean between the highest and lowest quoted selling prices on the applicable valuation date will satisfy all of the requirements of this paragraph (f)(2)(iv). In the case of the transfer of an interest in an entity (for example, a corporation or partnership) that is not actively traded, a description must be provided of any discount claimed in valuing the interests in the entity or any assets owned by such entity. In addition, if the value of the entity or of the interests in the entity is properly determined based on the net value of the assets held by the entity, a statement must be provided regarding the fair market value of 100 percent of the entity (determined without regard to any discounts in valuing the entity or any assets owned by the entity), the pro rata portion of the entity subject to the transfer, and the fair market value of the transferred interest as reported on the return. If 100 percent of the value of the entity is not disclosed, the taxpayer bears the burden

of demonstrating that the fair market value of the entity is properly determined by a method other than a method based on the net value of the assets held by the entity. If the entity that is the subject of the transfer owns an interest in another non-actively traded entity (either directly or through ownership of an entity), the information required in this paragraph (f)(2)(iv) must be provided for each entity if the information is relevant and material in determining the value of the interest; and

(v) A statement describing any position taken that is contrary to any proposed, temporary or final Treasury regulations or revenue rulings published at the time of the transfer (see § 601.601(d)(2) of this chapter).

(3) *Submission of appraisals in lieu of the information required under paragraph (f)(2)(iv) of this section.*—The requirements of paragraph (f)(2)(iv) of this section will be satisfied if the donor submits an appraisal of the transferred property that meets the following requirements—

(i) The appraisal is prepared by an appraiser who satisfies all of the following requirements:

(A) The appraiser is an individual who holds himself or herself out to the public as an appraiser or performs appraisals on a regular basis.

(B) Because of the appraiser's qualifications, as described in the appraisal that details the appraiser's background, experience, education, and membership, if any, in professional appraisal associations, the appraiser is qualified to make appraisals of the type of property being valued.

(C) The appraiser is not the donor or the donee of the property or a member of the family of the donor or donee, as defined in section 2032A(e)(2), or any person employed by the donor, the donee, or a member of the family of either; and

(ii) The appraisal contains all of the following:

(A) The date of the transfer, the date on which the transferred property was appraised, and the purpose of the appraisal.

(B) A description of the property.

(C) A description of the appraisal process employed.

(D) A description of the assumptions, hypothetical conditions, and any limiting conditions and restrictions on the transferred property that affect the analyses, opinions, and conclusions.

(E) The information considered in determining the appraised value, including in the case of an ownership interest in a business, all financial data that was used in determining the value of the interest that is sufficiently detailed so that another person can replicate the process and arrive at the appraised value.

(F) The appraisal procedures followed, and the reasoning that supports the analyses, opinions, and conclusions.

(G) The valuation method utilized, the rationale for the valuation method, and the procedure used in determining the fair market value of the asset transferred.

(H) The specific basis for the valuation, such as specific comparable sales or transactions, sales of similar interests, asset-based approaches, merger-acquisition transactions, etc.

(4) *Adequate disclosure of non-gift completed transfers or transactions.*—Completed transfers to members of the transferor's family, as defined in section 2032A(e)(2), that are made in the ordinary course of operating a business are deemed to be adequately disclosed under paragraph (f)(2) of this section, even if the transfer is not reported on a gift tax return, provided the transfer is properly reported by all parties for income tax purposes. For example, in the case of salary paid to a family member employed in a family owned business, the transfer will be treated as adequately disclosed for gift tax purposes if the item is properly reported by the business and the family member on their income tax returns. For purposes of this paragraph (f)(4), any other completed transfer that is reported, in its entirety, as not constituting a transfer by gift will be considered adequately disclosed under paragraph (f)(2) of this section only if the following information is provided on, or attached to, the return—

(i) The information required for adequate disclosure under paragraphs (f)(2)(i), (ii), (iii) and (v) of this section; and

(ii) An explanation as to why the transfer is not a transfer by gift under chapter 12 of the Internal Revenue Code.

(5) *Adequate disclosure of incomplete transfers.*—Adequate disclosure of a transfer that is reported as a completed gift on the gift tax return will commence the running of the period of limitations for assessment of gift tax on the transfer, even if the transfer is ultimately determined to be an incomplete gift for purposes of § 25.2511-2 of this chapter. For example, if an incomplete gift is reported as a completed gift on the gift tax return and is adequately disclosed, the period for assessment of the gift tax will begin to run when the return is filed, as determined under section 6501(b). Further, once the period of assessment for gift tax expires, the transfer will be subject to inclusion in the donor's gross estate for estate tax purposes only to

the extent that a completed gift would be so included. On the other hand, if the transfer is reported as an incomplete gift whether or not adequately disclosed, the period for assessing a gift tax with respect to the transfer will not commence to run even if the transfer is ultimately determined to be a completed gift. In that situation, the gift tax with respect to the transfer may be assessed at any time, up until three years after the donor files a return reporting the transfer as a completed gift with adequate disclosure.

(6) *Treatment of split gifts.*—If a husband and wife elect under section 2513 to treat a gift made to a third party as made one-half by each spouse, the requirements of this paragraph (f) will be satisfied with respect to the gift deemed made by the consenting spouse if the return filed by the donor spouse (the spouse that transferred the property) satisfies the requirements of this paragraph (f) with respect to that gift.

(7) *Examples.*—The following examples illustrate the rules of this paragraph (f):

*Example 1.* (i) *Facts.* In 2001, A transfers 100 shares of common stock of XYZ Corporation to A's child. The common stock of XYZ Corporation is actively traded on a major stock exchange. For gift tax purposes, the fair market value of one share of XYZ common stock on the date of the transfer, determined in accordance with § 25.2512-2(b) of this chapter (based on the mean between the highest and lowest quoted selling prices), is $150.00. On A's Federal gift tax return, Form 709, for the 2001 calendar year, A reports the gift to A's child of 100 shares of common stock of XYZ Corporation with a value for gift tax purposes of $15,000. A specifies the date of the transfer, recites that the stock is publicly traded, identifies the stock exchange on which the stock is traded, lists the stock's CUSIP number, and lists the mean between the highest and lowest quoted selling prices for the date of transfer.

(ii) *Application of the adequate disclosure standard.* A has adequately disclosed the transfer. Therefore, the period of assessment for the transfer under section 6501 will run from the time the return is filed (as determined under section 6501(b)).

*Example 2.* (i) *Facts.* On December 30, 2001, A transfers closely-held stock to B, A's child. A determined that the value of the transferred stock, on December 30, 2001, was $9,000. A made no other transfers to B, or any other donee, during 2001. On A's Federal gift tax return, Form 709, for the 2001 calendar year, A provides the information required under paragraph (f)(2) of this section such that the transfer is adequately disclosed. A claims an annual exclusion under section 2503(b) for the transfer.

(ii) *Application of the adequate disclosure standard.* Because the transfer is adequately disclosed under paragraph (f)(2) of this section, the period of assessment for the transfer will expire as prescribed by section 6501(b), notwithstanding that if A's valuation of the closely-held stock was correct, A was not required to file a gift tax return reporting the transfer under section 6019. After the period of assessment has expired on the transfer, the Internal Revenue Service is precluded from redetermining the amount of the gift for purposes of assessing gift tax or for purposes of determining the estate tax liability. Therefore, the amount of the gift as reported on A's 2001 Federal gift tax return may not be redetermined for purposes of determining A's prior taxable gifts (for gift tax purposes) or A's adjusted taxable gifts (for estate tax purposes).

*Example 3.* (i) *Facts.* A owns 100 percent of the common stock of X, a closely-held corporation. X does not hold an interest in any other entity that is not actively traded. In 2001, A transfers 20 percent of the X stock to B and C, A's children, in a transfer that is not subject to the special valuation rules of section 2701. The transfer is made outright with no restrictions on ownership rights, including voting rights and the right to transfer the stock. Based on generally applicable valuation principles, the value of X would be determined based on the net value of the assets owned by X. The reported value of the transferred stock incorporates the use of minority discounts and lack of marketability discounts. No other discounts were used in arriving at the fair market value of the transferred stock or any assets owned by X. On A's Federal gift tax return, Form 709, for the 2001 calendar year, A provides the information required under paragraph (f)(2) of this section including a statement reporting the fair market value of 100 percent of X (before taking into account any discounts), the pro rata portion of X subject to the transfer, and the reported value of the transfer. A also attaches a statement regarding the determination of value that includes a discussion of the discounts claimed and how the discounts were determined.

(ii) *Application of the adequate disclosure standard.* A has provided sufficient information such that the transfer will be considered adequately disclosed and the period of assessment for the transfer under section 6501 will run from the time the return is filed (as determined under section 6501(b)).

*Example 4.* (i) *Facts.* A owns a 70 percent limited partnership interest in PS. PS owns 40 percent of the stock in X, a closely-held

corporation. The assets of X include a 50 percent general partnership interest in PB. PB owns an interest in commercial real property. None of the entities (PS, X, or PB) is actively traded and, based on generally applicable valuation principles, the value of each entity would be determined based on the net value of the assets owned by each entity. In 2001, A transfers a 25 percent limited partnership interest in PS to B, A's child. On the Federal gift tax return, Form 709, for the 2001 calendar year, A reports the transfer of the 25 percent limited partnership interest in PS and that the fair market value of 100 percent of PS is $y and that the value of 25 percent of PS is $z, reflecting marketability and minority discounts with respect to the 25 percent interest. However, A does not disclose that PS owns 40 percent of X, and that X owns 50 percent of PB and that, in arriving at the $y fair market value of 100 percent of PS, discounts were claimed in valuing PS's interest in X, X's interest in PB, and PB's interest in the commercial real property.

(ii) *Application of the adequate disclosure standard.* The information on the lower tiered entities is relevant and material in determining the value of the transferred interest in PS. Accordingly, because A has failed to comply with requirements of paragraph (f)(2)(iv) of this section regarding PS's interest in X, X's interest in PB, and PB's interest in the commercial real property, the transfer will not be considered adequately disclosed and the period of assessment for the transfer under section 6501 will remain open indefinitely.

*Example 5.* The facts are the same as in *Example 4* except that A submits, with the Federal tax return, an appraisal of the 25 percent limited partnership interest in PS that satisfies the requirements of paragraph (f)(3) of this section in lieu of the information required in paragraph (f)(2)(iv) of this section. Assuming the other requirements of paragraph (f)(2) of this section are satisfied, the transfer is considered adequately disclosed and the period for assessment for the transfer under section 6501 will run from the time the return is filed (as determined under section 6501(b) of this chapter).

*Example 6.* A owns 100 percent of the stock of X Corporation, a company actively engaged in a manufacturing business. B, A's child, is an employee of X and receives an annual salary paid in the ordinary course of operating X Corporation. B reports the annual salary as income on B's income tax returns. In 2001, A transfers property to family members and files a Federal gift tax return reporting the transfers. However, A does not disclose the 2001 salary payments made to B. Because the salary payments were reported as income on B's income tax return, the salary payments are deemed to be adequately disclosed. The transfer of property to family members, other than the salary payments to B, reported on the gift tax return must satisfy the adequate disclosure requirements under paragraph (f)(2) of this section in order for the period of assessment under section 6501 to commence to run with respect to those transfers.

(8) *Effective date.*—This paragraph (f) is applicable to gifts made after December 31, 1996, for which the gift tax return for such calendar year is filed after December 3, 1999.

(g) *Listed transactions.*—(1) *In general.*—If a taxpayer is required to disclose a listed transaction under section 6011 and the regulations thereunder and does not do so in the time and manner required, then the time to assess any tax attributable to that listed transaction for the taxable year(s) to which the failure to disclose relates (as defined in paragraph (g)(3)(iii) of this section) will not expire before the earlier of one year after the date on which the taxpayer makes the disclosure described in paragraph (g)(5) of this section or one year after the date on which a material advisor makes a disclosure described in paragraph (g)(6) of this section. In no case will the operation of this paragraph (g) cause the period of limitations on assessment to expire any earlier than the period that would have otherwise applied under this section determined without regard to this paragraph (g)(1).

(2) *Limitations period if paragraph (g)(5) or (g)(6) is satisfied.*—If one of the disclosure provisions described in paragraphs (g)(5) or (6) of this section is satisfied, then the tax attributable to the listed transaction may be assessed at any time before the expiration of the limitations period that would have otherwise applied under this section (determined without regard to paragraph (g)(1) of this section) or the period ending one year after the date that one of the disclosure provisions described in paragraphs (g)(5) or (6) of this section was satisfied, whichever is later. If both disclosure provisions are satisfied, the one-year period will begin on the earlier of the dates on which the provisions were satisfied. Paragraph (g)(1) of this section does not apply to any period of limitations on assessment that expired before the date on which the failure to disclose the listed transaction under section 6011 occurred.

(3) *Definitions.*—(i) *Listed transaction.*—The term *listed transaction* means a transaction described in section 6707A(c)(2) of the Code and § 1.6011-4(b)(2) of this chapter.

(ii) *Material advisor.*—The term *material advisor* means a person described in section 6111(b)(1) of the Code and § 301.6111-3(b) of this chapter.

(iii) *Taxable year(s) to which the failure to disclose relates.*—The *taxable year(s) to which the failure to disclose relates* are each taxable year that the taxpayer participated (as defined under section 6011 and the regulations thereunder) in a transaction that was identified as a listed transaction and the taxpayer failed to disclose the listed transaction as required under section 6011. If the taxable year in which the taxpayer participated in the listed transaction is different from the taxable year in which the taxpayer is required to disclose the listed transaction under section 6011, the taxable year(s) to which the failure to disclose relates are each taxable year that the taxpayer participated in the transaction.

(4) *Application of paragraph with respect to pass-through entities.*—In the case of taxpayers who are partners in partnerships, shareholders in S corporations, or beneficiaries of trusts and are required to disclose a listed transaction under section 6011 and the regulations thereunder, paragraph (g)(1) of this section will apply to a particular partner, shareholder, or beneficiary if that particular partner, shareholder, or beneficiary does not disclose within the time and in the form and manner provided by section 6011 and § 1.6011-4(d) and (e), regardless of whether the partnership, S corporation, or trust or another partner, shareholder, or beneficiary discloses in accordance with section 6011 and the regulations thereunder. Similarly, because paragraph (g)(1) of this section applies on a taxpayer-by-taxpayer basis, the failure of a partnership, S corporation, or trust that has a disclosure obligation under section 6011 and that does not disclose within the time or in the form and manner provided by § 1.6011-4(d) and (e) will not cause paragraph (g)(1) of this section to apply to a partner, shareholder or beneficiary of the entity. Instead, the application of paragraph (g)(1) of this section to a partner, shareholder, or beneficiary will be determined based on whether the particular partner, shareholder, or beneficiary satisfied their disclosure obligation under section 6011 and the regulations thereunder.

(5) *Taxpayer's disclosure of a listed transaction that the taxpayer did not properly disclose under section 6011.*—(i) *In general.*—(A) *Method of disclosure.*—The taxpayer must complete the most current version of Form 8886, "Reportable Transaction Disclosure Statement" (or successor form), available on the date the taxpayer attempts to satisfy this paragraph (g)(5) in accordance with § 1.6011-4(d) and the instructions to the Form in effect on that date. The taxpayer must indicate on the Form 8886 that the form is being submitted for purposes of section 6501(c)(10) and the tax return(s) and taxable year(s) for which the taxpayer is making a section 6501(c)(10) disclosure. Disclosure under this paragraph (g)(5) will only be effective for the tax return(s) and taxable year(s) that the taxpayer specifies on the Form 8886 that he or she is attempting to disclose for purposes of section 6501(c)(10). If the Form 8886 contains a line for this purpose, then the taxpayer must complete the line in accordance with the instructions to that form. Otherwise, the taxpayer must include on the top of Page 1 of the Form 8886, and each copy of the form, the following statement: "*Section 6501(c)(10) Disclosure*" followed by the tax return(s) and taxable year(s) for which the taxpayer is making a section 6501(c)(10) disclosure. For example, if the taxpayer did not properly disclose its participation in a listed transaction the tax consequences of which were reflected on the taxpayer's Form 1040 for the 2005 taxable year, the taxpayer must include the following statement: "*Section 6501(c)(10) Disclosure; 2005 Form 1040*" on the form. The taxpayer must submit the properly completed Form 8886 and a cover letter, which must be completed in accordance with the requirements set forth in paragraph (g)(5)(i)(B) of this section, to the Office of Tax Shelter Analysis (OTSA). The taxpayer is permitted, but not required, to file an amended return with the Form 8886 and cover letter. Separate Forms 8886 and separate cover letters must be submitted for each listed transaction the taxpayer did not properly disclose under section 6011. If the taxpayer participated in one listed transaction over multiple years, the taxpayer may submit one Form 8886 (or successor form) and cover letter and indicate on that form all of the tax returns and taxable years for which the taxpayer is making a section 6501(c)(10) disclosure. If a taxpayer participated in more than one listed transaction, then the taxpayer must submit separate Forms 8886 (or successor form) for each listed transaction, unless the listed transactions are the same or substantially similar, in which case all the listed transactions may be reported on one Form 8886.

(B) *Cover letter.*—(1) A cover letter to which a Form 8886 is to be attached must identify the tax return(s) and taxable year(s) for which the taxpayer is making a section 6501(c)(10) disclosure and include the following statement signed under penalties of perjury by the taxpayer:

> Under penalties of perjury, I declare that I have examined this reportable transaction dis-

closure statement and, to the best of my knowledge and belief, this reportable transaction disclosure statement is true, correct, and complete.

(2) If the Form 8886 is prepared by a paid preparer, in addition to the statement under penalties of perjury signed by the taxpayer, the Form 8886 must also include the following statement signed under penalties of perjury by the paid preparer.

> Under penalties of perjury, I declare that I have examined this reportable transaction disclosure statement and, to the best of my knowledge and belief, this reportable transaction disclosure statement is true, correct, and complete. This declaration is based on all information of which I, as paid preparer, have any knowledge.

(C) *Taxpayer under examination or Appeals consideration.*—A taxpayer making a disclosure under paragraph (g)(5) of this section with respect to a taxable year under examination or Appeals consideration by the IRS must satisfy the requirements of paragraphs (g)(5)(i)(A) and (B) of this section and also submit a copy of the submission to the IRS examiner or Appeals officer examining or considering the taxable year(s) to which the disclosure under this paragraph (g) relates.

(D) *Date the one-year period will begin to run if paragraph (g)(5) satisfied.*—Unless an earlier expiration is provided for in paragraph (g)(6) of this section, the time to assess tax under this paragraph (g) will not expire before one year after the date on which the Secretary is furnished the information from the taxpayer that satisfies all of the requirements of paragraphs (g)(5)(i)(A) and (B) of this section and, if applicable, paragraph (g)(5)(i)(C) of this section. If the taxpayer does not satisfy all of the requirements on the same date, the one-year period will begin on the date that the IRS is furnished the information that, together with prior disclosures of information, satisfies the requirements of this paragraph (g)(5). For purposes of this paragraph (g)(5), the information is deemed furnished on the date the IRS receives the information.

(ii) *Exception for returns other than annual returns.*—The IRS may prescribe alternative procedures to satisfy the requirements of this paragraph (g)(5) in a revenue procedure, notice, or other guidance published in the Internal Revenue Bulletin for circumstances involving returns other than annual returns.

(6) *Material advisor's disclosure of a listed transaction not properly disclosed by a taxpayer under section 6011.*—(i) *In general.*—In response to a written request of the IRS under section 6112, a material advisor with respect to a listed transaction must furnish to the IRS the information described in section 6112 and § 301.6112-1(b) in the form and manner prescribed by section 6112 and § 301.6112-1(e). If the information the material advisor furnishes identifies the taxpayer as a person who entered into the listed transaction, regardless of whether the material advisor provides the information before or after the taxpayer's failure to disclose the listed transaction under section 6011, then the requirements of this paragraph (g)(6) will be satisfied for that taxpayer. The requirements of this paragraph (g)(6) will be considered satisfied even if the material advisor furnishes the information required under section 6112 to the IRS after the date prescribed in section 6708 or published guidance relating to section 6708.

(ii) *Paragraph (g)(6) not satisfied.*—(A) *Information not furnished by a material advisor or a person permitted to act on behalf of the material advisor.*—The requirements of this paragraph (g)(6) are not satisfied for a taxpayer unless the information is furnished by—

(1) A person who is a material advisor (as defined in paragraph (g)(3)(ii) of this section) with respect to the taxpayer,

(2) A person who is providing the information pursuant to § 301.6112-1(d) on behalf of a dissolved or liquidated material advisor with respect to the taxpayer, or

(3) a person who is providing the information on behalf of a material advisor with respect to the taxpayer under a designation agreement in accordance with § 301.6112-1(f).

(B) *No written request by IRS.*—The requirements of this paragraph (g)(6) are not satisfied unless the information is furnished in response to a written request made by the IRS to the material advisor under section 6112 (except as provided in § 301.6112-1(d) with respect to a list furnished to OTSA within 60 days after dissolution or liquidation of a material advisor).

(C) *Information furnished does not identify the taxpayer.*—The requirements of this paragraph (g)(6) are not satisfied for a taxpayer unless the information furnished identifies the taxpayer as a person who entered into the listed transaction.

(iii) *Date the one-year period will begin if paragraph (g)(6) is satisfied.*—Unless an earlier expiration is provided for in paragraph (g)(5) of this section, the time to assess tax under this paragraph (g) will expire one year after the date on which the material advisor satisfies the requirements of paragraph (g)(6)(i) of this section with respect to the taxpayer. For purposes of this paragraph (g)(6), information is deemed to be furnished on the date that, in response to a request under section 6112, the IRS receives the information from a material advisor that satisfies the requirements of paragraph (g)(6)(i) of this section with respect to the taxpayer.

(7) *Tax assessable under this section.*—If the period of limitations on assessment for a taxable year remains open under this section, the Secretary has authority to assess any tax with respect to the listed transaction in that year. This includes, but is not limited to, adjustments made to the tax consequences claimed on the return plus interest, additions to tax, additional amounts, and penalties that are related to the listed transaction or adjustments made to the tax consequences. This also includes any item to the extent the item is affected by the listed transaction even if it is unrelated to the listed transaction. An example of an item affected by, but unrelated to, a listed transaction is the threshold for the medical expense deduction under section 213 that varies if there is a change in an individual's adjusted gross income. An example of a penalty related to the listed transaction is the penalty under section 6707A for failure to file the disclosure statement reporting the taxpayer's participation in the listed transaction. Examples of penalties related to the adjustments made to the tax consequences are the accuracy-related penalties under sections 6662 and 6662A.

(8) *Examples.*—The rules of this paragraph (g) are illustrated by the following examples:

*Example 1. No requirement to disclose under section 6011.* P, an individual, is a partner in a partnership that entered into a transaction in 2001 that was the same as or substantially similar to the transaction identified as a listed transaction in Notice 2000-44 (2000-2 CB 255). P claimed a loss from the transaction on his Form 1040 for the tax year 2001. P filed the Form 1040 prior to June 14, 2002. P did not disclose his participation in the listed transaction because P was not required to disclose the transaction under the applicable section 6011 regulations (TD 8961), which were effective for any transaction entered into before January 1, 2001 and any transaction entered into on or after January 1, 2001 that was reported on a return of the taxpayer filed on or before June 14, 2002. Although the transaction was a listed transaction and P did not disclose the transaction, P had no obligation to include on any return or statement any information with respect to a listed transaction within the meaning of section 6501(c)(10) because TD 8961 only applied to corporations, not individuals. Accordingly, section 6501(c)(10) does not apply.

*Example 2. Taxable year to which the failure to disclose relates when transaction is identified as a listed transaction after first year of participation and the transaction must be disclosed with the return next filed.* (i) On December 30, 2003, Y, a corporation, enters into a transaction that at the time is not a reportable transaction. On March 15, 2004, Y timely files its 2003 Form 1120, reporting the tax consequences from the transaction. On April 1, 2004, the IRS issues Notice 2004-31 that identifies the transaction as a listed transaction. Y also reports tax consequences from the transaction on its 2004 Form 1120, which it timely filed on March 15, 2005. Y did not attach a completed Form 8886 to its 2004 Form 1120 and did not send a copy of the form to OTSA. The general three-year period of limitations on assessment for Y's 2003 and 2004 taxable years would expire on March 15, 2007, and March 17, 2008, respectively.

(ii) The period of limitations on assessment for Y's 2003 taxable year was open on the date the transaction was identified as a listed transaction. Under the applicable section 6011 regulations (TD 9108), which were effective for transactions entered into before August 3, 2007, Y should have disclosed its participation in the transaction with its next filed return, which was its 2004 Form 1120, but Y did not disclose its participation. Y's failure to disclose with the 2004 Form 1120 relates to taxable years 2003 and 2004. Section 6501(c)(10) operates to keep the period of limitations on assessment open for the 2003 and 2004 taxable years with respect to the listed transaction until at least one year after the date Y satisfies the requirements of paragraph (g)(5) of this section or a material advisor satisfies the requirements of paragraph (g)(6) of this section with respect to Y.

*Example 3. Taxable year to which the failure to disclose relates when transaction is identified as a listed transaction after the first year of participation and the transaction must be disclosed 90 days after the transaction became a listed transaction.* (i) In January 2015, A, a calendar year taxpayer, enters into a transaction that at the time is not a listed transaction. A reports the tax consequences from the transaction on its individual income tax return for 2015 timely filed on April 15, 2016. The time for the IRS to assess tax against A under the general three-year period of limitations for A's 2015 taxable year would

expire on April 15, 2019. A only participated in the transaction in 2015. On March 7, 2017, the IRS identifies the transaction as a listed transaction. A does not file the Form 8886 with OTSA by June 5, 2017.

(ii) The period of limitations on assessment for A's 2015 taxable year was open on the date the transaction was identified as a listed transaction. Under the current section 6011 regulations (TD 9350) which are effective for transactions entered into on or after August 3, 2007, A must disclose its participation in the transaction by filing a completed Form 8886 with OTSA on or before June 5, 2017, which is 90 days after the date the transaction became a listed transaction. A did not disclose the transaction as required. A's failure to disclose relates to taxable year 2015 even though the obligation to disclose did not arise until 2017. Section 6501(c)(10) operates to keep the period of limitations on assessment open for the 2015 taxable year with respect to the listed transaction until at least one year after the date A satisfies the requirements of paragraph (g)(5) of this section or a material advisor satisfies the requirements of paragraph (g)(6) of this section with respect to A.

*Example 4. Requirements of paragraph (g)(6) satisfied.* Same facts as *Example 3*, except that on April 5, 2019, the IRS hand delivers to Advisor J, who is a material advisor, a section 6112 request related to the listed transaction. Advisor J furnishes the required list with all the information required by section 6112 and § 301.6112-1, including all the information required with respect to A, to the IRS on May 8, 2019. The submission satisfies the requirements of paragraph (g)(6) even though Advisor J furnishes the information outside of the 20-business-day period provided in section 6708. Accordingly, under section 6501(c)(10), the period of limitations with respect to A's taxable year 2015 will end on May 8, 2020, one year after the IRS received the required information, unless the period of limitations remains open under another exception. Any tax for the 2015 taxable year not attributable to the listed transaction must be assessed by April 15, 2019.

*Example 5. Requirements of paragraph (g)(5) also satisfied.* Same facts as *Examples 3 and 4*, except that on May 23, 2019, A files a properly completed Form 8886 and signed cover letter with OTSA both identifying that the section 6501(c)(10) disclosure relates to A's Form 1040 for 2015. A satisfied the requirements of paragraph (g)(5) of this section as of May 23, 2019. Because the requirements of paragraph (g)(6) were satisfied first as described in *Example 4*, under section 6501(c)(10) the period of limitations will end on May 8, 2020 (one year after the requirements of paragraph (g)(6) were satisfied) instead of May 23, 2020 (one year after the requirements of paragraph (g)(5) were satisfied). Any tax for the 2015 taxable year not attributable to the listed transaction must be assessed by April 15, 2019.

*Example 6. Period to assess tax remains open under another exception.* Same facts as *Examples 3, 4, and 5*, except that on April 1, 2019, A signed Form 872, consenting to extend, without restriction, its period of limitations on assessment for taxable year 2015 under section 6501(c)(4) until July 15, 2020. In that case, although under section 6501(c)(10) the period of limitations would otherwise expire on May 8, 2020, the IRS may assess tax with respect to the listed transaction (as well as any other item on the return covered by the Form 872 extension) at any time up to and including July 15, 2020, pursuant to section 6501(c)(4). Section 6501(c)(10) operates to extend the assessment period but not to shorten any other applicable assessment period.

*Example 7. Requirements of (g)(5) not satisfied.* In 2015, X, a corporation, enters into a listed transaction. On March 15, 2016, X timely files its 2015 Form 1120, reporting the tax consequences from the transaction. X does not disclose the transaction as required under section 6011 when it files its 2015 return. The failure to disclose relates to taxable year 2015. On February 13, 2017, X completes and files a Form 8886 with respect to the listed transaction with OTSA but does not submit a cover letter, as required. The requirements of paragraph (g)(5) of this section have not been satisfied. Therefore, the time to assess tax against X with respect to the transaction for taxable year 2015 remains open under section 6501(c)(10).

*Example 8. Section 6501(c)(10) applies to keep one partner's period of limitations on assessment open.* T and S are partners in a partnership, TS, that enters into a listed transaction in 2015. T and S each receive a Schedule K-1 from TS on April 11, 2016. On April 15, 2016, TS, T and S each file their 2015 returns. Under the applicable section 6011 regulations, TS, T, and S each are required to disclose the transaction. TS attaches a completed Form 8886 to its 2015 Form 1065 and sends a copy of Form 8886 to OTSA. Neither T nor S files a disclosure statement with their respective returns nor sends a copy to OTSA on April 15, 2016. On May 17, 2016, T timely files a completed Form 8886 with OTSA pursuant to § 1.6011-4(e)(1). T's disclosure is timely because T received the Schedule K-1 within 10 calendar days before the due date of the return and, thus, T had 60 calendar days to file Form 8886 with OTSA. TS and T properly disclosed the transaction in accordance with the applicable regulations under section 6011, but S did not. S's failure to disclose relates to taxable year 2015. The time to assess tax with respect to the transaction against S for 2015 remains

**Limitations on Assessment and Collection**
See p. 20,601 for regulations not amended to reflect law changes
**67,027**

open under section 6501(c)(10) even though TS and T disclosed the transaction.

*Example 9. Section 6501(c)(10) satisfied before expiration of three-year period of limitations under section 6501(a).* Same facts as *Example 8*, except that on August 26, 2016, S satisfies the requirements of paragraph (g)(5) of this section. No material advisor satisfied the requirements of paragraph (g)(6) of this section with respect to S on a date earlier than August 26, 2016. Under section 6501(c)(10), the period of time in which the IRS may assess tax against S with respect to the listed transaction would expire no earlier than August 26, 2017, one year after the date S satisfied the requirements of paragraph (g)(5). As the general three-year period of limitations on assessment under section 6501(a) does not expire until April 15, 2019, the IRS will have until that date to assess any tax with respect to the listed transaction.

*Example 10. No section 6112 request.* B, a calendar year taxpayer, entered into a listed transaction in 2015. B did not comply with the applicable disclosure requirements under section 6011 for taxable year 2015; therefore, section 6501(c)(10) applies to keep the period of limitations on assessment open with respect to the tax related to the transaction until at least one year after B satisfies the requirements of paragraph (g)(5) of this section or a material advisor satisfies the requirements of paragraph (g)(6) of this section with respect to B. In June 2016, the IRS conducts a section 6700 investigation of Advisor K, who is a material advisor to B with respect to the listed transaction. During the course of the investigation, the IRS obtains the name, address, and TIN of all of Advisor K's clients who engaged in the transaction, including B. The information provided does not satisfy the requirements of paragraph (g)(6) with respect to B because the information was not provided pursuant to a section 6112 request. Therefore, the time to assess tax against B with respect to the transaction for taxable year 2015 remains open under section 6501(c)(10).

*Example 11. Section 6112 request but the requirements of paragraph (g)(6) are not satisfied with respect to B.* Same facts as *Example 10*, except that on January 9, 2017, the IRS sends by certified mail a section 6112 request to Advisor L, who is another material advisor to B with respect to the listed transaction. Advisor L furnishes some of the information required under section 6112 and §301.6112-1 to the IRS for inspection on January 17, 2017. The list includes information with respect to many clients of Advisor L, but it does not include any information with respect to B. The submission does not satisfy the requirements of paragraph (g)(6) of this section with respect to B. Therefore, the time to assess tax against B with respect to the transaction for taxable year 2015 remains open under section 6501(c)(10).

*Example 12. Section 6112 submission made before taxpayer failed to disclose a listed transaction.* Advisor M, who is a material advisor, advises C, an individual, in 2015 with respect to a transaction that is not a reportable transaction at that time. C files its return claiming the tax consequences of the transaction on April 15, 2016. The time for the IRS to assess tax against C under the general three-year period of limitations for C's 2015 taxable year would expire on April 15, 2019. The IRS identifies the transaction as a listed transaction on November 3, 2017. On December 7, 2017, the IRS hand delivers to Advisor M a section 6112 request related to the transaction. Advisor M furnishes the information to the IRS on December 29, 2017. The information contains all the required information with respect to Advisor M's clients, including C. C does not disclose the transaction on or before February 1, 2018, as required under section 6011 and the regulations under section 6011. Advisor M's submission under section 6112 satisfies the requirements of paragraph (g)(6) of this section even though it occurred prior to C's failure to disclose the listed transaction. Thus, under section 6501(c)(10), the period of limitations to assess tax against C with respect to the listed transaction will end on December 29, 2018 (one year after the requirements of paragraph (g)(6) of this section were satisfied), unless the period of limitations remains open under another exception.

*Example 13. Transaction removed from the category of listed transactions after taxpayer failed to disclose.* D, a calendar year taxpayer, entered into a listed transaction in 2015. D did not comply with the applicable disclosure requirements under section 6011 for taxable year 2015; therefore, section 6501(c)(10) applies to keep the period of limitations on assessment open with respect to the tax related to the transaction until at least one year after D satisfies the requirements of paragraph (g)(5) of this section or a material advisor satisfies the requirements of paragraph (g)(6) of this section with respect to D. In 2017, the IRS removes the transaction from the category of listed transactions because of a change in law. Section 6501(c)(10) continues to apply to keep the period of limitations on assessment open for D's taxable year 2015.

*Example 14. Taxes assessed with respect to the listed transaction.* (i) F, an individual, enters into a listed transaction in 2015. F files its 2015 Form 1040 on April 15, 2016, but does not disclose his participation in the listed transaction in accordance with section 6011 and the regulations under section 6011. F's failure to disclose relates to taxable year 2015. Thus, section 6501(c)(10) applies to keep the period of limita-

tions on assessment open with respect to the tax related to the listed transaction for taxable year 2015 until at least one year after the date F satisfies the requirements of paragraph (g)(5) of this section or a material advisor satisfies the requirements of paragraph (g)(6) of this section with respect to F.

(ii) On July 2, 2020, the IRS completes an examination of F's 2015 taxable year and disallows the tax consequences claimed as a result of the listed transaction. The disallowance of a loss increased F's adjusted gross income. Due to the increase of F's adjusted gross income, certain credits, such as the child tax credit, and exemption deductions were disallowed or reduced because of limitations based on adjusted gross income. In addition, F now is liable for the alternative minimum tax. The examination also uncovered that F claimed two deductions on Schedule C to which F was not entitled. Under section 6501(c)(10), the IRS can timely issue a statutory notice of deficiency (and assess in due course) against F for the deficiency resulting from (1) disallowing the loss, (2) disallowing the credits and exemptions to which F was not entitled based on F's increased adjusted gross income, and (3) being liable for the alternative minimum tax. In addition, the IRS can assess any interest and applicable penalties related to those adjustments, such as the accuracy-related penalty under sections 6662 and 6662A and the penalty under section 6707A for F's failure to disclose the transaction as required under section 6011 and the regulations under section 6011. The IRS cannot, however, pursuant to section 6501(c)(10), assess the increase in tax that would result from disallowing the two deductions on F's Schedule C because those deductions are not related to, or affected by, the adjustments concerning the listed transaction.

(9) *Effective/applicability date.*—The rules of this paragraph (g) apply to taxable years with respect to which the period of limitations on assessment under section 6501 (including subsection (c)(10)) did not expire before March 31, 2015. [Reg. §301.6501(c)-1.]

☐ [*T.D. 6172, 5-2-56. Amended by T.D. 6498, 10-24-60; T.D. 7838, 10-5-82; T.D. 8395, 1-28-92, T.D. 8845, 12-2-99 (corrected 1-6-2000) and T.D. 9718, 3-30-15 (corrected 4-27-2015).*]

**[Reg. §301.6501(d)-1]**

**§301.6501(d)-1. Request for prompt assessment.**—(a) Except as otherwise provided in section 6501(c), (e), or (f), any tax for which a return is required and for which:

(1) A decedent or an estate of a decedent may be liable, other than the estate tax imposed by chapter 11 of the Code, or

(2) A corporation which is contemplating dissolution, is in the process of dissolution, or has been dissolved, may be liable,

shall be assessed, or a proceeding in court without assessment for the collection of such tax shall be begun, within 18 months after the receipt of a written request for prompt assessment thereof.

(b) The executor, administrator, or other fiduciary representing the estate of the decedent, or the corporation, or the fiduciary representing the dissolved corporation, as the case may be, shall, after the return in question has been filed, file the request for prompt assessment in writing with the district director for the internal revenue district in which such return was filed. The request, in order to be effective, must be transmitted separately from any other document, must set forth the classes of tax and the taxable periods for which the prompt assessment is requested, and must clearly indicate that it is a request for prompt assessment under the provisions of section 6501(d). The effect of such a request is to limit the time in which an assessment of tax may be made, or a proceeding in court without assessment for collection of tax may be begun, to a period of 18 months from the date the request is filed with the proper district director. The request does not extend the time within which an assessment may be made, or a proceeding in court without assessment may be begun, beyond 3 years from the date the return was filed. This special period of limitations will not apply to any return filed after a request for prompt assessment has been made unless an additional request is filed in the manner provided herein.

(c) In the case of a corporation the 18-month period shall not apply unless:

(1) The written request notifies the district director that the corporation contemplates dissolution at or before the expiration of such 18-month period; the dissolution is in good faith begun before the expiration of such 18-month period; and the dissolution so begun is completed either before or after the expiration of such 18-month period; or

(2) The written request notifies the district director that a dissolution has in good faith been begun, and the dissolution is completed either before or after the expiration of such 18-month period; or

(3) A dissolution has been completed at the time the written request is made. [Reg. §301.6501(d)-1.]

☐ [*T.D. 6172, 5-2-56. Amended by T.D. 6425, 11-10-59 and T.D. 6498, 10-24-60.*]

[Reg. §301.6501(e)-1]

**§301.6501(e)-1. Omission from return.**—(a) *Income taxes.*—(1) *General rule.*—(i) If a taxpayer omits from the gross income stated in the return of a tax imposed by subtitle A of the Internal Revenue Code an amount properly includible therein that is in excess of 25 percent of the gross income so stated, the tax may be assessed, or a proceeding in court for the collection of that tax may be begun without assessment, at any time within 6 years after the return was filed.

(ii) For purposes of paragraph (a)(1)(i) of this section, the term *gross income*, as it relates to a trade or business, means the total of the amounts received or accrued from the sale of goods or services, to the extent required to be shown on the return, without reduction for the cost of those goods or services.

(iii) For purposes of paragraph (a)(1)(i) of this section, the term *gross income*, as it relates to any income other than from the sale of goods or services in a trade or business, has the same meaning as provided under section 61(a), and includes the total of the amounts received or accrued, to the extent required to be shown on the return. In the case of amounts received or accrued that relate to the disposition of property, and except as provided in paragraph (a)(1)(ii) of this section, *gross income* means the excess of the amount realized from the disposition of the property over the unrecovered cost or other basis of the property. Consequently, except as provided in paragraph (a)(1)(ii) of this section, an understated amount of gross income resulting from an overstatement of unrecovered cost or other basis constitutes an omission from gross income for purposes of section 6501(e)(1)(A)(i).

(iv) An amount shall not be considered as omitted from gross income if information sufficient to apprise the Commissioner of the nature and amount of the item is disclosed in the return, including any schedule or statement attached to the return.

(2) [Reserved]

(b) *Estate and gift taxes.*—(1) If the taxpayer omits from the gross estate as stated in the estate tax return, or from the total amount of the gifts made during the period for which the gift tax return was filed (see §25.6019-1 of this chapter) as stated in the gift tax return, an item or items properly includible therein the amount of which is in excess of 25 percent of the gross estate as stated in the estate tax return, or 25 percent of the total amount of the gifts as stated in the gift tax return, the tax may be assessed, or a proceeding in court for the collection thereof may be begun without assessment, at any time within 6 years after the estate tax or gift tax return, as applicable, was filed.

(2) For purposes of this paragraph (b), an item disclosed in the return or in any schedule or statement attached to the return in a manner sufficient to apprise the Commissioner of the nature and amount thereof shall not be taken into account in determining items omitted from the gross estate or total gifts, as the case may be. Further, there shall not be taken into account in computing the 25 percent omission from the gross estate stated in the estate tax return or from the total gifts stated in the gift tax return, any increases in the valuation of assets disclosed on the return.

(c) *Excise taxes.*—(1) *In general.*—If the taxpayer omits from a return of a tax imposed under a provision of subtitle D an amount properly includible thereon, which amount is in excess of 25 percent of the amount of tax reported thereon, the tax may be assessed or a proceeding in court for the collection thereof may be begun without assessment, at any time within 6 years after the return was filed. For special rules relating to chapter 41, 42, 43 and 44 taxes, see paragraphs (c)(2), (3), (4), and (5) of this section.

(2) *Chapter 41 excise taxes.*—If an organization discloses an expenditure in its return (or in a schedule or statement attached thereto) in a manner sufficient to apprise the Commissioner of the existence and nature of the expenditure, the three-year limitation on assessment and collection described in section 6501(a) shall apply with respect to any tax under chapter 41 arising from the expenditure. If a taxpayer fails to so disclose an expenditure in its return (or in a schedule or statement attached thereto), the tax arising from the expenditure not so disclosed may be assessed, or a proceeding in court for the collection of the tax may be begun without assessment, at any time within 6 years after the return was filed.

(3) *Chapter 42 excise taxes.*—(i) If a private foundation omits from its annual return with respect to the tax imposed by section 4940 an amount of tax properly includible therein that is in excess of 25 percent of the amount of tax imposed by section 4940 that is reported on the return, the tax may be assessed, or a proceeding in court for the collection of the tax may be begun without assessment, at any time within 6 years after the return was filed. If a private foundation discloses in its return (or in a schedule or statement

attached thereto) the nature, source, and amount of any income giving rise to any omitted tax, the tax arising from the income shall be counted as reported on the return in computing whether the foundation has omitted more than 25 percent of the tax reported on its return.

(ii) If a private foundation, trust, or other organization (as the case may be) discloses an item in its return (or in a schedule or statement attached thereto) in a manner sufficient to apprise the Commissioner of the existence and nature of the item, the three-year limitation on assessment and collection described in section 6501(a) shall apply with respect to any tax imposed under sections 4941(a), 4942(a), 4943(a), 4944(a), 4945(a), 4951(a), 4952(a), 4953 and 4958, arising from any transaction disclosed by the item. If a private foundation, trust, or other organization (as the case may be) fails to so disclose an item in its return (or in a schedule or statement attached thereto), the tax arising from any transaction not so disclosed may be assessed or a proceeding in court for the collection of the tax may be begun without assessment, at any time within 6 years after the return was filed.

(4) *Chapter 43 excise taxes.*—If a taxpayer discloses an item in its return (or in a schedule or statement attached thereto) in a manner sufficient to apprise the Commissioner of the existence and nature of the item, the three-year limitation on assessment and collection described in section 6501(a) shall apply with respect to any tax imposed under sections 4971(a), 4972, 4973,4974 and 4975(a), arising from any transaction disclosed by the item. If a taxpayer fails to so disclose an item in its return (or in a schedule or statement attached thereto), the tax arising from any transaction not so disclosed may be assessed, or a proceeding in court for the collection of the tax may be begun without assessment, at any time within 6 years after the return was filed. The applicable return for the tax under sections 4971, 4972, 4973 and 4974, is the return designated by the Commissioner for reporting the respective tax. The applicable return for the tax under section 4975 is the return filed by the plan used to report the act giving rise to the tax.

(5) *Chapter 44 excise taxes.*—If a real estate investment trust omits from its annual return with respect to the tax imposed by section 4981 an amount of tax properly includible therein that is in excess of 25 percent of the amount of tax imposed by section 4981 that is reported on the return, the tax may be assessed, or a proceeding in court for the collection of the tax may be begun without assessment, at any time within 6 years after the return was filed. If a real estate investment trust discloses in its return (or in a schedule or statement attached thereto) the nature, source, and amount of any income giving rise to any omitted tax, the tax arising from the income shall be counted as reported on the return in computing whether the trust has omitted more than 25 percent of the tax reported on its return.

(d) *Exception.*—The provisions of this section do not limit the application of section 6501(c).

(e) *Effective/applicability date.*—(1) *Income taxes.*—Paragraph (a) of this section applies to taxable years with respect to which the period for assessing tax was open on or after September 24, 2009.

(2) *Estate, gift and excise taxes.*—Paragraphs (b) through (d) of this section continue to apply as they did prior to being removed inadvertently on September 28, 2009. Specifically, paragraph (b) of this section applies to returns filed on or after May 2, 1956, except for the amendment to paragraph (b)(1) of this section that applies to returns filed on or after December 29, 1972. Paragraph (c) of this section applies to returns filed on or after October 7, 1982, except for the amendment to paragraph (c)(3)(ii) of this section that applies to returns filed on or after January 10, 2001. Paragraph (d) of this section applies to returns filed on or after May 2, 1956. [Reg. §301.6501(e)-1.]

☐ [*T.D.* 9511, 12-14-2010.]

### [Reg. §301.6501(f)-1]

**§301.6501(f)-1. Personal holding company tax.**—If a corporation which is a personal holding company for any taxable year fails to file with its income tax return for such year a schedule setting forth the items of gross income described in section 543(a) received by the corporation during such year, and the names and addresses of the individuals who owned, within the meaning of section 544, at any time during the last half of such taxable year, more than 50 percent in value of the outstanding capital stock of the corporation, the personal holding company tax for such year may be assessed, or a proceeding in court for the collection thereof may be begun without assessment, at any time within 6 years after the return for such year was filed. [Reg. §301.6501(f)-1.]

☐ [*T.D.* 6172, 5-2-56.]

**[Reg. § 301.6501(g)-1]**

**§ 301.6501(g)-1. Certain income tax returns of corporations.—**
(a) *Trusts or partnerships.*—If a taxpayer determines in good faith that it is a trust or partnership and files a return as such under subtitle A of the Code, and if the taxpayer is later held to be a corporation for the taxable year for which the return was filed, such return shall be deemed to be the return of the corporation for the purpose of section 6501.

(b) *Exempt organizations.*—If a taxpayer determines in good faith that it is an exempt organization and files a return as such under section 6033, and if the taxpayer is later held to be a taxable organization for the taxable year for which the return was filed, such return shall be deemed to be the return of the organization for the purpose of section 6501.

(c) *DISC.*—If a corporation determines in good faith that it is a DISC (as defined in section 992(a)(1)) for a taxable year and files a return as such pursuant to section 6011(c)(2), and if the corporation is thereafter held to be a corporation which is not a DISC for the taxable year for which the return was filed, then—

(1) Such return shall be deemed to be the return of the corporation for the purpose of section 6501.

(2) Such return if filed within the time required by section 6072(b) for filing a DISC return shall be deemed to be filed within the time required by section 6072(b) for filing of a return by a corporation which is not a DISC, and

(3) Interest on underpayment and overpayments allowed by chapter 67 of the Code and additions to the tax, additional amounts and assessable penalties allowed by Chapter 68 of the Code, when determined by reference to the time for filing of a return, shall be determined by reference to the time required by section 6072(b) for filing of a return by a DISC. [Reg. § 301.6501(g)-1.]

☐ [T.D. 6172, 5-2-56. *Amended by T.D. 6498, 10-24-60 and T.D. 7533,* 2-14-78.]

**[Reg. § 301.6501(h)-1]**

**§ 301.6501(h)-1. Net operating loss or capital loss carrybacks.**—In the case of a deficiency attributable to the application to the taxpayer of a net operating loss or capital loss carryback (including deficiencies which may be assessed pursuant to the provisions of section 6213(b)(2)), such deficiency may be assessed at any time before the expiration of the period within which a deficiency for the taxable year of the net operating loss or net capital loss which results in such carryback may be assessed. In the case of a deficiency attributable to the application of a net operating loss carryback, such deficiency may be assessed within 18 months after the date on which the taxpayer files in accordance with section 172(b)(3) a copy of the certification (with respect to such taxable year) issued under section 317 of the Trade Expansion Act of 1962, if later than the date prescribed by the preceding sentence. [Reg. § 301.6501(h)-1.]

☐ [T.D. 6425, 11-10-59. *Amended by T.D. 6730, 5-7-64 and T.D. 7301,* 1-3-74.]

**[Reg. § 301.6501(i)-1]**

**§ 301.6501(i)-1. Foreign tax carrybacks; taxable years beginning after December 31, 1957.**—With respect to taxable years beginning after December 31, 1957, a deficiency attributable to the application to the taxpayer of a carryback under section 904(d) (relating to carryback and carryover of excess foreign taxes), may be assessed at any time before the expiration of one year after the expiration of the period within which a deficiency may be assessed for the taxable year of the excess taxes described in section 904(d) which result in such carryback. [Reg. § 301.6501(i)-1.]

☐ [T.D. 6555, 3-14-61.]

**[Reg. § 301.6501(j)-1]**

**§ 301.6501(j)-1. Investment credit carryback; taxable years ending after December 31, 1961.**—With respect to taxable years ending after December 31, 1961, a deficiency attributable to the application to the taxpayer of an investment credit carryback may be assessed at any time before the expiration of the period within which a deficiency for the taxable year of the unused investment credit which results in such carryback may be assessed, or, with respect to any portion of an investment credit carryback from a taxable year attributable to a net operating loss or capital loss carryback from a subsequent taxable year, at any time before the expiration of the period within which a deficiency for such subsequent taxable year may be assessed. For purposes of this section a deficiency shall include a deficiency which may be assessed pursuant to the provisions of section 6213(b)(2), but only those arising with respect to applications for tentative carryback adjustments filed after November 2, 1966. [Reg. § 301.6501(j)-1.]

☐ [T.D. 7301, 1-3-74.]

**[Reg. § 301.6501(m)-1]**

**§ 301.6501(m)-1. Tentative carryback adjustment assessment period.**—(a) *Period of limitation after tentative carryback adjustment.*— (1) Under section 6501(m), in a case where an amount has been applied, credited, or refunded under section 6411, by reason of a net operating loss carryback, a capital loss carryback, an investment credit carryback, or a work incentive program credit carryback to a prior taxable year, the period described in section 6501(a) of the Code for assessing a deficiency for such prior taxable year is extended to include the period described in section 6501(h), (j) or (o), whichever is applicable; except that the amount which may be assessed solely by reason of section 6501(m) may not exceed the amount so applied, credited, or refunded under section 6411, reduced by any amount which may be assessed solely by reason of section 6501(h), (j) or (o), as the case may be.

(2) The application of this paragraph may be illustrated by the following example:

*Example.* Assume that M Corporation, which claims an unused investment credit of $50,000 for the calendar year 1968, files an application under section 6411 of the Code for an adjustment of its tax for 1965, and receives a refund of $50,000 in 1969. In 1971, it is determined that the amount of the unused investment credit for 1968 is $30,000 rather than $50,000. Moreover, it is determined that M Corporation would have owed $40,000 of additional tax for 1965 if it had properly reported certain income which it failed to include in its 1965 return. Assuming that M Corporation filed its 1968 return on March 15, 1969, and that the 3-year period described in section 6501(a) has not been extended, the period prescribed in section 6501(j) for assessing the excessive amount refunded, $20,000 (*i.e.,* $50,000, original amount refunded, less $30,000, correct amount of unused investment credit), does not expire until March 15, 1972, and $20,000 may be assessed on or before such date under section 6501(j). Under section 6501(m), M Corporation may be assessed on or before March 15, 1972, an amount not in excess of $30,000 ($50,000, the amount refunded under section 6411, minus $20,000, the amount which may be assessed solely by reason of section 6501(J)).

(b) *Effective date.*—The provisions of paragraph (a) of this section apply only with respect to applications under section 6411 filed after November 2, 1966. [Reg. § 301.6501(m)-1.]

☐ [T.D. 7301, 1-3-74.]

**[Reg. § 301.6501(n)-1]**

**§ 301.6501(n)-1. Special rules for chapter 42 and similar taxes.—**
(a) *Return filed by private foundation, plan, trust, or organization.*— (1) A return filed by a private foundation, plan, trust, or other organization (as the case may be) with respect to any act giving rise to a tax imposed by chapter 42 (other than a tax imposed by section 4940), or by section 4975 shall be considered, for purposes of section 6501, to be the return of all persons required to file a return with respect to any such tax arising from such act, notwithstanding that all such persons have not signed the return. In the case of a private foundation that files a Form 990-PF (or a Form 5227 in the case of a nonexempt foundation described in section 4947(a)(2)), which contains questions with respect to such taxes, the filing of such form by such foundation shall constitute the filing of a return with respect to any such act, even though the foundation incorrectly answered such questions.

(2) For purposes of section 4940, the return referred to in this section is the return filed by the private foundation for the taxable year for which the tax is imposed.

(b) *Failure of private foundation, plan, trust, or other organization to file.*—The period of limitations on assessment and collection described in section 6501 does not begin with respect to any person liable for tax under chapter 42 (other than section 4940) or section 4975 arising from a given act, where the private foundation, plan, trust, or other organization (as the case may be) has not filed its required return that reports such act for the year in which the act (or failure to act) giving rise to liability for such tax occurred.

(c) *Example.*—The provisions of this section may be illustrated by the following example:

*Example.* In 1973 D, an individual taxpayer who was a disqualified person under the provisions of section 4946(a)(1), participated in an act of self-dealing with a private foundation and incurred a tax under section 4941(a)(1). On May 15, 1974 the private foundation files a Form 990-PF and answers all the questions thereon with regard to any acts of self-dealing (as defined in section 4941(d)) in which it may have engaged in 1973. Assuming that the foundation's return was not a false or fraudulent return nor made with the willful attempt to defeat tax, the period of limitations on assessment and collection under section 6501(a) shall start with respect to any tax under section 4941(a) or section 4941(b) imposed on D arising out of that transaction with such foundation. [Reg. § 301.6501(n)-1.]

☐ [*T.D. 7838, 10-5-82. Amended by T.D. 8920, 1-9-2001.*]

### [Reg. § 301.6501(n)-2]

**§ 301.6501(n)-2. Certain contributions to section 501(c)(3) organizations.**—If a private foundation makes a contribution to a section 501(c)(3) organization as provided in section 4942(g)(3), and a deficiency of tax of such foundation occurs due to the failure of the section 501(c)(3) organization to make the distribution prescribed by section 4942(g)(3), then such deficiency may be assessed within one year after the expiration of the period within which a deficiency may be assessed for the taxable year with respect to which the contribution was made. [Reg. § 301.6501(n)-2.]

☐ [*T.D. 7838, 10-5-82.*]

### [Reg. § 301.6501(n)-3]

**§ 301.6501(n)-3. Certain set-asides described in section 4942(g)(2).**—Where a deficiency of tax of a private foundation results from the failure of an amount set aside by such foundation for a specific project to be treated as a qualifying distribution under section 4942(g)(2)(B)(ii)(II), such deficiency may be assessed within two years after the expiration of the period within which a deficiency may be assessed for the taxable year to which the amount set aside relates. [Reg. § 301.6501(n)-3.]

☐ [*T.D. 7838, 10-5-82.*]

### [Reg. § 301.6502-1]

**§ 301.6502-1. Collection after assessment.**—(a) *General rule.*—In any case in which a tax has been assessed within the applicable statutory period of limitations on assessment, a proceeding in court to collect the tax may be commenced, or a levy to collect the tax may be made, within 10 years after the date of assessment.

(b) *Agreement to extend the period of limitations on collection.*—The Secretary may enter into an agreement with a taxpayer to extend the period of limitations on collection in the following circumstances:

(1) *Extension agreement entered into in connection with an installment agreement.*—If the Secretary and the taxpayer enter into an installment agreement for the tax liability prior to the expiration of the period of limitations on collection, the Secretary and the taxpayer, at the time the installment agreement is entered into, may enter into a written agreement to extend the period of limitations on collection to a date certain. A written extension agreement entered into under this paragraph shall extend the period of limitations on collection until the 89th day after the date agreed upon in the written agreement.

(2) *Extension agreement entered into in connection with the release of a levy under section 6343.*—If the Secretary has levied on any part of the taxpayer's property prior to the expiration of the period of limitations on collection and the levy is subsequently released pursuant to section 6343 after the expiration of the period of limitations on collection, the Secretary and the taxpayer, prior to the release of the levy, may enter into a written agreement to extend the period of limitations on collection to a date certain. A written extension agreement entered into under this paragraph shall extend the period of limitations on collection until the date agreed upon in the extension agreement.

(c) *Proceeding in court for the collection of the tax.*—If a proceeding in court for the collection of a tax is begun within the period provided in paragraph (a) of this section (or within any extended period as provided in paragraph (b) of this section), the period during which the tax may be collected by levy is extended until the liability for the tax or a judgment against the taxpayer arising from the liability is satisfied or becomes unenforceable.

(d) *Effect of statutory suspensions of the period of limitations on collection if executed collection extension agreement is in effect.*—(1) Any statutory suspension of the period of limitations on collection tolls the running of the period of limitations on collection, as extended pursuant to an executed extension agreement under paragraph (b) of this section, for the amount of time set forth in the relevant statute.

(2) The following example illustrates the principle set forth in this paragraph (d):

*Example.* In June of 2003, the Internal Revenue Service (IRS) enters into an installment agreement with the taxpayer to provide for periodic payments of the taxpayer's timely assessed tax liabilities. At the time the installment agreement is entered into, the taxpayer and the IRS execute a written agreement to extend the period of limitations on collection. The extension agreement executed in connection with the installment agreement operates to extend the period of limitations on collection to the date agreed upon in the extension agreement, plus 89 days. Subsequently, and prior to the expiration of

the extended period of limitations on collection, the taxpayer files a bankruptcy petition under chapter 7 of the Bankruptcy Code and receives a discharge from bankruptcy a few months later. Assuming the tax is not discharged in the bankruptcy, section 6503(h) of the Internal Revenue Code operates to suspend the running of the previously extended period of limitations on collection for the period of time the IRS is prohibited from collecting due to the bankruptcy proceeding, and for 6 months thereafter. The new expiration date for the IRS to collect the tax is the date agreed upon in the previously executed extension agreement, plus 89 days, plus the period during which the IRS is prohibited from collecting due to the bankruptcy proceeding, plus 6 months.

(e) *Date when levy is considered made.*—The date on which a levy on property or rights to property is considered made is the date on which the notice of seizure required under section 6335(a) is given.

(f) *Effective date.*—This section is applicable on September 6, 2006. [Reg. § 301.6502-1.]

☐ [*T.D. 6172, 5-2-56. Amended by T.D. 7305, 3-14-74; T.D. 8391, 2-10-92 and T.D. 9284, 9-5-2006.*]

### [Reg. § 301.6503(a)-1]

**§ 301.6503(a)-1. Suspension of running of period of limitation; issuance of statutory notice of deficiency.**—(a) *General rule.*— (1) Upon the mailing of a notice of deficiency for income, estate, gift, chapter 41, 42, 43, or 44 tax under the provisions of section 6212, the period of limitation on assessment and collection of any deficiency is suspended for 90 days after the mailing of a notice of such deficiency if the notice of deficiency is addressed to a person within the States of the Union and the District of Columbia, or 150 days if such notice of deficiency is addressed to a person outside the States of the Union and the District of Columbia (not counting Saturday, Sunday, or a legal holiday in the District of Columbia as the 90th or 150th day), plus an additional 60 days thereafter in either case. If a proceeding in respect of the deficiency is placed on the docket of the Tax Court, the period of limitation is suspended until the decision of the Tax Court becomes final, and for an additional 60 days thereafter. If a notice of deficiency is mailed to a taxpayer within the period of limitation and the taxpayer does not appeal therefrom to the Tax Court, the notice of deficiency so given does not suspend the running of the period of limitation with respect to any additional deficiency shown to be due in a subsequent deficiency notice.

(2) This paragraph may be illustrated by the following example:

*Example.* A taxpayer filed a return for the calendar year 1973 on April 15, 1974; the notice of deficiency was mailed to him (at an address within the United States) on April 15, 1977; and he filed a petition with the Tax Court on July 14, 1977. The decision of the Tax Court became final on November 6, 1978. The running of the period of limitation for assessment is suspended from April 15, 1977, to January 5, 1979, which date is 60 days after the date (November 6, 1978), on which the decision became final. If in this example the taxpayer had failed to file a petition with the Tax Court, the running of the period of limitation for assessment would then be suspended from April 15, 1977 (the date of notice), to September 12, 1977 (that is, for the 90-day period in which he could file a petition with the Tax Court, and for 60 days thereafter).

(3) For provisions relating to suspension of the running of the period of limitation with respect to collection of "second tier" excise taxes (as defined in section 4963) until final resolution of a refund proceeding described in sections 4961 and 7422 for the determination of the taxpayer's liability for the second tier taxes, see § 53.4961-2(e)(4).

(b) *Corporations joining in consolidated return.*—If a notice under section 6212(a) with respect to a deficiency in tax imposed by subtitle A of the Code for any taxable year is mailed to a corporation, the suspension of the running of the period of limitations provided in section 6503(a)(1) shall apply in the case of corporations with which such corporation made a consolidated income tax return for such taxable year. Under § 1.1502-77(a) of this chapter (Income Tax Regulations), relating to consolidated returns, notices of deficiency are mailed only to the common parent. [Reg. § 301.6503(a)-1.]

☐ [*T.D. 6172, 5-2-56. Amended by T.D. 6498, 10-24-60; T.D. 7244, 12-29-72; T.D. 7838, 10-5-82 and T.D. 8084, 5-1-86.*]

### [Reg. § 301.6503(b)-1]

**§ 301.6503(b)-1. Suspension of running of period of limitation; assets of taxpayer in control or custody of court.**—Where all or substantially all of the assets of a taxpayer are in the control or custody of the court in any proceeding before any court of the United States, or of any State of the United States, or of the District of Columbia, the period of limitations on collection after assessment prescribed in section 6502 is suspended with respect to the outstanding amount due on the assessment for the period such assets are in the control or custody of the court, and for 6 months thereafter. In the case of an estate of a decedent or an incompetent, the period of limitations on collection is suspended only for periods beginning after November 2, 1966, during which assets are in the control or custody of a court, and for 6 months thereafter. [Reg. § 301.6503(b)-1.]

☐ [T.D. 6172, 5-2-56. *Amended by T.D. 7121, 6-2-71.*]

### [Reg. § 301.6503(c)-1]

**§ 301.6503(c)-1. Suspension of running of period of limitation; location of property outside the United States or removal of property from the United States; taxpayer outside of United States.**— (a) *Property located outside, or removed from, the United States prior to November 3, 1966.*—The running of the period of limitations on collection after assessment prescribed in section 6502 is suspended for the period of time, prior to November 3, 1966, that collection is hindered or delayed because property of the taxpayer is situated or held outside the United States or is removed from the United States. The total suspension of time under this provision shall not in the aggregate exceed 6 years. In any case in which the district director determines that collection is so hindered or delayed, he shall make and retain in the files of his office a written report which shall identify the taxpayer and the tax liability, shall show what steps were taken to collect the tax liability, shall state the grounds for his determination that property of the taxpayer is situated or held outside, or is removed from, the United States, and shall show the date on which it was first determined that collection was so hindered or delayed. The term "property" includes all property or rights to property, real or personal, tangible or intangible, belonging to the taxpayer. The suspension of the running of the period of limitations on collection shall be considered to begin on the date so determined by the district director. A copy of the report shall be mailed to the taxpayer at his last known address. For further guidance regarding the definition of last known address, see § 301.6212-2.

(b) *Taxpayer outside United States after November 2, 1966.*—The running of the period of limitations on collection after assessment prescribed in section 6502 (relating to collection after assessment) is suspended for the period after November 2, 1966, during which the taxpayer is absent from the United States if such period is a continuous period of absence from the United States extending for 6 months or more. In a case where the running of the period of limitations has been suspended under the first sentence of this paragraph and at the time of the taxpayer's return to the United States the period of limitations would expire before the expiration of 6 months from the date of his return, the period of limitations shall not expire until after 6 months from the date of the taxpayer's return. The taxpayer will be deemed to be absent from the United States for purposes of this section if he is generally and substantially absent from the United States, even though he makes casual temporary visits during the period. [Reg. § 301.6503(c)-1.]

☐ [T.D. 6172, 5-2-56. *Amended by T.D. 7121, 6-1-72. Amended by T.D. 8939, 1-11-2001.*]

### [Reg. § 301.6503(d)-1]

**§ 301.6503(d)-1. Suspension of running of period of limitation; extension of time for payment of estate tax.**—Where an estate is granted an extension of time as provided in section 6161(a)(2) or (b)(2), or under the provisions of section 6166, for payment of any estate tax, the running of the period of limitations for collection of such tax is suspended for the period of time for which the extension is granted. [Reg. § 301.6503(d)-1.]

☐ [T.D. 6172, 5-2-56. *Amended by T.D. 6425, 11-10-59 and T.D. 6498, 10-24-60.*]

### [Reg. § 301.6503(f)-1]

**§ 301.6503(f)-1. Suspension of running of period of limitation; wrongful seizure of property of third-party owner and discharge of lien for substitution of value.**—(a) *Wrongful seizure.*—The running of the period of limitations on collection after assessment prescribed in section 6502 (relating to collection after assessment) shall be suspended for a period equal to a period beginning on the date property (including money) is wrongfully seized or received by the appropriate official and ending on the date 30 days after the date on which the appropriate official returns the property pursuant to section 6343(b) (relating to authority to return property) or the date 30 days after the date on which a judgment secured pursuant to section 7426 (relating to civil actions by persons other than taxpayers) with respect to such property becomes final. The running of the period of limitations on collection after assessment shall be suspended under this section only with respect to the amount of such assessment which is equal to the amount of money or the value of specific property returned. This section applies in the case of property wrongfully seized or received after November 2, 1966. The following example illustrates the principles of this section:

*Example.* On June 1, 1968 (at which time 10 months remain before the period of limitations on collection after assessment will expire), the appropriate official wrongfully seizes $1,000 in B's account in Bank X and properly seizes $500 in taxpayer A's account in Bank Y in an attempt to satisfy A's assessed tax liability of $1,500. The appropriate official determines that the $1,000 seized in Bank X was not the property of taxpayer A and, on March 1, 1969, he returns the $1,000 to B. As a result of the wrongful seizure, the running of the period of limitations on collection after assessment of the amount owed by taxpayer A is suspended for the 9-month period (beginning June 1, 1968, when the money was wrongfully seized and ending March 1, 1969, when the money was returned to B), plus 30 days. Therefore, the period of limitations on collection after assessment prescribed in section 6502 will not expire until February 1, 1970, which is 10 months plus 30 days after the money was returned.

(b) *Discharge of wrongful lien for substitution of value.*—If a person other than the taxpayer submits a request in writing for a certificate of discharge for a filed Federal tax lien under section 6325(b)(4), the running of the period of limitations on collection after assessment under section 6502 for any liability listed in such notice of Federal tax lien shall be suspended for a period equal to the period beginning on the date the appropriate official receives a deposit or bond in the amount specified in § 301.6325-1(b)(4)(i) and ending on the date that is 30 days after the earlier of—

(1) The date the appropriate official no longer holds, or is deemed to no longer hold, within the meaning of paragraph (b)(4)(iv) of this section, any amount as a deposit or bond by reason of taking such actions as prescribed in sections 6325(b)(4)(B) and (C); or

(2) The date the judgment secured under section 7426(b)(5) becomes final.

(c) As used in this section, the term *appropriate official* means either the official or office identified in the relevant IRS Publication or, if such official or office is not so identified, the Secretary or his delegate.

(d) *Effective/applicability date.*—This section applies to any request for a certificate of discharge made after January 31, 2008. [Reg. § 301.6503(f)-1.]

☐ [T.D. 7121, 6-2-71. *Amended by T.D. 7838, 10-5-82 and T.D. 9378, 1-30-2008.*]

### [Reg. § 301.6503(g)-1]

**§ 301.6503(g)-1. Suspension pending correction.**—The running of the periods of limitations provided in sections 6501 and 6502 on the making of assessments, the collection by levy, or a proceeding in court in respect of any tax imposed by chapter 42 or section 507, 4971, or 4975 shall be suspended for any period described in section 507(g)(2) or during which the Commissioner has extended the time for making correction under section 4963(e)(1)(B). [Reg. § 301.6503(g)-1.]

☐ [T.D. 7838, 10-5-82. *Amended by T.D. 8084, 5-1-86.*]

### [Reg. § 301.6503(j)-1]

**§ 301.6503(j)-1. Suspension of running of period of limitations; extension in case of designated and related summonses.**— (a) *General rule.*—The running of the applicable period of limitations on assessment provided for in section 6501 is suspended with respect to any return of tax by a corporation that is the subject of a designated or related summons if a court proceeding is instituted with respect to that summons.

(b) *Period of suspension.*—The period of suspension is the time during which the running of the applicable period of limitations on assessment provided for in section 6501 is suspended under section 6503(j). If a court requires any compliance with a designated or related summons by ordering that any record, document, paper, object, or items be produced, or the testimony of any person be given, the period of suspension consists of the judicial enforcement period plus 120 days. If a court does not require any compliance with a designated or related summons, the period of suspension consists of the judicial enforcement period, and the period of limitations on assessment provided in section 6501 shall not expire before the 60th day after the close of the judicial enforcement period.

(c) *Definitions.*—(1) A *designated summons* is a summons issued to a corporation (or to any other person to whom the corporation has transferred records) with respect to any return of tax by such corporation for a taxable period for which such corporation is being examined under the coordinated industry case program or any other successor to the coordinated examination program if—

(i) The Division Commissioner and the Division Counsel of the Office of Chief Counsel (or their successors) for the organizations that have jurisdiction over the corporation whose tax liability is the subject of the summons have reviewed the summons before it is issued;

(ii) The Internal Revenue Service (IRS) issues the summons at least 60 days before the day the period prescribed in section 6501 for the assessment of tax expires (determined with regard to extensions); and

(iii) The summons states that it is a designated summons for purposes of section 6503(j).

(2) A *related summons* is any summons issued that—

(i) Relates to the same return of the corporation under examination as the designated summons; and

(ii) Is issued to any person, including the person to whom the designated summons was issued, during the 30-day period that begins on the day the designated summons is issued.

(3) The *judicial enforcement period* is the period that begins on the day on which a court proceeding is instituted with respect to a designated or related summons and ends on the day on which there is a final resolution as to the summoned person's response to that summons.

(4) *Court proceeding.*—(i) *In general.*—For purposes of this section, a *court proceeding* is a proceeding filed in a United States district court either to quash a designated or related summons under section 7609(b)(2) or to enforce a designated or related summons under section 7604. A court proceeding includes any collateral proceeding, such as a civil contempt proceeding.

(ii) *Date when proceeding is no longer pending.*—A proceeding to quash or to enforce a designated or related summons is no longer pending when all appeals (including review by the Supreme Court) are disposed of or after the expiration of the period in which an appeal may be taken or a request for further review (including review by the Supreme Court) may be made. If, however, following an enforcement order, a collateral proceeding is brought challenging whether the testimony given or production made by the summoned party fully satisfied the court order and whether sanctions should be imposed against the summoned party for a failure to so testify or produce, the proceeding to quash or to enforce the summons shall include the time from which the proceeding to quash or to enforce the summons was brought until the decision in the collateral proceeding becomes final. The decision becomes final on the date when all appeals (including review by the Supreme Court) are disposed of or when all appeal periods or all periods for further review (including review by the Supreme Court) expire. A decision in a collateral proceeding becomes final when all appeals (including review by the Supreme Court) are disposed of or when all appeal periods or all periods for further review (including review by the Supreme Court) expire.

(5) *Compliance.*—(i) *In general.*—*Compliance* is the giving of testimony or the performance of an act or acts of production, or both, in response to a court order concerning the designated or related summons and the determination that the terms of the court order have been satisfied.

(ii) *Date compliance occurs.*—Compliance with a court order that wholly denies enforcement of a designated or related summons is deemed to occur on the date when all appeals (including review by the Supreme Court) are disposed of or when the period in which an appeal may be taken or a request for further review (including review by the Supreme Court) may be made expires. Compliance with a court order that grants enforcement, in whole or in part, of a designated or related summons, occurs on the date the IRS determines that the testimony given, or the books, papers, records, or other data produced, or both, by the summoned party fully satisfy the court order concerning the summons. The IRS will determine whether there has been full compliance within a reasonable time, given the volume and complexity of the records produced, after the later of the giving of all testimony or the production of all records requested by the summons or required by any order enforcing any part of the summons. If, following an enforcement order, collateral proceedings are brought challenging whether the production made by the summoned party fully satisfied the court order and whether sanctions should be imposed against the summoned party for a failing to do so, the suspension of the periods of limitations shall continue until the order enforcing any part of the summons is fully complied with and the decision in the collateral proceeding becomes final. A decision in a collateral proceeding becomes final when all appeals are disposed of, the period in which an appeal may be taken has expired or the period in which a request for further review may be made has expired.

(6) *Final resolution* occurs when the designated or related summons or any order enforcing any part of the designated or related summons is fully complied with and all appeals or requests for further review are disposed of, the period in which an appeal may be

taken has expired or the period in which a request for further review may be made has expired.

(d) *Special rules.*—(1) *Number of summonses that may be issued.*—(i) *Designated summons.*—Only one designated summons may be issued in connection with the examination of a specific taxable year or other period of a corporation. A designated summons may cover more than one year or other period of a corporation. The designated summons may require production of information that was previously sought in a summons (other than a designated summons) issued in the course of the examination of that particular corporation if that information was not previously produced.

(ii) *Related summonses.*—There is no restriction on the number of related summonses that may be issued in connection with the examination of a corporation. As provided in paragraph (c)(2) of this section, however, a related summons must be issued within the 30-day period that begins on the date on which the designated summons to which it relates is issued and must relate to the same return as the designated summons. A related summons may request the same information as the designated summons.

(2) *Time within which court proceedings must be brought.*—In order for the period of limitations on assessment to be suspended under section 6503(j), a court proceeding to enforce or to quash a designated or related summons must be instituted within the period of limitations on assessment provided in section 6501 that is otherwise applicable to the tax return.

(3) *Computation of suspension period if multiple court proceedings are instituted.*—If multiple court proceedings are instituted to enforce or to quash a designated or one or more related summonses concerning the same tax return, the period of limitations on assessment is suspended beginning on the date the first court proceeding is brought. The suspension shall end on the date that is the latest date on which the judicial enforcement period, plus the 120 day or 60 day period (depending on whether the court requires any compliance) as provided in paragraph (b) of this section, expires with respect to each summons.

(4) *Effect on other suspension periods.*—(i) *In general.*—Suspensions of the period of limitations under section 6501 provided for under subsections 7609(e)(1) and (e)(2) do not apply to any summons that is issued pursuant to section 6503(j). The suspension under section 6503(j) of the running of the period of limitations on assessment under section 6501 is independent of, and may run concurrent with, any other suspension of the period of limitations on assessment that applies to the tax return to which the designated or related summons relates.

(ii) *Examples.*—The rules of paragraph (d)(4)(i) of this section are illustrated by the following examples:

*Example 1.* The period of limitations on assessment against Corporation P, a calendar year taxpayer, for its 2007 return is scheduled to end on March 17, 2011. (Ordinarily, Corporation P's returns are filed on March 15th of the following year, but March 15, 2008, was a Saturday, and Corporation P timely filed its return on the subsequent Monday, March 17, 2008, making March 17, 2011 the last day of the period of limitations on assessment for Corporation P's 2007 tax year.) On January 4, 2011, a designated summons is issued to Corporation P concerning its 2007 return. On March 3, 2011 (14 days before the period of limitations on assessment would otherwise expire with respect to Corporation P's 2007 return), a court proceeding is brought to enforce the designated summons issued to Corporation P. On June 6, 2011, the court orders Corporation P to comply with the designated summons. Corporation P does not appeal the court's order. On September 6, 2011, agents for Corporation P deliver material that they state are the records requested by the designated summons. On October 13, 2011, a final resolution to Corporation P's response to the designated summons occurs when it is determined that Corporation P has fully complied with the court's order. The suspension period applicable with respect to the designated summons issued to Corporation P consists of the judicial enforcement period (March 3, 2011, through October 13, 2011) and an additional 120-day period under section 6503(j)(1)(B), because the court required Corporation P to comply with the designated summons. Thus, the suspension period applicable with respect to the designated summons issued to Corporation P begins on March 3, 2011, and ends on February 10, 2012. Under the facts of this *Example 1*, the period of limitations on assessment against Corporation P further extends to February 24, 2012, to account for the additional 14 days that remained on the period of limitations on assessment under section 6501 when the suspension period under section 6503(j) began.

*Example 2.* Assume the same facts set forth in *Example 1*, except that in addition to the issuance of the designated summons and related enforcement proceedings, on April 5, 2011, a summons concerning Corporation P's 2007 return is issued and served on individual A, a third party. This summons is not a related summons because it was not issued during the 30-day period that began on the date the designated summons was issued. The third-party summons served on individual A is subject to the notice requirements of section 7609(a). Final resolution of individual A's response to this summons does not occur until February 15, 2012. Because there is no final resolution of individual A's response to this summons by October 5, 2011, which is six months from the date of service of the summons, the period of limitations on assessment against Corporation P is suspended under section 7609(e)(2) to the date on which there is a final resolution to that response for the purposes of section 7609(e)(2). Moreover, because final resolution to the summons served on individual A does not occur until after February 10, 2012, the end of the suspension period for the designated summons, the period of limita-

tions on assessment against Corporation P expires 14 days after the date that the final resolution as provided for in section 7609(e)(2) occurs with respect to the summons served on individual A.

(5) *Computation of 60-day period when last day of assessment period falls on a weekend or holiday.*—For purposes of paragraph (c)(1)(ii) of this section, in determining whether a designated summons has been issued at least 60 days before the date on which the period of limitations on assessment prescribed in section 6501 expires, the provisions of section 7503 apply when the last day of the assessment period falls on a Saturday, Sunday, or legal holiday.

(e) *Effective/applicability date.*—This section is applicable on July 31, 2009. [Reg. § 301.6503(j)-1.]

☐ [T.D. 9455, 7-30-2009.]

# LIMITATIONS ON CREDIT OR REFUND

## [Reg. § 301.6511(a)-1]

§ 301.6511(a)-1. Period of limitation on filing claim.—(a) In the case of any tax (other than a tax payable by stamp):

(1) If a return is filed, a claim for credit or refund of an overpayment must be filed by the taxpayer within 3 years from the time the return was filed or within 2 years from the time the tax was paid, whichever of such periods expires the later.

(2) If no return is filed, the claim for credit or refund of an overpayment must be filed by the taxpayer within 2 years from the time the tax was paid.

(b) In the case of any tax payable by means of a stamp, a claim for credit or refund of an overpayment of such tax must be filed by the taxpayer within 3 years from the time the tax was paid. For provisions relating to redemption of unused stamps, see section 6805.

(c) For limitations on allowance of credit or refund, special rules, and exceptions, see subsections (b) through (e) of section 6511. For limitations in the case of a petition to the Tax Court, see section 6512. For rules as to time return is deemed filed and tax considered paid, see section 6513. [Reg. § 301.6511(a)-1.]

☐ [T.D. 6172, 5-2-56. *Amended by T.D. 6425, 11-10-59.*]

## [Reg. § 301.6511(b)-1]

§ 301.6511(b)-1. Limitations on allowance of credits and refunds.—(a) *Effect of filing claim.*—Unless a claim for credit or refund of an overpayment is filed within the period of limitation prescribed in section 6511(a), no credit or refund shall be allowed or made after the expiration of such period.

(b) *Limit on amount to be credited or refunded.*—(1) In the case of any tax (other than a tax payable by stamp):

(i) If a return was filed, and a claim is filed within 3 years from the time the return was filed, the amount of the credit or refund shall not exceed the portion of the tax paid within the period, immediately preceding the filing of the claim, equal to 3 years plus the period of any extension of time for filing the return.

(ii) If a return was filed, and a claim is filed after the 3-year period described in subdivision (i) of this subparagraph but within 2 years from the time the tax was paid, the amount of the credit or refund shall not exceed the portion of the tax paid within the 2 years immediately preceding the filing of the claim.

(iii) If no return was filed, but a claim is filed, the amount of the credit or refund shall not exceed the portion of the tax paid within the 2 years immediately preceding the filing of the claim.

(iv) If no claim is filed, the amount of the credit or refund allowed or made by the district director or the director of the regional service center shall not exceed the amount that would have been allowable under the preceding subdivisions of this subparagraph if a claim had been filed on the date the credit or refund is allowed.

(2) In the case of a tax payable by stamp—

(i) If a claim is filed, the amount of the credit or refund shall not exceed the portion of the tax paid within the 3 years immediately preceding the filing of the claim.

(ii) If no claim is filed, the amount of the credit or refund allowed or made by the district director or the director of the regional service center shall not exceed the portion of the tax paid within the 3 years immediately preceding the allowance of the credit or refund. [Reg. § 301.6511(b)-1.]

☐ [T.D. 6172, 5-2-56. *Amended by T.D. 6425, 11-10-59, T.D. 6498, 10-24-60 and T.D. 6585, 12-27-61.*]

## [Reg. § 301.6511(c)-1]

§ 301.6511(c)-1. Special rules applicable in case of extension of time by agreement.—(a) *Scope.*—If, within the period prescribed in section 6511(a) for the filing of a claim for credit or refund, an

agreement extending the period of assessment of a tax has been made in accordance with the provisions of section 6501(c)(4), the special rules provided in this section become applicable. This section shall not apply to any claim filed, or credit or refund allowed if no claim is filed, either (1) prior to the execution of an agreement extending the period in which assessment may be made, or (2) more than 6 months after the expiration of the period within which an assessment may be made pursuant to the agreement or any extension thereof.

(b) *Period in which claim may be filed.*—Claim for credit or refund of an overpayment may be filed, or credit or refund may be allowed if no claim is filed, at any time within which an assessment may be made pursuant to an agreement, or any extension thereof, under section 6501(c)(4), and for 6 months thereafter.

(c) *Limit on amount to be credited or refunded.*—(1) If a claim is filed within the time prescribed in paragraph (b) of this section, the amount of the credit or refund allowed or made shall not exceed the portion of the tax paid after the execution of the agreement and before the filing of the claim, plus the amount that could have been properly credited or refunded under the provisions of section 6511(b)(2) if a claim had been filed on the date of the execution of the agreement.

(2) If no claim is filed, the amount of credit or refund allowed or made within the time prescribed in paragraph (b) of this section shall not exceed the portion of the tax paid after the execution of the agreement and before the making of the credit or refund, plus the amount that could have been properly credited or refunded under the provisions of section 6511(b)(2) if a claim had been filed on the date of the execution of the agreement.

(d) *Effective date of agreement.*—The agreement referred to in this section shall become effective when signed by the taxpayer and the district director or an assistant regional commissioner. [Reg. § 301.6511(c)-1.]

☐ [T.D. 6172, 5-2-56. *Amended by T.D. 6498, 10-24-60.*]

## [Reg. § 301.6511(d)-1]

§ 301.6511(d)-1. Overpayment of income tax on account of bad debts, worthless securities, etc.—(a)(1) If the claim for credit or refund relates to an overpayment of income tax on account of—

(i) The deductibility by the taxpayer, under section 166 or section 832(c), of a debt as a debt which became worthless, or, under section 165(g), of a loss from the worthlessness of a security, or

(ii) The effect that the deductibility of a debt or loss described in subdivision (i) of this subparagraph has on the application to the taxpayer of a carryover,

then in lieu of the 3-year period from the time the return was filed in which claim may be filed or credit or refund allowed, as prescribed in section 6511(a) or (b), the period shall be 7 years from the date prescribed by law for filing the return (determined without regard to any extension of time for filing such return) for the taxable year for which the claim is made or the credit or refund allowed or made.

(2) If the claim for credit or refund relates to an overpayment on account of the effect that the deductibility of a debt or loss, described in subparagraph (1) of this paragraph, has on the application to the taxpayer of a net operating loss carryback provided in section 172(b), the period within which claim for credit or refund may be filed shall be whichever of the following two periods expires later:

(i) Seven years from the last date prescribed for filing the return (determined without regard to any extension of time for filing such return) for the taxable year of the net operating loss which results in such carryback, or

(ii) The period which ends with the expiration of the period prescribed in section 6511(c) within which a claim for credit or refund may be filed with respect to the taxable year of the net operating loss which resulted in the carryback.

(3) In the case of a claim for credit or refund involving items described in this section, the amount of the credit or refund may exceed the portion of the tax paid within the period provided in section 6511(b)(2) or (c), whichever is applicable, to the extent of the amount of the overpayment attributable to the deductibility of items described in subparagraph (1) of this paragraph. If the claim involves an overpayment based not only on the deductibility of items described in subparagraph (1) of this paragraph but based also on other items, the credit or refund cannot exceed the sum of the following:

(i) The amount of the overpayment which is attributable to the deductibility of items described in subparagraph (1) of this paragraph, and

(ii) The balance of such overpayment up to a limit of the portion, if any, of the tax paid within the period provided in section 6511(b)(2) or (c), or within the period provided in any other applicable provision of law.

(4) If the claim involves an overpayment based not only on the deductibility of items described in subparagraph (1) of this paragraph but based also on other items, and if the claim with respect to any items is barred by the expiration of any applicable period of limitation, the portion of the overpayment attributable to the items not so barred shall be determined by treating the allowance of such items as the first adjustment to be made in computing such overpayment.

(b) If a claim for credit or refund is not filed within the applicable period described in paragraph (a) of this section, then credit or refund may be allowed or made only if claim therefor is filed or if such credit or refund is allowed within any period prescribed in section 6511(a), (b), or (c), whichever is applicable, subject to the provisions thereof limiting the amount of credit or refund in the case of a claim filed, or, if no claim was filed, in the case of credit or refund allowed within such applicable period as prescribed in section 6511(b) or (c).

(c) The provisions of this section and section 6511(d)(1) do not apply to an overpayment resulting from the deductibility of a debt that became partially worthless during the taxable year, but only to an overpayment resulting from the deductibility of a debt which became entirely worthless during such year.

(d) The provisions of paragraph (a) of this section with regard to an overpayment caused by the deductibility of a bad debt under section 166 or section 832(c), or of a loss from the worthlessness of a security under section 165(g), are likewise applicable to an overpayment caused by the effect that the deductibility of such bad debt or loss has on the application to the taxpayer of a carryover or of a carryback. [Reg. § 301.6511(d)-1.]

☐ [*T.D. 6172, 5-2-56. Amended by T.D. 6425, 11-10-59.*]

**[Reg. § 301.6511(d)-2]**

**§ 301.6511(d)-2. Overpayment of income tax on account of net operating loss or capital loss carrybacks.**—(a) *Special period of limitation.*—(1) If the claim for credit or refund relates to an overpayment of income tax attributable to a net operating loss carryback (provided in section 172(b)), or a capital loss carryback (provided in section 1212(a)), then in lieu of the 3-year period from the time the return was filed in which the claim may be filed or credit or refund allowed, as prescribed in section 6511(a) or (b), the period shall be whichever of the following 2 periods expires later:

(i) The period which ends with the expiration of the fifteenth day of the fortieth month (or thirty-ninth month, in the case of a corporation) following the end of the taxable year of the net operating loss or net capital loss which resulted in the carryback; or

(ii) The period which ends with the expiration of the period prescribed in section 6511(c) within which a claim for credit or refund may be filed with respect to the taxable year of the net operating loss or net capital loss which resulted in the carryback except that—

(a) With respect to an overpayment attributable to a net operating loss carryback to any year on account of a certification issued to the taxpayer under section 317 of the Trade Expansion Act of 1962, the period shall not expire before the expiration of the sixth month following the month in which such certification is issued to the taxpayer, and

(b) With respect to an overpayment attributable to the creation of, or an increase in, a net operating loss as a result of the elimination of excessive profits by a renegotiation (as defined in section 1481(a)(1)(A)), the period shall not expire before September 1, 1959, or the expiration of the twelfth month following the month in which the agreement or order for the elimination of such excessive profits becomes final, whichever is the later.

(2) In the case of a claim for credit or refund involving a net operating loss or capital loss carryback described in subparagraph (1) of this paragraph, the amount of the credit or refund may exceed the portion of the tax paid within the period provided in section

6511(b)(2) or (c), whichever is applicable, to the extent of the amount of the overpayment attributable to the carryback. If the claim involves an overpayment based not only on a net operating loss or capital loss carryback described in subparagraph (1) of this paragraph but based also on other items, the credit or refund cannot exceed the sum of the following:

(i) The amount of the overpayment which is attributable to the net operating loss or capital loss carryback, and

(ii) The balance of such overpayment up to a limit of the portion, if any, of the tax paid within the period provided in section 6511(b)(2) or (c), or within the period provided in any other applicable provision of law.

(3) If the claim involves an overpayment based not only on a net operating loss or capital loss carryback described in subparagraph (1) of this paragraph but based also on other items, and if the claim with respect to any items is barred by the expiration of any applicable period of limitation, the portion of the overpayment attributable to the items not so barred shall be determined by treating the allowance of such items as the first adjustment to be made in computing such overpayment. If a claim for credit or refund is not filed, and if credit or refund is not allowed, within the period prescribed in this paragraph, then credit or refund may be allowed or made only if claim therefor is filed, or if such credit or refund is allowed, within the period prescribed in section 6511(a), (b), or (c), whichever is applicable, subject to the provisions thereof limiting the amount of credit or refund in the case of a claim filed, or if no claim was filed, in case of credit or refund allowed, within such applicable period. For the limitations on the allowance of interest for an overpayment where credit or refund is subject to the provisions of this section, see section 6611(f).

(b) *Barred overpayments.*—(1) If the allowance of a credit or refund of an overpayment of tax attributable to a net operating loss carryback or capital loss carryback is otherwise prevented by the operation of any law or rule of law (other than section 7122, relating to compromises), such credit or refund may be allowed or made under the provisions of section 6511(d)(2)(B) if a claim therefor is filed within the period provided by section 6511(d)(2)(A) and paragraph (a) of this section for filing a claim for credit or refund of an overpayment attributable to a carryback. Similarly, if the allowance of an application, credit, or refund of a decrease in the tax determined under section 6411(b) is otherwise prevented by the operation of any law or rule of law (other than section 7122), such application, credit, or refund may be allowed or made if an application for a tentative carryback adjustment is filed within the period provided in section 6411(a). Thus, for example, even though the tax liability (not including the net operating loss deduction or capital loss carryback (or the effect of such deduction or carryback)) for a given taxable year has previously been litigated before the Tax Court, credit or refund of an overpayment may be allowed or made despite the provisions of section 6512(a), if claim for such credit or refund is filed within the period provided in section 6511(d)(2)(A) and paragraph (a) of this section. In the case of a claim for credit or refund of an overpayment attributable to a carryback, or in the case of an application for a tentative carryback adjustment, the determination of any court, including the Tax Court, in any proceeding in which the decision of the court has become final, shall be conclusive except with respect to the net operating loss deduction, and the effect of such deduction, or with respect to the determination of a short-term capital loss, and the effect of such short-term capital loss, to the extent that such deduction or short-term capital loss is affected by a carryback which was not in issue in such proceeding.

(2) For purposes of the special period of limitation for filing a claim for credit or refund of an overpayment of tax with respect to a computation year (as defined in section 1302(c)(1)) by an individual who has chosen to compute his tax under sections 1301 through 1305 (relating to income averaging), such claim is determined to relate to an overpayment attributable to a net operating loss carryback when such carryback relates to any base period year (as defined in section 1302(c)(3)). Thus, if (i) an individual has a net operating loss for a taxable year subsequent to a taxable year for which he had chosen the benefits of income averaging, and (ii) such net operating loss carryback is wholly utilized in any one or more of his base period years (which would result in an increased amount of averagable income for such computation year), the special period of limitation with respect to such individual's computation year applies and a timely claim for credit or refund with respect to the computation year may be filed. [Reg. § 301.6511(d)-2.]

☐ [*T.D. 6172, 5-2-56. Amended by T.D. 6425, 11-10-59, T.D. 6498, 10-24-60, T.D. 6730, 5-7-64, T.D. 7196, 7-12-72 and T.D. 7301, 1-3-74.*]

**[Reg. § 301.6511(d)-3]**

**§ 301.6511(d)-3. Special rules applicable to credit against income tax for foreign taxes.**—(a) *Period in which claim may be filed.*—In the case of an overpayment of income tax resulting from a credit, allowed under the provisions of section 901 or under the provisions of any treaty to which the United States is a party, for taxes paid or accrued to a foreign country or possession of the United States, a claim for credit or refund must be filed by the taxpayer within 10 years from the last date prescribed for filing the return (determined without regard to any extension of time for filing such return) for the taxable year with respect to which the claim is made. Such 10-year period shall be applied in lieu of the 3-year period prescribed in section 6511(a).

(b) *Limit on amount to be credited or refunded.*—In the case of a claim described in paragraph (a) of this section, the amount of the credit or refund allowed or made may exceed the portion of the tax paid within the period prescribed in section 6511(b) or (c), whichever is applicable, to the extent of the amount of the overpayment attributable to the allowance of a credit against income tax referred to in paragraph (a) of this section [Reg. §301.6511(d)-3.]

☐ [T.D. 6172, 5-2-56.]

**[Reg. §301.6511(d)-4]**

**§301.6511(d)-4. Overpayment of income tax on account of investment credit carryback.**—(a) *Special period of limitation.*—(1) If the claim for credit or refund relates to an overpayment of income tax attributable to an investment credit carryback, provided in section 46(b), then in lieu of the 3-year period from the time the return was filed in which the claim may be filed or credit refund allowed, as prescribed in section 6511(a) or (b), the period shall be whichever of the following 2 periods expires later:

(i) The period which ends with the expiration of the fifteenth day of the fortieth month (or thirty-ninth month, in the case of a corporation) following the end of the taxable year of the unused investment credit which resulted in the carryback (or, with respect to any portion of an investment credit carryback from a taxable year attributable to a net operating loss carryback or a capital loss carryback from a subsequent taxable year, the period which ends with the expiration of the fifteenth day of the fortieth month (or thirty-ninth month, in the case of a corporation) following the end of such subsequent taxable year); or

(ii) The period which ends with the expiration of the period prescribed in section 6511(c) within which a claim for credit or refund may be filed with respect to the taxable year of the unused investment credit which resulted in the carryback.

(2) In the case of a claim for credit or refund involving an investment credit carryback described in subparagraph (1) of this paragraph, the amount of the credit or refund may exceed the portion of the tax paid within the period provided in section 6511(b)(2) or (c), whichever is applicable, to the extent of the amount of the overpayment attributable to the carryback. If the claim involves an overpayment based not only on an investment credit carryback described in subparagraph (1) of this paragraph but based also on other items, the credit or refund cannot exceed the sum of the following:

(i) The amount of the overpayment which is attributable to the investment credit carryback, and

(ii) The balance of such overpayment up to a limit of the portion, if any, of the tax paid within the period provided in section 6511(b)(2) or (c), or within the period provided in any other applicable provision of law.

(3) If the claim involves an overpayment based not only on an investment credit carryback described in subparagraph (1) of this paragraph but based also on other items, and if the claim with respect to any items is barred by the expiration of any applicable period of limitation, the portion of the overpayment attributable to the items not so barred shall be determined by treating the allowance of such items as the first adjustment to be made in computing such overpayment. If a claim for credit or refund is not filed, and if credit or refund is not allowed, within the period prescribed in this paragraph, then credit or refund may be allowed or made only if claim therefor is filed, or if such credit or refund is allowed, within the period prescribed in section 6511(a), (b), or (c), whichever is applicable, subject to the provisions thereof limiting the amount of credit or refund in the case of a claim filed, or if no claim was filed, in case of credit or refund allowed, within such applicable period. For the limitations on the allowance of interest for an overpayment where credit or refund is subject to the provisions of this section, see section 6611(f).

(b) *Barred overpayments.*—If the allowance of a credit or refund of an overpayment of tax attributable to an investment credit carryback is otherwise prevented by the operation of any law or rule of law (other than section 7122, relating to compromises), such credit or refund may be allowed or made under the provisions of section 6511(d)(4)(B) if a claim therefor is filed within the period provided by section 6511(d)(4)(A) and paragraph (a) of this section for filing a claim for credit or refund of an overpayment attributable to a carryback. In the case of a claim for credit or refund of an overpayment attributable to a carryback, the determination of any court, including the Tax Court, in any proceeding in which the decision of the court has become final, shall not be conclusive with respect to the investment credit, and the effect of such credit, to the extent that such credit is affected by a carryback which was not in issue in such proceeding. [Reg. §301.6511(d)-4.]

☐ [T.D. 7301, 1-3-74.]

**[Reg. §301.6511(f)-1]**

**§301.6511(f)-1. Special rules for chapter 42 taxes.**—(a) *In general.*—Claims for credit or refund of an overpayment of any tax imposed by chapter 42 shall be filed by the taxpayer within 3 years from the time a return was filed by the private foundation or trust (as the case may be) with respect to such tax, or within 2 years from the time the tax was paid, whichever of such periods expire the later.

(b) *Examples.*—This section may be illustrated by the following examples:

*Example (1).* In 1972 D, an individual taxpayer who was a disqualified person under the provisions of section 4946(a)(1), participated in an act of self-dealing with a private foundation and incurred a tax under section 4941(a)(1). The private foundation files a Form 990-PF on May 15, 1973, and discloses thereon that it has engaged in an act of self-dealing with D. D files a Form 4720 on July 2, 1973, and pays the amount of tax imposed by section 4941(a) with respect to such act of self-dealing. For purposes of this section, the return was filed on May 15, 1973, and any claim for credit or refund by D must be filed by May 17, 1976 (May 15, 1976, was a Saturday).

*Example (2).* Assume the same facts as in example (1) except that D filed a Form 4720 on July 1, 1974, and pays the tax on that date. D must then file any claim for credit or refund by July 1, 1976. [Reg. §301.6511(f)-1.]

☐ [T.D. 7838, 10-5-82.]

**[Reg. §301.6512-1]**

**§301.6512-1. Limitations in case of petition to Tax Court.**—(a) *Effect of petition to Tax Court.*—(1) *General rule.*—If a person having a right to file a petition with the Tax Court with respect to a deficiency in income, estate, gift, or excise tax imposed by subtitle A or B, or chapter 41, 42, 43, or 44 of the Code has filed such petition within the time prescribed in section 6213(a), no credit or refund of income tax for the same taxable year, of gift tax for the same calendar year or calendar quarter, of estate tax in respect of the taxable estate of the same decedent, or of tax imposed by chapter 41, 42, 43, or 44 with respect to any act (or failure to act) to which such petition relates, in respect of which a district director or director of a service center (or a regional director of appeals) has determined the deficiency, shall be allowed or made, and no suit in any court for the recovery of any part of such tax shall be instituted by the taxpayer, except as to items set forth in paragraph (a)(2) of this section.

(2) *Exceptions.*—The exceptions to the rule stated in subparagraph (1) of this paragraph are as follows:

(i) An overpayment determined by a decision of the Tax Court which has become final;

(ii) Any amount collected in excess of an amount computed in accordance with the decision of the Tax Court which has become final; and

(iii) Any amount collected after the expiration of the period of limitation upon levying or beginning a proceeding in court for collection.

(b) *Overpayment determined by Tax Court.*—If the Tax Court finds that there is no deficiency and further finds that the taxpayer has made an overpayment of income tax for the same taxable year, of gift tax for the same calendar year or calendar quarter, of estate tax in respect of the taxable estate of the same decedent, or of tax imposed by chapter 41, 42, 43, or 44 with respect to any act (or failure to act) to which such petition relates, in respect of which a district director, or director of a service center (or a regional director of appeals) has determined the deficiency, or finds that there is a deficiency but that the taxpayer had made an overpayment of such tax, the overpayment determined by the Tax Court shall be credited or refunded to the taxpayer when the decision of the Tax Court has become final. (See section 7481, relating to the date when a Tax Court decision becomes final.) No such credit or refund shall be allowed or made of any portion of the tax unless the Tax Court determines as part of its decision that such portion was paid—

(1) After the mailing of the notice of deficiency, or

(2) Within the period which would be applicable under section 6511(b)(2), (c), (d), or (g) (see §§301.6511(b)-1, 301.6511(c)-1, 301.6511(d)-1, 301.6511(d)-2, and 301.6511(d)-3), if on the date of the

mailing of the notice of deficiency a claim had been filed (whether or not filed) stating the grounds upon which the Tax Court finds that there is an overpayment.

(c) *Jeopardy assessments.*—In the case of a jeopardy assessment made under section 6861(a), if the amount which should have been assessed as determined by a decision of the Tax Court which has become final is less than the amount already collected, the excess payment shall be credited or refunded subject to a determination being made by the Tax Court with respect to the time of payment as stated in paragraph (b) of this section.

(d) *Disallowance of deficiency by reviewing court.*—If the amount of the deficiency determined by the Tax Court (in a case where collection has not been stayed by the filing of a bond) is disallowed in whole or in part by the reviewing court, then the overpayment resulting from such disallowance shall be credited or refunded without the making of claim therefor, subject to a determination being made by the Tax Court with respect to the time of payment as stated in paragraph (b) of this section. (See section 7481, relating to date Tax Court decision becomes final.)

(e) *Collection in excess of amount determined by Tax Court.*—Where the amount collected is in excess of the amount computed in accordance with the decision of the Tax Court which has become final, the excess payment shall be credited or refunded within the period of limitation provided in section 6511.

(f) *Collection after expiration of statutory period.*—Where an amount is collected after the statutory period of limitation upon the beginning of levy or a proceeding in court for collection has expired (see section 6502, relating to collection after assessment), the taxpayer may file a claim for refund of the amount so collected within the period of limitation provided in section 6511. In any such case, the decision of the Tax Court as to whether the statutory period upon collection of the tax expired before notice of the deficiency was mailed shall, when the decision becomes final, be conclusive. [Reg. § 301.6512-1.]

☐ [*T.D.* 6172, 5-2-56. *Amended by T.D.* 7238, 12-28-72 *and T.D.* 7838, 10-5-82.]

### [Reg. § 301.6513-1]

**§ 301.6513-1. Time return deemed filed and tax considered paid.**—(a) *Early return or advance payment of tax.*—For purposes of section 6511, a return filed before the last day prescribed by law or regulations for the filing thereof shall be considered as filed on such last day. For purposes of section 6511(b)(2) and (c) and section 6512, payment of any portion of the tax made before the last day prescribed for payment shall be considered made on such last day. An extension of time for filing a return or for paying any tax, or an election to pay any tax in installments, shall not be given any effect in determining under this section the last day prescribed for filing a return or paying any tax.

(b) *Prepaid income tax.*—For purposes of section 6511 (relating to limitations on credit or refund) or section 6512 (relating to limitations in case of petition to Tax Court)—

(1) Any tax actually deducted and withheld at the source during any calendar year under chapter 24 of the Code (relating to collection of income tax at source on wages) shall, in respect of the recipient of the income, be deemed to have been paid by him on the 15th day of the fourth month following the close of his taxable year with respect to which such tax is allowable as a credit under section 31 (relating to tax withheld on wages),

(2) Any amount paid as estimated income tax for any taxable year shall be deemed to have been paid on the last day prescribed for filing the income tax return under section 6012 for such taxable year (determined without regard to any extension of time for filing such return), and

(3) Any tax withheld at the source on or after November 13, 1966, under chapter 3 of the Code (relating to tax withheld on nonresident aliens and foreign corporations and tax-free covenant bonds) shall, in respect of the recipient of the income, be deemed to have been paid by such recipient on the last day prescribed for filing his income tax return under section 6012 for the taxable year (determined without regard to any extension of time for filing such return) with respect to which such tax is allowable as a credit under section 1462 (relating to withheld tax as credit to recipient of income). Subparagraph (3) of this paragraph shall apply even though the recipient of the income has been granted under section 6012 and the regulations thereunder an exemption from the requirement of making an income tax return for the taxable year.

(c) *Return and payment of social security taxes and income tax withholding.*—Notwithstanding paragraph (a) of this section, if a return (or payment) on or after November 13, 1966, of tax imposed by chapter 3 of the Code (relating to withholding of tax on nonresident aliens and foreign corporations and tax-free covenant bonds), or if a return (or payment) of tax imposed by chapter 21 of the Code (relating to the Federal Insurance Contributions Act) or by chapter 24 of the Code (relating to the collection of income tax at source on wages), for any period ending with or within a calendar year is filed or paid before April 15 of the succeeding calendar year, for purposes of section 6511 (relating to limitations on credit or refund) the return shall be considered filed, or the tax considered paid, on April 15 of such succeeding calendar year.

(d) *Overpayment of income tax credited to estimated tax.*—If a taxpayer elects under the provisions of section 6402(b) to credit an overpayment of income tax for a taxable year against estimated tax for the succeeding taxable year, the amount so credited shall be considered a payment of income tax for such succeeding taxable year (whether or not claimed as a credit on the estimated tax return for such succeeding taxable year). If the treatment of such amount as a payment of income tax for the succeeding taxable year results in an overpayment for such succeeding taxable year, the period of limitations applicable to such overpayment is determined by reference to that taxable year. An election so to credit an overpayment of income tax precludes the allowance of a claim for credit or refund of such overpayment for the taxable year in which the overpayment arises. [Reg. § 301.6513-1.]

☐ [*T.D.* 6172, 5-2-56. *Amended by T.D.* 6498, 10-24-60 *and T.D.* 6922, 6-16-67.]

### [Reg. § 301.6514(a)-1]

**§ 301.6514(a)-1. Credits or refunds after period of limitation.**—(a) A refund of any portion of any internal revenue tax (or any interest, additional amount, addition to the tax, or assessable penalty) shall be considered erroneous and a credit of any such portion shall be considered void:

(1) If made after the expiration of the period of limitation prescribed by section 6511 for filing claim therefor, unless prior to the expiration of such period claim was filed, or

(2) In the case of a timely claim, if the credit or refund was made after the expiration of the period of limitation prescribed by section 6532(a) for the filing of suit, unless prior to the expiration of such period suit was begun.

(b) For procedure by the United States to recover erroneous refunds, see sections 6532(b) and 7405. [Reg. § 301.6514(a)-1.]

☐ [*T.D.* 6172, 5-2-56. *Amended by T.D.* 6498, 10-24-60.]

### [Reg. § 301.6514(b)-1]

**§ 301.6514(b)-1. Credit against barred liability.**—Any credit against a liability in respect of any taxable year shall be void if the collection of such liability would be barred by the applicable statute of limitations at the time such credit is made. [Reg. § 301.6514(b)-1.]

☐ [*T.D.* 6172, 5-2-56.]

# MITIGATION OF EFFECT OF PERIOD OF LIMITATIONS

### [Reg. § 301.6521-1]

**§ 301.6521-1. Mitigation of effect of limitation in case of related employee social security tax and self-employment tax.**—(a) Section 6521 may be applied in the correction of a certain type of error involving both the tax on self-employment income under section 1401 and the employee tax under section 3101 if the correction of the error as to one tax is, on the date the correction is authorized, prevented in whole or in part by the operation of any law or rule of law other than section 7122, relating to compromises. Examples of such law are sections 6212(c), 6401(a), 6501, 6511, 6512(a), 6514, 6532, 6901(c), (d) and (e), 7121, and 7459(e).

(b) If the liability for either tax with respect to which the error was made has been compromised under section 7122, the provisions of section 6521 limiting the correction with respect to the other tax do not apply.

(c) Section 6521 is not applicable if, on the date of the authorization, correction of the effect of the error is permissible as to both taxes without recourse to such section.

(d) If, because an amount of wages, as defined in section 3121(a), is erroneously treated as self-employment income, as defined in section 1402(b), or an amount of self-employment income is erroneously treated as wages, it is necessary in correcting the error to assess the correct tax and give a credit or refund for the amount of the tax erroneously paid, and if either, but not both, of such adjustments is prevented by any law or rule of law (other than section 7122), the amount of the assessment, or the amount of the credit or refund, authorized shall reflect the adjustment which would be made in respect of the other tax (either the tax on self-employment income under section 1401 or the employee tax under section 3101) but for the operation of such law or rule of law. For example, assume that during 1955 A paid $10 as tax on an amount erroneously treated as "wages", when such amount was actually self-employment income, and that credit or refund of the $10 is not barred. A should have paid a self-employment tax of $15 on the amount. If the assessment of the correct tax, that is, $15, is barred by the statute of limitations, no credit or refund of the $10 shall be made without offsetting against such $10 the $15, assessment of which is barred. Thus, no credit or refund in respect of the $10 can be made.

(e) As another example, assume that during 1955 a taxpayer reports wages of $4,200 and net earnings from self-employment of $900. By reason of the limitations of section 1402(b) he shows no self-employment income. Assume further that by reason of a final decision by the Tax Court of the United States, further adjustments to the taxpayer's income tax liability are barred. The question of the amount of his wages, as defined in section 3121, was not in issue in the Tax Court litigation, but it is subsequently determined (within the period of limitations applicable under the Federal Insurance Contributions Act) that $700 of the $4,200 reported as wages was not for employment as defined in section 3121(b). Therefore, the taxpayer is entitled to the allowance of a refund of the $14 tax paid on such remuneration under section 3101. The reduction of his wages from $4,200 to $3,500 would result in the determination of $700 self-employment income, the tax on which is $21 for the year. Under section 6521, the overpayment of $14 would be offset by the barred deficiency of $21, thus eliminating the refund otherwise allowable. If the facts were changed so that the taxpayer erroneously paid tax on self-employment income of $700, having been taxed on only $3,500 as wages, and within the period of limitations applicable under the Federal Insurance Contributions Act, it is determined that his wages were $4,200, the tax of $14 under section 3101, otherwise collectible, would be eliminated by offsetting under section 6521 the barred overpayment of $21. The balance of the barred overpayment, $7, cannot be credited or refunded.

(f) Another illustration of the operation of section 6521 is the case of a taxpayer who, for 1955, is erroneously taxed on $2,500 as wages, the tax on which is $50, and who reports no self-employment income. After the period of limitations has run on the refund of the tax under the Federal Insurance Contributions Act, it is determined that the amount treated as wages should have been reported as net earnings from self-employment. The taxpayer's self-employment income would then be $2,500 and the tax thereon would be $75. Assume that the period of limitations applicable to subtitle A of the Code has not expired, and that a notice of deficiency may properly be issued. Under section 6521, the amount of the deficiency of $75 must be reduced by the barred overpayment of $50. [Reg. § 301.6521-1.]

☐ [T.D. 6172, 5-2-56. *Amended by T.D. 6498, 10-24-60.*]

### [Reg. § 301.6521-2]

**§ 301.6521-2. Law applicable in determination of error.**—The question of whether there was an erroneous treatment of self-employment income or of wages is determined under the provisions of law and regulations applicable with respect to the year or other taxable period as to which the error was made. The fact that the error was in pursuance of an interpretation, either judicial or administrative, accorded such provisions of law and regulations at the time the action involved was taken is not necessarily determinative of this question. For example, if a later judicial decision authoritatively alters such interpretation so that such action is contrary to the applicable provisions of the law and regulations as later interpreted, the error comes within the scope of section 6521. [Reg. § 301.6521-2.]

☐ [T.D. 6172, 5-2-56.]

# PERIODS OF LIMITATION IN JUDICIAL PROCEEDINGS

### [Reg. § 301.6532-1]

**§ 301.6532-1. Periods of limitation on suits by taxpayers.**—(a) No suit or proceeding under section 7422(a) for the recovery of any internal revenue tax, penalty, or other sum shall be begun until whichever of the following first occurs:

(1) The expiration of 6 months from the date of the filing of the claim for credit or refund, or

(2) A decision is rendered on such claim prior to the expiration of 6 months after the filing thereof.

Except as provided in paragraph (b) of this section, no suit or proceeding for the recovery of any internal revenue tax, penalty, or other sum may be brought after the expiration of 2 years from the date of mailing by registered mail prior to September 3, 1958, or by either registered or certified mail on or after September 3, 1958, by a district director, a director of an internal revenue service center, or an assistant regional commissioner to a taxpayer of a notice of disallowance of the part of the claim to which the suit or proceeding relates.

(b) The 2-year period described in paragraph (a) of this section may be extended if an agreement to extend the running of the period of limitations is executed. The agreement must be signed by the taxpayer or by an attorney, agent, trustee, or other fiduciary on behalf of the taxpayer. If the agreement is signed by a person other than the taxpayer, it shall be accompanied by an authenticated copy of the power of attorney or other legal evidence of the authority of such person to act on behalf of the taxpayer. If the taxpayer is a corporation, the agreement should be signed with the corporate name followed by the signature of a duly authorized officer of the corporation. The agreement will not be effective until signed by a district director, a director of an internal revenue service center, or an assistant regional commissioner.

(c) The taxpayer may sign a waiver of the requirement that he be mailed a notice of disallowance. Such waiver is irrevocable and will commence the running of the 2-year period described in paragraph (a) of this section on the date the waiver is filed. The waiver shall set forth:

(1) The type of tax and the taxable period covered by the taxpayer's claim for refund;

(2) The amount of the claim;

(3) The amount of the claim disallowed;

(4) A statement that the taxpayer agrees the filing of the waiver will commence the running of the 2-year period provided for in section 6532(a)(1) as if a notice of disallowance had been sent the taxpayer by either registered or certified mail.

The filing of such a waiver prior to the expiration of 6 months from the date the claim was filed does not permit the filing of a suit for refund prior to the time specified in section 6532(a)(1) and paragraph (a) of this section.

(d) Any consideration, reconsideration, or other action with respect to a claim after the mailing by registered mail prior to September 3, 1958, or by either registered or certified mail on or after September 3, 1958, of a notice of disallowance or after the execution of a waiver referred to in paragraph (c) of this section, shall not extend the period for bringing suit or other proceeding under section 7422(a). [Reg. § 301.6532-1.]

☐ [T.D. 6172, 5-2-56. *Amended by T.D. 6425, 11-10-59 and T.D. 6827, 6-16-65.*]

### [Reg. § 301.6532-2]

**§ 301.6532-2. Periods of limitation on suits by the United States.**—The United States may not recover any erroneous refund by civil action under section 7405 unless such action is begun within 2 years after the making of such refund. However, if any part of the refund was induced by fraud or misrepresentation of a material fact, the action to recover the erroneous refund may be brought at any time within 5 years from the date the refund was made. [Reg. § 301.6532-2.]

☐ [T.D. 6172, 5-2-56.]

### [Reg. § 301.6532-3]

**§ 301.6532-3. Periods of limitation on suits by persons other than taxpayers.**—(a) *General rule.*—No suit or proceeding, except as otherwise provided in section 6532(c)(2) and paragraph (b) of this section, under section 7426 and § 301.7426-1 relating to civil actions by persons other than taxpayers, shall be begun after the expiration of 9 months from the date of levy or agreement under section 6325(b)(3) giving rise to such action.

(b) *Period when claim is filed.*—The 9-month period prescribed in section 6532(c)(1) and paragraph (a) of this section shall be extended to the shorter of,

(1) 12 months from the date of filing by a third party of a written request under § 301.6343-1(b)(2) for the return of property wrongfully levied upon, or

(2) 6 months from the date of mailing by registered or certified mail by the district director to the party claimant of a notice of disallowance of the part of the request to which the action relates.

A request which, under § 301.6343-1(b)(3), is not considered adequate does not extend the 9-month period described in paragraph (a) of this section.

(c) *Examples.*—The provisions of this section may be illustrated by the following examples:

*Example (1).* On June 1, 1970, a tax is assessed against A with respect to his delinquent tax liability. On July 19, 1970, a levy is wrongfully made upon certain tangible personal property of B's which is in A's possession at that time. On July 20, 1970, notice of seizure is given to A. Thus, under section 6502(b), July 20, 1970, is the date on which the levy is considered to be made. Unless a request for the return of property is sooner made to extend the 9-month period, no suit or proceeding under section 7426 may be begun by B after April 20, 1971, which is 9 months from the date of levy.

*Example (2).* Assume the same facts as in the preceding example except that, on August 3, 1970, B properly files a request for the return of his property wrongfully levied upon. Assume further that the district director mails, on March 1, 1971, a notice of disallowance of B's request for the return of the property. No suit or proceeding under section 7426 may be begun by B after August 3, 1971, which is 12 months from the date of filing a request for the return of property wrongfully levied upon.

*Example (3).* Assume the same facts as in the preceding example except that the notice of disallowance of B's request for the return of property wrongfully levied upon is mailed to B on November 12, 1970. Since the 6-month period from the mailing of the notice of disallowance expires before the 12-month period from the date of filing the request for the return of property which ends on August 3, 1971, no suit or proceeding under section 7426 may be begun by B after May 12, 1971, which is 6 months from the date of mailing the notice of disallowance. [Reg. § 301.6532-3.]

☐ [T.D. 7305, 3-14-74.]

## Interest

# INTEREST ON UNDERPAYMENTS

See p. 20,601 for regulations not amended to reflect law changes

### [Reg. § 20.6601-1]

**§ 20.6601-1. Interest on underpayment, nonpayment, or extensions of time for payment, of tax.**—For regulations concerning interest on underpayments, etc., see § 301.6601-1 of this chapter (Regulations on Procedure and Administration). [Reg. § 20.6601-1.]

☐ [T.D. 6296, 6-23-58.]

### [Reg. § 25.6601-1]

**§ 25.6601-1. Interest on underpayment, nonpayment, or extensions of time for payment, of tax.**—For regulations concerning interest on underpayment, nonpayment, or extensions of time for payment of tax, see § 301.6601-1 of this chapter(Regulations on Procedure and Administration). [Reg. § 25.6601-1.]

☐ [T.D. 6334, 10-14-58.]

### [Reg. § 53.6601-1]

**§ 53.6601-1. Interest on underpayment, nonpayment, or extensions of time for payment, of tax.**—For regulations concerning interest on underpayment, nonpayment, or extensions of time for payment of tax, see § 301.6601-1 of this chapter(Regulations on Procedure and Administration). [Reg. § 53.6601-1.]

☐ [T.D. 7368, 7-15-75.]

### [Reg. § 301.6601-1]

**§ 301.6601-1. Interest on underpayments.**—(a) *General rule.*—(1) Interest at the annual rate referred to in the regulations under section 6621 shall be paid on any unpaid amount of tax from the last date prescribed for payment of the tax (determined without regard to any extension of time for payment) to the date on which payment is received.

(2) For provisions requiring the payment of interest during the period occurring before July 1, 1975, see section 6601(a) prior to its amendment by section 7 of the Act of Jan. 3, 1975 (Pub. L. 93-625, 88 Stat. 2115).

(b) *Satisfaction by credits made after December 31, 1957.*—(1) *In general.*—If any portion of a tax is satisfied by the credit of an overpayment after December 31, 1957, interest shall not be imposed under section 6601 on such portion of the tax for any period during which interest on the overpayment would have been allowable if the overpayment had been refunded.

(2) *Examples.*—The provisions of this paragraph may be illustrated by the following examples:

*Example (1).* An examination of A's income tax returns for the calendar years 1955 and 1956 discloses an underpayment of $800 for 1955 and an overpayment of $500 for 1956. Interest under section 6601(a) ordinarily accrues on the underpayment of $800 from April 15, 1956, to the date of payment. However, the 1956 overpayment of $500 is credited after December 31, 1957, against the underpayment in accordance with the provisions of section 6402(a) and § 301.6402-1. Under such circumstances interest on the $800 underpayment runs from April 15, 1956, the last date prescribed for payment of the 1955 tax, to April 15, 1957, the date the overpayment of $500 was made. Since interest would have been allowed on the overpayment, if refunded, from April 15, 1957, to a date not more than 30 days prior to the date of the refund check, no interest is imposed after April 15, 1957, on $500, the portion of the underpayment satisfied by credit. Interest continues to run, however, on $300 (the $800 underpayment for 1955 less the $500 overpayment for 1956) to the date of payment.

*Example (2).* An examination of A's income tax returns for the calendar years 1956 and 1957 discloses an overpayment, occurring on April 15, 1957, of $700 for 1956 and an underpayment of $400 for 1957. After April 15, 1958, the last date prescribed for payment of the 1957 tax, the district director credits $400 of the overpayment against the underpayment. In such a case, interest will accrue upon the overpayment of $700 from April 15, 1957, to April 15, 1958, the due date of the amount against which the credit is taken. Interest will also accrue under section 6611 upon $300 ($700 overpayment less $400 underpayment) from April 15, 1958, to a date not more than 30 days prior to the date of the refund check. Since a refund of the portion of the overpayment credited against the underpayment would have resulted in interest running upon such portion from April 15, 1958, to a date not more than 30 days prior to the date of the refund check, no interest is imposed upon the underpayment.

(c) *Last date prescribed for payment.*—(1) In determining the last date prescribed for payment, any extension of time granted for payment of tax (including any postponement elected under section 6163(a)) shall be disregarded. The granting of an extension of time for the payment of tax does not relieve the taxpayer from liability for the payment of interest thereon during the period of the extension. Thus, except as provided in paragraph (b) of this section, interest at the annual rate referred to in the regulations under section 6621 is payable on any unpaid portion of the tax for the period during which such portion remains unpaid by reason of an extension of time for the payment thereof.

(2)(i) If a tax or portion thereof is payable in installments in accordance with an election made under section 6152(a) or 6156(a), the last date prescribed for payment of any installment of such tax or portion thereof shall be determined under the provisions of section 6152(b) or 6156(b), as the case may be, and interest shall run on any unpaid installment from such last date to the date on which payment is received. However in the event installment privileges are terminated for failure to pay an installment when due as provided by section 6152(d) and the time for the payment of any remaining installment is accelerated by the issuance of a notice and demand therefor, interest shall run on such unpaid installment from the date of the notice and demand to the date on which payment is received. But see section 6601(e)(4).

(ii) If the tax shown on a return is payable in installments, interest will run on any tax not shown on the return from the last date prescribed for payment of the first installment. If a deficiency is prorated to any unpaid installments, in accordance with section 6152(c), interest shall run on such prorated amounts from the date prescribed for the payment of the first installment to the date on which payment is received.

(3) If, by reason of jeopardy, a notice and demand for payment of any tax is issued before the last date otherwise prescribed for payment, such last date shall nevertheless be used for the purpose of the interest computation, and no interest shall be imposed for the period commencing with the date of the issuance of the notice and demand and ending on such last date. If the tax is not paid on or before such last date, interest will automatically accrue from such last date to the date on which payment is received.

(4) In the case of taxes payable by stamp and in all other cases where the last date for payment of the tax is not otherwise prescribed, such last date for the purpose of the interest computation shall be deemed to be the date on which the liability for the tax arose. However, such last date shall in no event be later than the date of issuance of a notice and demand for the tax.

(d) *Suspension of interest; waiver of restrictions on assessment.*—In the case of a deficiency determined by a district director (or an assistant regional commissioner, appellate) with respect to any income, estate, gift, or chapter 41, 42, 43, or 44 tax, if the taxpayer files with such internal revenue officer an agreement waiving the restrictions on assessment of such deficiency, and if notice and demand for payment of such deficiency is not made within 30 days after the filing of such waiver, no interest shall be imposed on the deficiency for the period beginning immediately after such 30th day and ending on the date notice and demand is made. In the case of an agreement with respect to a portion of the deficiency, the rules as set forth in this paragraph are applicable only to that portion of the deficiency to which the agreement relates.

(e) *Income tax reduced by carryback.*—(1) The carryback of a net operating loss, net capital loss, investment credit, or a work incentive program (WIN) credit shall not affect the computation of interest on any income tax for the period commencing with the last day prescribed for the payment of such tax and ending with the last day of the taxable year in which the loss or credit arises. For example, if the carryback of a net operating loss, a net capital loss, an investment credit, or a WIN credit to a prior taxable period eliminates or reduces a deficiency in income tax for that period, the full amount of the deficiency will nevertheless bear interest at the annual rate referred to in the regulations under section 6621 from the last date prescribed for payment of such tax until the last day of the taxable year in which the loss or credit arose. Interest will continue to run beyond such last day on any portion of the deficiency which is not eliminated by the carryback. With respect to any portion of an investment credit carryback or a WIN credit carryback from a taxable year attributable to a net operating loss carryback or a capital loss carryback from a subsequent taxable year, such investment credit carryback or WIN credit carryback shall not affect the computation of interest on any income tax for the period commencing with the last day prescribed for the payment of such tax and ending with the last day of such subsequent taxable year.

(2) Where an extension of time for payment of income tax has been granted under section 6164 to a corporation expecting a net operating loss carryback or a net capital loss carryback, interest is payable at the annual rate established under section 6621 on the amount of such unpaid tax from the last date prescribed for payment thereof without regard to such extension.

(3) Where there has been an allowance of an overpayment attributable to a net operating loss carryback, a capital loss carryback, or an investment credit carryback and all or part of such allowance is later determined to be excessive, interest shall be computed on the excessive amount from the last day of the year in which the net operating loss, net capital loss, or investment credit arose until the date on which the repayment of such excessive amount is received. Where there has been an allowance of an overpayment with respect to any portion of an investment credit carryback from a taxable year attributable to a net operating loss carryback or a capital loss carryback from a subsequent taxable year and all or part of such allowance is later determined to be excessive, interest shall be computed on the excessive amount from the last day of such subsequent taxable year until the date on which the repayment of such excessive amount is received.

(f) *Applicable rules.*—(1) Any interest prescribed by section 6601 shall be assessed and collected in the same manner as tax and shall be paid upon notice and demand by the district director or the director of the regional service center. Any reference in the Code (except in subchapter B, chapter 63, relating to deficiency procedures) to any tax imposed by the Code shall be deemed also to refer to the interest imposed by section 6601 on such tax. Interest on a tax may be assessed and collected at any time within the period of limitation on collection after assessment of the tax to which it relates. For rules relating to the period of limitation on collection after assessment, see section 6502.

(2) No interest under section 6601 shall be payable on any interest provided by such section. This paragraph (f)(2) shall not apply after December 31, 1982, with respect to interest accruing after such date, or accrued but unpaid on such date. See § 301.6622-1.

(3) Interest will not be imposed on any assessable penalty, addition to the tax (other than an addition to tax described in section 6601(e)(2)(B)), or additional amount if the amount is paid within 21 calendar days (10 business days if the amount assessed and shown on the notice and demand equals or exceeds $100,000) from the date of the notice and demand. If interest is imposed, it will be imposed only for the period from the date of the notice and demand to the date on which payment is received. This paragraph (f)(3) is applicable with respect to any notice and demand made after December 31, 1996.

(4) If notice and demand is made after December 31, 1996, for any amount and the amount is paid within 21 calendar days (10 business days if the amount assessed and shown on the notice and demand equals or exceeds $100,000) from the date of the notice and demand, interest will not be imposed for the period after the date of the notice and demand.

(5) For purposes of paragraphs (f)(3) and (4) of this section—

(i) The term *business day* means any day other than a Saturday, Sunday, legal holiday in the District of Columbia, or a statewide legal holiday in the state where the taxpayer resides or where the taxpayer's principal place of business is located. With respect to the tenth business day (after taking into account the first sentence of this paragraph (f)(5)(i)), see section 7503 relating to time for performance of acts where the last day falls on a statewide legal holiday in the state where the act is required to be performed.

(ii) The term *calendar day* means any day. With respect to the twenty-first calendar day, see section 7503 relating to time for performance of acts where the last day falls on a Saturday, Sunday, or legal holiday.

(6) No interest shall be imposed for failure to pay estimated tax as required by section 59 of the Internal Revenue Code of 1939 or section 6153 or 6154 of the Internal Revenue Code of 1954. [Reg. § 301.6601-1.]

☐ [*T.D.* 6234, 5-21-57. *Amended by T.D.* 6425, 11-10-59, *T.D.* 6498, 10-24-60, *T.D.* 6585, 12-27-61, *T.D.* 6730, 5-7-64, *T.D.* 7238, 12-28-72, *T.D.* 7301, 1-3-74, *T.D.* 7384, 10-21-75, *T.D.* 7838, 10-5-82; *T.D.* 7907, 8-22-83 *and T.D.* 8725, 7-21-97.]

### [Reg. § 301.6602-1]

**§ 301.6602-1. Interest on erroneous refund recoverable by suit.**—Any portion of an internal revenue tax (or any interest, assessable penalty, additional amount, or addition to tax) which has been erroneously refunded, and which is recoverable by a civil action pursuant to section 7405, shall bear interest at the annual rate referred to in the regulations under section 6621 from the date of the payment of the refund. [Reg. § 301.6602-1.]

☐ [*T.D.* 6234, 5-21-57. *Amended by T.D.* 7384, 10-21-75.]

# INTEREST ON OVERPAYMENTS

### [Reg. § 301.6611-1]

**§ 301.6611-1. Interest on overpayments.**—(a) *General rule.*—Except as otherwise provided, interest shall be allowed on any overpayment of any tax at the annual rate referred to in the regulations under section 6621 from the date of overpayment of the tax.

(b) *Date of overpayment.*—Except as provided in section 6401(a), relating to assessment and collection after the expiration of the applicable period of limitation, there can be no overpayment of tax until the entire tax liability has been satisfied. Therefore, the dates of overpayment of any tax are the date of payment of the first amount which (when added to previous payments) is in excess of the tax liability (including any interest, addition to the tax, or additional amount) and the dates of payment of all amounts subsequently paid with respect to such tax liability. For rules relating to the determination of the date of payment in the case of an advance payment of tax, a payment of estimated tax, and a credit for income tax withholding, see paragraph (d) of this section.

(c) *Examples.*—The application of paragraph (b) may be illustrated by the following examples:

*Example (1).* Corporation X files an income tax return on March 15, 1955, for the calendar year 1954 disclosing a tax liability of $1,000 and elects to pay the tax in installments. Subsequent to payment of the final installment, the correct tax liability is determined to be $900.

| Tax liability | |
| --- | --- |
| Assessed | $1,000 |
| Correct liability | 900 |
| Overassessment | 100 |

| Record of payments | |
| --- | --- |
| March 15, 1955 | $500 |
| June 15, 1955 | 500 |

Since the correct liability in this case is $900, the payment of $500 made on March 15, 1955, and $400 of the payment made on June 15, 1955, are applied in satisfaction of the tax liability. The balance of the payment made on June 15, 1955 ($100) constitutes the amount of the overpayment, and the date on which such payment was made would be the date of the overpayment from which interest would be computed.

**67,040**
**Determination of Interest Rate; Compounding of**
See p. 20,601 for regulations not amended to reflect law changes

*Example (2).* Corporation Y files an income tax return for the calendar year 1954 on March 15, 1955, disclosing a tax liability of $50,000, and elects to pay the tax in installments. On October 15, 1956, a deficiency in the amount of $10,000 is assessed and is paid in equal amounts on November 15 and November 26, 1956. On April 15, 1957, it is determined that the correct tax liability of the taxpayer for 1954 is only $35,000.

| Tax liability | |
|---|---|
| Original assessment | $50,000 |
| Deficiency assessment | 10,000 |
| Total assessed | 60,000 |
| Correct liability | 35,000 |
| Overassessment | 25,000 |

| Record of payments | |
|---|---|
| March 15, 1955 | $25,000 |
| June 15, 1955 | 25,000 |
| November 15, 1956 | 5,000 |
| November 26, 1956 | 5,000 |

Since the correct liability in this case is $35,000, the entire payment of $25,000 made on March 15, 1955, and $10,000 of the payment made on June 15, 1955, in satisfaction of the tax liability. The balance of the payment made on June 15, 1955 ($15,000), plus the amounts paid on November 15 ($5,000), and November 26, 1956 ($5,000), constitute the amount of the overpayment. The dates of the overpayments from which interest would be computed are as follows:

| Date | Amount of overpayment |
|---|---|
| June 15, 1955 | $15,000 |
| November 15, 1956 | 5,000 |
| November 26, 1956 | 5,000 |

The amount of any interest paid with respect to the deficiency of $10,000 is also an overpayment.

(d) *Advance payment of tax, payment of estimated tax, and credit for income tax withholding.*—In the case of an advance payment of tax, a payment of estimated income tax, or a credit for income tax withholding, the provisions of section 6513 (except the provisions of subsection (c) thereof), applicable in determining the date of payment of tax for purposes of the period of limitations on credit or refund, shall apply in determining the date of overpayment for purposes of computing interest thereon.

(e) *Refund of income tax caused by carryback.*—If any overpayment of tax imposed by subtitle A of the Code results from the carryback of a net operating loss, a net capital loss, an investment credit, or a work incentive (WIN) credit, such overpayment, for purposes of this section, shall be deemed not to have been made prior to the end of the taxable year in which the loss or credit arises, or, with respect to any portion of an investment credit carryback or a WIN credit carryback from a taxable year attributable to a net operating loss carryback or a capital loss carryback from a subsequent taxable year, such overpayment shall be deemed not to have been made prior to the close of such subsequent taxable year.

(f) *Refund of income tax caused by carryback of foreign taxes.*—For purposes of paragraph (a) of this section, any overpayment of tax resulting from a carryback of tax paid or accrued to foreign countries or possessions of the United States shall be deemed not to have been paid or accrued before the close of the taxable year under subtitle F of the Code of 1954 in which such taxes were in fact paid or accrued.

(g) *Period for which interest allowable in case of refunds.*—If an overpayment of tax is refunded, interest shall be allowed from the date of the overpayment to a date determined by the district director or the director of the regional service center, which shall be not more than 30 days prior to the date of the refund check. The acceptance of a refund check shall not deprive the taxpayer of the right to make a claim for any additional overpayment and interest thereon, provided the claim is made within the applicable period of limitation. However, if a taxpayer does not accept a refund check, no additional interest on the amount of the overpayment included in such check shall be allowed.

(h) *Period for which interest allowable in case of credits.*—(1) *General rule.*—If an overpayment of tax is credited, interest shall be allowed from the date of overpayment to the due date (as determined under subparagraph (2) of this paragraph) of the amount against which such overpayment is credited.

(2) *Determination of due date.*—(i) *In general.*—The term "due date", as used in this section, means the last day fixed by law or regulations for the payment of the tax (determined without regard to any extension of time), and not the date on which the district director or the director of the regional service center makes demand for the payment of the tax. Therefore, the due date of a tax (other than an additional assessment subject to the special rule provided by subdivision (iv) of this subparagraph) is the date fixed for the payment of the tax or the several installments thereof.

(ii) *Tax payable in installments.*—(a) *In general.*—In the case of a credit against a tax, where the taxpayer had properly elected to pay the tax in installments, the due date is the date prescribed for the payment of the installment against which the credit is applied.

(b) *Delinquent installment.*—If the taxpayer is delinquent in payment of an installment of tax and the notice and demand has been issued for the payment of the delinquent installment and the remaining installments, the due date of each remaining installment shall then be the date of such notice and demand.

(iii) *Tax or installment not yet due.*—If a taxpayer agrees to the crediting of an overpayment against tax or an installment of tax and the schedule of allowance is signed prior to the date on which such tax or installment would otherwise become due, then the due date of such tax or installment shall be the date on which such schedule is signed.

(iv) *Additional assessment satisfied by credit before January 1, 1958.*—In the case of a credit made before January 1, 1958, against an additional assessment, the due date of the tax satisfied by the credit is the date the additional assessment was made. For purposes of this subdivision, the term "additional assessment" means a further assessment of a tax of the same character previously paid in part, and includes the assessment of a deficiency as defined in section 6211.

(v) *Interest.*—In the case of a credit against interest that accrues for any period ending prior to January 1, 1983, the due date is the earlier of the date of assessment of such interest or December 31, 1982. In the case of a credit against interest that accrues for any period beginning on or after December 31, 1982, such interest is due as it economically accrues on a daily basis, rather than when it is assessed.

(vi) *Additional amount, addition to the tax, or assessable penalty.*—In the case of a credit against an additional amount, addition to the tax, or assessable penalty, the due date is the earlier of the date of assessment or the date from which such amount would bear interest if not satisfied by payment or credit.

(vii) *Estimated income tax for succeeding year.*—If the taxpayer elects to have all or part of the overpayment shown by his return applied to his estimated tax for his succeeding taxable year, no interest shall be allowed on such portion of the overpayment credited and such amount shall be applied as a payment on account of the estimated tax for such year or the installments thereof.

(i) [Reserved.]

(j) *Refund of overpayment.*—No interest shall be allowed on any overpayment of tax imposed by subtitle A of the Code if such overpayment is refunded—

(1) In the case of a return filed on or before the last date prescribed for filing the return of such tax (determined without regard to any extension of time for filing such return), within 45 days after such last date, or

(2) After December 17, 1966, in the case of a return filed after the last day prescribed for filing the return, within 45 days after the date on which the return is filed.

However, in the case of any overpayment of tax by an individual (other than an estate or trust and other than a nonresident alien individual) for a taxable year beginning in 1974, "60 days" shall be substituted for "45 days" each place it appears in this paragraph.

(k) *Effective date.*—Paragraphs (h)(2)(v) and (h)(2)(vi) of this section are effective for credits made on or after August 25, 1992. [Reg. §301.6611-1.]

☐ [*T.D.* 6234, 5-21-57. *Amended by T.D.* 6425, 11-10-59; *T.D.* 6498, 10-24-60; *T.D.* 6585, 12-27-61; *T.D.* 6730, 5-7-64; *T.D.* 7301, 1-3-74; *T.D.* 7384, 10-21-75 *and T.D.* 8524, 3-2-94.]

# DETERMINATION OF INTEREST RATE; COMPOUNDING OF INTEREST

[Reg. §301.6621-1]

§301.6621-1. Interest rate.—(a) *In general.*—The interest rate established under section 6621 shall be—

(1) On amounts outstanding before July 1, 1975, 6 percent per annum (or 4 percent in the case of certain extensions of time for payment of taxes as provided in sections 6601(b) and (j) prior to amendment by section 7(b) of the Act of Jan. 3, 1975 (Pub. L. 93-625,

88 Stat. 2115), and certain overpayments of the unrelated business income tax as provided in section 514(b)(3)(D), prior to its amendment by such Act).

| After | And before |
|---|---|
| June 30, 1975 | February 1, 1976 |
| January 31, 1976 | February 1, 1978 |
| January 31, 1978 | February 1, 1980 |
| January 31, 1980 | February 1, 1982 |
| January 31, 1982 | January 1, 1983 |

(3) On amounts outstanding after December 31, 1982, the adjusted rate established by the Commissioner under section 6621(b). This adjusted rate shall be published by the Commissioner in a Revenue Ruling. See §301.6622-1 for application of daily compounding in determining interest accruing after December 31, 1982. Because interest accruing after December 31, 1982, accrues at the prescribed rate per annum compounded daily, the effective annual percentage rate of interest will exceed the prescribed rate of interest.

(b) [Reserved]

(c) *Applicability of interest rate.*—(1) *Computation.*—Interest and additions to tax on any amount outstanding on a specific day shall be computed at the annual rate applicable on such day.

(2) *Additions to tax.*—Additions to tax under any section of the Code that refers to the annual rate established under this section, including sections 644(a)(2)(B), 4497(c)(2), 6654(a), and 6655(a) and (g), shall be computed at the same rate per annum as the interest rate set forth under paragraph (a) of this section.

(3) *Interest.*—Interest provided for under any section of the Code that refers to the annual rate established under this section, including sections 47(d)(3)(G), 167(q), 6332(c)(1), 6343(c), 6601(a), 6602, 6611(a), 7426(g), and section 1961(c)(1) or 2411 of Title 28 of the United States Code, shall be computed at the rate per annum set forth under paragraph (a) of this section.

(d) *Examples.*—The provisions of this section may be illustrated by the following examples. Example (6) illustrates the computation of interest for interest accruing after December 31, 1982.

*Example (1).* A, an individual, files an income tax return for the calendar year 1974 on April 15, 1975, showing a tax due of $1,000. A pays the $1,000 on September 1, 1975. Pursuant to section 6601(a), interest on the underpayment of $1,000 is computed at the rate of 6 percent per annum from April 15, 1975, to June 30, 1975, a total of 76 days. Interest for 63 days, from June 30, 1975, to September 1, 1975, shall be computed at the rate of 9 percent per annum.

*Example (2).* An executor of an estate is granted, in accordance with section 6161(a)(2)(A), a two-year extension of time for payment of the estate tax shown on the estate tax return, which tax was otherwise due on January 15, 1974. The tax is paid on January 15, 1976. Interest on the underpayment shall be computed at the rate of 4 percent per annum from January 15, 1974, to June 30, 1975, and at the rate of 9 percent per annum from June 30, 1975, to January 15, 1976.

*Example (3).* X, a corporation, files its 1973 corporate income tax return on March 15, 1974, and pays the balance of tax due shown thereon. On August 1, 1975, an assessment of a deficiency is made against X with respect to such tax. The deficiency is paid on October 1, 1975. Interest at the rate of 6 percent per annum is due on the deficiency from March 15, 1974, the due date of the return, to June 30, 1975, and at the rate of 9 percent per annum from June 30, 1975, to October 1, 1975.

*Example (4).* Y, an individual, files an amended individual income tax return on October 1, 1975, for the refund of an overpayment of income tax Y made on April 15, 1975. Interest is allowed on the overpayment to December 1, 1975. Pursuant to section 6611(a), interest is computed at the rate of 6 percent per annum from April 15, 1975, the date of overpayment, to June 30, 1975. Interest from June 30, 1975, to December 1, 1975, shall be computed at the rate of 9 percent per annum.

*Example (5).* A, an individual, is liable for an addition to tax under section 6654 for the underpayment of estimated tax from April 15, 1975 until January 15, 1976. The addition to tax shall be computed at the annual rate of 6 percent per annum from April 15, 1975, to June 30, 1975, and at the annual rate of 9 percent per annum from June 30, 1975, to January 15, 1976.

*Example (6).* B, an individual, files an income tax return for calendar year 1980 on April 15, 1981, showing a tax due of $1,000. B pays the $1,000 on March 1, 1983. Under section 6601(a), interest on the $1,000 underpayment is due from April 15, 1981, to March 1, 1983. Such interest is computed at the rate of 12 percent per annum, simple interest, from April 15, 1981, to January 31, 1982, and at the rate of 20 percent per annum, simple interest, from January 31, 1982, to December 31, 1982, and at the rate of 16 percent per annum, compounded daily, from December 31, 1982, to March 1, 1983. The total simple interest accrued but unpaid at the end of December 31, 1982, is

(2) On amounts outstanding—

| | Rate per annum (percent) |
|---|---|
| | 9 percent |
| | 7 percent |
| | 6 percent |
| | 12 percent |
| | 20 percent |

combined with the $1,000 underpayment for purposes of determining the amount of daily compounded interest to be charged from December 31, 1982, to March 1, 1983. [Reg. §301.6621-1.]

☐ [*T.D. 7384, 10-21-75. Amended by T.D. 7907, 8-22-83.*]

### [Reg. §301.6621-2T]

**§301.6621-2T. Questions and answers relating to the increased rate of interest on substantial underpayments attributable to certain tax motivated transactions (Temporary).**—The following questions and answers relate to the increased rate of interest on substantial underpayments attributable to certain tax motivated transactions as provided in section 6621(d) of the Internal Revenue Code of 1954, as added by section 144 of the Tax Reform Act of 1984 (Pub. L. 98-369, 98 Stat. 682):

Q-1. What is the annual interest rate under section 6621 for purposes of computing the amount of interest that must be paid under section 6601 (relating to interest on underpayments)?

A-1. In general, the annual interest rate for purposes of section 6601 is the adjusted rate of interest established under section 6621(b) and §301.6621-1 ("adjusted rate"). If, however, a tax motivated underpayment (as defined in A-2 of this section) for a taxable year is substantial (as defined in A-7 of this section), section 6621(d) provides that the annual rate of interest with respect to the tax motivated underpayment is 120 percent of the adjusted rate ("120 percent rate"), rounded to the nearest tenth of a percent.

Q-2. What is a tax motivated underpayment?

A-2. A tax motivated underpayment is the portion of a deficiency (as defined in section 6211) of tax imposed by subtitle A (income taxes) that is attributable to any of the following tax motivated transactions:

(1) Any instance in which the value of any property, or the adjusted basis of any property, claimed on a return is 150 percent or more of the amount determined to be the correct amount of such valuation or adjusted basis (*i.e.*, a valuation overstatement within the meaning of section 6659(c)(1));

(2) Any loss disallowed for any period by reason of section 465(a) or any amount included in gross income by reason of section 465(e);

(3) Any credit disallowed for any period by reason of section 46(c)(8) or section 48(d)(6);

(4) Any loss disallowed for any period with respect to a straddle, as defined in section 1092(c), but without regard to sections 1092(d) and (e);

(5) Any use of an accounting method that may result in a substantial distortion of income for any period (see A-3 of this section); and

(6) Any deduction disallowed with respect to any other tax motivated transaction (see A-4 of this section).

Q-3. What accounting methods may result in a substantial distortion of income for any period under A-2(5) of this section?

A-3. A deduction or credit disallowed, or income included, in any of the circumstances listed below shall be treated as attributable to the use of an accounting method that may result in a substantial distortion of income and shall thus be a tax motivated transaction that results in a tax motivated underpayment:

(1) Any deduction disallowed for any period by reason of section 464 or section 278(b), relating to certain expenses of farming syndicates;

(2) In the case of a taxpayer who computes taxable income using the cash receipts and disbursements method of accounting, any interest deduction disallowed for any period by reason of section 461(g), relating to prepaid interest, provided the interest is not paid with respect to indebtedness incurred in connection with (i) the purchase, refinancing, or improvement of the principal residence of the taxpayer, or (ii) the purchase of consumer goods by the taxpayer;

(3) Any interest deduction disallowed for any period because the amount of the claimed deduction was computed using a method resulting in an amount of interest for a period that exceeds the true cost of the indebtedness for the period computed by applying the effective rate of interest on the loan to the unpaid balance of the loan for that period (*i.e.*, the economic accrual of interest for the period), provided the interest is not accrued with respect to indebtedness incurred in connection with (i) the purchase, refinancing, or improvement of the principal residence of the taxpayer, or (ii) the purchase of consumer goods by the taxpayer (see Rev. Rul. 83-84, 1983-1 C.B. 97, and sections 163(e), 446(b), and 483);

(4) Any deduction disallowed for any period under section 709, relating to organization or syndication expenditures of a partnership;

(5) In the case of any expenditure described in section 248(b) that was incurred by an S corporation, any deduction disallowed because it exceeds the amount allowable under section 248, relating to organizational expenditures;

(6) Any deduction disallowed for any period under section 267(a), relating to transactions between related taxpayers;

(7) Any deduction disallowed for any period, or any income required to be included for any period, under section 467, relating to certain payments for the use of property or services;

(8) Any deduction disallowed for any period under section 461(i), relating to certain deductions of tax shelters; and

(9) In the case of a taxpayer who computes taxable income using the cash receipts and disbursements method of accounting, any deduction disallowed for any period because (i) the expenditure resulting in the deduction was a deposit rather than a payment, (ii) the expenditure was prepaid for tax avoidance purposes and not for a business purpose, or (iii) the deduction resulted in a material distortion of income (see, *e.g.*, Rev. Rul. 79-229, 1979-2 C.B. 210).

Q-4. Are any transactions other than those specified in A-2 of this section and those involving the use of accounting methods under circumstances specified in A-3 of this section considered tax motivated transactions under A-2(6) of this section?

A-4. Yes. Deductions disallowed under the following provisions are considered to be attributable to tax motivated transactions:

(1) Any deduction disallowed for any period under section 183, relating to an activity engaged in by an individual or an S corporation that is not engaged in for profit, and

(2) Any deduction disallowed for any period under section 165(c)(2), relating to any transaction not entered into for profit.

Q-5. How is the amount of a tax motivated underpayment determined?

A-5. Except as provided in A-6 of this section, the amount of a tax motivated underpayment is determined in the following manner:

(1) Calculate the amount of the tax liability for the taxable year as if all items of income, gain, loss, deduction, or credit, had been reported properly on the income tax return of the taxpayer ("total tax liability"); and

(2) Without taking into account any adjustments to items of income, gain, loss, deductions, or credit that are attributable to tax motivated transactions (as defined in A-2 through A-4 of this section), calculate the amount of the tax liability for the taxable year as if all other items of income, gain, loss, deduction, or credit had been reported properly on the income tax return of the taxpayer ("tax liability without regard to tax motivated transactions").

(3) The difference between the total tax liability and the tax liability without regard to tax motivated transactions is the amount of the tax motivated underpayment.

*Example.* Taxpayer A, a calendar year taxpayer, files his 1984 income tax return reporting $70,000 of taxable income and $23,171 of tax liability. On January 20, 1986, A enters into a closing agreement with the Internal Revenue Service that includes the following adjustments:

| | |
|---|---|
| Section 162 deduction disallowed (not tax motivated) . . . . . . . | $7,500 |
| Loss disallowed under section 465 (tax motivated—see A-2(2) of this section) . . . . . . . . . . . . . . . . . . . . . . . . . . . | $5,000 |
| Section 170 deduction disallowed because of a valuation overstatement (tax motivated—see A-2(1) of this section) . . . . | $10,000 |
| Loss disallowed with respect to a straddle as defined in section 1092(c) (tax motivated—see A-2 (4) of this section) . . . . . . . | $7,000 |
| Other adjustments (none of which are tax motivated) . . . . . . . | $4,000 |

The tax motivated underpayment is determined in the following manner:

| | | |
|---|---|---|
| 1. | $70,000 | reported taxable income |
| | + 33,500 | (add all adjustments to items of income, gain, loss, deduction, or credit (including tax motivated transactions subject to section 6621 (d))) |
| | $103,500 | tax = $39,685 ("total tax liability") |
| 2. | $ 70,000 | reported taxable income |
| | + 11,500 | (add adjustments to items of income, gain, loss, deduction, or credit other than those with respect to items that are tax motivated) |
| | $ 81,500 | tax = $28,691 ("tax liability without regard to tax motivated transactions") |

The tax motivated underpayment (*i.e.*, the underpayment attributable to tax motivated transactions) is $10,994 ($39,685 – $28,691). Accordingly, the interest on $10,994 would be computed at the 120 percent rate.

The remainder of the underpayment (*i.e.*, the underpayment not attributable to tax motivated transactions) is $5,520 ($28,691 (tax liability without regard to tax motivated items) – $23,171 (tax paid

with return)). The interest on $5,520 would be computed at the adjusted rate.

Q-6: How are the amounts of the tax motivated underpayment and the underpayment attributable to fraud or negligence determined if all or a portion of the taxpayer's underpayment is attributable to one or more tax motivated transactions and all or a portion is subject to the addition to tax imposed by section 6653(a)(2) (in the case of an underpayment attributable to negligence or intentional disregard) or section 6653(b)(2) (in the case of an underpayment attributable to fraud)?

A-6: If all or a portion of the taxpayer's underpayment is attributable to tax motivated transactions, and all or a portion is attributable to fraudulent or negligent items (*i.e.*, items that result in an underpayment subject to the addition to tax imposed by section 6653(a)(2) or (b)(2)), the amount of the tax motivated underpayment and the underpayment attributable to fraud or negligence is determined in the following manner:

(1) Determine the following amounts:

(i) The tax liability for the taxable year of the taxpayer as if all items of income, gain, loss, deduction, or credit had been reported properly on the income tax return of the taxpayer ("total tax liability");

(ii) The tax liability for the taxable year of the taxpayer as if all items of income, gain, loss, deduction, or credit without taking into account adjustments to items of income, gain, loss, deduction, or credit that are both (a) attributable to tax motivated transactions and (b) subject to section 6653(a)(2) or section 6653(b)(2), had been reported properly on the income tax return of the taxpayer ("tax liability without regard to fraudulent or negligent tax motivated items");

(iii) The tax liability for the taxable year of the taxpayer as if all items of income, gain, loss, deduction, or credit, without taking into account adjustments to items of income, gain, loss, deduction, or credit that are subject to section 6653(a)(2) or section 6653(b)(2), had been reported properly on the income tax return of the taxpayer ("tax liability without regard to fraudulent or negligent items");

(iv) The tax liability for the taxable year of the taxpayer as if all items of income, gain, loss, deduction, or credit, without taking into account adjustments to items of income, gain, loss, deduction, or credit that are either subject to section 6653(a)(2) or section 6653(b)(2) or attributable to tax motivated transactions, had been reported properly on the income tax return of the taxpayer ("tax liability without regard to tax motivated or fraudulent or negligent items").

(2) The tax motivated underpayment attributable to fraudulent or negligent items is the excess of the total tax liability over the tax liability determined without regard to fraudulent or negligent tax motivated items ((i)-(ii)).

(3) The tax motivated underpayment is the sum of (a) the tax motivated underpayment attributable to fraudulent or negligent items ((i)- (ii)) plus (b) the excess of the tax liability without regard to fraudulent or negligent items over the tax liability without regard to tax motivated or fraudulent or negligent items ((iii)-(iv)). Interest on this underpayment is computed at the 120 percent rate.

(4) The underpayment attributable to fraudulent or negligent items is the excess of the total tax liability over the tax liability without regard to fraudulent or negligent items ((i)-(iii)). The section 6653 addition to tax is 50 percent of the interest on this underpayment computed at the 120 percent rate on an amount equal to the tax motivated underpayment attributable to fraudulent or negligent items (computed in (2)) and at the adjusted rate on the remainder.

*Example.* Taxpayer A, a calendar year taxpayer, files his 1984 income tax return reporting $70,000 of taxable income and $23,171 of tax liability. On January 20, 1986, A enters into a closing agreement with the Internal Revenue Service that includes the following adjustments:

| | |
|---|---|
| Section 162 deduction disallowed (not tax motivated but fraudulent or negligent) . . . . . . . . . . . . . . . . . . . . . . . | $7,500 |
| Loss disallowed under section 465(a) (tax motivated—see A-2(2) of this section—and fraudulent or negligent) . . . . . . . . . . . . . | $5,000 |
| Section 170 deduction disallowed because of a valuation overstatement (tax motivated—see A-2(1) of this section—but not fraudulent or negligent) . . . . . . . . . . . . . . . . . . . . . . | $10,000 |
| Loss disallowed with respect to a straddle as defined in section 1092(c) (tax motivated—see A-2(4) of this section—but not fraudulent or negligent) . . . . . . . . . . . . . . . . . . . . . . | $7,000 |
| Other adjustments (none of which are tax motivated or fraudulent or negligent) . . . . . . . . . . . . . . . . . . . . . . . . . . . | $4,000 |

The tax motivated underpayment is determined in the following manner:

| | | |
|---|---|---|
| (1)(i) | $ 70,000 | reported taxable income |
| | + 33,500 | (add all adjustments) |
| | $103,500 | tax = $39,685 ("total tax liability") |
| (ii) | $ 70,000 | reported taxable income |

| | | |
|---|---:|---|
| | + 28,500 | (all adjustments other than those with respect to items that are both |
| | | tax motivated and fraudulent or negligent) |
| | $ 98,500 | tax = $37,185 ("tax liability without regard to fraudulent or negligent tax motivated items") |
| (iii) | $ 70,000 | reported taxable income |
| | + 21,000 | (all adjustments other than those with respect to items that are fraudulent or negligent) |
| | $ 91,000 | tax = $33,435 ("tax liability without regard to fraudulent or negligent items") |
| (iv) | $ 70,000 | reported taxable income |
| | + 4,000 | (all adjustments other than those with respect to items that are either tax |
| | | motivated or fraudulent or negligent) |
| | $ 74,000 | tax = $25,091 ("tax liability without regard to tax motivated or fraudulent or negligent items") |

(2) The tax motivated underpayment attributable to fraudulent or negligent items is $2,500 ((i)-(ii) or $39,685-$37,185).

(3) The tax motivated underpayment is $10,844 ((2) + (iii) − (iv)) or $2,500 + ($33,435 − $25,091)). Interest on $10,844 is computed at the 120 percent rate.

(4) The underpayment attributable to fraudulent or negligent items is $6,250 ((i) − (iii) or $39,685 − $33,435). The section 6653 addition to tax is 50 percent of the interest on $6,250, computed at the 120 percent rate on an amount equal to the tax motivated underpayment attributable to fraudulent or negligent items ($2,500) and at the adjusted rate on the remainder ($3,750).

(5) In summary, therefore, the total underpayment is $16,514 (total tax liability ($39,685) less reported tax liability ($23,171)) of which $10,844 accrues interest at the 120 percent rate and $5,670 ($16,514 − $10,844) accrues interest at the adjusted rate. In addition, $6,250 of the underpayment is subject to the section 6653(a)(2) or section 6653(b)(2) addition to tax. The underlying interest, upon which the addition to tax is based, is computed using the 120 percent rate for the portion of the underpayment subject to section 6621(d) ($2,500) and the adjusted rate for the portion that is not subject to section 6621(d) ($3,750).

Q-7. Does the 120 percent rate apply to all tax motivated underpayments?

A-7. No. The 120 percent rate applies only if the tax motivated underpayment for the taxable year is substantial. A tax motivated underpayment is substantial only if it exceeds $1,000. If, for example, a taxpayer has a $600 underpayment attributable to a valuation overstatement (within the meaning of section 6659(c)(1)) and a $500 underpayment attributable to a loss disallowed under section 465(a), the amount of the tax motivated underpayment is $1,100. Because the amount of the tax motivated underpayment is thus substantial, the 120 percent rate applies.

Q-8. How do carryovers affect the amount of the tax motivated underpayment and the amount of the underpayment attributable to fraudulent or negligent items?

A-8. For purposes of A-5 and A-6 of this section, a net operating loss carryover, capital loss carryover, or credit carryover is treated as a deduction or credit in the year in which taken into account. In any computation of tax liability required under A-5 or A-6 of this section (i.e., total tax liability, tax liability without regard to tax motivated transactions, etc.), the amount of such deduction or credit is the amount of the carryover determined as if the taxpayer had properly reported in each taxable year all items of income, gain, loss, deduction, or credit affecting the amount of the carryover other than adjustments of a type not taken into account in such computation of tax liability. A net operating loss carryback, capital loss carryback, or credit carryback is not taken into account, however, in determining the amount of the tax motivated underpayment or the amount of the underpayment attributable to fraud or negligence for periods before the last date prescribed for filing the income tax return for the taxable year in which the carryback arises (determined without regard to extensions).

Q-9. What amount is subject to the 120 percent rate if the amount of a taxpayer's unpaid tax for a year is less than the taxpayer's substantial tax motivated underpayment?

A-9. The 120 percent rate applies with respect to the lesser of—

(1) The amount of unpaid tax for the taxable year determined in accordance with § 301.6601-1; or

(2) The substantial tax motivated underpayment for the taxable year.

Q-10. What is the effective date for the 120 percent rate?

A-10. The 120 percent rate applies to interest accruing on a deficiency attributable to a substantial tax motivated underpayment after December 31, 1984, including interest accruing with respect to trans-

actions described in A-3 and A-4 of this section, regardless of the date prescribed for payment of the tax.

*Example.* Taxpayer A files his income tax return on April 15, 1983 (the last date prescribed for payment of tax for taxable year 1982 under section 6601). In January 1985, Taxpayer A files a petition in the Tax Court in response to a statutory notice of deficiency for taxable year 1982, which includes a tax motivated underpayment of $10,000. In September 1986, the Tax Court enters a decision for the Internal Revenue Service. Under section 6601, interest accrues at the adjusted rate, compounded daily, on tax motivated underpayments outstanding before January 1, 1985, and at the 120 percent rate, compounded daily, on amounts outstanding after December 31, 1984. The underpayment that is subject to the 120 percent rate includes both the $10,000 tax motivated underpayment and the interest that accrued on the underpayment at the adjusted rate from April 16, 1983, through December 31, 1984.

Q-11. Can a taxpayer stop the running of interest on a tax motivated underpayment by application of a remittance?

A-11. Yes. The running of interest on a tax liability stops on the date the remittance (either a payment of tax or a deposit in the nature of a cash bond) is received by the Internal Revenue Service, regardless of when the liability is assessed or the remittance is actually applied against the taxpayer's account. A taxpayer must make a remittance for both the tax liability and the interest that has accrued as of the date of remittance to stop the running of interest on both the tax liability and the accrued interest with respect to the liability. (See Rev. Proc. 84-58.) Taxpayers cannot make partial remittances applicable only to tax motivated underpayments. Under A-9 of this section, the 120 percent rate applies to the amount of unpaid tax to the extent that amount does not exceed the tax motivated underpayment. Therefore, a partial remittance is applied first to any tax due that is not attributable to a tax motivated underpayment. The excess of the partial remittance over tax that is not attributable to a tax motivated underpayment, if any, will then be applied to tax due that is attributable to a tax motivated underpayment.

Q-12. Does the 120 percent rate apply to interest accruing on interest, penalties, additional amounts, or additions to tax as provided in section 6601(e)(2)?

A-12. The 120 percent rate applies only to taxes imposed by subtitle A (income taxes) and to interest accrued with respect to such taxes. The penalties, additional amounts, and additions to tax specified in section 6601(e)(2) are not imposed by subtitle A and are not, therefore, included in the amount of a tax motivated underpayment. They are, however, included in the amount of unpaid tax for purposes of A-9 of this section.

*Example.* Taxpayer A, for taxable year 1984, has a $10,000 tax motivated underpayment and a $2,000 addition to tax for a total unpaid tax of $12,000. If A makes a $5,000 payment of tax, he will still have a $10,000 tax motivated underpayment but will now have only $7,000 of unpaid tax. Pursuant to A-9 of this section, therefore, the 120 percent rate would apply to the $7,000 of unpaid tax. [Temporary Reg. § 301.6621-2T.]

☐ [*T.D.* 7998, 12-26-84.]

### [Reg. § 301.6621-3]

**§ 301.6621-3. Higher interest rate payable on large corporate underpayments.**—(a) *In general.*—Section 6621 establishes the interest rate for purposes of computing the amount of interest that must be paid under section 6601, relating to interest on underpayments of tax. Section 6621(a)(2) provides that the underpayment rate is the sum of the Federal short-term rate (determined under section 6621(b)) plus 3 percentage points. That underpayment rate is referred to hereinafter as the "section 6621(a)(2) rate." Section 6621(c) and this section, however, provide that the underpayment rate on any large corporate underpayment is the sum of the Federal short-term rate (determined under section 6621(b)) plus 5 percentage points. This higher underpayment rate is referred to hereinafter as the "section 6621(c) rate." The section 6621(c) rate applies only for periods after the applicable date (as determined in paragraph (c) of this section).

(b) *Large corporate underpayment.*—(1) *Defined.*—For purposes of section 6621(c) and this section, "large corporate underpayment" means any underpayment of a tax by a C corporation for any taxable period if the amount of the threshold underpayment of the tax (as defined in paragraph (b)(2)(ii) of this section) for that taxable period exceeds $100,000.

(2) *Underpayment of a tax.*—(i) *In general.*—As used in section 6621(c) and this section, "underpayment of a tax" means the excess of a tax imposed by the Internal Revenue Code over the amount of such tax paid on or before the last date prescribed for payment. Except as provided in paragraph (b)(2)(ii) of this section, "tax" for such purposes includes interest, penalties, additional amounts, and additions to tax. *See* sections 6601(e)(1), 6665(a), and 6671(a). Thus, the section 6621(c) rate generally applies to any interest, penalties, additional

amounts, and additions to tax, as well as to the underlying tax with respect to which such amounts are imposed.

(ii) *Threshold underpayment of a tax.*—Solely for purposes of this section and not for any other purpose under section 6621(c) or elsewhere in the interpretation or administration of the federal tax laws, a "threshold underpayment of a tax" is the excess of a tax imposed by the Internal Revenue Code (exclusive of interest, penalties, additional amounts, and additions to tax) for the taxable period over the amount of such tax paid on or before the last date prescribed for payment. Thus, any payments made after the last date prescribed for payment (for example, by way of an amended return) will not affect the existence of a threshold underpayment. In determining whether there is a threshold underpayment, different types of taxes (such as income tax and FICA tax) and amounts that relate to different taxable periods are not added together.

(iii) *When determined.*—(A) *In general.*—The existence of a threshold underpayment of a tax and the amount of a large corporate underpayment are generally determined only when an assessment is made with respect to the taxable period. Thus, the amount of a deficiency or proposed deficiency set forth in a letter or notice pursuant to which the applicable date is determined (under paragraph (c) of this section) does not determine whether there is a large corporate underpayment.

(B) *Judicial determinations.*—Notwithstanding any prior assessment made with respect to a taxable period, the section 6621(c) rate does not apply if, after a federal court determines the taxpayer's liability for a period, the threshold underpayment for that taxable period does not exceed $100,000. See *Example 3* in paragraph (d) of this section.

(iv) *Special rule.*—The section 6621(c) rate is not used to compute the interest charges that a taxpayer timely assesses against itself in return for using a method of tax accounting or reporting that defers the payment of tax, such as the interest charges relating to passive foreign investment companies under section 1291(c) and installment obligations of nondealers under section 453A(c). However, to the extent such charges are not paid on or before the last date prescribed for payment and therefore become part of an underpayment of a tax, the section 6621(c) rate will apply to such amounts for periods after the applicable date (as determined in paragraph (c) of this section).

(3) *C corporation defined.*—For purposes of section 6621(c)(3)(A) and this section, "C corporation" means, with respect to any taxable period, a corporation that is a C corporation during any part of the taxable period. Interest on a large corporate underpayment for a taxable period continues to be imposed at the section 6621(c) rate even if during or after the taxable period—

(i) The taxpayer ceases to be a C corporation; or

(ii) The underpayment becomes the liability of a successor or transferee that is not a C corporation.

(4) *Taxable period.*—For purposes of section 6621(c) and this section, the "taxable period" is the taxable year in the case of any tax imposed by subtitle A of the Internal Revenue Code. In the case of any other tax, the "taxable period" is the period to which the underpayment relates. For example, the taxable period for an underpayment of FICA taxes is the calendar quarter. If the underpayment does not relate to a particular period (for example, in the case of certain transactional excise taxes), the "taxable period" is the period covered by a return on which the tax is required to be shown.

(5) *Last date prescribed for payment.*—For purposes of this section, the "last date prescribed for payment" means the last date prescribed for payment as determined, without regard to any extension of time, under section 6601(b).

(c) *Applicable date.*—(1) *In general.*—The section 6621(c) rate applies only to periods after the applicable date. Pursuant to the effective date of section 6621(c) and paragraph (e) of this section, however, the section 6621(c) rate will not apply prior to January 1, 1991, even if the applicable date is prior to December 31, 1990. A letter or notice relating to a particular type of tax creates an applicable date only for that type of tax. For example, a letter or notice with respect to FUTA tax will not create an applicable date with respect to income tax for the same taxable year.

(2) *When deficiency procedures apply.*—The applicable date, in the case of any underpayment of a tax to which the deficiency procedures of subchapter B of Chapter 63 of the Internal Revenue Code apply, is the 30th day after the earlier of—

(i) The date on which the Service sends the taxpayer the first letter of proposed deficiency that allows the taxpayer an opportunity

for administrative review in the Service's Office of Appeals (commonly called a "30-day letter"); or

(ii) The date on which the Service sends a deficiency notice under section 6212 of the Internal Revenue Code (commonly called a "90-day letter").

(3) *When deficiency procedures do not apply.*—The applicable date, in the case of any underpayment of a tax to which the deficiency procedures do not apply, is the 30th day after the date on which the Service sends the first letter or notice that notifies the taxpayer of an assessment or proposed assessment of the tax. In the case of income taxes, for example, the deficiency procedures do not apply to amounts shown as due on the taxpayer's return if the taxpayer fails to remit the full amount on or before the last date prescribed for payment, and to amounts attributable to mathematical or clerical errors on a return (unless a request for abatement is filed by the taxpayer under section 6213(b)). Because no 30-day letter or 90-day letter is issued to the taxpayer in such cases, the applicable date is the 30th day after the date on which an assessment notice under section 6303 of the Internal Revenue Code is sent.

(4) *Partnership items.*—For purposes of section 6621(c) and this paragraph (c), 60-day letters and the notices described in sections 6223(a)(1) and 6223(a)(2) (relating to administrative proceedings at the partnership level) are not treated as letters of proposed deficiency that allow the taxpayer an opportunity for administrative review in the Service's Office of Appeals, deficiency notices under section 6212 of the Internal Revenue Code, or letters or notices that notify the taxpayer of an assessment or proposed assessment of the tax. Thus, in the absence of any other letter or notice described in paragraph (c)(2) or (c)(3) of this section that establishes an earlier applicable date, the applicable date in the case of any underpayment of a tax attributable, in whole or in part, to a partnership item (as defined in section 6231(a)(3)) is the 30th day after the date on which the Service sends the first letter or notice that notifies the taxpayer of an assessment of the tax.

(5) *Exception for payment of amount shown as due.*—(i) *In general.*—A letter or notice will be disregarded for purposes of determining the applicable date if the taxpayer makes a payment equal to the amount shown as due in the letter or notice within 30 days from the date that the Service sends the letter or notice.

(ii) *Special transition rule.*—A letter or notice sent by the Service prior to January 1, 1991, will be disregarded by the Service for purposes of determining the applicable date if the taxpayer makes a payment on or before January 31, 1991, equal to the amount shown as due in the letter or notice plus a reasonable estimate of the interest payable on such amount computed by applying the section 6621(a)(2) rate. If the taxpayer has received two or more letters or notices with respect to the same tax for the same taxable period and pays the amount shown as due in the last letter or notice sent prior to December 19, 1990, (plus a reasonable estimate of the interest), all of the prior letters and notices with respect to the same tax for the same taxable period will be disregarded under this paragraph (c)(5)(ii). In the case of an assessment notice, the payment of the amount of interest shown as due on the last assessment notice sent to the taxpayer prior to December 19, 1990, will be treated as a payment of a reasonable estimate of the interest payable on the amount shown in that assessment notice or in any prior assessment notice sent with respect to the same tax for the same taxable period. The special transition rule in this paragraph (c)(5)(ii) applies even if the payment is not made within 30 days of the date on which the Service sent the letter or notice.

(iii) *Amount shown as due.*—For purposes of section 6621(c)(2)(B)(ii) and this paragraph (c)(5), the "amount shown as due" in any letter or notice means the total amount of tax, as well as any interest, penalties, additional amounts, and additions to tax that are set forth in the letter or notice. A deposit in the nature of a cash bond will not be considered a payment of the amount shown as due.

(6) *Exception for withdrawn letters and notices.*—(i) *Letters of proposed deficiency.*—A letter of proposed deficiency will be disregarded for purposes of determining the applicable date if the letter of proposed deficiency is issued as a result of an administrative error either to the wrong taxpayer or for the wrong taxable period.

(ii) *Deficiency notices.*—A deficiency notice under section 6212 of the Internal Revenue Code will be disregarded for purposes of determining the applicable date if the deficiency notice is rescinded under section 6212(d).

(iii) *Assessment letters and notices.*—A letter or notice that notifies the taxpayer of an assessment or proposed assessment of tax will be disregarded for purposes of determining the applicable date if the full amount of tax assessed is subsequently abated.

(d) *Examples.*—The application of this section may be illustrated by the following examples.

*Example 1.* V, a C corporation, timely files Form 941 on January 31, 1991, for the fourth quarter of 1990. On September 1, 1992, the Service sends V a section 6303 notice and demand reflecting an additional FICA tax liability for that quarter of $90,000. Interest computed at the section 6621(a)(2) rate totals $15,000 as of September 1, 1992. Accordingly, V's underpayment of FICA tax for the fourth quarter of 1990 exceeds $100,000. However, V's $90,000 threshold underpayment of FICA tax for that taxable period is less than $100,000, so that the section 6621(c) rate will not apply to the underpayment for that taxable period.

*Example 2.* (i) W, a C corporation, timely files its 1990 income tax return on March 15, 1991, showing a liability of $95,000, of which W pays only $35,000 with the return. On June 1, 1991, the Service sends W an assessment notice reflecting the balance due of $60,000 plus interest computed at the section 6621(a)(2) rate. W pays all amounts due on August 1, 1991. On July 1, 1993, the Service sends W a 90-day letter (without having sent a 30-day letter) reflecting an additional income tax deficiency of $85,000 for the taxable year 1990. W files a petition in the Tax Court within 90 days. In 1995, the Tax Court determines a $50,000 income tax deficiency (exclusive of interest, penalties, additional amounts, and additions to tax) for 1990, which the Service promptly assesses against W.

(ii) As a result of the combination of the failure to timely pay the $60,000 of income tax reported as due on the return and the Tax Court's determination of an additional deficiency of $50,000, W's threshold underpayment of income tax for 1990 is $110,000. Because W is a C corporation and the threshold underpayment for 1990 exceeds $100,000, the section 6621(c) rate applies to W's 1990 large corporate underpayment for periods after the applicable date.

(iii) The applicable date is July 1, 1991, the 30th day after the date on which the Service sent W the first assessment notice.

(iv) From March 16, 1991, through July 1, 1991, interest on W's 1990 underpayment of income tax (including any interest, penalties, additional amounts, and additions to tax) is computed at the section 6621(a)(2) rate. From July 2, 1991, such interest is computed at the section 6621(c) rate.

(v) If W had paid the amount shown as due on the June 1, 1991, assessment notice on or before June 30, 1991, instead of on August 1, 1991, the applicable date would have been July 31, 1993.

(vi) Assume that W had paid the amount shown as due on the June 1, 1991, assessment notice on or before June 30, 1991. If W had made a $40,000 deposit in the nature of a cash bond on July 15, 1993, the applicable date would be July 31, 1993. Moreover, the deposit would have no effect on the existence or amount of W's threshold underpayment or large corporate underpayment for 1990. In such a case, however, when the Service assesses the amount due from W in 1995, the deposit would be treated as a payment made as of July 15, 1993, for purposes of computing interest due after that date. As a result, interest would accrue after July 15, 1993, (at the section 6621(c) rate) only on the portion of W's 1990 underpayment that exceeds the $40,000 deposit amount.

*Example 3.* (i) X, a C corporation, filed its 1989 income tax return on September 17, 1990, pursuant to an automatic extension. X enclosed payment of the $7,500 balance reported on the return as due (plus interest). On January 1, 1992, the Service sends X a written notification that X's 1989 income tax return is being examined. This written notification also contains a request that X provide supplemental information with respect to particular deductions totalling $1.5 million. On July 1, 1993, the Service sends X a 30-day letter proposing a $450,000 deficiency (without any reference to penalties, additional amounts, additions to tax, and interest) with respect to 1989. On December 15, 1993, the Service sends X a 90-day letter asserting a deficiency of $300,000 (excluding penalties, additional amounts, additions to tax, and other interest). X does not file a Tax Court petition and the Service assesses the $300,000 (plus interest and penalties) on April 1, 1994. On April 5, 1994, X pays the full amount assessed. Thereafter, X timely files an administrative claim for refund and a refund suit in federal district court for the amounts assessed on April 1, 1994. On September 30, 1995, the federal district court determines that, exclusive of interest and penalties, X overpaid its 1989 income tax by $250,000.

(ii) The April 1, 1994, assessment establishes at that time that X's threshold underpayment of income tax for 1989 is $300,000. Because X is a C corporation and the threshold underpayment for 1989 exceeds $100,000, X's underpayment of income tax for 1989 is a large corporate underpayment to which the section 6621(c) rate applies for periods after the applicable date. X's decision to file a refund claim does not affect, in and of itself, either the existence of a threshold underpayment or the amount of X's large corporate underpayment.

(iii) For purposes of determining the amount of interest to assess on April 1, 1994, the applicable date is July 31, 1993, the 30th day after the date on which the Service sent X a 30-day letter. The January

1, 1992, notice of examination and request for additional information has no effect on the applicable date. Similarly, the September 30, 1995, federal district court decision has no effect on the applicable date.

(iv) From March 16, 1990, through July 31, 1993, interest on X's 1989 underpayment of income tax (including any interest, penalties, additional amounts, and additions to tax) is computed at the section 6621(a)(2) rate. From August 1, 1993, through April 5, 1994, such interest is computed at the section 6621(c) rate.

(v) Because of the federal district court's decision that X's underpayment, exclusive of interest and penalties, was only $50,000, X does not have a large corporate underpayment of income tax for 1989. Thus, the interest X paid with respect to the remaining $250,000 in taxes (exclusive of interest and penalties) becomes part of the overpayment and will be refunded. In addition, any interest computed at the section 6621(c) rate for the period from August 1, 1993, through April 5, 1994, should be recomputed at the section 6621(a)(2) rate and the difference refunded.

*Example 4.* (i) Y, a C corporation, timely filed its 1989 income tax return on March 15, 1990, and enclosed payment of the amount reported on the return as due. On May 1, 1990, the Service sent to Y an assessment notice for $1,000 resulting from a math error on Y's return. Y did not request an abatement of the assessment pursuant to section 6213(b). Instead, Y paid the $1,000, plus interest, on July 31, 1990. On March 31, 1992, the Service sends Y a 90-day letter showing an income tax deficiency for 1989 of $125,000 (exclusive of interest, penalties, additional amounts, and additions to tax). No 30-day letter had been issued previously to Y in connection with its 1989 taxable year. Y does not file a petition with the Tax Court, but files an amended return for 1989 on April 15, 1992, showing $30,000 of tax due. Y pays this amount (plus interest from March 15, 1990, computed at the section 6621(a)(2) rate) with the amended return. Shortly thereafter, the Service assesses the $125,000 deficiency (plus interest) and credits the April 15, 1992, payment against the assessment.

(ii) Y's threshold underpayment for 1989 is $125,000 notwithstanding Y's April 15, 1992, payment of $30,000. Because Y is a C corporation and the threshold underpayment for 1989 exceeds $100,000, Y has a large corporate underpayment of income tax for the taxable period 1989 to which the section 6621(c) rate applies for periods after the applicable date.

(iii) Because Y paid the $1,000 amount shown as due on the math error assessment notice (plus interest) on or before January 31, 1991, the applicable date is April 30, 1992, the 30th day after the 90-day letter is sent.

(iv) From March 16, 1990, through April 30, 1992, interest is computed on Y's underpayment of income tax (including any interest, penalties, additional amounts, and additions to tax) at the section 6621(a)(2) rate. From May 1, 1992, such interest is computed at the section 6621(c) rate.

(v) If Y had not paid the $1,000 amount shown as due on the math error assessment notice (plus interest) on or before January 31, 1991, the applicable date would have been May 31, 1990, and interest would be computed at the section 6621(c) rate beginning on January 1, 1991. If, however, Y had timely requested an abatement of the assessment under section 6213(b), the applicable date would be April 30, 1992.

*Example 5.* (i) Effective January 1, 1993, Y converts from a C corporation to an S corporation. On January 31, 1993, Y files its 1992 FUTA tax return and encloses a payment equal to the amount reported as due on the return. On March 15, 1993, Y files its 1992 income tax return and encloses a payment equal to the amount reported as due on the return. On August 1, 1993, the Service sends to Y an assessment notice for $150,000 of FUTA tax, plus interest, with respect to calendar year 1992. Y pays the full amount shown as due in the assessment notice on August 7, 1993. On January 1, 1995, Y files an amended income tax return for 1992 showing $15,000 of tax due. Y pays this amount with the amended return. On February 10, 1995, the Service sends Y an assessment notice for the interest payable on the $15,000. Y pays this interest on February 13, 1995.

(ii) Y's threshold underpayment of FUTA tax for 1992 is $150,000. Because Y was a C corporation in 1992 and the threshold underpayment of FUTA tax for 1992 exceeds $100,000, Y has a large corporate underpayment of FUTA tax. However, Y's threshold underpayment of income tax for the same taxable period (*i.e.*, calendar 1992) is $15,000, so that Y does not have a large corporate underpayment of income tax for that year.

(iii) Because Y pays within 30 days the amount shown as due on the August 1, 1993, assessment notice, there is no applicable date with respect to the large corporate underpayment of FUTA tax for 1992.

(iv) All of the interest payable with respect to the 1992 underpayments of FUTA and income taxes is computed at the section 6621(a)(2) rate.

(v) If Y had not paid the amount shown as due on the August 1, 1993, FUTA tax assessment notice within 30 days, the applicable date would have been August 31, 1993, (the 30th day after the assessment notice is sent). Thus, interest would have been computed at the section 6621(c) rate after that date, even though Y is not at that time a C corporation.

(vi) If the amended 1992 income tax return Y files on January 1, 1995, had shown $115,000 of tax due instead of $15,000, Y's threshold underpayment of income tax for 1992 would have been $115,000. Because Y was a C corporation in 1992 and the threshold underpayment of income tax for that year would have exceeded $100,000, Y would have a large corporate underpayment of income tax for that year. However, because Y would have paid the amount shown as due in the February 10, 1995, assessment notice within 30 days of when that assessment notice was sent, there would have been no applicable date with respect to that large corporate underpayment and the section 6621(c) rate would have not applied.

*Example 6.* (i) On August 1, 1990, the Service sent to Z, a C corporation, an assessment notice for $200,000 of income tax, plus $30,000 in interest and penalties, with respect to calendar year 1988. Subsequent assessment notices were sent to Z on September 12, 1990, October 10, 1990, and November 14, 1990, each including additional interest. The November 14, 1990, assessment notice provided that the total amount of tax, interest and penalties due was $242,000. On December 31, 1990, Z pays $230,000. On February 13, 1991, the Service sends Z an assessment notice for the remaining balance (plus additional interest thereon). On December 31, 1991, Z pays all amounts owed as of that date in connection with its 1988 income tax liability.

(ii) Z's threshold underpayment of income tax for 1988 is $200,000. Because Z is a C corporation and its threshold underpayment of income tax for 1988 exceeds $100,000, Z has a large corporate underpayment for 1988 to which the section 6621(c) rate applies for periods after the applicable date.

(iii) Notwithstanding Z's payment of $230,000 on December 31, 1990, the applicable date with respect to the large corporate underpayment of 1988 income tax is August 31, 1990, the 30th day after the date on which the Service sent the first assessment notice.

(iv) From March 16, 1989, to December 31, 1990, interest is computed on Z's underpayment of income tax (including any interest, penalties, additional amounts and additions to tax) at the section 6621(a)(2) rate. From January 1, 1991, through December 31, 1991, interest is computed on that underpayment at the section 6621(c) rate.

(v) If Z had paid on or before January 31, 1991, the full $242,000 shown as due on the November 14, 1990, assessment notice, the applicable date with respect to any remaining unpaid interest would have been March 15, 1991, the 30th day after the Service sent the February 13, 1991, assessments notice.

(vi) The same result as in paragraph (v) of this *Example 6* would apply if the November 14, 1990, assessment notice had provided that only $150,000 was due with respect to calendar year 1988 (as a result of a correction by the Service of an error in its original August 1,

1990, assessment, and not as a result of any payment by Z), and if Z had paid that $150,000 on or before January 31, 1991.

(e) *Effective Date.*—Section 6621(c) and this section are effective for determining interest for periods after December 31, 1990, regardless of the taxable period to which the underlying tax may relate and even if the applicable date is prior to December 31, 1990. [Reg. § 301.6621-3.]

☐ [*T.D. 8447,* 11-10-92.]

## [Reg. § 301.6622-1]

**§ 301.6622-1. Interest compounded daily.**—(a) *General rule.*—Effective for interest accruing after December 31, 1982, in computing the amount of any interest required to be paid under the Internal Revenue Code of 1954 or sections 1961(c)(1) or 2411 of Title 28, United States Code, by the Commissioner or by the taxpayer, or in computing any other amount determined by reference to such amount of interest, or by reference to the interest rate established under section 6621, such interest or such other amount shall be compounded daily by dividing such rate of interest by 365 (366 in a leap year) and compounding such daily interest rate each day.

(b) *Exception.*—Paragraph (a) of this section shall not apply for purposes of determining the amount of any addition to tax under sections 6654 or 6655 (relating to failure to pay estimated income tax).

(c) *Applicability to unpaid amounts on December 31, 1982.*—(1) *In general.*—The unpaid interest (or other amount) that shall be compounded daily includes the interest (or other amount) accrued but unpaid on December 31, 1982.

(2) *Illustration.*—The provisions of this (c) may be illustrated by the following example.

*Example.* Individual A files a tax return for calendar year 1981 on April 15, 1982, showing a tax due of $10,000. A pays $10,000 on December 31, 1982, but A does not pay any interest with respect to this underpayment until March 1, 1983, on which date A paid all amounts of interest with respect to the $10,000 underpayment of tax. On December 31, 1982, A's unsatisfied interest liability was $1,424.66 ($10,000 × 20 percent × 260/365 days). Interest, compounded daily, accrues on this unsatisfied interest obligation beginning on January 1, 1983, until March 1, 1983, the date the total interest obligation is satisfied. On March 1, 1983, the total interest obligation is $1,462.62, computed as follows:

| Item | Amount |
|---|---|
| Unpaid tax at December 31, 1982 | —0— |
| Unpaid interest at December 31, 1982 | $1,424.66 |
| Total unsatisfied obligation at December 31, 1982 | $1,424.66 |
| Interest from December 31, 1982, to March 1, 1983, at 16 percent per year compounded daily | $37.96 |
| Total due, March 1, 1983 | $1,462.62 |

[Reg. § 301.6622-1.]

☐ [*T.D. 7907,* 8-22-83.]

# Additions to the Tax, Additional Amounts, and Assessable Penalties

## ADDITIONS TO TAX AND ADDITIONAL AMOUNTS

See p. 20,601 for regulations not amended to reflect law changes

### [Reg. § 53.6651-1]

**§ 53.6651-1. Failure to file tax return or to pay tax.**—(a) *General rules.*—For general rules relating to the failure to file tax return or to pay tax, see the regulations under section 6651 contained in Part 301 of this chapter (Regulations on Procedure and Administration).

(b) *Special rule where foundation files return.*—(1) Except as provided in paragraph (b)(2) of this section, in the case of tax imposed by section 4941(a)(1) on any disqualified person, reasonable cause shall be presumed, for purposes of section 6651(a)(1), where the private foundation or trust described in section 4947(a)(2) files a return in good faith and such return indicates no tax liability with respect to such tax on the part of such disqualified person.

(2) Paragraph (b)(1) of this section shall not apply where the disqualified person knew of facts which, if known by the foundation, would have precluded the foundation from making the return, as filed, in good faith. [Reg. § 53.6651-1.]

☐ [*T.D. 7368,* 7-15-75.]

### [Reg. § 301.6651-1]

**§ 301.6651-1. Failure to file tax return or to pay tax.**—(a) *Addition to the tax.*—(1) *Failure to file tax return.*—In case of failure to file a return required under authority of—

(i) Subchapter A, chapter 61 of the Code, relating to returns and records (other than sections 6015 and 6016, relating to declarations of estimated tax, and part III thereof, relating to information returns);

(ii) Subchapter A, chapter 51 of the Code, relating to distilled spirits, wines, and beer;

(iii) Subchapter A, chapter 52 of the Code, relating to cigars, cigarettes, and cigarette papers and tubes; or

(iv) Subchapter A, chapter 53 of the Code, relating to machine guns, destructive devices, and certain other firearms; and

The regulations thereunder, on or before the date prescribed for filing (determined with regard to any extension of time for such filing), there shall be added to the tax required to be shown on the return the amount specified below unless the failure to file the return within the prescribed time is shown to the satisfaction of the district director, the director of the service center, or, as provided in paragraph (c) of this section, the Assistant Regional Commissioner (Alcohol, Tobacco and Firearms), to be due to reasonable cause and not to willful neglect. The amount to be added to the tax is 5 percent thereof if the failure is for not more than 1 month, with an additional 5 percent for each additional month or fraction thereof during which the failure continues, but not to exceed 25 percent in the aggregate. The amount of any addition under this subparagraph shall be reduced by the amount of the addition under subparagraph (2) of this paragraph for any month to which an addition to tax applies under both subparagraphs (1) and (2) of this paragraph (a).

(2) *Failure to pay tax shown on return.*—In case of failure to pay the amount shown as tax on any return (required to be filed after December 31, 1969, without regard to any extension of time for filing thereof) specified in subparagraph (1) of this paragraph on or before the date prescribed for payment of such tax (determined with regard to any extension of time for payment), there shall be added to the tax shown on the return the amount specified below unless the failure to pay the tax within the prescribed time is shown to the satisfaction of the district director or the director of the service center to be due to reasonable cause and not to willful neglect. Except as provided in paragraph (a)(4) of this section, the amount to be added to the tax is 0.5 percent of the amount of tax shown on the return if the failure is for not more than 1 month, with an additional 0.5 percent for each additional month or fraction thereof during which the failure continues, but not to exceed 25 percent in the aggregate.

(3) *Failure to pay tax not shown on return.*—In the case of failure to pay any amount of any tax required to be shown on a return specified in paragraph (a)(1) of this section that is not so shown (including an assessment made pursuant to section 6213(b)) within 21 calendar days from the date of the notice and demand (10 business days if the amount assessed and shown on the notice and demand equals or exceeds $100,000) with respect to any notice and demand made after December 31, 1996, there will be added to the amount stated in the notice and demand the amount specified below unless the failure to pay the tax within the prescribed time is shown to the satisfaction of the district director or the director of the service center to be due to reasonable cause and not to willful neglect. Except as provided in paragraph (a)(4) of this section, the amount to be added to the tax is 0.5 percent of the amount stated in the notice and demand if the failure is for not more than 1 month, with an additional 0.5 percent for each additional month or fraction thereof during which the failure continues, but not to exceed 25 percent in the aggregate. For purposes of this paragraph (a)(3), see § 301.6601-1(f)(5) for the definition of *calendar day* and *business day.*

(4) *Reduction of failure to pay penalty during the period an installment agreement is in effect.*—(i) *In general.*—In the case of a return filed by an individual on or before the due date for the return (including extensions)—

(A) The amount added to tax for a month or fraction thereof is determined by using 0.25 percent instead of 0.5 percent under paragraph (a)(2) of this section if at any time during the month an installment agreement under section 6159 is in effect for the payment of such tax; and

(B) The amount added to tax for a month or fraction thereof is determined by using 0.25 percent instead of 0.5 percent under paragraph (a)(3) of this section if at any time during the month an installment agreement under section 6159 is in effect for the payment of such tax.

(ii) *Effective date.*—This paragraph (a)(4) applies for purposes of determining additions to tax for months beginning after December 31, 1999.

(b) *Month defined.*—(1) If the date prescribed for filing the return or paying tax is the last day of a calendar month, each succeeding calendar month or fraction thereof during which the failure to file or pay tax continues shall constitute a month for purposes of section 6651.

(2) If the date prescribed for filing the return or paying tax is a date other than the last day of a calendar month, the period which terminates with the date numerically corresponding thereto in the succeeding calendar month and each such successive period shall constitute a month for purposes of section 6651. If, in the month of February, there is no date corresponding to the date prescribed for filing the return or paying tax, the period from such date in January through the last day of February shall constitute a month for purposes of section 6651. Thus, if a return is due on January 30, the first month shall end on February 28 (or 29 if a leap year), and the succeeding months shall end on March 30, April 30, etc.

(3) If a return is not timely filed or tax is not timely paid, the fact that the date prescribed for filing the return or paying tax, or the corresponding date in any succeeding calendar month, falls on a Saturday, Sunday, or a legal holiday is immaterial in determining the number of months for which the addition to the tax under section 6651 applies.

(c) *Showing of reasonable cause.*—(1) Except as provided in subparagraphs (3) and (4) of this paragraph, a taxpayer who wishes to avoid the addition to the tax for failure to file a tax return or pay tax must make an affirmative showing of all facts alleged as a reasonable cause for his failure to file such return or pay such tax on time in the form of a written statement containing a declaration that it is made under penalties of perjury. Such statement should be filed with the district director or the director of the service center with whom the return is required to be filed; *Provided,* That where special tax return of liquor dealers are delivered to an alcohol, tobacco and firearms officer working under the supervision of the Regional Director, Bureau of Alcohol, Tobacco and Firearms, such statement may be delivered with the return. If the district director, the director of the service center, or, where applicable, the Regional Director, Bureau of Alcohol, Tobacco and Firearms, determines that the delinquency was due to a reasonable cause and not to willful neglect, the addition to the tax will not be assessed. If the taxpayer exercised ordinary business care and prudence and was nevertheless unable to file the return within the prescribed time, then the delay is due to a reasonable cause. A failure to pay will be considered to be due to reasonable cause to the extent that the taxpayer has made a satisfactory showing that he exercised ordinary business care and prudence in providing for payment of his tax liability and was nevertheless either unable to pay the tax or would suffer an undue hardship (as described in § 1.6161-1(b) of this chapter) if he paid on the due date. In determining whether the taxpayer was unable to pay the tax in spite of the exercise of ordinary business care and prudence in providing for payment of his tax liability, consideration will be given to all the facts and circumstances of the taxpayer's financial situation, including the amount and nature of the taxpayer's expenditures in light of the income (or other amounts) he could, at the time of such expenditures, reasonably expect to receive prior to the date prescribed for the payment of the tax. Thus, for example, a taxpayer who incurs lavish or extravagant living expenses in an amount such that the remainder of his assets and anticipated income will be insufficient to pay his tax, has not exercised ordinary business care and prudence in providing for the payment of his tax liability. Further, a taxpayer who invests funds in speculative or illiquid assets has not exercised ordinary business care and prudence in providing for the payment of his tax liability unless, at the time of the investment, the remainder of the taxpayer's assets and estimated income will be sufficient to pay his tax or it can be reasonably foreseen that the speculative or illiquid investment made by the taxpayer can be utilized (by sale or as security for a loan) to realize sufficient funds to satisfy the tax liability. A taxpayer will be considered to have exercised ordinary business care and prudence if he made reasonable efforts to conserve sufficient assets in marketable form to satisfy his tax liability and nevertheless was unable to pay all or a portion of the tax when it became due.

(2) In determining if the taxpayer exercised ordinary business care and prudence in providing for the payment of his tax liability, consideration will be given to the nature of the tax which the taxpayer has failed to pay. Thus, for example, facts and circumstances which, because of the taxpayer's efforts to conserve assets in marketable form, may constitute reasonable cause for nonpayment of income taxes may not constitute reasonable cause for failure to pay over taxes described in section 7501 that are collected or withheld from any other person.

(3) If, for a taxable year ending on or after December 31, 1995, an individual taxpayer satisfies the requirement of § 1.6081-4(a) of this chapter (relating to automatic extension of time for filing an individual income tax return), reasonable cause will be presumed, for the period of the extension of time to file, with respect to any underpayment of tax if—

(i) The excess of the amount of tax shown on the individual income tax return over the amount of tax paid on or before the regular due date of the return (by virtue of tax withheld by the employer, estimated tax payments, and any payment with an application for extension of time to file pursuant to § 1.6081-4 of this chapter) is no greater than 10 percent of the amount of tax shown on the individual income tax return; and

(ii) Any balance due shown on the individual income tax return is remitted with the return.

(4) If, for a taxable year ending on or after December 31, 1972, a corporate taxpayer satisfies the requirements of § 1.6081-3(a) (relating to an automatic extension of time for filing a corporation income tax return), reasonable cause shall be presumed, for the period of the extension of time to file, with respect to any underpayment of tax if—

(i) The amount of tax (determined without regard to any prepayment thereof) shown on Form 7004, or the amount of tax paid on or before the regular due date of the return, is at least 90 percent of the amount of tax shown on the taxpayer's Form 1120, and

Reg. § 301.6651-1(c)(4)(i)

(ii) Any balance due shown on the Form 1120 is paid on, or before the due date of the return, including any extensions of time for filing.

(d) *Penalty imposed on net amount due.*—(1) *Credits against the tax.*—The amount of tax required to be shown on the return for purposes of section 6651(a)(1) and the amount shown as tax on the return for purposes of section 6651(a)(2) shall be reduced by the amount of any part of the tax which is paid on or before the date prescribed for payment of the tax and by the amount of any credit against the tax which may be claimed on the return.

(2) *Partial payments.*—(i) The amount of tax required to be shown on the return for purposes of section 6651(a)(2) shall, for the purpose of computing the addition for any month, be reduced by the amount of any part of the tax which is paid after the date prescribed for payment and on or before the first day of such month.

(ii) The amount of tax stated in the notice and demand for purposes of section 6651(a)(3) shall, for the purpose of computing the addition for any month, be reduced by the amount of any part of the tax which is paid before the first day of such month.

(e) *No addition to tax if fraud penalty assessed.*—No addition to the tax under section 6651 shall be assessed with respect to an underpayment of tax if a 50-percent addition to the tax for fraud is assessed with respect to the same underpayment under section 6653(b). See section 6653(d).

(f) *Examples.*—The provisions of this section may be illustrated by the following examples:

*Example (1).* (a) Under section 6072(a), income tax returns of individuals on a calendar year basis must be filed on or before the 15th day of April following the close of the calendar year. Assume an individual filed his income tax return for the calendar year 1969 on July 20, 1970, and the failure to file on or before the prescribed date is not due to reasonable cause. The tax shown on the return is $800 and a deficiency of $200 is subsequently assessed, making the tax required to be shown on the return, $1,000. Of this amount, $300 has been paid by withholding from wages and $400 has been paid as estimated tax. The balance due as shown on the return of $100 ($800 shown as tax on the return less $700 previously paid) is paid on August 21, 1970. The failure to pay on or before the prescribed date is not due to reasonable cause. There will be imposed, in addition to interest, an additional amount under section 6651(a)(2) of $2.50, which is 2.5 percent (2% for the 4 months from April 16 through August 15, and 0.5% for the fractional part of the month from August 16 through August 21) of the net amount due as shown on the return of $100 ($800 shown on the return less $700 paid on or before April 15). There will also be imposed an additional amount under section 6651(a)(1) of $58, determined as follows:

| | |
|---|---:|
| 20 percent (5% per month for the 3 months from April 16 through July 15 and 5% for the fractional part of the month from July 16 through July 20) of the net amount due of $300 ($1,000 required to be shown on the return less $700 paid on or before April 15) . . . . . . . . . . . . . | $60 |
| Reduced by the amount of the addition imposed under section 6651(a)(2) for those months . . . . . . . . . . . . . . . . . | 2 |
| Addition to tax under section 6651(a)(1) . . . . . . . . . . . . | $58 |

(b) A notice and demand for the $200 deficiency is issued on January 8, 1971, but the taxpayer does not pay the deficiency until December 23, 1971. In addition to interest there will be imposed an additional amount under section 6651(a)(3) of $10, determined as follows:

| | |
|---|---:|
| Addition computed without regard to limitation: | |
| 6 percent (5¹/₂% for the 11 months from January 19, 1971, through December 18, 1971, and 0.5% for the fractional part of the month from December 19 through December 23) of the amount stated in the notice and demand ($200) . . . . . . . . . . . . . . . | $12 |
| Limitation on addition: | |
| 25 percent of the amount stated in the notice and demand ($200) . . . . . . . . . . . | $50 |
| Reduced by the part of the addition under section 6651(a)(1) for failure to file attributable to the $200 deficiency (20% of $200) . . . . . . . . . . . . . . . . . . | $40 |
| Maximum amount of the addition under section 6651(a)(3) . . . . . . . . . . . . . . . . . . . . . . . . . . . . . . . . | $10 |

*Example (2).* An individual files his income tax return for the calendar year 1969 on December 2, 1970, and such delinquency is not due to reasonable cause. The balance due, as shown on the return, of $500 is paid when the return is filed on December 2, 1970. In addition to interest and the addition for failure to pay under section 6651(a)(2)

of $20, (8 months at 0.5% per month, 4%) there will also be imposed an additional amount under section 6651(a)(1) of $112.50, determined as follows:

| | |
|---|---:|
| Penalty at 5% for maximum of 5 months, 25% of $500 | $125.00 |
| Less reduction for the amount of the addition under section 6651(a)(2): | |
| Amount imposed under section 6651(a)(2) for failure to pay for the months in which there is also an addition for failure to file—2¹/₂ percent for the 5 months April 16 through September 15 of the net amount due ($500) . . . . . . . . . . . . . . . . . | $12.50 |
| Addition to tax under section 6651(a)(1) . . . . . . . . | $112.50 |

(g) *Treatment of returns prepared by the Secretary.*—(1) *In general.*—A return prepared by the Secretary under section 6020(b) will be disregarded for purposes of determining the amount of the addition to tax for failure to file any return pursuant to paragraph (a)(1) of this section. However, the return prepared by the Secretary will be treated as a return filed by the taxpayer for purposes of determining the amount of the addition to tax for failure to pay the tax shown on any return and for failure to pay the tax required to be shown on a return that is not so shown pursuant to paragraphs (a)(2) and (3) of this section, respectively.

(2) *Effective date.*—This paragraph (g) applies to returns the due date for which (determined without regard to extensions) is after July 30, 1996. [Reg. § 301.6651-1.]

☐ [*T.D.* 6268, 11-15-75. *Amended by T.D.* 6498, 10-24-60; *T.D.* 6585, 7-21-71; *T.D.* 7160, 2-1-72; *T.D.* 7260, 2-9-73; *T.D.* 8651, 1-3-96; *T.D.* 8703, 12-30-96; *T.D.* 8725, 7-21-97; *T.D.* 8895, 8-17-2000 *and T.D.* 9163, 12-6-2004.]

### [Reg. § 301.6652-1]

**§ 301.6652-1. Failure to file certain information returns.**—(a) *Returns with respect to payments made in calendar years after 1962.*—(1) *Payments of dividends, interest, or patronage dividends aggregating $10 or more.*—In the case of each failure to file a statement required by—

(i) Section 6042(a)(1), relating to information returns with respect to payments of dividends aggregating $10 or more in a calendar year, in effect with respect to payments made after December 31, 1962,

(ii) Section 6044(a)(1), relating to information returns with respect to certain payments by cooperatives aggregating $10 or more in a calendar year, in effect with respect to payments made on or after the first day of the first taxable year of the cooperative beginning after December 31, 1962, with respect to patronage occurring on or after such first day, or

(iii) Section 6049(a)(1), relating to information returns with respect to payments of interest aggregating $10 or more in a calendar year, in effect with respect to payments made after December 31, 1962, and the regulations under such section, within the time prescribed for filing such statement (determined with regard to any extension of time for filing), there shall be paid by the person failing to so file the statement $10 for each such statement not so filed. However, the total amount imposed on the delinquent person for all such failures under section 6652(a) and this section during any calendar year shall not exceed $25,000.

(2) *Other payments; statements with respect to tips.*—In the case of each failure—

(i) To file a statement of a payment made to another person required under authority of section 6041, relating to information returns with respect to certain information at source, or section 6051(d), relating to information returns with respect to payments of wages as defined in section 3401(a), or section 6050A(a), relating to information returns with respect to remuneration of certain crew members defined in section 3121(b)(20), or

(ii) To furnish a statement required under authority of section 6053(b), relating to statements furnished by employers with respect to tips, or section 6050A(b), relating to statements furnished by fishing boat operators with respect to remuneration of certain crew members, within the time prescribed by regulations under those sections for filing such statements (determined with regard to any extension of time for filing), there shall be paid by the person failing to so file the statement $1 for each such statement not so filed. However, the total amount imposed on the delinquent person for all such failure during any calendar year shall not exceed $1,000.

(b) *Returns with respect to payments made in calendar years before 1963 and to certain payments by cooperatives after 1962.*—In the case of each failure to file a statement, with respect to a payment to another person, required under authority of—

(1) Section 6041, relating to information returns with respect to certain information at source, in effect with respect to payments made before 1963,

(2) Section 6042(1), relating to information returns with respect to payments of corporate dividends, in effect with respect to payments made before 1963,

(3) Section 6044, relating to information returns with respect to payments of patronage dividends, in effect with respect to payments made by a cooperative with respect to patronage occurring before the first day of the first taxable year of the cooperative beginning after December 31, 1962, or

(4) Section 6051(d), relating to information returns with respect to payments of wages as defined in section 3401(a), in effect with respect to payments made before 1963,

and the regulations under such section, within the time prescribed for filing such statement (determined with regard to any extension of time for filing), there shall be paid by the person failing to so file such statement $1 for each such statement not so filed. However, the total amount imposed on the delinquent person for all such failures during any calendar year shall not exceed $1,000.

(c) *Returns with respect to reporting payments of wages in the form of group-term life insurance provided in a calendar year after December 31, 1963.*—In the case of each failure to file a return required by section 6052(a), relating to reporting payment of wages in the form of group-term life insurance provided for any employee on his life in a calendar year after December 31, 1963, and the regulations under such section, within the time prescribed for filing such return (determined with regard to any extension of time for filing), there shall be paid by the person failing to so file such return $10 for each such return not so filed. However, the total amount imposed on the delinquent person for all such failures under section 6652(a) and this section during any calendar year shall not exceed $25,000.

(d) *Returns with respect to transfer of stock or record title thereto pursuant to options exercised on or after January 1, 1964.*—In the case of each failure to file a statement of the transfer of stock or of record title thereto as required by section 6039(a) and the regulations under such section within the time prescribed for filing such statement (determined with regard to any extension of time for filing), there shall be paid by the corporation failing to so file such statement, $10 for each such statement not so filed. However, the total amount imposed on the delinquent corporation for all such failures under section 6652(a) and this section during any calendar year shall not exceed $25,000.

(e) *Manner of payment.*—The amount imposed under subsection (a), (b), or (c) of section 6652 and this section on any person shall be paid in the same manner as tax upon the issuance of a notice and demand therefor.

(f) *Showing of reasonable cause.*—The amount imposed by subsection (a), (b), or (c) of section 6652 shall not apply with respect to a failure to file a statement within the time prescribed if it is established to the satisfaction of the district director or the director of the internal revenue service center that such failure was due to reasonable cause and not to willful neglect. An affirmative showing of reasonable cause must be made in the form of a written statement, containing a declaration that it is made under the penalties of perjury, setting forth all the facts alleged as a reasonable cause.

(g) *Alcohol and tobacco taxes.*—For penalties for failure to file certain information returns with respect to alcohol and tobacco taxes, see, generally, subtitle E of the Code.

(h) *Tips.*—For regulations under section 6652(c) in respect of failure to report tips, see §31.6652-1 of this chapter (Employment Tax Regulations). [Reg. §301.6652-1.]

☐ [*T.D. 6268, 11-15-57. Amended by T.D. 6425, 11-10-59; T.D. 6585, 12-27-61; T.D. 6628, 12-27-62; T.D. 6887, 6-23-66; T.D. 7001, 1-17-69; T.D. 7127, 6-14-71 and T.D. 7716, 8-26-80.*]

### [Reg. §301.6652-2]

**§301.6652-2. Failure by exempt organizations and certain nonexempt organizations to file certain returns or to comply with section 6104(d) for taxable years beginning after December 31, 1969.**—(a) *Exempt organization or trust.*—In the case of a failure to file a return required by—

(1) Section 6033, relating to returns by exempt organizations, trusts described in section 4947(a)(1) and nonexempt private foundations,

(2) Section 6034, relating to returns by certain trusts, or

(3) Section 6043(b), relating to returns regarding the liquidation, dissolution, termination, or substantial contraction of an exempt organization, within the time and in the manner prescribed for filing such return (determined with regard to any extension of time for filing), unless it is shown that such failure is due to reasonable cause,

there shall be paid by the exempt organization or trust failing to file such return $10 for each day during which such failure continues. However, the total amount imposed on any exempt organization or trust under this paragraph for such failure with regard to any one return shall not exceed $5,000.

(b) *Managers.*—If an exempt organization or trust fails to file under section 6652(d)(1), the Commissioner may, by written demand, request that such organization or trust file the delinquent return within 90 days after the date of mailing of such demand, or within such additional period as the Commissioner shall determine is reasonable under the circumstances. If such organization or trust does not so file on or before the date specified in such demand, there shall be paid by the person or persons responsible for such failure to file $10 for each day after such date during which such failure continues, unless it is shown that such failure is due to reasonable cause. However, the total amount imposed under this paragraph on all persons responsible for such failure with regard to any one return shall not exceed $5,000.

(c) *Public inspection of private foundations' annual returns.*—(1) *In general.*—In the case of a failure to comply with the requirements of section 6104(d), relating to public inspection of private foundations' annual returns, within the time and in the manner prescribed for complying with section 6104(d), unless it is shown that such failure is due to reasonable cause, there shall be paid by the person or persons responsible for failing to comply with section 6104(d) $10 for each day during which such failure continues. However, the total amount imposed under this subparagraph on all persons responsible for any such failure with regard to any one annual return shall not exceed $5,000.

(2) *Amount imposed.*—The amount imposed under section 6652(d)(3) is $10 per day for a failure to comply with section 6104(d). For example, assume that an annual return must be filed by private foundation X on or before May 15, 1982, for the calendar year 1981. The foundation without reasonable cause does not comply with section 6104(d) by publishing notice of the availability of the annual return until July 30, 1982. In this case, the person failing to comply with section 6104(d) within the prescribed time is required to pay $760 for complying with section 6104(d) 76 days late.

(3) *Cross reference.*—For the penalty for willful failure to comply with section 6104(d), see §301.6685-1.

(d) *Special rules.*—For purposes of section 6652(d) and this section—

(1) *Person.*—The term "person" means any officer, director, trustee, employee, member, or other individual whose duty it is to perform the act in respect of which the violation occurs.

(2) *Liability.*—If more than one person (as defined in subparagraph (1) of this paragraph) is liable for a failure to file or to comply with section 6652(d)(2) or (3), all such persons shall be jointly and severally liable with respect to such failure.

(e) *Manner of payment.*—The amount imposed under section 6652(d) and this section on any exempt organization, trust, or person (as defined in paragraph (d)(1) of this section) shall be paid in the same manner as tax upon the issuance of a notice and demand therefor.

(f) *Showing of reasonable cause.*—No amount imposed by section 6652(d) shall apply with respect to a failure to file or comply under this section if it is established to the satisfaction of the district director or director of the internal revenue service center that such failure was due to reasonable cause. An affirmative showing of reasonable cause must be made in the form of a written statement containing a declaration by the appropriate person (as defined in paragraph (d)(1) of this section), or, in his absence, by any officer, director, or trustee of the organization, that the statement is made under the penalties of perjury, setting forth all the facts alleged as reasonable cause.

(g) *Group returns.*—If a central organization is authorized to file a group return on behalf of two or more of its local organizations for the taxable year in accordance with paragraph (d) of §1.6033-2 (Income Tax Regulations), the responsibility for timely filing of such a return is placed upon the central organization for purposes of this section. Consequently, the amount imposed by section 6652(d)(1) for failure to file the group return shall be paid by the central organization and the amount imposed by section 6652(d)(2) for failure to file the group return within the time prescribed by the Commissioner shall be paid by the person or persons responsible for filing the group return.

(h) *Effective date.*—This section shall apply for taxable years beginning after December 31, 1969. [Reg. §301.6652-2.]

☐ [*T.D. 7127, 6-14-71. Amended by T.D. 8026, 5-17-85.*]

[Reg. §301.6652-3]

**§301.6652-3. Failure to file information with respect to employee retirement benefit plan.**—(a) *Amount imposed.*—(1) *Annual registration statement.*—The plan administrator (within the meaning of section 414(g)) of an employee retirement benefit plan defined in §301.6057-1(a)(3) is liable for the amount imposed by section 6652(e)(1) in each case in which there is a failure to file information relating to the deferred vested retirement benefit of a plan participant, as required by section 6057(a) and §301.6057-1, at the time and place and in the manner prescribed therefor (determined without regard to any extension of time for filing). The amount imposed by section 6652(e)(1) on the plan administrator is $1 for each participant with respect to whom there is a failure to file the required information, multiplied by the number of days during which the failure continues. However, the total amount imposed by section 6652(e)(1) on the plan administrator with respect to a failure to file on behalf of a plan for a plan year shall not exceed $5,000.

(2) *Notification of change in status.*—The plan administrator (within the meaning of section 411(g)) of an employee retirement benefit plan defined in §301.6057-1(a)(3) is liable for the amount imposed by section 6652(e)(2) in each case in which there is a failure to file a notification of a change in plan status, as described in section 6057(b) and §301.6057-2, at the time and place and in the manner prescribed therefor (determined without regard to any extension of time for filing). The amount imposed by section 6652(e)(2) on the plan administrator is $1 for each day during which the failure to so file a notification of a change in plan status continues. However, the total amount imposed by section 6652(e)(2) on the plan administrator with respect to a failure to file a notification of a change in plan status shall not exceed $1,000.

(3) *Annual return of funded plan of deferred compensation.*—Under section 6652(f) the amount described in this subparagraph is imposed in each case in which there is a failure to file the annual return described in section 6058(a) on behalf of a plan described in §301.6058-1(a) at the time and in the manner prescribed therefor (determined with regard to any extension of time for filing). The employer maintaining the plan is liable for the amount imposed with respect to a failure to so file the annual return in each case in which the employer must file the return under §301.6058-1(a). The plan administrator (within the meaning of section 414(g)) is liable for the amount imposed in each case in which the plan administrator must file the return under §301.6058-1(a). In the case of an individual retirement account or annuity described in section 408, the individual described in §301.6058-1(d)(2) who must file the annual return under §301.6058-1(d) is liable for the amount imposed with respect to a failure to so file the annual return. The amount imposed is $10 for each day during which the failure to file the annual return on behalf of a plan for a year continues. However, the total amount imposed with respect to a failure to file on behalf of a plan for any year shall not exceed $5,000.

(4) *Actuarial statement in case of mergers.*—The plan administrator (within the meaning of section 414(g)) is liable for an amount imposed by section 6652(f) in each case in which there is a failure to file the actuarial statement described in section 6058(b) at the time and in the manner prescribed therefor (determined with regard to any extension of time for filing). The amount imposed by section 6652(f) on the plan administrator is $10 for each day during which the failure to file the statement with respect to a merger, consolidation or transfer of assets or liabilities continues. However, the amount imposed by section 6652(f) on the plan administrator with respect to a failure to file the statement with respect to a merger, consolidation or transfer shall not exceed $5,000.

(5) *Information relating to certain trusts and annuity and bond purchase plans.*—Under section 6652(f) the amount described in this subparagraph is imposed in each case in which there is a failure to file a return or statement required by section 6047 at the time and in the manner prescribed therefor in §1.6047-1 (determined without regard to any extension of time for filing). The amount is imposed upon the trustee of a trust described in section 401(a), custodian of a custodial account or issuer of an annuity contract, as the case may be (see §1.6047-1(a)(1) (i) and (ii)). The amount imposed by section 6652(f) is $10 for each day during which the failure to file with respect to a payee for a calendar year continues. However, the amount imposed with respect to a failure to file with respect to a payee for a calendar year shall not exceed $5,000.

(b) *Showing of reasonable cause.*—(1) No amount imposed by section 6652(e) shall apply with respect to a failure to file information relating to the deferred vested retirement benefit of a plan participant under section 6057(a), or a failure to give notice of a change in plan status under section 6057(b), if it is established to the satisfaction of the director of the internal revenue service center at which the information or notice is required to be filed that the failure was due to reasonable cause.

(2) No amount imposed by section 6652(f) shall apply with respect to a failure to file a return or statement required by section 6058 or 6047, or a failure to provide material items of information called for on such a return or statement, if it is established to the satisfaction of the appropriate district director or the director of the internal revenue service center at which the return or statement is required to be filed that the failure was due to reasonable cause.

(3) An affirmative showing of reasonable cause must be made in the form of a written statement setting forth all the facts alleged as reasonable cause. The statement must contain a declaration by the appropriate individual that the statement is made under the penalties of perjury.

(c) *Joint liability.*—If more than one person is responsible for a failure to comply with sections 6057(a) or (b) or section 6058(a) or (b) or section 6047, all such persons shall be jointly and severally liable with respect to the failure.

(d) *Manner of payment.*—An amount imposed under section 6652(e) or (f) and this section shall be paid in the same manner as a tax upon the issuance of notice and demand therefor.

(e) *Effective dates.*—(1) *Annual registration statement.*—With respect to the annual registration statement described in section 6057(a), this section is effective—

(i) In the case of a plan to which only one employer contributes, for plan years beginning after December 31, 1975, with respect to participants who separate from service covered by the plan in plan years beginning after that date, and

(ii) In the case of a plan to which more than one employer contributes, for plan years beginning after December 31, 1977, and with respect to participants who complete two consecutive one-year breaks in service under the plan in service computation periods beginning after December 31, 1974.

(2) *Notification of change in status.*—With respect to the notification of change in plan status required by section 6057(b), this section is effective with respect to a change in status occurring within plan years beginning after December 31, 1975.

(3) *Annual return of employee benefit plan.*—With respect to the annual return of employee benefit plan required by section 6058(a), this section is effective for plan years beginning after September 2, 1974.

(4) *Actuarial statement in case of mergers.*—With respect to the actuarial statement required by section 6058(b), this section is effective with respect to mergers, consolidations or transfers of assets or liabilities occurring after September 2, 1974.

(5) *Information relating to certain trusts and annuity and bond purchase plans.*—With respect to reports or statements required to be filed by section 6047 and the regulations thereunder, this section is effective with respect to calendar years ending after September 2, 1974. [Reg. §301.6652-3.]

☐ [*T.D.* 7561, 8-24-78.]

[Reg. §6a.6652(g)-1]

**§6a.6652(g)-1. Failure to make return or furnish statement required under section 6039C (Temporary).**—(a) *Amount imposed.*—In the case of each failure to meet the requirements of—

(1) Section 6039C, relating to information returns with respect to United States real property interests, or

(2) Section 6039C(b)(3), relating to statements to be provided to substantial investors in United States real property interests, on or before the date prescribed therefor (determined with regard to any extension of time for filing), the person failing to meet such requirement shall pay $25 for each day during which such failure continues.

(b) *Limitation.*—(1) *Domestic Corporations and Nominees.*—The maximum penalty which may be imposed under paragraph (a) of this section on a domestic corporation or nominee for failure to meet the requirements of section 6039C(a) for any calendar year is $25,000.

(2) *Partnerships, Trusts, Estates and Foreign Corporations.*—The maximum penalty which may be imposed on a partnership, trust, estate or foreign corporation for failure to meet the requirements of section 6039C(b) for any calendar year is $25,000.

(3) *Foreign persons holding U.S. real property interests and nominees.*—The maximum penalty which may be imposed on a foreign person holding a U.S. real property interest or on a nominee holding a U.S. real property interest for a foreign person for failure to meet

the requirements of section 6039C(c) for any calendar year is the lesser of $25,000 or 5 percent of the aggregate of the fair market value of the U.S. real property interests owned by such person at any time during such calendar year.

(c) *Definitions.*—(1) *Fair market value.*—The term "fair market value" as used in this section is defined in §6a.897-1 (in the *Federal Register* 47 FR 41541).

(2) *Failure.*—The term "failure to meet the requirements of section 6039C" includes the failure to file a return for any calendar year on the date prescribed therefor (determined with regard to any extension of time for such filing), or the omission on a return of one or more items of information required by section 6039C and the regulations thereunder to be provided on the return. It also includes the failure to furnish a statement required by section 6039C(b)(3). The failure to furnish a return required under section 6039C(b)(1) and the failure to furnish a statement to a substantial investor as required by section 6039C(b)(3), are separate failures for purposes of paragraph (a) of this section. Also, each failure to provide a statement to each substantial investor is a separate failure for purposes of paragraph (a). Thus, if an entity has 100 substantial investors as defined in section 6039C and fails to furnish any of the required statements to substantial investors, there are 100 separate failures to furnish the required statement.

(3) *Aggregate of the fair market value of the United States real property interests.*—The "aggregate of the fair market value of the U.S. real property interests" is the total of the fair market values of each U.S. real property interest owned at any time during the calendar year. Fair market value is determined as of December 31 of such year for property held at the end of the year and on the date of disposition for property disposed of during the year.

(d) *Attribution of ownership.*—For purposes of calculating the penalty limitation under §6a.6652(g)-1(b)(3) with respect to failure to meet the requirements of section 6039C(c), U.S. real property interests held by a partnership, trust, or estate shall be treated as owned proportionately by its partners or beneficiaries.

(e) *Exceptions.*—(1) *Provision of security.*—If a person otherwise required by section 6039C to file a return for a calendar year or furnish a statement to a substantial investor complies with the requirements of §6a.6039C-5 relating to furnishing security in lieu of filing such return, or its exempt, by virtue of §6a.6039C-5(f), from filing a return for such year with respect to its U.S. real property interests held, no penalty will be imposed under paragraph (a) of this section for failure to file such return or furnish such statement.

(2) *Showing of reasonable cause.*—No amount shall be imposed under paragraph (a) of this section for a failure described in such paragraph if it is established to the satisfaction of the director of the Internal Revenue Service Center, 11601 Roosevelt Boulevard, Philadelphia, Pennsylvania 19155 or in the case of returns concerning the Virgin Islands, the Commissioner of the Bureau of Internal Revenue, Tax Division, Charlotte Amalie, St. Thomas, V.I. 00801, that such failure is due to reasonable cause and not to willful neglect. An affirmative showing of reasonable cause must be made in the form of a written statement, made under the penalties of perjury, containing a declaration by the person failing to make a return or furnish a statement under section 6039C setting forth all the facts alleged as reasonable cause. Whether reasonable cause is shown may depend upon the subsection of section 6039C under which the failure occurs. However, the fact that stock of a foreign corporation, or any other interest in any entity to which this section applies, is registered in bearer form does not constitute reasonable cause under this paragraph (e)(2) for failure to comply with the requirements of section 6039C(b). Also, the fact that disclosure of ownership would contravene a secrecy law of any country does not constitute reasonable cause for failure to comply with the requirements of section 6039C(b). Where a return has been filed and there is an omission of one or more items of information required by section 6039C and the regulations thereunder, one of the facts to be considered in determining whether such failure is due to reasonable cause is the materialty of the item omitted.

(3) *Spouse or parent already filed with respect to same property.*—If an individual files a return with respect to all U.S. real property interests held by such individual in accordance with §6a.6039C-4(b), no penalty shall be imposed under this section on such individual's spouse or minor child for failure to file a return under §6a.6039C-4 with respect to the same property.

(f) *Manner of payment.*—The amount imposed under paragraph (a) of this section on any person shall be paid in the same manner as tax upon the issuance of a notice and demand therefor.

(g) *Examples.*—The provisions of this section may be illustrated by the following examples:

*Example (1).* Domestic corporation X is required under section 6039C(a) to make a return for calendar year 1982. X does not file such return on or before May 15, 1983 as required under §6a.6039C-1(c). The failure to file the return for calendar year 1982 continues throughout calendar years 1983, 1984, 1985, and 1986. The failure to file is not due to reasonable cause and no security has been furnished in lieu of filing. The maximum penalty which can be imposed on X for failure to file the 1982 return is $25,000, determined as follows:

| | Penalty incurred in given year | Cumulative penalty for failure to file 1982 return |
|---|---|---|
| Total penalty incurred in 1983: ($25 per day × 230 days) | $5,750 | $5,750 |
| Total penalty incurred in 1984 (a leap year): ($25 per day × 366 days) | $9,150 | $14,900 |
| Total penalty incurred in 1985: ($25 per day × 365 days) | $9,125 | $24,025 |
| Total penalty incurred in 1986: (lesser of $25 per day × 365 days or $975 (remaining penalty which may be imposed)) | $975 | $25,000 |

*Example (2).* The facts are the same as in example (1) except that X also fails to file a return under section 6039C(a) for calendar year 1983. The failure to file its return for calendar year 1983 continues throughout calendar years 1984, 1985, 1986 and 1987. The total penalty which may be imposed on X for failure to file its return for calendar year 1983 is $25,000. The amount of penalty which can be imposed on X in calendar years 1984, 1985, 1986 and 1987 is determined as follows:

| | Penalty for 1982 failure | Penalty for 1983 failure | Total Penalty for given year |
|---|---|---|---|
| **Penalty incurred in 1984 (a leap year):** | | | |
| for failure to file 1982 return ($25 per day × 366 days) | $9,150 | | |
| for failure to file 1983 return ($25 per day × 230 days) | | $5,750 | |
| Total | | | $14,900 |
| **Penalty incurred in 1985:** | | | |
| for failure to file 1982 return ($25 per day × 365 days) | $9,125 | | |
| for failure to file 1983 return ($25 per day × 365 days) | | $9,125 | |
| Total | | | $18,250 |
| **Penalty incurred in 1986:** | | | |
| for failure to file 1982 return (lesser of $25 per day × 365 days or $975 (remaining penalty which may be imposed)) | $975 | | |
| for failure to file 1983 return ($25 per day × 365 days) | | $9,125 | |
| Total | | | $10,100 |
| **Penalty incurred in 1987:** | | | |
| for failure to file 1983 return (lesser of $25 per day × 365 days or $1,000 (remaining penalty which may be imposed)) | | $1,000 | |
| Total | | | $1,000 |

*Example (3).* Foreign corporation Y is required under section 6039C(b)(1) to make a return for calendar year 1982. In addition, Y is required under section 6039C(b)(3) to furnish statements to each substantial investor in U.S. real property interests. Y has 10 such substantial investors. Y does not file such return on or before May 15, 1983 as required under §6a.6039C-1(c), nor does it furnish the required statements on or before January 31, 1983 as required under §6a.6039C-3(h). The failure to file the return for calendar year 1982 and to furnish the required statements for 1982 continues throughout calendar years 1984 and 1985. The failure to meet the requirements of section 6039C(b) are not due to reasonable cause and no security has been furnished in lieu of filing. The total penalty which can be

Penalty incurred in 1982:

| | |
|---|---:|
| for failure to file return ($25 per day × 230 days) . . . . . . . . . . . . . . . . . . . . . . . . . . . . . . . . . . . . . . . . | $5,750 |
| for each failure to furnish a statement required by section 6039C(b)(3) ($25 per day × 10 statements × the 334 days from February 1, 1983 to December 31, 1983 ($83,500) but not more than $19,250 (which when added to $5,750 would total $25,000)) | $19,250 |
| Total . . . . . . . . . . . . . . . . . . . . . . . . . . . . . . . . . . . . . . . . . . . . . . . . . . . . . . . . . . . . . . . . . . . | $25,000 |

Since Y has incurred the maximum penalty for failure to file its return and statements required for 1982 by the end of calendar year 1983, no further penalty for these failures is imposed.

*Example (4).* Under section 6039C(c) foreign person Y is required to make a return for calendar year 1982. Y does not file such return on May 15, 1983 and the failure is not due to reasonable cause. No security has been furnished in lieu of filing. All properties owned by Y in 1982 are U.S. real property interests. Y purchased property M in January 1982 when its fair market value was $10,000. In March, Y purchased property N when its fair market value was $15,000. In November, Y sold property M for $20,000. The fair market value of property N on December 31, 1982, was $20,000. The total of the fair market values of M and N (M as of the date of its sale and N as of December 31, 1982) is $40,000. The maximum penalty which may be imposed on Y for failure to meet the requirements of section 6039C(c) for any calendar year is the lesser of $25,000 or 5 percent of the aggregate of the fair market values of the U.S. real property interests owned by Y at any time during such calendar year. Since $2,000 (5 percent of $40,000) is less than $5,750 ($25 times 230 days, the number of days in calendar year 1983 for which the failure continues), the maximum penalty which may be imposed on Y in 1983 is $2,000. Since the maximum penalty for the failure to file the 1982 return is incurred in 1983, no amount may be imposed for Y's continuing failure to file the return for calendar year 1982 during calendar years after 1983.

(h) *Effective date.*—This section shall apply to 1980 and subsequent calendar years. The calendar year 1980 shall be treated as beginning on June 19, 1980 and ending on December 31, 1980. [Temporary Reg. §6a.6652(g)-1.]

☐ [T.D. 7866, 1-1-83.]

**[Reg. §301.6653-1]**

§301.6653-1. Failure to pay tax.—(a) *Negligence or intentional disregard of rules and regulations with respect to income or gift taxes.*—If any part of any underpayment, as defined in section 6653(c)(1) and paragraph (c)(1) of this section, of any income tax imposed by subtitle A or gift tax imposed by chapter 12 of subtitle B, of the Code, is due to negligence or intentional disregard of rules and regulations, but without intent to defraud, there shall be added to the tax an amount equal to 5 percent of the underpayment.

(b) *Fraud.*—(1) If any part of any underpayment of tax, as defined in section 6653(c) and paragraph (c) of this section, required to be shown on a return is due to fraud, there shall be added to the tax an amount equal to 50 percent of the underpayment.

(2) If a 50 percent addition to the tax for fraud is assessed under section 6653(b) with respect to an underpayment—

(i) The addition to the tax under section 6651, relating to failure to file a tax return, will not be assessed with respect to the same underpayment, and

(ii) In the case of the income taxes imposed by subtitle A and the gift tax imposed by chapter 12 of subtitle B, the 5 percent addition to the tax under section 6653(a), relating to negligence and intentional disregard of rules and regulations, will not be assessed with respect to the same underpayment.

(c) *Definition of underpayment.*—(1) *Income, estate, gift, and chapter 41, 42, 43, and 44 taxes.*—In the case of income, estate, gift, and chapter 41, 42, 43, and 44 taxes, an underpayment for purposes of section 6653 and this section is—

(i) The total amount of all deficiencies as defined in section 6211, if a return was filed on or before the last date (determined with regard to any extension of time) prescribed for filing such return, or

(ii) The amount of the tax imposed by subtitle A or B, or chapter 41, 42, 43, or 44, as the case may be, if a return was not filed on or before the last date (determined with regard to any extension of time) prescribed for filing such return.

However, for purposes of paragraph (c)(1)(i) of this section, any amount of additional tax shown on the amended return, so called, filed after the due date of the return is a deficiency.

imposed on Y for failure to file the return and statements required under section 6039C(b) for calendar year 1982 is $25,000. The amount of penalty incurred by Y in calendar year 1983 for failure to file the return and statements for calendar year 1982 is $25,000, determined as follows:

(2) *Other taxes.*—In the case of any tax other than an income, estate, gift or chapter 41, 42, 43, or 44 tax, an underpayment for purposes of section 6653 and this section is the amount by which the tax imposed exceeds—

(i) In the case of any tax with respect to which the taxpayer is required to file a return, the sum of (a) the amount shown as tax by the taxpayer upon his return filed in respect of such tax, but only if the return is filed on or before the last date (determined with regard to any extension of time) prescribed for filing such return, plus (b) any amount not shown on a return filed by the taxpayer which is paid in respect of such tax prior to the date prescribed for filing the return. The "amount shown as tax by the taxpayer upon his return" for the purposes of this subparagraph shall be determined without regard to any credit for an overpayment for any prior tax return period, and without regard to any adjustment made under section 6205(a), or section 6413(a), relating to special rules applicable to certain employment taxes.

(ii) In the case of any tax payable by stamp, the amount paid (on or before the date prescribed for payment) in respect of such tax. The amounts specified in subdivisions (i) and (ii) of this subparagraph shall be reduced, for purposes of determining the amount of the underpayment, by the amount of any rebates made. For purposes of this subparagraph, the term "rebates" means so much of an abatement, credit, refund, or other repayment as was made on the ground that the tax imposed was less than the excess of the amount specified in subdivision (i) or (ii) of this subparagraph, whichever is applicable, over any rebates previously made.

(d) *No delinquency penalty if fraud assessed.*—See paragraph (b)(2) of this section.

(e) *Failure to pay stamp tax.*—Any person (as defined in section 6671(b)) who willfully fails to pay any tax payable by stamp, coupons, tickets, books or other devices or methods prescribed by the Code or regulations promulgated thereunder, or willfully attempts in any manner to evade or defeat any such tax or the payment thereof, shall, in addition to other penalties provided by law, be liable to a penalty of 50 percent of the total amount of the underpayment of the tax.

(f) *Joint returns.*—No person filing a joint return shall be held liable for a fraud penalty except for his own personal fraudulent conduct. Thus, for the fraud penalty to apply to a taxpayer who files a joint return some part of the underpayment in such return must be due to the fraud of such taxpayer. A taxpayer shall not be subject to the fraud penalty solely by reason of the fraud of a spouse and his filing of a joint return with such spouse. [Reg. §301.6653-1.]

☐ [T.D. 6286, 11-15-57. Amended by T.D. 6498, 10-24-60, T.D. 7320, 8-5-74, T.D. 7498, 7-12-77 and T.D. 7838, 10-5-82.]

**[Reg. §1.6654-1]**

§1.6654-1. Addition to the tax in the case of an individual.—(a) *In general.*—(1) Section 6654 imposes an addition to the taxes under chapters 1 and 2 of the Code in the case of any underpayment of estimated tax by an individual (with certain exceptions described in section 6654(d)), including any underpayment of estimated qualified State individual income taxes which are treated pursuant to section 6361(a) as if they were imposed by chapter 1. This addition to the tax is in addition to any applicable criminal penalties and is imposed whether or not there was reasonable cause for the underpayment. The amount of the underpayment for any installment date is the excess of—

(i) The following percentages of the tax shown on the return for the taxable year or, if no return was filed, of the tax for such year, divided by the number of installment dates prescribed for such taxable year:

(A) 80 percent in the case of taxable years beginning after December 31, 1966, of individuals not referred to in section 6073(b) (relating to income from farming or fishing);

(B) 70 percent in the case of taxable years beginning before January 1, 1967, of such individuals; and

(C) 66⅔ percent in the case of individuals referred to in section 6073(b); over

(ii) The amount, if any, of the installment paid on or before the last day prescribed for such payment.

(2) The amount of the addition is determined at the annual rate referred to in the regulations under section 6621 upon the underpayment of any installment of estimated tax for the period from the date such installment is required to be paid until the 15th day of the fourth month following the close of the taxable year, or the date such underpayment is paid, whichever is earlier. For purposes of determining the period of the underpayment (i) the date prescribed for the payment of any installment of estimated tax shall be determined without regard to any extension of time, and (ii) a payment of estimated tax on any installment date, to the extent that it exceeds the amount of the installment determined under subparagraph (1)(i) of this paragraph for such installment date, shall be considered a payment of any previous underpayment.

(3) In determining the amount of the installment paid on or before the last day prescribed for payment thereof, the estimated tax shall be computed without any reduction for the amount which the taxpayer estimates as his credit under section 31 (relating to tax withheld at source on wages), and the amount of such credit shall be deemed a payment of estimated tax. An equal part of the amount of such credit shall be deemed paid on each installment date (determined under section 6153) for the taxable year unless the taxpayer establishes the dates on which all amounts were actually withheld. In the latter case, all amounts withheld shall be considered as payments of estimated tax on the dates such amounts were actually withheld. Under section 31 the entire amount withheld during a calendar year is allowed as a credit against the tax for the taxable year which begins in such calendar year. However, where more than one taxable year begins in any calendar year no portion of the amount withheld during the calendar year will be treated as a payment of estimated tax for any taxable year other than the last taxable year beginning in such calendar year. The rules prescribed in this subparagraph for determining the time as of which the amount withheld shall be deemed paid are applicable even though such amount was withheld during a taxable year preceding that for which the credit is allowed.

(4) The term "tax" when used in subparagraph (1)(i) of this paragraph shall mean—

(i) The tax imposed by chapter 1 of the Code (other than by section 56 or, for taxable years ending before September 30, 1968, the tax surcharge imposed by section 51), including any qualified State individual income taxes which are treated pursuant to section 6361(a) as if they were imposed by chapter 1, plus

(ii) For taxable years beginning after December 31, 1966, the tax imposed by chapter 2 of the Code, minus

(iii) All credits allowed by part IV, subchapter A of chapter 1, except the credit provided by section 31, relating to tax withheld at source on wages, minus

(iv) In the case of an individual who is subject to one or more qualified State individual incomes taxes, the sum of the credits allowed against such taxes pursuant to section 6362(b)(2)(B) or (C) or section 6362(c)(4) and paragraph (c) of §301.6362-4 of this chapter (Regulations on Procedure and Administration) (relating to the credit for income taxes of other States or political subdivisions thereof) and paragraph (c)(2) of §301.6361-1 (relating to the credit for tax withheld from wages on account of qualified State individual income taxes), and minus

(v) For taxable years ending after February 29, 1980, the individual's overpayment of windfall profit tax imposed by section 4986 of the Code for the taxable year. For this purpose, the amount of such overpayment is the sum of (A) the amount by which such individual's aggregate windfall profit tax liability for the taxable year as producer of crude oil is exceeded by withholding of windfall profit tax for the taxable year, and (B) any amount treated under section 6429 or 6430 as an overpayment of windfall profit tax for crude oil removed during the taxable year. The deemed payment date in section 4995(a)(4)(B) for the amount of windfall profit tax withheld with respect to payment for crude oil shall have no effect in the determination of the overpayment of windfall profit tax.

(b) *Statement relating to underpayment.*—If there has been an underpayment of estimated tax as of any installment date prescribed for its payment and the taxpayer believes that one or more of the exceptions described in §1.6654-2 precludes the assertion of the addition to the tax under section 6654, he should attach to his income tax return for the taxable year a Form 2210 showing the applicability of any exception upon which he relies.

(c) *Examples.*—The method prescribed in paragraph (a) of this section for computing the addition to the tax may be illustrated by the following examples:

*Example (1).* An individual taxpayer files his return for the calendar year 1972 on April 15, 1973 showing a tax (income and self-employment tax) of $30,000. He had paid a total of $20,000 of estimated tax in four installments of $5,000 on each of the four installment dates prescribed for such year. No other payments were made prior to the date the return was filed. Since the amount of each installment paid by the last date prescribed for payment thereof is less than one-quarter of 80 percent of the tax shown on the return, the addition to the tax is applicable in respect of the underpayment existing as of each installment date and is computed as follows:

| | |
|---|---:|
| (1) Amount of tax shown on return | $30,000 |
| (2) 80 percent of item (1) | 24,000 |
| (3) One-fourth of item (2) | $6,000 |
| (4) Deduct amount paid on each installment date | $5,000 |
| (5) Amount of underpayment for each installment date (item (3) minus item (4)) | $1,000 |
| (6) Addition to the tax: | |
| 1st installment—period 4-15-72 to 4-15-73 | $60 |
| 2nd installment—period 6-15-72 to 4-15-73 | 50 |
| 3rd installment—period 9-15-72 to 4-15-73 | 35 |
| 4th installment—period 1-15-73 to 4-15-73 | 15 |
| Total | $160 |

*Example (2).* An individual taxpayer files his return for the calendar year 1955 on April 15, 1956, showing a tax of $30,000. The requirements of section 6015(a) were first met after April 1 and before June 2, 1955, and a total of $18,000 of estimated tax was paid in three equal installments of $6,000 on each of the three installment dates prescribed for such year. Since the amount of each installment paid by the last date prescribed for payment thereof is less than one-third of 70 percent of the tax shown on the return, the addition to the tax is applicable in respect of the underpayment existing as of each installment date and is computed as follows:

| | |
|---|---:|
| (1) Amount of tax shown on return | $30,000 |
| (2) 70 percent of item (1) | 21,000 |
| (3) One-third of item (2) | $7,000 |
| (4) Deduct amount paid on each installment date | 6,000 |
| (5) Amount of underpayment for each installment date (item (3) minus item (4)) | $1,000 |
| (6) Addition to the tax: | |
| 1st installment—period 6/15/55 to 4/15/56 | $50 |
| 2nd installment—period 9/15/55 to 4/15/56 | 35 |
| 3rd installment—period 1/15/56 to 4/15/56 | 15 |
| Total | $100 |

[Reg. §1.6654-1.]

☐ [T.D. 6267, 11-13-57. *Amended by T.D. 6678, 9-30-63, T.D. 7384, 10-21-75, T.D. 7427, 8-9-76, T.D. 7577, 12-19-78 and T.D. 8016, 3-25-85.*]

### [Reg. §301.6654-1]

**§301.6654-1. Failure by individual to pay estimated income tax.**—For regulations under section 6654, see §§1.6654-1 to 1.6654-5, inclusive, of this chapter (Income Tax Regulations). [Reg. §301.6654-1.]

☐ [T.D. 6268, 11-15-57. *Republished in T.D. 6498, 10-24-60. Amended by T.D. 7282, 7-16-73.*]

### [Reg. §1.6654-2]

**§1.6654-2. Exceptions to imposition of the addition to the tax in the case of individuals.**—(a) *In general.*—The addition to the tax under section 6654 will not be imposed for any underpayment of any installment of estimated tax if, on or before the date prescribed for payment of the installment, the total amount of all payments of estimated tax made equals or exceeds the lesser of the amount in § 1.6654-2(a)(1) or the amount in § 1.6654-2(a)(2).

(1)(i) The amount which would have been required to be paid on or before the date prescribed for payment if estimated tax were the tax shown on the return for the preceding taxable year, provided that the preceding taxable year was a year of 12 months and a return showing a liability for tax was filed for such year. However, this subparagraph shall not apply with respect to any taxable year which ends on or after September 30, 1968, for which a tax is imposed by section 51 (relating to tax surcharge), in the case of a payment of estimated tax the time prescribed for payment of which is on or after September 15, 1968.

(ii) *Special rule for taxable years beginning in 2009.*—For any taxable year beginning in 2009, for a qualified individual, the amount described in paragraph (a)(1)(i) of this section is reduced to 90 percent of that amount.

(A) *Qualified individual* means any individual whose adjusted gross income shown on the individual's return for the preceding taxable year is less than $500,000 and who certifies, as prescribed in paragraph (a)(1)(ii)(D) of this section, that more than 50 percent of the gross income shown on the return for the preceding taxable year was income from a small business.

(B) *Income from a small business* means income from the operation of a bona fide trade or business of which the individual was an owner during calendar year 2009, and that on average had fewer than 500 employees in calendar year 2008.

(C) The trade or business may be organized as, or take the legal form of, a corporation, partnership, limited liability company, or sole proprietorship.

(D) A qualified individual shall file a certification of the individual's qualification in the manner and at the time prescribed by the Internal Revenue Service in forms, publications, or other guidance.

(2) The amount which would have been required to be paid on or before the date prescribed for payment if the estimated tax were an amount equal to a percentage of the tax computed by placing on an annual basis the taxable income for the calendar months in the taxable year ending before the month in which the installment is required to be paid. That percentage is 80 percent in the case of taxable years beginning after December 31, 1966, of individuals not referred to in section 6073(b) (relating to income from farming or fishing), 70 percent in the case of taxable years beginning before January 1, 1967, of such individuals, and 66²/3 percent in the case [of] individuals referred to in section 6073(b). With respect to taxable years beginning after December 31, 1966, the adjusted self-employment income shall be taken into account in determining the amount referred to in this subparagraph if net earnings from self-employment (as defined in section 1402(a)) for the taxable year equal or exceed $400. For purposes of this subparagraph—

(i) Taxable income shall be placed on an annualized basis—

(A) For taxable years beginning after 1976, by—

(1) Multiplying by 12 (or the number of months in the taxable year if less than 12) the adjusted gross income and the itemized deductions for the calendar months in the taxable year ending before the month in which the installment is required to be paid,

(2) Dividing the resulting amounts by the number of such calendar months,

(3) Increasing the amount of the annualized adjusted gross income by the unused zero bracket amount, if any, determined by reference to the annualized itemized deductions, or decreasing the amount of the annualized adjusted gross income by the excess itemized deductions, if any, determined by reference to the annualized itemized deductions (the amount resulting under this step is annualized tax table income), and

(4) Deducting from the annualized tax table income the deduction for personal exemptions (such personal exemptions being determined as of the date prescribed for payment of the installment). If the taxpayer would be eligible to use the tax tables on the basis of annualized tax table income, the amount which would have been required to be paid for purposes of this subparagraph may be determined by applying the tax tables to annualized tax table income, the amount resulting under (3).

(B) For taxable years beginning before 1977, by—

(1) Multiplying by 12 (or the number of months in the taxable year if less than 12) the taxable income (computed without the standard deduction and without the deduction for personal exemptions), or the adjusted gross income if the standard deduction is to be used for the calendar months in the taxable year ending before the month in which the installment is required to be paid,

(2) Dividing the resulting amount by the number of such calendar months, and

(3) Deducting from such amount the standard deduction, if applicable, and the deduction for personal exemptions (such personal exemptions being determined as of the date prescribed for payment of the installment).

(ii) The term "adjusted self-employment income" means—

(A) The net earnings from self-employment (as defined in section 1402(a)) for the calendar months in the taxable year ending before the month in which the installment is required to be paid, computed as if such months constituted the taxable year, but not more than

(B) The excess of—

(1) For taxable years beginning after 1966, $6,600,

(2) For taxable years beginning after 1971, $9,000,

(3) For taxable years beginning after 1972, $10,800,

(4) For taxable years beginning after 1973, $13,200 and

(5) For taxable years beginning after 1974, an amount equal to the contribution and benefit base (as determined under section 230 of the Social Security Act) which is effective for the calendar year in which the taxable year begins,

over the amount of the wages (within the meaning of section 1402(b)) for such calendar months placed on an annual basis. For this purpose, wages are annualized by multiplying by 12 (or the number of months in the case of a taxable year of less than 12 months) the wages for such calendar months and dividing the resulting amount by the number of such months.

(3) An amount equal to 90 percent of the tax computed, at the rates applicable to the taxable year, on the basis of the actual taxable income for the calendar months in the taxable year ending before the month in which the installment is required to be paid, as if such months constituted the entire taxable year. For taxable years beginning after December 31, 1966, such computation shall include the tax imposed by chapter 2 on the actual self-employment income for such months. For purposes of the subparagraph, the term "actual self-employment income" means—

(i) The net earnings from self-employment (as defined in section 1402(a)) for such calendar months, computed as if such months constituted the taxable year, but not more than

(ii) The excess of—

(A) For taxable years beginning after 1966, $6,600,

(B) For taxable years beginning after 1971, $9,000,

(C) For taxable years beginning after 1972, $10,800,

(D) For taxable years beginning after 1973, $13,200, and

(E) For taxable years beginning after 1974, an amount equal to the contribution and benefit base (as determined under section 230 of the Social Security Act) which is effective for the calendar year in which the taxable year begins,

over the amount of wages (within the meaning of section 1402(b)) for such months.

(4) The amount which would have been required to be paid on or before the date prescribed for payment if the estimated tax were an amount equal to a tax determined on the basis of the tax rates and the taxpayer's status with respect to personal exemptions under section 151 for the taxable year, but otherwise on the basis of the facts shown on the return for the preceding taxable year and the law applicable to such year, in the case of an individual required to file a return for such preceding taxable year.

In the case of a taxpayer whose taxable year consists of 52 or 53 weeks in accordance with section 441(f), the rules prescribed by § 1.441-2(c) shall be applicable in determining, for purposes of subparagraph (1) of this paragraph, whether a taxable year was a year of 12 months and, for purposes of subparagraphs (2) and (3) of this paragraph, the number of calendar months in a taxable year preceding the date prescribed for payment of an installment of estimated tax. For the rules to be applied in determining taxable income for any period described in subparagraphs (2) and (3) of this paragraph in the case of a taxpayer who employs accounting periods (e.g., thirteen 4-week periods or four 13-week periods) none of which terminates with the end of the applicable period described in subparagraph (2) or (3) of this paragraph, see paragraph (a)(5) of § 1.6655-2.

(b) *Meaning of terms.*—As used in this section and § 1.6654-3—

(1) The term "tax" means—

(i) The tax imposed by chapter 1 of the Code (other than by section 56), including any qualified State individual income taxes which are treated pursuant to section 6361(a) as if they were imposed by chapter 1, plus

(ii) For taxable years beginning after December 31, 1966, the tax imposed by chapter 2 of the Code, minus

(iii) The credits against tax allowed by part IV, subchapter A, chapter 1 of the Code, other than the credit against tax provided by section 31 (relating to tax withheld on wages), and without reduction for any payments of estimated tax, minus

(iv) In the case of an individual who is subject to one or more qualified State individual income taxes, the sum of the credits allowed against such taxes pursuant to section 6262(b)(2)(B) or (C) or section 6262(c)(4) and paragraph (c) of § 301.6362-4 of this chapter (Regulations on Procedure and Administration) (relating to the credit for income taxes of other States or political subdivisions thereof) and paragraph (c)(2) of § 301.6361-1 (relating to the credit for tax withheld from wages on account of qualified State individual income taxes), and minus

(v) For taxable years ending after February 29, 1980, the individual's overpayment of windfall profit tax imposed by section 4986 of the Code for the taxable year. For this purpose, the amount of such overpayment is the sum of (A) the amount by which such individual's aggregate windfall profit tax liability for the taxable year as producer of crude oil is exceeded by withholding of windfall profit tax for the taxable year, and (B) any amount treated under section 6429 or 6430 as an overpayment of windfall profit tax for crude oil removed during the taxable year. The deemed payment date in section 4995(a)(4)(B) for the amount of windfall profit tax withheld with respect to payments for crude oil shall have no effect in the determination of the overpayment of windfall profit tax.

(2) The credits against tax allowed by part IV, subchapter A, chapter 1 of the Code, are—

(i) In the case of the exception described in paragraph (a)(1) of this section, the credits shown on the return for the preceding taxable year,

(ii) In the case of the exceptions described in paragraph (a)(2) and (3) of this section, the credits computed under the law and rates applicable to the current taxable year, and

(iii) In the case of the exception described in paragraph (a)(4) of this section, the credits shown on the return for the preceding taxable year, except that if the amount of any such credit would be affected by any change in rates or status with respect to personal exemptions, the credits shall be determined by reference to the rates and status applicable to the current taxable year.

A change in rate may be either a change in the rate of tax, such as a change in the rate of tax imposed by section 1 or section 1401, or a change in a percentage affecting the computation of a credit, such as a change in the rate of withholding under chapter 3 of the Code or a change in the percentage of a qualified investment which is specified in section 46 for use in determining the amount of the investment credit allowed by section 38.

(3) The term "return for the preceding taxable year" means the income tax return for such year which is required by section 6012(a)(1) and, in the case of taxable years beginning after December 31, 1966, the self-employment tax return for such year which is required by section 6017.

(c) *Examples.*—The following examples illustrate the application of the exceptions to the imposition of the addition to the tax for an underpayment of estimated tax, in the case of an individual whose taxable year is the calendar year:

*Example (1).* A, a married man with one child and a dependent parent, files a joint return with his spouse, B, for 1955 on April 15, 1956, showing taxable income of $44,000 and a tax of $16,760. A and B had filed a joint declaration of estimated tax on April 15, 1955, showing an estimated tax of $10,000 which was paid in four equal installments of $2,500 each on April 15, June 15, and September 15, 1955, and January 15, 1956. The balance of $6,760 was paid with the return. A and B have an underpayment of estimated tax of $433 (¹/4 of 70 percent of $16,760, less $2,500) for each installment date. The 1954 calendar year return of A and B showed a liability of $10,000. Since the total amount of estimated tax paid by each installment date equalled the amount that would have been required to be paid on or before each of such dates if the estimated tax were the tax shown on the return for the preceding year, the exception described in paragraph (a)(1) of this section applies and no addition to the tax will be imposed.

*Example (2).* Assume the same facts as in example (1), except that the joint return of A and B for 1954 showed taxable income of $32,000 and a tax liability of $10,400. Assume further that only two personal exemptions under section 151 appeared on the 1954 return. The exception described in paragraph (a)(1) of this section would not apply. However, A and B are entitled to four exemptions under section 151 for 1955. Taxable income for 1954 based on four exemptions, but otherwise on the basis of the facts shown on the 1954 return, would be $30,800. The tax on such amount in the case of a joint return would be $9,836. Since the total amount of estimated tax paid by each installment date exceeds the amount which would have been required to be paid on or before each of such dates if the estimated tax were $9,836, the exception described in paragraph (a)(4) of this section applies and no addition to the tax will be imposed.

*Example (3).* C, who is self-employed (other than as a farmer or fisherman), has annualized taxable income of $6,900 for the period

January 1, 1967, through August 31, 1967, the income tax on which is $1,171. For the same period his net earnings from self-employment are $5,000 and his wages are $2,000. The estimated tax payments made by C for 1967 on or before September 15, 1967, total $1,200. For the purposes of the exception described in paragraph (a)(2) of this section, the adjusted self-employment income is $3,600, computed as follows:

| | |
|---|---:|
| (1) Net earnings from self-employment | $5,000 |
| (2) $6,600 minus annualized wages ($6,600 – 3,000 ($2,000 × 12 ÷ 8)) | 3,600 |
| (3) Lesser of (1) or (2) | 3,600 |

The tax on C's adjusted self-employment income would be $230.40 ($3,600 × 6.4 percent). Since the total amount of estimated tax paid on or before September 15, 1967, exceeds $1,121.12, that is, 80 percent of $1,401.40 ($1,171 + 230.40), the exception described in paragraph (a)(2) of this section applies and no addition to tax will be imposed.

*Example (4).* D, who is self-employed (other than as a farmer or fisherman), has actual taxable income of $3,800 for the period January 1, 1967, through August 31, 1967, the income tax on which is $586. For the same period his net earnings from self-employment are $5,000 and his wages are $2,000. The estimated tax payments made by D for 1967 on or before September 15, 1967, total $840. For the purposes of the exception described in paragraph (a)(3) of this section, the actual self-employment income for this period is $4,600, computed as follows:

| | |
|---|---:|
| (1) Net earnings from self-employment | $5,000 |
| (2) $6,600 minus wages ($6,600 – 2,000) | 4,600 |
| (3) Lesser of (1) or (2) | 4,600 |

The tax on D's actual self-employment income would be $294.40 ($4,600 × 6.4 percent). Since the total amount of estimated tax paid by September 15, 1967, exceeds $792.36, that is, 90 percent of $880.40 ($586 + 294.40); the exception described in paragraph (a)(3) of this section applies and no addition to tax will be imposed.

*Example (5).* E and F, his spouse, filed a joint return for the calendar year 1967 showing a tax liability of $10,000. The liability, attributable primarily to income received during the last quarter of the year, included both income and self-employment tax. Their aggregate payments of estimated tax on or before September 15, 1967, total $1,350, representing three installments of $450 paid on each of the first three installment dates prescribed for the taxable year. Since each installment paid, $450, was less than $2,000 (¹/4 of 80 percent of $10,000), there was an underpayment on each of the installment dates. Assume that the exceptions described in paragraph (a)(1) and (4) of this section do not apply. Actual taxable income for the three months ending March 31, 1967, was $2,000 and for the five months ending May 31, 1967, was $4,500. Actual self-employment income, for the same periods, was $2,000 and $4,000, respectively. Since the amounts paid by the April 15 and June 15 installment dates, $450 and $900, respectively, exceed $376.20 and $873.90, respectively (90 percent of the income tax on the actual taxable income of $2,000 and $4,500, respectively, determined on the basis of a joint return, and the self-employment tax on the actual self-employment income of $2,000 and $4,000, respectively), the exception described in paragraph (a)(3) of this section applies and no addition to the tax will be imposed for the underpayments on the April 15 and June 15 installment dates. For the eight months ending August 31, 1967, actual taxable income, assuming E and F did not elect to use the standard deduction, was $7,500; net earnings from self-employment were $6,000; and wages were $2,700. Since the total amount paid by the September 15 installment date, $1,350, was less than $1,381.14 (90 percent of the income tax on the actual taxable income of $7,500 determined on the basis of a joint return and the self-employment tax on actual self-employment income of $3,900 ($6,600 – 2,700)), the exception described in paragraph (a)(3) of this section does not apply to the September 15 installment. Furthermore, the exception described in paragraph (a)(2) of this section does not apply, as illustrated by the following computation:

| | | |
|---|---|---:|
| (1) | Income tax: | |
| | Taxable income for the period ending August 31, 1967 (without deduction for personal exemptions) on an annual basis ($8,700 × 12 ÷ 8) | $13,050.00 |
| | Deduction for two personal exemptions | 1,200.00 |
| | | 11,850.00 |
| | Tax on $11,850 (on the basis of a joint return) | 2,227.00 |
| (2) | Self-employment tax: | |
| | Net earnings from self-employment | 6,000.00 |
| | Adjusted self-employment income ($6,600 – 4,050 annualized wages ($2,700 × 12 ÷ 8)) | 2,550.00 |
| | Tax on adjusted self-employment income ($2,550 × 6.4 percent) | 163.20 |
| (3) | Total tax ($2,227.00 + 163.20) | $2,390.20 |

**Reg. § 1.6654-2(c)**

(4)    ³/₄ of 80 percent of $2,390.20 . . . . . . . . . .    1,434.12
          Amount paid by Sept. 15, 1967 . . . . . . . . .    1,350.00

An addition to the tax will thus be imposed for the underpayment of $1,550 ($2,000 − 450) on the September 15 installment.

*Example (6).* Assume the same facts as in example (5) and assume further that adjusted gross income for the eight months ending August 31, 1967, was $9,200 and the amount of deductions (other than the deduction for personal exemptions) not allowable in determining adjusted gross income aggregated only $500. If E and F elect, they may use the standard deduction in computing the tax for purposes of the exceptions described in paragraph (a)(2) and (3) of this section. Taxable income for purposes of the exception described in paragraph (a)(3) of this section would be reduced to $7,080 ($9,200 less $1,200 for two personal exemptions and $920 for the standard deduction). The income tax thereon is $1,205.20; income tax and self-employment tax total $1,454.80 ($1,205.20 + $249.60 ($3,900 × 6.4 percent)). Since the amount paid by the September 15 installment date, $1,350, exceeds $1,309.32 (90 percent of $1,454.80), the exception described in paragraph (a)(3) of this section applies. However, the exception described in paragraph (a)(2) of this section does not apply, as illustrated by the following computation:

Adjusted gross income for the period ending August 31,
   1967 . . . . . . . . . .    $9,200.00
Adjusted gross income annualized ($9,200 × 12 ÷ 8) .    13,800.00
Taxable income annualized ($13,800 minus $1,200 for
   two personal exemptions and $1,000 for the
   standard deduction) . . . . . . . . . . . . . . . . .    11,600.00
Income tax on $11,600 (on basis of a joint return) . . . .    2,172.00
Self-employment tax on adjusted self-employment
   income ($2,550 × 6.4 percent) . . . . . . . . . . . .    163.20
Total tax ($2,172.00 + 163.20) . . . . . . . . . . . .    $2,355.20
³/₄ of 80 percent of $2,335.20 . . . . . . . . . . . . .    1,401.12
Amount paid by Sept. 15, 1967 . . . . . . . . . . . .    1,350.00

*Example (7).* G was a married individual, 73 years of age, who filed a joint return with his wife, H, for the calendar year 1956. H, who was 70 years of age, had no income during the year. G had taxable income in the amount of $7,000 for the eight-month period ending on August 31, 1956, which included $2,000 of dividend income (after excluding $50 under section 116) and $900 of rental income. The $7,000 figure also reflected a deduction of $2,400 for personal exemptions ($600 × 4), since G and H are both over 65 years of age. The application of the exception described in paragraph (a)(2) of this section to an underpayment of estimated tax on the September 15 installment date may be illustrated by the following computation:

Taxable income for the period ending August 31, 1956
   (without deduction for personal exemptions) on an
   annual basis ($9,400 × 12 ÷ 8) . . . . . . . . . . .    $14,100.00
Deduction for personal exemptions . . . . . . . . . . .    2,400.00

Taxable income on an annual basis . . . . . . . . . . .    11,700.00
Tax (on the basis of a joint return) . . . . . . . . . . .    2,642.00
Dividends received for 8-month period . . . . . . . . .    2,050.00
Less: Amount excluded from gross income under section
   116 . . . . . . . . . . . . . . . . . . . . . . . .    50.00

Dividends included in gross income . . . . . . . . . . .    2,000.00
Dividend income annualized ($2,000 × 12 ÷ 8) . . . .    3,000.00
Dividends received credit under section 34 (4 percent of
   $3,000) . . . . . . . . . . . . . . . . . . . . . . .    120.00

Tax less dividends received credit . . . . . . . . . . .    2,522.00
Retirement income (as defined in section 37(c)) includes:
Dividend income (to extent included in gross income) .    2,000.00
Rental income . . . . . . . . . . . . . . . . . . . .    900.00

Total retirement income . . . . . . . . . . . . . . . .    $2,000.00
Limit on amount of retirement income under section 37(d)
   . . . . . . . . . . . . . . . . . . . . . . . . . .    1,200.00
Retirement income credit under section 37 (20 percent of
   $1,200) . . . . . . . . . . . . . . . . . . . . . . .    240.00

Tax less credits under section 34 and section 37 . . . .    2,282.00
Amount determined under the exception described in
   paragraph (a)(2) of this section (³/₄ of 70 percent of
   $2,282) . . . . . . . . . . . . . . . . . . . . . . .    1,198.05

*Example (8).* C, an unmarried individual for whom another taxpayer is entitled to a deduction under section 151(e), has adjusted gross income of $4,000 for the period January 1, 1977, through August 31, 1977. All of C's income is nonexempt interest. For the same period C, who is entitled to one personal exemption, has itemized deductions amounting to $300. C is entitled to no credits other than the general tax credit. C filed a declaration of estimated tax on April 15, 1977, and on or before September 15, 1977, makes estimated tax payments for 1977 which total $460. For purposes of determining whether the exception described in paragraph (a)(2) of this section applies, the following computations are necessary:

Adjusted gross income for the period ending August
   31, 1977, on an annual basis ($4,000 × 12 ÷ 8) . . .    $6,000
Itemized deductions for the period ending August 31,
   1977, on an annual basis ($300 × 12 ÷ 8) . . . . . .    450
Unused zero bracket amount computation required
   under section 63(e)(1)(D):
Zero bracket amount . . . . . . . . . . . . .    $2,200
Annualized itemized deductions . . . .    450

Unused zero bracket amount . . . . . . .    $1,750
Annualized adjusted gross income . . . . .    6,000
Plus: unused zero bracket amount . . . . .    1,750

Annualized tax table income . . . . . . . .    $7,750
Tax from tables . . . . . . . . . . .    757
Amount specified in paragraph (a)(2) of this section (³/₄
   × 80% × $757) . . . . . . . . . . . . . . . . . . .    454.20

The exception described in paragraph (a)(2) applies, and no addition to tax will be imposed.

*Example (9).* D, an unmarried taxpayer entitled to one exemption, has adjusted gross income of $16,000 and itemized deductions of $2,000 for the period January 1, 1977, through August 31, 1977. D has no net earnings from self-employment and is entitled to no credits other than the general tax credit. D files a declaration of estimated tax on April 15, 1977, and on or before September 15, 1977, makes estimated tax payments for 1977 which total $3,000. For purposes of determining whether the exception in paragraph (a)(2) of this section applies, the following computations are necessary:

Adjusted gross income for the period ending August 31, 1977, on
   an annual basis ($16,000 × 12 ÷ 8) . . . . . . . . .    $24,000
Itemized deductions for the period ending August 31, 1977, on an
   annual basis ($2,000 × 12 ÷ 8) . . . . . . . . . . .    3,000
Annualized itemized deductions . . . . . . . .    $3,000
Minus: zero bracket amount . . . . . . . . . .    2,200

Excess itemized deductions . . . . . . . . . . .    $ 800
Annualized adjusted gross income . . . . . . .    24,000
Minus: excess itemized deductions . . . . . . .    800

Annualized tax table income . . . . . . . . . . .    23,200
Minus: Personal exemption . . . . . . . . . . .    750

Annualized taxable income . . . . . . . . . . .    $22,450
Tax under section 1(c) on annualized taxable
   income . . . . . . . . . . . . . . . . . . .    5,325
Minus: general tax credit . . . . . . . . . . . .    180

Total . . . . . . . . . . . . . . . . . . . . . .    $5,145
Amount specified in paragraph (a)(2) of this
   section (³/₄ × 80% × $5,145) . . . . . . . . . . .    3,087

The exception described in paragraph (a)(2) does not apply.

(d) *Determination of taxable income for installment periods.*—(1) *In general.*—(i) In determining the applicability of the exceptions described in paragraph (a)(2) and (3) of this section, there must be an accurate determination of the amount of income and deductions for the calendar months in the taxable year preceding the installment date as of which the determination is made, that is, for the period terminating with the last day of the third, fifth, or eighth month of the taxable year. For example, a taxpayer distributes year-end bonuses to his employees but does not determine the amount of the bonuses until the last month of the taxable year. He may not deduct any portion of such year-end bonuses in determining his taxable income for any installment period other than the final installment period for the taxable year, since deductions are not allowable until paid or accrued, depending on the taxpayer's method of accounting.

(ii) If a taxpayer on an accrual method of accounting wishes to use either of the exceptions described in paragraph (a)(2) and (3) of this section, he must establish the amount of income and deductions for each applicable period. If his income is derived from a business in which the production, purchase, or sale of merchandise is an income-producing factor requiring the use of inventories, he will be unable to determine accurately the amount of his taxable income for the applicable period unless he can establish, with reasonable accuracy, his cost of goods sold for the applicable installment period. The cost of goods sold for such period shall be considered, unless a more exact determination is available, as such part of the cost of goods sold during the entire taxable year as the gross receipts from sales for such installment period is of gross receipts from sales for the entire taxable year.

(2) *Members of partnerships.*—The provisions of this subparagraph shall apply in determining the applicability of the exceptions described in paragraph (a)(2) and (3) of this section to an underpayment of estimated tax by a taxpayer who is a member of a partnership.

(i) For purposes of determining taxable income, there shall be taken into account—

(A) The partner's distributive share of partnership items set forth under section 702,

(B) The amount of any guaranteed payments under section 707(c), and

(C) Gains or losses on partnership distributions which are treated as gains or losses on sales of property.

(ii) For purposes of determining net earnings from self-employment (for taxable years beginning after December 31, 1966) there shall be taken into account—

(A) The partner's distributive share of income or loss, described in section 702(a)(9), subject to the special rules set forth in section 1402(a) and §§1.1402(a)-1 to 1.1402(a)-16, inclusive, and

(B) The amount of any guaranteed payments under section 707(c), except for payments received from a partnership not engaged in a trade or business within the meaning of section 1402(c) and §1.1402(c)-1.

In determining a partner's taxable income and, for taxable years beginning after December 31, 1966, net earnings from self-employment, for the months in his taxable year which precede the month in which the installment date falls, the partner shall take into account items set forth in sections 702 and 1402(a) for any partnership taxable year ending with or within his taxable year to the extent that such items are attributable to months in such partnership taxable year which precede the month in which the installment date falls. For special rules used in computing a partner's net earnings from self-employment in the case of the termination of his taxable year as a result of death, see section 1402(f) and §1.1402(f)-1. In addition, a partner shall include in his taxable income and, for taxable years beginning after December 31, 1966, net earnings from self-employment, for the months in his taxable year which precede the month in which the installment date falls guaranteed payments from the partnership to the extent that such guaranteed payments are includible in his taxable income for such months. See section 706(a), section 707(c), paragraph (c) of §1.707-1 and section 1402(a).

(iii) The provisions of subdivision (i)(A) and (B) and subdivision (ii) of this subparagraph may be illustrated by the following examples:

*Example (1)*. A, whose taxable year is the calendar year, is a member of a partnership whose taxable year ends on January 31. A must take into account, in determining his taxable income for the installment due on April 15, 1973, all of his distributive share of partnership items described in section 702 and the amount of any guaranteed payments made to him which were deductible by the partnership in the partnership taxable year beginning on February 1, 1972, and ending on January 31, 1973. A must take into account, in determining his net earnings from self-employment, his distributive share of partnership income or loss described in section 702(a)(9), subject to the special rules set forth in section 1402(a) and §§1.1402(a)-1 to 1.1402(a)-16, inclusive.

*Example (2)*. Assume that the taxable year of the partnership of which A, a calendar year taxpayer, is a member ends on June 30. A must take into account in the determination of his taxable income and net earnings from self-employment for the installment due on April 15, 1973, his distributive share of partnership items for the period July 1, 1972, through March 31, 1973; for the installment due on June 15, 1973, he must take into account such amounts for the period July 1, 1972, through May 31, 1973; and for the installment due on September 15, 1973, he must take into account such amounts for the entire partnership taxable year of July 1, 1972, through June 30, 1973 (the date on which the partnership taxable year ends).

(3) *Beneficiaries of estates and trusts.*—In determining the applicability of the exceptions described in paragraph (a)(2) and (3) of this section as of any installment date, the beneficiary of an estate or trust must take into account his distributable share of income from the estate or trust for the applicable period (whether or not actually distributed) if the trust or estate is required to distribute income to him currently. If the estate or trust is not required to distribute income currently, only the amounts actually distributed to the beneficiary during such period must be taken into account. If the taxable year of the beneficiary and the taxable year of the estate or trust are different, there shall be taken into account the beneficiary's distributable share of income, or the amount actually distributed to him as the case may be, during the months in the taxable year of the estate or trust ending within the taxable year of the beneficiary which precede the month in which the installment date falls. See subparagraph (2) of this paragraph for examples of a similar rule which is applied when a partner and the partnership of which he is a member have different taxable years.

(e) *Special rule in case of change from joint return or separate return for the preceding taxable year.*—(1) *Joint return to separate returns.*—In determining the applicability of the exceptions described in paragraph (a)(1) and (4) of this section to an underpayment of estimated tax, a taxpayer filing a separate return who filed a joint return for the

preceding taxable year shall be subject to the following rule: The tax—

(i) Shown on the return for the preceding taxable year, or

(ii) Based on the tax rates and personal exemptions for the current taxable year but otherwise determined on the basis of the facts shown on the return for the preceding taxable year, and the law applicable to such year, shall be that portion of the tax which bears the same ratio to the whole of the tax as the amount of the tax for which the taxpayer would have been liable bears to the sum of the taxes for which the taxpayer and his spouse would have been liable had each spouse filed a separate return for the preceding taxable year. For rules with respect to the allocation of joint payments of estimated tax, see §1.6654-2(e)(5).

(2) *Examples.*—The rule in paragraph (1) of this paragraph may be illustrated by the following examples:

*Example (1)*. H and W filed a joint return for the calendar year 1955 showing taxable income of $20,000 and a tax of $5,280. Of the $20,000 taxable income, $18,000 was attributable to H, and $2,000 was attributable to W. H and W filed separate returns for 1956. The tax shown on the return for the preceding taxable year, for purposes of determining the applicability of the exception described in paragraph (a)(1) of this section to an underpayment of estimated tax by H for 1956, is determined as follows:

| | |
|---|---:|
| Taxable income of H for 1955 . . . . . . . . . . . . . . . . . . | $18,000 |
| Tax on $18,000 (on basis of separate return) . . . . . . . . . | 6,200 |
| Taxable income of W for 1955 . . . . . . . | 2,000 |
| Tax on $2,000 (on basis of separate return) . . . . . . . . . . . | 400 |
| Aggregate tax of H and W (on basis of separate returns) . . | 6,600 |
| Portion of 1955 tax shown on joint return attributable to H (6200/6600 × 5280) . . . . . . . . . . . . . . . . . . . . . | 4,960 |

*Example (2)*. Assume the same facts as in example (1) and that H and W file a joint declaration of estimated tax for 1956 and pay estimated tax in amounts determined on the basis of their eligibility for three rather than two exemptions for 1956. H and W ultimately file separate income tax returns for 1956. Assume further that the exception described in paragraph (a)(1) of this section does not apply. The tax based on the tax rates and personal exemptions for 1956 but otherwise determined on the basis of the facts shown on the return for 1955 and the law applicable to 1955, for purposes of determining the applicability of the exception described in paragraph (a)(4) of this section to an underpayment of estimated tax by H for 1956, is determined as follows:

| | |
|---|---:|
| Taxable income of H and W for 1955 based on additional personal exemption for 1956 . . . . . . . . . . . . . . . | $19,400 |
| Tax on 1955 income based on joint return rate for 1956 . | 5,076 |
| Portion of 1955 tax attributable to H (computed as in example (1) but allowing benefit of additional exemption to H) . . . . . . . . . . . . . . . . . . . . . | 5,900/6,300 |
| Portion of tax attributable to H based on tax rates and personal exemptions for 1956 but otherwise on facts on 1955 return ($5,900/6,300 × $5,076) . . . . . . . . . | 4,754 |

*Example (3)*. Assume that H and W had the same taxable income in 1972 as in 1955, and that they filed a joint return for 1972 and separate returns for 1973. Assume further that H's taxable income for 1972 included net earnings from the self-employment in excess of the $9,000 maximum base for the self-employment tax for 1972, and that the joint return filed by H and W for 1972 showed tax under chapter 1 (other than section 56) and tax under chapter 2 totaling $5,055. The tax shown on the return for 1972, for purposes of determining the applicability of the exception described in paragraph (a)(1) of this section to an underpayment of estimated tax by H for 1973, is determined as follows:

| | |
|---|---:|
| Taxable income of H for 1972 . . . . . . . . . . . . . | $18,000 |
| Chapter 1 tax (other than section 56 tax) on $18,000 (on basis of separate return) . . . . . . . . . . . . . . | 5,170 |
| Self-employment income of H for 1972 . . . . . . . . . | 9,000 |
| Chapter 2 tax on $9,000 . . . . . . . . . . . . . . . . . | 675 |
| Total of such taxes . . . . . . . . . . . . . . . . . | $5,845 |
| Taxable income of W for 1972 . . . . . . . . . . . . . | 2,000 |
| Chapter 1 tax (other than section 56 tax) on $2,000 (on basis of separate return) . . . . . . . . . . . . . . | 310 |
| Aggregate tax of H and W (on basis of separate returns) . . . . . . . . . . . . . . . . . . . . . . . . | 6,155 |
| Portion of 1972 tax shown on joint return attributable to H (5845/6155 × $5,055) . . . . . . . . . . . . . . . | 4,800.40 |

(3) *Separate return to joint return.*—In the case of a taxpayer who files a joint return for the taxable year with respect to which there is an underpayment of estimated tax and who filed a separate return for the preceding taxable year—

(i) The tax shown on the return for the preceding taxable year, for purposes of determining the applicability of the exception described in paragraph (a)(1) of this section, shall be the sum of both the tax shown on the return of the taxpayer and the tax shown on the return of the taxpayer's spouse for such preceding year, and

(ii) The facts shown on both the taxpayer's return and the return of his spouse for the preceding taxable year shall be taken into account for purposes of determining the applicability of the exception described in paragraph (a)(4) of this section.

(4) *Example.*—The rules described in subparagraph (3) of this paragraph may be illustrated by the following example:

*Example.* H and W filed separate income tax returns for the calendar year 1954 showing tax liabilities of $2,640 and $350, respectively. In 1955 they married and participated in the filing of a joint return for that year. Thus, for the purpose of determining the applicability of the exceptions described in paragraph (a)(1) and (4) of this section to an underpayment of estimated tax for the year 1955, the tax shown on the return for the preceding taxable year is $2,990 ($2,640 plus $350).

(5) *Joint payments of estimated tax.*—(i) *In general.*—A husband and wife may make a joint payment of estimated tax even though they are not living together. However, a joint payment of estimated tax may not be made if the husband and wife are separated under a decree of divorce or of separate maintenance. A joint payment of estimated tax may not be made if the taxpayer's spouse is a nonresident alien (including a nonresident alien who is a bona fide resident of Puerto Rico or a possession to which section 931 applies during the entire taxable year), unless an election is in effect for the taxable year under section 6013(g) or (h) and the regulations. In addition, a joint payment of estimated tax may not be made if the taxpayer's spouse has a taxable year different from that of the taxpayer. If a joint payment of estimated tax is made, the amount estimated as the income tax imposed by chapter 1 of the Internal Revenue Code must be computed on the aggregate estimated taxable income of the spouses (see section 6013(d)(3) and §1.2-1), whereas, if applicable, the amount estimated as the self-employment tax imposed by chapter 2 of the Internal Revenue Code must be computed on the separate estimated self-employment income of each spouse. See sections 1401

and 1402 and §1.6017-1(b)(1). The liability with respect to the estimated tax, in the case of a joint payment, shall be joint and several.

(ii) *Application to separate returns.*—(A) Although a husband and wife may make a joint payment of estimated tax, they, nevertheless, can file separate returns. If they make a joint payment of estimated tax and file separate returns for the same taxable year with respect to which the joint payment was made, the payment made on account of the estimated tax for that taxable year may be treated as a payment on account of the tax liability of either the husband or wife for the taxable year, or may be divided between them in such manner as they may agree.

(B) In the event the husband and wife fail to agree to a division of the estimated tax payment, such payment shall be allocated between them in accordance with the following rule. The portion of such payment to be allocated to a taxpayer shall be that portion of the aggregate of all such payments as the amount of tax imposed by chapter 1 of the Internal Revenue Code shown on the separate return of the taxpayer (plus, if applicable, the amount of tax imposed by chapter 2 of the Internal Revenue Code shown on the return of the taxpayer) bears to the sum of the taxes imposed by chapter 1 of the Internal Revenue Code shown on the separate returns of the taxpayer and the spouse (plus, if applicable, the sum of the taxes imposed by chapter 2 of the Internal Revenue Code shown on the separate returns of the taxpayer and the spouse).

(6) *Example.*—The rule described in paragraph (e)(5) of this section may be illustrated by the following example:

*Example.* (i) H and W make a joint payment of estimated tax of $19,500 for the taxable year. H and W subsequently file separate returns for the taxable year showing tax imposed by chapter 1 of the Internal Revenue Code in the amount of $11,500 and $8,000, respectively. In addition, H's return shows a tax imposed by chapter 2 of the Internal Revenue Code in the amount of $500. H and W fail to agree to a division of the estimated tax paid. The amount of the aggregate estimated tax payments allocated to H is determined as follows:

(A) Chapter 1 tax shown on H's return ......................................................... $11,500
(B) Plus: Amount of tax imposed by chapter 2 shown on H's return ...................... .$500
(C) Total taxes imposed by chapter 1 and by chapter 2 shown on H's return ............ $12,000
(D) Amount of tax imposed by chapter 1 shown on W's return ............................ .$8,000
(E) Total taxes imposed by chapter 1 and by chapter 2 on both H's and W's returns .... $20,000
(F) Proportion of taxes shown on H's return to total amount of taxes shown on both H's and W's returns ........................................................................ ($12,000/$20,000) 60%
(G) Amount of estimated tax payments allocated to H (60% of $19,500) ................. $11,700

(ii) Accordingly, H's return would show a balance due in the amount of $300 ($12,000 taxes shown less $11,700 estimated tax allocated).

(7) *Death of spouse.*—(i) A joint payment of estimated tax may not be made after the death of either the husband or wife. However, if it is reasonable for a surviving spouse to assume that there will be filed a joint return for himself and the deceased spouse for his taxable year and the last taxable year of the deceased spouse, he may, in making a separate payment of estimated tax for his taxable year which includes the period comprising such last taxable year of his spouse, estimate the amount of the tax imposed by chapter 1 of the Internal Revenue Code on his and his spouse's taxable income on an aggregate basis and compute his estimated tax with respect to chapter 1 tax in the same manner as though a joint return had been filed.

(ii) If a husband and wife make a joint payment of estimated tax and thereafter one spouse dies, no further payments of joint estimated tax liability are required from the estate of the decedent. The surviving spouse, however, shall be liable for the payment of any subsequent installments of the joint estimated tax. For the purpose of making an amended payment of estimated tax by the surviving spouse, and the allocation of payments made pursuant to a joint payment of estimated tax between the surviving spouse and the legal representative of the decedent in the event a joint return is not filed, the payment of estimated tax may be divided between the decedent and the surviving spouse in such proportion as the surviving spouse and the legal representative of the decedent may agree.

(iii) If the surviving spouse and the legal representative of the decedent fail to agree to a division of a payment, such payment shall be allocated in accordance with the following rule. The portion of such payment to be allocated to the surviving spouse shall be that portion of the aggregate amount of such payments as the amount of tax imposed by chapter 1 of the Internal Revenue Code shown on the separate return of the surviving spouse (plus, if applicable, the amount of tax imposed by chapter 2 of the Internal Revenue Code shown on the return of the surviving spouse) bears to the sum imposed by chapter 1 of the Internal Revenue Code shown on the separate returns of the surviving spouse and of the decedent (plus, if applicable, the sum of the taxes imposed by chapter 2 of the Internal

Revenue Code shown on the returns of the surviving spouse and of the decedent); and the balance of such payments shall be allocated to the decedent. This rule may be illustrated by analogizing the surviving spouse described in this rule to H in the example contained in paragraph (e)(6) of this section and the decedent in this rule to W in that example.

(f) *Effective/applicability date.*—Paragraph (a)(1)(ii) of this section applies to any taxable year beginning in 2009 and does not apply to any taxable years beginning before or after 2009. [Reg. §1.6654-2.]

☐ [*T.D. 6267, 11-13-57. Amended by T.D. 6678, 9-30-63; T.D. 6777, 12-15-64; T.D. 7282, 7-16-73; T.D. 7427, 8-9-76; T.D. 7577, 12-19-78; T.D. 7585, 1-3-79; T.D. 8016, 3-25-85; T.D. 8996, 5-16-2002, T.D. 9224, 9-1-2005; T.D. 9480, 2-26-2010 and T.D. 9613, 2-25-2013.]*

### [Reg. §1.6654-3]

**§1.6654-3. Short taxable years of individuals.**—(a) *In general.*—The provisions of section 6654, with certain modifications relating to the application of section 6654(d), which are explained in paragraph (b) of this section, are applicable in the case of a short taxable year.

(b) *Rules as to application of section 6654(d).*—(1) In any case in which the taxable year for which an underpayment of estimated tax exists is a short taxable year due to a change in annual accounting periods, in determining the tax—

(i) Shown on the return for the preceding taxable year (for purposes of section 6654(d)(1)(A)), or

(ii) Based on the personal exemptions and rates for the current taxable year but otherwise on the basis of the facts shown on the return for the preceding taxable year, and the law applicable to such year (for purposes of section 6654(d)(4)),

the tax will be reduced by multiplying it by the number of months in the short taxable year and dividing the resulting amount by 12.

(2) If the taxable year for which an underpayment of estimated tax exists is a short taxable year due to a change in annual accounting periods, in annualizing the income for the months in the taxable year preceding an installment date, for purposes of section 6654(d)(2), the personal exemptions allowed as deductions under section 151 shall

be reduced to the same extent that they are reduced under section 443(c) in computing the tax for a short taxable year.

(3) If "the preceding taxable year" referred to in section 6654(d)(4) was a short taxable year, for purposes of determining the applicability of the exception described in section 6654(d)(4), the tax, computed on the basis of the facts shown on the return for the preceding year, shall be the tax computed on the annual basis in the manner described in section 443(b)(1) (prior to its reduction in the manner described in the last sentence thereof). If the tax rates or the taxpayer's status with respect to personal exemptions for the taxable year with respect to which the underpayment occurs differs from such rates or status applicable to the preceding taxable year, the tax determined in accordance with this subparagraph shall be recomputed to reflect the rates and status applicable to the year with respect to which the underpayment occurs. [Reg. § 1.6654-3.]

☐ [T.D. 6267, 11-13-57. Amended by T.D. 7427, 8-9-76 and T.D. 9224, 9-1-2005.]

### [Reg. §1.6654-4]

**§1.6654-4. [Reserved].**

☐ [Removed and reserved by T.D. 9849, 3-11-2019.]

### [Reg. §1.6654-5]

**§1.6654-5. Payments of estimated tax.**—(a) *In general.*—A payment of estimated tax by an individual shall be determined on Form 1040-ES. For the purpose of determining the estimated tax, the amount of gross income which the taxpayer can reasonably expect to receive or accrue, depending upon the method of accounting upon which taxable income is computed, and the amount of the estimated allowable deductions and credits to be taken into account in computing the amount of estimated tax, shall be determined upon the basis of the facts and circumstances existing at the time prescribed for determining the estimated tax, as well as those reasonably to be anticipated for the taxable year. If, therefore, the taxpayer is employed at the date prescribed for making an estimated tax payment at a given wage or salary, the taxpayer should presume, in the absence of circumstances indicating the contrary, for the purpose of the estimated tax payment that such employment will continue to the end of the taxable year at the wage or salary received by the taxpayer as of such date. In the case of income other than wages and salary, the regularity in the payment of income, such as dividends, interest, rents, royalties, and income arising from estates and trusts is a factor to be taken into consideration. Thus, if the taxpayer owns shares of stock in a corporation, and dividends have been paid regularly for several years upon the stock, the taxpayer should, in the absence of information indicating a change in the dividend policy, include the prospective dividends from the corporation for the taxable year as well as those actually received in such year prior to determining the estimated tax. In the case of a taxpayer engaged in business on his own account, there shall be made an estimate of gross income and deductions and credits in the light of the best available information affecting the trade, business, or profession.

(b) *Computation of estimated tax.*—In computing the estimated tax the taxpayer should take into account the taxes, credits, and other amounts listed in § 1.6654-1(a)(4). [Reg. § 1.6654-5.]

☐ [T.D. 9224, 9-1-2005.]

### [Reg. §1.6654-6]

**§1.6654-6. Nonresident alien individuals.**—(a) *In general.*—A nonresident alien individual is required to make a payment of estimated tax if that individual's gross income meets the requirements of section 6654 and § 1.6654-1. In making the determination under section 6654 as to whether the amount of the gross income of a nonresident alien individual is such as to require making a payment of estimated income tax, only the filing status relating to a single individual (other than a head of household) or to a married individual not entitled to file a joint return shall apply, unless an election is in effect for the taxable year under section 6013(g) or (h) and the regulations.

(b) *Determination of gross income.*—To determine the gross income of a nonresident alien individual who is not, or does not expect to be, a bona fide resident of Puerto Rico or a possession to which section 931 applies during the entire taxable year, see section 872 and §§ 1.872-1 and 1.872-2. To determine the gross income of a nonresident alien individual who is, or expects to be, a bona fide resident of Puerto Rico or a possession to which section 931 applies during the entire taxable year, see section 876 and the regulations. For rules for determining whether an individual is a bona fide resident of a United States possession (including Puerto Rico), see section 937 and the regulations. [Reg. § 1.6654-6.]

☐ [T.D. 9224, 9-1-2005.]

### [Reg. §1.6654-7]

**§1.6654-7. Applicability.**—Section 6654 is applicable only with respect to taxable years beginning after December 31, 1954. Section 294(d) of the Internal Revenue Code of 1939 shall continue in force with respect to taxable years beginning before January 1, 1955. [Reg. § 1.6654-7.]

☐ [T.D. 6267, 11-13-57. Amended by T.D. 7282, 7-16-73. Redesignated by T.D. 9224, 9-1-2005.]

### [Reg. §1.6655-0]

**§1.6655-0. Table of contents.**—This section lists the table of contents for §§ 1.6655–1 through 1.6655–7.

(C) Short taxable years.
(v) Distributive share of items
(A) Member of partnership.
(B) Treatment of subpart F income and income under section 936(h).
(1) General rule.
(2) Prior year safe harbor.
(i) General rule.
(ii) Special rule for noncontrolling shareholder.
(C) Dividends from closely held real estate investment trust.
(1) General rule.
(2) Closely held real estate investment trust.
(D) Other passthrough entities.
(vi) Alternative minimum taxable income exemption amount.
(vii) Examples.
(g) Items that substantially affect taxable income but cannot be determined accurately by the installment due date.
(1) In general.
(2) Example.
(h) Effective/applicability date.

§ 1.6655-3. *Adjusted seasonal installment method.*
(a) In general.
(b) Limitation on application of section.
(c) Determination of amount.
(d) Special rules.
(1) Base period percentage.
(2) Filing month.
(3) Application of the rules related to the annualized income installment method to the adjusted seasonal installment method.
(4) Alternative minimum tax.
(e) Example.
(f) Effective/applicability date.

§ 1.6655-4. *Large corporations.*
(a) Large corporation defined.
(b) Testing period.
(c) Computation of taxable income during testing period.
(1) Short taxable year.
(2) Computation of taxable income in taxable year when there occurs a transaction to which section 381 applies.
(d) Members of controlled group.
(1) In general.
(2) Aggregation.
(3) Allocation rule.
(4) Controlled group members.
(e) Effect on a corporation's taxable income of items that may be carried back or carried over from any other taxable year.
(f) Consolidated returns. [Reserved]
(g) Example.
(h) Effective/applicability date.

§ 1.6655-5. *Short taxable year.*
(a) In general.
(b) Exception to payment of estimated tax.
(c) Installment due dates.
(1) In general.
(i) Taxable year of at least four months but less than twelve months.
(ii) Exceptions.
(2) Early termination of taxable year.
(i) In general.
(ii) Exception.
(d) Amount due for required installment.
(1) In general.
(2) Tax shown on the return for the preceding taxable year.
(3) Applicable percentage.
(4) Applicable percentage for installment period in which taxpayer does not reasonably expect that the taxable year will be an early termination year.
(e) Examples.
(f) 52 or 53 week taxable year.
(g) Use of annualized income or seasonal installment method.
(1) In general.
(2) Computation of annualized income installment.
(3) Annualization period for final required installment.
(4) Examples.
(h) Effective/applicability date.

§ 1.6655-6. *Methods of accounting.*
(a) In general.
(b) Accounting method changes.
(c) Examples.
(d) Effective/applicability date.

§ 1.6655-7. *Addition to tax on account of excessive adjustment under section 6425.*
[Reg. § 1.6655–0.]

☐ [*T.D. 9347, 8-6-2007. Amended by T.D. 9870, 7-11-2019.*]

**[Reg. § 1.6655-1]**

**§ 1.6655-1. Addition to the tax in the case of a corporation.—**
(a) *In general.*—Section 6655 imposes an addition to the tax under chapter 1 of the Internal Revenue Code in the case of any underpayment of estimated tax by a corporation. An addition to tax due to the underpayment of estimated taxes is determined by applying the underpayment rate established under section 6621 to the amount of the underpayment, for the period of the underpayment. This addition to the tax is in addition to any applicable criminal penalties and is imposed whether or not there was reasonable cause for the underpayment.

(b) *Amount of underpayment.*—The amount of the underpayment for any required installment is the excess of—
(1) The required installment; over
(2) The amount, if any, of the installment paid on or before the last date prescribed for such payment.

(c) *Period of the underpayment.*—The period of the underpayment of any required installment runs from the date the installment was required to be paid to the 15th day of the 3rd month following the close of the taxable year, or to the date such underpayment is paid, whichever is earlier. For purposes of determining the period of the underpayment a payment of estimated tax will be credited against unpaid required installments in the order in which such installments are required to be paid.

(d) *Amount of required installment.*—(1) *In general.*—Except as otherwise provided in this section and §§ 1.6655-2 through 1.6655-7, the amount of any required installment is 25 percent of the lesser of—
(i) 100 percent of the tax shown on the return for the taxable year (or, if no return is filed, 100 percent of the tax for such year); or
(ii) 100 percent of the tax shown on the return for the preceding taxable year.

(2) *Exception.*—This paragraph (d)(1)(ii) does not apply if the preceding taxable year was not a taxable year of 12 months or the corporation did not file a return for the preceding taxable year showing a liability for tax.

(e) *Large corporation required to pay 100 percent of current year tax.*—(1) *In general.*—Except as provided in paragraph (e)(2) of this section, paragraph (d)(1)(ii) of this section does not apply in the case of a large corporation (as defined in § 1.6655-4).

(2) *May use last year's tax for first installment.*—Paragraph (e)(1) of this section does not apply for purposes of determining the amount of the 1st required installment for any taxable year. Any reduction in such 1st installment by reason of the preceding sentence is recaptured by increasing the amount of the next required installment determined under paragraph (d)(1)(i) of this section by the amount of such reduction and, if the next required installment is reduced by use of the annualized income installment method under § 1.6655-2 or the adjusted seasonal installment method under § 1.6655-3, by increasing subsequent required installments determined under paragraph (d)(1)(i) of this section to the extent that the reduction has not previously been recaptured.

(f) *Required installment due dates.*—(1) *Number of required installments.*—Unless otherwise provided, corporations must make 4 required installments for each taxable year.

(2) *Time for payment of installments.*—(i) *Calendar year.*—Unless otherwise provided, in the case of a calendar year taxpayer, the due dates of the required installments are as follows:

| | |
|---|---|
| 1st | April 15 |
| 2nd | June 15 |
| 3rd | September 15 |
| 4th | December 15 |

(ii) *Fiscal year.*—In the case of a taxpayer other than a calendar year taxpayer, the due dates of the required installments are as follows:

| | |
|---|---|
| 1st | 15th day of 4th month of the taxable year |
| 2nd | 15th day of 6th month of the taxable year |

3rd . . . . . .   15th day of 9th month of the taxable year
4th . . . . . .   15th day of 12th month of the taxable year

(iii) *Short taxable year.*—See §1.6655-5 for rules regarding required installments for corporations with a short taxable year.

(iv) *Partial month.*—Except as otherwise provided, for purposes of determining the due date of any required installment, a partial month is treated as a full month.

(g) *Definitions.*—(1) The term tax as used in this section and §§1.6655-2 through 1.6655-7 means the excess of—

(i) The sum of—

(A) The tax imposed by section 11, section 1201(a), or subchapter L of chapter 1 of the Internal Revenue Code, whichever is applicable;

(B) The tax imposed by section 55; plus

(C) The tax imposed by section 887; over

(ii) The credits against tax provided by part IV of subchapter A of chapter 1 of the Internal Revenue Code.

(2)(i) In the case of a foreign corporation subject to taxation under section 11, section 1201(a), or subchapter L of chapter 1 of the Internal Revenue Code, the tax imposed by section 881 is treated as a tax imposed by section 11.

(ii) In the case of a partnership that is treated, pursuant to regulations issued under section 1446(f)(2), as a corporation for purposes of this section, the tax imposed by section 1446 is treated as a tax imposed by section 11.

(iii) Unless otherwise provided in the Internal Revenue Code or Treasury regulations, for purposes of the definition of "tax" as used in this section, a recapture of tax, such as a recapture provided by section 50(a)(1)(A), and any other similar provision, is not considered to be a tax imposed by section 11.

(iv) For the purposes of paragraph (d) of this section, the return for the preceding taxable year is the Federal income tax return for such taxable year that is required by section 6012(a)(2). However, if an amended Federal income tax return has been filed before the due date of an installment, then the return for the preceding taxable year is the Federal income tax return as amended. If an amended Federal income tax return has been filed on or after the due date for an installment, then the return for the preceding taxable year does not include for such installment period the Federal income tax return as amended subsequent to the due date for such installment. Paragraph (d) of this section will apply without regard to whether the taxpayer's Federal income tax return for the preceding taxable year is filed in a timely manner.

(h) *Special rules for consolidated returns.*—For special rules relating to the determination of the amount of the underpayment in the case of a corporation whose income is included in a consolidated return, see §1.1502-5(b).

(i) *Overpayments applied to subsequent taxable year's estimated tax.*—(1) *In general.*—If a taxpayer elects under the provisions of sections 6402(b) and 6513(d) and the regulations to apply an overpayment in year one against the estimated tax liability for year two, the overpayment will be applied to the required installment payments for year two in the order due and to the extent necessary to satisfy such installments, similar to the manner in which an actual overpayment of one installment is carried forward to the next installment. No interest is accrued or paid on an overpayment if the election to apply the overpayment against estimated tax is made.

(2) *Subsequent examinations.*—If a deficiency is determined in an examination of a return for a taxable year that originally reflected an overpayment that was applied against estimated tax for the succeeding taxable year, interest on the deficiency will not begin to accrue on an amount applied until that amount is used to satisfy a required estimated tax payment in such taxable year. Regardless of whether the taxpayer anticipated the application of such overpayment from the prior taxable year in calculating and paying its required estimated tax installment liabilities for the current taxable year, the subsequently determined underpayment and interest computation thereon will not change the taxpayer's original election to apply the overpayment against the estimated tax liability of the succeeding taxable year. Any changes to the usage of the original overpayment from the prior taxable year are hypothetical only and solely for the purpose of computing deficiency interest. Overpayment interest will not be impacted. For further guidance, see Rev. Rul. 99-40 (1999-2 CB 441), (see §601.601(d)(2)(ii)(b) of this chapter).

(j) *Examples.*—The method prescribed in paragraphs (d) through (g) of this section is illustrated by the following examples:

*Example 1.* (i) X, a calendar year corporation, estimates its tax liability for its taxable year ending December 31, 2009, will be $85,000. X is not a large corporation as defined in section 6655(g)(2)

and §1.6655-4. X reported a liability of $74,900 on its return for the taxable year ended December 31, 2008, with no credits against tax. X paid four installments of estimated tax, each in the amount of $18,725 (25 percent of $74,900), on April 15, 2009, June 15, 2009, September 15, 2009, and December 15, 2009, respectively. X reported a tax liability of $88,900 on its return due March 15, 2010. X had a $5,000 credit against tax for tax year 2009 as provided by part IV of subchapter A of chapter 1 of the Internal Revenue Code. X did not underpay its estimated tax for tax year 2009 for any of the four installments, determined as follows:

(A) Tax as defined in paragraph (g) of this section for 2009 ($88,900-$5,000) = $83,900

(B) Tax as defined in paragraph (g) of this section for 2008 = $74,900

(C) 100% of the lesser of this paragraph (j), *Example 1* (i)(A) or (i)(B) = $74,900

(D) Amount of estimated tax required to be paid on or before each installment date (25% of $74,900) = $18,725

(E) Deduct amount paid on or before each installment date = $18,725

(F) Amount of underpayment for each installment date = $0

(ii) [Reserved].

*Example 2.* (i) *Facts.* Y, a calendar year corporation, estimates its tax liability for its taxable year ending December 31, 2009, will be $70,000. Y is not a large corporation as defined in section 6655(g)(2) and §1.6655-4. Y reported a Federal income tax liability of $90,000 for its taxable year ending December 31, 2008. Y paid no installment of estimated tax on or before April 15, 2009, June 15, 2009, or September 15, 2009, but made a payment of $63,000 on December 15, 2009. On March 15, 2010, Y filed its income tax return showing a tax of $70,000. Y had no credits against tax for tax year 2009. Of the $63,000 paid by Y on December 15, 2009, $17,500 is applied to each of the first three installments due on April 15, June 15, and September 15, 2009, and the remaining $10,500 is applied to the fourth installment. Y has an underpayment of estimated tax for each of the first three installments of $17,500 and for the fourth installment of $7,000. The addition to tax under section 6655(a) is computed as follows:

(A) Tax as defined in paragraph (g) of this section for 2009 = $70,000

(B) Tax as defined in paragraph (g) of this section for 2008 = $90,000

(C) 100% of the lesser of this paragraph (j), *Example 2* (i)(A) or (i)(B) = $70,000

(D) Amount of estimated tax required to be paid on or before each installment date (25% of $70,000) = $17,500

(E) Amount paid on or before the first, second, and third installment dates = $0

(F) Amount paid on or before the fourth installment date = $63,000

(G) Amount of underpayment for each of the first, second, and third installment dates = $17,500

(H) Amount of underpayment for the fourth installment date = $7,000

(ii) *Addition to tax.* Assuming that neither the annualized income installment method nor the adjusted seasonal installment method described in §§1.6655-2 and 1.6655-3 would result in a lower payment for any installment period, and the addition to tax is computed under section 6621(a)(2) at the rate of 8 percent per annum for the applicable periods of underpayment, the addition to tax is determined as follows:

(A) First installment (underpayment period 4-16-09 through 12-15-09), computed as $244/365 \times \$17,500 \times 8\% = \$936$

(B) Second installment (underpayment period 6-16-09 through 12-15-09), computed as $183/365 \times \$17,500 \times 8\% = \$702$

(C) Third installment (underpayment period 9-16-09 through 12-15-09), computed as $91/365 \times \$17,500 \times 8\% = \$349$

(D) Fourth installment (underpayment period 12-16-09 through 3-15-10), computed as $90/365 \times \$7,000 \times 8\% = \$138$

(E) Total of this paragraph (j), *Example 2* (ii)(A) through (D) = $2,125

(k) *Effective/applicability date.*—This section applies to taxable years beginning after September 6, 2007. [Reg. §1.6655-1.]

☐ [*T.D.* 6267, 11-13-57. *Amended by T.D.* 6768, 11-3-64, *T.D.* 7244, 12-29-72; *T.D.* 7384, 10-21-75 *and T.D.* 9347, 8-6-2007.]

**[Reg. §301.6655-1]**

**§301.6655-1.** *Failure by corporation to pay estimated income tax.*—(a) For regulations under section 6655, see §§1.6655-1 through 1.6655-7 of this chapter.

(b) Effective/applicability date: This section applies to taxable years beginning after September 6, 2007. [Reg. §301.6655-1.]

☐ [*T.D.* 6268, 11-15-57. *Amended by T.D.* 6498, 10-24-60; *T.D.* 7059, 9-16-70 *and T.D.* 9347, 8-6-2007.]

[Reg. §1.6655-2]

**§1.6655-2. Annualized income installment method.**—(a) *In general.*—In the case of any required installment, if the corporation establishes that the annualized income installment determined under this section, or the adjusted seasonal installment determined under §1.6655-3, is less than the amount determined under §1.6655-1—

(1) The amount of such required installment is the annualized income installment (or, if less, the adjusted seasonal installment); and

(2) Any reduction in a required installment resulting from the application of this section will be recaptured by increasing the amount of the next required installment determined under §1.6655-1 by the amount of such reduction (and, if the next required installment is similarly reduced, by increasing subsequent required installments to the extent that the reduction has not previously been recaptured).

(b) *Determination of annualized income installment—in general.*—In the case of any required installment, the annualized income installment is the excess (if any) of—

(1) The product of the applicable percentage and the tax (after reducing the annualized tax by the amount of any allowable credits) for the taxable year computed by annualizing the taxable income and alternative minimum taxable income—

(i) For the first 3 months of the taxable year, in the case of the first required installment;

(ii) For the first 3 months of the taxable year, in the case of the second required installment;

(iii) For the first 6 months of the taxable year, in the case of the third required installment; and

(iv) For the first 9 months of the taxable year, in the case of the fourth required installment; over

(2) The aggregate amount of any prior required installments for the taxable year.

(c) *Special rules.*—(1) *Applicable percentage.*—Except as otherwise provided in §1.6655-5(d) with respect to short taxable years—

| In the case of the following required installments: | The applicable percentage is: |
|---|---|
| 1st | 25% |
| 2nd | 50% |
| 3rd | 75% |
| 4th | 100% |

(2) *Partial month.*—Except as otherwise provided, for purposes of paragraph (b) of this section a partial month is treated as a month.

(3) *Annualization period not a short taxable year.*—An annualization period is not treated as a short taxable year for purposes of determining the taxable income of an annualization period.

(d) *Election of different annualization periods.*—(1) If the taxpayer timely files Form 8842, "Election to Use Different Annualization Periods for Corporate Estimated Tax," in accordance with section 6655(e)(2)(C)(iii), and elects Option 1—

(i) Paragraph (b)(1)(i) of this section will be applied by using the language "2 months" instead of "3 months";

(ii) Paragraph (b)(1)(ii) of this section will be applied by using the language "4 months" instead of "3 months";

(iii) Paragraph (b)(1)(iii) of this section will be applied by using the language "7 months" instead of "6 months"; and

(iv) Paragraph (b)(1)(iv) of this section will be applied by using the language "10 months" instead of "9 months".

(2) If the taxpayer timely files Form 8842, in accordance with section 6655(e)(2)(C)(iii), and elects Option 2—

(i) Paragraph (b)(1)(ii) of this section will be applied by using the language "5 months" instead of "3 months";

(ii) Paragraph (b)(1)(iii) of this section will be applied by using the language "8 months" instead of "6 months"; and

(iii) Paragraph (b)(1)(iv) of this section will be applied by using the language "11 months" instead of "9 months".

(3) The application of the annualized income installment method is illustrated by the following example:

*Example.* (i) ABC, a calendar year corporation, had a taxable year of less than twelve months for tax year 2008 and no credits against tax for tax year 2009. ABC made an estimated tax payment of $15,000 on the installment dates of April 15, 2009, June 15, 2009, September 15, 2009, and December 15, 2009, respectively. Assume that, under paragraph (d)(1) of this section, ABC elected Option 1 by timely filing Form 8842, in accordance with section 6655(e)(2)(C)(iii), and determined that its taxable income for the first 2, 4, 7 and 10 months was $25,000, $64,000, $125,000, and $175,000 respectively. The income for each period is annualized as follows:

$25,000 × 12/2 = $150,000
$64,000 × 12/4 = $192,000

$125,000 × 12/7 = $214,286
$175,000 × 12/10 = $210,000

(ii)(A) To determine whether the installment payment made on April 15, 2009, equals or exceeds the amount that would have been required to have been paid if the estimated tax were equal to 100 percent of the tax computed on the annualized income for the 2-month period, the following computation is necessary:

(1) Annualized income for the 2 month period = $150,000

(2) Tax on this paragraph (d)(3), *Example* (ii)(A)(1) = $41,750

(3) 100% of this paragraph (d)(3), *Example* (ii)(A)(2) = $41,750

(4) 25% of this paragraph (d)(3), *Example* (ii)(A)(3) = $10,438

(B) Because the total amount of estimated tax that was timely paid on or before the first installment date ($15,000) exceeds the amount required to be paid on or before this date if the estimated tax were 100 percent of the tax determined by placing on an annualized basis the taxable income for the first 2-month period ($10,438), the exception described in paragraphs (a) and (b) of this section applies, and no addition to tax will be imposed for the installment due on April 15, 2009.

(iii)(A) To determine whether the installment payments made on or before June 15, 2009, equal or exceed the amount that would have been required to have been paid if the estimated tax were equal to 100 percent of the tax computed on the annualized income for the 4-month period, the following computation is necessary:

(1) Annualized income for the 4 month period = $192,000

(2) Tax on this paragraph (d)(3), *Example* (iii)(A)(1) = $58,130

(3) 100% of this paragraph (d)(3), *Example* (iii)(A)(2) = $58,130

(4) 50% of this paragraph (d)(3), *Example* (iii)(A)(3) less $10,438 (amount due with the first installment) = $18,627

(B) Because the total amount of estimated tax actually paid on or before the second installment date ($19,562 ($15,000 second required installment payment plus $4,562 overpayment of first required installment)) exceeds the amount required to be paid on or before this date if the estimated tax were 100 percent of the tax determined by placing on an annualized basis the taxable income for the first 4-month period ($18,627), the exception described in paragraphs (a) and (b) of this section applies, and no addition to tax will be imposed for the installment due on June 15, 2009.

(iv)(A) To determine whether the installment payments made on or before September 15, 2009, equal or exceed the amount that would have been required to have been paid if the estimated tax were equal to 100 percent of the tax computed on the annualized income for the 7-month period, the following computation is necessary:

(1) Annualized income for the 7 month period = $214,286

(2) Tax on this paragraph (d)(3), *Example* (iv)(A)(1) = $66,821

(3) 100% of this paragraph (d)(3), *Example* (iv)(A)(2) = $66,821

(4) 75% of this paragraph (d)(3), *Example* (iv)(A)(3) less $29,065 (amount due with the first and second installment) = $21,051

(B) Because the total amount of estimated tax actually paid on or before the third installment date ($15,935 ($15,000 third required installment payment plus $935 overpayment of second required installment)) does not equal or exceed the amount required to be paid on or before this date if the estimated tax were 100 percent of the tax determined by placing on an annualized basis the taxable income for the first 7-month period ($21,051), the exception described in paragraphs (a) and (b) of this section does not apply, and an addition to tax will be imposed with respect to the underpayment of the September 15, 2009, installment unless another exception applies to this installment payment.

(v)(A) To determine whether the installment payments made on or before December 15, 2009, equal or exceed the amount that would have been required to have been paid if the estimated tax were equal to 100 percent of the tax computed on the annualized income for the 10-month period, the following computation is necessary:

(1) Annualized income for the 10 month period = $210,000

(2) Tax on this paragraph (d)(3), *Example* (v)(A)(1) = $65,150

(3) 100% of this paragraph (d)(3), *Example* (v)(A)(2) = $65,150

(4) 100% of this paragraph (d)(3), *Example* (v)(A)(3) less $50,116 (amount due with the first, second and third installment) = $15,034

(B) Because the total amount of estimated tax payments made on or before the fourth installment date that is available to be applied to the estimated tax due for the fourth installment ($9,884 ($15,000 fourth required installment payment less $5,116 underpayment for the third installment of estimated tax ($21,051 third installment of estimated tax due less $15,935 payments available to be applied to the third installment of estimated tax))) does not equal or exceed the amount required to be paid on or before this date if the estimated tax were 100 percent of the tax determined by placing on an annualized basis the taxable income for the first 10-month period ($15,034), the exception described in paragraphs (a) and (b) of this section does not apply, and an addition to tax will be imposed with respect to the underpayment of the December 15, 2009, installment unless another exception applies to this installment payment.

(vi) Assuming that no other exceptions apply and the addition to tax is computed under section 6621(a)(2) at the rate of 8 percent per annum for the applicable periods of underpayment, the amount of the addition to tax is as follows:

(A) First installment (no underpayment) = $0

(B) Second installment (no underpayment) = $0

(C) Third installment (underpayment period 9-16-09 through 12-15-09), computed as $91/365 \times \$5,116 \times 8\% = \$102$

(D) Fourth installment (underpayment period 12-16-09 through 3-15-10), computed as $90/365 \times \$5,150 \times 8\% = \$102$

(E) Total of this paragraph (d)(3), *Example* (vi)(A) through (D) = $204

(e) *52-53 week taxable year.*—(1) Generally, except as provided in the alternative rule in paragraph (e)(4) of this section, in the case of a taxpayer whose taxable year constitutes 52 or 53 weeks in accordance with section 441(f), the rules prescribed by § 1.441-2 are applicable in determining—

(i) Whether a taxable year is a taxable year of 12 months; and

(ii) When the 2-, 3- ,4-, 5-, 6-, 7-, 8-, 9-, 10-, or 11-month period (whichever is applicable) commences and ends for purposes of paragraphs (b)(1), (d)(1) and (d)(2) of this section.

(2) If a taxpayer employs four 13-week periods or thirteen 4-week accounting periods and the end of any accounting period employed by the taxpayer does not correspond to the end of the 2-, 3- ,4-, 5-, 6-, 7-, 8-, 9-, 10-, or 11-month period (whichever is applicable), then, provided the taxpayer has at least one full 4-week or 13-week accounting period, as appropriate, within the applicable period, annualized taxable income for the applicable period is—

(i) $[(x/(y*13))*z]$, in the case of a taxpayer using four 13-week periods, if—

(A) x = Taxable income for the number of full 13-week periods in the applicable period;

(B) y = The number of full 13-week periods in the applicable period; and

(C) z = The number of weeks in the taxable year; or

(ii) $[(x/(y*4))*z]$, in the case of a taxpayer using thirteen 4-week periods, if—

(A) x = Taxable income for the number of full 4-week periods in the applicable period;

(B) y = The number of full 4-week periods in the applicable period; and

(C) z = The number of weeks in the taxable year.

(3) If a taxpayer employs four 13-week periods and the taxpayer does not have at least one 13-week period within the applicable 2-, 3-, 4-, 5-, 6-, 7-, 8-, 9-, 10-, or 11-month period, the taxpayer is permitted to determine annualized taxable income for the applicable period based upon—

(i) The taxable income for the number of weeks in the applicable period; or

(ii) The taxable income for the full 13-week periods that end before the due date of the required installment.

(4) As an alternative to using the 52/53 week taxable year rules provided in paragraphs (e)(1), (e)(2), and (e)(3) of this section, a taxpayer whose taxable year constitutes 52 or 53 weeks in accordance with section 441(f) may base its annualization period on the month that ends closest to the end of its applicable 4-week period or 13-week period that ends within the applicable annualization period. This alternative may only be used if it is used for determining annualization periods for all required installments for the taxable year.

(5) The following examples illustrate the rules of this paragraph (e):

*Example 1*. Corporation ABC, an accrual method taxpayer, uses a 52/53 week year-end ending on the last Friday in December and uses four thirteen-week periods. For its year beginning December 28, 2007, ABC uses the annualized income installment method under section 6655(e)(2)(A)(i) to calculate all of its required installments. For purposes of computing its first and second required installments, the first 3 months of A's taxable year under paragraph (b)(1)(i) of this section will end on March 28th, the thirteenth Friday of ABC's taxable year. For purposes of its third required installment, the first 6 months of ABC's taxable year will end on June 27th, the twenty-sixth Friday of ABC's taxable year. For purposes of its fourth required installment, the first 9 months of ABC's taxable year will end on September 26th, the thirty-ninth Friday of ABC's taxable year.

*Example 2*. Same facts as *Example 1* except that ABC uses thirteen four-week periods and there are 52 weeks during ABC's taxable year beginning December 28, 2007, and ending December 26, 2008. For purposes of computing ABC's first and second required installments, ABC's annualized taxable income for the first three months will be the taxable income for the first three four-week periods of ABC's taxable year (December 28, 2007, through March 21, 2008) divided by 12 (number of full four-week periods in the first three months (3)

multiplied by 4) and multiplied by 52 (the number of weeks in the taxable year). For purposes of computing ABC's third required installment, ABC's annualized taxable income for the first six months will be the taxable income for the first six four-week periods of ABC's taxable year (December 28, 2007, through June 13, 2008) divided by 24 and multiplied by 52. For purposes of computing ABC's fourth required installment, ABC's annualized taxable income for the first nine months will be the taxable income for the first nine four-week periods of ABC's taxable year (December 28, 2007, through September 5, 2008) divided by 36 and multiplied by 52.

*Example 3*. Same facts as *Example 1* except that ABC uses the alternative method under paragraph (e)(4) of this section for computing its required installments for 2008. For purposes of computing its first and second required installments, the first three months of ABC's taxable year under paragraph (b)(1)(i) of this section will end on March 31, 2008, the month that ends closest to the end of ABC's applicable thirteen-week period for the first and second required installments. For purposes of ABC's third required installment, the first six months of ABC's taxable year will end on June 30, 2008, the month that ends closest to the end of ABC's applicable thirteen-week period for the third required installment. For purposes of ABC's fourth required installment, the first nine months of ABC's taxable year will end on September 30, 2008, the month that ends closest to the end of ABC's applicable thirteen-week period for the fourth required installment.

(f) *Determination of taxable income for an annualization period.*—(1) *In general.*—This paragraph (f) applies for purposes of determining the applicability of the exception described in paragraphs (a) and (b) of this section (relating to the annualization of income) and the exception described in § 1.6655-3 (relating to annualization of income for corporations with seasonal income). An item of income, deduction, gain or loss is to be taken into account in determining the taxable income and alternative minimum taxable income (and applicable tax and alternative minimum tax) for an annualization period in the manner provided in this paragraph (f). An item may not be taken into account in determining taxable income for any annualization period unless the item is properly taken into account by the last day of that annualization period and the item is properly taken into account in determining the taxpayer's taxable income and alternative minimum taxable income (and applicable tax and alternative minimum tax) for the taxable year that includes the annualization period.

(i) *Items of income.*—An item of income is taken into account in the annualization period in which the item is properly includible under the method of accounting employed by the taxpayer with respect to the item and in accordance with the appropriate provision of the Internal Revenue Code (for example, section 451 for accrual method taxpayers, section 453 for installment sales or section 460 for long-term contracts).

(ii) *Items of deduction.*—An item of deduction is taken into account in the annualization period in which the item is properly deductible under the method of accounting employed by the taxpayer with respect to the item and in accordance with the appropriate provision of the Internal Revenue Code (for example, under the cash receipts and disbursements method of accounting, the deduction must be paid under § 1.461-1(a)(1) and be otherwise deductible in computing taxable income; under an accrual method of accounting, the deduction must be incurred under § 1.461-1(a)(2) and be otherwise deductible in computing taxable income). Section 170(a)(2) and § 1.170A-11(b) (charitable contributions by accrual method corporations) and § 1.461-5 (recurring item exception) may not be taken into consideration by an accrual method taxpayer in any annualization period in determining whether an item of deduction has been incurred under § 1.461-1(a)(2) during that annualization period.

(iii) *Losses.*—An item of loss is to be taken into account during the annualization period in which events have occurred that permit the loss to be taken into account under the appropriate provision of the Internal Revenue Code.

(2) *Certain deductions required to be allocated in a reasonably accurate manner.*—(i) *In general.*—The following deductions allowed for a taxable year must be allocated throughout the taxable year in a reasonably accurate manner (as defined in paragraph (f)(2)(iii) of this section), regardless of the annualization period in which the item is paid or incurred:

(A) Real property tax deductions.

(B) Employee and independent contractor bonus compensation deductions (including the employer's share of employment taxes related to such compensation).

(C) Deductions under sections 404 (deferred compensation) and 419 (welfare benefit funds).

(D) Items allowed as a deduction for the taxable year by reason of section 170(a)(2) and § 1.170A-11(b) (certain charitable contributions by accrual method corporations), §1.461-5 (recurring item exception) or §1.263(a)-4(f) (12-month rule).

(E) Items of deduction designated by the Secretary by publication in the Internal Revenue Bulletin (see §601.601(d)(2)(ii)(b) of this chapter).

(ii) *Application of the reasonably accurate manner requirement to certain charitable contributions, recurring items, and 12-month rule items.* For purposes of paragraph (f)(2)(i)(D) of this section, the total amount of the item deducted in the computation of taxable income for the taxable year must be allocated in a reasonably accurate manner, notwithstanding the fact that section 170(a)(2) and §1.170A-11(b), §1.461-5, or §1.263(a)-4(f) applies to only a portion of the total amount of the item deducted for the taxable year. For example, if a portion of a taxpayer's rebate liabilities are deducted in the computation of taxable income under the recurring item exception, all rebate liabilities deducted in the computation of taxable income for the taxable year must be allocated in a reasonably accurate manner.

(iii) *Reasonably accurate manner defined.*—(A) An item is allocated throughout the taxable year in a reasonably accurate manner if the item is allocated ratably throughout the taxable year or if the allocation provides a reasonably accurate estimate of taxable income for the taxable year based upon the facts known as of the end of the annualization period. In determining that an allocation of an item provides a reasonably accurate estimate of taxable income for the taxable year, relevant considerations include—

(1) The extent to which the allocation is consistent with the taxpayer's accounting for the item on its non-tax books and records;

(2) The extent to which the allocable portion of the item becomes fixed and determinable (under §1.461-1(a)(2)) during the applicable annualization period; and

(3) The extent to which the allocation, if compared to the ratable allocation of the item, results in a better matching of the item of deduction to revenue, earnings, the use of property or the provision of services occurring during the annualization period.

(B) None of the relevant considerations above override the general requirement that the allocation must be done in a reasonably accurate manner based upon the facts known as of the end of the annualization period. For example, the fact that a liability for an annual expense becomes fixed and determinable during an annualization period will not establish that allocating all of the expense to that annualization period has been done in a reasonably accurate manner if the facts known as of the end of the annualization period indicate otherwise.

(iv) *Special rule for certain real property tax liabilities.*—Notwithstanding paragraph (f)(2)(iii) of this section, real property tax liabilities for which an election under section 461(c) is in effect must be allocated ratably throughout the taxable year for purposes of this section.

(v) *Examples.*—Unless otherwise stated, the following examples assume that the taxpayer uses the 3-3-6-9 annualization period:

*Example 1.* (i) Corporation ABC, a calendar year taxpayer, uses an accrual method of accounting and the annualized income installment method under section 6655(e)(2)(A)(i) to calculate all of its required installment payments for its 2008 taxable year. ABC has adopted a plan under which ABC pays an annual bonus to its employees. As of March 31, 2008, ABC estimates that it will pay a year-end bonus of $500,000 to its employees if earnings remain constant throughout the tax year. ABC does not pay any of the estimated bonus liability as of March 31, 2008. On October 31, 2008, ABC declares a $600,000 bonus to its employees which is paid out on November 15, 2008, and properly deducted in ABC's December 31, 2008, tax year. No other bonus liabilities are incurred by ABC during the tax year.

(ii) Under the general rule provided in paragraph (f)(2)(i) of this section, ABC is required to allocate its employee bonus liability in a reasonably accurate manner for annualization purposes. Under paragraph (f)(2)(iii) of this section, ABC's employee bonus liability will be deemed to be allocated in a reasonably accurate manner if the item is allocated ratably throughout the taxable year. Therefore, ABC is permitted to recognize a $150,000 bonus deduction (one quarter of the $600,000 bonus liability properly recognized by ABC in the tax year ending December 31, 2008) in the first annualization period ending March 31, 2008.

*Example 2.* (i) Corporation ABC, a calendar year taxpayer, uses an accrual method of accounting and the annualized income installment method under section 6655(e)(2)(A)(i) to calculate all of its required installment payments for its 2008 taxable year. ABC has adopted a plan under which ABC pays an annual bonus to its employees. ABC's employee bonus plan generally calls for an annual bonus equal to 2% of earnings. A bonus reserve for this amount is

reported each quarter in ABC's non-tax books and records. ABC's quarterly revenues throughout the year are $10,000,000; $6,000,000; $7,000,000; and $7,000,000 respectively. As of March 31, 2008, ABC estimates that it will pay a year-end bonus of $800,000 ($10,000,000 × 4 × 2%) to its employees if earnings remain constant throughout the year. ABC does not pay any of the estimated bonus payment as of March 31, 2008. On December 31, 2008, ABC declares a $600,000 bonus to its employees which is paid out on January 15, 2009, and properly deducted in ABC's December 31, 2008, tax year.

(ii) Under the general rule provided in paragraph (f)(2)(i) of this section, ABC must allocate its employee bonus liability in a reasonably accurate manner for annualization purposes. Under paragraph (f)(2)(iii) of this section, ABC's employee bonus liability will be deemed to be allocated in a reasonably accurate manner if the allocation provides a reasonable estimate of taxable income based upon the facts known as of the end of the annualization period. Based upon its earnings activities and other information available as of March 31, 2008, ABC estimated that its total deduction for employee bonuses for the taxable year ending December 31, 2008, would be $800,000 ($10,000,000 first quarter earnings × 4 × 2%). Allocating $200,000 ($10,000,000 × 2%) of ABC's annual bonus liability of $600,000 to ABC's first quarter based upon earnings during the quarter represents a better matching of ABC's bonus expense to earnings in the quarter as compared to allocating $150,000 to ABC's first quarter under a ratable accrual method and is consistent with the allocation provided in ABC's non-tax books and records. Accordingly, allocating ABC's employee bonus deductions based upon ABC's earnings will be considered allocated in a reasonably accurate manner.

*Example 3.* (i) Corporation ABC, a calendar year taxpayer, uses an accrual method of accounting and the annualized income installment method under section 6655(e)(2)(A)(i) to calculate all of its required installment payments for its 2008 taxable year. ABC has adopted a plan under which ABC pays a bonus to its employees each quarter based upon earnings for that quarter. On March 31, 2008, ABC pays out $2,000,000 to its employees as a quarterly bonus based upon the earnings of ABC for the period January 1, 2008, through March 31, 2008. The $2,000,000 bonus is recognized as an expense on ABC's audited financial statements in the quarter ending March 31, 2008. As of March 31, 2008, ABC anticipates that its earnings will continue throughout the year resulting in future quarterly bonus payments in 2008 similar to the $2,000,000 first quarter payment.

(ii) Under the general rule provided in paragraph (f)(2)(i) of this section, ABC is required to allocate its employee bonus liability in a reasonably accurate manner for annualization purposes. Under paragraph (f)(2)(iii) of this section, ABC's employee bonus liability will be deemed to be allocated in a reasonably accurate manner if the item is allocated ratably throughout the taxable year. Therefore, ABC may recognize a $500,000 bonus deduction (one quarter of the $2,000,000 bonus liability properly recognized by ABC in the tax year ending December 31, 2008) in the first annualization period ending March 31, 2008 (as well as one quarter of any additional bonus liability properly recognized by ABC in the tax year ending December 31, 2008).

(iii) In addition, paragraph (f)(2)(iii) of this section provides that an allocation will be considered reasonable if the allocation provides an accurate estimate of taxable income for the taxable year based upon the facts known as of the end of the annualization period. Based upon its earnings activities and other information available as of March 31, 2008, ABC estimates that its total deduction for employee bonuses for the taxable year ending December 31, 2008, would be $8,000,000. In addition, the $2,000,000 bonus liability became fixed and determinable during the first quarter. Allocating $2,000,000 to ABC's first quarter earnings is also consistent with ABC's non-tax books and records and represents a better matching of ABC's bonus expense to earnings in the quarter as compared to a ratable accrual. Accordingly, allocating ABC's bonus liability based upon earnings will be considered a reasonably accurate manner for estimated tax purposes.

*Example 4.* (i) Corporation ABC, a calendar year taxpayer, uses an accrual method of accounting with the recurring item exception and the annualized income installment method under section 6655(e)(2)(A)(i) to calculate all of its required installment payments for its 2009 taxable year. ABC regularly incurs rebate obligations related to the sale of its products. Rebate coupons that are received and validated by ABC are generally paid in the following month. During the tax year ending December 31, 2009, ABC received, validated and paid $400,000 in rebates. In addition, as of the end of December 31, 2009, ABC had received and validated $100,000 in rebate claims that were paid in January of 2010 and deducted in ABC's December 31, 2009, tax year under the recurring item exception. Therefore, ABC properly recognized a $500,000 rebate liability deduction on ABC's December 31, 2009, tax return.

(ii) Under the rule provided in paragraph (f)(2)(ii) of this section, an item must be allocated in a reasonably accurate manner if any portion of the item is deducted under the recurring item excep-

**Additions to Tax and Additional Amounts**
See p. 20,601 for regulations not amended to reflect law changes
**67,065**

tion. Therefore, ABC will be required to allocate its entire $500,000 rebate liability deduction in a reasonably accurate manner as defined in paragraph (f)(2)(iii) of this section.

(3) *Special rules.*—(i) *Advance payments under Rev. Proc. 2004-3.*—An advance payment for which the taxpayer uses the Deferral Method provided in section 5.02 of Rev. Proc. 2004-34 (2004-1 CB 991), (see § 601.601(d)(2)(ii)(b) of this chapter) is includible in computing taxable income for an annualization period in accordance with that method of accounting, except that any amount not included in computing taxable income by the end of the taxable year succeeding the taxable year of receipt is includible in computing taxable income on the last day of such succeeding taxable year.

(ii) *Extraordinary items.*—(A) *In general.*—In general, extraordinary items must be taken into account after annualizing the taxable income for the annualization period. For purposes of the preceding sentence an extraordinary item is any item identified in § 1.1502-76(b)(2)(ii)(C) (1), (2), (3), (4), (7), and (8), a net operating loss carryover, a section 481(a) adjustment, net gain or loss from the disposition of 25 percent or more of the fair market value of a taxpayer's business assets during a taxable year, and any other item designated by the Secretary by publication in the Internal Revenue Bulletin (see § 601.601(d)(2)(ii)(b) of this chapter).

(B) *De minimis extraordinary items.*—A taxpayer may treat any de minimis extraordinary item, other than a net operating loss carryover or section 481(a) adjustment, as an item under the general rule of paragraph (f)(1) of this section rather than an extraordinary item as provided for in paragraph (f)(3)(ii) of this section. A de minimis extraordinary item is any item identified in paragraph (f)(3)(ii)(A) of this section resulting from a transaction in which the total extraordinary items resulting from such transaction is less than $1,000,000.

(C) *Special rule for net operating loss deductions and section 481(a) adjustments.*—For purposes of paragraph (f)(3)(ii) of this section, a taxpayer must treat a net operating loss deduction and section 481(a) adjustment as extraordinary items arising on the first day of the tax year in which the item is taken into account in determining taxable income. Notwithstanding the preceding sentence, a taxpayer may choose to treat the portion of a section 481(a) adjustment recognized during the tax year of the accounting method change as an extraordinary item arising on the date the Form 3115, "Application for Change in Accounting Method," requesting the change was filed with the national office of the Internal Revenue Service.

(iii) *Credits.*—(A) *Current year credits.*—With respect to a current year credit, the items upon which the credit is computed are annualized, the amount of the credit is computed based on the annualized items, and the amount of the credit is deducted from the annualized tax. For example, for an annualization period consisting of three months in a full 12-month taxable year, the items upon which the credit is based that are taken into account for the three month period are multiplied by four, the credit is determined based on the annualized amount of the items, and the credit reduces the annualized tax.

(B) *Credit carryovers.*—Any credit carryover to the current taxable year is taken into account in computing an annualized income installment only after annualizing the taxable income for the annualization period and computing the applicable tax, and before applying the applicable percentage.

(iv) *Depreciation and amortization.*—(A) *Estimated annual depreciation and amortization.*—In general, in determining taxable income for any annualization period, a proportionate amount of the taxpayer's estimated annual depreciation and amortization (depreciation) expense may be taken into account. For purposes of the preceding sentence, estimated annual depreciation expense is the estimated depreciation expense to be properly taken into account in determining the taxpayer's taxable income for the taxable year. In determining the estimated annual depreciation expense, a taxpayer may take into account purchases, sales or other dispositions, changes in use, additional first-year depreciation and expense deductions and section 179 or any similar provision, and other events that, based on all the relevant information available as of the last day of the annualization period (such as capital spending budgets, financial statement data and projections, or similar reports that provide evidence of the taxpayer's capital spending plans for the current taxable year), are reasonably expected to occur or apply during the taxable year.

(B) *Safe harbors.*—(1) *Proportionate depreciation allowance.*—In determining taxable income for any annualization period, in lieu of the rule provided in paragraph (f)(3)(iv)(A) of this section a taxpayer may take into account a proportionate amount of the depreciation and amortization (depreciation) expense, including special depreciation and expense deductions such as those provided for in section

168(k) and section 179 or any similar provision, allowed for the taxable year from—

(i) Assets that were in service on the last day of the prior taxable year, are in service on the first day of the current taxable year, and that have not been disposed of during the annualization period;

(ii) Assets placed in service during the annualization period and have not been disposed of during that period; and

(iii) Assets that were in service on the last day of the prior taxable year and that are disposed of during the annualization period.

(2) *90 percent of preceding year's depreciation.*—In determining taxable income for any annualization period, in lieu of the general rule provided in paragraph (f)(3)(iv)(A) of this section, a proportionate amount of 90 percent of the amount of depreciation and amortization (depreciation) expense taken on the taxpayer's Federal income tax return for the preceding taxable year may be taken into account. If the taxpayer's preceding taxable year is less than 12 months (a short taxable year), the amount of depreciation expense taken into account is annualized by multiplying the depreciation and amortization for the short taxable year by 12, and dividing the result by the number of months in the short taxable year.

(3) *Safe harbor operational rules.*—If a taxpayer selects one of the two safe harbors provided in paragraph (f)(3)(iv)(B)(1) or paragraph (f)(3)(iv)(B)(2) of this section, the taxpayer must use that safe harbor for all depreciation expenses within the annualization period for the annualized income installment. However, a taxpayer may use either the method provided for in paragraph (f)(3)(iv)(A) of this section or a method provided for in this paragraph (f)(3)(iv)(B) of this section for each annualized income installment during the taxable year. For example, a taxpayer may use the safe harbor provided in paragraph (f)(3)(iv)(B)(1) of this section for its first annualized income installment and may use the general rule provided in paragraph (f)(3)(iv)(A) of this section for its second annualized income installment.

(C) *Short taxable years.*—If the taxable year is, or will be, a short taxable year (based on all relevant information available as of the last day of the annualization period), annual depreciation expense is computed using the rules applicable for computing depreciation during a short taxable year for purposes of determining the annual depreciation expense to be allocated to an annualization period. For this purpose, the rules applicable for computing depreciation during a short taxable year are applied on the basis of the date the taxable year is expected to end based on all relevant information available as of the last day of the annualization period. See Rev. Proc. 89-15 (1989-1 CB 816) for computing depreciation expense under section 168 (see § 601.601(d)(2)(ii)(b) of this chapter). An annualization period is not treated as a short taxable year for purposes of determining the depreciation expense for an annualization period. See paragraph (c)(3) of this section.

(v) *Distributive share of items.*—(A) *Member of partnership.*—In determining a partner's distributive share of partnership items that must be taken into account during an annualization period, the rules set forth in § 1.6654-2(d)(2) are applicable.

(B) *Treatment of subpart F income and income under section 936(h).*—(1) *General rule.*—Any amounts required to be included in gross income under section 936(h) or section 951(a), and credits properly allocable thereto, are taken into account in computing any annualized income installment in a manner similar to the manner under which partnership inclusions, and credits properly allocable thereto, are taken into account in accordance with paragraph (f)(3)(v)(A) of this section.

(2) *Prior year safe harbor.*—(i) *General rule.*—If a taxpayer elects to have the safe harbor in this paragraph (f)(3)(v)(B)(2) apply for any taxable year, then paragraph (f)(3)(v)(B)(1) of this section does not apply; and, for purposes of computing any annualized income installment for the taxable year, the taxpayer is treated as having received ratably during the taxable year items of income and credit described in paragraph (f)(3)(v)(B)(1) of this section in an amount equal to 115 percent of the amount of such items shown on the return of the taxpayer for the preceding taxable year (the second preceding taxable year in the case of the first and second required installments for such taxable year).

(ii) *Special rule for noncontrolling shareholder.*—If a taxpayer making the election under paragraph (f)(3)(v)(B)(2)(i) of this section is a noncontrolling shareholder of a corporation, paragraph (f)(3)(v)(B)(2)(i) of this section is applied with respect to items of such corporation by substituting "100 percent" for "115 percent". For purposes of paragraph (f)(3)(v)(B)(2)(ii) of this section, the term noncontrolling shareholder means, with respect to any corporation, a shareholder that, as of the beginning of the taxable year for which the installment is being made, does not own within the meaning of section 958(a), and is not treated as owning within the meaning of section 958(b), more than 50 percent by vote or value of the stock in the corporation.

(C) *Dividends from closely held real estate investment trust.*— (1) *General rule.*—Any dividend received from a closely held real estate investment trust by any person that owns, after the application of section 856(d)(5), 10 percent or more by vote or value of the stock or beneficial interests in the trust is taken into account in computing annualized income installments in a manner similar to the manner under which partnership income inclusions are taken into account.

(2) *Closely held real estate investment trust.*—For purposes of paragraph (f)(3)(v)(C)(1) of this section, the term closely held real estate investment trust means a real estate investment trust with respect to which 5 or fewer persons own, after the application of section 856(d)(5), 50 percent or more by vote or value of the stock or beneficial interests in the trust.

(D) *Other passthrough entities.*—A taxpayer's distributive share of items from a passthrough entity, other than those described in paragraphs (f)(3)(v)(A) and (f)(3)(v)(C) of this section, is taken into account in computing any annualized income installment in a manner similar to the manner under which partnership items are taken into account under paragraph (f)(3)(v)(A) of this section.

(vi) *Alternative minimum taxable income exemption amount.*— The alternative minimum taxable income exemption amount provided by section 55(d)(2) is applied after the alternative minimum taxable income for the annualization period is annualized.

(vii) *Examples.*—The provisions of this paragraph (f) are illustrated by the following examples. Unless otherwise stated, the following examples assume that the taxpayer uses the 3-3-6-9 annualization period.

*Example 1. Expense paid or incurred in the installment period.* Corporation ABC, a calendar year taxpayer, uses an accrual method of accounting and the annualized income installment method under section 6655(e)(2)(A)(i) to calculate all of its required installment payments for its 2008 taxable year. ABC has licensed technology from Corporation XYZ. Pursuant to the license agreement, ABC pays a license fee to XYZ equal to $.01 for every dollar of gross receipts earned by ABC. For 2008, ABC projects gross receipts of $200,000,000, of which $100,000,000 is earned by March 31, 2008. Pursuant to paragraph (f)(1) of this section, a license fee expense of $1,000,000 ($100,000,000 × $.01) is incurred by March 31, 2008, and may be taken into account for purposes of determining the taxable income to be annualized in computing ABC's first annualized income installment.

*Example 2. Expense not paid or incurred in the installment period.* Same facts as *Example 1* except that ABC does not earn any gross receipts by March 31, 2008. In accordance with paragraph (f)(1) of this section, because the license fee expense was not incurred under §1.461-1(a)(2) by the last day of the annualization period, no license fee expense is taken into account for purposes of determining the taxable income to be annualized in computing ABC's first annualized income installment, which is based on the income and deductions from the first three months of the taxable year.

*Example 3. Bad debt expense.* Corporation ABC, a calendar year taxpayer, uses an accrual method of accounting and the annualized income installment method under section 6655(e)(2)(A)(i) to calculate all of its required installment payments for its 2008 taxable year. As of December 31, 2007, ABC had a $100,000 account receivable due from XYZ related to the sale of goods from ABC to XYZ during 2007. On March 30, 2008, ABC determined that its receivable from XYZ was worthless under section 166 and the regulations. No other receivables were determined to be worthless between January 1, 2008, and March 31, 2008. In accordance with paragraph (f)(1) of this section, a $100,000 bad debt write-off is taken into account for purposes of determining the taxable income to be annualized in computing ABC's first annualized income installment.

*Example 4. Bad debt expense.* Same facts as *Example 3* except that ABC determines that the receivable from XYZ was worthless under section 166 and the regulations on April 10, 2008. As of March 31, 2008, ABC had not determined that any receivables were worthless under section 166 and the regulations. In accordance with paragraph (f)(1) of this section, the $100,000 bad debt expense attributable to the receivable from XYZ is not taken into account for purposes of determining the taxable income to be annualized in computing ABC's first annualized income installment, which is based on the income and deductions from the first three months of the taxable year, because the receivable from XYZ became worthless after the last day of the annualization period.

*Example 5. Employer deductions under section 404 and 419.* (i) Corporation ABC, a calendar year taxpayer, uses an accrual method of accounting and uses the annualized income installment method under section 6655(e)(2)(A)(i) to calculate all of its required installment payments for its 2008 taxable year. On March 1, 2008, the board of directors of ABC makes a binding, irrevocable commitment to fund a minimum contribution of $10,000,000 to ABC's qualified retirement plan by March 14, 2009. ABC remits a $1,000,000 payment to the retirement plan on March 1, 2008, and a $9,000,000 payment on March 3, 2009. ABC does not incur any other related retirement plan deductions during its 2008 taxable year.

(ii) Under the rule provided in paragraph (f)(2)(i) of this section, ABC's employer deduction for payment made to the qualified plan must be allocated throughout the tax year for estimated tax purposes in a reasonably accurate manner. Therefore, ABC will not be permitted to allocate the $10,000,000 deduction to its first installment period. Under paragraph (f)(2)(iii) of this section, ABC's qualified plan deduction will be deemed to be allocated in a reasonably accurate manner if the item is allocated ratably throughout the taxable year. Therefore, ABC will be permitted to allocate $2,500,000 of its qualified plan deduction in its first installment period.

*Example 6. Prepaid expense.* (i) Corporation ABC, a calendar year taxpayer, uses an accrual method of accounting and does not capitalize qualifying costs under the exception provided for in §1.263(a)-4(f). ABC uses the annualized income installment method under section 6655(e)(2)(A)(i) to calculate all of its required installment payments for its 2008 taxable year. On July 1, 2008, ABC purchases an annual business license from State X which permits ABC to operate its business in State X from July 1, 2008, through June 30, 2009. An annual payment of $12,000 is due on July 1, 2008, and ABC pays the fee on this date. ABC has not elected out of the 12-month rule provided by §1.263(a)-4(f) and therefore ABC is not required to capitalize any amount paid for the license and will recognize a $12,000 deduction for the tax year ending December 31, 2008, with respect to this license.

(ii) Under the rule provided in paragraph (f)(2)(ii) of this section, ABC's $12,000 business license expense must be allocated in a reasonably accurate manner because ABC utilizes the 12-month rule exception provided for in the §1.263(a)-4(f). Under paragraph (f)(2)(iii) of this section, ABC's deduction will be deemed to be allocated in a reasonably accurate manner if the item is allocated ratably throughout the taxable year. Therefore, ABC will be permitted to allocate $3,000 of its business license deduction in its first installment period.

*Example 7. Real property tax liability.* (i) Corporation ABC, a calendar year taxpayer, uses an accrual method of accounting and the annualized income installment method under section 6655(e)(2)(A)(i) to calculate all of its required installment payments for its 2008 taxable year. ABC owns real property in State Y and uses the real property in its trade or business. ABC incurs a $400,000 deduction for State Y real estate taxes during ABC's December 31, 2008, taxable year. ABC has elected to recognize its real property taxes ratably under section 461(c).

(ii) Under the rule provided in paragraph (f)(2)(i) of this section, ABC's $400,000 real property tax liabilities must be allocated in a reasonably accurate manner. However, paragraph (f)(2)(iv) of this section provides that with respect to real property taxes for which an election has been made under section 461(c), ratable accrual is the only method which will be considered a reasonably accurate method. Therefore, ABC will be required to allocate its $400,000 real property taxes ratably for estimated tax purposes and thus $100,000 will be allocated to the ABC's first annualized income installment.

*Example 8. NOL (Net Operating Loss) deduction.* Corporation ABC, a calendar year taxpayer, uses an accrual method of accounting and the annualized income installment method under section 6655(e)(2)(A)(i) to calculate all of its required installment payments for its 2008 taxable year. ABC has a net operating loss carryover to 2008 of $2,000,000. ABC's taxable income from January 1, 2008, through March 31, 2008, without regard to any net operating loss deduction, is $1,500,000 (pre-NOL taxable income). Under the special rule for net operating loss deductions provided in paragraph (f)(3)(ii) of this section, the NOL deduction is treated as an extraordinary item incurred on the first day of ABC's December 31, 2008, tax year. Therefore, the NOL deduction is taken into account after annualization for purposes of determining ABC's first annualized income installment.

*Example 9. Advance payment.* (i) Corporation ABC, a calendar year taxpayer, uses an accrual method of accounting and the annualized income installment method under section 6655(e)(2)(A)(i) to calculate all of its required installment payments for its 2008 and 2009 taxable years. ABC is in the business of giving dancing lessons and receives advance payments. For Federal income tax purposes, ABC uses the Deferral Method provided in section 5.02 of Rev. Proc. 2004-34 for the advance payments it receives for dance lessons. On November 1, 2008, ABC receives an advance payment of $2,400 for a 2-year contract commencing on November 1, 2008, and providing for up to 24 individual, 1-hour lessons. ABC provides 2 lessons in 2008, 12 lessons in 2009, and 10 lessons in 2010. ABC recognizes $200 in revenues in its financial statements for the last quarter of 2008. ABC recognizes $300 in revenues in its financial statements for each quarter of 2009 for a total of $1,200 in 2009. ABC recognizes the remaining $1,000 in revenues in its financial statements during 2010. For tax purposes, ABC recognizes $200 into revenue in 2008 and $2,200 into revenue in 2009 under Rev. Proc. 2004-34. See § 601.601(d)(2)(ii)(b).

(ii) Pursuant to paragraph (f)(3)(i)(B) of this section, ABC is not required to take into account any of the advance payment for purposes of computing any required installment payment for ABC's 2008 taxable year because no part of the $2,400 advance payment was recognized as income in ABC's financial statements during the first nine months of ABC's 2008 taxable year. In 2009, ABC must take into account $300 of revenue for purposes of computing its first and second required installment payments, $600 of revenue for purposes of computing its third required installment payment and $900 for purposes of computing its fourth required installment payment. Pursuant to paragraph (f)(3)(i)(B) of this section, the remaining deferred revenue is recognized on December 31, 2009, for purposes of computing ABC's annualized income installments for 2009.

*Example 10. Section 481(a) adjustment.* Corporation ABC, a calendar year taxpayer, uses an accrual method of accounting and the annualized income installment method under section 6655(e)(2)(A)(i) to calculate all of its required installment payments for its 2008 taxable year. On December 20, 2008, ABC files a Form 3115 requesting permission to change its method of accounting. The requested change results in a negative section 481(a) adjustment of $80,000. ABC subsequently receives the consent of the Commissioner to make the change and therefore, the negative $80,000 section 481(a) adjustment is properly recognized in ABC's tax return for the year ending December 31, 2008. Under paragraph (f)(3)(ii) of this section ABC is permitted to recognize the negative $80,000 section 481(a) adjustment as an extraordinary item occurring on January 1, 2008 (the first day of ABC's December 31, 2008, tax year), or December 20, 2008 (the date ABC filed the Form 3115). ABC chooses to recognize the negative $80,000 section 481(a) adjustment as an extraordinary item occurring in January 1, 2008. Accordingly, $80,000 of the negative section 481(a) adjustment is taken into account after annualization for purposes of determining ABC's first annualized income installment. In addition, under § 1.6655-6(b), ABC is required to use its new method of accounting as of January 1, 2008 for estimated tax purposes, consistent with the recognition of the section 481(a) adjustment for estimated tax purposes. Therefore, ABC will be required to use the new method of accounting in determining taxable income to be annualized in computing ABC's first annualized income installment.

*Example 11. Section 481(a) adjustment.* Corporation ABC, a calendar year taxpayer, uses an accrual method of accounting and uses the annualized income installment method under section 6655(e)(2)(A)(i) to calculate all of its required installment payments for its 2008 taxable year. On June 15, 2008, ABC files a Form 3115 requesting permission to change its method of accounting. The requested change results in a positive section 481(a) adjustment of $240,000. ABC subsequently receives the consent of the Commissioner to make the change and therefore, $60,000 of the section 481(a) adjustment (one quarter of the positive $240,000 section 481(a) adjustment) is properly recognized in ABC's tax return for the year ending December 31, 2008. Under paragraph (f)(3)(ii) of this section, ABC is permitted to recognize the positive $60,000 section 481(a) adjustment as an extraordinary item occurring on January 1, 2008 (the first day of ABC's December 31, 2008, tax year), or June 15, 2008 (the date ABC filed the Form 3115). ABC chooses to recognize the positive $60,000 section 481(a) adjustment as an extraordinary item occurring on June 15, 2008. Accordingly, the $60,000 positive section 481(a) adjustment is not taken into account for purposes of determining ABC's first annualized income installment. However, in all futures years any portion of the section 481(a) adjustment related to this change in method of accounting will be treated as an extraordinary item occurring on the first day of the tax year under paragraph (f)(3)(ii) of this section. In addition, under § 1.6655-6(b), ABC is required to use its new method of accounting as of June 15, 2008 for estimated tax purposes, consistent with the recognition of the section 481(a) adjustment for estimated tax purposes. Therefore, ABC will be required to use the new method of accounting (as of the beginning of the tax year) for purposes of determining taxable income to be annualized in computing ABC's third and fourth annualized income installments (which are based upon annualization periods that include June 15, 2008.)

*Example 12. Extraordinary item.* Corporation ABC, a calendar year taxpayer, uses an accrual method of accounting and the annualized income installment method under section 6655(e)(2)(A)(i) to calculate all of its required installment payments for its 2008 taxable year. On May 10, 2008, ABC reaches a settlement agreement with XYZ over a tort action filed by ABC. As a result, ABC receives a payment of $10,000,000 on June 15, 2006, that is recognized as income by ABC. The settlement of a tort action is an extraordinary item defined in paragraph (f)(3)(ii)(A) of this section. Accordingly, the $10,000,000 of income will be taken into account by ABC on May 10, 2008, for purposes of computing ABC's annualized income installments for 2008. Therefore, the $10,000,000 settlement will only be taken into account in computing ABC's third and fourth annualized income installments (which are based upon annualization periods that include May 10, 2008.) In addition, the $10,000,000 settlement income will be taken into account as an extraordinary item of income after annualization for purposes of determining ABC's third and fourth annualized installment payments.

*Example 13. Credit carryover.* Corporation ABC, a calendar year taxpayer, uses an accrual method of accounting and the annualized income installment method under section 6655(e)(2)(A)(i) to calculate all of its required installment payments for its 2008 taxable year. ABC projects its annualized tax for its 2008 taxable year, based on annualizing ABC's taxable income for its first annualization period from January 1, 2008, through March 31, 2008, to be $1,500,000 before reduction for any credits. ABC has an unused section 38 credit from 2007 for increasing research activities from 2007 of $500,000 that is carried over to 2008. For purposes of determining ABC's first annualized income installment, ABC's annualized tax for 2008 is $1,000,000, determined as the tax for the taxable year computed by placing on an annualized basis ABC's taxable income from its first annualization period from January 1, 2008, through March 31, 2008 ($1,500,000) reduced by the $500,000 credit carryover from 2007. Therefore, ABC's first required installment payment for 2008 is $250,000 ($1,000,000 × 25%).

*Example 14. Current year credit.* Corporation ABC, a calendar year taxpayer, uses an accrual method of accounting and the annualized income installment method under section 6655(e)(2)(A)(i) to calculate all of its required installment payments for its 2008 taxable year. ABC projects its annualized tax for its 2008 taxable year, based on annualizing ABC's taxable income for its first annualization period from January 1, 2008, through March 31, 2008, to be $2,000,000 before reduction for any credits. ABC has historically earned a section 41 credit for increasing research activities and, for 2008, ABC estimates that it will earn a credit for increasing research activities under section 41 of $1,200,000. However, pursuant to paragraph (f)(3)(iii) of this section, if ABC were to annualize all components involved in computing the current year credit based on ABC's activity from January 1, 2008, through March 31, 2008, ABC would generate a credit of $1,600,000 for 2008. For purposes of determining ABC's first annualized income installment, ABC's annualized tax for 2008 is $400,000, determined as the tax for the 2008 taxable year ($2,000,000) computed by placing on an annualized basis ABC's taxable income from its first annualization period January 1, 2008, through March 31, 2008, reduced by a $1,600,000 current year section 41 credit from increasing research activities. Therefore, ABC's first required installment payment for 2008 is $100,000 ($400,000 × 25%).

*Example 15. Current year credit.* Same facts as *Example 14* except that ABC does not begin any research activities until April 3, 2008, and will not incur any research expenses described in paragraph (f)(1)(ii) of this section. As a result, if ABC were to annualize all components involved in computing the current year credit based on ABC's activity from January 1, 2008, through March 31, 2008, ABC would generate no section 41 research credit for purposes of determining its first annualized income installment. Pursuant to paragraph (f)(3)(iii) of this section, ABC cannot take into account any credit for its first annualization period because ABC did not incur any qualified research expenses by the last day of the first annualization period. Accordingly, for purposes of determining ABC's first annualized income installment, ABC's annualized tax for its first annualization period January 1, 2008, through March 31, 2008, is $2,000,000. Therefore, ABC's first required installment payment for 2008 is $500,000 ($2,000,000 × 25%).

*Example 16. Depreciation and amortization expense.* Corporation ABC, a calendar year taxpayer that began business on January 2, 2007, adopted an accrual method of accounting and will use the annualized income installment method under section 6655(e)(2)(A)(i) to calculate all of its required installment payments for its 2008 taxable year. On January 2, 2007, ABC purchased and placed in service a tangible depreciable asset that costs $50,000 and is 5-year property under section 168(e). ABC depreciates its 5-year property placed in service in 2007 under the general depreciation system using the 200-percent declining balance method, a 5-year recovery period, and the half year convention. On January 2, 2008, ABC purchased and placed in service qualified Gulf Opportunity Zone property (GO Zone property) that costs $30,000 and is 5-year property under section 168(e). ABC will depreciate its 5-year property placed in service in 2008 under the general depreciation system using the 200-percent declining balance method, a 5-year recovery period, and the half-year convention. ABC will deduct the 50% additional first year depreciation deduction under section 1400N(d) with respect to the GO Zone property. For tax year 2007, ABC takes a depreciation deduction under section 168 of $10,000 ($50,000 × 20% = $10,000). ABC does not anticipate being subject to the mid-quarter convention for the 2008 taxable year, does not anticipate making any depreciation elections for any class of property, does not anticipate making a section 179 election, does not anticipate any sales or other dispositions of depreciable property, and no events have occurred, nor does ABC know, based on all relevant information available as of the due date of ABC's first required installment for 2008, of any event that will occur to cause ABC's 2008 taxable year to be a short taxable year. The optional amounts of depreciation expense ABC may take into account for its first annualized income installment for its 2008 taxable year are determined as follows:

(i) *General rule—Estimated annual depreciation.* In accordance with the general rule provided in paragraph (f)(3)(iv)(A) of this section, ABC may take a depreciation expense of $8,500 ($34,000 × 3/12 = $8,500) into account in computing ABC's January 1, 2008, through March 31, 2008, taxable income. ABC's estimated annual depreciation expense for 2008 of $34,000 is computed as follows: $15,000 for the 50% additional first year depreciation deduction under section 1400N(d) ($30,000 × 50% = $15,000) plus annual depreciation of $16,000 ($40,000 × 40% = $16,000) and $3,000 ($15,000 × 20% = $3,000). Under paragraphs (c)(3) and (f)(3)(iv)(C) of this section, ABC may not consider its first annualization period to be a short taxable year for purposes of determining the depreciation allowance for such annualization period.

(ii) *Safe Harbor—Proportionate depreciation allowance.* In accordance with the safe harbor provided in paragraph (f)(3)(iv)(B)(1) of this section, ABC may take a depreciation expense of $8,500 ($34,000 × 3/12 = $8,500) into account in computing ABC's January 1, 2008, through March 31, 2008, taxable income based on annual depreciation expense for 2008 of $34,000, computed as follows: $15,000 for the 50% additional first year depreciation deduction under section 1400N(d) ($30,000 × 50% = $15,000) plus annual depreciation of $16,000 ($40,000 × 40% = $16,000) and $3,000 ($15,000 × 20% = $3,000). Under paragraphs (c)(3) and (f)(3)(iv)(C) of this section, ABC may not consider its first annualization period to be a short taxable year for purposes of determining the depreciation allowance for such annualization period.

(iii) *Safe Harbor—90 percent of preceding year's depreciation.* In accordance with the safe harbor in paragraph (f)(3)(iv)(B)(2) of this section, ABC may take a depreciation expense of $2,250 ($10,000 prior year's depreciation × 90% = $9,000 × 3/12 = $2,250) into account in computing ABC's January 1, 2008, through March 31, 2008, taxable income. Under paragraphs (c)(3) and (f)(3)(iv)(C) of this section, ABC may not consider its first annualization period to be a short taxable year for purposes of determining the depreciation allowance for such annualization period.

(g) *Items that substantially affect taxable income but cannot be determined accurately by the installment due date.*—(1) *In general.*—In determining the applicability of the annualization exceptions described in paragraphs (a) and (b) of this section and § 1.6655-3, reasonable estimates may be made from existing data for items that substantially affect income if the amount of such items cannot be determined accurately by the installment due date. This paragraph (g) applies only to the inflation index for taxpayers using the dollar-value LIFO (last-in, first-out) inventory method, adjustments required under section 263A, the computation of a taxpayer's section 199 deduction, intercompany adjustments for taxpayers that file consolidated returns, the liquidation of a LIFO layer at the installment date that the taxpayer reasonably believes will be replaced at the end of the year, deferred gain on a qualifying conversion or exchange of property under sections 1031 and 1033 that the taxpayer reasonably believes will be replaced with qualifying replacement property, and any other item designated by the Secretary by publication in the Internal Revenue Bulletin (see § 601.601(d)(2)(ii)(b) of this chapter).

(2) *Example.*—The following example illustrates the rules of this paragraph (g):

*Example. Section 199 deduction.* Corporation ABC, a calendar year taxpayer, uses an accrual method of accounting and the annualized income installment method under section 6655(e)(2)(A)(i) to calculate all of its required installment payments for its 2008 taxable year. ABC engages in production activities that generate qualified production activities income (QPAI), as defined in § 1.199-1(c), and projects taxable income of $50,000 for its first annualization period from January 1, 2008, through March 31, 2008, without taking into account the section 199 deduction. During its first annualization period from January 1, 2008, through March 31, 2008, ABC incurs W-2 wages allocable to domestic production gross receipts pursuant to section 199(b)(2) of $10,000. Pursuant to paragraph (g)(1) of this section, ABC is permitted to take into account its estimated section 199 deduction before annualizing taxable income based on the lesser of its estimated QPAI or taxable income and W-2 wages for its first installment period for 2008. For the first installment period in 2008, ABC is

permitted to recognize a deduction under section 199 of $3,000 ($50,000 × .06 = $3,000) subject to the wage limitation of $5,000 (50 percent of $10,000 of W-2 wages incurred during the first installment period). Accordingly, ABC's annualized income for the first installment for 2008 is $188,000 (($50,000 - $3,000) × 12/3 = $188,000). The tax on $188,000 is $56,570 and ABC's first required installment for 2008 is $14,143 ($56,570 × .25 = $14,143).

(h) *Effective/applicability date.*—This section applies to taxable years beginning after September 6, 2007. [Reg. § 1.6655-2.]

☐ [*T.D. 6267*, 11-13-57. *Amended by T.D. 6293*, 5-20-58, *T.D. 6768*, 11-3-64, *T.D. 8996*, 5-16-2002, *T.D. 9347*, 8-6-2007 (*corrected 9-19-2007*) *and T.D. 9870*, 7-11-2019.]

### [Reg. § 1.6655-2T]

**§ 1.6655-2T. Safe harbor for certain installments of tax due before July 1, 1987 (temporary).**—(a) *Applicability.*—(1) *Safe harbor.*—The safe harbor provided by paragraph (b) of this section applies only to installment payments of corporate estimated tax required to be made before July 1, 1987, for taxable years beginning in 1987.

(2) *Subsequent payment.*—The requirement that a corporation using the safe harbor provided by this section make a timely subsequent installment payment in accordance with paragraph (c) of this section applies with respect to the corporation's first installment payment ("the subsequent installment payment") of estimated tax required to be made after the last payment computed under the safe harbor rule.

(3) *Section inapplicable to new corporation.*—This section shall not apply in the case of any corporation whose first taxable year began after December 31, 1986.

(b) *Safe harbor for use of annualization exception.*—(1) *In general.*—A corporation computing an installment payment of estimated tax using the annualization exception provided in section 6655(d)(3) will not be subject to an addition to tax under section 6655 with respect to an installment payment of estimated tax that satisfies the requirements of this paragraph (b), except as provided in paragraph (c) of this section. For purposes of this paragraph (b)—

(i) A corporation shall assume that its annualized taxable income for the current year equals or exceeds 120 percent of the taxable income shown on its return for the preceding taxable year, and

(ii) The term "tax" as used in section 6655(d)(3) shall be defined by reference to section 6655(f) without regard to section 6655(f)(1)(B) and (C) (that is, without regard to the alternative minimum tax imposed by section 55 or the environmental tax imposed by section 59A).

(2) *Special rules for determining taxable income for preceding year.*—For purposes of paragraph (b)(1)(i) of this section, the taxable income shown on the return of the corporation for its preceding taxable year shall be—

(i) Adjusted to eliminate any net operating loss deduction taken into account in that preceding year, and

(ii) Annualized, if that preceding year was of less than 12 months.

(3) *Credits taken into account.*—(i) *In general.*—In computing the amount of an installment payment under paragraph (b)(1) of this section, the corporation may take into account any credits against tax that are permitted to be taken into account under section 6655(d)(3) for the current taxable year.

(ii) *Foreign tax credit.*—For purposes of paragraph (b)(3)(i) of this section, the amount of foreign tax credit that is permitted to be taken into account for the current taxable year is equal to the foreign tax credit allowed for the preceding taxable year multiplied by the fraction specified in the following sentence. The numerator of the fraction is the highest tax rate applicable for the taxable year under section 11, as adjusted under section 15, and the denominator is 46 percent. This alternative computation of the foreign tax credit is applicable only for purposes of computing a safe harbor installment payment under paragraph (b) of this section and cannot be applied for other estimated tax purposes.

(4) *Net operating loss carryover.*—A corporation that has a net operating loss carryover as of the first day of the taxable year for which the estimated tax is being paid may use that carryover to reduce the annualized taxable income referred to in paragraph (b)(1)(i) of this section. For example, if a corporation with a net operating loss carryover of $3,000 had taxable income of $10,000 in 1986, it may use the carryover to reduce its annualized taxable income to $9,000 (($10,000 × 120%) – $3,000).

## Additions to Tax and Additional Amounts
### See p. 20,601 for regulations not amended to reflect law changes
**67,069**

(c) *Corporation must bring aggregate payments to required level through timely subsequent installment.*—(1) *In general.*—A corporation using the safe harbor provided by paragraph (b) of this section shall make a timely subsequent installment payment of estimated tax in an amount sufficient to satisfy the requirements of either paragraph (c)(3) or paragraph (c)(4) of this section.

(2) *Applicable percentage.*—For purposes of this paragraph (c), the applicable percentage is—

   (i) 45 percent (50 percent × 90 percent), if the subsequent installment payment is the second installment payment for the taxable year, or

   (ii) 67.5 percent (75 percent × 90 percent), if the subsequent installment payment is the third installment payment for the taxable year.

(3) *Annualization exception.*—The subsequent installment payment of a corporation satisfies the requirements of this paragraph (c)(3) if the amount of the payment is sufficient to satisfy the requirements of section 6655(d)(3) with respect to all applicable taxes specified in section 6655(f). Thus, the corporation must determine its annualized taxable income under section 6655(d)(3)(A)(ii) or (iii), whichever is applicable, and compute the resulting tax. The resulting tax shall include the alternative minimum tax under section 55 and the environmental tax under section 59A and may take credits into account to the extent permitted under section 6655(d)(3). The sum of this subsequent installment payment and the earlier installment payment or payments of the corporation must equal or exceed the applicable percentage of the tax so computed. In determining whether the corporation has satisfied the requirements of section 6655(d)(3)(A)(ii) or (iii) with respect to the subsequent installment, the safe harbor provided in paragraph (b)(1) of this section shall not apply.

(4) *Installment payments equal to applicable percentage of tax shown on return.*—The subsequent installment payment of a corporation satisfies the requirement of this paragraph (c)(4) if the sum of that payment and the earlier installment payment or payments of the corporation equals or exceeds the applicable percentage of the tax shown on the return of the corporation for the taxable year to which the installment payments relate. The tax shown on the return includes all taxes specified in section 6655(f).

(5) *Consequence of corporation's failure to satisfy requirements for subsequent installment.*—(i) *In general.*—If a corporation fails to satisfy the requirements set out in this paragraph (c), the corporation shall lose the benefit of the safe harbor provided by paragraph (b)(1) of this section.

   (ii) *Limit on penalty.*—The aggregate underpayment penalty with respect to any installment payment or payments for which a corporation loses the benefit of the safe harbor under paragraph (c)(5)(i) of this section shall be limited to the "shortfall penalty amount." The shortfall penalty amount is the penalty that would be imposed under section 6655(a) if there were an underpayment of the subsequent installment payment equal to the excess of—

     (A) The amount required to be paid, as determined under this paragraph (c), on or before the due date of the subsequent installment payment, over

     (B) The amount actually paid on or before such date with respect to the subsequent installment payment.
For purposes of this determination, the period of the underpayment shall run from the due date of the subsequent installment payment until the earlier of the dates specified in section 6655(c)(1) or (2).

   (iii) *Example.*—The provisions of this paragraph (c)(5) may be illustrated by the following example:

*Example.* Corporation M, which uses the calendar year as its taxable year, relies on the safe harbor provided by paragraph (b) of this section for its first two installment payments of estimated tax for 1987. M is required by this paragraph (c) to make a timely subsequent installment payment of $1,000,000 by September 15, 1987, but M's actual installment payment by that date is only $990,000. Because of this shortfall, M loses the benefit of the safe harbor and is subject to underpayment penalties with respect to the first two installments. The aggregate penalties with respect to those two installments, however, cannot exceed the amount of the underpayment penalty to which M would be subject if there were an underpayment of $10,000 with respect to the September 15, 1987, installment payment. Such penalties are independent of any penalty that may apply with respect to M's third installment payment under the normal rules of section 6655.

(d) *Example.*—The provisions of this section may be illustrated by the following example:

*Example.* (i) Corporation X (which is not a life insurance company) uses as its taxable year a fiscal year ending on January 31 and is required to pay an installment of estimated income tax by May 15, 1987, for its taxable year beginning on February 1, 1987. On its return for the taxable year ending January 31, 1987, which was a year of 12 months, X reported taxable income of $10,000,000 ($9,000,000 of which was ordinary income and $1,000,000 of which was net capital gain) and did not claim any net operating loss deduction. As of February 1, 1987, X has no net operating loss carryforwards and no credit carryforwards. X has no credits against tax that are permitted to be taken into account under section 6655(d)(3) for 1987. If X uses the safe harbor provided in paragraph (b)(1) of this section, X must make by May 15, 1987, an installment payment of estimated tax of at least $1,037,836, computed as follows:

| | | |
|---|---|---:|
| (1) | Taxable income shown on return for taxable year ending on January 31, 1987 . . . . . . . . . . . . . | $10,000,000 |
| (2) | Annualized taxable income for taxable year ending January 31, 1988, determined pursuant to paragraph (b)(1) of this section (Item (1) × 120%) . | |
| | . . . . . . . . . . . . . . . . . . . . . . . . . | $12,000,000 |
| | (Note: 120% × ordinary income of $9,000,000 = $10,800,000; | |
| | 120% × net capital gain of $1,000,000 = $1,200,000) | |
| (3) | Tax on annualized taxable income (Item 2) using rates under section 11 and 1201, taking into account section 15, applicable to the taxable year ending January 31, 1988 . . . . . . . . . . . . . . | $4,612,603 |
| (4) | Amount described in section 6655(d)(3)(A)(i) (Item (3) × 22.5%) . . . . . . . . . . . . . . . . . . | $1,037,836 |

   (ii) To preclude imposition of an addition to tax under section 6655 with respect to its May 15, 1987, installment payment, X must make by July 15, 1987, a second installment payment of estimated tax sufficient to bring its aggregate payments to the minimum level required under paragraph (c) of this section.

   (iii) X may satisfy the requirements of paragraph (c)(3) of this section by making a second installment payment sufficient to bring X within the exception provided in section 6655(d)(3). Thus, if X determines under that section that the aggregate of X's installment payments of estimated tax by July 15, 1987, must equal at least $3,000,000, X may obtain the benefit of the safe harbor provided in paragraph (b)(1) of this section with respect to the May 15, 1987, installment payment by making a timely second installment payment of $1,962,164 ($3,000,000 – $1,037,836).

   (iv) Even if X fails to satisfy the requirements of paragraph (c)(3) of this section, X may obtain the benefit of the safe harbor for the May 15, 1987, installment payment if X's second installment payment, when aggregated with the first payment, equals at least 45 percent of the tax (including the alternative minimum tax under section 55 and the environmental tax under section 59A) shown on X's return for X's taxable year beginning on February 1, 1987. Thus, if the tax shown on that return is $6,000,000, X's second installment payment under paragraph (c)(4) of this section must be at least $1,662,164, computed as follows:

| | | |
|---|---|---:|
| 45 percent of $6,000,000 | = | $2,700,000 |
| less first payment | | 1,037,836 |
| Minimum second installment | | $1,662,164 |

[Temporary Reg. § 1.6655-2T.]

☐ [*T.D.* 8132, 3-24-87.]

### [Reg. § 1.6655-3]

§ 1.6655-3. **Adjusted seasonal installment method.**—(a) *In general.*—In the case of any required installment, the amount of the adjusted seasonal installment is the excess (if any) of—

   (1) 100 percent of the amount determined under paragraph (c) of this section; over

   (2) The aggregate amount of all prior required installments for the taxable year.

(b) *Limitation on application of section.*—This section applies only if the base period percentage (as defined in section 6655(e)(3)(D)(i) and paragraph (d)(1) of this section) for any six consecutive months of the taxable year equals or exceeds seventy percent.

(c) *Determination of amount.*—The amount determined under this paragraph (c) for any installment will be determined in the following manner—

   (1) Take the taxable income for all months during the taxable year preceding the filing month;

   (2) Divide such amount by the base period percentage for all months during the taxable year preceding the filing month;

   (3) Determine the tax on the amount determined under paragraph (c)(2) of this section; and

   (4) Multiply the tax computed under paragraph (c)(3) of this section by the base period percentage for the filing month and all months during the taxable year preceding the filing month.

(d) *Special rules.*—(1) *Base period percentage.*—The base period percentage for any period of months is the average percent that the taxable income for the corresponding months in each of the three preceding taxable years bears to the taxable income for the three preceding taxable years. If there is no taxable income for the corresponding months, taxable income for this purpose is zero.

(2) *Filing month.*—The term filing month means the month in which the installment is required to be paid.

(3) *Application of the rules related to the annualized income installment method to the adjusted seasonal installment method.*—The rules governing the computation of taxable income (and resulting tax) for purposes of determining any required installment payment of estimated tax under the annualized income installment method under § 1.6655-2 apply to the computation of taxable income (and resulting tax) for purposes of determining any required installment payment of estimated tax under the adjusted seasonal installment method.

(4) *Alternative minimum tax.*—The amount determined under paragraph (c) of this section must properly take into account the amount of any alternative minimum tax under section 55 that would apply for the period of the computation. The amount of any alternative minimum tax that would apply is determined by applying to alternative minimum taxable income, tentative minimum tax, and alternative minimum tax, the rules described in paragraph (c) of this section for taxable income and tax.

(e) *Example.*—The provisions of this section may be illustrated by the following example:

*Example.* (i) X, a corporation that reports on a calendar year basis, expects to have an estimated tax liability of $1,200,000 for its taxable year ending December 31, 2009. On its 2008 tax return, X reports a tax liability of $652,800. X pays four installments of estimated tax, each in the amount of $250,000, $250,000, $250,000, and $450,000 on April 15, 2009, June 15, 2009, September 15, 2009, and December 15, 2009, respectively. X reports a tax liability of $1,152,600 on its return due March 15, 2010, with no credits against tax. Under the general provision of section 6655(b) and section 6655(d), there was an underpayment in the amount of $76,300 for the second installment through September 15, 2009, and $114,450 for the third installment through December 15, 2009, determined as follows:

(A) Tax as defined in section 6655(g) = $1,152,600

(B) 100% of this paragraph (e), *Example* (i)(A) = $1,152,600

(C) Amount of estimated tax required to be paid on or before the first installment (25% of $652,800) = $163,200

(D) Deduction of amount timely paid on or before the first installment due date under the general rule of section 6655(b) = $250,000

(E) Amount of overpaid estimated tax for the first installment date = $86,800

(F) Amount of estimated tax required to be paid on or before the second installment (25% of $1,152,600 plus the recapture amount under section 6655(d)(2)(B) of $124,950 (25% of $1,152,600 less $163,200)) = $413,100

(G) Deduction of amount paid on or before the due date of the second installment less amount applied towards the first installment under the general rule of section 6655(b) ($250,000 paid in each of the first and second installments less this paragraph (e), *Example* (i)(C)) = $336,800

(H) Amount of underpayment for the second installment date = $76,300

(I) Amount of estimated tax required to be paid on or before the third installment (25% of $1,152,600) = $288,150

(J) Deduction of amount paid on or before the due date of the third installment less amount applied towards the first and second installments under the general rule of section 6655(b) ($250,000 paid in each of the first, second, and third installments less this paragraph (e), *Example* (i)(C) less this paragraph (e), *Example* (i)(F)) = $173,700

(K) Amount of underpayment for the third installment date = $114,450

(L) Amount of estimated tax required to be paid on or before the fourth installment (25% of $1,152,600) = $288,150

(M) Deduction of amount paid on or before the due date of the fourth installment less amount applied towards the first, second, and third installments under the general rule of section 6655(b) ($250,000 paid in each of the first, second, and third installments plus $450,000 paid in the fourth installment less this paragraph (e), *Example* (i)(C) less this paragraph (e), *Example* (i)(F) less this paragraph (e), *Example* (i)(I)) = $335,550

(N) Amount of overpaid estimated tax for the fourth installment date = $47,400

(ii) X wants to determine if it qualifies for the adjusted seasonal installment method. X determines that its monthly taxable income for the preceding three taxable years and for the current taxable year 2009 is as follows:

| | January | February | March |
|---|---|---|---|
| 2006 | $100,000 | $90,000 | $80,000 |
| 2007 | 200,000 | 170,000 | 170,000 |
| 2008 | 410,000 | 350,000 | 330,000 |
| 2009 | 600,000 | 680,000 | 650,000 |

| | April | May | June |
|---|---|---|---|
| 2006 | $70,000 | $60,000 | $20,000 |
| 2007 | 130,000 | 125,000 | 45,000 |
| 2008 | 270,000 | 240,000 | 80,000 |
| 2009 | 560,000 | 460,000 | 170,000 |

| | July | August | September |
|---|---|---|---|
| 2006 | $10,000 | $10,000 | $10,000 |
| 2007 | 21,000 | 19,000 | 20,000 |
| 2008 | 40,000 | 40,000 | 40,000 |
| 2009 | 70,000 | 60,000 | 50,000 |

| | October | November | December |
|---|---|---|---|
| 2006 | $10,000 | $10,000 | $10,000 |
| 2007 | 20,000 | 20,000 | 20,000 |
| 2008 | 40,000 | 40,000 | 40,000 |
| 2009 | 40,000 | 30,000 | 20,000 |

(iii) X must initially determine if its base period percentage for the same 6 consecutive months of the 3 preceding taxable years equals or exceeds 70 percent (see section 6655(e)(3) and paragraphs (b) and (c) of this section). By using its taxable income for the first 6 months of 2006, 2007, and 2008, X qualifies for the adjusted seasonal installment method because its base period percentage is 87.5 percent (which exceeds 70 percent) computed as follows:

(A) Taxable income for first 6 months of 2006 = $420,000

(B) Total taxable income for 2006 = $480,000

(C) Divide this paragraph (e), *Example* (iii)(A) by this paragraph (e), *Example* (iii)(B) = .875

(D) Taxable income for first 6 months of 2007 = $840,000

(E) Total taxable income for 2007 = $960,000

(F) Divide this paragraph (e), *Example* (iii)(D) by this paragraph (e), *Example* (iii)(E) = .875

(G) Taxable income for first 6 months of 2008 = $1,680,000

(H) Total taxable income for 2008 = $1,920,000

(I) Divide this paragraph (e), *Example* (iii)(G) by this paragraph (e), *Example* (iii)(H) = .875

(J) Add this paragraph (e), *Example* (iii)(C), (F), and (I) = $2.625

(K) Divide this paragraph (e), *Example* (iii)(J) by 3 = .875

(iv) To determine the amount of the first installment under the rules of section 6655(e)(3) and paragraph (a) of this section, the following computation is necessary:

(A) Taxable income for first 3 months of 2009 = $1,930,000

(B) Taxable income for first 3 months of 2006 ($270,000) divided by total taxable income for 2006 ($480,000) = .5625

(C) Taxable income for first 3 months of 2007 ($540,000) divided by total taxable income for 2007 ($960,000) = .5625

(D) Taxable income for first 3 months of 2008 ($1,090,000) divided by total taxable income for 2008 ($1,920,000) = .5677

(E) Add this paragraph (e), *Example* (iv)(B), (C), and (D) and divide by 3 = .5642

(F) Divide this paragraph (e), *Example* (iv)(A) by this paragraph (e), *Example* (iv)(E) = $3,420,773

(G) Determine the tax on this paragraph (e), *Example* (iv)(F) = $1,163,049

(H) Taxable income for first 4 months of 2006 ($340,000) divided by total taxable income for 2006 ($480,000) = .7083

(I) Taxable income for first 4 months of 2007 ($670,000) divided by total taxable income for 2007 ($960,000) = .6979

(J) Taxable income for first 4 months of 2008 ($1,360,000) divided by total taxable income for 2008 (1,920,000) = .7083

(K) Add this paragraph (e), *Example* (iv)(H), (I), and (J) and divide by 3 = .7048

(L) Multiply this paragraph (e), *Example* (iv)(G) by this paragraph (e), *Example* (iv)(K) = $819,717

(M) 100% of this paragraph (e), *Example* (iv)(L) = $819,717

(N) Amount of all prior required installments for 2009 = $0

(O) Amount of adjusted seasonal installment for the first installment payment (this paragraph (e), *Example* (iv)(M) less this paragraph (e), *Example* (iv)(N)) = $819,717

(v) To determine the amount of the second installment under the rules of section 6655(e)(3) and paragraph (a) of this section, the following computation is necessary:

(A) Taxable income for first 5 months of 2009 = $2,950,000

(B) Taxable income for first 5 months of 2006 ($400,000) divided by total taxable income for 2006 ($480,000) = .8333

(C) Taxable income for first 5 months of 2007 ($795,000) divided by total taxable income for 2007 ($960,000) = .8281

(D) Taxable income for first 5 months of 2008 ($1,600,000) divided by total taxable income for 2008 ($1,920,000) = .8333

(E) Add this paragraph (e), *Example* (v)(B), (C), and (D) and divide by 3 = .8316

(F) Divide this paragraph (e), *Example* (v)(A) by this paragraph (e), *Example* (v)(E) = $3,547,379

(G) Determine the tax on this paragraph (e), *Example* (v)(F) = $1,206,109

(H) Taxable income for first 6 months of 2006 ($420,000) divided by total taxable income for 2006 ($480,000) = .875

(I) Taxable income for first 6 months of 2007 ($840,000) divided by total taxable income for 2007 ($960,000) = .875

(J) Taxable income for first 6 months of 2008 ($1,680,000) divided by total taxable income for 2008 ($1,920,000) = .875

(K) Add this paragraph (e), *Example* (v)(H), (I), and (J) and divide by 3 = .875

(L) Multiply this paragraph (e), *Example* (v)(G) by this paragraph (e), *Example* (v)(K) = $1,055,345

(M) 100% of this paragraph (e), *Example* (v)(L) = $1,055,345

(N) Amount of all prior required installments for 2009 = $163,200

(O) Amount of adjusted seasonal installment for the second installment payment (this paragraph (e), *Example* (v)(M) less this paragraph (e), *Example* (v)(N)) = $892,145

(vi) To determine the amount of the third installment under the rules of section 6655(e)(3) and paragraph (a) of this section, the following computation is necessary:

(A) Taxable income for first 8 months of 2009 = $3,250,000

(B) Taxable income for first 8 months of 2006 ($440,000) divided by total taxable income for 2006 ($480,000) = .9167

(C) Taxable income for first 8 months of 2007 ($880,000) divided by total taxable income for 2007 ($960,000) = .9167

(D) Taxable income for first 8 months of 2008 ($1,760,000) divided by total taxable income for 2008 ($1,920,000) = .9167

(E) Add this paragraph (e), *Example* (vi)(B), (C), and (D) and divide by 3 = .9167

(F) Divide this paragraph (e), *Example* (vi)(A) by this paragraph (e), *Example* (vi)(E) = $3,545,326

(G) Determine the tax on this paragraph (e), *Example* (vi)(F) = $1,205,411

(H) Taxable income for first 9 months of 2006 ($450,000) divided by total taxable income for 2006 ($480,000) = .9375

(I) Taxable income for first 9 months of 2007 ($900,000) divided by total taxable income for 2007 ($960,000) = .9375

(J) Taxable income for first 9 months of 2008 ($1,800,000) divided by total taxable income for 2008 ($1,920,000) = .9375

(K) Add this paragraph (e), *Example* (vi)(H), (I), and (J) and divide by 3 = .9375

(L) Multiply this paragraph (e), *Example* (vi)(G) by this paragraph (e), *Example* (vi)(K) = $1,130,073

(M) 100% of this paragraph (e), *Example* (vi)(L) = $1,130,073

(N) Amount of all prior required installments for 2009 = $576,300

(O) Amount of adjusted seasonal installment for the third installment payment (this paragraph (e), *Example* (vi)(M) less this paragraph (e), *Example* (vi)(N)) = $553,773

(vii) To determine the amount of the fourth installment under the rules of section 6655(e)(3) and paragraph (a) of this section, the following computation is necessary:

(A) Taxable income for first 11 months of 2009 = $3,370,000

(B) Taxable income for first 11 months of 2006 ($470,000) divided by total taxable income for 2006 ($480,000) = .9792

(C) Taxable income for first 11 months of 2007 ($940,000) divided by total taxable income for 2007 ($960,000) = .9792

(D) Taxable income for first 11 months of 2008 ($1,880,000) divided by total taxable income for 2008 ($1,920,000) = .9792

(E) Add this paragraph (e), *Example* (vii)(B), (C), and (D) and divide by 3 = .9792

(F) Divide this paragraph (e), *Example* (vii)(A) by this paragraph (e), *Example* (vii)(E) = $3,441,585

(G) Determine the tax on this paragraph (e), *Example* (vii)(F) = $1,170,139

(H) Taxable income for first 12 months of 2006 ($480,000) divided by total taxable income for 2006 ($480,000) = 1.0000

(I) Taxable income for first 12 months of 2007 ($960,000) divided by total taxable income for 2007 ($960,000) = 1.0000

(J) Taxable income for first 12 months of 2008 ($1,920,000) divided by total taxable income for 2008 ($1,920,000) = 1.0000

(K) Add this paragraph (e), *Example* (vii)(H), (I), and (J) and divide by 3 = 1.0000

(L) Multiply this paragraph (e), *Example* (vii)(G) by this paragraph (e), *Example* (vi)(K) = $1,170,139

(M) 100% of this paragraph (e), *Example* (vii)(L) = $1,170,139

(N) Amount of all prior required installments for 2009 = $864,450

(O) Amount of adjusted seasonal installment for the fourth installment payment (this paragraph (e), *Example* (vii)(M) less this paragraph (e), *Example* (vii)(N)) = $305,689

(viii) Because the total amount of each required estimated tax payment determined under section 6655(e)(3) and paragraph (a) of this section exceeds the amount of each required estimated tax payment determined under section 6655(d) and § 1.6655-1(d) and (e), the exception described in section 6655(e) and this section does not apply and the addition to the tax with respect to the underpayment for the June 15, 2009, and September 15, 2009, installments will be imposed unless another exception (for example, see section 6655(e)(2)) applies with respect to these installments.

(f) *Effective/applicability date.*—This section applies to taxable years beginning after September 6, 2007. [Reg. § 1.6655–3.]

☐ [T.D. 6267, 11-13-57. Amended by T.D. 9347, 8-6-2007.]

**[Reg. § 1.6655-4]**

**§ 1.6655-4. Large corporations.**—(a) *Large corporation defined.*—The term large corporation means any corporation (or a predecessor corporation) that had taxable income of at least $1,000,000 for any taxable year during the testing period. For purposes of this section, a predecessor corporation is the distributor or transferor corporation in a transaction to which section 381 (relating to carryovers in certain corporate acquisitions) applies.

(b) *Testing period.*—For purposes of paragraph (a) of this section, the term testing period means the 3 taxable years immediately preceding the taxable year for which estimated tax is being determined (the current taxable year) or, if less, the number of taxable years the taxpayer has been in existence.

(c) *Computation of taxable income during testing period.*—(1) *Short taxable year.*—In the case of a corporation (or predecessor corporation) that had a short taxable year during the testing period, for purposes of determining whether the $1,000,000 amount referred to in paragraph (a) of this section is equaled or exceeded, the taxable income for the short taxable year is computed by—

(i) Multiplying the taxable income for the short taxable year by 12; and

(ii) Dividing the resulting amount by the number of months in the short taxable year.

(2) *Computation of taxable income in taxable year when there occurs a transaction to which section 381 applies.*—(i) For purposes of determining whether an acquiring corporation had taxable income of $1,000,000 or more for a taxable year in which a section 381 transaction occurs, the acquiring corporation's taxable income will be the sum of—

(A) The taxable income of the acquiring corporation for its taxable year; plus

(B) The taxable income (or loss) of the distributor or transferor corporation for that portion of its taxable year corresponding to the acquiring corporation's taxable year up to and including the date of distribution or transfer (as defined in § 1.381(b)-1(b)).

(ii) For purposes of determining whether a transferor or distributor corporation had taxable income of $1,000,000 or more for a taxable year in which a section 381 transaction occurs, the distributor or transferor corporation's taxable income (or loss) is reduced by the amount of taxable income (or loss) that is included in the acquiring corporation's taxable income for the taxable year in which the distribution or transfer (as defined in § 1.381(b)-1(b)) occurs, as described in paragraph (c)(2)(i)(B) of this section.

(d) *Members of controlled group.*—(1) *In general.*—For purposes of applying paragraph (a) of this section, the taxable income of members of a controlled group of corporations (as defined in section 1563(a)) must be aggregated for each year of the testing period. The provisions of this section do not apply to a controlled group for any taxable year in which the aggregate taxable income of the members of the controlled group is less than $1,000,000.

(2) *Aggregation.*—For purposes of paragraph (d)(1) of this section, a taxable loss of any member of the controlled group for a taxable year during the testing period is not taken into account.

(3) *Allocation rule.*—If the aggregate taxable income of members of a controlled group computed pursuant to paragraph (d)(1) of this section exceeds $1,000,000 during the testing period, the $1,000,000 amount that is relevant for purposes of determining, under paragraph (a)(1) of this section, whether a corporation is a large corporation is divided equally among the component members of such group (including component members excluded pursuant to paragraph (d)(2) of this section) unless all of such component members consent to an apportionment plan providing for an alternative allocation of such amount. The procedure for making and filing this plan will be the same as the procedure used for making and filing an apportionment plan under section 1561. See section 1561 and the regulations.

(4) *Controlled group members.*—(i) In the case of any corporation that was a member of a controlled group of corporations at any time during the testing period but is not a member of such group during the taxable year involved, the taxable income of the former member for the testing period is determined as if such corporation were not a member of a group at any time during that period. With respect to the controlled group, the taxable income of its former member will not be taken into account in determining such group's taxable income for any taxable year during the testing period for purposes of applying paragraph (a)(1) of this section.

(ii) For purposes of paragraph (d)(4)(i) of this section, the determination of whether a corporation is a member of a controlled group during the testing period is based on whether the corporation was a member of the controlled group on the last day of the month preceding the due date of the required installment.

(e) *Effect on a corporation's taxable income of items that may be carried back or carried over from any other taxable year.*—In determining whether a corporation (or predecessor corporation) is a large corporation for its current taxable year, items that could offset taxable income during a taxable year included in the testing period (for example, those described in sections 172 and 1212) are not to be taken into account and the taxable income of a corporation for any taxable year during the testing period is determined without regard to items carried back or carried over from any other taxable year.

(f) *Consolidated returns.*—[Reserved].

(g) *Example.*—The provisions of this section may be illustrated by the following example:

*Example. Y Corporation and Z Corporation are calendar year taxpayers.* In 2008, Z acquires all of the assets of Y in a transaction to which section 381 applies. Z's taxable income for both 2006 and 2007 was less than $1,000,000. Y's taxable income for 2008 is determined under paragraph (c)(2) of this section to be $300,000 for that portion of Y's taxable year corresponding to Z's taxable year up to and including the date of transfer. Z's taxable income for 2008 is $800,000. Under the provisions of paragraph (c)(2) of this section, Z's 2008 taxable income for purposes of determining whether it is a large corporation for taxable year 2009 is $1,100,000 ($800,000 + $300,000). Thus, Z is a large corporation for the 2009 taxable year. In addition, if Z's 2008 taxable income, as determined under paragraph (c)(2) of this section, had been less than $1,000,000 but Y's taxable income in 2006 or 2007 had been $1,000,000 or more, Z would be a large corporation for taxable year 2009 because Y is a predecessor corporation.

(h) *Effective/applicability date.*—This section applies to taxable years beginning after September 6, 2007. [Reg. § 1.6655–4.]

☐ [*T.D. 9347, 8-6-2007.*]

**[Reg. § 1.6655-5]**

**§ 1.6655-5. Short taxable year.**—(a) *In general.*—Except as otherwise provided in this section, the provisions of section 6655 and these regulations are applicable in the case of a short taxable year (including an initial taxable year) for which a payment of estimated tax is required to be made.

(b) *Exception to payment of estimated tax.*—In the case of a short taxable year, no payment of estimated tax is required if—

(1) The short taxable year is a period of less than 4 full calendar months; or

(2) The tax shown on the return for such taxable year (or, if no return is filed, the tax) is less than $500.

(c) *Installment due dates.*—(1) *In general.*—(i) *Taxable year of at least four months but less than twelve months.*—Except as otherwise provided, in the case of a short taxable year, if such year results in a taxable year of four or more full calendar months but less than twelve full calendar months, the due dates prescribed in § 1.6655-1(f)(2) apply.

(ii) *Exceptions.*—(A) If the date determined under paragraph (c)(1)(i) of this section for the first required installment due during the taxpayer's short taxable year is earlier than the 15th day of the fourth month of the taxpayer's short taxable year, the taxpayer's first required installment is due on the first due date otherwise determined under paragraph (c)(1)(i) of this section that is on or after the 15th day of the fourth month of the short taxable year.

(B) A taxpayer with an initial short taxable year may make estimated tax payments as though it were a calendar year taxpayer until it files its tax return for its initial taxable year and will not be subject to an addition to tax under section 6655 for making estimated tax payments as though it were a calendar year taxpayer for the period beginning with its initial short taxable year to the time it files its tax return for its initial short taxable year if, when filing its tax return for its initial short taxable year, the taxpayer chooses to be a fiscal year taxpayer.

(2) *Early termination of taxable year.*—(i) *In general.*—Except as provided in paragraph (c)(2)(ii) of this section, if a taxable year ends early (for example, as a result of an acquisition or a change in taxable year), the due date for the final required installment is the date that would have been the due date of the next required installment if the event that gave rise to the short taxable year had not occurred.

(ii) *Exception.*—If the date determined under paragraph (c)(2)(i) of this section is within thirty days of the last day of the short taxable year, the due date for the final required installment is the fifteenth day of the second month following the month that includes the last day of the short taxable year.

(d) *Amount due for required installment.*—(1) *In general.*—The amount due for any required installment determined under section 6655(d)(1)(B)(i) for a short taxable year is 100% of the required annual payment for the short taxable year divided by the number of required installments due (as determined under this section) for the short taxable year.

(2) *Tax shown on the return for the preceding taxable year.*—If the current taxable year is a short taxable year, the amount due for any required installment determined under section 6655(d)(1)(B)(ii) is determined in the following manner—

(i) Take 100% of the tax shown on the return of the corporation for the preceding taxable year;

(ii) Multiply such amount by the number of full calendar months in the current short taxable year and divide by 12; and

(iii) Divide the amount determined under paragraph (d)(2)(ii) of this section by the number of required installments due (as determined under this section) for the current short taxable year.

(3) *Applicable percentage.*—In the case of any required installment determined under section 6655(e), the applicable percentage under section 6655(e)(2)(B)(ii) is—

(i) 25%, 50%, 75%, and 100% for the first, second, third, and fourth (last) required installments, respectively, if the taxpayer will have four required installments due for the short taxable year;

(ii) 33.33%, 66.67%, and 100% for the first, second, and third (last) required installments, respectively, if the taxpayer will have three required installments due for the short taxable year;

(iii) 50% and 100% for the first and second (last) required installments, respectively, if the taxpayer will have two required installments due for the short taxable year; or

(iv) 100% for the first (and last) required installment if the taxpayer will have one required installment for the short taxable year.

(4) *Applicable percentage for installment period in which taxpayer does not reasonably expect that the taxable year will be an early termination year.*—In the case of any required installment determined under section 6655(e) in which the taxpayer does not reasonably expect that the taxable year will be an early termination year, the applicable percentage under section 6655(e)(2)(B)(ii) is the applicable percentage provided by paragraph (d)(3)(i) of this section with the remaining balance of the estimated tax payment for the year due with the final installment.

(e) *Examples.*—The following examples illustrate the rules of this section:

(1) *Example 1. Short year of less than 4 months.*—Corporation A is a calendar year taxpayer that was acquired by corporation B, a member of a consolidated group (as defined in § 1.1502-1(h)) on April 16, 2009, resulting in A having a short taxable year from January 1, 2009, through April 16, 2009. Because A has a taxable year of less than four full calendar months, no estimated tax payments are required by A for the short taxable year.

(2) *Example 2. Initial short year with four required installments.*—Corporation B began business on January 9, 2009, and adopted a calendar year as its taxable year. B computes its required installments based on 100 percent of the tax shown on the return for the taxable year in accordance with section 6655(d)(1)(B)(i). Pursuant to § 1.6655-1(f)(2)(i), the due dates of B's required installments for B's initial taxable year from January 9, 2009, through December 31, 2009, are April 15, 2009, June 15, 2009, September 15, 2009, and December 15, 2009. Pursuant to paragraph (d)(1) of this section, the amount due with each required installment is 25% of the required annual payment for B's first required installment, 50% of the required annual payment for B's second required installment, 75% of the required annual payment for B's third required installment, and 100% of the required annual payment for B's fourth required installment.

(3) *Example 3. Initial short year with three required installments.*—Corporation C began business on February 12, 2009, and adopted a calendar year as its taxable year. C computes its required installments based on 100 percent of the tax shown on the return for the taxable year in accordance with section 6655(d)(1)(B)(i). Pursuant to § 1.6655-1(f)(2)(i), the due dates of C's required installments for C's initial taxable year from February 12, 2009, through December 31, 2009, are April 15, 2009, June 15, 2009, September 15, 2009, and December 15, 2009. However, in accordance with paragraph (c)(1)(ii)(A) of this section, C's first required installment is due June 15, 2009, because April 15, 2009, is earlier than the fifteenth day of the fourth month of C's taxable year. As a result, C's second required installment is due September 15, 2009, and C's third (and last) installment is due December 15, 2009. Pursuant to paragraph (d)(1) of this section, the amount due with each required installment is 33.33% of the required annual payment for C's first required installment, 66.67% of the required annual payment for C's second required installment, and 100% of the required annual payment for C's third (and last) required installment.

(4) *Example 4. Initial short year with two required installments.*—Same facts as *Example 3* except C began business on April 10, 2009. In accordance with paragraph (c)(1)(ii)(A) of this section, C's first required installment is due September 15, 2009, because April 15, 2009, and June 15, 2009, are earlier than the fifteenth day of the fourth month of C's taxable year. As a result, C's second (and last) required installment is due December 15, 2009. Pursuant to paragraph (d)(1) of this section, the amount due with each required installment is 50% of the required annual payment for C's first required installment, and 100% of the required annual payment for C's second (and last) required installment.

(5) *Example 5. Initial short year for fiscal year taxpayer with two required installments.*—Corporation D began business on February 12, 2009, and adopted a fiscal year ending October 31 as its taxable year. D computes its required installments based on 100 percent of the tax shown on the return for the taxable year in accordance with section 6655(d)(1)(B)(i). Pursuant to § 1.6655-1(f)(2)(ii), the due dates of D's required installments for D's initial taxable year from February 12, 2009, through October 31, 2009, are February 15, 2009, April 15, 2009, July 15, 2009, and October 15, 2009. However, in accordance with paragraph (c)(1)(ii)(A) of this section, D's first required installment is due July 15, 2009, because February 15, 2009, and April 15, 2009, are earlier than the fifteenth day of the fourth month of D's taxable year. As a result, D's second (and last) installment is due October 15, 2009. Pursuant to paragraph (d)(1) of this section, the amount due with each required installment is 50% of the required annual payment for

D's first required installment, and 100% of the required annual payment for D's second (and last) required installment.

(6) *Example 6. Initial short year for fiscal year taxpayer with one required installment.*—Same facts as *Example 5* except D corporation began business on May 11, 2009. In accordance with paragraph (c)(1)(ii)(A) of this section, D's first (and last) installment is due October 15, 2009, because July 15, 2009, is earlier than the fifteenth day of the fourth month of D's taxable year. Pursuant to paragraph (d)(1) of this section, the amount due with D's required installment is 100% of the required annual payment, computed as 100% divided by the number of required installments due for the short taxable year.

(7) *Example 7. Short termination year with three required installments.*—Corporation E is a calendar year taxpayer that computes its required installments based on 100 percent of the tax shown on the return for the taxable year in accordance with section 6655(d)(1)(B)(i). E computes its 2009 required installments based on a projected 2009 total tax liability of $600,000. On July 31, 2009, E is acquired by corporation F, a member of a consolidated group (as defined in § 1.1502-1(h)), resulting in E having a short taxable year from January 1, 2009, through July 31, 2009. E determines that its total tax liability for the short period is $350,000. The due dates for E's first and second required installments are April 15, 2009, and June 15, 2009, respectively. Pursuant to section 6655(d)(1)(A), E paid $150,000 with each required installment. Pursuant to paragraph (c)(2) of this section, E's third (and last) required installment of estimated tax is due on September 15, 2009, and the percentage of the required annual payment due with such installment is 100% pursuant to paragraph (d)(1) of this section. Accordingly, E is required to pay $50,000 with its final required installment on September 15, 2009 ($350,000 total tax liability for the short taxable year less prior installment payments of $300,000).

(8) *Example 8. Unexpected short termination year with three required installments using the annualization method.*—Same facts as *Example 7* except that E uses the annualized income installment method under section 6655(e)(2)(A)(i) to calculate all of its required installment payments for its 2009 taxable year. In addition, E does not reasonably expect until July 28, 2009, that it will have a short termination year caused by E being acquired by F on July 31, 2009. Had E known about its acquisition by F in the first quarter of 2009, E's applicable percentages for computing the amount of its three required installments would be 33.33%, 66.67%, and 100% for the first, second, and third (last) required installments, respectively, pursuant to paragraph (d)(3)(ii) of this section. However, because E had an unexpected short termination year that E was not aware of until after its second required installment payment, E's applicable percentages for computing the amount of its three required installment are 25%, 50%, and 100% for the first, second, and third (last) required installments, respectively, pursuant to paragraph (d)(4) of this section.

(9) *Example 9. Short termination year ending within 30 days of the regular final installment due date.*—Same facts as *Example 7* except that E is acquired by F on August 31, 2009. Pursuant to paragraph (c)(2)(ii) of this section, E's third (and last) required installment of estimated tax is due on October 15, 2009, because September 15, 2009, the date that would have been the due date of E's next required installment if F's acquisition of E had not occurred, is within thirty days of the last day of E's short taxable year, and 100% of the required annual payment is due with such installment.

(10) *Example 10. Short termination year ending within 30 days of the regular final installment due date.*—Corporation F is a calendar year taxpayer that computes its required installments based on 100 percent of the tax shown on the return for the taxable year in accordance with section 6655(d)(1)(B)(i). F computes its 2009 estimated tax payments based on a projected 2009 total tax liability of $900,000. On December 3, 2009, F is acquired by corporation G, a member of a consolidated group (as defined in § 1.1502-1(h)), resulting in F having a short taxable year from January 1, 2009, through December 3, 2009. F determined its total tax liability for the short period to be $800,000. The due dates for F's first, second, and third required installments are April 15, 2009, June 15, 2009, and September 15, 2009, respectively. Pursuant to section 6655(d)(1)(A), F paid $225,000 with each required installment. Pursuant to paragraph (c)(2)(ii) of this section, F's third (and last) required installment of estimated tax is due on February 15, 2010, and the percentage of the required annual payment due with such installment is 100% pursuant to paragraph (d)(1) of this section. However, because the due date for the fourth required installment falls on a legal holiday, F's required installment payment will be timely if paid on or before the first business day following the actual due date of the fourth required installment, that is, February 16, 2010. Accordingly, F is required to pay $125,000 with its final required installment on February 16, 2010 ($800,000 total tax liability for the short taxable year less prior installment payments of $675,000).

(11) *Example 11. Short termination year using the tax shown on the return for the preceding taxable year.*—Corporation G, a calendar year taxpayer, reported a tax liability of $75,000 on its return for the taxable year ending December 31, 2008, and is not a large corporation as defined in section 6655(g). On July 31, 2009, G makes a final distribution of its assets, in connection with a plan of complete liquidation, resulting in a short taxable year from January 1, 2009, through July 31, 2009. To satisfy the requirements of the exception described in section 6655(d)(1)(B)(ii) for payments determined by reference to the tax shown on the return of the corporation for the preceding taxable year, pursuant to paragraph (d)(2) of this section, G must pay in a proportionate amount of its 2008 tax liability based on the number of months in the current taxable year. Accordingly, G must pay $43,750 ($75,000 X 7/12) through payments of estimated tax payments in 2009, with $14,583 due on April 15, 2009, June 15, 2009, and September 15, 2009.

(12) *Example 12. Short termination year using the tax shown on the return for the preceding taxable year.*—Same facts as *Example 11* except that G makes a final distribution of its assets, in connection with a plan of complete liquidation, on October 1, 2009, resulting in a short taxable year from January 1, 2009, through October 1, 2009. To satisfy the requirements of the exception described in section 6655(d)(1)(B)(ii), G must pay $56,250 ($75,000 x 9/12) through payments of estimated tax in 2009, with $14,063 due on April 15, 2009, June 15, 2009, September 15, 2009, and December 15, 2009, respectively.

(13) *Example 13. Short initial year with three required installments resulting in an underpayment.*—(i) Corporation H began business on February 17, 2009, and adopted a calendar year. H computes its required installments based on 100 percent of the tax shown on the return for the taxable year in accordance with section 6655(d)(1)(B)(i). H estimated at the beginning of its short taxable year that its estimated tax liability for short taxable year February 17, 2009, through December 31, 2009, would be $180,000. H paid its first required installment of estimated tax of $60,000 on June 15, 2009, its second required installment of estimated tax of $60,000 on September 15, 2009, and its third (and last) required installment of estimated tax of $60,000 on December 15, 2009 ($180,000 total estimated tax liability for the short taxable year less prior installment payments of $120,000). H reported a tax liability of $240,000 on its return for the short period February 17, 2009, through December 31, 2009, with no credits against tax. There was an underpayment in the amount of $20,000 on the first installment date through September 15, 2009, $40,000 on the second installment date through December 15, 2009, and $60,000 on the third (and last) installment date through March 15, 2010, determined as follows:

(A) Tax as defined in section 6655(d)(1)(B)(i) = $240,000

(B) 100% of this paragraph (e), *Example 13* (A) = $240,000

(C) Amount of estimated tax required to be paid by the first installment date (33.33% of $240,000) = $80,000

(D) Amount of estimated tax required to be paid by the second installment date (66.67% of $240,000 less $80,000 (amount due with first installment)) = $80,000

(E) Amount of estimated tax required to be paid by the third installment date (100% of $240,000 less $160,000 (amount due with first and second installment)) = $80,000

(F) Deduction of amount paid on or before the first installment date = $60,000

(G) Amount of underpayment for the first installment date (this paragraph (e), *Example 13* (i)(C) minus this paragraph (e), *Example 13* (i)(F)) = $20,000

(H) Deduction of amount available for the second installment date ($60,000 second installment payment less this paragraph (e), *Example 13* (i)(G) applied towards the first installment underpayment) = $40,000

(I) Amount of underpayment for the second installment date (this paragraph (e), *Example 13* (i)(D) minus this paragraph (e), *Example 13* (i)(H)) = $40,000

(J) Deduction of amount available for the third installment date ($60,000 third installment payment less this paragraph (e), *Example 13* (i)(I) applied towards the second installment underpayment) = $20,000

(K) Amount of underpayment for the third installment date (this paragraph (e), *Example 1* (i)(E) minus this paragraph (e), *Example 13* (i)(J)) = $60,000

(ii) [Reserved].

(f) *52 or 53 week taxable year.*—For purposes of this section a taxable year of 52 or 53 weeks is deemed a period of 12 months in the case of a corporation that computes its taxable income in accordance with the election permitted by section 441(f).

(g) *Use of annualized income or seasonal installment method.*—(1) *In general.*—Regardless of the annual accounting period used by a corporation (for example, calendar year, fiscal year) the taxpayer may use the method described in §1.6655-2 (annualized income installment method) or §1.6655-3 (adjusted seasonal installment method) to compute its required installments of estimated tax when the current taxable year is a short taxable year.

(2) *Computation of annualized income installment.*—To the extent a short taxable year includes an annualization period elected by the taxpayer, the taxpayer computes its annualized income installment by determining the tax on the basis of such annualized income for the annualization period, divided by 12, multiplied by the number of months in the short taxable year, and multiplied by the applicable percentage for the required installment.

(3) *Annualization period for final required installment.*—For purposes of determining the final required installment (as described in paragraph (c)(2) of this section) for a short taxable year, annualized taxable income is determined by placing on an annualized basis the taxable income for the last complete annualization period that occurs within the short taxable year.

(4) *Examples.*—The provisions of paragraph (g) of this section may be illustrated by the following examples:

*Example 1.* Corporation X began business on February 12, 2009, and adopted a calendar year as its taxable year. X adopts an accrual method of accounting and uses the annualized income installment method under section 6655(e)(2)(A)(i) to calculate all of its required installment payments for its 2009 taxable year. Pursuant to §1.6655-1(f)(2)(i), the due dates of X's required installments for X's initial taxable year from February 12, 2009, through December 31, 2009, are April 15, 2009, June 15, 2009, September 15, 2009, and December 15, 2009. However, in accordance with paragraph (c)(1)(ii)(A) of this section, X's first required installment is due June 15, 2009. As a result, X's second required installment is due September 15, 2009, and X's third (and last) required installment is due December 15, 2009. The amount of X's first and second required installments are each based on annualizing X's taxable income from February 12, 2009, through April 30, 2009, (the first three months of X's taxable year) and X's third (and last) required installment is based on annualizing X's taxable income from February 12, 2009, through July 31, 2009 (the first six months of X's taxable year). Because X will have three required installments due for its short taxable year, pursuant to paragraph (d)(3)(ii) of this section, the applicable percentage is 33.33% for X's first required installment, 66.67% for X's second required installment, and 100% for X's third (and last) required installment.

*Example 2.* (i) Y, a calendar year corporation, made a final distribution of its assets, in connection with a plan of complete liquidation, on August 3, 2009. Y filed a timely election to use the alternative annualization periods described under section 6655(e)(2)(C)(i) and determined that its taxable income for the first 2, 4 and 7 months of the taxable year was $25,000, $50,000 and $140,000. The due dates for Y's required installments for its short taxable year January 1, 2009, through August 3, 2009, are April 15, 2009, June 15, 2009, and September 15, 2009. Y made installment payments of $10,000, $10,000, and $20,000, respectively, on April 15, 2009, June 15, 2009, and September 15, 2009. The taxable income for each period is annualized as follows:

$25,000 X 12/2 = $150,000

$50,000 X 12/4 = $150,000

$140,000 x 12/7 = $240,000

(ii)(A) To determine whether the first required installment equals or exceeds the amount that would have been required to have been paid if the estimated tax were equal to one hundred percent of the tax computed on the annualized income for the 2-month period taking into account the number of months in the short taxable year, the following computation is necessary:

(1) Annualized income for the 2 month period = $150,000

(2) Tax on this paragraph (g)(4), *Example 2* (ii)(A)(1) = $41,750

(3) Tax determined under this paragraph (g)(4), *Example 2* (ii)(A)(2) divided by 12 multiplied by 7 (the number of months in the short taxable year) = $24,354

(4) 100% of this paragraph (g)(4), *Example 2* (ii)(A)(3) = $24,354

(5) 33.33% of this paragraph (g)(4), *Example 2* (ii)(A)(4) = $8,117

(B) Because the total amount of estimated tax that is timely paid on or before the first installment date ($10,000) exceeds the amount required to be paid on or before this date if the estimated tax were one hundred percent of the tax determined by placing on an annualized basis the taxable income for the first 2-month period taking into account the number of months in the short taxable year, the exception described in §1.6655-2(a) applies and no addition to tax will be imposed for the installment due on April 15, 2009.

(iii)(A) To determine whether the required installments made on or before June 15, 2009, equal or exceed the amount that would have been required to have been paid if the estimated tax were equal to one hundred percent of the tax computed on the annualized income for the 4-month period taking into account the number of months in the short taxable year, the following computation is necessary:

(1) Annualized income for the 4 month period = $150,000

(2) Tax on this paragraph (g)(4), *Example 2* (iii)(A)(1) = $41,750

(3) Tax determined under this paragraph (g)(4), *Example 2* (iii)(A)(2) divided by 12 multiplied by 7 (the number of months in the short taxable year) = $24,354

(4) 100% of this paragraph (g)(4), *Example 2* (iii)(A)(3) = $24,354

(5) 66.67% of this paragraph (g)(4), *Example 2* (iii)(A)(4) less $8,117 (amount due with first installment) = $8,120

(B) Because the total amount of estimated tax available to apply towards the amount due for the second installment ($11,883 ($10,000 paid on the second installment date plus $1,883 overpayment of the first installment)) exceeds the amount required to be paid on or before this date if the estimated tax were one hundred percent of the tax determined by placing on an annualized basis the taxable income for the first 4-month period for the taxable year taking into account the number of months in the short taxable year, the exception described in § 1.6655-2(a) applies and no addition to tax will be imposed for the installment due on June 15, 2009.

(iv)(A) Pursuant to paragraph (c) and (d) of this section, the final required installment is due by September 15, 2009, and the applicable percentage due for the final required installment is 100%. To determine whether the installment payments made on or before September 15, 2009, equal or exceed the amount that would have been required to have been paid if the estimated tax were equal to one hundred percent of the tax computed on the annualized income for the 7-month period taking into account the number of months in the short taxable year, the following computation is necessary:

(1) Annualized income for the 7 month period = $240,000

(2) Tax on this paragraph (g)(4), *Example 2* (iv)(A)(1) = $76,850

(3) Tax determined under this paragraph (g)(4), *Example 2* (iv)(A)(2) divided by 12 multiplied by 7 (the number of months in the short taxable year) = $44,829

(4) 100% of this paragraph (g)(4), *Example 2* (iv)(A)(3) = $44,829

(5) 100% of this paragraph (g)(4), *Example 2* (iv)(A)(4) less $16,237 (amount due with first and second installment) = $28,592

(B) Because the total amount of estimated tax available to apply towards the amount due for the final installment ($23,763 ($20,000 that is timely paid on the third installment date plus $3,763 overpayment of the second installment)) does not exceed the amount required to be paid on or before this date if the estimated tax were one hundred percent of the tax determined by placing on an annualized basis the taxable income for the first 7-month period for the taxable year taking into account the number of months in the short taxable year, the exception described in § 1.6655-2(a) does not apply and an addition to tax will be imposed for the final installment due on September 15, 2009, unless another exception (for example, see section 6655(e)(3)) applies with respect to these installments.

(h) *Effective/applicability date.*—This section applies to taxable years beginning after September 6, 2007. [Reg. § 1.6655-5.]

☐ [*T.D. 9347, 8-6-2007. Amended by T.D. 9885, 12-2-2019.*]

### [Reg. § 1.6655-6]

**§ 1.6655-6. Methods of accounting.**—(a) *In general.*—In computing any required installment, a corporation must use the methods of accounting used in computing taxable income for the taxable year for which estimated tax is being determined (the current taxable year).

(b) *Accounting method changes.*—A taxpayer that changes its method of accounting with the consent of the Commissioner for the current taxable year must use the new method of accounting (as of the beginning of the taxable year) in the determination of taxable income for annualization periods ending on or after the date the related section 481(a) adjustment is treated as arising. See § 1.6655-2(f)(3)(ii)(C) for the date a section 481(a) adjustment is treated as arising. If the change in method of accounting does not result in a section 481(a) adjustment, the taxpayer may choose to use the new method of accounting (as of the beginning of the taxable year) in the determination of taxable income for all annualization periods during the year of change or only those annualization periods ending on or after the date the Form 3115 "Application for Change in Accounting Method" was filed with the national office of the Internal Revenue Service. This paragraph (b) only applies to the extent a taxpayer changes a method of accounting for the taxable year with the consent of the Commissioner. Therefore, a taxpayer may be subject to a section 6655 addition to tax for an underpayment of estimated tax if an underpayment results from a change in a method of accounting the taxpayer anticipates making for the taxable

year but for which the consent of the Commissioner is not subsequently received.

(c) *Example.*—The following example illustrates the rules of this section:

(1) *Example. Change of accounting method.* Corporation ABC, a calendar year taxpayer, uses an accrual method of accounting and the annualization method under section 6655(e)(2)(A)(i) to calculate all of its 2008 required installments. On June 15, 2008, ABC files a Form 3115 requesting permission to change its method of accounting for future litigation reserves for the tax year ending December 31, 2008. On February 15, 2009, ABC receives consent from the Commissioner to make the change for the tax year ending December 31, 2008. The change results in a positive section 481(a) adjustment of $100,000. Under the provisions of § 1.6655-2(f)(3)(ii) ABC chooses to treat the section 481(a) adjustment as arising on the date the Form 3115 is filed with the national office of the Internal Revenue Service. Therefore, ABC is required to use the new method of accounting (as of the beginning of the year) in the determination of taxable income for annualization periods ending on or after June 15, 2008.

(2) [Reserved.]

(d) *Effective/applicability date.*—This section applies to taxable years beginning after September 6, 2007. [Reg. § 1.6655-6.]

☐ [*T.D. 9347, 8-6-2007. Amended by T.D. 9870, 7-11-2019.*]

### [Reg. § 1.6655-7]

**§ 1.6655-7. Addition to tax on account of excessive adjustment under section 6425.**—(a) Section 6655(h) imposes an addition to the tax under chapter 1 of the Internal Revenue Code in the case of any excessive amount (as defined in paragraph (c) of this section) of an adjustment under section 6425 that is made before the 15th day of the third month following the close of a taxable year beginning after December 31, 1967. This addition to tax is imposed whether or not there was reasonable cause for an excessive adjustment.

(b) If the amount of an adjustment under section 6425 is excessive, there shall be added to the tax under chapter 1 of the Internal Revenue Code for the taxable year an amount determined at the annual rate referred to in the regulations under section 6621 upon the excessive amount from the date on which the credit is allowed or refund paid to the 15th day of the third month following the close of the taxable year. A refund is paid on the date it is allowed under section 6407.

(c) The excessive amount is equal to the lesser of the amount of the adjustment or the amount by which—

(1) The income tax liability (as defined in section 6425(c)) for the taxable year, as shown on the return for the taxable year; exceeds

(2) The estimated income tax paid during the taxable year, reduced by the amount of the adjustment.

(d) The computation of the addition to the tax imposed by section 6425 is made independent of, and does not affect the computation of, any addition to the tax that a corporation may otherwise owe for an underpayment of an installment of estimated tax.

(e) The following example illustrates the rules of this section:

*Example.* (i) Corporation X, a calendar year taxpayer, had an underpayment as defined in section 6655(b), for its fourth installment of estimated tax that was due on December 15, 2009, in the amount of $10,000. On January 4, 2010, X filed an application for adjustment of overpayment of estimated income tax for 2009 in the amount of $20,000.

(ii) On February 16, 2010, the Internal Revenue Service, in response to the application, refunded $20,000 to X. On March 15, 2010, X filed its 2009 tax return and made a payment in settlement of its total tax liability. Assuming that the addition to tax is computed under section 6621(a)(2) at a rate of 8% per annum for the applicable periods of underpayment, under section 6655(a), X is subject to an addition to tax in the amount of $197 (90/365 X $10,000 X 8%) on account of X's December 15, 2009, underpayment. Under section 6655(h), X is subject to an addition to tax in the amount of $118 (27/365 X $20,000 X 8%) on account of X's excessive adjustment under section 6425. In determining the amount of the addition to tax under section 6655(a) for failure to pay estimated income tax, the excessive adjustment under section 6425 is not taken into account.

(f) An adjustment is generally to be treated as a reduction of estimated income tax paid as of the date of the adjustment. However, for purposes of §§ 1.6655-1 through 1.6655-6, the adjustment is to be treated as if not made in determining whether there has been any underpayment of estimated income tax and, if there is an underpayment, the period during which the underpayment existed.

(g) Effective/applicability date: This section applies to taxable years beginning after September 6, 2007. [Reg. § 1.6655–7.]

☐ [*T.D. 7059, 9-16-70. Amended by T.D. 7384, 10-21-75. Redesignated and amended by T.D. 9347, 8-6-2007.*]

### [Reg. § 1.6655(e)-1]

**§ 1.6655(e)-1. Time and manner for making election under the Omnibus Budget Reconciliation Act of 1993.**—(a) *Description.*—Section 6655(e)(2)(C), as added by section 13225 of the Omnibus Budget Reconciliation Act of 1993 (Public Law 103-66, 107 Stat. 486), allows a corporate taxpayer to make an annual election to use a different annualization period to determine annualized income for purposes of paying any required installment of estimated income tax for a taxable year beginning after December 31, 1993.

(b) *Time and manner for making the election.*—An election under section 6655(e)(2)(C) must be made on or before the date required for the payment of the first required installment for the taxable year. For a calendar or fiscal year corporation, Form 8842, Election to Use Different Annualization Periods for Corporate Estimated Tax, must be filed by the 15th day of the 4th month of the taxable year for which the election is to apply. Form 8842 must be filed with the Internal Revenue Service Center where the corporation files its income tax return.

(c) *Revocability of election.*—The election described in this section is irrevocable.

(d) *Effective date.*—The rules set forth in this section are effective December 12, 1996. [Reg. § 1.6655(e)-1.]

☐ [T.D. 8688, 12-11-96.]

### [Reg. § 301.6656-1]

**§ 301.6656-1. Abatement of penalty.**—(a) *Exception for first time depositors of employment taxes.*—(1) *Waiver.*—The Secretary will generally waive the penalty imposed by section 6656(a) on a person's failure to deposit any employment tax under subtitle C of the Internal Revenue Code if—

(i) The failure is inadvertent;

(ii) The person meets the requirements referred to in section 7430(c)(4)(A)(ii) (relating to the net worth requirements applicable for awards of attorney's fees);

(iii) The failure occurs during the first quarter that the person is required to deposit any employment tax; and

(iv) The return of the tax is filed on or before the due date.

(2) *Inadvertent failure.*—For purposes of paragraph (a)(1)(i) of this section, the Secretary will determine if a failure to deposit is inadvertent based on all the facts and circumstances.

(b) *Deposit sent to Secretary.*—The Secretary may abate the penalty imposed by section 6656(a) if the first time a taxpayer is required to make a deposit, the amount required to be deposited is inadvertently sent to the Secretary rather than deposited by electronic funds transfer.

(c) *Effective/applicability date.*—This section applies to deposits and payments made after December 31, 2010. [Reg. § 301.6656-1.]

☐ [T.D. 8725, 7-21-97. Redesignated by T.D. 8947, 6-14-2001. Amended by T.D. 9507, 12-2-2010.]

### [Reg. § 301.6657-1]

**§ 301.6657-1. Bad checks.**—(a) *In general.*—Except as provided in paragraph (b) of this section, if a check or money order is tendered in the payment of any amount receivable under the Code, and such check or money order is not paid upon presentment, a penalty of one percent of the amount of the check or money order, in addition to any other penalties provided by law, shall be paid by the person who tendered such check or money order. If, however, the amount of the check or money order is less than $500, the penalty shall be $5 or the amount of the check or money order, whichever amount is the lesser. Such penalty shall be paid in the same manner as tax upon the issuance of a notice and demand therefor.

(b) *Reasonable cause.*—If payment is refused upon presentment of any check or money order and the person who tendered such check or money order establishes to the satisfaction of the district director that it was tendered in good faith with reasonable cause to believe that it would be duly paid, the penalty set forth in paragraph (a) of this section shall not apply. [Reg. § 301.6657-1.]

☐ [T.D. 6268, 11-15-57. Amended by T.D. 6586, 12-27-61.]

### [Reg. § 301.6659-1]

**§ 301.6659-1. Applicable rules.**—(a) *Additions treated as tax.*—Except as otherwise provided in the Code, any reference in the Code to "tax" shall be deemed also to be a reference to any addition to the tax, additional amount, or penalty imposed by chapter 68 of the Code with respect to such tax. Such additions to the tax, additional amounts, and penalties shall become payable upon notice and demand therefor and shall be assessed, collected, and paid in the same manner as taxes.

(b) *Additions to tax for failure to file return or pay tax.*—Any addition under section 6651 or section 6653 to a tax shall be considered a part of such tax for the purpose of the assessment and collection of such tax. For applicability of deficiency procedures to additions to the tax, see paragraph (c) of this section.

(c) *Deficiency procedures.*—(1) *Addition to the tax for failure to file tax return.*—Subchapter B, chapter 63, of the Code (deficiency procedures) applies to the additions to the income, estate, and gift taxes imposed by section 6651 for failure to file a tax return to the same extent that it applies to such taxes. Accordingly, if there is a deficiency (as defined in section 6211) in the tax (apart from the addition to the tax) where a return has not been timely filed, deficiency procedures apply to the addition to the tax under section 6651. If there is no deficiency in the tax where a return has not been timely filed, the addition to the tax under section 6651 may be assessed and collected without deficiency procedures. The provisions of this subparagraph may be illustrated by the following examples:

*Example (1).* A filed his income tax return for the calendar year 1955 on May 15, 1956, not having been granted an extension of time for such filing. His failure to file on time was not due to reasonable cause. The return showed a liability of $1,000 and it was determined that A is liable under section 6651 for an addition to such tax of $50 (5 percent a month for 1 month). The provisions of subchapter B of chapter 63 (deficiency procedures) do not apply to the assessment and collection of the addition to the tax since such provisions are not applicable to the tax with respect to which such addition was asserted, there being no statutory deficiency for purposes of section 6211.

*Example (2).* Assume the same facts as in Example (1) and assume further that a deficiency of $500 in tax and a further $25 addition to the tax under section 6651 is asserted against A for the calendar year 1955. Thus, the total addition to the tax under section 6651 is $75. Since the provisions of subchapter B of chapter 63 are applicable to the $500 deficiency, they likewise apply to the $25 addition to the tax asserted with respect to such deficiency (but not to the $50 addition to the tax under example (1)).

(2) *Additions to the tax for negligence or fraud.*—Subchapter B of chapter 63 (deficiency procedures) applies to all additions to the income, estate, and gift taxes imposed by section 6653(a) and (b) for negligence and fraud.

(3) *Additions to tax for failure to pay estimated income taxes.*—(i) *Return filed by taxpayer.*—The addition to the tax for underpayment of estimated income tax imposed by section 6654 (relating to failure by individuals to pay estimated income tax) or section 6655 (relating to failure by corporations to pay estimated income tax) is determined by reference to the tax shown on the return if a return is filed. Therefore, such addition may be assessed and collected without regard to the provisions of subchapter B of chapter 63 (deficiency procedures) if a return is filed since such provisions are not applicable to the assessment of the tax shown on the return. Further, since the additions to the tax imposed by section 6654 or 6655 are determined solely by reference to the amount of tax shown on the return if a return is filed, the assertion of a deficiency with respect to any tax not shown on such return will not make the provisions of subchapter B of chapter 63 (deficiency procedures) apply to the assessment and collection of any additions to the tax under section 6654 or 6655.

(ii) *No return filed by taxpayer.*—If the taxpayer has not filed a return and his entire income tax liability is asserted as a deficiency to which the provisions of subchapter B of chapter 63 apply, such provisions likewise will apply to any addition to such tax imposed by section 6654 or 6655. [Reg. § 301.6659-1.]

☐ [T.D. 6268, 11-16-57. Amended by T.D. 6498, 10-24-60 and T.D. 7838, 10-5-82.]

### [Reg. § 1.6662-0]

**§ 1.6662-0. Table of contents.**—This section lists the captions that appear in §§ 1.6662-1 through 1.6662-7.

*§ 1.6662-1. Overview of the accuracy-related penalty.*

*§ 1.6662-2. Accuracy-related penalty.*
  (a) In general.
  (b) Amount of penalty.
    (1) In general.
    (2) Increase in penalty for gross valuation misstatement.
  (c) No stacking of accuracy-related penalty components.
  (d) Effective dates.
    (1) Returns due before January 1, 1994.
    (2) Returns due after December 31, 1993.

(3) Special rules for tax shelter items.
(4) Special rule for reasonable basis.
(5) Returns filed after December 31, 2002.

§ 1.6662-3. *Negligence or disregard of rules or regulations.*
 (a) In general.
 (b) Definitions and rules.
  (1) Negligence.
  (2) Disregard of rules or regulations.
  (3) Reasonable basis.
 (c) Exception for adequate disclosure.
  (1) In general.
  (2) Method of disclosure.
 (d) Special rules in the case of carrybacks and carryovers.
  (1) In general.
  (2) Transition rule for carrybacks to pre-1990 years.
  (3) Example.

§ 1.6662-4. *Substantial understatement of income tax.*
 (a) In general.
 (b) Definitions and computational rules.
  (1) Substantial.
  (2) Understatement.
  (3) Amount of the tax required to be shown on the return.
  (4) Amount of the tax imposed which is shown on the return.
  (5) Rebate.
  (6) Examples.
 (c) Special rules in the case of carrybacks and carryovers.
  (1) In general.
  (2) Understatements for carryback years not reduced by amount of carrybacks.
  (3) Tainted items defined.
   (i) In general.
   (ii) Tax shelter items.
  (4) Transition rule for carrybacks to pre-1990 years.
  (5) Examples.
 (d) Substantial authority.
  (1) Effect of having substantial authority.
  (2) Substantial authority standard.
  (3) Determination of whether substantial authority is present.
   (i) Evaluation of authorities.
   (ii) Nature of analysis.
   (iii) Types of authority.
   (iv) Special rules.
    (A) Written determinations.
    (B) Taxpayer's jurisdiction.
    (C) When substantial authority determined.
   (v) Substantial authority for tax returns due before January 1, 1990.
 (e) Disclosure of certain information.
  (1) Effect of adequate disclosure.
  (2) Circumstances where disclosure will not have an effect.
  (3) Restriction for corporations.
 (f) Method of making adequate disclosure.
  (1) Disclosure statement.
  (2) Disclosure on return.
  (3) Recurring item.
  (4) Carrybacks and carryovers.
  (5) Pass-through entities.
 (g) Items relating to tax shelters.
  (1) In general.
   (i) Noncorporate taxpayers.
   (ii) Corporate taxpayers.
    (A) In general.
    (B) Special rule for transactions occurring prior to December 9, 1994.
   (iii) Disclosure irrelevant.
   (iv) Cross-reference.
  (2) Tax shelter.
   (i) In general.
   (ii) Principal purpose.
  (3) Tax shelter item.
  (4) Reasonable belief.
   (i) In general.
   (ii) Facts and circumstances; reliance on professional tax advisor.
  (5) Pass-through entities.

§ 1.6662-5. *Substantial and gross valuation misstatements under chapter 1.*
 (a) In general.

(b) Dollar limitation.
 (c) Special rules in the case of carrybacks and carryovers.
  (1) In general.
  (2) Transition rule for carrybacks to pre-1990 years.
 (d) Examples.
 (e) Definitions.
  (1) Substantial valuation misstatement.
  (2) Gross valuation misstatement.
  (3) Property.
 (f) Multiple valuation misstatements on a return.
  (1) Determination of whether valuation misstatements are substantial or gross.
  (2) Application of dollar limitation.
 (g) Property with a value or adjusted basis of zero.
 (h) Pass-through entities.
  (1) In general.
  (2) Example.
 (i) [Reserved]
 (j) Transactions between persons described in section 482 and net section 482 transfer price adjustments. [Reserved]
 (k) Returns affected.

§ 1.6662-5T. *Substantial and gross valuation misstatements under chapter 1 (Temporary).*
 (a) through (e)(3) [Reserved].
  (e)(4) Tests related to section 482.
   (i) Substantial valuation misstatement.
   (ii) Gross valuation misstatement.
   (iii) Property.
 (f) through (i) [Reserved].
 (j) Transactions between persons described in section 482 and net section 482 transfer price adjustments.

§ 1.6662-6. *Transactions between persons described in section 482 and net section 482 transfer price adjustments.*
 (a) In general.
  (1) Purpose and scope.
  (2) Reported results.
  (3) Identical terms used in the section 482 regulations.
 (b) The transactional penalty.
  (1) Substantial valuation misstatement.
  (2) Gross valuation misstatement.
  (3) Reasonable cause and good faith.
 (c) Net adjustment penalty.
  (1) Net section 482 adjustment.
  (2) Substantial valuation misstatement.
  (3) Gross valuation misstatement.
  (4) Setoff allocation rule.
  (5) Gross receipts.
  (6) Coordination with reasonable cause exception under section 6664(c).
  (7) Examples.
 (d) Amounts excluded from net section 482 adjustments.
  (1) In general.
  (2) Application of a specified section 482 method.
   (i) In general.
   (ii) Specified method requirement.
   (iii) Documentation requirement.
    (A) In general.
    (B) Principal documents.
    (C) Background documents.
  (3) Application of an unspecified method.
   (i) In general.
   (ii) Unspecified method requirement.
    (A) In general.
    (B) Specified method potentially applicable.
    (C) No specified method applicable.
   (iii) Documentation requirement.
    (A) In general.
    (B) Principal and background documents.
  (4) Certain foreign to foreign transactions.
  (5) Special rule.
  (6) Examples.
 (e) Special rules in the case of carrybacks and carryovers.
 (f) Rules for coordinating between the transactional penalty and the net adjustment penalty.
  (1) Coordination of a net section 482 adjustment subject to the net adjustment penalty and a gross valuation misstatement subject to the transactional penalty.

(2) Coordination of net section 482 adjustment subject to the net adjustment penalty and substantial valuation misstatements subject to the transactional penalty.

(3) Examples.

(g) Effective date.

**§1.6662-7. Omnibus Budget Reconciliation Act of 1993 changes to the accuracy-related penalty.**

(a) Scope.

(b) No disclosure exception for negligence penalty.

(c) Disclosure standard for other penalties is reasonable basis.

(d) Reasonable basis.

[Reg. §1.6662-0.]

□ [*T.D. 8381, 12-30-91. Amended by T.D. 8519, 1-27-94; T.D. 8533, 3-14-94; T.D. 8551, 7-5-94; T.D. 8617, 8-31-95; T.D. 8656, 2-8-96; T.D. 8790, 12-1-98 and T.D. 9109, 12-29-2003.*]

### [Reg. §1.6662-1]

**§1.6662-1. Overview of the accuracy-related penalty.**—Section 6662 imposes an accuracy-related penalty on any portion of an underpayment of tax required to be shown on a return that is attributable to one or more of the following:

(a) Negligence or disregard of rules or regulations;

(b) Any substantial understatement of income tax;

(c) Any substantial valuation misstatement under chapter 1;

(d) Any substantial overstatement of pension liabilities; or

(e) Any substantial estate or gift tax valuation understatement.

Sections 1.6662-1 through 1.6662-5 address only the first three components of the accuracy-related penalty, *i.e.*, the penalties for negligence or disregard of rules or regulations, substantial understatements of income tax, and substantial (or gross) valuation misstatements under chapter 1. The penalties for disregard of rules or regulations and for a substantial understatement of income tax may be avoided by adequately disclosing certain information as provided in §1.6662-3(c) and §§1.6662-4(e) and (f), respectively. The penalties for negligence and for a substantial (or gross) valuation misstatement under chapter 1 may not be avoided by disclosure. No accuracy-related penalty may be imposed on any portion of an underpayment if there was reasonable cause for, and the taxpayer acted in good faith with respect to, such portion. The reasonable cause and good faith exception to the accuracy-related penalty is set forth in §1.6664-4. [Reg. §1.6662-1.]

□ [*T.D. 8381, 12-30-91. Amended by T.D. 8617, 8-31-95.*]

### [Reg. §1.6662-2]

**§1.6662-2. Accuracy-related penalty.**—(a) *In general.*—Section 6662(a) imposes an accuracy-related penalty on any portion of an underpayment of tax (as defined in section 6664(a) and §1.6664-2) required to be shown on a return if such portion is attributable to one or more of the following types of misconduct:

(1) Negligence or disregard of rules or regulations (see §1.6662-3);

(2) Any substantial understatement of income tax (see §1.6662-4); or

(3) Any substantial (or gross) valuation misstatement under chapter 1 ("substantial valuation misstatement" or "gross valuation misstatement"), provided the applicable dollar limitation set forth in section 6662(e)(2) is satisfied (see §1.6662-5).

The accuracy-related penalty applies only in cases in which a return of tax is filed, except that the penalty does not apply in the case of a return prepared by the Secretary under the authority of section 6020(b). The accuracy-related penalty under section 6662 and the penalty under section 6651 for failure to timely file a return of tax may both be imposed on the same portion of an underpayment if a return is filed, but is filed late. The fact that a return is filed late, however, is not taken into account in determining whether an accuracy-related penalty should be imposed. No accuracy-related penalty may be imposed on any portion of an underpayment of tax on which the fraud penalty set forth in section 6663 is imposed.

(b) *Amount of penalty.*—(1) *In general.*—The amount of the accuracy-related penalty is 20 percent of the portion of an underpayment of tax required to be shown on a return that is attributable to any of the types of misconduct listed in paragraphs (a)(1) through (a)(3) of this section, except as provided in paragraph (b)(2) of this section.

(2) *Increase in penalty for gross valuation misstatement.*—In the case of a gross valuation misstatement, as defined in section 6662(h)(2) and §1.6662-5(e)(2), the amount of the accuracy-related penalty is 40 percent of the portion of an underpayment of tax required to be shown on a return that is attributable to the gross valuation misstatement, provided the applicable dollar limitation set forth in section 6662(e)(2) is satisfied.

(c) *No stacking of accuracy-related penalty components.*—The maximum accuracy-related penalty imposed on a portion of an underpayment may not exceed 20 percent of such portion (40 percent of the portion attributable to a gross valuation misstatement), notwithstanding that such portion is attributable to more than one of the types of misconduct described in paragraph (a) of this section. For example, if a portion of an underpayment of tax required to be shown on a return is attributable both to negligence and a substantial understatement of income tax, the maximum accuracy-related penalty is 20 percent of such portion. Similarly, the maximum accuracy-related penalty imposed on any portion of an underpayment that is attributable both to negligence and a gross valuation misstatement is 40 percent of such portion.

(d) *Effective dates.*—(1) *Returns due before January 1, 1994.*—Section 1.6662-3(c) and §§1.6662-4(e) and (f) (relating to methods of making adequate disclosure) (as contained in 26 CFR part 1 revised April 1, 1995) apply to returns the due date of which (determined without regard to extensions of time for filing) is after December 31, 1991, but before January 1, 1994. Except as provided in the preceding sentence and in paragraphs (d)(2), (3), and (4) of this section, §§1.6662-1 through 1.6662-5 apply to returns the due date of which (determined without regard to extensions of time for filing) is after December 31, 1989, but before January 1, 1994. To the extent the provisions of these regulations were not reflected in the statute as amended by the Omnibus Budget Reconciliation Act of 1989 (OBRA 1989), in Notice 90-20, 1990-1 C.B. 328, or in rules and regulations in effect prior to March 4, 1991 (to the extent not inconsistent with the statute as amended by OBRA 1989), these regulations will not be adversely applied to a taxpayer who took a position based upon such prior rules on a return filed before January 1, 1992.

(2) *Returns due after December 31, 1993.*—Except as provided in paragraphs (d)(3), (4) and (5) of this section and the last sentence of this paragraph (d)(2), the provisions of §§1.6662-1 through 1.6662-4 and §1.6662-7 (as revised to reflect the changes made to the accuracy-related penalty by the Omnibus Budget Reconciliation Act of 1993) and of §1.6662-5 apply to returns the due date of which (determined without regard to extensions of time for filing) is after December 31, 1993. These changes include raising the disclosure standard for the penalties for disregarding rules or regulations and for a substantial understatement of income tax from not frivolous to reasonable basis, eliminating the disclosure exception for the negligence penalty, and providing guidance on the meaning of reasonable basis. The Omnibus Budget Reconciliation Act of 1993 changes relating to the penalties for negligence or disregard of rules or regulations will not apply to returns (including qualified amended returns) that are filed on or before March 14, 1994, but the provisions of §§1.6662-1 through 1.6662-3 (as contained in 26 CFR part 1 revised April 1, 1995) relating to those penalties will apply to such returns.

(3) *Special rules for tax shelter items.*—Sections 1.6662-4(g)(1) and 1.6662-4(g)(4) apply to returns the due date of which (determined without regard to extensions of time for filing) is after September 1, 1995. Except as provided in the last sentence of this paragraph (d)(3), §§1.6662-4(g)(1) and 1.6662-4(g)(4) (as contained in 26 CFR part 1 revised April 1, 1995) apply to returns the due date of which (determined without regard to extensions of time for filing) is on or before September 1, 1995, and after December 31, 1989. For transactions occurring after December 8, 1994, §§1.6662-4(g)(1) and 1.6662-4(g)(2) (as contained in 26 CFR part 1 revised April 1, 1995) are applied taking into account the changes made to section 6662(d)(2)(C) (relating to the substantial understatement penalty for tax shelter items of corporations) by section 744 of Title VII of the Uruguay Round Agreements Act, Pub. L. 103-465 (108 Stat. 4809).

(4) *Special rules for reasonable basis.*—Section 1.6662-3(b)(3) applies to returns filed on or after December 2, 1998.

(5) *For returns filed after December 31, 2002.*—Sections 1.6662-3(a), 1.6662-3(b)(2) and 1.6662-3(c)(1) (relating to adequate disclosure) apply to returns filed after December 31, 2002, with respect to transactions entered into on or after January 1, 2003. Except as provided in paragraph (d)(1) of this section, §§1.6662-3(a), 1.6662-3(b)(2) and 1.6662-3(c)(1) (as contained in 26 CFR part 1 revised April 1, 2003) apply to returns filed with respect to transactions entered into prior to January 1, 2003. [Reg. §1.6662-2.]

[*T.D. 8381, 12-30-91. Amended by T.D. 8617, 8-31-95; T.D. 8790, 12-1-98 and T.D. 9109, 12-29-2003.*]

### [Reg. §1.6662-3]

**§1.6662-3. Negligence or disregard of rules or regulations.**—(a) *In general.*—If any portion of an underpayment, as defined in section 6664(a) and §1.6664-2, of any income tax imposed under subtitle A of the Internal Revenue Code that is required to be shown on a return is attributable to negligence or disregard of rules or regulations, there is added to the tax an amount equal to 20 percent of such portion. The penalty for disregarding rules or regulations does not apply, however, if the requirements of paragraph (c)(1) of this section are satisfied and the position in question is adequately disclosed as provided in paragraph (c)(2) of this section (and, if the position relates to a reportable transaction as defined in § 1.6011-4(b) (or § 1.6011-4T(b), as applicable), the transaction is disclosed in accordance with § 1.6011-4 (or § 1.6011-4T, as applicable)), or to the extent that the reasonable cause and good faith exception to this penalty set forth in § 1.6664-4 applies. In addition, if a position with respect to an item (other than with respect to a reportable transaction, as defined in § 1.6011-4(b) or § 1.6011-4T(b), as applicable) is contrary to a revenue ruling or notice (other than a notice of proposed rulemaking) issued by the Internal Revenue Service and published in the Internal Revenue Bulletin (see § 601.601(d)(2) of this chapter), this penalty does not apply if the position has a realistic possibility of being sustained on its merits. See § 1.6694-2(b) of the income tax return preparer penalty regulations for a description of the realistic possibility standard.

(b) *Definitions and rules.*—(1) *Negligence.*—The term "negligence" includes any failure to make a reasonable attempt to comply with the provisions of the internal revenue laws or to exercise ordinary and reasonable care in the preparation of a tax return. "Negligence" also includes any failure by the taxpayer to keep adequate books and records or to substantiate items properly. A return position that has a reasonable basis as defined in paragraph (b)(3) of this section is not attributable to negligence. Negligence is strongly indicated where—

(i) A taxpayer fails to include on an income tax return an amount of income shown on an information return, as defined in section 6724(d)(1);

(ii) A taxpayer fails to make a reasonable attempt to ascertain the correctness of a deduction, credit or exclusion on a return which would seem to a reasonable and prudent person to be "too good to be true" under the circumstances;

(iii) A partner fails to comply with the requirements of section 6222, which requires that a partner treat partnership items on its return in a manner that is consistent with the treatment of such items on the partnership return (or notify the Secretary of the inconsistency); or

(iv) A shareholder fails to comply with the requirements of section 6242, which requires that an S corporation shareholder treat subchapter S items on its return in a manner that is consistent with the treatment of such items on the corporation's return (or notify the Secretary of the inconsistency).

(2) *Disregard of rules or regulations.*—The term "disregard" includes any careless, reckless or intentional disregard of rules or regulations. The term "rules or regulations" includes the provisions of the Internal Revenue Code, temporary or final Treasury regulations issued under the Code, and revenue rulings or notices (other than notices of proposed rulemaking) issued by the Internal Revenue Service and published in the Internal Revenue Bulletin. A disregard of rules or regulations is "careless" if the taxpayer does not exercise reasonable diligence to determine the correctness of a return position that is contrary to the rule or regulation. A disregard is "reckless" if the taxpayer makes little or no effort to determine whether a rule or regulation exists, under circumstances which demonstrate a substantial deviation from the standard of conduct that a reasonable person would observe. A disregard is "intentional" if the taxpayer knows of the rule or regulation that is disregarded. Nevertheless, a taxpayer who takes a position (other than with respect to a reportable transaction, as defined in § 1.6011-4(b) or § 1.6011-4T(b), as applicable) contrary to a revenue ruling or notice has not disregarded the ruling or notice if the contrary position has a realistic possibility of being sustained on its merits.

(3) *Reasonable basis.*—Reasonable basis is a relatively high standard of tax reporting, that is, significantly higher than not frivolous or not patently improper. The reasonable basis standard is not satisfied by a return position that is merely arguable or that is merely a colorable claim. If a return position is reasonably based on one or more of the authorities set forth in § 1.6662-4(d)(3)(iii) (taking into account the relevance and persuasiveness of the authorities, and subsequent developments), the return position will generally satisfy the reasonable basis standard even though it may not satisfy the substantial authority standard as defined in § 1.6662-4(d)(2). (See § 1.6662-4(d)(3)(ii) for rules with respect to relevance, persuasiveness, subsequent developments, and use of a well-reasoned construction of an applicable statutory provision for purposes of the substantial understatement penalty.) In addition, the reasonable cause and good faith exception in § 1.6664-4 may provide relief from the penalty for negligence or disregard of rules or regulations, even if a return position does not satisfy the reasonable basis standard.

(c) *Exception for adequate disclosure.*—(1) *In general.*—No penalty under section 6662(b)(1) may be imposed on any portion of an underpayment that is attributable to a position contrary to a rule or regulation if the position is disclosed in accordance with the rules of paragraph (c)(2) of this section (and, if the position relates to a reportable transaction as defined in § 1.6011-4(b) (or § 1.6011-4T(b), as applicable), the transaction is disclosed in accordance with § 1.6011-4 (or § 1.6011-4T, as applicable)) and, in case of a position contrary to a regulation, the position represents a good faith challenge to the validity of the regulation. This disclosure exception does not apply, however, in the case of a position that does not have a reasonable basis or where the taxpayer fails to keep adequate books and records or to substantiate items properly.

(2) *Method of disclosure.*—Disclosure is adequate for purposes of the penalty for disregarding rules or regulations if made in accordance with the provisions of §§ 1.6662-4(f)(1), (3), (4) and (5), which permit disclosure on a properly completed and filed Form 8275 or 8275-R, as appropriate. In addition, the statutory or regulatory provision or ruling in question must be adequately identified on the Form 8275 or 8275-R, as appropriate. The provisions of § 1.6662-4(f)(2), which permit disclosure in accordance with an annual revenue procedure for purposes of the substantial understatement penalty, do not apply for purposes of this section.

(d) *Special rules in the case of carrybacks and carryovers*—.—(1) *In general.*—The penalty for negligence or disregard of rules or regulations applies to any portion of an underpayment for a year to which a loss, deduction or credit is carried, which portion is attributable to negligence or disregard of rules or regulations in the year in which the carryback or carryover of the loss, deduction or credit arises (the "loss or credit year").

(2) *Transition rule for carrybacks to pre-1990 years.*—A 20 percent penalty under section 6662(b)(1) is imposed on any portion of an underpayment for a carryback year, the return for which is due (without regard to extensions) before January 1, 1990, if—

(i) That portion is attributable to negligence or disregard of rules or regulations in a loss or credit year; and

(ii) The return for the loss or credit year is due (without regard to extensions) after December 31, 1989.

(3) *Example.*—The following example illustrates the provisions of paragraph (d) of this section. This example does not take into account the reasonable cause exception under § 1.6664-4.

*Example.* Corporation M is a C corporation. In 1990, M had a loss of $200,000 before taking into account a deduction of $350,000 that M claimed as an expense in careless disregard of the capitalization requirements of section 263 of the Code. M failed to make adequate disclosure of the item for 1990. M reported a $550,000 loss for 1990 and carried back the loss to 1987 and 1988. M had reported taxable income of $400,000 for 1987 and $200,000 for 1988, before application of the carryback. The carryback eliminated all of M's taxable income for 1987 and $150,000 of taxable income for 1988. After disallowance of the $350,000 expense deduction and allowance of a $35,000 depreciation deduction with respect to the capitalized amount, the correct loss for 1990 was determined to be $235,000. Because there is no underpayment for 1990, the penalty for negligence or disregard of rules or regulations does not apply for 1990. However, as a result of the 1990 adjustments, the loss carried back to 1987 is reduced from $550,000 to $235,000. After application of the $235,000 carryback, M has taxable income of $165,000 for 1987 and $200,000 for 1988. This adjustment results in underpayments for 1987 and 1988 that are attributable to the disregard of rules or regulations on the 1990 return. Therefore, the 20 percent penalty rate applies to the 1987 and 1988 underpayments attributable to the disallowed carryback. [Reg. § 1.6662-3.]

☐ [*T.D. 8381, 12-30-91. Amended by T.D. 8617, 8-31-95; T.D. 8790, 12-1-98 and T.D. 9109, 12-29-2003.*]

**[Reg. § 1.6662-4]**

**§ 1.6662-4. Substantial understatement of income tax.**—(a) *In general.*—If any portion of an underpayment, as defined in section 6664(a) and § 1.6664-2, of any income tax imposed under subtitle A of the Code that is required to be shown on a return is attributable to a substantial understatement of such income tax, there is added to the tax an amount equal to 20 percent of such portion. Except in the case of any item attributable to a tax shelter (as defined in paragraph (g)(2) of this section), an understatement is reduced by the portion of the understatement that is attributable to the tax treatment of an item for which there is substantial authority, or with respect to which there is adequate disclosure. General rules for determining the amount of an understatement are set forth in paragraph (b) of this section and more specific rules in the case of carrybacks and carryovers are set forth in paragraph (c) of this section. The rules for determining when substantial authority exists are set forth in

§1.6662-4(d). The rules for determining when there is adequate disclosure are set forth in §1.6662-4(e) and (f). This penalty does not apply to the extent that the reasonable cause and good faith exception to this penalty set forth in §1.6664-4 applies.

(b) *Definitions and computational rules.*—(1) *Substantial.*—An understatement (as defined in paragraph (b)(2) of this section) is "substantial" if it exceeds the greater of—

(i) 10 percent of the tax required to be shown on the return for the taxable year (as defined in paragraph (b)(3) of this section); or

(ii) $5,000 ($10,000 in the case of a corporation other than an S corporation (as defined in section 1361(a)(1)) or a personal holding company (as defined in section 542)).

(2) *Understatement.*—Except as provided in paragraph (c)(2) of this section (relating to special rules for carrybacks), the term "understatement" means the excess of—

(i) The amount of the tax required to be shown on the return for the taxable year (as defined in paragraph (b)(3) of this section), over

(ii) The amount of the tax imposed which is shown on the return for the taxable year (as defined in paragraph (b)(4) of this section), reduced by any rebate (as defined in paragraph (b)(5) of this section).

The definition of understatement also may be expressed as—

$$Understatement = X - (Y - Z)$$

where $X$ = the amount of the tax required to be shown on the return; $Y$ = the amount of the tax imposed which is shown on the return; and $Z$ = any rebate.

(3) *Amount of the tax required to be shown on the return.*—The "amount of the tax required to be shown on the return" for the taxable year has the same meaning as the "amount of income tax imposed" as defined in §1.6664-2(b).

(4) *Amount of the tax imposed which is shown on the return.*—The "amount of the tax imposed which is shown on the return" for the taxable year has the same meaning as the "amount shown as the tax by the taxpayer on his return," as defined in §1.6664-2(c), except that—

(i) There is no reduction for the excess of the amount described in §1.6664-2(c)(1)(i) over the amount described in §1.6664-2(c)(1)(ii), and

(ii) The tax liability shown by the taxpayer on his return is recomputed as if the following items had been reported properly:

(A) Items (other than tax shelter items as defined in §1.6662-4(g)(3)) for which there is substantial authority for the treatment claimed (as provided in §1.6662-4(d)).

(B) Items (other than tax shelter items as defined in §1.6662-4(g)(3)) with respect to which there is adequate disclosure (as provided in §1.6662-4(e) and (f)).

(C) Tax shelter items (as defined in §1.6662-4(g)(3)) for which there is substantial authority for the treatment claimed (as provided in §1.6662-4(d)), and with respect to which the taxpayer reasonably believed that the tax treatment of the items was more likely than not the proper tax treatment (as provided in §1.6662-4(g)(4)).

(5) *Rebate.*—The term "rebate" has the meaning set forth in §1.6664-2(e), except that—

(i) "Amounts not so shown previously assessed (or collected without assessment)" includes only amounts not so shown previously assessed (or collected without assessment) as a deficiency, and

(ii) The amount of the rebate is determined as if any items to which the rebate is attributable that are described in paragraph (b)(4) of this section had received the proper tax treatment.

(6) *Examples.*—The following examples illustrate the provisions of paragraph (b) of this section. These examples do not take into account the reasonable cause exception under §1.6664-4:

*Example 1.* In 1990, Individual A, a calendar year taxpayer, files a return for 1989, which shows taxable income of $18,200 and tax liability of $2,734. Subsequent adjustments on audit for 1989 increase taxable income to $51,500 and tax liability to $12,339. There was substantial authority for an item resulting in an adjustment that increases taxable income by $5,300. The item is not a tax shelter item. In computing the amount of the understatement, the amount of tax shown on A's return is determined as if the item for which there was

substantial authority had been given the proper tax treatment. Thus, the amount of tax that is treated as shown on A's return is $4,176, i.e., the tax on $23,500 ($18,200 taxable income actually shown on A's return plus $5,300, the amount of the adjustment for which there was substantial authority). The amount of the understatement is $8,163, i.e., $12,339 (the amount of tax required to be shown) less $4,176 (the amount of tax treated as shown on A's return after adjustment for the item for which there was substantial authority). Because the $8,163 understatement exceeds the greater of 10 percent of the tax required to be shown on the return for the year, i.e., $1,234 ($12,339 × .10) or $5,000, A has a substantial understatement of income tax for the year.

*Example 2.* Individual B, a calendar year taxpayer, files a return for 1990 that fails to include income reported on an information return, Form 1099, that was furnished to B. The Service detects this omission through its document matching program and assesses $3,000 in unreported tax liability. B's return is later examined and as a result of the examination the Service makes an adjustment to B's return of $4,000 in additional tax liability. Assuming there was neither substantial authority nor adequate disclosure with respect to the items adjusted, there is an understatement of $7,000 with respect to B's return. There is also an underpayment of $7,000. (See §1.6664-2.) The amount of the understatement is not reduced by imposition of a negligence penalty on the $3,000 portion of the underpayment that is attributable to the unreported income. However, if the Service does impose the negligence penalty on this $3,000 portion, the Service may only impose the substantial understatement penalty on the remaining $4,000 portion of the underpayment. (See §1.6662-2(c), which prohibits stacking of accuracy-related penalty components.)

(c) *Special rules in the case of carrybacks and carryovers.*—(1) *In general.*—The penalty for a substantial understatement of income tax applies to any portion of an underpayment for a year to which a loss, deduction or credit is carried that is attributable to a "tainted item" for the year in which the carryback or carryover of the loss, deduction or credit arises (the "loss or credit year"). The determination of whether an understatement is substantial for a carryback or carryover year is made with respect to the return of the carryback or carryover year. "Tainted items" are taken into account with items arising in a carryback or carryover year to determine whether the understatement is substantial for that year.

(2) *Understatements for carryback years not reduced by amount of carrybacks.*—The amount of an understatement for a carryback year is not reduced on account of a carryback of a loss, deduction or credit to that year.

(3) *Tainted items defined.*—(i) *In general.*—Except in the case of a tax shelter item (as defined in paragraph (g)(3) of this section), a "tainted item" is any item for which there is neither substantial authority nor adequate disclosure with respect to the loss or credit year.

(ii) *Tax shelter items.*—In the case of a tax shelter item (as defined in paragraph (g)(3) of this section), a "tainted item" is any item for which there is not, with respect to the loss or credit year, both substantial authority and a reasonable belief that the tax treatment is more likely than not the proper treatment.

(4) *Transition rule for carrybacks to pre-1990 years.*—A 20 percent penalty under section 6662(b)(2) is imposed on any portion of an underpayment for a carryback year, the return for which is due (without regard to extensions) before January 1, 1990, if—

(i) That portion is attributable to one or more "tainted items" (as defined in paragraph (c)(3) of this section) arising in a loss or credit year; and

(ii) The return for the loss or credit year is due (without regard to extensions) after December 31, 1989.

The preceding sentence applies only if the understatement in the carryback year is substantial. See *Example 2* in paragraph (c)(5) of this section.

(5) *Examples.*—The following examples illustrate the rules of paragraph (c) of this section regarding carrybacks and carryovers. These examples do not take into account the reasonable cause exception under §1.6664-4.

*Example 1.* (i) Corporation N, a calendar year taxpayer, is a C corporation. N was formed on January 1, 1987, and timely filed the following income tax returns:

| Tax Year | 1987 | 1988 | 1989 | 1990 |
|---|---|---|---|---|
| Taxable Income | $30,000 | $100,000 | ($300,000) | $50,000 (Before NOLCO) |
| Tax Liability | $4,575 | $22,250 | –0– | $ 7,500 (Before NOLCO) |

(ii) During 1990, N files Form 1139, Corporation Application for Tentative Refund, to carry back the NOL generated in 1989 (NOLCB). N received refunds of $4,575 for 1987 and $22,250 for 1988.

(iii) For tax year 1990, N carries over $50,000 of the 1989 loss to offset $50,000 of income earned in 1990 and reduce taxable income to zero. N would have reported $7,500 of tax liability for 1990 if it were

| | | |
|---|---|---|
| Taxable income per 1989 return . . . . . . . . . . . . . . . . . . . . . . . . . . . . . . . . . . . . | | ($300,000) |
| Adjustment: Unreported income . . . . . . . . . . . . . . . . . . . . . . . . . . . . . . . . . . . | | 310,000 |
| Corrected taxable income . . . . . . . . . . . . . . . . . . . . . . . . . . . . . . . . . . . . . . . . . | | $ 10,000 |
| Corrected tax liability . . . . . . . . . . . . . . . . . . . . . . . . . . . . . . . . . . . . | $1,500 | |

(v) There was not substantial authority for N's treatment of the items comprising the 1989 adjustment and N did not make adequate disclosure.

(vi) As a result of the adjustment to the 1989 return, N had an understatement of $4,575 for tax year 1987; an understatement of $22,250 for tax year 1988; an understatement of $1,500 for tax year 1989; and an understatement of $7,500 for tax year 1990. Only the $22,250 understatement for 1988 is a substantial understatement, i.e., it exceeds the greater of (a) $2,225 (10 percent of the tax required to be shown on the return for the taxable year (.10 × $22,250)) or (b) $10,000. The underpayment for 1988 is subject to a penalty rate of 20 percent.

*Example 2.* The facts are the same as in *Example 1*, except that in addition to examining the 1989 return, the Service also examines the 1987 return and makes an adjustment that results in an understatement. (This adjustment is unrelated to the adjustment on the 1987 return for the disallowance of the NOLCB from 1989.) If the understatement resulting from the adjustment to the 1987 return, when combined with the understatement resulting from the disallowance of the NOLCB from 1989, exceeds the greater of (a) 10 percent of the tax required to be shown on the return for 1987 or (b) $10,000, the underpayment for 1987 will also be subject to a substantial understatement penalty. The portion of the underpayment attributable to the adjustment unrelated to the disallowance of the NOLCB will be subject to a penalty rate of 25 percent under former section 6661. The portion of the underpayment attributable to the disallowance of the NOLCB will be subject to a penalty rate of 20 percent under section 6662.

*Example 3.* Individual P, a calendar year single taxpayer, files his 1990 return reporting taxable income of $10,000 and a tax liability of $1,504. An examination of the 1990 return results in an adjustment for unreported income of $25,000. There was not substantial authority for P's failure to report the income, and P did not make adequate disclosure with respect to the unreported income. P's correct tax liability for 1990 is determined to be $7,279, resulting in an understatement of $5,775 (the difference between the amount of tax required to be shown on the return ($7,279) and the tax shown on the return ($1,504)). Because the understatement exceeds the greater of (a) $728 (10 percent of the tax required to be shown on the return (.10 × $7,279)) or (b) $5,000, the understatement is substantial. Subsequently, P files his 1993 return showing a net operating loss. The loss is carried back to his 1990 return, reducing his taxable income for 1990 to zero. However, the amount of the understatement for 1990 is not reduced on account of the NOLCB to that year. P is subject to the 20 percent penalty rate under section 6662 on the underpayment attributable to the substantial understatement for 1990, notwithstanding that the tax required to be shown on the return for that year, after application of the NOLCB, is zero.

(d) *Substantial authority.*—(1) *Effect of having substantial authority.*—If there is substantial authority for the tax treatment of an item, the item is treated as if it were shown properly on the return for the taxable year in computing the amount of the tax shown on the return. Thus, for purposes of section 6662(d), the tax attributable to the item is not included in the understatement for that year. (For special rules relating to tax shelter items see § 1.6662-4(g).)

(2) *Substantial authority standard.*—The substantial authority standard is an objective standard involving an analysis of the law and application of the law to relevant facts. The substantial authority standard is less stringent than the more likely than not standard (the standard that is met when there is a greater than 50-percent likelihood of the position being upheld), but more stringent than the reasonable basis standard as defined in § 1.6662-3(b)(3). The possibility that a return will not be audited or, if audited, that an item will not be raised on audit, is not relevant in determining whether the substantial authority standard (or the reasonable basis standard) is satisfied.

(3) *Determination of whether substantial authority is present.*—(i) *Evaluation of authorities.*—There is substantial authority for the tax treatment of an item only if the weight of the authorities supporting the treatment is substantial in relation to the weight of authorities supporting contrary treatment. All authorities relevant to the tax treatment of an item, including the authorities contrary to the treatment, are taken into account in determining whether substantial authority exists. The weight of authorities is determined in light of the pertinent facts and circumstances in the manner prescribed by paragraph (d)(3)(ii) of this section. There may be substantial authority for more than one position with respect to the same item. Because the substantial authority standard is an objective standard, the taxpayer's belief that there is substantial authority for the tax treatment of an item is not relevant in determining whether there is substantial authority for that treatment.

(ii) *Nature of analysis.*—The weight accorded an authority depends on its relevance and persuasiveness, and the type of document providing the authority. For example, a case or revenue ruling having some facts in common with the tax treatment at issue is not particularly relevant if the authority is materially distinguishable on its facts, or is otherwise inapplicable to the tax treatment at issue. An authority that merely states a conclusion ordinarily is less persuasive than one that reaches its conclusion by cogently relating the applicable law to pertinent facts. The weight of an authority from which information has been deleted, such as a private letter ruling, is diminished to the extent that the deleted information may have affected the authority's conclusions. The type of document also must be considered. For example, a revenue ruling is accorded greater weight than a private letter ruling addressing the same issue. An older private letter ruling, technical advice memorandum, general counsel memorandum or action on decision generally must be accorded less weight than a more recent one. Any document described in the preceding sentence that is more than 10 years old generally is accorded very little weight. However, the persuasiveness and relevance of a document, viewed in light of subsequent developments, should be taken into account along with the age of the document. There may be substantial authority for the tax treatment of an item despite the absence of certain types of authority. Thus, a taxpayer may have substantial authority for a position that is supported only by a well-reasoned construction of the applicable statutory provision.

(iii) *Types of authority.*—Except in cases described in paragraph (d)(3)(iv) of this section concerning written determinations, only the following are authority for purposes of determining whether there is substantial authority for the tax treatment of an item: applicable provisions of the Internal Revenue Code and other statutory provisions; proposed, temporary and final regulations construing such statutes; revenue rulings and revenue procedures; tax treaties and regulations thereunder, and Treasury Department and other official explanations of such treaties; court cases; congressional intent as reflected in committee reports, joint explanatory statements of managers included in conference committee reports, and floor statements made prior to enactment by one of a bill's managers; General Explanations of tax legislation prepared by the Joint Committee on Taxation (the Blue Book); private letter rulings and technical advice memoranda issued after October 31, 1976; actions on decisions and general counsel memoranda issued after March 12, 1981 (as well as general counsel memoranda published in pre-1955 volumes of the Cumulative Bulletin); Internal Revenue Service information or press releases; and notices, announcements and other administrative pronouncements published by the Service in the Internal Revenue Bulletin. Conclusions reached in treatises, legal periodicals, legal opinions or opinions rendered by tax professionals are not authority. The authorities underlying such expressions of opinion where applicable to the facts of a particular case, however, may give rise to substantial authority for the tax treatment of an item. Notwithstanding the preceding list of authorities, an authority does not continue to be an authority to the extent it is overruled or modified, implicitly or explicitly, by a body with the power to overrule or modify the earlier authority. In the case of court decisions, for example, a district court opinion on an issue is not an authority if overruled or reversed by the United States Court of Appeals for such district. However, a Tax Court opinion is not considered to be overruled or modified by a court of appeals to which a taxpayer does not have a right of appeal, unless the Tax Court adopts the holding of the court of appeals. Similarly, a private letter ruling is not authority if revoked or if inconsistent with a subsequent proposed regulation, revenue ruling or other administrative pronouncement published in the Internal Revenue Bulletin.

(iv) *Special rules.*—(A) *Written determinations.*—There is substantial authority for the tax treatment of an item by a taxpayer if the treatment is supported by the conclusion of a ruling or a determination letter (as defined in § 301.6110-2(d) and (e)) issued to the taxpayer, by the conclusion of a technical advice memorandum in which the taxpayer is named, or by an affirmative statement in a revenue agent's report with respect to a prior taxable year of the taxpayer ("written determinations"). The preceding sentence does not apply, however, if—

(1) There was a misstatement or omission of a material fact or the facts that subsequently develop are materially different from the facts on which the written determination was based, or

(2) The written determination was modified or revoked after the date of issuance by—

(i) A notice to the taxpayer to whom the written determination was issued,

(ii) The enactment of legislation or ratification of a tax treaty,

(iii) A decision of the United States Supreme Court,

(iv) The issuance of temporary or final regulations, or

(v) The issuance of a revenue ruling, revenue procedure, or other statement published in the Internal Revenue Bulletin. Except in the case of a written determination that is modified or revoked on account of § 1.6662-4(d)(3)(iv)(A)(1), a written determination that is modified or revoked as described in § 1.6662-4(d)(3)(iv)(A)(2) ceases to be authority on the date, and to the extent, it is so modified or revoked. See section 6404(f) for rules which require the Secretary to abate a penalty that is attributable to erroneous written advice furnished to a taxpayer by an officer or employee of the Internal Revenue Service.

(B) *Taxpayer's jurisdiction.*—The applicability of court cases to the taxpayer by reason of the taxpayer's residence in a particular jurisdiction is not taken into account in determining whether there is substantial authority for the tax treatment of an item. Notwithstanding the preceding sentence, there is substantial authority for the tax treatment of an item if the treatment is supported by controlling precedent of a United States Court of Appeals to which the taxpayer has a right of appeal with respect to the item.

(C) *When substantial authority determined.*—There is substantial authority for the tax treatment of an item if there is substantial authority at the time the return containing the item is filed or there was substantial authority on the last day of the taxable year to which the return relates.

(v) *Substantial authority for tax returns due before January 1, 1990.*—There is substantial authority for the tax treatment of an item on a return that is due (without regard to extensions) after December 31, 1982 and before January 1, 1990, if there is substantial authority for such treatment under either the provisions of paragraph (d)(3)(iii) of this section (which set forth an expanded list of authorities) or of § 1.6661-3(b)(2) (which set forth a narrower list of authorities). Under either list of authorities, authorities both for and against the position must be taken into account.

(e) *Disclosure of certain information.*—(1) *Effect of adequate disclosure.*—Items for which there is adequate disclosure as provided in this paragraph (e) and in paragraph (f) of this section are treated as if such items were shown properly on the return for the taxable year in computing the amount of the tax shown on the return. Thus, for purposes of section 6662(d), the tax attributable to such items is not included in the understatement for that year.

(2) *Circumstances where disclosure will not have an effect.*—The rules of paragraph (e)(1) of this section do not apply where the item or position on the return —

(i) Does not have a reasonable basis (as defined in § 1.6662-3(b)(3));

(ii) Is attributable to a tax shelter (as defined in section 6662(d)(2)(C)(iii) and paragraph (g)(2) of this section); or

(iii) Is not properly substantiated, or the taxpayer failed to keep adequate books and records with respect to the item or position.

(3) *Restriction for corporations.*—For purposes of paragraph (e)(2)(i) of this section, a corporation will not be treated as having a reasonable basis for its tax treatment of an item attributable to a multi-party financing transaction entered into after August 5, 1997, if the treatment does not clearly reflect the income of the corporation.

(f) *Method of making adequate disclosure.*—(1) *Disclosure statement.*—Disclosure is adequate with respect to an item (or group of similar items, such as amounts paid or incurred for supplies by a taxpayer engaged in business) or a position on a return if the disclosure is made on a properly completed form attached to the return or to a qualified amended return (as defined in § 1.6664-2(c)(3)) for the taxable year. In the case of an item or position other than one that is contrary to a regulation, disclosure must be made on Form 8275 (Disclosure Statement); in the case of a position contrary to a regulation, disclosure must be made on Form 8275-R (Regulation Disclosure Statement).

(2) *Disclosure on return.*—The Commissioner may by annual revenue procedure (or otherwise) prescribe the circumstances under which disclosure of information on a return (or qualified amended return) in accordance with applicable forms and instructions is adequate. If the revenue procedure does not include an item, disclosure is adequate with respect to that item only if made on a properly completed Form 8275 or 8275-R, as appropriate, attached to the return for the year or to a qualified amended return.

(3) *Recurring item.*—Disclosure with respect to a recurring item, such as the basis of recovery property, must be made for each taxable year in which the item is taken into account.

(4) *Carrybacks and carryovers.*—Disclosure is adequate with respect to an item which is included in any loss, deduction or credit that is carried to another year only if made in connection with the return (or qualified amended return) for the taxable year in which the carryback or carryover arises (the "loss or credit year"). Disclosure is not also required in connection with the return for the taxable year in which the carryback or carryover is taken into account.

(5) *Pass-through entities.*—Disclosure in the case of items attributable to a pass-through entity (pass-through items) is made with respect to the return of the entity, except as provided in this paragraph (f)(5). Thus, disclosure in the case of pass-through items must be made on a Form 8275 or 8275-R, as appropriate, attached to the return (or qualified amended return) of the entity, or on the entity's return in accordance with the revenue procedure described in paragraph (f)(2) of this section, if applicable. A taxpayer (i.e., partner, shareholder, beneficiary, or holder of a residual interest in a REMIC) also may make adequate disclosure with respect to a pass-through item, however, if the taxpayer files a properly completed Form 8275 or 8275-R, as appropriate, in duplicate, one copy attached to the taxpayer's return (or qualified amended return) and the other copy filed with the Internal Revenue Service Center with which the return of the entity is required to be filed. Each Form 8275 or 8275-R, as appropriate, filed by the taxpayer should relate to the pass-through items of only one entity. For purposes of this paragraph (f)(5), a pass-through entity is a partnership, S corporation (as defined in section 1361(a)(1)), estate, trust, regulated investment company (as defined in section 851(a)), real estate investment trust (as defined in section 856(a)), or real estate mortgage investment conduit ("REMIC") (as defined in section 860D(a)).

(g) *Items relating to tax shelters.*—(1) *In general.*—(i) *Noncorporate taxpayers.*—Tax shelter items (as defined in paragraph (g)(3) of this section) of a taxpayer other than a corporation are treated for purposes of this section as if such items were shown properly on the return for a taxable year in computing the amount of the tax shown on the return, and thus the tax attributable to such items is not included in the understatement for the year, if—

(A) There is substantial authority (as provided in paragraph (d) of this section) for the tax treatment of that item; and

(B) The taxpayer reasonably believed at the time the return was filed that the tax treatment of that item was more likely than not the proper treatment.

(ii) *Corporate taxpayers.*—(A) *In general.*—Except as provided in paragraph (g)(1)(ii)(B) of this section, all tax shelter items (as defined in paragraph (g)(3) of this section) of a corporation are taken into account in computing the amount of any understatement.

(B) *Special rule for transactions occurring prior to December 9, 1994.*—The tax shelter items of a corporation arising in connection with transactions occurring prior to December 9, 1994 are treated for purposes of this section as if such items were shown properly on the return if the requirements of paragraph (g)(1)(i) are satisfied with respect to such items.

(iii) *Disclosure irrelevant.*—Disclosure made with respect to a tax shelter item of either a corporate or noncorporate taxpayer does not affect the amount of an understatement.

(iv) *Cross-reference.*—See § 1.6664-4(f) for certain rules regarding the availability of the reasonable cause and good faith exception to the substantial understatement penalty with respect to tax shelter items of corporations.

(2) *Tax shelter.*—(i) *In general.*—For purposes of section 6662(d), the term "tax shelter" means—

(A) A partnership or other entity (such as a corporation or trust),

(B) An investment plan or arrangement, or

(C) Any other plan or arrangement,

if the principal purpose of the entity, plan or arrangement, based on objective evidence, is to avoid or evade Federal income tax. The principal purpose of an entity, plan or arrangement is to avoid or evade Federal income tax if that purpose exceeds any other purpose. Typical of tax shelters are transactions structured with little or no motive for the realization of economic gain, and transactions that utilize the mismatching of income and deductions, overvalued assets or assets with values subject to substantial uncertainty, certain nonrecourse financing, financing techniques that do not conform to standard commercial business practices, or the mischaracterization of the substance of the transaction. The existence of economic substance does not of itself establish that a transaction is not a tax shelter if the transaction includes other characteristics that indicate it is a tax shelter.

(ii) *Principal purpose.*—The principal purpose of an entity, plan or arrangement is not to avoid or evade Federal income tax if the entity, plan or arrangement has as its purpose the claiming of exclusions from income, accelerated deductions or other tax benefits in a manner consistent with the statute and Congressional purpose. For example, an entity, plan or arrangement does not have as its principal purpose the avoidance or evasion of Federal income tax solely as a result of the following uses of tax benefits provided by the Internal Revenue Code: the purchasing or holding of an obligation bearing interest that is excluded from gross income under section 103; taking an accelerated depreciation allowance under section 168; taking the percentage depletion allowance under section 613 or section 613A; deducting intangible drilling and development costs as expenses under section 263(c); establishing a qualified retirement plan under sections 401-409; claiming the possession tax credit under section 936; or claiming tax benefits available by reason of an election under section 992 to be taxed as a domestic international sales corporation ("DISC"), under section 927(f)(1) to be taxed as a foreign sales corporation ("FSC"), or under section 1362 to be taxed as an S corporation.

(3) *Tax shelter item.*—An item of income, gain, loss, deduction or credit is a "tax shelter item" if the item is directly or indirectly attributable to the principal purpose of a tax shelter to avoid or evade Federal income tax. Thus, if a partnership is established for the principal purpose of avoiding or evading Federal income tax by acquiring and overstating the basis of property for purposes of claiming accelerated depreciation, the depreciation with respect to the property is a tax shelter item. However, a deduction claimed in connection with a separate transaction carried on by the same partnership is not a tax shelter item if the transaction does not constitute a plan or arrangement the principal purpose of which is to avoid or evade tax.

(4) *Reasonable belief.*—(i) *In general.*—For purposes of section 6662(d) and paragraph (g)(1)(i)(B) of this section (pertaining to tax shelter items of noncorporate taxpayers), a taxpayer is considered reasonably to believe that the tax treatment of an item is more likely than not the proper tax treatment if (without taking into account the possibility that a return will not be audited, that an issue will not be raised on audit, or that an issue will be settled)—

(A) The taxpayer analyzes the pertinent facts and authorities in the manner described in paragraph (d)(3)(ii) of this section, and in reliance upon that analysis, reasonably concludes in good faith that there is a greater than 50-percent likelihood that the tax treatment of the item will be upheld if challenged by the Internal Revenue Service; or

(B) The taxpayer reasonably relies in good faith on the opinion of a professional tax advisor, if the opinion is based on the tax advisor's analysis of the pertinent facts and authorities in the manner described in paragraph (d)(3)(ii) of this section and unambiguously states that the tax advisor concludes that there is a greater than 50-percent likelihood that the tax treatment of the item will be upheld if challenged by the Internal Revenue Service.

(ii) *Facts and circumstances; reliance on professional tax advisor.*— All facts and circumstances must be taken into account in determining whether a taxpayer satisfies the requirements of paragraph (g)(4)(i) of this section. However, in no event will a taxpayer be considered to have reasonably relied in good faith on the opinion of a professional tax advisor for purposes of paragraph (g)(4)(i)(B) of this section unless the requirements of §1.6664-4(c)(1) are met. The fact that the requirements of §1.6664-4(c)(1) are satisfied will not necessarily establish that the taxpayer reasonably relied on the opinion in good faith. For example, reliance may not be reasonable or in good faith if the taxpayer knew, or should have known, that the advisor lacked knowledge in the relevant aspects of Federal tax law.

(5) *Pass-through entities.*—In the case of tax shelter items attributable to a pass-through entity, the actions described in paragraphs (g)(4)(i)(A) and (B) of this section, if taken by the entity, are deemed to have been taken by the taxpayer and are considered in determining whether the taxpayer reasonably believed that the tax treatment of an item was more likely than not the proper tax treatment. [Reg. §1.6662-4.]

☐ [*T.D. 8381*, 12-30-91. *Amended by T.D. 8617*, 8-31-95; *T.D. 8790*, 12-1-98 *and T.D. 9109*, 12-29-2003.]

### [Reg. §1.6662-5]

**§1.6662-5. Substantial and gross valuation misstatements under chapter 1.**—(a) *In general.*—If any portion of an underpayment, as defined in section 6664(a) and §1.6664-2, of any income tax imposed under chapter 1 of subtitle A of the Code that is required to be shown on a return is attributable to a substantial valuation misstatement under chapter 1 ("substantial valuation misstatement"), there is added to the tax an amount equal to 20 percent of such portion. Section 6662(h) increases the penalty to 40 percent in the case of a gross valuation misstatement under chapter 1 ("gross valuation misstatement"). No penalty under section 6662(b)(3) is imposed, however, on a portion of an underpayment that is attributable to a substantial or gross valuation misstatement unless the aggregate of all portions of the underpayment attributable to substantial or gross valuation misstatements exceeds the applicable dollar limitation ($5,000 or $10,000), as provided in section 6662(e)(2) and paragraphs (b) and (f)(2) of this section. This penalty also does not apply to the extent that the reasonable cause and good faith exception to this penalty set forth in §1.6664-4 applies. There is no disclosure exception to this penalty.

(b) *Dollar limitation.*—No penalty may be imposed under section 6662(b)(3) for a taxable year unless the portion of the underpayment for that year that is attributable to substantial or gross valuation misstatements exceeds $5,000 ($10,000 in the case of a corporation other than an S corporation (as defined in section 1361(a)(1)) or a personal holding company (as defined in section 542)). This limitation is applied separately to each taxable year for which there is a substantial or gross valuation misstatement.

(c) *Special rules in the case of carrybacks and carryovers.*—(1) *In general.*—The penalty for a substantial or gross valuation misstatement applies to any portion of an underpayment for a year to which a loss, deduction or credit is carried that is attributable to a substantial or gross valuation misstatement for the year in which the carryback or carryover of the loss, deduction or credit arises (the "loss or credit year"), provided that the applicable dollar limitation set forth in section 6662(e)(2) is satisfied in the carryback or carryover year.

(2) *Transition rule for carrybacks to pre-1990 years.*—The penalty under section 6662(b)(3) is imposed on any portion of an underpayment for a carryback year, the return for which is due (without regard to extensions) before January 1, 1990, if—

(i) That portion is attributable to a substantial or gross valuation misstatement for a loss or credit year; and

(ii) The return for the loss or credit year is due (without regard to extensions) after December 31, 1989.

The preceding sentence applies only if the underpayment for the carryback year exceeds the applicable dollar limitation ($5,000, or $10,000 for most corporations). See *Example 3* in paragraph (d) of this section.

(d) *Examples.*—The following examples illustrate the provisions of paragraphs (b) and (c) of this section. These examples do not take into account the reasonable cause exception under §1.6664-4.

*Example 1.* Corporation Q is a C corporation. In 1990, the first year of its existence, Q had taxable income of $200,000 without considering depreciation of a particular asset. On its calendar year 1990 return, Q overstated its basis in this asset by an amount that caused a substantial valuation misstatement. The overstated basis resulted in depreciation claimed of $350,000, which was $250,000 more than the $100,000 allowable. Thus, on its 1990 return, Q showed a loss of $150,000. In 1991, Q had taxable income of $450,000 before application of the loss carryover, and Q claimed a carryover loss deduction under section 172 of $150,000, resulting in taxable income of $300,000 for 1991. Upon audit of the 1990 return, the basis of the asset was corrected, resulting in an adjustment of $250,000. For 1990, the underpayment resulting from the $100,000 taxable income (–$150,000 + $250,000) is attributable to the valuation misstatement. Assuming the underpayment resulting from the $100,000 taxable income exceeds the $10,000 limitation, the penalty will be imposed in 1990. For 1991, the elimination of the loss carryover results in additional taxable income of $150,000. The underpayment for 1991 resulting from that adjustment is also attributable to the substantial valuation misstatement on the 1990 return. Assuming the underpayment resulting from the $150,000 additional taxable income for 1991 exceeds the $10,000 limitation, the substantial valuation misstatement penalty also will be imposed for that year.

*Example 2.* (i) Corporation T is a C corporation. In 1990, the first year of its existence, T had a loss of $3,000,000 without considering depreciation of its major asset. On its calendar year 1990 return, T overstated its basis in this asset in an amount that caused a substantial valuation misstatement. This overstatement resulted in depreciation claimed of $3,500,000, which was $2,500,000 more than the $1,000,000 allowable. Thus, on its 1990 return, T showed a loss of $6,500,000. In 1991, T had taxable income of $4,500,000 before application of the carryover loss, but claimed a carryover loss deduction under section 172 in the amount of $4,500,000, resulting in taxable income of zero for that year and leaving a $2,000,000 carryover available. Upon audit of the 1990 return, the basis of the asset was corrected, resulting in an adjustment of $2,500,000.

(ii) For 1990, the underpayment is still zero (–$6,500,000 + $2,500,000 = – $4,000,000). Thus, the penalty does not apply in 1990. The loss for 1990 is reduced to $4,000,000.

(iii) For 1991, there is additional taxable income of $500,000 as a result of the reduction of the carryover loss ($4,500,000 reported income before carryover loss minus corrected carryover loss of $4,000,000 = $500,000). The underpayment for 1991 resulting from reduction of the carryover loss is attributable to the valuation misstatement on the 1990 return. Assuming the underpayment resulting from the $500,000 additional taxable income exceeds the $10,000 limitation, the substantial valuation misstatement penalty will be imposed in 1991.

*Example 3.* Corporation V is a C corporation. In 1990, V had a loss of $100,000 without considering depreciation of a particular asset which it had fully depreciated in earlier years. V had a depreciable basis in the asset of zero, but on its 1990 calendar year return erroneously claimed a basis in the asset of $1,250,000 and depreciation of $250,000. V reported a $350,000 loss for the year 1990, and carried back the loss to the 1987 and 1988 tax years. V had reported taxable income of $300,000 in 1987 and $200,000 in 1988, before application of the carryback. The $350,000 carryback eliminated all taxable income for 1987, and $50,000 of the taxable income for 1988. After disallowance of the $250,000 depreciation deduction for 1990, V still had a loss of $100,000. Because there is no underpayment for 1990, no valuation misstatement penalty is imposed for 1990. However, as a result of the 1990 depreciation adjustment, the carryback to 1987 is reduced from $350,000 to $100,000. After absorption of the $100,000 carryback, V has taxable income of $200,000 for 1987. This adjustment results in an underpayment for 1987 that is attributable to the valuation misstatement on the 1990 return. The valuation misstatement for 1990 is a gross valuation misstatement because the correct adjusted basis of the depreciated asset was zero. (See paragraph (e)(2) of this section.) Therefore, the 40 percent penalty rate applies to the 1987 underpayment attributable to the 1990 misstatement, provided that this underpayment exceeds $10,000. The adjustment also results in the elimination of any loss carryback to 1988 resulting in an increase in taxable income for 1988 of $50,000. Assuming the underpayment resulting from this additional $50,000 of income exceeds $10,000, the gross valuation misstatement penalty is imposed on the underpayment for 1988.

(e) *Definitions.*—(1) *Substantial valuation misstatement.*—There is a substantial valuation misstatement if the value or adjusted basis of any property claimed on a return of tax imposed under chapter 1 is 200 percent or more of the correct amount.

(2) *Gross valuation misstatement.*—There is a gross valuation misstatement if the value or adjusted basis of any property claimed on a return of tax imposed under chapter 1 is 400 percent or more of the correct amount.

(3) *Property.*—For purposes of this section, the term "property" refers to both tangible and intangible property. Tangible property includes property such as land, buildings, fixtures and inventory. Intangible property includes property such as goodwill, covenants not to compete, leaseholds, patents, contract rights, debts and choses in action.

(f) *Multiple valuation misstatements on a return.*—(1) *Determination of whether valuation misstatements are substantial or gross.*—The determination of whether there is a substantial or gross valuation misstatement on a return is made on a property-by-property basis. Assume, for example, that property A has a value of 60 but a taxpayer claims a value of 110, and that property B has a value of 40 but the taxpayer claims a value of 100. Because the claimed and correct values are compared on a property-by-property basis, there is a substantial valuation misstatement with respect to property B, but not with respect to property A, even though the claimed values (210) are 200 percent or more of the correct values (100) when compared on an aggregate basis.

(2) *Application of dollar limitation.*—For purposes of applying the dollar limitation set forth in section 6662(e)(2), the determination of the portion of an underpayment that is attributable to a substantial or gross valuation misstatement is made by aggregating all portions of the underpayment attributable to substantial or gross valuation misstatements. Assume, for example, that the value claimed for property C on a return is 250 percent of the correct value, and that the value claimed for property D on the return is 400 percent of the correct value. Because the portions of an underpayment that are attributable to a substantial or gross valuation misstatement on a return are aggregated in applying the dollar limitation, the dollar limitation is satisfied if the portion of the underpayment that is attributable to the misstatement of the value of property C, when aggregated with the portion of the underpayment that is attributable to the misstatement of the value of property D, exceeds $5,000 ($10,000 in the case of most corporations).

(g) *Property with a value or adjusted basis of zero.*—The value or adjusted basis claimed on a return of any property with a correct value or adjusted basis of zero is considered to be 400 percent or more of the correct amount. There is a gross valuation misstatement with respect to such property, therefore, and the applicable penalty rate is 40 percent.

(h) *Pass-through entities.*—(1) *In general.*—The determination of whether there is a substantial or gross valuation misstatement in the case of a return of a pass-through entity (as defined in §1.6662-4(f)(5)) is made at the entity level. However, the dollar limitation ($5,000 or $10,000, as the case may be) is applied at the taxpayer level (*i.e.*, with respect to the return of the shareholder, partner, beneficiary, or holder of a residual interest in a REMIC).

(2) *Example.*—The rules of paragraph (h)(1) of this section may be illustrated by the following example.

*Example.* Partnership P has two partners, individuals A and B. P claims a $40,000 basis in a depreciable asset which, in fact, has a basis of $15,000. The determination that there is a substantial valuation misstatement is made solely with reference to P by comparing the $40,000 basis claimed by P with P's correct basis of $15,000. However, the determination of whether the $5,000 threshold for application of the penalty has been reached is made separately for each partner. With respect to partner A, the penalty will apply if the portion of A's underpayment attributable to the passthrough of the depreciation deduction, when aggregated with any other portions of A's underpayment also attributable to substantial or gross valuation misstatements, exceeds $5,000 (assuming there is not reasonable cause for the misstatements (*see* §1.6664-4(c)).

(i) [Reserved]

(j) *Transactions between persons described in section 482 and net section 482 transfer price adjustments.*—[Reserved]

(k) *Returns affected.*—Except in the case of rules relating to transactions between persons described in section 482 and net section 482 transfer price adjustments, the provisions of section 6662(b)(3) apply to returns due (without regard to extensions of time to file) after December 31, 1989, notwithstanding that the original substantial or gross valuation misstatement occurred on a return that was due (without regard to extensions) before January 1, 1990. Assume, for example, that a calendar year corporation claimed a deduction on its 1990 return for depreciation of an asset with a basis of X. Also assume that it had reported the same basis for computing depreciation on its returns for the preceding 5 years and that the basis shown on the return each year was 200 percent or more of the correct basis. The corporation may be subject to a penalty for substantial valuation misstatements on its 1989 and 1990 returns, even though the original misstatement occurred prior to the effective date of sections 6662(b)(3) and (e). [Reg. §1.6662-5.]

☐ [T.D. 8381, 12-30-91.]

### [Reg. §1.6662-5T]

**§1.6662-5T. Substantial and gross valuation misstatements under chapter 1 (Temporary).**—(a) through (e)(3) [Reserved]. For further information, see §1.6662-5(a) through (e)(3).

(e)(4) *Tests related to section 482.*—(i) *Substantial valuation misstatement.*—There is a substantial valuation misstatement if there is a misstatement described in §1.6662-6(b)(1) or (c)(1) (concerning substantial valuation misstatements pertaining to transactions between related persons).

(ii) *Gross valuation misstatement.*—There is a gross valuation misstatement if there is a misstatement described in §1.6662-6(b)(2) or (c)(2) (concerning gross valuation misstatements pertaining to transactions between related persons).

(iii) *Property.*—For purposes of this section, the term *property* refers to both tangible and intangible property. Tangible property includes property such as money, land, buildings, fixtures and inventory. Intangible property includes property such as goodwill, covenants not to compete, leaseholds, patents, contract rights, debts, choses in action, and any other item of intangible property described in §1.482-4(b).

(f) through (h) [Reserved] For further information, see §1.6662-5(f) through (h).

(i) [Reserved].

(j) *Transactions between persons described in section 482 and net section 482 transfer price adjustments.*—For rules relating to the penalty imposed with respect to a substantial or gross valuation misstatement arising from a section 482 allocation, see §1.6662-6. [Temporary Reg. §1.6662-5T.]

☐ [*T.D. 8519, 1-27-94. Amended by T.D. 8656, 2-8-96.*]

### [Reg. §1.6662-6]

**§1.6662-6. Transactions between persons described in section 482 and net section 482 transfer price adjustments.**—(a) *In general.*—(1) *Purpose and scope.*—Pursuant to section 6662(e) a penalty is imposed on any underpayment attributable to a substantial valuation misstatement pertaining to either a transaction between persons described in section 482 (the transactional penalty) or a net section 482 transfer price adjustment (the net adjustment penalty). The penalty is equal to 20 percent of the underpayment of tax attributable to that substantial valuation misstatement. Pursuant to section 6662(h) the penalty is increased to 40 percent of the underpayment in the case of a gross valuation misstatement with respect to either penalty. Paragraph(b) of this section provides specific rules related to the transactional penalty. Paragraph (c) of this section provides specific rules related to the net adjustment penalty, and paragraph (d) of this section describes amounts that will be excluded for purposes of calculating the net adjustment penalty. Paragraph (e) of this section sets forth special rules in the case of carrybacks and carryovers. Paragraph (f) of this section provides coordination rules between penalties. Paragraph (g) of this section provides the effective date of this section.

(2) *Reported results.*—Whether an underpayment is attributable to a substantial or gross valuation misstatement must be determined from the results of controlled transactions that are reported on an income tax return, regardless of whether the amount reported differs from the transaction price initially reflected in the taxpayer's books and records. The results of controlled transactions that are reported on an amended return will be used only if the amended return is filed before the Internal Revenue Service has contacted the taxpayer regarding the corresponding original return. A written statement furnished by a taxpayer subject to the Coordinated Examination Program or a written statement furnished by the taxpayer when electing Accelerated Issue Resolution or similar procedures will be considered an amended return for purposes of this section if it satisfies either the requirements of a qualified amended return for purposes of §1.6664-2(c)(3) or such requirements as the Commissioner may prescribe by revenue procedure. In the case of a taxpayer that is a member of a consolidated group, the rules of this paragraph (a)(2) apply to the consolidated income tax return of the group.

(3) *Identical terms used in the section 482 regulations.*—For purposes of this section, the terms used in this section shall have the same meaning as identical terms used in regulations under section 482.

(b) *The transactional penalty.*—(1) *Substantial valuation misstatement.*—In the case of any transaction between related persons, there is a substantial valuation misstatement if the price for any property or services (or for the use of property) claimed on any return is 200 percent or more (or 50 percent or less) of the amount determined under section 482 to be the correct price.

(2) *Gross valuation misstatement.*—In the case of any transaction between related persons, there is a gross valuation misstatement if the price for any property or services (or for the use of property) claimed on any return is 400 percent or more (or 25 percent or less) of the amount determined under section 482 to be the correct price.

(3) *Reasonable cause and good faith.*—Pursuant to section 6664(c), the transactional penalty will not be imposed on any portion of an underpayment with respect to which the requirements of §1.6664-4 are met. In applying the provisions of §1.6664-4 in a case in which the taxpayer has relied on professional analysis in determining its transfer pricing, whether the professional is an employee of, or related to, the taxpayer is not determinative in evaluating whether the taxpayer reasonably relied in good faith on advice. A taxpayer

that meets the requirements of paragraph (d) of this section with respect to an allocation under section 482 will be treated as having established that there was reasonable cause and good faith with respect to that item for purposes of §1.6664-4. If a substantial or gross valuation misstatement under the transactional penalty also constitutes (or is part of) a substantial or gross valuation misstatement under the net adjustment penalty, then the rules of paragraph (d) of this section (and not the rules of §1.6664-4) will be applied to determine whether the adjustment is excluded from calculation of the net section 482 adjustment.

(c) *Net adjustment penalty.*—(1) *Net section 482 adjustment.*—For purposes of this section, the term *net section 482 adjustment* means the sum of all increases in the taxable income of a taxpayer for a taxable year resulting from allocations under section 482 (determined without regard to any amount carried to such taxable year from another taxable year) less any decreases in taxable income attributable to collateral adjustments as described in §1.482-1(g). For purposes of this section, amounts that meet the requirements of paragraph (d) of this section will be excluded from the calculation of the net section 482 adjustment. Substantial and gross valuation misstatements that are subject to the transactional penalty under paragraph (b)(1) or (2) of this section are included in determining the amount of the net section 482 adjustment. See paragraph (f) of this section for coordination rules between penalties.

(2) *Substantial valuation misstatement.*—There is a substantial valuation misstatement if a net section 482 adjustment is greater than the lesser of 5 million dollars or ten percent of gross receipts.

(3) *Gross valuation misstatement.*—There is a gross valuation misstatement if a net section 482 adjustment is greater than the lesser of 20 million dollars or twenty percent of gross receipts.

(4) *Setoff allocation rule.*—If a taxpayer meets the requirements of paragraph (d) of this section with respect to some, but not all of the allocations made under section 482, then for purposes of determining the net section 482 adjustment, setoffs, as taken into account under §1.482-1(g)(4), must be applied ratably against all such allocations. The following example illustrates the principle of this paragraph (c)(4):

*Example.* (i) The Internal Revenue Service makes the following section 482 adjustments for the taxable year:

| | | |
|---|---|---:|
| (1) | Attributable to an increase in gross income because of an increase in royalty payments . . . . . . . . . . . . . | $9,000,000 |
| (2) | Attributable to an increase in sales proceeds due to a decrease in the profit margin of a related buyer . . . . | 6,000,000 |
| (3) | Because of a setoff under §1.482-1(g)(4) . . . . . . . . | (5,000,000) |
| | Total section 482 adjustments . . . . . . . . . . . . . | 10,000,000 |

(ii) The taxpayer meets the requirements of paragraph (d) with respect to adjustment number one, but not with respect to adjustment number two. The five million dollar setoff will be allocated ratably against the nine million dollar adjustment ($9,000,000/$15,000,000 x $5,000,000 = $3,000,000) and the six million dollar adjustment ($6,000,000/$15,000,000 x $5,000,000 = $2,000,000). Accordingly, in determining the net section 482 adjustment, the nine million dollar adjustment is reduced to six million dollars ($9,000,000 - $3,000,000) and the six million dollar adjustment is reduced to four million dollars ($6,000,000 - $2,000,000). Therefore, the net section 482 adjustment equals four million dollars.

(5) *Gross receipts.*—For purposes of this section, gross receipts must be computed pursuant to the rules contained in §1.448-1T(f)(2)(iv), as adjusted to reflect allocations under section 482.

(6) *Coordination with reasonable cause exception under section 6664(c).*—Pursuant to section 6662(e)(3)(D), a taxpayer will be treated as having reasonable cause under section 6664(c) for any portion of an underpayment attributable to a net section 482 adjustment only if the taxpayer meets the requirements of paragraph (d) of this section with respect to that portion.

(7) *Examples.*—The principles of this paragraph (c) are illustrated by the following examples:

*Example 1.* (i) The Internal Revenue Service makes the following section 482 adjustments for the taxable year:

| | | |
|---|---|---:|
| (1) | Attributable to an increase in gross income because of an increase in royalty payments . | $2,000,000 |
| (2) | Attributable to an increase in sales proceeds due to a decrease in the profit margin of a related buyer | 2,500,000 |
| (3) | Attributable to a decrease in the cost of goods sold because of a decrease in the cost plus mark-up of a related seller . . . . . . . . . . . | 2,000,000 |
| | Total section 482 adjustments . . . . . . . . . . | 6,500,000 |

**67,086**
          **Additions to Tax and Additional Amounts**
See p. 20,601 for regulations not amended to reflect law changes

(ii) None of the adjustments are excluded under paragraph (d) of this section. The net section 482 adjustment ($6.5 million) is greater than five million dollars. Therefore, there is a substantial valuation misstatement.

*Example 2.* (i) The Internal Revenue Service makes the following section 482 adjustments for the taxable year:

| | | |
|---|---|---|
| (1) | Attributable to an increase in gross income because of an increase in royalty payments . | $11,000,000 |
| (2) | Attributable to an increase in sales proceeds due to a decrease in the profit margin of a related buyer . . . . . . . . . . . . . . . . . . . | 2,000,000 |
| (3) | Because of a setoff under §1.482-1(g)(4) . . . | (9,000,000) |
| | Total section 482 adjustments . . . . . . . . . | 4,000,000 |

(ii) The taxpayer has gross receipts of sixty million dollars after taking into account all section 482 adjustments. None of the adjustments are excluded under paragraph (d) of this section. The net section 482 adjustment ($4 million) is less than the lesser of five million dollars or ten percent of gross receipts ($60 million × 10% = $6 million). Therefore, there is no substantial valuation misstatement.

*Example 3.* (i) The Internal Revenue Service makes the following section 482 adjustments to the income of an affiliated group that files a consolidated return for the taxable year:

| | | |
|---|---|---|
| (1) | Attributable to Member A . . . . . . . . . . . . | $1,500,000 |
| (2) | Attributable to Member B . . . . . . . . . . . . | 1,000,000 |
| (3) | Attributable to Member C . . . . . . . . . . . . | 2,000,000 |
| | Total section 482 adjustments . . . . . . . . . | 4,500,000 |

(ii) Members A, B, and C have gross receipts of 20 million dollars, 12 million dollars, and 11 million dollars, respectively. Thus, the total gross receipts are 43 million dollars. None of the adjustments are excluded under paragraph (d) of this section. The net section 482 adjustment ($4.5 million) is greater than the lesser of five million dollars or ten percent of gross receipts ($43 million x 10% = $4.3 million). Therefore, there is a substantial valuation misstatement.

*Example 4.* (i) The Internal Revenue Service makes the following section 482 adjustments to the income of an affiliated group that files a consolidated return for the taxable year:

| | | |
|---|---|---|
| (1) | Attributable to Member A . . . . . . . . . . . . . . . . . . | $1,500,000 |
| (2) | Attributable to Member B . . . . . . . . . . . . . . . . . . | 3,000,000 |
| (3) | Attributable to Member C . . . . . . . . . . . . . . . . . . | 2,500,000 |
| | Total section 482 adjustments . . . . . . . . . | 7,000,000 |

(ii) Members A, B, and C have gross receipts of 20 million dollars, 35 million dollars, and 40 million dollars, respectively. Thus, the total gross receipts are 95 million dollars. None of the adjustments are excluded under paragraph (d) of this section. The net section 482 adjustment (7 million dollars) is greater than the lesser of five million dollars or ten percent of gross receipts ($95 million × 10% = $9.5 million). Therefore, there is a substantial valuation misstatement.

*Example 5.* (i) The Internal Revenue Service makes the following section 482 adjustments to the income of an affiliated group that files a consolidated return for the taxable year:

| | | |
|---|---|---|
| (1) | Attributable to Member A . . . . . . . . . . . . | $2,000,000 |
| (2) | Attributable to Member B . . . . . . . . . . . . | 1,000,000 |
| (3) | Attributable to Member C . . . . . . . . . . . . | 1,500,000 |
| | Total section 482 adjustments . . . . . . . . . | 4,500,000 |

(ii) Members A, B, and C have gross receipts of 10 million dollars, 35 million dollars, and 40 million dollars, respectively. Thus, the total gross receipts are 85 million dollars. None of the adjustments are excluded under paragraph (d) of this section. The net section 482 adjustment ($4.5 million) is less than the lesser of five million dollars or ten percent of gross receipts ($85 million x 10% = $8.5 million). Therefore, there is no substantial valuation misstatement even though individual member A's adjustment ($2 million) is greater than ten percent of its individual gross receipts ($10 million x 10% = $1 million).

(d) *Amounts excluded from net section 482 adjustments.*—(1) *In general.*—An amount is excluded from the calculation of a net section 482 adjustment if the requirements of paragraph (d)(2), (3), or (4) of this section are met with respect to that amount.

(2) *Application of a specified section 482 method.*—(i) *In general.*—An amount is excluded from the calculation of a net section 482 adjustment if the taxpayer establishes that both the specified method and documentation requirements of this paragraph (d)(2) are met with respect to that amount. For purposes of this paragraph (d), a method will be considered a specified method if it is described in the regulations under section 482 and the method applies to transactions of the type under review. An unspecified method is not considered a specified method. See §§ 1.482-3(e) and 1.482-4(d).

(ii) *Specified method requirement.*—(A) The specified method requirement is met if the taxpayer selects and applies a specified method in a reasonable manner. The taxpayer's selection and appli-

cation of a specified method is reasonable only if, given the available data and the applicable pricing methods, the taxpayer reasonably concluded that the method (and its application of that method) provided the most reliable measure of an arm's length result under the principles of the best method rule of § 1.482-1(c). A taxpayer can reasonably conclude that a specified method provided the most reliable measure of an arm's length result only if it has made a reasonable effort to evaluate the potential applicability of the other specified methods in a manner consistent with the principles of the best method rule. The extent of this evaluation generally will depend on the nature of the available data, and it may vary from case to case and from method to method. This evaluation may not entail an exhaustive analysis or detailed application of each method. Rather, after a reasonably thorough search for relevant data, the taxpayer should consider which method would provide the most reliable measure of an arm's length result given that data. The nature of the available data may enable the taxpayer to conclude reasonably that a particular specified method provides a more reliable measure of an arm's length result than one or more of the other specified methods, and accordingly no further consideration of such other specified methods is needed. Further, it is not necessary for a taxpayer to conclude that the selected specified method provides a more reliable measure of an arm's length result than any unspecified method. For examples illustrating the selection of a specified method consistent with this paragraph (d)(2)(ii), see § 1.482-8. Whether the taxpayer's conclusion was reasonable must be determined from all the facts and circumstances. The factors relevant to this determination include the following:

(1) The experience and knowledge of the taxpayer, including all members of the taxpayer's controlled group.

(2) The extent to which reliable data was available and the data was analyzed in a reasonable manner. A taxpayer must engage in a reasonably thorough search for the data necessary to determine which method should be selected and how it should be applied. In determining the scope of a reasonably thorough search for data, the expense of additional efforts to locate new data may be weighed against the likelihood of finding additional data that would improve the reliability of the results and the amount by which any new data would change the taxpayer's taxable income. Furthermore, a taxpayer must use the most current reliable data that is available before the end of the taxable year in question. Although the taxpayer is not required to search for relevant data after the end of the taxable year, the taxpayer must maintain as a principal document described in paragraph (d)(2)(iii)(B)(9) of this section any relevant data it obtains after the end of the taxable year but before the return is filed, if that data would help determine whether the taxpayer has reported its true taxable income.

(3) The extent to which the taxpayer followed the relevant requirements set forth in regulations under section 482 with respect to the application of the method.

(4) The extent to which the taxpayer reasonably relied on a study or other analysis performed by a professional qualified to conduct such a study or analysis, including an attorney, accountant, or economist. Whether the professional is an employee of, or related to, the taxpayer is not determinative in evaluating the reliability of that study or analysis, as long as the study or analysis is objective, thorough, and well reasoned. Such reliance is reasonable only if the taxpayer disclosed to the professional all relevant information regarding the controlled transactions at issue. A study or analysis that was reasonably relied upon in a prior year may reasonably be relied upon in the current year if the relevant facts and circumstances have not changed or if the study or analysis has been appropriately modified to reflect any change in facts and circumstances.

(5) If the taxpayer attempted to determine an arm's length result by using more than one uncontrolled comparable, whether the taxpayer arbitrarily selected a result that corresponds to an extreme point in the range of results derived from the uncontrolled comparables. Such a result generally would not likely be closest to an arm's length result. If the uncontrolled comparables that the taxpayer uses to determine an arm's length result are described in § 1.482-1(e)(2)(iii)(B), one reasonable method of selecting a point in the range would be that provided in § 1.482-1(e)(3).

(6) The extent to which the taxpayer relied on a transfer pricing methodology developed and applied pursuant to an Advance Pricing Agreement for a prior taxable year, or specifically approved by the Internal Revenue Service pursuant to a transfer pricing audit of the transactions at issue for a prior taxable year, provided that the taxpayer applied the approved method reasonably and consistently with its prior application, and the facts and circumstances surrounding the use of the method have not materially changed since the time of the IRS's action, or if the facts and circumstances have changed in a way that materially affects the reliability of the results, the taxpayer makes appropriate adjustments to reflect such changes.

*(7)* The size of a net transfer pricing adjustment in relation to the size of the controlled transaction out of which the adjustment arose.

*(B) Services cost method.*—A taxpayer's selection of the services cost method for certain services, described in §1.482-9(b), and its application of that method to a controlled services transaction will be considered reasonable for purposes of the specified method requirement only if the taxpayer reasonably allocated and apportioned costs in accordance with §1.482-9(k), and reasonably concluded that the controlled services transaction satisfies the requirements described in §1.482-9(b)(2). Whether the taxpayer's conclusion was reasonable must be determined from all the facts and circumstances. The factors relevant to this determination include those described in paragraph (d)(2)(ii)(A) of this section, to the extent applicable.

*(iii) Documentation requirement.*—(A) *In general.*—The documentation requirement of this paragraph (d)(2)(iii) is met if the taxpayer maintains sufficient documentation to establish that the taxpayer reasonably concluded that, given the available data and the applicable pricing methods, the method (and its application of that method) provided the most reliable measure of an arm's length result under the principles of the best method rule in §1.482-1(c), and provides that documentation to the Internal Revenue Service within 30 days of a request for it in connection with an examination of the taxable year to which the documentation relates. With the exception of the documentation described in paragraphs (d)(2)(iii)(B)(*9*) and (*10*) of this section, that documentation must be in existence when the return is filed. The district director may, in his discretion, excuse a minor or inadvertent failure to provide required documents, but only if the taxpayer has made a good faith effort to comply, and the taxpayer promptly remedies the failure when it becomes known. The required documentation is divided into two categories, principal documents and background documents as described in paragraphs (d)(2)(iii)(B) and (C) of this section.

*(B) Principal documents.*—The principal documents should accurately and completely describe the basic transfer pricing analysis conducted by the taxpayer. The documentation must include the following—

*(1)* An overview of the taxpayer's business, including an analysis of the economic and legal factors that affect the pricing of its property or services;

*(2)* A description of the taxpayer's organizational structure (including an organization chart) covering all related parties engaged in transactions potentially relevant under section 482, including foreign affiliates whose transactions directly or indirectly affect the pricing of property or services in the United States;

*(3)* Any documentation explicitly required by the regulations under section 482;

*(4)* A description of the method selected and an explanation of why that method was selected, including an evaluation of whether the regulatory conditions and requirements for application of that method, if any, were met;

*(5)* A description of the alternative methods that were considered and an explanation of why they were not selected;

*(6)* A description of the controlled transactions (including the terms of sale) and any internal data used to analyze those transactions. For example, if a profit split method is applied, the documentation must include a schedule providing the total income, costs, and assets (with adjustments for different accounting practices and currencies) for each controlled taxpayer participating in the relevant business activity and detailing the allocations of such items to that activity. Similarly, if a cost-based method (such as the cost plus method, the services cost method for certain services, or a comparable profits method with a cost-based profit level indicator) is applied, the documentation must include a description of the manner in which relevant costs are determined and are allocated and apportioned to the relevant controlled transaction.

*(7)* A description of the comparables that were used, how comparability was evaluated, and what (if any) adjustments were made;

*(8)* An explanation of the economic analysis and projections relied upon in developing the method. For example, if a profit split method is applied, the taxpayer must provide an explanation of the analysis undertaken to determine how the profits would be split;

*(9)* A description or summary of any relevant data that the taxpayer obtains after the end of the tax year and before filing a tax return, which would help determine if a taxpayer selected and applied a specified method in a reasonable manner; and

*(10)* A general index of the principal and background documents and a description of the recordkeeping system used for cataloging and accessing those documents.

*(C) Background documents.*—The assumptions, conclusions, and positions contained in principal documents ordinarily will be based on, and supported by, additional background documents. Documents that support the principal documentation may include the documents listed in §1.6038A-3(c) that are not otherwise described in paragraph (d)(2)(iii)(B) of this section. Every document listed in those regulations may not be relevant to pricing determinations under the taxpayer's specific facts and circumstances and, therefore, each of those documents need not be maintained in all circumstances. Moreover, other documents not listed in those regulations may be necessary to establish that the taxpayer's method was selected and applied in the way that provided the most reliable measure of an arm's length result under the principles of the best method rule in §1.482-1(c). Background documents need not be provided to the Internal Revenue Service in response to a request for principal documents. If the Internal Revenue Service subsequently requests background documents, a taxpayer must provide that documentation to the Internal Revenue Service within 30 days of the request. However, the district director may, in his discretion, extend the period for producing the background documentation.

*(D)* Satisfaction of the documentation requirements described in §1.482-7(k)(2) for the purpose of complying with the rules for CSAs under §1.482-7 also satisfies all of the documentation requirements listed in paragraph (d)(2)(iii)(B) of this section, except the requirements listed in paragraphs (d)(2)(iii)(B)(2) and (10) of this section, with respect to CSTs and PCTs described in §1.482-7(b)(1)(i) and (ii), provided that the documentation also satisfies the requirements of paragraph (d)(2)(iii)(A) of this section.

*(3) Application of an unspecified method.*—(i) *In general.*—An adjustment is excluded from the calculation of a net section 482 adjustment if the taxpayer establishes that both the unspecified method and documentation requirements of this paragraph (d)(3) are met with respect to that amount.

*(ii) Unspecified method requirement.*—(A) *In general.*—If a method other than a specified method was applied, the unspecified method requirement is met if the requirements of paragraph (d)(3)(ii)(B) or (C) of this section, as appropriate, are met.

*(B) Specified method potentially applicable.*—If the transaction is of a type for which methods are specified in the regulations under section 482, then a taxpayer will be considered to have met the unspecified method requirement if the taxpayer reasonably concludes, given the available data, that none of the specified methods was likely to provide a reliable measure of an arm's length result, and that it selected and applied an unspecified method in a way that would likely provide a reliable measure of an arm's length result. A taxpayer can reasonably conclude that no specified method was likely to provide a reliable measure of an arm's length result only if it has made a reasonable effort to evaluate the potential applicability of the specified methods in a manner consistent with the principles of the best method rule. However, it is not necessary for a taxpayer to conclude that the selected method provides a more reliable measure of an arm's length result than any other unspecified method. Whether the taxpayer's conclusion was reasonable must be determined from all the facts and circumstances. The factors relevant to this conclusion include those set forth in paragraph (d)(2)(ii) of this section.

*(C) No specified method applicable.*—If the transaction is of a type for which no methods are specified in the regulations under section 482, then a taxpayer will be considered to have met the unspecified method requirement if it selected and applied an unspecified method in a reasonable manner. For purposes of this paragraph (d)(3)(ii)(C), a taxpayer's selection and application is reasonable if the taxpayer reasonably concludes that the method (and its application of that method) provided the most reliable measure of an arm's length result under the principles of the best method rule in §1.482-1(c). However, it is not necessary for a taxpayer to conclude that the selected method provides a more reliable measure of an arm's length result than any other unspecified method. Whether the taxpayer's conclusion was reasonable must be determined from all the facts and circumstances. The factors relevant to this conclusion include those set forth in paragraph (d)(2)(ii) of this section.

*(iii) Documentation requirement.*—(A) *In general.*—The documentation requirement of this paragraph (d)(3) is met if the taxpayer maintains sufficient documentation to establish that the unspecified method requirement of paragraph (d)(3)(ii) of this section is met and provides that documentation to the Internal Revenue Service within 30 days of a request for it. That documentation must be in existence when the return is filed. The district director may, in his discretion, excuse a minor or inadvertent failure to provide required documents, but only if the taxpayer has made a good faith effort to comply, and the taxpayer promptly remedies the failure when it becomes known.

**Reg. §1.6662-6(d)(3)(iii)(A)**

(B) *Principal and background documents.*—See paragraphs (d)(2)(iii)(B) and (C) of this section for rules regarding these two categories of required documentation.

(4) *Certain foreign to foreign transactions.*—For purposes of calculating a net section 482 adjustment, any increase in taxable income resulting from an allocation under section 482 that is attributable to any controlled transaction solely between foreign corporations will be excluded unless the treatment of that transaction affects the determination of either corporation's income from sources within the United States or taxable income effectively connected with the conduct of a trade or business within the United States.

(5) *Special rule.*—If the regular tax (as defined in section 55(c)) imposed on the taxpayer is determined by reference to an amount other than taxable income, that amount shall be treated as the taxable income of the taxpayer for purposes of section 6662(e)(3). Accordingly, for taxpayers whose regular tax is determined by reference to an amount other than taxable income, the increase in that amount resulting from section 482 allocations is the taxpayer's net section 482 adjustment.

(6) *Examples.*—The principles of this paragraph (d) are illustrated by the following examples:

*Example 1.* (i) The Internal Revenue Service makes the following section 482 adjustments for the taxable year:

| | | |
|---|---|---|
| (1) | Attributable to an increase in gross income because of an increase in royalty payments . | $9,000,000 |
| (2) | Not a 200 percent or 400 percent adjustment | 2,000,000 |
| (3) | Attributable to a decrease in the cost of goods sold because of a decrease in the cost plus mark-up of a realted seller . . . . . . . . . . . . | 9,000,000 |
| | Total section 482 adjustments . . . . . . . . . . | 20,000,000 |

(ii) The taxpayer has gross receipts of 75 million dollars after all section 482 adjustments. The taxpayer establishes that for adjustments number one and three, it applied a transfer pricing method specified in section 482, the selection and application of the method was reasonable, it documented the pricing analysis, and turned that documentation over to the IRS within 30 days of a request. Accordingly, eighteen million dollars is excluded from the calculation of the net section 482 adjustment. Because the net section 482 adjustment is two million dollars, there is no substantial valuation misstatement.

*Example 2.* (i) The Internal Revenue Service makes the following section 482 adjustments for the taxable year:

| | | |
|---|---|---|
| (1) | Attributable to an increase in gross income because of an increase in royalty payments . | $9,000,000 |
| (2) | Attributable to an adjustment that is 200 percent or more of the correct section 482 price . . . . . . . . . . . . . . . . . . . . . . | 2,000,000 |
| (3) | Attributable to a decrease in the cost of goods sold because of a decrease in the cost plus mark-up of a related seller . . . . . . . . . . | 9,000,000 |
| | Total section 482 adjustments . . . . . . . . . | 20,000,000 |

(ii) The taxpayer has gross receipts of 75 million dollars after all section 482 adjustments. The taxpayer establishes that for adjustments number one and three it applied a transfer pricing method specified in section 482, the selection and application of the method was reasonable, it documented that analysis, and turned the documentation over to the IRS within 30 days. Accordingly, eighteen million dollars is excluded from the calculation of the section 482 transfer pricing adjustments for purposes of applying the five million dollar or 10% of gross receipts test. Because the net section 482 adjustment is only two million dollars, the taxpayer is not subject to the net adjustment penalty. However, the taxpayer may be subject to the transactional penalty on the underpayment of tax attributable to the two million dollar adjustment.

*Example 3.* CFC1 and CFC2 are controlled foreign corporations within the meaning of section 957. Applying section 482, the IRS disallows a deduction for 25 million dollars of the interest that CFC1 paid to CFC2, which results in CFC1's U.S. shareholder having a subpart F inclusion in excess of five million dollars. No other adjustments under section 482 are made with respect to the controlled taxpayers. However, the increase has no effect upon the determination of CFC1's or CFC2's income from sources within the United States or taxable income effectively connected with the conduct of a trade or business within the United States. Accordingly, there is no substantial valuation misstatement.

(e) *Special rules in the case of carrybacks and carryovers.*—If there is a substantial or gross valuation misstatement for a taxable year that gives rise to a loss, deduction or credit that is carried to another taxable year, the transactional penalty and the net adjustment penalty will be imposed on any resulting underpayment of tax in that other taxable year. In determining whether there is a substantial or gross valuation misstatement for a taxable year, no amount carried from another taxable year shall be included. The following example illustrates the principle of this paragraph (e):

*Example.* The Internal Revenue Service makes a section 482 adjustment of six million dollars in taxable year 1, no portion of which is excluded under paragraph (d) of this section. The taxpayer's income tax return for year 1 reported a loss of three million dollars, which was carried to taxpayer's year 2 income tax return and used to reduce income taxes otherwise due with respect to year 2. A determination is made that the six million dollar allocation constitutes a substantial valuation misstatement, and a penalty is imposed on the underpayment of tax in year 1 attributable to the substantial valuation misstatement and on the underpayment of tax in year 2 attributable to the disallowance of the net operating loss in year 2. For purposes of determining whether there is a substantial or gross valuation misstatement for year 2, the three million dollar reduction of the net operating loss will not be added to any section 482 adjustments made with respect to year 2.

(f) *Rules for coordinating between the transactional penalty and the net adjustment penalty.*—(1) *Coordination of a net section 482 adjustment subject to the net adjustment penalty and a gross valuation misstatement subject to the transactional penalty.*—In determining whether a net section 482 adjustment exceeds five million dollars or 10 percent of gross receipts, an adjustment attributable to a substantial or gross valuation misstatement that is subject to the transactional penalty will be taken into account. If the net section 482 adjustment exceeds five million dollars or ten percent of gross receipts, any portion of such amount that is attributable to a gross valuation misstatement will be subject to the transactional penalty at the forty percent rate, but will not also be subject to net adjustment penalty at a twenty percent rate. The remaining amount is subject to the net adjustment penalty at the twenty percent rate, even if such amount is less than the lesser of five million dollars or ten percent of gross receipts.

(2) *Coordination of net section 482 adjustment subject to the net adjustment penalty and substantial valuation misstatements subject to the transactional penalty.*—If the net section 482 adjustment exceeds twenty million dollars or 20 percent of gross receipts, the entire amount of the adjustment is subject to the net adjustment penalty at a forty percent rate. No portion of the adjustment is subject to the transactional penalty at a twenty percent rate.

(3) *Examples.*—The following examples illustrate the principles of this paragraph (f):

*Example 1.* (i) Applying section 482, the Internal Revenue Service makes the following adjustments for the taxable year:

| | | |
|---|---|---|
| (1) | Attributable to an adjustment that is 400 percent or more of the correct section 482 arm's length result . . . . . . . . . . . . . . . | $2,000,000 |
| (2) | Not a 200 or 400 percent adjustment . . . . . | 2,500,000 |
| | Total . . . . . . . . . . . . . . . . . . . . . . . . | 4,500,000 |

(ii) The taxpayer has gross receipts of 75 million dollars after all section 482 adjustments. None of the adjustments is excluded under paragraph (d) (Amounts excluded from net section 482 adjustments) of this section, in determining the five million dollar or 10% of gross receipts test under section 6662(e)(1)(B)(ii). The net section 482 adjustment (4.5 million dollars) is less than the lesser of five million dollars or ten percent of gross receipts ($75 million × 10% = $7.5 million). Thus, there is no substantial valuation misstatement. However, the two million dollar adjustment is attributable to a gross valuation misstatement. Accordingly, the taxpayer may be subject to a penalty, under section 6662(h), equal to 40 percent of the underpayment of tax attributable to the gross valuation misstatement of two million dollars. The 2.5 million dollar adjustment is not subject to a penalty under section 6662(b)(3).

*Example 2.* The facts are the same as in *Example 1*, except the taxpayer has gross receipts of 40 million dollars. The net section 482 adjustment ($4.5 million) is greater than the lesser of five million dollars or ten percent of gross receipts ($40 million × 10% = $4 million). Thus, the five million dollar or 10% of gross receipts test has been met. The two million dollar adjustment is attributable to a gross valuation misstatement. Accordingly, the taxpayer is subject to a penalty, under section 6662(h), equal to 40 percent of the underpayment of tax attributable to the gross valuation misstatement of two million dollars. The 2.5 million dollar adjustment is subject to a penalty under sections 6662(a) and 6662(b)(3), equal to 20 percent of the underpayment of tax attributable to the substantial valuation misstatement.

*Example 3.* (i) Applying section 482, the Internal Revenue Service makes the following transfer pricing adjustments for the taxable year:

| | | |
|---|---|---|
| (1) | Attributable to an adjustment that is 400 percent or more of the correct section 482 arm's length result . . . . . . . . . . . . . . . | $6,000,000 |
| (2) | Not a 200 or 400 percent adjustment . . . . . | 15,000,000 |
| | Total . . . . . . . . . . . . . . . . . . . . . . . . | 21,000,000 |

(ii) None of the adjustments are excluded under paragraph (d) (Amounts excluded from net section 482 adjustments) in determining the twenty million dollar or 20% of gross receipts test under section 6662(h). The net section 482 adjustment (21 million dollars) is greater than twenty million dollars and thus constitutes a gross valuation misstatement. Accordingly, the total adjustment is subject to the net adjustment penalty equal to 40 percent of the underpayment of tax attributable to the 21 million dollar gross valuation misstatement. The six million dollar adjustment will not be separately included for purposes of any additional penalty under section 6662.

(g) *Effective/applicability date.*—(1) *In general.*—This section is generally applicable on February 9, 1996. However, taxpayers may elect to apply this section to all open taxable years beginning after December 31, 1993.

(2) *Special rules.*—The provisions of paragraphs (d)(2)(ii)(B), (d)(2)(iii)(B)(4) and (d)(2)(iii)(B)(6) of this section are applicable for taxable years beginning after July 31, 2009. However, taxpayers may elect to apply the provisions of paragraphs (d)(2)(ii)(B), (d)(2)(iii)(B)(4) and (d)(2)(iii)(B)(6) of this section to earlier taxable years in accordance with the rules set forth in § 1.482-9(n)(2). [Reg. § 1.6662-6.]

☐ [*T.D. 8656*, 2-8-96. *Amended by T.D. 9278*, 7-31-2006; *T.D. 9441*, 12-31-2008; *T.D. 9456*, 7-31-2009 *and T.D. 9568*, 12-16-2011.]

### [Reg. § 1.6662-7]

**§ 1.6662-7. Omnibus Budget Reconciliation Act of 1993 changes to the accuracy-related penalty.**—(a) *Scope.*—The Omnibus Budget Reconciliation Act of 1993 made certain changes to the accuracy-related penalty in section 6662. This section provides rules reflecting those changes.

(b) *No disclosure exception for negligence penalty.*—The penalty for negligence in section 6662(b)(1) may not be avoided by disclosure of a return position.

(c) *Disclosure standard for other penalties is reasonable basis.*—The penalties for disregarding rules or regulations in section 6662(b)(1) and for a substantial understatement of income tax in section 6662(b)(2) may be avoided by adequate disclosure of a return position only if the position has at least a reasonable basis. See § 1.6662-3(c) and §§ 1.6662-4(e) and (f) for other applicable disclosure rules.

(d) *Reasonable basis.*—For purposes of §§ 1.6662-3(c) and 1.6662-4(e) and (f) (relating to methods of making adequate disclosure), the provisions of § 1.6662-3(b)(3) apply in determining whether a return position has a reasonable basis. [Reg. § 1.6662-7.]

☐ [*T.D. 8617*, 8-31-95. *Amended by T.D. 8790*, 12-1-98.]

### [Reg. § 1.6664-0]

☐ [*T.D. 8381*, 12-30-91. *Amended by T.D. 8519*, 1-27-94; *T.D. 8617*, 8-31-95; *T.D. 8656*, 2-8-96; *T.D. 8790*, 12-1-98; *T.D. 9109*, 12-29-2003 *and T.D. 9309*, 1-8-2007.]

### [Reg. § 1.6664-1]

**§ 1.6664-1. Accuracy-related and fraud penalties; definitions, effective date and special rules.**—(a) *In general.*—Section 6664(a) defines the term "underpayment" for purposes of the accuracy-related penalty under section 6662 and the fraud penalty under section 6663. The definition of "underpayment" of income taxes imposed under subtitle A is set forth in § 1.6664-2. Ordering rules for computing the total amount of accuracy-related and fraud penalties imposed with respect to a return are set forth in § 1.6664-3. Section 6664(c) provides a reasonable cause and good faith exception to the accuracy-related penalty. Rules relating to the reasonable cause and good faith exception are set forth in § 1.6664-4.

(b) *Effective date.*—(1) *In general.*—Sections 1.6664-1 through 1.6664-3 apply to returns the due date of which (determined without regard to extensions of time for filing) is after December 31, 1989.

(2) *Reasonable cause and good faith exception to section 6662 penalties.*—(i) *For returns due after September 1, 1995.*—Section 1.6664-4 applies to returns the due date of which (determined without regard to extensions of time for filing) is after September 1, 1995. Except as provided in the last sentence of this paragraph (b)(2), § 1.6664-4 (as contained in 26 CFR part 1 revised April 1, 1995) applies to returns the due date of which (determined without regard to extensions of time for filing) is on or before September 1, 1995, and after December 31, 1989. For transactions occurring after December 8, 1994, § 1.6664-4 (as contained in 26 CFR part 1 revised April 1, 1995) is applied taking into account the changes made to section 6662(d)(2)(C) (relating to the substantial understatement penalty for tax shelter items of corpo-

rations) by section 744 of Title VII of the Uruguay Round Agreements Act, Pub. L. 103-465 (108 Stat. 4809).

(ii) *For returns filed after December 31, 2002.*—Sections 1.6664-4(c) (relating to relying on opinion or advice) and (d) (relating to underpayments attributable to reportable transactions) apply to returns filed after December 31, 2002, with respect to transactions entered into on or after January 1, 2003. Except as provided in paragraph (b)(2)(i) of this section, § 1.6664-4 (as contained in 26 CFR part 1 revised April 1, 2003) applies to returns filed with respect to transactions entered into before January 1, 2003.

(3) *Qualified amended returns.*—Sections 1.6664-2(c)(1), (c) (2), (c) (3) (i) (A), (c) (3) (i) (B), (c) (3) (i) (C), (c) (3) (i) (D) (2), (c)(3)(i)(E), and (c)(4) are applicable for amended returns and requests for administrative adjustment filed on or after March 2, 2005. Sections 1.6664-2(c)(3)(i)(D)(1) and (c)(3)(ii)(B) and (C) are applicable for amended returns and requests for administrative adjustment filed on or after April 30, 2004. The applicability date for § 1.6664-2(c)(3)(ii)(A) varies depending upon which event occurs under § 1.6664-2(c)(3)(i). For purposes of § 1.6664-2(c)(3)(ii)(A), the date described in § 1.6664-2(c)(3)(i)(D)(1) is applicable for amended returns and requests for administrative adjustment filed on or after April 30, 2004. For purposes of § 1.6664-2(c)(3)(ii)(A), the dates described in § 1.6664-2(c)(3)(i)(A), (B), (C), (D)(2), and (E) are applicable for amended returns and requests for administrative adjustment filed on or after March 2, 2005. Section 1.6664-2(c)(1) through (c)(3), as contained in 26 CFR part 1 revised as of April 1, 2004 and as modified by Notice 2004-38, 2004-1 C.B. 949, applies with respect to returns and requests for administrative adjustment filed on or after April 30, 2004 and before March 2, 2005. Section 1.6664-2(c)(1) through (3), as contained in 26 CFR part 1 revised as of April 30, 2004, applies with respect to returns and requests for administrative adjustment filed before April 30, 2004. [Reg. § 1.6664-1.]

□ [*T.D. 8381*, 12-30-91. *Amended by T.D. 8617*, 8-31-95; *T.D. 9109*, 12-29-2003 *and T.D. 9309*, 1-8-2007.]

### [Reg. § 1.6664-2]

**§ 1.6664-2. Underpayment.**—(a) *Underpayment defined.*—In the case of income taxes imposed under subtitle A, an underpayment for purposes of section 6662, relating to the accuracy-related penalty, and section 6663, relating to the fraud penalty, means the amount by which any income tax imposed under this subtitle (as defined in paragraph (b) of the section) exceeds the excess of—

(1) The sum of—

(i) The amount shown as the tax by the taxpayer on his return (as defined in paragraph (c) of this section), plus

(ii) Amounts not so shown previously assessed (or collected without assessment) (as defined in paragraph (d) of this section), over

(2) The amount of rebates made (as defined in paragraph (e) of this section).

The definition of underpayment also may be expressed as—

$$Underpayment = W - (X + Y - Z),$$

where $W$ = the amount of income tax imposed; $X$ = the amount shown as the tax by the taxpayer on his return; $Y$ = amounts not so shown previously assessed (or collected without assessment); and $Z$ = the amount of rebates made.

(b) *Amount of income tax imposed.*—For purposes of paragraph (a) of this section, the "amount of income tax imposed" is the amount of tax imposed on the taxpayer under subtitle A for the taxable year, determined without regard to—

(1) The credits for tax withheld under sections 31 (relating to tax withheld on wages) and 33 (relating to tax withheld at source on nonresident aliens and foreign corporations);

(2) Payments of tax or estimated tax by the taxpayer;

(3) Any credit resulting from the collection of amounts assessed under section 6851 as the result of a termination assessment, or section 6861 as the result of a jeopardy assessment; and

(4) Any tax that the taxpayer is not required to assess on the return (such as the tax imposed by section 531 on the accumulated taxable income of a corporation).

(c) *Amount shown as the tax by the taxpayer on his return.*—(1) *Defined.*—For purposes of paragraph (a) of this section, the amount shown as the tax by the taxpayer on his return is the tax liability shown by the taxpayer on his return, determined without regard to the items listed in paragraphs (b)(1), (2), and (3) of this section, except that it is reduced by the excess of—

(i) The amounts shown by the taxpayer on his return as credits for tax withheld under section 31 (relating to tax withheld on wages) and section 33 (relating to tax withheld at source on nonresident aliens and foreign corporations), as payments of estimated tax,

or as any other payments made by the taxpayer with respect to a taxable year before filing the return for such taxable year, over

(ii) The amounts actually withheld, actually paid as estimated tax, or actually paid with respect to a taxable year before the return is filed for such taxable year.

(2) *Effect of qualified amended return.*—The amount shown as the tax by the taxpayer on his return includes an amount shown as additional tax on a qualified amended return (as defined in paragraph (c)(3) of this section), except that such amount is not included if it relates to a fraudulent position on the original return.

(3) *Qualified amended return defined.*—(i) *General rule.*—A qualified amended return is an amended return, or a timely request for an administrative adjustment under section 6227, filed after the due date of the return for the taxable year (determined with regard to extensions of time to file) and before the earliest of—

(A) The date the taxpayer is first contacted by the Internal Revenue Service (IRS) concerning any examination (including a criminal investigation) with respect to the return;

(B) The date any person is first contacted by the IRS concerning an examination of that person under section 6700 (relating to the penalty for promoting abusive tax shelters) for an activity with respect to which the taxpayer claimed any tax benefit on the return directly or indirectly through the entity, plan or arrangement described in section 6700(a)(1)(A);

(C) In the case of a pass-through item (as defined in § 1.6662-4(f)(5)), the date the pass-through entity (as defined in § 1.6662-4(f)(5)) is first contacted by the IRS in connection with an examination of the return to which the pass-through item relates;

(D)(1) The date on which the IRS serves a summons described in section 7609(f) relating to the tax liability of a person, group, or class that includes the taxpayer (or pass-through entity of which the taxpayer is a partner, shareholder, beneficiary, or holder of a residual interest in a REMIC) with respect to an activity for which the taxpayer claimed any tax benefit on the return directly or indirectly.

(2) The rule in paragraph (c)(3)(i)(D)(1) of this section applies to any return on which the taxpayer claimed a direct or indirect tax benefit from the type of activity that is the subject of the summons, regardless of whether the summons seeks the production of information for the taxable period covered by such return; and

(E) The date on which the Commissioner announces by revenue ruling, revenue procedure, notice, or announcement, to be published in the Internal Revenue Bulletin (see § 601.601(d)(2) of this chapter), a settlement initiative to compromise or waive penalties, in whole or in part, with respect to a listed transaction. This rule applies only to a taxpayer who participated in the listed transaction and for the taxable year(s) in which the taxpayer claimed any direct or indirect tax benefits from the listed transaction. The Commissioner may waive the requirements of this paragraph or identify a later date by which a taxpayer who participated in the listed transaction must file a qualified amended return in the published guidance announcing the listed transaction settlement initiative.

(ii) *Undisclosed listed transactions.*—An undisclosed listed transaction is a transaction that is the same as, or substantially similar to, a listed transaction within the meaning of § 1.6011-4(b)(2) (regardless of whether § 1.6011-4 requires the taxpayer to disclose the transaction) and was neither previously disclosed by the taxpayer within the meaning of § 1.6011-4 or § 1.6011-4T, nor disclosed under Announcement 2002-2 (2002-1 C.B. 304), (see § 601.601(d)(2)(ii) of this chapter) by the deadline therein. In the case of an undisclosed listed transaction for which a taxpayer claims any direct or indirect tax benefits on its return (regardless of whether the transaction was a listed transaction at the time the return was filed), an amended return or request for administrative adjustment under section 6227 will not be a qualified amended return if filed on or after the earliest of—

(A) The dates described in paragraph (c)(3)(i) of this section;

(B) The date on which the IRS first contacts any person regarding an examination of that person's liability under section 6707(a) with respect to the undisclosed listed transaction of the taxpayer; or

(C) The date on which the IRS requests, from any person who made a tax statement to or for the benefit of the taxpayer or from any person who gave the taxpayer material aid, assistance, or advice as described in section 6111(b)(1)(A)(i) with respect to the taxpayer, the information required to be included on a list under section 6112 relating to a transaction that was the same as, or substantially similar to, the undisclosed listed transaction, regardless of whether the taxpayer's information is required to be included on that list.

(4) *Special rules.*—(i) A qualified amended return includes an amended return that is filed to disclose information pursuant to §1.6662-3(c) or §1.6662-4(e) and (f) even though it does not report any additional tax liability. See §1.6662-3(c), §1.6662-4(f), and §1.6664-4(c) for rules relating to adequate disclosure.

(ii) The Commissioner may by revenue procedure prescribe the manner in which the rules of paragraph (c) of this section regarding qualified amended returns apply to particular classes of taxpayers.

(5) *Examples.* The following examples illustrate the provisions of paragraphs (c)(3) and (c)(4) of this section:

*Example 1.* T, an individual taxpayer, claimed tax benefits on its 2002 Federal income tax return from a transaction that is substantially similar to the transaction identified as a listed transaction in Notice 2002-65, 2002-2 C.B. 690 (Partnership Entity Straddle Tax Shelter). T did not disclose his participation in this transaction on a Form 8886, "Reportable Transaction Disclosure Statement," as required by §1.6011-4. On June 30, 2004, the IRS requested from P, T's material advisor, an investor list required to be maintained under section 6112. The section 6112 request, however, related to the type of transaction described in Notice 2003-81, 2003-2 C.B. 1223 (Tax Avoidance Using Offsetting Foreign Currency Option Contracts). T did not participate in (within the meaning of §1.6011-4(c)) a transaction described in Notice 2003-81. T may file a qualified amended return relating to the transaction described in Notice 2002-65 because T did not claim a tax benefit with respect to the listed transaction described in Notice 2003-81, which is the subject of the section 6112 request.

*Example 2.* The facts are the same as in *Example 1*, except that T's 2002 Federal income tax return reflected T's participation in the transaction described in Notice 2003-81. As of June 30, 2004, T may not file a qualified amended return for the 2002 tax year.

*Example 3.* (i) Corporation X claimed tax benefits from a transaction on its 2002 Federal income tax return. In October 2004, the IRS and Treasury Department identified the transaction as a listed transaction. In December 2004, the IRS contacted P concerning an examination of P's liability under section 6707(a) (as in effect prior to the amendment to section 6707 by section 816 of the American Jobs Creation Act of 2004 (the Jobs Act), Public Law 108-357 (118 Stat. 1418)). P is the organizer of a section 6111 tax shelter (as in effect prior to the amendment to section 6111 by section 815 of the Jobs Act) who provided representations to X regarding tax benefits from the transaction, and the IRS has contacted P about the failure to register that transaction. Three days later, X filed an amended return.

(ii) X's amended return is not a qualified amended return, because X did not disclose the transaction before the IRS contacted P. X's amended return would have been a qualified amended return if it was submitted prior to the date on which the IRS contacted P.

*Example 4.* The facts are the same as in *Example 3* except that, instead of contacting P concerning an examination under section 6707(a), in December 2004, the IRS served P with a John Doe summons described in section 7609(f) relating to the tax liability of participants in the type of transaction for which X claimed tax benefits on its return. X cannot file a qualified amended return after the John Doe summons has been served regardless of when, or whether, the transaction becomes a listed transaction.

*Example 5.* On November 30, 2003, the IRS served a John Doe summons described in section 7609(f) on Corporation Y, a credit card company. The summons requested the identity of, and information concerning, United States taxpayers who, during the taxable years 2001 and 2002, had signature authority over Corporation Y's credit cards issued by, through, or on behalf of certain offshore financial institutions. Corporation Y complied with the summons, and identified, among others, Taxpayer B. On May 31, 2004, before the IRS first contacted Taxpayer B concerning an examination of Taxpayer B's Federal income tax return for the taxable year 2002, Taxpayer B filed an amended return for that taxable year, that showed an increase in Taxpayer B's Federal income tax liability. Under paragraph (c)(3)(i)(D) of this section, the amended return is not a qualified amended return because it was not filed before the John Doe summons was served on Corporation Y.

*Example 6.* The facts are the same as in *Example 5*. Taxpayer B continued to maintain the offshore credit card account through 2003 and filed an original tax return for the 2003 taxable year claiming tax benefits attributable to the existence of the account. On March 21, 2005, Taxpayer B filed an amended return for the taxable year 2003, that showed an increase in Taxpayer B's Federal income tax liability. Under paragraph (c)(3)(i)(D) of this section, the amended return is not a qualified amended return because it was not filed before the John Doe summons for 2001 and 2002 was served on Corporation Y, and the return reflects benefits from the type of activity that is the subject of the John Doe summons.

*Example 7.* (i) On November 30, 2003, the IRS served a John Doe summons described in section 7609(f) on Corporation Y, a credit card company. The summons requested the identity of, and information

concerning, United States taxpayers who, during the taxable years 2001 and 2002, had signature authority over Corporation Y's credit cards issued by, through, or on behalf of certain offshore financial institutions. Taxpayer C did not have signature authority over any of Corporation Y's credit cards during either 2001 or 2002 and, therefore, was not a person described in the John Doe summons.

(ii) In 2003, Taxpayer C first acquired signature authority over a Corporation Y credit card issued by an offshore financial institution. Because Taxpayer C did not have signature authority during 2001 or 2002 over a Corporation Y credit card issued by an offshore financial institution, and was therefore not covered by the John Doe summons served on November 30, 2003, Taxpayer C's ability to file a qualified amended return for the 2003 taxable year is not limited by paragraph (c)(3)(i)(D) of this section.

(d) *Amounts not so shown previously assessed (or collected without assessment).*—For purposes of paragraph (a) of this section, "amounts not so shown previously assessed" means only amounts assessed before the return is filed that were not shown on the return, such as termination assessments under section 6851 and jeopardy assessments under section 6861 made prior to the filing of the return for the taxable year. For purposes of paragraph (a) of this section, the amount "collected without assessment" is the amount by which the total of the credits allowable under section 31 (relating to tax withheld on wages) and section 33 (relating to tax withheld at source on nonresident aliens and foreign corporations), estimated tax payments, and other payments in satisfaction of tax liability made before the return is filed, exceed the tax shown on the return (provided such excess has not been refunded or allowed as a credit to the taxpayer).

(e) *Rebates.*—The term "rebate" means so much of an abatement credit, refund or other repayment, as was made on the ground that the tax imposed was less than the excess of—

(1) The sum of—

(i) The amount shown as the tax by the taxpayer on his return, plus

(ii) Amounts not so shown previously assessed (or collected without assessment), over

(2) Rebates previously made.

(f) *Underpayments for certain carryback years not reduced by amount of carrybacks.*—The amount of an underpayment for a taxable year that is attributable to conduct proscribed by sections 6662 or 6663 is not reduced on account of a carryback of a loss, deduction or credit to that year. Such conduct includes negligence or disregard of rules or regulations; a substantial understatement of income tax; and a substantial (or gross) valuation misstatement under chapter 1, provided that the applicable dollar limitation is satisfied for the carryback year.

(g) *Examples.*—The following examples illustrate this section:

*Example 1.* Taxpayer's 1990 return showed a tax liability of $18,000. Taxpayer had no amounts previously assessed (or collected without assessment) and received no rebates of tax. Taxpayer claimed a credit in the amount of $23,000 for income tax withheld under section 3402, which resulted in a refund received of $5,000. It is later determined that the taxpayer should have reported additional income and that the correct tax for the taxable year is $25,500. There is an underpayment of $7,500, determined as follows:

| | | |
|---|---:|---:|
| Tax imposed under subtitle A | | $25,500 |
| Tax shown on return | $18,000 | |
| Tax previously assessed (or collected without assessment) | None | |
| Amount of rebates made | None | |
| Balance | | $18,000 |
| Underpayment | | $7,500 |

*Example 2.* The facts are the same as in *Example 1* except that the taxpayer failed to claim on the return a credit of $1,500 for income tax withheld. This $1,500 constitutes an amount collected without assessment as defined in paragraph (d) of this section. The underpayment is $6,000, determined as follows:

| | | |
|---|---:|---:|
| Tax imposed under subtitle A | | $25,500 |
| Tax shown on return | $18,000 | |
| Tax previously assessed (or collected without assessment) | 1,500 | |
| Amount of rebates made | None | |
| Balance | | $19,500 |
| Underpayment | | $6,000 |

*Example 3.* On Form 1040 filed for tax year 1990, taxpayer reported a tax liability of $10,000, estimated tax payments of $15,000, and received a refund of $5,000. Estimated tax payments actually made with respect to tax year 1990 were only $7,000. For purposes of determining the amount of underpayment subject to a penalty under section 6662 or section 6663, the tax shown on the return is $2,000 (reported tax liability of $10,000 reduced by the overstated estimated

tax of $8,000 ($15,000 – $7,000)). The underpayment is $8,000, determined as follows:

| | |
|---|---|
| Tax imposed under subtitle A | $10,000 |
| Tax shown on return | $2,000 |
| Tax previously assessed (or collected without assessment) | None |
| Amount of rebates made | None |
| Balance | $2,000 |
| Underpayment | $8,000 |

[Reg. § 1.6664-2.]

☐ [*T.D. 8381, 12-30-91. Amended by T.D. 9186, 3-1-2005 and T.D. 9309, 1-8-2007.*]

### [Reg. § 1.6664-3]

**§1.6664-3. Ordering rules for determining the total amount of penalties imposed.**—(a) *In general.*—This section provides rules for determining the order in which adjustments to a return are taken into account for the purpose of computing the total amount of penalties imposed under sections 6662 and 6663, where—

(1) There is at least one adjustment with respect to which no penalty has been imposed and at least one with respect to which a penalty has been imposed, or

(2) There are at least two adjustments with respect to which penalties have been imposed and they have been imposed at different rates.

This section also provides rules for allocating unclaimed prepayment credits to adjustments to a return.

(b) *Order in which adjustments are taken into account.*—In computing the portions of an underpayment subject to penalties imposed under sections 6662 and 6663, adjustments to a return are considered made in the following order:

(1) Those with respect to which no penalties have been imposed.

(2) Those with respect to which a penalty has been imposed at a 20 percent rate (*i.e.,* a penalty for negligence or disregard of rules or regulations, substantial understatement of income tax, or substantial valuation misstatement, under sections 6662(b)(1) through 6662(b)(3), respectively).

(3) Those with respect to which a penalty has been imposed at a 40 percent rate (*i.e.,* a penalty for a gross valuation misstatement under sections 6662(b)(3) and (h)).

(4) Those with respect to which a penalty has been imposed at a 75 percent rate (*i.e.,* a penalty for fraud under section 6663).

(c) *Manner in which unclaimed prepayment credits are allocated.*—Any income tax withholding or other payment made before a return was filed, that was neither claimed on the return nor previously allowed as a credit against the tax liability for the taxable year (an "unclaimed prepayment credit"), is allocated as follows—

(1) If an unclaimed prepayment credit is allocable to a particular adjustment, such credit is applied in full in determining the amount of the underpayment resulting from such adjustment.

(2) If an unclaimed prepayment credit is not allocable to a particular adjustment, such credit is applied in accordance with the ordering rules set forth in paragraph (b) of this section.

(d) *Examples.*—The following examples illustrate the rules of this §1.6664-3. These examples do not take into account the reasonable cause exception to the accuracy-related penalty under §1.6664-4.

*Example 1.* A and B, husband and wife, filed a joint federal income tax return for calendar year 1989, reporting taxable income of $15,800 and a tax liability of $2,374. A and B had no amounts previously assessed (or collected without assessment) and no rebates had been made. Subsequently, the return was examined and the following adjustments and penalties were agreed to:

| | |
|---|---|
| Adjustment #1 (No penalty imposed) | $1,000 |
| Adjustment #2 (Substantial understatement penalty imposed) | 40,000 |
| Adjustment # 3 (Civil fraud penalty imposed) | 45,000 |
| Total adjustments | $86,000 |
| Taxable income shown on return | 15,800 |
| Taxable income as corrected | $101,800 |

Computation of underpayment:

| | | |
|---|---|---|
| Tax imposed by subtitle A | | $25,828 |
| Tax shown on return | $2,374 | |
| Previous assessments | None | |
| Rebates | None | |
| Balance | | $2,374 |
| Underpayment | | $23,454 |

Computation of the portions of the underpayment on which penalties under section 6662(b)(2) and section 6663 are imposed:

*Step 1* Determine the portion, if any, of the underpayment on which no accuracy-related or fraud penalty is imposed:

| | |
|---|---|
| Taxable income shown on return | $15,800 |
| Adjustment #1 | 1,000 |
| "Adjusted" taxable income | $16,800 |
| Tax on "adjusted" taxable income | $2,524 |
| Tax shown on return | 2,374 |
| Portion of underpayment on which no penalty is imposed | $150 |

*Step 2* Determine the portion, if any, of the underpayment on which a penalty of 20 percent is imposed:

| | |
|---|---|
| "Adjusted" taxable income from step 1 | $16,800 |
| Adjustment #2 | 40,000 |
| "Adjusted" taxable income | $56,800 |
| Tax on "adjusted" taxable income | $11,880 |
| Tax on "adjusted" taxable income from step 1 | 2,524 |
| Portion of underpayment on which 20 percent penalty is imposed | $9,356 |

*Step 3* Determine the portion, if any, of the underpayment on which a penalty of 75 percent is imposed:

| | | |
|---|---|---|
| Total underpayment | | $23,454 |
| Less the sum of the portions of such underpayment determined in: | | |
| Step 1 | $150 | |
| Step 2 | $9,356 | |
| Total | | $9,506 |
| Portion of underpayment on which 75 percent penalty is imposed | | $13,948 |

*Example 2.* The facts are the same as in *Example 1* except that the taxpayers failed to claim on their return a credit of $1,500 for income tax withheld on unreported additional income that resulted in Adjustment #2. Because the unclaimed prepayment credit is allocable to Adjustment #2, the portion of the underpayment attributable to that adjustment is $7,856 ($9,356 – $1,500). The portions of the underpayment attributable to Adjustments #1 and #3 remain the same.

*Example 3.* The facts are the same as in *Example 1* except that the taxpayers made a timely estimated tax payment of $1,500 for 1989 which they failed to claim (and which the Service had not previously allowed). This unclaimed prepayment credit is not allocable to any particular adjustment. Therefore, the credit is allocated first to the portion of the underpayment on which no penalty is imposed ($150). The remaining amount ($1,350) is allocated next to the 20 percent penalty portion of the underpayment ($9,356). Thus, the portion of the underpayment that is not penalized is zero ($150 – $150), the portion subject to a 20 percent penalty is $8,006 ($9,356 – $1,350) and the portion subject to a 75 percent penalty is unchanged at $13,948. [Reg. § 1.6664-3.]

☐ [*T.D. 8381, 12-30-91.*]

### [Reg. § 1.6664-4]

**§1.6664-4. Reasonable cause and good faith exception to section 6662 penalties.**—(a) *In general.*—No penalty may be imposed under section 6662 with respect to any portion of an underpayment upon a showing by the taxpayer that there was reasonable cause for, and the taxpayer acted in good faith with respect to, such portion. Rules for determining whether the reasonable cause and good faith exception applies are set forth in paragraphs (b) through (h) of this section.

(b) *Facts and circumstances taken into account.*—(1) *In general.*—The determination of whether a taxpayer acted with reasonable cause and in good faith is made on a case-by-case basis, taking into account all pertinent facts and circumstances. (See paragraph (e) of this section for certain rules relating to a substantial understatement penalty attributable to tax shelter items of corporations.) Generally, the most important factor is the extent of the taxpayer's effort to assess the taxpayer's proper tax liability. Circumstances that may indicate reasonable cause and good faith include an honest misunderstanding of fact or law that is reasonable in light of all of the facts and circumstances, including the experience, knowledge, and education of the taxpayer. An isolated computational or transcriptional error generally is not inconsistent with reasonable cause and good faith. Reliance on an information return or on the advice of a professional tax advisor or an appraiser does not necessarily demonstrate reasonable cause and good faith. Similarly, reasonable cause and good faith is not necessarily indicated by reliance on facts that, unknown to the taxpayer, are incorrect. Reliance on an information return, professional advice, or other facts, however, constitutes reasonable cause and good faith if, under all the circumstances, such reliance was reasonable and the taxpayer acted in good faith. (See paragraph (c) of this section for certain rules relating to reliance on the advice of others.) For example, reliance on erroneous information (such as an error relating to the cost or adjusted basis of property, the date property was placed in service, or the amount of opening or closing inventory) inadvertently included in data compiled by the various divisions of a multidivisional corporation or in financial books and records prepared by those divisions generally indicates reasonable cause and good faith, provided the corporation employed internal controls and procedures, reasonable under the circumstances, that were designed to identify such factual errors. Reasonable cause and good faith ordinarily is not indicated by the mere fact that there is an appraisal of the value of property. Other factors to consider include the methodology and assumptions underlying the appraisal, the appraised value, the relationship between appraised value and purchase price, the circumstances under which the appraisal was obtained, and the appraiser's relationship to the taxpayer or to the activity in which the property is used. (See paragraph (g) of this section for certain rules relating to appraisals for charitable deduction property.) A taxpayer's reliance on erroneous information reported on a Form W-2, Form 1099, or other information return indicates reasonable cause and good faith, provided the taxpayer did not know or have reason to know that the information was incorrect. Generally, a taxpayer knows, or has reason to know, that the information on an information return is incorrect if such information is inconsistent with other information reported or otherwise furnished to the taxpayer, or with the taxpayer's knowledge of the transaction. This knowledge includes, for example, the taxpayer's knowledge of the terms of his employment relationship or of the rate of return on a payor's obligation.

(2) *Examples.*—The following examples illustrate this paragraph (b). They do not involve tax shelter items. (See paragraph (e) of this section for certain rules relating to the substantial understatement penalty attributable to the tax shelter items of corporations.)

*Example 1.* A, an individual calendar year taxpayer, engages B, a professional tax advisor, to give A advice concerning the deductibility of certain state and local taxes. A provides B with full details concerning the taxes at issue. B advises A that the taxes are fully deductible. A, in preparing his own tax return, claims a deduction for the taxes. Absent other facts, and assuming the facts and circumstances surrounding B's advice and A's reliance on such advice satisfy the requirements of paragraph (c) of this section, A is considered to have demonstrated good faith by seeking the advice of a professional tax advisor, and to have shown reasonable cause for any underpayment attributable to the deduction claimed for the taxes. However, if A had sought advice from someone that A knew, or should have known, lacked knowledge in the relevant aspects of Federal tax law, or if other facts demonstrate that A failed to act reasonably or in good faith, A would not be considered to have shown reasonable cause or to have acted in good faith.

*Example 2.* C, an individual, sought advice from D, a friend who was not a tax professional, as to how C might reduce his Federal tax obligations. D advised C that, for a nominal investment in Corporation X, D had received certain tax benefits which virtually eliminated D's Federal tax liability. D also named other investors who had received similar benefits. Without further inquiry, C invested in X and claimed the benefits that he had been assured by D were due him. In this case, C did not make any good faith attempt to ascertain the correctness of what D had advised him concerning his tax matters, and is not considered to have reasonable cause for the underpayment attributable to the benefits claimed.

*Example 3.* E, an individual, worked for Company X doing odd jobs and filling in for other employees when necessary. E worked irregular hours and was paid by the hour. The amount of E's pay check differed from week to week. The Form W-2 furnished to E reflected wages for 1990 in the amount of $29,729. It did not, however, include compensation of $1,467 paid for some hours E worked. Relying on the Form W-2, E filed a return reporting wages of $29,729. E had no reason to know that the amount reported on the Form W-2 was incorrect. Under the circumstances, E is considered to have acted in good faith in relying on the Form W-2 and to have reasonable cause for the underpayment attributable to the unreported wages.

*Example 4.* H, an individual, did not enjoy preparing his tax returns and procrastinated in doing so until April 15th. On April 15th, H hurriedly gathered together his tax records and materials, prepared a return, and mailed it before midnight. The return contained numerous errors, some of which were in H's favor and some of which were not. The net result of all the adjustments, however, was an underpayment of tax by H. Under these circumstances, H is not considered to have reasonable cause for the underpayment or to have acted in good faith in attempting to file an accurate return.

(c) *Reliance on opinion or advice.*—(1) *Facts and circumstances; minimum requirements.*—All facts and circumstances must be taken into account in determining whether a taxpayer has reasonably relied in good faith on advice (including the opinion of a professional tax advisor) as to the treatment of the taxpayer (or any entity, plan, or arrangement) under Federal tax law. For example, the taxpayer's education, sophistication and business experience will be relevant in determining whether the taxpayer's reliance on tax advice was reasonable and made in good faith. In no event will a taxpayer be considered to have reasonably relied in good faith on advice (including an opinion) unless the requirements of this paragraph (c)(1) are satisfied. The fact that these requirements are satisfied, however, will not necessarily establish that the taxpayer reasonably relied on the advice (including the opinion of a tax advisor) in good faith. For example, reliance may not be reasonable or in good faith if the taxpayer knew, or reasonably should have known, that the advisor lacked knowledge in the relevant aspects of Federal tax law.

(i) *All facts and circumstances considered.*—The advice must be based upon all pertinent facts and circumstances and the law as it relates to those facts and circumstances. For example, the advice must take into account the taxpayer's purposes (and the relative weight of such purposes) for entering into a transaction and for structuring a transaction in a particular manner. In addition, the requirements of this paragraph (c)(1) are not satisfied if the taxpayer fails to disclose a fact that it knows, or reasonably should know, to be relevant to the proper tax treatment of an item.

(ii) *No unreasonable assumptions.*—The advice must not be based on unreasonable factual or legal assumptions (including assumptions as to future events) and must not unreasonably rely on the representations, statements, findings, or agreements of the taxpayer or any other person. For example, the advice must not be based upon a representation or assumption which the taxpayer knows, or has reason to know, is unlikely to be true, such as an inaccurate representation or assumption as to the taxpayer's purposes for entering into a transaction or for structuring a transaction in a particular manner.

(iii) *Reliance on the invalidity of a regulation.*—A taxpayer may not rely on an opinion or advice that a regulation is invalid to establish that the taxpayer acted with reasonable cause and good faith unless the taxpayer adequately disclosed, in accordance with § 1.6662-3(c)(2), the position that the regulation in question is invalid.

(2) *Advice defined.*—Advice is any communication, including the opinion of a professional tax advisor, setting forth the analysis or conclusion of a person, other than the taxpayer, provided to (or for the benefit of) the taxpayer and on which the taxpayer relies, directly or indirectly, with respect to the imposition of the section 6662 accuracy-related penalty. Advice does not have to be in any particular form.

(3) *Cross-reference.*—For rules applicable to advisors, see e.g., §§ 1.6694-1 through 1.6694-3 (regarding preparer penalties), 31 CFR 10.22 (regarding diligence as to accuracy), 31 CFR 10.33 (regarding tax shelter opinions), and 31 CFR 10.34 (regarding standards for advising with respect to tax return positions and for preparing or signing returns).

(d) *Underpayments attributable to reportable transactions.*—If any portion of an underpayment is attributable to a reportable transaction, as defined in § 1.6011-4(b) (or § 1.6011-4T(b), as applicable), then failure by the taxpayer to disclose the transaction in accordance with § 1.6011-4 (or § 1.6011-4T, as applicable) is a strong indication that the taxpayer did not act in good faith with respect to the portion of the underpayment attributable to the reportable transaction.

(e) *Pass-through items.*—The determination of whether a taxpayer acted with reasonable cause and in good faith with respect to an underpayment that is related to an item reflected on the return of a pass-through entity is made on the basis of all pertinent facts and circumstances, including the taxpayer's own actions, as well as the actions of the pass-through entity.

(f) *Special rules for substantial understatement penalty attributable to tax shelter items of corporations.*—(1) *In general; facts and circumstances.*—The determination of whether a corporation acted with reasonable cause and in good faith in its treatment of a tax shelter item (as defined in § 1.6662-4(g)(3)) is based on all pertinent facts and circumstances. Paragraphs (f)(2), (3), and (4) of this section set forth rules that apply, in the case of a penalty attributable to a substantial understatement of income tax (within the meaning of section 6662(d)), in determining whether a corporation acted with reasonable cause and in good faith with respect to a tax shelter item.

(2) *Reasonable cause based on legal justification.*—(i) *Minimum requirements.*—A corporation's legal justification (as defined in paragraph (f)(2)(ii) of this section) may be taken into account, as appropriate, in establishing that the corporation acted with reasonable cause and in good faith in its treatment of a tax shelter item only if the authority requirement of paragraph (f)(2)(i)(A) of this section and the belief requirement of paragraph (f)(2)(i)(B) of this section are satisfied (the minimum requirements). Thus, a failure to satisfy the minimum requirements will preclude a finding of reasonable cause

and good faith based (in whole or in part) on the corporation's legal justification.

(A) *Authority requirement.*—The authority requirement is satisfied only if there is substantial authority (within the meaning of §1.6662-4(d)) for the tax treatment of the item.

(B) *Belief requirement.*—The belief requirement is satisfied only if, based on all facts and circumstances, the corporation reasonably believed, at the time the return was filed, that the tax treatment of the item was more likely than not the proper treatment. For purposes of the preceding sentence, a corporation is considered reasonably to believe that the tax treatment of an item is more likely than not the proper-tax treatment if (without taking into account the possibility that a return will not be audited, that an issue will not be raised on audit, or that an issue will be settled)—

(1) The corporation analyzes the pertinent facts and authorities in the manner described in §1.6662-4(d)(3)(ii), and in reliance upon that analysis, reasonably concludes in good faith that there is a greater than 50-percent likelihood that the tax treatment of the item will be upheld if challenged by the Internal Revenue Service; or

(2) The corporation reasonably relies in good faith on the opinion of a professional tax advisor, if the opinion is based on the tax advisor's analysis of the pertinent facts and authorities in the manner described in §1.6662-4(d)(3)(ii) and unambiguously states that the tax advisor concludes that there is a greater than 50-percent likelihood that the tax treatment of the item will be upheld if challenged by the Internal Revenue Service. (For this purpose, the requirements of paragraph (c) of this section must be met with respect to the opinion of a professional tax advisor.)

(ii) *Legal justification defined.*—For purposes of this paragraph (f), *legal justification* includes any justification relating to the treatment or characterization under the Federal tax law of the tax shelter item or of the entity, plan, or arrangement that gave rise to the tax benefit. Thus, a taxpayer's belief (whether independently formed or based on the advice of others) as to the merits of the taxpayer's underlying position is a legal justification.

(3) *Minimum requirements not dispositive.*—Satisfaction of the minimum requirements of paragraph (f)(2) of this section is an important factor to be considered in determining whether a corporate taxpayer acted with reasonable cause and in good faith, but is not necessarily dispositive. For example, depending on the circumstances, satisfaction of the minimum requirements may not be dispositive if the taxpayer's participation in the tax shelter lacked significant business purpose, if the taxpayer claimed tax benefits that are unreasonable in comparison to the taxpayer's investment in the tax shelter, or if the taxpayer agreed with the organizer or promoter of the tax shelter that the taxpayer would protect the confidentiality of the tax aspects of the structure of the tax shelter.

(4) *Other factors.*—Facts and circumstances other than a corporation's legal justification may be taken into account, as appropriate, in determining whether the corporation acted with reasonable cause

and in good faith with respect to a tax shelter item regardless of whether the minimum requirements of paragraph (f)(2) of this section are satisfied.

(g) *Transactions between persons described in section 482 and net section 482 transfer price adjustments.*—[Reserved]

(h) *Valuation misstatements of charitable deduction property.*—(1) *In general.*—There may be reasonable cause and good faith with respect to a portion of an underpayment that is attributable to a substantial (or gross) valuation misstatement of charitable deduction property (as defined in paragraph (h)(2) of this section) only if—

(i) The claimed value of the property was based on a qualified appraisal (as defined in paragraph (h)(2) of this section) by a qualified appraiser (as defined in paragraph (h)(2) of this section); and

(ii) In addition to obtaining a qualified appraisal, the taxpayer made a good faith investigation of the value of the contributed property.

(2) *Definitions.*—For purposes of this paragraph (h):

*Charitable deduction property* means any property (other than money or publicly traded securities, as defined in §1.170A-13(c)(7)(xi)) contributed by the taxpayer in a contribution for which a deduction was claimed under section 170.

*Qualified appraisal* means a qualified appraisal as defined in §1.170A-13(c)(3).

*Qualified appraiser* means a qualified appraiser as defined in §1.170A-13(c)(5).

(3) *Special rules.*—The rules of this paragraph (h) apply regardless of whether §1.170A-13 permits a taxpayer to claim a charitable contribution deduction for the property without obtaining a qualified appraisal. The rules of this paragraph (h) apply in addition to the generally applicable rules concerning reasonable cause and good faith. [Reg. §1.6664-4.]

☐ [*T.D.* 8381, 12-30-91. *Amended by T.D.* 8617, 8-31-95; *T.D.* 8790, 12-1-98 *and T.D.* 9109, 12-29-2003.]

### [Reg. §1.6664-4T]

**§1.6664-4T. Reasonable cause and good faith exception to section 6662 penalties.**—(a) through (e) [Reserved].

(f) *Transactions between persons described in section 482 and net section 482 transfer price adjustments.*—For purposes of applying the reasonable cause and good faith exception of section 6664(c) to net section 482 adjustments, the rules of §1.6662-6(d) apply. A taxpayer that does not satisfy the rules of §1.6662-6(d) for a net section 482 adjustment cannot satisfy the reasonable cause and good faith exception under section 6664(c). The rules of this section apply to underpayments subject to the transactional penalty in §1.6662-6(b). If the standards of the net section 482 penalty exclusion provisions under §1.6662-6(d) are met with respect to such underpayments, then the taxpayer will be considered to have acted with reasonable cause and good faith for purposes of this section. [Temporary Reg. §1.6664-4T.]

☐ [*T.D.* 8519, 1-27-94. *Amended by T.D.* 8656, 2-8-96.]

# ASSESSABLE PENALTIES

## General Provisions

### [Reg. §301.6671-1]

**§301.6671-1. Rules for application of assessable penalties.**—(a) *Penalty assessed as tax.*—The penalties and liabilities provided by subchapter B, chapter 68, of the Code (sections 6671 to 6675, inclusive) shall be paid upon notice and demand by the district director or the director of the regional service center and shall be assessed and collected in the same manner as taxes. Except as otherwise provided, any reference in the Code to "tax" imposed thereunder shall also be deemed to refer to the penalties and liabilities provided by subchapter B of chapter 68.

(b) *Person defined.*—For purposes of subchapter B of chapter 68, the term "person" includes an officer or employee of a corporation, or a member or employee of a partnership, who as such officer, employee, or member is under a duty to perform the act in respect of which the violation occurs. [Reg. §301.6671-1.]

☐ [*T.D.* 6268, 11-15-57. *Amended by T.D.* 6498, 10-24-60 *and T.D.* 6585, 12-27-61.]

### [Reg. §301.6672-1]

**§301.6672-1. Failure to collect and pay over tax, or attempt to evade or defeat tax.**—Any person required to collect, truthfully

account for, and pay over any tax imposed by the Code who willfully fails to collect such tax, or truthfully account for and pay over such tax, or willfully attempts in any manner to evade or defeat any such tax or the payment thereof, shall, in addition to other penalties, be liable to a penalty equal to the total amount of the tax evaded, or not collected, or not accounted for and paid over. The penalty imposed by section 6672 applies only to the collection, accounting for, or payment over of taxes imposed on a person other than the person who is required to collect, account for, and pay over such taxes. No penalty under section 6653, relating to failure to pay tax, shall be imposed for any offense to which this section is applicable. For further guidance regarding the determination of the proper address for mailing the notice required under section 6672(b)(1), see §301.6212-2. [Reg. §301.6672-1.]

☐ [*T.D.* 6268, 11-15-57. *Amended by T.D.* 8939, 1-11-2001.]

### [Reg. §301.6673-1]

**§301.6673-1. Damages assessable for instituting proceedings before the Tax Court merely for delay.**—Any damages awarded to the United States by the Tax Court under section 6673 against a taxpayer for instituting proceedings before the Tax Court merely for delay shall be assessed at the same time as the deficiency and shall be paid upon notice and demand from the district director or the director of the regional service center and shall be collected as a part of the tax. [Reg. § 301.6673-1.]

☐ *[T.D. 6268, 11-15-57. Amended by T.D. 6585, 12-27-61.]*

### [Reg. § 31.6674-1]

**§ 31.6674-1. Penalties for fraudulent statement or failure to furnish statement.**—Any person required to furnish a statement to an employee under the provisions of section 6051 or 6053(b) is subject to a civil penalty for willful failure to furnish such statement in the manner, at the time, and showing the information required under such section (or § 31.6051-1 or § 31.6053-2), or for willfully furnishing a false or fraudulent statement to an employee. The penalty for each such violation is $50, which shall be assessed and collected in the same manner as the tax imposed on employers under the Federal Insurance Contributions Act. See section 7204 for criminal penalty. [Reg. § 31.6674-1.]

☐ *[T.D. 6472, 6-22-60. Amended by T.D. 7001, 1-17-69.]*

### [Reg. § 301.6674-1]

**§ 301.6674-1. Fraudulent statement or failure to furnish statement to employee.**—For regulations under section 6674, see § 31.6674-1 of this chapter (Employment Tax Regulations). [Reg. § 301.6674-1.]

☐ *[T.D. 6268, 11-15-57. Amended by T.D. 6498, 10-24-60.]*

### [Reg. § 301.6678-1]

**§ 301.6678-1. Failure to furnish statements.**—(a) *In general.*—In the case of each failure to furnish a statement required—

(1) Under section 6042(c) and § 1.6042-4 to a person with respect to whom a return has been made under section 6042(a)(1), relating to information returns with respect to payments of dividends aggregating $10 or more in a calendar year,

(2) Under section 6044(e) and § 1.6044-5 to a person with respect to whom a return has been made under section 6044(a)(1), relating to information returns with respect to certain payments by cooperatives aggregating $10 or more in a calendar year,

(3) Under section 6049(c) and § 1.6049-3 to a person with respect to whom a return has been made under section 6049(a)(1), relating to information returns with respect to payments of interest aggregating $10 or more in a calendar year,

(4) Under section 6039(b) and § 1.6039-2 to a person with respect to whom a return has been made under section 6039(a), relating to information returns with respect to certain stock option transactions occurring in a calendar year, or

(5) Under section 6052(b) and § 1.6052-2 to a person with respect to whom a return has been made under section 6052(a), relating to information returns with respect to payment of wages in the form of group-term life insurance provided for an employee on his life, within the time prescribed for furnishing such statement (determined with regard to any extension of time for furnishing), there shall be paid by the person failing to so furnish the statement $10 for each such statement not so furnished. However, the total amount imposed on the delinquent person for all such failures during a calendar year shall not exceed $25,000.

(b) *Manner of payment.*—The penalty imposed under section 6678 and this section on any person shall be paid in the same manner as tax upon the issuance of a notice and demand therefor.

(c) *Showing of reasonable cause.*—The penalty imposed by section 6678 shall not apply with respect to a failure to furnish a statement within the time prescribed if it is established to the satisfaction of the district director or the director of the regional service center that such failure was due to reasonable cause and not to willful neglect. An affirmative showing of reasonable cause must be made in the form of a written statement, containing a declaration that it is made under the penalties of perjury, setting forth all the facts alleged as a reasonable cause. [Reg. § 301.6678-1.]

☐ *[T.D. 6628, 12-27-62. Amended by T.D. 6887, 6-23-66.]*

### [Reg. § 301.6679-1]

**§ 301.6679-1. Failure to file returns, etc. with respect to foreign corporations or foreign partnerships for taxable years beginning after September 3, 1982.**—(a) *Civil penalty.*—(1) *In general.*—In addition to any criminal penalty provided by law, each United States citizen, resident or person filing a separate or joint information return, or on whose behalf a return is filed, pursuant to sections 6035, 6046, or 6046A, and the regulations thereunder, who fails to file such a return within the time provided, or who files a return which does not show the required information, shall pay a penalty of $1,000, unless such failure is shown to be due to reasonable cause.

(2) *Joint return.*—The penalty imposed by section 6679 and this section shall apply to each United States citizen, resident, or person

filing a joint return pursuant to the provisions of section 6035, 6046, or 6046A, which does not show the required information.

(3) *Showing of reasonable cause.*—The district director, the director of the Internal Revenue service center, and the Director of International Operations are authorized to make the determination that such failure was due to a reasonable cause and that, accordingly, the penalty imposed by section 6679 shall not apply. An affirmative showing of reasonable cause must be made in the form of a written statement, containing a declaration that it is made under the penalties of perjury, setting forth all the facts alleged as a reasonable cause. If the taxpayer exercises ordinary business care and prudence and is nevertheless unable to furnish any item of information required under section 6035, 6046, or 6046A and the regulations thereunder, such failure shall be considered due to a reasonable cause. In determining the extent of a taxpayer's ability to obtain information, the percentage of stock owned by such taxpayer and the nature of the other interests in the foreign corporation will be considered.

(b) *Deficiency procedures not to apply.*—The penalty imposed by section 6679 may be assessed and collected without regard to the deficiency procedures provided by subchapter B of chapter 63 of the Code. [Reg. § 301.6679-1.]

☐ *[T.D. 6623, 11-30-62. Amended by T.D. 7288, 9-28-73; T.D. 7542, 4-28-78 and T.D. 8028, 6-3-85.]*

### [Reg. § 31.6682-1]

**§ 31.6682-1. False information with respect to withholding.**—(a) *Civil penalty.*—If any individual makes a statement under section 3402 (relating to income tax collected at source) which results in a lesser amount of income tax actually deducted and withheld than is properly allowable under section 3402 and, at the time the statement was made, there was no reasonable basis for the statement, the individual shall pay a penalty of $500 for the statement. There was a reasonable basis for a statement of the number of exemptions an individual claimed on a Form W-4, if the individual properly completed the Form W-4 by taking into account only allowable amounts for items which are allowable and by computing the number of exemptions in accordance with the instructions on the Form W-4. This penalty is in addition to any criminal penalty provided by law. This penalty may be assessed at any time after the statement is made, until the expiration of the applicable statute of limitations.

(b) *Deficiency procedures not to apply.*—The civil penalty imposed by section 6682 may be assessed and collected without regard to the deficiency procedures provided by subchapter B of chapter 63 of the Code. [Reg. § 31.6682-1.]

☐ *[T.D. 7963, 7-13-84.]*

### [Reg. § 301.6682-1]

**§ 301.6682-1. False information with respect to withholding allowances based on itemized deductions.**—For regulations under section 6682, see § 31.6682-1 of this chapter (Employment Tax Regulations). [Reg. § 301.6682-1.]

☐ *[T.D. 7065, 10-22-70.]*

### [Reg. § 301.6684-1]

**§ 301.6684-1. Assessable penalties with respect to liability for tax under chapter 42.**—(a) *In general.*—If any person (as defined in section 7701(a)(1)) becomes liable for tax under any section of chapter 42 (other than section 4940 or 4948(a)), relating to private foundations, by reason of any act or failure to act which is not due to reasonable cause and either—

(1) Such person has theretofore (at any time) been liable for tax under any section of such chapter (other than section 4940 or 4948(a)), or

(2) Such act or failure to act is both willful and flagrant, then such person shall be liable for a penalty equal to the amount of such tax.

(b) *Showing of reasonable cause.*—The penalty imposed by section 6684 shall not apply to any person with respect to a violation of any section of chapter 42 if it is established to the satisfaction of the district director or director of the internal revenue service center that such violation was due to reasonable cause. An affirmative showing of reasonable cause must be made in the form of a written statement, containing a declaration by such person that it is made under the penalties of perjury, setting forth all the facts alleged as reasonable cause.

(c) *Willful and flagrant.*—For purposes of this section, the term "willful and flagrant" has the same meaning as such term possesses in section 507(a)(2)(A) and the regulations thereunder.

(d) *Effective date.*—This section shall take effect on January 1, 1970. [Reg. § 301.6684-1.]

☐ [*T.D.* 7127, 6-14-71.]

### [Reg. § 301.6685-1]

**§ 301.6685-1. Assessable penalties with respect to private foundations' failure to comply with section 6104(d).**—(a) *In general.*—In addition to the penalty imposed by section 7207, relating to fraudulent returns, statements, or other documents, any person (as defined in paragraph (b) of this section) who is required to comply with the requirements of section 6104(d), relating to public inspection of private foundations' annual returns, and who fails so to comply, if such failure is willful, shall pay a penalty of $1,000 with respect to each such return with respect to which there is a failure so to comply.

(b) *Person.*—For purposes of this section, the term "person" means any officer, director, trustee, employee, member, or other individual whose duty it is to perform the act in respect of which the failure occurs.

(c) *Effective date.*—This section shall take effect on January 1, 1970.

(d) *Cross reference.*—For the amount imposed for failure to comply with section 6104(d), see paragraph (c) of § 301.6652-2. [Reg. § 301.6685-1.]

☐ [*T.D.* 7127, 6-14-71. *Amended by T.D.* 8026, 5-17-85.]

### [Reg. § 301.6686-1]

**§ 301.6686-1. Failure of DISC to file returns.**—(a) *In general.*—In addition to the penalty imposed by section 7203 (relating to willful failure to file a return, supply information, or pay tax) any person who is required to supply information or to file a return under section 6011(c) (relating to records and returns of DISC's) and who fails to supply such information or file such return at the time prescribed in sections 6072(b) and 1.6072-2(e) shall pay a penalty of $100 for each failure to supply information (provided that the total amount imposed on the delinquent person for all such failures during a calendar year shall not exceed $25,000) and a penalty of $1,000 with respect to each failure to file a return, unless it is shown that such failure is due to a reasonable cause.

(b) *Showing of reasonable cause.*—The penalty imposed by section 6686 shall not apply to any person with respect to a failure to supply information, or to file a return, under section 6011(c) if it is established to the satisfaction of the district director or director of the Internal Revenue Service Center that such failure was due to reasonable cause. An affirmative showing of reasonable cause must be made in the form of a written statement, which contains a declaration by such person that the statement is made under the penalties of perjury, and sets forth all the facts alleged as reasonable cause. [Reg. § 301.6686-1.]

☐ [*T.D.* 7533, 2-14-78.]

### [Reg. § 301.6688-1]

**§ 301.6688-1. Assessable penalties with respect to information required to be furnished with respect to possessions.**—(a) *In general.*—Each individual described in section 7654(a) who is subject to an information reporting requirement promulgated under the authority of section 937(c) or 7654 and who fails to fully satisfy such requirement within the time prescribed for reporting such information must, in addition to any criminal penalty provided by law, pay a penalty of $1000 for each such failure. Information reporting requirements promulgated under the authority of sections 937(c) and 7654(e) include the requirement for an individual to file Form 8898, "Statement for Individuals who Begin or End Bona Fide Residence in a U.S. Possession," under § 1.937-1(h) of this chapter, to report that he or she became or ceased to be a bona fide resident of a possession.

(b) *Manner of payment.*—The penalty set forth in paragraph (a) of this section must be paid in the same manner as tax upon the issuance of a notice and demand for the penalty.

(c) *Reasonable cause.*—(1) *In general.*—The penalty set forth in paragraph (a) of this section will not apply if it is established to the satisfaction of the *Commissioner* that the failure to file the information return or furnish the information within the prescribed time was due to reasonable cause and not to willful neglect. An individual who wishes to avoid the penalty must make an affirmative showing of all facts alleged as a reasonable cause for failure to file the information return on time, or furnish the information on time, in the form of a written statement containing a declaration that it is made under penalties of perjury. This statement must be filed with Internal Revenue Service Center where Form 8898 must be filed. In determining whether there was reasonable cause for failure to furnish the required information, account will be taken of the fact that the individual was unable to furnish the required information in spite of the exercise of ordinary business care and prudence in his effort to furnish the information. An individual will be considered to have exercised ordinary business care and prudence in his effort to furnish the required information if he made reasonable efforts to furnish the information but was unable to do so because of a lack of sufficient facts on which to make a proper determination.

(d) *Effective/applicability date.*—This section applies to taxable years ending after April 9, 2008. [Reg. § 301.6688-1.]

☐ [*T.D.* 7385, 10-18-75. *Amended by T.D.* 9194, 4-6-2005 *and T.D.* 9391, 4-4-2008 (*corrected* 5-13-2008).]

### [301.6689-1]

**§ 301.6689-1. Failure to file notice of redetermination of foreign income taxes.**—(a) *Application of civil penalty.*—If a foreign tax redetermination occurs, and the taxpayer failed to notify the Internal Revenue Service (IRS) on or before the date and in the manner prescribed in § 1.905-4 of this chapter, or as required under section 404A(g)(2), for giving notice of a foreign tax redetermination, then, unless paragraph (d) of this section applies, there is added to the deficiency (or the imputed underpayment as determined under section 6225) attributable to such redetermination an amount determined under paragraph (b) of this section. Subchapter B of chapter 63 of the Internal Revenue Code (relating to deficiency proceedings) does not apply with respect to the assessment of the amount of the penalty.

(b) *Amount of the penalty.*—The amount of the penalty shall be equal to—

(1) Five percent of the deficiency (or imputed underpayment) if the failure is for not more than one month; plus

(2) An additional five percent of the deficiency (or imputed underpayment) for each month (or fraction thereof) during which the failure continues, but not to exceed in the aggregate twenty-five percent of the deficiency (or imputed underpayment).

(c) *Foreign tax redetermination defined.*—For purposes of this section, a foreign tax redetermination is any redetermination for which a notice is required under sections 905(c) or 404A(g)(2). See § § 1.905-3 through 1.905-5 of this chapter for rules relating to the notice requirement under section 905(c).

(d) *Reasonable cause.*—The penalty set forth in this section shall not apply if it is established to the satisfaction of the IRS that the failure to file the notification within the prescribed time was due to reasonable cause and not due to willful neglect. An affirmative showing of reasonable cause must be made in the form of a written statement that sets forth all the facts alleged as reasonable cause for the failure to file the notification on time and that contains a declaration by the taxpayer that the statement is made under the penalties of perjury. This statement must be filed with the Internal Revenue Service Center in which the notification was required to be filed. The taxpayer must file this statement with the notice required under section 905(c) or 404A(g)(2). If the taxpayer exercised ordinary business care and prudence and was nevertheless unable to file the notification within the prescribed time, then the delay will be considered to be due to reasonable cause and not willful neglect.

(e) *Applicability date.*—This section applies to foreign tax redeterminations occurring in taxable years ending on or after December 16, 2019, and to foreign tax redeterminations of foreign corporations occurring in taxable years that end with or within a taxable year of a United States shareholder ending on or after December 16, 2019. [Reg. § 301.6689-1.]

☐ [*T.D.* 9922, 11-2-2020.]

### [Reg. § 301.6690-1]

**§ 301.6690-1. Penalty for fraudulent statement or failure to furnish statement to plan participant.**—(a) *Penalty.*—Any plan administrator required by section 6057(e) and § 301.6058-1(d) to furnish a statement of deferred vested retirement benefit to a plan participant is subject to a penalty of $50 in each case in which the administrator (1) willfully fails to furnish the statement to the participant in the manner, at the time, and showing the information required by section 6057(e) and § 301.6057-1(e) or (2) willfully furnishes a false or fraudulent statement to the participant. The penalty shall be assessed and collected in the same manner as the tax imposed on employers under the Federal Insurance Contributions Act.

(b) *Effective date.*—This section shall take effect on September 2, 1974. [Reg. § 301.6690-1.]

☐ [*T.D.* 7561, 8-24-78.]

[Reg. § 301.6692-1]

**§ 301.6692-1. Failure to file actuarial report.**—(a) *Penalty.*—In each case in which the plan administrator (within the meaning of section 414(g)) of a defined benefit plan to which the minimum funding standards of section 412 apply fails to file the actuarial report described in section 6059 and § 301.6059-1 within the time prescribed, the plan administrator shall pay a penalty of $1,000. A failure to provide a material item of information called for in the actuarial report is considered a failure to file the report. For this purpose, the signature of an enrolled actuary (see § 301.6059-1(d)) is considered a material item of information. Further, for any report filed for a plan year ending after January 25, 1982, if the actuary seeks to materially qualify a statement required by § 301.6059-1(c)(4) or (5) there is a failure to provide a material item of information called for in the report. For rules relating to statements not considered as materially qualifying the required statements, see § 301.6059-1(d).

(b) *Failure to make actuarial valuation.*—Section 412(c)(9) and the regulations thereunder prescribe the time for making an actuarial valuation of a defined benefit plan. For purposes of this section, the failure to base information called for in the actuarial report upon an actuarial valuation of the plan which is made within the time prescribed by section 412(c)(9) and the regulations thereunder is considered a failure to file the actuarial report.

(c) *Showing of reasonable cause.*—The penalty imposed by this section does not apply if it is established to the satisfaction of the appropriate district director or the director of the Internal Revenue Service Center at which the actuarial report is required to be filed that the failure to file the report was due to reasonable cause. An affirmative showing of reasonable cause must be made in the form of a written statement setting forth all the facts alleged as reasonable cause. The statement must contain a declaration by the appropriate individual that the statement is made under the penalties of perjury.

(d) *Joint liability.*—If more than one person is responsible as a plan administrator for a failure to file the actuarial report, all such persons are jointly and severally liable with respect to the failure.

(e) *Manner of payment.*—The penalty imposed for the failure to file an actuarial report shall be paid in the same manner as a tax upon the issuance of notice and demand therefor.

(f) *Effective dates.*—In the case of a plan in existence on January 1, 1974, this section is effective beginning with the first plan year beginning after December 31, 1975, for which the minimum funding standards of section 412 apply to the plan. In the case of a plan not in existence on January 1, 1974, this section is effective beginning with the first plan year beginning after September 2, 1974, for which the minimum funding standards apply to the plan. [Reg. § 301.6692-1.]

☐ [*T.D.* 7798, 11-23-81.]

[Reg. § 301.6693-1]

**§ 301.6693-1. Penalty for failure to provide reports and documents concerning individual retirement accounts or annuities.**—(a) *In general.*—(1) *Annual reports, etc.*—The trustee of an individual retirement account described in section 408(a), or the issuer of an individual retirement annuity described in section 408(b), who fails to furnish or file a report or any other document required under section 408(i) and § 1.408-5 within the time and in the manner prescribed for furnishing or filing such item shall pay a penalty of $10 for each failure unless it is shown that such failure is due to reasonable cause.

(2) *Disclosure statements.*—The trustee of an individual retirement account described in section 408(a), or the issuer of an individual retirement annuity described in section 408(b), who fails to furnish or file a disclosure statement, a governing instrument, an amendment to either, or any other document required under section 408(i) and § 1.408-6, within the time and in the manner prescribed for furnishing or filing such item, shall pay a penalty of $10 for each failure unless it is shown that such failure is due to reasonable cause.

(b) *Showing of reasonable cause.*—The penalty imposed by section 6693 shall not apply to any person with respect to a failure to furnish or file a report, statement, or other document within the time and in the manner prescribed if it is established to the satisfaction of the district director that such failure was due to reasonable cause. An affirmative showing of reasonable cause must be made in the form of a written statement, containing a declaration by such person that it is made under the penalties of perjury and setting forth all the facts alleged to constitute reasonable cause.

(c) *Deficiency procedures not to apply.*—The penalty imposed by section 6693 may be assessed and collected without regard to the deficiency procedures provided by subchapter B of chapter 63 of the Code.

(d) *Other penalties.*—The penalties of section 6693 and this section are in lieu of any penalty imposed by section 6652(f) for violation of section 6047(d), with respect to any failure to furnish or file described in this section.

(e) *Effective date.*—This section shall take effect on January 1, 1975. [Reg. § 301.6693-1.]

☐ [*T.D.* 7730, 10-31-80.]

[Reg. § 1.6694-0]

**§ 1.6694-0. Table of contents.**—This section lists the captions that appear in § § 1.6694-1 through 1.6694-4.

(1) Proscribed conduct.
(2) Special rule for corporations, partnerships, and other firms.
(b) Willful attempt to understate liability.
(c) Reckless or intentional disregard.
(d) Examples.
(e) Rules or regulations.
(f) Section 6694(b) penalty reduced by section 6694(a) penalty.
(g) Effective/applicability date.

*§1.6694-4 Extension of period of collection when tax return preparer pays 15 percent of a penalty for understatement of taxpayer's liability and certain other procedural matters.*

(a) In general.
(b) Tax return preparer must bring suit in district court to determine liability for penalty.
(c) Suspension of running of period of limitations on collection.
(d) Effective/applicability date.
[Reg. §1.6694-0.]

☐ *T.D. 8382, 12-30-91. Amended by T.D. 9436, 12-15-2008.]*

**[Reg. §1.6694-1]**

**§1.6694-1. Section 6694 penalties applicable to tax return preparers.**—(a) *Overview.*—(1) *In general.*—Sections 6694(a) and (b) impose penalties on tax return preparers for conduct giving rise to certain understatements of liability on a return (including an amended or adjusted return) or claim for refund. For positions other than those with respect to tax shelters (as defined in section 6662(d)(2)(C)(ii)) and reportable transactions to which section 6662A applies, the section 6694(a) penalty is imposed in an amount equal to the greater of $1,000 or 50 percent of the income derived (or to be derived) by the tax return preparer for an understatement of tax liability that is due to an undisclosed position for which the tax return preparer did not have substantial authority or due to a disclosed position for which there is no reasonable basis. For positions with respect to tax shelters (as defined in section 6662(d)(2)(C)(ii)) or reportable transactions to which section 6662A applies, the section 6694(a) penalty is imposed in an amount equal to the greater of $1,000 or 50 percent of the income derived (or to be derived) by the tax return preparer for an understatement of tax liability for which it is not reasonable to believe that the position would more likely than not be sustained on its merits. The section 6694(b) penalty is imposed in an amount equal to the greater of $5,000 or 50 percent of the income derived (or to be derived) by the tax return preparer for an understatement of liability with respect to tax that is due to a willful attempt to understate tax liability or that is due to reckless or intentional disregard of rules or regulations. Refer to §1.6694-2 for rules relating to the penalty under section 6694(a). Refer to §1.6694-3 for rules relating to the penalty under section 6694(b).

(2) *Date return is deemed prepared.*—For purposes of the penalties under section 6694, a return or claim for refund is deemed prepared on the date it is signed by the tax return preparer. If a signing tax return preparer within the meaning of §301.7701-15(b)(1) of this chapter fails to sign the return, the return or claim for refund is deemed prepared on the date the return or claim is filed. See §1.6695-1 of this section. In the case of a nonsigning tax return preparer within the meaning of §301.7701-15(b)(2) of this chapter, the relevant date is the date the nonsigning tax return preparer provides the tax advice with respect to the position giving rise to the understatement. This date will be determined based on all the facts and circumstances.

(b) *Tax return preparer.*—(1) *In general.*—For purposes of this section, "tax return preparer" means any person who is a tax return preparer within the meaning of section 7701(a)(36) and §301.7701-15 of this chapter. An individual is a tax return preparer subject to section 6694 if the individual is primarily responsible for the position(s) on the return or claim for refund giving rise to an understatement. See §301.7701-15(b)(3). There is only one individual within a firm who is primarily responsible for each position on the return or claim for refund giving rise to an understatement. In the course of identifying the individual who is primarily responsible for the position, the Internal Revenue Service (IRS) may advise multiple individuals within the firm that it may be concluded that they are the individual within the firm who is primarily responsible. In some circumstances, there may be more than one tax return preparer who is primarily responsible for the position(s) giving rise to an understatement if multiple tax return preparers are employed by, or associated with, different firms.

(2) *Responsibility of signing tax return preparer.*—If there is a signing tax return preparer within the meaning of §301.7701-15(b)(1) of this chapter within a firm, the signing tax return preparer generally will be considered the person who is primarily responsible for all of the positions on the return or claim for refund giving rise to an

understatement unless, based upon credible information from any source, it is concluded that the signing tax return preparer is not primarily responsible for the position(s) on the return or claim for refund giving rise to an understatement. In that case, a nonsigning tax return preparer within the signing tax return preparer's firm (as determined in paragraph (b)(3) of this section) will be considered the tax return preparer who is primarily responsible for the position(s) on the return or claim for refund giving rise to an understatement.

(3) *Responsibility of nonsigning tax return preparer.*—If there is no signing tax return preparer within the meaning of §301.7701-15(b)(1) of this chapter for the return or claim for refund within the firm or if, after the application of paragraph (b)(2) of this section, it is concluded that the signing tax return preparer is not primarily responsible for the position, the nonsigning tax return preparer within the meaning of §301.7701-15(b)(2) of this chapter within the firm with overall supervisory responsibility for the position(s) giving rise to the understatement generally will be considered the tax return preparer who is primarily responsible for the position for purposes of section 6694 unless, based upon credible information from any source, it is concluded that another nonsigning tax return preparer within that firm is primarily responsible for the position(s) on the return or claim for refund giving rise to the understatement.

(4) *Responsibility of signing and nonsigning tax return preparer.*—If the information presented would support a finding that, within a firm, either the signing tax return preparer or a nonsigning tax return preparer is primarily responsible for the position(s) giving rise to the understatement, the penalty may be assessed against either one of the individuals, but not both, as the primarily responsible tax return preparer.

(5) *Tax return preparer and firm responsibility.*—To the extent provided in §§1.6694-2(a)(2) and 1.6694-3(a)(2), an individual and the firm that employs the individual, or the firm of which the individual is a partner, member, shareholder, or other equity holder, both may be subject to penalty under section 6694 with respect to the position(s) on the return or claim for refund giving rise to an understatement. If an individual (other than the sole proprietor) who is employed by a sole proprietorship is subject to penalty under section 6694, the sole proprietorship is considered a "firm" for purposes of this paragraph (b).

(6) *Examples.*—The provisions of paragraph (b) of this section are illustrated by the following examples:

*Example 1.* Attorney A provides advice to Client C concerning the proper treatment of an item with respect to which all events have occurred on C's tax return. In preparation for providing that advice, A seeks advice regarding the proper treatment of the item from Attorney B, who is within the same firm as A, but A is the attorney who signs C's return as a tax return preparer. B provides advice on the treatment of the item upon which A relies. B's advice is reflected on C's tax return but no disclosure was made in accordance with §1.6694-2(d)(3). The advice constitutes preparation of a substantial portion of the return within the meaning of §301.7701-15(b)(3). The IRS later challenges the position taken on the tax return, giving rise to an understatement of liability. For purposes of the regulations under section 6694, A is initially considered the tax return preparer with respect to C's return, and the IRS advises A that A may be subject to the penalty under section 6694 with respect to C's return. Based upon information received from A or another source, it may be concluded that B, rather than A, had primary responsibility for the position taken on the return that gave rise to the understatement and may be subject to penalty under section 6694 instead of A.

*Example 2.* Same as *Example 1*, except that neither Attorney A nor any other source produce credible information that Attorney B had primary responsibility for the position on the return giving rise to an understatement. Attorney A is the tax return preparer who may be subject to penalty under section 6694 with respect to C's return.

*Example 3.* Same as *Example 1*, except that neither Attorney A nor any other attorney within A's firm signs Client C's return as a tax return preparer. Attorney B is the nonsigning tax return preparer within the firm with overall supervisory responsibility for the position giving rise to an understatement. Accordingly, B is the tax return preparer who is primarily responsible for the position on C's return giving rise to an understatement and may be subject to penalty under section 6694.

*Example 4.* Same as *Example 1*, except Attorney D, who works for a different firm than A, also provides advice on the same position upon which A relies. It may be concluded that D is also primarily responsible for the position on the return and may be subject to penalty under section 6694.

*Example 5.* Same as *Example 1*, except Attorney B is able to present credible information that A is also responsible for the position on C's return giving rise to an understatement. The IRS may conclude between A and B, the two responsible persons for the position, who is primarily responsible and may assess a section 6694 penalty against A or B, but not both, as the primarily responsible tax return preparer.

(c) *Understatement of liability.*—For purposes of this section, an "understatement of liability" exists if, viewing the return or claim for refund as a whole, there is an understatement of the net amount payable with respect to any tax imposed by the Internal Revenue Code (Code), or an overstatement of the net amount creditable or refundable with respect to any tax imposed by the Code. The net amount payable in a taxable year with respect to the return for which the tax return preparer engaged in conduct proscribed by section 6694 is not reduced by any carryback. Tax imposed by the Code does not include additions to the tax, additional amounts, and assessable penalties imposed by subchapter 68 of the Code. Except as provided in paragraph (d) of this section, the determination of whether an understatement of liability exists may be made in a proceeding involving the tax return preparer that is separate and apart from any proceeding involving the taxpayer.

(d) *Abatement of penalty where taxpayer's liability not understated.*—If a penalty under section 6694(a) or (b) concerning a return or claim for refund has been assessed against one or more tax return preparers, and if it is established at any time in a final administrative determination or a final judicial decision that there was no understatement of liability relating to the position(s) on the return or claim for refund, then—

(1) The assessment shall be abated; and

(2) If any amount of the penalty was paid, that amount shall be refunded to the person or persons who so paid, as if the payment were an overpayment of tax, without consideration of any period of limitations.

(e) *Verification of information furnished by taxpayer or other party.*—(1) *In general.*—For purposes of sections 6694(a) and (b) (including demonstrating that a position complied with relevant standards under section 6694(a) and demonstrating reasonable cause and good faith under §1.6694-2(e)), the tax return preparer generally may rely in good faith without verification upon information furnished by the taxpayer. A tax return preparer also may rely in good faith and without verification upon information and advice furnished by another advisor, another tax return preparer or other party (including another advisor or tax return preparer at the tax return preparer's firm). The tax return preparer is not required to audit, examine or review books and records, business operations, documents, or other evidence to verify independently information provided by the taxpayer, advisor, other tax return preparer, or other party. The tax return preparer, however, may not ignore the implications of information furnished to the tax return preparer or actually known by the tax return preparer. The tax return preparer must make reasonable inquiries if the information as furnished appears to be incorrect or incomplete. Additionally, some provisions of the Code or regulations require that specific facts and circumstances exist (for example, that the taxpayer maintain specific documents) before a deduction or credit may be claimed. The tax return preparer must make appropriate inquiries to determine the existence of facts and circumstances required by a Code section or regulation as a condition of the claiming of a deduction or credit.

(2) *Verification of information on previously filed returns.*—For purposes of section 6694(a) and (b) (including meeting the reasonable to believe that the position would more likely than not be sustained on its merits and reasonable basis standards in §§1.6694-2(b) and (d)(2), and demonstrating reasonable cause and good faith under §1.6694-2(e)), a tax return preparer may rely in good faith without verification upon a tax return that has been previously prepared by a taxpayer or another tax return preparer and filed with the IRS. For example, a tax return preparer who prepares an amended return (including a claim for refund) need not verify the positions on the original return. The tax return preparer, however, may not ignore the implications of information furnished to the tax return preparer or actually known by the tax return preparer. The tax return preparer must make reasonable inquiries if the information as furnished appears to be incorrect or incomplete. The tax return preparer must confirm that the position being relied upon has not been adjusted by examination or otherwise.

(3) *Examples.*—The provisions of this paragraph (e) are illustrated by the following examples:

*Example 1.* During an interview conducted by Preparer E, a taxpayer stated that he had made a charitable contribution of real estate in the amount of $50,000 during the tax year, when in fact he had not made this charitable contribution. E did not inquire about the existence of a qualified appraisal or complete a Form 8283, Noncash Charitable Contributions, in accordance with the reporting and substantiation requirements under section 170(f)(11). E reported

a deduction on the tax return for the charitable contribution, which resulted in an understatement of liability for tax, and signed the tax return as the tax return preparer. E is subject to a penalty under section 6694.

*Example 2.* While preparing the 2008 tax return for an individual taxpayer, Preparer F realizes that the taxpayer did not provide a Form 1099-INT, "Interest Income", for a bank account that produced significant taxable income in 2007. When F inquired about any other income, the taxpayer furnished the Form 1099-INT to F for use in preparation of the 2008 tax return. F did not know that the taxpayer owned an additional bank account that generated taxable income for 2008, and the taxpayer did not reveal this information to the tax return preparer notwithstanding F's general inquiry about any other income. F signed the taxpayer's return as the tax return preparer. F is not subject to a penalty under section 6694.

*Example 3.* In preparing a tax return, for purposes of determining the deductibility of a contribution by an employer for a qualified pension plan, Accountant G relies on a computation of the section 404 limit on deductible amounts made by the enrolled actuary for the plan. On the basis of this calculation, G completed and signed the tax return. It is later determined that there is an understatement of liability for tax that resulted from the overstatement of the section 404 limit on deductible amounts made by the actuary. G had no reason to believe that the actuary's calculation of the limit on deductible contributions was incorrect or incomplete, and the calculation appeared reasonable on its face. G was also not aware at the time the return was prepared of any reason why the actuary did not know all of the relevant facts or that the calculation of the limit on deductible contributions was no longer reliable due to developments in the law since the time the calculation was given. G is not subject to a penalty under section 6694. The actuary, however, may be subject to penalty under section 6694 if the calculation provided by the actuary constitutes a substantial portion of the tax return within the meaning of §301.7701-15(b)(3) of this chapter.

(f) *Income derived (or to be derived) with respect to the return or claim for refund.*—(1) *In general.*—For purposes of sections 6694(a) and (b), *income derived (or to be derived)* means all compensation the tax return preparer receives or expects to receive with respect to the engagement of preparing the return or claim for refund or providing tax advice (including research and consultation) with respect to the position(s) taken on the return or claim for refund that gave rise to the understatement. In the situation of a tax return preparer who is not compensated directly by the taxpayer, but rather by a firm that employs the tax return preparer or with which the tax return preparer is associated, *income derived (or to be derived)* means all compensation the tax return preparer receives from the firm that can be reasonably allocated to the engagement of preparing the return or claim for refund or providing tax advice (including research and consultation) with respect to the position(s) taken on the return or claim for refund that gave rise to the understatement. In the situation where a firm that employs the individual tax return preparer (or the firm of which the individual tax return preparer is a partner, member, shareholder, or other equity holder) is subject to a penalty under section 6694(a) or (b) pursuant to the provisions in §§1.6694-2(a)(2) or 1.6694-3(a)(2), *income derived (or to be derived)* means all compensation the firm receives or expects to receive with respect to the engagement of preparing the return or claim for refund or providing tax advice (including research and consultation) with respect to the position(s) taken on the return or claim for refund that gave rise to the understatement.

(2) *Compensation.*—(i) *Multiple engagements.*—For purposes of applying paragraph (f)(1) of this section, if the tax return preparer or the tax return preparer's firm has multiple engagements related to the same return or claim for refund, only those engagements relating to the position(s) taken on the return or claim for refund that gave rise to the understatement are considered for purposes of calculating the income derived (or to be derived) with respect to the return or claim for refund.

(ii) *Reasonable allocation.*—For purposes of applying paragraph (f)(1) of this section, only compensation for tax advice that is given with respect to events that have occurred at the time the advice is rendered and that relates to the position(s) giving rise to the understatement will be taken into account for purposes of calculating the section 6694(a) and (b) penalties. If a lump sum fee is received that includes amounts not taken into account under the preceding sentence, the amount of income derived will be based on a reasonable allocation of the lump sum fee between the tax advice giving rise to the penalty and the advice that does not give rise to the penalty.

(iii) *Fee refunds.*—For purposes of applying paragraph (f)(1) of this section, a refund to the taxpayer of all or part of the amount paid to the tax return preparer or the tax return preparer's firm will not reduce the amount of the section 6694 penalty assessed. A refund in this context does not include a discounted fee or alternative billing arrangement for the services provided.

(iv) *Reduction of compensation.*—For purposes of applying paragraph (f)(1) of this section, it may be concluded based upon information provided by the tax return preparer or the tax return preparer's firm that an appropriate allocation of compensation attributable to the position(s) giving rise to the understatement on the return or claim for refund is less than the total amount of compensation associated with the engagement. For example, the number of hours of the engagement spent on the position(s) giving rise to the understatement may be less than the total hours associated with the engagement. If this is concluded, the amount of the penalty will be calculated based upon the compensation attributable to the position(s) giving rise to the understatement. Otherwise, the total amount of compensation from the engagement will be the amount of income derived for purposes of calculating the penalty under section 6694.

(3) *Individual and firm allocation.*—If both an individual within a firm and a firm that employs the individual (or the firm of which the individual is a partner, member, shareholder, or other equity holder) are subject to a penalty under section 6694(a) or (b) pursuant to the provisions in §§ 1.6694-2(a)(2) or 1.6694-3(a)(2), the amount of penalties assessed against the individual and the firm shall not exceed 50 percent of the income derived (or to be derived) by the firm from the engagement of preparing the return or claim for refund or providing tax advice (including research and consultation) with respect to the position(s) taken on the return or claim for refund that gave rise to the understatement. The portion of the total amount of the penalty assessed against the individual tax return preparer shall not exceed 50 percent of the individual's compensation as determined under paragraphs (f)(1) and (2) of this section.

(4) *Examples.*—The provisions of this paragraph (f) are illustrated by the following examples:

*Example 1.* Signing Tax Return Preparer H is engaged by a taxpayer and paid a total of $21,000. Of this amount, $20,000 relates to research and consultation regarding a transaction that is later reported on a return, and $1,000 is for the activities relating to the preparation of the return. Based on H's hourly rates, a reasonable allocation of the amount of compensation related to the advice rendered prior to the occurrence of events that are the subject of the advice is $5,000. The remaining compensation of $16,000 is considered to be compensation related to the advice rendered after the occurrence of events that are the subject of the advice and return preparation. The income derived by H with respect to the return for purposes of computing the penalty under section 6694(a) is $16,000, and the amount of the penalty imposed under section 6694(a) is $8,000.

*Example 2.* Accountants I, J, and K are employed by Firm L. I is a principal manager of Firm L and provides corporate tax advice for the taxpayer after all events have occurred subject to an engagement for corporate tax advice. J provides international tax advice for the taxpayer after all events have occurred subject to a different engagement for international tax advice. K prepares and signs the taxpayer's return under a general tax services engagement. I's advice is the source of an understatement on the return and the advice constitutes preparation of a substantial portion of the return within the meaning of § 301.7701-15(b) of this chapter. I is the nonsigning tax return preparer within the firm with overall supervisory responsibility for the position on the taxpayer's return giving rise to an understatement. Thus, I is the tax return preparer who is primarily responsible for the position on the taxpayer's return giving rise to the understatement. Because K's signature as the signing tax return preparer is on the return, the IRS advises K that K may be subject to the section 6694(a) penalty. K provides credible information that I is the tax return preparer with primary responsibility for the position that gave rise to the understatement. The IRS, therefore, assesses the section 6694 penalty against I. The portion of the total amount of the penalty allocable to I does not exceed 50 percent of that part of I's compensation that is attributable to the corporate tax advice engagement. In the event that Firm L is also liable under the provisions in § 1.6694-2(a)(2), the IRS assesses the section 6694 penalty in an amount not exceeding 50 percent of Firm L's firm compensation based on the engagement relating to the corporate tax advice services provided by I where there is no applicable reduction in compensation pursuant to § 1.6694-1(f)(2)(iii).

*Example 3.* Same facts as *Example 2*, except that I provides the advice on the corporate matter when the events have not yet occurred. I's advice is the cause of an understatement position on the return, but I is not a tax return preparer pursuant to § 301.7701-15(b)(2) or (3) of this chapter. K is not limited to reliance on persons who provide post-transactional advice if such reliance is reasonable and in good faith. Further, K has reasonable cause because K relied on I for the advice on the corporate tax matter. I, K and Firm L are not liable for the section 6694 penalty.

*Example 4.* Attorney M is an employee of Firm N with a salary of $75,000 per year. M performs tax preparation work for Client O. Client O's return contains a position that results in an understatement subject to the section 6694 penalty. M spent 100 hours on the position (out of a total 2,000 billed during the year). The total fees earned by Firm N with respect to the position reflected on Client O's return are $50,000. If M is subject to the penalty, the penalty amount computed under the 50 percent of income standard is .5 × (100/2000) × $75,000 = $1,875. If Firm N is subject to the penalty, the penalty amount computed under the 50% of income standard is .5 × $50,000 = $25,000, less any penalty amount imposed against M. If a penalty of $1,875 was assessed against M and Firm N was subject to the penalty, a penalty of $23,125 would be the amount of penalty assessed against Firm N.

(g) *Effective/applicability date.*—This section is applicable to returns and claims for refund filed, and advice provided, after December 31, 2008. [Reg. § 1.6694-1.]

☐ [*T.D.* 7519. *Amended by T.D.* 7572, 11-15-78; *T.D.* 8382, 12-30-91 and *T.D.* 9436, 12-15-2008 (*corrected* 1-28-2009).]

### [Reg. § 20.6694-1]

**§ 20.6694-1. Section 6694 penalties applicable to tax return preparer.**—(a) *In general.*—For general definitions regarding section 6694 penalties applicable to preparers of estate tax returns or claims for refund, see § 1.6694-1 of this chapter.

(b) *Effective/applicability date.*—Paragraph (a) of this section is applicable to returns and claims for refund filed, and advice provided, after December 31, 2008. [Reg. § 20.6694-1.]

☐ [*T.D.* 9436, 12-15-2008 (*corrected* 1-28-2009).]

### [Reg. § 25.6694-1]

**§ 25.6694-1. Section 6694 penalties applicable to tax return preparer.**—(a) *In general.*—For general definitions regarding section 6694 penalties applicable to preparers of gift tax returns or claims for refund, see § 1.6694-1 of this chapter.

(b) *Effective/applicability date.*—Paragraph (a) of this section is applicable to returns and claims for refund filed, and advice provided, after December 31, 2008. [Reg. § 25.6694-1.]

☐ [*T.D.* 9436, 12-15-2008 (*corrected* 1-28-2009).]

### [Reg. § 26.6694-1]

**§ 26.6694-1. Section 6694 penalties applicable to tax return preparer.**—(a) *In general.*—For general definitions regarding section 6694 penalties applicable to preparers of generation-skipping transfer tax returns or claims for refund, see § 1.6694-1 of this chapter.

(b) *Effective/applicability date.*—Paragraph (a) of this section is applicable to returns and claims for refund filed, and advice provided, after December 31, 2008. [Reg. § 26.6694-1.]

☐ [*T.D.* 9436, 12-15-2008 (*corrected* 1-28-2009).]

### [Reg. § 31.6694-1]

**§ 31.6694-1. Section 6694 penalties applicable to tax return preparer.**—(a) *In general.*—For general definitions regarding section 6694 penalties applicable to preparers of employment tax returns or claims for refund of employment tax under chapters 21 through 25 of subtitle C of the Internal Revenue Code, see § 1.6694-1 of this chapter.

(b) *Effective/applicability date.*—Paragraph (a) of this section is applicable to returns and claims for refund filed, and advice provided, after December 31, 2008. [Reg. § 31.6694-1.]

☐ [*T.D.* 9436, 12-15-2008 (*corrected* 1-28-2009).]

### [Reg. § 40.6694-1]

**§ 40.6694-1. Section 6694 penalties applicable to tax return preparer.**—(a) *In general.*—For general definitions regarding section 6694 penalties applicable to preparers of returns or claims for refund of any tax to which this part 40 applies, see § 1.6694-1 of this chapter.

(b) *Effective/applicability date.*—This section is applicable to returns and claims for refund filed, and advice provided, after December 31, 2008. [Reg. § 40.6694-1.]

☐ [*T.D.* 9436, 12-15-2008 (*corrected* 1-28-2009).]

### [Reg. § 41.6694-1]

**§ 41.6694-1. Section 6694 penalties applicable to tax return preparer.**—(a) *In general.*—For general definitions regarding section 6694 penalties applicable to preparers of tax returns or claims for refund, see § 1.6694-1 of this chapter.

(b) *Effective/applicability date.*—This section is applicable to returns and claims for refund filed, and advice provided, after December 31, 2008. [Reg. § 41.6694-1.]

☐ [*T.D.* 9436, 12-15-2008.]

**[Reg. § 44.6694-1]**

**§ 44.6694-1. Section 6694 penalties applicable to tax return preparer.**—(a) *In general.*—For general definitions regarding section 6694 penalties applicable to preparers of wagering tax returns or claims for refund under sections 4401 or 4411, see § 1.6694-1 of this chapter.

(b) *Effective/applicability date.*—This section is applicable to returns and claims for refund filed, and advice provided, after December 31, 2008. [Reg. § 44.6694-1.]

☐ [*T.D.* 9436, 12-15-2008.]

**[Reg. § 53.6694-1]**

**§ 53.6694-1. Section 6694 penalties applicable to tax return preparer.**—(a) *In general.*—For general definitions regarding section 6694 penalties applicable to preparers of tax returns or claims for refund under Chapter 42 of the Internal Revenue Code, see § 1.6694-1 of this chapter.

(b) *Effective/applicability date.*—Paragraph (a) of this section is applicable to returns and claims for refund filed, and advice provided, after December 31, 2008. [Reg. § 53.6694-1.]

☐ [*T.D.* 9436, 12-15-2008.]

**[Reg. § 54.6694-1]**

**§ 54.6694-1. Section 6694 penalties applicable to tax return preparer.**—(a) *In general.*—For general definitions regarding section 6694 penalties applicable to preparers of tax returns or claims for refund of tax under Chapter 43 of subtitle D, see § 1.6694-1 of this chapter.

(b) *Effective/applicability date.*—Paragraph (a) of this section is applicable to returns and claims for refund filed, and advice provided, after December 31, 2008. [Reg. § 54.6694-1.]

☐ [*T.D.* 9436, 12-15-2008.]

**[Reg. § 55.6694-1]**

**§ 55.6694-1. Section 6694 penalties applicable to tax return preparer.**—(a) *In general.*—For general definitions regarding section 6694 penalties applicable to preparers of tax returns or claims for refund of tax under chapter 44 of Subtitle D see § 1.6694-1 of this chapter.

(b) *Effective/applicability date.*—Paragraph (a) of this section is applicable to returns and claims for refund filed, and advice provided, after December 31, 2008. [Reg. § 55.6694-1.]

☐ [*T.D.* 9436, 12-15-2008.]

**[Reg. § 56.6694-1]**

**§ 56.6694-1. Section 6694 penalties applicable to tax return preparer.**—(a) *In general.*—For general definitions regarding section 6694 penalties applicable to preparers of tax returns or claims for refund of tax under chapter 41 of subtitle D see § 1.6694-1 of this chapter.

(b) *Effective/applicability date.*—Paragraph (a) of this section is applicable to returns and claims for refund filed, and advice provided, after December 31, 2008. [Reg. § 56.6694-1.]

☐ [*T.D.* 9436, 12-15-2008.]

**[Reg. § 156.6694-1]**

**§ 156.6694-1. Section 6694 penalties applicable to tax return preparer.**—(a) *In general.*—For general definitions regarding section 6694 penalties applicable to preparers of tax returns or claims for refund for tax under section 5881 of the Internal Revenue Code, see § 1.6694-1 of this chapter.

(b) *Effective/applicability date.*—Paragraph (a) of this section is applicable to returns and claims for refund filed, and advice provided, after December 31, 2008. [Reg. § 156.6694-1.]

☐ [*T.D.* 9436, 12-15-2008.]

**[Reg. § 157.6694-1]**

**§ 157.6694-1. Section 6694 penalties applicable to tax return preparer.**—(a) *In general.*—For general definitions regarding section 6694 penalties applicable to preparers of tax returns or claims for refund for tax under section 5891 of the Internal Revenue Code see § 1.6694-1 of this chapter.

(b) *Effective/applicability date.*—Paragraph (a) of this section is applicable to returns and claims for refund filed, and advice provided, after December 31, 2008. [Reg. § 157.6694-1.]

☐ [*T.D.* 9436, 12-15-2008.]

**[Reg. § 1.6694-2]**

**§ 1.6694-2. Penalty for understatement due to an unreasonable position.**—(a) *In general.*—(1) *Proscribed conduct.*—Except as otherwise provided in this section, a tax return preparer is liable for a penalty under section 6694(a) equal to the greater of $1,000 or 50 percent of the income derived (or to be derived) by the tax return preparer for any return or claim for refund that it prepares that results in an understatement of liability due to a position if the tax return preparer knew (or reasonably should have known) of the position and either—

(i) The position is with respect to a tax shelter (as defined in section 6662(d)(2)(C)(ii)) or a reportable transaction to which section 6662A applies, and it was not reasonable to believe that the position would more likely than not be sustained on its merits;

(ii) The position was not disclosed as provided in this section, the position is not with respect to a tax shelter (as defined in section 6662(d)(2)(C)(ii)) or a reportable transaction to which section 6662A applies, and there was not substantial authority for the position; or

(iii) The position (other than a position with respect to a tax shelter or a reportable transaction to which section 6662A applies) was disclosed as provided in this section but there was no reasonable basis for the position.

(2) *Special rule for corporations, partnerships, and other firms.*—A firm that employs a tax return preparer subject to a penalty under section 6694(a) (or a firm of which the individual tax return preparer is a partner, member, shareholder or other equity holder) is also subject to penalty if, and only if—

(i) One or more members of the principal management (or principal officers) of the firm or a branch office participated in or knew of the conduct proscribed by section 6694(a);

(ii) The corporation, partnership, or other firm entity failed to provide reasonable and appropriate procedures for review of the position for which the penalty is imposed; or

(iii) The corporation, partnership, or other firm entity disregarded its reasonable and appropriate review procedures through willfulness, recklessness, or gross indifference (including ignoring facts that would lead a person of reasonable prudence and competence to investigate or ascertain) in the formulation of the advice, or the preparation of the return or claim for refund, that included the position for which the penalty is imposed.

(b) *Reasonable to believe that the position would more likely than not be sustained on its merits.*—(1) *In general.*—If a position is with respect to a tax shelter (as defined in section 6662(d)(2)(C)(ii)) or a reportable transaction to which section 6662A applies, it is "reasonable to believe that a position would more likely than not be sustained on its merits" if the tax return preparer analyzes the pertinent facts and authorities and, in reliance upon that analysis, reasonably concludes in good faith that the position has a greater than 50 percent likelihood of being sustained on its merits. In reaching this conclusion, the possibility that the position will not be challenged by the Internal Revenue Service (IRS) (for example, because the taxpayer's return may not be audited or because the issue may not be raised on audit) is not to be taken into account. The analysis prescribed by § 1.6662-4(d)(3)(ii) (or any successor provision) for purposes of determining whether substantial authority is present applies for purposes of determining whether the more likely than not standard is satisfied. Whether a tax return preparer meets this standard will be determined based upon all facts and circumstances, including the tax return preparer's diligence. In determining the level of diligence in a particular situation, the tax return preparer's experience with the area of Federal tax law and familiarity with the taxpayer's affairs, as well as the complexity of the issues and facts, will be taken into account. A tax return preparer may reasonably believe that a position more likely than not would be sustained on its merits despite the absence of other types of authority if the position is supported by a well-reasoned construction of the applicable statutory provision. For purposes of determining whether it is reasonable to believe that the position would more likely than not be sustained on the merits, a tax return preparer may rely in good faith without verification upon information furnished by the taxpayer and information and advice furnished by another advisor, another tax return preparer, or other party (including another advisor or tax return preparer at the tax return preparer's firm), as provided in §§ 1.6694-1(e) and 1.6694-2(e)(5).

(2) *Authorities.*—The authorities considered in determining whether a position satisfies the more likely than not standard are

those authorities provided in § 1.6662-4(d)(3)(iii) (or any successor provision).

(3) *Written determinations.*—The tax return preparer may avoid the section 6694(a) penalty by taking the position that the tax return preparer reasonably believed that the taxpayer's position satisfies the "more likely than not" standard if the taxpayer is the subject of a "written determination" as provided in § 1.6662-4(d)(3)(iv)(A).

(4) *Taxpayer's jurisdiction.*—The applicability of court cases to the taxpayer by reason of the taxpayer's residence in a particular jurisdiction is not taken into account in determining whether it is reasonable to believe that the position would more likely than not be sustained on the merits. Notwithstanding the preceding sentence, the tax return preparer may reasonably believe that the position would more likely than not be sustained on the merits if the position is supported by controlling precedent of a United States Court of Appeals to which the taxpayer has a right of appeal with respect to the item.

(5) *When "more likely than not" standard must be satisfied.*—For purposes of this section, the requirement that a position satisfies the "more likely than not" standard must be satisfied on the date the return is deemed prepared, as prescribed by § 1.6694-1(a)(2).

(c) [Reserved].

(d) *Exception for adequate disclosure of positions with a reasonable basis.*—(1) *In general.*—The section 6694(a) penalty will not be imposed on a tax return preparer if the position taken (other than a position with respect to a tax shelter or a reportable transaction to which section 6662A applies) has a reasonable basis and is adequately disclosed within the meaning of paragraph (c)(3) of this section. For an exception to the section 6694(a) penalty for reasonable cause and good faith, see paragraph (e) of this section.

(2) *Reasonable basis.*—For purposes of this section, "reasonable basis" has the same meaning as in § 1.6662-3(b)(3) or any successor provision of the accuracy-related penalty regulations. For purposes of determining whether the tax return preparer has a reasonable basis for a position, a tax return preparer may rely in good faith without verification upon information furnished by the taxpayer and information and advice furnished by another advisor, another tax return preparer, or other party (including another advisor or tax return preparer at the tax return preparer's firm), as provided in §§ 1.6694-1(e) and 1.6694-2(e)(5).

(3) *Adequate disclosure.*—(i) *Signing tax return preparers.*—In the case of a signing tax return preparer within the meaning of § 301.7701-15(b)(1) of this chapter, disclosure of a position (other than a position with respect to a tax shelter or a reportable transaction to which section 6662A applies) for which there is a reasonable basis but for which there is not substantial authority is adequate if the tax return preparer meets any of the following standards:

(A) The position is disclosed in accordance with § 1.6662-4(f) (which permits disclosure on a properly completed and filed Form 8275, "Disclosure Statement," or Form 8275-R, "Regulation Disclosure Statement," as appropriate, or on the tax return in accordance with the annual revenue procedure described in § 1.6662-4(f)(2));

(B) The tax return preparer provides the taxpayer with the prepared tax return that includes the disclosure in accordance with § 1.6662-4(f); or

(C) For returns or claims for refund that are subject to penalties pursuant to section 6662 other than the accuracy-related penalty attributable to a substantial understatement of income tax under section 6662(b)(2) and (d), the tax return preparer advises the taxpayer of the penalty standards applicable to the taxpayer under section 6662. The tax return preparer must also contemporaneously document the advice in the tax return preparer's files.

(ii) *Nonsigning tax return preparers.*—In the case of a nonsigning tax return preparer within the meaning of § 301.7701-15(b)(2) of this chapter, disclosure of a position (other than a position with respect to a tax shelter or a reportable transaction to which section 6662A applies) that satisfies the reasonable basis standard but does not satisfy the substantial authority standard is adequate if the position is disclosed in accordance with § 1.6662-4(f) (which permits disclosure on a properly completed and filed Form 8275 or Form 8275-R, as applicable, or on the return in accordance with an annual revenue procedure described in § 1.6662-4(f)(2)). In addition, disclosure of a position is adequate in the case of a nonsigning tax return preparer if, with respect to that position, the tax return preparer complies with the provisions of paragraph (d)(3)(ii)(A) or (B) of this section, whichever is applicable.

(A) *Advice to taxpayers.*—If a nonsigning tax return preparer provides advice to the taxpayer with respect to a position (other than a position with respect to a tax shelter or a reportable transaction to

which section 6662A applies) for which there is a reasonable basis but for which there is not substantial authority, disclosure of that position is adequate if the tax return preparer advises the taxpayer of any opportunity to avoid penalties under section 6662 that could apply to the position, if relevant, and of the standards for disclosure to the extent applicable. The tax return preparer must also contemporaneously document the advice in the tax return preparer's files. The contemporaneous documentation should reflect that the affected taxpayer has been advised by a tax return preparer in the firm of the potential penalties and the opportunity to avoid penalty through disclosure.

(B) *Advice to another tax return preparer.*—If a nonsigning tax return preparer provides advice to another tax return preparer with respect to a position (other than a position with respect to a tax shelter or a reportable transaction to which section 6662A applies) for which there is a reasonable basis but for which there is not substantial authority, disclosure of that position is adequate if the tax return preparer advises the other tax return preparer that disclosure under section 6694(a) may be required. The tax return preparer must also contemporaneously document the advice in the tax return preparer's files. The contemporaneous documentation should reflect that the tax return preparer outside the firm has been advised that disclosure under section 6694(a) may be required. If the advice is to another nonsigning tax return preparer within the same firm, contemporaneous documentation is satisfied if there is a single instance of contemporaneous documentation within the firm.

(iii) *Requirements for advice.*—For purposes of satisfying the disclosure standards of paragraphs (d)(3)(i)(C) and (ii) of this section, each return position for which there is a reasonable basis but for which there is not substantial authority must be addressed by the tax return preparer. The advice to the taxpayer with respect to each position, therefore, must be particular to the taxpayer and tailored to the taxpayer's facts and circumstances. The tax return preparer is required to contemporaneously document the fact that the advice was provided. There is no general pro forma language or special format required for a tax return preparer to comply with these rules. A general disclaimer will not satisfy the requirement that the tax return preparer provide and contemporaneously document advice regarding the likelihood that a position will be sustained on the merits and the potential application of penalties as a result of that position. Tax return preparers, however, may rely on established forms or templates in advising clients regarding the operation of the penalty provisions of the Internal Revenue Code. A tax return preparer may choose to comply with the documentation standard in one document addressing each position or in multiple documents addressing all of the positions.

(iv) *Pass-through entities.*—Disclosure in the case of items attributable to a pass-through entity is adequate if made at the entity level in accordance with the rules in § 1.6662-4(f)(5) or at the entity level in accordance with the rules in paragraphs (d)(3)(i) or (ii) of this section.

(v) *Examples.*—The provisions of paragraph (d)(3) of this section are illustrated by the following examples:

*Example 1.* An individual taxpayer hires Accountant R to prepare its income tax return. A particular position taken on the tax return does not have substantial authority although there is a reasonable basis for the position. The position is not with respect to a tax shelter or a reportable transaction to which section 6662A applies. R prepares and signs the tax return and provides the taxpayer with the prepared tax return that includes the Form 8275, "Disclosure Statement," disclosing the position taken on the tax return. The individual taxpayer signs and files the tax return without disclosing the position. The IRS later challenges the position taken on the tax return, resulting in an understatement of liability. R is not subject to a penalty under section 6694.

*Example 2.* Attorney S advises a large corporate taxpayer concerning the proper treatment of complex entries on the corporate taxpayer's tax return. S has reason to know that the tax attributable to the entries is a substantial portion of the tax required to be shown on the tax return within the meaning of § 301.7701-15(b)(3). When providing the advice, S concludes that one position does not have substantial authority, although the position meets the reasonable basis standard. The position is not with respect to a tax shelter or a reportable transaction to which section 6662A applies. S advises the corporate taxpayer that the position lacks substantial authority and the taxpayer may be subject to an accuracy-related penalty under section 6662 unless the position is disclosed in a disclosure statement included in the return. S also documents the fact that this advice was contemporaneously provided to the corporate taxpayer at the time the advice was provided. Neither S nor any other attorney within S's firm signs the corporate taxpayer's return as a tax return preparer, but the advice by S constitutes preparation of a substantial portion of the tax return, and S is the individual with overall supervisory responsibility for the position giving rise to the understatement. Thus, S is a tax return preparer for purposes of section 6694. S, however, will not be subject to a penalty under section 6694.

(e) *Exception for reasonable cause and good faith.*—The penalty under section 6694(a) will not be imposed if, considering all the facts and circumstances, it is determined that the understatement was due to reasonable cause and that the tax return preparer acted in good faith. Factors to consider include:

(1) *Nature of the error causing the understatement.*—The error resulted from a provision that was complex, uncommon, or highly technical, and a competent tax return preparer of tax returns or claims for refund of the type at issue reasonably could have made the error. The reasonable cause and good faith exception, however, does not apply to an error that would have been apparent from a general review of the return or claim for refund by the tax return preparer.

(2) *Frequency of errors.*—The understatement was the result of an isolated error (such as an inadvertent mathematical or clerical error) rather than a number of errors. Although the reasonable cause and good faith exception generally applies to an isolated error, it does not apply if the isolated error is so obvious, flagrant, or material that it should have been discovered during a review of the return or claim for refund. Furthermore, the reasonable cause and good faith exception does not apply if there is a pattern of errors on a return or claim for refund even though any one error, in isolation, would have qualified for the reasonable cause and good faith exception.

(3) *Materiality of errors.*—The understatement was not material in relation to the correct tax liability. The reasonable cause and good faith exception generally applies if the understatement is of a relatively immaterial amount. Nevertheless, even an immaterial understatement may not qualify for the reasonable cause and good faith exception if the error or errors creating the understatement are sufficiently obvious or numerous.

(4) *Tax return preparer's normal office practice.*—The tax return preparer's normal office practice, when considered together with other facts and circumstances, such as the knowledge of the tax return preparer, indicates that the error in question would occur rarely and the normal office practice was followed in preparing the return or claim for refund in question. Such a normal office practice must be a system for promoting accuracy and consistency in the preparation of returns or claims for refund and generally would include, in the case of a signing tax return preparer, checklists, methods for obtaining necessary information from the taxpayer, a review of the prior year's return, and review procedures. Notwithstanding these rules, the reasonable cause and good faith exception does not apply if there is a flagrant error on a return or claim for refund, a pattern of errors on a return or claim for refund, or a repetition of the same or similar errors on numerous returns or claims for refund.

(5) *Reliance on advice of others.*—For purposes of demonstrating reasonable cause and good faith, a tax return preparer may rely without verification upon advice and information furnished by the taxpayer and information and advice furnished by another advisor, another tax return preparer or other party, as provided in § 1.6694-1(e). The tax return preparer may rely in good faith on the advice of, or schedules or other documents prepared by, the taxpayer, another advisor, another tax return preparer, or other party (including another advisor or tax return preparer at the tax return preparer's firm), who the tax return preparer had reason to believe was competent to render the advice or other information. The advice or information may be written or oral, but in either case the burden of establishing that the advice or information was received is on the tax return preparer. A tax return preparer is not considered to have relied in good faith if—

(i) The advice or information is unreasonable on its face;

(ii) The tax return preparer knew or should have known that the other party providing the advice or information was not aware of all relevant facts; or

(iii) The tax return preparer knew or should have known (given the nature of the tax return preparer's practice), at the time the return or claim for refund was prepared, that the advice or information was no longer reliable due to developments in the law since the time the advice was given.

(6) *Reliance on generally accepted administrative or industry practice.*—The tax return preparer reasonably relied in good faith on generally accepted administrative or industry practice in taking the position that resulted in the understatement. A tax return preparer is not considered to have relied in good faith if the tax return preparer knew or should have known (given the nature of the tax return preparer's practice), at the time the return or claim for refund was prepared, that the administrative or industry practice was no longer reliable due to developments in the law or IRS administrative practice since the time the practice was developed.

(f) *Effective/applicability date.*—This section is applicable to returns and claims for refund filed, and advice provided, after December 31, 2008. [Reg. § 1.6694-2.]

☐ [*T.D. 7519, 11-17-77. Amended by T.D. 8382, 12-30-91 and T.D. 9436, 12-15-2008 (corrected 1-28-2009).*].

### [Reg. § 20.6694-2]

**§ 20.6694-2. Penalties for understatement due to an unreasonable position.**—(a) *In general.*—A person who is a tax return preparer of any return or claim for refund of estate tax under chapter 11 of subtitle B of the Internal Revenue Code (Code) shall be subject to penalties under section 6694(a) of the Code in the manner stated in § 1.6694-2 of this chapter.

(b) *Effective/applicability date.*—This section is applicable to returns and claims for refund filed, and advice provided, after December 31, 2008. [Reg. § 20.6694-2.]

☐ [*T.D. 9436, 12-15-2008.*]

### [Reg. § 25.6694-2]

**§ 25.6694-2. Penalties for understatement due to an unreasonable position.**—(a) *In general.*—A person who is a tax return preparer of any return or claim for refund of gift tax under chapter 12 of subtitle B of the Internal Revenue Code (Code) shall be subject to penalties under section 6694(a) of the Code in the manner stated in § 1.6694-2 of this chapter.

(b) *Effective/applicability date.*—This section is applicable to returns and claims for refund filed, and advice provided, after December 31, 2008. [Reg. § 25.6694-2.]

☐ [*T.D. 9436, 12-15-2008.*]

### [Reg. § 26.6694-2]

**§ 26.6694-2. Penalties for understatement due to an unreasonable position.**—(a) *In general.*—A person who is a tax return preparer of any return or claim for refund of generationskipping transfer tax under chapter 13 of subtitle B of the Internal Revenue Code (Code) shall be subject to penalties under section 6694(a) of the Code in the manner stated in § 1.6694-2 of this chapter.

(b) *Effective/applicability date.*—This section is applicable to returns and claims for refund filed, and advice provided, after December 31, 2008. [Reg. § 26.6694-2.]

☐ [*T.D. 9436, 12-15-2008.*]

### [Reg. § 31.6694-2]

**§ 31.6694-2. Penalties for understatement due to an unreasonable position.**—(a) *In general.*—A person who is a tax return preparer of any return or claim for refund of employment tax under chapters 21 through 25 of subtitle C of the Internal Revenue Code (Code) shall be subject to penalties under section 6694(a) of the Code in the manner stated in § 1.6694-2 of this chapter.

(b) *Effective/applicability date.*—This section is applicable to returns and claims for refund filed, and advice provided, after December 31, 2008. [Reg. § 31.6694-2.]

☐ [*T.D. 9436, 12-15-2008.*]

### [Reg. § 40.6694-2]

**§ 40.6694-2. Penalties for understatement due to an unreasonable position.**—(a) *In general.*—A person who is a tax return preparer of any return or claim for refund of any tax to which this part 40 applies shall be subject to penalties under section 6694(a) in the manner stated in § 1.6694-2 of this chapter.

(b) *Effective/applicability date.*—This section is applicable to returns and claims for refund filed, and advice provided, after December 31, 2008. [Reg. § 40.6694-2.]

☐ [*T.D. 9436, 12-15-2008 (corrected 1-28-2009).*]

### [Reg. § 41.6694-2]

**§ 41.6694-2. Penalties for understatement due to an unreasonable position.**—(a) *In general.*—A person who is a tax return preparer of any return or claim for refund of excise tax under section 4481 shall be subject to penalties under section 6694(a) in the manner stated in § 1.6694-2 of this chapter.

(b) *Effective/applicability date.*—This section is applicable to returns and claims for refund filed, and advice provided, after December 31, 2008. [Reg. § 41.6694-2.]

☐ [*T.D. 9436, 12-15-2008.*]

**[Reg. § 44.6694-2]**

**§ 44.6694-2. Penalties for understatement due to an unreasonable position.**—(a) *In general.*—A person who is a tax return preparer of any return or claim for refund of tax on wagers under sections 4401 or 4411 shall be subject to penalties under section 6694(a) in the manner stated in § 1.6694-2 of this chapter.

(b) *Effective/applicability date.*—This section is applicable to returns and claims for refund filed, and advice provided, after December 31, 2008. [Reg. § 44.6694-2.]

☐ [*T.D.* 9436, 12-15-2008.]

**[Reg. § 53.6694-2]**

**§ 53.6694-2. Penalties for understatement due to an unreasonable position.**—(a) *In general.*—A person who is a tax return preparer of any return or claim for refund of tax under Chapter 42 of the Internal Revenue Code (Code) shall be subject to penalties under section 6694(a) of the Code in the manner stated in § 1.6694-2 of this chapter.

(b) *Effective/applicability date.*—This section is applicable to returns and claims for refund filed, and advice provided, after December 31, 2008. [Reg. § 53.6694-2.]

☐ [*T.D.* 9436, 12-15-2008.]

**[Reg. § 54.6694-2]**

**§ 54.6694-2. Penalties for understatement due to an unreasonable position.**—(a) *In general.*—A person who is a tax return preparer of any return or claim for refund of tax under chapter 43 of subtitle D of the Internal Revenue Code (Code) shall be subject to penalties under section 6694(a) of the Code in the manner stated in § 1.6694-2 of this chapter.

(b) *Effective/applicability date.*—This section is applicable to returns and claims for refund filed, and advice provided, after December 31, 2008. [Reg. § 54.6694-2.]

☐ [*T.D.* 9436, 12-15-2008.]

**[Reg. § 55.6694-2]**

**§ 55.6694-2. Penalties for understatement due to an unreasonable position.**—(a) *In general.*—A person who is a tax return preparer of any return or claim for refund of excise tax under chapter 44 of subtitle D of the Internal Revenue Code (Code) shall be subject to penalties under section 6694(a) of the Code in the manner stated in § 1.6694-2 of this chapter.

(b) *Effective/applicability date.*—This section is applicable to returns and claims for refund filed, and advice provided, after December 31, 2008. [Reg. § 55.6694-2.]

☐ [*T.D.* 9436, 12-15-2008.]

**[Reg. § 56.6694-2]**

**§ 56.6694-2. Penalties for understatement due to an unreasonable position.**—(a) *In general.*—A person who is a tax return preparer of any return or claim for refund of excise tax under chapter 41 of subtitle D of the Internal Revenue Code (Code) shall be subject to penalties under section 6694(a) of the Code in the manner stated in § 1.6694-2 of this chapter.

(b) *Effective/applicability date.*—This section is applicable to returns and claims for refund filed, and advice provided, after December 31, 2008. [Reg. § 56.6694-2.]

☐ [*T.D.* 9436, 12-15-2008.]

**[Reg. § 156.6694-2]**

**§ 156.6694-2. Penalties for understatement due to an unreasonable position.**—(a) *In general.*—A person who is a tax return preparer of any return or claim for refund of tax under section 5881 of the Internal Revenue Code (Code) shall be subject to penalties under section 6694(a) of the Code in the manner stated in § 1.6694-2 of this chapter.

(b) *Effective/applicability date.*—This section is applicable to returns and claims for refund filed, and advice provided, after December 31, 2008. [Reg. § 156.6694-2.]

☐ [*T.D.* 9436, 12-15-2008.]

**[Reg. § 157.6694-2]**

**§ 157.6694-2. Penalties for understatement due to an unreasonable position.**—(a) *In general.*—A person who is a tax return preparer of any return or claim for refund of tax under section 5891 of the Internal Revenue Code (Code) shall be subject to penalties under section 6694(a) of the Code in the manner stated in § 1.6694-2 of this chapter.

(b) *Effective/applicability date.*—This section is applicable to returns and claims for refund filed, and advice provided, after December 31, 2008. [Reg. § 157.6694-2.]

☐ [*T.D.* 9436, 12-15-2008.]

**[Reg. § 1.6694-3]**

**§ 1.6694-3. Penalty for understatement due to willful, reckless, or intentional conduct.**—(a) *In general.*—(1) *Proscribed conduct.*—A tax return preparer is liable for a penalty under section 6694(b) equal to the greater of $5,000 or 50 percent of the income derived (or to be derived) by the tax return preparer if any part of an understatement of liability for a return or claim for refund that is prepared is due to—

(i) A willful attempt by a tax return preparer to understate in any manner the liability for tax on the return or claim for refund; or

(ii) Any reckless or intentional disregard of rules or regulations by a tax return preparer.

(2) *Special rule for corporations, partnerships, and other firms.*—A firm that employs a tax return preparer subject to a penalty under section 6694(b) (or a firm of which the individual tax return preparer is a partner, member, shareholder or other equity holder) is also subject to penalty if, and only if—

(i) One or more members of the principal management (or principal officers) of the firm or a branch office participated in or knew of the conduct proscribed by section 6694(b);

(ii) The corporation, partnership, or other firm entity failed to provide reasonable and appropriate procedures for review of the position for which the penalty is imposed; or

(iii) The corporation, partnership, or other firm entity disregarded its reasonable and appropriate review procedures through willfulness, recklessness, or gross indifference (including ignoring facts that would lead a person of reasonable prudence and competence to investigate or ascertain) in the formulation of the advice, or the preparation of the return or claim for refund, that included the position for which the penalty is imposed.

(b) *Willful attempt to understate liability.*—A preparer is considered to have willfully attempted to understate liability if the preparer disregards, in an attempt wrongfully to reduce the tax liability of the taxpayer, information furnished by the taxpayer or other persons. For example, if a preparer disregards information concerning certain items of taxable income furnished by the taxpayer or other persons, the preparer is subject to the penalty. Similarly, if a taxpayer states to a preparer that the taxpayer has only two dependents, and the preparer reports six dependents on the return, the preparer is subject to the penalty.

(c) *Reckless or intentional disregard.*—(1) Except as provided in paragraphs (c)(2) and (c)(3) of this section, a preparer is considered to have recklessly or intentionally disregarded a rule or regulation if the preparer takes a position on the return or claim for refund that is contrary to a rule or regulation (as defined in paragraph (f)[(e)] of this section) and the preparer knows of, or is reckless in not knowing of, the rule or regulation in question. A preparer is reckless in not knowing of a rule or regulation if the preparer makes little or no effort to determine whether a rule or regulation exists, under circumstances which demonstrate a substantial deviation from the standard of conduct that a reasonable preparer would observe in the situation.

(2) A tax return preparer is not considered to have recklessly or intentionally disregarded a rule or regulation if the position contrary to the rule or regulation has a reasonable basis as defined in § 1.6694-2(d)(2) and is adequately disclosed in accordance with §§ 1.6694-2(d)(3)(i)(A) or (C) or 1.6694-2(d)(3)(ii). In the case of a position contrary to a regulation, the position must represent a good faith challenge to the validity of the regulation and, when disclosed in accordance with §§ 1.6694-2(d)(3)(i)(A) or (C) or 1.6694-2(d)(3)(ii), the tax return preparer must identify the regulation being challenged. For purposes of this section, disclosure on the return in accordance with an annual revenue procedure under § 1.6662-4(f)(2) is not applicable.

(3) In the case of a position contrary to a revenue ruling or notice (other than a notice of proposed rulemaking) published by the Internal Revenue Service in the Internal Revenue Bulletin, a tax return preparer also is not considered to have recklessly or intentionally disregarded the ruling or notice if the position meets the substantial authority standard described in § 1.6662-4(d) and is not with respect to a reportable transaction to which section 6662A applies.

(d) *Examples.*—The provisions of paragraphs (b) and (c) of this section are illustrated by the following examples:

*Example 1.* A taxpayer provided Preparer T with detailed check registers reflecting personal and business expenses. One of the expenses was for domestic help, and this expense was identified as personal on the check register. T knowingly deducted the expenses of the taxpayer's domestic help as wages paid in the taxpayer's business. T is subject to the penalty under section 6694(b).

*Example 2.* A taxpayer provided Preparer U with detailed check registers to compute the taxpayer's expenses. U, however, knowingly overstated the expenses on the return. After adjustments by the examiner, the tax liability increased significantly. Because U disregarded information provided in the check registers, U is subject to the penalty under section 6694(b).

*Example 3.* Preparer V prepares a taxpayer's return in 2009 and encounters certain expenses incurred in the purchase of a business. Final regulations provide that such expenses incurred in the purchase of a business must be capitalized. One U.S. Tax Court case decided in 2006 has expressly invalidated that portion of the regulations. There are no courts that ruled favorably with respect to the validity of that portion of the regulations and there are no other authorities existing on the issue. Under these facts, V will have a reasonable basis for the position as defined in § 1.6694-2(d)(2) and will not be subject to the section 6694(b) penalty if the position is adequately disclosed in accordance with paragraph (c)(2) of this section because the position represents a good faith challenge to the validity of the regulations.

(e) *Rules or regulations.*—The term *rules or regulations* includes the provisions of the Internal Revenue Code (Code), temporary or final Treasury regulations issued under the Code, and revenue rulings or notices (other than notices of proposed rulemaking) issued by the Internal Revenue Service and published in the Internal Revenue Bulletin.

(f) *Section 6694(b) penalty reduced by section 6694(a) penalty.*—The amount of any penalty to which a tax return preparer may be subject under section 6694(b) for a return or claim for refund is reduced by any amount assessed and collected against the tax return preparer under section 6694(a) for the same position on a return or claim for refund.

(g) *Effective/applicability date.*—This section is applicable to returns and claims for refund filed, and advice provided, after December 31, 2008.

(h) *Burden of proof.*—In any proceeding with respect to the penalty imposed by section 6694(b), the Government bears the burden of proof on the issue of whether the preparer willfully attempted to understate the liability for tax. See section 7427. The preparer bears the burden of proof on such other issues as whether—

(1) The preparer recklessly or intentionally disregarded a rule or regulation;

(2) A position contrary to a regulation represents a good faith challenge to the validity of the regulation; and

(3) Disclosure was adequately made in accordance with paragraph (e) of this section. [Reg. § 1.6694-3.]

☐ [*T.D.* 8382, 12-30-91. *Amended by T.D.* 9436, 12-15-2008 (*corrected* 1-28-2009).]

### [Reg. § 20.6694-3]

**§ 20.6694-3. Penalty for understatement due to willful, reckless, or intentional conduct.**—(a) *In general.*—A person who is a tax return preparer of any return or claim for refund of estate tax under chapter 11 of subtitle B of the Internal Revenue Code (Code) shall be subject to penalties under section 6694(b) of the Code in the manner stated in § 1.6694-3 of this chapter.

(b) *Effective/applicability date.*—This section is applicable to returns and claims for refund filed, and advice provided, after December 31, 2008. [Reg. § 20.6694-3.]

☐ [*T.D.* 9436, 12-15-2008.]

### [Reg. § 25.6694-3]

**§ 25.6694-3. Penalty for understatement due to willful, reckless, or intentional conduct.**—(a) *In general.*—A person who is a tax return preparer of any return or claim for refund of gift tax under chapter 12 of subtitle B of the Internal Revenue Code (Code) shall be subject to penalties under section 6694(b) of the Code in the manner stated in § 1.6694-3 of this chapter.

(b) *Effective/applicability date.*—This section is applicable to returns and claims for refund filed, and advice provided, after December 31, 2008. [Reg. § 25.6694-3.]

☐ [*T.D.* 9436, 12-15-2008.]

### [Reg. § 26.6694-3]

**§ 26.6694-3. Penalty for understatement due to willful, reckless, or intentional conduct.**—(a) *In general.*—A person who is a tax return preparer of any return or claim for refund of generation-skip-

ping transfer tax under chapter 13 of subtitle B of the Internal Revenue Code (Code) shall be subject to penalties under section 6694(b) of the Code in the manner stated in § 1.6694-3 of this chapter.

(b) *Effective/applicability date.*—This section is applicable to returns and claims for refund filed, and advice provided, after December 31, 2008. [Reg. § 26.6694-3.]

☐ [*T.D.* 9436, 12-15-2008.]

### [Reg. § 31.6694-3]

**§ 31.6694-3. Penalty for understatement due to willful, reckless, or intentional conduct.**—(a) *In general.*—A person who is a tax return preparer of any return or claim for refund of employment tax under chapters 21 through 25 of subtitle C of the Internal Revenue Code (Code) shall be subject to penalties under section 6694(b) of the Code in the manner stated in § 1.6694-3 of this chapter.

(b) *Effective/applicability date.*—This section is applicable to returns and claims for refund filed, and advice provided, after December 31, 2008. [Reg. § 31.6694-3.]

☐ [*T.D.* 9436, 12-15-2008 (*corrected* 1-28-2009).]

### [Reg. § 40.6694-3]

**§ 40.6694-3. Penalty for understatement due to willful, reckless, or intentional conduct.**—(a) *In general.*—A person who is a tax return preparer of any return or claim for refund of any tax to which this part 40 applies shall be subject to penalties under section 6694(b) in the manner stated in § 1.6694-3 of this chapter.

(b) *Effective/applicability date.*—This section is applicable to returns and claims for refund filed, and advice provided, after December 31, 2008. [Reg. § 40.6694-3.]

☐ [*T.D.* 9436, 12-15-2008 (*corrected* 1-28-2009).]

### [Reg. § 41.6694-3]

**§ 41.6694-3. Penalty for understatement due to willful, reckless, or intentional conduct.**—(a) *In general.*—A person who is a tax return preparer of any return or claim for refund of excise tax under section 4481 shall be subject to penalties under section 6694(b) in the manner stated in § 1.6694-3 of this chapter.

(b) *Effective/applicability date.*—This section is applicable to returns and claims for refund filed, and advice provided, after December 31, 2008. [Reg. § 41.6694-3.]

☐ [*T.D.* 9436, 12-15-2008.]

### [Reg. § 44.6694-3]

**§ 44.6694-3. Penalty for understatement due to willful, reckless, or intentional conduct.**—(a) *In general.*—A person who is a tax return preparer of any return or claim for refund of tax on wagers under sections 4401 or 4411 shall be subject to penalties under section 6694(b) in the manner stated in § 1.6694-3 of this chapter.

(b) *Effective/applicability date.*—This section is applicable to returns and claims for refund filed, and advice provided, after December 31, 2008. [Reg. § 44.6694-3.]

☐ [*T.D.* 9436, 12-15-2008.]

### [Reg. § 53.6694-3]

**§ 53.6694-3. Penalty for understatement due to willful, reckless, or intentional conduct.**—(a) *In general.*—A person who is a tax return preparer of any return or claim for refund of tax under Chapter 42 of the Internal Revenue Code (Code) shall be subject to penalties under section 6694(b) of the Code in the manner stated in § 1.6694-3 of this chapter.

(b) *Effective/applicability date.*—This section is applicable to returns and claims for refund filed, and advice provided, after December 31, 2008. [Reg. § 53.6694-3.]

☐ [*T.D.* 9436, 12-15-2008.]

### [Reg. § 54.6694-3]

**§ 54.6694-3. Penalty for understatement due to willful, reckless, or intentional conduct.**—(a) *In general.*—A person who is a tax return preparer of any return or claim for refund of excise tax under chapter 43 of subtitle D of the Internal Revenue Code (Code) shall be subject to penalties under section 6694(b) of the Code in the manner stated in § 1.6694-3 of this chapter.

(b) *Effective/applicability date.*—This section is applicable to returns and claims for refund filed, and advice provided, after December 31, 2008. [Reg. § 54.6694-3.]

☐ [*T.D.* 9436, 12-15-2008.]

**[Reg. § 55.6694-3]**

**§ 55.6694-3. Penalty for understatement due to willful, reckless, or intentional conduct.**—(a) *In general.*—A person who is a tax return preparer of any return or claim for refund of tax under chapter 44 of subtitle D of the Internal Revenue Code (Code) shall be subject to penalties under section 6694(b) of the Code in the manner stated in § 1.6694-3 of this chapter.

(b) *Effective/applicability date.*—This section is applicable to returns and claims for refund filed, and advice provided, after December 31, 2008. [Reg. § 55.6694-3.]

☐ [*T.D.* 9436, 12-15-2008.]

**[Reg. § 56.6694-3]**

**§ 56.6694-3. Penalty for understatement due to willful, reckless, or intentional conduct.**—(a) *In general.*—A person who is a tax return preparer of any return or claim for refund of tax under chapter 41 of subtitle D of the Internal Revenue Code (Code) shall be subject to penalties under section 6694(b) of the Code in the manner stated in § 1.6694-3 of this chapter.

(b) *Effective/applicability date.*—This section is applicable to returns and claims for refund filed, and advice provided, after December 31, 2008. [Reg. § 56.6694-3.]

☐ [*T.D.* 9436, 12-15-2008.]

**[Reg. § 156.6694-3]**

**§ 156.6694-3. Penalty for understatement due to willful, reckless, or intentional conduct.**—(a) *In general.*—A person who is a tax return preparer of any return or claim for refund of tax under section 5881 of the Internal Revenue Code (Code) shall be subject to penalties under section 6694(b) of the Code in the manner stated in § 1.6694-3 of this chapter.

(b) *Effective/applicability date.*—This section is applicable to returns and claims for refund filed, and advice provided, after December 31, 2008. [Reg. § 156.6694-3.]

☐ [*T.D.* 9436, 12-15-2008.]

**[Reg. § 157.6694-3]**

**§ 157.6694-3. Penalty for understatement due to willful, reckless, or intentional conduct.**—(a) *In general.*—A person who is a tax return preparer of any return or claim for refund of tax under section 5891 of the Internal Revenue Code (Code) shall be subject to penalties under section 6694(b) of the Code in the manner stated in § 1.6694-3 of this chapter.

(b) *Effective/applicability date.*—This section is applicable to returns and claims for refund filed, and advice provided, after December 31, 2008. [Reg. § 157.6694-3.]

☐ [*T.D.* 9436, 12-15-2008.]

**[Reg. § 1.6694-4]**

**§ 1.6694-4. Extension of period of collection when tax return preparer pays 15 percent of a penalty for understatement of taxpayer's liability and certain other procedural matters.**—(a) *In general.*—(1) The Internal Revenue Service (IRS) will investigate the preparation by a tax return preparer of a return of tax under the Internal Revenue Code (Code) or claim for refund of tax under the Code as described in § 301.7701-15(b)(4) of this chapter, and will send a report of the examination to the tax return preparer before the assessment of either—

(i) A penalty for understating tax liability due to a position for which either it was not reasonable to believe that the position would more likely than not be sustained on its merits under section 6694(a) or no substantial authority, as applicable (or not a reasonable basis for disclosed positions); or

(ii) A penalty for willful understatement of liability or reckless or intentional disregard of rules or regulations under section 6694(b).

(2) Unless the period of limitations (if any) under section 6696(d) may expire without adequate opportunity for assessment, the IRS will also send, before assessment of either penalty, a 30-day letter to the tax return preparer notifying him of the proposed penalty or penalties and offering an opportunity to the tax return preparer to request further administrative consideration and a final administrative determination by the IRS concerning the assessment. If the tax return preparer then makes a timely request, assessment may not be made until the IRS makes a final administrative determination adverse to the tax return preparer.

(3) If the IRS assesses either of the two penalties described in section 6694(a) and section 6694(b), it will send to the tax return preparer a statement of notice and demand, separate from any notice of a tax deficiency, for payment of the amount assessed.

(4) Within 30 days after the day on which notice and demand of either of the two penalties described in section 6694(a) and section 6694(b) is made against the tax return preparer, the tax return preparer must either—

(i) Pay the entire amount assessed (and may file a claim for refund of the amount paid at any time not later than 3 years after the date of payment); or

(ii) Pay an amount which is not less than 15 percent of the entire amount assessed with respect to each return or claim for refund and file a claim for refund of the amount paid.

(5) If the tax return preparer pays an amount and files a claim for refund under paragraph (a)(4)(ii) of this section, the IRS may not make, begin, or prosecute a levy or proceeding in court for collection of the unpaid remainder of the amount assessed until the later of—

(i) A date which is more than 30 days after the earlier of—

(A) The day on which the tax return preparer's claim for refund is denied; or

(B) The expiration of 6 months after the day on which the tax return preparer filed the claim for refund; and

(ii) Final resolution of any proceeding begun as provided in paragraph (b) of this section.

(6) The IRS may counterclaim in any proceeding begun as provided in paragraph (b) of this section for the unpaid remainder of the amount assessed. Final resolution of a proceeding includes any settlement between the IRS and the tax return preparer, any final determination by a court (for which the period for appeal, if any, has expired) and, generally, the types of determinations provided under section 1313(a) (relating to taxpayer deficiencies). Notwithstanding section 7421(a) (relating to suits to restrain assessment or collection), the beginning of a levy or proceeding in court by the IRS in contravention of paragraph (a)(5) of this section may be enjoined by a proceeding in the proper court.

(b) *Preparer must bring suit in district court to determine liability for penalty.*—The IRS may proceed with collection of the amount of the penalty not paid under paragraph (a)(4)(ii) of this section if the preparer fails to begin a proceeding for refund in the appropriate United States district court within 30 days after the earlier of—

(1) The day on which the preparer's claim for refund filed under paragraph (a)(4)(ii) of this section is denied; or

(2) The expiration of 6 months after the day on which the preparer filed the claim for refund.

(c) *Suspension of running of period of limitations on collection.*—The running of the period of limitations provided in section 6502 on the collection by levy or by a proceeding in court of the unpaid amount of a penalty or penalties described in section 6694(a) or section 6694(b) is suspended for the period during which the IRS, under paragraph (a)(5) of this section, may not collect the unpaid amount of the penalty or penalties by levy or a proceeding in court.

(d) *Effective/applicability date.*—This section is applicable to returns and claims for refund filed, and advice provided, after December 31, 2008. [Reg. § 1.6694-4.]

☐ [*T.D.* 8382, 12-30-91. *Amended by T.D.* 9436, 12-15-2008.]

**[Reg. § 20.6694-4]**

**§ 20.6694-4. Extension of period of collection when preparer pays 15 percent of a penalty for understatement of taxpayer's liability and certain other procedural matters.**—(a) *In general.*—For rules relating to the extension of the period of collection when a tax return preparer who prepared a return or claim for refund for estate tax under chapter 11 of subtitle B of the Internal Revenue Code pays 15 percent of a penalty for understatement of the taxpayer's liability, and procedural matters relating to the investigation, assessment and collection of the penalties under sections 6694(a) and (b), the rules under § 1.6694-4 of this chapter will apply.

(b) *Effective/applicability date.*—This section is applicable to returns and claims for refund filed, and advice provided, after December 31, 2008. [Reg. § 20.6694-4.]

☐ [*T.D.* 9436, 12-15-2008.]

**[Reg. § 25.6694-4]**

**§ 25.6694-4. Extension of period of collection when tax return preparer pays 15 percent of a penalty for understatement of taxpayer's liability and certain other procedural matters.**—(a) *In general.*—For rules for the extension of period of collection when a tax return preparer who prepared a return or claim for refund for gift tax under chapter 12 of subtitle B of the Internal Revenue Code pays 15 percent of a penalty for understatement of taxpayer's liability, and procedural matters relating to the investigation, assessment and collection of the penalties under section 6694(a) and (b), the rules under § 1.6694-4 of this chapter will apply.

(b) *Effective/applicability date.*—This section is applicable to returns and claims for refund filed, and advice provided, after December 31, 2008. [Reg. § 25.6694-4.]

☐ [*T.D.* 9436, 12-15-2008.]

### [Reg. § 26.6694-4]

**§ 26.6694-4. Extension of period of collection when preparer pays 15 percent of a penalty for understatement of taxpayer's liability and certain other procedural matters.**—(a) *In general.*—For rules relating to the extension of period of collection when a tax return preparer who prepared a return or claim for refund for generation-skipping transfer tax under chapter 13 of subtitle B of the Internal Revenue Code pays 15 percent of a penalty for understatement of taxpayer's liability, and procedural matters relating to the investigation, assessment and collection of the penalties under section 6694(a) and (b), the rules under § 1.6694-4 of this chapter will apply.

(b) *Effective/applicability date.*—This section is applicable to returns and claims for refund filed, and advice provided, after December 31, 2008. [Reg. § 26.6694-4.]

☐ [*T.D.* 9436, 12-15-2008.]

### [Reg. § 31.6694-4]

**§ 31.6694-4. Extension of period of collection when tax return preparer pays 15 percent of a penalty for understatement of taxpayer's liability and certain other procedural matters.**—(a) *In general.*—For rules relating to the extension of period of collection when a tax return preparer who prepared a return or claim for refund for employment tax under chapters 21 through 25 of subtitle C of the Internal Revenue Code pays 15 percent of a penalty for understatement of taxpayer's liability and procedural matters relating to the investigation, assessment and collection of the penalties under section 6694(a) and (b), the rules under § 1.6694-4 of this chapter will apply.

(b) *Effective/applicability date.*—This section is applicable to returns and claims for refund filed, and advice provided, after December 31, 2008. [Reg. § 31.6694-4.]

☐ [*T.D.* 9436, 12-15-2008.]

### [Reg. § 40.6694-4]

**§ 40.6694-4. Extension of period of collection when tax return preparer pays 15 percent of a penalty for understatement of taxpayer's liability and certain other procedural matters.**—(a) *In general.*—For rules relating to the extension of period of collection when a tax return preparer who prepared a return or claim for refund of any tax to which this part 40 applies pays 15 percent of a penalty for understatement of taxpayer's liability and procedural matters relating to the investigation, assessment and collection of the penalties under section 6694(a) and (b), the rules under § 1.6694-4 of this chapter will apply.

(b) *Effective/applicability date.*—This section is applicable to returns and claims for refund filed, and advice provided, after December 31, 2008. [Reg. § 40.6694-4.]

☐ [*T.D.* 9436, 12-15-2008 (*corrected* 1-28-2009).]

### [Reg. § 41.6694-4]

**§ 41.6694-4. Extension of period of collection when preparer pays 15 percent of a penalty for understatement of taxpayer's liability and certain other procedural matters.**—(a) *In general.*—For rules relating to the extension of period of collection when a tax return preparer who prepared a return or claim for refund for excise tax under section 4481 pays 15 percent of a penalty for understatement of taxpayer's liability, and procedural matters relating to the investigation, assessment and collection of the penalties under section 6694(a) and (b), the rules under § 1.6694-4 of this chapter will apply.

(b) *Effective/applicability date.*—This section is applicable to returns and claims for refund filed, and advice provided, after December 31, 2008. [Reg. § 41.6694-4.]

☐ [*T.D.* 9436, 12-15-2008.]

### [Reg. § 44.6694-4]

**§ 44.6694-4. Extension of period of collection when preparer pays 15 percent of a penalty for understatement of taxpayer's liability and certain other procedural matters.**—(a) *In general.*—For rules relating to the extension of period of collection when a tax return preparer who prepared a return or claim for refund for tax on wagers under sections 4401 or 4411 pays 15 percent of a penalty for understatement of taxpayer's liability and procedural matters relating to the investigation, assessment and collection of the penalties under section 6694(a) and (b), the rules under § 1.6694-4 of this chapter will apply.

(b) *Effective/applicability date.*—This section is applicable to returns and claims for refund filed, and advice provided, after December 31, 2008. [Reg. § 44.6694-4.]

☐ [*T.D.* 9436, 12-15-2008.]

### [Reg. § 53.6694-4]

**§ 53.6694-4. Extension of period of collection when tax return preparer pays 15 percent of a penalty for understatement of taxpayer's liability and certain other procedural matters.**—(a) *In general.*—For rules relating to the extension of period of collection when a tax return preparer who prepared a return or claim for refund of tax under Chapter 42 of the Internal Revenue Code pays 15 percent of a penalty for understatement of taxpayer's liability and procedural matters relating to the investigation, assessment and collection of the penalties under section 6694(a) and (b), the rules under § 1.6694-4 of this chapter will apply.

(b) *Effective/applicability date.*—This section is applicable to returns and claims for refund filed, and advice provided, after December 31, 2008. [Reg. § 53.6694-4.]

☐ [*T.D.* 9436, 12-15-2008.]

### [Reg. § 54.6694-4]

**§ 54.6694-4. Extension of period of collection when tax return preparer pays 15 percent of a penalty for understatement of taxpayer's liability and certain other procedural matters.**—(a) *In general.*—For rules relating to the extension of period of collection when a tax return preparer who prepared a return or claim for refund for tax under chapter 43 of subtitle D of the Internal Revenue Code pays 15 percent of a penalty for understatement of taxpayer's liability, and procedural matters relating to the investigation, assessment and collection of the penalties under section 6694(a) and (b), the rules under § 1.6694-4 of this chapter will apply.

(b) *Effective/applicability date.*—This section is applicable to returns and claims for refund filed, and advice provided, after December 31, 2008. [Reg. § 54.6694-4.]

☐ [*T.D.* 9436, 12-15-2008.]

### [Reg. § 55.6694-4]

**§ 55.6694-4. Extension of period of collection when tax return preparer pays 15 percent of a penalty for understatement of taxpayer's liability and certain other procedural matters.**—(a) *In general.*—For rules relating to the extension of period of collection when a tax return preparer who prepared a return or claim for refund for excise tax under chapter 44 of subtitle D of the Internal Revenue Code pays 15 percent of a penalty for understatement of taxpayer's liability and procedural matters relating to the investigation, assessment and collection of the penalties under section 6694(a) and (b), the rules under § 1.6694-4 of this chapter will apply.

(b) *Effective/applicability date.*—This section is applicable to returns and claims for refund filed, and advice provided, after December 31, 2008. [Reg. § 55.6694-4.]

☐ [*T.D.* 9436, 12-15-2008.]

### [Reg. § 56.6694-4]

**§ 56.6694-4. Extension of period of collection when tax return preparer pays 15 percent of a penalty for understatement of taxpayer's liability and certain other procedural matters.**—(a) *In general.*—For rules relating to the extension of period of collection when a tax return preparer who prepared a return or claim for refund for tax under chapter 41 of subtitle D of the Internal Revenue Code pays 15 percent of a penalty for understatement of taxpayer's liability and procedural matters relating to the investigation, assessment and collection of the penalties under section 6694(a) and (b), the rules under § 1.6694-4 of this chapter will apply.

(b) *Effective/applicability date.*—This section is applicable to returns and claims for refund filed, and advice provided, after December 31, 2008. [Reg. § 56.6694-4.]

☐ [*T.D.* 9436, 12-15-2008.]

### [Reg. § 156.6694-4]

**§ 156.6694-4. Extension of period of collection when tax return preparer pays 15 percent of a penalty for understatement of taxpayer's liability and certain other procedural matters.**—(a) *In general.*—For rules relating to the extension of period of collection when a tax return preparer who prepared a return or claim for refund for tax under section 5881 of the Internal Revenue Code pays 15 percent of a penalty for understatement of taxpayer's liability and procedural matters relating to the investigation, assessment and collection of the penalties under section 6694(a) and (b), the rules under § 1.6694-4 of this chapter will apply.

(b) *Effective/applicability date.*—This section is applicable to returns and claims for refund filed, and advice provided, after December 31, 2008. [Reg. § 156.6694-4.]

□ [*T.D.* 9436, 12-15-2008.]

### [Reg. §157.6694-4]

**§157.6694-4. Extension of period of collection when preparer pays 15 percent of a penalty for understatement of taxpayer's liability and certain other procedural matters.**—(a) *In general.*—For rules relating to the extension of period of collection when a tax return preparer who prepared a return or claim for refund for tax under section 5891 of the Internal Revenue Code pays 15 percent of a penalty for understatement of taxpayer's liability and procedural matters relating to the investigation, assessment and collection of the penalties under section 6694(a) and (b), the rules under § 1.6694-4 of this chapter will apply.

(b) *Effective/applicability date.*—This section is applicable to returns and claims for refund filed, and advice provided, after December 31, 2008. [Reg. § 157.6694-4.]

□ [*T.D.* 9436, 12-15-2008.]

### [Reg. §1.6695-1]

**§1.6695-1. Other assessable penalties with respect to the preparation of tax returns for other persons.**—(a) *Failure to furnish copy to taxpayer.*—(1) A person who is a signing tax return preparer as described in § 301.7701-15(b)(1) of this chapter of any return of tax or claim for refund of tax under the Internal Revenue Code (Code), and who fails to satisfy the requirements imposed by section 6107(a) and § 1.6107-1(a) to furnish a copy of the return or claim for refund to the taxpayer (or nontaxable entity), shall be subject to a penalty of $50 for such failure, with a maximum penalty of $25,000 per person imposed with respect to each calendar year, unless it is shown that the failure is due to reasonable cause and not due to willful neglect.

(2) No penalty may be imposed under section 6695(a) and paragraph (a)(1) of this section upon a tax return preparer who furnishes a copy of the return or claim for refund to taxpayers who—

(i) Hold an elected or politically appointed position with the government of the United States or a state or political subdivision thereof; and

(ii) In order faithfully to carry out their official duties, have so arranged their affairs that they have less than full knowledge of the property that they hold or of the debts for which they are responsible, if information is deleted from the copy in order to preserve or maintain this arrangement.

(b) *Failure to sign return.*—(1) An individual who is a signing tax return preparer as described in § 301.7701-15(b)(1) of this chapter with respect to a return of tax or claim for refund of tax under the Code as described in § 301.7701-15(b)(4) that is not signed electronically shall sign the return or claim for refund after it is completed and before it is presented to the taxpayer (or nontaxable entity) for signature. For rules covering electronically signed returns, see paragraph (b)(2) of this section. If the signing tax return preparer is unavailable for signature, another tax return preparer shall review the entire preparation of the return or claim for refund, and then shall sign the return or claim for refund. The tax return preparer shall sign the return in the manner prescribed by the Commissioner in forms, instructions, or other appropriate guidance.

(2) In the case of electronically signed tax returns, the signing tax return preparer need not sign the return prior to presenting a completed copy of the return to the taxpayer. The signing tax return preparer, however, must furnish all of the information that will be transmitted as the electronically signed tax return to the taxpayer contemporaneously with furnishing the Form 8879, "IRS e-file Signature Authorization," or other similar Internal Revenue Service (IRS) e-file signature form. The information may be furnished on a replica of an official form. The signing tax return preparer shall electronically sign the return in the manner prescribed by the Commissioner in forms, instructions, or other appropriate guidance.

(3) An individual required by this paragraph (b) to sign a return or claim for refund shall be subject to a penalty of $50 for each failure to sign, with a maximum of $25,000 per person imposed with respect to each calendar year, unless it is shown that the failure is due to reasonable cause and not due to willful neglect. If the tax return preparer asserts reasonable cause for failure to sign, the IRS will require a written statement to substantiate the tax return preparer's claim of reasonable cause. For purposes of this paragraph (b), reasonable cause is a cause that arises despite ordinary care and prudence exercised by the individual tax return preparer.

(4) *Examples.*—The application of this paragraph (b) is illustrated by the following examples:

*Example 1.* Law Firm A employs B, a lawyer, to prepare for compensation estate tax returns and claims for refund of taxes. Firm A is engaged by C to prepare a Federal estate tax return. Firm A assigns B to prepare the return. B obtains the information necessary for completing the return from C and makes determinations with respect to the proper application of the tax laws to such information in order to determine the estate's tax liability. B then forwards such information to D, a computer tax service that performs the mathematical computations and prints the return by means of computer processing. D then sends the completed estate tax return to B who reviews the accuracy of the return. B is the individual tax return preparer who is primarily responsible for the overall accuracy of the estate tax return. B must sign the return as tax return preparer in order to not be subject to the section 6695(b) penalty.

*Example 2.* Partnership E is a national accounting firm that prepares returns and claims for refund of taxes for compensation. F and G, employees of Partnership E, are involved in preparing the Form 990-T, Exempt Organization Business Income Tax Return, for H, a tax exempt organization. After they complete the return, including the gathering of the necessary information, analyzing the proper application of the tax laws to such information, and the performance of the necessary mathematical computations, I, a supervisory employee of Partnership E, reviews the return. As part of this review, I reviews the information provided and the application of the tax laws to this information. The mathematical computations and carriedforward amounts are reviewed by J, an employee of Partnership E. The policies and practices of Partnership E require that K, a partner, finally review the return. The scope of K's review includes reviewing the information provided and applying to this information his knowledge of H's affairs, observing that Partnership E's policies and practices have been followed, and making the final determination with respect to the proper application of the tax laws to determine H's tax liability. K may or may not exercise these responsibilities, or may exercise them to a greater or lesser extent, depending on the degree of complexity of the return, his confidence in I (or F and G), and other factors. K is the individual tax return preparer who is primarily responsible for the overall accuracy of H's return. K must sign the return as tax return preparer in order to not be subject to the section 6695(b) penalty.

*Example 3.* L corporation maintains an office in Seattle, Washington, for the purpose of preparing partnership returns for compensation. L makes compensatory arrangements with individuals (but provides no working facilities) in several states to collect information from partners of a partnership and to make decisions with respect to the proper application of the tax laws to the information in order to prepare the partnership return and calculate the partnership's distributive items. M, an individual, who has such an arrangement in Los Angeles with L, collects information from N, the general partner of a partnership, and completes a worksheet kit supplied by L that is stamped with M's name and an identification number assigned to M by L. In this process, M classifies this information in appropriate categories for the preparation of the partnership return. The completed worksheet kit signed by M is then mailed to L. O, an employee in L's office, reviews the worksheet kit to make sure it was properly completed. O does not review the information obtained from N for its validity or accuracy. O may, but did not, make the final decision with respect to the proper application of tax laws to the information provided. The data from the worksheet is entered into a computer and the return form is completed. The return is prepared for submission to N with filing instructions. M is the individual tax return preparer primarily responsible for the overall accuracy of the partnership return. M must sign the return as tax return preparer in order to not be subject to the section 6695(b) penalty.

*Example 4.* P employs R, S, and T to prepare gift tax returns for taxpayers. After R and S have collected the information from a taxpayer and applied the tax laws to the information, the return form is completed by a computer service. On the day the returns prepared by R and S are ready for their signatures, R is away from the city for 1 week on another assignment and S is on detail to another office in the same city for the day. T may sign the gift tax returns prepared by R, provided that T reviews the information obtained by R relative to the taxpayer, and T reviews the preparation of each return prepared by R. T may not sign the returns prepared by S because S is available.

(5) *Effective/applicability date.*—This paragraph (b) is applicable to returns and claims for refund filed after December 31, 2008.

(c) *Failure to furnish identifying number.*—(1) A person who is a signing tax return preparer as described in § 301.7701-15(b)(1) of this chapter of any return of tax under the Code or claim for refund of tax under the Code, and who fails to satisfy the requirement of section 6109(a)(4) and § 1.6109-2(a) to furnish one or more identifying numbers of signing tax return preparers or persons employing the signing tax return preparer (or with which the signing tax return preparer is associated) on a return or claim for refund after it is completed and before it is presented to the taxpayer (or nontaxable entity) for signature shall be subject to a penalty of $50 for each failure, with a maximum of $25,000 per person imposed with respect to each calendar year, unless it is shown that the failure is due to reasonable cause and not due to willful neglect.

(2) No more than one penalty of $50 may be imposed under section 6695(c) and paragraph (c)(1) of this section with respect to a single return or claim for refund.

(d) *Failure to retain copy or record.*—(1) A person who is a signing tax return preparer as described in §301.7701-15(b)(1) of this chapter of any return of tax under the Code or claim for refund of tax under the Code, and who fails to satisfy the requirements imposed upon him or her by section 6107(b) and §1.6107-1(b) and (c) (other than the record requirement described in both §1.6107-1(b)(2) and (3)) to retain and make available for inspection a copy of the return or claim for refund, or to include the return or claim for refund in a record of returns and claims for refund and make the record available for inspection, shall be subject to a penalty of $50 for the failure, unless it is shown that the failure is due to reasonable cause and not due to willful neglect.

(2) A person may not, for returns or claims for refund presented to the taxpayers (or nontaxable entities) during each calendar year, be subject to more than $25,000 in penalties under section 6695(d) and paragraph (d)(1) of this section.

(e) *Failure to file correct information returns.*—A person who is subject to the reporting requirements of section 6060 and §1.6060-1 and who fails to satisfy these requirements shall pay a penalty of $50 for each such failure, with a maximum of $25,000 per person imposed for each calendar year, unless such failure was due to reasonable cause and not due to willful neglect.

(f) *Negotiation of check.*—(1) No person who is a tax return preparer as described in §301.7701-15 of this chapter may endorse or otherwise negotiate, directly or through an agent, a check (including an electronic version of a check) for the refund of tax under the Code that is issued to a taxpayer other than the tax return preparer if the person was a tax return preparer of the return or claim for refund which gave rise to the refund check. A tax return preparer will not be considered to have endorsed or otherwise negotiated a check for purposes of this paragraph (f)(1) solely as a result of having affixed the taxpayer's name to a refund check for the purpose of depositing the check into an account in the name of the taxpayer or in the joint names of the taxpayer and one or more other persons (excluding the tax return preparer) if authorized by the taxpayer or the taxpayer's recognized representative.

(2) Section 6695(f) and paragraphs (f)(1) and (3) of this section do not apply to a tax return preparer-bank that—

(i) Cashes a refund check and remits all of the cash to the taxpayer or accepts a refund check for deposit in full to a taxpayer's account, so long as the bank does not initially endorse or negotiate the check (unless the bank has made a loan to the taxpayer on the basis of the anticipated refund); or

(ii) Endorses a refund check for deposit in full to a taxpayer's account pursuant to a written authorization of the taxpayer (unless the bank has made a loan to the taxpayer on the basis of the anticipated refund).

(3) A tax return preparer-bank may also subsequently endorse or negotiate a refund check as a part of the checkclearing process through the financial system after initial endorsement or negotiation.

(4) The tax return preparer shall be subject to a penalty of $500 for each endorsement or negotiation of a check prohibited under section 6695(f) and paragraph (f)(1) of this section.

(g) *Effective/applicability date.*—This section is applicable to returns and claims for refund filed after December 31, 2008. [Reg. §1.6695-1.]

☐ [*T.D. 7519, 11-17-77. Amended by T.D. 7640, 8-21-79; T.D. 8549, 6-28-94; T.D. 8689, 12-11-96; T.D. 8803, 12-30-98; T.D. 8893, 7-17-2000; T.D. 9053, 4-23-2003; T.D. 9119, 3-24-2004 and T.D. 9436, 12-15-2008 (corrected 1-28-2009).*]

**[Reg. §20.6695-1]**

**§20.6695-1. Other assessable penalties with respect to the preparation of tax returns for other persons.**—(a) *In general.*—A person who is a tax return preparer of any return or claim for refund of estate tax under chapter 11 of subtitle B of the Internal Revenue Code (Code) shall be subject to penalties for failure to furnish a copy to the taxpayer under section 6695(a) of the Code, failure to sign the return under section 6695(b) of the Code, failure to furnish an identification number under section 6695(c) of the Code, failure to retain a copy or list under section 6695(d) of the Code, failure to file a correct information return under section 6695(e) of the Code, and negotiation of a check under section 6695(f) of the Code, in the manner stated in §1.6695-1 of this chapter.

(b) *Effective/applicability date.*—This section is applicable to returns and claims for refund filed after December 31, 2008. [Reg. §20.6695-1.]

☐ [*T.D. 9436, 12-15-2008.*]

**[Reg. §25.6695-1]**

**§25.6695-1. Other assessable penalties with respect to the preparation of tax returns for other persons.**—(a) *In general.*—A person who is a tax return preparer of any return or claim for refund of gift tax under chapter 12 of subtitle B of the Internal Revenue Code (Code) shall be subject to penalties for failure to furnish a copy to the taxpayer under section 6695(a) of the Code, failure to sign the return under section 6695(b) of the Code, failure to furnish an identification number under section 6695(c) of the Code, failure to retain a copy or list under section 6695(d) of the Code, failure to file a correct information return under section 6695(e) of the Code, and negotiation of a check under section 6695(f) of the Code, in the manner stated in §1.6695-1 of this chapter.

(b) *Effective/applicability date.*—This section is applicable to returns and claims for refund filed after December 31, 2008. [Reg. §25.6695-1.]

☐ [*T.D. 9436, 12-15-2008.*]

**[Reg. §26.6695-1]**

**§26.6695-1. Other assessable penalties with respect to the preparation of tax returns for other persons.**—(a) *In general.*—A person who is a tax return preparer of any return or claim for refund of generation-skipping transfer tax under chapter 13 of subtitle B of the Internal Revenue Code (Code) shall be subject to penalties for failure to furnish a copy to the taxpayer under section 6695(a) of the Code, failure to sign the return under section 6695(b) of the Code, failure to furnish an identification number under section 6695(c) of the Code, failure to retain a copy or list under section 6695(d) of the Code, failure to file a correct information return under section 6695(e) of the Code, and negotiation of a check under section 6695(f) of the Code, in the manner stated in §1.6695-1 of this chapter.

(b) *Effective/applicability date.*—This section is applicable to returns and claims for refund filed after December 31, 2008. [Reg. §26.6695-1.]

☐ [*T.D. 9436, 12-15-2008.*]

**[Reg. §31.6695-1]**

**§31.6695-1. Other assessable penalties with respect to the preparation of tax returns for other persons.**—(a) *In general.*—A person who is a tax return preparer of any return or claim for refund of employment tax under chapters 21 through 25 of subtitle C of the Internal Revenue Code (Code) shall be subject to penalties for failure to furnish a copy to the taxpayer under section 6695(a) of the Code, failure to sign the return under section 6695(b) of the Code, failure to furnish an identification number under section 6695(c) of the Code, failure to retain a copy or list under section 6695(d) of the Code, failure to file a correct information return under section 6695(e) of the Code, and negotiation of a check under section 6695(f) of the Code, in the manner stated in §1.6695-1 of this chapter.

(b) *Effective/applicability date.*—This section is applicable to returns and claims for refund filed after December 31, 2008. [Reg. §31.6695-1.]

☐ [*T.D. 9436, 12-15-2008.*]

**[Reg. §40.6695-1]**

**§40.6695-1. Other assessable penalties with respect to the preparation of tax returns for other persons.**—(a) *In general.*—A person who is a tax return preparer of any return or claim for refund of any tax to which this part 40 applies shall be subject to penalties for failure to furnish a copy to the taxpayer under section 6695(a) of the Internal Revenue Code (Code), failure to sign the return under section 6695(b) of the Code, failure to furnish an identification number under section 6695(c) of the Code, failure to retain a copy or list under section 6695(d) of the Code, failure to file a correct information return under section 6695(e) of the Code, and negotiation of a check under section 6695(f) of the Code, in the manner stated in §6695-1 of this chapter.

(b) *Effective/applicability date.*—This section is applicable for returns and claims for refund filed after December 31, 2008. [Reg. §40.6695-1.]

☐ [*T.D. 9436, 12-15-2008 (corrected 1-28-2009).*]

**[Reg. §41.6695-1]**

**§41.6695-1. Other assessable penalties with respect to the preparation of tax returns for other persons.**—(a) *In general.*—A person who is a tax return preparer of any return or claim for refund of excise tax under section 4481 of the Internal Revenue Code (Code) shall be subject to penalties for failure to furnish a copy to the taxpayer under section 6695(a) of the Code, failure to sign a return under section 6695(b) of the Code, failure to furnish an identification number under section 6695(c) of the Code, failure to retain a copy or list under section 6695(d) of the Code, failure to file a correct information return under section 6695(e) of the Code, and negotiation of a check under section 6695(f) of the Code, in the manner stated in § 6695-1 of this chapter.

(b) *Effective/applicability date.*—This section is applicable to returns and claims for refund filed after December 31, 2008. [Reg. § 41.6695-1.]

☐ [*T.D.* 9436, 12-15-2008 (*corrected* 1-28-2009).]

### [Reg. § 44.6695-1]

**§ 44.6695-1. Other assessable penalties with respect to the preparation of tax returns for other persons.**—(a) *In general.*—A person who is a tax return preparer of any return or claim for refund of tax on wagers under sections 4401 or 4411 of the Internal Revenue Code (Code) shall be subject to penalties for failure to furnish a copy to the taxpayer under section 6695(a) of the Code, failure to sign the return under section 6695(b) of the Code, failure to furnish an identification number under section 6695(c) of the Code, failure to retain a copy or list under section 6695(d) of the Code, failure to file a correct information return under section 6695(e) of the Code, and negotiation of a check under section 6695(f) of the Code, in the manner stated in § 6695-1 of this chapter.

(b) *Effective/applicability date.*—This section is applicable to returns and claims for refund filed after December 31, 2008. [Reg. § 44.6695-1.]

☐ [*T.D.* 9436, 12-15-2008 (*corrected* 1-28-2009).]

### [Reg. § 53.6695-1]

**§ 53.6695-1. Other assessable penalties with respect to the preparation of tax returns or claims for refund for other persons.**.—(a) *In general.*—A person who is a tax return preparer of any return or claim for refund of tax under Chapter 42 of the Internal Revenue Code (Code) shall be subject to penalties for failure to furnish a copy to the taxpayer under section 6695(a) of the Code, failure to sign the return under section 6695(b) of the Code, failure to furnish an identification number under section 6695(c) of the Code, failure to retain a copy or list under section 6695(d) of the Code, failure to file a correct information return under section 6695(e) of the Code, and negotiation of a check under section 6695(f) of the Code, in the manner stated in § 1.6695-1 of this chapter.

(b) *Effective/applicability date.*—This section is applicable to returns and claims for refund filed after December 31, 2008. [Reg. § 53.6695-1.]

☐ [*T.D.* 9436, 12-15-2008.]

### [Reg. § 54.6695-1]

**§ 54.6695-1. Other assessable penalties with respect to the preparation of tax returns for other persons.**—(a) *In general.*—A person who is a tax return preparer of any return or claim for refund of tax under chapter 43 of subtitle D of the Internal Revenue Code (Code) shall be subject to penalties for failure to furnish a copy to the taxpayer under section 6695(a) of the Code, failure to sign the return under section 6695(b) of the Code, failure to furnish an identification number under section 6695(c) of the Code, failure to retain a copy or list under section 6695(d) of the Code, failure to file a correct information return under section 6695(e) of the Code, and negotiation of a check under section 6695(f) of the Code, in the manner stated in § 1.6695-1 of this chapter.

(b) *Effective/applicability date.*—This section is applicable to returns and claims for refund filed after December 31, 2008. [Reg. § 54.6695-1.]

☐ [*T.D.* 9436, 12-15-2008.]

### [Reg. § 55.6695-1]

**§ 55.6695-1. Other assessable penalties with respect to the preparation of tax returns or claims for refund for other persons.**—(a) *In general.*—A person who is a tax return preparer of any return or claim for refund of tax under chapter 44 of subtitle D of the Internal Revenue Code (Code) shall be subject to penalties for failure to furnish a copy to the taxpayer under section 6695(a) of the Code, failure to sign the return under section 6695(b) of the Code, failure to furnish an identification number under section 6695(c) of the Code, failure to retain a copy or list under section 6695(d) of the Code, failure to file a correct information return under section 6695(e) of the

Code, and negotiation of a check under section 6695(f) of the Code, in the manner stated in § 1.6695-1 of this chapter.

(b) *Effective/applicability date.*—This section is applicable to returns and claims for refund filed after December 31, 2008. [Reg. § 55.6695-1.]

☐ [*T.D.* 9436, 12-15-2008.]

### [Reg. § 56.6695-1]

**§ 56.6695-1. Other assessable penalties with respect to the preparation of tax returns or claims for refund for other persons.**—(a) *In general.*—A person who is a tax return preparer of any return or claim for refund of tax under chapter 41 of subtitle D of the Internal Revenue Code (Code) shall be subject to penalties for failure to furnish a copy to the taxpayer under section 6695(a) of the Code, failure to sign the return under section 6695(b) of the Code, failure to furnish an identification number under section 6695(c) of the Code, failure to retain a copy or list under section 6695(d) of the Code, failure to file a correct information return under section 6695(e) of the Code, and negotiation of a check under section 6695(f) of the Code, in the manner stated in § 1.6695-1 of this chapter.

(b) *Effective/applicability date.*—This section is applicable to returns and claims for refund filed after December 31, 2008. [Reg. § 56.6695-1.]

☐ [*T.D.* 9436, 12-15-2008.]

### [Reg. § 156.6695-1]

**§ 156.6695-1. Other assessable penalties with respect to the preparation of tax returns or claims for refund for other persons.**—(a) *In general.*—A person who is a tax return preparer of any return or claim for refund of tax under section 5881 of the Internal Revenue Code (Code) shall be subject to penalties for failure to furnish a copy to the taxpayer under section 6695(a) of the Code, failure to sign the return under section 6695(b) of the Code, failure to furnish an identification number under section 6695(c) of the Code, failure to retain a copy or list under section 6695(d) of the Code, failure to file a correct information return under section 6695(e) of the Code, and negotiation of a check under section 6695(f) of the Code, in the manner stated in § 1.6695-1 of this chapter.

(b) *Effective/applicability date.*—This section is applicable to returns and claims for refund filed after December 31, 2008. [Reg. § 156.6695-1.]

☐ [*T.D.* 9436, 12-15-2008.]

### [Reg. § 157.6695-1]

**§ 157.6695-1. Other assessable penalties with respect to the preparation of tax returns or claims for refund for other persons.**—(a) *In general.*—A person who is a tax return preparer of any return or claim for refund of tax under section 5891 of the Internal Revenue Code (Code) shall be subject to penalties for failure to furnish a copy to the taxpayer under section 6695(a) of the Code, failure to sign the return under section 6695(b) of the Code, failure to furnish an identification number under section 6695(c) of the Code, failure to retain a copy or list under section 6695(d) of the Code, failure to file a correct information return under section 6695(e) of the Code, and negotiation of a check under section 6695(f) of the Code, in the manner stated in § 1.6695-1 of this chapter.

(b) *Effective/applicability date.*—This section is applicable to returns and claims for refund filed after December 31, 2008. [Reg. § 157.6695-1.]

☐ [*T.D.* 9436, 12-15-2008.]

### [Reg. § 1.6695-2]

**§ 1.6695-2. Tax return preparer due diligence requirements for certain credits.**—(a) *Penalty for failure to meet due diligence requirements.*—(1) *In general.*—A person who is a tax return preparer (as defined in section 7701(a)(36)) of a tax return or claim for refund under the Internal Revenue Code who determines the taxpayer's eligibility to file as head of household under section 2(b), or who determines the taxpayer's eligibility for, or the amount of, the child tax credit (CTC)/additional child tax credit (ACTC) under section 24, the American opportunity tax credit (AOTC) under section 25A(i), or the earned income credit (EIC) under section 32, and who fails to satisfy the due diligence requirements of paragraph (b) of this section will be subject to a penalty as prescribed in section 6695(g) (indexed for inflation under section 6695(h)) for each failure. A separate penalty applies to a tax return preparer with respect to the head of household filing status determination and to each applicable credit claimed on a return or claim for refund for which the due diligence requirements of this section are not satisfied and for which the exception to penalty provided by paragraph (d) of this section does not apply.

(2) *Examples.*—The provisions of paragraph (a)(1) of this section are illustrated by the following examples:

(i) *Example 1.* Preparer A prepares a federal income tax return for a taxpayer claiming the CTC and the AOTC. Preparer A did not meet the due diligence requirements under this section with respect to the CTC or the AOTC claimed on the taxpayer's return. Unless the exception to penalty provided by paragraph (d) of this section applies, Preparer A is subject to two penalties under section 6695(g): one for failure to meet the due diligence requirements for the CTC and a second penalty for failure to meet the due diligence requirements for the AOTC.

(ii) *Example 2.* Preparer B prepares a federal income tax return for a taxpayer claiming the CTC and the AOTC. Preparer B did not meet the due diligence requirements under this section with respect to the CTC claimed on the taxpayer's return, but Preparer B did meet the due diligence requirements under this section with respect to the AOTC claimed on the taxpayer's return. Unless the exception to penalty provided by paragraph (d) of this section applies, Preparer B is subject to one penalty under section 6695(g) for the failure to meet the due diligence requirements for the CTC. Preparer B is not subject to a penalty under section 6695(g) for failure to meet the due diligence requirements for the AOTC.

(iii) *Example 3.* Preparer C prepares a federal income tax return for a taxpayer using the head of household filing status and claiming the CTC and the AOTC. Preparer C did not meet the due diligence requirements under this section with respect to the head of household filing status and the CTC claimed on the taxpayer's return. Preparer C did meet the due diligence requirements under this section with respect to the AOTC claimed on the taxpayer's return. Unless the exception to penalty provided by paragraph (d) of this section applies, Preparer C is subject to two penalties under section 6695(g) for the failure to meet the due diligence requirements: one for the head of household filing status and one for the CTC. Preparer C is not subject to a penalty under section 6695(g) for failure to meet the due diligence requirements for the AOTC.

(b) *Due diligence requirements.*—A preparer must satisfy the following due diligence requirements:

(1) *Completion and submission of Form 8867.*—(i) The tax return preparer must complete Form 8867, "Paid Preparer's Due Diligence Checklist," or complete such other form and provide such other information as may be prescribed by the Internal Revenue Service (IRS), and—

(A) In the case of a signing tax return preparer electronically filing the tax return or claim for refund, must electronically file the completed Form 8867 (or successor form) with the tax return or claim for refund;

(B) In the case of a signing tax return preparer not electronically filing the tax return or claim for refund, must provide the taxpayer with the completed Form 8867 (or successor form) for inclusion with the filed tax return or claim for refund; or

(C) In the case of a nonsigning tax return preparer, must provide the signing tax return preparer with the completed Form 8867 (or successor form), in either electronic or non-electronic format, for inclusion with the filed tax return or claim for refund.

(ii) The tax return preparer's completion of Form 8867 must be based on information provided by the taxpayer to the tax return preparer or otherwise reasonably obtained or known by the tax return preparer.

(2) *Computation of credit or credits.*—(i) When computing the amount of a credit or credits described in paragraph (a) of this section to be claimed on a return or claim for refund, the tax return preparer must either—

(A) Complete the worksheet in the Form 1040, 1040A, 1040EZ, and/or Form 8863 instructions or such other form including such other information as may be prescribed by the IRS applicable to each credit described in paragraph (a) of this section claimed on the return or claim for refund; or

(B) Otherwise record in one or more documents in the tax return preparer's paper or electronic files the tax return preparer's computation of the credit or credits claimed on the return or claim for refund, including the method and information used to make the computations.

(ii) The tax return preparer's completion of an applicable worksheet described in paragraph (b)(2)(i)(A) of this section (or other record of the tax return preparer's computation of the credit or credits permitted under paragraph (b)(2)(i)(B) of this section) must be based on information provided by the taxpayer to the tax return preparer or otherwise reasonably obtained or known by the tax return preparer.

(3) *Knowledge.*—(i) *In general.*—The tax return preparer must not know, or have reason to know, that any information used by the tax return preparer in determining the taxpayer's eligibility to file as head of household or in determining the taxpayer's eligibility for, or the amount of, any credit described in paragraph (a) of this section and claimed on the return or claim for refund is incorrect. The tax return preparer may not ignore the implications of information furnished to, or known by, the tax return preparer, and must make reasonable inquiries if a reasonable and well-informed tax return preparer knowledgeable in the law would conclude that the information furnished to the tax return preparer appears to be incorrect, inconsistent, or incomplete. The tax return preparer must also contemporaneously document in the preparer's paper or electronic files any inquiries made and the responses to those inquiries.

(ii) *Examples.*—The provisions of paragraph (b)(3)(i) of this section are illustrated by the following examples:

(A) *Example 1.* In 2018, Q, a 22-year-old taxpayer, engages Preparer C to prepare Q's 2017 federal income tax return. Q completes Preparer C's standard intake questionnaire and states that Q has never been married and has two sons, ages 10 and 11. Based on the intake sheet and other information that Q provides, including information that shows that the boys lived with Q throughout 2017, Preparer C believes that Q may be eligible to claim each boy as a qualifying child for purposes of the EIC and the CTC. However, Q provides no information to Preparer C, and Preparer C does not have any information from other sources, to verify the relationship between Q and the boys. To meet the knowledge requirement in paragraph (b)(3) of this section, Preparer C must make reasonable inquiries to determine whether each boy is a qualifying child of Q for purposes of the EIC and the CTC, including reasonable inquiries to verify Q's relationship to the boys, and Preparer C must contemporaneously document these inquiries and the responses.

(B) *Example 2.* Assume the same facts as in *Example 1* of paragraph (b)(3)(ii)(A) of this section. In addition, as part of preparing Q's 2017 federal income tax return, Preparer C made sufficient reasonable inquiries to verify that the boys were Q's legally adopted children. In 2019, Q engages Preparer C to prepare Q's 2018 federal income tax return. When preparing Q's 2018 federal income tax return, Preparer C is not required to make additional inquiries to determine each boy's relationship to Q for purposes of the knowledge requirement in paragraph (b)(3) of this section.

(C) *Example 3.* In 2018, R, an 18-year-old taxpayer, engages Preparer D to prepare R's 2017 federal income tax return. R completes Preparer D's standard intake questionnaire and states that R has never been married, has one child, an infant, and that R and R's infant lived with R's parents during part of the 2017 tax year. R also provides Preparer D with a Form W-2 showing that R earned $10,000 during 2017. R provides no other documents or information showing that R earned any other income during the tax year. Based on the intake sheet and other information that R provides, Preparer D believes that R may be eligible to claim the infant as a qualifying child for the EIC and the CTC. To meet the knowledge requirement in paragraph (b)(3) of this section, Preparer D must make reasonable inquiries to determine whether R is eligible to claim these credits, including reasonable inquiries to verify that R is not a qualifying child of R's parents (which would make R ineligible to claim the EIC) or a dependent of R's parents (which would make R ineligible to claim the CTC), and Preparer D must contemporaneously document these inquiries and the responses.

(D) *Example 4.* Assume the same facts as the facts in *Example 3* of paragraph (b)(3)(ii)(C) of this section. In addition, Preparer D previously prepared the 2017 joint federal income tax return for R's parents. Based on information provided by R's parents, Preparer D has determined that R is not eligible to be claimed as a dependent or as a qualifying child for purposes of the EIC or the CTC on R's parents' return. Therefore, for purposes of the knowledge requirement in paragraph (b)(3) of this section, Preparer D is not required to make additional inquiries to determine that R is not R's parents' qualifying child or dependent.

(E) *Example 5.* In 2019, S engages Preparer E to prepare S's 2018 federal income tax return. During Preparer E's standard intake interview, S states that S has never been married and that S's niece and nephew lived with S for part of the 2018 tax year. Preparer E believes S may be eligible to file as head of household and claim each of these children as a qualifying child for purposes of the EIC and the CTC, but the information furnished to Preparer E is incomplete. To meet the knowledge requirement in paragraph (b)(3) of this section, Preparer E must make reasonable inquiries to determine whether S is eligible to file as head of household and whether each child is a qualifying child for purposes of the EIC and the CTC, including reasonable inquiries about the children's residency, S's relationship to the children, the children's income, the sources of support for the children, and S's contribution to the payment of costs related to operating the household, and Preparer E must contemporaneously document these inquiries and the responses.

(F) *Example 6.* Assume the same facts as the facts in *Example 5* of paragraph (b)(3)(ii)(E) of this section. In addition, Preparer E knows from prior social interactions with S that the children resided with S for more than one-half of the 2018 tax year and that the children did not provide over one-half of their own support for the 2018 tax year. To meet the knowledge requirement in paragraph (b)(3) of this section, Preparer E must make the same reasonable inquiries to determine whether S is eligible to file as head of household and whether each child is a qualifying child for purposes of the EIC and the CTC as discussed in *Example 5* of this section, and Preparer E must contemporaneously document these inquiries and the responses.

(G) *Example 7.* W engages Preparer F to prepare W's federal income tax return. During Preparer F's standard intake interview, W states that W is 50 years old, has never been married, and has no children. W further states to Preparer F that during the tax year W was self-employed, earned $10,000 from W's business, and had no business expenses or other income. Preparer F believes W may be eligible for the EIC. To meet the knowledge requirement in paragraph (b)(3) of this section, Preparer F must make reasonable inquiries to determine whether W is eligible for the EIC, including reasonable inquiries to determine whether W's business income and expenses are correct, and Preparer F must contemporaneously document these inquiries and the responses.

(H) *Example 8.* Y, who is 32 years old, engages Preparer G to prepare Y's federal income tax return. Y completes Preparer G's standard intake questionnaire and states that Y has never been married. As part of Preparer G's client intake process, Y provides Preparer G with a copy of the Form 1098-T Y received showing that University M billed $4,000 of qualified tuition and related expenses for Y's enrollment or attendance at the university and that Y was at least a half-time undergraduate student. Preparer G believes that Y may be eligible for the AOTC. To meet the knowledge requirement in paragraph (b)(3) of this section, Preparer G must make reasonable inquiries to determine whether Y is eligible for the AOTC, as Form 1098-T does not contain all the information needed to determine eligibility for the AOTC or to calculate the amount of the credit if Y is eligible, and contemporaneously document these inquiries and the responses.

(4) *Retention of records.*—(i) The tax return preparer must retain—

(A) A copy of the completed Form 8867 (or successor form);

(B) A copy of each completed worksheet required under paragraph (b)(2)(i)(A) of this section (or other record of the tax return preparer's computation permitted under paragraph (b)(2)(i)(B) of this section); and

(C) A record of how and when the information used to complete Form 8867 and the applicable worksheets required under paragraph (b)(2)(i)(A) of this section (or other record of the tax return preparer's computation permitted under paragraph (b)(2)(i)(B) of this section) was obtained by the tax return preparer, including the identity of any person furnishing the information, as well as a copy of any document that was provided by the taxpayer and on which the tax return preparer relied to complete Form 8867 and/or an applicable worksheet required under paragraph (b)(2)(i)(A) of this section (or other record of the tax return preparer's computation permitted under paragraph (b)(2)(i)(B) of this section).

(ii) The items in paragraph (b)(4)(i) of this section must be retained for three years from the latest of the following dates, as applicable:

(A) The due date of the tax return (determined without regard to any extension of time for filing);

(B) In the case of a signing tax return preparer electronically filing the tax return or claim for refund, the date the tax return or claim for refund was filed;

(C) In the case of a signing tax return preparer not electronically filing the tax return or claim for refund, the date the tax return or claim for refund was presented to the taxpayer for signature; or

(D) In the case of a nonsigning tax return preparer, the date the nonsigning tax return preparer submitted to the signing tax return preparer that portion of the tax return or claim for refund for which the nonsigning tax return preparer was responsible.

(iii) The items in paragraph (b)(4)(i) of this section may be retained on paper or electronically in the manner prescribed in applicable regulations, revenue rulings, revenue procedures, or other appropriate guidance (see §601.601(d)(2) of this chapter).

(c) *Special rule for firms.*—A firm that employs a tax return preparer subject to a penalty under section 6695(g) is also subject to penalty if, and only if—

(1) One or more members of the principal management (or principal officers) of the firm or a branch office participated in or,

prior to the time the return was filed, knew of the failure to comply with the due diligence requirements of this section;

(2) The firm failed to establish reasonable and appropriate procedures to ensure compliance with the due diligence requirements of this section; or

(3) The firm disregarded its reasonable and appropriate compliance procedures through willfulness, recklessness, or gross indifference (including ignoring facts that would lead a person of reasonable prudence and competence to investigate) in the preparation of the tax return or claim for refund with respect to which the penalty is imposed.

(d) *Exception to penalty.*—The section 6695(g) penalty will not be applied with respect to a particular tax return or claim for refund if the tax return preparer can demonstrate to the satisfaction of the IRS that, considering all the facts and circumstances, the tax return preparer's normal office procedures are reasonably designed and routinely followed to ensure compliance with the due diligence requirements of paragraph (b) of this section, and the failure to meet the due diligence requirements of paragraph (b) of this section with respect to the particular tax return or claim for refund was isolated and inadvertent. The preceding sentence does not apply to a firm that is subject to the penalty as a result of paragraph (c) of this section.

(e) *Applicability date.*—The rules of this section apply to tax returns and claims for refund for tax years beginning after December 31, 2015, that are prepared on or after December 5, 2016. However, the rules relating to the determination of a taxpayer's eligibility to file as head of household under section 2(b) apply to tax returns and claims for refund for tax years beginning after December 31, 2017, that are prepared on or after November 7, 2018.

☐ [*T.D.* 8905, 10-16-2000. *Amended by T.D.* 9436, 12-15-2008, *T.D.* 9570, 12-19-2011, *T.D.* 9799, 12-2-2016 *and T.D.* 9842, 11-5-2018 (*corrected* 12-14-2018).]

### [Reg. §1.6696-1]

**§1.6696-1. Claims for credit or refund by tax return preparers or appraisers.**—(a) *Notice and demand.*—(1) The Internal Revenue Service (IRS) shall issue to each tax return preparer or appraiser one or more statements of notice and demand for payment for all penalties assessed against the tax return preparer or appraiser under section 6694 and §1.6694-1, under section 6695 and §1.6695-1, or under section 6695A (and any subsequently issued regulations).

(2) For the definition of the term "tax return preparer", see section 7701(a)(36) and §301.7701-15 of this chapter. A person who prepares a claim for credit or refund under this section for another person, however, is not, with respect to that preparation, a tax return preparer as defined in section 7701(a)(36) and §301.7701-15 of this chapter.

(b) *Claim filed by tax return preparer or appraiser.*—A claim for credit or refund of a penalty (or penalties) assessed against a tax return preparer or appraiser under section 6694 and §1.6694-1, under section 6695 and §1.6695-1, or under section 6695A (and any subsequently issued regulations) may be filed under this section only by the tax return preparer or the appraiser (or the tax return preparer's or appraiser's estate) against whom the penalty (or penalties) is assessed and not by, for example, the tax return preparer's or appraiser's employer. This paragraph (b) is not intended, however, to impose any restrictions on the preparation of this claim for credit or refund. The claim may be prepared by the tax return preparer's or appraiser's employer or by other persons. In all cases, however, the claim for credit or refund shall contain the information specified in paragraph (d) of this section and, as required by paragraph (d) of this section, shall be verified by a written declaration by the tax return preparer or appraiser that the information is provided under penalty of perjury.

(c) *Separation and consolidation of claims.*—(1) Unless paragraph (c)(2) of this section applies, a tax return preparer shall file a separate claim for each penalty assessed in each statement of notice and demand issued to the tax return preparer.

(2) A tax return preparer may file one or more consolidated claims for any or all penalties imposed on the tax return preparer by a single IRS campus or office under section 6695(a) and §1.6695-1(a) (relating to failure to furnish copy of return to taxpayer), section 6695(b) and §1.6695-1(b) (relating to failure to sign), section 6695(c) and §1.6695-1(c) (relating to failure to furnish identifying number), or under section 6695(d) and §1.6695-1(d) (relating to failure to retain copy of return or record), whether the penalties are asserted on a single or on separate statements of notice and demand. In addition, a tax return preparer may file one consolidated claim for any or all penalties imposed on the tax return preparer by a single IRS campus or office under section 6695(e) and §1.6695-1(e) (relating to failure to

file correct information return), which are asserted on a single statement of notice and demand.

(d) *Content of claim.*—Each claim for credit or refund for any penalty (or penalties) paid by a tax return preparer under section 6694 and §1.6694-1, or under section 6695 and §1.6695-1, or paid by an appraiser under section 6695A (and any subsequently issued regulations) shall include the following information, verified by a written declaration by the tax return preparer or appraiser that the information is provided under penalty of perjury:

(1) The tax return preparer's or appraiser's name.

(2) The tax return preparer's or appraiser's identification number. If the tax return preparer or appraiser is—

  (i) An individual (not described in paragraph (d)(2)(iii) of this section) who is a citizen or resident of the United States, the tax return preparer's or appraiser's social security account number (or such alternative number as may be prescribed by the IRS in forms, instructions, or other appropriate guidance) shall be provided;

  (ii) An individual who is not a citizen or resident of the United States and also was not employed by another tax return preparer or appraiser to prepare the document (or documents) with respect to which the penalty (or penalties) was assessed, the tax return preparer's or appraiser's employer identification number shall be provided; or

  (iii) A person (whether an individual, corporation, or partnership) that employed one or more persons to prepare the document (or documents) with respect to which the penalty (or penalties) was assessed, the tax return preparer's or appraiser's employer identification number shall be provided.

(3) The tax return preparer's or appraiser's address where the IRS mailed the statement (or statements) of notice and demand and, if different, the tax return preparer's or appraiser's address shown on the document (or documents) with respect to which the penalty (or penalties) was assessed.

(4)(i) The address of the IRS campus or office that issued the statement (or statements) of notice and demand for payment of the penalty (or penalties).

  (ii) The date (or dates) and identifying number (or numbers) of the statement (or statements) of notice and demand.

(5)(i) The identification, by amount, type, and document to which related, of each penalty included in the claim. Each document referred to in the preceding sentence shall be identified by the form title or number, by the taxpayer's (or nontaxable entity's) name and taxpayer identification number, and by the taxable year to which the document relates.

  (ii) The date (or dates) of payment of the amount (or amounts) of the penalty (or penalties) included in the claim.

  (iii) The total amount claimed.

(6) A statement setting forth in detail—

  (i) Each ground upon which each penalty overpayment claim is based; and

  (ii) Facts sufficient to apprise the IRS of the exact basis of each such claim.

(e) *Form for filing claim.*—Notwithstanding §301.6402-2(c) of this chapter, Form 6118, "Claim for Refund of Tax Return Preparer and Promoter Penalties," is the form prescribed for making a claim as provided in this section with respect to penalties under sections 6694 and 6695. Form 843, Claim for Refund and Request for Abatement, is the form prescribed for making a claim as provided in this section with respect to a penalty under section 6695A.

(f) *Place for filing claim.*—A claim filed under this section shall be filed with the IRS campus or office that issued to the tax return preparer or appraiser the statement (or statements) of notice and demand for payment of the penalty (or penalties) included in the claim.

(g) *Time for filing claim.*—(1)(i) Except as provided in section 6694(c)(1) and §1.6694-4(a)(4)(ii) and (5), and in section 6694(d) and §1.6694-1(d):

  (A) A claim for a penalty paid by a tax return preparer under section 6694 and §1.6694-1, or under section 6695 and §1.6695-1, or by an appraiser under section 6695A (and any subsequently issued regulations) shall be filed within three years from the date the payment was made.

  (B) A consolidated claim, permitted under paragraph (c)(2) of this section, shall be filed within three years from the first date of payment of any penalty included in the claim.

  (ii) For purposes of this paragraph (g)(1), payment is considered made on the date payment is received by the IRS or, if applicable, on the date an amount is credited in satisfaction of the penalty.

(2) For purposes of determining whether a claim is timely filed, the rules under sections 7502 and 7503 and the provisions of §§1.7502-1, 1.7502-2, and 1.7503-1 apply.

(h) *Application of refund to outstanding liability of tax return preparer or appraiser.*—The IRS may, within the applicable period of limitations, credit any amount of an overpayment by a tax return preparer or appraiser of a penalty (or penalties) paid under section 6694 and §1.6694-1, under section 6695 and §1.6695-1, or under section 6695A (and any subsequently issued regulations) against any outstanding liability for any tax (or for any interest, additional amount, addition to the tax, or assessable penalty) owed by the tax return preparer or appraiser making the overpayment. If a portion of an overpayment is so credited, only the balance will be refunded to the tax return preparer or appraiser.

(i) *Interest.*—(1) Section 6611 and §301.6611-1 of this chapter apply to the payment by the IRS of interest on an overpayment by a tax return preparer or appraiser of a penalty (or penalties) paid under section 6694 and §1.6694-1, under section 6695 and §1.6695-1, or under section 6695A (and any subsequently issued regulations).

(2) Section 6601 and §301.6601-1 of this chapter apply to the payment of interest by a tax return preparer or appraiser to the IRS on any penalty (or penalties) assessed against the tax return preparer under section 6694 and §1.6694-1, under section 6695 and §1.6695-1, or under section 6695A (and any subsequently issued regulations).

(j) *Suits for refund of penalty.*—(1) A tax return preparer or appraiser may not maintain a civil action for the recovery of any penalty paid under section 6694 and §1.6694-1, under section 6695 and §1.6695-1, or under section 6695A(and any subsequently issued regulations), unless the tax return preparer or appraiser has previously filed a claim for credit or refund of the penalty as provided in this section (and the court has jurisdiction of the proceeding). See sections 6694(c) and 7422.

(2)(i) Except as provided in section 6694(c)(2) and §1.6694-4(b), the periods of limitation contained in section 6532 and §301.6532-1 of this chapter apply to a tax return preparer's or appraiser's suit for the recovery of any penalty paid under section 6694 and §1.6694-1, under section 6695 and §1.6695-1, or under section 6695A (and any subsequently issued regulations).

  (ii) The rules under section 7503 and §301.7503-1 of this chapter apply to the timely commencement by a tax return preparer or appraiser of a suit for the recovery of any penalty paid under section 6694 and §1.6694-1, under section 6695 and §1.6695-1, or under section 6695A (and any subsequently issued regulations).

(k) *Effective/applicability date.*—This section is applicable to returns and claims for refund filed, and advice provided, after December 31, 2008. [Reg. §1.6696-1.]

☐ [*T.D. 7621, 5-11-79. Amended by T.D. 9436, 12-15-2008 (corrected 1-28-2009).*]

### [Reg. §20.6696-1]

**§20.6696-1. Claims for credit or refund by tax return preparers or appraisers.**—(a) *In general.*—For rules for claims for credit or refund by a tax return preparer who prepared a return or claim for refund for estate tax under chapter 11 of subtitle B of the Internal Revenue Code, or by an appraiser that prepared an appraisal in connection with such a return or claim for refund under section 6695A, the rules under §1.6696-1 of this chapter will apply.

(b) *Effective/applicability date.*—This section is applicable to returns and claims for refund filed, and advice provided, after December 31, 2008. [Reg. §20.6696-1.]

☐ [*T.D. 9436, 12-15-2008.*]

### [Reg. §25.6696-1]

**§25.6696-1. Claims for credit or refund by tax return preparers.**—(a) *In general.*—For rules for claims for credit or refund by a tax return preparer who prepared a return or claim for refund for gift tax under chapter 12 of subtitle B of the Internal Revenue Code, or by an appraiser that prepared an appraisal in connection with such a return or claim for refund under section 6695A, the rules under §1.6696-1 of this chapter will apply.

(b) *Effective/applicability date.*—This section is applicable to returns and claims for refund filed, and advice provided, after December 31, 2008. [Reg. §25.6696-1.]

☐ [*T.D. 9436, 12-15-2008.*]

### [Reg. §26.6696-1]

**§26.6696-1. Claims for credit or refund by tax return preparers.**—(a) *In general.*—For rules for claims for credit or refund by a tax return preparer who prepared a return or claim for refund for generation-skipping transfer tax under chapter 13 of subtitle B of the Internal Revenue Code, or by an appraiser that prepared an appraisal in connection with such a return or claim for refund under section 6695A, the rules under §1.6696-1 of this chapter will apply.

(b) *Effective/applicability date.*—This section is applicable to returns and claims for refund filed, and advice provided, after December 31, 2008. [Reg. § 26.6696-1.]

☐ [*T.D.* 9436, 12-15-2008.]

### [Reg. § 31.6696-1]

**§ 31.6696-1. Claims for credit or refund by tax return preparers.**—(a) *In general.*—For rules for claims for credit or refund by a tax return preparer who prepared a return or claim for refund for employment tax under chapters 21 through 25 of subtitle C of the Internal Revenue Code, the rules under § 1.6696-1 of this chapter will apply.

(b) *Effective/applicability date.*—This section is applicable to returns and claims for refund filed, and advice provided, after December 31, 2008. [Reg. § 31.6696-1.]

☐ [*T.D.* 9436, 12-15-2008.]

### [Reg. § 40.6696-1]

**§ 40.6696-1. Claims for credit or refund by tax return preparers.**—(a) *In general.*—The rules under § 1.6696-1 of this chapter will apply for claims for credit or refund by a tax return preparer who prepared a return or claim for refund of any tax to which this part 40 applies.

(b) *Effective/applicability date.*—This section is applicable to returns and claims for refund filed, and advice provided, after December 31, 2008. [Reg. § 40.6696-1.]

☐ [*T.D.* 9436, 12-15-2008 (*corrected* 1-28-2009).]

### [Reg. § 41.6696-1]

**§ 41.6696-1. Claims for credit or refund by tax return preparers.**—(a) *In general.*—For rules for claims for credit or refund by a tax return preparer who prepared a return or claim for refund for excise tax under section 4481, the rules under § 1.6696-1 of this chapter will apply.

(b) *Effective/applicability date.*—This section is applicable to returns and claims for refund filed, and advice provided, after December 31, 2008. [Reg. § 41.6696-1.]

☐ [*T.D.* 9436, 12-15-2008.]

### [Reg. § 44.6696-1]

**§ 44.6696-1. Claims for credit or refund by tax return preparers.**—(a) *In general.*—For rules for claims for credit or refund by a tax return preparer who prepared a return or claim for refund for tax on wagers under sections 4401 or 4411, the rules under § 1.6696-1 of this chapter will apply.

(b) *Effective/applicability date.*—This section is applicable to returns and claims for refund filed, and advice provided, after December 31, 2008. [Reg. § 44.6696-1.]

☐ [*T.D.* 9436, 12-15-2008.]

### [Reg. § 53.6696-1]

**§ 53.6696-1. Claims for credit or refund by tax return preparers.**—(a) *In general.*—For rules for claims for credit or refund by a tax return preparer who prepared a return or claim for refund for tax under Chapter 42 of the Internal Revenue Code, the rules under § 1.6696-1 of this chapter will apply.

(b) *Effective/applicability date.*—This section is applicable to returns and claims for refund filed, and advice provided, after December 31, 2008. [Reg. § 53.6696-1.]

☐ [*T.D.* 9436, 12-15-2008.]

### [Reg. § 54.6696-1]

**§ 54.6696-1. Claims for credit or refund by tax return preparers.**—(a) *In general.*—For rules for claims for credit or refund by a tax return preparer who prepared a return or claim for refund for excise tax under chapter 43 of subtitle D of the Internal Revenue Code, the rules under § 1.6696-1 of this chapter will apply.

(b) *Effective/applicability date.*—This section is applicable to returns and claims for refund filed, and advice provided, after December 31, 2008. [Reg. § 54.6696-1.]

☐ [*T.D.* 9436, 12-15-2008.]

### [Reg. § 55.6696-1]

**§ 55.6696-1. Claims for credit or refund by tax return preparers.**—(a) *In general.*—For rules for claims for credit or refund by a tax return preparer who prepared a return or claim for refund for tax under chapter 44 of subtitle D of the Internal Revenue Code, the rules under § 1.6696-1 of this chapter will apply.

(b) *Effective/applicability date.*—This section is applicable to returns and claims for refund filed, and advice provided, after December 31, 2008. [Reg. § 55.6696-1.]

☐ [*T.D.* 9436, 12-15-2008.]

### [Reg. § 56.6696-1]

**§ 56.6696-1. Claims for credit or refund by tax return preparers.**—(a) *In general.*—For rules relating to claims for credit or refund by a tax return preparer who prepared a return or claim for refund for tax under chapter 41 of subtitle D of the Internal Revenue Code, the rules under § 1.6696-1 of this chapter will apply.

(b) *Effective/applicability date.*—This section is applicable to returns and claims for refund filed, and advice provided, after December 31, 2008. [Reg. § 56.6696-1.]

☐ [*T.D.* 9436, 12-15-2008.]

### [Reg. § 156.6696-1]

**§ 156.6696-1. Claims for credit or refund by tax return preparers.**—(a) *In general.*—For rules for claims for credit or refund by a tax return preparer who prepared a return or claim for refund for tax under section 5881 of the Internal Revenue Code, the rules under § 1.6696-1 of this chapter will apply.

(b) *Effective/applicability date.*—This section is applicable to returns and claims for refund filed, and advice provided, after December 31, 2008. [Reg. § 156.6696-1.]

☐ [*T.D.* 9436, 12-15-2008.]

### [Reg. § 157.6696-1]

**§ 157.6696-1. Claims for credit or refund by tax return preparers.**—(a) *In general.*—For rules for claims for credit or refund by a tax return preparer who prepared a return or claim for refund for tax under section 5891 of the Internal Revenue Code, the rules under § 1.6696-1 of this chapter will apply.

(b) *Effective/applicability date.*—This section is applicable to returns and claims for refund filed, and advice provided, after December 31, 2008. [Reg. § 157.6696-1.]

☐ [*T.D.* 9436, 12-15-2008.]

### [Reg. § 301.6707-1]

**§ 301.6707-1. Failure to furnish information regarding reportable transactions.**—(a)(1) *In general.*—A material advisor who is required to file a return under section 6111(a) of the Internal Revenue Code (Code) with respect to any reportable transaction who fails to file a timely return in accordance with § 301.6111-3(e) or who files a return with false or incomplete information with respect to the reportable transaction will be subject to a penalty. A material advisor who fails to file a timely return or who files a false or incomplete return with respect to more than one reportable transaction will be subject to a separate section 6707 penalty for each transaction.

(i) *Reportable transactions.*—The amount of the penalty for failing to timely file a return under section 6111(a), or filing the return with false or incomplete information with respect to any reportable transaction other than a listed transaction is $50,000.

(ii) *Listed transactions.*—(A) *In general.*—The amount of the penalty for failing to timely file a return under section 6111(a), or filing the return with false or incomplete information with respect to a listed transaction is the greater of $200,000 or 50 percent of the gross income derived by the material advisor with respect to aid, assistance, or advice that is provided with respect to the listed transaction before the date the return is filed under section 6111.

(B) *Intentional action or failure.*—If the failure or action subject to the penalty is with respect to a listed transaction and is intentional, the penalty is the greater of $200,000 or 75 percent of the gross income derived by the material advisor with respect to aid, assistance, or advice that is provided with respect to the listed transaction before the date the return is filed under section 6111.

(C) *Transaction that is both a listed transaction and reportable transaction other than a listed transaction.*—In the case of a penalty imposed under section 6707 with respect to a transaction that is both a listed transaction and a reportable transaction other than a listed transaction, the penalty under this paragraph (a)(1)(ii), and not the penalty under paragraph (a)(1)(i) of this section, will apply.

(2) *Gross income derived by the material advisor.*—For purposes of calculating the amount of the penalty with respect to a listed transaction, the gross income derived by the material advisor will be determined in accordance with § 301.6111-3(b)(3)(ii) of this chapter. If a person is a material advisor with regard to more than one type of

listed transaction, the gross income derived from each type of listed transaction will be considered separately and will not be aggregated to determine the amount of any section 6707 penalty for failing to make a proper return under section 6111(a). Further, only gross income derived from listed transactions for which the advisor is a material advisor under section 6111 is taken into account for purposes of computing the penalty.

(b) *Definitions.*—(1) *Derive.*—The term "derive" is defined in §301.6111-3(c)(3).

(2) *False information.*—For purposes of this section, the term "false information: means information provided on a Form 8918, "Material Advisor Disclosure Statement" (or successor form), filed with the Internal Revenue Service (IRS) that is untrue or incorrect when the Form 8918 (or successor form) was filed. False information does not include information provided on a Form 8918 (or successor form) filed with the IRS that is immaterial or that is untrue or incorrect due to a mistake or accident after the exercise of reasonable care.

(3) *Incomplete information.*—For purposes of this section, the term "incomplete information" means a Form 8918 (or successor form) filed with the IRS that does not provide the information required under §301.6111-3(d). A Form 8918 (or successor form) filed with the IRS will not be considered incomplete when the information not provided on the form is immaterial or was not provided due to mistake or accident after the exercise of reasonable care. Whether information is immaterial will be determined based upon the facts and circumstances surrounding each failure to file or filing of an incomplete return. A material advisor who completes the form to the best of the material advisor's ability and knowledge after the exercise of reasonable effort to obtain the information will not be considered to have filed incomplete information within the meaning of this section. A Form 8918 (or successor form) will be considered to provide incomplete information when it omits information required to be provided under §301.6111-3(d) or contains a statement that the omitted information will be provided upon request.

(4) *Intentional.*—For purposes of this section, the failure to timely file a return or the submission of a return with false or incomplete information is intentional if—

(i) The material advisor knew of the obligation to file a return and knowingly did not timely file a return with the IRS; or

(ii) The material advisor filed a return knowing that it was false or incomplete.

(5) *Listed transaction.*—The term "listed transaction" is defined in section 6707A(c)(2) of the Code and §1.6011-4(b)(2) of this chapter.

(6) *Material Advisor.*—The term "material advisor" is defined in section 6111(b)(1) of the Code and §301.6111-3(b).

(7) *Reportable transaction.*—The term "reportable transaction" is defined in section 6707A(c)(1) of the Code and §1.6011-4(b)(1) of this chapter.

(c) *Assessment of penalty.*—(1) *Intentional failure determined based on all the facts and circumstances.*—Whether a material advisor intentionally failed to timely file a return or intentionally filed a false or incomplete return will be determined based upon all the facts and circumstances surrounding the non-filing or filing of a false and/or incomplete return. The higher penalty under the flush language of section 6707(b)(2) will not apply to any material advisor whose failure to timely file or whose furnishing of false or incomplete information was unintentional. The failure to timely file a return, or filing a return with false or incomplete information, will be considered unintentional if the material advisor subsequently files a true and complete return prior to the earlier of the date that any taxpayer files a Form 8886, "Reportable Transaction Disclosure Statement" (or successor form) identifying the material advisor with respect to the reportable transaction in question, or the date the IRS contacts the material advisor concerning the reportable transaction.

(2) *Individual liability in the case of more than one material advisor.*—If there is more than one material advisor who is responsible for filing a return under section 6111 with respect to the same reportable transaction, a separate penalty under section 6707 may be assessed against each material advisor who fails to timely file or files a return with false or incomplete information. The determination of whether the failure or action subject to the penalty is intentional will be made individually for each material advisor.

(3) *Designation agreements.*—A material advisor who is required to file a return under section 6111 and who is a party to a designation agreement within the meaning of §301.6111-3(f) is subject to a penalty under section 6707 if the designated material advisor fails to file a return timely or files a return with false or incomplete information.

In the case of a listed transaction, if the designated material advisor fails to file a return timely, or files a return with false or incomplete information, the nondesignated material advisor who is a party to the designation agreement will not be treated as intentionally failing to file the return, or intentionally filing a return with false or incomplete information, unless the nondesignated material advisor knew or should have known that the designated material advisor would fail to file a true and complete return timely.

(d) *Examples.*—The rules of paragraphs (a) through (c) of this section are illustrated by the following examples:

*Example 1.* Advisor A becomes a material advisor as defined under section 6111(b)(1) and §301.6111-3(b) in the fourth quarter of 2014 with respect to a reportable transaction other than a listed transaction, and Advisor B also becomes a material advisor in the same quarter with respect to the same reportable transaction. Advisors A and B fail to timely file the Form 8918 with respect to the reportable transaction. Under paragraph (a)(1)(ii) of this section, the penalty for failure by a material advisor to timely disclose a reportable transaction other than a listed transaction is $50,000. Because the section 6707 penalty applies to each material advisor independently under paragraph (c)(2) of this section, Advisors A and B each are subject to a section 6707 penalty of $50,000.

*Example 2.* Same as *Example 1*, except that Advisor B timely files the Form 8918. Advisors A and B did not enter into a designation agreement. Accordingly, paragraph (c)(3) of this section does not apply and only Advisor A is subject to a $50,000 section 6707 penalty.

*Example 3.* Advisor C becomes a material advisor to Client X on January 5, 2015, with respect to a listed transaction. Advisor C derives $400,000 in gross income from his advice to Client X because he expects to receive that amount from Client X, even though he has not yet received that amount. On January 5, 2016, Advisor C becomes a material advisor to Client Y with respect to the same type of listed transaction. Advisor C derives $100,000 in gross income from his advice to Client Y because he expects to receive that amount from Client Y, even though he has not yet received that amount. At no time did Advisor C file a Form 8918 to disclose the listed transaction. For purposes of this example, assume that Advisor C's failure to file a Form 8918 was unintentional. Therefore, under paragraph (c)(2) of this section, Advisor C is subject to a section 6707 penalty based on the gross income derived from Client X and Client Y. Accordingly, Advisor C is subject to a penalty of $250,000 (50 percent of $500,000, the gross income derived from Clients X and Y).

*Example 4.* Same as *Example 3*, except that the gross income Advisor C expects to receive from his advice to Client Y (a C corporation) is $20,000. Because the material advisor fee threshold is not satisfied with respect to Client Y, Advisor C is not a material advisor to Client Y with respect to the listed transaction. Advisor C is, however, a material advisor with respect to Client X with respect to the same listed transaction. Therefore, Advisor C is subject to a section 6707 penalty with respect to the failure to timely file a Form 8918 disclosing the listed transaction. Although Advisor C provided advice with respect to two transactions that are the same type of listed transaction, Advisor C was only a material advisor with respect to advice provided to Client X. Therefore, under paragraph (c)(2) of this section Advisor C is subject to a section 6707 penalty based only on the gross income derived from Client X. Accordingly, Advisor C is subject to a penalty of $200,000 (50 percent of $400,000, the gross income derived from Client X).

*Example 5.* Same as *Example 3*, except that Advisor C files a Form 8918 disclosing the listed transaction on November 16, 2015. Because Advisor C becomes a material advisor to Client X on January 5, 2015, the Form 8918 is required to be filed on or before April 30, 2015 (the last day of the month that follows the end of the calendar quarter in which the advisor became a material advisor with regard to the reportable transaction). See §301.6111-3(e). Therefore, Advisor C did not timely file the Form 8918. Advisor C is subject to a $200,000 penalty under section 6707 for his unintentional failure because, as of the date he filed the Form 8918, the gross income Advisor C had received or expected to receive with respect to advice relating to a listed transaction that was not disclosed only included $400,000 of gross income for advice to Client X. By the time that Advisor C provides advice to Client Y on January 5, 2016, Advisor C has disclosed the listed transaction.

*Example 6.* Same as *Example 3*, except that Advisor C files the Form 8918 on February 16, 2016, disclosing the listed transaction. Because Advisor C first becomes a material advisor with respect to the listed transaction on January 5, 2015, the Form 8918 is required to be filed on or before April 30, 2015 regardless of the fact that Advisor C is also a material advisor to a second client, Client Y, with respect to the same listed transaction. This is because under the facts of *Example 3*, Advisor C "becomes" a material advisor on January 5, 2015. The date on which a material advisor "becomes" a material advisor is determinative of the due date for the Form 8918 under §301.6111-3(e). Therefore, when Advisor C files the Form 8918 on February 16, 2016, the form is not timely filed under section 6111. Under paragraph (c)(2) of this section, Advisor C is subject to a penalty under section 6707 of $250,000 (50 percent of $500,000) because, as of the date that the Form 8918 was filed, the gross income that Advisor C received or expected to receive as a material advisor with respect to a listed transaction that was not disclosed included gross income for advice to both Client X ($400,000) and Client Y ($100,000).

*Example 7.* Advisor D becomes a material advisor as defined under section 6111(b)(1) and § 301.6111-3(b) in the first quarter of 2016 with respect to a reportable transaction other than a listed transaction. Advisor D does not file a Form 8918 by April 30, 2016. The transaction is then identified as a listed transaction in published guidance on July 7, 2016. Advisor D knew that he had a new obligation to file a Form 8918 by October 31, 2016, and intentionally fails to file the Form 8918. Advisor D is subject to only one penalty, in the amount of the greater of $200,000, or 75 percent of the gross income he derived from the transaction, for intentionally failing to disclose the listed transaction in accordance with § 301.6111-3(d)(1) and (e).

*Example 8.* Same as *Example 7*, except that Advisor D filed a Form 8918 disclosing the listed transaction on October 15, 2016. As a result of that disclosure, Advisor D is not subject to the section 6707 penalty amount described in § 301.6707-1(a)(1)(ii). However, because Advisor D did not timely file a Form 8918 by April 30, 2016, the due date for the Form 8918 with respect to the reportable transaction for which Advisor D became a material advisor in the first quarter of 2016, Advisor D is subject to a section 6707 penalty of $50,000 as described in § 301.6707-1(a)(1)(i). The disclosure of the listed transaction does not correct Advisor D's initial failure to disclose the reportable transaction by April 30, 2016.

(e) *Rescission authority.*—(1) *In general.*—The Commissioner (or the Commissioner's delegate) may rescind the section 6707 penalty if—

(i) The violation relates to a reportable transaction that is not a listed transaction; and

(ii) Rescinding the penalty would promote compliance with the requirements of the Code and effective tax administration.

(2) *Requesting rescission.*—The Secretary may prescribe the procedures for a material advisor to request rescission of a section 6707 penalty by guidance published in the Internal Revenue Bulletin.

(3) *Factors that weigh in favor of granting rescission.*—In determining whether rescission would promote compliance with the requirements of the Code and effective tax administration, the Commissioner (or the Commissioner's delegate) will take into account the following list of factors that weigh in favor of granting rescission. This is not an exclusive list, and no single factor will be determinative of whether to grant rescission in any particular case. Rather, the Commissioner (or the Commissioner's delegate) will consider and weigh all relevant factors, regardless of whether the factor is included in this list.

(i) The material advisor, upon becoming aware of the failure to disclose a reportable transaction in accordance with section 6111 and the regulations thereunder, filed a complete and proper, albeit untimely, Form 8918 (or successor form). This factor weighs in favor of rescission if circumstances suggest that the material advisor did not delay in filing an untimely but properly completed Form 8918 (or successor form) until after the IRS had taken steps to identify the person as a material advisor with respect to the reportable transaction. For instance, this factor will weigh strongly in favor of rescission if the material advisor files the Form 8918 (or successor form) prior to the date the IRS contacts the material advisor concerning the reportable transaction. However, this factor will not weigh in favor of rescission if the facts and circumstances indicate that the material advisor delayed filing the Form 8918 (or successor form) until after a taxpayer files a Form 8886 (or successor form) identifying the material advisor with respect to the reportable transaction in question.

(ii) The material advisor's failure to disclose the reportable transaction properly was due to an unintentional mistake of fact that existed despite the material advisor's reasonable attempts to ascertain the correct facts with respect to the transaction.

(iii) The material advisor has an established history of properly disclosing other reportable transactions and complying with other tax laws, including compliance with any requests made by the IRS under section 6112, if applicable.

(iv) The material advisor demonstrates that the failure to include on any return or statement any information required to be disclosed under section 6111 arose from events beyond the material advisor's control.

(v) The material advisor cooperates with the IRS by providing timely information with respect to the transaction at issue that the Commissioner (or the Commissioner's delegate) may request in consideration of the rescission request. In considering whether a material advisor cooperates with the IRS, the Commissioner (or the Commissioner's delegate) will take into account whether the material advisor

meets the deadlines described in guidance published in the Internal Revenue Bulletin for complying with requests for additional information.

(vi) Assessment of the penalty weighs against equity and good conscience, including whether the material advisor demonstrates that there was reasonable cause for, and the material advisor acted in good faith with respect to, the failure to timely file or to include on any return any information required to be disclosed under section 6111. An important factor in determining reasonable cause and good faith is the extent of the material advisor's efforts to determine whether there was a requirement to file the return required under section 6111. The presence of reasonable cause, however, will not necessarily be determinative of whether to grant rescission.

(4) *Absence of favorable factors weighs against rescission.*—The absence of facts establishing the factors described in paragraph (e)(3) of this section weighs against granting rescission. The presence or absence of any one of these factors, however, will not necessarily be determinative of whether to grant rescission; rather the determination will be made in consideration of all of the factors and any other facts and circumstances.

(5) *Factors not considered.*—In determining whether to grant rescission, the Commissioner (or the Commissioner's delegate) will not consider doubt as to collectability of, or liability for, the penalties (except that the Commissioner (or the Commissioner's delegate) may consider doubt as to liability to the extent it is a factor in the determination of reasonable cause and good faith).

(f) *Effective/applicability date.*—The rules of this section apply to returns the due date for which is after July 31, 2014. [Reg. § 301.6707-1.]

☐ [T.D. 9686, 7-30-2014.]

**[Reg. § 301.6707A-1]**

**§ 301.6707A-1. Failure to include on any return or statement any information required to be disclosed under section 6011 with respect to a reportable transaction.**—(a) *In general.*—Any person who fails to include on any return or statement any information required to be disclosed under section 6011 with respect to a reportable transaction may be subject to a monetary penalty. Subject to maximum and minimum limits, the penalty for failure to include information with respect to any reportable transaction is 75 percent of the decrease in tax shown on the return as a result of the transaction or the decrease that would have resulted from the transaction if it were respected for Federal tax purposes. The penalty for failure to include information with respect to a listed transaction shall not exceed $100,000 for a natural person and $200,000 for all other persons. The penalty for failure to include information with respect to any other reportable transaction shall not exceed $10,000 for a natural person and $50,000 for all other persons. The penalty with respect to any reportable transaction shall not be less than $5,000 for a natural person and $10,000 for all other persons. The section 6707A penalty is in addition to any other penalty that may be imposed.

(b) *Definitions.*—(1) *Reportable transaction.*—The term "reportable transaction" is defined in section 6707A(c)(1) of the Code and § 1.6011-4(b)(1) of this chapter.

(2) *Listed transaction.*—The term "listed transaction" is defined in section 6707A(c)(2) of the Code and § 1.6011-4(b)(2) of this chapter.

(3) *Return.*—For purposes of this section, the term *return* means an original return, amended return, or application for tentative refund, except where otherwise indicated. As used in examples, the term *return* means an original return, except where otherwise indicated.

(c) *Assessment of the penalty.*—(1) *In general.*—The Internal Revenue Service may assess a penalty under section 6707A with respect to each failure to disclose a reportable transaction within the time and in the form and manner provided by §§ 1.6011-4(d) and 1.6011-4(e) of this chapter or pursuant to the time, form, and manner stated in other published guidance. Section 1.6011-4(e) provides, in part, that a taxpayer must attach a disclosure statement to the taxpayer's return for each taxable year for which the taxpayer participates in a reportable transaction. A taxpayer also must attach a disclosure statement to each amended return that reflects the taxpayer's participation in a reportable transaction and, if a reportable transaction results in a loss that is carried back to a prior year, a taxpayer must attach a disclosure statement to the taxpayer's application for tentative refund or amended return for that prior year. In addition, a copy of the disclosure statement must be sent to the IRS Office of Tax Shelter Analysis (OTSA) at the same time that any disclosure statement is first filed by the taxpayer pertaining to a particular reportable transaction. Nonetheless, a taxpayer who is required to disclose a transaction by filing Form 8886, "Reportable Transaction Disclosure Statement," (or successor form) with a return and who is also required to disclose the transaction by filing that form with OTSA, is subject to only a single section 6707A penalty for failure to make either one or both of those disclosures. If section 6011 and the regulations thereunder require a disclosure statement to be filed at the time that a return is filed, the disclosure statement is considered to be timely filed if it is filed at the same time as the return, even if the return is filed untimely after its due date (including extensions).

(2) *Examples.*—The rules of paragraph (c)(1) of this section are illustrated by the following examples:

*Example 1.* Taxpayer T is required to attach a Form 8886 to its return for the 2008 taxable year and to send a copy of the Form 8886 to OTSA at the time it files its return. Taxpayer T fails to attach the Form 8886 to its return and fails to send a copy of the Form 8886 to OTSA. Taxpayer T is subject to a single penalty under section 6707A for failure to disclose because Taxpayer T failed to comply with the disclosure requirements of section 6011 as described in § § 1.6011-4(d) and 1.6011-4(e) of this chapter. A penalty under section 6707A also would apply if Taxpayer T had failed to comply with only one of the two requirements.

*Example 2.* Same as *Example 1*, except that Taxpayer T also subsequently files an amended return for 2008 that reflects Taxpayer T's participation in the reportable transaction described in *Example 1*. Taxpayer T fails to attach a Form 8886 to the amended return as required by § 1.6011-4(e)(1) of this chapter. Taxpayer T is subject to an additional penalty under section 6707A for failing to disclose a reportable transaction on the amended return for 2008.

*Example 3.* In November 2009, Taxpayer U participates in a reportable transaction resulting in a loss. On March 15, 2010, Taxpayer U files its 2009 return, on which it reports the loss and to which it fails to attach a Form 8886. One month later, Taxpayer U files an amended return for 2008, on which it carries back the loss and to which it fails to attach a Form 8886. Section 1.6011-4(e)(1) of this chapter requires Taxpayer U to attach a Form 8886 to its amended return for the 2008 taxable year. Taxpayer U is subject to two penalties under section 6707A: one for the failure to attach Form 8886 to its amended return for 2008 and another for the failure to attach Form 8886 to its 2009 return.

*Example 4.* Taxpayer V participates in a nonlisted reportable transaction and is required to attach a Form 8886 to its return for the 2009 taxable year that is due on March 15, 2010. Taxpayer V timely files its return but fails to attach the Form 8886 to its return. After the due date of Taxpayer V's return and without an extension of time to file, Taxpayer V files an amended return relating to the 2009 taxable year to which Taxpayer V attaches the Form 8886. Taxpayer V is subject to a penalty under section 6707A for failure to disclose because Taxpayer V failed to comply with the disclosure requirements of section 6011 (described in § 1.6011-4(e)(1) of this chapter) by not attaching a Form 8886 to its original return for the 2009 taxable year that was timely filed on or before the due date of March 15, 2010. An additional penalty under section 6707A would apply if Taxpayer V had failed to attach a Form 8886 to its amended return.

*Example 5.* Shareholder W, a shareholder in an S Corporation, receives a timely Schedule K-1, "Shareholder's Share of Income, Deductions, Credits, etc.," on April 10, 2009, and determines that she is required to attach a Form 8886 to her individual income tax return for the 2008 taxable year. Shareholder W fails to attach the Form 8886 to her 2008 individual income tax return but files a proper and complete Form 8886 with OTSA on June 12, 2009. Section 1.6011-4(e)(1) of this chapter provides that if a taxpayer who is a partner in a partnership, a shareholder in an S corporation, or a beneficiary of a trust receives a timely Schedule K-1 less than 10 calendar days before the due date of the taxpayer's return (including extensions) and, based on receipt of the timely Schedule K-1, the taxpayer determines that the taxpayer participated in a reportable transaction, the disclosure statement will not be considered late if the taxpayer discloses the reportable transaction by filing a disclosure statement with OTSA within 60 calendar days after the due date of the taxpayer's return (including extensions). Accordingly, Shareholder W is not subject to a penalty under section 6707A for failure to disclose.

*Example 6.* In July 2008, Taxpayer X participates in Transaction Z, a transaction that is not reportable as of April 15, 2009, the date Taxpayer X files his individual income tax return for 2008. On July 15, 2009, Transaction Z is identified as a transaction of interest. Section 1.6011-4(e)(2)(i) of this chapter provides that if a transaction that is not otherwise a reportable transaction becomes a listed transaction or a transaction of interest after the taxpayer has filed a tax return (including an amended return) reflecting the taxpayer's participation in the listed transaction or transaction of interest and before the end of the period of limitations for assessment of tax for any taxable year in which the taxpayer participated in the listed transaction or transaction of interest, then a disclosure statement must be filed with OTSA within 90 calendar days after the date on which the transaction became a listed transaction or transaction of interest, regardless of whether the taxpayer participated in the transaction in the year the transaction became a listed transaction or a transaction of interest. Taxpayer X fails to file a Form 8886 with OTSA by October 13, 2009, 90 calendar days after the date that the transaction was identified as a transaction of interest. Accordingly, Taxpayer X is subject to a penalty under section 6707A.

*Example 7.* Taxpayer Y is required to attach a Form 8886 to its return for the 2008 taxable year with respect to participation in a listed transaction. Taxpayer Y attaches the Form 8886 to its timely filed return. The Form 8886, however, does not describe all of the potential tax benefits expected to result from this transaction and states that information will be provided upon request. Because the Form 8886 does not describe all of the potential tax benefits expected to result from the transaction and merely provides that the information will be provided upon request, the Form 8886 filed by Taxpayer Y is incomplete and does not satisfy the requirements set forth in § 1.6011-4(d) of this chapter. Taxpayer Y is subject to a penalty under section 6707A for failure to disclose in the appropriate manner.

(d) *Calculation of the penalty.*—(1) *Decrease in tax.*—(i) *In general.*—(A) As used in this section, the phrase *decrease in tax shown on the return as a result of the transaction or the decrease that would have resulted from the transaction if it were respected for Federal tax purposes* means the sum of:

(1) The excess of the amount of the tax that would have been shown on the return if the return did not reflect the taxpayer's participation in the reportable transaction over the tax actually reported on the return reflecting participation in the reportable transaction; and

(2) Any other tax that results from participation in the reportable transaction but was not reported on the taxpayer's return.

(B) The amount of tax that would have been shown on the return if it did not reflect the taxpayer's participation in the reportable transaction includes adjustments that result mechanically from backing out the reportable transaction, such as tax items affected by an increase in adjusted gross income resulting from not participating in the transaction. The calculation of the penalty is unaffected by whether a taxpayer's tax liability is ultimately settled with the IRS for a different amount or whether the taxpayer subsequently reports a different amount of tax on an amended return, because these amounts do not enter into the calculation of the decrease in tax shown on the return (or returns) to which the penalty relates.

(ii) *Subsequently identified transactions.*—If the taxpayer fails to file, as required by § 1.6011-4(a) of this chapter, a complete and proper disclosure statement disclosing participation in a listed transaction or transaction of interest with respect to more than one return in the time prescribed under § 1.6011-4(e)(2)(i) of this chapter, the amount of the penalty will be computed by aggregating the decrease in tax shown on each return for which the period of limitations on assessment remains open.

(iii) *Penalty for failure to report to the SEC.*—In the case of a penalty imposed under section 6707A(e) for failure to disclose liability for certain penalties in reports to the Securities and Exchange Commission (SEC), the amount of the penalty will be determined under section 6707A(b) and this paragraph (d), regardless of whether the penalty that the taxpayer failed to disclose is imposed under section 6707A, 6662A, or 6662(h).

(iv) *Minimum and maximum amount of the penalty.*—The limitations on the minimum and maximum penalty amounts described in paragraph (a) of this section apply separately to each failure to disclose that is subject to a penalty.

(2) *No tax required to be shown on return.*—For returns with respect to which disclosure is required but on which no tax is required to be shown (for example, returns of passthrough entities), the minimum penalty amount will be imposed for the failure to disclose.

(3) *Examples.*—The rules in paragraphs (d)(1) and (2) of this section are illustrated by the following examples:

(i) Example 1. Taxpayer X, a natural person, participated in a listed transaction involving a Roth IRA and filed a return reflecting participation in the transaction. X failed to disclose participation in the listed transaction as required by the regulations under section 6011. As a result of the transaction, X was liable under section 4973 for a $10,000 excise tax for excess contributions to X's Roth IRA. On X's return reflecting participation in the listed transaction, X correctly reported $25,000 of income tax, none of which was attributable to the listed transaction, but failed to report the excise tax. If X had not participated in the listed transaction, the excise tax under section 4973 would not have applied and X's income tax would have remained $25,000. There would, therefore, be no difference between the tax on the return as filed and the tax on the return if it did not reflect participation in the transaction. The excise tax, however, is another tax that resulted from participation in the transaction but was not reported on X's return, as described in paragraph (d)(1)(i)(B) of this section. Therefore, under paragraph (d)(1) of this section, the decrease in tax resulting from the listed transaction is $10,000. This amount is determined by adding zero (the excess of the amount of tax that would have been shown on X's return if the return did not reflect X's participation in the transaction over the tax X actually reported on the return reflecting X's participation in the transaction) and $10,000 (the amount of excise tax that resulted from participation in the transaction but was not reported on the return). The amount of the penalty under section 6707A is $7,500, which amount is 75 percent of the $10,000 decrease in tax.

(ii) Example 2. Taxpayer X participated in a listed transaction that resulted in a $40,000 decrease in the tax shown on the return reflecting participation in the transaction. X failed to disclose its participation in the transaction as required by the regulations under section 6011 and is, therefore, subject to a penalty under section 6707A. After weighing litigating hazards and other costs of litigation, the IRS Office of Appeals agreed to settle X's deficiency for $20,000. For purposes of calculating the amount of the penalty under paragraph (d)(1) of this section, the settlement does not affect the decrease in tax shown on X's return as a result of the listed transaction which remains $40,000. The amount of X's penalty under section 6707A is $30,000, which amount is 75 percent of the $40,000 decrease in tax.

(iii) *Example 3.* For the 2018 tax year, Taxpayer X, a natural person, failed to disclose participation in a reportable transaction that is not a listed transaction and, therefore, is subject to a penalty under section 6707A. After offsetting gross income with the losses generated in the reportable transaction, X's return reported adjusted gross income of $100,000. The return also reported $12,000 of medical expenses, $4,500 of which were deductible after applying the 7.5 percent floor in section 213(a) and (f). If X's return had not reflected participation in the reportable transaction, X's adjusted gross income would have been $140,000 and the deductible medical expenses would be limited to $1,500 ($3,000 less than the deductible amount claimed). Under paragraph (d)(1) of this section, the decrease in tax shown on X's return as a result of X's participation in the reportable transaction takes into account both the tax on the additional $40,000 in adjusted gross income had X not participated in the reportable transaction and the tax on the $3,000 adjustment to X's deductible medical expenses caused by the increase in adjusted gross income.

(iv) *Example 4.* Taxpayer X, a natural person, timely filed X's 2019 return and reported income tax of $40,000. X did not participate in a reportable transaction in 2019. X participated in a listed transaction in 2020, but failed to file a complete and proper disclosure statement with X's 2020 return as required by the regulations under section 6011. As filed, the 2020 return reports that X owes no tax and has a loss of $10,000. If the tax consequences of the listed transaction were not reflected on the 2020 return, the return would show income tax of $15,000 and no loss. X files an amended return for the 2019 tax year on which the only amendment is to carry back the $10,000 loss reported on the 2020 tax return to the 2019 tax year. The loss carryback reduces X's tax liability for 2019 by $3,000 to $37,000. X fails to file a complete and proper disclosure statement with the 2019 amended return as required by the regulations under section 6011. Two penalties under section 6707A apply: one for X's failure to disclose participation in a listed transaction reflected on the 2020 return and another for the failure to disclose participation in the same listed transaction reflected on the 2019 amended return. Under paragraph (d)(1) of this section, the decrease in tax on the 2020 return resulting from the listed transaction is $15,000, which is the excess of the amount of tax that would have been shown on X's 2020 return if that return did not reflect X's participation in the listed transaction over the tax X actually reported on the 2020 return. The amount of the section 6707A penalty with respect to the 2020 return is $11,250, which amount is 75 percent of the decrease in tax. Under paragraph (d)(1) of this section, the decrease in tax on the 2019 amended return that results from the listed transaction is $3,000. This amount is computed by determining the excess of the amount of tax that would have been shown on X's 2019 amended return if that return did not reflect X's participation in the listed transaction over the tax X actually reported on the 2019 amended return reflecting the loss carryback resulting from X's participation in the listed transaction in 2020. See paragraph (c) of this section. However, because X is a natural person, and because 75 percent of the $3,000 decrease in tax is less than $5,000, which is the minimum penalty under paragraph (a) of this section and section 6707A(b)(3), the section 6707A penalty with respect to the failure to disclose the listed transaction with respect to the 2019 amended return is $5,000. Accordingly, X is subject to a $11,250 section 6707A penalty for failure to disclose participation in a listed transaction reflected on the 2020 return and a $5,000 section 6707A penalty for failure to disclose participation in a listed transaction reflected on the 2019 amended return.

(v) Example 5. Taxpayer X, a corporation, timely files its 2019, 2020, and 2021 returns, each of which reflects participation in the same transaction. In 2023, the transaction becomes a listed transaction. When the transaction at issue became listed, the periods of limitations on assessment on X's 2020 and 2021 tax year were open, but the period of limitations on assessment on X's 2019 tax year was closed. Pursuant to §1.6011-4(a) and (e)(2)(i) of this chapter, X is required to file a single disclosure statement reflecting its participation in the listed transaction 90 calendar days after the date on which the transaction becomes a listed transaction. X failed to file a disclosure statement as required. Pursuant to paragraph (d)(1)(ii) of this section, the section 6707A penalty is computed by aggregating the decrease in tax shown on the 2020 return and the decrease in tax shown on the 2021 return. Because the period of limitations on assessment for X's 2019 tax year was closed at the time the transaction became listed, the decrease in tax shown on the 2019 return as a result of X's participation in the listed transaction is not taken into account in computing the amount of the penalty. The decreases in tax shown on the returns as a result of X's participation in the transaction are $265,000 in tax year 2020 and $7,000 in tax year 2021. Under paragraph (d)(1) of this section, the total decrease in tax shown is computed by adding the decrease in tax for 2020 and the decrease in tax for 2021, which is $272,000. Seventy-five percent of that amount is $204,000. Because X is a corporation, the maximum penalty amount is $200,000 under paragraph (a) of this section and section 6707A(b)(2)(A). Accordingly, X is subject to a section 6707A penalty of $200,000, rather than $204,000.

(vi) *Example 6.* Taxpayer X, a natural person, files X's 2019 return reflecting participation in a reportable transaction that is not a listed transaction, but fails to disclose the transaction as required by the regulations under section 6011. The decrease in tax with respect to X's 2019 return as a result of participation in the reportable transaction is $20,000. X files an amended 2019 return to include a net operating loss carried forward from a prior year, which X inadvertently failed to include when filing the original 2019 return. The amended return reflects participation in the same reportable transaction, but X again fails to disclose the transaction as required by the regulations under section 6011. The decrease in tax with respect to the amended 2019 return as a result of participation in the transaction is also $20,000. X is subject to two separate 6707A penalties: one for the failure to disclose the reportable transaction with respect to the tax benefits from the reportable transaction reflected on the original 2019 return and one for the failure to disclose the reportable transaction with respect to the tax benefits from the reportable transaction reflected on the amended 2019 return. Seventy-five percent of the $20,000 decrease in tax shown on the original 2019 return is $15,000 and on the amended 2019 return is another $15,000. However, because X is a natural person, the amount of the penalty for failure to disclose is limited to the maximum amount of $10,000 under §301.6707A-1(a) and section 6707A(b)(2)(B). Accordingly, the amount of the section 6707A penalty for the 2019 original return is $10,000 and the amount of the section 6707A penalty for the 2019 amended return is also $10,000, for a total penalty of $20,000.

(vii) *Example 7.* Taxpayer X, a natural person, timely files X's 2019 return on April 15, 2020, reflecting participation in a transaction that was not identified as a reportable transaction when X filed the return, the only year X participated in the transaction. In early 2021, the IRS identifies the transaction as a listed transaction. X fails to disclose the listed transaction as required by the regulations under section 6011. In late 2021, X files an amended 2019 income tax return to claim deductions that had been omitted from the originally filed 2019 return. The amended 2019 return reflects X's participation in the listed transaction. X does not disclose the listed transaction when filing the amended 2019 return. The decrease in tax resulting from X's participation in the transaction is $100,000 with respect to the original 2019 return and $80,000 with respect to the 2019 amended return. Pursuant to §1.6011-4(e)(2)(i) of this chapter, X was required to file a disclosure statement reflecting X's participation in the listed transaction if the period of limitations on assessment of tax remained open for any taxable year in which the taxpayer participated in the listed transaction. When the transaction at issue became listed, the period of limitations on assessment on X's 2019 tax year was open. Pursuant to §1.6011-4(e)(1) of this chapter, X was also required to disclose participation in the transaction when the 2019 amended return was filed because the transaction was a listed transaction at that time. X is subject to two penalties under section 6707A: one for the failure to disclose participation in a listed transaction reflected on X's original 2019 return within 90 calendar days of the date the transaction became a listed transaction as required by §1.6011-4(e)(2)(i) of this chapter and another for the failure to disclose participation in the same listed transaction reflected on the 2019 amended return. Seventy-five percent of this decrease in tax with respect to the original 2019 return is $75,000 (75 percent of $100,000) and with respect to the 2019 amended return is $60,000 (75 percent of $80,000). Pursuant to paragraph (d)(1)(iv) of this section, because X is subject to two separate penalties, the maximum penalty amount of $100,000 under § 301.6707A-1(a) and section 6707A(b)(2)(A) applies separately to each penalty and does not operate to reduce the amount of the X's 6707A penalties.

(viii) *Example 8.* Under § 1.6011-4 of this chapter, Partnership M is required to attach a disclosure statement to its Form 1065, U.S. Return of Partnership Income, for the 2020 taxable year. M fails to do so and is, therefore, subject to a penalty under section 6707A. No tax is required to be shown on M's Form 1065. Pursuant to § 301.6707A-1(d)(2), M is subject to the minimum section 6707A penalty of $10,000. The partners of Partnership M may have separate disclosure obligations as required by the regulations under section 6011 and would be subject to separate section 6707A penalties if they fail to comply with the disclosure requirements.

(ix) *Example 9.* In tax year 2019, Taxpayer X participated in a listed transaction that resulted in a $150,000 deduction. X's gross income for 2019 before the listed transaction deduction is $100,000. X uses $100,000 of the deduction resulting in zero tax liability for 2019. X carried over to tax year 2020 the remaining $50,000 net operating loss that was not used in 2019. X's gross income for tax year 2020 is $200,000 but as a result of the $50,000 net operating loss carryover, X reports $150,000 adjusted gross income. Pursuant to § 1.6011-4 of this chapter, X is required to disclose participation in the listed transaction for both 2019 and 2020, but X fails to make the required disclosures and is therefore subject to the section 6707A penalty for each failure. The decrease in tax on the 2019 return is the amount of tax on $100,000 because that is the difference between the amount of tax that would have been shown on the return if it did not reflect participation in the listed transaction and the tax actually reported. No other tax resulted from X's participation in the listed transaction. The amount of the penalty with respect to X's failure to disclose with respect to 2019 will be 75 percent of the decrease in tax. The decrease in tax on the 2020 return is the difference between the tax shown on the return as filed and the tax that would be shown if the $50,000 net operating loss was not used, including any changes to the amount of tax that are only indirectly connected with the listed transaction. The amount of the penalty with respect to X's failure to disclose with respect to 2020 will be 75 percent of the decrease in tax, subject to the minimum and maximum penalty amount limitations.

(x) *Example 10.* In tax year 2020, Taxpayer X, a natural person, participated in a listed transaction that resulted in a $50,000 deduction. X also has a net operating loss carryover of $150,000 from 2019. X uses the deduction of $50,000 and a portion of the net operating loss carryover resulting in zero tax liability for 2020. X carries over the remaining net operating loss to tax year 2021. X's gross income for 2021 is $250,000, but as a result of the net operating loss carryover, X reports reduced adjusted gross income of $150,000. Pursuant to § 1.6011-4 of this chapter, X is required to disclose participation in the listed transaction for both 2020 and 2021, but X fails to make the required disclosures and is subject to the section 6707A penalty for each failure. The decrease in tax on the 2020 return that results from the reportable transaction is zero. Because X has $150,000 of a net operating loss carryover not attributable to the reportable transaction, X's tax without the benefits of the reportable transaction is the same as the tax shown on the 2020 return as filed. Because X is a natural person, the minimum penalty of $5,000 under § 301.6707A-1(a) and section 6707A(b)(3) will apply for the failure to disclose the listed transaction with the 2020 return. The decrease in tax on the 2021 return is the difference between the tax shown on the return as filed and the tax that would be shown if X had only $50,000 of net operating loss to carry over to 2021 (i.e., if X had not offset $50,000 of its 2020 gross income with the deduction resulting from the reportable transaction and thus had used $100,000 of its net operating loss carryover in 2020), including any changes to the amount of tax that are only indirectly connected with the listed transaction. The amount of the penalty with respect to the disclosure relating to 2021 will be 75 percent of this decrease in tax, subject to the minimum and maximum penalty amount limitations.

(xi) *Example 11.* Taxpayer X, a public corporation required to file periodic reports under section 13 or 15(d) of the Securities Exchange Act of 1934, timely filed its 2019 return reflecting tax benefits from a reportable transaction that is not a listed transaction and properly disclosed the transaction in accordance with the regulations under section 6011. In 2023, as a result of an examination of X's 2019 return, the IRS imposes a penalty under section 6662A with respect to the reportable transaction. The decrease in tax for purposes of paragraph (d)(1) of this section is $190,000. As a person who is required to file periodic reports under section 13 or 15(d) of the Securities Exchange Act of 1934, X is required, pursuant to section 6707A(e), to disclose the penalty imposed under section 6662A to the Securities and Exchange Commission in 2023, which X failed to do. X's failure to disclose the section 6662A penalty is treated as a failure to disclose to which section 6707A(b) applies. Thus, X is subject to a penalty under section 6707A(e), which equals 75 percent of the decrease in tax

resulting from the transaction. The decrease in tax resulting from the reportable transaction was $190,000, 75 percent of which is $142,500. Because X is a corporation and the transaction is not a listed transaction, the amount of the penalty is limited to $50,000 under paragraph (a) of this section and section 6707A(b)(2)(B). Therefore, rather than $142,500, X is subject to a $50,000 section 6707A penalty for failure to disclose the section 6662A penalty to the SEC.

(e) *Rescission authority.*—(1) *In general.*—The Commissioner (or the Commissioner's delegate) may rescind the section 6707A penalty if—

    (i) The violation relates to a reportable transaction that is not a listed transaction; and

    (ii) Rescinding the penalty would promote compliance with the requirements of the Code and effective tax administration.

(2) *Requesting rescission.*—The Secretary may prescribe the procedures for a taxpayer to request rescission of a section 6707A penalty with respect to a reportable transaction other than a listed transaction by publishing a revenue procedure or other guidance in the Internal Revenue Bulletin.

(3) *Factors that weigh in favor of granting rescission.*—In determining whether rescission would promote compliance with the requirements of the Internal Revenue Code and effective tax administration, the Commissioner (or the Commissioner's delegate) will take into account the following list of factors that weigh in favor of granting rescission. This is not an exclusive list and no single factor will be determinative of whether to grant rescission in any particular case. Rather, the Commissioner (or the Commissioner's delegate) will consider and weigh all relevant factors, regardless of whether the factor is included in this list.

    (i) The taxpayer, upon becoming aware that it failed, in whole or in part, to disclose a reportable transaction in accordance with the requirements of § 1.6011-4 of this chapter, filed a complete and proper, albeit untimely, Form 8886 (or successor form), as required by § 1.6011-4. If the penalty is due to the taxpayer's failure to file Form 8886 (or successor form) with a return , in order for an untimely disclosure to weigh in favor of rescission, the taxpayer must file an amended return with the appropriate Service Center and attach a complete and proper Form 8886 (or successor form) to that amended return. The amended return filed with the untimely Form 8886 (or successor form) must not reflect any other changes to the return that it amends, and the taxpayer must, in the space provided for an explanation of changes on the amended return, state the reason for filing the amended return. If the penalty is due to the taxpayer's failure to file Form 8886 (or successor form) with OTSA, in order for an untimely disclosure to weigh in favor of rescission, the taxpayer must file a complete and proper Form 8886 (or successor form) with OTSA. If the taxpayer fails to file a complete and proper Form 8886 (or successor form) with the return and also fails to file a copy of the complete and proper Form 8886 (or successor form) with OTSA, incurring one penalty for both failures, then the taxpayer must, in the manner prescribed in this paragraph (e)(3)(i), file complete and proper Forms 8886 with both the Service Center and OTSA in order for the untimely disclosures to weigh in favor of rescission. This factor will weigh heavily in favor of rescission provided that—

    (A) The taxpayer files the Form 8886 prior to the date the IRS first contacts the taxpayer (including contacts by the IRS with any partnership in which the taxpayer is a partner, any S corporation in which the taxpayer is a shareholder, or any trust in which the taxpayer is a beneficiary) concerning a tax examination for the tax period in which the taxpayer participated in the reportable transaction; and

    (B) Other circumstances suggest that the taxpayer did not delay filing an untimely but properly completed Form 8886 until after the IRS had taken steps to identify the taxpayer's participation in the reportable transaction in question.

    (ii) The failure, in whole or in part, to disclose in accordance with the requirements of § 1.6011-4 of this chapter was due to an unintentional mistake of fact that existed despite the taxpayer's reasonable attempts to ascertain the correct facts with respect to the transaction.

    (iii) The taxpayer has an established history of properly disclosing other reportable transactions and complying with other tax laws.

    (iv) The taxpayer demonstrates that the failure to include on any return or statement any information required to be disclosed under section 6011 arose from events beyond the taxpayer's control.

    (v) The taxpayer cooperates with the IRS by providing timely information with respect to the transaction at issue that the Commissioner (or the Commissioner's delegate) may request in consideration of the rescission request. In considering whether a taxpayer cooperates with the IRS, the Commissioner (or the Commissioner's delegate) will take into account whether the taxpayer meets the deadlines described in Rev. Proc. 2007-21 (2007-1 CB 613) (or successor document) (see §601.601(d)(2)(ii)(b) of this chapter) for complying with requests for additional information.

(vi) Assessment of the penalty weighs against equity and good conscience, including whether the taxpayer demonstrates that there was reasonable cause for, and the taxpayer acted in good faith with respect to, the failure to timely file or to include on any return any information required to be disclosed under section 6011. An important factor in determining reasonable cause and good faith is the extent of the taxpayer's efforts to ensure that persons who prepared the taxpayer's return were informed of the taxpayer's participation in the reportable transactions; this factor will be disregarded, however, if the persons who prepared the taxpayer's return were material advisors with respect to the reportable transaction. The presence of reasonable cause, however, will not necessarily be determinative of whether to grant rescission.

(4) *Absence of favorable factors weighs against rescission.*—The absence of facts establishing the factors described in paragraph (e)(3) of this section weighs against granting rescission. The absence of any one of these factors, however, will not necessarily be determinative of whether to grant rescission.

(5) *Factors not considered.*—In determining whether to grant rescission, the Commissioner (or the Commissioner's delegate) will not consider collectability of, or doubt as to liability for, the penalties (except that the Commissioner may consider doubt as to liability to the extent it is a factor in the determination of reasonable cause and good faith).

(6) *Example.*—The following example illustrates the rules of paragraph (e)(3) of this section:

*Example.* In 2008, Taxpayer Z participated in a nonlisted reportable transaction for the first time. Under §1.6011-4(e)(1) of this chapter, he was required to attach a complete and proper Form 8886 to his 2008 return, due on April 15, 2009, and to file a copy of the Form 8886 with OTSA. Taxpayer Z timely filed his 2008 return but failed to attach a Form 8886 to his return or file a Form 8886 with OTSA. On June 1, 2009, Taxpayer Z discovered his error. On June 8, 2009, Taxpayer Z filed an amended return for tax year 2008 and attached a complete and proper Form 8886 that disclosed his participation in the reportable transaction. The amended return reflected no changes from the original return and explained that the sole purpose of the amended return was to correct Taxpayer Z's failure to file a Form 8886 with his original return. On June 8, 2009, Taxpayer Z also filed a copy of the complete and proper Form 8886 with OTSA. The IRS later notified Taxpayer Z that he was subject to a penalty under section 6707A because he failed to comply with the disclosure requirements of section 6011 by not attaching Form 8886 to his return for the 2008 taxable year. The IRS properly assessed the penalty under section 6707A and, on October 15, 2010, issued notice and demand. On November 1, 2010, in accordance with Rev. Proc. 2007-21, Taxpayer Z submitted a written request for rescission of the assessed penalty. The fact that Taxpayer Z filed an untimely Form 8886 shortly after discovery of his error but before the IRS first contacted him concerning his return for the 2008 taxable year will weigh heavily in favor of rescission.

(f) *Reports to the Securities and Exchange Commission (SEC).*—(1) *In general.*—Under section 6707A(e), a taxpayer who is required to file periodic reports under section 13 or section 15(d) of the Securities Exchange Act of 1934 (or is required to be consolidated with another person for purposes of these reports) must disclose in certain reports, as provided in revenue procedures or other guidance published pursuant to paragraph (f)(2) of this section, the requirement to pay each of the following penalties:

(i) The penalty imposed by section 6707A(a) for failure to disclose a listed transaction.

(ii) The accuracy-related penalty imposed by section 6662A(a) at the 30-percent rate determined under section 6662A(c) for a reportable transaction understatement with respect to which the relevant facts affecting the tax treatment of the reportable transaction were not adequately disclosed in accordance with regulations prescribed under section 6011.

(iii) The accuracy-related penalty imposed by section 6662(a) at the 40-percent rate determined under section 6662(h) for a gross valuation misstatement, if the taxpayer (but for the exclusionary rule of section 6662A(e)(2)(C)(ii)) would have been subject to the accuracy-related penalty under section 6662A(a) at the 30-percent rate determined under section 6662A(c).

(iv) The penalty described in paragraph (f)(3) of this section for failure to disclose in periodic reports filed with the SEC the requirement to pay any of the penalties described in paragraphs (f)(1)(i) through (iii) or paragraph (f)(3) of this section.

(2) *Manner and content of disclosure.*—The Secretary may, by publishing a revenue procedure or other guidance in the Internal Reve-

nue Bulletin, prescribe the manner in which the disclosure under paragraph (f)(1) of this section must be made, including identification of the specific SEC form and section thereof in which the taxpayer must make the disclosure as well as specification of the timing and contents of the disclosure.

(3) *Penalty for failure to disclose in SEC filings.*—Any taxpayer who is required to file periodic reports under section 13 or section 15(d) of the Securities Exchange Act of 1934 (or is required to file consolidated reports with another person) may be subject to a penalty under section 6707A(b) for each failure to disclose the requirement to pay a penalty identified in paragraphs (f)(1)(i) through (iii) of this section in the manner specified by revenue procedure or other guidance published in the Internal Revenue Bulletin. The taxpayer also may be subject to an additional penalty under section 6707A(b) for each failure to disclose a penalty arising under this section in the manner specified by revenue procedure or other guidance published in the Internal Revenue Bulletin. The penalty provided by this paragraph (f)(3) will be rescinded if the IRS rescinds in full the penalty for failing to disclose under section 6011 the reportable transaction underlying the penalty provided by this section. Otherwise, the penalty provided by this paragraph (f)(3) is not subject to rescission.

(g) *Applicability date.*—(1) This section applies to penalties assessed after *March 26, 2019.*

(2) For penalties assessed before *March 26, 2019,* §301.6707A-1 (as contained in 26 CFR part 1, revised April 2018) shall apply. [Reg. §301.6707A-1.]

☐ [*T.D.* 9550, 9-1-2011. *Amended by T.D.* 9853, 3-25-2019.]

**[Reg. §301.6708-1]**

**§301.6708-1. Failure to maintain lists of advisees with respect to reportable transactions.**—(a) *In general.*—Any person who is required to maintain a list under section 6112 who, upon written request for the list, fails to make the list available to the Secretary within 20 business days after the date of the request shall be subject to a penalty in the amount of $10,000 for each subsequent calendar day on which the person fails to furnish a list containing the information and in the form required by section 6112 and its corresponding regulations. The penalty will not be imposed on any particular day or days for which the person establishes that the failure to comply on that day is due to reasonable cause.

(b) *Calculation of the 20-business-day period.*—The 20-business-day period shall begin on the first business day after the earliest of the date that the IRS—

(1) Mails a request for the list required to be maintained under section 6112(a) by certified or registered mail to the person required to maintain the list;

(2) Hand delivers the written request to the person required to maintain the list; or

(3) Leaves the written request with an individual 18 years old or older at the usual place of business of the person required to maintain the list.

(c) *Making a list available.*—(1) A person who is required to maintain a list required by section 6112 may make the list available by mailing or delivering it to the IRS within 20 business days after the date of the list request. Section 7502 and the regulations thereunder shall apply to this section.

(2) A person who is required to maintain a list required by section 6112 may also make the list available to the IRS by making it available for inspection and copying during normal business hours, as provided by section 6112, or by another agreed-upon method, on an agreed-upon date that falls within the 20-business-day period following the list request.

(3) *Extension.*—(i) *In general.*—Upon a showing of good cause by the person prior to the expiration of the 20-business-day period following a list request, the IRS may, in its discretion, agree to extend the period within which to make all or part of the list available. For purposes of this paragraph, "good cause" is shown if the person establishes that the 20-business-day deadline cannot reasonably be met despite diligent efforts by the person to maintain the materials constituting a list and to make that list available to the IRS in the time and manner required by the Secretary under section 6112.

(ii) *Requesting an extension.*—Any request for an extension of the 20-business-day period must be made in writing to the person at the IRS who requested the list. The person requesting an extension must briefly describe the information and documents that comprise the list as required by section 6112; explain the circumstances that would warrant additional time; propose a schedule to complete the production of the list; state that to the best of the person's knowledge, as of the date of the list request, all information and records relating to the list under the person's possession, custody, or control had been maintained in accordance with procedures and policies that are consistent with sections 6001 and 6112 of the Internal Revenue Code; and state that the extension request is not being made to avoid the person's list maintenance obligations imposed by section 6112 and its corresponding regulations. The IRS may, in its discretion, grant the person's extension request in full or in part. The IRS will consider whether granting an extension may impair its ability to make a timely assessment against any of the participants in the transaction associated with the requested list. The IRS will not grant an extension if it determines that a significant reason for the extension request is to delay producing the list. A pending extension request by itself does not constitute reasonable cause for purposes of section 6708.

(4) *Examples.*—The following examples illustrate paragraph (c)(3)(i) and (ii) of this section. These examples are intended to illustrate how the facts and circumstances in paragraph (c)(3)(i) and (ii) of this section may apply; in any given case, however, all of the facts and circumstances must be analyzed.

*Example 1.* (i) Firm A is a large law firm that is a material advisor. Firm A conducts annual sessions to educate its professionals about reportable transactions and the firm's obligations related to those reportable transactions. Firm A instructs its professionals to provide information on tax engagements that involve reportable transactions and to provide the documents required to be maintained under sections 6001 and 6112 to Firm A's compliance officer for list maintenance purposes. Firm A's policy provides that, for each engagement involving a reportable transaction, one firm professional will send an email to the firm's compliance officer about the engagement and then direct a subordinate to send the documents required to be maintained to the firm's compliance officer. Firm A has policies and procedures in place to monitor compliance with these rules and to address non-compliance.

(ii) Firm A receives a request from the IRS for a section 6112 list. In compiling its list to turn over to the IRS during the 20-business-day period following the list request, Firm A discovers that, with respect to one reportable transaction, a subordinate did not provide the documentation required by Firm A's policy. In addition, Firm A experiences difficulty locating the required documents as both the professional and the subordinate who worked on the matter are no longer employed by Firm A, requiring the firm to undertake an extensive search for the information responsive to the list request. Firm A also seeks the information from the firm's clients. Despite these efforts, Firm A reasonably determined that it will not be able to respond timely to the request. Within the 20-business-day period, Firm A notifies the IRS, in writing, of the difficulties it is experiencing and requests an additional 10 business days to locate and produce the information for this one transaction. Within the 20-business-day period, Firm A makes all other required list information available to the IRS, together with a description of the information that is being searched for, all statements required by these regulations, and a proposed schedule to produce the missing information.

(iii) Under these circumstances, Firm A demonstrated that it could not reasonably make the portion of the list relating to the one transaction available within the 20-business-day period and thus qualified for an extension. Firm A had established policies and procedures reasonably designed and implemented to ensure and monitor compliance with the requirements of section 6112 and address non-compliance. Because the facts and circumstances indicate that Firm A made diligent efforts to maintain the materials constituting the list in a readily accessible form and as otherwise required under section 6112, the requested 10-business-day extension with respect to the portion of the list relating to the one transaction where records were not maintained in accordance with the firm's policies and procedures should be granted.

*Example 2.* (i) Assume the same facts set forth in example one, except that, in the process of compiling the list to comply with the list maintenance request, Firm A first becomes aware that a firm professional did not send an email to the firm's compliance officer about a transaction subject to the list maintenance request and did not direct a subordinate to send to the firm's compliance officer the information required to be maintained with respect to the transaction. Assume further that Firm A had a robust section 6112 compliance monitoring program in place and despite this, the firm did not know that the professional did not follow firm policies and procedures with respect to this transaction. The professional who worked on the matter is no longer employed by Firm A, causing Firm A difficulty in locating the required information and in ascertaining whether the professional in question failed to comply with Firm A's list maintenance policies with respect to any other reportable transactions. Firm A is searching its records to locate information responsive to the list request and to ensure that no other reportable transactions were omitted from the list. Firm A estimates that it will take an additional 20 business days after the 20th business day to retrieve the missing information and

provide IRS with the additional information responsive to the list request. Within the 20-business-day period, Firm A notifies the IRS, in writing, of the difficulties it is experiencing and requests an additional 20 business days to locate and produce the information for this one transaction and for any other reportable transactions omitted from the list as a result of the inaction by the professional in question. Within the 20-business-day period, Firm A makes all other required list information available to the IRS, together with a description of the information that is being searched for, all statements required by these regulations, and a proposed schedule to produce the missing documents.

(ii) Under these facts and circumstances, Firm A demonstrated that it could not reasonably, within the 20-business-day period, make available the portion of the list relating to one or possibly more transactions omitted from the list because of the inaction of the professional in question. Firm A therefore qualifies for an extension. Firm A had established policies and procedures reasonably designed and implemented to ensure and monitor compliance with the requirements of section 6112 and address non-compliance. Because the facts and circumstances indicate that Firm A made diligent efforts to maintain the materials constituting the list in a readily accessible form and as otherwise required under section 6112, the requested 20-business-day extension with respect to the portion of the list relating to the one known omitted transaction and to any other omitted reportable transactions resulting from the inaction of the professional in question should be granted.

(d) *Failure to make list available.*—A failure to make the list available includes any failure to furnish the requested list to the IRS in a timely manner and in the form required under section 6112 and its corresponding regulations. Examples of failures to make a list available include instances in which a person fails to furnish any list; furnishes an incomplete list; or furnishes a list, whether or not complete, after the time required by this section.

(e) *Computation of penalty.*—(1) *In general.*—The penalty imposed by section 6708 accrues daily, beginning on the first calendar day after the expiration of the 20-business-day period following a written list request, and continues for each calendar day thereafter until the person's failure to furnish a list in the form required by section 6112 and its corresponding regulations ends. If the list is delivered or mailed to the IRS outside of the 20-business-day period, the penalty shall not apply on the day the list is delivered to the IRS or, if the list is mailed, the day the list is received by the IRS.

(2) *Computation of penalty after grant of extension.*—If the IRS grants an extension of the 20-business-day period pursuant to paragraph (c)(3) of this section, the penalty imposed by section 6708 accrues daily, beginning on the first calendar day after the extension period expires, and continues for each calendar day thereafter until the person's failure to furnish a list in the form required by section 6112 and its corresponding regulations ends. If the list is delivered or mailed to the IRS outside of the period of extension, the penalty shall not apply on the day the list is delivered to the IRS or, if the list is mailed, the day the list is received by the IRS.

(3) *Designation agreements and concurrent application of penalty.*—If material advisors with respect to the same reportable transaction enter into a designation agreement pursuant to section 6112(b)(2) and § 301.6112-1(f), separate penalties will be imposed on designated material advisors and nondesignated material advisors who are parties to the designation agreement for their respective periods of failure or noncompliance with a list request. A penalty will continue to accrue against a material advisor who is a party to a designation agreement until such time when a list complying with the requirements of section 6112 and its corresponding regulations is furnished by that material advisor or any other material advisor who is a party to the designation agreement.

(4) *Example.*—The following example illustrates paragraph (e) of this section.

*Example.* The IRS hand delivers a written request for the list required to be maintained under section 6112 to Firm B, a material advisor, on Friday, March 10, 2017. Firm B must make the list available to the IRS on or before Friday, April 7, 2017, the 20th business day after the request was hand delivered. If Firm B fails to make the list available to the IRS by that day, absent reasonable cause or the IRS's grant of an extension of the response time, the $10,000-per-day penalty begins on Saturday, April 8, 2017. The $10,000 per day penalty will continue for each subsequent calendar day until Firm B makes the complete list available, except for those days for which Firm B demonstrates reasonable cause. If Firm B hand delivers a complete copy of the requested list to the IRS on the morning of Tuesday, April 11, 2017, absent reasonable cause or the IRS's prior grant of an extension for the response time, a penalty of $30,000 will be imposed upon Firm B (for April 8, 9, and 10). See

**Reg. §301.6708-1(e)(4)**

paragraphs (g) and (h) of this section for an explanation of reasonable cause.

(f) *Definitions.*—For purposes of this section, the following definitions apply:

(1) *Material advisor* means a person described in section 6111 and § 301.6111-3(b).

(2) *Business day* means every calendar day other than a Saturday, Sunday, or legal holiday within the meaning of section 7503.

(3) *Reportable transaction* means a transaction described in section 6707A(c)(1) and section 1.6011-4(b)(1).

(4) *Listed transaction* means a transaction described in section 6707A(c)(2) and § 1.6011-4(b)(2) of this chapter.

(g) *Reasonable cause – general applicability.*—(1) *Overview.*—The section 6708 penalty will not be imposed for any day or days for which the person shows that the failure to make a complete list available to the IRS was due to reasonable cause. The determination of whether a person had reasonable cause is made on a case-by-case and day-by-day basis, taking into account all the relevant facts and circumstances. Facts and circumstances relevant to a material advisor's reasonable cause for failing to make available the list on a specific day include facts and circumstances arising after the request for the list. The person's showing of reasonable cause should relate to each specific day or days for which the person failed to make available the requested list. Factors establishing reasonable cause include, but are not limited to, factors identified in paragraphs (g) and (h) of this section.

(2) *Good-faith factors.*—The most important factors to establish reasonable cause are those that reflect the extent of the person's good-faith efforts to comply with section 6112. The following factors, which are not exclusive, will be considered in determining whether a person has made a good-faith effort to comply with the section 6112 requirements:

(i) The person's efforts to determine or assess its status as a material advisor as defined by section 6111;

(ii) The person's efforts to determine the information and documentation required to be maintained under section 6112;

(iii) The person's efforts to meet its obligations to maintain a readily producible list as required by section 6112;

(iv) The person's efforts, upon receiving the list request, to make the list available to the IRS within the 20-business-day period (or extended period) under paragraphs (a), (b), and (c)(3) of this section; and

(v) The person's efforts to ensure that the list furnished to the IRS is accurate and complete.

(3) *Ordinary business care.*—The exercise of ordinary business care may constitute reasonable cause. To show ordinary business care, the person may, for example, show that the person established, and adhered to, procedures reasonably designed and implemented to ensure compliance with the section 6112 requirements. In all instances when ordinary business care is claimed as constituting reasonable cause, a person must show that the person took immediate steps, upon discovering any failure relating to the list, to correct the failure. A person's failure to take immediate steps to correct a failure related to the list upon discovering the failure is a factor weighing against a conclusion that the person exercised ordinary business care. Notwithstanding the occurrence of an isolated and inadvertent failure, a person still may be able to demonstrate that the person exercised ordinary business care, considering all the relevant facts and circumstances, but only if the person had established and adhered to procedures reasonably designed and implemented to ensure compliance with the section 6112 requirements.

(4) *Supervening events.*—A person may establish reasonable cause for one or more days for which, considering all the relevant facts and circumstances, the failure to timely furnish the list required by section 6112 was due solely to a supervening event beyond the person's control. Events beyond a person's control may include fire, flood, storm, or other casualty; illness; theft; or other similarly unexpected event that damages or impairs the person's relevant business records or system for processing and providing these records, or that affects the person's ability to maintain the section 6112 list or make it available to the IRS. Reasonable cause may be established only for the period that a person who exercised ordinary business care would need to provide the list from alternative records in existence, or make the list available, under the specific facts and circumstances.

(5) *Reliance on opinion or advice.*—(i) *In general.*—A person may rely on an independent tax professional's advice to establish reasonable cause. The reliance, however, must be reasonable and in good faith, in light of all the other facts and circumstances. For a person to be considered to have relied on the advice, the advice must have been received by the person before the date the list is required to be made available to the IRS. If the person received advice from an independent tax professional, the person's reliance on that advice will be considered reasonable only if the independent tax professional reasonably believed that it is more likely than not that the person does not have an obligation imposed by section 6112. For example, this advice may conclude that the person is not a material advisor; that the transaction upon which the person provided material aid, assistance, or advice is not a reportable transaction for which a list was required to be maintained as of the date of the advice; that the information and documents to be produced constitute the required list; or that the information or documents withheld by the person are not required to be produced. The advice must also take into account and consider all relevant facts and circumstances, not rely on unreasonable legal or factual assumptions, not rely on or take into account the possibility that a list request may not be made, and not rely on unreasonable representations or statements of the person seeking the advice. Advice from a tax professional who is not independent may be considered in determining reasonable cause if, in light of and in relation to all the other facts and circumstances, taking into account such advice is reasonable. However, by itself, advice from a tax professional who is not independent is not sufficient to establish reasonable cause. Independent tax professional advice is not required to establish reasonable cause and the failure to obtain advice from an independent tax professional does not preclude a finding of reasonable cause if, based on the totality of all of the relevant facts and circumstances, reasonable cause has been established.

(ii) *Independent tax professional.*—For purposes of this section, an independent tax professional is a person who is knowledgeable in the relevant aspects of Federal tax law and who is not a material advisor with respect to the specific transaction that is the subject of the list request. For advice related to a listed transaction, a person who is a material advisor with respect to any transaction that is the same as or substantially similar to the type of transaction that is the subject of the list request will not be considered an independent tax professional.

(6) *Examples.*—The following examples illustrate this paragraph (g). These examples are intended to illustrate how the facts and circumstances in paragraphs (g)(2) through (g)(5) of this section may apply; in any given case, however, all of the facts and circumstances must be analyzed.

*Example 1.* On August 11, 2017, the IRS sends a list request via certified mail to Firm C, a material advisor. Firm C consists of a sole practitioner, X, who is away from the office on vacation on this date. X has arranged for a colleague, Y, to review Firm C's mail, email, and telephone messages daily during his absence. X returns to the office the day after his vacation ends, on September 5, 2017, and immediately contacts the IRS to notify it of his absence. Firm C makes a complete list available to the IRS on September 19, 2017, 10 business days after he has returned from vacation. Firm C establishes that X was on vacation at the time the list request was sent to Firm C, and Firm C promptly furnished the requested list in a manner and time period reflecting ordinary business care and prudence upon X's return to the office. Under these circumstances, Firm C is considered to have made a good-faith effort to comply with the section 6112 requirements. Firm C has established reasonable cause for the entire period between the expiration of the 20-business-day period following the list request and the date the list was made available to the IRS. See paragraphs (g)(2) and (3) of this section.

*Example 2.* On March 3, 2017, the IRS hand delivers to Firm D, a material advisor, a list request related to a transaction believed by the IRS to have been implemented in November 2008 by a group of Firm D's clients (the advisees). Firm D's involvement in the transaction included implementing the transaction on behalf of some but not all of the advisees. Firm D timely makes the requested list available to the IRS. Upon review, the IRS determines that the information furnished by Firm D appears to be accurate, but the IRS believes that some of the information is incomplete because it does not contain information about certain individuals who were identified through other investigative means as Firm D's clients who may have engaged in the transaction. In response to a follow-up inquiry by the IRS, Firm D establishes, however, that it is not a material advisor with respect to these taxpayers. Under these circumstances, Firm D has furnished the list as required by section 6112. Because the list was complete when furnished, Firm D need not make a showing of reasonable cause. See paragraph (g)(1) of this section.

*Example 3.* The IRS sends a list request by certified mail to Firm E, a material advisor. Firm E maintains the materials responsive to the list request on a portable data storage device. Under Firm E's established procedures for maintaining section 6112 lists, once the transaction is completed, paper documents are scanned and saved electronically according to Firm E's records management procedures. Under Firm E's records management procedures, after the scanning

**Reg. § 301.6708-1(f)**

process is completed, Firm E sends the paper documents to an off-site storage facility. Three days before the 20th business day following the date of the written request, the electronic data is permanently destroyed. Firm E contacts the IRS representative listed as a contact person on the section 6112 list request to advise him that the relevant data was permanently destroyed. Firm E establishes that it exercised ordinary business care but that the data was nevertheless destroyed due to circumstances outside of its control. Under these circumstances, Firm E has reasonable cause for the period of time that Firm E cannot respond to the list request due to circumstances out of Firm E's control. The reasonable cause exception, however, will only be available to Firm E for the period of time that a person who exercises ordinary business care would need to obtain the materials that are part of the list, including in this case paper documents from the off-site storage facility, and furnish the list to the IRS. See paragraphs (g)(3) and (4) of section.

*Example 4.* On February 2, 2017, the IRS hand delivers a list request to Firm F, a material advisor. Firm F filed with the IRS the disclosure statement required by section 6111 for the reportable transaction that is the subject of the list request but did not maintain the section 6112 list documentation in a readily accessible format after filing the section 6111 statement. On March 3, 2017, the 20th business day (due to the Presidents' Day holiday) after the list request is delivered to Firm F, Firm F contacts the IRS to ask for additional time to comply with the list request, stating that it could not gather the list information together in 20 business days. Because Firm F is not able to show that it made diligent efforts to maintain the materials constituting the list in a readily accessible form, the IRS should not grant Firm F an extension of time. See paragraph (c)(3) of this section. Further, Firm F does not have reasonable cause because it has failed to demonstrate a good-faith effort to comply with the section 6112 requirements and ordinary business care. See paragraphs (g)(2) and (3) of this section.

*Example 5.* On August 11, 2017, the IRS sends a list request, via certified mail, to Firm G, a material advisor. Firm G consists of a sole practitioner, P. Firm G maintains the materials responsive to the list request electronically. Generally, under Firm G's records management procedures, once a transaction is completed, the documents related to that transaction are scanned and then saved electronically consistent with IRS guidance on maintaining books and records in electronic form. P is aware of the list request but ignores it. On September 24, 2017, the 13th calendar day after the 20-business-day period following the list request (due to the Labor Day holiday), P suffers a temporary but debilitating illness that lasts 22 days. Following the illness, P immediately returns to work. After returning to work, P continues to ignore the list request. In this situation, the facts and circumstances indicate that Firm G does not have reasonable cause for any day in which there was a failure to make the list available to the IRS, including the 22 days due to the intervening event, because the failure was not due solely to the supervening event occurring on September 24, 2017. Firm G did not make a good-faith effort to make the list available to the IRS before or after the supervening event occurred. Firm G is liable for the $10,000 per day penalty from the first day following the expiration of the 20-business-day period until but not including the day that Firm G furnishes the list to the IRS. See paragraphs (g)(2) and (4) of this section.

*Example 6.* On August 11, 2017, the IRS sends a list request, via certified mail, to Firm H, a material advisor. Firm H, consists of a sole practitioner, P. Firm H maintains the materials responsive to the list request electronically. Generally, under Firm H's records management procedures, once the transaction is completed, the documents are scanned and then saved electronically consistent with IRS guidance on maintaining books and records in electronic form. P is aware of the list request and begins compiling the documents to respond to the IRS within the 20–business-day period ending on September 11, 2017 (due to the Labor Day holiday). Before responding to the list request, P suffers a temporary but debilitating illness on September 3, 2017, that lasts through September 19, 2017. Upon returning to work on September 20, 2017, P contacts the IRS to explain that P experienced a temporary but debilitating illness from September 3, 2017, through September 19, 2017, and that P has returned to the office and intends to furnish the list to the IRS within a short period of time. Firm H furnishes the list to the IRS on September 22, 2017. In this situation, the facts and circumstances indicate that Firm H has reasonable cause for the period from September 12, 2017 until September 21, 2017, attributable to P's illness. The failure to furnish the list in a timely fashion was solely attributable to the supervening event occurring on September 3, 2017, and Firm H promptly furnished the requested list in a manner and time period reflecting ordinary business care upon P's return to the office. Firm H is considered to have made a good-faith effort to comply with the section 6112 requirements. Firm H has established reasonable cause for the entire period between the expiration of the 20-business-day period following the list request and the date Firm H furnished the list to the IRS. See paragraphs (g)(2) and (4) of this section.

*Example 7.* Firm I receives a list request for transactions that are the same or substantially similar to the listed transaction described in Notice 2002-21, 2002-1 CB 730. Firm I will be considered a material advisor with respect to a particular transaction for which it provided advice if the transaction is the same as or substantially similar to the transaction described in Notice 2002-21. Firm I, however, is unsure whether the transaction is the same as or substantially similar to the transaction described in this Notice. Firm I obtains an opinion from Firm L, a law firm, on this issue. P, a partner in Firm L, provided tax advice to clients who invested in other Notice 2002-21 transactions, including how to report the purported tax benefits from the transaction on their income tax returns, and Firm L is a material advisor with respect to those transactions. Because Firm L is a material advisor with respect to the type of transaction that is the same as or substantially similar to the transaction described in Notice 2002-21, Firm L is not considered an independent tax professional under paragraph (g)(5)(ii) of this section. Therefore, Firm I cannot rely on advice provided by Firm L to establish reasonable cause under this paragraph (g). The IRS may consider Firm L's advice in determining reasonable cause in light of other facts and circumstances, but Firm L's advice, without more, is not sufficient to establish reasonable cause because P is not an independent tax professional under paragraph (g)(5)(ii) of this section.

*Example 8.* Firm J, a law firm, provides advice to various clients of the firm regarding the potential tax benefits of a reportable transaction under § 1.6011-4(b)(5) of this chapter (involving a section 165 loss) and is a material advisor with respect to that transaction. Firm J also provides advice to Firm M, an accounting firm, regarding the same transaction. Firm M then advises various Firm M clients regarding this same transaction, and is a material advisor. The transaction is not a listed transaction. Firm N, a law firm that is not associated with Firm J and has not provided advice with respect to the same transaction to Firm M, has provided advice to its own clients regarding other transactions subject to § 1.6011-4(b)(5) of this chapter, but not the particular transaction that was the subject of Firm J's advice to Firm M. The IRS hand delivers a list request to Firm M, the subject of which is the transaction regarding which Firm J provided advice to Firm M. Before the expiration of the 20-business-day period, Firm M seeks advice from Firm J and Firm N about the propriety of withholding certain documents related to the transaction. Because Firm J provided advice with respect to the particular transaction that is the subject of the list request, Firm J is not an independent tax professional under paragraph (g)(5)(ii) of this section. Although Firm N has provided advice on a transaction that is considered a reportable transaction under § 1.6011-4(b)(5) of this chapter, Firm N is considered to be an independent tax professional under paragraph (g)(5)(ii) of this section because Firm N did not provide material assistance with respect to the particular transaction that is the subject of the list request.

(h) *Reasonable cause – special considerations.*—(1) *Material advisor no longer in existence.*—If a material advisor has dissolved, been liquidated, or otherwise is no longer in existence, the person required by section 6112 to maintain the list (the "responsible person") is subject to the penalty for failing to make the list available. In considering whether a responsible person or successor in interest has reasonable cause for any failure to timely make the list available to the IRS, the IRS will consider all of the facts and circumstances, including those facts and circumstances relating to the dissolution, liquidation, and winding up of the original material advisor's business and any efforts the original material advisor made to comply with the section 6112 requirements before the dissolution or liquidation. When appropriate or applicable, due diligence, if any, performed by a responsible person or successor in interest will be considered, and due consideration will be given for acts taken by that person to minimize the potential for violating the section 6112 requirements.

(2) *Review by IRS.*—Whether reasonable cause exists for a period of time will be determined based on all the relevant facts and circumstances, including facts and circumstances arising after the request for the list. If a material advisor establishes that, in its efforts to comply with the provisions of section 6112 and its corresponding regulations, it acted in good faith, as defined in paragraph (g)(2) of this section, the material advisor will be deemed to have reasonable cause for the periods of time the IRS takes to review a furnished list for compliance with the section 6112 requirements and to inform the material advisor of any identified failures in the list. If the material advisor does not establish that it acted in good faith the IRS will not consider the time it takes to review the list or inform the material advisor of identified failures as a factor in determining whether the material advisor has reasonable cause for that period.

(3) *Examples.*—The following examples illustrate paragraph (h)(2) of this section.

*Example 1.* On February 2, 2017, the IRS hand delivers a list request to Firm O, a material advisor. On March 3, 2017, the 20th business day (due to the Presidents' Day holiday) after the list request is delivered to Firm O, Firm O sends a list to the IRS that was contemporaneously prepared after Firm O issued advice with respect to the reportable transaction and continuously maintained in accordance with the requirements of section 6112 and the related regulations. Before sending the list, a supervisor at Firm O carefully reviewed the list to verify that it was comprehensive and accurate. The IRS completes its review on March 23, 2017, and determines that the list is not complete because Firm O furnished a draft copy of the tax opinion, rather than the final document, which Firm O had mistakenly misfiled. After Firm O is notified of the missing information, Firm O immediately furnishes a complete copy of the final version of the tax opinion. Firm O made a good-faith effort to comply with the section 6112 requirements, including its efforts to ensure that the list that was furnished to the IRS was accurate and complete. Firm O has reasonable cause for the entire period between the expiration of the 20-business-day period following the list request and the date it furnished the complete list to the IRS.

*Example 2.* On February 2, 2017, the IRS hand delivers a list request to Firm P, a material advisor. Firm P's involvement in the reportable transaction included implementing the transaction on behalf of some but not all of Firm P's clients. On March 3, 2017, the 20th business day (due to the Presidents' Day holiday) after the list request is delivered to Firm P, Firm P sends the list to the IRS. The IRS completes its review on March 23, 2017. The IRS believes the client list is incomplete because it does not contain information about certain individuals who were identified through other investigative means as clients of Firm P who may have engaged in the transaction. On March 27, 2017, in response to a follow-up inquiry by the IRS, Firm P establishes that it is not a material advisor with respect to these taxpayers. Therefore, the March 3, 2017 list was complete and accurate when first furnished. Under these circumstances, Firm P has timely furnished the list as required by section 6112. Because Firm P complied with the requirements of section 6112 no penalty applies, and Firm P does not need to establish reasonable cause for the period from March 4, 2017, through March 27, 2017, when the IRS was reviewing the list.

*Example 3.* On February 2, 2017, the IRS hand delivers a list request to Firm Q, a material advisor. On March 3, 2017, the 20th business day (due to the Presidents' Day holiday) after the list request is delivered to Firm Q, Firm Q sends the list to the IRS. Firm Q had not maintained a list contemporaneously after issuing the advice with respect to the reportable transaction, and created the list during the 20 business days before providing the list to the IRS. To meet the 20-business-day deadline, a supervisor did not review the final list before sending it to the IRS. The IRS completes its review on March 23, 2017, and determines that the list is not complete because it does not include 15 persons for whom Firm Q acted as a material advisor with respect to the reportable transaction. Firm Q furnishes the additional information on March 27, 2017. Because Firm Q is not able to show that it made diligent efforts to maintain the materials constituting the list in a readily accessible form and that it made a reasonable effort to ensure that the list that was furnished to the IRS was accurate and complete, Firm Q cannot establish that it exhibited a good-faith effort to comply with the section 6112 requirements. Firm Q does not have reasonable cause for its failure to furnish the complete list from March 4, 2017, through March 26, 2017.

*Example 4.* Within the 20-business-day period following a list request, Firm R sends four boxes of documents comprising the required list to the IRS using a commercial delivery service. The IRS receives only three of the boxes because box 4 was erroneously self-addressed using Firm R's office address. Box 4 arrives at Firm R's office on January 6, 2017, the 2nd calendar day after the 20th business day after the list request was made. Firm R immediately recognizes its clerical error, promptly contacts the IRS, and resends the original and unopened box 4, properly addressed, to the IRS together with documentation supporting the error. The IRS receives box 4 on January 9, 2017. Under these circumstances, Firm R has reasonable cause for the late delivery of box 4 because it made a good-faith attempt to timely comply with the list request and immediately corrected an inadvertent error upon its discovery. As a result, no penalty will be imposed based on the delay in providing box 4. If, after inspection, the IRS determines that, even with the contents of box 4, the list is incomplete or defective, Firm R must establish reasonable cause for the incomplete nature of the list or the defect to avoid imposition of a penalty for the period beginning January 5, 2017, until but not including the day that Firm R furnishes the list to the IRS.

*Example 5.* (i) Firm S is a large law firm that is a material advisor. Firm S conducts annual sessions to educate its professionals about reportable transactions and the firm's obligations related to those reportable transactions. Firm S instructs its professionals to provide information on tax engagements that involve reportable transactions and to provide the documents required to be maintained under section 6112 to Firm S's compliance officer for list maintenance

purposes. Firm S's policy provides that, for each engagement involving a reportable transaction, one firm professional will send an email to the firm's compliance officer about the engagement and then direct a subordinate to send to the firm's compliance officer the documents required to be maintained.

(ii) Firm S receives a request from the IRS for a section 6112 list. In compiling its list to turn over to the IRS during the 20-business-day period, Firm S asks all professionals to ensure that they have reported all engagements involving a reportable transaction to the firm's compliance officer. Before submission to the IRS, a Firm S supervisor reviews the list to ensure completeness. Firm S has no reason to know of any deficiencies, and in compiling its list, Firm S discovers no deficiencies.

(iii) Upon review of the list, the IRS determines that the information furnished by Firm S appears to be accurate, but the IRS believes that some of the information is incomplete because it does not contain information about an individual who may have engaged in the transaction and who was identified through other investigative means as Firm S's client. In response to a follow-up inquiry by the IRS, Firm S immediately reviews its files and discovers that a former Firm S professional, who is no longer employed by Firm S, provided material advice to the individual with respect to carrying out a reportable transaction, but did not send an email to the firm's compliance officer about the transaction or direct a subordinate to send the documents required to be maintained to the firm's compliance officer. Firm S immediately furnishes the missing information and documents related to the identified omission to the IRS.

(iv) Firm S establishes that the professional in question ordinarily complied with Firm S's list maintenance procedures and that Firm S had no reason to know of this one omission or to suspect that the professional had failed to report any reportable transactions to the firm's compliance officer in accordance with the firm's policies. Firm S also immediately undertakes a thorough search of its electronic and paper files to locate any additional reportable transactions relating to the professional in question that may have been omitted from the list. Under these circumstances, Firm S has demonstrated that it has acted in good faith in its efforts to comply with section 6112 and is deemed to have reasonable cause for the period of time the IRS took to review the furnished list and to inform the material advisor of the identified failure in the list. See paragraph (h)(2) of this section. The reasonable cause exception, however, will only be available to Firm S with respect to the omission identified by the IRS for the period of time that a person who exercises ordinary business care would need to obtain the information and documents related to the identified omission. See paragraph (g)(3) of this section. With respect to any other omissions related to the same professional and not identified by the IRS, the reasonable cause exception will only be available to Firm S for the period of time that a person who exercises ordinary business care would need to ascertain whether any other reportable transactions were omitted from the list and to obtain the information and documents related to any such omissions. See paragraph (g)(3) of this section.

(i) *Effective/applicability date.*—This section applies to all requests for lists required to be maintained under section 6112, including lists that persons were required to maintain under section 6112(a) as in effect before October 22, 2004, made on or after April 28, 2016. [Reg. § 301.6708-1.]

☐ [*T.D. 9764*, 4-27-2016.]

**[Reg. § 301.6708-1T]**

**§ 301.6708-1T. Failure to maintain list of investors in potentially abusive tax shelters (Temporary).**—The following questions and answers issued under section 6708 of the Internal Revenue Code of 1954, as added by section 142 of the Tax Reform Act of 1984 (Pub. L. No. 98-369; 98 Stat. 683), relate to the penalty for failure to maintain a list of investors in potentially abusive tax shelters.

Q-1. What penalties are provided with respect to the failure properly to maintain a list of persons who acquire interests in potentially abusive tax shelters?

A-1. Any organizer (as defined in A-5 of § 301.6112-1T) of a tax shelter (as defined in A-3 of § 301.6112-1T) or seller (as defined in A-6 of § 301.6112-1T) of interests in a tax shelter who fails to meet any requirement imposed by section 6112 regarding the requirement to maintain a list of persons who have acquired interests in a tax shelter shall pay a penalty of $50 for each investor with respect to whom there is such a failure, unless it is shown that the failure is due to reasonable cause and not due to willful neglect. For example, if an organizer who is required to maintain a list identifying each of 100 persons who acquired interests in a tax shelter fails to maintain the list, the organizer will be liable for a penalty of $5,000 ($50 × 100 persons), unless the organizer can show the failure was due to reasonable cause and not due to willful neglect. As another example, if a seller is required to maintain a list identifying each of 100 persons who acquired interests in a tax shelter from the seller and fails properly to maintain such list by omitting the TIN of each person, the seller will be liable for a penalty of $5,000 ($50 × 100 persons), unless the seller can show the failure was due to reasonable cause and not due to willful neglect.

Q-2. If an organizer or seller properly maintains a list, but fails to make the list available to the Internal Revenue Service upon request, will the organizer or seller be subject to a penalty?

A-2. Yes. A penalty applies if an organizer or seller fails to meet any requirement imposed by section 6112, including the requirement, upon request, to make the list available to the Internal Revenue Service as soon as practicable, but in any event within 10 calendar days. (See A-21 of §301.6112-1T). The amount of the penalty is $50 for each person required to be on the list at the time of the request by the Internal Revenue Service. Assume, for example, that an organizer of a tax shelter properly maintains a list of 200 persons who have acquired interests in a tax shelter and that the Internal Revenue Service requests the organizer to provide the list. If the organizer fails to provide the list to the Internal Revenue Service as soon as practicable (as required by A-21 of §301.6112-1T), or in a form that enables the Internal Revenue Service to obtain the required information without undue delay or difficulty (as required by A-16 of §301.6112-1T), the organizer will be liable for a penalty of $10,000 ($50 × 200 persons), unless the organizer can show that the failure to provide the list was due to reasonable cause and not to willful neglect.

Q-3. If an organizer or seller is required to maintain lists for more than one tax shelter in which the same person has acquired interests, how does the penalty apply if the organizer or seller fails to identify the person on each of the lists?

A-3. A separate $50 penalty applies with respect to the list for each tax shelter on which the person who acquired interests is not identified.

Q-4. Is there a limitation on the amount of the penalty imposed on a seller or organizer required to maintain a list of persons who have acquired interests in a tax shelter?

A-4. Yes. The maximum penalty that may be imposed on a person for any calendar year may not exceed $50,000.

Q-5. How does the calendar year limitation apply?

A-5. A separate $50,000 limitation applies to each calendar year in which a failure occurs, and to each tax shelter for which a list is required to be maintained. See A-6 of this section for special rules for determining how the $50,000 limitation applies to a designated person who fails properly to maintain a list of investors.

*Example (1).* Assume that A, an organizer of a tax shelter, fails to maintain and to provide to the Internal Revenue Service a list of 900 persons who acquired interests in the tax shelter in 1986. In addition, assume that A again fails to maintain and to provide the list of 900 investors upon request in 1987. A is subject to a penalty of $45,000 (900 persons × $50) for each calendar year in which there is a failure to comply with the requirements of section 6112. Thus, A is subject to $45,000 in penalties for the failures to maintain and to provide the list in 1986, and $45,000 in penalties for the failures to maintain and to provide the list in 1987, unless A can show reasonable cause for the failures.

*Example (2).* Assume that B, an organizer of Tax Shelter I, fails to provide a list of 1,500 persons who acquired interests in the tax shelter to the Internal Revenue Service upon request in 1987. Assume also that B, an organizer of Tax Shelter II, fails to provide a list of 2,000 persons who acquired interests in Tax Shelter II to the Internal Revenue Service upon request in 1987. Because the $50,000 calendar year limitation applies separately with respect to each tax shelter for which a list must be maintained, B is subject to a penalty of $50,000 for failing to provide the list for Tax Shelter I in 1987 and a $50,000 penalty for failing to provide the list for Tax Shelter II in 1987.

Q-6. How does the penalty apply to a designated person?

A-6. Separate penalties, each with its own $50,000 calendar year limitation, apply with respect to the portion of the list kept by the designated person in that person's capacity as organizer and to each portion of the list kept by the designated person in that person's capacity as the designated person with respect to each organizer and seller who signed the agreement under A-12 of §301.6112-1T and for whom the designated person is responsible for complying with the requirements of section 6112.

*Example.* Assume that X, an organizer and seller, sells interests in a tax shelter directly to 750 investors in 1985. In addition, assume that A, an agent of X, negotiates for X sales of interests in the tax shelter to an additional 500 persons in 1985. If no agreement to designate X is made pursuant to A-11 of §301.6112-1T, X would be required to maintain a list of the 1,250 investors who acquired interests in the tax shelter (see paragraph (a) of A-8 of §301.6112-1T) and A would be required to maintain a list of the 500 persons who acquired interests through A (see A-10 of §301.6112-1T). If, therefore, neither X nor A complied with the requirements of section 6112 in 1985, X would be

liable for $50,000 in penalties ($50 × 1,250 investors, subject to the $50,000 maximum) and A would be liable for $25,000 in penalties ($50 × 500 investors). Assume, however, that X and A enter into a written agreement to designate X to maintain the list for the tax shelter. Pursuant to that agreement, A submits to X all of the required information regarding the sales to the 500 persons otherwise required to be maintained on A's list and provides the notice required by A-13 of §301.6112-1T to each person. In 1986, X fails to provide any list of investors to the Internal Revenue Service upon request. For calendar year 1986, X is liable for penalties of $50,000 in in X's capacity as an organizer ($50 × 1,250 persons, subject to the $50,000 maximum). In addition, X, as the person designated to maintain the list for A, is liable for penalties of $25,000 for failing properly to maintain A's list of investors ($50 × 500 persons). A would not be liable for any penalties.

Q-7. If an organizer or seller is subject to a penalty with respect to a tax shelter under section 6708, may the organizer or seller also be liable for other fines or penalties with respect to the tax shelter?

A-7. Yes. The penalty imposed by section 6708 is in addition to any other penalty provided by law. If, for example, an organizer of a tax shelter is subject to a penalty under section 6700 for promoting an abusive tax shelter, the organizer also would be liable for any applicable penalties for failing properly to maintain a list for the tax shelter. Similarly, if an organizer or seller fails to furnish a list upon request by the Internal Revenue Service, the organizer or seller may be subject both to the fine under section 7203 for the willful failure to supply information, and to the penalty for failing properly to maintain a list for the tax shelter.

Q-8. When is the penalty under section 6708 effective?

A-8. The penalty under section 6708 applies with respect to any interest in a tax shelter which is required to be included on a list under section 6112. See A-22 of §301.6112-1T.
[Temporary Reg. §301.6708-1T.]

☐ [T.D. 7969, 8-24-84.]

### [Reg. §1.6709-1T]

**§1.6709-1T. Penalties with respect to mortgage credit certificates.**—(a) *Material misstatement.*—(1) *Negligence.*—If any person makes a material misstatement in any affidavit or other statement under penalty of perjury made with respect to the issuance of a mortgage credit certificate and such misstatement is due to the negligence of that person, that person shall pay a penalty of $1,000 for each mortgage credit certificate with respect to which that misstatement was made.

(2) *Fraud.*—If a misstatement described in subparagraph (1) is due to fraud on the part of the person making the misstatement, that person shall pay a penalty of $10,000 for each mortgage credit certificate with respect to which the fraudulent misstatement was made. The penalty imposed by this paragraph (a)(2) is in addition to any criminal penalty.

(b) *Reports.*—(1) Any person required by §1.25-8T to file a report with respect to any mortgage credit certificate who fails to file the report at the time and in the manner required by §1.25-8T shall pay a penalty of $200 for each mortgage credit certificate with respect to which that failure occurred. The preceding sentence shall not apply if it is shown that such failure is due to reasonable cause and not to willful neglect.

(2) In the case of any report required under §1.25-8T(b), the aggregate amount of the penalty imposed by this paragraph shall not exceed $2,000. [Temporary Reg. §1.6709-1T.]

☐ [T.D. 8023, 5-3-85.]

### [Reg. §301.6712-1]

**§301.6712-1. Failure to disclose treaty-based return positions.**—(a) *Penalty imposed.*—A taxpayer who fails in a material way to disclose one or more positions taken for a taxable year, as required by section 6114 and the regulations thereunder, is subject to a separate penalty for each failure to disclose a position taken with respect to each separate payment or separate income item in the amount of—

(1) For a corporation taxable as such under the Code, $10,000; or

(2) For all other taxpayers, $1,000.

The penalty imposed by this section may be imposed more than once for a single taxable year if a taxpayer has failed to disclose one or more positions taken with respect to more than one separate payment or separate income item and may be imposed in addition to any other penalty imposed by law. For this purpose, separate payments or income items of the same type (*e.g.*, interest payments) received from the same ultimate payor (*e.g.*, the obligor on the note) will be treated as separate payments or income items (and not aggregated). However, for purposes of determining the number of separate penalties to be imposed under this section, the District Director shall have the discretion to aggregate separate payments or income items, in whole or in part, in accordance with the rules for aggregation of such items for purposes of reporting, as described in §301.6114-1(d).

(b) *Penalty waived.*—Pursuant to the authority contained in section 6712 (b) of the Code, the penalty imposed by paragraph (a) of this section may be waived, in whole or in part, if it is established to the satisfaction of the Assistant Commissioner (International), the district director or the director of the Internal Revenue Service Center that the taxpayer's failure to disclose the required information was not due to willful neglect. An affirmative showing of lack of willful neglect must be made in the form of a written statement that sets forth all the facts alleged to show lack of willful neglect and contains a declaration by such person that the statement is made under the penalties of perjury.

(c) *Manner of payment.*—The penalty set forth in paragraph (a) of this section shall be paid in the same manner as tax upon the issuance of a notice and demand thereof.

(d) *Effective date.*—This section is effective for taxable years of the taxpayer for which the due date for filing returns (without extension) occurs after December 31, 1988. [Reg. §301.6712-1.]

☐ [*T.D. 8292, 3-13-90.*]

### [Reg. §48.6715-1]

**§48.6715-1. Penalty for misuse of dyed fuel.**—(a) *In general.*—If any person willfully alters, or attempts to alter, the strength or composition of any dye or marking done pursuant to §48.4082-1 in any dyed fuel, then section 6715(a)(3) provides that such person shall pay a penalty in addition to any tax. The penalty imposed by section 6715(a)(3) will not apply in the following cases:

(1) Diesel fuel or kerosene that satisfies the dyeing and marking requirements of §48.4082-1(b) and (c) is blended with any undyed liquid and the resulting product satisfies the dyeing and marking requirements of §48.4082-1(b) and (c).

(2) Diesel fuel or kerosene that satisfies the dyeing and marking requirements of §48.4082-1(b) and (c) is blended with any other liquid (other than diesel fuel or kerosene) that contains the type and amount of dye and marker required for diesel fuel or kerosene dyed and marked in accordance with §48.4082-1(b) and (c).

(3) The alteration or attempted alteration occurs in an exempt area of Alaska after September 30, 1996.

(4) Diesel fuel or kerosene that does not satisfy the dyeing and marking requirements of §48.4082-1(b) and (c) is blended with diesel fuel or kerosene that satisfies the dyeing and marking requirements of §48.4082-1(b) and (c) and the blending occurs as part of a use described in §48.4082-4(c) or §48.6427-8(b)(1)(vii)(C) or (D).

(b) *Effective date.*—This section is effective January 1, 1994. [Reg. §48.6715-1.]

☐ [*T.D. 8659, 3-13-96. Amended by T.D. 8685, 11-8-96; T.D. 8748, 12-31-97 and T.D. 8879, 3-30-2000.*]

## Failure to File Certain Information Returns or Statements

(iv) Additional requirements.

(v) Failures to which a solicitation relates.

(vi) Exceptions and limitations.

(2) Manner of making annual solicitations—by mail or telephone.

(i) By mail.

(ii) By telephone.

(f) Acting in a responsible manner—special rules for incorrect TINs.

(1) In general.

(i) Initial solicitation.

(ii) First annual solicitation.

(iii) Second annual solicitation.

(iv) Additional requirements.

(2) Manner of making annual solicitation if notified pursuant to section 3406(a)(1)(B) and the regulations thereunder.

(3) Manner of making annual solicitation if notified pursuant to section 6721.

(4) Failures to which a solicitation relates.

(5) Exceptions and limitations.

(g) Due diligence safe harbor.

(1) In general.

(2) Special rules relating to TINs.

(3) Effective dates.

(h) Transitional rules for information returns required to be filed (or payee statements required to be furnished) after December 31, 1989 (without regard to extensions), and on or before April 22, 1991.

(1) In general.

(2) Special rule on TINs.

(i) [Reserved].

(j) Failures to which this section relates.

(k) Examples.

(l) [Reserved].

(m) Procedure for seeking a waiver.

(n) Manner of payment.

[Reg. § 301.6721-0.]

☐ [*T.D. 8386*, 12-27-91. *Amended by T.D. 8734*, 10-6-97 (T.D. 8804 delayed the effective date of T.D. 8734 from January 1, 1999, to January 1, 2000; T.D. 8856 further delayed the effective date of T.D. 8734 until January 1, 2001).]

**[Reg. § 301.6721-1]**

**§ 301.6721-1. Failure to file correct information returns.—** (a) *Imposition of penalty.*—(1) *General rule.*—A penalty of $50 is imposed for each information return (as defined in section 6724(d)(1) and paragraph (g) of this section) with respect to which a failure (as defined in section 6721(a)(2) and paragraph (a)(2) of this section) occurs. No more than one penalty will be imposed under this paragraph (a)(1) with respect to a single information return even though there may be more than one failure with respect to such return. The total amount imposed on any person for all failures during any calendar year with respect to all information returns shall not exceed $250,000. See paragraph (b) of this section for a reduction in the penalty when the failures are corrected within specified periods. See paragraph (c) of this section for an exception to the penalty for inconsequential errors or omissions. See paragraph (d) of this section for an exception to the penalty for a *de minimis* number of failures. See paragraph (e) of this section for lower limitations to the $250,000 maximum penalty. See paragraph (f) of this section for higher penalties when a failure is due to intentional disregard of the requirement to file timely correct information returns. See paragraph (a)(1) of § 301.6724-1 for waiver of the penalty for a failure that is due to reasonable cause.

(2) *Failures subject to the penalty.*—The failures to which section 6721(a) and paragraph (a)(1) of this section apply are—

(i) A failure to file an information return on or before the required filing date ("failure to file timely"), and

(ii) A failure to include all of the information required to be shown on the return or the inclusion of incorrect information ("failure to include correct information"). A failure to file timely includes a failure to file in the required manner, for example, on magnetic media or in other machine-readable form as provided under section 6011(e). However, no penalty is imposed under paragraph (a)(1) of this section solely by reason of any failure to comply with the requirements of section 6011(e)(2), except to the extent that such a failure occurs with respect to more than 250 information returns (the 250-threshold requirement) or in the case of a partnership with more than 100 partners, more than 100 information returns (the 100-threshold requirement) (collectively, the threshold requirements). Each Schedule K-1 considered in applying the 100-threshold requirement

will be treated as a separate information return. These threshold requirements apply separately to each type of information return required to be filed. Further, these threshold requirements apply separately to original and corrected returns. Thus, for example, if a filer files 300 returns on Form 1099-DIV and later files 70 corrected returns on Form 1099-DIV, the corrected returns may be filed either on the prescribed paper form (because they fall below the 250-threshold requirement) or on magnetic media or other machine-readable form. Filers who are required to file information returns on magnetic media and who file such information returns electronically are considered to have satisfied the magnetic media filing requirement. Except as provided in paragraph (c)(1) of this section, a failure to include correct information encompasses a failure to include the information required by applicable information reporting statutes or by any administrative pronouncements issued thereunder (such as regulations, revenue rulings, revenue procedures, or information reporting forms and form instructions). A failure to include information in the correct format may be either a failure to file timely an information return or a failure to include correct information on an information return. For example, an error on a magnetic media submission to the Internal Revenue Service that prevents processing by the Internal Revenue Service may constitute a failure to file timely. However, if information is set forth on the wrong field of the magnetic media submission, such an error may constitute a failure to file timely or a failure to include correct information, depending upon the extent of the failure.

(b) *Reduction in the penalty when a correction is made within specified periods.*—(1) *Correction within 30 days.*—The penalty imposed under section 6721(a) for a failure to file timely or for a failure to include correct information shall be $15 in lieu of $50 if the failure is corrected on or before the 30th day after the required filing date ("within 30 days"). The total amount imposed on a person for all failures during any calendar year that are corrected within 30 days shall not exceed $75,000.

(2) *Correction after 30 days but on or before August 1.*—The penalty imposed under section 6721(a) for a failure to file timely or for a failure to include correct information shall be $30 in lieu of $50 if the failure is corrected after the 30-day period described in paragraph (b)(1) of this section but on or before August 1 of the year in which the required filing date occurs ("after 30 days but on or before August 1"). (See paragraph (b)(6) of this section for an exception to the provisions of this paragraph (b)(2) for returns that are not due on February 28 or March 15.) The total amount imposed on a person for all failures during any calendar year corrected after 30 days but on or before August 1 shall not exceed $150,000.

(3) *Required filing date defined.*—The term "required filing date" means the date prescribed for filing an information return with the Internal Revenue Service (or the Social Security Administration in the case of Forms W-2) determined with regard to any extension of time for filing.

(4) *Penalty amount for return with multiple failures.*—If a return is subject to a penalty for more than one failure, and the penalty amounts for the failures differ, the higher penalty amount will be imposed.

(5) *Examples.*—The provisions of paragraphs (a) and (b)(1) through (4) of this section may be illustrated by the following examples. These examples do not take into account any possible application of the *de minimis* exception under paragraph (d) of this section, the lower small business limitations under paragraph (e) of this section, the penalty for intentional disregard under paragraph (f) of this section, or the reasonable cause waiver under paragraph (a) of § 301.6724-1:

*Example 1.* Corporation R fails to file timely 11,000 Forms 1099-MISC (relating to miscellaneous income) for the 1990 calendar year. Five thousand of these returns are filed with correct information within 30 days, and 6,000 after 30 days but on or before August 1, 1991. For the same year R fails to file timely 400 Forms 1099-INT (relating to payments of interest) which R eventually files on September 28, 1991, after the period for reduction of the penalty has elapsed. R is subject to a penalty of $20,000 for the 400 forms which were not filed by August 1 ($50 × 400 = $20,000), $150,000 for the 6,000 forms filed after 30 days ($30 × 6,000 = $180,000, limited to $150,000 under paragraph (b)(2) of this section), and $75,000 for the 5,000 forms filed within 30 days ($15 × 5,000 = $75,000), for a total penalty of $245,000.

*Example 2.* Corporation T fails to file timely 6,000 Forms 1099-MISC for the 1990 calendar year. T files the 6000 Forms 1099-MISC on September 1, 1991. Because T does not correct the failure by August 1, 1991, T is subject to a penalty of $250,000, the maximum penalty under paragraph (a) of this section. Without the limitation of paragraph (a), T would be subject to a $300,000 penalty ($50 × 6,000 = $300,000).

*Example 3.* Corporation U files timely 300 Forms 1099-MISC on paper for the 1990 calendar year with correct information. Under section 6011(e)(2) a person required to file at least 250 returns during a calendar year must file those returns on magnetic media. U does not correct its failures to file these returns on magnetic media by August 1, 1991. It is therefore subject to a penalty for a failure to file timely under paragraph (a)(2) of this section. However, pursuant to section 6724(c) and paragraph (a)(2) of this section, the penalty for a failure to file timely on magnetic media applies only to the extent the number of returns exceeds 250. As U was required to file 300 returns on magnetic media, U is subject to a penalty of $2,500 for 50 returns ($50 × 50 = $2,500).

*Example 4.* Corporation V files 300 Forms 1099-MISC on paper for the 1990 calendar year. The forms were filed on March 15, 1991, rather than on the required filing date of February 28, 1991. Under section 6011(e)(2), a person required to file at least 250 returns during a calendar year must file those returns on magnetic media. V does not correctly file these returns on magnetic media by August 1, 1991. V is subject to a penalty of $3,750 for filing 250 of the returns late ($15 × 250) and $2,500 for failing to file 50 returns on magnetic media ($50 × 50) for a total penalty of $6,250.

(6) *Application to returns not due on February 28 or March 15.*—For returns that are not due on February 28 or March 15 (for example, Forms 8300 reporting certain cash payments of $10,000 or more), the penalty is $15 if the failure is corrected within 30 days. If the failure is corrected after 30 days, the penalty is $50 rather than $30. There is no period during which the penalty is reduced to $30 under paragraph (b)(2) of this section.

(c) *Exception for inconsequential errors or omissions.*—(1) *In general.*— An inconsequential error or omission is not considered a failure to include correct information. For purposes of this paragraph (c)(1), the term "inconsequential error or omission" means any failure that does not prevent or hinder the Internal Revenue Service from processing the return, from correlating the information required to be shown on the return with the information shown on the payee's tax return, or from otherwise putting the return to its intended use. See paragraph (g)(5) of this section for the definition of "payee."

(2) *Errors or omissions that are never inconsequential.*—Errors or omissions relating to the following are never inconsequential—

(i) A taxpayer identification number;

(ii) A surname of a payee (*i.e.*, the person required to be furnished a copy of the information set forth on an information return); and

(iii) Any monetary amounts.
The Internal Revenue Service may, by administrative pronouncement, specify other types of errors or omissions that are never inconsequential.

(3) *Examples.*—The provisions of this paragraph (c) may be illustrated by the following examples, which do not take into account any possible application of the penalty for intentional disregard under paragraph (f) of this section or the reasonable cause waiver under paragraph (a) of § 301.6724-1:

*Example 1.* A filer files a Form 1099-MISC (relating to miscellaneous income) with the Internal Revenue Service. The Form 1099-MISC is complete and correct except that the word "street" is misspelled in the payee's address. The error does not prevent or hinder the Internal Revenue Service from processing the return, from correlating the information required to be shown on the return with the information shown on the payee's tax return, or from otherwise putting the return to its intended use. Therefore, no penalty is imposed under paragraph (a) of this section.

*Example 2.* A filer files a Form 1099-MISC with the Internal Revenue Service. The Form 1099-MISC is complete and correct except that the payee's first name, William, is misspelled as "Willaim." The error does not prevent or hinder the Internal Revenue Service from processing the return, from correlating the information required to be shown on the return with the information shown on the payee's tax return, or from otherwise putting the return to its intended use. See paragraph (c)(2) of this section. Therefore, no penalty is imposed under paragraph (a) of this section.

*Example 3.* A filer files a Form 1099-MISC with the Internal Revenue Service. The Form 1099-MISC is complete and correct except that the payee's name, "John Doe," is misspelled as "John Ode." Under paragraph (c)(2) of this section, supplying an incorrect surname for a payee is never considered an inconsequential error. Therefore, a penalty is imposed under paragraph (a) of this section.

(d) *Exception for a de minimis number of failures.*—(1) *Requirements.*—The penalty under paragraph (a) of this section is not imposed for a *de minimis* number of failures to include correct information if the filer corrects such failures on or before August 1 of the year in which the required filing date occurs. (See paragraph

(d)(4) of this section for special rules relating to returns that are not due on February 28 or March 15.)

(2) *Calculation of the de minimis exception.*—The number of returns to which the *de minimis* exception applies for any calendar year shall not exceed the greater of 10 or one-half of one percent of the total number of all information returns the filer is required to file during the year. If the number of returns on which the filer fails to include correct information exceeds the number of returns to which the *de minimis* exception applies, the *de minimis* exception applies to those returns that will afford the filer the greatest reduction in penalty. The *de minimis* exception applies to failures to include correct information that exist after the application (if any) of the waiver for reasonable cause under section 6724(a) and § 301.6724-1. Returns to which the *de minimis* exception applies are treated as having been originally filed with correct information.

(3) *Examples.*—The provisions of this paragraph (d) may be illustrated by the following examples. In each of the examples, the failures to file and to include correct information are subject to penalty under paragraph (a) of this section. The examples do not take into account any possible application of paragraph (f) of this section or the reasonable cause waiver under paragraph (a) of § 301.6724-1 of this section.

*Example 1.* Corporation T files timely 10,000 Forms 1099-INT (relating to payments of interest) for 1990 by February 28, 1991. The 10,000 returns are all the information returns that T is required to file during the 1991 calendar year. Of the returns filed, 70 contained incorrect information. T corrects the failures on July 12, 1991. No penalty is imposed for 50 of the failures (i.e., the greater of 10 or .005 × 10,000 = 50) even though the total failures, 70, exceed the number to which the *de minimis* exception may apply. The $30 penalty under paragraph (b)(2) of this section is imposed, in lieu of $50, for the remaining 20 failures, which were corrected after 30 days but on or before August 1, resulting in a total penalty of $600 ($30 × 20 = $600).

*Example 2.* Corporation U files timely 9,500 Forms 1099-INT for 1990 by February 28, 1991, the required filing date. Fifty of these returns contain incorrect information with respect to which U files correct information on August 1, 1991. U also files 500 Forms 1099-INT for 1990 on August 30, 1991, after the required filing date. The 10,000 returns are all the information returns that U is required to file during the 1991 calendar year. The calculation of the *de minimis* exception is based on the 10,000 returns required to be filed during the 1991 calendar year even though 500 of the returns filed during the year were not filed timely. Therefore, the number of failures for which the *de minimis* exception applies is 50, and accordingly no penalty is imposed for the 50 Forms 1099-INT that were corrected on August 1, 1991. However, the $50 penalty under paragraph (a)(1) of this section is imposed for each failure to file timely, resulting in a total penalty of $25,000 ($50 × 500 = $25,000).

*Example 3.* Corporation V files timely 9,950 Forms 1099-INT for 1990 by February 28, 1991. However, V fails to file timely 50 of its Forms 1099-INT. The 10,000 returns are all the information returns that V is required to file during the 1991 calendar year. Upon discovering the error, V files the 50 returns within 30 days of February 28, 1991. The 50 returns are complete and correct except that V fails to include the taxpayer identification numbers of the payees on the returns. V files corrected returns on August 1, 1991. Absent application of the *de minimis* exception, the penalty imposed for the failure to include correct information would be $1,500 ($30 × 50 = $1,500). Because the incorrect returns are corrected on August 1, the 50 forms are treated under the *de minimis* exception as originally filed with correct information, and therefore no penalty is imposed under paragraph (a) of this section for the failure to include correct information. Nevertheless, the penalty under paragraph (a) of this section is imposed for the failure to file timely the 50 returns because the *de minimis* exception does not apply to the penalty for the failure to file timely. Hence, a penalty of $750 ($15 × 50 = $750) is imposed.

*Example 4.* Corporation W files timely 100 Forms 1099-DIV and files an additional 50 Forms 1099-DIV late, but within 30 days of February 28, 1991. These are all the information returns that W was required to file during the 1991 calendar year. W discovers errors on 10 of the returns that were filed timely, and on 5 of the returns that were filed late. W corrects all the errors on August 1. The *de minimis* exception applies to 10 of the corrected returns. The exception will be allocated to the 10 returns that were filed timely with incorrect information because that allocation is most favorable to W (*i.e.*, applying the exception to a return filed late with incorrect information would save W $15, by reducing the penalty on that return from $30 to $15, but applying the exception to a return filed timely would save W $30, by reducing the penalty on that return from $30 to $0). (See paragraph (b)(4) of this section.)

(4) *Nonapplication to returns not due on February 28 or March 15.*—The exception for a *de minimis* number of failures provided in paragraph (d)(1) of this section does not apply to failures with respect to

returns that are not due on February 28 or March 15 (for example, Forms 8300 reporting certain cash payments of $10,000 or more). Nevertheless, the returns that are not due on February 28 or March 15 are included in the total number of all information returns that the filer is required to file during a year for purposes of calculating the number of the returns subject to the *de minimis* exception under paragraph (d)(2) of this section.

(e) *Lower limitations on the $250,000 maximum penalty amount with respect to persons with gross receipts of not more than $5,000,000.*—(1) *In general.*—If a person meets the gross receipts test (as defined in paragraph (e)(2) of this section) for any calendar year, the total amount of the penalty imposed on such person for all failures described in section 6721(a)(2) and paragraph (a)(2) of this section during such calendar year shall not exceed $100,000. The total amount of the penalty imposed under paragraph (b)(1) of this section for failures corrected within 30 days shall not exceed $25,000 for such calendar year. The total amount of the penalty imposed under paragraph (b)(2) of this section for failures corrected after 30 days but on or before August 1 shall not exceed $50,000 for such calendar year.

(2) *Gross receipts test.*—A person meets the gross receipts test for any calendar year if the average annual gross receipts for such person for the three most recent taxable years ending before such calendar year do not exceed $5,000,000. For purposes of determining the amount of gross receipts during the three most recent taxable years, the rules of section 448(c)(2) and (3) shall apply.

(f) *Higher penalty for intentional disregard of requirement to file timely correct information returns.*—(1) *Application of section 6721(e).*—If a failure is due to intentional disregard of the requirement to file timely or to include correct information on a return as described in paragraph (g) of this section, the amount of the penalty imposed under paragraph (a) of this section shall be determined under paragraph (f)(4) of this section.

(2) *Meaning of "intentional disregard".*—A failure is due to intentional disregard if it is a knowing or willful—

(i) Failure to file timely, or

(ii) Failure to include correct information.

Whether a person knowingly or willfully fails to file timely or fails to include correct information is determined on the basis of all the facts and circumstances in the particular case.

(3) *Facts and circumstances considered.*—The facts and circumstances that are considered in determining whether a failure is due to intentional disregard include, but are not limited to—

(i) Whether the failure to file timely or the failure to include correct information is part of a pattern of conduct by the person who filed the return of repeatedly failing to file timely or repeatedly failing to include correct information;

(ii) Whether correction was promptly made upon discovery of the failure;

(iii) Whether the filer corrects a failure to file or a failure to include correct information within 30 days after the date of any written request from the Internal Revenue Service to file or to correct; and

(iv) Whether the amount of the information reporting penalties is less than the cost of complying with the requirement to file timely or to include correct information on an information return.

(4) *Amount of the penalty.*—If one or more failures to file timely or to include correct information are due to intentional disregard of the requirement to file timely or to include correct information, then, with respect to each such failure determined under this paragraph (f)—

(i) Paragraphs (b), (d), and (e) of this section shall not apply;

(ii) The $250,000 limitation under paragraph (a) of this section shall not apply, and the penalty under this paragraph (f) shall not be taken into account in applying the $250,000 limitation (or any similar limitation under paragraph (b) or (e) of this section) to penalties not determined under this paragraph (f);

(iii) The penalty imposed under paragraph (a) of this section shall be $100 or, if greater, the statutory percentage; and

(iv) The term "statutory percentage" means—

(A) In the case of a return other than a return required under section 6045(a), 6041A(b), 6050H, 6050I (for amounts received after November 5, 1990), 6050J, 6050K, or 6050L, 10 percent of the aggregate dollar amount of the items required to be reported correctly,

(B) In the case of a return required to be filed by section 6045(a), 6050K, or 6050L, 5 percent of the aggregate dollar amount of the items required to be reported correctly, or

(C) In the case of a return required to be filed under section 6050I(a) with respect to amounts received after November 5, 1990, for any transaction (or related transactions), the greater of $25,000 or the

amount of cash (within the meaning of section 6050I(d)) received in such transaction to the extent the amount of such cash does not exceed $100,000.

(5) *Computation of the penalty; aggregate dollar amount of the items required to be reported correctly.*—The aggregate dollar amount used in computing the penalty under this paragraph (f) is the amount that is not reported or is reported incorrectly. If the intentional disregard relates to a dollar amount, the statutory percentage is applied to the difference between the dollar amount reported and the amount required to be reported correctly. If the intentional disregard relates to any other item on the return, the statutory percentage is applied to the aggregate amount of items required to be reported correctly. In determining the aggregate amount of items required to be reported correctly, no item shall be taken into account more than once. For example, if a filer willfully fails to file a Form 1099-INT on which $800 of interest and $160 of Federal income tax withheld (*i.e.*, backup withholding) is required to be reported, only the $800 amount is taken into account in computing the penalty.

(6) *Examples.*—The provisions of this paragraph (f) may be illustrated by the following examples:

*Example 1.* On December 1, 1990, Automobile dealer P receives $55,000 from an individual for the purchase of an automobile in a transaction subject to reporting under section 6050I. The individual presents documents to P that identify him as "John Doe." However, P completes the Form 8300 (relating to cash received in a trade or business) and reflects the name of a cartoon character as the payor. Because P knew at the time of filing the Form 8300 that the payor's name was not the name of the cartoon character, he willfully failed to include correct information as described under paragraph (f)(2) of this section. Therefore, the penalty under paragraph (f)(4) of this section is imposed for the intentional disregard of the requirement to include correct information. The amount used in computing the penalty under paragraph (f)(5) of this section is $55,000 (*i.e.*, the amount required to be reported on the return with respect to which the payee is not correctly identified). The amount of the penalty determined under paragraph (f)(4)(ii)(C) of this section is $55,000 (*i.e.*, the greater of $25,000 or the amount of cash received in the transaction up to $100,000).

*Example 2.* On December 1, 1990, Individual B contacts his agent, F, to act as his intermediary in the purchase of an automobile. B gives F $20,000 and requests F to purchase the automobile in F's name, which F does. F prepares the Form 8300 as required under section 6050I, but in the area designated for the name of the payor, F writes "confidential." Because F knew at the time the return was filed that it contained incomplete information, the penalty under paragraph (f)(4) of this section is imposed for the intentional disregard of the requirement to include correct information. The amount used in computing the penalty under paragraph (f)(5) of this section is $20,000 (*i.e.*, the amount required to be reported on the return with respect to which the payee is not correctly identified). The amount of the penalty determined under paragraph (f)(4)(ii)(C) of this section is $25,000 (*i.e.*, the greater of $25,000 or the amount of cash received in the transaction up to $100,000).

*Example 3.* Corporation M deliberately does not include $5,000 of dividends on a Form 1099-DIV (relating to payments of dividends) on which a total of $200,000 (including the $5,000 dividends) is required to be reported under section 6042(a). Because the failure was deliberate, Corporation M's failure is due to intentional disregard of the requirement to include correct information. Accordingly, the amount of the penalty imposed under paragraph (a) is determined under paragraph (f)(4) of this section. Because the Form 1099-DIV is required to be filed under section 6042(a), under paragraph (f)(4)(ii)(A) the amount of the penalty with respect to such failure is 10 percent of the aggregate dollar amount of the items that were required to be but that were not reported correctly. Under paragraph (f)(5) of this section, $5,000 is the difference between the dollar amount reported and the amount required to be reported correctly. Therefore, the amount of the penalty is $500 ($5,000 × .10 = $500).

*Example 4.* Form 8027 requires certain large food and beverage establishments to report certain information with respect to tips. The form requires (among other things) that the establishment report its gross receipts from food and beverage operations. Establishment A, in intentional disregard of the information reporting requirement, reported gross receipts of $1,000,000, when the correct amount was $1,500,000. The significance of the gross receipts reporting requirement is that section 6053(c)(3)(A) requires an establishment to allocate as tips among its employees the excess of 8 percent of its gross receipts over the aggregate amount reported by employees to the establishment as tips under section 6053(a). A's misstatement of its gross receipts caused A to show $80,000 on the Form 8027 as 8 percent of its gross receipts, rather than the correct amount of $120,000. A correctly reported the amount of tips reported to it by employees under section 6053(a) as $80,000. Thus A reported the excess of 8 percent of its gross receipts over tips reported to it as zero, rather than as the correct amount of $40,000. The requirement of reporting gross receipts is considered merely a step in the computation of the excess of 8 percent of gross receipts over tips reported to A under section 6053(a), so that the penalty for intentional disregard will be $4,000 (*i.e.,* 10 percent of the difference between the $40,000 required to be reported as the excess of 8 percent of gross receipts over tips reported under section 6053(a), and the zero amount actually reported).

(g) *Definitions.*—(1) *Information return.*—For purposes of this section the term "information return" means any statement described in paragraph (g)(2) of this section, any return described in paragraph (g)(3) of this section, and any other items described in paragraph (g)(4) of this section.

(2) *Statements.*—The statements subject to this section are the statements required by—

(i) Section 6041(a) or (b) (relating to certain information at source, generally reported on Form 1099-MISC, "Miscellaneous Income"; Form W-2, "Wage and Tax Statement"; Form W-2G, "Certain Gambling Winnings"; and Form 1099-INT, "Interest Income");

(ii) Section 6042(a)(1) (relating to payments of dividends, generally reported on Form 1099-DIV, "Dividends and Distributions");

(iii) Section 6044(a)(1) (relating to payments of patronage dividends, generally reported on Form 1099-PATR, "Taxable Distributions Received From Cooperatives");

(iv) Section 6049(a) (relating to payments of interest, generally reported on Form 1099-INT or Form 1099-OID, "Original Issue Discount");

(v) Section 6050A(a) (relating to reporting requirements of certain fishing boat operators, generally reported on Form 1099-MISC);

(vi) Section 6050N(a) (relating to payments of royalties, generally reported on Form 1099-MISC);

(vii) Section 6051(d) (relating to information returns with respect to income tax withheld, generally reported on Form W-2);

(viii) Section 6050R (relating to returns relating to certain purchases of fish, generally reported on Form 1099-MISC);

(ix) Section 110(d) (relating to qualified lessee construction allowances for shortterm leases, generally reported by attaching a statement to an income tax return);

(x) Section 408(i) (relating to reports with respect to individual retirement accounts or annuities on Form 1099-R, "Distributions From Pensions, Annuities, Retirement or Profit-Sharing Plans, IRAs, Insurance Contracts, etc."); or

(xi) Section 6047(d) (relating to reports by employers, plan administrators, etc., on Form 1099-R).

(3) *Returns.*—The returns subject to this section are the returns required by—

(i) Section 6041A(a) or (b) (relating to returns of direct sellers, generally reported on Form 1099-MISC);

(ii) Section 6043A(a) (relating to returns relating to taxable mergers and acquisitions);

(iii) Section 6045(a) or (d) (relating to returns of brokers, generally reported on Form 1099-B, "Proceeds From Broker and Barter Exchange Transactions," for broker transactions; Form 1099-S, "Proceeds From Real Estate Transactions," for gross proceeds from the sale or exchange of real estate; and Form 1099-MISC for certain substitute payments and payments to attorneys);

(iv) Section 6045B(a) (relating to returns relating to actions affecting basis of specified securities);

(v) Section 6050H(a) or (h)(1) (relating to mortgage interest received in trade or business from individuals, generally reported on Form 1098, "Mortgage Interest Statement");

(vi) Section 6050I(a) or (g)(1) (relating to cash received in trade or business, etc., generally reported on Form 8300, "Report of Cash Payments Over $10,000 Received In a Trade or Business");

(vii) Section 6050J(a) (relating to foreclosures and abandonments of security, generally reported on Form 1099-A, "Acquisition or Abandonment of Secured Property");

(viii) Section 6050K(a) (relating to exchanges of certain partnership interests, generally reported on Form 8308, "Report of a Sale or Exchange of Certain Partnership Interests");

(ix) Section 6050L(a) (relating to returns relating to certain dispositions of donated property, generally reported on Form 8282, "Donee Information Return");

(x) Section 6050P (relating to returns relating to the cancellation of indebtedness by certain financial entities, generally reported on Form 1099-C, "Cancellation of Debt");

(xi) Section 6050Q (relating to certain long-term care benefits, generally reported on Form 1099-LTC, "Long-Term Care and Accelerated Death Benefits");

(xii) Section 6050S (relating to returns relating to payments for qualified tuition and related expenses, generally reported on Form 1098-E, "Student Loan Interest Statement," or Form 1098-T, "Tuition Statement");

(xiii) Section 6050T (relating to returns relating to credit for health insurance costs of eligible individuals, generally reported on Form 1099-H, "Health Coverage Tax Credit (HCTC) Advance Payments");

(xiv) Section 6052(a) (relating to reporting payment of wages in the form of group-life insurance, generally reported on Form W-2);

(xv) Section 6050V (relating to returns relating to applicable insurance contracts in which certain exempt organizations hold interests, generally reported on Form 8921, "Applicable Insurance Contract Information Return");

(xvi) Section 6053(c)(1) (relating to reporting with respect to certain tips, generally reported on Form 8027, "Employer's Annual Information Return of Tip Income and Allocated Tips");

(xvii) Section 1060(b) (relating to reporting requirements of transferors and transferees in certain asset acquisitions, generally reported on Form 8594, "Asset Acquisition Statement"), or section 1060(e) (relating to information required in the case of certain transfers of interests in entities (effective for acquisitions after October 9, 1990, except any acquisition pursuant to a written binding contract in effect on October 9, 1990, and at all times thereafter before such acquisition)));

(xviii) Section 4101(d) (relating to information reporting with respect to fuel oils (effective for information returns required to be filed after November 30, 1990));

(xix) Section 338(h)(10)(C) (relating to information required to be furnished to the Secretary in case of elective recognition of gain or loss (effective for acquisitions after October 9, 1990, except any acquisition pursuant to a written binding contract in effect on October 9, 1990, and at all times thereafter before such acquisition));

(xx) Section 264(f)(5)(A)(iv) (relating to reporting with respect to certain life insurance and annuity contracts);

(xxi) Section 6050U (relating to charges or payments for qualified long-term care insurance contracts under combined arrangements, generally reported on Form 1099-R);

(xxii) Section 6039(a) (relating to returns required with respect to certain options);

(xxiii) Section 6050W (relating to information returns with respect to payments made in settlement of payment card and third party network transactions);

(xxiv) Section 6055 (relating to information returns reporting minimum essential coverage); or

(xxv) Section 6056 (relating to information returns reporting on offers of health insurance coverage by applicable large employer members).

(4) *Other items.*—The term *information return* also includes any form, statement, or schedule required to be filed with the Internal Revenue Service with respect to any amount from which tax is required to be deducted and withheld under chapter 3 of the Internal Revenue Code (or from which tax would be required to be so deducted and withheld but for an exemption under the Internal Revenue Code or any treaty obligation of the United States), generally Forms 1042-S, "Foreign Person's U.S. Source Income Subject to Withholding," and 8805, "Foreign Partner's Information Statement of Section 1446 Withholding Tax." The provisions of this paragraph (g)(4) referring to Form 8805, shall apply to partnership taxable years beginning after May 18, 2005, or such earlier time as the regulations under §§ 1.1446-1 through 1.1446-5 of this chapter apply by reason of an election under § 1.1446-7 of this chapter.

(5) *Payee.*—For purposes of section 6721 the term "payee" means any person who is required to receive a copy of the information set forth on an information return by the filer of the return as defined in section 6724(d)(1).

(6) *Filer.*—For purposes of this section the term "filer" means a person that is required to file an information return as defined in paragraph (g)(1) of this section under the applicable information reporting section described in paragraph (g)(2) through (4) of this section. [Reg. § 301.6721-1.]

☐ [*T.D. 8386, 12-27-91. Amended by T.D. 8843, 11-10-99; T.D. 9200, 5-13-2005; T.D. 9496, 8-13-2010; T.D. 9504, 10-12-2010 and T.D. 9660, 3-5-2014.*]

### [Reg. § 301.6722-1]

**§ 301.6722-1. Failure to furnish correct payee statements.**— (a) *Imposition of penalty.*—(1) *General rule.*—A penalty of $50 is imposed for each payee statement (as defined in section 6722(d)(2)) with respect to which a failure (as defined in section 6722(a) and paragraph (a)(2) of this section) occurs. No more than one penalty will be imposed under this paragraph (a) with respect to a single payee statement even though there may be more than one failure with respect to such statement. However, the penalty shall apply to failures on composite substitute payee statements as though each type of payment and other required information were furnished on separate statements. A "composite substitute payee statement" is a single document created by a filer to reflect several types of payments made to the same payee. The total amount imposed on any person for all failures during any calendar year with respect to all payee statements shall not exceed $100,000. See section 6722(c) and paragraph (c) of this section for higher penalties when a failure is due to intentional disregard of the requirement to furnish timely correct payee statements. See paragraph (a)(1) of § 301.6724-1 for a waiver of the penalty for a failure that is due to reasonable cause.

(2) *Failures subject to the penalty.*—The failures to which section 6722(a) and paragraph (a)(1) of this section apply are—

(i) A failure to furnish a payee statement on or before the prescribed date therefor to the person to whom such statement is required to be furnished ("failure to furnish timely"), and

(ii) A failure to include all of the information required to be shown on a payee statement or the inclusion of incorrect information ("failure to include correct information").

A failure to furnish timely includes a failure to furnish a written statement to the payee in a statement mailing as required under sections 6042(c), 6044(e), 6049(c), and 6050N(b), as well as a failure to furnish the statement on a form acceptable to the Internal Revenue Service. Except as provided in paragraph (b) of this section, a failure to include correct information encompasses a failure to include the information required by applicable information reporting statutes or by any administrative pronouncements issued thereunder (such as regulations, revenue rulings, revenue procedures, or information reporting forms).

(b) *Exception for inconsequential errors or omissions.*—(1) *In general.*—An inconsequential error or omission is not considered a failure to include correct information. For purposes of this paragraph (b), the term "inconsequential error or omission" means any failure that cannot reasonably be expected to prevent or hinder the payee from timely receiving correct information and reporting it on his or her return or from otherwise putting the statement to its intended use.

(2) *Errors or omissions that are never inconsequential.*—Errors or omissions relating to the following are never inconsequential:

(i) A dollar amount,

(ii) The significant items in the address of a payee, which is the address provided by the payee to the filer,

(iii) The appropriate form for the information provided (*i.e.*, whether or not the form is an acceptable substitute for an official form of the Internal Revenue Service), and

(iv) The manner of furnishing a statement required under sections 6042(c), 6044(e), 6049(e), and 6050N(b).

The Internal Revenue Service may, by administrative pronouncement, specify other types of errors or omissions that are never inconsequential.

(3) *Examples.*—The provisions of this paragraph (b) may be illustrated by the following examples which do not take into account any possible application of the penalty for intentional disregard under paragraph (c) of this section or the reasonable cause waiver under paragraph (a) of § 301.6724-1:

*Example 1.* A payor furnishes a statement with respect to a Form 1099-MISC (relating to miscellaneous income). The payee statement is complete and correct, except the word "boulevard" is misspelled in the payee's address. The error cannot reasonably be expected to prevent or hinder the payee from timely receiving correct information and reporting it on his or her tax return or from otherwise putting the statement to its intended use. Therefore, no penalty is imposed under paragraph (a) of this section.

*Example 2.* Assume the same facts as in *Example 1*, except that the only error on the payee statement is that the payee's street address, 4821 Grant Boulevard, is reported incorrectly as 8421 Grant Boulevard. A penalty is imposed under paragraph (a) of this section with respect to the payee statement because the error can reasonably be expected to prevent or hinder the payee from timely receiving correct information and reporting it on his or her tax return or from otherwise putting the statement to its intended use.

(c) *Higher penalty for intentional disregard of requirement to furnish timely correct payee statements.*—(1) *Application of section 6722(c).*—If a failure is due to intentional disregard of the requirement to furnish timely correct payee statements, the amount of the penalty shall be determined under paragraph (c)(2) of this section. Whether a failure is due to intentional disregard of the requirement to furnish timely

correct payee statements is based upon the facts and circumstances surrounding the failure. The facts and circumstances considered include those under § 301.6721-1(f)(3), which shall apply in determining whether a failure under this section is due to intentional disregard.

(2) *Amount of the penalty.*—If one or more failures under paragraph (a) of this section are due to intentional disregard of the requirement to furnish timely payee statements or of the requirement to include correct information, then, with respect to each such failure determined under this paragraph (c)(2)—

(i) The $100,000 limitation under paragraph (a) of this section shall not apply and the penalty under this paragraph (c)(2) shall not be taken into account in applying the $100,000 limitation to penalties not determined under this paragraph (c)(2);

(ii) The penalty imposed under paragraph (a) of this section shall be $100 or, if greater, the statutory percentage; and

(iii) The term "statutory percentage" means—

(A) In the case of a payee statement other than a statement required under section 6045(b), 6041A(e) (in respect of a return required under section 6041A(b)), 6050H(d), 6050J(e), 6050K(b), or 6050L(c), 10 percent of the aggregate dollar amount of the items required to be reported correctly, or

(B) In the case of a payee statement required under section 6045(b), 6050K(b), or 6050L(c), 5 percent of the aggregate dollar amount of the items required to be reported correctly.

(3) *Computation of the penalty; aggregate dollar amount of items required to be shown correctly.*—The aggregate dollar amount used in computing the penalty under this paragraph (c) is the amount that is not reported or is reported incorrectly. If the intentional disregard relates to a dollar amount, the statutory percentage is applied to the difference between the dollar amount reported and the amount required to be reported correctly. If the intentional disregard relates to any other item on the return, the statutory percentage is applied to the aggregate amount of items required to be reported correctly. In determining such amount the same item shall be counted only once. For example, if a filer willfully fails to furnish a Form 1099-INT on which $800 of interest and $160 of Federal income tax withheld (*i.e.*, backup withholding) is required to be shown, only the $800 amount is taken into account in computing the penalty.

(d) *Definitions.*—(1) *Payee.*—See § 301.6721-1(g)(5) for the definition of "payee."

(2) *Payee statement.*—The term *payee statement* means any statement required to be furnished under—

(i) Section 6031(b) or (c), 6034A, or 6037(b) (relating to statements furnished by certain pass-thru entities, generally a Schedule K-1 (Form 1065), "Partner's Share of Income, Deductions, Credits, etc.," for section 6031(b) or (c), a copy of the Schedule K-1 (Form 1041), "Beneficiary's Share of Income, Deductions, Credits, etc.," for section 6034A, and a copy of Schedule K-1 (Form 1120S), "Shareholder's Share of Income, Deductions, Credits, etc.," for section 6037(b));

(ii) Section 6039(b) (relating to information required in connection with certain options);

(iii) Section 6041(d) (relating to information at source, generally the recipient copy of Form 1099-MISC, "Miscellaneous Income"; Form W-2, "Wage and Tax Statement"; Form 1099-INT, "Interest Income"; and the winner's copies of Form W-2G, "Certain Gambling Winnings");

(iv) Section 6041A(e) (relating to returns regarding payments of remuneration for services and direct sales, generally the recipient copy of Form 1099-MISC);

(v) Section 6042(c) (relating to returns regarding payments of dividends and corporate earnings and profits, generally the recipient copy of Form 1099-DIV, "Dividends and Distributions");

(vi) Section 6043A(b) or (d) (relating to returns relating to taxable mergers and acquisitions);

(vii) Section 6044(e) (relating to returns regarding payments of patronage dividends, generally the recipient copy of Form 1099-PATR, "Taxable Distributions Received From Cooperatives");

(viii) Section 6045(b) or (d) (relating to returns of brokers, generally the recipient copy of Form 1099-B, "Proceeds From Broker and Barter Exchange Transactions," for broker transactions; the transferor copy of Form 1099-S, "Proceeds From Real Estate Transactions," for reporting proceeds from real estate transactions; and the recipient copy of Form 1099-MISC for certain substitute payments and payments to attorneys);

(ix) Section 6045A (relating to information required in connection with transfers of covered securities to brokers);

(x) Section 6045B(c) or (e) (relating to returns relating to actions affecting basis of specified securities);

(xi) Section 6049(c) (relating to returns regarding payments of interest, generally the recipient copy of Form 1099-INT or Form 1099-OID, "Original Issue Discount");

(xii) Section 6050A(b) (relating to reporting requirements of certain fishing boat operators, generally the recipient copy of Form 1099-MISC);

(xiii) Section 6050H(d) or (h)(2) (relating to returns relating to mortgage interest received in trade or business from individuals, generally the payor copy of Form 1098, "Mortgage Interest Statement");

(xiv) Section 6050I(e), (g)(4), or (g)(5) (relating to returns relating to cash received in trade or business, etc., generally a copy of Form 8300, "Report of Cash Payments Over $10,000 Received In a Trade or Business");

(xv) Section 6050J(e) (relating to returns relating to foreclosures and abandonments of security, generally the borrower copy of Form 1099-A, "Acquisition or Abandonment of Secured Property");

(xvi) Section 6050K(b) (relating to returns relating to exchanges of certain partnership interests, generally a copy of Form 8308, "Report of a Sale or Exchange of Certain Partnership Interests");

(xvii) Section 6050L(c) (relating to returns relating to certain dispositions of donated property, generally a copy of Form 8282, "Donee Information Return");

(xviii) Section 6050N(b) (relating to returns regarding payments of royalties, generally the recipient copy of Form 1099-MISC);

(xix) Section 6050P(d) (relating to returns relating to the cancellation of indebtedness by certain financial entities, generally the recipient copy of Form 1099-C, "Cancellation of Debt");

(xx) Section 6050Q(b) (relating to certain long-term care benefits, generally the policyholder and insured copies of Form 1099-LTC, "Long-Term Care and Accelerated Death Benefits");

(xxi) Section 6050R(c) (relating to returns relating to certain purchases of fish, generally the recipient copy of Form 1099-MISC);

(xxii) Section 6051 (relating to receipts for employees, generally the employee copy of Form W-2);

(xxiii) Section 6052(b) (relating to returns regarding payment of wages in the form of group-term life insurance, generally the employee copy of Form W-2);

(xxiv) Section 6053(b) or (c) (relating to reports of tips, generally the employee copy of Form W-2);

(xxv) Section 6048(b)(1)(B) (relating to foreign trust reporting requirements, generally copies of the owner and beneficiary statements of Form 3520-A, "Annual Information Return of Foreign Trust With a U.S. Owner");

(xxvi) Section 408(i) (relating to reports with respect to individual retirement plans on the recipient copies of Form 1099-R, "Distributions From Pensions, Annuities, Retirement or Profit-Sharing Plans, IRAs, Insurance Contracts, etc.");

(xxvii) Section 6047(d) (relating to reports by plan administrators on the recipient copies of Form 1099-R);

(xxviii) Section 6050S(d) (relating to returns relating to qualified tuition and related expenses, generally the borrower copy of Form 1098-E, "Student Loan Interest Statement," or the student copy of Form 1098-T, "Tuition Statement");

(xxix) Section 264(f)(5)(A)(iv) (relating to reporting with respect to certain life insurance and annuity contracts);

(xxx) Section 6050T (relating to returns relating to credit for health insurance costs of eligible individuals, generally the recipient copy of Form 1099-H, "Health Coverage Tax Credit (HCTC) Advance Payments");

(xxxi) Section 6050U (relating to charges or payments for qualified long-term care insurance contracts under combined arrangements, generally the recipient copy of Form 1099-R);

(xxxii) Section 6050W (relating to information returns with respect to payments made in settlement of payment card and third party network transactions);

(xxxiii) Section 6055 (relating to information returns reporting minimum essential coverage); or

(xxxiv) Section 6056 (relating to information returns reporting on offers of health insurance coverage by applicable large employer members).

(3) *Other items.*—The term *payee statement* also includes any form, statement, or schedule required to be furnished to the recipient of any amount from which tax is required to be deducted and withheld under chapter 3 of the Internal Revenue Code (or from which tax would be required to be so deducted and withheld but for an exemption under the Internal Revenue Code or any treaty obligation of the United States) (generally the recipient copy of Form 1042-S, "Foreign Person's U.S. Source Income subject to Withholding," or Form 8805, "Foreign Partner's Information Statement of Section 1446 Withholding Tax.")

(e) *Effective/Applicability date.*—The reference in paragraph (d)(3) of this section to Form 8805 shall apply to partnership taxable years beginning after April 29, 2008. [Reg. § 301.6722-1.]

☐ [*T.D.* 8386, 12-27-91. *Amended by T.D.* 9394, 4-28-2008; *T.D.* 9496, 8-13-2010; *T.D.* 9504, 10-12-2010 *and T.D.* 9660, 3-5-2014.]

[Reg. § 301.6723-1]

**§ 301.6723-1. Failure to comply with other information reporting requirements.**—(a) *Imposition of penalty.*—(1) *General rule.*—A penalty of $50 is imposed for each failure to comply timely with a specified information reporting requirement(as defined in paragraph (a)(4) of this section) or for each failure to include correct specified information. Multiple penalties are imposed with respect to a document with failures to comply with more than one of the requirements set forth in paragraph (a)(4) of this section or multiple instances of failures to comply with any one of these requirements. Nonetheless, if a failure that occurs with respect to any requirement defined in paragraph (a)(4) of this section would be subject to a penalty under both paragraph (a)(2)(i) and paragraph (a)(2)(ii) of this section, no more than one penalty is imposed for such failure. The total amount imposed on any person for all failures during any calendar year with respect to all specified information reporting requirements shall not exceed $100,000. See paragraph (a) of § 301.6724-1 for the waiver of the penalty for a failure that is due to reasonable cause.

(2) *Failures subject to the penalty.*—The failures to which paragraph (a)(1) of this section apply are—

(i) A failure to comply timely with a specified information reporting requirement on or before the date prescribed therefor ("failure to comply timely"), and

(ii) A failure to include all the information required by a specified information reporting requirement or the inclusion of incorrect information ("failure to include correct information").

(3) *Exception for inconsequential errors or omissions.*—An inconsequential error or omission is not considered a failure to comply with a specified information reporting requirement. For purposes of paragraph (a)(3) of this section, an error or omission is considered inconsequential if it does not frustrate the purpose or use for which the information is intended.

(4) *Specified information reporting requirement defined.*—For purposes of section 6723 and this section, a "specified information reporting requirement" means—

(i) The requirement to provide the notice under section 6050X(c)(1) (relating to the requirement that a transferor notify the partnership of an exchange of a partnership interest);

(ii) Any requirement contained in the regulations under section 6109 that a person—

(A) Include his or her taxpayer identification number ("TIN") on any return, statement, or other document (other than an information return or payee statement),

(B) Include on any return, statement, or other document (other than an information return or payee statement) made with respect to another person the TIN of such person, or

(C) Furnish his or her TIN to another person;

(iii) Any requirement contained in the regulations under section 215 that a person—

(A) Furnish his or her TIN to another person, or

(B) Include on his or her return the TIN of another person; and

(iv) The requirement under section 6109(e) that a person include the TIN of any dependent on his or her return.

(b) *Examples.*—The provisions of paragraph (a) of this section may be illustrated by the following examples which do not take into account the reasonable cause waiver under section 6724(a) and paragraph (a)(1) of § 301.6724-1.

*Example 1.* Individual A, who has two dependents ages 7 and 9, files his 1990 Form 1040 in 1991. The Form 1040 requires him to provide the TINs of his two dependents, which A fails to do. Because A fails to comply timely with two requirements to include on his return the TIN of another person, a $50 penalty under paragraph (a) of this section is imposed on A for each of the two failures, for a total penalty of $100.

*Example 2.* In 1991 Individual B opens with Bank X an account which pays reportable interest under section 6049. When B opens the account, Bank X requests that B provide his TIN on a Form W-9. B does not provide his TIN as required by § 301.6109-1(b). As a result B fails to comply timely with a specified information reporting requirement under paragraph (a) of this section for furnishing his TIN to another person. Therefore, a $50 penalty is imposed on B under paragraph (a) of this section for the failure. See section 6721(a) for the penalty to which X may be subject if X files a Form 1099-INT (relating to payments of interest) for calendar year 1991 without B's TIN. See section 3406(a)(1)(A) which requires X to impose backup withholding on reportable payments of interest to B's account.

*Example 3.* In 1991 Individual C is a nonresident alien with an account inside the U.S. with Bank Z. The account pays interest that would be reportable under section 6049 but for the fact that it is paid to a nonresident alien. Under section 6109 and § 301.6109-1(b), Bank Z is required to request the TIN from C. C claims that he is a nonresident alien and that his account is not subject to information reporting under section 6049. Because of this, C contends he is not required to provide any TIN information. As a result of this discussion, Bank Z then requests C to provide it with a Form W-8 in order for C to certify that he is a nonresident alien which C fails to do. C fails to comply timely with a specified information reporting requirement under paragraph (a) of this section to furnish his TIN to another person. Therefore, a penalty is imposed on C under paragraph (a) of this section for the failure. See section 6721(a) for the penalty that may be imposed on Z if Z files a Form 1099-INT for calendar year 1991 without C's TIN. See section 3406(a)(1)(A) under which Z is required to impose backup withholding on reportable payment of interest to C's account.

*Example 4.* In 1991 Partnership D opens with Bank Y an account that pays reportable interest under section 6049. When D opens the account, Y requests the partnership's employer identification number (EIN) on a Form W-9 as required under § 301.6109-1(b). The partnership provides its EIN on the Form W-9. Y files an information return with respect to D for the 1991 calendar year. Subsequently, the Internal Revenue Service later notifies Y that D's EIN is incorrect as defined under section 3406 and § 35a.3406-1(a)(6). D fails to comply timely with a specified reporting requirement under paragraph (a) of this section of furnishing its correct EIN to another person. Therefore, a penalty is imposed on D under paragraph (a) of this section for the failure. See section 6721(a) for the penalty to which Y may be subject if Y files a Form 1099-INT for calendar year 1991 without D's correct EIN. See section 3406(a)(1)(B), which requires Y to impose backup withholding on reportable payments of interest to B's account when the Internal Revenue Service or a broker has notified Y that the EIN is incorrect. [Reg. § 301.6723-1.]

☐ [*T.D.* 8386, 12-27-91.]

**[Reg. § 301.6724-1]**

**§ 301.6724-1. Reasonable cause.**—(a) *Waiver of the penalty.*—(1) *General rule.*—The penalty for a failure relating to an information reporting requirement(as defined in paragraph (j) of this section) is waived if the failure is due to reasonable cause and is not due to willful neglect.

(2) *Reasonable cause defined.*—The penalty is waived for reasonable cause only if the filer establishes that either—

(i) There are significant mitigating factors with respect to the failure, as described in paragraph (b) of this section; or

(ii) The failure arose from events beyond the filer's control ("impediment"), as described in paragraph (c) of this section. Moreover, the filer must establish that the filer acted in a responsible manner, as described in paragraph (d) of this section, both before and after the failure occurred. Thus, if the filer establishes that there are significant mitigating factors for a failure but is unable to establish that the filer acted in a responsible manner, the mitigating factors will not be sufficient to obtain a waiver of the penalty. Similarly, if the filer establishes that a failure arose from an impediment but is unable to establish that the filer acted in a responsible manner, the impediment will not be sufficient to obtain a waiver of the penalty. See paragraph (g) of this section for the reasonable cause safe harbor for persons who exercise due diligence.

(b) *Significant mitigating factors.*—In order to establish reasonable cause under this paragraph (b), the filer must satisfy paragraph (d) of this section and must show that there are significant mitigating factors for the failure. The mitigating factors include, but are not limited to—

(1) The fact that prior to the failure the filer was never required to file the particular type of return or furnish the particular type of statement with respect to which the failure occurred, or

(2) The fact that the filer has an established history of complying with the information reporting requirement with respect to which the failure occurred. In determining whether the filer has such an established history, significant consideration is given to—

(i) Whether the filer has incurred any penalty under §§ 301.6721-1, 301.6722-1, or 301.6723-1 in prior years for the failure (or under parallel provisions of prior law), and

(ii) If the filer has incurred any such penalty in prior years, the extent of the filer's success in lessening its error rate from year to year.

A filer may treat as a penalty not incurred any penalty under sections 6721 through 6723 that was self-assessed under section 6724(c)(3) and

any penalty under section 6676(b) that was self-assessed under section 6676(d), prior to amendment or repeal by the Omnibus Budget Reconciliation Act of 1989. See paragraph (c)(5) of this section for the application of this paragraph (b) to failures attributable to the actions of a filer's agent.

(c) *Events beyond the filer's control.*—(1) *In general.*—In order to establish reasonable cause under this paragraph (c)(1), the filer must satisfy paragraph (d) of this section and must show that the failure was due to events beyond the filer's control. Events which are generally considered beyond the filer's control include but are not limited to—

(i) The unavailability of the relevant business records (as described in paragraph (c)(2) of this section),

(ii) An undue economic hardship relating to filing on magnetic media (as described in paragraph (c)(3) of this section),

(iii) Certain actions of the Internal Revenue Service (as described in paragraph (c)(4) of this section),

(iv) Certain actions of an agent (as described in paragraph (c)(5) of this section), and

(v) Certain actions of the payee or any other person providing necessary information with respect to the return or payee statement (as described in paragraph (c)(6) of this section).

(2) *Unavailability of the relevant business records.*—In order to establish reasonable cause under paragraph (c)(1) of this section due to the unavailability of the relevant business records, the filer's business records must have been unavailable under such conditions, in such manner, and for such period as to prevent timely compliance (ordinarily at least a 2-week period prior to the due date (with regard to extensions) of the required return or the required date (with regard to extensions) for furnishing the payee statement), and the unavailability must have been caused by a supervening event. A "supervening event" includes, but is not limited to—

(i) A fire or other casualty that damages or impairs the filer's relevant business records or the filer's system for processing and filing such records;

(ii) A statutory or regulatory change that has a direct impact upon data processing and that is made so close to the time that the return or payee statement is required that, for all practical purposes, the change cannot be complied with; or

(iii) The unavoidable absence (*e.g.*, due to death or serious illness) of the person with the sole responsibility for filing a return or furnishing a payee statement.

(3) *Undue economic hardship relating to filing on magnetic media.*—In order to establish reasonable cause under paragraph (c)(1) of this section due to an undue economic hardship for filing on magnetic media, the filer must show that it failed to file on magnetic media because the filer lacked the necessary hardware. For purposes of this paragraph (c)(3), the filer will not be considered to have acted in a responsible manner under paragraph (d) of this section unless—

(i) The filer attempted on a timely basis to contract out the magnetic media filing;

(ii) The cost of filing on magnetic media was prohibitive as determined at least 45 days before the due date of the returns (without regard to extensions) (90 days for information returns the due date for which (without regard to extensions) is after December 31, 1989, and by or before February 28, 1991 (March 15, 1991, for Forms 1042S));

(iii) The cost was supported by a minimum of two cost estimates from unrelated parties; and

(iv) The filer filed the returns on paper. Reasonable cause will not ordinarily be established under this paragraph (c)(3) if a filer received a reasonable cause waiver in any prior year under paragraph (c)(1) of this section due to an undue economic hardship relating to filing on magnetic media.

(4) *Actions of the Internal Revenue Service.*—In order to establish reasonable cause under paragraph (c)(1) of this section due to certain actions of the Internal Revenue Service, a filer must show that the failure was due to the filer's reasonable reliance on erroneous written information from the Internal Revenue Service. Reasonable reliance means that the filer relied in good faith on the information. The filer shall not be considered to have relied in good faith if the Internal Revenue Service was not aware of all the facts when it provided the information to the filer. In order to substantiate reasonable cause under this paragraph (c)(4), the filer must provide a copy of the written information provided by the Internal Revenue Service and, if applicable, the filer's written request for the information.

(5) *Actions of agent—imputed reasonable cause.*—In order to establish reasonable cause under paragraph (c)(1) of this section due to actions of an agent, the filer must show the following:

(i) The filer exercised reasonable business judgment in contracting with the agent to file timely correct returns or furnish timely correct payee statements with respect to which the failure occurred. This includes contracting with the agent and providing the proper information sufficiently in advance of the due date of the return or statement to permit timely filing of correct returns or timely furnishing of correct payee statements; and

(ii) The agent satisfied the reasonable cause criteria set forth in paragraph (b) or one of the reasonable cause criteria set forth in paragraph (c)(2) through (6) of this section.

(6) *Actions of the payee or any other person.*—In order to establish reasonable cause under paragraph (c)(1) of this section due to the actions of the payee or any other person, such as a broker as defined in section 6045(c) providing information with respect to the return or payee statement, the filer must show either—

(i) That the failure resulted from the failure of the payee, or any other person required to provide information necessary for the filer to comply with the information reporting requirements ("any other person"), to provide information to the filer, or

(ii) That the failure resulted from incorrect information provided by the payee (or any other person) upon which information the filer relied in good faith.

To substantiate reasonable cause under this paragraph (c)(6), the filer must provide documentary evidence upon request of the Internal Revenue Service showing that the failure was attributable to the payee (or any other person). See paragraph (d)(2) of this section for special rules relating to the availability of a waiver where the filer's failure relates to a taxpayer identification number (TIN), and the failure is attributable to actions of the payee described in paragraph (c) (6)(i) or (ii) of this section.

(d) *Responsible manner.*—(1) *In general.*—Acting in a responsible manner means—

(i) That the filer exercised reasonable care, which is that standard of care that a reasonably prudent person would use under the circumstances in the course of its business in determining its filing obligations and in handling account information such as account numbers and balances, and

(ii) That the filer undertook significant steps to avoid or mitigate the failure, including, where applicable—

(A) Requesting appropriate extensions of time to file, when practicable, in order to avoid the failure,

(B) Attempting to prevent an impediment or a failure, if it was foreseeable,

(C) Acting to remove an impediment or the cause of a failure, once it occurred, and

(D) Rectifying the failure as promptly as possible once the impediment was removed or the failure was discovered.

Ordinarily, a rectification is considered prompt if it is made within 30 days after the date the impediment is removed or the failure is discovered or on the earliest date thereafter on which a regular submission of corrections is made. Submissions will be considered regular only if made at intervals of 30 days or less. A failure may be rectified by filing or correcting the information return, furnishing or correcting the payee statement, or by providing or correcting the information to satisfy the specified information reporting requirement with respect to which the failure occurs. Paragraph (d)(ii)(D) of this section does not apply with respect to information the filer is prohibited from altering under specific information reporting rules. See § 1.6045-4(i)(5) of this chapter.

(2) *Special rule for filers seeking a waiver pursuant to paragraph (c)(6) of this section.*—A filer seeking a waiver for reasonable cause pursuant to paragraph (c)(6) of this section with respect to a failure resulting from a missing or an incorrect TIN will be deemed to have acted in a responsible manner in compliance with this paragraph (d) only if the filer satisfies the requirements of paragraph (e) of this section (relating to missing TINs) or paragraph (f) of this section (relating to incorrect TINs), whichever is applicable.

(e) *Acting in a responsible manner—special rules for missing TINs.*—(1) *In general.*—A filer that is seeking a waiver for reasonable cause under paragraph (c)(6) of this section will satisfy paragraph (d)(2) of this section with respect to establishing that a failure to include a TIN on an information return resulted from the failure of the payee to provide information to the filer (*i.e.*, a missing TIN) only if the filer makes the initial and, if required, the annual solicitations described in this paragraph (e) (required solicitations). For purposes of this section, a number is treated as a "missing TIN" if the number does not contain nine digits or includes one or more alpha characters (a character or symbol other than an Arabic numeral) as one of the nine digits. A solicitation means a request by the filer for the payee to furnish a correct TIN. See paragraph (f) of this section for the rules that a filer must follow to establish that the filer acted in a responsible manner with respect to providing incorrect TINs on information returns. See paragraph (e)(1)(vi)(A) of this section for alternative

solicitation requirements. See paragraph (g) of this section for the safe harbor due diligence rules. See paragraph (h) of this section for the rule applicable to failures with respect to information returns the due date for which (without regard to extensions) is after December 31, 1989, and on or before April 22, 1991.

(i) *Initial solicitation.*—An initial solicitation for a payee's correct TIN must be made at the time an account is opened. The term "account" includes accounts, relationships, and other transactions. However, a filer is not required to make an initial solicitation under this paragraph (e)(1)(i) with respect to a new account if the filer has the payee's TIN and uses that TIN for all accounts of the payee. For example, see § 31.3406(h)-3(a) of this chapter. Further, a filer is not required to make an initial solicitation under this paragraph (e)(1)(i) with respect to accounts for which the filer filed an information return subject to paragraph (h) of this section. For purposes of this section, the initial solicitation requirement is deemed to have been met with respect to accounts opened after December 31, 1989, and on or before April 22, 1991. If the account is opened in person, the initial solicitation may be made by oral or written request, such as on an account creation document. If the account is opened by mail, telephone, or other electronic means, the TIN may be requested through such communications. If the account is opened by the payee's completing and mailing an application furnished by the filer that requests the payee's TIN, the initial solicitation requirement is considered met. If a TIN is not received as a result of an initial solicitation, the filer may be required to make additional solicitations ("annual solicitations").

(ii) *First annual solicitation.*—Except as provided in paragraph (e)(1)(vi) of this section, a filer must undertake an annual solicitation if a TIN is not received as a result of an initial solicitation (or if the filer was not required to make an initial solicitation under paragraph (e)(1)(i) of this section and the filer has not received a payee's TIN). The first annual solicitation must be made on or before December 31 of the year in which the account is opened (for accounts opened before December) or January 31 of the following year (for accounts opened in the preceding December) ("annual solicitation period").

(iii) *Second annual solicitation.*—If the TIN is not received as a result of the first annual solicitation, the filer must undertake a second annual solicitation. The second annual solicitation must be made after the expiration of the annual solicitation period and on or before December 31 of the year immediately succeeding the calendar year in which the account is opened.

(iv) *Additional requirements.*—After receiving a TIN, a filer must include that TIN on any information returns the original due date of which (with regard to extensions) is after the date that the filer receives the TIN.

(v) *Failures to which a solicitation relates.*—The initial and first annual solicitations relate to failures on returns filed for the year in which an account is opened. The second annual solicitation relates to failures on returns filed for the year immediately following the year in which an account is opened and for succeeding calendar years.

(vi) *Exceptions and limitations.*—(A) The solicitation requirements under this paragraph (e) do not apply to the extent an information reporting provision under which a return, as defined in paragraph (g) of § 301.6721-1, is filed provides specific requirements relating to the manner or the time period in which a TIN must be solicited. In that event, the requirements of this paragraph (e) will be satisfied only if the filer complies with the manner and time period requirements of the specific information reporting provision and the provisions of this paragraph (e) to the extent applicable. Also, see section 3406(e) which provides rules on the manner and time period in which a TIN must be provided for certain accounts with respect to interest, dividends, patronage dividends, and amounts subject to broker reporting.

(B) An annual solicitation is not required to be made for a year under this paragraph (e) with respect to an account if no payments are made to the account for such year or if no return as defined in paragraph (g) of § 301.6721-1 is required to be filed for the account for the year.

(C) If a filer fails to make one (or more) of the required solicitations under paragraphs (e)(1)(i), (ii), and (iii) of this section, the filer may satisfy the requirements of this section by—

(1) Making two consecutive annual solicitations in subsequent years ("make-up solicitations"), and

(2) Satisfying paragraph (e)(1)(iv) of this section.

For example, a filer who has made none of the required solicitations may satisfy the requirements of this section by making two consecutive solicitations. In determining whether a filer has made two consecutive solicitations, years to which paragraph (e)(1)(vi)(B) of this section applies shall be disregarded. If a filer fails to make the initial solicitation under paragraph (e)(1)(i) of this section, the make-up solicitations described in this paragraph (e)(1)(vi)(C) may be made in the years in which the first and second annual solicitations are required to be made; however, the penalty will apply with respect to the year in which the filer failed to make the initial solicitation. The penalty will apply to failures with respect to years for which a required solicitation is not made and to failures with respect to all subsequent years until the filer conducts its make-up solicitations. The penalty will not apply with respect to the year in which the first make-up solicitation is made (unless it is also the year in which the filer fails to make its initial solicitation) if the second make-up solicitation is made in the following year.

(D) A financial institution is not required to make an annual solicitation by mail on accounts with "stop-mail" or "hold-mail" instructions, provided the filer furnishes the solicitation material to the payee in the same manner as it furnishes other mail.

(E) A filer is not required to make annual solicitations on accounts with respect to which the filer undertook two consecutive annual mailings by December 31, 1989, under Q/A-5 through Q/A-7B or under Q/A-56 of §35a.9999-1 of the Temporary Employment Tax Regulations under the Interest and Dividend Tax Compliance Act of 1983, as provided under section 6676(b) (prior to its amendment by the Omnibus Budget Reconciliation Act of 1989).

(F) A filer is not required to make annual solicitations by mail on accounts with respect to which the filer has an undeliverable address, *i.e.*, where other mailings to that address have been returned to the filer because the address was incorrect and no new address has been provided to the filer.

(G) Except as provided in paragraph (e)(1)(vi)(A) and (C) of this section, no more than two annual solicitations are required under this paragraph (e) in order for a filer to establish reasonable cause.

(2) *Manner of making annual solicitations—by mail or telephone.*—(i) *By mail.*—A mail solicitation must include—

(A) A letter informing the payee that he or she must provide his or her TIN and that he or she is subject to a $50 penalty imposed by the Internal Revenue Service under section 6723 if he or she fails to furnish his or her TIN,

(B) A Form W-9 or an acceptable substitute form, as defined in §31.3406(h)-3(a), (b), or (c) of this chapter, on which the payee may provide the TIN, and

(C) A return envelope for the payee to provide the TIN which may be, but is not required to be, postage prepaid.

(ii) *By telephone.*—An annual solicitation may be made by telephone if the solicitation procedure is reasonably designed and carried out in a manner that is conducive to obtaining the TIN. An annual solicitation is made pursuant to this paragraph (e)(2)(ii) for a failure if the filer—

(A) Completes a call to each person with a missing TIN and speaks to an adult member of the household, or to an officer of the business or the organization,

(B) Requests the TIN of the payee,

(C) Informs the payee that he or she is subject to a $50 penalty imposed by the Internal Revenue Service under section 6723 if he or she fails to furnish his or her TIN,

(D) Maintains contemporaneous records showing that the solicitation was properly made, and

(E) Provides such contemporaneous records to the Internal Revenue Service upon request.

(f) *Acting in a responsible manner—special rules for incorrect TINS.*—(1) *In general.*—A filer that is seeking a waiver for reasonable cause under paragraph (c)(6) of this section will satisfy paragraph (d)(2) of this section with respect to establishing that a failure resulted from incorrect information provided by the payee or any other person (*i.e.*, inclusion of an incorrect TIN) on an information return only if the filer makes the initial and annual solicitations described in this paragraph (f). See paragraph (e)(1) of this section for the definition of the term "solicitation." See paragraph (f)(5)(i) of this section for alternative solicitation requirements. See paragraph (g) of this section for the safe harbor due diligence rules. See paragraph (h) of this section for the rule applicable to failures with respect to information returns the due date for which (without regard to extensions) is after December 31, 1989, and on or before April 22, 1991.

(i) *Initial solicitation.*—An initial solicitation for a payee's correct TIN must be made at the time the account is opened. The term "account" includes accounts, relationships, and other transactions. However, a filer is not required to make an initial solicitation under this paragraph (f)(1)(i) with respect to a new account if the filer has the payee's TIN and uses that TIN for all accounts of the payee. For example, see §31.3406(h)-3(a) of this chapter. Further, a filer is not required to make an initial solicitation under this paragraph (f)(1)(i) with respect to accounts for which the filer filed an information return subject to paragraph (h) of this section. For purposes of this

section, the initial solicitation requirement is deemed to have been met with respect to accounts opened after December 31, 1989, and on or before April 22, 1991. No additional solicitation is required after the filer receives the TIN unless the Internal Revenue Service or, in some cases, a broker notifies the filer that the TIN is incorrect. Following such notification the filer may be required to make an annual solicitation to obtain the correct TIN as provided in paragraph (f)(1)(ii) and (iii) of this section.

(ii) *First annual solicitation.*—Except as provided in paragraph (f)(5) of this section, a filer must undertake an annual solicitation only if the payor has been notified of an incorrect TIN and such account contains the incorrect TIN at the time of the notification. The first annual solicitation must be made as required by paragraph (f)(2) or (3) of this section, whichever applies. An account contains an incorrect TIN at the time of notification if the name and number combination on the account matches the name and number combination set forth on the notice from the Internal Revenue Service or a broker. A filer may be notified of an incorrect TIN by the Internal Revenue Service or by a broker pursuant to section 3406(a)(1)(B), or by a penalty notice issued by the Internal Revenue Service pursuant to section 6721. Except as otherwise provided in this section, the annual solicitation required by this paragraph (f) must be made on or before December 31 of the year in which the filer is notified of the incorrect TIN or by January 31 of the following year if the filer is notified of an incorrect TIN in the preceding December.

(iii) *Second annual solicitation.*—A filer must undertake a second annual solicitation as required by paragraph (f)(2) or (3) of this section, whichever applies, if the filer is notified in any year following the year of the notification described in paragraph (f)(1)(ii) of this section that the account of a payee contains an incorrect TIN, as described in paragraph (f)(1)(ii) of this section.

(iv) *Additional requirements.*—Upon receipt of a TIN, a filer must include that TIN on any information returns the original due date of which (with regard to extensions) is after the date that the filer receives the TIN.

(2) *Manner of making annual solicitation if notified pursuant to section 6721.*—A filer that has been notified of an incorrect TIN by a penalty notice or other notification pursuant to section 6721 may satisfy the solicitation requirement of this paragraph (f) either by mail, in the manner set forth in paragraph (e)(2)(i) of this section; by telephone, in the manner set forth in paragraph (e)(2)(ii) of this section; or by requesting the TIN in person.

(3) *Coordination with solicitations under section 3406(a)(1)(b).*—(i) A filer that has been notified of an incorrect TIN pursuant to section 3406(a)(1)(B) (except filers to which §31.3406(d)-5(b)(4)(i)(A) of this chapter applies) will satisfy the solicitation requirement of this paragraph (f) only if it makes a solicitation in the manner and within the time period required under §31.3406(d)-5(d)(2)(i) or (g)(1)(ii) of this chapter, whichever applies.

(ii) A filer that has been notified of an incorrect TIN by a notice pursuant to section 6721 (except filers to which §31.3406(d)-5(b)(4)(i)(A) of this chapter applies) is not required to make the annual solicitation of this paragraph (f) if—

(A) The filer has received an effective notice pursuant to section 3406(a)(1)(B) with respect to the same payee, either during the same calendar year or for information returns filed for the same year; and

(B) The filer makes a solicitation in the manner and within the time period required under §31.3406(d)-5(d)(2)(i) or (g)(1)(ii) of this chapter, whichever applies, before the filer is required to make the annual solicitation of this paragraph (f).

(iii) A filer that has been notified of an incorrect TIN by a notice pursuant to section 6721 with respect to a fiduciary or nominee account to which §31.3406(d)-5(b)(4)(i)(A) of this chapter applies is required to make the annual solicitation of this paragraph (f).

(4) *Failures to which a solicitation relates.*—The initial solicitation relates to failures on returns filed for the year an account is opened and for any succeeding year that precedes the year in which the filer receives a notification of an incorrect TIN. The first and second annual solicitations relate to failures on returns filed for the year in which a notification of an incorrect TIN is received. The second solicitation also relates to failures on returns filed for succeeding calendar years.

(5) *Exceptions and limitations.*—(i) The solicitation requirements under this paragraph (f) do not apply to the extent that an information reporting provision under which a return, as defined in paragraph (g) of §301.6721-1, is filed provides specific requirements relating to the manner or the time period in which a TIN must be solicited. In that event, the requirements of this paragraph (f) will be satisfied only if the filer complies with the manner and time period

requirement under the specific information reporting provisions and this paragraph (f), to the extent applicable.

(ii) An annual solicitation is not required to be made for a year under this paragraph (f) with respect to an account if no payments are made to the account for such year or if no return as defined in paragraph (g) of § 301.6721-1 is required to be filed for the account for such year.

(iii) If a filer fails to make one (or more) of the required solicitations under paragraph (f)(1)(i), (ii), and (iii) of this section, the filer may satisfy the requirements of this section by:

(A) Making two consecutive annual solicitations in subsequent years ("make-up solicitations"), and

(B) Satisfying paragraph (f)(1)(iv) of this section.

For example, a filer who has made none of the required solicitations may satisfy the requirements of this section by making two consecutive solicitations. In determining whether a filer has made two consecutive solicitations, years to which paragraph (f)(5)(ii) of this section applies are disregarded. If a filer fails to make the initial solicitation under paragraph (f)(1)(i) of this section, the make-up solicitations described in this paragraph (f)(5)(iii) may be made in the years in which the first and second annual solicitations are required to be made; however, the penalty will apply with respect to the year in which the filer failed to make the initial solicitation. The penalty will apply to failures in years in which a required solicitation is not made and to failures with respect to all subsequent years until the filer conducts its make-up solicitations. The penalty will not apply with respect to the year in which the first make-up solicitation is made (unless it is also the year in which the filer fails to make the initial solicitation) if the second make-up solicitation is made in the following year.

(iv) A financial institution is not required to make an annual solicitation by mail on accounts with "stop-mail" or "hold-mail" instructions, provided the filer furnishes the solicitation material to the payee in the same manner as it furnishes other mail.

(v) A filer is not required to make annual solicitations by mail on accounts with respect to which the filer has an undeliverable address, *i.e.*, where other mailings to that address have been returned to the filer because the address was incorrect and no new address has been provided to the filer.

(vi) In general, except as provided in paragraph (f)(5)(i) and (iii) of this section, no more than two annual solicitations are required under this paragraph (f) in order for a filer to establish reasonable cause. However, a filer who complies with this paragraph (f) during a calendar year after receiving a notice under section 6721 and who later during the same calendar year receives a notice pursuant to section 3406 may be required to undertake additional annual mailings in such calendar year pursuant to section 3406(a)(1)(B) in order to satisfy the annual solicitation requirement in paragraph (f)(3) of this section.

(g) *Due diligence safe harbor.*—(1) *In general.*—A filer may establish reasonable cause with respect to a failure relating to an information reporting requirement as described in paragraph (j) of this section if the filer exercises due diligence with respect to failures described in sections 6721 through 6723.

(2) *Special rules relating to TINs.*—The following questions and answers provide guidance on the exercise of due diligence for an exception to a penalty under sections 6721 through 6723 for a failure to provide a correct TIN on any information return (as defined in § 301.6721-1(g)), payee statement (as defined in § 301.6722-1(d)), document (as described in § 301.6723-1(a)(4)), or the failure merely to provide a TIN as described in § 301.6723-1(a)(4)(ii).

GENERAL RULE

Q-1. Is a payor subject to a penalty for a failure to provide a correct TIN on an information return with respect to a reportable interest or dividend payment if the payee has certified, under penalties of perjury, that the TIN furnished to the payor is the payee's correct number, the payor provided that number on an information return, and the number is later determined not to be the payee's correct number?

A-1. A payor is not subject to a penalty for failure to provide the payee's correct TIN on an information return, if the payee has certified, under penalties of perjury, that the TIN provided to the payor was his correct number, and the payor included such number on the information return before being notified by the Internal Revenue Service (IRS) (or a broker) that the number is incorrect.

DUE DILIGENCE DEFINED FOR ACCOUNTS OPENED AND INSTRUMENTS ACQUIRED AFTER DECEMBER 31, 1983

Q-2. In order for a payor of a reportable interest or dividend payment (other than in a window transaction) to be considered to have exercised due diligence in furnishing the correct TIN of a payee

with respect to an account opened or an instrument acquired after December 31, 1983, what actions must the payor take?

A-2. (1) In general, the payor of an account or instrument that is not a pre-1984 account nor a window transaction must use a TIN provided by the payee under penalties of perjury on information returns filed with the IRS to satisfy the due diligence requirement. Therefore, if a payor permits a payee to open an account without obtaining the payee's TIN under penalties of perjury and files an information return with the IRS with a missing or an incorrect TIN, the payor will be liable for the $50 penalty for the year with respect to which such information return is filed. However, in its administrative discretion, the IRS will not enforce the penalty with respect to a calendar year if the certified TIN is obtained after the account is opened and before December 31 of such year, provided that the payor exercises due diligence in processing such number, i.e., the payor uses the same care in processing the TIN provided by the payee that a reasonably prudent payor would use in the course of the payor's business in handling account information such as account numbers and balances.

(2) Once notified by the IRS (or a broker) that a number is incorrect, a payor is liable for the penalty for all prior years in which an information return was filed with that particular incorrect number if the payor has not exercised due diligence with respect to such years. A pre-existing certified TIN does not constitute an exercise of due diligence after the IRS or a broker notifies the payor that the number is incorrect unless the payor undertakes the actions described in § 31.3406(d)-5(d)(2)(i) of this chapter with respect to accounts receiving reportable payments described in section 3406(b)(1) and reported on information returns described in sections 6724(d)(1)(A)(i) through (iv).

Q-3. Is a payor as described in A-2 liable for the penalty if the payor obtained a certified TIN from a payee but inadvertently processed the name or number incorrectly on the information return?

A-3. Yes. The payor is liable for the penalty unless the payor exercised that degree of care in processing the TIN and name and in furnishing it on the information return that a reasonably prudent payor would use in the course of the payor's business in handling account information, such as account numbers and account balances.

SPECIAL RULES

Q-4. With respect to an instrument transferred without the assistance of a broker, is a payor liable for the penalty for filing an information return with a missing or an incorrect TIN if the payor records on its books a transfer of a readily tradable instrument in a transaction in which the payor was not a party?

A-4. Generally, a payor as described in Q-4 will be considered to have exercised due diligence with respect to a readily tradable instrument that is not part of a pre-1984 account with the payor if the payor records on its books a transfer in which the payor was not a party. This exception applies until the calendar year in which the payor receives a certified TIN from the payee.

Q-5. Is the payor described in A-4 required to solicit the TIN of a payee of an account with a missing TIN in order to be considered as having exercised due diligence in a subsequent calendar year?

A-5. There is no requirement on the payor to solicit the TIN in order to be considered to have exercised due diligence in a subsequent calendar year under the rule set forth in A-4.

Q-6. Is a payor as described in Q-4 considered to have exercised due diligence if the payee provides a TIN to the payor (whether or not certified), the payor uses that number on the information return filed for the payee, and the number is later determined to be incorrect?

A-6. A payor as described in Q-4 who records on its books a transfer in which it was not a party is considered to have exercised due diligence under the rule set forth in A-4 where the transfer is accompanied with a TIN provided that the payor uses the same care in processing the TIN provided by a payee that a reasonably prudent payor would use in the course of the payor's business in handling account information, such as account numbers and account balances. Thus, a payor will not be liable for the penalty if the payor uses the TIN provided by the payee on information returns that it files, even if the TIN provided by the payee is later determined to be incorrect. However, a payor will not be considered as having exercised due diligence under A-4 after the IRS or a broker notifies the payor that the number is incorrect unless the payor undertakes the required additional actions described in the second paragraph of A-2.

Q-7. Is a payor liable for a penalty for filing an information return with a missing or an incorrect TIN with respect to a post-1983 account or instrument if the payor could have met the due diligence requirements but for the fact that the payor incurred an undue hardship?

A-7. A payor of a post-1983 account or instrument is not liable for a penalty under section 6721(a) for filing an information return with a missing or an incorrect TIN if the IRS determines that the payor could have satisfied the due diligence requirements but for the fact that the payor incurred an undue hardship. An undue hardship is an extraordinary or unexpected event such as the destruction of records or place of business of the payor by fire or other casualty (or the place of business of the payor's agent who under a pre-existing written contract had agreed to fulfill the payor's due diligence obligations with respect to the account subject to the penalty and there was no means for the obligations to be performed by another agent or the payor). Undue hardship will also be found to exist if the payor could have met the due diligence requirements only by incurring an extraordinary cost.

Q-8. How does a payor obtain a determination from the IRS that the payor has met the undue hardship exception to the penalty under section 6721(a) for the failure to include the correct TIN on an information return for the year with respect to which the payor is subject to the penalty?

A-8. A determination of undue hardship may be established only by submitting a written statement to the IRS signed under penalties of perjury that sets forth all the facts and circumstances that make an affirmative showing that the payor could have satisfied the due diligence requirements but for the occurrence of an undue hardship. Thus, the statement must describe the undue hardship and make an affirmative showing that the payor either was in the process of exercising or stood ready to exercise due diligence when the undue hardship occurred. A payor may request an undue hardship determination from the district director or the director of the Internal Revenue Service Center where the payor is required to remit the penalty under section 6721(a).

Q-9. Is a pre-1984 account or instrument of a payor that is exchanged for an account or instrument of another payor as a result of a merger of the other payor or acquisition of the accounts or instruments of such payor transformed into a post-1983 account or instrument if the merger or acquisition occurs after December 31, 1983?

A-9. No. A pre-1984 account or instrument that is exchanged for another account or instrument pursuant to a statutory merger or the acquisition of accounts or instruments is not transformed into a post-1983 account or instrument because the exchange occurs without the participation of the payee.

Q-10. May the acquiring taxpayer described in A-9 rely upon the business records and past procedures of the merged payor or the payor whose accounts or instruments were acquired in order to establish that due diligence has been exercised on the acquired pre-1984 and post-1983 accounts or instruments?

A-10. Yes. The acquiring payor may rely upon the business records and past procedures of the merged payor or of the payor whose accounts or instruments were acquired in order to establish due diligence to avoid the penalty under section 6721(a) with respect to information returns that have been or will be filed.

Q-11. To what extent may a payor rely on the due diligence rules set forth in §§ 35a.9999-1, 35a.9999-2, and 35a.9999-3 of this chapter in effect prior to January 1, 2001 (see §§ 35a.9999-1, 35a.9999-2, and 35a.9999-3 as contained in 26 CFR part 35a, revised April 1, 1999)?

A-11. A payor may rely on the due diligence rules set forth in §§ 35a.9999-1, 35a.9999-2, and 35a.9999-3 of this chapter in effect prior to January 1, 2001 (see §§ 35a.9999-1, 35a.9999-2, and 35a.9999-3 as contained in 26 CFR part 35a, revised April 1, 1999) solely for the definitions of terms or phrases used in this paragraph (g)(2).

(3) *Effective dates.*—This paragraph (g) is effective for information returns (as defined in section 6724(d)(1)) required to be filed, payee statements (as defined in section 6724(d)(2)) required to be furnished, and specified information (as described in section 6724(d)(3)) required to be reported after December 31, 2000. See § 301.6724-1(g) in effect prior to January 1, 2001 (see § 301.6724-1(g) as contained in 26 CFR part 301, revised April 1, 1999) for substantially similar rules applicable prior to January 1, 2001.

(h) *Transitional rules for information returns required to be filed (or payee statements required to be furnished) after December 31, 1989 (without regard to extensions), and on or before April 22, 1991.*—(1) *In general.*— With respect to information returns required to be filed (or payee statements required to be furnished) after December 31, 1989 (without regard to extensions), and on or before April 22, 1991, a filer will be deemed to have satisfied reasonable cause if, with respect to the failure, the filer would have satisfied reasonable cause under sections 6721, 6722, or 6723 (prior to their amendment by the Omnibus Budget Reconciliation Act of 1989) and the regulations thereunder.

(2) *Special rule on TINs.*—With respect to information returns required to be filed after December 31, 1989 (without regard to extensions), and on or before April 22, 1991, which contain a missing or an incorrect TIN, a filer will be deemed to have satisfied reasonable cause if, at the time the account was opened, the filer—

(i) Exercised due diligence or fulfilled the requirements of Q/A-56 of § 35a.9999-1 of this chapter as in effect on December 31, 1989,

as provided under section 6676(b) (prior to its repeal by the Omnibus Budget Reconciliation Act of 1989),

(ii) Requested the TIN according to the regulations under the section requiring the filing of the information return, but if none, under section 6109, or

(iii) Would have satisfied reasonable cause under section 6676(a) (prior to its repeal by the Omnibus Budget Reconciliation Act of 1989).

(i) [*Reserved.*]

(j) *Failures to which this section relates.*—For purposes of this section, a failure relating to an information reporting requirement means—

(1) A failure described under § 301.6721-1(a)(2) relating to the failure to file timely correct information returns as defined in section 6724(d)(1),

(2) A failure described under § 301.6722-1(a)(2) relating to the failure to furnish timely a correct payee statement as defined in section 6724(d)(2), and

(3) A failure described under § 301.6723-1(a)(2) relating to the failure to timely comply with and to include correct specified information as defined in section 6724(d)(3).

(k) *Examples.*—The provisions of this section may be illustrated by the following examples:

*Example (1).* (i) On August 1, 1991, Individual A, an independent contractor, establishes a relationship ("an account") with Institution L, which pays A amounts reportable under section 6041. When A opens the account L requests that A supply his TIN on the account creation document. A fails to provide his TIN. On October 1, 1991, L mails a solicitation for A's TIN that satisfies the requirement of paragraph (e)(1)(ii) of this section. A does not provide a TIN to L during 1991. L timely files an information return subject to section 6721, that does not contain A's TIN, for payments made during the 1991 calendar year with respect to A's account. A penalty is imposed on L pursuant to paragraph (a)(2) of § 301.6721-1 for L's failure to file a correct information return because A's TIN was not shown on the return. The penalty will be waived, however, if L establishes that the failure was due to reasonable cause as defined in this section.

(ii) To establish reasonable cause under this section, L must satisfy both paragraphs (c)(6) and (d) of this section. The criteria for obtaining a waiver under these paragraphs are as follows:

(A) L acted in a responsible manner in attempting to satisfy the information reporting requirement as described in paragraph (d) of this section, and

(B) L demonstrates that the failure arose from events beyond L's control, as described in paragraph (c)(6) of this section.

(iii) Pursuant to paragraph (d)(2) of this section, L may demonstrate that it acted in a responsible manner only by complying with paragraph (e) of this section. Paragraph (e) of this section requires a filer to request a TIN at the time the account is opened (the initial solicitation) and, if the filer does not receive the TIN at that time, to solicit the TIN on or before December 31 of the year the account is opened (for accounts opened before December) or January 31 of the following year (for accounts in the preceding December) (the annual solicitation). Because L has performed these solicitations within the time and in the manner prescribed by paragraph (e) of this section, L has acted in a responsible manner as described in paragraph (d) of this section. L satisfies paragraph (c)(6) of this section because, under the facts, L can show that the failure was caused by A's failure to provide a TIN, an event beyond L's control. As a result, L has established reasonable cause under paragraph (a)(2) of this section. Therefore, the penalty imposed under paragraph (a)(2) of § 301.6721-1 for the failure on the 1991 information return is waived. See section 3406(a)(1)(A) which requires L to impose backup withholding on reportable payments to A if L has not received A's TIN.

*Example (2).* (i) On August 1, 1991, Individual B opens an account with Bank M, which pays B interest reportable under section 6049. When B opens the account, M requests that B supply his TIN on the account creation document. B provides his TIN to M. On February 28, 1992, M includes the TIN that B provided on the Form 1099-INT for the 1991 calendar year. In October 1992 the Internal Revenue Service, pursuant to section 3406(a)(1)(B), notifies M that the 1991 return filed for B contains an incorrect TIN. In April 1993 a penalty is imposed on M pursuant to paragraph (a)(2) of § 301.6721-1 for M's failure to file a correct information return for the 1991 calendar year, *i.e.*, the return did not contain B's correct TIN. The penalty will be waived, however, if M establishes that the failure was due to reasonable cause as defined in this section.

(ii) To establish reasonable cause under this section, M must satisfy the criteria in both paragraphs (c)(6) and (d) of this section. Pursuant to paragraph (d)(2) of this section, M can demonstrate that it acted in a responsible manner only if M complies with paragraph (f) of this section. Paragraph (f) of this section requires a filer to request a TIN at the time the account is opened, an initial solicitation. Under paragraph (f)(4) of this section the initial solicitation relates to failures on returns filed for the year an account is opened. Because M performed the initial solicitation in 1991 in the time and manner prescribed in paragraph (f)(1)(i) of this section and reflected the TIN received from B on the 1991 return as required by paragraph (f)(1)(iv) of this section, M has acted in a responsible manner as described in paragraph (d) of this section. M satisfies paragraph (c)(6) of this section because, under the facts, M can show that the failure was

| 1991 | 2/92 |
|------|------|
| account opened (solicits TIN) | 1991 return |

| 4/93 | 10/93 |
|------|-------|
| 6721 penalty notice for 1991 return | B-notice w/respect to 1992 return |

(ii) The facts are the same as in *Example 2.* Under §31.3406(d)-5(d)(2)(i) of this chapter and paragraph (f)(3) of this section, within 15 days of the October 1992 notification of the incorrect TIN from the Internal Revenue Service, M solicits the correct TIN from B. B fails to respond. M timely files the return for 1992 with respect to the account setting forth B's incorrect TIN. In October 1993 the Internal Revenue Service notifies M pursuant to section 3406(a)(1)(B) that the 1992 return contains an incorrect TIN. In April 1994, a penalty is imposed on M pursuant to paragraph (a)(2) of §301.6721-1 for M's failure to include B's correct TIN on the return for 1992. The penalty will be waived, however, if M establishes that the failure was due to reasonable cause as defined in this section.

(iii) M must satisfy the reasonable cause criteria in paragraphs (c)(6) and (d) of this section. M may demonstrate that it acted in a responsible manner as required under paragraph (d) of this section only by complying with paragraph (f) of this section. Paragraph (f) of

| 1991 | 2/92 |
|------|------|
| account opened (solicits TIN) | 1991 return filed |

| 4/93 | 10/93 |
|------|-------|
| 6721 penalty notice for 1991 return | B-notice w/respect to 1992 return |

(ii) The facts are the same as in *Example 3.* M timely solicits B's TIN in October 1993, which B fails to provide. M files the return for 1993 with the incorrect TIN. In April 1995 the Internal Revenue Service informs M that the 1993 return contains an incorrect TIN. M does not solicit a TIN from B in 1994 and files a return for 1994 with B's incorrect TIN. M seeks a waiver of the penalty under paragraph (a)(2) of §301.6721-1 for reasonable cause. M must satisfy the reasonable cause criteria in paragraphs (c)(6) and (d) of this section. Because M made the initial and two annual solicitations as required by paragraph (f) of this section, M has demonstrated that it acted in a responsible manner and is not required to solicit B's TIN in 1994. See paragraph (f)(5)(iv) of this section. M satisfies paragraph (c)(6) of this section because, under the facts, M can show that the failure was caused by B's failure to provide his correct TIN, an event beyond M's control. Therefore, M has established reasonable cause under paragraph (a)(2) of this section.

*Example 5.* In 1992, Mortgage Finance Company N lends money to C to purchase property in a transaction subject to reporting under

| 10/91 | 2/92 |
|-------|------|
| account opened (solicits TIN) | 1991 return filed |

| 4/93 | 10/93 |
|-------|-------|
| 6721 penalty notice | B-notice w/respect to 1992 return |

(ii) On October 1, 1991, Individual E opens an account with Institution R, which pays E amounts reportable under section 6049. When E opens the account, R requests that E supply his TIN on an account creation document, which E does. Pursuant to paragraph (f)(1)(iv) of this section, R uses the TIN furnished by E on the information return filed for the 1991 calendar year. In October 1992 the Internal Revenue Service notifies R pursuant to section 3406(a)(1)(B) that the information return filed for E for the 1991 calendar year contained an incorrect TIN. At the time R receives this notification, E's account contains the incorrect TIN. On December 31, 1992, R telephones E pursuant to paragraphs (f)(2) and (e)(2)(ii) of this section and receives different TIN information from E. R uses this information on the return that it files timely for E for the 1992 calendar year, *i.e.,* in February 1993.

(iii) In April 1993, the Internal Revenue Service notifies R pursuant to paragraph (a)(2) of §301.6721-1 that the information return filed for the 1991 calendar year contains an incorrect TIN. The penalty will be waived, however, if R establishes the failure was due to reasonable cause as defined in this section.

(iv) To establish reasonable cause under this section, R must satisfy the criteria in both paragraphs (c)(6) and (d)(2) of this section. Pursuant to paragraph (d)(2) of this section, R can demonstrate that it acted in a responsible manner only if it complies with paragraph (f) of this section. R solicited E's TIN at the time the account was opened (initial solicitation). Under paragraphs (d)(2) and (f)(4) of this section,

caused by B's failure to provide a correct TIN, an event beyond M's control. As a result, M has established reasonable cause under paragraph (a)(2) of this section. Therefore, the penalty imposed under paragraph (a)(2) of §301.6721-1 for the failure on the 1991 information return is waived. See section 3406(a)(1)(B) which requires M to impose backup withholding on reportable payments to B if M has not received B's correct TIN.

*Example (3).* (i) *Table.*

| 10/92 | 2/93 |
|-------|------|
| B-notice w/respect to 1991 return | 1992 return filed |

| 2/93 | 4/94 |
|------|------|
| 1993 return filed | 6721 penalty notice for 1992 return |

this section requires a filer to make an initial solicitation for a TIN when an account is opened. Further, a filer must make an annual solicitation for a TIN by mail within 15 business days after the date that the Internal Revenue Service notifies the filer of an incorrect TIN pursuant to section 3406(a)(1)(B). M made the initial solicitation for the TIN in 1991 and, after being notified of the incorrect TIN in October 1992, the first annual solicitation within the time and manner prescribed by §31.3406(d)-5(d)(2)(i) of this chapter and paragraph (f)(1)(ii) and (2) of this section. M acted in a responsible manner. M satisfies paragraph (c)(6) of this section because, under the facts, M can show that the failure was caused by B's failure to provide his correct TIN, an event beyond M's control. As a result M has established reasonable cause under paragraph (a)(2) of this section. Therefore, the penalty imposed under paragraph (a)(2) of §301.6721-1 for the failure on the 1992 return is waived due to reasonable cause.

*Example (4).* (i) *Table.*

| 10/92 | 2/93 |
|-------|------|
| B-notice w/respect to 1991 return | 1992 return filed |

| 2/94 | 4/94 |
|------|------|
| 1993 return filed | 6721 penalty notice for 1992 return |

section 6050H and to section 6721. As part of the transaction, C gives N a promissory note providing for repayment of principal and the payment of interest. At the time C incurs the obligation N requests C's TIN, as required under §1.6050H-2(f) of this chapter. C fails to provide the TIN as required by §1.6050H-2(f) of this chapter. N sends solicitations by mail in 1992 and 1993 for the missing TIN, which C fails to provide. However, for 1994 M fails to send the solicitation required by §1.6050H-2(f) of this chapter. N files returns for the 1992, 1993, and 1994 calendar years pursuant to section 6050H without C's TIN. Although N made the initial and the first annual solicitations in 1992 and the second annual solicitation in 1993, N did not solicit the TIN in 1994 as required under section 6050H, which requires continued annual solicitations until the TIN is obtained. Therefore, under paragraph (e)(1)(vi)(A) of this section the penalty imposed under paragraph (a) of §301.6721-1 for the 1994 information return is not waived.

*Example (6).* (i) *Table.*

| 10/92 | 2/93 |
|-------|------|
| B-notice w/respect to 1991 return | 1992 return filed |

| 2/94 | 4/94 |
|------|------|
| 1993 return filed | 6721 penalty notice for 1992 return |

the initial solicitation relates to failures on returns filed for the year in which an account is opened (*i.e.,* 1991) and for subsequent years until the calendar year in which the filer receives a notification of an incorrect TIN pursuant to section 3406. Because E failed to provide the correct TIN upon request, the failure arose from events beyond R's control as described in paragraph (c)(6) of this section. Therefore, the penalty with respect to the failure on the 1991 calendar year information return is waived due to reasonable cause.

*Example (7).* (i) The facts are the same as in *Example 6.* In April 1994 the Internal Revenue Service notifies R pursuant to paragraph (a)(2) of §301.6721-1 that the information return filed for the 1992 calendar year for E contained an incorrect TIN.

(ii) To establish reasonable cause for the failure under this section, R must satisfy the criteria in both paragraphs (c)(6) and (d)(2) of this section. Pursuant to paragraph (d)(2) of this section R may establish that it acted in a responsible manner only by complying with paragraph (f) of this section. Pursuant to paragraph (f)(1)(ii) of this section, R must make an annual solicitation after being notified of an incorrect TIN if the payee's account contains the incorrect TIN at the time of the notification. Paragraph (f)(3) of this section provides that if the filer is notified pursuant to section 3406(a)(1)(B) the time and manner of making an annual solicitation is that required under §31.3406(d)-5(g)(1)(ii) of this chapter. Section 31.3406(d)-5(g)(1)(ii) of this chapter requires R to notify E by mail within 15 business days after the date of the notice from the Internal Revenue Service, which

R failed to do. As a result, R has failed to act in a responsible manner with respect to the failure on the 1992 information return, and the penalty will not be waived due to reasonable cause.

(l) [*Reserved.*]

(m) *Procedure for seeking a waiver.*—In seeking an administrative determination that the failure was due to reasonable cause and not willful neglect, the filer must submit a written statement to the district director or the director of the Internal Revenue Service Center where the returns, as defined in section 6724(d), are required to be filed. The statement must—

(1) State the specific provision under which the waiver is being requested, *i.e.*, paragraph (b) or under paragraph (c)(2) through (6),

(2) Set forth all the facts alleged as the basis for reasonable cause,

(3) Contain the signature of the person required to file the return, and

(4) Contain a declaration that it is made under penalties of perjury.

See § 1.6061-1 of the Income Tax Regulations for the rules on the signing of returns.

(n) *Manner of payment.*—The penalty due under sections 6721 through 6723 shall be paid upon notice and demand by Internal Revenue Service, and in the same manner as a tax liability is paid. [Reg. § 301.6724-1.]

☐ [*T.D. 8386, 12-27-91. Amended by T.D. 8409, 4-10-92; T.D. 8734, 10-6-97; T.D. 8804, 12-30-98; T.D. 8856, 12-29-99; T.D. 9055, 4-28-2003; T.D. 9136, 7-12-2004 and T.D. 9699, 10-24-2014.*]

# General Provisions Relating to Stamps

See p. 20,601 for regulations not amended to reflect law changes

### [Reg. § 301.6801-1]

**§ 301.6801-1. Authority for establishment, alteration, and distribution.**—(a) *Establishment and alteration.*—The Commissioner may establish, and from time to time alter, renew, replace, or change the form, style, character, material, and device of any stamp, mark, or label under any provision of the law relating to internal revenue.

(b) *Preparation and distribution of forms, stamps and dies.*—The Commissioner shall prepare and distribute all the instructions, directions, forms, blanks, and stamps; and shall provide proper and sufficient adhesive stamps and other stamps or dies for expressing and denoting the several stamp taxes. [Reg. § 301.6801-1.]

### [Reg. § 301.6802-1]

**§ 301.6802-1. Supply and distribution.**—(a) *Postmaster General.*—The Commissioner shall furnish to the Postmaster General, without prepayment, a suitable quantity of adhesive stamps (other than the stamps on playing cards), coupons, tickets, or such other devices as may be prescribed pursuant to section 6302(b) (authorizing a discretionary method for collecting certain specified taxes) or chapter 69 of the Code, to be distributed to, and kept on sale by, the various postmasters in the United States in all post offices of the first and second classes, and such post offices of the third and fourth classes as are located in county seats or Postmaster General as necessary.

(b) *Designated depositary of the United States.*—The district director for the district in which any designated depositary of the United States is located shall furnish to such designated depositary, without prepayment, a suitable quantity of adhesive stamps to be kept on sale by the designated depositary.

(c) *State agents.*—Any person who is duly appointed and acting as agent of any State for the sale of stock transfer stamps of such State may make application to the district director for the district in which the State agent is located, to be designated for the purpose of being furnished without prepayment, for sale, stamps to be used in payment of the tax imposed by section 4301. The application shall contain the location and post office address of the State agent, and the maximum amount of stamps he desires to maintain on hand. A copy of the agent's appointment as State agent should be attached to the application. [Reg. § 301.6802-1.]

### [Reg. § 301.6803-1]

**§ 301.6803-1. Accounting and safeguarding.**—In cases coming within the provisions of section 6802(2) and (3) and paragraphs (b) and (c) of § 301.6802-1, the district director may require a bond in such amount as he deems advisable, conditioned for the faithful return, whenever so required, of all quantities or amounts of adhesive stamps undisposed of and for the payment monthly for all quantities or amounts of adhesive stamps sold or not remaining on hand. Such bond shall be furnished in accordance with the provisions contained in section 7101 and § 301.7101-1. [Reg. § 301.6803-1.]

### [Reg. § 301.6804-1]

**§ 301.6804-1. Attachment and cancellation.**—For provisions relating to the attachment and cancellation of specific stamps used with respect to a particular tax, see the regulations relating to such tax. [Reg. § 301.6804-1.]

### [Reg. § 301.6805-1]

**§ 301.6805-1. Redemption of stamps.**—(a) *Authorization.*—(1) Upon receipt of satisfactory evidence of the facts by the district director or director of the service center, he may make allowance for or redeem stamps issued under the authority of any internal revenue law if—

(i) The stamps have been spoiled, destroyed, or rendered useless or unfit for the purpose intended, or

(ii) The owner of the stamps has no use therefor.

(2) If a stamp has been in use for any period of time, it may not be redeemed under section 6805. Similarly, no allowance shall be made for stamps which have been lost or stolen.

(b) *Method and conditions of allowance.*—Such allowance or redemption may be made, either by giving other stamps in lieu of the stamps so allowed for or redeemed, or by refunding the amount or value to the owner thereof, deducting therefrom, in case of repayment, the percentage, if any, allowed to the purchaser thereof. Claims for the redemption of or allowance for stamps shall be made on Form 843 and filed with the district director or director of the service center within three years from the date of the purchase of the stamps from the Government. The stamps for which redemption or allowance is claimed shall be submitted with the claim. If the stamps are destroyed or damaged to the extent that they cannot be presented for redemption or allowance, proof satisfactory to the district director or director of the service center that they have been destroyed or so damaged must accompany the claim before allowance or redemption shall be made. In any case where the actual date of purchase of the stamps from the Government cannot be established, it must be definitely shown in the claim whether they were so purchased within three years prior to the date of filing of the claim.

(c) *Time for filing claims.*—No claim for the redemption of, or allowance for, stamps shall be allowed under this section unless presented within 3 years after the purchase of such stamps from the Government.

(d) *Finality of decisions.*—The findings of fact in and the decision of the district director or director of the service center upon the merits of any claim presented under or authorized by this section, shall in the absence of fraud or mistake in mathematical calculation, be final and not subject to revision by any accounting officer. [Reg. § 301.6805-1.]

☐ [*T.D. 7188, 6-29-72.*]

### [Reg. § 301.6806-1]

**§ 301.6806-1. Posting occupational tax stamps.**—For provisions relating to the posting of specific stamps used with respect to a particular tax, other than a special tax under subchapter B of chapter 35, subchapter B of chapter 36, or subtitle E, see the regulations relating to such tax. For penalties for failure to post occupational tax stamps, see section 7273. [Reg. § 301.6806-1.]

☐ [*T.D. 7188, 6-29-72.*]

# Jeopardy, Receiverships, Etc.

## JEOPARDY

## Termination of Taxable Year

See p. 20,601 for regulations not amended to reflect law changes

**[Reg. §1.6851-1]**

**§1.6851-1. Termination assessments of income tax.—** (a) *Authority for making.*—(1) *In general.*—This section applies to assessments authorized by a district director under section 6851(a) (hereinafter referred to as termination assessments). The district director shall immediately authorize a termination assessment of the income tax for the current or preceding taxable year if the district director finds that a taxpayer designs to do an act which would tend to prejudice proceedings to collect the income tax for such year or years unless such proceedings are brought without delay. In addition, the district director shall immediately authorize such a termination assessment if the district director determines that the taxpayer designs to do any act which would tend to render such proceedings wholly or partially ineffective unless brought without delay. A termination assessment will be made if collection is determined to be in jeopardy because at least one of the following conditions exists:

(i) The taxpayer is or appears to be designing quickly to depart from the United States or to conceal himself or herself.

(ii) The taxpayer is or appears to be designing quickly to place his, her, or its property beyond the reach of the Government either by removing it from the United States, by concealing it, by dissipating it, or by transferring it to other persons.

(iii) The taxpayer's financial solvency is or appears to be imperiled.

Paragraph (a)(1)(iii) of this section does not include cases where the taxpayer becomes insolvent by virtue of the accrual of the proposed assessment of tax, and penalty, if any. A tax assessed under this section shall become immediately due and payable and the district director shall serve upon such taxpayer notice and demand for immediate payment of such tax.

(2) *Computation of tax.*—If a termination assessment of the income tax for the current year is made, the income tax for such year shall be computed for the period beginning on the first day of such year and ending on the day of the assessment. A credit shall be allowed for any tax for the taxable year previously assessed under section 6851. The taxpayer is entitled to a deduction for the personal exemptions (as limited in the case of certain nonresident aliens) without any proration for or because of the short taxable period.

(3) *Taxable year not affected by termination.*—Notwithstanding any termination assessment a taxpayer shall file a return in accordance with section 6012 and the regulations thereunder for the taxpayer's full taxable year. The term "full taxable year" means the taxpayer's usual annual accounting period determined without regard to any action under section 6851 and this section. The return shall show all items of gross income, deductions, and credits for such taxable year. Any tax collected as a result of a termination assessment will be applied against the tax due for the taxpayer's full taxable year. Except as provided in §1.6851-2 (relating to departing aliens), no return is required to be filed for a terminated period other than a full taxable year.

(4) *Evidence of compliance with income tax obligations.*—Citizens of the United States or of possessions of the United States departing from the United States or its possessions will not be required to procure certificates of compliance or to present any other evidence of compliance with income tax obligations. However, for the rules relating to the furnishing of evidence of compliance with the income tax obligations by certain departing aliens, see §1.6851-2.

(5) *Section 6851 inapplicable where section 6861 applies.*—No termination assessment for the preceding taxable year shall be made after the due date of the taxpayer's return for such year (determined with regard to extensions of time to file such return).

(b) *Notice of deficiency.*—Where notice and demand for payment (following a termination assessment) takes place after February 28, 1977, the district director shall, within 60 days after the later of—

(1) The date the taxpayer files a return for the full taxable year; or

(2) The due date of such return (determined with regard to extensions).

send the taxpayer a notice of deficiency under section 6212(a). The amount of the deficiency shall be computed in accordance with section 6211 and the regulations thereunder. In applying section 6211, the tax imposed and the amount shown upon the return shall be determined on the basis of the taxpayer's full taxable year. Thus, for example assume that on November 1, 1979, a termination assessment against A, a calendar year taxpayer, is made in the amount of $18,000. The termination assessment is for the period from January 1, 1979 through November 1, 1979. Further assume that on or before April 15, 1980, A files a form 1040 showing an income tax liability for the full year 1979 of $10,000. If the district director determines A's liability for tax for 1979 is $16,000, a notice of deficiency for $6,000 shall be sent to A on or before June 14, 1980. Assuming that the district director had collected the $18,000 assessed, $2,000 shall be refunded.

(c) *Immediate payment.*—The district director shall make demand for immediate payment of the amount of the termination assessment, and the taxpayer shall immediately pay such amount or shall immediately file the bond provided in section 6863.

(d) *Abatement.*—The provisions of §§301.6861-1(e) and 301.6861-1(f) relating to the abatement of jeopardy assessments, shall apply to assessments made under section 6851. [Reg. §1.6851-1.]

☐ [T.D. 6426, 11-30-59. *Amended by T.D. 7575, 12-15-78.*]

**[Reg. §301.6851-1]**

**§301.6851-1. Termination of taxable year.**—For regulations under section 6851, see §§1.6851-1 to 1.6851-3, inclusive, of this chapter (Income Tax Regulations). [Reg. §301.6851-1.]

☐ [T.D. 6227, 3-29-57. *Amended by T.D. 6498, 10-24-60.*]

**[Reg. §1.6851-2]**

**§1.6851-2. Certificates of compliance with income tax laws by departing aliens.**—(a) *In general.*—(1) *Requirement.*—The rules of this section are applicable, except as otherwise expressly provided, to any alien who departs from the United States or any of its possessions after January 20, 1961. Except as provided in subparagraph (2) of this paragraph, no such alien, whether resident or nonresident, may depart from the United States unless he first procures a certificate that he has complied with all of the obligations imposed upon him by the income tax laws. In order to procure such a certificate, an alien who intends to depart from the United States (i) must file with the district director for the internal revenue district in which he is located the statements or returns required by paragraph (b) of this section to be filed before obtaining such certificate, (ii) must appear before such district director if the district director deems it necessary, and (iii) must pay any taxes required under paragraph (b) of this section to be paid before obtaining the certificate. Either such certificate of compliance, properly executed, or evidence that the alien is excepted under subparagraph (2) of this paragraph from obtaining the certificate must be presented at the point of departure. An alien who presents himself at the point of departure without a certificate of compliance, or evidence establishing that such a certificate is not required, will be subject at such departure point to examination by an internal revenue officer or employee and to the completion of returns and statements and payment of taxes as required by paragraph (b) of this section.

(2) *Exceptions.*—(i) *Employees of foreign governments or international organizations.*—(a) *Diplomatic representatives, their families and servants.*—(1) Representatives of foreign governments bearing diplomatic passports, whether accredited to the United States or other countries, and members of their households shall not, upon departure from the United States or any of its possessions, be examined as to their liability for United States income tax or be required to obtain a certificate of compliance. If a foreign government does not issue diplomatic passports but merely indicates on passports issued to members of its diplomatic service the status of the bearer as a member of such service, such passports are considered as diplomatic passports for income tax purposes.

(2) Likewise, the servant of a diplomatic representative who accompanies any individual bearing a diplomatic passport upon departure from the United States or any of its possessions shall not be required, upon such departure, to obtain a certificate of compliance or to submit to examination as to his liability for United States income tax. If the departure of such a servant from the United States or any of its possessions is not made in the company of an individual bearing a diplomatic passport, the servant is required to obtain a

certificate of compliance. However, such certificate will be issued to him on Form 2063 without examination as to his income tax liability upon presentation to the district director for the internal revenue district in which the servant is located of a letter from the chief of the diplomatic mission to which the servant is attached certifying (i) that the name of the servant appears on the "White List," a list of employees of diplomatic missions, and (ii) that the servant is not obligated to the United States for any income tax, and will not be so obligated up to and including the intended date of departure.

(b) *Other employees.*—Any employee of an international organization or of a foreign government (other than a diplomatic representative to whom (a) of this subdivision applies) whose compensation for official services rendered to such organization or government is excluded from gross income under section 893 and who has received no gross income from sources within the United States, and any member of his household who has received no gross income from sources within the United States, shall not, upon departure from the United States or any of its possessions after November 30, 1962 be examined as to his liability for United States income tax or be required to obtain a certificate of compliance.

(c) *Effect of waiver.*—An alien who has filed with the Attorney General the waiver provided for under section 247(b) of the Immigration and Nationality Act (8 U.S.C. 1257(b)) is not entitled to the exception provided by this subdivision.

(ii) *Alien students, industrial trainees, and exchange visitors.*—A certificate of compliance shall not be required, and examination as to United States income tax liability shall not be made, upon the departure from the United States or any of its possessions of—

(A) An alien student, industrial trainee, or exchange visitor, and any spouse and children of that alien, admitted solely on an F-1, F-2, H-3, H-4, J-1 or J-2 visa, who has received no gross income from sources inside the United States other than—

(1) Allowances to cover expenses incident to study or training in the United States (including expenses for travel, maintenance, and tuition);

(2) The value of any services or accommodations furnished incident to such study or training;

(3) Income derived in accordance with the employment authorizations in 8 CFR 274a.12(b) and (c) that apply to the alien's visa; or

(4) Interest on deposits described in section 871(i)(2)(A); or

(B) An alien student, and any spouse or children of that alien admitted solely on an M-1 or M-2 visa, who has received no gross income from sources inside the United States other than income derived in accordance with the employment authorization in 8 CFR 274a.12(c)(6) or interest on deposits described in section 871(i)(2)(A).

(b) *Issuance of certificate of compliance.*—(1) *In general.*—(i) Upon the departure of an alien required to secure a certificate of compliance under paragraph (a) of this section, the district director shall determine whether the departure of such alien jeopardizes the collection of any income tax for the current or the preceding taxable year, but the district director may determine that jeopardy does not exist in some cases. If the district director finds that the departure of such an alien results in jeopardy, the taxable period of the alien will be terminated, and the alien will be required to file returns and make payment of tax in accordance with subparagraph (3)(iii) of this paragraph. On the other hand, if the district director finds that the departure of the alien does not result in jeopardy, the alien will be required to file the statement on returns required by subparagraph (2) or (3)(ii) of this paragraph, but will not be required to pay income tax before the usual time for payment.

(ii) The departure of an alien who is a resident of the United States or a possession thereof (or treated as a resident under section 6013(g) or (h)) and who intends to continue such residence (or treatment as a resident) shall be treated as not resulting in jeopardy, and thus not requiring termination of his taxable period, except when the district director has information indicating that the alien intends by such departure to avoid the payment of his income tax. In the case of a nonresident alien (including a resident alien discontinuing residence), the fact that the alien intends to depart from the United States will justify termination of his taxable period unless the alien establishes to the satisfaction of the district director that he intends to return to the United States and that his departure will not jeopardize collection of the tax. The determination of whether the departure of the alien results in jeopardy will be made on examination of all the facts in the case. Evidence tending to establish that jeopardy does not result from the departure of the alien may be provided, for example, by information showing that the alien is engaged in trade or business in the United States or that he leaves sufficient property in the United States to secure payment of his income tax for the taxable year and of any income tax for the preceding year which remains unpaid.

(2) *Alien having no taxable income and resident alien whose taxable period is not terminated.*—A statement on Form 2063 shall be filed with the district director by every alien required to obtain a certificate of compliance—

(i) Who is a resident of the United States and whose taxable period is not terminated either because he has had no taxable income for the taxable year up to and including the date of his departure (and for the preceding taxable year where the period for making the income tax return for such year has not expired) or because, although he has had taxable income for such period or periods, the district director has not found that his departure jeopardizes collection of the tax on such income; or

(ii) Who is not a resident of the United States and who has had no taxable income for the taxable year up to and including the date of his departure (and for the preceding taxable year where the period for making the income tax return for such year has not expired).

Any alien described in subdivision (i) or (ii) of this subparagraph who is in default in making return of, or paying, income tax for any taxable year shall, in addition, file with the district director any returns which have not been made as required and pay to the district director the amount of any tax for which he is in default. Upon compliance by an alien with the foregoing requirements of this subparagraph, the district director shall execute and issue to the alien the certificate of compliance attached to Form 2063. The certificate of compliance so issued shall be effective for all departures of the alien during his current taxable year, subject to revocation upon any subsequent departure should the district director have reason to believe that such subsequent departure would result in jeopardy. The statement required of a resident alien under this subparagraph, if made before January 21, 1961, with respect to a departure after January 20, 1961, may be made on a Form 1040C in lieu of a Form 2063.

(3) *Nonresident alien having taxable income and resident alien whose taxable period is terminated.*—(i) *Nonresident alien having taxable income.*—Every nonresident alien required to obtain a certificate of compliance (but not described in subparagraph (2) of this paragraph) who wishes to establish that his departure does not result in jeopardy shall furnish to the district director such information as may be required for the purpose of determining whether the departure of the alien jeopardizes collection of the income tax and thus requires termination of his taxable period.

(ii) *Nonresident alien whose taxable period is not terminated.*—Every nonresident alien described in subdivision (i) of this subparagraph whose taxable period is not terminated upon departure shall file with the district director—

(a) A return in duplicate on Form 1040C for the taxable year of his intended departure, showing income received, and reasonably expected to be received, during the entire taxable year within which the departure occurs; and

(b) Any income tax returns which have not been filed as required.

Upon compliance by the alien with the foregoing requirements of this subdivision, and the payment of any income tax for which he is in default, the district director shall execute and issue to the alien the certificate of compliance on the duplicate copy of Form 1040C. The certificate of compliance so issued shall be effective for all departures of the alien during his current taxable year, subject to revocation by the district director upon any subsequent departure if the taxable period of the alien is terminated on such subsequent departure.

(iii) *Alien (whether resident or nonresident) whose taxable period is terminated.*—Every alien required to obtain a certificate of compliance, whether resident or nonresident, whose taxable period is terminated upon departure shall file with the district director—

(a) A return in duplicate on Form 1040C for the short taxable period resulting from such termination, showing income received, and reasonably expected to be received, during the taxable year up to and including the date of departure;

(b) Where the period for filing has not expired, the return required under section 6012 and § 1.6012-1 for the preceding taxable years; and

(c) Any other income tax returns which have not been filed as required.

Upon compliance with the foregoing requirements of this subdivision, and payment of the income tax required to be shown on the returns filed pursuant to (a) and (b) of this subdivision and of any income tax due and owing for prior years, the departing alien will be issued the certificate of compliance on the duplicate copy of Form 1040C. The certificate of compliance so issued shall be effective only for the specific departure with respect to which it is issued. A departing alien may postpone payment of the tax required to be shown on the returns filed in accordance with (a) and (b) of this subdivision until the usual time of payment by furnishing a bond as provided in §301.6863-1 of this chapter (regulations on procedure and administration).

(4) *Joint return on Form 1040C.*—A departing alien may not file a joint return on Form 1040C unless—

(i) Such alien and his spouse may reasonably be expected to be eligible to file a joint return at the normal close of their taxable periods for which the return is made; and

(ii) If the taxable period of such alien is terminated, the taxable periods of both spouses are so terminated as to end at the same time.

(5) *Annual return.*—Notwithstanding that Form 1040C has been filed for either the entire taxable year of departure or for a terminated period, the return required under section 6012 and §1.6012-1 for such taxable year shall be filed. Any income tax paid on income shown on the return on Form 1040C shall be applied against the tax determined to be due on the income required to be shown on the subsequent return under section 6012 and §1.6012-1. [Reg. §1.6851-2.]

☐ [*T.D. 6426, 11-30-59. Amended by T.D. 6537, 1-19-61; T.D. 6620, 11-29-62; T.D. 7575, 12-15-78; T.D. 7670, 1-30-80; T.D. 8332, 1-25-91 and T.D. 8526, 3-2-94.*]

### [Reg. §1.6851-3]

**§1.6851-3. Furnishing of bond to insure payment; cross reference.**—See section 6863 and §301.6863-1 of this chapter (regulations on procedure and administration) for rules relating to the furnishing of bond to stay collection. [Reg. §1.6851-3.]

☐ [*T.D. 6426, 11-30-59. Amended by T.D. 7575, 12-15-78.*]

### [Reg. §301.6852-1]

**§301.6852-1. Termination assessments of tax in the case of flagrant political expenditures of section 501(c)(3) organizations.**—

(a) *Authority for making.*—Any assessment under section 6852 as a result of a flagrant violation by a section 501(c)(3) organization of the prohibition against making political expenditures must be authorized by the District Director.

(b) *Determination of income tax.*—An organization shall be subject to an assessment of income tax under section 6852 only if the flagrant violation of the prohibition against making political expenditures results in revocation of the organization's tax exemption under section 501(a) because it is not described in section 501(c)(3). An organization subject to such an assessment is not liable for income taxes for any period prior to the effective date of the revocation of the organization's tax exemption.

(c) *Payment.*—Where a District Director has made a determination of income tax under paragraph (b) of this section or of section 4955 excise tax, notwithstanding any other provision of law, any tax will become immediately due and payable. The taxpayer is required to pay the amount of the assessment within 10 days after the District Director sends the notice and demand for immediate payment regardless of the filing of an administrative appeal or of a court petition. Regardless of filing an administrative appeal or of petitioning a court, enforced collection action may proceed after the 10-day payment period unless the taxpayer posts the bond described in section 6863. For purposes of collection procedures such as section 6331 (regarding levy), assessments under the authority of paragraph (a) of this section do not constitute situations in which the collection of such tax is in jeopardy and, therefore, do not suspend normal collection procedures.

(d) *Effective date.*—This section is effective December 5, 1995. [Reg. §301.6852-1.]

☐ [*T.D. 8628, 12-4-95.*]

## Jeopardy Assessments

### [Reg. §301.6861-1]

**§301.6861-1. Jeopardy assessments of income, estate, gift, and certain excise taxes.**—(a) *Authority for making.*—If a district director or director of a service center believes that the assessment or collection of a deficiency in income, estate, gift, or chapter 41, 42, 43, or 44 tax will be jeopardized by delay, then the director is required to assess such deficiency immediately, together with the interest, additional amounts, and additions to the tax provided by law. A district director will make an assessment under this section if collection is determined to be in jeopardy because at least one of the conditions described in §1.6851-1(a)(1)(i), (ii), or (iii) (relating to termination assessments) exists. A jeopardy assessment may be made before or after the mailing of the notice of deficiency provided by section 6212. However, a jeopardy assessment for a taxable year under section 6861 cannot be made after a decision of the Tax Court with respect to such taxable year has become final (see section 7481) or after the taxpayer has filed a petition for review of the decision of the Tax Court with respect to such taxable year. In the case of a deficiency determined by a decision of the Tax Court which has become final or with respect to which the taxpayer has filed a petition for review and has not filed a bond as provided in section 7485, assessment may be made in accordance with the provisions of section 6215, without regard to section 6861.

(b) *Amount of jeopardy assessment.*—If a notice of a deficiency is mailed to the taxpayer before it is discovered that delay would jeopardize the assessment or collection of the tax, a jeopardy assessment may be made in an amount greater or less than that included in the deficiency notice. If a deficiency is assessed on account of jeopardy after the decision of the Tax Court is rendered, the jeopardy assessment may be made only with respect to the deficiency determined by the Tax Court.

(c) *Jurisdiction of Tax Court.*—If the jeopardy assessment is made before the notice in respect of the tax to which the jeopardy assessment relates has been mailed pursuant to section 6212(a), the district director shall, within 60 days after the making of the assessment, send the taxpayer a notice of deficiency pursuant to such subsection. The taxpayer may file a petition with the Tax Court for a redetermination of the amount of the deficiency within the time prescribed in section 6213(a). If the petition of the taxpayer is filed with the Tax Court, either before or after the making of the jeopardy assessment, the Commissioner, through his counsel, is required to notify the Tax Court of such assessment or of any abatement thereof, and the Tax Court has jurisdiction to redetermine the amount of the deficiency,

together with all other amounts assessed at the same time in connection therewith.

(d) *Payment and collection of jeopardy assessment.*—After a jeopardy assessment has been made, the district director is required to send notice and demand to the taxpayer for the amount of the jeopardy assessment. Regardless of whether the taxpayer has filed a petition with the Tax Court, he is required to make payment of the amount of such assessment (to the extent that it has not been abated) within 10 days after the sending of notice and demand by the district director, unless before the expiration of such 10-day period he files with the district director a bond as provided in section 6863. Section 6331 provides that, if the district director makes a finding that the collection of the tax is in jeopardy, he may make demand for immediate payment of the amount of the jeopardy assessment and, in such case, the taxpayer shall immediately pay such amount or shall immediately file the bond provided in section 6863. If a petition is not filed with the Tax Court within the period prescribed in section 6213(a), the district director will be so advised, and, if collection of the deficiency has been stayed by the timely filing of a bond as provided in section 6863, he should then give notice and make demand for payment of the amount assessed plus interest. After the Tax Court has rendered its decision and such decision has become final, the district director will be notified of the action taken. He will then send notice and demand for payment of the unpaid portion of the amount determined by the Tax Court, the collection of which has been stayed by the bond. If the amount of the jeopardy assessment is less than the amount determined by the Tax Court, the difference will be assessed and collected as part of the tax upon the issuance of a notice and demand therefor. If the amount of the jeopardy assessment is in excess of the amount determined by the Tax Court, the unpaid portion of such excess will be abated. If any part of the excess amount has been paid, it will be credited or refunded to the taxpayer as provided in section 6402, without the filing of claim therefor.

(e) *Abatement of excessive assessment.*—The district director or the director of the regional service center may, at any time before the decision of the Tax Court is rendered, abate a jeopardy assessment in whole or in part if the district director believes that such assessment is excessive in amount.

(f) *Abatement if jeopardy does not exist.*—(1) The district director or the director of the regional service center may abate a jeopardy assessment in whole or in part, if it is shown to his satisfaction that jeopardy does not exist. An abatement may not be made under this paragraph after a decision of the Tax Court in respect of the deficiency has been rendered or, if no petition is filed with such court, after the expiration of the period for filing such petition.

(2) After abatement of a jeopardy assessment in whole or in part, a deficiency may be assessed and collected in the manner authorized by law as if the jeopardy assessment or part thereof so abated had not existed. If a notice of deficiency has been sent to the taxpayer before the abatement of the jeopardy assessment in whole or in part, whether such notice was sent before or after the making of the assessment, such abatement will not affect the validity of the notice or of any proceedings for redetermination based thereon. The period of limitation on the making of assessments and the beginning of levy or a proceeding in court for collection in respect of any deficiency shall be determined as if the jeopardy assessment so abated had not been made, except that the running of such period shall in any event be suspended for the period from the date of such jeopardy assessment until the expiration of the tenth day after the date on which such jeopardy assessment is abated in whole or in part. The provisions of this subparagraph may be illustrated by the following example:

*Example.* On March 18, 1958, 28 days before the last day of the 3-year period of limitations on assessment, a jeopardy assessment is made in respect of a proposed deficiency. On May 2, 1958, before the mailing of the notice of deficiency provided by section 6861(b), this assessment is abated. By virtue of this subparagraph, the last day of the period of limitations for the making of an assessment is June 9, 1958, that is, the thirty-eighth day after the date of the abatement. If the notice of deficiency provided for in section 6861(b) had been sent before the abatement, the running of the period of limitations on assessment would have been suspended pursuant to the provisions of section 6503(a).

(3) See section 7429 with respect to requesting the district director to review the making of the jeopardy assessment.

(g) *Special rules for chapters 42 and 43 taxes.*—For purposes of paragraph (a) of this section, the amount of a deficiency with respect to any tax imposed by section 4941(a), 4942(a), 4943(a), 4944(a), 4945(a), 4951(a), 4952(a), 4955(a), 4971(a) or 4975(a) shall include the amount of additional tax imposed by section 4941(b), 4942(b), 4943(b), 4944(b), 4945(b), 4951(b), 4952(b), 4955(b), 4971(b), or 4975(b) for failure to correct the act (or failure to act) which gave rise to liability for the initial tax. [Reg. § 301.6861-1.]

☐ [*T.D. 6227, 3-29-57. Amended by T.D. 6585, 12-27-61; T.D. 7575, 12-15-78; T.D. 7838, 10-5-82; T.D. 8084, 5-1-86 and T.D. 8628, 12-4-95.*]

### [Reg. § 301.6862-1]

**§ 301.6862-1. Jeopardy assessment of taxes other than income, estate, gift, and certain excise taxes.**—(a) If the district director believes that the collection of any tax (other than income, estate, gift, chapter 41, 42, 43, or 44 tax) will be jeopardized by delay, the director shall, whether or not the time otherwise prescribed by law for filing the return or paying such tax has expired, immediately assess such tax, together with all interest, additional amounts and additions to the tax provided by law. A district director will make an assessment under this section if collection is determined to be in jeopardy because at least one of the conditions described in § 1.6851-1(a)(1)(i), (ii), or (iii) (relating to termination assessments) exists. For example, assume that a taxpayer incurs on January 18, 1977, liability for tax imposed by section 4061, that the last day on which return and payment of such tax is required to be made is May 2, 1977, and that on January 18, 1977 the district director determines that collection of such tax would be jeopardized by delay. In such case, the district director shall immediately assess the tax.

(b) The tax, interest, additional amounts, and additions to the tax will, upon assessment, become immediately due and payable, and the district director shall, without delay, issue a notice and demand for payment thereof in full. Upon failure or refusal to pay the amount demanded, collection thereof by levy shall be lawful without regard to the 10-day period provided in section 6331(a). However, the collection of the whole or any part of the amount of the jeopardy assessment may be stayed by timely filing with the district director a bond as provided in section 6863.

(c) See section 7429 with respect to requesting the district director to review the making of the jeopardy assessment. [Reg. § 301.6862-1.]

☐ [*T.D. 6227, 3-29-57. Amended by T.D. 7575, 12-15-78 and T.D. 7838, 10-5-82.*]

### [Reg. § 301.6863-1]

**§ 301.6863-1. Stay of collection of jeopardy assessments; bond to stay collection.**—(a) *General rule.*—(1) The collection of an assessment under section 6851, 6861, or 6862 (referred to as a "jeopardy assessment" for purposes of this section), or under section 6852 (referred to as a political assessment for purposes of this section) of any tax may be stayed by filing with the district director a bond on the form to be furnished by the district director upon request.

(2) The bond may be filed—

(i) At any time before the time collection by levy is authorized under section 6331(a), or

(ii) After collection by levy is authorized and before levy is made on any property or rights to property, or

(iii) In the discretion of the district director, after any such levy has been made and before the expiration of the period of limitations on collection.

(3) The bond made must be in an amount equal to the portion (including interest thereon to the date of payment as calculated by the district director) of the jeopardy assessment or political assessment collection of which is sought to be stayed. See section 7101 and § 301.7101-1, relating to the form of bond and the sureties thereon. The bond shall be conditioned upon the payment of the amount (together with interest thereon), the collection of which is stayed, at the time at which, but for the making of the jeopardy assessment, such amount would be due.

(4) Upon the filing of a bond in accordance with this section, the collection of so much of the assessment as is covered by the bond will be stayed. The taxpayer may at any time waive the stay of collection of the whole or any part of the amount covered by the bond. If as a result of such waiver any part of the amount covered by the bond is paid, or if any portion of the jeopardy assessment or political assessment is abated by the district director, then the bond shall at the request of the taxpayer be proportionately reduced.

(b) *Additional conditions applicable to income, estate, gift, and chapter 41, 42, 43 and 44 tax assessments.*—In the case of a jeopardy assessment or political assessment of income, estate, gift, chapter 41, 42, 43, or 44 tax, the bond must be conditioned upon the payment of so much of the amount included therein as is not abated by a decision of the Tax Court which has become final, together with the interest on such amount. If the Tax Court determines that the amount assessed is greater than the correct amount of the tax, the bond will be proportionately reduced at the request of the taxpayer after the Tax Court renders its decision. If the bond is given before the taxpayer has filed his petition with the Tax Court, it must contain a further condition that if a petition is not filed before the expiration of the period provided in section 6213(a) for the filing of such petition the amount stayed by the bond will be paid upon notice and demand at any time after the expiration of such period, together with interest thereon at the annual rate referred to in the regulations under section 6621 from the date of the jeopardy (or political assessment) notice and demand to the date of the notice and demand made after the expiration of the period for filing petition with the Tax Court. [Reg. § 301.6863-1.]

☐ [*T.D. 6227, 3-29-57. Amended by T.D. 6498, 10-24-60; T.D. 7384, 10-21-75; T.D. 7575, 12-15-78; T.D. 7838, 10-5-82 and T.D. 8628, 12-4-95.*]

### [Reg. § 301.6863-2]

**§ 301.6863-2. Collection of jeopardy assessment; stay of sale of seized property pending Tax Court decision.**—(a) *General rule.*—In the case of an assessment under section 6851, 6852, 6861, or 6862, any property seized for the collection of such assessment shall not (except as provided in paragraph (b) of this section) be sold until the latest of the following occurs:

(1) The period provided in section 7429(a)(2) to request the district director to review the action taken expires.

(2) The period provided in section 7429(b)(1) to file an action in U.S. District Court expires if a request for a redetermination is made to the district director.

(3) The U.S. District Court judgment in such action becomes final, if a civil action is begun in accordance with section 7429(b).

(4) In addition to the occurrences described in paragraphs (a)(1), (2), and (3) of this section in the case of an assessment of income, estate, gift, chapter 41, 42, 43, or 44 excise taxes, until the latest of the following occurs:

(i) The expiration of the period provided in section 6213(a) within which the taxpayer may file a petition with the Tax Court; or

(ii) The decision of the Tax Court becomes final, if a petition for redetermination is filed with the Tax Court (whether before or after the making of the assessment).

However, notwithstanding paragraph (a)(4)(i) of this section, in the case of a termination assessment under section 6851, property seized may be sold after the due date (determined with extensions) of the taxpayer's return if the taxpayer does not file a return by such date. Furthermore, for the purposes of paragraph (a)(4)(ii) of this section, a petition will not operate as a further stay of the sale of the seized property unless the taxpayer files a bond as provided in section 7485.

(b) *Exceptions.*—Notwithstanding the provisions of paragraph (a) of this section, any property seized may be sold—

(1) If the taxpayer files with the district director a written consent to the sale, or

(2) If the district director determines that the expenses of conservation and maintenance of the property will greatly reduce the net proceeds from the sale of such property, or

(3) If the property is of a type to which section 6336 (relating to sale of perishable goods) is applicable. [Reg. § 301.6863-2.]

☐ [*T.D. 6227, 3-29-57. Amended by T.D. 7575, 12-15-78 and T.D. 8628,12-4-95.*]

# Special Rules with Respect to Certain Cash

[Reg. § 301.6867-1]

**§301.6867-1. Presumptions where owner of large amount of cash is not identified.**—(a) *General rule.*—For purposes of section 6851 (relating to termination assessments) and section 6861 (relating to jeopardy assessments), if cash in excess of $10,000 is found in the physical possession of an individual who does not claim either ownership of that cash or ownership by some other person whose identity the Commissioner can readily ascertain and who acknowledges ownership of that cash as of the date the cash was found, then, it shall be presumed that—

(1) The cash represents gross income of an unknown single individual; and

(2) That the collection of tax on that income will be jeopardized by delay.

(b) *Rules for assessment.*—The Commissioner may make an assessment pursuant to section 6851 or section 6861, as appropriate, using the rules for assessment specified in this paragraph. In the case of any assessment resulting from the application of paragraph (a) of this section—

(1) The entire amount of cash is treated as taxable income for the taxable year in which the cash is found;

(2) The income is treated as taxable at the highest rate of tax specified in section 1 of the Internal Revenue Code; and

(3) Except as provided in paragraph (c), the possessor of the cash is treated (solely with respect to that cash) as the taxpayer for purposes of chapters 63 and 64 and section 7429(a)(1) of the Internal Revenue Code.

(c) *Effect of later substitution of true owner.*—(1) *In general.*—If an assessment resulting from the application of paragraph (a) of this section is later abated and replaced by an assessment against the true owner of the cash, the later assessment is treated for purposes of all laws relating to lien, levy, and collection as relating back to the date of the original assessment. Notwithstanding the preceding sentence, any notice and review provided for by section 7429 and the notice of deficiency issued to the true owner relative to the later assessment are to be made within the prescribed time limits, using the actual date of the later assessment against the true owner.

(2) *Example.*—The provisions of paragraph (c)(1) of this section may be illustrated by the following example:

*Example.* On June 5, 1994, A is found in possession of a bag, containing $200,000, which A claims he was holding for a friend whose name A cannot remember. Because A does not claim ownership of the cash and does not provide the name of the true owner so that the Commissioner can identify the true owner and have that person acknowledge ownership of the cash, it is presumed that the cash represents gross income of an individual for calendar year 1994, and that the collection of tax on that gross income will be jeopardized by delay. Accordingly, on June 17, 1994, a termination assessment under section 6851 is made against A, in his capacity as possessor of the cash. On June 21, 1994, the written statement of information provided for by section 7429(a)(1) is given to A. No request for review under section 7429(a)(2) is made by the true owner within 30 days after the day on which A was furnished the written statement provided for in section 7429(a)(1). Subsequently, individual B comes to the Service and states that he is the owner of the cash. On September 2, 1994, the Service determines that B was the true owner of the cash on June 5, 1994. On September 9, 1994, the Service abates the termination assessment made against A solely as possessor of cash and, after determining that jeopardy exists, replaces it with a termination assessment under section 6851 against B. The lien against B that arises under section 6321 is treated as arising on June 17, 1994. However, within 5 days after September 9, 1994, the Service must give B the written statement of information required by section 7429(a)(1) so that B can make a request for review under section 7429(a)(2). In addition, a notice of deficiency must be sent to B within 60 days after the later of the due date or the actual filing of B's tax return for 1994, as required by section 6851(b).

(d) *Rights of possessor of cash.*—(1) *Action permitted.*—Section 6867 provides that the possessor of cash is treated as the taxpayer for purposes of chapter 63 (relating to assessment) and chapter 64 (relating to collection) of the Internal Revenue Code. Accordingly, the possessor of cash may file a petition with the United States Tax Court, within the applicable time limits, challenging the notice of

deficiency issued to the possessor solely in that person's capacity as possessor of cash.

(2) *Actions not permitted.*—Section 6867 provides that the possessor of cash is treated as the taxpayer solely for purposes of section 7429(a)(1), and is entitled to the written statement of information provided for by that section. The possessor of cash is not treated as the taxpayer for purposes of sections 7429(a)(2) and 7429(b), relating to administrative and judicial review of termination and jeopardy assessments, and may not maintain an action under section 7429 for such review. The possessor of cash is not treated as the taxpayer for purposes of section 7422, relating to civil actions for refund, or chapter 65 of the Internal Revenue Code, relating to abatements, credits, and refunds, and may not institute a suit for refund in district court after the deficiency has been collected.

(e) *Rights of true owner of cash.*—(1) *Actions permitted.*—The true owner of cash may request administrative review under section 7429(a)(2) and may maintain a civil action under section 7429(b) for judicial review of an assessment under section 6851 or section 6861 made against the possessor solely in that person's capacity as possessor of cash. Such an action, however, must be preceded by a request for review under section 7429(a)(2) made by the true owner within 30 days after the day on which the possessor is furnished the written statement provided for in section 7429(a)(1). In addition, after the deficiency asserted against the possessor of cash has been levied upon, the true owner of cash may bring an action in federal district court to recover the cash, as provided in section 7426, relating to civil actions by persons other than taxpayers. See, however, section 6532(c), relating to the 9-month statute of limitations for suits under section 7426. In addition, the true owner of cash, with the permission of the court, may appear before the United States Tax Court in any proceeding that may be filed by the possessor of the cash challenging the notice of deficiency issued to the possessor solely in that person's capacity as possessor of the cash.

(2) *Actions not permitted.*—The true owner of cash may not file a petition with the United States Tax Court challenging the notice of deficiency issued to the possessor solely in that person's capacity as possessor of cash. Notwithstanding the preceding sentence, the true owner of cash may file a petition with the United States Tax Court challenging any notice of deficiency issued to the true owner following the abatement of the assessment made against the possessor of cash.

(f) *Definitions.*—For the purposes of this section and section 6867—

(1) *Cash.*—The term *cash* includes any cash equivalents.

(2) *Cash equivalent.*—(i) *In general.*—The term *cash equivalent* includes foreign currency, any bearer obligation, and any medium of exchange that is of a type that has been frequently used in illegal activities, as listed in paragraph (f)(2)(ii) of this section.

(ii) *Specific cash equivalents.*—For purposes of paragraph (f)(2)(i), the following are also cash equivalents—

(A) Coins;

(B) Precious metals;

(C) Jewelry;

(D) Precious stones;

(E) Postage stamps;

(F) Traveler's checks in any form;

(G) Negotiable instruments (including personal checks, business checks, official bank checks, cashier's checks, notes, and money orders) that are either in bearer form, endorsed without restriction, made out to a fictitious payee, or otherwise in such form that title thereto passes upon delivery;

(H) Incomplete instruments (including personal checks, business checks, official bank checks, cashier's checks, notes, and money orders) signed but with the payee's name omitted; and

(I) Securities or stock in bearer form or otherwise in such form that title thereto passes upon delivery.

(iii) *Value of cash equivalents.*—A cash equivalent is taken into account at its fair market value except in the case of a bearer obligation, in which case it is taken into account at its face value.

(3) *Possessor of cash.*—An individual is considered to be the possessor of cash if the cash is found on that individual's person or in

that individual's possession or is found in any object, container, vehicle, or area under that individual's custody or control.

(4) *True owner of the cash.*—The true owner of cash is the individual who beneficially owns the cash on the date such cash is found in the physical possession of the individual described in paragraph (f)(3) of this section. An agent, bailee, or other custodian of the cash is not the true owner of cash. A true owner of cash does not include an individual who, subsequent to the date on which the cash is found in the physical possession of the individual described in paragraph (f)(3) of this section, obtains ownership of the cash by purchase, subrogation, descent, or other means.

(g) *Effective date.*—This section is effective with respect to cash found in the physical possession of an individual on or after August 3, 1995. [Reg. §301.6867-1.]

☐ [T.D. 8605, 8-2-95.]

# RECEIVERSHIPS, ETC.

## [Reg. §301.6871(a)-1]

**§301.6871(a)-1. Immediate assessment of claims for income, estate, and gift taxes in bankruptcy and receivership proceedings.**— (a) Upon (1) the adjudication of bankruptcy of any taxpayer in any liquidating proceeding, (2) the filing with a court of competent jurisdiction or (where approval is required by the Bankruptcy Act, 11 U.S.C. chs. 1-14) the approval of a petition of, or the approval of a petition against, any taxpayer in any other proceeding under the Bankruptcy Act, or (3) the appointment of any receiver for any taxpayer in a receivership proceeding before any court of the United States or of any State or Territory or of the District of Columbia, the district director shall immediately assess any deficiency of income, estate, or gift tax (together with all interest, additional amounts, or additions to the tax provided by law), determined by him, if such deficiency has not heretofore been assessed in accordance with law. Such assessment shall be made immediately, whether or not a notice of deficiency has been issued, and without regard to the restrictions upon assessments under section 6213.

(b) As used in this section and §§301.6871(a)-2 to 301.6873-1, inclusive, the term "proceeding under the Bankruptcy Act" includes a proceeding under chapters I to VII, inclusive, of the Bankruptcy Act, or under section 75 or 77 (11 U.S.C. 203, 205), or chapters X to XIII, inclusive, of such Act, or any other proceeding under the Act. [Reg. §301.6871(a)-1.]

☐ [T.D. 6227, 3-29-57. *Amended by T.D.* 6425, 11-10-59 *and T.D.* 6498, 10-24-60.]

## [Reg. §301.6871(a)-2]

**§301.6871(a)-2. Collection of assessed taxes in bankruptcy and receivership proceedings.**—(a) During a proceeding under the Bankruptcy Act (11 U.S.C. chs. 1-14) or a receivership proceeding in either a Federal or State court, generally the assets of the taxpayer are under the control of the court in which such proceeding is pending, and the collection of taxes cannot be made by levying upon such assets. However, any assets which under applicable provisions of law are not under the control of the court may be subject to levy. See paragraph (b) of this section and §301.6871(b)-1 with respect to claims for such taxes. See section 6873 with respect to collection of unpaid claims.

(b) District directors should, promptly after ascertaining the existence of any outstanding liability against a taxpayer in any proceeding under the Bankruptcy Act or in any receivership proceeding, and in any event within the time limited by the appropriate provisions of the Bankruptcy Act, or by the appropriate orders of the court in which such proceeding is pending, file proof of claim covering such liability in the court in which such proceeding is pending. Such proof of claim should be filed whether the unpaid taxes involved have been assessed or not, except in cases where the instructions of the Commissioner direct otherwise; for example, where the payment of the taxes is secured by a sufficient bond. At the same time proof of claim is filed with the bankruptcy or receivership court, the district director will send notice and demand for payment to the taxpayer, together with a copy of such proof of claim.

(c) Under sections 3466 and 3467 of the Revised Statutes (31 U.S.C. 191, 192) and section 64 of the Bankruptcy Act, 11 U.S.C. 104, taxes are entitled to the priority over other claims therein specified, and the trustee, receiver, debtor in possession, or other person designated as in control of the assets of the debtor by the court in which the proceeding under the Bankruptcy Act or receivership proceeding is pending, may be held personally liable for failure on his part to protect the priority of the Government respecting taxes of which he has notice. Sections 75(l), 77(e), 199, 337(2), 455, and 659(6) of the Bankruptcy Act (11 U.S.C. 203(l), 205(e), 599, 737(2), 855, and 1059(6)) also contain provisions with respect to the rights of the United States relative to priority of payment. For the filing of returns by a trustee in bankruptcy or by a receiver, see section 6012(b)(3) and 28 U.S.C. 960. Bankruptcy courts have jurisdiction under the Bankruptcy Act to determine all disputes regarding the amount and validity of taxes claimed in a proceeding under the Bankruptcy Act. A proceeding under the Bankruptcy Act or receivership proceeding does not discharge any portion of a claim of the United States for taxes except in the case of a proceeding under section 77 or chapter X of the Bankruptcy Act. However, the claim may be settled or compromised as in other cases in court.

(d) For the requirement that a receiver, trustee in bankruptcy, or other like fiduciary give notice as to his qualification as such, see section 6036 and the regulations thereunder. [Reg. §301.6871(a)-2.]

☐ [T.D. 6227, 3-29-57. *Amended by T.D.* 6498, 10-24-60.]

## [Reg. §301.6871(b)-1]

**§301.6871(b)-1. Claims for income, estate, and gift taxes in proceedings under the Bankruptcy Act and receivership proceedings; claim filed despite pendency of Tax Court proceedings.**—(a) If it is determined that a deficiency is due in respect of income, estate, or gift tax and the taxpayer has filed a petition with the Tax Court before (1) the adjudication of bankruptcy in any liquidating proceeding, (2) the filing with a court of competent jurisdiction or (where approval is required by the Bankruptcy Act (11 U.S.C. chs. 1-14)) the approval of a petition of, or the approval of a petition against, any taxpayer in any other proceeding under the Bankruptcy Act, or (3) the appointment of a receiver, the trustee, receiver, debtor in possession, or other like fiduciary, may, upon his own motion, be made a party to the Tax Court proceeding and thereafter may prosecute the appeal before the Tax Court as to that particular determination. No petition shall be filed with the Tax Court for a redetermination of the deficiency after the adjudication of bankruptcy, the filing or (where approval is required by the Bankruptcy Act) the approval of a petition of, or the approval of a petition against, any taxpayer in any other bankruptcy proceeding, or the appointment of the receiver.

(b) Even though the determination of a deficiency is pending before the Tax Court for redetermination, proof of claim for the amount of such deficiency may be filed with the court in which the proceeding under the Bankruptcy Act or receivership proceeding is pending without awaiting final decision of the Tax Court. In case of a final decision of the Tax Court before the payment or the disallowance of the claim in the proceeding under the Bankruptcy Act or receivership proceeding, a copy of the Tax Court's decision may be filed by the district director with the court in which such proceeding is pending.

(c) While a district director is required by section 6871(a) and paragraph (a) of §301.6871(a)-1 to make immediate assessment of any deficiency, such assessment is not made as a jeopardy assessment within the meaning of section 6861, and consequently the provisions of that section do not apply to any assessment made under section 6871. Therefore, the notice of deficiency provided in section 6861(b) will not be mailed. Although such notice will not be issued, a letter will be sent to the taxpayer or to the trustee, receiver, debtor in possession, or other like fiduciary, notifying him in detail how the deficiency was computed, that he may furnish evidence showing wherein the deficiency is incorrect, and that upon request he will be granted a conference by the district director with respect to such deficiency. However, such letter will not provide for such a conference where a petition was filed with the Tax Court before (1) the adjudication of bankruptcy in a liquidating proceeding, (2) the filing with a court of competent jurisdiction or (where approval is required by the Bankruptcy Act), the approval of a petition of, or the approval of a petition against, any taxpayer in any other proceeding under the Bankruptcy Act, or (3) the appointment of a receiver. [Reg. §301.6871(b)-1.]

☐ [T.D. 6227, 3-29-57. *Amended by T.D.* 6425, 11-10-59 *and T.D.* 6498, 10-24-60.]

## [Reg. §301.6872-1]

**§301.6872-1. Suspension of running of period of limitations on assessment.**—If any fiduciary in any proceeding under the Bankruptcy Act (11 U.S.C. chs. 1-14), including a trustee, receiver, or debtor in possession or a receiver in any other court proceeding is required, pursuant to section 6036, to give notice in writing to the district director of his qualification as such, then the running of the period of limitations on assessment shall be suspended from the date the proceeding is instituted to the date such notice is received by the district director, and for an additional 30 days thereafter. However, the suspension under this section of the running of the period of limitation on assessment shall in no case exceed 2 years. [Reg. §301.6872-1.]

☐ [*T.D. 6227, 3-29-57. Amended by T.D. 6948, 10-24-60.*]

### [Reg. §301.6873-1]

**§301.6873-1. Unpaid claims in bankruptcy or receivership proceedings.**—(a) If any portion of the claim allowed by the court in a receivership proceeding, or in any proceeding under the Bankruptcy Act (11 U.S.C. chs. 1-14), remains unpaid after the termination of such proceeding, the district director will send notice and demand for payment thereof to the taxpayer. Such unpaid portion with interest as provided in section 6601 may be collected from the taxpayer by levy or proceeding in court within the period of limitation for collection after assessment. For the general rule as to such period of limitation, see section 6502, and for suspensions of the running of the period provided in section 6502, see, for example, section 6503. For suspensions under other provisions of law, see, for example,

section 11f of the Bankruptcy Act (11 U.S.C. 29(f)). Extension of time for the payment of such unpaid amount may be granted in the same manner and subject to the same provisions and limitations as provided in section 6161(c).

(b) Section 6873 is applicable only where a claim for taxes is allowed in a receivership proceeding or in a proceeding under the Bankruptcy Act. Claims for taxes, interest, additional amounts, or additions to the tax may be collectible in equity or under other provisions of law although no claim was allowed in the proceeding because, for example, such items were not included in a proof of claim filed in the proceeding or no proof of claim was filed. Except in the case of a proceeding under section 77 or chapter X of the Bankruptcy Act, a tax or a liability in respect thereof is not discharged by a proceeding under such Act, whether or not a claim is filed in such proceeding, and provisions suspending the running of the period of limitation on the collection of taxes are applicable, whether or not a claim is filed in such proceeding. [Reg. §301.6873-1.]

☐ [*T.D. 6227, 3-29-57.*]

# Transferees and Fiduciaries

See p. 20,601 for regulations not amended to reflect law changes

### [Reg. §301.6901-1]

**§301.6901-1. Procedure in the case of transferred assets.**—(a) *Method of collection.*—(1) *Income, estate, and gift taxes.*—The amount for which a transferee of property of—

(i) A taxpayer, in the case of a tax imposed by subtitle A (relating to income taxes),

(ii) A decedent, in the case of the estate tax imposed by chapter 11 of the Code, or

(iii) A donor, in the case of the gift tax imposed by chapter 12 of the Code, is liable, at law or in equity, and the amount of the personal liability of a fiduciary under section 3467 of the Revised Statutes, as amended (31 U.S.C. 192), in respect of the payment of such taxes, whether shown on the return of the taxpayer or determined as a deficiency in the tax, shall be assessed against such transferee or fiduciary and paid and collected in the same manner and subject to the same provisions and limitations as in the case of a deficiency in the tax with respect to which such liability is incurred, except as hereinafter provided.

(2) *Other taxes.*—The liability, at law or in equity, of a transferee of property of any person liable in respect of any other tax, in any case where the liability of the transferee arises on the liquidation of a corporation or partnership, or a corporate reorganization within the meaning of section 368(a), shall be assessed against such transferee and paid and collected in the same manner and subject to the same provisions and limitations as in the case of the tax with respect to which such liability is incurred, except as hereinafter provided.

(3) *Applicable provisions.*—The provisions of the Code made applicable by section 6901(a) to the liability of a transferee or fiduciary referred to in subparagraphs (1) and (2) of this paragraph include the provisions relating to:

(i) Delinquency in payment after notice and demand and the amount of interest attaching because of such delinquency;

(ii) The authorization of distraint and proceedings in court for collection;

(iii) The prohibition of claims and suits for refund; and

(iv) In any instance in which the liability of a transferee or fiduciary is one referred to in subparagraph (1) of this paragraph, the filing of a petition with the Tax Court of the United States and the filing of a petition for review of the Tax Court's decision.
For detailed provisions relating to assessments, collections, and refunds, see chapters 63, 64, and 65 of the Code, respectively.

(b) *Definition of transferee.*—As used in this section, the term "transferee" includes an heir, legatee, devisee, distributee of an estate of a deceased person, the shareholder of a dissolved corporation, the assignee or donee of an insolvent person, the successor of a corporation, a party to a reorganization as defined in section 368, and all other classes of distributees. Such term also includes, with respect to the gift tax, a donee (without regard to the solvency of the donor) and, with respect to the estate tax, any person who, under section 6324(a)(2), is personally liable for any part of such tax.

(c) *Period of limitation on assessment.*—The period of limitation for assessment of the liability of a transferee or of a fiduciary is as follows:

(1) *Initial transferee.*—In the case of the liability of an initial transferee, one year after the expiration of the period of limitation for assessment against the taxpayer in the case of a tax imposed by

subtitle A (relating to income taxes), the executor in the case of the estate tax imposed by Chapter 11, or the donor in the case of the gift tax imposed by Chapter 12, each of which for purposes of this section is referred to as the "taxpayer" (see subchapter A of Chapter 66 of the Code).

(2) *Transferee of transferee.*—In the case of the liability of a transferee of a transferee, one year after the expiration of the period of limitation for assessment against the preceding transferee, or three years after the expiration of the period of limitation for assessment against the taxpayer, whichever of such periods first expires.

(3) *Court proceeding against taxpayer or last preceding transferee.*—If, before the expiration of the period specified in subparagraph (1) or subparagraph (2) of this paragraph (whichever is applicable), a court proceeding against the taxpayer or last preceding transferee for the collection of the tax or liability in respect thereof, respectively, has been begun within the period of limitation for the commencement of such proceeding, then within one year after the return of execution in such proceeding.

(4) *Fiduciary.*—In the case of the liability of a fiduciary, not later than one year after the liability arises or not later than the expiration of the period for collection of the tax in respect of which such liability arises, whichever is later.

(d) *Extension by agreement.*—(1) *Extension of time for assessment.*—The time prescribed by section 6901 for the assessment of the liability of a transferee or fiduciary may, prior to the expiration of such time, be extended for any period of time agreed upon in writing by the transferee or fiduciary and the district director or an assistant regional commissioner. The extension shall become effective when the agreement has been executed by both parties. The period agreed upon may be extended by subsequent agreements in writing made before the expiration of the period previously agreed upon.

(2) *Extension of time for credit or refund.*—(i) For the purpose of determining the period of limitation on credit or refund to the transferee or fiduciary of overpayments made by such transferee or fiduciary or overpayments made by the taxpayer to which such transferee or fiduciary may be legally entitled to credit or refund, an agreement and any extension thereof referred to in subparagraph (1) of this paragraph shall be deemed an agreement and extension thereof for purposes of section 6511(c) (relating to limitations on credit or refund in case of extension of time by agreement).

(ii) For the purpose of determining the limit specified in section 6511(c)(2) on the amount of the credit or refund, if the agreement is executed after the expiration of the period of limitation for assessment against the taxpayer with reference to whom the liability of such transferee or fiduciary arises, the periods specified in section 6511(b)(2) shall be increased by the period from the date of such expiration to the date the agreement is executed. The application of this subdivision may be illustrated by the following example:

*Example.* Assume that Corporation A files its income tax return on March 15, 1955, for the calendar year 1954, showing a liability of $100,000 which is paid with the return. The period within which an assessment may be made against Corporation A expires on March 15, 1958. Corporation B is a transferee of Corporation A. An agreement is executed on October 9, 1958, extending beyond its normal expiration date of March 15, 1959, the period within which an assessment may be made against Corporation B. Under section 6511(c)(2) and section 6511(b)(2)(A) the portion of an overpayment, paid before the execution of an agreement extending the period for assessment, may not be credited or refunded unless paid within three years prior to the date on which the agreement is executed. However, as applied to Corporation B such 3-year period is increased under section 6901(d)(2) to include the period from March 15, 1958, to October 9, 1958, the date on which the agreement was executed.

(e) *Period of assessment against taxpayer.*—For the purpose of determining the period of limitation for assessment against a transferee or a fiduciary, if the taxpayer is deceased, or, in the case of a corporation, has terminated its existence, the period of limitation for assessment against the taxpayer shall be the period that would be in effect had the death or termination of existence not occurred.

(f) *Suspension of running of period of limitations.*—In the cases of the income, estate, and gift taxes, if a notice of the liability of a transferee or the liability of a fiduciary has been mailed to such transferee or to such fiduciary under the provisions of section 6212, then the running of the statute of limitations shall be suspended for the period during which assessment is prohibited in respect of the liability of the transferee or fiduciary (and in any event, if a proceeding in respect of the liability is placed on the docket of the Tax Court, until the decision of the Tax Court becomes final), and for 60 days thereafter. [Reg. §301.6901-1.]

☐ [*T.D. 6246, 8-2-57. Amended by T.D. 6498, 10-24-60 and T.D. 6585, 12-27-61.*]

### [Reg. §301.6902-1]

§301.6902-1. Burden of proof.—In proceedings before the Tax Court the burden of proof shall be upon the Commissioner to show that a petitioner is liable as a transferee of property of a taxpayer, but not to show that the taxpayer was liable for the tax. [Reg. §301.6902-1.]

☐ [*T.D. 6246, 8-2-57.*]

### [Reg. §301.6903-1]

§301.6903-1. Notice of fiduciary relationship.—(a) *Rights and obligations of fiduciary.*—Every person acting for another person in a fiduciary capacity shall give notice thereof to the district director in writing. As soon as such notice is filed with the district director such fiduciary must, except as otherwise specifically provided, assume the powers, rights, duties, and privileges of the taxpayer with respect to the taxes imposed by the Code. If the person is acting as a fiduciary for a transferee or other person subject to the liability specified in section 6901, such fiduciary is required to assume the powers, rights, duties, and privileges of the transferee or other person under that section. The amount of the tax or liability is ordinarily not collectible from the personal estate of the fiduciary but is collectible from the estate of the taxpayer or from the estate of the transferee or other person subject to the liability specified in section 6901.

(b) *Manner of notice.*—(1) *Notices filed before April 24, 2002.*—This paragraph (b)(1) applies to notices filed before April 24, 2002. The notice shall be signed by the fiduciary, and shall be filed with the Internal Revenue Service office where the return of the person for whom the fiduciary is acting is required to be filed. The notice must state the name and address of the person for whom the fiduciary is acting, and the nature of the liability of such person; that is, whether it is a liability for tax, and, if so, the type of tax, the year or years involved, or a liability at law or in equity of a transferee of property of a taxpayer, or a liability of a fiduciary under section 3467 of the Revised Statutes, as amended (31 U.S.C. 192) in respect of the payment of any tax from the estate of the taxpayer. Satisfactory evidence of the authority of the fiduciary to act for any other person in a fiduciary capacity must be filed with and made a part of the notice. If the fiduciary capacity exists by order of court, a certified copy of the order may be regarded as satisfactory evidence. When the fiduciary capacity has terminated, the fiduciary, in order to be relieved of any further duty or liability as such, must file with the Internal Revenue Service office with whom the notice of fiduciary relationship was filed written notice that the fiduciary capacity has terminated as to him, accompanied by satisfactory evidence of the termination of the fiduciary capacity. The notice of termination should state the name and address of the person, if any, who has been substituted as fiduciary. Any written notice disclosing a fiduciary relationship which has been filed with the Commissioner under the Internal Revenue Code of 1939 or any prior revenue law shall be considered as sufficient notice within the meaning of section 6903. Any satisfactory evidence of the authority of the fiduciary to act for another person already filed with the Commissioner or district director need not be resubmitted.

(2) *Notices filed on or after April 24, 2002.*—This paragraph (b)(2) applies to notices filed on or after April 24, 2002. The notice shall be signed by the fiduciary, and shall be filed with the Internal Revenue

Service Center where the return of the person for whom the fiduciary is acting is required to be filed. The notice must state the name and address of the person for whom the fiduciary is acting, and the nature of the liability of such person; that is, whether it is a liability for tax, and if so, the type of tax, the year or years involved, or a liability at law or in equity of a transferee of property of a taxpayer, or a liability of a fiduciary under 31 U.S.C. 3713(b), in respect of the payment of any tax from the estate of the taxpayer. The fiduciary must retain satisfactory evidence of his or her authority to act for any other person in a fiduciary capacity as long as the evidence may become material in the administration of any internal revenue law.

(c) *Where notice is not filed.*—If the notice of the fiduciary capacity described in paragraph (b) of this section is not filed with the district director before the sending of notice of a deficiency by registered mail or certified mail to the last known address of the taxpayer (see section 6212), or the last known address of the transferee or other person subject to liability (see section 6901(g)), no notice of the deficiency will be sent to the fiduciary. For further guidance regarding the definition of last known address, see §301.6212-2. In such a case the sending of the notice to the last known address of the taxpayer, transferee, or other person, as the case may be, will be a sufficient compliance with the requirements of the Code, even though such taxpayer, transferee, or other person is deceased, or is under a legal disability, or, in the case of a corporation, has terminated its existence. Under such circumstances, if no petition is filed with the Tax Court of the United States within 90 days after the mailing of the notice (or within 150 days after mailing in the case of such a notice addressed to a person outside the States of the Union and the District of Columbia) to the taxpayer, transferee, or other person, the tax, or liability under section 6901, will be assessed immediately upon the expiration of such 90-day or 150-day period, and demand for payment will be made. See paragraph (a) of §301.6213-1 with respect to the expiration of such 90-day or 150-day period.

(d) *Definition of fiduciary.*—The term "fiduciary" is defined in section 7701(a)(6) to mean a guardian, trustee, executor, administrator, receiver, conservator, or any person acting in any fiduciary capacity for any person.

(e) *Applicability of other provisions.*—This section, relating to the provisions of section 6903, shall not be taken to abridge in any way the powers and duties of fiduciaries provided for in other sections of the Code. [Reg. §301.6903-1.]

☐ [*T.D. 6246, 8-2-57. Amended by T.D. 6498, 10-24-60; T.D. 6585, 12-27-61; T.D. 8939, 1-11-2001; T.D. 8989, 4-23-2002 and T.D. 9040, 1-30-2003.*]

### [Reg. §20.6905-1]

§20.6905-1. Discharge of executor from personal liability for decedent's income and gift taxes.—For regulations concerning the discharge of an executor from personal liability for a decedent's income and gift taxes, see §301.6905-1 of this chapter (Regulations on Procedure and Administration). [Reg. §20.6905-1.]

☐ [*T.D. 7238, 12-28-72.*]

### [Reg. §25.6905-1]

§25.6905-1. Discharge of executor from personal liability for decedent's income and gift taxes.—For regulations concerning the discharge of an executor from personal liability for a decedent's income and gift taxes, see §301.6905-1 of this chapter (Regulations on Procedure and Administration). [Reg. §25.6905-1.]

☐ [*T.D. 7238, 12-28-72.*]

### [Reg. §301.6905-1]

§301.6905-1. Discharge of executor from personal liability for decedent's income and gift taxes.—(a) *Discharge of liability.*—With respect to decedents dying after December 31, 1970, the executor of a decedent's estate may make written application to the applicable internal revenue officer with whom the estate tax return is required to be filed, as provided in §20.6091-1 of this chapter, for a determination of the income or gift taxes imposed upon the decedent by subtitle A or by chapter 12 of the Code, and for a discharge of personal liability therefrom. If no estate tax return is required to be filed, then such application should be filed where the decedent's final income tax return is required to be filed. The application must be filed after the return with respect to such income or gift taxes is filed. Within 9 months (1 year with respect to the estate of a decedent dying before January 1, 1974) after receipt of the application, the executor shall be notified of the amount of the income or gift tax and, upon payment thereof, he will be discharged from personal liability for any deficiency in income or gift tax thereafter found to be due. If no such notification is received, the executor is discharged at the end of such 9-month (1 year with respect to the estate of a decedent dying before January 1, 1974) period from personal liability for any deficiency thereafter found to be due. The discharge of the executor under this section from personal liability applies only to him in his personal capacity and to his personal assets. The discharge is not applicable to his liability as executor to the extent of the assets of the estate in his possession or control. Further, the discharge does not operate as a release of any part of the property from the lien provided under section 6321 or the special lien provided under subsection (a) or (b) of section 6324.

(b) *Definition of "executor.".*—For purposes of this section, the term "executor" means the executor or administrator of the decedent appointed, qualified, and acting within the United States.

(c) *Cross reference.*—For provisions concerning the discharge of the executor from personal liability for estate taxes imposed by chapter 11 of the Code, see section 2204 and the regulations thereunder. [Reg. §301.6905-1.]

☐ [T.D. 7238, 12-28-72.]

# Licensing and Registration

### [Reg. §301.7001-1]

§301.7001-1. **License to collect foreign items.**—(a) *In general.*—Any bank or agent undertaking as a matter of business or for profit the collection of foreign items must obtain a license from the district director for the district in which is located its principal place of business within the United States. For definitions of the terms "foreign item" and "collection", see paragraph (b) of this section.

(b) *Definitions.*—(1) *Foreign item.*—The term "foreign item", as used in this section, means any item of interest upon the bonds of a foreign country or of a nonresident foreign corporation not having a fiscal or paying agent in the United States (including Puerto Rico as if a part of the United States), or any item of dividends upon the stock of such corporation.

(2) *Collection.*—The term "collection", as used in this section, includes the following:

(i) The payment by the licensee of the foreign item in cash;

(ii) The crediting by the licensee of the account of the person presenting the foreign item;

(iii) The tentative crediting by the licensee of the account of the person presenting the foreign item until the amount of the foreign item is received by the licensee from abroad; and

(iv) The receipt of foreign items by the licensee for the purpose of transmitting them abroad for deposits.

(c) *Application for license.*—Application for the license required by paragraph (a) of this section shall be made in writing and shall contain the following information:

(1) The name and present business of the person, partnership (including names of all partners), or corporation applying for the license;

(2) The address of the applicant's principal place of business in the United States and of any branch offices in the United States;

(3) The date on which the applicant intends to commence the collection of foreign items; and

(4) An estimate of the aggregate amount of annual collections of foreign items (in dollars).

The application shall be signed by the applicant (a partner, in the case of a partnership, or an officer, in the case of a corporation).

(d) *Issuance of license.*—The license will be issued by the district director in letter form without cost to the licensee.

(e) *Previous license holders.*—Any person who has been issued a license under the corresponding provision of the Internal Revenue Code of 1939, or any prior revenue law, is not required to renew such license under this section.

(f) *Returns of information as to foreign items.*—For provisions relating to the filing of returns as to foreign items, see section 6041(b) and §1.6041-4 of this chapter (Income Tax Regulations). [Reg. §301.7001-1.]

☐ [T.D. 6450, 2-3-60. *Amended by T.D. 6498, 10-24-60.*]

# Bonds

### [Reg. §20.7101-1]

§20.7101-1. **Form of bonds.**—See paragraph (b) of §20.6165-1 for provisions relating to the bond required in any case in which the payment of the tax attributable to a reversionary or remainder interest has been postponed under the provisions of §20.6163-1. For further provisions relating to bonds, see §20.6165-1 of these regulations and the regulations under section 7101 contained in Part 301 of this chapter (Regulations on Procedure and Administration). [Reg. §20.7101-1.]

☐ [T.D. 6296, 6-23-58. *Amended by T.D. 6600, 5-28-62.*]

### [Reg. §25.7101-1]

§25.7101-1. **Form of bonds.**—For provisions relating to form of bonds, see the regulations under section 7101 contained in Part 301 of this chapter (Regulations on Procedure and Administration). [Reg. §25.7101-1.]

☐ [T.D. 6334, 10-14-58. *Amended by T.D. 6600, 5-28-62.*]

### [Reg. §53.7101-1]

§53.7101-1. **Form of bonds.**—For provisions relating to form of bonds, see the regulations under section 7101 contained in Part 301 of this chapter (Regulations on Procedure and Administration). [Reg. §53.7101-1.]

☐ [T.D. 7368, 7-15-75.]

### [Reg. §301.7101-1]

§301.7101-1. **Form of bond and surety required.**—(a) *In general.*—Any person required to furnish a bond under the provisions of the Code (other than section 6803(a)(1), relating to bonds required of certain postmasters before June 6, 1972, and section 7485, relating to bonds to stay assessment and collection of a deficiency pending review of a Tax Court decision), or under any rules or regulations

prescribed under the Code, shall (except as provided in paragraph (d) of this section) execute such bond;

(1) On the appropriate form prescribed by the Internal Revenue Service (which may be obtained from the district director), and

(2) With satisfactory surety.

For provisions as to what will be considered "satisfactory surety", see paragraph (b) of this section. The bonds referred to in this paragraph shall be drawn in favor of the United States.

(b) *Satisfactory surety.*—(1) *Approved surety company or bonds or notes of the United States.*—For purposes of paragraph (a) of this section, a bond shall be considered executed with satisfactory surety if:

(i) It is executed by a surety company holding a certificate of authority from the Secretary as an acceptable surety on Federal bonds; or

(ii) It is secured by bonds or notes of the United States as provided in 6 U.S.C. 15 (see 31 CFR Part 225).

(2) *Other surety acceptable in discretion of district director.*—Unless otherwise expressly provided in the Code, or the regulations thereunder, a bond may, in the discretion of the district director, be considered executed with satisfactory surety if, in lieu of being executed or secured as provided in subparagraph (1) of this paragraph, it is—

(i) Executed by a corporate surety (other than a surety company), provided such corporate surety establishes that it is within its corporate powers to act as surety for another corporation or an individual;

(ii) Executed by two or more individual sureties, provided such individual sureties meet the conditions contained in subparagraph (3) of this paragraph;

(iii) Secured by a mortgage on real or personal property;

(iv) Secured by a certified, cashier's, or treasurer's check drawn on any bank or trust company incorporated under the laws of the United States or any State, Territory, or possession of the United

States, or by a United States postal, bank, express, or telegraph money order;

(v) Secured by corporate bonds or stocks, or by bonds issued by a State or political subdivision thereof, of recognized stability; or

(vi) Secured by any other acceptable collateral.

Collateral shall be deposited with the district director or, in his discretion, with a responsible financial institution acting as escrow agent.

(3) *Conditions to be met by individual sureties.*—If a bond is executed by two or more individual sureties, the following conditions must be met by each such individual surety:

(i) He must reside within the State in which the principal place of business or legal residence of the primary obligor is located;

(ii) He must have property subject to execution of a current market value, above all encumbrances, equal to at least the penalty of the bond;

(iii) All real property which he offers as security must be located in the State in which the principal place of business or legal residence of the primary obligor is located;

(iv) He must agree not to mortgage, or otherwise encumber, any property offered as security while the bond continues in effect without first securing the permission of the district director; and

(v) He must file with the bond, and annually thereafter so long as the bond continues in effect, an affidavit as to the adequacy of his security, executed on the appropriate form furnished by the district director.

Partners may not act as sureties upon bonds of their partnership. Stockholders of a corporate principal may be accepted as sureties provided their qualifications as such are independent of their holding of the stock of the corporation.

(4) *Adequacy of surety.*—No surety or security shall be accepted if it does not adequately protect the interest of the United States.

(c) *Bonds required by Internal Revenue Code of 1939.*—This section shall also apply in the case of bonds required under the Internal Revenue Code of 1939 (other than sections 1423(b) and 1145) or under the regulations under such Code.

(d) *Bonds required under subtitle E and chapter 75 of the Internal Revenue Code of 1954.*—Bonds required under subtitle E and chapter 75, subtitle F, of the Internal Revenue Code of 1954 (or under the corresponding provisions of the Internal Revenue Code of 1939) shall be in such form and with such surety or sureties as are prescribed in the regulations in Subchapter E of this Chapter (Alcohol, Tobacco, and other Excise Taxes). [Reg. § 301.7101-1.]

☐ [*T.D.* 6443, 1-7-60. *Amended by T.D.* 6498, 10-24-60 *and T.D.* 7239, 12-27-72.]

**[Reg. § 301.7102-1]**

**§ 301.7102-1. Single bond in lieu of multiple bonds.**—(a) *In general.*—Except as provided in paragraph (b) of this section, a person who is required, or authorized, under the Internal Revenue Code of 1954 (other than sections 6803(a)(1) and 7485), or under any rules or regulations under the Code, to execute two or more bonds may, in the discretion of the district director, furnish a single bond in lieu of such two or more bonds but only if such single bond meets all the conditions and requirements prescribed for each of the separate bonds which it replaces. This section shall also apply in the case of bonds required or authorized under the Internal Revenue Code of 1939 (other than sections 1423(b) and 1145) or under the regulations under such Code.

(b) *Bonds required under subtitle E and chapter 75 of the Internal Revenue Code of 1954.*—In the case of bonds required under subtitle E and chapter 75, subtitle F, of the Internal Revenue Code of 1954 (or under the corresponding provisions of the Internal Revenue Code of 1939), a single bond will not be accepted in lieu of two or more bonds except as provided in the regulations in Subchapter E of this Chapter (Alcohol, Tobacco, and other Excise Taxes). [Reg. § 301.7102-1.]

☐ [*T.D.* 6443, 1-7-60. *Amended by T.D.* 6498, 10-24-60.]

# Closing Agreements and Compromises

See p. 20,601 for regulations not amended to reflect law changes

**[Reg. § 301.7121-1]**

**§ 301.7121-1. Closing agreements.**—(a) *In general.*—The Commissioner may enter into a written agreement with any person relating to the liability of such person (or of the person or estate for whom he acts) in respect of any internal revenue tax for any taxable period ending prior or subsequent to the date of such agreement. A closing agreement may be entered into in any case in which there appears to be an advantage in having the case permanently and conclusively closed, or if good and sufficient reasons are shown by the taxpayer for desiring a closing agreement and it is determined by the Commissioner that the United States will sustain no disadvantage through consummation of such an agreement.

(b) *Scope of closing agreement.*—(1) *In general.*—A closing agreement may be executed even though under the agreement the taxpayer is not liable for any tax for the period to which the agreement relates. There may be a series of closing agreements relating to the tax liability for a single period.

(2) *Taxable periods ended prior to due date of closing agreement.*—Closing agreements with respect to taxable periods ended prior to the date of the agreement may relate to the total tax liability of the taxpayer or to one or more separate items affecting the tax liability of the taxpayer, as, for example, the amount of gross income, deduction for losses, depreciation, depletion, the year in which an item of income is to be included in gross income, the year in which an item of loss is to be deducted, or the value of property on a specific date. A closing agreement may also be entered into for the purpose of allowing a deficiency dividend deduction under section 547. In addition, a closing agreement constitutes a determination as defined by section 1313.

(3) *Taxable periods ending subsequent to date of closing agreement.*—Closing agreements with respect to taxable periods ending subsequent to the date of the agreement may relate to one or more separate items affecting the tax liability of the taxpayer.

(4) *Illustration.*—The provisions of this paragraph may be illustrated by the following example:

*Example.* A owns 500 shares of stock in the XYZ Corporation which he purchased prior to March 1, 1913. A is considering selling 200 shares of such stock but is uncertain as to the basis of the stock for the purpose of computing gain. Either prior or subsequent to the sale, a closing agreement may be entered into determining the market value of such stock as of March 1, 1913, which represents the basis for determining gain if it exceeds the adjusted basis otherwise determined as of such date. Not only may the closing agreement determine the basis for computing gain on the sale of the 200 shares of stock, but such an agreement may also determine the basis (unless or until the law is changed to require the use of some other factor to determine basis) of the remaining 300 shares of stock upon which gain will be computed in a subsequent sale.

(c) *Finality.*—A closing agreement which is approved within such time as may be stated in such agreement, or later agreed to, shall be final and conclusive, and, except upon a showing of fraud or malfeasance, or misrepresentation of a material fact—

(1) The case shall not be reopened as to the matters agreed upon or the agreement modified by any officer, employee, or agent of the United States, and

(2) In any suit, action, or proceeding, such agreement, or any determination, assessment, collection, payment, abatement, refund, or credit made in accordance therewith, shall not be annulled, modified, set aside, or disregarded.

However, a closing agreement with respect to a taxable period ending subsequent to the date of the agreement is subject to any change in, or modification of, the law enacted subsequent to the date of the agreement and made applicable to such taxable period, and each closing agreement shall so recite.

(d) *Procedure with respect to closing agreements.*—(1) *Submission of request.*—A request for a closing agreement which relates to a prior taxable period may be submitted at any time before a case with respect to the tax liability involved is docketed in the Tax Court of the United States. All closing agreements shall be executed on forms prescribed by the Internal Revenue Service. The procedure with respect to request for closing agreements shall be under such rules as may be prescribed from time to time by the Commissioner in accordance with the regulations under this section.

(2) *Collection, credit, or refund.*—Any tax or deficiency in tax determined pursuant to a closing agreement shall be assessed and collected, and any overpayment determined pursuant thereto shall be credited or refunded, in accordance with the applicable provisions of law. [Reg. § 301.7121-1.]

☐ [*T.D.* 6450, 2-3-60. *Amended by T.D.* 6498, 10-24-60.]

**[Reg. § 301.7122-0]**

**§ 301.7122-0. Table of contents.**—This section lists the major captions that appear in the regulations under § 301.7122-1.

[Reg. § 301.7122-0.]

☐ [*T.D.* 9007, 7-18-2002.]

**[Reg. § 301.7122-1]**

**§ 301.7122-1. Compromises.**—**(a)** *In general.*—(1) If the Secretary determines that there are grounds for compromise under this section, the Secretary may, at the Secretary's discretion, compromise any civil or criminal liability arising under the internal revenue laws prior to reference of a case involving such a liability to the Department of Justice for prosecution or defense.

(2) An agreement to compromise may relate to a civil or criminal liability for taxes, interest, or penalties. Unless the terms of the offer and acceptance expressly provide otherwise, acceptance of an offer to compromise a civil liability does not remit a criminal liability, nor does acceptance of an offer to compromise a criminal liability remit a civil liability.

**(b)** *Grounds for compromise.*—(1) *Doubt as to liability.*—Doubt as to liability exists where there is a genuine dispute as to the existence or amount of the correct tax liability under the law. Doubt as to liability does not exist where the liability has been established by a final court decision or judgment concerning the existence or amount of the liability. See paragraph (f)(4) of this section for special rules applicable to rejection of offers in cases where the Internal Revenue Service (IRS) is unable to locate the taxpayer's return or return information to verify the liability.

(2) *Doubt as to collectibility.*—Doubt as to collectibility exists in any case where the taxpayer's assets and income are less than the full amount of the liability.

(3) *Promote effective tax administration.*—(i) A compromise may be entered into to promote effective tax administration when the Secretary determines that, although collection in full could be achieved, collection of the full liability would cause the taxpayer economic hardship within the meaning of § 301.6343-1.

(ii) If there are no grounds for compromise under paragraphs (b)(1), (2), or (3)(i) of this section, the IRS may compromise to promote effective tax administration where compelling public policy or equity considerations identified by the taxpayer provide a sufficient basis for compromising the liability. Compromise will be justified only where, due to exceptional circumstances, collection of the full liability would undermine public confidence that the tax laws are being administered in a fair and equitable manner. A taxpayer proposing compromise under this paragraph (b)(3)(ii) will be expected to demonstrate circumstances that justify compromise even though a similarly situated taxpayer may have paid his liability in full.

(iii) No compromise to promote effective tax administration may be entered into if compromise of the liability would undermine compliance by taxpayers with the tax laws.

**(c)** *Special rules for evaluating offers to compromise.*—(1) *In general.*—Once a basis for compromise under paragraph (b) of this section has been identified, the decision to accept or reject an offer to compromise, as well as the terms and conditions agreed to, is left to the discretion of the Secretary. The determination whether to accept or reject an offer to compromise will be based upon consideration of all the facts and circumstances, including whether the circumstances of a particular case warrant acceptance of an amount that might not otherwise be acceptable under the Secretary's policies and procedures.

(2) *Doubt as to collectibility.*—(i) *Allowable Expenses.*—A determination of doubt as to collectibility will include a determination of ability to pay. In determining ability to pay, the Secretary will permit taxpayers to retain sufficient funds to pay basic living expenses. The determination of the amount of such basic living expenses will be founded upon an evaluation of the individual facts and circumstances presented by the taxpayer's case. To guide this determination, guidelines published by the Secretary on national and local living expense standards will be taken into account.

(ii) *Nonliable spouses.*—(A) *In general.*—Where a taxpayer is offering to compromise a liability for which the taxpayer's spouse has no liability, the assets and income of the nonliable spouse will not be considered in determining the amount of an adequate offer. The assets and income of a nonliable spouse may be considered, however, to the extent property has been transferred by the taxpayer to the nonliable spouse under circumstances that would permit the IRS to effect collection of the taxpayer's liability from such property (e.g., property that was conveyed in fraud of creditors), property has been transferred by the taxpayer to the nonliable spouse for the purpose of removing the property from consideration by the IRS in evaluating the compromise, or as provided in paragraph (c)(2)(ii)(B) of this section. The IRS also may request information regarding the assets and income of the nonliable spouse for the purpose of verifying the amount of and responsibility for expenses claimed by the taxpayer.

(B) *Exception.*—Where collection of the taxpayer's liability from the assets and income of the nonliable spouse is permitted by applicable state law (e.g., under state community property laws), the assets and income of the nonliable spouse will be considered in determining the amount of an adequate offer except to the extent that the taxpayer and the nonliable spouse demonstrate that collection of such assets and income would have a material and adverse impact on the standard of living of the taxpayer, the nonliable spouse, and their dependents.

(3) *Compromises to promote effective tax administration.*—(i) Factors supporting (but not conclusive of) a determination that collection would cause economic hardship within the meaning of paragraph (b)(3)(i) of this section include, but are not limited to—

(A) Taxpayer is incapable of earning a living because of a long term illness, medical condition, or disability, and it is reasonably foreseeable that taxpayer's financial resources will be exhausted providing for care and support during the course of the condition;

(B) Although taxpayer has certain monthly income, that income is exhausted each month in providing for the care of dependents with no other means of support; and

(C) Although taxpayer has certain assets, the taxpayer is unable to borrow against the equity in those assets and liquidation of those assets to pay outstanding tax liabilities would render the taxpayer unable to meet basic living expenses.

(ii) Factors supporting (but not conclusive of) a determination that compromise would undermine compliance within the meaning of paragraph (b)(3)(iii) of this section include, but are not limited to—

(A) Taxpayer has a history of noncompliance with the filing and payment requirements of the Internal Revenue Code;

(B) Taxpayer has taken deliberate actions to avoid the payment of taxes; and

(C) Taxpayer has encouraged others to refuse to comply with the tax laws.

(iii) The following examples illustrate the types of cases that may be compromised by the Secretary, at the Secretary's discretion, under the economic hardship provisions of paragraph (b)(3)(i) of this section:

*Example 1.* The taxpayer has assets sufficient to satisfy the tax liability. The taxpayer provides full time care and assistance to her dependent child, who has a serious long-term illness. It is expected that the taxpayer will need to use the equity in his assets to provide for adequate basic living expenses and medical care for his child. The taxpayer's overall compliance history does not weigh against compromise.

*Example 2.* The taxpayer is retired and his only income is from a pension. The taxpayer's only asset is a retirement account, and the funds in the account are sufficient to satisfy the liability. Liquidation of the retirement account would leave the taxpayer without an adequate means to provide for basic living expenses. The taxpayer's overall compliance history does not weigh against compromise.

*Example 3.* The taxpayer is disabled and lives on a fixed income that will not, after allowance of basic living expenses, permit full payment of his liability under an installment agreement. The taxpayer also owns a modest house that has been specially equipped to accommodate his disability. The taxpayer's equity in the house is sufficient to permit payment of the liability he owes. However, because of his disability and limited earning potential, the taxpayer is unable to obtain a mortgage or otherwise borrow against this equity. In addition, because the taxpayer's home has been specially equipped to accommodate his disability, forced sale of the taxpayer's residence would create severe adverse consequences for the taxpayer. The taxpayer's overall compliance history does not weigh against compromise.

(iv) The following examples illustrate the types of cases that may be compromised by the Secretary, at the Secretary's discretion, under the public policy and equity provisions of paragraph (b)(3)(ii) of this section:

*Example 1.* In October of 1986, the taxpayer developed a serious illness that resulted in almost continuous hospitalizations for a number of years. The taxpayer's medical condition was such that during this period the taxpayer was unable to manage any of his financial affairs. The taxpayer has not filed tax returns since that time. The taxpayer's health has now improved and he has promptly begun to attend to his tax affairs. He discovers that the IRS prepared a substitute for return for the 1986 tax year on the basis of information returns it had received and had assessed a tax deficiency. When the taxpayer discovered the liability, with penalties and interest, the tax bill is more than three times the original tax liability. The taxpayer's overall compliance history does not weigh against compromise.

*Example 2.* The taxpayer is a salaried sales manager at a department store who has been able to place $2,000 in a tax-deductible IRA account for each of the last two years. The taxpayer learns that he can earn a higher rate of interest on his IRA savings by moving those savings from a money management account to a certificate of deposit at a different financial institution. Prior to transferring his savings, the taxpayer submits an e-mail inquiry to the IRS at its Web Page, requesting information about the steps he must take to preserve the tax benefits he has enjoyed and to avoid penalties. The IRS responds in an answering e-mail that the taxpayer may withdraw his IRA savings from his neighborhood bank, but he must redeposit those savings in a new IRA account within 90 days. The taxpayer withdraws the funds and redeposits them in a new IRA account 63 days later. Upon audit, the taxpayer learns that he has been misinformed about the required rollover period and that he is liable for additional taxes, penalties and additions to tax for not having redeposited the amount within 60 days. Had it not been for the erroneous advice that is reflected in the taxpayer's retained copy of the IRS e-mail response to his inquiry, the taxpayer would have redeposited the amount within the required 60-day period. The taxpayer's overall compliance history does not weigh against compromise.

(d) *Procedures for submission and consideration of offers.*—(1) *In general.*—An offer to compromise a tax liability pursuant to section 7122 must be submitted according to the procedures, and in the form and manner, prescribed by the Secretary. An offer to compromise a tax liability must be made in writing, must be signed by the taxpayer under penalty of perjury, and must contain all of the information prescribed or requested by the Secretary. However, taxpayers submitting offers to compromise liabilities solely on the basis of doubt as to liability will not be required to provide financial statements.

(2) *When offers become pending and return of offers.*—An offer to compromise becomes pending when it is accepted for processing. The IRS may not accept for processing any offer to compromise a liability following reference of a case involving such liability to the Department of Justice for prosecution or defense. If an offer accepted for processing does not contain sufficient information to permit the IRS to evaluate whether the offer should be accepted, the IRS will request that the taxpayer provide the needed additional information. If the taxpayer does not submit the additional information that the IRS has requested within a reasonable time period after such a request, the IRS may return the offer to the taxpayer. The IRS may also return an offer to compromise a tax liability if it determines that the offer was submitted solely to delay collection or was otherwise nonprocessable. An offer returned following acceptance for processing is deemed pending only for the period between the date the offer is accepted for processing and the date the IRS returns the offer to the taxpayer. See paragraphs (f)(5)(ii) and (g)(4) of this section for rules regarding the effect of such returns of offers.

(3) *Withdrawal.*—An offer to compromise a tax liability may be withdrawn by the taxpayer or the taxpayer's representative at any time prior to the IRS' acceptance of the offer to compromise. An offer will be considered withdrawn upon the IRS' receipt of written notification of the withdrawal of the offer either by personal delivery or certified mail, or upon issuance of a letter by the IRS confirming the taxpayer's intent to withdraw the offer.

(e) *Acceptance of an offer to compromise a tax liability.*—(1) An offer to compromise has not been accepted until the IRS issues a written notification of acceptance to the taxpayer or the taxpayer's representative.

(2) As additional consideration for the acceptance of an offer to compromise, the IRS may request that taxpayer enter into any collateral agreement or post any security which is deemed necessary for the protection of the interests of the United States.

(3) Offers may be accepted when they provide for payment of compromised amounts in one or more equal or unequal installments.

(4) If the final payment on an accepted offer to compromise is contingent upon the immediate and simultaneous release of a tax lien in whole or in part, such payment must be made in accordance with the forms, instructions, or procedures prescribed by the Secretary.

(5) Acceptance of an offer to compromise will conclusively settle the liability of the taxpayer specified in the offer. Compromise with one taxpayer does not extinguish the liability of, nor prevent the IRS from taking action to collect from, any person not named in the offer who is also liable for the tax to which the compromise relates. Neither the taxpayer nor the Government will, following acceptance of an offer to compromise, be permitted to reopen the case except in instances where—

(i) False information or documents are supplied in conjunction with the offer;

(ii) The ability to pay or the assets of the taxpayer are concealed; or

(iii) A mutual mistake of material fact sufficient to cause the offer agreement to be reformed or set aside is discovered.

(6) *Opinion of Chief Counsel.*—Except as otherwise provided in this paragraph (e)(6), if an offer to compromise is accepted, there will be placed on file the opinion of the Chief Counsel for the IRS with respect to such compromise, along with the reasons therefor. However, no such opinion will be required with respect to the compromise of any civil case in which the unpaid amount of tax assessed (including any interest, additional amount, addition to the tax, or assessable penalty) is less than $50,000. Also placed on file will be a statement of—

(i) The amount of tax assessed;

(ii) The amount of interest, additional amount, addition to the tax, or assessable penalty, imposed by law on the person against whom the tax is assessed; and

(iii) The amount actually paid in accordance with the terms of the compromise.

(f) *Rejection of an offer to compromise.*—(1) An offer to compromise has not been rejected until the IRS issues a written notice to the taxpayer or his representative, advising of the rejection, the reason(s) for rejection, and the right to an appeal.

(2) The IRS may not notify a taxpayer or taxpayer's representative of the rejection of an offer to compromise until an independent administrative review of the proposed rejection is completed.

(3) No offer to compromise may be rejected solely on the basis of the amount of the offer without evaluating that offer under the provisions of this section and the Secretary's policies and procedures regarding the compromise of cases.

(4) *Offers based upon doubt as to liability.*—Offers submitted on the basis of doubt as to liability cannot be rejected solely because the IRS is unable to locate the taxpayer's return or return information for verification of the liability.

(5) *Appeal of rejection of an offer to compromise.*—(i) *In general.*—The taxpayer may administratively appeal a rejection of an offer to compromise to the IRS Office of Appeals (Appeals) if, within the 30-day period commencing the day after the date on the letter of rejection, the taxpayer requests such an administrative review in the manner provided by the Secretary.

(ii) *Offer to compromise returned following a determination that the offer was nonprocessable, a failure by the taxpayer to provide requested information, or a determination that the offer was submitted for purposes of delay.*—Where a determination is made to return offer documents because the offer to compromise was nonprocessable, because the taxpayer failed to provide requested information, or because the IRS determined that the offer to compromise was submitted solely for purposes of delay under paragraph (d)(2) of this section, the return of the offer does not constitute a rejection of the offer for purposes of this provision and does not entitle the taxpayer to appeal the matter to Appeals under the provisions of this paragraph (f)(5). However, if the offer is returned because the taxpayer failed to provide requested financial information, the offer will not be returned until a managerial review of the proposed return is completed.

(g) *Effect of offer to compromise on collection activity.*—(1) *In general.*—The IRS will not levy against the property or rights to property of a taxpayer who submits an offer to compromise, to collect the liability that is the subject of the offer, during the period the offer is pending, for 30 days immediately following the rejection of the offer, and for any period when a timely filed appeal from the rejection is being considered by Appeals.

(2) *Revised offers submitted following rejection.*—If, following the rejection of an offer to compromise, the taxpayer makes a good faith revision of that offer and submits the revised offer within 30 days

after the date of rejection, the IRS will not levy to collect from the taxpayer the liability that is the subject of the revised offer to compromise while that revised offer is pending.

(3) *Jeopardy.*—The IRS may levy to collect the liability that is the subject of an offer to compromise during the period the IRS is evaluating whether that offer will be accepted if it determines that collection of the liability is in jeopardy.

(4) *Offers to compromise determined by IRS to be nonprocessable or submitted solely for purposes of delay.*—If the IRS determines, under paragraph (d)(2) of this section, that a pending offer did not contain sufficient information to permit evaluation of whether the offer should be accepted, that the offer was submitted solely to delay collection, or that the offer was otherwise nonprocessable, then the IRS may levy to collect the liability that is the subject of that offer at any time after it returns the offer to the taxpayer.

(5) *Offsets under section 6402.*—Notwithstanding the evaluation and processing of an offer to compromise, the IRS may, in accordance with section 6402, credit any overpayments made by the taxpayer against a liability that is the subject of an offer to compromise and may offset such overpayments against other liabilities owed by the taxpayer to the extent authorized by section 6402.

(6) *Proceedings in court.*—Except as otherwise provided in this paragraph (g)(6), the IRS will not refer a case to the Department of Justice for the commencement of a proceeding in court, against a person named in a pending offer to compromise, if levy to collect the liability is prohibited by paragraph (g)(1) of this section. Without regard to whether a person is named in a pending offer to compromise, however, the IRS may authorize the Department of Justice to file a counterclaim or third-party complaint in a refund action or to join that person in any other proceeding in which liability for the tax that is the subject of the pending offer to compromise may be established or disputed, including a suit against the United States under 28 U.S.C. 2410. In addition, the United States may file a claim in any bankruptcy proceeding or insolvency action brought by or against such person.

(h) *Deposits.*—Sums submitted with an offer to compromise a liability or during the pendency of an offer to compromise are considered deposits and will not be applied to the liability until the offer is accepted unless the taxpayer provides written authorization for application of the payments. If an offer to compromise is withdrawn, is determined to be nonprocessable, or is submitted solely for purposes of delay and returned to the taxpayer, any amount tendered with the offer, including all installments paid on the offer, will be refunded without interest. If an offer is rejected, any amount tendered with the offer, including all installments paid on the offer, will be refunded, without interest, after the conclusion of any review sought by the taxpayer with Appeals. Refund will not be required if the taxpayer has agreed in writing that amounts tendered pursuant to the offer may be applied to the liability for which the offer was submitted.

(i) *Statute of limitations.*—(1) *Suspension of the statute of limitations on collection.*—The statute of limitations on collection will be suspended while levy is prohibited under paragraph (g)(1) of this section.

(2) *Extension of the statute of limitations on assessment.*—For any offer to compromise, the IRS may require, where appropriate, the extension of the statute of limitations on assessment. However, in any case where waiver of the running of the statutory period of limitations on assessment is sought, the taxpayer must be notified of the right to refuse to extend the period of limitations or to limit the extension to particular issues or particular periods of time.

(j) *Inspection with respect to accepted offers to compromise.*—For provisions relating to the inspection of returns and accepted offers to compromise, see section 6103(k)(1).

(k) *Effective date.*—This section applies to offers to compromise pending on or submitted on or after July 18, 2002. [Reg. § 301.7122-1.]

☐ [*T.D. 9007, 7-18-2002 (corrected 8-19-2002).*]

# Crimes, Other Offenses, and Forfeitures

## CRIMES

### General Provisions

See p. 20,601 for regulations not amended to reflect law changes

**[Reg. § 301.7207-1]**

**§ 301.7207-1. Fraudulent returns, statements, or other documents.**—Any person who willfully delivers or discloses to any officer or employee of the Internal Revenue Service any list, return, account, statement, or other document known by him to be fraudulent or to be false as to any material matter, shall be fined not more than $1,000, or imprisoned not more than 1 year, or both. Any person required pursuant to section 6047(b) or (c) or section 6104(d), to furnish information to any officer or employee of the Internal Revenue Service or any other person who willfully furnishes to such officer or employee of the Internal Revenue Service or such other person any information known by him to be fraudulent or to be false as to any material matter shall be fined not more than $1,000, or imprisoned not more than 1 year, or both. [Reg. § 301.7207-1.]

☐ [*T.D. 6498, 10-24-60. Amended by T.D. 6677, 9-16-63, T.D. 7127, 6-14-71, and T.D. 8026, 5-17-85.*]

**[Reg. § 301.7214-1]**

**§ 301.7214-1. Offenses by officers and employees of the United States.**—Any officer or employee of the United States acting in connection with any revenue law of the United States required to make a written report under the provisions of section 7214(a)(8) shall submit such report to the Commissioner, or to a regional commissioner or district director. [Reg. § 301.7214-1.]

☐ [*T.D. 6498, 10-24-60.*]

**[Reg. § 301.7216-0]**

**§ 301.7216-0. Table of contents.**—This section lists captions contained in §§ 301.7216-1 through 301.7216-3.

(d) *Effective date.*
[Reg. § 301.7216-0.]

☐ [*T.D. 9375, 1-3-2008. Amended by T.D. 9478, 12-29-2009 and T.D. 9608, 12-26-2012.*]

**[Reg. § 301.7216-1]**

**§ 301.7216-1. Penalty for disclosure or use of tax return information.**—(a) *In general.*—Section 7216(a) prescribes a criminal penalty for tax return preparers who knowingly or recklessly disclose or use tax return information for a purpose other than preparing a tax return. A violation of section 7216 is a misdemeanor, with a maximum penalty of up to one year imprisonment or a fine of not more than $1,000, or both, together with the costs of prosecution. Section 7216(b) establishes exceptions to the general rule in section 7216(a) prohibiting disclosure and use. Section 7216(b) also authorizes the Secretary to promulgate regulations prescribing additional permitted disclosures and uses. Section 6713(a) prescribes a related civil penalty for disclosures and uses that constitute a violation of section 7216. The penalty for violating section 6713 is $250 for each prohibited disclosure or use, not to exceed a total of $10,000 for a calendar year. Section 6713(b) provides that the exceptions in section 7216(b) also apply to section 6713. Under section 7216(b), the provisions of section 7216(a) will not apply to any disclosure or use permitted under regulations prescribed by the Secretary.

(b) *Definitions.*—For purposes of section 7216 and §§ 301.7216-1 through 301.7216-3:

(1) *Tax return.*—The term *tax return* means any return (or amended return) of income tax imposed by chapter 1 of the Internal Revenue Code.

(2) *Tax return preparer.*—(i) *In general.*—The term *tax return preparer* means:

(A) Any person who is engaged in the business of preparing or assisting in preparing tax returns;

(B) Any person who is engaged in the business of providing auxiliary services in connection with the preparation of tax returns, including a person who develops software that is used to prepare or file a tax return and any Authorized IRS *e-file* Provider;

(C) Any person who is otherwise compensated for preparing, or assisting in preparing, a tax return for any other person; or

(D) Any individual who, as part of their duties of employment with any person described in paragraph (b)(2)(i)(A), (B), or (C) of this section performs services that assist in the preparation of, or assist in providing auxiliary services in connection with the preparation of, a tax return.

(ii) *Business of preparing returns.*—A person is engaged in the business of preparing tax returns as described in paragraph (b)(2)(i)(A) of this section if, in the course of the person's business, the person holds himself out to tax return preparers or taxpayers as a person who prepares tax returns or assists in preparing tax returns, whether or not tax return preparation is the person's sole business activity and whether or not the person charges a fee for tax return preparation services.

(iii) *Providing auxiliary services.*—A person is engaged in the business of providing auxiliary services in connection with the preparation of tax returns as described in paragraph (b)(2)(i)(B) of this section if, in the course of the person's business, the person holds himself out to tax return preparers or to taxpayers as a person who performs auxiliary services, whether or not providing the auxiliary services is the person's sole business activity and whether or not the person charges a fee for the auxiliary services. Likewise, a person is engaged in the business of providing auxiliary services if, in the course of the person's business, the person receives a taxpayer's tax return information from another tax return preparer pursuant to the provisions of § 301.7216-2(d)(2).

(iv) *Otherwise compensated.*—A tax return preparer described in paragraph (b)(2)(i)(C) of this section includes any person who—

(A) Is compensated for preparing a tax return for another person, but not in the course of a business; or

(B) Is compensated for helping, on a casual basis, a relative, friend, or other acquaintance to prepare their tax return.

(v) *Exclusions.*—A person is not a tax return preparer merely because he leases office space to a tax return preparer, furnishes credit to a taxpayer whose tax return is prepared by a tax return preparer, furnishes information to a tax return preparer at the taxpayer's request, furnishes access (free or otherwise) to a separate person's tax return preparation website through a hyperlink on his own website, or otherwise performs some service that only incidentally relates to the preparation of tax returns.

(vi) *Examples.*—The application of § 301.7216-1(b)(2) may be illustrated by the following examples:

*Example 1.* Bank B is a tax return preparer within the meaning of paragraph (b)(2)(i)(A) of this section, and an Authorized IRS *e-file* Provider. B employs one individual, Q, to solicit the necessary tax return information for the preparation of a tax return; another individual, R, to prepare the return on the basis of the information that is furnished; a secretary, S, who types the information on the returns into a computer; and an administrative assistant, T, who uses a computer to file electronic versions of the tax returns. Under these circumstances, only R is a tax return preparer for purposes of section 7701(a)(36), but all four employees are tax return preparers for purposes of section 7216, as provided in paragraph (b) of this section.

*Example 2.* Tax return preparer P contracts with department store D to rent space in D's store. D advertises that taxpayers who use P's services may charge the cost of having their tax return prepared to their charge account with D. Under these circumstances, D is not a tax return preparer because it provides space, credit, and services only incidentally related to the preparation of tax returns.

(3) *Tax return information.*—(i) *In general.*—The term *tax return information* means any information, including, but not limited to, a taxpayer's name, address, or identifying number, which is furnished in any form or manner for, or in connection with, the preparation of a tax return of the taxpayer. This information includes information that the taxpayer furnishes to a tax return preparer and information furnished to the tax return preparer by a third party. Tax return information also includes information the tax return preparer derives or generates from tax return information in connection with the preparation of a taxpayer's return.

(A) Tax return information can be provided directly by the taxpayer or by another person. Likewise, tax return information includes information received by the tax return preparer from the IRS in connection with the processing of such return, including an acknowledgment of acceptance or notice of rejection of an electronically filed return.

(B) Tax return information includes statistical compilations of tax return information, even in a form that cannot be associated with, or otherwise identify, directly or indirectly, a particular taxpayer. See § 301.7216-2(o) for limited use of tax return information to make statistical compilations without taxpayer consent and to use the statistical compilations for limited purposes.

(C) Tax return information does not include information identical to any tax return information that has been furnished to a tax return preparer if the identical information was obtained otherwise than in connection with the preparation of a tax return.

(D) Information is considered "in connection with tax return preparation," and therefore tax return information, if the taxpayer would not have furnished the information to the tax return preparer but for the intention to engage, or the engagement of, the tax return preparer to prepare the tax return.

(ii) *Examples.*—The application of this paragraph (b)(3) may be illustrated by the following examples:

*Example 1.* Taxpayer A purchases computer software designed to assist with the preparation and filing of her income tax return. When A loads the software onto her computer, it prompts her to register her purchase of the software. In this situation, the software provider is a tax return preparer under paragraph (b)(2)(i)(B) of this section and the information that A provides to register her purchase is tax return information because she is providing it in connection with the preparation of a tax return.

*Example 2.* Corporation A is a brokerage firm that maintains a website through which its clients may access their accounts, trade stocks, and generally conduct a variety of financial activities. Through its website, A offers its clients free access to its own tax preparation software. Taxpayer B is a client of A and has furnished A his name, address, and other information when registering for use of A's website to use A's brokerage services. In addition, A has a record of B's brokerage account activity, including sales of stock, dividends paid, and IRA contributions made. B uses A's tax preparation software to prepare his tax return. The software populates some fields on B's return on the basis of information A already maintains in its databases. A is a tax return preparer within the meaning of paragraph (b)(2)(i)(B) of this section because it has prepared and provided software for use in preparing tax returns. The information in A's databases that the software accesses to populate B's return, *i.e.,* the registration information and brokerage account activity, is not tax return information because A did not receive that information in connection with the preparation of a tax return. Once A uses the information to populate the return, however, the information associated with the return becomes tax return information. If A retains the information in a form in which A can identify that the information was used in connection with the preparation of a return, the information in that form is tax return information. If, however, A retains the information in a database in which A cannot identify whether the information was used in connection with the preparation of a return, then that information is not tax return information.

(4) *Use.*—(i) *In general.*—Use of tax return information includes any circumstance in which a tax return preparer refers to, or relies upon, tax return information as the basis to take or permit an action.

(ii) *Example.*—The application of this paragraph (b)(4) may be illustrated by the following example:

*Example.* Preparer G is a tax return preparer as defined by paragraph (b)(2)(i)(A) of this section. If G determines, upon preparing a return, that the taxpayer is eligible to make a contribution to an individual retirement account (IRA), G will ask whether the taxpayer desires to make a contribution to an IRA. G does not ask about IRAs in cases in which the taxpayer is not eligible to make a contribution. G is using tax return information when it asks whether a taxpayer is interested in making a contribution to an IRA because G is basing the inquiry upon knowledge gained from information that the taxpayer furnished in connection with the preparation of the taxpayer's return.

(5) *Disclosure.*—The term *disclosure* means the act of making tax return information known to any person in any manner whatever. To the extent that a taxpayer's use of a hyperlink results in the transmission of tax return information, this transmission of tax return information is a disclosure by the tax return preparer subject to penalty under section 7216 if not authorized by regulation.

(6) *Hyperlink.*—For purposes of section 7216, a hyperlink is a device used to transfer an individual using tax preparation software from a tax return preparer's webpage to a webpage operated by another person without the individual having to separately enter the web address of the destination page.

(7) *Request for consent.*—A request for consent includes any effort by a tax return preparer to obtain the taxpayer's consent to use or disclose the taxpayer's tax return information. The act of supplying a taxpayer with a paper or electronic form that meets the requirements of a revenue procedure published pursuant to § 301.7216-3(a) is a request for a consent. When a tax return preparer requests a taxpayer's consent, any associated efforts of the tax return preparer, including, but not limited to, verbal or written explanations of the form, are part of the request for consent.

(c) *Gramm-Leach-Bliley Act.*—Any applicable requirements of the Gramm-Leach-Bliley Act, Public Law 106-102 (113 Stat. 1338), do not supersede, alter, or affect the requirements of section 7216 and §§ 301.7216-1 through 301.7216-3. Similarly, the requirements of section 7216 and §§ 301.7216-1 through 301.7216-3 do not override any requirements or restrictions of the Gramm-Leach-Bliley Act, which are in addition to the requirements or restrictions of section 7216 and §§ 301.7216-1 through 301.7216-3.

(d) *Effective/applicability date.*—This section applies to disclosures or uses of tax return information occurring on or after January 1, 2009. [Reg. § 301.7216-1.]

☐ [*T.D. 7310, 3-27-74. Amended by T.D. 9375, 1-3-2008.*]

### [Reg. § 301.7216-2]

**§ 301.7216-2. Permissible disclosures or uses without consent of the taxpayer.**—(a) *Disclosure pursuant to other provisions of the Internal Revenue Code.*—The provisions of section 7216(a) and § 301.7216-1 shall not apply to any disclosure of tax return information if the disclosure is made pursuant to any other provision of the Internal Revenue Code or the regulations thereunder.

(b) *Disclosures to the IRS.*—The provisions of section 7216(a) and § 301.7216-1 shall not apply to any disclosure of tax return information to an officer or employee of the IRS.

(c) *Disclosures or uses for preparation of a taxpayer's return.*—(1) *Updating Taxpayers' Tax Return Preparation Software.*—If a tax return preparer provides software to a taxpayer that is used in connection with the preparation or filing of a tax return, the tax return preparer may use the taxpayer's tax return information to update the taxpayer's software for the purpose of addressing changes in IRS forms, e-file specifications and administrative, regulatory and legislative guidance or to test and ensure the software's technical capabilities without the taxpayer's consent under § 301.7216-3.

(2) *Tax return preparers located within the same firm in the United States.*—If a taxpayer furnishes tax return information to a tax return preparer located within the United States, including any territory or possession of the United States, an officer, employee, or member of a tax return preparer may use the tax return information, or disclose the tax return information to another officer, employee, or member of the same tax return preparer, for the purpose of performing services that assist in the preparation of, or assist in providing auxiliary

services in connection with the preparation of, the taxpayer's tax return. If an officer, employee, or member to whom the tax return information is to be disclosed is located outside of the United States or any territory or possession of the United States, the taxpayer's consent under § 301.7216-3 prior to any disclosure is required.

(3) *Furnishing tax return information to tax return preparers located outside the United States.*—If a taxpayer initially furnishes tax return information to a tax return preparer located outside of the United States or any territory or possession of the United States, an officer, employee, or member of a tax return preparer may use tax return information, or disclose any tax return information to another officer, employee, or member of the same tax return preparer, for the purpose of performing services that assist in the preparation of, or assist in providing auxiliary services in connection with the preparation of, the tax return of a taxpayer by or for whom the information was furnished without the taxpayer's consent under § 301.7216-3.

(4) *Examples.*—The following examples illustrate this paragraph (c):

*Example 1.* Preparer P provides tax return preparation software to Taxpayer T for T to use in the preparation of its 2009 income tax return. For the 2009 tax year, and using T's tax return information furnished while registering for the software, P would like to update the tax return preparation software that T is using to account for last minute changes made to the tax laws for the 2009 tax year. P is not required to obtain T's consent to update the tax return preparation software. P may perform a software update regardless of whether the software update will affect T's particular return preparation activities.

*Example 2.* T is a client of Firm, which is a tax return preparer. E, an employee at Firm's State A office, receives tax return information from T for use in preparing T's income tax return. E discloses the tax return information to P, an employee in Firm's State B office; P uses the tax return information to process T's income tax return. Firm is not required to receive T's consent under § 301.7216-3 prior to E's disclosure of T's tax return information to P because the tax return information is disclosed to an employee employed by the same tax return preparer located within the United States.

*Example 3.* Same facts as *Example 2* except T's tax return information is disclosed to FE who is located in Firm's Country F office. FE uses the tax return information to process T's income tax return. After processing, FE returns the processed tax return information to E in Firm's State A office. Because FE is outside of the United States, Firm is required to obtain T's consent under § 301.7216-3 prior to E's disclosure of T's tax return information to FE.

*Example 4.* T, Firm's client, is temporarily located in Country F. She initially furnishes her tax return information to employee FE in Firm's Country F office for the purpose of having Firm prepare her U.S. income tax return. FE makes the substantive determinations concerning T's tax liability and forwards T's tax return information to FP, an employee in Firm's Country P office, for the purpose of processing T's tax return information. FP processes the return information and forwards it to Partner at Firm's State A office in the United States for review and delivery to T. Because T initially furnished the tax return information to a tax return preparer outside of the United States, T's prior consent for disclosure or use under § 301.7216-3 was not required. An officer, employee, or member of Firm in the United States may use T's tax return information or disclose the tax return information to another officer, employee, or member of Firm without T's prior consent under § 301.7216-3 as long as any disclosure or use of T's tax return information is within the United States. Firm is required to receive T's consent under § 301.7216-3 prior to any subsequent disclosure of T's tax return information to a tax return preparer located outside of the United States.

(d) *Disclosures to other tax return preparers.*—(1) *Preparer-to-preparer disclosures.*—Except as limited in paragraph (d)(2) of this section, an officer, employee, or member of a tax return preparer may disclose tax return information of a taxpayer to another tax return preparer (other than an officer, employee, or member of the same tax return preparer) located in the United States (including any territory or possession of the United States) for the purpose of preparing or assisting in preparing a tax return, or obtaining or providing auxiliary services in connection with the preparation of any tax return, so long as the services provided are not substantive determinations or advice affecting the tax liability reported by taxpayers. A substantive determination involves an analysis, interpretation, or application of the law. The authorized disclosures permitted under this paragraph (d)(1) include one tax return preparer disclosing tax return information to another tax return preparer for the purpose of having the second tax return preparer transfer that information to, and compute the tax liability on, a tax return of the taxpayer by means of electronic, mechanical, or other form of tax return processing service. The authorized disclosures permitted under this paragraph (d)(1) also include disclosures by a tax return preparer to an Authorized IRS *e-file* Provider for the purpose of electronically filing the return with the IRS. Authorized disclosures also include disclosures by a tax return preparer to a second tax return preparer for the purpose of making information concerning the return available to the taxpayer. This would include, for example, whether the return has been accepted or rejected by the IRS, or the status of the taxpayer's refund. Except as provided in paragraph (c) of this section, a tax return preparer may not disclose tax return information to another tax return preparer for the purpose of the second tax return preparer providing substantive determinations without first receiving the taxpayer's consent in accordance with the rules under § 301.7216-3.

(2) *Disclosures to contractors.*—A tax return preparer may disclose tax return information to a person under contract with the tax return preparer in connection with the programming, maintenance, repair, testing, or procurement of equipment or software used for purposes of tax return preparation only to the extent necessary for the person to provide the contracted services, and only if the tax return preparer ensures that all individuals who are to receive disclosures of tax return information receive a written notice that informs them of the applicability of sections 6713 and 7216 to them and describes the requirements and penalties of sections 6713 and 7216. Contractors receiving tax return information pursuant to this section are tax return preparers under section 7216 because they are performing auxiliary services in connection with tax return preparation. See § 301.7216-1(b)(2)(i)(B) and (D).

(3) *Examples.*—The following examples illustrate this paragraph (d):

*Example 1.* E, an employee at Firm's State A office, receives tax return information from T for Firm's use in preparing T's income tax return. E makes substantive determinations and forwards the tax return information to P, an employee at Processor; Processor is located in State B. P places the tax return information on the income tax return and furnishes the finished product to E. E is not required to receive T's prior consent under § 301.7216-3 before disclosing T's tax return information to P because Processor's services are not substantive determinations and the tax return information remained in the United States at Processor's State B office during the entire course of the tax return preparation process.

*Example 2.* Firm, a tax return preparer, offers income tax return preparation services. Firm's contract with its software provider, Contractor, requires Firm to periodically randomly select certain taxpayers' tax return information solely for the purpose of testing the reliability of the software sold to Firm. Under its agreement with Contractor, Firm discloses tax return information to Contractor's employee, C, who services Firm's contract without providing Contractor or C with a written notice that describes the requirements of and penalties under sections 7216 and 6713. C uses the tax return information solely for quality assurance purposes. Firm's disclosure of tax return information to C was an impermissible disclosure because Firm failed to ensure that C received a written notice that describes the requirements and penalties of sections 7216 and 6713.

*Example 3.* E, an employee of Firm in State A in the United States, receives tax return information from T for use in preparing T's income tax return. After E enters T's tax return information into Firm's computer, that information is stored on a computer server that is physically located in State A. Firm contracts with Contractor, located in Country F, to prepare its clients' tax returns. FE, an employee of Contractor, uses a computer in Country F and inputs a password to view T's income tax information stored on the computer server in State A to prepare T's tax return. A computer program permits FE to view T's tax return information, but prohibits FE from downloading or printing out T's tax return information from the computer server. Because Firm is disclosing T's tax return information outside of the United States, Firm is required to obtain T's consent under § 301.7216-3 prior to the disclosure to FE. As provided in § 301.7216-3(b)(5), however, Firm may not obtain consent to disclose T's social security number (SSN) to a tax return preparer located outside of the United States or any territory or possession of the United States.

*Example 4.* A, an employee at Firm A, receives tax return information from T for Firm's use in preparing T's income tax return. A forwards the tax return information to B, an employee at another firm, Firm B, to obtain advice on the issue of whether T may claim a deduction for a certain business expense. A is required to receive T's prior consent under § 301.7216-3 before disclosing T's tax return information to B because B's services involve a substantive determination affecting the tax liability that T will report.

(e) *Disclosure or use of information in the case of related taxpayers.*—(1) In preparing a tax return of a second taxpayer, a tax return preparer may use, and may disclose to the second taxpayer in the form in which it appears on the return, any tax return information that the tax return preparer obtained from a first taxpayer if—

(i) The second taxpayer is related to the first taxpayer within the meaning of paragraph (e)(2) of this section;

(ii) The first taxpayer's tax interest in the information is not adverse to the second taxpayer's tax interest in the information; and

(iii) The first taxpayer has not expressly prohibited the disclosure or use.

(2) For purposes of paragraph (e)(1)(i) of this section, a taxpayer is related to another taxpayer if they have any one of the following relationships: husband and wife, child and parent, grandchild and grandparent, partner and partnership, trust or estate and beneficiary, trust or estate and fiduciary, corporation and shareholder, or members of a controlled group of corporations as defined in section 1563.

(3) See § 301.7216-3 for disclosure or use of tax return information of the taxpayer in preparing the tax return of a second taxpayer when the requirements of this paragraph are not satisfied.

(f) *Disclosure pursuant to an order of a court, or an administrative order, demand, request, summons or subpoena which is issued in the performance of its duties by a Federal or State agency, the United States Congress, a professional association ethics committee or board, or the Public Company Accounting Oversight Board.*—The provisions of section 7216(a) and § 301.7216-1 will not apply to any disclosure of tax return information if the disclosure is made pursuant to any one of the following documents:

(1) The order of any court of record, Federal, State, or local.

(2) A subpoena issued by a grand jury, Federal or State.

(3) A subpoena issued by the United States Congress.

(4) An administrative order, demand, summons or subpoena that is issued in the performance of its duties by—

(i) Any Federal agency as defined in 5 U.S.C. 551(1) and 5 U.S.C. 552(f), or

(ii) A State agency, body, or commission charged under the laws of the State or a political subdivision of the State with the licensing, registration, or regulation of tax return preparers.

(5) A written request from a professional association ethics committee or board investigating the ethical conduct of the tax return preparer.

(6) A written request from the Public Company Accounting Oversight Board in connection with an inspection under section 104 of the Sarbanes-Oxley Act of 2002, 15 U.S.C. 7214, or an investigation under section 105 of such Act, 15 U.S.C. 7215, for use in accordance with such Act.

(g) *Disclosure for use in securing legal advice, Treasury investigations or court proceedings.*—A tax return preparer may disclose tax return information—

(1) To an attorney for purposes of securing legal advice;

(2) To an employee of the Treasury Department for use in connection with any investigation of the tax return preparer (including investigations relating to the tax return preparer in its capacity as a practitioner) conducted by the IRS or the Treasury Department; or

(3) To any officer of a court for use in connection with proceedings involving the tax return preparer (including proceedings involving the tax return preparer in its capacity as a practitioner), or the return preparer's client, before the court or before any grand jury that may be convened by the court.

(h) *Certain disclosures by attorneys and accountants.*—The provisions of section 7216(a) and § 301.7216-1 shall not apply to any disclosure of tax return information permitted by this paragraph (h).

(1)(i) A tax return preparer who is lawfully engaged in the practice of law or accountancy and prepares a tax return for a taxpayer may use the taxpayer's tax return information, or disclose the information to another officer, employee or member of the tax return preparer's law or accounting firm, consistent with applicable legal and ethical responsibilities, who may use the tax return information for the purpose of providing other legal or accounting services to the taxpayer. As an example, a lawyer who prepares a tax return for a taxpayer may use the tax return information of the taxpayer for, or in connection with, rendering legal services, including estate planning or administration, or preparation of trial briefs or trust instruments, for the taxpayer or the estate of the taxpayer. In addition, the lawyer who prepared the tax return may disclose the tax return information to another officer, employee or member of the same firm for the purpose of providing other legal services to the taxpayer. As another example, an accountant who prepares a tax return for a taxpayer may use the tax return information, or disclose it to another officer, employee or member of the firm, for use in connection with the preparation of books and records, working papers, or accounting statements or reports for the taxpayer. In the normal course of rendering the legal or accounting services to the taxpayer, the attorney or accountant may make the tax return information available to third parties, including stockholders, management, suppliers, or lenders, consistent with the applicable legal and ethical responsibilities, unless the taxpayer directs otherwise. For rules regarding disclosures outside of the United States, see §301.7216-2(c) and (d).

(ii) A tax return preparer's law or accounting firm does not include any related or affiliated firms. For example, if law firm A is affiliated with law firm B, officers, employees and members of law firm A must receive a taxpayer's consent under §301.7216-3 before disclosing the taxpayer's tax return information to an officer, employee or member of law firm B.

(2) A tax return preparer who is lawfully engaged in the practice of law or accountancy and prepares a tax return for a taxpayer may, consistent with the applicable legal and ethical responsibilities, take the tax return information into account, and may act upon it, in the course of performing legal or accounting services for a client other than the taxpayer, or disclose the information to another officer, employee or member of the tax return preparer's law or accounting firm to enable that other officer, employee or member to take the information into account, and act upon it, in the course of performing legal or accounting services for a client other than the taxpayer. This is permissible when the information is, or may be, relevant to the subject matter of the legal or accounting services for the other client, and consideration of the information by those performing the services is necessary for the proper performance of the services. In no event, however, may the tax return information be disclosed to a person who is not an officer, employee or member of the law or accounting firm, unless the disclosure is exempt from the application of section 7216(a) and §301.7216-1 by reason of another provision of §§301.7216-2 or 301.7216-3.

(3) *Examples.*—The application of this paragraph may be illustrated by the following examples:

*Example 1.* A, a member of an accounting firm, renders an opinion on a financial statement of M Corporation that is part of a registration statement filed with the Securities and Exchange Commission. After the registration statement is filed, but before its effective date, B, a member of the same accounting firm, prepares an income tax return for N Corporation. In the course of preparing N's income tax return, B discovers that N does business with M and concludes that the information given by N should be considered by A to determine whether the financial statement opined on by A contains an untrue statement of material fact or omits a material fact required to keep the statement from being misleading. B discloses to A the tax return information of N for this purpose. A determines that there is an omission of material fact and that an amended statement should be filed. A so advises M and the Securities and Exchange Commission. A explains that the omission was revealed as a result of confidential information that came to A's attention after the statement was filed, but A does not disclose the identity of the taxpayer or the tax return information itself. Section 7216(a) and §301.7216-1 do not apply to B's disclosure of N's tax return information to A and A's use of the information in advising M and the Securities and Exchange Commission of the necessity for filing an amended statement. Section 7216(a) and §301.7216-1 would apply to a disclosure of N's tax return information to M or to the Securities and Exchange Commission unless the disclosure is exempt from the application of section 7216(a) and §301.7216-1 by reason of another provision of either this section or §301.7216-3.

*Example 2.* A, a member of an accounting firm, is conducting an audit of M Corporation, and B, a member of the same accounting firm, prepares an income tax return for D, an officer of M. In the course of preparing the return, B obtains information from D indicating that D, pursuant to an arrangement with a supplier doing business with M, has been receiving from the supplier a percentage of the amounts that the supplier invoices to M. B discloses this information to A who, acting upon it, searches in the course of the audit for indications of a kickback scheme. As a result, A discovers information from audit sources that independently indicate the existence of a kickback scheme. Without revealing the tax return information A has received from B, A brings to the attention of officers of M the audit information indicating the existence of the kickback scheme. Section 7216(a) and §301.7216-1 do not apply to B's disclosure of D's tax return information to A, A's use of D's information in the course of the audit, and A's disclosure to M of the audit information indicating the existence of the kickback scheme. Section 7216(a) and §301.7216-1 would apply to a disclosure to M, or to any other person not an employee or member of the accounting firm, of D's tax return information furnished to B.

(i) *Corporate fiduciaries.*—A trust company, trust department of a bank, or other corporate fiduciary that prepares a tax return for a taxpayer for whom it renders fiduciary, investment, or other custodial or management services may, unless the taxpayer directs otherwise—

(1) Disclose or use the taxpayer's tax return information in the ordinary course of rendering such services to or for the taxpayer; or

(2) Make the information available to the taxpayer's attorney, accountant, or investment advisor.

(j) *Disclosure to taxpayer's fiduciary.*—If, after furnishing tax return information to a tax return preparer, the taxpayer dies or becomes incompetent, insolvent, or bankrupt, or the taxpayer's assets are placed in conservatorship or receivership, the tax return preparer may disclose the information to the duly appointed fiduciary of the taxpayer or his estate, or to the duly authorized agent of the fiduciary.

(k) *Disclosure or use of information in preparation or audit of State or local tax returns or assisting a taxpayer with foreign country tax obligations.*—The provisions of paragraphs (c) and (d) of this section shall apply to the disclosure by any tax return preparer of any tax return information in the preparation of, or in connection with the preparation of, any tax return of the taxpayer under the law of any State or political subdivision thereof, of the District of Columbia, of any territory or possession of the United States, or of a country other than the United States. The provisions of section 7216(a) and §301.7216-1 shall not apply to the use by any tax return preparer of any tax return information in the preparation of, or in connection with the preparation of, any tax return of the taxpayer under the law of any State or political subdivision thereof, of the District of Columbia, of any territory or possession of the United States, or of a country other than the United States. The provisions of section 7216(a) and §301.7216-1 shall not apply to the disclosure or use by any tax return preparer of any tax return information in the audit of, or in connection with the audit of, any tax return of the taxpayer under the law of any State or political subdivision thereof, the District of Columbia, or any territory or possession of the United States.

(l) *Payment for tax preparation services.*—A tax return preparer may use and disclose, without the taxpayer's written consent, tax return information that the taxpayer provides to the tax return preparer to pay for tax preparation services to the extent necessary to process or collect the payment. For example, if the taxpayer gives the tax return preparer a credit card to pay for tax preparation services, the tax return preparer may disclose the taxpayer's name, credit card number, credit card expiration date, and amount due for tax preparation services to the credit card company, as necessary, to process the payment. Any tax return information that the taxpayer did not give the tax return preparer for the purpose of making payment for tax preparation services may not be used or disclosed by the tax return preparer without the taxpayer's prior written consent, unless otherwise permitted under another provision of this section.

(m) *Retention of records.*—A tax return preparer may retain tax return information of a taxpayer, including copies of tax returns, in paper or electronic format, prepared on the basis of the tax return information, and may use the information in connection with the preparation of other tax returns of the taxpayer or in connection with an examination by the Internal Revenue Service of any tax return or subsequent tax litigation relating to the tax return. The provisions of paragraph (n) of this section regarding the transfer of a taxpayer list also apply to the transfer of any records and related papers to which this paragraph applies.

(n) *Lists for solicitation of tax return preparation business.*—(1) A tax return preparer, other than a person who is a tax return preparer solely because the person provides auxiliary services as defined in §301.7216-1(b)(2)(iii), may compile and maintain a separate list containing solely items of tax return information. The following items of tax return information are permissible: the names, mailing addresses, e-mail addresses, phone numbers, taxpayer entity classification (including "individual" or the specific type of business entity), and income tax return form number (for example, Form 1040-EZ) of taxpayers whose tax returns the tax return preparer has prepared or processed. The Internal Revenue Service may issue guidance, by publication in the Internal Revenue Bulletin (see §601.601(d)(2)(ii)(*b*) of this chapter), describing other types of information that may be included in a list compiled and maintained pursuant to this paragraph. This list may be used by the compiler solely to contact the taxpayers on the list for the purpose of providing tax information and general business or economic information or analysis for educational purposes, or soliciting additional tax return preparation services. The list may not be used to solicit any service or product other than tax return preparation services. The compiler of the list may not transfer the taxpayer list, or any part thereof, to any other person unless the transfer takes place in conjunction with the sale or other disposition of the compiler's tax return preparation business. Due diligence conducted prior to a proposed sale of a compiler's tax return preparation business is in conjunction with the sale or other disposition of a compiler's tax return preparation business and will not constitute a transfer of the list if conducted pursuant to a written agreement that requires confidentiality of the tax return information disclosed and expressly prohibits the further disclosure or use of the tax return information for any purpose other than that related to the purchase of the tax return preparation business. A person who acquires a taxpayer list, or a part thereof, in conjunction with a sale or other disposition of a tax return preparation business falls under the provisions of this paragraph with respect to the list. The term *list*, as used in this paragraph (n), includes any record or system whereby the types of information expressly authorized for inclusion in a taxpayer list pursuant to the terms of this paragraph (n) are retained. The provisions of this paragraph (n) also apply to the transfer of any records and related papers to which this paragraph (n) applies.

(2) *Examples.*—The following examples illustrate this paragraph (n):

*Example 1.* Preparer A is a tax return preparer as defined by § 301.7216-1(b)(2)(i)(A). Preparer A's office is located in southeast Pennsylvania, and Preparer A prepares federal and state income tax returns for taxpayers who live in Pennsylvania, New Jersey, Maryland, and Delaware. Preparer A maintains a list of taxpayer clients containing the information allowed by this paragraph (n). Preparer A provides quarterly state income tax information updates to his individual taxpayer clients by e-mail or U.S. mail. To ensure that his clients only receive the information updates that are relevant to them, Preparer A uses his list to direct his outreach efforts towards the relevant clients by searching his list to filter it by zip code and income tax return form number (Form 1040 and corresponding state income tax return form number). Preparer A may use the list information in this manner without taxpayer consent because he is providing tax information for educational or informational purposes and is targeting clients based solely upon tax return information that is authorized by this paragraph (n) (by zip code, which is part of a taxpayer's address, and by income tax return form number). Without taxpayer consent, Preparer A also may deliver this information to his clients by e-mail, U.S. mail, or other method of delivery that uses only information authorized by this paragraph (n).

*Example 2.* Preparer B is a tax return preparer as defined by § 301.7216-1(b)(2)(i)(A). Preparer B maintains a list of taxpayer clients containing the information allowed by this paragraph (n). Preparer B provides monthly federal income tax information updates in the form of a newsletter to all of her taxpayer clients by e-mail or U.S. mail. When Preparer B hires a new employee who participates or assists in tax return preparation, she announces that hire in the newsletter for the month that follows the hiring. Each announcement includes a photograph of the new employee, the employee's name, the employee's telephone number, a brief listing of the employee's qualifications, and a brief listing of the employee's employment responsibilities. Preparer B may use the tax return information described in this paragraph (n) in this manner without taxpayer consent because she is providing tax information for educational or informational purposes to provide general federal income tax information updates. Preparer B may include the new employee announcements in the form described because this is considered tax information for informational purposes, provided the announcements do not contain solicitations for non-tax return preparation services. Without taxpayer consent, Preparer B also may deliver this information to her clients by e-mail, U.S. mail, or other method of delivery that uses only information authorized by this paragraph (n).

(o) *Producing statistical information in connection with tax return preparation business.*—(1) A tax return preparer may use tax return information, subject to the limitations specified in this paragraph (o), to produce a statistical compilation of data described in § 301.7216-1(b)(3)(i)(B). The purpose for and disclosure or use of the statistical compilation requiring data acquired during the tax return preparation process must relate directly to the internal management or support of the tax return preparer's tax return preparation business, or to bona fide research or public policy discussions concerning state or federal taxation. A tax return preparer may not disclose the statistical compilation, or any part thereof, to any other person unless disclosure of the statistical compilation is anonymous as to taxpayer identity, does not disclose an aggregate figure containing data from fewer than ten tax returns, and is in direct support of the tax return preparer's tax return preparation business or of bona fide research or public policy discussions concerning state or federal taxation. A statistical compilation is anonymous as to taxpayer identity if it is in a form which cannot be associated with, or otherwise identify, directly or indirectly, a particular taxpayer. For purposes of this paragraph, marketing and advertising is in direct support of the tax return preparer's tax return preparation business provided the marketing and advertising is not false, misleading, or unduly influential. This paragraph, however, does not authorize the disclosure or use in marketing or advertising of any statistical compilations, or part thereof, that identify dollar amounts of refunds, credits, or deductions associated with tax returns, or percentages relating thereto, whether or not the data are statistical, averaged, aggregated, or anonymous. Disclosures made in support of fundraising activities

conducted by volunteer return preparation programs and other organizations described in section 501(c) of the Internal Revenue Code (Code) in direct support of their tax return preparation businesses are not marketing and advertising under this paragraph. A tax return preparer who produces a statistical compilation of data described in § 301.7216-1(b)(3)(i)(B) may disclose the compilation to comply with financial accounting or regulatory reporting requirements whether or not the statistical compilation is anonymous as to taxpayer identity or discloses an aggregate figure containing data from fewer than ten tax returns.

(2) A tax return preparer may not sell or exchange for value a statistical compilation of data described in § 301.7216-1(b)(3)(i)(B), in whole or in part, except in conjunction with the transfer of assets made pursuant to the sale or other disposition of the tax return preparer's tax return preparation business. The provisions of paragraph (n) of this section regarding the transfer of a taxpayer list also apply to the transfer of any statistical compilations of data to which this paragraph applies. A person who acquires a statistical compilation, or a part thereof, pursuant to the operation of this paragraph (o) or in conjunction with a sale or other disposition of a tax return preparation business is subject to the provisions of this paragraph with respect to the compilation.

(3) *Examples.*—The following examples illustrate this paragraph (o):

*Example 1.* Preparer A is a tax return preparer as defined by § 301.7216-1(b)(2)(i)(A). In 2009, A used tax return information to produce a statistical compilation of data for both internal management purposes and to support A's tax return preparation business. The statistical compilation included an aggregate figure containing the information that A prepared 32 S corporation tax returns in 2009. In 2010, A decided to embark upon a new marketing campaign emphasizing its experience preparing small business tax returns. In the campaign, A discloses the aggregate figure containing the number of S corporation tax returns prepared in 2009. A's disclosure does not include any information that can be associated with or identify any specific taxpayers. A may disclose the anonymous statistical compilation without taxpayer consent.

*Example 2.* Preparer B is a tax return preparer as defined by § 301.7216-1(b)(2)(i)(A). In 2010, in support of B's tax return preparation business, B wants to advertise that the average tax refund obtained for its clients in 2009 was $2,800. B may not disclose this information because it contains a statistical compilation reflecting average refund amounts.

*Example 3.* Preparer C is a tax return preparer as defined by § 301.7216-1(b)(2)(i)(A) and is a volunteer income tax assistance program. In 2010, in support of C's tax return preparation business, C submits a grant application to a charitable foundation to fund C's operations providing free tax return preparation services to low- and moderate-income families. In support of C's request, C includes anonymous statistical data consisting of aggregated figures containing data from ten or more tax returns showing that, in 2009, C provided services to 500 taxpayers, that 95 percent of the taxpayer population served by C received the Earned Income Tax Credit (EITC), and that the average amount of the EITC received was $3,300. Despite the fact that this information constitutes an average credit amount, C may disclose the information to the charitable foundation because disclosures made in support of fundraising activities conducted by volunteer income tax assistance programs and other organizations described in section 501(c) of the Code in direct support of their tax return preparation business are not considered marketing and advertising for purposes of § 301.7216-2(o)(1).

*Example 4.* Preparer D is a tax return preparer as defined by § 301.7216-1(b)(2)(i)(A). In December 2009, D produced an anonymous statistical compilation of tax return information obtained during the 2009 filing season. In 2010, D wants to disclose portions of the anonymous statistical compilation from aggregated figures containing data from ten or more tax returns in connection with the marketing of its financial advisory and asset planning services. D is required to receive taxpayer consent under § 301.7216-3 before disclosing the tax return information contained in the anonymous statistical compilation because the disclosure is not being made in support of D's tax return preparation business.

(p) *Disclosure or use of information for quality, peer, or conflict reviews.*—(1) The provisions of section 7216(a) and § 301.7216-1 shall not apply to any disclosure for the purpose of a quality or peer review to the extent necessary to accomplish the review. A quality or peer review is a review that is undertaken to evaluate, monitor, and improve the quality and accuracy of a tax return preparer's tax preparation, accounting, or auditing services. A quality or peer review may be conducted only by attorneys, certified public accountants, enrolled agents, and enrolled actuaries who are eligible to practice before the Internal Revenue Service. See Department of the Treasury Circular 230, 31 CFR part 10. Tax return information may also be disclosed to persons who provide administrative or support services to an individual who is conducting a quality or peer review under this paragraph (p), but only to the extent necessary for the reviewer to conduct the review. Tax return information gathered in conducting a review may be used only for purposes of a review. No tax return information identifying a taxpayer may be disclosed in any evaluative reports or recommendations that may be accessible to any person other than the reviewer or the tax return preparer being reviewed. The tax return preparer being reviewed will maintain a record of the review, including the information reviewed and the identity of the persons conducting the review. After completion of the review, no documents containing information that may identify any taxpayer by name or identification number may be retained by a reviewer or by the reviewer's administrative or support personnel.

(2) The provisions of section 7216(a) and §301.7216-1 shall not apply to any disclosure necessary to accomplish a conflict review. A conflict review is a review undertaken to comply with requirements established by any federal, state, or local law, agency, board or commission, or by a professional association ethics committee or board, to either identify, evaluate, or monitor actual or potential legal and ethical conflicts of interest that may arise when a tax return preparer is employed or acquired by another tax return preparer, or to identify, evaluate, or monitor actual or potential legal and ethical conflicts of interest that may arise when a tax return preparer is considering engaging a new client. Tax return information gathered in conducting a conflict review may be used only for purposes of a conflict review. No tax return information identifying a taxpayer may be disclosed in any evaluative reports or recommendations that may be accessible to any person other than those responsible for identifying, evaluating, or monitoring legal and ethical conflicts of interest. No tax return information identifying a taxpayer may be disclosed outside of the United States or a territory or possession of the United States unless the disclosing and receiving tax return preparers have procedures in place that are consistent with good business practices and designed to maintain the confidentiality of the disclosed tax return information.

(3) Any person (including administrative and support personnel) receiving tax return information in connection with a quality, peer, or conflict review is a tax return preparer for purposes of sections 7216(a) and 6713(a). Tax return information disclosed and used for purposes of a quality, peer, or conflict review shall not be disclosed or used for any other purpose.

(q) *Disclosure to report the commission of a crime.*—The provisions of section 7216(a) and §301.7216-1 shall not apply to the disclosure of any tax return information to the proper Federal, State, or local official in order, and to the extent necessary, to inform the official of activities that may constitute, or may have constituted, a violation of any criminal law or to assist the official in investigating or prosecuting a violation of criminal law. A disclosure made in the bona fide but mistaken belief that the activities constituted a violation of criminal law is not subject to section 7216(a) and §301.7216-1.

(r) *Disclosure of tax return information due to a tax return preparer's incapacity or death.*—In the event of incapacity or death of a tax return preparer, disclosure of tax return information may be made for the purpose of assisting the tax return preparer or his legal representative (or the representative of a deceased tax return preparer's estate) in operating the business. Any person receiving tax return information under the provisions of this paragraph (r) is a tax return preparer for purposes of sections 7216(a) and 6713(a).

(s) *Effective/applicability date.*—Paragraphs (n), (o), and (p) of this section apply to disclosures or uses of tax return information occurring on or after December 28, 2012. All other paragraphs of this section apply to disclosures or uses of tax return information occurring on or after January 1, 2009. [Reg. §301.7216-2.]

☐ [T.D. 7310, 3-27-74. *Amended by T.D. 7676, 2-20-80; T.D. 7708, 7-24-80; T.D. 7498, 3-7-84; T.D. 8383, 12-26-91; T.D. 8427, 8-17-92; T.D. 9375, 1-3-2008; T.D. 9478, 12-29-2009 and T.D. 9608, 12-26-2012.]*

### [Reg. §301.7216-3]

**§301.7216-3. Disclosure or use permitted only with the taxpayer's consent.**—(a) *In general.*—(1) *Taxpayer consent.*—Unless section 7216 or §301.7216-2 specifically authorizes the disclosure or use of tax return information, a tax return preparer may not disclose or use a taxpayer's tax return information prior to obtaining a written consent from the taxpayer, as described in this section. A tax return preparer may disclose or use tax return information as the taxpayer directs as long as the preparer obtains a written consent from the taxpayer as provided in this section. The consent must be knowing and voluntary. Except as provided in paragraph (a)(2) of this section, conditioning the provision of any services on the taxpayer's furnishing consent will make the consent involuntary, and the consent will not satisfy the requirements of this section.

(2) *Taxpayer consent to a tax return preparer furnishing tax return information to another tax return preparer.*—(i) A tax return preparer may condition its provision of preparation services upon a taxpayer's consenting to disclosure of the taxpayer's tax return information to another tax return preparer for the purpose of performing services that assist in the preparation of, or provide auxiliary services in connection with the preparation of, the tax return of the taxpayer.

(ii) *Example.*—The application of this paragraph (a)(2) may be illustrated by the following example:

*Example.* Preparer P, who is located within the United States, is retained by Company C to provide tax return preparation services for employees of Company C. An employee of Company C, Employee E, works for C outside of the United States. To provide tax return preparation services for E, P requires the assistance of and needs to disclose E's tax return information to a tax return preparer who works for P's affiliate located in the country where E works. P may condition its provision of tax return preparation services upon E consenting to the disclosure of E's tax return information to the tax return preparer in the country where E works.

(3) *The form and contents of taxpayer consents.*—(i) *In general.*—All consents to disclose or use tax return information must satisfy the following requirements—

(A) A taxpayer's consent to a tax return preparer's disclosure or use of tax return information must include the name of the tax return preparer and the name of the taxpayer.

(B) If a taxpayer consents to a disclosure of tax return information, the consent must identify the intended purpose of the disclosure. Except as provided in §301.7216-3(a)(3)(iii), if a taxpayer consents to a disclosure of tax return information, the consent must also identify the specific recipient (or recipients) of the tax return information. If the taxpayer consents to use of tax return information, the consent must describe the particular use authorized. For example, if the tax return preparer intends to use tax return information to generate solicitations for products or services other than tax return preparation, the consent must identify each specific type of product or service for which the tax return preparer may solicit use of the tax return information. Examples of products or services that must be identified include, but are not limited to, balance due loans, mortgage loans, mutual funds, individual retirement accounts, and life insurance.

(C) The consent must specify the tax return information to be disclosed or used by the return preparer.

(D) If a tax return preparer to whom the tax return information is to be disclosed is located outside of the United States, the taxpayer's consent under §301.7216-3 prior to any disclosure is required. See §301.7216-2(c) and (d).

(E) A consent to disclose or use tax return information must be signed and dated by the taxpayer.

(ii) *The form and contents of taxpayer consents with respect to taxpayers filing a return in the Form 1040 series - guidance describing additional requirements for taxpayer consents with respect to Form 1040 series filers.*—The Secretary may issue guidance, by publication in the Internal Revenue Bulletin (see §601.601(d)(2)(ii)(b) of this chapter), describing additional requirements for tax return preparers regarding the format and content of consents to disclose and use tax return information with respect to taxpayers filing a return in the Form 1040 series, *e.g.,* Form 1040, Form 1040NR, Form 1040A, or Form 1040EZ.

(iii) *The form and contents of taxpayer consents with respect to all other taxpayers.*—A consent to disclose or use tax return information with respect to a taxpayer not filing a return in the Form 1040 series may be in any format, including an engagement letter to a client, as long as the consent complies with the requirements of §301.7216-3(a)(3)(i). Additionally, the requirements of §301.7216-3(c)(1) are inapplicable to consents to disclose or use tax return information with respect to taxpayers not filing a return in the Form 1040 series. Solely for purposes of a consent issued under §301.7216-3(a)(3)(iii), in lieu of identifying specific recipients of an intended disclosure under §301.7216-3(a)(3)(i)(B), a consent may allow disclosure to a descriptive class of entities engaged by a taxpayer or the taxpayer's affiliate for purposes of services in connection with the preparation of tax returns, audited financial statements, or other financial statements or financial information as required by a government authority, municipality or regulatory body.

(iv) *Examples.*—The application of §301.7216-3(a)(3)(iii) may be illustrated by the following examples:

*Example 1.* Consistent with applicable legal and ethical responsibilities, Preparer Z sends its client, a corporation, Taxpayer C, an engagement letter. Part of the engagement letter requests the consent of Taxpayer C for the purpose of disclosing tax return information to an investment banking firm to assist the investment banking firm in securing long term financing for Taxpayer C. The engagement letter includes language and information that meets the requirements of §301.7216-3(a)(3)(i), including: (I) Preparer Z's name, Taxpayer C's name, and a signature and date line for Taxpayer C; and (II) a statement that "Taxpayer C authorizes Preparer Z to disclose the portions of Taxpayer C's 2009 tax return information to the firm retained by Taxpayer C necessary for the purposes of assisting Taxpayer C secure long term financing." The engagement letter satisfies the requirements of §301.7216-3(a)(3) for the disclosure of the information provided therein for the specific purpose stated.

*Example 2.* Consistent with applicable legal and ethical responsibilities, Preparer N sends its client, a corporation, Taxpayer D, an engagement letter. Part of the engagement letter requests the consent of Taxpayer D for the purpose of disclosing tax return information to Preparer N's affiliated firms located outside of the United States for the purposes of preparation of Taxpayer D's 2009 tax return. The engagement letter includes language and information that meets the requirements of §301.7216-3(a)(3)(i), including: (I) Preparer N's name, Taxpayer D's name, and a signature and date line for Taxpayer D; (II) a statement that "Taxpayer D authorizes Preparer N to disclose Taxpayer D's 2009 tax return information to Preparer N's affiliates located outside of the United States for the purposes of assisting Preparer N prepare Taxpayer D's 2009 tax return"; and (III) a statement that, in providing consent, Taxpayer D acknowledges that its tax return information for 2009 will be disclosed to tax return preparers located abroad. The engagement letter satisfies the requirements of §301.7216-3(a)(3) for the disclosure of the information provided therein for the specific purpose stated.

(b) *Timing requirements and limitations.*—(1) *No retroactive consent.*—A taxpayer must provide written consent before a tax return preparer discloses or uses the taxpayer's tax return information.

(2) *Time limitations on requesting consent in solicitation context.*—A tax return preparer may not request a taxpayer's consent to disclose or use tax return information for purposes of solicitation of business unrelated to tax return preparation after the tax return preparer provides a completed tax return to the taxpayer for signature.

(3) *No requests for consent after an unsuccessful request.*—With regard to tax return information for each income tax return that a tax return preparer prepares, if a taxpayer declines a request for consent to the disclosure or use of tax return information for purposes of solicitation of business unrelated to tax return preparation, the tax return preparer may not solicit from the taxpayer another consent for a purpose substantially similar to that of the rejected request.

(4) *No consent to the disclosure of a taxpayer's social security number to a return preparer outside of the United States with respect to a taxpayer filing a return in the Form 1040 Series.*—(i) *In general.*—Except as provided in paragraph (b)(4)(ii) of this section, a tax return preparer located within the United States, including any territory or possession of the United States, may not obtain consent to disclose the taxpayer's social security number (SSN) with respect to a taxpayer filing a return in the Form 1040 Series, for example, Form 1040, Form 1040NR, Form 1040A, or Form 1040EZ, to a tax return preparer located outside of the United States or any territory or possession of the United States. Thus, if a tax return preparer located within the United States (including any territory or possession of the United States) obtains consent from an individual taxpayer to disclose tax return information to another tax return preparer located outside of the United States, as provided under §§301.7216-2(c) and 301.7216-2(d), the tax return preparer located in the United States may not disclose the taxpayer's SSN, and the tax return preparer must redact or otherwise mask the taxpayer's SSN before the tax

return information is disclosed outside of the United States. If a tax return preparer located within the United States initially receives or obtains a taxpayer's SSN from another tax return preparer located outside of the United States, however, the tax return preparer within the United States may, without consent, retransmit the taxpayer's SSN to the tax return preparer located outside the United States that initially provided the SSN to the tax return preparer located within the United States. For purposes of this section, a tax return preparer located outside of the United States does not include a tax return preparer who is continuously and regularly employed in the United States or any territory or possession of the United States and who is in a temporary travel status outside of the United States.

(ii) *Exception.*—A tax return preparer located within the United States, including any territory or possession of the United States, may obtain consent to disclose the taxpayer's SSN to a tax return preparer located outside of the United States or any territory or possession of the United States only if the tax return preparer within the United States discloses the SSN to a tax return preparer outside of the United States through the use of an adequate data protection safeguard as defined by the Secretary in guidance published in the Internal Revenue Bulletin (see §601.601(d)(2)(ii)(b) of this chapter) and verifies the maintenance of the adequate data protection safeguards in the request for the taxpayer's consent pursuant to the specifications described by the Secretary in guidance published in the Internal Revenue Bulletin.

(5) *Duration of consent.*—A consent document may specify the duration of the taxpayer's consent to the disclosure or use of tax return information. If a consent agreed to by the taxpayer does not specify the duration of the consent, the consent to the disclosure or use of tax return information will be effective for a period of one year from the date the taxpayer signed the consent.

(c) *Special rules.*—(1) *Multiple disclosures within a single consent form or multiple uses within a single consent form.*—A taxpayer may consent to multiple uses within the same written document, or multiple disclosures within the same written document. A single written document, however, cannot authorize both uses and disclosures; rather one written document must authorize the uses and another separate written document must authorize the disclosures. Furthermore, a consent that authorizes multiple disclosures or multiple uses must specifically and separately identify each disclosure or use. See §301.7216-3(a)(3)(iii) for an exception to this rule for certain taxpayers.

(2) *Disclosure of entire return.*—A consent may authorize the disclosure of all information contained within a return. A consent authorizing the disclosure of an entire return must provide that the taxpayer has the ability to request a more limited disclosure of tax return information as the taxpayer may direct.

(3) *Copy of consent must be provided to taxpayer.*—The tax return preparer must provide a copy of the executed consent to the taxpayer at the time of execution. The requirements of this paragraph (c)(3) may also be satisfied by giving the taxpayer the opportunity, at the time of executing the consent, to print the completed consent or save it in electronic form.

(d) *Effective/applicability date.*—This section applies to disclosures or uses of tax return information occurring on or after January 1, 2009. [Reg. §301.7216-3.]

☐ [*T.D. 7310, 3-27-74. Amended by T.D. 9375, 1-3-2008; T.D. 9409, 7-1-2008 and T.D. 9437, 12-15-2008.*]

## Penalties Applicable to Certain Taxes

**[Reg. §301.7231-1]**

**§301.7231-1. Failure to obtain license for collection of foreign items.**—For provisions relating to the obtaining of a license for the collection of foreign items, see section 7001 and §301.7001-1. [Reg. §301.7231-1.]

☐ [*T.D. 6498, 10-24-60.*]

**[Reg. §44.7262-1]**

**§44.7262-1. Failure to pay special tax.**—Any person liable for the special tax who does any act which makes him liable for such tax, without having paid the tax, is, besides being liable for the tax, subject to a fine of not less than $1,000 and not more than $5,000. [Reg. §44.7262-1.]

☐ [*T.D. 6370.*]

# OTHER OFFENSES

**[Reg. §301.7269-1]**

**§301.7269-1. Failure to produce records.**—Whoever fails to comply with any duty imposed upon him by section 6018, 6036 (in the case of an executor), or 6075(a), or, having in his possession or control any record, file, or paper, containing or supposed to contain

any information concerning the estate or the decedent, or, having in his possession or control any property comprised in the gross estate of the decedent, fails to exhibit the same upon request of any officer or employee of the Internal Revenue Service who desires to examine the same in the performance of his duties under chapter 11 of the Code (relating to estate taxes) shall be liable to a penalty of not exceeding $500, to be recovered with costs of suit, in a civil action in the name of the United States. [Reg. § 301.7269-1.]

☐ [T.D. 6498, 10-24-60.]

### [Reg. § 301.7272-1]

**§ 301.7272-1. Penalty for failure to register.**—(a) Any person who fails to register with the district director as required by the Code or by regulations issued thereunder shall be liable to a penalty of $50 except that on and after September 3, 1958, this section shall not apply to persons required to register under subtitle E of the Code, or persons engaging in a trade or business on which a special tax is imposed by such subtitle.

(b) For provisions relating to registration under sections 4101, 4412, 4455, 4722, 4753, and 4804(d), see the regulations relating to the particular tax. For regulations under section 7011, see § 301.7011-1. [Reg. § 301.7272-1.]

☐ [T.D. 6498, 10-24-60.]

# FORFEITURES

## Provisions Common to Forfeitures

### [Reg. § 301.7304-1]

**§ 301.7304-1. Penalty for fraudulently claiming drawback.**— Whenever any person fraudulently claims or seeks to obtain an allowance of drawback on goods, wares, or merchandise on which no internal tax shall have been paid, or fraudulently claims any greater allowance of drawback than the tax actually paid, he shall forfeit triple the amount wrongfully or fraudulently claimed or sought to be obtained, or the sum of $500, at the election of the district director. [Reg. § 301.7304-1.]

### [Reg. § 301.7321-1]

**§ 301.7321-1. Seizure of property.**—Any property subject to forfeiture to the United States under any provision of the Code may be seized by the district director or assistant regional commissioner(alcohol, tobacco, and firearms). Upon seizure of property by the district director he shall notify the assistant regional commissioner (alcohol, tobacco, and firearms) for the region wherein the district is located who will take charge of the property and arrange for its disposal or retention under the provisions of law and regulations applicable thereto. [Reg. § 301.7321-1.]

☐ [T.D. 6498, 10-24-60. Amended by T.D. 7188, 6-28-72.]

### [Reg. § 301.7322-1]

**§ 301.7322-1. Delivery of seized property to United States marshal.**—Any forfeitable property which may be seized under the provisions of the Code may, at the option of the assistant regional commissioner (alcohol, tobacco, and firearms), be delivered to the United States marshal of the judicial district wherein the property was seized, and remain in the care and custody and under the control of such marshal, pending the disposal thereof as provided by law. [Reg. § 301.7322-1.]

☐ [T.D. 7188, 6-28-72.]

### [Reg. § 301.7324-1]

**§ 301.7324-1. Special disposition of perishable goods.**—For regulations relating to the disposal of perishable goods, see § 172.30 of this chapter (Disposition of Seized Personal Property). [Reg. § 301.7324-1.]

☐ [T.D. 6498, 10-24-60.]

### [Reg. § 301.7325-1]

**§ 301.7325-1. Personal property valued at $2,500 or less.**—For regulations relating to the forfeiture of personal property valued at $2,500 or less, see Part 172 of this chapter (Disposition of Seized Personal Property). [Reg. § 301.7325-1.]

☐ [T.D. 6498, 10-24-60.]

## Judiciary Proceedings

# CIVIL ACTIONS BY THE UNITED STATES

### See p. 20,601 for regulations not amended to reflect law changes

### [Reg. § 301.7401-1]

**§ 301.7401-1. Authorization.**—(a) In general.—No civil action for the collection or recovery of taxes, or of any fine, penalty, or forfeiture, shall be commenced unless the Commissioner (or the Director, Alcohol, Tobacco and Firearms Division, with respect to the provisions of subtitle E of the Code), or the Chief Counsel for the Internal Revenue Service or his delegate authorizes or sanctions the proceedings and the Attorney General or his delegate directs that the action be commenced.

(b) Property held by banks.—The Commissioner shall not authorize or sanction any civil action for the collection or recovery of taxes, or of any fine, penalty, or forfeiture, from any deposits held in a foreign office of a bank engaged in the banking business in the United States or a possession of the United States unless the Commissioner believes—

(1) That the taxpayer is within the jurisdiction of a United States court at the time the civil action is authorized or sanctioned and that the bank is in possession of (or obligated with respect to) deposits of the taxpayer in an office of the bank outside the United States or a possession of the United States; or

(2) That the taxpayer is not within the jurisdiction of a United States court at the time the civil action is authorized or sanctioned, that the bank is in possession of (or obligated with respect to) deposits of the taxpayer in an office outside the United States or a possession of the United States, and that such deposits consist, in whole or in part, of funds transferred from the United States or a possession of the United States in order to hinder or delay the collection of a tax imposed by the Code.

For purposes of this paragraph, the term "possession of the United States" includes Guam, the Midway Islands, the Panama Canal Zone, the Commonwealth of Puerto Rico, American Samoa, the Virgin Islands, and Wake Island. [Reg. § 301.7401-1.]

☐ [T.D. 6498, 10-24-60. Amended by T.D. 6746, 7-20-64; T.D. 6902, 12-13-66 and T.D. 7188, 6-28-72.]

### [Reg. § 301.7403-1]

**§ 301.7403-1. Action to enforce lien or to subject property to payment of tax.**—(a) Civil actions.—In any case where there has been a refusal or neglect to pay any tax, or to discharge any liability in respect thereof, whether or not levy has been made, the Attorney General or his delegate, at the request of the Commissioner (or the Director, Bureau of Alcohol, Tobacco, and Firearms, or the Chief Counsel for the Bureau, with respect to the provisions of subtitle E of the Code), or the Chief Counsel for the Internal Revenue Service or his delegate, may direct a civil action to be filed in a district court of the United States to enforce the lien of the United States under the Code with respect to such tax or liability or to subject any property, of whatever nature, of the delinquent, or in which he has any right, title or interest, to the payment of such tax or liability. In any such proceeding, at the instance of the United States, the court may appoint a receiver to enforce the lien, or, upon certification by the Commissioner or the Chief Counsel for the Internal Revenue Service during the pendency of such proceedings that it is in the public interest, may appoint a receiver with all the powers of a receiver in equity.

(b) Bid by the United States.—If property is sold to satisfy a first lien held by the United States, the United States may bid at the sale a sum which does not exceed the amount of its lien and the expenses of the sale. See also 31 U.S.C. 195. [Reg. § 301.7403-1.]

☐ [T.D. 6498, 10-24-60. Amended by T.D. 6902, 12-13-66 and T.D. 7305, 3-14-74.]

### [Reg. § 301.7404-1]

**§ 301.7404-1. Authority to bring civil action for estate taxes.**— (a) If the estate tax imposed by chapter 11 of the Code is not paid on or before the last date prescribed for payment, the district director shall proceed to collect the tax under the provisions of general law; or appropriate proceedings in the name of the United States may be commenced in any court having jurisdiction to subject the property of the decedent to be sold under the judgment or decree of the court.

(b) The remedy by action provided in section 7404 is not exclusive. The district director may proceed to collect the tax by levy, as provided in section 6331, on any or all property or rights to property of the estate, or collection may be enforced by an appropriate action against the executor, certain transferees, trustees, and beneficiaries for their personal liability. See §20.2002-1 of this chapter (Estate Tax Regulations). [Reg. §301.7404-1.]

☐ [*T.D.* 6498, 10-24-60.]

### [Reg. §301.7406-1]

**§301.7406-1. Disposition of judgments and moneys received.—** All judgments and moneys recovered or received for taxes, costs, forfeitures, and penalties shall be paid to the district director as collections of internal revenue taxes. [Reg. §301.7406-1.]

☐ [*T.D.* 6498, 10-24-60.]

### [Reg. §301.7409-1]

**§301.7409-1. Action to enjoin flagrant political expenditures of section 501(c)(3) organizations.—**(a) *Letter to organization.—*When the Assistant Commissioner (Employee Plans and Exempt Organizations) concludes that a section 501(c)(3) organization has engaged in flagrant political intervention and is likely to continue to engage in political intervention that involves political expenditures, the Assistant Commissioner (Employee Plans and Exempt Organizations) shall send a letter to the organization providing it with the facts based on which the Service believes that the organization has been engaging in flagrant political intervention and is likely to continue to engage in political intervention that involves political expenditures. The organization will have 10 calendar days after the letter is sent to

respond by establishing that it will immediately cease engaging in political intervention, or by providing the Service with sufficient information to refute the Service's evidence that it has been engaged in flagrant political intervention. The Internal Revenue Service will not proceed to seek an injunction under section 7409 until after the close of this 10-day response period.

(b) *Determination by Commissioner.—*If the organization does not respond within 10 calendar days to the letter under paragraph (a) of this section in a manner sufficient to dissuade the Assistant Commissioner (Employee Plans and Exempt Organizations) of the need for an injunction, the file will be forwarded to the Commissioner of Internal Revenue. The Commissioner of Internal Revenue will personally determine whether to forward to the Department of Justice a recommendation that it immediately bring an action to enjoin the organization from making further political expenditures. The Commissioner may also recommend that the court action include any other action that is appropriate in ensuring that the assets of the section 501(c)(3) organization are preserved for section 501(c)(3) purposes. The authority of the Commissioner to make the determinations described in this paragraph may not be delegated to any other persons.

(c) *Flagrant political intervention.—*For purposes of this section, *flagrant political intervention* is defined as participation in, or intervention in (including the publication and distribution of statements), any political campaign by a section 501(c)(3) organization on behalf of (or in opposition to) any candidate for public office in violation of the prohibition on such participation or intervention in section 501(c)(3) and the regulations thereunder if the participation or intervention is flagrant.

(d) *Effective date.—*This section is effective December 5, 1995. [Reg. §301.7409-1.]

☐ [*T.D.* 8628, 12-4-95.]

# PROCEEDINGS BY TAXPAYERS AND THIRD PARTIES

### [Reg. §301.7422-1]

**§301.7422-1. Special rules for certain excise taxes imposed by chapter 42 or 43.—**(a) *Finality of refund proceeding.—*For purposes of sections 4941, 4942, 4943, 4944, 4945, 4951, 4952, 4955, 4958, 4961, 4963, 4971, and 4975, and the regulations thereunder, a decision in a suit for refund instituted under the provisions of this section shall be final—

(1) Upon the expiration of the time allowed for filing a notice of appeal from a decision of the United States Claims Court or of the United States District Court, if no timely notice of appeal is filed; or

(2) Upon the expiration of the time allowed for filing a petition for certiorari from a decision of the United States Claims Court, or from a decision of the United States District Court, which has been affirmed or the appeal dismissed by the United States Court of Appeals, if no timely petition for certiorari is filed; or

(3) If a petition for certiorari has been filed, thirty days from the denial of such petition; or

(4) Thirty days from the date of a decision of the United States Supreme Court if no timely petition for rehearing is filed; however, if a timely petition for rehearing from such a decision is filed, and is denied, thirty days from the denial thereof; or

(5) If a decision is entered upon a rehearing or if a decision is modified or reversed as the result of a decision of a higher court, upon the expiration, with respect to the decision on rehearing or the modified or reversed decision, of periods similar to those provided in subparagraphs (1) through (4).

(b) *Right to bring action.—*With respect to any taxable event, payment of the full amount of first tier tax for the taxable period shall constitute sufficient payment in order to maintain an action under this section with respect to the second tier tax.

(c) *Limitation on suit for refund.—*No suit may be maintained under this section for the credit or refund of any tax imposed under section 4941, 4942, 4943, 4944, 4945, 4951, 4952, 4955, 4958, 4971, or 4975 with respect to any taxable event unless—

(1) No other suit has been maintained for credit or refund of any tax imposed by such sections with respect to such taxable event; and

(2) No petition has been filed in the Tax Court with respect to a deficiency in any tax imposed by such sections with respect to such taxable event.

(d) *Final determination of issues.—*For purposes of this section, any suit for the credit or refund of any tax imposed under section 4941, 4942, 4943, 4944, 4945, 4951, 4952, 4955, 4958, 4971, or 4975, together

with a supplemental proceeding (if any) under section 4961(b), with respect to any taxable event, shall constitute a suit to determine all questions with respect to any other tax imposed with respect to such taxable event under such sections. Consequently, failure by the parties to the suit to bring before the Court any question described in the preceding sentence shall constitute a bar to the question.

(e) *Definitions.—*For definitions of the terms "taxable event," "first tier tax," and "second tier tax," see §53.4963-1. [Reg. §301.7422-1.]

☐ [*T.D.* 7838, 10-5-82. *Amended by T.D.* 8084, 5-1-86; *T.D.* 8628, 12-4-95 *and T.D.* 8920, 1-9-2001.]

### [Reg. §301.7423-1]

**§301.7423-1. Repayments to officers or employees.—**The Commissioner is authorized to repay to any officer or employee of the United States the full amount of such sums of money as may be recovered against him in any court, for any internal revenue taxes collected by him, with the cost and expense of suit, and all damages and costs recovered against any officer or employee of the United States in any suit brought against him by reason of anything done in the official performance of his duties under the Code. [Reg. §301.7423-1.]

☐ [*T.D.* 6498, 10-24-60.]

### [Reg. §301.7424-2]

**§301.7424-2. Intervention.—**If the United States is not a party to a civil action or suit, the United States may intervene in such action or suit to assert any lien arising under title 26 of the United States Code on the property which is the subject of such action or suit. The provisions of section 2410 of title 28 of the United States Code (except subsection (b)) and of section 1444 of title 28 of the United States Code shall apply in any case in which the United States intervenes as if the United States had originally been named a defendant in such action or suit. If the application of the United States to intervene is denied, the adjudication in such civil action or suit shall have no effect upon such lien. [Reg. §301.7424-2.]

☐ [*T.D.* 7305, 3-14-74.]

### [Reg. §301.7425-1]

**§301.7425-1. Discharge of liens; scope and application; judicial proceedings.—**(a) *In general.—*A tax lien of the United States, or a title derived from the enforcement of a tax lien of the United States, may be discharged or divested under local law only in the manner prescribed in section 2410 of Title 28 of the United States Code or in the manner prescribed in section 7425 of the Internal Revenue Code. Section 7425(a) contains provisions relating to the discharge of a lien when the United States is not joined as a party in the judicial proceedings described in subsection (a) of section 2410 of Title 28 of the United States Code. These judicial proceedings are plenary in nature and proceed on formal pleadings. Section 7425(b) contains provisions relating to the discharge of a lien or a title derived from the enforcement of a lien in the event of a nonjudicial sale with respect to the property involved. Section 7425(c) contains special rules relating to the notice of sale requirements contained in section 7425(b). Section 301.7425-2 contains rules with respect to the nonjudicial sales described in section 7425(b). Paragraph(a) of §301.7425-3 contains rules with respect to the notice of sale provisions of section 7425(c)(1). Paragraph (b) of §301.7425-3 contains rules relating to the consent to sale provisions of section 7425(c)(2). Paragraph (c) of §301.7425-3 contains rules relating to the sale of perishable goods provisions of section 7425(c)(3). Paragraph (d) of §301.7425-3 contains the requirements with respect to the contents of a notice of sale. Section 301.7425-4 prescribes rules with respect to the redemption of real property by the United States.

(b) *Effective date.*—The provisions of section 7425, as added by the Federal Tax Lien Act of 1966, are effective with respect to sales described in section 7425 occurring after November 2, 1966. The notice of sale provisions of section 7425(c)(1) or (3) do not apply to sales occurring after November 2, 1966, if the seller of the property performed an act before November 3, 1966, which act at the time of performance was required and effective under local law with respect to the sale. An example of such an act is publication of a notice of the sale in a local newspaper before November 3, 1966, if local law requires such publication before a sale and the publication is effective under local law. Accordingly, in such a case, it is not necessary to notify the Internal Revenue Service pursuant to the provisions of section 7425(c)(1) or (3). With respect to a notice of sale required under section 7425(c)(1) or (3)—

(1) Any notice of sale given to an office of the Internal Revenue Service or the Treasury Department during the period November 3, 1966, through December 21, 1966, shall be considered as adequate;

(2) Any notice of sale given during the period December 22, 1966, through January 31, 1968, which complies with the provisions of either—

(i) Revenue Procedure 67-25, 1967-1 C.B. 626 (based on Technical Information Release 873, dated December 22, 1966), or

(ii) Section 301.7425-3,

shall be considered as adequate; and

(3) Any notice of sale given after January 31, 1968, which complies with the provisions of §301.7425-3 shall be considered as adequate.

(c) *Judicial proceedings.*—(1) *In general.*—Section 7425(a) provides rules, where the United States is not joined as a party, to determine the effect of a judgment in any civil action or suit described in subsection (a) of section 2410 of title 28 of the United States Code (relating to joinder of the United States in certain proceedings), or a judicial sale pursuant to such a judgment, with respect to property on which the United States has or claims a lien under the provisions of this title. If the United States is improperly named as a party to a judicial proceeding, the effect is the same as if the United States were not joined.

(2) *Notice of lien filed when the proceeding is commenced.*—Where the United States is not properly joined as a party in the court proceeding and a notice of lien has been filed in accordance with section 6323(f) or (g) in the place provided by law for such filing at the time the action or suit is commenced, a judgment or judicial sale pursuant to such a judgment shall be made subject to and without disturbing the lien of the United States.

(3) *Notice of lien not filed when the proceeding is commenced.*— (i) *General rule.*—Where the United States is not joined as a party in the court proceeding and either a notice of lien has not been filed in accordance with section 6323(f) or (g) in the place provided by law for such filing at the time the action or suit is commenced, or the law makes no provision for that filing, a judgment or judicial sale pursuant to such a judgment shall have the same effect with respect to the discharge or divestment of the lien of the United States as may be provided with respect to these matters by the local law of the place where the property is situated.

(ii) *Examples.*—The provisions of subparagraph (3) may be illustrated by the following examples:

*Example (1).* A, the first mortgagee of an apartment building located in State Y, commenced a foreclosure action on the mortgage prior to the time that a notice of a Federal tax lien, on that building, had been filed. Under the law of Y, junior liens on real property are discharged by a judicial sale pursuant to a judgment in a foreclosure

action. Therefore, the Federal tax lien on the building will be discharged by the judicial sale. This result is the same whether the tax lien arose before or after the date of commencement of the foreclosure action and whether notice of the tax lien was filed at any time after commencement of the foreclosure action.

*Example (2).* On January 10, 1969, B dies testate and devises Blackacre to C. At B's death, Blackacre is subject to a first mortgage held by D. Realty is subject to administration as part of a decedent's estate under the laws of State X. However, C takes possession of Blackacre with the assent of E, the executor of B's estate. On January 5, 1970, D commences a foreclosure action on the mortgage. Under the law of X, junior liens on real property are discharged by a judicial sale pursuant to a judgment in a foreclosure action. After commencement of the proceedings, an assessment for estate taxes is made and, thereafter, a notice of lien is filed in accordance with section 6323. The special lien on Blackacre, arising at the date of B's death, for estate taxes under section 6324(a) will be discharged by the judicial sale because there are no provisions for filing a notice thereof under law and junior liens are discharged by the sale under local law. The lien is discharged even though the executor failed to obtain a discharge of his personal liability under section 2204. Furthermore, the general lien on Blackacre under section 6321 will be discharged by the judicial sale because the foreclosure action was commenced prior to the time that a notice of lien was filed.

(4) *Proceeds of a judicial sale.*—If a judicial sale of property pursuant to a judgment in any civil action or suit to which the United States is not a party discharges a lien of the United States arising under the provisions of the Internal Revenue Code of 1954, the United States may claim the proceeds of the sale (exclusive of costs) prior to the time that distribution of the proceeds is ordered. The claim of the United States in such a case is treated as having the same priority with respect to the proceeds as the lien had with respect to the property which was discharged from the lien by the judicial sale. [Reg. §301.7425-1.]

☐ [T.D. 7430, 5-20-75.]

**[Reg. §301.7425-2]**

**§301.7425-2. Discharge of liens; nonjudicial sales.**—(a) *In general.*—Section 7425(b) contains provisions with respect to the effect on the interest of the United States in property in which the United States has or claims a lien, or a title derived from the enforcement of a lien, of a sale made pursuant to—

(1) An instrument creating a lien on the property sold,

(2) A confession of judgment on the obligation secured by an instrument creating a lien on the property sold, or

(3) A statutory lien on the property sold.

For purposes of this section, such a sale is referred to as a "nonjudicial sale." The term "nonjudicial sale" includes, but is not limited to, the divestment of the taxpayer's interest in property which occurs by operation of law, by public or private sale, by forfeiture, or by termination under provisions contained in a contract for a deed or a conditional sales contract. Under section 7425(b)(1), if a notice of lien is filed in accordance with section 6323(f) or (g), or the title derived from the enforcement of a lien is recorded as provided by local law, more than 30 days before the date of sale, and the appropriate district director is not given notice of the sale (in the manner prescribed in §301.7425-3), the sale shall be made subject to and without disturbing the lien or title of the United States. Under section 7425(b)(2)(C), in any case in which notice of the sale is given to the district director not less than 25 days prior to the date of sale (in the manner prescribed in section 7425(c)(1)), the sale shall have the same effect with respect to the discharge or divestment of the lien or title as may be provided by local law with respect to other junior liens or other titles derived, from the enforcement of junior liens. A nonjudicial sale pursuant to a lien which is junior to a tax lien does not divest the tax lien, even though notice of the nonjudicial sale is given to the appropriate district director. However, under the provisions of section 6325(b) and §301.6325-1, a district director may discharge the property from a tax lien, including a tax lien which is senior to another lien upon the property.

(b) *Date of sale.*—In the case of a nonjudicial sale subject to the provisions of section 7425(b), in order to compute any period of time determined with reference to the date of sale, the date of sale shall be determined in accordance with the following rules:

(1) In the case of divestment of junior liens on property resulting directly from a public sale, the date of sale is deemed to be the date the public sale is held, regardless of the date under local law on which junior liens on the property are divested or the title to the property is transferred,

(2) In the case of divestment of junior liens on property resulting directly from a private sale, the date of sale is deemed to be the date title to the property is transferred, regardless of the date junior liens on the property are divested under local law, and

(3) In the case of divestment of junior liens on property not resulting directly from a public or private sale, the date of sale is deemed to be the date on which junior liens on the property are divested under local law.

For provisions relating to the right of redemption of the United States, see section 7425(d) and §301.7425-4.

(c) *Examples.*—The provisions of this section may be illustrated by the following examples:

*Example (1).* (i) Under the law of State M, upon entry of judgment, the judgment creditor obtains a statutory lien upon the real property of the judgment debtor, and certain procedures are provided by which the judgment creditor may execute by public sale upon such real property. These procedures provide, among other things, for notification by personal service or registered or certified mail to other lien creditors, if any, and publication of a notice of the sale in a local newspaper. After the expiration of a prescribed period of time after such notification and publication, the sheriff of the county where the real property is located may sell the property at public sale. After payment of the amount bid at the public sale, the sheriff issues to the purchaser a deed to the real property, and the interests of junior lienors in the property are divested.

(ii) For purposes of this section, such an execution sale is a nonjudicial sale described in section 7425(b) because the sale is made pursuant to a statutory lien on the property sold. The date of sale, for purposes of computing a period of time determined with reference to the date of sale, is the date on which the public sale is held because junior liens on the real property are divested directly as a result of the public sale. This result obtains even though the junior liens are legally divested on a later date when the sheriff issues the deed.

*Example (2).* (i) Under the law of State N, mortgages on real property may contain a power of sale which authorizes the mortgagee, upon breach by the mortgagor of one of the conditions of the mortgage, to have the mortgaged property sold at public sale. This public sale must be preceded by notice by advertisement in a local newspaper, and the time, place, description of the property, and other terms of the sale must be specified. The purchaser at such a public sale obtains a title to the real property which is not subject to a right of redemption by the mortgagor and which divests the interests of the junior lienors in the property.

(ii) For purposes of this section, a sale pursuant to such a power of sale is a nonjudicial sale described in section 7425(b) because the sale is made pursuant to the mortgage instrument which created a lien on the property sold. The date of the sale, for purposes of computing a period of time determined with reference to the date of sale, is the date of the public sale because junior liens on the property are divested directly as a result of the public sale.

*Example (3).* Assume the same facts as in example (2) except that the purchaser at the public sale obtains a title which is defeasible by the exercise of a right of redemption in the mortgagor. The purchaser's title divests the interests of junior lienors in the property as of the time of public sale. The interests of junior lienors in the property revive if the mortgagor exercises his right of redemption. The date of the sale, for purposes of computing a period of time determined with reference to the date of sale, is the date of the public sale because junior liens on the property are divested directly as a result of the public sale although such junior liens may be revived by a subsequent redemption by the mortgagor.

*Example (4).* (i) Under the law of State O, upon breach by a mortgagor of real property of one of the conditions of the mortgage, the mortgagee may foreclose the mortgage by securing possession of the property by one of several procedures provided by statute. These procedures are generally referred to as "strict foreclosure." In order for a foreclosure to be effective under these procedures, a certificate attesting the fact of entry must be recorded with the proper registrar of deeds within 30 days after the mortgagee enters the property. During the one-year period following the date on which the certificate of entry is recorded, the mortgagor or a junior lienor may redeem the property by paying the mortgagee the amount of the mortgage obligation. If, during such one-year period the property is not redeemed and the mortgagee's possession is continued, the interests of the mortgagor and the junior lienors in the property are divested as of the date such one-year period expires.

(ii) For purposes of this section, such a foreclosure procedure is a nonjudicial sale described in section 7425(b) because it results in the divestment of the mortgagor's interest in the property by operation of law pursuant to the mortgage which created a lien on the property. In addition, because there is no public or private sale which directly results in the divestment of junior liens on the property, the date of sale, for purposes of computing a period of time determined with reference to the date of sale, is the date on which the one-year period following the recording of the certificate of entry expires.

*Example (5).* The law of State P contains a procedure which permits a county to collect a delinquent tax assessment with respect to real property by the means of a tax sale of the property. First, a notice of a public auction with respect to the tax assessment on the real property is published in a local newspaper. At the public auction, the purchaser, upon payment of the delinquent taxes and interest, obtains from the county tax collector a tax certificate with respect to the real property. Because the obtaining of this tax certificate does not directly result in the divestment of either the owner's title or junior liens with respect to the property, the public auction is not a nonjudicial sale described in section 7425(b). At any time before a tax deed with respect to the property is issued by the clerk of the county court, the owner or any holder of a lien or other interest with respect to the property may obtain the tax certificate by paying the holder of the tax certificate the amount of the taxes, interest, and costs. After a date which is two years after the date on which the tax assessment became delinquent, the holder of the tax certificate may request the clerk of the county court to have the property advertised for sale. After advertisement of the sale, the clerk of the county court conducts a public sale of the real property and the purchaser obtains a tax deed. The interests of all junior lienors in the property are divested and the property is not subject to a right of redemption under the law of State P. For purposes of this section, this public sale is considered to be a nonjudicial sale described in section 7425(b) because the sale is made pursuant to a statutory lien on the property sold. The date of the sale, for purposes of computing a period of time determined with reference to the date of sale, is the date on which the public sale is held at which the purchaser obtains a tax deed as this sale directly results in the divestment of junior liens on the property.

*Example (6).* The law of State Q contains a provision which permits a county to collect a delinquent tax assessment with respect to real property by the means of a tax sale of the property. After public notice is given, a "tax sale" of the real property is conducted. Upon payment of the delinquent taxes and interest, a purchaser obtains a tax certificate with respect to the real property. If there is no purchaser at the tax sale, the property is deemed to be bid in by the State. Because the obtaining of this tax certificate by a purchaser or State Q does not directly result in the divestment of either the owner's title or junior liens with respect to the property, the tax sale is not a nonjudicial sale described in section 7425(b). Following the tax sale, there is a three year period during which any person having an interest in the property may redeem the property by paying the holder of the tax certificate the amount of taxes, interest, and costs. Unless redeemed, the holder of the tax certificate may obtain an absolute title at the expiration of the period of redemption provided he serves a notice of the expiration of the redemption period upon the owner at least 60 days prior to the date of expiration. Because there is no public or private sale which directly results in the divestment of junior liens on the property, the date of sale, for purposes of computing a period of time determined with reference to the date of sale, is the date on which the holder of the tax certificate obtains absolute title. [Reg. §301.7425-2.]

☐ [*T.D. 7430, 8-19-76.*]

**[Reg. §301.7425-3]**

**§301.7425-3. Discharge of liens; special rules.**—(a) *Notice of sale requirements.*—(1) *In general.*—Except in the case of the sale of perishable goods described in paragraph (c) of this section, a notice (as described in paragraph (d) of this section) of a nonjudicial sale shall be given, in writing by registered or certified mail or by personal service, not less than 25 days prior to the date of sale (determined under the provisions of §301.7425-2(b)), to the Internal Revenue Service (IRS) official, office and address specified in IRS Publication 786, "Instructions for Preparing a Notice of Nonjudicial Sale of Property and Application for Consent to Sale," or any successor publication. The relevant IRS publications may be downloaded from the IRS internet site at *www.irs.gov*. Under this section, a notice of sale is not effective if it is given to an office other than the office listed in the relevant publication. The provisions of sections 7502 (relating to timely mailing treated as timely filing) and 7503 (relating to time for performance of acts where the last day falls on Saturday, Sunday, or a legal holiday) apply in the case of notices required to be made under this paragraph.

(2) *Postponement of scheduled sale.*—(i) *Where notice of sale is given.*—In the event that notice of a sale is given in accordance with subparagraph (1) of this paragraph with respect to a scheduled sale which is postponed to a later time or date, the seller of the property is required to give notice of the postponement to the IRS in the same manner as is required under local law with respect to other secured creditors. For example, assume that in State M local law requires that in the event of a postponement of a scheduled foreclosure sale of real property, an oral announcement of the postponement at the place and time of the scheduled sale constitutes sufficient notice to secured creditors of the postponement. Accordingly, if at the place and time of a scheduled sale in State M an oral announcement of the postponement is made, the Internal Revenue Service is considered to have notice of the postponement for the purpose of this subparagraph.

Reg. §301.7425-3(a)(2)(i)

(ii) *Where notice of sale is not given.*—In the event that—

(A) Notice of a nonjudicial sale would not be required under subparagraph (1) of this paragraph if the sale were held on the originally scheduled date,

(B) Because of a postponement of the scheduled sale, more than 30 days elapse between the originally scheduled date of the sale and the date of the sale, and

(C) A notice of lien with respect to the property to be sold is filed more than 30 days before the date of the sale,

notice of the sale is required to be given to the IRS in accordance with the provisions of subparagraph (1) of this paragraph. In any case in which notice of sale is required to be given with respect to a scheduled sale, and notice of the sale is not given, any postponement of the scheduled sale does not affect the rights of the United States under section 7425(b).

(iii) *Examples.*—The provisions of subdivision (ii) of this subparagraph may be illustrated by the following examples:

*Example (1).* A nonjudicial sale of Blackacre, belonging to A, a delinquent taxpayer, is scheduled for December 2, 1968. As no notice of lien is filed applicable to Blackacre more than 30 days before December 2, 1968, no notice of sale is given to the IRS. On December 2, 1968, the sale of Blackacre is postponed until January 15, 1969. A notice of lien with respect to Blackacre is properly filed on January 2, 1969. The sale of Blackacre is held on January 15, 1969. Even though more than 30 days elapsed between the originally scheduled date of the sale (December 2, 1968) and the date of the sale (January 15, 1969), no notice of sale is required to be given to the IRS because the notice of lien was not filed more than 30 days before the date of the sale.

*Example (2).* Assume the same facts as in example (1) except that a notice of lien is filed on November 29, 1968 in accordance with section 6323. Because more than 30 days elapsed between the originally scheduled date of the sale and the date of the sale, and the notice of lien is filed (on November 29, 1968) more than 30 days before the date of the sale (January 15, 1969), notice of the sale, in accordance with the provisions of subparagraph (1) of this paragraph, is required to be given to the IRS.

*Example (3).* A nonjudicial sale of Whiteacre, belonging to B, a delinquent taxpayer, is scheduled for December 2, 1968. A notice of lien applicable to Whiteacre is filed on November 12, 1968 in accordance with section 6323. As the notice of lien was not filed more than 30 days before December 2, 1968, no notice of sale is given to the IRS. On December 2, 1968, the sale of Whiteacre is postponed until December 20, 1968. The sale of Whiteacre is held on December 20, 1968. Even though more than 30 days elapsed between the date notice of lien was filed (November 12, 1968) and the date of the sale (December 20, 1968), no notice of sale is required to be given to the IRS because not more than 30 days elapsed between the date of the originally scheduled sale (December 2, 1968) and the date the sale was actually held (December 20, 1968).

(b) *Consent to sale.*—(1) *In general.*—Notwithstanding the notice of sale provisions of paragraph (a) of this section, a nonjudicial sale of property shall discharge or divest the property of the lien and title of the United States if the IRS consents to the sale of the property free of the lien or title. Pursuant to section 7425(c)(2), where adequate protection is afforded the lien or title of the United States, the IRS may, in its discretion, consent with respect to the sale of property in appropriate cases. Such consent shall be effective only if given in writing and shall be subject to such limitations and conditions as the IRS may require. However, the IRS may not consent to a sale of property under this section after the date of sale, as determined under §301.7425-2(b). For provisions relating to the authority of the IRS to release a lien or discharge property subject to a tax lien, see section 6325 and the section 6325 regulations.

(2) *Application for consent.*—Any person desiring the IRS's consent to sell property free of a tax lien or a title derived from the enforcement of a tax lien of the United States in the property shall submit to the IRS, at the office and address specified in the relevant IRS publications, a written application, in triplicate, declaring that it is made under penalties of perjury, and requesting that such consent be given. The application shall contain the information required in the case of a notice of sale, as set forth in paragraph (d)(1) of this section, and, in addition, shall contain a statement of the reasons why the consent is desired.

(c) *Sale of perishable goods.*—(1) *In general.*—A notice (as described in paragraph (d) of this section) of a nonjudicial sale of perishable goods (as defined in paragraph (c)(2) of this section) shall be given in writing, by registered or certified mail or delivered by personal service, at any time before the sale, to the IRS official and office specified in the relevant IRS publications, at the address specified in such publications. Under this section, a notice of sale is not effective if it is given to an office other than the office listed in the relevant

publication. If a notice of a nonjudicial sale is timely given in the manner described in this paragraph, the nonjudicial sale shall discharge or divest the tax lien, or a title derived from the enforcement of a tax lien, of the United States in the property. The provisions of sections 7502 (relating to timely mailing treated as timely filing) and 7503 (relating to time for performance of acts where the last day falls on Saturday, Sunday, or a legal holiday) apply in the case of notices required to be made under this paragraph. The seller of the perishable goods shall hold the proceeds (exclusive of costs) of the sale as a fund, for not less than 30 days after the date of the sale, subject to the liens and claims of the United States, in the same manner and with the same priority as the liens and claims of the United States had with respect to the property sold. If the seller fails to hold the proceeds of the sale in accordance with the provisions of this paragraph and if the IRS asserts a claim to the proceeds within 30 days after the date of sale, the seller shall be personally liable to the United States for an amount equal to the value of the interest of the United States in the fund. However, even if the proceeds of the sale are not so held by the seller, but all the other provisions of this paragraph are satisfied, the buyer of the property at the sale takes the property free of the liens and claims of the United States. In the event of a postponement of the scheduled sale of perishable goods, the seller is not required to notify the IRS of the postponement. For provisions relating to the authority of the IRS to release a lien or discharge property subject to a tax lien, see section 6325 and the regulations.

(2) *Definition of perishable goods.*—For the purpose of this paragraph, the term "perishable goods" means any tangible personal property which, in the reasonable view of the person selling the property, is liable to perish or become greatly reduced in price or value by keeping, or cannot be kept without great expense.

(d) *Content of notice of sale.*—(1) *In general.*—With respect to a notice of sale described in paragraph (a) or (c) of this section, the notice will be considered adequate if it contains the information described in subdivision (i), (ii), (iii), and (iv) of this subparagraph.

(i) The name and address of the person submitting the notice of sale;

(ii) A copy of each Notice of Federal Tax Lien (Form 668) affecting the property to be sold, or the following information as shown on each such Notice of Federal Tax Lien—

(A) The IRS office named thereon,

(B) The name and address of the taxpayer, and

(C) The date and place of filing of the notice;

(iii) With respect to the property to be sold, the following information—

(A) A detailed description, including location, of the property affected by the notice (in the case of real property, the street address, city, and State and the legal description contained in the title or deed to the property and, if available, a copy of the abstract of title),

(B) The date, time, place, and terms of the proposed sale of the property, and

(C) In the case of a sale of perishable property described in paragraph (c) of this section, a statement of the reasons why the property is believed to be perishable; and

(iv) The approximate amount of the principal obligation, including interest, secured by the lien sought to be enforced and a description of the other expenses (such as legal expenses, selling costs, etc.) which may be charged against the sale proceeds.

(2) *Inadequate notice.*—Except as otherwise provided in this paragraph, a notice of sale described in paragraph (a) of this section that does not contain the information described in paragraph (d)(1) of this section shall be considered inadequate by the IRS. If the IRS determines that the notice is inadequate, the IRS will give written notification of the items of information which are inadequate to the person who submitted the notice. A notice of sale that does not contain the name and address of the person submitting such notice shall be considered to be inadequate for all purposes without notification of any specific inadequacy. In any case where a notice of sale does not contain the information required under paragraph (d)(1)(ii) of this section with respect to a Notice of Federal Tax Lien, the IRS may give written notification of such omission without specification of any other inadequacy and such notice of sale shall be considered inadequate for all purposes. In the event the IRS gives notification that the notice of sale is inadequate, a notice complying with the provisions of this section (including the requirement that the notice be given not less than 25 days prior to the sale in the case of a notice described in paragraph (a) of this section) must be given. However, in accordance with the provisions of paragraph (b)(1) of this section, in such a case the IRS may, in its discretion, consent to the sale of the property free of the lien or title of the United States even though notice of the sale is given less than 25 days prior to the sale. In any case where the person who submitted a timely notice, which indicates his name and

address, does not receive more than 5 days prior to the date of sale written notification from the IRS that the notice is inadequate, the notice shall be considered adequate for purposes of this section.

(3) *Acknowledgment of notice.*—If a notice of sale described in paragraph (a) or (c) of this section is submitted in duplicate to the IRS with a written request that receipt of the notice be acknowledged and returned to the person giving the notice, this request will be honored by the IRS. The acknowledgment by the IRS will indicate the date and time of the receipt of the notice.

(4) *Disclosure of adequacy of notice.*—The IRS is authorized to disclose, to any person who has a proper interest, whether an adequate notice of sale was given under paragraph (d)(1) of this section. Any person desiring this information should submit to the IRS a written request that clearly describes the property sold or to be sold, identifies the applicable notice of lien, gives the reasons for requesting the information, and states the name and address of the person making the request. The request should be submitted to the IRS official, office and address specified in IRS Publication 4235, "Technical Services (Advisory) Group Addresses," or any successor publication. The relevant IRS publications may be downloaded from the IRS internet site at *www.irs.gov*.

(e) *Effective/applicability date.*—These regulations are effective on July 8, 2008. [Reg. § 301.7425-3.]

☐ [*T.D. 7430, 8-19-76. Amended by T.D. 9344, 7-19-2007 and T.D. 9410, 7-7-2008.*]

### [Reg. § 301.7425-4]

**§ 301.7425-4. Discharge of liens; redemption by United States.**— (a) *Right to redeem.*—(1) *In general.*—In the case of a nonjudicial sale of real property to satisfy a lien prior to the tax lien or a title derived from the enforcement of a tax lien, the district director may redeem the property within the redemption period (as described in subparagraph (2) of this paragraph). The right of redemption of the United States exists under section 7425(d) even though the district director has consented to the sale under section 7425(c)(2) and § 301.7425-3(b). For purposes of this section, the term "nonjudicial sale" shall have the same meaning as used in paragraph (a) of § 301.7425-2.

(2) *Redemption period.*—For purposes of this section, the redemption period shall be—

(i) The period beginning with the date of the sale (as determined under paragraph (b) of § 301.7425-2) and ending with the 120th day after such date, or

(ii) The period for redemption of real property allowable, with respect to other secured creditors, under the local law of the place where the real property is located, whichever expires later. Whichever period is applicable, section 7425 and this section shall govern the amount to be paid and the procedure to be followed.

(3) *Limitations.*—In the event a sale does not ultimately discharge the property from the tax lien (whether by reason of local law or the provisions of section 7425(b)), the provisions of this section do not apply because the tax lien will continue to attach to the property after the sale. In a case in which the Internal Revenue Service is not entitled to a notice of sale under section 7425(b) and § 301.7425-3, the United States does not have a right of redemption under section 7425(d). However, in such a case, if a tax lien has attached to the property at the time of sale, the United States has the same right of redemption, if any, which is afforded to any similar creditors under the local law of the place in which the property is situated.

(b) *Amount to be paid.*—(1) *In general.*—In any case in which a district director exercises the right to redeem real property under section 7425(d), the amount to be paid is the sum of the following amounts—

(i) The actual amount paid for the property (as determined under subparagraph (2) of this paragraph) being redeemed (which, in the case of a purchaser who is the holder of the lien being foreclosed, shall include the amount of the obligation secured by such lien to the extent legally satisfied by reason of the sale);

(ii) Interest on the amount paid (described in subdivision (i) of this subparagraph) at the sale by the purchaser of the real property computed at the rate of 6 percent per annum for the period from the date of the sale (as determined under paragraph (b) of § 301.7425-2) to the date of redemption;

(iii) The amount, if any, equal to the excess of (A) the expenses necessarily incurred to maintain such property (as determined under subparagraph (3) of this paragraph) by the purchaser (and his successor in interest, if any) over (B) the income from such property realized by the purchaser (and his successor in interest, if any) plus a reasonable rental value of such property (to the extent the property is used by or with the consent of the purchaser or his

successor in interest or is rented at less than its reasonable rental value); and

(iv) With respect to a redemption made after December 31, 1976, the amount, if any, of a payment made by the purchaser or his successor in interest after the foreclosure sale to a holder of a senior lien (to the extent provided under subparagraph (4) of this paragraph).

(2) *Actual amount paid.*—(i) The actual amount paid for property by a purchaser, other than the holder of the lien being foreclosed, is the amount paid by him at the sale. For purposes of this subdivision, the amount paid by the purchaser at the sale includes deferred payments upon the bid price. The actual amount paid does not include costs and expenses incurred prior to the foreclosure sale by the purchaser except to the extent such expenses are included in the amount bid and paid for the property. For example, the actual amount paid does not normally include the expenses of the purchaser such as title searches, professional fees, or interest on debt incurred to obtain funds to purchase the property.

(ii) In the case of a purchaser who is the holder of the lien being foreclosed, the actual amount paid is the sum of (A) the amount of the obligation sucured by such lien to the extent legally satisfied by reason of the sale and (B) any additional amount bid and paid at the sale. For purposes of this section, a purchaser who acquires title as a result of a nonjudicial foreclosure sale is treated as the holder of the lien being foreclosed if a lien (or any interest reserved, created, or conveyed as security for the payment of a debt or fulfullment of other obligation) held by him is partially or fully satisfied by reason of the foreclosure sale. For example, a person whose title is derived from a tax deed issued under local law shall be treated as a purchaser who is the holder of the lien foreclosed in a case where a tax certificate, evidencing a lien on the property arising from the payment of property taxes, ripens into title. The amount paid by a purchaser at the sale includes deferred payments upon any portion of the bid price which is in excess of the amount of the lien being foreclosed. The actual amount paid does not include costs and expenses incurred prior to the foreclosure sale by the purchaser except to the extent such expenses are included in the amount of the lien being foreclosed which is legally satisfied by reason of the sale or in the amount bid and paid at the sale. Where the lien being foreclosed attaches to other property not subject to the foreclosure sale, the amount legally satisfied by reason of the sale does not include the amount of such lien that attaches to the other property. However, for purposes of the preceding sentence, the amount of the lien that attaches to the other property shall be considered to be equal to the amount by which the value of the other property exceeds the amount of any other senior lien on that property. Where, after the sale, the holder of the lien being foreclosed has the right to the unpaid balance of the amount due him, the amount legally satisfied by reason of the sale does not include the amount of such lien to the extent a deficiency judgment may be obtained therefor. However, for purposes of the preceding sentence, an amount, with respect to which the holder of the lien being foreclosed would otherwise have a right to a deficiency judgment, shall be considered to be legally satisfied by reason of the foreclosure sale to the extent that the holder has waived his right to a deficiency judgment prior to the foreclosure sale. For this purpose, the waiver must be in writing and legally binding upon the foreclosing lienholder as of the time the sale is concluded. If, prior to the foreclosure, payments have been made by the foreclosing lienhold to a holder of a superior lien, the payments are included in the actual amount paid to the extent they give rise to an interest which is legally satisfied by reason of the foreclosure sale.

(3) *Excess expenses incurred by purchaser.*—(i) Expenses necessarily incurred in connection with the property after the foreclosure sale and before redemption by the United States are taken into account in determining if there are excess expenses payable under subparagraph (1)(iii) of this paragraph. Expenses incurred by the purchaser prior to the foreclosure sale are not considered under this subparagraph. (See subparagraph (2)(ii) of this paragraph for circumstances under which such expenses may be included in the amount to be paid.) Expenses necessarily incurred in connection with the property include, for example, rental agent commissions, repair and maintenance expenses, utilities expenses, legal fees incurred after the foreclosure sale and prior to redemption in defending the title acquired through the foreclosure sale, and a proportionate amount of casualty insurance premiums and ad valorem taxes. Improvements made to the property are not considered as an expense unless the amounts incurred for such improvements are necessarily incurred to maintain the property.

(ii) At any time prior to the expiration of the redemption period applicable under paragraph (a)(2) of this section, the district director may, by certified or registered mail or hand delivery, request a written itemized statement of the amount claimed by the purchaser or his successor in interest to be payable under subparagraph (1)(iii) of this paragraph. Unless the purchaser or his successor in interest furnishes the written itemized statement within 15 days after the request is made by the district director, it shall be presumed that no amount is payable for expenses in excess of income and the Internal Revenue Service shall tender only the amount otherwise payable under subparagraph (1) of this paragraph. If a purchaser or his or her successor in interest has failed to furnish the written itemized statement within 15 days after the request is made by the district director, or there is a disagreement as to the amount properly payable under paragraph (b)(1)(iii) of this section, or if there were additional excess expenses that were not claimed in the original itemized statement, the purchaser or his or her successor in interest may submit a written itemized statement to the district director within 30 days after the date of redemption. If the purchaser or his or her successor in interest fails to timely submit such a written itemized statement, no amount shall be payable for expenses in excess of income.

(4) *Payments made by purchaser or his successor in interest to a senior lienor.*—(i) The amount to be paid upon a redemption by the United States made after December 31, 1976, shall include the amount of a payment made by the purchaser or his successor in interest to a holder of a senior lien to the extent a request for the reimbursement thereof (made in accordance with subdivision (ii) of this subparagraph) is approved as provided under subdivision (iii) of this subparagraph. This subparagraph applies only to a payment made after the foreclosure sale and before the redemption to a holder of a lien that was, immediately prior to the foreclosure sale, superior to the lien foreclosed. A payment of principal or interest to a senior lienor shall be taken into account. Generally, the portion, if any, of a payment which is to be held in escrow for the payment of an expense, such as hazard insurance or real property taxes, is not considered under this subparagraph. However, a payment by the escrow agent of a real property tax or special assessment lien, which was senior to the lien foreclosed, shall be considered to be a payment made by the purchaser or his successor in interest for purposes of this subparagraph. With respect to real property taxes assessed after the foreclosure sale, see subparagraph (3)(i) of this paragraph, relating to excess expenses incurred by the purchaser.

(ii) Before the expiration of the redemption period applicable under paragraph (a)(2) of this section, the district director shall, in any case where a redemption is contemplated, send notice to the purchaser (or his successor in interest of record) by certified or registered mail or hand delivery of his right under this subparagraph to request reimbursement (payable in the event the right to redeem under section 7425(d) is exercised) for a payment made to a senior lienor. No later than 15 days after the notice from the district director is sent, the request for reimbursement shall be mailed or delivered to the office specified in such notice and shall consist of—

(A) A written itemized statement, signed by the claimant, of the amount claimed with respect to a payment made to a senior lienor, together with the supporting evidence requested in the notice from the district director, and

(B) A waiver or other document that will be effective upon redemption by the United States to discharge the property from, or transfer to the United States, any interest in or lien on the property that may arise under local law with respect to the payment made to a senior lienor.

Upon a showing of reasonable cause, a district director may, in his discretion and at any time before the expiration of the applicable period for redemption, grant an extension for a reasonable period of time to submit, amend, or supplement a request for reimbursement. Unless a request for reimbursement is timely submitted (determined with regard to any extension of time granted), no amount shall be payable to the purchaser or his successor in interest on account of a payment made to a senior lienor if the right to redeem under section 7425(d) is exercised. A waiver or other document submitted pursuant to this subdivision shall be treated as effective only to the extent of the amount included in the redemption price under this subparagraph. If the right to redeem is not exercised or a request for reimbursement is withdrawn, the district director shall, by certified or registered mail or hand delivery, return to the purchaser or his successor any waiver or other document submitted pursuant to this subdivision as soon as is practicable.

(iii) A request for reimbursement submitted in accordance with subdivision (ii) of this subparagraph shall be considered to be approved for the total amount claimed by the purchaser, and payable in the event the right to redeem is exercised, unless the district director sends notice to the claimant, by certified or registered mail or hand delivery, of the denial of the amount claimed within 30 days after receipt of the request or 15 days before expiration of the applicable period for redemption, whichever is later. The notification of denial shall state the grounds for denial. If such notice of denial is given, the request for reimbursement for a payment made to a senior lienor shall be treated as having been withdrawn by the purchaser or

his successor and the Internal Revenue Service shall tender only the amount otherwise payable under subparagraph (1) of this paragraph. If a request for reimbursement is treated as having been withdrawn under the preceding sentence, payment for amounts described in this subparagraph may, in the discretion of the district director, be made after the redemption upon the resolution of the disagreement as to the amount properly payable under paragraph (1)(iv) of this paragraph.

(5) *Examples.*—The provisions of subparagraph (1)(i) of this paragraph may be illustrated by the following examples:

*Example (1).* A, a delinquent taxpayer, owns Blackacre located in State X upon which B holds a mortgage. After the mortgage is properly recorded, a notice of tax lien is filed under section 6323(f) which is applicable to Blackacre. Subsequently, A defaults on the mortgage and B forecloses on the mortgage which has an outstanding obligation in the amount of $100,000. At the foreclosure sale, B bids $50,000 and obtains title to Blackacre as a result of the sale. At the time of the foreclosure sale, Blackacre has a fair market value of $75,000. Under the laws of State X, the mortgage obligation is fully satisfied by operation of the foreclosure sale per se and the mortgagee cannot obtain a deficiency judgment. Under paragraph (b)(1)(i) of this section, the district director must pay $100,000 in order to redeem Blackacre.

*Example (2).* Assume the same facts as in example (1) except that under the laws of State X, the amount bid is the amount of the obligation legally satisfied as a result of the foreclosure sale, and in the case in which the amount of the obligation exceeds the amount bid, the mortgagee has the right to a judgment for the deficiency computed as the difference between the amount of the obligation and the amount bid. B does not waive, prior to the foreclosure sale, his right to a deficiency judgment. In such a case, the district director must, under paragraph (b)(1)(i) of this section, pay $50,000 in order to redeem Blackacre, whether or not B seeks a judgment for the deficiency.

*Example (3).* C, a delinquent taxpayer, owns Greenacre located in State Y upon which D holds a first mortgage and E holds a second mortgage. After the mortgages are properly recorded, a notice of tax lien is filed under section 6323(f) which is applicable to Greenacre. Subsequently, C defaults on both mortgages and E pays $5,000 to D, which is the portion of D's obligation which is in default. The second mortgage held by E is an outstanding obligation in the amount of $100,000. Under the laws of State Y, E may treat the amount paid to D as an addition to his second mortgage upon foreclosure by him. E forecloses upon the security interest held by him. At the foreclosure sale, E bids $50,000 and obtains title to Greenacre subject to D's mortgage as a result of the foreclosure sale. Under the laws of State Y, the mortgage obligation legally satisfied is the amount bid and E has the right to a judgment for a deficiency in the amount of $55,000 ($100,000 plus $5,000 less $50,000). In such a case, the district director must, under paragraph (b)(1)(i) of this section, pay $50,000 in order to redeem Greenacre, whether or not E seeks a judgment for the deficiency.

*Example (4).* The law of State Z contains a procedure which permits a county to collect a delinquent tax assessment with respect to real property by the means of a "tax sale" of the property. Pursuant to this procedure, a public auction is conducted on January 15, 1970, to collect the delinquent property taxes assessed against Whiteacre, which is owned by F. At the auction, a bid of $1,000 (representing the tax, costs, and interest due at the time of the auction) is made by G. Subsequently, G pays the amount bid to the county and obtains a tax certificate with respect to Whiteacre. Under this tax sale procedure, the obtaining of the tax certificate does not directly result in the divestment of either F's title or any junior liens on Whiteacre. On January 15, 1973, the period under this tax sale procedure during which F could have redeemed Whiteacre expires. Further, more than 30 days before January 15, 1973, a notice of tax lien affecting Whiteacre is filed under section 6323(f) with respect to F's delinquent Federal income taxes. Under the state tax sale procedure, the amount which would be required to be paid by F to G on January 15, 1973, to redeem Whiteacre is $1,350 (the $1,000 amount bid, interest of $300, and costs of $50). However, Whiteacre is not redeemed by F under the state procedure and, on January 16, 1973, G obtains a tax deed to Whiteacre. Under the law of State Z, the issuance of the tax deed results in the divestment of F's title and junior liens on Whiteacre. Thus, under §301.7425-2(b), the date of sale is January 16, 1973, for purposes of section 7425(b). The amount legally satisfied by reason of the sale is the amount G is entitled to receive, immediately prior to the expiration of the period for redemption under the law of State Z, if Whiteacre were redeemed at such time. Thus, the district director must, under paragraph (b)(1)(i) of this section pay $1,350 in order to redeem Whiteacre.

(c) *Certificate of redemption.*—(1) *In general.*—If a district director exercises the right of redemption of the United States described in paragraph (a) of this section, he shall apply to the officer designated by local law, if any, for the documents necessary to evidence the fact of redemption and to record title to the redeemed property in the name of the United States. If no such officer has been designated by local law or if the officer designated by local law fails to issue the necessary documents, the district director is authorized to issue a certificate of redemption for the property redeemed by the United States.

(2) *Filing.*—The district director shall, without delay, cause either the documents issued by the local officer or the certificate of redemption executed by the district director to be filed with the local office where certificates of redemption are generally filed. If a certificate of redemption is issued by the district director and if the State in which the real property redeemed by the United States is situated has no office with which certificates of redemption may be filed, the district director shall file the certificate of redemption in the office of the clerk of the United States district court for the judicial district in which the redeemed property is situated.

(3) *Effect of certificate of redemption.*—A certificate of redemption executed pursuant to paragraph (c)(1) of this section shall constitute *prima facie* evidence of the regularity of the redemption. When a certificate of redemption is recorded, it shall transfer to the United States all the rights, title, and interest in and to the redeemed property acquired by the person, from whom the district director redeemed the property, by virtue of the sale of the property. Therefore, if under local law the purchaser takes title free of liens junior to the lien of the foreclosing lienholder, the United States takes title free of such junior liens upon redemption of the property. If a certificate of redemption has been erroneously prepared and filed because the redemption was not effective, the district director shall issue a document revoking such certificate of redemption and such document shall be conclusively binding upon the United States against a purchaser of the property or a holder of a lien upon the property.

(4) *Application for release of right of redemption.*—Upon application of a party with a proper interest in the real property sold in a nonjudicial sale described in section 7425(b) and § 301.7425-2 which real property is subject to the right of redemption of the United States described in this section, the district director may, in his discretion, release the right of redemption with respect to the property. The application for the release shall be submitted in writing to a district director and shall contain such information as the district director may require. If the district director determines that the right of redemption of the United States is without value, no amount shall be required to be paid with respect to the release of the right of redemption. [Reg. § 301.7425-4.]

☐ [T.D. 7430, 8-19-76. Amended by T.D. 8596, 6-1-95.]

### [Reg. § 301.7426-1]

**§ 301.7426-1. Civil actions by persons other than taxpayers.**— (a) *Actions permitted.*—(1) *Wrongful levy.*—(i) *In general.*—If a levy has been made on property or property has been sold pursuant to a levy, any person (other than the person against whom is assessed the tax out of which such levy arose) may bring a civil action against the United States in a district court of the United States based upon such person's claim—

(A) That such person has an interest in, or lien on, such property which is senior to the interest of the United States; and

(B) That such property was wrongfully levied upon.

(ii) *Debt owed by another Federal agency.*—Section 7426 and this paragraph (a) apply when a levy is made by the Internal Revenue Service on a debt owed to a taxpayer by another Federal agency. By contrast, section 7426 and this paragraph (a) do not apply if the Internal Revenue Service requests payment from another Federal agency pursuant to a request for setoff.

(2) *Surplus proceeds.*—If property has been sold pursuant to levy, any person (other than the person against whom is assessed the tax out of which such levy arose) may bring a civil action against the United States in a district court of the United States based upon such person's claim that he—

(i) Has an interest in or lien on such property junior to that of the United States; and

(ii) Is entitled to the surplus proceeds of such sale.

(3) *Substituted sale proceeds.*—Any person who claims to be legally entitled to all or any part of the amount which is held as a fund from the sale of property pursuant to an agreement described in section 6325(b)(3) may bring a civil action against the United States in a district court of the United States to obtain the relief provided by section 7426(b)(4). It is not necessary that the claimant be a party to the agreement which provides for the substitution of the sale proceeds for the property subject to the lien.

(4) *Substitution of value.*—A person who obtains a certificate of discharge under section 6325(b)(4) with respect to any property may, within 120 days after the day on which the certificate is issued, bring a civil action against the United States in a district court of the United States for a determination of whether the value of the interest of the United States (if any) in such property is less than the value determined by the appropriate official. A civil action under this provision shall be the exclusive judicial remedy for a person other than the taxpayer who obtains a certificate of discharge for a filed notice of Federal tax lien.

(b) *Adjudication.*—(1) *Wrongful levy.*—If the court determines that property has been wrongfully levied upon, the court may—

(i) Grant an injunction to prohibit the enforcement of such levy or to prohibit a sale of such property if such sale would irreparably injure rights in the property which are superior to the rights of the United States in such property; or

(ii) Order the return of specific property if the United States is in possession of such property; or

(iii) Grant a judgment for the amount of money levied upon; or

(iv) Grant a judgment for an amount not exceeding the amount received by the United States from the sale of such property (which, in the case of property declared purchased by the United States at a sale, shall be the greater of the minimum amount determined pursuant to section 6335(e) or the amount received by the United States from the resale of such property). For purposes of this paragraph, a levy is wrongful against a person (other than the taxpayer against whom the assessment giving rise to the levy is made) if (*a*) the levy is upon property exempt from levy under section 6334, or (*b*) the levy is upon property in which the taxpayer had no interest at the time the lien arose or thereafter, or (*c*) the levy is upon property with respect to which such person is a purchaser against whom the lien is invalid under section 6323 or 6324(a)(2) or (b), or (*d*) the levy or sale pursuant to levy will or does effectively destroy or otherwise irreparably injure such person's interest in the property which is senior to the Federal tax lien. A levy may be wrongful against a holder of a senior lien upon the taxpayer's property under certain circumstances although legal rights to enforce his interest survive the levy procedure. For example, the levy may be wrongful against such a person if the property is an obligation which is collected pursuant to the levy rather than sold and nothing thereafter remains for the senior lienholder, or the property levied upon is of such a nature that when it is sold at a public sale the property subject to the senior lien is not available for the senior lienholder as a realistic source for the enforcement of his interest. Some of the factors which should be taken into account in determining whether property remains or will remain a realistic source from which the senior lienholder may realize collection are: (*1*) the nature of the property, (*2*) the number of purchasers, (*3*) the value of each unit sold or to be sold, (*4*) whether, as a direct result of the distraint sale, the costs of realizing collection from the security have been or will be so substantially increased as to render the security substantially valueless as a source of collection, and (*5*) whether the property subject to the distraint sale constitutes substantially all of the property available as security for the payment of the indebtedness to the senior lienholder.

(2) *Example.*—The provisions of subparagraph (1) of this paragraph may be illustrated by the following example:

*Example.* On April 10, 1972, A makes a $10,000 loan to B which is partially secured by a $5,000 obligation owed to B by C. Under local law, A's security interest in the obligation owed to B by C is protected against a subsequent judgment lien arising out of an unsecured obligation. Thus, under section 6323(h)(1), A's security interest exists as of April 10, 1972, for purposes of determining priorities against a tax lien under section 6323. On April 17, 1972, an assessment of $6,000 is made against B with respect to his delinquent Federal tax liability. Thereafter, notice of lien is filed pursuant to section 6323(f) with respect to B's delinquent tax liability. On July 10, 1972, a notice of levy is served upon C to reach the amount owed by him to B. C pays over the $5,000 obligation in satisfaction of the levy and, under local law, the obligation is discharged as to A. Because the levy effectively destroyed A's senior security interest in the obligation owed to B by C, the levy is wrongful as to A for purposes of section 7426. Under these circumstances, the levy is wrongful with respect to A even if, under local law, A may have a cause of action in contract against B for the $10,000 loan or may have a cause of action in tort against C for the amount of the $5,000 payment which defeated A's security interest in the obligation owed by C to B.

(3) *Surplus proceeds.*—If the court determines that the interest or lien of any party to an action under section 7426 was transferred to the proceeds of a sale of the property, the court may grant a judgment in an amount equal to all or any part of the amount of the surplus proceeds of such sale. The term "surplus proceeds" means

those proceeds realized on a sale of property remaining after application of the provisions of section 6342(a).

(4) *Substituted sale proceeds.*—If the court determines that a party has an interest in or lien on the amount held as a fund pursuant to an agreement described in section 6325(b)(3), the court may grant a judgment in an amount equal to all or any part of the amount of such fund.

(5) *Substitution of value.*—If the court determines that the determination by the appropriate official of the value of the interest of the United States in the property exceeds the actual value of such interest, the court may grant a judgment ordering a refund of the amount deposited, or a release of the bond, to the extent that the aggregate of those amounts exceeds the value as determined by the court.

(c) *Effective date.*—Paragraph (a)(1) of this section is effective as of December 23, 1993.

(d) Paragraphs (a)(4) and (b)(5) of this section apply to any request for a certificate of discharge made after January 31, 2008. [Reg. §301.7426-1.]

□ [*T.D. 7305, 3-14-74. Amended by T.D. 8541, 5-20-94 and T.D. 9378, 1-30-2008.*]

### [Reg. §301.7426-2]

**§301.7426-2. Recovery of damages in certain cases.**—(a) *In general.*—In addition to remedies related to wrongful levy set forth in §301.7426-1(b), if a district court of the United States finds in any action brought under section 7426 that any officer or employee of the Internal Revenue Service recklessly or intentionally, or by reason of negligence, disregarded any provision of this title, the United States shall be liable to the plaintiff for damages. The plaintiff has a duty to mitigate damages. The total amount of damages recoverable under this section is the lesser of $1,000,000 ($100,000 in the case of negligence), or the sum of—

(1) Actual, direct economic damages as defined in §301.7433-1(b) sustained as a proximate result of the reckless, intentional, or negligent actions of the officer or employee, reduced by the amount of any damages awarded under §301.7426-1(b); and

(2) Costs of the action as defined in §301.7433-1(c).

(b) *Administrative remedies must be exhausted.*—The court may not award a judgment for damages under paragraph (a) of this section unless the court determines that the plaintiff has filed an administrative claim pursuant to paragraph (d) of this section, and has satisfied the requirements of paragraph (c) of this section.

(c) *No request for damages in a district court of the United States prior to filing an administrative claim.*—(1) Except as provided in paragraph (c)(2) of this section, no request for damages under paragraph (a) of this section shall be maintained in any district court of the United States before the earlier of the following dates—

(i) The date the decision is rendered on a claim filed in accordance with paragraph (d) of this section; or

(ii) The date that is six months after the date an administrative claim is filed in accordance with paragraph (d) of this section.

(2) If an administrative claim is filed in accordance with paragraph (d) of this section during the last six months of the period of limitations described in paragraph (f) of this section, the claimant may file an action in a district court of the United States any time after the administrative claim is filed and before the expiration of the period of limitations.

(d) *Procedures for an administrative claim.*—(1) *Manner.*—An administrative claim for the lesser of $1,000,000 ($100,000 in the case of negligence) or actual, direct economic damages as defined in §301.7433-1(b) shall be in writing to the Area Director, Attn: Compliance Technical Support Manager of the area in which the taxpayer currently resides.

(2) *Form.*—The administrative claim shall include—

(i) The name, taxpayer identification number, current address and current home and work telephone numbers (indicating any convenient times to be contacted) of the person making the claim;

(ii) The grounds, in reasonable detail, for the claim (include copies of any available substantiating documentation or correspondence with the Internal Revenue Service);

(iii) A description of the damages incurred by the claimant filing the claim (include copies of any available substantiating documentation or evidence);

(iv) The dollar amount of the claim, including any damages that have not yet been incurred but which are reasonably foreseeable (include copies of any available substantiating documentation or evidence); and

(v) The signature of the claimant or duly authorized representative.

(3) *Duly authorized representative.*—For purposes of this paragraph (d), a duly authorized representative is any attorney, certified public accountant, enrolled actuary, or any other person permitted to represent the claimant before the Internal Revenue Service who is not disbarred or suspended from practice before the Internal Revenue Service and who has a written power of attorney executed to the claimant.

(e) *No liability for damages for any sum in excess of the dollar amount sought in the administrative claim.*—See §301.7433-1(f).

(f) *Period of limitations.*—(1) *Time for filing.*—A civil action under paragraph (a) of this section must be brought in a district court of the United States within two years after the date the cause of action accrues.

(2) *Right of action accrues.*—A cause of action under paragraph (a) of this section accrues when the plaintiff has had a reasonable opportunity to discover all essential elements of a possible cause of action.

(g) *Recovery of costs under section 7430.*—See §301.7433-1(h).

(h) *Effective date.*—This section is applicable March 25, 2003. [Reg. §301.7426-2.]

□ [*T.D. 9050, 3-24-2003.*]

### [Reg. §301.7429-1]

**§301.7429-1. Review of jeopardy and termination assessment and jeopardy levy procedures; information to taxpayer.**—Not later than 5 days after the day on which an assessment is made under section 6851(a), 6852(a), 6861(a), or 6862, or a levy is made under section 6331(a) without complying with the notice before levy provisions of section 6331(d), the district director shall provide the taxpayer a written statement setting forth the information upon which the district director relies in authorizing such assessment or levy. [Reg. §301.7429-1.]

□ [*T.D. 7575, 12-15-78. Amended by T.D. 8453, 12-11-92.*]

### [Reg. §301.7429-2]

**§301.7429-2. Review of jeopardy and termination assessment and jeopardy levy procedures.**—(a) *Request for administrative review.*—Any request for the review of a jeopardy or termination assessment or jeopardy levy provided for by section 7429(a)(2) shall be filed with the district director within 30 days after the statement described in §301.7429-1 is given to the taxpayer. However, if no statement is given within the 5 day period described in §301.7429-1, any request for review of the jeopardy or termination assessment or jeopardy levy shall be filed within 35 days after the date such assessment or levy is made. Such request shall be in writing, shall state fully the reasons for the request, and shall be supported by such evidence as will enable the district director to make the redetermination described in section 7429(a)(3).

(b) *Administrative review.*—In determining whether the assessment is reasonable and the amount assessed is appropriate, or whether the jeopardy levy is reasonable, the district director shall take into account not only information available at the time the assessment or jeopardy levy is made but also information which subsequently becomes available.

(c) *Abatement of assessment.*—For rules relating to the abatement of assessments made under sections 6851 and 6861 see §§301.6861-1(e), 301.6861-1(f) and 1.6851-1(d) of this chapter. [Reg. §301.7429-2.]

□ [*T.D. 7575, 12-15-78. Amended by T.D. 8453, 12-11-92.*]

### [Reg. §301.7429-3]

**§301.7429-3. Review of jeopardy and termination assessment and jeopardy levy procedures; judicial action.**—(a) *Time for bringing judicial action.*—An action for judicial review described in section 7429(b) may be instituted by the taxpayer during the period beginning on the earlier of—

(1) The date the district director notifies the taxpayer of the determination described in section 7429(a)(3) and ending on the 90th day thereafter; or

(2) The 16th day after the request described in section 7429(a)(2) was made by the taxpayer and ending on the 90th day thereafter.

(b) *Extension of period for judicial review.*—The United States Government may not by itself seek an extension of the 20 day period described in section 7429(b)(3), but it may join with the taxpayer in seeking such an extension.

(c) *Jurisdiction for determination.*—In general, the United States district courts will have exclusive jurisdiction over any civil action for a determination described in section 7429(b). However, if a petition for

**Proceedings by Taxpayers and Third Parties**
See p. 20,601 for regulations not amended to reflect law changes
**67,169**

a redetermination of a deficiency has been timely filed with the Tax Court prior to the making of an assessment or levy that is subject to the section 7429 review procedures, and one or more of the taxes and tax periods before the Tax Court as a result of the petition is also included in the written statement that was provided to the taxpayer, then the Tax Court will have jurisdiction concurrent with the district courts over any civil action for a judicial determination with respect to all the taxes and tax periods included in the written statement. In all other cases, the appropriate United States district court continues to have exclusive jurisdiction over such an action. [Reg. § 301.7429-3.]

☐ [*T.D. 7575, 12-15-78. Amended by T.D. 8453, 12-11-92.*]

### [Reg. § 301.7430-0]

**§ 301.7430-0. Table of contents.**—This section lists the captions that appear in § § 301.7430-1 through 301.7430-6.

(e) Time for filing claim for administrative costs.

(f) Effective date.

[Reg. § 301.7430-0.]

☐ [T.D. 8542, 6-6-94. *Amended by T.D. 8725, 7-21-97 and T.D. 9756,* 2-29-2016.]

### [Reg. § 301.7430-1]

**§ 301.7430-1. Exhaustion of administrative remedies.**—(a) *In general.*—Section 7430(b)(1) provides that a court shall not award reasonable litigation costs in any civil tax proceeding under section 7430(a) unless the court determines that the prevailing party has exhausted the administrative remedies available to the party within the Internal Revenue Service. This section sets forth the circumstances in which such administrative remedies shall be deemed to have been exhausted.

(b) *Requirements.*—(1) *In general.*—A party has not exhausted the administrative remedies available within the Internal Revenue Service with respect to any tax matter for which an Appeals office conference is available under §§ 601.105 and 601.106 of this chapter (other than a tax matter described in paragraph (c) of this section) unless—

(i) The party, prior to filing a petition in the Tax Court or a civil action for refund in a court of the United States (including the Court of Federal Claims), participates, either in person or through a qualified representative described in § 601.502 of this chapter, in an Appeals office conference; or

(ii) If no Appeals office conference is granted, the party, prior to the issuance of a statutory notice in the case of a petition in the Tax Court or the issuance of a notice of disallowance in the case of a civil action for refund in a court of the United States (including the Court of Federal Claims)—

(A) Requests an Appeals office conference in accordance with §§ 601.105 and 601.106 of this chapter or any successor published guidance; and

(B) Files a written protest if a written protest is required to obtain an Appeals office conference.

(2) *Participates.*—For purposes of this section, a party or qualified representative of the party described in § 601.502 of this chapter participates in an Appeals office conference if the party or qualified representative discloses to the Appeals office all relevant information regarding the party's tax matter to the extent such information and its relevance were known or should have been known to the party or qualified representative at the time of such conference.

(3) *Tax matter.*—For purposes of this section, "tax matter" means a matter in connection with the determination, collection or refund of any tax, interest, penalty, addition to tax or additional amount under the Internal Revenue Code.

(4) *Failure to agree to extension of time for assessments.*—Any failure by the prevailing party to agree to an extension of the time for the assessment of any tax will not be taken into account for purposes of determining whether the prevailing party has exhausted the administrative remedies available to the party within the Internal Rrevenue Service.

(c) *Revocation of a determination that an organization is described in section 501(c)(3).*—A party has not exhausted the administrative remedies available within the Internal Revenue Service with respect to a revocation of a determination that an organization described in section 501(c)(3) unless, prior to filing a declaratory judgment action under section 7428, the party has exhausted its administrative remedies in accordance with section 7428, and any regulations, rules, and revenue procedures thereunder.

(d) *Actions involving summonses, levies, liens, jeopardy and termination assessments, etc.*—(1) A party has not exhausted the administrative remedies available within the Internal Revenue Service with respect to a matter other than one to which paragraph (b) or (c) of this section applies (including summonses, levies, liens, and jeopardy and termination assessments) unless, prior to filing an action in a court of the United States (including the Tax Court and the Court of Federal Claims)—

(i) The party follows all applicable Internal Revenue Service procedures for contesting the matter (including filing a written protest or claim, requesting an administrative appeal, and participating in an administrative hearing or conference); or

(ii) If there are no applicable Internal Revenue Service procedures, the party submits to the Area Director of the area having jurisdiction over the dispute a written claim for relief reciting facts and circumstances sufficient to show the nature of the relief requested and that the party is entitled to the requested relief, and the Area Director denies the claim for relief in writing or fails to act on the claim within a reasonable period after the claim is received by the Area Director.

(2) For purposes of paragraph (d)(1)(ii) of this section, a *reasonable period* is—

(i) The 5-day period preceding the filing of a petition to quash an administrative summons issued under section 7609;

(ii) The 5-day period preceding the filing of a wrongful levy action in which a demand for the return of property is made;

(iii) The period expressly provided for administrative review of the party's claim by an applicable provision of the Internal Revenue Code that expressly provides for the pursuit of administrative remedies (such as the 16-day period provided under section 7429(b)(1)(B) relating to review of jeopardy assessment procedures); or

(iv) The 60-day period following receipt of the claim for relief in all other cases.

(e) *Actions involving willful violations of the automatic stay under section 362 or the discharge provisions under section 524 of the Bankruptcy Code.*—(1) *Section 7433 claims.*—A party has not exhausted administrative remedies within the Internal Revenue Service with respect to asserted violations of the automatic stay under section 362 of the Bankruptcy Code or the discharge provisions under section 524 of the Bankruptcy Code unless it files an administrative claim for damages or for relief from a violation of section 362 or 524 of the Bankruptcy Code with the Chief, Local Insolvency Unit, for the judicial district in which the bankruptcy petition that is the basis for the asserted automatic stay or discharge violation was filed pursuant to § 301.7433-2(e) and satisfies the other conditions set forth in § 301.7433-2(d) prior to filing a petition under section 7433.

(2) *Section 362(h) claims.*—A party has not exhausted administrative remedies within the Internal Revenue Service with respect to asserted violations of the automatic stay under section 362 of the Bankruptcy Code unless it files an administrative claim for relief from a violation of section 362 of the Bankruptcy Code with the Chief, Local Insolvency Unit, for the judicial district in which the bankruptcy petition that is the basis for the asserted automatic stay violation was filed pursuant to § 301.7433-2(e) and satisfies the other conditions set forth in § 301.7433-2(d) prior to filing a petition under section 362(h) of the Bankruptcy Code.

(f) *Exception to requirement that party pursue administrative remedies.*—If the conditions set forth in paragraph (f)(1), (f)(2), (f)(3), or (f)(4) of this section are satisfied, a party's administrative remedies within the Internal Revenue Service shall be deemed to have been exhausted for purposes of section 7430.

(1) The Internal Revenue Service notifies the party in writing that the pursuit of administrative remedies in accordance with paragraphs (b), (c), and (d) of this section is unnecessary.

(2) In the case of a petition in the Tax Court—

(i) The party did not receive a notice of proposed deficiency (30-day letter) prior to the issuance of the statutory notice and the failure to receive such notice was not due to actions of the party (such as a failure to supply requested information or a current mailing address to the Internal Revenue Service office or service center having jurisdiction over the tax matter); and

(ii) The party does not refuse to participate in an Appeals office conference while the case is in docketed status.

(3) In the case of a civil action for refund involving a tax matter other than a tax matter described in paragraph (e)[(f)](4) of this section, the party—

(i) Participates in an Appeals office conference with respect to the tax matter prior to issuance of a statutory notice of deficiency with respect to such tax matter; or

(ii) Did not receive written notification that an Appeals office conference was available prior to issuance of a notice of disallowance and the failure to receive such a notification was not due to the actions of the party (such as the failure to supply requested information or a current mailing address to the Internal Revenue Service office or service center having jurisdiction over the tax matter); or

(iii) Did not receive either written or oral notification that an Appeals office conference had been granted within six months from the date of the filing of the claim for refund and the failure to receive such notice was not due to actions of the party (such as the failure to supply requested information or a current mailing address to the Internal Revenue Service office or service center having jurisdiction over the tax matter).

(4) In the case of a civil action for refund involving a tax matter under sections 6703 or 6694—

(i) The party did not receive a notice of proposed disallowance prior to issuance of a notice of disallowance and the failure to receive such notice was not due to the actions of the party (such as the failure to supply requested information or a current mailing address to the Internal Revenue Service office or service center having jurisdiction over the tax matter); or

(ii) During the six-month period following the day on which the party's claim for refund is filed, the party's claim for refund is not denied, and the Internal Revenue Service has failed to process the claim with due diligence.

(g) *Examples.*—The provisions of this section may be illustrated by the following examples:

*Example 1.* Taxpayer A exchanges property held for investment for similar property and claims that the gain on the exchange is not recognized under section 1031. The Internal Revenue Service conducts a field examination and determines that there has not been a like-kind exchange. No agreement is reached on the matter and a notice of proposed deficiency (30-day letter) is sent to A. A does not file a request for an Appeals office conference. A pays the amount of the proposed deficiency and files a claim for refund. A notice of proposed disallowance is issued by the Internal Revenue Service. A does not request an Appeals office conference and, instead, files a civil action for refund in a United States District Court. A has not exhausted the administrative remedies available within the Internal Revenue Service.

*Example 2.* Assume the same facts as in *Example 1* except that, after receiving the notice of proposed deficiency (30-day letter), A files a request for an Appeals office conference. No agreement is reached at the conference. A pays the amount of the proposed deficiency and files a claim for refund. A notice of proposed disallowance is issued by the Internal Revenue Service. A does not request an Appeals office conference and files a civil action for refund in a United States District Court. A has exhausted the administrative remedies available within the Internal Revenue Service.

*Example 3.* Assume the same facts as in *Example 1* except A first requests an Appeals office conference after A's receipt of the notice of proposed disallowance. A is granted an Appeals office conference and A participates in such conference. A has exhausted the administrative remedies available within the Internal Revenue Service.

*Example 4.* Taxpayer B receives a notice of proposed deficiency (30-day letter) after completion of a field examination. B provided to the Internal Revenue Service during the examination all relevant information under the taxpayer's control and all relevant legal arguments supporting the taxpayer's position. B properly requests an Appeals office conference. The Appeals office, to obtain an additional period of time to consider the tax matter, requests that B sign Form 872 to extend the time for an assessment of tax, but B declines. Appeals then denies the request for a conference and issues a notice of deficiency. B has exhausted the administrative remedies available within the Internal Revenue Service.

*Example 5.* Taxpayer C receives a notice of proposed deficiency (30-day letter) and a written statement that C need not file a written protest or request an Appeals office conference since a conference will not be granted. C files a petition in the Tax Court after receiving the statutory notice of deficiency. C's administrative remedies within the Internal Revenue Service are deemed to have been exhausted.

*Example 6.* On January 2, the Internal Revenue Service serves a summons issued under section 7609 on third-party recordkeeper D to produce records of taxpayer E. On January 5, notice of the summons is given to E. The last day on which E may file a petition in a court of the United States to quash the summons is January 25. Thereafter, E files a written claim for relief with the Internal Revenue Service office having jurisdiction over the matter together with a copy of the summons. The claim and copy are received by the Internal Revenue Service office on January 20. On January 25, E files a petition to quash the summons. E has exhausted the administrative remedies available within the Internal Revenue Service.

*Example 7.* A notice of Federal tax lien is filed in County M on March 3, in the name of F. On April 2, F pays the entire liability thereby satisfying the lien. On May 2, F files a written claim with the Internal Revenue Service office having jurisdiction over the tax matter demanding a certificate of release of lien. Thereafter, F provides the Internal Revenue Service office with a copy of the notice of Federal tax lien and a copy of the cancelled check in satisfaction of the lien, which are received by the district director on May 15. F's claim is deemed to have been filed on May 15. Accordingly, F must wait until after July 14 (60 days following the filing of the claim for relief on May 15) to commence an action, in order to have exhausted the administrative remedies available within the Internal Revenue Service.

*Example 8.* A revenue officer seizes an automobile to effect collection of G's liability on January 10. On January 22, H submits a written claim to the Internal Revenue Service office having jurisdiction over the tax matter claiming that H purchased the automobile from G for an adequate consideration before the tax lien against G arose, and demands immediate return of the automobile. A copy of the title certificate and H's cancelled check are submitted with the claim. The claim is received by the Internal Revenue Service office on January 25. On January 30, H brings a wrongful levy action. H has exhausted the administrative remedies available within the Internal Revenue Service.

*Example 9.* The Internal Revenue Service issues a revenue ruling which holds that ear piercing does not affect a function or structure of the body within the meaning of section 213 and therefore is not deductible. Taxpayer I deducts the costs of ear piercing and, following an examination, receives a notice of proposed deficiency (30-day letter) disallowing the treatment of these costs. Because of the revenue ruling, I believes a conference would not aid in the resolution of the tax dispute. Accordingly, I does not request an Appeals office conference. After receiving a statutory notice of deficiency, I files a petition in the Tax Court. I has not exhausted the administrative remedies available within the Internal Revenue Service. The issuance of a revenue ruling covering the same fact situation but taking a contrary position does not constitute notification by the Internal Revenue Service to I that the pursuit of administrative remedies is unnecessary. Similarly, the issuance to I of a private letter ruling or technical advice does not constitute notification by the Internal Revenue Service that the pursuit of administrative remedies is unnecessary.

*Example 10.* Taxpayer J is assessed a penalty under section 6701 for aiding in the understatement of the tax liability of another person. J pays 15% of the penalty in accordance with section 6703 and files a claim for refund on June 15. J is not issued a notice of proposed disallowance and thus cannot participate in an Appeals office conference within six months of the filing of the claim for refund. J brings an action on December 23. J has exhausted the administrative remedies available within the Internal Revenue Service.

*Example 11.* Taxpayer K receives a notice of proposed deficiency (30-day letter) and neither requests nor participates in an Appeals office conference. The Service then issues a statutory notice of deficiency (90-day letter). Upon receiving the statutory notice, and after filing a petition with the Tax Court, K requests an Appeals office conference. K has not exhausted the administrative remedies available within the Internal Revenue Service because the request for an Appeals office conference was made after the issuance of the statutory notice.

(h) *Effective date.*—This section applies to court proceedings described in section 7430 filed in a court of the United States (including the Tax Court and the Court of Federal Claims) after May 7, 1992. [Reg. § 301.7430-1.]

☐ [*T.D. 7950, 4-16-83. Amended by T.D. 8543, 6-6-94; T.D. 8725, 7-21-97 T.D. 9050, 3-24-2003 and T.D. 9756, 2-29-2016.*]

### [Reg. § 301.7430-2]

**§ 301.7430-2. Requirements and procedures for recovery of reasonable administrative costs.**—(a) *Introduction.*—Section 7430(a)(1) provides for the recovery, under certain circumstances, of reasonable administrative costs incurred in connection with an administrative proceeding before the Internal Revenue Service. Paragraph (b) of this section lists the requirements that a taxpayer must meet to be entitled to an award of reasonable administrative costs from the Internal Revenue Service. Paragraph (c) of this section describes the procedures that a taxpayer must follow to recover reasonable administrative costs. Paragraphs (b) and (c) apply to requests for administrative costs regarding all administrative proceedings within the Internal Revenue Service.

(b) *Requirements for recovery.*—(1) *Determination by the Internal Revenue Service.*—The Internal Revenue Service will grant a taxpayer's request for recovery of reasonable administrative costs incurred in connection with an administrative proceeding under section 7430 and this section only if—

(i) *Jurisdiction.*—The underlying substantive issues or the issue of reasonable administrative costs are not, and have never been, before any court of the United States (including the Tax Court or United States Court of Federal Claims) with jurisdiction over those issues;

(ii) *Administrative proceeding.*—The costs were incurred in connection with an administrative proceeding as defined in § 301.7430-3(a);

(iii) *Administrative proceeding date.*—The costs were incurred on or after the administrative proceeding date as defined in § 301.7430-3(c);

(iv) *Reasonable administrative costs.*—The costs were reasonable administrative costs as defined in § 301.7430-4;

(v) *Prevailing party.*—The taxpayer is a prevailing party as defined in § 301.7430-5;

(vi) *Not unreasonably protracted.*—The administrative proceeding was not unreasonably protracted by the taxpayer as discussed in paragraph (d) of this section; and

(vii) *Procedural requirements.*—The taxpayer follows the procedures set forth in paragraph (c) of this section.

(2) *Determination by court.*—Although the Internal Revenue Service will not grant a request for reasonable administrative costs where the requirements of paragraph (b)(1)(i) of this section are not met, a taxpayer may file a claim for reasonable administrative costs with the court with jurisdiction over the judicial proceeding. The court may award the taxpayer reasonable administrative costs under section 7430(a). Under section 7430(c)(4)(C)(ii), where the final determination with respect to the tax, interest, or penalty at issue is made by a court, the court determines whether the taxpayer qualifies as a prevailing party. Thus, where the requirements of paragraph (b)(1)(i) of this section are not met, the taxpayer's only possibility of obtaining an award of reasonable administrative costs is to obtain an award of these costs from the court. In the event the court awards reasonable administrative costs, it may also award litigation costs for the reasonable costs of pursuing the claim for reasonable administrative costs, provided the requirements under section 7430 regarding an award of reasonable administrative costs are satisfied with respect to these costs. A claim filed with the court should be made in accordance with the rules of the court.

(c) *Procedure for recovering reasonable administrative costs.*—(1) *In general.*—The Internal Revenue Service will not award administrative costs under section 7430 unless the taxpayer files a written request to recover reasonable administrative costs in accordance with the provisions of this section.

(2) *Where request must be filed.*—A request required by paragraph (c)(1) of this section must be filed with the Internal Revenue Service personnel who have jurisdiction over the tax matter underlying the claim for the costs, except that requests with respect to administrative proceedings defined by §301.7430-8(c) should be made to the Chief, Local Insolvency Unit. However, if those persons are unknown to the taxpayer making the request, the taxpayer may send the request to the Internal Revenue Service office that considered the underlying matter.

(3) *Contents of request.*—The request must be in writing and must contain the following statements, affidavits, documentation, and information with regard to the taxpayer's administrative proceeding—

(i) *Statements*—

(A) A statement that the underlying substantive issues or the issue of reasonable administrative costs are not, and have never been, before any court of the United States (including the Tax Court or United States Court of Federal Claims) with jurisdiction over those issues;

(B) A clear and concise statement of the reasons why the taxpayer alleges that the position of the Internal Revenue Service in the administrative proceeding was not substantially justified. For administrative proceedings commenced after July 30, 1996, if the taxpayer alleges that the Internal Revenue Service did not follow any applicable published guidance, the statement must identify all applicable published guidance that the taxpayer alleges that the Internal Revenue Service did not follow. For purposes of this paragraph (c)(3)(i)(B), the term applicable published guidance means final or temporary regulations, revenue rulings, revenue procedures, information releases, notices, announcements, and, if issued to the taxpayer, private letter rulings, technical advice memoranda, and determination letters. Also, for purposes of this paragraph (c)(3)(i)(B), the term administrative proceeding includes only those administrative proceedings or portions of administrative proceedings occurring on or after the administrative proceeding date as defined in §301.7430-3(c). For costs incurred after January 18, 1999, if the taxpayer alleges that the United States has lost in courts of appeal for other circuits on substantially similar issues, the taxpayer must provide, for each such case, the full name of the case, volume and pages of the reporter in which the opinion appears, the circuit in which the case was decided, and the year of the opinion;

(C) A statement sufficient to demonstrate that the taxpayer has substantially prevailed as to the amount in controversy or with respect to the most significant issue or set of issues presented in the proceeding;

(D) A statement that the taxpayer has not unreasonably protracted the portion of the administrative proceeding for which the taxpayer is requesting costs; and

(E) A statement supported by a detailed affidavit executed by the taxpayer or the taxpayer's representative that sets forth the nature and amount of each specific item of reasonable administrative costs for which the taxpayer is seeking recovery. This statement must identify whether the representation is on a pro bono basis as defined

in §301.7430-4(d) and, if so, to whom payment should be made. Specifically, the statement must direct whether payment should be made to the taxpayer's representative or to the representative's employer.

(ii) *Affidavit or affidavits*—

(A) An affidavit executed by the taxpayer stating that the taxpayer meets the net worth and size limitations of §301.7430-5(f);

(B) An affidavit supporting the statement described in paragraph (c)(3)(i)(E) of this section; and

(C) For costs incurred after January 18, 1999, if more than $125 per hour (as adjusted for an increase in the cost of living pursuant to §301.7430-4(b)(3)) is claimed for the fees of a representative in connection with the administrative proceeding, an affidavit is necessary stating that a special factor described in §301.7430-4(b)(3) is applicable, such as the difficulty of the issues presented in the case or the lack of local availability of tax expertise. If a special factor is claimed based on specialized skills and distinctive knowledge as described in §301.7430-4(b)(2)(ii), the affidavit should state—

(1) Why the specialized skills and distinctive knowledge were necessary in the representation;

(2) That there is a limited availability of representatives possessing these specialized skills and distinctive knowledge; and

(3) How the representative's education and experience qualifies the representative as someone with the necessary specialized skills and distinctive knowledge.

(iii) *Documentation and information*—

(A) A copy of the billing records of the representative for the requested fees; and

(B) An address at which the taxpayer wishes to receive notice of the determination of the Internal Revenue Service with regard to the request for reasonable administrative costs.

(C) In cases of pro bono representation, time records similar to billing records, detailing the time spent and work completed, must be submitted for the requested fees.

(4) *Form of Request.*—No specific form is required for the request other than one that satisfies the requirements of paragraph (c)(3) of this section. Where practicable the required statements may be included in a single document. Similarly, where practicable, the required affidavits may be combined in a single affidavit to the extent they are to be executed by the same person.

(5) *Period for requesting costs from the Internal Revenue Service.*—To recover reasonable administrative costs pursuant to section 7430 and this section, the taxpayer must file a written request for costs within 90 days after the date the final adverse decision of the Internal Revenue Service with respect to all tax, additions to tax, interest, and penalties at issue in the administrative proceeding is mailed or otherwise furnished to the taxpayer. For purposes of this section, *interest* means the interest that is specifically at issue in the administrative proceeding independent of the taxpayer's objections to the underlying tax, additions to tax, and penalties imposed. The final decision of the Internal Revenue Service for purposes of this section is the document that resolves the taxpayer's liability with regard to all tax, additions to tax, interest, and penalties at issue in the administrative proceeding (such as a Form 870 or closing agreement), or a notice of assessment for that liability (such as the notice and demand under section 6303), whichever is earlier mailed or otherwise furnished to the taxpayer. For purposes of this section, if the 90th day falls on a Saturday, Sunday, or a legal holiday, the 90-day period shall end on the next succeeding day that is not a Saturday, Sunday, or a legal holiday as defined by section 7503.

(6) *Notice.*—The Internal Revenue Service is authorized, but not required, to notify the taxpayer of its decision to grant or deny (in whole or in part) an award for reasonable administrative costs under section 7430 and this section by certified mail or registered mail. If the Internal Revenue Service does not respond on the merits to a request by the taxpayer for an award of reasonable administrative costs filed under paragraph (c)(1) of this section within 6 months after the request is filed, the Internal Revenue Service's failure to respond may be considered by the taxpayer as a decision of the Internal Revenue Service denying an award for reasonable administrative costs.

(7) *Appeal to Tax Court.*—A taxpayer may appeal a decision by the Internal Revenue Service denying (in whole or in part) a request for reasonable administrative costs under section 7430 and this section by filing a petition for reasonable administrative costs with the Tax Court. The petition must be in accordance with the Tax Court's Rules of Practice and Procedure and must be filed with the Tax Court after the Internal Revenue Service denies (in whole or in part) the taxpayer's request for reasonable administrative costs. Once a notice of decision denying (in whole or in part) an award for reasonable

administrative costs is mailed by the Internal Revenue Service via certified mail or registered mail as required by paragraph (c)(6) of this section, a taxpayer may obtain judicial review of that decision by filing a petition for review with the Tax Court prior to the 91st day after the mailing of the notice of decision.

(d) *Unreasonable protraction of administrative proceeding.*—An award of reasonable administrative costs will not be made where the taxpayer unreasonably protracted the administrative proceeding. However, a taxpayer that unreasonably protracted only a portion of the administrative proceeding, but not other portions of the administrative proceeding, may recover reasonable administrative costs for the portion(s) of the administrative proceeding that the taxpayer did not unreasonably protract, if the requirements of paragraph (b)(1) of this section are otherwise satisfied.

(e) The following examples primarily illustrate paragraph (a) of this section:

*Example 1.* Taxpayer A receives a notice of proposed deficiency (30-day letter). A requests and is granted Appeals office consideration. The administrative file contains certain documents provided by A as substantiation for the tax matters at issue. Appeals determines that the information submitted is insufficient. Appeals then issues a notice of deficiency. After receiving the notice of deficiency but before the 90-day period for filing a petition with the Tax Court has expired, and before filing a petition with the Tax Court, A convinces Appeals that the information previously submitted and reviewed by Appeals is sufficient and, therefore, the notice of deficiency is incorrect and A owes no additional tax. Pursuant to section 6212(d), the notice of deficiency is rescinded. Appeals then closes the case showing a zero deficiency and mails A a notice to this effect. Assuming that Appeals did not rely on any new information provided by A in rescinding the notice of deficiency and that all of the other requirements of section 7430 are satisfied, A may recover reasonable administrative costs incurred after the date of the 30-day letter (the administrative proceeding date as defined in Treas. Reg. §301.7430-3(c)). To recover these costs, A must file a request for administrative costs with the Appeals office personnel who settled A's tax matter, or if that person is unknown to A, with the Area Director of the area that considered the underlying matter, within 90 days after the date of mailing of the Office of Appeals' final decision that A owes no additional tax.

*Example 2.* Taxpayer B files a request for an abatement of interest pursuant to section 6404 and the regulations thereunder. The Area Director issues a notice of proposed disallowance of the abatement request (akin to a 30-day letter). B requests and is granted Appeals office consideration. No agreement is reached with Appeals and the Office of Appeals issues a notice of disallowance of the abatement request. B does not file suit in the Tax Court, but instead contacts the Appeals office within 180 days after the mailing date of the notice of disallowance of the abatement request to attempt to reverse the decision. B convinces the Appeals office that the notice of disallowance is in error. The Appeals office agrees to abate the interest and mails the taxpayer a notification of this decision. The mailing date of the notification from Appeals of the decision to abate interest commences the 90-day period from which the taxpayer may request administrative costs. Assuming that Appeals did not rely on any new information provided by B in reversing its notice of disallowance, and that all of the other requirements of section 7430 are satisfied, B may recover reasonable administrative costs incurred after the date the Area Director issued the notice of proposed disallowance of the abatement request (the administrative proceeding date as defined in Treas. Reg. §301.7430-3(c)). To recover these costs, B must file a request for costs with the Appeals office personnel who settled B's tax matter, or if that person is unknown to B, with the Area Director of the area that considered the underlying matter within 90 days after the date of mailing of the Office of Appeals' final decision that B is entitled to abatement of interest.

*Example 3.* Taxpayer C receives a notice of proposed adjustment and employment tax 30-day letter. C requests and is granted Appeals office consideration. The administrative file contains certain documents provided by C to support C's position in the tax matters at issue. Appeals determines that the documents submitted are insufficient. Appeals then issues a notice of determination of worker classification. After receiving the notice of determination of worker classification but before the 90-day period for filing a petition with the Tax Court has expired, C convinces Appeals that the documents previously submitted and reviewed by Appeals adequately support its position and, therefore, C owes no additional employment tax. Appeals then closes the case showing a zero tax adjustment and mails C a no-change letter. Assuming that Appeals did not rely on any new information provided by C in reversing its notice of determination of worker classification, and that all of the other requirements of section 7430 are satisfied, C may recover reasonable administrative costs incurred after the date of the notice of proposed adjustment and 30-day letter (the administrative proceeding date as

defined in Treas. Reg. §301.7430-3(c)). To recover these costs, C must file a request for administrative costs with the Appeals office personnel who settled C's tax matter, or if that person is unknown to C, with the Area Director of the area that considered the underlying matter, within 90 days after the date of mailing of the Office of Appeals' final decision that C owes no additional tax. [Reg. §301.7430-2.]

☐ [*T.D. 8542, 6-6-94. Amended by T.D. 8725, 7-21-97 T.D. 9050, 3-24-2003 and T.D. 9756, 2-29-2016.*]

**[Reg. §301.7430-3]**

**§301.7430-3. Administrative proceeding and administrative proceeding date.**—(a) *Administrative proceeding.*—For purposes of section 7430, an administrative proceeding generally means any procedure or other action before the Internal Revenue Service that is commenced after November 10, 1988. However, an administrative proceeding does not include—

(1) Proceedings involving matters of general application, including hearings on regulations, comments on forms, or proceedings involving revenue rulings or revenue procedures;

(2) Proceedings involving requests for private letter rulings or similar determinations;

(3) Proceedings involving technical advice memoranda, except those submitted after the administrative proceeding date (as defined in paragraph (c) of this section); and

(4) Proceedings in connection with collection actions (as defined in paragraph (b) of this section), including proceedings under section 7432 or 7433, except proceedings brought under section 7433(e) and §301.7433-2 or proceedings otherwise described in §301.7430-8(c). See §301.7430-8.

(b) *Collection action.*—A collection action generally includes any action taken by the Internal Revenue Service to collect a tax (or any interest, additional amount, addition to tax, or penalty, together with any costs in addition to the tax) or any action taken by a taxpayer in response to the Internal Revenue Service's act or failure to act in connection with the collection of a tax (including any interest, additional amount, addition to tax, or penalty, together with any costs in addition to the tax). A collection action for purposes of section 7430 and this section includes any action taken by the Internal Revenue Service under Chapter 64 of Subtitle F to collect a tax. Collection actions also include collection due process hearings under sections 6320 and 6330 (unless the underlying tax liability is properly at issue), and those actions taken by a taxpayer to remedy the Internal Revenue Service's failure to release a lien under section 6325 or to remedy any unauthorized collection action as described by section 7433, except those collection actions described by section 7433(e). An action or procedure directly relating to a claim for refund after payment of an assessed tax is not a collection action.

(c) *Administrative proceeding date.*—(1) *General rule.*—For purposes of section 7430 and the regulations thereunder, the term *administrative proceeding date* means the earlier of—

(i) The date of the receipt by the taxpayer of the notice of the decision of the Internal Revenue Service Office of Appeals;

(ii) The date of the notice of deficiency; or

(iii) The date on which the first letter of proposed deficiency that allows the taxpayer an opportunity for administrative review in the Internal Revenue Service Office of Appeals is sent.

(2) *Notice of the decision of the Internal Revenue Service Office of Appeals.*—For purposes of section 7430 and the regulations thereunder, a notice of the decision of the Internal Revenue Service Office of Appeals is the final written document, mailed or delivered to the taxpayer, that is signed by an individual in the Office of Appeals who has been delegated the authority to settle the dispute on behalf of the Commissioner, and states or indicates that the notice is the final determination of the entire case. A notice of claim disallowance issued by the Office of Appeals is a notice of the decision of the Internal Revenue Service Office of Appeals. Solely for purposes of determining the administrative proceeding date, a notice of deficiency issued by the Office of Appeals is not a notice of the decision of the Internal Revenue Service Office of Appeals.

(3) *Notice of deficiency.*—A notice of deficiency is a notice described in section 6212(a), including a notice rescinded pursuant to section 6212(d). For purposes of determining reasonable administrative costs under section 7430 and the regulations thereunder, the following will be treated as a notice of deficiency:

(i) A notice of final partnership administrative adjustment described in section 6223(a)(2).

(ii) A notice of determination of worker classification issued pursuant to section 7436.

(iii) A final notice of determination denying innocent spouse relief issued pursuant to section 6015.

(4) *First letter of proposed deficiency that allows the taxpayer an opportunity for administrative review in the Office of Appeals.*—Generally, the first letter of proposed deficiency that allows the taxpayer an opportunity for administrative review in the Office of Appeals is the first letter issued to the taxpayer that describes the proposed adjustments and advises the taxpayer of the opportunity to contact the Office of Appeals. It also may be a claim disallowance or the first letter of determination that allows the taxpayer an opportunity for administrative review in the Office of Appeals.

(d) *Examples.*—The provisions of this section are illustrated by the following examples:

*Example 1.* Taxpayer A receives a notice of proposed deficiency (30-day letter). A files a request for and is granted an Appeals office conference. At the Appeals conference no agreement is reached on the tax matters at issue. The Office of Appeals then issues a notice of deficiency. Upon receiving the notice of deficiency, A does not file a petition with the Tax Court. Instead, A pays the deficiency and files a claim for refund. The claim for refund is considered by the Internal Revenue Service and the Area Director issues a notice of proposed claim disallowance. A requests and is granted Appeals office consideration. A convinces Appeals that A's claim is correct and Appeals allows A's claim. A may recover reasonable administrative costs incurred on or after the date of the notice of proposed deficiency (30-day letter), but only if the other requirements of section 7430 and the regulations thereunder are satisfied. A cannot recover costs incurred prior to the date of the 30-day letter because these costs were incurred before the administrative proceeding date.

*Example 2.* Taxpayer B files an individual income tax return showing a balance due. No payment is made with the return and the Internal Revenue Service assesses the amount shown on the return. The Internal Revenue Service issues a Notice Of Intent to Levy And Notice Of Your Right To A Hearing pursuant to sections 6330(a) and 6331(d). B timely requests and is granted a Collection Due Process (CDP) hearing. In connection with the CDP hearing, B enters into an installment agreement as a collection alternative. The costs that B incurred in connection with the CDP hearing were not incurred in an administrative proceeding, but rather in a collection action. Accordingly, B may not recover those costs as reasonable administrative costs under section 7430 and the regulations thereunder. [Reg. § 301.7430-3.]

☐ [*T.D. 8542, 6-6-94. Amended by T.D. 9050, 3-24-2003 and T.D. 9756, 2-29-2016.*]

### [Reg. § 301.7430-4]

**§ 301.7430-4. Reasonable administrative costs.**—(a) *In general.*—For purposes of section 7430 and the regulations thereunder, reasonable administrative costs are any costs described in paragraph (b) of this section that are incurred in connection with an administrative proceeding (as defined in § 301.7430-3(a)) and incurred on or after the administrative proceeding date (as defined in § 301.7430-3(c)).

(b) *Costs described.*—(1) *In general.*—The costs described in this paragraph are the reasonable and necessary amount of costs incurred by the taxpayer to present the taxpayer's position with respect to the merits of the tax controversy or the recovery of reasonable administrative costs. These costs include—

(i) Any administrative fees or similar charges imposed by the Internal Revenue Service;

(ii) Reasonable expenses of expert witnesses;

(iii) Reasonable costs of any study, analysis, engineering report, test or project that is necessary for, and incurred in preparation of, the taxpayer's case; and

(iv) Reasonable fees paid or incurred for the services of a representative (as defined in paragraph (b)(2) of this section) in connection with the administrative proceeding.

(2) *Representative and specially qualified representative.*—(i) *Representative.*—A representative is a person compensated for services rendered in connection with the administrative proceeding, who is authorized to practice before the Internal Revenue Service or the Tax Court.

(ii) *Specially qualified representative.*—For purposes of paragraphs (b)(3)(iii) and (c)(2)(ii) of this section, a specially qualified representative is a representative (as defined in paragraph (b)(2)(i) of this section) possessing a distinctive knowledge or a unique and specialized skill that is necessary to adequately represent the taxpayer in the proceeding. Examples of a unique and specialized skill or distinctive knowledge would be an identifiable practice specialty such as patent law or knowledge of a foreign law or language where that specialty or knowledge is necessary to adequately represent the taxpayer in the proceeding. For purposes of this paragraph, neither knowledge of tax law nor experience in representing taxpayers before the Internal Revenue Service is considered distinctive knowl-

edge or a unique and specialized skill. An extraordinary level of general representational knowledge and ability that is useful in all proceedings is not considered, in and of itself, distinctive knowledge or a unique and specialized skill. Specially qualified representatives also do not include those who have a distinctive knowledge of the underlying subject matter of the controversy in circumstances where that distinctive knowledge could reasonably be supplied through the use of an expert, or could readily be obtained through literature pertaining to the subject.

(3) *Limitation on fees for a representative.*—(i) *In general.*—Except as otherwise provided in this section, fees incurred after January 18, 1999, and described in paragraph (b)(1)(iv) of this section that are recoverable under section 7430 and the regulations thereunder as reasonable administrative costs may not exceed $125 per hour (as adjusted for an increase in the cost of living and, if appropriate, a special factor adjustment).

(ii) *Cost of living adjustment.*—The Internal Revenue Service will make a cost of living adjustment to the $125 per hour limitation for fees incurred in any calendar year beginning after December 31, 1996. The cost of living adjustment will be an amount equal to $125 multiplied by the cost of living adjustment determined under section 1(f)(3) for the calendar year (substituting "calendar year 1995" for "calendar year 1992" in section 1(f)(3)(B)). If the dollar limitation as adjusted by this cost of living increase is not a multiple of $10, the dollar amount will be rounded to the nearest multiple of $10 (rounding up if the amount is a multiple of $5).

(iii) *Special factor adjustment.*—(A) *In general.*—If the presence of a special factor is demonstrated by the taxpayer, the amount reimbursable is the amount of reasonable fees paid or incurred by the taxpayer in connection with the proceeding for the services of a representative as defined in paragraph (b)(2)(i) of this section.

(B) *Special factor.*—A *special factor* is a factor, other than an increase in the cost of living, that justifies an increase in the $125 per hour limitation of section 7430(c)(1)(B)(iii). The undesirability of the case, the work and the ability of counsel, the results obtained, and customary fees and awards in other cases, are factors applicable to a broad spectrum of litigation and do not constitute special factors for the purpose of increasing the $125 per hour limitation. By contrast, the limited availability of a specially qualified representative for the proceeding, the limited local availability of tax expertise, and the difficulty of the issues are special factors justifying an increase in the $125 per hour limitation.

(C) *Limited availability.*—Limited availability of a specially qualified representative is established by demonstrating that a specially qualified representative for the proceeding is not available at the $125 per hour rate (as adjusted for an increase in the cost of living). The representative's special qualification must be based on nontax expertise. Initially, this showing may be made by submission of an affidavit signed by the taxpayer or by the taxpayer's counsel, that in a case similar to the taxpayer's, a specially qualified representative that practices within a reasonable distance from the taxpayer's principal residence or principal office would normally charge a client similar to the taxpayer at a rate in excess of this amount. If the Internal Revenue Service challenges this initial showing, the taxpayer may submit additional evidence to establish the limited availability of a specially qualified representative at the rate specified above.

(D) *Limited local availability of tax expertise.*—Limited local availability of tax expertise is established by demonstrating that a representative possessing tax expertise is not available in the taxpayer's geographical area. Initially, this showing may be made by submission of an affidavit signed by the taxpayer, or by the taxpayer's counsel, that no representative possessing tax expertise practices within a reasonable distance from the taxpayer's principal residence or principal office. The hourly rate charged by representatives in the geographical area is not relevant in determining whether tax expertise is locally available. If the Internal Revenue Service challenges this initial showing, the taxpayer may submit additional evidence to establish the limited local availability of a representative possessing tax expertise.

(E) *Difficulty of the issues.*—In determining whether the difficulty of the issues justifies an increase in the $125 per hour limitation on the applicable hourly rate, the Internal Revenue Service will consider the following factors:

(1) The number of different provisions of law involved in each issue.

(2) The complexity of the particular provision or provisions of law involved in each issue.

(3) The number of factual issues present in the proceeding.

*(4)* The complexity of the factual issues present in the proceeding.

*(F) Example.*—The provisions of this section are illustrated by the following example:

*Example.* Taxpayer A is represented by B, a CPA and attorney with a LL.M. Degree in Taxation with Highest Honors who regularly handles cases dealing with TEFRA partnership issues. B represents A in an administrative proceeding involving TEFRA partnership issues that is subject to the provisions of this section. Assuming A qualifies for an award of reasonable administrative costs by meeting the requirements of section 7430, the amount of the award attributable to the fees of B may not exceed the $125 per hour limitation (as adjusted for an increase in the cost of living), absent a special factor. B is not a specially qualified representative because extraordinary knowledge of the tax laws does not constitute distinctive knowledge or a unique and specialized skill constituting a special factor. A higher rate may be justified by another special factor, that is, the limited local availability of tax expertise or the difficulty of the issues.

(c) *Certain costs excluded.*—(1) *Costs not incurred in an administrative proceeding.*—Costs that are not reasonable administrative costs for purposes of section 7430 include any costs incurred in connection with a proceeding that is not an administrative proceeding within the meaning of § 301.7430-3.

(2) *Costs incurred in an administrative proceeding but not reasonable.*—(i) *In general.*—Costs incurred in an administrative proceeding that are incurred on or after the administrative proceeding date, and that are otherwise described in paragraph (b) of this section, are not recoverable unless they are reasonable in both nature and amount. For example, costs normally included in the hourly rate of the representative by the custom and usage of the representative's profession, when billed separately, are not recoverable separate and apart from the representative's hourly rate. These costs typically include costs such as secretarial and overhead expenses. In contrast, costs that are normally billed separately may be reasonable administrative costs that may be recoverable in addition to the representative's hourly rate. Therefore, necessary costs incurred for travel; expedited mail delivery; messenger service; expenses while on travel; long distance telephone calls; and necessary copying fees imposed by the Internal Revenue Service, any court, bank or other third party, when normally billed separately from the representative's hourly rate, may be reasonable administrative costs.

(ii) *Special Rule for Expert Witness' Fees on Issue of Prevailing Market Rates.*—Under paragraph (b)(3)(iii)(C) of this section, the taxpayer may initially establish a limited availability of specially qualified representatives for the proceeding by submission of an affidavit signed by the taxpayer or by the taxpayer's representative. The Internal Revenue Service may endeavor to rebut the affidavit submitted on this issue by demonstrating either that a specially qualified representative was not necessary to represent the taxpayer in the proceeding, that the taxpayer's representative is not a specially qualified representative or that the prevailing rate for specially qualified representatives does not exceed $125 per hour (as adjusted for an increase in the cost of living). Unless the Internal Revenue Service endeavors to demonstrate that the prevailing rate for specially qualified representatives does not exceed $125 per hour (as adjusted for an increase in the cost of living), fees for expert witnesses used to establish prevailing market rates are not included in the term reasonable administrative costs.

(3) *Litigation costs.*—Litigation costs are not reasonable administrative costs because they are not incurred in connection with an administrative proceeding. Litigation costs include—

(i) Costs incurred in connection with the preparation and filing of a petition with the United States Tax Court or in connection with the commencement of any other court proceeding; and

(ii) Costs incurred after the filing of a petition with the United States Tax Court or after the commencement of any other court proceeding.

(4) *Examples.*—The provisions of this section are illustrated by the following examples:

*Example 1.* After incurring fees for representation during the Internal Revenue Service's examination of A's income tax return, A receives a notice of proposed deficiency (30-day letter). A files a request for and is granted an Appeals office conference. At the conference no agreement is reached on the tax matters at issue. The Internal Revenue Service then issues a notice of deficiency. Upon receiving the notice of deficiency, A discontinues A's administrative efforts and files a petition with the Tax Court. A's costs incurred before the date of the mailing of the 30-day letter are not reasonable administrative costs because they were incurred before the adminis-

trative proceeding date. Similarly, A's costs incurred in connection with the preparation and filing of a petition with the Tax Court are litigation costs and not reasonable administrative costs.

*Example 2.* Assume the same facts as in *Example 1* except that after A receives the notice of deficiency, in addition to petitioning the Tax Court, A recontacts Appeals and A convinces Appeals that the information previously submitted during the review by Appeals is sufficient and, therefore, the notice of deficiency is incorrect and A owes no additional tax. The Internal Revenue Service and A agree to a stipulated decision in the Tax Court case to reflect Appeals' decision. The Tax Court enters the decision. If A seeks administrative costs, A may recover costs incurred after the date of the mailing of the 30-day letter, costs incurred in recontacting Appeals after the issuance of the notice of deficiency, and costs incurred up to the time the Tax Court petition was filed, as reasonable administrative costs, but only if the other requirements of section 7430 and the regulations thereunder are satisfied. The costs incurred before the date of the mailing of the 30-day letter are not reasonable administrative costs because they were incurred before the administrative proceeding date, as set forth in § 301.7430-3(c)(1)(iii). A's costs incurred in connection with the filing of a petition with the Tax Court are not reasonable administrative costs because those costs are litigation costs. Similarly, A's costs incurred after the filing of the petition are not reasonable administrative costs, as they are litigation costs.

(d) *Pro bono representation.*—(1) *In general.*—Fees recoverable under section 7430 and the regulations thereunder as reasonable administrative costs may exceed the attorneys' fees paid or incurred by the prevailing party if such fees are less than the reasonable attorneys' fees because an individual is representing the prevailing party on a pro bono basis. In addition to attorneys' fees, reasonable costs incurred or paid by the individual providing the pro bono representation that are normally billed separately also may be recovered under this section. The Treasury Department and the Internal Revenue Service may, in revenue rulings, notices, or other guidance published in the Internal Revenue Bulletin, provide for additional rules that apply for awards of costs for pro bono representation for purposes of this paragraph (d).

(2) *Requirements.*—Pro bono representation is established by demonstrating—

(i) Representation was provided for no fee or for a fee that (taking into account all the facts and circumstances) constitutes a nominal fee;

(ii) The representative intended to provide representation for no fee or for a nominal fee from the commencement of the representation. Intent to provide representation for no fee or for a nominal fee may be demonstrated through documentation such as a retainer agreement. An individual will not be considered to have represented a client on a pro bono basis if the facts demonstrate that the individual anticipated a fee greater than a nominal fee or provided representation on a contingency fee basis. The fact that the representative intended to seek recovery of fees under section 7430 will not prevent the representative from satisfying this requirement.

(3) *Nominal fee.*—A *nominal fee* is defined as a fee that is insignificantly small or minimal. A nominal fee is a trivial payment, bearing no relation to the value of the representation provided, taking into account all the facts and circumstances.

(4) *Payment when representation provided at no charge or for a nominal fee.*—A prevailing party who receives representation at no charge or for a nominal fee and who satisfies the requirements under this section is eligible to receive reasonable fees in excess of the fees actually paid or incurred. Payment will be made to the representative or the representative's employer.

(5) *Recordkeeping.*—Contemporaneous records must be maintained, demonstrating the work performed and the time allocated to each task. These records should contain similar information to billing records.

(6) *Examples.*—The provisions of this section are illustrated by the following example:

*Example 1.* Taxpayer A, an attorney, files a petition with the Tax Court and pays a $60 filing fee. A appears pro se in the court proceeding. If A prevails, he will not be entitled to an award of reasonable litigation costs for his services. A is rendering services on his own behalf, not providing pro bono representation. His lost opportunity costs are not compensable under section 7430. A may recover the filing fee as a litigation cost, but only if the other requirements of section 7430 and the regulations thereunder are satisfied. [Reg. § 301.7430-4.]

☐ [*T.D. 8542, 6-6-94. Amended by T.D. 8725, 7-21-97 and T.D. 9756, 2-29-2016.*]

[Reg. §301.7430-5]

**§301.7430-5. Prevailing party.**—(a) *In general.*—For purposes of an award of reasonable administrative costs under section 7430 in the case of administrative proceedings commenced after July 30, 1996, a taxpayer is a prevailing party (other than by reason of section 7430(c)(4)(E)) only if—

(1) At least one issue (other than recovery of administrative costs) remains in dispute as of the date that the Internal Revenue Service takes a position in the administrative proceeding, as described in paragraph (b) of this section;

(2) The position of the Internal Revenue Service was not substantially justified;

(3) The taxpayer substantially prevails as to the amount in controversy or with respect to the most significant issue or set of issues presented; and

(4) The taxpayer satisfies the net worth and size limitations referenced in paragraph (f) of this section.

(b) *Position of the Internal Revenue Service.*—The position of the Internal Revenue Service in an administrative proceeding is the position taken by the Internal Revenue Service as of the earlier of—

(1) The date of the receipt by the taxpayer of the notice of the decision of the Internal Revenue Service Office of Appeals; or

(2) The date of the notice of deficiency or any date thereafter.

(c) *Examples.*—The provisions of this section may be illustrated by the following examples:

*Example 1.* Taxpayer A receives a notice of proposed deficiency (30-day letter). A pays the amount of the proposed deficiency and files a claim for refund. A's claim is considered and a notice of proposed claim disallowance is issued by the Area Director. A does not request an Appeals office conference and the Area Director issues a notice of claim disallowance. A then files suit in a United States District Court. A cannot recover reasonable administrative costs because the notice of claim disallowance is not a notice of the decision of the Internal Revenue Service Office of Appeals or a notice of deficiency. Accordingly, the Internal Revenue Service has not taken a position in the administrative proceeding pursuant to section 7430(c)(7)(B).

*Example 2.* Taxpayer B receives a notice of proposed deficiency (30-day letter). B disputes the proposed adjustments and requests an Appeals office conference. The Appeals office determines that B has no additional tax liability. B requests administrative costs from the date of the 30-day letter. B is not the prevailing party and may not recover administrative costs because all of the proposed adjustments in the case were resolved as of the date that the Internal Revenue Service took a position in the administrative proceeding.

(d) *Substantially justified.*—(1) *In general.*—The position of the Internal Revenue Service is substantially justified if it has a reasonable basis in both fact and law. A significant factor in determining whether the position of the Internal Revenue Service is substantially justified as of a given date is whether, on or before that date, the taxpayer has presented all relevant information under the taxpayer's control and relevant legal arguments supporting the taxpayer's position to the appropriate Internal Revenue Service personnel. The appropriate Internal Revenue Service personnel are personnel responsible for reviewing the information or arguments, or personnel who would transfer the information or arguments in the normal course of procedure and administration to the personnel who are responsible.

(2) *Position in courts of appeal.*—Whether the United States has won or lost an issue substantially similar to the one in the taxpayer's case in courts of appeal for circuits other than the one to which the taxpayer's case would be appealable should be taken into consideration in determining whether the Internal Revenue Service's position was substantially justified.

(3) *Example.*—The provisions of this section (d) are illustrated by the following example:

*Example.* The Internal Revenue Service, in the conduct of a correspondence examination of taxpayer A's individual income tax return, requests substantiation from A of claimed medical expenses. A does not respond to the request and the Internal Revenue Service issues a notice of deficiency. After receiving the notice of deficiency, A presents sufficient information and arguments to convince a tax compliance officer that the notice of deficiency is incorrect and that A owes no tax. The revenue agent then closes the case showing no deficiency. Although A incurred costs after the issuance of the notice of deficiency, A is unable to recover these costs because, as of the date these costs were incurred, A had not presented relevant information under A's control and relevant legal arguments supporting A's position to the appropriate Internal Revenue Service personnel.

Accordingly, the position of the Internal Revenue Service was substantially justified at the time the costs were incurred.

(4) *Included costs.*—(i) An award of reasonable administrative costs shall only include costs incurred on or after the administrative proceeding date as defined in section 301.7430-3(c) of this chapter.

(ii) If the Internal Revenue Service takes a position in an administrative proceeding, as defined in paragraph (b) of this section, and the position is not substantially justified, the taxpayer may be permitted to recover costs incurred before the position was taken, but not before the dates set forth in this paragraph (d)(4).

(5) *Examples.*—The provisions of this section may be illustrated by the following examples:

*Example 1.* Pursuant to section 6672, taxpayer D receives from the Area Director Collection Operations (Collection) a proposed assessment of trust fund taxes (Trust Fund Recovery Penalty). D requests and is granted Appeals office consideration. Appeals considers the issues and decides to uphold Collection's recommended assessment. Appeals notifies D of this decision in writing. Collection then assesses the tax and notice and demand is made. D timely pays the minimum amount required to commence a court proceeding, files a claim for refund, and furnishes the required bond. Collection disallows the claim, but Appeals, on reconsideration, reverses its original position, thus upholding D's position. If Appeals' initial determination was not substantially justified, D may recover administrative costs incurred on or after the mailing of the proposed assessment of trust fund taxes, because the proposed assessment is the first determination letter that allows the taxpayer an opportunity for administrative review in the Internal Revenue Service Office of Appeals.

*Example 2.* Taxpayer E receives a notice of proposed deficiency (30-day letter). E pays the amount of the proposed deficiency and files a claim for refund. E's claim is considered and a notice of proposed disallowance is issued by the Area Director. E requests and is granted Appeals office consideration. No agreement is reached with Appeals and the Office of Appeals issues a notice of claim disallowance. E does not file suit in a United States District Court but instead contacts the Appeals office to attempt to reverse the decision. E convinces the Appeals officer that the notice of claim disallowance is in error. The Appeals officer then abates the assessment. E may recover reasonable administrative costs if the position taken in the notice of claim disallowance issued by the Office of Appeals was not substantially justified and the other requirements of section 7430 and the regulations thereunder are satisfied. If so, E may recover administrative costs incurred from the mailing date of the 30-day letter because the requirements of paragraph (c)(2) of this section are met. E cannot recover the costs incurred prior to the mailing of the 30-day letter because they were incurred before the administrative proceeding date.

(6) *Exception.*—If the position of the Internal Revenue Service was substantially justified with respect to some issues in the proceeding and not substantially justified with respect to the remaining issues, any award of reasonable administrative costs to the taxpayer may be limited to only reasonable administrative costs attributable to those issues with respect to which the position of the Internal Revenue Service was not substantially justified. If the position of the Internal Revenue Service was substantially justified for only a portion of the period of the proceeding and not substantially justified for the remaining portion of the proceeding, any award of reasonable administrative costs to the taxpayer may be limited to only reasonable administrative costs attributable to that portion during which the position of the Internal Revenue Service was not substantially justified. Where an award of reasonable administrative costs is limited to that portion of the administrative proceeding during which the position of the Internal Revenue Service was not substantially justified, whether the position of the Internal Revenue Service was substantially justified is determined as of the date any cost is incurred.

(7) *Presumption.*—If the Internal Revenue Service did not follow any applicable published guidance in an administrative proceeding commenced after July 30, 1996, the position of the Internal Revenue Service, on those issues to which the guidance applies and for all periods during which the guidance was not followed, will be presumed not to be substantially justified. This presumption may be rebutted. For purposes of this paragraph (d)(7), the term *applicable published guidance* means final or temporary regulations, revenue rulings, revenue procedures, information releases, notices, and announcements published in the Internal Revenue Bulletin and, if issued to or with respect to the taxpayer, private letter rulings, technical advice memoranda, and determination letters (§601.601(d)(2) of this chapter). Also, for purposes of this paragraph (d)(7), the term administrative proceeding includes only those administrative proceedings or portions of administrative proceedings occurring on or after the administrative proceeding date as defined in §301.7430-3(c).

## Proceedings by Taxpayers and Third Parties
### See p. 20,601 for regulations not amended to reflect law changes
**67,177**

(e) *Amount in controversy.*—The amount in controversy shall include the amount in issue as of the administrative proceeding date as increased by any amounts subsequently placed in issue by any party. The amount in controversy is determined without increasing or reducing the amount in controversy for amounts of loss, deduction, or credit carried over from years not in issue.

(f) *Most significant issue or set of issues presented.*—(1) *In general.*—Where the taxpayer has not substantially prevailed with respect to the amount in controversy the taxpayer may nonetheless be a prevailing party if the taxpayer substantially prevails with respect to the most significant issue or set of issues presented. The issues presented include those raised as of the administrative proceeding date and those raised subsequently. Only in a multiple issue proceeding can a most significant issue or set of issues presented exist. However, not all multiple issue proceedings contain a most significant issue or set of issues presented. An issue or set of issues constitutes the most significant issue or set of issues presented if, despite involving a lesser dollar amount in the proceeding than the other issue or issues, it objectively represents the most significant issue or set of issues for the taxpayer or the Internal Revenue Service. This may occur because of the effect of the issue or set of issues on other transactions or other taxable years of the taxpayer or related parties.

(2) *Example.*—The provisions of this section may be illustrated by the following example:

*Example.* In the purchase of an ongoing business, Taxpayer F obtains from the previous owner of the business a covenant not to compete for a period of five years. On audit of F's individual income tax return for the year in which the business was acquired, the Internal Revenue Service challenges the basis assigned to the covenant not to compete and a deduction taken as a business expense for a seminar attended by F. Both parties agree that the covenant not to compete is amortizable over a period of five years; however, the Internal Revenue Service asserts that the proper basis of the covenant is $25,000, while F asserts the basis is $50,000 and claims a deduction of $10,000 in the year in which the business was acquired. F deducted $12,000 for the seminar. The Internal Revenue Service determines that the deduction for the seminar should be disallowed entirely. In the notice of deficiency, the Internal Revenue Service adjusts the amortization deduction to reflect the change to the basis of the covenant not to compete, and disallows the seminar expense. Thus, of the two adjustments determined for the year under audit, the adjustment attributable to the disallowance of the seminar is larger than that attributable to the covenant not to compete. Due to the impact on the next succeeding four years, however, the covenant not to compete adjustment is the most significant issue to both F and the Internal Revenue Service.

(g) *Net worth and size limitations.*—(1) *Individuals.*—A taxpayer who is a natural person meets the net worth and size limitations of this paragraph if the taxpayer's net worth does not exceed two million dollars. For purposes of determining net worth, individuals filing a joint return, and jointly incurring administrative or litigation costs shall have their net worth determined jointly, with all assets and liabilities treated as joint for purposes of the net worth evaluation, and applying a joint cap of four million dollars. Individuals who file a joint return, but incur separate administrative or litigation costs, by retaining separate representation, and/or seeking individual administrative review or petitioning the court individually, such as under section 6015, shall have their net worth determined separately, with only those assets and liabilities reasonably attributable to each spouse considered against separate caps of two million dollars per spouse.

(2) *Estates and trusts.*—An estate or a trust meets the net worth and size limitations of this paragraph if the estate or trust's net worth does not exceed two million dollars. The net worth of an estate shall be determined as of the date of the decedent's death provided the date of death is prior to the date the court proceeding is commenced. The net worth of a trust shall be determined as of the last day of the last taxable year involved in the proceeding.

(3) *Others.*—(i) A taxpayer that is a partnership, corporation, association, unit of local government, or organization (other than an organization described in paragraph (g)(4) of this section) meets the net worth and size limitations of this paragraph if, as of the administrative proceeding date:

(A) The taxpayer's net worth does not exceed seven million dollars; and

(B) The taxpayer does not have more than 500 employees.

(ii) A taxpayer who is a natural person and owns an unincorporated business is subject to the net worth and size limitations contained in paragraph (g)(3)(i) of this section if the tax at issue (or any interest, additional amount, addition to tax, or penalty, together with any costs in addition to the tax) relates directly to the business activities of the unincorporated business.

(4) *Special rule for charitable organizations and certain cooperatives.*—An organization described in section 501(c)(3) exempt from taxation under section 501(a), or a cooperative association as defined in section 15(a) of the Agricultural Marketing Act, 12 U.S.C. 1141j(a) (as in effect on October 22, 1986), meets the net worth and size limitations of this paragraph if, as of the administrative proceeding date, the organization or cooperative association does not have more than 500 employees.

(5) *Special rule for TEFRA partnership proceedings.*—(i) In cases involving partnerships subject to the unified audit and litigation procedures of subchapter C of chapter 63 of the Internal Revenue Code (TEFRA partnership cases), the TEFRA partnership meets the net worth and size limitations requirements of this paragraph (g) if, on the administrative proceeding date—

(A) The partnership's net worth does not exceed seven million dollars; and

(B) The partnership does not have more than 500 employees.

(ii) In addition, each partner requesting fees pursuant to section 7430 must meet the appropriate net worth and size limitations set forth in paragraph (g)(1), (g)(2), or (g)(3) of this section. For example, if a partner is an individual, his or her net worth must not exceed two million dollars as of the administrative proceeding date. If the partner is a corporation, its net worth must not exceed seven million dollars and it must not have more than 500 employees.

(6) *Determining net worth.*—For purposes of determining net worth under this paragraph (g), assets are valued based on the cost of their acquisition.

(h) *Determination of prevailing party.*—If the final decision with respect to the tax, interest, or penalty is made at the administrative level, the determination of whether a taxpayer is a prevailing party shall be made by agreement of the parties, or absent an agreement, by the Internal Revenue Service. See § 301.7430-2(c)(7) regarding the right to appeal the decision of the Internal Revenue Service denying (in whole or in part) a request for reasonable administrative costs to the Tax Court. [Reg. § 301.7430-5.]

☐ [*T.D. 8542, 6-6-94. Amended by T.D. 8725, 7-21-97 and T.D. 9756, 2-29-2016.*]

### [Reg. § 301.7430-6]

**§ 301.7430-6. Effective/applicability dates.**—Sections 301.7430-2 through 301.7430-6, other than §§ 301.7430-2(b)(2), (c)(3)(i)(B), (c)(3)(i)(E), (c)(3)(ii)(C), (c)(3)(iii)(C), (c)(5), (c)(7), and (e); §§ 301.7430-3(c)(1), (c)(3), (c)(4), and (d); §§ 301.7430-4(b)(3)(i), (b)(3)(ii), (b)(3)(iii)(B), (b)(3)(iii)(C), (b)(3)(iii)(D), (b)(3)(iii)(E), (b)(3)(iii)(F), (c)(2)(ii), (c)(4), and (d); and §§ 301.7430-5(a), (b), (c)(3), (d)(2), (d)(3), (d)(4), (d)(5), (d)(7), (f)(2), (g)(1), (g)(2), (g)(3), (g)(5), and (g)(6) apply to claims for reasonable administrative costs filed with the Internal Revenue Service after December 23, 1992, with respect to costs incurred in administrative proceedings commenced after November 10, 1988. Section 301.7430-2(c)(5) is applicable to costs incurred and services performed in cases in which the petition was filed on or after March 1, 2016, except for the last two sentences, which are applicable March 23, 1993. Sections 301.7430-2(b)(2), and (c)(3)(i)(B) (except the last sentence); 301.7430-4(b)(3)(ii), (b)(3)(iii)(C) (except the first two sentences), and (c)(2)(ii) (except for references to the statutory cap as $125); and 301.7430-5(a) (except the parenthetical of 5(a) and all of 5(a)(1)), and the first and last sentence of (d)(7) are applicable for administrative proceedings commenced after July 30, 1996. Sections 301.7430-1(e), 301.7430-2(c)(2), 7430-3(a)(4) and (b) are applicable with respect to actions taken by the Internal Revenue Service after July 22, 1998. The last sentence of § 301.7430-2(c)(3)(i)(B), the first two sentences of § 301.7430-2(b)(3)(iii)(C), §§ 301.7430-2(c)(3)(i)(E), (c)(3)(ii)(C), (c)(3)(iii)(C), (c)(7), (e); 301.7430-3(c)(1), (c)(3), (c)(4), (d); Reg. § 301.7430-4(b)(3)(i),(b)(3)(iii)(B), (b)(3)(iii)(E), (b)(3)(iii)(F), (c)(2)(ii)(to the extent it references the statutory cap as $125), (c)(4), (d); the parenthetical of § 301.7430-5(a) and §§ 301.7430-5(a)(1), (b), (d)(2), (d)(3), (d)(4), (d)(5), (d)(7), except the first and last sentences, (f)(2), (g)(1), (g)(2), (g)(3), (g)(5), and (g)(6)apply to costs incurred and services performed in cases in which the petition was filed on or after March 1, 2016. [Reg. § 301.7430-6.]

☐ [*T.D. 8542, 6-6-94. Amended by T.D. 8725, 7-21-97, T.D. 9050, 3-24-2003 and T.D. 9756, 2-29-2016.*]

### [Reg. § 301.7430-7]

**§ 301.7430-7. Qualified offers.**—(a) *In general.*—Section 7430(c)(4)(E) (the qualified offer rule) provides that a party to a court proceeding satisfying the timely filing and net worth requirements of section 7430(c)(4)(A)(ii) shall be treated as the prevailing party if the liability of the taxpayer pursuant to the judgment in the proceeding (determined without regard to interest) is equal to or less than the liability of the taxpayer which would have been so determined if the United States had accepted the last qualified offer of the party as defined in section 7430(g). For purposes of this section, the term *judgment* means the cumulative determinations of the court concerning the adjustments at issue and litigated to a determination in the court proceeding. In making the comparison between the liability under the qualified offer and the liability under the judgment, the taxpayer's liability under the judgment is further modified by the provisions of paragraph (b)(3) of this section. The provisions of the qualified offer rule do not apply if the taxpayer's liability under the judgment, as modified by the provisions of paragraph (b)(3) of this section, is determined exclusively pursuant to a settlement, or to any proceeding in which the amount of tax liability is not in issue, including any declaratory judgment proceeding, any proceeding to enforce or quash any summons issued pursuant to the Internal Revenue Code (Code), and any action to restrain disclosure under section 6110(f). If the qualified offer rule applies to the court proceeding, the determination of whether the liability under the qualified offer would have equaled or exceeded the liability pursuant to the judgment is made by reference to the last qualified offer made with respect to the tax liability at issue in the administrative or court proceeding. An award of reasonable administrative and litigation costs under the qualified offer rule only includes those costs incurred on or after the date of the last qualified offer and is limited to those costs attributable to the adjustments at issue at the time the last qualified offer was made that were included in the court's judgment other than by reason of settlement. The qualified offer rule is inapplicable to reasonable administrative or litigation costs otherwise awarded to a taxpayer who is a prevailing party under any other provision of section 7430(c)(4). This section sets forth the requirements to be satisfied for a taxpayer to be treated as a prevailing party by reason of the taxpayer making a qualified offer, as well as the circumstances leading to the application of the exceptions, special rules, and coordination provisions of the qualified offer rule. Furthermore, this section sets forth the elements necessary for an offer to be treated as a qualified offer under section 7430(g).

(b) *Requirements for treatment as a prevailing party based upon having made a qualified offer.*—(1) *In general.*—In order to be treated as a prevailing party by reason of having made a qualified offer, the liability of the taxpayer for the type or types of tax and the taxable year or years at issue in the proceeding (as calculated pursuant to paragraph (b)(2) of this section), based on the last qualified offer (as defined in paragraph (c) of this section) made by the taxpayer in the court or administrative proceeding, must equal or exceed the liability of the taxpayer pursuant to the judgment by the court for the same type or types of tax and the same taxable year or years (as calculated pursuant to paragraph (b)(3) of this section). Furthermore, the taxpayer must meet the timely filing and net worth requirements of section 7430(c)(4)(A)(ii). If all of the adjustments subject to the last qualified offer are settled prior to the entry of the judgment by the court, the taxpayer is not a prevailing party by reason of having made a qualified offer. The taxpayer may, however, still qualify as a prevailing party if the requirements of section 7430(c)(4)(A) are met. If one or more adjustments covered by a qualified offer (see paragraph (c)(3)) are settled following a ruling by the court that substantially resolves those adjustments, then those adjustments will not be treated as having been settled prior to the entry of the judgment by the court and instead will be treated as amounts included in the judgment as a result of the court's determinations. For purposes of the preceding sentence, rulings relating to discovery, admissibility of evidence, and burden of proof are not rulings that substantially resolve adjustments covered by a qualified offer.

(2) *Liability under the last qualified offer.*—For purposes of paragraph (b)(1) of this section, the taxpayer's liability under the last qualified offer is the change in the taxpayer's liability that would have resulted if the United States had accepted the taxpayer's last qualified offer on all of the adjustments that were at issue in the administrative or court proceeding at the time that the offer was made compared to the amount shown on the return or returns (or as previously adjusted). The portion of a taxpayer's liability that is attributable to adjustments raised by either party after the making of the last qualified offer is not included in the calculation of the liability under that offer. The taxpayer's liability under the last qualified offer is calculated without regard to adjustments that the parties have stipulated will be resolved in accordance with the outcome of a separate pending Federal, state, or other judicial or administrative proceeding. For example, the parties may stipulate that the taxpayer's liability will be resolved in accordance with the outcome of an alternative dispute resolution proceeding or a separate court proceeding, such as a probate, tort liability, or trademark action.

Furthermore, the taxpayer's liability under the last qualified offer is calculated without regard to interest, unless the taxpayer's liability for, or entitlement to, interest is a contested issue in the administrative or court proceeding and is one of the adjustments included in the last qualified offer.

(3) *Liability pursuant to the judgment.*—For purposes of paragraph (b)(1) of this section, the taxpayer's liability pursuant to the judgment is the change in the taxpayer's liability resulting from amounts contained in the judgment as a result of the court's determinations, and amounts contained in settlements not included in the judgment, that are attributable to all adjustments that were included in the last qualified offer compared to the amount shown on the return or returns (or as previously adjusted). This liability includes amounts attributable to adjustments included in the last qualified offer and settled by the parties prior to the entry of judgment regardless of whether those amounts are actually included in the judgment entered by the court. The taxpayer's liability pursuant to the judgment does not include amounts attributable to adjustments that are not included in the last qualified offer, even if those amounts are actually included in the judgment entered by the court. The taxpayer's liability under the judgment is calculated without regard to adjustments that the parties have stipulated will be resolved in accordance with the outcome of a separate pending Federal, state, or other judicial or administrative proceeding. Furthermore, the taxpayer's liability pursuant to the judgment is calculated without regard to interest, unless the taxpayer's liability for, or entitlement to, interest is a contested issue in the administrative or court proceeding and is one of the adjustments included in the last qualified offer. Where adjustments raised by either party subsequent to the making of the last qualified offer are included in the judgment entered by the court, or are settled prior to the court proceeding, the taxpayer's liability pursuant to the judgment is calculated by treating the subsequently raised adjustments as if they had never been raised.

(c) *Qualified offer.*—(1) *In general.*—A qualified offer is defined in section 7430(g) to mean a written offer which—

(i) Is made by the taxpayer to the United States during the qualified offer period;

(ii) Specifies the offered amount of the taxpayer's liability (determined without regard to interest, unless interest is a contested issue in the proceeding);

(iii) Is designated at the time it is made as a qualified offer for purposes of section 7430(g); and

(iv) By its terms, remains open during the period beginning on the date it is made and ending on the earliest of the date the offer is rejected, the date the trial begins, or the 90th day after the date the offer is made.

(2) *To the United States.*—(i) A qualified offer is made to the United States when it is delivered to the office or personnel within the Internal Revenue Service, Office of Appeals, Office of Chief Counsel (including field personnel) or Department of Justice that has jurisdiction over the tax matter at issue in the administrative or court proceeding. If those offices or persons are unknown to the taxpayer making the qualified offer, the taxpayer may deliver the offer to the appropriate office, as follows:

(A) If the taxpayer's initial pleading in a court proceeding has been answered, the taxpayer may deliver the offer to the office that filed the answer.

(B) If the taxpayer's petition in the Tax Court has not yet been answered, the taxpayer may deliver the offer to the Office of Chief Counsel, 1111 Constitution Avenue, NW., Washington, DC 20224.

(C) If the taxpayer's initial pleading in any Federal court, other than the Tax Court, has not yet been answered, the taxpayer may deliver the offer to the Attorney General of the United States, 950 Pennsylvania Ave., NW., Washington, DC 20530-0001. For a suit brought in a United States district court, a copy of the offer should also be delivered to the United States Attorney for the district in which the suit was brought.

(D) In any other situation, the taxpayer may deliver the offer to the office that sent the taxpayer the first letter of proposed deficiency which allows the taxpayer an opportunity for administrative review in the Internal Revenue Service Office of Appeals.

(ii) Until an offer is received by the appropriate personnel or office under this paragraph (c)(2), it is not considered to have been made, with the following exception. If the offer is deposited in the United States mail, in an envelope or other appropriate wrapper, postage prepaid, properly addressed to the appropriate personnel or office under this paragraph (c)(2), the date of the United States postmark stamped on the cover in which the offer is mailed shall be deemed to be the date of receipt of that offer by the addressee. If any offer is deposited with a designated delivery service, as defined in section 7502(f)(2), in lieu of the United States mail, the provisions of section 7502(f)(1) shall apply in determining whether that offer qualifies for this exception.

(3) *Specifies the offered amount.*—A qualified offer specifies the offered amount if it clearly specifies the amount for the liability of the taxpayer, calculated as set forth in paragraph (b)(2) of this section. The offer may be a specific dollar amount of the total liability or a percentage of the adjustments at issue in the proceeding at the time the offer is made. This amount must be with respect to all of the adjustments at issue in the administrative or court proceeding at the time the offer is made and only those adjustments. The specified amount must be an amount, the acceptance of which by the United States will fully resolve the taxpayer's liability, and only that liability (determined without regard to adjustments that the parties have stipulated will be resolved in accordance with the outcome of a separate pending Federal, state, or other judicial or administrative proceeding, or interest, unless interest is a contested issue in the proceeding) for the type or types of tax and the taxable year or years at issue in the proceeding. In cases involving multiple tax years, if adjustments in different tax years arise from separate and distinct issues such that the resolution of issues in one or more tax years will not affect the taxpayer's liability in one or more of the other tax years in the proceeding, then a qualified offer may be made for less than all of the tax years involved. A qualified offer, however, must resolve all of the issues for the tax years covered by the offer and also must cover all tax years in the proceeding affected by those issues. A tax year (affected year) is affected by an issue if the treatment of the issue in another tax year involved in the proceeding necessarily affects the treatment of the issue in the affected year.

(4) *Designated at the time it is made as a qualified offer.*—An offer is not a qualified offer unless it designates in writing at the time it is made that it is a qualified offer for purposes of section 7430(g). An offer made at a time when one or more adjustments not included in the first letter of proposed deficiency which allows the taxpayer an opportunity for administrative review in the Internal Revenue Service Office of Appeals have been raised by the taxpayer and remain unresolved, is not considered to be a qualified offer unless contemporaneously or prior to the making of the offer, the taxpayer has provided the United States with the substantiation and legal and factual arguments necessary to allow for informed consideration of the merits of those adjustments. For example, a taxpayer will be considered to have provided the United States with the necessary substantiation and legal and factual arguments if the taxpayer (or a recognized representative of the taxpayer described in § 601.502 of this chapter) participates in an Appeals office conference, participates in an Area Counsel conference, or confers with the Department of Justice, and at that time, discloses all relevant information. All relevant information includes, but is not limited to, the legal and factual arguments supporting the taxpayer's position on any adjustments raised by the taxpayer after the issuance of the first letter of proposed deficiency which allows the taxpayer an opportunity for administrative review in the Internal Revenue Service Office of Appeals. A taxpayer has disclosed all relevant information if the taxpayer has supplied sufficient information to allow informed consideration of the taxpayer's tax matter to the extent the information and its relevance were known or should have been known to the taxpayer at the time of the conference.

(5) *Remains open.*—A qualified offer must, by its terms, remain open for acceptance by the United States from the date it is made, as defined in paragraph (c)(2)(ii) of this section, until the earliest of the date it is rejected in writing by a person with authority to reject the offer, the date the trial begins, or the 90th day after being received by the United States. The offer, by its written terms, may remain open after the occurrence of one or more of the above-referenced events. Once made, the period during which a qualified offer remains open may be extended by the taxpayer prior to its expiration, but an extension cannot be used to make an offer meet the minimum period for remaining open required by this paragraph (c)(5).

(6) *Last qualified offer.*—A taxpayer may make multiple qualified offers during the qualified offer period. For purposes of the comparison under paragraph (b) of this section, the making of a qualified offer supersedes any previously made qualified offers. In making the comparison described in paragraph (b) of this section, only the qualified offer made most closely in time to the end of the qualified offer period is compared to the taxpayer's liability under the judgment.

(7) *Qualified offer period.*—To constitute a qualified offer, an offer must be made during the qualified offer period. The qualified offer period begins on the date on which the first letter of proposed deficiency which allows the taxpayer an opportunity for administrative review in the Internal Revenue Service Office of Appeals is sent to the taxpayer. For this purpose, the date of the notice of claim

disallowance will begin the qualified offer period in a refund case. If there has been no notice of claim disallowance in a refund case, the qualified offer period begins on the date on which the answer or other responsive pleading is filed with the court. The qualified offer period ends on the date which is thirty days before the date the case is first set for trial. In determining when the qualified offer period ends for cases in the Tax Court and other Federal courts using calendars for trial, a case will be considered set for trial on the date scheduled for the calendar call. A case may be removed from a trial calendar at any time. Thus, a case may be removed from a trial calendar before the date that precedes by thirty days the date scheduled for that trial calendar. The qualified offer period does not end until the case remains on a trial calendar on the date that precedes by 30 days the scheduled date of the calendar call for that trial session. The qualified offer period may not be extended beyond the periods set forth in this paragraph (c)(7), although the period during which a qualified offer remains open may extend beyond the end of the qualified offer period.

(8) *Interest as a contested issue.*—To constitute a qualified offer, an offer must specify the offered amount of the taxpayer's liability (determined without regard to interest, unless interest is a contested issue in the proceeding), as provided in paragraphs (c)(1)(ii) and (c)(3) of this section. Therefore, a qualified offer generally may only include an offer to compromise tax, penalties, additions to the tax, and additional amounts. Interest may only be included in a qualified offer if interest is a contested issue in the proceeding. For purposes of this section, interest is a contested issue in the proceeding only if the court in which the proceeding could be brought would have jurisdiction to determine the amount of interest due on the underlying tax, penalties, additions to the tax, and additional amounts. Examples of proceedings in which interest might be a contested issue include proceedings in which the increased interest rate for large corporate underpayments under section 6621(c) is imposed by the Internal Revenue Service and interest abatement proceedings brought under section 6404. Interest is not a contested issue in the proceeding if the court that would have jurisdiction over the proceeding would not have jurisdiction to determine the amount or rate of interest, regardless of whether the taxpayer attempts to raise interest as an issue in the proceeding. Consequently, interest will not be a contested issue in the vast majority of tax cases because they merely involve the straightforward application of statutory interest under section 6601. Accordingly, in those cases, interest may not be included in the offer.

(d) [Reserved].

(e) *Examples.*—The following examples illustrate the provisions of this section:

*Example 1. Definition of a judgment.* The Internal Revenue Service (IRS) audits Taxpayer A for year X and issues a notice of proposed deficiency (30-day letter) proposing to disallow deductions 1, 2, 3, and 4. A files a protest and participates in a conference with the Internal Revenue Service Office of Appeals (Appeals). Appeals allows deduction 1, and issues a statutory notice of deficiency for deductions 2, 3, and 4. A's petition to the United States Tax Court for year X never mentions deduction 2. Prior to trial, A concedes deduction 3. After the trial, the Tax Court issues an opinion allowing A to deduct a portion of deduction 4. As used in paragraph (a) of this section, the term judgment means the cumulative determinations of the court concerning the adjustments at issue in the court proceeding. Thus, the term judgment does not include deduction 1 because it was never at issue in the court proceeding. Similarly, the term judgment does not include deduction 2 because it was not placed at issue by A in the court proceeding. Although deduction 3 was at issue in the court proceeding, it is not included in the term judgment because it was not determined by the court, but rather by concession or settlement. For purposes of section 7430(c)(4)(E), the term judgment only includes the portion of deduction 4 disallowed by the Tax Court.

*Example 2. Liability under the offer and liability under the judgment.* Assume the same facts as in *Example 1* except that A makes a qualified offer after the Appeals conference, which is not accepted by the IRS. A's offer is with respect to all adjustments at issue at that time. Those adjustments are deductions 2, 3, and 4. At the conclusion of the litigation, A's entitlement to an award based upon the qualified offer will depend, among other things, on a comparison of the change in A's liability for income tax for year X resulting from the judgment of the Tax Court with the change that would have resulted had the IRS accepted A's qualified offer. In making this comparison, the term judgment (as discussed in *Example 1*) is modified by including the amounts of settled or conceded adjustments that were at issue at the time the qualified offer was made. Any settled or conceded adjustments that were not at issue at the time the qualified offer was made, either because the settlement or concession occurred before the offer or because the adjustment was not raised until after the offer, are not included in the comparison. Thus, A's offer on deductions 2, 3, and 4 is compared with the change in A's liability resulting from the Tax Court's determination of deduction 4, and the concessions of issues 2 and 3 by A.

*Example 3. Offer must resolve full liability.* Assume the same facts as in *Example 2* except that A's offer after the Appeals conference explicitly states that it is only with respect to adjustments 2 and 3 and not with respect to adjustment 4. Even if A's liability pursuant to the judgment, calculated under paragraph (b)(3) of this section as illustrated in *Example 2*, is equal to or less than it would have been had the IRS accepted A's offer after the Appeals conference, A is not a prevailing party under section 7430(c)(4)(E). A qualified offer must include all adjustments at issue at the time the offer is made. Since A's offer excluded adjustment 4, which was an adjustment at issue at the time the offer was made, it does not constitute a qualified offer pursuant to paragraph (b)(2) of this section.

*Example 4. Offer must resolve full liability.* Assume the same facts as in *Example 1*, except that A makes a qualified offer that is accepted by the IRS. After the offer is accepted, A attempts to reduce the amount A will pay pursuant to the offer by applying net operating loss carryovers to the years in issue. Because the net operating losses were not at issue when the offer was made, A's offer was a qualified offer. Whether A is entitled to apply net operating losses to reduce the amount stated in the offer will depend upon the application of contract principles, local court rules, and, because net operating losses are at issue, section 6511(d) and related provisions.

*Example 5. Qualified offer rule for multiple tax years, partial resolution offer is a qualified offer.* Taxpayer B receives a notice of deficiency for taxable years 2001, 2002, and 2003. For 2001, the statutory notice disallows business deductions. For 2002, the statutory notice increases income for unreported lottery winnings. For 2003, the statutory notice disallows a child care credit. B submits a qualified offer only with respect to 2002. Since the adjustments for the three tax years are separate and distinct, B may submit a qualified offer for a single year. If B's liability under the judgment is equal to or less than the qualified offer with respect to 2002, irrespective of 2001 and 2003, B is a prevailing party for 2002 for purposes of section 7430(g). Assuming B satisfies the remaining requirements of section 7430, B may recover reasonable administrative and litigation costs that are attributable to 2002 from the date of the qualified offer. To qualify for any costs with respect to 2001 or 2003, B must satisfy the requirements of section 7430(c)(4).

*Example 6. Qualified offer rule for multiple tax years, partial resolution offer is not a qualified offer.* Assume the same facts as in *Example 5* except that with respect to 2002, in addition to increasing B's income for the unreported lottery winnings, the statutory notice also disallows a charitable contribution deduction. B submits a settlement offer that purports to be a qualified offer, but only covers the unreported lottery winnings. B's offer is not a qualified offer because it does not address the charitable contribution issue, and thus, does not fully resolve B's liability for 2002.

*Example 7. Qualified offer rule for multiple tax years, partial resolution offer is not a qualified offer.* Taxpayer C receives a notice of deficiency for taxable years 2001, 2002, and 2003 adjusting the amount of a depreciation deduction due to the Internal Revenue Service's increase to the recovery period. C submits a settlement offer relating only to 2003 that purports to be a qualified offer. C's offer is not a qualified offer because the issue in the three tax years is not separable given that the treatment of the issue in one of the years necessarily affects the treatment of the issue in the other years, and C's offer only applies to one of the years in the proceeding. In cases involving multiple tax years with nonseparable tax issues affecting all tax years, an offer is not a qualified offer unless it resolves the liability for all tax years at issue in the administrative or judicial proceeding.

*Example 8. Qualified offer rule inapplicable when all issues settled.* Taxpayer D receives a notice of proposed deficiency (30-day letter) proposing to disallow both a personal interest deduction in the amount of $10,000 (Adjustment 1), and a charitable contribution deduction in the amount of $2,000 (Adjustment 2), and to include in income $4,000 of unreported interest income (Adjustment 3). D timely files a protest with Appeals. At the Appeals conference, D presents substantiation for the charitable contribution and presents arguments that the interest paid was deductible mortgage interest and that the interest received was held in trust for Taxpayer E. At the conference, D also provides the Appeals officer assigned to D's case a written offer to settle the case for a deficiency of $2,000, exclusive of interest. The offer states that it is a qualified offer for purposes of section 7430(g) and that it will remain open for acceptance by the IRS for a period in excess of 90 days. After considering D's substantiation and arguments, the Appeals Officer accepts the $2,000 offer to settle the case in full. Although D's offer is a qualified offer, because all three adjustments contained in the qualified offer were settled, the qualified offer rule is inapplicable.

*Example 9. Qualified offer rule inapplicable when all issues contained in the qualified offer are settled; subsequently raised adjustments ignored.* Assume the same facts as in *Example 8* except that D's qualified offer was for a deficiency of $1,800 and the IRS rejected that offer. Subsequently, the IRS issued a statutory notice of deficiency disallowing the three adjustments contained in *Example 8*, and, in addition, disallowing a home office expense in the amount of $5,000 (Adjustment 4). After petitioning the Tax Court, D presents the field attorney assigned to the case with a written offer, which is not designated as a qualified offer for purposes of section 7430(g), to settle the three adjustments that had been the subject of the qualified offer, plus adjustment 4, for a total deficiency of $2,500. After negotiating with D, a settlement is reached on the three adjustments that were the subject of the rejected qualified offer, for a deficiency of $1,800. Adjustment 4 is litigated in the Tax Court and the court determines that D is entitled to the full $5,000 deduction for that adjustment. Consequently, a decision is entered by the Tax Court reflecting the $1,800 settlement amount, which matches exactly the amount of D's only qualified offer in the case. Although the determined liability for adjustments 1, 2, and 3, equals that of the rejected qualified offer, because all three adjustments contained in the qualified offer were settled, the qualified offer rule is inapplicable.

*Example 10. Exclusion of adjustments made after the qualified offer is made.* Assume the same facts as in *Example 9* except the settlement is reached only on adjustments 1 and 2, for a liability of $1,500. Adjustments 3 and 4 are tried in the Tax Court and in accordance with the court's opinion, the taxpayer has a $300 deficiency attributable to Adjustment 3, and a $1,550 deficiency attributable to adjustment 4. Consequently, a decision is entered reflecting the $1,500 settled amount, the $300 liability on adjustment 3, and the $1,550 liability on adjustment 4. The $3,350 deficiency reflected in the Tax Court's decision exceeds the last (and only) qualified offer made by D. For purposes of determining whether D is a prevailing party as a result of having made a qualified offer in the proceeding, the liability attributable to adjustment 4, which was raised after the last qualified offer was made, is not included in the comparison of D's liability under the judgment with D's offered liability under the last qualified offer. Thus, D's $1,800 liability under the judgment, as modified for purposes of the qualified offer rule comparison, is equal to D's offered liability under the last qualified offer. Because D's liability under the last qualified offer equals or exceeds D's liability under the judgment, as calculated under paragraph (b)(3) of this section, D is a prevailing party for purposes of section 7430. Assuming D satisfies the remaining requirements of section 7430, D may recover those reasonable administrative and litigation costs attributable to adjustment 3. To qualify for any further award of reasonable administrative and litigation costs, D must satisfy the requirements of section 7430(c)(4)(A).

*Example 11. Qualified offer in a refund case.* Taxpayer E timely files an amended return claiming a refund of $1,000. This refund claim results from several omitted deductions which, if allowed, would reduce E's tax liability from $10,000 to $9,000. E receives a notice of claim disallowance and files a complaint with the appropriate United States District Court. Subsequently, E makes a qualified offer for a refund of $500. The offer is rejected and after trial the court finds E is entitled to a refund of $700. The change in E's liability from the tax shown on the return that would have resulted from the acceptance of E's qualified offer is a reduction in that liability of $500. The change in E's liability from the tax shown on the return resulting from the judgment of the court is a reduction in that liability of $700. Because E's liability under the qualified offer exceeds E's liability under the judgment, E is a prevailing party for purposes of section 7430. Assuming E satisfies the remaining requirements of section 7430, E may recover those reasonable litigation costs incurred on or after the date of the qualified offer. To qualify for any further award of reasonable administrative and litigation costs E must satisfy the requirements of section 7430(c)(4)(A).

*Example 12. End of qualified offer period when case is removed from Tax Court trial calendar more than 30 days before scheduled trial calendar.* Taxpayer F has petitioned the Tax Court in response to the issuance of a notice of deficiency. F receives notice that the case will be heard on the July trial session in F's city of residence. The scheduled date for the calendar call for that trial session is July 1st. On May 15th, F's motion to remove the case from the July trial session and place it on the October trial session for that city is granted. The scheduled date for the calendar call for the October trial session is October 1st. On May 31st, F delivers a qualified offer to the field attorney assigned to the case. On August 31st, F delivers a revised qualified offer to the field attorney assigned to the case. Neither offer is accepted. The case is tried during the October trial session, and at some time thereafter, a decision is entered by the court. Assume the judgment in the case, as calculated under paragraph (b)(3) of this section, is greater than the amount offered, as calculated under paragraph (b)(2) of this section, in the qualified offer delivered on May 31st, but less than the amount offered, as similarly calculated, in the qualified offer delivered on August 31st. Because the qualified offer period did not end until September 1st, and the offer of August 31st otherwise satisfied the requirements of paragraph (c) of this section, the offer delivered on August 31st is a qualified offer. Furthermore, because the August 31st qualified offer is closer in time to the end of the qualified offer period than the May 31st qualified offer, the August 31st qualified offer is the last qualified offer made by F. Consequently, the August 31st offer is the qualified offer that is compared to the judgment for purposes of determining whether F is a prevailing party under section 7430(c)(4)(E). Because F's liability under the August 31st qualified offer equals or exceeds F's liability under the judgment as calculated under paragraph (b)(3) of this section, F is a prevailing party for purposes of section 7430.

*Example 13. End of qualified offer period when case is removed from Tax Court trial calendar less than 30 days before scheduled trial calendar.* Assume the same facts as in *Example 12* except that F's motion was granted on June 15th. Because the qualified offer period ended on June 1st when the case remained on the July trial session on the date that preceded by 30 days the scheduled date of the calendar call for that trial session, the offer delivered on May 31st was F's last qualified offer. The August 31st offer is not a qualified offer for purposes of this rule. Consequently, F is not a prevailing party under the qualified offer rule. Therefore, F must satisfy the requirements of section 7430(c)(4)(A) to qualify for any award of reasonable administrative and litigation costs.

*Example 14. When a qualified offer can be made and to whom it must be made.* During the examination of Taxpayer G's return, the IRS issues a notice of deficiency without having first issued a 30-day letter. After receiving the notice of deficiency G timely petitions the Tax Court. The next day G mails an offer to the office that issued the notice of deficiency, which offer satisfies the requirements of paragraphs (c)(3) through (6) of this section. This is the only written offer made by G during the administrative or court proceeding, and by its terms it is to remain open for a period in excess of 90 days after the date of mailing to the office issuing the notice of deficiency. The office that issued the notice of deficiency transmitted the offer to the field attorney with jurisdiction over the Tax Court case. After answering the case, the field attorney refers the case to Appeals pursuant to Rev. Proc. 87-24 (1987-1 C.B. 720). See §601.601(d)(2)(ii)(*b*) of this chapter. After careful consideration, Appeals rejects the offer and holds a conference with G during which some adjustments are settled. The remainder of the adjustments are tried in the Tax Court and G's liability resulting from the Tax Court's determinations, when added to G's liability resulting from the settled adjustments, is less than G's liability would have been under the offer rejected by Appeals. Because the Tax Court case had not yet been answered when the offer was sent, G properly mailed the offer to the office that issued the notice of deficiency. Thus, G's offer satisfied the requirements of paragraph (c)(2) of this section. Furthermore, even though G did not receive a 30-day letter, G's offer was made after the beginning of the qualified offer period, satisfying the requirements of paragraph (c)(7) of this section, because the issuance of the statutory notice provided G with notice of the IRS's determination of a deficiency, and the docketing of the case provided G with an opportunity for administrative review in the Internal Revenue Service Office of Appeals under Rev. Proc. 87-24. See §601.601(d)(2)(ii)(*b*) of this chapter. Because G's offer satisfied all of the requirements of paragraph (c) of this section, the offer was a qualified offer and G is a prevailing party.

*Example 15. Substitution of parties permitted under last qualified offer.* Taxpayer H receives a 30-day letter and participates in a conference with the Office of Appeals but no agreement is reached. Subsequently, H receives a notice of deficiency and petitions the Tax Court. Upon receiving the Internal Revenue Service's answer to the petition, H sends a qualified offer to the field attorney who signed the answer, by United States mail. The qualified offer stated that it would remain open for more than 90 days. Thirty days after making the offer, H dies and, on motion under Rule 63(a) of the Tax Court's Rules of Practice and Procedure by H's personal representative, I is substituted for H as a party in the Tax Court proceeding. I makes no qualified offers to settle the case and the case proceeds to trial, with the Tax Court issuing an opinion partially in favor of I. Even though I was not a party when the qualified offer was made by H, that offer constitutes a qualified offer because by its terms, when made, it was to remain open until at least the earlier of the date it is rejected, the date of trial, or 90 days. If the liability of I under the qualified offer, as determined under paragraph (b)(2) of this section, equals or exceeds the liability under the judgment of the Tax Court, as determined under paragraph (b)(3) of this section, I will be a prevailing party for purposes of an award of reasonable litigation costs under section 7430.

*Example 16. Qualified offer may not compromise interest unless it is a contested issue.* Taxpayer J receives a notice of deficiency making an adjustment resulting in a deficiency in tax of $6,500 plus a penalty of $500. Interest is not a contested issue in the proceeding. Within the qualified offer period, J submits a written offer to settle the case for a deficiency of $1,000, including all taxes, penalties, and interest. The offer states that it is a qualified offer for purposes of section 7430(g) and that it will remain open for acceptance by the Internal Revenue

Service for a period of 90 days. Section 7430(g)(2)(B) and paragraph (c)(3) of this section state that the amount of a qualified offer must be without regard to interest unless interest is at issue in the proceeding. Since J's offer attempts to compromise interest, which is not a contested issue in the proceeding, it is not a qualified offer.

*Example 17. Qualified offer based on new defense or legal theory.* Taxpayers K and L received a statutory notice of deficiency for tax year 2005, a tax year when they were married and filed a joint income tax return. Taxpayer K files a separate petition claiming innocent spouse relief and simultaneously submits an offer purporting to be a qualified offer. The offer states that K is entitled to innocent spouse relief and offers to settle the 2005 deficiency as to K. K's innocent spouse claim was not raised during K and L's audit, nor was it raised during their appeals conference. Additionally, at no time prior to or contemporaneously with submitting the offer did K file with the Internal Revenue Service a Form 8857, Request for Innocent Spouse Relief, or otherwise provide the information specified in §1.6015-5(a) of this chapter. K's offer is not a qualified offer because K did not file a Form 8857 or otherwise provide substantiation or legal and factual arguments necessary to allow for informed consideration of the merits of the innocent spouse claim as required by paragraph (c)(4) of this section, contemporaneously with the offer or prior to making the offer.

(f) *Effective/applicability date.*—This section is applicable with respect to qualified offers made in administrative or court proceedings described in section 7430 after December 24, 2003, except that paragraph (c)(8) is effective as of March 1, 2016. [Reg. §301.7430-7.]

☐ [T.D. 9106, 12-24-2003 (*corrected* 1-27-2004). *Amended by* T.D. 9756, 2-29-2016]

## [Reg. §301.7430-8]

**§301.7430-8. Administrative costs incurred in damage actions for violations of section 362 or 524 of the Bankruptcy Code.**—(a) *In general.*—The Internal Revenue Service may grant a taxpayer's request for recovery of reasonable administrative costs incurred in connection with the administrative proceeding before the Internal Revenue Service relating to the willful violation of section 362 or 524 of the Bankruptcy Code only if the taxpayer is a prevailing party.

(b) *Prevailing party.*—A taxpayer is a prevailing party for purposes of this section only if—

(1) The taxpayer satisfies the net worth and size limitations in paragraph (f) of §301.7430-5;

(2) The taxpayer establishes that in connection with the collection of his or her federal tax an officer or employee of the Internal Revenue Service has willfully violated a provision of section 362 or 524 of the Bankruptcy Code; and

(3) The position of the Internal Revenue Service in the proceeding was not substantially justified.

(c) *Administrative proceeding.*—For purposes of this section, an administrative proceeding is a proceeding related to an administrative claim presented to the Internal Revenue Service seeking relief from a violation of section 362 or 524 of the Bankruptcy Code by the Internal Revenue Service or recovery of damages from the Internal Revenue Service under §301.7433-2(e).

(d) *Costs incurred after filing of bankruptcy petition.*—Administrative costs may be recovered only if incurred on or after the date of filing of the bankruptcy petition that formed the basis for the stay on collection under Bankruptcy Code section 362 or the discharge injunction under Bankruptcy Code section 524, as the case might be.

(e) *Time for filing claim for administrative costs.*—(1) For purposes of this section, the taxpayer must file a claim for administrative costs before the Internal Revenue Service not later than 90 days after the date the Internal Revenue Service mails to the taxpayer, or otherwise notifies the taxpayer of, the decision regarding the claim for relief from or damages relating to a violation of the collection stay or the discharge injunction.

(2) If the Internal Revenue Service denies the claim for administrative costs in whole or in part, the taxpayer must file a petition with the Bankruptcy Court for administrative costs no later than 90 days after the date on which the denial of the claim for administrative costs is mailed, or otherwise furnished, to the taxpayer. If the Internal Revenue Service does not respond on the merits to a request by the taxpayer for an award of reasonable administrative costs within six months after such request is filed, the Internal Revenue Service's failure to respond may be considered by the taxpayer as a denial of an award of reasonable administrative costs.

(3) For purposes of paragraphs (e)(1) and (2) of this section, if the 90th day falls on a Saturday, Sunday, or a legal holiday, the 90-day period shall end on the next succeeding day which is not a Saturday, Sunday, or a legal holiday. The term legal holiday means a legal holiday in the District of Columbia. If the request for costs is to

be filed with the Internal Revenue Service at an office of the Internal Revenue Service located outside the District of Columbia, the term legal holiday also means a statewide legal holiday in the state where such office is located.

(f) *Effective date.*—This section is applicable with respect to actions taken by the Internal Revenue Service after July 22, 1998. [Reg. § 301.7430-8.]

☐ [*T.D. 9050, 3-24-2003.*]

### [Reg. § 301.7432-1]

**§ 301.7432-1. Civil cause of action for failure to release a lien.**—(a) *In general.*—If any officer or employee of the Internal Revenue Service knowingly, or by reason of negligence, fails to release a lien on property of the taxpayer in accordance with section 6325 of the Internal Revenue Code, such taxpayer may bring a civil action for damages against the United States in federal district court. The total amount of damages recoverable is the sum of:

(1) the actual, direct economic damages sustained by the taxpayer which, but for the officer's or the employee's knowing or negligent failure to release the lien under section 6325, would not have been sustained; and

(2) costs of the action.

The amount of actual, direct economic damages that are recoverable is reduced to the extent such damages reasonably could have been mitigated by the plaintiff. An action for damages filed in federal district court may not be maintained unless the taxpayer has filed an administrative claim pursuant to paragraph (f) of this section and has waited the period required under paragraph (e) of this section.

(b) *Finding of satisfaction or unenforceability.*—For purposes of this section, a finding under section 6325(a)(1) that the liability for the amount assessed, together with all interest in respect thereof, has been fully satisfied or has become legally unenforceable is treated as made on the earlier of:

(1) the date on which the district director of the district in which the taxpayer currently resides or the district in which the lien was filed finds full satisfaction or legal unenforceability; or

(2) the date on which such district director receives a request for a certificate of release of lien in accordance with § 401.6325-1(f), together with any information which is reasonably necessary for the district director to conclude that the lien has been fully satisfied or is legally unenforceable.

(c) *Actual, direct economic damages.*—(1) *Definition.*—Actual, direct economic damages are actual pecuniary damages sustained by the taxpayer that would not have been sustained but for an officer's or an employee's failure to release a lien in accordance with section 6325 of the Internal Revenue Code. Injuries such as inconvenience, emotional distress and loss of reputation are compensable only to the extent that they result in actual pecuniary damages.

(2) *Litigation costs and administrative costs not recoverable.*—Litigation costs and administrative costs described in this paragraph are not recoverable as actual, direct economic damages. Litigation costs may be recoverable under section 7430 (*see* paragraph (j) of this section) or, solely to the extent described in paragraph (d) of this section, as costs of the action.

(i) *Litigation costs.*—For purposes of this paragraph, litigation costs are any costs incurred pursuing litigation for relief from the failure to release a lien, including costs incurred pursuing a civil action in federal district court under paragraph (a) of this section. Litigation costs include the following:

(A) Court costs;

(B) Expenses of expert witnesses in connection with a court proceeding;

(C) Cost of any study, analysis, engineering report, test, or project prepared for a court proceeding; and

(D) Fees paid or incurred for the services of attorneys, or other individuals authorized to practice before the court, in connection with a court proceeding.

(ii) *Administrative costs.*—For purposes of this section, administrative costs are any costs incurred pursuing administrative relief from the failure to release a lien, including costs incurred pursuing an administrative claim for damages under paragraph (f) of this section. The term administrative costs includes:

(A) Any administrative fees or similar charges imposed by the Internal Revenue Service; and

(B) Expenses, costs, and fees described in paragraph (c)(2)(i) of this section incurred in pursuing administrative relief.

(d) *Costs of the action.*—Costs of the action recoverable as damages under this section are limited to the following costs:

(1) Fees of the clerk and marshall;

(2) Fees of the court reporter for all or any part of the stenographic transcript necessarily obtained for use in the case;

(3) Fees and disbursements for printing and witnesses;

(4) Fees for exemplification and copies of paper necessarily obtained for use in the case;

(5) Docket fees; and

(6) Compensation of court appointed experts and interpreters.

(e) *No civil action in federal district court prior to filing an administrative claim.*—(1) Except as provided in paragraph (e)(2) of this section, no action under paragraph (a) of this section shall be maintained in any federal district court before the earlier of the following dates:

(i) The date a decision is rendered on a claim filed in accordance with paragraph (f) of this section; or

(ii) The date 30 days after the date an administrative claim is filed in accordance with paragraph (f) of this section.

(2) If an administrative claim is filed in accordance with paragraph (f) of this section during the last 30 days of the period of limitations described in paragraph (i) of this section, the taxpayer may file an action in federal district court any time after the administrative claim is filed and before the expiration of the period of limitations, without waiting for 30 days to expire or for a decision to be rendered on the claim.

(f) *Procedures for an administrative claim.*—(1) *Manner.*—An administrative claim for actual, direct economic damages as defined in paragraph (c) of this section shall be sent in writing to the district director (marked for the attention of the Chief, Special Procedures Function) in the district in which the taxpayer currently resides or the district in which the notice of federal tax lien was filed.

(2) *Form.*—The administrative claim shall include:

(i) The name, current address, current home and work telephone numbers and any convenient times to be contacted, and taxpayer identification number of the taxpayer making the claim;

(ii) A copy of the notice of federal tax lien affecting the taxpayer's property, if available;

(iii) A copy of the request for release of lien made in accordance with section 401.6325-1(f) of the Code of Federal Regulations, if applicable;

(iv) The grounds, in reasonable detail, for the claim (include copies of any available substantiating documentation or correspondence with the Internal Revenue Service);

(v) A description of the injuries incurred by the taxpayer filing the claim (include copies of any available substantiating documentation or evidence);

(vi) The dollar amount of the claim, including any damages that have not yet been incurred but that are reasonably foreseeable (include copies of any available substantiating documentation or evidence); and

(vii) The signature of the taxpayer or duly authorized representative.

For purposes of this paragraph, a duly authorized representative is any attorney, certified public accountant, enrolled actuary, or any other person permitted to represent the taxpayer before the Internal Revenue Service who is not disbarred or suspended from practice before the Internal Revenue Service and who has a written power of attorney executed by the taxpayer.

(g) *Notice of failure to release lien.*—An administrative claim under paragraph (f) of this section shall be considered a notice of failure to release a lien.

(h) *No action in federal district court for any sum in excess of the dollar amount sought in the administrative claim.*—No action for actual, direct economic damages under paragraph (a) of this section shall be instituted in federal district court for any sum in excess of the amount (already incurred and estimated) of the administrative claim filed under paragraph (f) of this section, except where the increased amount is based upon newly discovered evidence not reasonably discoverable at the time the administrative claim was filed, or upon allegation and proof of intervening facts relating to the amount of the claim.

(i) *Period of limitations.*—(1) *Time of filing.*—A civil action under paragraph (a) of this section must be brought in federal district court within 2 years after the date the cause of action accrues.

(2) *Cause of action accrues.*—A cause of action accrues when the taxpayer has had a reasonable opportunity to discover all essential elements of a possible cause of action.

(j) *Recovery of costs under section 7430.*—Reasonable litigation costs, including attorney's fees, not recoverable under this section may be recoverable under section 7430. If following the Internal Revenue Service's denial of an administrative claim on the grounds that the Internal Revenue Service did not violate section 7432(a), a taxpayer brings a civil action for damages in a district court of the United States, and establishes entitlement to damages under this section, substantially prevails with respect to the amount of damages in controversy, and meets the requirements of section 7430(c)(4)(A)(iii) (relating to notice and net worth requirements), the taxpayer will be considered a "prevailing party" for purposes of section 7430. Such taxpayer, therefore, will generally be entitled to attorney's fees and other reasonable litigation costs not recoverable under this section. For purposes of this paragraph, if the Internal Revenue Service does not respond on the merits to an administrative claim for damages within 30 days after the claim is filed, the Internal Revenue Service's failure to respond shall be considered a denial of the administrative claim on the grounds that the Internal Revenue Service did not violate section 7432(a). Administrative costs, including attorney's fees incurred pursuing an administrative claim under paragraph (f) of this section, are not recoverable under section 7430.

(k) *Effective date.*—This section applies with respect to civil actions under section 7432 filed in federal district court after January 30, 1992. [Reg. § 301.7432-1.]

☐ [T.D. 8393, 1-29-92.]

### [Reg. § 301.7433-1]

**§ 301.7433-1. Civil cause of action for certain unauthorized collection actions.**—(a) *In general.*—If, in connection with the collection of a federal tax with respect to a taxpayer, an officer or an employee of the Internal Revenue Service recklessly or intentionally, or by reason of negligence, disregards any provision of the Internal Revenue Code or any regulation promulgated under the Internal Revenue Code, such taxpayer may bring a civil action for damages against the United States in federal district court. The taxpayer has a duty to mitigate damages. The total amount of damages recoverable is the lesser of $1,000,000 ($100,000 in the case of negligence), or the sum of:

(1) the actual, direct economic damages sustained as a proximate result of the reckless or intentional actions of the officer or employee; and

(2) costs of the action.

An action for damages filed in federal district court may not be maintained unless the taxpayer has filed an administrative claim pursuant to paragraph (e) of this section, and has waited for the period required under paragraph (d) of this section.

(b) *Actual, direct economic damages.*—(1) *Definition.*—Actual, direct economic damages are actual pecuniary damages sustained by the taxpayer as the proximate result of the reckless or intentional, or negligent, actions of an officer or an employee of the Internal Revenue Service. Injuries such as inconvenience, emotional distress and loss of reputation are compensable only to the extent that they result in actual pecuniary damages.

(2) *Litigation costs and administrative costs not recoverable.*—Litigation costs and administrative costs are not recoverable as actual, direct economic damages. Litigation costs may be recoverable under section 7430 (*see* paragraph (h) of this section) or, solely to the extent described in paragraph (c) of this section, as costs of the action.

(i) *Litigation costs.*—For purposes of this paragraph, litigation costs are any costs incurred pursuing litigation for relief from the action taken by the officer or employee of the Internal Revenue Service, including costs incurred pursuing a civil action in federal district court under paragraph (a) of this section. The term litigation costs includes the following:

(A) Court costs;

(B) Expenses of expert witnesses in connection with a court proceeding;

(C) Cost of any study, analysis, engineering report, test, or project prepared for a court proceeding; and

(D) Fees paid or incurred for the services of attorneys, or other individuals authorized to practice before the court, in connection with a court proceeding.

(ii) *Administrative costs.*—For purposes of this section, administrative costs are any costs incurred pursuing administrative relief from the action taken by an officer or employee of the Internal Revenue Service, including costs incurred pursuing an administrative claim for damages under paragraph (e) of this section. The term administrative costs includes:

(A) Any administrative fees or similar charges imposed by the Internal Revenue Service; and

(B) Expenses, costs, and fees described in paragraph (b)(2)(i) of this section incurred pursuing administrative relief.

(c) *Costs of the action.*—Costs of the action recoverable as damages under this section are limited to the following costs:

(1) Fees of the clerk and marshall;

(2) Fees of the court reporter for all or any part of the stenographic transcript necessarily obtained for use in the case;

(3) Fees and disbursements for printing and witnesses;

(4) Fees for exemplification and copies of paper necessarily obtained for use in the case;

(5) Docket fees; and

(6) Compensation of court appointed experts and interpreters.

(d) *No civil action in federal district court prior to filing an administrative claim.*—(1) Except as provided in paragraph (d)(2) of this section, no action under paragraph (a) of this section shall be maintained in any federal district court before the earlier of the following dates:

(i) The date the decision is rendered on a claim filed in accordance with paragraph (e) of this section; or

(ii) The date six months after the date an administrative claim is filed in accordance with paragraph (e) of this section.

(2) If an administrative claim is filed in accordance with paragraph (e) of this section during the last six months of the period of limitations described in paragraph (g) of this section, the taxpayer may file an action in federal district court any time after the administrative claim is filed and before the expiration of the period of limitations.

(e) *Procedures for an administrative claim.*—(1) *Manner.*—An administrative claim for the lesser of $1,000,000 ($100,000 in the case of negligence) or actual, direct economic damages as defined in paragraph (b) of this section shall be sent in writing to the Area Director, Attn: Compliance Technical Support Manager of the area in which the taxpayer currently resides.

(2) *Form.*—The administrative claim shall include:

(i) The name, current address, current home and work telephone numbers and any convenient times to be contacted, and taxpayer identification number of the taxpayer making the claim;

(ii) The grounds, in reasonable detail, for the claim (include copies of any available substantiating documentation or correspondence with the Internal Revenue Service);

(iii) A description of the injuries incurred by the taxpayer filing the claim (include copies of any available substantiating documentation or evidence);

(iv) The dollar amount of the claim, including any damages that have not yet been incurred but which are reasonably foreseeable (include copies of any available substantiating documentation or evidence); and

(v) The signature of the taxpayer or duly authorized representative.

For purposes of this paragraph, a duly authorized representative is any attorney, certified public accountant, enrolled actuary, or any other person permitted to represent the taxpayer before the Internal Revenue Service who is not disbarred or suspended from practice before the Internal Revenue Service and who has a written power of attorney executed by the taxpayer.

(f) *No action in federal district court for any sum in excess of the dollar amount sought in the administrative claim.*—No action for actual, direct economic damages under paragraph (a) of this section shall be instituted in federal district court for any sum in excess of the amount (already incurred and estimated) of the administrative claim filed under paragraph (e) of this section, except where the increased amount is based upon newly discovered evidence not reasonably discoverable at the time the administrative claim was filed, or upon allegation and proof of intervening facts relating to the amount of the claim.

(g) *Period of limitations.*—(1) *Time for filing.*—A civil action under paragraph (a) of this section must be brought in federal district court within 2 years after the date the cause of action accrues.

(2) *Right of action accrues.*—A cause of action under paragraph (a) of this section accrues when the taxpayer has had a reasonable opportunity to discover all essential elements of a possible cause of action.

(h) *Recovery of costs under section 7430.*—Reasonable litigation costs, including attorney's fees, not recoverable under this section may be recoverable under section 7430. If following the Internal Revenue Service's denial of an administrative claim on the grounds that the Internal Revenue Service did not violate section 7433(a), a taxpayer brings a civil action for damages in a district court of the United States, and establishes entitlement to damages under this section, substantially prevails with respect to the amount of damages in controversy and meets the requirements of section 7430(c)(4)(A)(iii) (relating to notice and net worth requirements), the taxpayer will be considered a "prevailing party" for purposes of section 7430. Such taxpayer, therefore, will generally be entitled to attorney's fees and other reasonable litigation costs not recoverable under this section.

For purposes of this paragraph, if the Internal Revenue Service does not respond on the merits to an administrative claim for damages within six months after the claim is filed, the Internal Revenue Service's failure to respond shall be considered a denial of the claim on the grounds that the Internal Revenue Service did not violate section 7433(a). Administrative costs, including attorney's fees incurred pursuing an administrative claim under paragraph (e) of this section, are not recoverable under section 7430.

(i) *Effective dates.*—The portions of this section relating to reckless or intentional acts are applicable to actions taken by Internal Revenue Service officials after July 30, 1996. The portions of this section relating to negligent acts are applicable to actions taken by the Internal Revenue Service officials after July 22, 1998. [Reg. § 301.7433-1.]

☐ [*T.D. 8392, 1-29-92. Amended by T.D. 9050, 3-24-2003.*]

### [Reg. § 301.7433-2]

**§ 301.7433-2. Civil cause of action for violation of section 362 or 524 of the Bankruptcy Code.**—(a) *In general.*—(1) If, in connection with the collection of a federal tax with respect to a taxpayer, an officer or employee of the Internal Revenue Service willfully violates any provision of section 362 (relating to the automatic stay) or section 524 (relating to discharge) of title 11, United States Code, or any regulation promulgated under such provision, the taxpayer may file a petition for damages against the United States in Federal bankruptcy court. The taxpayer has a duty to mitigate damages. The total amount of damages recoverable under this section is the lesser of $1,000,000, or the sum of—

(i) Actual, direct economic damages sustained as a proximate result of the willful actions of the officer or employee; and

(ii) Costs of the action.

(2) An action under this section constitutes the exclusive remedy under the Internal Revenue Code for violations of sections 362 and 524 of the Bankruptcy Code. In addition, taxpayers injured by violations of section 362 of the Bankruptcy Code may maintain actions under section 362(h) of the Bankruptcy Code (relating to an individual injured by a willful violation of the stay). However, any administrative or litigation costs in connection with an action under section 362(h) may be awarded, if at all, only under section 7430 of the Internal Revenue Code.

(b) *Actual, direct economic damages.*—(1) *Definition.*—See § 301.7433-1(b)(1).

(2) *Litigation costs and administrative costs not recoverable as actual, direct economic damages.*—Litigation costs and administrative costs are not recoverable as actual, direct economic damages. These costs may be recoverable under section 7430 (see paragraph (h) of this section), or, solely to the extent described in paragraph (c) of this section, as costs of the action.

(c) *Costs of the action.*—Costs of the action recoverable as damages under this section are limited to the costs set forth in § 301.7433-1(c).

(d) *No civil action in federal bankruptcy court prior to filing an administrative claim.*—(1) *In general.*—Except as provided in paragraph (d)(2) of this section, no action under paragraph (a)(1) of this section shall be maintained in any bankruptcy court before the earlier of the following dates—

(i) The date the decision is rendered on a claim filed in accordance with paragraph (e) of this section; or

(ii) The date that is six months after the date an administrative claim is filed in accordance with paragraph (e) of this section.

(2) *When administrative claim filed in last six months of period of limitations.*—If an administrative claim is filed in accordance with paragraph (e) of this section during the last six months of the period of limitations described in paragraph (g) of this section, the taxpayer may petition the bankruptcy court any time after the administrative claim is filed and before the expiration of the period of limitations.

(e) *Procedures for an administrative claim.*—(1) *Manner.*—An administrative claim for the lesser of $1,000,000 or actual, direct economic damages as defined in paragraph (b) of this section shall be sent in writing to the Chief, Local Insolvency Unit, for the judicial district in which the taxpayer filed the underlying bankruptcy case giving rise to the alleged violation.

(2) *Form.*—The administrative claim shall include—

(i) The name, taxpayer identification number, current address, and current home and work telephone numbers (with an identification of any convenient times to be contacted) of the taxpayer making the claim;

(ii) The location of the bankruptcy court in which the underlying bankruptcy case was filed and the case number of the case in which the violation occurred;

(iii) A description, in reasonable detail, of the violation (include copies of any available substantiating documentation or correspondence with the Internal Revenue Service);

(iv) A description of the injuries incurred by the taxpayer filing the claim (include copies of any available substantiating documentation or evidence);

(v) The dollar amount of the claim, including any damages that have not yet been incurred but which are reasonably foreseeable (include copies of any available documentation or evidence); and

(vi) The signature of the taxpayer or duly authorized representative.

(3) *Duly authorized representative defined.*—For purposes of this paragraph (e), a duly authorized representative is any attorney, certified public accountant, enrolled actuary, or any other person permitted to represent the taxpayer before the Internal Revenue Service who is not disbarred or suspended from practice before the Internal Revenue Service and who has a written power of attorney executed by the taxpayer.

(f) *No action in bankruptcy court for any sum in excess of the dollar amount sought in the administrative claim.*—No action for actual, direct economic damages under paragraph (a) of this section may be instituted in federal bankruptcy court for any sum in excess of the amount (already incurred and estimated) of the administrative claim filed under paragraph (e) of this section, except where the increased amount is based upon newly discovered evidence not reasonably discoverable at the time the administrative claim was filed, or upon allegation and proof of intervening facts relating to the amount of the claim.

(g) *Period of limitations.*—(1) *Time for filing.*—A petition for damages under paragraph (a) of this section must be filed in bankruptcy court within two years after the date the cause of action accrues.

(2) *Right of action accrues.*—A cause of action under paragraph (a) of this section accrues when the taxpayer has had a reasonable opportunity to discover all essential elements of a possible cause of action.

(h) *Recovery of litigation costs and administrative costs under section 7430.*—(1) *In general.*—Litigation costs, as defined in § 301.7433-1(b)(2)(i), including attorneys fees, not recoverable under this section may be recoverable under section 7430 if a taxpayer challenges in whole or in part an Internal Revenue Service denial of an administrative claim for damages by filing a petition in the bankruptcy court. If, following the Internal Revenue Service's denial of an administrative claim for damages, a taxpayer files a petition in the bankruptcy court challenging that denial in whole or in part, substantially prevails with respect to the amount of damages in controversy, and meets the requirements of section 7430(c)(4)(A)(ii) (relating to net worth and size requirements), the taxpayer will be considered a prevailing party for purposes of section 7430, unless the Internal Revenue Service establishes that the position of the Internal Revenue Service in the proceeding was substantially justified. Such taxpayer will generally be entitled to attorneys' fees and other reasonable litigation costs not recoverable under this section. For purposes of this paragraph (h), if the Internal Revenue Service does not respond on the merits to an administrative claim for damages within six months after the claim is filed, the Internal Revenue Service's failure to respond will be considered a denial of the claim on the grounds that the Internal Revenue Service did not willfully violate Bankruptcy Code section 362 or 524.

(2) *Administrative costs.*—(i) *In general.*—Administrative costs, as defined in § 301.7433-1(b)(2)(ii), including attorneys' fees, not recoverable under this section may be recoverable under section 7430. See § 301.7430-8.

(ii) *Limitation regarding recoverable administrative costs.*—Administrative costs may be awarded only if incurred on or after the date of filing of the bankruptcy petition that formed the basis for the stay on collection under Bankruptcy Code section 362 or the discharge injunction under Bankruptcy Code section 524, as the case might be.

(i) *Effective date.*—This section is applicable to actions taken by the Internal Revenue Service officials after July 22, 1998. [Reg. § 301.7433-2.]

☐ [*T.D. 9050, 3-24-2003.*]

# THE TAX COURT

## Procedure

### [Reg. § 301.7452-1]

**§ 301.7452-1. Representation of parties.**—The Commissioner shall be represented by the Chief Counsel for the Internal Revenue Service in the same manner before the Tax Court as he has heretofore been represented in proceedings before such Court. The taxpayer shall continue to be represented in accordance with the rules of practice prescribed by the Court. [Reg. § 301.7452-1.]

☐ [*T.D. 6498, 10-24-60.*]

### [Reg. § 301.7454-1]

**§ 301.7454-1. Burden of proof in fraud and transferee cases.**—In any proceeding involving the issue whether the petitioner has been guilty of fraud with intent to evade tax, the burden of proof in respect of such issue shall be upon the Commissioner. [Reg. § 301.7454-1.]

☐ [*T.D. 6498, 10-24-60.*]

### [Reg. § 301.7454-2]

**§ 301.7454-2. Burden of proof in foundation manager, etc. cases.**—(a) *Foundation manager.*—In any proceeding involving the issue whether a foundation manager as defined in section 4946(b) has "knowingly" participated in an act of self-dealing within the meaning of section 4941, participated in an investment which jeopardizes the carrying out of exempt purposes within the meaning of section 4944, or agreed to the making of a taxable expenditure within the meaning of section 4945 or whether an organization manager (as defined in section 4958(f)(2) has "knowingly" participated in an excess benefit transaction (as defined in section 4958(c), the burden of proof in respect of such issue shall be upon the Commissioner.

(b) *Trustee of a black lung benefit trust.*—In any proceeding involving the issue whether a trustee of a trust described in section 501(c)(21) has "knowingly" participated in an act of self-dealing within the meaning of section 4951 or agreed to the making of a taxable expenditure within the meaning of section 4952, the burden of proof in respect of such issue shall be upon the Commissioner. [Reg. § 301.7454-2.]

☐ [*T.D. 7838, 10-5-82. Amended by T.D. 8920, 1-9-2001.*]

### [Reg. § 301.7456-1]

**§ 301.7456-1. Administration of oaths and procurement of testimony; production of records of foreign corporations, foreign trusts or estates and nonresident alien individuals.**—Upon motion and notice by the Commissioner and upon good cause shown therefor, the Tax Court or any division thereof shall order any foreign corporation, foreign trust or estate, or nonresident alien individual, who has filed a petition with the Tax Court, to produce, or, upon satisfactory proof to the Tax Court or any of its divisions that the petitioner is unable to produce, to make available to the Commissioner, and, in either case, to permit the inspection, copying, or photographing of, such books, records, documents, memoranda, correspondence and other papers, wherever situated, as the Tax Court or any of its divisions may deem relevant to the proceedings and which are in the possession, custody or control of the petitioner, or of any person directly or indirectly under his control or having control over him or subject to the same common control. [Reg. § 301.7456-1.]

☐ [*T.D. 6498, 10-24-60.*]

### [Reg. § 301.7457-1]

**§ 301.7457-1. Witness fees.**—Any witness summoned for the Commissioner or whose deposition is taken under section 7456 shall receive the same fees and mileage as witnesses in courts of the United States. Such fees and mileage and the expense of taking any such deposition shall be paid by the Commissioner out of any moneys appropriated for the collection of internal revenue taxes, and may be paid in advance. [Reg. § 301.7457-1.]

☐ [*T.D. 6498, 10-24-60.*]

### [Reg. § 301.7458-1]

**§ 301.7458-1. Hearings.**—Notice and opportunity to be heard upon any proceeding instituted before the Tax Court shall be given to the taxpayer and the Commissioner. If an opportunity to be heard upon the proceeding is given before a division of the Tax Court, neither the taxpayer nor the Commissioner shall be entitled to notice and opportunity to be heard before the Tax Court upon review, except upon a specific order to the chief judge. [Reg. § 301.7458-1.]

☐ [*T.D. 6498, 10-24-60.*]

### [Reg. § 301.7461-1]

**§ 301.7461-1. Publicity of proceedings.**—All reports of the Tax Court and all evidence received by the Tax Court and its divisions, including a transcript of the stenographic report of the hearings, shall be public records open to the inspection of the public; except that after the decision of the Tax Court in any proceeding has become final the Tax Court may, upon motion of the taxpayer or the Commissioner, permit the withdrawal by the party entitled thereto of the originals of books, documents, and records, and of models, diagrams, and other exhibits, introduced in evidence before the Tax Court or any of its divisions; or the Tax Court may, on its own action, make such other disposition thereof as it deems advisable. [Reg. § 301.7461-1.]

☐ [*T.D. 6498, 10-24-60.*]

## Declaratory Judgments

### [Reg. § 1.7476-1]

**§ 1.7476-1. Interested parties.**—(a) *In general.*—(1) *Notice requirement.*—Before the Internal Revenue Service can issue an advance determination as to the qualified status of certain retirement plans, the applicant must provide the Internal Revenue Service with satisfactory evidence that such applicant has notified the persons who qualify as interested parties, under regulations prescribed under section 7476(b)(1) of the Code, of the application for such determination. See section 3001(a) of the Employee Retirement Income Security Act of 1974 (88 Stat. 995). For the rules for giving notice to interested parties, see § 1.7476-2 and paragraph (o) of § 601.201 of this chapter (Statement of Procedural Rules).

(2) *Declaratory judgments.*—Section 7476 provides a procedure for obtaining a declaratory judgment by the Tax Court with respect to the initial or continuing qualification under subchapter D of chapter 1 of the Code of a retirement plan defined in section 7476(d), in the case of an actual controversy involving:

(i) A determination by the Internal Revenue Service with respect to the initial qualification or continuing qualification under such subchapter of such a plan, or

(ii) A failure by the Internal Revenue Service to make a determination with respect to—

(A) Such initial qualification of such a plan, or

(B) Such continuing qualification of such a plan, if the controversy arises from a plan amendment or plan termination.

Under section 7476(d) the term "retirement plan" means a pension, profit-sharing, or stock bonus plan described in section 401(a), or a trust which is part of such a plan, an annuity plan described in section 403(a), or a bond purchase plan described in section 405(a). This procedure is available only to the employer, the plan administrator as defined in section 414(g), an employee who qualifies as an interested party as defined in this section, or the Pension Benefit Guaranty Corporation, where such person has an actual controversy involving a determination described in paragraph (a)(2)(i) of this section, or failure to make a determination described in paragraph (a)(2)(ii) of this section. In the case of an application for such a determination, this procedure is available only if such determination or failure to make such determination is with respect to an application described in paragraph (b)(7) of this section. In addition, in the case of such an application, if a petitioner was the applicant for the determination, the Tax Court may hold, under section 7476(b)(2), the filing of a pleading for a declaratory judgment to be premature unless the petitioner establishes to the satisfaction of the Tax Court that such petitioner has caused the interested parties to be notified in accordance with this section and § 1.7476-2.

(b) *Interested parties.*—(1) *In general.*—If paragraphs (b)(2), (3), (4), and (5) of this section do not apply, then, except as otherwise provided in paragraphs (b)(6)(i), (ii), and (iii) of this section, the following persons shall be interested parties with respect to an application for an advance determination as to the qualified status of a retirement plan:

(i) All present employees of the employer who are eligible to participate in the plan (as defined in paragraph (d)(2) of this section), and

(ii) All other present employees of the employer whose principal place of employment (as defined in paragraph (d)(3) of this section) is the same as the principal place of employment of any employee described in paragraph (b)(1)(i) of this section.

(2) *Certain plans covering a principal owner.*—Notwithstanding paragraph (b)(1) of this section, where—

(i) A principal owner (within the meaning of paragraph (d)(2) of § 1.414(c)-3) of the employer or of a common parent of the employer (where the employer is a member of a parent-subsidiary group of trades or businesses under common control under section 414(b) or (c)) is eligible to participate in the plan, and

(ii) the number of employees employed by such employer (including all employees who by reason of section 414(b) or (c) are treated as employees of such employer) is 100 or less,
then except as otherwise provided in paragraphs (b)(6)(i), (ii), and (iv) of this section, all present employees of the employer shall be interested parties with respect to an application for an advance determination as to the qualified status of the retirement plan.

(3) *Certain plan amendments.*—In the case of an application for an advance determination as to whether a plan amendment affects the continuing qualification of a plan, if—

(i) there is outstanding a favorable determination letter for a plan year to which section 410 applies, and

(ii) the amendment does not alter the participation provisions of the plan,
then paragraphs (b)(1) and (2) of this section shall not apply, and all present employees of the employer who are eligible to participate in the plan (as defined in paragraph (d)(2) of this section), shall be interested parties. For the purpose of this paragraph (b)(3), if qualification of the plan is dependent upon benefits under the plan integrating with those benefits provided under the Social Security Act or a similar program, and if such integration results in excluding any employee or could possibly result in any participant's benefit being reduced to zero and the amendment alters contributions to or the amount of benefits payable under the plan, then the amendment shall be considered to alter the participation provisions of the plan.

(4) *Collectively bargained plans.*—In the case of an application with respect to a plan described in section 413(a) (relating to collectively bargained plans), paragraphs (b)(1), (2) and (3) of this section shall not apply and all present employees covered by a collective-bargaining agreement pursuant to which the plan is maintained shall be interested parties.

(5) *Plan terminations.*—In the case of an application for an advance determination with respect to whether a plan termination affects the continuing qualification of a retirement plan, paragraphs (b)(1), (2), (3) and (4) of this section shall not apply, and all present employees with accrued benefits under the plan, all former employees with vested benefits under the plan, and all beneficiaries of deceased former employees currently receiving benefits under the plan, shall be interested parties.

(6) *Exceptions.*—(i) In the case of an application to which paragraph (b)(1) or (2) of this section applies, an employee who is not eligible to participate in the plan shall not be an interested party if such employee is excluded from consideration for purposes of section 410(b)(1) by reason of section 410(b)(2)(B) or (C).

(ii) In the case of an application to which paragraph (b)(1) or (2) of this section applies, an employee who is not eligible to participate in the plan shall not be an interested party if such plan meets the eligibility standards of section 410(b)(1)(A).

(iii) In the case of an application to which paragraph (b)(1) of this section applies, an employee who is not eligible to participate in the plan shall not be an interested party with respect to such plan if such employee is eligible to participate in any other plan of the employer with respect to which a favorable determination letter is outstanding (whether or not issued pursuant to an application to which this section applies), or in such a plan of another employer whose employees, by reason of section 414(b) or (c), are treated as employees of the employer making the application.

(iv) In the case of an application to which paragraph (b)(2) of this section applies, an employee who is not eligible to participate in the plan shall not be an interested party with respect to such plan if such employee is eligible to participate in a plan described in section 413(a) (relating to collectively bargained plans) maintained by the employer with respect to which a favorable determination letter is outstanding (whether or not issued pursuant to an application to which this section applies), or in such a plan of another employer whose employees, by reason of section 414(b) or (c), are treated as employees of the employer making the application.

(7) *Applicability.*—Paragraph (b) of this section shall only apply in the case of an application made to the Internal Revenue Service requesting an advance determination that a retirement plan as defined in section 7476(d) and paragraph (a) of this section meets the requirements for qualification for a plan year or years to which section 410 applies to such plan. See paragraph (c)(4) and (5) of this section for special rules in respect of years to which section 410 applies.

(c) *Special rules.*—For purposes of paragraph (b) of this section and § 1.7476-2—

(1) *Time of determination.*—The status of an individual as an interested party and as a present employee or former employee shall be determined as of a date determined by the applicant, which date shall not be earlier than five business days before the first date on which the notice of the application is given to interested parties pursuant to § 1.7476-2 nor later than the date on which such notice is given.

(2) *Controlled groups, etc.*—An individual shall be considered to be an employee of an employer if such employee is treated as that employer's employee under section 414(b) or (c).

(3) *Self-employed individuals.*—A self-employed individual shall be considered an employee.

(4) *Years to which section 410 relates.*—For purposes of paragraph (b)(7) of this section, section 410 shall be considered to apply to a plan year if an election has been made under section 1017(d) of the Employee Retirement Income Security Act of 1974 to have section 410 apply to such plan year, whether or not the election is conditioned upon the issuance by the Commissioner of a favorable determination letter.

(5) *Government, church plans, etc.*—In the case of an organization described in section 410(c)(1), section 410 will be considered to apply to a plan year of such organization for any plan year to which section 410(c)(2) applies to such plan.

(d) *Definitions.*—For the purposes of paragraph (b) of this section and § 1.7476-2—

(1) *Employer.*—The term "employer" includes all employers who maintain the plan with respect to which an advance determination applies. A sole proprietor shall be considered such person's own employer and a partnership is considered to be the employer of each of the partners.

(2) *Eligible to participate.*—For purposes of this section, an employee is eligible to participate in a plan if such employee—

(i) is a participant in the plan,

(ii) would be a participant in the plan if such employee met the minimum age and service requirements of the plan or

(iii) would be a participant in the plan upon making mandatory employee contributions.
In applying this paragraph (d)(2), plan provisions (with respect to which the determination regarding qualification is to be based) not in effect on the first date on which notice is given to interested parties shall be treated as though they were in effect on such date.

(3) *Place of employment.*—A place of employment includes all worksites within a plant, installation, store, office, or similar facility. Any employee who has no principal place of employment shall be treated as though such employee's principal place of employment is that place to which such employee regularly reports to the employer.

(e) *Effective date.*—The provisions of this section apply to applications referred to in paragraph (a) of this section made on or after June 21, 1976. [Reg. § 1.7476-1.]

☐ [T.D. 7421, 5-20-76. *Amended by T.D.* 8179, 3-1-88 *and T.D.* 9006, 7-18-2002.]

**[Reg. § 301.7476-1]**

**§ 301.7476-1. Declaratory judgments.**—See the regulations under section 7476 contained in Part 1 of this chapter (Income Tax Regulations) for provisions relating to declaratory judgments, for provisions relating to the qualification of an employee as an "interested party", and for a requirement that the applicant for an advance determination by the Internal Revenue Service of the qualification of certain retirement plans give notice of such application to interested parties. [Reg. § 301.7476-1.]

☐ [T.D. 7421, 5-20-76.]

**[Reg. § 1.7476-2]**

**§ 1.7476-2. Notice to interested parties.**—(a) *In general.*—Any person applying to a district director for a determination described in paragraph (b)(7) of §1.7476-1 shall cause notice of the application to be given to persons who qualify as interested parties under §1.7476-1 with respect to the application, whether or not such application is received by the Internal Revenue Service before the date on which section 410 applies to the plan.

(b) *Nature of notice.*—The notice required by this section shall—

(1) Contain the information and be given within the time period prescribed in §601.201(o)(3) of this chapter; and

(2) Be given in a manner prescribed in paragraph (c) of this section.

(c) *Method of giving notice.*—(1) In the case of a present employee, former employee, or beneficiary who is an interested party, the notice may be provided by any method reasonably calculated to ensure that each interested party is notified of the application for a determination. If an interested party who is a present employee is in a unit of employees covered by a collective-bargaining agreement between employee representatives and one or more employers, notice shall also be given to the collective-bargaining representative of such interested party by any method that satisfies this paragraph. Whether the notice is provided in a manner that satisfies the requirements of this paragraph is determined on the basis of all the relevant facts and circumstances. Because the facts and circumstances differ depending on the interested party, it may be necessary to use more than one method of delivery in order to ensure timely and adequate notice to all interested parties.

(2) If the notice to interested parties is delivered using an electronic medium under an electronic system that satisfies the applicable notice requirements of §1.401(a)-21 of this chapter, the notice is deemed to be provided in a manner that satisfies the requirements of paragraph (c)(1) of this section.

(d) *Examples.*—The principles of this section are illustrated by the following examples:

*Example 1.* (i) Employer A is amending Plan C and applying for a determination letter. Plan C is not maintained pursuant to one or more collective bargaining agreements and is not being terminated. As part of the determination letter application process, Employer A provides the notice required under this section to interested parties. For present employees, Employer A provides the notice by posting the notice at those locations within the principal places of employment of the interested parties which are customarily used for employer notices to employees with regard to employment and employee benefit matters.

(ii) In this *Example 1*, Employer A satisfies the notice to interested parties requirement described in this section.

*Example 2.* (i) Employer B is amending Plan D and applying for a determination letter. As part of the determination letter application process, Employer B provides the notice required under this section to interested parties.

(ii) Employer B has multiple worksites. Employer B's employees located at worksites 1 through 4 have reasonable access to computers at their workplace. However, Employer B's employees located at worksite 5 do not have access to computers.

(iii) For present employees with reasonable access to computers (worksites 1 through 4), Employer B provides the notice by posting the notice on Employer B's web site (Internet or intranet). Employees at worksites 1 through 4 customarily receive employer notification with regard to employment and employee benefit matters from the Employer B's web site. For present employees without access to computers (worksite 5), Employer B provides the notice by posting the notice at worksite 5 in a location that is customarily used for employer notices to employees with regard to employment and employee benefit matters.

(iv) Employer B also sends the notice by e-mail to each collective-bargaining representative of interested parties who are present employees of Employer B covered by a collective-bargaining agreement between employee representatives and Employer B, using the e-mail address previously provided to Employer B by such collective-bargaining representative.

(v) In this *Example 2*, Employer B satisfies the notice to interested parties requirement described in this section.

*Example 3.* (i) Employer C is terminating Plan E and applying for a determination letter as to whether the plan termination affects the continuing qualification of Plan E. As part of the determination letter application process, Employer C provides the notice required under this section to interested parties.

(ii) All of Employer C's employees have reasonable access to computers. Each employee has an e-mail address where he or she can receive messages from Employer C. Employees of Employer C customarily receive employer notices regarding employment and employee benefit matters by e-mail.

(iii) For present employees, Employer C provides the notice by sending the notice by e-mail.

(iv) Employer C also sends the notice by e-mail to each collective-bargaining representative of interested parties who are present employees of Employer C covered by a collective-bargaining agreement between employee representatives and Employer C, using the e-mail address previously provided to Employer C by such collective-bargaining representative.

(v) In addition, Employer C sends the notice by e-mail to each interested party who is a former employee or beneficiary, using the e-mail address previously provided to Employer C by such interested party. For any former employee or beneficiary who did not provide an e-mail address, Employer C sends the notice by regular mail to the last known address of such former employee or beneficiary.

(vi) In this *Example 3*, Employer C satisfies the notice to interested parties requirement described in this section.

(e) *Effective date.*—(1) The provisions of this section shall apply to applications referred to in §1.7476-1 (a) made on or after January 1, 2003.

(2) For applications made on or after June 21, 1976 and before January 1, 2003, §1.7476-2 (as it appeared in the April 1, 2002 edition of 26 CFR part 1) applies. [Reg. §1.7476-2.]

☐ [T.D. 7421, 5-20-76. *Amended by T.D.* 9006, 7-18-2002 *and T.D.* 9294, 10-19-2006.]

**[Reg. §1.7476-3]**

**§1.7476-3. Notice of determination.**—(a) *In general.*—Under section 7476(b)(5), if a district director sends to the employer, the plan administrator, an interested party with respect to the plan, or the Pension Benefit Guaranty Corporation (or in the case of certain individuals who qualify as interested parties under paragraph (b) of §1.7476-1, to the person described under paragraph (c) of this section as the representative of such individuals) by certified or registered mail a notice of determination with respect to the qualification of a retirement plan described in section 7476(d), no proceeding for a declaratory judgment by the United States Tax Court with respect to the qualification of such plan may be initiated by such person unless the pleading initiating such proceeding is filed by such person with such Court before the ninety-first day after the day after such notice is mailed.

(b) *Address for notice of determination.*—(1) *Applicant.*—In the case of the applicant for a determination, a notice of determination referred to in section 7476(b)(5) shall be sufficient if mailed to such person at the address set forth on the application for the determination.

(2) *Interested party.*—In the case of an interested party or parties who, pursuant to section 3001(b) of the Employee Retirement Income Security Act of 1974 (88 Stat. 995), submitted a comment to a district director with respect to the qualification of the plan, a notice of determination referred to in section 7476(b)(5) shall be sufficient if mailed to the address designated in the comment as the address to which correspondence should be sent.

(c) *Representative of interested parties.*—(1) In the case of an interested party who, in accordance with section 3001(b) of the Employee Retirement Income Security Act of 1974 (88 Stat. 995), requests the Secretary of Labor to submit a comment to a district director on matters respecting the qualification of the plan, where pursuant to such request such Secretary does in fact submit such a comment, the Administrator of Pension and Welfare Benefit Programs, Department of Labor, shall be the representative of such interested party for purposes of receiving the notice referred to in section 7476(b)(5) with respect to those matters on which the Secretary of Labor commented.

(2) In the event a single comment with respect to the qualification of the plan is submitted to a district director by two or more interested parties, the representative designated in the comment for receipt of correspondence shall be the representative of all the interested parties submitting the comment for purposes of receiving the notice referred to in section 7476(b)(5) on behalf of all of them. Such designated representative must be either one of the interested parties who submitted the comment or a person described in paragraph (e)(6)(i), (ii) or (iii) of §601.201 of this chapter (Statement of Procedural Rules). If one person is not designated in the comment as the representative for receipt of correspondence, a notice of determination mailed to any interested party who submitted the comment shall be notice to all the interested parties who submitted the comment for purposes of section 7476(b)(5). [Reg. §1.7476-3.]

☐ [T.D. 7421, 5-20-76.]

**[Reg. §301.7477-1]**

**§301.7477-1. Declaratory judgments relating to the value of certain gifts for gift tax purposes.**—(a) *In general.*—If the adjustment(s) proposed by the Internal Revenue Service (IRS) will not result in any deficiency in or refund of the donor's gift tax liability for the calendar year, and if the requirements contained in paragraph (d) of this section are satisfied, then the declaratory judgment procedure under section 7477 is available to the donor for determining the amount of one or more of the donor's gifts during that calendar year for Federal gift tax purposes.

(b) *Declaratory judgment procedure.*—(1) *In general.*—If a donor does not resolve a dispute with the IRS concerning the value of a transfer for gift tax purposes at the Examination level, the donor will be sent a notice of preliminary determination of value (Letter 950-G or such other document as may be utilized by the IRS for this purpose from time to time, but referred to in this section as Letter 950-G), inviting the donor to file a formal protest and to request consideration by the appropriate IRS Appeals office. See §§ 601.105 and 601.106 of this chapter. Subsequently, the donor will be sent a notice of determination of value (Letter 3569, or such other document as may be utilized from time to time by the IRS for this purpose in cases where no deficiency or refund would result, but referred to in this section as Letter 3569) if—

(i) The donor requests Appeals consideration in writing within 30 calendar days after the mailing date of the Letter 950-G, or by such later date as determined pursuant to IRS procedures, and the matter is not resolved by Appeals;

(ii) The donor does not request Appeals consideration within the time provided in paragraph (b)(1)(i) of this section; or

(iii) The IRS does not issue a Letter 950-G in circumstances described in paragraph (d)(4)(iv) of this section.

(2) *Notice of determination of value.*—The Letter 3569 will notify the donor of the adjustment(s) proposed by the IRS, and will advise the donor that the donor may contest the determination made by the IRS by filing a petition with the Tax Court before the 91st day after the date on which the Letter 3569 was mailed to the donor by the IRS.

(3) *Tax Court petition.*—If the donor does not file a timely petition with the Tax Court, the IRS determination as set forth in Letter 3569 will be considered the final determination of value, as defined in sections 2504(c) and 2001(f). If the donor files a timely petition with the Tax Court, the Tax Court will determine whether the donor has exhausted available administrative remedies. Under section 7477, the Tax Court is not authorized to issue a declaratory judgment unless the Tax Court finds that the donor has exhausted all administrative remedies within the IRS. See paragraph (d)(4) of this section regarding the exhaustion of administrative remedies.

(c) *Adjustments subject to declaratory judgment procedure.*—The declaratory judgment procedures set forth in this section apply to adjustments involving all issues relating to the transfer, including without limitation valuation issues and legal issues involving the interpretation and application of the gift tax law.

(d) *Requirements for declaratory judgment procedure.*—(1) *In general.*—The declaratory judgment procedure provided in this section is available to a donor with respect to a transfer only if all the requirements of paragraphs (d)(2) through (5) of this section with regard to that transfer are satisfied.

(2) *Reporting.*—The transfer is shown or disclosed on the return of tax imposed by chapter 12 for the calendar year during which the transfer was made or on a statement attached to such return. For purposes of this paragraph (d)(2), the term *return of tax imposed by chapter 12* means the last gift tax return (Form 709, "United States Gift (and Generation-Skipping Transfer) Tax Return" or such other form as may be utilized for this purpose from time to time by the IRS) for the calendar year filed on or before the due date of the return, including extensions granted if any, or, if a timely return is not filed, the first gift tax return for that calendar year filed after the due date. For purposes of satisfying this requirement, the transfer need not be reported in a manner that constitutes adequate disclosure within the meaning of § 301.6501(c)-1(e) or (f) (and thus for which, under §§ 20.2001-1(b) and 25.2504-2(b) of this chapter, the period during which the IRS may adjust the value of the gift will not expire). The issuance of a Letter 3569 with regard to a transfer disclosed on a return does not constitute a determination by the IRS that the transfer was adequately disclosed, or otherwise cause the period of limitations on assessment to commence to run with respect to that transfer. In addition, in the case of a transfer that is shown on the return, the IRS may in its discretion defer until a later time making a determination with regard to such transfer. If the IRS exercises its discretion to defer such determination in that case, the transfer will not be addressed in the Letter 3569 (if any) sent to the donor currently, and the donor is not yet eligible for a declaratory judgment with regard to that transfer under section 7477.

(3) *IRS determination and actual controversy.*—The IRS makes a determination regarding the gift tax treatment of the transfer that results in an actual controversy. The IRS makes a determination that

results in an actual controversy with respect to a transfer by mailing a Letter 3569 to the donor, thereby notifying the donor of the adjustment(s) proposed by the IRS with regard to that transfer and of the donor's rights under section 7477.

(4) *Exhaustion of administrative remedies.*—(i) *In general.*—The Tax Court determines whether the donor has exhausted all administrative remedies available within the IRS for resolving the controversy.

(ii) *Appeals office consideration.*—For purposes of this section, the IRS will consider a donor to have exhausted all administrative remedies if, prior to filing a petition in Tax Court (except as provided in paragraphs (d)(4)(iii) and (iv) of this section), the donor, or a qualified representative of the donor described in § 601.502 of this chapter, timely requests consideration by Appeals and participates fully (within the meaning of paragraph (d)(4)(vi) of this section) in the Appeals consideration process. A timely request for consideration by Appeals is a written request from the donor for Appeals consideration made within 30 days after the mailing date of the Letter 950-G, or by such later date for responding to the Letter 950-G as is agreed to between the donor and the IRS.

(iii) *Request for Appeals office consideration not granted.*—If the donor, or a qualified representative of the donor described in § 601.502 of this chapter, timely requests consideration by Appeals and Appeals does not grant that request, the IRS nevertheless will consider the donor to have exhausted all administrative remedies within the IRS for purposes of section 7477 upon the issuance of the Letter 3569, provided that the donor, or a qualified representative of the donor described in § 601.502 of this chapter, after the filing of a petition in Tax Court for a declaratory judgment pursuant to section 7477, participates fully (within the meaning of paragraph (d)(4)(vi) of this section) in the Appeals office consideration if offered by the IRS while the case is in docketed status.

(iv) *No Letter 950-G issued.*—If the IRS does not issue a Letter 950-G to the donor prior to the issuance of Letter 3569, the IRS nevertheless will consider the donor to have exhausted all administrative remedies within the IRS for purposes of section 7477 upon the issuance of the Letter 3569, provided that—

(A) The IRS decision not to issue the Letter 950-G was not due to actions or inactions of the donor (such as a failure to supply requested information or a current mailing address to the Area Director having jurisdiction over the tax matter); and

(B) The donor, or a qualified representative of the donor described in § 601.502 of this chapter, after the filing of a petition in Tax Court for a declaratory judgment pursuant to section 7477, participates fully (within the meaning of paragraph (d)(4)(vi) of this section) in the Appeals office consideration if offered by the IRS while the case is in docketed status.

(v) *Failure to agree to extension of time for assessment.*—For purposes of section 7477, the donor's refusal to agree to an extension of the time under section 6501 within which gift tax with respect to the transfer at issue (if any) may be assessed will not be considered by the IRS to constitute a failure by the donor to exhaust all administrative remedies available to the donor within the IRS.

(vi) *Participation in Appeals consideration process.*—For purposes of this section, the donor or a qualified representative of the donor described in § 601.502 of this chapter participates fully in the Appeals consideration process if the donor or the qualified representative timely submits all information related to the transfer that is requested by the IRS in connection with the Appeals consideration and discloses to the Appeals office all relevant information regarding the controversy to the extent such information and its relevance is known or should be known by the donor or the qualified representative during the time the issue is under consideration by Appeals.

(5) *Timely petition in Tax Court.*—The donor files a pleading with the Tax Court requesting a declaratory judgment under section 7477. This pleading must be filed with the Tax Court before the 91st day after the date of mailing of the Letter 3569 by the IRS to the donor. The pleading must be in the form of a petition subject to Tax Court Rule 211(d).

(e) *Examples.*—The following examples illustrate the provisions of this section, and assume that in each case the Tax Court petition is filed on or after September 9, 2009. These examples, however, do not address any other situations that might affect the Tax Court's jurisdiction over the proceeding:

*Example 1. Exhaustion of administrative remedies.* The donor (D) timely files a Form 709, "United States Gift (and Generation-Skipping Transfer) Tax Return," on which D reports D's completed gift of closely held stock. After conducting an examination, the IRS concludes that the value of the stock on the date of the gift is greater than the value reported on the return. Because the amount of D's available applicable credit amount under section 2505 is sufficient to cover any resulting tax liability, no gift tax deficiency will result from the adjustment. D is unable to resolve the matter with the IRS examiner. The IRS sends a Letter 950-G to D informing D of the proposed adjustment. D, within 30 calendar days after the mailing date of the letter, submits a written request for Appeals consideration. During the Appeals process, D provides to the Appeals office all additional information (if any) requested by Appeals relevant to the determination of the value of the stock in a timely fashion. The Appeals office and D are unable to reach an agreement regarding the value of the stock as of the date of the gift. The Appeals office sends D a notice of determination of value (Letter 3569). For purposes of section 7477, the IRS will consider D to have exhausted all available administrative remedies within the IRS, and thus will not contest the allegation in D's petition that D has exhausted all such administrative remedies.

*Example 2. Exhaustion of administrative remedies.* Assume the same facts as in *Example 1*, except that D does not timely request consideration by Appeals after receiving the Letter 950-G. A Letter 3569 is mailed to D more than 30 days after the mailing of the Letter 950-G and prior to the expiration of the period of limitations for assessment of gift tax. D timely files a petition in Tax Court pursuant to section 7477. After the case is docketed, D requests Appeals consideration. In this situation, because D did not respond timely to the Letter 950-G with a written request for Appeals consideration, the IRS will not consider D to have exhausted all administrative remedies available within the IRS for purposes of section 7477 prior to filing the petition in Tax Court, and thus may contest any allegation in D's petition that D has exhausted all such administrative remedies.

*Example 3. Exhaustion of administrative remedies.* D timely files a Form 709 on which D reports D's completed gifts of interests in a family limited partnership. After conducting an examination, the IRS proposes to adjust the value of the gifts as reported on the return. No gift tax deficiency will result from the adjustments, however, because D has a sufficient amount of available applicable credit amount under section 2505. D declines to consent to extend the time for the assessment of gift tax with respect to the gifts at issue. Because of the pending expiration of the period of limitation on assessment within which a gift tax, if any, could be assessed, the IRS determines that there is not adequate time for Appeals consideration. Accordingly, the IRS mails to D a Letter 3569, even though a Letter 950-G had not first been issued to D. D timely files a petition in Tax Court pursuant to section 7477. After the case is docketed in Tax Court, D is offered the opportunity for Appeals to consider any dispute regarding the determination and participates fully in the Appeals consideration process. However, the Appeals office and D are unable to resolve the issue. The IRS will consider D to have exhausted all administrative remedies available within the IRS, and thus will not assert that D has not exhausted all such administrative remedies.

*Example 4. Legal issue.* D transfers nonvested stock options to a trust for the benefit of D's child. D timely files a Form 709 reporting the transfer as a completed gift for Federal gift tax purposes and complies with the adequate disclosure requirements for purposes of triggering the commencement of the applicable statute of limitations. Pursuant to §301.6501(c)-1(f)(5), adequate disclosure of a transfer that is reported as a completed gift on the Form 709 will commence the running of the period of limitations for assessment of gift tax on D, even if the transfer is ultimately determined to be an incomplete gift for purposes of §25.2511-2 of this chapter. After conducting an examination, the IRS concurs with the reported valuation of the stock options, but concludes that the reported transfer is not a completed gift for Federal gift tax purposes. D is unable to resolve the matter with the IRS examiner. The IRS sends a Letter 950-G to D, who timely mails a written request for Appeals consideration. Assuming that the IRS mails to D a Letter 3569 with regard to this transfer, and that D complies with the administrative procedures set forth in this section, including the exhaustion of all administrative remedies available within the IRS, then D may file a petition for declaratory judgment with the Tax Court pursuant to section 7477.

*Example 5. Transfers in controversy.* On April 16, 2007, D timely files a Form 709 on which D reports gifts made in 2006 of fractional interests in certain real property and of interests in a family limited partnership (FLP). However, although the gifts are disclosed on the return, the return does not contain information sufficient to constitute adequate disclosure under §301.6501(c)-1(e) or (f) for purposes of the application of the statute of limitations on assessment of gift tax with respect to the reported gifts. The IRS conducts an examination and concludes that the value of both the interests in the real property and the FLP interests on the date(s) of the transfers are greater than the values reported on the return. No gift tax deficiency will result from the adjustments because D has a sufficient amount of remaining applicable credit amount under section 2505. However, D does not agree with the adjustments. The IRS sends a Letter 950-G to D informing D of the proposed adjustments in the value of the reported gifts. D, within 30 calendar days after the mailing date of the letter, submits a written request for Appeals consideration. The Appeals office and D are unable to reach an agreement regarding the value of any of the gifts. In the exercise of its discretion, the IRS decides to resolve currently only the value of the real property interests, and to defer the resolution of the value of the FLP interests. On May 28, 2009, the Appeals office sends D a Letter 3569 addressing only the value of the gifts of interests in the real property. Because none of the gifts reported on the return filed on April 16, 2007, were adequately disclosed for purposes of §301.6501(c)-1(e) or (f), the period of limitations during which the IRS may adjust the value of those gifts has not begun to run. Accordingly, the Letter 3569 is timely mailed. If D timely files a petition in Tax Court pursuant to section 7477 with regard to the value of the interests in the real property, then, assuming the other requirements of section 7477 are satisfied with regard to those interests, the Tax Court's declaratory judgment, once it becomes final, will determine the value of the gifts of the interests in the real property. Because the IRS has not yet put the gift tax value of the interests in the FLP into controversy, the procedure under section 7477 is not yet available with regard to those gifts.

(f) *Effective/applicability date.*—This section applies to civil proceedings described in section 7477 filed in the United States Tax Court on or after September 9, 2009. [Reg. §301.7477-1.]

☐ [T.D. 7596, 2-22-79. *Amended by* T.D. 7954, 5-7-84 *and* T.D. 9460, 9-8-2009 (*corrected* 10-26-2009).]

# COURT REVIEW OF TAX COURT PROCEEDINGS

**[Reg. §301.7481-1]**

**§301.7481-1. Date when Tax Court decision becomes final; decision modified or reversed.**—(a) *Upon mandate of Supreme Court.*—Under section 7481(3)(A) of the Code, if the Supreme Court directs that the decision of the Tax Court be modified or reversed, the decision of the Tax Court rendered in accordance with the mandate of the Supreme Court shall become final upon the expiration of 30 days from the time it was rendered, unless within 30 days either the Commissioner or the taxpayer has instituted proceedings to have such decision corrected to accord with the mandate, in which event the decision of the Tax Court shall become final when so corrected.

(b) *Upon mandate of the Court of Appeals.*—Under section 7481(3)(B) of the Code, if the decision of the Tax Court is modified or reversed by the United States Court of Appeals, and if—

(i) The time allowed for filing a petition for certiorari has expired and no such petition has been duly filed, or

(ii) The petition for certiorari has been denied, or

(iii) The decision of the United States Court of Appeals has been affirmed by the Supreme Court, then the decision of the Tax Court rendered in accordance with the mandate of the United States Court of Appeals shall become final on the expiration of 30 days from the time such decision of the Tax Court was rendered, unless within such 30 days either the Commissioner or the taxpayer has instituted proceedings to have such decision corrected so that it will accord with the mandate, in which event the decision of the Tax Court shall become final when so corrected. [Reg. §301.7481-1.]

☐ [T.D. 6498, 10-24-60.]

**[Reg. §301.7482-1]**

**§301.7482-1. Courts of review; venue.**—Under section 7482(b)(2) of the Code, decisions of the Tax Court may be reviewed by any United States Court of Appeals which may be designated by the Commissioner and the taxpayer by stipulation in writing. [Reg. §301.7482-1.]

☐ [T.D. 6498, 10-24-60.]

**[Reg. §301.7483-1]**

**§301.7483-1. Petition for review.**—The decision of the Tax Court may be reviewed by a United States Court of Appeals as provided in section 7482 of the Code if a petition for such review is filed by either the Commissioner or the taxpayer within 3 months after the decision is rendered. If, however, a petition for such review is so filed by one party to the proceeding, a petition for review of the decision of the Tax Court may be filed by any other party to the proceeding within 4 months after such decision is rendered. [Reg. §301.7483-1.]

☐ [T.D. 6498, 10-24-60.]

[Reg. § 301.7484-1]

**§ 301.7484-1. Change of incumbent in office.**—When the incumbent of the office of Commissioner changes, no substitution of the name of his successor shall be required in proceedings pending before any appellate court reviewing the action of the Tax Court. [Reg. § 301.7484-1.]

□ [*T.D. 6498, 10-24-60.*]

# Miscellaneous Provisions

[Reg. § 301.7502-1]

**§ 301.7502-1. Timely mailing of documents and payments treated as timely filing and paying.**—(a) *General rule.*—Section 7502 provides that, if the requirements of that section are met, a document or payment is deemed to be filed or paid on the date of the postmark stamped on the envelope or other appropriate wrapper (envelope) in which the document or payment was mailed. Thus, if the envelope that contains the document or payment has a timely postmark, the document or payment is considered timely filed or paid even if it is received after the last date, or the last day of the period, prescribed for filing the document or making the payment. Section 7502 does not apply in determining whether a failure to file a return or pay a tax has continued for an additional month or fraction thereof for purposes of computing the penalties and additions to tax imposed by section 6651. Except as provided in section 7502(e) and § 301.7502-2, relating to the timely mailing of deposits, and paragraph (d) of this section, relating to electronically filed documents, section 7502 is applicable only to those documents or payments as defined in paragraph (b) of this section and only if the document or payment is mailed in accordance with paragraph (c) of this section and is delivered in accordance with paragraph (e) of this section.

(b) *Definitions.*—(1) *Document defined.*—(i) The term *document*, as used in this section, means any return, claim, statement, or other document required to be filed within a prescribed period or on or before a prescribed date under authority of any provision of the internal revenue laws, except as provided in paragraph (b) (1) (ii), (iii), or (iv) of this section.

(ii) The term does not include returns, claims, statements, or other documents that are required under any provision of the internal revenue laws or the regulations thereunder to be delivered by any method other than mailing.

(iii) The term does not include any document filed in any court other than the Tax Court, but the term does include any document filed with the Tax Court, including a petition and a notice of appeal of a decision of the Tax Court.

(iv) The term does not include any document that is mailed to an authorized financial institution under section 6302. However, see § 301.7502-2 for special rules relating to the timeliness of deposits and documents required to be filed with deposits.

(2) *Claims for refund.*—(i) *In general.*—In the case of certain taxes, a return may constitute a claim for credit or refund. Section 7502 is applicable to the determination of whether a claim for credit or refund is timely filed for purposes of section 6511(a) if the conditions of section 7502 are met, irrespective of whether the claim is also a return. For rules regarding claims for refund on late filed tax returns, see paragraph (f) of this section. Section 7502 is also applicable when a claim for credit or refund is delivered after the last day of the period specified in section 6511(b)(2)(A) or in any other corresponding provision of law relating to the limit on the amount of credit or refund that is allowable.

(ii) *Example.*—The rules of paragraph (b)(2)(i) of this section are illustrated by the following example:

*Example.* (A) Taxpayer A, an individual, mailed his 2004 Form 1040, "U.S. Individual Income Tax Return," on May 10, 2005, but no tax was paid at that time because the tax liability disclosed by the return had been completely satisfied by the income tax that had been withheld on A's wages. On April 15, 2008, A mails, in accordance with the requirements of this section, a Form 1040X, "Amended U.S. Individual Income Tax Return," claiming a refund of a portion of the tax that had been paid through withholding during 2004. The date of the postmark on the envelope containing the claim for refund is April 15, 2008. The claim is received by the IRS on April 18, 2008.

(B) Under section 6511(a), A's claim for refund is timely if filed within three years from May 10, 2005, the date on which A's 2004 return was filed. As a result of the limitations of section 6511(b)(2)(A), if A's claim is not filed within three years after April 15, 2005, the date on which A is deemed under section 6513 to have paid his 2004 tax, A is not entitled to any refund. Because A's claim for refund is postmarked and mailed in accordance with the requirements of this section and is delivered after the last day of the period specified in section 6511(b)(2)(A), section 7502 is applicable and the claim is deemed to have been filed on April 15, 2008.

(3) *Payment defined.*—(i) The term *payment*, as used in this section, means any payment required to be made within a prescribed period or on or before a prescribed date under the authority of any provision of the internal revenue laws, except as provided in paragraph (b)(3)(ii), (iii), (iv), or (v) of this section.

(ii) The term does not include any payment that is required under any provision of the internal revenue laws or the regulations thereunder to be delivered by any method other than mailing. See, for example, section 6302(h) and the regulations thereunder regarding electronic funds transfer.

(iii) The term does not include any payment, whether it is made in the form of currency or other medium of payment, unless it is actually received and accounted for. For example, if a check is used as the form of payment, this section does not apply unless the check is honored upon presentation.

(iv) The term does not include any payment to any court other than the Tax Court.

(v) The term does not include any deposit that is required to be made with an authorized financial institution under section 6302. However, see § 301.7502-2 for rules relating to the timeliness of deposits.

(4) *Last date or last day prescribed.*—As used in this section, the term *the last date, or the last day of the period, prescribed for filing the document or making the payment* includes any extension of time granted for that action. When the last date, or the last day of the period, prescribed for filing the document or making the payment falls on a Saturday, Sunday or legal holiday, section 7503 applies. Therefore, in applying the rules of this paragraph (b)(4), the next succeeding day that is not a Saturday, Sunday, or legal holiday is treated as the last date, or the last day of the period, prescribed for filing the document or making the payment. Also, when the last date, or the last day of the period, prescribed for filing the document or making the payment falls within a period disregarded under section 7508 or section 7508A, the next succeeding day after the expiration of the section 7508 period or section 7508A period that is not a Saturday, Sunday, or legal holiday is treated as the last date, or the last day of the period, prescribed for filing the document or making the payment.

(c) *Mailing requirements.*—(1) *In general.*—Section 7502 does not apply unless the document or payment is mailed in accordance with the following requirements:

(i) *Envelope and address.*—The document or payment must be contained in an envelope, properly addressed to the agency, officer, or office with which the document is required to be filed or to which the payment is required to be made.

(ii) *Timely deposited in U.S. mail.*—The document or payment must be deposited within the prescribed time in the mail in the United States with sufficient postage prepaid. For this purpose, a document or payment is deposited in the mail in the United States when it is deposited with the domestic mail service of the U.S. Postal Service. The domestic mail service of the U.S. Postal Service, as defined by the Domestic Mail Manual as incorporated by reference in the postal regulations, includes mail transmitted within, among, and between the United States of America, its territories and possessions, and Army post offices (APO), fleet post offices (FPO), and the United Nations, NY. (See Domestic Mail Manual, section G011.2.1, as incorporated by reference in 39 CFR 111.1.) Section 7502 does not apply to any document or payment that is deposited with the mail service of any other country.

(iii) *Postmark.*—(A) *U.S. Postal Service postmark.*—If the postmark on the envelope is made by the U.S. Postal Service, the postmark must bear a date on or before the last date, or the last day of the period, prescribed for filing the document or making the payment. If the postmark does not bear a date on or before the last date, or the last day of the period, prescribed for filing the document or making the payment, the document or payment is considered not to be timely filed or paid, regardless of when the document or payment is deposited in the mail. Accordingly, the sender who relies upon the applicability of section 7502 assumes the risk that the postmark will bear a date on or before the last date, or the last day of the period, prescribed for filing the document or making the payment. See, however, paragraph (c)(2) of this section with respect to the use of registered mail or certified mail to avoid this risk. If the postmark on the envelope is made by the U.S. Postal Service but is not legible, the person who is required to file the document or make the payment has the burden of proving the date that the postmark was made. Furthermore, if the envelope that contains a document or payment has a timely postmark made by the U.S. Postal Service, but it is received after the time when a document or payment postmarked and mailed at that time would ordinarily be received, the sender may be required to prove that it was timely mailed.

(B) *Postmark made by other than U.S. Postal Service.—(1) In general.*—If the postmark on the envelope is made other than by the U.S. Postal Service—

(i) The postmark so made must bear a legible date on or before the last date, or the last day of the period, prescribed for filing the document or making the payment; and

(ii) The document or payment must be received by the agency, officer, or office with which it is required to be filed not later than the time when a document or payment contained in an envelope that is properly addressed, mailed, and sent by the same class of mail would ordinarily be received if it were postmarked at the same point of origin by the U.S. Postal Service on the last date, or the last day of the period, prescribed for filing the document or making the payment.

(2) *Document or payment received late.*—If a document or payment described in paragraph (c)(1)(iii)(B)(*1*) is received after the time when a document or payment so mailed and so postmarked by the U.S. Postal Service would ordinarily be received, the document or payment is treated as having been received at the time when a document or payment so mailed and so postmarked would ordinarily be received if the person who is required to file the document or make the payment establishes—

(i) That it was actually deposited in the U.S. mail before the last collection of mail from the place of deposit that was postmarked (except for the metered mail) by the U.S. Postal Service on or before the last date, or the last day of the period, prescribed for filing the document or making the payment;

(ii) That the delay in receiving the document or payment was due to a delay in the transmission of the U.S. mail; and

(iii) The cause of the delay.

(3) *U.S. and non-U.S. postmarks.*—If the envelope has a postmark made by the U.S. Postal Service in addition to a postmark not so made, the postmark that was not made by the U.S. Postal Service is disregarded, and whether the envelope was mailed in accordance with this paragraph (c)(1)(iii)(B) will be determined solely by applying the rule of paragraph (c)(1)(iii)(A) of this section.

(2) *Registered or certified mail.*—If the document or payment is sent by U.S. registered mail, the date of registration of the document or payment is treated as the postmark date. If the document or payment is sent by U.S. certified mail and the sender's receipt is postmarked by the postal employee to whom the document or payment is presented, the date of the U.S. postmark on the receipt is treated as the postmark date of the document or payment. Accordingly, the risk that the document or payment will not be postmarked on the day that it is deposited in the mail may be eliminated by the use of registered or certified mail.

(3) *Private delivery services.*—Under section 7502(f)(1), a service of a private delivery service (PDS) may be treated as an equivalent to United States mail for purposes of the postmark rule if the Commissioner determines that the service satisfies the conditions of section 7502(f)(2). Thus, the Commissioner may, in guidance published in the Internal Revenue Bulletin (see § 601.601(d)(2)(ii)(b) of this chapter), prescribe procedures and additional rules to designate a service of a PDS for purposes of the postmark rule of section 7502(a).

(d) *Electronically filed documents.—(1) In general.*—A document filed electronically with an electronic return transmitter (as defined in paragraph (d)(3)(i) of this section and authorized pursuant to paragraph (d)(2) of this section) in the manner and time prescribed by the Commissioner is deemed to be filed on the date of the electronic postmark (as defined in paragraph (d)(3)(ii) of this section) given by the authorized electronic return transmitter. Thus, if the electronic postmark is timely, the document is considered filed timely although it is received by the agency, officer, or office after the last date, or the last day of the period, prescribed for filing such document.

(2) *Authorized electronic return transmitters.*—The Commissioner may enter into an agreement with an electronic return transmitter or prescribe in forms, instructions, or other appropriate guidance the procedures under which the electronic return transmitter is authorized to provide taxpayers with an electronic postmark to acknowl-

edge the date and time that the electronic return transmitter received the electronically filed document.

(3) *Definitions.*—(i) *Electronic return transmitter.*—For purposes of this paragraph (d), the term *electronic return transmitter* has the same meaning as contained in section 3.01(4) of Rev. Proc. 2000-31 (2000-31 I.R.B. 146 (July 31, 2000)) (see § 601.601(d)(2) of this chapter) or in procedures prescribed by the Commissioner.

(ii) *Electronic postmark.*—For purposes of this paragraph (d), the term *electronic postmark* means a record of the date and time (in a particular time zone) that an authorized electronic return transmitter receives the transmission of a taxpayer's electronically filed document on its host system. However, if the taxpayer and the electronic return transmitter are located in different time zones, it is the taxpayer's time zone that controls the timeliness of the electronically filed document.

(e) *Delivery.—(1) General rule.*—Except as provided in section 7502(f) and paragraphs (c)(3) and (d) of this section, section 7502 is not applicable unless the document or payment is delivered by U.S. mail to the agency, officer, or office with which the document is required to be filed or to which payment is required to be made.

(2) *Exceptions to actual delivery.*—(i) *Registered and certified mail.*—In the case of a document (but not a payment) sent by registered or certified mail, proof that the document was properly registered or that a postmarked certified mail sender's receipt was properly issued and that the envelope was properly addressed to the agency, officer, or office constitutes prima facie evidence that the document was delivered to the agency, officer, or office. Other than direct proof of actual delivery, proof of proper use of registered or certified mail, and proof of proper use of a duly designated PDS as provided for by paragraph (e)(2)(ii) of this section, are the exclusive means to establish prima facie evidence of delivery of a document to the agency, officer, or office with which the document is required to be filed. No other evidence of a postmark or of mailing will be prima facie evidence of delivery or raise a presumption that the document was delivered.

(ii) *Equivalents of registered and certified mail.*—Under section 7502(f)(3), the Secretary may extend the prima facie evidence of delivery rule of section 7502(c)(1)(A) to a service of a designated PDS, which is substantially equivalent to United States registered or certified mail. Thus, the Commissioner may, in guidance published in the Internal Revenue Bulletin (see § 601.601(d)(2)(ii)(b) of this chapter), prescribe procedures and additional rules to designate a service of a PDS for purposes of demonstrating prima facie evidence of delivery of a document pursuant to section 7502(c).

(f) *Claim for credit or refund on late filed tax return.—(1) In general.*—Generally, an original income tax return may constitute a claim for credit or refund of income tax. See § 301.6402-3(a)(5). Other original tax returns can also be considered claims for credit or refund if the liability disclosed on the return is less than the amount of tax that has been paid. If section 7502 would not apply to a return (but for the operation of paragraph (f)(2) of this section) that is also considered a claim for credit or refund because the envelope that contains the return does not have a postmark dated on or before the due date of the return, section 7502 will apply separately to the claim for credit or refund if—

(i) The date of the postmark on the envelope is within the period that is three years (plus the period of any extension of time to file) from the day the tax is paid or considered paid (see section 6513), and the claim for credit or refund is delivered after this three-year period; and

(ii) The conditions of section 7502 are otherwise met.

(2) *Filing date of late filed return.*—If the conditions of paragraph (f)(1) of this section are met, the late filed return will be deemed filed on the postmark date.

(3) *Example.*—The rules of this paragraph (f) are illustrated by the following example:

*Example.* (i) Taxpayer A, an individual, mailed his 2001 Form 1040, "U.S. Individual Income Tax Return," on April 15, 2005, claiming a refund of amounts paid through withholding during 2001. The date of the postmark on the envelope containing the return and claim for refund is April 15, 2005. The return and claim for refund are received by the Internal Revenue Service (IRS) on April 18, 2005. Amounts withheld in 2001 exceeded A's tax liability for 2001 and are treated as paid on April 15, 2002, pursuant to section 6513.

(ii) Even though the date of the postmark on the envelope is after the due date of the return, the claim for refund and the late filed return are treated as filed on the postmark date for purposes of this paragraph (f). Accordingly, the return will be treated as filed on April 15, 2005. In addition, the claim for refund will be treated as timely filed on April 15, 2005. Further, the entire amount of the refund attributable to withholding is allowable as a refund under section 6511(b)(2)(A).

(g) *Effective date.*—(1) *In general.*—Except as provided in paragraphs (g) (2) and (3) of this section, the rules of this section apply to any payment or document mailed and delivered in accordance with the requirements of this section in an envelope bearing a postmark dated after January 11, 2001.

(2) *Claim for credit or refund on late filed tax return.*—Paragraph (f) of this section applies to any claim for credit or refund on a late filed tax return described in paragraph (f) (1) of this section except for those claims for credit or refund which (without regard to paragraph (f) of this section) were barred by the operation of section 6532(a) or any other law or rule of law (including res judicata) as of January 11, 2001.

(3) *Electronically filed documents.*—This section applies to any electronically filed return, claim, statement, or other document transmitted to an electronic return transmitter that is authorized to provide an electronic postmark pursuant to paragraph (d) (2) of this section after January 11, 2001.

(4) *Registered or certified mail as the means to prove delivery of a document.*—Section 301.7502-1(e)(2) will apply to all documents mailed after September 21, 2004. [Reg. § 301.7502-1.]

☐ [*T.D. 6232, 5-2-57. Amended by T.D. 6292, 4-18-58; T.D. 6444, 1-14-60; T.D. 6498, 10-24-60; T.D. 8807, 1-14-99; T.D. 8932, 1-10-2001 and T.D. 9543, 8-22-2011.*]

### [Reg. § 301.7503-1]

**§ 301.7503-1. Time for performance of acts where last day falls on Saturday, Sunday, or legal holiday.**—(a) *In general.*—Section 7503 provides that when the last day prescribed under authority of any internal revenue law for the performance of any act falls on a Saturday, Sunday, or legal holiday, such act shall be considered performed timely if performed on the next succeeding day which is not a Saturday, Sunday, or legal holiday. For this purpose, any authorized extension of time shall be included in determining the last day for performance of any act. Section 7503 is applicable only in case an act is required under authority of any internal revenue law to be performed on or before a prescribed date or within a prescribed period. For example, if the 2-year period allowed by section 6532(a)(1) to bring a suit for refund of any internal revenue tax expires on Thursday, November 23, 1995 (Thanksgiving Day), the suit will be timely if filed on Friday, November 24, 1995, in the Court of Federal Claims, or in a district court. Section 7503 applies to acts to be performed by the taxpayer (such as, the filing of any return of, and the payment of, any income, estate, or gift tax; the filing of a petition with the Tax Court for redetermination of a deficiency, or for review of a decision rendered by such Court; the filing of a claim for credit or refund of any tax) and acts to be performed by the Commissioner, a district director, or the director of a regional service center (such as, the giving of any notice with respect to, or making any demand for the payment of, any tax; the assessment or collection of any tax).

(b) *Legal holidays.*—For the purpose of section 7503, the term *legal holiday* includes the legal holidays in the District of Columbia as found in D.C. Code Ann. 28-2701. In the case of any return, statement, or other document required to be filed, or any other act required under the authority of the internal revenue laws to be performed, at an office of the Internal Revenue Service, or any other office or agency of the United States, located outside the District of Columbia but within an internal revenue district, the term *legal holiday* includes, in addition to the legal holidays in the District of Columbia, any statewide legal holiday of the state where the act is required to be performed. If the act is performed in accordance with law at an office of the Internal Revenue Service or any other office or agency of the United States located in a territory or possession of the United States, the term *legal holiday* includes, in addition to the legal holidays in the District of Columbia, any legal holiday that is recognized throughout the territory or possession in which the office is located. [Reg. § 301.7503-1.]

☐ [*T.D. 6232, 5-2-57. Amended by T.D. 6498, 10-24-60; T.D. 6585, 12-27-61; T.D. 7309, 3-27-74 and T.D. 8681, 8-13-96.*]

### [Reg. § 301.7505-1]

**§ 301.7505-1. Sale of personal property acquired by the United States.**—(a) *Sale.*—(1) *In general.*—Any personal property (except bonds, notes, checks, and other securities) acquired by the United States in payment of or as security for debts arising under the internal revenue laws may be sold by the district director who acquired such property for the United States. United States Savings Bonds shall not be sold by the district director but shall be trans-

ferred to the appropriate office of the Treasury Department for redemption. Other bonds, notes, checks, and other securities shall be disposed of in accordance with instructions issued by the Commissioner.

(2) *Time, place, manner, and terms of sale.*—The time, place, manner, and terms of sale of personal property acquired for the United States shall be as follows:

(i) *Time, notice, and place of sale.*—The property may be sold at any time after it has been acquired by the United States. A public notice of sale shall be posted at the post office nearest the place of sale and in at least two other public places. The notice shall specify the property to be sold and the time, place, manner, and conditions of sale. In addition, the district director may use such other methods of advertising as he believes will result in obtaining the highest price for the property. The place of sale shall be within the internal revenue district where the property was originally acquired by the United States. However, if the district director believes that a substantially higher price may be obtained, the sale may be held outside his district.

(ii) *Rejection of bids and adjournment of sale.*—The internal revenue officer conducting the sale reserves the right to reject any and all bids and withdraw the property from the sale. When it appears to the internal revenue officer conducting the sale that an adjournment of the sale will best serve the interest of the United States, he may order the sale adjourned from time to time. If the sale is adjourned for more than 30 days in the aggregate, public notice of the sale must again be given in accordance with subdivision (i) of this subparagraph.

(iii) *Liquidated damages.*—The notice shall state whether, in the case of default in payment of the bid price, any amount deposited with the United States will be retained as liquidated damages. In case liquidated damages are provided, the amount thereof shall not exceed $200.

(3) *Agreement to bid.*—The district director may, before giving notice of sale, solicit offers from prospective bidders and enter into agreements with such persons that they will bid at least a specified amount in case the property is offered for sale. In such cases, the district director may also require such persons to make deposits to secure the performance of their agreements. Any such deposit, but not more than $200, shall be retained as liquidated damages in case such person fails to bid the specified amount and the property is not sold for as much as the amount specified in such agreement.

(4) *Terms of payment.*—The property shall be offered for sale upon whichever of the following terms is fixed by the district director in the public notice of sale—

(i) Payment in full upon acceptance of the highest bid, without regard to the amount of such bid, or

(ii) If the aggregate price of all property purchased by a successful bidder at the sale is more than $200, an initial payment of $200 or 20 percent of the purchase price, whichever is the greater, and payment of the balance (including all costs incurred for the protection or preservation of the property subsequent to the sale and prior to final payment) within a specified period, not to exceed one month from the date of the sale.

(5) *Method of sale.*—The property may be sold either—

(i) At public auction, at which open competitive bids shall be received, or

(ii) At public sale under sealed bids.

(6) *Sales under sealed bids.*—The following rules, in addition to the other rules provided in this paragraph, shall be applicable to public sales under sealed bids:

(i) *Invitation to bidders.*—Bids shall be solicited through a public notice of sale.

(ii) *Form for use by bidders.*—A bid shall be submitted on a form which will be furnished by the district director upon request. The form shall be completed in accordance with the instructions thereon.

(iii) *Remittance with bid.*—If the total bid is $200 or less, the full amount of the bid shall be submitted therewith. If the total bid is more than $200, 20 percent of such bid or $200, whichever is greater, shall be submitted therewith. Such remittance shall be by a certified, cashier's, or treasurer's check drawn on any bank or trust company incorporated under the laws of the United States or under the laws of any State, Territory, or possession of the United States, or by a United States postal, bank, express, or telegraph money order.

(iv) *Time for receiving and opening bids.*—Each bid shall be submitted in a securely sealed envelope. The bidder shall indicate in the upper left hand corner of the envelope his name and address and the time and place of sale as announced in the public notice of sale. A bid will not be considered unless it is received by the internal revenue officer conducting the sale prior to the opening of the bids. The bids will be opened at the time and place stated in the notice of sale, or at the time fixed in the announcement of the adjournment of the sale.

(v) *Consideration of bids.*—The internal revenue officer conducting the sale shall have the right to waive any technical defects in a bid. After the opening, examination, and consideration of all bids, the internal revenue officer conducting the sale shall announce the amount of the highest bid or bids and the name of the successful bidder or bidders, unless in the opinion of the officer a higher price can be obtained for the property than has been bid. In the event the highest bids are equal in amount (and unless in the opinion of the internal revenue officer conducting the sale a higher price can be obtained for the property than has been bid), the officer shall determine the successful bidder by drawing lots. Any remittance submitted in connection with an unsuccessful bid shall be returned to the bidder at the conclusion of the sale.

(vi) *Withdrawal of bids.*—A bid may be withdrawn on written or telegraphic request received from the bidder prior to the time fixed for opening the bids. A technical defect in a bid confers no right on the bidder for the withdrawal of his bid after it has been opened.

(7) *Payment of bid price.*—All payments for property sold pursuant to this section shall be made by cash or by a certified, cashier's, or treasurer's check drawn on any bank or trust company incorporated under the laws of the United States or under the laws of any State, Territory, or possession of the United States, or by a United States postal, bank, express, or telegraph money order. If payment in full is required upon acceptance of the highest bid, the payment shall be made at such time. If payment in full is not made at such time, the internal revenue officer conducting the sale may forthwith proceed again to sell the property in the manner provided in subparagraph (5) of this paragraph. If deferred payment is permitted, the initial payment shall be made upon acceptance of the bid, and the balance shall be paid on or before the date fixed for payment thereof. Any remittance submitted with a successful sealed bid shall be applied toward the purchase price.

(8) *Delivery and removal of personal property.*—The risk of loss is on the purchaser of the property upon acceptance of his bid. Possession of any property shall not be delivered to the purchaser until the purchase price has been paid in full. If payment of part of the purchase price for the property is deferred, the United States will retain possession of such property as security for the payment of the balance of the purchase price and, as agent for the purchaser, will cause the property to be cared for until the purchase price has been paid in full or the sale is declared null and void for failure to make full payment of the purchase price. In such case, all charges and expenses incurred in caring for the property after acceptance of the bid shall be borne by the purchaser.

(9) *Certificate of sale.*—The internal revenue officer conducting the sale shall issue a certificate of sale to the purchaser upon payment in full of the purchase price.

(b) *Accounting.*—In case of the resale of such property, the proceeds of the sale shall be paid into the Treasury as internal revenue collections, and there shall be rendered by the district director a distinct account of all charges incurred in such sale. For additional accounting rules, see section 7809 and the instructions thereunder. [Reg. § 301.7505-1.]

☐ [*T.D. 6232, 5-2-57. Amended by T.D. 7305, 3-14-75.*]

### [Reg. § 301.7506-1]

**§ 301.7506-1. Administration of real estate acquired by the United States.**—(a) *Persons charged with.*—The district director for the internal revenue district in which the property is situated shall have charge of all real estate which is or shall become the property of the United States by judgment of forfeiture under the internal revenue laws, or which has been or shall be assigned, set off, or conveyed by purchase or otherwise to the United States in payment of debts or penalties arising under the laws relating to internal revenue, or which has been or shall be vested in the United States by mortgage, or other security for payment of such debts, or which has been redeemed by the United States, or which has been or shall be acquired by the United States in payment of or as security for debts arising under the internal revenue laws, and of all trusts created for the use of the United States in payment of such debts due the United States.

(b) *Sale.*—The district director for the internal revenue district in which the property is situated may sell any real estate owned or held by the United States as aforesaid, subject to the following rules—

(1) *Property purchases at sale under levy.*—If the property was acquired as a result of being declared purchased for the United States at a sale under section 6335, relating to sale of seized property, the property shall not be sold until after the expiration of 120 days (or 1 year in the case of such sale under levy before November 3, 1966) after such sale under levy.

(2) *Notice of sale.*—A notice of sale shall be published in some newspaper published or generally circulated within the county where the property is situated, or a notice shall be posted at the post office nearest the place where the property is situated and in at least two other public places. The notice shall specify the property to be sold and the time, place, manner and conditions of sale. In addition, the district director may use other methods of advertising and of giving notice of sale if he believes such method will enhance the possibility of obtaining a higher price for the property.

(3) *Time and place of sale.*—The time of the sale shall be not less than 20 days from the date of giving public notice of sale under subparagraph (2) of this paragraph. The place of sale shall be within the county where the property is situated. However, if the district director believes a substantially better price may be obtained, he may hold the sale outside such county.

(4) *Rejection of bids and adjournment of sale.*—The internal revenue officer conducting the sale reserves the right to reject any and all bids and withdraw the property from the sale. When it appears to the internal revenue officer conducting the sale that an adjournment of the sale will best serve the interests of the United States, he may order the sale adjourned from time to time. If the sale is adjourned for more than 30 days in the aggregate, public notice of the sale must be given again in accordance with subparagraph (2) of this paragraph.

(5) *Liquidated damages.*—The notice shall state whether, in the case of default in payment of the bid price, any amount deposited with the United States will be retained as liquidated damages. In case liquidated damages are provided, the amount thereof shall not exceed $200.

(6) *Agreement to bid.*—The district director may, before giving notice of sale, solicit offers from prospective bidders and enter into agreements with such persons that they will bid at least a specified amount in case the property is offered for sale. In such cases, the district director may also require such persons to make deposits to secure the performance of their agreements. Any such deposit, but not more than $200, shall be retained as liquidated damages in case such person fails to bid the specified amount and the property is not sold for as much as the amount specified in such agreement.

(7) *Terms.*—The property shall be offered for sale upon whichever of the following terms is fixed by the district director in the public notice of sale:

(i) Payment in full upon acceptance of the highest bid, or

(ii) If the price of the property purchased by a successful bidder at the sale is more than $200, an initial payment of $200 or 20 percent of the purchase price, whichever is the greater, and payment of the balance within a specified period, not to exceed one month from the date of the sale.

(8) *Method of sale.*—The property may be sold either—

(i) At public auction, at which open competitive bids shall be received, or

(ii) At public sale under sealed bids.

(9) *Sales under sealed bids.*—The following rules, in addition to the other rules provided in this paragraph, shall be applicable at public sales under sealed bids:

(i) *Invitation to bidders.*—Bids shall be solicited through a public notice of sale.

(ii) *Form for use by bidders.*—A bid shall be submitted on a form which will be furnished by the district director upon request. The form shall be completed in accordance with the instructions thereon.

(iii) *Remittance with bid.*—If the total bid is $200 or less, the full amount of the bid shall be submitted therewith. If the total bid is more than $200, 20 percent of such bid or $200, whichever is greater, shall be submitted therewith. Such remittance shall be by a certified, cashier's, or treasurer's check drawn on any bank or trust company incorporated under the laws of the United States or under the laws of any State, Territory, or possession of the United States, or by a United States postal, bank, express, or telegraph money order.

(iv) *Time for receiving and opening bids.*—Each bid shall be submitted in a securely sealed envelope. The bidder shall indicate in the upper left hand corner of the envelope his name and address and the time and place of sale as announced in the public notice of sale. A bid shall not be considered unless it is received by the internal revenue officer conducting the sale prior to the opening of the bids. The bids will be opened at the time and place stated in the notice of sale, or at the time fixed in the announcement of the adjournment of the sale.

(v) *Consideration of bids.*—The internal revenue officer conducting the sale shall have the right to waive any technical defects in a bid. After the opening, examination, and consideration of all bids, the internal revenue officer conducting the sale shall announce the amount of the highest bid or bids and the name of the successful bidder or bidders, unless in the opinion of the officer a higher price can be obtained for the property than has been bid. In the event the highest bids are equal in amount (and unless in the opinion of the internal revenue officer conducting the sale a higher price can be obtained for the property than has been bid), the officer shall determine the successful bidder by drawing lots. Any remittance submitted in connection with an unsuccessful bid shall be returned to the bidder at the conclusion of the sale.

(vi) *Withdrawal of bids.*—A bid may be withdrawn on written or telegraphic request received from the bidder prior to the time fixed for opening the bids. A technical defect in a bid confers no right on the bidder for the withdrawal of his bid after it has been opened.

(10) *Payment of bid price.*—All payments for property sold pursuant to this section shall be made by cash or by a certified, cashier's or treasurer's check drawn on any bank or trust company incorporated under the laws of the United States or under the laws of any State, Territory, or possession of the United States, or by a United States postal, bank, express, or telegraph money order. If payment in full is required upon acceptance of the highest bid, the payment shall be made at such time. If payment in full is not made at such time, the internal revenue officer conducting the sale may forthwith proceed again to sell the property in the manner provided in subparagraph (8) of this paragraph. If deferred payment is permitted, the initial payment shall be made upon acceptance of the bid, and the balance shall be paid on or before the date fixed for payment thereof. Any remittance submitted with a successful sealed bid shall be applied toward the purchase price.

(11) *Deed.*—Upon payment in full of the purchase price, the district director shall execute a quitclaim deed to the purchaser.

(c) *Lease.*—Until real estate is sold, the district director for the internal revenue district in which the property is situated may, in accordance with instructions issued by the Commissioner, lease such property.

(d) *Release to debtor.*—In cases where real estate has or may become the property of the United States by conveyance or otherwise, in payment of or as security for a debt arising under the laws relating to internal revenue, and such debt shall have been paid, together with the interest thereon (at the rate of one percent per month), to the United States within two years from the date of the acquisition of such real estate, the district director for the internal revenue district in which the property is located may release by deed or otherwise convey such real estate to the debtor from whom it was taken, or to his heirs or other legal representatives. If property is declared purchased by the United States under section 6335, then, for the purpose of this paragraph, the date of such declaration shall be deemed to be the date of acquisition of such real estate.

(e) *Accounting.*—The district director for the internal revenue district in which the property is situated shall, in accordance with section 7809 and the instructions thereunder, account for the proceeds of all sales or leases of the property and all expenses connected with the maintenance, sale, or lease of the property.

(f) *Authority of Commissioner.*—Notwithstanding the other paragraphs of this section, the Commissioner may, when he deems it advisable, take charge of and assume responsibility for any real estate to which this section is applicable. In such case, the Commissioner will notify in writing the district director for the internal revenue district in which the property is situated. In any case where a single parcel of real estate is situated in more than one internal revenue district, the Commissioner may designate in writing a district director who shall have charge of and be responsible for the entire property. [Reg. § 301.7506-1.]

☐ [*T.D. 6232, 5-2-57. Amended by T.D. 7027, 2-26-70 and T.D. 7305, 3-14-74.*]

**[Reg. § 301.7507-1]**

**§ 301.7507-1. Banks and trust companies covered.**—(a) Section 7507 applies to any national bank, or bank or trust company organized under State law, a substantial portion of the business of which

consists of receiving deposits and making loans and discounts, and which has—

(1) Ceased to do business by reason of insolvency or bankruptcy, or

(2) Been released or discharged from its liability to its depositors for any part of their deposit claims, and the depositors have accepted in lieu thereof a lien upon its subsequent earnings or claims against its assets either (i) segregated and held by it for benefit of the depositors or (ii) transferred to an individual or corporate trustee or agent who liquidates, holds or operates the assets for the benefit of the depositors.

(b) As used in this section and §§ 301.7507-2 to 301.7507-11, inclusive:

(1) The term "bank", unless otherwise indicated by the context, means any national bank, or bank or trust company organized under State law, within the scope of section 7507.

(2) The terms "statute of limitations" and "limitations" mean all applicable provisions of law (including section 7507) which impose, change, or affect the limitations, conditions, or requirements relative to the allowance of refunds and abatements or the assessment or collection of tax, as the case may be.

(3) The term "segregated assets" includes transferred or trusteed assets, or assets set aside or earmarked, to all or a portion of which, or the proceeds of which, the depositors are absolutely or conditionally entitled.

(4) The term *ceased to do business* means the bank no longer accepts deposits or makes loans and discounts, and is winding up its affairs and is in the process of liquidating its assets to pay depositors. A bank will not be considered to have ceased to do business on account of a transaction in which the bank—

(i) Transfers assets and liabilities to a Bridge Bank in a transfer described in § 1.597-4 of this chapter;

(ii) Transfers assets and liabilities to any person in a transaction to which section 381(a) applies or in which the transferee receives property with a transferred basis;

(iii) Transfers assets or liabilities to any person in a transaction in which Federal Financial Assistance (as defined in section 597) is provided to any party to the transaction, unless all the Federal Financial Assistance is deposit insurance under § 301.7507-9(d); or

(iv) Transfers assets or liabilities to any person in a transaction similar to any transaction described in paragraphs (b)(4)(i) through (iii) of this section. This paragraph (b)(4) applies to taxable years ending on or after April 22, 1992. [Reg. § 301.7507-1.]

☐ [*T.D. 6232, 5-2-57. Amended by T.D. 6498, 10-24-60 and T.D. 8641, 12-20-95.*]

**[Reg. § 301.7507-2]**

**§ 301.7507-2. Scope of section generally.**—(a) *Purpose.*—Section 7507 is intended to assist depositors of a bank which had ceased to do business by reason of insolvency to recover their deposits, by prohibiting collection of taxes of the bank which would diminish the assets necessary for payment of its depositors and also assist depositors of banks which are in financial difficulties but which, in certain conditions, continue in business.

(b) *Requisites of application.*—In order that section 7507 shall operate in a case where the bank continues business it is necessary that the depositors shall agree to accept, in lieu of all or a part of their deposit claims as such, claims against segregated assets, or a lien upon subsequent earnings of the bank, or both. When such an agreement exists, no tax diminishing such assets or earnings, or both, otherwise available and necessary for payment of depositors, may be collected therefrom. If, under such an agreement, the depositors have the right also to look to the unsegregated assets of the bank for recovery, in whole or in part, the unsegregated assets are likewise, until they exceed the amount of the depositors' claims chargeable thereto, unavailable for tax collection. Any tax of such a bank, or part of any tax, which is once uncollectible under section 7507, cannot thereafter be collected except from any residue of segregated assets remaining after claims of depositors against such assets have been paid.

(c) *Interest.*—For the purposes of section 7507, depositors' claims include bona fide interest, either on the deposits as such, or on the claims accepted in lieu of deposits as such.

(d) *Limitations on immunity.*—Section 7507 is not primarily intended for the relief of banks as such. It does not prevent tax collection, from assets not necessary, or not available, for payment of depositors, from a bank within section 7507(a), at any time within the statute of limitations. In other words, the immunity of such a bank is not complete, but ceases whenever, within the statutory period for collection, it becomes possible to make collection without diminishing assets necessary for payment of depositors. In the case of a bank within section 7507(b), any immunity to which the bank is entitled is absolute except as to segregated assets. Any tax coming within such immunity may never be collected. With respect to segregated assets, such a bank is subject to the same rule as a bank within section 7507(a), that is to say, after claims of depositors against segregated assets have been paid, any surplus is subject, within the statute of limitations, to collection of any tax, due at any time, the collection of which was suspended by the section. The section is not for the relief of creditors other than depositors, although it may incidentally operate for their benefit. See § 301.7507-4 and paragraph (b) of § 301.7507-9. [Reg. § 301.7507-2.]

☐ [T.D. 6232, 5-2-57. Amended by T.D. 6498, 10-24-60.]

### [Reg. § 301.7507-3]

§ 301.7507-3. **Segregated or transferred assets.**—(a) *In general.*—In a case involving segregated or transferred assets, it is not necessary, for application of section 7507, that the assets shall technically constitute a trust fund. It is sufficient that segregated assets be definitely separated from other assets of the bank and that transferred assets be definitely separated both from other assets of the bank and from other assets held or owned by the trustee or agent to whom assets of the bank have been transferred; that the bank be wholly or partially released from liability for repayment of deposits as such; and that the depositors have claims against the separated assets. Any excess of separated assets, over the amount necessary for payment of such depositors will be available for tax collection after full payment of depositors' claims under the agreement against such assets. But see § 301.7507-9.

(b) *Corporate transferees.*—Where the segregated assets are transferred to a separate corporate trustee or corporate agent, the assets and earnings therefrom are within the protection of the section, until full payment of depositors' claims against such assets and earnings, no matter by whom the stock of such corporation is held, and no matter whether the assets be liquidated or operated or held for benefit of the depositors. [Reg. § 301.7507-3.]

☐ [T.D. 6232, 5-2-57. Amended by T.D. 6498, 10-24-60.]

### [Reg. § 301.7507-4]

§ 301.7507-4. **Unsegregated assets.**—(a) *Depositors' claims against assets.*—(1) Claims of depositors, to the extent that they are to be satisfied out of segregated assets, will not be considered in determining the availability of unsegregated assets for tax collection. If depositors have agreed to accept payment out of segregated assets only, collection of tax from unsegregated assets will not diminish the assets available and necessary for payment of the depositors' claims. Thus, it may be possible to collect taxes from the unsegregated assets of the bank although the segregated assets are immune under the section.

(2) If the unsegregated assets of the bank are subject to any portion of the depositors' claims, such unsegregated assets will be within the immunity of the section only to the extent necessary to satisfy the claims to which such assets are subject. Taxes will still be collectible from the unsegregated assets to the extent of the amount by which the total value of such assets exceeds the liability to depositors to be satisfied therefrom. Therefore, if, for example, in the case of a bank having a tax liability, not previously immune under the section, of $50,000, the deposit claims against the bank are in the amount of $75,000, and the assets available for satisfaction of deposit claims amount to $100,000, the $50,000 tax is collectible to the extent of the $25,000 excess of assets over deposit claims. Collection is not to be postponed until the full amount of the tax is collectible.

(b) *Depositors' claims against earnings.*—Even though under a bona fide agreement a bank has been released from depositors' claims as to unsegregated assets, if all or a portion of its earnings are subject to depositors' claims, all assets the earnings from which, in whole or part, are charged with the payment of depositors' claims, will be immune from tax collection. But see paragraph (a) of § 301.7507-5. [Reg. § 301.7507-4.]

☐ [T.D. 6232, 5-2-57.]

### [Reg. § 301.7507-5]

§ 301.7507-5. **Earnings.**—(a) *Availability for tax collection.*—Earnings of a bank within section 7507(b), whether from segregated or unsegregated assets, which are necessary for, applicable to, and actually used for, payment of depositors' claims under an agreement, are within the immunity of the section. If only a portion or percentage of income from segregated or unsegregated assets is available and necessary for payment of depositors' claims, the remaining income is available for tax collection. Earnings of the bank's first fiscal year ending after the making of the agreement not applicable to payment of depositors will be assumed to be applicable for collection of any tax due prior to subsequent to execution of the agreement. Earnings of subsequent fiscal periods from unsegregated assets not applicable to depositors' claims will be assumed to be applicable to

payment of taxes as to which immunity under the section has not previously attached. Earnings from segregated assets are available for collection of tax, whether previously uncollectible under the section or not, after depositors' claims against such assets have been paid in full. See paragraph (a) of § 301.7507-3 and paragraph (a) of § 301.7507-9.

(b) *Tax computation.*—The fact that earnings of a given year may be wholly or partly unavailable under section 7507 for collection of taxes does not exempt the income for that year, or any part thereof, from tax liability. The section affects collectibility only, and is not concerned with taxability. Accordingly, the taxpayer's income tax return shall correctly compute the tax liability, even though in the opinion of the taxpayer it is immune from tax collection under the section. The tax shall be determined with respect to the entire gross income and not merely with respect to the portion of the earnings out of which tax may be collected. As to establishment of immunity from tax collection see § 301.7507-7.

*Example.* (1) An agreement, executed in the year 1954 between a bank and its depositors, provides (i) that certain assets are to be segregated for the benefit of the depositors who have waived (as claims against unsegregated assets of the bank) a percentage of the deposits; (ii) that 40 percent of the bank's net earnings, for years beginning with 1954, from unsegregated assets, shall be paid to the depositors until the portion of their claims waived with respect to unsegregated assets of the bank has been paid; and (iii) that the unsegregated assets shall not be subject to depositors' claims. The net income of the bank for the calendar year 1954 is $10,000, $4,000 produced by the segregated, and $6,000 produced by the unsegregated assets. Such amount shall be considered the net earnings for the purpose of section 7507 in computing the portion of the earnings to be paid to depositors. The bank has an outstanding tax liability for prior years of $7,000. The income tax liability of the bank for 1954 is 30 percent of $10,000, or $3,000, making a total outstanding tax liability of $10,000. The portion of the earnings of the bank for 1954 remaining after provision for depositors is $3,600 ($6,000 less 40 percent thereof, or $2,400). It will be assumed that of the total outstanding tax liability of $10,000, $3,600 may be assessed and collected, leaving $6,400 to be collected from any excess of the segregated assets after claims of depositors against such segregated assets have been paid in full. No part of the $6,400 immune from collection from 1954 earnings may be collected thereafter from unsegregated assets of the bank or earnings therefrom, so that except for any possible surplus of the segregated assets the $6,400 is uncollectible.

(2) In the year 1955, the earnings are again $10,000, $4,000 from segregated and $6,000 from unsegregated assets, as in 1954. However, the return filed shows income of $5,000 and a tax liability of $1,500. An investigation shows the true income to be $10,000, on which the tax is $3,000. The full $3,000 will be assumed to be collectible. The $600 difference between $3,600 (the excess of earnings from unsegregated assets over the amount going to the depositors), and the $3,000 tax for 1955, is not available for collection of the tax for prior years, which became immune as described above, but may be available for collection of tax for subsequent years.

(c) No significance attaches to the selection of the years 1954 and 1955 in the example set forth in paragraph (b) of this section. The rules indicated by the example are equally applicable to subsequent or prior years not excluded by limitations. [Reg. § 301.7507-5.]

☐ [T.D. 6232, 5-2-57. Amended by T.D. 6498, 10-24-60.]

### [Reg. § 301.7507-6]

§ 301.7507-6. **Abatement and refund.**—(a) An assessment or collection, no matter when made, if contrary to section 7507, is subject to abatement or refund within the applicable statutory period of limitations.

(b) Collection from a bank within section 7507(b) which diminishes assets necessary for payment of depositors, if made prior to agreement with depositors, is not contrary to the section, and affords no ground for refund.

(c) Any abatement or refund is subject to existing statutory periods of limitation, which periods are not suspended or extended by section 7507. In order to secure a refund of any taxes paid for any taxable year during the period of immunity the bank must file claim therefor. [Reg. § 301.7507-6.]

☐ [T.D. 6232, 5-2-57.]

### [Reg. § 301.7507-7]

§ 301.7507-7. **Establishment of immunity.**—(a) The mere allegation of insolvency, or that depositors have claims against segregated or other assets or earnings, will not of itself secure immunity from tax collection. It must be affirmatively established to the satisfaction of the district director that collection of tax will be contrary to section 7507. See also § 301.7507-8.

(b) Any claim, by a bank, of immunity under section 7507(b), shall be supported by a statement, under oath or affirmation, which shall show: (1) The total of depositors' claims outstanding, and (2) separately and in detail, the amount of each of the following, and the amount of depositors' claims properly chargeable against each: (i) Segregated or transferred assets; (ii) unsegregated assets; (iii) estimated future average annual earnings and profits; (iv) amount collectible from shareholders; and (v) any other resources available for payment of depositors' claims. The detail shall show the full amount of depositors' claims chargeable against each of the items in subdivisions (i) to (v), inclusive, of this paragraph even though part or all of the amount chargeable against a particular item is also chargeable against some other item or items. There shall also be filed a copy of any agreement between the bank and its depositors, and any other agreement or document bearing on the claim of immunity. The statement shall show the basis, as "book", "market", etc., of valuation of the assets. [Reg. §301.7507-7.]

☐ [*T.D. 6232, 5-2-57. Amended by T.D. 6498, 10-24-60.*]

### [Reg. §301.7507-8]

**§301.7507-8. Procedure during immunity.**—(a) *Statements to be filed.*—As long as complete or partial immunity is claimed, a bank within section 7507(b) shall file with each income tax return a statement as required by §301.7507-7, in duplicate, and shall also file such additional statements as the district director may require. Whether or not additional statements shall be required, and the frequency thereof, will depend on the circumstances, including the financial status and apparent prospects of the bank, and the time which is available for assessment and collection. If a copy of an agreement or document has once been filed, a copy of the same agreement or document need not again be filed with a subsequent statement, if it is shown by the subsequent statement, when and where and with what return the copy was filed. In case of amendment a copy of the amendment must be filed with the return for the taxable year in which the amendment is made.

(b) *Failure to file.*—Failure of a bank to file any required statement will be treated as indicating that the bank is not entitled to immunity. [Reg. §301.7507-8.]

☐ [*T.D. 6232, 5-2-57.*]

### [Reg. §301.7507-9]

**§301.7507-9. Termination of immunity.**—(a) *In general.*—(1) In the case of a bank within section 7507(a), immunity will end whenever, and to the extent that, taxes may be assessed and collected, within the applicable limitation periods as extended by section 7507, without diminishing the assets available and necessary for payment of depositors. Immunity of a bank within section 7507(b) is terminated, as to segregated assets, whenever claims of depositors against such assets have been paid in full. See §301.7507-3. As to segregated assets, the termination of immunity is complete, and any balance remaining after payment of depositors is available, within statutory limitations, for collection of tax due at any time. However, taxes of the bank will be collectible from segregated assets only to the extent that the bank has a legal or equitable interest therein. Assets as to which there has been a complete conveyance for benefit of depositors, and the bank has bona fide been divested of all legal and equitable interest, are not available for collection of the bank's tax liability.

(2) As to unsegregated assets of a bank within section 7507(b), immunity terminates only as to taxes thereafter becoming due. When taxes are once immune from collection, the immunity as to unsegregated assets is absolute. But see paragraph (a) of §301.7507-4.

(b) *General creditors.*—While the immunity from tax collection is for protection of depositors, and not for benefit of general creditors, in some cases the immunity will not end until the assets are sufficient to cover indebtedness of creditors generally. This situation will exist where under applicable law the claims of general creditors are on a parity with those of depositors, so that to pay depositors in full it is necessary to pay all creditors in full.

(c) *Shareholder liability.*—In determining the sufficiency of the assets to satisfy the depositors' claims, shareholders' liability to the extent collectible shall be treated as available assets. See §301.7507-7.

(d) *Deposit insurance.*—Deposit insurance payable to depositors shall not be treated as an asset of the bank and shall be disregarded in determining the sufficiency of the assets to meet the claims of depositors. For taxable years ending on or after April 22, 1992, deposit insurance does not include Federal Financial Assistance (as defined in section 597) and other payments described in section 597(a) prior to its amendment by the Financial Institutions Reform, Recovery, and Enforcement Act of 1989 and, therefore, such pay-

ments must be taken into account to determine whether a bank's assets are sufficient to meet claims of depositors.

(e) *Notice by bank.*—A bank within section 7507(b), upon termination of immunity with respect to (1) earnings, (2) segregated or transferred assets, or (3) unsegregated assets, shall immediately notify the district director of internal revenue for the internal revenue district in which the taxpayer's returns were filed of such termination of immunity. See paragraph (b) of §301.7507-8.

(f) *Payment by bank.*—As immunity terminates with respect to any assets, it will be the duty of the bank, without notice from the district director, to make payment of taxes collectible from such assets. [Reg. §301.7507-9.]

☐ [*T.D. 6232, 5-2-57. Amended by T.D. 6498, 10-24-60 and T.D. 8641, 12-20-95.*]

### [Reg. §301.7507-10]

**§301.7507-10. Collection of tax after termination of immunity.**—If, in the case of a bank within section 7507(b), segregated assets (including earnings therefrom), in excess of those necessary for payment of outstanding deposits become available, such excess of segregated assets shall be applied toward satisfaction of accumulated outstanding taxes previously immune under the section, and not barred by the statute of limitations. But see §301.7507-3. Where sufficient segregated or unsegregated assets are available, statutory interest shall be collected with the tax. When unsegregated assets or earnings therefrom previously immune become available for tax collection, they will be available only for collection of taxes (including interest and other additions) becoming due after immunity ceases. See the example in paragraph (b) of §301.7507-5. [Reg. §301.7507-10.]

☐ [*T.D. 6232, 5-2-57. Amended by T.D. 6498, 10-24-60.*]

### [Reg. §301.7507-11]

**§301.7507-11. Exception of employment taxes.**—The immunity granted by section 7507 does not apply to taxes imposed by chapter 21 or chapter 23 of the Code. [Reg. §301.7507-11.]

☐ [*T.D. 6232, 5-2-57. Amended by T.D. 6498, 10-24-60.*]

### [Reg. §301.7508-1]

**§301.7508-1. Time for performing certain acts postponed by reason of service in a combat zone.**—(a) *General rule.*—The period of time that may be disregarded for performing certain acts under section 7508 applies to acts described in section 7508(a)(1) and to other acts specified in a revenue ruling, revenue procedure, notice, or other guidance published in the Internal Revenue Bulletin (see §601.601(d)(2) of this chapter).

(b) *Effective date.*—This section applies to any period for performing an act that has not expired before December 30, 1999. [Reg. §301.7508-1.]

☐ [*T.D. 8911, 12-14-2000.*]

### [Reg. §301.7508A-1]

**§301.7508A-1. Postponement of certain tax-related deadlines by reasons of a federally declared disaster or terroristic or military action.**—(a) *Scope.*—This section provides rules by which the Internal Revenue Service (IRS) may postpone deadlines for performing certain acts with respect to taxes other than taxes not administered by the IRS such as firearms tax (chapter 32, section 4181); harbor maintenance tax (chapter 36, section 4461); and alcohol and tobacco taxes (subtitle E).

(b) *Postponed deadlines.*—(1) *In general.*—In the case of a taxpayer determined by the Secretary to be affected by a federally declared disaster (as defined in section 1033(h)(3)) or a terroristic or military action (as defined in section 692(c)(2)), the Secretary may specify a postponement period (as defined in paragraph (d)(1) of this section) of up to one year that may be disregarded in determining under the internal revenue laws, in respect of any tax liability of the affected taxpayer (as defined in paragraph (d)(1) of this section)—

(i) Whether any or all of the acts described in paragraph (c) of this section were performed within the time prescribed;

(ii) The amount of interest, penalty, additional amount, or addition to the tax; and

(iii) The amount of credit or refund.

(2) *Effect of postponement period.*—When an affected taxpayer is required to perform a tax-related act by a due date that falls within the postponement period, the affected taxpayer is eligible for postponement of time to perform the act until the last day of the period. The affected taxpayer is eligible for relief from interest, penalties,

additional amounts, or additions to tax during the postponement period.

(3) *Interaction between postponement period and extensions of time to file or pay.*—(i) *In general.*—The postponement period under section 7508A runs concurrently with extensions of time to file and pay, if any, under other sections of the Internal Revenue Code.

(ii) *Original due date prior to, but extended due date within, the postponement period.*—When the original due date precedes the first day of the postponement period and the extended due date falls within the postponement period, the following rules apply. If an affected taxpayer received an extension of time to file, filing will be timely on or before the last day of the postponement period, and the taxpayer is eligible for relief from penalties or additions to tax related to the failure to file during the postponement period. Similarly, if an affected taxpayer received an extension of time to pay, payment will be timely on or before the last day of the postponement period, and the taxpayer is eligible for relief from interest, penalties, additions to tax, or additional amounts related to the failure to pay during the postponement period.

(4) *Due date not extended.*—The postponement of the deadline of a tax-related act does not extend the due date for the act, but merely allows the IRS to disregard a time period of up to one year for performance of the act. To the extent that other statutes may rely on the date a return is due to be filed, the postponement period will not change the due date of the return.

(5) *Additional relief.*—The rules of this paragraph (b) demonstrate how the IRS generally implements section 7508A. The IRS may determine, however, that additional relief to taxpayers is appropriate and may provide additional relief to the extent allowed under section 7508A. To the extent that the IRS grants additional relief, the IRS will provide specific guidance on the scope of relief in the manner provided in paragraph (e) of this section.

(c) *Acts for which a period may be disregarded.*—(1) *Acts performed by taxpayers.*—Paragraph (b) of this section applies to the following acts performed by affected taxpayers (as defined in paragraph (d)(1) of this section)—

(i) Filing any return of income tax, estate tax, gift tax, generation-skipping transfer tax, excise tax (other than firearms tax (chapter 32, section 4181); harbor maintenance tax (chapter 36, section 4461); and alcohol and tobacco taxes (subtitle E)), or employment tax (including income tax withheld at source and income tax imposed by subtitle C or any law superseded thereby);

(ii) Paying any income tax, estate tax, gift tax, generation-skipping transfer tax, excise tax (other than firearms tax (chapter 32, section 4181); harbor maintenance tax (chapter 36, section 4461); and alcohol and tobacco taxes (subtitle E)), employment tax (including income tax withheld at source and income tax imposed by subtitle C or any law superseded thereby), any installment of those taxes (including payment under section 6159 relating to installment agreements), or of any other liability to the United States in respect thereof, but not including deposits of taxes pursuant to section 6302 and the regulations under section 6302;

(iii) Making contributions to a qualified retirement plan (within the meaning of section 4974(c)) under section 219(f)(3), 404(a)(6), 404(h)(1)(B), or 404(m)(2); making distributions under section 408(d)(4); recharacterizing contributions under section 408A(d)(6); or making a rollover under section 402(c), 403(a)(4), 403(b)(8), or 408(d)(3);

(iv) Filing a petition with the Tax Court, or for review of a decision rendered by the Tax Court;

(v) Filing a claim for credit or refund of any tax;

(vi) Bringing suit upon a claim for credit or refund of any tax; and

(vii) Any other act specified in a revenue ruling, revenue procedure, notice, announcement, news release, or other guidance published in the Internal Revenue Bulletin (see § 601.601(d)(2) of this chapter).

(2) *Acts performed by the government.*—Paragraph (b) of this section applies to the following acts performed by the government—

(i) Assessing any tax;

(ii) Giving or making any notice or demand for the payment of any tax, or with respect to any liability to the United States in respect of any tax;

(iii) Collecting by the Secretary, by levy or otherwise, of the amount of any liability in respect of any tax;

(iv) Bringing suit by the United States, or any officer on its behalf, in respect of any liability in respect of any tax;

(v) Allowing a credit or refund of any tax; and

(vi) Any other act specified in a revenue ruling, revenue procedure, notice, or other guidance published in the Internal Revenue Bulletin (see § 601.601(d)(2) of this chapter).

(d) *Definitions.*—(1) *Affected taxpayer* means—

(i) Any individual whose principal residence (for purposes of section 1033(h)(4)) is located in a covered disaster area;

(ii) Any business entity or sole proprietor whose principal place of business is located in a covered disaster area;

(iii) Any individual who is a relief worker affiliated with a recognized government or philanthropic organization and who is assisting in a covered disaster area;

(iv) Any individual whose principal residence (for purposes of section 1033(h)(4)), or any business entity or sole proprietor whose principal place of business is not located in a covered disaster area, but whose records necessary to meet a deadline for an act specified in paragraph (c) of this section are maintained in a covered disaster area;

(v) Any estate or trust that has tax records necessary to meet a deadline for an act specified in paragraph (c) of this section and that are maintained in a covered disaster area;

(vi) The spouse of an affected taxpayer, solely with regard to a joint return of the husband and wife; or

(vii) Any individual, business entity, or sole proprietorship not located in a covered disaster area, but whose records necessary to meet a deadline for an act specified in paragraph (c) of this section are located in the covered disaster area;

(viii) Any individual visiting the covered disaster area who was killed or injured as a result of the disaster; or

(ix) Any other person determined by the IRS to be affected by a federally declared disaster (within the meaning of section 1033(h)(3)).

(2) *Covered disaster area* means an area of a federally declared disaster (within the meaning of section 1033(h)(3)) to which the IRS has determined paragraph (b) of this section applies.

(3) *Postponement period* means the period of time (up to one year) that the IRS postpones deadlines for performing tax-related acts under section 7508A.

(e) *Notice of postponement of certain acts.*—If a tax-related deadline is postponed under section 7508A and this section, the IRS will publish a revenue ruling, revenue procedure, notice, announcement, news release, or other guidance (see § 601.601(d)(2) of this chapter) describing the acts postponed, the postponement period, and the location of the covered disaster area. Guidance under this paragraph (e) will be published as soon as practicable after the occurrence of a terrorist or military action or declaration of a federally declared disaster.

(f) *Examples.*—The rules of this section are illustrated by the following examples:

*Example 1.* (i) Corporation X, a calendar year taxpayer, has its principal place of business in County M in State W. Pursuant to a timely filed request for extension of time to file, Corporation X's 2008 Form 1120, "U.S. Corporation Income Tax Return," is due on September 15, 2009. Also due on September 15, 2009, is Corporation X's third quarter estimated tax payment for 2009. Corporation X's 2009 third quarter Form 720, "Quarterly Federal Excise Tax Return," and third quarter Form 941, "Employer's Quarterly Federal Tax Return," are due on October 31, 2009. In addition, Corporation X has an employment tax deposit due on September 15, 2009.

(ii) On September 1, 2009, a hurricane strikes County M in State W. On September 7, 2009, certain counties in State W (including County M) are determined to be disaster areas within the meaning of section 1033(h)(3) that are eligible for assistance by the Federal government under the Stafford Act. Also on September 7, 2009, the IRS determines that County M in State W is a covered disaster area and publishes guidance announcing that the time period for affected taxpayers to file returns, pay taxes, and perform other time-sensitive acts falling on or after September 1, 2009, and on or before November 30, 2009, has been postponed to November 30, 2009, pursuant to section 7508A.

(iii) Because Corporation X's principal place of business is in County M, Corporation X is an affected taxpayer. Accordingly, Corporation X's 2008 Form 1120 will be timely if filed on or before November 30, 2009. Corporation X's 2009 third quarter estimated tax payment will be timely if made on or before November 30, 2009. In addition, pursuant to paragraph (c) of this section, Corporation X's 2009 third quarter Form 720 and third quarter Form 941 will be timely if filed on or before November 30, 2009. However, because deposits of taxes are excluded from the scope of paragraph (c) of this section, Corporation X's employment tax deposit is due on September 15, 2009. In addition, Corporation X's deposits relating to the third quarter Form 720 are not postponed. Absent reasonable cause, Corporation X is subject to the failure to deposit penalty under section 6656 and accrual of interest.

*Example 2.* The facts are the same as in *Example 1*, except that because of the severity of the hurricane, the IRS determines that postponement of government acts is necessary. During 2009, Corporation X's 2005 Form 1120 is being examined by the IRS. Pursuant to a timely filed request for extension of time to file, Corporation X timely filed its 2005 Form 1120 on September 15, 2006. Without application of this section, the statute of limitation on assessment for the 2005 income tax year will expire on September 15, 2009. However, pursuant to paragraph (c) of this section, assessment of tax is one of the government acts for which up to one year may be disregarded. Because September 15, 2009, falls within the period in which government acts are postponed, the statute of limitation on assessment for Corporation X's 2005 income tax will expire on November 30, 2009. Because Corporation X did not timely file an extension of time to pay, payment of its 2005 income tax was due on March 15, 2006. As such, Corporation X will be subject to the failure to pay penalty and related interest beginning on March 15, 2006. The due date for payment of Corporation X's 2005 income tax preceded the postponement period. Therefore, Corporation X is not entitled to the suspension of interest or penalties during the disaster period with respect to its 2005 income tax liability.

*Example 3.* The facts are the same as in *Example 2*, except that the examination of the 2005 taxable year was completed earlier in 2009, and on July 28, 2009, the IRS mailed a statutory notice of deficiency to Corporation X. Without application of this section, Corporation X has 90 days (or until October 26, 2009) to file a petition with the Tax Court. However, pursuant to paragraph (c) of this section, filing a petition with the Tax Court is one of the taxpayer acts for which a period of up to one year may be disregarded. Because Corporation X is an affected taxpayer, Corporation X's petition to the Tax Court will be timely if filed on or before November 30, 2009, the last day of the postponement period.

*Example 4.* (i) H and W, individual calendar year taxpayers, intend to file a joint Form 1040, "U.S. Individual Income Tax Return," for the 2008 taxable year and are required to file a Schedule H, "Household Employment Taxes." The joint return is due on April 15, 2009. H and W's principal residence is in County M in State Q.

(ii) On April 2, 2009, a severe ice storm strikes County M. On April 5, 2009, certain counties in State Q (including County M) are determined to be disaster areas within the meaning of section 1033(h)(3) that are eligible for assistance by the Federal government under the Stafford Act. Also on April 5, 2009, the IRS determines that County M in State Q is a covered disaster area and publishes guidance announcing that the time period for affected taxpayers to file returns, pay taxes, and perform other time-sensitive acts falling on or after April 2, 2009, and on or before June 2, 2009, has been postponed to June 2, 2009.

(iii) Because H and W's principal residence is in County M, H and W are affected taxpayers. April 15, 2009, the due date for the filing of H and W's 2008 Form 1040 and Schedule H, falls within the postponement period described in the IRS published guidance. Thus, H and W's return will be timely if filed on or before June 2, 2009. If H and W request an extension of time to file under section 6081 on or before June 2, 2009, the extension is deemed to have been filed by April 15, 2009. Thus, H and W's return will be timely if filed on or before October 15, 2009.

(iv) April 15, 2009, is also the due date for the payment due on the return. This date falls within the postponement period described in the IRS published guidance. Thus, the payment of tax due with the return will be timely if paid on or before June 2, 2009, the last day of the postponement period. If H and W fail to pay the tax due on the 2008 Form 1040 by June 2, 2009, and do not receive an extension of time to pay under section 6161, H and W will be subject to failure to pay penalties and accrual of interest beginning on June 3, 2009.

*Example 5.* (i) H and W, residents of County D in State G, intend to file an amended return to request a refund of 2008 taxes. H and W timely filed their 2008 income tax return on April 15, 2009. Under section 6511(a), H and W's amended 2008 tax return must be filed on or before April 16, 2012 (because April 15, 2012, falls on a Sunday, H and W's amended return was due to be filed on April 16, 2012).

(ii) On April 2, 2012, an earthquake strikes County D. On April 6, 2012, certain counties in State G (including County D) are determined to be disaster areas within the meaning of section 1033(h)(3) that are eligible for assistance by the Federal government under the Stafford Act. Also on April 6, 2012, the IRS determines that County D in State G is a covered disaster area and publishes guidance announcing that the time period for affected taxpayers to file returns, pay taxes, and perform other time-sensitive acts falling on or after April 2, 2012, and on or before October 2, 2012, has been postponed to October 2, 2012.

(iii) Under paragraph (c) of this section, filing a claim for refund of tax is one of the taxpayer acts for which the IRS may disregard a period of up to one year. The postponement period for this disaster begins on April 2, 2012, and ends on October 2, 2012. Accordingly, H

and W's claim for refund for 2008 taxes will be timely if filed on or before October 2, 2012. Moreover, in applying the lookback period in section 6511(b)(2)(A), which limits the amount of the allowable refund, the period from October 2, 2012, back to April 2, 2012, is disregarded under paragraph (b)(1)(iii) of this section. Thus, if the claim is filed on or before October 2, 2012, amounts deemed paid on April 15, 2009, under section 6513(b), such as estimated tax and tax withheld from wages, will have been paid within the lookback period of section 6511(b)(2)(A).

*Example 6.* (i) A is an unmarried, calendar year taxpayer whose principal residence is located in County W in State Q. A intends to file a Form 1040 for the 2008 taxable year. The return is due on April 15, 2009. A timely files Form 4868, "Application for Automatic Extension of Time to File U.S. Individual Income Tax Return." Due to A's timely filing of Form 4868, the extended filing deadline for A's 2008 tax return is October 15, 2009. Because A timely requested an extension of time to file, A will not be subject to the failure to file penalty under section 6651(a)(1), if A files the 2008 Form 1040 on or before October 15, 2009. However, A failed to pay the tax due on the return by April 15, 2009, and did not receive an extension of time to pay under section 6161. Absent reasonable cause, A is subject to the failure to pay penalty under section 6651(a)(2) and accrual of interest.

(ii) On September 30, 2009, a blizzard strikes County W. On October 5, 2009, certain counties in State Q (including County W) are determined to be disaster areas within the meaning of section 1033(h)(3) that are eligible for assistance by the Federal government under the Stafford Act. Also on October 5, 2009, the IRS determines that County W in State Q is a covered disaster area and announces that the time period for affected taxpayers to file returns, pay taxes, and perform other time-sensitive acts falling on or after September 30, 2009, and on or before December 2, 2009, has been postponed to December 2, 2009.

(iii) Because A's principal residence is in County W, A is an affected taxpayer. Because October 15, 2009, the extended due date to file A's 2008 Form 1040, falls within the postponement period described in the IRS's published guidance, A's return is timely if filed on or before December 2, 2009. However, the payment due date, April 15, 2009, preceded the postponement period. Thus, A will continue to be subject to failure to pay penalties and accrual of interest during the postponement period.

*Example 7.* (i) H and W, individual calendar year taxpayers, intend to file a joint Form 1040 for the 2008 taxable year. The joint return is due on April 15, 2009. After credits for taxes withheld on wages and estimated tax payments, H and W owe tax for the 2008 taxable year. H and W's principal residence is in County J in State W.

(ii) On March 3, 2009, severe flooding strikes County J. On March 6, 2009, certain counties in State W (including County J) are determined to be disaster areas within the meaning of section 1033(h)(3) that are eligible for assistance by the Federal government under the Stafford Act. Also on March 6, 2009, the IRS determines that County J in State W is a covered disaster area and publishes guidance announcing that the time period for affected taxpayers to file returns, pay taxes, and perform other time-sensitive acts falling on or after March 3, 2009, and on or before June 1, 2009, has been postponed to June 1, 2009.

(iii) Because H and W's principal residence is in County J, H and W are affected taxpayers. April 15, 2009, the due date for filing the 2008 joint return, falls within the postponement period described in the IRS published guidance. Therefore, H and W's joint return without extension will be timely if filed on or before June 1, 2009. Similarly, H and W's 2008 income taxes will be timely paid if paid on or before June 1, 2009.

(iv) On April 30, 2009, H and W timely file Form 4868, "Application for Automatic Extension of Time to File U.S. Individual Income Tax Return." H and W's extension will be deemed to have been filed on April 15, 2009. Thus, H and W's 2008 income tax return will be timely if filed on or before October 15, 2009.

(v) H and W did not request or receive an extension of time to pay. Therefore, the payment of tax due with the 2008 joint return will be timely if paid on or before June 1, 2009. If H and W fail to pay the tax due on the 2008 joint return by June 1, 2009, H and W will be subject to failure to pay penalties and accrual of interest beginning on June 2, 2009.

*Example 8.* (i) H and W, individual calendar year taxpayers, entered into an installment agreement with respect to their 2006 tax liabilities. H and W's installment agreement required H and W to make regularly scheduled installment payments on the 15th day of the month for the next 60 months. H and W's principal residence is in County K in State X.

(ii) On May 1, 2009, severe flooding strikes County K. On May 5, 2009, certain counties in State X including County K) are determined by the Federal government to be disaster areas within the meaning of section 1033(h)(3), and are eligible for assistance under the Stafford Act. Also on May 5, 2009, the IRS determines that County K in State

X is a covered disaster area and publishes guidance announcing that the time period for affected taxpayers to file returns, pay taxes, and perform other time-sensitive acts falling on or after May 1, 2009, and on or before July 1, 2009, has been postponed to July 1, 2009.

(iii) Because H and W's principal residence is in County K, H and W are affected taxpayers. Pursuant to the IRS's grant of relief under section 7508A, H and W's installment agreement payments that become due during the postponement period are suspended until after the postponement period has ended. H and W will be required to resume payments no later than August 15, 2009. Skipped payments will be tacked on at the end of the installment payment period. Because the installment agreement pertains to prior year tax liabilities, interest and penalties will continue to accrue. H and W may, however, be entitled to abatement of the failure to pay penalties incurred during the postponement period upon establishing reasonable cause.

(g) *Effective/applicability date.*—This section applies to disasters declared after January 15, 2009. [Reg. § 301.7508A-1.]

☐ [*T.D.* 8911, 12-14-2000 (*corrected* 2-14-2001). *Amended by T.D.* 9443, 1-14-2009 (*corrected* 12-16-2009).]

### [Reg. § 301.7510-1]

**§ 301.7510-1. Exemption from tax of domestic goods purchased for the United States.**—For any regulations under section 7510, see the applicable regulations with respect to the various taxes. [Reg. § 301.7510-1.]

☐ [*T.D.* 6232, 5-2-57.]

### [Reg. § 301.7512-1]

**§ 301.7512-1. Separate accounting for certain collected taxes.**— (a) *Scope.*—The provisions of section 7512 and this section apply to—

(1) The following taxes imposed by subtitle C of the Code in respect of wages or compensation paid after February 11, 1958, for pay periods beginning after such date:

(i) The employee tax imposed by section 3101 of chapter 21 (Federal Insurance Contributions Act),

(ii) The employee tax imposed by section 3201 of chapter 22 (Railroad Retirement Tax Act), and

(iii) The income tax required to be withheld on wages by section 3402 of chapter 24 (Collection of Income Tax at Source on Wages); and

(2) The following taxes imposed by chapter 33 of the Code in respect of taxable payments made, except as otherwise specifically provided in this subparagraph, after February 11, 1958:

(i) The taxes imposed by section 4231(1), (2), and (3) on amounts paid for admissions, and the tax imposed by section 4231(6) on amounts paid for admission, refreshment, service, or merchandise, at any roof garden, cabaret, or other similar place, to the extent that such tax on amounts paid on or after January 1, 1959, is required to be collected by the proprietor of the roof garden, cabaret, or similar place from a concessionaire in such establishment,

(ii) The taxes imposed by section 4241 on amounts paid as club dues,

(iii) The taxes imposed by section 4251 on amounts paid for communications services or facilities,

(iv) The tax imposed by section 4261 on amounts paid for transportation of persons and the tax imposed by section 4271 on amounts paid before August 1, 1958, for the transportation of property, and

(v) The tax imposed by section 4286 on amounts collected for the use of safe deposit boxes.

(b) *Requirement.*—If the district director determines that any person required to collect, account for, and pay over any tax described in paragraph (a) of this section has, at the time and in the manner prescribed by law or regulations, failed to collect, truthfully account for, or pay over any such tax, or make deposits, payments, or returns of any such tax, such person, if notified to do so by the district director in accordance with section 7512 and paragraph (d) of this section, shall—

(1) Collect, at the times and in the manner provided by the law and the regulations in respect of the various taxes described in paragraph (a) of this section, all of the taxes described in such paragraph which become collectible by him after receipt of such notice;

(2) Deposit the taxes so collected, not later than the end of the second banking day after collection, with a bank, as defined in section 581, in a separate account established in accordance with paragraph (c) of this section; and

(3) Keep in such account the taxes so deposited until payment thereof is made to the United States as required by the law and the regulations in respect of such taxes.

The separate accounting requirements contained in subparagraphs (1), (2), and (3) of this paragraph are applicable, in the case of the taxes described in paragraph (a)(1) of this section, to taxes with respect to wages or compensation paid after receipt of the notice from the district director, irrespective of whether such wages or compensation was earned prior to or after receipt of the notice; and, in the case of the taxes described in paragraph (a)(2) of this section, to taxes with respect to taxable payments made after receipt of the notice from the district director, irrespective of whether the transactions with respect to which such payments were made occurred prior to or after receipt of the notice.

(c) *Trust fund account.*—The separate bank account referred to in paragraph (b) of this section shall be established under the designation, "(Name of person required to establish account), Trustee, Special Fund in Trust for U.S. under sec. 7512, I.R.C.". The taxes deposited in such account shall constitute a fund in trust for the United States payable only to the Internal Revenue Service on demand by the trustee.

(d) *Notice.*—Notice to any person requiring his compliance with the provisions of section 7512(b) and this section shall be in writing and shall be delivered in hand to such person by an internal revenue officer or employee. In the case of a trade or business carried on other than as a sole proprietorship, such as a corporation, partnership, or trust, notice delivered in hand to an officer, partner, or trustee shall be deemed to be notice delivered in hand to such corporation, partnership, or trust and to all officers, partners, trustees, and employees thereof.

(e) *Cancellation of notice.*—The district director may relieve a person to whom notice requiring separate accounting has been given pursuant to section 7512 and this section from further compliance with such separate accounting requirements whenever he is satisfied that such person will comply with all requirements of the Code and the regulations applicable, in respect of the taxes to which the notice relates, in the case of persons not required to comply with the provisions of section 7512(b). Notice of cancellation of the requirement for separate accounting shall be made in writing and shall take effect at such time as is specified in the notice of cancellation.

(f) *Penalties.*—For criminal penalty for failure to comply with any provision of section 7512, see section 7215. For criminal penalties for failure to file return, supply information, or pay tax, for failure to collect or pay over tax, and for attempt to evade or defeat tax, see sections 7203, 7202, and 7201, respectively. [Reg. § 301.7512-1.]

☐ [*T.D.* 6299, 6-30-58. *Amended by T.D.* 6444, 1-14-60.]

### [Reg. § 301.7513-1]

**§ 301.7513-1. Reproduction of returns and other documents.**— (a) *In general.*—The Commissioner, district directors, and other authorized officers and employees of the Internal Revenue Service may contract with any Federal agency or any person to have such agency or person process films and other photoimpressions of any return, statement, document, or of any card, record, or other matter, and make reproductions from such films and photoimpressions.

(b) *Safeguards.*—(1) *By private contractor.*—Any person entering into a contract with the Internal Revenue Service for the performance of any of the services described in paragraph (a) of this section shall agree to comply, and to assume responsibility for compliance by his employees, with the following requirements:

(i) The films or photoimpressions, and reproductions made therefrom, shall be used only for the purpose of carrying out the provisions of the contract, and information contained in such material shall be treated as confidential and shall not be divulged or made known in any manner to any person except as may be necessary in the performance of the contract;

(ii) All the services shall be performed under the supervision of the person with whom the contract is made or his responsible employees;

(iii) All material received for processing and all processed and reproduced material shall be kept in a locked and fireproof compartment in a secure place when not being worked upon;

(iv) All spoilage of reproductions made from the film or photoimpressions supplied to the contractor shall be destroyed, and a statement under the penalties of perjury shall be submitted to the Internal Revenue Service that such destruction has been accomplished; and

(v) All film, photoimpressions, and reproductions made therefrom, shall be transmitted to the Internal Revenue Service by personal delivery, first-class mail, parcel post, or express.

(2) *By Federal agency.*—Any Federal agency entering into a contract with the Internal Revenue Service for the performance of any services described in paragraph (a) of this section, shall treat as

confidential all material processed or reproduced pursuant to such contract.

(3) *Inspection.*—The Internal Revenue Service shall have the right to send its officers and employees into the offices and plants of Federal agencies and other contractors for inspection of the facilities and operations provided for the performance of any work contracted or to be contracted for under this section.

(4) *Criminal sanctions.*—For penalty provisions relating to the unauthorized use and disclosure of information in violation of the provisions of this section, see section 7213(c).

(c) *Legal status of reproductions.*—Section 7513 provides that any reproduction made in accordance with such section of any return, document, or other matter shall have the same legal status as the original and requires that any such reproduction shall, if properly authenticated, be admissible in evidence in any judicial or administrative proceeding, as if it were the original, whether or not the original is in existence. [Reg. §301.7513-1.]

☐ [*T.D. 6444, 1-14-60. Amended by T.D. 6498, 10-24-60.*]

**[Reg. §301.7514-1]**

**§301.7514-1. Seals of office.**—(a) *Establishment of seals.*—(1) *Commissioner of Internal Revenue.*—There is hereby established in and for the office of the Commissioner of Internal Revenue an official seal. The seal is described as follows, and illustrated below: A circle within which shall appear that part of the seal of the Treasury Department represented by the shield and side wreaths. Exterior to this circle and within a circumscribed circle in the form of a rope shall appear in the upper part the words "OFFICE OF" and in the lower part the words "COMMISSIONER OF INTERNAL REVENUE."

(2) *Establishment of uniform seal.*—(i) In addition to the seals of office prescribed for those offices set forth in paragraphs (a)(3) through (8) of this section, a uniform seal for use by any office of internal revenue is established. The uniform seal is described as follows, and is illustrated in this paragraph (a)(2)(i). A circle within which shall appear that part of the seal of the Treasury Department represented by the shield with a dark background. Exterior to this circle and within a circumscribed circle forming the exterior of the seal shall appear words describing the specific office of internal revenue authorized to use the seal under this section. This paragraph (a)(2) is effective on October 27, 1995. The uniform seal is as follows:

(ii) The uniform seal may be used by any office of internal revenue set forth in paragraphs (a)(3) through (8) of this section, and any other office designated by the Commissioner to use a seal, including the following internal revenue offices resulting from a reorganization of the IRS that will be implemented beginning October 1, 1995:

*Office of Regional Commissioner for:*
  Midstates Region (Dallas)
  Northeast Region (Manhattan)
  Southeast Region (Atlanta)
  Western Region (San Francisco)
*Office of District Director for:*
  Arkansas-Oklahoma District (Oklahoma City)
  Brooklyn District
  Central California District (San Jose)
  Connecticut-Rhode Island District (Hartford)
  Delaware-Maryland District (Baltimore)
  Georgia District (Atlanta)
  Gulf Coast District (New Orleans)
  Houston District
  Illinois District (Chicago)
  Indiana District (Indianapolis)
  Kansas-Missouri District (St. Louis)
  Kentucky-Tennessee District (Nashville)
  Los Angeles District
  Manhattan District
  Michigan District (Detroit)
  Midwest District (Milwaukee)
  New Jersey District (Newark)
  New England District (Boston)
  North Central District (St. Paul)
  North Florida District (Jacksonville)
  North-South Carolina District (Greensboro)
  North Texas District (Dallas)
  Northern California District (Oakland)
  Ohio District (Cincinnati)
  Pacific-Northwest District (Seattle)
  Pennsylvania District (Philadelphia)
  Rocky Mountain District (Denver)
  South Florida District (Fort Lauderdale)
  South Texas District (Austin)
  Southern California District (Laguna Niguel)
  Southwest District (Phoenix)
  Upstate New York District (Buffalo)
  Virginia-West Virginia District (Richmond)
*Office of Director of Computing Centers in:*
  Detroit                 Martinsburg
  Memphis
*Office of Director of Submission Processing Centers in:*
  Austin                  Kansas City
  Cincinnati              Ogden
  Memphis
*Office of Director of Customer Service Centers in:*
  Andover                 Jacksonville
  Atlanta                 Kansas City
  Austin                  Memphis
  Baltimore               Nashville
  Brookhaven              Ogden
  Buffalo                 Philadelphia
  Cincinnati              Pittsburgh
  Cleveland               Portland, OR
  Dallas                  Richmond
  Denver                  St. Louis
  Fresno                  Seattle.
  Indianapolis

(3) *District directors of internal revenue.*—(i) There is hereby established an official seal in and for each of the offices of district director of internal revenue listed in subdivision (ii) of this subparagraph. The seal is described as follows, and one such seal is illustrated below: A circle within which shall appear that part of the seal of the Treasury Department represented by the shield and side wreaths. Exterior to this circle and within a circumscribed circle in the form of a rope shall appear in the upper part the words "DISTRICT DIRECTOR OF INTERNAL REVENUE" and in the lower part the location of the office for which the seal is established.

(ii) The offices of district director of internal revenue for which seals are established in subdivision (i) of this subparagraph are as follows:

* * *

[Asterisks represent list of District Directors' offices.]

(iii) There is hereby established an official seal in and for each of the offices of district director of internal revenue listed in paragraph (a)(2)(iv) of this section. The seal is described as follows, and one such seal is illustrated below: A circle within which shall appear that part of the seal of the Treasury Department represented by the shield. Exterior to this circle and within a circumscribed circle in the form of a rope shall appear in the upper part the words "DISTRICT DIRECTOR OF INTERNAL REVENUE" and in the lower part the location of the office for which the seal is established.

(iv) The offices of district director of internal revenue for which seals are established in paragraph (a)(2)(iii) of this section are as follows:

District Director of Internal Revenue, Laguna Niguel, CA.,

District Director of Internal Revenue, Sacramento, CA.,

District Director of Internal Revenue, San Jose Dist.

(v) There is hereby established an official seal in and for the office of district director of internal revenue listed in paragraph (a)(2)(vi) of this section. The seal is described as follows, and illustrated below: A circle within which shall appear the Internal Revenue emblem. Exterior to this circle and within a circumscribed circle in the form of a rope shall appear in the upper part the words "DISTRICT DIRECTOR OF INTERNAL REVENUE" and in the lower part the location of the office for which the seal is established.

(vi) The office of district director of internal revenue for which the seal is established in paragraph (a)(2)(v) of this section is as follows:
District Director of Internal Revenue, Las Vegas, Nevada.

(4) *Assistant Commissioner (International).*—There is hereby established in and for the office of the Assistant Commissioner (International) an official seal. The seal is described as follows, and illustrated below: A circle within which shall appear that part of the seal of the Treasury Department represented by the shield and side wreaths. Exterior to this circle and within a circumscribed circle in the form of a rope shall appear in the upper part the words "ASSISTANT COMMISSIONER (INTERNATIONAL)" and in the lower part "Washington, D.C. Internal Revenue Service".

(5) *Regional commissioners of internal revenue.*—(i) There is hereby established an official seal in and for each of the offices of regional commissioner of internal revenue listed in subdivision (ii) of this subparagraph. The seal is described as follows, and one such seal is illustrated below: A circle within which shall appear that part of the seal of the Treasury Department represented by the shield and side wreaths. Exterior to this circle and within a circumscribed circle in the form of a rope shall appear in the upper part the words "REGIONAL COMMISSIONER OF INTERNAL REVENUE" and in the lower part the title of the region for which the seal is established.

(ii) The offices of the regional commissioner of internal revenue for which seals are established in subdivision (i) of this subparagraph are as follows:

Regional Commissioner of Internal Revenue, Central Region.

Regional Commissioner of Internal Revenue, Mid-Atlantic Region.

Regional Commissioner of Internal Revenue, Midwest Region.

Regional Commissioner of Internal Revenue, North-Atlantic Region.

Regional Commissioner of Internal Revenue, Southeast Region.

Regional Commissioner of Internal Revenue, Southwest Region.

Regional Commissioner of Internal Revenue, Western Region.

(6) *Directors of internal revenue service centers.*—(i) There is hereby established an official seal in and for each of the offices of director of internal revenue service center listed in subdivision (ii) of this subparagraph. The seal is described as follows, and one such seal is illustrated below: A circle within which shall appear that part of the seal of the Treasury Department represented by the shield and side wreaths. Exterior to this circle and within a circumscribed circle in the form of a rope shall appear in the upper part the words "DIRECTOR, INTERNAL REVENUE SERVICE CENTER" and in the lower part the name of the region and the name of the principal city in or near which the service center is located.

(ii) The offices of director of internal revenue service center for which seals are established in subdivision (i) of this subparagraph are as follows:

Director, Internal Revenue Service Center, Central Region, Covington, Ky.

Director, Internal Revenue Service Center, Mid-Atlantic Region, Philadelphia, Pa.

Director, Internal Revenue Service Center, Midwest Region, Kansas City, Mo.

Director, Internal Revenue Service Center, North-Atlantic Region, Andover, Mass.

Director, Internal Revenue Service Center, North-Atlantic Region, Brookhaven, N.Y.

Director, Internal Revenue Service Center, Southeast Region, Chamblee, Ga.

Director, Internal Revenue Service Center, Southeast Region, Memphis, Tenn.

Director, Internal Revenue Service Center, Southwest Region, Austin, Tex.

Director, Internal Revenue Service Center, Western Region, Fresno, Calif.

Director, Internal Revenue Service Center, Southwest Region, Ogden, Utah.

(7) *Director of Internal Revenue Computing Center.*—There is hereby established in and for the office of the Director of the Internal Revenue Computing Center an official seal. The seal is described as follows, and illustrated below: A circle within which shall appear that part of the seal of the Treasury Department represented by the shield. Exterior to this circle and within a circumscribed circle in the form of a rope shall appear in the upper part the words "DIRECTOR, INTERNAL REVENUE SERVICE" and in the lower part "Detroit Computing Center Detroit, Michigan".

(8) *Director of Internal Revenue Compliance Center.*—There is hereby established in and for the office of the Director of the Internal Revenue Compliance Center an official seal. The seal is described as follows, and illustrated below: A circle within which shall appear that part of the seal of the Treasury Department represented by the shield and side wreaths. Exterior to this circle and within a circumscribed circle in the form of a rope shall appear in the upper part the words "DIRECTOR, INTERNAL REVENUE COMPLIANCE CENTER" and in the lower part "Southwest Region Austin, Tex".

(b) *Custody of seal.*—Each seal established by this section shall be in the custody of the officer for whose office such seal is established.

(c) *Use of official seal.*—Each seal of office established by this section may be affixed in lieu of the seal of the Treasury Department to any certificate or attestation required to be made by the officer for whose office such seal is established in authentication of originals and copies of books, records, papers, writings, and documents of the Internal Revenue Service in the custody of such officer, for all purposes, including the purposes of 28 U.S.C. 1733(b), Rule 44 of the Federal Rules of Civil Procedure, and Rule 27 of the Federal Rules of Criminal Procedure, except that—

(1) No such seal shall be affixed to material to be published in the Federal Register, and

(2) The seal of the office of a district director of internal revenue or the Director of International Operations shall not be affixed to the certification of copies of books, records, papers, writings, or documents in his custody in any case in which, pursuant to Executive order, Treasury decision, or Part 601 of this chapter (Statement of Procedural Rules), such copies may be furnished to applicants only by the Commissioner.

(d) *Judicial notice.*—In accordance with the provisions of section 7514, judicial notice shall be taken of the seals established under this section. [Reg. §301.7514-1.]

☐ [*T.D.* 6422, 10-28-59. *Amended by T.D.* 6442, 1-5-60; *T.D.* 6498, 10-24-60; *T.D.* 6585, 12-27-61; *T.D.* 6626, 12-26-62; *T.D.* 6698, 12-27-63; *T.D.* 6833, 7-6-65; *T.D.* 6974, 10-2-68; *T.D.* 7147, 10-22-71, *T.D.* 8414, 4-23-92; *and T.D.* 8625, 10-26-95.]

**[Reg. §301.7516-1]**

**§301.7516-1. Training and training aids on request.**—The Commissioner is authorized, within his discretion, upon written request, to admit employees and officials of any State, the Commonwealth of

Puerto Rico, any possession of the United States, any political subdivision or instrumentality of any of the foregoing, the District of Columbia, or any foreign government to training courses conducted by the Internal Revenue Service, and to supply them with texts and other training aids. Requests for such training or training aids should be addressed to the Commissioner of Internal Revenue, Washington, D.C. 20224, Attention: A: T, except that requests involving officials or visitors of foreign governments should be addressed to the Commissioner of Internal Revenue, Washington, D.C. 20224, Attention: C: FA. The Commissioner may require payment from the party or parties making the request of a reasonable fee not to exceed the cost of the training and training aids supplied pursuant to such request. [Reg. § 301.7516-1.]

☐ [*T.D. 6713, 3-23-64. Amended by T.D. 6790, 1-4-65.*]

### [Reg. § 301.7517-1]

**§ 301.7517-1. Furnishing on request of statement explaining estate or gift valuation.**—(a) *In general.*—Section 7517 requires the Service to furnish to a taxpayer, at the request of that taxpayer, a statement explaining the estate, gift or generation-skipping transfer valuation of any item contained on a return filed by the taxpayer as to which a determination or proposed determination of value has been made. The request must be filed no later than the latest time to file a claim for refund of the tax which is dependent on the value with respect to which the determination has been made. The request should be filed with the district director's office that has jurisdiction over the return of the taxpayer.

(b) *Effective date.*—(1) *Estates of decedents.*—Section 7517 applies to estates of decedents dying after December 31, 1976.

(2) *Gifts.*—Section 7517 applies to gifts made after December 31, 1976.

(3) *Generation-skipping transfer.*—Section 7517 applies to any generation-skipping transfer subject to chapter 13 [Reg. § 301.7517-1.]

☐ [*T.D. 7757, 1-16-81.*]

### [Reg. § 1.7519-0T]

**§ 1.7519-0T. Table of contents (temporary).**—This section lists the captions that appear in the temporary regulations under section 7519.

[Temporary Reg. § 1.7519-0T.]

☐ [*T.D. 8205, 5-24-88.*]

### [Reg. § 1.7519-1T]

**§ 1.7519-1T. Required payments for entities electing not to have required year (temporary).**—(a) *In general.*—(1) *Applicability.*—This section applies to any taxable year that a partnership or S corporation has an election under section 444 in effect (an "applicable election year").

(2) *Returns and required payments.*—For each applicable election year, a partnership or S corporation must—

(i) File a return as provided in § 1.7519-2T (a)(2), and

(ii) Make a required payment (as defined in paragraph (a)(3) of this section) as provided in § 1.7519-2T.

However, if the required payment for an applicable election year is not more than $500 and the partnership or S corporation has not been required to make a required payment for a prior year, the partnership or S corporation should not make a required payment for such applicable election year.

(3) *Required payment.*—The term "required payment" means, with respect to any applicable election year, an amount equal to the excess of—

(i) The product of the applicable percentage of the adjusted highest section 1 rate, multiplied by the net base year income (as defined in paragraph (b)(5) of this section) of the entity, over

(ii) The cumulative amount of required payments actually made for all preceding applicable election years (reduced by the cumulative amount of such payments refundable under section 7519(c) for all such preceding years).

Furthermore, the amount of the required payment is determined without regard to the required payment of any other partnership or S corporation. See example (3) in paragraph (d) of this section.

(4) *Examples.*—The provisions of paragraph (a) of this section may be illustrated by the following examples.

*Example (1).* A, a partnership, makes a section 444 election to retain its taxable year ending September 30. For A's first applicable election year, A's required payment, as defined in paragraph (a)(3) of this section, is $400. Thus, A does not have to make a required payment for that year. However, A is required to file the return prescribed by § 1.7519-2T (a)(2).

*Example (2).* The facts are the same as in example (1), and, in addition to those facts, for A's second applicable election year, the amount determined under paragraph (a)(3)(i) of this section is $800. Because A did not actually make a required payment for A's first applicable election year, A's required payment is $800 for its second applicable election year. Since the required payment is greater than $500, A must make a required payment for its second applicable election year. Furthermore, A must file the return prescribed by §1.7519-2T (a)(2).

*Example (3).* The facts are the same as in example (2), and, in addition to those facts, for A's third applicable election year, the amount determined under paragraph (a)(3)(i) is $1,200. Thus, A's required payment is $400 ($1,200 determined under paragraph (a)(3)(i) of this section less $800 determined under paragraph (a)(3)(ii) of this section). Although A's required payment for its third applicable election year is not more than $500, A must make its required payment for such year because the required payment for a preceding applicable election year exceeded $500. A must also file the return prescribed by §1.7519-2T (a)(2) for its third applicable election year.

(b) *Definitions and special rules.*—(1) *Applicable percentage.*—(i) *In general.*—Except as provided in paragraph (b)(1)(ii) of this section, the term "applicable percentage" means the percentage determined in accordance with the following table:

| If the applicable election year of the partnership or S corporation begins during: | The applicable percentage is: |
| --- | --- |
| 1987 | 25 |
| 1988 | 50 |
| 1989 | 75 |
| 1990 or thereafter | 100 |

(ii) *Exception for certain applicable election years beginning after 1987.*—[Reserved.]

(iii) *Example.*—The provisions of paragraph (b) (1) of this section may be illustrated by the following example.

*Example.* B is a corporation that has historically used a June 30 taxable year. For its taxable year beginning July 1, 1987, B elects to be an S corporation and elects under section 1.444-1T (b)(3) to retain its June 30 taxable year. Had B changed to a calendar year, its required year under section 1378, B's shareholders would not have been entitled to the 4-year spread under section 806(e)(2)(C) of the Tax Reform Act of 1986 because B was not an S corporation for its taxable year beginning in 1986. Nevertheless, for purposes of determining the required payment for B's applicable election year beginning July 1, 1987, the applicable percentage is 25 percent.

(2) *Adjusted highest section 1 rate.*—(i) *General rule.*—For any applicable election year, the term "adjusted highest section 1 rate" means the highest rate of tax under section 1 applicable to the period defined in paragraph (b)(2)(ii) of this section, plus 1 percentage point. Notwithstanding the preceding sentence, the adjusted highest section 1 rate is 36 percent for applicable election years beginning in 1987. For purposes of this section, the highest rate of tax is determined without regard to the effect of section 1(g), relating to the phaseout of the 15-percent rate and personal exemptions.

(ii) *Period for determining highest section 1 rate.*—For purposes of paragraph (b)(2)(i) of this section, the period for determining the highest rate of tax under section 1 is the 12 month period that—

(A) Ends with the required taxable year for the applicable election year, and

(B) Includes the end of the base year.

For example, assume that a partnership's applicable election year begins on October 1, 1988 and that the required taxable year for such applicable election year is December 31. Based upon these facts, the period for determining the highest section 1 rate is the 12-month period ending December 31, 1988.

(3) *Base year.*—The term "base year" means, with respect to any applicable election year, the taxable year of the partnership or S corporation preceding such applicable election year.

(4) *Special rules for certain applicable election years.*—(i) *First applicable election year of new entities.*—If an applicable election year is a partnership's or S corporation's first year in existence (*i.e.,* the partnership or S corporation is newly formed and therefore does not have a base year), the required payment for such applicable election year is zero.

(ii) *Applicable election years ending prior to the required taxable year.*—If a partnership or S corporation makes a section 444 election and the resulting applicable election year (the "first applicable election year") of the partnership or S corporation ends prior to the last day of the required year, the required payment for the first applicable

election year is zero. See example (5) in paragraph (b)(5)(vi) of this section.

(5) *Net base year income.*—(i) *In general.*—Except as provided in paragraph (b)(5)(v) of this section (relating to short base years), the net base year income of a partnership or S corporation is the sum of—

(A) The deferral ratio multiplied by the partnership's or S corporation's net income for the base year, plus

(B) The excess (if any) of—

(1) The deferral ratio multiplied by the aggregate amount of applicable payments made by the partnership or S corporation during the base year, over

(2) The aggregate amount of such applicable payments made during the deferral period of the base year.

The term "deferral ratio" means the ratio which the number of months in the deferral period (as defined in §1.444-1T (b)(4)) of the applicable election year bears to 12 months.

(ii) *Partnership net income.*—For purposes of paragraph (b)(5)(i) of this section—

(A) *In general.*—The net income of the partnership is the amount (not below zero) determined by taking into account the aggregate amount of the partnership's items described in section 702(a), except for—

(1) Credits,

(2) Tax-exempt income, and

(3) Guaranteed payments under section 707(c).

(B) *Treatment of deductions and losses.*—For purposes of determining the aggregate amount of partnership items, deductions and losses are treated as negative income. Thus, for example, if under section 702(a) a partnership has $1,000 of ordinary taxable income, $500 of specially allocated deductions, and $300 of capital loss, the net income of the partnership is $200 ($1,000 – $500 – $300).

(C) *Partner limitations disregarded.*—Any limitation on the amount of a partnership item described in section 702(a) which may be taken into account for purposes of computing the taxable income of a partner shall be disregarded in computing the net income of the partnership.

(iii) *S corporation net income.*—For purposes of paragraph (b)(5)(i) of this section—

(A) *In general.*—The net income of an S corporation is the amount (not below zero) determined by taking into account the aggregate amount of the S corporation's items described in section 1366(a)(other than credits and tax-exempt income). If the S corporation was a C corporation for the base year, the taxable income of the C corporation shall be treated as the net income of the S corporation for such year.

(B) *Treatment of deductions and losses.*—For purposes of determining the aggregate amount of S corporation items, deductions and losses are treated as negative income. Thus, for example, if under section 1366(a) an S corporation has $2,000 of ordinary taxable income, $1,000 of deductions described in section 1366 (a)(1)(A) of the Code, and $500 of capital loss, the net income of the S corporation is $500 ($2,000 – $1,000 – $500).

(C) *Shareholder limitations disregarded.*—Any limitation on any amount described in section 1366(a) which may be taken into account for purposes of computing the taxable income of a shareholder shall be disregarded in computing the net income of the S corporation.

(iv) *Applicable payments.*—(A) *In general.*—The term "applicable payment" means any amount deductible in the base year that is includible at any time, directly or indirectly, in the gross income of a taxpayer that during the base year is a partner or shareholder.

(B) *Exceptions.*—The term "applicable payment" does not include any guaranteed payments under section 707(c).

(C) *Special rule for corporation electing S status.*—If an S corporation was a C corporation for the base year, the corporation shall be treated as if it were an S corporation for the base year for purposes of determining the amount of applicable payments under this section. Thus, amounts deductible by the C corporation in the base year that are includible at any time in the gross income of a taxpayer that is a shareholder during the base year are treated as if from an S corporation, and therefore within the meaning of the term "applicable payments."

(D) *Special rules for certain payments.*—(1) *Certain indirect payments.*—For purposes of paragraph (b)(5)(iv)(A) of this section, an amount is indirectly includible in the gross income of a partner or shareholder of a partnership or S corporation that has a section 444 election in effect (an electing partnership or S corporation) if the amount is includible in the gross income of a—

(i) The spouse (other than a spouse who is legally separated from the partner or shareholder under a decree of divorce or separate maintenance) or child (under age 14) of such partner or shareholder, or

(ii) A corporation more than 50 percent (measured by fair market value) of which is owned in the aggregate by partners or shareholders (and individuals related under paragraph (b)(5)(iv)(D)(1)(i) of this section to any such partners or shareholders), of the electing partnership or S corporation, or

(iii) A partnership more than 50 percent of the profits and capital of which is owned in the aggregate by partners or shareholders (and individuals related under paragraph (b)(5)(iv)(D)(1)(i) of this section to any such partners or shareholders) of the electing partnership or S corporation, or

(iv) A trust more than 50 percent of the beneficial ownership of which is owned in the aggregate by partners or shareholders (and individuals related under paragraph (b)(5)(iv)(D)(1)(i) of this section to any such partners or shareholders), of the electing partnership or S corporation.

For purposes of this paragraph (b)(5)(iv)(D)(1), ownership by any person described in this paragraph (b)(5)(iv)(D)(1) shall be treated as ownership by the partners or shareholders of the electing partnership or S corporation. This paragraph (b)(5)(iv)(D)(1) does not apply to amounts deductible by a partnership or S corporation that has made a section 444 election (the "deducting partnership") and included in the gross income of a partnership or S corporation defined in paragraphs (b)(5)(iv)(D)(1)(ii) or (iii) of this section (the "including partnership"), if the including partnership has the same taxable year as the deducting partnership and the including partnership has a section 444 election in effect. Furthermore, notwithstanding the general effective date provided in §1.7519-3T, this paragraph (b)(5)(iv)(D)(1) is effective for amounts deductible on or after June 1, 1988.

(2) *Payments by a downstream controlled partnership.*—(i) *In general.*—If a partnership or S corporation has made a section 444 election, any amounts deducted by a downstream controlled partnership will be considered deducted by the partnership or S corporation that has made the section 444 election for purposes of determining the applicable payments of the partnership or S corporation that has made the section 444 election.

(ii) *Definition of a downstream controlled partnership.*—If a partnership or S corporation that has made a section 444 election owns more than 50 percent of a partnership's profits and capital, such owned partnership is considered a downstream controlled partnership for purposes of paragraph (b)(5)(iv)(D)(2)(i) of this section. Furthermore, if more than 50 percent of a partnership's profits and capital are owned by a downstream controlled partnership, such owned partnership is considered a downstream controlled partnership for purposes of paragraph (b)(5)(iv)(D)(2)(i) of this section.

(3) *Examples.*—The provisions of this paragraph (b)(5)(iv)(D) may be illustrated by the following examples.

*Example (1).* I1 and I2, calendar year individuals, own 100 percent of the profits and capital of C1, a partnership. In addition to owning C1, I1 and I2 also own 100 percent of the profits and capital of C2, a calendar year partnership. For its taxable years beginning February 1, 1987, 1988, and 1989, C1 has a section 444 election in effect to use a January 31 taxable year. During its base years beginning February 1, 1986, 1987, and 1988, C1 deducted $10,000, $11,000, and $12,000, respectively that was included in C2's gross income. Furthermore, of the $12,000 deducted by C1 for its taxable year beginning February 1, 1988, $7,000 was deducted during the period June 1, 1988 to January 31, 1989. Pursuant to paragraph (b)(5)(iv)(D)(1) of this section, the $7,000 deducted by C1 on or after June 1, 1988, and included in C2's gross income is considered an applicable payment for C1's base year beginning February 1, 1988. Amounts deducted by C1 prior to June 1, 1988, are not subject to paragraph (b)(5)(iv)(D)(1) of this section.

*Example (2).* The facts are the same as in example (1), except that I1 and I2 own only 51 percent of C2's profits and capital. Since the two partners in C1 (*i.e.*, I1 and I2) own more than 50 percent of C2's profits and capital, C2 is considered controlled by the partners of C1 pursuant to paragraph (b)(5)(iv)(D)(1)(iii) of this section. Thus, the conclusions in example (1) are unchanged. Furthermore, if the $7,000 deducted by C1 was included in the income of a partnership more than 50 percent of the profits and capital of which is owned by C2, such $7,000 would be considered an applicable payment for its base year beginning February 1, 1988.

*Example (3).* The facts are the same as in example (1), except that for its taxable years beginning February 1, 1987, 1988, and

1989, C2 has a section 444 election in effect to use a January 31 taxable year. Since both C1 and C2 have the same taxable year and both have section 444 elections in effect, paragraph (b)(5)(iv)(D)(1) of this section does not apply to the $7,000 deducted by C1 for its base year beginning February 1, 1988.

*Example (4).* I3 and I4, calendar year individuals, own 100 percent of the profits and capital of C3, a partnership. C3 has made a section 444 election to retain a year ending June 30 for its taxable year beginning July 1, 1987. Furthermore, C3 owns more than 50 percent of the profits and capital of C4, a partnership that historically used a June 30 taxable year. Pursuant to §1.706-3T(b), C4 retains its year ending June 30 for its taxable year beginning July 1, 1987. For its taxable year beginning July 1, 1986, C4 deducted $20,000 that was included in I3's gross income. Pursuant to paragraph (b)(5)(iv)(D)(2) of this section, the $20,000 deducted by C4 is considered an applicable payment by C3 for its base year beginning July 1, 1986.

*Example (5).* The facts are the same as in example (4), except that the $20,000 deducted by C4 is included in the gross income of a calendar year partnership 100 percent owned by I3 and I4. Pursuant to paragraphs (b)(5)(iv)(D)(1) and (2) of this section, the $20,000 deducted by C4 is considered an applicable payment by C3 for its base year beginning July 1, 1986.

*Example (6).* The facts are the same as in example (4), except that instead of directly owning a portion of C4, C3 owns more than 50 percent of the profits and capital of C5. Furthermore, C5 owns more than 50 percent of the profits and capital of C4. Pursuant to paragraph (b)(5)(iv)(D)(2)(ii) of this section, both C5 and C4 are considered downstream controlled partnerships of C3. Thus, pursuant to paragraph (b)(5)(iv)(D)(2)(i) of this section, the $20,000 deducted by C4 is considered an applicable payment by C3 for its base year beginning July 1, 1986.

(v) *Special rule for base year of less than twelve months.*—(A) *In general.*—If a base year is a taxable year of less than twelve months (a "short base year"), net base year income for such year is an amount equal to the excess, if any, of—

(1) The deferral ratio multiplied by the annualized short base year income, over

(2) Applicable payments made during the deferral period of the applicable election year following the base year.

(B) *Annualized short base year income.*—The annualized short base year income is determined by—

(1) Increasing the net income for the short base year by applicable payments deductible in the short base year, and

(2) Multiplying the short base year income as increased in paragraph (b)(5)(v)(B)(1) of this section by twelve, and dividing the result by the number of months in the short base year.

(vi) *Examples.*—The provisions of paragraph (b)(5) of this section may be illustrated by the following examples.

*Example (1).* D, a partnership, is owned 10 percent by a C corporation with a September 30 taxable year and 90 percent by calendar year individuals. D has historically used a September 30 taxable year. For its taxable year beginning October 1, 1987, D makes a section 444 election to retain its September 30 taxable year. For the base year from October 1, 1986 to September 30, 1987, D has net income of $200,000 and no applicable payments. D's deferral ratio is $3/12$ (the ratio of the number of months in the deferral period to 12 months). Based upon these facts, D has net base year income of $50,000 ($200,000 × $3/12$).

*Example (2).* The facts are the same as in example (1) except that D's net income for the base year is $140,000, after applicable payments of $60,000. Of the applicable payments $15,000 were deductible during the deferral period of the base year. Based upon these facts, D has net base year income of $35,000, determined as follows:

| | | |
|---|---|---|
| Net income . . . . . . . . . . . . . | $140,000 | |
| multiplied by deferral ratio . . . | × $3/12$ | |
| | | $35,000 |
| Plus the excess, if any, of | | |
| applicable payments . . . . . . . | $60,000 | |
| multiplied by deferral ratio . . . | × $3/12$ | |
| | $15,000 | |
| over aggregate amount of applicable payments deductible during deferral period of base year | $15,000 | —0— |
| Net base year income . . . . . . . . . . . . . . . . . . . | | $35,000 |

*Example (3).* The facts are the same as in example (2) except that of the $60,000 applicable payments only $10,000 are deductible during the deferral period of the base year. Based on these facts, D has net base year income of $40,000, determined as follows:

| | |
|---|---|
| Net income . . . . . . . . . . . . . . . . | $140,000 |
| multiplied by deferral ratio . . . . . | × $3/12$ |

| | | $35,000 |
|---|---|---|
| plus the excess, if any, of applicable payments . . . . . . . . . . . . . . . . | $60,000 | |
| multiplied by deferral ratio . . . . . | × 3/12 | |
| | | $15,000 |
| over aggregate amount of applicable payments deductible during deferral period of base year . . . . . . . . . . . . . . . . . . | $10,000 | |
| | | $5,000 |
| Net base year income . . . . . . . . . . . . . . . . . . . . | | $40,000 |

*Example (4).* E is a C corporation that has historically used a January 31 taxable year. For its taxable year beginning February 1, 1987, E makes an election to be an S corporation and also makes a section 444 election to retain its January 31 taxable year. E's taxable income for the taxable year beginning February 1, 1986 to January 31, 1987 is $120,000. Pursuant to paragraph (b)(5)(iii)(A) of this section, the base year for X's first applicable election year is the taxable year beginning February 1, 1986 and ending January 31, 1987. Thus, E's net income for the base year is $120,000. During the base year, E pays its sole shareholder, A, a salary of $5,000 a month plus a $30,000 bonus on January 15, 1987. Thus, under paragraph (b)(5)(iv)(C) of this section, E's applicable payments for the base year are $90,000, of which $55,000 are applicable payments deductible during the deferral period of the base year (February 1 to December 31, 1986). Based upon these facts, E's net base year income is $137,500, determined as follows:

| | | |
|---|---|---|
| Net income . . . . . . . . . . . . | $120,000 | |
| multiplied by deferral ratio | × 11/12 | |
| | | $110,000 |
| plus the excess, if any, of applicable payments . . . . . | $90,000 | |
| multiplied by the deferral ratio . . . . . . . . . . . . . | × 11/12 | |
| | $82,500 | |
| over aggregate amount of applicable payments deductible during deferral period of base year . . . . . . . . . . . . . . | $55,000 | $27,500 |
| Net base year income . . . . . . . . . . . . . . . . . . . | | $137,500 |

*Example (5).* E, a corporation that has historically used a taxable year ending July 31, makes an election to be an S corporation for its taxable year beginning August 1, 1987. For that year, E also makes a section 444 election to use a taxable year ending September 30. Thus, E has two applicable election years beginning in 1987, the first beginning August 1, 1987 and ending September 30, 1987, and the second beginning October 1, 1987 and ending September 30, 1988. E's required year under section 1378 is the calendar year. Because E's first applicable election year ends prior to the last day of E's required year (*i.e.,* December 31, 1987), the required payment for E's first applicable election year is zero. However, E is required to file a return for such year as provided in § 1.7519-2T.

*Example (6).* The facts are the same as in example (5). E's second applicable election year is the year from October 1, 1987 to September 30, 1988, and the base year for the second applicable election year is a period of less than 12 months (*i.e.,* August 1, 1987 to September 30, 1987). Thus, E must compute its net base year income using the special rule for short base years provided in paragraph (b)(5)(v) of this section. Assume E's net income for the short base year is $50,000, and E's applicable payments for the short base year are $15,000. Pursuant to paragraph (b)(5)(v)(B) of this section, E's annualized short base year net income is $390,000 ($65,000 × 12/2). Furthermore, assume E's applicable payments for the deferral period of its second applicable election year are $20,000. Based on these facts, the net base year income for the applicable election year beginning October 1, 1987 is $77,500, computed as follows:

| | | |
|---|---|---|
| Annualized short base year income . . . . . . . . . . . . . . | $390,000 | |
| multiplied by deferral ratio . . . . . . . | × 3/12 | |
| | | $97,500 |
| less: | | |
| applicable payments for deferral period . . . . . . . . . . | | $20,000 |
| Net base year income . . . . . . . . . . . . . . . . . . . | | $77,500 |

(c) *Refunds of required payments.*—A partnership or S corporation is entitled to make a claim for refund, in accordance with the procedures provided in § 1.7519-2T(a)(6), if—

(1) The amount specified in paragraph (a)(3)(i) of this section is less than the amount specified in paragraph (a)(3)(ii) of this section; or

(2) The partnership or S corporation terminates its section 444 election, within the meaning of § 1.444-1T(a)(5).

(d) *Examples.*—The provisions of this section may be illustrated by the following examples.

*Example (1).* G, a partnership, is owned 10 percent by a C corporation with a June 30 taxable year, and 90 percent by calendar year individuals. G has historically used a June 30 taxable year. For its taxable year beginning July 1, 1987, G makes a section 444 election to retain its June 30 taxable year. For the base year from July 1, 1986 to June 30, 1987, G has net income of $300,000 and no applicable payments. G's deferral ratio is 6/12 (the ratio of the number of months in the deferral period to 12 months). Based on these facts, G's net base year income is $150,000 ($300,000 × 6/12). Thus, G's required payment for its first applicable election year is $13,500 ($150,000 of net base year income multiplied by 9 percent (the product of the applicable percentage for 1987, 25 percent, and the highest section 1 rate for 1987, 36 percent)).

*Example (2).* The facts are the same as in example (1). In addition, G continues its section 444 election for the taxable year beginning July 1, 1988, and G's net base year income for the year beginning July 1, 1987 is $150,000. The required payment for G's second applicable election year is $8,250 ($150,000 of net base year income multiplied by 14.5 percent (the product of the applicable percentage for 1988 applicable election years, 50 percent, and the adjusted highest section 1 rate for 1988, 29 percent) less G's $13,500 required payment for the first applicable election year).

*Example (3).* H, a partnership with a taxable year ending September 30, desires to make a section 444 election for its taxable year beginning October 1, 1987. H is 15 percent owned by I, a partnership with a taxable year ending September 30, and 85 percent owned by calendar year individuals. Assume H and I are qualified to make section 444 elections as a result of the "same taxable year exception" provided in § 1.444-2T(e). If H and I make section 444 elections, they must each make a required payment (assuming the amount computed under paragraph (a)(3) of this section is greater than $500). Pursuant to paragraph (a)(3) of this section, the required payments of H and I are calculated independent of each other. Thus, in determining the amount of its required payment, I may not exclude its income attributable to H, even though H must also make a required payment on the same income.

*Example (4).* The facts are the same as in example (1) except that H is 90 percent owned by I and 10 percent owned by calendar year individuals. Pursuant to § 1.706-3T, if I makes a section 444 election to retain its taxable year ending September 30, H's required year will be September 30, because H's majority interest partner will have a September 30 taxable year. Thus, H is not required to make a section 444 election and a required payment in order to use a September 30 taxable year. I, however, must make a required payment. [Temporary Reg. § 1.7519-1T.]

☐ [T.D. 8205, 5-24-88.]

### [Reg. § 1.7519-2T]

**§ 1.7519-2T. Required payments—procedures and administration (temporary).**—(a) *Payment and return required.*—(1) *In general.*—With respect to any taxable year for which a partnership or S corporation has a section 444 election in effect (an "applicable election year"), the partnership or S corporation shall file a return as provided in paragraphs (a)(2) and (3) of this section and make a payment, if required, as provided in paragraph (a)(4) of this section.

(2) *Return required.*—(i) *In general.*—A return showing the required payment shall be made, even if the required payment for the applicable election year is zero. For an applicable election year beginning in 1987, the return shall be made on Form 720, "Quarterly Federal Excise Tax Return." For an applicable election year beginning after 1987, the return shall also be made on Form 720 unless another form is prescribed by the Commissioner.

(ii) *Procedure if amount for applicable election year (and all preceding years) is not greater than $500.*—If a partnership or S corporation is not required to make a payment under section 7519 for an applicable election year, the partnership or S corporation should type or legibly print "zero" on the appropriate line of the prescribed form.

(3) *Time and place for filing return.*—(i) *Applicable election years beginning in 1987.*—For an applicable election year beginning in 1987, the Form 720 must be filed with the Service Center indicated by the instructions for the Form 720. The date for filing such form is as follows—

(A) *Taxpayers that would otherwise file Form 720 for the second quarter of 1988.*—Taxpayers that are required, without regard to this section, to file Form 720 for the second quarter of 1988 (*e.g.,* taxpayers reporting liability for manufacturers excise tax) must file Form 720 by the normal due date of such form for the second quarter of 1988. Thus, such taxpayers must generally file Form 720 on or before July 31, 1988. However, if such taxpayers must also report tax imposed by section 4251 (relating to communications services tax), sections 4261 and 4271 (relating to air transportation tax), or section 4986 (relating to windfall profits tax) for the second quarter of 1988, they must file Form 720 on or before August 31, 1988.

(B) *Other taxpayers.*—Taxpayers that are not described in paragraph (a)(3)(i)(A) of this section (*i.e.*, taxpayers that but for this section would not be required to file Form 720 for the second quarter of 1988) must file Form 720 on or before July 31, 1988.

(ii) *Applicable election years beginning after 1987.*—(A) *Return made on Form 720.*—[Reserved].

(B) *Return made on form other than Form 720.*—For an applicable election year beginning after 1987, the return showing the required payment is to be filed with the Service Center indicated by the instructions for the form prescribed for payment. The return must be filed on or before the date prescribed by the instructions to the form.

(iii) *Special rule for back-up section 444 election.*—See § 1.444-3T(b)(4)(iii) for a special rule that may extend the due date for filing a return required by paragraph (a)(2) of this section.

(4) *Time and place for making required payment.*—(i) *Applicable election years beginning in 1987.*—For an applicable election year beginning in 1987, the required payment is due and payable without assessment and notice on or before the date the taxpayer's Form 720 for the second quarter is due (as specified in paragraph (a)(3) of this section). The required payment must be paid by check or money order, and such check or money order must indicate the partnership's or S corporation's taxpayer identification number and must include the statement: "IRS NO. 11 PAYMENT." The check or money order must be sent, together with Form 720, to the Service Center indicated by the instructions for the Form 720.

(ii) *Applicable election years beginning after 1987.*—For an applicable election year beginning after 1987, the required payment is due and payable without assessment or notice, on or before May 15 of the calendar year following the calendar year in which the applicable election year begins.

(iii) *Special rule for back-up section 444 election.*—See § 1.444-3T(b)(4)(iii) for a special rule that may extend the due date for making a required payment.

(5) *Penalties for failure to pay.*—In the case of any failure by a partnership or S corporation to pay the required payment on or before the date prescribed in paragraph (a)(4) of this section, there shall be assessed on such partnership or S corporation a penalty of 10 percent of the underpayment. For purposes of this section, the term "underpayment" means the excess of the amount of the payment required under this section over the amount (if any) of such payment paid on or before the date prescribed in paragraph (a)(4) of this section.

(6) *Refund of required payment.*—(i) *In general.*—If a partnership or S corporation is entitled to make a claim for refund pursuant to § 1.7519-1T(c), such partnership or S corporation should file a claim for refund, as provided in paragraph (a)(6)(ii) of this section. However, in no event shall a refund be made prior to April 15 of the second calendar year that follows the calendar year in which an applicable election year begins. For example, assume a partnership made a section 444 election to retain its taxable year for its taxable year beginning October 1, 1987, and as a result made a required payment for such year. Further assume that the partnership terminates its election for its taxable year beginning October 1, 1988. Based on these facts, the partnership will be entitled to a refund, but no earlier than April 15, 1989.

(ii) *Procedures for claiming refund.*—[Reserved].

(iii) *Interest on refund.*—No interest shall be allowed with respect to any refund of a required payment under § 1.7519-1T(c).

(b) *Assessment and collection of payment.*—A required payment shall be assessed and collected in the same manner as if it were a tax imposed by subtitle C. Furthermore, no deduction shall be allowable to a partnership or S corporation (or their owners) with respect to the required payment.

(c) *Termination due to willful failure.*—See § 1.444-1T(a)(5)(i)(C), which provides that willful failure to comply with the requirements of this section will result in the termination of the section 444 election.

(d) *Negligence and fraud penalties made applicable.*—For purposes of section 6653, relating to additions to tax for negligence and fraud, any payment required by this section shall be treated as a tax. [Temporary Reg. § 1.7519-2T.]

☐ [*T.D.* 8205, 5-24-88.]

**[Reg. §1.7519-3T]**

**§1.7519-3T. Effective date (temporary).**—The provisions of §§1.7519-1T through 1.7519-3T are effective for taxable years beginning after December 31, 1986. [Temporary Reg. §1.7519-3T.]

☐ [*T.D.* 8205, 5-24-88.]

**[Reg. §1.7520-1]**

**§1.7520-1. Valuation of annuities, unitrust interests, interests for life or terms of years, and remainder or reversionary interests.**—(a) *General actuarial valuations.*—(1) Except as otherwise provided in this section and in §1.7520-3 (relating to exceptions to the use of prescribed tables under certain circumstances), in the case of certain transactions after April 30, 1989, subject to income tax, the fair market value of annuities, interests for life or for a term of years (including unitrust interests), remainders, and reversions is their present value determined under this section. See §20.2031-7(d) of this chapter (and, for periods prior to May 1, 2009, §20.2031-7A) for the computation of the value of annuities, unitrust interests, life estates, terms for years, remainders, and reversions, other than interests described in paragraphs (a)(2) and (a)(3) of this section.

(2) For a transfer to a pooled income fund, see §1.642(c)-6(e) (or, for periods prior to May 1, 2009, §1.642(c)-6A) with respect to the valuation of the remainder interest.

(3) For a transfer to a charitable remainder annuity trust after April 30, 1989, see §1.664-2 with respect to the valuation of the remainder interest. See §1.664-4 with respect to the valuation of the remainder interest in property transferred to a charitable remainder unitrust.

(b) *Components of valuation.*—(1) *Interest rate component.*—(i) *Section 7520 Interest rate.*—The section 7520 interest rate is the rate of return, rounded to the nearest two-tenths of one percent, that is equal to 120 percent of the applicable Federal mid-term rate, compounded annually, for purposes of section 1274(d)(1), for the month in which the valuation date falls. In rounding the rate to the nearest two-tenths of a percent, any rate that is midway between one two-tenths of a percent and another is rounded up to the higher of those two rates. For example, if 120 percent of the applicable Federal mid-term rate is 10.30, the section 7520 interest rate component is 10.4. The section 7520 interest rate is published monthly by the Internal Revenue Service in the Internal Revenue Bulletin (see §601.601(d)(2)(ii)(*b*) of this chapter).

(ii) *Valuation date.*—Except as provided in §1.7520-2, the valuation date is the date on which the transaction takes place.

(2) *Mortality component.*—The mortality component reflects the mortality data most recently available from the United States census. As new mortality data becomes available after each decennial census, the mortality component described in this section will be revised and the revised mortality component tables will be published in the regulations at that time. For transactions with valuation dates on or after May 1, 2009, the mortality component table (Table 2000CM) is contained in §20.2031-7(d)(7) of this chapter. See §20.2031-7A for mortality component tables applicable to transactions for which the valuation date falls before May 1, 2009.

(c) *Tables.*—The present value on the valuation date of an annuity, life estate, term of years, remainder, or reversion is computed by using the section 7520 interest rate component that is described in paragraph (b)(1) of this section and the mortality component that is described in paragraph (b)(2) of this section. Actuarial factors for determining these present values are included in tables in these regulations and in publications by the Internal Revenue Service. If a special factor is required in order to value an interest, the Internal Revenue Service will furnish the factor upon a request for a ruling. The request for a ruling must be accompanied by a recitation of the facts, including the date of birth for each measuring life and copies of relevant instruments. A request for a ruling must comply with the instructions for requesting a ruling published periodically in the Internal Revenue Bulletin (see Rev. Proc. 94-1, 1994-1 I.R.B. 10, and subsequent updates, and §§601.201 and 601.601(d)(2)(ii)(*b*) of this chapter) and include payment of the required user fee.

(1) *Regulation sections containing tables with interest rates between 0.2 and 14 percent for valuation dates on or after May 1, 2009.*—Section 1.642(c)-6(e)(6) contains Table S used for determining the present value of a single life remainder interest in a pooled income fund as defined in §1.642(c)-5. See §1.642(c)-6A for actuarial factors for one life applicable to valuation dates before May 1, 2009. Section 1.664-4(e)(6) contains Table F (payout factors) and Table D (actuarial factors used in determining the present value of a remainder interest postponed for a term of years). Section 1.664-4(e)(7) contains Table U(1) (unitrust single life remainder factors). These tables are used in

determining the present value of a remainder interest in a charitable remainder unitrust as defined in §1.664-3. See §1.664-4A for unitrust single life remainder factors applicable to valuation dates before May 1, 2009. Section 20.2031-7(d)(6) of this chapter contains Table B (actuarial factors used in determining the present value of an interest for a term of years), Table J (term certain annuity beginning-of-interval adjustment factors), and Table K (annuity end-of-interval adjustment factors). Section 20.2031-7(d)(7) contains Table S (single life remainder factors), and Table 2000CM (mortality components). These tables are used in determining the present value of annuities, life estates, remainders, and reversions. See §20.2031-7A for single life remainder factors for one life and mortality components applicable to valuation dates before May 1, 2009.

(2) *Internal Revenue Service publications containing tables with interest rates between 0.2 and 22 percent for valuation dates on or after May 1, 2009.*—The following documents are available, at no charge, electronically via the IRS Internet site at *www.irs.gov*:

(i) Internal Revenue Service Publication 1457, "Actuarial Valuations Version 3A" (2009). This publication includes tables of valuation factors, as well as examples that show how to compute other valuation factors, for determining the present value of annuities, life estates, terms of years, remainders, and reversions, measured by one or two lives. These factors must also be used in the valuation of interests in a charitable remainder annuity trust as defined in §1.664-2 and a pooled income fund as defined in §1.642(c)-5.

(ii) Internal Revenue Service Publication 1458, "Actuarial Valuations Version 3B" (2009). This publication includes term certain tables and tables of one and two life valuation factors for determining the present value of remainder interests in a charitable remainder unitrust as defined in §1.664-3.

(iii) Internal Revenue Service Publication 1459, "Actuarial Valuations Version 3C" (2009). This publication includes tables for computing depreciation adjustment factors. See §1.170A-12.

(d) *Effective/applicability dates.*—This section applies on and after May 1, 2009. [Reg. §1.7520-1.]

☐ [*T.D.* 8540, 6-9-94. *Amended by T.D.* 8819, 4-29-99; *T.D.* 8886, 6-9-2000; *T.D.* 9448, 5-1-2009; *and T.D.* 9540, 8-9-2011.]

**[Reg. §20.7520-1]**

**§20.7520-1. Valuation of annuities, unitrust interests, interests for life or terms of years, and remainder or reversionary interests.**—(a) *General actuarial valuations.*—(1) Except as otherwise provided in this section and in §20.7520-3 (relating to exceptions to the use of prescribed tables under certain circumstances), in the case of estates of decedents with valuation dates after April 30, 1989, the fair market value of annuities, interests for life or for a term of years (including unitrust interests), remainders, and reversions is their present value determined under this section. See §20.2031-7(d) (and, for periods prior to May 1, 2009, §20.2031-7A) for the computation of the value of annuities, unitrust interests, life estates, terms for years, remainders, and reversions, other than interests described in paragraphs (a)(2) and (a)(3) of this section.

(2) In the case of a transfer to a pooled income fund, see §1.642(c)-6(e) of this chapter (or, for periods prior to May 1, 2009, §1.642(c)-6A) with respect to the valuation of the remainder interest.

(3) In the case of a transfer to a charitable remainder annuity trust with a valuation date after April 30, 1989, see §1.664-2 of this chapter with respect to the valuation of the remainder interest. See §1.664-4 of this chapter with respect to the valuation of the remainder interest in property transferred to a charitable remainder unitrust.

(b) *Components of valuation.*—(1) *Interest rate component.*—(i) *Section 7520 Interest rate.*—The section 7520 interest rate is the rate of return, rounded to the nearest two-tenths of one percent, that is equal to 120 percent of the applicable Federal mid-term rate, compounded annually, for purposes of section 1274(d)(1), for the month in which the valuation date falls. In rounding the rate to the nearest two-tenths of a percent, any rate that is midway between one two-tenths of a percent and another is rounded up to the higher of those two rates. For example, if 120 percent of the applicable Federal mid-term rate is 10.30, the section 7520 interest rate component is 10.4. The section 7520 interest rate is published monthly by the Internal Revenue Service in the Internal Revenue Bulletin (See §601.601(d)(2)(ii)(*b*) of this chapter).

(ii) *Valuation date.*—Generally, the valuation date is the date on which the transfer takes place. For estate tax purposes, the valuation date is the date of the decedent's death, unless the executor elects the alternate valuation date in accordance with section 2032, in which event, and under the limitations prescribed in section 2032 and

the regulations thereunder, the valuation date is the alternate valuation date. For special rules in the case of charitable transfers, see §20.7520-2.

(2) *Mortality component.*—The mortality component reflects the mortality data most recently available from the United States census. As new mortality data becomes available after each decennial census, the mortality component described in this section will be revised and the revised mortality component tables will be published in the regulations at that time. For decedent's estates with valuation dates on or after May 1, 2009, the mortality component table (Table 2000CM) is contained in §20.2031-7(d)(7). See §20.2031-7A for mortality component tables applicable to decedent's estates with valuation dates before May 1, 2009.

(c) *Tables.*—The present value on the valuation date of an annuity, life estate, term of years, remainder, or reversion is computed by using the section 7520 interest rate component that is described in paragraph (b)(1) of this section and the mortality component that is described in paragraph (b)(2) of this section. Actuarial factors for determining these present values are included in tables in these regulations and in publications by the Internal Revenue Service. If a special factor is required in order to value an interest, the Internal Revenue Service will furnish the factor upon a request for a ruling. The request for a ruling must be accompanied by a recitation of the facts, including the date of birth for each measuring life and copies of relevant instruments. A request for a ruling must comply with the instructions for requesting a ruling published periodically in the Internal Revenue Bulletin (see Rev. Proc. 94-1, 1994-1 I.R.B. 10, and the first Rev. Proc. published each year, and §§601.201 and 601.601(d)(2)(ii)(*b*) of this chapter) and include payment of the required user fee.

(1) *Regulation sections containing tables with interest rates between 0.2 and 14 percent for valuation dates on or after May 1, 2009.*—Section 1.642(c)-6(e)(6) of this chapter contains Table S used for determining the present value of a single life remainder interest in a pooled income fund as defined in §1.642(c)-5. See §1.642(c)-6A for single life remainder factors applicable to valuation dates before May 1, 2009. Section 1.664-4(e)(6) contains Table F (payout factors) and Table D (actuarial factors used in determining the present value of a remainder interest postponed for a term of years). Section 1.664-4(e)(7) contains Table U(1) (unitrust single life remainder factors). These tables are used in determining the present value of a remainder interest in a charitable remainder unitrust as defined in §1.664-3. See §1.664-4A for unitrust single life remainder factors applicable to valuation dates before May 1, 2009. Section 20.2031-7(d)(6) contains Table B (actuarial factors used in determining the present value of an interest for a term of years), Table K (annuity end-of-interval adjustment factors), and Table J (term certain annuity beginning-of-interval adjustment factors). Section 20.2031-7(d)(7) contains Table S (single life remainder factors), and Table 2000CM (mortality components). These tables are used in determining the present value of annuities, life estates, remainders, and reversions. See §20.2031-7A for single life remainder factors applicable to valuation dates before May 1, 2009.

(2) *Internal Revenue Service publications containing tables with interest rates between 0.2 and 22 percent for valuation dates on or after May 1, 2009.*—The following documents are available, at no charge, electronically via the IRS Internet site at *www.irs.gov*:

(i) Internal Revenue Service Publication 1457, "Actuarial Valuations Version 3A" (2009). This publication includes tables of valuation factors, as well as examples that show how to compute other valuation factors, for determining the present value of annuities, life estates, terms of years, remainders, and reversions, measured by one or two lives. These factors may also be used in the valuation of interests in a charitable remainder annuity trust as defined in §1.664-2 of this chapter and a pooled income fund as defined in §1.642(c)-5.

(ii) Internal Revenue Service Publication 1458, "Actuarial Valuations Version 3B" (2009). This publication includes term certain tables and tables of one and two life valuation factors for determining the present value of remainder interests in a charitable remainder unitrust as defined in §1.664-3 of this chapter.

(iii) Internal Revenue Service Publication 1459, "Actuarial Valuations Version 3C" (2009). This publication includes tables for computing depreciation adjustment factors. See §1.170A-12 of this chapter.

(d) *Effective/applicability dates.*—This section applies on and after May 1, 2009. [Reg. §20.7520-1.]

☐ [*T.D.* 8540, 6-9-94. *Amended by T.D.* 8819, 4-29-99; *T.D.* 8886, 6-9-2000; *T.D.* 9448, 5-1-2009; *and T.D.* 9540, 8-9-2011.]

[Reg. § 25.7520-1]

**§ 25.7520-1. Valuation of annuities, unitrust interests, interests for life or terms of years, and remainder or reversionary interests.**—(a) *General actuarial valuations.*—(1) Except as otherwise provided in this section and in § 25.7520-3(b) (relating to exceptions to the use of prescribed tables under certain circumstances), in the case of certain gifts after April 30, 1989, the fair market value of annuities, interests for life or for a term of years (including unitrust interests), remainders, and reversions is their present value determined under this section. See § 20.2031-7(d) of this chapter (and, for periods prior to May 1, 2009, § 20.2031-7A) for the computation of the value of annuities, unitrust interests, life estates, terms for years, remainders, and reversions, other than interests described in paragraphs (a)(2) and (a)(3) of this section.

(2) In the case of a gift to a beneficiary of a pooled income fund, see § 1.642(c)-6(e) of this chapter (or, for periods prior to May 1, 2009, § 1.642(c)-6A) with respect to the valuation of the remainder interest.

(3) In the case of a gift to a beneficiary of a charitable remainder annuity trust after April 30, 1989, see § 1.664-2 of this chapter with respect to the valuation of the remainder interest. See § 1.664-4 of this chapter (Income Tax Regulations) with respect to the valuation of the remainder interest in property transferred to a charitable remainder unitrust.

(b) *Components of valuation.*—(1) *Interest rate component.*— (i) *Section 7520 interest rate.*—The section 7520 interest rate is the rate of return, rounded to the nearest two-tenths of one percent, that is equal to 120 percent of the applicable Federal mid-term rate, compounded annually, for purposes of section 1274(d)(1), for the month in which the valuation date falls. In rounding the rate to the nearest two-tenths of a percent, any rate that is midway between one two-tenths of a percent and another is rounded up to the higher of those two rates. For example, if 120 percent of the applicable Federal mid-term rate is 10.30, the section 7520 interest rate component is 10.4. The section 7520 interest rate is published monthly by the Internal Revenue Service in the Internal Revenue Bulletin (See § 601.601(d)(2)(ii)(*b*) of this chapter.)

(ii) *Valuation date.*—Generally, the valuation date is the date on which the gift is made. For gift tax purposes, the valuation date is the date on which the gift is complete under § 25.2511-2. For special rules in the case of charitable transfers, see § 25.7520-2.

(2) *Mortality component.*—The mortality component reflects the mortality data most recently available from the United States census. As new mortality data becomes available after each decennial census, the mortality component described in this section will be revised and the revised mortality component tables will be published in the regulations at that time. For gifts with valuation dates on or after May 1, 2009, the mortality component table (Table 2000CM) is contained in § 20.2031-7(d)(7). See § 20.2031-7A of this chapter for mortality component tables applicable to gifts for which the valuation date falls before May 1, 2009.

(c) *Tables.*—The present value on the valuation date of an annuity, life estate, term of years, remainder, or reversion is computed by using the section 7520 interest rate component that is described in paragraph (b)(1) of this section and the mortality component that is described in paragraph (b)(2) of this section. Actuarial factors for determining these present values are included in tables in these regulations and in publications by the Internal Revenue Service. If a special factor is required in order to value an interest, the Internal Revenue Service will furnish the factor upon a request for a ruling. The request for a ruling must be accompanied by a recitation of the facts, including the date of birth for each measuring life and copies of relevant instruments. A request for a ruling must comply with the instructions for requesting a ruling published periodically in the Internal Revenue Bulletin (see Rev. Proc. 94-1, 1994-1 I.R.B. 10, and subsequent updates, and §§ 601.201 and 601.601(d)(2)(ii)(*b*) of this chapter) and include payment of the required user fee.

(1) *Regulation sections containing tables with interest rates between 0.2 and 14 percent for valuation dates on or after May 1, 2009.*—Section 1.642(c)-6(e)(6) of this chapter contains Table S used for determining the present value of a single life remainder interest in a pooled income fund as defined in § 1.642(c)-5. See § 1.642(c)-6A for single life remainder factors applicable to valuation dates before May 1, 2009. Section 1.664-4(e)(6) contains Table F (payout factors) and Table D (actuarial factors used in determining the present value of a remainder interest postponed for a term of years). Section 1.664-4(e)(7) contains Table U(1) (unitrust single life remainder factors). These tables are used in determining the present value of a remainder interest in a charitable remainder unitrust as defined in § 1.664-3. See § 1.664-4A for unitrust single life remainder factors applicable to valuation dates before May 1, 2009. Section 20.2031-7(d)(6) of this chapter contains Table B (actuarial factors used in determining the present value of an interest for a term of years), Table K (annuity end-of-interval adjustment factors), and Table J (term certain annuity beginning-of-interval adjustment factors). Section 20.2031-7(d)(7) contains Table S (single life remainder factors), and Table 2000CM (mortality components). These tables are used in determining the present value of annuities, life estates, remainders, and reversions. See § 20.2031-7A for single life remainder factors and mortality components applicable to valuation dates before May 1, 2009.

(2) *Internal Revenue Service publications containing tables with interest rates between 0.2 and 22 percent for valuation dates on or after May 1, 2009.*—The following documents are available, at no charge, electronically via the IRS Internet site at *www.irs.gov*:

(i) Internal Revenue Service Publication 1457, "Actuarial Valuations Version 3A" (2009). This publication includes tables of valuation factors, as well as examples that show how to compute other valuation factors, for determining the present value of annuities, life estates, terms of years, remainders, and reversions, measured by one or two lives. These factors may also be used in the valuation of interests in a charitable remainder annuity trust as defined in § 1.664-2 and a pooled income fund as defined in § 1.642(c)-5 of this chapter.

(ii) Internal Revenue Service Publication 1458, "Actuarial Valuations Version 3B" (2009). This publication includes term certain tables and tables of one and two life valuation factors for determining the present value of remainder interests in a charitable remainder unitrust as defined in § 1.664-3 of this chapter.

(iii) Internal Revenue Service Publication 1459, "Actuarial Valuations Version 3C" (2009). This publication includes tables for computing depreciation adjustment factors. See § 1.170A-12 of this chapter.

(d) *Effective/applicability dates.*—This section applies on and after May 1, 2009. [Reg. § 25.7520-1.]

☐ [*T.D.* 8540, 6-9-94. *Amended by T.D.* 8819, 4-29-99 (corrected 6-21-99); *T.D.* 8886, 6-9-2000; *T.D.* 9448, 5-1-2009 *and T.D.* 9540, 8-9-2011.]

[Reg. § 1.7520-2]

**§ 1.7520-2. Valuation of charitable interests.**—(a) *In general.*— (1) *Valuation.*—Except as otherwise provided in this section and in § 1.7520-3 (relating to exceptions to the use of prescribed tables under certain circumstances), the fair market value of annuities, interests for life or for a term of years, remainders, and reversions for which an income tax charitable deduction is allowable is the present value of such interests determined under § 1.7520-1.

(2) *Prior-month election rule.*—If any part of the property interest transferred qualifies for an income tax charitable deduction under section 170(c), the taxpayer may elect (under paragraph (b) of this section) to compute the present value of the interest transferred by use of the section 7520 interest rate for the month during which the interest is transferred or the section 7520 interest rate component for either of the 2 months preceding the month during which the interest is transferred. Paragraph (b) of this section explains how a prior-month election is made. The interest rate for the month so elected is the applicable section 7520 interest rate. If the actuarial factor for either or both of the 2 months preceding the month during which the interst is transferred is based on a mortality experience that is different from the mortality experience at the date of the transfer and if the taxpayer elects to use the section 7520 rate for a prior month with the different mortality experience, the taxpayer must use the actuarial factor derived from the mortality experience in effect during the month of the section 7520 rate elected. All actuarial computations relating to the transfer must be made by applying the interest rate component and the mortality component of the month elected by the taxpayer.

(3) *Transfers of more than one interest in the same property.*—If a taxpayer transfers more than one interest in the same property at the same time, for purposes of valuing the transferred interests, the taxpayer must use the same interest rate and mortality component for each interest in the property transferred. If more than one interest in the same property is transferred in two or more separate transfers at different times, the value of each interest is determined by the use of the interest rate component and mortality component in effect during the month of the transfer of that interest or, if applicable under paragraph (a)(2) of this section, either of the two months preceding the month of the transfer.

(4) *Information required with tax return.*—The following information must be attached to the income tax return (or to the amended return) if the taxpayer claims a charitable deduction for the present value of a temporary or remainder interest in property—

(i) A complete description of the interest that is transferred, including a copy of the instrument of transfer;

(ii) The valuation date of the transfer;

(iii) The names and identification numbers of the beneficiaries of the transferred interest;

(iv) The names and birthdates of any measuring lives, a description of any relevant terminal illness condition of any measuring life, and (if applicable) an explanation of how any terminal illness condition was taken into account in valuing the interest; and

(v) A computation of the deduction showing the applicable section 7520 interest rate that is used to value the transferred interest.

(5) *Place for filing returns.*—See section 6091 of the Internal Revenue Code and the regulations thereunder for the place for filing the return or other document required by this section.

(b) *Election of interest rate component.*—(1) *Time for making election.*—A taxpayer makes a prior-month election under paragraph (a)(2) of this section by attaching the information described in paragraph (b)(2) of this section to the taxpayer's income tax return or to an amended return for that year that is filed within 24 months after the later of the date the original return for the year was filed or the due date for filing the return.

(2) *Manner of making election.*—A statement that the prior-month election under section 7520(a) of the Internal Revenue Code is being made and that identifies the elected month must be attached to the income tax return (or to the amended return).

(3) *Revocability.*—The prior-month election may be revoked by filing an amended return within 24 months after the later of the date the original return of tax for the year was filed or the due date for filing the return. The revocation must be filed in the place referred to in paragraph (a)(5) of this section.

(c) *Effective dates.*—Paragraph (a) of this section is effective as of May 1, 1989. Paragraph (b) of this section is effective for elections made after June 10, 1994. [Reg. § 1.7520-2.]

☐ [T.D. 8540, 6-9-94.]

### [Reg. § 20.7520-2]

**§ 20.7520-2. Valuation of charitable interests.**—(a) *In general.*—(1) *Valuation.*—Except as otherwise provided in this section and in § 20.7520-3 (relating to exceptions to the use of prescribed tables under certain circumstances), the fair market value of annuities, interests for life or for a term of years, remainders, and reversions for which an estate tax charitable deduction is allowable is the present value of such interests determined under § 20.7520-1.

(2) *Prior-month election rule.*—If any part of the property interest transferred qualifies for an estate tax charitable deduction under section 2055 or 2106, the executor may compute the present value of the transferred interest by use of the section 7520 interest rate for the month during which the interest is transferred or the section 7520 interest rate for either of the 2 months preceding the month during which the interest is transferred. Paragraph (b) of this section explains how a prior-month election is made. The interest rate for the month so elected is the applicable section 7520 interest rate. If the executor elects the alternate valuation date under section 2032 and also elects to use the section 7520 interest rate for either of the 2 months preceding the month in which the interest is transferred, the month so elected (either of the 2 months preceding the month in which the alternate valuation date falls) is the valuation date. If the actuarial factor for either or both of the 2 months preceding the month during which the interest is transferred is based on a mortality experience that is different from the mortality experience at the date of the transfer and if the executor elects to use the section 7520 rate for a prior month with the different mortality experience, the executor must use the actuarial factor derived from the mortality experience in effect during the month of the section 7520 rate elected. All actuarial computations relating to the transfer must be made by applying the interest rate component and the mortality component of the month elected by the executor.

(3) *Transfers of more than one interest in the same property.*—If a decedent's estate includes the transfer of more than one interest in the same property, the executor must, for purposes of valuing the transferred interests, use the same interest rate and mortality components for each interest in the property transferred.

(4) *Information required with tax return.*—The following information must be attached to the estate tax return (or be filed subsequently as supplemental information to the return) if the estate claims a charitable deduction for the present value of a temporary or remainder interest in property—

(i) A complete description of the interest that is transferred, including a copy of the instrument of transfer;

(ii) The valuation date of the transfer;

(iii) The names and identification numbers of the beneficiaries of the transferred interest;

(iv) The names and birthdates of any measuring lives, a description of any relevant terminal illness condition of any measuring life, and (if applicable) an explanation of how any terminal illness condition was taken into account in valuing the interest; and

(v) A computation of the deduction showing the applicable section 7520 interest rate that is used to value the transferred interest.

(5) *Place for filing returns.*—See section 6091 of the Internal Revenue Code and the regulations thereunder for the place for filing the return or other document required by this section.

(b) *Election of interest rate component.*—(1) *Time for making election.*—An executor makes a prior-month election under paragraph (a)(2) of this section by attaching the information described in paragraph (b)(2) of this section to the decedent's estate tax return or by filing a supplemental statement of the election information within 24 months after the later of the date the original estate tax return was filed or the due date for filing the return.

(2) *Manner of making election.*—A statement that the prior-month election under section 7520(a) of the Internal Revenue Code is being made and that identifies the elected month must be attached to the estate tax return (or by subsequently filing the statement as supplemental information to the return).

(3) *Revocability.*—The prior-month election may be revoked by filing a statement of supplemental information within 24 months after the later of the date the original return of tax for the decedent's estate was filed or the due date for filing the return. The revocation must be filed in the place referred to in paragraph (a)(5) of this section.

(c) *Effective dates.*—Paragraph (a) of this section is effective as of May 1, 1989. Paragraph (b) of this section is effective for elections made after June 10, 1994. [Reg. § 20.7520-2.]

☐ [T.D. 8540, 6-9-94.]

### [Reg. § 25.7520-2]

**§ 25.7520-2. Valuation of charitable interests.**—(a) *In general.*—(1) *Valuation.*—Except as otherwise provided in this section and in § 25.7520-3 (relating to exceptions to the use of prescribed tables under certain circumstances), the fair market value of annuities, interests for life or for a term of years, remainders, and reversions for which a gift tax charitable deduction is allowable is the present value of such interests determined under § 25.7520-1.

(2) *Prior-month election rule.*—If any part of the property interest transferred qualifies for a gift tax charitable deduction under section 2522, the donor may elect to compute the present value of the interest transferred by use of the section 7520 interest rate for the month during which the gift is made or the section 7520 interest rate for either of the 2 months preceding the month during which the gift is made. Paragraph (b) of this section explains how a prior-month election is made. The interest rate for the month so elected is the applicable section 7520 interest rate. If the actuarial factor for either or both of the 2 months preceding the month during which the gift is made is based on a mortality experience that is different from the mortality experience at the date of the gift and if the donor elects to use the section 7520 rate for a prior month with the different mortality experience, the donor must use the actuarial factor derived from the mortality experience in effect during the month of the section 7520 rate elected. All actuarial computations relating to the gift must be made by applying the interest rate component and the mortality component of the month elected by the donor.

(3) *Gifts of more than one interest in the same property.*—If a donor makes a gift of more than one interest in the same property at the same time, the donor must, for purposes of valuing the gifts, use the same interest rate and mortality components for the gift of each interest in the property. If the donor has made gifts of more than one interest in the same property at different times, the donor must determine the value of the gift by the use of the interest rate component and mortality component in effect during the month of that gift or, if applicable under paragraph (a)(2) of this section, either of the two months preceding the month of the gift.

(4) *Information required with tax return.*—The following information must be attached to the gift tax return (or to the amended return) if the donor claims a charitable deduction for the present value of a temporary or remainder interest in property—

(i) A complete description of the interest that is transferred, including a copy of the instrument of transfer;

(ii) The valuation date of the transfer;

(iii) The names and identification numbers of the beneficiaries of the transferred interest;

(iv) The names and birthdates of any measuring lives, a description of any relevant terminal illness condition of any measuring life, and (if applicable) an explanation of how any terminal illness condition was taken into account in valuing the interest; and

(v) A computation of the deduction showing the applicable section 7520 interest rate that is used to value the transferred interest.

(5) *Place for filing returns.*—See section 6091 of the Internal Revenue Code and the regulations thereunder for the place for filing the return or other document required by this section.

(b) *Election of interest rate component.*—(1) *Time for making election.*—A taxpayer makes a prior-month election under paragraph (a)(2) of this section by attaching the information described in paragraph (b)(2) of this section to the donor's gift tax return or to an amended return for that year that is filed within 24 months after the later of the date the original return for the year was filed or the due date for filing the return.

(2) *Manner of making election.*—A statement that the prior-month election under section 7520(a) of the Internal Revenue Code is being made and that identifies the elected month must be attached to the gift tax return (or to the amended return).

(3) *Revocability.*—The prior-month election may be revoked by filing an amended return within 24 months after the later of the date the original return of tax for that year was filed or the due date for filing the return. The revocation must be filed in the place referred to in paragraph (a)(5) of this section.

(c) *Effective dates.*—Paragraph (a) of this section is effective as of May 1, 1989. Paragraph (b) of this section is effective for elections made after June 10, 1994. [Reg. § 25.7520-2.]

☐ [T.D. 8540, 6-9-94.]

### [Reg. § 1.7520-3]

**§ 1.7520-3. Limitation on the application of section 7520.**— (a) *Internal Revenue Code sections to which section 7520 does not apply.*— Section 7520 of the Internal Revenue Code does not apply for purposes of—

(1) Part I, subchapter D of subtitle A (section 401 et. seq.), relating to the income tax treatment of certain qualified plans. (However, section 7520 does apply to the estate and gift tax treatment of certain qualified plans and for purposes of determining excess accumulations under section 4980A);

(2) Sections 72 and 101(b), relating to the income taxation of life insurance, endowment, and annuity contracts, unless otherwise provided for in the regulations under sections 72, 101, and 1011 (see, particularly, §§ 1.101-2(e)(1)(iii)(*b*)(2), and 1.1011-2(c), *Example 8*);

(3) Sections 83 and 451, unless otherwise provided for in the regulations under those sections;

(4) Section 457, relating to the valuation of deferred compensation, unless otherwise provided for in the regulations under section 457;

(5) Sections 3121(v) and 3306(r), relating to the valuation of deferred amounts, unless otherwise provided for in the regulations under those sections;

(6) Section 6058, relating to valuation statements evidencing compliance with qualified plan requirements, unless otherwise provided for in the regulations under section 6058;

(7) Section 7872, relating to income and gift taxation of interest-free loans and loans with below-market interest rates, unless otherwise provided for in the regulations under section 7872; or

(8) Section 2702(a)(2)(A), relating to the value of a nonqualified retained interest upon a transfer of an interest in trust to or for the benefit of a member of the transferor's family; and

(9) Any other sections of the Internal Revenue Code to the extent provided by the Internal Revenue Service in revenue rulings or revenue procedures. (See §§ 601.201 and 601.601 of this chapter.)

(b) *Other limitations on the application of section 7520.*—(1) *In general.*—(i) *Ordinary beneficial interests.*—For purposes of this section:

(A) An *ordinary annuity interest* is the right to receive a fixed dollar amount at the end of each year during one or more measuring lives or for some other defined period. A standard section 7520 annuity factor for an ordinary annuity interest represents the present worth of the right to receive $1.00 per year for a defined period, using the interest rate prescribed under section 7520 for the appropriate month. If an annuity interest is payable more often than annually or is payable at the beginning of each period, a special adjustment must be made in any computation with a standard section 7520 annuity factor.

(B) An *ordinary income interest* is the right to receive the income from, or the use of, property during one or more measuring lives or for some other defined period. A standard section 7520 income factor for an ordinary income interest represents the present

worth of the right to receive the use of $1.00 for a defined period, using the interest rate prescribed under section 7520 for the appropriate month.

(C) An *ordinary remainder or reversionary interest* is the right to receive an interest in property at the end of one or more measuring lives or some other defined period. A standard section 7520 remainder factor for an ordinary remainder or reversionary interest represents the present worth of the right to receive $1.00 at the end of a defined period, using the interest rate prescribed under section 7520 for the appropriate month.

(ii) *Certain restricted beneficial interests.*—A *restricted beneficial interest* is an annuity, income, remainder, or reversionary interest that is subject to a contingency, power, or other restriction, whether the restriction is provided for by the terms of the trust, will, or other governing instrument or is caused by other circumstances. In general, a standard section 7520 annuity, income, or remainder factor may not be used to value a restricted beneficial interest. However, a special section 7520 annuity, income, or remainder factor may be used to value a restricted beneficial interest under some circumstances. See paragraph (b)(4) *Example 2* of this section, which illustrates a situation where a special section 7520 actuarial factor is needed to take into account the shorter life expectancy of the terminally ill measuring life. See § 1.7520-1(c) for requesting a special factor from the Internal Revenue Service.

(iii) *Other beneficial interests.*—If, under the provisions of this paragraph (b), the interest rate and mortality components prescribed under section 7520 are not applicable in determining the value of any annuity, income, remainder, or reversionary interest, the actual fair market value of the interest (determined without regard to section 7520) is based on all of the facts and circumstances if and to the extent permitted by the Internal Revenue Code provision applicable to the property interest.

(2) *Provisions of governing instrument and other limitations on source of payment.*—(i) *Annuities.*—A standard section 7520 annuity factor may not be used to determine the present value of an annuity for a specified term of years or the life of one or more individuals unless the effect of the trust, will, or other governing instrument is to ensure that the annuity will be paid for the entire defined period. In the case of an annuity payable from a trust or other limited fund, the annuity is not considered payable for the entire defined period if, considering the applicable section 7520 interest rate at the valuation date of the transfer, the annuity is expected to exhaust the fund before the last possible annuity payment is made in full. For this purpose, it must be assumed that it is possible for each measuring life to survive until age 110. For example, for a fixed annuity payable annually at the end of each year, if the amount of the annuity payment (expressed as a percentage of the initial corpus) is less than or equal to the applicable section 7520 interest rate at the date of the transfer, the corpus is assumed to be sufficient to make all payments. If the percentage exceeds the applicable section 7520 interest rate and the annuity is for a definite term of years, multiply the annual annuity amount by the Table B term certain annuity factor, as described in § 1.7520-1(c)(1), for the number of years of the defined period. If the percentage exceeds the applicable section 7520 interest rate and the annuity is payable for the life of one or more individuals, multiply the annual annuity amount by the Table B annuity factor for 110 years minus the age of the youngest individual. If the result exceeds the limited fund, the annuity may exhaust the fund, and it will be necessary to calculate a special section 7520 annuity factor that takes into account the exhaustion of the trust or fund. This computation would be modified, if appropriate, to take into account annuities with different payment terms. See § 25.7520-3(b)(2)(v) *Example 5* of this chapter, which provides an illustration involving an annuity trust that is subject to exhaustion.

(ii) *Income and similar interests.*—(A) *Beneficial enjoyment.*—A standard section 7520 income factor for an ordinary income interest may not be used to determine the present value of an income or similar interest in trust for a term of years or for the life of one or more individuals unless the effect of the trust, will, or other governing instrument is to provide the income beneficiary with that degree of beneficial enjoyment of the property during the term of the income interest that the principles of the law of trusts accord to a person who is unqualifiedly designated as the income beneficiary of a trust for a similar period of time. This degree of beneficial enjoyment is provided only if it was the transferor's intent, as manifested by the provisions of the governing instrument and the surrounding circumstances, that the trust provide an income interest for the income beneficiary during the specified period of time that is consistent with the value of the trust corpus and with its preservation. In determining whether a trust arrangement evidences that intention, the treatment required or permitted with respect to individual items must be considered in relation to the entire system provided for in the administration of the subject trust. Similarly, in determining the present value of the right to use tangible property (whether or not in trust) for one or more measuring lives or for some other specified period of time, the interest rate component prescribed under section 7520 and §1.7520-1 may not be used unless, during the specified period, the effect of the trust, will or other governing instrument is to provide the beneficiary with that degree of use, possession, and enjoyment of the property during the term of interest that applicable state law accords to a person who is unqualifiedly designated as a life tenant or term holder for a similar period of time.

(B) *Diversions of income and corpus.*—A standard section 7520 income factor for an ordinary income interest may not be used to value an income interest or similar interest in property for a term of years or for one or more measuring lives if—

(1) The trust, will, or other governing instrument requires or permits the beneficiary's income or other enjoyment to be withheld, diverted, or accumulated for another person's benefit without the consent of the income beneficiary; or

(2) The governing instrument requires or permits trust corpus to be withdrawn from the trust for another person's benefit during the income beneficiary's term of enjoyment without the consent of and accountability to the income beneficiary for such diversion.

(iii) *Remainder and reversionary interests.*—A standard section 7520 remainder interest factor for an ordinary remainder or reversionary interest may not be used to determine the present value of a remainder or reversionary interest (whether in trust or otherwise) unless, consistent with the preservation and protection that the law of trusts would provide for a person who is unqualifiedly designated as the remainder beneficiary of a trust for a similar duration, the effect of the administrative and dispositive provisions for the interest or interests that precede the remainder or reversionary interest is to assure that the property will be adequately preserved and protected (e.g., from erosion, invasion, depletion, or damage) until the remainder or reversionary interest takes effect in possession and enjoyment. This degree of preservation and protection is provided only if it was the transferor's intent, as manifested by the provisions of the arrangement and the surrounding circumstances, that the entire disposition provide the remainder or reversionary beneficiary with an undiminished interest in the property transferred at the time of the termination of the prior interest.

(iv) *Pooled income fund interests.*—In general, pooled income funds are created and administered to achieve a special rate of return. A beneficial interest in a pooled income fund is not ordinarily valued using a standard section 7520 income or remainder interest factor. The present value of a beneficial interest in a pooled income fund is determined according to rules and special remainder factors prescribed in §1.642(c)-6 and, when applicable, the rules set forth in paragraph (b)(3) of this section, if the individual who is the measuring life is terminally ill at the time of the transfer.

(3) *Mortality component.*—The mortality component prescribed under section 7520 may not be used to determine the present value of an annuity, income interest, remainder interest, or reversionary interest if an individual who is a measuring life is terminally ill at the time of the transaction. For purposes of this paragraph (b)(3), an individual who is known to have an incurable illness or other deteriorating physical condition is considered terminally ill if there is at least a 50 percent probability that the individual will die within 1 year. However, if the individual survives for eighteen months or longer after the date of the transaction, that individual shall be presumed to have not been terminally ill at the time of the transaction unless the contrary is established by clear and convincing evidence.

(4) *Examples.*—The provisions of this paragraph (b) are illustrated by the following examples:

*Example 1. Annuity funded with unproductive property.* The taxpayer transfers corporation stock worth $1,000,000 to a trust. The trust provides for a 6 percent ($60,000 per year) annuity in cash or other property to be paid to a charitable organization for 25 years and for the remainder to be distributed to the donor's child. The trust specifically authorizes, but does not require, the trustee to retain the shares of stock. The section 7520 interest rate for the month of the transfer is 8.2 percent. The corporation has paid no dividends on this stock during the past 5 years, and there is no indication that this policy will change in the near future. Under applicable state law, the corporation is considered to be a sound investment that satisfies fiduciary standards. Therefore, the trust's sole investment in this corporation is not expected to adversely affect the interest of either the annuitant or the remainder beneficiary. Considering the 6 percent annuity payout rate and the 8.2 percent section 7520 interest rate, the trust corpus is considered sufficient to pay this annuity for the entire 25-year term of the trust, or even indefinitely. Although it appears

that neither beneficiary would be able to compel the trustee to make the trust corpus produce investment income, the annuity interest in this case is considered to be an ordinary annuity interest, and the standard section 7520 annuity factor may be used to determine the present value of the annuity. In this case, the section 7520 annuity factor would represent the right to receive $1.00 per year for a term of 25 years.

*Example 2. Terminal illness.* The taxpayer transfers property worth $1,000,000 to a charitable remainder unitrust described in section 664(d)(2) and §1.664-3. The trust provides for a fixed-percentage 7 percent unitrust benefit (each annual payment is equal to 7 percent of the trust assets as valued at the beginning of each year) to be paid quarterly to an individual beneficiary for life and for the remainder to be distributed to a charitable organization. At the time the trust is created, the individual beneficiary is age 60 and has been diagnosed with an incurable illness and there is at least a 50 percent probability of the individual dying within 1 year. Assuming the presumption in paragraph (b)(3) of this section does not apply, because there is at least a 50 percent probability that this beneficiary will die within 1 year, the standard section 7520 unitrust remainder factor for a person age 60 from the valuation tables may not be used to determine the present value of the charitable remainder interest. Instead, a special unitrust remainder factor must be computed that is based on the section 7520 interest rate and that takes into account the projection of the individual beneficiary's actual life expectancy.

(5) *Additional limitations.*—Section 7520 does not apply to the extent as may otherwise be provided by the Commissioner.

(c) *Effective date.*—Section 1.7520-3(a) is effective as of May 1, 1989. The provisions of paragraph (b) of this section are effective with respect to transactions after December 13, 1995. [Reg. §1.7520-3.]

☐ [*T.D.* 8540, 6-9-94. Amended by *T.D.* 8630, 12-12-95.]

**[Reg. §20.7520-3]**

**§20.7520-3. Limitation on the application of section 7520.**—(a) *Internal Revenue Code sections to which section 7520 does not apply.*—Section 7520 of the Internal Revenue Code does not apply for purposes of—

(1) Part I, subchapter D of subtitle A (section 401 et. seq.), relating to the income tax treatment of certain qualified plans. (However, section 7520 does apply to the estate and gift tax treatment of certain qualified plans and for purposes of determining excess accumulations under section 4980A);

(2) Sections 72 and 101(b), relating to the income taxation of life insurance, endowment, and annuity contracts, unless otherwise provided for in the regulations under sections 72, 101, and 1011 (see, particularly, §§1.101-2(e)(1)(iii)(*b*)(2), and 1.1011-2(c), *Example 8*);

(3) Sections 83 and 451, unless otherwise provided for in the regulations under those sections;

(4) Section 457, relating to the valuation of deferred compensation, unless otherwise provided for in the regulations under section 457;

(5) Sections 3121(v) and 3306(r), relating to the valuation of deferred amounts, unless otherwise provided for in the regulations under those sections;

(6) Section 6058, relating to valuation statements evidencing compliance with qualified plan requirements, unless otherwise provided for in the regulations under section 6058;

(7) Section 7872, relating to income and gift taxation of interest-free loans and loans with below-market interest rates, unless otherwise provided for in the regulations under section 7872; or

(8) Section 2702(a)(2)(A), relating to the value of a nonqualified retained interest upon a transfer of an interest in trust to or for the benefit of a member of the transferor's family; and

(9) Any other sections of the Internal Revenue Code to the extent provided by the Internal Revenue Service in revenue rulings or revenue procedures. (See §§601.201 and 601.601 of this chapter).

(b) *Other limitations on the application of section 7520.*—(1) *In general.*—(i) *Ordinary beneficial interests.*—For purposes of this section:

(A) An *ordinary annuity interest* is the right to receive a fixed dollar amount at the end of each year during one or more measuring lives or for some other defined period. A standard section 7520 annuity factor for an ordinary annuity interest represents the present worth of the right to receive $1.00 per year for a defined period, using the interest rate prescribed under section 7520 for the appropriate month. If an annuity interest is payable more often than annually or is payable at the beginning of each period, a special adjustment must be made in any computation with a standard section 7520 annuity factor.

(B) An *ordinary income interest* is the right to receive the income from or the use of property during one or more measuring lives or for some other defined period. A standard section 7520 income factor for an ordinary income interest represents the present worth of the right to receive the use of $1.00 for a defined period, using the interest rate prescribed under section 7520 for the appropriate month.

(C) An *ordinary remainder or reversionary interest* is the right to receive an interest in property at the end of one or more measuring lives or some other defined period. A standard section 7520 remainder factor for an ordinary remainder or reversionary interest represents the present worth of the right to receive $1.00 at the end of a defined period, using the interest rate prescribed under section 7520 for the appropriate month.

(ii) *Certain restricted beneficial interests.*—A *restricted beneficial interest* is an annuity, income, remainder, or reversionary interest that is subject to any contingency, power, or other restriction, whether the restriction is provided for by the terms of the trust, will, or other governing instrument or is caused by other circumstances. In general, a standard section 7520 annuity, income, or remainder factor may not be used to value a restricted beneficial interest. However, a special section 7520 annuity, income, or remainder factor may be used to value a restricted beneficial interest under some circumstances. See paragraphs (b)(2)(v) *Example 4* and (b)(4) *Example 1* of this section, which illustrate situations where special section 7520 actuarial factors are needed to take into account limitations on beneficial interests. See § 20.7520-1(c) for requesting a special factor from the Internal Revenue Service.

(iii) *Other beneficial interests.*—If, under the provisions of this paragraph (b), the interest rate and mortality components prescribed under section 7520 are not applicable in determining the value of any annuity, income, remainder, or reversionary interest, the actual fair market value of the interest (determined without regard to section 7520) is based on all of the facts and circumstances if and to the extent permitted by the Internal Revenue Code provision applicable to the property interest.

(2) *Provisions of governing instrument and other limitations on source of payment.*—(i) *Annuities.*—A standard section 7520 annuity factor may not be used to determine the present value of an annuity for a specified term of years or the life of one or more individuals unless the effect of the trust, will, or other governing instrument is to ensure that the annuity will be paid for the entire defined period. In the case of an annuity payable from a trust or other limited fund, the annuity is not considered payable for the entire defined period if, considering the applicable section 7520 interest rate at the valuation date of the transfer, the annuity is expected to exhaust the fund before the last possible annuity payment is made in full. For this purpose, it must be assumed that it is possible for each measuring life to survive until age 110. For example, for a fixed annuity payable annually at the end of each year, if the amount of the annuity payment (expressed as a percentage of the initial corpus) is less than or equal to the applicable section 7520 interest rate at the date of the transfer, the corpus is assumed to be sufficient to make all payments. If the percentage exceeds the applicable section 7520 interest rate and the annuity is for a definite term of years, multiply the annual annuity amount by the Table B term certain annuity factor, as described in § 20.7520-1(c)(1), for the number of years of the defined period. If the percentage exceeds the applicable section 7520 interest rate and the annuity is payable for the life of one or more individuals, multiply the annual annuity amount by the Table B annuity factor for 110 years minus the age of the youngest individual. If the result exceeds the limited fund, the annuity may exhaust the fund, and it will be necessary to calculate a special section 7520 annuity factor that takes into account the exhaustion of the trust or fund. This computation would be modified, if appropriate, to take into account annuities with different payment terms. See § 25.7520-3(b)(2)(v) *Example 5* of this chapter, which provides an illustration involving an annuity trust that is subject to exhaustion.

(ii) *Income and similar interests.*—(A) *Beneficial enjoyment.*—A standard section 7520 income factor for an ordinary income interest may not be used to determine the present value of an income or similar interest in trust for a term of years, or for the life of one or more individuals, unless the effect of the trust, will, or other governing instrument is to provide the income beneficiary with that degree of beneficial enjoyment of the property during the term of the income interest that the principles of the law of trusts accord to a person who is unqualifiedly designated as the income beneficiary of a trust for a similar period of time. This degree of beneficial enjoyment is provided only if it was the transferor's intent, as manifested by the provisions of the governing instrument and the surrounding circumstances, that the trust provide an income interest for the income beneficiary during the specified period of time that is consistent with the value of the trust corpus and with its preservation. In determining whether a trust arrangement evidences that intention, the treatment required or permitted with respect to individual items must be considered in relation to the entire system provided for in the administration of the subject trust. Similarly, in determining the present value of the right to use tangible property (whether or not in trust) for one or more measuring lives or for some other specified period of time, the interest rate component prescribed under section 7520 and § 1.7520-1 of this chapter may not be used unless, during the specified period, the effect of the trust, will, or other governing instrument is to provide the beneficiary with that degree of use, possession, and enjoyment of the property during the term of interest that applicable state law accords to a person who is unqualifiedly designated as a life tenant or term holder for a similar period of time.

(B) *Diversions of income and corpus.*—A standard section 7520 income factor for an ordinary income interest may not be used to value an income interest or similar interest in property for a term of years, or for one or more measuring lives, if—

(1) The trust, will, or other governing instrument requires or permits the beneficiary's income or other enjoyment to be withheld, diverted, or accumulated for another person's benefit without the consent of the income beneficiary; or

(2) The governing instrument requires or permits trust corpus to be withdrawn from the trust for another person's benefit without the consent of the income beneficiary during the income beneficiary's term of enjoyment and without accountability to the income beneficiary for such diversion.

(iii) *Remainder and reversionary interests.*—A standard section 7520 remainder interest factor for an ordinary remainder or reversionary interest may not be used to determine the present value of a remainder or reversionary interest (whether in trust or otherwise) unless, consistent with the preservation and protection that the law of trusts would provide for a person who is unqualifiedly designated as the remainder beneficiary of a trust for a similar duration, the effect of the administrative and dispositive provisions for the interest or interests that precede the remainder or reversionary interest is to assure that the property will be adequately preserved and protected (e.g., from erosion, invasion, depletion, or damage) until the remainder or reversionary interest takes effect in possession and enjoyment. This degree of preservation and protection is provided only if it was the transferor's intent, as manifested by the provisions of the arrangement and the surrounding circumstances, that the entire disposition provide the remainder or reversionary beneficiary with an undiminished interest in the property transferred at the time of the termination of the prior interest.

(iv) *Pooled income fund interests.*—In general, pooled income funds are created and administered to achieve a special rate of return. A beneficial interest in a pooled income fund is not ordinarily valued using a standard section 7520 income or remainder interest factor. The present value of a beneficial interest in a pooled income fund is determined according to rules and special remainder factors prescribed in § 1.642(c)-6 of this chapter and, when applicable, the rules set forth under paragraph (b)(3) of this section if the individual who is the measuring life is terminally ill at the time of the transfer.

(v) *Examples.*—The provisions of this paragraph (b)(2) are illustrated by the following examples:

*Example 1. Unproductive property.* A died, survived by B and C. B died two years after A. A's will provided for a bequest of corporation stock in trust under the terms of which all of the trust income was paid to B for life. After the death of B, the trust terminated and the trust property was distributed to C. The trust specifically authorized, but did not require, the trustee to retain the shares of stock. The corporation paid no dividends on this stock during the 5 years before A's death and the 2 years before B's death. There was no indication that this policy would change after A's death. Under applicable state law, the corporation is considered to be a sound investment that satisfies fiduciary standards. The facts and circumstances, including applicable state law, indicate that B did not have the legal right to compel the trustee to make the trust corpus productive in conformity with the requirements for a lifetime trust income interest under applicable local law. Therefore, B's life income interest in this case is considered nonproductive. Consequently, B's income interest may not be valued actuarially under this section.

*Example 2. Beneficiary's right to make trust productive.* The facts are the same as in *Example 1*, except that the trustee is not specifically authorized to retain the shares of stock. Further, the terms of the trust specifically provide that B, the life income beneficiary, may require the trustee to make the trust corpus productive consistent with income yield standards for trusts under applicable state law. Under that law, the minimum rate of income that a productive trust may produce is substantially below the section 7520 interest rate for the month of A's death. In this case, because B has the right to compel the trustee to make the trust productive for purposes of applicable local law during the beneficiary's lifetime, the income interest is considered an ordinary income interest for purposes of this paragraph, and the standard section 7520 life income interest factor may be used to determine the present value of B's income interest.

*Example 3. Discretionary invasion of corpus.* The decedent, A, transferred property to a trust under the terms of which all of the trust income is to be paid to A's child for life and the remainder of the trust is to be distributed to a grandchild. The trust authorizes the trustee without restriction to distribute corpus to A's surviving spouse for the spouse's comfort and happiness. In this case, because the trustee's power to invade trust corpus is unrestricted, the exercise of the power could result in the termination of the income interest at any time. Consequently, the income interest is not considered an ordinary income interest for purposes of this paragraph, and may not be valued actuarially under this section.

*Example 4. Limited invasion of corpus.* The decedent, A, bequeathed property to a trust under the terms of which all of the trust income is to be paid to A's child for life and the remainder is to be distributed to A's grandchild. The trust authorizes the child to withdraw up to $5,000 per year from the trust corpus. In this case, the child's power to invade trust corpus is limited to an ascertainable amount each year. Annual invasions of any amount would be expected to progressively diminish the property from which the child's income is paid. Consequently, the income interest is not considered an ordinary income interest for purposes of this paragraph, and the standard section 7520 income interest factor may not be used to determine the present value of the income interest. Nevertheless, the present value of the child's income interest is ascertainable by making a special actuarial calculation that would take into account not only the initial value of the trust corpus, the section 7520 interest rate for the month of the transfer, and the mortality component for the child's age, but also the assumption that the trust corpus will decline at the rate of $5,000 each year during the child's lifetime. The child's right to receive an amount not in excess of $5,000 per year may be separately valued in this instance and, assuming the trust corpus would not exhaust before the child would attain age 110, would be considered an ordinary annuity interest.

*Example 5. Power to consume.* The decedent, A, devised a life estate in 3 parcels of real estate to A's surviving spouse with the remainder to a child, or, if the child doesn't survive, to the child's estate. A also conferred upon the spouse an unrestricted power to consume the property, which includes the right to sell part or all of the property and to use the proceeds for the spouse's support, comfort, happiness, and other purposes. Any portion of the property or its sale proceeds remaining at the death of the surviving spouse is to vest by operation of law in the child at that time. The child predeceased the surviving spouse. In this case, the surviving spouse's power to consume the corpus is unrestricted, and the exercise of the power could entirely exhaust the remainder interest during the life of the spouse. Consequently, the remainder interest that is includible in the child's estate is not considered an ordinary remainder interest for purposes of this paragraph and may not be valued actuarially under this section.

(3) *Mortality component.*—(i) *Terminal illness.*—Except as provided in paragraph (b)(3)(ii) of this section, the mortality component prescribed under section 7520 may not be used to determine the present value of an annuity, income interest, remainder interest, or reversionary interest if an individual who is a measuring life is terminally ill at the time of the decedent's death. For purposes of this paragraph (b)(3), an individual who is known to have an incurable illness or other deteriorating physical condition is considered terminally ill if there is at least a 50 percent probability that the individual will die within 1 year. However, if the individual survives for eighteen months or longer after the date of the decedent's death, that individual shall be presumed to have not been terminally ill at the date of death unless the contrary is established by clear and convincing evidence.

(ii) *Terminal illness exceptions.*—In the case of the allowance of the credit for tax on a prior transfer under section 2013, if a final determination of the federal estate tax liability of the transferor's estate has been made under circumstances that required valuation of the life interest received by the transferee, the value of the property transferred, for purposes of the credit allowable to the transferee's estate, shall be the value determined previously in the transferor's estate. Otherwise, for purposes of section 2013, the provisions of paragraph (b)(3)(i) of this section shall govern in valuing the property transferred. The value of a decedent's reversionary interest under sections 2037(b) and 2042(2) shall be determined without regard to the physical condition, immediately before the decedent's death, of the individual who is the measuring life.

(iii) *Death resulting from common accidents.*—The mortality component prescribed under section 7520 may not be used to determine the present value of an annuity, income interest, remainder interest, or reversionary interest if the decedent, and the individual

who is the measuring life, die as a result of a common accident or other occurrence.

(4) *Examples.*—The provisions of paragraph (b)(3) of this section are illustrated by the following examples:

*Example 1. Terminal illness.* The decedent bequeaths $1,000,000 to a trust under the terms of which the trustee is to pay $103,000 per year to a charitable organization during the life of the decedent's child. Upon the death of the child, the remainder in the trust is to be distributed to the decedent's grandchild. The child, who is age 60, has been diagnosed with an incurable illness, and there is at least a 50 percent probability of the child dying within 1 year. Assuming the presumption provided for in paragraph (b)(3)(i) of this section does not apply, the standard life annuity factor for a person age 60 may not be used to determine the present value of the charitable organization's annuity interest because there is at least a 50 percent probability that the child, who is the measuring life, will die within 1 year. Instead, a special section 7520 annuity factor must be computed that takes into account the projection of the child's actual life expectancy.

*Example 2. Deaths resulting from common accidents, etc.* The decedent's will establishes a trust to pay income to the decedent's surviving spouse for life. The will provides that, upon the spouse's death or, if the spouse fails to survive the decedent, upon the decedent's death the trust property is to pass to the decedent's children. The decedent and the decedent's spouse die simultaneously in an accident under circumstances in which it was impossible to determine who survived the other. Even if the terms of the will and applicable state law presume that the decedent died first with the result that the property interest is considered to have passed in trust for the benefit of the spouse for life, after which the remainder is to be distributed to the decedent's children, the spouse's life income interest may not be valued by use of the mortality component described under section 7520. The result would be the same even if it was established that the spouse survived the decedent.

(5) *Additional limitations.*—Section 7520 does not apply to the extent as may otherwise be provided by the Commissioner.

(c) *Effective date.*—Section § 20.7520-3(a) is effective as of May 1, 1989. The provisions of paragraph (b) of this section are effective with respect to estates of decedents dying after December 13, 1995. [Reg. § 20.7520-3.]

☐ [*T.D.* 8540, 6-9-94. *Amended by T.D.* 8630, 12-12-95.]

**[Reg. § 25.7520-3]**

**§ 25.7520-3. Limitation on the application of section 7520.**—(a) *Internal Revenue Code sections to which section 7520 does not apply.*—Section 7520 of the Internal Revenue Code does not apply for purposes of—

(1) Part I, subchapter D of subtitle A (section 401 et. seq.), relating to the income tax treatment of certain qualified plans. (However, section 7520 does apply to the estate and gift tax treatment of certain qualified plans and for purposes of determining excess accumulations under section 4980A);

(2) Sections 72 and 101(b), relating to the income taxation of life insurance, endowment, and annuity contracts, unless otherwise provided for in the regulations under sections 72, 101, and 1011 (see, particularly, § § 1.101-2(e)(1)(iii)(*b*)(2), and 1.1011-2(c), *Example 8*);

(3) Sections 83 and 451, unless otherwise provided for in the regulations under those sections;

(4) Section 457, relating to the valuation of deferred compensation, unless otherwise provided for in the regulations under section 457;

(5) Sections 3121(v) and 3306(r), relating to the valuation of deferred amounts, unless otherwise provided for in the regulations under those sections;

(6) Section 6058, relating to valuation statements evidencing compliance with qualified plan requirements, unless otherwise provided for in the regulations under section 6058;

(7) Section 7872, relating to income and gift taxation of interest-free loans and loans with below-market interest rates, unless otherwise provided for in the regulations under section 7872; or

(8) Section 2702(a)(2)(A), relating to the value of a nonqualified retained interest upon a transfer of an interest in trust to or for the benefit of a member of the transferor's family; and

(9) Any other section of the Internal Revenue Code to the extent provided by the Internal Revenue Service in revenue rulings or revenue procedures. (See § § 601.201 and 601.601 of this chapter).

(b) *Other limitations on the application of section 7520.*—(1) *In general.*—(i) *Ordinary beneficial interests.*—For purposes of this section:

(A) An *ordinary annuity interest* is the right to receive a fixed dollar amount at the end of each year during one or more measuring lives or for some other defined period. A standard section 7520 annuity factor for an ordinary annuity interest represents the present worth of the right to receive $1.00 per year for a defined period, using the interest rate prescribed under section 7520 for the appropriate month. If an annuity interest is payable more often than annually or is payable at the beginning of each period, a special adjustment must be made in any computation with a standard section 7520 annuity factor.

(B) An *ordinary income interest* is the right to receive the income from or the use of property during one or more measuring lives or for some other defined period. A standard section 7520 income factor for an ordinary income interest represents the present worth of the right to receive the use of $1.00 for a defined period, using the interest rate prescribed under section 7520 for the appropriate month. However, in the case of certain gifts made after October 8, 1990, if the donor does not retain a qualified annuity, unitrust, or reversionary interest, the value of any interest retained by the donor is considered to be zero if the remainder beneficiary is a member of the donor's family. See § 25.2702-2.

(C) An *ordinary remainder or reversionary interest* is the right to receive an interest in property at the end of one or more measuring lives or some other defined period. A standard section 7520 remainder factor for an ordinary remainder or reversionary interest represents the present worth of the right to receive $1.00 at the end of a defined period, using the interest rate prescribed under section 7520 for the appropriate month.

(ii) *Certain restricted beneficial interests.*—A *restricted beneficial interest* is an annuity, income, remainder, or reversionary interest that is subject to any contingency, power, or other restriction, whether the restriction is provided for by the terms of the trust, will, or other governing instrument or is caused by other circumstances. In general, a standard section 7520 annuity, income, or remainder factor may not be used to value a restricted beneficial interest. However, a special section 7520 annuity, income, or remainder factor may be used to value a restricted beneficial interest under some circumstances. See paragraphs (b)(2)(v) *Example 5* and (b)(4) of this section, which illustrate situations in which special section 7520 actuarial factors are needed to take into account limitations on beneficial interests. See § 25.7520-1(c) for requesting a special factor from the Internal Revenue Service.

(iii) *Other beneficial interests.*—If, under the provisions of this paragraph (b), the interest rate and mortality components prescribed under section 7520 are not applicable in determining the value of any annuity, income, remainder, or reversionary interest, the actual fair market value of the interest (determined without regard to section 7520) is based on all of the facts and circumstances if and to the extent permitted by the Internal Revenue Code provision applicable to the property interest.

(2) *Provisions of governing instrument and other limitations on source of payment.*—(i) *Annuities.*—A standard section 7520 annuity factor may not be used to determine the present value of an annuity for a specified term of years or the life of one or more individuals unless the effect of the trust, will, or other governing instrument is to ensure that the annuity will be paid for the entire defined period. In the case of an annuity payable from a trust or other limited fund, the annuity is not considered payable for the entire defined period if, considering the applicable section 7520 interest rate on the valuation date of the transfer, the annuity is expected to exhaust the fund before the last possible annuity payment is made in full. For this purpose, it must be assumed that it is possible for each measuring life to survive until age 110. For example, for a fixed annuity payable annually at the end of each year, if the amount of the annuity payment (expressed as a percentage of the initial corpus) is less than or equal to the applicable section 7520 interest rate at the date of the transfer, the corpus is assumed to be sufficient to make all payments. If the percentage exceeds the applicable section 7520 interest rate and the annuity is for a definite term of years, multiply the annual annuity amount by the Table B term certain annuity factor, as described in § 25.7520-1(c)(1), for the number of years of the defined period. If the percentage exceeds the applicable section 7520 interest rate and the annuity is payable for the life of one or more individuals, multiply the annual annuity amount by the Table B annuity factor for 110 years minus the age of the youngest individual. If the result exceeds the limited fund, the annuity may exhaust the fund, and it will be necessary to calculate a special section 7520 annuity factor that takes into account the exhaustion of the trust or fund. This computation would be modified, if appropriate, to take into account annuities with different payment terms.

(ii) *Income and similar interests.*—(A) *Beneficial enjoyment.*—A standard section 7520 income factor for an ordinary income interest is not to be used to determine the present value of an income or similar interest in trust for a term of years or for the life of one or more individuals unless the effect of the trust, will, or other governing instrument is to provide the income beneficiary with that degree of beneficial enjoyment of the property during the term of the income interest that the principles of the law of trusts accord to a person who is unqualifiedly designated as the income beneficiary of a trust for a similar period of time. This degree of beneficial enjoyment is provided only if it was the transferor's intent, as manifested by the provisions of the governing instrument and the surrounding circumstances, that the trust provide an income interest for the income beneficiary during the specified period of time that is consistent with the value of the trust corpus and with its preservation. In determining whether a trust arrangement evidences that intention, the treatment required or permitted with respect to individual items must be considered in relation to the entire system provided for in the administration of the subject trust. Similarly, in determining the present value of the right to use tangible property (whether or not in trust) for one or more measuring lives or for some other specified period of time, the interest rate component prescribed under section 7520 and § 1.7520-1 of this chapter may not be used unless, during the specified period, the effect of the trust, will or other governing instrument is to provide the beneficiary with that degree of use, possession, and enjoyment of the property during the term of interest that applicable state law accords to a person who is unqualifiedly designated as a life tenant or term holder for a similar period of time.

(B) *Diversions of income and corpus.*—A standard section 7520 income factor for an ordinary income interest may not be used to value an income interest or similar interest in property for a term of years, or for one or more measuring lives, if—

(1) The trust, will, or other governing instrument requires or permits the beneficiary's income or other enjoyment to be withheld, diverted, or accumulated for another person's benefit without the consent of the income beneficiary; or

(2) The governing instrument requires or permits trust corpus to be withdrawn from the trust for another person's benefit without the consent of the income beneficiary during the income beneficiary's term of enjoyment and without accountability to the income beneficiary for such diversion.

(iii) *Remainder and reversionary interests.*—A standard section 7520 remainder interest factor for an ordinary remainder or reversionary interest may not be used to determine the present value of a remainder or reversionary interest (whether in trust or otherwise) unless, consistent with the preservation and protection that the law of trusts would provide for a person who is unqualifiedly designated as the remainder beneficiary of a trust for a similar duration, the effect of the administrative and dispositive provisions for the interest or interests that precede the remainder or reversionary interest is to assure that the property will be adequately preserved and protected (e.g., from erosion, invasion, depletion, or damage) until the remainder or reversionary interest takes effect in possession and enjoyment. This degree of preservation and protection is provided only if it was the transferor's intent, as manifested by the provisions of the arrangement and the surrounding circumstances, that the entire disposition provide the remainder or reversionary beneficiary with an undiminished interest in the property transferred at the time of the termination of the prior interest.

(iv) *Pooled income fund interests.*—In general, pooled income funds are created and administered to achieve a special rate of return. A beneficial interest in a pooled income fund is not ordinarily valued using a standard section 7520 income or remainder interest factor. The present value of a beneficial interest in a pooled income fund is determined according to rules and special remainder factors prescribed in § 1.642(c)-6 of this chapter and, when applicable, the rules set forth under paragraph (b)(3) of this section if the individual who is the measuring life is terminally ill at the time of the transfer.

(v) *Examples.*—The provisions of this paragraph (b)(2) are illustrated by the following examples:

*Example 1. Unproductive property.* The donor transfers corporation stock to a trust under the terms of which all of the trust income is payable to A for life. Considering the applicable federal rate under section 7520 and the appropriate life estate factor for a person A's age, the value of A's income interest, if valued under this section, would be $10,000. After A's death, the trust is to terminate and the trust property is to be distributed to B. The trust specifically authorizes, but does not require, the trustee to retain the shares of stock. The corporation has paid no dividends on this stock during the past 5 years, and there is no indication that this policy will change in the near future. Under applicable state law, the corporation is considered to be a sound investment that satisfies fiduciary standards. The facts and circumstances, including applicable state law, indicate that the income beneficiary would not have the legal right to compel the trustee to make the trust corpus productive in conformity with the requirements for a lifetime trust income interest under applicable local law. Therefore, the life income interest in this case is considered nonproductive. Consequently, A's income interest may not be valued actuarially under this section.

*Example 2. Beneficiary's right to make trust productive.* The facts are the same as in *Example 1*, except that the trustee is not specifically authorized to retain the shares of corporation stock. Further, the terms of the trust specifically provide that the life income beneficiary may require the trustee to make the trust corpus productive consistent with income yield standards for trusts under applicable state law. Under that law, the minimum rate of income that a productive trust may produce is substantially below the section 7520 interest rate on the valuation date. In this case, because A, the income beneficiary, has the right to compel the trustee to make the trust productive for purposes of applicable local law during A's lifetime, the income interest is considered an ordinary income interest for purposes of this paragraph, and the standard section 7520 life income factor may be used to determine the value of A's income interest. However, in the case of gifts made after October 8, 1990, if the donor was the life income beneficiary, the value of the income interest would be considered to be zero in this situation. See § 25.2702-2.

*Example 3. Annuity trust funded with unproductive property.* The donor, who is age 60, transfers corporation stock worth $1,000,000 to a trust. The trust will pay a 6 percent ($60,000 per year) annuity in cash or other property to the donor for 10 years or until the donor's prior death. Upon the termination of the trust, the trust property is to be distributed to the donor's child. The section 7520 rate for the month of the transfer is 8.2 percent. The corporation has paid no dividends on the stock during the past 5 years, and there is no indication that this policy will change in the near future. Under applicable state law, the corporation is considered to be a sound investment that satisfies fiduciary standards. Therefore, the trust's sole investment in this corporation is not expected to adversely affect the interest of either the annuity beneficiary or the remainder beneficiary. Considering the 6 percent annuity payout rate and the 8.2

percent section 7520 interest rate, the trust corpus is considered sufficient to pay this annuity for the entire 10-year term of the trust, or even indefinitely. The trust specifically authorizes, but does not require, the trustee to retain the shares of stock. Although it appears that neither beneficiary would be able to compel the trustee to make the trust corpus produce investment income, the annuity interest in this case is considered to be an ordinary annuity interest, and a section 7520 annuity factor may be used to determine the present value of the annuity. In this case, the section 7520 annuity factor would represent the right to receive $1.00 per year for a term of 10 years or the prior death of a person age 60.

*Example 4. Unitrust funded with unproductive property.* The facts are the same as in *Example 3*, except that the donor has retained a unitrust interest equal to 7 percent of the value of the trust property, valued as of the beginning of each year. Although the trust corpus is nonincome-producing, the present value of the donor's retained unitrust interest may be determined by using the section 7520 unitrust factor for a term of years or a prior death.

*Example 5. Eroding corpus in an annuity trust.* (i) The donor, who is age 60 and in normal health, transfers property worth $1,000,000 to a trust on or after May 1, 2009, but before 2019. The trust will pay a 10 percent ($100,000 per year) annuity to a charitable organization for the life of the donor, payable annually at the end of each period, and the remainder then will be distributed to the donor's child. The section 7520 rate for the month of the transfer is 6.8 percent. First, it is necessary to determine whether the annuity may exhaust the corpus before all annuity payments are made. Because it is assumed that any measuring life may survive until age 110, any life annuity could require payments until the measuring life reaches age 110. Based on a section 7520 interest rate of 6.8 percent, the determination of whether the annuity may exhaust the corpus before the termination of the annuity interest is made as follows:

| | |
|---|---:|
| Age to which life annuity may continue . . . . . . . . . . . . . . . . . . . . . | 110 |
| less: Age of measuring life at date of transfer . . . . . . . . . . . . . . . . . | 60 |
| Number of years annuity may continue . . . . . . . . . . . . . . . | 50 |
| Annual annuity payment . . . . . . . . . . . . . . . . . . . . . . . . . | $100,000.00 |
| times: Annuity factor for 50 years derived from Table B (1 - .037277 / .068) . . . . . . . . . . . . . . . . | 14.1577 |
| Present value of term certain annuity . . . . . . . . . . . . . . . . . . | $1,415,770.00 |

(ii) Because the present value of an annuity for a term of 50 years exceeds the corpus, the annuity may exhaust the trust before all payments are made. Consequently, the annuity must be valued as an annuity payable for a term of years or until the prior death of the annuitant, with the term of years determined by when the fund will be exhausted by the annuity payments.

(iii) The annuity factor for a term of years at 6.8 percent is derived by subtracting the applicable remainder factor in Table B (see § 20.2031-7(d)(6)) from 1.000000 and then dividing the result by .068. An annuity of $100,000 payable at the end of each year for a period that has an annuity factor of 10.0 would have a present value exactly equal to the principal available to pay the annuity over the term. The annuity factor for 17 years is 9.8999 and the annuity factor for 18 years is 10.2059. Thus, it is determined that the $1,000,000 initial transfer will be sufficient to make 17 annual payments of $100,000, but not to make the entire 18th payment. The present value of an annuity of $100,000 payable at the end of each year for 17 years is $100,000 times 9.8999 or $989,990. The remaining amount is $10,010.00. Of the initial corpus amount, $10,010.00 is not needed to make payments for 17 years, so this amount, as accumulated for 18 years, will be available for the final payment. The 18-year accumulation factor is $(1 + 0.068)^{18}$ or 3.268004, so the amount available in 18 years is $10,010.00 times 3.268004 or $32,712.72. Therefore, for purposes of analysis, the annuity payments are considered to be composed of two distinct annuity components. The two annuity components taken together must equal the total annual amount of $100,000. The first annuity component is the exact amount that the trust will have available for the final payment, $32,712.72. The second annuity component then must be $100,000 minus $32,712.72, or $67,287.28. Specifically, the initial corpus will be able to make payments of $67,287.28 per year for 17 years plus payments of $32,712.72 per year for 18 years. The total annuity is valued by adding the value of the two separate annuity components.

(iv) Based on Table H of Publication 1457, Actuarial Valuations Version 3A, which may be obtained from the IRS Internet site, the present value of an annuity of $67,287.28 per year payable for 17 years or until the prior death of a person aged 60 is $597,013.12 ($67,287.28 X 8.8726). The present value of an annuity of $32,712.72 per year payable for 18 years or until the prior death of a person aged 60 is $296,887.56 ($32,712.72 X 9.0756). Thus, the present value of the charitable annuity interest is $893,900.68 ($597,013.12 + $296,887.56).

(3) *Mortality component.*—The mortality component prescribed under section 7520 may not be used to determine the present value of an annuity, income interest, remainder interest, or reversionary interest if an individual who is a measuring life dies or is terminally ill at the time the gift is completed. For purposes of this paragraph (b)(3), an individual who is known to have an incurable illness or other deteriorating physical condition is considered terminally ill if there is at least a 50 percent probability that the individual will die within 1 year. However, if the individual survives for eighteen months or longer after the date the gift is completed, that individual shall be presumed to have not been terminally ill at the date the gift was completed unless the contrary is established by clear and convincing evidence.

(4) *Example.*—The provisions of paragraph (b)(3) of this section are illustrated by the following example:

*Example. Terminal illness.* The donor transfers property worth $1,000,000 to a child on or after May 1, 2009 but before 2019, in exchange for the child's promise to pay the donor $80,000 per year for the donor's life, payable annually at the end of each period. The donor is age 75 but has been diagnosed with an incurable illness and has at least a 50 percent probability of dying within 1 year. The section 7520 interest rate for the month of the transfer is 7.6 percent, and the standard annuity factor at that interest rate for a person age 75 in normal health is 6.6493 (1 - .49465 / .076). Thus, if the donor were not terminally ill, the present value of the annuity would be $531,944.00 ($80,000 X 6.6493). Assuming the presumption provided in paragraph (b)(3) of this section does not apply, because there is at least a 50 percent probability that the donor will die within 1 year, the standard section 7520 annuity factor may not be used to determine the present value of the donor's annuity interest. Instead, a special section 7520 annuity factor must be computed that takes into account the projection of the donor's actual life expectancy.

(5) *Additional limitations.*—Section 7520 does not apply to the extent as may otherwise be provided by the Commissioner.

(c) *Effective/applicability dates.*—Section 25.7520-3(a) is effective as of May 1, 1989. The provisions of paragraph (b) of this section, except *Example 5* in paragraph (b)(2)(v) and paragraph (b)(4), are effective with respect to gifts made after December 13, 1995. *Example 5* in paragraph (b)(2)(v) and paragraph (b)(4) are effective with respect to gifts made on or after May 1, 2009. [Reg. § 25.7520-3.]

□ [*T.D. 8540, 6-9-94. Amended by T.D. 8630, 12-12-95; T.D. 8819, 4-29-99; T.D. 8886, 6-9-2000; T.D. 9448, 5-1-2009 and T.D. 9540, 8-9-2011.*]

### [Reg. §1.7520-4]

**§1.7520-4. Transitional rules.**—(a) *Reliance.*—If the valuation date is after April 30, 1989, and before June 10, 1994, a taxpayer can rely on Notice 89-24, 1989-1 C.B. 660, or Notice 89-60, 1989-1 C.B. 700 (See §601.601(d)(2)(ii)(*b*) of this chapter), in valuing the transferred interest.

(b) *Effective date.*—This section is effective as of May 1, 1989. [Reg. §1.7520-4.]

□ [*T.D. 8540, 6-9-94.*]

### [Reg. §20.7520-4]

**§20.7520-4. Transitional rules.**—(a) *Reliance.*—If the valuation date is after April 30, 1989, and before June 10, 1994, an executor can rely on Notice 89-24, 1989-1 C.B. 660, or Notice 89-60, 1989-1 C.B. 700 (See §601.601(d)(2)(ii)(*b*) of this chapter), in valuing the transferred interest.

(b) *Effective date.*—This section is effective as of May 1, 1989. [Reg. §20.7520-4.]

□ [*T.D. 8540, 6-9-94.*]

### [Reg. §25.7520-4]

**§25.7520-4. Transitional rules.**—(a) *Reliance.*—If the valuation date is after April 30, 1989, and before June 10, 1994, a donor can rely on Notice 89-24, 1989-1 C.B. 660, or Notice 89-60, 1989-1 C.B. 700 (See §601.601(d)(2)(ii)(*b*) of this chapter), in valuing the transferred interest.

(b) *Transfers in 1989.*—If a donor transferred an interest in property by gift after December 31, 1988, and before May 1, 1989, retaining an interest in the same property and, after April 30, 1989, and before January 1, 1990, transferred the retained interest in the property, the donor may, at the donor's option, value the transfer of the retained interest under either §25.2512-5(d) or §25.2512-5A(d).

(c) *Effective date.*—This section is effective as of May 1, 1989. [Reg. §25.7520-4.]

□ [*T.D. 8540, 6-9-94.*]

# Discovery of Liability and Enforcement of Title

# EXAMINATION AND INSPECTION

**See p. 20,601 for regulations not amended to reflect law changes**

### [Reg. §301.7601-1]

**§301.7601-1. Canvass of districts for taxable persons and objects.**—Each district director shall, to the extent he deems it practicable, cause officers or employees under his supervision and control to proceed, from time to time, through his district and inquire after and concerning all persons therein who may be liable to pay any internal revenue tax, and all persons owning or having the care and management of any objects with respect to which any tax is imposed. [Reg. §301.7601-1.]

□ [*T.D. 6421, 10-23-59. Amended by T.D. 7188, 6-28-72 and T.D. 7297, 12-18-73.*]

**»»→ Caution: The Treasury Department has identified Reg. §301.7602-1, as amended by T.D. 9778, as a significant tax regulation that imposes an undue financial burden on U.S. taxpayers and/or adds undue complexity to the federal tax laws, pursuant to Executive Order 13789 (issued April 21, 2017) (Notice 2017-38, I.R.B. 2017-30). In a subsequent report, issued October 4, 2017, Treasury recommended planned actions that would reduce the burden of these regulations.**

### [Reg. §301.7602-1]

**§301.7602-1. Examination of books and witnesses.**—(a) *In general.*—For the purpose of ascertaining the correctness of any return, making a return where none has been made, determining the liability of any person for any internal revenue tax (including any interest, additional amount, addition to the tax, or civil penalty) or the liability at law or in equity of any transferee or fiduciary of any person in respect of any internal revenue tax, collecting any such liability or inquiring into any offense connected with the administration or enforcement of the internal revenue laws, any authorized officer or employee of the Internal Revenue Service may examine any books, papers, records or other data which may be relevant or material to such inquiry; and take such testimony of the person concerned, under oath, as may be relevant to such inquiry.

(b) *Summons.*—(1) *In general.*—For the purposes described in §301.7602-1(a), the Commissioner is authorized to summon the person liable for tax or required to perform the act, or any officer or employee of such person or any person having possession, custody, or care of books of accounts containing entries relating to the business of the person liable for tax or required to perform the act, or any other person deemed proper, to appear before one or more officers or employees of the Internal Revenue Service at a time and place named in the summons and to produce such books, papers, records, or other data, and to give such testimony, under oath, as may be relevant or material to such inquiry; and take such testimony of the person concerned, under oath, as may be relevant or material to such inquiry. This summons power may be used in an investigation of either civil or criminal tax-related liability. The Commissioner may designate one or more officers or employees of the IRS as the individuals before whom a person summoned pursuant to section 6420(e)(2), 6421(g)(2), 6427(j)(2), or 7602 shall appear. Any such officer or employee is authorized to take testimony under oath of the person summoned and to receive and examine books, papers, records, or other data produced in compliance with the summons.

(2) *Officer or employee of the IRS.*—For purposes of this paragraph (b), officer or employee of the IRS means all officers and employees of the United States, who are engaged in the administration and enforcement of the internal revenue laws or any other laws administered by the IRS, and who are appointed or employed by, or subject to the directions, instructions, or orders of the Secretary of the Treasury or the Secretary's delegate. An officer or employee of the IRS, for purposes of this paragraph (b), shall include an officer or employee of the Office of Chief Counsel.

(3) *Participation of a person described in section 6103(n).*—For purposes of this paragraph (b), a person authorized to receive returns or return information under section 6103(n) and §301.6103(n)-1(a) of the regulations may receive and review books, papers, records, or other data produced in compliance with a summons and, in the presence and under the guidance of an IRS officer or employee, participate fully in the interview of a witness summoned by the IRS to provide testimony under oath. Fully participating in an interview includes, but is not limited to, receipt, review, and use of summoned books, papers, records, or other data; being present during summons interviews; questioning the person providing testimony under oath; and asking a summoned person's representative to clarify an objection or assertion of privilege.

(c) *Proscription on issuing of administrative summons when a Justice Department referral is in effect.*—(1) *In general.*—The Commissioner may neither issue a summons under this title nor initiate a proceeding to enforce a previously issued summons by way of section 7604 with respect to any person whose tax liability is in issue, if a Justice Department referral is in effect with respect to that person for that liability.

(2) *Justice Department referral in effect.*—A Justice Department referral is in effect with respect to any person when:

(i) The Secretary recommends, within the meaning of this paragraph, that the Attorney General either commence a grand jury investigation of or criminal prosecution of such person for any alleged offense connected with the administration or enforcement of the internal revenue laws, or

(ii) The Attorney General (or Deputy Attorney General or Assistant Attorney General) under section 6103(h)(3)(B) requests in writing that the Secretary disclose a return of, or return information relating to, such person. The request must set forth that the need for disclosure is for the purpose of a grand jury investigation of or potential or pending criminal prosecution of such person for any alleged offense connected with the administration or enforcement of the internal revenue laws.

The referral is effective at the time the document recommending criminal prosecution or grand jury investigation is signed by the Secretary or upon the Secretary's receipt of the section 6103(h)(3)(B) request.

(3) *Cessation of Justice Department referral.*—A Justice Department referral ceases to be in effect with respect to a person:

(i) When the Secretary receives written notification from the Attorney General that the Justice Department:

(A) Will not prosecute that person for any offense connected with the administration or enforcement of the internal revenue laws that gave rise to the referral under paragraph (2)(i) of this section, or

(B) Will not authorize a grand jury investigation of that person with respect to such offense, or

(C) Will discontinue any grand jury investigation of that person with respect to such offense;

(ii) When a final disposition with respect to a criminal proceeding brought against that person has been made; or

(iii) When the Secretary receives written notification from the Attorney General, Deputy Attorney General, or an Assistant Attorney General, that the Justice Department will not prosecute such person for any offense connected with the administration or enforcement of the internal revenue laws, based upon a previous request for disclosure under section 6103(h)(3)(B).

(4) *Taxable years and taxes imposed by separate chapters of the Code treated separately.*—(i) *In general.*—For purposes of this section, each taxable period (or, if there is no taxable period, each taxable event) and each tax imposed by a separate chapter of the Code is treated separately.

(ii) *Examples.*—The following examples illustrate the application of this paragraph (c)(4):

*Example (1).* A Justice Department referral is in effect for D's criminal evasion of income tax for the taxable year 1979. The Commissioner may issue a summons respecting D's 1980 criminal and/or civil tax liability. The Commissioner may not issue a summons respecting D's 1979 income tax liability.

*Example (2).* A referral has been made to the Department of Justice for the criminal prosecution of F with regard to F's income tax liability for the taxable year 1978. The Commissioner may issue a summons respecting F's gift tax liability for the taxable year 1978.

*Example (3).* A referral has been made to the Department of Justice for a grand jury investigation respecting G's 1980 income tax liability. The Commissioner may issue a summons related to an investigation of G's liability for Federal Insurance Contribution Act (FICA) taxes for the taxable year 1980.

*Example (4).* A referral has been made to the Department of Justice respecting J's criminal evasion of windfall profit tax for all quarters of the calendar year 1982. The Commissioner may issue a summons respecting J's liability for highway motor vehicle use tax covering the same periods.

*Example (5).* A referral has been made to the Department of Justice for a grand jury investigation respecting L's 1983 income tax liability. The Commissioner may issue a summons related to the investigation of L's liability under sections 6700 (abusive tax shelter promoter penalty) and 7408 of the Code for his conduct during 1983.

(d) *Applicability date.*—This section is applicable after September 3, 1982, except for paragraphs (b)(1) and (2) of this section which are applicable on and after April 1, 2005 and paragraph (b)(3) of this section which applies to summons interviews conducted on or after July 14, 2016. For rules under paragraphs (b)(1) and (2) that are applicable to summonses issued on or after September 10, 2002 or under paragraph (b)(3) that are applicable to summons interviews conducted on or after June 18, 2014, see 26 CFR 301.7602-1T (revised as of April 1, 2016). [Reg. §301.7602-1.]

☐ [*T.D. 6421, 10-23-59. Amended by T.D. 6498, 10-24-60, T.D. 7188, 6-28-72, T.D. 7297, 12-18-73; T.D. 8091, 6-24-86; T.D. 9015, 9-9-2002, T.D. 9195, 3-31-2005 and T.D. 9778, 7-12-2016.*]

**[Reg. §301.7602-2]**

**§301.7602-2. Third party contacts.**—(a) *In general.*—Subject to the exceptions in paragraph (f) of this section, no officer or employee of the Internal Revenue Service (IRS) may contact any person other than the taxpayer with respect to the determination or collection of such taxpayer's tax liability without giving the taxpayer reasonable notice in advance that such contacts may be made. A record of persons so contacted must be made and given to the taxpayer upon the taxpayer's request.

(b) *Third-party contact defined.*—Contacts subject to section 7602(c) and this regulation shall be called "third-party contacts." A third-party contact is a communication which—

(1) Is initiated by an IRS employee;

(2) Is made to a person other than the taxpayer;

(3) Is made with respect to the determination or collection of the tax liability of such taxpayer;

(4) Discloses the identity of the taxpayer being investigated; and

(5) Discloses the association of the IRS employee with the IRS.

(c) *Elements of third-party contact explained.*—(1) *Initiation by an IRS employee.*—(i) *Explanation.*—(A) *Initiation.*—An IRS employee initiates a communication whenever it is the employee who first tries to communicate with a person other than the taxpayer. Returning unsolicited telephone calls or speaking with persons other than the taxpayer as part of an attempt to speak to the taxpayer are not initiations of third-party contacts.

(B) *IRS employee.*—For purposes of this section, an IRS employee includes all officers and employees of the IRS, the Chief Counsel of the IRS and the National Taxpayer Advocate, as well as a person described in section 6103(n), an officer or employee of such person, or a person who is subject to disclosure restrictions pursuant to a written agreement in connection with the solicitation of an agreement described in section 6103(n) and its implementing regulations. No inference about the employment or contractual relationship of such other persons with the IRS may be drawn from this regulation for any purpose other than the requirements of section 7602(c).

(ii) *Examples.*—The following examples illustrate this paragraph (c)(1):

*Example 1.* An IRS employee receives a message to return an unsolicited call. The employee returns the call and speaks with a person who reports information about a taxpayer who is not meeting his tax responsibilities. Later, the employee makes a second call to the person and asks for more information. The first call is not a contact initiated by an IRS employee. Just because the employee must return the call does not change the fact that it is the other person, and not the employee, who initiated the contact. The second call, however, is initiated by the employee and so meets the first element.

*Example 2.* An IRS employee wants to hire an appraiser to help determine the value of a taxpayer's oil and gas business. At the initial interview, the appraiser signs an agreement that prohibits him from disclosing return information of the taxpayer except as allowed by the agreement. Once hired, the appraiser initiates a contact by calling an industry expert in Houston and discusses the taxpayer's business. The IRS employee's contact with the appraiser does not meet the first element of a third-party contact because the appraiser is treated, for section 7602(c) purposes only, as an employee of the IRS. For the same reason, however, the appraiser's call to the industry expert does meet the first element of a third-party contact.

*Example 3.* A revenue agent trying to contact the taxpayer to discuss the taxpayer's pending examination twice calls the taxpayer's place of business. The first call is answered by a receptionist who states that the taxpayer is not available. The IRS employee leaves a message with the receptionist stating only his name and telephone number, and asks that the taxpayer call him. The second call is answered by the office answering machine, on which the IRS employee leaves the same message. Neither of these phone calls meets the first element of a third-party contact because the IRS employee is trying to initiate a communication with the taxpayer and not a person other than the taxpayer. The fact that the IRS employee must either speak with a third party (the receptionist) or leave a message on the answering machine, which may be heard by a third party, does not mean that the employee is initiating a communication with a person other than the taxpayer. Both the receptionist and the answering machine are only intermediaries in the process of reaching the taxpayer.

(2) *Person other than the taxpayer.*—(i) *Explanation.*—The phrases "person other than the taxpayer" and "third party" are used interchangeably in this section, and do not include—

(A) An officer or employee of the IRS, as defined in paragraph (c)(1)(i)(B) of this section, acting within the scope of his or her employment;

(B) Any computer database or web site regardless of where located and by whom maintained, including databases or web sites maintained on the Internet or in county courthouses, libraries, or any other real or virtual site; or

(C) A current employee, officer, or fiduciary of a taxpayer when acting within the scope of his or her employment or relationship with the taxpayer. Such employee, officer, or fiduciary shall be conclusively presumed to be acting within the scope of his or her employment or relationship during business hours on business premises.

(ii) *Examples.*—: The following examples illustrate this paragraph (c)(2):

*Example 1.* A revenue agent examining a taxpayer's return speaks with another revenue agent who has previously examined the same taxpayer about a recurring issue. The revenue agent has not contacted a "person other than the taxpayer" within the meaning of section 7602(c).

*Example 2.* A revenue agent examining a taxpayer's return speaks with one of the taxpayer's employees on business premises during business hours. The employee is conclusively presumed to be acting within the scope of his employment and is therefore not a "person other than the taxpayer" for section 7602(c) purposes.

*Example 3.* A revenue agent examining a corporate taxpayer's return uses a commercial online research service to research the corporate structure of the taxpayer. The revenue agent uses an IRS account, logs on with her IRS user name and password, and uses the name of the corporate taxpayer in her search terms. The revenue agent later explores several Internet web sites that may have information relevant to the examination. The searches on the commercial online research service and Internet web sites are not contacts with "persons other than the taxpayer."

(3) *With respect to the determination or collection of the tax liability of such taxpayer.*—(i) *Explanation.*—(A) *With respect to.*—A contact is "with respect to" the determination or collection of the tax liability of such taxpayer when made for the purpose of either determining or collecting a particular tax liability and when directly connected to that purpose. While a contact made for the purpose of determining a particular taxpayer's tax liability may also affect the tax liability of one or more other taxpayers, such contact is not for that reason alone a contact "with respect to" the determination or collection of those other taxpayers' tax liabilities. Contacts to determine the tax status of a pension plan under chapter 1, subchapter D (Deferred Compensation) of the Internal Revenue Code, are not "with respect to" the determination of plan participants' tax liabilities. Contacts to determine the tax status of a bond issue under chapter 1, subchapter B, Part IV (Tax Exemption Requirements for State and Local Bonds) of the Internal Revenue Code, are not "with respect to" the determination of the bondholders' tax liabilities. Contacts to determine the tax status of an organization under chapter 1, subchapter F (Exempt Organizations) of the Internal Revenue Code, are not "with respect to" the determination of the contributors' liabilities, nor are any similar determinations "with respect to" any persons with similar relationships to the taxpayer whose tax liability is being determined or collected.

(B) *Determination or collection.*—A contact is with respect to the "determination or collection" of the tax liability of such taxpayer when made during the administrative determination or collection process. For purposes of this paragraph (c) only, the administrative determination or collection process may include any administrative action to ascertain the correctness of a return, make a return when none has been filed, or determine or collect the tax liability of any person as a transferee or fiduciary under chapter 71 of Title 26.

(C) *Tax liability.*—A *tax liability* means the liability for any tax imposed by Title 26 of the United States Code (including any interest, additional amount, addition to the tax, or penalty) and does not include the liability for any tax imposed by any other jurisdiction nor any liability imposed by other Federal statutes.

(D) *Such taxpayer.*—A contact is with respect to the determination or collection of the tax liability of "such taxpayer" when made while determining or collecting the tax liability of a particular, identified taxpayer. Contacts made during an investigation of a particular, identified taxpayer are third-party contacts only as to the particular, identified taxpayer under investigation and not as to any other taxpayer whose tax liabilities might be affected by such contacts.

(ii) *Examples.*—The following examples illustrate the operation of this paragraph (c)(3):

*Example 1.* As part of a compliance check on a return preparer, an IRS employee visits the preparer's office and reviews the preparer's client files to ensure that the proper forms and records have been created and maintained. This contact is not a third-party contact "with respect to" the preparer's clients because it is not for the purpose of determining the tax liability of the preparer's clients, even though the agent might discover information that would lead the agent to recommend an examination of one or more of the preparer's clients.

*Example 2.* A revenue agent is assigned to examine a taxpayer's return, which was prepared by a return preparer. As in all such examinations, the revenue agent asks the taxpayer routine questions about what information the taxpayer gave the preparer and what advice the preparer gave the taxpayer. As a result of the examination, the revenue agent recommends that the preparer be investigated for penalties under section 6694 or 6695. Neither the examination of the taxpayer's return nor the questions asked of the taxpayer are "with respect to" the determination of the preparer's tax liabilities within the meaning of section 7602(c) because the purpose of the contacts was to determine the taxpayer's tax liability, even though the agent discovered information that may result in a later investigation of the preparer.

*Example 3.* To help identify taxpayers in the florist industry who may not have filed proper returns, an IRS employee contacts a company that supplies equipment to florists and asks for a list of its customers in the past year in order to cross-check the list against filed returns. The employee later contacts the supplier for more information about one particular florist who the employee believes did not file a proper return. The first contact is not a contact with respect to the determination of the tax liability of "such taxpayer" because no particular taxpayer has been identified for investigation at the time the contact is made. The later contact, however, is with respect to the determination of the tax liability of "such taxpayer" because a particular taxpayer has been identified. The later contact is also "with respect to" the determination of that taxpayer's liability because, even though no examination has been opened on the taxpayer, the information sought could lead to an examination.

*Example 4.* A revenue officer, trying to collect the trust fund portion of unpaid employment taxes of a corporation, begins to investigate the liability of two corporate officers for the section 6672 Trust Fund Recovery Penalty (TFRP). The revenue officer obtains the signature cards for the corporation's bank accounts from the corporation's bank. The contact with the bank to obtain the signature cards is a contact with respect to the determination of the two identified corporate officers' tax liabilities because it is directly connected to the purpose of determining a tax liability of two identified taxpayers. It is not, however, a contact with respect to any other person not already under investigation for TFRP liability, even though the signature cards might identify other potentially liable persons.

*Example 5.* The IRS is asked to rule on whether a certain pension plan qualifies under section 401 so that contributions to the pension plan are excludable from the employees' incomes under section 402 and are also deductible from the employer's income under section 404. Contacts made with the plan sponsor (and with persons other than the plan sponsor) are not contacts "with respect to" the determination of the tax liabilities of the pension plan participants because the purpose of the contacts is to determine the status of the plan, even though that determination may affect the participants' tax liabilities.

*Example 6(a).* The IRS audits a TEFRA partnership at the partnership (entity) level pursuant to sections 6221 through 6233. The tax treatment of partnership items is at issue, but the respective tax liabilities of the partners may be affected by the results of the TEFRA partnership audit. With respect to the TEFRA partnership, contacts made with employees of the partnership acting within the scope of their duties or any partner are not section 7602(c) contacts because they are considered the equivalent of contacting the partnership. Contacts relating to the tax treatment of partnership items made with persons other than the employees of the partnership who are acting within the scope of their duties or the partners are section 7602(c) contacts with respect to the TEFRA partnership, and reasonable advance notice should be provided by sending the appropriate Letter 3164 to the partnership's tax matters partner (TMP). Individual partners who are merely affected by the partnership audit but who are not identified as subject to examination with respect to their individual tax liabilities need not be sent Letters 3164.

*Example 6(b).* In the course of an audit of a TEFRA partnership at the partnership (entity) level, the IRS intends to contact third parties regarding transactions between the TEFRA partnership and specific, identified partners. In addition to the partnership's TMP, the specific, identified partners should also be provided advance notice of any third-party contacts relating to such transactions.

(4) *Discloses the identity of the taxpayer being investigated.*—(i) *Explanation.*—An IRS employee discloses the taxpayer's identity whenever the employee knows or should know that the person being contacted can readily ascertain the taxpayer's identity from the information given by the employee.

(ii) *Examples.*—The following examples illustrate this paragraph (c)(4):

*Example 1.* A revenue agent seeking to value the taxpayer's condominium calls a real estate agent and asks for a market analysis of the taxpayer's condominium, giving the unit number of the taxpayer's condominium. The revenue agent has revealed the identity of the taxpayer, regardless of whether the revenue agent discloses the name of the taxpayer, because the real estate agent can readily ascertain the taxpayer's identity from the address given.

*Example 2.* A revenue officer seeking to value the taxpayer's condominium calls a real estate agent and, without identifying the taxpayer's unit, asks for the sales prices of similar units recently sold and listing prices of similar units currently on the market. The revenue officer has not revealed the identity of the taxpayer because the revenue officer has not given any information from which the real estate agent can readily ascertain the taxpayer's identity.

(5) *Discloses the association of the IRS employee with the IRS.*—An IRS employee discloses his association with the IRS whenever the

employee knows or should know that the person being contacted can readily ascertain the association from the information given by the employee.

(d) *Pre-contact notice.*—(1) *In general.*—An officer or employee of the IRS may not make third-party contacts without providing reasonable notice in advance to the taxpayer that contacts may be made. The pre-contact notice may be given either orally or in writing. If written notice is given, it may be given in any manner that the IRS employee responsible for giving the notice reasonably believes will be received by the taxpayer in advance of the third-party contact. Written notice is deemed reasonable if it is—

(i) Mailed to the taxpayer's last known address;

(ii) Given in person;

(iii) Left at the taxpayer's dwelling or usual place of business; or

(iv) Actually received by the taxpayer.

(2) *Pre-contact notice not required.*—Pre-contact notice under this section need not be provided to a taxpayer for third-party contacts of which advance notice has otherwise been provided to the taxpayer pursuant to another statute, regulation or administrative procedure. For example, Collection Due Process notices sent to taxpayers pursuant to section 6330 and its regulations constitute reasonable advance notice that contacts with third parties may be made in order to effectuate a levy.

(e) *Post-contact reports.*—(1) *Requested reports.*—A taxpayer may request a record of persons contacted in any manner that the Commissioner reasonably permits. The Commissioner may set reasonable limits on how frequently taxpayer requests need be honored. The requested report may be mailed either to the taxpayer's last known address or such other address as the taxpayer specifies in the request.

(2) *Contents of record.*—(i) *In general.*—The record of persons contacted should contain information, if known to the IRS employee making the contact, which reasonably identifies the person contacted. Providing the name of the person contacted fully satisfies the requirements of this section, but this section does not require IRS employees to solicit identifying information from a person solely for the purpose of the post-contact report. The record need not contain any other information, such as the nature of the inquiry or the content of the third party's response. The record need not report multiple contacts made with the same person during a reporting period.

(ii) *Special rule for employees.*—For contacts with the employees, officers; or fiduciaries of any entity who are acting within the scope of their employment or relationship, it is sufficient to record the entity as the person contacted. A fiduciary, officer or employee shall be conclusively presumed to be acting within the scope of his employment or relationship during business hours or on business premises. For purposes of this paragraph (e)(2)(ii), the term *entity* means any business (whether operated as a sole proprietorship, disregarded entity under §301.7701-2 of the regulations, or otherwise), trust, estate, partnership, association, company, corporation, or similar organization.

(3) *Post-contact record not required.*—A post-contact record under this section need not be made, or provided to a taxpayer, for third-party contacts of which the taxpayer has already been given a similar record pursuant to another statute, regulation, or administrative procedure.

(4) *Examples.*—The following examples illustrate this paragraph (e):

*Example 1.* An IRS employee trying to find a specific taxpayer's assets in order to collect unpaid taxes talks to the owner of a marina. The employee asks whether the taxpayer has a boat at the marina. The owner gives his name as John Doe. The employee may record the contact as being with John Doe and is not required by this regulation to collect or record any other identifying information.

*Example 2.* An IRS employee trying to find a specific taxpayer and his assets in order to collect unpaid taxes talks to a person at 502 Fernwood. The employee asks whether the taxpayer lives next door at 500 Fernwood, as well as where the taxpayer works, what kind of car the taxpayer drives and whether the camper parked in front of 500 Fernwood belongs to the taxpayer. The person does not disclose his name. The employee may record the contact as being with a person at 502 Fernwood. If the employee then makes the same inquiries of another person on the street in front of 500 Fernwood, and does not learn that person's name, the latter contact may be reported as being with a person on the street in front of 500 Fernwood.

*Example 3.* An IRS employee examining a return obtains loan documents from a bank where the taxpayer applied for a loan. After reviewing the documents, the employee talks with the loan officer at the bank who handled the application. The employee has contacted

only one "person other than the taxpayer." The bank and not the loan officer is the "person other than the taxpayer" for section 7602(c) purposes. The contact with the loan officer is treated as a contact with the bank because the loan officer was an employee of the bank and was acting within the scope of her employment with the bank.

*Example 4.* An IRS employee issues a summons to a third party with respect to the determination of a taxpayer's liability and properly follows the procedures for such summonses under section 7609, which requires that a copy of the summons be given to the taxpayer. This third-party contact need not be maintained in a record of contacts available to the taxpayer because providing a copy of the third-party summons to the taxpayer pursuant to section 7609 satisfies the post-contact recording and reporting requirement of this section.

*Example 5.* An IRS employee serves a levy on a third party with respect to the collection of a taxpayer's liability. The employee provides the taxpayer with a copy of the notice of levy form that shows the identity of the third party. This third-party contact need not be maintained in a record of contacts available to the taxpayer because providing a copy of the notice of levy to the taxpayer satisfies the post-contact recording and reporting requirement of this section.

(f) *Exceptions.*—(1) *Authorized by taxpayer.*—(i) *Explanation.*—Section 7602(c) does not apply to contacts authorized by the taxpayer. A contact is "authorized" within the meaning of this section if—

(A) The contact is with the taxpayer's authorized representative, that is, a person who is authorized to speak or act on behalf of the taxpayer, such as a person holding a power of attorney, a corporate officer, a personal representative, an executor or executrix, or an attorney representing the taxpayer; or

(B) The taxpayer or the taxpayer's authorized representative requests or approves the contact.

(ii) *No prevention or delay of contact.*—This section does not entitle any person to prevent or delay an IRS employee from contacting any individual or entity.

(2) *Jeopardy.*—(i) *Explanation.*—Section 7602(c) does not apply when the IRS employee making a contact has good cause to believe that providing the taxpayer with either a general pre-contact notice or a record of the specific person contacted may jeopardize the collection of any tax. For purposes of this section only, good cause includes a reasonable belief that providing the notice or record will lead to—

(A) Attempts by any person to conceal, remove, destroy, or alter records or assets that may be relevant to any tax examination or collection activity;

(B) Attempts by any person to prevent other persons, through intimidation, bribery, or collusion, from communicating any information that may be relevant to any tax examination or collection activity; or

(C) Attempts by any person to flee, or otherwise avoid testifying or producing records that may be relevant to any tax examination or collection activity.

(ii) *Record of contact.*—If the circumstances described in this paragraph (f)(2) exist, the IRS employee must still make a record of the person contacted, but the taxpayer need not be provided the record until it is no longer reasonable to believe that providing the record would cause the jeopardy described.

(3) *Reprisal.*—(i) *In general.*—Section 7602(c) does not apply when the IRS employee making a contact has good cause to believe that providing the taxpayer with either a general pre-contact notice or a specific record of the person being contacted may cause any person to harm any other person in any way, whether the harm is physical, economic, emotional or otherwise. A statement by the person contacted that harm may occur against any person is sufficient to constitute good cause for the IRS employee to believe that reprisal may occur. The IRS employee is not required to further question the contacted person about reprisal or otherwise make further inquiries regarding the statement.

(ii) *Examples.*—The following examples illustrate this paragraph (f)(3):

*Example 1.* An IRS employee seeking to collect unpaid taxes is told by the taxpayer that all the money in his and his brother's joint bank account belongs to the brother. The IRS employee contacts the brother to verify this information. The brother refuses to confirm or deny the taxpayer's statement. He states that he does not believe that reporting the contact to the taxpayer would result in harm to anyone but further states that he does not want his name reported to the taxpayer because it would appear that he gave information. This contact is not excepted from the statute merely because the brother asks that his name be left off the list of contacts.

*Example 2.* Assume the same facts as in *Example 1*, except that the brother states that he fears harm from the taxpayer should the taxpayer learn of the contact, even though the brother gave no information. This contact is excepted from the statute because the third party has expressed a fear of reprisal. The IRS employee is not required to make further inquiry into the nature of the brothers' relationship or otherwise question the brother's fear of reprisal.

*Example 3.* An IRS employee is examining a joint return of a husband and wife, who recently divorced. From reading the court divorce file, the IRS employee learns that the divorce was acrimonious and that the ex-husband once violated a restraining order issued to protect the ex-wife. This information provides good cause for the IRS employee to believe that reporting contacts which might disclose the ex-wife's location may cause reprisal against any person. Therefore, when the IRS employee contacts the ex-wife's new employer to verify salary information provided by the ex-wife, the IRS employee has good cause not to report that contact to the ex-husband, regardless of whether the new employer expresses concern about reprisal against it or its employees.

(4) *Pending criminal investigations.*—(i) *IRS criminal investigations.*—Section 7602(c) does not apply to contacts made during an investigation, or inquiry to determine whether to open an investigation, when the investigation or inquiry is—

(A) Made against a particular, identified taxpayer for the primary purpose of evaluating the potential for criminal prosecution of that taxpayer; and

(B) Made by an IRS employee whose primary duties include either identifying or investigating criminal violations of the law.

(ii) *Other criminal investigations.*—Section 7602(c) does not apply to contacts which, if reported to the taxpayer, could interfere with a known pending criminal investigation being conducted by law enforcement personnel of any local, state, Federal, foreign or other governmental entity.

(5) *Governmental entities.*—Section 7602(c) does not apply to any contact with any office of any local, state, Federal or foreign governmental entity except for contacts concerning the taxpayer's business with the government office contacted, such as the taxpayer's contracts with or employment by the office. The term *office* includes any agent or contractor of the office acting in such capacity.

(6) *Confidential informants.*—Section 7602(c) does not apply when the employee making the contact has good cause to believe that providing either the pre-contact notice or the record of the person contacted would identify a confidential informant whose identity would be protected under section 6103(h)(4).

(7) *Nonadministrative contacts.*—(i) *Explanation.*—Section 7602(c) does not apply to contacts made in the course of a pending court proceeding.

(ii) *Examples.*—The following examples illustrate this paragraph (f)(7):

*Example 1.* An attorney for the Office of Chief Counsel needs to contact a potential witness for an upcoming Tax Court proceeding involving the 1997 and 1998 taxable years of the taxpayer. Section 7602(c) does not apply because the contact is being made in the course of a pending court proceeding.

*Example 2.* While a Tax Court case is pending with respect to a taxpayer's 1997 and 1998 income tax liabilities, a revenue agent is conducting an examination of the taxpayer's excise tax liabilities for the fiscal year ending 1999. Any third-party contacts made by the revenue agent with respect to the excise tax liabilities would be subject to the requirements of section 7602(c) because the Tax Court proceeding does not involve the excise tax liabilities.

*Example 3.* A taxpayer files a Chapter 7 bankruptcy petition and receives a discharge. A revenue officer contacts a third party in order to determine whether the taxpayer has any exempt assets against which the IRS may take collection action to enforce its federal tax lien. At the time of the contact, the bankruptcy case has not been closed. Although the bankruptcy proceeding remains pending, the purpose of this contact relates to potential collection action by the IRS, a matter not before or related to the bankruptcy court proceeding.

(g) *Effective date.*—This section is applicable on December 18, 2002. [Reg. § 301.7602-2.]

☐ [*T.D. 9028, 12-17-2002.*]

### [Reg. § 301.7603-1]

§ 301.7603-1. **Service of summons.**—(a) *In general.*—(1) *Hand delivery or delivery to place of abode.*—Except as otherwise provided in paragraph (a)(2) of this section, a summons issued under section 6420(e)(2), 6421(g)(2), 6427(j)(2), or 7602 shall be served by an attested

copy delivered in hand to the person to whom it is directed, or left at such person's last and usual place of abode.

(2) *Summonses issued to third-party recordkeepers.*—A summons issued under section 6420(e)(2), 6421(g)(2), 6427(j)(2), or 7602 for the production of records (or testimony about such records) by a third-party recordkeeper, as described in section 7603(b)(2) and § 301.7603-2, may also be served by certified or registered mail to the third-party recordkeeper's last known address, as defined in § 301.6212-2. If service to a third-party recordkeeper is made by certified or registered mail, the date of service is the date on which the summons is mailed.

(b) *Persons who may serve a summons.*—The officers and employees of the Internal Revenue Service whom the Commissioner has designated to carry out the authority described in § 301.7602-1(b) to issue a summons are authorized to serve a summons issued under section 6420(e)(2), 6421(g)(2), 6427(j)(2), or 7602.

(c) *Effect of certificate of service.*—The certificate of service signed by the person serving the summons shall be evidence of the facts it states on the hearing of an application for the enforcement of the summons.

(d) *Sufficiency of description of summoned records.*—When a summons requires the production of records, it shall be sufficient if such records are described with reasonable certainty.

(e) *Records.*—For purposes of this section and § 301.7603-2, the term records includes books, papers, or other data.

(f) *Effective/applicability date.*—This section is applicable on April 30, 2008. [Reg. § 301.7603-1.]

☐ [*T.D. 6421, 10-23-59. Amended by T.D. 7188, 6-28-72; T.D. 7297, 12-18-73 and T.D. 9395, 4-29-2008.*]

### [Reg. § 301.7603-2]

§ 301.7603-2. **Third-party recordkeepers.**—(a) *Definitions.*—(1) *Accountant.*—A person is an accountant under section 7603(b)(2)(F) for purposes of determining whether that person is a third-party recordkeeper if, on the date the records described in the summons were created, the person was registered, licensed, or certified as an accountant under the authority of any state, commonwealth, territory, or possession of the United States, or of the District of Columbia.

(2) *Attorney.*—A person is an attorney under section 7603(b)(2)(E) for purposes of determining whether that person is a third-party recordkeeper if, on the date the records described in the summons were created, the person was registered, licensed, or certified as an attorney under the authority of any state, commonwealth, territory, or possession of the United States, or of the District of Columbia.

(3) *Credit cards.*—(i) *Person extending credit through credit cards.*—The term *person extending credit through the use of credit cards or similar devices* under section 7603(b)(2)(C) generally includes any person who issues a credit card. The term does not include a seller of goods or services who honors credit cards issued by other parties but who does not extend credit through the use of credit cards or similar devices.

(ii) *Devices similar to credit cards.*—An object is a device similar to a credit card under section 7603(b)(2)(C) only if it is physical in nature, such as a charge plate or similar device that may be tendered to obtain an extension of credit. Thus, a person who extends credit by requiring customers to sign sales slips without requiring the use of, or reference to, a physical object issued by that person is not a third-party recordkeeper under section 7603(b)(2)(C).

(iii) *Debit cards.*—A debit card is not a credit card or similar device because a debit card is not tendered to obtain an extension of credit.

(4) *Enrolled agent.*—A person is an enrolled agent under section 7603(b)(2)(I) for purposes of determining whether that person is a third-party recordkeeper if the person is enrolled as an agent authorized to practice before the Internal Revenue Service pursuant to Circular 230, 31 CFR Part 10.

(5) *Owner or developer of certain computer code and data.*—An owner or developer of computer software source code under section 7603(b)(2)(J) is a third-party recordkeeper when summoned to produce a computer software source code (as defined in section 7612(d)(2)), or an executable code and associated data described in section 7612(b)(1)(A)(ii), even if that person did not make or keep records of another person's business transactions or affairs.

**Reg. § 301.7603-2(a)(5)**

(b) *When third-party recordkeeper status arises.*—(1) *In general.*—Except as provided in paragraph (a)(5) of this section, a person listed in section 7603(b)(2) is a third-party recordkeeper for purposes of section 7609(c)(2)(E) and §301.7603-1 only if the summons served on that person seeks records (or testimony regarding such records) of a third party's business transactions or affairs and such recordkeeper made or kept the records in the capacity of a third-party recordkeeper. For instance, an accountant is not a third-party recordkeeper (by reason of being an accountant) with respect to the accountant's records of a sale of property by the accountant to another person. Similarly, a credit card issuer is not a third-party recordkeeper (by reason of being a person extending credit through the use of credit cards or similar devices) with respect to—

(i) Records relating to non-credit card transactions, such as a cash sale by the issuer to a holder of the issuer's credit card; or

(ii) Records relating to transactions involving the use of another issuer's credit card.

(2) *Examples.*—The rules of paragraph (b)(1) of this section are illustrated by the following examples:

*Example 1.* V issues a credit card (the V card) that is honored by R, a retailer. When using the V card, C, a customer, signs a sales slip in triplicate. C, R, and V each retain one copy. Only the copy held by V is held by a third-party recordkeeper under section 7603(b)(2), even though R may issue its own credit card.

*Example 2.* R, a retailer, issues its own credit card (the R card) to C, a customer. When C makes a credit purchase from R using the R card, C signs a sales slip in duplicate. C and R each retain one copy. Because R keeps the copy in its capacity as credit card issuer, as well as in its capacity as a retailer, it is a third-party recordkeeper under section 7603(b)(2) with respect to its copy of the sales slip.

(c) *Effective/applicability date.*—This section is applicable on April 30, 2008. [Reg. §301.7603-2.]

☐ [T.D. 9395, 4-29-2008.]

### [Reg. §301.7604-1]

**§301.7604-1. Enforcement of summons.**—(a) *In general.*—Whenever any person summoned under section 6420(e)(2), 6421(f)(2), or 7602 neglects or refuses to obey such summons, or to produce books, papers, records, or other data, or to give testimony, as required, application may be made to the judge of the district court or to a United States commissioner for the district within which the person so summoned resides or is found for an attachment against him as for a contempt.

(b) *Persons who may apply for an attachment.*—The officers and employees of the Internal Revenue Service whom the Commissioner has designated to carry out the authority given him by §301.7602-1(b) to issue a summons are authorized to apply for an attachment as provided in paragraph (a) of this section. [Reg. §301.7604-1.]

☐ [T.D. 6421, 10-23-59. *Amended by T.D. 7297, 12-18-73.*]

### [Reg. §301.7605-1]

**§301.7605-1. Time and place of examination.**—(a) *Time and place of examination to be reasonable.*—(1) *In general.*—The time and place of examination pursuant to the provisions of sections 6420(e)(2), 6421(g)(2), 6427(j)(2), or 7602 of the Internal Revenue Code are to be fixed by an officer or employee of the Internal Revenue Service, and officers and employees are to endeavor to schedule a time and place that are reasonable under the circumstances. This section sets forth general criteria for the Service to apply in determining whether a particular time and place for an examination are reasonable under the circumstances. Officers and employees should exercise sound judgment in applying these criteria to the circumstances at hand and should balance convenience of the taxpayer with the requirements of sound and efficient tax administration.

(2) *International examinations.*—Except for the provisions of paragraph (b)(2) of this section, this section does not apply to examinations that fall under the jurisdiction of the Office of the Assistant Commissioner (International).

(3) *Criminal investigations.*—Except for the provisions of paragraph (b)(2) of this section, this section does not apply to criminal investigations.

(b) *Time of examination.*—(1) *Date and time of examination.*—It is reasonable for the Service to schedule the day (or days) for an examination during a normally scheduled workday (or workdays) of the Service, during the Service's normal business hours. It is reasonable for the Service to schedule examinations throughout the year, without regard to seasonal fluctuations in the businesses of particular taxpayers or their representatives. However, the Service will work with taxpayers or their representatives to try to minimize any adverse effects in scheduling the date and time of an examination.

(2) *Date of appearance when summons is used.*—If a summons is issued under authority of section 7602(a)(2) of the Internal Revenue Code, or under the corresponding authority of sections 6420(e)(2), 6421(g)(2), or 6427(j)(2), the date fixed for appearance before an officer or employee of the Service must be no less than 10 days from the date of the summons.

(c) *Type of examination.*—(1) *In general.*—The Service will determine whether an examination will be an office examination (*i.e.*, an examination conducted at a Service office) or a field examination (*i.e.*, an examination conducted at the taxpayer's residence or place of business, or some other location that is not a Service office), based upon the complexity of the return and which form of examination will be more conducive to effective and efficient tax administration.

(2) *Office examination held in location other than Service office in case of clear need.*—The Service will grant a request to hold an office examination at a location other than a Service office in a case of clear need, such as when it would be unreasonably difficult for the taxpayer to travel to a Service office because of the taxpayer's advanced age or infirm physical condition, or when the taxpayer's books, records, and source documents are too cumbersome for the taxpayer to bring to a Service office.

(d) *Place of examination.*—(1) *In general.*—The Service generally will make an initial determination of the place for an examination, including the Internal Revenue Service district to which an examination will be assigned, based upon the address shown on the return for the period selected for examination. Requests by taxpayers to transfer the place of examination will be resolved on a case-by-case basis, using the criteria set forth in paragraph (e) of this section.

(2) *Office examinations.*—(i) *In general.*—An office examination of an individual or sole proprietorship generally is based on the residence of the individual taxpayer. An office examination of a taxpayer that is an entity generally is based on the location where the taxpayer entity's original books, records, and source documents are maintained. An office examination generally will take place at the closest Service office within the district encompassing the taxpayer's residence or at the closest Service office within the district where the taxpayer entity's books, records, and source documents are maintained. It generally is not reasonable for the Service to require a taxpayer to attend an examination at an office within an assigned district other than the closest Service office.

(ii) *Exception.*—If the office within the assigned district closest to an individual taxpayer's residence or the location where a taxpayer entity's books, records and source documents are maintained does not have an examination group or the appropriate personnel to conduct the examination, it generally is reasonable for the Service to require the taxpayer to attend an examination at the closest Service office within the assigned district that has an examination group or the appropriate personnel.

(iii) *Travel considerations.*—In scheduling office examinations, the Service in appropriate circumstances will take into account the distance a taxpayer would have to travel.

(3) *Field examinations.*—(i) *In general.*—A field examination will generally take place at the location where the taxpayer's original books, records, and source documents pertinent to the examination are maintained. In the case of a sole proprietorship or taxpayer entity, this will usually be the taxpayer's principal place of business.

(ii) *Exception for certain small businesses.*—If an examination is scheduled by the Service at the taxpayer's place of business and the taxpayer represents to the Service in writing that conducting the examination at the place of business would essentially require the business to close or would unduly disrupt business operations, the Service, upon verification, will change the place of examination to a Service office within the district where the taxpayer's books, records, and source documents are maintained.

(iii) *Site visitations.*—Regardless of where an examination takes place, the Service may visit the taxpayer's place of business or residence to establish facts that can only be established by direct visit, such as inventory or asset verification. The Service generally will visit for these purposes on a normal workday of the Service during the Service's normal duty hours.

(e) *Requests by taxpayers to change place of examination.*—(1) *In general.*—The Service will consider, on a case-by-case basis, written requests by taxpayers or their representatives to change the place that the Service has set for an examination. In considering these requests, the Service will take into account the following factors—

(i) The location of the taxpayer's current residence;

(ii) The location of the taxpayer's current principal place of business;

(iii) The location at which the taxpayer's books, records, and source documents are maintained;

(iv) The location at which the Service can perform the examination most efficiently;

(v) The Service resources available at the location to which the taxpayer has requested a transfer; and

(vi) Other factors that indicate that conducting the examination at a particular location could pose undue inconvenience to the taxpayer.

(2) *Circumstances in which the Service normally will permit transfers.*—A request by a taxpayer to transfer the place of examination will generally be granted under the following circumstances:

(i) *Office examination.*—(A) If the current residence of the taxpayer, in the case of an individual or sole proprietorship, or the location where the taxpayer's books, records, and source documents are maintained, in the case of a taxpayer entity, is closer to a different Service office in the same district as the office where the examination has been scheduled, the Service normally will agree to transfer the examination to the closer Service office.

(B) If the current residence of a taxpayer, in the case of an individual or sole proprietorship, or the location where a taxpayer entity's books, records, and source documents are maintained, is in a district other than the district where the examination has been scheduled, the Service normally will agree to transfer the examination to the closest Service office in the other district.

(ii) *Field examinations.*—(A) If a taxpayer does not reside at the residence where an examination has been scheduled, the Service will agree to transfer the examination to the taxpayer's current residence.

(B) If, in the case of an individual, a sole proprietorship, or a taxpayer entity, the taxpayer's books, records, and source documents are maintained at a location other than the location where the examination has been scheduled, the Service will agree to transfer the examination to the location where the taxpayer's books, records, and source documents are maintained.

(3) *Transfer for convenience of taxpayer's representative.*—The location of the place of business of a taxpayer's representative will generally not be considered in determining the place for an examination. However, the Service in its sole discretion may determine, based on the factors described in paragraph (e)(1) of this section, to transfer the place of examination to the representative's office.

(4) *Transfer within thirteen months of expiration of limitations period.*—If any applicable period of limitations on assessment or collection provided in the Internal Revenue Code will expire within thirteen months from the date of a taxpayer's request to transfer the place of an examination, the Service may require, as a condition for an otherwise permissible transfer, that the taxpayer first agree in writing to extend the limitations period for up to one year.

(5) *Transfer to office with insufficient resources.*—The Service is not required to transfer an examination to an office or district that does not have adequate resources to conduct the examination.

(f) *Safety of Service officers and employees.*—Notwithstanding any other provision of this regulation, officers and employees of the Service may decline to conduct an examination at a particular location if it appears that the possibility of physical danger may exist at that location. In these circumstances, the Service may transfer an examination to a Service office and take any other steps reasonably necessary to protect its officers and employees.

(g) *Transfers initiated by Service.*—Nothing in this section shall be interpreted as precluding the Service from initiating the transfer of an examination if the transfer would promote the effective and efficient conduct of the examination. Should a taxpayer request that such a transfer not be made, the Service will consider the request according to the principles and criteria set forth in paragraph (e) of this section.

(h) *Restrictions on examination of taxpayer.*—No taxpayer shall be subjected to unnecessary examination or investigations, and only one inspection of a taxpayer's books of account shall be made for each taxable year unless the taxpayer requests otherwise or unless an authorized internal revenue officer, after investigation, notifies the taxpayer in writing that an additional inspection is necessary. The inspection of a taxpayer's books of account pursuant to the procedures of § 1.1441-4(b)(3) and (4) is not an inspection of a taxpayer's books of account for purposes of section 7605(b) and this section.

(i) *Restriction on examination of churches.*—(1) *In general.*—This section imposes certain restrictions upon the examination of the books of account and religious activities of a church or convention or

association of churches for the purpose of determining whether such organization may be engaged in activities the income from which is subject to tax under section 511 as unrelated business taxable income. The purposes of these restrictions are to protect such organizations from undue interference in their internal financial affairs through unnecessary examinations to determine the existence of unrelated business taxable income, and to limit the scope of examination for this purpose to matters directly relevant to a determination of the existence or amount of such income. This section also imposes additional restrictions upon other examinations of such organizations.

(2) *Books of account.*—No examination of the books of account of an organization which claims to be a church or a convention or association of churches shall be made except after the giving of notice as provided in this subparagraph and except to the extent necessary (i) to determine the initial or continuing qualification of the organization under section 501(c)(3); (ii) to determine whether the organization qualifies as one, contributions to which are deductible under section 170, 545, 556, 642, 2055, 2106, or 2522; (iii) to obtain information for the purpose of ascertaining or verifying payments made by the organization to another person in determining the tax liability of the recipient, such as payments of salaries, wages, or other forms of compensation; or (iv) to determine the amount of tax, if any, imposed by the Code upon such organization. No examination of the books of account of a church or convention or association of churches shall be made unless the Regional Commissioner believes that such examination is necessary and so notifies the organization in writing at least 30 days in advance of examination. The Regional Commissioner will conclude that such examination is necessary only after reasonable attempts have been made to obtain information from the books of account by written request and the Regional Commissioner has determined that the information cannot be fully or satisfactorily obtained in that manner. In any examination of a church or convention or association of churches for the purpose of determining unrelated business income tax liability pursuant to such notice, no examination of the books of account of the organization shall be made except to the extent necessary to determine such liability.

(3) *Religious activities.*—No examination of the religious activities of an organization which claims to be a church or convention or association of churches shall be made except (i) to the extent necessary to determine the initial or continuing qualification of the organization under section 501(c)(3); (ii) to determine whether the organization qualifies as one, contributions to which are deductible under section 170, 545, 556, 642, 2055, 2106, or 2522; or (iii) to determine whether the organization is a church or convention or association of churches subject to the provisions of part III of subchapter F of chapter 1. The requirements of subparagraph (2) of this paragraph that the Regional Commissioner give notice prior to examination of the books of account of an organization do not apply to an examination of the religious activities of the organization for any purpose described in this subparagraph. Once it has been determined that the organization is a church or convention or association of churches, no further examination of its religious activities may be made in connection with determining its liability, if any, for unrelated business income tax.

(4) *Effective date.*—The provisions of this paragraph shall apply to audits and examinations of taxable years beginning after December 31, 1969.

(j) *Effective date.*—Paragraphs (a) through (g) of this section, inclusive, are effective for examinations scheduled after April 2, 1993. [Reg. § 301.7605-1.]

☐ [*T.D. 6421, 10-23-59. Amended by T.D. 6498, 10-24-60; T.D. 7146, 10-26-71; T.D. 7977, 9-19-84; T.D. 8297, 4-2-90 and T.D. 8469, 4-2-93.*]

**[Reg. § 301.7606-1]**

**§ 301.7606-1. Entry of premises for examination of taxable objects.**—Any officer or employee of the Internal Revenue Service may, in the performance of his duty, enter in the daytime any building or place where any articles or objects subject to tax are made, produced, or kept, so far as it may be necessary for the purpose of examining said articles or objects and also enter at night any such building or place, while open, for a similar purpose. [Reg. § 301.7606-1.]

☐ [*T.D. 6421, 10-23-59. Amended by T.D. 7297, 12-18-73.*]

**[Reg. § 301.7609-1]**

**§ 301.7609-1. Special procedures for third-party summonses.**—(a) *In general.*—(1) Section 7609 requires the Internal Revenue Service (IRS) to follow special procedures when summoning a third party's testimony, records, or computer software source code. Except as provided in § 301.7609-2(b), the IRS must provide notice of a third-party summons to any person identified in the summons, other than the person summoned. A person entitled to notice of a third-party summons may intervene in any proceeding brought to enforce the summons or may bring a proceeding to quash the summons, regardless of whether they receive notice of the summons from the IRS pursuant to section 7609(a) and § 301.7609-2.

(2) Neither section 7609 nor the regulations hereunder limit the IRS's ability to obtain information, other than by summons, through formal or informal procedures authorized by sections 7601 and 7602.

(b) *Cross references.*—See § 301.7609-2 for rules relating to persons who must be notified of a third-party summons and exceptions to the notification requirements. See § 301.7609-3 for rules relating to the rights and duties of summoned parties. See § 301.7609-4 for rules relating to actions to quash a summons or to intervene in a summons enforcement proceeding. See § 301.7609-5 for rules relating to the suspension of periods of limitations.

(c) *Records.*—For purposes of § § 301.7609-1 through 301.7609-5, the term *records* includes books, papers, or other data.

(d) *Effective/applicability date.*—This section is applicable on April 30, 2008. [Reg. § 301.7609-1.]

☐ [*T.D.* 7899, 7-18-83. *Amended by T.D.* 8091, 6-24-86 *and T.D.* 9395, 4-29-2008.]

### [Reg. § 301.7609-2]

**§ 301.7609-2. Notification of persons identified in third-party summonses.**—(a) *In general.*—(1) *Persons entitled to notice.*—Except as provided in § 301.7609- 2(b), the Internal Revenue Service (IRS) shall give notice of a third-party summons to any person, other than the person summoned, who is identified in the summons. The only persons so identified are the person with respect to whose liability the summons is issued and any other person identified in the description of summoned records or testimony. For example, if the IRS issues a summons to a bank with respect to the liability of C that requires the production of account records of A and B, both of whom are named in the summons, the IRS must notify A, B and C of the summons.

(2) *Time for providing notice.*—If notice is required by this paragraph, such notice must be given within three days of the date on which the summons is served on the third party, but no later than 23 days prior to the date fixed in the summons as the date on which the examination of the summoned person or records is scheduled.

(3) *Methods for serving notice.*—Notice may be served by hand delivery to any person entitled to notice or by leaving notice at such person's last and usual place of abode. Notice also may be served by certified or registered mail to the person's last known address, as defined in § 301.6212-2. If service to a person entitled to notice is made by certified or registered mail, the date of service is the date on which the notice is mailed.

(4) *Content of the notice.*—Notice required to be given to any person entitled to notice must be accompanied by a copy of the summons that has been served and must include an explanation of the right to bring a proceeding to quash the summons. The copy of the summons accompanying the notice is not required to contain the attestation that appears pursuant to section 7603 on the copy of the summons served on the summoned person.

(b) *Exceptions.*—The IRS is not required to provide notice to persons identified in the following third-party summonses:

(1) *Summons served on the taxpayer.*—The IRS is not required to provide notice of a summons served on the person with respect to whose liability the summons was issued, or any officer or employee of such person.

(2) *Existence of records.*—The IRS is not required to provide notice in the case of a summons issued to determine whether or not records of the business transactions or affairs of a person identified in the summons have been made or kept.

(3) *Numbered account or similar arrangement.*—The IRS is not required to provide notice in the case of a summons issued solely to determine the identity of a person having a numbered account or similar arrangement with a bank or other institution. An account is a numbered account or similar arrangement within the meaning of this paragraph if it is an account through which a person may authorize transactions solely through the use of a number, symbol, code name, or other device not involving the disclosure of the person's identity. The term *person having a numbered account or similar arrangement* includes the person who opened the account and any person authorized to access the account or to receive records or statements concerning it.

(4) *Summonses in aid of the collection of liabilities.*—(i) *In general.*—The IRS is not required to provide notice in the case of a summons

issued in aid of the collection of liabilities. A summons is in aid of the collection of liabilities within the meaning of this paragraph if it is issued in connection with the collection of—

(A) An assessment or judgment against the person with respect to whose liability the summons is issued; or

(B) The liability determined at law or in equity of any transferee or fiduciary of a person described in paragraph (b)(4)(i)(A) of this section.

(ii) *Examples.*—The rules of paragraph (b)(4) of this section are illustrated by the following examples:

*Example 1.* A third-party summons is issued to a bank to determine the amount held in an account in the name of A, against whom unpaid income taxes have been assessed. Notice of the summons is not required to be given to A or any other person identified in the summons because the summons is issued in connection with the collection of taxes that have been assessed.

*Example 2.* A third-party summons is issued to determine whether assessments should be made against A, who is potentially liable for a trust fund recovery penalty under section 6672 with respect to the assessed but unpaid withholding tax liability of employer E. The summons is captioned: In the matter of A. Notice of the summons must be provided to A and to any other persons identified in the summons because the summons was issued with respect to A's potential, unassessed liability under section 6672.

(5) *Summonses issued by a criminal investigator.*—The IRS is not required to provide notice in the case of a summons issued by a criminal investigator to a person other than a third-party recordkeeper, as defined in section 7603(b). For purposes of section 7609(c)(2)(E), a summons issued by a criminal investigator is any summons issued as part of a criminal investigation by an IRS officer or employee having authority to conduct a criminal investigation and to issue a summons.

(6) *John Doe summons.*—The IRS is not required to provide notice in the case of a John Doe summons issued under section 7609(f).

(7) *Summons issued pursuant to a court order to prevent spoliation of evidence.*—The IRS is not required to provide notice in the case of a summons for which a court determines there is reasonable cause to believe the giving of notice may lead to attempts to conceal, destroy, or alter records relevant to the examination, to prevent communication of information from other persons through intimidation, bribery, or collusion, or to flee to avoid prosecution, testifying, or production of records.

(c) *Effective/applicability date.*—This section is applicable on April 30, 2008. [Reg. § 301.7609-2.]

☐ [*T.D.* 7899, 7-18-83. *Amended by T.D.* 8091, 6-24-86 *and T.D.* 9395, 4-29-2008.]

### [Reg. § 301.7609-3]

**§ 301.7609-3. Duty of and protection for the summoned party.**—(a) *Duty of the summoned party.*—Upon receipt of a summons, the summoned party must begin to assemble the summoned records. The summoned party must be prepared to produce the summoned records on the date on which the summons states that they are to be examined, regardless of the institution or anticipated institution of a proceeding to quash or the summoned party's intervention in a proceeding to quash, as allowed under section 7609(b)(2)(C).

(b) *Disclosing summoned party not liable.*—(1) *In general.*—A summoned party, or an agent or employee thereof, who makes a disclosure of records or gives testimony as required by a summons in good faith reliance on the certificate of the Secretary (as defined in paragraph (b)(2) of this section) or an order of a court requiring production of records or giving of testimony, will not be liable for any claim arising from such disclosure brought by any customer, any party with respect to whose tax liability the summons was issued, or any other person.

(2) *Certificate of the Secretary.*—The Secretary may issue to the summoned party a certificate if the person with respect to whose liability the summons was issued expressly consents to the examination of the records summoned and the taking of testimony. The Secretary also may issue to the summoned party a certificate stating that—

(i) The 20-day period within which a person entitled to notice of the summons may institute a proceeding to quash the summons has expired; and

(ii) No proceeding has been instituted within that period.

(c) *Reimbursement of costs.*—Summoned third parties may be entitled to reimbursement of their costs of assembling and preparing to produce summoned records, to the extent allowed by section 7610 and § 301.7610-1.

(d) *Notification of suspension of periods of limitations in connection with a John Doe summons.*—(1) *Requirement of notification.*—If any periods of limitations are suspended under section 7609(e)(2) and §301.7609-5(d) with respect to a John Doe summons described in section 7609(f), the summoned party is required under section 7609(i)(4) to provide notice of such suspension to all persons with respect to whose liability the summons was issued.

(2) *Content of notification.*—A summoned party required to notify a person of the suspension of the periods of limitations shall provide the following information to such person—

(i) A John Doe summons was served on the summoned party seeking records that may be relevant to the person's tax liability;

(ii) The date on which the summons was served;

(iii) The tax period(s) to which the summons relates;

(iv) Six months has passed since service of the summons and the summoned party's response to the summons has not been finally resolved;

(v) The periods of limitations under section 6501 (relating to assessment and collection) and section 6531 (relating to criminal prosecution), have been suspended; and

(vi) The date on which suspension of the periods of limitations under sections 6501 and 6531 began.

(3) *Time and manner of notification.*—The notification must be made in writing and may be delivered in person, by mail sent to the address last known by the summoned party, or by use of any electronic means of transmission. Notification should be made as soon as possible after the suspension of the periods of limitations begins. Failure by a summoned party to give notice of the suspension of periods of limitations as required by section 7609(i)(4) does not prevent the suspension of the periods of limitations under section 7609(e)(2).

(e) *Effective/applicability date.*—This section is applicable on April 30, 2008. [Reg. §301.7609-3.]

☐ [*T.D. 7899, 7-18-83. Amended by T.D. 8091, 6-24-86 and T.D. 9395, 4-29-2008.*]

### [Reg. §301.7609-4]

**§301.7609-4. Right to intervene; right to institute a proceeding to quash.**—(a) *Intervention in proceeding with respect to enforcement of a summons.*—Under section 7609(b)(1), a person entitled to notice of a summons under section 7609(a) and §301.7609-2 is entitled to intervene in any proceeding brought under section 7604 with respect to the enforcement of that summons.

(b) *Right to institute a proceeding to quash.*—(1) *In general.*—Under section 7609(b), a person entitled to notice of a summons under section 7609(a) and §301.7609-2 may institute a proceeding to quash the summons in the United States district court for the district in which the summoned person resides or is found.

(2) *Requirements for a proceeding to quash.*—To institute a proceeding to quash a summons, a person entitled to notice of the summons must, not later than the 20th day following the day the notice of the summons was served on or mailed to such person—

(i) File a petition to quash a summons in the name of the person entitled to notice of the summons in the proper district court;

(ii) Notify the Internal Revenue Service (IRS) by sending a copy of that petition to quash by registered or certified mail to the IRS employee and office designated in the notice of summons to receive the copy; and

(iii) Notify the summoned person by sending by registered or certified mail a copy of the petition to quash to the summoned person.

(3) *Failure to give timely notice.*—If a person entitled to notice of the summons fails to give proper and timely notice to either the summoned person or the IRS in the manner described in this paragraph, that person has failed to institute a proceeding to quash and the district court lacks jurisdiction to hear the proceeding. For example, if the person entitled to notice mails a copy of the petition to the summoned person, but fails to mail a copy of the petition to the designated IRS employee and office, the person entitled to notice has failed to institute a proceeding to quash. Similarly, if the person entitled to notice mails a copy of such petition to the summoned person but, instead of sending a copy of the petition by registered or certified mail to the designated IRS employee and office, the person entitled to notice provides the designated IRS employee and office the petition by some other means, the person entitled to notice has failed to institute a proceeding to quash.

(4) *Failure to institute a proceeding to quash.*—If a person entitled to notice fails to institute a proceeding to quash within 20 days following the day the notice of the summons was served on or mailed to such person, the IRS may examine the summoned records and take summoned testimony following the 23rd day after notice of the summons was served on or mailed to the person entitled to notice.

(c) *Presumption no notice has been mailed.*—Section 7609(b)(2)(B) permits a person entitled to notice to institute a proceeding to quash by filing a petition in district court and notifying both the IRS and the summoned person. Unless the person entitled to notice has notified both the IRS and the summoned person in the appropriate manner, the person entitled to notice has failed to institute a proceeding to quash. For the purpose of permitting the IRS to examine the summoned witnesses and records, it is presumed that the notification was not timely mailed if the copy of the petition was not delivered to the summoned person or to the person and office designated to receive the notice on behalf of the IRS within three days after the close of the 20-day period allowed for instituting a proceeding to quash.

(d) *Effective/applicability date.*—This section is applicable on April 30, 2008. [Reg. §301.7609-4.]

☐ [*T.D. 7899, 7-18-83. Amended by T.D. 8091, 6-24-86 and T.D. 9395, 4-29-2008.*]

### [Reg. §301.7609-5]

**§301.7609-5. Suspension of periods of limitations.**—(a) *In general.*—Except in the case of a summons that is a designated or related summons described in section 6503(j), the following rules relating to the suspension of certain periods of limitations apply to all third-party summonses subject to the notice requirements of section 7609(a) and to all John Doe summonses subject to the requirements of section 7609(f).

(b) *Intervention in an action to enforce the summons.*—(1) *In general.*—If a person entitled to notice of a summons under section 7609(a) and §301.7609-2 with respect to whose liability the summons was issued, or such person's agent, nominee, or other person acting under the direction or control of the person entitled to notice, takes any action to intervene in a proceeding with respect to enforcement of such summons brought pursuant to section 7604, that person's periods of limitations under sections 6501 (relating to assessment and collection) and 6531 (relating to criminal prosecutions) for the tax period or periods that are the subject of the summons are suspended for the period during which such proceeding is pending.

(2) *Action to intervene.*—A person entitled to notice takes any action to intervene in a proceeding to enforce a summons within the meaning of §301.7609-4(a) on the date when a motion to intervene is filed with the court.

(c) *Institution of a proceeding to quash a summons.*—(1) *In general.*—If a person entitled to notice of a summons under section 7609(a) and §301.7609-2 with respect to whose liability the summons was issued, or such person's agent, nominee, or other person acting under the direction or control of the such person, takes any action described in §301.7609-4(b) to institute a proceeding to quash such summons, that person's periods of limitations under sections 6501 and 6531 for the tax period or periods that are the subject of the summons are suspended for the period during which such proceeding is pending.

(2) *Action to institute a proceeding to quash a summons.*—A person entitled to notice takes any action to institute a proceeding to quash if he or she files a petition to quash the summons in any district court, regardless of whether the timely filing requirements of section 7609(b)(2)(A) or the notice requirements of section 7609(b)(2)(B) are satisfied. For example, a person entitled to notice takes an action to institute a proceeding to quash a summons for purposes of this section if that person files a petition to quash the summons in district court and notifies the summoned person by sending a copy of the petition by registered or certified mail, but fails to mail a copy of that notice to the appropriate Internal Revenue Service (IRS) person and office.

(d) *Summoned party's failure to finally resolve the response to a summons after six months from service.*—(1) *In general.*—If a third party's response to a summons for which the IRS was required to provide notice to persons identified in the summons, or to a John Doe summons described in section 7609(f), is not finally resolved within six months after the date of service of the summons, the periods of limitations are suspended under sections 6501 and 6531, for the person with respect to whose liability the summons was issued and for any person whose identity is sought to be obtained by a John Doe summons, for the tax period or periods that are the subject of the summons. The suspension shall begin on the date which is six months after the service of the summons and shall end on the date on which there is a final resolution of the summoned party's response to the summons.

*(2) Example.*—The rules of paragraph (d)(1) of this section are illustrated by the following example:

A John Doe summons is issued on April 1, 2004, to the promoter of a tax shelter and seeks the names of all participants in the shelter in order to investigate the participants' income tax liabilities for 2001 and 2002. The district court approves service of the summons on April 30, 2004, and the summons is served on the promoter on May 3, 2004. The promoter does not provide the names of the participants. The periods of limitations for the participants' income tax liabilities and criminal prosecution for 2001 and 2002 are suspended under section 7609(e)(2) beginning on November 3, 2004, the date which is six months after the date the John Doe summons was served until the date on which the promoter's response to the summons is finally resolved.

*(e) Definitions.*—(1) *Agent, nominee, etc.*—A person is the agent, nominee, or other person of a person entitled to notice under section 7609(a) and § 301.7609-2, and is acting under the direction or control of the person entitled to notice for purposes of section 7609(e)(1), if the person entitled to notice has the ability in fact or at law to cause the agent, nominee or other person, to take the actions permitted under section 7609(b).

*(2) Period during which a proceeding is pending.*—(i) *Intervention in an enforcement proceeding.*—The period during which the periods of limitations under sections 6501 and 6531 are suspended under section 7609(e)(1) begins on the date any person described in paragraph (b) of this section intervenes in an action to enforce the summons. The periods of limitations remain suspended until all appeals are disposed of, or until the expiration of the period during which an appeal may be taken or a request for further review may be made. The periods of limitations remain suspended for the period during which a proceeding is pending, regardless of compliance (or partial compliance) with the summons during that period. If, following issuance of an order to enforce a third-party summons, a collateral proceeding is brought challenging whether production made by the summoned party fully satisfied the court order and whether sanctions should be imposed against the summoned party for a failure to satisfy that order, the periods of limitations remain suspended until all appeals of the collateral proceeding are disposed of, or until the expiration of the period during which an appeal may be taken or a request for further review of the collateral proceeding may be made. Any collateral proceeding to the original proceeding shall be considered to be a continuation of the original proceeding.

(ii) *Proceeding to quash a summons.*—The period during which the periods of limitations under sections 6501 and 6531 are suspended under section 7609(e)(1) begins on the date any person described in paragraph (c) of this section files a petition to quash the summons in district court. The periods of limitations remain suspended until all appeals are disposed of, or until expiration of the period in which an appeal may be taken or a request for further review may be made. The periods of limitations remain suspended for the period during which a proceeding is pending, regardless of compliance (or partial compliance) with the summons during that period.

(iii) *Examples.*—The rules of paragraph (e)(2) are illustrated by the following examples:

*Example 1.* A revenue agent issues a summons to A, an accountant for B, requiring production of records relating to B's income tax liabilities for 2002. The summons is served on A on March 1, 2004. B files a petition to quash the summons in district court on March 15, 2004. The district court dismisses B's petition on July 1, 2004. B fails to appeal this decision by filing a notice of appeal within 60 days from the date of the district court's order of dismissal. The revenue agent notifies A that B did not appeal the district court's order. A turns over all of the records requested in the summons. The periods of limitations applicable to B for 2002 under sections 6501 and 6531 are suspended under section 7609(e)(1) from March 15, 2004, the date B filed a petition to quash, until August 30, 2004, the last day on which B could have filed a notice of appeal.

*Example 2.* A revenue agent issues a summons to A, an accountant for B, requiring production of records relating to B's income tax liabilities for 2003. The summons is served on A on June 1, 2005. B files an untimely petition to quash the summons in district court on June 29, 2005. The district court dismisses B's petition on July 29, 2005. B does not file an appeal of the district court's order. The periods of limitations applicable to B for 2003 under sections 6501 and 6531 are suspended under section 7609(e)(1) from June 29, 2005, the date B filed an untimely petition to quash, until September 27, 2005, the last day on which B could have filed a notice of appeal.

*(3) Final resolution of the summoned third party's response to a summons.*—For purposes of section 7609(e)(2)(B), final resolution with respect to a summoned party's response to a third-party summons occurs when the summons or any order enforcing any part of the summons is fully complied with and all appeals or requests for further review are disposed of, the period in which an appeal may be taken has expired or the period in which a request for further review may be made has expired. The determination of whether there has been full compliance will be made within a reasonable time, given the volume and complexity of the records produced, after the later of the giving of all testimony or the production of all records requested by the summons or required by any order enforcing any part of the summons. If, following an enforcement order, collateral proceedings are brought challenging whether the production made by the summoned party fully satisfied the court order and whether sanctions should be imposed against the summoned party for a failing to do so, the suspension of the periods of limitations shall continue until the summons or any order enforcing any part of the summons is fully complied with and the decision in the collateral proceeding becomes final. A decision in a collateral proceeding becomes final when all appeals are disposed of, the period in which an appeal may be taken has expired or the period in which a request for further review may be made has expired.

*(f) Effective/applicability date.*—This section is applicable on April 30, 2008. [Reg. § 301.7609-5.]

☐ [*T.D. 7899, 7-18-83. Amended by T.D. 8091, 6-24-86 and T.D. 9395, 4-29-2008.*]

### [Reg. § 301.7610-1]

**§ 301.7610-1. Fees and costs for witnesses.**—*(a) Introduction.*—Section 7610 provides that the Internal Revenue Service may make payments to certain persons who are asked to give information to the Service. Under section 7610 witnesses generally will not be reimbursed for actual expenses incurred but instead will be paid in accordance with the payment rates established by regulations. Paragraph (b) of this section contains elaborations of certain terms found in section 7610 and definitions of other terms used in the regulations under section 7610(a)(2); and paragraphs (c) and (d) contain rules and rates applicable to payments under section 7610. Section 7610 and its regulations are effective for summonses issued after February 28, 1977, except as otherwise provided.

*(b) Definitions.*—(1) *Directly incurred costs.*—Directly incurred costs are costs incurred solely, immediately, and necessarily as a consequence of searching for, reproducing, or transporting records in order to comply with a summons. They do not include a proportionate allocation of fixed costs, such as overhead, equipment depreciation, etc. However, where a third party's records are stored at an independent storage facility that charges the third party a search fee to search for, reproduce, or transport particular records requested, these fees are considered to be directly incurred by the summoned third party.

*(2) Reproduction costs.*—Reproduction costs are costs incurred in making copies or duplicates of summoned documents, transcripts, and other similar material.

*(3) Search costs.*—Search costs include only the total cost of personnel time directly incurred in searching for records or information and the cost of retrieving information stored by computer. Salaries of persons locating and retrieving summoned material are not includible in search costs. Also, search costs do not include salaries, fees, or similar expenditures for analysis of material or for managerial or legal advice, expertise, or research, or time spent for these activities.

*(4) Third party.*—A third party is any person served with a summons, other than a person with respect to whose liability a summons is issued, or an officer, employee, agent, accountant, or attorney of that person.

*(5) Third party records.*—Third party records are books, papers, records or other data in which the person with respect to whose liability a summons is issued does not have a proprietary interest at the time the summons is served.

*(6) Transportation costs.*—Transportation costs include only costs incurred to transport personnel to search for records or information requested and costs incurred solely by the need to transport the summoned material to the place of examination. These costs do not include the cost of transporting the summoned witness for appearance at the place of examination. See paragraph (c)(2) of this section for payment of travel expenses.

*(c) Conditions and rates of payments.*—(1) *Basis for payment.*—Payment for search, reproduction, and transportation costs will be made only to third parties served with a summons to produce third party records or information and only for material requested by the summons. Payment will be made only for these costs that are both directly incurred and reasonably necessary. Search, reproduction, and transportation costs must be considered separately in determin-

ing whether costs are reasonably necessary. No payment will be made until the third party has satisfactorily complied with the summons and has submitted an itemized bill or invoice showing specific details concerning the costs to the Internal Revenue Service employee before whom the third party was summoned. If a third party charges any other person for any cost for which the third party is seeking payment from the Service, the amount charged to the other person must be subtracted from the amount the Internal Revenue Service may pay.

(2) *Payment rates.*—The following rates are established:

(i) *Search costs.*—(A) For the total amount of personnel time required to locate records or information, $8.50 per person hour for summonses issued after July 19, 1983. For summonses issued on or before such date, $5.00 per person hour.

(B) For retrieval of information stored by computer in the format in which it is normally produced, actual costs, based on computer time and necessary supplies, except that personnel time for computer search is payable only under subparagraph (2)(i)(A) of this paragraph.

(ii) *Reproductions costs.*—(A) For copies of documents, $.20 per page for summonses issued after July 19, 1983. For copies of documents issued on or before such date, $.10 per page.

(B) For photographs, films and other materials, actual cost, except that personnel time is payable only under subparagraph (2)(i)(A) of this paragraph.

(iii) *Transportation costs.*—For transportation costs, actual cost, except that personnel time is payable only under subparagraph (2)(i)(A) of this paragraph.

(d) *Appearance fees and allowances.*—(1) *In general.*—Under Section 7610(a)(1) and this paragraph, the Service shall pay a summoned person certain fees and allowances. No payments will be made until after the party summoned appears and has submitted any necessary receipts or other evidence of cost to the Service employee before whom the person was summoned. This paragraph is effective with respect to appearances made after October 26, 1978.

(2) *Attendance fees.*—A summoned person shall be paid an attendance fee for each day's attendance. A summoned person shall also be paid the attendance fee for the time necessarily occupied in going to and returning from the place of attendance at the beginning and end of the attendance or at any time during the attendance. The attendance fee is the higher of $30 per day or the amount paid under 28 U.S.C. 1821(b) to witnesses in attendance at courts of the United States at the time of the summoned person's appearance.

(3) *Travel allowances.*—A summoned person who travels by common carrier shall be paid for the actual expenses of travel on the basis of the means of transportation reasonably utilized and the distance necessarily traveled to and from the summoned person's residence by the shortest practical route in going to and returning from the place of attendance. Such a summoned person shall utilize a common carrier at the most economical rate reasonably available. A receipt or other evidence of actual cost shall be furnished. A travel allowance equal to the mileage allowance which the Administrator of General Services has prescribed, under 5 U.S.C. 5704, for official travel of employees of the Federal Government shall be paid to each summoned person who travels by privately owned vehicle. That rate is $.20 per mile as of April 20, 1980. Computation of mileage under this paragraph shall be made on the basis of a uniform table of distances adopted by the Administrator of General Services. Toll charges for toll roads, bridges, tunnels, and ferries, taxicab fares between places of lodging and carrier terminals, and parking fees (upon presentation of a valid parking receipt) shall be paid in full to a summoned person incurring those expenses.

(4) *Subsistence allowances.*—A subsistence allowance shall be paid to a summoned person (other than a summoned person who is incarcerated) when an overnight stay is required at the place of attendance because the place is so far removed from the residence of the summoned person as to prohibit return thereto from day to day. A subsistence allowance for a summoned person shall be paid in an amount not to exceed the maximum per diem allowance prescribed by the Administrator of General Services, under 5 U.S.C. 5702(a), for official travel in the area of attendance by employees of the Federal Government. As of April 30, 1979, that maximum per diem allowance is $35 per day. A subsistence allowance for a summoned person attending in an area designated by the Administrator of General Services as a high-cost area shall be paid in an amount not to exceed the maximum actual subsistence allowance prescribed by the Administrator, under 5 U.S.C. 5702(c)(B), for official travel in that area by employees of the Federal Government. As of April 30, 1979, maximum rates of up to $50 per day have been prescribed by the Admin-

istrator for certain areas. An alien who has been paroled into the United States for prosecution, under section 212(d)(5) of the Immigration and Nationality Act (8 U.S.C. 1182(d)(5)), or an alien who either has admitted belonging to a class of aliens who are deportable or has been determined under section 242(b) of that Act (8 U.S.C. 1252(b)) to be deportable, shall be ineligible to receive the fees or allowances provided for under section 7610(a)(1). [Reg. § 301.7610-1.]

☐ [*T.D.* 7899, 7-18-83.]

## [Reg. § 301.7611-1]

**§ 301.7611-1. Questions and answers relating to church tax inquiries and examinations.—**

*Church tax inquiry*

Q-1: When may the Internal Revenue Service begin an inquiry of a church's tax liability?

A-1: Under section 7611 of the Internal Revenue Code, the Internal Revenue Service may begin a church tax inquiry only when the appropriate Regional Commissioner (or higher Treasury official) reasonably believes, on the basis of facts and circumstances recorded in writing, that the organization (1) may not qualify for tax exemption as a church; (2) may be carrying on an unrelated trade or business (within the meaning of section 513); or (3) may be otherwise engaged in activities subject to tax. Information received by the Internal Revenue Service at its request may not be used to form the basis of a reasonable belief to begin a church tax inquiry, unless the Service's request is made within the procedures of section 7611, is a request permitted by these questions and answers to be made without application of the procedures of section 7611, or is a request to which the procedures of section 7611 do not apply.

Q-2: What is a church tax inquiry within the meaning of section 7611?

A-2: A church tax inquiry is any inquiry to a church (other than a routine request described in Q and A-4, an inquiry described in Q and A-5, an investigation described in Q and A-6 or an examination described in Qs and As 10 and 14), to serve as a basis for determining whether the organization qualifies for tax exemption as a church or whether it is carrying on an unrelated trade or business or is otherwise engaged in activities subject to tax. An inquiry is considered to commence when the Internal Revenue Service requests information or materials from a church of a type contained in church records. The term "church tax inquiry" does not include routine requests for information or inquiries regarding matters which do not primarily concern the tax status or liability of the church itself. See Q and A-4 with respect to routine requests regarding, among other things, withholding responsibilities for income tax or FICA (social security) tax liabilities. See Q and A-6 with respect to the types of investigations, other than routine requests, that are outside the scope of the procedures of section 7611. See Q and A-5 with respect to requests for third party records that are outside the scope of the procedures of section 7611.

Q-3: What is a "church" for purposes of the church tax inquiry and examination procedures of section 7611?

A-3: Solely for purposes of applying the procedures of section 7611, and as used in these questions and answers, the term "church" includes any organization claiming to be a church and any convention or association of churches. For purposes of the procedures of section 7611 and these questions and answers a church does not include separately incorporated church-supported schools or other organizations incorporated separately from the church.

*Routine requests*

Q-4: What is a routine request to a church that is outside the scope of and does not necessitate application of the procedures set forth in section 7611?

A-4: Routine requests to a church will not be considered to commence a church tax inquiry and will not necessitate application of the procedures set forth in section 7611. Routine requests for this purpose include (but are not limited to) questions regarding (1) the filing or failure to file any tax return or information return by the church; (2) compliance with income tax or FICA (social security) tax withholding responsibilities by the church; (3) any supplemental information needed to complete the mechanical processing of any incomplete or incorrect return filed by the church; (4) information necessary to process applications for exempt status and letter ruling requests; (5) information necessary to process and update periodically a church's (i) registrations for tax-free transactions (excise tax), (ii) elections for exemption from windfall profit tax, or (iii) employment tax exemption requests; (6) information identifying a church that is used to update the Cumulative List of Tax Exempt Organizations (Publication No. 78) and other computer files; and (7) confirmation that a specific business is or is not owned or operated by a church.

*Third party records*

Q-5: To what extent may the Internal Revenue Service gain access to third party records?

A-5: The Internal Revenue Service may request a church to provide information necessary to locate third-party records (for instance, bank records), including information regarding the church's chartered name, state and year of incorporation, and location of checking and savings accounts, without application of the procedures of section 7611.

Records (for instance, cancelled checks or other records in the possession of a bank) held by third party recordkeepers, as defined in section 7609, are not considered church records. Thus, subject to the provisions set forth in section 7609 regarding third party summonses, access is permitted to such records without regard to the requirements of the procedures set forth in section 7611. The Internal Revenue Service is generally required, under other rules, to inform a church of any Internal Revenue Service requests for materials.

Third party materials may be acquired without application of the procedures of section 7611; however, a determination that a church is not entitled to an exemption, or an assessment of tax for unrelated business income against a church, may not be made solely on the basis of third party records, without first complying with the requirements of two notices and offering of a conference (see Qs and As 9 and 10) pursuant to the procedures set forth in section 7611. This limitation does not apply to assessments of tax other than income tax resulting from loss of exemption or for unrelated business income (for instance, assessments of social security or other employment taxes). Third party bank records will not be used in a manner inconsistent with the procedures set forth in section 7611 or in these questions and answers.

*Scope of section 7611*

Q-6: What types of investigations, other than routine requests and requests for information necessary to locate and examine third party records, and examination of those records, are outside the scope of the procedures of section 7611?

A-6: The church inquiry and examination procedures described in section 7611 do not apply to (1) any inquiry or examination relating to the tax liability of any person other than a church; (2) any termination assessment under section 6851 or 6852, or jeopardy assessment under section 6861; or (3) any case involving a knowing failure to file a return or a willful attempt to defeat or evade tax (including but not limited to any case involving a failure by the church to withhold or pay social security or other employment taxes or income tax required to be withheld from wages). Additionally, the church inquiry and examination procedures do not apply to any criminal investigations.

The church tax inquiry and examination procedures also do not apply to inquiries or examinations which relate primarily to the tax status (including, but not limited to, social security or self-employment tax or income tax required to be withheld from wages) or liability of persons other than the church (including, but not limited to, the tax status or liability of a contributor or contributors to the church), rather than the tax status or liability of the church itself. These may include, but are not limited to: (1) inquiries or examinations regarding the inurement of church funds to a particular individual or individuals or to another organization, which may result in the denial of all or part of such individual's or organization's deduction for charitable contributions to a church; (2) inquiries or examinations regarding the assignment of income or services or contributions to a church; and (3) inquiries or examinations regarding a vow of poverty by an individual or individuals followed by a transfer of property or an assignment of income or services to a church. Inquiries may be made to a church regarding these matters without being considered to have commenced a church tax inquiry under section 7611, and an examination of church records may be made relating to these issues (including enforcement of a summons for access to such records) without application of the requirements contained in section 7611 applicable to church tax inquiries and examinations. Such examinations are subject to the general rules regarding examinations of taxpayer books and records.

Q-7: What action may be taken if the church or its agents fail to respond to routine requests, or questions regarding other individuals' or organizations' tax liabilities?

A-7: Repeated (two or more) failures by a church or its agents to reply to routine requests (see Q and A-4) will be considered by the appropriate Internal Revenue Service Regional Commissioner to be a reasonable basis for commencement of a church tax inquiry under the church tax inquiry and examination procedures of section 7611. The failure of a church to respond to repeated requests for information regarding individuals' or other organizations' tax liabilities (see Q and A-6) will be considered a reasonable basis for commencement of a church tax inquiry. Failure by a church to provide information necessary to locate third-party records (see Q and A-5) will be a factor, but not a conclusive factor, in determining if there is reasonable cause for commencing a church tax inquiry. For this purpose, a failure to respond to a request means either that no response has been made or that the response does not make a reasonable attempt to submit the information called for by the specific language of the request.

Q-8: Where an inquiry or examination is outside the scope of and does not necessitate application of the procedures of section 7611, what are the limitations on the Internal Revenue Service's actions?

A-8: Inquiries or examinations which are outside the scope of the procedures of section 7611 and therefore are conducted without application of the procedures of section 7611 (for instance, those addressed in Q and A-6) will be limited to the determination of facts and circumstances specifically relating to the tax liabilities of the individuals or other organizations in question. For example, in a case against an individual or other organization, information may be requested or church records examined, if pertinent, regarding amounts of money, property, or services transferred to the individual or individuals in question (including, but not limited to wages, loans, or noncontractual transfers), the use of church funds for personal expenses, or other similar matters, without having to follow the church tax inquiry and examination procedures. As one example, in an assignment of income case against an individual or other organization, information could be requested or church records examined if relevant to an individual's assignment of particular income, donation of property, or transfer of a business to a church. However, without following the church tax inquiry and examination procedures, no examination of a contributor or membership list in the possession of the church will be made, other than under the applicable procedures of section 7611, for the purpose of determining the overall financial structure of the church, merely because such structure was relevant to the church's qualification as a tax-exempt entity and therefore indirectly relevant to the validity of contributors' deductions in general. Inquiries or examinations regarding individuals' or other organizations' tax liabilities will not be used in a manner inconsistent with the procedures set forth in section 7611 or in these questions and answers.

*Notice requirements*

Q-9: What satisfies the inquiry notice requirement (first notice) upon commencement of a church tax inquiry?

A-9: Upon commencing a church tax inquiry, the appropriate Regional Commissioner is required to provide written notice to the church of the beginning of the inquiry. This notice will include (1) an explanation of the concerns which gave rise to the inquiry and the general subject matter of the inquiry, which is sufficiently specific to allow the church to understand the particular area of church activities or behavior which is at issue; (2) a general explanation of the provisions of the Internal Revenue Code which authorize the inquiry or which may otherwise be involved in the inquiry; and (3) a general explanation of applicable administrative and constitutional provisions with respect to the inquiry, including the right to a conference with the Internal Revenue Service before an examination of church records is commenced. The inquiry notice (first notice) will generally request information in an effort to alleviate the concerns which gave rise to the inquiry.

However, the Internal Revenue Service is not precluded from expanding its inquiry beyond the concerns expressed in the inquiry notice (first notice) as a result of facts and circumstances which subsequently come to its attention (including, where appropriate, an expansion of an unrelated business income inquiry to include questions of tax-exempt status, and vice-versa).

The inquiry notice requirement (first notice) does not require the Internal Revenue Service to share particular items of evidence with the church, or to identify its sources of information regarding church activities, if providing such information would be damaging to the inquiry or to the sources of information. For example, in an inquiry regarding unrelated business income, the Internal Revenue Service might state that its inquiry was prompted by a local newspaper advertisement regarding a church-owned business. However, the Internal Revenue Service would not be required to reveal the existence or identity of any so-called "informers" within a church (including present or former employees).

Q-10: What must be done to satisfy the examination notice requirement (second notice) before commencing an examination of church records or religious activities with respect to an examination conducted under section 7611?

A-10: Where an examination is conducted under section 7611, church records or religious activities of a church may be examined only if, at least 15 days prior to the examination, written notice of the proposed examination is provided to the church and to the appropriate Regional Counsel. This notice is in addition to the notice of commencement of inquiry (first notice) previously provided to the church.

The notice of examination (second notice) is required to include (1) a copy of the church tax inquiry notice (first notice) previously provided to the church; (2) a description of the church records and activities sought to be examined; and (3) a copy of all documents which were collected or prepared by the Internal Revenue Service for use in the examination, and which are required to be disclosed under the Freedom of Information Act (5 U.S.C. § 552) as supplemented by section 6103 of the Code (relating to disclosure and confidentiality of tax return information). The documents to be supplied under this provision will be limited to documents specifically concerning the church whose records are to be examined and will not include documents relating to other inquiries or examinations or to Internal Revenue Service practices and procedures in general. Disclosure to the church will be subject to restrictions regarding the disclosure of the existence or identity of informants. Although a description of materials to be examined will be provided in the notice of examination (second notice), the description does not restrict the ability of the Internal Revenue Service to examine church records or religious activities which are not specifically mentioned in the notice of examination (second notice) but which are properly within the scope of the examination. Thus, the Internal Revenue Service is not precluded from expanding its inquiry beyond the concerns expressed in the examination notice (second notice) as a result of facts and circumstances which subsequently come to its attention (including, where appropriate, an expansion of an unrelated business income examination to include questions of tax-exempt status, and vice versa).

At the time the notice of examination (second notice) is provided to the church, a copy of the same notice will be provided to the appropriate Regional Counsel. The Regional Counsel is then allowed 15 days from issuance of the second notice in which to file an advisory objection to the examination. (This is concurrent with the 15-day period during which an examination of church records is prohibited pending a request for a conference.)

As part of the notice of examination (second notice), the church will be offered an opportunity to meet with an Internal Revenue Service official to discuss the concerns which gave rise to the inquiry and the general subject matter of the inquiry. An examination will not begin until 15 days after the mailing of the notice of examination (second notice). The organization may request a conference at any time prior to beginning of the examination and a conference so requested will be scheduled within a reasonable time after the request is made.

The purpose of the conference is to remind the church, in general terms, of the stages of the church tax inquiry and examination procedures and to discuss the relevant issues that may arise as part of the inquiry, in an effort to resolve the issues of tax exemption or liability without the necessity of an examination of church records or activities. Information properly excludable from a written notice of examination (second notice) (including information regarding the identity of third-party witnesses or evidence provided by such witnesses) is not a subject for discussion at, and will not be revealed during, a conference.

Once a conference request is timely made, an examination will begin only following the conference. The conference requirement may not be utilized to delay an examination beyond the time reasonably necessary to prepare for and hold the conference. The holding of one conference with the church will be sufficient to satisfy the requirements of section 7611 and these questions and answers.

*Action after issuance of notice*

Q-11: What action may be taken after issuance of the examination notice (second notice)?

A-11: After the examination notice (second notice) is issued, the organization may request a conference as described in Q and A-10 (see Q and A-12 with respect to time for issuance of examination notice). If the matters of concern which gave rise to the issuance of the examination notice (second notice) are resolved at the conference, it may be determined that an examination is not necessary. If the matters of concern are not resolved at the conference, or if the organization does not request a conference, the examination will ordinarily begin.

The examination will be conducted under the Internal Revenue Service's general examination procedures and the procedures of section 7611. The outcome of such an examination will ordinarily be: (1) no change in tax-exempt status or tax liability; (2) no change in such status or liability, conditioned on compliance with a request to modify in future tax periods matters such as internal accounting practices and procedures or coupled with a caution to refrain from increasing certain activities limited by the Internal Revenue Code, such as lobbying programs aimed at influencing legislation; (3) a proposal to revoke tax-exempt status; (4) a proposal asserting unrelated business income tax liability; or (5) a proposal asserting liability for other taxes.

In certain exceptional circumstances the Internal Revenue Service may, in lieu of an examination, propose to revoke the organization's exemption based upon the facts and circumstances which form the basis for a reasonable belief to commence an inquiry under section 7611 and any other appropriate information that becomes apparent as a result of the inquiry, the conference, or both.

Pursuant to section 7611(d), the Regional Counsel is required to approve, in writing, certain final determinations that are within the scope of section 7611 and adversely affect tax-exempt status or increase any tax liability. The Regional Counsel will review and approve (1) a determination that an organization is not entitled to tax-exempt status; (2) a determination that an organization is not entitled to receive tax-deductible contributions; or (3) the issuance of a notice of tax deficiency to a church arising out of an inquiry or examination or, in cases where deficiency procedures are inapplicable, the assessment of any underpayment of tax by the church arising out of an inquiry or examination. The Regional Counsel will also state in writing that there has been substantial compliance with section 7611, when applicable.

*Procedural time limitations*

Q-12: When may the notice of examination (second notice) be sent?

A-12: The notice of examination (second notice) may be mailed to a church not less than 15 days after the notice of commencement of a church tax inquiry (first notice). Thus, at least 30 days must pass between the first notice and the actual examination of church records since an examination may not begin until 15 days after the notice of examination (second notice). For example, if notice of commencement of an inquiry is mailed to a church on March 1st, the notice of proposed examination may be mailed to the church no earlier than the 15th day after the date of the inquiry notice, or March 16th. If the notice of examination (second notice) was mailed March 16th, no examination of church records may be made prior to day 30; thus, the earliest date the examination may commence is March 31st. If an organization does not request a conference prior to day 30, the Internal Revenue Service may proceed to examine church records and complete its investigation or make a determination based on the information already in its possession.

Q-13: What is the limitation on the amount of time the Internal Revenue Service has to complete inquiries and examinations?

A-13: The Internal Revenue Service is required to complete any church inquiry or examination, and to make a final determination with respect thereto, not later than two years after the date on which the notice of examination (second notice) is mailed to the church. The running of this two-year period is suspended for any period during which (1) a judicial proceeding brought by the church or its officials or agents against the Internal Revenue Service with respect to the church tax inquiry or examination is pending or being appealed (even though section 7611 (e)(2) describes the exclusive remedy for a violation of the church tax inquiry and examination procedures; see Q and A-17); (2) a judicial proceeding brought by the Internal Revenue Service against the church (or any official or agent thereof) to compel compliance with any reasonable request for examination of church records or religious activities is pending or being appealed; or (3) the Internal Revenue Service is unable to take actions with respect to the church tax inquiry or examination by reason of an order issued in a suit under section 7609 involving access to records held by third-party recordkeepers. The two-year period is also suspended for any period in excess of 20 days (but not in excess of 6 months) in which the church or its agents fail to comply with any reasonable request for church records or other information. The two-year period may be extended by mutual agreement of the church and the Internal Revenue Service.

In cases where the inquiry is not followed by an examination notice (second notice), the inquiry must be concluded and a final determination made within 90 days of the date of the notice of inquiry (first notice). This 90-day period is suspended during any period for which the two year period for duration of a church examination would be suspended; except that the 90-day period will not be suspended because of the church's failure to comply with requests for information made prior to the notice of examination (second notice).

**Reg. § 301.7611-1**

Q-13a: When do the church tax inquiry and church tax examination periods commence and conclude?

A-13a: A church tax inquiry commences when the church tax inquiry notice (first notice) is mailed. A church tax inquiry must be concluded not later than 90 days after the church tax inquiry notice (first notice) date. The period is counted from the day after the inquiry notice (first notice) is mailed. A church tax inquiry is concluded when the results of the inquiry or the notice of examination, as appropriate, is mailed. For example, if the inquiry notice (first notice) is mailed on November 1, 1985, the church tax inquiry must be concluded, in the absence of a permissible suspension of the period (see Q and A-13), on or before January 30, 1986.

A church tax examination commences when the church tax examination notice (second notice) is mailed. A church tax examination must be concluded not later than the date which is 2 years after the examination notice (second notice) date. The period is counted from the day after the examination notice (second notice) is mailed. A church tax examination is concluded when the final determination is mailed. For example, if the examination notice is mailed on November 16, 1985, the final determination must be made, in the absence of a permissible suspension of the period (see Q and A-13), on or before November 16, 1987.

*Examination of records or religious activities*

Q-14: To what extent may church records or religious activities of a church be examined?

A-14: In cases conducted under section 7611, an examination of church records may be made only after complying with the notice provisions of section 7611 (see Qs and As 9, 10 and 12) unless the church files a written waiver of the provisions of section 7611 or a part thereof. In cases conducted under section 7611 where no written waiver has been filed, church records may be examined only to the extent necessary to determine the liability for, and the amount of, any Federal tax. This includes examinations (1) to determine the initial or continuing qualification of the organization whose records are being examined as a tax-exempt church under section 501(c)(3); (2) to determine whether the organization qualifies to receive tax-deductible contributions under section 170(c); or (3) to determine the amount of tax (including unrelated business income tax), if any, which is to be imposed on the organization.

Church records include all regularly kept church corporate and financial records including (but not limited to) corporate minute books, contributor or membership lists, and any materials which qualified as church books of account under section 7605(c), as in effect on December 31, 1984. Church records include private correspondence between a church and its members that is in the possession of the church. However, church records do not include records previously filed with a public official or newspapers or newsletters distributed generally to church members.

The religious activities of an organization claiming to be a church (see Q and A-3 for a definition of the term "church" as used in section 7611 and in these questions and answers) may be examined only to the extent necessary to determine if the organization actually is a church exempt from tax. This includes a determination of the organization's qualification as a church for any period.

*Limitations on period of assessment or proceedings for collections without assessment*

Q-15: What are the special limitations on the period of assessment or proceedings for collection without assessment?

A-15: The special limitation periods for church tax liabilities are described below and are not to be construed to increase an otherwise applicable limitation period. Thus, a three-year limitation period would apply where a church filed a tax return before an examination was held and did not substantially understate income. No limitation period is to apply in any case of fraud, willful tax evasion, or knowing failure to file a return which should have been filed.

In the case of any church tax examination with respect to the revocation of tax-exempt status under section 501(a), any tax imposed by chapter 1 (other than section 511) may be assessed, or a proceeding in court for collection of such tax may be begun without assessment, only for the three most recently completed taxable years preceding the examination notice date (*i.e.*, the date the notice of examination is mailed to the church). If an organization is not a church exempt from tax under section 501(a) for any of the three years described in the preceding sentence, then the period of assessment will apply to the six most recently completed taxable years ending before the examination notice date.

For examinations concerning qualification for tax-exempt status, the examination is limited initially to an examination of church records which are relevant to a determination of tax status or liability for the three most recently completed taxable years ending before the examination notice date. If it is determined that an organization is not a church exempt from tax for one or more of the three most recently completed taxable years and no return has been filed for the three years ending before the three most recently completed taxable

years, an examination of relevant records may be made, as part of the same examination, for the six most recently completed taxable years ending before the examination notice date. (This assumes that no returns were filed for any of the three years to which the examination is to be extended. If a return was timely filed for any such year, the filing of that return determines the applicable statute of limitations for that year in the absence of other factors, for example, fraud, willful tax evasion or substantial understatement, which ordinarily would extend the statute of limitations.)

For purposes of section 7611(d)(2)(A) and this question and answer, an organization is determined not to be a church exempt from tax for one or more of the three most recently completed taxable years ending before the examination notice date, when the appropriate Regional Commissioner approves, in writing, the completed findings of the examining agent that the organization is not a church exempt from tax for one or more of such years. Such approval may not be delegated by the Regional Commissioner to a subordinate official. The completed findings of the examining agent, as approved by the appropriate Regional Commissioner for this purpose, do not constitute a final revenue agent's report under section 7611(g).

Church records of a year earlier than the third or sixth completed taxable year, as applicable, may be examined if material to a determination of tax-exempt status during the applicable three or six year period.

For examinations concerning unrelated business taxable income, where no return has been filed by the church, tax may be assessed or collected for the six most recently completed taxable years ending before the examination notice date. Church records of a year earlier than the sixth year may be examined if material to a determination of unrelated business income tax liability during the six year period.

For examinations involving issues other than revocation of exempt status or unrelated business income (*e.g.*, examinations relating to social security or other employment taxes), no limitation period is to apply if no return has been filed.

The applicable limitation period may be extended by mutual agreement of the church and the Internal Revenue Service.

*Multiple examinations*

Q-16: What are the special multiple examination rules applicable to churches?

A-16: The Assistant Commissioner (Employee Plans and Exempt Organizations) is required to approve, in writing, any second inquiry or examination of a church, if the second inquiry or examination is to be undertaken within five years of an earlier inquiry or examination and if the earlier inquiry or examination did not result in either (1) revocation of tax exemption, notice of deficiency or an assessment of tax, or (2) a request for any significant changes in church operational practices (including the adequacy or sufficiency of records maintained to reflect income). The Assistant Commissioner's approval is required only if the second inquiry or examination involves the same or similar issues as the earlier inquiry or examination. The 5-year period is counted from the examination notice date of the earlier examination or, if no notice of examination was mailed, the inquiry notice date of the earlier examination. This 5-year period is to be suspended for periods during which the two-year period for completion of an examination is suspended (as described in Q and A-13) unless the prior examination was actually concluded within 2 years of the notice of examination.

In determining whether the second church tax inquiry or examination involves the same or similar issues as the preceding inquiry or examination, the substantive factual issues involved in the two examinations, rather than legal classifications, will govern. For example, where a prior examination and a current examination of unrelated business income involve income from different sources, the current examination involves different issues than the prior examination and the approval of the Assistant Commissioner (Employee Plans and Exempt Organizations) is not necessary.

*Remedy for violations of section 7611*

Q-17: What remedy is available for a violation of the church inquiry and examination procedures?

A-17: The exclusive remedy for any Internal Revenue Service violation of the church tax inquiry and examination procedures is as follows: Failure to comply substantially with the requirements that (1) two notices be sent to the church; (2) the Regional Commissioner approve the commencement of a church tax inquiry; or (3) an offer of a conference with the church be made (and a conference held if timely requested), will result in a stay of proceedings in a summons proceeding to gain access to church records (but not in dismissal of such proceeding), until these requirements are satisfied. The two-year limitation on duration of a church tax examination will not be suspended during stays of summons proceedings resulting from violations described above; however, violations may be corrected without regard to the otherwise applicable time limits prescribed under the procedures of section 7611. In determining whether a stay is necessary, a court must consider the good faith effort of the

Internal Revenue Service and the effect of any violation of the proper examination procedures.

Section 7611(e)(2) provides that no suit may be maintained and no defense may be raised, other than a stay in a summons enforcement proceeding, by reason of any noncompliance with the requirements of section 7611. Thus, failure to comply with any of these requirements may not be raised as a defense or affirmative ground for relief in any judicial proceeding including, but not limited to, a summons proceeding to gain access to church records; a declaratory judgment proceeding involving a determination of tax-exempt status under section 7428; a proceeding to collect unpaid tax; or a deficiency or refund proceeding. Additionally, failure to substantially comply with the requirements that two notices be sent, that the Regional Commissioner approve an inquiry, and that a conference be offered (and the conference held if requested) may not be raised as a defense or as an affirmative ground for relief in a summons proceeding or any other judicial proceeding other than as specifically set forth above. Therefore, a church or its representatives will not be able to litigate the issue of the reasonableness of the appropriate Regional Commissioner's belief in approving the commencement of a church tax inquiry (*i.e.,* that the church may not be tax-exempt or may be engaged in taxable activities) in a summons proceeding or any other judicial proceeding. The church retains the right to raise any substan-

tive or procedural argument which would be available to taxpayers generally in an appropriate proceeding.

*Effective date*

Q-18: What is the effective date of the church examination procedures?

A-18: The procedures set forth in section 7611 apply to all tax inquiries and examinations beginning after December 31, 1984. The procedures of section 7605 will apply to any examination commenced before January 1, 1985. Any activities commenced after December 31, 1984, that would constitute a new inquiry or new examination must comply with the procedures of section 7611.

*Application to Section 4958*

Q-19: When do the church tax inquiry and examination procedures described in section 7611 apply to a determination of whether there was an excess benefit transaction described in section 4958?

A-19: See §53.4958-8(b) of this chapter for rules governing the interaction between section 4958 excise taxes on excess benefit transactions and section 7611 church tax inquiry and examination procedures. [Reg. §301.7611-1.]

☐ [*T.D.* 8013, 3-7-85. *Amended by T.D.* 8077, 2-20-86; *T.D.* 8628, 12-4-95; *T.D.* 8920, 1-9-2001 (*corrected* 3-1-2001) *and T.D.* 8978, 1-22-2002 (*corrected* 3-18-2002).]

# GENERAL POWERS AND DUTIES

## [Reg. §301.7621-1]

**§301.7621-1. Internal revenue districts.**—For delegation to the Secretary of authority to prescribe internal revenue districts for the purpose of administering the internal revenue laws, see Executive Order No. 10289, dated September 17, 1951 (16 F.R. 9499), as made applicable to the Code by Executive Order No. 10574, dated November 5, 1954 (19 F.R. 7249). [Reg. §301.7621-1.]

☐ [*T.D. 6421,* 10-23-59. *Amended by T.D. 6498,* 10-24-60.]

## [Reg. §301.7622-1]

**§301.7622-1. Authority to administer oaths and certify.**—The officers and employees of the Internal Revenue Service whom the Commissioner has designated are authorized to administer such oaths or affirmations and to certify to such papers as may be necessary under the internal revenue laws or regulations issued thereunder, except that the authority to certify shall not be construed as applying to those papers or documents the certification of which is authorized by separate order or directive. [Reg. §301.7622-1.]

☐ [*T.D. 6421,* 10-23-59. *Amended by T.D. 6498,* 10-24-60; *T.D. 6585,* 12-27-61; *T.D. 7188,* 6-28-72; *T.D. 7297,* 12-18-73 *and T.D. 7359,* 5-30-75.]

## [Reg. §301.7623-1]

**§301.7623-1. General rules, submitting information on underpayments of tax or violations of the internal revenue laws, and filing claims for award.**—(a) *In general.*—In cases in which awards are not otherwise provided for by law, the Whistleblower Office may pay an award under section 7623(a), in a suitable amount, for information necessary for detecting underpayments of tax or detecting and bringing to trial and punishment persons guilty of violating the internal revenue laws or conniving at the same. In cases that satisfy the requirements of section 7623(b)(5) and (b)(6) and in which the Internal Revenue Service (IRS) proceeds with an administrative or judicial action based on information provided by an individual, the Whistleblower Office must determine and pay an award under section 7623(b)(1), (2), or (3). The awards provided for by section 7623 and this paragraph must be paid from collected proceeds, as defined in §301.7623-2(d).

(b) *Eligibility to file claim for award.*—(1) *In general.*—Any individual, other than an individual described in paragraph (b)(2) of this section, is eligible to file a claim for award and to receive an award under section 7623 and §§301.7623-1 through 301.7623-4.

(2) *Ineligible whistleblowers.*—The Whistleblower Office will reject any claim for award filed by an ineligible whistleblower and will provide written notice of the rejection to the whistleblower. The following individuals are not eligible to file a claim for award or receive an award under section 7623 and §§301.7623-1 through 301.7623-4—

(i) An individual who is an employee of the Department of Treasury or was an employee of the Department of Treasury when the individual obtained the information on which the claim is based;

(ii) An individual who obtained the information through the individual's official duties as an employee of the Federal Govern-

ment, or who is acting within the scope of those official duties as an employee of the Federal Government;

(iii) An individual who is or was required by Federal law or regulation to disclose the information or who is or was precluded by Federal law or regulation from disclosing the information;

(iv) An individual who obtained or had access to the information based on a contract with the Federal Government; or

(v) An individual who filed a claim for award based on information obtained from an ineligible whistleblower for the purpose of avoiding the rejection of the claim that would have resulted if the claim was filed by the ineligible whistleblower.

(c) *Submission of information and claims for award.*—(1) *Submitting information.*—To be eligible to receive an award under section 7623 and §§301.7623-1 through 301.7623-4, a whistleblower must submit to the IRS specific and credible information that the whistleblower believes will lead to collected proceeds from one or more persons whom the whistleblower believes have failed to comply with the internal revenue laws. In general, a whistleblower's submission should identify the person(s) believed to have failed to comply with the internal revenue laws and should provide substantive information, including all available documentation, that supports the whistleblower's allegations. Information that identifies a pass-through entity will be considered to also identify all persons with a direct or indirect interest in the entity. Information that identifies a member of a firm who promoted another identified person's participation in a transaction described and documented in the information provided will be considered to also identify the firm and all other members of the firm. Submissions that provide speculative information or that do not provide specific and credible information regarding tax underpayments or violations of internal revenue laws do not provide a basis for an award. If documents or supporting evidence are known to the whistleblower but are not in the whistleblower's control, then the whistleblower should describe the documents or supporting evidence and identify their location to the best of the whistleblower's ability. If all available information known to the whistleblower is not provided to the IRS by the whistleblower, then the whistleblower bears the risk that this information might not be considered by the Whistleblower Office for purposes of an award.

(2) *Filing claim for award.*—To claim an award under section 7623 and §§301.7623-1 through 301.7623-4 for information provided to the IRS, a whistleblower must file a formal claim for award by completing and sending Form 211, "Application for Award for Original Information," to the Internal Revenue Service, Whistleblower Office, at the address provided on the form, or by complying with other claim filing procedures as may be prescribed by the IRS in other published guidance. The Form 211 should be completed in its entirety and should include the following information—

(i) The date of the claim;

(ii) The whistleblower's name;

(iii) The whistleblower's address and telephone number;

(iv) The whistleblower's date of birth;

(v) The whistleblower's taxpayer identification number; and

(vi) An explanation of how the information on which the claim is based came to the attention and into the possession of the whistleblower, including, as available, the date(s) on which the whistleblower acquired the information and a complete description of the whistleblower's present or former relationship (if any) to person(s) identified on the Form 211.

(3) *Under penalty of perjury.*—No award may be made under section 7623(b) unless the information on which the award is based is submitted to the IRS under penalty of perjury. All claims for award under section 7623 and §§ 301.7623-1 through 301.7623-4 must be accompanied by an original signed declaration under penalty of perjury, as follows: "I declare under penalty of perjury that I have examined this application, my accompanying statement, and supporting documentation and aver that such application is true, correct, and complete, to the best of my knowledge." This requirement precludes the filing of a claim for award by a person serving as a representative of, or in any way on behalf of, another individual. Claims filed by more than one whistleblower (joint claims) must be signed by each individual whistleblower under penalty of perjury.

(4) *Perfecting claim for award.*—If a whistleblower files a claim for award that does not include information described under paragraph (c)(2) of this section, does not contain specific and credible information as described in paragraph (c)(1) of this section, or is based on information that was not submitted under penalty of perjury as required by paragraph (c)(3) of this section, the Whistleblower Office may reject the claim or notify the whistleblower of the deficiencies and provide the whistleblower an opportunity to perfect the claim for award. If a whistleblower does not perfect the claim for award within the time period specified by the Whistleblower Office, then the Whistleblower Office may reject the claim. If the Whistleblower Office rejects a claim, then the Whistleblower Office will provide notice of the rejection to the whistleblower pursuant to the rules of § 301.7623-3(b)(3) or (c)(7). If the Whistleblower Office rejects a claim for the reasons described in this paragraph, then the whistleblower may perfect and resubmit the claim.

(d) *Request for assistance.*—(1) *In general.*—The Whistleblower Office, the IRS, or IRS Office of Chief Counsel may request the assistance of a whistleblower or the whistleblower's legal representative. Any assistance shall be at the direction and control of the Whistleblower Office, the IRS, or the IRS Office of Chief Counsel assigned to the matter. See § 301.6103(n)-2 for rules regarding written contracts among the IRS, whistleblowers, and legal representatives of whistleblowers.

(2) *No agency relationship.*—Submitting information, filing a claim for award, or responding to a request for assistance does not create an agency relationship between a whistleblower and the Federal Government, nor does a whistleblower or the whistleblower's legal representative act in any way on behalf of the Federal Government.

(e) *Confidentiality of whistleblowers.*—Under the informant's privilege, the IRS will use its best efforts to protect the identity of whistleblowers. In some circumstances, the IRS may need to reveal a whistleblower's identity, for example, when it is determined that it is in the best interests of the Government to use a whistleblower as a witness in a judicial proceeding. In those circumstances, the IRS will make every effort to notify the whistleblower before revealing the whistleblower's identity.

(f) *Effective/applicability date.*—This rule is effective on August 12, 2014. This rule applies to information submitted on or after August 12, 2014, and to claims for award under sections 7623(a) and 7623(b) that are open as of August 12, 2014. [Reg. § 301.7623-1.]

☐ [*T.D. 6421*, 10-23-59. *Amended by T.D. 6498*, 10-24-60; *T.D. 7188*, 6-28-72; *T.D. 7297*, 12-18-73; *T.D. 8737*, 10-10-97; *T.D. 8780*, 8-20-98; *T.D. 9580*, 2-21-2012 *and T.D. 9687*, 8-7-2014.]

### [Reg. § 301.7623-2]

**§ 301.7623-2. Definitions.**—(a) *Action.*—(1) *In general.*—For purposes of section 7623(b) and §§ 301.7623-1 through 301.7623-4, the term *action* means an administrative or judicial action.

(2) *Administrative action.*—For purposes of section 7623(b) and §§ 301.7623-1 through 301.7623-4, the term *administrative action* means all or a portion of an Internal Revenue Service (IRS) civil or criminal proceeding against any person that may result in collected proceeds, as defined in paragraph (d) of this section, including, for example, an examination, a collection proceeding, a status determination proceeding, or a criminal investigation.

(3) *Judicial action.*—For purposes of section 7623(b) and §§ 301.7623-1 through 301.7623-4, the term *judicial action* means all or a portion of a proceeding against any person in any court that may result in collected proceeds, as defined in paragraph (d) of this section.

(b) *Proceeds based on.*—(1) *In general.*—For purposes of section 7623(b) and §§ 301.7623-1 through 301.7623-4, the IRS *proceeds based on* information provided by a whistleblower when the information provided substantially contributes to an action against a person identified by the whistleblower. For example, the IRS proceeds based on the information provided when the IRS initiates a new action, expands the scope of an ongoing action, or continues to pursue an ongoing action, that the IRS would not have initiated, expanded the scope of, or continued to pursue, but for the information provided. The IRS does not proceed based on information when the IRS analyzes the information provided or investigates a matter raised by the information provided.

(2) *Examples.*—The provisions of paragraph (b)(1) of this section may be illustrated by the following examples:

*Example 1.* Information provided to the IRS by a whistleblower, under section 7623 and § 301.7623-1, identifies a taxpayer, describes and documents specific facts relating to the taxpayer's foreign sales in Country A, and, based on those facts, alleges that the taxpayer was not entitled to a foreign tax credit relating to its foreign sales in Country A. The IRS receives the information after having already initiated an examination of the taxpayer. The IRS's audit plan includes foreign tax credit issues but focuses on taxpayer's foreign sales in Country B and does not specifically address the taxpayer's foreign sales in Country A. Based on the information provided, the IRS expands the examination of the foreign tax credit issue to include consideration of the amount of foreign tax credit relating to the taxpayer's foreign sales in Country A. For purposes of section 7623 and §§ 301.7623-1 through 301.7623-4, the portion of the IRS's examination of the taxpayer relating to the foreign tax credit issue with respect to Country A is an administrative action with which the IRS proceeds based on the information provided by the whistleblower because the information provided substantially contributed to the action by causing the expansion of the IRS's examination.

*Example 2.* Information provided to the IRS by a whistleblower, under section 7623 and § 301.7623-1, identifies a taxpayer, describes and documents specific facts relating to the taxpayer's activities, and, based on those facts, alleges that the taxpayer owed additional taxes in Year 1. The IRS proceeds with an examination of the taxpayer for Year 1 based on the information provided by the whistleblower. The IRS discovers that the taxpayer engaged in the same activities in Year 2 and expands the examination to Year 2. In the course of the examination, the IRS obtains, through the issuance of Information Document Requests (IDRs) and summonses, additional facts that are unrelated to the activities described in the information provided by the whistleblower. Based on these additional facts, the IRS expands the scope of the examination of the taxpayer for both Year 1 and Year 2. For purposes of section 7623 and §§ 301.7623-1 through 301.7623-4, the portion of the IRS's examination relating to the activities described and documented in the information provided is an administrative action with which the IRS proceeds based on information provided by the whistleblower because the information provided substantially contributed to the action by causing the expansion of the IRS's examination of Year 1 and Year 2. The portions of the IRS's examination of the taxpayer in both Year 1 and Year 2 relating to the additional facts obtained through the issuance of IDRs and summonses are not actions with which the IRS proceeds based on the information provided by the whistleblower because the information provided did not substantially contribute to the action.

*Example 3.* Information provided to the IRS by a whistleblower, under section 7623 and § 301.7623-1, identifies a taxpayer, describes and documents specific facts relating to the taxpayer's activities, and, based on those facts, alleges that the taxpayer owed additional taxes in Year 1. The IRS receives the information after having already initiated an examination of the taxpayer for Year 1. During the examination, the information is provided to the Exam team and the Exam team uses the information provided to confirm the correctness of adjustments made based on other information. Although the whistleblower's information confirms the correctness of the IRS's adjustments, the IRS does not rely on the whistleblower's information when it makes the adjustments, nor does the information cause the IRS to expand the scope of its examination. The whistleblower's information merely supports information independently obtained by the IRS. For purposes of section 7623 and §§ 301.7623-1 through 301.7623-4, the IRS's examination is not an administrative action with which the IRS proceeds based on information provided by the whistleblower because the information provided did not substantially contribute to the action.

*Example 4.* Same facts as *Example 3.* During the examination, however, the Exam team identifies inconsistencies between the information provided by the whistleblower and other information already in the Exam team's possession. The Exam team uses the information provided by the whistleblower to make additional adjustments that it would not have made based solely on the other information. For purposes of section 7623 and §§ 301.7623-1 through 301.7623-4, the portion of the IRS's examination relating to the additional adjustments is an administrative action with which the IRS proceeds based on information provided by the whistleblower because the information provided substantially contributed to the action.

(c) *Related action.*—(1) *In general.*—For purposes of section 7623(b) and §§301.7623-1 through 301.7623-4, the term *related action* means an action against a person other than the person(s) identified in the information provided and subject to the original action(s), when—

(i) The facts relating to the underpayment of tax or violations of the internal revenue laws by the other person are substantially the same as the facts described and documented in the information provided (with respect to the person(s) subject to the original action);

(ii) The IRS proceeds with the action against the other person based on the specific facts described and documented in the information provided; and

(iii) The other, unidentified person is related to the person identified in the information provided. For purposes of this paragraph, an unidentified person is related to the person identified in the information provided if the IRS can identify the unidentified person using the information provided (without first having to use the information provided to identify any other person or having to independently obtain additional information).

(2) *Examples.*—The provisions of paragraph (c)(1) of this section may be illustrated by the following examples:

*Example 1.* Information provided to the IRS by a whistleblower, under section 7623 and §301.7623-1, identifies a taxpayer (Taxpayer 1), describes and documents specific facts relating to Taxpayer 1's activities, and, based on those facts, alleges tax underpayments by Taxpayer 1. The information provided also identifies an accountant (CPA 1) and describes and documents specific facts relating to CPA 1's contribution to the activities of Taxpayer 1 that the whistleblower alleges resulted in tax underpayments. The IRS proceeds with an examination of Taxpayer 1 based on the information provided by the whistleblower. Using the information provided, the IRS obtains CPA 1's client list and identifies two taxpayer/clients of CPA 1 (Taxpayer 2 and Taxpayer 3) that appear to have engaged in activities similar to Taxpayer 1. The IRS proceeds with an examination of Taxpayer 2 and finds that Taxpayer 2 engaged in the same activities as those described in the information provided with respect to Taxpayer 1. The IRS proceeds with an examination of Taxpayer 3 and finds that Taxpayer 3 engaged in different activities from those described in the information provided with respect to Taxpayer 1. For purposes of section 7623 and §§301.7623-1 through 301.7623-4, the examination of Taxpayer 2 is a related action because it satisfies the conditions of paragraph (c)(1) of this section. The examination of Taxpayer 3 is not a related action because the relevant facts are not substantially the same as the facts relevant to the examination of Taxpayer 1.

*Example 2.* Same facts as *Example 1.* Using the information provided by the whistleblower, the IRS identifies a co-promoter of CPA 1 (CPA 2) that appears to have engaged in activities similar to CPA 1. CPA 2 is not a member of CPA 1's firm. The IRS subsequently obtains the client list of CPA 2 and identifies a taxpayer/client of CPA 2 (Taxpayer 4) that appears to have engaged in activities similar to Taxpayer 1. The IRS proceeds with an examination of Taxpayer 4 and finds that Taxpayer 4 engaged in the same activities as those described in the information provided with respect to Taxpayer 1, and that CPA 2 contributed to the activities in the same way as described in the information provided with respect to CPA 1. The IRS proceeds with an examination of CPA 2's liability for promoter penalties under section 6700 in connection with the activities described in the information provided with respect to Taxpayer 1 and CPA 1. For purposes of section 7623 and §§301.7623-1 through 301.7623-4, the examination of CPA 2 is a related action because it satisfies the conditions of paragraph (c)(1) of this section. The examination of Taxpayer 4 is not a related action because Taxpayer 4 was not related to a person identified in the information provided. CPA 2 was not identified in the information provided and the IRS first had to identify CPA 2 before identifying Taxpayer 4 and proceeding with the examination of Taxpayer 4.

*Example 3.* Same facts as *Example 1.* An accountant (CPA 3) is a member of CPA 1's firm. Using the information provided by the whistleblower, the IRS obtains the client list of CPA 3 and identifies a taxpayer/client of CPA 3 (Taxpayer 5) that appears to have engaged in activities similar to Taxpayer 1. The IRS proceeds with an examination of Taxpayer 5 and finds that Taxpayer 5 engaged in the same activities as those described in the information provided with respect to Taxpayer 1, and that CPA 3 contributed to the activities in the same way as described in the information provided with respect to CPA 1. For purposes of section 7623 and §§301.7623-1 through 301.7623-4, the examination of Taxpayer 5 is a related action because Taxpayer 5 is related to CPA 3, a person considered to be identified in the information provided under §301.7623-1(c)(1), and the facts relating to Taxpayer 5 are substantially the same as the facts described

and documented in the information provided. An IRS examination of CPA 3's liability for promoter penalties under section 6700, based on the facts described and documented in the information provided with respect to Taxpayer 1 and CPA 1, is an administrative action based on the information provided.

*Example 4.* Information provided to the IRS by a whistleblower, under section 7623 and §301.7623-1, identifies a taxpayer (Taxpayer 1), describes and documents specific facts relating to Taxpayer 1's activities, and, in particular, Taxpayer 1's participation in a transaction. Based on those facts, the whistleblower alleges that Taxpayer 1 owed additional taxes. The IRS proceeds with an examination of Taxpayer 1 based on the information provided by the whistleblower. The IRS identifies the other parties to the transaction described in the information provided (Taxpayer 2 and Taxpayer 3). The IRS proceeds with examinations of Taxpayer 2 and Taxpayer 3 relating to their participation in the transaction described in the information provided. For purposes of section 7623 and §§301.7623-1 through 301.7623-4, the IRS's examinations of Taxpayer 2 and Taxpayer 3 relating to the activities described and documented in the information provided are related actions because they satisfy the conditions of paragraph (c)(1) of this section.

(d) *Collected proceeds.*—(1) *In general.*—For purposes of section 7623 and §§301.7623-1 through 301.7623-4, the terms *proceeds of amounts collected* and *collected proceeds* (collectively, *collected proceeds*) include: tax, penalties, interest, additions to tax, and additional amounts collected because of the information provided; amounts collected prior to receipt of the information if the information provided results in the denial of a claim for refund that otherwise would have been paid; and a reduction of an overpayment credit balance used to satisfy a tax liability incurred because of the information provided. Collected proceeds are limited to amounts collected under the provisions of title 26, United States Code.

(2) *Refund netting.*—(i) *In general.*—If any portion of a claim for refund that is substantively unrelated to the information provided is—

(A) Allowed, and

(B) Used to satisfy a tax liability attributable to the information provided instead of refunded to the taxpayer, then the allowed but non-refunded amount constitutes collected proceeds.

(ii) *Example.*—The provisions of paragraph (d)(2)(i) of this section may be illustrated by the following example:

*Example.* Information provided to the IRS by a whistleblower, under section 7623 and §301.7623-1, identifies a corporate taxpayer (Corporation), describes and documents specific facts relating to Corporation's activities, and, based on those facts, alleges that Corporation owed additional taxes. Based on the information provided by the whistleblower, the IRS proceeds with an examination of Corporation and determines adjustments that would result in an unpaid tax liability of $500,000. During the examination, Corporation informally claims a refund of $400,000 based on adjustments to items of income and expense that are wholly unrelated to the information provided by the whistleblower. The IRS agrees to the unrelated adjustments. The IRS nets the adjustments and determines a tax deficiency of $100,000. Thereafter, Corporation makes full payment of the $100,000 deficiency. For purposes of section 7623 and §§301.7623-1 through 301.7623-4, the collected proceeds include the $400,000 informally claimed as a refund and netted against the adjustments attributable to the information provided, as well as the $100,000 paid by Corporation.

(3) *Amended returns.*—Amounts collected based on amended returns constitute collected proceeds if—

(i) The IRS proceeds based on the information provided;

(ii) As a result, the person subject to the action(s) with which the IRS proceeds files amended returns; and

(iii) The amounts collected based on the amended returns relate to the activities or facts described in the information provided.

(4) *Criminal fines.*—Criminal fines deposited into the Crime Victims Fund are not collected proceeds and cannot be used for payment of awards.

(5) *Computation of collected proceeds.*—(i) *In general.*—Pursuant to §301.7623-4(d)(1), the IRS cannot make an award payment until there has been a final determination of tax. For purposes of determining the amount of an award under section 7623 and §§301.7623-1 through 301.7623-4, after there has been a final determination of tax as defined in §301.7623-4(d)(2), the IRS will compute the amount of collected proceeds based on all information known with respect to the taxpayer's account, including with respect to all tax attributes, as of the date the computation is made.

(ii) *Post-determination proceeds.*—If, based on all information known with respect to the taxpayer's account as of the date of the computation described in paragraph (d)(5)(i) of this section, there is a possibility that the IRS may collect additional proceeds, then the Whistleblower Office will continue to monitor the case. If the Whistleblower Office identifies additional collected proceeds, then the IRS will compute and pay accordingly.

(iii) *Partial collection.*—If the IRS does not collect the full amount of taxes, penalties, interest, additions to tax, and additional amounts assessed against the taxpayer, then any amounts that the IRS does collect will constitute collected proceeds in the same proportion that the adjustments attributable to the information provided bear to the total adjustments.

(e) *Amount in dispute and gross income.*—(1) *In general.*—Section 7623(b) applies with respect to any action against any taxpayer in which the tax, penalties, interest, additions to tax, and additional amounts in dispute exceed $2,000,000 but, if the taxpayer is an individual, then only if the taxpayer's gross income exceeds $200,000 in at least one taxable year subject to the action.

(2) *Amount in dispute.*—(i) *In general.*—For purposes of section 7623(b)(5) and §§ 301.7623-1 through 301.7623-4, the term *amount in dispute* means the greater of the maximum total of tax, penalties, interest, additions to tax, and additional amounts that resulted from the action(s) with which the IRS proceeded based on the information provided, or the maximum total of such amounts that were stated in formal positions taken by the IRS in the action(s). The IRS will compute the amount in dispute, for purposes of award determinations described in § 301.7623-3(c)(6), when there has been a final determination of tax as defined in § 301.7623-4(d)(2).

(ii) *Examples.*—The provisions of paragraph (e)(2)(i) of this section may be illustrated by the following examples:

*Example 1.* Information provided to the IRS by a whistleblower, under section 7623 and § 301.7623-1, identifies a corporate taxpayer, describes and documents specific facts relating to the taxpayer's activities, and, based on those facts, alleges that the taxpayer owed additional taxes. The IRS proceeds with an examination of the taxpayer based on the information provided by the whistleblower; makes adjustments to items of income and expense and allows certain credits; and, ultimately, determines a deficiency against the taxpayer of $1,900,000 and issues the taxpayer a statutory notice of deficiency. The taxpayer petitions the notice to the United States Tax Court. The Tax Court sustains the IRS's position resulting in a deficiency of $1,900,000. Following the final determination of tax, the IRS computes that the total of tax, penalties, interest, additions to tax, and additional amounts that resulted from the action was $2,500,000. For purposes of section 7623 and §§ 301.7623-1 through 301.7623-4, the amount in dispute is $2,500,000.

*Example 2.* Same facts as *Example 1*, except the IRS determines a deficiency of $1,500,000; the Tax Court sustains the deficiency of $1,500,000; and, following the final determination of tax, the IRS computes that the total of tax, penalties, interest, additions to tax, and additional amounts that resulted from the action was $1,750,000. For purposes of section 7623 and §§ 301.7623-1 through 301.7623-4, the amount in dispute is $1,750,000.

*Example 3.* Same facts as *Example 1*, except the IRS determines a deficiency of $2,100,000; the Tax Court redetermines a deficiency of $1,500,000; and, following the final determination of tax, the IRS computes that the total of tax, penalties, interest, additions to tax, and additional amounts that resulted from the action was $1,750,000. For purposes of section 7623 and §§ 301.7623-1 through 301.7623-4, the amount in dispute is $2,100,000.

(3) *Gross income.*—For purposes of section 7623(b)(5) and §§ 301.7623-1 through 301.7623-4, the term *gross income* has the same meaning as provided under section 61(a). The IRS will compute the individual taxpayer's gross income, for purposes of award determinations described in § 301.7623-3(c)(6), when there has been a final determination of tax as defined in § 301.7623-4(d)(2).

(f) *Effective/applicability date.*—This rule is effective on August 12, 2014. This rule applies to information submitted on or after August 12, 2014, and to claims for award under sections 7623(a) and 7623(b) that are open as of August 12, 2014. [Reg. § 301.7623-2.]

☐ [T.D. 9687, 8-7-2014 (*corrected* 9-25-2014).]

### [Reg. § 301.7623-3]

**§ 301.7623-3. Whistleblower administrative proceedings and appeals of award determinations.**—(a) *In general.*—The Whistleblower Office will pay awards under section 7623(a) and determine and pay awards under section 7623(b) in whistleblower administrative proceedings pursuant to the rules of this section. The whistleblower administrative proceedings described in this section are administrative proceedings pertaining to tax administration for purposes of section 6103(h)(4). See § 301.6103(h)(4)-1 for additional rules regard-

ing disclosures of return information in whistleblower administrative proceedings. The Whistleblower Office may determine awards for claims involving multiple actions in a single whistleblower administrative proceeding. For purposes of the whistleblower administrative proceedings for rejections and denials, described in paragraphs (b)(3), (c)(7), and (c)(8) of this section, the Internal Revenue Service (IRS) may rely on the whistleblower's description of the amount owed by the taxpayer(s). The IRS may, however, rely on other information as necessary (for example, when the alleged amount in dispute is below the $2 million threshold of section 7623(b)(5)(B), but the actual amount in dispute is above the threshold).

(b) *Awards under section 7623(a).*—(1) *Preliminary award recommendation.*—In cases in which the Whistleblower Office recommends payment of an award under section 7623(a), the Whistleblower Office will communicate a preliminary award recommendation under section 7623(a) and §§ 301.7623-1 through 301.7623-4 to the whistleblower by sending a preliminary award recommendation letter that states the Whistleblower Office's preliminary computation of the amount of collected proceeds, recommended award percentage, recommended award amount (even in cases when the application of § 301.7623-4 results in a reduction of the recommended award amount to zero), and a list of the factors that contributed to the recommended award percentage. The whistleblower administrative proceeding described in paragraphs (b)(1) and (2) of this section begins on the date the Whistleblower Office sends the preliminary award recommendation letter. If the whistleblower believes that the Whistleblower Office erred in evaluating the information provided, the whistleblower has 30 days from the date the Whistleblower Office sends the preliminary award recommendation to submit comments to the Whistleblower Office (this period may be extended at the sole discretion of the Whistleblower Office). The Whistleblower Office will review all comments submitted timely by the whistleblower (or the whistleblower's legal representative, if any) and pay an award, pursuant to paragraph (b)(2) of this section.

(2) *Decision letter.*—At the conclusion of the process described in paragraph (b)(1) of this section, and when there is a final determination of tax, as defined in § 301.7623-4(d)(2), the Whistleblower Office will pay an award under section 7623(a) and §§ 301.7623-1 through 301.7623-4. The Whistleblower Office will communicate the amount of the award to the whistleblower in a decision letter.

(3) *Rejections and denials.*—If the Whistleblower Office rejects a claim for award under section 7623(a), pursuant to § 301.7623-1(b) or (c), or if the IRS either did not proceed based on information provided by the whistleblower, as defined in § 301.7623-2(b), or did not collect proceeds, as defined in § 301.7623-2(d), then the Whistleblower Office will not apply the rules of paragraphs (b)(1) or (2) of this section. The Whistleblower Office will provide written notice to the whistleblower of the rejection or denial of any award and, in the case of a rejection, the written notice will state the basis for the rejection.

(c) *Awards under section 7623(b).*—(1) *Preliminary award recommendation.*—For claims under section 7623(b) other than those described in paragraphs (c)(7) and (c)(8) of this section (rejections and denials), the Whistleblower Office will prepare a preliminary award recommendation based on the Whistleblower Office's review of the administrative claim file and the application of the rules of section 7623 and §§ 301.7623-1 through 301.7623-4 to the facts of the case. See paragraph (e)(2) of this section for a description of the administrative claim file. The whistleblower administrative proceeding described in paragraphs (c)(1) through (6) of this section begins on the date the Whistleblower Office sends the preliminary award recommendation letter. The preliminary award recommendation is not a determination letter within the meaning of paragraph (c)(6) of this section and cannot be appealed to Tax Court under section 7623(b)(4) and paragraph (d) of this section. The preliminary award recommendation will notify the whistleblower that the IRS cannot determine or pay any award until there is a final determination of tax, as defined in § 301.7623-4(d)(2).

(2) *Contents of preliminary award recommendation.*—The Whistleblower Office will communicate the preliminary award recommendation under section 7623(b) to the whistleblower by sending—

(i) A preliminary award recommendation letter that describes the whistleblower's options for responding to the preliminary award recommendation;

(ii) A summary report that states a preliminary computation of the amount of collected proceeds, the recommended award percentage, the recommended award amount (even in cases when the application of section 7623(b)(2) or section 7623(b)(3) results in a reduction of the recommended award amount to zero), and a list of the factors that contributed to the recommended award percentage;

(iii) An award consent form; and

(iv) A confidentiality agreement.

(3) *Opportunity to respond to preliminary award recommendation.*—The whistleblower will have 30 days (this period may be extended at the sole discretion of the Whistleblower Office) from the date the Whistleblower Office sends the preliminary award recommendation letter to respond to the preliminary award recommendation in one of the following ways—

(i) If the whistleblower takes no action, then the Whistleblower Office will make an award determination, pursuant to paragraph (c)(6) of this section;

(ii) If the whistleblower signs, dates, and returns the award consent form agreeing to the preliminary award recommendation and waiving any and all administrative and judicial appeal rights, then the Whistleblower Office will make an award determination, pursuant to paragraph (c)(6) of this section;

(iii) If the whistleblower signs, dates, and returns the confidentiality agreement, then the Whistleblower Office will provide the whistleblower with a detailed award report, and an opportunity to review documents supporting the report pursuant to paragraphs (c)(4) and (5) of this section, and any comments submitted by the whistleblower will be added to the administrative claim file; or

(iv) If the whistleblower submits comments on the preliminary award recommendation to the Whistleblower Office, but does not sign, date, and return the confidentiality agreement, then the comments will be added to the administrative claim file and reviewed by the Whistleblower Office in making an award determination, pursuant to paragraph (c)(6) of this section.

(4) *Detailed report.*—(i) *Contents of detailed report.*—If the whistleblower signs, dates, and returns the confidentiality agreement accompanying the preliminary award recommendation under section 7623(b), pursuant to paragraph (c)(3) of this section, then the Whistleblower Office will send the whistleblower—

(A) A detailed report that states a preliminary computation of the amount of collected proceeds, the recommended award percentage, and the recommended award amount, and provides a full explanation of the factors that contributed to the recommended award percentage;

(B) Instructions for scheduling an appointment for the whistleblower (and the whistleblower's legal representative, if any) to review information in the administrative claim file that is not protected by one or more common law or statutory privileges; and

(C) An award consent form.

(ii) *Opportunity to respond to detailed report.*—The whistleblower will have 30 days (this period may be extended at the sole discretion of the Whistleblower Office) from the date the Whistleblower Office sends the detailed report to respond in one of the following ways—

(A) If the whistleblower takes no action, then the Whistleblower Office will make an award determination, pursuant to paragraph (c)(6) of this section;

(B) If the whistleblower requests an appointment to review information from the administrative claim file that is not protected from disclosure by one or more common law or statutory privileges, then a meeting will be arranged pursuant to paragraph (c)(5) of this section;

(C) If the whistleblower does not request an appointment but does submit comments on the detailed report to the Whistleblower Office, then the comments will be added to the administrative claim file and reviewed by the Whistleblower Office in making an award determination pursuant to paragraph (c)(6) of this section; or

(D) If the whistleblower signs, dates, and returns the award consent form agreeing to the preliminary award recommendation and waiving any and all administrative and judicial appeal rights, then the Whistleblower Office will make an award determination, pursuant to paragraph (c)(6) of this section.

(iii) *Additional rules.*—The detailed report is not a determination letter within the meaning of paragraph (c)(6) of this section and cannot be appealed to Tax Court under section 7623(b)(4) and paragraph (d) of this section. The detailed report will notify the whistleblower that the IRS cannot determine or pay any award until there is a final determination of tax, as defined in § 301.7623-4(d)(2).

(5) *Opportunity to review documents supporting award report recommendations.*—Appointments for the whistleblower (and the whistleblower's legal representative, if any) to review information from the administrative claim file that is not protected from disclosure by one or more common law or statutory privileges will be held at the Whistleblower Office in Washington, D.C., unless the Whistleblower Office, in its sole discretion, decides to hold the meeting at another location. At the appointment, the Whistleblower Office will provide for viewing the information from the administrative claim file. The Whistleblower Office will supervise the whistleblower's review of the information and the whistleblower will not be permitted to make copies of any documents or other information. The whistleblower will have 30 days (this period may be extended at the sole discretion of the Whistleblower Office) from the date of the appointment to submit comments on the detailed report and the documents reviewed at the appointment to the Whistleblower Office. All comments will be added to the administrative claim file and reviewed by the Whistleblower Office in making an award determination, pursuant to paragraph (c)(6) of this section.

(6) *Determination letter.*—After the whistleblower's participation in the whistleblower administrative proceeding, pursuant to paragraph (c) of this section, has concluded, and there is a final determination of tax, as defined in § 301.7623-4(d)(2), a Whistleblower Office official will determine the amount of the award under section 7623(b)(1), (2), or (3), and § § 301.7623-1 through 301.7623-4, based on the official's review of the administrative claim file. The Whistleblower Office will communicate the award to the whistleblower in a determination letter, stating the amount of the award. If, however, the whistleblower has executed an award consent form agreeing to the amount of the award and waiving the whistleblower's right to appeal the award determination, pursuant to section 7623(b)(4) and paragraph (d) of this section, then the Whistleblower Office will not send the whistleblower a determination letter and will make payment of the award as promptly as circumstances permit.

(7) *Rejections.*—A rejection is a determination that relates solely to the whistleblower and the information on the face of the claim that pertains to the whistleblower. If the Whistleblower Office rejects a claim for award under section 7623(b), pursuant to § 301.7623-1(b) or (c), then the Whistleblower Office will not apply the rules of paragraphs (c)(1) through (6) of this section. The Whistleblower Office will send to the whistleblower a preliminary rejection letter that states the basis for the rejection of the claim. The whistleblower administrative proceeding described in this paragraph begins on the date the Whistleblower Office sends the preliminary rejection letter. If the whistleblower believes that the Whistleblower Office erred in evaluating the information provided, the whistleblower has 30 days from the date the Whistleblower Office sends the preliminary rejection letter to submit comments to the Whistleblower Office (this period may be extended at the sole discretion of the Whistleblower Office). The Whistleblower Office will review all comments submitted timely by the whistleblower (or the whistleblower's legal representative, if any) and, following that review, the Whistleblower Office will either provide written notice to the whistleblower of the rejection of the claim, including the basis for the rejection, or apply the rules of paragraphs (c)(1) through (c)(6) of this section.

(8) *Denials.*—A denial is a determination that relates to or implicates taxpayer information. If, with respect to a claim for award under section 7623(b), the IRS either did not proceed based on the information provided by the whistleblower, as defined in § 301.7623-2(b), or did not collect proceeds, as defined in § 301.7623-2(d), then the Whistleblower Office will not apply the rules of paragraphs (c)(1) through (6) of this section. The Whistleblower Office will send to the whistleblower a preliminary denial letter that states the basis for the denial of the claim. The whistleblower administrative proceeding described in this paragraph begins on the date the Whistleblower Office sends the preliminary denial letter. If the whistleblower believes that the Whistleblower Office erred in evaluating the information provided, the whistleblower has 30 days from the date the Whistleblower Office sends the preliminary denial letter to submit comments to the Whistleblower Office (this period may be extended at the sole discretion of the Whistleblower Office). The Whistleblower Office will review all comments submitted timely by the whistleblower (or the whistleblower's legal representative, if any) and, following that review, the Whistleblower Office will either provide written notice to the whistleblower of the denial of any award, including the basis for the denial, or apply the rules of paragraphs (c)(1) through (c)(6) of this section.

(d) *Appeal of award determination.*—Any determination regarding an award under section 7623(b)(1), (2), or (3) may, within 30 days of such determination, be appealed to the Tax Court.

(e) *Administrative record.*—(1) *In general.*—The administrative record comprises all information contained in the administrative claim file that is relevant to the award determination and not protected by one or more common law or statutory privileges.

(2) *Administrative claim file.*—The administrative claim file will include the following materials relating to the action(s) to which the determination relates—

(i) The Form 211, "Application for Award for Original Information," filed by the whistleblower and all information provided by the whistleblower (whether provided with the whistleblower's original submission or through a subsequent contact with the IRS).

(ii) Copies of all debriefing notes and recorded interviews held with the whistleblower (and the whistleblower's legal representative, if any).

(iii) Form(s) 11369, "Confidential Evaluation Report on Claim for Award," including narratives prepared by the relevant IRS office(s), explaining the whistleblower's contributions to the actions and documenting the actions taken by the IRS in the case(s). The Form 11369 will refer to and incorporate additional documents relating to the issues raised by the claim, as appropriate, including, for example, relevant portions of revenue agent reports, copies of agreements entered into with the taxpayer(s), tax returns, and activity records.

(iv) Copies of all contracts entered into among the IRS, the whistleblower, and the whistleblower's legal representative (if any), and an explanation of the cooperation provided by the whistleblower (or the whistleblower's legal representative, if any) under the contract.

(v) Any information that reflects actions by the whistleblower that may have had a negative impact on the IRS's ability to examine the taxpayer(s).

(vi) All correspondence and documents sent by the Whistleblower Office to the whistleblower.

(vii) All notes, memoranda, and other documents made by officers and employees of the Whistleblower Office and considered by the official making the award determination.

(viii) All correspondence and documents received by the Whistleblower Office from the whistleblower (and the whistleblower's legal representative, if any) in the course of the whistleblower administrative proceeding.

(ix) All other information considered by the official making the award determination.

(f) *Effective/applicability date.*—This rule is effective on August 12, 2014. This rule applies to information submitted on or after August 12, 2014, and to claims for award under sections 7623(a) and 7623(b) that are open as of August 12, 2014. [Reg. § 301.7623-3.]

☐ [T.D. 9687, 8-7-2014.]

### [Reg. § 301.7623-4]

**§301.7623-4. Amount and payment of award.**—(a) *In general.*— The Whistleblower Office will pay all awards under section 7623(a) and determine and pay all awards under section 7623(b). For all awards under section 7623 and §§ 301.7623-1 through 301.7623-4, the Whistleblower Office will—

(1) Analyze the claim by applying the rules provided in paragraph (c) of this section to the information contained in the administrative claim file to determine an award percentage; and

(2) Multiply the award percentage by the amount of collected proceeds. If the award determination arises out of a single whistleblower administrative proceeding involving multiple actions, the Whistleblower Office may determine separate award percentages on an action-by-action basis and apply the separate award percentages to the collected proceeds attributable to the corresponding actions. The Internal Revenue Service (IRS) will pay all awards in accordance with the rules provided in paragraph (d) of this section. All relevant factors will be taken into account by the Whistleblower Office in determining whether an award will be paid and, if so, the amount of the award. No person is authorized under this section to make any offer or promise or otherwise bind the Whistleblower Office with respect to the amount or payment of an award.

(b) *Factors used to determine award percentage.*—(1) *Positive factors.*— The application of the following non-exclusive factors may support increasing an award percentage under paragraphs (c)(1) or (2) of this section—

(i) The whistleblower acted promptly to inform the IRS or the taxpayer of the tax noncompliance.

(ii) The information provided identified an issue or transaction of a type previously unknown to the IRS.

(iii) The information provided identified taxpayer behavior that the IRS was unlikely to identify or that was particularly difficult to detect through the IRS's exercise of reasonable diligence.

(iv) The information provided thoroughly presented the factual details of tax noncompliance in a clear and organized manner, particularly if the manner of the presentation saved the IRS work and resources.

(v) The whistleblower (or the whistleblower's legal representative, if any) provided exceptional cooperation and assistance during the pendency of the action(s).

(vi) The information provided identified assets of the taxpayer that could be used to pay liabilities, particularly if the assets were not otherwise known to the IRS.

(vii) The information provided identified connections between transactions, or parties to transactions, that enabled the IRS to understand tax implications that might not otherwise have been understood by the IRS.

(viii) The information provided had an impact on the behavior of the taxpayer, for example by causing the taxpayer to promptly correct a previously-reported improper position.

(2) *Negative factors.*—The application of the following non-exclusive factors may support decreasing an award percentage under paragraphs (c)(1) or (2) of this section—

(i) The whistleblower delayed informing the IRS after learning the relevant facts, particularly if the delay adversely affected the IRS's ability to pursue an action or issue.

(ii) The whistleblower contributed to the underpayment of tax or tax noncompliance identified.

(iii) The whistleblower directly or indirectly profited from the underpayment of tax or tax noncompliance identified, but did not plan and initiate the actions that led to the underpayment of tax or actions described in section 7623(a)(2).

(iv) The whistleblower (or the whistleblower's legal representative, if any) negatively affected the IRS's ability to pursue the action(s), for example by disclosing the existence or scope of an enforcement activity.

(v) The whistleblower (or the whistleblower's legal representative, if any) violated instructions provided by the IRS, particularly if the violation caused the IRS to expend additional resources.

(vi) The whistleblower (or the whistleblower's legal representative, if any) violated the terms of the confidentiality agreement described in § 301.7623-3(c)(2)(iv).

(vii) The whistleblower (or the whistleblower's legal representative, if any) violated the terms of a contract entered into with the IRS pursuant to § 301.6103(n)-2.

(viii) The whistleblower provided false or misleading information or otherwise violated the requirements of section 7623(b)(6)(C) or § 301.7623-1(c)(3).

(c) *Amount of award percentage.*—(1) *Award for substantial contribution.*—(i) *In general.*—If the IRS proceeds with any administrative or judicial action based on information brought to the IRS's attention by a whistleblower, such whistleblower shall, subject to paragraphs (c)(2) and (3) of this section, receive as an award at least 15 percent but not more than 30 percent of the collected proceeds resulting from the action (including any related actions) or from any settlement in response to such action. The amount of any award under this paragraph depends on the extent of the whistleblower's substantial contribution to the action(s). See paragraph (c)(4) of this section for rules regarding multiple whistleblowers.

(ii) *Computational framework.*—Starting the analysis at 15 percent, the Whistleblower Office will analyze the administrative claim file using the factors listed in paragraph (b)(1) of this section to determine whether the whistleblower merits an increased award percentage of 22 percent or 30 percent. The Whistleblower Office may increase the award percentage based on the presence and significance of positive factors. The Whistleblower Office will then analyze the contents of the administrative claim file using the factors listed in paragraph (b)(2) of this section to determine whether the whistleblower merits a decreased award percentage of 15 percent, 18 percent, 22 percent, or 26 percent. The Whistleblower Office may decrease the award percentage based on the presence and significance of negative factors. Although the factors listed in paragraphs (b)(1) and (2) of this section are described as positive and negative factors, the Whistleblower Office's analysis cannot be reduced to a mathematical equation. The factors are not exclusive and are not weighted and, in a particular case, one factor may override several others. The presence and significance of positive factors may offset the presence and significance of negative factors. But the absence of negative factors does not constitute a positive factor.

(iii) *Examples.*—The operation of the provisions of paragraph (c)(1)(ii) of this section may be illustrated by the following examples. The examples are intended to illustrate the operation of the computational framework. The examples provide simplified descriptions of the facts relating to the claims for award, the information provided, and the facts relating to the underlying tax cases. The application of section 7623(b)(1) and paragraph (c)(1)(ii) of this section will depend on the specific facts of each case.

*Example 1.* Facts. Whistleblower A, an employee in Corporation's sales department, submitted to the IRS a claim for award under section 7623 and information indicating that Corporation improperly claimed a credit in tax year 2006. Whistleblower A's information consisted of numerous non-privileged documents relevant to Corporation's eligibility for the credit. Whistleblower A's original submission also included an analysis of the documents, as well as information about meetings in which the claim for credit was discussed. When interviewed by the IRS, Whistleblower A clarified ambiguities in the original submission, answered questions about Corporation's business and accounting practices, and identified potential sources to corroborate the information.

Some of the documents provided by Whistleblower A were not included in Corporation's general record-keeping system and their existence may not have been easily uncovered through normal IRS examination procedures. Corporation initially denied the facts revealed in the information provided by Whistleblower A, which were essential to establishing the impropriety of the claim for credit. IRS examination of Corporation's return confirmed that the credit was improperly claimed by Corporation in tax year 2006, as alleged by Whistleblower A. Corporation agreed to the ensuing assessments of tax and interest and paid the liabilities in full.

*Analysis.* In this case, Whistleblower A provided specific and credible information that formed the basis for action by the IRS. Whistleblower A provided information that was difficult to detect, provided useful assistance to the IRS, and helped the IRS sustain the assessment. Based on the presence and significance of these positive factors, viewed against all the specific facts relevant to Corporation's 2006 tax year, the Whistleblower Office could increase the award percentage to 22 percent of collected proceeds. If, however, Whistleblower A's claim reflected negative factors, for example Whistleblower A violated instructions provided by the IRS and the violation caused the IRS to expend additional resources, then the Whistleblower Office could, based on this negative factor, reduce the award percentage to 18 or 15 percent (but not to lower than 15 percent of collected proceeds).

*Example 2.* Facts. Whistleblower B, an employee of Financial Advisory Firm 1 (Firm 1), submitted to the IRS a claim for award under section 7623 and information indicating that Firm 1 helped clients engage in activities that were intended to, and did, result in substantial tax underpayments. The activities were designed to avoid detection by the IRS, and prior IRS audits of several clients of Firm 1 had failed to detect underpayments of tax. Whistleblower B learned of the activities after being reassigned to a new position with Firm 1. Whistleblower B provided the information to the IRS soon after he understood the scope, nature and impact of the activities. The information provided consisted of numerous documents containing client profiles and marketing strategies, as well as descriptions of the transactions and structures used by Firm 1 and its clients to obscure the clients' identities and to generate the substantial tax underpayments. Whistleblower B also provided an analysis of the documents, as well as information about meetings in which the transactions and structures were discussed. When interviewed by the IRS, Whistleblower B clarified ambiguities in the original submission, answered questions about Firm 1's execution of specific client transactions, and identified potential sources to corroborate the information provided. Whistleblower B also notified the IRS of steps taken by Firm 1 to limit the disclosure of information requested by the IRS, enabling the IRS to obtain full disclosure of the information through the targeted use of summonses.

*Analysis.* Ultimately, the IRS collected tax, penalties, and interest from Firm 1 and multiple clients. In addition, Treasury and the IRS issued a notice identifying the impropriety of the transactions and structures employed by Firm 1 and its clients. Whistleblower B provided specific and credible information that formed the basis for action by the IRS. The information provided identified transactions that were difficult to detect. Whistleblower B acted promptly after he understood the activities at issue and he provided useful assistance to the IRS. Whistleblower B's assistance, and the information he provided, helped the IRS overcome the efforts made to obscure the activities and the clients' identities. And the information provided by Whistleblower B contributed to the decision to issue the notice, which may have a positive effect on client behavior and save IRS resources. Based on the presence and significance of these positive factors, the Whistleblower Office could increase the award percentage to 30 percent of collected proceeds. If Whistleblower B directly or indirectly profited from Firm 1's and the clients' activities resulting in the tax underpayments, then the Whistleblower Office could, based on this negative factor, reduce the award percentage to 26, 22, 18 percent or 15 percent (but not to lower than 15 percent of collected proceeds).

(2) *Award for less substantial contribution.*—(i) *In general.*—If the Whistleblower Office determines that the action described in paragraph (c)(1) of this section is based principally on disclosures of specific allegations resulting from a judicial or administrative hearing; a government report, hearing, audit, or investigation; or the news media, then the Whistleblower Office will determine an award of no more than 10 percent of the collected proceeds resulting from

the action (including any related actions) or from any settlement in response to such action. If the whistleblower is the original source of the information from which the disclosures of specific allegations resulted, however, then the award percentage will be determined under paragraph (c)(1) of this section.

(ii) *Computational framework.*—The Whistleblower Office will analyze the administrative claim file to determine—

(A) Whether the claim involves specific allegations regarding a tax underpayment or a violation of the internal revenue laws that reasonably may be inferred to have resulted from a judicial or administrative hearing; a government report, hearing, audit, or investigation; or the news media;

(B) Whether the action described in paragraph (c)(1) of this section was based principally on the disclosure of the specific allegations; and

(C) Whether the whistleblower was the original source of the information that gave rise to the specific allegations. If the Whistleblower Office determines that the action was based principally on disclosures of specific allegations, as stated in paragraph (c)(2)(ii)(B) of this section, and that the whistleblower was not the original source of the information, then, starting at 1 percent, the Whistleblower Office will analyze the administrative claim file using the factors listed in paragraph (b)(1) of this section to determine whether the whistleblower merits an increased award percentage of 4 percent, 7 percent, or 10 percent. The Whistleblower Office will then determine whether the whistleblower merits a decreased award percentage of zero, 1 percent, 4 percent, or 7 percent using the factors listed in paragraph (b)(2) of this section. The Whistleblower Office may increase the award percentage based on the presence and significance of positive factors and may decrease (to zero) the award percentage based on the presence and significance of negative factors. Like the analysis described in paragraph (c)(1)(ii) of this section, the Whistleblower Office's analysis cannot be reduced to a mathematical equation. The factors are not exclusive and are not weighted and, in a particular case, one factor may override several others. The presence and significance of positive factors may offset the presence and significance of negative factors. But the absence of negative factors does not constitute a positive factor.

(iii) *Example.*—The operation of the provisions of paragraph (c)(2)(ii) of this section may be illustrated by the following example. The example is intended to illustrate the operation of the computational framework. The example provides a simplified description of the facts relating to the claim for award, the information provided, and the facts relating to the underlying tax case(s). The application of section 7623(b)(2) and paragraph (c)(2)(ii) of this section will depend on the specific facts of each case.

*Example.* Facts. Whistleblower A submitted to the IRS a claim for award under section 7623 and information indicating that Taxpayer B was the defendant in a criminal prosecution for embezzlement. Whistleblower A's information further indicated that evidence presented at Taxpayer B's trial revealed Taxpayer B's efforts to conceal the embezzled funds by depositing them in bank accounts of entities controlled by Taxpayer B. Taxpayer B's failure to pay tax on the embezzled funds was not explicitly stated during the judicial hearing, but could be reasonably inferred from the facts and circumstances, including Taxpayer B's efforts to conceal the funds.

*Analysis.* In this case, Whistleblower A's information is based principally on disclosures of specific allegations resulting from a judicial hearing. Absent information demonstrating that the investigation leading to the embezzlement charge was based on information provided by Whistleblower A, section 7623(b)(2) and paragraph (c)(2) of this section apply to the determination of Whistleblower A's award. In this case, there is no reason for the Whistleblower Office to increase the applicable award percentage above 1 percent, the starting point for its analysis, given the absence of positive factors. Accordingly, Whistleblower A may receive an award of 1 percent of collected proceeds.

(3) *Reduction in award and denial of award.*—(i) *In general.*—If the Whistleblower Office determines that a claim for award is brought by a whistleblower who planned and initiated the actions, transaction, or events (underlying acts) that led to the underpayment of tax or actions described in section 7623(a)(2), then the Whistleblower Office may appropriately reduce the amount of the award percentage that would otherwise result under section 7623(b)(1) and paragraph (c)(1) of this section or section 7623(b)(2) and paragraph (c)(2) of this section, as applicable. The Whistleblower Office will deny an award if the whistleblower is convicted of criminal conduct arising from his or her role in planning and initiating the underlying acts.

(ii) *Threshold determination.*—A whistleblower *planned and initiated* the underlying acts if the whistleblower—

(A) Designed, structured, drafted, arranged, formed the plan leading to, or otherwise planned, an underlying act,

(B) Took steps to start, introduce, originate, set into motion, promote or otherwise initiate an underlying act, and

(C) Knew or had reason to know that an underpayment of tax or actions described in section 7623(a)(2) could result from planning and initiating the underlying act.

(D) The whistleblower need not have been the sole person involved in planning and initiating the underlying acts. A whistleblower who merely furnishes typing, reproducing, or other mechanical assistance in implementing one or more underlying acts will not be treated as initiating any underlying act. A whistleblower who is a junior employee acting at the direction, and under the control, of a senior employee will not be treated as initiating any underlying act.

(E) If the Whistleblower Office determines that a whistleblower has satisfied this initial threshold of planning and initiating, the Whistleblower Office will then reduce the award amount based on the extent of the whistleblower's planning and initiating, pursuant to paragraph (c)(3)(iii) of this section.

(iii) *Computational framework.*—After determining the award percentage that would otherwise result from the application of section 7623(b)(1) and paragraph (c)(1) of this section or section 7623(b)(2) and paragraph (c)(2) of this section, as applicable, the Whistleblower Office will analyze the administrative claim file to make the threshold determination described in paragraph (c)(3)(ii) of this section. If the whistleblower is determined to have planned and initiated the underlying acts, then the Whistleblower Office will reduce the award based on the extent of the whistleblower's planning and initiating. The Whistleblower Office's analysis and the amount of the appropriate reduction determined in a particular case cannot be reduced to a mathematical equation. To determine the appropriate award reduction, the Whistleblower Office will—

(A) Categorize the whistleblower's role as a planner and initiator as primary, significant, or moderate; and

(B) Appropriately reduce the award percentage that would otherwise result from the application of section 7623(b)(1) and paragraph (c)(1) of this section or section 7623(b)(2) and paragraph (c)(2) of this section, as applicable, by 67 percent to 100 percent in the case of a primary planner and initiator, by 34 percent to 66 percent in the case of a significant planner and initiator, or by 0 percent to 33 percent in the case of a moderate planner and initiator. If the whistleblower is convicted of criminal conduct arising from his or her role in planning and initiating the underlying acts, then the Whistleblower Office will deny an award without regard to whether the Whistleblower Office categorized the whistleblower's role as a planner and initiator as primary, significant, or moderate.

(iv) *Factors demonstrating the extent of a whistleblower's planning and initiating.*—The application of the following non-exclusive factors may support a determination of the extent of a whistleblower's planning and initiating of the underlying acts—

(A) The whistleblower's role as a planner and initiator. Was the whistleblower the sole decision-maker or one of several contributing planners and initiators? To what extent was the whistleblower acting under the direction and control of a supervisor?

(B) The nature of the whistleblower's planning and initiating activities. Was the whistleblower involved in legitimate tax planning activities? Did the whistleblower take steps to hide the actions at the planning stage? Did the whistleblower commit any identifiable misconduct (legal, ethical, etc.)?

(C) The extent to which the whistleblower knew or should have known that tax noncompliance could result from the course of conduct.

(D) The extent to which the whistleblower acted in furtherance of the noncompliance, including, for example, efforts to conceal or disguise the transaction.

(E) The whistleblower's role in identifying and soliciting others to participate in the actions reported, whether as parties to a common transaction or as parties to separate transactions.

(v) *Examples.*—The operation of the provisions of paragraphs (c)(3)(ii) and (iii) of this section may be illustrated by the following examples. These examples are intended to illustrate the operation of the computational framework. The examples provide simplified descriptions of the facts relating to the claim for award, the information provided, and the facts relating to the underlying tax case. The application of section 7623(b)(3) and paragraph (c)(3) of this section will depend on the specific facts of each case.

*Example* 1. Facts. Whistleblower A is employed as a junior associate in a law firm and is responsible for performing research and drafting activities for, and under the direction and control of, partners of the law firm. Whistleblower A performed research on financial products for Partner B that Partner B used in advising a client (Corporation 1) on a financial strategy. After Corporation 1 executed the strategy, Whistleblower A submitted a claim for award under section 7623 along with information about the strategy to the IRS. The IRS initiated an examination of Corporation 1 based on Whistleblower A's information, determined deficiencies in tax and penalties, and ultimately assessed and collected the tax and penalties as determined.

Analysis. Whistleblower A did nothing to design or set into motion Corporation 1's activities. Whistleblower A did not know or have reason to know that an underpayment of tax or actions described in section 7623(a)(2) could result from the research and drafting activities. Accordingly, as a threshold matter, Whistleblower A was not a planner and initiator of Corporation 1's strategy, and the award that would otherwise be determined based on the application of section 7623(b)(1) and paragraph (c)(1) of this section is not subject to reduction under section 7623(b)(3) and paragraph (c)(3) of this section.

*Example 2.* Facts. Whistleblower C is employed in the human resources department of a corporation (Corporation 2). Corporation 2 tasked Whistleblower C with hiring a large number of temporary employees to meet Corporation 2's seasonal business demands. Whistleblower C organized, scheduled, and conducted job fairs and job interviews to hire the seasonal employees. Whistleblower C was not responsible for, had no knowledge of, and played no part in, classifying the seasonal employees for Federal income tax purposes. Whistleblower C later discovered, however, that Corporation 2 classified the seasonal employees as independent contractors. After discovering the misclassification, Whistleblower C submitted a claim for award under section 7623 along with non-privileged information describing the employee misclassification to the IRS. The IRS initiated an examination of Corporation 2 based on Whistleblower C's information, determined deficiencies in tax and penalties, and ultimately assessed and collected the tax and penalties as determined.

Analysis. The award that would otherwise be determined based on the application of section 7623(b)(1) and paragraph (c)(1) of this section would not be subject to a reduction under section 7623(b)(3) and paragraph (c)(3) of this section because Whistleblower C did not satisfy the requirements of the threshold determination of a planner and initiator. Whistleblower C did not know and had no reason to know that her actions could result in an underpayment of tax or actions described in section 7623(a)(2) or that Corporation 2 would misclassify the employees as independent contractors.

*Example 3.* Facts. Whistleblower D is employed as a supervisor in the finance department of a corporation (Corporation 3) and is responsible for planning Corporation 3's overall financial strategy. Pursuant to the overall financial strategy, Whistleblower D and others at Corporation 3, in good faith but incorrectly, planned tax-advantaged transactions. Whistleblower D and others at Corporation 3 prepared documents needed to execute the transactions. After Corporation 3 executed the transactions, Whistleblower D reached the conclusion that the tax consequences claimed were incorrect and Whistleblower D submitted a claim for award under section 7623 along with non-privileged information about the transactions to the IRS. The IRS initiated an examination of Corporation 3 based on Whistleblower D's information, determined deficiencies in tax and penalties, and ultimately assessed and collected the tax and penalties as determined.

Analysis. The award that would otherwise be determined based on the application of section 7623(b)(1) and paragraph (c)(1) of this section would be subject to an appropriate reduction under section 7623(b)(3) and paragraph (c)(3) of this section because Whistleblower D satisfies the requirements of the threshold determination of a planner and initiator. Whistleblower D planned the transactions, prepared the necessary documents, and knew that an underpayment of tax could result from the transactions. Whistleblower D was not the sole planner and initiator of Corporation 3's transactions. Whistleblower D did nothing to conceal Corporation 3's activities. Corporation 3 had a good faith basis for claiming the disallowed tax benefits. On the basis of those facts, Whistleblower D was a moderate-level planner and initiator. Accordingly, the Whistleblower Office will exercise its discretion to reduce Whistleblower D's award by 0 to 33 percent.

*Example 4.* Facts. Same facts as *Example 3*, except that Whistleblower D independently planned a high-risk tax avoidance transaction and prepared draft documents to execute the transaction. Whistleblower D presented the transaction, along with the draft documents, to Corporation 3's Chief Financial Officer. Without the further involvement of Whistleblower D, Corporation 3's Chief Financial Officer, Chief Executive Officer, and Board of Directors subsequently approved the execution of the transaction. After Corporation 3 executed the transaction, Whistleblower D submitted a claim for award under section 7623 along with non-privileged information about the transaction to the IRS. The IRS initiated an examination of Corporation 3 based on Whistleblower D's information, determined deficiencies in tax and penalties, and ultimately assessed and collected the tax and penalties as determined.

Analysis. The award that would otherwise be determined based on the application of section 7623(b)(1) and paragraph (c)(1) of this section would be subject to an appropriate reduction under section 7623(b)(3) and paragraph (c)(3) of this section because Whistleblower D satisfies the requirements of the threshold determination of a planner and initiator. Whistleblower D planned the transaction, prepared the necessary documents, and knew that an underpayment of tax or actions described in section 7623(a)(2) could result from the transaction. Working independently, Whistleblower D designed and took steps to effectuate the transaction while knowing that the planning and initiating of the transaction was likely to result in tax noncompliance. Whistleblower D, however, did not approve the execution of the transaction by Corporation 3 and, therefore, was not a decision-maker. On the basis of these facts, Whistleblower D was a significant-level planner and initiator. Accordingly, the Whistleblower Office will exercise its discretion to reduce Whistleblower D's award by 34 to 66 percent.

*Example 5.* Facts. Whistleblower E is a financial planner. Whistleblower E designed a financial product that the IRS identified as an abusive tax avoidance transaction. Whistleblower E marketed the transaction to taxpayers, facilitated their participation in the transaction, and, initially, took steps to disguise the transaction. After several taxpayers had participated in the transaction, Whistleblower E submitted a claim for award under section 7623 along with non-privileged information to the IRS about the transaction and the participating taxpayers. The IRS initiated an examination of the identified taxpayers based on Whistleblower E's information, determined deficiencies in tax and penalties, and ultimately assessed and collected the tax and penalties as determined. Whistleblower E was not criminally prosecuted.

Analysis. The award that would otherwise be determined based on the application of section 7623(b)(1) and paragraph (c)(1) of this section would be subject to an appropriate reduction under section 7623(b)(3) and paragraph (c)(3) of this section because Whistleblower E satisfies the requirements of the threshold determination of a planner and initiator. Whistleblower E designed the financial product, marketed and facilitated its use by taxpayers, and knew that an underpayment of tax or actions described in section 7623(a)(2) could result from the transaction. Whistleblower E was the sole designer of the transaction, solicited clients to participate in the transaction, and facilitated and attempted to conceal their participation in the transaction. Whistleblower E knew that the planning and initiating of the taxpayers' participation in the transaction was likely to result in an underpayment of tax or actions described in section 7623(a)(2). On the basis of these facts, Whistleblower E was a primary-level planner and initiator. Accordingly, the Whistleblower Office will exercise its discretion to reduce Whistleblower E's award by 67 to 100 percent.

(4) *Multiple whistleblowers.*—If two or more independent claims relate to the same collected proceeds, then the Whistleblower Office may evaluate the contribution of each whistleblower to the action(s) that resulted in collected proceeds. The Whistleblower Office will determine whether the information submitted by each whistleblower would have been obtained by the IRS as a result of the information previously submitted by any other whistleblower. If the Whistleblower Office determines that multiple whistleblowers submitted information that would not have been obtained based on a prior submission, then the Whistleblower Office will determine the amount of each whistleblower's award based on the extent to which each whistleblower contributed to the action(s). The aggregate award amount in cases involving two or more independent claims that relate to the same collected proceeds will not exceed the maximum award amount that could have resulted under section 7623(b)(1) or section 7623(b)(2), as applicable, subject to the award reduction provisions of section 7623(b)(3), if a single claim had been submitted.

(d) *Payment of Award.*—(1) *In general.*—The IRS will pay any award determined under section 7623 and §§ 301.7623-1 through 301.7623-4 to the whistleblower(s) that filed the corresponding claim for award. Payment of an award will be made as promptly as the circumstances permit, but not until there has been a final determination of tax with respect to the action(s), as defined in paragraph (d)(2) of this section, the Whistleblower Office has determined the award, and all appeals of the Whistleblower Office's determination are final or the whistleblower has executed an award consent form agreeing to the amount of the award and waiving the whistleblower's right to appeal the determination.

(2) *Final determination of tax.*—(i) *In general.*—For purposes of §§ 301.7623-1 through 301.7623-4, a *final determination of tax* means that the proceeds resulting from the action(s) subject to the award determination have been collected and either the statutory period for filing a claim for refund has expired or the taxpayer(s) subject to the action(s) and the IRS have agreed with finality to the tax or other liabilities for the period(s) at issue and the taxpayer(s) have waived

the right to file a claim for refund. A final determination of tax does not preclude a subsequent final determination of tax if the IRS proceeds based on the information provided following the payment, denial, or rejection of an award.

(ii) *Example.*—The provisions of paragraph (d)(2)(i) of this section, regarding subsequent final determination of tax, may be illustrated by the following example:

*Example.* Information provided to the IRS by a whistleblower, under section 7623 and § 301.7623-1, identifies a taxpayer (Corporation 1), describes and documents specific facts relating to Corporation 1's activities, and, based on those facts, alleges that Corporation 1 owed additional taxes in Year 1. The Whistleblower Office processes the incoming claim and provides the information to an IRS Operating Division (Operating Division 1). Operating Division 1 reviews the claim and the allegations and ultimately decides not to proceed with an action against Corporation 1. Operating Division 1 conveys its determination not to proceed with an action against Corporation 1 to the Whistleblower Office on a Form 11369 along with all of the relevant supporting documents. The Whistleblower Office provides written notice to the whistleblower, denying any award pursuant to § 301.7623-3(c)(8), and the whistleblower does not appeal the notice to Tax Court within 30 days.

Two months after the Whistleblower Office denies the award, the Whistleblower Office recognizes a potential connection between the information provided and a recently-initiated, ongoing, examination of a second taxpayer by a second IRS Operating Division (Operating Division 2). The Whistleblower Office provides the information to Operating Division 2. Operating Division 2 evaluates the information and proceeds with an action against Taxpayer 2 based on the information provided. Ultimately, Operating Division 2 assesses and collects taxes resulting from the action and totaling $3 million. Following the conclusion of the whistleblower's participation in a whistleblower administrative proceeding described in § 301.7623-3(c) and the expiration of the statutory period for filing a claim for refund by Taxpayer 2, the Whistleblower Office determines the amount of the award and communicates the award to the whistleblower in a determination letter. The whistleblower may appeal the notice to the Tax Court within 30 days.

(3) *Joint Whistleblowers.*—If multiple whistleblowers jointly submit a claim for award, the IRS will pay any award in equal shares to the joint whistleblowers unless the joint whistleblowers specify a different allocation in a written agreement, signed by all the joint whistleblowers and notarized, and submitted with the claim for award. The aggregate award payment in cases involving joint whistleblowers will be within the award percentage range of section 7623(b)(1) or section 7623(b)(2), as applicable, and subject to the award reduction provisions of section 7623(b)(3).

(4) *Deceased Whistleblower.*—If a whistleblower dies before or during the whistleblower administrative proceeding, the Whistleblower Office may substitute an executor, administrator, or other legal representative on behalf of the deceased whistleblower for purposes of conducting the whistleblower administrative proceeding.

(5) *Tax treatment of award.*—All awards are includible in gross income and subject to current Federal tax reporting and withholding requirements.

(e) *Effective/applicability date.*—This rule is effective on August 12, 2014. This rule applies to information submitted on or after August 12, 2014, and to claims for award under section 7623(b) that are open as of August 12, 2014. [Reg. § 301.7623-4.]

☐ [*T.D. 9687, 8-7-2014.*]

**[Reg. § 301.7624-1]**

**§ 301.7624-1. Reimbursement to State and local law enforcement agencies.**—(a) *In general.*—The Internal Revenue Service may reimburse a State or local law enforcement agency for expenses, such as salaries, overtime pay, per diem, and similar reasonable expenses, incurred in an investigation in which information is furnished to the Service that substantially contributes to the recovery of Federal taxes imposed with respect to illegal drug or related money laundering activities. The amount of reimbursement that may be paid shall not exceed the limits specified in paragraphs (e)(2) and (e)(3) of this section.

(b) *Information that substantially contributes to recovery of taxes.*—(1) *Definition.*—The Service generally will consider that information furnished by a State or local law enforcement agency substantially contributed to the recovery of taxes with respect to illegal drug or related money laundering activities provided the information was not already in the possession of the Service at the time the information is furnished by the State or local law enforcement agency, and

(i) concerns a taxpayer who is not under examination or investigation by the Service at the time the information is furnished or has not already been selected by the Service for examination or investigation in the near future, or

(ii) concerns a taxpayer who is under examination or has been selected for examination at the time the information is furnished but the information furnished would not normally have been discovered in the course of an ordinary investigation or examination by the Service. Also, information will generally be considered as substantially contributing to the recovery of taxes if it leads to the discovery of hidden assets owned by the taxpayer which are used to satisfy the taxpayer's assessed but otherwise uncollectable Federal tax liability with respect to illegal drug or related money laundering activities.

For purposes of this paragraph (b), information includes, but is not limited to, tax years of violations, aliases, addresses, social security numbers and/or employer identification numbers, financial data (bank accounts, assets, etc.) and their location, and any documentation that substantiates allegations concerning tax liability (books and records) and its location.

(2) *Examples.*

*Example (1).* A local police department's narcotics division has been gathering information on a suspected local drug dealer for approximately six months. Because this person is very cautious when handling narcotics, the local police have been unsuccessful in catching this person in possession of drugs. Rather than drop the case, the narcotics detective turns over to the local IRS Criminal Investigation Division (CID) office information concerning this person. At the time the information is furnished, the Service is unaware of this person's suspected involvement in drugs and has no reason to suspect that this person's Federal income tax returns are incorrect. Upon examination of this person's returns for three open years, the Service determines that additional Federal income taxes and civil penalties of approximately $20,000 per year are due because of unreported income from drug dealing. Because the taxpayer was not under examination and was not reasonably anticipated to have been examined prior to receipt of the information, the Service will consider that the information furnished by the local police department substantially contributed to the recovery of approximately $60,000 in taxes with respect to illegal drug activities.

*Example (2).* Assume the same facts as example (1) except that at the time the information is turned over to the Service, the Service was already aware of the extent of this person's involvement in drug dealing, either through information developed in the course of examinations of other taxpayers or through information received from other sources, and had already selected this person's returns for examination although the person had not yet been contacted by the Service. In this case, the information provided by the local police department did not substantially contribute to the recovery of taxes from this person because the information was already known to the Service.

*Example (3).* A state or local police officer is conducting ordinary traffic patrol. The officer stops a vehicle for speeding and reckless driving. The officer recognizes the driver as a known narcotics dealer. In the vehicle is a brief case containing $75,000 in cash, but no trace of narcotics is found. The driver claims the cash was won in a high stakes poker game. The officer arrests the driver for traffic violations and takes the briefcase into custody for safe keeping. The local police department cannot seize the money because they cannot tie it to a narcotics transaction. Instead, they immediately inform the local CID office of their find. At the time this information is furnished to the Service, there is an unpaid assessed liability of $300,000 in Federal taxes and penalties owed by the dealer with respect to illegal drug activities that the Service has been unable to collect. Therefore, the Service immediately seizes the $75,000 in cash in partial payment of the tax liability. The Service will consider that the information furnished by the police department substantially contributed to the recovery of $75,000 in taxes with respect to drug related activities.

*Example (4).* Through information furnished by a reliable informant, a local police department learns that a known racketeer and suspected drug dealer maintains a second set of books and records in a safe at home. The local police obtain a search warrant and find a set of books revealing that this person has been using a legitimate business operation to launder money derived from both prostitution and drug dealing. At the time these records are turned over to the

local CID office, the taxpayer is already under examination for tax evasion. However, based on the information contained in this second set of books, the Service is able to collect additional taxes and civil penalties in the amount of $1 million in connection with these illegal activities. The Service will consider that this information substantially contributed to the recovery of $1 million in taxes with respect to money laundering in connection with illegal drug activities because, even though the taxpayer was already under examination, the information provided by the local police would normally not have been discovered by the Service in the course of an ordinary investigation.

(c) *Application for reimbursement.*—An agency that intends to apply for reimbursement under the provisions of this section must indicate this intent to the Service at the time the information is first provided to the Service. A final application for reimbursement of expenses must be submitted on Form 211A, State or Local Law Enforcement Application for Reimbursement, to the Chief, Criminal Investigation Division of the Internal Revenue Service district in which the taxpayer is located. Copies of Forms 9061, DAG-71, or other claim for an equitable share of asset forfeitures in the case must also be furnished with Form 211A.

(d) *Time for filing application for reimbursement.*—An application for reimbursement may be filed by an agency at the time the information is first provided or as soon as practicable after submitting information to the Service. However, it must be filed not later than 30 days after the Service notifies the agency pursuant to section 7624(b) of the amount of taxes collected as a result of the information provided. If an application for reimbursement is filed by more than one agency with respect to taxes recovered from a taxpayer, the Service will use discretion in determining an equitable amount of reimbursement allocated to each agency based on all relevant factors. In no event, however, shall the aggregate of the amounts paid by the Service to two or more agencies exceed the amount specified in paragraph (e)(3) of this section.

(e) *Amount and payment of reimbursement.*—(1) *De minimis rule.*— No reimbursement shall be paid under section 7624 or this section to a State or local law enforcement agency in any case where the taxes recovered total less than $50,000.

(2) *Taxes recovered.*—For purposes of section 7624 and this section, the terms "taxes" recovered and "sum" recovered mean additional Federal taxes, civil penalties, and additions to tax collected (less any subsequent refund to the taxpayer) with respect to illegal drug or related money laundering activities, but not additional interest or criminal fines that may be collected.

(3) *Limitation on reimbursement.*—The amount of reimbursement payable under section 7624 and this section shall not exceed 10 percent of any taxes recovered.

(4) *No duplicate reimbursement.*—A State or local law enforcement agency shall not receive reimbursement under section 7624 or this section for any expenses incurred in the investigation of a taxpayer which have been or will be reimbursed under any other program or arrangement including, but not limited to, Federal or State forfeiture programs, State revenue laws, or Federal and State equitable sharing arrangements.

(5) *Time of payment.*—No payment of any reimbursement under this section will be made to a State or local law enforcement agency before the later of final expiration of the applicable period of limitations for filing a claim for refund by the taxpayer of the taxes recovered as provided in subchapter B of chapter 66 of the Code or the determination of the taxpayer's tax liability, as defined in section 1313(a). However, reimbursement may be made earlier but only if the agency provides adequate indemnification against loss by the Service due to a refund to the taxpayer of Federal taxes recovered.

(6) *Applicability.*—The provisions of section 7624 apply only to State and local law enforcement agencies within the United States and the District of Columbia.

(f) *Effective date.*—This section applies with respect to information first provided to the Service by a State or local law enforcement agency after February 16, 1989. [Reg. §301.7624-1.]

☐ [T.D. 8415, 4-23-92.]

# POSSESSIONS

[Reg. §301.7654-1]

**§301.7654-1. Coordination of U.S. and Guam individual income taxes.**—(a) *Application of section.*—(1) *Scope.*—Section 7654 and this section set forth the general procedures to be followed by the Government of the United States and the Government of Guam in the

division between the two governments of revenue derived from collections of the income taxes imposed for any taxable year beginning after December 31, 1972, with respect to any individual described in subparagraph (2) of this paragraph and paragraph(e) of this section. To the extent that section 7654 and this section are inconsistent with the provisions of section 30 of the Organic Act of

Guam (48 U.S.C. 1421h), relating to duties and taxes to be covered into the treasury of Guam and held in account for the Government of Guam, such section 30 is superseded.

(2) *Individuals covered.*—Paragraph (b) of this section applies only to an individual who, for a taxable year, is described in paragraph (a)(2) of §1.935-1 of this chapter (Income Tax Regulations) and has (or in the case of a joint return, such individual and his spouse have)—

    (i) Adjusted gross income of $50,000 or more, and

    (ii) Gross income of $5,000 or more from sources within the jurisdiction (either the United States or Guam) other than the jurisdiction with which the individual is required to file his income tax return under paragraph (b) of §1.935-1 of this chapter.

For the determination of gross income and adjusted gross income see sections 61 and 62, and the regulations thereunder, or, when applicable, the corresponding provisions as made applicable in Guam by the Guam Territorial income tax (48 U.S.C. 1421i). For purposes of this subparagraph, gross income consisting of compensation for military or naval service shall be taken into account notwithstanding section 514 of the Soldiers' and Sailors' Civil Relief Act of 1940 (50 App. U.S.C. 574). However, see paragraph (e) of this section.

(b) *Allocation of tax.*—(1) Net collections of income taxes imposed for each taxable year beginning after December 31, 1972, with respect to each individual described in paragraph (a)(2) of this section for such year shall be divided between the United States and Guam by the Commissioner of Internal Revenue and the Commissioner of Revenue and Taxation of Guam as follows:

    (i) Net collections attributable to income from sources within the United States shall be covered into the Treasury of the United States,

    (ii) Net collections attributable to income from sources within Guam shall be covered into the treasury of Guam, and

    (iii) Net collections not described in subdivision (i) or (ii) of this subparagraph (i.e., net collections attributable to income from sources other than within the United States or Guam) shall be covered into the treasury of the jurisdiction (either the United States or Guam) with which the individual is required to file his return under paragraph (b) of §1.935-1 of this chapter for such year.

(2) The amount of tax of any individual for a taxable year which shall be allocated to Guam for purposes of determining the portion of the net collections from such individual which shall be covered into the treasury of Guam by the United States for such year shall be that amount which bears the same ratio to such amount of tax as the adjusted gross income of that individual for such year which is allocable to sources in Guam bears to the total adjusted gross income of such individual for such year. For purposes of such allocation by the United States, the adjusted gross income of the taxpayer shall be determined by taking into account any compensation of any member of the Armed Forces for services performed in Guam the withheld tax on which is paid into the treasury of Guam pursuant to paragraph (e) of this section. The amount of tax of any individual for any taxable year which shall be allocated to the United States for purposes of determining the portion of the net collections from such individual which shall be covered into the Treasury of the United States by Guam for such year shall be that amount which bears the same ratio to such amount of tax as the adjusted gross income of that individual for such year which is allocable to sources in the United States bears to the total adjusted gross income of such individual for such year.

(c) *Definitions and special rules.*—For purposes of this section—

(1) *Net collections.*—(i) In determining net collections for a taxable year, appropriate adjustment between the two jurisdictions shall be made on a proportionate basis for underpayments of income taxes for such taxable year, credits allowed against the income tax for such taxable year (other than the credit for taxes withheld under section 3402 on wages), and refunds made of income taxes paid with respect to such taxable year. Thus, if a net operating loss results in a carryback to an earlier taxable year which gives rise to a refund for that earlier year, an adjustment must be made based upon the proportion which the amount of tax covered by one jurisdiction into the treasury of the other jurisdiction for that earlier year bears to the total amount of tax paid for that earlier year, even though the loss may have resulted from activities in one jurisdiction and the income, against which the loss was offset, was earned in the other jurisdiction. Similar adjustments must be made for foreign tax credit carrybacks even though different jurisdictions are involved. If, for example, an individual pays income tax of $30,000 to the United States for 1974 and $10,000 of such tax is covered into the treasury of Guam, and if for 1975 such individual has a net operating loss attributable to a trade or business carried on in the United States which loss is carried back to 1974 and gives rise to a refund of $15,000 by the United States, Guam must cover into the Treasury of the United States the

amount of $5,000 which is the adjustment based upon the refund ($15,000 × $10,000/$30,000 = $5,000).

    (ii) Tax withheld from the compensation of any member of the Armed Forces described in paragraph (a)(2) of this section which is paid to Guam pursuant to section 7654(d) and paragraph (e) of this section shall be taken into account in determining the amount required to be covered into the treasury of Guam under paragraph (b)(1)(ii) of this section.

    (iii) For purposes of this subparagraph, any underpayment of tax is treated as attributable on a pro rata basis to income from sources within the United States, Guam, and sources other than within the United States or Guam, respectively, and is divided between the United States and Guam under the rules in paragraph (b) of this section.

(2) *Income taxes.*—The term "income taxes" means—

    (i) With respect to taxes imposed by the United States, the income taxes imposed by chapter 1 of the Code, and

    (ii) With respect to taxes imposed by Guam, the Guam Territorial income tax (48 U.S.C. 1421i).

(3) *Source rules.*—The determination of the source of income shall be based on the principles contained in sections 861 through 863, and the regulations thereunder, or, when applicable, in those sections as made applicable in Guam by the Guam Territorial income tax. For such purposes the provisions of section 514 of the Soldiers' and Sailors' Civil Relief Act of 1940 (50 App. U.S.C. 574) relating to the determination of the source of income of members of the Armed Forces shall not be taken into account. For purposes of this subparagraph, the provisions in section 935(c) treating Guam as part of the United States, and vice versa, do not apply. For definition of the terms "United States" and "Guam" (see section 7701(a)(9) of the Code and section 2 of the Organic Act of Guam (48 U.S.C. 1421).

(d) *Information return.*—Each individual described in paragraph (a)(2) of this section for a taxable year who is required by paragraph (b)(1) of §1.935-1 of this chapter to file his return of income for such year with the United States shall timely file a properly executed Form 5074 (Allocation of Individual Income Tax to Guam) by attaching such form to his income tax return. Each individual described in paragraph (a)(2) of this section for a taxable year who is required by paragraph (b)(1) of §1.935-1 of this chapter to file his return of income for such year with Guam shall timely file such information as may be required by the Commissioner of Revenue and Taxation with respect to his income derived from sources within the United States. See section 6688 and §301.6688-1 for the penalty for failure to comply with this paragraph.

(e) *Military personnel in Guam.*—The Commissioner of Internal Revenue shall arrange to pay to Guam the amount of the taxes deducted and withheld by the United States under section 3402 from wages paid to members of the Armed Forces who are stationed in Guam but who have no income tax liability to Guam with respect to such wages by reason of section 514 of the Soldiers' and Sailors' Civil Relief Act of 1940 (50 App. U.S.C. 574). Section 514 of that Act provides in effect that for purposes of the taxation of income by Guam a person shall not be deemed to have lost a residence or domicile in the United States solely by reason of being absent therefrom in compliance with military or naval orders and the compensation for military or naval service of such a person who is not a resident of, or domiciled in, Guam shall not be deemed income for services performed within, or from sources within, Guam. Any amount paid to Guam under this paragraph in respect of a member of the Armed Forces described in paragraph (a)(2) of this section shall be taken into account in determining the amount required to be covered into the treasury of Guam under paragraph (b)(1)(ii) of this section. For purposes of this paragraph, the term "Armed Forces of the United States" has the meaning provided by §301.7701-8 of this chapter. This paragraph does not apply to wages for services performed in Guam by members of the Armed Forces of the United States which are not compensation for military or naval service. In determining the amount of tax to be covered into the treasury of Guam under this paragraph with respect to remuneration for services performed in Guam by members of the Armed Forces of the United States, the special procedure agreed upon with the Department of Defense in 1951 shall not apply to remuneration paid after December 31, 1974. Under that procedure the tax withheld under section 3402 upon such remuneration for services performed in Guam during April and October of each year was to be projected for the appropriate six-month period of which the base month is a part, thereby arriving at an estimated figure for semiannual withholding tax to be covered over.

(f) *Transfers of funds.*—The transfers of funds between the United States and Guam required to effectuate the provisions of this section shall be made when convenient for the two governments, but not less frequently than once in each calendar year. In complying with paragraph (b) of this section, only net balances will be transferred between the two governments. Further, amounts transferred pursuant to paragraph (b) of this section may be determined on the basis of estimates rather than the actual amounts derived from information furnished by taxpayers, except that the net collections for 1973 and every third calendar year thereafter are to be transferred on the basis of the information furnished by taxpayers pursuant to paragraph (d) of this section. In order to facilitate the transfer of funds pursuant to this section, the Commissioner of Internal Revenue and the Commissioner of Revenue and Taxation of Guam shall exchange such information, including copies of income tax returns, as will ensure that the provisions of section 7654 and this section are being properly implemented. [Reg. § 301.7654-1.]

☐ [*T.D.* 7385, 10-18-75.]

# Definitions

See p. 20,601 for regulations not amended to reflect law changes

### [Reg. § 1.7701-1]

**§ 1.7701-1. Definitions; spouse, husband and wife, husband, wife, marriage.**—(a) *In general.*—For the definition of the terms spouse, husband and wife, husband, wife, and marriage, see § 301.7701-18 of this chapter.

(b) *Applicability date.*—The rules of this section apply to taxable years ending on or after September 2, 2016. [Reg. § 1.7701-1.]

☐ [*T.D.* 9785, 8-31-2016.]

### [Reg. § 20.7701-1]

**§ 20.7701-1. Tax return preparer.**—(a) *In general.*—For the definition of a tax return preparer, see § 301.7701-15 of this chapter.

(b) *Effective/applicability date.*—This section is applicable to returns and claims for refund filed, and advice provided, after December 31, 2008. [Reg. § 20.7701-1.]

☐ [*T.D.* 9436, 12-15-2008.]

### [Reg. § 25.7701-1]

**§ 25.7701-1. Tax return preparer.**—(a) *In general.*—For the definition of a tax return preparer, see § 301.7701-15 of this chapter.

(b) *Effective/applicability date.*—This section is applicable to returns and claims for refund filed, and advice provided, after December 31, 2008. [Reg. § 25.7701-1.]

☐ [*T.D.* 9436, 12-15-2008.]

### [Reg. § 26.7701-1]

**§ 26.7701-1. Tax return preparer.**—(a) *In general.*—For the definition of a tax return preparer, see § 301.7701-15 of this chapter.

(b) *Effective/applicability date.*—This section is applicable to returns and claims for refund filed, and advice provided, after December 31, 2008. [Reg. § 26.7701-1.]

☐ [*T.D.* 9436, 12-15-2008.]

### [Reg. § 31.7701-1]

**§ 31.7701-1. Tax return preparer.**—(a) *In general.*—For the definition of a tax return preparer, see § 301.7701-15 of this chapter.

(b) *Effective/applicability date.*—This section is applicable to returns and claims for refund filed, and advice provided, after December 31, 2008. [Reg. § 31.7701-1.]

☐ [*T.D.* 9436, 12-15-2008.]

### [Reg. § 40.7701-1]

**§ 40.7701-1. Tax return preparer.**—(a) *In general.*—For the definition of a tax return preparer, see § 301.7701-15 of this chapter.

(b) *Effective/applicability date.*—This section is applicable to returns and claims for refund filed, and advice provided, after December 31, 2008. [Reg. § 40.7701-1.]

☐ [*T.D.* 9436, 12-15-2008.]

### [Reg. § 41.7701-1]

**§ 41.7701-1. Tax return preparer.**—(a) *In general.*—For the definition of a tax return preparer, see § 301.7701-15 of this chapter.

(b) *Effective/applicability date.*—This section is applicable to returns and claims for refund filed, and advice provided, after December 31, 2008. [Reg. § 41.7701-1.]

☐ [*T.D.* 9436, 12-15-2008.]

### [Reg. § 44.7701-1]

**§ 44.7701-1. Tax return preparer.**—(a) *In general.*—For the definition of a tax return preparer, see § 301.7701-15 of this chapter.

(b) *Effective/applicability date.*—This section is applicable to returns and claims for refund filed, and advice provided, after December 31, 2008. [Reg. § 44.7701-1.]

☐ [*T.D.* 9436, 12-15-2008.]

### [Reg. § 53.7701-1]

**§ 53.7701-1. Tax return preparer.**—(a) *In general.*—For the definition of a tax return preparer, see § 301.7701-15 of this chapter.

(b) *Effective/applicability date.*—This section is applicable to returns and claims for refund filed, and advice provided, after December 31, 2008. [Reg. § 53.7701-1.]

☐ [*T.D.* 9436, 12-15-2008.]

### [Reg. § 54.7701-1]

**§ 54.7701-1. Tax return preparer.**—(a) *In general.*—For the definition of a tax return preparer, see § 301.7701-15 of this chapter.

(b) *Effective/applicability date.*—This section is applicable to returns and claims for refund filed, and advice provided, after December 31, 2008. [Reg. § 54.7701-1.]

☐ [*T.D.* 9436, 12-15-2008.]

### [Reg. § 55.7701-1]

**§ 55.7701-1. Tax return preparer.**—(a) *In general.*—For the definition of a tax return preparer, see § 301.7701-15 of this chapter.

(b) *Effective/applicability date.*—This section is applicable to returns and claims for refund filed, and advice provided, after December 31, 2008. [Reg. § 55.7701-1.]

☐ [*T.D.* 9436, 12-15-2008.]

### [Reg. § 56.7701-1]

**§ 56.7701-1. Tax return preparer.**—(a) *In general.*—For the definition of a tax return preparer, see § 301.7701-15 of this chapter.

(b) *Effective/applicability date.*—This section is applicable to returns and claims for refund filed, and advice provided, after December 31, 2008. [Reg. § 56.7701-1.]

☐ [*T.D.* 9436, 12-15-2008.]

### [Reg. § 156.7701-1]

**§ 156.7701-1. Tax return preparer.**—(a) *In general.*—For the definition of a tax return preparer, see § 301.7701-15 of this chapter.

(b) *Effective/applicability date.*—This section is applicable to returns and claims for refund filed, and advice provided, after December 31, 2008. [Reg. § 156.7701-1.]

☐ [*T.D.* 9436, 12-15-2008.]

### [Reg. § 157.7701-1]

**§ 157.7701-1. Tax return preparer.**—(a) *In general.*—For the definition of a tax return preparer, see § 301.7701-15 of this chapter.

(b) *Effective/applicability date.*—This section is applicable to returns and claims for refund filed, and advice provided, after December 31, 2008. [Reg. § 157.7701-1.]

☐ [*T.D.* 9436, 12-15-2008.]

### [Reg. § 301.7701-1]

**§ 301.7701-1. Classification of organizations for federal tax purposes.**—(a) *Organizations for federal tax purposes.*—(1) *In general.*—The Internal Revenue Code prescribes the classification of various organizations for federal tax purposes. Whether an organization is an entity separate from its owners for federal tax purposes is a matter of federal tax law and does not depend on whether the organization is recognized as an entity under local law.

**(2)** *Certain joint undertakings give rise to entities for federal tax purposes.*—A joint venture or other contractual arrangement may create a separate entity for federal tax purposes if the participants carry on a trade, business, financial operation, or venture and divide the profits therefrom. For example, a separate entity exists for federal tax purposes if co-owners of an apartment building lease space and in addition provide services to the occupants either directly or through an agent. Nevertheless, a joint undertaking merely to share expenses does not create a separate entity for federal tax purposes. For example, if two or more persons jointly construct a ditch merely to drain surface water from their properties, they have not created a separate entity for federal tax purposes. Similarly, mere co-ownership of property that is maintained, kept in repair, and rented or leased does not constitute a separate entity for federal tax purposes. For example, if an individual owner, or tenants in common, of farm property lease it to a farmer for a cash rental or a share of the crops, they do not necessarily create a separate entity for federal tax purposes.

**(3)** *Certain local law entities not recognized.*—An entity formed under local law is not always recognized as a separate entity for federal tax purposes. For example, an organization wholly owned by a State is not recognized as a separate entity for federal tax purposes if it is an integral part of the State. Similarly, tribes incorporated under section 17 of the Indian Reorganization Act of 1934, as amended, 25 U.S.C. 477, or under section 3 of the Oklahoma Indian Welfare Act, as amended, 25 U.S.C. 503, are not recognized as separate entities for federal tax purposes.

**(4)** *Single owner organizations.*—Under §§ 301.7701-2 and 301.7701-3, certain organizations that have a single owner can choose to be recognized or disregarded as entities separate from their owners.

**(b)** *Classification of organizations.*—The classification of organizations that are recognized as separate entities is determined under §§ 301.7701-2, 301.7701-3, and 301.7701-4 unless a provision of the Internal Revenue Code (such as section 860A addressing Real Estate Mortgage Investment Conduits (REMICs)) provides for special treatment of that organization. For the classification of organizations as trusts, see § 301.7701-4. That section provides that trusts generally do not have associates or an objective to carry on business for profit. Sections 301.7701-2 and 301.7701-3 provide rules for classifying organizations that are not classified as trusts.

**(c)** *Cost sharing arrangements.*—A cost sharing arrangement that is described in § 1.482-7 of this chapter, including any arrangement that the Commissioner treats as a CSA under § 1.482-7(b)(5) of this chapter, is not recognized as a separate entity for purposes of the Internal Revenue Code. See § 1.482-7 of this chapter for the rules regarding CSAs.

**(d)** *Domestic and foreign business entities.*—See § 301.7701-5 for the rules that determine whether a business entity is domestic or foreign.

**(e)** *State.*—For purposes of this section and § 301.7701-2, the term *State* includes the District of Columbia.

**(f)** *Effective/applicability dates.*—Except as provided in the following sentence, the rules of this section are applicable as of January 1, 1997. The rules of paragraph (c) of this section are applicable on January 5, 2009. [Reg. § 301.7701-1.]

☐ [*T.D.* 6503, 11-15-80. *Amended by T.D.* 6797, 2-2-65; *T.D.* 7515, 10-17-77; *T.D.* 8697, 12-17-96; *T.D.* 9153, 8-11-2004; *T.D.* 9246, 1-27-2006; *T.D.* 9441, 12-31-2008 *and T.D.* 9568, 12-16-2011.]

### [Reg. § 305.7701-1]

**§ 305.7701-1. Definition of Indian tribal government (Temporary).**—**(a)** *Definition.*—A governing body of a tribe, band, pueblo, community, village, or group of native American Indians, or Alaska Natives, qualifies as an Indian tribal government upon determination by the Internal Revenue Service that the governing body exercises governmental functions. Designation of a governing body as an Indian tribal government will be by revenue procedure. If a governing body is not currently designated by the applicable revenue procedure as an Indian tribal government, and such governing body believes that it qualifies for such designation, the governing body may apply for a ruling from the Internal Revenue Service. In order to qualify as an Indian tribal government, for purposes of section 7701(a)(40) and this section, such governing body must receive a favorable ruling from the Internal Revenue Service. The request for a ruling shall be made in accordance with all applicable procedural rules set forth in the Statement of Procedural Rules (26 CFR Part 601) and any applicable revenue procedures relating to the submission of ruling requests. The request shall be submitted to the Internal Revenue Service, Associate Chief Counsel (Technical), Attention:

CC:IND:S, Room 6545, 1111 Constitution Avenue, N.W., Washington, D.C. 20224.

**(b)** *Effective date.*—The provisions of this section are effective after December 31, 1982. [Temporary Reg. § 305.7701-1.]

☐ [*T.D.* 7952, 5-4-84.]

### [Reg. § 20.7701-2]

**§ 20.7701-2. Definitions; spouse, husband and wife, husband, wife, marriage.**—**(a)** *In general.*—For the definition of the terms spouse, husband and wife, husband, wife, and marriage, see § 301.7701-18 of this chapter.

**(b)** *Applicability date.*—The rules of this section apply to taxable years ending on or after September 2, 2016. [Reg. § 20.7701-2.]

☐ [*T.D.* 9785, 8-31-2016.]

### [Reg. § 25.7701-2]

**§ 25.7701-2. Definitions; spouse, husband and wife, husband, wife, marriage.**—**(a)** *In general.*—For the definition of the terms spouse, husband and wife, husband, wife, and marriage, see § 301.7701-18 of this chapter.

**(b)** *Applicability date.*—The rules of this section apply to taxable years ending on or after September 2, 2016. [Reg. § 25.7701-2.]

☐ [*T.D.* 9785, 8-31-2016.]

### [Reg. § 26.7701-2]

**§ 26.7701-2. Definitions; spouse, husband and wife, husband, wife, marriage.**—**(a)** *In general.*—For the definition of the terms spouse, husband and wife, husband, wife, and marriage, see § 301.7701-18 of this chapter.

**(b)** *Applicability date.*—The rules of this section apply to taxable years ending on or after September 2, 2016. [Reg. § 26.7701-2.]

☐ [*T.D.* 9785, 8-31-2016.]

### [Reg. § 31.7701-2]

**§ 31.7701-2. Definitions; spouse, husband and wife, husband, wife, marriage.**—**(a)** *In general.*—For the definition of the terms spouse, husband and wife, husband, wife, and marriage, see § 301.7701-18 of this chapter.

**(b)** *Applicability date.*—The rules of this section apply to taxable years ending on or after September 2, 2016. [Reg. § 31.7701-2.]

☐ [*T.D.* 9785, 8-31-2016.]

### [Reg. § 301.7701-2]

**§ 301.7701-2. Business entities; definitions.**—**(a)** *Business entities.*—For purposes of this section and § 301.7701-3, a *business entity* is any entity recognized for federal tax purposes (including an entity with a single owner that may be disregarded as an entity separate from its owner under § 301.7701-3) that is not properly classified as a trust under § 301.7701-4 or otherwise subject to special treatment under the Internal Revenue Code. A business entity with two or more members is classified for federal tax purposes as either a corporation or a partnership. A business entity with only one owner is classified as a corporation or is disregarded; if the entity is disregarded, its activities are treated in the same manner as a sole proprietorship, branch, or division of the owner. But see paragraphs (c)(2)(iii) through (vi) of this section for special rules that apply to an eligible entity that is otherwise disregarded as an entity separate from its owner.

**(b)** *Corporations.*—For federal tax purposes, the term *corporation* means—

**(1)** A business entity organized under a Federal or State statute, or under a statute of a federally recognized Indian tribe, if the statute describes or refers to the entity as incorporated or as a corporation, body corporate, or body politic;

**(2)** An association (as determined under § 301.7701-3);

**(3)** A business entity organized under a State statute, if the statute describes or refers to the entity as a joint-stock company or joint-stock association;

**(4)** An insurance company;

**(5)** A State-chartered business entity conducting banking activities, if any of its deposits are insured under the Federal Deposit Insurance Act, as amended, 12 U.S.C. 1811 et seq., or a similar federal statute;

**(6)** A business entity wholly owned by a State or any political subdivision thereof, or a business entity wholly owned by a foreign government or any other entity described in § 1.892-2T;

(7) A business entity that is taxable as a corporation under a provision of the Internal Revenue Code other than section 7701(a)(3); and

(8) *Certain foreign entities.*—(i) *In general.*—Except as provided in paragraphs (b)(8)(ii) and (d) of this section, the following business entities formed in the following jurisdictions:

American Samoa, Corporation
Argentina, Sociedad Anonima
Australia, Public Limited Company
Austria, Aktiengesellschaft
Barbados, Limited Company
Belgium, Societe Anonyme
Belize, Public Limited Company
Bolivia, Sociedad Anonima
Brazil, Sociedade Anonima
Bulgaria, Aktsionerno Druzhestvo
Canada, Corporation and Company
Chile, Sociedad Anonima
People's Republic of China, Gufen Youxian Gongsi
Republic of China (Taiwan), Ku-fen Yu-hsien Kung-szu
Colombia, Sociedad Anonima
Costa Rica, Sociedad Anonima
Cyprus, Public Limited Company
Czech Republic, Akciova Spolecnost
Denmark, Aktieselskab
Ecuador, Sociedad Anonima or Compania Anonima
Egypt, Sharikat Al-Mossahamah
El Salvador, Sociedad Anonima
Estonia, Aktsiaselts
European Economic Area/European Union, Societas Europaea
Finland, Julkinen Osakeyhtio/Publikt Aktiebolag
France, Societe Anonyme
Germany, Aktiengesellschaft
Greece, Anonymos Etairia
Guam, Corporation
Guatemala, Sociedad Anonima
Guyana, Public Limited Company
Honduras, Sociedad Anonima
Hong Kong, Public Limited Company
Hungary, Reszvenytarsasag
Iceland, Hlutafelag
India, Public Limited Company
Indonesia, Perseroan Terbuka
Ireland, Public Limited Company
Israel, Public Limited Company
Italy, Societa per Azioni
Jamaica, Public Limited Company
Japan, Kabushiki Kaisha
Kazakstan, Ashyk Aktsionerlik Kogham
Republic of Korea, Chusik Hoesa
Latvia, Akciju Sabiedriba
Liberia, Corporation
Liechtenstein, Aktiengesellschaft
Lithuania, Akcine Bendroves
Luxembourg, Societe Anonyme
Malaysia, Berhad
Malta, Public Limited Company
Mexico, Sociedad Anonima
Morocco, Societe Anonyme
Netherlands, Naamloze Vennootschap
New Zealand, Limited Company
Nicaragua, Compania Anonima
Nigeria, Public Limited Company
Northern Mariana Islands, Corporation
Norway, Allment Aksjeselskap
Pakistan, Public Limited Company
Panama, Sociedad Anonima
Paraguay, Sociedad Anonima
Peru, Sociedad Anonima
Philippines, Stock Corporation
Poland, Spolka Akcyjna
Portugal, Sociedade Anonima
Puerto Rico, Corporation
Romania, Societate pe Actiuni
Russia, Otkrytoye Aktsionernoy Obshchestvo
Saudi Arabia, Sharikat Al-Mossahamah
Singapore, Public Limited Company
Slovak Republic, Akciova Spolocnost
Slovenia, Delniska Druzba
South Africa, Public Limited Company
Spain, Sociedad Anonima
Surinam, Naamloze Vennootschap
Sweden, Publika Aktiebolag
Switzerland, Aktiengesellschaft
Thailand, Borisat Chamkad (Mahachon)
Trinidad and Tobago, Limited Company
Tunisia, Societe Anonyme
Turkey, Anonim Sirket
Ukraine, Aktsionerne Tovaristvo Vidkritogo Tipu
United Kingdom, Public Limited Company
United States Virgin Islands, Corporation
Uruguay, Sociedad Anonima
Venezuela, Sociedad Anonima or Compania Anonima

(ii) *Clarification of list of corporations in paragraph (b)(8)(i) of this section.*—(A) *Exceptions in certain cases.*—The following entities will not be treated as corporations under paragraph (b)(8)(i) of this section:

*(1)* With regard to Canada, a Nova Scotia Unlimited Liability Company (or any other company or corporation all of whose owners have unlimited liability pursuant to federal or provincial law).

*(2)* With regard to India, a company deemed to be a public limited company solely by operation of Section 43A(1) (relating to corporate ownership of the company), section 43A(1A) (relating to annual average turnover), or section 43A(1B) (relating to ownership interests in other companies) of the Companies Act, 1956 (or any combination of these), provided that the organizational documents of such deemed public limited company continue to meet the requirements of section 3(1)(iii) of the Companies Act, 1956.

*(3)* With regard to Malaysia, a Sendirian Berhad.

(B) *Inclusions in certain cases.*—With regard to Mexico, the term Sociedad Anonima includes a Sociedad Anonima that chooses to apply the variable capital provision of Mexican corporate law (Sociedad Anonima de Capital Variable).

(iii) *Public companies.*—For purposes of paragraph (b)(8)(i) of this section, with regard to Cyprus, Hong Kong, and Jamaica, the term Public Limited Company includes any Limited Company that is not defined as a private company under the corporate laws of those jurisdictions. In all other cases, where the term Public Limited Company is not defined, that term shall include any Limited Company defined as a public company under the corporate laws of the relevant jurisdiction.

(iv) *Limited companies.*—For purposes of this paragraph (b)(8), any reference to a Limited Company includes, as the case may be, companies limited by shares and companies limited by guarantee.

(v) *Multilingual countries.*—Different linguistic renderings of the name of an entity listed in paragraph (b)(8)(i) of this section shall be disregarded. For example, an entity formed under the laws of Switzerland as a Societe Anonyme will be a corporation and treated in the same manner as an Aktiengesellschaft.

(9) *Business entities with multiple charters.*—(i) An entity created or organized under the laws of more than one jurisdiction if the rules of this section would treat it as a corporation with reference to any one of the jurisdictions in which it is created or organized. Such an entity may elect its classification under §301.7701-3, subject to the limitations of those provisions, only if it is created or organized in each jurisdiction in a manner that meets the definition of an eligible entity in §301.7701-3(a). The determination of a business entity's corporate or non-corporate classification is made independently from the determination of whether the entity is domestic or foreign. See §301.7701-5 for the rules that determine whether a business entity is domestic or foreign.

(ii) *Examples.*—The following examples illustrate the rule of this paragraph (b)(9):

*Example 1.* (i) *Facts.* X is an entity with a single owner organized under the laws of Country A as an entity that is listed in paragraph (b)(8)(i) of this section. Under the rules of this section, such an entity is a corporation for Federal tax purposes and under §301.7701-3(a) is unable to elect its classification. Several years after its formation, X files a certificate of domestication in State B as a limited liability company (LLC). Under the laws of State B, X is considered to be created or organized in State B as an LLC upon the filing of the certificate of domestication and is therefore subject to the laws of State B. Under the rules of this section and §301.7701-3, an LLC with a single owner organized only in State B is disregarded as an entity separate from its owner for Federal tax purposes (absent an election to be treated as an association). Neither Country A nor State B law requires X to terminate its charter in Country A as a result of the domestication, and in fact X does not terminate its Country A charter. Consequently, X is now organized in more than one jurisdiction.

(ii) *Result.* X remains organized under the laws of Country A as an entity that is listed in paragraph (b)(8)(i) of this section, and as such, it is an entity that is treated as a corporation under the rules of this section. Therefore, X is a corporation for Federal tax purposes because the rules of this section would treat X as a corporation with reference to one of the jurisdictions in which it is created or organized. Because X is organized in Country A in a manner that does not meet the definition of an eligible entity in § 301.7701-3(a), it is unable to elect its classification.

*Example 2.* (i) *Facts.* Y is an entity that is incorporated under the laws of State A and has two shareholders. Under the rules of this section, an entity incorporated under the laws of State A is a corporation for Federal tax purposes and under § 301.7701-3(a) is unable to elect its classification. Several years after its formation, Y files a certificate of continuance in Country B as an unlimited company. Under the laws of Country B, upon filing a certificate of continuance, Y is treated as organized in Country B. Under the rules of this section and § 301.7701-3, an unlimited company organized only in Country B that has more than one owner is treated as a partnership for Federal tax purposes (absent an election to be treated as an association). Neither State A nor Country B law requires Y to terminate its charter in State A as a result of the continuance, and in fact Y does not terminate its State A charter. Consequently, Y is now organized in more than one jurisdiction.

(ii) *Result.* Y remains organized in State A as a corporation, an entity that is treated as a corporation under the rules of this section. Therefore, Y is a corporation for Federal tax purposes because the rules of this section would treat Y as a corporation with reference to one of the jurisdictions in which it is created or organized. Because Y is organized in State A in a manner that does not meet the definition of an eligible entity in § 301.7701-3(a), it is unable to elect its classification.

*Example 3.* (i) *Facts.* Z is an entity that has more than one owner and that is recognized under the laws of Country A as an unlimited company organized in Country A. Z is organized in Country A in a manner that meets the definition of an eligible entity in § 301.7701-3(a). Under the rules of this section and § 301.7701-3, an unlimited company organized only in Country A with more than one owner is treated as a partnership for Federal tax purposes (absent an election to be treated as an association). At the time Z was formed, it was also organized as a private limited company under the laws of Country B. Z is organized in Country B in a manner that meets the definition of an eligible entity in § 301.7701-3(a). Under the rules of this section and § 301.7701-3, a private limited company organized only in Country B is treated as a corporation for Federal tax purposes (absent an election to be treated as a partnership). Thus, Z is organized in more than one jurisdiction. Z has not made any entity classification elections under § 301.7701-3.

(ii) *Result.* Z is organized in Country B as a private limited company, an entity that is treated (absent an election to the contrary) as a corporation under the rules of this section. However, because Z is organized in each jurisdiction in a manner that meets the definition of an eligible entity in § 301.7701-3(a), it may elect its classification under § 301.7701-3, subject to the limitations of those provisions.

*Example 4.* (i) *Facts.* P is an entity with more than one owner organized in Country A as a general partnership. Under the rules of this section and § 301.7701-3, an eligible entity with more than one owner in Country A is treated as a partnership for federal tax purposes (absent an election to be treated as an association). P files a certificate of continuance in Country B as an unlimited company. Under the rules of this section and § 301.7701-3, an unlimited company in Country B with more than one owner is treated as a partnership for federal tax purposes (absent an election to be treated as an association). P is not required under either the laws of Country A or Country B to terminate the general partnership in Country A, and in fact P does not terminate its Country A partnership. P is now organized in more than one jurisdiction. P has not made any entity classification elections under § 301.7701-3.

(ii) *Result.* P's organization in both Country A and Country B would result in P being classified as a partnership. Therefore, since the rules of this section would not treat P as a corporation with reference to any jurisdiction in which it is created or organized, it is not a corporation for federal tax purposes.

(c) *Other business entities.*—For federal tax purposes—

(1) The term *partnership* means a business entity that is not a corporation under paragraph (b) of this section and that has at least two members.

(2) *Wholly owned entities.*—(i) *In general.*—Except as otherwise provided in this paragraph (c), a business entity that has a single

owner and is not a corporation under paragraph (b) of this section is disregarded as an entity separate from its owner.

(ii) *Special rule for certain business entities.*—If the single owner of a business entity is a bank (as defined in section 581, or, in the case of a foreign bank, as defined in section 585(a)(2)(B) without regard to the second sentence thereof), then the special rules applicable to banks under the Internal Revenue Code will continue to apply to the single owner as if the wholly owned entity were a separate entity. For this purpose, the special rules applicable to banks under the Internal Revenue Code do not include the rules under sections 864(c), 882(c), and 884.

(iii) *Tax liabilities of certain disregarded entities.*—(A) *In general.*—An entity that is disregarded as separate from its owner for any purpose under this section is treated as an entity separate from its owner for purposes of—

(1) Federal tax liabilities of the entity with respect to any taxable period for which the entity was not disregarded;

(2) Federal tax liabilities of any other entity for which the entity is liable; and

(3) Refunds or credits of Federal tax.

(B) *Examples.*—The following examples illustrate the application of paragraph (c)(2)(iii)(A) of this section:

*Example 1.* In 2006, X, a domestic corporation that reports its taxes on a calendar year basis, merges into Z, a domestic LLC wholly owned by Y that is disregarded as an entity separate from Y, in a state law merger. X was not a member of a consolidated group at any time during its taxable year ending in December 2005. Under the applicable state law, Z is the successor to X and is liable for all of X's debts. In 2009, the Internal Revenue Service (IRS) seeks to extend the period of limitations on assessment for X's 2005 taxable year. Because Z is the successor to X and is liable for X's 2005 taxes that remain unpaid, Z is the proper party to sign the consent to extend the period of limitations.

*Example 2.* The facts are the same as in *Example 1*, except that in 2007, the IRS determines that X miscalculated and underreported its income tax liability for 2005. Because Z is the successor to X and is liable for X's 2005 taxes that remain unpaid, the deficiency may be assessed against Z and, in the event that Z fails to pay the liability after notice and demand, a general tax lien will arise against all of Z's property and rights to property.

(iv) *Special rule for employment tax purposes.*—(A) *In general.*—Except as provided in paragraph (c)(2)(iv)(C) of this section, paragraph (c)(2)(i) of this section (relating to certain wholly owned entities) does not apply to taxes imposed under Subtitle C—Employment Taxes and Collection of Income Tax (Chapters 21, 22, 23, 23A, 24, and 25 of the Internal Revenue Code).

(B) *Treatment of entity.*—Except as provided in paragraph (c)(2)(iv)(C) of this section, an entity that is disregarded as an entity separate from its owner for any purpose under this section is treated as a corporation with respect to taxes imposed under Subtitle C—Employment Taxes and Collection of Income Tax (Chapters 21, 22, 23, 23A, 24, and 25 of the Internal Revenue Code). For special rules regarding the application of certain employment tax exceptions, see §§ 31.3121(b)(3)-1(d), 31.3127-1(b), and 31.3306(c)(5)-1(d) of this chapter.

(C) *Special rules.*—(1) Paragraphs (c)(2)(iv)(A) and (B) of this section do not apply to withholding requirements imposed by section 3406 (backup withholding). Thus, in the case of an entity that is disregarded as an entity separate from its owner for any purpose under this section, the owner is subject to the withholding requirements imposed by section 3406 (backup withholding).

(2) Paragraph (c)(2)(i) of this section applies to taxes imposed under subtitle A of the Code, including Chapter 2—Tax on Self-Employment Income. Thus, an entity that is treated in the same manner as a sole proprietorship under paragraph (a) of this section is not treated as a corporation for purposes of employing its owner; instead, the entity is disregarded as an entity separate from its owner for this purpose and is not the employer of its owner. The owner will be subject to self-employment tax on self-employment income with respect to the entity's activities. Also, if a partnership is the owner of an entity that is disregarded as an entity separate from its owner for any purpose under this section, the entity is not treated as a corporation for purposes of employing a partner of the partnership that owns the entity; instead, the entity is disregarded as an entity separate from the partnership for this purpose and is not the employer of any partner of the partnership that owns the entity. A partner of a partnership that owns an entity that is disregarded as an entity separate from its owner for any purpose under this section is subject to the same self-employment tax rules as a partner of a partnership that does not own an entity that is disregarded as an entity separate from its owner for any purpose under this section.

(D) *Example.*—The following example illustrates the application of paragraph (c)(2)(iv) of this section:

*Example.* (i) LLCA is an eligible entity owned by individual A and is generally disregarded as an entity separate from its owner for Federal tax purposes. However, LLCA is treated as an entity separate from its owner for purposes of subtitle C of the Internal Revenue Code. LLCA has employees and pays wages as defined in sections 3121(a), 3306(b), and 3401(a).

(ii) LLCA is subject to the provisions of subtitle C of the Internal Revenue Code and related provisions under 26 CFR subchapter C, Employment Taxes and Collection of Income Tax at Source, parts 31 through 39. Accordingly, LLCA is required to perform such acts as are required of an employer under those provisions of the Internal Revenue Code and regulations thereunder that apply. All provisions of law (including penalties) and the regulations prescribed in pursuance of law applicable to employers in respect of such acts are applicable to LLCA. Thus, for example, LLCA is liable for income tax withholding, Federal Insurance Contributions Act (FICA) taxes, and Federal Unemployment Tax Act (FUTA) taxes. See sections 3402 and 3403 (relating to income tax withholding); 3102(b) and 3111 (relating to FICA taxes), and 3301 (relating to FUTA taxes). In addition, LLCA must file under its name and EIN the applicable Forms in the 94X series, for example, Form 941, "Employer's Quarterly Employment Tax Return," Form 940, "Employer's Annual Federal Unemployment Tax Return;" file with the Social Security Administration and furnish to LLCA's employees statements on Forms W-2, "Wage and Tax Statement;" and make timely employment tax deposits. See § § 31.6011(a)-1, 31.6011(a)-3, 31.6051-1, 31.6051-2, and 31.6302-1 of this chapter.

(iii) A is self-employed for purposes of subtitle A, chapter 2, Tax on Self-Employment Income, of the Internal Revenue Code. Thus, A is subject to tax under section 1401 on A's net earnings from self-employment with respect to LLCA's activities. A is not an employee of LLCA for purposes of subtitle C of the Internal Revenue Code. Because LLCA is treated as a sole proprietorship of A for income tax purposes, A is entitled to deduct trade or business expenses paid or incurred with respect to activities carried on through LLCA, including the employer's share of employment taxes imposed under sections 3111 and 3301, on A's Form 1040, Schedule C, "Profit or Loss for Business (Sole Proprietorship)."

(v) *Special rule for certain excise tax purposes.*—(A) *In general.*—Paragraph (c)(2)(i) of this section (relating to certain wholly owned entities) does not apply for purposes of—

(1) Federal tax liabilities imposed by Chapters 31, 32 (other than section 4181), 33, 34, 35, 36 (other than section 4461), 38, and 49 of the Internal Revenue Code, or any floor stocks tax imposed on articles subject to any of these taxes;

(2) Collection of tax imposed by Chapters 33 and 49 of the Internal Revenue Code;

(3) Registration under sections 4101, 4222, and 4412;

(4) Claims of a credit (other than a credit under section 34), refund, or payment related to a tax described in paragraph (c)(2)(v)(A)(1) of this section or under section 6426 or 6427; and

(5) Assessment and collection of an assessable payment imposed by section 4980H and reporting required by section 6056.

(B) *Treatment of entity.*—An entity that is disregarded as an entity separate from its owner for any purpose under this section is treated as a corporation with respect to items described in paragraph (c)(2)(v)(A) of this section.

(C) *Example.*—The following example illustrates the provisions of this paragraph (c)(2)(v):

*Example.* (i) LLCB is an eligible entity that has a single owner, B. LLCB is generally disregarded as an entity separate from its owner. However, under paragraph (c)(2)(v) of this section, LLCB is treated as an entity separate from its owner for certain purposes relating to excise taxes.

(ii) LLCB mines coal from a coal mine located in the United States. Section 4121 of chapter 32 of the Internal Revenue Code imposes a tax on the producer's sale of such coal. Section 48.4121-1(a) of this chapter defines a "producer" generally as the person in whom is vested ownership of the coal under state law immediately after the coal is severed from the ground. LLCB is the person that owns the coal under state law immediately after it is severed from the ground. Under paragraph (c)(2)(v)(A)(1) of this section, LLCB is the producer of the coal and is liable for tax on its sale of such coal under chapter 32 of the Internal Revenue Code. LLCB must report and pay tax on Form 720, "Quarterly Federal Excise Tax Return," under its own name and taxpayer identification number.

(iii) LLCB uses undyed diesel fuel in an earthmover that is not registered or required to be registered for highway use. Such use is an off-highway business use of the fuel. Under section 6427(l), the ultimate purchaser is allowed to claim an income tax credit or payment related to the tax imposed on diesel fuel used in an off-highway business use. Under paragraph (c)(2)(v) of this section, for purposes of the credit or payment allowed under section 6427(l), LLCB is the person that could claim the amount on its Form 720 or on a Form 8849, "Claim for Refund of Excise Taxes." Alternatively, if LLCB did not claim a payment during the time prescribed in section 6427(i)(2) for making a claim under section 6427, §1.34-1 of this chapter provides that B, the owner of LLCB, could claim the income tax credit allowed under section 34 for the nontaxable use of diesel fuel by LLCB.

(iv) Assume the same facts as in paragraph (c)(2)(v)(C) *Example* (i) and (ii) of this section. If LLCB does not pay the tax on its sale of coal under chapter 32 of the Internal Revenue Code, any notice of lien the Internal Revenue Service files will be filed as if LLCB were a corporation.

(vi) *Special rule for reporting under section 6038A.*—(A) *In general.*—An entity that is disregarded as an entity separate from its owner for any purpose under this section is treated as an entity separate from its owner and classified as a corporation for purposes of section 6038A if—

(1) The entity is a domestic entity; and

(2) One foreign person has direct or indirect sole ownership of the entity.

(B) *Definitions.*—(1) *Indirect sole ownership.*—For purposes of paragraph (c)(2)(vi)(A)(2) of this section, indirect sole ownership means ownership by one person entirely through one or more other entities disregarded as entities separate from their owners or through one or more grantor trusts, regardless of whether any such disregarded entity or grantor trust is domestic or foreign.

(2) *Entity disregarded as separate from its owner.*—For purposes of paragraph (c)(2)(vi)(B)(1) of this section, an entity disregarded as an entity separate from its owner is an entity described in paragraph (c)(2)(i) of this section.

(3) *Grantor trust.*—For purposes of paragraph (c)(2)(vi)(B)(1) of this section, a grantor trust is any portion of a trust that is treated as owned by the grantor or another person under subpart E of subchapter J of chapter 1 of the Code.

(C) *Taxable year.*—The taxable year of an entity classified as a corporation for section 6038A purposes pursuant to paragraph (c)(2)(vi)(A) of this section is—

(1) The same as the taxable year of the foreign person described in paragraph (c)(2)(vi)(A)(2) of this section, if that foreign person has a U.S. income tax or information return filing obligation for its taxable year; or

(2) The calendar year, if paragraph (c)(2)(vi)(C)(1) of this section does not apply, unless otherwise provided in forms, instructions, or published guidance.

(d) *Special rule for certain foreign business entities.*—(1) *In general.*—Except as provided in paragraph (d)(3) of this section, a foreign business entity described in paragraph (b)(8)(i) of this section will not be treated as a corporation under paragraph (b)(8)(i) of this section if—

(i) The entity was in existence on May 8, 1996;

(ii) The entity's classification was relevant (as defined in §301.7701-3(d)) on May 8, 1996;

(iii) No person (including the entity) for whom the entity's classification was relevant on May 8, 1996, treats the entity as a corporation for purposes of filing such person's federal income tax returns, information returns, and withholding documents for the taxable year including May 8, 1996;

(iv) Any change in the entity's claimed classification within the sixty months prior to May 8, 1996, occurred solely as a result of a change in the organizational documents of the entity, and the entity and all members of the entity recognized the federal tax consequences of any change in the entity's classification within the sixty months prior to May 8, 1996;

(v) A reasonable basis (within the meaning of section 6662) existed on May 8, 1996, for treating the entity as other than a corporation; and

(vi) Neither the entity nor any member was notified in writing on or before May 8, 1996, that the classification of the entity was under examination (in which case the entity's classification will be determined in the examination).

(2) *Binding contract rule.*—If a foreign business entity described in paragraph (b)(8)(i) of this section is formed after May 8, 1996, pursuant to a written binding contract (including an accepted bid to develop a project) in effect on May 8, 1996, and all times thereafter, in which the parties agreed to engage (directly or indirectly) in an active and substantial business operation in the jurisdiction in which the

entity is formed, paragraph (d)(1) of this section will be applied to that entity by substituting the date of the entity's formation for May 8, 1996.

(3) *Termination of grandfather status.*—(i) *In general.*—An entity that is not treated as a corporation under paragraph (b)(8)(i) of this section by reason of paragraph (d)(1) or (d)(2) of this section will be treated permanently as a corporation under paragraph (b)(8)(i) of this section from the earliest of:

(A) The effective date of an election to be treated as an association under § 301.7701-3;

(B) A termination of the partnership under section 708(b)(1)(B) (regarding sale or exchange of 50 percent or more of the total interest in an entity's capital or profits within a twelve month period);

(C) A division of the partnership under section 708(b)(2)(B); or

(D) The date any person or persons, who were not owners of the entity as of November 29, 1999, own in the aggregate a 50 percent or greater interest in the entity.

(ii) *Special rule for certain entities.*—For purposes of paragraph (d)(2) of this section, paragraph (d)(3)(i)(B) of this section shall not apply if the sale or exchange of interests in the entity is to a related person (within the meaning of sections 267(b) and 707(b)) and occurs no later than twelve months after the date of the formation of the entity.

(e) *Effective/applicability date.*—(1) Except as otherwise provided in this paragraph (e), the rules of this section apply as of January 1, 1997, except that paragraph (b)(6) of this section applies on or after January 14, 2002, to a business entity wholly owned by a foreign government regardless of any prior entity classification, and paragraph (c)(2)(ii) of this section applies to taxable years beginning after January 12, 2001. The reference to the Finnish, Maltese, and Norwegian entities in paragraph (b)(8)(i) of this section is applicable on November 29, 1999. The reference to the Trinidadian entity in paragraph (b)(8)(i) of this section applies to entities formed on or after November 29, 1999. Any Maltese or Norwegian entity that becomes an eligible entity as a result of paragraph (b)(8)(i) of this section in effect on November 29, 1999, may elect by February 14, 2000, to be classified for Federal tax purposes as an entity other than a corporation retroactive to any period from and including January 1, 1997. Any Finnish entity that becomes an eligible entity as a result of paragraph (b)(8)(i) of this section in effect on November 29, 1999, may elect by February 14, 2000, to be classified for Federal tax purposes as an entity other than a corporation retroactive to any period from and including September 1, 1997. However, paragraph (d)(3)(i)(D) of this section applies on or after October 22, 2003.

(2) Paragraph (c)(2)(iii) of this section applies on and after September 14, 2009. For rules that apply before September 14, 2009, see 26 CFR part 301, revised as of April 1, 2009.

(3)(i) *General rule.*—Except as provided in paragraph (e)(3)(ii) of this section, the rules of paragraph (b)(9) of this section apply as of August 12, 2004, to all business entities existing on or after that date.

(ii) *Transition rule.*—For business entities created or organized under the laws of more than one jurisdiction as of August 12, 2004, the rules of paragraph (b)(9) of this section apply as of May 1, 2006. These entities, however, may rely on the rules of paragraph (b)(9) of this section as of August 12, 2004.

(4) The reference to the Estonian, Latvian, Liechtenstein, Lithuanian, and Slovenian entities in paragraph (b)(8)(i) of this section applies to such entities formed on or after October 7, 2004, and to any such entity formed before such date from the date any person or persons, who were not owners of the entity as of October 7, 2004, own in the aggregate a 50 percent or greater interest in the entity. The reference to the European Economic Area/European Union entity in paragraph (b)(8)(i) of this section applies to such entities formed on or after October 8, 2004.

(5)(i) Except as provided in this paragraph (e)(5), paragraph (c)(2)(iv) of this section applies with respect to wages paid on or after January 1, 2009.

(ii) Paragraph (c)(2)(iv)(B) applies with respect to wages paid on or after September 14, 2009. For rules that apply before September 14, 2009, see 26 CFR part 301 revised as of April 1, 2009.

(iii) Paragraph (c)(2)(iv)(C)(*1*) of this section applies with respect to wages paid on or after November 1, 2011. For rules that apply before November 1, 2011, see 26 CFR part 301, revised as of April 1, 2011. However, taxpayers may apply paragraph (c)(2)(iv)(C)(*1*) of this section with respect to wages paid on or after January 1, 2009.

(6)(i) Except as provided in this paragraph (e)(6), paragraph (c)(2)(v) of this section applies to liabilities imposed and actions first

required or permitted in periods beginning on or after January 1, 2008.

(ii) Paragraphs (c)(2)(v)(B) and (c)(2)(v)(C) *Example* (iv) of this section apply on and after September 14, 2009.

(iii) Paragraph (c)(2)(v)(A)(5) of this section applies for periods after December 31, 2014.

(iv) References to Chapter 49 in paragraph (c)(2)(v) of this section apply to taxes imposed on amounts paid on or after July 1, 2012.

(7) The reference to the Bulgarian entity in paragraph (b)(8)(i) of this section applies to such entities formed on or after January 1, 2007, and to any such entity formed before such date from the date that, in the aggregate, a 50 percent or more interest in such entity is owned by any person or persons who were not owners of the entity as of January 1, 2007. For purposes of the preceding sentence, the term *interest* means—

(i) In the case of a partnership, a capital or profits interest; and

(ii) In the case of a corporation, an equity interest measured by vote or value.

(8) Paragraph (c)(2)(iv)(C)(2) of this section applies on the later of—

(i) August 1, 2016; or

(ii) The first day of the latest-starting plan year beginning after May 4, 2016, and on or before May 4, 2017, of an affected plan (based on the plans adopted before, and the plan year in effect as of, May 4, 2016) sponsored by an entity that is disregarded as an entity separate from its owner for any purpose under this section. For rules that apply before the applicability date of paragraph (c)(2)(iv)(C)(2) of this section, see 26 CFR part 301 revised as of April 1, 2016. For the purposes of this paragraph (e)(8)—

(A) An affected plan includes any qualified plan, health plan, or section 125 cafeteria plan if the plan benefits participants whose employment status is affected by paragraph (c)(2)(iv)(C)(2) of this section;

(B) A qualified plan means a plan, contract, pension, or trust described in paragraph (A) or (B) of section 219(g)(5) (other than paragraph (A)(iii)); and

(C) A health plan means an arrangement described under § 1.105-5 of this chapter.

(9) *Reporting required under section 6038A.*—Paragraph (c)(2)(vi) of this section applies to taxable years of entities beginning after December 31, 2016, and ending on or after December 13, 2017. [Reg. § 301.7701-2.]

☐ [*T.D.* 6503, 11-15-60. *Amended by T.D.* 6797, 2-2-65; *T.D.* 7515, 10-17-77; *T.D.* 7889, 4-25-83; *T.D.* 8475, 5-13-93; *T.D.* 8697, 12-17-96 (*corrected* 4-3-2008); *T.D.* 8844, 11-26-99; *T.D.* 9012, 7-31-2002; *T.D.* 9093, 10-21-2003; *T.D.* 9153, 8-11-2004; *T.D.* 9183, 2-24-2005 *T.D.* 9197, 4-13-2005; *T.D.* 9235, 12-15-2005; *T.D.* 9246, 1-27-2006; *T.D.* 9356, 8-15-2007; *T.D.* 9388, 3-20-2008; *T.D.* 9433, 11-26-2008; *T.D.* 9462, 9-11-2009; *T.D.* 9553, 10-25-2011; *T.D.* 9554, 10-31-2011; *T.D.* 9596, 6-22-2012; *T.D.* 9655, 2-10-2014, *T.D.* 9670, 6-25-2014, *T.D.* 9766, 5-3-2016, *T.D.* 9796, 12-12-2016 and *T.D.* 9869, 6-28-2019.]

### [Reg. § 301.7701-3]

**§ 301.7701-3. Classification of certain business entities.**—(a) *In general.*—A business entity that is not classified as a corporation under § 301.7701-2(b)(1), (3), (4), (5), (6), (7), or (8) (an *eligible entity*) can elect its classification for federal tax purposes as provided in this section. An eligible entity with at least two members can elect to be classified as either an association (and thus a corporation under § 301.7701-2(b)(2)) or a partnership, and an eligible entity with a single owner can elect to be classified as an association or to be disregarded as an entity separate from its owner. Paragraph (b) of this section provides a default classification for an eligible entity that does not make an election. Thus, elections are necessary only when an eligible entity chooses to be classified initially as other than the default classification or when an eligible entity chooses to change its classification. An entity whose classification is determined under the default classification retains that classification (regardless of any changes in the members' liability that occurs at any time during the time that the entity's classification is relevant as defined in paragraph (d) of this section) until the entity makes an election to change that classification under paragraph (c)(1) of this section. Paragraph (c) of this section provides rules for making express elections, including a rule under which a domestic eligible entity that elects to be classified as an association consents to be subject to the dual consolidated loss rules of section 1503(d). Paragraph (e) of this section provides special rules for classifying entities resulting from partnership terminations and divisions under section 708(b). Paragraph (f) of this section sets forth the effective date of this section and a special rule relating to prior periods.

(b) *Classification of eligible entities that do not file an election.*—(1) *Domestic eligible entities.*—Except as provided in paragraph (b)(3) of this section, unless the entity elects otherwise, a domestic eligible entity is—

(i) A partnership if it has two or more members; or

(ii) Disregarded as an entity separate from its owner if it has a single owner.

(2) *Foreign eligible entities.*—(i) *In general.*—Except as provided in paragraph (b)(3) of this section, unless the entity elects otherwise, a foreign eligible entity is—

(A) A partnership if it has two or more members and at least one member does not have limited liability;

(B) An association if all members have limited liability; or

(C) Disregarded as an entity separate from its owner if it has a single owner that does not have limited liability.

(ii) *Definition of limited liability.*—For purposes of paragraph (b)(2)(i) of this section, a member of a foreign eligible entity has limited liability if the member has no personal liability for the debts of or claims against the entity by reason of being a member. This determination is based solely on the statute or law pursuant to which the entity is organized, except that if the underlying statute or law allows the entity to specify in its organizational documents whether the members will have limited liability, the organizational documents may also be relevant. For purposes of this section, a member has personal liability if the creditors of the entity may seek satisfaction of all or any portion of the debts or claims against the entity from the member as such. A member has personal liability for purposes of this paragraph even if the member makes an agreement under which another person (whether or not a member of the entity) assumes such liability or agrees to indemnify that member for any such liability.

(3) *Existing eligible entities.*—(i) *In general.*—Unless the entity elects otherwise, an eligible entity in existence prior to the effective date of this section will have the same classification that the entity claimed under §§301.7701-1 through 301.7701-3 as in effect on the date prior to the effective date of this section; except that if an eligible entity with a single owner claimed to be a partnership under those regulations, the entity will be disregarded as an entity separate from its owner under this paragraph (b)(3)(i). For special rules regarding the classification of such entities prior to the effective date of this section, see paragraph (h)(2) of this section.

(ii) *Special rules.*—For purposes of paragraph (b)(3)(i) of this section, a foreign eligible entity is treated as being in existence prior to the effective date of this section only if the entity's classification was relevant (as defined in paragraph (d) of this section) at any time during the sixty months prior to the effective date of this section. If an entity claimed different classifications prior to the effective date of this section, the entity's classification for purposes of paragraph (b)(3)(i) of this section is the last classification claimed by the entity. If a foreign eligible entity's classification is relevant prior to the effective date of this section, but no federal tax or information return is filed or the federal tax or information return does not indicate the classification of the entity, the entity's classification for the period prior to the effective date of this section is determined under the regulations in effect on the date prior to the effective date of this section.

(c) *Elections.*—(1) *Time and place for filing.*—(i) *In general.*—Except as provided in paragraphs (c)(1)(iv) and (v) of this section, an eligible entity may elect to be classified other than as provided under paragraph (b) of this section, or to change its classification, by filing Form 8832, Entity Classification Election, with the service center designated on Form 8832. An election will not be accepted unless all of the information required by the form and instructions, including the taxpayer identifying number of the entity, is provided on Form 8832. See §301.6109-1 for rules on applying for and displaying Employer Identification Numbers.

(ii) *Further notification of elections.*—An eligible entity required to file a Federal tax or information return for the taxable year for which an election is made under §301.7701-3(c)(1)(i) must attach a copy of its Form 8832 to its Federal tax or information return for that year. If the entity is not required to file a return for that year, a copy of its Form 8832 ("Entity Classification Election") must be attached to the Federal income tax or information return of any direct or indirect owner of the entity for the taxable year of the owner that includes the date on which the election was effective. An indirect owner of the entity does not have to attach a copy of the Form 8832 to its return if an entity in which it has an interest is already filing a copy of the Form 8832 with its return. If an entity, or one of its direct or indirect owners, fails to attach a copy of a Form 8832 to its return as directed in this section, an otherwise valid election under §301.7701-3(c)(1)(i) will not be invalidated, but the non-filing party may be subject to

penalties, including any applicable penalties if the Federal tax or information returns are inconsistent with the entity's election under §301.7701-3(c)(1)(i). In the case of returns for taxable years beginning after December 31, 2002, the copy of Form 8832 attached to a return pursuant to this paragraph (c)(1)(ii) is not required to be a signed copy.

(iii) *Effective date of election.*—An election made under paragraph (c)(1)(i) of this section will be effective on the date specified by the entity on Form 8832 or on the date filed if no such date is specified on the election form. The effective date specified on Form 8832 can not be more than 75 days prior to the date on which the election is filed and can not be more than 12 months after the date on which the election is filed. If an election specifies an effective date more than 75 days prior to the date on which the election is filed, it will be effective 75 days prior to the date it was filed. If an election specifies an effective date more than 12 months from the date on which the election is filed, it will be effective 12 months after the date it was filed. If an election specifies an effective date before January 1, 1997, it will be effective as of January 1, 1997. If a purchasing corporation makes an election under section 338 regarding an acquired subsidiary, an election under paragraph (c)(1)(i) of this section for the acquired subsidiary can be effective no earlier than the day after the acquisition date (within the meaning of section 338(h)(2)).

(iv) *Limitation.*—If an eligible entity makes an election under paragraph (c)(1)(i) of this section to change its classification (other than an election made by an existing entity to change its classification as of the effective date of this section), the entity cannot change its classification by election again during the sixty months succeeding the effective date of the election. However, the Commissioner may permit the entity to change its classification by election within the sixty months if more than fifty percent of the ownership interests in the entity as of the effective date of the subsequent election are owned by persons that did not own any interests in the entity on the filing date or on the effective date of the entity's prior election. An election by a newly formed eligible entity that is effective on the date of formation is not considered a change for purposes of this paragraph (c)(1)(iv).

(v) *Deemed elections.*—(A) *Exempt organizations.*—An eligible entity that has been determined to be, or claims to be, exempt from taxation under section 501(a) is treated as having made an election under this section to be classified as an association. Such election will be effective as of the first day for which exemption is claimed or determined to apply, regardless of when the claim or determination is made, and will remain in effect unless an election is made under paragraph (c)(1)(i) of this section after the date the claim for exempt status is withdrawn or rejected or the date the determination of exempt status is revoked.

(B) *Real estate investment trusts.*—An eligible entity that files an election under section 856(c)(1) to be treated as a real estate investment trust is treated as having made an election under this section to be classified as an association. Such election will be effective as of the first day the entity is treated as a real estate investment trust.

(C) *S corporations.*—An eligible entity that timely elects to be an S corporation under section 1362(a)(1) is treated as having made an election under this section to be classified as an association, provided that (as of the effective date of the election under section 1362(a)(1)) the entity meets all other requirements to qualify as a small business corporation under section 1361(b). Subject to §301.7701-3(c)(1)(iv), the deemed election to be classified as an association will apply as of the effective date of the S corporation election and will remain in effect until the entity makes a valid election, under §301.7701-3(c)(1)(i), to be classified as other than an association.

(vi) *Examples.*—The following examples illustrate the rules of this paragraph (c)(1):

*Example 1.* On July 1, 1998, X, a domestic corporation, purchases a 10% interest in Y, an eligible entity formed under Country A law in 1990. The entity's classification was not relevant to any person for federal tax or information purposes prior to X's acquisition of an interest in Y. Thus, Y is not considered to be in existence on the effective date of this section for purposes of paragraph (b)(3) of this section. Under the applicable Country A statute, all members of Y have limited liability as defined in paragraph (b)(2)(ii) of this section. Accordingly, Y is classified as an association under paragraph (b)(2)(i)(B) of this section unless it elects under this paragraph (c) to be classified as a partnership. To be classified as a partnership as of July 1, 1998, Y must file a Form 8832 by September 14, 1998. See paragraph (c)(1)(i) of this section. Because an election cannot be effective more than 75 days prior to the date on which it is filed, if Y files its Form 8832 after September 14, 1998, it will be classified as an association from July 1, 1998, until the effective date of the election. In that case, it could not change its classification by election under this paragraph (c) during the sixty months succeeding the effective date of the election.

*Example 2.* (i) Z is an eligible entity formed under Country B law and is in existence on the effective date of this section within the meaning of paragraph (b)(3) of this section. Prior to the effective date of this section, Z claimed to be classified as an association. Unless Z files an election under this paragraph (c), it will continue to be classified as an association under paragraph (b)(3) of this section.

(ii) Z files a Form 8832 pursuant to this paragraph (c) to be classified as a partnership, effective as of the effective date of this section. Z can file an election to be classified as an association at any time thereafter, but then would not be permitted to change its classification by election during the sixty months succeeding the effective date of that subsequent election.

(2) *Authorized signatures.*—(i) *In general.*—An election made under paragraph (c)(1)(i) of this section must be signed by—

(A) Each member of the electing entity who is an owner at the time the election is filed; or

(B) Any officer, manager, or member of the electing entity who is authorized (under local law or the entity's organizational documents) to make the election and who represents to having such authorization under penalties of perjury.

(ii) *Retroactive elections.*—For purposes of paragraph (c)(2)(i) of this section, if an election under paragraph (c)(1)(i) of this section is to be effective for any period prior to the time that it is filed, each person who was an owner between the date the election is to be effective and the date the election is filed, and who is not an owner at the time the election is filed, must also sign the election.

(iii) *Changes in classification.*—For paragraph (c)(2)(i) of this section, if an election under paragraph (c)(1)(i) of this section is made to change the classification of an entity, each person who was an owner on the date that any transactions under paragraph (g) of this section are deemed to occur, and who is not an owner at the time the election is filed, must also sign the election. This paragraph (c)(2)(iii) applies to elections filed on or after November 29, 1999.

(3) *Consent to be subject to section 1503(d).*—(i) *Rule.*—A domestic eligible entity that elects to be classified as an association consents to be treated as a dual resident corporation for purposes of section 1503(d) (such an entity, a *domestic consenting corporation*), for any taxable year for which it is classified as an association and the condition set forth in § 1.1503(d)-1(c)(1) of this chapter is satisfied.

(ii) *Transition rule — deemed consent.*—If, as a result of the applicability date (see paragraph (c)(3)(iii) of this section) relating to paragraph (c)(3)(i) of this section, a domestic eligible entity that is classified as an association has not consented to be treated as a domestic consenting corporation pursuant to paragraph (c)(3)(i) of this section, then the domestic eligible entity is deemed to consent to be so treated as of its first taxable year beginning on or after December 20, 2019. The first sentence of this paragraph (c)(3)(ii) does not apply if the domestic eligible entity elects, on or after December 20, 2018 and effective before its first taxable year beginning on or after December 20, 2019, to be classified as a partnership or disregarded entity such that it ceases to be a domestic eligible entity that is classified as an association. For purposes of the election described in the second sentence of this paragraph (c)(3)(ii), the sixty month limitation under paragraph (c)(1)(iv) of this section is waived.

(iii) *Applicability date.*—The sixth sentence of paragraph (a) of this section and paragraph (c)(3)(i) of this section apply to a domestic eligible entity that on or after December 20, 2018 files an election to be classified as an association (regardless of whether the election is effective before December 20, 2018). Paragraph (c)(3)(ii) of this section applies as of December 20, 2018.

(d) *Special rules for foreign eligible entities.*—(1) *Definition of relevance.*—(i) *General rule.*—For purposes of this section, a foreign eligible entity's classification is relevant when its classification affects the liability of any person for federal tax or information purposes. For example, a foreign entity's classification would be relevant if U.S. income was paid to the entity and the determination by the withholding agent of the amount to be withheld under chapter 3 of the Internal Revenue Code (if any) would vary depending upon whether the entity is classified as a partnership or as an association. Thus, the classification might affect the documentation that the withholding agent must receive from the entity, the type of tax or information return to file, or how the return must be prepared. The date that the classification of a foreign eligible entity is relevant is the date an event occurs that creates an obligation to file a federal tax return, information return, or statement for which the classification of the

entity must be determined. Thus, the classification of a foreign entity is relevant, for example, on the date that an interest in the entity is acquired which will require a U.S. person to file an information return on Form 5471.

(ii) *Deemed relevance.*—(A) *General rule.*—For purposes of this section, except as provided in paragraph (d)(1)(ii)(B) of this section, the classification for Federal tax purposes of a foreign eligible entity that files Form 8832, "Entity Classification Election", shall be deemed to be relevant only on the date the entity classification election is effective.

(B) *Exception.*—If the classification of a foreign eligible entity is relevant within the meaning of paragraph (d)(1)(i) of this section, then the rule in paragraph (d)(1)(ii)(A) of this section shall not apply.

(2) *Entities the classification of which has never been relevant.*—If the classification of a foreign eligible entity has never been relevant (as defined in paragraph (d)(1) of this section), then the entity's classification will initially be determined pursuant to the provisions of paragraph (b)(2) of this section when the classification of the entity first becomes relevant (as defined in paragraph (d)(1)(i) of this section).

(3) *Special rule when classification is no longer relevant.*—If the classification of a foreign eligible entity is not relevant (as defined in paragraph (d)(1) of this section) for 60 consecutive months, then the entity's classification will initially be determined pursuant to the provisions of paragraph (b)(2) of this section when the classification of the foreign eligible entity becomes relevant (as defined in paragraph (d)(1)(i) of this section). The date that the classification of a foreign entity is not relevant is the date an event occurs that causes the classification to no longer be relevant, or, if no event occurs in a taxable year that causes the classification to be relevant, then the date is the first day of that taxable year.

(4) *Effective date.*—Paragraphs (d)(1)(ii), (d)(2), and (d)(3) of this section apply on or after October 22, 2003.

(e) *Coordination with section 708(b).*—Except as provided in § 301.7701-2(d)(3) (regarding termination of grandfather status for certain foreign business entities), an entity resulting from a transaction described in section 708(b)(1)(B) (partnership termination due to sales or exchanges) or section 708(b)(2)(B) (partnership division) is a partnership.

(f) *Changes in number of members of an entity.*—(1) *Associations.*—The classification of an eligible entity as an association is not affected by any change in the number of members of the entity.

(2) *Partnerships and single member entities.*—An eligible entity classified as a partnership becomes disregarded as an entity separate from its owner when the entity's membership is reduced to one member. A single member entity disregarded as an entity separate from its owner is classified as a partnership when the entity has more than one member. If an elective classification change under paragraph (c) of this section is effective at the same time as a membership change described in this paragraph (f)(2), the deemed transactions in paragraph (g) of this section resulting from the elective change preempt the transactions that would result from the change in membership.

(3) *Effect on sixty month limitation.*—A change in the number of members of an entity does not result in the creation of a new entity for purposes of the sixty month limitation on elections under paragraph (c)(1)(iv) of this section.

(4) *Examples.*—The following examples illustrate the application of this paragraph (f):

*Example 1.* A, a U.S. person, owns a domestic eligible entity that is disregarded as an entity separate from its owner. On January 1, 1998, B, a U.S. person, buys a 50 percent interest in the entity from A. Under this paragraph (f), the entity is classified as a partnership when B acquires an interest in the entity. However, A and B elect to have the entity classified as an association effective on January 1, 1998. Thus, B is treated as buying shares of stock on January 1, 1998. (Under paragraph (c)(1)(iv) of this section, this election is treated as a change in classification so that the entity generally cannot change its classification by election again during the sixty months succeeding the effective date of the election.) Under paragraph (g)(1) of this section, A is treated as contributing the assets and liabilities of the entity to the newly formed association immediately before the close of December 31, 1997. Because A does not retain control of the association as required by section 351, A's contribution will be a taxable event. Therefore, under section 1012, the association will take a fair market value basis in the assets contributed by A, and A will have a fair market value basis in the stock received. A will have no additional gain upon the sale of stock to *B*, and *B* will have a cost basis in the stock purchased from *A*.

*Example 2.* (i) On April 1, 1998, *A* and *B*, U.S. persons, form *X*, a foreign eligible entity. *X* is treated as an association under the default provisions of paragraph (b)(2)(i) of this section, and *X* does not make an election to be classified as a partnership. *A* subsequently purchases all of *B*'s interest in *X*.

(ii) Under paragraph (f)(1) of this section, *X* continues to be classified as an association. *X*, however, can subsequently elect to be disregarded as an entity separate from *A*. The sixty month limitation of paragraph (c)(1)(iv) of this section does not prevent *X* from making an election because *X* has not made a prior election under paragraph (c)(1)(i) of this section.

*Example 3.* (i) On April 1, 1998, *A* and *B*, U.S. persons, form *X*, a foreign eligible entity. *X* is treated as an association under the default provisions of paragraph (b)(2)(i) of this section, and *X* does not make an election to be classified as a partnership. On January 1, 1999, *X* elects to be classified as a partnership effective on that date. Under the sixty month limitation of paragraph (c)(1)(iv) of this section, *X* cannot elect to be classified as an association until January 1, 2004 (i.e., sixty months after the effective date of the election to be classified as a partnership).

(ii) On June 1, 2000, *A* purchases all of *B*'s interest in *X*. After *A*'s purchase of *B*'s interest, *X* can no longer be classified as a partnership because *X* has only one member. Under paragraph (f)(2) of this section, *X* is disregarded as an entity separate from *A* when *A* becomes the only member of *X*. *X*, however, is not treated as a new entity for purposes of paragraph (c)(1)(iv) of this section. As a result, the sixty month limitation of paragraph (c)(1)(iv) of this section continues to apply to *X*, and *X* cannot elect to be classified as an association until January 1, 2004 (i.e., sixty months after January 1, 1999, the effective date of the election by *X* to be classified as a partnership).

(5) *Effective date.*—This paragraph (f) applies as of November 29, 1999.

(g) *Elective changes in classification.*—(1) *Deemed treatment of elective change.*—(i) *Partnership to association.*—If an eligible entity classified as a partnership elects under paragraph (c)(1)(i) of this section to be classified as an association, the following is deemed to occur: The partnership contributes all of its assets and liabilities to the association in exchange for stock in the association, and immediately thereafter, the partnership liquidates by distributing the stock of the association to its partners.

(ii) *Association to partnership.*—If an eligible entity classified as an association elects under paragraph (c)(1)(i) of this section to be classified as a partnership, the following is deemed to occur: The association distributes all of its assets and liabilities to its shareholders in liquidation of the association, and immediately thereafter, the shareholders contribute all of the distributed assets and liabilities to a newly formed partnership.

(iii) *Association to disregarded entity.*—If an eligible entity classified as an association elects under paragraph (c)(1)(i) of this section to be disregarded as an entity separate from its owner, the following is deemed to occur: The association distributes all of its assets and liabilities to its single owner in liquidation of the association.

(iv) *Disregarded entity to an association.*—If an eligible entity that is disregarded as an entity separate from its owner elects under paragraph (c)(1)(i) of this section to be classified as an association, the following is deemed to occur: The owner of the eligible entity contributes all of the assets and liabilities of the entity to the association in exchange for stock of the association.

(2) *Effect of elective changes.*—(i) *In general.*—The tax treatment of a change in the classification of an entity for federal tax purposes by election under paragraph (c)(1)(i) of this section is determined under all relevant provisions of the Internal Revenue Code and general principles of tax law, including the step transaction doctrine.

(ii) *Adoption of plan of liquidation.*—For purposes of satisfying the requirement of adoption of a plan of liquidation under section 332, unless a formal plan of liquidation that contemplates the election to be classified as a partnership or to be disregarded as an entity separate from its owner is adopted on an earlier date, the making, by an association, of an election under paragraph (c)(1)(i) of this section to be classified as a partnership or to be disregarded as an entity separate from its owner is considered to be the adoption of a plan of liquidation immediately before the deemed liquidation described in paragraph (g)(1)(ii) or (iii) of this section. This paragraph (g)(2)(ii) applies to elections filed on or after December 17, 2001. Taxpayers may apply this paragraph (g)(2)(ii) retroactively to elections filed before December 17, 2001, if the corporate owner claiming treatment under section 332 and its subsidiary making the election take consis-

tent positions with respect to the federal tax consequences of the election.

(3) *Timing of election.*—(i) *In general.*—An election under paragraph (c)(1)(i) of this section that changes the classification of an eligible entity for federal tax purposes is treated as occurring at the start of the day for which the election is effective. Any transactions that are deemed to occur under this paragraph (g) as a result of a change in classification are treated as occurring immediately before the close of the day before the election is effective. For example, if an election is made to change the classification of an entity from an association to a partnership effective on January 1, the deemed transactions specified in paragraph (g)(1)(ii) of this section (including the liquidation of the association) are treated as occurring immediately before the close of December 31 and must be reported by the owners of the entity on December 31. Thus, the last day of the association's taxable year will be December 31 and the first day of the partnership's taxable year will be January 1.

(ii) *Coordination with section 338 election.*—A purchasing corporation that makes a qualified stock purchase of an eligible entity taxed as a corporation may make an election under section 338 regarding the acquisition if it satisfies the requirements for the election, and may also make an election to change the classification of the target corporation. If a taxpayer makes an election under section 338 regarding its acquisition of another entity taxable as a corporation and makes an election under paragraph (c) of this section for the acquired corporation (effective at the earliest possible date as provided by paragraph (c)(1)(iii) of this section), the transactions under paragraph (g) of this section are deemed to occur immediately after the deemed asset purchase by the new target corporation under section 338.

(iii) *Application to successive elections in tiered situations.*—When elections under paragraph (c)(1)(i) of this section for a series of tiered entities are effective on the same date, the eligible entities may specify the order of the elections on Form 8832. If no order is specified for the elections, any transactions that are deemed to occur in this paragraph (g) as a result of the classification change will be treated as occurring first for the highest tier entity's classification change, then for the next highest tier entity's classification change, and so forth down the chain of entities until all the transactions under this paragraph (g) have occurred. For example, Parent, a corporation, wholly owns all of the interest of an eligible entity classified as an association (S1), which wholly owns another eligible entity classified as an association (S2), which wholly owns another eligible entity classified as an association (S3). Elections under paragraph (c)(1)(i) of this section are filed to classify S1, S2, and S3 each as disregarded as an entity separate from its owner effective on the same day. If no order is specified for the elections, the following transactions are deemed to occur under this paragraph (g) as a result of the elections, with each successive transaction occurring on the same day immediately after the preceding transaction: S1 is treated as liquidating into Parent, then S2 is treated as liquidating into Parent, and finally S3 is treated as liquidating into Parent.

(4) *Effective date.*—Except as otherwise provided in paragraph (g)(2)(ii) of this section, this paragraph (g) applies to elections that are filed on or after November 29, 1999. Taxpayers may apply this paragraph (g) retroactively to elections filed before November 29, 1999 if all taxpayers affected by the deemed transactions file consistently with this paragraph (g).

(h) *Effective date.*—(1) *In general.*—Except as otherwise provided in this section, the rules of this section are applicable as of January 1, 1997.

(2) *Prior treatment of existing entities.*—In the case of a business entity that is not described in § 301.7701-2(b)(1), (3), (4), (5), (6), or (7), and that was in existence prior to January 1, 1997, the entity's claimed classification(s) will be respected for all periods prior to January 1, 1997, if—

(i) The entity had a reasonable basis (within the meaning of section 6662) for its claimed classification;

(ii) The entity and all members of the entity recognized the federal tax consequences of any change in the entity's classification within the sixty months prior to January 1, 1997; and

(iii) Neither the entity nor any member was notified in writing on or before May 8, 1996, that the classification of the entity was under examination (in which case the entity's classification will be determined in the examination).

(3) *Deemed elections for S corporations.*—Paragraph (c)(1)(v)(C) of this section applies to timely S corporation elections under section 1362(a) filed on or after July 20, 2004. Eligible entities that filed timely S elections before July 20, 2004 may also rely on the provisions of the regulation. [Reg. § 301.7701-3.]

☐ [*T.D. 6503, 11-15-60. Amended by T.D. 8632, 12-19-95; T.D. 8697, 12-17-96; T.D. 8767, 3-23-98; T.D. 8827, 7-12-99 (corrected 10-29-99); T.D. 8844, 11-26-99; T.D. 8970, 12-14-2001; T.D. 9093, 10-21-2003; T.D. 9100, 12-18-2003; T.D. 9139, 7-19-2004; T.D. 9153, 8-11-2004; T.D. 9203, 5-20-2005 T.D. 9300, 12-7-2006 and T.D. 9896, 4-7-2020.*]

## [Reg. § 301.7701-4]

**§ 301.7701-4. Trusts.**—(a) *Ordinary trusts.*—In general, the term "trust" as used in the Internal Revenue Code refers to an arrangement created either by a will or by an inter vivos declaration whereby trustees take title to property for the purpose of protecting or conserving it for the beneficiaries under the ordinary rules applied in chancery or probate courts. Usually the beneficiaries of such a trust do no more than accept the benefits thereof and are not the voluntary planners or creators of the trust arrangement. However, the beneficiaries of such a trust may be the persons who create it and it will be recognized as a trust under the Internal Revenue Code if it was created for the purpose of protecting or conserving the trust property for beneficiaries who stand in the same relation to the trust as they would if the trust had been created by others for them. Generally speaking, an arrangement will be treated as a trust under the Internal Revenue Code if it can be shown that the purpose of the arrangement is to vest in trustees responsibility for the protection and conservation of property for beneficiaries who cannot share in the discharge of this responsibility and, therefore, are not associates in a joint enterprise for the conduct of business for profit.

(b) *Business trusts.*—There are other arrangements which are known as trusts because the legal title to property is conveyed to trustees for the benefit of beneficiaries, but which are not classified as trusts for purposes of the Internal Revenue Code because they are not simply arrangements to protect or conserve the property for the beneficiaries. These trusts, which are often known as business or commercial trusts, generally are created by the beneficiaries simply as a device to carry on a profit-making business which normally would have been carried on through business organizations that are classified as corporations or partnerships under the Internal Revenue Code. However, the fact that the corpus of the trust is not supplied by the beneficiaries is not sufficient reason in itself for classifying the arrangement as an ordinary trust rather than as an association or partnership. The fact that any organization is technically cast in the trust form, by conveying title to property to trustees for the benefit of persons designated as beneficiaries, will not change the real character of the organization if the organization is more properly classified as a business entity under § 301.7701-2.

(c) *Certain investment trusts.*—(1) An "investment" trust will not be classified as a trust if there is a power under the trust agreement to vary the investment of the certificate holders. *See Commissioner v. North American Bond Trust,* 122 F. 2d 545 [41-2 USTC ¶9644](2d Cir. 1941), *cert. denied,* 314 U.S. 701 (1942). An investment trust with a single class of ownership interests, representing undivided beneficial interests in the assets of the trust, will be classified as a trust if there is no power under the trust agreement to vary the investment of the certificate holders. An investment trust with multiple classes of ownership interests ordinarily will be classified as a business entity under § 301.7701-2; however, an investment trust with multiple classes of ownership interests, in which there is no power under the trust agreement to vary the investment of the certificate holders, will be classified as a trust if the trust is formed to facilitate direct investment in the assets of the trust and the existence of multiple classes of ownership interests is incidental to that purpose.

(2) The provisions of paragraph (c)(1) of this section may be illustrated by the following examples:

*Example (1):* A corporation purchases a portfolio of residential mortgages and transfers the mortgages to a bank under a trust agreement. At the same time, the bank as trustee delivers to the corporation certificates evidencing rights to payments from the pooled mortgages; the corporation sells the certificates to the public. The trustee holds legal title to the mortgages in the pool for the benefit of the certificate holders but has no power to reinvest proceeds attributable to the mortgages in the pool or to vary investments in the pool in any other manner. There are two classes of certificates. Holders of class A certificates are entitled to all payments of mortgage principal, both scheduled and prepaid, until their certificates are retired; holders of class B certificates receive payments of principal only after all class A certificates have been retired. The different rights of the class A and class B certificates serve to shift to the holders of the class A certificates, in addition to the earlier scheduled payments of principal, the risk that mortgages in the pool will be prepaid so that the holders of the class B certificates will have "call protection" (freedom from premature termination of their interests on account of prepayments). The trust thus serves to create investment interests with respect to the mortgages held by the trust that differ significantly from direct investment in the mortgages. As a

consequence, the existence of multiple classes of trust ownership is not incidental to any purpose of the trust to facilitate direct investment, and, accordingly, the trust is classified as a business entity under § 301.7701-2.

*Example (2):* Corporation M is the originator of a portfolio of residential mortgages and transfers the mortgages to a bank under a trust agreement. At the same time, the bank as trustee delivers to M certificates evidencing rights to payments from the pooled mortgages. The trustee holds legal title to the mortgages in the pool for the benefit of the certificate holders, but has no power to reinvest proceeds attributable to the mortgages in the pool or to vary investments in the pool in any other manner. There are two classes of certificates. Holders of class C certificates are entitled to receive 90 percent of the payments of principal and interest on the mortgages; class D certificate holders are entitled to receive the other ten percent. The two classes of certificates are identical except that, in the event of a default on the underlying mortgages, the payment rights of class D certificate holders are subordinated to the rights of class C certificate holders. M sells the class C certificates to investors and retains the class D certificates. The trust has multiple classes of ownership interests, given the greater security provided to holders of class C certificates. The interests of certificate holders, however, are substantially equivalent to undivided interests in the pool of mortgages, coupled with a limited recourse guarantee running from M to the holders of class C certificates. In such circumstances, the existence of multiple classes of ownership interests is incidental to the trust's purpose of facilitating direct investment in the assets of the trust. Accordingly, the trust is classified as a trust.

*Example (3):* A promoter forms a trust in which shareholders of a publicly traded corporation can deposit their stock. For each share of stock deposited with the trust, the participant receives two certificates that are initially attached, but may be separated and traded independently of each other. One certificate represents the right to dividends and the value of the underlying stock up to a specified amount; the other certificate represents the right to appreciation in the stock's value above the specified amount. The separate certificates represent two different classes of ownership interest in the trust, which effectively separate dividend rights on the stock held by the trust from a portion of the right to appreciation in the value of such stock. The multiple classes of ownership interests are designed to permit investors, by transferring one of the certificates and retaining the other, to fulfill their varying investment objectives of seeking primarily either dividend income or capital appreciation from the stock held by the trust. Given that the trust serves to create investment interests with respect to the stock held by the trust that differ significantly from direct investment in such stock, the trust is not formed to facilitate direct investment in the assets of the trust. Accordingly, the trust is classified as a business entity under § 301.7701-2.

*Example (4):* Corporation N purchases a portfolio of bonds and transfers the bonds to a bank under a trust agreement. At the same time, the trustee delivers to N certificates evidencing interests in the bonds. These certificates are sold to public investors. Each certificate represents the right to receive a particular payment with respect to a specific bond. Under section 1286, stripped coupons and stripped bonds are treated as separate bonds for federal income tax purposes. Although the interest of each certificate holder is different from that of each other certificate holder, and the trust thus has multiple classes of ownership, the multiple classes simply provide each certificate holder with a direct interest in what is treated under section 1286 as a separate bond. Given the similarity of the interests acquired by the certificate holders to the interests that could be acquired by direct investment, the multiple classes of trust interests merely facilitate direct investment in the assets held by the trust. Accordingly, the trust is classified as a trust.

(d) *Liquidating trusts.*—Certain organizations which are commonly known as liquidating trusts are treated as trusts for purposes of the Internal Revenue Code. An organization will be considered a liquidating trust if it is organized for the primary purpose of liquidating and distributing the assets transferred to it, and if its activities are all reasonably necessary to, and consistent with, the accomplishment of that purpose. A liquidating trust is treated as a trust for purposes of the Internal Revenue Code because it is formed with the objective of liquidating particular assets and not as an organization having as its purpose the carrying on of a profit-making business which normally would be conducted through business organizations classified as corporations or partnerships. However, if the liquidation is unreasonably prolonged or if the liquidation purpose becomes so obscured by business activities that the declared purpose of liquidation can be said to be lost or abandoned, the status of the organization will no longer be that of a liquidating trust. Bondholders' protective committees, voting trusts, and other agencies formed to protect the interests of security holders during insolvency, bankruptcy, or corporate reorganization proceedings are analogous to liquidating trusts but if subsequently utilized to further the control or profitable operation of a going business on a permanent continuing basis, they will lose their classification as trusts for purposes of the Internal Revenue Code.

(e) *Environmental remediation trusts.*—(1) An environmental remediation trust is considered a trust for purposes of the Internal Revenue Code. For purposes of this paragraph (e), an organization is an environmental remediation trust if the organization is organized under state law as a trust; the primary purpose of the trust is collecting and disbursing amounts for environmental remediation of an existing waste site to resolve, satisfy, mitigate, address, or prevent the liability or potential liability of persons imposed by federal, state, or local environmental laws; all contributors to the trust have (at the time of contribution and thereafter) actual or potential liability or a reasonable expectation of liability under federal, state, or local environmental laws for environmental remediation of the waste site; and the trust is not a qualified settlement fund within the meaning of § 1.468B-1(a) of this chapter. An environmental remediation trust is classified as a trust because its primary purpose is environmental remediation of an existing waste site and not the carrying on of a profit-making business that normally would be conducted through business organizations classified as corporations or partnerships. However, if the remedial purpose is altered or becomes so obscured by business or investment activities that the declared remedial purpose is no longer controlling, the organization will no longer be classified as a trust. For purposes of this paragraph (e), environmental remediation includes the costs of assessing environmental conditions, remedying and removing environmental contamination, monitoring remedial activities and the release of substances, preventing future releases of substances, and collecting amounts from persons liable or potentially liable for the costs of these activities. For purposes of this paragraph (e), persons have potential liability or a reasonable expectation of liability under federal, state, or local environmental laws for remediation of the existing waste site if there is authority under a federal, state, or local law that requires or could reasonably be expected to require such persons to satisfy all or a portion of the costs of the environmental remediation.

(2) Each contributor (grantor) to the trust is treated as the owner of the portion of the trust contributed by that grantor under rules provided in section 677 and § 1.677(a)-1(d) of this chapter. Section 677 and § 1.677(a)-1(d) of this chapter provide rules regarding the treatment of a grantor as the owner of a portion of a trust applied in discharge of the grantor's legal obligation. Items of income, deduction, and credit attributable to an environmental remediation trust are not reported by the trust on Form 1041, but are shown on a separate statement to be attached to that form. See § 1.671-4(a) of this chapter. The trustee must also furnish to each grantor a statement that shows all items of income, deduction, and credit of the trust for the grantor's taxable year attributable to the portion of the trust treated as owned by the grantor. The statement must provide the grantor with the information necessary to take the items into account in computing the grantor's taxable income, including information necessary to determine the federal tax treatment of the items (for example, whether an item is a deductible expense under section 162(a) or a capital expenditure under section 263(a)) and how the item should be taken into account under the economic performance rules of section 461(h) and the regulations thereunder. See § 1.461-4 of this chapter for rules relating to economic performance.

(3) All amounts contributed to an environmental remediation trust by a grantor (cash-out grantor) who, pursuant to an agreement with the other grantors, contributes a fixed amount to the trust and is relieved by the other grantors of any further obligation to make contributions to the trust, but remains liable or potentially liable under the applicable environmental laws, will be considered amounts contributed for remediation. An environmental remediation trust agreement may direct the trustee to expend amounts contributed by a cash-out grantor (and the earnings thereon) before expending amounts contributed by other grantors (and the earnings thereon). A cash-out grantor will cease to be treated as an owner of a portion of the trust when the grantor's portion is fully expended by the trust.

(4) The provisions of this paragraph (e) may be illustrated by the following example:

*Example.* (a) *X, Y,* and *Z* are calendar year corporations that are liable for the remediation of an existing waste site under applicable federal environmental laws. On June 1, 1996, pursuant to an agreement with the governing federal agency, *X, Y,* and *Z* create an environmental remediation trust within the meaning of paragraph (e)(1) of this section to collect funds contributed to the trust by *X, Y,* and *Z* and to carry out the remediation of the waste site to the satisfaction of the federal agency. *X, Y,* and *Z* are jointly and severally liable under the federal environmental laws for the remediation of the waste site, and the federal agency will not release *X, Y,* or *Z* from liability until the waste site is remediated to the satisfaction of the agency.

(b) The estimated cost of the remediation is $20,000,000. *X, Y,* and *Z* agree that, if *Z* contributes $1,000,000 to the trust, *Z* will not be required to make any additional contributions to the trust, and *X* and *Y* will complete the remediation of the waste site and make additional contributions if necessary.

(c) On June 1, 1996, *X, Y,* and *Z* each contribute $1,000,000 to the trust. The trust agreement directs the trustee to spend *Z*'s contributions to the trust and the income allocable to *Z*'s portion before spending *X*'s and *Y*'s portions. On November 30, 1996, the trustee disburses $2,000,000 for remediation work performed from June 1, 1996, through September 30, 1996. For the six-month period ending November 30, 1996, the interest earned on the funds in the trust was $75,000, which is allocated in equal shares of $25,000 to *X*'s, *Y*'s, and *Z*'s portions of the trust.

(d) *Z* made no further contributions to the trust. Pursuant to the trust agreement, the trustee expended *Z*'s portion of the trust before expending *X*'s and *Y*'s portion. Therefore, *Z*'s share of the remediation disbursement made in 1996 is $1,025,000 ($1,000,000 contribution by *Z* plus $25,000 of interest allocated to *Z*'s portion of the trust). *Z* takes the $1,025,000 disbursement into account under the appropriate federal tax accounting rules. In addition, *X*'s share of the remediation disbursement made in 1996 is $487,500, and *Y*'s share of the remediation disbursement made in 1996 is $487,500. *X* and *Y* take their respective shares of the disbursement into account under the appropriate federal tax accounting rules.

(e) The trustee made no further remediation disbursements in 1996, and *X* and *Y* made no further contributions in 1996. From December 1, 1996, to December 31, 1996, the interest earned on the funds remaining in the trust was $5,000, which is allocated $2,500 to *X*'s portion and $2,500 to *Y*'s portion. Accordingly, for 1996, *X* and *Y* each had interest income of $27,500 from the trust and *Z* had interest income of $25,000 from the trust.

(5) This paragraph (e) is applicable to trusts meeting the requirements of paragraph (e)(1) of this section that are formed on or after May 1, 1996. This paragraph (e) may be relied on by trusts formed before May 1, 1996, if the trust has at all times met all requirements of this paragraph (e) and the grantors have reported items of income and deduction consistent with this paragraph (e) on original or amended returns. For trusts formed before May 1, 1996, that are not described in the preceding sentence, the Commissioner may permit by letter ruling, in appropriate circumstances, this paragraph (e) to be applied subject to appropriate terms and conditions.

(f) *Effective date.*—The rules of this section generally apply to taxable years beginning after December 31, 1960. Paragraph (e)(5) of this section contains rules of applicability for paragraph (e) of this section. In addition, the last sentences of paragraphs (b), (c)(1), and (c)(2) *Example 1* and *Example 3* of this section are effective as of January 1, 1997. [Reg. § 301.7701-4.]

☐ [*T.D.* 6503, 11-15-60. *Amended by T.D.* 8080, 3-21-86; *T.D.* 8668, 4-30-96 *and T.D.* 8697, 12-17-96.]

## [Reg. § 301.7701-5]

**§ 301.7701-5. Domestic and foreign business entities.**— (a) *Domestic and foreign business entities.*—A business entity (including an entity that is disregarded as separate from its owner under § 301.7701-2(c)) is domestic if it is created or organized as any type of entity (including, but not limited to, a corporation, unincorporated association, general partnership, limited partnership, and limited liability company) in the United States, or under the law of the United States or of any State. Accordingly, a business entity that is created or organized both in the United States and in a foreign jurisdiction is a domestic entity. A business entity (including an entity that is disregarded as separate from its owner under § 301.7701-2(c)) is foreign if it is not domestic. The determination of whether an entity is domestic or foreign is made independently from the determination of its corporate or noncorporate classification. See §§ 301.7701-2 and 301.7701-3 for the rules governing the classification of entities.

(b) *Examples.*—The following examples illustrate the rules of this section:

*Example 1.* (i) *Facts.* Y is an entity that is created or organized under the laws of Country A as a public limited company. It is also an entity that is organized as a limited liability company (LLC) under the laws of State B. Y is classified as a corporation for Federal tax purposes under the rules of §§ 301.7701-2, and 301.7701-3.

(ii) *Result.* Y is a domestic corporation because it is an entity that is classified as a corporation and it is organized as an entity under the laws of State B.

*Example 2.* (i) *Facts.* P is an entity with more than one owner organized under the laws of Country A as an unlimited company. It is also an entity that is organized as a general partnership under the laws of State B. P is classified as a partnership for Federal tax purposes under the rules of §§ 301.7701-2, and 301.7701-3.

(ii) *Result.* P is a domestic partnership because it is an entity that is classified as a partnership and it is organized as an entity under the laws of State B.

(c) *Effective date.*—(1) *General rule.*—Except as provided in paragraph (c)(2) of this section, the rules of this section apply as of August 12, 2004, to all business entities existing on or after that date.

(2) *Transition rule.*—For business entities created or organized under the laws of more than one jurisdiction as of August 12, 2004, the rules of this section apply as of May 1, 2006. These entities, however, may rely on the rules of this section as of August 12, 2004. [Reg. § 301.7701-5.]

☐ [*T.D. 6503,* 11-15-60. *Amended by T.D. 8813,* 2-1-99; *T.D. 9153,* 8-11-2004 *and T.D. 9246,* 1-27-2006.]

### [Reg. § 301.7701-6]

**§301.7701-6. Definitions; person, fiduciary.**—(a) *Person.*—The term *person* includes an individual, a corporation, a partnership, a trust or estate, a joint-stock company, an association, or a syndicate, group, pool, joint venture, or other unincorporated organization or group. The term also includes a guardian, committee, trustee, executor, administrator, trustee in bankruptcy, receiver, assignee for the benefit of creditors, conservator, or any person acting in a fiduciary capacity.

(b) *Fiduciary.*—(1) *In general.*—Fiduciary is a term that applies to persons who occupy positions of peculiar confidence toward others, such as trustees, executors, and administrators. A fiduciary is a person who holds in trust an estate to which another has a beneficial interest, or receives and controls income of another, as in the case of receivers. A committee or guardian of the property of an incompetent person is a fiduciary.

(2) *Fiduciary distinguished from agent.*—There may be a fiduciary relationship between an agent and a principal, but the word agent does not denote a fiduciary. An agent having entire charge of property, with authority to effect and execute leases with tenants entirely on his own responsibility and without consulting his principal, merely turning over the net profits from the property periodically to his principal by virtue of authority conferred upon him by a power of attorney, is not a fiduciary within the meaning of the Internal Revenue Code. In cases when no legal trust has been created in the estate controlled by the agent and attorney, the liability to make a return rests with the principal.

(c) *Effective date.*—The rules of this section are effective as of January 1, 1997. [Reg. § 301.7701-6.]

☐ [*T.D. 6503,* 11-15-60. *Amended by T.D. 8697,* 12-17-96.]

### [Reg. § 301.7701-7]

**§301.7701-7. Trusts—domestic and foreign.**—(a) *In general.*—(1) A trust is a United States person if—

(i) A court within the United States is able to exercise primary supervision over the administration of the trust (court test); and

(ii) One or more United States persons have the authority to control all substantial decisions of the trust (control test).

(2) A trust is a United States person for purposes of the Internal Revenue Code (Code) on any day that the trust meets both the court test and the control test. For purposes of the regulations in this chapter, the term *domestic trust* means a trust that is a United States person. The term *foreign trust* means any trust other than a domestic trust.

(3) Except as otherwise provided in part I, subchapter J, chapter 1 of the Code, the taxable income of a foreign trust is computed in the same manner as the taxable income of a nonresident alien individual who is not present in the United States at any time. Section 641(b). Section 7701(b) is not applicable to trusts because it only applies to individuals. In addition, a foreign trust is not considered to be present in the United States at any time for purposes of section 871(a)(2), which deals with capital gains of nonresident aliens present in the United States for 183 days or more.

(b) *Applicable law.*—The terms of the trust instrument and applicable law must be applied to determine whether the court test and the control test are met.

(c) *The court test.*—(1) *Safe harbor.*—A trust satisfies the court test if—

(i) The trust instrument does not direct that the trust be administered outside of the United States;

(ii) The trust in fact is administered exclusively in the United States; and

(iii) The trust is not subject to an automatic migration provision described in paragraph (c)(4)(ii) of this section.

(2) *Example.*—The following example illustrates the rule of paragraph (c)(1) of this section:

*Example.* A creates a trust for the equal benefit of A's two children, B and C. The trust instrument provides that DC, a State Y corporation, is the trustee of the trust. State Y is a state within the United States. DC administers the trust exclusively in State Y and the trust instrument is silent as to where the trust is to be administered. The trust is not subject to an automatic migration provision described in paragraph (c)(4)(ii) of this section. The trust satisfies the safe harbor of paragraph (c)(1) of this section and the court test.

(3) *Definitions.*—The following definitions apply for purposes of this section:

(i) *Court.*—The term *court* includes any federal, state, or local court.

(ii) *The United States.*—The term *the United States* is used in this section in a geographical sense. Thus, for purposes of the court test, the United States includes only the States and the District of Columbia. See section 7701(a)(9). Accordingly, a court within a territory or possession of the United States or within a foreign country is not a court within the United States.

(iii) *Is able to exercise.*—The term *is able to exercise* means that a court has or would have the authority under applicable law to render orders or judgments resolving issues concerning administration of the trust.

(iv) *Primary supervision.*—The term *primary supervision* means that a court has or would have the authority to determine substantially all issues regarding the administration of the entire trust. A court may have primary supervision under this paragraph (c)(3)(iv) notwithstanding the fact that another court has jurisdiction over a trustee, a beneficiary, or trust property.

(v) *Administration.*—The term *administration* of the trust means the carrying out of the duties imposed by the terms of the trust instrument and applicable law, including maintaining the books and records of the trust, filing tax returns, managing and investing the assets of the trust, defending the trust from suits by creditors, and determining the amount and timing of distributions.

(4) *Situations that cause a trust to satisfy or fail to satisfy the court test.*—(i) Except as provided in paragraph (c)(4)(ii) of this section, paragraphs (c)(4)(i)(A) through (D) of this section set forth some specific situations in which a trust satisfies the court test. The four situations described are not intended to be an exclusive list.

(A) *Uniform Probate Code.*—A trust meets the court test if the trust is registered by an authorized fiduciary or fiduciaries of the trust in a court within the United States pursuant to a state statute that has provisions substantially similar to Article VII, *Trust Administration,* of the Uniform Probate Code, 8 Uniform Laws Annotated 1 (West Supp. 1998), available from the National Conference of Commissioners on Uniform State Laws, 676 North St. Clair Street, Suite 1700, Chicago, Illinois 60611.

(B) *Testamentary trust.*—In the case of a trust created pursuant to the terms of a will probated within the United States (other than an ancillary probate), if all fiduciaries of the trust have been qualified as trustees of the trust by a court within the United States, the trust meets the court test.

(C) *Inter vivos trust.*—In the case of a trust other than a testamentary trust, if the fiduciaries and/or beneficiaries take steps with a court within the United States that cause the administration of the trust to be subject to the primary supervision of the court, the trust meets the court test.

(D) *A United States court and a foreign court are able to exercise primary supervision over the administration of the trust.*—If both a United States court and a foreign court are able to exercise primary supervision over the administration of the trust, the trust meets the court test.

(ii) *Automatic migration provisions.*—Notwithstanding any other provision in this section, a court within the United States is not considered to have primary supervision over the administration of the trust if the trust instrument provides that a United States court's attempt to assert jurisdiction or otherwise supervise the administration of the trust directly or indirectly would cause the trust to migrate from the United States. However, this paragraph (c)(4)(ii) will not apply if the trust instrument provides that the trust will migrate from the United States only in the case of foreign invasion of the United States or widespread confiscation or nationalization of property in the United States.

(5) *Examples.*—The following examples illustrate the rules of this paragraph (c):

*Example 1. A*, a United States citizen, creates a trust for the equal benefit of *A*'s two children, both of whom are United States citizens. The trust instrument provides that *DC*, a domestic corporation, is to act as trustee of the trust and that the trust is to be administered in Country *X*, a foreign country. *DC* maintains a branch office in Country *X* with personnel authorized to act as trustees in Country *X*. The trust instrument provides that the law of State *Y*, a state within the United States, is to govern the interpretation of the trust. Under the law of Country *X*, a court within Country *X* is able to exercise primary supervision over the administration of the trust. Pursuant to the trust instrument, the Country *X* court applies the law of State *Y* to the trust. Under the terms of the trust instrument the trust is administered in Country *X*. No court within the United States is able to exercise primary supervision over the administration of the trust. The trust fails to satisfy the court test and therefore is a foreign trust.

*Example 2. A*, a United States citizen, creates a trust for *A*'s own benefit and the benefit of *A*'s spouse, *B*, a United States citizen. The trust instrument provides that the trust is to be administered in State *Y*, a state within the United States, by *DC*, a State *Y* corporation. The trust instrument further provides that in the event that a creditor sues the trustee in a United States court, the trust will automatically migrate from State *Y* to Country *Z*, a foreign country, so that no United States court will have jurisdiction over the trust. A court within the United States is not able to exercise primary supervision over the administration of the trust because the United States court's jurisdiction over the administration of the trust is automatically terminated in the event the court attempts to assert jurisdiction. Therefore, the trust fails to satisfy the court test from the time of its creation and is a foreign trust.

(d) *Control test.*—(1) *Definitions.*—(i) *United States person.*—The term *United States person* means a United States person within the meaning of section 7701(a)(30). For example, a domestic corporation is a United States person, regardless of whether its shareholders are United States persons.

(ii) *Substantial decisions.*—The term *substantial decisions* means those decisions that persons are authorized or required to make under the terms of the trust instrument and applicable law and that are not ministerial. Decisions that are ministerial include decisions regarding details such as the bookkeeping, the collection of rents, and the execution of investment decisions. Substantial decisions include, but are not limited to, decisions concerning—

(A) Whether and when to distribute income or corpus;

(B) The amount of any distributions;

(C) The selection of a beneficiary;

(D) Whether a receipt is allocable to income or principal;

(E) Whether to terminate the trust;

(F) Whether to compromise, arbitrate, or abandon claims of the trust;

(G) Whether to sue on behalf of the trust or to defend suits against the trust;

(H) Whether to remove, add, or replace a trustee;

(I) Whether to appoint a successor trustee to succeed a trustee who has died, resigned, or otherwise ceased to act as a trustee, even if the power to make such a decision is not accompanied by an unrestricted power to remove a trustee, unless the power to make such a decision is limited such that it cannot be exercised in a manner that would change the trust's residency from foreign to domestic, or vice versa; and

(J) Investment decisions; however, if a United States person under section 7701(a)(30) hires an investment advisor for the trust, investment decisions made by the investment advisor will be considered substantial decisions controlled by the United States person if the United States person can terminate the investment advisor's power to make investment decisions at will.

(iii) *Control.*—The term *control* means having the power, by vote or otherwise, to make all of the substantial decisions of the trust, with no other person having the power to veto any of the substantial decisions. To determine whether United States persons have control, it is necessary to consider all persons who have authority to make a substantial decision of the trust, not only the trust fiduciaries.

(iv) *Safe harbor for certain employee benefit trusts and investment trusts.*—Notwithstanding the provisions of this paragraph (d), the trusts listed in this paragraph (d)(1)(iv) are deemed to satisfy the control test set forth in paragraph (a)(1)(ii) of this section, provided that United States trustees control all of the substantial decisions made by the trustees of the trust—

(A) A qualified trust described in section 401(a);

(B) A trust described in section 457(g);

(C) A trust that is an individual retirement account described in section 408(a);

(D) A trust that is an individual retirement account described in section 408(k) or 408(p);

(E) A trust that is a Roth IRA described in section 408A;

(F) A trust that is an education individual retirement account described in section 530;

(G) A trust that is a voluntary employees' beneficiary association described in section 501(c)(9);

(H) A group trust described in Rev. Rul. 81-100 (1981-1 C.B. 326) (See § 601.601(d)(2) of this chapter);

(I) An investment trust classified as a trust under § 301.7701-4(c), provided that the following conditions are satisfied—

(1) All trustees are United States persons and at least one of the trustees is a bank, as defined in section 581, or a United States Government-owned agency or United States Government-sponsored enterprise;

(2) All sponsors (persons who exchange investment assets for beneficial interests with a view to selling the beneficial interests) are United States persons; and

(3) The beneficial interests are widely offered for sale primarily in the United States to United States persons;

(J) Such additional categories of trusts as the Commissioner may designate in revenue procedures, notices, or other guidance published in the Internal Revenue Bulletin (see § 601.601(d)(2)(ii)(*b*)).

(v) *Examples.*—The following examples illustrate the rules of paragraph (d)(1) of this section:

*Example 1.* Trust is a testamentary trust with three fiduciaries, *A*, *B*, and *C*. *A* and *B* are United States citizens, and *C* is a nonresident alien. No persons except the fiduciaries have authority to make any decisions of the trust. The trust instrument provides that no substantial decisions of the trust can be made unless there is unanimity among the fiduciaries. The control test is not satisfied because United States persons do not control all the substantial decisions of the trust. No substantial decisions can be made without *C*'s agreement.

*Example 2.* Assume the same facts as in *Example 1*, except that the trust instrument provides that all substantial decisions of the trust are to be decided by a majority vote among the fiduciaries. The control test is satisfied because a majority of the fiduciaries are United States persons and therefore United States persons control all the substantial decisions of the trust.

*Example 3.* Assume the same facts as in *Example 2*, except that the trust instrument directs that *C* is to make all of the trust's investment decisions, but that *A* and *B* may veto *C*'s investment decisions. *A* and *B* cannot act to make the investment decisions on their own. The control test is not satisfied because the United States persons, *A* and *B*, do not have the power to make all of the substantial decisions of the trust.

*Example 4.* Assume the same facts as in *Example 3*, except *A* and *B* may accept or veto *C*'s investment decisions and can make investments that *C* has not recommended. The control test is satisfied because the United States persons control all substantial decisions of the trust.

*Example 5. X*, a foreign corporation, conducts business in the United States through various branch operations. *X* has United States employees and has established a trust as part of a qualified employee benefit plan under section 401(a) for these employees. The trust is established under the laws of State *A*, and the trustee of the trust is *B*, a United States bank governed by the laws of State *A*. *B* holds legal title to the trust assets for the benefit of the trust beneficiaries. A plan committee makes decisions with respect to the plan and the trust. The plan committee can direct *B*'s actions with regard to those decisions and under the governing documents *B* is not liable for those decisions. Members of the plan committee consist of United States persons and nonresident aliens, but nonresident aliens make up a majority of the plan committee. Decisions of the plan committee are made by majority vote. In addition, *X* retains the power to terminate the trust and to replace the United States trustee or to appoint additional trustees. This trust is deemed to satisfy the control test under paragraph (d)(1)(iv) of this section because *B*, a United States person, is the trust's only trustee. Any powers held by the plan committee or *X* are not considered under the safe harbor of paragraph (d)(1)(iv) of this section. In the event that *X* appoints additional trustees including foreign trustees, any powers held by such trustees must be considered in determining whether United States trustees control all substantial decisions made by the trustees of the trust.

(2) *Replacement of any person who had authority to make a substantial decision of the trust.*—(i) *Replacement within 12 months.*—In the event of an inadvertent change in any person that has the power to make a substantial decision of the trust that would cause the domestic or foreign residency of the trust to change, the trust is allowed 12 months from the date of the change to make necessary changes either

with respect to the persons who control the substantial decisions or with respect to the residence of such persons to avoid a change in the trust's residency. For purposes of this section, an inadvertent change means the death, incapacity, resignation, change in residency or other change with respect to a person that has a power to make a substantial decision of the trust that would cause a change to the residency of the trust but that was not intended to change the residency of the trust. If the necessary change is made within 12 months, the trust is treated as retaining its pre-change residency during the 12-month period. If the necessary change is not made within 12 months, the trust's residency changes as of the date of the inadvertent change.

(ii) *Request for extension of time.*—If reasonable actions have been taken to make the necessary change to prevent a change in trust residency, but due to circumstances beyond the trust's control the trust is unable to make the modification within 12 months, the trust may provide a written statement to the district director having jurisdiction over the trust's return setting forth the reasons for failing to make the necessary change within the required time period. If the district director determines that the failure was due to reasonable cause, the district director may grant the trust an extension of time to make the necessary change. Whether an extension of time is granted is in the sole discretion of the district director and, if granted, may contain such terms with respect to assessment as may be necessary to ensure that the correct amount of tax will be collected from the trust, its owners, and its beneficiaries. If the district director does not grant an extension, the trust's residency changes as of the date of the inadvertent change.

(iii) *Examples.*—The following examples illustrate the rules of paragraphs (d)(2)(i) and (ii) of this section:

*Example 1.* A trust that satisfies the court test has three fiduciaries, *A*, *B*, and *C*. *A* and *B* are United States citizens and *C* is a nonresident alien. All decisions of the trust are made by majority vote of the fiduciaries. The trust instrument provides that upon the death or resignation of any of the fiduciaries, *D*, is the successor fiduciary. *A* dies and *D* automatically becomes a fiduciary of the trust. When *D* becomes a fiduciary of the trust, *D* is a nonresident alien. Two months after *A* dies, *B* replaces *D* with *E*, a United States person. Because *D* was replaced with *E* within 12 months after the date of *A*'s death, during the period after *A*'s death and before *E* begins to serve, the trust satisfies the control test and remains a domestic trust.

*Example 2.* Assume the same facts as in *Example 1* except that at the end of the 12-month period after *A*'s death, *D* has not been replaced and remains a fiduciary of the trust. The trust becomes a foreign trust on the date *A* died unless the district director grants an extension of the time period to make the necessary change.

(3) *Automatic migration provisions.*—Notwithstanding any other provision in this section, United States persons are not considered to control all substantial decisions of the trust if an attempt by any governmental agency or creditor to collect information from or assert a claim against the trust would cause one or more substantial decisions of the trust to no longer be controlled by United States persons.

(4) *Examples.*—The following examples illustrate the rules of this paragraph (d):

*Example 1.* *A*, a nonresident alien individual, is the grantor and, during *A*'s lifetime, the sole beneficiary of a trust that qualifies as an individual retirement account (IRA). *A* has the exclusive power to make decisions regarding withdrawals from the IRA and to direct its investments. The IRA's sole trustee is a United States person within the meaning of section 7701(a)(30). The control test is satisfied with respect to this trust because the special rule of paragraph (d)(1)(iv) of this section applies.

*Example 2.* *A*, a nonresident alien individual, is the grantor of a trust and has the power to revoke the trust, in whole or in part, and revest assets in *A*. *A* is treated as the owner of the trust under sections 672(f) and 676. *A* is not a fiduciary of the trust. The trust has one trustee, *B*, a United States person, and the trust has one beneficiary, *C*. *B* has the discretion to distribute corpus or income to *C*. In this case, decisions exercisable by *A* to have trust assets distributed to *A* are substantial decisions. Therefore, the trust is a foreign trust because *B* does not control all substantial decisions of the trust.

*Example 3.* A trust, Trust *T*, has two fiduciaries, *A* and *B*. Both *A* and *B* are United States persons. *A* and *B* hire *C*, an investment advisor who is a foreign person, and may terminate *C*'s employment at will. The investment advisor makes the investment decisions for the trust. *A* and *B* control all other decisions of the trust. Although *C* has the power to make investment decisions, *A* and *B* are treated as controlling these decisions. Therefore, the control test is satisfied.

*Example 4.* *G*, a United States citizen, creates a trust. The trust provides for income to *A* and *B* for life, remainder to *A*'s and *B*'s descendants. *A* is a nonresident alien and *B* is a United States person.

The trustee of the trust is a United States person. The trust instrument authorizes *A* to replace the trustee. The power to replace the trustee is a substantial decision. Because *A*, a nonresident alien, controls a substantial decision, the control test is not satisfied.

(e) *Effective date.*—(1) *General rule.*—Except for the election to remain a domestic trust provided in paragraph (f) of this section and except as provided in paragraph (e)(3) of this section, this section is applicable to taxable years ending after February 2, 1999. This section may be relied on by trusts for taxable years beginning after December 31, 1996, and also may be relied on by trusts whose trustees have elected to apply sections 7701(a)(30) and (31) to the trusts for taxable years ending after August 20, 1996, under section 1907(a)(3)(B) of the Small Business Job Protection Act of 1996, (the SBJP Act) Public Law 104-188, 110 Stat. 1755 (26 U.S.C. 7701 note).

(2) *Trusts created after August 19, 1996.*—If a trust is created after August 19, 1996, and before April 5, 1999, and the trust satisfies the control test set forth in the regulations project REG-251703-96 published under section 7701(a)(30) and (31) (1997-1 C.B. 795) (See § 601.601(d)(2) of this chapter), but does not satisfy the control test set forth in paragraph (d) of this section, the trust may be modified to satisfy the control test of paragraph (d) by December 31, 1999. If the modification is completed by December 31, 1999, the trust will be treated as satisfying the control test of paragraph (d) for taxable years beginning after December 31, 1996, (and for taxable years ending after August 20, 1996, if the election under section 1907(a)(3)(B) of the SBJP Act has been made for the trust).

(3) *Effective date of safe harbor for certain employee benefit trusts and investment trusts.*—Paragraphs (d)(1)(iv) and (v) *Examples 1* and *5* of this section apply to trusts for taxable years beginning on or after August 9, 2001. Paragraphs (d)(1)(iv) and (v) *Examples 1* and *5* of this section may be relied on by trusts for taxable years beginning after December 31, 1996, and also may be relied on by trusts whose trustees have elected to apply sections 7701(a)(30) and (31) to the trusts for taxable years ending after August 20, 1996, under section 1907(a)(3)(B) of the SBJP Act.

(f) *Election to remain a domestic trust.*—(1) *Trusts eligible to make the election to remain domestic.*—A trust that was in existence on August 20, 1996, and that was treated as a domestic trust on August 19, 1996, as provided in paragraph (f)(2) of this section, may elect to continue treatment as a domestic trust notwithstanding section 7701(a)(30)(E). This election is not available to a trust that was wholly-owned by its grantor under subpart E, part I, subchapter J, chapter 1, of the Code on August 20, 1996. The election is available to a trust if only a portion of the trust was treated as owned by the grantor under subpart E on August 20, 1996. If a partially-owned grantor trust makes the election, the election is effective for the entire trust. Also, a trust may not make the election if the trust has made an election pursuant to section 1907(a)(3)(B) of the SBJP Act to apply the new trust criteria to the first taxable year of the trust ending after August 20, 1996, because that election, once made, is irrevocable.

(2) *Determining whether a trust was treated as a domestic trust on August 19, 1996.*—(i) *Trusts filing Form 1041 for the taxable year that includes August 19, 1996.*—For purposes of the election, a trust is considered to have been treated as a domestic trust on August 19, 1996, if: the trustee filed a Form 1041, "U.S. Income Tax Return for Estates and Trusts," for the trust for the period that includes August 19, 1996 (and did not file a Form 1040NR, "U.S. Nonresident Alien Income Tax Return," for that year); and the trust had a reasonable basis (within the meaning of section 6662) under section 7701(a)(30) prior to amendment by the SBJP Act (prior law) for reporting as a domestic trust for that period.

(ii) *Trusts not filing a Form 1041.*—Some domestic trusts are not required to file Form 1041. For example, certain group trusts described in Rev. Rul. 81-100 (1981-1 C.B. 326) (See § 601.601(d)(2) of this chapter) consisting of trusts that are parts of qualified retirement plans and individual retirement accounts are not required to file Form 1041. Also, a domestic trust whose gross income for the taxable year is less than the amount required for filing an income tax return and that has no taxable income is not required to file a Form 1041. Section 6012(a)(4). For purposes of the election, a trust that filed neither a Form 1041 nor a Form 1040NR for the period that includes August 19, 1996, will be considered to have been treated as a domestic trust on August 19, 1996, if the trust had a reasonable basis (within the meaning of section 6662) under prior law for being treated as a domestic trust for that period and for filing neither a Form 1041 nor a Form 1040NR for that period.

(3) *Procedure for making the election to remain domestic.*—(i) *Required Statement.*—To make the election, a statement must be filed with the Internal Revenue Service in the manner and time described in this section. The statement must be entitled "Election to

Remain a Domestic Trust under Section 1161 of the Taxpayer Relief Act of 1997," be signed under penalties of perjury by at least one trustee of the trust, and contain the following information—

(A) A statement that the trust is electing to continue to be treated as a domestic trust under section 1161 of the Taxpayer Relief Act of 1997;

(B) A statement that the trustee had a reasonable basis (within the meaning of section 6662) under prior law for treating the trust as a domestic trust on August 19, 1996. (The trustee need not explain the reasonable basis on the election statement.);

(C) A statement either that the trust filed a Form 1041 treating the trust as a domestic trust for the period that includes August 19, 1996, (and that the trust did not file a Form 1040NR for that period), or that the trust was not required to file a Form 1041 or a Form 1040NR for the period that includes August 19, 1996, with an accompanying brief explanation as to why a Form 1041 was not required to be filed; and

(D) The name, address, and employer identification number of the trust.

(ii) *Filing the required statement with the Internal Revenue Service.*—(A) Except as provided in paragraphs (f)(3)(ii)(E) through (G) of this section, the trust must attach the statement to a Form 1041. The statement may be attached to either the Form 1041 that is filed for the first taxable year of the trust beginning after December 31, 1996 (1997 taxable year), or to the Form 1041 filed for the first taxable year of the trust beginning after December 31, 1997 (1998 taxable year). The statement, however, must be filed no later than the due date for filing a Form 1041 for the 1998 taxable year, plus extensions. The election will be effective for the 1997 taxable year, and thereafter, until revoked or terminated. If the trust filed a Form 1041 for the 1997 taxable year without the statement attached, the statement should be attached to the Form 1041 filed for the 1998 taxable year.

(B) If the trust has insufficient gross income and no taxable income for its 1997 or 1998 taxable year, or both, and therefore is not required to file a Form 1041 for either or both years, the trust must make the election by filing a Form 1041 for either the 1997 or 1998 taxable year with the statement attached (even though not otherwise required to file a Form 1041 for that year). The trust should only provide on the Form 1041 the trust's name, name and title of fiduciary, address, employer identification number, date created, and type of entity. The statement must be attached to a Form 1041 that is filed no later than October 15, 1999.

(C) If the trust files a Form 1040NR for the 1997 taxable year based on application of new section 7701(a)(30)(E) to the trust, and satisfies paragraph (f)(1) of this section, in order for the trust to make the election the trust must file an amended Form 1040NR return for the 1997 taxable year. The trust must note on the amended Form 1040NR that it is making an election under section 1161 of the Taxpayer Relief Act of 1997. The trust must attach to the amended Form 1040NR the statement required by paragraph (f)(3)(i) of this section and a completed Form 1041 for the 1997 taxable year. The items of income, deduction and credit of the trust must be excluded from the amended Form 1040NR and reported on the Form 1041. The amended Form 1040NR for the 1997 taxable year, with the statement and the Form 1041 attached, must be filed with the Philadelphia Service Center no later than the due date, plus extensions, for filing a Form 1041 for the 1998 taxable year.

(D) If a trust has made estimated tax payments as a foreign trust based on application of section 7701(a)(30)(E) to the trust, but has not yet filed a Form 1040NR for the 1997 taxable year, when the trust files its Form 1041 for the 1997 taxable year it must note on its Form 1041 that it made estimated tax payments based on treatment as a foreign trust. The Form 1041 must be filed with the Philadelphia Service Center (and not with the service center where the trust ordinarily would file its Form 1041).

(E) If a trust forms part of a qualified stock bonus, pension, or profit sharing plan, the election provided by this paragraph (f) must be made by attaching the statement to the plan's annual return required under section 6058 (information return) for the first plan year beginning after December 31, 1996, or to the plan's information return for the first plan year beginning after December 31, 1997. The statement must be attached to the plan's information return that is filed no later than the due date for filing the plan's information return for the first plan year beginning after December 31, 1997, plus extensions. The election will be effective for the first plan year beginning after December 31, 1996, and thereafter, until revoked or terminated.

(F) Any other type of trust that is not required to file a Form 1041 for the taxable year, but that is required to file an information return (for example, Form 5227) for the 1997 or 1998 taxable year must attach the statement to the trust's information return for the 1997 or 1998 taxable year. However, the statement must be attached to an information return that is filed no later than the due date for filing the trust's information return for the 1998 taxable year, plus

extensions. The election will be effective for the 1997 taxable year, and thereafter, until revoked or terminated.

(G) A group trust described in Rev. Rul. 81-100 consisting of trusts that are parts of qualified retirement plans and individual retirement accounts (and any other trust that is not described above and that is not required to file a Form 1041 or an information return) need not attach the statement to any return and should file the statement with the Philadelphia Service Center. The trust must make the election provided by this paragraph (f) by filing the statement by October 15, 1999. The election will be effective for the 1997 taxable year, and thereafter, until revoked or terminated.

(iii) *Failure to file the statement in the required manner and time.*— If a trust fails to file the statement in the manner or time provided in paragraphs (f)(3)(i) and (ii) of this section, the trustee may provide a written statement to the district director having jurisdiction over the trust setting forth the reasons for failing to file the statement in the required manner or time. If the district director determines that the failure to file the statement in the required manner or time was due to reasonable cause, the district director may grant the trust an extension of time to file the statement. Whether an extension of time is granted shall be in the sole discretion of the district director. However, the relief provided by this paragraph (f)(3)(iii) is not ordinarily available if the statute of limitations for the trust's 1997 taxable year has expired. Additionally, if the district director grants an extension of time, it may contain terms with respect to assessment as may be necessary to ensure that the correct amount of tax will be collected from the trust, its owners, and its beneficiaries.

(4) *Revocation or termination of the election.*—(i) *Revocation of election.*—The election provided by this paragraph (f) to be treated as a domestic trust may only be revoked with the consent of the Commissioner. See sections 684, 6048, and 6677 for the federal tax consequences and reporting requirements related to the change in trust residence.

(ii) *Termination of the election.*—An election under this paragraph (f) to remain a domestic trust terminates if changes are made to the trust subsequent to the effective date of the election that result in the trust no longer having any reasonable basis (within the meaning of section 6662) for being treated as a domestic trust under section 7701(a)(30) prior to its amendment by the SBJP Act. The termination of the election will result in the trust changing its residency from a domestic trust to a foreign trust on the effective date of the termination of the election. See sections 684, 6048, and 6677 for the federal tax consequences and reporting requirements related to the change in trust residence.

(5) *Effective date.*—This paragraph (f) is applicable beginning on February 2, 1999. [Reg. § 301.7701-7.]

☐ [*T.D. 8813, 2-1-99. Amended by T.D. 8962, 8-8-2001.*]

### [Reg. § 301.7701-8]

**§ 301.7701-8. Military or naval forces and Armed Forces of the United States.**—The term "military or naval forces of the United States" and the term "Armed Forces of the United States" each includes all regular and reserve components of the uniformed services which are subject to the jurisdiction of the Secretary of Defense, the Secretary of the Army, the Secretary of the Navy, or the Secretary of the Air Force. The terms also include the Coast Guard. The members of such forces include commissioned officers and the personnel below the grade of commissioned officer in such forces. [Reg. § 301.7701-8.]

☐ [*T.D. 6503, 11-15-60.*]

### [Reg. § 301.7701-9]

**§ 301.7701-9. Secretary or his delegate.**—(a) The term "Secretary or his delegate" means the Secretary of the Treasury, or any officer, employee, or agency of the Treasury Department duly authorized by the Secretary (directly, or indirectly by one or more redelegations of authority) to perform the function mentioned or described in the context, and the term "or his delegate" when used in connection with any other official of the United States shall be similarly construed.

(b) In any case in which a function is vested by the Internal Revenue Code of 1954 or any other statute in the Secretary or his delegate, and Treasury regulations or Treasury decisions approved by the Secretary or his delegate provide that such function may be performed by the Commissioner, assistant commissioner, regional commissioner, assistant regional commissioner, district director, director of a regional service center, or by a designated officer or employee in the office of any such officer, such provision in the regulations or Treasury decision shall constitute a delegation by the Secretary of the authority to perform such function to the designated officer or employee. If such authority is delegated to any officer or employee performing services under the supervision and control of the Commissioner, such provision in the regulations or Treasury decision shall constitute a delegation by the Secretary to the Commissioner of the authority to perform such function and a redelegation thereof by the Commissioner to the designated officer or employee.

(c) An officer or employee, including the Commissioner, authorized by regulations or Treasury decision to perform a function shall have authority to redelegate the performance of such function to any officer or employee performing services under his supervision and control, unless such power to so redelegate is prohibited or restricted by proper order or directive. The Commissioner may also redelegate authority to perform such function to other officers or employees under his supervision and control and, to the extent he deems proper, may authorize further redelegation of such authority.

(d) The Commissioner may prescribe such limitations as he deems proper on the extent to which any officer or employee under his supervision and control shall perform any such function, but, in the case of an officer or employee designated in regulations or Treasury decision as authorized to perform such function, such limitations shall not render invalid any performance by such officer or employee of the function which, except for such limitations, such officer or employee is authorized to perform by such regulations or Treasury decision in effect at the time the function is performed. [Reg. §301.7701-9.]

☐ [*T.D. 6503, 11-15-60. Amended by T.D. 6585, 12-27-61.*]

### [Reg. §301.7701-10]

**§301.7701-10. District director.**—The term "district director" means the district director of internal revenue for an internal revenue district. The term also includes the Assistant Commissioner(International). [Reg. §301.7701-10.]

☐ [*T.D. 6503, 11-15-60. Amended by T.D. 8411, 4-24-92.*]

### [Reg. §301.7701-11]

**§301.7701-11. Social security number.**—For purposes of this chapter, the term "social security number" means the taxpayer identifying number of an individual or estate which is assigned pursuant to section 6011(b) or corresponding provisions of prior law, or pursuant to section 6109, and in which nine digits are separated by hyphens as follows: 000-00-0000. Such term does not include a number with a letter as a suffix which is used to identify an auxiliary beneficiary under the social security program. The terms "account number" and "social security number" refer to the same number. [Reg. §301.7701-11.]

☐ [*T.D. 6606, 8-24-62. Amended by T.D. 7306, 3-14-74.*]

### [Reg. §301.7701-12]

**§301.7701-12. Employer identification number.**—For purposes of this chapter, the term "employer identification number" means the taxpayer identifying number of an individual or other person(whether or not an employer) which is assigned pursuant to section 6011(b) or corresponding provisions of prior law, or pursuant to section 6109, and in which nine digits are separated by a hyphen, as follows: 00-0000000. The terms "employer identification number" and "identification number" (defined in §31.0-2(a)(11) of this chapter (Employment Tax Regulations)) refer to the same number. [Reg. §301.7701-12.]

☐ [*T.D. 6606, 8-24-62. Amended by T.D. 7306, 3-14-74.*]

### [Reg. §301.7701-13A]

**§301.7701-13A. Post-1969 domestic building and loan association.**—(a) *In general.*—For taxable years beginning after July 11, 1969, the term "domestic building and loan association" means a domestic building and loan association, a domestic savings and loan association, a Federal savings and loan association, and any other savings institution chartered and supervised as a savings and loan or similar association under Federal or State law which meets the supervisory test (described in paragraph (b) of this section), the business operations test (described in paragraph (c) of this section), and the assets test (described in paragraph (d) of this section). For the definition of the term "domestic building and loan association" for taxable years beginning after October 16, 1962, and before July 12, 1969, see §301.7701-13.

(b) *Supervisory test.*—A domestic building and loan association must be either (1) an insured institution within the meaning of section 401(a) of the National Housing Act (12 U.S.C. 1724(a)) or (2) subject by law to supervision and examination by State or Federal authority having supervision over such associations. An "insured institution" is one the accounts of which are insured by the Federal Savings and Loan Insurance Corporation.

(c) *Business operations test.*—(1) *In general.*—An association must utilize its assets so that its business consists principally of acquiring the savings of the public and investing in loans. The requirement of this paragraph is referred to in this section as the business operations test. The business of acquiring the savings of the public and investing in loans includes ancillary or incidental activities which are directly and primarily related to such acquisition and investment, such as advertising for savings, appraising property on which loans are to be made by the association, and inspecting the progress of construction in connection with construction loans. Even though an association meets the supervisory test described in paragraph (b) of this section and the assets test described in paragraph (d) of this section, it will nevertheless not qualify as a domestic building and loan association if it does not meet the requirements of both subparagraphs (2) and (3) of this paragraph, relating, respectively, to acquiring the savings of the public and investing in loans.

(2) *Acquiring the savings of the public.*—The requirement that an association's business (other than investing in loans) must consist principally of acquiring the savings of the public ordinarily will be considered to be met if savings are acquired in all material respects in conformity with the rules and regulations of the Federal Home Loan Bank Board or substantially equivalent rules of a State law or supervisory authority. Alternatively, such requirement will be considered to be met if more than 75 percent of the dollar amount of the total deposits, withdrawable shares, and other obligations of the association are held during the taxable year by the general public, as opposed to amounts deposited or held by family or related business groups or persons who are officers or directors of the association. However, the preceding sentence shall not apply if the dollar amount of other obligations of the association outstanding during the taxable year exceeds 25 percent of the dollar amount of the total deposits, withdrawable shares, and other obligations of the association outstanding during such year. For purposes of this subparagraph, the term "other obligations" means notes, bonds, debentures, or other obligations, or other securities (except capital stock), issued by an association in conformity with the rules and regulations of the Federal Home Loan Bank Board or substantially equivalent rules of a State law or supervisory authority. The term "other obligations" does not include an advance made by a Federal Home Loan Bank under the authority of section 10 or 10b of the Federal Home Loan Bank Act (12 U.S.C. 1430, 1430b) as amended and supplemented. Both percentages specified in this subparagraph shall be computed either as of the close of the taxable year or, at the option of the taxpayer, on the basis of the average of the dollar amounts of the total deposits, withdrawable shares, and other obligations of the association held during the taxable year. Such averages shall be determined by computing each percentage specified either as of the close of each month, as of the close of each quarter, or semiannually during the taxable year and by using the yearly average of the monthly, quarterly, or semiannual percentages obtained. The method selected must be applied uniformly for the taxable year to both percentages, but the method may be changed from year to year.

(3) *Investing in loans.*—(i) *In general.*—The requirement that an association's business (other than acquiring the savings of the public) must consist principally of investing in loans will be considered to be met for a taxable year only if more than 75 percent of the gross income of the association consists of—

(a) Interest or dividends on assets defined in subparagraphs (1), (2), and (3) of paragraph (e) of this section,

(b) Interest on loans,

(c) Income attributable to the portion of property used in the association's business, as defined in paragraph (e)(11) of this section,

(d) So much of the amount of premiums, discounts, commissions, or fees (including late charges and penalties) on loans which have at some time been held by the association, or for which firm commitments have been issued, as is not in excess of 20 percent of the gross income of the association,

(e) Net gain from sales and exchanges of governmental obligations, as defined in paragraph (e)(2) of this section, or

(f) Income, gain or loss attributable to foreclosed property, as defined in paragraph (e)(9) of this section, but not including such income, gain or loss which, pursuant to section 595 and the regulations thereunder, is not included in gross income.

Examples of types of income which would cause an association to fail to meet the requirements of this subparagraph if, in the aggregate, they equal or exceed 25 percent of gross income, are: the excess of gains over losses from sales of real property (other than foreclosed property); rental income (other than on foreclosed property and the portion of property used in the association's business); premiums, commissions, and fees (other than commitment fees) on loans which have never been held by the association; and insurance brokerage fees.

(ii) *Computation of gross income.*—For purposes of this subparagraph, gross income is computed without regard to—

(a) Gain or loss on the sale or exchange of the portion of property used in the association's business as defined in paragraph (e)(11) of this section,

(b) Gain or loss on the sale or exchange of the rented portion of property used as the principal or branch office of the association, as defined in paragraph (e)(11) of this section, and

(c) Gains or losses on sales of participations and loans, other than governmental obligations defined in paragraph (e)(2) of this section.

For purposes of this subparagraph, gross income is also computed without regard to items of income which an association establishes arise out of transactions which are necessitated by exceptional circumstances and which are not undertaken as recurring business activities for profit. Thus, for example, an association would meet the investing in loans requirement if it can establish that it would otherwise fail to meet that requirement solely because of the receipt of a non-recurring item of income due to exceptional circumstances. For this purpose, transactions necessitated by an excess of demand for loans over savings capital in the association's area are not to be deemed to be necessitated by exceptional circumstances. For purposes of (c) of this subdivision, the term "sales of participations" means sales by an association of interests in loans, which sales meet the requirements of the regulations of the Federal Home Loan Bank Board relating to sale of participations, or which meet substantially equivalent requirements of State law or regulations relating to sales of participations.

(iii) *Reporting requirement.*—In the case of income tax returns for taxable years beginning after July 11, 1969, there is required to be filed with the return a statement showing the amount of gross income for the taxable year in each of the categories described in subdivision (i), of this subparagraph.

(d) *60 percent of assets test.*—At least 60 percent of the amount of the total assets of a domestic building and loan association must consist of the assets defined in paragraph (e) of this section. The percentage specified in this paragraph is computed as of the close of the taxable year or, at the option of the taxpayer, may be computed on the basis of the average assets outstanding during the taxable year. Such average is determined by making the appropriate computation described in this section either as of the close of each month, as of the close of each quarter, or semiannually during the taxable year and by using the yearly average of the monthly, quarterly, or semiannual percentage obtained for each category of assets defined in paragraph (e) of this section. The method selected must be applied uniformly for the taxable year to all categories of assets, but the method may be changed from year to year. For purposes of this paragraph, it is immaterial whether the association originated the loans defined in subparagraphs (4) through (8) and (10) of paragraph (e) of this section or purchased or otherwise acquired them in whole or in part from another. See paragraph (f) of this section for definition of certain terms used in this paragraph and in paragraph (e) of this section, and for the determination of amount and character of loans.

(e) *Assets defined.*—The assets defined in this paragraph are—

(1) *Cash.*—The term "cash" means cash on hand, and time or demand deposits with, or withdrawable accounts in, other financial institutions.

(2) *Governmental obligations.*—The term "governmental obligations" means—

(i) Obligations of the United States,

(ii) Obligations of a State or political subdivision of a State, and

(iii) Stock or obligations of a corporation which is an instrumentality of the United States, a State, or a political subdivision of a State,

other than obligations the interest on which is excludable from gross income under section 103 and the regulations thereunder.

(3) *Deposit insurance company securities.*—The term "deposit insurance company securities" means certificates of deposit in, or obligations of a corporation organized under a State law which specifically authorizes such corporation to insure the deposits or share accounts of member associations.

(4) *Passbook loan.*—The term "passbook loan" means a loan to the extent secured by a deposit, withdrawable share, or savings account in the association, or share of a member of the association, with respect to which a distribution is allowable as a deduction under section 591.

(5) *Residential real property loan.*—[Reserved]

(6) *Church loan.*—[Reserved]

(7) *Urban renewal loan.*—[Reserved]

(8) *Institutional loan.*—[Reserved]

(9) *Foreclosed property.*—[Reserved]

(10) *Educational loan.*—[Reserved]

(11) *Property used in the association's business.*—(i) *In general.*—The term "property used in the association's business" means land, buildings, furniture, fixtures, equipment, leasehold interests, leasehold improvements, and other assets used by the association in the conduct of its business of acquiring the savings of the public and investing in loans. Real property held for the purpose of being used primarily as the principal or branch office of the association constitutes property used in the association's business so long as it is reasonably anticipated that such property will be occupied for such use by the association, or that construction work preparatory to such occupancy will be commenced thereon, within 2 years after acquisition of the property. Stock of a wholly owned subsidiary corporation which has as its exclusive activity the ownership and management of property more than 50 percent of the fair rental value of which is used as the principal or branch office of the association constitutes property used in such business. Real property held by an association for investment or sale, even for the purpose of obtaining mortgage loans thereon, does not constitute property used in the association's business.

(ii) *Property rented to others.*—Except as provided in the second sentence of subdivision (i) of this subparagraph, property or a portion thereof rented by the association to others does not constitute property used in the association's business. However, if the fair rental value of the rented portion of a single piece of real property (including appurtenant parcels) used as the principal or branch office of the association constitutes less than 50 percent of the fair rental value of such piece of property, or if such property has an adjusted basis of not more than $150,000, the entire property shall be considered used in such business. If such rented portion constitutes 50 percent or more of the fair rental value of such piece of property, and such property has an adjusted basis of more than $150,000, an allocation of its adjusted basis is required. The portion of the total adjusted basis of such piece of property which is deemed to be property used in the association's business shall be equal to an amount which bears the same ratio to such total adjusted basis as the amount of the fair rental value of the portion used as the principal or branch office of the association bears to the total fair rental value of such property. In the case of all property other than real property used or to be used as the principal or branch office of the association, if the fair rental value of the rented portion thereof constitutes less than 15 percent of the fair rental value of such property, the entire property shall be considered used in the association's business. If such rented portion constitutes 15 percent or more of the fair rental value of such property, an allocation of its adjusted basis (in the same manner as required for real property used as the principal or branch office) is required.

(12) *Regular or residual interest in a REMIC.*—(i) *In general.*—If for any calendar quarter at least 95 percent of a REMIC's assets (as determined in accordance with § 1.860F-4(e)(1)(ii) or § 1.6049-7(f)(3) of this chapter) are assets defined in paragraph (e)(1) through (e)(11) of this section, then for that calendar quarter all the regular and residual interests in that REMIC are treated as assets defined in this paragraph (e). If less than 95 percent of a REMIC's assets are assets defined in paragraph (e)(1) through (e)(11) of this section, the percentage of each REMIC regular or residual interest treated as an asset defined in this paragraph (e) is equal to the percentage of the REMIC's assets that are assets defined in paragraph (e)(1) through (e)(11) of this section. See § § 1.860F-4(e)(1)(ii)(B) and 1.6049-7(f)(3) of this chapter for information required to be provided to regular and residual interest holders if the 95 percent test is not met.

(ii) *Loans secured by manufactured housing.*—For purposes of paragraph (e)(12)(i) of this section, a loan secured by manufactured housing treated as a single family residence under section 25(e)(10) is an asset defined in paragraph (e)(1) through (e)(11) of this section.

(f) *Special rules.*—[Reserved][Reg. § 301.7701-13A.]

☐ [*T.D. 7622, 5-15-79. Amended by T.D. 8458, 12-23-92.*]

**[Reg. § 301.7701-14]**

**§ 301.7701-14. Cooperative bank.**—For taxable years beginning after October 16, 1962, the term "cooperative bank" means an institution without capital stock organized and operated for mutual purposes without profit which meets the supervisory test, the business operations test, and the various assets tests specified in paragraphs (d) through (h) of § 301.7701-13, employing the rules and definitions of paragraphs (j) through (l) of that section. In applying paragraphs (b) through (l) of such section any references to an "association" or to a "domestic building and loan association" shall be deemed to be a reference to a cooperative bank. [Reg. § 301.7701-14.]

☐ [*T.D. 6766, 10-30-64.*]

### [Reg. § 301.7701-15]

**§ 301.7701-15. Tax return preparer.**—(a) *In general.*—A *tax return preparer* is any person who prepares for compensation, or who employs one or more persons to prepare for compensation, all or a substantial portion of any return of tax or any claim for refund of tax under the Internal Revenue Code (Code).

(b) *Definitions.*—(1) *Signing tax return preparer.*—A *signing tax return preparer* is the individual tax return preparer who has the primary responsibility for the overall substantive accuracy of the preparation of such return or claim for refund.

(2) *Nonsigning tax return preparer.*—(i) *In general.*—A *nonsigning tax return preparer* is any tax return preparer who is not a signing tax return preparer but who prepares all or a substantial portion of a return or claim for refund within the meaning of paragraph (b)(3) of this section with respect to events that have occurred at the time the advice is rendered. In determining whether an individual is a nonsigning tax return preparer, time spent on advice that is given after events have occurred that represents less than 5 percent of the aggregate time incurred by such individual with respect to the position(s) giving rise to the understatement shall not be taken into account. Notwithstanding the preceding sentence, time spent on advice before the events have occurred will be taken into account if all facts and circumstances show that the position(s) giving rise to the understatement is primarily attributable to the advice, the advice was substantially given before events occurred primarily to avoid treating the person giving the advice as a tax return preparer, and the advice given before events occurred was confirmed after events had occurred for purposes of preparing a tax return. Examples of nonsigning tax return preparers are tax return preparers who provide advice (written or oral) to a taxpayer (or to another tax return preparer) when that advice leads to a position or entry that constitutes a substantial portion of the return within the meaning of paragraph(b)(3) of this section.

(ii) *Examples.*—The provisions of this paragraph (b)(2) are illustrated by the following examples:

*Example 1.* Attorney A, an attorney in a law firm, provides legal advice to a large corporate taxpayer regarding a completed corporate transaction. The advice provided by A is directly relevant to the determination of an entry on the taxpayer's return, and this advice leads to a position(s) or entry that constitutes a substantial portion of the return. A, however, does not prepare any other portion of the taxpayer's return and is not the signing tax return preparer of this return. A is considered a nonsigning tax return preparer.

*Example 2.* Attorney B, an attorney in a law firm, provides legal advice to a large corporate taxpayer regarding the tax consequences of a proposed corporate transaction. Based upon this advice, the corporate taxpayer enters into the transaction. Once the transaction is completed, the corporate taxpayer does not receive any additional advice from B with respect to the transaction. B did not provide advice with respect to events that have occurred and is not considered a tax return preparer.

*Example 3.* The facts are the same as *Example 2*, except that Attorney B provides supplemental advice to the corporate taxpayer on a phone call after the transaction is completed. Attorney B did not provide advice before the corporate transaction occurred with the primary intent to avoid being treated as a tax return preparer. The time incurred on this supplemental advice by B represented less than 5 percent of the aggregate amount of time spent by B providing tax advice on the position. B is not considered a tax return preparer.

(3) *Substantial portion.*—(i) Only a person who prepares all or a substantial portion of a return or claim for refund shall be considered to be a tax return preparer of the return or claim for refund. A person who renders tax advice on a position that is directly relevant to the determination of the existence, characterization, or amount of an entry on a return or claim for refund will be regarded as having prepared that entry. Whether a schedule, entry, or other portion of a return or claim for refund is a substantial portion is determined based upon whether the person knows or reasonably should know that the tax attributable to the schedule, entry, or other portion of a return or claim for refund is a substantial portion of the tax required to be shown on the return or claim for refund. A single tax entry may constitute a substantial portion of the tax required to be shown on a return. Factors to consider in determining whether a schedule, entry,

or other portion of a return or claim for refund is a substantial portion include but are not limited to—

(A) the size and complexity of the item relative to the taxpayer's gross income; and

(B) the size of the understatement attributable to the item compared to the taxpayer's reported tax liability.

(ii)(A) For purposes of applying the rules of paragraph (b)(3)(i) of this section to a nonsigning tax return preparer within the meaning of paragraph (b)(2) of this section only, the schedule or other portion is not considered to be a substantial portion if the schedule, entry, or other portion of the return or claim for refund involves amounts of gross income, amounts of deductions, or amounts on the basis of which credits are determined that are—

(1) Less than $10,000; or

(2) Less than $400,000 and also less than 20 percent of the gross income as shown on the return or claim for refund (or, for an individual, the individual's adjusted gross income).

(B) If more than one schedule, entry or other portion is involved, all schedules, entries or other portions shall be aggregated in applying the de minimis rule in paragraph (b)(3)(ii)(A) of this section.

(C) The de minimis rule in paragraph (b)(3)(ii)(A) of this section shall not apply to a signing tax return preparer within the meaning of paragraph (b)(1) of this section.

(iii) A tax return preparer with respect to one return is not considered to be a tax return preparer of another return merely because an entry or entries reported on the first return may affect an entry reported on the other return, unless the entry or entries reported on the first return are directly reflected on the other return and constitute a substantial portion of the other return. For example, the sole preparer of a partnership return of income or small business corporation income tax return is considered a tax return preparer of a partner's or a shareholder's return if the entry or entries on the partnership or small business corporation return reportable on the partner's or shareholder's return constitute a substantial portion of the partner's or shareholder's return.

(iv) *Examples.*—The provisions of this paragraph (b)(3) are illustrated by the following examples:

*Example 1.* Accountant C prepares a Form 8886, "Reportable Transaction Disclosure Statement", that is used to disclose reportable transactions. C does not prepare the tax return or advise the taxpayer regarding the tax return reporting position of the transaction to which the Form 8886 relates. The preparation of the Form 8886 is not directly relevant to the determination of the existence, characterization, or amount of an entry on a tax return or claim for refund. Rather, the Form 8886 is prepared by C to disclose a reportable transaction. C has not prepared a substantial portion of the tax return and is not considered a tax return preparer under section 6694.

*Example 2.* Accountant D prepares a schedule for an individual taxpayer's Form 1040, "U.S. Individual Income Tax Return", reporting $4,000 in dividend income and gives oral or written advice about Schedule A, which results in a claim of a medical expense deduction totaling $5,000, but does not sign the tax return. D is not a nonsigning tax return preparer because the total aggregate amount of the deductions is less than $10,000.

(4) *Return and claim for refund.*—(i) *Return.*—For purposes of this section, a return of tax is a return (including an amended or adjusted return) filed by or on behalf of a taxpayer reporting the liability of the taxpayer for tax under the Code, if the type of return is identified in published guidance in the Internal Revenue Bulletin. A return of tax also includes any information return or other document identified in published guidance in the Internal Revenue Bulletin and that reports information that is or may be reported on another taxpayer's return under the Code if the information reported on the information return or other document constitutes a substantial portion of the taxpayer's return within the meaning of paragraph (b)(3) of this section.

(ii) *Claim for refund.*—For purposes of this section, a claim for refund of tax includes a claim for credit against any tax that is included in published guidance in the Internal Revenue Bulletin. A claim for refund also includes a claim for payment under section 6420, 6421, or 6427.

(c) *Mechanical or clerical assistance.*—A person who furnishes to a taxpayer or other tax return preparer sufficient information and advice so that completion of the return or claim for refund is largely a mechanical or clerical matter is considered a tax return preparer, even though that person does not actually place or review placement of information on the return or claim for refund. See also paragraph (b)(3) of this section.

(d) *Qualifications.*—A person may be a tax return preparer without regard to educational qualifications and professional status requirements.

(e) *Outside the United States.*—A person who prepares a return or claim for refund outside the United States is a tax return preparer, regardless of the person's nationality, residence, or the location of the person's place of business, if the person otherwise satisfies the definition of *tax return preparer.* Notwithstanding the provisions of §301.6109-1(g), the person shall secure an employer identification number if the person is an employer of another tax return preparer, is a partnership in which one or more of the general partners is a tax return preparer, is a firm in which one or more of the equity holders is a tax return preparer, or is an individual not employed by another tax return preparer.

(f) *Persons who are not tax return preparers.*—(1) The following persons are not tax return preparers:

(i) An official or employee of the Internal Revenue Service (IRS) performing official duties.

(ii) Any individual who provides tax assistance under a Volunteer Income Tax Assistance (VITA) program established by the IRS, but only with respect to those returns prepared as part of the VITA program.

(iii) Any organization sponsoring or administering a VITA program established by the IRS, but only with respect to that sponsorship or administration.

(iv) Any individual who provides tax counseling for the elderly under a program established pursuant to section 163 of the Revenue Act of 1978, but only with respect to those returns prepared as part of that program.

(v) Any organization sponsoring or administering a program to provide tax counseling for the elderly established pursuant to section 163 of the Revenue Act of 1978, but only with respect to that sponsorship or administration.

(vi) Any individual who provides tax assistance as part of a qualified Low-Income Taxpayer Clinic (LITC), as defined by section 7526, subject to the requirements of paragraphs (f)(2) and (3) of this section, but only with respect to those returns and claims for refund prepared as part of the LITC program.

(vii) Any organization that is a qualified LITC, as defined by section 7526, subject to the requirements of paragraphs (f)(2) and (3) of this section.

(viii) An individual providing only typing, reproduction, or other mechanical assistance in the preparation of a return or claim for refund.

(ix) An individual preparing a return or claim for refund of a taxpayer, or an officer, a general partner, member, shareholder, or employee of a taxpayer, by whom the individual is regularly and continuously employed or compensated or in which the individual is a general partner.

(x) An individual preparing a return or claim for refund for a trust, estate, or other entity of which the individual either is a fiduciary or is an officer, general partner, or employee of the fiduciary.

(xi) An individual preparing a claim for refund for a taxpayer in response to—

(A) A notice of deficiency issued to the taxpayer; or

(B) A waiver of restriction on assessment after initiation of an audit of the taxpayer or another taxpayer if a determination in the audit of the other taxpayer affects, directly or indirectly, the liability of the taxpayer for tax.

(xii) A person who prepares a return or claim for refund for a taxpayer with no explicit or implicit agreement for compensation, even if the person receives an insubstantial gift, return service, or favor.

(2) Paragraphs (f)(1)(vi) and (vii) of this section apply only if any assistance with a return of tax or claim for refund is directly related to a controversy with the IRS for which the qualified LITC is providing assistance or is an ancillary part of a LITC program to inform individuals for whom English is a second language about their rights and responsibilities under the Code.

(3) Notwithstanding paragraph (f)(2) of this section, paragraphs (f)(1)(vi) and (f)(1)(vii) of this section do not apply if an LITC charges a separate fee or varies a fee based on whether the LITC provides assistance with a return of tax or claim for refund under the Code or if the LITC charges more than a nominal fee for its services.

(4) For purposes of paragraph (f)(1)(ix) of this section, the employee of a corporation owning more than 50 percent of the voting power of another corporation, or the employee of a corporation more than 50 percent of the voting power of which is owned by another corporation, is considered the employee of the other corporation as well.

(5) For purposes of paragraph (f)(1)(x) of this section, an estate, guardianship, conservatorship, committee, or any similar arrangement for a taxpayer under a legal disability (such as a minor, an incompetent, or an infirm individual) is considered a trust or estate.

(6) *Examples.*—The mechanical assistance exception described in paragraph (f)(1)(viii) of this section is illustrated by the following examples:

*Example 1.* A reporting agent received employment tax information from a client from the client's business records. The reporting agent did not render any tax advice to the client or exercise any discretion or independent judgment on the client's underlying tax positions. The reporting agent processed the client's information, signed the return as authorized by the client pursuant to Form 8655, Reporting Agent Authorization, and filed the client's return using the information supplied by the client. The reporting agent is not a tax return preparer.

*Example 2.* A reporting agent rendered tax advice to a client on determining whether its workers are employees or independent contractors for Federal tax purposes. For compensation, the reporting agent received employment tax information from the client, processed the client's information and filed the client's return using the information supplied by the client. The reporting agent is a tax return preparer.

(g) *Effective/applicability date.*—This section is applicable to returns and claims for refund filed, and advice provided, after December 31, 2008. [Reg. §301.7701-15.]

☐ [*T.D.* 7519, 11-17-77. *Amended by T.D.* 7675, 2-20-80; *T.D.* 9026, 12-17-2002 *and T.D.* 9436, 12-15-2008 (*corrected* 1-28-2009).]

### [Reg. §301.7701-16]

**§301.7701-16. Other terms.**—For a definition of the term "withholding agent" see §1.1441-7(a). Any other terms that are defined in section 7701 and that are not defined in §§301.7701-1 to 301.7701-15, inclusive, shall, when used in this chapter, have the meanings assigned to them in section 7701. [Reg. §301.7701-16.]

☐ [*T.D.* 6606, 8-24-62. *Amended by T.D.* 6766, 10-30-64, *T.D.* 7519, 11-17-77 *and T.D.* 7977, 9-19-84.]

### [Reg. §301.7701-17T]

**§301.7701-17T. Collective-bargaining plans and agreements (Temporary).**—

Q-1: How did the Tax Reform Act of 1984 (TRA of 1984) change the laws with respect to plans that are maintained pursuant to collective bargaining agreements?

A-1: (a) Many of the requirements and rules applicable to deferred compensation and welfare benefit plans are different for plans maintained pursuant to a collective bargaining agreement. Prior to the TRA of 1984, the Internal Revenue Code provided no clear definition of an employee representative or whether there is a collective bargaining agreement between such employee representative and one or more employers.

(b) Section 526(c) of the TRA of 1984 added a new condition under a new section 7701(a)(46) that must be satisfied in order for a plan to be considered to be a plan maintained pursuant to a collective bargaining agreement between employee representatives and one or more employers for purposes of the Code after March 31, 1984. If more than one-half of the membership of an organization is comprised of owners, officers, and executives of employers covered by the plan, then such organization is not an employee representative for purposes of determining whether a plan is to be treated as maintained pursuant to a collective bargaining agreement between employee representatives and one or more employers. Whether an individual is an owner, officer or executive is to be determined separately with respect to each employer. Additionally, section 7701(a)(46) provides that the Internal Revenue Service shall make the determination for purposes of the Code as to whether there is a collective bargaining agreement between employee representatives and one or more employers.

Q-2: If an organization does not fail to be an employee representative under the 50 percent or less test of section 7701(a)(46), is a plan maintained pursuant to an agreement between such organization and one or more employers necessarily treated, under the Code, as a plan maintained pursuant to a collective bargaining agreement between an employee representative and one or more employers?

A-2: (a) No.

(b) Specific Code provisions generally require other conditions than that in section 7701(a)(46) to be satisfied in order for a plan to be considered to be collectively-bargained. For example, in order for a plan to be described in section 413(a), the Secretary of Labor must find that the plan is maintained pursuant to a collective bargaining agreement between employee representatives and one or more employers.

(c) Even if (1) the finding in the example in the preceding paragraph (b) is made by the Secretary of Labor, (2) the union has been recognized as exempt under section 501(c)(5), and (3) the percentage condition in section 7701(a)(46) is satisfied, the Internal Revenue Service has the authority, pursuant to section 7701(a)(46), to determine whether there is a collective bargaining agreement under the Code. [Temporary Reg. §301.7701-17T.]

☐ [*T.D.* 8073, 1-29-86.]

### [Reg. §301.7701-18]

**§301.7701-18. Definitions; spouse, husband and wife, husband, wife, marriage.**—(a) *In general.*—For federal tax purposes, the terms *spouse, husband,* and *wife* mean an individual lawfully married to another individual. The term *husband and wife* means two individuals lawfully married to each other.

(b) *Persons who are lawfully married for federal tax purposes.*—(1) *In general.*—Except as provided in paragraph (b)(2) of this section regarding marriages entered into under the laws of a foreign jurisdiction, a marriage of two individuals is recognized for federal tax purposes if the marriage is recognized by the state, possession, or territory of the United States in which the marriage is entered into, regardless of domicile.

(2) *Foreign marriages.*—Two individuals who enter into a relationship denominated as marriage under the laws of a foreign jurisdiction are recognized as married for federal tax purposes if the relationship would be recognized as marriage under the laws of at least one state, possession, or territory of the United States, regardless of domicile.

(c) *Persons who are not lawfully married for federal tax purposes.*—The terms *spouse, husband,* and *wife* do not include individuals who have entered into a registered domestic partnership, civil union, or other similar formal relationship not denominated as a marriage under the law of the state, possession, or territory of the United States where such relationship was entered into, regardless of domicile. The term *husband and wife* does not include couples who have entered into such a formal relationship, and the term *marriage* does not include such formal relationships.

(d) *Applicability date.*—The rules of this section apply to taxable years ending on or after September 2, 2016. [Reg. §301.7701-18.]

☐ [*T.D.* 9785, 8-31-2016.]

### [Reg. §301.7701(b)-0]

**§301.7701(b)-0. Outline of regulations provisions for section 7701(b)-1 through (b)-9.**—This section lists the paragraphs contained in §§301.7701(b)-1 through 301.7701(b)-9.

*§301.7701(b)-1. Resident alien.*
  (a) Scope.
  (b) Lawful permanent resident.
    (1) Green card test.
    (2) Rescission of resident status.
    (3) Administrative or judicial determination of abandonment of resident status.
  (c) Substantial presence test.
    (1) In general.
    (2) Determination of presence.
      (i) Physical presence.
      (ii) United States.
    (3) Current year.
    (4) Thirty-one day minimum.
  (d) Application of section 7701(b) to the possessions and territories.
    (1) Application to aliens.
    (2) Non-application to citizens.
  (e) Examples.

*§301.7701(b)-2. Closer connection exception.*
  (a) In general.
  (b) Foreign country.
  (c) Tax home.
    (1) Definition.
    (2) Duration and nature of tax home.
  (d) Closer connection to a foreign country.
    (1) In general.
    (2) Permanent home.
  (e) Special rule.
  (f) Closer connection exception unavailable.
  (g) Filing requirements.

*§301.7701(b)-3. Days of presence in the United States that are excluded for purposes of section 7701(b).*
  (a) In general.
  (b) Exempt individuals.
    (1) In general.

    (2) Foreign government-related individual.
      (i) In general.
      (ii) Definition of international organization.
      (iii) Full-time diplomatic or consular status.
    (3) Teacher or trainee.
    (4) Student.
    (5) Professional athlete.
    (6) Substantial compliance.
    (7) Limitation on teacher or trainee and student exemptions.
      (i) Teacher or trainee limitation in general.
      (ii) Special teacher or trainee limitation for section 872(b)(3) compensation.
      (iii) Limitation on student exemption.
      (iv) Transition rule.
      (v) Examples.
    (8) Immediate family.
  (c) Medical condition.
    (1) In general.
    (2) Intent to leave the United States.
    (3) Preexisting medical condition.
    (4) Examples.
  (d) Days in transit.
  (e) Regular commuters from Mexico or Canada.
    (1) General rule.
    (2) Definitions.
    (3) Examples.
  (f) Determination of excluded days applies beyond year of determination.

*§301.7701(b)-4. Residency time periods.*
  (a) First year of residency.
  (b) Last year of residency.
    (1) General rule.
    (2) Exceptions.
  (c) Rules relating to residency starting date and residency termination date.
    (1) De minimis presence.
    (2) Proration.
    (3) Residency starting date for certain individuals.
      (i) In general.
      (ii) Determination of presence.
      (iii) Thirty-one day period.
      (iv) Period of continuous presence.
      (v) Election procedure.
        (A) Filing requirements.
        (B) Election on behalf of a dependent child.
        (C) Statement.
      (vi) Penalty for failure to comply with filing requirements.
        (A) General rule.
        (B) Exception.
  (d) Examples.
  (e) No lapse.
    (1) Residency in prior year.
    (2) Residency in following year.
    (3) Special rule.
    (4) Example.

*§301.7701(b)-5. Coordination with section 877.*
  (a) General rule.
  (b) Tax imposed.
  (c) Example.

*§301.7701(b)-6. Taxable year.*
  (a) In general.
  (b) Examples.

*§301.7701(b)-7. Coordination with income tax treaties.*
  (a) Consistency requirement.
    (1) Application.
    (2) Computation of tax liability.
    (3) Other Internal Revenue Code purposes.
    (4) Special rules for S corporations. [Reserved]
  (b) Filing requirements.
  (c) Contents of statement.
    (1) In general.
      (i) Returns due after December 15, 1997.
      (ii) Earlier returns.
    (2) Controlled foreign corporation shareholders.
    (3) S corporation shareholders. [Reserved]
  (d) Relationship to section 6114(a) treaty-based return positions.
  (e) Examples.

*§ 301.7701(b)-8. Procedural rules.*

  (a) Who must file.

    (1) Closer connection exception.

    (2) Exempt individuals and individuals with a medical condition.

    (3) De minimis presence and residency starting and termination dates.

  (b) Contents of statement.

    (1) Closer connection exception.

      (i) Returns due after December 15, 1997.

      (ii) Earlier returns.

    (2) Exempt individuals and individuals with a medical condition.

      (i) Returns due after December 15, 1997.

      (ii) Earlier returns.

    (3) De minimis presence and residency starting and termination dates.

  (c) How to file.

  (d) Penalty for failure to file statement.

    (1) General rule.

    (2) Exception.

  (e) Filing requirement disregarded.

*§ 301.7701(b)-9. Effective dates of § § 301.7701(b)-1 through 301.7701(b)-7.*

  (a) In general.

  (b) Special rules.

    (1) Green card test-residency starting date.

    (2) Substantial presence test-years included.

    (3) Professional athletes.

    (4) Procedural rules and filing requirements. [Reg. § 301.7701(b)-0.]

  ☐ [T.D. 8411, 4-24-92. Amended by T.D. 8733, 10-6-97.]

### [Reg. § 301.7701(b)-1]

**§ 301.7701(b)-1. Resident alien.**—(a) *Scope.*—Section 301.7701(b)-1(b) provides rules for determining whether an alien individual is a lawful permanent resident of the United States. Section 301.7701(b)-1(c) provides rules for determining if an alien individual satisfies the substantial presence test. Section 301.7701(b)-2 provides rules for determining when an alien individual will be considered to maintain a tax home in a foreign country and to have a closer connection to that foreign country. Section 301.7701(b)-3 provides rules for determining if an individual is an exempt individual because of his or her status as a foreign government-related individual, teacher, trainee, student, or professional athlete. Section 301.7701(b)-3 also provides rules for determining whether an individual may exclude days of presence in the United States because the individual was unable to leave the United States because of a medical condition. Section 301.7701(b)-4 provides rules for determining an individual's residency starting and termination dates. Section 301.7701(b)-5 provides rules for applying section 877 to a nonresident alien individual. Section 301.7701(b)-6 provides rules for determining the taxable year of an alien. Section 301.7701(b)-7 provides rules for determining the effect of these regulations on rules in tax conventions to which the United States is a party. Section 301.7701(b)-8 provides procedural rules for establishing that an individual is a nonresident alien. Section 301.7701(b)-9 provides the effective dates of section 7701(b) and the regulations under that section. Unless the context indicates otherwise, the regulations under § § 301.7701(b)-1 through 301.7701(b)-9 apply for purposes of determining whether a United States citizen is also a resident of the United States. (This determination may be relevant, for example, to the application of section 861(a)(1) which treats income from interest-bearing obligations of residents as income from sources within the United States.) The regulations do not apply and § § 1.871-2 and 1.871-5 of this chapter continue to apply for purposes of the bona fide residence test of section 911. See § 1.911-2(c) of this chapter. For purposes of determining whether an individual is a resident of the United States for estate and gift tax purposes, see § 20.0-1(b)(1) and (2) and § 25.2501-1(b) of this chapter, respectively.

  (b) *Lawful permanent resident.*—(1) *Green card test.*—An alien is a resident alien with respect to a calendar year if the individual is a lawful permanent resident at any time during the calendar year. A lawful permanent resident is an individual who has been lawfully granted the privilege of residing permanently in the United States as an immigrant in accordance with the immigration laws. Resident status is deemed to continue unless it is rescinded or administratively or judicially determined to have been abandoned.

  (2) *Rescission of resident status.*—Resident status is considered to be rescinded if a final administrative or judicial order of exclusion or deportation is issued regarding the alien individual. For purposes of this paragraph, the term "final judicial order" means an order that is no longer subject to appeal to a higher court of competent jurisdiction.

  (3) *Administrative or judicial determination of abandonment of resident status.*—An administrative or judicial determination of abandonment of resident status may be initiated by the alien individual, the Immigration and Naturalization Service (INS), or a consular officer. If the alien initiates this determination, resident status is considered to be abandoned when the individual's application for abandonment (INS Form I-407) or a letter stating the alien's intent to abandon his or her resident status, with the Alien Registration Receipt Card (INS Form I-151 or Form I-551) enclosed, is filed with the INS or a consular officer. If INS replaces any of the form numbers referred to in this paragraph or § 301.7701(b)-2(f), refer to the comparable INS replacement form number. For purposes of this paragraph, an alien individual shall be considered to have filed a letter stating the intent to abandon resident status with the INS or a consular office if such letter is sent by certified mail, return receipt requested (or a foreign country's equivalent thereof). A copy of the letter, along with proof that the letter was mailed and received, should be retained by the alien individual. If the INS or a consular officer initiates this determination, resident status will be considered to be abandoned upon the issuance of a final administrative order of abandonment. If an individual is granted an appeal to a federal court of competent jurisdiction, a final judicial order is required.

  (c) *Substantial presence test.*—(1) *In general.*—An alien individual is a resident alien if the individual meets the substantial presence test. An individual satisfies this test if he or she has been present in the United States on at least 183 days during a three year period that includes the current year. For purposes of this test, each day of presence in the current year is counted as a full day. Each day of presence in the first preceding year is counted as one-third of a day and each day of presence in the second preceding year is counted as one-sixth of a day. For purposes of this paragraph, any fractional days resulting from the above calculations will not be rounded to the nearest whole number. (See § 301.7701(b)-9(b)(2) for transitional rules for calendar years 1985 and 1986.)

  (2) *Determination of presence.*—(i) *Physical presence.*—For purposes of the substantial presence test, an individual shall be treated as present in the United States on any day that he or she is physically present in the United States at any time during the day. (But see § 301.7701(b)-3 relating to days of presence that may be excluded.)

  (ii) *United States.*—For purposes of section 7701(b) and the regulations thereunder, the term "United States" when used in a geographical sense includes the states and the District of Columbia. It also includes the territorial waters of the United States and the seabed and subsoil of those submarine areas which are adjacent to the territorial waters of the United States and over which the United States has exclusive rights, in accordance with international law, with respect to the exploration and exploitation of natural resources. It does not include the possessions and territories of the United States or the air space over the United States.

  (3) *Current year.*—The term "current year" means any calendar year for which an alien individual is determining his or her resident status.

  (4) *Thirty-one day minimum.*—If an individual is not physically present for more than 30 days during the current year, the substantial presence test will not be applied for that year even if the three-year total is 183 or more days. For purposes of the substantial presence test, it is irrelevant that an individual was not present for more than 30 days in the first or second year preceding the current year.

  (d) *Application of section 7701(b) to the possessions and territories.*—(1) *Application to aliens for purposes of mirror systems.*—Section 7701(b) provides the basis for determining whether an alien individual is a resident of a United States possession or territory that administers income tax laws that are identical (except for the substitution of the name of the possession or territory for the term "United States" where appropriate) to those in force in the United States, for purposes of applying such laws with respect to income tax liability incurred to such possession or territory.

  (2) *Non-application for bona fide resident determination.*—Section 7701(b) does not provide the basis for determining whether an individual (including an alien individual) is a bona fide resident of a United States possession or territory for Federal income tax purposes. For the applicable rules for making this determination, see section 937(a) and § 1.937-1 of this chapter.

  (e) *Examples.*—This section may be illustrated by the following examples:

*Example 1.* B, an alien individual, is present in the United States for 122 days in the current year. He was present in the United States for 122 days in the first preceding calendar year and for 122 days in the second preceding calendar year. In determining his status for the current year, B counts all 122 days in the United States in the current year plus $1/3$ of the 122 days in the United States in the first preceding calendar year (40 $2/3$ days) and $1/6$ of the 122 days in the United States during the second preceding calendar year (20 $1/3$ days). The total of 122 + 40 $2/3$ + 20 $1/3$ equals 183 days. B meets the substantial presence test and is a resident alien for the current year.

*Example 2.* C, an alien individual, is present in the United States for 25 days during the current year. She was present in the United States for 365 days during the first preceding year and 365 days during the second preceding year. The substantial presence test does not apply because C is present in the United States for fewer than 31 days during the current year.

*Example 3.* D, an alien individual, is present in the United States for 170 days during the current year. He was present in the United States for 30 days during the first preceding year and 30 days during the second preceding year. In determining his status for the current year, D counts all 170 days in the United States in the current year plus $1/3$ of the 30 days in the United States in the first preceding calendar year (10 days) and $1/6$ of the 30 days in the United States during the second preceding calendar year (5 days). The total of 170 + 10 + 5 equals 185 days. D meets the substantial presence test and is a resident alien for the current year notwithstanding the fact that he was present in the United States for fewer than 31 days in each of the two preceding years. [Reg. §301.7701(b)-1.]

□ [*T.D. 8411, 4-24-92. Amended by T.D. 9194, 4-6-2005 and T.D. 9391, 4-4-2008.*]

### [Reg. §301.7701(b)-2]

**§301.7701(b)-2. Closer connection exception.**—(a) *In general.*—An alien individual who meets the substantial presence test may nevertheless be considered a nonresident alien for the current year if the following conditions are satisfied—

(1) The individual is present in the United States for fewer than 183 days in the current year;

(2) The individual maintains a tax home in a foreign country during the current year; and

(3) Except as provided in paragraph (e) of this section, the individual has a closer connection during the current year to a single foreign country in which he or she maintains a tax home than to the United States.

(b) *Foreign country.*—For purposes of section 7701(b) and the regulations thereunder, the term "foreign country" when used in a geographical sense includes any territory under the sovereignty of the United Nations or a government other than that of the United States. It includes the territorial waters of the foreign country (determined in accordance with the laws of the United States), and the seabed and subsoil of those submarine areas which are adjacent to the territorial waters of the foreign country and over which the foreign country has exclusive rights, in accordance with international law, with respect to the exploration and exploitation of natural resources. It also includes the possessions and territories of the United States.

(c) *Tax home.*—(1) *Definition.*—For purposes of section 7701(b) and the regulations under that section, the term "tax home" has the same meaning that it has for purposes of section 162(a)(2) (relating to travel expenses while away from home). Thus, an individual's tax home is considered to be located at the individual's regular or principal (if more than one regular) place of business. If the individual has no regular or principal place of business because of the nature of the business, or because the individual is not engaged in carrying on any trade or business within the meaning of section 162(a), then the individual's tax home is the individual's regular place of abode in a real and substantial sense.

(2) *Duration and nature of tax home.*—The tax home maintained by the alien individual must be in existence for the entire current year. The tax home must be located in the same foreign country for which the individual is claiming to have the closer connection described in paragraph (d) of this section.

(d) *Closer connection to a foreign country.*—(1) *In general.*—For purposes of section 7701(b) and the regulations under that section, an alien individual will be considered to have a closer connection to a foreign country than the United States if the individual or the Commissioner establishes that the individual has maintained more significant contacts with the foreign country than with the United States. In determining whether an individual has maintained more significant contacts with a foreign country than the United States, the facts and circumstances to be considered include, but are not limited to, the following—

(i) The location of the individual's permanent home;

(ii) The location of the individual's family;

(iii) The location of personal belongings, such as automobiles, furniture, clothing and jewelry owned by the individual and his or her family;

(iv) The location of social, political, cultural or religious organizations with which the individual has a current relationship;

(v) The location where the individual conducts his or her routine personal banking activities;

(vi) The location where the individual conducts business activities (other than those that constitute the individual's tax home);

(vii) The location of the jurisdiction in which the individual holds a driver's license;

(viii) The location of the jurisdiction in which the individual votes;

(ix) The country of residence designated by the individual on forms and documents; and

(x) The types of official forms and documents filed by the individual, such as Form 1078 (Certificate of Alien Claiming Residence in the United States), Form W-8 (Certificate of Foreign Status) or Form W-9 (Payee's Request for Taxpayer Identification Number).

(2) *Permanent home.*—For purposes of paragraph (d)(1)(i) of this section, it is immaterial whether a permanent home is a house, an apartment, or a furnished room. It is also immaterial whether the home is owned or rented by the alien individual. It is material, however, that the dwelling be available at all times, continuously, and not solely for stays of short duration.

(e) *Special rule.*—An alien individual may demonstrate in one year that he or she has a closer connection to two foreign countries (but no more than two) if he or she satisfies all of the following conditions—

(1) The individual maintains a tax home beginning on the first day of the current year in one foreign country;

(2) The individual changes his or her tax home during the current year to a second foreign country;

(3) The individual continues to maintain his or her tax home in the second foreign country for the remainder of the current year;

(4) The individual has a closer connection to each foreign country than to the United States for the period during which the individual maintains a tax home in that foreign country; and

(5) The individual is subject to taxation as a resident pursuant to the internal laws of either foreign country for the entire year or subject to taxation as a resident in both foreign countries for the period during which the individual maintains a tax home in each foreign country.

(f) *Closer connection exception unavailable.*—An alien individual who has personally applied, or taken other affirmative steps, to change his or her status to that of a permanent resident during the current year or has an application pending for adjustment of status during the current year will not be eligible for the closer connection exception. Affirmative steps to change status to that of a permanent resident include, but are not limited to, the following—

(1) The filing of Immigration and Naturalization Form I-508 (Waiver of Immunities) by the alien;

(2) The filing of Immigration and Naturalization Form I-485 (Application for Status as Permanent Resident) by the alien;

(3) The filing of Immigration and Naturalization Form I-130 (Petition for Alien Relative) on behalf of the alien;

(4) The filing of Immigration and Naturalization Form I-140 (Petition for Prospective Immigrant Employee) on behalf of the alien;

(5) The filing of Department of Labor Form ETA-750 (Application for Alien Employment Certification) on behalf of the alien; or

(6) The filing of Department of State Form OF-230 (Application for Immigrant Visa and Alien Registration) by the alien.

(g) *Filing requirements.*—See §301.7701(b)-8 with regard to the statement that must be filed by an alien individual claiming the closer connection exception. [Reg. §301.7701(b)-2.]

□ [*T.D. 8411, 4-24-92.*]

### [Reg. §301.7701(b)-3]

**§301.7701(b)-3. Days of presence in the United States that are excluded for purposes of section 7701(b).**—(a) *In general.*—In computing days of presence in the United States, an alien is considered to be present if the individual is physically present in the United States at any time during the day (see §301.7701(b)-1(c)(2)(i)). However, for purposes of section 7701(b) and the regulations under that section, the following days shall be excluded and will not count as days of presence in the United States—

(1) Any day that an individual is present in the United States as an exempt individual;

(2) Any day that an individual is prevented from leaving the United States because of a medical condition that arose while the individual was present in the United States—

(3) Any day that an individual is in transit between two points outside the United States; and

(4) Any day on which a regular commuter residing in Canada or Mexico commutes to and from employment in the United States.

(b) *Exempt individuals.*—(1) *In general.*—An exempt individual is an individual who is either a—

(i) Foreign government-related individual as defined in paragraph (b)(2) of this section;

(ii) Teacher or trainee as defined in paragraph (b)(3) of this section;

(iii) Student as defined in paragraph (b)(4) of this section; or

(iv) Professional athlete as defined in paragraph (b)(5) of this section.

(2) *Foreign government-related individual.*—(i) *In general.*—A foreign government-related individual is an individual (and that individual's immediate family) who is temporarily present in the United States—

(A) as a full-time employee of an international organization;

(B) by reason of diplomatic status; or

(C) by reason of a visa that the Secretary of the Treasury or his or her delegate (after consultation with the Secretary of State when appropriate) determines represents full-time diplomatic or consular status. An individual described in this paragraph shall be considered to be temporarily present in the United States if the individual is not a lawful permanent resident as described in § 301.7701(b)-1(b)(1), regardless of the actual amount of time that the individual is present in the United States.

(ii) *Definition of international organization.*—The term "international organization" means any public international organization that has been designated by the President by Executive Order as being entitled to enjoy the privileges, exemptions, and immunities provided for in the International Organizations Act (22 U.S.C. 288). An individual described in paragraph (b)(2)(i) of this section will be a full-time employee of an international organization if that individual's employment with the organization is consistent with an employment schedule of a person with a standard full-time work schedule with the organization.

(iii) *Full-time diplomatic or consular status.*—An individual is considered to have full-time diplomatic or consular status if—

(A) The individual has been accredited by a foreign government recognized de jure or de facto by the United States;

(B) The individual intends to engage primarily in official activities for that foreign government while in the United States; and

(C) The individual has been recognized by the President, or by the Secretary of State, or by a consular officer acting on behalf of the Secretary of State, as being entitled to such status.

(3) *Teacher or trainee.*—A teacher or trainee includes any individual (and that individual's immediate family), other than a student, who is admitted temporarily to the United States as a nonimmigrant under section 101(a)(15)(J) (relating to the admission of teachers and trainees into the United States) or section 101(a)(15)(Q) (relating to the admission of participants in international cultural exchange programs) of the Immigration and Nationality Act (8 U.S.C. 1101(a)(15)(J), (Q)) and who substantially complies with the requirements of being admitted.

(4) *Student.*—A student is any individual (and that individual's immediate family) who is admitted temporarily to the United States as a nonimmigrant under section 101(a)(15)(F) or (M) (relating to the admission of students into the United States) or as a student under section 101(a)(15)(J) (relating to the admission of teachers and trainees into the United States) or section 101(a)(15)(Q) (relating to the admission of participants in international cultural exchange programs) of the Immigration and Nationality Act (8 U.S.C. 1101(a)(15)(F), (J), (M), (Q)) who substantially complies with the requirements of being admitted. For rules concerning taxation of certain nonresident students or trainees, see section 871(c) and § 1.871-9(a) of this chapter.

(5) *Professional athlete.*—A professional athlete is an individual who is temporarily present in the United States to compete in a charitable sports event described in section 274(l)(1)(B). For purposes of computing the days of presence in the United States, only days on which the athlete actually competes in a charitable sports event described in section 274(l)(1)(B) shall be excluded. Thus, days on which the individual is present to practice for the event, to perform promotional or other activities related to the event, or to travel

between events shall be included for purposes of the substantial presence test.

(6) *Substantial compliance.*—An individual described in paragraph (b)(3) or (4) of this section will be deemed to comply substantially with the visa requirements relevant to residence for tax purposes if the individual has not engaged in activities that are prohibited by the Immigration and Nationality Act and the regulations thereunder and could result in the loss of F, J or M visa status. An individual will not be deemed to comply substantially with the visa requirements relevant to residence for tax purposes merely by showing that the individual's visa has not been revoked. An independent determination of substantial compliance may be made by the Internal Revenue Service for any individual claiming to be an exempt individual under paragraph (b)(3) or (4) of this section. For example, if an individual with an F visa (student visa) is found to have accepted unauthorized employment or to have maintained a course of study that is not considered by the Internal Revenue Service to be full-time, the individual will not be considered to comply substantially with the individual's visa requirements regardless of whether the individual's visa has been revoked.

(7) *Limitation on teacher or trainee and student exemptions.*—(i) *Teacher or trainee limitation in general.*—Except as otherwise provided, an individual shall not exclude days of presence as a teacher or trainee if the individual has been exempt as a teacher, trainee, or student for any part of two of the six preceding calendar years.

(ii) *Special teacher or trainee limitation for section 872 (b)(3) compensation.*—If—

(A) A teacher or trainee receives compensation in the current year and all of that compensation is described in section 872(b)(3);

(B) That individual was present in the United States as a teacher or trainee in any prior year within the last 6 years; and

(C) During each prior year (within the 6 year period) in which the individual was present as a teacher or trainee, the individual received compensation all of which was described in section 872(b)(3);

then that individual shall include days of presence as a teacher or trainee in the current year only if the individual has been exempt as a teacher, trainee, or student for any part of four of the six preceding calendar years.

(iii) *Limitation on student exemption.*—An individual will not be able to exclude days of presence as a student if the individual has been exempt as a teacher, trainee, or student for any part of more than five calendar years, unless it is established to the satisfaction of the district director that the individual does not intend to reside permanently in the United States and has substantially complied with the requirements of the student visa providing for the individual's temporary presence in the United States. For purposes of this paragraph (b)(7), the facts and circumstances to be considered in determining if an individual has demonstrated an intent to reside permanently in the United States include (but are not limited to)—

(A) Whether the individual has maintained a closer connection with a foreign country as described in § 301.7701(b)-2; and

(B) Whether the individual has taken affirmative steps within the meaning of paragraph (f) of § 301.7701(b)-2 to adjust the individual's status from nonimmigrant to lawful permanent resident.

(iv) *Transition rule.*—The rules in this paragraph (b)(7) relating to stated periods of exempt status apply only for those stated periods that occur after 1984. Thus, for example, an alien who is present as a student during the calendar years 1982-1990 will not be subject to the five year rule for students until 1990.

(v) *Examples.*—The following examples illustrate the application of paragraphs (b)(7)(i) and (ii) of this section:

*Example 1.* B is temporarily present in the United States during the current year as a teacher, within the meaning of section 101(a)(15)(J) of the Immigration and Nationality Act. B does not receive compensation described in section 872(b)(3) in the current year. B has been treated as an exempt student for the past three years. Although this is the first year that B is seeking to be exempt as a teacher, he will not be considered an exempt individual for the year because he has been exempt as a student for at least two of the past six years.

*Example 2.* C is temporarily present in the United States during the current year as a teacher and receives compensation described in section 872(b)(3) in the current year. C has been treated as an exempt teacher for the past two years but C's compensation for those years was not described in section 872(b)(3). C will not be considered an exempt individual for the current year because she has been exempt as a teacher for at least two of the past six years.

*Example 3.* The facts are the same as in *Example 2,* except that all of C's compensation for the two preceding years was described in section 872(b)(3). C will be considered to be an exempt individual for the current year because she has not been exempt as a student, teacher or trainee for four of the six preceding calendar years.

*Example 4.* D is temporarily present in the United States during the current year as a teacher, within the meaning of section 101(a)(15)(J) of the Immigration and Nationality Act. D does not receive compensation described in section 872(b)(3) in the current year. D entered the United States in December of the second preceding year and intends to remain in the United States until June of the current year. D will not be considered an exempt individual for the current year because he has been exempt as a teacher for at least two of the past six years.

(8) *Immediate family.*—The immediate family of an exempt individual includes the individual's spouse and unmarried children (whether by blood or adoption) but only if the spouse's or unmarried children's visa status are derived from and dependent on the visa classification of the exempt individual. For the purposes of this paragraph, the term "unmarried children" means those children who are under 21 years of age, who reside regularly in the household of the exempt individual, and who are not members of some other household. The immediate family of an exempt individual does not include the attendants, servants, and personal employees of that individual.

(c) *Medical condition.*—(1) *In general.*—An individual will not be considered present on any day that the individual intends to leave and is unable to leave the United States because of a medical condition or medical problem that arose while the individual was present in the United States. A day of presence will not be excluded if the individual, who was initially prevented from leaving, is subsequently able to leave the United States and then remains in the United States beyond a reasonable period for making arrangements to leave the United States. A day will also not be excluded if the medical condition arose during a prior stay in the United States (whether or not days of presence during the prior stay were excluded) and the alien returns to the United States for treatment of the medical condition or medical problem that arose during the prior stay.

(2) *Intent to leave the United States.*—For purposes of paragraph (c)(1) of this section, whether an individual intends to leave the United States on a particular day will be determined based on all the facts and circumstances. Thus, if at the time an individual's medical condition or medical problem arose, the individual was present in the United States for a definite purpose which by its nature could be accomplished within the United States during a period of time that would not cause the individual to be a resident under the substantial presence test, the individual may be able to establish that he or she intended to leave the United States. However, if the individual's purpose is of such a nature that an extended period of time would be required for its accomplishment (sufficient to cause the individual to be a resident under the substantial presence test), the individual would not be able to establish the requisite intent to leave the United States. If the individual is present in the United States for no particular purpose or a purpose by its nature that does not require a specific period of time to accomplish, the determination of whether the individual has the requisite intent to leave the United States will depend on all the surrounding facts and circumstances. In the case of an individual adjudicated mentally incompetent, proof of intent to leave the United States may be determined by analyzing the incompetent's pattern of behavior prior to the adjudication of incompetence. Generally, an individual will be presumed to have intended to leave during a period of illness if the individual leaves the United States within a reasonable period of time (time to make arrangements to leave) after becoming physically able to leave.

(3) *Pre-existing medical condition.*—A medical condition or problem will not be considered to arise while the individual is present in the United States, if the condition or problem existed prior to the individual's arrival in the United States, and the individual was aware of the condition or problem, regardless of whether the individual required treatment for the condition or problem when the individual entered the United States.

(4) *Examples.*—The following examples illustrate the application of this paragraph (c):

*Example 1.* B is in a serious automobile accident in the United States on March 25. B intended to leave the United States on March 31 (as evidenced by an airline ticket), but was unable to leave on that date as a result of the injuries suffered in the accident. B recovered from the injuries and was able to leave and did leave the United States on May 31. B's presence in the United States during the period

from April 1 through May 31 will not be counted as days of presence in the United States.

*Example 2.* The facts are the same as in *Example 1,* except that B's return flight (as evidenced by an airline ticket) was scheduled for May 31. Because B did not intend to leave the United States until May 31, B may not exclude any days of presence in the United States.

(d) *Days in transit.*—An alien individual may exclude days of presence in the United States if the individual is in transit between two foreign points, and is physically present in the United States for fewer than 24 hours. For purposes of this paragraph, an individual will be considered to be in transit if the individual pursues activities that are substantially related to completing his or her travel to a foreign point of destination. For example, an alien who travels between airports in the United States in order to change planes en route to the individual's destination will be considered to be in transit. However, if the individual attends a business meeting while he or she is present in the United States, whether or not that meeting is within the confines of the airport, the individual will not be considered to be in transit. For purposes of this paragraph, the term "foreign point" means any areas that are not included within the definition of the term "United States" provided in § 301.7701(b)-1(c)(2)(ii).

(e) *Regular commuters from Mexico or Canada.*—(1) *General rule.*—An alien individual will not be considered to be present in the United States on days that the individual commutes to the United States from the individual's residence in Mexico or Canada if the individual regularly commutes from Mexico or Canada. An alien individual will be considered to commute regularly if the individual commutes to the individual's location of employment or self-employment in the United States from his or her residence in Mexico or Canada on more than 75% of the workdays during the working period.

(2) *Definitions.*—(i) The term "commutes" means to travel to employment or self-employment and to return to one's residence within a 24-hour period.

(ii) The term "workdays" means days on which the individual works in the United States or Canada or Mexico.

(iii) The term "working period" means the period beginning with the first day in the current year on which the individual is physically present in the United States for purposes of engaging in employment or self-employment and ending on the last day in the current year on which the individual is physically present in the United States for purposes of engaging in that employment or self-employment. If the nature of the employment or self-employment is such that it requires the individual to be present in the United States only on a seasonal or cyclical basis, the working period will begin with the first day of the season or cycle on which the individual is present in the United States for purposes of engaging in that employment or self-employment and end on the last day of the season or cycle on which the individual is present in the United States for the purpose of engaging in that employment or self-employment. Thus, there may be more than one working period in a calendar year and a working period may begin in one calendar year and end in the following calendar year.

(3) *Examples.*—The following examples illustrate the operation of this paragraph (e):

*Example 1.* B lives in Mexico and is employed by Corporation X in its office in Mexico. B was temporarily assigned to X's office in the United States. B's employment in the United States office began on February 1, 1988, and continued through June 1, 1988. On June 2, B resumed his employment in Mexico. On 59 days in the period beginning on February 1, 1988, and ending on June 1, 1988, B travelled each morning from his residence in Mexico to X Corporation's United States office for the purpose of engaging in his employment with X Corporation. B returned to his residence in Mexico on each of those evenings. On seven days in the period from February 1, 1988, through June 1, 1988, B worked in X's Mexico office. B is not considered to have been present in the United States on any of the days that he travelled to X's United States office for the purpose of engaging in employment with Corporation X because he commuted to his place of employment within the United States on more than 75% of the workdays during the working period (59 workdays in the United States/66 workdays in the working period = 89.4%).

*Example 2.* C, who lives in Canada, contracted with a resort located in the United States to provide snow-skiing instructions for the resort's customers for two skiing seasons, the first beginning on November 15, 1987, and ending on March 15, 1988, and the second beginning on November 15, 1988, and ending on March 15, 1989. On 90 days in each of the two skiing seasons, C travelled in the morning from Canada to the resort to provide skiing instructions pursuant to the contract. C returned to Canada on each of those evenings. On 20 days during each of the two skiing seasons, C worked in Canada. C is not considered to have been present in the United States on any of the days that she travelled to the United States to provide ski instructions in either the first working period beginning on November 15, 1987, and ending on March 15, 1988, or the second working period beginning on November 15, 1988, and ending on March 15, 1989, because she commuted to her employment within the United States on more than 75% of the workdays during each of the working periods (90 workdays in the United States / 110 workdays in the working period = 81.8%).

*Example 3.* D, who lives in Canada, is the sole proprietor of a wholesale lumber business with offices in both the United States and Canada. Beginning on January 4, 1988, and ending on February 12, 1988, D commuted to work in his United States office on 30 days. Beginning on February 15, 1988, and ending on March 25, 1988, D commuted to work in his Canadian office on 30 days. Beginning on March 28, 1988, and ending on May 27, 1988, D commuted to work in his United States office on 45 days. Subsequent to May 27, D did not commute to the United States on any other days in 1988. D is considered to have been present in the United States on each day that he travelled to his office in the United States because D did not commute to the United States office on more than 75% of the workdays during the working period beginning on January 4, 1988, and ending on May 27, 1988 (75 workdays in the United States / 105 workdays in the working period = 71.4%).

(f) *Determination of excluded days applies beyond year of determination.*—If a day of presence is excluded under this section, then that day shall not be taken into account in the current year or the first or second preceding year. [Reg. § 301.7701(b)-3.]

☐ [*T.D. 8411, 4-24-92. Amended by T.D. 8733, 10-6-97.*]

**[Reg. § 301.7701(b)-4]**

§301.7701(b)-4. Residency time periods.—(a) *First year of residency.*—An alien individual who was not a United States resident during the preceding calendar year and who is a United States resident for the current year will begin to be a resident for tax purposes on the alien's residency starting date. The residency starting date for an alien who meets the substantial presence test is the first day during the calendar year on which the individual is present in the United States. The residency starting date for an alien who meets the lawful permanent resident test (green card test), described in paragraph (b)(1) of §301.7701(b)-1, is the first day during the calendar year in which the individual is physically present in the United States as a lawful permanent resident. The residency starting date for an alien who satisfies both the substantial presence test and the green card test will be the earlier of the first day the individual is physically present in the United States as a lawful permanent resident of the United States or the first day during the year that the individual is present for purposes of the substantial presence test. (See § 301.7701(b)-9(b)(1) for the transitional rule relating to the residency starting date of an alien individual who was a lawful permanent resident in 1984. See also § 301.7701(b)-3 for days that may be excluded.)

(b) *Last year of residency.*—(1) *General rule.*—An alien individual who is a United States resident during the current year but who is not a United States resident at any time during the following calendar year will cease to be a resident for tax purposes on the individual's residency termination date. Generally, the residency termination date will be the last day of the calendar year.

(2) *Exceptions.*—Notwithstanding paragraph (b)(1) of this section, the residency termination date for an alien individual who meets the substantial presence test is the last day during the calendar year that the individual is physically present in the United States if the individual establishes that, for the remainder of the calendar year, the individual's tax home was in a foreign country and he or she maintained a closer connection (within the meaning of § 301.7701(b)-2(d)) to that foreign country than to the United States. Similarly, the residency termination date for an alien who meets the green card test is the first day during the calendar year that the alien is no longer a lawful permanent resident if the individual establishes that, for the remainder of the calendar year, his or her tax home was in a foreign country and he or she maintained a closer connection to that foreign country than to the United States. The residency termination date for an alien who satisfies both the substantial presence test and the green card test for the current year, will be the later of the first day the individual is no longer a lawful permanent resident of the United States or the last day the individual was physically present in the United States if the alien establishes that, for the remainder of the calendar year, his or her tax home was in a foreign country and he or she maintained a closer connection to that foreign country than to the United States. It is immaterial whether the individual's tax home was in the United States, or that the individual had a closer connection to the United States than to the foreign country, prior to the date of his or her departure from the United

States or the date on which the individual was no longer a lawful permanent resident, whichever is applicable.

(c) *Rules relating to residency starting date and residency termination date.*—(1) *De minimis presence.*—An alien individual may be present in the United States for up to 10 days without triggering the residency starting date (for purposes of the substantial presence test) or extending the residency termination date (for purposes of the substantial presence test) if the individual is able to establish that, during that period, the individual's tax home was in a foreign country and he or she maintained a closer connection to that foreign country than to the United States. Days from more than one period of presence may be disregarded for purposes of determining an individual's residency starting date or termination date so long as the total is not more than 10 days. However, an individual may not disregard any days that occur in a period of consecutive days of presence, if all the days that occur during that period cannot be excluded. An individual must include days of presence for purposes of determining whether the individual meets the substantial presence test even though the days may be disregarded for purposes of determining the individual's residency starting date or residency termination date.

(2) *Proration.*—If an individual's residency starting date does not fall on the first day of the tax year, or the individual's residency termination date does not fall on the last day of the tax year, the individual's income tax liability should be calculated in accordance with §1.871-13 of this chapter dealing with the taxation of individuals who change residence status during the taxable year.

(3) *Residency starting date for certain individuals.*—(i) *In general.*—If an alien individual (who otherwise does not meet the substantial presence test or the green card test for the current year) is physically present in the United States for at least 31 consecutive days during the current year, and also for a period of continuous presence beginning with the first day of that thirty-one day period (see paragraph (c)(3)(iii) of this section), then the individual may elect to be treated as a resident during the current year. The individual's residency starting date shall be the first day of that thirty-one day period, if—

(A) The individual was not a resident of the United States under the substantial presence test or the green card test in the year preceding the current year; and

(B) The individual is a resident of the United States in the subsequent year under the substantial presence test (whether or not the individual is also a resident of the United States under the green card test).

(ii) *Determination of presence.*—Except as otherwise provided in paragraph (c)(3)(iii) of this section, an individual shall be treated as present in the United States on any day that the individual is physically present in the United States at any time during the day.

(iii) *Thirty-one day period.*—For purposes of this paragraph (c)(3), the term "thirty-one day period" means any period of 31 consecutive days during which an individual is physically present in the United States during each day of the period.

(iv) *Period of continuous presence.*—For purposes of this paragraph (c)(3), the term "continuous presence" means a period of presence in the United States that includes 75 percent of the days in the current year beginning with (and including) the first day of the individual's thirty-one day period of presence. Only for purposes of the continuous presence requirement, an individual will be deemed to be present in the United States for up to 5 days on which the individual is absent from the United States. These days will not be deemed to be days of presence for purposes of the thirty-one day period of presence requirement. If an individual is present for more than one thirty-one day period of presence and satisfies the continuous presence requirement with regard to each period, the individual's residency starting date shall be the first day of the first thirty-one day period of presence. If an individual is present for more than one thirty-one day period of presence but satisfies the continuous presence requirement only for a later thirty-one day period, the individual's residency starting date shall be the first day of the later thirty-one day period of presence. For purposes of this paragraph (c)(3), days of presence that are otherwise excluded under section 7701(b)(3)(D)(i) and § 301.7701(b)-3(a)(1) (exempt individual), (a)(2) (medical condition), (a)(3) (in transit between two foreign points), and (a)(4) (regular commuter) shall not be counted as days of presence for purposes of either the thirty-one day period or continuous presence requirement.

(v) *Election procedure.*—(A) *Filing requirements.*—An alien individual shall make an election to be treated as a resident under paragraph (c)(3) of this section by attaching a statement (described in paragraph (c)(3)(v)(C) of this section) to the individual's income tax return (Form 1040) for the taxable year for which the election is to be in effect (the election year). The alien individual may not make this election until such time as he has satisfied the substantial presence test for the year following the election year. If an alien individual has not satisfied the substantial presence test for the year following the election year as of the due date (not including extensions) of the tax return for the election year, the alien individual may request an extension of time for filing the return until a reasonable period after he or she has satisfied such test, provided that the individual pays with his or her extension application the amount of tax he or she expects to owe for the election year computed as if he or she were a nonresident alien throughout the election year. An election made under paragraph (c)(3) of this section may not be revoked without the approval of the Commissioner or his delegate.

(B) *Election on behalf of a dependent child.*—An individual may make an election on behalf of a dependent child (as defined in paragraphs (1) and (2) of section 152(a), without regard to section 152(b)(3)) if the individual is qualified to make an election on his or her own behalf, the child qualifies to make an election under this paragraph (c)(3), and the child is not required by section 6012 to file a United States income tax return for the year for which the election is to be effective.

(C) *Statement.*—The statement required by paragraph (c)(3)(v)(A) of this section shall include the name and address of the alien individual and contain a signed declaration that the election is being made. If the individual is also making an election on behalf of any dependent children, then the statement must include the required information with respect to those children. The statement must specify—

(1) That the alien individual was not a resident in the year immediately preceding the election year;

(2) That the alien individual is a resident under the substantial presence test in the year following the election year;

(3) The individual's number of days of presence in the United States during the year following the election year;

(4) The date or dates of the alien individual's thirty-one day period of presence and period of continuous presence in the United States during the election year; and

(5) The date or dates of absence from the United States during the election year that are deemed to be days of presence.

(vi) *Penalty for failure to comply with filing requirements.*— (A) *General rule.*—If an individual fails to comply with the election procedure of paragraph (c)(3)(v) of this section, the individual must file his or her income tax return for the current year as a nonresident alien.

(B) *Exception.*—The penalty described in paragraph (c)(3)(vi)(A) of this section shall not apply if the individual can show by clear and convincing evidence that he or she took reasonable actions to become aware of the filing requirements and significant affirmative steps to comply with the requirements. An individual who requests an extension of time to file his or her income tax return pursuant to paragraph (c)(3)(v) of this section will be considered to have taken significant affirmative steps to comply with the requirement that the individual pay his or her tax determined as if the individual were a nonresident alien if the individual paid with his or her extension application at least 90 percent of the amount of the tax the individual actually owed for the election year computed as if he or she were a nonresident alien throughout the election year.

(d) *Examples.*—The following examples illustrate the operation of this section:

*Example 1.* B, a citizen of foreign country X, is an alien who has never before been a United States resident for tax purposes. B comes to the United States on January 6, 1985, to attend a business meeting and returns to country X on January 10, 1985. B is able to establish a closer connection to country X for the period January 6-10. On March 1, 1985, B moves to the United States and resides here until August 20, 1985, when he returns to country X. On December 12, 1985, B comes to the United States for pleasure and stays here until December 16, 1985 when he returns to country X. B is able to establish a closer connection to country X for the period December 12-16. B is not a United States resident for tax purposes during the following year and can establish a closer connection to country X for the remainder of calendar year 1985. B is a resident of the United States under the substantial presence test because B is present in the United States for 183 days (5 days in January plus 173 days for the period March 1-August 20 plus 5 days in December). B's residency starting date is March 1, 1985, and his residency termination date is August 20, 1985.

*Example 2.* The facts are the same as in *Example 1,* except that B remains in the United States until December 17, 1985, and is able to establish a closer connection to country X for the period December 18 through 31. B's residency termination date is December 17, 1985.

*Example 3.* C, a citizen of foreign country Y, is an alien who has never before been a United States resident for tax purposes. C comes to the United States for the first time on February 10, 1985, and attends a business conference until February 24, 1985, when she returns to country Y. On April 20, 1985, C enters the United States as a lawful permanent resident. On November 10, 1985, C ceases to be a lawful permanent resident but stays on in the United States until November 20, 1985 when she returns to country Y. On December 8, 1985, C comes to the United States and stays here until December 17, 1985 when she returns to country Y. She can establish a closer connection to country Y for that period. C is not a resident of the United States during the following calendar year and can establish a closer connection to country Y for the remainder of calendar year 1985. C qualifies as a United States resident under both the green card test and the substantial presence test. C's residency starting date under the green card test is April 20, 1985. Under the substantial presence test, C's residency starting date is February 10, 1985, because she is present for more than ten days in February and cannot take advantage of the de minimis presence rule. Therefore, C's residency starting date is February 10, 1985. C's residency termination date under the green card test is November 10, 1985. Her residency termination date under the substantial presence test is November 20, because B can disregard ten days of presence in December. Thus, her residency termination date is November 20, 1985, the later of her residency termination date under the substantial presence test or the green card test.

*Example 4.* The facts are the same as in *Example 3,* except that C is initially present in the United States on business from February 5 to February 9, 1985. C is able to establish a closer connection to country Y for that period. C may take advantage of only ten days of de minimis presence and may exclude days from a continuous period of presence only if she can exclude all the days that occur during that period. Thus, C may choose either of the following periods of residency: residency starting date February 5, 1985, and residency termination date November 20, 1985, or residency starting date April 20, 1985, and residency termination date December 17, 1985.

*Example 5.* D, a citizen of foreign country Z, is an alien who has never before been a United States resident for tax purposes. D comes to the United States on November 1, 1985 and is present in the United States on 31 consecutive days (from November 1 through December 1, 1985). D returns to country Z on December 1 and does not come back to the United States until December 17, 1985. He remains in the United States for the rest of 1986. During 1986, D is a resident of the United States under the substantial presence test. D may elect to be treated as a resident of the United States for 1985 because he was present in the United States in 1985 for a 31 consecutive day period of presence (November 1 through December 1, 1985) and for at least 75 percent of the days following (and including) the first day of D's 31 consecutive day period of presence (46 total days of presence in the United States/61 days in the period from November 1 through December 31 = 75.4%). If D makes the election to be treated as a resident, his residency starting date will be November 1, 1985.

*Example 6.* The facts are the same as in *Example 5,* except that D is absent from the United States on December 24, 25, 29, 30 and 31. D may make the election to be treated as a resident for 1985 because up to five days of absence will be deemed to be days of presence for purposes of the continuous presence requirement.

*Example 7.* F, a citizen of foreign country M, is an alien individual who has never before been a United States resident for tax purposes. F comes to the United States on January 1, 1985 and remains in the United States through January 31, 1985, when she returns to country M. F comes back to the United States on October 1, 1985 and is present in the United States through November 1, 1985. From November 1, 1985 through December 31, 1985, F is present in the United States for 38 days. Although F satisfies two 31 consecutive day periods of presence, (January 1 through January 31 and October 1 through November 1), she satisfies the continuous presence requirement only with regard to the later period of presence (69 total days of presence/92 days in the period from October 1 through December 31 = 75%). Thus, if F makes the election to be treated as a resident, his residency starting date is October 1, 1985.

(e) *No lapse.*—(1) *Residency in prior year.*—An alien individual who was a United States resident during any part of the preceding calendar year and who is a United States resident for any part of the current year will be considered to be taxable as a resident at the beginning of the current year. For purposes of this paragraph (e)(1), it is immaterial whether an individual is considered to be a resident under the substantial presence test or the green card test.

(2) *Residency in following year.*—An alien individual who is a United States resident for any part of the current year and who is also a United States resident for any part of the following year (regardless of whether the individual has a closer connection to a foreign country

than the United States during the current year) will be taxable as a resident through the end of the current year. For purposes of this paragraph (e)(2), it is immaterial whether an individual is considered to be a resident under the substantial presence test or the green card test.

(3) *Special rule.*—If an individual meets the green card test for the current year but is not physically present in the United States during the current year, then the individual's residency starting date shall be the first day of the following year.

(4) *Example.*—The following example illustrates the application of this paragraph (e).

*Example.* B, an alien individual who is a citizen of foreign country M, comes to the United States for the first time on May 1, 1985, and remains in the United States until November 5, 1985, when he returns to country M. B comes back to the United States on March 5, 1986 as a lawful permanent resident and remains in the United States until September 10, 1986, when he ceases to be a lawful permanent resident and returns to country M. B is not a resident in calendar year 1987. B's United States residency in calendar year 1985 continues through December 31, 1985, because he is a United States resident in the following calendar year. In calendar year 1986, B's United States residency is deemed to begin on January 1, 1986 because B qualified as a resident in the preceding calendar year. Thus, B's residency period in the United States begins on May 1, 1985, and ends on September 10, 1986. [Reg. § 301.7701(b)-4.]

□ [*T.D.* 8411, 4-24-92.]

### [Reg. § 301.7701(b)-5]

**§ 301.7701(b)-5. Coordination with section 877.**—(a) *General rule.*—An alien individual will be subject to United States income tax in the manner provided by section 877, regardless of whether the individual has a tax avoidance motive, if—

(1) The alien individual is a resident alien of the United States for at least three consecutive calendar years (the initial residency period) beginning after December 31, 1984;

(2) The period of residence for each of the three consecutive calendar years includes at least 183 days;

(3) The alien is once again taxed as a nonresident (including an individual taxed as a nonresident under § 301.7701(b)-7(a)(1); and

(4) The alien then becomes a resident of the United States before the close of the third calendar year beginning after the individual's residency termination date in the initial residency period.

(b) *Tax imposed.*—The tax provided for under paragraph (a) of this section will be imposed for the intervening period of nonresidency only if the amount of tax would exceed the amount of tax that would be imposed under section 871, relating to the taxation of nonresident aliens.

(c) *Example.*—The following example illustrates the application of this section.

*Example.* B, a citizen of foreign country F, enters the United States on April 1, 1985, as a lawful permanent resident. On August 1, 1987, B ceases to be a lawful permanent resident and returns to country F. B meets the initial residency period requirement because he is a resident of the United States for at least 183 days in each of three consecutive years (1985, 1986 and 1987). B returns to the United States on October 5, 1990, as a lawful permanent resident. Because B became a resident of the United States before the close of the third calendar year (1990) beginning after the close of the initial residency period (August 1, 1987), he is subject to tax under section 877(b) for the intervening period of nonresidency, August 2, 1987 through October 4, 1990, if the amount of the tax imposed under section 877 is more than the tax imposed under section 871. [Reg. § 301.7701(b)-5.]

□ [*T.D.* 8411, 4-24-92.]

### [Reg. § 301.7701(b)-6]

**§ 301.7701(b)-6. Taxable year.**—(a) *In general.*—An alien individual who has not established a fiscal year as his or her taxable year prior to the period that the individual is subject to United States income tax as a resident or a nonresident shall adopt the calendar year as his or her taxable year. An alien who has established a fiscal year in a foreign country prior to the period that the individual is subject to United States income tax may adopt the calendar year as his or her taxable year for United States income tax purposes without requesting a change in accounting period. An individual will be considered to have established a fiscal year (whether in the United States or a foreign country) if the annual accounting period on which the individual computes his or her income is a fiscal year, the individual keeps his or her books in accordance with that fiscal year, and the requirements of section 441 and § 1.441-1(b) of this chapter are otherwise satisfied. An alien who has established a fiscal year and is a resident alien during the calendar year will be treated as a

resident alien with respect to any portion of his or her taxable year (beginning with the individual's residency starting date and ending with the individual's residency termination date) that falls within such calendar year. Once the individual has established either a fiscal or calendar year taxable year for any period for which the individual is subject to United States income tax, the individual may not change that taxable year without the approval of the Secretary. See section 442.

(b) *Examples.*—The following examples illustrate the operation of this section:

*Example 1.* B, a citizen and resident of foreign country F, was engaged in a United States business during 1982 and filed a return on a fiscal year basis. B's fiscal year runs from October 1 to September 30. B comes to the United States on March 8, 1985 and remains in the United States until October 10, 1985, when he returns to country F. B maintains a closer connection to and his tax home in Country F for the remainder of calendar year 1985. B, who is not a United States resident at any time in 1986, is a United States resident for the period that begins on March 8, 1985, and ends on October 10, 1985. B has adopted a fiscal year taxable year for purposes of computing his United States income tax liability. For his fiscal year that ends on September 30, 1985, B will be taxed as a United States resident for the period that begins on March 8, 1985 and ends on September 30, 1985. For his fiscal year that ends on September 30, 1986, B will only be taxed as a United States resident for the period that begins on October 1, 1985 and ends on October 10, 1985.

*Example 2.* The facts are the same as in *Example 1,* except that B's 1982 business was a country F business established on a fiscal year basis and at no time prior to 1985 was B subject to United States income tax. B may adopt a calendar year as his taxable year for United States income tax purposes without requesting a change of accounting period. B continues to use a fiscal year as his taxable year. For his fiscal year that ends on September 30, 1985, B will be taxed as a United States resident for the period that begins on March 8, 1985 and ends September 30, 1985. For his fiscal year that ends on September 30, 1986, B will be taxed as a United States resident for the period that begins on October 1, 1985 and ends on October 10, 1985.

*Example 3.* The facts are the same as in *Example 1,* except that B's 1982 business was a country F business established on a fiscal year basis and at no time prior to 1985 was B subject to United States income tax. B may adopt a calendar year as his taxable year for United States income tax purposes without requesting a change of accounting period. B adopts a calendar year as his taxable year for 1985. For his calendar year taxable year ending on December 31, 1985, B will be taxed as a United States resident for the period that begins on March 8, 1985, and ends on October 10, 1985. [Reg. § 301.7701(b)-6.]

□ [*T.D.* 8411, 4-24-92. *Amended by T.D.* 8996, 5-16-2002.]

### [Reg. § 301.7701(b)-7]

**§ 301.7701(b)-7. Coordination with income tax treaties.**—(a) *Consistency requirement.*—(1) *Application.*—The application of this section shall be limited to an alien individual who is a dual resident taxpayer pursuant to a provision of a treaty that provides for resolution of conflicting claims of residence by the United States and its treaty partner. A "dual resident taxpayer" is an individual who is considered a resident of the United States pursuant to the internal laws of the United States and also a resident of a treaty country pursuant to the treaty partner's internal laws. If the alien individual determines that he or she is a resident of the foreign country for treaty purposes, and the alien individual claims a treaty benefit (as a nonresident of the United States) so as to reduce the individual's United States income tax liability with respect to any item of income covered by an applicable tax convention during a taxable year in which the individual was considered a dual resident taxpayer, then that individual shall be treated as a nonresident alien of the United States for purposes of computing that individual's United States income tax liability under the provisions of the Internal Revenue Code and the regulations thereunder (including the withholding provisions of section 1441 and the regulations under that section in cases in which the dual resident taxpayer is the recipient of income subject to withholding) with respect to that portion of the taxable year the individual was considered a dual resident taxpayer.

(2) *Computation of tax liability.*—If an alien individual is a dual resident taxpayer, then the rules on residency provided in the convention shall apply for purposes of determining the individual's residence for all purposes of that treaty.

(3) *Other Code purposes.*—Generally, for purposes of the Internal Revenue Code other than the computation of the individual's United States income tax liability, the individual shall be treated as a United States resident. Therefore, for example, the individual shall be treated as a United States resident for purposes of determining whether a

foreign corporation is a controlled foreign corporation under section 957 or whether a foreign corporation is a foreign personal holding company under section 552. In addition, the application of paragraph (a)(2) of this section does not affect the determination of the individual's residency time periods under § 301.7701(b)-4.

(4) *Special rules for S corporations.*—[Reserved]

(b) *Filing requirements.*—An alien individual described in paragraph (a) of this section who determines his or her U.S. tax liability as if he or she were a nonresident alien shall make a return on Form 1040NR on or before the date prescribed by law (including extensions) for making an income tax return as a nonresident. The individual shall prepare a return and compute his or her tax liability as a nonresident alien. The individual shall attach a statement (in the form required in paragraph (c) of this section) to the Form 1040NR. The Form 1040NR and the attached statement, shall be filed with the Internal Revenue Service Center, Philadelphia, PA 19255. The filing of a Form 1040NR by an individual described in paragraph (a) of this section may affect the determination by the Immigration and Naturalization Service as to whether the individual qualifies to maintain a residency permit.

(c) *Contents of statement.*—(1) *In general.*—(i) *Returns due after December 15, 1997.*—The statement filed by an individual described in paragraph (a)(1) of this section, for a return relating to a taxable year for which the due date (without extensions) is after December 15, 1997, must be in the form of a fully completed Form 8833 (Treaty-Based Return Position Disclosure Under Section 6114 or 7701(b)) or appropriate successor form. See section 6114 and § 301.6114-1 for rules relating to other treaty-based return positions taken by the same taxpayer.

(ii) *Earlier returns.*—For returns relating to taxable years for which the due date for filing returns (without extensions) is on or before December 15, 1997, the statement filed by the individual described in paragraph (a)(1) of this section must contain the information in accordance with paragraph (c)(1) of this section in effect prior to December 15, 1997 (see § 301.7701(b)-7(c)(1) as contained in 26 CFR part 301, revised April 1, 1997).

(2) *Controlled foreign corporation shareholders.*—If the taxpayer who claims a treaty benefit as a nonresident of the United States is a United States shareholder in a controlled foreign corporation (CFC), as defined in section 957 or section 953(c), and there are no other United States shareholders in that CFC, then for purposes of paragraph (c)(1) of this section, the approximate amount of subpart F income (as defined in section 952) that would have been included in the taxpayer's income may be determined based on the audited foreign financial statements of the CFC.

(3) *S corporation shareholders.*—[Reserved]

(d) *Relationship to section 6114(a) treaty-based return positions.*—The statement required by paragraph (b) of this section will be considered disclosure for purposes of section 6114 and § 301.6114-1(a), but only if the statement is in the form required by paragraph (c) of this section. If the taxpayer fails to file the statement required by paragraph (b) of this section on or before the date prescribed in paragraph (b) of this section, the taxpayer will be subject to the penalties imposed by section 6712. See section 6712 and § 301.6712-1.

(e) *Examples.*—The following examples illustrate the application of this section:

*Example 1.* B, an alien individual, is a resident of foreign country X, under X's internal law. Country X is a party to an income tax convention with the United States. B is also a resident of the United States under the Internal Revenue Code. B is considered to be a resident of country X under the convention. The convention does not specifically deal with characterization of foreign corporations as controlled foreign corporations or the taxability of United States shareholders on inclusions of subpart F income, but it provides, in an "Other Income" article similar to Article 21 of the 1981 draft of the United States Model Income Tax Convention (U.S. Model), that items of income of a resident of country X that are not specifically dealt with in the convention shall be taxable only in country X. B owns 80% of the one class of stock of foreign corporation R. The remaining 20% is owned by C, a United States citizen who is unrelated to B. In 1985, corporation R's only income is interest that is foreign personal holding company income under § 1.954A-2 of this chapter. Because the United States-X income tax convention does not deal with characterization of foreign corporations as controlled foreign corporations, United States internal income tax law applies. Therefore, B and C are United States shareholders within the meaning of § 1.951-1(g) of this chapter, corporation R is a controlled foreign corporation within the meaning of § 1.957-1 of this chapter, and corporation R's income is included in C's income as subpart F income under § 1.951-1 of this

chapter. B may avoid current taxation on his share of the subpart F inclusion by filing as a nonresident (*i.e.*, by following the procedure in § 301.7701(b)-7(b)).

*Example 2.* The facts are the same as in *Example 1*, except that B also earns United States source dividend income. The United States-X income tax convention provides that the rate of United States tax on United States source dividends paid to residents of country X shall not exceed 15 percent of the gross amount of the dividends. B's United States tax liability with respect to the dividends would be smaller if he were treated as a resident alien, subject to tax on a net basis (*i.e.*, after the allowance of deductions) than if he were treated as a nonresident alien. If, however, B chooses to file as a nonresident in order to claim treaty benefits with respect to his share of R's subpart F income, his overall United States tax liability, including the portion attributable to the dividends, must be determined as if he were a nonresident alien.

*Example 3.* C, a married alien individual with three children, is a resident of foreign country Y, under Y's internal law. Country Y is a party to an income tax convention with the United States. C is also a resident of the United States under the Internal Revenue Code. C is considered to be a resident of country Y under the convention. The convention specifically covers, among other items of income, personal services income, dividends and interest. C is sent by her country Y employer to work in the United States from January 1, 1985 until December 31, 1985. During 1985, C also earns United States source dividends and interest and incurs mortgage interest expenses on her personal residence. The United States-Y treaty provides that remuneration for personal services performed in the United States by a country Y resident is exempt from United States tax if, among other things, the individual performing such services is present in the United States for a period that is not in excess of 183 days. The treaty provides that the rate of United States tax on United States source dividends paid to residents of Y shall not exceed 15 percent of the gross amount of the dividends and it exempts residents of Y from United States tax on United States source interest. In filing her 1985 tax return, C may choose to file either as a resident alien without claiming any treaty benefits or as a nonresident alien if she desires to claim any treaty benefit. C files as a nonresident (*i.e.*, by following the procedure described in § 301.7701(b)-7(b)). Because C does not satisfy the requirements of the United States-Y treaty with regard to exempting personal services income from United States tax, C will be taxed on her personal services income at graduated rates under section 1 of the Code pursuant to section 871(b) of the Code. She will not be entitled to deduct her mortgage interest expenses or to claim more than one personal exemption because she is taxed as a nonresident alien under the Code by virtue of her decision to claim treaty benefits, and section 873 of the Code denies nonresidents the deduction for personal residence mortgage interest expense and generally limits them to only one personal exemption. C will be subject to a tax of 15 percent of the gross amount of her dividend income under section 871(a) of the Code as modified by the treaty, and she will be exempt from tax on her interest income. C is not entitled to file a joint return with her spouse even if he is a resident alien under the Code for 1985.

*Example 4.* The facts are the same as in *Example 3*, except that C does not choose to claim treaty benefits with respect to any items of income covered by the treaty (*i.e.*, she files as a resident). Therefore, she is taxed as a resident under the Code and pays tax at graduated rates on her personal services income, dividends, and interest. In addition, she is entitled to deduct her mortgage interest expenses and to take personal exemptions for her spouse and three children. C will be entitled to file a joint return with her spouse if he is a resident alien for 1985 or, if he is a nonresident alien, C and her spouse may elect to file a joint return pursuant to section 6013. [Reg. § 301.7701(b)-7.]

☐ [T.D. 8411, 4-24-92. Amended by T.D. 8733, 10-6-97.]

### [Reg. § 301.7701(b)-8]

**§ 301.7701(b)-8. Procedural rules.**—(a) *Who must file.*—(1) *Closer connection exception.*—An alien individual who otherwise meets the substantial presence test must file a statement to explain the basis of the individual's claim that he or she is able to satisfy the closer connection exception described in § 301.7701(b)-2.

(2) *Exempt individuals and individuals with a medical condition.*—An alien individual must file a statement to explain the basis of the individual's claim that he or she is able to exclude days of presence in the United States because the individual—

(i) Is an exempt individual as described in § 301.7701(b)-3(b)(3) (teacher/trainee) or (b)(4) (student);

(ii) Is an exempt individual described in § 301.7701(b)-3(b)(5) (professional athlete); or

(iii) Has a medical condition or problem as described in § 301.7701(b)-3(c).

(3) *De minimis presence and residency starting and termination dates.*—A statement must be filed by an individual who is seeking to establish—

(i) That a period of de minimis presence of ten or fewer days should be disregarded for purposes of the individual's residency starting or termination date; or

(ii) A residency termination date.

(b) *Contents of statement.*—(1) *Closer connection exception.*—(i) *Returns due after December 15, 1997.*—The statement filed by an individual described in paragraph (a)(1) of this section, for a return relating to a taxable year for which the due date (without extensions) is after December 15, 1997, must be in the form of a fully completed Form 8840 (Closer Connection Exception Statement) or appropriate successor form.

(ii) *Earlier returns.*—For returns relating to taxable years for which the due date for filing returns (without extensions) is on or before December 15, 1997, the statement filed by the individual described in paragraph (a)(1) of this section must contain the information in accordance with paragraph (b)(1) of this section in effect prior to December 15, 1997 (see § 301.7701(b)-8(b)(1) as contained in 26 CFR Part 301, revised April 1, 1997).

(2) *Exempt individuals and individuals with a medical condition.*—(i) *Returns due after December 15, 1997.*—The statement filed by an individual described in paragraph (a)(2) of this section, for a return relating to a taxable year for which the due date (without extensions) is after December 15, 1997, must be in the form of a fully completed Form 8843 (Statement for Exempt Individuals and Individuals with a Medical Condition) or appropriate successor form.

(ii) *Earlier returns.*—For returns relating to taxable years for which the due date for filing returns (without extensions) is on or before December 15, 1997, the statement filed by the individual described in paragraph (a)(2) of this section must contain the information in accordance with paragraph (b)(2) of this section in effect prior to December 15, 1997 (see § 301.7701(b)-8(b)(2) as contained in 26 CFR Part 301, revised April 1, 1997).

(3) *De minimis presence and residency starting and termination dates.*—The statement filed by an individual described in paragraph (a)(3) of this section shall be dated, signed by the individual seeking to exclude de minimis presence for purposes of the individual's residency starting or termination date or to establish a residency termination date, and verified by a declaration that the statement is made under the penalty of perjury. The statement shall contain the information described in paragraphs (b)(1)(i), (ii) and (iii) of this section and the following information (as applicable)—

(i) The first day that the individual was present in the United States during the current year;

(ii) The last day that the individual was present in the United States during the current year;

(iii) Dates of de minimis presence that the individual is seeking to exclude from his or her residency starting or termination dates;

(iv) Sufficient facts to establish that the individual has maintained his or her tax home in and a closer connection to a foreign country during a period of de minimis presence;

(v) Sufficient facts to establish that the individual has maintained his or her tax home in and a closer connection to a foreign country following the individual's last day of presence in the United States during the current year or following the abandonment or rescission of the individual's status as a lawful permanent resident during the current year;

(vi) Date that the individual's status as a lawful permanent resident was abandoned or rescinded; and

(vii) Sufficient facts (including copies of relevant documents) to establish that the individual's status as lawful permanent resident has been abandoned or rescinded.

(c) *How to file.*—Individuals described in paragraph (a) of this section who are required to make a return on Form 1040 or 1040NR pursuant to paragraph (a) or (b) of § 1.6012-1 of this chapter must attach the statement described in paragraph (b) of this section to their return for the taxable year for which the statement is relevant. An individual who is not required to file either Form 1040 or 1040NR must file the statement with the Internal Revenue Service Center, Philadelphia, PA 19255 on or before the date prescribed by law (including extensions) for making an income tax return as a nonresident for the calendar year for which the statement applies. The statement may be signed and filed for the taxpayer by the taxpayer's agent in accordance with § 1.6061-1 of this chapter.

(d) *Penalty for failure to file statement.*—(1) *General rule.*—If an individual is required to file a statement pursuant to paragraph (a)(1), (a)(2)(ii), (a)(2)(iii) or (a)(3) of this section and fails to file such statement on or before the date prescribed by paragraph (c) of this section, the individual will not be eligible for the closer connection exception described in § 301.7701(b)-2 and will be required to include all days of presence in the United States (calculated without the benefit of §§ 301.7701(b)-3(b)(5), 301.7701(b)-3(c), and 301.7701(b)-4(c)(1)) for purposes of the substantial presence test and for determining the individual's residency starting and termination dates. If an individual is considered to be a resident because of this paragraph and the individual is also a resident of a country with which the United States has an income tax convention pursuant to that convention, the individual shall be treated in the manner provided in § 301.7701(b)-7(a) (relating to the treatment of individuals who are dual residents).

(2) *Exception.*—The penalty described in paragraph (d)(1) of this section shall not apply if the individual can show by clear and convincing evidence that he or she took reasonable actions to become aware of the filing requirements and significant affirmative steps to comply with those requirements.

(e) *Filing requirement disregarded.*—Notwithstanding paragraph (d) of this section, the Secretary or his or her delegate may in their sole discretion, when it is in the best interest of the government to do so and based on all of the facts and circumstances, disregard the individual's failure to file timely the statement described in paragraph (a) of this section in determining the individual's days of presence in the United States. [Reg. § 301.7701(b)-8.]

☐ [*T.D. 8411, 4-24-92. Amended by T.D. 8733, 10-6-97.*]

**[Reg. § 301.7701(b)-9]**

**§ 301.7701(b)-9. Effective/applicability dates of §§ 301.7701(b)-1 through 301.7701(b)-7.**—(a) *In general.*—Except as indicated in paragraph (b) of this section, §§ 301.7701(b)-1 through 301.7701(b)-7 apply to taxable years beginning after December 31, 1984. For the rules applicable to earlier taxable years, see §§ 1.871-2 through 1.871-5 of this chapter.

(b) *Special rules.*—(1) *Green card test-residency starting date.*—If an alien was a lawful permanent resident throughout 1984 (regardless of whether the individual was physically present in the United States), or was physically present in the United States at any time during 1984 while a lawful permanent resident, the individual will be considered to have been a resident of the United States during 1984 for purposes of applying the provisions of section 7701(b)(2)(A) and § 301.7701(b)-4 such that the individual will, if he meets the substantial presence or green card test in 1985, be considered a resident of the United States as of January 1, 1985, regardless of when the individual was first present in the United States in 1985.

(2) *Substantial presence test-years included.*—For purposes of applying the substantial presence test for calendar years 1985 and 1986, days of presence in 1984 will only be counted for aliens who had been residents under prior law (§§ 1.871-2 through 1.871-5 of this chapter) at the end of calendar year 1984. Days of presence in 1983 will only be counted for aliens who had been residents under prior law at the end of both calendar year 1983 and 1984.

(3) *Professional athletes.*—For purposes of applying the substantial presence test, only days of presence in the United States after October 22, 1986, shall be excluded for individuals described in § 301.7701(b)-3(b)(5) (professional athletes).

(4) *Procedural rules and filing requirements.*—The procedural rules and filing requirements described in §§ 301.7701(b)-7(b) and 301.7701(b)-8 shall apply to taxable years beginning after December 31, 1991.

(5) *Possessions and territories.*—For purposes of applying section 7701(b) and the regulations under that section, § 301.7701(b)-1(d) applies to taxable years ending after April 9, 2008. [Reg. § 301.7701(b)-9.]

☐ [*T.D. 8411, 4-24-92. Amended by T.D. 9391, 4-4-2008.*]

**[Reg. § 301.7701(i)-0]**

**§ 301.7701(i)-0. Outline of taxable mortgage pool provisions.**— This section lists the major paragraphs contained in §§ 301.7701(i)-1 through 301.7701(i)-4.

*§ 301.7701(i)-1. Definition of a taxable mortgage pool.*
(a) Purpose.
(b) In general.
(c) Asset composition tests.
  (1) Determination of amount of assets.
  (2) Substantially all.
    (i) In general.
    (ii) Safe harbor.
  (3) Equity interests in pass-through arrangements.

(4) Treatment of certain credit enhancement contracts.
   (i) In general.
   (ii) Credit enhancement contract defined.
(5) Certain assets not treated as debt obligations.
   (i) In general.
   (ii) Safe harbor.
     (A) In general.
     (B) Payments with respect to a mortgage defined.
     (C) Entity treated as not anticipating payments.
(d) Real estate mortgages or interests therein defined.
  (1) In general.
  (2) Interests in real property and real property defined.
   (i) In general.
   (ii) Manufactured housing.
  (3) Principally secured by an interest in real property.
   (i) Tests for determining whether an obligation is principally secured.
     (A) The 80 percent test.
     (B) Alternative test.
   (ii) Obligations secured by real estate mortgages (or interests therein), or by combinations of real estate mortgages (or interests therein) and other assets.
     (A) In general.
     (B) Example.
(e) Two or more maturities.
  (1) In general.
  (2) Obligations that are allocated credit risk unequally.
  (3) Examples.
(f) Relationship test.
  (1) In general.
  (2) Payments on asset obligations defined.
  (3) Safe harbor for entities formed to liquidate assets.
(g) Anti-avoidance rules.
  (1) In general.
  (2) Certain investment trusts.
  (3) Examples.

**§ 301.7701(i)-2. Special rules for portions of entities.**
(a) Portion defined.
(b) Certain assets and rights to assets disregarded.
  (1) Credit enhancement assets.
  (2) Assets unlikely to service obligations.
  (3) Recourse.
(c) Portion as obligor.
  (1) In general.
  (2) Example.

**§ 301.7701(i)-3. Effective dates and duration of taxable mortgage pool classification.**
(a) Effective dates.
(b) Entities in existence on December 31, 1991.
  (1) In general.
  (2) Special rule for certain transfers.
  (3) Related debt obligation.
  (4) Example.
(c) Duration of taxable mortgage pool classification.
  (1) Commencement and duration.
  (2) Testing day defined.

**§ 301.7701(i)-4. Special rules for certain entities.**
(a) States and municipalities.
  (1) In general.
  (2) Governmental purpose.
  (3) Determinations by the Commissioner.
(b) REITs. [Reserved]
(c) Subchapter S corporations.
  (1) In general.
  (2) Portion of an S corporation treated as a separate corporation.
[Reg. § 301.7701(i)-0.]
☐ [T.D. 8610, 8-4-95.]

### [Reg. § 301.7701(i)-1]

**§ 301.7701(i)-1. Definition of a taxable mortgage pool.—**
(a) *Purpose.*—This section provides rules for applying section 7701(i), which defines taxable mortgage pools. The purpose of section 7701(i) is to prevent income generated by a pool of real estate mortgages from escaping Federal income taxation when the pool is used to issue multiple class mortgage-backed securities. The regulations in this section and in §§ 301.7701(i)-2 through 301.7701(i)-4 are to be applied in accordance with this purpose. The taxable mortgage pool provi-

sions apply to entities or portions of entities that qualify for REMIC status but do not elect to be taxed as REMICs as well as to certain entities or portions of entities that do not qualify for REMIC status.

(b) *In general.*—(1) A taxable mortgage pool is any entity or portion of an entity (as defined in § 301.7701(i)-2) that satisfies the requirements of section 7701(i)(2)(A) and this section as of any testing day (as defined in § 301.7701(i)-3(c)(2)). An entity or portion of an entity satisfies the requirements of section 7701(i)(2)(A) and this section if substantially all of its assets are debt obligations, more than 50 percent of those debt obligations are real estate mortgages, the entity is the obligor under debt obligations with two or more maturities, and payments on the debt obligations under which the entity is obligor bear a relationship to payments on the debt obligations that the entity holds as assets.

(2) Paragraph (c) of this section provides the tests for determining whether substantially all of an entity's assets are debt obligations and for determining whether more than 50 percent of its debt obligations are real estate mortgages. Paragraph (d) of this section defines real estate mortgages for purposes of the 50 percent test. Paragraph (e) of this section defines two or more maturities and paragraph (f) of this section provides rules for determining whether debt obligations bear a relationship to the assets held by an entity. Paragraph (g) of this section provides anti-avoidance rules. Section 301.7701(i)-2 provides rules for applying section 7701(i) to portions of entities and § 301.7701(i)-3 provides effective dates. Section 301.7701(i)-4 provides special rules for certain entities. For purposes of the regulations under section 7701(i), the term entity includes a portion of an entity (within the meaning of section 7701(i)(2)(B)), unless the context clearly indicates otherwise.

(c) *Asset composition tests.*—(1) *Determination of amount of assets.*—An entity must use the Federal income tax basis of an asset for purposes of determining whether substantially all of its assets consist of debt obligations (or interests therein) and whether more than 50 percent of those debt obligations (or interests) consist of real estate mortgages (or interests therein). For purposes of this paragraph, an entity determines the basis of an asset with the assumption that the entity is not a taxable mortgage pool.

(2) *Substantially all.*—(i) *In general.*—Whether substantially all of the assets of an entity consist of debt obligations (or interests therein) is based on all the facts and circumstances.

(ii) *Safe harbor.*—Notwithstanding paragraph (c)(2)(i) of this section, if less than 80 percent of the assets of an entity consist of debt obligations (or interests therein), then less than substantially all of the assets of the entity consist of debt obligations (or interests therein).

(3) *Equity interests in pass-through arrangements.*—The equity interest of an entity in a partnership, S corporation, trust, REIT, or other pass-through arrangement is deemed to have the same composition as the entity's share of the assets of the pass-through arrangement. For example, if an entity's stock interest in a REIT has an adjusted basis of $20,000, and the assets of the REIT consist of equal portions of real estate mortgages and other real estate assets, then the entity is treated as holding $10,000 of real estate mortgages and $10,000 of other real estate assets.

(4) *Treatment of certain credit enhancement contracts.*—(i) *In general.*—A credit enhancement contract (as defined in paragraph (c)(4)(ii) of this section) is not treated as a separate asset of an entity for purposes of the asset composition tests set forth in section 7701(i)(2)(A)(i), but instead is treated as part of the asset to which it relates. Furthermore, any collateral supporting a credit enhancement contract is not treated as an asset of an entity solely because it supports the guarantee represented by that contract.

(ii) *Credit enhancement contract defined.*—For purposes of this section, a credit enhancement contract is any arrangement whereby a person agrees to guarantee full or partial payment of the principal or interest payable on a debt obligation (or interest therein) or on a pool of such obligations (or interests), or full or partial payment on one or more classes of debt obligations under which an entity is the obligor, in the event of defaults or delinquencies on debt obligations, unanticipated losses or expenses incurred by the entity, or lower than expected returns on investments. Types of credit enhancement contracts may include, but are not limited to, pool insurance contracts, certificate guarantee insurance contracts, letters of credit, guarantees, or agreements whereby an entity, a mortgage servicer, or other third party agrees to make advances (regardless of whether, under the terms of the agreement, the payor is obligated, or merely permitted, to make those advances). An agreement by a debt servicer to advance to an entity out of its own funds an amount to make up for delinquent payments on debt obligations is a credit enhancement contract. An agreement by a debt servicer to pay taxes and hazard insurance premiums on property securing a debt obligation, or other expenses incurred to protect an entity's security interests in the collateral in the event that the debtor fails to pay such taxes, insurance premiums, or other expenses, is a credit enhancement contract.

(5) *Certain assets not treated as debt obligations.*—(i) *In general.*—For purposes of section 7701(i)(2)(A), real estate mortgages that are seriously impaired are not treated as debt obligations. Whether a mortgage is seriously impaired is based on all the facts and circumstances including, but not limited to: the number of days delinquent, the loan-to-value ratio, the debt service coverage (based upon the operating income from the property), and the debtor's financial position and stake in the property. However, except as provided in paragraph (c)(5)(ii) of this section, no single factor in and of itself is determinative of whether a loan is seriously impaired.

(ii) *Safe harbor.*—(A) *In general.*—Unless an entity is receiving or anticipates receiving payments with respect to a mortgage, a single family residential real estate mortgage is seriously impaired if payments on the mortgage are more than 89 days delinquent, and a multi-family residential or commercial real estate mortgage is seriously impaired if payments on the mortgage are more than 59 days delinquent. Whether an entity anticipates receiving payments with respect to a mortgage is based on all the facts and circumstances.

(B) *Payments with respect to a mortgage defined.*—For purposes of paragraph (c)(5)(ii)(A) of this section, payments with respect to a mortgage mean any payments on the mortgage as defined in paragraph (f)(2)(i) of this section if those payments are substantial and relatively certain as to amount and any payments on the mortgage as defined in paragraph (f)(2)(ii) or (iii) of this section.

(C) *Entity treated as not anticipating payments.*—With respect to any testing day (as defined in §301.7701(i)-3(c)(2)), an entity is treated as not having anticipated receiving payments on the mortgage as defined in paragraph (f)(2)(i) of this section if 180 days after the testing day, and despite making reasonable efforts to resolve the mortgage, the entity is not receiving such payments and has not entered into any agreement to receive such payments.

(d) *Real estate mortgages or interests therein defined.*—(1) *In general.*—For purposes of section 7701(i)(2)(A)(i), the term real estate mortgages (or interests therein) includes all—

(i) Obligations (including participations or certificates of beneficial ownership therein) that are principally secured by an interest in real property (as defined in paragraph (d)(3) of this section);

(ii) Regular and residual interests in a REMIC; and

(iii) Stripped bonds and stripped coupons (as defined in section 1286(e)(2) and (3)) if the bonds (as defined in section 1286(e)(1)) from which such stripped bonds or stripped coupons arose would have qualified as real estate mortgages or interests therein.

(2) *Interests in real property and real property defined.*—(i) *In general.*—The definition of interests in real property set forth in §1.856-3(c) of this chapter and the definition of real property set forth in §1.856-3(d) of this chapter apply to define those terms for purposes of paragraph (d) of this section.

(ii) *Manufactured housing.*—For purposes of this section, the definition of real property includes manufactured housing, provided the properties qualify as single family residences under section 25(e)(10) and without regard to the treatment of the properties under state law.

(3) *Principally secured by an interest in real property.*—(i) *Tests for determining whether an obligation is principally secured.*—For purposes of paragraph (d)(1) of this section, an obligation is principally secured by an interest in real property only if it satisfies either the test set out in paragraph (d)(3)(i)(A) of this section or the test set out in paragraph (d)(3)(i)(B) of this section.

(A) *The 80 percent test.*—An obligation is principally secured by an interest in real property if the fair market value of the interest in real property (as defined in paragraph (d)(2) of this section) securing the obligation was at least equal to 80 percent of the adjusted issue price of the obligation at the time the obligation was originated (that is, the issue date). For purposes of this test, the fair market value of the real property interest is first reduced by the amount of any lien on the real property interest that is senior to the obligation being tested, and is reduced further by a proportionate amount of any lien that is in parity with the obligation being tested.

(B) *Alternative test.*—An obligation is principally secured by an interest in real property if substantially all of the proceeds of the obligation were used to acquire, improve, or protect an interest in real property that, at the origination date, is the only security for the obligation. For purposes of this test, loan guarantees made by Federal, state, local governments or agencies, or other third party credit enhancement, are not viewed as additional security for a loan. An

obligation is not considered to be secured by property other than real property solely because the obligor is personally liable on the obligation.

(ii) *Obligations secured by real estate mortgages (or interests therein), or by combinations of real estate mortgages (or interests therein) and other assets.*—(A) *In general.*—An obligation secured only by real estate mortgages (or interests therein), as defined in paragraph (d)(1) of this section, is treated as an obligation secured by an interest in real property to the extent of the value of the real estate mortgages (or interests therein). An obligation secured by both real estate mortgages (or interests therein) and other assets is treated as an obligation secured by an interest in real property to the extent of both the value of the real estate mortgages (or interests therein) and the value of so much of the other assets that constitute real property. Thus, under this paragraph, a collateralized mortgage obligation may be an obligation principally secured by an interest in real property. This section is applicable only to obligations issued after December 31, 1991.

(B) *Example.*—The following example illustrates the principles of this paragraph (d)(3)(ii):

*Example.* At the time it is originated, an obligation has an adjusted issue price of $300,000 and is secured by a $70,000 loan principally secured by an interest in a single family home, a fifty percent co-ownership interest in a $400,000 parcel of land, and $80,000 of stock. Under paragraph (d)(3)(ii)(A) of this section, the obligation is treated as secured by interests in real property and under paragraph (d)(3)(i)(A) of this section, the obligation is treated as principally secured by interests in real property.

(e) *Two or more maturities.*—(1) *In general.*—For purposes of section 7701(i)(2)(A)(ii), debt obligations have two or more maturities if they have different stated maturities or if the holders of the obligations possess different rights concerning the acceleration of or delay in the maturities of the obligations.

(2) *Obligations that are allocated credit risk unequally.*—Debt obligations that are allocated credit risk unequally do not have, by that reason alone, two or more maturities. Credit risk is the risk that payments of principal or interest will be reduced or delayed because of a default on an asset that supports the debt obligations.

(3) *Examples.*—The following examples illustrate the principles of this paragraph (e):

*Example 1.* (i) Corporation M transfers a pool of real estate mortgages to a trustee in exchange for Class A bonds and a certificate representing the residual beneficial ownership of the pool. All Class A bonds have a stated maturity of March 1, 2002, but if cash flows from the real estate mortgages and investments are sufficient, the trustee may select one or more bonds at random and redeem them earlier.

(ii) The Class A bonds do not have different maturities. Each outstanding Class A bond has an equal chance of being redeemed because the selection process is random. The holders of the Class A bonds, therefore, have identical rights concerning the maturities of their obligations.

*Example 2.* (i) Corporation N transfers a pool of real estate mortgages to a trustee in exchange for Class C bonds, Class D bonds, and a certificate representing the residual beneficial ownership of the pool. The Class D bonds are subordinate to the Class C bonds so that cash flow shortfalls due to defaults or delinquencies on the real estate mortgages are borne first by the Class D bond holders. The terms of the bonds are otherwise identical in all relevant aspects except that the Class D bonds carry a higher coupon rate because of the subordination feature.

(ii) The Class C bonds and the Class D bonds share credit risk unequally because of the subordination feature. However, neither this difference, nor the difference in interest rates, causes the bonds to have different maturities. The result is the same if, in addition to the other terms described in paragraph (i) of this *Example 2*, the Class C bonds are accelerated as a result of the issuer becoming unable to make payments on the Class C bonds as they become due.

(f) *Relationship test.*—(1) *In general.*—For purposes of section 7701(i)(2)(A)(iii), payments on debt obligations under which an entity is the obligor (liability obligations) bear a relationship to payments (as defined in paragraph (f)(2) of this section) on debt obligations an entity holds as assets (asset obligations) if under the terms of the liability obligations (or underlying arrangement) the timing and amount of payments on the liability obligations are in large part determined by the timing and amount of payments or projected payments on the asset obligations. For purposes of the relationship test, any payment arrangement, including a swap or other hedge, that achieves a substantially similar result is treated as satisfying the test. For example, any arrangement where the timing and amount of payments on liability obligations are determined by reference to a group of assets (or an index or other type of model) that has an expected payment experience similar to that of the asset obligations is treated as satisfying the relationship test.

(2) *Payments on asset obligations defined.*—For purposes of section 7701(i)(2)(A)(iii) and this section, payments on asset obligations include—

(i) A payment of principal or interest on an asset obligation, including a prepayment of principal, a payment under a credit enhancement contract (as defined in paragraph (c)(4)(ii) of this section) and a payment from a settlement at a discount (other than a substantial discount);

(ii) A payment from a settlement at a substantial discount, but only if the settlement is arranged, whether in writing or otherwise, prior to the issuance of the liability obligations; and

(iii) A payment from the foreclosure on or sale of an asset obligation, but only if the foreclosure or sale is arranged, whether in writing or otherwise, prior to the issuance of the liability obligations.

(3) *Safe harbor for entities formed to liquidate assets.*—Payments on liability obligations of an entity do not bear a relationship to payments on asset obligations of the entity if—

(i) The entity's organizational documents manifest clearly that the entity is formed for the primary purpose of liquidating its assets and distributing proceeds of liquidation;

(ii) The entity's activities are all reasonably necessary to and consistent with the accomplishment of liquidating assets;

(iii) The entity plans to satisfy at least 50 percent of the total issue price of each of its liability obligations having a different maturity with proceeds from liquidation and not with scheduled payments on its asset obligations; and

(iv) The terms of the entity's liability obligations (or underlying arrangement) provide that within three years of the time it first acquires assets to be liquidated the entity either—

(A) Liquidates; or

(B) Begins to pass through without delay all payments it receives on its asset obligations (less reasonable allowances for expenses) as principal payments on its liability obligations in proportion to the adjusted issue prices of the liability obligations.

(g) *Anti-avoidance rules.*—(1) *In general.*—For purposes of determining whether an entity meets the definition of a taxable mortgage pool, the Commissioner can disregard or make other adjustments to a transaction (or series of transactions) if the transaction (or series) is entered into with a view to achieving the same economic effect as that of an arrangement subject to section 7701(i) while avoiding the application of that section. The Commissioner's authority includes treating equity interests issued by a non-REMIC as debt if the entity issues equity interests that correspond to maturity classes of debt.

(2) *Certain investment trusts.*—Notwithstanding paragraph (g)(1) of this section, an ownership interest in an entity that is classified as a trust under § 301.7701-4(c) will not be treated as a debt obligation of the trust.

(3) *Examples.*—The following examples illustrate the principles of this paragraph (g):

*Example 1.* (i) Partnership P, in addition to its other investments, owns $10,000,000 of mortgage pass-through certificates guaranteed by FNMA (FNMA Certificates). On May 15, 1997, Partnership P transfers the FNMA Certificates to Trust 1 in exchange for 100 Class A bonds and Certificate 1. The Class A bonds, under which Trust 1 is the obligor, have a stated principal amount of $5,000,000 and bear a relationship to the FNMA Certificates (within the meaning of § 301.7701(i)-1(f)). Certificate 1 represents the residual beneficial ownership of the FNMA Certificates.

(ii) On July 5, 1997, with a view to avoiding the application of section 7701(i), Partnership P transfers Certificate 1 to Trust 2 in exchange for 100 Class B bonds and Certificate 2. The Class B bonds, under which Trust 2 is the obligor, have a stated principal amount of $5,000,000, bear a relationship to the FNMA Certificates (within the meaning of § 301.7701(i)-1(f)), and have a different maturity than the Class A bonds (within the meaning of § 301.7701(i)-1(e)). Certificate 2 represents the residual beneficial ownership of Certificate 1.

(iii) For purposes of determining whether Trust 1 is classified as a taxable mortgage pool, the Commissioner can disregard the separate existence of Trust 2 and treat Trust 1 and Trust 2 as a single trust.

*Example 2.* (i) Corporation Q files a consolidated return with its two wholly-owned subsidiaries, Corporation R and Corporation S. Corporation R is in the business of building and selling single family homes. Corporation S is in the business of financing sales of those homes.

(ii) On August 10, 1998, Corporation S transfers a pool of its real estate mortgages to Trust 3, taking back Certificate 3 which represents beneficial ownership of the pool. On September 25, 1998, with a view to avoiding the application of section 7701(i), Corporation R issues bonds that have different maturities (within the meaning of

§ 301.7701(i)-1(e)) and that bear a relationship (within the meaning of § 301.7701(i)-1(f)) to the real estate mortgages in Trust 3. The holders of the bonds have an interest in a credit enhancement contract that is written by Corporation S and collateralized with Certificate 3.

(iii) For purposes of determining whether Trust 3 is classified as a taxable mortgage pool, the Commissioner can treat Trust 3 as the obligor of the bonds issued by Corporation R.

*Example 3.* (i) Corporation X, in addition to its other assets, owns $110,000,000 in Treasury securities. From time to time, Corporation X acquires pools of real estate mortgages, which it immediately uses to issue multiple-class debt obligations.

(ii) On October 1, 1996, Corporation X transfers $20,000,000 in Treasury securities to Trust 4 in exchange for Class C bonds, Class D bonds, Class E bonds, and Certificate 4. Trust 4 is the obligor of the bonds. The different classes of bonds have the same stated maturity date, but if cash flows from the Trust 4 assets exceed the amounts needed to make interest payments, the trustee uses the excess to retire the classes of bonds in alphabetical order. Certificate 4 represents the residual beneficial ownership of the Treasury securities.

(iii) With a view to avoiding the application of section 7701(i), Corporation X reserves the right to replace any Trust 4 asset with real estate mortgages or guaranteed mortgage pass-through certificates. In the event the right is exercised, cash flows on the real estate mortgages and guaranteed pass-through certificates will be used in the same manner as cash flows on the Treasury securities. Corporation X exercises this right of replacement on February 1, 1997.

(iv) For purposes of determining whether Trust 4 is classified as a taxable mortgage pool, the Commissioner can treat February 1, 1997, as a testing day (within the meaning of § 301.7701(i)-3(c)(2)). The result is the same if Corporation X has an obligation, rather than a right, to replace the Trust 4 assets with real estate mortgages and guaranteed pass-through certificates.

*Example 4.* (i) Corporation Y, in addition to its other assets, owns $1,900,000 in obligations secured by personal property. On November 1, 1995, Corporation Y begins negotiating a $2,000,000 loan to individual A. As security for the loan, A offers a first deed of trust on land worth $1,700,000.

(ii) With a view to avoiding the application of section 7701(i), Corporation Y induces A to place the land in a partnership in which A will have a 95 percent interest and agrees to accept the partnership interest as security for the $2,000,000 loan. Thereafter, the loan to A, together with the $1,900,000 in obligations secured by personal property, are transferred to Trust 5 and used to issue bonds that have different maturities (within the meaning of § 301.7701(i)-1(e)) and that bear a relationship (within the meaning of § 301.7701(i)-1(f)) to the $1,900,000 in obligations secured by personal property and the loan to A.

(iii) For purposes of determining whether Trust 5 is a taxable mortgage pool, the Commissioner can treat the loan to A as an obligation secured by an interest in real property rather than as an obligation secured by an interest in a partnership.

*Example 5.* (i) Corporation Z, in addition to its other assets, owns $3,000,000 in notes secured by interests in retail shopping centers. Partnership L, in addition to its other assets, owns $20,000,000 in notes that are principally secured by interests in single family homes and $3,500,000 in notes that are principally secured by interests in personal property.

(ii) On December 1, 1995, Partnership L asks Corporation Z for two separate loans, one in the amount of $9,375,000 and another in the amount of $625,000. Partnership L offers to collateralize the $9,375,000 loan with $10,312,500 of notes secured by interests in single family homes and the $625,000 loan with $750,000 of notes secured by interests in personal property. Corporation Z has made similar loans to Partnership L in the past.

(iii) With a view to avoiding the application of section 7701(i), Corporation Z induces Partnership L to accept a single $10,000,000 loan and to post as collateral $7,500,000 of the notes secured by interests in single family homes and all $3,500,000 of the notes secured by interests in personal property. Ordinarily, Corporation Z would not make a loan on these terms. Thereafter, the loan to Partnership L, together with the $3,000,000 in notes secured by interests in retail shopping centers, are transferred to Trust 6 and used to issue bonds that have different maturities (within the meaning of § 301.7701(i)-1(e)) and that bear a relationship (within the meaning of § 301.7701(i)-1(f)) to the loans secured by interests in retail shopping centers and the loan to Partnership L.

(iv) For purposes of determining whether Trust 6 is a taxable mortgage pool, the Commissioner can treat the $10,000,000 loan to Partnership L as consisting of a $9,375,000 obligation secured by interests in real property and a $625,000 obligation secured by interests in personal property. Under § 301.7701(i)-1(d)(3)(ii)(A), the notes secured by single family homes are treated as $7,500,000 of interests in real property. Under § 301.7701(i)-1(d)(3)(i)(A), $7,500,000 of interests in real property are sufficient to treat a $9,375,000 obligation as principally secured by an interest in real property ($7,500,000 equals 80 percent of $9,375,000). [Reg. § 301.7701(i)-1.]

☐ [T.D. 8610, 8-4-95.]

### [Reg. § 301.7701(i)-2]

**§ 301.7701(i)-2. Special rules for portions of entities.**—(a) *Portion defined.*—Except as provided in paragraph (b) of this section and § 301.7701(i)-1, a portion of an entity includes all assets that support one or more of the same issues of debt obligations. For this purpose, an asset supports a debt obligation if, under the terms of the debt obligation (or underlying arrangement), the timing and amount of payments on the debt obligation are in large part determined, either directly or indirectly, by the timing and amount of payments or projected payments on the asset or a group of assets that includes the asset. Indirect payment arrangements include, for example, a swap or other hedge, or arrangements where the timing and amount of payments on the debt obligations are determined by reference to a group of assets (or an index or other type of model) that has an expected payment experience similar to that of the assets. For purposes of this paragraph, the term payments includes all proceeds and receipts from an asset.

(b) *Certain assets and rights to assets disregarded.*—(1) *Credit enhancement assets.*—An asset that qualifies as a credit enhancement contract (as defined in § 301.7701(i)-1(c)(4)(ii)) is not included in a portion as a separate asset, but is treated as part of the assets in the portion to which it relates under § 301.7701(i)-1(c)(4)(i). An asset that does not qualify as a credit enhancement contract (as defined in § 301.7701(i)-1(c)(4)(ii)), but that nevertheless serves the same function as a credit enhancement contract, is not included in a portion as a separate asset or otherwise.

(2) *Assets unlikely to service obligations.*—A portion does not include assets that are unlikely to produce any significant cash flows for the holders of the debt obligations. This paragraph applies even if the holders of the debt obligations are legally entitled to cash flows from the assets. Thus, for example, even if the sale of a building would cause a series of debt obligations to be redeemed, the building is not included in a portion if it is not likely to be sold.

(3) *Recourse.*—An asset is not included in a portion solely because the holders of the debt obligations have recourse to the holder of that asset.

(c) *Portion as obligor.*—(1) *In general.*—For purposes of section 7701(i)(2)(A)(ii), a portion of an entity is treated as the obligor of all debt obligations supported by the assets in that portion.

(2) *Example.*—The following example illustrates the principles of this section:

*Example.* (i) Corporation Z owns $1,000,000,000 in assets including an office complex and $90,000,000 of real estate mortgages.

(ii) On November 30, 1998, Corporation Z issues eight classes of bonds, Class A through Class H. Each class is secured by a separate letter of credit and by a lien on the office complex. One group of the real estate mortgages supports Class A through Class D, another group supports Class E through Class G, and a third group supports Class H. It is anticipated that the cash flows from each group of mortgages will service its related bonds.

(iii) Each of the following constitutes a separate portion of Corporation Z: the group of mortgages supporting Class A through Class D; the group of mortgages supporting Class E through Class G; and the group of mortgages supporting Class H. No other asset is included in any of the three portions notwithstanding the lien of the bonds on the office complex and the fact that Corporation Z is the issuer of the bonds. The letters of credit are treated as incidents of the mortgages to which they relate.

(iv) For purposes of section 7701(i)(2)(A)(ii), each portion described above is treated as the obligor of the bonds of that portion, notwithstanding the fact that Corporation Z is the legal obligor with respect to the bonds. [Reg. § 301.7701(i)-2.]

☐ [T.D. 8610, 8-4-95.]

### [Reg. § 301.7701(i)-3]

**§ 301.7701(i)-3. Effective dates and duration of taxable mortgage pool classification.**—(a) *Effective dates.*—Except as otherwise provided, the regulations under section 7701(i) are effective and applicable September 6, 1995.

(b) *Entities in existence on December 31, 1991.*—(1) *In general.*—For transitional rules concerning the application of section 7701(i) to entities in existence on December 31, 1991, see section 675(c) of the Tax Reform Act of 1986.

(2) *Special rule for certain transfers.*—A transfer made to an entity on or after September 6, 1995, is a substantial transfer for purposes of section 675(c)(2) of the Tax Reform Act of 1986 only if—

(i) The transfer is significant in amount; and

(ii) The transfer is connected to the entity's issuance of related debt obligations (as defined in paragraph (b)(3) of this section) that have different maturities (within the meaning of § 301.7701-1(e)).

(3) *Related debt obligation.*—A related debt obligation is a debt obligation whose payments bear a relationship (within the meaning of § 301.7701-1(f)) to payments on debt obligations that the entity holds as assets.

(4) *Example.*—The following example illustrates the principles of this paragraph (b):

*Example.* On December 31, 1991, Partnership Q holds a pool of real estate mortgages that it acquired through retail sales of single family homes. Partnership Q raises $10,000,000 on October 25, 1996, by using this pool to issue related debt obligations with multiple maturities. The transfer of the $10,000,000 to Partnership Q is a substantial transfer (within the meaning of § 301.7701(i)-3(b)(2)).

(c) *Duration of taxable mortgage pool classification.*—(1) *Commencement and duration.*—An entity is classified as a taxable mortgage pool on the first testing day that it meets the definition of a taxable mortgage pool. Once an entity is classified as a taxable mortgage pool, that classification continues through the day the entity retires its last related debt obligation.

(2) *Testing day defined.*—A testing day is any day on or after September 6, 1995, on which an entity issues a related debt obligation (as defined in paragraph (b)(3) of this section) that is significant in amount. [Reg. § 301.7701(i)-3.]

☐ [T.D. 8610, 8-4-95.]

### [Reg. § 301.7701(i)-4]

**§ 301.7701(i)-4. Special rules for certain entities.**—(a) *States and municipalities.*—(1) *In general.*—Regardless of whether an entity satisfies any of the requirements of section 7701(i)(2)(A), an entity is not classified as a taxable mortgage pool if—

(i) The entity is a State, territory, a possession of the United States, the District of Columbia, or any political subdivision thereof (within the meaning of § 1.1031(b) of this chapter), or is empowered to issue obligations on behalf of one of the foregoing;

(ii) The entity issues the debt obligations in the performance of a governmental purpose; and

(iii) The entity holds the remaining interests in all assets that support those debt obligations until the debt obligations issued by the entity are retired.

(2) *Governmental purpose.*—The term governmental purpose means an essential governmental function within the meaning of section 115. A governmental purpose does not include the mere packaging of debt obligations for re-sale on the secondary market even if any profits from the sale are used in the performance of an essential governmental function.

(3) *Determinations by the Commissioner.*—If an entity is not described in paragraph (a)(1) of this section, but has a similar purpose, then the Commissioner may determine that the entity is not classified as a taxable mortgage pool.

(b) *REITs.*—[Reserved]

(c) *Subchapter S corporations.*—(1) *In general.*—An entity that is classified as a taxable mortgage pool may not elect to be an S corporation under section 1362(a) or maintain S corporation status.

(2) *Portion of an S corporation treated as a separate corporation.*—An S corporation is not treated as a member of an affiliated group under section 1361(b)(2)(A) solely because a portion of the S corporation is treated as a separate corporation under section 7701(i). [Reg. § 301.7701(i)-4.]

☐ [T.D. 8610, 8-4-95.]

### [Reg. § 1.7701(l)-0]

**§ 1.7701(l)-0. Table of contents.**—This section lists captions that appear in § § 1.7701(l)-1 and 1.7701(l)-3:

(i) Defined.

(ii) Determination.

(3) Benefited stock.

(c) Recharacterization of certain fast-pay arrangements.

(1) Scope.

(2) Recharacterization.

(i) Relationship between benefited shareholders and fast-pay shareholders.

(ii) Relationship between benefited shareholders and corporation.

(iii) Relationship between fast-pay shareholders and corporation.

(3) Other rules.

(i) Character of the financing instruments.

(ii) Multiple types of benefited stock.

(iii) Transactions affecting benefited stock.

(A) Sale of benefited stock.

(B) Transactions other than sales.

(iv) Adjustment to basis for amounts accrued or paid in taxable years ending before February 27, 1997.

(d) Prohibition against affirmative use of recharacterization by taxpayers.

(e) Examples.

(f) Reporting requirement.

(1) Filing requirements.

(i) In general.

(ii) Controlled foreign corporation.

(iii) Foreign personal holding company.

(iv) Passive foreign investment company.

(2) Statement.

(g) Effective date.

(1) In general.

(2) Election to limit taxable income attributable to a recharacterized fast-pay arrangement for periods before April 1, 2000.

(i) Limit.

(ii) Adjustment and statement.

(iii) Examples.

(3) Rule to comply with this section.

(4) Reporting requirements.

[Reg. § 1.7701(l)-0.]

☐ [*T.D. 8853, 1-7-2000.*]

**[Reg. § 1.7701(l)-1]**

**§ 1.7701(l)-1. Conduit financing arrangements.**—Section 7701(l) authorizes the issuance of regulations that recharacterize any multiple-party financing transaction as a transaction directly among any two or more of such parties where the Secretary determines that such recharacterization is appropriate to prevent avoidance of any tax imposed by title 26 of the United States Code. [Reg. § 1.7701(l)-1.]

☐ [*T.D. 8611, 8-10-95. Amended by T.D. 8735, 10-6-97.*]

**[Reg. § 1.7701(l)-3]**

**§ 1.7701(l)-3. Recharacterizing financing arrangements involving fast-pay stock.**—(a) *Purpose and scope.*—This section is intended to prevent the avoidance of tax by persons participating in fast-pay arrangements (as defined in paragraph (b)(1) of this section) and should be interpreted in a manner consistent with this purpose. This section applies to all fast-pay arrangements. Paragraph (c) of this section recharacterizes certain fast-pay arrangements to ensure the participants are taxed in a manner reflecting the economic substance of the arrangements. Paragraph (f) of this section imposes reporting requirements on certain participants.

(b) *Definitions.*—(1) *Fast-pay arrangement.*—A fast-pay arrangement is any arrangement in which a corporation has fast-pay stock outstanding for any part of its taxable year.

(2) *Fast-pay stock.*—(i) *Defined.*—Stock is fast-pay stock if it is structured so that dividends (as defined in section 316) paid by the corporation with respect to the stock are economically (in whole or in part) a return of the holder's investment (as opposed to only a return on the holder's investment). Unless clearly demonstrated otherwise, stock is presumed to be fast-pay stock if—

(A) It is structured to have a dividend rate that is reasonably expected to decline (as opposed to a dividend rate that is reasonably expected to fluctuate or remain constant); or

(B) It is issued for an amount that exceeds (by more than a de minimis amount, as determined under the principles of § 1.1273-1(d)) the amount at which the holder can be compelled to dispose of the stock.

(ii) *Determination.*—The determination of whether stock is fast-pay stock is based on all the facts and circumstances, including any related agreements such as options or forward contracts. A related agreement includes any direct or indirect agreement or understanding, oral or written, between the holder of the stock and the issuing corporation, or between the holder of the stock and one or more other shareholders in the corporation. To determine if it is fast-pay stock, stock is examined when issued, and, for stock that is not fast-pay stock when issued, when there is a significant modification in the terms of the stock or the related agreements or a significant change in the relevant facts and circumstances. Stock is not fast-pay stock solely because a redemption is treated as a dividend as a result of section 302(d) unless there is a principal purpose of achieving the same economic and tax effect as a fast-pay arrangement.

(3) *Benefited stock.*—With respect to any fast-pay stock, all other stock in the corporation (including other fast-pay stock having any significantly different characteristics) is benefited stock.

(c) *Recharacterization of certain fast-pay arrangements.*—(1) *Scope.*—This paragraph (c) applies to any fast-pay arrangement—

(i) In which the corporation that has outstanding fast-pay stock is a regulated investment company (RIC) (as defined in section 851) or a real estate investment trust (REIT) (as defined in section 856); or

(ii) If the Commissioner determines that a principal purpose for the structure of the fast-pay arrangement is the avoidance of any tax imposed by the Internal Revenue Code. Application of this paragraph (c)(1)(ii) is at the Commissioner's discretion, and a determination under this paragraph (c)(1)(ii) applies to all parties to the fast-pay arrangement, including transferees.

(2) *Recharacterization.*—A fast-pay arrangement described in paragraph (c)(1) of this section is recharacterized as an arrangement directly between the benefited shareholders and the fast-pay shareholders. The inception and resulting relationships of the recharacterized arrangement are deemed to be as follows:

(i) *Relationship between benefited shareholders and fast-pay shareholders.*—The benefited shareholders issue financial instruments (the financing instruments) directly to the fast-pay shareholders in exchange for cash equal to the fair market value of the fast-pay stock at the time of issuance (taking into account any related agreements). The financing instruments have the same terms (other than issuer) as the fast-pay stock. Thus, for example, the timing and amount of the payments made with respect to the financing instruments always match the timing and amount of the distributions made with respect to the fast-pay stock.

(ii) *Relationship between benefited shareholders and corporation.*—The benefited shareholders contribute to the corporation the cash they receive for issuing the financing instruments. Distributions made with respect to the fast-pay stock are distributions made by the corporation with respect to the benefited shareholders' benefited stock.

(iii) *Relationship between fast-pay shareholders and corporation.*—For purposes of determining the relationship between the fast-pay shareholders and the corporation, the fast-pay stock is ignored. The corporation is the paying agent of the benefited shareholders with respect to the financing instruments.

(3) *Other rules.*—(i) *Character of the financing instruments.*—The character of a financing instrument (for example, stock or debt) is determined under general tax principles and depends on all the facts and circumstances.

(ii) *Multiple types of benefited stock.*—If any benefited stock has any significantly different characteristics from any other benefited stock, the recharacterization rules of this paragraph (c) apply among the different types of benefited stock as appropriate to match the economic substance of the fast-pay arrangement.

(iii) *Transactions affecting benefited stock.*—(A) *Sale of benefited stock.*—If one person sells benefited stock to another—

(1) In addition to any consideration actually paid and received for the benefited stock, the buyer is deemed to pay and the seller is deemed to receive the amount necessary to terminate the seller's position in the financing instruments at fair market value; and

(2) The buyer is deemed to issue financing instruments to the fast-pay shareholders in exchange for the amount necessary to terminate the seller's position in the financing instruments.

(B) *Transactions other than sales.*—Except for transactions subject to paragraph (c)(3)(iii)(A) of this section, in the case of any transaction affecting benefited stock, the parties to the transaction must make appropriate adjustments to properly take into account the fast-pay arrangement as characterized under paragraph (c)(2) of this section.

(iv) *Adjustment to basis for amounts accrued or paid in taxable years ending before February 27, 1997.*—In the case of a fast-pay arrangement involving amounts accrued or paid in taxable years ending before February 27, 1997, and recharacterized under this paragraph (c), a benefited shareholder must decrease its basis in any benefited stock (as determined under paragraph (c)(2)(ii) of this section) by the amount (if any) that—

(A) Its income attributable to the benefited stock (reduced by deductions attributable to the financing instruments) for taxable years ending before February 27, 1997, computed by recharacterizing the fast-pay arrangement under this paragraph (c) and by treating the financing instruments as debt; exceeds

(B) Its income attributable to such stock for taxable years ending before February 27, 1997, computed without applying the rules of this paragraph (c).

(d) *Prohibition against affirmative use of recharacterization by taxpayers.*—A taxpayer may not use the rules of paragraph (c) of this section if a principal purpose for using such rules is the avoidance of any tax imposed by the Internal Revenue Code. Thus, with respect to such taxpayer, the Commissioner may depart from the rules of this section and recharacterize (for all purposes of the Internal Revenue Code) the fast-pay arrangement in accordance with its form or its economic substance. For example, if a foreign person acquires fast-pay stock in a REIT and a principal purpose for acquiring such stock is to reduce United States withholding taxes by applying the rules of paragraph (c) of this section, the Commissioner may, for purposes of determining the foreign person's United States tax consequences (including withholding tax), depart from the rules of paragraph (c) of this section and treat the foreign person as holding fast-pay stock in the REIT.

(e) *Examples.*—The following examples illustrate the rules of paragraph (c) of this section:

*Example 1. Decline in dividend rate*—(i) *Facts.* Corporation X issues 100 shares of A Stock and 100 shares of B Stock for $1,000 per share. By its terms, a share of B Stock is reasonably expected to pay a $110 dividend in years 1 through 10 and a $30 dividend each year thereafter. If X liquidates, the holder of a share of B Stock is entitled to a preference equal to the share's issue price. Otherwise, the B Stock cannot be redeemed at either X's or the shareholder's option.

(ii) *Analysis.* When issued, the B Stock has a dividend rate that is reasonably expected to decline from an annual rate of 11 percent of its issue price to an annual rate of 3 percent of its issue price. Since the B Stock is structured to have a declining dividend rate, the B Stock is fast-pay stock, and the A Stock is benefited stock.

*Example 2. Issued at a premium*—(i) *Facts.* The facts are the same as in *Example 1* of this paragraph (e) except that a share of B Stock is reasonably expected to pay an annual $110 dividend as long as it is outstanding, and Corporation X has the right to redeem the B Stock for $400 a share at the end of year 10.

(ii) *Analysis.* The B Stock is structured so that the issue price of the B Stock ($1,000) exceeds (by more than a de minimis amount) the price at which the holder can be compelled to dispose of the stock ($400). Thus, the B Stock is fast-pay stock, and the A Stock is benefited stock.

*Example 3. Planned section 302(d) redemptions*—(i) *Facts.* Corporation L, a subchapter C corporation, issues 220 shares of common stock for $1,000 per share. No other stock is authorized, but L can issue warrants entitling the holder to acquire L common stock for $3,000 per share until such time as L adopts a plan of liquidation. L can adopt a plan of liquidation if approved by 90 percent of its shareholders. Half of L's stock is purchased by Corporation M, and half by Organization N, which is tax exempt. At the time of purchase, M and N agree that for a period of ten years L will annually redeem (and N will tender) ten shares of stock in exchange for $12,100 and ten warrants. It is anticipated that, under sections 302 and 301, the annual payment to N will be a distribution of property that is a dividend.

(ii) *Analysis.* Considering all the facts and circumstances, including the agreement between M and N, L's redemption of N's stock is undertaken with a principal purpose of achieving the same economic and tax effect as a fast-pay arrangement. Thus, N's stock is fast-pay stock, M's stock is benefited stock, and the parties have entered into a fast-pay arrangement. Because L is neither a RIC nor a REIT, whether this fast-pay arrangement is recharacterized under paragraph (c) of this section depends on whether the Commissioner determines, under paragraph (c)(1)(ii) of this section, that a principal purpose for the structure of the fast-pay arrangement is the avoidance of any tax imposed by the Internal Revenue Code.

*Example 4. Recharacterization illustrated*—(i) *Facts.* On formation, REIT Y issues 100 shares of C Stock and 100 shares of D Stock for $1,000 per share. By its terms, a share of D Stock is reasonably

expected to pay a $110 dividend in years 1 through 10 and a $30 dividend each year thereafter. In years 1 through 10, persons holding a majority of the D Stock must consent before Y may take any action that would result in Y liquidating or dissolving, merging or consolidating, losing its REIT status, or selling substantially all of its assets. Thereafter, Y may take these actions without consent so long as the D Stock shareholders receive $400 in exchange for their D Stock.

(ii) *Analysis.* When issued, the D Stock has a dividend rate that is reasonably expected to decline from an annual rate of 11 percent of its issue price to an annual rate of 3 percent of its issue price. In addition, the $1,000 issue price of a share of D Stock exceeds the price at which the shareholder can be compelled to dispose of the stock ($400). Thus, the D Stock is fast-pay stock, and the C Stock is benefited stock. Because Y is a REIT, the fast-pay arrangement is recharacterized under paragraph (c) of this section.

(iii) *Recharacterization.* The fast-pay arrangement is recharacterized as follows:

(A) Under paragraph (c)(2)(i) of this section, the C Stock shareholders are treated as issuing financing instruments to the D Stock shareholders in exchange for $100,000 ($1,000, the fair market value of each share of D Stock, multiplied by 100, the number of shares).

(B) Under paragraph (c)(2)(ii) of this section, the C Stock shareholders are treated as contributing $200,000 to Y (the $100,000 received for the financing instruments, plus the $100,000 actually paid for the C Stock) in exchange for the C Stock.

(C) Under paragraph (c)(2)(ii) of this section, each distribution with respect to the D Stock is treated as a distribution with respect to the C Stock.

(D) Under paragraph (c)(2)(iii) of this section, the C Stock shareholders are treated as making payments with respect to the financing instruments, and Y is treated as the paying agent of the financing instruments for the C Stock shareholders.

*Example 5. Transfer of benefited stock illustrated*—(i) *Facts.* The facts are the same as in *Example 4* of this paragraph (e). Near the end of year 5, a person holding one share of C Stock sells it for $1,300. The buyer is unrelated to REIT Y or to any of the D Stock shareholders. At the time of the sale, the amount needed to terminate the seller's position in the financing instruments at fair market value is $747.

(ii) *Benefited shareholder's treatment on sale.* Under paragraph (c)(3)(iii)(A) of this section, the seller's amount realized is $2,047 ($1,300, the amount actually received, plus $747, the amount necessary to terminate the seller's position in the financing instruments at fair market value). The seller's gain on the sale of the common stock is $47 ($2,047, the amount realized, minus $2,000, the seller's basis in the common stock). The seller has no income or deduction with respect to terminating its position in the financing instruments.

(iii) *Buyer's treatment on purchase.* Under paragraph (c)(3)(iii)(A) of this section, the buyer's basis in the share of D Stock is $2,047 ($1,300, the amount actually paid, plus $747, the amount needed to terminate the seller's position in the financing instruments at fair market value). Under paragraph (c)(3)(iii)(B) of this section, simultaneous with the sale, the buyer is treated as issuing financing instruments to the fast-pay shareholders in exchange for $747, the amount necessary to terminate the seller's position in the financing instruments at fair market value.

*Example 6. Fast-pay arrangement involving amounts accrued or paid in a taxable year ending before February 27, 1997*—(i) *Facts.* Y is a calendar year taxpayer. In June 1996, Y acquires shares of REIT T benefited stock for $15,000. In December 1996, Y receives dividends of $100. Under the recharacterization rules of paragraph (c)(2) of this section, Y's 1996 income attributable to the benefited stock is $1,200, Y's 1996 deduction attributable to the financing instruments is $500, and Y's basis in the benefited stock is $25,000.

(ii) *Analysis.* Under paragraph (c)(3)(iv) of this section, Y's basis in the benefited stock is reduced by $600. This is the amount by which Y's 1996 income from the fast-pay arrangement as recharacterized under this section ($1,200 of income attributable to the benefited stock less $500 of deductions attributable to the financing instruments), exceeds Y's 1996 income from the fast-pay arrangement as not recharacterized under this section ($100 of income attributable to the benefited stock). Thus, in 1997 when the fast-pay arrangement is recharacterized, Y's basis in the benefited stock is $24,400.

(f) *Reporting requirement.*—(1) *Filing requirements.*—(i) *In general.*— A corporation that has fast-pay stock outstanding at any time during the taxable year must attach the statement described in paragraph (f)(2) of this section to its federal income tax return for such taxable year. This paragraph (f)(1)(i) does not apply to a corporation described in paragraphs (f)(1)(ii), (iii), or (iv) of this section.

(ii) *Controlled foreign corporation.*—In the case of a controlled foreign corporation (CFC), as defined in section 957, that has fast-pay stock outstanding at any time during its taxable year (during which time it was a CFC), each controlling United States shareholder (within the meaning of §1.964-1(c)(5)) must attach the statement described in paragraph (f)(2) of this section to the shareholder's Form

5471 for the CFC's taxable year. The provisions of section 6038 and the regulations under section 6038 apply to any statement required by this paragraph (f)(1)(ii).

(iii) *Foreign personal holding company.*—In the case of a foreign personal holding company (FPHC), as defined in section 552, that has fast-pay stock outstanding at any time during its taxable year (during which time it was a FPHC), each United States citizen or resident who is an officer, director, or 10-percent shareholder (within the meaning of section 6035(e)(1)) of such FPHC must attach the statement described in paragraph (f)(2) of this section to his or her Form 5471 for the FPHC's taxable year. The provisions of sections 6035 and 6679 and the regulations under sections 6035 and 6679 apply to any statement required by this paragraph (f)(1)(iii).

(iv) *Passive foreign investment company.*—In the case of a passive foreign investment company (PFIC), as defined in section 1297, that has fast-pay stock outstanding at any time during its taxable year (during which time it was a PFIC), each shareholder that has elected (under section 1295) to treat the PFIC as a qualified electing fund and knows or has reason to know that the PFIC has outstanding fast-pay stock must attach the statement described in paragraph (f)(2) of this section to the shareholder's Form 8621 for the PFIC's taxable year. Each shareholder owning 10 percent or more of the shares of the PFIC (by vote or value) is presumed to know that the PFIC has issued fast-pay stock. The provisions of sections 1295(a)(2) and 1298(f) and the regulations under those sections (including §1.1295-1T(f)(2)) apply to any statement required by this paragraph (f)(1)(iv).

(2) *Statement.*—The statement required under this paragraph (f) must say, "This fast-pay stock disclosure statement is required by §1.7701(l)-3(f) of the income tax regulations." The statement must also identify the corporation that has outstanding fast-pay stock and must contain the date on which the fast-pay stock was issued, the terms of the fast-pay stock, and (to the extent the filing person knows or has reason to know such information) the names and taxpayer identification numbers of the shareholders of any stock that is not traded on an established securities market (as described in §1.7704-1(b)).

(g) *Effective date.*—(1) *In general.*—Except as provided in paragraph (g) (4) of this section (relating to reporting requirements), this section applies to taxable years ending after February 26, 1997. Thus, all amounts accrued or paid during the first taxable year ending after February 26, 1997, are subject to this section.

(2) *Election to limit taxable income attributable to a recharacterized fast-pay arrangement for periods before April 1, 2000.*—(i) *Limit.*—For periods before April 1, 2000, provided the shareholder recharacterizes the fast-pay arrangement consistently for all such periods, a shareholder may limit its taxable income attributable to a fast-pay arrangement recharacterized under paragraph (c) of this section to the taxable income that results if the fast-pay arrangement is recharacterized under either—

(A) Notice 97-21, 1997-1 C.B. 407, see §601.601(d)(2) of this chapter; or

(B) Paragraph (c) of this section, computed by assuming the financing instruments are debt.

(ii) *Adjustment and statement.*—A shareholder that limits its taxable income to the amount determined under paragraph (g)(2)(i)(A) of this section must include as an adjustment to taxable income the excess, if any, of the amount determined under paragraph (g)(2)(i)(B) of this section, over the amount determined under paragraph (g)(2)(i)(A) of this section. This adjustment to taxable income must be made in the shareholder's first taxable year that includes April 1, 2000. A shareholder to which this paragraph (g)(2)(ii) applies must include a statement in its books and records

identifying each fast-pay arrangement for which an adjustment must be made and providing the amount of the adjustment for each such fast-pay arrangement.

(iii) *Examples.*—The following examples illustrate the rules of this paragraph (g)(2). For purposes of these examples, assume that a shareholder may limit its taxable income under this paragraph (g)(2) for periods before January 1, 2000.

*Example 1. Fast-pay arrangement recharacterized under Notice 97-21; REIT holds third-party debt*—(i) *Facts.* (A) REIT Y is formed on January 1, 1997, at which time it issues 1,000 shares of fast-pay stock and 1,000 shares of benefited stock for $100 per share. Y and all of its shareholders are U.S. persons and have calendar taxable years. All shareholders of Y have elected to accrue market discount based on a constant interest rate, to include the market discount in income as it accrues, and to amortize bond premium.

(B) For years 1 through 5, the fast-pay stock has an annual dividend rate of $17 per share ($17,000 for all fast-pay stock); in later years, the fast-pay stock has an annual dividend rate of $1 per share ($1,000 for all fast-pay stock). At the end of year 5, and thereafter, a share of fast-pay stock can be acquired by Y in exchange for $50 ($50,000 for all fast-pay stock).

(C) On the day Y is formed, it acquires a five-year mortgage note (the note) issued by an unrelated third party for $200,000. The note provides for annual interest payments on December 31 of $18,000 (a coupon interest rate of 9.00 percent, compounded annually), and one payment of principal at the end of 5 years. The note can be prepaid, in whole or in part, at any time.

(ii) *Recharacterization under Notice 97-21*—(A) *In general.* One way to recharacterize the fast-pay arrangement under Notice 97-21 is to treat the fast-pay shareholders and the benefited shareholders as if they jointly purchased the note from the issuer with the understanding that over the five-year term of the note the benefited shareholders would use their share of the interest to buy (on a dollar-for-dollar basis) the fast-pay shareholders' portion of the note. The benefited shareholders' and the fast-pay shareholders' yearly taxable income under Notice 97-21 can then be calculated after determining their initial portions of the note and whether those initial portions are purchased at a discount or premium.

(B) *Determining initial portions of the debt instrument.* The fast-pay shareholders' and the benefited shareholders' initial portions of the note can be determined by comparing the present values of their expected cash flows. As a group, the fast-pay shareholders expect to receive cash flows of $135,000 (five annual payments of $17,000, plus a final payment of $50,000). As a group, the benefited shareholders expect to receive cash flows of $155,000 (five annual payments of $1,000, plus a final payment of $150,000). Using a discount rate equal to the yield to maturity (as determined under §1.1272-1(b)(1)(i)) of the mortgage note (9.00 percent, compounded annually), the present value of the fast-pay shareholders' cash flows is $98,620, and the present value of the benefited shareholders' cash flows is $101,380. Thus, the fast-pay shareholders initially acquire 49 percent of the note at a $1,380 premium (that is, they paid $100,000 for $98,620 of principal in the note). The benefited shareholders initially acquire 51 percent of the note at a $1,380 discount (that is, they paid $100,000 for $101,380 of principal in the note). Under section 171, the fast-pay shareholders' premium is amortizable based on their yield in their initial portion of the note (8.574 percent, compounded annually). The benefited shareholders' discount accrues based on the yield in their initial portion of the note (9.353 percent, compounded annually).

(C) *Taxable income under Notice 97-21*— (1) *Fast-pay shareholders.* Under Notice 97-21, the fast-pay shareholders compute their taxable income attributable to the fast-pay arrangement for periods before January 1, 2000, by subtracting the amortizable premium from the accrued interest on the fast-pay shareholders' portion of the note. For purposes of paragraph (g)(2)(i)(A) of this section, the fast-pay shareholders' taxable income as a group is as follows:

| Taxable Period | Interest Income | Amortizable Premium | Taxable Income |
|---|---|---|---|
| 1/1/97 - 12/31/97 . . . . . . . . . . . . . | $8,876 | ($302) | $8,574 |
| 1/1/98 - 12/31/98 . . . . . . . . . . . . . | $8,145 | ($293) | $7,852 |
| 1/1/99 - 12/31/99 . . . . . . . . . . . . . | $7,348 | ($281) | $7,067 |
| | $24,369 | ($876) | $23,493 |

(2) *Benefited shareholders.* Under Notice 97-21, the benefited shareholders compute their taxable income attributable to the fast-pay arrangement for periods before January 1, 2000, by adding the accrued discount to the accrued interest on the benefited sharehold-

ers' portion of the note. For purposes of paragraph (g)(2)(i)(A) of this section, the benefited shareholders' taxable income as a group is as follows:

| Taxable Period | Interest Income | Accrued Discount | Taxable Income |
|---|---|---|---|
| 1/1/97 - 12/31/97 . . . . . . . . . . . . . | $9,124 | $229 | $9,353 |
| 1/1/98 - 12/31/98 . . . . . . . . . . . . . | $9,855 | $251 | $10,106 |
| 1/1/99 - 12/31/99 . . . . . . . . . . . . . | $10,652 | $274 | $10,926 |
| | $29,631 | $754 | $30,385 |

*(iii) Taxable income under the recharacterization of this section*—(A) *Fast-pay shareholders.* Under paragraphs (c) and (g)(2)(i)(B) of this section, the fast-pay shareholders' taxable income attributable to the fast-pay arrangement for periods before January 1, 2000, is the interest deemed paid on the financing instruments. For purposes of paragraph (g)(2)(i)(B) of this section, the fast-pay shareholders' taxable income as a group is as follows:

| Taxable Period | Taxable Income |
|---|---|
| 1/1/97 - 12/31/97 | $8,574 |
| 1/1/98 - 12/31/98 | $7,852 |
| 1/1/99 - 12/31/99 | $7,067 |
| | $23,493 |

(B) *Benefited shareholders.* Under paragraphs (c) and (g)(2)(i)(B) of this section, the benefited shareholders compute their taxable income attributable to the fast-pay arrangement for periods before January 1, 2000, by subtracting the interest deemed paid on the financing instruments from the dividends actually and deemed paid on the benefited stock. For purposes of paragraph (g)(2)(i)(B) of this section, the benefited shareholders' taxable income as a group is as follows:

| Taxable Period | Dividends Paid On Benefited Stock | Interest Paid On Financing Instruments | Taxable Income |
|---|---|---|---|
| 1/1/97 - 12/31/97 | $18,000 | ($8,574) | $9,426 |
| 1/1/98 - 12/31/98 | $18,000 | ($7,852) | $10,148 |
| 1/1/99 - 12/31/99 | $18,000 | ($7,067) | $10,933 |
| | $54,000 | ($23,493) | $30,507 |

*(iv) Limit on taxable income under paragraph (g)(2)(i) of this section*—(A) *Fast-pay shareholders.* For periods before January 1, 2000, the fast-pay shareholders have the same taxable income under the recharacterization of Notice 97-21 and paragraph (g)(2)(i)(A) of this section ($23,493) as they have under the recharacterization of paragraphs (c) and (g)(2)(i)(B) of this section ($23,493). Thus, under paragraph (g)(2)(i) of this section, the fast-pay shareholders may limit their taxable income attributable to the fast-pay arrangement for periods before January 1, 2000, to $23,493 (as a group).

(B) *Benefited shareholders.* For periods before January 1, 2000, the benefited shareholders have taxable income attributable to the fast-pay arrangement of $30,385 under the recharacterization of Notice 97-21 and paragraph (g)(2)(i)(A) of this section, and taxable income of $30,507 under the recharacterization of paragraphs (c) and (g)(2)(i)(B) of this section. Thus, under paragraph (g)(2)(i) of this section, the benefited shareholders may limit their taxable income attributable to the fast-pay arrangement for periods before January 1, 2000, to either $30,385 (as a group) or $30,507 (as a group).

*(v) Adjustment to taxable income under paragraph (g)(2)(ii) of this section.* Under paragraph (g)(2)(ii) of this section, any benefited shareholder that limited its taxable income to the amount determined under paragraph (g)(2)(i)(A) of this section must include as an adjustment to taxable income the excess, if any, of the amount determined under paragraph (g)(2)(i)(B) of this section, over the amount determined under paragraph (g)(2)(i)(A) of this section. If all benefited shareholders limited their taxable income to the amount determined under paragraph (g)(2)(i)(A) of this section, then as a group their adjustment to income is $122 ($30,507, minus $30,385). Each shareholder must include its adjustment in income for the taxable year that includes January 1, 2000.

*Example 2. REIT holds debt issued by a benefited shareholder*—(i) *Facts.* The facts are the same as in *Example 1* of this paragraph (g)(2) except that corporation Z holds 800 shares (80 percent) of the benefited stock, and Z, instead of a third party, issues the mortgage note acquired by Y.

(ii) *Recharacterization under Notice 97-21.* Because Y holds a debt instrument issued by Z, the fast-pay arrangement is recharacterized under Notice 97-21 as an arrangement in which Z issued one or more instruments directly to the fast-pay shareholders and the other benefited shareholders.

(A) *Fast-pay shareholders.* Consistent with this recharacterization, Z is treated as issuing a debt instrument to the fast-pay shareholders for $100,000. The debt instrument provides for five annual payments of $17,000 and an additional payment of $50,000 in year five. Thus, the debt instrument's yield to maturity is 8.574 percent per annum, compounded annually.

(B) *Benefited shareholders.* Z is also treated as issuing a debt instrument to the other benefited shareholders for $20,000 (200 shares multiplied by $100, or 20 percent of the $100,000 paid to Y by the benefited shareholders as a group). This debt instrument provides for five annual payments of $200 and an additional payment of $30,000 in year five. The debt instrument's yield to maturity is 9.304 percent per annum, compounded annually.

(C) *Issuer's interest expense under Notice 97-21.* Under Notice 97-21, Z's interest expense attributable to the fast-pay arrangement for periods before January 1, 2000, equals the interest accrued on the debt instrument held by the fast-pay shareholders, plus the interest accrued on the debt instrument held by the benefited shareholders other than Z. For purposes of paragraph (g)(2)(i)(A) of this section, Z's interest expense is as follows:

| Taxable Period | Accrued Interest Fast-pay Shareholders | Accrued Interest Other Benefited Shareholders | Total Interest Expense |
|---|---|---|---|
| 1/1/97 - 12/31/97 | ($8,574) | ($1,861) | ($10,435) |
| 1/1/98 - 12/31/98 | ($7,852) | ($2,015) | ($9,867) |
| 1/1/99 - 12/31/99 | ($7,067) | ($2,184) | ($9,251) |
| | ($23,493) | ($6,060) | ($29,553) |

(iii) *Recharacterization under this section.* Under paragraphs (c) and (g)(2)(i)(B) of this section, Z's taxable income attributable to the fast-pay arrangement for periods before January 1, 2000, equals Z's share of the dividends actually and deemed paid on the benefited stock (80 percent of the outstanding benefited stock), reduced by the sum of the interest accrued on the note held by Y and the interest accrued on the financing instruments deemed to have been issued by Z. For purposes of paragraph (g)(2)(i)(B) of this section, Z's taxable income is as follows:

| Taxable Period | Dividends Benefited Stock | Accrued Interest On Debt Held By Y | Accrued Interest Financing Instruments | Taxable Expense |
|---|---|---|---|---|
| 1/1/97 - 12/31/97 | $14,400 | ($18,000) | ($6,859) | ($10,459) |
| 1/1/98 - 12/31/98 | $14,400 | ($18,000) | ($6,281) | ($9,881) |
| 1/1/99 - 12/31/99 | $14,400 | ($18,000) | ($5,654) | ($9,254) |
| | $43,200 | ($54,000) | ($18,794) | ($29,594) |

(iv) *Limit on taxable income under this paragraph (g)(2).* For periods before January 1, 2000, Z has a taxable loss attributable to the fast-pay arrangement of $29,553 under the recharacterization of Notice 97-21 and paragraph (g)(2)(i)(A) of this section, and a taxable loss of $29,594 under the recharacterization of paragraphs (c) and (g)(2)(i)(B) of this section. Thus, under paragraph (g)(2)(i) of this section, Z may report a taxable loss attributable to the fast-pay arrangement for periods before January 1, 2000, of either $29,553 or $29,594. Under paragraph (g)(2)(ii), Z has no adjustment to its taxable income for its taxable year that includes January 1, 2000.

(3) *Rule to comply with this section.*—To comply with this section for each taxable year in which it failed to do so, a taxpayer should file an amended return. For taxable years ending before January 10, 2000, a taxpayer that has complied with Notice 97-21, 1997-1 C.B. 407 (see § 601.601(d)(2) of this chapter), for all such taxable years is consid-

ered to have complied with this section and limited its taxable income under paragraph (g)(2)(i)(A) of this section.

(4) *Reporting requirements.*—The reporting requirements of paragraph (f) of this section apply to taxable years (of the person required to file the statement) ending after January 10, 2000. [Reg. § 1.7701(l)-3.]

☐ [*T.D.* 8853, 1-7-2000.]

## [Reg. § 1.7701(l)-4]

**§ 1.7701(l)-4. Rules regarding inversion transactions.—** (a) *Overview.*—This section provides rules applicable to United States shareholders of controlled foreign corporations after certain inversion transactions. Paragraph (b) of this section defines specified transactions and provides the scope of the rules in this section. Paragraph (c) of this section provides rules recharacterizing certain specified transactions. Paragraph (d) of this section sets forth rules governing transactions that affect the stock of an expatriated foreign subsidiary following a recharacterized specified transaction. Paragraph (e) of this section sets forth a rule concerning the treatment of amounts included in income as a result of a specified transaction as foreign personal holding company income. Paragraph (f) of this section sets forth definitions that apply for purposes of this section. Paragraph (g) of this section sets forth examples illustrating these rules. Paragraph (h) of this section provides applicability dates. See § 1.367(b)-4(e) and (f) for rules concerning certain other exchanges after an inversion transaction. See also § 1.956-2(a)(4), (c)(5), and (d)(2) for additional rules applicable to United States property held by controlled foreign corporations after an inversion transaction.

(b) *Specified transaction.*—(1) *In general.*—Except as provided in paragraph (b)(2) of this section, paragraph (c) of this section applies to specified transactions. For purposes of this section, a *specified transaction* is, with respect to an expatriated foreign subsidiary, a transaction in which stock of the expatriated foreign subsidiary is issued or transferred to a person that immediately before the issuance or transfer is a specified related person, provided the transaction occurs during the applicable period. However, a specified transaction does not include a transaction in which stock of the expatriated foreign subsidiary is deemed issued pursuant to section 304.

(2) *Exceptions.*—Paragraph (c) of this section does not apply to a specified transaction—

(i) That is a fast-pay arrangement that is recharacterized under § 1.7701(l)-3(c)(2);

(ii) In which the specified stock was transferred by a shareholder of the expatriated foreign subsidiary, and the shareholder either—

(A) Pursuant to § 1.367(b)-4(e)(1), both—

(1) Included in gross income as a deemed dividend the section 1248 amount attributable to the specified stock; and

(2) After taking into account the increase in basis provided in § 1.367(b)-2(e)(3)(ii) resulting from the deemed dividend (if any), recognized all realized gain with respect to the stock that otherwise would not have been recognized; or

(B) Included in gross income all of the gain recognized on the transfer of the specified stock (including gain included in gross income as a dividend pursuant to section 964(e), section 1248(a), or section 356(a)(2)); or

(iii) In which—

(A) Immediately after the specified transaction and any related transaction, the expatriated foreign subsidiary is a controlled foreign corporation;

(B) The post-transaction ownership percentage with respect to the expatriated foreign subsidiary is at least 90 percent of the pre-transaction ownership percentage with respect to the expatriated foreign subsidiary; and

(C) The post-transaction ownership percentage with respect to any lower-tier expatriated foreign subsidiary is at least 90 percent of the pre-transaction ownership percentage with respect to the lower-tier expatriated foreign subsidiary. See *Example 3* and *Example 4* of paragraph (g) of this section.

(c) *Recharacterization of specified transactions.*—(1) *In general.*—Except as otherwise provided, a specified transaction that is recharacterized under this paragraph (c) is recharacterized for all purposes of the Internal Revenue Code as of the date on which the specified transaction occurs, unless and until the rules of paragraph (d) of this section apply to alter or terminate the recharacterization. For purposes of paragraphs (c)(2) and (3) and (d) of this section, stock is considered owned by a section 958(a) U.S. shareholder if it is owned within the meaning of section 958(a) by the section 958(a) U.S. shareholder.

(2) *Specified transactions through stock issuance.*—A specified transaction in which the specified stock is issued by an expatriated foreign subsidiary to a specified related person is recharacterized as follows—

(i) The transferred property is treated as having been transferred by the specified related person to the persons that were section 958(a) U.S. shareholders of the expatriated foreign subsidiary immediately before the specified transaction, in proportion to the stock of the expatriated foreign subsidiary owned by each section 958(a) U.S. shareholder, in exchange for deemed instruments in the section 958(a) U.S. shareholders; and

(ii) The transferred property treated as transferred to the section 958(a) U.S. shareholders pursuant to paragraph (c)(2)(i) of this section is treated as having been contributed by the section 958(a) U.S. shareholders (through intermediate entities, if any, in exchange for equity in the intermediate entities) to the expatriated foreign subsidiary in exchange for deemed issued stock in the expatriated foreign subsidiary. See *Example 1*, *Example 2*, and *Example 6* of paragraph (g) of this section.

(3) *Specified transactions through shareholder transfer.*—A specified transaction in which specified stock is transferred by shareholders of the expatriated foreign subsidiary to a specified related person is recharacterized as follows—

(i) The transferred property is treated as having been transferred by the specified related person to the persons that were section 958(a) U.S. shareholders of the expatriated foreign subsidiary immediately before the specified transaction, in proportion to the specified stock owned by each section 958(a) U.S. shareholder, in exchange for deemed instruments in the section 958(a) U.S. shareholders; and

(ii) To the extent the section 958(a) U.S. shareholders are not the transferring shareholders, the transferred property treated as transferred to the section 958(a) U.S. shareholders pursuant to paragraph (c)(3)(i) of this section is treated as having been contributed by the section 958(a) U.S. shareholders (through intermediate entities, if any, in exchange for equity in the intermediate entities) to the transferring shareholder in exchange for equity in the transferring shareholder. See *Example 5* of paragraph (g) of this section.

(4) *Treatment of deemed instruments following a recharacterized specified transaction.*—(i) *Deemed instruments.*—The deemed instruments described in paragraphs (c)(2) and (3) of this section have the same terms as the specified stock issued or transferred pursuant to the specified transaction (that is, the disregarded specified stock), other than the issuer. When a distribution is made with respect to the disregarded specified stock, matching seriatim distributions with respect to the deemed issued stock are treated as made by the expatriated foreign subsidiary, through intermediate entities, if any, to the section 958(a) U.S. shareholders, which, in turn, then are treated as making corresponding payments with respect to the deemed instruments to the specified related person.

(ii) *Paying agent.*—The expatriated foreign subsidiary is treated as the paying agent of the section 958(a) U.S. shareholder with respect to the deemed instruments treated as issued by the section 958(a) U.S. shareholder to the specified related person.

(d) *Transactions affecting ownership of stock of an expatriated foreign subsidiary following a recharacterized specified transaction.*—(1) *Transfers of stock other than specified stock.*—When, after a specified transaction with respect to an expatriated foreign subsidiary that is recharacterized under paragraph (c)(2) or (3) of this section, stock of the expatriated foreign subsidiary, other than disregarded specified stock, that is owned by a section 958(a) U.S. shareholder is transferred, the deemed issued stock treated as owned by the section 958(a) U.S. shareholder as a result of the specified transaction continues to be treated as directly owned by the holder, as are the deemed instruments treated as issued to the specified related person as a result of the specified transaction.

(2) *Transactions in which the expatriated foreign subsidiary ceases to be a foreign related person.*—When, after a specified transaction with respect to an expatriated foreign subsidiary that is recharacterized under paragraph (c)(2) or (3) of this section, there is a transaction that affects the ownership of the stock (including disregarded specified stock) of the expatriated foreign subsidiary, and, immediately after the transaction, the expatriated foreign subsidiary is not a foreign related person (determined without taking into account the recharacterization under paragraph (c)(2) or (3) of this section), then, immediately before the transaction—

(i) Each section 958(a) U.S. shareholder that is treated as owning deemed issued stock in the expatriated foreign subsidiary under paragraph (c)(2) or (3) of this section is treated as transferring the deemed issued stock (after the deemed issued stock is deemed to be transferred to the section 958(a) U.S. shareholder through intermediate entities, if any, in redemption of equity deemed issued by the intermediate entities pursuant to paragraph (c)(2) or (3) of this section) to the specified related person that is treated as holding the deemed instruments issued by the section 958(a) U.S. shareholder under paragraph (c)(2) or (3) of this section, in redemption of the deemed instruments; and

(ii) The deemed issued stock that is treated as transferred pursuant to paragraph (d)(2)(i) of this section is treated as recapitalized into the disregarded specified stock actually held by the specified related person, which immediately thereafter is treated as specified stock owned by the specified related person for all purposes of the Internal Revenue Code. See *Example 8*, *Example 9*, and *Example 12* of paragraph (g) of this section.

(3) *Transfers in which disregarded specified stock ceases to be held by a foreign related person, specified related person, or expatriated entity.*— When, after a specified transaction with respect to an expatriated foreign subsidiary that is recharacterized under paragraph (c)(2) or (3) of this section, there is a direct or indirect transfer of the disregarded specified stock in the expatriated foreign subsidiary, and immediately after the transfer, the expatriated foreign subsidiary is a foreign related person, then, to the extent that, as a result of the transfer, the disregarded specified stock is actually held (determined without taking into account the recharacterization under paragraph (c)(2) or (3) of this section) by a person that is not a foreign related person, a specified related person, or an expatriated entity, immediately before the transfer—

(i) Each section 958(a) U.S. shareholder that is treated as owning all or a portion of the deemed issued stock in the expatriated foreign subsidiary is treated as transferring the deemed issued stock that is allocable to the transferred disregarded specified stock that is out-of-group transferred disregarded specified stock (after the deemed issued stock is deemed to be transferred to the section 958(a) U.S. shareholder through intermediate entities, if any, in redemption of equity deemed issued by the intermediate entities pursuant to paragraph (c)(2) or (3) of this section) to the specified related person that is treated as holding the deemed instruments allocable to the out-of-group transferred disregarded specified stock, in redemption of the deemed instruments that are allocable to the out-of-group transferred disregarded specified stock; and

(ii) The deemed issued stock that is treated as transferred pursuant to paragraph (d)(3)(i) of this section is treated as recapitalized into the disregarded specified stock actually held by the specified related person, which immediately thereafter is treated as specified stock owned by the specified related person for all purposes of the Internal Revenue Code. See *Example 7* and *Example 11* of paragraph (g) of this section.

(4) *Certain direct transfers of disregarded specified stock to which unwind rules do not apply.*—When a specified related person directly transfers the disregarded specified stock of the expatriated foreign subsidiary and paragraphs (d)(2) and (3) of this section do not apply with respect to the transfer, the specified related person is deemed to transfer the deemed instruments allocable to the transferred disregarded specified stock, whether it is in-group transferred disregarded specified stock or out-of-group transferred disregarded specified stock, to the transferee of the specified stock, in lieu of the disregarded specified stock, in exchange for the consideration provided by the transferee for the disregarded specified stock. See *Example 10* of paragraph (g) of this section.

(5) *Determination of deemed issued stock and deemed instruments allocable to transferred disregarded specified stock.*—(i) *Out-of-group transfers of disregarded specified stock.*—For purposes of paragraphs (d)(3) and (4) of this section, the portion of the deemed issued stock treated as owned, and of the deemed instruments treated as issued, by each section 958(a) U.S. shareholder as a result of the specified transaction that is allocable to out-of-group transferred disregarded specified stock is the amount that is proportionate to the ratio of the amount of the out-of-group transferred disregarded specified stock to the amount of disregarded specified stock of the expatriated foreign subsidiary that is actually held by the specified related person immediately before the transfer referred to in paragraph (d)(3) or (4) of this section as a result of the specified transaction.

(ii) *In-group direct transfers of disregarded specified stock.*—For purposes of paragraph (d)(4) of this section, the portion of the deemed issued stock treated as owned by each section 958(a) U.S. shareholder as a result of the specified transaction that is allocable to in-group transferred disregarded specified stock is the amount that is proportionate to the ratio of the amount of the in-group transferred disregarded specified stock to the amount of disregarded specified stock of the expatriated foreign subsidiary that is actually held by the specified related person immediately before the transfer described in paragraph (d)(4) of this section as a result of the specified transaction.

(e) *Certain exception from foreign personal holding company income not available.*—An amount included in the gross income of a controlled foreign corporation as a dividend with respect to stock transferred in a specified transaction does not qualify for the exception from foreign personal holding company income provided by section 954(c)(6) (to the extent in effect).

(f) *Definitions.*—In addition to the definitions in §1.7874-12, the following definitions and special rules apply for purposes of this section:

(1) *Deemed instruments* mean, with respect to a specified transaction, instruments deemed issued by a section 958(a) U.S. shareholder in exchange for transferred property in the specified transaction.

(2) *Deemed issued stock* means, with respect to a specified transaction, stock of an expatriated foreign subsidiary deemed issued to a section 958(a) U.S. shareholder (or an intermediate entity) in the specified transaction.

(3) *Disregarded specified stock* means, with respect to a specified transaction, specified stock that is actually held by a specified related person but that is disregarded for all purposes of the Internal Revenue Code pursuant to paragraph (c)(2) or (3) of this section.

(4) *Indirect ownership.*—To determine indirect ownership of the stock of a corporation for purposes of calculating a pre-transaction ownership percentage or post-transaction ownership percentage with respect to that corporation, the principles of section 958(a) apply without regard to whether an intermediate entity is foreign or domestic. For this purpose, stock of the corporation that is directly or indirectly (applying the principles of section 958(a) without regard to whether an intermediate entity is foreign or domestic) owned by a domestic corporation that is an expatriated entity is not treated as indirectly owned by a non-EFS foreign related person.

(5) *In-group transferred disregarded specified stock* means disregarded specified stock that is directly transferred to a foreign related person, a specified related person, or an expatriated entity.

(6) A *lower-tier expatriated foreign subsidiary* means an expatriated foreign subsidiary, stock of which is directly or indirectly owned by an expatriated foreign subsidiary.

(7) *Out-of-group transferred disregarded specified stock* means disregarded specified stock that, as a result of a transfer of disregarded specified stock, is actually held by a person that is not a foreign related person, a specified related person, or an expatriated entity.

(8) *Pre-transaction ownership percentage* means, with respect to a corporation, 100 percent less the percentage of stock (by value) in the corporation that, immediately before a specified transaction and any related transaction, is owned, in the aggregate, directly or indirectly by non-EFS foreign related persons.

(9) *Post-transaction ownership percentage* means, with respect to a corporation, 100 percent less the percentage of stock (by value) in the corporation that, immediately after the specified transaction and any related transaction, is owned, in the aggregate, directly or indirectly by non-EFS foreign related persons.

(10) A *section 958(a) U.S. shareholder* means, with respect to an expatriated foreign subsidiary, a United States shareholder with respect to the expatriated foreign subsidiary that owns (within the meaning of section 958(a)) stock of the expatriated foreign subsidiary and that is an expatriated entity.

(11) *Specified stock* means the stock of the expatriated foreign subsidiary that is issued or transferred to a specified related person in a specified transaction.

(12) *Transferred property* means the property transferred by the specified related person in exchange for specified stock in a specified transaction.

(g) *Examples.*—The following examples illustrate the regulations described in this section. Except as otherwise provided, FA, a foreign corporation, wholly owns DT, a domestic corporation, which, in turn, wholly owns FT, a foreign corporation that is a controlled foreign corporation. FA also wholly owns FS, a foreign corporation that is a controlled foreign corporation for its taxable year beginning January 1, 2017, but not for prior taxable years. FA acquired DT in an inversion transaction that was completed on January 1, 2015. Accordingly, DT is the domestic entity and a section 958(a) U.S. shareholder with respect to FT, FT is an expatriated foreign subsidiary, and FA and FS are non-EFS foreign related persons and specified related persons. All entities have a calendar year tax year for U.S. tax purposes.

*Example 1.* (i) *Facts.* On February 1, 2015, FA acquires $6x of FT stock, representing 60% of the total voting power and value of the stock of FT, from FT in a stock issuance, in exchange for $6x of cash.

(ii) *Analysis.* (A) Under paragraph (b) of this section, FA's acquisition of the FT specified stock from FT is a specified transaction because stock of an expatriated foreign subsidiary was issued to a specified related person (FA) during the applicable period. Furthermore, the exceptions to recharacterization in paragraph (b)(2) of this section do not apply to the transaction.

(B) FA's acquisition of the FT specified stock is recharacterized under paragraphs (c)(1) and (2) of this section as follows, with the result that FT continues to be a CFC even before its taxable year beginning January 1, 2017:

(1) DT is treated as having issued deemed instruments to FA in exchange for $6x of cash.

(2) DT is treated as having contributed the $6x of cash to FT in exchange for deemed issued stock of FT.

(C) Under paragraph (c)(4)(i) of this section, any distribution with respect to the FT specified stock issued to FA will be treated as a distribution to DT, which, in turn, will be treated as making a matching distribution with respect to the deemed instruments that DT is treated as having issued to FA. Under paragraph (c)(4)(ii) of this section, FT is treated as the paying agent of DT with respect to the deemed instruments issued by DT to FA.

*Example 2.* (i) *Facts.* DT owns stock of FT representing 60% of the total voting power and value of the stock of FT, and the remaining stock of FT, representing 40% of the total voting power and value, is owned by USP, a domestic corporation that is not an expatriated entity. On February 1, 2015, FA acquires $6x of FT stock, representing 60% of the total voting power and value of the stock of FT, from FT in a stock issuance, in exchange for $6x of cash.

(ii) *Analysis.* (A) Under paragraph (b) of this section, FA's acquisition of the FT specified stock from FT is a specified transaction because stock of an expatriated foreign subsidiary was issued to a specified related person (FA) during the applicable period. Furthermore, the exceptions to recharacterization in paragraph (b)(2) of this section do not apply to the transaction.

(B) FA's acquisition of the FT specified stock is recharacterized under paragraphs (c)(1) and (2) of this section as follows, with the result that FT continues to be a CFC even before its taxable year beginning January 1, 2017:

(1) DT is treated as having issued deemed instruments to FA in exchange for $6x of cash.

(2) DT is treated as having contributed the $6x of cash to FT in exchange for deemed issued stock of FT.

(3) DT is treated as owning $8.40x of the stock of FT, representing 84% of the total voting power and value of the stock of FT. USP owns $1.60x of the stock of FT, representing 16% of the total voting power and value of the stock of FT.

(C) Under paragraph (c)(4)(i) of this section, any distribution with respect to the FT specified stock issued to FA will be treated as a distribution to DT, which, in turn, will be treated as making a matching distribution with respect to the deemed instruments that DT is treated as having issued to FA. Under paragraph (c)(4)(ii) of this section, FT is treated as the paying agent of DT with respect to the deemed instruments issued by DT to FA.

*Example 3.* (i) *Facts.* DT owns stock of FT representing 50% of the total voting power and value of the $8x of stock of FT outstanding, and the remaining stock of FT, representing 50% of the total voting power and value, is owned by USP, a domestic corporation that is not an expatriated entity. On April 30, 2016, FA and USP each simultaneously acquire $1x of FT stock from FT in a stock issuance, in exchange for $1x of cash each.

(ii) *Analysis.* (A) Under paragraph (b) of this section, FA's acquisition of the FT specified stock from FT is a specified transaction because stock of an expatriated foreign subsidiary was issued to a specified related person (FA) during the applicable period.

(B) However, the specified transaction is not recharacterized under paragraphs (c)(1) and (2) of this section because the exception in paragraph (b)(2)(iii) of this section applies. The exception applies because FT remains a controlled foreign corporation immediately after the specified transaction and any related transaction, and the post-transaction ownership percentage with respect to FT is 90% (90%/100%), or at least 90%, of the pre-transaction ownership percentage with respect to FT. The rule in paragraph (b)(2)(iii)(C) of this section does not apply because there is no lower-tier expatriated foreign subsidiary. Although FA (a non-EFS foreign related person) indirectly owns $4x of FT stock both immediately before and after the specified transaction and any related transaction, all of that stock is directly owned by DT (a domestic corporation), and as a result, under paragraph (f)(4) of this section, none of that stock is treated as directly or indirectly owned by FA for purposes of calculating the pre-transaction ownership percentage and the post-transaction ownership percentage with respect to FT. Accordingly, under paragraph (f)(8) of this section, the pre-transaction ownership percentage with respect to FT (100% less the percentage of stock (by value) in FT that, immediately before the specified transaction with respect to FT and any related transaction, is owned by non-EFS foreign related persons) is 100 (100% - 0%). Under paragraph (f)(9) of this section, the post-transaction ownership percentage with respect to FT (100% less the percentage of stock (by value) in FT that, immediately after the

specified transaction with respect to FT and any related transaction, is owned by non-EFS foreign related persons) is 90 (100% - 10% ($1x/$10x)).

*Example 4.* (i) *Facts.* On February 1, 2015, FA acquires 60% of the FT stock owned by DT in exchange for $2.40x of cash in a fully taxable transaction. DT recognizes and includes in income all of the gain (including any gain treated as a deemed dividend pursuant to section 1248(a)) with respect to the FT stock transferred to FA.

(ii) *Analysis.* (A) Under paragraph (b) of this section, FA's acquisition of the FT specified stock is a specified transaction because stock of an expatriated foreign subsidiary was transferred to a specified related person (FA) during the applicable period.

(B) However, the specified transaction is not recharacterized under paragraphs (c)(1) and (c)(3) of this section because the exception in paragraph (b)(2)(ii) of this section applies. The exception applies because DT recognizes and includes in income all of the gain (including any gain treated as a deemed dividend pursuant to section 1248(a)) with respect to the FT specified stock transferred to FA.

*Example 5.* (i) *Facts.* On February 1, 2015, DT and FA organize FPRS, a foreign partnership, with nominal capital. DT transfers all of the stock of FT to FPRS in exchange for 40% of the capital and profits interests in the partnership. Furthermore, FA contributes property to FPRS in exchange for the other 60% of the capital and profits interests.

(ii) *Analysis.* (A) Under paragraph (b) of this section, DT's transfer of the FT specified stock is a specified transaction, because stock of an expatriated foreign subsidiary was transferred to a specified related person (FPRS) during the applicable period. The exceptions to recharacterization in paragraph (b)(2) of this section do not apply to the transaction.

(B) DT's transfer of the FT specified stock is recharacterized under paragraphs (c)(1) and (c)(3) of this section as follows, with the result that FT continues to be a CFC even before its taxable year beginning January 1, 2017:

(1) FPRS is treated as having issued 40% of its capital and profits interests to DT in exchange for deemed instruments treated as having been issued by DT.

(2) DT is treated as continuing to own all of the stock of FT, as well as the FPRS interests.

(C) Under paragraph (c)(4)(i) of this section, any distribution with respect to the FT specified stock transferred to FPRS will be treated as a distribution to DT, which, in turn, will be treated as making a matching distribution with respect to the deemed instruments that DT is treated as having issued to FPRS. Under paragraph (c)(4)(ii) of this section, FT is treated as the paying agent of DT with respect to the deemed instruments issued by DT to FPRS.

*Example 6.* (i) *Facts.* DT wholly owns FT2, a foreign corporation that is a controlled foreign corporation. FT and FT2 each own 50% of the capital and profits interests in DPRS, a domestic partnership. DPRS wholly owns FT3, a foreign corporation that is a controlled foreign corporation. FT2 and FT3 are expatriated foreign subsidiaries. On April 30, 2016, FS acquires $9x of the stock of each of FT and FT2, representing 9% of the total voting power and value of the stock of FT and FT2, from FT and FT2, respectively, in a stock issuance, in exchange for cash of $9x each. Also on April 30, 2016, in a related transaction, FS acquires $9x of the stock of FT3, representing 9% of the total voting power and value of the stock of FT3, from FT3 in a stock issuance, in exchange for cash of $9x.

(ii) *Analysis.* (A) Under paragraph (b) of this section, the acquisitions by FS of the specified stock of each of FT, FT2, and FT3 from FT, FT2, and FT3 are specified transactions with respect to each of FT, FT2, and FT3, respectively, because stock of an expatriated foreign subsidiary was issued to a specified related person (FS) during the applicable period.

(B) If FS had acquired only stock of FT and FT2, and had not acquired stock of FT3 in a related transaction, the specified transactions resulting from the acquisitions with respect to FT and FT2 would not have been recharacterized under paragraphs (c)(1) and (2) of this section, because the exception from recharacterization in paragraph (b)(2)(iii) of this section would have applied. FT and FT2 remain controlled foreign corporations immediately after each specified transaction and any related transaction. Under paragraph (f)(9) of this section, the post-transaction ownership percentage with respect to each of FT, FT2, and FT3 (a lower-tier expatriated foreign subsidiary of FT and FT2) would have been 91% ((100% - 9%)/(100% - 0%)), or at least 90%, of the pre-transaction ownership percentage determined under paragraph (f)(8) of this section with respect to each of FT, FT2, and FT3 (100%).

(C) However, for the specified transactions with respect to FT, FT2, and FT3, the post-transaction ownership percentage determined under paragraph (f)(9) of this section with respect to FT3 (the lower-tier expatriated foreign subsidiary of FT and FT2), 100% less the percentage of stock (by value) in FT3 that, immediately after each of the specified transactions with respect to each of FT and FT2 and any related transaction, is owned by the non-EFS foreign related persons, is 82.81 (100%-(9%x50%x91%)-(9%x50%x91%)-9%). Accordingly, the post-transaction ownership percentage with respect to FT3 is 82.81% (82.81/(100%-0%)), which is less than 90%, of the pre-transaction ownership percentage determined under paragraph (f)(8) of this section with respect to FT3. Thus, the exception from recharacterization in paragraph (b)(2)(iii) of this section does not apply with respect to the specified transactions with respect to FT, FT2, or FT3.

(D) The specified transactions with respect to FT and FT2 are recharacterized under paragraphs (c)(1) and (2) of this section as follows:

(1) DT is treated as having issued 2 deemed instruments worth $9x each to FA in exchange for $18x ($9x + $9x) of cash.

(2) DT is treated as having contributed $9x of cash to each of FT and FT2 in exchange for deemed issued stock of FT and FT2.

(3) DT is treated as continuing to own all of the stock of FT and FT2.

(E) Under paragraph (c)(4)(i) of this section, any distribution with respect to the FT and FT2 specified stock issued to FS will be treated as a distribution to DT, which, in turn, will be treated as making a matching distribution with respect to the deemed instruments that DT is treated as having issued to FS. Under paragraph (c)(4)(ii) of this section, FT and FT2 are treated as the paying agents of DT with respect to the deemed instruments issued by DT to FS.

(F) The specified transaction with respect to FT3 is recharacterized under paragraphs (c)(1) and (2) of this section as follows:

(1) DPRS is treated as having issued a deemed instrument worth $9x to FA in exchange for $9x of cash.

(2) DPRS is treated as having contributed $9x of cash to FT3 in exchange for deemed issued stock of FT3.

(3) DPRS is treated as continuing to own all of the stock of FT3.

(G) Under paragraph (c)(4)(i) of this section, any distribution with respect to the FT3 specified stock issued to FS will be treated as a distribution to DPRS, which, in turn, will be treated as making a matching distribution with respect to the deemed instruments that DPRS is treated as having issued to FS. Under paragraph (c)(4)(ii) of this section, FT3 is treated as the paying agent of DPRS with respect to the deemed instrument issued by DPRS to FS.

*Example 7.* (i) *Facts.* The facts are the same as in *Example 1* of this paragraph (g). On April 30, 2016, FA transfers $4x of the FT disregarded specified stock that it acquired on February 1, 2015 to USP, a domestic corporation that is not an expatriated entity, in exchange for $4x of cash.

(ii) *Results.* After the transfer, FT remains a foreign related person. Therefore, paragraph (d)(2) of this section does not apply. However, the $4x of FT disregarded specified stock transferred to USP ceases to be held by a foreign related person, a specified related person, or an expatriated entity (determined without taking into account paragraph (c)(2) or (3) of this section). Therefore, under paragraph (d)(3) of this section, immediately before the transfer of the disregarded specified stock, DT is deemed to transfer $4x ($6x x ($4x/$6x)) of the FT deemed issued stock that it is treated as owning to FA, the specified related person, in redemption of $4x ($6x x ($4x/$6x)) of the DT deemed instruments that FA is treated as owning, and the $4x of FT deemed issued stock deemed transferred to FA is deemed recapitalized into disregarded specified stock actually held by FA, which is thereafter treated as owned by FA for all purposes of the Code until the transfer to USP.

*Example 8.* (i) *Facts.* The facts are the same as in *Example 7* of this paragraph (g), except that on April 30, 2016, FA transfers all $6x of the FT disregarded specified stock to USP in exchange for $6x of cash.

(ii) *Results.* After the transfer, FT ceases to be a foreign related person (determined without taking into account paragraph (c)(2) or (3) of this section). Therefore, under paragraph (d)(2) of this section, immediately before the transfer of the disregarded specified stock, DT is deemed to transfer the $6x of FT deemed issued stock that it is treated as owning to FA, the specified related person, in redemption of the $6x of DT deemed instruments that FA is treated as owning, and the $6x of FT deemed issued stock deemed transferred to FA is deemed recapitalized into disregarded specified stock actually held by FA, which is thereafter treated as owned by FA for all purposes of the Code until the transfer to USP.

*Example 9.* (i) *Facts.* The facts are the same as in *Example 7* of this paragraph (g), except that on April 30, 2016, FA transfers $5.5x of the FT disregarded specified stock to USP in exchange for $5.5x of cash.

(ii) *Results.* After the transfer, FT ceases to be a foreign related person (determined without taking into account paragraph (c)(2) or (3) of this section). Therefore, under paragraph (d)(2) of this section, immediately before the transfer of the disregarded specified stock, DT is deemed to transfer the $6x of FT deemed issued stock that it is treated as owning to FA, the specified related person, in redemption of the $6x of DT deemed instruments that FA is treated as owning, and the $6x of FT deemed issued stock deemed transferred to FA is

deemed recapitalized into disregarded specified stock actually held by FA, which is thereafter treated as owned by FA for all purposes of the Code and $5.5x of which is transferred to USP. The remaining $0.5x of the specified stock continues to be treated as owned by FA for all purposes of the Code.

*Example 10.* (i) *Facts.* The facts are the same as in *Example 1* of this paragraph (g). On April 30, 2016, FA transfers $5x of the FT disregarded specified stock that it acquired on February 1, 2015 to DS, a domestic corporation wholly owned by DT, in exchange for $5x of cash.

(ii) *Results.* After the transfer, FT remains a foreign related person because DS is wholly owned by DT. Therefore, paragraph (d)(2) of this section does not apply. Furthermore, the $5x of FT disregarded specified stock is not, as a result of the transfer, held by a person that is not a foreign related person, a specified related person, or an expatriated entity. Therefore, paragraph (d)(3) of this section does not apply. Because FA, a specified related person, directly transferred disregarded specified stock of FT in a transaction to which paragraphs (d)(2) and (3) of this section do not apply, under paragraph (d)(4) of this section, FA is treated as transferring the $5x of deemed instruments of DT allocable to the $5x of in-group transferred disregarded specified stock ($6x x ($5x/$6x)) to DS.

*Example 11.* (i) *Facts.* On February 11, 2015, FA acquires $6x of FT stock, representing 60% of the total voting power and value of the stock of FT, from FT in a stock issuance, in exchange for $6x of cash. The $6x of FT stock is specified stock, and the transaction is recharacterized under paragraph (c)(2) of this section. See *Example 1* of this paragraph (g). On April 30, 2016, FA transfers stock of FS representing 60% of the total voting power and value of the stock of FS to USP, a domestic corporation that is not an expatriated entity. As a result of the transfer, FS ceases to be a foreign related person.

(ii) *Results.* After the February 1, 2015 transfer, FT remains a foreign related person because the FT stock is acquired by FS, a foreign related person with respect to DT at that time. Therefore, paragraph (d)(2) of this section does not apply. However, after the April 30, 2016 transfer, because FS ceases to be a foreign related person, it ceases to be a specified related person. Furthermore, the $6x of disregarded specified stock held before the transaction continues to be held by FS after the transaction, and therefore is not held by a foreign related person, a specified related person, or an expatriated entity after the transaction. Accordingly, under paragraph (d)(3) of this section, immediately before the transfer of FS disregarded specified stock, DT is deemed to transfer $6x ($6x x ($6x/$6x)) of the FT deemed issued stock that it is treated as owning to FS, the specified related person, in redemption of $6x ($6x x ($6x/$6x)) of the DT deemed instruments that FS is treated as owning, and the $6x of FT deemed issued stock deemed transferred to FS is deemed recapitalized into disregarded specified stock actually held by FS, which thereafter is treated as owned by FS for all purposes of the Code, including after the transfer of 60% of the FS stock to USP.

*Example 12.* (i) *Facts.* The facts are the same as in *Example 1* of this paragraph (g). On April 30, 2016, FP, a foreign corporation that is not a foreign related person acquires $15x of FT stock, representing 60% of the total voting power and value of the stock of FT, from FT in a stock issuance, in exchange for $15x of cash.

(ii) *Results.* After the transaction, FT ceases to be a foreign related person. Therefore, under paragraph (d)(2) of this section, immediately before the issuance of FT stock to FP, DT is deemed to transfer the $6x of FT deemed issued stock that it is treated as owning to FA, the specified related person, in redemption of the $6x of DT deemed instruments that FA is treated as owning, and the $6x of FT deemed issued stock deemed transferred to FA is deemed recapitalized into disregarded specified stock actually held by FA, which thereafter is treated as owned by FA for all purposes of the Code.

*Example 13.* (i) *Facts.* The facts are the same as in *Example 1* of this paragraph (g). On April 30, 2016, FS acquires $4x of the FT stock owned by DT in exchange for $4x of cash in a fully taxable transaction. DT recognizes and includes in income all of the gain (including any gain treated as a deemed dividend pursuant to section 1248(a)) with respect to the FT stock transferred to FS.

(ii) *Results.* (A) The transfer of FT stock by DT to FS is a specified transaction, but it is not recharacterized under paragraphs (c)(1) and (3) of this section because the exception in paragraph (b)(2)(ii) of this section applies. See *Example 4* of this paragraph (g).

(B) After the transfer, FT remains a foreign related person. Therefore, paragraph (d)(2) of this section does not apply. The disregarded specified stock of FT is not, as a result of the transfer, held by a person that is not a foreign related person, a specified related person, or an expatriated entity. Therefore, paragraph (d)(3) of this section does not apply. There has been no direct transfer of specified stock. Therefore, paragraph (d)(4) of this section also does not apply.

(C) Under paragraph (d)(1) of this section, the $6x of deemed issued stock treated as owned by DT as a result of the specified transaction in which FA acquired FT stock continues to be treated as owned by DT, and the $6x of deemed instruments treated as issued by DT to FA continue to be treated as owned by FA.

(h) *Applicability date.*—Except as otherwise provided in this paragraph (h), this section applies to specified transactions completed on or after September 22, 2014, but only if the inversion transaction was completed on or after September 22, 2014. Paragraph (b)(2)(ii)(A)(2) of this section applies to specified transactions completed on or after November 19, 2015, but only if the inversion transaction was completed on or after September 22, 2014. Paragraphs (d) and (f)(5), (7), and (10) of this section apply to specified transactions completed on or after April 4, 2016, but only if the inversion transaction was completed on or after September 22, 2014. For inversion transactions completed on or after September 22, 2014, however, taxpayers may elect to apply paragraphs (d) and (f)(5), (7), and (10) of this section to specified transactions completed before April 4, 2016. In addition, for inversion transactions completed on or after September 22, 2014, in lieu of applying paragraphs (d) and (f)(5) and (7) of this section to specified transactions completed on or after September 22, 2014, and before April 4, 2016, taxpayers may elect to apply the principles of § 1.7701(l)-3(c)(3)(iii). Furthermore, for inversion transactions completed on or after September 22, 2014, in lieu of applying paragraph (f)(10) of this section to specified transactions completed on or after September 22, 2014, and before April 4, 2016, taxpayers may elect to define a section 958(a) U.S. shareholder as a United States shareholder with respect to the expatriated foreign subsidiary that owns (within the meaning of section 958(a)) stock in the expatriated foreign subsidiary, but only if such United States shareholder is related (within the meaning of section 267(b) or 707(b)(1)) to the specified related person or is under the same common control (within the meaning of section 482) as the specified related person. [Reg. § 1.7701(l)-4.]

☐ [*T.D.* 9834, 7-11-2018.]

### [Reg. § 1.7702-0.]

**§1.7702-0. Table of contents.**—This section lists the captions that appear in § § 1.7702-1, 1.7702-2, and 1.7702-3.

*§ 1.7702-1 Mortality charges.*
(a) General rule.
(b) Reasonable mortality charges.
  (1) Actually expected to be imposed.
  (2) Limit on charges.
(c) Safe harbors.
  (1) 1980 C.S.O. Basic Mortality Tables.
  (2) Unisex tables and smoker/nonsmoker tables.
  (3) Certain contracts based on 1958 C.S.O. table.
(d) Definitions.
  (1) Prevailing commissioners' standard tables.
  (2) Substandard risk.
  (3) Nonparticipating contract.
  (4) Charge reduction mechanism.
  (5) Plan of insurance.
(e) Effective date.

*§ 1.7702-2 Attained age of the insured under a life insurance contract.*
(a) In general.
(b) Contract insuring a single life.
(c) Contract insuring multiple lives on a last-to-die basis.
  (1) In general.
  (2) Modifications to cash value and future mortality charges upon the death of insured.
(d) Contract insuring multiple lives on a first-to-die basis.
(e) Examples.
(f) Effective dates.
  (1) In general.
  (2) Contracts issued before the general effective date.

*§ 1.7702-3 Definitions.*
(a) In general.
(b) Cash value.
  (1) In general.
  (2) Amounts excluded from cash value.
(c) Death benefit.
  (1) In general.
  (2) Qualified accelerated death benefit treated as death benefit.
(d) Qualified accelerated death benefit.
  (1) In general.
  (2) Determination of present value of the reduction in death benefit.
  (3) Examples.
(e) Terminally ill defined.
(f) Certain other additional benefits.
  (1) In general.
  (2) Examples.

(g) Adjustments under section 7702 (f) (7).
(h) Cash surrender value.
  (1) In general.
  (2) For purposes of section 7702 (f) (7).
(i) Net surrender value.
(j) Effective date and special rules.
  (1) In general.
  (2) Provision of certain benefits before July 1, 1993.
    (i) Not treated as cash value.
    (ii) No effect on date of issuance.
    (iii) Special rule for addition of benefit or loan provision after December 15, 1992.
  (3) Addition of qualified accelerated death benefit.
  (4) Addition of other additional benefits.
[Reg. § 1.7702-0.]

☐ [*T.D.* 9287, 9-12-2006.]

### [Reg. § 1.7702-2]

**§1.7702-2. Attained age of the insured under a life insurance contract.**—(a) *In general.*—This section provides guidance on determining the attained age of an insured under a contract that is a life insurance contract under the applicable law, for purposes of determining the guideline level premium of the contract under section 7702(c) (4), applying the cash value corridor of section 7702(d) or applying the computational rules of section 7702(e), as applicable.

(b) *Contract insuring a single life.*—(1) If a contract insures the life of a single individual, either of the following two ages may be treated as the attained age of the insured with respect to that contract—
  (i) The insured's age determined by reference to the individual's actual birthday as of the date of determination (actual age); or
  (ii) The insured's age determined by reference to contract anniversary (rather than the individual's actual birthday), so long as the age assumed under the contract (contract age) is within 12 months of the actual age as of that date.
  (2) Once determined under paragraph (b)(1) of this section, the attained age with respect to an individual insured under a contract changes annually. Moreover, the same attained age must be used for purposes of applying sections 7702(c) (4), 7702(d), and 7702(e), as applicable.

(c) *Contract insuring multiple lives on a last-to-die basis.*—(1) *In general.*—Except as provided in paragraph (c)(2) of this section, if a contract insures the lives of more than one individual on a last-to-die basis, the attained age of the insured is determined by applying paragraph (b) of this section as if the youngest individual were the only insured under the contract for purposes of sections 7702(c) (4), 7702(d), and 7702(e), as applicable.

  (2) *Modifications to cash value and future mortality charges upon the death of insured.*—If both the cash value and future mortality charges under a contract change by reason of the death of one or more insureds to no longer take into account the attained age of the deceased insured or insureds, the youngest surviving insured shall thereafter be treated as the only insured under the contract.

(d) *Contract insuring multiple lives on a first-to-die basis.*—If a contract insures the lives of more than one individual on a first-to-die basis, the attained age of the insured is determined by applying paragraph (b) of this section as if the oldest individual were the only insured under the contract for purposes of sections 7702(c) (4), 7702(d), and 7702(e), as applicable.

(e) *Examples.*—The following examples illustrate the determination of the attained age of the insured for purposes of sections 7702(c)(4), 7702(d), and 7702(e), as applicable. The examples are as follows:

*Example 1.* (i) X was born on May 1, 1947. X became 60 years old on May 1, 2007. On January 1, 2008, X purchases from IC a contract insuring X's life. January 1 is the contract anniversary date for all future years. IC determines X's annual premiums on an age-last-birthday basis. Based on the method used by IC to determine age, X has an attained age of 60 for the first contract year, 61 for the second contract year, and so on.

(ii) Section 1.7702-2(b)(1) permits the determination of attained age under either of two alternative approaches. Section 1.7702-2(b)(1)(i) provides that, if a contract insures the life of a single insured individual, the attained age may be determined by reference to the individual's actual birthday as of the date of determination. Under this provision, X has an attained age of 60 for the first contract year, 61 for the second contract year, and so on. Alternatively, § 1.7702-2(b)(1)(ii) provides that the insured's age may be determined by reference to contract anniversary (rather than the individual's actual birthday), so long as the age assumed under the contract is within 12 months of the actual age as of that date. If IC determines X's attained age under

§ 1.7702-2(b)(1)(ii), X likewise has an attained age of 60 for the first contract year, 61 for the second contract year, and so on. Whichever provision IC uses to determine X's attained age must be used consistently from year to year for purposes of sections 7702 (c) (4), 7702(d), and 7702(e), as applicable.

*Example 2.* (i) The facts are the same as in *Example 1* except that, under the contract, X's annual premiums are determined on an age-nearest-birthday basis. X's nearest birthday to January 1, 2008, is May 1, 2008, when X will become 61 years old. Based on the method used by IC to determine age, X has an attained age of 61 for the first contract year, 62 for the second contract year, and so on.

(ii) Section 1.7702-2(b)(1) permits the determination of attained age under either of two alternative approaches. Section 1.7702-2(b)(1)(i) provides that, if a contract insures the life of a single insured individual, the attained age may be determined by reference to the individual's actual birthday as of the date of determination. Under this provision, X has an attained age of 60 for the first contract year, 61 for the second contract year, and so on. Alternatively, § 1.7702-2(b)(1)(ii) provides that the insured's age may be determined by reference to contract anniversary (rather than the individual's actual birthday), so long as the age assumed under the contract is within 12 months of the actual age as of that date. If IC determines X's attained age under § 1.7702-2(b)(1)(ii), X has an attained age of 61 for the first contract year, 62 for the second contract year, and so on. Whichever provision IC uses to determine X's attained age must be used consistently from year to year for purposes of sections 7702 (c) (4), 7702(d), and 7702(e), as applicable.

*Example 3.* (i) The facts are the same as in *Example 1* except that the face amount of the contract is increased on May 15, 2011. During the contract year beginning January 1, 2011, the age assumed under the contract on an age-last-birthday basis is 63 years. However, X has an actual age of 64 as of the date the face amount of the contract is increased.

(ii) Section 1.7702-2(b)(1)(ii) provides that the insured's age may be determined by reference to contract anniversary (rather than the individual's actual birthday), so long as the age assumed under the contract is within 12 months of the actual age. Section 1.7702-2(b)(2) provides that, once determined under paragraph (b)(1) of this section, the attained age with respect to an individual insured under a contract changes annually. Accordingly, X continues to be 63 years old throughout the contract year beginning January 1, 2011, for purposes of sections 7702(c)(4), 7702(d), and 7702 (e), as applicable.

*Example 4.* (i) The facts are the same as in *Example 1* except that in addition to X (born in 1947), the insurance contract also insures the life of Y, born on September 1, 1942. The death benefit will be paid when the second of the two insureds dies.

(ii) Section 1.7702-2 (c) (1) provides that if a life insurance contract insures the lives of more than one individual on a last-to-die basis, the attained age of the insured is determined by applying § 1.7702-2(b) as if the youngest individual were the only insured under the contract. Because X is younger than Y, the attained age of X must be used for purposes of sections 7702 (c) (4), 7702(d), and 7702(e), as applicable.

*Example 5.* (i) The facts are the same as *Example 4* except that X (the younger of the two insureds) dies in 2012. After X's death, both the cash value and mortality charges of the life insurance contract are adjusted to take into account only the life of Y.

(ii) Section 1.7702-2 (c) (1) provides that if a life insurance contract insures the lives of more than one individual on a last-to-die basis, the attained age of the insured is determined by applying § 1.7702-2(b) as if the youngest individual were the only insured under the contract. Paragraph (c)(2) of this section provides that if both the cash value and future mortality charges under a contract change by reason of the death of an insured to no longer take into account the attained age of the deceased insured, the youngest surviving insured is thereafter treated as the only insured under the contract. Because both the cash value and mortality charges are adjusted after X's death to take into account only the life of Y, only the attained age of Y is taken into account after X's death for purposes of sections 7702(c) (4), 7702(d), and 7702 (e), as applicable.

*Example 6.* (i) The facts are the same as *Example 1* except that in addition to X (born in 1947), the insurance contract also insures the life of Z, born on September 1, 1952. The death benefit will be paid when the first of the two insureds dies.

(ii) Section 1.7702-2(d) provides that if a life insurance contract insures the lives of more than one individual on a first-to-die basis, the attained age of the insured is determined by applying § 1.7702-2(b) as if the oldest individual were the only insured under the contract. Because X is older than Z, the attained age of X must be used for purposes of sections 7702 (c) (4), 7702(d), and 7702 (e), as applicable.

(f) *Effective dates.*—(1) *In general.*—Except as provided in paragraph (f)(2) of this section, these regulations apply to all life insurance contracts that are either—

(i) Issued after December 31, 2008; or

(ii) Issued on or after October 1, 2007 and based upon the 2001 CSO tables.

(2) *Contracts issued before the general effective date.*—Pursuant to section 7805(b)(7), a taxpayer may apply these regulations retroactively for contracts issued before October 1, 2007, provided that the taxpayer does not later determine qualification of those contracts in a manner that is inconsistent with these regulations. [Reg. § 1.7702-2.]

☐ [*T.D. 9287, 9-12-2006.*]

### [Reg. § 1.7702B-1]

**§ 1.7702B-1. Consumer protection provisions.**—(a) *In general.*—Under sections 7702B(b)(1)(F), 7702B(g), and 4980C, qualified long-term care insurance contracts and issuers of those contracts are required to satisfy certain provisions of the Long-Term Care Insurance Model Act (Model Act) and Long-Term Care Insurance Model Regulation (Model Regulation) promulgated by the National Association of Insurance Commissioners (NAIC), as adopted as of January 1993. The requirements for qualified long-term care insurance contracts under section 7702B(b)(1)(F) and (g) relate to guaranteed renewal or noncancellability, prohibitions on limitations and exclusions, extension of benefits, continuation or conversion of coverage, discontinuance and replacement of policies, unintentional lapse, disclosure, prohibitions against post-claims underwriting, minimum standards, inflation protection, prohibitions against pre-existing conditions exclusions and probationary periods, and prior hospitalization. The requirements for qualified long-term care insurance contracts under section 4980C relate to application forms and replacement coverage, reporting requirements, filing requirements for marketing, standards for marketing, appropriateness of recommended purchase, standard format outline of coverage, delivery of a shopper's guide, right to return, outline of coverage, certificates under group plans, policy summary, monthly reports on accelerated death benefits, and incontestability period.

(b) *Coordination with State requirements.*—(1) *Contracts issued in a State that imposes more stringent requirements.*—If a State imposes a requirement that is more stringent than the analogous requirement imposed by section 7702B(g) or 4980C, then, under section 4980C(f), compliance with the more stringent requirement of State law is considered compliance with the parallel requirement of section 7702B(g) or 4980C. The principles of paragraph (b)(3) of this section apply to any case in which a State imposes a requirement that is more stringent than the analogous requirement imposed by section 7702B(g) or 4980C (as described in this paragraph (b)(1)), but in which there has been a failure to comply with that State requirement.

(2) *Contracts issued in a State that has adopted the model provisions.*—If a State imposes a requirement that is the same as the parallel requirement imposed by section 7702B(g) or 4980C, compliance with that requirement of State law is considered compliance with the parallel requirement of section 7702B(g) or 4980C, and failure to comply with that requirement of State law is considered failure to comply with the parallel requirement of section 7702B(g) or 4980C.

(3) *Contracts issued in a State that has not adopted the model provisions or more stringent requirements.*—If a State has not adopted the Model Act, the Model Regulation, or a requirement that is the same as or more stringent than the analogous requirement imposed by section 7702B(g) or 4980C, then the language, caption, format, and content requirements imposed by sections 7702B(g) and 4980C with respect to contracts, applications, outlines of coverage, policy summaries, and notices will be considered satisfied for a contract subject to the law of that State if the language, caption, format, and content are substantially similar to those required under the parallel provision of the Model Act or Model Regulation. Only nonsubstantive deviations are permitted in order for language, caption, format, and content to be considered substantially similar to the requirements of the Model Act or Model Regulation.

(c) *Effective date.*—This section applies with respect to contracts issued after December 10, 1999. [Reg. § 1.7702B-1.]

☐ [*T.D. 8792, 12-9-98.*]

### [Reg. § 1.7702B-2]

**§ 1.7702B-2. Special rules for pre-1997 long-term care insurance contracts.**—(a) *Scope.*—The definitions and special provisions of this section apply solely for purposes of determining whether an insurance contract (other than a qualified long-term care insurance contract described in section 7702B(b) and any regulations issued thereunder) is treated as a qualified long-term care insurance contract for purposes of the Internal Revenue Code under section 321(f)(2) of the Health Insurance Portability and Accountability Act of 1996 (Public Law 104-191).

(b) *Pre-1997 long-term care insurance contracts.*—(1) *In general.*—A pre-1997 long-term care insurance contract is treated as a qualified long-term care insurance contract, regardless of whether the contract satisfies section 7702B(b) and any regulations issued thereunder.

(2) *Pre-1997 long-term care insurance contract defined.*—A pre-1997 long-term care insurance contract is any insurance contract with an issue date before January 1, 1997, that met the long-term care insurance requirements of the State in which the contract was sitused on the issue date. For this purpose, the long-term care insurance requirements of the State are the State laws (including statutory and administrative law) that are intended to regulate insurance coverage that constitutes "long-term care insurance" (as defined in section 4 of the National Association of Insurance Commissioners (NAIC) Long-Term Care Insurance Model Act, as in effect on August 21, 1996), regardless of the terminology used by the State in describing the insurance coverage.

(3) *Issue date of a contract.*—(i) *In general.*—Except as otherwise provided in this paragraph (b)(3), the issue date of a contract is the issue date assigned to the contract by the insurance company. In no event is the issue date earlier than the date the policyholder submitted a signed application for coverage to the insurance company. If the period between the date the signed application is submitted to the insurance company and the date coverage under the contract actually becomes effective is substantially longer than under the insurance company's usual business practice, then the issue date is the later of the date coverage under the contract becomes effective or the issue date assigned to the contract by the insurance company. A policyholder's right to return a contract within a free-look period following delivery for a full refund of any premiums paid is not taken into account in determining the contract's issue date.

(ii) *Special rule for group contracts.*—The issue date of a group contract (including any certificate issued thereunder) is the date on which coverage under the group contract becomes effective.

(iii) *Exchange of contract or certain changes in a contract treated as a new issuance.*—For purposes of this paragraph (b)(3)—

(A) A contract issued in exchange for an existing contract after December 31, 1996, is considered a contract issued after that date;

(B) Any change described in paragraph (b)(4) of this section is treated as the issuance of a new contract with an issue date no earlier than the date the change goes into effect; and

(C) If a change described in paragraph (b)(4) of this section occurs with regard to one or more, but fewer than all, of the certificates evidencing coverage under a group contract, then the insurance coverage under the changed certificates is treated as coverage under a newly issued group contract (and the insurance coverage provided by any unchanged certificate continues to be treated as coverage under the original group contract).

(4) *Changes treated as the issuance of a new contract.*—(i) *In general.*—For purposes of paragraph (b)(3) of this section, except as provided in paragraph (b)(4)(ii) of this section, the following changes are treated as the issuance of a new contract—

(A) A change in the terms of a contract that alters the amount or timing of an item payable by either the policyholder (or certificate holder), the insured, or the insurance company;

(B) A substitution of the insured under an individual contract; or

(C) A change (other than an immaterial change) in the contractual terms, or in the plan under which the contract was issued, relating to eligibility for membership in the group covered under a group contract.

(ii) *Exceptions.*—For purposes of this paragraph (b)(4), the following changes are not treated as the issuance of a new contract—

(A) A policyholder's exercise of any right provided under the terms of the contract as in effect on December 31, 1996, or a right required by applicable State law to be provided to the policyholder;

(B) A change in the mode of premium payment (for example, a change from monthly to quarterly premiums);

(C) In the case of a policy that is guaranteed renewable or noncancellable, a classwide increase or decrease in premiums;

(D) A reduction in premiums due to the purchase of a long-term care insurance contract by a family member of the policyholder;

(E) A reduction in coverage (with a corresponding reduction in premiums) made at the request of a policyholder;

(F) A reduction in premiums as a result of extending to an individual policyholder a discount applicable to similar categories of individuals pursuant to a premium rate structure that was in effect

on December 31, 1996, for the issuer's pre-1997 long-term care insurance contracts of the same type;

(G) The addition, without an increase in premiums, of alternative forms of benefits that may be selected by the policyholder;

(H) The addition of a rider (including any similarly identifiable amendment) to a pre-1997 long-term care insurance contract in any case in which the rider, if issued as a separate contract of insurance, would itself be a qualified long-term care insurance contract under section 7702B and any regulations issued thereunder (including the consumer protection provisions in section 7702B(g) to the extent applicable to the addition of a rider);

(I) The deletion of a rider or provision of a contract that prohibited coordination of benefits with Medicare (often referred to as an HHS (Health and Human Services) rider);

(J) The effectuation of a continuation or conversion of coverage right that is provided under a pre-1997 group contract and that, in accordance with the terms of the contract as in effect on December 31, 1996, provides for coverage under an individual contract following an individual's ineligibility for continued coverage under the group contract; and

(K) The substitution of one insurer for another insurer in an assumption reinsurance transaction.

(5) *Examples.*—The following examples illustrate the principles of this paragraph (b):

*Example 1.* (i) On December 3, 1996, A, an individual, submits a signed application to an insurance company to purchase a nursing home contract that meets the long-term care insurance requirements of the State in which the contract is sitused. The insurance company decides on December 20, 1996, that it will issue the contract, and assigns December 20, 1996, as the issue date for the contract. Under the terms of the contract, A's insurance coverage becomes effective on January 1, 1997. The company delivers the contract to A on January 3, 1997. A has the right to return the contract within 15 days following delivery for a refund of all premiums paid.

(ii) Under paragraph (b)(3)(i) of this section, the issue date of the contract is December 20, 1996. Thus, the contract is a pre-1997 long-term care insurance contract that is treated as a qualified long-term care insurance contract.

*Example 2.* (i) The facts are the same as in *Example 1*, except that the insurance coverage under the contract does not become effective until March 1, 1997. Under the insurance company's usual business practice, the period between the date of the application and the date the contract becomes effective is 30 days or less.

(ii) Under paragraph (b)(3)(i) of this section, the issue date of the contract is March 1, 1997. Thus, the contract is not a pre-1997 long-term care insurance contract, and, accordingly, the contract must meet the requirements of section 7702B(b) and any regulations issued thereunder to be a qualified long-term care insurance contract.

*Example 3.* (i) B, an individual, is the policyholder under a long-term care insurance contract purchased in 1995. On June 15, 2000, the insurance coverage and premiums under the contract are increased by agreement between B and the insurance company.

(ii) Under paragraph (b)(4)(i)(A) of this section, a change in the terms of a contract that alters the amount or timing of an item payable by the policyholder or the insurance company is treated as the issuance of a new contract. Thus, B's coverage is treated as coverage under a contract issued on June 15, 2000, and, accordingly, the contract must meet the requirements of section 7702B(b) and any regulations issued thereunder in order to be a qualified long-term care insurance contract.

*Example 4.* (i) C, an individual, is the policyholder under a long-term care insurance contract purchased in 1994. At that time and through December 31, 1996, the contract met the long-term care insurance requirements of the State in which the contract was sitused. In 1996, the policy was amended to add a provision requiring the policyholder to be offered the right to increase dollar limits for inflation every three years (without the policyholder being required to pass a physical or satisfy any other underwriting requirements). During 2002, C elects to increase the amount of insurance coverage (with a resulting premium increase) pursuant to the inflation provision.

(ii) Under paragraph (b)(4)(ii)(A) of this section, an increase in the amount of insurance coverage at the election of the policyholder (without the insurance company's consent and without underwriting or other limitations on the policyholder's rights) pursuant to a pre-1997 inflation provision is not treated as the issuance of a new contract. Thus, C's contract continues to be a pre-1997 long-term care insurance contract that is treated as a qualified long-term care insurance contract.

(c) *Effective date.*—This section is applicable January 1, 1999. [Reg. § 1.7702B-2.]

□ [T.D. 8792, 12-9-98.]

**[Reg. § 1.7703-1]**

**§1.7703-1. Determination of marital status.**—(a) *General rule.*—The determination of whether an individual is married shall be made as of the close of his taxable year unless his spouse dies during his taxable year, in which case such determination shall be made as of the time of such death; and, except as provided in paragraph (b) of this section, an individual shall be considered as married even though living apart from his spouse unless legally separated under a decree of divorce or separate maintenance. The provisions of this paragraph may be illustrated by the following examples:

*Example (1).* Taxpayer A and his wife B both make their returns on a calendar year basis. In July 1954, they enter into a separation agreement and thereafter live apart, but no decree of divorce or separate maintenance is issued until March 1955. If A itemizes and claims his actual deductions on his return for the calendar year 1954, B may not elect the standard deduction on her return since B is considered as married to A (although permanently separated by agreement) on the last day of 1954.

*Example (2).* Taxpayer A makes his returns on the basis of a fiscal year ending June 30. His wife B makes her returns on the calendar year basis. A died in October 1954. In such case, since A and B were married as of the date of death, B may not elect the standard deduction for the calendar year 1954 if the income of A for the short taxable year ending with the date of his death is determined without regard to the standard deduction.

(b) *Certain married individuals living apart.*—(1) For purposes of part IV of subchapter B of chapter 1 of the Code, an individual is not considered as married for taxable years beginning after December 31, 1969, if (i) such individual is married (within the meaning of paragraph (a) of this section) but files a separate return; (ii) such individual maintains as his home a household which constitutes for more than one-half of the taxable year the principal place of abode of a dependent (*a*) who (within the meaning of section 152 and the regulations thereunder) is a son, stepson, daughter, or stepdaughter of the individual, and (*b*) with respect to whom such individual is entitled to a deduction for the taxable year under section 151; (iii) such individual furnishes over half of the cost of maintaining such household during the taxable year; and (iv) during the entire taxable year such individual's spouse is not a member of such household.

(2) For purposes of subparagraph (1)(ii)(*a*) of this paragraph, a legally adopted son or daughter of an individual, a child (described in paragraph (c)(2) of §1.152-2) who is a member of an individual's household if placed with such individual by an authorized placement agency (as defined in paragraph (c)(2) of §1.152-2) for legal adoption by such individual, or a foster child (described in paragraph (c)(4) of §1.152-2) of an individual if such child satisfies the requirements of section 152(a)(9) of the Code and paragraph (b) of §1.152-1 with respect to such individual, shall be treated as a son or daughter of such individual by blood.

(3) For purposes of subparagraph (1)(ii) of this paragraph, the household must actually constitute the home of the individual for his taxable year. However, a physical change in the location of such home will not prevent an individual from qualifying for the treatment provided in subparagraph (1) of this paragraph. It is not sufficient that the individual maintain the household without being its occupant. The individual and the dependent described in subparagraph (1)(ii)(*a*) of this paragraph must occupy the household for more than one-half of the taxable year of the individual. However, the fact that such dependent is born or dies within the taxable year will not prevent an individual from qualifying for such treatment if the household constitutes the principal place of abode of such dependent for the remaining or preceding part of such taxable year. The individual and such dependent will be considered as occupying the household during temporary absences from the household due to special circumstances. A nonpermanent failure to occupy the common abode by reason of illness, education, business, vacation, military service, or a custody agreement under which a child or stepchild is absent for less than 6 months in the taxable year of the taxpayer, shall be considered a temporary absence due to special circumstances. Such absence will not prevent an individual from qualifying for the treatment provided in subparagraph (1) of this paragraph if (i) it is reasonable to assume that such individual or the dependent will return to the household and (ii) such individual continues to maintain such household or a substantially equivalent household in anticipation of such return.

(4) An individual shall be considered as maintaining a household only if he pays more than one-half of the cost thereof for his taxable year. The cost of maintaining a household shall be the expenses incurred for the mutual benefit of the occupants thereof by reason of its operation as the principal place of abode of such occupants for such taxable year. The cost of maintaining a household shall not include expenses otherwise incurred. The expenses of maintaining a household include property taxes, mortgage interest, rent, utility charges, upkeep and repairs, property insurance, and food consumed on the premises. Such expenses do not include the cost of clothing, education, medical treatment, vacations, life insurance, and transportation. In addition, the cost of maintaining a household shall not include any amount which represents the value of services rendered in the household by the taxpayer or by a dependent described in subparagraph (1)(ii)(*a*) of this paragraph.

(5) For purposes of subparagraph (1)(iv) of this paragraph, an individual's spouse is not a member of the household during a taxable year if such household does not constitute such spouse's place of abode at any time during such year. An individual's spouse will be considered to be a member of the household during temporary absences from the household due to special circumstances. A nonpermanent failure to occupy such household as his abode by reason of illness, education, business, vacation, or military service shall be considered a mere temporary absence due to special circumstances.

(6) The provisions of this paragraph may be illustrated by the following example:

*Example.* Taxpayer A, married to B at the close of the calendar year 1971, his taxable year, is living apart from B, but A is not legally separated from B under a decree of divorce or separate maintenance. A maintains a household as his home which is for 7 months of 1971 the principal place of abode of C, his son, with respect to whom A is entitled to a deduction under Section 151. A pays for more than one-half of the cost of maintaining that household. At no time during 1971 was B a member of the household occupied by A and C. A files a separate return for 1971. Under these circumstances, A is considered as not married under section 143(b) for purposes of the standard deduction. Even though A is married and files a separate return A may claim for 1971 as his standard deduction the larger of the low income allowance up to a maximum of $1,050 consisting of both the basic allowance and additional allowance (rather than the basic allowance only subject to the $500 limitation applicable to a separate return of a married individual) or the percentage standard deduction subject to the $1,500 limitation (rather than the $750 limitation applicable to a separate return of a married individual). See §1.141-1. For purposes of the provisions of part IV of subchapter B of chapter 1 of the Code and the regulations thereunder, A is treated as unmarried. [Reg. §1.7703-1.]

☐ [T.D. 6272, 11-25-57. *Amended by* T.D. 7123, 6-8-71. *Redesignated by* T.D. 8712, 1-10-97.]

**[Reg. § 1.7704-1]**

**§1.7704-1. Publicly traded partnerships.**—(a) *In general.*—(1) *Publicly traded partnership.*—A domestic or foreign partnership is a publicly traded partnership for purposes of section 7704(b) and this section if—

(i) Interests in the partnership are traded on an established securities market; or

(ii) Interests in the partnership are readily tradable on a secondary market or the substantial equivalent thereof.

(2) *Partnership interest.*—(i) *In general.*—For purposes of section 7704(b) and this section, an interest in a partnership includes—

(A) Any interest in the capital or profits of the partnership (including the right to partnership distributions); and

(B) Any financial instrument or contract the value of which is determined in whole or in part by reference to the partnership (including the amount of partnership distributions, the value of partnership assets, or the results of partnership operations).

(ii) *Exception for non-convertible debt.*—For purposes of section 7704(b) and this section, an interest in a partnership does not include any financial instrument or contract that—

(A) Is treated as debt for federal tax purposes; and

(B) Is not convertible into or exchangeable for an interest in the capital or profits of the partnership and does not provide for a payment of equivalent value.

(iii) *Exception for tiered entities.*—For purposes of section 7704(b) and this section, an interest in a partnership or a corporation (including a regulated investment company as defined in section 851 or a real estate investment trust as defined in section 856) that holds an interest in a partnership (lower-tier partnership) is not considered an interest in the lower-tier partnership.

(3) *Definition of transfer.*—For purposes of section 7704(b) and this section, a transfer of an interest in a partnership means a transfer in any form, including a redemption by the partnership or the entering into of a financial instrument or contract described in paragraph (a)(2)(i)(B) of this section.

(b) *Established securities market.*—For purposes of section 7704(b) and this section, an established securities market includes—

(1) A national securities exchange registered under section 6 of the Securities Exchange Act of 1934 (15 U.S.C. 78f);

(2) A national securities exchange exempt from registration under section 6 of the Securities Exchange Act of 1934 (15 U.S.C. 78f) because of the limited volume of transactions;

(3) A foreign securities exchange that, under the law of the jurisdiction where it is organized, satisfies regulatory requirements that are analogous to the regulatory requirements under the Securities Exchange Act of 1934 described in paragraph (b)(1) or (2) of this section (such as the London International Financial Futures Exchange; the Marche a Terme International de France; the International Stock Exchange of the United Kingdom and the Republic of Ireland, Limited; the Frankfurt Stock Exchange; and the Tokyo Stock Exchange;

(4) A regional or local exchange; and

(5) An interdealer quotation system that regularly disseminates firm buy or sell quotations by identified brokers or dealers by electronic means or otherwise.

(c) *Readily tradable on a secondary market or the substantial equivalent thereof.*—(1) *In general.*—For purposes of section 7704(b) and this section, interests in a partnership that are not traded on an established securities market (within the meaning of section 7704(b) and paragraph (b) of this section) are readily tradable on a secondary market or the substantial equivalent thereof if, taking into account all of the facts and circumstances, the partners are readily able to buy, sell, or exchange their partnership interests in a manner that is comparable, economically, to trading on an established securities market.

(2) *Secondary market or the substantial equivalent thereof.*—For purposes of paragraph (c)(1) of this section, interests in a partnership are readily tradable on a secondary market or the substantial equivalent thereof if—

(i) Interests in the partnership are regularly quoted by any person, such as a broker or dealer, making a market in the interests;

(ii) Any person regularly makes available to the public (including customers or subscribers) bid or offer quotes with respect to interests in the partnership and stands ready to effect buy or sell transactions at the quoted prices for itself or on behalf of others;

(iii) The holder of an interest in the partnership has a readily available, regular, and ongoing opportunity to sell or exchange the interest through a public means of obtaining or providing information of offers to buy, sell, or exchange interests in the partnership; or

(iv) Prospective buyers and sellers otherwise have the opportunity to buy, sell, or exchange interests in the partnership in a time frame and with the regularity and continuity that is comparable to that described in the other provisions of this paragraph (c)(2).

(3) *Secondary market safe harbors.*—The fact that a transfer of a partnership interest is not within one or more of the safe harbors described in paragraph (e), (f), (g), (h), or (j) of this section is disregarded in determining whether interests in the partnership are readily tradable on a secondary market or the substantial equivalent thereof.

(d) *Involvement of the partnership required.*—For purposes of section 7704(b) and this section, interests in a partnership are not traded on an established securities market within the meaning of paragraph (b)(5) of this section and are not readily tradable on a secondary market or the substantial equivalent thereof within the meaning of paragraph (c) of this section (even if interests in the partnership are traded or readily tradable in a manner described in paragraph (b)(5) or (c) of this section) unless—

(1) The partnership participates in the establishment of the market or the inclusion of its interests thereon; or

(2) The partnership recognizes any transfers made on the market by—

(i) Redeeming the transferor partner (in the case of a redemption or repurchase by the partnership); or

(ii) Admitting the transferee as a partner or otherwise recognizing any rights of the transferee, such as a right of the transferee to receive partnership distributions (directly or indirectly) or to acquire an interest in the capital or profits of the partnership.

(e) *Transfers not involving trading.*—(1) *In general.*—For purposes of section 7704(b) and this section, the following transfers (private transfers) are disregarded in determining whether interests in a partnership are readily tradable on a secondary market or the substantial equivalent thereof—

(i) Transfers in which the basis of the partnership interest in the hands of the transferee is determined, in whole or in part, by reference to its basis in the hands of the transferor or is determined under section 732;

(ii) Transfers at death, including transfers from an estate or testamentary trust;

(iii) Transfers between members of a family (as defined in section 267(c)(4));

(iv) Transfers involving the issuance of interests by (or on behalf of) the partnership in exchange for cash, property, or services;

(v) Transfers involving distributions from a retirement plan qualified under section 401(a) or an individual retirement account;

(vi) Block transfers (as defined in paragraph (e)(2) of this section);

(vii) Transfers pursuant to a right under a redemption or repurchase agreement (as defined in paragraph (e) (3) of this section) that is exercisable only—

(A) Upon the death, disability, or mental incompetence of the partner; or

(B) Upon the retirement or termination of the performance of services of an individual who actively participated in the management of, or performed services on a full-time basis for, the partnership;

(viii) Transfers pursuant to a closed end redemption plan (as defined in paragraph (e)(4) of this section);

(ix) Transfers by one or more partners of interests representing in the aggregate 50 percent or more of the total interests in partnership capital and profits in one transaction or a series of related transactions; and

(x) Transfers not recognized by the partnership (within the meaning of paragraph (d)(2) of this section).

(2) *Block transfers.*—For purposes of paragraph (e)(1)(vi) of this section, a block transfer means the transfer by a partner and any related persons (within the meaning of section 267(b) or 707(b)(1)) in one or more transactions during any 30 calendar day period of partnership interests representing in the aggregate more than 2 percent of the total interests in partnership capital or profits.

(3) *Redemption or repurchase agreement.*—For purposes of section 7704(b) and this section, a redemption or repurchase agreement means a plan of redemption or repurchase maintained by a partnership whereby the partners may tender their partnership interests for purchase by the partnership, another partner, or a person related to another partner (within the meaning of section 267(b) or 707(b)(1)).

(4) *Closed end redemption plan.*—For purposes of paragraph (e)(1)(viii) of this section, a redemption or repurchase agreement (as defined in paragraph (e)(3) of this section) is a closed end redemption plan only if—

(i) The partnership does not issue any interest after the initial offering (other than the issuance of additional interests prior to August 5, 1988); and

(ii) No partner or person related to any partner (within the meaning of section 267(b) or 707(b)(1)) provides contemporaneous opportunities to acquire interests in similar or related partnerships which represent substantially identical investments.

(f) *Redemption and repurchase agreements.*—For purposes of section 7704(b) and this section, the transfer of an interest in a partnership pursuant to a redemption or repurchase agreement (as defined in paragraph (e)(3) of this section) that is not described in paragraph (e)(1)(vii) or (viii) of this section is disregarded in determining whether interests in the partnership are readily tradable on a secondary market or the substantial equivalent thereof only if—

(1) The redemption or repurchase agreement provides that the redemption or repurchase cannot occur until at least 60 calendar days after the partner notifies the partnership in writing of the partner's intention to exercise the redemption or repurchase right;

(2) Either—

(i) The redemption or repurchase agreement requires that the redemption or repurchase price not be established until at least 60 calendar days after receipt of such notification by the partnership or the partner; or

(ii) The redemption or repurchase price is established not more than four times during the partnership's taxable year; and

(3) The sum of the percentage interests in partnership capital or profits transferred during the taxable year of the partnership (other than in private transfers described in paragraph (e) of this section) does not exceed 10 percent of the total interests in partnership capital or profits.

(g) *Qualified matching services.*—(1) *In general.*—For purposes of section 7704(b) and this section, the transfer of an interest in a partnership through a qualified matching service is disregarded in determining whether interests in the partnership are readily tradable on a secondary market or the substantial equivalent thereof.

(2) *Requirements.*—A matching service is a qualified matching service only if—

(i) The matching service consists of a computerized or printed listing system that lists customers' bid and/or ask quotes in order to match partners who want to sell their interests in a partnership (the selling partner) with persons who want to buy those interests;

(ii) Matching occurs either by matching the list of interested buyers with the list of interested sellers or through a bid and ask process that allows interested buyers to bid on the listed interest;

(iii) The selling partner cannot enter into a binding agreement to sell the interest until the 15th calendar day after the date information regarding the offering of the interest for sale is made available to potential buyers and such time period is evidenced by contemporaneous records ordinarily maintained by the operator at a central location;

(iv) The closing of the sale effected by virtue of the matching service does not occur prior to the 45th calendar day after the date information regarding the offering of the interest for sale is made available to potential buyers and such time period is evidenced by contemporaneous records ordinarily maintained by the operator at a central location;

(v) The matching service displays only quotes that do not commit any person to buy or sell a partnership interest at the quoted price (nonfirm price quotes) or quotes that express interest in partnership interest without an accompanying price (nonbinding indications of interest) and does not display quotes at which any person is committed to buy or sell a partnership interest at the quoted price (firm quotes);

(vi) The selling partner's information is removed from the matching service within 120 calendar days after the date information regarding the offering of the interest for sale is made available to potential buyers and, following any removal (other than removal by reason of a sale of any part of such interest) of the selling partner's information from the matching service, no offer to sell an interest in the partnership is entered into the matching service by the selling partner for at least 60 calendar days; and

(vii) The sum of the percentage interests in partnership capital or profits transferred during the taxable year of the partnership (other than in private transfers described in paragraph (e) of this section) does not exceed 10 percent of the total interests in partnership capital or profits.

(3) *Closing.*—For purposes of paragraph (g)(2)(iv) of this section, the closing of a sale occurs no later than the earlier of—

(i) The passage of title to the partnership interest;

(ii) The payment of the purchase price (which does not include the delivery of funds to the operator of the matching service or other closing agent to hold on behalf of the seller pending closing); or

(iii) The date, if any, that the operator of the matching service (or any person related to the operator within the meaning of section 267(b) or 707(b)(1)) loans, advances, or otherwise arranges for funds to be available to the seller in anticipation of the payment of the purchase price.

(4) *Optional features.*—A qualified matching service may be sponsored or operated by a partner of the partnership (either formally or informally), the underwriter that handled the issuance of the partnership interests, or an unrelated third party. In addition, a qualified matching service may offer the following features—

(i) The matching service may provide prior pricing information, including information regarding resales of interests and actual prices paid for interests; a description of the business of the partnership; financial and reporting information from the partnership's financial statements and reports; and information regarding material events involving the partnership, including special distributions, capital distributions, and refinancings or sales of significant portions of partnership assets;

(ii) The operator may assist with the transfer documentation necessary to transfer the partnership interest;

(iii) The operator may receive and deliver funds for completed transactions; and

(iv) The operator's fee may consist of a flat fee for use of the service, a fee or commission based on completed transactions, or any combination thereof.

(h) *Private placements.*—(1) *In general.*—For purposes of section 7704(b) and this section, except as otherwise provided in paragraph (h) (2) of this section, interests in a partnership are not readily tradable on a secondary market or the substantial equivalent thereof if—

(i) All interests in the partnership were issued in a transaction (or transactions) that was not required to be registered under the Securities Act of 1933 (15 U.S.C. 77a et seq.); and

(ii) The partnership does not have more than 100 partners at any time during the taxable year of the partnership.

(2) *Exception for certain offerings outside of the United States.*—Paragraph (h) (1) of this section does not apply to the offering and sale of interests in a partnership that was not required to be regis-

tered under the Securities Act of 1933 by reason of Regulation S (17 CFR 230.901 through 230.904) unless the offering and sale of the interests would not have been required to be registered under the Securities Act of 1933 if the interests had been offered and sold within the United States.

(3) *Anti-avoidance rule.*—For purposes of determining the number of partners in the partnership under paragraph (h)(1)(ii) of this section, a person (beneficial owner) owning an interest in a partnership, grantor trust, or S corporation (flow-through entity), that owns, directly or through other flow-through entities, an interest in the partnership, is treated as a partner in the partnership only if—

(i) Substantially all of the value of the beneficial owner's interest in the flow-through entity is attributable to the flow-through entity's interest (direct or indirect) in the partnership; and

(ii) A principal purpose of the use of the tiered arrangement is to permit the partnership to satisfy the 100 partner limitation in paragraph (h)(1)(ii) of this section.

(i) [Reserved].

(j) *Lack of actual trading.*—(1) *General rule.*—For purposes of section 7704(b) and this section, interests in a partnership are not readily tradable on a secondary market or the substantial equivalent thereof if the sum of the percentage interests in partnership capital or profits transferred during the taxable year of the partnership (other than in transfers described in paragraph (e), (f), or (g) of this section) does not exceed 2 percent of the total interests in partnership capital or profits.

(2) *Examples.*—The following examples illustrate the rules of this paragraph (j):

*Example 1. Calculation of percentage interest transferred.* (i) ABC, a calendar year limited partnership formed in 1996, has 9,000 units of limited partnership interests outstanding at all times during 1997, representing in the aggregate 95 percent of the total interests in capital and profits of ABC. The remaining 5 percent is held by the general partner.

(ii) During 1997, the following transactions occur with respect to the units of ABC's limited partnership interests—

(A) 800 units are sold through the use of a qualified matching service that meets the requirements of paragraph (g) of this section;

(B) 50 units are sold through the use of a matching service that does not meet the requirements of paragraph (g) of this section; and

(C) 500 units are transferred as a result of private transfers described in paragraph (e) of this section.

(iii) The private transfers of 500 units and the sale of 800 units through a qualified matching service are disregarded under paragraph (j)(1) of this section for purposes of applying the 2 percent rule. As a result, the total percentage interests in partnership capital and profits transferred for purposes of the 2 percent rule is .528 percent, determined by—

(A) Dividing the number of units sold through a matching service that did not meet the requirements of paragraph (g) of this section (50) by the total number of outstanding limited partnership units (9,000); and

(B) Multiplying the result by the percentage of total interests represented by limited partnership units (95 percent) ([50/9,000]x .95 = .528 percent).

*Example 2. Application of the 2 percent rule.* (i) ABC operates a service consisting of computerized video display screens on which subscribers view and publish nonfirm price quotes that do not commit any person to buy or sell a partnership interest and unpriced indications of interest in a partnership interest without an accompanying price. The ABC service does not provide firm quotes at which any person (including the operator of the service) is committed to buy or sell a partnership interest. The service may provide prior pricing information, including information regarding resales of interests and actual prices paid for interests; transactional volume information; and information on special or capital distributions by a partnership. The operator's fee may consist of a flat fee for use of the service; a fee based on completed transactions, including, for example, the number of nonfirm quotes or unpriced indications of interest entered by users of the service; or any combination thereof.

(ii) The ABC service is not an established securities market for purposes of section 7704(b) and this section. The service is not an interdealer quotation system as defined in paragraph (b)(5) of this section because it does not disseminate firm buy or sell quotations. Therefore, partnerships whose interests are listed and transferred on the ABC service are not publicly traded for purposes of section 7704(b) and this section as a result of such listing or transfers if the sum of the percentage interests in partnership capital or profits transferred during the taxable year of the partnership (other than in transfers described in paragraph (e), (f), or (g) of this section) does not exceed 2 percent of the total interests in partnership capital or profits. In addition, assuming the ABC service complies with the necessary requirements, the service may qualify as a matching service described in paragraph (g) of this section.

(k) *Percentage interests in partnership capital or profits.*—(1) *Interests considered.*—(i) *General rule.*—Except as otherwise provided in this paragraph (k), for purposes of this section, the total interests in partnership capital or profits are determined by reference to all outstanding interests in the partnership.

(ii) *Exceptions.*—(A) *General partner with greater than 10 percent interest.*—If the general partners and any person related to the general partners (within the meaning of section 267(b) or 707(b)(1)) own, in the aggregate, more than 10 percent of the outstanding interests in partnership capital or profits at any one time during the taxable year of the partnership, the total interests in partnership capital or profits are determined without reference to the interests owned by such persons.

(B) *Derivative interests.*—Any partnership interests described in paragraph (a)(2)(i)(B) of this section are taken into account for purposes of determining the total interests in partnership capital or profits only if and to the extent that the partnership satisfies paragraph (d)(1) or (2) of this section.

(2) *Monthly determination.*—For purposes of this section, except in the case of block transfers (as defined in paragraph (e)(2) of this section), the percentage interests in partnership capital or profits represented by partnership interests that are transferred during a taxable year of the partnership is equal to the sum of the percentage interests transferred for each calendar month during the taxable year of the partnership in which a transfer of a partnership interest occurs (other than a private transfer as described in paragraph (e) of this section). The percentage interests in capital or profits of interests transferred during a calendar month is determined by reference to the partnership interests outstanding during that month.

(3) *Monthly conventions.*—For purposes of paragraph (k) (2) of this section, a partnership may use any reasonable convention in determining the interests outstanding for a month, provided the convention is consistently used by the partnership from month to month during a taxable year and from year to year. Reasonable conventions include, but are not limited to, a determination by reference to the interests outstanding at the beginning of the month, on the 15th day of the month, or at the end of the month.

(4) *Block transfers.*—For purposes of paragraph (e)(2) of this section (defining block transfers), the partnership must determine the percentage interests in capital or profits for each transfer of an interest during the 30 calendar day period by reference to the partnership interests outstanding immediately prior to such transfer.

(5) *Example.*—The following example illustrates the rules of this paragraph (k):

*Example. Conventions.* (i) ABC limited partnership, a calendar year partnership formed in 1996, has 1,000 units of limited partnership interests outstanding on January 1, 1997, representing in the aggregate 95 percent of the total interests in capital and profits of ABC. The remaining 5 percent is held by the general partner.

(ii) The following transfers take place during 1997—

(A) On January 15, 10 units of limited partnership interests are sold in a transaction that is not a private transfer;

(B) On July 10, 1,000 additional units of limited partnership interests are issued by the partnership (the general partner's percentage interest is unchanged); and

(C) On July 20, 15 units of limited partnership interests are sold in a transaction that is not a private transfer.

(iii) For purposes of determining the sum of the percentage interests in partnership capital or profits transferred, ABC chooses to use the end of the month convention. The percentage interests in partnership capital and profits transferred during January is .95 percent, determined by dividing the number of transferred units (10) by the total number of limited partnership units (1,000) and multiplying the result by the percentage of total interests represented by limited partnership units ([10/1,000] x .95). The percentage interests in partnership capital and profits transferred during July is .7125 percent ([15/2,000] x .95). ABC is not required to make determinations for the other months during the year because no transfers of partnership interests occurred during such months. ABC may qualify for the 2 percent rule for its 1997 taxable year because less than 2 percent (.95 percent + .7125 percent = 1.6625 percent) of its total interests in partnership capital and profits was transferred during that year.

(iv) If ABC had chosen to use the beginning of the month convention, the interests in capital or profits sold during July would have been 1.425 percent ([15/1,000] x .95) and ABC would not have satisfied the 2 percent rule for its 1997 taxable year because 2.375

percent (.95 + 1.425) of ABC's interests in partnership capital and profits was transferred during that year.

(l) *Effective date.*—(1) *In general.*—Except as provided in paragraph (1)(2) of this section, this section applies to taxable years of a partnership beginning after December 31, 1995.

(2) *Transition period.*—For partnerships that were actively engaged in an activity before December 4, 1995, this section applies to taxable years beginning after December 31, 2005, unless the partnership adds a substantial new line of business after December 4, 1995, in which case this section applies to taxable years beginning on or after the addition of the new line of business. Partnerships that qualify for this transition period may continue to rely on the provisions of Notice 88-75 (1988-2 C.B. 386) (see §601.601(d)(2) of this chapter) for guidance regarding the definition of readily tradable on a secondary market or the substantial equivalent thereof for purposes of section 7704(b).

(3) *Substantial new line of business.*—For purposes of paragraph (1)(2) of this section—

(i) Substantial is defined in §1.7704-2(c); and

(ii) A new line of business is defined in §1.7704-2(d), except that the applicable date is "December 4, 1995" instead of "December 17, 1987".

(4) *Termination under section 708(b)(1)(B).*—The termination of a partnership under section 708(b)(1)(B) due to the sale or exchange of 50 percent or more of the total interests in partnership capital and profits is disregarded in determining whether a partnership qualifies for the transition period provided in paragraph (1)(2) of this section. [Reg. §1.7704-1.]

☐ [T.D. 8629, 11-29-95.]

### [Reg. §1.7704-2]

**§1.7704-2. Transition provisions.**—(a) *Transition rule.*—(1) *Statutory dates.*—Section 7704 generally applies to taxable years beginning after December 31, 1987. In the case of an existing partnership, however, section 7704 and the regulations thereunder apply to taxable years beginning after December 31, 1997.

(2) *Effective date of regulations.*—These regulations apply to taxable years beginning after December 31, 1991.

(b) *Existing partnership.*—(1) *In general.*—For purposes of §1.7704-2, the term "existing partnership" means any partnership if:

(i) The partnership was a publicly traded partnership (within the meaning of section 7704(b)) on December 17, 1987;

(ii) A registration statement indicating that the partnership was to be a publicly traded partnership was filed with the Securities and Exchange Commission (SEC) with respect to the partnership on or before December 17, 1987; or

(iii) With respect to the partnership, an application was filed with a state regulatory commission on or before December 17, 1987, seeking permission to restructure a portion of a corporation as a publicly traded partnership.

(2) *Changed status of an existing partnership.*—A partnership will not qualify as an existing partnership after a new line of business is substantial.

(c) *Substantial.*—(1) *In general.*—A new line of business is substantial as of the earlier of—

(i) The taxable year in which the partnership derives more than 15 percent of its gross income from that line of business; or

(ii) The taxable year in which the partnership directly uses in that line of business more than 15 percent (by value) of its total assets.

(2) *Timing Rule.*—If a substantial new line of business is added during the taxable year (*e.g.*, by acquisition), the line of business is treated as substantial as of the date it is added; otherwise a substantial new line of business is treated as substantial as of the first day of the taxable year in which it becomes substantial.

(d) *New Line of Business.*—(1) *In general.*—A new line of business is any business activity of the partnership not closely related to a preexisting business of the partnership to the extent that the activity generates income other than "qualifying income" within the meaning of section 7704 and the regulations thereunder.

(2) *Pre-existing business.*—A business activity is a pre-existing business of the partnership if—

(i) The partnership was actively engaged in the activity on or before December 17, 1987; or

(ii) The partnership is actively engaged in the business activity that was specifically described as a proposed business activity of the partnership in a registration statement or amendment thereto filed on behalf of the partnership with the SEC on or before December 17, 1987. For this purpose, a specific description does not include a general grant of authority to conduct any business.

(3) *Closely related.*—All of the facts and circumstances will determine whether a new business activity is closely related to a pre-existing business of the partnership. The following factors, among others, will help to establish that a new business activity is closely related to a pre-existing business of the partnership and therefore is not a new line of business:

(i) The activity provides products or services very similar to the products or services provided by the pre-existing business.

(ii) The activity markets products and services to the same class of customers as that of the pre-existing business.

(iii) The activity is of a type that is normally conducted in the same business location as the pre-existing business.

(iv) The activity requires the use of similar operating assets as those used in the pre-existing business.

(v) The activity's economic success depends on the success of the pre-existing business.

(vi) The activity is of a type that would normally be treated as a unit with the pre-existing business in the business, accounting records.

(vii) If the activity and the pre-existing business are regulated or licensed, they are regulated or licensed by the same or similar governmental authority.

(viii) The United States Bureau of the Census assigns the activity the same four-digit Industry Number Standard Identification Code ("Industry SIC Code") as the pre-existing business. Such Codes are set forth in the Executive Office of the President, Office of Management and Budget, Standard Industrial Classification Manual, prepared, and from time to time revised, by the Statistical Policy Division of the United States Office of Management and Budget. For example, if a partnership's pre-existing business is manufacturing steam turbines and then the partnership begins an activity manufacturing hydraulic turbines, both activities would be assigned the same Industry SIC Code, 3511—Steam, Gas, and Hydraulic Turbines, and Turbine Generator Set Units. In the case of a pre-existing business or activity that is listed under the Industry SIC Code, 9999—Nonclassifiable Establishments—or under a miscellaneous category (e.g., most Industry SIC Codes ending in a "9" are miscellaneous categories), the similarity of the SIC Codes is ignored as a factor in determining whether the activity is closely related to the pre-existing business. The dissimilarity of the SIC Codes is considered in determining whether the business activity is closely related to the pre-existing line of business.

(e) *Activities conducted through controlled corporations.*—(1) *In general.*—An activity conducted by a corporation controlled by an existing partnership may be treated as an activity of the existing partnership if the effect of the arrangement is to permit the partnership to engage in an activity the income from which is not subject to a corporate-level tax and which would be a new line of business if conducted directly by the partnership. This determination is based upon all facts and circumstances.

(2) *Safe harbor.*—(i) *In general.*—This paragraph (e)(2) provides a safe harbor for activities of a corporation controlled by an existing partnership. An activity conducted by a corporation controlled by an existing partnership is not deemed to be an activity of the partnership for purposes of determining whether an existing partnership has added a new line of business if no more than 10% of the gross income that the partnership derives from the corporation during the taxable year is section 7704(d) qualifying income that is recharacterized as nonqualifying income under paragraphs (e)(2)(ii) and (iii) of this section. The Internal Revenue Service will not presume that an activity conducted through a corporation controlled by an existing partnership is an activity of the partnership solely because the partnership fails to satisfy the requirements of this paragraph (e)(2)(i).

(ii) *Recharacterization of qualifying income.*—Gross income received by a partnership from a controlled corporation that would be qualifying income under section 7704(d) is subject to recharacterization as nonqualifying income if the amount is deductible in computing the income of the controlled corporation.

(iii) *Extent of recharacterization.*—The amount of income described in paragraph (e)(2)(ii) of this section that is recharacterized as nonqualifying income is:

(A) The amount described in paragraph (e)(2)(ii) of this section; multiplied by

(B) The controlled corporation's taxable income (determined without regard to deductions for amounts paid to the partnership) that would not be qualifying income within the meaning of section 7704(d) if earned directly by the partnership; divided by

(C) The controlled corporation's taxable income (determined without regard to deductions for amounts paid to the partnership).

(3) *Control.*—For purposes of paragraphs (e)(1) and (2) of this section, control of a corporation is determined generally under the rules of section 304(c). However, the application of section 304(c) is modified to apply only to partners who own five percent or more by value (directly or indirectly) of the existing partnership unless a principal purpose of the arrangement is to avoid tax at the corporate level.

(4) *Example.*—The following example illustrates the application of this paragraph (e):

*Example.* (i) PTP, an existing partnership, acquired all the stock of X corporation on January 1, 1993. During PTP's 1993 taxable year it received $185,000 of dividends and $15,000 of interest from X. Determined without regard to interest paid to PTP, X's taxable income during that period was $500,000 none of which was "qualifying income" within the meaning of section 7704 and the regulations thereunder. In computing the income of X, the $15,000 of interest paid to PTP is deductible.

(ii) Under paragraph (e)(2)(ii) of this section, all $15,000 of PTP's interest income was nonqualifying income ($15,000 × 500,000/500,000). Under paragraph (e)(2) of this section, however, the activities of X will not be considered to be activities of PTP for the 1993 taxable year because no more than 10 percent of the gross income that PTP derived from X would be treated as other than qualifying income (15,000/200,000 = 7.5%).

(f) *Activities conducted through tiered partnerships.*—An activity conducted by a partnership in which an existing partnership holds an interest (directly or through another partnership) will be considered an activity of the existing partnership.

(g) *Exceptions.*—(1) *Coordination with gross income requirements of section 7704(c)(2).*—A partnership that is either an existing partnership as of December 31, 1997, or an existing partnership that ceases to qualify as an existing partnership is subject to section 7704 and the regulations thereunder. Section 7704(a) does not apply to these partnerships, however, if these partnerships meet the gross income requirements of paragraphs (c)(1) and (2) of section 7704. For purposes of applying section 7704(c)(1) and (2) to these partnerships, the only taxable years that must be tested are those beginning on and after the earlier of—

(i) January 1, 1998; or

(ii) The day on which the partnership ceases to qualify as an existing partnership because of the addition of a new line of business; or

(iii) The first day of the first taxable year in which a new line of business becomes substantial (if the new line of business becomes substantial after the year in which it is added).

(2) *Specific exceptions.*—In determining whether a partnership is an existing partnership for purposes of section 7704, the following events do not in themselves terminate the status of existing partnerships:

(i) Termination of the partnership under section 708(b)(1)(B) due to the sale or exchange of 50 percent or more of the total interests in partnership capital and profits;

(ii) Issuance of additional partnership units; and

(iii) Dropping a line of business. This event, however, could affect an existing partnership's status indirectly. For example, dropping one line of business could change the composition of the partnership's gross income. The change in composition could make a new line of business "substantial," under paragraph (c) of this section, and terminate the partnership's status. *See* paragraph (b)(2) of this section.

(h) *Examples.*—The following examples illustrate the application of this section:

*Example 1.* (i) On December 17, 1987, PTP, a calendar-year publicly traded partnership, owned and operated citrus groves. On March 1, 1993, PTP purchased a processing business involving frozen citrus products. In the partnership's 1993 taxable year, the partnership directly used in the processing business more than 15 percent (by value) of its total assets.

(ii) The citrus grove activities provide different products from the processing activities, are marketed to customers different from the customers of the processing activities, require different types of operating assets, are not commonly conducted at the same location, are not commonly treated as a unit in accounting records, do not depend upon one another for economic success, and do not have the same Industry SIC Code. Under the facts and circumstances, the processing business is not closely related to the citrus grove operation and is a new line of business under paragraph (d)(1) of this section.

(iii) The assets of the partnership used in the new line of business are substantial under paragraph (c)(2) of this section. Because PTP added a substantial new line of business after December 17, 1987, paragraph (b)(2) of this section terminates PTP's status as an existing partnership on March 1, 1993.

*Example 2.* (i) On December 17, 1987, PTP, a calendar-year publicly traded partnership, owned and operated retirement centers that serve the elderly. Each center contains three sections—

(A) A residential section, which includes suites of rooms, dining facilities, lounges, and gamerooms;

(B) An assisted-living section, which provides laundry and housekeeping services, health monitoring, and emergency care; and

(C) A nursing section, which provides private and semiprivate rooms, dining facilities, examination and treatment rooms, drugs, medical equipment, and physical, speech, and occupational therapy.

(ii) The business activities of each section constitute pre-existing businesses of PTP under paragraph (d)(2) of this section, because PTP was actively engaged in the activities on or before December 17, 1987.

(iii) The nursing sections primarily furnish health care. They employ nurses and therapists, are subject to federal, state, and local licensing requirements, and may charge certain costs to government programs like Medicare and Medicaid.

(iv) In 1993, PTP acquired new nursing homes that treat inpatient adults of all ages. The nursing homes provide private and semiprivate rooms, dining facilities, examination and treatment rooms, drugs, medical equipment, and physical, speech, and occupational therapy. The nursing homes primarily furnish health care. They employ nurses and therapists, are subject to federal, state, and local licensing requirements, and may charge certain costs to government programs like Medicare and Medicaid.

(v) PTP's new nursing homes and old nursing sections provide very similar services, market to very similar customers, use similar types of property and personnel, and are licensed by the same regulatory agencies. The nursing homes and old nursing sections have the same Industry SIC Code. Under these facts and circumstances, the new nursing homes are closely related to a pre-existing business of the partnership. Accordingly, under paragraph (d)(1) of this section, the acquisition of the new nursing homes is not the addition of a new line of business.

(vi) PTP was a publicly traded partnership on December 17, 1987, and was an existing partnership under paragraph (b)(1)(i) of this section. Because PTP has added no substantial new line of business after December 17, 1987, paragraph (b)(2) of this section does not terminate PTP's status as an existing partnership.

*Example 3.* (i) On December 17, 1987, PTP, a calendar-year publicly traded partnership, owned and operated cable television systems in the northeastern United States. PTP's registration statement described as its proposed business activities the ownership and operation of cable television systems, any ancillary operations, and any business permitted by the laws of the state in which PTP was formed.

(ii) PTP's cable systems include cables strung along telephone lines, converter boxes in subscribers' homes, other types of cable equipment, satellite dishes that receive programs broadcast by various television networks, and channels that carry public service announcements of local interest. Subscribers pay the systems a fee for the right to receive both the local announcements and the network signals relayed through the cables. Those fees constitute PTP's primary revenue. The systems operate under franchise agreements negotiated with each municipality in which they do business.

(iii) On September 1, 1993, PTP purchased a television station in the northwestern United States. The station owns broadcasting facilities, satellite dishes that receive programs broadcast by the station's network, and a studio that produces programs of interest to the area that receives the station's broadcasts. Fees from advertisers constitute the station's primary revenue. The station operates under a license from the Federal Communications Commission.

(iv) In the partnership's 1993 taxable year, the station generated less than 15 percent of PTP's gross income and constituted less than 15 percent of its total assets (by value). In PTP's 1994 taxable year, the station generated more than 15 percent of PTP's gross income.

(v) The cable systems relay signals through cables to subscribers and earn revenue from subscriber fees; the station broadcasts signals to the general public and earns revenue by selling air time for commercials. Despite certain similarities, the two types of activities generally require different operating assets and earn income from different sources. They are regulated by different agencies. They are not commonly conducted at the same location and do not generally depend upon one another for their economic success. They have different Industry SIC Codes. Under the facts and circumstances, the television station activities are not closely related to PTP's pre-existing business, the cable system activities.

(vi) As of December 17, 1987, PTP did not own and operate any television station. PTP's registration statement specifically described

as its proposed business activities only the ownership and operation of cable television systems and any ancillary operations. For purposes of paragraph (d)(2) of this section, a specific description does not include PTP's general authority to carry on any business permitted by the state of its formation. Therefore, the television station line of business was not specifically described as a proposed business activity of PTP in its registration statement. PTP's acquisition of the television station business activity constitutes a new line of business under paragraph (d)(1) of this section.

(vii) PTP was a publicly traded partnership on December 17, 1987, and was an existing partnership under paragraph (b)(1)(i) of this section. PTP added a new line of business in 1993, but that line of business was not substantial under paragraph (c) of this section, and thus PTP remained an existing partnership for its 1993 taxable year. In 1994, the new line of business became substantial because it generated more than 15 percent of PTP's gross income. Paragraph (b)(2) of this section therefore terminates PTP's existing partnership status as of January 1, 1994, the first day of the first taxable year beginning after December 31, 1987, in which PTP's new line of business became substantial. [Reg. § 1.7704-2.]

☐ [*T.D.* 8450, 12-10-92.]

### [Reg. § 301.7704-2]

**§ 301.7704-2. Transition provisions.**—See the regulations under section 7704 contained in part 1 of this chapter for a definition of the "substantial new line of business" that an "existing" publicly traded partnership cannot enter without forfeiting its partnership status under the transition provisions applicable to section 7704. [Reg. § 301.7704-2.]

☐ [*T.D.* 8450,12-10-92.]

### [Reg. § 1.7704-3]

**§ 1.7704-3. Qualifying income.**—(a) *Certain investment income.*— (1) *In general.*—For purposes of section 7704(d)(1), qualifying income includes capital gain from the sale of stock, income from holding annuities, income from notional principal contracts (as defined in § 1.446-3), and other substantially similar income from ordinary and routine investments to the extent determined by the Commissioner. Income from a notional principal contract is included in qualifying income only if the property, income, or cash flow that measures the amounts to which the partnership is entitled under the contract would give rise to qualifying income if held or received directly by the partnership.

(2) *Limitations.*—Qualifying income described in paragraph (a)(1) of this section does not include income derived in the ordinary course of a trade or business. For purposes of the preceding sentence, income derived from an asset with respect to which the partnership is a broker, market maker, or dealer is income derived in the ordinary course of a trade or business; income derived from an asset with respect to which the taxpayer is a trader or investor is not income derived in the ordinary course of a trade or business.

(b) *Calculation of gross income and qualifying income.*—(1) *Treatment of losses.*—Except as otherwise provided in this section, in computing the gross income and qualifying income of a partnership for purposes of section 7704(c)(2) and this section, losses do not enter into the computation.

(2) *Certain positions that are marked to market.*—Gain recognized with respect to a position that is marked to market (for example, under section 475(f), 1256, 1259, or 1296) shall not fail to be qualifying income solely because there is no sale or disposition of the position.

(3) *Certain items of ordinary income.*—Gain recognized with respect to a capital asset shall not fail to be qualifying income solely because it is characterized as ordinary income under section 475(f), 988, 1258, or 1296.

(4) *Straddles.*—In computing the gross income and qualifying income of a partnership for purposes of section 7704(c)(2) and this section, a straddle (as defined in section 1092(c)) shall be treated as set forth in this paragraph (b)(4). For purposes of the preceding sentence, two or more straddles that are part of a larger straddle shall be treated as a single straddle. The amount of the gain from any straddle to be taken into account shall be computed as follows:

(i) *Straddles other than mixed straddle accounts.*—With respect to each straddle (whether or not a straddle during the taxable year) other than a mixed straddle account, the amount of gain taken into account shall be the excess, if any, of gain recognized during the taxable year with respect to property that was at any time a position in that straddle over any loss recognized during the taxable year with respect to property that was at any time a position in that straddle (including loss realized in an earlier taxable year).

(ii) *Mixed straddle accounts.*—With respect to each mixed straddle account (as defined in §1.1092(b)-4T(b)), the amount of gain taken into account shall be the annual account gain for that mixed straddle account, computed pursuant to §1.1092(b)-4T(c)(2).

(5) *Certain transactions similar to straddles.*—In computing the gross income and qualifying income of a partnership for purposes of section 7704(c)(2) and this section, related interests in property (whether or not personal property as defined in section 1092(d)(1)) that produce a substantial diminution of the partnership's risk of loss similar to that of a straddle (as defined in section 1092(c)) shall be combined so that the amount of gain taken into account by the partnership in computing its gross income shall be the excess, if any, of gain recognized during the taxable year with respect to such interests over any loss recognized during the taxable year with respect to such interests.

(6) *Wash sale rule.*—(i) *Gain not taken into account.*—Solely for purposes of section 7704(c)(2) and this section, if a partnership recognizes gain in a section 7704 wash sale transaction with respect to one or more positions in either a straddle (as defined in section 1092(c)) or an arrangement described in paragraph (b)(5) of this section, then the gain shall not be taken into account to the extent of the amount of unrecognized loss (as of the close of the taxable year) in one or more offsetting positions of the straddle or arrangement described in paragraph (b)(5) of this section.

(ii) *Section 7704 wash sale transaction.*—For purposes of this paragraph (b)(6), a section 7704 wash sale transaction is a transaction in which—

(A) A partnership disposes of one or more positions of a straddle (as defined in section 1092(c)) or one or more related positions described in paragraph (b)(5) of this section; and

(B) The partnership acquires a substantially similar position or positions within a period beginning 30 days before the date of the disposition and ending 30 days after such date.

(c) *Effective date.*—This section applies to taxable years of a partnership beginning on or after December 17, 1998. However, a partnership may apply this section in its entirety for all of the partnership's open taxable years beginning after any earlier date selected by the partnership. [Reg. §1.7704-3.]

☐ [T.D. 8799, 12-16-98.]

**[Reg. §1.7704-4]**

**§1.7704-4. Qualifying income – mineral and natural resources.**—(a) *In general.*—For purposes of section 7704(d)(1)(E), qualifying income is income and gains from qualifying activities with respect to minerals or natural resources as defined in paragraph (b) of this section. Qualifying activities are section 7704(d)(1)(E) activities (as described in paragraph (c) of this section) and intrinsic activities (as described in paragraph (d) of this section).

(b) *Mineral or natural resource.*—The term mineral or natural resource (including fertilizer, geothermal energy, and timber) means any product of a character with respect to which a deduction for depletion is allowable under section 611, except that such term does not include any product described in section 613(b)(7)(A) or (B) (soil, sod, dirt, turf, water, mosses, or minerals from sea water, the air, or other similar inexhaustible sources). For purposes of this section, the term mineral or natural resource does not include industrial source carbon dioxide, fuels described in section 6426(b) through (e), any alcohol fuel defined in section 6426(b)(4)(A), or any biodiesel fuel as defined in section 40A(d)(1).

(c) *Section 7704(d)(1)(E) activities.*—(1) *Definition.*—Section 7704(d)(1)(E) activities include the exploration, development, mining or production, processing, refining, transportation, or marketing of any mineral or natural resource. Solely for purposes of section 7704(d), such terms are defined as provided in this paragraph (c).

(2) *Exploration.*—An activity constitutes exploration if it is performed to ascertain the existence, location, extent, or quality of any deposit of mineral or natural resource before the beginning of the development stage of the natural deposit including by—

(i) Drilling an exploratory or stratigraphic type test well;

(ii) Conducting drill stem and production flow tests to verify commerciality of the deposit;

(iii) Conducting geological or geophysical surveys;

(iv) Interpreting data obtained from geological or geophysical surveys; or

(v) For minerals, testpitting, trenching, drilling, driving of exploration tunnels and adits, and similar types of activities described in Rev. Rul. 70-287 (1970-1 CB 146), (see §601.601(d)(2)(ii)(b) of this chapter) if conducted prior to development activities with respect to the minerals.

(3) *Development.*—An activity constitutes development if it is performed to make accessible minerals or natural resources, including by—

(i) Drilling wells to access deposits of minerals or natural resources;

(ii) Constructing and installing drilling, production, or dual purpose platforms in marine locations, or any similar supporting structures necessary for extraordinary non-marine terrain (such as swamps or tundra);

(iii) Completing wells, including by installing lease and well equipment, such as pumps, flow lines, separators, and storage tanks, so that wells are capable of producing oil and gas, and the production can be removed from the premises;

(iv) Performing a development technique such as, for minerals other than oil and natural gas, stripping, benching and terracing, dredging by dragline, stoping, and caving or room-and-pillar excavation, and for oil and natural gas, fracturing; or

(v) Constructing and installing gathering systems and custody transfer stations.

(4) *Mining or production.*—An activity constitutes mining or production if it is performed to extract minerals or natural resources from the ground including by operating equipment to extract minerals or natural resources from mines and wells, or to extract minerals or natural resources from the waste or residue of prior mining or production allowable under this section. The recycling of scrap or salvaged metals or minerals from previously manufactured products or manufacturing processes is not considered to be the extraction of ores or minerals from waste or residue.

(5) *Processing.*—An activity constitutes processing if it is performed to convert raw mined or harvested products or raw well effluent to substances that can be readily transported or stored, as described in this paragraph (c)(5).

(i) *Natural gas.*—An activity constitutes processing of natural gas if it is performed to—

(A) Purify natural gas, including by removal of oil or condensate, water, or non-hydrocarbon gases (such as carbon dioxide, hydrogen sulfide, nitrogen, and helium); and

(B) Separate natural gas into its constituents which are normally recovered in a gaseous phase (methane and ethane) and those which are normally recovered in a liquid phase (propane, butane, pentane, and heavier streams).

(ii) *Crude oil.*—An activity constitutes processing of crude oil if it is performed to separate produced fluids by passing crude oil through mechanical separators to remove gas, placing crude oil in settling tanks to recover basic sediment and water, dehydrating crude oil, and operating heater-treaters that separate raw oil well effluent into crude oil, natural gas, and salt water.

(iii) *Ores and minerals other than natural gas or crude oil.*—An activity constitutes processing of ores and minerals other than natural gas or crude oil if it meets the definition of mining processes under §1.613-4(f)(1)(ii), without regard to §1.613-4(f)(2)(iv).

(iv) *Timber.*—An activity constitutes processing of timber if it is performed to modify the physical form of timber, including by the application of heat or pressure to timber, without adding any foreign substances. Processing of timber does not include activities that add chemicals or other foreign substances to timber to manipulate its physical or chemical properties, such as using a digester to produce pulp. Products that result from timber processing include wood chips, sawdust, rough lumber, kiln-dried lumber, veneers, wood pellets, wood bark, and rough poles. Products that are not the result of timber processing include pulp, paper, paper products, treated lumber, oriented strand board/plywood, and treated poles.

(6) *Refining.*—An activity constitutes refining if the activity is set forth in this paragraph (c)(6).

(i) *Natural gas and crude oil.*—(A) The refining of natural gas and crude oil includes the further physical or chemical conversion or separation processes of products resulting from activities listed in paragraph (c)(5)(i) and (ii) of this section, and the blending of petroleum hydrocarbons, to the extent they give rise to a product listed in paragraph (c)(5)(i) or (ii) of this section or to the products of a type produced in a petroleum refinery or natural gas processing plant listed in this paragraph (c)(6)(i)(A). Refining of natural gas and crude oil also includes the further physical or chemical conversion or separation processes and blending of the products listed in this paragraph (c)(6)(i)(A), to the extent that the resulting product is also listed in this paragraph (c)(6)(i)(A). The following products are of a type produced in a petroleum refinery or natural gas processing plant:

(1) Ethane.

*(2)* Ethylene.

*(3)* Propane.

*(4)* Propylene.

*(5)* Normal butane.

*(6)* Butylene.

*(7)* Isobutane.

*(8)* Isobutene.

*(9)* Isobutylene.

*(10)* Pentanes plus.

*(11)* Unfinished naphtha.

*(12)* Unfinished kerosene and light gas oils.

*(13)* Unfinished heavy gas oils.

*(14)* Unfinished residuum.

*(15)* Reformulated gasoline with fuel ethanol.

*(16)* Reformulated other motor gasoline.

*(17)* Conventional gasoline with fuel ethanol – Ed55 and lower gasoline.

*(18)* Conventional gasoline with fuel ethanol – greater than Ed55 gasoline.

*(19)* Conventional gasoline with fuel ethanol – other conventional finished gasoline.

*(20)* Reformulated blendstock for oxygenate (RBOB).

*(21)* Conventional blendstock for oxygenate (CBOB).

*(22)* Gasoline treated as blendstock (GTAB).

*(23)* Other motor gasoline blending components defined as gasoline blendstocks as provided in §48.4081-1(c)(3) of this chapter.

*(24)* Finished aviation gasoline and blending components.

*(25)* Special naphthas (solvents).

*(26)* Kerosene-type jet fuel.

*(27)* Kerosene.

*(28)* Distillate fuel oil (heating oils, diesel fuel, and ultra-low sulfur diesel fuel).

*(29)* Residual fuel oil.

*(30)* Lubricants (lubricating base oils).

*(31)* Asphalt and road oil (atmospheric or vacuum tower bottom).

*(32)* Waxes.

*(33)* Petroleum coke.

*(34)* Still gas.

*(35)* Naphtha less than 401°F end-point.

*(36)* Other products of a refinery that the Commissioner may identify through published guidance.

(B) For purposes of this section, the products listed in this paragraph (c)(6)(i)(B) are not products of refining:

*(1)* Heat, steam, or electricity produced by processing or refining.

*(2)* Products that are obtained from third parties or produced onsite for use in the refinery, such as hydrogen, if excess amounts are sold.

*(3)* Any product that results from further chemical change of a product listed in paragraph (c)(6)(i)(A) of this section that does not result in the same or another product listed in paragraph (c)(6)(i)(A) of this section (for example, production of petroleum coke from heavy (refinery) residuum qualifies, but any upgrading of petroleum coke (such as to calcined coke) does not qualify because it is further chemically changed and does not result in the same or another product listed in paragraph (c)(6)(i)(A) of this section).

*(4)* Plastics or similar petroleum derivatives.

(ii) *Ores and minerals other than natural gas or crude oil.*— (A) An activity constitutes refining of ores and minerals other than natural gas or crude oil if it is one of the various processes performed subsequent to mining processes (as defined in paragraph (c)(5)(iii) of this section) to eliminate impurities or foreign matter and which are necessary steps in achieving a high degree of purity from metallic ores and minerals which are not customarily sold in the form of the crude mineral product, as specified in paragraph (c)(6)(ii)(B) of this section. Refining processes include: fine pulverization, electrowinning, electrolytic deposition, roasting, thermal or electric smelting, or substantially equivalent processes or combinations of processes used to separate or extract the specified metals listed in paragraph (c)(6)(ii)(B) of this section from the ore for the primary purpose of producing a purer form of the metal, as for example the smelting of concentrates to produce Doré bars or refining of blister copper.

(B) For purposes of this section, the specified metallic ores or minerals which are not customarily sold in the form of the crude mineral product are—

*(1)* Lead;

*(2)* Zinc;

*(3)* Copper;

*(4)* Gold;

*(5)* Silver; and

*(6)* Any other ores or minerals that the Commissioner may identify through published guidance.

(C) Refining does not include the introduction of additives that remain in the metal, for example, in the manufacture of alloys of gold. Also, the application of nonmining processes as defined in §1.613-4(g) in order to produce a specified metal that is considered a waste or by-product of production from a non-specified mineral deposit is not considered refining for purposes of this section.

(7) *Transportation.*—(i) *General rule.*—An activity constitutes transportation if it is performed to move minerals or natural resources, and products under paragraph (c)(4), (5), or (6) of this section, including by pipeline, marine vessel, rail, or truck. Except as provided in paragraph (c)(7)(ii) of this section, transportation does not include the movement of minerals or natural resources, and products produced under paragraph (c)(4), (5), or (6) of this section, directly to retail customers or to a place that sells or dispenses to retail customers. Retail customers do not include a person who acquires oil or gas for refining or processing, or a utility. Transportation includes the following activities:

(A) Providing storage services.

(B) Providing terminalling services, including the following: receiving products from pipelines, marine vessels, railcars, or trucks; storing products; loading products to pipelines, marine vessels, railcars, or trucks for distribution; testing and treating, as well as blending and additization, if income from such activities would be qualifying income pursuant to paragraph (c)(10)(iv) and (v) of this section; and separating and selling excess renewable identification numbers acquired as part of additization services to comply with environmental regulations.

(C) Moving or carrying (whether by owner or operator) products via pipelines, gathering systems, and custody transfer stations.

(D) Operating marine vessels (including time charters), railcars, or trucks.

(E) Providing compression services to a pipeline.

(F) Liquefying or regasifying natural gas.

(ii) *Transportation to retail customers or to a place that sells to retail customers.*—Transportation includes the movement of minerals or natural resources, and products under paragraph (c)(4), (5), or (6) of this section, via pipeline to a place that sells to retail customers. Transportation also includes the movement of liquefied petroleum gas via trucks, rail cars, or pipeline to a place that sells to retail customers or directly to retail customers.

(8) *Marketing.*—(i) *General rule.*—An activity constitutes marketing if it is the bulk sale of minerals or natural resources, and products under paragraph (c)(4), (5), or (6) of this section. Except as provided in paragraph (c)(8)(ii) of this section, marketing does not include retail sales (sales made in small quantities directly to end users), which includes the operation of gasoline service stations, home heating oil delivery services, and local natural gas delivery services.

(ii) *Retail sales of liquefied petroleum gas.*—Retail sales of liquefied petroleum gas are included in marketing.

(iii) *Certain activities that facilitate sale.*—Marketing also includes certain activities that facilitate sales that constitute marketing under paragraphs (c)(8)(i) and (ii) of this section, including packaging, as well as and blending and additization, if income from blending and additization would be qualifying income pursuant to paragraph (c)(10)(iv) and (v) of this section.

(9) *Fertilizer.*—[Reserved]

(10) *Additional activities.*—The following types of income as described in paragraph (c)(10)(i) through (v) of this section will be considered derived from a section 7704(d)(1)(E) activity.

(i) *Cost reimbursements.*—If the partnership is in the trade or business of performing a section 7704(d)(1)(E) activity, qualifying income includes income received to reimburse the partnership for its costs in performing that section 7704(d)(1)(E) activity, whether imbedded in the rate the partnership charges or separately itemized. Reimbursable costs may include the cost of designing, constructing, installing, inspecting, maintaining, metering, monitoring, or relocating an asset used in that section 7704(d)(1)(E) activity, or providing office functions necessary to the operation of that section 7704(d)(1)(E) activity (such as staffing, purchasing supplies, billing, accounting, and financial reporting). For example, a pipeline operator that charges a customer for its cost to build, repair, or schedule flow on the pipelines that it operates will have qualifying income from such activity whether or not it itemizes those costs when it bills the customer.

(ii) *Hedging.*—[Reserved]

(iii) *Passive Interests.*—Qualifying income includes income and gains from a passive interest or non-operating interest, including production royalties, minimum annual royalties, net profits interests, delay rentals, and lease-bonus payments, if the interest is in a mineral or natural resource as defined in paragraph (b) of this section. Payments received on a production payment will not be qualifying income if they are properly treated as loan payments under section 636.

(iv) *Blending.*—Qualifying income includes income and gains from performing blending activities or services with respect to products under paragraph (c)(4), (5), or (6) of this section, so long as the products being blended are component parts of the same mineral or natural resource. For purposes of this paragraph (c)(10)(iv), products of oil and natural gas will be considered as from the same natural resource. Blending does not include combining different minerals or natural resources or products thereof together. However, see paragraph (c)(10)(v) of this section for rules concerning additization.

(v) *Additization.*—Qualifying income includes income and gains from providing additization services with respect to products under paragraph (c)(4), (5), or (6) of this section to the extent specifically permitted in this paragraph (c)(10)(v). The addition of additives described in paragraph (c)(10)(v)(A) through (C) of this section is permissible if the additives aid in the transportation of a product, enhance or protect the intrinsic properties of a product, or are necessary as required by federal, state, or local law (for example, to meet environmental standards), but only if such additives do not create a new product.

(A) The addition of additives to products of natural gas and crude oil is permissible, provided that such additives constitute less than 5 percent (except that ethanol or biodiesel may be up to 20 percent) of the total volume for products of natural gas and crude oil and are added into the product by the terminal operator or upstream of the terminal operator.

(B) In the case of ores and minerals other than natural gas or crude oil, the addition of incidental amounts of material such as paper dots to identify shipments, antifreeze to aid in shipping, or compounds to allay dust as required by law or reduce losses during shipping is permissible.

(C) In the case of timber, additization of incidental amounts to comply with government regulations is permissible, to the extent such additization does not create a new product. For example, the pressure treatment of wood is impermissible because it creates a new product.

(d) *Intrinsic activities.*—(1) *General requirements.*—An activity is an intrinsic activity only if the activity is specialized to support a section 7704(d)(1)(E) activity, is essential to the completion of the section 7704(d)(1)(E) activity, and requires the provision of significant services to support the section 7704(d)(1)(E) activity. Whether an activity is an intrinsic activity is determined on an activity-by-activity basis.

(2) *Specialization.*—An activity is a specialized activity if—

(i) The partnership provides personnel (including employees of the partnership, an affiliate, subcontractor, or independent contractor performing work on behalf of the partnership) to support a section 7704(d)(1)(E) activity and those personnel have received training in order to support the section 7704(d)(1)(E) activity that is unique to the mineral or natural resource industry and of limited utility other than to perform or support a section 7704(d)(1)(E) activity; and

(ii) To the extent that the activity involves the sale, provision, or use of specific property, either—

(A) The property is primarily tangible property that is dedicated to, and has limited utility outside of, section 7704(d)(1)(E) activities and is not easily converted (as determined based on all the facts and circumstances, including the cost to convert the property) to another use other than supporting or performing the section 7704(d)(1)(E) activities (except that the use of non-specialized property typically used incidentally in operating a business will not cause a partnership to fail this paragraph (d)(2)(ii)(A)); or

(B) If the property is used as an injectant to perform a section 7704(d)(1)(E) activity that is also commonly used outside of section 7704(d)(1)(E) activities (such as water and lubricants), the partnership provides the injectants exclusively to those engaged in section 7704(d)(1)(E) activities; the partnership is also in the trade or business of collecting, cleaning, recycling, or otherwise disposing of injectants after use in accordance with Federal, state, or local regulations concerning waste products from mining or production activities; and the partnership operates its injectant delivery and disposal services within the same geographic area.

(3) *Essential.*—(i) An activity is essential to the section 7704(d)(1)(E) activity if it is required to—

(A) Physically complete a section 7704(d)(1)(E) activity (including in a cost-effective manner, such as by making the activity economically viable), or

(B) Comply with Federal, state, or local law regulating the section 7704(d)(1)(E) activity.

(ii) Legal, financial, consulting, accounting, insurance, and other similar services do not qualify as essential to a section 7704(d)(1)(E) activity.

(4) *Significant services.*—(i) An activity requires significant services to support the section 7704(d)(1)(E) activity if those services must be conducted on an ongoing or frequent basis by the partnership's personnel at the site or sites of the section 7704(d)(1)(E) activities. Alternatively, those services may be conducted offsite if the services are performed on an ongoing or frequent basis and are offered to those engaged in one or more section 7704(d)(1)(E) activities. If the services are monitoring, those services must be offered exclusively to those engaged in one or more section 7704(d)(1)(E) activities. Whether services are conducted on an ongoing or frequent basis is determined based on all the facts and circumstances, including recognized best practices in the relevant industry.

(ii) Personnel perform significant services only if those services are necessary for the partnership to perform an activity that is essential to the section 7704(d)(1)(E) activity, or to support the section 7704(d)(1)(E) activity. Personnel include employees of the partnership, an affiliate, subcontractor, or independent contractor performing work on behalf of the partnership.

(iii) Services are not significant services with respect to a section 7704(d)(1)(E) activity if the services principally involve the design, construction, manufacturing, repair, maintenance, lease, rent, or temporary provision of property.

(e) *Interpretations of section 611 and section 613.*—This section and interpretations of this section have no effect on interpretations of sections 611 and 613, or other sections of the Code, or the regulations thereunder; however, this section incorporates some of the interpretations under section 611 and 613 and the regulations thereunder as provided in this section.

(f) *Examples.*—The following examples illustrate the provisions of this section:

*Example 1. Petrochemical products sourced from an oil and gas well.* (i) Z, a publicly traded partnership, chemically converts a mixture of ethane and propane (obtained from physical separation of natural gas) into ethylene and propylene through use of a steam cracker. Z sells the ethylene and propylene in bulk to a third party.

(ii) Ethylene and propylene are products of refining as provided in paragraph (c)(6)(i) of this section; therefore, Z is engaged in a section 7704(d)(1)(E) activity. The income Z receives from the sale of ethylene and propylene is qualifying income for purposes of section 7704(d)(1)(E).

*Example 2. Petroleum streams chemically converted into refinery grade olefins byproducts.* (i) Y, a publicly traded partnership, owns a petroleum refinery. The refinery physically separates crude oil, obtaining heavy gas oil. The refinery then uses a catalytic cracking unit to chemically convert the heavy gas oil into a liquid stream suitable for gasoline blending and a gas stream containing ethane, ethylene, and other gases. The refinery also further physically separates the gas stream, resulting in refinery-grade ethylene. Y sells the ethylene in bulk to a third party.

(ii) Y's activities give rise to products of refining as provided in paragraph (c)(6)(i) of this section; therefore, Y is engaged in a section 7704(d)(1)(E) activity. The income Y receives from the sales of ethylene is qualifying income for purposes of section 7704(d)(1)(E).

*Example 3. Converting methane gas into synthetic fuels through chemical change.* (i) Y, a publicly traded partnership, chemically converts methane into methanol and synthesis gas, and further chemically converts those products into gasoline and diesel fuel. Y receives income from bulk sales of gasoline and diesel created during the conversion processes, as well as from sales of methanol.

(ii) With respect to the production of gasoline or diesel from methane, gasoline and diesel are products of refining as provided in paragraph (c)(6)(i) of this section; therefore, Y is engaged in a section 7704(d)(1)(E) activity. Y's income from the sale of gasoline and diesel is qualifying income for purposes of section 7704(d)(1)(E).

(iii) The income from the sale of methanol, an intermediate product in the conversion process, is not qualifying income for purposes of section 7704(d)(1)(E) because methanol is not a product of processing or refining as defined in paragraph (c)(5) and (6) of this section.

*Example 4. Converting methanol into gasoline and diesel.* (i) Assume the same facts as in *Example 3* of this paragraph (f), except Y purchases methanol and synthesis gas and chemically converts the methanol and synthesis gas into gasoline and diesel.

(ii) The chemical conversion of methanol and synthesis gas into gasoline and diesel is not refining as provided in paragraph (c)(6)(i) of this section because it is not the physical or chemical conversion or the separation or blending of products listed in paragraph (c)(6)(i)(A) of this section. Accordingly, the income from the sales of the gasoline and diesel is not qualifying income for purposes of section 7704(d)(1)(E).

*Example 5. Delivery of refined products.* (i) X, a publicly traded partnership, sells diesel to a government entity at wholesale prices and delivers those goods in bulk.

(ii) X's sale of a refined product to the government entity is a section 7704(d)(1)(E) activity because it is a bulk transportation and sale as described in paragraph (c)(7) and (8) of this section and is not a retail sale.

*Example 6. Constructing a pipeline.* (i) X, a publicly traded partnership, operates interstate and intrastate natural gas pipelines. Y, a corporation, is a construction firm. X pays Y to build a pipeline. X later seeks reimbursement for its cost to build the pipeline from A, a refiner who contracts with X to transport gasoline.

(ii) X, as an operator of pipelines, is engaged in transportation pursuant to paragraph (c)(7)(i)(C) of this section. The reimbursement X receives from A for X's cost to build the pipeline is qualifying income pursuant to paragraph (c)(10)(i) of this section because X receives the income to reimburse X for its costs in performing X's transportation activity and reimbursable costs may include construction costs. In contrast, Y is not in the trade or business of performing a 7704(d)(1)(E) activity, thus income Y received from X for building the pipeline is not qualifying income to Y.

*Example 7. Delivery of water.* (i) X, a publicly traded partnership, owns interstate and intrastate natural gas pipelines. X built a water delivery pipeline along the existing right of way for its natural gas pipeline to deliver water to A for use in A's fracturing activity. A uses the delivered water in fracturing to develop A's natural gas reserve in a cost-efficient manner. X earns income for transporting natural gas in the pipelines and for delivery of water.

(ii) X's income from transporting natural gas in its interstate and intrastate pipelines is qualifying income for purposes of section 7704(c) because transportation of natural gas is a section 7704(d)(1)(E) activity as provided in paragraph (c)(7)(i)(C) of this section.

(iii) The income X obtains from its water delivery services is not a section 7704(d)(1)(E) activity as provided in paragraph (c) of this section. However, because X's water delivery supports A's development of natural gas, a section 7704(d)(1)(E) activity, X's income from water delivery services may be qualifying income for purposes of section 7704(c) if the water delivery service is an intrinsic activity as provided in paragraph (d) of this section. An activity is an intrinsic activity if the activity is specialized to support the section 7704(d)(1)(E) activity, is essential to the completion of the section 7704(d)(1)(E) activity, and requires the provision of significant services to support the section 7704(d)(1)(E) activity. Under paragraph (d)(2)(ii)(B) of this section, the provision of water for use as an injectant in a section 7704(d)(1)(E) activity is specialized to that activity only if the partnership (1) provides the water exclusively to those engaged in section 7704(d)(1)(E) activities, (2) is also in the trade or business of cleaning, recycling, or otherwise disposing of water after use in accordance with Federal, state, or local regulations concerning waste products from mining or production activities, and (3) operates these disposal services within the same geographic area as that in which it delivers water. Because X does not perform such disposal services, X's water delivery activities are not specialized to support the section 7704(d)(1)(E) activity. Thus, X's water delivery is not an intrinsic activity. Accordingly, X's income from the delivery of water is not qualifying income for purposes of section 7704(c).

*Example 8. Delivery of water and recovery and recycling of flowback.* (i) Assume the same facts as in *Example 7* of this paragraph (f), except that X also collects and treats flowback at the drilling site in accordance with state regulations as part of its water delivery services and transports the treated flowback away from the site. In connection with these services, X provides personnel to perform these services on an ongoing or frequent basis that is consistent with best industry practices. X has provided these personnel with specialized training regarding the recovery and recycling of flowback produced during the development of natural gas, and this training is of limited utility other than to perform or support the development of natural gas.

(ii) The income X obtains from its water delivery services is not a section 7704(d)(1)(E) activity as provided in paragraph (c) of this section. However, because X's water delivery supports A's development of natural gas, a section 7704(d)(1)(E) activity, X's income from water delivery services may be qualifying income for purposes of section 7704(c) if the water delivery service is an intrinsic activity as provided in paragraph (d) of this section.

(iii) An activity is an intrinsic activity if the activity is specialized to support the section 7704(d)(1)(E) activity, is essential to the comple-

tion of the section 7704(d)(1)(E) activity, and requires the provision of significant services to support the section 7704(d)(1)(E) activity. Under paragraph (d)(2)(ii)(B) of this section, the provision of water for use as an injectant in a section 7704(d)(1)(E) activity is specialized to that activity only if the partnership (1) provides the water exclusively to those engaged in section 7704(d)(1)(E) activities, (2) is also in the trade or business of cleaning, recycling, or otherwise disposing of water after use in accordance with Federal, state, or local regulations concerning waste products from mining or production activities, and (3) operates these disposal services within the same geographical area as where it delivers water. X's provision of personnel is specialized because those personnel received training regarding the recovery and recycling of flowback produced during the development of natural gas, and this training is of limited utility other than to perform or support the development of natural gas. The provision of water is also specialized because water is an injectant used to perform a section 7704(d)(1)(E) activity, and X also collects and treats flowback in accordance with state regulations as part of its water delivery services. Therefore, X meets the specialization requirement. The delivery of water is essential to support A's development activity because the water is needed for use in fracturing to develop A's natural gas reserve in a cost-efficient manner. Finally, the water delivery and recovery and recycling activities require significant services to support the development activity because X's personnel provide services necessary for the partnership to perform the support activity at the development site on an ongoing or frequent basis that is consistent with best industry practices. Because X's delivery of water and X's collection, transport, and treatment of flowback is a specialized activity, is essential to the completion of a section 7704(d)(1)(E) activity, and requires significant services, the delivery of water and the transport and treatment of flowback is an intrinsic activity. X's income from the delivery of water and the collection, treatment, and transport of flowback is qualifying income for purposes of section 7704(c).

(g) *Effective/applicability date and transition rule.*—(1) *In general.*—Except as provided in paragraph (g)(2) of this section, this section applies to income earned by a partnership in a taxable year beginning on or after January 19, 2017. Paragraph (g)(2) of this section applies during the period that ends on the last day of the partnership's taxable year that includes January 19, 2027 (Transition Period).

(2) *Income during Transition Period.*—A partnership may treat income from an activity as qualifying income during the Transition Period if—

(i) The partnership received a private letter ruling from the IRS holding that the income from that activity is qualifying income;

(ii) Prior to May 6, 2015, the partnership was publicly traded, engaged in the activity, and treated the activity as giving rise to qualifying income under section 7704(d)(1)(E), and that income was qualifying income under the statute as reasonably interpreted prior to May 6, 2015;

(iii) Prior to May 6, 2015, the partnership was publicly traded and had entered into a binding agreement for construction of assets to be used in such activity that would give rise to income that was qualifying income under the statute as reasonably interpreted prior to May 6, 2015; or

(iv) The partnership is publicly traded and engages in the activity after May 6, 2015 but before January 19, 2017, and the income from that activity is qualifying income under the proposed regulations (REG-132634-14) contained in the Internal Revenue Bulletin (IRB) 2015-21 (see https://www.irs.gov/pub/irs-irbs/irb15-21.pdf).

(3) *Relief from technical termination.*—In the event of a technical termination under section 708(b)(1)(B) of a partnership that satisfies the requirements of paragraph (g)(2) of this section without regard to the technical termination, the resulting partnership will be treated as the partnership that satisfies the requirements of paragraph (g)(2) of this section for purposes of applying the Transition Period. [Reg. §1.7704-4.]

☐ [*T.D.* 9817, 1-19-2017.]

**[Reg. §301.7705-1]**

**§301.7705-1. Certified professional employer organization.**—(a) *In general.*—The definitions set forth in this section apply for purposes of this section, §§31.3511-1 and 301.7705-2, and sections 3302(h), 3303(a)(4), 6053(c)(8), and 7528(b)(4).

(b) *Definitions.*—(1) *Certified professional employer organization* (CPEO) means a person that applies to be certified as a CPEO in accordance with §301.7705-2(a) and has been certified by the Internal Revenue Service (IRS) as meeting the requirements of §301.7705-2. For purposes of §301.7705-2(g)(2), the term CPEO also includes the person before it applied for certification and while its application is pending with the IRS. For all other purposes, a person is a CPEO as of the effective date of its certification (as specified in the certification notice described in § 301.7705-2(a)(2)) and until its certification is revoked by the IRS (as described in § 301.7705-2(n)) or, if earlier and applicable, until the CPEO voluntarily terminates its certification in the time and manner prescribed by the Commissioner in further guidance.

(2) *CPEO applicant* means a person that has applied to be certified as a CPEO in accordance with § 301.7705-2(a) and whose application is pending with the IRS.

(3) *CPEO contract* means a service contract between a CPEO and a customer that is in writing and provides that, with respect to an individual providing services to the customer, the CPEO will—

(i) Assume responsibility for payment of wages to the individual, without regard to the receipt or adequacy of payment from the customer for the services;

(ii) Assume responsibility for reporting, withholding, and paying any applicable federal employment taxes with respect to the individual's wages, without regard to the receipt or adequacy of payment from the customer for the services;

(iii) Assume responsibility for any employee benefits that the service contract may require the CPEO to provide to the individual, without regard to the receipt or adequacy of payment from the customer for such benefits;

(iv) Assume responsibility for recruiting, hiring, and firing the individual in addition to the customer's responsibility for recruiting, hiring, and firing the individual;

(v) Maintain employee records relating to the individual; and

(vi) Agree to be treated as a CPEO for purposes of section 3511 with respect to the individual.

(4) *Certified public accountant (CPA)* means a certified public accountant who—

(i) With respect to a CPEO applicant or CPEO, is independent of the CPEO applicant or CPEO (as prescribed by the American Institute of Certified Public Accountants' Professional Standards, Code of Professional Conduct, and its interpretations and rulings);

(ii) Is not currently under suspension or disbarment from practice before the IRS;

(iii) Is duly qualified to practice as a CPA in any state;

(iv) Files with the IRS a written declaration that he or she is currently qualified to practice as a CPA in any state; and

(v) Meets such other requirements as the Commissioner may prescribe in further guidance.

(5) *Covered employee* means, with respect to a customer, any individual (other than a self-employed individual, as defined in paragraph (b)(14) of this section) who performs services for the customer and who is covered by a CPEO contract between the CPEO and the customer.

(6) *Customer.*—(i) *In general.*—Except as provided in paragraph (b)(6)(ii) of this section, a customer is any person who enters into a CPEO contract with a CPEO.

(ii) *Persons who are not customers.*—A provider of payroll services that uses its own EIN for filing federal employment tax returns on behalf of its clients (or that used its own EIN immediately prior to entering into a service contract with the CPEO) is not a customer, even if it has entered into a service contract with the CPEO that meets all of the requirements for a CPEO contract described in paragraph (b)(3) of this section other than being a contract between a CPEO and a customer.

(7) *Federal employment taxes* mean the taxes imposed by subtitle C of the Internal Revenue Code.

(8) *Guidance* includes guidance published in the Federal Register or Internal Revenue Bulletin, as well as administrative guidance such as forms, instructions, publications, or other guidance on the *irs.gov* Web site.

(9) *Partnership* means a business entity (as described in § 301.7701-2(a)) that is classified as a partnership for federal tax purposes under § § 301.7701-1, 301.7701-2, and 301.7701-3. Accordingly, any references to a managing member or general partner of a partnership mean a managing member or general partner of an entity that is classified as a partnership for federal tax purposes.

(10) *Precursor entity.*—(i) *In general.*—A precursor entity means, with respect to a CPEO applicant, any related entity of the CPEO applicant that is or was a provider of payroll services that—

(A) Has made a substantial asset transfer to the CPEO applicant during the calendar year in which the CPEO applicant applies for certification or any of the three preceding calendar years or plans to make such a substantial asset transfer while the application for certification is pending or in the 12-month period following the date of the CPEO applicant's application for certification; or

(B) Has ceased operations or dissolved during the calendar year in which the CPEO applicant applied for certification or any of the three preceding calendar years.

(ii) *Related.*—For purposes of this paragraph (b)(10), a provider of payroll services is considered a related entity of a CPEO applicant if it is a related entity within the meaning of paragraph (b)(12) of this section or if it would be or would have been such a related entity based on the ownership and responsible individuals of the provider of payroll services at the time of its substantial asset transfer, ceasing of operations, or dissolution, as applicable, and the ownership and responsible individuals of the CPEO applicant at the time of its application.

(11) *Provider of payroll services* means a person that provides federal employment tax administration, payroll services, or other similar federal employment tax-related compliance services to clients, including, but not limited to, collecting, reporting, and paying federal employment taxes with respect to wages or compensation paid by the person to individuals performing services for the clients. A provider of payroll services includes, but is not limited to, a CPEO.

(12) *Related entity* means, with respect to a CPEO applicant or CPEO, any person that meets one or more of the following criteria:

(i) The person is a member of a controlled group of which the CPEO applicant or CPEO is also a member. Additionally, CPEO applicants and CPEOs that, but for their status as disregarded entities would separately be members of a controlled group, are treated as members of a controlled group for purposes of this paragraph (b)(12)(i). For purposes of this paragraph (b)(12)(i), controlled group has the meaning given to such term by sections 414(b) and (c) and § § 1.414(b)-1 and 1.414(c)-1 through 1.414(c)-6 of this chapter, except that—

(A) With respect to a person that is not a provider of payroll services "more than 50 percent" will be substituted for "at least 80 percent" each place it appears in section 1563(a) (which is cross-referenced in section 414(b) and § 1.414(c)-2 of this chapter); and

(B) With respect to a person that is a provider of payroll services, "more than 5 percent" will be substituted for "at least 80 percent" each place it appears in section 1563(a) and § 1.414(c)-2 of this chapter; or

(ii) The person is a provider of payroll services and—

(A) A majority of the directors or a majority of the officers (as described in paragraph (b)(13)(ii) of this section) of the CPEO applicant or CPEO are directors or officers (as described in paragraph (b)(13)(ii) of this section), respectively, of the provider of payroll services; or

(B) An individual is a responsible individual of both the provider of payroll services and the CPEO applicant or CPEO by reason of paragraph (b)(13)(i) of this section.

(13) *Responsible individual* means, with respect to a CPEO applicant or CPEO, (or, for purposes of paragraph (b)(10)(ii) or (b)(12)(ii) of this section, a provider of payroll services), the following individuals:

(i) Any individual who owns, directly or indirectly, applying the constructive ownership rules of section 1563(e) with respect to stock ownership and substituting the term "interest" for the term "stock" and the term "partnership" for the term "corporation" used in that section, as appropriate for purposes of determining whether an interest in a partnership is indirectly owned by any person, 33 percent or more of—

(A) In the case of a corporation, the total combined voting power of all classes of stock entitled to vote of such corporation or the total value of shares of all classes of stock of such corporation; or

(B) In the case of a partnership, the capital interest or profits interest of such partnership.

(ii) Any individual who is a director or an officer. For purposes of this paragraph (b)(13)(ii), a director is a voting member of the governing body (that is, the board of directors or equivalent controlling body authorized under state law to make governance decisions on behalf of the organization), and the officers are determined by reference to the organizing document, bylaws, or resolutions of the governing body, or otherwise designated consistent with state law. Officers may include individuals such as a president, vice-president, secretary, and treasurer.

(iii) Any individual who, regardless of title, has ultimate responsibility for implementing the decisions of the organization's governing body. An individual who serves with the title of chief executive officer, executive director, and/or president has this ultimate responsibility. An individual with this ultimate responsibility may include an individual who is not treated as an employee of the organization. If this ultimate responsibility resides with two or more individuals (for example, co-presidents), who may exercise such responsibility in concert or individually, then each such individual is a responsible individual.

(iv) Any individual who, regardless of title, has ultimate responsibility for supervising the management, administration, or operation of the organization. An individual who serves with the title of chief operating officer has this ultimate responsibility. An individual with this ultimate responsibility may include an individual who is not treated as an employee of the organization. If this ultimate responsibility resides with two or more individuals, who may exercise such responsibility in concert or individually, then each such individual is a responsible individual.

(v) Any individual who, regardless of title, has ultimate responsibility for managing the organization's finances. An individual who serves with the title of chief financial officer or treasurer has this ultimate responsibility. An individual with this ultimate responsibility may include an individual who is not treated as an employee of the organization. If this ultimate responsibility resides with two or more individuals who may exercise the responsibility in concert or individually, then each such individual is a responsible individual.

(vi) In the case of a partnership, any individual who is a managing member or general partner.

(vii) In the case of a sole proprietorship, the sole proprietor.

(viii) In the case of a disregarded entity owned by a corporation or partnership, the responsible individuals of that corporation or partnership.

(ix) In the case of a disregarded entity owned by an individual, the individual owner.

(x) Any other individual with primary responsibility for the organization's federal employment tax compliance.

(14) *Self-employed individual* means an individual with net earnings from self-employment (as defined in section 1402(a) without regard to the exceptions thereunder) derived from providing services covered by a CPEO contract, whether such net earnings from self-employment are derived from providing services as a non-employee to a customer of the CPEO, from the individual's own trade or business as a sole proprietor customer of the CPEO, or as an individual who is a partner in a partnership that is a customer of the CPEO, but only with regard to such net earnings.

(15) *Substantial asset transfer* means any transfer of 35 percent or more of the value of the operating assets of the person making the transfer, whether through one or a series of transactions and whether accomplished through sale, lease, gift, assignment, succession, merger, consolidation, corporate separation, or any other means. For purposes of this paragraph (b)(15), operating assets include both tangible and intangible resources related to the conduct of the person's trade or business, including, but not limited to, such intangible assets as contracts, agreements, receivables, employees, and goodwill (which includes the value of a trade or business based on expected continued customer patronage due to its name, reputation, or any other factors). In the case of a contract described in section 7705(e)(2) or a service agreement described in § 31.3504-2(b)(2) of this chapter entered into by a provider of payroll services, even if the contract or agreement is not sold, gifted, assigned, or otherwise formally transferred to a CPEO applicant, it will be considered transferred from the provider of payroll services to the CPEO applicant if the CPEO applicant reports, withholds, or pays, under its employer identification number (EIN), any applicable federal employment taxes with respect to the wages of any individuals covered by the contract or agreement.

(16) *Work site* means a physical location at which an individual regularly performs services for a customer of a CPEO or, if there is no such location, the location from which the customer assigns work to the individual. A work site may not be the individual's residence or a telework site unless the customer requires the individual to work at that site. For purposes of this paragraph (b)(16), work sites that are contiguous locations will be treated as a single physical location and thus a single work site, and noncontiguous locations will be treated as separate physical locations and thus separate work sites, except as provided in the next sentence. A CPEO customer may treat noncontiguous locations as a single physical location and thus a single work site if each of the locations is separated by less than 35 miles from every other location in the single work site and all locations in the single work site operate in the same industry. For purposes of the preceding sentence, the determination of the industry of a work site is based on the nature of the CPEO customer's work at that work site, irrespective of work performed by other entities at the same site. When treating noncontiguous locations as a single physical location and thus a single work site, one noncontiguous location cannot be included in more than one work site. For example, assume there are three noncontiguous locations, A, B, and C, operating in the same industry and that B is 20 miles east from A and C is 20 miles east from B. A CPEO customer would not be permitted to treat these three locations as a single work site but would be permitted to treat either A and B as a single work site or B and C as a single work site.

(17) *Work site employee.*—(i) *In general.*—A work site employee means, with respect to a customer, a covered employee who performs services for such customer at a work site where at least 85 percent of the individuals performing services for the customer are covered employees of the customer.

(ii) *Self-employed individuals.*—Solely for purposes of determining whether the 85 percent threshold described in paragraph (b)(17)(i) of this section is met, a self-employed individual described in paragraph (b)(14) of this section is treated as a covered employee if such individual would be a covered employee but for the exclusion of self-employed individuals from the definition of covered employee in paragraph (b)(5) of this section.

(iii) *Excluded employees.*—In determining whether the 85 percent threshold described in paragraph (b)(17)(i) of this section is met, an individual who is an excluded employee described in section 414(q)(5) is not treated as either an individual providing services or a covered employee.

(iv) *Treatment for calendar quarter.*—A covered employee will be considered a work site employee for the entirety of a calendar quarter if the employee qualifies as a work site employee at any time during that quarter.

(v) *Separate determination for each work site.*—The determination of whether a covered employee is a work site employee is made separately with regard to each work site at which the covered employee regularly provides services and for each customer for which the covered employee is providing services. A covered employee may be determined to be a work site employee of more than one work site during a calendar quarter.

(vi) *Good faith determination respected.*—A CPEO's determination that a covered employee is a work site employee will be respected if the CPEO has made a good faith determination that the covered employee meets the requirements of section 7705(e), this paragraph (b)(17), and any further guidance related to work site employee determinations.

(c) *Applicability date.*—The rules in this section apply on and after May 3, 2019. [Reg. § 301.7705-1.]

☐ [*T.D.* 9860, 5-23-2019.]

### [Reg. § 301.7705-2]

**§ 301.7705-2. CPEO certification process.**—(a) *Application requirement and certification.*—(1) *Application.*—To be certified as a certified professional employer organization (CPEO), a person must submit a properly completed and executed application for certification as a CPEO in the time and manner prescribed by, and providing such information as required by, this section and any further guidance issued by the Commissioner. In addition, the applicant's responsible individuals must submit such information as is specified in this section and further guidance.

(2) *Notice.*—A CPEO applicant will be notified by the Internal Revenue Service (IRS) whether its application for certification has been approved or denied, and, if approved, the effective date of certification. If the IRS denies the application, the IRS will inform the CPEO applicant of the reason(s) for denial. If the IRS denies an application for certification, or if the CPEO applicant withdraws an application for certification, the CPEO applicant may reapply for certification in such time and manner, and must include such information, as the Commissioner may prescribe in further guidance.

(3) *Public disclosure of certification.*—If the IRS approves a CPEO applicant's application for certification, the IRS will make available to the public the name and address of the CPEO, as well as the effective date of its certification, in the time and manner described in further guidance.

(4) *Effective date of certification.*—A CPEO's certification will be effective as of the effective date of certification specified in the notice described in paragraph (a)(2) of this section and in the public disclosure described in paragraph (a)(3) of this section and will continue in effect until the effective date of the revocation of the CPEO's certification, if any, as described in paragraph (n) of this section or, if earlier, the date that the CPEO voluntarily terminates its certification in the time and manner prescribed by the Commissioner in further guidance.

(b) *Requirements for certification.*—To receive and maintain certification, a CPEO applicant or CPEO must meet the requirements described in this section, as well as any additional requirements the Commissioner may prescribe in further guidance. In addition, any precursor entities, related entities, and responsible individuals of the CPEO applicant or CPEO must meet any requirements applicable to them described in this section and in further guidance. The IRS may deny an application for certification or revoke or suspend a CPEO's certification if a CPEO applicant or CPEO, or one or more of its precursor entities, related entities, or responsible individuals, fails to meet any applicable requirement described in this section or other applicable guidance, and the IRS will do so if the IRS determines, in its sole discretion, that such failure presents a material risk to the IRS's collection of federal employment taxes. In determining whether one or more failures to meet the requirements described in this section presents a material risk to the IRS's collection of federal employment taxes, the IRS generally will consider all relevant facts and circumstances, including the size, scope, nature, significance, recurrence, and timing of and reason for the failure and, in the case of a CPEO, any prior failures of the CPEO to meet the requirements of this section.

(c) *Suitability.*—(1) *In general.*—The IRS may deny an application for certification or revoke or suspend a CPEO's certification for any of the following reasons:

(i) The CPEO applicant or CPEO, or any of its precursor entities, related entities, or responsible individuals, has failed to pay any applicable federal, state, or local taxes or file any required federal, state, or local tax or information returns in a timely and accurate manner, unless the failure is determined to be due to reasonable cause and not due to willful neglect.

(ii) The CPEO applicant or CPEO, or any of its precursor entities, related entities, or responsible individuals, has been charged with or convicted of any criminal offense under the laws of the United States or of a state or political subdivision thereof, or is the subject of an active IRS criminal investigation.

(iii) The CPEO applicant or CPEO, or any of its precursor entities, related entities, or responsible individuals, has been sanctioned, or had a license, registration, or accreditation (including a license, registration, or accreditation relating to its status or ability to operate as a professional employer organization) denied, suspended, or revoked, by a court of competent jurisdiction, licensing board, assurance or other professional organization, or federal or state agency, court, body, board, or other authority for any misconduct that involves dishonesty, fraud, or breach of trust or that otherwise bears upon the suitability of the CPEO applicant or CPEO to perform its professional functions (including, but not limited to, any civil or criminal penalty described in 42 U.S.C. 503(k)(1)(D) imposed by state law).

(iv) The CPEO applicant or CPEO, or any of its precursor entities, related entities, or responsible individuals, is listed on any sanctions list compiled by the Office of Foreign Assets Control (OFAC) within the Department of Treasury, including, but not limited to, the OFAC Consolidated Sanctions List and the OFAC Specially Designated Nationals List.

(v) The CPEO applicant or CPEO, or any of its precursor entities, related entities, or responsible individuals, fails to demonstrate a history of financial responsibility, which the IRS may assess by checks on credit history and other similar indicators.

(vi) The CPEO applicant or CPEO and the responsible individuals of the CPEO applicant or CPEO fail to demonstrate adequate collective knowledge or experience with respect to:

(A) Federal or state employment tax reporting, depositing, and withholding requirements;

(B) Handling of and accounting for payroll, tax payments, and other funds on behalf of others;

(C) Effective recordkeeping systems;

(D) Retention of qualified personnel and legal advisors as needed; and

(E) General business and risk management.

(vii) The CPEO applicant or CPEO, or any of its responsible individuals, gives false or misleading information (including by intentionally omitting relevant information), or participates in any way in the giving of false or misleading information, to the IRS, knowing, or having reason to know, that the information is false or misleading. For the purpose of this paragraph (c)(1)(vii), "information" includes (but is not limited to) facts or other matters contained in testimony, federal tax returns, and financial statements and opinions regarding such statements; applications for certification (and all accompanying documentation); affidavits, declarations, assertions, attestations, statements, and agreements; and periodic verifications that the requirements of this section continue to be met; and any other information that is required to be provided by this section, section 3511(g), §31.3511-1 of this chapter, or further guidance.

(2) *Must be a business entity or sole proprietorship.*—(i) *In general.*—A CPEO must be a business entity described in §301.7701-2(a) or a sole proprietorship. Accordingly, a CPEO may not be an entity classified as a trust under §301.7701-4.

(ii) *Ownership by a United States person.*—In addition, a sole proprietorship or a business entity that is disregarded as an entity separate from its owner for federal tax purposes under §§301.7701-2 and 301.7701-3 (without regard to the special rule in

§301.7701-2(c)(2)(iv) that provides that such entities are corporations for federal employment tax purposes) must be wholly owned directly (including through one or more disregarded entities organized in the United States, in the case of a business entity) by a United States person (as defined in section 7701(a)(30)).

(iii) *Treatment as separate member of a controlled group.*—Except as provided in paragraph (h) of this section, a CPEO applicant or CPEO that otherwise qualifies as a member of a controlled group (within the meaning of sections 414(b) and (c) and §§1.414(b)-1 and 1.414(c)-1 through 1.414(c)-6 of this chapter) but for its status as an entity disregarded as separate from its owner for federal tax purposes under §§301.7701-2 and 301.7701-3, is treated as a separate member of a controlled group for purposes of this section, §301.7705-1, section 3511, §31.3511-1 of this chapter, and section 7705.

(3) *Authorization to investigate suitability.*—A CPEO applicant or CPEO, and each of its responsible individuals, must take such actions as are necessary to authorize the IRS to investigate the accuracy of statements and submissions, including waiving confidentiality and privilege when necessary (*i.e.*, in situations in which the IRS is otherwise unable to obtain or confirm information necessary to evaluate a CPEO applicant's or CPEO's qualification for certification), and to conduct comprehensive background checks, including, but not limited to, Federal Bureau of Investigation or other similar criminal background checks, checks on tax compliance, professional experience (including through the contact of third-party references), credit history, and professional sanctions. In addition, a CPEO applicant or CPEO, and any of its responsible individuals, must provide the IRS with such additional information as the IRS may request to facilitate such background investigations. Each responsible individual of a CPEO applicant or CPEO must also submit fingerprints in the time and manner and under the circumstances prescribed by the Commissioner in further guidance.

(d) *Business location.*—(1) *State of organization.*—A CPEO applicant or CPEO must be created or organized in the United States or under the law of the United States or of any state.

(2) *Business location in the United States.*—A CPEO applicant or CPEO must have one or more established, physical business locations in the United States at which regular operations of an activity that constitutes a trade or business within the United States (within the meaning of section 864(b)) take place and at which a significant portion of its CPEO-related functions are carried on and administrative records are kept.

(3) *United States responsible individuals.*—A majority of the CPEO applicant's or CPEO's responsible individuals must be citizens or residents of the United States.

(4) *Use of financial institution.*—A CPEO applicant or CPEO must use only financial institutions described in section 265(b)(5) to hold substantially all of its cash and cash equivalents, receive payments from customers, and pay wages and federal employment taxes.

(e) *Financial statements.*—(1) *CPEOs.*—By the last day of the sixth month after the end of each fiscal year, and beginning with the first fiscal year that ends after the CPEO's effective date of certification, a CPEO must cause to be prepared and provided to the IRS—

(i) A copy of its annual audited financial statements for the fiscal year;

(ii) An opinion of a certified public accountant (CPA) that such financial statements are presented fairly and in accordance with generally accepted accounting principles (GAAP); and

(iii) A statement in the Note to the Financial Statements covered by the CPA opinion that the CPEO's annual audited financial statements reflect positive working capital or, only if the CPEO satisfies the requirements of paragraph (e)(3) of this section, reflect negative working capital, with such statement in either case setting forth in detail a calculation of the CPEO's working capital as reflected in the annual audited financial statements (a working capital statement).

(2) *CPEO applicants.*—(i) *In general.*—A CPEO applicant must cause to be prepared and provided to the IRS, with its application, a copy of its annual audited financial statements, an opinion with respect to such financial statements, and a working capital statement (each as described in paragraph (e)(1) of this section) for the most recently completed fiscal year as of the date it applies for certification. Notwithstanding the preceding sentence, if a CPEO applicant applies for certification before the last day of the sixth month following its most recently completed fiscal year, and the audit of the financial statements for that fiscal year has not yet been completed at the time of application, a CPEO applicant must provide to the IRS, with its application, the financial statements, opinion, and working

capital statement described in paragraph (e)(1) of this section for the immediately preceding fiscal year, if any, and must subsequently provide to the IRS the financial statements, opinion, and working capital statement for the most recently completed fiscal year by the last day of the sixth month after such fiscal year ends. In addition, for any fiscal year that ends after the CPEO applicant applies for certification and on or before the effective date of certification, if applicable, the CPEO applicant must provide the audited financial statements, opinion, and working capital statement by the last day of the sixth month after such fiscal year ends. The obligation to provide the annual audited financial statements described in the preceding sentence continues to apply even if the CPEO applicant is certified as a CPEO prior to the date the annual audited financial statements are provided.

(ii) *Newly established CPEO applicants.*—In addition to the requirements in paragraph (e)(2)(i) of this section, a CPEO applicant that was not operating as a provider of payroll services for all or part of its most recently completed fiscal year as of the date it applies for certification must provide a copy of the annual audited financial statements of any precursor entity, if one exists, an opinion with respect to such financial statements, and a working capital statement (each as described in paragraph (e)(1) of this section) for the precursor entity's most recently completed fiscal year as of the date of the application for certification in such time and manner as the Commissioner may prescribe in further guidance, as well as such additional information as the Commissioner may prescribe in further guidance.

(3) *Exception to positive working capital requirement.*—A CPEO applicant or CPEO with annual audited financial statements for a fiscal year that do not reflect positive working capital will not fail to meet the requirements of paragraph (e)(1)(iii) of this section if—

(i) The CPEO applicant or CPEO has negative working capital for no more than two consecutive fiscal quarters of that fiscal year, as demonstrated by the financial statements (for the final fiscal quarter in the fiscal year) and the statements described in paragraph (f)(1)(ii) of this section (for any other fiscal quarter), as applicable;

(ii) The CPEO applicant or CPEO, or its CPA, provides, in such time and manner as the Commissioner may prescribe in further guidance, an explanation to the IRS describing the reason for the failure; and

(iii) The IRS determines, in its sole discretion, that the failure does not present a material risk to the IRS's collection of federal employment taxes.

(4) *Completed fiscal year.*—For purposes of this paragraph (e), a fiscal year will be considered completed once the last day of that fiscal year has ended, regardless of whether the CPEO applicant or CPEO was in operation or certified for all 12 months of the fiscal year or the fiscal year consisted of fewer than 12 months.

(f) *Quarterly assertions and attestations.*—(1) *CPEOs.*—By the last day of the second month after the end of each calendar quarter, and beginning with the first calendar quarter that ends after the CPEO's effective date of certification, a CPEO must provide the following to the IRS:

(i) An assertion, signed by a responsible individual under penalties of perjury, stating that the CPEO has withheld and made deposits of all federal employment taxes (other than taxes imposed by chapter 23 of the Code) as required by subtitle C for such calendar quarter and an examination level attestation from a CPA stating that such assertion is fairly stated in all material respects.

(ii) A statement signed by a responsible individual under penalties of perjury verifying that the CPEO has positive working capital (as determined in accordance with GAAP) at the end of the most recently completed fiscal quarter, as well as such additional financial information that the Commissioner may specify in further guidance.

(2) *Exceptions.*—(i) *Immaterial failures.*—A CPEO will not fail to meet the requirements of paragraph (f)(1)(i) of this section if the CPA examination level attestation indicates that the CPEO has failed to withhold or make deposits in certain immaterial respects, provided that—

(A) The attestation provides a summary of the immaterial failures that were found;

(B) The attestation states that the failures were immaterial and isolated and do not reflect a meaningful lapse in compliance with federal employment tax withholding and deposit requirements; and

(C) The IRS determines, in its sole discretion, that the isolated and immaterial failures identified by the CPA do not present a material risk to the IRS's collection of federal employment taxes.

(ii) *Negative working capital.*—A CPEO with negative working capital at the end of a fiscal quarter will not fail to meet the requirements of paragraph (f)(1)(ii) of this section if—

(A) The CPEO does not have negative working capital at the end of the two fiscal quarters immediately preceding such fiscal quarter, as demonstrated by the annual audited financial statements described in paragraph (e)(1) of this section, if available, or the statements described in paragraph (f)(1)(ii) of this section;

(B) The CPEO provides an explanation to the IRS describing the reason for such negative working capital in such time and manner as the Commissioner may prescribe in further guidance; and

(C) The IRS determines, in its sole discretion, that the negative working capital does not present a material risk to the IRS's collection of federal employment taxes.

(3) *CPEO applicants.*—(i) *In general.*—By the last day of the second month after the end of each calendar quarter, beginning with the most recently completed calendar quarter as of the date of a CPEO applicant's application for certification and ending with the most recently completed calendar quarter as of the effective date of certification (if applicable), a CPEO applicant must provide to the IRS the assertion, examination level attestation, and working capital statement described in paragraph (f)(1) of this section, subject to the exceptions described in paragraph (f)(2) of this section (though substituting "CPEO applicant" for "CPEO").

(ii) *Newly established CPEO applicants.*—A CPEO applicant that was not operating as a provider of payroll services during the most recently completed calendar quarter as of the date of its application for certification or during any calendar quarter that ends while its application for certification is pending must provide to the IRS the assertion, examination level attestation, and working capital statement described in paragraph (f)(1) of this section with respect to any precursor entity, if applicable, in such time and manner as the Commissioner may prescribe in further guidance, as well as such additional information as the Commissioner may prescribe in further guidance.

(g) *Bond.*—(1) *In general.*—A CPEO must post a bond (or bonds, as described in paragraph (g)(3) of this section) from a qualified surety (as described in paragraph (g)(6) of this section) for the payment of federal employment taxes, issued in the form and containing the terms prescribed by the Commissioner in this paragraph (g) and in further guidance and in an amount described in paragraph (g)(2) of this section.

(2) *Bond amount.*—(i) *In general.*—The amount of the bond (or bonds, as described in paragraph (g)(3) of this section) must be, for each period beginning on April 1 of any calendar year and ending on March 31 of the following calendar year (or, in the case of a newly certified CPEO, beginning with the effective date of certification and ending on the subsequent March 31) (the bond period), at least equal to the greater of—

(A) Five percent of the CPEO's liability under section 3511 (or, if applicable, the liability described in paragraph (g)(2)(ii) of this section) during the calendar year preceding the beginning of the bond period, but not more than $1,000,000; or

(B) $50,000.

(ii) *Amount of bond in first and second year as a CPEO.*—If a CPEO does not have any liability under section 3511 for all or a portion of a preceding calendar year because the CPEO was not certified as a CPEO for all or a portion of that preceding calendar year, the liability applied for purposes of paragraph (g)(2)(i)(A) of this section for the entirety or portion of the preceding calendar year during which the CPEO was not certified will be the federal employment tax liability of the CPEO, and of any precursor entity of the CPEO described in § 301.7705-1(b)(10)(i)(A), that results from one or more service agreements described in § 31.3504-2(b)(2) of this chapter. With respect to the federal employment tax liability of such precursor entity during a preceding calendar year, for purposes of paragraph (g)(2)(i)(A) of this section, the liability will be applied only to the extent it results from service agreements that have been transferred or are intended to be transferred by the precursor entity to the CPEO at the time the bond amount is determined. For purposes of this paragraph (g)(2)(ii), an entity is considered a precursor entity of a CPEO described in § 301.7705-1(b)(10)(i)(A) if it was determined to be its precursor entity under that section at the time it was a CPEO applicant.

(iii) *One continuous obligation.*—The bond, any riders thereto, and any strengthening bonds posted to satisfy the requirements of this section are considered one continuous obligation of the surety for unpaid tax liabilities accrued by the CPEO under subtitle C from the effective date of the bond until the bond is superseded or cancelled.

**Reg. § 301.7705-2(g)(2)(iii)**

*(3) Increase in bond amount.*—*(i) In general.*—A CPEO must determine if an increase in the bond amount is necessary for each new bond period. If a CPEO's liability under section 3511 (or, if applicable, the liability described in paragraph (g)(2)(ii) of this section) for the preceding calendar year results in a minimum required bond amount specified in paragraph (g)(2) of this section that exceeds the current amount of the bond, the CPEO must increase the amount of its bond with respect to the new bond period in order to meet the minimum required bond amount specified in paragraph (g)(2) of this section. To increase the bond amount, a CPEO may amend an existing bond through the use of a rider, or post a strengthening, superseding, or new bond, where applicable, and in such time and manner as the Commissioner may prescribe in further guidance.

*(ii) To reflect adjustment or assessment.*—Subject to the limit in paragraph (g)(2)(i)(A) of this section, if, during the bond period, the CPEO or the IRS determines that the applicable federal employment tax liability for the preceding calendar year was higher than the amount reported and paid and on which the bond amount for the bond period was based (and the applicable party makes an adjustment or assessment reflecting such determination), a CPEO must increase the amount of its bond to meet the minimum required bond amount specified in paragraph (g)(2) of this section through the use of a rider, or by posting a strengthening, superseding, or new bond in such time and manner as the Commissioner may prescribe in further guidance.

*(4) Cancellation.*—*(i) Notice.*—A bond required under this paragraph (g) must provide that it may be cancelled by the surety only after the surety gives written notice of such cancellation to the IRS and the CPEO in such time and manner as the Commissioner may prescribe in further guidance.

*(ii) New or superseding bond required.*—If a CPEO either receives notice of cancellation from the surety provider of its bond, or gives notice to the IRS of the CPEO's intent to cancel the bond, the CPEO must post a new or superseding bond for the minimum required bond amount specified in paragraph (g)(2) of this section in such time and manner as the Commissioner may prescribe in further guidance.

*(iii) Ongoing liability.*—A bond required under this paragraph (g) must provide that, if a surety cancels the bond without issuing a superseding bond to the CPEO, the surety will, notwithstanding the cancellation, remain liable for all federal employment tax liability accrued by the CPEO during the period beginning with the effective date of the first bond issued by the surety to the CPEO in any consecutive series of bonds issued by that surety prior to cancellation and ending with the cancellation of the bond (the total bond period), up to the penal amount of the bond at the time of the cancellation. A cancelling surety will remain liable as described in this paragraph (g)(4)(iii) for federal employment tax liability accrued during the total bond period up to the penal amount of the bond for as long as the Commissioner may assess and collect taxes for such period under sections 6501 and 6502.

*(5) No posting of collateral.*—*(i) In general.*—Except as provided in paragraph (g)(5)(iii) of this section, a CPEO must meet the bond requirements of this paragraph (g) without posting collateral.

*(ii) Surety's retention of the right to seek collateral by itself not a violation of paragraph (g)(5)(i) of this section.*—A surety's retention of the right to seek collateral, as long as no collateral is actually required by the surety or posted by the CPEO, does not violate the rule in paragraph (g)(5)(i).

*(iii) Exceptions to no collateral requirement.*—The Commissioner may provide exceptions to the rule in paragraph (g)(5)(i) of this section in further guidance published in the Internal Revenue Bulletin.

*(6) Requirements for surety.*—Any surety that issues a bond required by this paragraph (g) to a CPEO must be a surety company that holds a certificate of authority from the Secretary as an acceptable surety on federal bonds and meets such other requirements as the Commissioner may prescribe in further guidance.

*(7) Bond definitions.*—*(i) Rider.*—A rider is an amendment to an existing bond that increases the bond amount. The rider must apply to liabilities that arise on or after the effective date of the bond that the rider amends. The surety remains liable under the existing bond, as amended by the rider, for the assessment and collection periods applicable to the CPEO under sections 6501 and 6502, respectively, with respect to any taxable period that occurs during the term of the bond unless and until the bond is superseded.

*(ii) Strengthening bond.*—A strengthening bond is an additional bond posted in the incremental amount of the increase so that the strengthening bond together with the existing bond equal the total minimum required bond amount specified in paragraph (g)(2) of this section. The strengthening bond must apply to liabilities that arise on or after the effective date of the bond it strengthens. Both the strengthening bond and the bond it strengthens must remain in effect, and the surety remains liable under both bonds for the assessment and collection periods applicable to the CPEO under sections 6501 and 6502, respectively, with respect to any taxable period that occurs during the term of the bonds, unless and until the bonds are superseded.

*(iii) New bond.*—A new bond is a bond posted for the total required bond amount, and a new bond may only be posted upon the CPEO's initial certification or immediately following cancellation of an existing bond. In the case of a cancellation of an existing bond, the effective date of the new bond must be no later than the effective date of the cancellation of the existing bond, and the surety providing the existing (now cancelled) bond remains liable for liabilities that accrued during the term of the cancelled bond for the assessment and collection periods applicable to the CPEO under sections 6501 and 6502, respectively, with respect to any taxable period that occurred during the term of that bond.

*(iv) Superseding bond.*—A superseding bond is a bond posted for the total minimum required bond amount specified in paragraph (g)(2) of this section, not just for an incremental increase. Upon execution of the superseding bond, the superseded bond is no longer in effect, and the surety that provided the superseded bond is no longer liable under the superseded bond. The superseding bond must apply to liabilities that arise on or after the effective date of the superseded bond.

*(h) Controlled group.*—All CPEO applicants and CPEOs that are members of a controlled group within the meaning of sections 414(b) and (c), and §§1.414(b)-1 and 1.414(c)-1 through 1.414(c)-6 of this chapter, will be treated as a single CPEO applicant or CPEO for purposes of paragraphs (e) (other than (e)(1)(iii)), (f) (other than (f)(1)(ii)), and (g) of this section.

*(i) Consents to disclose.*—To receive and maintain certification, a CPEO applicant or CPEO must provide such consents for the IRS to disclose confidential tax information to its customers, and to other persons as necessary to carry out the purposes of these regulations, that relates to its certification and obligations to report, deposit, and pay federal employment taxes as the Commissioner may require in further guidance.

*(j) Periodic verification.*—A CPEO must periodically verify that it continues to meet the requirements of this section in the time and manner prescribed by the Commissioner in further guidance.

*(k) Notification of material changes.*—A CPEO applicant or CPEO must notify the IRS, in the time and manner prescribed by the Commissioner in further guidance, of any change that materially affects the continuing accuracy of any agreement or information that was previously made or provided to the IRS.

*(l) Accrual method of accounting.*—A CPEO must compute its taxable income using an accrual method of accounting or, if applicable, another method that the Commissioner provides for in further guidance.

*(m) Compliance with reporting obligations.*—*(1) In general.*—A CPEO must agree to make reports to the IRS and to its clients as provided in section 3511(g) and §31.3511-1 of this chapter, including filing all federal employment tax returns and information returns as required.

*(2) Filing on magnetic media.*—A CPEO must file all returns, schedules, reports, and other forms and documents on magnetic media when required by section 3511(g) and §31.3511-1 of this chapter, other Treasury regulations, or other guidance.

*(n) Suspension and revocation.*—*(1) In general.*—The IRS may suspend or revoke the certification of any CPEO, in the time and manner and under the circumstances prescribed by the Commissioner in this section and in further guidance, as a result of one or more failures to meet any of the requirements for CPEOs described in this section, section 3511(g), §31.3511-1 of this chapter, and any further guidance and will suspend or revoke certification if the IRS determines, in its sole discretion, that such failure(s) present a material risk to the IRS's collection of federal employment taxes. See paragraph (b) of this section for the factors the IRS will consider in determining whether one or more failures to meet any of the requirements described in this section presents a material risk to the IRS's collection of federal employment taxes.

*(2) Suspension.*—Section 3511 will not apply to any contract described in section 7705(e)(2) into which the CPEO enters while its certification is suspended.

(3) *Revocation.*—If an organization's certification as a CPEO is revoked, the organization will not be considered a CPEO for purposes of section 3511 unless and until it again applies to be certified as a CPEO in accordance with paragraph (a) of this section and is again certified by the IRS as meeting the requirements of this section. An organization whose certification as a CPEO has been revoked may not reapply to be certified as a CPEO until one year has passed after the effective date of its revocation.

(4) *Disclosure of suspension and revocation.*—(i) *Notification by the CPEO.*—An organization whose certification as a CPEO has been suspended or revoked must notify its customers of such suspension or revocation in the time and manner prescribed by the Commissioner in further guidance.

(ii) *Disclosure by the IRS.*—If the IRS suspends or revokes an organization's certification as a CPEO, the IRS will make available to the public the fact of such suspension or revocation in the time and manner described in further guidance. The IRS may also separately notify the organization's customers of such suspension or revocation.

(o) *Applicability date.*—The rules in this section apply on and after May 3, 2019. [Reg. § 301.7705-2.]

☐ [*T.D.* 9860, 5-23-2019.]

# General Rules

# APPLICATION OF INTERNAL REVENUE LAWS

See p. 20,601 for regulations not amended to reflect law changes

## [Reg. § 801.1]

**§ 801.1. Balanced performance measurement system; in general.**—(a) *In general.*—(1) The regulations in this part 801 implement the provisions of sections 1201 and 1204 of the Internal Revenue Service Restructuring and Reform Act of 1998 (Public Law 105-106, 112 Stat. 685, 715-716, 722) (the Act) and provide rules relating to the establishment by the Internal Revenue Service (IRS) of a balanced performance measurement system.

(2) Modern management practice and various statutory and regulatory provisions require the IRS to set performance goals for organizational units and to measure the results achieved by those units with respect to those goals. To fulfill these requirements, the IRS has established a balanced performance measurement system, composed of three elements: Customer Satisfaction Measures; Employee Satisfaction Measures; and Business Results Measures. The IRS is likewise required to establish a performance evaluation system for individual employees.

(b) [Reserved]. [Reg. § 801.1.]

☐ [*T.D.* 9227, 10-14-2005. *Redesignated and amended by T.D.* 9426, 10-10-2008.]

## [Reg. § 801.2]

**§ 801.2. Measuring organizational performance.**—The performance measures that comprise the balanced measurement system will, to the maximum extent possible, be stated in objective, quantifiable, and measurable terms and will be used to measure the overall performance of various operational units within the IRS. In addition to implementing the requirements of the Act, the measures described here will, where appropriate, be used in establishing performance goals and making performance evaluations established, inter alia, under Division E, National Defense Authorization Act for Fiscal Year 1996 (the Clinger-Cohen Act of 1996) (Public Law 104-106, 110 Stat. 186, 679); the Government Performance and Results Act of 1993 (Public Law 103-62, 107 Stat. 285); and the Chief Financial Officers Act of 1990 (Public Law 101-576, 108 Stat. 2838). Thus, organizational measures of customer satisfaction, employee satisfaction, and business results (including quality and quantity measures as described in § 801.6T) may be used to evaluate the performance of or to impose or suggest production goals for, any organizational unit. [Reg. § 801.2.]

☐ [*T.D.* 9227, 10-14-2005. *Redesignated and amended by T.D.* 9426, 10-10-2008.]

## [Reg. § 801.3]

**§ 801.3. Measuring employee performance.**—(a) *In general.*—All employees of the IRS will be evaluated according to the critical elements and standards or such other performance criteria as may be established for their positions. In accordance with the requirements of 5 U.S.C. 4312, 4313, and 9508 and section 1201 of the Act, the performance criteria for each position as are appropriate to that position, will be composed of elements that support the organizational measures of Customer Satisfaction, Employee Satisfaction, and Business Results; however, such organizational measures will not directly determine the evaluation of individual employees.

(b) *Fair and equitable treatment of taxpayers.*—In addition to all other criteria required to be used in the evaluation of employee performance, all employees of the IRS will be evaluated on whether they provided fair and equitable treatment to taxpayers.

(c) *Senior Executive Service and special positions.*—Employees in the Senior Executive Service will be rated in accordance with the requirements of 5 U.S.C. 4312 and 4313 and employees selected to fill positions under 5 U.S.C. 9503 will be evaluated pursuant to work-plans, employment agreements, performance agreements, or similar documents entered into between the IRS and the employee.

(d) *General workforce.*—The performance evaluation system for all other employees will—

(1) Establish one or more retention standards for each employee related to the work of the employee and expressed in terms of individual performance;

(2) Require periodic determinations of whether each employee meets or does not meet the employee's established retention standards;

(3) Require that action be taken in accordance with applicable laws and regulations, with respect to employees whose performance does not meet the established retention standards;

(4) Establish goals or objectives for individual performance consistent with the IRS's performance planning procedures;

(5) Use such goals and objectives to make performance distinctions among employees or groups of employees; and

(6) Use performance assessments as a basis for granting employee awards, adjusting an employee's rate of basic pay, and other appropriate personnel actions, in accordance with applicable laws and regulations.

(e) *Limitations.*—(1) No employee of the IRS may use records of tax enforcement results (as described in § 801.6) to evaluate any other employee or to impose or suggest production quotas or goals for any employee.

(i) For purposes of the limitation contained in this paragraph (e), *employee* has the meaning as defined in 5 U.S.C. 2105(a).

(ii) For purposes of the limitation contained in this paragraph (e), *evaluate* includes any process used to appraise or measure an employee's performance for purposes of providing the following:

(A) Any required or requested performance rating.

(B) A recommendation for an award covered by Chapter 45 of Title 5; 5 U.S.C. 5384; or section 1201(a) of the Act.

(C) An assessment of an employee's qualifications for promotion, reassignment, or other change in duties.

(D) An assessment of an employee's eligibility for incentives, allowances, or bonuses.

(E) Ranking of employees for release/recall and reductions in force.

(2) Employees who are responsible for exercising judgment with respect to tax enforcement results in cases concerning one or more taxpayers may be evaluated on work done on such cases only in the context of their critical elements and standards.

(3) Performance measures based in whole or in part on quantity measures (as described in § 801.6) will not be used to evaluate the performance of any non-supervisory employee who is responsible for exercising judgment with respect to tax enforcement results (as described in § 801.6). [Reg. § 801.3.]

☐ [*T.D.* 9227, 10-14-2005. *Redesignated and amended by T.D.* 9426, 10-10-2008.]

## [Reg. § 801.4]

**§ 801.4. Customer satisfaction measures.**—The customer satisfaction goals and accomplishments of operating units within the IRS will be determined on the basis of information gathered through various methods. For example, questionnaires, surveys and other types of information gathering mechanisms may be employed to gather data regarding customer satisfaction. Information to measure customer satisfaction for a particular work unit will be gathered from a statistically valid sample of the customers served by that operating unit and will be used to measure, among other things, whether those customers believe that they received courteous, timely, and professional treatment by the IRS personnel with whom they dealt. Customers will be permitted to provide information requested for these purposes under conditions that guarantee them anonymity. For purposes of this section, customers may include individual taxpayers, organizational units, or employees within the IRS and external groups affected by the services performed by the IRS operating unit. [Reg. § 801.4.]

☐ [*T.D.* 9227, 10-14-2005. *Redesignated by T.D.* 9426, 10-10-2008.]

### [Reg. § 801.5]

**§ 801.5. Employee satisfaction measures.**—(a) The employee satisfaction numerical ratings to be given to a Business Operating Division (BOD) or equivalent office within the IRS will be determined on the basis of information gathered through various methods. For example, questionnaires, surveys, and other information gathering mechanisms may be employed to gather data regarding satisfaction. The information gathered will be used to measure, among other factors bearing upon employee satisfaction, the quality of supervision, and the adequacy of training and support services. All full and part-time permanent employees of a BOD or equivalent office who are in pay and duty status will have an opportunity to provide information regarding employee satisfaction under conditions that guarantee them confidentiality.

(b) This section applies to the reporting of employee satisfaction information that occurs on or after March 7, 2018. [Reg. § 801.5.]

☐ [*T.D.* 9227, 10-14-2005. *Redesignated by T.D.* 9426, 10-10-2008. *Amended by T.D.* 9703, 11-12-2014 *and T.D.* 9831, 3-6-2018.]

### [Reg. § 801.6]

**§ 801.6. Business results measures.**—(a) *In general.*—The business results measures will consist of numerical scores determined under the quality measures and the quantity measures described elsewhere in this section.

(b) *Quality measures.*—Quality measures will be determined on the basis of a review by a specially dedicated staff within the IRS of a statistically valid sample of work items handled by certain functions or organizational units determined by the Commissioner or his delegate such as the following:

(1) *Examination and collection units and Automated Collection System Units (ACS).*—The quality review of the handling of cases involving particular taxpayers will focus on such factors as whether IRS personnel devoted an appropriate amount of time to a matter, properly analyzed the facts, and complied with statutory, regulatory, and IRS procedures, including timeliness, adequacy of notifications, and required contacts with taxpayers.

(2) *Toll-free telephone sites.*—The quality review of telephone services will focus on such factors as whether IRS personnel provided accurate tax law and account information.

(3) *Other work units.*—The quality review of other work units will be determined according to criteria prescribed by the Commissioner or his delegate.

(c) *Quantity measures.*—Quantity measures will consist of outcome-neutral production and resource data that does not contain information regarding the tax enforcement result reached in any case that involves particular taxpayers. Examples of quantity measures include, but are not limited to—

(1) Cases started;

(2) Cases closed;

(3) Work items completed;

(4) Customer education, assistance, and outreach efforts completed;

(5) Time per case;

(6) Direct examination time/out of office time;

(7) Cycle time;

(8) Number or percentage of overage cases;

(9) Inventory information;

(10) Toll-free level of access; and

(11) Talk time.

(d) *Definitions.*—(1) *Tax enforcement results.*—A tax enforcement result is the outcome produced by an IRS employee's exercise of judgment in recommending or determining whether or how the IRS should pursue enforcement of the tax laws. Examples of tax enforcement results include a lien filed, a levy served, a seizure executed, the amount assessed, the amount collected, and a fraud referral. Examples of data that are not tax enforcement results include a quantity measure and data derived from a quality review or from a review of an employee's or a work unit's work on a case, such as the number or percentage of cases in which correct examination adjustments were proposed or appropriate lien determinations were made.

(2) *Records of tax enforcement results.*—Records of tax enforcement results are data, statistics, compilations of information or other numerical or quantitative recordations of the tax enforcement results reached in one or more cases. Such records may be used for purposes such as forecasting, financial planning, resource management, and the formulation of case selection criteria. Records of tax enforcement results may be used to develop methodologies and algorithms for use in selecting tax returns to audit. Records of tax enforcement results do not include tax enforcement results of individual cases when used to determine whether an employee exercised appropriate judgment in pursuing enforcement of the tax laws based upon a review of the employee's work on that individual case. [Reg. § 801.6.]

☐ [*T.D.* 9227, 10-14-2005. *Redesignated by T.D.* 9426, 10-10-2008.]

### [Reg. § 801.7]

**§ 801.7. Examples.**—(a) The rules of § 801.3 are illustrated by the following examples:

*Example 1.* (i) Each year Division A's Examination and Collection functions develop detailed workplans that set goals for specific activities (e.g., number of audits or accounts closed) and for other quantity measures such as cases started, cycle time, overage cases, and direct examination time. These quantity measure goals are developed nationally and by Area Office based on budget allocations, available resources, historical experience, and planned improvements. These plans also include information on measures of quality, customer satisfaction, and employee satisfaction. Results are updated monthly to reflect how each organizational unit is progressing against its workplan, and this information is shared with all levels of management.

(ii) Although specific workplans are not developed at the Territory level, Headquarters management expects the Area Directors to use the information in the Area plans to guide the activity in their Territories. For 2005, Area Office 1's workplan has a goal to close 1,000 examinations of small business corporations and 120,000 taxpayer delinquent accounts (TDAs), and there are 10 Exam Territories and 12 Collection Territories in Area Office 1. While taking into account the mix and priority of workload, and available staffing and grade levels, the Examination Area Director communicates to the Territory Managers the expectation that, on average, each Territory should plan to close about 100 cases. The Collection Area Director similarly communicates to each Territory the expectation that, on average, they will close about 10,000 TDAs, subject to similar factors of workload mix and staffing.

(iii) Similar communications then occur at the next level of management between Territory Managers and their Group Managers, and between Group Managers and their employees. These communications will emphasize the overall goals of the organization and each employee's role in meeting those goals. The communications will include expectations regarding the average number of case closures that would have to occur to reach those goals, taking into account the fact that each employee's actual closures will vary based upon the facts and circumstances of specific cases.

(iv) Setting these quantity measure goals, and the communication of those goals, is permissible because case closures are a quantity measure. Case closures are an example of outcome-neutral production data that does not specify the outcome of any specific case such as the amount assessed or collected.

*Example 2.* In conducting a performance evaluation, a supervisor is permitted to take into consideration information the supervisor has developed showing that the employee failed to propose an appropriate adjustment to tax liability in one of the cases the employee examined, provided that information is derived from a review of the work done on the case. All information derived from such a review of individual cases handled by the employee, including time expended, issues raised, and enforcement outcomes reached should be considered and discussed with the employee and used in evaluating the employee.

*Example 3.* When assigning a case, a supervisor is permitted to discuss with the employee the merits, issues, and development of techniques of the case based upon a review of the case file.

*Example 4.* A supervisor is not permitted to establish a goal for proposed adjustments in a future examination.

(b) [Reserved].

[Reg. § 801.7.]

☐ [*T.D.* 9227, 10-14-2005. *Redesignated and amended by T.D.* 9426, 10-10-2008.]

### [Reg. § 801.8]

**§ 801.8. Effective/applicability dates.**—The provisions of § § 801.1 through 801.7 apply on or after October 17, 2005. [Reg. § 801.8.]

☐ [*T.D.* 9227, 10-14-2005. *Redesignated and amended by T.D.* 9426, 10-10-2008.]

**[Reg. §31.7805-1]**

**§31.7805-1. Promulgation of regulations.**—In pursuance of section 7805 of the Internal Revenue Code of 1954, the foregoing regulations are hereby prescribed. (See §31.0-3 of Subpart A of the regulations in this part relating to the scope of the regulations.) [Reg. §31.7805-1.]

☐ [T.D. 6472, 6-22-60.]

**[Reg. §301.7805-1]**

**§301.7805-1. Rules and regulations.**—(a) *Issuance.*—The Commissioner, with the approval of the Secretary, shall prescribe all needful rules and regulations for the enforcement of the Code (except where this authority is expressly given by the Code to any person other than an officer or employee of the Treasury Department), including all rules and regulations as may be necessary by reason of any alteration of law in relation to internal revenue.

(b) *Retroactivity.*—The Commissioner, with the approval of the Secretary, may prescribe the extent, if any, to which any regulation or Treasury decision relating to the internal revenue laws shall be applied without retroactive effect. The Commissioner may prescribe the extent, if any, to which any ruling relating to the internal revenue laws, issued by or pursuant to authorization from him, shall be applied without retroactive effect.

(c) *Preparation and distribution of regulations, forms, stamps, and other matters.*—The Commissioner, under the direction of the Secretary, shall prepare and distribute all the instructions, regulations, directions, forms, blanks, stamps, and other matters pertaining to the assessment and collection of internal revenue. [Reg. §301.7805-1.]

☐ [T.D. 6498, 10-24-60.]

**[Reg. §301.7811-1]**

**§301.7811-1. Authority to issue taxpayer assistance orders.**—(a) *Authority to issue.*—(1) *In general.*—When an application for a taxpayer assistance order (TAO) is filed by the taxpayer or the taxpayer's authorized representative in the form, manner and time specified in paragraph (b) of this section, the National Taxpayer Advocate (NTA) may issue a TAO if, in the determination of the NTA, the taxpayer is suffering or is about to suffer a significant hardship as a result of the manner in which the internal revenue laws are being administered by the Internal Revenue Service (IRS), including action or inaction on the part of the IRS.

(2) *The National Taxpayer Advocate defined.*—The term *National Taxpayer Advocate* includes any designee of the NTA, such as a Local Taxpayer Advocate.

(3) *Issuance without a written application.*—The NTA may issue a TAO in the absence of a written application by the taxpayer under section 7811(a).

(4) *Significant hardship.*—(i) *Determination required.*—Before a TAO may be issued, the NTA is required to make a determination regarding significant hardship.

(ii) *Term defined.*—The term *significant hardship* means a serious privation caused or about to be caused to the taxpayer as the result of the particular manner in which the revenue laws are being administered by the IRS. Significant hardship includes situations in which a system or procedure fails to operate as intended or fails to resolve the taxpayer's problem or dispute with the IRS. A significant hardship also includes, but is not limited to:

(A) An immediate threat of adverse action;

(B) A delay of more than 30 days in resolving taxpayer account problems;

(C) The incurring by the taxpayer of significant costs (including fees for professional representation) if relief is not granted; or

(D) Irreparable injury to, or a long-term adverse impact on, the taxpayer if relief is not granted.

(iii) *A delay of more than 30 days in resolving taxpayer account problems is further defined.*—A delay of more than 30 days in resolving taxpayer account problems exists under the following conditions:

(A) When a taxpayer does not receive a response by the date promised by the IRS; or

(B) When the IRS has established a normal processing time for taking an action and the taxpayer experiences a delay of more than 30 days beyond the normal processing time.

(iv) *Examples of significant hardship.*—The provisions of this section are illustrated by the following examples:

*Example 1. Immediate threat of adverse action.* The IRS serves a levy on A's bank account. A needs the bank funds to pay for a medically necessary surgical procedure that is scheduled to take place in one week. If the levy is not released, A will lack the funds necessary to have the procedure. A is experiencing an immediate threat of adverse action.

*Example 2. Delay of more than 30 days.* B files a Form 4506, "Request for a Copy of Tax Return." B does not receive the photocopy of the tax return after waiting more than 30 days beyond the normal time for processing. B is experiencing a delay of more than 30 days.

*Example 3. Significant costs.* The IRS sends XYZ, Inc. a notice requesting payment of the outstanding employment taxes and penalties owed by XYZ, Inc. The notice indicates that XYZ, Inc. has small employment tax balances with respect to 12 employment tax quarters totaling $10X. XYZ, Inc. provides documentation to the IRS which it contends shows that if all payments were applied to each quarter correctly, there would be no balance due. The IRS requests additional records and documentation. Because there are 12 quarters involved, to comply with this request XYZ, Inc. asserts that it will need to hire an accountant, who estimates he will charge at least $5X to organize all the records and provide a detailed analysis of how to apply the deposits and payments. XYZ, Inc. is facing significant costs.

*Example 4. Irreparable injury.* D has arranged with a bank to refinance his mortgage to lower his monthly payment. D is unable to make the current monthly payment. Unless the monthly payment amount is lowered, D will lose his residence to foreclosure. The IRS refuses to subordinate the Federal tax lien, as permitted by section 6325(d), or discharge the property subject to the lien, as permitted by section 6325(b). As a result, the bank will not allow D to refinance. D is facing an irreparable injury if relief is not granted.

(5) *Distinction between significant hardship and the issuance of a TAO.*—A finding that a taxpayer is suffering or about to suffer a significant hardship as a result of the manner in which the internal revenue laws are being administered by the IRS will not automatically result in the issuance of a TAO. After making a determination of significant hardship, the NTA must determine whether the facts and the law support relief for the taxpayer. In cases where any IRS employee is not following applicable published administrative guidance (including the Internal Revenue Manual), the NTA shall construe the factors taken into account in determining whether to issue a TAO in the manner most favorable to the taxpayer.

(b) *Generally.*—A TAO is an order by the NTA to the IRS. The IRS will comply with a TAO unless it is appealed and then modified or rescinded by the NTA, the Commissioner, or the Deputy Commissioner. If a TAO is modified or rescinded by the Commissioner or the Deputy Commissioner, a written explanation of the reasons for the modification or rescission must be provided to the NTA. The NTA may not make a substantive determination of any tax liability. A TAO is also not intended to be a substitute for an established administrative or judicial review procedure, but rather is intended to supplement existing procedures if a taxpayer is about to suffer or is suffering a significant hardship. A request for a TAO shall be made on a Form 911, "Request for Taxpayer Advocate Service Assistance (And Application for Taxpayer Assistance Order)" (or other specified form) or in a written statement that provides sufficient information for the Taxpayer Advocate Service (TAS) to determine the nature of the harm or the need for assistance. A taxpayer's right to administrative or judicial review will not be diminished or expanded in any way as a result of the taxpayer's seeking assistance from TAS.

(c) *Contents of Taxpayer Assistance Orders.*—After establishing that the taxpayer is facing significant hardship and determining that the facts and law support relief to the taxpayer, the NTA may issue a TAO ordering the IRS within a specified time to—

(1) *Release a levy.*—Release levied property (to the extent that the IRS may by law release such property); or

(2) *Take certain other actions.*—Cease any action, take any action as permitted by law, or refrain from taking any action with respect to a taxpayer pursuant to—

(i) Chapter 64 (relating to collection);

(ii) Chapter 70, subchapter B (relating to bankruptcy and receiverships);

(iii) Chapter 78 (relating to discovery of liability and enforcement of title); or

(iv) Any other provision of the internal revenue laws specifically described by the NTA in the TAO.

(3) *Expedite, review, or reconsider an action at a higher level.*—Although the NTA may not make the substantive determination, a TAO may be issued to require the IRS to expedite, reconsider, or review at a higher level an action taken with respect to a determination or collection of a tax liability.

(4) *Examples.*—The following examples assume the existence of significant hardship:

*Example 1.* J contacts a Local Taxpayer Advocate because a wage levy is causing financial difficulties. The NTA determines that the levy should be released as it is causing economic hardship (within the meaning of section 6343(a)(1)(D) and § 301.6343-1(b)(4)). The NTA may issue a TAO ordering the IRS to release the levy in whole or in part by a specified date.

*Example 2.* The IRS rejects K's offer in compromise. K files a Form 911, "Request for Taxpayer Advocate Service Assistance (And Application for Taxpayer Assistance Order)." The NTA discovers facts that support acceptance of the offer in compromise. The NTA may issue a TAO ordering the IRS to reconsider its rejection of the offer or to review the rejection of the offer at a higher level. The TAO may include the NTA's analysis of and recommendation for resolving the case.

*Example 3.* L files a protest requesting Appeals consideration of IRS's proposed denial of L's request for innocent spouse relief. Appeals advises L that it is going to issue a Final Determination denying the request for innocent spouse relief. L files a Form 911, "Request for Taxpayer Advocate Service Assistance (And Application for Taxpayer Assistance Order)." The NTA reviews the administrative record and concludes that the facts support granting innocent spouse relief. The NTA may issue a TAO ordering Appeals to refrain from issuing a Final Determination and reconsider or review at a higher level its decision to deny innocent spouse relief. The TAO may include the NTA's analysis of and recommendation for resolving the case.

(d) *Issuance.*—A TAO may be issued to any office, operating division, or function of the IRS. A TAO shall apply to persons performing services under a qualified tax collection contract (as defined in section 6306(b)) to the same extent and in the same manner as the order applies to IRS employees. A TAO will not be issued to IRS Criminal Investigation division (CI), or any successor IRS division responsible for the criminal investigation function, if the action ordered in the TAO could reasonably be expected to impede a criminal investigation. CI will determine whether the action ordered in the TAO could reasonably be expected to impede an investigation. Generally, a TAO may not be issued to the Office of Chief Counsel.

(e) *Suspension of statutes of limitations.*—(1) *In general.*—The running of the applicable period of limitations for any action which is the subject of a taxpayer assistance order shall be suspended for the period beginning on the date the Ombudsman receives an application for a taxpayer assistance order in the form, manner, and time specified in paragraph (b) of this section and ending on the date on which the Ombudsman makes a determination with respect to the application, and for any additional period specified by the Ombudsman in an order issued pursuant to a taxpayer's application. For the purpose of computing the period suspended, all calendar days except the date of receipt of the application shall be included.

(2) *Date of decision.*—The "date on which the Ombudsman makes a decision with respect to the application" is the date on which the taxpayer's request for a taxpayer assistance order is denied, or agreement is reached with the involved function of the Service, or a taxpayer assistance order is issued (except that when the taxpayer assistance order is reviewed by an official who may modify or rescind the taxpayer assistance order as provided in paragraph (d)

of this section, the decision date is the date on which such review is completed).

(3) *Periods suspended.*—The periods of limitations which are suspended under section 7811(d) are those which apply to the taxable periods to which the application for a taxpayer assistance order relate or the taxable periods specifically indicated in the terms of a taxpayer assistance order.

*Example (1).* On August 31, 1989, the Internal Revenue Service levies on funds in the taxpayer's checking account. On September 1, 1989, (at which time 7 months remain before the period of limitations on collection after assessment will expire on April 1, 1990) the Ombudsman receives the taxpayer's written application for a taxpayer assistance order. Subsequently, on September 6, 1989, the Ombudsman determines that the levy has caused a significant hardship and the Internal Revenue Service function which served the levy agrees to release the levy. The levy is released. As a result of the application and the decision by the Ombudsman and the involved function of the Service resolving the hardship, the statute of limitations on collection after assessment is suspended from the date the Ombudsman received the application, September 1, 1989, until the date on which the decision was made to release the levy, September 6, 1989. Therefore, the statute of limitations on collection after assessment will not expire until after April 6, 1990, which is 7 months plus 5 days after the date on which the application for a taxpayer assistance order was received by the Ombudsman.

*Example (2).* The facts are the same as in example (1) except that the Internal Revenue Service function which served the levy does not agree to release the levy, and the Ombudsman, having made a determination that the levy is causing a significant hardship, issues a taxpayer assistance order on September 6, 1989, in which the levy is ordered to be released and specifies that the statute of limitations on collection after assessment is suspended for an additional 15 days. The period of limitations on collection after assessment will therefore not expire until after April 21, 1990, which is 7 months and 20 days (5 days plus 15 days) after the application for the taxpayer assistance order was received by the Ombudsman.

*Example (3).* The facts are the same as in example (2) except that the Ombudsman does not specifically suspend the statute of limitations on collection after assessment for an additional number of days in the taxpayer assistance order, but rather the function seeks modification or rescission of the taxpayer assistance order and the appropriate official charged with that responsibility completes his consideration of the assistance order on September 8, 1989. The period of limitations on collection after assessment will therefore not expire until after April 8, 1990, which is 7 months and 7 days after the application for the taxpayer assistance order was received by the Ombudsman.

(4) *Absence of a written application.*—The statute of limitations is not suspended in cases where the Ombudsman issues an order in the absence of a written application for relief by the taxpayer or the taxpayer's duly authorized representative.

(f) *Effective/applicability date.*—These regulations are applicable for TAOs issued on or after April 1, 2011 except that paragraph (e) of this section is applicable beginning March 20, 1992. [Reg. § 301.7811-1.]

☐ [*T.D. 8246, 3-21-89. Amended by T.D. 8403, 3-20-92, T.D. 9519, 4-1-2011.*]

# PROVISIONS AFFECTING MORE THAN ONE SUBTITLE

[Reg. § 305.7871-1]

**§ 305.7871-1. Indian tribal governments treated as States for certain purposes (Temporary).**—(a) *In general.*—An Indian tribal government, as defined in section 7701(a)(40) and the regulations thereunder, shall be treated as a State, and a subdivision of an Indian tribal government, as determined under section 7871(d) and paragraph(e) of this section, shall be treated as a political subdivision of a State, under the following sections and regulations thereunder—

(1) Section 170 (relating to income tax deductions for charitable, etc., contributions and gifts), sections 2055 and 2106(a)(2) (relating to estate tax deductions for transfers of public, charitable and religious uses), and section 2522 (relating to gift tax deductions for charitable and similar gifts), for purposes of determining whether and in what amount any contribution or transfer to or for the use of an Indian tribal government (or subdivision thereof) is deductible;

(2) Section 164 (relating to deductions for taxes);

(3) Section 511 (a)(2)(B) (relating to the taxation of colleges and universities which are agencies or instrumentalities of governments or their political subdivisions);

(4) Section 37(e)(9)(A) (relating to certain public retirement systems);

(5) Section 41(c)(4) (defining "State" for purposes of credit for contributions to candidates for public offices);

(6) Section 117(b)(2)(A) (relating to scholarships and fellowship grants);

(7) Section 403(b)(1)(A)(ii) (relating to the taxation of contributions of certain employers for employee annuities);

(8) Chapter 41 of the Code (relating to tax on excess expenditures to influence legislation); and

(9) Subchapter A of chapter 42 of the Code (relating to private foundations).

(b) *Special rule for excise tax provisions.*—An Indian tribal government shall be treated as a State, and a subdivision of an Indian tribal government shall be treated as a political subdivision of a State, for purposes of any exemption from, credit or refund of, or payment with respect to, an excise tax imposed on a transaction under—

(1) Chapter 31 of the Code (relating to tax on special fuels);

(2) Chapter 32 of the Code (relating to manufacturers excise taxes);

(3) Subchapter B of chapter 33 of the Code (relating to communications excise tax); and

(4) Subchapter D of chapter 36 of the Code (relating to tax on use of certain highway vehicles),

if, in addition to satisfying all requirements applicable to a similar transaction involving a State (or political subdivision thereof) under the Code, the transaction involves the exercise of an essential governmental function of the Indian tribal government, as defined in paragraph (d) of this section.

(c) *Special rule for tax-exempt bonds.*—An Indian tribal government shall be treated as a State and a subdivision of an Indian tribal government shall be treated as a political subdivision of a State for purposes of any obligation issued by such government or subdivision under section 103 (relating to interest on certain governmental obligations) if such obligation is part of an issue substantially all of the proceeds of which are to be used in the exercise of an essential governmental function, as defined in paragraph (d) of this section. For purposes of section 7871 and this section, the "substantially all" test is the same as that provided in § 1.103-8(a)(1)(i). An Indian tribal government shall not be treated as a State and a subdivision of an Indian tribal government shall not be treated as a political subdivision of a State, however, for issues of the following private activity bonds—

(1) An industrial development bond (as defined in section 103(b)(2));

(2) An obligation described in section 103(l)(1)(A) (relating to scholarship bonds); or

(3) A mortgage subsidy bond (as defined in section 103A(b)(1), without regard to section 103A(b)(2)).

(d) *Essential governmental function.*—For purposes of section 7871 and this section, an essential governmental function of an Indian tribal government (or portion thereof) is a function of a type which is—

(1) Eligible for funding under 25 U.S.C. 13 and the regulations thereunder;

(2) Eligible for grants or contracts under 25 U.S.C. 450(f), (g), and (h) and the regulations thereunder; or

(3) An essential governmental function under section 115 and the regulations thereunder when conducted by a State or political subdivision thereof.

(e) *Treatment of subdivisions of Indian tribal governments as political subdivisions.*—A subdivision of an Indian tribal government shall be treated as a political subdivision of a State for purposes of section 7871 and this section if the Internal Revenue Service determines that the subdivision has been delegated the right to exercise one or more of the substantial governmental functions of the Indian tribal government. Designation of a subdivision of an Indian tribal government as a political subdivision of a State will be by revenue procedure. If a subdivision of an Indian tribal government is not currently designated by the applicable revenue procedure as a political subdivision of a State, and such subdivision believes that it qualifies for such designation, the subdivision may apply for a ruling from the Internal Revenue Service. In order to qualify as a political subdivision of a State, for purposes of section 7871 and this section, such subdivision must receive a favorable ruling from the Internal Revenue Service. The request for a ruling shall be made in accordance with all applicable procedural rules set forth in the Statement of Procedural Rules (26 CFR Part 601) and any applicable revenue procedures relating to submission of ruling requests. The request shall be submitted to the Internal Revenue Service, Associate Chief Counsel (Technical), Attention: CC:IND:S, Room 6545, 1111 Constitution Ave., N.W., Washington, D.C. 20224.

(f) *Effective dates.*—(1) *In general.*—Except as provided in paragraph (f)(2) of this section, the provisions of this section are effective after December 31, 1982.

(2) *Specific effective dates.*—Specific provisions of this section are effective as follows:

(i) Provisions relating to Chapter 1 of the Internal Revenue Code of 1954 (other than section 103 and section 37(e)(9)(A)) shall apply to taxable years beginning after December 31, 1982, and before January 1, 1985;

(ii) Provisions relating to section 37(e)(9)(A) shall apply to taxable years beginning after December 31, 1982, and before January 1, 1984;

(iii) Provisions relating to section 103 shall apply to obligations issued after December 31, 1982, and before January 1, 1985;

(iv) Provisions relating to chapter 11 of the Code shall apply to estates of decedents dying after December 31, 1982, and before January 1, 1985;

(v) Provisions relating to chapter 12 of the Code shall apply to gifts made after December 31, 1982, and before January 1, 1985; and

(vi) Provisions relating to taxes imposed by subtitle D of the Code shall take effect on January 1, 1983 and shall cease to apply at the close of December 31, 1984. [Temporary Reg. § 305.7871-1.]

☐ [*T.D.* 7952, 5-4-84.]

### [Reg. § 1.7872-5]

**§ 1.7872-5. Exempted loans.**—(a) *In general.*—(1) *General rule.*—Except as provided in paragraph (a)(2) of this section, notwithstanding any other provision of section 7872 and the regulations under that section, section 7872 does not apply to the loans listed in paragraph (b) of this section because the interest arrangements do not have a significant effect on the Federal tax liability of the borrower or the lender.

(2) *No exemption for tax avoidance loans.*—If a taxpayer structures a transaction to be a loan described in paragraph (b) of this section and one of the principal purposes of so structuring the transaction is the avoidance of Federal tax, then the transaction will be recharacterized as a tax avoidance loan as defined in section 7872(c)(1)(D).

(b) *List of exemptions.*—Except as provided in paragraph (a) of this section, the following transactions are exempt from section 7872:

(1) through (15) [Reserved]. For further guidance, see § 1.7872-5T(b)(1) through (15).

(16) An exchange facilitator loan (within the meaning of § 1.468B-6(c)(1)) if the amount of the exchange funds (as defined in § 1.468B-6(b)(2)) treated as loaned does not exceed $2,000,000 and the duration of the loan is 6 months or less. The Commissioner may increase this $2,000,000 loan exemption amount in published guidance of general applicability, see § 601.601(d)(2) of this chapter.

(c) [Reserved]. For further guidance, see § 1.7872-5T(c).

(d) *Effective/applicability date.*—This section applies to exchange facilitator loans issued on or after October 8, 2008. [Reg. § 1.7872-5.]

☐ [*T.D.* 9413, 7-9-2008.]

### [Reg. § 1.7872-5T]

**§ 1.7872-5T. Exempted loans (temporary).**—(a) *In general.*—(1) *General rule.*—Except as provided in paragraph (a) (2) of this section, notwithstanding any other provision of section 7872 and the regulations thereunder, section 7872 does not apply to the loans listed in paragraph (b) of this section because the interest arrangements do not have a significant effect on the Federal tax liability of the borrower or the lender.

(2) *No exemption for tax avoidance loans.*—If a taxpayer structures a transaction to be a loan described in paragraph (b) of this section and one of the principal purposes of so structuring the transaction is the avoidance of Federal tax, then the transaction will be recharacterized as a tax avoidance loan as defined in section 7872(c)(1)(D).

(b) *List of exemptions.*—Except as provided in paragraph (a) of this section, the following transactions are exempt from section 7872:

(1) Loans which are made available by the lender to the general public on the same terms and conditions and which are consistent with the lender's customary business practice;

(2) Accounts or withdrawable shares with a bank (as defined in section 581), or an institution to which section 591 applies, or a credit union, made in the ordinary course of its business;

(3) Acquisitions of publicly traded debt obligations for an amount equal to the public trading price at the time of acquisition;

(4) Loans made by a life insurance company (as defined in section 816(a)), in the ordinary course of its business, to an insured, under a loan right contained in a life insurance policy and in which the cash surrender values are used as collateral for the loans;

(5) Loans subsidized by the Federal, State (including the District of Columbia), or Municipal government (or any agency or instrumentality thereof), and which are made available under a program of general application to the public;

(6) Employee-relocation loans that meet the requirements of paragraph (c)(1) of this section;

(7) Obligations the interest on which is excluded from gross income under section 103;

(8) Obligations of the United States government;

(9) Gift loans to a charitable organization (described in section 170(c)), but only if at no time during the taxable year will the aggregate outstanding amount of loans by the lender to that organization exceed $250,000. Charitable organizations which are effectively controlled, within the meaning of section 1.482-1(a)(1), by the same person or persons shall be considered one charitable organization for purposes of this limitation.

(10) Loans made to or from a foreign person that meet the requirements of paragraph (c)(2) of this section;

(11) Loans made by a private foundation or other organization described in section 170(c), the primary purpose of which is to accomplish one or more of the purposes described in section 170(c)(2)(B);

(12) Indebtedness subject to section 482, but such indebtedness is exempt from the application of section 7872 only during the interest-free period, if any, determined under § 1.482-2(a)(1)(iii) with respect to intercompany trade receivables described in § 1.482-2(a)(1)(ii)(A)(*ii*). See also § 1.482-2(a)(3);

(13) All money, securities, and property—

(i) Received by a futures commission merchant or registered broker/dealer or by a clearing organization (A) to margin, guarantee or secure contracts for future delivery on or subject to the rules of a qualified board or exchange (as defined in section 1256(g)(7)), or (B) to purchase, margin, guarantee or secure options contracts traded on or subject to the rules of a qualified board or exchange, so long as the amounts so received to purchase, margin, guarantee or secure such contracts for future delivery or such options contracts are reasonably necessary for such purposes and so long as any commissions received by the futures commission merchant, registered broker/dealer, or clearing organization are not reduced for those making deposits of money, and all money accruing to account holders as the result of such futures and options contracts or

(ii) Received by a clearing organization from a member thereof as a required deposit to a clearing fund, guaranty fund, or similar fund maintained by the clearing organization to protect it against defaults by members.

(14) Loans the interest arrangements of which the taxpayer is able to show have no significant effect of any Federal tax liability of the lender or the borrower, as described in paragraph (c)(3) of this section; and

(15) Loans, described in revenue rulings or revenue procedures issued under section 7872(g)(1)(C), if the Commissioner finds that the factors justifying an exemption for such loans are sufficiently similar to the factors justifying the exemptions contained in this section.

(c) *Special rules.*—(1) *Employee-relocation loans.*—(i) *Mortgage loans.*—In the case of a compensation-related loan to an employee, where such loan is secured by a mortgage on the new principal residence (within the meaning of section 217 and the regulations thereunder) of the employee, acquired in connection with the transfer of that employee to a new principal place of work (which meets the requirements in section 217(c) and the regulations thereunder), the loan will be exempt from section 7872 if the following conditions are satisfied:

(A) The loan is a demand loan or is a term loan the benefits of the interest arrangements of which are not transferable by the employee and are conditioned on the future performance of substantial services by the employee;

(B) The employee certifies to the employer that the employee reasonably expects to be entitled to and will itemize deductions for each year the loan is outstanding; and

(C) The loan agreement requires that the loan proceeds be used only to purchase the new principal residence of the employee.

(ii) *Bridge loans.*—In the case of a compensation-related loan to an employee which is not described in paragraph (c)(1)(i) of this section, and which is used to purchase a new principal residence (within the meaning of section 217 and the regulations thereunder) of the employee acquired in connection with the transfer of that employee to a new principal place of work (which meets the requirements in section 217(c) and the regulations thereunder), the loan will be exempt from section 7872 if the following conditions are satisfied:

(A) The conditions contained in paragraphs (c)(1)(i)(A), (B), and (C) of this section;

(B) The loan agreement provides that the loan is payable in full within 15 days after the date of the sale of the employee's immediately former principal residence;

(C) The aggregate principal amount of all outstanding loans described in this paragraph (c)(1)(ii) to an employee is no greater than the employer's reasonable estimate of the amount of the equity of the employee and the employee's spouse in the employee's immediately former principal residence; and

(D) The employee's immediately former principal residence is not converted to business or investment use.

(2) *Below-market loans involving foreign persons.*—(i) Section 7872 shall not apply to a below-market loan (other than a compensation-related loan or a corporation-shareholder loan where the borrower is a shareholder that is not a C corporation as defined in section 1361(a)(2)) if the lender is a foreign person and the borrower is a U.S. person unless the interest income imputed to the foreign lender (without regard to this paragraph) would be effectively connected with the conduct of a U.S. trade or business within the meaning of

section 864(c) and the regulations thereunder and not exempt from U.S. income taxation under an applicable income tax treaty.

(ii) Section 7872 shall not apply to a below-market loan where both the lender and the borrower are foreign persons unless the interest income imputed to the lender (without regard to this paragraph) would be effectively connected with the conduct of a U.S. trade or business within the meaning of section 864(c) and the regulations thereunder and not exempt from U.S. income taxation under an applicable income tax treaty.

(iii) For purposes of this section, the term "foreign person" means any person that is not a U.S. person.

(3) *Loans without significant tax effect.*—Whether a loan will be considered to be a loan the interest arrangements of which have a significant effect on any Federal tax liability of the lender or the borrower will be determined according to all of the facts and circumstances. Among the factors to be considered are—

(i) whether items of income and deduction generated by the loan offset each other;

(ii) the amount of such items;

(iii) the cost to the taxpayer of complying with the provisions of section 7872 if such section were applied; and

(iv) any non-tax reasons for deciding to structure the transaction as a below-market loan rather than a loan with interest at a rate equal to or greater than the applicable Federal rate and a payment by the lender to the borrower. [Temporary Reg. § 1.7872-5T.]

☐ [T.D. 8045, 8-15-85. *Amended by T.D. 8093, 7-9-86 and T.D. 8204, 5-20-88.*]

### [Reg. § 1.7872-15]

**§ 1.7872-15. Split-dollar loans.**—(a) *General rules.*—(1) *Introduction.*—This section applies to split-dollar loans as defined in paragraph (b)(1) of this section. If a split-dollar loan is not a below-market loan, then, except as provided in this section, the loan is governed by the general rules for debt instruments (including the rules for original issue discount (OID) under sections 1271 through 1275 and the regulations thereunder). If a split-dollar loan is a below-market loan, then, except as provided in this section, the loan is governed by section 7872. The timing, amount, and characterization of the imputed transfers between the lender and borrower of a below-market split-dollar loan depend upon the relationship between the parties and upon whether the loan is a demand loan or a term loan. For additional rules relating to the treatment of split-dollar life insurance arrangements, see § 1.61-22.

(2) *Loan treatment.*—(i) *General rule.*—A payment made pursuant to a split-dollar life insurance arrangement is treated as a loan for Federal tax purposes, and the owner and non-owner are treated, respectively, as the borrower and the lender, if—

(A) The payment is made either directly or indirectly by the non-owner to the owner (including a premium payment made by the non-owner directly or indirectly to the insurance company with respect to the policy held by the owner);

(B) The payment is a loan under general principles of Federal tax law or, if it is not a loan under general principles of Federal tax law (for example, because of the nonrecourse nature of the obligation or otherwise), a reasonable person nevertheless would expect the payment to be repaid in full to the non-owner (whether with or without interest); and

(C) The repayment is to be made from, or is secured by, the policy's death benefit proceeds, the policy's cash surrender value, or both.

(ii) *Payments that are only partially repayable.*—For purposes of § 1.61-22 and this section, if a non-owner makes a payment pursuant to a split-dollar life insurance arrangement and the non-owner is entitled to repayment of some but not all of the payment, the payment is treated as two payments: one that is repayable and one that is not. Thus, paragraph (a)(2)(i) of this section refers to the repayable payment.

(iii) *Treatment of payments that are not split-dollar loans.*—See § 1.61-22(b)(5) for the treatment of payments by a non-owner that are not split-dollar loans.

(iv) *Examples.*—The provisions of this paragraph (a)(2) are illustrated by the following examples:

*Example 1.* Assume an employee owns a life insurance policy under a split-dollar life insurance arrangement, the employer makes premium payments on this policy, there is a reasonable expectation that the payments will be repaid, and the repayments are secured by the policy. Under paragraph (a)(2)(i) of this section, each premium payment is a loan for Federal tax purposes.

*Example 2.* (i) Assume an employee owns a life insurance policy under a split-dollar life insurance arrangement and the employer makes premium payments on this policy. The employer is entitled to be repaid 80 percent of each premium payment, and the repayments are secured by the policy. Under paragraph (a)(2)(ii) of this section, the taxation of 20 percent of each premium payment is governed by §1.61-22(b)(5). If there is a reasonable expectation that the remaining 80 percent of a payment will be repaid in full, then, under paragraph (a)(2)(i) of this section, the 80 percent is a loan for Federal tax purposes.

(ii) If less than 80 percent of a premium payment is reasonably expected to be repaid, then this paragraph (a)(2) does not cause any of the payment to be a loan for Federal tax purposes. If the payment is not a loan under general principles of Federal tax law, the taxation of the entire premium payment is governed by §1.61-22(b)(5).

(3) *No de minimis exceptions.*—For purposes of this section, section 7872 is applied to a split-dollar loan without regard to the de minimis exceptions in section 7872(c)(2) and (3).

(4) *Certain interest provisions disregarded.*—(i) *In general.*—If a split-dollar loan provides for the payment of interest and all or a portion of the interest is to be paid directly or indirectly by the lender (or a person related to the lender), then the requirement to pay the interest (or portion thereof) is disregarded for purposes of this section. All of the facts and circumstances determine whether a payment to be made by the lender (or a person related to the lender) is sufficiently independent from the split-dollar loan for the payment to not be an indirect payment of the interest (or a portion thereof) by the lender (or a person related to the lender).

(ii) *Examples.*—The provisions of this paragraph (a)(4) are illustrated by the following examples:

*Example 1*—(i) On January 1, 2009, Employee *B* issues a split-dollar term loan to Employer *Y*. The split-dollar term loan provides for five percent interest, compounded annually. Interest and principal on the split-dollar term loan are due at maturity. On January 1, 2009, *B* and *Y* also enter into a fully vested non-qualified deferred compensation arrangement that will provide a payment to *B* in an amount equal to the accrued but unpaid interest due at the maturity of the split-dollar term loan.

(ii) Under paragraph (a)(4)(i) of this section, *B*'s requirement to pay interest on the split-dollar term loan is disregarded for purposes of this section, and the split-dollar term loan is treated as a loan that does not provide for interest for purposes of this section.

*Example 2*—(i) On January 1, 2004, Employee *B* and Employer *Y* enter into a fully vested non-qualified deferred compensation arrangement that will provide a payment to *B* equal to *B*'s salary in the three years preceding the retirement of *B*. On January 1, 2009, *B* and *Y* enter into a split-dollar life insurance arrangement and, under the arrangement, *B* issues a split-dollar term loan to *Y* on that date. The split-dollar term loan provides for five percent interest, compounded annually. Interest and principal on the split-dollar term loan are due at maturity. Over the period in which the non-qualified deferred compensation arrangement is effective, the terms and conditions of *B*'s non-qualified deferred compensation arrangement do not change in a way that indicates that the payment of the non-qualified deferred compensation is related to *B*'s requirement to pay interest on the split-dollar term loan. No other facts and circumstances exist to indicate that the payment of the non-qualified deferred compensation is related to *B*'s requirement to pay interest on the split-dollar term loan.

(ii) The facts and circumstances indicate that the payment by *Y* of non-qualified deferred compensation is independent from *B*'s requirement to pay interest under the split-dollar term loan. Under paragraph (a)(4)(i) of this section, the fully vested non-qualified deferred compensation does not cause *B*'s requirement to pay interest on the split-dollar term loan to be disregarded for purposes of this section. For purposes of this section, the split-dollar term loan is treated as a loan that provides for stated interest of five percent, compounded annually.

(b) *Definitions.*—For purposes of this section, the terms *split-dollar life insurance arrangement*, *owner*, and *non-owner* have the same meanings as provided in §1.61-22(b) and (c). In addition, the following definitions apply for purposes of this section:

(1) A *split-dollar loan* is a loan described in paragraph (a)(2)(i) of this section.

(2) A *split-dollar demand loan* is any split-dollar loan that is payable in full at any time on the demand of the lender (or within a reasonable time after the lender's demand).

(3) A *split-dollar term loan* is any split-dollar loan other than a split-dollar demand loan. See paragraph (e)(5) of this section for special rules regarding certain split-dollar term loans payable on the death of an individual, certain split-dollar term loans conditioned on the future performance of substantial services by an individual, and gift split-dollar term loans.

(c) *Interest deductions for split-dollar loans.*—The borrower may not deduct any qualified stated interest, OID, or imputed interest on a split-dollar loan. See sections 163(h) and 264(a). In certain circumstances, an indirect participant may be allowed to deduct qualified stated interest, OID, or imputed interest on a deemed loan. See paragraph (e)(2)(iii) of this section (relating to indirect loans).

(d) *Treatment of split-dollar loans providing for nonrecourse payments.*—(1) *In general.*—Except as provided in paragraph (d)(2) of this section, if a payment on a split-dollar loan is nonrecourse to the borrower, the payment is a contingent payment for purposes of this section. See paragraph (j) of this section for the treatment of a split-dollar loan that provides for one or more contingent payments.

(2) *Exception for certain loans with respect to which the parties to the split-dollar life insurance arrangement make a representation.*—(i) *Requirement.*—An otherwise noncontingent payment on a split-dollar loan that is nonrecourse to the borrower is not a contingent payment under this section if the parties to the split-dollar life insurance arrangement represent in writing that a reasonable person would expect that all payments under the loan will be made.

(ii) *Time and manner for providing written representation.*—The Commissioner may prescribe the time and manner for providing the written representation required by paragraph (d)(2)(i) of this section. Until the Commissioner prescribes otherwise, the written representation that is required by paragraph (d)(2)(i) of this section must meet the requirements of this paragraph (d)(2)(ii). Both the borrower and the lender must sign the representation not later than the last day (including extensions) for filing the Federal income tax return of the borrower or lender, whichever is earlier, for the taxable year in which the lender makes the first split-dollar loan under the split-dollar life insurance arrangement. This representation must include the names, addresses, and taxpayer identification numbers of the borrower, lender, and any indirect participants. Unless otherwise stated therein, this representation applies to all subsequent split-dollar loans made pursuant to the split-dollar life insurance arrangement. Each party should retain an original of the representation as part of its books and records and should attach a copy of this representation to its Federal income tax return for any taxable year in which the lender makes a loan to which the representation applies.

(e) *Below-market split-dollar loans.*—(1) *Scope.*—(i) *In general.*—This paragraph (e) applies to below-market split-dollar loans enumerated under section 7872(c)(1), which include gift loans, compensation-related loans, and corporation-shareholder loans. The characterization of a split-dollar loan under section 7872(c)(1) and of the imputed transfers under section 7872(a)(1) and (b)(1) depends upon the relationship between the lender and the borrower or the lender, borrower, and any indirect participant. For example, if the lender is the borrower's employer, the split-dollar loan is generally a compensation-related loan, and any imputed transfer from the lender to the borrower is generally a payment of compensation. The loans covered by this paragraph (e) include indirect loans between the parties. See paragraph (e)(2) of this section for the treatment of certain indirect split-dollar loans. See paragraph (f) of this section for the treatment of any stated interest or OID on split-dollar loans. See paragraph (j) of this section for additional rules that apply to a split-dollar loan that provides for one or more contingent payments.

(ii) *Significant-effect split-dollar loans.*—If a direct or indirect below-market split-dollar loan is not enumerated in section 7872(c)(1)(A), (B), or (C), the loan is a significanteffect loan under section 7872(c)(1)(E).

(2) *Indirect split-dollar loans.*—(i) *In general.*—If, based on all the facts and circumstances, including the relationship between the borrower or lender and some third person (the indirect participant), the effect of a below-market split-dollar loan is to transfer value from the lender to the indirect participant and from the indirect participant to the borrower, then the below-market split-dollar loan is restructured as two or more successive below-market loans (the deemed loans) as provided in this paragraph (e)(2). The transfers of value described in the preceding sentence include (but are not limited to) a gift, compensation, a capital contribution, and a distribution under section 301 (or, in the case of an S corporation, under section 1368). The deemed loans are—

(A) A deemed below-market split-dollar loan made by the lender to the indirect participant; and

(B) A deemed below-market split-dollar loan made by the indirect participant to the borrower.

(ii) *Application.*—Each deemed loan is treated as having the same provisions as the original loan between the lender and borrower, and section 7872 is applied to each deemed loan. Thus, for example, if, under a split-dollar life insurance arrangement, an employer (lender) makes an interest-free split-dollar loan to an employee's child (borrower), the loan is restructured as a deemed compensation-related below-market split-dollar loan from the lender to the employee (the indirect participant) and a second deemed gift below-market split-dollar loan from the employee to the employee's child. In appropriate circumstances, section 7872(d)(1) may limit the interest that accrues on a deemed loan for Federal income tax purposes. For loan arrangements between husband and wife, see section 7872(f)(7).

(iii) *Limitations on investment interest for purposes of section 163(d)*.—For purposes of section 163(d), the imputed interest from the indirect participant to the lender that is taken into account by the indirect participant under this paragraph (e)(2) is not investment interest to the extent of the excess, if any, of—

(A) The imputed interest from the indirect participant to the lender that is taken into account by the indirect participant; over

(B) The imputed interest to the indirect participant from the borrower that is recognized by the indirect participant.

(iv) *Examples*.—The provisions of this paragraph (e)(2) are illustrated by the following examples:

*Example 1*. (i) On January 1, 2009, Employer *X* and Individual *A* enter into a split-dollar life insurance arrangement under which *A* is named as the policy owner. *A* is the child of *B*, an employee of *X*. On January 1, 2009, *X* makes a $30,000 premium payment, repayable upon demand without interest. Repayment of the premium payment is fully recourse to *A*. The payment is a below-market split-dollar demand loan. *A*'s net investment income for 2009 is $1,100, and there are no other outstanding loans between *A* and *B*. Assume that the blended annual rate for 2009 is 5 percent, compounded annually.

(ii) Based on the relationships among the parties, the effect of the below-market split-dollar loan from *X* to *A* is to transfer value from *X* to *B* and then to transfer value from *B* to *A*. Under paragraph (e)(2) of this section, the below-market split-dollar loan from *X* to *A* is restructured as two deemed below-market split-dollar demand loans: a compensation-related below-market split-dollar loan between *X* and *B* and a gift below-market split-dollar loan between *B* and *A*. Each of the deemed loans has the same terms and conditions as the original loan.

(iii) Under paragraph (e)(3) of this section, the amount of forgone interest deemed paid to *B* by *A* in 2009 is $1,500 ([$30,000 × 0.05] – 0). Under section 7872(d)(1), however, the amount of forgone interest deemed paid to *B* by *A* is limited to $1,100 (*A*'s net investment income for the year). Under paragraph (e)(2)(iii) of this section, *B*'s deduction under section 163(d) in 2009 for interest deemed paid on *B*'s deemed loan from *X* is limited to $1,100 (the interest deemed received from *A*).

*Example 2*. (i) The facts are the same as the facts in *Example 1*, except that *T*, an irrevocable life insurance trust established for the benefit of *A* (*B*'s child), is named as the policy owner. *T* is not a grantor trust.

(ii) Based on the relationships among the parties, the effect of the below-market split-dollar loan from *X* to *T* is to transfer value from *X* to *B* and then to transfer value from *B* to *T*. Under paragraph (e)(2) of this section, the below-market split-dollar loan from *X* to *T* is restructured as two deemed below-market split-dollar demand loans: a compensation-related below-market split-dollar loan between *X* and *B* and a gift below-market split-dollar loan between *B* and *T*. Each of the deemed loans has the same terms and conditions as the original loan.

(iii) Under paragraph (e)(3) of this section, the amount of forgone interest deemed paid to *B* by *T* in 2009 is $1,500 ([$30,000 × 0.05] – 0). Section 7872(d)(1) does not apply because *T* is not an individual. The amount of forgone interest deemed paid to *B* by *T* is $1,500. Under paragraph (e)(2)(iii) of this section, *B*'s deduction under section 163(d) in 2009 for interest deemed paid on *B*'s deemed loan from *X* is $1,500 (the interest deemed received from *T*).

(3) *Split-dollar demand loans*.—(i) *In general*.—This paragraph (e)(3) provides rules for testing split-dollar demand loans for sufficient interest, and, if the loans do not provide for sufficient interest, rules for the calculation and treatment of forgone interest on these loans. See paragraph (g) of this section for additional rules that apply to a split-dollar loan providing for certain variable rates of interest.

(ii) *Testing for sufficient interest*.—Each calendar year that a split-dollar demand loan is outstanding, the loan is tested to determine if the loan provides for sufficient interest. A split-dollar demand loan provides for sufficient interest for the calendar year if the rate (based on annual compounding) at which interest accrues on the loan's adjusted issue price during the year is no lower than the blended annual rate for the year. (The Internal Revenue Service publishes the blended annual rate in the Internal Revenue Bulletin in July of each year (see § 601.601(d)(2)(ii) of this chapter).) If the loan does not provide for sufficient interest, the loan is a below-market split-dollar demand loan for that calendar year. See paragraph

(e)(3)(iii) of this section to determine the amount and treatment of forgone interest for each calendar year the loan is below-market.

(iii) *Imputations*.—(A) *Amount of forgone interest*.—For each calendar year, the amount of forgone interest on a split-dollar demand loan is treated as transferred by the lender to the borrower and as retransferred as interest by the borrower to the lender. This amount is the excess of—

(1) The amount of interest that would have been payable on the loan for the calendar year if interest accrued on the loan's adjusted issue price at the blended annual rate (determined in paragraph (e)(3)(ii) of this section) and were payable annually on the day referred to in paragraph (e)(3)(iii)(B) of this section; over

(2) Any interest that accrues on the loan during the year.

(B) *Timing of transfers of forgone interest*.—(1) *In general*.—Except as provided in paragraphs (e)(3)(iii)(B)(2) and (3) of this section, the forgone interest (as determined under paragraph (e)(3)(iii)(A) of this section) that is attributable to a calendar year is treated as transferred by the lender to the borrower (and retransferred as interest by the borrower to the lender) on the last day of the calendar year and is accounted for by each party to the split-dollar loan in a manner consistent with that party's method of accounting.

(2) *Exception for death, liquidation, or termination of the borrower*.—In the taxable year in which the borrower dies (in the case of a borrower who is a natural person) or is liquidated or otherwise terminated (in the case of a borrower other than a natural person), any forgone interest is treated, for both the lender and the borrower, as transferred and retransferred on the last day of the borrower's final taxable year.

(3) *Exception for repayment of below-market split-dollar loan*.—Any forgone interest is treated, for both the lender and the borrower, as transferred and retransferred on the day the split-dollar loan is repaid in full.

(4) *Split-dollar term loans*.—(i) *In general*.—Except as provided in paragraph (e)(5) of this section, this paragraph (e)(4) provides rules for testing split-dollar term loans for sufficient interest and, if the loans do not provide for sufficient interest, rules for imputing payments on these loans. See paragraph (g) of this section for additional rules that apply to a split-dollar loan providing for certain variable rates of interest.

(ii) *Testing a split-dollar term loan for sufficient interest*.—A split-dollar term loan is tested on the day the loan is made to determine if the loan provides for sufficient interest. A split-dollar term loan provides for sufficient interest if the imputed loan amount equals or exceeds the amount loaned. The imputed loan amount is the present value of all payments due under the loan, determined as of the date the loan is made, using a discount rate equal to the AFR in effect on that date. The AFR used for purposes of the preceding sentence must be appropriate for the loan's term (short-term, mid-term, or long-term) and for the compounding period used in computing the present value. See section 1274(d)(1). If the split-dollar loan does not provide for sufficient interest, the loan is a below-market split-dollar term loan subject to paragraph (e)(4)(iv) of this section.

(iii) *Determining loan term*.—This paragraph (e)(4)(iii) provides rules to determine the term of a split-dollar term loan for purposes of paragraph (e)(4)(ii) of this section. The term of the loan determined under this paragraph (e)(4)(iii) (other than paragraph (e)(4)(iii)(C) of this section) applies to determine the split-dollar loan's term, payment schedule, and yield for all purposes of this section.

(A) *In general*.—Except as provided in paragraph (e)(4)(iii)(B), (C), (D) or (E) of this section, the term of a split-dollar term loan is based on the period from the date the loan is made until the loan's stated maturity date.

(B) *Special rules for certain options*.—(1) *Payment schedule that minimizes yield*.—If a split-dollar term loan is subject to one or more unconditional options that are exercisable at one or more times during the term of the loan and that, if exercised, require payments to be made on the split-dollar loan on an alternative payment schedule (for example, an option to extend or an option to call a split-dollar loan), then the rules of this paragraph (e)(4)(iii)(B)(1) determine the term of the loan. However, this paragraph (e)(4)(iii)(B)(1) applies only if the timing and amounts of the payments that comprise each payment schedule are known as of the issue date. For purposes of determining a split-dollar loan's term, the borrower is projected to exercise or not exercise an option or combination of options in a manner that minimizes the loan's overall yield. Similarly, the lender is projected to exercise or not exercise an option or combination of options in a manner that minimizes the loan's overall yield. If different projected patterns of exercise or non-exercise produce the same minimum yield, the parties are projected to exercise or not exercise an option or combination of options in a manner that produces the longest term.

(2) *Change in circumstances.*—If the borrower (or lender) does or does not exercise the option as projected under paragraph (e)(4)(iii)(B)(*1*) of this section, the split-dollar loan is treated for purposes of this section as retired and reissued on the date the option is or is not exercised for an amount of cash equal to the loan's adjusted issue price on that date. The reissued loan must be retested using the appropriate AFR in effect on the date of reissuance to determine whether it is a below-market loan.

(3) *Examples.*—The following examples illustrate the rules of this paragraph (e)(4)(iii)(B):

*Example 1.* Employee *B* issues a 10-year split-dollar term loan to Employer *Y*. *B* has the right to prepay the loan at the end of year 5. Interest is payable on the split-dollar loan at 1 percent for the first 5 years and at 10 percent for the remaining 5 years. Under paragraph (e)(4)(iii)(B)(*1*) of this section, this arrangement is treated as a 5-year split-dollar term loan from *Y* to *B*, with interest payable at 1 percent.

*Example 2.* The facts are the same as the facts in *Example 1*, except that *B* does not in fact prepay the split-dollar loan at the end of year 5. Under paragraph (e)(4)(iii)(B)(*2*) of this section, the first loan is treated as retired at the end of year 5 and a new 5-year split-dollar term loan is issued at that time, with interest payable at 10 percent.

*Example 3.* Employee *A* issues a 10-year split-dollar term loan on which the lender, Employer *X*, has the right to demand payment at the end of year 2. Interest is payable on the split-dollar loan at 7 percent each year that the loan is outstanding. Under paragraph (e)(4)(iii)(B)(*1*) of this section, this arrangement is treated as a 10-year split-dollar term loan because the exercise of *X*'s put option would not reduce the yield of the loan (the yield of the loan is 7 percent, compounded annually, whether or not *X* demands payment).

(C) *Split-dollar term loans providing for certain variable rates of interest.*—If a split-dollar term loan is subject to paragraph (g) of this section (a split-dollar loan that provides for certain variable rates of interest), the term of the loan for purposes of paragraph (e)(4)(ii) of this section is determined under paragraph (g)(3)(ii) of this section.

(D) *Split-dollar loans payable upon the death of an individual.*—If a split-dollar term loan is described in paragraph (e)(5)(ii)(A) or (v)(A) of this section, the term of the loan for purposes of paragraph (e)(4)(ii) of this section is determined under paragraph (e)(5)(ii)(C) or (v)(B)(2) of this section, whichever is applicable.

(E) *Split-dollar loans conditioned on the future performance of substantial services by an individual.*—If a split-dollar term loan is described in paragraph (e)(5)(iii)(A)(*1*) or (v)(A) of this section, the term of the loan for purposes of paragraph (e)(4)(ii) of this section is determined under paragraph (e)(5)(iii)(C) or (v)(B)(2) of this section, whichever is applicable.

(iv) *Timing and amount of imputed transfer in connection with below-market split-dollar term loans.*—If a split-dollar term loan is a below-market loan, then the rules applicable to below-market term loans under section 7872 apply. In general, the loan is recharacterized as consisting of two portions: an imputed loan amount (as defined in paragraph (e)(4)(ii) of this section) and an imputed transfer from the lender to the borrower. The imputed transfer occurs at the time the loan is made (for example, when the lender makes a premium payment on a life insurance policy) and is equal to the excess of the amount loaned over the imputed loan amount.

(v) *Amount treated as OID.*—In the case of any below-market split-dollar term loan described in this paragraph (e)(4), for purposes of applying sections 1271 through 1275 and the regulations thereunder, the issue price of the loan is the amount determined under §1.1273-2, reduced by the amount of the imputed transfer described in paragraph (e)(4)(iv) of this section. Thus, the loan is generally treated as having OID in an amount equal to the amount of the imputed transfer described in paragraph (e)(4)(iv) of this section, in addition to any other OID on the loan (determined without regard to section 7872(b)(2)(A) or this paragraph (e)(4)).

(vi) *Example.*—The provisions of this paragraph (e)(4) are illustrated by the following example:

*Example.* (i) On July 1, 2009, Corporation *Z* and Shareholder *A* enter into a split-dollar life insurance arrangement under which *A* is named as the policy owner. On July 1, 2009, *Z* makes a $100,000 premium payment, repayable without interest in 15 years. Repayment of the premium payment is fully recourse to *A*. The premium payment is a split-dollar term loan. Assume the long-term AFR

(based on annual compounding) at the time the loan is made is 7 percent.

(ii) Based on a 15-year term and a discount rate of 7 percent, compounded annually (the long-term AFR), the present value of the payments under the loan is $36,244.60, determined as follows: $100,000/[1+(0.07/1)]^{15}$. This loan is a below-market split-dollar term loan because the imputed loan amount of $36,244.60 (the present value of the amount required to be repaid to *Z*) is less than the amount loaned ($100,000).

(iii) In accordance with section 7872(b)(1) and paragraph (e)(4)(iv) of this section, on the date that the loan is made, *Z* is treated as transferring to *A* $63,755.40 (the excess of $100,000 (amount loaned) over $36,244.60 (imputed loan amount)). Under section 7872 and paragraph (e)(1)(i) of this section, *Z* is treated as making a section 301 distribution to *A* on July 1, 2009, of $63,755.40. *Z* must take into account as OID an amount equal to the imputed transfer. See §1.1272-1 for the treatment of OID.

(5) *Special rules for certain split-dollar term loans.*—(i) *In general.*—This paragraph (e)(5) provides rules for split-dollar loans payable on the death of an individual, split-dollar loans conditioned on the future performance of substantial services by an individual, and gift term loans. These split-dollar loans are split-dollar term loans for purposes of determining whether the loan provides for sufficient interest. If, however, the loan is a below-market split-dollar loan, then, except as provided in paragraph (e)(5)(v) of this section, forgone interest is determined annually, similar to a demand loan, but using an AFR that is appropriate for the loan's term and that is determined when the loan is issued.

(ii) *Split-dollar loans payable not later than the death of an individual.*—(A) *Applicability.*—This paragraph (e)(5)(ii) applies to a split-dollar term loan payable not later than the death of an individual.

(B) *Treatment of loan.*—A split-dollar loan described in paragraph (e)(5)(ii)(A) of this section is tested under paragraph (e)(4)(ii) of this section to determine if the loan provides for sufficient interest. If the loan provides for sufficient interest, then section 7872 does not apply to the loan, and the interest on the loan is taken into account under paragraph (f) of this section. If the loan does not provide for sufficient interest, then section 7872 applies to the loan, and the loan is treated as a below-market demand loan subject to paragraph (e)(3)(iii) of this section. For each year that the loan is outstanding, however, the rate used in the determination of forgone interest under paragraph (e)(3)(iii) of this section is not the blended annual rate but rather is the AFR (based on annual compounding) appropriate for the loan's term as of the month in which the loan is made. See paragraph (e)(5)(ii)(C) of this section to determine the loan's term.

(C) *Term of loan.*—For purposes of paragraph (e)(5)(ii)(B) of this section, the term of a split-dollar loan payable on the death of an individual (including the death of the last survivor of a group of individuals) is the individual's life expectancy as determined under the appropriate table in §1.72-9 on the day the loan is made. If a split-dollar loan is payable on the earlier of the individual's death or another term determined under paragraph (e)(4)(iii) of this section, the term of the loan is whichever term is shorter.

(D) *Retirement and reissuance of loan.*—If a split-dollar loan described in paragraph (e)(5)(ii)(A) of this section remains outstanding longer than the term determined under paragraph (e)(5)(ii)(C) of this section because the individual outlived his or her life expectancy, the split-dollar loan is treated for purposes of this section as retired and reissued as a split-dollar demand loan at that time for an amount of cash equal to the loan's adjusted issue price on that date. However, the loan is not retested at that time to determine whether the loan provides for sufficient interest. For purposes of determining forgone interest under paragraph (e)(5)(ii)(B) of this section, the appropriate AFR for the reissued loan is the AFR determined under paragraph (e)(5)(ii)(B) of this section on the day the loan was originally made.

(iii) *Split-dollar loans conditioned on the future performance of substantial services by an individual.*—(A) *Applicability.*—(*1*) *In general.*—This paragraph (e)(5)(iii) applies to a split-dollar term loan if the benefits of the interest arrangements of the loan are not transferable and are conditioned on the future performance of substantial services (within the meaning of section 83) by an individual.

(*2*) *Exception.*—Notwithstanding paragraph (e)(5)(iii)(A)(*1*) of this section, this paragraph (e)(5)(iii) does not apply to a split-dollar loan described in paragraph (e)(5)(v)(A) of this section (regarding a split-dollar loan that is payable on the later of a term certain and the date on which the condition to perform substantial future services by an individual ends).

(B) *Treatment of loan.*—A split-dollar loan described in paragraph (e)(5)(iii)(A)(1) of this section is tested under paragraph (e)(4)(ii) of this section to determine if the loan provides for sufficient interest. Except as provided in paragraph (e)(5)(iii)(D) of this section, if the loan provides for sufficient interest, then section 7872 does not apply to the loan and the interest on the loan is taken into account under paragraph (f) of this section. If the loan does not provide for sufficient interest, then section 7872 applies to the loan and the loan is treated as a below-market demand loan subject to paragraph (e)(3)(iii) of this section. For each year that the loan is outstanding, however, the rate used in the determination of forgone interest under paragraph (e)(3)(iii) of this section is not the blended annual rate but rather is the AFR (based on annual compounding) appropriate for the loan's term as of the month in which the loan is made. See paragraph (e)(5)(iii)(C) of this section to determine the loan's term.

(C) *Term of loan.*—The term of a split-dollar loan described in paragraph (e)(5)(iii)(A)(1) of this section is based on the period from the date the loan is made until the loan's stated maturity date. However, if a split-dollar loan described in paragraph (e)(5)(iii)(A)(1) of this section does not have a stated maturity date, the term of the loan is presumed to be seven years.

(D) *Retirement and reissuance of loan.*—If a split-dollar loan described in paragraph (e)(5)(iii)(A)(1) of this section remains outstanding longer than the term determined under paragraph (e)(5)(iii)(C) of this section because of the continued performance of substantial services, the split-dollar loan is treated for purposes of this section as retired and reissued as a split-dollar demand loan at that time for an amount of cash equal to the loan's adjusted issue price on that date. The loan is retested at that time to determine whether the loan provides for sufficient interest.

(iv) *Gift split-dollar term loans.*—(A) *Applicability.*—This paragraph (e)(5)(iv) applies to gift split-dollar term loans.

(B) *Treatment of loan.*—A split-dollar loan described in paragraph (e)(5)(iv)(A) of this section is tested under paragraph (e)(4)(ii) of this section to determine if the loan provides for sufficient interest. If the loan provides for sufficient interest, then section 7872 does not apply to the loan and the interest on the loan is taken into account under paragraph (f) of this section. If the loan does not provide for sufficient interest, then section 7872 applies to the loan and the loan is treated as a below-market demand loan subject to paragraph (e)(3)(iii) of this section. For each year that the loan is outstanding, however, the rate used in the determination of forgone interest under paragraph (e)(3)(iii) of this section is not the blended annual rate but rather is the AFR (based on annual compounding) appropriate for the loan's term as of the month in which the loan is made. See paragraph (e)(5)(iv)(C) of this section to determine the loan's term.

(C) *Term of loan.*—For purposes of paragraph (e)(5)(iv)(B) of this section, the term of a gift split-dollar term loan is the term determined under paragraph (e)(4)(iii) of this section.

(D) *Limited application for gift split-dollar term loans.*—The rules of paragraph (e)(5)(iv)(B) of this section apply to a gift split-dollar term loan only for Federal income tax purposes. For purposes of Chapter 12 of the Internal Revenue Code (relating to the gift tax), gift below-market split-dollar term loans are treated as term loans under section 7872(b) and paragraph (e)(4) of this section. See section 7872(d)(2).

(v) *Split-dollar loans payable on the later of a term certain and another specified date.*—(A) *Applicability.*—This paragraph (e)(5)(v) applies to any split-dollar term loan payable upon the later of a term certain or—

(1) The death of an individual; or

(2) For a loan described in paragraph (e)(5)(iii)(A)(1) of this section, the date on which the condition to perform substantial future services by an individual ends.

(B) *Treatment of loan.*—(1) *In general.*—A split-dollar loan described in paragraph (e)(5)(v)(A) of this section is a split-dollar term loan, subject to paragraph (e)(4) of this section.

(2) *Term of the loan.*—The term of a split-dollar loan described in paragraph (e)(5)(v)(A) of this section is the term certain.

(3) *Appropriate AFR.*—The appropriate AFR for a split-dollar loan described in paragraph (e)(5)(v)(A) of this section is based on a term of the longer of the term certain or the loan's expected term as determined under either paragraph (e)(5)(ii) or (iii) of this section, whichever is applicable.

(C) *Retirement and reissuance.*—If a split-dollar loan described in paragraph (e)(5)(v)(A) of this section remains outstanding longer than the term certain, the split-dollar loan is treated for

purposes of this section as retired and reissued at the end of the term certain for an amount of cash equal to the loan's adjusted issue price on that date. The reissued loan is subject to paragraph (e)(5)(ii) or (iii) of this section, whichever is applicable. However, the loan is not retested at that time to determine whether the loan provides for sufficient interest. For purposes of paragraph (e)(3)(iii) of this section, the appropriate AFR for the reissued loan is the AFR determined under paragraph (e)(5)(v)(B)(3) of this section on the day the loan was originally made.

(vi) *Example.*—The provisions of this paragraph (e)(5) are illustrated by the following example:

*Example.* (i) On January 1, 2009, Corporation $Y$ and Shareholder $B$, a 65 year-old male, enter into a split-dollar life insurance arrangement under which $B$ is named as the policy owner. On January 1, 2009, $Y$ makes a $100,000 premium payment, repayable, without interest, from the death benefits of the underlying contract upon $B$'s death. The premium payment is a split-dollar term loan. Repayment of the premium payment is fully recourse to $B$. Assume the long-term AFR (based on annual compounding) at the time of the loan is 7 percent. Both $Y$ and $B$ use the calendar year as their taxable years.

(ii) Based on Table 1 in §1.72-9, the expected term of the loan is 15 years. Under paragraph (e)(5)(ii)(C) of this section, the long-term AFR (based on annual compounding) is the appropriate test rate. Based on a 15-year term and a discount rate of 7 percent, compounded annually (the long-term AFR), the present value of the payments under the loan is $36,244.60, determined as follows: $100,000/[1+(0.07/1)]^{15}$. Under paragraph (e)(5)(ii)(B) of this section, this loan is a below-market split-dollar term loan because the imputed loan amount of $36,244.60 (the present value of the amount required to be repaid to $Y$) is less than the amount loaned ($100,000).

(iii) Under paragraph (e)(5)(ii)(B) of this section, the amount of forgone interest for 2009 (and each subsequent full calendar year that the loan remains outstanding) is $7,000, which is the amount of interest that would have been payable on the loan for the calendar year if interest accrued on the loan's adjusted issue price ($100,000) at the long-term AFR (7 percent, compounded annually). Under section 7872 and paragraph (e)(1)(i) of this section, on December 31, 2009, $Y$ is treated as making a section 301 distribution to $B$ of $7,000. In addition, $Y$ has $7,000 of imputed interest income for 2009.

(f) *Treatment of stated interest and OID for split-dollar loans.*—(1) *In general.*—If a split-dollar loan provides for stated interest or OID, the loan is subject to this paragraph (f), regardless of whether the split-dollar loan has sufficient interest. Except as otherwise provided in this section, split-dollar loans are subject to the same Internal Revenue Code and regulatory provisions for stated interest and OID as other loans. For example, the lender of a split-dollar loan that provides for stated interest must account for any qualified stated interest (as defined in §1.1273-1(c)) under its regular method of accounting (for example, an accrual method or the cash receipts and disbursements method). See §1.446-2 to determine the amount of qualified stated interest that accrues during an accrual period. In addition, the lender must account under §1.1272-1 for any OID on a split-dollar loan. However, §1.1272-1(c) does not apply to any split-dollar loan. See paragraph (h) of this section for a subsequent waiver, cancellation, or forgiveness of stated interest on a split-dollar loan.

(2) *Term, payment schedule, and yield.*—The term of a split-dollar term loan determined under paragraph (e)(4)(iii) of this section (other than paragraph (e)(4)(iii)(C) of this section) applies to determine the split-dollar loan's term, payment schedule, and yield for all purposes of this section.

(g) *Certain variable rates of interest.*—(1) *In general.*—This paragraph (g) provides rules for a split-dollar loan that provides for certain variable rates of interest. If this paragraph (g) does not apply to a variable rate split-dollar loan, the loan is subject to the rules in paragraph (j) of this section for split-dollar loans that provide for one or more contingent payments.

(2) *Applicability.*—(i) *In general.*—Except as provided in paragraph (g)(2)(ii) of this section, this paragraph (g) applies to a split-dollar loan that is a variable rate debt instrument (within the meaning of §1.1275-5) and that provides for stated interest at a qualified floating rate (or rates).

(ii) *Interest rate restrictions.*—This paragraph (g) does not apply to a split-dollar loan if, as a result of interest rate restrictions (such as an interest rate cap), the expected yield of the loan taking the restrictions into account is significantly less than the expected yield of the loan without regard to the restrictions. Conversely, if reasonably symmetric interest rate caps and floors or reasonably symmetric governors are fixed throughout the term of the loan, these restrictions generally do not prevent this paragraph (g) from applying to the loan.

(3) *Testing for sufficient interest.*—(i) *Demand loan.*—For purposes of paragraph (e)(3)(ii) of this section (regarding testing a split-dollar demand loan for sufficient interest), a split-dollar demand loan is treated as if it provided for a fixed rate of interest for each accrual period to which a qualified floating rate applies. The projected fixed rate for each accrual period is the value of the qualified floating rate as of the beginning of the calendar year that contains the last day of the accrual period.

(ii) *Term loan.*—For purposes of paragraph (e)(4)(ii) of this section (regarding testing a split-dollar term loan for sufficient interest), a split-dollar term loan subject to this paragraph (g) is treated as if it provided for a fixed rate of interest for each accrual period to which a qualified floating rate applies. The projected fixed rate for each accrual period is the value of the qualified floating rate on the date the split-dollar term loan is made. The term of a split-dollar loan that is subject to this paragraph (g)(3)(ii) is determined using the rules in § 1.1274-4(c)(2). For example, if the loan provides for interest at a qualified floating rate that adjusts at varying intervals, the term of the loan is determined by reference to the longest interval between interest adjustment dates. See paragraph (e)(5) of this section for special rules relating to certain split-dollar term loans, such as a split-dollar term loan payable not later than the death of an individual.

(4) *Interest accruals and imputed transfers.*—For purposes of paragraphs (e) and (f) of this section, the projected fixed rate or rates determined under paragraph (g)(3) of this section are used for purposes of determining the accrual of interest each period and the amount of any imputed transfers. Appropriate adjustments are made to the interest accruals and any imputed transfers to take into account any difference between the projected fixed rate and the actual rate.

(5) *Example.*—The provisions of this paragraph (g) are illustrated by the following example:

*Example.* (i) On January 1, 2010, Employer *V* and Employee *F* enter into a split-dollar life insurance arrangement under which *F* is named as the policy owner. On January 1, 2010, *V* makes a $100,000 premium payment, repayable in 15 years. The premium payment is a split-dollar term loan. Under the arrangement between the parties, interest is payable on the split-dollar loan each year on January 1, starting January 1, 2011, at a rate equal to the value of 1-year LIBOR as of the payment date. The short-term AFR (based on annual compounding) at the time of the loan is 7 percent. Repayment of both the premium payment and the interest due thereon is nonrecourse to *F*. However, the parties made a representation under paragraph (d)(2) of this section. Assume that the value of 1-year LIBOR on January 1, 2010, is 8 percent, compounded annually.

(ii) The loan is subject to this paragraph (g) because the loan is a variable rate debt instrument that bears interest at a qualified floating rate. Because the interest rate is reset each year, under paragraph (g)(3)(ii) of this section, the short-term AFR (based on annual compounding) is the appropriate test rate used to determine whether the loan provides for sufficient interest. Moreover, under paragraph (g)(3)(ii) of this section, to determine whether the loan provides for sufficient interest, the loan is treated as if it provided for a fixed rate of interest equal to 8 percent, compounded annually. Based on a discount rate of 7 percent, compounded annually (the short-term AFR), the present value of the payments under the loan is $109,107.91. The loan provides for sufficient interest because the loan's imputed loan amount of $109,107.91 (the present value of the payments) is more than the amount loaned of $100,000. Therefore, the loan is not a below-market split-dollar term loan, and interest on the loan is taken into account under paragraph (f) of this section.

(h) *Adjustments for interest paid at less than the stated rate.*—(1) *Application.*—(i) *In general.*—To the extent required by this paragraph (h), if accrued but unpaid interest on a split-dollar loan is subsequently waived, cancelled, or forgiven by the lender, then the waiver, cancellation, or forgiveness is treated as if, on that date, the interest had in fact been paid to the lender and retransferred by the lender to the borrower. The amount deemed transferred and retransferred is determined under paragraph (h)(2) or (3) of this section. Except as provided in paragraph (h)(1)(iv) of this section, the amount treated as retransferred by the lender to the borrower under paragraph (h)(2) or (3) of this section is increased by the deferral charge determined under paragraph (h)(4) of this section. To determine the character of any retransferred amount, see paragraph (e)(1)(i) of this section. See § 1.61-22(b)(6) for the treatment of amounts other than interest on a split-dollar loan that are waived, cancelled, or forgiven by the lender.

(ii) *Certain split-dollar term loans.*—For purposes of this paragraph (h), a split-dollar term loan described in paragraph (e)(5) of this section (for example, a split-dollar term loan payable not later than the death of an individual) is subject to the rules of paragraph (h)(3) of this section.

(iii) *Payments treated as a waiver, cancellation, or forgiveness.*—For purposes of this paragraph (h), if a payment by the lender (or a person related to the lender) to the borrower is, in substance, a waiver, cancellation, or forgiveness of accrued but unpaid interest, the payment by the lender (or person related to the lender) is treated as an amount retransferred to the borrower by the lender under this paragraph (h) and is subject to the deferral charge in paragraph (h)(4) of this section to the extent that the payment is, in substance, a waiver, cancellation, or forgiveness of accrued but unpaid interest.

(iv) *Treatment of certain nonrecourse split-dollar loans.*—For purposes of this paragraph (h), if the parties to a split-dollar life insurance arrangement make the representation described in paragraph (d)(2) of this section and the interest actually paid on the split-dollar loan is less than the interest required to be accrued on the split-dollar loan, the excess of the interest required to be accrued over the interest actually paid is treated as waived, cancelled, or forgiven by the lender under this paragraph (h). However, the amount treated as retransferred under paragraph (h)(1)(i) of this section is not increased by the deferral charge in paragraph (h)(4) of this section.

(2) *Split-dollar term loans.*—In the case of a split-dollar term loan, the amount of interest deemed transferred and retransferred for purposes of paragraph (h)(1) of this section is determined as follows:

(i) If the loan's stated rate is less than or equal to the appropriate AFR (the AFR used to test the loan for sufficient interest under paragraph (e) of this section), the amount of interest deemed transferred and retransferred pursuant to this paragraph (h) is the excess of the amount of interest payable at the stated rate over the interest actually paid.

(ii) If the loan's stated rate is greater than the appropriate AFR (the AFR used to test the loan for sufficient interest under paragraph (e) of this section), the amount of interest deemed transferred and retransferred pursuant to this paragraph (h) is the excess, if any, of the amount of interest payable at the AFR over the interest actually paid.

(3) *Split-dollar demand loans.*—In the case of a split-dollar demand loan, the amount of interest deemed transferred and retransferred for purposes of paragraph (h)(1) of this section is equal to the aggregate of—

(i) For each year that the split-dollar demand loan was outstanding in which the loan was a below-market split-dollar demand loan, the excess of the amount of interest payable at the stated rate over the interest actually paid allocable to that year; plus

(ii) For each year that the split-dollar demand loan was outstanding in which the loan was not a below-market split-dollar demand loan, the excess, if any, of the amount of interest payable at the appropriate rate used for purposes of imputation for that year over the interest actually paid allocable to that year.

(4) *Deferral charge.*—The Commissioner may prescribe the method for determining the deferral charge treated as retransferred by the lender to the borrower under paragraph (h)(1) of this section. Until the Commissioner prescribes otherwise, the deferral charge is determined under paragraph (h)(4)(i) of this section for a split-dollar term loan subject to paragraph (h)(2) of this section and under paragraph (h)(4)(ii) of this section for a split-dollar demand loan subject to paragraph (h)(3) of this section.

(i) *Split-dollar term loan.*—The deferral charge for a split-dollar term loan subject to paragraph (h)(2) of this section is determined by multiplying the hypothetical underpayment by the applicable underpayment rate, compounded daily, for the period from the date the split-dollar loan was made to the date the interest is waived, cancelled, or forgiven. The hypothetical underpayment is equal to the amount determined under paragraph (h)(2) of this section, multiplied by the highest rate of income tax applicable to the borrower (for example, the highest rate in effect under section 1 for individuals) for the taxable year in which the split-dollar term loan was made. The applicable underpayment rate is the average of the quarterly underpayment rates in effect under section 6621(a)(2) for the period from the date the split-dollar loan was made to the date the interest is waived, cancelled, or forgiven.

(ii) *Split-dollar demand loan.*—The deferral charge for a split-dollar demand loan subject to paragraph (h)(3) of this section is the sum of the following amounts determined for each year the loan was outstanding (other than the year in which the waiver, cancellation, or forgiveness occurs): For each year the loan was outstanding, multiply the hypothetical underpayment for the year by the applicable underpayment rate, compounded daily, for the applicable period. The hypothetical underpayment is equal to the amount determined under paragraph (h)(3) of this section for each year, multiplied by the highest rate of income tax applicable to the borrower for that year (for example, the highest rate in effect under section 1 for individuals). The applicable underpayment rate is the average of the quarterly underpayment rates in effect under section 6621(a)(2) for the applicable period. The applicable period for a year is the period of time from the last day of that year until the date the interest is waived, cancelled, or forgiven.

(5) *Examples.*—The provisions of this paragraph (h) are illustrated by the following examples:

*Example 1.* (i) On January 1, 2009, Employer *Y* and Employee *B* entered into a split-dollar life insurance arrangement under which *B* is named as the policy owner. On January 1, 2009, *Y* made a $100,000 premium payment, repayable on December 31, 2011, with interest of 5 percent, compounded annually. The premium payment is a split-dollar term loan. Assume the short-term AFR (based on annual compounding) at the time the loan was made was 5 percent. Repayment of both the premium payment and the interest due thereon was fully recourse to *B*. On December 31, 2011, *Y* is repaid $100,000 but *Y* waives the remainder due on the loan ($15,762.50). Both *Y* and *B* use the calendar year as their taxable years.

(ii) When the split-dollar term loan was made, the loan was not a below-market loan under paragraph (e)(4)(ii) of this section. Under paragraph (f) of this section, *Y* was required to accrue compound interest of 5 percent each year the loan remained outstanding. *B*, however, was not entitled to any deduction for this interest under paragraph (c) of this section.

(iii) Under paragraph (h)(1) of this section, the waived amount is treated as if, on December 31, 2011, it had in fact been paid to *Y* and was then retransferred by *Y* to *B*. The amount deemed transferred to *Y* and retransferred to *B* equals the excess of the amount of interest payable at the stated rate ($15,762.50) over the interest actually paid ($0), or $15,762.50. In addition, the amount deemed retransferred to *B* is increased by the deferral charge determined under paragraph (h)(4) of this section. Because of the employment relationship between *Y* and *B*, the total retransferred amount is treated as compensation paid by *Y* to *B*.

*Example 2.* (i) On January 1, 2009, Employer *Y* and Employee *B* entered into a split-dollar life insurance arrangement under which *B* is named as the policy owner. On January 1, 2009, *Y* made a $100,000 premium payment, repayable on the demand of *Y*, with interest of 7 percent, compounded annually. The premium payment is a split-dollar demand loan. Assume the blended annual rate (based on annual compounding) in 2009 was 5 percent and in 2010 was 6 percent. Repayment of both the premium payment and the interest due thereon was fully recourse to *B*. On December 31, 2010, *Y* demands repayment and is repaid its $100,000 premium payment in full; however, *Y* waives all interest due on the loan. Both *Y* and *B* use the calendar year as their taxable years.

(ii) For each year that the split-dollar demand loan was outstanding, the loan was not a below-market loan under paragraph (e)(3)(ii) of this section. Under paragraph (f) of this section, *Y* was required to accrue compound interest of 7 percent each year the loan remained outstanding. *B*, however, was not entitled to any deduction for this interest under paragraph (c) of this section.

(iii) Under paragraph (h)(1) of this section, a portion of the waived interest is treated as if, on December 31, 2010, it had in fact been paid to *Y* and was then retransferred by *Y* to *B*. The amount of interest deemed transferred to *Y* and retransferred to *B* equals the excess, if any, of the amount of interest payable at the blended annual rate for each year the loan is outstanding over the interest actually paid with respect to that year. For 2009, the interest payable at the blended annual rate is $5,000 ($100,000 × 0.05). For 2010, the interest payable at the blended annual rate is $6,000 ($100,000 × 0.06). Therefore, the amount of interest deemed transferred to *Y* and retransferred to *B* equals $11,000. In addition, the amount deemed retransferred to *B* is increased by the deferral charge determined under paragraph (h)(4) of this section. Because of the employment relationship between *Y* and *B*, the total retransferred amount is treated as compensation paid by *Y* to *B*.

(i) [Reserved]

(j) *Split-dollar loans that provide for contingent payments.*—(1) *In general.*—Except as provided in paragraph (j)(2) of this section, this paragraph (j) provides rules for a split-dollar dollar loan that provides for one or more contingent payments. This paragraph (j), rather than § 1.1275-4, applies to split-dollar loans that provide for one or more contingent payments.

(2) *Exceptions.*—(i) *Certain contingencies.*—For purposes of this section, a split-dollar loan does not provide for contingent payments merely because—

(A) The loan provides for options described in paragraph (e)(4)(iii)(B) of this section (for example, certain call options, put options, and options to extend); or

(B) The loan is described in paragraph (e)(5) of this section (relating to certain split-dollar term loans, such as a split-dollar term loan payable not later than the death of an individual).

(ii) *Insolvency and default.*—For purposes of this section, a payment is not contingent merely because of the possibility of impairment by insolvency, default, or similar circumstances. However, if any payment on a split-dollar loan is nonrecourse to the borrower, the payment is a contingent payment for purposes of this paragraph (j) unless the parties to the arrangement make the written representation provided for in paragraph (d)(2) of this section.

(iii) *Remote and incidental contingencies.*—For purposes of this section, a payment is not a contingent payment merely because of a contingency that, as of the date the split-dollar loan is made, is either remote or incidental (within the meaning of § 1.1275-2(h)).

(iv) *Exceptions for certain split-dollar loans.*—This paragraph (j) does not apply to a split-dollar loan described in § 1.1272-1(d) (certain debt instruments that provide for a fixed yield) or a split-dollar loan described in paragraph (g) of this section (relating to split-dollar loans providing for certain variable rates of interest).

(3) *Contingent split-dollar method.*—(i) *In general.*—If a split-dollar loan provides for one or more contingent payments, then the parties account for the loan under the contingent split-dollar method. In general, except as provided in this paragraph (j), this method is the same as the noncontingent bond method described in § 1.1275-4(b).

(ii) *Projected payment schedule.*—(A) *Determination of schedule.*—No comparable yield is required to be determined. The projected payment schedule for the loan includes all noncontingent payments and a projected payment for each contingent payment. The projected payment for a contingent payment is the lowest possible value of the payment. The projected payment schedule, however, must produce a yield that is not less than zero. If the projected payment schedule produces a negative yield, the schedule must be reasonably adjusted to produce a yield of zero.

(B) *Split-dollar term loans payable upon the death of an individual.*—If a split-dollar term loan described in paragraph (e)(5)(ii)(A) or (v)(A)(1) of this section provides for one or more contingent payments, the projected payment schedule is determined based on the term of the loan as determined under paragraph (e)(5)(ii)(C) or (v)(B)(2) of this section, whichever is applicable.

(C) *Certain split-dollar term loans conditioned on the future performance of substantial services by an individual.*—If a split-dollar term loan described in paragraph (e)(5)(iii)(A)(1) or (v)(A)(2) of this section provides for one or more contingent payments, the projected payment schedule is determined based on the term of the loan as determined under paragraph (e)(5)(iii)(C) or (v)(B)(2) of this section, whichever is applicable.

(D) *Demand loans.*—If a split-dollar demand loan provides for one or more contingent payments, the projected payment schedule is determined based on a reasonable assumption as to when the lender will demand repayment.

(E) *Borrower/lender consistency.*—Contrary to § 1.1275-4(b)(4)(iv), the lender rather than the borrower is required to determine the projected payment schedule and to provide the schedule to the borrower and to any indirect participant as described in paragraph (e)(2) of this section. The lender's projected payment schedule is used by the lender, the borrower, and any indirect participant to compute interest accruals and adjustments.

(iii) *Negative adjustments.*—If the issuer of a split-dollar loan is not allowed to deduct interest or OID (for example, because of section 163(h) or 264), then the issuer is not required to include in income any negative adjustment carryforward determined under § 1.1275-4(b)(6)(iii)(C) on the loan, except to the extent that at maturity the total payments made over the life of the loan are less than the issue price of the loan.

(4) *Application of section 7872.*—(i) *Determination of below-market status.*—The yield based on the projected payment schedule determined under paragraph (j)(3) of this section is used to determine whether the loan is a below-market split-dollar loan under paragraph (e) of this section.

(ii) *Adjustment upon the resolution of a contingent payment.*—To the extent that interest has accrued under section 7872 on a split-dollar loan and the interest would not have accrued under this paragraph (j) in the absence of section 7872, the lender is not required to recognize income under § 1.1275-4(b) for a positive adjustment and the borrower is not treated as having interest expense for a positive adjustment. To the same extent, there is a reversal of the tax consequences imposed under paragraph (e) of this section for the prior imputed transfer from the lender to the borrower. This reversal is taken into account in determining adjusted gross income.

(5) *Examples.*—The following examples illustrate the rules of this paragraph (j). For purposes of this paragraph (j)(5), assume that the contingent payments are neither remote nor incidental. The examples are as follows:

*Example 1.* (i) On January 1, 2010, Employer *T* and Employee *G* enter into a splitdollar life insurance arrangement under which *G* is named as the policy owner. On January 1, 2010, *T* makes a $100,000 premium payment. On December 31, 2013, *T* will be repaid an amount equal to the premium payment plus an amount based on the increase, if any, in the price of a specified commodity for the period the loan is outstanding. The premium payment is a split-dollar term loan. Repayment of both the premium payment and the interest due thereon is recourse to *G*. Assume that the appropriate AFR for this loan, based on annual compounding, is 7 percent. Both *T* and *G* use the calendar year as their taxable years.

(ii) Under this paragraph (j), the split-dollar term loan between *T* and *G* provides for a contingent payment. Therefore, the loan is subject to the contingent split-dollar method. Under this method, the projected payment schedule for the loan provides for a noncontingent payment of $100,000 and a projected payment of $0 for the contingent payment (because it is the lowest possible value of the payment) on December 31, 2013.

(iii) Based on the projected payment schedule and a discount rate of 7 percent, compounded annually (the appropriate AFR), the present value of the payments under the loan is $76,289.52. Under paragraphs (e)(4) and (j)(4)(i) of this section, the loan does not provide for sufficient interest because the loan's imputed loan amount of $76,289.52 (the present value of the payments) is less than the amount loaned of $100,000. Therefore, the loan is a below-market split-dollar term loan and the loan is recharacterized as consisting of two portions: an imputed loan amount of $76,289.52 and an imputed transfer of $23,710.48 (amount loaned of $100,000 minus the imputed loan amount of $76,289.52).

(iv) In accordance with section 7872(b)(1) and paragraph (e)(4)(iv) of this section, on the date the loan is made, *T* is treated as transferring to *G* $23,710.48 (the imputed transfer) as compensation. In addition, *T* must take into account as OID an amount equal to the imputed transfer. See § 1.1272-1 for the treatment of OID.

*Example 2.* (i) Assume, in addition to the facts in *Example 1*, that on December 31, 2013, *T* receives $115,000 (its premium payment of $100,000 plus $15,000).

(ii) Under the contingent split-dollar method, when the loan is repaid, there is a $15,000 positive adjustment ($15,000 actual payment minus $0 projected payment). Under paragraph (j)(4) of this section, because *T* accrued imputed interest under section 7872 on this split-dollar loan to *G* and this interest would not have accrued in the absence of section 7872, *T* is not required to include the positive adjustment in income, and *G* is not treated as having interest expense for the positive adjustment. To the same extent, *T* must include in income, and *G* is entitled to deduct, $15,000 to reverse their respective prior tax consequences imposed under paragraph (e) of this section (*T*'s prior deduction for imputed compensation deemed paid to *G* and *G*'s prior inclusion of this amount). *G* takes the reversal into account in determining adjusted gross income. That is, the $15,000 is an "above-the-line" deduction, whether or not *G* itemizes deductions.

*Example 3.* (i) Assume the same facts as in *Example 2*, except that on December 31, 2013, *T* receives $127,000 (its premium payment of $100,000 plus $27,000).

(ii) Under the contingent split-dollar method, when the loan is repaid, there is a $27,000 positive adjustment ($27,000 actual payment minus $0 projected payment). Under paragraph (j)(4) of this section, because *T* accrued imputed interest of $23,710.48 under section 7872 on this split-dollar loan to *G* and this interest would not have accrued in the absence of section 7872, *T* is not required to include $23,710.48 of the positive adjustment in income, and *G* is not treated as having interest expense for the positive adjustment. To the same extent, in 2013, *T* must include in income, and *G* is entitled to deduct, $23,710.48 to reverse their respective prior tax consequences imposed under paragraph (e) of this section (*T*'s prior deduction for imputed compensation deemed paid to *G* and *G*'s prior inclusion of this amount). *G* and *T* take these reversals into account in determining adjusted gross income. Under the contingent split-dollar method, *T* must include in income $3,289.52 upon resolution of the contingency ($27,000 positive adjustment minus $23,710.48).

(k) *Payment ordering rule.*—For purposes of this section, a payment made by the borrower to or for the benefit of the lender pursuant to a split-dollar life insurance arrangement is applied to all direct and indirect split-dollar loans in the following order—

(1) A payment of interest to the extent of accrued but unpaid interest (including any OID) on all outstanding split-dollar loans in the order the interest accrued;

(2) A payment of principal on the outstanding split-dollar loans in the order in which the loans were made;

(3) A payment of amounts previously paid by a non-owner pursuant to a split-dollar life insurance arrangement that were not reasonably expected to be repaid by the owner; and

(4) Any other payment with respect to a split-dollar life insurance arrangement, other than a payment taken into account under paragraphs (k)(1), (2), and (3) of this section.

(l) [Reserved]

(m) *Repayments received by a lender.*—Any amount received by a lender under a life insurance contract that is part of a split-dollar life insurance arrangement is treated as though the amount had been paid to the borrower and then paid by the borrower to the lender. Any amount treated as received by the borrower under this paragraph (m) is subject to other provisions of the Internal Revenue Code as applicable (for example, sections 72 and 101(a)). The lender must take the amount into account as a payment received with respect to a split-dollar loan, in accordance with paragraph (k) of this section. No amount received by a lender with respect to a split-dollar loan is treated as an amount received by reason of the death of the insured.

(n) *Effective date.*—(1) *General rule.*—This section applies to any split-dollar life insurance arrangement entered into after September 17, 2003. For purposes of this section, an arrangement is entered into as determined under § 1.61-22(j)(1)(ii).

(2) *Modified arrangements treated as new arrangements.*—If an arrangement entered into on or before September 17, 2003 is materially modified (within the meaning of § 1.61-22(j)(2)) after September 17, 2003, the arrangement is treated as a new arrangement entered into on the date of the modification. [Reg. § 1.7872-15.]

☐ [*T.D. 9092, 9-11-2003.*]

**[Reg. § 1.7872-16]**

**§ 1.7872-16. Loans to an exchange facilitator under § 1.468B-6.**—(a) *Exchange facilitator loans.*—This section provides rules in applying section 7872 to an exchange facilitator loan (within the meaning of § 1.468B-6(c)(1)). For purposes of this section, the terms *deferred exchange, exchange agreement, exchange facilitator, exchange funds, qualified intermediary, replacement property*, and *taxpayer* have the same meanings as in § 1.468B-6(b).

(b) *Treatment as demand loans.*—For purposes of section 7872, except as provided in paragraph (d) of this section, an exchange facilitator loan is a demand loan.

(c) *Treatment as compensation-related loans.*—If an exchange facilitator loan is a below-market loan, the loan is a compensation-related loan under section 7872(c)(1)(B).

(d) *Applicable Federal rate (AFR) for exchange facilitator loans.*—For purposes of section 7872, in the case of an exchange facilitator loan, the applicable Federal rate is the lower of the short-term AFR in effect under section 1274(d)(1) (as of the day on which the loan is made), compounded semiannually, or the 91-day rate. For purposes of the preceding sentence, the 91-day rate is equal to the investment rate on a 13-week (generally 91-day) Treasury bill with an issue date that is the same as the date that the exchange facilitator loan is made or, if the two dates are not the same, with an issue date that most closely precedes the date that the exchange facilitator loan is made.

(e) *Use of approximate method permitted.*—The taxpayer and exchange facilitator may use the approximate method to determine the amount of forgone interest on any exchange facilitator loan.

(f) *Exemption for certain below-market exchange facilitator loans.*—If an exchange facilitator loan is a below-market loan, the loan is not eligible for the exemptions from section 7872 listed under § 1.7872-5T. However, the loan may be eligible for the exemption from section 7872 under § 1.7872-5(b)(16) (relating to exchange facilitator loans in which the amount treated as loaned does not exceed $2,000,000).

(g) *Effective/applicability date.*—This section applies to exchange facilitator loans issued on or after October 8, 2008.

(h) *Example.*—The provisions of this section are illustrated by the following example:

*Example.* (i) T enters into a deferred exchange with QI, a qualified intermediary. The exchange is governed by an exchange agreement. The exchange funds held by QI pursuant to the exchange agreement are treated as loaned to QI under § 1.468B-6(c)(1). The loan between T and QI is an exchange facilitator loan. The exchange agreement between T and QI provides that no earnings will be paid to T. On December 1, 2008, T transfers property to QI, QI transfers the property to a purchaser for $2,100,000, and QI deposits $2,100,000 in a money market account. On March 1, 2009, QI uses $2,100,000 of the funds in the account to purchase replacement property identified by T, and transfers the replacement property to T. The amount loaned for purposes of section 7872 is $2,100,000 and the loan is outstanding for three months. For purposes of section 7872, under paragraph (d) of this section, T uses the 91-day rate, which is 4 percent, compounded semi-annually. T uses the approximate method for purposes of section 7872.

(ii) Under paragraphs (b) and (c) of this section, the loan from T to QI is a compensation-related demand loan. Because there is no interest payable on the loan from T to QI, the loan is a below-market loan under section 7872. The loan is not exempt under §1.7872-5(b)(16) because the amount treated as loaned exceeds $2,000,000. Under section 7872(e)(2), the amount of forgone interest on the loan for 2008 is $7000 ($2,100,000*.04/2*1/6). Under section 7872(e)(2), the amount of forgone interest for 2009 is $14,000 ($2,100,000*.04/2*2/6). The $7000 for 2008 is deemed transferred as compensation by T to QI and retransferred as interest by QI to T on December 31, 2008. The $14,000 for 2009 is deemed transferred as compensation by T to QI and retransferred as interest by QI to T on March 1, 2009. [Reg. §1.7872-16.]

☐ [T.D. 9413, 7-9-2008.]

### [Reg. §1.7874-1]

**§1.7874-1. Disregard of affiliate-owned stock.**—(a) *Scope.*—Section 7874(c)(2)(A) provides that stock of the foreign acquiring corporation held by members of the expanded affiliated group shall not be taken into account in determining ownership for purposes of section 7874(a)(2)(B)(ii). This section provides rules under section 7874(c)(2)(A). The rules provided in this section are also subject to section 7874(c)(4). For definitions that apply for purposes of this section, see 1.7874-12.

(b) *General rule.*—Except as provided in paragraph (c) of this section, for purposes of determining the ownership percentage described in section 7874(a)(2)(B)(ii), stock held by one or more members of the EAG is not included in either the numerator or the denominator of the ownership fraction.

(c) *Exceptions to general rule.*—(1) *Overview.*—Stock held by one or more members of the EAG shall be included in the denominator, but not in the numerator, of the ownership fraction, if the domestic entity acquisition qualifies as an *internal group restructuring* or results in a *loss of control*, as described in paragraph (c)(2) and (c)(3) of this section. For rules addressing the interaction of this section and other rules, see paragraph (d) of this section.

(2) *Internal group restructuring.*—For purposes of paragraph (c)(1) of this section, a domestic entity acquisition qualifies as an internal group restructuring if:

(i) Before the domestic entity acquisition, 80 percent or more of the stock (by vote and value) or the capital and profits interest, as applicable, of the domestic entity was held directly or indirectly by the corporation that is the common parent of the EAG after the acquisition; and

(ii) After the domestic entity acquisition, 80 percent or more of the stock (by vote and value) of the foreign acquiring corporation is held directly or indirectly by such common parent.

(iii) *Special rule.*—If §1.7874-6(c)(2) applies for purposes of applying section 7874(c)(2)(A) and this section, then, for purposes of paragraph (c)(2) of this section (and so much of paragraph (c)(1) of this section as relates to paragraph (c)(2) of this section), the determination of the EAG after the domestic entity acquisition, as well as the determination of stock held by one or more members of the EAG after the domestic entity acquisition, is made without regard to one or more transfers (other than by issuance), in a transaction (or series of transactions) after and related to the acquisition, of stock of the acquiring foreign corporation by one or more members of the foreign-parented group described in §1.7874-6(c)(2)(i).

(3) *Loss of control.*—For purposes of paragraph (c)(1) of this section, the domestic entity acquisition results in a loss of control if after the acquisition, the former domestic entity shareholders or former domestic entity partners do not hold, in the aggregate, directly or indirectly, more than 50 percent of the stock (by vote or value) of any member of the EAG.

(d) *Interaction of expanded affiliated group rules with other rules.*—(1) *Exclusion rules.*—Stock that is excluded from the denominator of the ownership fraction pursuant to §1.7874-4(b), 1.7874-7(b), 1.7874-8(b), 1.7874-9(b), or section 7874(c)(4) is taken into account for purposes of determining whether an entity is a member of the expanded affiliated group for purposes of applying section 7874(c)(2)(A) and paragraph (b) of this section and determining whether a domestic entity acquisition qualifies as an internal group restructuring or results in a loss of control, as described in paragraphs (c)(2) and (3) of this section, respectively. However, such stock is excluded from the denominator of the ownership fraction regardless of whether it otherwise would be included in the denomi-

nator of the ownership fraction as a result of the application of paragraph (c) of this section. See *Example 8* and *Example 9* of §1.7874-4(i) for illustrations of the application of this paragraph (d)(1).

(2) *NOCD rule.*—Stock of the foreign acquiring corporation treated as received by former domestic entity shareholders or former domestic entity partners, as applicable, under §1.7874-10(b) is not taken into account for purposes of determining whether an entity is a member of the expanded affiliated group for purposes of applying section 7874(c)(2)(A) and paragraph (b) of this section and determining whether a domestic entity acquisition qualifies as an internal group restructuring or results in a loss of control, as described in paragraphs (c)(2) and (3) of this section, respectively. However, such stock is included in the numerator and denominator of the ownership fraction, except to the extent that it is treated as held by a member of the EAG and is excluded from the numerator or both the numerator and the denominator, as applicable, under section 7874(c)(2)(A) or paragraphs (b) or (c) of this section.

(e) *Treatment of certain hook stock.*—This paragraph applies to stock of a corporation that is held by an entity in which at least 50 percent of the stock (by vote or value) or at least 50 percent of the capital or profits interest, as applicable, in such entity, is held directly or indirectly by the corporation. The stock to which this paragraph applies shall not be included in either the numerator or denominator of any fraction for the following purposes:

(1) For applying paragraph (c)(1) of this section; and

(2) For determining whether the domestic entity acquisition qualifies as an internal group restructuring (described in paragraph (c)(2) of this section) or results in a loss of control (described in paragraph (c)(3) of this section).

(f) *Stock held by a partnership.*—For purposes of this section, each partner in a partnership shall be treated as holding its proportionate share of stock held by the partnership, as determined under the rules and principles of sections 701 through 777.

(g) *Treatment of transactions related to the acquisition.*—Except as provided in paragraph (c)(2)(iii) of this section, all transactions that are related to an acquisition are taken into account in applying this section.

(h) *Examples.*—The application of this section is illustrated by the following examples. It is assumed that all transactions in the examples occur after March 4, 2003. In all the examples, if an entity or other person is not described as either domestic or foreign, it may be either domestic or foreign. In addition, each entity has only a single class of equity outstanding. Finally, the analysis of the following examples is limited to a discussion of issues under section 7874, even though the examples may raise other issues (for example, under section 367).

*Example 1. Disregard of hook stock*—(i) *Facts.* USS, a domestic corporation, has 100 shares of stock outstanding. USS's stock is held by a group of individuals. Pursuant to a plan, USS forms FS, a foreign corporation, and transfers to FS the stock of several wholly owned foreign corporations, in exchange for 90 shares of FS stock. FS then forms Merger Sub, a domestic corporation. Under a merger agreement and state law, Merger Sub merges into USS, with USS surviving the merger. In exchange for their USS stock, the former shareholders of USS receive, in the aggregate, 100 shares of newly issued FS stock. As a result of the merger FS holds 100 percent of the USS stock. USS continues to hold 90 shares of FS stock.

(ii) *Analysis.* FS has indirectly acquired substantially all the properties held directly or indirectly by USS pursuant to a plan. After the acquisition, the former shareholders of USS hold 100 shares of FS stock by reason of holding stock in USS, and USS holds 90 shares of FS stock. Under paragraph (b) of this section, the 90 shares of FS stock held by USS, a member of the EAG, are not included in either the numerator or the denominator of the ownership fraction. Accordingly, the ownership fraction is 100/100. If the condition in section 7874(a)(2)(B)(iii) is satisfied, FS is a surrogate foreign corporation which is treated as a domestic corporation under section 7874(b).

*Example 2. Internal group restructuring; wholly owned corporation*—(i) *Facts.* P, a corporation, owns all 100 outstanding shares of USS, a domestic corporation. USS forms FS, a foreign corporation, and transfers all its assets to FS in exchange for all 100 shares of the stock of FS, in a reorganization described in section 368(a)(1). P exchanges its USS stock for FS stock under section 354.

(ii) *Analysis.* FS has directly acquired substantially all the properties held directly or indirectly by USS pursuant to a plan. The acquisition is an internal group restructuring described in paragraph (c)(2) of this section because P, the common parent of the EAG after the acquisition, held directly or indirectly 80 percent or more of the stock (by vote and value) of USS before the acquisition, and after the acquisition, P holds directly or indirectly 80 percent or more of the stock (by vote and value) of FS. Accordingly, under paragraph (c)(1) of this section, the FS stock held by P is included in the denominator, but not in the numerator of the ownership fraction. Therefore, the ownership fraction is 0/100. FS is not a surrogate foreign corporation.

*Example 3. Internal group restructuring; wholly owned corporation*—(i) *Facts.* The facts are the same as in *Example 2,* except that USS does not transfer any of its assets to FS. Instead, P transfers all 100 shares of USS stock to FS in exchange for all 100 shares of FS stock.

(ii) *Analysis.* FS has indirectly acquired substantially all the properties held directly or indirectly by USS pursuant to a plan. The acquisition is an internal group restructuring described in paragraph (c)(2) of this section because P, the common parent of the EAG after the acquisition, held directly or indirectly 80 percent or more of the stock (by vote and value) of USS before the acquisition, and after the acquisition, P holds directly or indirectly 80 percent or more of the stock (by vote and value) of FS. Accordingly, under paragraph (c)(1) of this section, the FS stock held by P is included in the denominator, but not in the numerator of the ownership fraction. Accordingly, the ownership fraction is 0/100. FS is not a surrogate foreign corporation.

*Example 4. Internal group restructuring; less than wholly owned corporation*—(i) *Facts.* The facts are the same as in *Example 3,* except that P holds 85 shares of USS stock. The remaining 15 shares of USS stock are held by A, a person unrelated to P. P and A transfer their shares of USS stock to FS in exchange for 85 and 15 shares of FS stock, respectively.

(ii) *Analysis.* FS has indirectly acquired substantially all the properties held directly or indirectly by USS pursuant to a plan. The acquisition is an internal group restructuring described in paragraph (c)(2) of this section because P, the common parent of the EAG after the acquisition, held directly or indirectly 80 percent or more of the stock (by vote and value) of USS before the acquisition, and after the acquisition P holds directly or indirectly 80 percent or more of the stock (by vote and value) of FS. Therefore, under paragraph (c)(1) of this section, the FS stock held by P is included in the denominator, but not in the numerator of the ownership fraction. Accordingly, the ownership fraction is 15/100. FS is not a surrogate foreign corporation.

*Example 5. Internal group restructuring exception not applicable; less than 80 percent owned corporation*—(i) *Facts.* The facts are the same as in *Example 2,* except that P owns 55 shares of USS stock, and A, a person unrelated to P, holds 45 shares of USS stock. P and A exchange their shares of USS stock for 55 shares and 45 shares of FS stock, respectively.

(ii) *Analysis.* FS has acquired substantially all the properties held directly or indirectly by USS pursuant to a plan. P, the common parent of the EAG after the acquisition, did not hold directly or indirectly 80 percent or more of the stock (by vote and value) of USS before the acquisition, and after the acquisition P does not hold directly or indirectly 80 percent or more of the stock (by vote and value) of FS. Thus, the acquisition is not an internal group restructuring described in paragraph (c)(1) of this section, and the general rule of paragraph (b) of this section applies. Under paragraph (b) of this section, the FS stock held by P, a member of the EAG, is not included in either the numerator or the denominator of the ownership fraction. Accordingly, the ownership fraction is 45/45. If the condition in section 7874(a)(2)(B)(iii) is satisfied, FS is a surrogate foreign corporation which is treated as a domestic corporation under section 7874(b).

*Example 6. Internal group restructuring; hook stock*—(i) *Facts.* USS, a domestic corporation, has 100 shares of stock outstanding. P, a corporation, holds 80 shares of USS stock. The remaining 20 shares of USS stock are held by A, a person unrelated to P. USS owns all 30 outstanding shares of FS, a foreign corporation. Pursuant to a plan, FS forms Merger Sub, a domestic corporation. Under a merger agreement and state law, Merger Sub merges into USS, with USS surviving the merger as a subsidiary of FS. In exchange for their USS stock, P and A, the former shareholders of USS, respectively receive 56 and 14 shares of FS stock. USS continues to hold 30 shares of FS stock.

(ii) *Analysis.* FS has indirectly acquired substantially all the properties held directly or indirectly by USS pursuant to a plan. Under paragraph (b) of this section, the shares of FS stock held by P and USS, both of which are members of the EAG, are not included in either the numerator or denominator of the ownership fraction, unless the acquisition results in an internal group restructuring or loss of control of USS such that the exception of paragraph (c)(1) of this section applies. In determining whether the acquisition of USS is an internal group restructuring, under paragraph (e)(2) of this section, the FS stock held by USS is disregarded. Because P held directly or indirectly 80 percent or more of the stock (by vote and value) of USS before the acquisition, and after the acquisition P holds directly or indirectly 80 percent or more of the stock (by vote and value) of FS (when disregarding the FS stock held by USS), the acquisition is an internal group restructuring and the exception of paragraph (c)(1) of

this section applies. Accordingly, when determining whether FS is a surrogate foreign corporation, the FS stock held by P is included in the denominator, but not the numerator of the ownership fraction. However, under paragraph (b) of this section, the FS stock held by USS is not included in either the numerator or denominator of the ownership fraction. Accordingly, the ownership fraction is 14/70, or 20 percent, since only the stock held by A is included in the numerator, and the stock held by both P and A is included in the denominator. Accordingly, FS is not a surrogate foreign corporation.

*Example 7. Loss of control*—(i) *Facts.* P, a corporation, holds all the outstanding stock of USS, a domestic corporation. B, a corporation unrelated to P, holds all 60 outstanding shares of FS, a foreign corporation. P transfers to FS all the outstanding stock of USS in exchange for 40 newly issued shares of FS.

(ii) *Analysis.* FS has indirectly acquired substantially all the properties held directly or indirectly by USS pursuant to a plan. After the acquisition, B holds 60 percent of the outstanding shares of the FS stock. Accordingly, B, FS and USS are members of an EAG. After the acquisition, P does not hold directly or indirectly more than 50 percent of the stock (by vote or value) of any member of the EAG and, thus, the acquisition results in a loss of control described in paragraph (c)(3) of this section. Accordingly, under paragraph (c)(1) of this section, the FS stock owned by B is included in the denominator, but not in the numerator, of the ownership fraction. Therefore, the ownership fraction is 40/100. FS is not a surrogate foreign corporation.

*Example 8. Internal group restructuring; partnership*—(i) *Facts.* LLC, a Delaware limited liability company, is engaged in the conduct of a trade or business. P, a corporation, holds 90 percent of the interests of LLC. A, a person unrelated to P, holds 10 percent of the interests of LLC. LLC has not elected to be treated as an association taxable as a corporation. P and A transfer their interests in LLC to FS, a newly formed foreign corporation, in exchange for 90 shares and 10 shares, respectively, of FS's stock, which are all of the outstanding shares of FS. Accordingly, LLC becomes a disregarded entity.

(ii) *Analysis.* Prior to the FS's acquisition of the interests of LLC, LLC was a domestic partnership for Federal income tax purposes. FS has acquired substantially all the properties constituting a trade or business of LLC pursuant to a plan. After the acquisition, P holds 90 percent of FS's stock (by vote and value) by reason of holding a capital and profits interest in LLC, and A holds 10 percent of FS's stock (by vote and value) by reason of holding a capital and profits interest in LLC. The internal group restructuring exception under paragraph (c)(2) of this section applies, because before the acquisition, P held 80 percent or more of the capital and profits interest in LLC, and after the acquisition, P holds 80 percent or more of the stock (by vote and value) of FS. Under paragraph (c)(1) of this section, the FS stock held by P is included in the denominator, but not the numerator, of the ownership fraction. Accordingly, the ownership fraction is 10/100. FS is not a surrogate foreign corporation.

(i) *Applicability dates.*—(1) *In general.*—Except as otherwise provided, this section shall apply to domestic entity acquisitions completed on or after May 20, 2008. This section shall not, however, apply to a domestic entity acquisition that was completed on or after May 20, 2008, provided such acquisition was entered into pursuant to a written agreement which was (subject to customary conditions) binding prior to May 20, 2008, and at all times thereafter (binding commitment). For purposes of the preceding sentence, a binding commitment shall include entering into options and similar interests in connection with one or more written agreements described in the preceding sentence. Notwithstanding the general application of this paragraph, taxpayers may elect to apply this section to domestic entity acquisitions completed before May 20, 2008, but must apply it consistently to all acquisitions within its scope. Paragraph (f) of this section shall apply to acquisitions completed on or after June 7, 2012. See § 1.7874-1T(f), as contained in 26 CFR part 1 revised as of April 1, 2012, for domestic entity acquisitions completed before June 7, 2012.

(2) *Applicability date of certain provisions of this section.*—Except as provided in this paragraph (i)(2), paragraph (c)(2)(iii) of this section applies to domestic entity acquisitions completed on or after April 4, 2016. Except as provided in this paragraph (i)(2), paragraph (d) of this section (interaction of EAG rules with other rules) applies to domestic entity acquisitions completed on or after July 12, 2018. See §§ 1.7874-4(h) and 1.7874-7T(e), as contained in 26 CFR part 1 revised as of April 1, 2017, for certain coordination rules for domestic entity acquisitions completed before July 12, 2018. Except as provided in this paragraph (i)(2), paragraph (g) of this section applies to domestic entity acquisitions completed on or after September 22, 2014. For domestic entity acquisitions completed before April 4, 2016, however, taxpayers may elect to consistently apply paragraphs (c)(2)(iii) and (g) of this section, and § 1.7874-6(c)(2), (d)(2), and (f)(2)(ii). In addition, for domestic entity acquisitions completed before July 12,

2018, taxpayers may elect to consistently apply paragraph (d) of this section. [Reg. § 1.7874-1.]

☐ [T.D. 9399, 5-19-2008. *Amended by T.D. 9453, 6-9-2009; T.D. 9591, 6-7-2012, T.D. 9654, 1-16-2014, T.D. 9761, 4-4-2016; T.D. 9812, 1-13-2017 and T.D. 9834, 7-11-2018.*]

### [Reg. § 1.7874-2]

**§ 1.7874-2. Surrogate foreign corporation.**—(a) *Scope.*—This section provides rules for determining whether a foreign corporation is treated as a surrogate foreign corporation under section 7874(a)(2)(B). Paragraph (b) of this section provides definitions and special rules. Paragraph (c) of this section provides rules to determine whether a foreign corporation has acquired properties held by a domestic corporation (or a partnership). Paragraph (d) of this section provides rules that apply when two or more foreign corporations complete, in the aggregate, a domestic entity acquisition. Paragraph (e) of this section provides rules that apply when, pursuant to a plan, a single foreign corporation completes more than one domestic entity acquisition. Paragraph (f) of this section provides rules to identify the stock of a foreign corporation that is held by reason of holding stock in a domestic corporation (or an interest in a domestic partnership). Paragraph (g) of this section provides rules that treat certain publicly traded foreign partnerships as foreign corporations for purposes of section 7874. Paragraph (h) of this section provides rules concerning the treatment of certain options (or similar interests) for purposes of section 7874. Paragraph (i) of this section provides rules that treat certain interests (including debt, stock, or a partnership interest) as stock of a foreign corporation for purposes of section 7874. Paragraph (j) of this section provides rules concerning the conversion of a foreign corporation to a domestic corporation by reason of section 7874(b). Paragraph (k) of this section provides examples that illustrate the rules of this section. Paragraph (l) of this section provides the applicability dates of this section. For additional definitions that apply for purposes of this section, see § 1.7874-12.

(b) *Definitions and special rules.*—In addition to the definitions in § 1.7874-12, the following definitions and special rules apply for purposes of this section.

(1) The rules of this section are subject to section 7874(c)(4).

(2) References to *properties held* by a domestic corporation include properties held directly or indirectly by the domestic corporation.

(3) The rules and principles of sections 701 through 777 shall be applied for purposes of determining a proportionate amount (or share) of properties held by a partnership (such as stock).

(4) Any reference to the acquisition of properties held by a domestic corporation (or a partnership) includes a direct or indirect acquisition of such properties.

(5) In the case of an acquisition of stock of a domestic corporation or an interest in a partnership, the proportionate amount of properties held by the domestic corporation (or the partnership) that is treated as indirectly acquired shall, as applicable, be determined at the time of the acquisition based on the relative value of—

(i) The stock acquired compared to all outstanding stock of the domestic corporation; or

(ii) The interest acquired compared to all interests in the partnership.

(6) The determination of whether a foreign corporation is a surrogate foreign corporation is made after the domestic entity acquisition. A foreign corporation that is treated as a surrogate foreign corporation (including a surrogate foreign corporation treated as a domestic corporation described in section 7874(b)) shall continue to be treated as a surrogate foreign corporation (or a domestic corporation), even if the conditions of section 7874(a)(2)(B)(ii) and (iii) are not satisfied at a later date.

(7) A *former initial acquiring corporation shareholder* of an initial acquiring corporation means any person that held stock in the initial acquiring corporation before the subsequent acquisition, including any person that holds stock in the initial acquiring corporation both before and after the subsequent acquisition.

(8) An *initial acquisition* means, with respect to a subsequent acquisition, a domestic entity acquisition occurring, pursuant to a plan that includes the subsequent acquisition (or a series of related transactions), before the subsequent acquisition.

(9) An *initial acquiring corporation* means, with respect to an initial acquisition, the foreign acquiring corporation.

(10) A *subsequent acquisition* means, with respect to an initial acquisition, a transaction occurring, pursuant to a plan that includes the initial acquisition (or a series of related transactions), after the initial acquisition in which a foreign corporation directly or indirectly acquires (within the meaning of paragraph (c)(4)(ii) of this section) substantially all of the properties held directly or indirectly by the initial acquiring corporation.

(11) A *subsequent acquiring corporation* means, with respect to a subsequent acquisition, the foreign corporation that directly or indirectly acquires substantially all of the properties held directly or indirectly by the initial acquiring corporation.

(12) *Special rule regarding initial acquisitions.*—With respect to an initial acquisition, the determination of the ownership percentage described in section 7874(a)(2)(B)(ii) is made without regard to the subsequent acquisition and all related transactions occurring after the subsequent acquisition.

(13) *Special rule regarding subsequent acquisitions.*—With respect to a subsequent acquisition (or a similar acquisition under the principles of paragraph (c)(4)(i) of this section) that is an inversion transaction, the applicable period begins on the first date that properties are acquired as part of the initial acquisition.

(c) *Acquisition of properties.*—(1) *Indirect acquisition of properties.*—For purposes of section 7874(a)(2)(B)(i), an indirect acquisition of properties held by a domestic corporation (or a partnership) includes, but is not limited to, the acquisitions described in paragraphs (c)(1)(i) through (iv) of this section. An acquisition of less than all of the stock of a domestic corporation (or interests in a partnership) shall constitute an indirect acquisition of a proportionate amount of the properties held by the domestic corporation or the partnership. See paragraph (b)(8) of this section for rules determining the proportionate amount of properties indirectly acquired.

(i) An acquisition of stock of a domestic corporation. See *Example 1* of paragraph (k) of this section for an illustration of the rules of this paragraph (c)(1)(i).

(ii) An acquisition of an interest in a partnership. See *Example 2* of paragraph (k) of this section for an illustration of the rules of this paragraph (c)(1)(ii).

(iii) An acquisition by a corporation (acquiring corporation) of properties held by a domestic corporation (or a partnership) in exchange for stock of a foreign corporation (foreign issuing corporation) that is part of the expanded affiliated group that includes the acquiring corporation after the acquisition shall be treated as an acquisition by the foreign issuing corporation. See *Example 3* of paragraph (k) of this section for an illustration of the rules of this paragraph (c)(1)(iii).

(iv) An acquisition by a partnership (acquiring partnership) of properties held by a domestic corporation (or a partnership) in exchange for stock of a foreign corporation that is part of the expanded affiliated group that would include the acquiring partnership after the acquisition (if the partnership were a corporation) shall be treated as an acquisition by the foreign issuing corporation.

(2) *Acquisition of stock of a foreign corporation.*—Except as provided in paragraph (c)(4) of this section, an acquisition of stock of a foreign corporation that owns directly or indirectly stock of a domestic corporation (or an interest in a partnership) shall not constitute an indirect acquisition of any properties held by the domestic corporation (or the partnership). See *Example 4* of paragraph (k) of this section for an illustration of the rules of this paragraph (c)(2).

(3) *Downstream transactions.*—An acquisition by a corporation of its stock from another corporation or a partnership (for example, as a result of a downstream merger) is an acquisition of the other corporation's or partnership's properties for purposes of section 7874(a)(2)(B)(i).

(4) *Multiple-step acquisitions.*—(i) *Rule.*—A subsequent acquisition is treated as a domestic entity acquisition, and the subsequent acquiring corporation is treated as a foreign acquiring corporation. See *Example 21* of paragraph (k) of this section for an illustration of this rule. See also paragraph (f)(1)(iv) of this section (treating certain stock of the subsequent acquiring corporation as stock of a foreign corporation that is held by reason of holding stock of, or a partnership interest in, the domestic entity).

(ii) *Acquisition of property pursuant to a subsequent acquisition.*—In determining whether a foreign corporation directly or indirectly acquires substantially all of the properties held directly or indirectly by an initial acquiring corporation, the principles of section 7874(a)(2)(B)(i) apply, including paragraph (c) of this section other than paragraph (c)(2) of this section. For this purpose, the principles of paragraph (c)(1) of this section, including paragraph (b)(5) of this section, apply by substituting the term "foreign" for "domestic" wherever it appears.

(iii) *Additional related transactions.*—If, pursuant to the same plan (or a series of related transactions), a foreign corporation directly or indirectly acquires (under the principles of paragraph (c)(4)(ii) of this section) substantially all of the properties directly or indirectly held by a subsequent acquiring corporation in a transaction occurring after the subsequent acquisition, then the principles of paragraph (c)(4)(i) of this section apply to such transaction (and any subsequent transaction or transactions occurring pursuant to the plan (or the series of related transactions)).

(d) *Acquisitions by multiple foreign corporations.*—If, pursuant to a plan (or a series of related transactions), two or more foreign corporations complete, in the aggregate, a domestic entity acquisition, then each foreign corporation shall be treated as completing the acquisition for purposes of determining whether such foreign corporation is treated as a surrogate foreign corporation. See *Examples 5* and *6* of paragraph (k) of this section for illustrations of the rules of this paragraph (d).

(e) *Acquisitions of multiple domestic entities.*—If, pursuant to a plan (or a series of related transactions), a foreign corporation completes two or more domestic entity acquisitions involving domestic corporations and/or domestic partnerships (domestic entities), then, for purposes of section 7874(a)(2)(B)(ii), the acquisitions shall be treated as a single acquisition and the domestic entities shall be treated as a single domestic entity. If the transaction involves one or more domestic corporations and one or more domestic partnerships, the stock of the foreign corporation held by former domestic entity shareholders and former domestic entity partners by reason of holding stock or a partnership interest in the domestic entities shall be aggregated for purposes of determining whether the ownership condition of section 7874(a)(2)(B)(ii) is satisfied. See *Example 7* of paragraph (k) of this section for an illustration of the rules of this paragraph (e).

(f) *Stock held by reason of holding stock in a domestic corporation or an interest in a domestic partnership.*—(1) *Certain transactions.*—For purposes of section 7874(a)(2)(B)(ii), stock of a foreign corporation that is held by reason of holding stock in a domestic corporation (or an interest in a domestic partnership) includes, but is not limited to, the stock described in paragraphs (f)(1)(i) through (iv) of this section.

(i) Stock of a foreign corporation received in exchange for, or with respect to, stock of a domestic corporation.

(ii) Stock of a foreign corporation received in exchange for, or with respect to, an interest in a domestic partnership.

(iii) To the extent that paragraph (f)(1)(ii) of this section does not apply, stock of a foreign corporation received by a domestic partnership in exchange for all or part of its properties. In such a case, each partner in the domestic partnership shall be treated as holding its proportionate share of the stock of the foreign corporation by reason of holding an interest in the domestic partnership.

(iv) Stock of a subsequent acquiring corporation received by a former initial acquiring corporation shareholder pursuant to a subsequent acquisition in exchange for, or with respect to, stock of an initial acquiring corporation that is held by reason of holding stock of, or a partnership interest in, a domestic entity.

(2) *Transactions involving other property.*—(i) *Stock of a domestic corporation.*—If, pursuant to the same transaction, stock of a foreign corporation is received in exchange for, or with respect to, stock of a domestic corporation and other property, the stock of the foreign corporation that was received in exchange for, or with respect to, the stock of the domestic corporation shall be determined based on the relative value of the stock of the domestic corporation compared to the aggregate value of such stock and the other property.

(ii) *Interest in a domestic partnership.*—If, pursuant to the same transaction, stock of a foreign corporation is received in exchange for, or with respect to, an interest in a domestic partnership and other property, the stock of the foreign corporation that was received in exchange for, or with respect to, the interest in the domestic partnership shall be determined based on the relative value of the interest in the domestic partnership compared to the aggregate value of such interest and the other property.

(3) See *Examples 8* through *10* of paragraph (k) of this section for illustrations of the rules of this paragraph (f).

(g) *Publicly traded foreign partnerships.*—(1) *Treatment as a foreign corporation.*—For purposes of section 7874, a publicly traded foreign partnership described in paragraph (g)(2) of this section shall be treated as a foreign corporation that is organized in the foreign country in which, or under the law of which, the publicly traded foreign partnership was created or organized, and the partnership interests in the publicly traded foreign partnership shall be treated as stock of the foreign corporation. For purposes of determining whether the foreign corporation shall be treated as a surrogate foreign corporation, a deemed acquisition of assets and liabilities by reason of §1.708-1(b)(4) shall not constitute an acquisition described in section 7874(a)(2)(B)(i).

(2) *Publicly traded foreign partnership.*—A publicly traded foreign partnership described in this paragraph (g)(2) is any foreign partner-

ship that would, but for section 7704(c), be treated as a corporation under section 7704(a)—

(i) At the time of the domestic entity acquisition; or

(ii) At any time after the domestic entity acquisition pursuant to a plan that existed at the time of the domestic entity acquisition. For this purpose, a plan shall be deemed to exist at the time of the domestic entity acquisition if the foreign partnership would, but for section 7704(c), be treated as a corporation under section 7704(a) at any time during the two-year period following the completion of the domestic entity acquisition.

(3) *Surrogate foreign corporation to which section 7874(b) applies.*—If paragraph (g)(1) of this section applies to a publicly traded foreign partnership and the foreign corporation is a surrogate foreign corporation to which section 7874(b) applies, the publicly traded foreign partnership shall be treated as a domestic corporation for purposes of the Internal Revenue Code (Code). See paragraph (g)(6) of this section for the timing and treatment of the conversion of the publicly traded foreign partnership to a domestic corporation. See *Example 11* of paragraph (k) of this section for an illustration of the rules of this paragraph (g)(3).

(4) *Surrogate foreign corporation to which section 7874(b) does not apply.*—If paragraph (g)(1) of this section applies to a publicly traded foreign partnership and the foreign corporation is a surrogate foreign corporation to which section 7874(b) does not apply, the publicly traded foreign partnership shall continue to be treated as a foreign partnership for purposes of the Code, but section 7874(a)(1) shall apply to any expatriated entity (as defined in section 7874(a)(2)(A)). See *Example 13* of paragraph (k) of this section for an illustration of the rules of this paragraph (g)(4).

(5) *Foreign corporation not treated as a surrogate foreign corporation.*—If paragraph (g)(1) of this section applies to a publicly traded foreign partnership and the foreign corporation is not treated as a surrogate foreign corporation, the status of the publicly traded foreign partnership as a foreign partnership shall not be affected by section 7874. See *Example 12* of paragraph (k) of this section for an illustration of the rules of this paragraph (g)(5).

(6) *Conversion to a domestic corporation.*—Except for purposes of determining whether the publicly traded foreign partnership is a surrogate foreign corporation, if paragraph (g)(1) of this section applies to a publicly traded foreign partnership and the foreign corporation is a surrogate foreign corporation to which section 7874(b) applies, then at the later of the end of the day immediately preceding the first date properties are acquired as part of the domestic entity acquisition or immediately after the formation of the publicly traded foreign partnership, the publicly traded foreign partnership shall be treated as transferring all of its assets and liabilities to a newly formed domestic corporation in exchange solely for stock of the domestic corporation, and then distributing such stock to its partners in proportion to their partnership interests in liquidation of the partnership. The treatment of the transfer of assets and liabilities to the domestic corporation and the distribution of the stock of the domestic corporation to the partners in liquidation of the partnership shall be determined under all relevant provisions of the Code and general tax principles.

(h) *Options.*—(1) *Value.*—Except to the extent otherwise provided in this paragraph (h), for purposes of section 7874, including for purposes of determining the membership of an expanded affiliated group under section 7874(c)(1), an option with respect to a corporation or partnership will be treated as stock in the corporation, or an interest in the partnership, as applicable, with a value equal to the holder's claim on the equity of the corporation or partnership. For this purpose, claim on the equity equals the value of the stock or partnership interest that may be acquired pursuant to the option, less the exercise price (but in no case is a claim on the equity less than zero). Also for this purpose, the equity of the corporation or partnership shall not include the amount of any property the holder of the option would be required to provide to the corporation or partnership under the terms of the option if such option were exercised. See *Example 14* and *Example 16* of paragraph (k) of this section for illustrations of the rules of this paragraph (h)(1).

(2) *Voting power.*—Except to the extent otherwise provided in this paragraph (h), for purposes of determining the voting power of a foreign corporation under section 7874, including for purposes of determining the membership of an expanded affiliated group under section 7874(c)(1), an option will be treated as exercised only if a principal purpose of the issuance or transfer of the option is to avoid the foreign corporation being treated as a surrogate foreign corporation.

(3) *Timing.*—For purposes of this paragraph (h), the value of the holder's claim on the equity is determined—

(i) In the case of a domestic corporation or a domestic partnership, immediately before the domestic entity acquisition.

(ii) In the case of a foreign corporation or foreign partnership, immediately after the domestic entity acquisition.

(4) *Certain options disregarded.*—The rules of paragraph (h)(1) of this section shall not apply to an option if—

(i) A principal purpose of the issuance or acquisition of the option is to avoid the foreign corporation being treated as a surrogate foreign corporation, or

(ii) At the time of the domestic entity acquisition, the probability of the option being exercised is remote.

(5) *Options and interests similar to an option.*—For purposes of this paragraph (h), an option includes an interest similar to an option. Examples of options (including interests similar to options) include, but are not limited to, a warrant, a convertible debt instrument, an instrument other than debt that is convertible into stock or a partnership interest, a put, stock or a partnership interest subject to risk of forfeiture, a contract to acquire or sell stock or a partnership interest, and an exchangeable share or exchangeable partnership interest.

(6) *Multiple claims on equity.*—Paragraph (h)(1) of this section shall not apply to an option to the extent treating the option as stock or a partnership interest would duplicate a shareholder's or partner's claim on the equity of the corporation or partnership by reason of holding stock in the corporation or an interest in the partnership. See *Example 15* of paragraph (k) of this section for an illustration of the rules of this paragraph (h)(6).

(i) *Interests treated as stock of a foreign corporation.*—(1) *Stock or other interests.*—If the conditions of paragraphs (i)(1)(i) and (ii) of this section are satisfied, then, for purposes of section 7874, any interest (including stock or a partnership interest) that is not otherwise treated as stock of a foreign corporation (including under paragraph (h) of this section) shall be treated as stock of the foreign corporation. See *Examples 17* and *18* of paragraph (k) of this section for illustrations of the rules of this paragraph (i)(1).

(i) The interest provides the holder distribution rights that are substantially similar in all material respects to the distribution rights provided by stock in the foreign corporation. For this purpose, distribution rights include rights to dividends (or partnership distributions), distributions in redemption of the interest (in whole or in part), distributions in liquidation, or other similar distributions that represent a return on, or of, the holder's investment in the interest.

(ii) Treating the interest as stock of the foreign corporation has the effect of treating the foreign corporation as a surrogate foreign corporation under section 7874(a)(2)(B).

(2) *Creditor claims.*—(i) *Domestic corporation.*—For purposes of section 7874, if, immediately prior to the first date properties are acquired as part of a domestic entity acquisition, a domestic corporation is in a title 11 or similar case (as defined in section 368(a)(3)), or the liabilities of the domestic corporation exceed the value of its assets, then each creditor of the domestic corporation shall be treated as a shareholder of the domestic corporation and any claim of the creditor against the domestic corporation shall be treated as stock of the domestic corporation. See *Example 19* of paragraph (k) of this section for an illustration of the rules of this paragraph (i)(2)(i).

(ii) *Domestic or foreign partnership.*—For purposes of section 7874, if, immediately prior to the first date properties are acquired as part of a domestic entity acquisition, a partnership (foreign or domestic) is in a title 11 or similar case (as defined in section 368(a)(3)), or the liabilities of the partnership exceed the value of its assets, then each creditor of the partnership shall be treated as a partner in the partnership and any claim of the creditor against the partnership shall be treated as an interest in the partnership.

(iii) *Treatment of creditor as shareholder or partner.*—A creditor that is treated as a shareholder or partner under paragraph (i)(2)(i) or (ii) of this section shall be treated as a shareholder or partner for all purposes of section 7874. See, for example, §1.7874-1(c) and paragraph (f) of this section. See *Example 19* of paragraph (k) of this section for an illustration of the rules of this paragraph (i)(2)(iii).

(j) *Application of section 7874(b).*—(1) *Conversion to a domestic corporation.*—Except for purposes of determining whether a foreign corporation is treated as a surrogate foreign corporation, the conversion of a foreign corporation to a domestic corporation by reason of section 7874(b) shall constitute a reorganization described in section 368(a)(1)(F) that occurs at the later of the end of the day immediately preceding the first date properties are acquired as part of the domestic entity acquisition or immediately after the formation of the foreign corporation. See, for example, §§1.367(b)-2 and 1.367(b)-3 for certain consequences of the reorganization. The treatment of all other aspects of the conversion shall be determined under the relevant

provisions of the Code and general tax principles. See *Example 20* of paragraph (k) of this section for an illustration of the rules of this paragraph (j)(1).

(2) *Entity classification.*—A foreign corporation that is treated as a domestic corporation under section 7874(b) is not an eligible entity as defined in §301.7701-3(a), and therefore may not elect to be classified as other than an association (and thus cannot be treated as other than a corporation) for Federal tax purposes.

(3) *Application of section 367.*—If a foreign corporation is treated as a domestic corporation under section 7874(b), section 367 shall not apply to any transfer of property by a United States person to such foreign corporation as part of the domestic entity acquisition. However, section 367 shall apply to the conversion of the foreign corporation to a domestic corporation. See paragraph (j)(1) of this section. See *Example 20* of paragraph (k) of this section for an illustration of the rules of this paragraph (j)(3).

(k) *Examples.*—(1) *Assumed facts.*—Except as otherwise stated, assume the following for purposes of the examples included in paragraph (k)(2) of this section.

(i) DC1 and DC2 are domestic corporations.

(ii) FA, FP, F1, F2, F3, and F4 are foreign corporations organized in Country A.

(iii) DPS is a domestic partnership that conducts a trade or business.

(iv) FPS is a foreign partnership that is not publicly traded.

(v) Under the terms of the partnership agreements of DPS and FPS, each partner's share in the partnership's items of income, gain, deduction, and loss is determined in accordance with the partner's partnership interest percentage in the partnership, as stated in the examples.

(vi) A, B, and C are unrelated individuals.

(vii) Each entity has a single class of equity outstanding and is unrelated to all other entities.

(viii) All transactions are completed pursuant to a plan.

(ix) All acquisitions of properties are completed after March 4, 2003.

(x) Section 7874(c)(4) does not apply, and no option is issued or acquired with a principal purpose to avoid a foreign corporation being treated as a surrogate foreign corporation.

(2) *Examples.*—The following examples illustrate the rules of this section.

*Example 1. Acquisition of stock of a domestic corporation.* (i) *Facts.* FA acquires 25% of the outstanding stock of DC1.

(ii) *Analysis.* Under paragraph (c)(1)(i) of this section, for purposes of section 7874(a)(2)(B)(i), FA is treated as acquiring 25% of the properties held by DC1 on the date of the stock acquisition.

*Example 2. Acquisition of a partnership interest.* (i) *Facts.* DPS wholly owns DC1. FA acquires a 40% interest in DPS.

(ii) *Analysis.* Under paragraph (c)(1)(ii) of this section, for purposes of section 7874(a)(2)(B)(i), FA is treated as acquiring 40 percent of the DC1 stock held by DPS on the date of the acquisition of the partnership interest. Further, under paragraph (c)(1)(i) of this section, for purposes of section 7874(a)(2)(B)(i), FA is treated as acquiring 40% of the properties held by DC1 on the date of the acquisition of the partnership interest.

*Example 3. Acquisition of stock by a subsidiary.* (i) *Facts.* FP wholly owns FA. FA acquires all the outstanding stock of DC1 in exchange solely for FP stock. FP and FA are members of the same expanded affiliated group after the acquisition.

(ii) *Analysis.* Under paragraph (c)(1)(i) of this section, for purposes of section 7874(a)(2)(B)(i), FA is treated as acquiring 100% of the properties held by DC1 on the date of the stock acquisition. Further, under paragraph (c)(1)(iii) of this section, for purposes of section 7874(a)(2)(B)(i), FP is also treated as acquiring 100% of the properties held by DC1 on the date of the stock acquisition. The result would be the same if instead FA had directly acquired all the properties held by DC1 in exchange for FP stock.

*Example 4. Acquisition of stock of a foreign corporation.* (i) *Facts.* FP wholly owns DC1. FA acquires all of the outstanding stock of FP.

(ii) *Analysis.* Under paragraph (c)(2) of this section, for purposes of section 7874(a)(2)(B)(i), FA is not treated as acquiring any properties held by DC1 on the date of the acquisition of the FP stock.

*Example 5. Acquisition of stock by multiple foreign corporations.* (i) *Facts.* Pursuant to the same plan, the shareholders of DC1 transfer all of their DC1 stock equally to F1, F2, F3, and F4 in exchange solely for stock of each foreign corporation.

(ii) *Analysis.* Under paragraph (c)(1)(i) of this section, in the aggregate F1, F2, F3, and F4 are treated as acquiring substantially all of the properties held by DC1. Because the acquisition was pursuant to the same plan, under paragraph (d) of this section, F1, F2, F3, and F4 are each treated as acquiring substantially all of the properties held by DC1 for purposes of determining whether each foreign corporation shall be treated as a surrogate foreign corporation.

*Example 6. Acquisition of assets by multiple foreign corporations.* (i) *Facts.* Individual A wholly owns DC1. DC1 forms F1, F2, F3, and F4, and transfers an equal portion of its properties to each corporation in exchange solely for stock of the corporation. Pursuant to the same plan DC1 then distributes the stock of each foreign corporation to individual A.

(ii) *Analysis.* Because pursuant to the same plan F1, F2, F3, and F4 acquired, in the aggregate, substantially all of the properties held by DC1, under paragraph (d) of this section, F1, F2, F3, and F4 are each treated as acquiring substantially all of the properties held by DC1 for purposes of determining whether each foreign corporation shall be treated as a surrogate foreign corporation.

*Example 7. Acquisition of multiple domestic corporations.* (i) *Facts.* Individual A wholly owns DC1, and individual B wholly owns DC2. Pursuant to the same plan, individuals A and B transfer all of their DC1 stock and DC2 stock to FA, a newly formed corporation, in exchange solely for all 100 shares of FA stock outstanding.

(ii) *Analysis.* Under paragraph (c)(1)(i) of this section, for purposes of section 7874(a)(2)(B)(i), FA is treated as acquiring all of the properties held by DC1 and DC2 on the date of the stock acquisition. Under paragraph (e) of this section, because pursuant to the same plan FA acquired substantially all of the properties held by DC1 and DC2, for purposes of determining whether FA shall be treated as a surrogate foreign corporation, DC1 and DC2 shall be treated as a single domestic corporation, of which individuals A and B are former domestic entity shareholders. Thus, individuals A and B are treated as holding all 100 shares of the FA stock by reason of holding stock of such domestic corporation, and the ownership fraction under section 7874(a)(2)(B)(ii) is 100/100, or 100%.

*Example 8. Exchange of stock and other property.* (i) *Facts.* Individual A wholly owns DC1 and F1. DC1 has a $40x value and F1 has a $60x value. Individual A transfers all of the DC1 stock and F1 stock to FA, a newly formed corporation, in exchange solely for FA stock.

(ii) *Analysis.* Under paragraphs (f)(1)(i) and (f)(2)(i) of this section, for purposes of section 7874(a)(2)(B)(ii), individual A is considered to hold 40% of the FA stock by reason of holding stock in DC1 ($100x FA stock multiplied by $40x/$100x, the relative value of the DC1 stock to all the property transferred by A to FA).

*Example 9. Stock received as a distribution.* (i) *Facts.* Pursuant to a divisive reorganization described in section 368(a)(1)(D), DC1 contributes substantially all of its properties to FA, a newly formed corporation, in exchange solely for FA stock and then distributes the FA stock to its shareholders in a transaction qualifying under section 355.

(ii) *Analysis.* Under paragraph (f)(1)(i) of this section, for purposes of section 7874(a)(2)(B)(ii), the FA stock received by the DC1 shareholders as a distribution with respect to the DC1 stock is considered held by reason of holding stock in DC1. The result would be the same if the transaction did not qualify as a reorganization (for example, if the distribution were subject to sections 301 and 311(b)).

*Example 10. Incorporation of a partnership trade or business.* (i) *Facts.* Individuals A and B equally own DPS. DPS transfers substantially all of its properties constituting a trade or business to FA, a newly formed corporation, solely in exchange for FA stock. DPS retains the FA stock after the transaction.

(ii) *Analysis.* Under paragraph (f)(1)(iii) of this section, for purposes of section 7874(a)(2)(B)(ii), individuals A and B are treated as holding a proportionate amount (that is, an equal amount) of the FA stock held by DPS by reason of holding an interest in DPS.

*Example 11. Publicly traded foreign partnership treated as domestic corporation.* (i) *Facts.* Pursuant to a plan, DC1 and individual B organize a limited liability company (HPS) under the law of Country A. DC1 owns 90% of the membership interests in HPS, and B owns 10% of the membership interests in HPS. HPS is a foreign eligible entity under §301.7701-2, and DC1 and B make an election under §301.7701-3 to treat HPS as a partnership for Federal tax purposes as of the date of the formation of HPS. HPS forms DC2. One day after the formation of HPS, DC2 merges with and into DC1. Pursuant to the merger agreement, the DC1 shareholders exchange their DC1 stock solely for membership interests in HPS. After the merger HPS wholly owns DC1, and the former domestic entity shareholders of DC1 own a greater than 80% interest in HPS by reason of holding stock of DC1. Public trading of the HPS ownership interests begins the day after the date on which the merger is completed. HPS is not treated as a corporation under section 7704(a) by reason of section 7704(c). If HPS were a corporation, the condition of section 7874(a)(2)(B)(iii) would be satisfied.

(ii) *Analysis.* HPS is a publicly traded foreign partnership that is described in paragraph (g)(2) of this section. Therefore, under paragraph (g)(1) of this section, for purposes of section 7874, HPS is treated as a foreign corporation organized under the law of Country A and the membership interests in HPS are treated as stock of the

foreign corporation. The foreign corporation is treated as a surrogate foreign corporation under section 7874(a)(2)(B) because, pursuant to the merger, HPS acquired substantially all of the properties held by DC1, the former domestic entity shareholders of DC1 hold at least 60% of the stock of the foreign corporation by reason of holding stock of DC1, and the expanded affiliated group that includes the foreign corporation does not have substantial business activities in Country A when compared to the total business activities of the expanded affiliated group. Further, because the former domestic entity shareholders of DC1 hold at least 80% of the stock of the foreign corporation by reason of holding stock of DC1, section 7874(b) applies to the surrogate foreign corporation, and therefore HPS is treated as a domestic corporation for purposes of the Code. Under paragraph (g)(6) of this section, except for purposes of determining whether HPS is a surrogate foreign corporation, at the end of the day immediately preceding the date of the merger of DC2 with and into DC1, HPS is treated as transferring all of its assets and liabilities to a new domestic corporation in exchange solely for stock of the domestic corporation. HPS is then treated as proportionately distributing such stock to its membership interest holders in liquidation of the partnership. In addition, as a result of the merger of DC2 with and into DC1, the former domestic entity shareholders of DC1 shall be treated as receiving stock of a domestic corporation in exchange for their DC1 stock.

*Example 12. Publicly traded foreign partnership not treated as a surrogate foreign corporation.* (i) *Facts.* The facts are the same as in *Example 11* of this section, except that, after the domestic entity acquisition, the expanded affiliated group that includes HPS (treated as a foreign corporation for this purpose) has substantial business activities in Country A when compared to the total business activities of the expanded affiliated group.

(ii) *Analysis.* Under paragraph (g)(1) of this section, for purposes of section 7874, HPS is treated as a foreign corporation and the membership interests in HPS are treated as stock of the foreign corporation. However, the foreign corporation is not treated as a surrogate foreign corporation under section 7874(a)(2)(B) because, after the domestic entity acquisition, the expanded affiliated group that includes HPS has substantial business activities in Country A when compared to the total business activities of the expanded affiliated group. Therefore, under paragraph (g)(5) of this section, section 7874 does not apply and the status of HPS as a foreign partnership is not affected. In addition, DC1 is not treated as an expatriated entity under section 7874(a) by reason of the domestic entity acquisition.

*Example 13. Publicly traded foreign partnership treated as a surrogate foreign corporation but not as a domestic corporation.* (i) *Facts.* FPS is a publicly traded foreign partnership organized in Country A that, by reason of section 7704(c), is not treated as a corporation under section 7704(a). FPS acquires all the stock of DC1 in exchange for partnership interests in FPS. After the acquisition, the former domestic entity shareholders of DC1 hold a 75%-interest in FPS by reason of holding DC1 stock. After the acquisition, the expanded affiliated group that includes FPS (treated as a foreign corporation for this purpose) does not have substantial business activities in Country A when compared to the total business activities of the expanded affiliated group.

(ii) *Analysis.* Under paragraph (g)(1) of this section, for purposes of section 7874, FPS is treated as a foreign corporation and the partnership interests in FPS are treated as stock of the foreign corporation. FPS is treated as a surrogate foreign corporation because the conditions of section 7874(a)(2)(B) are satisfied. However, because the former domestic entity shareholders of DC1 hold less than an 80%-interest in FPS by reason of holding DC1 stock, section 7874(b) does not apply to FPS. Therefore, under paragraph (g)(4) of this section FPS continues to be treated as a foreign partnership for purposes of the Code, but section 7874(a)(1) applies to DC1 and any other expatriated entity.

*Example 14. Warrant to acquire stock from the foreign corporation.* (i) *Facts.* Individual A wholly owns DC1. DC1 has a $200x value. Individual B wholly owns FA. The value of B's FA stock is $400x. Individual C holds a warrant to acquire FA stock from FA at an exercise price of $20x. Individual A transfers all of its DC1 stock to FA in exchange solely for FA stock with a value of $200x. At the time of the transfer, the FA stock that individual C can acquire pursuant to the warrant has a $70x value.

(ii) *Analysis.* Under paragraphs (h)(1) of this section, for purposes of section 7874, individual C is treated as owning FA stock with a $50x value. This amount represents individual C's claim on the equity of FA after the domestic entity acquisition ($70x value of FA stock that may be acquired pursuant to the warrant, less the $20x exercise price), without taking into account the $20x individual C would be required to provide to FA upon the exercise of the warrant. Thus, for purposes of section 7874, the value of the stock of FA immediately after the transaction is $650x ($600x of FA stock, plus C's $50x claim on the equity of FA). C's warrant is not taken into account for purposes of determining the voting power of FA under section 7874.

*Example 15. Option to acquire stock from another shareholder.* (i) *Facts.* The facts are the same as in *Example 14* except that, instead of holding a warrant issued by FA, individual C holds an option to acquire FA stock from individual B for an exercise price of $20x. At the time of the domestic entity acquisition, the FA stock that individual C can acquire under the option has a $70x value.

(ii) *Analysis.* Under paragraph (h)(6) of this section, for purposes of section 7874, individual C is not treated as owning FA stock by reason of holding the option because treating the option as FA stock would have the effect of partially duplicating individual B's claim on the equity of FA at the time of the domestic entity acquisition by reason of holding FA stock. However, all of the FA stock owned by individual B will be taken into account for purposes of section 7874. C's warrant is not taken into account for purposes of determining voting power of FA under section 7874.

*Example 16. Warrant to acquire stock from the domestic corporation.* (i) *Facts.* A DC1 employee holds a warrant to acquire DC1 stock from DC1. In connection with the domestic entity acquisition by FA of substantially all of the properties held by DC1, the DC1 employee receives a warrant from FA to acquire 15 shares of FA stock in exchange for the warrant to acquire DC1 stock.

(ii) *Analysis.* Under paragraphs (h)(1) of this section, for purposes of section 7874, the warrant held by the DC1 employee is treated as DC1 stock with a value equal to the employee's claim on the equity of DC1 immediately before the domestic entity acquisition. Further, for purposes of section 7874, the DC1 employee is treated as holding FA stock with a value equal to the employee's claim on the equity of FA after the domestic entity acquisition by reason of holding the warrant to acquire DC1 stock (treated as DC1 stock for this purpose). The option held by the DC1 employee is not taken into account for purposes of determining the voting power of FA under section 7874.

*Example 17. Stock in a subsidiary treated as stock of a foreign parent corporation.* (i) *Facts.* (A) Individuals A and B equally own DC1. FA, a newly formed corporation, issues stock in a public offering for cash. FA contributes part of the cash from the public offering to DC2, a newly formed corporation, in exchange for all the stock of DC2. DC2 merges with and into DC1 with DC1 surviving. Pursuant to the merger agreement, individuals A and B exchange their DC1 stock for cash and shares of class B stock of DC1. Following the merger FA owns all the class A stock of DC1. FA does not hold significant assets other than the class A stock of DC1. Individuals A and B own all the class B stock of DC1. DC1 has no other class of stock outstanding.

(B) The class B stock entitles individuals A and B to dividend distributions approximately equal to any dividend distributions made by FA with respect to its publicly traded stock. In certain circumstances, the class B stock also permits individuals A and B to require DC1 to redeem the stock at fair market value. The class B stock does not provide individuals A and B voting rights with respect to FA.

(ii) *Analysis.* The dividend rights provided by the class B stock are substantially similar in all material respects to the dividend rights provided by the FA stock. In addition, because FA does not hold significant assets other than the class A stock, the value of the class B stock held by individuals A and B is approximately equal to the value of a corresponding amount of publicly traded FA stock. The distribution rights on liquidation (or redemption) provided by the class B stock, therefore, are substantially similar in all material respects to the distribution rights on liquidation (or redemption) provided by the FA stock. As a result, the distribution rights provided by the class B stock are substantially similar in all material respects to the distribution rights provided by the publicly traded FA stock. Thus, if treating the class B stock as FA stock would have the effect of treating FA as a surrogate foreign corporation, under paragraph (i)(1) of this section the class B stock will be treated as FA stock for purposes of section 7874.

*Example 18. Partnership interest treated as stock of foreign acquiring corporation.* (i) *Facts.* (A) Individuals A and B equally own DC1. FA, a newly formed corporation, issues stock in a public offering for cash. Individuals A and B and FA organize FPS. FA transfers part of the cash from the public offering to FPS in exchange for a class A partnership interest. FA does not hold any significant assets other than the class A partnership interest. Individuals A and B transfer their DC1 stock to FPS in exchange for class B partnership interests.

(B) The class B partnership interests entitle individuals A and B to cash distributions from FPS approximately equal to any dividend distributions made by FA with respect to its publicly traded stock. In certain circumstances, the class B partnership interests also permit individuals A and B to require FPS to redeem the interests in exchange for cash equal to the value of an amount of FA stock as determined on the redemption date. The class B partnership interests do not provide individuals A or B voting rights with respect to FA.

(ii) *Analysis.* The non-liquidating distribution rights provided by the class B partnership interests are substantially similar in all material respects to the dividend rights provided by the FA stock. Because FA does not hold any significant assets other than the class A partnership interest, the value of the class B partnership interests held by individuals A and B is approximately equal to a corresponding amount of FA stock. The distribution rights on liquidation (or redemption) provided by the class B partnership interests, therefore, are substantially similar in all material respects to distribution rights on liquidation (or redemption) provided by the FA stock. Thus, the distribution rights provided by the class B partnership interests are substantially similar in all material respects to the distribution rights provided by the publicly traded FA stock. As a result, if treating the class B partnership interests as FA stock would have the effect of treating FA as a surrogate foreign corporation, under paragraph (i)(1) of this section the class B partnership interests will be treated as FA stock for purposes of section 7874.

*Example 19. Creditor treated as a shareholder.* (i) *Facts.* Individuals A and B equally own DC1. The liabilities of DC1 exceed the value of its assets. Pursuant to a plan, FA, a newly formed corporation, acquires substantially all of the properties held by DC1 in exchange solely for FA stock. Pursuant to the plan, the DC1 stock held by individuals A and B is cancelled, and the creditors of DC1 receive all the FA stock in exchange for their claims against DC1.

(ii) *Analysis.* Because immediately before the first date on which properties are acquired as part of the domestic entity acquisition the liabilities of DC1 exceed the value of its assets, under paragraph (i)(2)(i) of this section, for purposes of section 7874, the creditors of DC1 are treated as shareholders of DC1 and the creditors' claims against DC1 are treated as DC1 stock. Therefore, for purposes of section 7874(a)(2)(B)(ii), the FA stock received by the creditors of DC1 by reason of their claims against DC1 is considered held by former domestic entity shareholders of DC1 by reason of holding DC1 stock.

*Example 20. Conversion to a domestic corporation and application of section 367.* (i) *Facts.* Individuals A and B are United States persons and equally own DC1. Pursuant to a plan, individuals A and B transfer their DC1 stock to FA in exchange solely for 80% of the outstanding FA stock. After the acquisition, the expanded affiliated group that includes FA does not have substantial business activities in Country A when compared to the total business activities of the expanded affiliated group.

(ii) *Analysis.* Under paragraph (c)(1)(i) of this section, for purposes of section 7874(a)(2)(B)(i), FA is treated as acquiring all of the properties held by DC1 on the date of the stock acquisition. After the acquisition, the former domestic entity shareholders of DC1 own 80% of the stock of FA by reason of holding DC1 stock. Therefore, FA is a surrogate foreign corporation that is treated as a domestic corporation under section 7874(b). Under paragraph (j)(1) of this section, except for purposes of determining whether FA is treated as a surrogate foreign corporation, the conversion of FA to a domestic corporation constitutes a reorganization described in section 368(a)(1)(F) that occurs at the end of the day immediately preceding the date of the stock acquisition. Section 367 applies to the conversion of FA to a domestic corporation. See, for example, § § 1.367(b)-2 and 1.367(b)-3 for the consequences of the conversion. Under paragraph (j)(3) of this section, section 367 does not apply to the transfers of DC1 stock by individuals A and B to FA.

*Example 21. Application of multiple-step acquisition rule*—(i) *Facts.* Individual A owns all 70 shares of stock of DC1, a domestic corporation. Individual B owns all 30 shares of stock of F1, a foreign corporation that is a tax resident (as described in § 1.7874-3(d)(11)) of Country X. Pursuant to a reorganization described in section 368(a)(1)(D), DC1 transfers all of its properties to F1 solely in exchange for 70 newly issued voting shares of F1 stock (DC1 acquisition) and distributes the F1 stock to Individual A in liquidation pursuant to section 361(c)(1). Pursuant to a plan that includes the DC1 acquisition, F2, a newly formed foreign corporation that is also a tax resident of Country X, acquires 100 percent of the stock of F1 solely in exchange for 100 newly issued shares of F2 stock (F1 acquisition). After the F1 acquisition, Individual A owns 70 shares of F2 stock, Individual B owns 30 shares of F2 stock, F2 owns all 100 shares of F1 stock, and F1 owns all the properties held by DC1 immediately before the DC1 acquisition. In addition, the form of the transaction is respected for U.S. federal income tax purposes.

(ii) *Analysis*—(A) The DC1 acquisition is a domestic entity acquisition, and F1 is a foreign acquiring corporation, because F1 directly acquires 100 percent of the properties of DC1. In addition, the 70 shares of F1 stock received by A pursuant to the DC1 acquisition in exchange for Individual A's DC1 stock are stock of a foreign corporation that is held by reason of holding stock in DC1. As a result, those 70 shares are included in both the numerator and the denominator of the ownership fraction when applying section 7874 to the DC1 acquisition.

(B) The DC1 acquisition is also an initial acquisition because it is a domestic entity acquisition that, pursuant to a plan that includes the F1 acquisition, occurs before the F1 acquisition (which, as described in paragraph (ii)(C) of this *Example 21*, is a subsequent acquisition). Thus, F1 is the initial acquiring corporation.

(C) The F1 acquisition is a subsequent acquisition because it occurs, pursuant to a plan that includes the DC1 acquisition, after the DC1 acquisition and, pursuant to the F1 acquisition, F2 acquires 100 percent of the stock of F1 and therefore is treated under paragraph (c)(4)(ii) of this section (which applies the principles of section 7874(a)(2)(B)(i) with certain modifications) as indirectly acquiring substantially all of the properties held directly or indirectly by F1. Thus, F2 is the subsequent acquiring corporation.

(D) Under paragraph (c)(4)(i) of this section, the F1 acquisition is treated as a domestic entity acquisition, and F2 is treated as a foreign acquiring corporation. In addition, under paragraph (f)(1)(iv) of this section, the 70 shares of F2 stock received by Individual A (a former initial acquiring corporation shareholder) pursuant to the F1 acquisition in exchange for Individual A's F1 stock are stock of a foreign corporation that is held by reason of holding stock in DC1. As a result, those 70 shares are included in both the numerator and the denominator of the ownership fraction when applying section 7874 to the F1 acquisition.

(l) *Applicability date.*—(1) *In general.*—This section applies to domestic entity acquisitions completed on or after June 7, 2012. For domestic entity acquisitions completed prior to June 7, 2012, see § 1.7874-2T(o), as contained in 26 CFR part 1, revised as of April 1, 2012.

(2) *Applicability date of certain provisions of this section.*— Paragraphs (a), (b)(7) through (13), (c)(2) and (4), and (f)(1)(iv) of this section, as well as the introductory text of paragraph (f)(1) and *Example 21* of paragraph (k)(2), apply to domestic entity acquisitions completed on or after April 4, 2016. [Reg. § 1.7874-2.]

☐ [*T.D. 9591, 6-7-2012. Amended by T.D. 9761, 4-4-2016 and T.D. 9834, 7-11-2018.*]

### [Reg. § 1.7874-3]

**§ 1.7874-3. Substantial business activities.**—(a) *Scope.*—This section provides rules regarding when an expanded affiliated group will be considered to have substantial business activities in the relevant foreign country when compared to the total business activities of the expanded affiliated group for purposes of section 7874(a)(2)(B)(iii). Paragraph (b) of this section describes the general rule for determining whether the expanded affiliated group has substantial business activities in the relevant foreign country when compared to its total business activities. Paragraph (c) of this section describes certain items that are not taken into account as located or derived in the relevant foreign country. Paragraph (d) of this section provides definitions and certain rules of application. Paragraph (e) of this section provides rules regarding the treatment of partnerships for purposes of this section. Paragraph (f) of this section provides the effective/applicability dates.

(b) *General rule.*—The expanded affiliated group will be considered to have substantial business activities in the relevant foreign country on the completion date when compared to the total business activities of the expanded affiliated group only if, subject to paragraph (c) of this section, each of the requirements of this paragraph (b) are satisfied.

(1) *Group employees.*—(i) *Number of employees.*—The number of group employees based in the relevant foreign country is at least 25 percent of the total number of group employees on the applicable date.

(ii) *Employee compensation.*—The employee compensation incurred with respect to group employees based in the relevant foreign country is at least 25 percent of the total employee compensation incurred with respect to all group employees during the testing period.

(2) *Group assets.*—The value of the group assets located in the relevant foreign country is at least 25 percent of the total value of all group assets on the applicable date.

(3) *Group income.*—The group income derived in the relevant foreign country is at least 25 percent of the total group income during the testing period.

(4) *Tax residence of foreign acquiring corporation.*—The foreign acquiring corporation is a tax resident of the relevant foreign country. However, this paragraph (b)(4) does not apply if the relevant foreign country does not impose corporate income tax.

(c) *Items not to be considered.*—(1) *General rule.*—Except to the extent provided in paragraph (c)(2) of this section, the following items are not taken into account in the numerator, but are taken into account in the denominator, for each of the tests described in paragraphs (b)(1) through (3) of this section:

(i) Any group assets, group employees, or group income attributable to business activities that are associated with properties or liabilities the transfer of which is disregarded under section 7874(c)(4).

(ii) Any group assets or group employees located in, or group income derived in, the relevant foreign country as part of a plan with a principal purpose of avoiding the purposes of section 7874.

(iii) Any group assets or group employees located in, or group income derived in, the relevant foreign country if such group assets or group employees, or the business activities to which such group income is attributable, are subsequently transferred to another country in connection with a plan that existed at the time of the domestic entity acquisition.

(2) *Transfers of properties to the expanded affiliated group.*—Any group assets, group employees, or group income attributable to business activities that are associated with property that is transferred to the expanded affiliated group in a transfer that is disregarded under section 7874(c)(4) are not taken into account in the numerator or the denominator for each of the tests described in paragraphs (b)(1) through (3) of this section.

(d) *Definitions and special rules.*—In addition to the definitions in § 1.7874-12, the following definitions and special rules apply for purposes of this section.

(1) The term *applicable date* means either of the following dates, applied consistently for all purposes of this section:

(i) The completion date; or

(ii) The last day of the month immediately preceding the month that includes the completion date.

(2) The term *employee compensation* means all amounts incurred by members of the expanded affiliated group that directly relate to services performed by group employees (including, for example, wages, salaries, deferred compensation, employee benefits, and employer payroll taxes). Employee compensation with respect to a particular group employee is treated as incurred when it would be deductible by the employer as compensation, and the amount of employee compensation equals the amount that would be deductible by the employer as compensation. Both the timing and the amount of the deduction for employee compensation must be determined for all group employees under U.S. federal income tax principles or for all group employees based on the relevant tax laws. Employee compensation is determined in U.S. dollars, translated, if necessary, using the weighted average exchange rate (as defined in § 1.989(b)-1) for the testing period.

(3) The term *group assets* means tangible personal property or real property used or held for use in the active conduct of a trade or business by members of the expanded affiliated group, provided such property is either owned or, in the circumstances described below, rented by members of the expanded affiliated group at the close of the completion date. A group asset is considered to be located in the relevant foreign country only if the asset was physically present in such country at the close of the completion date and the asset was physically present in such country for more time than in any other country during the testing period. Notwithstanding the foregoing, a group asset that is mobile in nature and is used in a transportation activity, such as a vessel, an aircraft, or a motor vehicle, is considered to be located in the relevant foreign country if the asset was physically present in such country for more time than in any other country during the testing period, regardless of whether the asset was physically present in such country at the close of the completion date. Group assets must be valued on a gross basis (that is, not reduced by liabilities) by consistently using for all group assets of the expanded affiliated group either the adjusted tax basis or fair market value determined in U.S. dollars, translated, if necessary, at the spot rate determined under the principles of § 1.988-1(d)(1), (2), and (4). Tangible personal property or real property that is rented by members of the expanded affiliated group from a person other than a member of the expanded affiliated group is also treated as a group asset, provided such property is used in the active conduct of a trade or business and is being rented by members of the expanded affiliated group at the close of the completion date. For purposes of this section, a group asset that is rented is valued at eight times the net annual rent paid or accrued with respect to the property by members of the expanded affiliated group.

(4) The term *group employees* means all individuals who are employees of members of the expanded affiliated group. Whether individuals are employees must be determined for all members of the expanded affiliated group under U.S. federal tax principles or for all members of the expanded affiliated group based on the relevant

tax laws. A group employee is considered to be based in the relevant foreign country only if the employee spent more time providing services in such country than in any other single country during the testing period.

(5) The term *group income* means gross income of members of the expanded affiliated group from transactions occurring in the ordinary course of business with customers that are not related persons. Group income must be determined consistently for all members of the expanded affiliated group either under U.S. federal income tax principles or as reflected in the relevant financial statements. Group income is translated into U.S. dollars, if necessary, using the weighted average exchange rate (as defined in §1.989(b)-1) for the testing period. Group income is considered derived in the relevant foreign country only if it is derived from a transaction with a customer located in such country.

(6) The term *net annual rent* means the annual rent paid or accrued with respect to property, less any payments received or accrued from subleasing such property (or other similar arrangement).

(7) The term *related person* has the meaning specified in section 954(d)(3), except that section 954(d)(3) is applied by substituting "one or more members of the expanded affiliated group" for "a controlled foreign corporation" and "the controlled foreign corporation" each place they appear.

(8) The term *relevant financial statements* means financial statements prepared consistently for all members of the expanded affiliated group in accordance with either U.S. Generally Accepted Accounting Principles (U.S. GAAP) or the International Financial Reporting Standards (IFRS) used for the expanded affiliated group's consolidated financial statements, but, if, after the domestic entity acquisition, financial statements will not be prepared consistently for all members of the expanded affiliated group in accordance with either U.S. GAAP or IFRS, then, for each member, financial statements prepared in accordance with either U.S. GAAP or IFRS. The relevant financial statements must take into account all items of income generated by all members of the expanded affiliated group for the entire testing period.

(9) The term *relevant foreign country* means the foreign country in which, or under the law of which, the foreign acquiring corporation was created or organized.

(10) The term *relevant tax law* means, for purposes of determining whether a particular individual who performs services for a member of the expanded affiliated group is an employee for purposes of paragraph (d)(6) of this section and the timing and amount of employee compensation for a particular employee of a member of the expanded affiliated group for purposes of paragraph (d)(3) of this section, the tax law to which the member is subject. Notwithstanding the foregoing, if the tax law to which a member is subject does not distinguish between whether an individual is an employee, or, for example, an independent contractor, then for this purpose the relevant tax law is considered to be U.S. federal tax law.

(11) The term *tax resident* means, with respect to a foreign country, a body corporate liable to tax under the laws of the country as a resident.

(12) The term *testing period* means the one-year period ending on the applicable date.

(e) *Treatment of partnerships.*—(1) *Stock held by a partnership.*—In determining the members of the expanded affiliated group for purposes of this section, each partner in a partnership, as determined without regard to the application of paragraph (e)(2) of this section, shall be treated as holding its proportionate share of the stock held by the partnership, as determined under the rules and principles of sections 701 through 777.

(2) *Business activities of a partnership.*—For purposes of this section, if one or more members of the expanded affiliated group, as determined after the application of paragraph (e)(1) of this section, own, in the aggregate, more than 50 percent (by value) of the interests in a partnership, the partnership will be treated as a corporation that is a member of the expanded affiliated group. Thus, all items of such a partnership are taken into account for purposes of this section. No items of a partnership are taken into account for purposes of this section unless the partnership is treated as a member of the expanded affiliated group pursuant to this paragraph (e)(2).

(f) *Applicability dates.*—(1) *General rule.*—Except as otherwise provided in paragraph (f)(2) of this section, this section applies to domestic entity acquisitions that are completed on or after June 3, 2015. For domestic entity acquisitions completed before June 3, 2015, see §1.7874-3T as contained in 26 CFR part 1 revised as of April 1, 2016.

(2) *Paragraphs (b)(4), (d)(8), and (d)(11) of this section.*—The first sentence of paragraph (b)(4) of this section applies to domestic entity

acquisitions completed on or after November 19, 2015, and the second sentence applies to domestic entity acquisitions completed on or after July 12, 2018. Paragraph (d)(8) of this section applies to domestic entity acquisitions completed on or after April 4, 2016. Paragraph (d)(11) of this section applies to domestic entity acquisitions completed on or after July 12, 2018. For domestic entity acquisitions completed on or after June 3, 2015, and before April 4, 2016, however, taxpayers may elect to apply paragraph (d)(8) of this section. For domestic entity acquisitions completed on or after November 19, 2015, and before July 12, 2018, taxpayers may elect to apply the second sentence of paragraph (b)(4) and paragraph (d)(11) of this section. [Reg. §1.7874-3.]

☐ [*T.D.* 9720, 6-3-2015. *Amended by T.D.* 9761, 4-4-2016 *and T.D.* 9834, 7-11-2018.]

**[Reg. §1.7874-4]**

**§1.7874-4. Disregard of certain stock related to the domestic entity acquisition.**—(a) *Scope.*—This section identifies certain stock of the foreign acquiring corporation that is disregarded in determining the ownership fraction and modifies the scope of section 7874(c)(2)(B). Paragraph (b) of this section sets forth the general rule that certain stock of the foreign acquiring corporation, and only such stock, is treated as stock described in section 7874(c)(2)(B) and therefore is excluded from the denominator of the ownership fraction. Paragraph (c) of this section identifies the stock of the foreign acquiring corporation that is subject to paragraph (b) of this section. Paragraph (d) of this section provides a de minimis exception to the application of the general exclusion rule of paragraph (b) of this section. Paragraph (e) of this section provides rules for transfers of stock of the foreign acquiring corporation in satisfaction of, or in exchange for the assumption of, one or more obligations of the transferor. Paragraph (f) of this section provides rules for certain transfers of stock of the foreign acquiring corporation involving multiple properties or obligations. Paragraph (g) of this section provides rules for the treatment of partnerships, and paragraph (h) of this section provides definitions. Paragraph (h) of this section provides definitions. Paragraph (i) of this section provides examples illustrating the application of the rules of this section. Paragraph (j) of this section provides dates of applicability. See §1.7874-1(d)(1) for rules addressing the interaction of this section with the expanded affiliated group rules of section 7874(c)(2)(A) and §1.7874-1.

(b) *Exclusion of disqualified stock under section 7874(c)(2)(B).*—Except as provided in paragraph (d) of this section, disqualified stock (as determined under paragraph (c) of this section) is treated as stock described in section 7874(c)(2)(B) and therefore is not included in the denominator of the ownership fraction. Section 7874(c)(2)(B) shall not apply to exclude stock from the denominator of the ownership fraction that is not disqualified stock.

(c) *Disqualified stock.*—(1) *General rule.*—Except as provided in paragraph (c)(2) of this section, disqualified stock is stock of the foreign acquiring corporation (other than stock described in §1.7874-2(f)) that is transferred in an exchange described in paragraph (c)(1)(i) or (ii) of this section that is related to the domestic entity acquisition. This paragraph (c) applies without regard to whether the stock of the foreign acquiring corporation is publicly traded at the time of the transfer or at any other time.

(i) *Exchanged for nonqualified property.*—The stock is transferred to a person other than the domestic entity in exchange for nonqualified property. See *Example 1, Example 2, Example 6, Example 8,* and *Example 9* of paragraph (i) of this section for illustrations of the application of this paragraph (c)(1)(i).

(ii) *Exchanged for property with associated obligations.*—(A) *General rule.*—Subject to the limitation provided in in paragraph (c)(1)(ii)(B) of this section, the stock is transferred by a person (transferor) to another person (transferee) in exchange for property (exchanged property) and, pursuant to the same plan (or series of related transactions), the transferee subsequently transfers such stock (or, if the transferee exchanges such stock for other property, such other property) in satisfaction of, or in exchange for the assumption of, one or more obligations of the transferee or a person related (within the meaning of section 267 or 707(b)) to the transferee. See *Example 6* and *Example 10* of paragraph (i) of this section for illustrations of the application of paragraph (c)(1)(ii) of this section.

(B) *Limitation.*—The amount of stock treated as transferred in an exchange described in paragraph (c)(2)(ii)(A) of this section shall not exceed—

(1) With respect to a transferee that is the domestic entity, the proportionate share of obligations associated with the exchanged property (determined based on the fair market value of the exchanged property relative to the fair market value of all properties with which the obligations are associated) that, pursuant to the same

plan (or series of related transactions), is not assumed by the transferor.

(2) With respect to any other transferee, the proportionate share of obligations associated with the exchanged property (determined based on the fair market value of the exchanged property relative to the fair market value of all properties with which the obligations are associated) that, pursuant to the same plan (or series of related transactions), is not assumed by the transferor, multiplied by a fraction, the numerator of which is the amount of exchanged property that is qualified property, and the denominator of which is the total amount of exchanged property.

(C) *Associated obligations.*—For purposes of paragraph (c)(1)(ii) of this section, an obligation is associated with property if, for example, the obligation arose from the conduct of a trade or business in which the property has been used, regardless of whether the obligation is a non-recourse obligation.

(2) *Stock transferred in an exchange that does not increase the fair market value of the assets or decrease the amount of liabilities of the foreign acquiring corporation.*—Stock is disqualified stock only to the extent that the transfer of the stock in the exchange increases the fair market value of the assets of the foreign acquiring corporation or decreases the amount of its liabilities. This paragraph (c)(2) is applied to an exchange without regard to any other exchange described in paragraph (c)(1)(i) or (ii) of this section or any other transaction related to the domestic entity acquisition. See *Example 4* and *Example 7* of paragraph (i) of this section for illustrations of the application of this paragraph (c)(2).

(d) *Exception to exclusion of disqualified stock.*—(1) *De minimis ownership.*—Except as provided in paragraph (d)(2) of this section, paragraph (b) of this section does not apply if both:

(i) The ownership percentage described in section 7874(a)(2)(B)(ii), determined without regard to the application of paragraph (b) of this section and §§ 1.7874-7(b) and 1.7874-10(b), is less than five (by vote and value); and

(ii) On the completion date, each five percent former domestic entity shareholder or five percent former domestic entity partner, as applicable, owns (applying the attribution rules of section 318(a) with the modifications described in section 304(c)(3)(B)) less than five percent (by vote and value) of the stock of (or a partnership interest in) each member of the expanded affiliated group. For this purpose, a five percent former domestic entity shareholder (or five percent former domestic entity partner) is a former domestic entity shareholder (or former domestic entity partner) that, before the domestic entity acquisition, owned (applying the attribution rules of section 318(a) with the modifications described in section 304(c)(3)(B)) at least five percent (by vote and value) of the stock of (or a partnership interest in) the domestic entity. See *Example 5* of this paragraph (i) for an illustration of this paragraph (d).

(2) *Stock issued to avoid the purposes of section 7874.*—The exception in paragraph (d)(1) of this section does not apply to disqualified stock that is transferred in a transaction (or series of transactions) related to the domestic entity acquisition with a principal purpose of avoiding the purposes of section 7874.

(e) *Satisfaction or assumption of obligations.*—Except to the extent stock is treated as disqualified stock as a result of being described in paragraph (c)(1)(ii) of this section, this paragraph (e) applies if, in a transaction related to the domestic entity acquisition, stock of the foreign acquiring corporation is transferred to a person other than the domestic entity in exchange for the satisfaction or the assumption of one or more obligations of the transferor. In such a case, solely for purposes of this section, the stock of the foreign acquiring corporation is treated as if it is transferred in exchange for an amount of cash equal to the fair market value of such stock.

(f) *Transactions involving multiple properties.*—For purposes of this section, if stock and other property are exchanged for qualified property and nonqualified property, the stock is treated as transferred in exchange for the qualified property or nonqualified property, respectively, based on the relative fair market value of the property. See also § 1.7874-2(f)(2) (allocating stock of a foreign acquiring corporation between an interest in the domestic entity and other property).

(g) *Treatment of partnerships.*—For purposes of this section, if one or more members of the expanded affiliated group own, in the aggregate, more than 50 percent (by value) of the interests in a partnership, such partnership is treated as a corporation that is a member of the expanded affiliated group.

(h) *Definitions.*—In addition to the definitions in § 1.7874-12, the following definitions apply for purposes of this section:

(1) *Marketable securities* has the meaning set forth in section 453(f)(2), except that the term marketable securities does not include stock of a corporation or an interest in a partnership that becomes a member of the expanded affiliated group in a transaction (or series of transactions) related to the domestic entity acquisition. See *Example 4* of paragraph (i) of this section for an illustration of this paragraph (h)(1).

(2) *Nonqualified property* is property described in paragraphs (h)(2)(i) through (iv) of this section. Thus, stock in a corporation or an interest in a partnership is nonqualified property to the extent provided in paragraph (h)(2)(ii) or (iv) of this section. Qualified property is property other than nonqualified property.

(i) Cash or cash equivalents.

(ii) Marketable securities, within the meaning of paragraph (h)(1) of this section.

(iii) An obligation owed by any of the following:

(A) A member of the expanded affiliated group, unless the holder of the obligation immediately before the domestic entity acquisition and any related transaction (or its successor) is a member of the expanded affiliated group after the domestic entity acquisition and all related transactions. See *Example 6* of paragraph (i) of this section for an illustration of this paragraph (h)(2)(iii)(A).

(B) A former domestic entity shareholder or former domestic entity partner of the domestic entity that owns (applying the attribution rules of section 318(a) with the modifications described in section 304(c)(3)(B)) at least five percent (by vote or value) of the stock of, or partnership interests in, the domestic entity before the domestic entity acquisition.

(C) A person, other than a member of the expanded affiliated group, that, before or after the domestic entity acquisition, either owns (applying the attribution rules of section 318(a) with the modifications described in section 304(c)(3)(B)) at least five percent (by vote or value) of the stock of (or partnership interests in) or is related (within the meaning of section 267 or 707(b)) to—

(1) A member of the expanded affiliated group; or

(2) A person described in paragraph (h)(2)(iii)(B) of this section.

(iv) Any other property acquired with a principal purpose of avoiding the purposes of section 7874, regardless of whether the transaction involves an indirect transfer of property described in paragraph (h)(2)(i), (ii), or (iii) of this section. See *Example 2* and *Example 3* of paragraph (i) of this section for illustrations of the application of this paragraph (h)(2)(iv).

(3) An *obligation* means any fixed or contingent obligation to make a payment or provide value without regard to whether the obligation is otherwise taken into account for purposes of the Internal Revenue Code. An obligation includes, but is not limited to, a debt obligation, an environmental obligation, a tort obligation, a contract obligation (including an obligation to provide goods or services), a pension obligation, an obligation under a short sale, and an obligation under derivative financial instruments such as options, forward contracts, futures contracts, and swaps. An obligation does not include any obligation treated as stock for purposes of section 7874 (see, for example, § 1.7874-2(i), which treats certain interests, including certain creditor claims, as stock).

(4) A *transfer* is, with respect to stock of the foreign acquiring corporation, an issuance, sale, distribution, exchange, or any other disposition of such stock.

(i) *Examples.*—The following examples illustrate the application of the rules of this section. For purposes of the examples, unless otherwise indicated, assume the following facts in addition to the facts stated in the examples:

(1) FA, FMS, FS, and FT are foreign corporations, all of which have only one class of stock issued and outstanding;

(2) DMS and DT are domestic corporations;

(3) P and R are corporations that may be either domestic or foreign;

(4) PRS is a partnership with individual partners;

(5) The de minimis ownership exception in paragraph (d)(1) of this section does not apply;

(6) None of the shareholders or partners in the entities described in the examples are related persons with respect to each other;

(7) All transactions described in each example occur pursuant to the same plan;

(8) No property is acquired with a principal purpose of avoiding the purposes of section 7874;

(9) FA, FMS, FS, and FT are tax residents in the same foreign country;

(10) For purposes of determining the ownership fraction, no shares of FA stock are excluded from the denominator pursuant to § 1.7874-7(b) (which disregards stock attributable to passive assets); and

**Reg. § 1.7874-4(i)(10)**

(11) For purposes of determining the ownership fraction, no shares of FA stock are treated as received by former shareholders of DT pursuant to §1.7874-10(b) (which disregards certain distributions).

*Example 1. Stock transferred in exchange for marketable securities*—(i) *Facts.* Individual A wholly owns DT. PRS transfers marketable securities (within the meaning of paragraph (h)(1) of this section) to FA, a newly formed corporation, in exchange solely for 25 shares of FA stock. Then Individual A transfers all the DT stock to FA in exchange solely for 75 shares of FA stock.

(ii) *Analysis.* Under paragraph (h)(2)(ii) of this section, the marketable securities constitute nonqualified property. Accordingly, the 25 shares of FA stock transferred by FA to PRS in exchange for the marketable securities constitute disqualified stock described in paragraph (c)(1) of this section by reason of paragraph (c)(1)(i) of this section. Paragraph (c)(2) of this section does not reduce the amount of disqualified stock described in paragraph (c)(1)(i) of this section because the transfer of FA stock in exchange for the marketable securities increases the fair market value of the assets of FA by the fair market value of the marketable securities transferred. Under paragraph (b) of this section, the 25 shares of FA stock transferred to PRS are not included in the denominator of the ownership fraction. See also section 7874(c)(4). Accordingly, the only FA stock included in the ownership fraction is the FA stock transferred to Individual A in exchange for the DT stock, and that FA stock is included in both the numerator and the denominator of the ownership fraction. Thus, the ownership fraction is 75/75.

*Example 2. Stock transferred in exchange for property acquired with a principal purpose of avoiding the purposes of section 7874*—(i) *Facts.* Individual A wholly owns DT. PRS transfers marketable securities (within the meaning of paragraph (h)(1) of this section) to FT, a newly formed corporation, in exchange solely for all the FT stock. Then PRS transfers the FT stock to FA, a newly formed corporation, in exchange solely for 25 shares of FA stock. Finally, Individual A transfers all the DT stock to FA in exchange solely for 75 shares of FA stock. FA acquires the FT stock with a principal purpose of avoiding the purposes of section 7874.

(ii) *Analysis.* Under paragraph (h)(2)(iv) of this section, the FT stock constitutes nonqualified property because a principal purpose of FA acquiring the FT stock is to avoid the purposes of section 7874. Accordingly, the 25 shares of FA stock transferred by FA to PRS in exchange for the FT stock constitute disqualified stock described in paragraph (c)(1) of this section by reason of paragraph (c)(1)(i) of this section. Paragraph (c)(2) of this section does not reduce the amount of disqualified stock described in paragraph (c)(1)(i) of this section because the transfer of FA stock in exchange for the FT stock increases the fair market value of FA's assets by the fair market value of the FT stock. Under paragraph (b) of this section, the 25 shares of FA stock transferred to PRS are not included in the denominator of the ownership fraction. Furthermore, even in the absence of paragraph (h)(2)(iv) of this section, the transfer of marketable securities to FT would be disregarded pursuant to section 7874(c)(4). Accordingly, the only FA stock included in the ownership fraction is the FA stock transferred to Individual A in exchange for the DT stock, and that FA stock is included in both the numerator and the denominator of the ownership fraction. Thus, the ownership fraction is 75/75.

*Example 3. Stock transferred in exchange for property acquired with a principal purpose of avoiding the purposes of section 7874*—(i) *Facts.* DT is a publicly traded corporation. PRS is a foreign partnership that is unrelated to DT. PRS transfers certain business assets (PRS properties) to FA, a newly formed foreign corporation, in exchange solely for 25 shares of FA stock. The shareholders of DT transfer all of their DT stock to FA in exchange solely for the remaining 75 shares of FA stock (DT acquisition). None of the PRS properties is property described in paragraph (h)(2)(i) through (iii) of this section, but FA acquires the PRS properties with a principal purpose of avoiding the purposes of section 7874.

(ii) *Analysis.* Under paragraph (h)(2)(iv) of this section, the PRS properties transferred to FA constitute nonqualified property, because FA acquires the PRS properties in a transaction related to the DT acquisition with a principal purpose of avoiding the purposes of section 7874. Accordingly, the 25 shares of FA stock transferred by FA to PRS in exchange for the PRS properties constitute disqualified stock described in paragraph (c)(1) of this section by reason of paragraph (c)(1)(i) of this section. Paragraph (c)(2) of this section does not apply to reduce the amount of disqualified stock described in paragraph (c)(1)(i) of this section because the transfer of FA stock in exchange for the PRS properties increases the fair market value of FA's assets by the fair market value of the PRS properties. Accordingly, pursuant to paragraph (b) of this section, the 25 shares of FA stock transferred to PRS in exchange for the PRS properties are not included in the denominator of the ownership fraction. Furthermore, even in the absence of paragraph (h)(2)(iv) of this section, the transfer of the PRS properties to FA would be disregarded pursuant to section

7874(c)(4). Therefore, the only FA stock included in the ownership fraction is the FA stock transferred to the former domestic entity shareholders of DT in exchange for their DT stock, and that FA stock is included in both the numerator and the denominator of the ownership fraction. Thus, the ownership fraction is 75/75.

*Example 4. Stock transferred in exchange for stock of a foreign corporation that becomes a member of the expanded affiliated group*—(i) *Facts.* FT, a publicly traded corporation, forms FA, and then FA forms DMS and FMS. FMS merges with and into FT, with FT surviving the merger (FMS-FT merger). Pursuant to the FMS-FT merger, the FT shareholders exchange their FT stock solely for 100 shares of FA stock and FT becomes a wholly owned subsidiary of FA. Following the FMS-FT merger, DMS merges with and into DT, also a publicly traded corporation, with DT surviving the merger (DT acquisition). Pursuant to the DT acquisition, the DT shareholders exchange their DT stock solely for the remaining 100 shares of FA stock, and DT becomes a wholly owned subsidiary of FA. After the completion of the plan, FA wholly owns FT and DT, DMS and FMS cease to exist, and the stock of FA is publicly traded.

(ii) *Analysis.* Because FT becomes a member of the expanded affiliated group that includes FA in a transaction related to the DT acquisition, the FT stock does not constitute marketable securities (within the meaning of paragraph (h)(1) of this section) and therefore does not constitute nonqualified property pursuant to paragraph (h)(2)(ii) of this section. Accordingly, no FA stock is disqualified stock described in paragraph (c)(1) of this section and therefore the FA stock transferred in exchange for the FT stock and DT stock is included in the denominator of the ownership fraction. Thus, the ownership fraction is 100/200.

(iii) *Alternative facts.* The facts are the same as in paragraph (i) of this *Example 4*, except that, instead of undertaking the FMS-FT merger, FT merges with and into FA with FA surviving the merger (FT-FA merger). Pursuant to the FT-FA merger, the FT shareholders exchange their FT stock solely for 100 shares of FA stock. At the time of the FT-FA merger, FT does not hold nonqualified property and has no obligations. Accordingly, FA stock transferred by FA to FT in exchange for the property of FT is not disqualified stock described in paragraph (c)(1) of this section. Furthermore, pursuant to paragraph (c)(2) of this section, the 100 shares of FA stock transferred by FT to the shareholders of FT in exchange for their FT stock do not constitute disqualified stock described in paragraph (c)(1) of this section. Although the FT stock is nonqualified property (the FT stock constitutes marketable securities within the meaning of paragraph (h)(2)(ii) of this section because the stock of FT is publicly traded and FT is not a member of the expanded affiliated group that includes FA after the DT acquisition), under paragraph (c)(2) of this section, the transfer of FA stock by FT to the shareholders of FT neither increases the fair market value of the assets of FA nor decreases the liabilities of FA. Accordingly, no FA stock is disqualified stock described in paragraph (c)(1) of this section and, therefore, the FA stock transferred in exchange for the assets of FT and the DT stock is included in the denominator of the ownership fraction. Thus, the ownership fraction is 100/200.

*Example 5. De minimis exception*—(i) *Facts.* Individual A wholly owns DT. The fair market value of the DT stock is $100x. PRS transfers $96x of cash to FA, a newly formed corporation, in exchange solely for 96 shares of FA stock. Then Individual A transfers the DT stock to FA in exchange for $96x of cash and 4 shares of FA stock (DT acquisition).

(ii) *Analysis.* Under paragraph (h)(2)(i) of this section, cash constitutes nonqualified property. Accordingly, the 96 shares of FA stock transferred by FA to PRS in exchange for $96x of cash constitute disqualified stock described in paragraph (c)(1) of this section by reason of paragraph (c)(1)(i) of this section. Furthermore, paragraph (c)(2) of this section does not reduce the amount of disqualified stock described in paragraph (c)(1)(i) of this section because the transfer of FA stock in exchange for $96x of cash increases the fair market value of the assets of FA by $96x. However, without regard to the application of paragraph (b) of this section and §§1.7874-7(b) and 1.7874-10T(b), the ownership percentage described in section 7874(a)(2)(B)(ii) would be less than 5 (by vote and value), or 4 (4/100, or 4 shares of FA stock held by Individual A by reason of owning the DT stock, determined under §1.7874-2(f)(2), over 100 shares of FA stock outstanding after the DT acquisition). Furthermore, after the DT acquisition and all related transactions, Individual A owns less than 5% (by vote and value, applying the attribution rules of section 318(a) with the modifications described in section 304(c)(3)(B)) of the stock of FA and DT (the members of the expanded affiliated group that includes FA). Accordingly, the de minimis exception in paragraph (d)(1) of this section applies and therefore paragraph (b) of this section does not apply to exclude the FA stock transferred to PRS from the denominator of the ownership fraction. Therefore, the FA stock transferred to Individual A and PRS is included in the denominator of the ownership fraction. Thus, the ownership fraction is 4/100.

*Example 6. Obligation of the expanded affiliated group satisfied with stock*—(i) *Facts.* Individual A wholly owns DT. The stock of DT held by Individual A has a fair market value of $75x. Individual A also holds an obligation of DT with a value and face amount of $25x. DT holds property with a value of $100x, and the $25x obligation is associated with the property. FA, a newly formed corporation, transfers 100 shares of FA stock to Individual A in exchange for all the DT stock and the $25x obligation of DT.

(ii) *Analysis.* Under paragraph (h)(2)(iii)(A) of this section, the $25x obligation of DT constitutes nonqualified property because DT is a member of the expanded affiliated group that includes FA, and Individual A (the holder of the obligation immediately before the domestic entity acquisition and any related transaction) is not a member of the EAG after the domestic entity acquisition and all related transactions. Thus, the shares of FA stock transferred by FA to Individual A in exchange for the obligation of DT constitute disqualified stock described in paragraph (c)(1) of this section by reason of paragraph (c)(1)(i) of this section. Under §1.7874-2(f)(2), Individual A is treated as receiving 75 shares of FA stock in exchange for the DT stock (100 x $75x/$100x) and 25 shares of FA stock in exchange for the obligation of DT (100 x $25x/$100x). Thus, 25 shares of FA stock constitute disqualified stock described in paragraph (c)(1) of this section by reason of paragraph (c)(1)(i) of this section. Paragraph (c)(2) of this section does not reduce the amount of disqualified stock described in paragraph (c)(1)(i) of this section because the transfer of FA stock for the $25x obligation increases the fair market value of FA's assets by $25x. Therefore, under paragraph (b) of this section, the 25 shares of FA stock transferred to Individual A in exchange for the obligation of DT are not included in the denominator of the ownership fraction. Accordingly, the only FA stock included in the ownership fraction is the 75 shares of FA stock transferred to Individual A in exchange for the DT stock, and that FA stock is included in both the numerator and the denominator of the ownership fraction. Thus, the ownership fraction is 75/75.

(iii) *Alternative facts.* The facts are the same as in paragraph (i) of this *Example 6*, except that instead of acquiring the stock of DT and the $25x obligation of DT, FA acquires the $100x of property from DT in exchange solely for 100 shares of FA stock. DT distributes 75 shares of FA stock to Individual A in exchange for Individual A's DT stock and transfers 25 shares of FA stock to Individual A in satisfaction of DT's obligation to Individual A, and liquidates. The 25 shares of FA stock transferred by FA to DT in exchange for the property of DT and then transferred by DT in satisfaction of DT's obligation to Individual A constitute disqualified stock described in paragraph (c)(1) of this section by reason of paragraph (c)(1)(ii) of this section. Paragraph (c)(2) of this section does not reduce the amount of disqualified stock described in paragraph (c)(1)(ii) of this section because the transfer of FA stock in exchange for the property of DT increases the fair market value of FA's assets by $100x (although the amount of disqualified stock is limited to 25 shares of FA stock in this case). Therefore, under paragraph (b) of this section, the 25 shares of FA stock that constitute disqualified stock are not included in the denominator of the ownership fraction. Accordingly, only 75 shares of FA stock are included in the ownership fraction, and that FA stock is included in both the numerator and the denominator of the ownership fraction. Thus, the ownership fraction is 75/75.

*Example 7. "Over-the-top" stock transfer*—(i) *Facts.* Individual A wholly owns DT. Individual B holds all 100 outstanding shares of FA stock. Individual C acquires 20 shares of FA stock from Individual B for cash, and then FA acquires all of the stock of DT from Individual A in exchange solely for 100 shares of FA stock.

(ii) *Analysis.* Under paragraph (h)(2)(i) of this section, cash constitutes nonqualified property. Accordingly, absent the application of paragraph (c)(2) of this section, the 20 shares of FA stock transferred by Individual B to Individual C in exchange for cash would constitute disqualified stock described in paragraph (c)(1) of this section by reason of paragraph (c)(1)(i) of this section. Nevertheless, because Individual B's sale of FA stock neither increases the assets of FA nor decreases the liabilities of FA, such FA stock is not disqualified stock by reason of paragraph (c)(2) of this section. Accordingly, paragraph (b) of this section does not apply to exclude the 20 shares of FA stock sold by Individual B to Individual C, and that FA stock is included in the denominator of the ownership fraction. The 100 shares of FA stock received by Individual A are the only shares included in the numerator of the ownership fraction. Thus, the ownership fraction is 100/200.

*Example 8. Interaction with internal group restructuring rule*—(i) *Facts.* P holds 85 shares of DT stock. The remaining 15 shares of DT stock are held by Individual A. P and Individual A transfer their shares of DT stock to FA, a newly formed corporation, in exchange for 85 and 15 shares of FA stock, respectively (DT acquisition), and PRS transfers $75x of cash to FA in exchange for the remaining 75 shares of FA stock.

(ii) *Analysis.* Under paragraph (h)(2)(i) of this section, cash constitutes nonqualified property. Accordingly, the 75 shares of FA stock

transferred by FA to PRS in exchange for $75x of cash constitute disqualified stock described in paragraph (c)(1) of this section by reason of paragraph (c)(1)(i) of this section. Furthermore, paragraph (c)(2) of this section does not reduce the amount of disqualified stock described in paragraph (c)(1)(i) of this section because the transfer of FA stock in exchange for $75x of cash increases the fair market value of the assets of FA by $75x. Therefore, under paragraph (b) of this section, the 75 shares of FA stock transferred to PRS are not included in the denominator of the ownership fraction. Although PRS's shares of FA stock are excluded from the denominator of the ownership fraction under paragraph (b) of this section, under §1.7874-1(d)(1), such shares of FA stock nonetheless are taken into account for purposes of determining whether P is a member of the expanded affiliated group that includes FA and for purposes of determining whether the DT acquisition qualifies as an internal group restructuring. Because P holds 48.6% of the FA stock (85/175) after the DT acquisition and all transactions related to the DT acquisition, it is not a member of the expanded affiliated group that includes FA. In addition, the DT acquisition does not qualify as an internal group restructuring described in §1.7874-1(c)(2) because P does not hold, directly or indirectly, 80% or more of the shares of FA stock (by vote and value) after the DT acquisition and all transactions related to the DT acquisition. Therefore, the FA stock held by P (along with the FA stock held by Individual A) is included in the numerator and the denominator of the ownership fraction. Thus, the ownership fraction is 100/100.

*Example 9. Interaction with loss of control rule*—(i) *Facts.* P wholly owns DT. P transfers all of its shares of DT stock to FA, a newly formed corporation, in exchange for 49 shares of FA stock (DT acquisition), and R transfers marketable securities (within the meaning of paragraph (h)(1) of this section) to FA in exchange for the remaining 51 shares of FA stock.

(ii) *Analysis.* Under paragraph (h)(2)(ii) of this section, the marketable securities constitute nonqualified property. Accordingly, the shares of FA stock transferred by FA to R in exchange for the marketable securities constitute disqualified stock described in paragraph (c)(1) of this section by reason of paragraph (c)(1)(i) of this section. Paragraph (c)(2) of this section does not reduce the amount of disqualified stock described in paragraph (c)(1)(i) of this section because the transfer of FA stock in exchange for the marketable securities increases the fair market value of the assets of FA by the fair market value of the marketable securities transferred. Therefore, under paragraph (b) of this section, the shares of FA stock transferred to R are not included in the denominator of the ownership fraction. Although under paragraph (b) of this section R's shares of FA stock are excluded from the denominator of the ownership fraction, under §1.7874-1(d)(1), such stock is taken into account for purposes of determining whether P or R is a member of the expanded affiliated group that includes FA. Because P holds 49% of the shares of FA stock (49/100), P is not a member of the expanded affiliated group that includes FA, and P's FA stock is included in both the numerator and the denominator of the ownership fraction. Because R holds 51% of the shares of FA stock (51/100), R is a member of the expanded affiliated group that includes FA and, before taking into account §1.7874-1(c), R's FA stock would be excluded from the numerator and denominator of the ownership fraction under section 7874(c)(2)(A) and §1.7874-1(b). However, the DT acquisition results in a loss of control described in §1.7874-1(c)(3) because P does not hold, in the aggregate, directly or indirectly, more than 50% of the shares of stock (by vote or value) of R, FA, or DT after the acquisition. Accordingly, the FA stock held by R would be included in the denominator of the ownership fraction under §1.7874-1(c)(1). Nevertheless, the FA stock held by R is excluded from the denominator of the ownership fraction under paragraph (b) of this section and §1.7874-1(d)(1). Thus, the ownership fraction is 49/49.

(iii) *Alternative facts.* The facts are the same as in paragraph (i) of this *Example 9*, except that, in exchange for 51 shares of FA stock, R transfers marketable securities (within the meaning of paragraph (h)(1) of this section) with a value equal to that of 16 shares of FA stock and qualified property (within the meaning of paragraph (h)(2) of this section) with a value equal to that of 35 shares of FA stock. Accordingly, 16 of the 51 shares of FA stock transferred to R constitute disqualified stock described in paragraph (c)(1) of this section by reason of paragraph (c)(1)(i) of this section, and 35 of such shares do not constitute disqualified stock. Paragraph (c)(2) of this section does not reduce the amount of disqualified stock described in paragraph (c)(1)(i) of this section because the transfer of FA stock in exchange for the marketable securities increases the fair market value of the assets of FA by the fair market value of the marketable securities transferred. Therefore, under paragraph (b) of this section, 16 of the 51 shares of FA stock transferred to R are not included in the denominator of the ownership fraction. Although 16 of the 51 shares of FA stock that are transferred to R are excluded from the denominator of the ownership fraction, under §1.7874-1(d)(1), all 51 of R's shares of FA stock are taken into account for purposes of determining whether P or R is a member of the expanded affiliated group that includes FA. Because P holds 49% of the shares of FA stock (49/100), it is not a member of the expanded affiliated group that includes FA, and its FA stock is included in both the numerator and the denominator of the ownership fraction. Because R holds 51% of the shares of FA stock (51/100), it is a member of the expanded affiliated group that includes FA and, before taking into account § 1.7874-1(c), its FA stock is excluded from the numerator and denominator of the ownership fraction under section 7874(c)(2)(A) and § 1.7874-1(b). However, the DT acquisition results in a loss of control described in § 1.7874-1(c)(3) because P does not hold, in the aggregate, directly or indirectly, more than 50% of the shares of stock (by vote or value) of R, FA, or DT after the acquisition. Accordingly, the 51 shares of FA stock held by R would be included in the denominator of the ownership fraction under § 1.7874-1(c)(1). Nevertheless, the 16 shares of FA stock that constitute disqualified stock are excluded from the denominator of the ownership fraction under paragraph (b) of this section and § 1.7874-1(d)(1). In addition, the 35 shares of FA stock received by R that do not constitute disqualified stock are included in the denominator. Thus, the ownership fraction is 49/84.

*Example 10. Stock issued in lieu of assuming associated obligation*—(i) *Facts.* Individual A wholly owns DT. The stock of DT has a fair market value of $100x. Individual B wholly owns FT, a foreign corporation, which conducts two businesses, Business C and Business D. Business C comprises property with a gross fair market value of $70x and $20x of associated obligations. Business D comprises property with a gross fair market value of $45x and $35x of associated obligations. Individual A transfers all of the shares of DT stock to FA, a newly formed corporation, in exchange for $100x of FA stock (DT acquisition). In transactions related to the DT acquisition, FA acquires all of the Business C property from FT in exchange for $70x of FA stock and then FT transfers $30x of the FA stock to its creditors in satisfaction of $30x of its obligations. None of the Business C property is nonqualified property.

(ii) *Analysis.* Under paragraph (c)(1) of this section by reason of paragraph (c)(1)(ii) of this section, the $30x of FA stock transferred to FT (the transferee) in exchange for the Business C property (the exchanged property) and then transferred by FT in satisfaction of $30x of its obligations is disqualified stock, except to the extent limited by paragraph (c)(1)(ii)(B) of this section. Under paragraph (c)(1)(ii)(B)(*1*) of this section, the proportionate share of obligations associated with the exchanged property that is not assumed by FA must be determined. The proportionate share of obligations associated with the exchanged property is $20x, calculated as $20x (the obligations associated with the Business C properties) multiplied by $70x/$70x (the fair market value of the exchanged property, $70x, relative to the fair market value of all the Business C property, $70x). The proportionate share of obligations associated with the exchanged property that is not assumed by FA is $20x, calculated as the proportionate share of obligations associated with the exchanged property ($20x) less the obligations assumed by FA ($0x). Under paragraph (c)(1)(ii)(B)(*2*) of this section, the amount of disqualified stock is limited to the proportionate share of obligations associated with the exchanged property that is not assumed ($20x) multiplied by a fraction, which in this case is $70x/$70x (the amount of exchanged property that is qualified property, $70x, divided by the total amount of exchanged property, $70x). Accordingly, $20x of FA stock is disqualified stock under paragraph (c)(1) of this section by reason of paragraph (c)(1)(ii) of this section. Paragraph (c)(2) of this section does not reduce the amount of disqualified stock described in paragraph (c)(1)(ii) of this section because the transfer of the FA stock in exchange for the exchanged property increases the fair market value of FA's assets by $70x (although the amount of disqualified stock is limited to $20x of FA stock in this case). Therefore, under paragraph (b) of this section, the $20x of FA stock that constitutes disqualified stock is not included in the denominator of the ownership fraction. Accordingly, only $150x of FA stock is included in the denominator of the ownership fraction, calculated as the $100x of FA stock received by Individual A plus the $70x of FA stock received by FT less the $20x FA stock that is disqualified stock. Thus, the ownership fraction is $100x/$150x. The result would be the same if, in transactions related to the DT acquisition, FT instead sold the $30x of FA stock for $30x cash and then transferred the cash in satisfaction of $30x of its obligations.

(iii) *Alternative facts.* The facts are the same as in paragraph (i) of this *Example 10*, except that FA acquires only $42x of the Business C property in exchange for $30x of FA stock and the assumption of $12x of the obligations associated with the Business C property. Under paragraph (c)(1) of this section by reason of paragraph (c)(1)(ii) of this section, the $30x of FA stock transferred to FT (the transferee) in exchange for the Business C property (the exchanged property) and then transferred by FT in satisfaction of $30x of its obligations is disqualified stock, except to the extent limited by paragraph (c)(1)(ii)(B) of this section. Under paragraph (c)(1)(ii)(B)(*1*)

of this section, the proportionate share of obligations associated with the exchanged property that is not assumed by FA must be determined. The proportionate share of obligations associated with the exchanged property is $12x, calculated as $20x (the obligations associated with the Business C property) multiplied by $42x/$70x (the fair market value of the exchanged property, $42x, relative to the fair market value of all the Business C property, $70x). The proportionate share of obligations associated with the exchanged property that is not assumed by FA is $0, calculated as the proportionate share of obligations associated with the exchanged property ($12x) less the obligations assumed by FA ($12x). Accordingly, as a result of the application of paragraph (c)(1)(ii)(B)(*2*) of this section, no FA stock is disqualified stock under paragraph (c)(1) of this section by reason of paragraph (c)(1)(ii) of this section. As a result, $130x of FA stock is included in the denominator of the ownership fraction, calculated as the $100x of FA stock received by Individual A plus the $30x of FA stock received by FT. Thus, the ownership fraction is $100x/$130x.

(j) *Applicability dates.*—(1) *General rule.*—Except to the extent otherwise provided in paragraph (j) of this section, this section applies to domestic entity acquisitions completed on or after September 17, 2009. Paragraphs (h)(1) and (h)(2)(iv) of this section apply to domestic entity acquisitions completed on or after November 19, 2015. Paragraph (d)(1)(i) of this section applies to domestic entity acquisitions completed on or after April 4, 2016. Paragraphs (c)(1)(ii), (h)(2)(iii), and (h)(3) of this section apply to domestic entity acquisitions completed on or after January 13, 2017. For domestic entity acquisitions completed before November 19, 2015, see § 1.7874-4T(i)(6) and (i)(7)(iv) (the predecessors of paragraphs (h)(1) and (h)(2)(iv) of this section) as contained in 26 CFR part 1 revised as of April 1, 2016. For domestic entity acquisitions completed on or after September 22, 2014, and before April 4, 2016, see § 1.7874-4T(d)(1)(i) as contained in 26 CFR part 1 revised as of April 1, 2016. For domestic entity acquisitions completed before January 13, 2017, see § 1.7874-4T(c)(1)(ii), (i)(7)(iii) (the predecessor of paragraph (h)(2)(iii) of this section), and (i)(8) (the predecessor of paragraph (h)(3) of this section) as contained in 26 CFR part 1 revised as of April 1, 2016. Paragraph (d)(1)(ii) of this section applies to domestic entity acquisitions completed on or after July 12, 2018, though taxpayers may elect to consistently apply paragraph (d)(1)(ii) of this section to domestic entity acquisitions completed before July 12, 2018. For domestic entity acquisitions completed before July 12, 2018, see § 1.7874-4(d)(1)(ii) as contained in 26 CFR part 1 revised as of April 1, 2017.

(2) *Transitional rules for domestic entity acquisitions completed on or after September 17, 2009, but before January 16, 2014.*—For domestic entity acquisitions completed on or after September 17, 2009, but before January 16, 2014, except as provided in paragraph (j)(3) of this section, this section shall be applied with the following modifications:

(i) Nonqualified property does not include property described in paragraph (h)(2)(iii) of this section.

(ii) A transfer is limited to an issuance of stock of the foreign acquiring corporation.

(iii) The determination of whether stock of the foreign acquiring corporation is described in paragraph (c)(1) of this section is made without regard to paragraphs (c)(1)(ii), (c)(2), and (e) of this section.

(iv) Paragraph (d) of this section and § 1.7874-1(d)(1) do not apply.

(3) *Election for domestic entity acquisitions completed on or after September 17, 2009, and before January 13, 2017.*—If, pursuant to paragraph (j)(1) or (2) of this section, a paragraph of this section would not otherwise apply to a domestic entity acquisition completed on or after September 17, 2009, and before January 13, 2017 (transition period), a taxpayer may elect to apply the paragraph if the taxpayer applies the paragraph consistently to all acquisitions completed during the transition period. The election is made by applying the paragraph to all such acquisitions on a timely filed original return (including extensions) or an amended return filed no later than six months after January 13, 2017. A separate statement or form evidencing the election need not be filed. [Reg. § 1.7874-4.]

☐ [T.D. 9812, 1-13-2017 (corrected 9-6-2017). Amended by T.D. 9834, 7-11-2018.]

### [Reg. § 1.7874-5]

**§ 1.7874-5. Effect of certain transfers of stock related to the acquisition.**—(a) *General rule.*—Stock of a foreign acquiring corporation that is described in section 7874(a)(2)(B)(ii) shall not cease to be so described as a result of any subsequent transfer of the stock by the former domestic entity shareholder or former domestic entity partner that received such stock, even if the subsequent transfer is related to the domestic entity acquisition.

(b) *Example.*—The rule of this section is illustrated by the following example:

*Example.* (i) *Facts.* Individual A wholly owns DT, a domestic corporation. FA, a newly formed foreign corporation, acquires all of the stock of DT from Individual A in exchange solely for 100 shares of FA stock. Pursuant to a binding commitment that was entered into in connection with FA's acquisition of the DT stock, Individual A sells 25 shares of FA stock to B, an unrelated person, in exchange for cash. For federal income tax purposes, the form of the steps of the transaction is respected.

(ii) *Analysis.* Under § 1.7874-2(f)(1), the 100 shares of FA stock received by Individual A are stock of a foreign corporation (FA) that is held by reason of holding stock in a domestic corporation (DT). Accordingly, such stock is described in section 7874(a)(2)(B)(ii). Under paragraph (a) of this section, all 100 shares of FA stock retain their status as being described in section 7874(a)(2)(B)(ii), even though Individual A sells 25 of the 100 shares in connection with the acquisition described in section 7874(a)(2)(B)(i) pursuant to the binding commitment. Therefore, all 100 of the shares of FA stock are included in both the numerator and denominator of the ownership fraction.

(c) *Certain transfers involving expanded affiliated group members.*—For rules addressing whether certain stock is treated as held by members of the expanded affiliated group for purposes of applying section 7874(c)(2)(A) and § 1.7874-1, see § 1.7874-6.

(d) *Definitions.*—The definitions provided in § 1.7874-12 apply for purposes of this section.

(e) *Applicability dates.*—This section applies to domestic entity acquisitions that are completed on or after January 16, 2014. [Reg. § 1.7874-5.]

☐ *[T.D. 9812, 1-13-2017. Amended by T.D. 9834, 7-11-2018.]*

### [Reg. § 1.7874-6]

**§ 1.7874-6. Stock transferred by members of the EAG.—**
(a) *Scope.*—This section provides rules regarding whether transferred stock is treated as held by members of the EAG for purposes of applying section 7874(c)(2)(A) and § 1.7874-1. Paragraph (b) of this section sets forth the general rule under which transferred stock is not treated as held by members of the EAG for purposes of applying section 7874(c)(2)(A) and § 1.7874-1. Paragraph (c) of this section provides exceptions to the general rule. Paragraph (d) of this section provides rules regarding the treatment of partnerships, and paragraph (e) of this section provides rules regarding transactions related to the acquisition. Paragraph (f) of this section provides definitions. Paragraph (g) of this section provides examples illustrating the application of the rules of this section. Paragraph (h) of this section provides dates of applicability.

(b) *General rule.*—Except as provided in paragraph (c) of this section, transferred stock is not treated as held by members of the EAG for purposes of applying section 7874(c)(2)(A) and § 1.7874-1. Transferred stock that is not treated as held by members of the EAG for purposes of applying section 7874(c)(2)(A) and § 1.7874-1 is included in the numerator and the denominator of the ownership fraction. See § 1.7874-5(a).

(c) *Exceptions.*—Transferred stock is treated as held by members of the EAG for purposes of applying section 7874(c)(2)(A) and § 1.7874-1 if paragraph (c)(1) or (2) of this section applies. Transferred stock that is treated as held by members of the EAG for purposes of applying section 7874(c)(2)(A) and § 1.7874-1 is excluded from the numerator of the ownership fraction and, depending upon the application of § 1.7874-1(c), may be excluded from the denominator of the ownership fraction. See §§ 1.7874-1(b) and (c).

(1) *Transfers involving a U.S.-parented group.*—This paragraph (c)(1) applies if the following conditions are satisfied:

(i) Before the domestic entity acquisition, the transferring corporation is a member of a U.S.-parented group.

(ii) After the domestic entity acquisition, each of the transferring corporation (or its successor), any person that holds transferred stock, and the foreign acquiring corporation are members of a U.S.-parented group the common parent of which—

(A) Before the domestic entity acquisition, was a member of the U.S.-parented group described in paragraph (c)(1)(i) of this section; or

(B) Is a corporation that was formed in a transaction related to the domestic entity acquisition, provided that, immediately after the corporation was formed (and without regard to any related transactions), the corporation was a member of the U.S.-parented group described in paragraph (c)(1)(i) of this section.

(2) *Transfers involving a foreign-parented group.*—This paragraph (c)(2) applies if the following conditions are satisfied:

(i) Before the domestic entity acquisition, the transferring corporation and the domestic entity are members of the same foreign-parented group.

(ii) After the domestic entity acquisition, the transferring corporation—

(A) Is a member of the EAG; or

(B) Would be a member of the EAG absent one or more transfers (other than by issuance), in a transaction (or series of transactions) after and related to the domestic entity acquisition, of stock of the foreign acquiring corporation by one or more members of the foreign-parented group described in paragraph (c)(2)(i) of this section.

(d) *Treatment of partnerships.*—(1) *Stock held by a partnership.*—For purposes of this section, each partner in a partnership, as determined without regard to the application of paragraph (d)(2) of this section, is treated as holding its proportionate share of the stock held by the partnership, as determined under the rules and principles of sections 701 through 777.

(2) *Partnership treated as corporation.*—For purposes of this section, if one or more members of an affiliated group, as determined after the application of paragraph (d)(1) of this section, own, in the aggregate, more than 50 percent (by value) of the interests in a partnership, the partnership will be treated as a corporation that is a member of the affiliated group.

(e) *Treatment of transactions related to the acquisition.*—Except as provided in paragraphs (c)(1)(ii)(B) and (c)(2)(ii)(B) of this section, all transactions that are related to a domestic entity acquisition are taken into account in applying this section.

(f) *Definitions.*—In addition to the definitions provided in § 1.7874-12, the following definitions apply for purposes of this section.

(1) A *foreign-parented group* means an affiliated group that has a foreign corporation as the common parent corporation. A *member of the foreign-parented group* is an entity included in the foreign-parented group.

(2) *Transferred stock.*—(i) *In general.*—Transferred stock means stock of the foreign acquiring corporation described in section 7874(a)(2)(B)(ii) that is received by a transferring corporation and, in a transaction (or series of transactions) related to the domestic entity acquisition, is subsequently transferred.

(ii) *Special rule.*—This paragraph (f)(2)(ii) applies in certain cases in which a transferring corporation receives stock of the foreign acquiring corporation described in section 7874(a)(2)(B)(ii) that has the same terms as other stock of the foreign acquiring corporation that is received by the transferring corporation in a transaction (or series of transactions) related to the domestic entity acquisition or that is owned by the transferring corporation prior to the domestic entity acquisition (the stock described in this sentence, collectively, *fungible stock*). Pursuant to this paragraph (f)(2)(ii), if, in a transaction (or series of transactions) related to the domestic entity acquisition, the transferring corporation subsequently transfers less than all of the fungible stock, a pro rata portion of the stock subsequently transferred is treated as consisting of stock of the foreign acquiring corporation described in section 7874(a)(2)(B)(ii). The pro rata portion is based, at the time of the subsequent transfer, on the relative fair market value of the fungible stock that is stock of the foreign acquiring corporation described in section 7874(a)(2)(B)(ii) to the fair market value of all the fungible stock.

(3) A *transferring corporation* means a corporation that is a former domestic entity shareholder or former domestic entity partner.

(4) A *U.S.-parented group* means an affiliated group that has a domestic corporation as the common parent corporation. A *member of the U.S.-parented group* is an entity included in the U.S.-parented group, including the common parent corporation.

(g) *Examples.*—The following examples illustrate the application of this section.

*Example 1. U.S.-parented group exception not available*—(i) *Facts.* USP, a domestic corporation wholly owned by Individual A, owns all the stock of DT, a domestic corporation, as well as other property. The DT stock does not represent substantially all of the property of USP for purposes of section 7874. Pursuant to a reorganization described in section 368(a)(1)(D), USP transfers all the DT stock to FA, a newly formed foreign corporation, in exchange for 100 shares of FA stock (DT acquisition) and distributes the FA stock to Individual A pursuant to section 361(c)(1).

(ii) *Analysis.* The 100 FA shares received by USP are stock of a foreign acquiring corporation described in section 7874(a)(2)(B)(ii) and, under § 1.7874-5(a), the shares retain their status as such even though USP subsequently distributes the shares to Individual A pursuant to section 361(c)(1). Thus, the 100 FA shares are included in the ownership fraction, unless the shares are treated as held by members of the EAG for purposes of applying section 7874(c)(2)(A) and §1.7874-1 and are excluded from the ownership fraction under those rules. For purposes of applying section 7874(c)(2)(A) and §1.7874-1, the 100 FA shares, which constitute transferred stock under paragraph (f)(2) of this section, are treated as held by members of the EAG only if an exception in paragraph (c) of this section applies. See paragraph (b) of this section. The U.S.-parented group exception described in paragraph (c)(1) of this section does not apply. Although before the DT acquisition, USP (the transferring corporation) is a member of a U.S.-parented group of which USP is the common parent, after the DT acquisition, and taking into account all transactions related to the acquisition, each of USP, Individual A (the person that holds the transferred stock), and FA (the foreign acquiring corporation) are not members of a U.S.-parented group described in paragraph (c)(1)(ii)(A) or (B) of this section. Accordingly, because the 100 FA shares are not treated as held by members of the EAG, those shares are included in the numerator and the denominator of the ownership fraction. Therefore, the ownership fraction is 100/100.

*Example 2. U.S.-parented group exception available*—(i) *Facts.* USP, a domestic corporation wholly owned by Individual A, owns all the stock of USS, a domestic corporation, and USS owns all the stock of FT, a foreign corporation. FT owns all the stock of DT, a domestic corporation. FT does not own any other property and has no liabilities. Pursuant to a reorganization described in section 368(a)(1)(F), FT transfers all of its DT stock to FA, a newly formed foreign corporation, in exchange for 100 shares of FA stock (DT acquisition) and distributes the FA stock to USS in liquidation pursuant to section 361(c)(1). In a transaction after and related to the DT acquisition, USP sells 60 percent of the stock of USS (by vote and value) to Individual B.

(ii) *Analysis.* The 100 FA shares received by FT are stock of a foreign acquiring corporation described in section 7874(a)(2)(B)(ii) and, under §1.7874-5(a), the shares retain their status as such even though FT subsequently distributes the shares to USS pursuant to section 361(c)(1). Thus, the 100 FA shares are included in the ownership fraction, unless the shares are treated as held by members of the EAG for purposes of applying section 7874(c)(2)(A) and §1.7874-1 and are excluded from the ownership fraction under those rules. For purposes of applying section 7874(c)(2)(A) and §1.7874-1, the 100 FA shares, which constitute transferred stock under paragraph (f)(2) of this section, are treated as held by members of the EAG only if an exception in paragraph (c) of this section applies. See paragraph (b) of this section. The U.S.-parented group exception described in paragraph (c)(1) of this section applies. The requirement set forth in paragraph (c)(1)(i) of this section is satisfied because before the DT acquisition, FT (the transferring corporation) is a member of a U.S.-parented group of which USP is the common parent (the USP group). The requirement set forth in paragraph (c)(1)(ii) of this section is satisfied because after the DT acquisition, and taking into account all transactions related to the acquisition, each of FA (which is both the successor to FT, the transferring corporation, and the foreign acquiring corporation) and USS (the person that holds the transferred stock) are members of a U.S.-parented group of which USS (a member of the USP group before the DT acquisition) is the common parent. Moreover, the DT acquisition qualifies as an internal group restructuring under §1.7874-1(c)(2). The requirement set forth in §1.7874-1(c)(2)(i) is satisfied because before the DT acquisition, 80 percent or more of the stock (by vote and value) of DT was held directly or indirectly by USS (the corporation that after the acquisition, and taking into account all transactions related to the acquisition, is the common parent of the EAG). The requirement set forth in §1.7874-1(c)(2)(ii) is satisfied because after the acquisition, and taking into account all transactions related to the acquisition, 80 percent or more of the stock (by vote and value) of FA (the foreign acquiring corporation) is held directly or indirectly by USS. Therefore, the 100 FA shares are excluded from the numerator, but included in the denominator, of the ownership fraction. Accordingly, the ownership fraction is 0/100.

*Example 3. U.S.-parented group exception available*—(i) *Facts.* USP, a domestic corporation wholly owned by Individual A, owns all the stock of USS, a domestic corporation, and USS owns all the stock of DT, also a domestic corporation. DT owns all the stock of FT, a foreign corporation. The FT stock represents substantially all of the property of DT for purposes of section 7874. Pursuant to a reorganization described in section 368(a)(1)(D), DT transfers all the FT stock to FA, a newly formed foreign corporation, in exchange for 100 shares of FA stock (DT acquisition) and distributes the FA stock to USS pursuant to section 361(c)(1). In a related transaction, USS distributes all the FA stock to USP under section 355(c)(1). Lastly, in another related transaction and pursuant to a divisive reorganization described in section 368(a)(1)(D), USP transfers all the stock of USS and FA to DP, a newly formed domestic corporation, in exchange for

all the stock of DP and distributes the DP stock to Individual A pursuant to section 361(c)(1).

(ii) *Analysis.* The 100 FA shares received by USS are stock of a foreign acquiring corporation described in section 7874(a)(2)(B)(ii) and, under §1.7874-5(a), the shares retain their status as such even though USS subsequently transfers the shares to USP. Thus, the 100 FA shares are included in the ownership fraction, unless the shares are treated as held by members of the EAG for purposes of applying section 7874(c)(2)(A) and §1.7874-1 and are excluded from the ownership fraction under those rules. For purposes of applying section 7874(c)(2)(A) and §1.7874-1, the 100 FA shares, which constitute transferred stock under paragraph (f)(2) of this section, are treated as held by members of the EAG only if an exception in paragraph (c) of this section applies. See paragraph (b) of this section. The U.S.-parented group exception described in paragraph (c)(1) of this section applies. The requirement set forth in paragraph (c)(1)(i) of this section is satisfied because before the DT acquisition, USS (the transferring corporation) is a member of a U.S.-parented group of which USP is the common parent (the USP group). The requirement set forth in paragraph (c)(1)(ii) of this section is satisfied because after the DT acquisition, and taking into account all transactions related to the acquisition, each of USS, DP (the person that holds the transferred stock), and FA (the foreign acquiring corporation) are members of a U.S.-parented group of which DP (a corporation that was formed in a transaction related to the DT acquisition and that, immediately after it was formed (but without regard to any related transactions) was a member of the USP group) is the common parent. Therefore, the 100 FA shares are excluded from the numerator and the denominator of the ownership fraction. Accordingly, the ownership fraction is 0/0.

*Example 4. Foreign-parented group exception*—(i) *Facts.* Individual A owns all the stock of FT, a foreign corporation, and FT owns all the stock of DT, a domestic corporation. FT does not own any other property and has no liabilities. Pursuant to a reorganization described in section 368(a)(1)(F), FT transfers all the stock of DT to FA, a newly formed foreign corporation, in exchange for 100 shares of FA stock (DT acquisition) and distributes the FA stock to Individual A in liquidation pursuant to section 361(c)(1).

(ii) *Analysis.* The 100 FA shares received by FT are stock of a foreign acquiring corporation described in section 7874(a)(2)(B)(ii) and, under §1.7874-5(a), the shares retain their status as such even though FT subsequently distributes the shares to Individual A pursuant to section 361(c)(1). Thus, the 100 FA shares are included in the ownership fraction, unless the shares are treated as held by members of the EAG of purposes of applying section 7874(a)(2)(A) and §1.7874-1 and are excluded from the ownership fraction under those rules. For purposes of applying section 7874(c)(2)(A) and §1.7874-1, the 100 FA shares, which constitute transferred stock under paragraph (f)(2) of this section, are treated as held by members of the EAG only if an exception in paragraph (c) of this section applies. See paragraph (b) of this section. The foreign-parented group exception described in paragraph (c)(2) of this section applies. The requirement set forth in paragraph (c)(2)(i) of this section is satisfied because before the DT acquisition, FT (the transferring corporation) and DT are members of the foreign-parented group of which FT is the common parent. The requirement set forth in paragraph (c)(2)(ii) of this section is satisfied because after the acquisition, and taking into account all transactions related to the acquisition, FT would be a member of the EAG absent the distribution of the FA shares pursuant to section 361(c)(1). Moreover, the DT acquisition qualifies as an internal group restructuring under §1.7874-1(c)(2). The requirement set forth in §1.7874-1(c)(2)(i) is satisfied because before the acquisition, 80 percent or more of the stock (by vote and value) of DT was held directly or indirectly by FT, the corporation that, without regard to the distribution of the FA shares pursuant to section 361(c)(1), would be common parent of the EAG after the acquisition. See §1.7874-1(c)(2)(iii). The requirement set forth in §1.7874-1(c)(2)(ii) is satisfied because after the acquisition, but without regard to the distribution of the FA shares pursuant to the section 361(c)(1) distribution, FT would directly or indirectly hold 80 percent or more of the stock (by vote and value) of FA (the foreign acquiring corporation). See §1.7874-1(c)(2)(iii). Therefore, the 100 FA shares are excluded from the numerator, but included in the denominator, of the ownership fraction. Accordingly, the ownership fraction is 0/100.

(iii) *Alternative facts.* The facts are the same as in paragraph (i) of this *Example 4*, except that in a transaction after and related to the DT acquisition, FA issues 200 shares of FA stock to Individual B in exchange for qualified property (within the meaning of §1.7874-4(h)(2)). The foreign-parented group exception does not apply because after the acquisition, and taking into account FA's issuance of the 200 FA shares to Individual B, FT would not be a member of the EAG absent FT's distribution of the 100 FA shares pursuant to section 361(c)(1). Accordingly, the 100 FA shares received by FT are not treated as held by a member of the EAG for purposes of applying section 7874(c)(2)(A) and §1.7874-1. As a result, the ownership fraction is 100/300.

(h) *Applicability dates.*—Except as otherwise provided in this paragraph (h), this section applies to domestic entity acquisitions completed on or after September 22, 2014. Paragraphs (d)(2) and (f)(2)(ii) of this section apply to domestic entity acquisitions completed on or after April 4, 2016. Taxpayers, however, may elect either to apply paragraph (c)(2) of this section to domestic entity acquisitions completed before September 22, 2014, or to consistently apply paragraphs (c)(2), (d)(2), and (f)(2)(ii) of this section and §§1.7874-1(c)(2)(iii) and (g) to domestic entity acquisitions completed before April 4, 2016. [Reg. §1.7874-6.]

☐ [T.D. 9834, 7-11-2018.]

**[Reg. §1.7874-7]**

**§1.7874-7. Disregard of certain stock attributable to passive assets.**—(a) *Scope.*—This section identifies certain stock of a foreign acquiring corporation that is attributable to passive assets and that is disregarded in determining the ownership fraction by value. Paragraph (b) of this section sets forth the general rule regarding when stock of a foreign acquiring corporation is excluded from the denominator of the ownership fraction under this section. Paragraph (c) of this section provides a de minimis exception to the application of the general rule of paragraph (b) of this section. Paragraph (d) of this section provides rules for the treatment of partnerships, and paragraph (e) of this section provides definitions. Paragraph (f) of this section provides examples illustrating the application of the rules of this section. Paragraph (g) of this section provides dates of applicability. The rules provided in this section are also subject to section 7874(c)(4). See §1.7874-1(d)(1) for rules addressing the interaction of this section with the expanded affiliated group rules of section 7874(c)(2)(A) and §1.7874-1.

(b) *General rule.*—If, on the completion date, more than fifty percent of the gross value of all foreign group property constitutes foreign group nonqualified property, then, for purposes of determining the ownership percentage by value (but not vote) described in section 7874(a)(2)(B)(ii), stock of the foreign acquiring corporation is excluded from the denominator of the ownership fraction in an amount equal to the product of—

(1) The value of stock of the foreign acquiring corporation, other than stock that is described in section 7874(a)(2)(B)(ii) and stock that is excluded from the denominator of the ownership fraction under §1.7874-1(b), §1.7874-4(b), §1.7874-8(b), §1.7874-9(b), or section §7874(c)(4); and

(2) The foreign group nonqualified property fraction.

(c) *De minimis ownership.*—Paragraph (b) of this section does not apply if—

(1) The ownership percentage described in section 7874(a)(2)(B)(ii), determined without regard to the application of paragraph (b) of this section and §§1.7874-4(b) and 1.7874-10(b), is less than five (by vote and value); and

(2) On the completion date, each five percent former domestic entity shareholder or five percent former domestic entity partner, as applicable, owns (applying the attribution rules of section 318(a) with the modifications described in section 304(c)(3)(B)) less than five percent (by vote and value) of the stock of (or a partnership interest in) each member of the expanded affiliated group. For this purpose, a five percent former domestic entity shareholder (or five percent former domestic entity partner) is a former domestic entity shareholder (or former domestic entity partner) that, before the domestic entity acquisition, owned (applying the attribution rules of section 318(a) with the modifications described in section 304(c)(3)(B)) at least five percent (by vote and value) of the stock of (or a partnership interest in) the domestic entity.

(d) *Treatment of partnerships.*—For purposes of this section, if one or more members of the modified expanded affiliated group own, in the aggregate, more than 50 percent (by value) of the interests in a partnership, the partnership is treated as a corporation that is a member of the modified expanded affiliated group.

(e) *Definitions.*—In addition to the definitions provided in §1.7874-12, the following definitions apply for purposes of this section.

(1) *Foreign group nonqualified property.*—(i) *General rule.*—Foreign group nonqualified property means foreign group property described in §1.7874-4(h)(2), other than the following:

(A) Property that gives rise to income described in section 954(h), determined—

*(1)* In the case of property held by a foreign corporation, by substituting the term "foreign corporation" for the term "controlled foreign corporation;" and

*(2)* In the case of property held by a domestic corporation, by substituting the term "domestic corporation" for the term "controlled foreign corporation," without regard to the phrase "other than the United States" in section 954(h)(3)(A)(ii)(I), and without regard to any inference that the tests in section 954(h) should be calculated or determined without taking transactions with customers located in the United States into account.

(B) Property that gives rise to income described in section 954(i), determined by substituting the term "foreign corporation" for the term "controlled foreign corporation."

(C) Property that gives rise to income described in section 1297(b)(2)(A) or (B) (determined without regard to other passive foreign investment company rules).

(D) Property held by a domestic corporation that is subject to tax as an insurance company under subchapter L of chapter 1 of subtitle A of the Internal Revenue Code, provided that the property is required to support, or is substantially related to, the active conduct of an insurance business.

(ii) *Special rule.*—Foreign group nonqualified property also means any foreign group property that, in a transaction related to the domestic entity acquisition, is acquired in exchange for other property, including cash, if such other property would be described in paragraph (e)(1)(i) of this section had the transaction not occurred.

(2) *Foreign group property* means any property (including excluded property, as described in paragraph (e)(3)(ii) of this section)) held on the completion date by the modified expanded affiliated group, other than—

(i) Property that is directly or indirectly acquired in the domestic entity acquisition;

(ii) Stock or a partnership interest in a member of the modified expanded affiliated group; and

(iii) An obligation of a member of the modified expanded affiliated group.

(3) *Foreign group nonqualified property fraction.*—(i) *In general.*—Foreign group nonqualified property fraction means a fraction calculated with the following numerator and denominator:

(A) The numerator of the fraction is the gross value of all foreign group nonqualified property, other than excluded property (as described in paragraph (e)(3)(ii) of this section).

(B) The denominator of the fraction is the gross value of all foreign group property, other than excluded property (as described in paragraph (e)(3)(ii) of this section)

(ii) *Excluded property.*—For purposes of paragraph (e)(3) of this section, excluded property means property that gives rise to stock that is excluded from the ownership fraction with respect to the domestic entity acquisition under §1.7874-4(b), §1.7874-8(b), §1.7874-9(b), or section 7874(c)(4). For this purpose, only property that was directly or indirectly acquired in a prior domestic entity acquisition (as described in §1.7874-8(g)(4)) or covered foreign acquisition (as described in §1.7874-9(d)(4)) with respect to the domestic entity acquisition may be considered to give rise to stock that is excluded from the ownership fraction with respect to the domestic entity acquisition under §1.7874-8(b) or §1.7874-9(b). If only a portion of the consideration provided in a prior domestic entity acquisition or covered foreign acquisition consisted of stock of the foreign acquiring corporation, then only a pro rata portion of a property directly or indirectly acquired in the prior domestic entity acquisition or covered foreign acquisition may be considered excluded property, based on a fraction the numerator of which is the amount of the consideration that consisted of stock of the foreign acquiring corporation and the denominator of which is the total amount of consideration.

(4) *Modified expanded affiliated group* means, with respect to a domestic entity acquisition, the group described in either paragraph (e)(4)(i) of this section or paragraph (e)(4)(ii) of this section. A *member of the modified expanded affiliated group* is an entity included in the modified expanded affiliated group.

(i) When the foreign acquiring corporation is not the common parent corporation of the expanded affiliated group, the expanded affiliated group determined as if the foreign acquiring corporation was the common parent corporation.

(ii) When the foreign acquiring corporation is the common parent corporation of the expanded affiliated group, the expanded affiliated group.

(f) *Examples.*—The following examples illustrate the rules of this section.

*Example 1. Application of general rule*—(i) *Facts.* Individual A owns all 20 shares of the sole class of stock of FA, a foreign corporation. FA acquires all the stock of DT, a domestic corporation, solely in exchange for 76 shares of newly issued FA stock (DT acquisition). In a transaction related to the DT acquisition, FA issues 4 shares of stock to Individual A in exchange for Asset A, which has a gross value of $50x. On the completion date, in addition to the DT stock and Asset A, FA holds Asset B, which has a gross value of $150x, and Asset C, which has a gross value of $100x. Assets A and B, but not Asset C, are nonqualified property (within the meaning of § 1.7874-4(h)(2)). Further, Asset C was not acquired in a transaction related to the DT acquisition.

(ii) *Analysis.* The 4 shares of FA stock issued to Individual A in exchange for Asset A are disqualified stock under § 1.7874-4(c) and are excluded from the denominator of the ownership fraction pursuant to § 1.7874-4(b). Furthermore, additional shares of FA stock are excluded from the denominator of the ownership fraction pursuant to paragraph (b) of this section. This is because on the completion date, the gross value of all foreign group property is $300x (the sum of the gross values of Assets A, B, and C), the gross value of all foreign group nonqualified property is $200x (the sum of the gross values of Assets A and B), and thus 66.67% of the gross value of all foreign group property constitutes foreign group nonqualified property ($200x/$300x). Because FA has only one class of stock outstanding, the shares of FA stock that are excluded from the denominator of the ownership fraction pursuant to paragraph (b) of this section are calculated by multiplying 20 shares of FA stock (100 shares less the 76 shares described in section 7874(a)(2)(B)(ii) and the 4 shares of disqualified stock) by the foreign group nonqualified property fraction. The numerator of the foreign group nonqualified property fraction is $150x (the gross value of Asset B) and the denominator is $250x (the sum of the gross values of Assets B and C). Asset A is not taken into account for purposes of the foreign group nonqualified property fraction because it gives rise to FA stock that is excluded under § 1.7874-4(b) (4 shares) and, as a result, is excluded property. Accordingly, 12 shares of FA stock are excluded from the denominator of the ownership fraction pursuant to paragraph (b) of this section (20 shares multiplied by $150x/$250x). Thus, a total of 16 shares are excluded from the denominator of the ownership fraction (4 + 12). As a result, the ownership fraction by value is 76/84.

*Example 2. Application of de minimis exception*—(i) *Facts.* Individual A owns all 96 shares of the sole class of stock of FA, a foreign corporation. Individual B wholly owns DT, a domestic corporation. Individuals A and B are not related. FA acquires all the stock of DT solely in exchange for 4 shares of newly issued FA stock (DT acquisition). On the completion date, in addition to all of the stock of DT, FA holds Asset A, which is nonqualified property (within the meaning of § 1.7874-4(h)(2)).

(ii) *Analysis.* Without regard to the application of §§ 1.7874-4(b) and 1.7874-10(b) as well as paragraph (b) of this section, the ownership percentage described in section 7874(a)(2)(B)(ii) would be less than 5 (by vote and value), or 4 (4/100, or 4 shares of FA stock held by Individual B by reason of owning the DT stock, determined under § 1.7874-2(f)(2), over 100 shares of FA stock outstanding after the DT acquisition). Furthermore, on the completion date, Individual B owns less than 5% (by vote and value) of the stock of FA and DT (the members of the expanded affiliated group). Accordingly, the de minimis exception in paragraph (c) of this section applies. Therefore, paragraph (b) of this section does not apply and the ownership fraction is 4/100.

*Example 3. Foreign acquiring corporation not common parent of EAG*—(i) *Facts.* FP, a foreign corporation, owns all 85 shares of the sole class of stock of FA, a foreign corporation. FA acquires all the stock of DT, a domestic corporation, solely in exchange for 65 shares of newly issued FA stock (DT acquisition). On the completion date, FA, in addition to all of the stock of DT, owns Asset A, which has a gross value of $40x, and Asset B, which has a gross value of $45x. Moreover, on the completion date, in addition to the 85 shares of FA stock, FP owns Asset C, which has a gross value of $10x. Assets A and C, but not Asset B, are nonqualified property (within the meaning of § 1.7874-4(h)(2)). Further, Asset B was not acquired in a transaction related to the DT acquisition in exchange for nonqualified property.

(ii) *Analysis.* Under paragraph (e)(2) of this section, Assets A and B, but not Asset C, are foreign group property. Although Asset C is held on the completion date by FP, a member of the expanded affiliated group, Asset C is not foreign group property because FP is not a member of the modified expanded affiliated group. This is the case because if the expanded affiliated group were determined based on FA as the common parent corporation, FP would not be a member of such expanded affiliated group (see paragraph (e)(4)(i) of this section). Under paragraph (e)(1) of this section, Asset A, but not Asset B, is foreign group nonqualified property. Therefore, on the completion date, the gross value of all foreign group property is $85x (the sum of the gross values of Assets A and B), and the gross value of all foreign group nonqualified property is $40x (the gross value of Asset A). Accordingly, on the completion date, only 47.06% of the gross value of all foreign group property constitutes foreign group nonqualified property ($40x/$85x). Consequently, paragraph (b) of this section does not apply to exclude any FA stock from the denominator of the ownership fraction.

*Example 4. Coordination with serial acquisition rule*—(i) *Facts.* Individual A owns all 30 shares of the sole class of stock of FA, a foreign corporation. In Year 1, FA acquires all the stock of DT1, a domestic corporation, solely in exchange for 40 shares of newly issued FA stock (DT1 acquisition). In Year 2, FA acquires all the stock of DT2, a domestic corporation, solely in exchange for 50 shares of newly issued FA stock (DT2 acquisition). On the completion date for the DT2 acquisition, in addition to the DT2 stock, FA holds Asset A, which has a gross value of $15x, Asset B, which has a gross value of $15x, and all the stock of DT1, which has a gross value of $40x. At all times, DT1 holds only Asset C, which has a gross value of $30x, and Asset D, which has a gross value of $10x. Assets A and C, but not Assets B and D, are nonqualified property (within the meaning of § 1.7874-4(h)(2)). In addition, at all times, the fair market value of each share of FA stock is $1x. Further, there have been no redemptions of FA stock subsequent to the DT1 acquisition. Lastly, under § 1.7874-8, the DT1 acquisition is a prior domestic entity acquisition with respect to the DT2 acquisition and $40x of FA stock is excluded from the denominator of the ownership fraction with respect to the DT2 acquisition.

(ii) *Analysis.* Shares of FA stock are excluded from the denominator of the ownership fraction pursuant to paragraph (b) of this section. This is because on the completion date, the gross value of all foreign group property is $70x (the sum of the gross values of Assets A, B, C, and D), the gross value of all foreign group nonqualified property is $45x (the sum of the gross values of Assets A and C), and thus 64.29% of the gross value of all foreign group property constitutes foreign group nonqualified property ($45x/$70x). The shares of FA stock that are excluded from the denominator of the ownership fraction pursuant to paragraph (b) of this section are calculated by multiplying $30x ($120x, the value of all the shares of FA stock, less $50x, the value of the stock described in section 7874(a)(2)(B)(ii), less $40x, the value of the stock excluded under § 1.7874-8(b)) by the foreign group nonqualified property fraction. The property taken into account for purposes of determining the foreign group nonqualified property fraction is Asset A and Asset B. Asset C and Asset D are not taken into account for purposes of the foreign group nonqualified property fraction because they are excluded property. This is because FA indirectly acquired the Assets in the DT1 acquisition (a prior domestic entity acquisition with respect to the DT2 acquisition) and, as a result of that acquisition, $40x of FA stock is excluded from the denominator of the ownership fraction with respect to the DT2 acquisition under § 1.7874-8(b). Thus, the numerator of the foreign group nonqualified property fraction is $15x (the gross value of Asset A) and the denominator is $30x (the sum of the gross values of Asset A, $15x, and Asset B, $15x). Accordingly, $15x of FA stock is excluded from the denominator of the ownership fraction pursuant to paragraph (b) of this section ($30x multiplied by $15x/$30x). Thus, a total of $55x of FA stock is excluded from the denominator of the ownership fraction ($40x + $15x), making the denominator $65x ($120x - $55x). As a result, the ownership percentage with respect to the DT2 acquisition by value is 76.92 ($50x/$65x).

(iii) *Alternative facts.* The facts are the same as in paragraph (i) of this *Example 4*, except as follows. Initially, there are 40 shares of FA stock outstanding, all of which are owned by Individual A. At all times, the gross value of asset D is $20x. In the DT1 acquisition, FA acquires all the stock of DT1 ($50x fair market value) solely in exchange for 40 shares of newly issued FA stock and $10x of other property. As in paragraph (i) of this Example 4, shares of FA stock are excluded from the denominator of the ownership fraction pursuant to paragraph (b) of this section. This is because on the completion date, the gross value of all foreign group property is $80x (the sum of the gross values of Assets A, B, C, and D), the gross value of all foreign group nonqualified property is $45x (the sum of the gross values of Assets A and C), and thus 56.25% of the gross value of all foreign group property constitutes foreign group nonqualified property ($45x/$80x). The shares of FA stock that are excluded from the denominator of the ownership fraction pursuant to paragraph (b) of this section are calculated by multiplying $40x ($130x, the value of all the shares of FA stock, less $50x, the value of the stock described in section 7874(a)(2)(B)(ii), less $40x, the value of the stock excluded under § 1.7874-8(b)) by the foreign group nonqualified property fraction. The property taken into account for purposes of determining the foreign group nonqualified property fraction is Asset A, Asset B, and the portion of Asset C and Asset D that is not excluded property. Eighty percent of each of Asset C and Asset D are considered excluded property because FA indirectly acquired Asset C and Asset D in the DT1 acquisition (a prior domestic entity acquisition with respect to the DT2 acquisition); as a result of that acquisition, $40x of FA stock is excluded from the denominator of the ownership fraction with respect to the DT2 acquisition under § 1.7874-8(b); and 80% of the consideration provided in the DT1 acquisition consisted of stock of FA ($40x/$50x). Thus, the numerator of the foreign group nonqualified property fraction is $21x (the sum of the gross values of Asset A, $15x, and the portion of Asset C that is not excluded property, $6x) and the denominator is $40x (the sum of the gross values of Asset A, $15x, Asset B, $15x, and the portion of Asset C and Asset D that is not excluded property, $6x and $4x, respectively). Accordingly, $21x of FA stock is excluded from the denominator of the ownership fraction pursuant to paragraph (b) of this section ($40x multiplied by $21x/$40x). Thus, a total of $61x of FA stock is excluded from the denominator of the ownership fraction pursuant to paragraph (b) of this section ($40x + $21x), making the denominator $69x ($130x - $61x). As a result, the ownership percentage with respect to D2 acquisition by value is 72.46 ($50x/$69x).

(g) *Applicability dates.*—This section applies to domestic entity acquisitions completed on or after July 12, 2018. For domestic entity acquisitions completed before July 12, 2018, see §1.7874-7T, as contained in 26 CFR part 1 revised as of April 1, 2017. However, to the extent this section differs from §1.7874-7T, as contained in 26 CFR part 1 revised as of April 1, 2017, taxpayers may elect to consistently apply the differences to domestic entity acquisitions completed before July 12, 2018. [Reg. §1.7874-7.]

☐ [T.D. 9834, 7-11-2018.]

### [Reg. §1.7874-8]

**§1.7874-8. Disregard of certain stock attributable to serial acquisitions.**—(a) *Scope.*—This section identifies stock of a foreign acquiring corporation that is disregarded in determining an ownership fraction by value because it is attributable to certain prior domestic entity acquisitions. Paragraph (b) of this section sets forth the general rule regarding the amount of stock of a foreign acquiring corporation that is excluded from the denominator of the ownership fraction by value under this section, and paragraphs (c) through (f) of this section provide rules for determining this amount. Paragraph (g) provides definitions. Paragraph (h) of this section provides examples illustrating the application of the rules of this section. Paragraph (i) of this section provides dates of applicability. This section applies after taking into account §1.7874-2(e). See §1.7874-1(d)(1) for rules addressing the interaction of this section with the expanded affiliated group rules of section 7874(c)(2)(A) and §1.7874-1.

(b) *General rule.*—This paragraph (b) applies to a domestic entity acquisition (relevant domestic entity acquisition) when the foreign acquiring corporation (including a predecessor, as defined in §1.7874-10(f)(1)) has completed one or more prior domestic entity acquisitions. When this paragraph (b) applies, then, for purposes of determining the ownership percentage by value (but not vote) described in section 7874(a)(2)(B)(ii), stock of the foreign acquiring corporation is excluded from the denominator of the ownership fraction in an amount equal to the sum of the excluded amounts computed separately with respect to each prior domestic entity acquisition and each relevant share class.

(c) *Computation of excluded amounts.*—With respect to each prior domestic entity acquisition and each relevant share class, the excluded amount is the product of—

(1) The total number of prior acquisition shares, reduced by the sum of the number of allocable redeemed shares for all redemption testing periods; and

(2) The fair market value of a single share of stock of the relevant share class on the completion date of the relevant domestic entity acquisition.

(d) *Computation of allocable redeemed shares.*—(1) *In general.*—With respect to each prior domestic entity acquisition and each relevant share class, the allocable redeemed shares, determined separately for each redemption testing period, is the product of the number of redeemed shares during the redemption testing period and the redemption fraction.

(2) *Redemption fraction.*—The redemption fraction is determined separately with respect to each prior domestic entity acquisition, each relevant share class, and each redemption testing period, as follows:

(i) The numerator is the total number of prior acquisition shares, reduced by the sum of the number of allocable redeemed shares for all prior redemption testing periods.

(ii) The denominator is the sum of—

(A) The number of outstanding shares of the foreign acquiring corporation stock as of the end of the last day of the redemption testing period; and

(B) The number of redeemed shares during the redemption testing period.

(e) *Rules for determining redemption testing periods.*—(1) *In general.*—Except as provided in paragraph (e)(2) of this section, a redemption testing period with respect to a prior domestic entity acquisition is the period beginning on the day after the completion date of the prior domestic entity acquisition and ending on the day prior to the completion date of the relevant domestic entity acquisition.

(2) *Election to use multiple redemption testing periods.*—A foreign acquiring corporation may establish a reasonable method for dividing the period described in paragraph (e)(1) of this section into shorter periods (each such shorter period, a redemption testing period). A reasonable method would include a method based on a calendar convention (for example, daily, monthly, quarterly, or yearly), or on a convention that triggers the start of a new redemption testing period whenever a share issuance occurs that exceeds a certain threshold. In order to be reasonable, the method must be consistently applied with respect to all prior domestic entity acquisitions and all relevant share classes.

(f) *Appropriate adjustments required to take into account share splits and similar transactions.*—For purposes of this section, appropriate adjustments must be made to take into account changes in a foreign acquiring corporation's capital structure, including, for example, stock splits, reverse stock splits, stock distributions, recapitalizations, and similar transactions. Thus, for example, in determining the total number of prior acquisition shares with respect to a relevant share class, appropriate adjustments must be made to take into account a stock split with respect to that relevant share class that occurs after the completion date with respect to a prior domestic entity acquisition.

(g) *Definitions.*—In addition to the definitions provided in §1.7874-12, the following definitions apply for purposes of this section.

(1) A *binding contract* means an instrument enforceable under applicable law against the parties to the instrument. The presence of a condition outside the control of the parties (including, for example, regulatory agency approval) does not prevent an instrument from being a binding contract. Further, the fact that insubstantial terms remain to be negotiated by the parties to the contract, or that customary conditions remain to be satisfied, does not prevent an instrument from being a binding contract. A tender offer that is subject to section 14(d) of the Securities and Exchange Act of 1934, (15 U.S.C. 78n(d)(1)), and Regulation 14D (17 CFR 240.14d-1 through 240.14d-103) and that is not pursuant to a binding contract, is treated as a binding contract made on the date of its announcement, notwithstanding that it may be modified by the offeror or that it is not enforceable against the offerees.

(2) A *relevant share class* means, with respect to a prior domestic entity acquisition, each separate legal class of shares in the foreign acquiring corporation from which prior acquisition shares were issued. See also paragraph (f) of this section (requiring appropriate adjustments in certain cases).

(3) *Total number of prior acquisition shares* means, with respect to a prior domestic entity acquisition and each relevant share class, the total number of shares of stock of the foreign acquiring corporation that were described in section 7874(a)(2)(B)(ii) as a result of that acquisition (without regard to whether the 60 percent test of section 7874(a)(2)(B)(ii) was satisfied), other than stock treated as received by former domestic entity shareholders or former domestic entity partners under §1.7874-10(b) or section 7874(c)(4), adjusted as appropriate under paragraph (f) of this section.

(4) A *prior domestic entity acquisition.*—(i) *General rule.*—Except as provided in this paragraph (g)(4), a prior domestic entity acquisition means, with respect to a relevant domestic entity acquisition, a domestic entity acquisition that occurred within the 36-month period ending on the signing date of the relevant domestic entity acquisition.

(ii) *Exception.*—A domestic entity acquisition is not a prior domestic entity acquisition if it is described in paragraph (g)(4)(ii)(A) or (B) of this section.

(A) *De minimis.*—A domestic entity acquisition is described in this paragraph (g)(4)(ii)(A) if—

(1) The ownership percentage described in section 7874(a)(2)(B)(ii) with respect to the domestic entity acquisition was less than five (by vote and value); and

(2) The fair market value of the stock of the foreign acquiring corporation described in section 7874(a)(2)(B)(ii) as a result of the domestic entity acquisition (without regard to whether the 60 percent test of section 7874(a)(2)(B)(ii) was satisfied) did not exceed $50 million, as determined on the completion date with respect to the domestic entity acquisition.

(B) *Foreign-parented group.*—A domestic entity acquisition is described in this paragraph (g)(4)(ii)(B) if—

(1) Before the domestic entity acquisition and any related transaction, the domestic entity was a member of a foreign-parented group (as described in §1.7874-6(f)(1)); and

(2) The domestic entity acquisition qualified for the internal group restructuring exception under §1.7874-1(c)(2).

(5) A *redeemed share* means a share of stock in a relevant share class that was redeemed (within the meaning of section 317(b)).

(6) A *signing date* means the first date on which the contract to effect the relevant domestic entity acquisition is a binding contract, or if another binding contract to effect a substantially similar acquisition was terminated with a principal purpose of avoiding section 7874, the first date on which such other contract was a binding contract.

(h) *Examples.*—The following examples illustrate the rules of this section.

*Example 1. Application of general rule*—(i) *Facts.* Individual A wholly owns DT1, a domestic corporation. Individual B owns all 100 shares of the sole class of stock of FA, a foreign corporation. In Year 1, FA acquires all the stock of DT1 solely in exchange for 100 shares of newly issued FA stock (DT1 acquisition). On the completion date with respect to the DT1 acquisition, the fair market value of each share of FA stock is $1x. In Year 3, FA enters into a binding contract to acquire all the stock of DT2, a domestic corporation wholly owned by Individual C. Thereafter, FA acquires all the stock of DT2 solely in exchange for 150 shares of newly issued FA stock (DT2 acquisition). On the completion date with respect to the DT2 acquisition, the fair market value of each share of FA stock is $1.50x. FA did not complete the DT1 acquisition and DT2 acquisition pursuant to a plan (or series of related transactions) for purposes of applying §1.7874-2(e). In addition, there have been no redemptions of FA stock subsequent to the DT1 acquisition.

(ii) *Analysis.* The DT1 acquisition is a prior domestic entity acquisition with respect to the DT2 acquisition (the relevant domestic entity acquisition) because the DT1 acquisition occurred within the 36-month period ending on the signing date with respect to the DT2 acquisition. Accordingly, paragraph (b) of this section applies to the DT2 acquisition. As a result, and because there were no redemptions of FA stock, the excluded amount is $150x, calculated as 100 (the total number of prior acquisition shares) multiplied by $1.50x (the fair market value of a single share of FA stock on the completion date with respect to the DT2 acquisition). Accordingly, the numerator of the ownership fraction by value is $225x (the fair market value of the stock of FA that, with respect to the DT2 acquisition, is described in section 7874(a)(2)(B)(ii)) (150 shares x $1.50x per share). In addition, the denominator of the ownership fraction is $375x (calculated as $525x, the fair market value of all 350 shares of FA stock as of the completion date with respect to the DT2 acquisition, less $150x, the excluded amount). Therefore, the ownership percentage by value is 60 ($225x divided by $375x).

*Example 2. Effect of certain redemptions*—(i) *Facts.* The facts are the same as in paragraph (i) of *Example 1* of this paragraph (h), except that in Year 2 FA redeems 50 shares of its stock (the Year 2 redemption).

(ii) *Analysis.* As is the case in paragraph (ii) of *Example 1* of this paragraph (h), the DT1 acquisition is a prior domestic entity acquisition with respect to the DT2 acquisition (the relevant domestic entity acquisition), and paragraph (b) of this section thus applies to the DT2 acquisition. Because of the Year 2 redemption, the allocable redeemed shares, and thus the redemption fraction, must be calculated. For this purpose, the redemption testing period is the period beginning on the day after the completion date with respect to the DT1 acquisition and ending on the day prior to the completion date with respect to the DT2 acquisition. The redemption fraction for the redemption testing period is thus 100/200, calculated as 100 (the total number of prior acquisition shares) divided by 200 (150, the number of outstanding shares of FA stock on the last day of the redemption testing period, plus 50, the number of redeemed shares during the redemption testing period), and the allocable redeemed shares for the redemption testing period is 25, calculated as 50 (the number of redeemed shares during the redemption testing period) multiplied by 100/200 (the redemption fraction for the redemption testing period). As a result, the excluded amount is $112.50x, calculated as 75 (100, the total number of prior acquisition shares, less 25, the allocable redeemed shares) multiplied by $1.50x (the fair market value of a single share of FA stock on the completion date with respect to the DT2 acquisition). Accordingly, the numerator of the ownership fraction by value is $225x (the fair market value of the stock of FA that, with respect to the DT2 acquisition, is described in section 7874(a)(2)(B)(ii)) (150 shares x $1.50x per share), and the denominator of the ownership fraction is $337.50x (calculated as $450x, the fair market value of all 300 shares of FA stock as of the completion date with respect to the DT2 acquisition, less $112.50x, the excluded amount). Therefore, the ownership percentage by value is 66.67 ($225x divided by $337.50x).

*Example 3. Stock split*—(i) *Facts.* The facts are the same as in paragraph (i) of *Example 2* of this paragraph (h), except as follows. After the Year 2 redemption, but before the DT2 acquisition, FA undergoes a stock split and, as a result, each of the 150 shares of FA stock outstanding are converted into two shares (Year 2 stock split). Further, pursuant to the DT2 acquisition, FA acquires all the stock of DT2 solely in exchange for 300 shares of newly issued FA stock. Moreover, on the completion date with respect to the DT2 acquisition, the fair market value of each share of FA stock is $0.75x.

(ii) *Analysis.* As is the case in paragraph (ii) of *Example 1* of this paragraph (h), the DT1 acquisition is a prior domestic entity acquisition with respect to the DT2 acquisition (the relevant domestic entity acquisition), and paragraph (b) of this section applies to the DT2 acquisition. In addition, as is the case in paragraph (ii) of *Example 2* of this paragraph (h), the redemption testing period is the period beginning on the day after the completion date with respect to the DT1 acquisition and ending on the day prior to the completion date with respect to the DT2 acquisition. To calculate the redemption fraction, the total number of prior acquisition shares and the number of redeemed shares during the redemption testing period must be appropriately adjusted to take into account the Year 2 stock split. See paragraph (f) of this section. In this case, the appropriate adjustment is to increase the total number of prior acquisition shares from 100 to 200 and to increase the number of redeemed shares during the redemption testing period from 50 to 100. Thus, the redemption fraction for the redemption testing period is 200/400, calculated as 200 (the total number of prior acquisition shares) divided by 400 (300, the number of outstanding shares of FA stock on the last day of the redemption testing period, plus 100, the number of redeemed shares during the redemption testing period), and the allocable redeemed shares for the redemption testing period is 50, calculated as 100 (the number of redeemed shares during the redemption testing period) multiplied by 200/400 (the redemption fraction for the redemption testing period). In addition, for purposes of calculating the excluded amount, the total number of prior acquisition shares must be adjusted from 100 to 200. See paragraph (f) of this section. Accordingly, the excluded amount is $112.50x, calculated as 150 (200, the total number of prior acquisition shares, less 50, the allocable redeemed shares) multiplied by $0.75x (the fair market value of a single share of FA stock on the completion date with respect to the DT2 acquisition). Consequently, the numerator of the ownership fraction by value is $225x (the fair market value of the stock of FA that, with respect to the DT2 acquisition, is described in section 7874(a)(2)(B)(ii)) (300 shares x $0.75x per share), and the denominator of the ownership fraction is $337.50x (calculated as $450x, the fair market value of all 600 shares of FA stock as of the completion date with respect to the DT2 acquisition, less $112.50x, the excluded amount). Therefore, the ownership percentage by value is 66.67 ($225 divided by $337.50x).

(i) *Applicability dates.*—Except as provided in this paragraph (i), this section applies to domestic entity acquisitions completed on or after April 4, 2016, regardless of when a prior domestic entity acquisition was completed. Paragraphs (g)(3) and (g)(4)(ii) of this section apply to domestic entity acquisitions completed on or after July 12, 2018. However, taxpayers may elect to consistently apply paragraphs (g)(3) and (g)(4)(ii) of this section to domestic entity acquisitions completed on or after April 4, 2016, and before July 12, 2018. For domestic entity acquisitions completed on or after April 4, 2016, and before July 12, 2018, see §1.7874-8T(g)(3) and (g)(4)(ii) as contained in 26 CFR part 1 revised as of April 1, 2017. [Reg. §1.7874-8.]

☐ [*T.D.* 9834, 7-11-2018.]

**[Reg. §1.7874-9]**

**§1.7874-9. Disregard of certain stock in third-country transactions.**—(a) *Scope.*—This section identifies certain stock of a foreign acquiring corporation that is disregarded in determining the ownership fraction. Paragraph (b) of this section provides a rule that, in a third-country transaction, excludes from the denominator of the ownership fraction stock in the foreign acquiring corporation held by former shareholders of an acquired foreign corporation by reason of holding certain stock in that foreign corporation. Paragraph (c) of this section defines a third-country transaction, and paragraph (d) of this section provides other definitions. Paragraph (e) of this section provides operating rules. Paragraph (f) of this section provides an example illustrating the application of the rules of this section. Paragraph (g) of this section provides the dates of applicability. See §1.7874-1(d)(1) for rules addressing the interaction of this section with the expanded affiliated group rules of section 7874(c)(2)(A) and §1.7874-1.

(b) *Exclusion of certain stock of a foreign acquiring corporation from the ownership fraction.*—When a domestic entity acquisition is a third-country transaction, stock of the foreign acquiring corporation held by reason of holding stock in the acquired foreign corporation (within the meaning of paragraph (e)(4) of this section) is, to the extent the stock otherwise would be included in the denominator of the ownership fraction, excluded from the denominator of the ownership fraction pursuant to this paragraph.

(c) *Third-country transaction.*—A domestic entity acquisition is a third-country transaction if the following requirements are satisfied:

(1) The foreign acquiring corporation completes a covered foreign acquisition pursuant to a plan (or series of related transactions) that includes the domestic entity acquisition.

(2) After the covered foreign acquisition and all related transactions are complete, the foreign acquiring corporation is not a tax resident of the foreign country in which the acquired foreign corporation was a tax resident before the covered foreign acquisition and all related transactions.

(3) The ownership percentage described in section 7874(a)(2)(B)(ii), determined without regard to the application of paragraph (b) of this section, is at least 60.

(d) *Definitions.*—In addition to the definitions provided in §1.7874-12, the following definitions apply for purposes of this section.

(1) A *foreign acquisition* means a transaction in which a foreign acquiring corporation directly or indirectly acquires substantially all of the properties held directly or indirectly by an acquired foreign corporation (within the meaning of paragraph (e)(2) of this section).

(2) An *acquired foreign corporation* means a foreign corporation whose properties are acquired in a foreign acquisition.

(3) *Foreign ownership percentage* means, with respect to a foreign acquisition, the percentage of stock (by vote or value) of the foreign acquiring corporation held by reason of holding stock in the acquired foreign corporation (within the meaning of paragraph (e)(3) of this section).

(4) *Covered foreign acquisition.*—(i) *In general.*—Except as provided in paragraphs (d)(4)(ii) and (iii) of this section, a covered foreign acquisition means a foreign acquisition in which, after the acquisition and all related transactions are complete, the foreign ownership percentage is at least 60.

(ii) *Substantial business activities exception.*—A foreign acquisition is not a covered foreign acquisition if, on the completion date, the following requirements are satisfied:

(A) The foreign acquiring corporation is a tax resident of a foreign country.

(B) The expanded affiliated group has substantial business activities in the country in which the foreign acquiring corporation is a tax resident when compared to the total business activities of the expanded affiliated group. For this purpose, the principles of §1.7874-3 apply and the determination of whether there are substantial business activities is made without regard to the domestic entity acquisition.

(iii) *No income tax exception.*—A foreign acquisition is not a covered foreign acquisition if—

(A) Before the acquisition and all related transactions, the acquired foreign corporation was created or organized in, or under the law of, a foreign country that does not impose corporate income tax and was not a tax resident of any other foreign country; and

(B) After the acquisition and all related transactions are complete, the foreign acquiring corporation is created or organized in, or under the law of, a foreign country that does not impose corporate income tax and is not a tax resident of any other foreign country.

(5) A *tax resident* of a foreign country has the meaning set forth in §1.7874-3(d)(11).

(e) *Operating rules.*—The following rules apply for purposes of this section.

(1) *Acquisition of multiple foreign corporations that are tax residents of the same foreign country.*—When multiple foreign acquisitions occur pursuant to the same plan (or a series of related transactions) and two or more of the acquired foreign corporations were tax residents of the same foreign country before the foreign acquisitions and all related transactions, then those foreign acquisitions are treated as a single foreign acquisition and those acquired foreign corporations are treated as a single acquired foreign corporation for purposes of this section.

(2) *Acquisition of properties of an acquired foreign corporation.*—For purposes of determining whether a foreign acquisition occurs, the principles of section 7874(a)(2)(B)(i) and §1.7874-2(c) and (d) (regarding acquisitions of properties of a domestic entity and acquisitions by multiple foreign corporations) apply with the following modifications:

(i) The principles of §1.7874-2(c)(1) (providing rules for determining whether there is an indirect acquisition of properties of a domestic entity), including §1.7874-2(b)(5) (providing rules for determining the proportionate amount of properties indirectly acquired), apply by substituting the term "foreign" for "domestic" wherever it appears.

(ii) The principles of §1.7874-2(c)(2) (regarding acquisitions of stock of a foreign corporation that owns a domestic entity) apply by substituting the term "domestic" for "foreign" wherever it appears.

(3) *Computation of foreign ownership percentage.*—For purposes of determining a foreign ownership percentage, the principles of all rules applicable to calculating an ownership percentage apply (including §§1.7874-2, 1.7874-4, 1.7874-5, 1.7874-7, and section 7874(c)(4)) with the following modifications:

(i) Stock of a foreign acquiring corporation described in section 7874(a)(2)(B)(ii) is not taken into account.

(ii) The principles of this section, section 7874(c)(2)(A), and §§1.7874-1, 1.7874-6, 1.7874-8, and 1.7874-10 do not apply.

(iii) The principles of §1.7874-7 apply by, in addition to the exclusions listed in §1.7874-7(e)(2)(i) through (iii), also excluding from the definition of foreign group property any property held directly or indirectly by the acquired foreign corporation immediately before the foreign acquisition and directly or indirectly acquired in the foreign acquisition.

(4) *Stock held by reason of holding stock in an acquired foreign corporation.*—For purposes of determining stock of a foreign acquiring corporation held by reason of holding stock in an acquired foreign corporation, the principles of section 7874(a)(2)(B)(ii) and §§1.7874-2(f) and 1.7874-5 apply.

(5) *Change in the tax residency of a foreign corporation.*—For purposes of this section, a change in a country in which a foreign corporation is a tax resident is treated as a transaction. Further, for purposes of this section, if a foreign acquiring corporation changes the country in which it is a tax resident in a manner that would not otherwise be considered to result in a foreign acquisition (for example, by changing where it is managed and controlled), then the foreign acquiring corporation is treated as—

(i) Both an acquired foreign corporation and a foreign acquiring corporation; and

(ii) Directly or indirectly acquiring all of the properties held directly or indirectly by the acquired foreign corporation solely in exchange for stock of the foreign acquiring corporation.

(f) *Example.*—The following example illustrates the rules of this section.

*Example. Third-country transaction*—(i) *Facts.* FA, a newly formed foreign corporation that is a tax resident of Country Y, acquires all the stock of DT, a domestic corporation that is wholly owned by Individual A, solely in exchange for 65 shares of newly issued FA stock (DT acquisition). Pursuant to a plan that includes the DT acquisition, FA acquires all the stock of FT, a foreign corporation that is a tax resident of Country X and wholly owned by Individual B, solely in exchange for the remaining 35 shares of newly issued FA stock (FT acquisition). After the FT acquisition and all related transactions, the expanded affiliated group does not have substantial business activities in Country Y when compared to the total business activities of the expanded affiliated group, as determined under the principles of §1.7874-3 and without regard to the DT acquisition.

(ii) *Analysis.* As described in paragraphs (A) through (C) of this *Example*, the requirements set forth in paragraphs (c)(1) through (3) of this section are satisfied and, as result, the DT acquisition is a third-country transaction.

(A) The FT acquisition is a foreign acquisition because, pursuant to the FT acquisition, FA (a foreign acquiring corporation) acquires 100 percent of the stock of FT and is thus treated as indirectly acquiring 100 percent of the properties held by FT (an acquired foreign corporation). See §1.7874-2(c)(1) and paragraph (e)(2) of this section. Moreover, Individual B is treated as receiving 35 shares of FA stock by reason of holding stock in FT. See §1.7874-2(f)(1)(i) and paragraph (e)(4) of this section. As a result, not taking into account the 65 shares of FA stock held by Individual A (a former domestic entity shareholder), 100 percent (35/35) of the stock of FA is held by reason of holding stock in FT and, thus, the foreign ownership percentage is 100. See paragraph (e)(3) of this section. Accordingly, the FT acquisition is a covered foreign acquisition. Therefore, because the FT acquisition occurs pursuant to a plan that includes the DT acquisition, the requirement set forth in paragraph (c)(1) of this section is satisfied.

(B) The requirement set forth in paragraph (c)(2) of this section is satisfied because, after the FT acquisition and all related transactions, the foreign country in which FA is a tax resident (Country Y) is different than the foreign country in which FT was a resident (Country X) before the FT acquisition and all related transactions.

(C) The requirement set forth in paragraph (c)(3) of this section is satisfied because, not taking into account paragraph (b) of this section, the ownership fraction is 65/100 and the ownership percentage is 65.

(D) Because the DT acquisition is a third-country transaction, the 35 shares of FA stock held by reason of holding stock in FT are excluded from the denominator of the ownership fraction. See paragraph (b) of this section. As a result, the ownership fraction is 65/65 and the ownership percentage is 100. The result would be the same if instead FA had directly acquired all of the properties held by FT in exchange for FA stock, for example, in a transaction that would qualify for U.S. federal income tax purposes as an asset reorganization under section 368.

(iii) *Alternative facts.* The facts are the same as in paragraph (i) of this example, except that before the FT acquisition, but in a transaction related to the FT acquisition, FT becomes a tax resident of Country Y by reincorporating in Country Y. As is the case in paragraph (ii) of this *Example*, the requirements set forth in paragraphs (c)(1) and (3) of this section are satisfied. The requirement set forth in paragraph (c)(2) of this section is satisfied because, after the FT acquisition and any related transactions, the foreign country of which FA is a tax resident (Country Y) is different than the foreign country of which FT was a tax resident (Country X) before the FT acquisition and the reincorporation. See paragraph (e)(5) of this section. Accordingly, the DT acquisition is a third-country transaction and the consequences are the same as in paragraph (ii)(D) of this *Example*.

(iv) *Alternative facts.* The facts are the same as in paragraph (i) of this *Example*, except that, instead of FA acquiring all of the stock of FT, FS, a newly formed foreign corporation that is wholly owned by FA and that is a tax resident of Country X, acquires all the stock of FT solely in exchange for 35 shares of newly issued FA stock (FT acquisition). As a result of the FT acquisition, FS and FA are each treated as indirectly acquiring 100 percent of the properties held by FT. See § 1.7874-2(c)(1)(i) and (iii) and paragraph (e)(2) of this section. Accordingly, each of FS's and FA's indirect acquisition of properties of FT (an acquired foreign corporation) is a foreign acquisition. However, FS's indirect acquisition of FT's properties is not a covered foreign acquisition because no shares of FS stock are held by reason of holding stock in FT; thus, with respect to this foreign acquisition, the foreign ownership percentage is zero. See § 1.7874-2(f) and paragraphs (e)(3) and (4) of this section. FA's indirect acquisition of FT's properties is a covered foreign acquisition because 35 shares of FA stock (the shares received by Individual B) are held by reason of holding stock in FT; thus, the foreign ownership percentage is 100 percent (35/35). See § 1.7874-2(f)(1)(i) and paragraphs (e)(3) and (4) of this section. Accordingly, because the FT acquisition occurs pursuant to a plan that includes the DT acquisition, the requirement set forth in paragraph (c)(1) of this section is satisfied. Further, as is the case in paragraphs (ii)(B) through (C) of this *Example*, the requirements set forth in paragraphs (c)(2) and (3) of this section are satisfied. Therefore, the DT acquisition is a third-country transaction and the consequences are the same as in paragraph (ii)(D) of this *Example*.

(g) *Applicability dates.*—This section applies to domestic entity acquisitions completed on or after July 12, 2018. For domestic entity acquisitions completed before July 12, 2018, see § 1.7874-9T, as contained in 26 CFR part 1 revised as of April 1, 2017. However, to the extent this section differs from § 1.7874-9T, as contained in 26 CFR part 1 revised as of April 1, 2017, taxpayers may elect to consistently apply the differences to domestic entity acquisitions completed before July 12, 2018. [Reg. § 1.7874-9.]

☐ [T.D. 9834, 7-11-2018.]

**[Reg. § 1.7874-10]**

**§ 1.7874-10. Disregard of certain distributions.**—(a) *Scope.*—This section identifies distributions made by a domestic entity that are disregarded in determining an ownership fraction. Paragraph (b) of this section provides the general rule that former domestic entity shareholders or former domestic entity partners are treated as receiving additional stock of the foreign acquiring corporation when the domestic entity has made non-ordinary course distributions (NOCDs). Paragraph (c) of this section identifies distributions that, in whole or in part, are outside the scope of this section. Paragraph (d) of this section provides a de minimis exception to the application of the general rule in paragraph (b) of this section. Paragraph (e) of this section provides rules concerning the treatment of distributions made by a predecessor, and paragraph (f) of this section provides rules for identifying a predecessor. Paragraph (g) of this section provides a special rule for certain distributions described in section 355. Paragraph (h) of this section provides rules regarding the allocation of NOCD stock. Paragraph (i) of this section addresses cases in which there are multiple foreign acquiring corporations, and paragraph (j) of this section addresses cases in which multiple domestic entities are treated as a single domestic entity. Paragraph (k) of this section provides definitions. Paragraph (l) of this section provides dates of applicability. See § 1.7874-1(d)(2) for rules addressing the interaction of this section with the expanded affiliated group rules of section 7874(c)(2)(A) and § 1.7874-1.

(b) *General rule regarding NOCDs.*—Except as provided in paragraph (d) of this section, for purposes of determining the ownership

percentage by value (but not vote) described in section 7874(a)(2)(B)(ii), former domestic entity shareholders or former domestic entity partners, as applicable, are treated as receiving, by reason of holding stock or partnership interests in a domestic entity, stock of the foreign acquiring corporation with a fair market value equal to the amount of the non-ordinary course distributions (NOCDs), determined as of the date of the distributions, made by the domestic entity during the look-back period. The stock of the foreign acquiring corporation treated as received under this paragraph (b) (NOCD stock) is in addition to stock of the foreign acquiring corporation otherwise treated as received by the former domestic entity shareholders or former domestic entity partners by reason of holding stock or partnership interests in the domestic entity.

(c) *Distributions that are not NOCDs.*—If only a portion of a distribution is an NOCD, section 7874(c)(4) may apply to the remainder of the distribution. This section does not, however, create a presumption that section 7874(c)(4) applies to the remainder of the distribution.

(d) *De minimis exception to the general rule.*—Paragraph (b) of this section does not apply if—

(1) The ownership percentage described in section 7874(a)(2)(B)(ii), determined without regard to the application of paragraph (b) of this section and § § 1.7874-4(b) and 1.7874-7(b), is less than five (by vote and value); and

(2) On the completion date, each five percent former domestic entity shareholder or five percent former domestic entity partner, as applicable, owns (applying the attribution rules of section 318(a) with the modifications described in section 304(c)(3)(B)) less than five percent (by vote and value) of the stock of (or a partnership interest in) each member of the expanded affiliated group. For this purpose, a five percent former domestic entity shareholder (or five percent former domestic entity partner) is a former domestic entity shareholder (or former domestic entity partner) that, before the domestic entity acquisition, owned (applying the attribution rules of section 318(a) with the modifications described in section 304(c)(3)(B)) at least five percent (by vote and value) of the stock of (or a partnership interest in) the domestic entity.

(e) *Treatment of distributions made by a predecessor.*—For purposes of this section, a corporation or a partnership (relevant entity), including a domestic entity, is treated as making the following distributions made by a predecessor with respect to the relevant entity:

(1) A distribution made before the predecessor acquisition with respect to the predecessor; and

(2) A distribution made in connection with the predecessor acquisition to the extent the property distributed is directly or indirectly provided by the predecessor. See paragraph (k)(1)(iv) of this section.

(f) *Rules for identifying a predecessor.*—(1) *Definition of predecessor.*— A corporation or a partnership (tentative predecessor) is a predecessor with respect to a relevant entity if—

(i) The relevant entity completes a predecessor acquisition; and

(ii) After the predecessor acquisition and all related transactions are complete, the tentative predecessor ownership percentage is at least 10.

(2) *Definition of predecessor acquisition.*—(i) *In general.*—Predecessor acquisition means a transaction in which a relevant entity directly or indirectly acquires substantially all of the properties held directly or indirectly by a tentative predecessor.

(ii) *Acquisition of properties of a tentative predecessor.*—For purposes of determining whether a predecessor acquisition occurs, the principles of section 7874(a)(2)(B)(i) apply, including § 1.7874-2(c) other than § 1.7874-2(c)(2) and (4) (regarding acquisitions of properties of a domestic entity), without regard to whether the tentative predecessor is domestic or foreign.

(iii) *Lower-tier entities of a predecessor.*—If, before a predecessor acquisition and all related transactions, the predecessor held directly or indirectly stock in a corporation or an interest in a partnership, then, for purposes of this section, the relevant entity is not considered to directly or indirectly acquire the properties held directly or indirectly by the corporation or partnership.

(3) *Definition of tentative predecessor ownership percentage.*—Tentative predecessor ownership percentage means, with respect to a predecessor acquisition, the percentage of stock or partnership interests (by value) in a relevant entity held by reason of holding stock or partnership interests in the tentative predecessor. For purposes of computing the tentative predecessor ownership percentage, the following rules apply:

(i) For purposes of determining the stock or partnership interests in a relevant entity held by reason of holding stock or partnership interests in the tentative predecessor, the principles of section 7874(a)(2)(B)(ii) and §§1.7874-2(f)(1)(i) through (iii) and 1.7874-5 apply.

(ii) For purposes of determining the stock or partnership interests in a relevant entity included in the numerator of the fraction used to compute the tentative predecessor ownership percentage, the rules of paragraph (f)(3)(i) of this section apply, and all the rules applicable to calculating the numerator of an ownership fraction with respect to a domestic entity acquisition apply, except that—

(A) The principles of section 7874(c)(2)(A) and §§1.7874-1 and 1.7874-6 do not apply; and

(B) The principles of paragraph (b) of this section do not apply.

(iii) For purposes of determining stock or partnership interests in a relevant entity included in the denominator of the fraction used to compute the tentative predecessor ownership percentage, the principles of section 7874(a)(2)(B)(ii) and all rules applicable to calculating the denominator of an ownership fraction with respect to a domestic entity acquisition apply, except that—

(A) The principles of section 7874(c)(2)(A) and §§1.7874-1 and 1.7874-6 do not apply; and

(B) The principles of §§1.7874-4 and 1.7874-7 through 1.7874-9 do not apply.

(g) *Rule regarding direction of a section 355 distribution.*—For purposes of this section, if a domestic corporation (distributing corporation) distributes the stock of another domestic corporation (controlled corporation) pursuant to a transaction described in section 355, and, immediately before the distribution, the fair market value of the stock of the controlled corporation owned by the distributing corporation and any related person (determined under section 7874(d)(3), without regard to whether the person is foreign) represents more than 50 percent of the fair market value of the stock of the distributing corporation, then, the controlled corporation is deemed, on the date of the distribution, to have distributed the stock of the distributing corporation. The deemed distribution is equal to the fair market value of the stock of the distributing corporation (but not taking into account the fair market value of the stock of the controlled corporation) on the date of the distribution.

(h) *Allocation of NOCD stock.*—NOCD stock is allocated among the former domestic entity shareholders or former domestic entity partners, as applicable, based on the amount of NOCDs that the former domestic entity shareholders or former domestic entity partners, as applicable, are treated as having received under this paragraph (h). Under this paragraph (h), a pro rata portion of each distribution during a look-back year is treated as comprising an NOCD with respect to the look-back year, based on a fraction the numerator of which is the amount of NOCDs during the look-back year and the denominator of which is the amount of distributions during the look-back year. Thus, each former domestic entity shareholder or former domestic entity partner, as applicable, is treated as receiving an amount of NOCD stock equal to the amount of NOCDs treated as received by the former domestic entity shareholder or former domestic entity partner, as applicable.

(i) *Multiple foreign acquiring corporations.*—If there are multiple foreign acquiring corporations with respect to a domestic entity acquisition, then the foreign acquiring corporation or corporations as to which NOCD stock is considered comprised is based on the proportion of consideration directly or indirectly provided by a foreign acquiring corporation in the domestic entity acquisition relative to the total amount of consideration directly or indirectly provided by the foreign acquiring corporations in the domestic entity acquisition. For purposes of this paragraph (i), consideration is not considered directly provided by a foreign acquiring corporation if it was indirectly provided by another foreign acquiring corporation. In addition, for purposes of this paragraph (i), consideration provided in the domestic entity acquisition does not include money or other property described in paragraph (k)(1)(iii) of this section.

(j) *Multiple domestic entities.*—If pursuant to §1.7874-2(e) two or more domestic entities are treated as a single domestic entity, then the determination of the amount of NOCDs made by the single domestic entity is made by—

(1) Applying the rules of this section to each domestic entity on a separate basis, with the result that the amount of NOCDs made by each domestic entity is separately computed; and

(2) Treating the amount of NOCDs made by the single domestic entity as the sum of the separately computed NOCDs made by each domestic entity.

(k) *Definitions.*—In addition to the definitions provided in §1.7874-12, the following definitions apply for purposes of this section.

(1) A *distribution* means the following:

(i) Any distribution made by a corporation with respect to its stock other than—

(A) A distribution to which section 305 applies;

(B) A distribution to which section 304(a)(1) applies; and

(C) Except as provided in paragraphs (k)(1)(iii) and (iv) of this section, a distribution pursuant to section 361(c)(1) (other than a distribution to which section 355 applies).

(ii) Any distribution by a partnership (other than a distribution pursuant to section 752(b) to the extent that the transaction giving rise to such distribution does not reduce the partnership's value).

(iii) In the case of a domestic entity, a transfer of money or other property to the former domestic entity shareholders or former domestic entity partners that is made in connection with the domestic entity acquisition to the extent the money or other property is directly or indirectly provided by the domestic entity.

(iv) In the case of a predecessor, a transfer of money or other property to the former owners of the predecessor that is made in connection with the predecessor acquisition to the extent the money or other property is directly or indirectly provided by the predecessor.

(2) *Distribution history period.*—(i) *In general.*—Except as provided in paragraph (k)(2)(ii) or (iii) of this section, a distribution history period means, with respect to a look-back year, the 36-month period preceding the start of the look-back year.

(ii) *Formation date less than 36 months but at least 12 months before look-back year.*—If the formation date is less than 36 months, but at least 12 months, before the start of a look-back year, then the distribution history period with respect to that look-back year means the entire period, starting with the formation date, that precedes the start of the look-back year.

(iii) *Formation date less than 12 months before look-back year.*—If the formation date is less than 12 months before the start of a look-back year, then there is no distribution history period with respect to that look-back year.

(3) *Formation date* means, with respect to a domestic entity, the date that the domestic entity was created or organized, or, if earlier, the earliest date that any predecessor of the domestic entity was created or organized.

(4) *Look-back period* means, with respect to a domestic acquisition, the 36-month period ending on the completion date or, if shorter, the entire period, starting with the formation date, that ends on the completion date.

(5) *Look-back year* means, with respect to a look-back period, the following:

(i) If the look-back period is 36 months, the three consecutive 12-month periods that comprise the look-back period.

(ii) If the look-back period is less than 36 months, but at least 24 months—

(A) The 12-month period that ends on the completion date;

(B) The 12-month period that immediately precedes the period described in paragraph (k)(5)(ii)(A) of this section; and

(C) The period, if any, that immediately precedes the period described in paragraph (k)(5)(ii)(B) of this section.

(iii) If the look-back period is less than 24 months, but at least 12 months—

(A) The 12-month period that ends on the completion date; and

(B) The period, if any, that immediately precedes the period described in paragraph (k)(5)(iii)(A) of this section.

(iv) If the look-back period is less than 12 months, the entire period, starting with the formation date, that ends on the completion date.

(6) *NOCDs* mean, with respect to a look-back year, the excess of all distributions made during the look-back year over the NOCD threshold for the look-back year.

(7) *NOCD threshold* means, with respect to a look-back year, the following:

(i) If the look-back year has at least a 12-month distribution history period, 110 percent of the sum of all distributions made during the distribution history period multiplied by a fraction. The numerator of the fraction is the number of days in the look-back year and the denominator is the number of days in the distribution history period with respect to the look-back year.

(ii) If the look-back year has no distribution history period, zero.

(l) *Applicability date.*—This section applies to domestic entity acquisitions completed on or after July 12, 2018. For domestic entity acquisitions completed before July 12, 2018, see § 1.7874-10T, as contained in 26 CFR part 1 revised as of April 1, 2017. However, to the extent this section differs from § 1.7874-10T, as contained in 26 CFR part 1 revised as of April 1, 2017, taxpayers may elect to consistently apply the differences to domestic entity acquisitions completed before July 12, 2018. [Reg. § 1.7874-10.]

☐ [*T.D.* 9834, 7-11-2018.]

### [Reg. § 1.7874-11]

**§ 1.7874-11. Rules regarding inversion gain.**—(a) *Scope.*—This section provides rules for determining the inversion gain of an expatriated entity for purposes of section 7874. Paragraph (b) of this section provides rules for determining the inversion gain of an expatriated entity. Paragraph (c) of this section provides special rules with respect to certain foreign partnerships in which an expatriated entity owns an interest. Paragraph (d) of this section provides additional definitions. Paragraph (e) of this section provides an example that illustrates the rules of this section. Paragraph (f) of this section provides the applicability dates.

(b) *Inversion gain.*—(1) *General rule.*—Except as provided in paragraphs (b)(2) and (3) of this section, inversion gain includes income (including an amount treated as a dividend under section 78) or gain recognized by an expatriated entity for any taxable year that includes any portion of the applicable period by reason of a direct or indirect transfer of stock or other properties or license of any property either as part of the domestic entity acquisition, or after such acquisition if the transfer or license is to a specified related person.

(2) *Exception for property described in section 1221(a)(1).*—Inversion gain does not include income or gain recognized by reason of the transfer or license, after the domestic entity acquisition, of property that is described in section 1221(a)(1) in the hands of the transferor or licensor.

(3) *Treatment of partnerships.*—Except to the extent provided in paragraph (c) of this section and section 7874(e)(2), inversion gain does not include income or gain recognized by reason of the transfer or license of property by a partnership.

(c) *Transfers and licenses by partnerships.*—If a partnership that is a foreign related person transfers or licenses property, a partner of the partnership shall be treated as having transferred or licensed its proportionate share of that property, as determined under the rules and principles of sections 701 through 777, for purposes of determining the inversion gain of an expatriated entity. See section 7874(e)(2) for rules regarding the treatment of transfers and licenses by domestic partnerships and transfers of interests in certain domestic partnerships.

(d) *Definitions.*—The definitions provided in § 1.7874-12 apply for purposes of this section.

(e) *Example.*—The following example illustrates the rules of this section.

*Example*—(i) *Facts.* On July 1, 2016, FA, a foreign corporation, acquires all the stock of DT, a domestic corporation, in an inversion transaction. When the inversion transaction occurred, DT wholly owned FS, a foreign corporation that is a controlled foreign corporation (within the meaning of section 957(a)). During the applicable period, FS sells to FA property that is not described in section 1221(a)(1) in the hands of FS. Under section 951(a)(1)(A), DT has a $80x gross income inclusion that is attributable to FS's gain from the sale of the property. Under section 960(a)(1), DT is deemed to have paid $20x of the post-1986 foreign income taxes of FS by reason of this income inclusion and includes $20x in gross income as a deemed dividend under section 78. Accordingly, DT recognizes $100x ($80x + $20x) of gross income because of FS's sale of property to FA.

(ii) *Analysis.* Pursuant to section 7874(a)(2)(A), DT is an expatriated entity. Under paragraph (b)(1) of this section, DT's $100x gross income recognized under sections 951(a)(1)(A) and 78 is inversion gain, because it is income recognized by an expatriated entity during the applicable period by reason of an indirect transfer of property by DT (through its wholly-owned CFC, FS) after the inversion transaction to a specified related person (FA). Sections 7874(a)(1) and (e) therefore prevent the use of certain tax attributes (such as net operating losses) to reduce the U.S. tax owed with respect to DT's $100x gross income recognized under sections 951(a)(1)(A) and 78.

(f) *Applicability dates.*—Except as otherwise provided in this paragraph (f), this section applies to transfers and licenses of property completed on or after November 19, 2015, but only if the inversion transaction was completed on or after September 22, 2014. For inversion transactions completed on or after September 22, 2014, however, taxpayers may elect to apply paragraph (b) of this section by excluding the phrase "(including an amount treated as a dividend under section 78)" for transfers and licenses of property completed on or after November 19, 2015, and before April 4, 2016. [Reg. § 1.7874-11.]

☐ [*T.D.* 9834, 7-11-2018.]

### [Reg. § 1.7874-12]

**§ 1.7874-12. Definitions.**—(a) *Definitions.*—Except as otherwise provided, the following definitions apply for purposes of this section and §§ 1.367(b)-4, 1.956-2, 1.7701(l)-4, and 1.7874-1 through 1.7874-11.

(1) An *affiliated group* has the meaning set forth in section 1504(a) but without regard to section 1504(b)(3), except that section 1504(a) is applied by substituting "more than 50 percent" for "at least 80 percent" each place it appears. A *member of the affiliated group* is an entity included in the affiliated group.

(2) The *applicable period* means, with respect to an inversion transaction, the period described in section 7874(d)(1). However, see also § 1.7874-2(b)(13) in the case of a subsequent acquisition (or a similar acquisition under the principles of § 1.7874-2(c)(4)(i)) that is an inversion transaction.

(3) The *completion date* means, with respect to a domestic entity acquisition, the date that the domestic entity acquisition and all transactions related to the domestic entity acquisition are complete.

(4) A *controlled foreign corporation* (or *CFC*) has the meaning provided in section 957.

(5) A *domestic entity acquisition* means an acquisition described in section 7874(a)(2)(B)(i).

(6) A *domestic entity* means, with respect to a domestic entity acquisition, a domestic corporation or domestic partnership described in section 7874(a)(2)(B)(i). A reference to a domestic entity includes a successor to such domestic corporation or domestic partnership, including a corporation that succeeds to and takes into account amounts with respect to the domestic entity pursuant to section 381.

(7) An *expanded affiliated group* (or *EAG*) means, with respect to a domestic entity acquisition, an affiliated group that includes the foreign acquiring corporation, determined as of the completion date. A *member of the EAG* is an entity included in the EAG, and a reference to a member of the EAG includes a predecessor with respect to such member.

(8) An *expatriated entity* means, with respect to an inversion transaction—

(i) The domestic entity; and

(ii) A United States person that, on any date on or after the completion date, is or was related (within the meaning of section 267(b) or 707(b)(1)) to the domestic entity.

(9) *Expatriated foreign subsidiary.*—(i) *General rule.*—Except as provided in paragraph (a)(9)(ii) of this section, an expatriated foreign subsidiary means a foreign corporation that is a CFC (determined without applying subparagraphs (A), (B), and (C) of section 318(a)(3) so as to consider a United States person as owning stock which is owned by a person who is not a United States person) and in which an expatriated entity is a United States shareholder (determined without applying subparagraphs (A), (B), and (C) of section 318(a)(3) so as to consider a United States person as owning stock which is owned by a person who is not a United States person).

(ii) *Exception to the general rule.*—A foreign corporation is not an expatriated foreign subsidiary if, with respect to the inversion transaction as a result of which the foreign corporation otherwise would be an expatriated foreign subsidiary—

(A) On the completion date, the foreign corporation was both a CFC (determined without applying subparagraphs (A), (B), and (C) of section 318(a)(3) so as to consider a United States person as owning stock which is owned by a person who is not a United States person) and a member of the EAG; and

(B) On or before the completion date, the domestic entity was not a United States shareholder (determined without applying subparagraphs (A), (B), and (C) of section 318(a)(3) so as to consider a United States person as owning stock which is owned by a person who is not a United States person) with respect to the foreign corporation.

(10) A *foreign acquiring corporation* means, with respect to a domestic entity acquisition, the foreign corporation described in section 7874(a)(2)(B). A reference to a foreign acquiring corporation includes a successor to the foreign acquiring corporation, including a corporation that succeeds to and takes into account amounts with respect to the foreign acquiring corporation pursuant to section 381.

(11) A *foreign related person* means, with respect to an inversion transaction, a foreign person that is related (within the meaning of section 267(b) or 707(b)(1)) to, or under the same common control as (within the meaning of section 482), a person that is an expatriated entity with respect to the inversion transaction.

**IRS Procedure on Requests for Disclosure**
**67,337**
See p. 20,601 for regulations not amended to reflect law changes

(12) A *former domestic entity partner* of a domestic entity that is a domestic partnership is any person that held an interest in the partnership before the domestic entity acquisition, including any person that holds an interest in the partnership both before and after the domestic entity acquisition.

(13) A *former domestic entity shareholder* of a domestic entity that is a domestic corporation is any person that held stock in the domestic corporation before the domestic entity acquisition, including any person that holds stock in the domestic corporation both before and after the domestic entity acquisition.

(14) An *interest in a partnership* includes a capital or profits interest.

(15) An *inversion transaction* means a domestic entity acquisition in which the foreign acquiring corporation is treated as a surrogate foreign corporation under section 7874(a)(2)(B), taking into account section 7874(a)(3).

(16) A *non-EFS foreign related person* means, with respect to an inversion transaction, a foreign related person that is not an expatriated foreign subsidiary.

(17) The *ownership fraction* means, with respect to a domestic entity acquisition, the ownership percentage described in section 7874(a)(2)(B)(ii), expressed as a fraction.

(18) A *specified related person* means, with respect to an inversion transaction—

(i) A non-EFS foreign related person;

(ii) A domestic partnership in which a non-EFS foreign related person is a partner; and

(iii) A domestic trust of which a non-EFS foreign related person is a beneficiary.

(19) A *United States person* means a person described in section 7701(a)(30).

(20) A *United States shareholder* has the meaning provided in section 951(b).

(b) *Applicability dates.*—Except as otherwise provided in this paragraph (b), this section applies to domestic entity acquisitions completed on or after September 22, 2014. The following apply to domestic entity acquisitions completed on or after April 4, 2016: paragraph (a)(8) of this section; in paragraph (a)(6) of this section, the phrase ", including a corporation that succeeds to and takes into account amounts with respect to the domestic entity pursuant to section 381"; and the second sentence of paragraph (a)(10) of this section. For domestic entity acquisitions completed on or after September 22, 2014, and before April 4, 2016, however, taxpayers, may elect to apply the provisions in the immediately prior sentence. [Reg. § 1.7874-12.]

☐ [*T.D. 9834, 7-11-2018.*]

# Regulations Not Issued Under Specific Code Sections
# IRS PROCEDURE ON REQUESTS FOR DISCLOSURE

See p. 20,601 for regulations not amended to reflect law changes

[Reg. § 301.9000-1]

**§ 301.9000-1. Definitions when used in §§ 301.9000-1 through 301.9000-6.**—(a) *IRS records or information* means any material (including copies thereof) contained in the files (including paper, electronic or other media files) of the Internal Revenue Service (IRS), any information relating to material contained in the files of the IRS, or any information acquired by an IRS officer or employee, while an IRS officer or employee, as a part of the performance of official duties or because of that IRS officer's or employee's official status with respect to the administration of the internal revenue laws or any other laws administered by or concerning the IRS. IRS records or information includes, but is not limited to, returns and return information as those terms are defined in section 6103(b)(1) and (2) of the Internal Revenue Code (Code), tax convention information as defined in section 6105 of the Code, information gathered during Bank Secrecy Act and money laundering investigations, and personnel records and other information pertaining to IRS officers and employees. IRS records and information also includes information received, generated or collected by an IRS contractor pursuant to the contractor's contract or agreement with the IRS. The term does not include records or information obtained by IRS officers and employees, solely for the purpose of a federal grand jury investigation, while under the direction and control of the United States Attorney's Office. The term IRS records or information nevertheless does include records or information obtained by the IRS before, during, or after a Federal grand jury investigation if the records or information are obtained—

(1) At the administrative stage of a criminal investigation (prior to the initiation of the grand jury);

(2) From IRS files (such as transcripts or tax returns); or

(3) For use in a subsequent civil investigation.

(b) *IRS officers and employees* means all officers and employees of the United States appointed by, employed by, or subject to the directions, instructions, or orders of the Commissioner or IRS Chief Counsel and also includes former officers and employees.

(c) *IRS contractor* means any person, including the person's current and former employees, maintaining IRS records or information pursuant to a contract or agreement with the IRS, and also includes former contractors.

(d) A *request* is any request for testimony of an IRS officer, employee or contractor or for production of IRS records or information, oral or written, by any person, which is not a demand.

(e) A *demand* is any subpoena or other order of any court, administrative agency or other authority, or the Congress, or a committee or subcommittee of the Congress, and any notice of deposition (either upon oral examination or written questions), request for admissions, request for production of documents or things, written interrogatories to parties, or other notice of, request for, or service for discovery in a matter before any court, administrative agency or other authority.

(f) An *IRS matter* is any matter before any court, administrative agency or other authority in which the United States, the Commissioner, the IRS, or any IRS officer or employee acting in an official capacity, or any IRS officer or employee (including an officer or employee of IRS Office of Chief Counsel) in his or her individual capacity if the United States Department of Justice or the IRS has agreed to represent or provide representation to the IRS officer or employee, is a party and that is directly related to official business of the IRS or to any law administered by or concerning the IRS, including, but not limited to, judicial and administrative proceedings described in section 6103(h)(4) and (I)(4) of the Internal Revenue Code.

(g) An *IRS congressional matter* is any matter before the Congress, or a committee or subcommittee of the Congress, that is related to the administration of the internal revenue laws or any other laws administered by or concerning the IRS, or to IRS records or information.

(h) A *non-IRS matter* is any matter that is not an IRS matter or an IRS congressional matter.

(i) A *testimony authorization* is a written instruction or oral instruction memorialized in writing within a reasonable period by an authorizing official that sets forth the scope of and limitations on proposed testimony and/or disclosure of IRS records or information issued in response to a request or demand for IRS records or information. A testimony authorization may grant or deny authorization to testify or disclose IRS records or information and may make an authorization effective only upon the occurrence of a precedent condition, such as the receipt of a consent complying with the provisions of section 6103(c) of the Internal Revenue Code. To authorize testimony means to issue the instruction described in this paragraph (i).

(j) An *authorizing official* is a person with delegated authority to authorize testimony and the disclosure of IRS records or information. [Reg. § 301.9000-1.]

☐ [*T.D. 6920, 6-7-67. Amended by 37 F.R. 2481, 2-1-72; T.D. 7188, 6-28-72; T.D. ATF-33, 10-6-76 and T.D. 9178, 2-11-2005.*]

[Reg. § 301.9000-2]

**§ 301.9000-2. Considerations in responding to a request or demand for IRS records or information.**—(a) *Situations in which disclosure shall not be authorized.*—Authorizing officials shall not permit testimony or disclosure of IRS records or information in response to requests or demands if testimony or disclosure of IRS records or information would—

(1) Violate a Federal statute including, but not limited to, sections 6103 or 6105 of the Internal Revenue Code (Code), the Privacy Act of 1974 (5 U.S.C. 552a), or a rule of procedure, such as the grand jury secrecy rule, Fed. R. Crim. P. 6(e);

(2) Violate a specific Federal regulation, including, but not limited to, 31 CFR 103.53;

(3) Reveal classified national security information, unless properly declassified;

(4) Reveal the identity of an informant; or

(5) Reveal investigatory records or information compiled for law enforcement purposes that would permit interference with law enforcement proceedings or would disclose investigative techniques

and procedures, the effectiveness of which could thereby be impaired.

(b) *Assertion of privileges.*—Any applicable privilege or protection under law may be asserted in response to a request or demand for testimony or disclosure of IRS records or information, including, but not limited to, the following—

(1) Attorney-client privilege;

(2) Attorney work product doctrine; and

(3) Deliberative process (executive) privilege.

(c) *Non-IRS matters.*—If any person makes a request or demand for IRS records or information in connection with a non-IRS matter, authorizing officials shall take into account the following additional factors in responding to the request or demand—

(1) Whether the requester is a Federal agency, or a state or local government or agency thereof;

(2) Whether the demand was issued by a Federal or state court, administrative agency or other authority;

(3) The potential effect of the case on the administration of the internal revenue laws or any other laws administered by or concerning the IRS;

(4) The importance of the legal issues presented;

(5) Whether the IRS records or information are available from other sources;

(6) The IRS's anticipated commitment of time and anticipated expenditure of funds necessary to comply with the request or demand;

(7) The number of similar requests and their cumulative effect on the expenditure of IRS resources;

(8) Whether the request or demand allows a reasonable time for compliance (generally, at least fifteen business days);

(9) Whether the testimony or disclosure is appropriate under the rules of procedure governing the case or matter in which the request or demand arises;

(10) Whether the request or demand involves expert witness testimony;

(11) Whether the request or demand is for the testimony of an IRS officer, employee or contractor who is without personal knowledge of relevant facts;

(12) Whether the request or demand is for the testimony of a presidential appointee or senior executive and whether the testimony of a lower-level official would suffice;

(13) Whether the procedures in §301.9000-5 have been followed; and

(14) Any other relevant factors that may be brought to the attention of the authorizing official. [Reg. §301.9000-2.]

☐ [*T.D.* 9178, 2-11-2005.]

### [Reg. §301.9000-3]

**§301.9000-3. Testimony authorizations.**—(a) *Prohibition on disclosure of IRS records or information without testimony authorization.*—Except as provided in paragraph (b) of this section, when a request or demand for IRS records or information is made, no IRS officer, employee or contractor shall testify or disclose IRS records or information to any court, administrative agency or other authority, or to the Congress, or to a committee or subcommittee of the Congress without a testimony authorization. However, an IRS officer, employee or contractor may appear in person to advise that he or she is awaiting instructions from an authorizing official with respect to the request or demand.

(b) *Exceptions.*—No testimony authorization is required in the following circumstances—

(1) To respond to a request or demand for IRS records or information by the attorney or other government representative representing the IRS in a particular IRS matter;

(2) To respond solely in writing, under the direction of the attorney or other government representative, to requests and demands in IRS matters, including, but not limited to, admissions, document production, and written interrogatories to parties;

(3) To respond to a request or demand issued to a former IRS officer, employee or contractor for expert or opinion testimony if the testimony sought from the former IRS officer, employee or contractor involves general knowledge (such as information contained in published procedures of the IRS or the IRS Office of Chief Counsel) gained while the former IRS officer, employee or contractor was employed or under contract with the IRS; or

(4) If a more specific procedure established by the Commissioner governs the disclosure of IRS records or information. These procedures include, but are not limited to, those relating to: procedures pursuant to §601.702(d) of this chapter; Freedom of Information Act requests pursuant to 5 U.S.C. 552; Privacy Act of 1974 requests pursuant to 5 U.S.C. 552a; disclosures to state tax agencies

pursuant to section 6103(d) of the Internal Revenue Code (Code) and disclosures to the United States Department of Justice pursuant to an ex parte order under section 6103(i)(1) of the Code.

(c) *Disclosures of IRS records or information with or without testimony authorization must be permitted under other applicable law.*—Any disclosure of IRS records or information that is otherwise permissible under this section must not be prohibited under applicable law. For example, in a case in which returns and return information may be disclosed, the disclosure must be authorized under section 6103, even if any required testimony authorization is obtained. If tax convention information (as defined under section 6105) may be disclosed, in deciding whether the disclosure is authorized, the authorizing official must coordinate the disclosure with the U.S. Competent Authority. [Reg. §301.9000-3.]

☐ [*T.D.* 9178, 2-11-2005.]

### [Reg. §301.9000-4]

**§301.9000-4. Procedure in the event of a request or demand for IRS records or information.**—(a) *Purpose and scope.*—This section prescribes procedures to be followed by IRS officers, employees and contractors upon receipt of a request or demand in matters in which a testimony authorization is or may be required.

(b) *Notification of the Disclosure Officer.*—Except as provided in paragraphs (c), (d), and (e) of this section, an IRS officer, employee or contractor who receives a request or demand for IRS records or information for which a testimony authorization is or may be required shall notify promptly the disclosure officer servicing the IRS officer's, employee's or contractor's geographic area. The IRS officer, employee or contractor shall await instructions from the authorizing official concerning the response to the request or demand. An IRS officer, employee, or contractor who receives a request or demand in one of the following matters should not notify the disclosure officer, but should follow the instructions in paragraph (c), (d), or (e) of this section, as applicable:

(1) United States Tax Court cases.

(2) Personnel matters, labor relations matters, government contract matters, matters related to informant claims or matters related to the rules of *Bivens v. Six Unknown Named Agents of Federal Bureau of Narcotics*, 403 U.S. 388 (1971) (Bivens matters), or matters under the Federal Tort Claims Act (FTCA).

(3) IRS congressional matters.

(c) *Requests or demands in United States Tax Court cases.*—An IRS officer, employee or contractor who receives a request or demand for IRS records or Information on behalf of a petitioner in a United States Tax Court case shall notify promptly the IRS Office of Chief Counsel attorney assigned to the case. The IRS Office of Chief Counsel attorney shall notify promptly the authorizing official. The IRS officer, employee or contractor who received the request or demand shall await instructions from the authorizing official.

(d) *Requests or demands in personnel, labor relations, government contract, Bivens or FTCA matters, or matters related to informant claims.*—An IRS officer, employee or contractor who receives a request or demand, on behalf of an appellant, grievant, complainant or representative, for IRS records or information in a personnel, labor relations, government contract, Bivens or FTCA matter, or matter related to informant claims, shall notify promptly the IRS Associate Chief Counsel (General Legal Services) attorney assigned to the case. If no IRS Associate Chief Counsel (General Legal Services) attorney is assigned to the case, the IRS officer, employee or contractor shall notify promptly the IRS Associate Chief Counsel (General Legal Services) attorney servicing the geographic area. The IRS Associate Chief Counsel (General Legal Services) attorney shall notify promptly the authorizing official. The IRS officer, employee or contractor who received the request or demand shall await instructions from the authorizing official.

(e) *Requests or demands in IRS congressional matters.*—An IRS officer, employee or contractor who receives a request or demand in an IRS congressional matter shall notify promptly the IRS Office of Legislative Affairs. The IRS officer, employee or contractor who received the request or demand shall await instructions from the authorizing official.

(f) *Opposition to a demand for IRS records or information in IRS and non-IRS matters.*—If, in response to a demand for IRS records or information, an authorizing official has not had a sufficient opportunity to issue a testimony authorization, or determines that the demand for IRS records or information should be denied, the authorizing official shall request the government attorney or other representative of the government to oppose the demand and respectfully inform the court, administrative agency or other authority, by appropriate action, that the authorizing official either has not yet issued a testimony authorization, or has issued a testimony authorization to the IRS officer, employee or contractor that denies permission to testify or disclose the IRS records or information. If the authorizing official denies authorization in whole or in part, the government attorney or other representative of the government shall inform the court, administrative agency or other authority of the reasons the authorizing official gives for not authorizing the testimony or the disclosure of the IRS records or information or take other action in opposition as may be appropriate (including, but not limited to, filing a motion to quash or a motion to remove to Federal court).

(g) *Procedure in the event of an adverse ruling.*—In the event the court, administrative agency, or other authority rules adversely with respect to the refusal to disclose the IRS records or information pursuant to the testimony authorization, or declines to defer a ruling until a testimony authorization has been received, the IRS officer, employee or contractor who has received the request or demand shall, pursuant to this section, respectfully decline to testify or disclose the IRS records or information.

(h) *Penalties.*—Any IRS officer or employee who discloses IRS records or information without following the provisions of this section or §301.9000-3, may be subject to administrative discipline, up to and including dismissal. Any IRS officer, employee or contractor may be subject to applicable contractual sanctions and civil or criminal penalties, including prosecution under 5 U.S.C. 552a(i), for willful disclosure in an unauthorized manner of information protected by the Privacy Act of 1974, or under section 7213 of the Internal Revenue Code, for willful disclosure in an unauthorized manner of return information.

(i) *No creation of benefit or separate privilege.*—Nothing in §§301.9000-1 through 301.9000-3, this section, and §§301.9000-5 and 301.9000-6, creates, is intended to create, or may be relied upon to create, any right or benefit, substantive or procedural, enforceable at law by a party against the United States. Nothing in these regulations creates a separate privilege or basis to withhold IRS records or information. [Reg. §301.9000-4.]

☐ [*T.D.* 9178, 2-11-2005.]

### [Reg. §301.9000-5]

**§301.9000-5. Written statement required for requests or demands in non-IRS matters.**—(a) *Written statement.*—A request or demand for IRS records or information for use in a non-IRS matter shall be accompanied by a written statement made by or on behalf of the party seeking the testimony or disclosure of IRS records or information, setting forth—

(1) A brief description of the parties to and subject matter of the proceeding and the issues;

(2) A summary of the testimony, IRS records or information sought, the relevance to the proceeding, and the estimated volume of IRS records involved;

(3) The time that will be required to present the testimony (on both direct and cross examination);

(4) Whether any of the IRS records or information is a return or is return information (as defined in section 6103(b) of the Internal Revenue Code (Code)), or tax convention information (as defined in section 6105(c)(1) of the Code), and the statutory authority for the disclosure of the return or return information (and, if no consent to disclose pursuant to section 6103(c) of the Code accompanies the request or demand, the reason consent is not necessary);

(5) Whether a declaration of an IRS officer, employee or contractor under penalties of perjury pursuant to 28 U.S.C. 1746 would suffice in lieu of deposition or trial testimony;

(6) Whether deposition or trial testimony is necessary in a situation in which IRS records may be authenticated without testimony under applicable rules of evidence and procedure;

(7) Whether IRS records or information are available from other sources; and

(8) A statement that the request or demand allows a reasonable time (generally at least fifteen business days) for compliance.

(b) *Permissible waiver of statement.*—The requirement of a written statement in paragraph (a) of this section may be waived by the authorizing official for good cause. [Reg. §301.9000-5.]

☐ [*T.D.* 9178, 2-11-2005.]

### [Reg. §301.9000-6]

**§301.9000-6. Examples.**—The following examples illustrate the provisions of §§301.9000-1 through 301.9000-5:

*Example 1.* A taxpayer sues a practitioner in state court for malpractice in connection with the practitioner's preparation of a Federal income tax return. The taxpayer subpoenas an IRS employee to testify concerning the IRS employee's examination of the taxpayer's

Federal income tax return. The taxpayer provides the statement required by §301.9000-5. This is a non-IRS matter. A testimony authorization would be required for the IRS employee to testify. (In addition, the taxpayer would be required to execute an appropriate consent under section 6103(c) of the Code). The IRS would oppose the IRS employee's appearance in this case because the IRS is a disinterested party with respect to the dispute and would consider the commitment of resources to comply with the subpoena inappropriate.

*Example 2.* In a state judicial proceeding concerning child support, the child's custodiel parent subpoenas for a deposition an IRS agent who is examining certain post-divorce Federal income tax returns of the non-custodial parent. This is a non-IRS matter. The custodial parent submits with the subpoena the statement required by §301.9000-5 stating as the reason for the lack of taxpayer consent to disclosure that the non-custodial parent has refused to provide the consent (both a consent from the taxpayer complying with section 6103(c) and a testimony authorization would be required prior to the IRS agent testifying at the deposition). If taxpayer consent is obtained, the IRS may provide a declaration or certified return information of the taxpayer. A deposition would be unnecessary under the circumstances.

*Example 3.* The chairperson of a congressional committee requests the appearance of an IRS employee before the committee and committee staff to submit to questioning by committee staff concerning the procedures for processing Federal employment tax returns. This is an IRS congressional matter. Even though questioning would not involve the disclosure of returns or return information, the questioning would involve the disclosure of IRS records or information; therefore, a testimony authorization would be required. The IRS employee must contact the IRS Office of Legislative Affairs for instructions before appearing.

*Example 4.* The IRS opens a criminal investigation as to the tax liabilities of a taxpayer. This is an IRS matter. During the criminal investigation, the IRS refers the matter to the United States Department of Justice, requesting the institution of a Federal grand jury to investigate further potential criminal tax violations. The United States Department of Justice approves the request and initiates a grand jury investigation. The grand jury indicts the taxpayer. During the taxpayer's trial, the taxpayer subpoenas an IRS special agent for testimony regarding the investigation. The records and information collected during the administrative stage of the investigation, including the taxpayer's tax returns from IRS files, are IRS records and information. A testimony authorization is required for the IRS special agent to testify regarding this information. However, no IRS testimony authorization is required regarding the information collected by the IRS special agent when the IRS special agent was acting under the direction and control of the United States Attorney's Office in the Federal grand jury investigation. That information is not IRS records or information within the meaning of §301.9000-1(a). Disclosure of that information should be coordinated with the United States Attorney's Office.

*Example 5.* The United States Department of Justice attorney representing the IRS in a suit for refund requests testimony from an IRS revenue agent. This is an IRS matter. A testimony authorization would not be required for the IRS revenue agent to testify because the testimony was requested by the government attorney.

*Example 6.* In response to a request by the taxpayer's counsel to interview an IRS revenue agent who was involved in a case at the administrative level, the United States Department of Justice attorney representing the IRS in a suit for refund asks that the IRS revenue agent be made available to be interviewed. This is an IRS matter. A testimony authorization would be required for the IRS agent to testify because the testimony was first requested by taxpayer's counsel.

*Example 7.* A state assistant attorney general, acting in accordance with a recommendation from his state's department of revenue, is prosecuting a taxpayer under a state criminal law proscribing the intentional failure to file a state income tax return. The assistant attorney general serves an IRS employee with a subpoena to testify concerning the taxpayer's Federal income tax return filing history. This is a non-IRS matter. This is also a state judicial proceeding pertaining to tax administration within the meaning of section 6103(h)(4) and (b)(4). As such, the requirements of section 6103(h)(4) apply. A testimony authorization would be required for the testimony demand in the subpoena.

*Example 8.* A former IRS revenue agent is requested to testify in a divorce proceeding. The request seeks testimony explaining the meaning of entries appearing on one party's transcript of account, which is already in the possession of the parties. This is a non-IRS matter. No testimony authorization is required because the testimony requested from the former IRS employee involves general knowledge gained while the former IRS revenue agent was employed with the IRS.

**67,340**
**Extension of Time for Making Elections**
See p. 20,601 for regulations not amended to reflect law changes

*Example 9.* A Department of Justice attorney requests an IRS employee to testify in a refund suit involving Taxpayer A. The testimony may include tax convention information, as defined in section 6105, which was originally obtained by the IRS from a treaty partner in connection with a tax case against Taxpayer B. While no testimony authorization is necessary, because the testimony is being requested by government counsel in a tax matter, the IRS employee may not testify (or otherwise disclose IRS records or information) without coordinating with the U.S. Competent Authority, as disclosure of tax convention information is governed by section 6105. The disclosure must also meet the requirements in section 6103(h)(4).

*Example 10.* In a state court tort action, Defendant subpoenas IRS for Plaintiff's federal income tax returns for particular taxable years. This is a non-IRS matter. The Disclosure Officer instructs Defendant that the IRS has established procedures for obtaining copies of Federal income tax returns. Section 601.702(d)(1) of this chapter establishes the procedures for obtaining Federal tax returns by requiring written requests for copies of tax returns using IRS Form 4506, "Request for Copy of Tax Return." At Defendant's request, Plaintiff executes Form 4506, naming Defendant's counsel as designee, and the form is properly submitted to IRS. A testimony authorization would not be required to disclose Plaintiff's returns to Defendant's counsel.

[Reg. § 301.9000-6.]

☐ [*T.D.* 9178, 2-11-2005.]

### [Reg. § 301.9000-7]

**§ 301.9000-7. Effective date.**—These regulations are applicable on February 14, 2005.

☐ [*T.D.* 9178, 2-11-2005.]

# EXTENSION OF TIME FOR MAKING ELECTIONS

### [Reg. § 301.9100-0]

**§ 301.9100-0. Outline of regulations.**—This section lists the paragraphs in § § 301.9100-1 through 301.9100-3.

§ 301.9100-1. *Extensions of time to make elections.*
  (a) Introduction.
  (b) Terms.
  (c) General standards for relief.
  (d) Exceptions.
  (e) Effective dates.

§ 301.9100-2. *Automatic extensions.*
  (a) Automatic 12-month extension.
    (1) In general.
    (2) Elections eligible for automatic 12-month extension.
  (b) Automatic 6-month extension.
  (c) Corrective action.
  (d) Procedural requirements.
  (e) Examples.

§ 301.9100-3. *Other extensions.*
  (a) In general.
  (b) Reasonable action and good faith.
    (1) In general.
    (2) Reasonable reliance on a qualified tax professional.
    (3) Taxpayer deemed to have not acted reasonably or in good faith.
  (c) Prejudice to the interests of the Government.
    (1) In general.
      (i) Lower tax liability.
      (ii) Closed years.
    (2) Special rules for accounting method regulatory elections.
    (3) Special rules for accounting period regulatory elections.
  (d) Effect of amended returns.
    (1) Second examination under section 7605(b).
    (2) Suspension of the period of limitations under section 6501(a).
  (e) Procedural requirements.
    (1) In general.
    (2) Affidavit and declaration from taxpayer.
    (3) Affidavits and declarations from other parties.
    (4) Other information.
    (5) Filing instructions.
  (f) Examples.

[Reg. § 301.9100-0.]

☐ [*T.D.* 8742, 12-30-97.]

### [Reg. § 301.9100-1]

**§ 301.9100-1. Extensions of time to make elections.**—(a) *Introduction.*—The regulations under this section and § § 301.9100-2 and 301.9100-3 provide the standards the Commissioner will use to determine whether to grant an extension of time to make a regulatory election. The regulations under this section and § 301.9100-2 also provide an automatic extension of time to make certain statutory elections. An extension of time is available for elections that a taxpayer is otherwise eligible to make. However, the granting of an extension of time is not a determination that the taxpayer is otherwise eligible to make the election. Section 301.9100-2 provides automatic extensions of time for making regulatory and statutory elections when the deadline for making the election is the due date of the return or the due date of the return including extensions. Section 301.9100-3 provides extensions of time for making regulatory elections that do not meet the requirements of § 301.9100-2.

(b) *Terms.*—The following terms have the meanings provided below—

*Election* includes an application for relief in respect of tax; a request to adopt, change, or retain an accounting method or accounting period; but does not include an application for an extension of time for filing a return under section 6081.

*Regulatory election* means an election whose due date is prescribed by a regulation published in the Federal Register, or a revenue ruling, revenue procedure, notice, or announcement published in the Internal Revenue Bulletin (see § 601.601(d)(2) of this chapter).

*Statutory election* means an election whose due date is prescribed by statute.

*Taxpayer* means any person within the meaning of section 7701(a)(1).

(c) *General standards for relief.*—The Commissioner in exercising the Commissioner's discretion may grant a reasonable extension of time under the rules set forth in § § 301.9100-2 and 301.9100-3 to make a regulatory election, or a statutory election (but no more than 6 months except in the case of a taxpayer who is abroad), under all subtitles of the Internal Revenue Code except subtitles E, G, H, and I.

(d) *Exceptions.*—Notwithstanding the provisions of paragraph (c) of this section, an extension of time will not be granted—

  (1) For elections under section 4980A(f)(5); or

  (2) For elections that are expressly excepted from relief or where alternative relief is provided by a statute, a regulation published in the Federal Register, or a revenue ruling, revenue procedure, notice, or announcement published in the Internal Revenue Bulletin (see § 601.601(d)(2) of this chapter).

(e) *Effective dates.*—In general, this section and § § 301.9100-2 and 301.9100-3 apply to all requests for an extension of time submitted to the Internal Revenue Service (IRS) on or after December 31, 1997. However, the automatic 12-month and 6-month extensions provided in § 301.9100-2 apply to elections for which corrective action is taken on or after December 31, 1997. For other requests for an extension of time, see § § 301.9100-1T through 301.9100-3T in effect prior to December 31, 1997. (§ § 301.9100-1T through 301.9100-3T as contained in the 26 CFR part 1 edition revised as of April 1, 1997). [Reg. § 301.9100-1.]

☐ [*T.D.* 8378, 12-21-91. *Amended by T.D.* 8481, 6-29-93 *and T.D.* 8742, 12-30-97.]

### [Reg. § 301.9100-2]

**§ 301.9100-2. Automatic extensions.**—(a) *Automatic 12-month extension.*—(1) *In general.*—An automatic extension of 12 months from the due date for making a regulatory election is granted to make elections described in paragraph (a) of this section provided the taxpayer takes corrective action as defined in paragraph (c) of this section within that 12-month extension period. For purposes of this paragraph (a), the due date for making a regulatory election is the extended due date of the return if the due date of the election is the due date of the return or the due date of the return including extensions and the taxpayer has obtained an extension of time to file the return. This extension is available regardless of whether the taxpayer timely filed its return for the year the election should have been made.

(2) *Elections eligible for automatic 12-month extension.*—The following regulatory elections are eligible for the automatic 12-month extension described in paragraph (a)(1) of this section—

(i) The election to use other than the required taxable year under section 444;

(ii) The election to use the last-in, first-out (LIFO) inventory method under section 472;

(iii) The 15-month rule for filing an exemption application for a section 501(c)(9), 501(c) (17), or 501(c) (20) organization under section 505;

(iv) The 15-month rule for filing an exemption application for a section 501(c)(3) organization under section 508;

(v) The election to be treated as a homeowners association under section 528;

(vi) The election to adjust basis on partnership transfers and distributions under section 754;

(vii) The estate tax election to specially value qualified real property (where the Internal Revenue Service (IRS) has not yet begun an examination of the filed return) under section 2032A(d)(1)

(viii) The chapter 14 gift tax election to treat a qualified payment right as other than a qualified payment under section 2701(c)(3)(C)(i); and

(ix) The chapter 14 gift tax election to treat any distribution right as a qualified payment under section 2701(c)(3)(C)(ii).

(b) *Automatic 6-month extension .*—An automatic extension of 6 months from the due date of a return excluding extensions is granted to make regulatory or statutory elections whose due dates are the due date of the return or the due date of the return including extensions provided the taxpayer timely filed its return for the year the election should have been made and the taxpayer takes corrective action as defined in paragraph (c) of this section within that 6-month extension period. This paragraph (b) does not apply to regulatory or statutory elections that must be made by the due date of the return excluding extensions.

(c) *Corrective action .*—For purposes of this section, corrective action means taking the steps required to file the election in accordance with the statute or the regulation published in the Federal Register, or the revenue ruling, revenue procedure, notice, or announcement published in the Internal Revenue Bulletin (see § 601.601(d)(2) of this chapter). For those elections required to be filed with a return, corrective action includes filing an original or an amended return for the year the regulatory or statutory election should have been made and attaching the appropriate form or statement for making the election. Taxpayers who make an election under an automatic extension (and all taxpayers whose tax liability would be affected by the election) must file their return in a manner that is consistent with the election and comply with all other requirements for making the election for the year the election should have been made and for all affected years; otherwise, the IRS may invalidate the election.

(d) *Procedural requirements .*—Any return, statement of election, or other form of filing that must be made to obtain an automatic extension must provide the following statement at the top of the document: "FILED PURSUANT TO § 301.9100-2". Any filing made to obtain an automatic extension must be sent to the same address that the filing to make the election would have been sent had the filing been timely made. No request for a letter ruling is required to obtain an automatic extension. Accordingly, user fees do not apply to taxpayers taking corrective action to obtain an automatic extension.

(e) *Examples .*—The following examples illustrate the provisions of this section:

*Example 1. Automatic 12-month extension.* Taxpayer A fails to make an election described in paragraph (a)(2) of this section when filing A's 1997 income tax return on March 16, 1998, the due date of the return. This election does not affect the tax liability of any other taxpayer. The applicable regulation requires that the election be made by attaching the appropriate form to a timely filed return including extensions. In accordance with paragraphs (a) and (c) of this section, A may make the regulatory election by taking the corrective action of filing an amended return with the appropriate form by March 15, 1999 (12 months from the March 16, 1998 due date of the return). If A obtained a 6-month extension to file its 1997 income tax return, A may make the regulatory election by taking the corrective action of filing an amended return with the appropriate form by September 15, 1999 (12 months from the September 15, 1998 extended due date of the return).

*Example 2. Automatic 6-month extension.* Taxpayer B fails to make an election not described in paragraph (a)(2) of this section when filing B's 1997 income tax return on March 16, 1998, the due date of the return. This election does not affect the tax liability of any other taxpayer. The applicable regulation requires that the election be made by attaching the appropriate form to a timely filed return including extensions. In accordance with paragraphs (b) and (c) of this section, B may make the regulatory election by taking the corrective action of filing an amended return with the appropriate form by

September 15, 1998 (6 months from the March 16, 1998 due date of the return).
[Reg. § 301.9100-2.]

☐ [*T.D. 8742, 12-30-97.*]

### [Reg. § 301.9100-3]

**§ 301.9100-3. Other extensions.**—(a) *In general.*—Requests for extensions of time for regulatory elections that do not meet the requirements of § 301.9100-2 must be made under the rules of this section. Requests for relief subject to this section will be granted when the taxpayer provides the evidence (including affidavits described in paragraph (e) of this section) to establish to the satisfaction of the Commissioner that the taxpayer acted reasonably and in good faith, and the grant of relief will not prejudice the interests of the Government.

(b) *Reasonable action and good faith.*—(1) *In general.*—Except as provided in paragraphs (b)(3)(i) through (iii) of this section, a taxpayer is deemed to have acted reasonably and in good faith if the taxpayer—

(i) Requests relief under this section before the failure to make the regulatory election is discovered by the Internal Revenue Service (IRS);

(ii) Failed to make the election because of intervening events beyond the taxpayer's control;

(iii) Failed to make the election because, after exercising reasonable diligence (taking into account the taxpayer's experience and the complexity of the return or issue), the taxpayer was unaware of the necessity for the election;

(iv) Reasonably relied on the written advice of the Internal Revenue Service (IRS); or

(v) Reasonably relied on a qualified tax professional, including a tax professional employed by the taxpayer, and the tax professional failed to make, or advise the taxpayer to make, the election.

(2) *Reasonable reliance on a qualified tax professional.*—For purposes of this paragraph (b), a taxpayer will not be considered to have reasonably relied on a qualified tax professional if the taxpayer knew or should have known that the professional was not—

(i) Competent to render advice on the regulatory election; or

(ii) Aware of all relevant facts.

(3) *Taxpayer deemed to have not acted reasonably or in good faith.*—For purposes of this paragraph (b), a taxpayer is deemed to have not acted reasonably and in good faith if the taxpayer—

(i) Seeks to alter a return position for which an accuracy-related penalty has been or could be imposed under section 6662 at the time the taxpayer requests relief (taking into account any qualified amended return filed within the meaning of § 1.6664-2(c)(3) of this chapter) and the new position requires or permits a regulatory election for which relief is requested;

(ii) Was informed in all material respects of the required election and related tax consequences, but chose not to file the election; or

(iii) Uses hindsight in requesting relief. If specific facts have changed since the due date for making the election that make the election advantageous to a taxpayer, the IRS will not ordinarily grant relief. In such a case, the IRS will grant relief only when the taxpayer provides strong proof that the taxpayer's decision to seek relief did not involve hindsight.

(c) *Prejudice to the interests of the Government.*—(1) *In general.*—The Commissioner will grant a reasonable extension of time to make a regulatory election only when the interests of the Government will not be prejudiced by the granting of relief. This paragraph (c) provides the standards the Commissioner will use to determine when the interests of the Government are prejudiced.

(i) *Lower tax liability.*—The interests of the Government are prejudiced if granting relief would result in a taxpayer having a lower tax liability in the aggregate for all taxable years affected by the election than the taxpayer would have had if the election had been timely made (taking into account the time value of money). Similarly, if the tax consequences of more than one taxpayer are affected by the election, the Government's interests are prejudiced if extending the time for making the election may result in the affected taxpayers, in the aggregate, having a lower tax liability than if the election had been timely made.

(ii) *Closed years.*—The interests of the Government are ordinarily prejudiced if the taxable year in which the regulatory election should have been made or any taxable years that would have been affected by the election had it been timely made are closed by the period of limitations on assessment under section 6501(a) before the taxpayer's receipt of a ruling granting relief under this section. The IRS may condition a grant of relief on the taxpayer providing the IRS with a statement from an independent auditor (other than an auditor providing an affidavit pursuant to paragraph (e)(3) of this section) certifying that the interests of the Government are not prejudiced under the standards set forth in paragraph (c)(1)(i) of this section.

(2) *Special rules for accounting method regulatory elections.*—The interests of the Government are deemed to be prejudiced except in unusual and compelling circumstances if the accounting method regulatory election for which relief is requested—

(i) Is subject to the procedure described in §1.4461(e)(3)(i) of this chapter (requiring the advance written consent of the Commissioner);

(ii) Requires an adjustment under section 481(a) (or would require an adjustment under section 481(a) if the taxpayer changed to the method of accounting for which relief is requested in a taxable year subsequent to the taxable year the election should have been made);

(iii) Would permit a change from an impermissible method of accounting that is an issue under consideration by examination, an appeals office, or a federal court and the change would provide a more favorable method or more favorable terms and conditions than if the change were made as part of an examination; or

(iv) Provides a more favorable method of accounting or more favorable terms and conditions if the election is made by a certain date or taxable year.

(3) *Special rules for accounting period regulatory elections.*—The interests of the Government are deemed to be prejudiced except in unusual and compelling circumstances if an election is an accounting period regulatory election (other than the election to use other than the required taxable year under section 444) and the request for relief is filed more than 90 days after the due date for filing the Form 1128, Application to Adopt, Change, or Retain a Tax Year (or other required statement).

(d) *Effect of amended returns-.*—(1) *Second examination under section 7605(b).*—Taxpayers requesting and receiving an extension of time under this section waive any objections to a second examination under section 7605(b) for the issue(s) that is the subject of the relief request and any correlative adjustments.

(2) *Suspension of the period of limitations under section 6501(a).*—A request for relief under this section does not suspend the period of limitations on assessment under section 6501(a). Thus, for relief to be granted, the IRS may require the taxpayer to consent under section 6501(c)(4) to an extension of the period of limitations on assessment for the taxable year in which the regulatory election should have been made and any taxable years that would have been affected by the election had it been timely made.

(e) *Procedural requirements.*—(1) *In general.*—Requests for relief under this section must provide evidence that satisfies the requirements in paragraphs (b) and (c) of this section, and must provide additional information as required by this paragraph (e).

(2) *Affidavit and declaration from taxpayer.*—The taxpayer, or the individual who acts on behalf of the taxpayer with respect to tax matters, must submit a detailed affidavit describing the events that led to the failure to make a valid regulatory election and to the discovery of the failure. When the taxpayer relied on a qualified tax professional for advice, the taxpayer's affidavit must describe the engagement and responsibilities of the professional as well as the extent to which the taxpayer relied on the professional. The affidavit must be accompanied by a dated declaration, signed by the taxpayer, which states: "Under penalties of perjury, I declare that I have examined this request, including accompanying documents, and, to the best of my knowledge and belief, the request contains all the relevant facts relating to the request, and such facts are true, correct, and complete." The individual who signs for an entity must have personal knowledge of the facts and circumstances at issue.

(3) *Affidavits and declarations from other parties.*—The taxpayer must submit detailed affidavits from the individuals having knowledge or information about the events that led to the failure to make a valid regulatory election and to the discovery of the failure. These individuals must include the taxpayer's return preparer, any individual (including an employee of the taxpayer) who made a substantial contribution to the preparation of the return, and any accountant or attorney, knowledgeable in tax matters, who advised the taxpayer with regard to the election. An affidavit must describe the engagement and responsibilities of the individual as well as the advice that the individual provided to the taxpayer. Each affidavit must include the name, current address, and taxpayer identification number of the individual, and be accompanied by a dated declaration, signed by the individual, which states: "Under penalties of perjury, I declare that I have examined this request, including accompanying documents, and, to the best of my knowledge and belief, the request

contains all the relevant facts relating to the request, and such facts are true, correct, and complete."

(4) *Other information.*—The request for relief filed under this section must also contain the following information—

(i) The taxpayer must state whether the taxpayer's return(s) for the taxable year in which the regulatory election should have been made or any taxable years that would have been affected by the election had it been timely made is being examined by a district director, or is being considered by an appeals office or a federal court. The taxpayer must notify the IRS office considering the request for relief if the IRS starts an examination of any such return while the taxpayer's request for relief is pending;

(ii) The taxpayer must state when the applicable return, form, or statement used to make the election was required to be filed and when it was actually filed;

(iii) The taxpayer must submit a copy of any documents that refer to the election;

(iv) When requested, the taxpayer must submit a copy of the taxpayer's return for any taxable year for which the taxpayer requests an extension of time to make the election and any return affected by the election; and

(v) When applicable, the taxpayer must submit a copy of the returns of other taxpayers affected by the election.

(5) *Filing instructions.*—A request for relief under this section is a request for a letter ruling. Requests for relief should be submitted in accordance with the applicable procedures for requests for a letter ruling and must be accompanied by the applicable user fee.

(f) *Examples.*—The following examples illustrate the provisions of this section:

*Example 1. Taxpayer discovers own error.* Taxpayer A prepares A's 1997 income tax return. A is unaware that a particular regulatory election is available to report a transaction in a particular manner. A files the 1997 return without making the election and reporting the transaction in a different manner. In 1999, A hires a qualified tax professional to prepare A's 1999 return. The professional discovers that A did not make the election. A promptly files for relief in accordance with this section. Assume paragraphs (b)(3)(i) through (iii) of this section do not apply. Under paragraph (b)(3)(i) of this section, A is deemed to have acted reasonably and in good faith because A requested relief before the failure to make the regulatory election was discovered by the IRS.

*Example 2. Reliance on qualified tax professional.* Taxpayer B hires a qualified tax professional to advise B on preparing B's 1997 income tax return. The professional was competent to render advice on the election and B provided the professional with all the relevant facts. The professional fails to advise B that a regulatory election is necessary in order for B to report income on B's 1997 return in a particular manner. Nevertheless, B reports this income in a manner that is consistent with having made the election. In 2000, during the examination of the 1997 return by the IRS, the examining agent discovers that the election has not been filed. B promptly files for relief in accordance with this section, including attaching an affidavit from B's professional stating that the professional failed to advise B that the election was necessary. Assume paragraphs (b)(3)(i) through (iii) of this section do not apply. Under paragraph (b)(1)(v) of this section, B is deemed to have acted reasonably and in good faith because B reasonably relied on a qualified tax professional and the tax professional failed to advise B to make the election.

*Example 3. Accuracy-related penalty.* Taxpayer C reports income on its 1997 income tax return in a manner that is contrary to a regulatory provision. In 2000, during the examination of the 1997 return, the IRS raises an issue regarding the reporting of this income on C's return and asserts the accuracy-related penalty under section 6662. C requests relief under this section to elect an alternative method of reporting the income. Under paragraph (b)(3)(i) of this section, C is deemed to have not acted reasonably and in good faith because C seeks to alter a return position for which an accuracy-related penalty could be imposed under section 6662.

*Example 4. Election not requiring adjustment under section 481(a).* Taxpayer D prepares D's 1997 income tax return. D is unaware that a particular accounting method regulatory election is available. D files D's 1997 return without making the election and uses another permissible method of accounting. The applicable regulation provides that the election is made on a cut-off basis (without an adjustment under section 481(a)). In 1998, D requests relief under this section to make the election under the regulation. If D were granted an extension of time to make the election, D would pay no less tax than if the election had been timely made. Assume that paragraphs (c)(2)(i), (iii), and (iv) of this section do not apply. Under paragraph (c)(2)(ii) of this section, the interests of the Government are not deemed to be prejudiced because the election does not require an adjustment under section 481(a).

*Example 5. Election requiring adjustment under section 481(a).* The facts are the same as in *Example 4* of this paragraph (f) except that the applicable regulation provides that the election requires an adjustment under section 481(a). Under paragraph (c)(2)(ii) of this section, the interests of the Government are deemed to be prejudiced except in unusual or compelling circumstances.

*Example 6. Under examination by the IRS.* A regulation permits an automatic change in method of accounting for an item on a cut-off basis. Taxpayer E reports income on E's 1997 income tax return using an impermissible method of accounting for the item. In 2000, during the examination of the 1997 return by the IRS, the examining agent notifies E in writing that its method of accounting for the item is an issue under consideration. Any change from the impermissible method made as part of an examination is made with an adjustment under section 481(a). E requests relief under this section to make the change pursuant to the regulation for 1997. The change on a cut-off basis under the regulation would be more favorable than if the change were made with an adjustment under section 481(a) as part of an examination. Under paragraph (c)(2)(iii) of this section, the interests of the Government are deemed to be prejudiced except in unusual and compelling circumstances because E seeks to change from an impermissible method of accounting that is an issue under consideration in the examination on a basis that is more favorable than if the change were made as part of an examination.
[Reg. §301.9100-3.]

☐ [T.D. 8742, 12-30-97.]

# ELECTIONS UNDER ECONOMIC RECOVERY TAX ACT OF 1981

[Reg. §301.9100-4T]

**§301.9100-4T. Time and manner of making certain elections under the Economic Recovery Tax Act of 1981 (Temporary).—**

(a) *Miscellaneous elections.*—(1) *Elections to which this paragraph applies.*—This paragraph applies to the following elections provided under the Economic Recovery Tax Act of 1981:

| Section of Act | Section of Code | Description of Election | Availability of Election |
|---|---|---|---|
| 201(a) | 168(b)(3) | Different recovery period. | Property placed in service after 1980. |
| 201(a) | 168(d)(2)(A) | Inclusion in income of entire proceeds of disposition. | Property placed in service after 1980. |
| 201(a) | 168(e)(2) | Exclusion of property from recovery system. | Property placed in service after 1980. |
| 201(a) | 168(f)(2)(C) | Different recovery period for property used outside U.S. | Property placed in service after 1980. |
| 202(a) | 179 | Expensing certain depreciable property. | Taxable years beginning after 1981. |
| 237 | 474 | For small business to use one inventory pool when LIFO is elected. | Taxable years beginning after 1981. |
| 266(a) | | Deferral of commencement of amortization period for motor carrier operating authority. | Taxable years ending after June 30, 1980. |
| 508(c) | | Application of Title V of the Act to all regulated futures contracts or positions held on June 23, 1981. | Property held on June 23, 1981. |
| 509 | | Application of Code sec. 1256 and extension of time for payment of tax for all regulated futures contracts held at any time during taxable year that includes June 23, 1981. | Property held during taxable year that includes June 23, 1981. |

(2) *Time for making elections.*—(i) *In general.*—Except as otherwise provided in this paragraph (a)(2), the elections specified in paragraph (a)(1) of this section shall be made by the later of—

(A) The due date (taking extensions into account) of the income tax return for the taxable year for which the election is to be effective, or

(B) April 15, 1982.

(ii) *No extension of time for payment.*—Payments of tax due shall be made in accordance with chapter 62 of the Code.

(iii) *Elections under section 508(c) or 509 of the Act.*—Elections under section 508(c) or 509 of the Act shall be made by the due date (taking extensions into account) of the income tax return for the taxable year for which the election is to be effective.

(3) *Manner of making elections.*—The elections specified in paragraph (a)(1) of this section shall be made by attaching a statement to the income tax return (or amended return) for the taxable year for which the election is made. Except as otherwise provided in the return or in the instructions accompanying the return for the taxable year, the statement shall—

(i) Contain the name, address, and taxpayer identification number of the electing taxpayer,

(ii) Identify the election,

(iii) Indicate the section of the Code (or, if the provision is not codified, the section of the Act) under which the election is being made,

(iv) Specify the period for which the election is being made and the property to which the election is to apply, and

(v) Provide any information required by the relevant statutory provisions and any information necessary to show that the taxpayer is entitled to make the election.

(b) *Designation of principal campaign committee.*—This paragraph applies to the designation of a principal campaign committee under section 527(h) of the Code, as added by section 128 of the Act. References in this section to "elections" include designations under section 527 (h). Under that provision a candidate for Congress may designate one committee as the candidate's principal campaign committee. The political organization taxable income of that committee shall be taxed at the appropriate rates under section 11(b); that income is ordinarily taxed at the highest rate specified in section 11(b). The candidate shall designate the principal campaign committee by filing a statement of designation with the income tax return of the committee for the first taxable year of the committee ending after 1981 for which the designation is to be effective. The return and the statement shall be filed by the due date (taking extensions into account) of the return. The rules of section 21 (relating to effects of changes in rates during a taxable year) shall apply in the case of any taxable year beginning before 1982 for which a designation is made. The statement of designation shall be signed by the candidate and shall—

(1) Contain the name, address, and taxpayer identification number of the candidate and of the committee,

(2) Identify the statement as a designation under section 527(h) of the Code, and

(3) Designate the committee as the principal campaign committee of the candidate.

The candidate shall attach to the statement a copy of the statement of designation filed with the Federal Election Commission.

(c) *Election to be treated as a qualified fund for purposes of the research credit.*—This paragraph applies to the election provided under section 44F(e)(4) of the Code, as added by section 221(a) of the Act. The election to be treated as a qualified fund for purposes of the research credit may be made effective as of any date after June 30, 1981, and before January 1, 1986. An organization shall make this election by filing with the service center with which it files its annual return a statement signed by a person authorized to act on behalf of the organization. That statement shall—

(1) Contain the name, address, and taxpayer identification number of the electing organization and of the organization that established and maintains the electing organization,

(2) Identify the election as an election under section 44F(e)(4) of the Code,

(3) Specify the date on which the election is to become effective (in the case of elections filed before February 1, 1982, not earlier than the date that is 7 months before the date on which the election is filed; in the case of elections filed after January 31, 1982, not earlier than the date on which the election is filed), and

(4) Provide all information necessary to show that the organization is entitled to make the election.

(d) *Election to treat qualified subchapter S trust as grantor trust.*—This paragraph applies to the election provided under section 1371(g)(2) of the Code, as added by section 234(b) of the Act. The election to treat a qualified subchapter S trust as a grantor trust described in section 1371(e)(1)(A) of the Code is available for taxable years beginning after 1981. The beneficiary of the trust (or the legal representative of the beneficiary) shall make this election by signing and filing with the service center with which the subchapter S corporation files its income tax return a statement that—

(1) Contains the name, address, and taxpayer identification number of the beneficiary, the trust, and the subchapter S corporation,

(2) Identifies the election as an election under section 1371(g)(2) of the Code,

(3) Specifies the date on which the election is to become effective (not earlier than 60 days before the date on which the election is filed), and

(4) Provides all information necessary to show that the beneficiary is entitled to make the election.

Note that this election does not itself constitute an election as to the status of the corporation; the corporation must make the election provided in section 1372(a) to be treated as an electing small business corporation.

(e) *Election to have Code section 422A apply to options granted before 1981.*—This paragraph applies to the election provided under section 251(c)(1)(B) of the Act to have Code section 422A apply to certain options granted before 1981. A corporation may make only one election under this provision. Thus, a corporation that makes an election under this provision with respect to certain options granted before 1981 may not make any subsequent election under this provision with respect to other options granted before 1981. An election under this provision shall be made no later than the due date (taking extensions into account) of the income tax return of the corporation for its first taxable year during which either an option subject to the election or an option subject to the rules of section 422A of the Code is exercised. In any event, no election under this provision will be permitted after the due date (taking extensions into account) of the income tax return for the taxable year including December 31, 1982. A corporation shall make this election by attaching to its income tax return (or amended return) a statement that—

(1) Contains the name, address, and taxpayer identification number of the corporation,

(2) Identifies the election as an election under section 251(c)(1)(B) of the Economic Recovery Tax Act of 1981,

(3) Specifies the options to which the election applies, and

(4) Provides all information necessary to show that the corporation is entitled to make the election.

(f) *Election to increase basis of property on which additional estate tax is imposed.*—This paragraph applies to the election provided under section 1016 (c) of the Code, as amended by section 421(g) of the Act. The election to increase the basis of property on which additional

estate tax is imposed is available with respect to the estates of decedents dying after 1981. The qualified heir shall make this election by filing with the Form 706-A (Additional Estate Tax Return) a statement that—

(1) Contains the name, address, and taxpayer identification number of the qualified heir and of the estate,

(2) Identifies the election as an election under section 1016(c) of the Code,

(3) Specifies the property with respect to which the election is made, and

(4) Provides any additional information required by the instructions accompanying Form 706-A.

A qualified heir making an election under this paragraph must pay interest on the additional estate tax from the date that is 9 months after the date of the decedent's death to the date of the payment of the additional estate tax.

(g) *Revocation of elections.*—Elections under paragraph (f) of this section are irrevocable. Other elections made under this section may be revoked only with the consent of the Commissioner. An application for consent to revoke an election shall be signed by the applicant and filed with the service center with which the election was filed and shall—

(1) Contain the name, address, and taxpayer identification number of all parties identified in connection with the election,

(2) Identify the election being revoked by reference to the section of the Code or Act under which the election was made,

(3) Specify the scope of the election, and

(4) Explain why the applicant seeks to revoke the election.

(h) *Additional information required.*—If later regulations issued under the section of the Code or Act under which the election was made require the furnishing of information in addition to that which was furnished with the statement of election and an office of the Internal Revenue Service requests the taxpayer to provide the additional information, the taxpayer shall furnish the additional information in a statement filed with that office of the Internal Revenue Service within 60 days after the request is made. This statement shall also—

(1) Contain the name, address, and taxpayer identification numbers of all parties identified in connection with the election,

(2) Identify the election by reference to the section of the Code or Act under which the election was made, and

(3) Specify the scope of the election.

If the additional information is not provided within 60 days after the request is made, the election may, at the discretion of the Commissioner, be held invalid.

(i) *Effective date.*—This section applies to elections made after August 12, 1981. [Temporary Reg. § 301.9100-4T.]

☐ [T.D. 7793, 10-29-81. Redesignated by T.D. 8435, 9-18-92. *Amended by T.D. 9481, 4-7-2010.*]

# ELECTIONS UNDER TAX EQUITY AND FISCAL RESPONSIBILITY ACT OF 1982

## [Reg. § 301.9100-5T]

**§ 301.9100-5T. Time and manner of making certain elections under the Tax Equity and Fiscal Responsibility Act of 1982 (Tempo-** rary).—(a) *Miscellaneous elections.*—(1) *Elections to which this paragraph applies.*—This paragraph applies to the following elections provided under the Tax Equity and Fiscal Responsibility Act of 1982.

| Section of Act | Section of Code | Description of Election | Availability of Election |
|---|---|---|---|
| 201(c) | 58(i)(1) | Optional 10-year write off of certain tax preferences. | Taxable years beginning after Dec. 31, 1982. |
| 201(c)(1) | 58(i)(4) | Intangible drilling and development costs. | Taxable years beginning after Dec. 31, 1982. |
| 205(a) | 48(q) | Reduced investment credit in lieu of basis adjustment. | Generally to period beginning after Dec. 31, 1982. |
| 256(f) | 820 | Insurance company revocation of election under section 820. | Contracts which took effect in 1980 or 1981. |

(2) *Time for making elections.*—(i) *In general.*—Except as otherwise provided in paragraph (a)(2) of this section, the elections specified in paragraph (a)(1) of this section shall be made by the later of—

(A) The due date (taking extensions into account) of the income tax return for the taxable year for which the election is to be effective, or

(B) April 15, 1983.

(ii) *No extensions of time for payment.*—Payments of tax due shall be made in accordance with chapter 62 of the Code.

(iii) *Election by insurance companies relating to repeal of section 820.*—Elections under section 256(f) of the Act, relating to special rule allowing reinsured insurance company to revoke an election under section 820, must be made before March 5, 1983.

(3) *Manner of making elections.*—The elections specified in paragraph (a)(1) of this section shall be made by attaching a statement to the income tax return (or amended return) for the taxable year for which the election is made. Except as otherwise provided in the

return or in the instructions accompanying the return for the taxable year, the statement shall—

(i) Contain the name, address, and taxpayer identification number of the electing taxpayer,

(ii) Identify the election,

(iii) Indicate the section of the Code (or, if the provision is not codified, the section of the Act) under which the election is being made,

(iv) Specify the period for which the election is being made and the property to which the election is to apply, and

(v) Provide any information required by the relevant statutory provisions and any information necessary to show that the taxpayer is entitled to make the election.

(b) *Special rules for reduced investment credit in lieu of basis adjustment.*—(1) *Appropriate return.*—For purposes of section 48(q) of the Code and paragraph (a)(2)(i)(A) and (3) of this section the term "income tax return for the taxable year for which the election is effective" with respect to any property is the tax return for the taxable year in which such property is placed in service, or in the case of property to which an election under section 46(d) (relating to qualified progress expenditures) applies, the appropriate return is the return for the first taxable year for which qualified progress expenditures were taken into account with respect to such property.

(2) *Applicability of election.*—In general, the election under section 48(q) is applicable to periods beginning after December 31, 1982 under rules similar to the rules of section 48(m) of the Code. However, the election does not apply to property excepted by section 205(c)(1)(B) of the Act.

(c) *Election by a reinsurer to make installment payments of taxes owed resulting from the repeal of section 820.*—This paragraph applies to the election by an insurance company provided under section 256(e) of the Act. A reinsurer that is a calendar year taxpayer shall be considered to have made an election under section 256(e) of the Act if by March 15, 1983 it files its income tax return (or an application on Form 7004 for an automatic extension of time to file its income tax return), with the statement required to be filed under this paragraph attached and, unless the reinsurer is making a further election under section 256(e)(2)(B) of the Act, pays one-third of the amount described in section 256(e)(1) of the Act by March 15, 1983. A reinsurer making an election under section 256(e)(2)(B) of the Act must pay one-sixth of the amount described in section 256(e)(1) of the Act by March 15, 1983 and one-sixth of such amount by June 15, 1983. The statement required to be filed under this paragraph shall—

(1) Contain the name, address, and taxpayer identification number of the corporation,

(2) Identify the election as an election under section 256(e) of the Act, and section 256(e)(2)(B) if applicable, and

(3) Provide all information necessary to show the taxpayer is entitled to make the election.

For provisions relating to the use of authorized financial institutions in depositing the taxes, see § 1.6302-1.

(d) [Reserved].

(e) *Additional information required.*—If later regulations issued under the section of the Code or Act under which the election was made require the furnishing of information in addition to that which was furnished with the statement of election and an office of the Internal Revenue Service requests the taxpayer to provide the additional information, the taxpayer shall furnish the additional information in a statement filed with that office of the Internal Revenue Service within 60 days after the request is made. This statement shall also—

(1) Contain the name, address, and taxpayer identification numbers of all parties identified in connection with the election,

(2) Identify the election by reference to the section of the Code or Act under which the election was made, and

(3) Specify the scope of the election.

If the additional information is not provided within 60 days after the request is made, the election may, at the discretion of the Commissioner, be held valid.

[(f)] *Effective date.*—This section applies to elections made after September 3, 1982. [Temporary Reg. § 301.9100-5T.]

☐ [*T.D. 7870, 1-12-83. Redesignated by T.D. 8435, 9-18-92. Amended by T.D. 8952, 6-25-2001.*]

# ELECTIONS UNDER DEFICIT REDUCTION ACT OF 1984

**[Reg. § 301.9100-6T]**

**§ 301.9100-6T. Time and manner of making certain elections under the Deficit Reduction Act of 1984 (Temporary).—**

(a) *Miscellaneous elections.*—(1) *Elections to which this paragraph applies.*—This paragraph applies to the following elections provided under the Deficit Reduction Act of 1984 (the Act):

TABLE 1 TO PARAGRAPH (a)(1)

| Section of Act | Section of Code | Description of Election | Availability of Election |
|---|---|---|---|
| 31(a) and 31(g)(16) | 168(j)(4)(E)(ii) | Election by certain 501(c)(12) organizations to be treated as taxable organizations and to have certain arbitrage profits taxed | Generally for property placed in service after May 23, 1983, or leased after such date |
| 31(f) | 46(e)(4)(C) | Election by section 593 organizations not to apply section 46(e)(4)(A) | Generally for property placed in service after November 5, 1983, or leased after such date |
| 41(a) | 1282(b)(2) | Election to have section 1281 apply to all short-term obligations acquired on or after the first day of the first taxable year to which the election relates (but not to obligations acquired before July 19, 1984) | Taxable years ending after July 18, 1984, with respect to obligations acquired after such date |
| 41(a) | 1283(c)(2) | Election to have section 1283(c)(1) not apply to all obligations acquired on or after the first day of the first taxable year to which the election relates (but not to obligations acquired before July 19, 1984) | Taxable years ending after July 18, 1984, with respect to obligations acquired after such date |
| 113 | 48(r) | Election by all persons having an ownership interest in a sound recording to treat such recording as 3-year recovery property | Property placed in service after March 15, 1984 |
| 431(e)(2) | 46(c)(8) and (9), 48(d)(6), 47(d)(1) and (2) | Election to apply the investment tax credit at risk rules as modified by the Tax Reform Act of 1984 to all transactions covered by section 211(f) of the Economic Recovery Tax Act of 1981 | Generally to property placed in service between February 18, 1981, and July 19, 1984 |
| 712(l)(7)(B) | 304 | Election to apply certain technical corrections of section 304 to all transfers covered by the changes made to section 304 by the Tax Equity and Fiscal Responsibility Act of 1982 | Stock acquired after August 31, 1982, and before June 19, 1984 |
| 712(l)(7)(C)(ii) | 304 | Election with respect to bank holding companies to apply certain technical corrections of section 304 to stock acquired after June 18, 1984 | Generally to transfers to bank holding companies formed pursuant to application filed with Federal Reserve Board before June 18, 1984 |
| 1066 | 163(d) | Elections to treat certain income from S corporations for purposes of section 163(d), as such income would have been treated prior to the Subchapter S Revision Act of 1982 | With respect to S corporation taxable years beginning in 1983 or 1984 |
| 1078 | | Election to exclude from gross income payments from U.S. Forest Service as result of restricting motorized traffic in the Boundary Waters Canoe Area | Payments in taxable years beginning after December 31, 1979 |

(2) *Time for making elections.*—(i) *In general.*—Except as otherwise provided in this paragraph (a)(2), the elections specified in paragraph (a)(1) of this section shall be made by the later of—

(A) The due date (taking extensions into account) of the tax return for the first taxable year for which the election is to be effective, or

(B) April 15, 1985 (in which case the election generally must be made by amended return).

(ii) *No extension of time for payment.*—Payments of tax due shall be made in accordance with chapter 62 of the Code.

(iii) [Reserved]

(iv) *Time for making the election to exclude from gross income payments received from the U.S. Forest Service as a result of the restriction of motorized traffic in the Boundary Waters Canoe Area.*—Elections under section 1078 of the Act shall be made by the later of the expiration of the period for making a claim for credit or refund of the tax imposed by chapter 1 of the Code for the taxable year in which the reinvestment of the payment occurred, or July 18, 1985. Amended returns for years after the year for which the election is made must be filed if making this election affects the tax liability for such years.

(3) *Manner of making elections.*—(i) *In general.*—The elections specified in paragraph (a)(1) of this section shall be made by attaching a statement to the tax return for the taxable year in which the election is made. If because of paragraph (a)(2)(i)(B) the election may be filed after the due date of the tax return for the first taxable year for which the election is to be effective, such election must be attached to a tax return or amended return for the taxable year to which the election relates. Except as otherwise provided in the return or in the instructions accompanying the return for the taxable year, the statement shall—

(A) Contain the name, address, and taxpayer identification number of the electing taxpayer,

(B) Identify the election,

(C) Indicate the section of the Code (or, if the provision is not codified, the section of the Act) under which the election is made,

(D) Specify, as applicable, the period for which the election is being made and/or the property or other items to which the election is to apply, and

(E) Provide any information required by the relevant statutory provisions and any information necessary to show that the taxpayer is entitled to make the election.

(ii) *Special rules for making the election with respect to sound recordings.*—The election under section 48(r), as amended by section 113 of the Act, shall be made separately for each sound recording and must be made by all persons having an ownership interest in the sound recording. In the case of an ownership interest held by a partnership or an S corporation, the partnership or S corporation shall make the election. Each person making the election shall do so in accordance with paragraph (a)(2) and (3) of this section, and shall identify in the statement described in paragraph (a)(3) of this section the persons with ownership interests in the sound recording, and shall state that each such person is making the election with respect to that sound recording.

(iii) *Special rules for making the election with respect to redemption through use of related corporations.*—For either election available under section 712(l)(7) of the Act (relating to redemptions through related corporations) to be effective, such election must be made jointly by both the issuing and acquiring corporations. The election is made jointly when both the issuing and acquiring corporations make the election in accordance with paragraph (a)(2) and (3) of this section.

(iv) *Special rules for making the election for investment tax credit at risk rules.*—The election under section 431(e)(2) of the Act is made by filing an amended return for the first taxable year ending after February 18, 1981, during which taxable year property, to which the amendments made by section 211(f) of the Economic Recovery Tax Act of 1981 apply, was placed in service. If that taxable year is a closed year, the election is made by filing an amended return for the first succeeding open taxable year, but in such event this election can be made only if the aggregate amount of the investment tax credit that would have been allowable in the closed years had the election been effective for those years is greater than or equal to the amount of the investment tax credits actually claimed in the closed years. In the case of partnerships and S corporations, the election under section 431(e) is made, respectively, at the partner or the shareholder

level. Any election made under section 431(e) shall apply to all property of the taxpayer to which the amendments made by section 211(f) of the Economic Recovery Tax Act of 1981 apply. Amended returns must be filed for any year the tax liability for which is affected by making this election.

(4) *Revocation.*—The elections under Act sections 31(a), 31(g)(16), 31(f), 41(a) (Code section 1283(b)(2)), 113, 431(e)(2), and 712(l)(7)(B) and (C)(ii) are irrevocable. Elections under Act sections 41(a) (Code sections 1282(b)(2) and 1283(c)(2)), 1066, and 1078 are revocable only with the consent of the Commissioner.

(b) *Church or qualified church-controlled organization's election of exemption from social security taxes under chapter 21.*—(1) *In general.*—This paragraph applies to the election under section 3121(w) of the Code, as added by section 2603(b) of the Act, by a church or qualified church-controlled organization (as defined in section 3121(w)(3)) that service performed in the employ of such church or organization shall be excluded from employment for purposes of title II of the Social Security Act and chapter 21 of the Internal Revenue Code. Any election made under section 3121(w) shall apply to all service performed on or after January 1, 1984, by employees of such church or organization (whether or not they were employees on that date or on the date the election is made). Employees of the electing church or organization are subject to the provisions of chapter 2 of the Code (relating to the tax on self-employment income) as amended by section 2603(c)(2) and (d)(2) of the Act for service performed for such church or organization on or after January 1, 1984.

(2) *Time for making the election.*—Any election under section 3121(w) by a church or qualified church-controlled organization for which a quarterly employment tax return for the tax imposed under section 3111 is due (or would be due but for the election) on October 31, 1984, must be made on or before October 30, 1984. Any election under section 3121(w) by a church or organization for which the first quarterly employment tax return for the tax imposed under section 3111 is due (or would be due but for this election) after October 31, 1984, must be made on or before the day before the first date that such tax return would be due from the church or organization (disregarding any extension of such due date). A purported election filed after the date prescribed in this paragraph (b)(2) shall be void.

(3) *Manner of making the election.*—To make an election under section 3121(w), a church or qualified church-controlled organization must certify that it is opposed for religious reasons to the payment of the tax imposed by section 3111 (relating to the employer tax) of the Code. The election and certification are made by executing and filing Form 8274 in accordance with the form and its instructions. The form shall be signed by an official authorized to sign tax returns for the church or organization. Where tax imposed by section 3111 is reported (or would be reported but for this election) with respect to more than one church or organization on a single quarterly employment tax return, and the election under section 3121(w) is made, then all of the churches and organizations covered by the last such return filed before such election was made for which the time for making the election has not expired shall be covered by the election unless specifically excluded by stating such exclusion in the election.

(4) *Refunds of FICA taxes paid.*—Where a church or qualified church-controlled organization makes a timely election under section 3121(w), a refund, without interest, shall be made to such church or organization of any taxes paid under sections 3101 and 3111 with respect to service performed after December 31, 1983, covered by the election. However, the refund will be made only if the church or organization agrees on its claim for the refund to pay to each employee covered by the election the portion of the refund attributable to the tax imposed on the wages of the employee by section 3101. The employee may not receive any other refund of such taxes. The claim for refund shall be made by the church or organization by filing Form 843 with the service center where the Form 941 on which the taxes subject to refund was filed. Form 843 shall be executed in accordance with the form and its instructions, and also in accordance with the instructions to Form 8274 that relate to Form 843.

(5) *Irrevocability of election except by Commissioner.*—An election under section 3121 shall be irrevocable by the electing church or organization. The Commissioner, however, shall permanently revoke the election if the church or organization fails to furnish the information required under section 6051 to the Internal Revenue Service for a period of 2 years or more and also fails to furnish such information

within 60 days after a written request therefor is made by the Internal Revenue Service.

(c) *Election to issue taxable student loan bonds.*—This paragraph applies to the election by an issuer to issue taxable student loan bonds under section 625(c) of the Act. The election is available for obligations issued after December 31, 1983, and is made by filing a statement and necessary attachments with the Internal Revenue Service Center, Philadelphia, PA 19255, prior to the issuance of such taxable bonds. The statement shall identify the election as made under section 625(c) of the Tax Reform Act of 1984 and shall contain the name, address and taxpayer identification number of the issuer, and the total purchase price, face amount and interest rate of the issue, bond issuance costs, amounts allocated to reasonably required reserve or replacement funds, and the date of issue. The issuer shall attach to the statement of election a copy of previous Internal Revenue Service correspondence relating to the tax exempt status of the issuing authority and a statement containing the total purchase price, face amount, interest rate, bond issuance costs, amounts allocated to reasonably required reserve or replacement funds, and the date of issuance of outstanding tax exempt issues of student loan bonds of the issuer. With respect to outstanding tax exempt issues of student loan bonds of the issuer issued after December 31, 1982, the issuer may alternatively attach copies of the Form 8038 filed with respect to such issues. Each taxable student loan bond must state on its face that the interest paid on such bond is subject to federal income taxation. An election with respect to an issue is irrevocable once made.

(d) [Reserved.]

(e) *Election not to claim the credit for alcohol used as fuel.*—The election under section 40(f) (as added by section 474(k) of the Act) not to claim the alcohol fuels credit is available for taxable years beginning after December 31, 1983, and shall be made for the taxable year, in which such credit is determined by not claiming such credit on an original return or amended return at any time before the expiration of the 3-year period beginning on the last date prescribed by law for filing the return for the taxable year (determined without regard for extensions). The election may be revoked within the 3-year period by filing an amended return and claiming the credit on the return.

(f) *Protective election to adopt LIFO method.*—(1) *Time for making the election.*—A protective election in connection with the enactment of section 95 of the Act to adopt the LIFO method of accounting for inventory under section 472 of the Code can only be made for the taxpayer's first taxable year beginning after July 18, 1984, and must be made on or before the due date (including extensions) of the tax return for such taxable year. Once made, the election is irrevocable unless the Commissioner authorizes the use of another inventory method (see § 1.472-5).

(2) *Manner for making a protective election.*—The protective election is made by completing all line items on a current Form 970 and indicating that the election is a protective election filed in connection with the enactment of section 95 of the Tax Reform Act of 1984. The Form 970 must be attached to the taxpayer's income tax return for the taxable year for which the protective election is made. The LIFO method adopted under the protective election must be consistent in all respects with the taxpayer's LIFO method used in the taxpayer's most recently completed taxable year for which the LIFO method was used. In completing the current Form 970, the taxpayer shall specify the method of inventory valuation that the taxpayer would have used, the opening LIFO inventory for the taxable year for which the protective election is made, and the section 481 adjustment that would be required, as if the taxpayer were not on the LIFO method for the taxable year immediately preceding the taxable year for which the protective election is made.

(g) *Election by an estate or trust to recognize gain or loss on the distribution of property (other than cash) to a beneficiary.*—This paragraph applies to the election made by a trust or estate to recognize gain or loss on the distribution of property (other than cash) to a beneficiary under section 643(d) of the Code as amended by section 81 of the Act. The election is available for distributions made after June 1, 1984, in taxable years ending after such date. The election must be made by the fiduciary who is required to make the return of the estate or trust under section 641 and § 1.641(b)-2. The election shall be made by such fiduciary on the tax return of the estate or trust for the taxable year with respect to which the distribution of property was made and must be filed by the due date (including extensions) of such return. Until the Form 1041, U.S. Fiduciary Income Tax Return is revised, the election should be made by including the gain or loss on the Schedule D (or other appropriate schedule, if applicable) of the Form 1041 and attaching the statement described in paragraph (a)(3) of this section to the tax return on which the election is made and including on that statement the name and taxpayer identification number of the distributee. For distributions made after June 1, 1984,

and before July 18, 1984, the election must be filed by the later of the due date (including extensions) of the tax return of the estate or trust for the taxable year with respect to which the distribution was made or January 1, 1985. For those distributions, the fiduciary may make the election in the manner described above on a tax return, or amended return, for the year with respect to which the distribution was made. An election under section 643(d) may be revoked only with the consent of the Commissioner. The request for revocation of an election should be made by the fiduciary in the form of a ruling request and must contain the information required by regulations and revenue procedures pertaining thereto.

(h) *Election to treat a stapled foreign entity as a subsidiary.*—This paragraph applies to the election, provided under section 136(c)(6) of the Act, to treat a foreign corporation which was a stapled entity with a domestic corporation as of June 30, 1983, as being owned (to the extent of its stapled interests) by the domestic corporation with which it is stapled. This treatment, if so elected, is in lieu of the treatment prescribed in section 269B(a)(1) of the Code, as added by the Act. This election may be made by the domestic corporation with which the foreign entity is stapled. The election may not be made by the foreign entity or by shareholders of the domestic corporation. This election must be made no later than January 14, 1985, and may be revoked only with the consent of the Commissioner. This election shall be effective after December 31, 1986. The domestic corporation shall make this election by filing with the service center with which the domestic corporation files its income tax return a statement that—

(1) Contains the name, address, and taxpayer identification number of the domestic corporation,

(2) Identifies the election as made under section 136(c)(6) of the Tax Reform Act of 1984, and

(3) Identifies the foreign entity and the interests in the foreign entity which constitute stapled interests with respect to the stock of the domestic corporation, and specifies the date on which those interests became stapled interests.

If this election is not made, the foreign corporation (interests in which were stapled interests as of June 30, 1983) will be treated as a domestic corporation, effective January 1, 1987, under section 269B(a)(1) of the Code.

(i) *Election to treat certain section 1248 amounts as included in gross income under section 951(a)(1)(A).*—This paragraph applies to the elections, provided under section 133(d)(3) of the Act, to treat amounts included in the gross income of any person as a dividend by reason of section 1248(a) or (f) after October 9, 1975, and before July 19, 1985, as an amount included in the gross income of such person under section 951(a)(1)(A). The election with respect to transactions to which section 1248(a) applies may be made by the foreign corporation described in section 1248(a) (or its successor in interest). The election with respect to transactions to which section 1248(f) applies may be made by the domestic corporation described in section 1248(f)(1) (or its successor in interest). Neither election may be made by an affected shareholder of any such corporation (unless the shareholder is the successor in interest). This election must be made no later than January 14, 1985, and shall apply with respect to all transactions to which section 1248(a) or (f) applies that occurred after October 9, 1975, and before July 19, 1984. Once made, the election may be revoked only with the consent of the Commissioner. A foreign corporation shall make this election by filing the statement described in this paragraph with the Internal Revenue Service Center, Philadelphia, PA 19255. A domestic corporation shall make this election by filing the statement described in this paragraph with the service center with which the domestic corporation files its income tax return. In either case, the statement shall—

(1) Contain the name, address, and taxpayer identification number (if any) of the corporation making the election,

(2) Identify the election as made under section 133(d)(3) of the Tax Reform Act of 1984, and

(3) Identify all of the transactions (including the date of each transaction), shareholders involved in those transactions, and amounts to which the election applies.

(j) *Special election for computing investment company taxable income.*—This paragraph applies to the election by a regulated investment company provided under section 1071(b) of the Act, which added section 852(b)(2)(F) to the Code. Under section 852(b)(2)(F), the taxable income of a regulated investment company shall be computed without regard to Section 454(b) (relating to short-term obligations issued on a discount basis) if the company so elects. The election may be made only for taxable years beginning after December 31, 1978. A regulated investment company shall make the election by computing taxable income without regard to section 454(b) on its return for the first taxable year for which it desires the election to apply and shall attach the statement described in paragraph (a)(3) of this section to the return on which the election is made. A regulated investment company shall make the election by the time set forth in paragraph (a)(2) of this section. Once made, the election applies to the first taxable year for which it is made and to all subsequent taxable years and cannot be revoked without the consent of the Commissioner.

(k) *Election of extension of time for payment of estate tax for interests in certain holding companies.*—An election under section 6166(b)(8), as added by section 1021(a) of the Act, or under section 1021(d)(2) of the Act, shall be made by including on the notice of election under section 6166 required by § 20.6166-1(b) a statement that an election is being made under section 6166(b)(8) or section 1021(d)(2) of the Act (whichever is applicable) and the facts which formed the basis for the executor's conclusion that the estate qualified for such election. If a taxpayer makes an election described in this paragraph (k), then the special 4-percent interest rate of section 6601(j) and the 5-year deferral of principal payments of section 6166(a)(3) are not available. Thus, the first installment of tax is due on the date prescribed by section 6151(a) and subsequent installments bear interest at the rate determined under section 6621. If the executor makes an election described in this paragraph (k) and the notice of election under section 6166 fails to state the amount of tax to be paid in installments or the number of installments, then the election is presumed to be for the maximum amount so payable and for payment thereof in 10 equal annual installments, beginning on the date prescribed in section 6151(a). The elections described under this paragraph (k) are available for estates of decedents dying after July 18, 1984.

(l) *Subchapter S election by commodities dealers and options dealers.*— This paragraph applies to a commodities dealer or options dealer referred to in section 102(d)(3) of the Act (relating to the election by such a dealer to be an S corporation) whose taxable year is the calendar year and that was a small business corporation (as defined in section 1361(b) of the Code) as of January 1, 1984. The election by such a dealer under section 102(d)(3) of the Act shall be made in the manner prescribed by section 1362 and the regulations thereunder, except that the election under section 102(d)(3) must be made before October 2, 1984. In addition to making the election in the manner prescribed under such section 1362 and the regulations thereunder, the commodities dealer or options dealer must indicate on Form 2553

that the election is made under section 102(d)(3) of the Act. Although section 102(d)(3) of the Act applies to dealers not covered by this paragraph, and such dealers may make an election under such section 102(d)(3), guidelines for making such an election are not provided in this paragraph and are forthcoming.

(m) *Election with respect to treatment of S termination year.*—For the election provided under section 1362(e)(3), as amended by section 721(h) of the Act, see § 18.1362-4 of this chapter.

(n) *Election to be an S corporation; certain short taxable years.*—For the election provided under section 1362(b), as amended by section 721(l) of the Act, see § 18.1362-1(b) of this chapter.

(o) *Election with respect to subchapter S passive investment income rules.*—For the election provided under 721(i) of the Act which amends section 6(b) of the Subchapter S Revision Act of 1982, see § 18.1362-5 of this chapter.

(p) *Election with respect to subchapter S distributions during certain post-termination transition periods.*—For the election provided under section 1371(e), as amended by section 721(o) of the Act, see § 18.1371-1 of this chapter.

(q) *No elections for closed year.*—Any election under this section which is allowed to be made by filing an amended return may only be made if the period for making a claim for refund or credit with respect to the taxable year for which such election is to be effective has not expired. This paragraph shall not apply to the election under paragraph (a)(2)(iv) of this section with respect to the election under section 1078 of the Act.

(r) *Additional information required.*—Later regulations or revenue procedures issued under provisions of the Code or Act covered by this section may require the furnishing of information in addition to that which was furnished with the statement of election described herein. In such event the later regulations or revenue procedures will provide guidance with respect to the furnishing of such additional information. [Temporary Reg. § 301.9100-6T.]

☐ [T.D. 7976, 9-5-84. *Amended by* T.D. 8062, 11-5-85. *Redesignated by* T.D. 8435, 9-18-92. *Amended by* T.D. 9172, 1-3-2005 *and* T.D. 9911, 10-9-2020.]

# ELECTIONS UNDER TAX REFORM ACT OF 1986

### [Reg. § 301.9100-7T]

**§ 301.9100-7T. Time and manner of making certain elections under the Tax Reform Act of 1986 (Temporary).**—(a) *Miscellaneous elections.*—(1) *Elections to which this paragraph applies.*—This paragraph applies to the elections set forth below provided under the Tax Reform Act of 1986 (the Act). General rules regarding the time for making the elections are provided in paragraph (a)(2) of this section. General rules regarding the manner for making the elections are

provided in paragraph (a)(3) of this section. Special rules regarding the time and manner for making certain elections are contained in paragraphs (a)—(i) of this section. If a special rule applies to one of the elections listed below, a cross-reference to the special rule is shown in brackets at the end of the description of the "Availability of Election." Paragraph (j) of this section provides that additional information with respect to elections may be required by future regulations or revenue procedures.

| Section of Act | Section of Code | Description of Election | Availability of Election |
|---|---|---|---|
| 201(a) | 168(b)(5) | Election to depreciate property using the straight line method of recovery with respect to one or more classes of property for any taxable year. | Property placed in service after 12-31-86. Election must be made for taxable year in which property is placed in service. Election shall apply to all property in the class placed in service during the taxable year for which the election is made. |
| 201(a) | 168(f)(1) | Election to exclude certain property from the accelerated cost recovery system. | Property placed in service after 12-31-86. Election must be made for taxable year in which property is placed in service. |
| 201(a) | 168(g)(7) | Election to use alternative depreciation system with respect to one or more classes of property for any taxable year (except for residential rental or nonresidential real property where the election may be made separately with respect to each property). | Property placed in service after 12-31-86. Election must be made for taxable year in which property is placed in service. Except for residential rental or nonresidential real property, election shall apply to all property in the class placed in service during the taxable year for which the election is made. |
| 201(a), 1802(a) | 168(h)(6)(F)(ii), 168(j) (as in effect before October 22, 1986) | Election by a tax-exempt controlled entity to treat any gain recognized by the tax-exempt parent on any disposition of an interest in the tax-exempt controlled entity (and to treat any dividends or interest received or accrued from the tax-exempt controlled entity) as unrelated business taxable income under Code section 511 in order for the tax-exempt controlled entity to not be treated as a tax-exempt entity (or as a successor to a tax-exempt entity). | Property placed in service after 9-27-85, but can apply to property placed in service before such date if the tax-exempt controlled entity so elects. [See paragraph (a)(3)(ii) of this section.] |
| 203(a)(1)(B) | — | Election to apply Act section 201 (including all elections within section 201). | Property placed in service after 7-31-86 and before 1-1-87. |

| Section of Act | Section of Code | Description of Election | Availability of Election |
|---|---|---|---|
| 204(e) | — | Election to have Act section 201 either (i) not apply to any property placed in service during 1987 or 1988 which is replacement property for property lost, damaged or destroyed in a flood which occurred 11-3-85 through 11-7-85 and which was declared a natural disaster area by the President of the United States, or (ii) apply to all such replacement property placed in service during 1985 or 1986. | (i) Property placed in service during 1987 or 1988; or (ii) property placed in service during 1985 or 1986. |
| 243(a) | — | Election to begin the 60 month amortization period with the first month of the taxpayer's first taxable year beginning after 11-19-82 in lieu of the 11-19-82 date or the bus operating authority acquisition date. | Bus operating authorities held on 11/19/82, or acquired after that date under a written contract that was binding on that date. |
| 243(b) | — | Election to begin the 60 month amortization period on the first month of the taxpayer's first taxable year beginning after the deregulation month in lieu of the deregulation month. | Freight forwarder operating authorities held at the beginning of the 60 month period applicable to the taxpayer (i.e., the deregulation date or the first month of the first taxable year beginning after the deregulation date). |
| 243(a), (b) | — | Election by a qualified corporate taxpayer to allocate a portion of the cost basis of a qualified acquiring corporation in the stock of an acquired corporation to the basis of the authority. | For bus operating authorities: authorities held on 11/19/82, or acquired after that date under a written contract that was binding on that date. For freight forwarders: authorities held at the beginning of the 60-month period applicable to the taxpayer. |
| 252(a) | 42(f)(1) | Election concerning beginning of credit period for low-income housing credit. | Buildings placed in service after 12-31-86 and before 1-1-90 (before 1-1-91 for buildings described in Code section 42(n)(2)(B)). [See paragraph (b) of this section.] |
| 252(a) | 42(g)(1) | Election concerning qualified low-income housing project to either satisfy the 20-50 or the 40-60 occupancy test. | Buildings placed in service after 12-31-86 and before 1-1-90 (before 1-1-91 for buildings described in Code section 42(n)(2)(B)). [See paragraph (b) of this section.] |
| 252(a) | 42(i)(2) | Election to reduce eligible basis by outstanding balance of Federal loan subsidy. | Buildings placed in service after 12-31-86 and before 1-1-90 (before 1-1-91 for buildings described in Code section 42(n)(2)(B)). [See paragraph (b) of this section.] |
| 252(a) | 42(j)(5) | Election to have certain partnerships treated as the taxpayer eligible for low-income housing credit. | Buildings placed in service after 12-31-86 and before 1-1-90 (before 1-1-91 for buildings described in Code section 42(n)(2)(B)). [See paragraph (b) of this section.] |
| 311(d)(2) | — | Revocation of prior election under Code section 631(a). | Election for taxable years beginning before 1-1-87 may be revoked for taxable years ending after 12-31-86. |
| 411(b)(1) | 263(i) | For intangible drilling and development costs paid or incurred with respect to an oil, gas, or geothermal well located outside the United States, election to include such costs in adjusted basis for purposes of computing the amount of any deduction under Code section 611 (without regard to section 613). | Costs paid or incurred after 12-31-86 in taxable years ending after such date. [See paragraph (a)(2)(iii) of this section.] |
| 411(b)(2) | 616(d) | For expenditures paid or incurred with respect to the development of a mine or other natural deposit (other than an oil, gas, or geothermal well) located outside the United States, election to include such expenditures paid or incurred during the taxable year for which made in adjusted basis for purposes of computing the amount of any deduction under Code section 611 (without regard to section 613). | Costs paid or incurred after 12-31-86 in taxable years ending after such date. [See paragraph (a)(2)(iv) of this section.] |
| 411(b)(2) | 617(h) | For expenditures paid or incurred before the development stage for the purpose of ascertaining the existence, location, extent or quality of any deposit of ore or other mineral deposit (other than an oil, gas or geothermal well) located outside the United States, election to include all such expenditures, paid or incurred during the taxable year or any subsequent taxable year with respect to any such deposit, in adjusted basis for purposes of computing the amount of any deduction under Code section 611 (without regard to section 613). | Costs paid or incurred after 12-31-86 in taxable years ending after such date. [See paragraph (a)(2)(v) of this section.] |
| 501(a) | 469(j)(9) | Election to increase basis of property by amount of disallowed credit for purposes of determining gain or loss from a disposition of property used in a passive activity. | Taxable years beginning after 12-31-86. [See paragraph (a)(3)(iii) of this section.] |
| 614(b) | 1059(c)(4) | Election to determine whether a dividend is extraordinary by reference to the fair market value of the share of stock with respect to which the dividend was received. | Dividends declared after July 18, 1986 in taxable years ending after such date. |

| Section of Act | Section of Code | Description of Election | Availability of Election |
|---|---|---|---|
| 644(d) | 216(b)(3) | Election by a cooperative housing corporation to allocate real estate taxes or interest or both to each tenant-stockholder's dwelling unit in a manner which reasonably reflects the cost to the corporation of the tenant-stockholder's dwelling unit. | Taxable years beginning after 12-31-86. [See paragraph (a)(3)(iv) of this section.] |
| 646 | — | Election by an entity to be treated as a trust under the Internal Revenue Code if such entity was created in 1906 as a common law trust and governed by the trust laws of the State of Minnesota, receives royalties from iron ore leases, and income interests in the entity are publicly traded on a national stock exchange. | The election is effective beginning on first day of the first taxable year beginning after October 22, 1986 and following the year in which the election is made. Such election must be made by the board of trustees of such entity and must be accompanied by a written agreement signed by the board of trustees of the entity. |
| 651 | 4982(e)(4) | Election by a regulated investment company to use taxable years ending on 11-30 or 12-31 for purposes of computing capital gain net income under Code section 4982. | Calendar years beginning after 12/31/86. [See paragraph (a)(2)(vi) of this section.] |
| 701(a) | 56(f)(3)(B) | Election to have amount of net book income be equal to amount of earnings and profits. | Taxable years beginning after 12-31-86. |
| 801(a) | 448(d)(4) | Election of common parent of an affiliated group that all members of such group be treated as one taxpayer if substantially all the activities of all members of the affiliated group involve performance of services in the same field. | Taxable years beginning after 12-31-86. |
| 801(d)(2) | — | Election to continue using the cash method of accounting for loans, leases and related party transactions. | Loans, leases and related party transactions entered into before 9-26-85. |
| 802 | 474 | Election by certain small businesses to use the simplified dollar-value LIFO method. | Taxable years beginning after 12-31-86. [See paragraph (a)(3)(v) of this section.] |
| 803(a) | 263A(d)(3) | Election to have rules of Code section 263A (relating to capitalization and inclusion in inventory costs of certain expenses) not apply to any plant or animal produced in any farming business conducted by the electing taxpayer. | Unless consent is obtained from the Commissioner, the first taxable year beginning after 12-31-86 during which the taxpayer engages in a farming business. [See paragraph (c) of this section.] |
| 806(e)(2)(C) | — | Election to have net income for the short taxable year of a partnership or S corporation which results from the required change in accounting period included entirely in income for such short taxable year. | Partner and shareholder taxable years beginning after 12-31-86 with or within which the short taxable year created under section 806 of the Act ends. [See paragraph (d) of this section.] |
| — | — | Election to reduce partnership or S corporation income for the short taxable year resulting from a required change in accounting period under section 806 of the Act by an unamortized adjustment amount existing as of October 22, 1986, where such adjustment was required to effectuate a previous accounting period change under Rev. Proc. 72-51, 1972-2 C.B. 832 or Rev. Proc. 83-25, 1983-1 C.B. 689. | Short taxable years of partnerships or S corporations beginning after 12-31-86. [See paragraph (e) of this section.] |
| 811(a) | 453C(b)(2)(B) | Election to compute adjusted bases using depreciation deduction used under Code section 312(k). | Taxable years ending after 12-31-86 with respect to dispositions made after 2-28-86. |
| 811(a) | 453C(e)(4) | Election to have Code section 453C not apply to obligations arising from sales of timeshares and unimproved residential lots to individuals. | Taxable years ending after 12-31-86 with respect to dispositions made after 2-28-86. [See paragraph (a)(3)(vi) of this section.] |
| 905(a) | 165(l)(1) | Election to treat amount of reasonably estimated loss on a deposit in insolvent or bankrupt qualified financial institution as a loss described in Code section 165(c)(3) and incurred in the taxable year. | Taxable years beginning after 12-31-82. [See paragraph (f) of this section.] |
| 905(c) | — | Election to apply Code section 451(f) (relating to treatment of interest on frozen deposits in certain financial institutions). | Taxable years beginning after 12-31-82 and before 1-1-87. |
| 1301(b) | 141(b)(9) | Election by issuer of tax-exempt bonds to treat a portion of an issue as a qualified 501(c)(3) bond if such portion would have qualified as a 501(c)(3) bond had it been issued separately. | Bonds issued after 8-15-86. [See paragraph (g) of this section.] |
| 1301(b) | 142(d)(1) | Election by issuer of tax-exempt bonds for residential rental property to satisfy either the 20-50 or the 40-60 occupancy test. | Bonds issued after 8-15-86. [See paragraph (g) of this section.] |
| 1301(b) | 142(d)(4)(B) | Election by issuer of tax-exempt bonds for residential rental property to treat the project as a deep rent skewed project. | Bonds issued after 8-15-86. [See paragraph (g) of this section.] |
| 1301(b) | 143(k)(9)(D)(iii) | Election to treat limited equity cooperative housing as residential rental property and not as owner-occupied housing. | Bonds issued after 8-15-86 and before 1-1-89. [See paragraph (g) of this section.] |

| Section of Act | Section of Code | Description of Election | Availability of Election |
|---|---|---|---|
| 1301(b) | 145(d) | Election by issuer of tax-exempt bonds to have Code section 145 not apply to the issue if the issue is an issue of exempt facility bonds or qualified redevelopment bonds, to which the volume cap applies. | Bonds issued after 8-15-86. [See paragraph (g) of this section.] |
| 1301(b) | 147(b)(4)(A) | Election by issuer of qualified 501(c)(3) bonds to have such bonds treated as meeting the limitation on maturity requirements of Code section 147(b)(1) if the requirements of section 147(b)(4)(B) are met. | Bonds issued after 8-15-86. [See paragraph (g) of this section.] |
| 1704(b) | — | Election to revoke prior election under Code section 1402(e) (relating to exemption from social security taxes for certain clergy). | Remuneration received in taxable years ending on or after October 22, 1986. [See paragraph (h) of this section.] |
| 1801(a) | 168(i) (as in effect before October 22, 1986) | Election to make finance leasing rules inapplicable to property which would otherwise be subject to them under the transitional rules of section 12(c)(1) of the Tax Reform Act of 1984. | Personal property leased under certain lease agreements effective on or after 1-1-84. [See paragraph (a)(3)(vii) of this section.] |
| 1804(e)(4) | — | Election by a common parent of an affiliated group to apply amendments made by the Tax Reform Act of 1984 for taxable years beginning after 12-31-83. | Groups which include a corporation which on 6-22-84 is a member of the group which files a consolidated return for such corporation's taxable year which includes 6-22-84. |
| 1807(a)(7) | 468B | Election to treat a qualified payment made to a court-ordered fund as a payment made to a designated settlement fund. | Generally, liabilities arising out of personal injury, death or property damage that are incurred after 7-18-84 under law in effect before the enactment of Code section 461(h). Election is made for the taxable year in which qualified payments are made to a designated settlement fund. |
| 1809(e)(2) | 48(b)(2) | Election by lessee and lessor not to apply the rule of Code section 48(b)(2) concerning the date leased property is treated as originally placed in service. | Property originally placed in service after 4-11-84 (as determined under Code section 48(b) prior to its amendment by section 114(a) of the Tax Reform Act of 1984). [See paragraph (a)(3)(viii) of this section.] |
| 1810(l)(4) | 7701(b) | Election to be treated as a resident alien. | Taxable years beginning after December 31, 1984. [See paragraph (a)(3)(ix) of this section.] |
| 1879(p)(1) | 83(c)(3) | Election to treat certain stock acquired upon the exercise of nonqualified stock options as subject to a substantial risk of forfeiture by reason of Code section 83(c)(3) even though the transfer of stock pursuant to such exercise occurred before 1-1-82, the effective date of section 83(c)(3). | Transfers of stock described in section 1879(p)(1) of the Act. [See paragraphs (a)(2)(vii) and (a)(3)(x) of this section.] |
| 1882(c) | 3121(w)(2) | Election to revoke prior election under Code section 3121(w) (relating to exemption from social security taxes for certain churches and qualified church-controlled organizations). | Remuneration paid after 12-31-86 unless such electing church or church-controlled organization had withheld and paid over all employment taxes due, as if such election had never been in effect during the period from the stated effective date of the election being revoked through 12-31-86. [See paragraph (i) of this section.] |

(2) *Time for making elections.*—(i) *In general.*—Except as otherwise provided in this section, the elections specified in paragraph (a)(1) of this section shall be made by the later of—

(A) The due date (taking extensions into account) of the tax return for the first taxable year for which the election is to be effective, or

(B) April 15, 1987 (in which case the election generally must be made by amended return).

(ii) *No extension of time for payment.*—Payments of tax due shall be made in accordance with chapter 62 of the Code.

(iii) *Time for making the election with respect to foreign intangible drilling costs.*—With respect to the election under Act section 411(b)(1) (Code section 263(i)(2)(A)), the election shall be made on a property-by-property basis for each oil, gas, or geothermal property (as defined in Code section 614). The election shall be made by the due date (taking extensions into account) of the income tax return for the first taxable year in which the taxpayer pays or incurs any cost with respect to the development of such property for which the election is available.

(iv) *Time for making the election with respect to foreign development expenditures.*—With respect to the election under Act section 411(b)(2) (Code section 616(d)(2)(A)), the election shall be made for each mine or other natural deposit not later than the time prescribed by law for filing the income tax return (taking extensions into account) for the taxable year to which such election is applicable.

(v) *Time for making the election with respect to foreign exploration expenditures.*—With respect to the election under Act section 411(b)(2)

(Code section 617(h)(2)(A)), the election may be made at any time before the expiration of the period prescribed for filing a claim for credit or refund of the tax imposed by chapter 1 of the Code for the first taxable year for which the taxpayer desires the election to be applicable.

(vi) *Time for making certain elections by regulated investment companies.*—The election under Act section 651 (Code section 4982(e)(4)) shall be made on a statement attached to the form prescribed by the Internal Revenue Service which is used to report and pay the excise tax liability under section 4982. The election shall be filed on or before the later of—

(A) March 15 of the first calendar year beginning after the end of the first excise tax period for which the election is to be effective, or

(B) If the regulated investment company has been granted an extension of time to file a return for the excise tax under Code section 4982 for such excise tax period, the due date (including extensions thereof) for such return.

The statement of election under section 4982(e)(4) shall be attached to the prescribed form regardless of whether the regulated investment company is liable for the excise tax imposed by section 4982 for the excise tax period in question.

(vii) *Time for making the election with respect to certain nonqualified stock options.*—The election under section 1879(p)(1) of the Act (Code section 83(c)(3)) shall be made—

(A) By April 21, 1987, in any case in which the operation of any law or rule of law on or before such date would prevent the credit or refund of any overpayment of tax resulting from such election, and

(B) By no later than any date after April 21, 1987 on which the operation of any law or rule of law would prevent the credit or refund of any overpayment of tax resulting from such election.

(3) *Manner of making elections.*—(i) *In general.*—Except as otherwise provided in this section, the elections specified in paragraph (a)(1) of this section shall be made by attaching a statement to the tax return for the taxable year for which the election is to be effective. If because of paragraph (a)(2)(i)(B) of this section the election may be filed after the due date of the tax return for the first taxable year for which the election is to be effective, such statement must be attached to a tax return or amended return for the taxable year to which the election relates. Except as otherwise provided in the return or in the instructions accompanying the return for the taxable year, the statement shall—

(A) Contain the name, address and taxpayer identification number of the electing taxpayer,

(B) Identify the election,

(C) Indicate the section of the Code (or, if the provision is not codified, the section of the Act) under which the election is made,

(D) Specify, as applicable, the period for which the election is being made and/or the property or other items to which the election is to apply, and

(E) Provide any information required by the relevant statutory provisions and any information necessary to show that the taxpayer is entitled to make the election.

(ii) *Special rules for making the transitional rule elections with respect to certain tax-exempt controlled entities.*—The irrevocable election under Act sections 201(a) and 1802(a) (Code sections 168(h)(6)(F)(ii) and 168(j), as in effect before October 22, 1986), shall be made by the tax-exempt controlled entity at the time and in the manner described in paragraphs (a)(2) and (a)(3)(i) of this section. A copy of the election statement filed by the tax-exempt controlled entity shall also be attached to the Federal tax returns (*e.g.,* Form 990 or 5500) of each of the tax-exempt shareholders or beneficiaries of the controlled entity.

(iii) *Special rule for making the election with respect to gain or loss from a disposition of property used in a passive activity.*—The election under Act section 501(a) (Code section 469(j)(9)) shall be made on the form prescribed by the Internal Revenue Service for computing the taxpayer's passive activity loss and credit for the taxable year in which the property is disposed.

(iv) *Special rules for making the election with respect to cooperative housing corporations.*—The election under Act section 644(d) (Code section 216(b)(3)(B)(ii)) may be made by a cooperative housing corporation with respect to its real estate taxes or interest or both. The election is available for any taxable year beginning after December 31, 1986, if the cooperative housing corporation has, by January 31 of the year following the first calendar year that includes any period to which the election applies, furnished to each tenant-stockholder during that period a written statement showing the amount of the allocation (or allocations) under section 216(b)(3)(B)(i) attributable to such tenant-stockholder's dwelling unit (or units) for that period. Any cooperative housing corporation making the election shall do so in accordance with paragraph (a)(2) and (3) of this section and shall identify in the statement described in paragraph (a)(3) of this section whether the election is for real estate taxes or interest or both.

(v) *Special rules for making the election with respect to the simplified dollar-value LIFO method.*—The election under Act section 802 (Code section 474) may be made only if the taxpayer files with the taxpayer's income tax return for the taxable year as of the close of which the method is first to be used a statement of the taxpayer's election to use the simplified dollar-value LIFO inventory method. The statement shall be on Form 970 pursuant to the instructions to the form and to the requirements of the regulations under section 474, or in such other manner as may be acceptable to the Commissioner.

(vi) *Special rules for making election to have section 453C not apply to obligations arising from sales of timeshares and unimproved residential lots to individuals.*—The election under Act section 811(a) (Code section 453C(e)(4)) to have section 453C not apply to obligations arising from sales of timeshares and unimproved residential lots to individuals may be made with respect to any obligation, or with respect to a class of such obligations. In the case of an election made with respect to a class of obligations, such election shall describe the class of obligations with such specificity as to make the class readily identifiable.

(vii) *Special rules for making certain finance leasing transitional rule elections.*—The election relating to finance leases under Act section 1801(a)(1) (Code section 168(i) as in effect before October 22, 1986) shall be made by the lessor under a lease agreement subject to the finance lease rules of section 168(i) of the Code, as in effect before October 22, 1986, by noting this election in the books and records relating to the lease agreement within 12 months after February 5, 1987.

(viii) *Special rules for making the election relating to the date leased property is treated as originally placed in service.*—The election under Act section 1809(e)(2) (Code section 48(b)(2)) must be made jointly by the lessee and the lessor. The election is made jointly when both the lessee and the lessor make the election in accordance with paragraphs (a)(2) and (a)(3)(i) of this section. In addition to the other information required to be provided under paragraph (a)(3)(i) of this section, the statement described therein shall include a copy of the lease agreement and shall be signed by both the lessee and the lessor.

(ix) *Special rules for making the election to be treated as a resident alien.*—The election under Act section 1810 (l)(4) (Code section 7701(b)) to be treated as a resident under Code section 7701(b) shall be made by an alien individual by attaching a statement to the individual's income tax return (Form 1040), for the taxable year for which the election is to be in effect (the election year). The alien individual may not make this election until such time as he has satisfied the substantial presence test of Code section 7701(b)(1)(A)(ii) for the year following the election year. If an alien individual has not satisfied the substantial presence test for the year following the election year as of the due date (without regard to extensions) of the tax return for the election year, the alien individual may request an extension of time for filing the return until after he has satisfied such test, provided that he pays with his extension application the amount of tax he expects to owe for the election year, computed as if he were a nonresident alien throughout the election year. The statement shall include the name and address of the alien individual and contain a signed declaration that the election is being made. It must specify—

(A) That the alien individual was not a resident in the year immediately preceding the election year;

(B) That the alien individual is a resident in the year immediately following the election year under the substantial presence test and the individual's number of days of presence in the United States during such year;

(C) The date or dates of the alien individual's 31 consecutive day period of presence and continuous presence in the United States during the election year; and

(D) The date or dates of absence from the United States during the election year that are deemed to be days of presence.

(x) *Special rules for making the election with respect to the treatment of the exercise of certain nonqualified stock options.*—The election under Act section 1879(p)(1) (Code section 83(c)(3)) is made by filing on Form 1040X a claim for credit or refund of the overpayment of tax resulting from the election. In order to satisfy the requirements of § 301.6402-2(b)(1) (relating to grounds set forth in claim), the claim for credit or refund must set forth—

(A) The date on which the option was granted,

(B) The name of the corporation which granted the option,

(C) The date on which the stock was transferred pursuant to the exercise of the option,

(D) The fair market value of such stock on December 4, 1973,

(E) The fair market value on July 1, 1974 of the stock received upon the reorganization of the corporation which granted the option, and

(F) The date on which the taxpayer sold substantially all of the stock received in such reorganization.

The taxpayer shall file a single claim for credit or refund of the entire overpayment of tax resulting from the election under Act section 1879(p)(1).

(4) *Revocation.*—(i) *Irrevocable elections.*—The elections described in this section under Act sections 201(a) (Code sections 168(b)(5), 168(f)(1), 168(g)(7), and 168(h)(6)(F)(ii)), 203(a)(1)(B), 252(a) (Code sections 42(f)(1), 42(g)(1), 42(i)(2), and 42(j)(5)), 411(b)(1) (Code section 263(i)), 411(b)(2)(A) (Code section 616(d)(2)(A)), 501(a) (Code section 469(j)(9)), 801(d)(2), 905(c), 1301(b) (Code sections 141(b)(9), 142(d)(1), 142(d)(4)(B), 143(k)(9)(D)(iii), 145(d), and 147(b)(4)(A)), 1704(b), 1802(a) (Code section 168(j) as in effect before October 22, 1986), 1804(e)(4), 1879(p)(1) (Code section 83(c)(3)), and 1882(c) (Code section 3121(w)(2)) are irrevocable.

(ii) *Elections revocable with the consent of the Commissioner.*—The elections described in this section under Act sections 204(e), 243(a), 243(b), 243(a)(b), 411(b)(2)(B) (Code section 617(h)(2)(A)), 614(b) (Code section 1059(c)(4)), 644(d) (Code section 216(b)(3)), 646, 651 (Code section 4982(e)(4)(B)), 701(a) (Code section 56(f)(3)(B)), 801(a) (Code section 448(d)(4)), 802 (Code section 474), 803(a) (Code section 263A(d)(3)), 806(e)(2)(C) (and the election described in H.R. Rep. No. 99-841 at II-320), 811(a) (Code sections 453C(b)(2)(B)(i) and

453C(e)(4)), (Code sections 585(c)(3)(B)(ii) and 585(c)(4)), 905(a) (Code section 165(l)(1)), 1801(a) (Code section 168(i) as in effect before October 22, 1986), 1807(a)(7) (Code section 468B), 1809(e)(2) (Code section 48(b)(2)), and 1810(l)(4) (Code section 7701(b)) are revocable only with the consent of the Commissioner.

(iii) *Freely revocable elections.*—The election described in this section under Act section 311(d)(2) is freely revocable.

(b) *Elections with respect to low-income housing credit.*—The elections under Act section 252(a) (Code sections 42(f)(1), 42(g)(1), 42(i)(2), and 42(j)(5)) must be made for the taxable year in which the project is placed in service and shall be made in the certification required to be filed pursuant to section 42(l)(1).

(c) *Election to have the rules of section 263A (relating to capitalization and inclusion in inventory costs of certain expenses) not apply to any plant or animal produced in any farming business conducted by the electing taxpayer.*—(1) *In general.*—This paragraph applies to the election under Act section 803(a) (Code section 263A(d)(3)) to have the rules of section 263A (relating to capitalization and inclusion in inventory costs of certain expenses) not apply to any plant or animal produced in any farming business conducted by the electing taxpayer. The election is available to taxpayers engaged in the business of farming, including producers of agricultural crops, livestock, nursery stock, sod, trees bearing fruit, nuts or other crops, and ornamental trees (for purposes of section 263A, an evergreen tree that is more than 6 years old at the time it is severed from the roots shall not be treated as an ornamental tree). The election is not available to a corporation, partnership, or tax shelter that is required to use the accrual method of accounting under section 447 or section 448(a)(3), or farming syndicates (as defined in section 464(c)), or with respect to the planting, cultivation, maintenance or development of pistachio trees. In addition, the election does not apply with respect to costs incurred for the planting, cultivation, maintenance or development of any citrus or almond grove incurred during the 4-taxable-year period beginning with the taxable year in which such grove was planted. If a citrus or almond grove is planted in more than one taxable year, the portion of the grove planted in one taxable year is treated as a separate grove for this purpose.

(2) *Time and manner of making the election.*—Unless consent is obtained from the Commissioner, the election may only be made for the taxpayer's first taxable year that begins after December 31, 1986, and during which the taxpayer engages in a farming business. The election shall be made on the Schedule E, F or other schedule required to be attached to the income tax return for the first taxable year for which the election is effective. In the case of a partnership or S corporation, the election must be made at the partner or shareholder level.

(3) *Election treated as if made if certain requirements satisfied.*—A taxpayer eligible to make the election under section 263A(d)(3) shall be treated as having made the election if such taxpayer reports income and expenses in accordance with the rules under the election on a timely filed income tax return.

(4) *Revocation.*—Once the election is made, it is revocable only with the consent of the Commissioner.

(5) *Special rules for treatment of expenses.*—If the election is made, the plant or animal produced is treated as section 1245 property and gain is recaptured (treated as ordinary income) in the amount of deductions which, but for the election, would have been required to be capitalized with respect to the plant or animal. If the taxpayer or a related person makes the election, a non-accelerated method of depreciation (as defined in section 168(g)(2)) shall be applied to all property used predominantly in any farming business of the taxpayer or related person and placed in service in any taxable year during which the election is in effect. For purposes of this election, related party means: (i) the members of the taxpayer's family (defined for this purpose to include the spouse of the taxpayer and any of his or her children who have not reached the age of 18 as of the last day of the taxable year); (ii) any corporation (including an S corporation) 50 percent or more of the value of which is owned directly or indirectly (through the application of section 318) by the taxpayer or members of the taxpayer's family; (iii) any corporation that is a member of the same controlled group (within the meaning of section 1563) as the taxpayer; and (iv) any partnership if 50 percent or more of the value of the interests in such partnership is owned directly or indirectly (through the application of section 318) by the taxpayer or members of the taxpayer's family.

(d) *Election with respect to the treatment of net income for the short taxable year resulting from a required change in accounting period.*—This paragraph applies to the election under section 806(e)(2)(C) of the Act. Net income for the short taxable year resulting from a required change in accounting period under the provisions of section 806 of

the Act which is to be included ratably in the partners' and S corporation shareholders' income for the first four taxable years (including the short taxable year) beginning after December 31, 1986, or included entirely in income for the short taxable year at the election of the partner or shareholder, shall be taken into account in accordance with section 702 (with respect to partners) and section 1366 (with respect to S corporation shareholders).

(e) *Election with respect to reducing partnership or S corporation income for the short taxable year resulting from a required change in accounting period under section 806 of the Act by an unamortized adjustment amount existing as of October 22, 1986.*—(1) *In general.*—This paragraph applies to the election described in H.R. Rep. No. 99-841 at II-320.

(2) *Partnerships or S corporations that make the election to reduce income for the short taxable year by an unamortized adjustment amount existing as of October 22, 1986.*—Where a partnership or S corporation elects to reduce its income for the short taxable year required under the provisions of section 806 of the Act by the unamortized adjustment amount existing as of October 22, 1986, in accordance with paragraph (a) of this section, the income for the short taxable year (reduced by the unamortized adjustment amount) may then be subject to the election, under section 806(e)(2)(C) of the Act, by partners and S corporation shareholders to include all the net income for the short taxable year entirely in income for the partners' or shareholders' taxable year with or within which the short taxable year ends.

(3) *Partnership or S corporations that do not make the election to reduce income for the short taxable year by an unamortized adjustment amount existing as of October 22, 1986.*—Where a partnership or S corporation does not elect to reduce its income for the short taxable year created by the provisions of section 806 of the Act by the unamortized adjustment amount existing as of October 22, 1986, as provided in paragraph (a) of this section, the short taxable year required under the provisions of section 806 of the Act shall be considered one taxable year for purposes of amortizing the adjustment amount under the requirements of Rev. Proc. 72-51, 1972-2 C.B. 832, or Rev. Proc. 83-25, 1983-1 C.B. 689. The net income of the partnership or S corporation after reduction by the adjustment amount for the short taxable year may then be subject to the election under section 806(e)(2)(C) of the Act by partners or S corporation shareholders to include all the net income for the short taxable year entirely in income for the partners' or shareholders' taxable year with or within which the short taxable year of the partnership or S corporation ends.

(f) *Cross-reference.*—See § 301.9100-8(d) for rules on both the election under section 905(a) of the Act, relating to section 165(l)(1), and the related election under section 165(l)(5), added by section 1009(d) of the Technical and Miscellaneous Revenue Act of 1988, 102 Stat. 3342. An election under section 165(l) is available only to qualified individuals and, in general, applies to reasonably estimated losses on deposits in an insolvent or bankrupt financial institution.

(g) *Elections with respect to certain bonds.*—The elections under Act section 1301(b) (Code sections 141(b)(9), 142(d)(1), 142(d)(4)(B), 143(k)(9)(D)(iii), 145(d), and 147(b)(4)(A)) must be made in the bond indenture or a related document (as defined in § 1.103-13(b)(8)) on or before the date of issue. With respect to obligations issued on or before March 9, 1987, these elections must be made on or before March 9, 1987, and need not be made in the bond indenture or a related document, but must be made in writing and retained as part of the issuer's books and records.

(h) *Revocation of the election for exemption from social security taxes by certain clergy.*—(1) *In general.*—This paragraph applies to the election under Act section 1704(b) to revoke an election under section 1402(e)(1) of the Code by a duly ordained, commissioned, or licensed minister of a church, a member of a religious order (other than a member of a religious order who has taken a vow of poverty as a member of such order), or a Christian Science practitioner. Only elections which are effective for the taxable year containing October 22, 1986 may be revoked under this paragraph.

(2) *Time for revoking the election.*—The election shall be revoked by filing Form 2031 before the date on which the individual becomes entitled to benefits under section 202(a) or 223 of the Social Security Act (without regard to section 202(j)(1) or 223(b) of such Act), and no later than the due date of the Federal income tax return (including any extension thereof) for the individual's first taxable year beginning after October 22, 1986.

(3) *Manner of revoking the election.*—To revoke an election under section 1402(e)(1), the individual shall file Form 2031 in accordance with the instructions accompanying that form. The revocation shall be made effective, as designated by the individual on the form, either with respect to the individual's first taxable year ending on or after

October 22, 1986, or with respect to the individual's first taxable year beginning after October 22, 1986.

(4) *Special rules for payment of self-employment taxes with respect to certain taxable years ending on or after October 22, 1986.*—(i) *Elections filed after the due date of the Federal income tax return.*—If Form 2031 is filed on or after the due date of the Federal income tax return (including any extension thereof) for the individual's first taxable year ending on or after October 22, 1986, and the election made therein is effective with respect to that taxable year, Form 2031 shall be accompanied by an amended Federal income tax return for such taxable year together with payment in full of an amount equal to the total of the taxes that would have been imposed by section 1401 of the Code with respect to all of the individual's income derived in that taxable year which would have constituted net earnings from self-employment for purposes of chapter 2 of subtitle A of the Code (notwithstanding paragraph (4) or (5) of section 1402(c)) but for the exemption under section 1402(e)(1).

(ii) *Elections filed before the due date of the Federal income tax return.*—If Form 2031 is filed before the due date of the Federal income tax return (including any extension thereof) for the individual's first taxable year ending on or after October 22, 1986, and the election is effective with respect to that taxable year, payment in full of an amount equal to the total of the taxes that would have been imposed by section 1401 of the Code with respect to all of the individual's income derived in that taxable year which would have constituted net earnings from self-employment for purposes of chapter 2 of subtitle A of the Code (notwithstanding paragraph (4) or (5) of section 1402(c)) but for the exemption under section 1402(e)(1) shall be made:

(A) In the case of Forms 2031 that are filed on or before the date on which the individual's Federal income tax return for such first taxable year is filed, with the individual's Federal income tax return for such taxable year; and

(B) In the case of Forms 2031 that are filed after the date on which the individual's Federal income tax return for such first taxable year is filed, with an amended Federal income tax return for that taxable year filed on or before the due date for the individual's Federal income tax return (including any extension thereof) for such taxable year.

(iii) *Interest on amounts paid after the due date of the Federal income tax return.*—If any amount of tax imposed by section 1401 for an individual's taxable year with respect to which an election under this paragraph (h) is effective is paid after the due date of the individual's Federal income tax return (without regard to extensions) for such taxable year, interest will be assessed on such tax from the due date of such return (without regard to extensions) to the date on which such tax is paid.

(5) *Revocability of the revocation of the election.*—Once having filed Form 2031, the individual may not thereafter file an application for an exemption under section 1402(e)(1).

(6) *Effective date of this provision.*—This provision shall apply with respect to remuneration received in the taxable years for which the individual designates the revocation to be effective, as described in paragraph (h)(3) of this section, and with respect to monthly insurance benefits payable under title II of the Social Security Act on the basis of the wages and self-employment income of any individual for months in or after the calendar year in which such individual's application for revocation is effective (and lump-sum death payments payable under such title on the basis of such wages and self-employment income in the case of deaths occurring in or after such calendar year).

(i) *Revocation of the election for exemption from social security taxes by certain churches or qualified church-controlled organizations.*—(1) *In general.*—This paragraph applies to the election under Act section 1882 (Code section 3121(w)(2)) to revoke an election under section 3121(w) by a church or qualified church-controlled organization (as defined in section 3121(w)(3)).

(2) *Time and manner of revoking the election.*—The revocation described in this paragraph (i) shall be made by filing a Form 941 on or before the due date for filing Form 941 (without regard to extensions) for the first quarter for which the revocation is to be effective, accompanied by payment in full of the taxes that would be due for that quarter had there been no election under section 3121(w). See paragraph (i)(4) of this section for the effective date of revocations made under this paragraph (i).

(3) *Revocability of the revocation of the election.*—Once an election under section 3121(w) is revoked under this paragraph (i), a new election under section 3121(w) may not be made.

(4) *Effective date of this paragraph.*—A revocation made under this paragraph (i) shall be effective for the quarter of the calendar year covered by the Form 941 on which the revocation is made in accordance with paragraph (i)(2) of this section and all subsequent quarters. However, no revocation shall be effective prior to January 1, 1987 unless such electing church or church-controlled organization had withheld and paid over all employment taxes due, as if such election had never been in effect, during the period from the effective date of the election being revoked through December 31, 1986.

(j) *Additional information required.*—Later regulations or revenue procedures issued under provisions of the Code or Act covered by this section may require the furnishing of information in addition to that which was furnished with the statement of election described in this section. In such event, the later regulations or revenue procedures will provide guidance with respect to the furnishing of such additional information. (26 U.S.C. 7805). [Temporary Reg. § 301.9100-7T.]

☐ [*T.D. 8124, 2-4-87. Amended by T.D. 8180, 2-29-88 and T.D. 8267, 9-21-89. Redesignated and amended by T.D. 8435, 9-18-92. Amended by T.D. 8513, 12-28-93; T.D. 8530, 3-17-94 and T.D. 8644, 12-26-95.*]

# ELECTIONS UNDER TECHNICAL AND MISCELLANEOUS REVENUE ACT OF 1988

### [Reg. § 301.9100-8]

**§ 301.9100-8. Time and manner of making certain elections under the Technical and Miscellaneous Revenue Act of 1988.**—(a) *Miscellaneous elections.*—(1) *Elections to which this paragraph applies.*—This paragraph applies to the elections set forth below provided under the Technical and Miscellaneous Revenue Act of 1988, 102 Stat. 3342 (the Act). General rules regarding the time for making the elections are provided in paragraph (a)(2) of this section. General rules regarding the manner for making the elections are provided in paragraph (a)(3) of this section. Special rules regarding the time and manner for making certain elections are contained in paragraphs (a) through (i) of this section. In this paragraph (a)(1), a cross-reference to a special rule applicable to an election is shown in brackets at the end of the description of the "Availability of Election." Paragraph (j) of this section lists certain elections provided under the Act that are not addressed in this section. Paragraph (k) of this section provides that additional information with respect to elections may be required by future regulations or revenue procedures.

| Section of Act | Section of Code | Description of Election | Availability of Election |
|---|---|---|---|
| 1002(a) (11)(A) | 168(b)(2) | Election to depreciate property using the 150 percent declining balance method for one or more classes of property for any taxable year. | For property placed in service after December 31, 1986, the election must be made for the taxable year in which the property is placed in service. For taxable years ending before January 1, 1989, taxpayers have until January 22, 1990 to amend their returns to elect the 150 percent declining balance method, regardless of whether the taxpayer had used or elected to use a different method for property placed in service during those taxable years. The election will apply to all property in the class placed in service during the taxable year for which the election is made. |
| 1002(a) (23)(B) | 168(d) (3)(B) | Election to disregard property placed in service and disposed of in the same taxable year in applying the 40 percent test to determine if the mid-quarter convention applies. | Available for property placed in service in taxable years beginning on or before March 31, 1988. Election will apply to all property placed in service and disposed of during the taxable year for which the election is made. |

| Section of Act | Section of Code | Description of Election | Availability of Election |
|---|---|---|---|
| 1002(l) (1)(A) | 42(b)(2) (A)(ii) | Election to use the applicable percentage for a month other than the month in which a building is placed in service. | Available for qualified buildings placed in service after December 31, 1987 and with respect to which either a binding agreement is made as to the allocable credit dollar amount or tax-exempt bonds are issued. [See paragraph (b) of this section.] |
| 1002(l) (2)(B) | 42(f)(1) | Election to defer the beginning of the credit period for the low-income housing credit. | Available for qualified buildings placed in service after December 31, 1986. |
| 1002(l) (4) | 42(d)(3) (B) | Election to exclude excess costs of disproportionate units. | Available for qualified buildings placed in service after December 31, 1986. |
| 1002(l) (12) | 42(g)(3) (B)(i) | Election to aggregate buildings in a low-income housing project to satisfy the minimum set-aside requirement elected under section 42(g)(1) of the Code. | Available for qualified buildings placed in service after December 31, 1986. |
| 1002(l) (19)(B) | 42(i) (2)(B) | Election to reduce eligible basis by outstanding balance of Federal loan subsidy or proceeds of tax- exempt obligation. | Available for qualified buildings placed in service after December 31, 1986. |
| 1005(c) (11) | 469, 163 | Election to treat certain carryovers of disallowed investment interest expense as passive activity deductions for the first taxable year beginning after December 31, 1986. | Available for investment interest that is disallowed for the last taxable year beginning before January 1, 1987, and is properly allocable to a passive activity for the first taxable year beginning after December 31, 1986. [See paragraph (c) of this section.] |
| 1006(d) (15) | 382 | As a general rule, a firm commitment underwriter of an offering of a loss corporation's stock made before September 19, 1986 (January 1, 1989, for an institution described in section 591) is not treated as acquiring underwritten stock if it is disposed of pursuant to the offering on or before 60 days after the initial offering. The loss corporation may elect not to apply the general rule. | Available to any loss corporation to which the general rule would otherwise apply. The election is to be made by filing a statement with the District Director with whom the loss corporation would file its Federal income tax return. The statement must identify the election as an election under section 1006(d)(15) of the Act and must (1) contain the taxpayer's name, address, and employee identification number, (2) identify the transaction to which the election relates, (3) represent that the conditions for making the election have been satisfied, and (4) be signed by a person authorized to sign the Federal income tax return of the loss corporation. |
| 1006(j) (1)(C) | 171(e) | Election to reduce interest payments received on certain bonds by allocable bond premium in accordance with section 171(e) of the Code. | Available for obligations acquired after October 22, 1986, and before January 1, 1988. |
| 1006(t) (18)(B) | 860F(e) | Election not to treat a REMIC (real estate mortgage investment conduit) as a partnership for purposes of determining who may sign the REMIC return. | Available for REMICs with a start-up date (as defined in section 860G(a)(9) of the Code, as in effect on November 9, 1988) before November 10, 1988. The election is made by attaching a statement to the amended tax return for tax year 1987 or to the tax return for the first taxable year for which the election is to be effective. |
| 1008(c) (4)(A) | 460(b)(3) | Election not to discount an amount received or accrued after completion of a contract to its value as of the completion of the contract for purposes of applying the look-back method. | Effective as if included in the Tax Reform Act of 1986 (1986 Act) (available for contracts entered into after February 28, 1986). The election must be made on a contract-by-contract basis by attaching a statement to the tax return for the first year after completion in which the taxpayer includes in income any adjustments to the contract price or deducts any adjustments to contract costs (or, if later, the first tax return filed after October 23, 1989). |
| 1009(d) | 165(l) | Election to treat amount of reasonably estimated loss on a deposit in an insolvent or bankrupt qualified financial institution as a loss described in either section 165(c)(2) or (3) of the Code and incurred in the taxable year for which the election is made. | Available for taxable years beginning after December 31, 1981. [See paragraph (d) of this section.] |
| 1010(f) (1) | 831(b) (2)(A) | Election for insurance companies other than life to use alternative tax under certain circumstances. | Available for taxable years beginning after December 31, 1986. |
| 1010(f) (2) | 835(a) | Election for an interinsurer or reciprocal under- writer mutual insurance company subject to section 831(a) of the Code to be subject to section 835(b) limitation. | Available for taxable years beginning after December 31, 1986. |
| 1011(a) | 219(g)(4) | Election to treat a married individual as not married for purposes of certain contributions made to an individual retirement plan for 1987. | Available to a married individual who (1) was an active participant during 1987, (2) lived apart from the other spouse during the entire 1987 calendar year, (3) filed a separate income tax return for 1987, (4) had adjusted gross income of not more than $35,000 for 1987, and (5) made a contribution to an individual retirement plan for 1987. |
| 1012(d) (4) | 865(f) | Election to treat an affiliate and its wholly-owned subsidiaries as one corporation. | Shareholder-level election, available, subject to certain conditions, to United States residents selling stock in an affiliate which is a foreign corporation. Available for taxable years beginning after December 31, 1986. |
| 1012(d) (6) | 865(g)(3) | Election to treat a corporation and its wholly-owned subsidiaries as one corporation. | Shareholder-level election, available only to individual bona fide residents of Puerto Rico, if the corporate group is engaged in active trade or business in Puerto Rico and meets a gross income test. Available for taxable years beginning after December 31, 1986. |

| Section of Act | Section of Code | Description of Election | Availability of Election |
|---|---|---|---|
| 1012(d) (8) | 865(h)(2) | Election to apply treaty source rule to treat gain from a sale of an intangible or of stock in a foreign corporation as foreign source. | Taxpayer election for treatment of gain on the disposition of certain stocks and intangibles. Available for taxable years beginning after December 31, 1986. |
| 1012(l) (2) | 245(a) (10) | Election to apply treaty source rules to treat dividends received from a qualified 10-percent owned foreign corporation as foreign source. | Available to corporations for distributions out of earnings and profits for taxable years beginning after December 31, 1986. |
| 1012(n) (3) | 936 | Election to reduce the amount of qualified possession source investment income for certain corporations that fail the 75 percent active trade or business income requirement of section 936(a)(2)(B) of the Code due to section 1231(d) of the 1986 Act. | Corporate-level election, available for any taxable year beginning in 1987 or 1988. |
| 1012(bb) (4) | 904(g) (10) | Election to apply treaty source rules (in lieu of rules in section 904(g) of the Code) to treat an amount derived from a U.S.-owned foreign corporation as foreign source. | Available generally beginning July 18, 1984 (the amendment is to take effect as if included in the amendment made in section 121 of the Tax Reform Act of 1984). |
| 1014(c) (1) | 664(b) | Election by a beneficiary of a trust to which section 664 of the Code applies to obtain certain benefits of section 1403(c)(2) of the 1986 Act, relating to the ratable inclusion of certain income over 4 taxable years. | Available for taxable years beginning after December 31, 1986, provided the trust was required to change its taxable year under section 1403(a) of the 1986 Act. Election is made by attaching a statement to an amended return for the trust beneficiary's first taxable year beginning after December 31, 1986. Amended return must be filed on or before January 22, 1990. If no such election is filed, the benefits of section 1403(c)(2) are waived. |
| 1014(c) (2) | 652 662 | Election by any trust beneficiary (other than a beneficiary of a trust to which section 664 of the Code applies), to waive the benefits of section 1403(c)(2) of the 1986 Act. | Available for taxable years beginning after December 31, 1986. Election is made by attaching a statement to an amended return for the trust beneficiary's first taxable year beginning after December 31, 1986. Amended return must be filed on or before January 22, 1990. |
| 1014(d) (3)(B); 1014(d) (4) | 643(g) (2) | Election to have certain payments of estimated tax made by a trust or estate treated as paid by the beneficiary. | Available for taxable years beginning after December 31, 1986. In the case of an estate, the election is available only for a taxable year reasonably expected to be the estate's last taxable year. Election must be made by the fiduciary of the trust or estate on or before the 65th day after the close of the taxable year for which the election is made. The election must be made by that date by filing Form 1041-T with the Internal Revenue Service Center where the trust's return for such taxable year is required to be filed. The trust's return (or amended return) for that year must include a copy of the Form 1041-T. |
| 2004(j) (1) | 1503(e) | Election, made by an affiliated group filing a consolidated return upon the disposition of intragroup stock on or before December 15, 1987, to reduce the disposing member's basis in the indebtedness of the subsidiary member whose stock has been disposed of, in lieu of taking into account as negative basis the "unrecaptured amount" allocable to the stock disposed of. | Available to an affiliated group filing a consolidated return in which a member disposes of intragroup stock on or before December 15, 1987. |
| 2004(m) (5) | 384 | Election to have amendments (to the limitation on use of preacquisition losses to offset corporate built-in gains) made by section 2004(m) of the Act not apply in any case where the acquisition date is before March 31, 1988. | Available when the acquisition date is before March 31, 1988. Election must be made not later than the later of the due date (including extensions) for filing the return for the taxable year of the acquiring corporation in which the acquisition date occurs or March 10, 1989. |
| 4004(a) | 42(j) (5)(B) | Election to have certain partnerships not treated as the taxpayer to which the low-income housing credit is allowable. | Available for qualified buildings placed in service after December 31, 1986, and owned by partnerships with 35 or more partners. [See paragraph (b) of this section.] |
| 4008(b) | 41(h) | Election to have the research credit under section 41 of the Code not apply for any taxable year. | Available in any taxable year beginning after December 31, 1988. The election is made by not claiming the research credit on an original return, or by filing an amended return on which no research credit is claimed, at any time before the expiration of the 3-year period beginning on the last day prescribed by law for filing the return for the taxable year (determined without regard to extensions). The election may be revoked within the above-described 3-year period by filing an amended return on which the credit is claimed. |
| 5012(e) (4) | 7702A (c)(3) 72(e) | Election to recognize gain on exchange of life insurance contracts to avoid the characterization of life insurance contract as a modified endowment contract. | Available for contracts entered into after June 20, 1988, and before November 6, 1988, which are exchanged before February 10, 1989. |

## Technical and Miscellaneous Revenue Act Elections
### See p. 20,601 for regulations not amended to reflect law changes

67,357

| Section of Act | Section of Code | Description of Election | Availability of Election |
|---|---|---|---|
| 5031(a) | 7520(a) | Election to use 120 percent of the Applicable Federal Midterm rate for either of the two months preceding a valuation date in valuing certain interests transferred to charity for which an income, estate, or gift tax charitable deduction is allowable. | Available in cases where the valuation date occurs on or after May 1, 1989. The election is made by attaching a statement to the last income, estate, or gift tax return filed before the due date, or if a timely return is not filed, the first return filed after the due date. The statement shall contain the following: (1) a statement that an election under section 7520(a) is being made; (2) the transferor's name and taxpayer identification number as they appear on the return; (3) a description of the interest being valued; (4) the recipients, beneficiaries, or donees of the transferred interest; (5) the date of the transfer; (6) the Applicable Federal Midterm rate that is used to value the transferred interest and the month to which the rate pertains. |
| 5033(a)(2) | 2056A(d) | Election to treat a trust for the benefit of a surviving spouse who is not a U.S. citizen as a Qualified Domestic Trust, transfers to which are deductible under section 2056(a) of the Code. | Available in the case of estates of decedents dying after November 11, 1988. The election is made by the executor on the last Federal estate tax return filed by the executor before the due date of the return, or if a timely return is not filed by the executor, on the first estate tax return filed by the executor after the due date. However, elections made on or after May 5, 1991, may not be made on any return filed more than one year after the time prescribed for filing the return (including extensions). |
| 6006(a) | 1(i)(7) | Election to include certain unearned income of a child on the parent's return. | Available for taxable years beginning after December 31, 1988. The election must be made in the manner prescribed by the appropriate forms for the parent's return for the year for which the election is effective. The election must be made by the due date (taking extensions into account) of such tax return. |
| 6011 | 121(d)(9) | Election to exclude gain on the sale of a principal residence by certain incapacitated taxpayers age 55 or over. | Election may be made for a sale or exchange after September 30, 1988, by a taxpayer who becomes physically or mentally incapable of self-care and meets the required use rule provided in section 121(d)(9) of the Code. For the time and manner of making the election see § 1.121-4 of the Income Tax Regulations. |
| 6026(a) | 263A(h) | Election for certain authors, photographers, and artists to apply the exemption from the uniform capitalization rules for the first taxable year ending after November 10, 1988. | Available for the first taxable year ending after November 10, 1988. An eligible taxpayer will be treated as having made the election if the taxpayer reports income and expenses for the first taxable year ending after November 10, 1988 in accordance with the exemption from section 263A of the Code. |
| 6026(b)(1) | 263A(d)(1) | Revocation of prior election under section 263A(d)(3) of the Code (relating to the capitalization of certain expenses for the production of animals). | Election for any taxable year beginning before January 1, 1989, may be revoked for the first taxable year beginning after December 31, 1988. |
| 6026(c) | 263A(d)(3)(B) | Election by eligible taxpayers not to have section 263A of the Code apply to costs incurred in the planting, cultivation, maintenance, or development of pistachio trees. | Available without the consent of the Commissioner for the first taxable year beginning after December 31, 1986, during which the taxpayer engages in the planting, cultivation, maintenance, or development of pistachio trees. Consent must be obtained from the Commissioner for the election to be made for any subsequent taxable year. |
| 6152(a) 6152(c)(3) | 2056(b)(7)(C)(ii) | Election to treat a survivor annuity payable to a surviving spouse that is otherwise deductible under section 2056(b)(7)(C) of the Code as a nondeductible terminable interest. | Available in the case of estates of decedents dying after December 31, 1981, and in no event will the time for making the election expire before November 11, 1990. [See paragraph (e) of this section.] |
| 6152(b) 6152(c)(3) | 2523(f)(6)(B) | Election to treat a joint and survivor annuity in which the donee spouse has a survivorship interest that is otherwise deductible under section 2523(f)(6)(A) of the Code as a nondeductible terminable interest. | Available in the case of transfers made after December 31, 1981, and in no event will the time for making the election expire before November 11, 1990. [See paragraph (f) of this section.] |
| 6152(c)(2) | 2056(b)(7)(C)(ii) 2523(f) (6)(B) | Election to treat as deductible for estate or gift tax purposes under sections 2056(b)(7)(C) or 2523(f)(6) of the Code, respectively, a survivor's annuity payable to a surviving spouse reported on an estate or gift tax return filed prior to November 11, 1988, as a nondeductible terminable interest. | Available to estates of decedents dying after December 31, 1981, or to transfers made after December 31, 1981, where: (1) the estate or gift tax return was filed prior to November 11, 1988; (2) the annuity was not deducted on the return as qualified terminable interest property under sections 2056(b)(7) or 2523(f) of the Code; and (3) the executor or donor elects to treat the interest as a deductible terminable interest under sections 2056(b)(7)(C) or 2523(f)(6) prior to November 11, 1990. [See paragraph (g) of this section.] |
| 6180(b)(1) | 142(i)(2) | Election by a nongovernmental owner of a highspeed intercity rail facility not to claim any deduction under section 167 or 168 of the Code and any credit under subtitle A, in order for the facility to be described in section 142(a)(11). | Available for bonds issued after November 10, 1988. [See paragraph (h) of this section.] |
| 6181(c)(2) | 148(f)(4)(A) | One-time election by the issuer of tax-exempt bonds outstanding as of November 11, 1988, other than private activity bonds, to apply the amendments made by section 148(b) of the Code to amounts deposited after such date in bona fide debt service funds. | Available for bonds outstanding as of November 11, 1988. The election must be made in writing on the later of March 21, 1990 or the first date any payment is required under section 148(f) of the Code. The election should be retained as part of the issuer's books and records (as defined in § 1.103-10(b)(2)(vi) of the regulations) of the bond issue to which it relates. |

| Section of Act | Section of Code | Description of Election | Availability of Election |
|---|---|---|---|
| 6277 | 382 383 | Election by a loss corporation that otherwise qualifies for the exception of section 621(f)(5) of the 1986 Act not to apply that exception. That exception provides for the inapplicability, in certain situations, of the amendments to sections 382 and 383 of the Code made by the 1986 Act (relating to limitation of corporate attributes after an ownership change). That exception applies with respect to a loss corporation's ownership change resulting from a reorganization described in section 368(a)(1)(G) of the Code or from an exchange of debt for stock in a Title 11 or similar case if a petition was filed with the court before August 14, 1986. | Available for ownership changes described in section 621(f)(5) of the 1986 Act, if a petition was filed with the court before August 14, 1986. The election is to be made by filing a statement with the District Director with whom the loss corporation would file its Federal income tax return. The statement must identify the election as an election under section 6277 of the Act and must (1) contain the taxpayer's name, address, and employee identification number, (2) identify the transaction to which the election relates, (3) represent that the conditions for making the election have been satisfied, and (4) be signed by a person authorized to sign the Federal income tax return of the loss corporation. |
| 8007(a)(1) | 3127 | Election to be exempted from the taxes imposed by sections 3101 and 3111 of the Code. | An individual employer and an employee, both of whom are members of a recognized religious sect or a division thereof described in section 1402(g)(1) of the Code and adherents of established tenets or teachings of such sect or division, may, if both qualify and make elections, obtain exemptions from the taxes imposed by sections 3101 and 3111. [See paragraph (i) of this section.] |

(2) *Time for making elections.*—(i) *In general.*—Except as otherwise provided in this section, the elections described in paragraph (a)(1) of this section must be made by the later of—

(A) The due date (taking into account any extensions of time to file obtained by the taxpayer) of the tax return for the first taxable year for which the election is effective, or

(B) January 22, 1990 (in which case the election generally must be made by amended return).

(ii) *No extension of time for payment.*—Payments of tax due must be made in accordance with chapter 62 of the Code.

(3) *Manner of making elections.*—Except as otherwise provided in this section, the elections described in paragraph (a)(1) of this section must be made by attaching a statement to the tax return for the first taxable year for which the election is to be effective. If such tax return is filed prior to the making of the election, the statement must be attached to an amended tax return of the first taxable year for which the election is to be effective. Except as otherwise provided in the return or in the instructions accompanying the return for the taxable year, the statement must—

(i) Contain the name, address and taxpayer identification number of the electing taxpayer;

(ii) Identify the election;

(iii) Indicate the section of the Code (or, if the provision is not codified, the section of the Act) under which the election is made;

(iv) Specify, as applicable, the period for which the election is being made and the property or other items to which the election is to apply; and

(v) Provide any information required by the relevant statutory provisions and any information requested in applicable forms and instructions, such as the information necessary to show that the taxpayer is entitled to make the election.

Notwithstanding the foregoing, an amended return need not be filed for an election made prior to October 23, 1989 if the taxpayer made the election in a reasonable manner.

(4) *Revocation.*—(i) *Irrevocable elections.*—The elections described in this section that are made under the following sections of the Act are irrevocable: 1002(a)(11)(A) (Code section 168(b)(2)), 1002(a)(23)(B), 1002(l)(1)(A) (Code section 42(b)(2)(A)(ii)), 1002(l)(2)(B) (Code section 42(f)(1)), 1005(c)(11), 1008(c)(4)(A) (Code section 460(b)(3)), 1014(c)(1), 1014(c)(2), 1014(d)(3)(B) and 1014(d)(4) (Code section 643(g)(2)), 2004(m)(5), 4004(a) (Code section 42(j)(5)(B)), 5033(a)(2) (Code section 2056A(d)), 6006(a) (Code section 1(i)(7)), 6026(a) (Code section 263A(h)), 6026(b)(1) (Code section 263A(d)(1)), 6152(a) and 6152(c)(3) (Code section 2056(b)(7)(C)(ii)), 6152(b) and 6152(c)(3) (Code section 2523(f)(6)(B)), 6152(c)(2) (Code sections 2056(b)(7)(C)(ii) and 2523(f)(6)(B)), and 6180(b)(1) (Code section 142(i)(2)).

(ii) *Elections revocable with the consent of the Commissioner.*—The elections described in this section that are made under the following sections of the Act are revocable only with the consent of the Commissioner: 1006(d)(15), 1006(j)(1)(C), 1006(t)(18)(B), 1009(d) (Code section 165(l)), 1010(f)(1) (Code section 831(b)(2)(A)), 1010(f)(2) (Code section 835(a)), 1012(d)(4) (Code section 865(f)), 1012(d)(6) (Code section 865(g)(3)), 1012(d)(8) (Code section 865(h)(2)), 1012(l)(2) (Code section 245(a)(10)), 1012(n)(3), 1012(bb)(4) (Code section 904(g)(10)), 2004(j)(1), 5031(a) (Code section 7520(a)), 6026(c) (Code section 263A(d)(3)(B)), and 6277.

(iii) *Freely revocable elections.*—The election described in this section that is made under section 6011 of the Act is revocable without the consent of the Commissioner. (See section 121(c) of the Code and §1.121-4 of the regulations.)

(b) *Elections with respect to the low-income housing credit.*—The elections under sections 42(d)(3)(B), 42(f)(1), 42(g)(3)(B)(i), 42(i)(2)(B), and 42(j)(5)(B) of the Code generally must be made for the taxable year in which the building is placed in service, or the succeeding taxable year if the section 42(f)(1) election is made to defer the start of the credit period, and must be made in the certification required to be filed pursuant to section 42(l)(1) and (2), as amended by the Act. The election under section 42(j)(5)(B) of the Code must be made by the later of the due date of the certification or January 22, 1990. The election under section 42(b)(2)(A)(ii) must be made in accordance with the requirements of Notice 89-1, 1989-2 I.R.B. 10.

(c) *Election to treat certain carryovers of disallowed investment interest expense as passive activity deductions.*—The requirements of paragraphs (a)(2) and (3) of this section do not apply to an election under section 1005(c)(11) of the Act. Instead, the election must be made at the time and in the manner prescribed in Notice 89-36, 1989-13 I.R.B. 6. Thus, the election must be made before the filing deadline specified in Notice 89-36 by amending previously filed returns to reflect any change in the computation of tax liability that results from the election.

(d) *Election with respect to the treatment of reasonably estimated losses in an insolvent or bankrupt financial institution.*—(1) *In general.*—This paragraph (d) applies to an election under section 905(a) of the 1986 Act, and to an election under section 1009(d) of the Act, both relating to section 165(l) of the Code. If—

(i) As of the close of the taxable year, it can reasonably be estimated that there is a loss on a deposit (within the meaning of section 165(l)(4)) of a qualified individual (as defined in section 165(l)(2)) in a qualified financial institution (as defined in section 165(l)(3)), and

(ii) Such loss is on account of the bankruptcy or insolvency of such institution, then the qualified individual may elect under either section 165(l)(1) or (5) (but not both), to treat the amount (subject to the applicable limitations if under section 165(l)(5)) so estimated for that taxable year as a loss described in either section 165(c)(3), relating to casualty losses, or section 165(c)(2), relating to transactions entered into for profit, and incurred during the taxable year.

The election will apply to all losses of the qualified individual on deposits in the institution with respect to which an election is made. For additional information and examples of the application of the election rules, see Notice 89-28, 1989-12 I.R.B. 72. This paragraph (d) includes the procedural and the principal substantive rules first issued in Notice 89-28. For specific rules relating to an election under section 165(l)(5), see paragraph (d)(2) of this section.

(2) *Specific rules relating to the section 165(l)(5) election.*—(i) *Applicability.*—An election under section 165(l)(5) of the Code may be made only if no part of the taxpayer's deposits in the financial institution is federally insured. Generally, this requirement will be met only in cases in which none of the deposits in the financial institution are federally insured.

(ii) *Dollar limitations.*—An election under section 165(l)(5) of the Code is limited to $20,000 ($10,000 in the case of a separate return by a married individual) in aggregate losses on deposits in any one financial institution. The applicable dollar limit must be reduced by the amount of any insurance proceeds that can reasonably be expected to be received under any state law.

(3) *Time and manner of determining loss and making the election.*—(i) *Year of election and determination of loss.*—A qualified individual may make an election under section 165(l) of the Code either for the first taxable year in which a reasonable estimate of the loss can be made or for a later taxable year that is prior to the taxable year in which the loss is sustained. The amount of the loss is determined by the difference between a taxpayer's basis in the deposits and the amount that is reasonably estimated to be recovered, taking into account all facts and circumstances reasonably available to the taxpayer as of the date the election is made. A reasonable estimate might be based, for example, on the percentage of total deposits likely to be recovered by the depositors according to a determination made by the regulatory authority or trustee having responsibility over the institution. In addition, the taxpayer's basis in the deposits must be reduced to the extent that a loss is claimed.

(ii) *Time and manner of making election.*—A qualified individual may make an election under section 165(l) of the Code on—

(A) The income tax return for the taxable year with respect to which the taxpayer made a reasonable estimate of the loss;

(B) An amended income tax return for a taxable year described in paragraph (d)(3)(ii)(A) of this section, if the period prescribed for filing a claim for refund or credit for that taxable year has not yet expired; or, if applicable,

(C) An amended income tax return for a taxable year (beginning after December 31, 1981) described in paragraph (d)(3)(ii)(A) of this section, whether or not the claim for refund or credit is barred by another provision of law, but only if the amended return is properly filed on or before November 9, 1989.

(iii) *Information to include with election.*—The election should include any information requested in the applicable forms and instructions (e.g., Form 4684, Casualties and Thefts). If the applicable form(s) and instructions do not make reference to or request information concerning this election, the taxpayer should, on an appropriate line or space clearly indicate the name of the financial institution, include the following language: "Insolvent Financial Institution Election," and include the calculation of the reasonably estimated loss claimed.

(4) *Revocability of the election.*—(i) *In general.*—If a taxpayer desires to revoke an election under section 165(1) of the Code, the taxpayer must request, in writing, the consent of the Secretary setting forth the pertinent facts surrounding the election and the reasons for requesting a revocation.

(ii) *Exception.*—With respect to an election made under section 165(l)(1) of the Code prior to November 9, 1989, a qualified individual may revoke such election without securing the prior consent of the Secretary but only if the taxpayer makes an election under section 165(l)(5) by November 9, 1989, in the manner prescribed in paragraph (d)(3) of this section.

(5) *Effective date.*—Paragraph (d) of this section is generally effective for elections made under section 165(l) of the Code on or after November 10, 1988. However, an election filed prior to February 24, 1989, that is made in any reasonable manner will be effective.

(e) *Election to treat a survivor annuity payable to a surviving spouse as a nondeductible terminable interest.*—Where the time for making the election under section 2056(b)(7)(C)(ii) of the Code to treat the survivor annuity as nondeductible otherwise expires before November 11, 1990, the election may be made before November 11, 1990, by filing with the Service Center where the original return was filed supplemental information under §20.6081-1(c) of the Estate Tax Regulations containing:

(1) A statement that the election under section 2056(b)(7)(C)(ii) of the Code is being made;

(2) The applicable revised schedules;

(3) A recomputation of the tax due; and

(4) Payment of any additional tax due.

(f) *Election to treat a joint and survivor annuity in which the donee spouse has a survivor interest as a nondeductible terminable interest.*—Where the time for making the election under section 2523(f)(6)(B) of the Code to treat the interest as nondeductible otherwise expires before November 11, 1990, the election may be made before November 11, 1990, by filing with the appropriate Service Center an original return (or an amended return if an original return was filed) containing:

(1) A statement that the election under section 2523(f)(6)(B) is being made;

(2) A recomputation of the tax due; and

(3) Payment of any additional tax due.

(g) *Election to treat survivor's annuity payable to the surviving spouse as qualified terminable interest property deductible under sections 2056(b)(7)(C) or 2523(f)(6) of the Code in the case of a return filed prior to November 11, 1988.*—(1) In the case of an estate tax election under section 2056(b)(7)(C) the election is made by filing with the Service Center where the estate tax return was filed supplemental information under §20.6081-1(c) of the Estate Tax Regulations (and timely claim for refund under section 6511 of the Code, if applicable) containing:

(i) A statement that the election under section 6152(c)(2) of the Technical and Miscellaneous Revenue Act of 1988 is being made;

(ii) The applicable revised schedules; and

(iii) A recomputation of the estate's tax liability showing the amount of any refund due.

(2) In the case of a gift tax election under section 2523(f)(6) of the Code, the election is made by filing with the Service Center where the original return was filed an amended return (and timely claim for refund under section 6511, if applicable) containing:

(i) A statement that the election under section 6152(c)(2) of the Technical and Miscellaneous Revenue Act of 1988 is being made;

(ii) The applicable revised schedules; and

(iii) A recomputation of the gift tax liability showing the amount of any refund due.

(h) *Elections with respect to certain nongovernmentally owned rail facilities.*—(1) *In general.*—This paragraph applies to the election under section 6180(b)(1) of the Act (Code section 142(i)(2)) not to claim a deduction under section 167 or 168 of the Code or any credit with respect to certain bond-financed property. An electing owner that is not a governmental unit must make the election at the time the loan agreement with the issuer of the bond is executed. The election must be signed by the owner and include—

(i) A description of the property with respect to which the election is being made;

(ii) The name, address, and taxpayer identification number of the issuing authority;

(iii) The name, address, and taxpayer identification number of the electing owner; and

(iv) The date and face amount of the issue used to provide the property.

(2) *Other requirements.*—The electing owner must provide a copy of the election to the issuing authority and to any person purchasing the facilities during the period the bonds are outstanding or within 6 years after the last bond that is part of the issue is retired. The electing owner, purchaser, and all successors in interest to the electing owner or purchaser must each retain the original election document or a copy thereof in its records until 6 years after the later of the date the last bond that is part of the issue is retired or the date such owner, purchaser or successor in interest ceases to own the facilities. The issuer must retain a copy of the election until 6 years after the date the last bond that is part of the issue is retired. In addition, while the facilities are nongovernmentally owned, any publicly recorded document with respect to the facilities must state that neither the electing owner, nor any person purchasing the facilities during the period the bonds are outstanding or within 6 years after the date the last bond that is part of the issue is retired, nor any successor in interest to the electing owner or such purchaser, may claim any deduction under section 167 or 168 of the Code or any credit with respect to the facilities.

(3) *Election is binding on purchasers and successors.*—The election is binding at all times on any person purchasing the facilities during the period the bonds are outstanding or within 6 years after the date the last bond that is part of the issue is retired and on all successors in interest to the electing owner and such purchaser.

(i) *Election under section 3127 of the Code to be exempted from the taxes imposed by sections 3111 and 3101.*—(1) *Application for exemption.*—To be exempt from the taxes imposed under section 3111 and 3101 of the Code with regard to wages paid after December 31, 1988, an individual who is an employer and his or her employee must each file an application on the prescribed form with the Internal Revenue Service office designated in the instructions relating to the application for exemption.

(2) *Approval of application for exemption.*—The application for exemption by the individual employer or the employee will be approved only if:

(i) The application contains or is accompanied by the evidence described in section 1402(g)(1)(A) of the Code and a waiver described in section 1402(g)(1)(B);

(ii) The Secretary of Health and Human Services makes the findings described in section 1402(g)(1)(C), (D), and (E) with respect to the religious sect or division described in section 1402(g)(1) of which the individual employer and employee are members; and

(iii) No benefit or other payment referred to in section 1402(g)(1)(B) became payable (or, but for sections 203 or 222(b) of the Social Security Act, would have become payable) to the employee filing the application at or before the time of the filing.

(3) *Effective period of exemption.*—The election provided in paragraph (h)(1) of this section will apply with respect to wages paid by such individual employer during the period commencing with the first day of the first calendar quarter, after the quarter in which such application is filed, throughout which such individual employer or employee meets the applicable requirements specified in paragraphs (h)(2) and (h)(3).

(4) *Termination of election.*—The exemption granted under section 3127 of the Code will end on the last day of the calendar quarter preceding the first calendar quarter thereafter in which:

(i) Such individual employer or the employee involved ceases to meet the applicable requirements of paragraphs (h)(2) and (h)(3), or

(ii) The sect or division thereof of which such individual employer or employee is a member is found by the Secretary of Health and Human Services to have failed to meet the requirements of section 3127(b)(2).

(5) *Both the individual employer and employee must qualify and elect.*—The exemption from the taxes imposed under sections 3101 and 3111 of the Code is applicable only if both the individual employer and the employee qualify and make the election under the provisions of section 3127.

(j) *Certain elections not addressed in this section.*—Elections under the Act that are not addressed in this section include:

(1) An election relating to the effective date of certain source rules under section 861(a) of the Code (section 1012(g)(1) of the Act);

(2) An election relating to transitional rules for interest allocation under section 864(e) of the Code (section 1012(h)(7) of the Act);

(3) An election relating to the chain deficit rules under section 952(c)(1)(C) of the Code (section 1012(i)(25) of the Act);

(4) An election relating to the definition of a passive foreign investment company in section 1296 of the Code (section 1012(p)(27) of the Act);

(5) An election by a shareholder of a qualified electing fund under section 1291(d)(2)(B) of the Code (section 1012(p)(28) of the Act);

(6) An election to be treated as a qualified electing fund under section 1295 of the Code (section 6127 of the Act);

(7) An election relating to treatment of an insurance branch as a separate corporation under section 964(d) of the Code (section 6129 of the Act);

(8) An election relating to certain regulated futures contracts and nonequity options under section 988(c)(1)(D) of the Code (section 6130(b) of the Act);

(9) An election relating to certain qualified funds under section 988(c)(1)(E) of the Code (section 6130(b) of the Act);

(10) An election under section 952(c)(1)(B) of the Code to apply section 953(a) without regard to the same country exception (section 6131(a) of the Act);

(11) An election relating to treatment of a foreign insurance company as a domestic corporation under section 953(d) of the Code (section 6135 of the Act).

Guidance concerning the elections described in this paragraph (j) will generally be provided in regulations to be issued under the relevant Code sections. With respect to certain elections described in this paragraph (j), preliminary guidance has been published. See Notice 88-125, 1988-52 I.R.B. 4, for guidance with respect to the election described in paragraph (j)(6) of this section, relating to the qualified electing fund election. See Notice 88-124, 1988-51 I.R.B. 6, for guidance with respect to the elections described in paragraph (j)(8) and (9) of this section, relating to section 988(c)(1)(D) and (E) of the Code.

(k) *Additional information required.*—Later regulations or revenue procedures issued under provisions of the Code or Act covered by this section may require the furnishing of information in addition to that which was furnished with the statement of election described in this section. In that event, the later regulations or revenue procedures will provide guidance with respect to the furnishing of additional information. [Reg. §301.9100-8.]

☐ [*T.D. 8267, 9-21-89. Redesignated and amended by T.D. 8435, 9-18-92.*]

# ELECTIONS UNDER THE BANK HOLDING COMPANY ACT OF 1976

## [Reg. §301.9100-9T]

**§301.9100-9T. Election by a bank holding company to forego grandfather provision for all property representing pre-June 30, 1968, activities (Temporary).**—(a) *In general.*—For purposes of sections 1101 through 1103 and 6158 of the Code, a bank holding company may elect under section 1103(g) to have the determination of whether property is prohibited property or is property eligible to be distributed without recognition of gain under section 1101(b)(1) made under the Bank Holding Company Act (12 U.S.C. 1841 et seq.) as if the Act did not contain the proviso of section 4(a)(2) thereof.

(b) *Manner of making election.*—The election under section 1103(g) shall be made in a written statement filed with the Federal Reserve Board indicating that by resolution of its board of directors, the bank holding company is electing to apply the provisions of section 1103(g). In addition, the bank holding company shall indicate on its income tax return for each taxable year in which the election applies to a distribution or sale of property (in the manner specified in the Internal Revenue Service's instructions for the preparation of the return) that it has made the election under section 1103(g). The election shall be considered to be made on the date on which the written statement is received by the Federal Reserve Board.

(c) *Scope of election.*—The election under section 1103(g) applies to all determinations of whether property is prohibited property or is property eligible to be distributed without recognition of gain under section 1101(b)(1).

(d) *Election; binding effect.*—An election made under section 1103(g) is irrevocable.

(e) *Final certification.*—An election under section 1103(g) shall not apply unless the final certification referred to in section 1101(e) or section 6158(c)(2), as the case may be, includes a certification by the Federal Reserve Board that the bank holding company has disposed of either all banking property or all nonbanking property (including property described in the proviso of section 4(a)(2) of the Bank Holding Company Act).

(f) *Conditional certification.*—A certification by the Federal Reserve Board under section 1101(a)(1)(B), 1101(b)(1)(B), 1101(c)(2)(C), 1101(c)(3)(C), or 6158(a) that is conditioned upon the bank holding company's making an election under section 1103(g) shall not be considered to be made before the distribution or sale unless the certification and the election are made before the distribution or sale. [Temporary Reg. §301.9100-9T.]

☐ [*T.D. 7570, 11-7-78. Redesignated by T.D. 8435, 9-18-92.*]

## [Reg. §301.9100-10T]

**§301.9100-10T. Election by certain family-owned bank holding companies to divest all banking or nonbanking property (Temporary).**—(a) *In general.*—For purposes of sections 1101 through 1103 and 6158 of the Code, a bank holding company may elect under section 1103(h) to have the determination of whether property is prohibited property or is property eligible to be distributed without recognition of gain under section 1101(b)(1) made under the Bank Holding Company Act (12 U.S.C. 1841 et seq.) as if the Act did not contain clause (ii) of section 4(c) thereof.

(b) *Manner of making election.*—The election under section 1103(h) shall be made in a written statement filed with the Federal Reserve Board indicating that by resolution of its board of directors, the bank holding company is electing to apply the provisions of section 1103(h). In addition, the bank holding company shall indicate on its income tax return for each taxable year in which the election applies to a distribution or sale of property (in the manner specified in the Internal Revenue Service's instructions for the preparation of the return) that it has made the election under section 1103(h). The election shall be considered to be made on the date on which the written statement is received by the Federal Reserve Board.

(c) *Scope of election.*—The election under section 1103(h) applies to all determinations of whether property is prohibited property or is property eligible to be distributed without recognition of gain under section 1101(b)(1).

(d) *Election; binding effect.*—An election made under section 1103(h) is irrevocable.

(e) *Final certification.*—An election under section 1103(h) shall not apply unless the final certification referred to in section 1101(e) or section 6158(c)(2), as the case may be, includes a certification by the

Federal Reserve Board that the bank holding company has disposed of either all banking property or all nonbanking property.

(f) *Conditional certification.*—A certification by the Federal Reserve Board under section 1101(a)(1)(B), 1101(b)(1)(B), 1101(c)(2)(C), 1101(c)(3)(C), or 6158(a) that is conditioned upon the bank holding company's making an election under section 1103(h) shall not be considered to be made before the distribution or sale unless the certification and the election are made before the distribution or sale. [Temporary Reg. § 301.9100-10T.]

☐ [*T.D. 7570, 11-7-78. Redesignated by T.D. 8435, 9-18-92.*]

### [Reg. § 301.9100-11T]

**§ 301.9100-11T. Election by a qualified bank holding corporation to pay in installments the tax attributable to sales under the Bank Holding Company Act (Temporary).**—(a) *In general.*—Under section 6158(a) of the Code, a qualified bank holding corporation may elect to pay in installments the tax under chapter 1 of the Code attributable to the sale of bank property or prohibited property (as those terms are defined in section 6158(f)(2) and (3)) if—

(1) It meets the conditions described in paragraph (b) of this section, and

(2) It files an election in accordance with the rules set forth in paragraph (c) of this section.

(b) *Conditions.*—(1) The sale of bank property or prohibited property must take place after July 7, 1970.

(2) The Federal Reserve Board must certify before the sale of the bank property or prohibited property that the divestiture of such property is necessary or appropriate to effectuate section 4 or the policies of the Bank Holding Company Act (12 U.S.C. 1841 et seq.).

(3) If bank property is sold, the qualified bank holding corporation (or a corporation having control of it or a subsidiary of it) must not have—

(i) Previously elected to apply section 6158 to a sale of prohibited property, or

(ii) Previously distributed prohibited property under section 1101(a).

(4) If prohibited property is sold, the qualified bank holding corporation (or a corporation having control of it or a subsidiary of it) must not have—

(i) Previously elected to apply section 6158 to a sale of bank property, or

(ii) Previously distributed bank property under section 1101(b).

(5) The qualified bank holding corporation must not have elected to return the income from the sale under the installment provisions of section 453.

(c) *Time and manner of making election.*—(1) Except as provided in paragraph (c)(2) of this section, a qualified bank holding corporation shall make the election under section 6158(a) by—

(i) Attaching a statement to its income tax return for the taxable year in which the prohibited property or bank property is sold showing the tax computation under paragraph (f) of this section and the amount of the installment paid with the return, and

(ii) Entering the amount of the installment payment followed by the words "computed under section 6158" in the appropriate place on the tax return.

(2) If the qualified bank holding corporation filed its income tax return for the year of sale before February 6, 1979 (without electing under section 6158(a)), then it shall make the election under section 6158(a) by attaching a statement to its claim for credit or refund (amended tax return) for its overpayment of income tax attributable to the application of section 6158 showing the tax computation under paragraph (f) of this section and entering the amount of the credit or refund followed by the words "attributable to the application of section 6158" in the appropriate place on the claim. In order for the election to be effective, the claim must be filed before the earlier of—

(i) The expiration of the period of limitation for the filing of the claim, or

(ii) February 6, 1979.

(d) *Scope of election.*—An election under section 6158 will apply only to the particular sale or sales of property with respect to which the election is being made.

(e) *Special rule for certifying sales.*—For purposes of section 6158(a) and paragraph (b)(2) of this section, in the case of a sale which takes place after July 7, 1970, and before January 1, 1977, a certification by the Federal Reserve Board shall be treated as made before the sale if application for such certification was made before January 1, 1977.

(f) *Tax attributable to sales.*—The tax under chapter 1 of the Code attributable to sales with respect to which an election under section 6158 has been made shall be the amount, if any, by which the tax under chapter 1 on the taxable income of the qualified bank holding corporation (computed without regard to section 6158) for the taxable year during which the sales occur exceeds the greater of—

(1) The tax under chapter 1 for such year on the taxable income of the corporation exclusive of gains on sales of property with respect to which an election under section 6158 has been made, or

(2) The tax under chapter 1 for such year on the taxable income of the corporation exclusive of gains and losses on all sales of the type of property (either bank property or prohibited property) with respect to which an election under section 6158 has been made. [Temporary Reg. § 301.9100-11T.]

☐ [*T.D. 7570, 11-7-78. Redesignated by T.D. 8435, 9-18-92.*]

# ELECTIONS UNDER TAX REFORM ACT OF 1976

### [Reg. § 301.9100-12T]

**§ 301.9100-12T. Various elections under the Tax Reform Act of 1976 (Temporary).**—(a) *Elections covered by temporary rules.*—The sec-

tions of the Internal Revenue Code of 1954, or of the Tax Reform Act of 1976, to which this section applies and under which an election or notification may be made pursuant to the procedures described in paragraphs (b) and (d) are as follows:

| Section | Description of Election | Availability of Election |
|---|---|---|
| *(1) First Category* | | |
| 167(o) of Code | Substantially rehabilitated historic property. | Additions to capital account occurring after June 30, 1976, and before July 1, 1981. |
| 172(b)(3)(E)[(C)] of Code | Forego of carryback period. | Any taxable year ending after December 31, 1975. |
| 402(e)(4)(L) of Code | Lump sum distributions from qualified plans. | Distributions and payments made after December 31, 1975, in taxable years beginning after such date. |
| 451(e) of Code | Livestock sold on account of drought. | Any taxable year beginning after December 31, 1975. |
| 812(b)(3) of Code | Forego of carryback period by life insurance companies. | Any taxable year ending after December 31, 1975. |
| 819A of Code | Contiguous country branches of domestic life insurance companies. | All taxable years beginning after December 31, 1975. |
| 825(d)(2) of Code | Forego of carryback period by mutual insurance companies. | Any taxable year ending after December 31, 1975. |
| 911(e) of Code | Foregoing of benefits of section 911. | All taxable years beginning after December 31, 1975. |
| *(2) Second Category* | | |
| 185(d) of Code | Amortization of railroad grading and tunnel bores. | All taxable years beginning after December 31, 1974. |
| 1057 of Code | Transfer to foreign trusts etc. | Any transfer of property after October 2, 1975. |

(b) *Time for making election or serving notice.*—(1) *Category (1).*—A taxpayer may make an election under any section referred to in paragraph (a)(1) of this section for the first taxable year for which the election is required to be made or for the taxable year selected by the

**67,362**
**Elections Under the Bankruptcy Tax Act of 1980**
See p. 20,601 for regulations not amended to reflect law changes

taxpayer when the choice of the taxable year is optional. The election must be made by the later of the time, including extensions thereof, prescribed by law for filing income tax returns for such taxable year or March 8, 1977.

(2) *Category (2).*—A taxpayer may make an election under any section referred to in paragraph (a)(2) for the first taxable year for which the election is allowed or for the taxable year selected by the taxpayer when the choice of the taxable year is optional. The election must be made (i) for any taxable year ending before December 31, 1976, for which a return has been filed before January 31, 1977, by filing an amended return, provided that the period of limitation for filing claim for credit or refund of overpayment of tax, determined from the time the return was filed, has not expired or (ii) for all other years by filing the income tax return for the year for which the election is made not later than the time, including extensions thereof, prescribed by law for filing income tax returns for such year.

(c) *Certain other elections.*—The elections described in this paragraph shall be made in the manner and within the time prescribed herein and in paragraph (d) of this section.

(1) The following elections under the Tax Reform Act of 1976 shall be made:

| (i) | Sec. 207 (c)(3) of Act. | Change from static value method of accounting. | All taxable years beginning after December 31, 1976. |
|---|---|---|---|

by filing Form 3115 with the National Office of the Internal Revenue Service before October 5, 1977.

| (ii) | Sec. 604 of Act. | Travel expenses of State legislators. | All taxable years beginning before January 1, 1976. |
|---|---|---|---|

by filing an amended return for any taxable year for which the period for assessing or collecting a deficiency has not expired before October 4, 1976, by the last day for filing a claim for refund or credit for the taxable year but in no event shall such day be earlier than October 4, 1977.

| (iii) | Sec. 804(e)(2) of Act. | Retroactive applications of amendments to property described in section 50(a) of Code. | Certain taxable years beginning before January 1, 1975. |
|---|---|---|---|

by filing amended returns before October 5, 1977, for all taxable years to which applicable for which the period of limitation for filing claim for credit or refund for overpayment of tax has not expired.

| (iv) | Sec. 1608(d)(2) of Act. | Election as a result of determination as defined in section 859(c) of the Code. | Determinations made after October 4, 1976. |
|---|---|---|---|

by filing a statement with the district director for the district in which the taxpayer maintains its principal place of business within 60 days after such determination.

| (v) | Sec. 2103 of Act. | Treatment of certain 1972 disaster losses. | Any taxable year in which payment is received or indebtedness is forgiven. |
|---|---|---|---|

by filing a return for the taxable year or an amended return by the last day for making a claim for credit or refund for the taxable year but in no event shall such day be earlier than October 4, 1977.

(2) [Deleted].

(3) The election provided for in section 167(e)(3) of the Code shall be made in accordance with §1.167(e)-1(d) except that the election shall be applicable for the first taxable year of the taxpayer beginning after December 31, 1975.

(d) *Manner of making election.*—Unless otherwise provided in the return or in a form accompanying a return for the taxable year, the elections described in paragraphs (a) and (c) (except paragraphs (c)(1)(i) and (c)(5)) shall be made by a statement attached to the return (or amended return) for the taxable year. The statement required when making an election pursuant to this section shall indicate the section under which the election is being made and shall set forth information to identify the election, the period for which it applies, and the taxpayer's basis or entitlement for making the election.

(e) *Effect of election.*—(1) *Consent to revoke required.*—Except where otherwise provided by statute or except as provided in subparagraph (2) of this paragraph, an election to which this section applies made in accordance with this section shall be binding unless consent to revoke the election is obtained from the Commissioner. An application for consent to revoke the election will not be accepted before the promulgation of the permanent regulations relating to the section of the Code or Act under which the election is made. Such regulations will provide a reasonable period of time within which taxpayers will be permitted to apply for consent to revoke the election.

(2) *Revocation without consent.*—An election to which this section applies, made in accordance with this section, may be revoked without the consent of the Commissioner not later than 90 days after the permanent regulations relating to the section of the Code or Act under which the election is made are filed with the office of the Federal Register, provided such regulations grant taxpayers blanket permission to revoke that election within such time without the consent of the Commissioner. Such blanket permission to revoke an election will be provided by the permanent regulations in the event of a determination by the Secretary or his delegate that such regulations contain provisions that may not reasonably have been anticipated by taxpayers at the time of making such election.

(f) *Furnishing of supplementary information required.*—If the permanent regulations which are issued under the section of the Code or Act referred to in this section to which the election relates require the furnishing of information in addition to that which was furnished with the statement of election filed pursuant to paragraph (d) of this section, the taxpayer must furnish such additional information in a statement addressed to the district director, or the director of the regional service center, with whom the election was filed. This statement must clearly identify the election and the taxable year for which it was made. If such information is not provided the election may, at the discretion of the Commissioner, be held invalid. [Temporary Reg. §301.9100-12T.]

☐ [*T.D.* 7459, 1-4-77. *Amended by T.D.* 7478, 4-5-77; *T.D.* 7670, 1-30-80; *T.D.* 7673, 2-7-80; *T.D.* 7692, 4-7-80; *T.D.* 7743, 12-19-80 *and T.D.* 8308, 8-30-90. *Redesignated by T.D.* 8435, 9-18-92.]

# ELECTIONS UNDER THE BANKRUPTCY TAX ACT OF 1980

## [Reg. §301.9100-14T]

**§301.9100-14T. Individual's election to terminate taxable year when case commences (Temporary).**—(a) *Scope.*—The regulations prescribed in this section provide rules for making the election under section 1398(d)(2) to terminate the taxable year of an individual taxpayer.

(b) *Availability of election.*—This election is available to an individual taxpayer in a case commenced after March 24, 1981, under chapter 7 (relating to liquidations) or chapter 11 (relating to reorganizations) of title 11 of the United States Code. If the case is dismissed, the taxpayer cannot make the election, and an election previously made will be void. For purposes of this section, a partnership is not treated as an individual. If the taxpayer making the election is married (within the meaning of section 143), the election is available to the taxpayer's spouse, but only if the spouse is eligible to file, and does file, a joint return with the taxpayer for the taxable year ended as a result of the election.

(c) *Effect of election.*—The election terminates the taxable year of the taxpayer (and of a spouse who joins in the election) on the day before the commencement date of the case. A new taxable year begins on the commencement date and (unless terminated earlier) ends on the date on which the taxpayer's taxable year in which the case commenced would have ended if the election had not been made.

(d) *Time and manner.*—A taxpayer to whom the election is available makes the election by filing a return for the short taxable year ending the day before commencement of the case (the "first short taxable year") on or before the 15th day of the fourth full month following the end of that first short taxable year. The spouse of such a taxpayer makes the election by making a joint return with the taxpayer for that first short taxable year within the time prescribed in the preceding sentence. To facilitate processing, the taxpayer should write "SECTION 1398 ELECTION" at the top of the return. A taxpayer may also make the election by attaching a statement of election to an application for extension of time for filing a return that satisfies the requirements under section 6081 for the first short taxable year. The application for extension must be submitted under section 6081 on or before the due date of the return for the first short taxable year. The statement must state that the taxpayer elects under section 1398(d)(2) to close his or her taxable year as of the day before commencement of the case. If the taxpayer's spouse elects to close his or her taxable year, the spouse must join in the application for extension and in the statement of election. If a joint return is not filed for the first short taxable year, the election of the spouse made with the application is void.

(e) *Irrevocability of election.*—The election is irrevocable.

(f) *Subsequent bankruptcy case of debtor's spouse.*—If a case under chapter 7 or chapter 11 of title 11 of the United States Code commences with respect to the spouse of a debtor to whom an election under this section was available, the spouse can make an election under this section even if the spouse's case commences in the same taxable year in which the debtor's case commences. The spouse can make the election whether or not the spouse previously joined in the debtor's election. If the spouse joined in the debtor's election, or if the debtor did not make the election, the debtor may join in the spouse's election, assuming the debtor is otherwise eligible to file a joint return with the spouse.

(g) *Example.*—(1) Assume that husband and wife are calendar-year taxpayers, that a bankruptcy case involving only the husband commences on March 1, 1982, and that a bankruptcy case involving only the wife commences on October 10, 1982.

(2) If the husband does not make an election, his taxable year would not be affected; *i.e.*, it does not terminate on February 28. If the husband does make an election, his first short taxable year would be January 1 through February 28; his second short taxable year would begin March 1. The tax return for his first short taxable year would be due on June 15. The wife could join in the husband's election, but only if they file a joint return for the taxable year January 1 through February 28.

(3) The wife could elect to terminate her taxable year on October 9. If she did, and if the husband had not made an election or if the wife had not joined in the husband's election, she would have two taxable years in 1982—the first from January 1 through October 9, and the second from October 10 through December 31. The tax return for her first short taxable year would be due on February 15, 1983. If the husband had not made an election to terminate his taxable year on February 28, the husband could join in an election by his wife, but only if they file a joint return for the taxable year January 1 through October 9. If the husband had made an election but the wife had not joined in the husband's election, the husband could not join in an election by the wife to terminate her taxable year on October 9, since they could not file a joint return for such year.

(4) If the wife makes the election relating to her own bankruptcy case, and had joined the husband in making an election relating to his case, she would have two additional taxable years with respect to her 1982 income and deductions—the second short taxable year would be March 1 through October 9, and the third short taxable year would be October 10 through December 31. The husband could join in the wife's election if they file a joint return for the second short taxable year. If the husband joins in the wife's election, they could file joint returns for the short taxable year ending December 31, but would not be required to do so. [Temporary Reg. § 301.9100-14T.]

☐ [*T.D. 7775, 5-1-81. Redesignated by T.D. 8435, 9-18-92.*]

### [Reg. § 301.9100-15T]

**§ 301.9100-15T. Election to use retroactive effective date (Temporary).**—(a) *Scope.*—The regulations prescribed in this section provide rules for making the election to use a retroactive effective date under section 7(f) of the Bankruptcy Tax Act of 1980.

(b) *Availability of election.*—The election is available to the debtor (or debtors) in a case under title 11 of the United States Code (or a receivership, foreclosure, or similar proceeding in a Federal or State court) that commences after September 30, 1979, and before January 1, 1981. The court must approve the election. For purposes of this paragraph (b), a receivership, foreclosure, or similar proceeding before a Federal or State agency involving a financial institution to which section 585 or 593 applies shall be treated as a proceeding before a court.

(c) *Effect of election.*—(1) *In general.*—An election under this section changes the effective date of certain amendments to the Code made by the Bankruptcy Tax Act of 1980. The amendments affected by an election under this section are listed in paragraph (c)(2) and (3) of this section. If the election is made, all of the amendments listed in paragraph (c)(2) and (3) of this section apply to all transactions in the case (or similar proceeding) and to all parties in respect of all transactions in the case (or similar proceeding). Thus, the debtor may not elect to have only certain of the amendments apply to transactions in the case (or similar proceeding) and may not elect to have the amendments apply only to certain transactions in the case (or similar proceeding). An election under this section will not make the amend-

ments listed in paragraph (c)(2) and (3) applicable to transactions occurring prior to commencement of the case (or similar proceeding) or transactions not in the case (or similar proceeding).

(2) *Amendments affected.*—An election under this section changes the effective date of the amendments to the following sections:

(i) 111, relating to recovery of bad debts, prior taxes and delinquency amounts,

(ii) 302, relating to the repeal of special treatment for certain railroad redemptions,

(iii) 312, relating to the effect of debt discharge on earnings and profits,

(iv) 337, relating to the application of the 12-month liquidation rule,

(v) 351, relating to certain transfers to controlled corporations,

(vi) 354 (other than the amendment made by section 6(i)(2) of the Bankruptcy Tax Act of 1980), 355, 357, 368, and 381, relating to corporate reorganizations,

(vii) 382, relating to special limitations on net operating loss carryover,

(viii) 542, relating to the personal holding company tax, and

(ix) 703, relating to elections of partnerships.

(3) *Other amendments affected in part.*—Subject to the transitional rule of section 7(a)(2) of the Bankruptcy Tax Act of 1980, an election under this section changes the effective date of the amendments to sections 108 and 1017, relating to the tax treatment of discharge of indebtedness.

(4) *Substitution of effective dates.*—The election under this section changes the effective date of the amendments listed in paragraph (c)(2) and (3) of this section by substituting "September 30, 1979" for "December 31, 1980" wherever it appears in section 7(a), (c), and (d) of the Bankruptcy Tax Act of 1980.

(d) *Time and manner.*—(1) *Time and place.*—A debtor makes the election under this section by filing the written statement and evidence of court approval required under paragraph (d)(2) and (3) of this section on or before November 2, 1981, with the District Director or the Director of the Internal Revenue Service Center with whom an income tax return for the debtor would be filed if it were due on the date the election is filed. The election shall be considered to be made on the date on which the written statement and evidence of court approval is filed. The debtor should attach a copy of the statement and evidence of court approval to the next income tax return filed on or after the date the election is made.

(2) *Statement.*—The written statement must be signed by the debtor (or a person duly authorized to sign the income tax return of the debtor) and must contain the following:

(i) the name, address, and taxpayer identification number of the debtor,

(ii) a statement that the debtor is making the election under section 7(f) of the Bankruptcy Tax Act of 1980, and

(iii) information (including the date of commencement) sufficient to identify the bankruptcy case or similar proceeding.

(3) *Evidence of court approval.*—The evidence of court approval (or of approval of an agency in certain proceedings described in paragraph (b) of this section) must be a copy of an order or other document properly signed by the judge or other presiding officer. In addition to information identifying the debtor and the case or proceeding over which the officer presides, the order or other document must state that the court (or agency, as the case may be) approves the election of the debtor under section 7(f) of the Bankruptcy Tax Act of 1980.

(e) *Revocability.*—An election under this section may be revoked only with the consent of the Commissioner. A request for revocation can be made only with approval of the court (or agency). [Temporary Reg. § 301.9100-15T.]

☐ [*T.D. 7775, 5-1-81. Redesignated by T.D. 8435, 9-18-92.*]

### [Reg. § 301.9100-21]

**§ 301.9100-21. References to other temporary elections under various tax acts.**—Regulations regarding elections under various other tax acts are found at the following sections in title 26 of the Code of Federal Regulations:

| Section of 26 CFR | Description of Election |
|---|---|
| 5c.168(f)(8)-2 | Election to characterize transaction as a section 168(f)(8) lease, under the Economic Recovery Tax Act of 1981. |
| 5c.1256-1 | Election with respect to property held on June 23, 1981, under section 508(c) of the Economic Recovery Tax Act of 1981. |
| 5c.1256-2 | Election with respect to taxable years beginning before June 23, 1981, and ending after June 22, 1981, under section 509 of the Economic Recovery Tax Act of 1981. |

| | |
|---|---|
| 7.48-1 | Election to have investment credit for movie and television films determined in accordance with previous litigation, under the Tax Reform Act of 1976. |
| 7.48-2 | Election of forty-percent method of determining investment credit for movie and television films placed in service in a taxable year beginning before January 1, 1975, under the Tax Reform Act of 1976. |
| 7.48-3 | Election to apply the amendments made by sections 804(a) and (b) of the Tax Reform Act of 1976 to property described in section 50(a) of the Code. |
| 7.57(d)-1 | Election with respect to straight line recovery of intangibles, under the Tax Reform Act of 1976. |
| 11.402(a)(4)(B)-1 | Election to treat an amount as a lump sum distribution, under the Employee Retirement Income Security Act of 1974. |
| 11.410-1 | Election by church to have participation, vesting, funding, etc., provisions apply, under the Employee Retirement Income Security Act of 1974. |
| 11.412(c)-7 | Election to treat certain retroactive plan amendments as made on the first day of the plan year, under the Employee Retirement Income Security Act of 1974. |
| 11.412(c)-11 | Election with respect to bonds, under the Employee Retirement Income Security Act of 1974. |
| 11.415(c)(4)-1 | Special elections for section 403(b) annuity contracts purchased by educational institutions, hospitals and home health service agencies, under the Employee Retirement Income Security Act of 1974. |
| 12.4 | Election of Class Life Asset Depreciation Range System (ADR), under the Revenue Act of 1971. |
| 12.7 | Election to be treated as a DISC, under the Revenue Act of 1971. |
| 12.8 | Elections with respect to net leases of real property, under the Revenue Act of 1971. |
| 12.9 | Election to postpone determination with respect to the presumption described in section 183(d), under the Revenue Act of 1971. |
| 15.1-1 | Elections to deduct, relating to exploration expenditures in the case of mining. |
| 15.1-2 | Revocation of election to deduct, relating to exploration expenditures in the case of mining. |
| 15.1-3 | Elections as to methods of recapture, relating to exploration expenditures in the case of mining. |
| 18.1361-1 | Election to treat qualified subchapter S trust as a trust described in section 1361(c)(2)(A)(i), under the Subchapter S Revision Act of 1982. |
| 18.1362-1 | Election to be an S corporation, under the Subchapter S Revision Act of 1982. |
| 18.1362-3 | Revocation of election, under the Subchapter S Revision Act of 1982. |
| 18.1362-5 | Election not to have new passive income rules apply during 1982, under the Subchapter S Revision Act of 1982. |
| 18.1371-1 | Election to treat distributions as dividends during certain post-termination transition periods, under the Subchapter S Revision Act of 1982. |
| 18.1377-1 | Election to terminate year, under the Subchapter S Revision Act of 1982. |
| 18.1379-2 | Special rules for all elections, consents, and refusals, under the Subchapter S Revision Act of 1982. |
| 22.0 | Certain estate tax elections under the Economic Recovery Tax Act of 1981. |
| 23.1 | Election and eligibility to treat interests in property held jointly on December 31, 1976, as qualified joint interests, under the Revenue Act of 1978. |

[Reg. § 301.9100-21.]

☐ [*T.D. 8435, 9-18-92.*]

### [Reg. § 301.9100-22]

**§ 301.9100-22. Time, form, and manner of making the election under section 1101(g)(4) of the Bipartisan Budget Act of 2015 for returns filed for partnership taxable years beginning after November 2, 2015 and before January 1, 2018.**—(a) *Election.*—Pursuant to section 1101(g)(4) of the Bipartisan Budget Act of 2015, Public Law 114-74 (BBA), a partnership may elect at the time and in such form and manner as described in this section for amendments made by section 1101 of the BBA, except section 6221(b) as added by the BBA, to apply to any return of the partnership filed for an eligible taxable year as defined in paragraph (d) of this section. An election is valid only if made in accordance with this section. Once made, an election may only be revoked with the consent of the Internal Revenue Service (IRS). An election is not valid if it frustrates the purposes of section 1101 of the BBA. A partnership may not request an extension of time under § 301.9100-3 for an election described in this section.

(b) *Election on notification by the IRS.*—(1) *Time for making the election.*—Except as described in paragraph (c) of this section, an election under this section must be made within 30 days of the date of notification to a partnership, in writing, that a return of the partnership for an eligible taxable year has been selected for examination (a notice of selection for examination).

(2) *Form and manner of making the election.*—(i) *In general.*—The partnership makes an election under this section by providing a written statement with the words "Election under Section 1101(g)(4)" written at the top that satisfies the requirements of paragraph (b)(2) of this section to the individual identified in the notice of selection for examination as the IRS contact regarding the examination.

(ii) *Statement requirements.*—A statement making an election under this section must be in writing and be dated and signed by the tax matters partner, as defined under section 6231(a)(7) (prior to amendment by the BBA), and the applicable regulations, or an individual who has the authority to sign the partnership return for the taxable year under section 6063, the regulations thereunder, and applicable forms and instructions. The fact that an individual dates and signs the statement making the election described in this paragraph (b) shall be prima facie evidence that the individual is authorized to make the election on behalf of the partnership. A statement making an election must include—

(A) The partnership's name, taxpayer identification number, and the partnership taxable year for which the election described in this paragraph (b) is being made;

(B) The name, taxpayer identification number, address, and daytime telephone number of the individual who signs the statement;

(C) Language indicating that the partnership is electing application of section 1101(c) of the BBA for the partnership return for the eligible taxable year identified in the notice of selection for examination;

(D) The information required to properly designate the partnership representative as defined by section 6223 as amended by the BBA, which must include the name, taxpayer identification number, address, and daytime telephone number of the partnership representative and any additional information required by applicable regulations, forms and instructions, and other guidance issued by the IRS;

(E) The following representations—

(1) The partnership is not insolvent and does not reasonably anticipate becoming insolvent before resolution of any adjustment with respect to the partnership taxable year for which the election described in this paragraph (b) is being made;

(2) The partnership has not filed, and does not reasonably anticipate filing, voluntarily a petition for relief under title 11 of the United States Code;

(3) The partnership is not subject to, and does not reasonably anticipate becoming subject to, an involuntary petition for relief under title 11 of the United States Code; and

(4) The partnership has sufficient assets, and reasonably anticipates having sufficient assets, to pay a potential imputed underpayment with respect to the partnership taxable year that may be determined under subchapter C of chapter 63 of the Internal Revenue Code as amended by the BBA; and

(F) A representation, signed under penalties of perjury, that the individual signing the statement is duly authorized to make the election described in this paragraph (b) and that, to the best of the individual's knowledge and belief, all of the information contained in the statement is true, correct, and complete.

(iii) *Notice of Administrative Proceeding.*—Upon receipt of the election described in this paragraph (b), the IRS will promptly mail a notice of administrative proceeding to the partnership and the partnership representative, as required under section 6231(a)(1) as amended by the BBA. Notwithstanding the preceding sentence, the IRS will not mail the notice of administrative proceeding before the date that is 30 days after receipt of the election described in paragraph (b) of this section.

(c) *Election for the purpose of filing an administrative adjustment request (AAR) under section 6227 as amended by the BBA.*—(1) *In general.*—A partnership that has not been issued a notice of selection for examination as described in paragraph (b)(1) of this section may make an election with respect to a partnership return for an eligible taxable year for the purpose of filing an AAR under section 6227 as amended by the BBA. Once an election under this paragraph (c) is made, all of the amendments made by section 1101 of the BBA, except section 6221(b) as added by the BBA, apply with respect to the partnership taxable year for which such election is made.

(2) *Time for making the election.*—No election under this paragraph (c) may be made before January 1, 2018.

(3) *Form and manner of making an election.*—An election under this paragraph (c) must be made in the manner prescribed by the IRS for that purpose in accordance with applicable regulations, forms and instructions, and other guidance issued by the IRS.

(4) *Effect of filing an AAR before January 1, 2018.*—Except in the case of an election made in accordance with paragraph (b) of this section, an AAR filed on behalf of a partnership before January 1, 2018, is deemed for purposes of paragraph (d)(2) of this section, to be an AAR filed under section 6227(c) (prior to amendment by the BBA) or an amended return of partnership income, as applicable.

(d) *Eligible taxable year.*—(1) *In general.*—For purposes of this section, the term *eligible taxable year* means any partnership taxable year beginning after November 2, 2015 and before January 1, 2018, except as provided in paragraph (d)(2) of this section.

(2) *Exception if AAR or amended return filed or deemed filed.*—Notwithstanding paragraph (d)(1) of this section, a partnership taxable year is not an eligible taxable year for purposes of this section if for the partnership taxable year—

(i) The tax matters partner has filed an AAR under section 6227(c) (prior to amendment by the BBA),

(ii) The partnership is deemed to have filed an AAR under section 6227(c) (prior to the amendment by the BBA) in accordance with paragraph (c)(4) of this section, or

(iii) An amended return of partnership income has been filed or has been deemed to be filed under paragraph (c)(4) of this section.

(e) *Applicability date.*—These regulations are applicable to returns filed for partnership taxable years beginning after November 2, 2015 and before January 1, 2018. [Reg. § 301.9100-22.]

☐ [*T.D.* 9839, 8-6-2018.]

# USE OF MAGNETIC TAPES

### [Reg. § 1.9101-1]

**§ 1.9101-1. Permission to submit information required by certain returns and statements on magnetic tape.**—In any case where the use of a Form 1087 or 1099 is required by the regulations under this part for the purpose of making a return or reporting information, such requirement may be satisfied by submitting the information required by such form on magnetic tape or by other media, provided that the prior consent of the Commissioner or other authorized officer or employee of the Internal Revenue Service has been ob-

tained. Applications for such consent must be filed in accordance with procedures established by the Internal Revenue Service. In any case where the use of Form W-2 is required for the purpose of making a return or reporting information, such requirement may be satisfied by submitting the information required by such form on magnetic tape or other approved media, provided that the prior consent of the Commissioner of Social Security (or other authorized officer or employee thereof) has been obtained. [Reg. § 1.9101-1.]

☐ [*T.D.* 6883, 5-2-66. *Amended by T.D.* 7580, 12-20-78.]

# GROUP HEALTH PLAN REQUIREMENTS

### [Reg. § 54.9801-1]

**§ 54.9801-1. Basis and scope.**—(a) *Statutory basis.*—This section and sections 54.9801-2 through 54.9801-6, 54.9802-1, 54.9802-2, 54.9802-3T, 54.9811-1, 54.9812-1T, 54.9831-1, and 54.9833-1 (portability sections) implement Chapter 100 of Subtitle K of the Internal Revenue Code of 1986.

(b) *Scope.*—A group health plan or health insurance issuer offering group health insurance coverage may provide greater rights to participants and beneficiaries than those set forth in the portability and market reform sections of this part 54. This part 54 sets forth minimum requirements for group health plans and group health insurance issuers offering group health insurance coverage concerning certain consumer protections of the Health Insurance Portability and Accountability Act (HIPAA), including special enrollment periods and the prohibition against discrimination based on a health factor, as amended by the Patient Protection and Affordable Care Act (Affordable Care Act). Other consumer protection provisions, including other protections provided by the Affordable Care Act and the Mental Health Parity and Addiction Equity Act, are set forth in this part 54.

(c) *Similar Requirements under the Employee Retirement Income Security Act and the Public Health Service Act.*—Sections 701, 702, 703, 711,

712, 732, and 733 of the Employee Retirement Income Security Act of 1974 and sections 2701, 2702, 2704, 2705, 2721, and 2791 of the Public Health Service Act impose requirements similar to those imposed under Chapter 100 of Subtitle K with respect to health insurance issuers offering group health insurance coverage. See 29 CFR Part 2590 and 45 CFR Parts 144, 146, and 148. See also Part B of Title XXVII of the Public Health Service Act and 45 CFR Part 148 for other rules applicable to health insurance offered in the individual market (defined in § 54.9801-2). [Reg. § 54.9801-1.]

☐ [*T.D.* 9166, 12-29-2004. *Amended by T.D.* 9299, 12-12-2006; *T.D.* 9427, 10-17-2008; *T.D.* 9464, 10-1-2009 *and T.D.* 9656, 2-20-2014.]

### [Reg. § 54.9801-2]

**§ 54.9801-2. Definitions.**—Unless otherwise provided, the definitions in this section govern in applying the provisions of sections 9801 through 9815 and 9831 through 9833.

*Affiliation period* means a period of time that must expire before health insurance coverage provided by an HMO becomes effective, and during which the HMO is not required to provide benefits.

*COBRA* definitions:

(1) *COBRA* means Title X of the Consolidated Omnibus Budget Reconciliation Act of 1985, as amended.

(2) *COBRA continuation coverage* means coverage, under a group health plan, that satisfies an applicable COBRA continuation provision.

(3) *COBRA continuation provision* means section 4980B (other than paragraph (f)(1) of section 4980B insofar as it relates to pediatric vaccines), sections 601-608 of ERISA, or Title XXII of the PHS Act.

(4) *Exhaustion of COBRA continuation coverage* means that an individual's COBRA continuation coverage ceases for any reason other than either failure of the individual to pay premiums on a timely basis, or for cause (such as making a fraudulent claim or an intentional misrepresentation of a material fact in connection with the plan). An individual is considered to have exhausted COBRA continuation coverage if such coverage ceases —

(i) Due to the failure of the employer or other responsible entity to remit premiums on a timely basis;

(ii) When the individual no longer resides, lives, or works in the service area of an HMO or similar program (whether or not within the choice of the individual) and there is no other COBRA continuation coverage available to the individual; or

(iii) When the individual incurs a claim that would meet or exceed a lifetime limit on all benefits and there is no other COBRA continuation coverage available to the individual.

*Condition* means a *medical condition*.

*Creditable coverage* means *creditable coverage* within the meaning of § 54.9801-4(a).

*Dependent* means any individual who is or may become eligible for coverage under the terms of a group health plan because of a relationship to a participant.

*Employee Retirement Income Security Act of 1974 (ERISA)* means the Employee Retirement Income Security Act of 1974, as amended (29 U.S.C. 1001 *et seq.*).

*Enroll* means to become covered for benefits under a group health plan (that is, when coverage becomes effective), without regard to when the individual may have completed or filed any forms that are required in order to become covered under the plan. For this purpose, an individual who has health coverage under a group health plan is enrolled in the plan regardless of whether the individual elects coverage, the individual is a dependent who becomes covered as a result of an election by a participant, or the individual becomes covered without an election.

*Enrollment date* means the first day of coverage or, if there is a waiting period, the first day of the waiting period. If an individual receiving benefits under a group health plan changes benefit packages, or if the plan changes group health insurance issuers, the individual's enrollment date does not change.

*Excepted benefits* means the benefits described as excepted in § 54.9831(c).

*First day of coverage* means, in the case of an individual covered for benefits under a group health plan, the first day of coverage under the plan and, in the case of an individual covered by health insurance coverage in the individual market, the first day of coverage under the policy or contract.

*Genetic information* has the meaning given the term in § 54.9802-3T(a)(3).

*Group health insurance coverage* means health insurance coverage offered in connection with a group health plan. Individual health insurance coverage reimbursed by the arrangements described in 29 CFR 2510.3-1(l) is not offered in connection with a group health plan, and is not group health insurance coverage, provided all the conditions in 29 CFR 2510.3-1(l) are satisfied.

*Group health plan* or *plan* means a *group health plan* within the meaning of § 54.9831-1(a).

*Group market* means the market for health insurance coverage offered in connection with a group health plan. (However, certain very small plans may be treated as being in the individual market, rather than the group market; see the definition of *individual market* in this section.)

*Health insurance coverage* means benefits consisting of medical care (provided directly, through insurance or reimbursement, or otherwise) under any hospital or medical service policy or certificate, hospital or medical service plan contract, or HMO contract offered by a health insurance issuer. Health insurance coverage includes group health insurance coverage, individual health insurance coverage, and short-term, limited-duration insurance. However, benefits described in § 54.9831(c)(2) are not treated as benefits consisting of medical care.

*Health insurance issuer* or *issuer* means an insurance company, insurance service, or insurance organization (including an HMO) that is required to be licensed to engage in the business of insurance in a state and that is subject to state law that regulates insurance (within the meaning of section 514(b)(2) of ERISA). Such term does not include a group health plan.

*Health maintenance organization* or *HMO* means—

(1) A federally qualified health maintenance organization (as defined in section 1301(a) of the PHS Act);

(2) An organization recognized under state law as a health maintenance organization; or

(3) A similar organization regulated under state law for solvency in the same manner and to the same extent as such a health maintenance organization.

*Individual health insurance coverage* means health insurance coverage offered to individuals in the individual market, but does not include short-term, limited-duration insurance. Individual health insurance coverage can include dependent coverage.

*Individual market* means the market for health insurance coverage offered to individuals other than in connection with a group health plan. Unless a state elects otherwise in accordance with section 2791(e)(1)(B)(ii) of the PHS Act, such term also includes coverage offered in connection with a group health plan that has fewer than two participants who are current employees on the first day of the plan year.

*Issuer* means a *health insurance issuer*.

*Late enrollee* means an individual whose enrollment in a plan is a late enrollment.

*Late enrollment* means enrollment of an individual under a group health plan other than on the earliest date on which coverage can become effective for the individual under the terms of the plan; or through special enrollment. (For rules relating to special enrollment, see § 54.9801-6.) If an individual ceases to be eligible for coverage under a plan, and then subsequently becomes eligible for coverage under the plan, only the individual's most recent period of eligibility is taken into account in determining whether the individual is a late enrollee under the plan with respect to the most recent period of coverage. Similar rules apply if an individual again becomes eligible for coverage following a suspension of coverage that applied generally under the plan.

*Medical care* has the meaning given such term by section 213(d), determined without regard to section 213(d)(1)(C) and so much of section 213(d)(1)(D) as relates to qualified long-term care insurance.

*Medical condition* or *condition* means any condition, whether physical or mental, including, but not limited to, any condition resulting from illness, injury (whether or not the injury is accidental), pregnancy, or congenital malformation. However, genetic information is not a condition.

*Participant* means *participant* within the meaning of section 3(7) of ERISA.

*Placement, or being placed, for adoption* means the assumption and retention of a legal obligation for total or partial support of a child by a person with whom the child has been placed in anticipation of the child's adoption. The child's placement for adoption with such person ends upon the termination of such legal obligation.

*Plan year* means the year that is designated as the plan year in the plan document of a group health plan, except that if the plan document does not designate a plan year or if there is no plan document, the plan year is —

(1) The deductible or limit year used under the plan;

(2) If the plan does not impose deductibles or limits on a yearly basis, then the plan year is the policy year;

(3) If the plan does not impose deductibles or limits on a yearly basis, and either the plan is not insured or the insurance policy is not renewed on an annual basis, then the plan year is the employer's taxable year; or

(4) In any other case, the plan year is the calendar year.

*Preexisting condition exclusion* means a limitation or exclusion of benefits (including a denial of coverage) based on the fact that the condition was present before the effective date of coverage (or if coverage is denied, the date of the denial) under a group health plan or group or individual health insurance coverage (or other coverage provided to Federally eligible individuals pursuant to 45 CFR part 148), whether or not any medical advice, diagnosis, care, or treatment was recommended or received before that day. A preexisting condition exclusion includes any limitation or exclusion of benefits (including a denial of coverage) applicable to an individual as a result of information relating to an individual's health status before the individual's effective date of coverage (or if coverage is denied, the date of the denial) under a group health plan, or group or individual health insurance coverage (or other coverage provided to Federally eligible individuals pursuant to 45 CFR part 148), such as a condition identified as a result of a pre-enrollment questionnaire or physical examination given to the individual, or review of medical records relating to the pre-enrollment period.

*Public health plan* means *public health plan* within the meaning of § 54.9801-4(a)(1)(ix).

*Public Health Service Act (PHS Act)* means the Public Health Service Act (42 U.S.C. 201, *et seq.*).

*Short-term, limited-duration insurance* means health insurance coverage provided pursuant to a contract with an issuer that:

(1) Has an expiration date specified in the contract that is less than 12 months after the original effective date of the contract and, taking into account renewals or extensions, has a duration of no longer than 36 months in total;

(2) With respect to policies having a coverage start date before January 1, 2019, displays prominently in the contract and in any application materials provided in connection with enrollment in such coverage in at least 14 point type the language in the following Notice 1, excluding the heading "Notice 1," with any additional information required by applicable state law:

Notice 1:

This coverage is not required to comply with certain federal market requirements for health insurance, principally those contained in the Affordable Care Act. Be sure to check your policy carefully to make sure you are aware of any exclusions or limitations regarding coverage of preexisting conditions or health benefits (such as hospitalization, emergency services, maternity care, preventive care, prescription drugs, and mental health and substance use disorder services). Your policy might also have lifetime and/or annual dollar limits on health benefits. If this coverage expires or you lose eligibility for this coverage, you might have to wait until an open enrollment period to get other health insurance coverage. Also, this coverage is not "minimum essential coverage." If you don't have minimum essential coverage for any month in 2018, you may have to make a payment when you file your tax return unless you qualify for an exemption from the requirement that you have health coverage for that month.;

(3) With respect to policies having a coverage start date on or after January 1, 2019, displays prominently in the contract and in any application materials provided in connection with enrollment in such coverage in at least 14 point type the language in the following Notice 2, excluding the heading "Notice 2," with any additional information required by applicable state law:

Notice 2:

This coverage is not required to comply with certain federal market requirements for health insurance, principally those contained in the Affordable Care Act. Be sure to check your policy carefully to make sure you are aware of any exclusions or limitations regarding coverage of preexisting conditions or health benefits (such as hospitalization, emergency services, maternity care, preventive care, prescription drugs, and mental health and substance use disorder services). Your policy might also have lifetime and/or annual dollar limits on health benefits. If this coverage expires or you lose eligibility for this coverage, you might have to wait until an open enrollment period to get other health insurance coverage.

(4) If a court holds the 36-month maximum duration provision set forth in paragraph (1) of this definition or its applicability to any person or circumstances invalid, the remaining provisions and their applicability to other people or circumstances shall continue in effect.

*Significant break in coverage* means a *significant break in coverage* within the meaning of §54.9801-4(b)(2)(iii).

*Special enrollment* means enrollment in a group health plan under the rights described in §54.9801-6 or in group health insurance coverage under the rights described in 29 CFR 2590.701-6 or 45 CFR 146.117.

*State health benefits risk pool* means a *state health benefits risk pool* within the meaning of §54.9801-4(a)(1)(vii).

*Travel insurance* means insurance coverage for personal risks incident to planned travel, which may include, but is not limited to, interruption or cancellation of trip or event, loss of baggage or personal effects, damages to accommodations or rental vehicles, and sickness, accident, disability, or death occurring during travel, provided that the health benefits are not offered on a stand-alone basis and are incidental to other coverage. For this purpose, the term travel insurance does not include major medical plans that provide comprehensive medical protection for travelers with trips lasting 6 months or longer, including, for example, those working overseas as an expatriate or military personnel being deployed.

*Waiting period* means *waiting period* within the meaning of §54.9815-2708(b).

[Reg. §54.9801-2.]

☐ [T.D. 9166, 12-29-2004. *Amended by* T.D. 9299, 12-12-2006; T.D. 9427, 10-17-2008; T.D. 9464, 10-1-2009; T.D. 9491, 6-22-2010, T.D. 9656, 2-20-2014, T.D. 9744, 11-13-2015, T.D. 9791, 10-28-2016, T.D. 9837, 8-1-2018 *and* T.D. 9867, 6-13-2019.]

**[Reg. §54.9801-3]**

**§54.9801-3. Limitations on preexisting condition exclusion period.**—(a) *Preexisting condition exclusion defined.*—(1) A *preexisting*

*condition exclusion* means a *preexisting condition exclusion* within the meaning of §54.9801-2.

(2) *Examples.*—The rules of this paragraph (a)(1) are illustrated by the following examples:

*Example 1.* (i) *Facts.* A group health plan provides benefits solely through an insurance policy offered by Issuer *S*. At the expiration of the policy, the plan switches coverage to a policy offered by Issuer *T*. Issuer *T*'s policy excludes benefits for any prosthesis if the body part was lost before the effective date of coverage under the policy.

(ii) *Conclusion.* In this *Example 1*, the exclusion of benefits for any prosthesis if the body part was lost before the effective date of coverage is a preexisting condition exclusion because it operates to exclude benefits for a condition based on the fact that the condition was present before the effective date of coverage under the policy. The exclusion of benefits, therefore, is prohibited.

*Example 2.* (i) *Facts.* A group health plan provides coverage for cosmetic surgery in cases of accidental injury, but only if the injury occurred while the individual was covered under the plan.

(ii) *Conclusion.* In this *Example 2*, the plan provision excluding cosmetic surgery benefits for individuals injured before enrolling in the plan is a preexisting condition exclusion because it operates to exclude benefits relating to a condition based on the fact that the condition was present before the effective date of coverage. The plan provision, therefore, is prohibited.

*Example 3.* (i) *Facts.* A group health plan provides coverage for the treatment of diabetes, generally not subject to any requirement to obtain an approval for a treatment plan. However, if an individual was diagnosed with diabetes before the effective date of coverage under the plan, diabetes coverage is subject to a requirement to obtain approval of a treatment plan in advance.

(ii) *Conclusion.* In this *Example 3*, the requirement to obtain advance approval of a treatment plan is a preexisting condition exclusion because it limits benefits for a condition based on the fact that the condition was present before the effective date of coverage. The plan provision, therefore, is prohibited.

*Example 4.* (i) *Facts.* A group health plan provides coverage for three infertility treatments. The plan counts against the three-treatment limit benefits provided under prior health coverage.

(ii) *Conclusion.* In this *Example 4*, counting benefits for a specific condition provided under prior health coverage against a treatment limit for that condition is a preexisting condition exclusion because it operates to limit benefits for a condition based on the fact that the condition was present before the effective date of coverage. The plan provision, therefore, is prohibited.

*Example 5.* (i) *Facts.* When an individual's coverage begins under a group health plan, the individual generally becomes eligible for all benefits. However, benefits for pregnancy are not available until the individual has been covered under the plan for 12 months.

(ii) *Conclusion.* In this *Example 5*, the requirement to be covered under the plan for 12 months to be eligible for pregnancy benefits is a subterfuge for a preexisting condition exclusion because it is designed to exclude benefits for a condition (pregnancy) that arose before the effective date of coverage. The plan provision, therefore, is prohibited.

*Example 6.* (i) *Facts.* A group health plan provides coverage for medically necessary items and services, generally including treatment of heart conditions. However, the plan does not cover those same items and services when used for treatment of congenital heart conditions.

(ii) *Conclusion.* In this *Example 6*, the exclusion of coverage for treatment of congenital heart conditions is a preexisting condition exclusion because it operates to exclude benefits relating to a condition based on the fact that the condition was present before the effective date of coverage. The plan provision, therefore, is prohibited.

*Example 7.* (i) *Facts.* A group health plan generally provides coverage for medically necessary items and services. However, the plan excludes coverage for the treatment of cleft palate.

(ii) *Conclusion.* In this *Example 7*, the exclusion of coverage for treatment of cleft palate is not a preexisting condition exclusion because the exclusion applies regardless of when the condition arose relative to the effective date of coverage. The plan provision, therefore, is not prohibited. (But see 45 CFR 147.150, which may require coverage of cleft palate as an essential health benefit for health insurance coverage in the individual or small group market, depending on the essential health benefits benchmark plan as defined in 45 CFR 156.20).

*Example 8.* (i) *Facts.* A group health plan provides coverage for treatment of cleft palate, but only if the individual being treated has been continuously covered under the plan from the date of birth.

(ii) *Conclusion.* In this *Example 8*, the exclusion of coverage for treatment of cleft palate for individuals who have not been covered under the plan from the date of birth operates to exclude benefits in relation to a condition based on the fact that the condition was present before the effective date of coverage. The plan provision, therefore, is prohibited.

(b) *General rules.—See* section 2704 of the Public Health Service Act, incorporated into section 9815 of the Code, and its implementing regulations for rules prohibiting the imposition of a preexisting condition exclusion. [Reg. §54.9801-3.]

☐ [*T.D. 9166, 12-29-2004. Amended by T.D. 9491, 6-22-2010, T.D. 9656, 2-20-2014 and T.D. 9744, 11-13-2015.*]

### [Reg. §54.9801-4]

**§54.9801-4. Rules relating to creditable coverage.**—(a) *General rules.*—(1) *Creditable coverage.*—For purposes of this section, except as provided in paragraph (a)(2) of this section, the term *creditable coverage* means coverage of an individual under any of the following:

(i) A group health plan as defined in §54.9831-1(a).

(ii) Health insurance coverage as defined in §54.9801-2 (whether or not the entity offering the coverage is subject to Chapter 100 of Subtitle K, and without regard to whether the coverage is offered in the group market, the individual market, or otherwise).

(iii) Part A or B of Title XVIII of the Social Security Act (Medicare).

(iv) Title XIX of the Social Security Act (Medicaid), other than coverage consisting solely of benefits under section 1928 of the Social Security Act (the program for distribution of pediatric vaccines).

(v) Title 10 U.S.C. Chapter 55 (medical and dental care for members and certain former members of the uniformed services, and for their dependents; for purposes of Title 10 U.S.C. Chapter 55, *uniformed services* means the armed forces and the Commissioned Corps of the National Oceanic and Atmospheric Administration and of the Public Health Service).

(vi) A medical care program of the Indian Health Service or of a tribal organization.

(vii) A state health benefits risk pool. For purposes of this section, a *state health benefits risk pool* means —

(A) An organization qualifying under section 501(c)(26);

(B) A qualified high risk pool described in section 2744(c)(2) of the PHS Act; or

(C) Any other arrangement sponsored by a state, the membership composition of which is specified by the state and which is established and maintained primarily to provide health coverage for individuals who are residents of such state and who, by reason of the existence or history of a medical condition —

(1) Are unable to acquire medical care coverage for such condition through insurance or from an HMO, or

(2) Are able to acquire such coverage only at a rate which is substantially in excess of the rate for such coverage through the membership organization.

(viii) A health plan offered under Title 5 U.S.C. Chapter 89 (the Federal Employees Health Benefits Program).

(ix) A public health plan. For purposes of this section, a *public health plan* means any plan established or maintained by a state, the U.S. government, a foreign country, or any political subdivision of a state, the U.S. government, or a foreign country that provides health coverage to individuals who are enrolled in the plan.

(x) A health benefit plan under section 5(e) of the Peace Corps Act (22 U.S.C. 2504(e)).

(xi) Title XXI of the Social Security Act (State Children's Health Insurance Program).

(2) *Excluded coverage.*—Creditable coverage does not include coverage of solely excepted benefits (described in §54.9831-1).

(b) *Counting creditable coverage rules superseded by prohibition on preexisting condition exclusion.*—See section 2704 of the Public Health Service Act, incorporated into section 9815 of the Code, and its implementing regulations for rules prohibiting the imposition of a preexisting condition exclusion. [Reg. §54.9801-4.]

☐ [*T.D. 9166, 12-29-2004. Amended by T.D. 9656, 2-20-2014.*]

### [Reg. §54.9801-5]

**§54.9801-5. Evidence of creditable coverage.**—(a) *In general.*— The rules for providing certificates of creditable coverage and demonstrating creditable coverage have been superseded by the prohibition on preexisting condition exclusions. *See* section 2704 of the Public Health Service Act, incorporated into section 9815 of the Code, and its implementing regulations for rules prohibiting the imposition of a preexisting condition exclusion.

(b) *Applicability.*—The provisions of this section apply beginning December 31, 2014. [Reg. §54.9801-5.]

☐ [*T.D. 9166, 12-29-2004. Amended by T.D. 9656, 2-20-2014.*]

### [Reg. §54.9801-6]

**§54.9801-6. Special enrollment periods.**—(a) *Special enrollment for certain individuals who lose coverage.*—(1) *In general.*—A group health plan is required to permit current employees and dependents (as defined in §54.9801-2) who are described in paragraph (a)(2) of this section to enroll for coverage under the terms of the plan if the conditions in paragraph (a)(3) of this section are satisfied. The special enrollment rights under this paragraph (a) apply without regard to the dates on which an individual would otherwise be able to enroll under the plan. (See section 701(f)(1) of ERISA and section 2701(f)(1) of the PHS Act, under which this obligation is also imposed on a health insurance issuer offering group health insurance coverage.)

(2) *Individuals eligible for special enrollment.*—(i) *When employee loses coverage.*—A current employee and any dependents (including the employee's spouse) each are eligible for special enrollment in any benefit package under the plan (subject to plan eligibility rules conditioning dependent enrollment on enrollment of the employee) if —

(A) The employee and the dependents are otherwise eligible to enroll in the benefit package;

(B) When coverage under the plan was previously offered, the employee had coverage under any group health plan or health insurance coverage; and

(C) The employee satisfies the conditions of paragraph (a)(3)(i), (ii), or (iii) of this section and, if applicable, paragraph (a)(3)(iv) of this section.

(ii) *When dependent loses coverage.*—(A) A dependent of a current employee (including the employee's spouse) and the employee each are eligible for special enrollment in any benefit package under the plan (subject to plan eligibility rules conditioning dependent enrollment on enrollment of the employee) if —

(1) The dependent and the employee are otherwise eligible to enroll in the benefit package;

(2) When coverage under the plan was previously offered, the dependent had coverage under any group health plan or health insurance coverage; and

(3) The dependent satisfies the conditions of paragraph (a)(3)(i), (ii), or (iii) of this section and, if applicable, paragraph (a)(3)(iv) of this section.

(B) However, the plan is not required to enroll any other dependent unless that dependent satisfies the criteria of this paragraph (a)(2)(ii), or the employee satisfies the criteria of paragraph (a)(2)(i) of this section.

(iii) *Examples.*—The rules of this paragraph (a)(2) are illustrated by the following examples:

*Example 1.* (i) *Facts.* Individual A works for Employer X. A, A's spouse, and A's dependent children are eligible but not enrolled for coverage under X's group health plan. A's spouse works for Employer Y and at the time coverage was offered under X's plan, A was enrolled in coverage under Y's plan. Then, A loses eligibility for coverage under Y's plan.

(ii) *Conclusion.* In this *Example 1*, because A satisfies the conditions for special enrollment under paragraph (a)(2)(i) of this section, A, A's spouse, and A's dependent children are eligible for special enrollment under X's plan.

*Example 2.* (i) *Facts.* Individual A and A's spouse are eligible but not enrolled for coverage under Group Health Plan P maintained by A's employer. When A was first presented with an opportunity to enroll A and A's spouse, they did not have other coverage. Later, A and A's spouse enroll in Group Health Plan Q maintained by the employer of A's spouse. During a subsequent open enrollment period in P, A and A's spouse did not enroll because of their coverage under Q. They then lose eligibility for coverage under Q.

(ii) *Conclusion.* In this *Example 2*, because A and A's spouse were covered under Q when they did not enroll in P during open enrollment, they satisfy the conditions for special enrollment under paragraphs (a)(2)(i) and (ii) of this section. Consequently, A and A's spouse are eligible for special enrollment under P.

*Example 3.* (i) *Facts.* Individual B works for Employer X. B and B's spouse are eligible but not enrolled for coverage under X's group health plan. B's spouse works for Employer Y and at the time coverage was offered under X's plan, B's spouse was enrolled in self-only coverage under Y's group health plan. Then, B's spouse loses eligibility for coverage under Y's plan.

(ii) *Conclusion.* In this *Example 3*, because B's spouse satisfies the conditions for special enrollment under paragraph (a)(2)(ii) of this section, both B and B's spouse are eligible for special enrollment under X's plan.

*Example 4.* (i) *Facts.* Individual A works for Employer X. X maintains a group health plan with two benefit packages — an HMO option and an indemnity option. Self-only and family coverage are available under both options. *A* enrolls for self-only coverage in the HMO option. *A*'s spouse works for Employer *Y* and was enrolled for self-only coverage under *Y*'s plan at the time coverage was offered under *X*'s plan. Then, *A*'s spouse loses coverage under *Y*'s plan. *A* requests special enrollment for *A* and *A*'s spouse under the plan's indemnity option.

(ii) *Conclusion*. In this *Example 4*, because *A*'s spouse satisfies the conditions for special enrollment under paragraph (a)(2)(ii) of this section, both *A* and *A*'s spouse can enroll in either benefit package under *X*'s plan. Therefore, if *A* requests enrollment in accordance with the requirements of this section, the plan must allow *A* and *A*'s spouse to enroll in the indemnity option.

(3) *Conditions for special enrollment.*—(i) *Loss of eligibility for coverage.*—In the case of an employee or dependent who has coverage that is not COBRA continuation coverage, the conditions of this paragraph (a)(3)(i) are satisfied at the time the coverage is terminated as a result of loss of eligibility (regardless of whether the individual is eligible for or elects COBRA continuation coverage). Loss of eligibility under this paragraph (a)(3)(i) does not include a loss due to the failure of the employee or dependent to pay premiums on a timely basis or termination of coverage for cause (such as making a fraudulent claim or an intentional misrepresentation of a material fact in connection with the plan). Loss of eligibility for coverage under this paragraph (a)(3)(i) includes (but is not limited to) —

(A) Loss of eligibility for coverage as a result of legal separation, divorce, cessation of dependent status (such as attaining the maximum age to be eligible as a dependent child under the plan), death of an employee, termination of employment, reduction in the number of hours of employment, and any loss of eligibility for coverage after a period that is measured by reference to any of the foregoing;

(B) In the case of coverage offered through an HMO, or other arrangement, in the individual market that does not provide benefits to individuals who no longer reside, live, or work in a service area, loss of coverage because an individual no longer resides, lives, or works in the service area (whether or not within the choice of the individual);

(C) In the case of coverage offered through an HMO, or other arrangement, in the group market that does not provide benefits to individuals who no longer reside, live, or work in a service area, loss of coverage because an individual no longer resides, lives, or works in the service area (whether or not within the choice of the individual), and no other benefit package is available to the individual; and

(D) A situation in which a plan no longer offers any benefits to the class of similarly situated individuals (as described in §54.9802-1(d)) that includes the individual.

(ii) *Termination of employer contributions.*—In the case of an employee or dependent who has coverage that is not COBRA continuation coverage, the conditions of this paragraph (a)(3)(ii) are satisfied at the time employer contributions towards the employee's or dependent's coverage terminate. Employer contributions include contributions by any current or former employer that was contributing to coverage for the employee or dependent.

(iii) *Exhaustion of COBRA continuation coverage.*—In the case of an employee or dependent who has coverage that is COBRA continuation coverage, the conditions of this paragraph (a)(3)(iii) are satisfied at the time the COBRA continuation coverage is exhausted. For purposes of this paragraph (a)(3)(iii), an individual who satisfies the conditions for special enrollment of paragraph (a)(3)(i) of this section, does not enroll, and instead elects and exhausts COBRA continuation coverage satisfies the conditions of this paragraph (a)(3)(iii). (*Exhaustion of COBRA continuation coverage* is defined in §54.9801-2.)

(iv) *Written statement.*—A plan may require an employee declining coverage (for the employee or any dependent of the employee) to state in writing whether the coverage is being declined due to other health coverage only if, at or before the time the employee declines coverage, the employee is provided with notice of the requirement to provide the statement (and the consequences of the employee's failure to provide the statement). If a plan requires such a statement, and an employee does not provide it, the plan is not required to provide special enrollment to the employee or any dependent of the employee under this paragraph (a)(3). A plan must treat an employee as having satisfied the plan requirement permitted under this paragraph (a)(3)(iv) if the employee provides a written statement that coverage was being declined because the employee or dependent had other coverage; a plan cannot require anything more for the employee to satisfy the plan's requirement to provide a written statement. (For example, the plan cannot require that the statement be notarized.)

(v) The rules of this paragraph (a)(3) are illustrated by the following examples:

*Example 1.* (i) *Facts.* Individual *D* enrolls in a group health plan maintained by Employer *Y*. At the time *D* enrolls, *Y* pays 70 percent of the cost of employee coverage and *D* pays the rest. *Y* announces that beginning January 1, *Y* will no longer make employer contributions towards the coverage. Employees may maintain coverage, however, if they pay the total cost of the coverage.

(ii) *Conclusion.* In this *Example 1*, employer contributions towards *D*'s coverage ceased on January 1 and the conditions of paragraph (a)(3)(ii) of this section are satisfied on this date (regardless of whether *D* elects to pay the total cost and continue coverage under *Y*'s plan).

*Example 2.* (i) *Facts.* A group health plan provides coverage through two options — Option 1 and Option 2. Employees can enroll in either option only within 30 days of hire or on January 1 of each year. Employee *A* is eligible for both options and enrolls in Option 1. Effective July 1 the plan terminates coverage under Option 1 and the plan does not create an immediate open enrollment opportunity into Option 2.

(ii) *Conclusion.* In this *Example 2*, *A* has experienced a loss of eligibility for coverage that satisfies paragraph (a)(3)(i) of this section, and has satisfied the other conditions for special enrollment under paragraph (a)(2)(i) of this section. Therefore, if *A* satisfies the other conditions of this paragraph (a), the plan must permit *A* to enroll in Option 2 as a special enrollee. (*A* may also be eligible to enroll in another group health plan, such as a plan maintained by the employer of *A*'s spouse, as a special enrollee.) The outcome would be the same if Option 1 was terminated by an issuer and the plan made no other coverage available to *A*.

*Example 3.* (i) *Facts.* Individual *C* is covered under a group health plan maintained by Employer *X*. While covered under *X*'s plan, *C* was eligible for but did not enroll in a plan maintained by Employer *Z*, the employer of *C*'s spouse. *C* terminates employment with *X* and loses eligibility for coverage under *X*'s plan. *C* has a special enrollment right to enroll in *Z*'s plan, but *C* instead elects COBRA continuation coverage under *X*'s plan. *C* exhausts COBRA continuation coverage under *X*'s plan and requests special enrollment in *Z*'s plan.

(ii) *Conclusion.* In this *Example 3*, *C* has satisfied the conditions for special enrollment under paragraph (a)(3)(iii) of this section, and has satisfied the other conditions for special enrollment under paragraph (a)(2)(i) of this section. The special enrollment right that *C* had into *Z*'s plan immediately after the loss of eligibility for coverage under *X*'s plan was an offer of coverage under *Z*'s plan. When *C* later exhausts COBRA coverage under *X*'s plan, *C* has a second special enrollment right in *Z*'s plan.

(4) *Applying for special enrollment and effective date of coverage.*—(i) A plan or issuer must allow an employee a period of at least 30 days after an event described in paragraph (a)(3) of this section to request enrollment (for the employee or the employee's dependent).

(ii) Coverage must begin no later than the first day of the first calendar month beginning after the date the plan or issuer receives the request for special enrollment.

(b) *Special enrollment with respect to certain dependent beneficiaries.*—(1) *In general.*—A group health plan that makes coverage available with respect to dependents is required to permit individuals described in paragraph (b)(2) of this section to be enrolled for coverage in a benefit package under the terms of the plan. Paragraph (b)(3) of this section describes the required special enrollment period and the date by which coverage must begin. The special enrollment rights under this paragraph (b) apply without regard to the dates on which an individual would otherwise be able to enroll under the plan. (See 29 CFR 2590.701-6(b) and 45 CFR 146.117(b), under which this obligation is also imposed on a health insurance issuer offering group health insurance coverage.)

(2) *Individuals eligible for special enrollment.*—An individual is described in this paragraph (b)(2) if the individual is otherwise eligible for coverage in a benefit package under the plan and if the individual is described in paragraph (b)(2)(i), (ii), (iii), (iv), (v), or (vi) of this section.

(i) *Current employee only.*—A current employee is described in this paragraph (b)(2)(i) if a person becomes a dependent of the individual through marriage, birth, adoption, or placement for adoption.

(ii) *Spouse of a participant only.*—An individual is described in this paragraph (b)(2)(ii) if either —

(A) The individual becomes the spouse of a participant; or

(B) The individual is a spouse of a participant and a child becomes a dependent of the participant through birth, adoption, or placement for adoption.

Reg. §54.9801-6(b)(2)(ii)(B)

(iii) *Current employee and spouse.*—A current employee and an individual who is or becomes a spouse of such an employee, are described in this paragraph (b)(2)(iii) if either —

(A) The employee and the spouse become married; or

(B) The employee and spouse are married and a child becomes a dependent of the employee through birth, adoption, or placement for adoption.

(iv) *Dependent of a participant only.*—An individual is described in this paragraph (b)(2)(iv) if the individual is a dependent (as defined in §54.9801-2) of a participant and the individual has become a dependent of the participant through marriage, birth, adoption, or placement for adoption.

(v) *Current employee and a new dependent.*—A current employee and an individual who is a dependent of the employee, are described in this paragraph (b)(2)(v) if the individual becomes a dependent of the employee through marriage, birth, adoption, or placement for adoption.

(vi) *Current employee, spouse, and a new dependent.*—A current employee, the employee's spouse, and the employee's dependent are described in this paragraph (b)(2)(vi) if the dependent becomes a dependent of the employee through marriage, birth, adoption, or placement for adoption.

(3) *Applying for special enrollment and effective date of coverage.*—(i) *Request.*—A plan must allow an individual a period of at least 30 days after the date of the marriage, birth, adoption, or placement for adoption (or, if dependent coverage is not generally made available at the time of the marriage, birth, adoption, or placement for adoption, a period of at least 30 days after the date the plan makes dependent coverage generally available) to request enrollment (for the individual or the individual's dependent).

(ii) *Reasonable procedures for special enrollment.*—[Reserved.]

(iii) *Date coverage must begin.*—(A) *Marriage.*—In the case of marriage, coverage must begin no later than the first day of the first calendar month beginning after the date the plan (or any issuer offering health insurance coverage under the plan) receives the request for special enrollment.

(B) *Birth, adoption, or placement for adoption.*—Coverage must begin in the case of a dependent's birth on the date of birth and in the case of a dependent's adoption or placement for adoption no later than the date of such adoption or placement for adoption (or, if dependent coverage is not made generally available at the time of the birth, adoption, or placement for adoption, the date the plan makes dependent coverage available).

(4) *Examples.*—The rules of this paragraph (b) are illustrated by the following examples:

*Example 1.* (i) *Facts.* An employer maintains a group health plan that offers all employees employee-only coverage, employee-plus-spouse coverage, or family coverage. Under the terms of the plan, any employee may elect to enroll when first hired (with coverage beginning on the date of hire) or during an annual open enrollment period held each December (with coverage beginning the following January 1). Employee *A* is hired on September 3. *A* is married to *B*, and they have no children. On March 15 in the following year a child *C* is born to *A* and *B*. Before that date, *A* and *B* have not been enrolled in the plan.

(ii) *Conclusion.* In this *Example 1*, the conditions for special enrollment of an employee with a spouse and new dependent under paragraph (b)(2)(vi) of this section are satisfied. If *A* satisfies the conditions of paragraph (b)(3) of this section for requesting enrollment timely, the plan will satisfy this paragraph (b) if it allows *A* to enroll either with employee-only coverage, with employee-plus-spouse coverage (for *A* and *B*), or with family coverage (for *A*, *B*, and *C*). The plan must allow whatever coverage is chosen to begin on March 15, the date of *C*'s birth.

*Example 2.* (i) *Facts.* Individual *D* works for Employer *X*. *X* maintains a group health plan with two benefit packages - an HMO option and an indemnity option. Self-only and family coverage are available under both options. *D* enrolls for self-only coverage in the HMO option. Then, a child, *E*, is placed for adoption with *D*. Within 30 days of the placement of *E* for adoption, *D* requests enrollment for *D* and *E* under the plan's indemnity option.

(ii) *Conclusion.* In this *Example 2*, *D* and *E* satisfy the conditions for special enrollment under paragraphs (b)(2)(v) and (b)(3) of this section. Therefore, the plan must allow *D* and *E* to enroll in the indemnity coverage, effective as of the date of the placement for adoption.

(c) *Notice of special enrollment.*—At or before the time an employee is initially offered the opportunity to enroll in a group health plan,

the plan must furnish the employee with a notice of special enrollment that complies with the requirements of this paragraph (c).

(1) *Description of special enrollment rights.*—The notice of special enrollment must include a description of special enrollment rights. The following model language may be used to satisfy this requirement:

If you are declining enrollment for yourself or your dependents (including your spouse) because of other health insurance or group health plan coverage, you may be able to enroll yourself and your dependents in this plan if you or your dependents lose eligibility for that other coverage (or if the employer stops contributing towards your or your dependents' other coverage). However, you must request enrollment within [insert "30 days" or any longer period that applies under the plan] after your or your dependents' other coverage ends (or after the employer stops contributing toward the other coverage).

In addition, if you have a new dependent as a result of marriage, birth, adoption, or placement for adoption, you may be able to enroll yourself and your dependents. However, you must request enrollment within [insert "30 days" or any longer period that applies under the plan] after the marriage, birth, adoption, or placement for adoption.

To request special enrollment or obtain more information, contact [insert the name, title, telephone number, and any additional contact information of the appropriate plan representative].

(2) *Additional information that may be required.*—The notice of special enrollment must also include, if applicable, the notice described in paragraph (a)(3)(iv) of this section (the notice required to be furnished to an individual declining coverage if the plan requires the reason for declining coverage to be in writing).

(d) *Treatment of special enrollees.*—(1) If an individual requests enrollment while the individual is entitled to special enrollment under either paragraph (a) or (b) of this section, the individual is a special enrollee, even if the request for enrollment coincides with a late enrollment opportunity under the plan. Therefore, the individual cannot be treated as a late enrollee.

(2) Special enrollees must be offered all the benefit packages available to similarly situated individuals who enroll when first eligible. For this purpose, any difference in benefits or cost-sharing requirements for different individuals constitutes a different benefit package. In addition, a special enrollee cannot be required to pay more for coverage than a similarly situated individual who enrolls in the same coverage when first eligible.

(3) The rules of this section are illustrated by the following example:

*Example.* (i) *Facts.* Employer *Y* maintains a group health plan that has an enrollment period for late enrollees every November 1 through November 30 with coverage effective the following January 1. On October 18, Individual *B* loses coverage under another group health plan and satisfies the requirements of paragraphs (a)(2), (3), and (4) of this section. *B* submits a completed application for coverage on November 2.

(ii) *Conclusion.* In this *Example*, *B* is a special enrollee. Therefore, even though *B*'s request for enrollment coincides with an open enrollment period, *B*'s coverage is required to be made effective no later than December 1 (rather than the plan's January 1 effective date for late enrollees).

[Reg. §54.9801-6.]

☐ [*T.D.* 9166, 12-29-2004. *Amended by T.D.* 9656, 2-20-2014.]

**[Reg. §54.9802-1]**

**§54.9802-1. Prohibiting discrimination against participants and beneficiaries based on a health factor.**—(a) *Health factors.*—(1) The term *health factor* means, in relation to an individual, any of the following health status-related factors:

(i) Health status;

(ii) Medical condition (including both physical and mental illnesses), as defined in §54.9801-2;

(iii) Claims experience;

(iv) Receipt of health care;

(v) Medical history;

(vi) Genetic information, as defined in §54.9802-3T.

(vii) Evidence of insurability; or

(viii) Disability.

(2) Evidence of insurability includes —

(i) Conditions arising out of acts of domestic violence; and

(ii) Participation in activities such as motorcycling, snowmobiling, all-terrain vehicle riding, horseback riding, skiing, and other similar activities.

(3) The decision whether health coverage is elected for an individual (including the time chosen to enroll, such as under special enrollment or late enrollment) is not, itself, within the scope of any health factor. (However, under §54.9801-6, a plan must treat special enrollees the same as similarly situated individuals who are enrolled when first eligible.)

(b) *Prohibited discrimination in rules for eligibility.*—(1) *In general.*— (i) A group health plan, and a health insurance issuer offering health insurance coverage in connection with a group health plan, may not establish any rule for eligibility (including continued eligibility) of any individual to enroll for benefits under the terms of the plan or group health insurance coverage that discriminates based on any health factor that relates to that individual or a dependent of that individual. This rule is subject to the provisions of paragraph (b)(2) of this section (explaining how this rule applies to benefits), paragraph (d) of this section (containing rules for establishing groups of similarly situated individuals), paragraph (e) of this section (relating to nonconfinement, actively-at-work, and other service requirements), paragraph (f) of this section (relating to wellness programs), and paragraph (g) of this section (permitting favorable treatment of individuals with adverse health factors).

(ii) For purposes of this section, rules for eligibility include, but are not limited to, rules relating to—

(A) Enrollment;

(B) The effective date of coverage;

(C) Waiting (or affiliation) periods;

(D) Late and special enrollment;

(E) Eligibility for benefit packages (including rules for individuals to change their selection among benefit packages);

(F) Benefits (including rules relating to covered benefits, benefit restrictions, and cost-sharing mechanisms such as coinsurance, copayments, and deductibles), as described in paragraphs (b)(2) and (3) of this section;

(G) Continued eligibility; and

(H) Terminating coverage (including disenrollment) of any individual under the plan.

(iii) The rules of this paragraph (b)(1) are illustrated by the following examples:

*Example 1.* (i) *Facts.* An employer sponsors a group health plan that is available to all employees who enroll within the first 30 days of their employment. However, employees who do not enroll within the first 30 days cannot enroll later unless they pass a physical examination.

(ii) *Conclusion.* In this *Example 1*, the requirement to pass a physical examination in order to enroll in the plan is a rule for eligibility that discriminates based on one or more health factors and thus violates this paragraph (b)(1).

*Example 2.* (i) *Facts.* Under an employer's group health plan, employees who enroll during the first 30 days of employment (and during special enrollment periods) may choose between two benefit packages: an indemnity option and an HMO option. However, employees who enroll during late enrollment are permitted to enroll only in the HMO option and only if they provide evidence of good health.

(ii) *Conclusion.* In this *Example 2*, the requirement to provide evidence of good health in order to be eligible for late enrollment in the HMO option is a rule for eligibility that discriminates based on one or more health factors and thus violates this paragraph (b)(1). However, if the plan did not require evidence of good health but limited late enrollees to the HMO option, the plan's rules for eligibility would not discriminate based on any health factor, and thus would not violate this paragraph (b)(1), because the time an individual chooses to enroll is not, itself, within the scope of any health factor.

*Example 3.* (i) *Facts.* Under an employer's group health plan, all employees generally may enroll within the first 30 days of employment. However, individuals who participate in certain recreational activities, including motorcycling, are excluded from coverage.

(ii) *Conclusion.* In this *Example 3*, excluding from the plan individuals who participate in recreational activities, such as motorcycling, is a rule for eligibility that discriminates based on one more health factors and thus violates this paragraph (b)(1).

*Example 4.* (i) *Facts.* A group health plan applies for a group health policy offered by an issuer. As part of the application, the issuer receives health information about individuals to be covered under the plan. Individual *A* is an employee of the employer maintaining the plan. *A* and *A*'s dependents have a history of high health claims. Based on the information about *A* and *A*'s dependents, the issuer excludes *A* and *A*'s dependents from the group policy it offers to the employer.

(ii) *Conclusion.* See *Example 4* in 29 CFR 2590.702(b)(1) and 45 CFR 146.121(b)(1) for a conclusion that the exclusion by the issuer of *A* and *A*'s dependents from coverage is a rule for eligibility that discriminates based on one or more health factors and violates rules under 29 CFR 2590.702(b)(1) and 45 CFR 146.121(b)(1) similar to the rules under this paragraph (b)(1). (If the employer is a small employer under 45 CFR 144.103 (generally, an employer with 50 or fewer employees), the issuer also may violate 45 CFR 146.150, which requires issuers to offer all the policies they sell in the small group market on a guaranteed available basis to all small employers and to accept every eligible individual in every small employer group.) If the plan provides coverage through this policy and does not provide equivalent coverage for *A* and *A*'s dependents through other means, the plan violates this paragraph (b)(1).

(2) *Application to benefits.*—(i) *General rule.*—(A) Under this section, a group health plan is not required to provide coverage for any particular benefit to any group of similarly situated individuals.

(B) However, benefits provided under a plan must be uniformly available to all similarly situated individuals (as described in paragraph (d) of this section). Likewise, any restriction on a benefit or benefits must apply uniformly to all similarly situated individuals and must not be directed at individual participants or beneficiaries based on any health factor of the participants or beneficiaries (determined based on all the relevant facts and circumstances). Thus, for example, a plan may limit or exclude benefits in relation to a specific disease or condition, limit or exclude benefits for certain types of treatments or drugs, or limit or exclude benefits based on a determination of whether the benefits are experimental or not medically necessary, but only if the benefit limitation or exclusion applies uniformly to all similarly situated individuals and is not directed at individual participants or beneficiaries based on any health factor of the participants or beneficiaries. In addition, a plan or issuer may require the satisfaction of a deductible, copayment, coinsurance, or other cost-sharing requirement in order to obtain a benefit if the limit or cost-sharing requirement applies uniformly to all similarly situated individuals and is not directed at individual participants or beneficiaries based on any health factor of the participants or beneficiaries. In the case of a cost-sharing requirement, see also paragraph (b)(2)(ii) of this section, which permits variances in the application of a cost-sharing mechanism made available under a wellness program. (Whether any plan provision or practice with respect to benefits complies with this paragraph (b)(2)(i) does not affect whether the provision or practice is permitted under ERISA, the Affordable Care Act (including the requirements related to essential health benefits), the Americans with Disabilities Act, or any other law, whether State or Federal.)

(C) For purposes of this paragraph (b)(2)(i), a plan amendment applicable to all individuals in one or more groups of similarly situated individuals under the plan and made effective no earlier than the first day of the first plan year after the amendment is adopted is not considered to be directed at any individual participants or beneficiaries.

(D) The rules of this paragraph (b)(2)(i) are illustrated by the following examples:

*Example 1.* (i) *Facts.* A group health plan applies a $10,000 annual limit on a specific covered benefit that is not an essential health benefit to each participant or beneficiary covered under the plan. The limit is not directed at individual participants or beneficiaries.

(ii) *Conclusion.* In this *Example 1*, the limit does not violate this paragraph (b)(2)(i) because coverage of the specific, non-essential health benefit up to $10,000 is available uniformly to each participant and beneficiary under the plan and because the limit is applied uniformly to all participants and beneficiaries and is not directed at individual participants or beneficiaries.

*Example 2.* (i) *Facts.* A group health plan has a $500 deductible on all benefits for participants covered under the plan. Participant *B* files a claim for the treatment of AIDS. At the next corporate board meeting of the plan sponsor, the claim is discussed. Shortly thereafter, the plan is modified to impose a $2,000 deductible on benefits for the treatment of AIDS, effective before the beginning of the next plan year.

(ii) *Conclusion.* The facts of this *Example 2* strongly suggest that the plan modification is directed at *B* based on *B*'s claim. Absent outweighing evidence to the contrary, the plan violates this paragraph (b)(2)(i).

*Example 3.* (i) A group health plan applies for a group health policy offered by an issuer. Individual *C* is covered under the plan and has an adverse health condition. As part of the application, the issuer receives health information about the individuals to be covered, including information about *C*'s adverse health condition. The policy form offered by the issuer generally provides benefits for the adverse health condition that *C* has, but in this case the issuer offers the plan a policy modified by a rider that excludes benefits for *C* for that condition. The exclusionary rider is made effective the first day of the next plan year.

(ii) *Conclusion.* See *Example 3* in 29 CFR 2590.702(b)(2)(i) and 45 CFR 146.121(b)(2)(i) for a conclusion that the issuer violates rules under 29 CFR 2590.702(b)(2)(i) and 45 CFR 146.121(b)(2)(i) similar to the rules under this paragraph (b)(2)(i) because benefits for C's condition are available to other individuals in the group of similarly situated individuals that includes C but are not available to C. Thus, the benefits are not uniformly available to all similarly situated individuals. Even though the exclusionary rider is made effective the first day of the next plan year, because the rider does not apply to all similarly situated individuals, the issuer violates the rules under 29 CFR 2590.702(b)(2)(i) and 45 CFR 146.121(b)(2)(i). If the plan provides coverage through this policy and does not provide equivalent coverage for C through other means, the plan violates this paragraph (b)(2)(i).

*Example 4.* (i) *Facts.* A group health plan has a $2,000 lifetime limit for the treatment of temporomandibular joint syndrome (TMJ). The limit is applied uniformly to all similarly situated individuals and is not directed at individual participants or beneficiaries.

(ii) *Conclusion.* In this *Example 4*, the limit does not violate this paragraph (b)(2)(i) because $2,000 of benefits for the treatment of TMJ are available uniformly to all similarly situated individuals and a plan may limit benefits covered in relation to a specific disease or condition if the limit applies uniformly to all similarly situated individuals and is not directed at individual participants or beneficiaries. (However, applying a lifetime limit on TMJ may violate PHS Act section 2711 and its implementing regulations, if TMJ coverage is an essential health benefit, depending on the essential health benefits benchmark plan as defined in 45 CFR 156.20. This example does not address whether the plan provision is permissible under any other applicable law, including PHS Act section 2711 or the Americans with Disabilities Act.)

*Example 5.* (i) *Facts.* A group health plan applies a $2 million lifetime limit on all benefits. However, the $2 million lifetime limit is reduced to $10,000 for any participant or beneficiary covered under the plan who has a congenital heart defect.

(ii) *Conclusion.* In this *Example 5*, the lower lifetime limit for participants and beneficiaries with a congenital heart defect violates this paragraph (b)(2)(i) because benefits under the plan are not uniformly available to all similarly situated individuals and the plan's lifetime limit on benefits does not apply uniformly to all similarly situated individuals. Additionally, this plan provision is prohibited under PHS Act section 2711 and its implementing regulations because it imposes a lifetime limit on essential health benefits.

*Example 6.* (i) *Facts.* A group health plan limits benefits for prescription drugs to those listed on a drug formulary. The limit is applied uniformly to all similarly situated individuals and is not directed at individual participants or beneficiaries.

(ii) *Conclusion.* In this *Example 6*, the exclusion from coverage of drugs not listed on the drug formulary does not violate this paragraph (b)(2)(i) because benefits for prescription drugs listed on the formulary are uniformly available to all similarly situated individuals and because the exclusion of drugs not listed on the formulary applies uniformly to all similarly situated individuals and is not directed at individual participants or beneficiaries.

*Example 7.* (i) *Facts.* Under a group health plan, doctor visits are generally subject to a $250 annual deductible and 20 percent coinsurance requirement. However, prenatal doctor visits are not subject to any deductible or coinsurance requirement. These rules are applied uniformly to all similarly situated individuals and are not directed at individual participants or beneficiaries.

(ii) *Conclusion.* In this *Example 7*, imposing different deductible and coinsurance requirements for prenatal doctor visits and other visits does not violate this paragraph (b)(2)(i) because a plan may establish different deductibles or coinsurance requirements for different services if the deductible or coinsurance requirement is applied uniformly to all similarly situated individuals and is not directed at individual participants or beneficiaries.

(ii) *Exception for wellness programs.*—A group health plan may vary benefits, including cost-sharing mechanisms (such as a deductible, copayment, or coinsurance), based on whether an individual has met the standards of a wellness program that satisfies the requirements of paragraph (f) of this section.

(iii) *Specific rule relating to source-of-injury exclusions.*—(A) If a group health plan generally provides benefits for a type of injury, the plan may not deny benefits otherwise provided for treatment of the injury if the injury results from an act of domestic violence or a medical condition (including both physical and mental health conditions). This rule applies in the case of an injury resulting from a medical condition even if the condition is not diagnosed before the injury.

(B) The rules of this paragraph (b)(2)(iii) are illustrated by the following examples:

*Example 1.* (i) *Facts.* A group health plan generally provides medical/surgical benefits, including benefits for hospital stays, that are medically necessary. However, the plan excludes benefits for self-inflicted injuries or injuries sustained in connection with attempted suicide. Because of depression, Individual D attempts suicide. As a result, D sustains injuries and is hospitalized for treatment of the injuries. Under the exclusion, the plan denies D benefits for treatment of the injuries.

(ii) *Conclusion.* In this *Example 1*, the suicide attempt is the result of a medical condition (depression). Accordingly, the denial of benefits for the treatments of D's injuries violates the requirements of this paragraph (b)(2)(iii) because the plan provision excludes benefits for treatment of an injury resulting from a medical condition.

*Example 2.* (i) *Facts.* A group health plan provides benefits for head injuries generally. The plan also has a general exclusion for any injury sustained while participating in any of a number of recreational activities, including bungee jumping. However, this exclusion does not apply to any injury that results from a medical condition (nor from domestic violence). Participant E sustains a head injury while bungee jumping. The injury did not result from a medical condition (nor from domestic violence). Accordingly, the plan denies benefits for E's head injury.

(ii) *Conclusion.* In this *Example 2*, the plan provision that denies benefits based on the source of an injury does not restrict benefits based on an act of domestic violence or any medical condition. Therefore, the provision is permissible under this paragraph (b)(2)(iii) and does not violate this section. (However, if the plan did not allow E to enroll in the plan (or applied different rules for eligibility to E) because E frequently participates in bungee jumping, the plan would violate paragraph (b)(1) of this section.)

(c) *Prohibited discrimination in premiums or contributions.*—(1) *In general.*—(i) A group health plan may not require an individual, as a condition of enrollment or continued enrollment under the plan, to pay a premium or contribution that is greater than the premium or contribution for a similarly situated individual (described in paragraph (d) of this section) enrolled in the plan based on any health factor that relates to the individual or a dependent of the individual.

(ii) Discounts, rebates, payments in kind, and any other premium differential mechanisms are taken into account in determining an individual's premium or contribution rate. (For rules relating to cost-sharing mechanisms, see paragraph (b)(2) of this section (addressing benefits).)

(2) *Rules relating to premium rates.*—(i) *Group rating based on health factors not restricted under this section.*—Nothing in this section restricts the aggregate amount that an employer may be charged for coverage under a group health plan. But see §54.9802-3T(b), which prohibits adjustments in group premium or contribution rates based on genetic information.

(ii) *List billing based on a health factor prohibited.*—However, a group health plan may not quote or charge an employer (or an individual) a different premium for an individual in a group of similarly situated individuals based on a health factor. (But see paragraph (g) of this section permitting favorable treatment of individuals with adverse health factors.)

(iii) *Examples.*—The rules of this paragraph (c)(2) are illustrated by the following examples:

*Example 1.* (i) *Facts.* An employer sponsors a group health plan and purchases coverage from a health insurance issuer. In order to determine the premium rate for the upcoming plan year, the issuer reviews the claims experience of individuals covered under the plan. The issuer finds that Individual F had significantly higher claims experience than similarly situated individuals in the plan. The issuer quotes the plan a higher per-participant rate because of F's claims experience.

(ii) *Conclusion.* See *Example 1* in 29 CFR 2590.702(c)(2) and 45 CFR 146.121(c)(2) for a conclusion that the issuer does not violate the provisions of 29 CFR 2590.702(c)(2) and 45 CFR 146.121(c)(2) similar to the provisions of this paragraph (c)(2) because the issuer blends the rate so that the employer is not quoted a higher rate for F than for a similarly situated individual based on F's claims experience. (However, those examples conclude that if the issuer used genetic information in computing the group rate, it would violate 29 CFR 2590.702-1(b) or 45 CFR 146.122(b).)

*Example 2.* (i) *Facts.* Same facts as *Example 1*, except that the issuer quotes the employer a higher premium rate for F, because of F's claims experience, than for a similarly situated individual.

(ii) *Conclusion.* See *Example 2* in 29 CFR 2590.702(c)(2) and 45 CFR 146.121(c)(2) for a conclusion that the issuer violates provisions of 29 CFR 2590.702(c)(2) and 45 CFR 146.121(c)(2) similar to the provisions of this paragraph (c)(2). Moreover, even if the plan purchased the policy based on the quote but did not require a higher participant contribution for F than for a similarly situated individual, see *Example 2* in 29 CFR 2590.702(c)(2) and 45 CFR 146.121(c)(2) for a conclusion that the issuer would still violate 29 CFR 2590.702(c)(2) and 45 CFR 146.121(c)(2) (but in such a case the plan would not violate this paragraph (c)(2)).

(3) *Exception for wellness programs.*—Notwithstanding paragraphs (c)(1) and (2) of this section, a plan may vary the amount of premium or contribution it requires similarly situated individuals to pay based on whether an individual has met the standards of a wellness program that satisfies the requirements of paragraph (f) of this section.

(d) *Similarly situated individuals.*—The requirements of this section apply only within a group of individuals who are treated as similarly situated individuals. A plan may treat participants as a group of similarly situated individuals separate from beneficiaries. In addition, participants may be treated as two or more distinct groups of similarly situated individuals and beneficiaries may be treated as two or more distinct groups of similarly situated individuals in accordance with the rules of this paragraph (d). Moreover, if individuals have a choice of two or more benefit packages, individuals choosing one benefit package may be treated as one or more groups of similarly situated individuals distinct from individuals choosing another benefit package.

(1) *Participants.*—Subject to paragraph (d)(3) of this section, a plan may treat participants as two or more distinct groups of similarly situated individuals if the distinction between or among the groups of participants is based on a bona fide employment-based classification consistent with the employer's usual business practice. Whether an employment-based classification is bona fide is determined on the basis of all the relevant facts and circumstances. Relevant facts and circumstances include whether the employer uses the classification for purposes independent of qualification for health coverage (for example, determining eligibility for other employee benefits or determining other terms of employment). Subject to paragraph (d)(3) of this section, examples of classifications that, based on all the relevant facts and circumstances, may be bona fide include full-time versus part-time status, different geographic location, membership in a collective bargaining unit, date of hire, length of service, current employee versus former employee status, and different occupations. However, a classification based on any health factor is not a bona fide employment-based classification, unless the requirements of paragraph (g) of this section are satisfied (permitting favorable treatment of individuals with adverse health factors).

(2) *Beneficiaries.*—(i) Subject to paragraph (d)(3) of this section, a plan may treat beneficiaries as two or more distinct groups of similarly situated individuals if the distinction between or among the groups of beneficiaries is based on any of the following factors:

(A) A bona fide employment-based classification of the participant through whom the beneficiary is receiving coverage;

(B) Relationship to the participant (for example, as a spouse or as a dependent child);

(C) Marital status;

(D) With respect to children of a participant, age or student status; or

(E) Any other factor if the factor is not a health factor.

(ii) Paragraph (d)(2)(i) of this section does not prevent more favorable treatment of individuals with adverse health factors in accordance with paragraph (g) of this section.

(3) *Discrimination directed at individuals.*—Notwithstanding paragraphs (d)(1) and (2) of this section, if the creation or modification of an employment or coverage classification is directed at individual participants or beneficiaries based on any health factor of the participants or beneficiaries, the classification is not permitted under this paragraph (d), unless it is permitted under paragraph (g) of this section (permitting favorable treatment of individuals with adverse health factors). Thus, if an employer modified an employment-based classification to single out, based on a health factor, individual participants and beneficiaries and deny them health coverage, the new classification would not be permitted under this section.

(4) *Examples.*—The rules of this paragraph (d) are illustrated by the following examples:

*Example 1.* (i) *Facts.* An employer sponsors a group health plan for full-time employees only. Under the plan (consistent with the employer's usual business practice), employees who normally work at least 30 hours per week are considered to be working full-time. Other employees are considered to be working part-time. There is no evidence to suggest that the classification is directed at individual participants or beneficiaries.

(ii) *Conclusion.* In this *Example 1*, treating the full-time and part-time employees as two separate groups of similarly situated individuals is permitted under this paragraph (d) because the classification

is bona fide and is not directed at individual participants or beneficiaries.

*Example 2.* (i) *Facts.* Under a group health plan, coverage is made available to employees, their spouses, and their children. However, coverage is made available to a child only if the child is under age 26 (or under age 29 if the child is continuously enrolled full-time in an institution of higher learning (full-time students)). There is no evidence to suggest that these classifications are directed at individual participants or beneficiaries.

(ii) *Conclusion.* In this *Example 2*, treating spouses and children differently by imposing an age limitation on children, but not on spouses, is permitted under this paragraph (d). Specifically, the distinction between spouses and children is permitted under paragraph (d)(2) of this section and is not prohibited under paragraph (d)(3) of this section because it is not directed at individual participants or beneficiaries. It is also permissible to treat children who are under age 26 (or full-time students under age 29) as a group of similarly situated individuals separate from those who are age 26 or older (or age 29 or older if they are not full-time students) because the classification is permitted under paragraph (d)(2) of this section and is not directed at individual participants or beneficiaries.

*Example 3.* (i) *Facts.* A university sponsors a group health plan that provides one health benefit package to faculty and another health benefit package to other staff. Faculty and staff are treated differently with respect to other employee benefits such as retirement benefits and leaves of absence. There is no evidence to suggest that the distinction is directed at individual participants or beneficiaries.

(ii) *Conclusion.* In this *Example 3*, the classification is permitted under this paragraph (d) because there is a distinction based on a bona fide employment-based classification consistent with the employer's usual business practice and the distinction is not directed at individual participants and beneficiaries.

*Example 4.* (i) *Facts.* An employer sponsors a group health plan that is available to all current employees. Former employees may also be eligible, but only if they complete a specified number of years of service, are enrolled under the plan at the time of termination of employment, and are continuously enrolled from that date. There is no evidence to suggest that these distinctions are directed at individual participants or beneficiaries.

(ii) *Conclusion.* In this *Example 4*, imposing additional eligibility requirements on former employees is permitted because a classification that distinguishes between current and former employees is a bona fide employment-based classification that is permitted under this paragraph (d), provided that it is not directed at individual participants or beneficiaries. In addition, it is permissible to distinguish between former employees who satisfy the service requirement and those who do not, provided that the distinction is not directed at individual participants or beneficiaries. (However, former employees who do not satisfy the eligibility criteria may, nonetheless, be eligible for continued coverage pursuant to a COBRA continuation provision or similar State law.)

*Example 5.* (i) *Facts.* An employer sponsors a group health plan that provides the same benefit package to all seven employees of the employer. Six of the seven employees have the same job title and responsibilities, but Employee G has a different job title and different responsibilities. After G files an expensive claim for benefits under the plan, coverage under the plan is modified so that employees with G's job title receive a different benefit package that includes a higher deductible than in the benefit package made available to the other six employees.

(ii) *Conclusion.* Under the facts of this *Example 5*, changing the coverage classification for G based on the existing employment classification for G is not permitted under this paragraph (d) because the creation of the new coverage classification for G is directed at G based on one or more health factors.

(e) *Nonconfinement and actively-at-work provisions.*—(1) *Nonconfinement provisions.*—(i) *General rule.*—Under the rules of paragraphs (b) and (c) of this section, a plan may not establish a rule for eligibility (as described in paragraph (b)(1)(ii) of this section) or set any individual's premium or contribution rate based on whether an individual is confined to a hospital or other health care institution. In addition, under the rules of paragraphs (b) and (c) of this section, a plan may not establish a rule for eligibility or set any individual's premium or contribution rate based on an individual's ability to engage in normal life activities, except to the extent permitted under paragraphs (e)(2)(ii) and (3) of this section (permitting plans, under certain circumstances, to distinguish among employees based on the performance of services).

(ii) *Examples.*—The rules of this paragraph (e)(1) are illustrated by the following examples:

*Example 1.* (i) *Facts.* Under a group health plan, coverage for employees and their dependents generally becomes effective on the first day of employment. However, coverage for a dependent who is confined to a hospital or other health care institution does not become effective until the confinement ends.

(ii) *Conclusion.* In this *Example 1*, the plan violates this paragraph (e)(1) because the plan delays the effective date of coverage for dependents based on confinement to a hospital or other health care institution.

*Example 2.* (i) *Facts.* In previous years, a group health plan has provided coverage through a group health insurance policy offered by Issuer *M*. However, for the current year, the plan provides coverage through a group health insurance policy offered by Issuer *N*. Under Issuer *N*'s policy, items and services provided in connection with the confinement of a dependent to a hospital or other health care institution are not covered if the confinement is covered under an extension of benefits clause from a previous health insurance issuer.

(ii) *Conclusion.* See *Example 2* in 29 CFR 2590.702(e)(1) and 45 CFR 146.121(e)(1) for a conclusion that Issuer *N* violates provisions of 29 CFR 2590.702(e)(1) and 45 CFR 146.121(e)(1) similar to the provisions of this paragraph (e)(1) because the group health insurance coverage restricts benefits based on whether a dependent is confined to a hospital or other health care institution that is covered under an extension of benefits from a previous issuer. See *Example 2* in 29 CFR 2590.702(e)(1) and 45 CFR 146.121(e)(1) for the additional conclusions that under State law Issuer *M* may also be responsible for providing benefits to such a dependent; and that in a case in which Issuer *N* has an obligation under 29 CFR 2590.702(e)(1) or 45 CFR 146.121(e)(1) to provide benefits and Issuer *M* has an obligation under State law to provide benefits, any State laws designed to prevent more than 100% reimbursement, such as State coordination-of-benefits laws, continue to apply.

(2) *Actively-at-work and continuous service provisions.*—(i) *General rule.*—(A) Under the rules of paragraphs (b) and (c) of this section and subject to the exception for the first day of work described in paragraph (e)(2)(ii) of this section, a plan may not establish a rule for eligibility (as described in paragraph (b)(1)(ii) of this section) or set any individual's premium or contribution rate based on whether an individual is actively at work (including whether an individual is continuously employed), unless absence from work due to any health factor (such as being absent from work on sick leave) is treated, for purposes of the plan, as being actively at work.

(B) The rules of this paragraph (e)(2)(i) are illustrated by the following examples:

*Example 1.* (i) *Facts.* Under a group health plan, an employee generally becomes eligible to enroll 30 days after the first day of employment. However, if the employee is not actively at work on the first day after the end of the 30-day period, then eligibility for enrollment is delayed until the first day the employee is actively at work.

(ii) *Conclusion.* In this *Example 1*, the plan violates this paragraph (e)(2) (and thus also violates paragraph (b) of this section). However, the plan would not violate paragraph (e)(2) or (b) of this section if, under the plan, an absence due to any health factor is considered being actively at work.

*Example 2.* (i) *Facts.* Under a group health plan, coverage for an employee becomes effective after 90 days of continuous service; that is, if an employee is absent from work (for any reason) before completing 90 days of service, the beginning of the 90-day period is measured from the day the employee returns to work (without any credit for service before the absence).

(ii) *Conclusion.* In this *Example 2*, the plan violates this paragraph (e)(2) (and thus also paragraph (b) of this section) because the 90-day continuous service requirement is a rule for eligibility based on whether an individual is actively at work. However, the plan would not violate this paragraph (e)(2) or paragraph (b) of this section if, under the plan, an absence due to any health factor is not considered an absence for purposes of measuring 90 days of continuous service. (In addition, any eligibility provision that is time-based must comply with the requirements of PHS Act section 2708 and its implementing regulations.)

(ii) *Exception for the first day of work.*—(A) Notwithstanding the general rule in paragraph (e)(2)(i) of this section, a plan may establish a rule for eligibility that requires an individual to begin work for the employer sponsoring the plan (or, in the case of a multiemployer plan, to begin a job in covered employment) before coverage becomes effective, provided that such a rule for eligibility applies regardless of the reason for the absence.

(B) The rules of this paragraph (e)(2)(ii) are illustrated by the following examples:

*Example 1.* (i) *Facts.* Under the eligibility provision of a group health plan, coverage for new employees becomes effective on the first day that the employee reports to work. Individual *H* is scheduled to begin work on August 3. However, *H* is unable to begin

work on that day because of illness. *H* begins working on August 4, and *H*'s coverage is effective on August 4.

(ii) *Conclusion.* In this *Example 1*, the plan provision does not violate this section. However, if coverage for individuals who do not report to work on the first day they were scheduled to work for a reason unrelated to a health factor (such as vacation or bereavement) becomes effective on the first day they were scheduled to work, then the plan would violate this section.

*Example 2.* (i) *Facts.* Under a group health plan, coverage for new employees becomes effective on the first day of the month following the employee's first day of work, regardless of whether the employee is actively at work on the first day of the month. Individual *J* is scheduled to begin work on March 24. However, *J* is unable to begin work on March 24 because of illness. *J* begins working on April 7 and *J*'s coverage is effective May 1.

(ii) *Conclusion.* In this *Example 2*, the plan provision does not violate this section. However, as in *Example 1*, if coverage for individuals absent from work for reasons unrelated to a health factor became effective despite their absence, then the plan would violate this section.

(3) *Relationship to plan provisions defining similarly situated individuals.*—(i) Notwithstanding the rules of paragraphs (e)(1) and (2) of this section, a plan may establish rules for eligibility or set any individual's premium or contribution rate in accordance with the rules relating to similarly situated individuals in paragraph (d) of this section. Accordingly, a plan may distinguish in rules for eligibility under the plan between full-time and part-time employees, between permanent and temporary or seasonal employees, between current and former employees, and between employees currently performing services and employees no longer performing services for the employer, subject to paragraph (d) of this section. However, other Federal or State laws (including the COBRA continuation provisions and the Family and Medical Leave Act of 1993) may require an employee or the employee's dependents to be offered coverage and set limits on the premium or contribution rate even though the employee is not performing services.

(ii) The rules of this paragraph (e)(3) are illustrated by the following examples:

*Example 1.* (i) *Facts.* Under a group health plan, employees are eligible for coverage if they perform services for the employer for 30 or more hours per week or if they are on paid leave (such as vacation, sick, or bereavement leave). Employees on unpaid leave are treated as a separate group of similarly situated individuals in accordance with the rules of paragraph (d) of this section.

(ii) *Conclusion.* In this *Example 1*, the plan provisions do not violate this section. However, if the plan treated individuals performing services for the employer for 30 or more hours per week, individuals on vacation leave, and individuals on bereavement leave as a group of similarly situated individuals separate from individuals on sick leave, the plan would violate this paragraph (e) (and thus also would violate paragraph (b) of this section) because groups of similarly situated individuals cannot be established based on a health factor (including the taking of sick leave) under paragraph (d) of this section.

*Example 2.* (i) *Facts.* To be eligible for coverage under a bona fide collectively bargained group health plan in the current calendar quarter, the plan requires an individual to have worked 250 hours in covered employment during the three-month period that ends one month before the beginning of the current calendar quarter. The distinction between employees working at least 250 hours and those working less than 250 hours in the earlier three-month period is not directed at individual participants or beneficiaries based on any health factor of the participants or beneficiaries.

(ii) *Conclusion.* In this *Example 2*, the plan provision does not violate this section because, under the rules for similarly situated individuals allowing full-time employees to be treated differently than part-time employees, employees who work at least 250 hours in a three-month period can be treated differently than employees who fail to work 250 hours in that period. The result would be the same if the plan permitted individuals to apply excess hours from previous periods to satisfy the requirement for the current quarter.

*Example 3.* (i) *Facts.* Under a group health plan, coverage of an employee is terminated when the individual's employment is terminated, in accordance with the rules of paragraph (d) of this section. Employee *B* has been covered under the plan. *B* experiences a disabling illness that prevents *B* from working. *B* takes a leave of absence under the Family and Medical Leave Act of 1993. At the end of such leave, *B* terminates employment and consequently loses coverage under the plan. (This termination of coverage is without regard to whatever rights the employee (or members of the employee's family) may have for COBRA continuation coverage.)

(ii) *Conclusion.* In this *Example 3*, the plan provision terminating *B*'s coverage upon *B*'s termination of employment does not violate this section.

*Example 4.* (i) *Facts.* Under a group health plan, coverage of an employee is terminated when the employee ceases to perform services for the employer sponsoring the plan, in accordance with the rules of paragraph (d) of this section. Employee *C* is laid off for three months. When the layoff begins, *C*'s coverage under the plan is terminated. (This termination of coverage is without regard to whatever rights the employee (or members of the employee's family) may have for COBRA continuation coverage.)

(ii) *Conclusion.* In this *Example 4*, the plan provision terminating *C*'s coverage upon the cessation of *C*'s performance of services does not violate this section.

(f) *Nondiscriminatory wellness programs - in general.*—A wellness program is a program of health promotion or disease prevention. Paragraphs (b)(2)(ii) and (c)(3) of this section provide exceptions to the general prohibitions against discrimination based on a health factor for plan provisions that vary benefits (including cost-sharing mechanisms) or the premium or contribution for similarly situated individuals in connection with a wellness program that satisfies the requirements of this paragraph (f).

(1) *Definitions.*—The definitions in this paragraph (f)(1) govern in applying the provisions of this paragraph (f).

(i) *Reward.*—Except where expressly provided otherwise, references in this section to an individual obtaining a reward include both obtaining a reward (such as a discount or rebate of a premium or contribution, a waiver of all or part of a cost-sharing mechanism, an additional benefit, or any financial or other incentive) and avoiding a penalty (such as the absence of a premium surcharge or other financial or nonfinancial disincentive). References in this section to a plan providing a reward include both providing a reward (such as a discount or rebate of a premium or contribution, a waiver of all or part of a cost-sharing mechanism, an additional benefit, or any financial or other incentive) and imposing a penalty (such as a surcharge or other financial or nonfinancial disincentive).

(ii) *Participatory wellness programs.*—If none of the conditions for obtaining a reward under a wellness program is based on an individual satisfying a standard that is related to a health factor (or if a wellness program does not provide a reward), the wellness program is a participatory wellness program. Examples of participatory wellness programs are:

(A) A program that reimburses employees for all or part of the cost for membership in a fitness center.

(B) A diagnostic testing program that provides a reward for participation in that program and does not base any part of the reward on outcomes.

(C) A program that encourages preventive care through the waiver of the copayment or deductible requirement under a group health plan for the costs of, for example, prenatal care or well-baby visits. (Note that, with respect to non-grandfathered plans, §54.9815-2713T requires benefits for certain preventive health services without the imposition of cost sharing.)

(D) A program that reimburses employees for the costs of participating, or that otherwise provides a reward for participating, in a smoking cessation program without regard to whether the employee quits smoking.

(E) A program that provides a reward to employees for attending a monthly, no-cost health education seminar.

(F) A program that provides a reward to employees who complete a health risk assessment regarding current health status, without any further action (educational or otherwise) required by the employee with regard to the health issues identified as part of the assessment. (*See also* §54.9802-3T for rules prohibiting collection of genetic information.)

(iii) *Health-contingent wellness programs.*—A health-contingent wellness program is a program that requires an individual to satisfy a standard related to a health factor to obtain a reward (or requires an individual to undertake more than a similarly situated individual based on a health factor in order to obtain the same reward). A health-contingent wellness program may be an activity-only wellness program or an outcome-based wellness program.

(iv) *Activity-only wellness programs.*—An activity-only wellness program is a type of health-contingent wellness program that requires an individual to perform or complete an activity related to a health factor in order to obtain a reward but does not require the individual to attain or maintain a specific health outcome. Examples include walking, diet, or exercise programs, which some individuals may be unable to participate in or complete (or have difficulty participating in or completing) due to a health factor, such as severe asthma, pregnancy, or a recent surgery. *See* paragraph (f)(3) of this section for requirements applicable to activity-only wellness programs.

(v) *Outcome-based wellness programs.*—An outcome-based wellness program is a type of health-contingent wellness program that requires an individual to attain or maintain a specific health outcome (such as not smoking or attaining certain results on biometric screenings) in order to obtain a reward. To comply with the rules of this paragraph (f), an outcome-based wellness program typically has two tiers. That is, for individuals who do not attain or maintain the specific health outcome, compliance with an educational program or an activity may be offered as an alternative to achieve the same reward. This alternative pathway, however, does not mean that the overall program, which has an outcome-based component, is not an outcome-based wellness program. That is, if a measurement, test, or screening is used as part of an initial standard and individuals who meet the standard are granted the reward, the program is considered an outcome-based wellness program. For example, if a wellness program tests individuals for specified medical conditions or risk factors (including biometric screening such as testing for high cholesterol, high blood pressure, abnormal body mass index, or high glucose level) and provides a reward to individuals identified as within a normal or healthy range for these medical conditions or risk factors, while requiring individuals who are identified as outside the normal or healthy range (or at risk) to take additional steps (such as meeting with a health coach, taking a health or fitness course, adhering to a health improvement action plan, complying with a walking or exercise program, or complying with a health care provider's plan of care) to obtain the same reward, the program is an outcome-based wellness program. *See* paragraph (f)(4) of this section for requirements applicable to outcome-based wellness programs.

(2) *Requirement for participatory wellness programs.*—A participatory wellness program, as described in paragraph (f)(1)(ii) of this section, does not violate the provisions of this section only if participation in the program is made available to all similarly situated individuals, regardless of health status.

(3) *Requirements for activity-only wellness programs.*—A health-contingent wellness program that is an activity-only wellness program, as described in paragraph (f)(1)(iv) of this section, does not violate the provisions of this section only if all of the following requirements are satisfied:

(i) *Frequency of opportunity to qualify.*—The program must give individuals eligible for the program the opportunity to qualify for the reward under the program at least once per year.

(ii) *Size of reward.*—The reward for the activity-only wellness program, together with the reward for other health-contingent wellness programs with respect to the plan, must not exceed the applicable percentage (as defined in paragraph (f)(5) of this section) of the total cost of employee-only coverage under the plan. However, if, in addition to employees, any class of dependents (such as spouses, or spouses and dependent children) may participate in the wellness program, the reward must not exceed the applicable percentage of the total cost of the coverage in which an employee and any dependents are enrolled. For purposes of this paragraph (f)(3)(ii), the cost of coverage is determined based on the total amount of employer and employee contributions towards the cost of coverage for the benefit package under which the employee is (or the employee and any dependents are) receiving coverage.

(iii) *Reasonable design.*—The program must be reasonably designed to promote health or prevent disease. A program satisfies this standard if it has a reasonable chance of improving the health of, or preventing disease in, participating individuals, and it is not overly burdensome, is not a subterfuge for discriminating based on a health factor, and is not highly suspect in the method chosen to promote health or prevent disease. This determination is based on all the relevant facts and circumstances.

(iv) *Uniform availability and reasonable alternative standards.*—The full reward under the activity-only wellness program must be available to all similarly situated individuals.

(A) Under this paragraph (f)(3)(iv), a reward under an activity-only wellness program is not available to all similarly situated individuals for a period unless the program meets both of the following requirements:

*(1)* The program allows a reasonable alternative standard (or waiver of the otherwise applicable standard) for obtaining the reward for any individual for whom, for that period, it is unreasonably difficult due to a medical condition to satisfy the otherwise applicable standard; and

*(2)* The program allows a reasonable alternative standard (or waiver of the otherwise applicable standard) for obtaining the reward for any individual for whom, for that period, it is medically inadvisable to attempt to satisfy the otherwise applicable standard.

(B) While plans and issuers are not required to determine a particular reasonable alternative standard in advance of an individual's request for one, if an individual is described in either paragraph (f)(3)(iv)(A)(*1*) or (*2*) of this section, a reasonable alternative standard must be furnished by the plan or issuer upon the individual's request or the condition for obtaining the reward must be waived.

(C) All the facts and circumstances are taken into account in determining whether a plan or issuer has furnished a reasonable alternative standard, including but not limited to the following:

(*1*) If the reasonable alternative standard is completion of an educational program, the plan or issuer must make the educational program available or assist the employee in finding such a program (instead of requiring an individual to find such a program unassisted), and may not require an individual to pay for the cost of the program.

(*2*) The time commitment required must be reasonable (for example, requiring attendance nightly at a one-hour class would be unreasonable).

(*3*) If the reasonable alternative standard is a diet program, the plan or issuer is not required to pay for the cost of food but must pay any membership or participation fee.

(*4*) If an individual's personal physician states that a plan standard (including, if applicable, the recommendations of the plan's medical professional) is not medically appropriate for that individual, the plan or issuer must provide a reasonable alternative standard that accommodates the recommendations of the individual's personal physician with regard to medical appropriateness. Plans and issuers may impose standard cost sharing under the plan or coverage for medical items and services furnished pursuant to the physician's recommendations.

(D) To the extent that a reasonable alternative standard under an activity-only wellness program is, itself, an activity-only wellness program, it must comply with the requirements of this paragraph (f)(3) in the same manner as if it were an initial program standard. (Thus, for example, if a plan or issuer provides a walking program as a reasonable alternative standard to a running program, individuals for whom it is unreasonably difficult due to a medical condition to complete the walking program (or for whom it is medically inadvisable to attempt to complete the walking program) must be provided a reasonable alternative standard to the walking program.) To the extent that a reasonable alternative standard under an activity-only wellness program is, itself, an outcome-based wellness program, it must comply with the requirements of paragraph (f)(4) of this section, including paragraph (f)(4)(iv)(D).

(E) If reasonable under the circumstances, a plan or issuer may seek verification, such as a statement from an individual's personal physician, that a health factor makes it unreasonably difficult for the individual to satisfy, or medically inadvisable for the individual to attempt to satisfy, the otherwise applicable standard of an activity-only wellness program. Plans and issuers may seek verification with respect to requests for a reasonable alternative standard for which it is reasonable to determine that medical judgment is required to evaluate the validity of the request.

(v) *Notice of availability of reasonable alternative standard.*—The plan or issuer must disclose in all plan materials describing the terms of an activity-only wellness program the availability of a reasonable alternative standard to qualify for the reward (and, if applicable, the possibility of waiver of the otherwise applicable standard), including contact information for obtaining a reasonable alternative standard and a statement that recommendations of an individual's personal physician will be accommodated. If plan materials merely mention that such a program is available, without describing its terms, this disclosure is not required. Sample language is provided in paragraph (f)(6) of this section, as well as in certain examples of this section.

(vi) *Example.*—The provisions of this paragraph (f)(3) are illustrated by the following example:

*Example.* (i) *Facts.* A group health plan provides a reward to individuals who participate in a reasonable specified walking program. If it is unreasonably difficult due to a medical condition for an individual to participate (or if it is medically inadvisable for an individual to attempt to participate), the plan will waive the walking program requirement and provide the reward. All materials describing the terms of the walking program disclose the availability of the waiver.

(ii) *Conclusion.* In this *Example*, the program satisfies the requirements of paragraph (f)(3)(iii) of this section because the walking program is reasonably designed to promote health and prevent disease. The program satisfies the requirements of paragraph (f)(3)(iv) of this section because the reward under the program is available to all similarly situated individuals. It accommodates individuals for whom it is unreasonably difficult to participate in the walking program due to a medical condition (or for whom it would be medically inadvisable to attempt to participate) by providing them with the reward even if they do not participate in the walking program (that is, by waiving the condition). The plan also complies with the disclo-

sure requirement of paragraph (f)(3)(v) of this section. Thus, the plan satisfies paragraphs (f)(3)(iii), (iv), and (v) of this section.

(4) *Requirements for outcome-based wellness programs.*—A health-contingent wellness program that is an outcome-based wellness program, as described in paragraph (f)(1)(v) of this section, does not violate the provisions of this section only if all of the following requirements are satisfied:

(i) *Frequency of opportunity to qualify.*—The program must give individuals eligible for the program the opportunity to qualify for the reward under the program at least once per year.

(ii) *Size of reward.*—The reward for the outcome-based wellness program, together with the reward for other health-contingent wellness programs with respect to the plan, must not exceed the applicable percentage (as defined in paragraph (f)(5) of this section) of the total cost of employee-only coverage under the plan. However, if, in addition to employees, any class of dependents (such as spouses, or spouses and dependent children) may participate in the wellness program, the reward must not exceed the applicable percentage of the total cost of the coverage in which an employee and any dependents are enrolled. For purposes of this paragraph (f)(4)(ii), the cost of coverage is determined based on the total amount of employer and employee contributions towards the cost of coverage for the benefit package under which the employee is (or the employee and any dependents are) receiving coverage.

(iii) *Reasonable design.*—The program must be reasonably designed to promote health or prevent disease. A program satisfies this standard if it has a reasonable chance of improving the health of, or preventing disease in, participating individuals, and it is not overly burdensome, is not a subterfuge for discriminating based on a health factor, and is not highly suspect in the method chosen to promote health or prevent disease. This determination is based on all the relevant facts and circumstances. To ensure that an outcome-based wellness program is reasonably designed to improve health and does not act as a subterfuge for underwriting or reducing benefits based on a health factor, a reasonable alternative standard to qualify for the reward must be provided to any individual who does not meet the initial standard based on a measurement, test, or screening that is related to a health factor, as explained in paragraph (f)(4)(iv) of this section.

(iv) *Uniform availability and reasonable alternative standards.*—The full reward under the outcome-based wellness program must be available to all similarly situated individuals.

(A) Under this paragraph (f)(4)(iv), a reward under an outcome-based wellness program is not available to all similarly situated individuals for a period unless the program allows a reasonable alternative standard (or waiver of the otherwise applicable standard) for obtaining the reward for any individual who does not meet the initial standard based on the measurement, test, or screening, as described in this paragraph (f)(4)(iv).

(B) While plans and issuers are not required to determine a particular reasonable alternative standard in advance of an individual's request for one, if an individual is described in paragraph (f)(4)(iv)(A) of this section, a reasonable alternative standard must be furnished by the plan or issuer upon the individual's request or the condition for obtaining the reward must be waived.

(C) All the facts and circumstances are taken into account in determining whether a plan or issuer has furnished a reasonable alternative standard, including but not limited to the following:

(*1*) If the reasonable alternative standard is completion of an educational program, the plan or issuer must make the educational program available or assist the employee in finding such a program (instead of requiring an individual to find such a program unassisted), and may not require an individual to pay for the cost of the program.

(*2*) The time commitment required must be reasonable (for example, requiring attendance nightly at a one-hour class would be unreasonable).

(*3*) If the reasonable alternative standard is a diet program, the plan or issuer is not required to pay for the cost of food but must pay any membership or participation fee.

(*4*) If an individual's personal physician states that a plan standard (including, if applicable, the recommendations of the plan's medical professional) is not medically appropriate for that individual, the plan or issuer must provide a reasonable alternative standard that accommodates the recommendations of the individual's personal physician with regard to medical appropriateness. Plans and issuers may impose standard cost sharing under the plan or coverage for medical items and services furnished pursuant to the physician's recommendations.

(D) To the extent that a reasonable alternative standard under an outcome-based wellness program is, itself, an activity-only wellness program, it must comply with the requirements of paragraph (f)(3) of this section in the same manner as if it were an initial program standard. To the extent that a reasonable alternative standard under an outcome-based wellness program is, itself, another outcome-based wellness program, it must comply with the requirements of this paragraph (f)(4), subject to the following special rules:

(1) The reasonable alternative standard cannot be a requirement to meet a different level of the same standard without additional time to comply that takes into account the individual's circumstances. For example, if the initial standard is to achieve a BMI less than 30, the reasonable alternative standard cannot be to achieve a BMI less than 31 on that same date. However, if the initial standard is to achieve a BMI less than 30, a reasonable alternative standard for the individual could be to reduce the individual's BMI by a small amount or small percentage, over a realistic period of time, such as within a year.

(2) An individual must be given the opportunity to comply with the recommendations of the individual's personal physician as a second reasonable alternative standard to meeting the reasonable alternative standard defined by the plan or issuer, but only if the physician joins in the request. The individual can make a request to involve a personal physician's recommendations at any time and the personal physician can adjust the physician's recommendations at any time, consistent with medical appropriateness.

(E) It is not reasonable to seek verification, such as a statement from an individual's personal physician, under an outcome-based wellness program that a health factor makes it unreasonably difficult for the individual to satisfy, or medically inadvisable for the individual to attempt to satisfy, the otherwise applicable standard as a condition of providing a reasonable alternative to the initial standard. However, if a plan or issuer provides an alternative standard to the otherwise applicable measurement, test, or screening that involves an activity that is related to a health factor, then the rules of paragraph (f)(3) of this section for activity-only wellness programs apply to that component of the wellness program and the plan or issuer may, if reasonable under the circumstances, seek verification that it is unreasonably difficult due to a medical condition for an individual to perform or complete the activity (or it is medically inadvisable to attempt to perform or complete the activity). (For example, if an outcome-based wellness program requires participants to maintain a certain healthy weight and provides a diet and exercise program for individuals who do not meet the targeted weight, a plan or issuer may seek verification, as described in paragraph (f)(3)(iv)(D) of this section, if reasonable under the circumstances, that a second reasonable alternative standard is needed for certain individuals because, for those individuals, it would be unreasonably difficult due to a medical condition to comply, or medically inadvisable to attempt to comply, with the diet and exercise program, due to a medical condition.)

(v) *Notice of availability of reasonable alternative standard.*—The plan or issuer must disclose in all plan materials describing the terms of an outcome-based wellness program, and in any disclosure that an individual did not satisfy an initial outcome-based standard, the availability of a reasonable alternative standard to qualify for the reward (and, if applicable, the possibility of waiver of the otherwise applicable standard), including contact information for obtaining a reasonable alternative standard and a statement that recommendations of an individual's personal physician will be accommodated. If plan materials merely mention that such a program is available, without describing its terms, this disclosure is not required. Sample language is provided in paragraph (f)(6) of this section, as well as in certain examples of this section.

(vi) *Examples.*—The rules of this paragraph (f)(4) are illustrated by the following examples:

*Example 1 - Cholesterol screening with reasonable alternative standard to work with personal physician.* (i) *Facts.* A group health plan offers a reward to participants who achieve a count under 200 on a total cholesterol test. If a participant does not achieve the targeted cholesterol count, the plan allows the participant to develop an alternative cholesterol action plan in conjunction with the participant's personal physician that may include recommendations for medication and additional screening. The plan allows the physician to modify the standards, as medically necessary, over the year. (For example, if a participant develops asthma or depression, requires surgery and convalescence, or some other medical condition or consideration makes completion of the original action plan inadvisable or unreasonably difficult, the physician may modify the original action plan.) All plan materials describing the terms of the program include the following statement: "Your health plan wants to help you take charge of your health. Rewards are available to all employees who participate in our Cholesterol Awareness Wellness Program. If your total cholesterol count is under 200, you will receive the reward. If not, you will still have an opportunity to qualify for the reward. We

will work with you and your doctor to find a Health Smart program that is right for you." In addition, when any individual participant receives notification that his or her cholesterol count is 200 or higher, the notification includes the following statement: "Your plan offers a Health Smart program under which we will work with you and your doctor to try to lower your cholesterol. If you complete this program, you will qualify for a reward. Please contact us at [contact information] to get started."

(ii) *Conclusion.* In this *Example 1*, the program is an outcome-based wellness program because the initial standard requires an individual to attain or maintain a specific health outcome (a certain cholesterol level) to obtain a reward. The program satisfies the requirements of paragraph (f)(4)(iii) of this section because the cholesterol program is reasonably designed to promote health and prevent disease. The program satisfies the requirements of paragraph (f)(4)(iv) of this section because it makes available to all participants who do not meet the cholesterol standard a reasonable alternative standard to qualify for the reward. Lastly, the plan also discloses in all materials describing the terms of the program and in any disclosure that an individual did not satisfy the initial outcome-based standard the availability of a reasonable alternative standard (including contact information and the individual's ability to involve his or her personal physician), as required by paragraph (f)(4)(v) of this section. Thus, the program satisfies the requirements of paragraphs (f)(4)(iii), (iv), and (v) of this section.

*Example 2 - Cholesterol screening with plan alternative and no opportunity for personal physician involvement.* (i) *Facts.* Same facts as *Example 1*, except that the wellness program's physician or nurse practitioner (rather than the individual's personal physician) determines the alternative cholesterol action plan. The plan does not provide an opportunity for a participant's personal physician to modify the action plan if it is not medically appropriate for that individual.

(ii) *Conclusion.* In this *Example 2*, the wellness program does not satisfy the requirements of paragraph (f)(4)(iii) of this section because the program does not accommodate the recommendations of the participant's personal physician with regard to medical appropriateness, as required under paragraph (f)(4)(iv)(C)(3) of this section. Thus, the program is not reasonably designed under paragraph (f)(4)(iii) of this section and is not available to all similarly situated individuals under paragraph (f)(4)(iv) of this section. The notice also does not provide all the content required under paragraph (f)(4)(v) of this section.

*Example 3 - Cholesterol screening with plan alternative that can be modified by personal physician.* (i) *Facts.* Same facts as *Example 2*, except that if a participant's personal physician disagrees with any part of the action plan, the personal physician may modify the action plan at any time, and the plan discloses this to participants.

(ii) *Conclusion.* In this *Example 3*, the wellness program satisfies the requirements of paragraph (f)(4)(iii) of this section because the participant's personal physician may modify the action plan determined by the wellness program's physician or nurse practitioner at any time if the physician states that the recommendations are not medically appropriate, as required under paragraph (f)(4)(iv)(C)(3) of this section. Thus, the program is reasonably designed under paragraph (f)(4)(iii) of this section and is available to all similarly situated individuals under paragraph (f)(4)(iv) of this section. The notice, which includes a statement that recommendations of an individual's personal physician will be accommodated, also complies with paragraph (f)(4)(v) of this section.

*Example 4 - BMI screening with walking program alternative.* (i) *Facts.* A group health plan will provide a reward to participants who have a body mass index (BMI) that is 26 or lower, determined shortly before the beginning of the year. Any participant who does not meet the target BMI is given the same discount if the participant complies with an exercise program that consists of walking 150 minutes a week. Any participant for whom it is unreasonably difficult due to a medical condition to comply with this walking program (and any participant for whom it is medically inadvisable to attempt to comply with the walking program) during the year is given the same discount if the participant satisfies an alternative standard that is reasonable taking into consideration the participant's medical situation, is not unreasonably burdensome or impractical to comply with, and is otherwise reasonably designed based on all the relevant facts and circumstances. All plan materials describing the terms of the wellness program include the following statement: "Fitness is Easy! Start Walking! Your health plan cares about your health. If you are considered overweight because you have a BMI of over 26, our Start Walking program will help you lose weight and feel better. We will help you enroll. (**If your doctor says that walking isn't right for you, that's okay too. We will work with you (and, if you wish, your own doctor) to develop a wellness program that is.)" Participant E is unable to achieve a BMI that is 26 or lower within the plan's timeframe and receives notification that complies with paragraph (f)(4)(v) of this section. Nevertheless, it is unreasonably difficult due to a medical condition for E to comply with the walking program. E proposes a program based on the recommendations of E's physician. The plan agrees to make the same discount available to E that is available to other participants in the BMI program or the alternative walking program, but only if E actually follows the physician's recommendations.

(ii) *Conclusion*. In this *Example 4*, the program is an outcome-based wellness program because the initial standard requires an individual to attain or maintain a specific health outcome (a certain BMI level) to obtain a reward. The program satisfies the requirements of paragraph (f)(4)(iii) of this section because it is reasonably designed to promote health and prevent disease. The program also satisfies the requirements of paragraph (f)(4)(iv) of this section because it makes available to all individuals who do not satisfy the BMI standard a reasonable alternative standard to qualify for the reward (in this case, a walking program that is not unreasonably burdensome or impractical for individuals to comply with and that is otherwise reasonably designed based on all the relevant facts and circumstances). In addition, the walking program is, itself, an activity-only standard and the plan complies with the requirements of paragraph (f)(3) of this section (including the requirement of paragraph (f)(3)(iv) that, if there are individuals for whom it is unreasonably difficult due to a medical condition to comply, or for whom it is medically inadvisable to attempt to comply, with the walking program, the plan provide a reasonable alternative to those individuals). Moreover, the plan satisfies the requirements of paragraph (f)(4)(v) of this section because it discloses, in all materials describing the terms of the program and in any disclosure that an individual did not satisfy the initial outcome-based standard, the availability of a reasonable alternative standard (including contact information and the individual's option to involve his or her personal physician) to qualify for the reward or the possibility of waiver of the otherwise applicable standard. Thus, the program satisfies the requirements of paragraphs (f)(4)(iii), (iv), and (v) of this section.

*Example 5 - BMI screening with alternatives available to either lower BMI or meet personal physician's recommendations*. (i) Facts. Same facts as *Example 4* except that, with respect to any participant who does not meet the target BMI, instead of a walking program, the participant is expected to reduce BMI by one point. At any point during the year upon request, any individual can obtain a second reasonable alternative standard, which is compliance with the recommendations of the participant's personal physician regarding weight, diet, and exercise as set forth in a treatment plan that the physician recommends or to which the physician agrees. The participant's personal physician is permitted to change or adjust the treatment plan at any time and the option of following the participant's personal physician's recommendations is clearly disclosed.

(ii) *Conclusion*. In this *Example 5*, the reasonable alternative standard to qualify for the reward (the alternative BMI standard requiring a one-point reduction) does not make the program unreasonable under paragraph (f)(4)(iii) or (iv) of this section because the program complies with paragraph (f)(4)(iv)(C)(4) of this section by allowing a second reasonable alternative standard to qualify for the reward (compliance with the recommendations of the participant's personal physician, which can be changed or adjusted at any time). Accordingly, the program continues to satisfy the applicable requirements of paragraph (f) of this section.

*Example 6 - Tobacco use surcharge with smoking cessation program alternative*. (i) Facts. In conjunction with an annual open enrollment period, a group health plan provides a premium differential based on tobacco use, determined using a health risk assessment. The following statement is included in all plan materials describing the tobacco premium differential: "Stop smoking today! We can help! If you are a smoker, we offer a smoking cessation program. If you complete the program, you can avoid this surcharge." The plan accommodates participants who smoke by facilitating their enrollment in a smoking cessation program that requires participation at a time and place that are not unreasonably burdensome or impractical for participants, and that is otherwise reasonably designed based on all the relevant facts and circumstances, and discloses contact information and the individual's option to involve his or her personal physician. The plan pays for the cost of participation in the smoking cessation program. Any participant can avoid the surcharge for the plan year by participating in the program, regardless of whether the participant stops smoking, but the plan can require a participant who wants to avoid the surcharge in a subsequent year to complete the smoking cessation program again.

(ii) *Conclusion*. In this *Example 6*, the premium differential satisfies the requirements of paragraphs (f)(4)(iii), (iv), and (v). The program is an outcome-based wellness program because the initial standard for obtaining a reward is dependent on the results of a health risk assessment (a measurement, test, or screening). The program is reasonably designed under paragraph (f)(4)(iii) because the plan provides a reasonable alternative standard (as required under

paragraph (f)(4)(iv) of this section) to qualify for the reward to all tobacco users (a smoking cessation program). The plan discloses, in all materials describing the terms of the program, the availability of the reasonable alternative standard (including contact information and the individual's option to involve his or her personal physician). Thus, the program satisfies the requirements of paragraphs (f)(4)(iii), (iv), and (v) of this section.

*Example 7 - Tobacco use surcharge with alternative program requiring actual cessation*. (i) Facts. Same facts as *Example 6*, except the plan does not provide participant F with the reward in subsequent years unless F actually stops smoking after participating in the tobacco cessation program.

(ii) *Conclusion*. In this *Example 7*, the program is not reasonably designed under paragraph (f)(4)(iii) of this section and does not provide a reasonable alternative standard as required under paragraph (f)(4)(iv) of this section. The plan cannot cease to provide a reasonable alternative standard merely because the participant did not stop smoking after participating in a smoking cessation program. The plan must continue to offer a reasonable alternative standard whether it is the same or different (such as a new recommendation from F's personal physician or a new nicotine replacement therapy).

*Example 8 - Tobacco use surcharge with smoking cessation program alternative that is not reasonable*. (i) Facts. Same facts as *Example 6*, except the plan does not facilitate participant F's enrollment in a smoking cessation program. Instead the plan advises F to find a program, pay for it, and provide a certificate of completion to the plan.

(ii) *Conclusion*. In this *Example 8*, the requirement for F to find and pay for F's own smoking cessation program means that the alternative program is not reasonable. Accordingly, the plan has not offered a reasonable alternative standard that complies with paragraphs (f)(4)(iii) and (iv) of this section and the program fails to satisfy the requirements of paragraph (f) of this section.

(5) *Applicable percentage*.—(i) For purposes of this paragraph (f), the applicable percentage is 30 percent, except that the applicable percentage is increased by an additional 20 percentage points (to 50 percent) to the extent that the additional percentage is in connection with a program designed to prevent or reduce tobacco use.

(ii) The provisions of this paragraph (f)(5) are illustrated by the following examples:

*Example 1*. (i) *Facts*. An employer sponsors a group health plan. The annual premium for employee-only coverage is $6,000 (of which the employer pays $4,500 per year and the employee pays $1,500 per year). The plan offers employees a health-contingent wellness program with several components, focused on exercise, blood sugar, weight, cholesterol, and blood pressure. The reward for compliance is an annual premium rebate of $600.

(ii) *Conclusion*. In this *Example 1*, the reward for the wellness program, $600, does not exceed the applicable percentage of 30 percent of the total annual cost of employee-only coverage, $1,800. ($6,000 × 30% = $1,800.)

*Example 2*. (i) *Facts*. Same facts as *Example 1*, except the wellness program is exclusively a tobacco prevention program. Employees who have used tobacco in the last 12 months and who are not enrolled in the plan's tobacco cessation program are charged a $1,000 premium surcharge (in addition to their employee contribution towards the coverage). (Those who participate in the plan's tobacco cessation program are not assessed the $1,000 surcharge.)

(ii) *Conclusion*. In this *Example 2*, the reward for the wellness program (absence of a $1,000 surcharge), does not exceed the applicable percentage of 50 percent of the total annual cost of employee-only coverage, $3,000. ($6,000 × 50% = $3,000.)

*Example 3*. (i) *Facts*. Same facts as *Example 1*, except that, in addition to the $600 reward for compliance with the health-contingent wellness program, the plan also imposes an additional $2,000 tobacco premium surcharge on employees who have used tobacco in the last 12 months and who are not enrolled in the plan's tobacco cessation program. (Those who participate in the plan's tobacco cessation program are not assessed the $2,000 surcharge.)

(ii) *Conclusion*. In this *Example 3*, the total of all rewards (including absence of a surcharge for participating in the tobacco program) is $2,600 ($600 + $2,000 = $2,600), which does not exceed the applicable percentage of 50 percent of the total annual cost of employee-only coverage ($3,000); and, tested separately, the $600 reward for the wellness program unrelated to tobacco use does not exceed the applicable percentage of 30 percent of the total annual cost of employee-only coverage ($1,800).

*Example 4*. (i) *Facts*. An employer sponsors a group health plan. The total annual premium for employee-only coverage (including both employer and employee contributions towards the coverage) is $5,000. The plan provides a $250 reward to employees who complete a health risk assessment, without regard to the health issues identified as part of the assessment. The plan also offers a Healthy

Heart program, which is a health-contingent wellness program, with an opportunity to earn a $1,500 reward.

(ii) *Conclusion.* In this *Example 4,* even though the total reward for all wellness programs under the plan is $1,750 ($250 + $1,500 = $1,750, which exceeds the applicable percentage of 30 percent of the cost of the annual premium for employee-only coverage ($5,000 × 30% = $1,500), only the reward offered for compliance with the health-contingent wellness program ($1,500) is taken into account in determining whether the rules of this paragraph (f)(5) are met. (The $250 reward is offered in connection with a participatory wellness program and therefore is not taken into account.) Accordingly, the health-contingent wellness program offers a reward that does not exceed the applicable percentage of 30 percent of the total annual cost of employee-only coverage.

(6) *Sample language.*—The following language, or substantially similar language, can be used to satisfy the notice requirement of paragraphs (f)(3)(v) or (f)(4)(v) of this section: "Your health plan is committed to helping you achieve your best health. Rewards for participating in a wellness program are available to all employees. If you think you might be unable to meet a standard for a reward under this wellness program, you might qualify for an opportunity to earn the same reward by different means. Contact us at [insert contact information] and we will work with you (and, if you wish, with your doctor) to find a wellness program with the same reward that is right for you in light of your health status."

(g) *More favorable treatment of individuals with adverse health factors permitted.*—(1) *In rules for eligibility.*—(i) Nothing in this section prevents a group health plan from establishing more favorable rules for eligibility (described in paragraph (b)(1) of this section) for individuals with an adverse health factor, such as disability, than for individuals without the adverse health factor. Moreover, nothing in this section prevents a plan from charging a higher premium or contribution with respect to individuals with an adverse health factor if they would not be eligible for the coverage were it not for the adverse health factor. (However, other laws, including State insurance laws, may set or limit premium rates; these laws are not affected by this section.)

(ii) The rules of this paragraph (g)(1) are illustrated by the following examples:

*Example 1.* (i) *Facts.* An employer sponsors a group health plan that generally is available to employees, spouses of employees, and dependent children until age 26. However, dependent children who are disabled are eligible for coverage beyond age 26.

(ii) *Conclusion.* In this Example 1, the plan provision allowing coverage for disabled dependent children beyond age 26 satisfies this paragraph (g)(1) (and thus does not violate this section).

*Example 2.* (i) *Facts.* An employer sponsors a group health plan, which is generally available to employees (and members of the employee's family) until the last day of the month in which the employee ceases to perform services for the employer. The plan generally charges employees $50 per month for employee-only coverage and $125 per month for family coverage. However, an employee who ceases to perform services for the employer by reason of disability may remain covered under the plan until the last day of the month that is 12 months after the month in which the employee ceased to perform services for the employer. During this extended period of coverage, the plan charges the employee $100 per month for employee-only coverage and $250 per month for family coverage. (This extended period of coverage is without regard to whatever rights the employee (or members of the employee's family) may have for COBRA continuation coverage.)

(ii) *Conclusion.* In this *Example 2,* the plan provision allowing extended coverage for disabled employees and their families satisfies this paragraph (g)(1) (and thus does not violate this section). In addition, the plan is permitted, under this paragraph (g)(1), to charge the disabled employees a higher premium during the extended period of coverage.

*Example 3.* (i) *Facts.* To comply with the requirements of a COBRA continuation provision, a group health plan generally makes COBRA continuation coverage available for a maximum period of 18 months in connection with a termination of employment but makes the coverage available for a maximum period of 29 months to certain disabled individuals and certain members of the disabled individual's family. Although the plan generally requires payment of 102 percent of the applicable premium for the first 18 months of COBRA continuation coverage, the plan requires payment of 150 percent of the applicable premium for the disabled individual's COBRA continuation coverage during the disability extension if the disabled individual would not be entitled to COBRA continuation coverage but for the disability.

(ii) *Conclusion.* In this *Example 3,* the plan provision allowing extended COBRA continuation coverage for disabled individuals satisfies this paragraph (g)(1) (and thus does not violate this section).

In addition, the plan is permitted, under this paragraph (g)(1), to charge the disabled individuals a higher premium for the extended coverage if the individuals would not be eligible for COBRA continuation coverage were it not for the disability. (Similarly, if the plan provided an extended period of coverage for disabled individuals pursuant to State law or plan provision rather than pursuant to a COBRA continuation coverage provision, the plan could likewise charge the disabled individuals a higher premium for the extended coverage.)

(2) *In premiums or contributions.*—(i) Nothing in this section prevents a group health plan from charging individuals a premium or contribution that is less than the premium (or contribution) for similarly situated individuals if the lower charge is based on an adverse health factor, such as disability.

(ii) The rules of this paragraph (g)(2) are illustrated by the following example:

*Example.* (i) *Facts.* Under a group health plan, employees are generally required to pay $50 per month for employee-only coverage and $125 per month for family coverage under the plan. However, employees who are disabled receive coverage (whether employee-only or family coverage) under the plan free of charge.

(ii) *Conclusion.* In this *Example,* the plan provision waiving premium payment for disabled employees is permitted under this paragraph (g)(2) (and thus does not violate this section).

(h) *No effect on other laws.*—Compliance with this section is not determinative of compliance with any provision of ERISA (including the COBRA continuation provisions) or any other State or Federal law, such as the Americans with Disabilities Act. Therefore, although the rules of this section would not prohibit a plan from treating one group of similarly situated individuals differently from another (such as providing different benefit packages to current and former employees), other Federal or State laws may require that two separate groups of similarly situated individuals be treated the same for certain purposes (such as making the same benefit package available to COBRA qualified beneficiaries as is made available to active employees). In addition, although this section generally does not impose new disclosure obligations on plans, this section does not affect any other laws, including those that require accurate disclosures and prohibit intentional misrepresentation.

(i) *Applicability dates.*—This section applies for plan years beginning on or after July 1, 2007. [Reg. §54.9802-1.]

☐ [*T.D. 8931, 1-5-2001 (corrected 3-8-2001). Amended by T.D. 9298, 12-12-2006 (corrected 2-21-2007); T.D. 9464, 10-1-2009; T.D. 9620, 5-29-2013 and T.D. 9656, 2-20-2014.*]

### [Reg. §54.9802-2]

**§54.9802-2. Special rules for certain church plans.**—(a) *Exception for certain church plans.*—(1) *Church plans in general.*—A church plan described in paragraph (b) of this section is not treated as failing to meet the requirements of section 9802 or §54.9802-1 solely because the plan requires evidence of good health for coverage of individuals under plan provisions described in paragraph (b)(2) or (3) of this section.

(2) *Health insurance issuers.*—See sections 2702 and 2721(b)(1)(B) of the Public Health Service Act (42 U.S.C. 300gg-2 and 300gg-21(b)(1)(B)) and 45 CFR 146.121, which require health insurance issuers providing health insurance coverage under a church plan that is a group health plan to comply with nondiscrimination requirements similar to those that church plans are required to comply with under section 9802 and §54.9802-1 except that those nondiscrimination requirements do not include an exception for health insurance issuers comparable to the exception for church plans under section 9802(c) and this section.

(b) *Church plans to which this section applies.*—(1) *Church plans with certain coverage provisions in effect on July 15, 1997.*—This section applies to any church plan (as defined in section 414(e)) for a plan year if, on July 15, 1997 and at all times thereafter before the beginning of the plan year, the plan contains either the provisions described in paragraph (b)(2) of this section or the provisions described in paragraph (b)(3) of this section.

(2) *Plan provisions applicable to individuals employed by employers of 10 or fewer employees and self-employed individuals.*—(i) A plan contains the provisions described in this paragraph (b)(2) if it requires evidence of good health of both—

(A) Any employee of an employer of 10 or fewer employees (determined without regard to section 414(e)(3)(C), under which a church or convention or association of churches is treated as the employer); and

(B) Any self-employed individual.

(ii) A plan does not contain the provisions described in this paragraph (b)(2) if the plan contains only one of the provisions described in this paragraph (b)(2). Thus, for example, a plan that requires evidence of good health of any self-employed individual, but not of any employee of an employer with 10 or fewer employees, does not contain the provisions described in this paragraph (b)(2). Moreover, a plan does not contain the provision described in paragraph (b)(2)(i)(A) of this section if the plan requires evidence of good health of any employee of an employer of fewer than 10 (or greater than 10) employees. Thus, for example, a plan does not contain the provision described in paragraph (b)(2)(i)(A) of this section if the plan requires evidence of good health of any employee of an employer with five or fewer employees.

(3) *Plan provisions applicable to individuals who enroll after the first 90 days of initial eligibility.*—(i) A plan contains the provisions described in this paragraph (b)(3) if it requires evidence of good health of any individual who enrolls after the first 90 days of initial eligibility under the plan.

(ii) A plan does not contain the provisions described in this paragraph (b)(3) if it provides for a longer (or shorter) period than 90 days. Thus, for example, a plan requiring evidence of good health of any individual who enrolls after the first 120 days of initial eligibility under the plan does not contain the provisions described in this paragraph (b)(3).

(c) *Examples.*—The rules of this section are illustrated by the following examples:

*Example 1.* (i) *Facts.* A church organization maintains two church plans for entities affiliated with the church. One plan is a group health plan that provides health coverage to all employees (including ministers and lay workers) of any affiliated church entity that has more than 10 employees. The other plan is Plan O, which is a group health plan that is not funded through insurance coverage and that provides health coverage to any employee (including ministers and lay workers) of any affiliated church entity that has 10 or fewer employees and any self-employed individual affiliated with the church (including a self-employed minister of the church). Plan O requires evidence of good health in order for any individual of a church entity that has 10 or fewer employees to be covered and in order for any self-employed individual to be covered. On July 15, 1997 and at all times thereafter before the beginning of the plan year, Plan O has contained all the preceding provisions.

(ii) *Conclusion.* In this *Example 1*, because Plan O contains the plan provisions described in paragraph (b)(2) of this section and because those provisions were in the plan on July 15, 1997 and at all times thereafter before the beginning of the plan year, Plan O will not be treated as failing to meet the requirements of section 9802 or §54.9802-1 for the plan year solely because the plan requires evidence of good health for coverage of the individuals described in those plan provisions.

*Example 2.* (i) *Facts.* A church organization maintains Plan P, which is a church plan that is not funded through insurance coverage and that is a group health plan providing health coverage to individuals employed by entities affiliated with the church and self-employed individuals affiliated with the church (such as ministers). On July 15, 1997 and at all times thereafter before the beginning of the plan year, Plan P has required evidence of good health for coverage of any individual who enrolls after the first 90 days of initial eligibility under the plan.

(ii) *Conclusion.* In this *Example 2*, because Plan P contains the plan provisions described in paragraph (b)(3) of this section and because those provisions were in the plan on July 15, 1997 and at all times thereafter before the beginning of the plan year, Plan P will not be treated as failing to meet the requirements of section 9802 or §54.9802-1 for the plan year solely because the plan requires evidence of good health for coverage of individuals enrolling after the first 90 days of initial eligibility under the plan.

(d) *Applicability date.*—This section is applicable to plan years beginning on or after July 1, 2007. [Reg. §54.9802-2.]

☐ [*T.D.* 9299, 12-12-2006.]

### [Reg. §54.9802-3T]

**§54.9802-3T. Standards relating to benefits for mothers and newborns (temporary).**—(a) *Definitions.*—Unless otherwise provided, the definitions in this paragraph (a) govern in applying the provisions of this section.

(1) *Collect* means, with respect to information, to request, require, or purchase such information.

(2) *Family member* means, with respect to an individual —

(i) A dependent (as defined for purposes of §54.9801-2) of the individual; or

(ii) Any other person who is a first-degree, second-degree, third-degree, or fourthdegree relative of the individual or of a depen-

dent of the individual. Relatives by affinity (such as by marriage or adoption) are treated the same as relatives by consanguinity (that is, relatives who share a common biological ancestor). In determining the degree of the relationship, relatives by less than full consanguinity (such as half-siblings, who share only one parent) are treated the same as relatives by full consanguinity (such as siblings who share both parents).

(A) First-degree relatives include parents, spouses, siblings, and children.

(B) Second-degree relatives include grandparents, grandchildren, aunts, uncles, nephews, and nieces.

(C) Third-degree relatives include great-grandparents, great-grandchildren, great aunts, great uncles, and first cousins.

(D) Fourth-degree relatives include great-great grandparents, great-great grandchildren, and children of first cousins.

(3) *Genetic information* means—

(i) Subject to paragraphs (a)(3)(ii) and (a)(3)(iii) of this section, with respect to an individual, information about—

(A) The individual's genetic tests (as defined in paragraph (a)(5) of this section);

(B) The genetic tests of family members of the individual;

(C) The manifestation (as defined in paragraph (a)(6) of this section) of a disease or disorder in family members of the individual; or

(D) Any request for, or receipt of, genetic services (as defined in paragraph (a)(4) of this section), or participation in clinical research which includes genetic services, by the individual or any family member of the individual.

(ii) The term *genetic information* does not include information about the sex or age of any individual.

(iii) The term *genetic information* includes—

(A) With respect to a pregnant woman (or a family member of the pregnant woman), genetic information of any fetus carried by the pregnant woman; and

(B) With respect to an individual (or a family member of the individual) who is utilizing an assisted reproductive technology, genetic information of any embryo legally held by the individual or family member.

(4) *Genetic services* means—

(i) A genetic test, as defined in paragraph (a)(5) of this section;

(ii) Genetic counseling (including obtaining, interpreting, or assessing genetic information); or

(iii) Genetic education.

(5)(i) *Genetic test* means an analysis of human DNA, RNA, chromosomes, proteins, or metabolites, if the analysis detects genotypes, mutations, or chromosomal changes. However, a genetic test does not include an analysis of proteins or metabolites that is directly related to a manifested disease, disorder, or pathological condition. Accordingly, a test to determine whether an individual has a BRCA1 or BRCA2 variant is a genetic test. Similarly, a test to determine whether an individual has a genetic variant associated with hereditary nonpolyposis colorectal cancer is a genetic test. However, an HIV test, complete blood count, cholesterol test, liver function test, or test for the presence of alcohol or drugs is not a genetic test.

(ii) The rules of this paragraph (a)(5) are illustrated by the following example:

*Example.* (i) *Facts.* Individual A is a newborn covered under a group health plan. A undergoes a phenylketonuria (PKU) screening, which measures the concentration of a metabolite, phenylalanine, in A's blood. In PKU, a mutation occurs in the phenylalanine hydroxylase (PAH) gene which contains instructions for making the enzyme needed to break down the amino acid phenylalanine. Individuals with the mutation, who have a deficiency in the enzyme to break down phenylalanine, have high concentrations of phenylalanine.

(ii) *Conclusion.* In this *Example*, the PKU screening is a genetic test with respect to A because the screening is an analysis of metabolites that detects a genetic mutation.

(6)(i) *Manifestation* or *manifested* means, with respect to a disease, disorder, or pathological condition, that an individual has been or could reasonably be diagnosed with the disease, disorder, or pathological condition by a health care professional with appropriate training and expertise in the field of medicine involved. For purposes of this section, a disease, disorder, or pathological condition is not manifested if a diagnosis is based principally on genetic information.

(ii) The rules of this paragraph (a)(6) are illustrated by the following examples:

*Example 1.* (i) *Facts.* Individual A has a family medical history of diabetes. A begins to experience excessive sweating, thirst, and fatigue. A's physician examines A and orders blood glucose testing (which is not a genetic test). Based on the physician's examination, A's symptoms, and test results that show elevated levels of blood glucose, A's physician diagnoses A as having adult onset diabetes mellitus (Type 2 diabetes).

(ii) *Conclusion.* In this *Example 1,* A has been diagnosed by a health care professional with appropriate training and expertise in the field of medicine involved. The diagnosis is not based principally on genetic information. Thus, Type 2 diabetes is manifested with respect to A.

*Example 2.* (i) *Facts.* Individual B has several family members with colon cancer. One of them underwent genetic testing which detected a mutation in the MSH2 gene associated with hereditary nonpolyposis colorectal cancer (HNPCC). B's physician, a health care professional with appropriate training and expertise in the field of medicine involved, recommends that B undergo a targeted genetic test to look for the specific mutation found in B's relative to determine if B has an elevated risk for cancer. The genetic test with respect to B showed that B also carries the mutation and is at increased risk to develop colorectal and other cancers associated with HNPCC. B has a colonoscopy which indicates no signs of disease, and B has no symptoms.

(ii) *Conclusion.* In this *Example 2,* because B has no signs or symptoms of colorectal cancer, B has not been and could not reasonably be diagnosed with HNPCC. Thus, HNPCC is not manifested with respect to B.

*Example 3.* (i) *Facts.* Same facts as *Example 2,* except that B's colonoscopy and subsequent tests indicate the presence of HNPCC. Based on the colonoscopy and subsequent test results, B's physician makes a diagnosis of HNPCC.

(ii) *Conclusion.* In this *Example 3,* HNPCC is manifested with respect to B because a health care professional with appropriate training and expertise in the field of medicine involved has made a diagnosis that is not based principally on genetic information.

*Example 4.* (i) *Facts.* Individual C has a family member that has been diagnosed with Huntington's Disease. A genetic test indicates that C has the Huntington's Disease gene variant. At age 42, C begins suffering from occasional moodiness and disorientation, symptoms which are associated with Huntington's Disease. C is examined by a neurologist (a physician with appropriate training and expertise for diagnosing Huntington's Disease). The examination includes a clinical neurological exam. The results of the examination do not support a diagnosis of Huntington's Disease.

(ii) *Conclusion.* In this *Example 4,* C is not and could not reasonably be diagnosed with Huntington's Disease by a health care professional with appropriate training and expertise. Therefore, Huntington's Disease is not manifested with respect to C.

*Example 5.* (i) *Facts.* Same facts as *Example 4,* except that C exhibits additional neurological and behavioral symptoms, and the results of the examination support a diagnosis of Huntington's Disease with respect to C.

(ii) *Conclusion.* In this *Example 5,* C could reasonably be diagnosed with Huntington's Disease by a health care professional with appropriate training and expertise. Therefore, Huntington's Disease is manifested with respect to C.

(7) *Underwriting purposes* has the meaning given in paragraph (d)(1) of this section.

(b) *No group-based discrimination based on genetic information.*— (1) *In general.*—For purposes of this section, a group health plan must not adjust premium or contribution amounts for any employer, or any group of similarly situated individuals under the plan, on the basis of genetic information. For this purpose, "similarly situated individuals" are those described in § 54.9802-1(d).

(2) *Rule of construction.*—Nothing in paragraph (b)(1) of this section (or in paragraph (d)(1) or (d)(2) of this section) limits the ability of a group health plan to increase the premium for an employer or for a group of similarly situated individuals under the plan based on the manifestation of a disease or disorder of an individual who is enrolled in the plan. In such a case, however, the manifestation of a disease or disorder in one individual cannot also be used as genetic information about other group members to further increase the premium for an employer or a group of similarly situated individuals under the plan.

(3) *Examples.*—The rules of this paragraph (b) are illustrated by the following examples:

*Example 1.* (i) *Facts.* An employer sponsors a group health plan that provides coverage through a health insurance issuer. In order to determine the premium rate for the upcoming plan year, the issuer reviews the claims experience of individuals covered under the plan and other health status information of the individuals, including genetic information. The issuer finds that three individuals covered under the plan had unusually high claims experience. In addition, the issuer finds that the genetic information of two other individuals indicates the individuals have a higher probability of developing certain illnesses although the illnesses are not manifested at this time. The issuer quotes the plan a higher per-participant rate because of both the genetic information and the higher claims experience.

(ii) *Conclusion.* See *Example 1* in 29 CFR 2590.702-1(b)(3) or 45 CFR 146.122(b)(3) for a conclusion that the issuer violates the provisions of 29 CFR 2590.702-1(b) or 45 CFR 146.122(b) similar to the requirements of this paragraph (b) because the issuer adjusts the premium based on genetic information. However, if the adjustment related solely to claims experience, the adjustment would not violate the requirements of 29 CFR 2590.702-1 or 45 CFR 146.122 similar to the requirements of this section (nor would it violate the requirements of paragraph (c) of 29 CFR 2590.702 or 45 CFR 146.121 similar to the requirements of paragraph (c) of § 54.9802-1, which prohibits discrimination in individual premiums or contributions based on a health factor but permits increases in the group rate based on a health factor).

*Example 2.* (i) *Facts.* An employer sponsors a group health plan that provides coverage through a health insurance issuer. In order to determine the premium rate for the upcoming plan year, the issuer reviews the claims experience of individuals covered under the plan and other health status information of the individuals, including genetic information. The issuer finds that Employee A has made claims for treatment of polycystic kidney disease. A also has two dependent children covered under the plan. The issuer quotes the plan a higher per-participant rate because of both A's claims experience and the family medical history of A's children (that is, the fact that A has the disease).

(ii) *Conclusion.* See *Example 2* in 29 CFR 2590.702-1(b)(3) or 45 CFR 146.122(b)(3) for a conclusion that the issuer violates the provisions of 29 CFR 2590.702-1(b) or 45 CFR 146.122(b) similar to the requirements of this paragraph (b) because, by taking the likelihood that A's children may develop polycystic kidney disease into account in computing the rate for the plan, the issuer adjusts the premium based on genetic information relating to a condition that has not been manifested in A's children. However, the issuer does not violate the requirements of 29 CFR 2590.702-1(b) or 45 CFR 146.122(b) similar to the requirements of this paragraph (b) by increasing the premium based on A's claims experience.

(c) *Limitation on requesting or requiring genetic testing.*—(1) *General rule.*—Except as otherwise provided in this paragraph (c), a group health plan must not request or require an individual or a family member of the individual to undergo a genetic test.

(2) *Health care professional may recommend a genetic test.*—Nothing in paragraph (c)(1) of this section limits the authority of a health care professional who is providing health care services to an individual to request that the individual undergo a genetic test.

(3) *Examples.*—The rules of paragraphs (c)(1) and (c)(2) of this section are illustrated by the following examples:

*Example 1.* (i) *Facts.* Individual A goes to a physician for a routine physical examination. The physician reviews A's family medical history and A informs the physician that A's mother has been diagnosed with Huntington's Disease. The physician advises A that Huntington's Disease is hereditary and recommends that A undergo a genetic test.

(ii) *Conclusion.* In this *Example 1,* the physician is a health care professional who is providing health care services to A. Therefore, the physician's recommendation that A undergo the genetic test does not violate this paragraph (c).

*Example 2.* (i) *Facts.* Individual B is covered by a health maintenance organization (HMO). B is a child being treated for leukemia. B's physician, who is employed by the HMO, is considering a treatment plan that includes six-mercaptopurine, a drug for treating leukemia in most children. However, the drug could be fatal if taken by a small percentage of children with a particular gene variant. B's physician recommends that B undergo a genetic test to detect this variant before proceeding with this course of treatment.

(ii) *Conclusion.* In this *Example 2,* even though the physician is employed by the HMO, the physician is nonetheless a health care professional who is providing health care services to B. Therefore, the physician's recommendation that B undergo the genetic test does not violate this paragraph (c).

(4) *Determination regarding payment.*—(i) *In general..*—As provided in this paragraph (c)(4), nothing in paragraph (c)(1) of this section precludes a plan from obtaining and using the results of a genetic test in making a determination regarding payment. For this purpose, "payment" has the meaning given such term in 45 CFR 164.501 of the privacy regulations issued under the Health Insurance Portability and Accountability Act. Thus, if a plan conditions payment for an item or service based on its medical appropriateness and the medical appropriateness of the item or service depends on the genetic makeup of a patient, then the plan is permitted to condition payment for the item or service on the outcome of a genetic test. The plan may also refuse payment if the patient does not undergo the genetic test.

(ii) *Limitation.*—A plan is permitted to request only the minimum amount of information necessary to make a determination regarding payment. The minimum amount of information necessary is determined in accordance with the minimum necessary standard in 45 CFR 164.502(b) of the privacy regulations issued under the Health Insurance Portability and Accountability Act.

(iii) *Examples.*—See paragraph (e) of this section for examples illustrating the rules of this paragraph (c)(4), as well as other provisions of this section.

(5) *Research exception.*—Notwithstanding paragraph (c)(1) of this section, a plan may request, but not require, that a participant or beneficiary undergo a genetic test if all of the conditions of this paragraph (c)(5) are met:

(i) *Research in accordance with Federal regulations and applicable State or local law or regulations.*—The plan makes the request pursuant to research, as defined in 45 CFR 46.102(d), that complies with 45 CFR Part 46 or equivalent Federal regulations, and any applicable State or local law or regulations for the protection of human subjects in research.

(ii) *Written request for participation in research.*—The plan makes the request in writing, and the request clearly indicates to each participant or beneficiary (or, in the case of a minor child, to the legal guardian of the beneficiary) that—

(A) Compliance with the request is voluntary; and

(B) Noncompliance will have no effect on eligibility for benefits (as described in § 54.9802-1(b)(1)) or premium or contribution amounts.

(iii) *Prohibition on underwriting.*—No genetic information collected or acquired under this paragraph (c)(5) can be used for underwriting purposes (as described in paragraph (d)(1) of this section).

(iv) *Notice to Federal agencies.*—The plan completes a copy of the "Notice of Research Exception under the Genetic Information Nondiscrimination Act" authorized by the Secretary and provides the notice to the address specified in the instructions thereto.

(d) *Prohibitions on collection of genetic information.*—(1) *For underwriting purposes.*—(i) *General rule.*—A group health plan must not collect (as defined in paragraph (a)(1) of this section) genetic information for underwriting purposes. See paragraph (e) of this section for examples illustrating the rules of this paragraph (d)(1), as well as other provisions of this section.

(ii) *Underwriting purposes defined.*—Subject to paragraph (d)(1)(iii) of this section, *underwriting purposes* means, with respect to any group health plan, or health insurance coverage offered in connection with a group health plan—

(A) Rules for, or determination of, eligibility (including enrollment and continued eligibility) for benefits under the plan or coverage as described in § 54.9802-1(b)(1)(ii) (including changes in deductibles or other cost-sharing mechanisms in return for activities such as completing a health risk assessment or participating in a wellness program);

(B) The computation of premium or contribution amounts under the plan or coverage (including discounts, rebates, payments in kind, or other premium differential mechanisms in return for activities such as completing a health risk assessment or participating in a wellness program);

(C) The application of any preexisting condition exclusion under the plan or coverage; and

(D) Other activities related to the creation, renewal, or replacement of a contract of health insurance or health benefits.

(iii) *Medical appropriateness.*—If an individual seeks a benefit under a group health plan, the plan may limit or exclude the benefit based on whether the benefit is medically appropriate, and the determination of whether the benefit is medically appropriate is not within the meaning of underwriting purposes. Accordingly, if an individual seeks a benefit under the plan and the plan conditions the benefit based on its medical appropriateness and the medical appropriateness of the benefit depends on genetic information of the individual, then the plan is permitted to condition the benefit on the genetic information. A plan is permitted to request only the minimum amount of genetic information necessary to determine medical appropriateness. The plan may deny the benefit if the patient does not provide the genetic information required to determine medical appropriateness. If an individual is not seeking a benefit, the medical appropriateness exception of this paragraph (d)(1)(iii) to the definition of underwriting purposes does not apply. See paragraph (e) of this section for examples illustrating the medical appropriateness provisions of this paragraph (d)(1)(iii), as well as other provisions of this section.

(2) *Prior to or in connection with enrollment.*—(i) *In general.*—A group health plan must not collect genetic information with respect to any individual prior to that individual's effective date of coverage under that plan, nor in connection with the rules for eligibility (as defined in § 54.9802-1(b)(1)(ii)) that apply to that individual. Whether or not an individual's information is collected prior to that individual's effective date of coverage is determined at the time of collection.

(ii) *Incidental collection exception.*—(A) *In general.*—If a group health plan obtains genetic information incidental to the collection of other information concerning any individual, the collection is not a violation of this paragraph (d)(2), as long as the collection is not for underwriting purposes in violation of paragraph (d)(1) of this section.

(B) *Limitation.*—The incidental collection exception of this paragraph (d)(2)(ii) does not apply in connection with any collection where it is reasonable to anticipate that health information will be received, unless the collection explicitly states that genetic information should not be provided.

(3) *Examples.*—The rules of this paragraph (d) are illustrated by the following examples:

*Example 1.* (i) *Facts.* A group health plan provides a premium reduction to enrollees who complete a health risk assessment. The health risk assessment is requested to be completed after enrollment. Whether or not it is completed or what responses are given on it has no effect on an individual's enrollment status, or on the enrollment status of members of the individual's family. The health risk assessment includes questions about the individual's family medical history.

(ii) *Conclusion.* In this *Example 1*, the health risk assessment includes a request for genetic information (that is, the individual's family medical history). Because completing the health risk assessment results in a premium reduction, the request for genetic information is for underwriting purposes. Consequently, the request violates the prohibition on the collection of genetic information in paragraph (d)(1) of this section.

*Example 2.* (i) *Facts.* The same facts as *Example 1*, except there is no premium reduction or any other reward for completing the health risk assessment.

(ii) *Conclusion.* In this *Example 2*, the request is not for underwriting purposes, nor is it prior to or in connection with enrollment. Therefore, it does not violate the prohibition on the collection of genetic information in this paragraph (d).

*Example 3.* (i) *Facts.* A group health plan requests that enrollees complete a health risk assessment prior to enrollment, and includes questions about the individual's family medical history. There is no reward or penalty for completing the health risk assessment.

(ii) *Conclusion.* In this *Example 3*, because the health risk assessment includes a request for genetic information (that is, the individual's family medical history), and requests the information prior to enrollment, the request violates the prohibition on the collection of genetic information in paragraph (d)(2) of this section. Moreover, because it is a request for genetic information, it is not an incidental collection under paragraph (d)(2)(ii) of this section.

*Example 4.* (i) *Facts.* The facts are the same as in *Example 1*, except there is no premium reduction or any other reward given for completion of the health risk assessment. However, certain people completing the health risk assessment may become eligible for additional benefits under the plan by being enrolled in a disease management program based on their answers to questions about family medical history. Other people may become eligible for the disease management program based solely on their answers to questions about their individual medical history.

(ii) *Conclusion.* In this *Example 4*, the request for information about an individual's family medical history could result in the individual being eligible for benefits for which the individual would not otherwise be eligible. Therefore, the questions about family medical history on the health risk assessment are a request for genetic information for underwriting purposes and are prohibited under this paragraph (d). Although the plan conditions eligibility for the disease management program based on determinations of medical appropriateness, the exception for determinations of medical appropriateness does not apply because the individual is not seeking benefits.

*Example 5.* (i) *Facts.* A group health plan requests enrollees to complete two distinct health risk assessments (HRAs) after and unrelated to enrollment. The first HRA instructs the individual to answer only for the individual and not for the individual's family. The first HRA does not ask about any genetic tests the individual has undergone or any genetic services the individual has received. The plan offers a reward for completing the first HRA. The second HRA asks about family medical history and the results of genetic tests the individual has undergone. The plan offers no reward for completing the second HRA and the instructions make clear that completion of the second HRA is wholly voluntary and will not affect the reward given for completion of the first HRA.

(ii) *Conclusion.* In this *Example 5*, no genetic information is collected in connection with the first HRA, which offers a reward, and no benefits or other rewards are conditioned on the request for genetic information in the second HRA. Consequently, the request for genetic information in the second HRA is not for underwriting purposes, and the two HRAs do not violate the prohibition on the collection of genetic information in this paragraph (d).

*Example 6.* (i) *Facts.* A group health plan waives its annual deductible for enrollees who complete an HRA. The HRA is requested to be completed after enrollment. Whether or not the HRA is completed or what responses are given on it has no effect on an individual's enrollment status, or on the enrollment status of members of the individual's family. The HRA does not include any direct questions about the individual's genetic information (including family medical history). However, the last question reads, "Is there anything else relevant to your health that you would like us to know or discuss with you?"

(ii) *Conclusion.* In this *Example 6*, the plan's request for medical information does not explicitly state that genetic information should not be provided. Therefore, any genetic information collected in response to the question is not within the incidental collection exception and is prohibited under this paragraph (d).

*Example 7.* (i) *Facts.* Same facts as *Example 6*, except that the last question goes on to state, "In answering this question, you should not include any genetic information. That is, please do not include any family medical history or any information related to genetic testing, genetic services, genetic counseling, or genetic diseases for which you believe you may be at risk."

(ii) *Conclusion.* In this *Example 7*, the plan's request for medical information explicitly states that genetic information should not be provided. Therefore, any genetic information collected in response to the question is within the incidental collection exception. However, the plan may not use any genetic information it obtains incidentally for underwriting purposes.

*Example 8.* (i) *Facts.* Issuer M acquires Issuer N. M requests N's records, stating that N should not provide genetic information and should review the records to excise any genetic information. N assembles the data requested by M and, although N reviews it to delete genetic information, the data from a specific region included some individuals' family medical history. Consequently, M receives genetic information about some of N's covered individuals.

(ii) *Conclusion.* In this *Example 8*, M's request for health information explicitly stated that genetic information should not be provided. See *Example 8* in 29 CFR 2590.702-1(d)(3) or 45 CFR 146.122(d)(3) for a conclusion that the collection of genetic information was within the incidental collection exception of 29 CFR 2590.702-1(d)(2)(ii) or 45 CFR 146.122(d)(ii) similar to the incidental exception of paragraph (d)(2)(ii) of this section. See *Example 8* in 29 CFR 2590.702-1(d)(3) or 45 CFR 146.122(d)(3) also for a caveat that M may not use the genetic information it obtained incidentally for underwriting purposes.

(e) *Examples regarding determinations of medical appropriateness.*— The application of the rules of paragraphs (c) and (d) of this section to plan determinations of medical appropriateness is illustrated by the following examples:

*Example 1.* (i) *Facts.* Individual A's group health plan covers genetic testing for celiac disease for individuals who have family members with this condition. After A's son is diagnosed with celiac disease, A undergoes a genetic test and promptly submits a claim for the test to A's issuer for reimbursement. The issuer asks A to provide the results of the genetic test before the claim is paid.

(ii) *Conclusion.* See *Example 1* in 29 CFR 2590.702-1(e) or 45 CFR 146.122(e) for a conclusion under the rules of paragraph (c)(4) of 29 CFR 2590.702-1 or 45 CFR 146.122 similar to the rules of paragraph (c)(4) of this section that the issuer is permitted to request only the minimum amount of information necessary to make a decision regarding payment. Because the results of the test are not necessary for the issuer to make a decision regarding the payment of A's claim, the conclusion in *Example 1* in 29 CFR 2590.702-1(e) or 45 CFR 146.122(e) concludes that the issuer's request for the results of the genetic test violates paragraph (c) of 29 CFR 2590.702-1 or 45 CFR 146.122 similar to paragraph (c) of this section.

*Example 2.* (i) *Facts.* Individual B's group health plan covers a yearly mammogram for participants and beneficiaries starting at age 40, or at age 30 for those with increased risk for breast cancer, including individuals with BRCA1 or BRCA2 gene mutations. B is 33 years old and has the BRCA2 mutation. B undergoes a mammogram and promptly submits a claim to B's plan for reimbursement. Following an established policy, the plan asks B for evidence of increased risk of breast cancer, such as the results of a genetic test or a family history of breast cancer, before the claim for the mammogram is paid.

This policy is applied uniformly to all similarly situated individuals and is not directed at individuals based on any genetic information.

(ii) *Conclusion.* In this *Example 2*, the plan does not violate paragraphs (c) or (d) of this section. Under paragraph (c), the plan is permitted to request and use the results of a genetic test to make a determination regarding payment, provided the plan requests only the minimum amount of information necessary. Because the medical appropriateness of the mammogram depends on the genetic makeup of the patient, the minimum amount of information necessary includes the results of the genetic test. Similarly, the plan does not violate paragraph (d) of this section because the plan is permitted to request genetic information in making a determination regarding the medical appropriateness of a claim if the genetic information is necessary to make the determination (and if the genetic information is not used for underwriting purposes).

*Example 3.* (i) *Facts.* Individual C was previously diagnosed with and treated for breast cancer, which is currently in remission. In accordance with the recommendation of C's physician, C has been taking a regular dose of tamoxifen to help prevent a recurrence. C's group health plan adopts a new policy requiring patients taking tamoxifen to undergo a genetic test to ensure that tamoxifen is medically appropriate for their genetic makeup. In accordance with, at the time, the latest scientific research, tamoxifen is not helpful in up to 7 percent of breast cancer patients, those with certain variations of the gene for making the CYP2D6 enzyme. If a patient has a gene variant making tamoxifen not medically appropriate, the plan does not pay for the tamoxifen prescription.

(ii) *Conclusion.* In this *Example 3*, the plan does not violate paragraph (c) of this section if it conditions future payments for the tamoxifen prescription on C's undergoing a genetic test to determine what genetic markers C has for making the CYP2D6 enzyme. Nor does the plan violate paragraph (c) of this section if the plan refuses future payment if the results of the genetic test indicate that tamoxifen is not medically appropriate for C.

*Example 4.* (i) *Facts.* A group health plan offers a diabetes disease management program to all similarly situated individuals for whom it is medically appropriate based on whether the individuals have or are at risk for diabetes. The program provides enhanced benefits related only to diabetes for individuals who qualify for the program. The plan sends out a notice to all participants that describes the diabetes disease management program and explains the terms for eligibility. Individuals interested in enrolling in the program are advised to contact the plan to demonstrate that they have diabetes or that they are at risk for diabetes. For individuals who do not currently have diabetes, genetic information may be used to demonstrate that an individual is at risk.

(ii) *Conclusion.* In this *Example 4*, the plan may condition benefits under the disease management program upon a showing by an individual that the individual is at risk for diabetes, even if such showing may involve genetic information, provided that the plan requests genetic information only when necessary to make a determination regarding whether the disease management program is medically appropriate for the individual and only requests the minimum amount of information necessary to make that determination.

*Example 5.* (i) *Facts.* Same facts as *Example 4*, except that the plan includes a questionnaire that asks about the occurrence of diabetes in members of the individual's family as part of the notice describing the disease management program.

(ii) *Conclusion.* In this *Example 5*, the plan violates the requirements of paragraph (d)(1) of this section because the requests for genetic information are not limited to those situations in which it is necessary to make a determination regarding whether the disease management program is medically appropriate for the individuals.

*Example 6.* (i) *Facts.* Same facts as *Example 4*, except the disease management program provides an enhanced benefit in the form of a lower annual deductible to individuals under the program; the lower deductible applies with respect to all medical expenses incurred by the individual. Thus, whether or not a claim relates to diabetes, the individual is provided with a lower deductible based on the individual providing the plan with genetic information.

(ii) *Conclusion.* In this *Example 6*, because the enhanced benefits include benefits not related to the determination of medical appropriateness, making available the enhanced benefits is within the meaning of underwriting purposes. Accordingly, the plan may not request or require genetic information (including family history information) in determining eligibility for enhanced benefits under the program because such a request would be for underwriting purposes and would violate paragraph (d)(1) of this section.

(f) *Effective/applicability date.*—This section applies for plan years beginning on or after December 7, 2009.

(g) *Expiration date.*—This section expires on or before October 1, 2012. [Temporary Reg. § 54.9802-3T.]

☐ [*T.D.* 9464, 10-1-2009.]

⟫→ *Caution: Reg. §54.9802-4, below, as added by T.D. 9867, applies to plan years beginning on or after January 1, 2020.*

[Reg. §54.9802-4]

**§54.9802-4. Special Rule Allowing Integration of Health Reimbursement Arrangements (HRAs) and Other Account-Based Group Health Plans with Individual Health Insurance Coverage and Medicare and Prohibiting Discrimination In HRAs and Other Account-Based Group Health Plans.**—(a) *Scope.*—This section applies to health reimbursement arrangements (HRAs) and other account-based group health plans, as defined in §54.9815-2711(d)(6)(i) of this chapter. For ease of reference, the term "HRA" is used in this section to include other account-based group health plans. For related regulations, see 26 CFR 1.36B-2(c)(3)(i) and (c)(5), 29 CFR 2510.3-1(l), and 45 CFR 155.420.

(b) *Purpose.*—This section provides the conditions that an HRA must satisfy in order to be integrated with individual health insurance coverage for purposes of Public Health Service Act (PHS Act) sections 2711 and 2713 and §54.9815-2711(d)(4) of this chapter (referred to as an individual coverage HRA). This section also allows an individual coverage HRA to be integrated with Medicare for purposes of PHS Act sections 2711 and 2713 and §54.9815-2711(d)(4), subject to the conditions provided in this section (see paragraph (e) of this section). Some of the conditions set forth in this section specifically relate to compliance with PHS Act sections 2711 and 2713 and some relate to the effect of having or being offered an individual coverage HRA on eligibility for the premium tax credit under section 36B. In addition, this section provides conditions that an individual coverage HRA must satisfy in order to comply with the nondiscrimination provisions in section 9802 and PHS Act section 2705 (which is incorporated in section 9815) and that are consistent with the provisions of the Patient Protection and Affordable Care Act, Public Law 111–148 (124 Stat. 119 (2010)), and the Health Care and Education Reconciliation Act of 2010, Public Law 111–152 (124 Stat. 1029 (2010)), each as amended, that are designed to create a competitive individual market. These conditions are intended to prevent an HRA plan sponsor from intentionally or unintentionally, directly or indirectly, steering any participants or dependents with adverse health factors away from its traditional group health plan, if any, and toward individual health insurance coverage.

(c) *General rule.*—An HRA will be considered to be integrated with individual health insurance coverage for purposes of PHS Act sections 2711 and 2713 and §54.9815-2711(d)(4) of this chapter and will not be considered to discriminate in violation of section 9802 and PHS Act section 2705 solely because it is integrated with individual health insurance coverage, provided that the conditions of this paragraph (c) are satisfied. See paragraph (e) of this section for how these conditions apply to an individual coverage HRA integrated with Medicare. For purposes of this section, medical care expenses means medical care expenses as defined in §54.9815-2711(d)(6)(ii) of this chapter and Exchange means Exchange as defined in 45 CFR 155.20.

(1) *Enrollment in individual health insurance coverage.*—(i) *In general.*—The HRA must require that the participant and any dependent(s) are enrolled in individual health insurance coverage that is subject to and complies with the requirements in PHS Act section 2711 (and §54.9815-2711(a)(2) of this chapter) and PHS Act section 2713 (and §54.9815-2713(a)(1) of this chapter), for each month that the individual(s) are covered by the HRA. For purposes of this paragraph (c), all individual health insurance coverage, except for individual health insurance coverage that consists solely of excepted benefits, is treated as being subject to and complying with PHS Act sections 2711 and 2713. References to individual health insurance coverage in this paragraph (c) do not include individual health insurance coverage that consists solely of excepted benefits.

(ii) *Forfeiture.*—The HRA must provide that if any individual covered by the HRA ceases to be covered by individual health insurance coverage, the HRA will not reimburse medical care expenses that are incurred by that individual after the individual health insurance coverage ceases. In addition, if the participant and all dependents covered by the participant's HRA cease to be covered by individual health insurance coverage, the participant must forfeit the HRA. In either case, the HRA must reimburse medical care expenses incurred by the individual prior to the cessation of individual health insurance coverage to the extent the medical care expenses are otherwise covered by the HRA, but the HRA may limit the period to submit medical care expenses for reimbursement to a reasonable specified time period. If a participant or dependent loses coverage under the HRA for a reason other than cessation of individual health insurance coverage, COBRA and other continuation coverage requirements may apply.

(iii) *Grace periods and retroactive termination of individual health insurance coverage.*—In the event an individual is initially enrolled in individual health insurance coverage and subsequently timely fails

to pay premiums for the coverage, with the result that the individual is in a grace period, the individual is considered to be enrolled in individual health insurance coverage for purposes of this paragraph (c)(1) and the individual coverage HRA must reimburse medical care expenses incurred by the individual during that time period to the extent the medical care expenses are otherwise covered by the HRA. If the individual fails to pay the applicable premium(s) by the end of the grace period and the coverage is cancelled or terminated, including retroactively, or if the individual health insurance coverage is cancelled or terminated retroactively for some other reason (for example, a rescission), an individual coverage HRA must require that a participant notify the HRA that coverage has been cancelled or terminated and the date on which the cancellation or termination is effective. After the individual coverage HRA has received the notice of cancellation or termination, the HRA may not reimburse medical care expenses incurred on and after the date the individual health insurance coverage was cancelled or terminated, which is considered to be the date of termination of coverage under the HRA.

(2) *No traditional group health plan may be offered to same participants.*—To the extent a plan sponsor offers any class of employees (as defined in paragraph (d) of this section) an individual coverage HRA, the plan sponsor may not also offer a traditional group health plan to the same class of employees, except as provided in paragraph (d)(5) of this section. For purposes of this section, a traditional group health plan is any group health plan other than either an account-based group health plan or a group health plan that consists solely of excepted benefits. Therefore, a plan sponsor may not offer a choice between an individual coverage HRA or a traditional group health plan to any participant or dependent.

(3) *Same terms requirement.*—(i) *In general.*—If a plan sponsor offers an individual coverage HRA to a class of employees described in paragraph (d) of this section, the HRA must be offered on the same terms to all participants within the class, except as provided in paragraphs (c)(3)(ii) through (vi) and (d)(5) of this section.

(ii) *Carryover amounts, salary reduction arrangements, and transfer amounts.*—Amounts that are not used to reimburse medical care expenses for any plan year that are made available to participants in later plan years are disregarded for purposes of determining whether an HRA is offered on the same terms, provided that the method for determining whether participants have access to unused amounts in future years, and the methodology and formula for determining the amounts of unused funds which they may access in future years, is the same for all participants in a class of employees. In addition, the ability to pay the portion of the premium for individual health insurance coverage that is not covered by the HRA, if any, by using a salary reduction arrangement under section 125 is considered to be a term of the HRA for purposes of this paragraph (c)(3). Therefore, an HRA is not provided on the same terms unless the salary reduction arrangement, if made available to any participant in a class of employees, is made available on the same terms to all participants (other than former employees, as defined in paragraph (c)(3)(iv) of this section) in the class of employees. Further, to the extent that a participant in an individual coverage HRA was previously covered by another HRA and the current individual coverage HRA makes available amounts that were not used to reimburse medical care expenses under the prior HRA (transferred amounts), the transferred amounts are disregarded for purposes of determining whether the HRA is offered on the same terms, provided that if the HRA makes available transferred amounts, it does so on the same terms for all participants in the class of employees.

(iii) *Permitted variation.*—An HRA does not fail to be provided on the same terms solely because the maximum dollar amount made available to participants in a class of employees to reimburse medical care expenses for any plan year increases in accordance with paragraph (c)(3)(iii)(A) or (B) of this section.

(A) *Variation due to number of dependents.*—An HRA does not fail to be provided on the same terms to participants in a class of employees solely because the maximum dollar amount made available to those participants to reimburse medical care expenses for any plan year increases as the number of the participant's dependents who are covered under the HRA increases, so long as the same maximum dollar amount attributable to the increase in family size is made available to all participants in that class of employees with the same number of dependents covered by the HRA.

(B) *Variation due to age.*—An HRA does not fail to be provided on the same terms to participants in a class of employees solely because the maximum dollar amount made available under the terms of the HRA to those participants to reimburse medical care expenses for any plan year increases as the age of the participant increases, so long as the requirements in paragraphs (c)(3)(iii)(B)(1)

***⤞ Caution: Reg. §54.9802-4, below, as added by T.D. 9867, applies to plan years beginning on or after January 1, 2020.***

and (2) of this section are satisfied. For the purpose of this paragraph (c)(3)(iii)(B), the plan sponsor may determine the age of the participant using any reasonable method for a plan year, so long as the plan sponsor determines each participant's age for the purpose of this paragraph (c)(3)(iii)(B) using the same method for all participants in the class of employees for the plan year and the method is determined prior to the plan year.

*(1)* The same maximum dollar amount attributable to the increase in age is made available to all participants who are the same age.

*(2)* The maximum dollar amount made available to the oldest participant(s) is not more than three times the maximum dollar amount made available to the youngest participant(s).

(iv) *Former employees.*—An HRA does not fail to be treated as provided on the same terms if the plan sponsor offers the HRA to some, but not all, former employees within a class of employees. However, if a plan sponsor offers the HRA to one or more former employees within a class of employees, the HRA must be offered to the former employee(s) on the same terms as to all other employees within the class, except as provided in paragraph (c)(3)(ii) of this section. For purposes of this section, a former employee is an employee who is no longer performing services for the employer.

(v) *New employees or new dependents.*—For a participant whose coverage under the HRA becomes effective later than the first day of the plan year, the HRA does not fail to be treated as being provided on the same terms to the participant if the maximum dollar amount made available to the participant either is the same as the maximum dollar amount made available to participants in the participant's class of employees whose coverage became effective as of the first day of the plan year, or is pro-rated consistent with the portion of the plan year in which the participant is covered by the HRA. Similarly, if the HRA provides for variation in the maximum amount made available to participants in a class of employees based on the number of a participant's dependents covered by the HRA, and the number of a participant's dependents covered by the HRA changes during a plan year (either increasing or decreasing), the HRA does not fail to be treated as being provided on the same terms to the participant if the maximum dollar amount made available to the participant either is the same as the maximum dollar amount made available to participants in the participant's class of employees who had the same number of dependents covered by the HRA on the first day of the plan year or is pro-rated for the remainder of the plan year after the change in the number of the participant's dependents covered by the HRA consistent with the portion of the plan year in which that number of dependents are covered by the HRA. The method the HRA uses to determine amounts made available for participants whose coverage under the HRA is effective later than the first day of the plan year or who have changes in the number of dependents covered by the HRA during a plan year must be the same for all participants in the class of employees and the method must be determined prior to the beginning of the plan year.

(vi) *HSA-compatible HRAs.*—An HRA does not fail to be treated as provided on the same terms if the plan sponsor offers participants in a class of employees a choice between an HSA-compatible individual coverage HRA and an individual coverage HRA that is not HSA compatible, provided both types of HRAs are offered to all participants in the class of employees on the same terms. For the purpose of this paragraph (c)(3)(vi), an HSA-compatible individual coverage HRA is an individual coverage HRA that is limited in accordance with applicable guidance under section 223 such that an individual covered by such an HRA is not disqualified from being an eligible individual under section 223.

(vii) *Examples.*—The following examples illustrate the provisions of this paragraph (c)(3), without taking into account the provisions of paragraph (d) of this section. In each example, the HRA is an individual coverage HRA that has a calendar year plan year and may reimburse any medical care expenses, including premiums for individual health insurance coverage (except as provided in paragraph (c)(3)(vii)(E) of this section (*Example 5*)). Further, in each example, assume the HRA is offered on the same terms, except as otherwise specified in the example and that no participants or dependents are Medicare beneficiaries.

(A) *Example 1: Carryover amounts permitted*—*(1) Facts.* For 2020 and again for 2021, Plan Sponsor A offers all employees $7,000 each in an HRA, and the HRA provides that amounts that are unused at the end of a plan year may be carried over to the next plan year, with no restrictions on the use of the carryover amounts compared to the use of newly available amounts. At the end of 2020, some employees have used all of the funds in their HRAs, while other employees have balances remaining that range from $500 to $1,750 that are carried over to 2021 for those employees.

*(2) Conclusion.* The same terms requirement of this paragraph (c)(3) is satisfied in this paragraph (c)(3)(vii)(A) (*Example 1*) for 2020 because Plan Sponsor A offers all employees the same amount, $7,000, in an HRA for that year. The same terms requirement is also satisfied for 2021 because Plan Sponsor A again offers all employees the same amount for that year, and the carryover amounts that some employees have are disregarded in applying the same terms requirement because the amount of the carryover for each employee (that employee's balance) and each employee's access to the carryover amounts is based on the same terms.

(B) *Example 2: Employees hired after the first day of the plan year*—*(1) Facts.* For 2020, Plan Sponsor B offers all employees employed on January 1, 2020, $7,000 each in an HRA for the plan year. Employees hired after January 1, 2020, are eligible to enroll in the HRA with an effective date of the first day of the month following their date of hire, as long as they have enrolled in individual health insurance coverage effective on or before that date, and the amount offered to these employees is pro-rated based on the number of months remaining in the plan year, including the month which includes their coverage effective date.

*(2) Conclusion.* The same terms requirement of this paragraph (c)(3) is satisfied in this paragraph (c)(3)(vii)(B) (*Example 2*) for 2020 because Plan Sponsor B offers all employees employed on the first day of the plan year the same amount, $7,000, in an HRA for that plan year and all employees hired after January 1, 2020, a pro-rata amount based on the portion of the plan year during which they are enrolled in the HRA.

(C) *Example 3: HRA amounts offered vary based on number of dependents*—*(1) Facts.* For 2020, Plan Sponsor C offers its employees the following amounts in an HRA: $1,500, if the employee is the only individual covered by the HRA; $3,500, if the employee and one dependent are covered by the HRA; and $5,000, if the employee and more than one dependent are covered by the HRA.

*(2) Conclusion.* The same terms requirement of this paragraph (c)(3) is satisfied in this paragraph (c)(3)(vii)(C) (*Example 3*) because paragraph (c)(3)(iii)(A) of this section allows the maximum dollar amount made available in an HRA to increase as the number of the participant's dependents covered by the HRA increases and Plan Sponsor C makes the same amount available to each employee with the same number of dependents covered by the HRA.

(D) *Example 4: HRA amounts offered vary based on increases in employees' ages*—*(1) Facts.* For 2020, Plan Sponsor D offers its employees the following amounts in an HRA: $1,000 each for employees age 25 to 35; $2,000 each for employees age 36 to 45; $2,500 each for employees age 46 to 55; and $4,000 each for employees over age 55.

*(2) Conclusion.* The same terms requirement of this paragraph (c)(3) is not satisfied in this paragraph (c)(3)(vii)(D) (*Example 4*) because the terms of the HRA provide the oldest participants (those over age 55) with more than three times the amount made available to the youngest participants (those ages 25 to 35), in violation of paragraph (c)(3)(iii)(B)(2) of this section.

(E) *Example 5: Application of same terms requirement to premium only HRA*—*(1) Facts.* For 2020, Plan Sponsor E offers its employees an HRA that reimburses only premiums for individual health insurance coverage, up to $10,000 for the year. Employee A enrolls in individual health insurance coverage with a $5,000 premium for the year and is reimbursed $5,000 from the HRA. Employee B enrolls in individual health insurance coverage with an $8,000 premium for the year and is reimbursed $8,000 from the HRA.

*(2) Conclusion.* The same terms requirement of this paragraph (c)(3) is satisfied in this paragraph (c)(3)(vii)(E) (*Example 5*) because Plan Sponsor E offers the HRA on the same terms to all employees, notwithstanding that some employees receive a greater amount of reimbursement than others based on the cost of the individual health insurance coverage selected by the employee.

(4) *Opt out.*—Under the terms of the HRA, a participant who is otherwise eligible for coverage must be permitted to opt out of and waive future reimbursements on behalf of the participant and all dependents eligible for the HRA from the HRA once, and only once, with respect to each plan year. The HRA may establish timeframes for enrollment in (and opting out of) the HRA but, in general, the opportunity to opt out must be provided in advance of the first day of the plan year. For participants who become eligible to participate in the HRA on a date other than the first day of the plan year (or who become eligible fewer than 90 days prior to the plan year or for whom the notice under paragraph (c)(6) of this section is required to be provided as set forth in paragraph (c)(6)(i)(C) of this section), or for a dependent who newly becomes eligible during the plan year, this opportunity must be provided during the applicable HRA enrollment period(s) established by the HRA for these individuals. Further, under the terms of the HRA, upon termination of employment, for a participant who is covered by the HRA, either the remaining

>>> *Caution: Reg. §54.9802-4, below, as added by T.D. 9867, applies to plan years beginning on or after January 1, 2020.*

amounts in the HRA must be forfeited or the participant must be permitted to permanently opt out of or waive future reimbursements from the HRA on behalf of the participant and all dependents covered by the HRA.

(5) *Reasonable procedures for coverage substantiation.*—(i) *Substantiation of individual health insurance coverage for the plan year.*—The HRA must implement, and comply with, reasonable procedures to substantiate that participants and each dependent covered by the HRA are, or will be, enrolled in individual health insurance coverage for the plan year (or for the portion of the plan year the individual is covered by the HRA, if applicable). The HRA may establish the date by which this substantiation must be provided, but, in general, the date may be no later than the first day of the plan year. However, for a participant who is not eligible to participate in the HRA on the first day of the plan year (or who becomes eligible fewer than 90 days prior to the plan year or for whom the notice under paragraph (c)(6) of this section is required to be provided as set forth in paragraph (c)(6)(i)(C) of this section), the HRA may establish the date by which this substantiation must be provided, but that date may be no later than the date the HRA coverage begins. Similarly, for a participant who adds a new dependent during the plan year, the HRA may establish the date by which this substantiation must be provided, but the date may be no later than the date the HRA coverage for the new dependent begins; however, to the extent the dependent's coverage under the HRA is effective retroactively, the HRA may establish a reasonable time by which this substantiation is required, but must require it be provided before the HRA will reimburse any medical care expense for the newly added dependent. The reasonable procedures an HRA may use to implement the substantiation requirement set forth in this paragraph (c)(5)(i) may include a requirement that a participant substantiate enrollment by providing either:

(A) A document from a third party (for example, the issuer or an Exchange) showing that the participant and any dependents covered by the HRA are, or will be, enrolled in individual health insurance coverage (for example, an insurance card or an explanation of benefits document pertaining to the relevant time period or documentation from the Exchange showing that the individual has completed the application and plan selection); or

(B) An attestation by the participant stating that the participant and dependent(s) covered by the HRA are, or will be, enrolled in individual health insurance coverage, the date coverage began or will begin, and the name of the provider of the coverage.

(ii) *Coverage substantiation with each request for reimbursement of medical care expenses.*—Following the initial substantiation of coverage, with each new request for reimbursement of an incurred medical care expense for the same plan year, the HRA may not reimburse a participant for any medical care expenses unless, prior to each reimbursement, the participant substantiates that the individual on whose behalf medical care expenses are requested to be reimbursed continues to be enrolled in individual health insurance coverage for the month during which the medical care expenses were incurred. The HRA must implement, and comply with, reasonable procedures to satisfy this requirement. This substantiation may be in the form of a written attestation by the participant, which may be part of the form used to request reimbursement, or a document from a third party (for example, a health insurance issuer) showing that the participant or the dependent, if applicable, are or were enrolled in individual health insurance coverage for the applicable month.

(iii) *Reliance on substantiation.*—For purposes of this paragraph (c)(5), an HRA may rely on the participant's documentation or attestation unless the HRA, its plan sponsor, or any other entity acting in an official capacity on behalf of the HRA has actual knowledge that any individual covered by the HRA is not, or will not be, enrolled in individual health insurance coverage for the plan year (or applicable portion of the plan year) or the month, as applicable.

(6) *Notice requirement.*—(i) *Timing.*—The HRA must provide a written notice to each participant:

(A) At least 90 calendar days before the beginning of each plan year for any participant who is not described in either paragraph (c)(6)(i)(B) or (C) of this section;

(B) No later than the date on which the HRA may first take effect for the participant, for any participant who is not eligible to participate at the beginning of the plan year (or is not eligible to participate at the time the notice is provided at least 90 calendar days before the beginning of the plan year pursuant to paragraph (c)(6)(i)(A) of this section); or

(C) No later than the date on which the HRA may first take effect for the participant, for any participant who is employed by an employer that is first established less than 120 days before the

beginning of the first plan year of the HRA; this paragraph (c)(6)(i)(C) applies only with respect to the first plan year of the HRA.

(ii) *Content.*—The notice must include all the information described in this paragraph (c)(6)(ii) (and may include any additional information that does not conflict with that information). To the extent that the Departments of the Treasury, Labor and Health and Human Services provide model notice language for certain elements of this required notice, HRAs are permitted, but not required, to use the model language.

(A) A description of the terms of the HRA, including the maximum dollar amount available for each participant (including the self-only HRA amount available for the plan year (or the maximum dollar amount available for the plan year if the HRA provides for reimbursements up to a single dollar amount regardless of whether a participant has self-only or other than self-only coverage)), any rules regarding the proration of the maximum dollar amount applicable to any participant (or dependent, if applicable) who is not eligible to participate in the HRA for the entire plan year, whether (and which of) the participant's dependents are eligible for the HRA, a statement that there are different kinds of HRAs (including a qualified small employer health reimbursement arrangement) and the HRA being offered is an individual coverage HRA, a statement that the HRA requires the participant and any covered dependents to be enrolled in individual health insurance coverage (or Medicare Part A and B or Medicare Part C, if applicable), a statement that the coverage in which the participant and any covered dependents must be enrolled cannot be short-term, limited-duration insurance or consist solely of excepted benefits, if the HRA is subject to the Employee Retirement Income Security Act (ERISA), a statement that individual health insurance coverage in which the participant and any covered dependents are enrolled is not subject to ERISA, if the conditions under 29 CFR 2510.3-1(l) are satisfied, the date as of which coverage under the HRA may first become effective (both for participants whose coverage will become effective on the first day of the plan year and for participants whose HRA coverage may become effective at a later date), the dates on which the HRA plan year begins and ends, and the dates on which the amounts newly made available under the HRA will be made available.

(B) A statement of the right of the participant to opt out of and waive future reimbursements from the HRA, as set forth under paragraph (c)(4) of this section.

(C) A description of the potential availability of the premium tax credit if the participant opts out of and waives future reimbursements from the HRA and the HRA is not affordable for one or more months under § 1.36B-2(c)(5) of this chapter, a statement that even if the participant opts out of and waives future reimbursements from an HRA, the offer will prohibit the participant (and, potentially, the participant's dependents) from receiving a premium tax credit for the participant's coverage (or the dependent's coverage, if applicable) on an Exchange for any month that the HRA is affordable under § 1.36B-2(c)(5) of this chapter, a statement describing how the participant may find assistance with determining affordability, a statement that, if the participant is a former employee, the offer of the HRA does not render the participant (or the participant's dependents, if applicable) ineligible for the premium tax credit regardless of whether it is affordable under § 1.36B-2(c)(5) of this chapter, and a statement that if the participant or dependent is enrolled in Medicare, he or she is ineligible for the premium tax credit without regard to the offer or acceptance of the HRA;

(D) A statement that if the participant accepts the HRA, the participant may not claim a premium tax credit for the participant's Exchange coverage for any month the HRA may be used to reimburse medical care expenses of the participant, and a premium tax credit may not be claimed for the Exchange coverage of the participant's dependents for any month the HRA may be used to reimburse medical care expenses of the dependents.

(E) A statement that the participant must inform any Exchange to which the participant applies for advance payments of the premium tax credit of the availability of the HRA; the self-only HRA amount available for the HRA plan year (or the maximum dollar amount available for the plan year if the HRA provides for reimbursements up to a single dollar amount regardless of whether a participant has self-only or other than self-only coverage) as set forth in the written notice in accordance with paragraph (c)(6)(ii)(A) of this section; whether the HRA is also available to the participant's dependents and if so, which ones; the date as of which coverage under the HRA may first become effective; the date on which the plan year begins and the date on which it ends; and whether the participant is a current employee or former employee.

(F) A statement that the participant should retain the written notice because it may be needed to determine whether the

>>>→ *Caution: Reg. §54.9802-4, below, as added by T.D. 9867, applies to plan years beginning on or after January 1, 2020.*

participant is allowed a premium tax credit on the participant's individual income tax return.

(G) A statement that the HRA may not reimburse any medical care expense unless the substantiation requirement set forth in paragraph (c)(5)(ii) of this section is satisfied and a statement that the participant must also provide the substantiation required by paragraph (c)(5)(i) of this section.

(H) A statement that if the individual health insurance coverage (or coverage under Medicare Part A and B or Medicare Part C) of a participant or dependent ceases, the HRA will not reimburse any medical care expenses that are incurred by the participant or dependent, as applicable, after the coverage ceases, and a statement that the participant must inform the HRA if the participant's or dependent's individual health insurance coverage (or coverage under Medicare Part A and B or Medicare Part C) is cancelled or terminated retroactively and the date on which the cancellation or termination is effective.

(I) The contact information (including a phone number) for an individual or a group of individuals who participants may contact in order to receive additional information regarding the HRA. The plan sponsor may determine which individual or group of individuals is best suited to be the specified contact.

(J) A statement of availability of a special enrollment period to enroll in or change individual health insurance coverage, through or outside of an Exchange, for the participant and any dependents who newly gain access to the HRA and are not already covered by the HRA.

(d) *Classes of employees.*—(1) *In general.*—This paragraph (d) sets forth the rules for determining classes of employees. Paragraph (d)(2) of this section sets forth the specific classes of employees; paragraph (d)(3) of this section sets forth a minimum class size requirement that applies in certain circumstances; paragraph (d)(4) of this section sets forth rules regarding the definition of "full-time employees," "part-time employees," and "seasonal employees"; paragraph (d)(5) of this section sets forth a special rule for new hires; and paragraph (d)(6) of this section addresses student premium reduction arrangements. For purposes of this section, including determining classes under this paragraph (d), the employer is the common law employer and is determined without regard to the rules under sections 414(b), (c), (m), and (o) that would treat the common law employer as a single employer with certain other entities.

(2) *List of classes.*—Participants may be treated as belonging to a class of employees based on whether they are, or are not, included in the classes described in this paragraph (d)(2). If the individual coverage HRA is offered to former employees, former employees are considered to be in the same class in which they were included immediately before separation from service. Before each plan year, a plan sponsor must determine for the plan year which classes of employees it intends to treat separately and the definition of the relevant class(es) it will apply, to the extent these regulations permit a choice. After the classes and the definitions of the classes are established for a plan year, a plan sponsor may not make changes to the classes of employees or the definitions of those relevant classes with respect to that plan year.

(i) Full-time employees, defined at the election of the plan sponsor to mean either full-time employees under section 4980H (and §54.4980H-1(a)(21) of this chapter) or employees who are not part-time employees (as described in §1.105-11(c)(2)(iii)(C) of this chapter);

(ii) Part-time employees, defined at the election of the plan sponsor to mean either employees who are not full-time employees under section 4980H (and under §54.4980H-1(a)(21) of this chapter (which defines full-time employee)) or employees who are part-time employees as described in §1.105-11(c)(2)(iii)(C) of this chapter;

(iii) Employees who are paid on a salary basis;

(iv) Non-salaried employees (such as, for example, hourly employees);

(v) Employees whose primary site of employment is in the same rating area as defined in 45 CFR 147.102(b);

(vi) Seasonal employees, defined at the election of the plan sponsor to mean seasonal employees as described in either §54.4980H-1(a)(38) or §1.105-11(c)(2)(iii)(C) of this chapter;

(vii) Employees included in a unit of employees covered by a particular collective bargaining agreement (or an appropriate related participation agreement) in which the plan sponsor participates (as described in §1.105-11(c)(2)(iii)(D) of this chapter);

(viii) Employees who have not satisfied a waiting period for coverage (if the waiting period complies with §54.9815-2708 of this chapter);

(ix) Non-resident aliens with no U.S.-based income (as described in §1.105-11(c)(2)(iii)(E) of this chapter);

(x) Employees who, under all the facts and circumstances, are employees of an entity that hired the employees for temporary placement at an entity that is not the common law employer of the employees and that is not treated as a single employer with the entity that hired the employees for temporary placement under section 414(b), (c), (m), or (o); or

(xi) A group of participants described as a combination of two or more of the classes of employees set forth in paragraphs (d)(2)(i) through (x) of this section.

(3) *Minimum class size requirement.*—(i) *In general.*—If a class of employees is subject to the minimum class size requirement as set forth in this paragraph (d)(3), the class must consist of at least a minimum number of employees (as described in paragraphs (d)(3)(iii) and (iv) of this section), otherwise, the plan sponsor may not treat that class as a separate class of employees. Paragraph (d)(3)(ii) of this section sets forth the circumstances in which the minimum class size requirement applies to a class of employees, paragraph (d)(3)(iii) of this section sets forth the rules for determining the applicable class size minimum, and paragraph (d)(3)(iv) of this section sets forth the rules for a plan sponsor to determine if it satisfies the minimum class size requirement with respect to a class of employees.

(ii) *Circumstances in which minimum class size requirement applies.*—(A) The minimum class size requirement applies only if a plan sponsor offers a traditional group health plan to one or more classes of employees and offers an individual coverage HRA to one or more other classes of employees.

(B) The minimum class size requirement does not apply to a class of employees offered a traditional group health plan or a class of employees offered no coverage.

(C) The minimum class size requirement applies to a class of employees offered an individual coverage HRA if the class is full-time employees, part-time employees, salaried employees, non-salaried employees, or employees whose primary site of employment is in the same rating area (described in paragraph (d)(2)(i), (ii), (iii), (iv), or (v) of this section, respectively, and referred to collectively as the applicable classes or individually as an applicable class), except that:

*(1)* In the case of the class of employees whose primary site of employment is in the same rating area (as described in paragraph (d)(2)(v) of this section), the minimum class size requirement does not apply if the geographic area defining the class is a State or a combination of two or more entire States; and

*(2)* In the case of the classes of employees that are full-time employees and part-time employees (as described in paragraphs (d)(2)(i) and (ii) of this section, respectively), the minimum class size requirement applies only to those classes (and the classes are only applicable classes) if the employees in one such class are offered a traditional group health plan while the employees in the other such class are offered an individual coverage HRA. In such a case, the minimum class size requirement applies only to the class offered an individual coverage HRA.

(D) A class of employees offered an individual coverage HRA is also subject to the minimum class size requirement if the class is a class of employees created by combining at least one of the applicable classes (as defined in paragraph (d)(3)(ii)(C) of this section) with any other class, except that the minimum class size requirement shall not apply to a class that is the result of a combination of one of the applicable classes and a class of employees who have not satisfied a waiting period (as described in paragraph (d)(2)(viii) of this section).

(iii) *Determination of the applicable class size minimum.*—(A) *In general.*—The minimum number of employees that must be in a class of employees that is subject to the minimum class size requirement (the applicable class size minimum) is determined prior to the beginning of the plan year for each plan year of the individual coverage HRA and is:

*(1)* 10, for an employer with fewer than 100 employees;

*(2)* A number, rounded down to a whole number, equal to 10 percent of the total number of employees, for an employer with 100 to 200 employees; and

*(3)* 20, for an employer with more than 200 employees.

(B) *Determining employer size.*—For purposes of this paragraph (d)(3), the number of employees of an employer is determined in advance of the plan year of the HRA based on the number of employees that the employer reasonably expects to employ on the first day of the plan year.

(iv) *Determining if a class satisfies the applicable class size minimum.*—For purposes of this paragraph (d)(3), whether a class of employees satisfies the applicable class size minimum for a plan year of the individual coverage HRA is based on the number of employ-

*»»→ Caution: Reg. §54.9802-4, below, as added by T.D. 9867, applies to plan years beginning on or after January 1, 2020.*

ees in the class offered the individual coverage HRA as of the first day of the plan year. Therefore, this determination is not based on the number of employees that actually enroll in the individual coverage HRA, and this determination is not affected by changes in the number of employees in the class during the plan year.

(4) *Consistency requirement.*—For any plan year, a plan sponsor may define "full-time employee," "part-time employee," and "seasonal employee" in accordance with the relevant provisions of sections 105(h) or 4980H, as set forth in paragraphs (d)(2)(i), (ii), and (vi) of this section, if:

(i) To the extent applicable under the HRA for the plan year, each of the three classes of employees are defined in accordance with section 105(h) or each of the three classes of employees are defined in accordance with section 4980H for the plan year; and

(ii) The HRA plan document sets forth the applicable definitions prior to the beginning of the plan year to which the definitions will apply.

(5) *Special rule for new hires.*—(i) *In general.*—Notwithstanding paragraphs (c)(2) and (3) of this section, a plan sponsor that offers a traditional group health plan to a class of employees may prospectively offer the employees in that class of employees who are hired on or after a certain future date (the new hire date) an individual coverage HRA (with this group of employees referred to as the new hire subclass), while continuing to offer employees in that class of employees who are hired before the new hire date a traditional group health plan (with the rule set forth in this sentence referred to as the special rule for new hires). For the new hire subclass, the individual coverage HRA must be offered on the same terms to all participants within the subclass, in accordance with paragraph (c)(3) of this section. In accordance with paragraph (c)(2) of this section, a plan sponsor may not offer a choice between an individual coverage HRA or a traditional group health plan to any employee in the new hire subclass or to any employee in the class who is not a member of the new hire subclass.

(ii) *New hire date.*—A plan sponsor may set the new hire date for a class of employees prospectively as any date on or after January 1, 2020. A plan sponsor may set different new hire dates prospectively for separate classes of employees.

(iii) *Discontinuation of use of special rule for new hires and multiple applications of the special rule for new hires.*—A plan sponsor may discontinue use of the special rule for new hires at any time for any class of employees. In that case, the new hire subclass is no longer treated as a separate subclass of employees. In the event a plan sponsor applies the special rule for new hires to a class of employees and later discontinues use of the rule to the class of employees, the plan sponsor may later apply the rule if the application of the rule would be permitted under the rules for initial application of the special rule for new hires. If a plan sponsor, in accordance with the requirements for the special rule for new hires, applies the rule to a class of employees subsequent to any prior application and discontinuance of the rule to that class, the new hire date must be prospective.

(iv) *Application of the minimum class size requirement under the special rule for new hires.*—The minimum class size requirement set forth in paragraph (d)(3) of this section does not apply to the new hire subclass. However, if a plan sponsor subdivides the new hire subclass subsequent to creating the new hire subclass, the minimum class size requirement set forth in paragraph (d)(3) of this section applies to any class of employees created by subdividing the new hire subclass, if the minimum class size requirement otherwise applies.

(6) *Student employees offered student premium reduction arrangements.*—For purposes of this section, if an institution of higher education (as defined in the Higher Education Act of 1965) offers a student employee a student premium reduction arrangement, the employee is not considered to be part of the class of employees to which the employee would otherwise belong. For the purpose of this paragraph (d)(6) and paragraph (f)(1) of this section, a student premium reduction arrangement is defined as any program offered by an institution of higher education under which the cost of insured or self-insured student health coverage is reduced for certain students through a credit, offset, reimbursement, stipend or similar arrangement. A student employee offered a student premium reduction arrangement is also not counted for purposes of determining the applicable class size minimum under paragraph (d)(3)(iii) of this section. If a student employee is not offered a student premium reduction arrangement (including if the student employee is offered an individual coverage HRA instead), the student employee is considered to be part of the class of employees to which the employee otherwise belongs and is

counted for purposes of determining the applicable class size minimum under paragraph (d)(3)(iii) of this section.

(e) *Integration of Individual Coverage HRAs with Medicare.*—(1) *General rule.*—An individual coverage HRA will be considered to be integrated with Medicare (and deemed to comply with PHS Act sections 2711 and 2713 and §54.9815-2711(d)(4) of this chapter), provided that the conditions of paragraph (c) of this section are satisfied, subject to paragraph (e)(2) of this section. Nothing in this section requires that a participant and his or her dependents all have the same type of coverage; therefore, an individual coverage HRA may be integrated with Medicare for some individuals and with individual health insurance coverage for others, including, for example, a participant enrolled in Medicare Part A and B or Part C and his or her dependents enrolled in individual health insurance coverage.

(2) *Application of conditions in paragraph (c) of this section.*—(i) *In general.*—Except as provided in paragraph (e)(2)(ii) of this section, in applying the conditions of paragraph (c) of this section with respect to integration with Medicare, a reference to "individual health insurance coverage" is deemed to refer to coverage under Medicare Part A and B or Part C. References in this section to integration of an HRA with Medicare refer to integration of an individual coverage HRA with Medicare Part A and B or Part C.

(ii) *Exceptions.*—For purposes of the statement regarding ERISA under the notice content element under paragraph (c)(6)(ii)(A) of this section and the statement regarding the availability of a special enrollment period under the notice content element under paragraph (c)(6)(ii)(J) of this section, the term individual health insurance coverage means only individual health insurance coverage and does not also mean coverage under Medicare Part A and B or Part C.

(f) *Examples.*—(1) *Examples regarding classes and the minimum class size requirement.*—The following examples illustrate the provisions of paragraph (c)(3) of this section, taking into account the provisions of paragraphs (d)(1) through (4) and (d)(6) of this section. In each example, the HRA is an individual coverage HRA that may reimburse any medical care expenses, including premiums for individual health insurance coverage and it is assumed that no participants or dependents are Medicare beneficiaries.

(i) *Example 1: Collectively bargained employees offered traditional group health plan; non-collectively bargained employees offered HRA*—(A) *Facts.* For 2020, Plan Sponsor A offers its employees covered by a collective bargaining agreement a traditional group health plan (as required by the collective bargaining agreement) and all other employees (non-collectively bargained employees) each an HRA on the same terms.

(B) *Conclusion.* The same terms requirement of paragraph (c)(3) of this section is satisfied in this paragraph (f)(1)(i) (*Example 1*) because collectively bargained and non-collectively bargained employees may be treated as different classes of employees, one of which may be offered a traditional group health plan and the other of which may be offered an individual coverage HRA, and Plan Sponsor A offers the HRA on the same terms to all participants who are non-collectively bargained employees. The minimum class size requirement does not apply to this paragraph (f)(1)(i) (*Example 1*) even though Plan Sponsor A offers one class a traditional group health plan and one class the HRA because collectively bargained and non-collectively bargained employees are not applicable classes that are subject to the minimum class size requirement.

(ii) *Example 2: Collectively bargained employees in one unit offered traditional group health plan and in another unit offered HRA*—(A) *Facts.* For 2020, Plan Sponsor B offers its employees covered by a collective bargaining agreement with Local 100 a traditional group health plan (as required by the collective bargaining agreement), and its employees covered by a collective bargaining agreement with Local 200 each an HRA on the same terms (as required by the collective bargaining agreement).

(B) *Conclusion.* The same terms requirement of paragraph (c)(3) of this section is satisfied in this paragraph (f)(1)(ii) (*Example 2*) because the employees covered by the collective bargaining agreements with the two separate bargaining units (Local 100 and Local 200) may be treated as two different classes of employees and Plan Sponsor B offers an HRA on the same terms to the participants covered by the agreement with Local 200. The minimum class size requirement does not apply to this paragraph (f)(1)(ii) (*Example 2*) even though Plan Sponsor B offers the Local 100 employees a traditional group health plan and the Local 200 employees an HRA because collectively bargained employees are not applicable classes that are subject to the minimum class size requirement.

(iii) *Example 3: Employees in a waiting period offered no coverage; other employees offered an HRA*—(A) *Facts.* For 2020, Plan Sponsor C offers its employees who have completed a waiting period that

⋙→ *Caution: Reg. §54.9802-4, below, as added by T.D. 9867, applies to plan years beginning on or after January 1, 2020.*

complies with the requirements for waiting periods in § 54.9815-2708 of this chapter each an HRA on the same terms and does not offer coverage to its employees who have not completed the waiting period.

(B) *Conclusion.* The same terms requirement of paragraph (c)(3) of this section is satisfied in this paragraph (f)(1)(iii) (*Example 3*) because employees who have completed a waiting period and employees who have not completed a waiting period may be treated as different classes and Plan Sponsor C offers the HRA on the same terms to all participants who have completed the waiting period. The minimum class size requirement does not apply to this paragraph (f)(1)(iii) (*Example 3*) because Plan Sponsor C does not offer at least one class of employees a traditional group health plan and because the class of employees who have not completed a waiting period and the class of employees who have completed a waiting period are not applicable classes that are subject to the minimum class size requirement.

(iv) *Example 4: Employees in a waiting period offered an HRA; other employees offered a traditional group health plan*—(A) *Facts.* For 2020, Plan Sponsor D offers its employees who have completed a waiting period that complies with the requirements for waiting periods in § 54.9815-2708 of this chapter a traditional group health plan and offers its employees who have not completed the waiting period each an HRA on the same terms.

(B) *Conclusion.* The same terms requirement of paragraph (c)(3) of this section is satisfied in this paragraph (f)(1)(iv) (*Example 4*) because employees who have completed a waiting period and employees who have not completed a waiting period may be treated as different classes and Plan Sponsor D offers an HRA on the same terms to all participants who have not completed the waiting period. The minimum class size requirement does not apply to this paragraph (f)(1)(iv) (*Example 4*) even though Plan Sponsor D offers employees who have completed a waiting period a traditional group health plan and employees who have not completed a waiting period an HRA because the class of employees who have not completed a waiting period is not an applicable class that is subject to the minimum class size requirement (nor is the class made up of employees who have completed the waiting period).

(v) *Example 5: Staffing firm employees temporarily placed with customers offered an HRA; other employees offered a traditional group health plan*—(A) *Facts.* Plan Sponsor E is a staffing firm that places certain of its employees on temporary assignments with customers that are not the common law employers of Plan Sponsor E's employees or treated as a single employer with Plan Sponsor E under section 414(b), (c), (m), or (o) (unrelated entities); other employees work in Plan Sponsor E's office managing the staffing business (non-temporary employees). For 2020, Plan Sponsor E offers its employees who are on temporary assignments with customers each an HRA on the same terms. All other employees are offered a traditional group health plan.

(B) *Conclusion.* The same terms requirement of paragraph (c)(3) of this section is satisfied in this paragraph (f)(1)(v) (*Example 5*) because the employees who are hired for temporary placement at an unrelated entity and non-temporary employees of Plan Sponsor E may be treated as different classes of employees and Plan Sponsor E offers an HRA on the same terms to all participants temporarily placed with customers. The minimum class size requirement does not apply to this paragraph (f)(1)(v) (*Example 5*) even though Plan Sponsor E offers one class a traditional group health plan and one class the HRA because the class of employees hired for temporary placement is not an applicable class that is subject to the minimum class size requirement (nor is the class made up of non-temporary employees).

(vi) *Example 6: Staffing firm employees temporarily placed with customers in rating area 1 offered an HRA; other employees offered a traditional group health plan*—(A) *Facts.* The facts are the same as in paragraph (f)(1)(v) of this section (*Example 5*), except that Plan Sponsor E has work sites in rating area 1 and rating area 2, and it offers its 10 employees on temporary assignments with a work site in rating area 1 an HRA on the same terms. Plan Sponsor E has 200 other employees in rating areas 1 and 2, including its non-temporary employees in rating areas 1 and 2 and its employees on temporary assignments with a work site in rating area 2, all of whom are offered a traditional group health plan.

(B) *Conclusion.* The same terms requirement of paragraph (c)(3) of this section is not satisfied in this paragraph (f)(1)(vi) (*Example 6*) because, even though the employees who are temporarily placed with customers generally may be treated as employees of a different class, because Plan Sponsor E is also using a rating area to identify the class offered the HRA (which is an applicable class for the minimum class size requirement) and is offering one class the HRA and another class the traditional group health plan, the minimum class size requirement applies to the class offered the HRA, and the

class offered the HRA fails to satisfy the minimum class size requirement. Because Plan Sponsor E employs 210 employees, the applicable class size minimum is 20, and the HRA is offered to only 10 employees.

(vii) *Example 7: Employees in State 1 offered traditional group health plan; employees in State 2 offered HRA*—(A) *Facts.* Plan Sponsor F employs 45 employees whose work site is in State 1 and 7 employees whose primary site of employment is in State 2. For 2020, Plan Sponsor F offers its 45 employees in State 1 a traditional group health plan, and each of its 7 employees in State 2 an HRA on the same terms.

(B) *Conclusion.* The same terms requirement of paragraph (c)(3) of this section is satisfied in this paragraph (f)(1)(vii) (*Example 7*) because Plan Sponsor F offers the HRA on the same terms to all employees with a work site in State 2 and that class is a permissible class under paragraph (d) of this section. This is because employees whose work sites are in different rating areas may be considered different classes and a plan sponsor may create a class of employees by combining classes of employees, including by combining employees whose work site is in one rating area with employees whose work site is in a different rating area, or by combining all employees whose work site is in a state. The minimum class size requirement does not apply to this paragraph (f)(1)(vii) (*Example 7*) because the minimum class size requirement does not apply if the geographic area defining a class of employees is a state or a combination of two or more entire states.

(viii) *Example 8: Full-time seasonal employees offered HRA; all other full-time employees offered traditional group health plan; part-time employees offered no coverage*—(A) *Facts.* Plan Sponsor G employs 6 full-time seasonal employees, 75 full-time employees who are not seasonal employees, and 5 part-time employees. For 2020, Plan Sponsor G offers each of its 6 full-time seasonal employees an HRA on the same terms, its 75 full-time employees who are not seasonal employees a traditional group health plan, and offers no coverage to its 5 part-time employees.

(B) *Conclusion.* The same terms requirement of paragraph (c)(3) of this section is satisfied in this paragraph (f)(1)(viii) (*Example 8*) because full-time seasonal employees and full-time employees who are not seasonal employees may be considered different classes and Plan Sponsor G offers the HRA on the same terms to all full-time seasonal employees. The minimum class size requirement does not apply to the class offered the HRA in this paragraph (f)(1)(viii) (*Example 8*) because part-time employees are not offered coverage and full-time employees are not an applicable class subject to the minimum class size requirement if part-time employees are not offered coverage.

(ix) *Example 9: Full-time employees in rating area 1 offered traditional group health plan; full-time employees in rating area 2 offered HRA; part-time employees offered no coverage*—(A) *Facts.* Plan Sponsor H employs 17 full-time employees and 10 part-time employees whose work site is in rating area 1 and 552 full-time employees whose work site is in rating area 2. For 2020, Plan Sponsor H offers its 17 full-time employees in rating area 1 a traditional group health plan and each of its 552 full-time employees in rating area 2 an HRA on the same terms. Plan Sponsor H offers no coverage to its 10 part-time employees in rating area 1. Plan Sponsor H reasonably expects to employ 569 employees on the first day of the HRA plan year.

(B) *Conclusion.* The same terms requirement of paragraph (c)(3) of this section is satisfied in this paragraph (f)(1)(ix) (*Example 9*) because employees whose work sites are in different rating areas may be considered different classes and Plan Sponsor H offers the HRA on the same terms to all full-time employees in rating area 2. The minimum class size requirement applies to the class offered the HRA in this paragraph (f)(1)(ix) (*Example 9*) because the minimum class size requirement applies to a class based on a geographic area unless the geographic area is a state or a combination of two or more entire states. However, the minimum class size requirement applies only to the class offered the HRA, and Plan Sponsor H offers the HRA to the 552 full-time employees in rating area 2 on the first day of the plan year, satisfying the minimum class size requirement (because the applicable class size minimum for Plan Sponsor H is 20).

(x) *Example 10: Employees in rating area 1 offered HRA; employees in rating area 2 offered traditional group health plan*—(A) *Facts.* The facts are the same as in paragraph (f)(1)(ix) of this section (*Example 9*) except that Plan Sponsor H offers its 17 full-time employees in rating area 1 the HRA and offers its 552 full-time employees in rating area 2 the traditional group health plan.

(B) *Conclusion.* The same terms requirement of paragraph (c)(3) of this section is not satisfied in this paragraph (f)(1)(x) (*Example 10*) because, even though employees whose work sites are in different rating areas generally may be considered different classes and Plan Sponsor H offers the HRA on the same terms to all participants in rating area 1, the HRA fails to satisfy the minimum class size require-

⟫→ *Caution: Reg. §54.9802-4, below, as added by T.D. 9867, applies to plan years beginning on or after January 1, 2020.*

ment. Specifically, the minimum class size requirement applies to this paragraph (f)(1)(x) (*Example 10*) because the minimum class size requirement applies to a class based on a geographic area unless the geographic area is a state or a combination of two or more entire states. Further, the applicable class size minimum for Plan Sponsor H is 20 employees, and the HRA is only offered to the 17 full-time employees in rating area 1 on the first day of the HRA plan year.

(xi) *Example 11: Employees in State 1 and rating area 1 of State 2 offered HRA; employees in all other rating areas of State 2 offered traditional group health plan*—(A) *Facts.* For 2020, Plan Sponsor I offers an HRA on the same terms to a total of 200 employees it employs with work sites in State 1 and in rating area 1 of State 2. Plan Sponsor I offers a traditional group health plan to its 150 employees with work sites in other rating areas in State 2. Plan Sponsor I reasonably expects to employ 350 employees on the first day of the HRA plan year.

(B) *Conclusion.* The same terms requirement of paragraph (c)(3) of this section is satisfied in this paragraph (f)(1)(xi) (*Example 11*). Plan Sponsor I may treat all of the employees with a work site in State 1 and rating area 1 of State 2 as a class of employees because employees whose work sites are in different rating areas may be considered different classes and a plan sponsor may create a class of employees by combining classes of employees, including by combining employees whose work site is in one rating area with a class of employees whose work site is in a different rating area. The minimum class size requirement applies to the class of employees offered the HRA (made up of employees in State 1 and in rating area 1 of State 2) because the minimum class size requirement applies to a class based on a geographic area unless the geographic area is a state or a combination of two or more entire states. In this case, the class is made up of a state plus a rating area which is not the entire state. However, this class satisfies the minimum class size requirement because the applicable class size minimum for Plan Sponsor I is 20, and Plan Sponsor I offered the HRA to 200 employees on the first day of the plan year.

(xii) *Example 12: Salaried employees offered a traditional group health plan; hourly employees offered an HRA*—(A) *Facts.* Plan Sponsor J has 163 salaried employees and 14 hourly employees. For 2020, Plan Sponsor J offers its 163 salaried employees a traditional group health plan and each of its 14 hourly employees an HRA on the same terms. Plan Sponsor J reasonably expects to employ 177 employees on the first day of the HRA plan year.

(B) *Conclusion.* The same terms requirement of paragraph (c)(3) of this section is not satisfied in this paragraph (f)(1)(xii) (*Example 12*) because, even though salaried and hourly employees generally may be considered different classes and Plan Sponsor J offers the HRA on the same terms to all hourly employees, the HRA fails to satisfy the minimum class size requirement. Specifically, the minimum class size requirement applies in this paragraph (f)(1)(xii) (*Example 12*) because employees who are paid on a salaried basis and employees who are not paid on a salaried basis are applicable classes subject to the minimum class size requirement. Because Plan Sponsor J reasonably expects to employ between 100 and 200 employees on the first day of the plan year, the applicable class size minimum is 10 percent, rounded down to a whole number. Ten percent of 177 total employees, rounded down to a whole number is 17, and the HRA is offered to only 14 hourly employees.

(xiii) *Example 13: Part-time employees and full-time employees offered different HRAs; no traditional group health plan offered* —(A) *Facts.* Plan Sponsor K has 50 full-time employees and 7 part-time employees. For 2020, Plan Sponsor K offers its 50 full-time employees $2,000 each in an HRA otherwise provided on the same terms and each of its 7 part-time employees $500 in an HRA otherwise provided on the same terms. Plan Sponsor K reasonably expects to employ 57 employees on the first day of the HRA plan year.

(B) *Conclusion.* The same terms requirement of paragraph (c)(3) of this section is satisfied in this paragraph (f)(1)(xiii) (*Example 13*) because full-time employees and part-time employees may be treated as different classes and Plan Sponsor K offers an HRA on the same terms to all the participants in each class. The minimum class size requirement does not apply to either the full-time class or the part-time class because (although in certain circumstances the minimum class size requirement applies to a class of full-time employees and a class of part-time employees) Plan Sponsor K does not offer any class of employees a traditional group health plan, and the minimum class size requirement applies only when, among other things, at least one class of employees is offered a traditional group health plan while another class is offered an HRA.

(xiv) *Example 14: No employees offered an HRA*—(A) *Facts.* The facts are the same facts as in paragraph (f)(1)(xiii) of this section (*Example 13*), except that Plan Sponsor K offers its full-time employees a traditional group health plan and does not offer any group health plan (either a traditional group health plan or an HRA) to its part-time employees.

(B) *Conclusion.* The regulations set forth under this section do not apply to Plan Sponsor K because Plan Sponsor K does not offer an individual coverage HRA to any employee.

(xv) *Example 15: Full-time employees offered traditional group health plan; part-time employees offered HRA*—(A) *Facts.* The facts are the same as in paragraph (f)(1)(xiii) of this section (*Example 13*), except that Plan Sponsor K offers its full-time employees a traditional group health plan and offers each of its part-time employees $500 in an HRA and otherwise on the same terms.

(B) *Conclusion.* The same terms requirement of paragraph (c)(3) of this section is not satisfied in this paragraph (f)(1)(xv) (*Example 15*) because, even though the full-time employees and the part-time employees generally may be treated as different classes, in this paragraph (f)(1)(xv) (*Example 15*), the minimum class size requirement applies to the part-time employees, and it is not satisfied. Specifically, the minimum class size requirement applies to the part-time employees because that requirement applies to an applicable class offered an HRA when one class is offered a traditional group health plan while another class is offered an HRA, and to the part-time and full-time employee classes when one of those classes is offered a traditional group health plan while the other is offered an HRA. Because Plan Sponsor K reasonably expects to employ fewer than 100 employees on the first day of the HRA plan year, the applicable class size minimum for Plan Sponsor K is 10 employees, but Plan Sponsor K offered the HRA only to its 7 part-time employees.

(xvi) *Example 16: Satisfying minimum class size requirement based on employees offered HRA*—(A) *Facts.* Plan Sponsor L employs 78 full-time employees and 12 part-time employees. For 2020, Plan Sponsor L offers its 78 full-time employees a traditional group health plan and each of its 12 part-times employees an HRA on the same terms. Only 6 part-time employees enroll in the HRA. Plan Sponsor L reasonably expects to employ fewer than 100 employees on the first day of the HRA plan year.

(B) *Conclusion.* The same terms requirement of paragraph (c)(3) of this section is satisfied in this paragraph (f)(1)(xvi) (*Example 16*) because full-time employees and part-time employees may be treated as different classes, Plan Sponsor L offers an HRA on the same terms to all the participants in the part-time class, and the minimum class size requirement is satisfied. Specifically, whether a class of employees satisfies the applicable class size minimum is determined as of the first day of the plan year based on the number of employees in a class that is offered an HRA, not on the number of employees who enroll in the HRA. The applicable class size minimum for Plan Sponsor L is 10 employees, and Plan Sponsor L offered the HRA to its 12 part-time employees.

(xvii) *Example 17: Student employees offered student premium reduction arrangements and same terms requirement*—(A) *Facts.* Plan Sponsor M is an institution of higher education that offers each of its part-time employees an HRA on the same terms, except that it offers its parttime employees who are student employees a student premium reduction arrangement, and the student premium reduction arrangement provides different amounts to different part-time student employees.

(B) *Conclusion.* The same terms requirement of paragraph (c)(3) of this section is satisfied in this paragraph (f)(1)(xvii) (*Example 17*) because Plan Sponsor M offers the HRA on the same terms to its part-time employees who are not students and because the part-time student employees offered a student premium reduction arrangement (and their varying HRAs) are not taken into account as part-time employees for purposes of determining whether a class of employees is offered an HRA on the same terms.

(xiii) *Example 18: Student employees offered student premium reduction arrangements and minimum class size requirement*—(A) *Facts.* Plan Sponsor N is an institution of higher education with 25 hourly employees. Plan Sponsor N offers 15 of its hourly employees, who are student employees, a student premium reduction arrangement and it wants to offer its other 10 hourly employees an HRA for 2022. Plan Sponsor N offers its salaried employees a traditional group health plan. Plan Sponsor N reasonably expects to have 250 employees on the first day of the 2022 HRA plan year, 15 of which will have offers of student premium reduction arrangements.

(B) *Conclusion.* The same terms requirement of paragraph (c)(3) of this section is not satisfied in this paragraph (f)(1)(xviii) (*Example 18*). The minimum class size requirement will apply to the class of hourly employees to which Plan Sponsor N wants to offer the HRA because Plan Sponsor N offers a class of employees a traditional group health plan and another class the HRA, and the minimum class size requirement generally applies to a class of hourly employees offered an HRA. Plan Sponsor N's applicable class size minimum is 20 because Plan Sponsor N reasonably expects to employ 235 employees on the first day of the plan year (250 employees minus 15 employees receiving a student premium reduction arrangement).

>>>→ *Caution: Reg. §54.9802-4, below, as added by T.D. 9867, applies to plan years beginning on or after January 1, 2020.*

Plan Sponsor N may not offer the HRA to its hourly employees because the 10 employees offered the HRA as of the first day of the plan year does not satisfy the applicable class size minimum.

(2) *Examples regarding special rule for new hires.*—The following examples illustrate the provisions of paragraph (c)(3) of this section, taking into account the provisions of paragraph (d) of this section, in particular the special rule for new hires under paragraph (d)(5) of this section. In each example, the HRA is an individual coverage HRA that has a calendar year plan year and may reimburse any medical care expenses, including premiums for individual health insurance coverage. The examples also assume that no participants or dependents are Medicare beneficiaries.

(i) *Example 1: Application of special rule for new hires to all employees*—(A) *Facts.* For 2021, Plan Sponsor A offers all employees a traditional group health plan. For 2022, Plan Sponsor A offers all employees hired on or after January 1, 2022, an HRA on the same terms and continues to offer the traditional group health plan to employees hired before that date. On the first day of the 2022 plan year, Plan Sponsor A has 2 new hires who are offered the HRA.

(B) *Conclusion.* The same terms requirement of paragraph (c)(3) of this section is satisfied in this paragraph (f)(2)(i) (*Example 1*) because, under the special rule for new hires in paragraph (d)(5) of this section, the employees newly hired on and after January 1, 2022, may be treated as a new hire subclass, Plan Sponsor A offers the HRA on the same terms to all participants in the new hire subclass, and the minimum class size requirement does not apply to the new hire subclass.

(ii) *Example 2: Application of special rule for new hires to full-time employees*—(A) *Facts.* For 2021, Plan Sponsor B offers a traditional group health plan to its full-time employees and does not offer any coverage to its part-time employees. For 2022, Plan Sponsor B offers full-time employees hired on or after January 1, 2022, an HRA on the same terms, continues to offer its full-time employees hired before that date a traditional group health plan, and continues to offer no coverage to its part-time employees. On the first day of the 2022 plan year, Plan Sponsor B has 2 new hire, full-time employees who are offered the HRA.

(B) *Conclusion.* The same terms requirement of paragraph (c)(3) of this section is satisfied in this paragraph (f)(2)(ii) (*Example 2*) because, under the special rule for new hires in paragraph (d)(5) of this section, the full-time employees newly hired on and after January 1, 2022, may be treated as a new hire subclass and Plan Sponsor B offers the HRA on the same terms to all participants in the new hire subclass. The minimum class size requirement does not apply to the new hire subclass.

(iii) *Example 3: Special rule for new hires impermissibly applied retroactively*—(A) *Facts.* For 2025, Plan Sponsor C offers a traditional group health plan to its full-time employees. For 2026, Plan Sponsor C wants to offer an HRA to its full-time employees hired on and after January 1, 2023, while continuing to offer a traditional group health plan to its full-time employees hired before January 1, 2023.

(B) *Conclusion.* The special rule for new hires under paragraph (d)(5) of this section does not apply in this paragraph (f)(2)(iii) (*Example 3*) because the rule must be applied prospectively. That is, Plan Sponsor C may not, in 2026, choose to apply the special rule for new hires retroactive to 2023. If Plan Sponsor C were to offer an HRA in this way, it would fail to satisfy the conditions under paragraphs (c)(2) and (3) of this section because the new hire subclass would not be treated as a subclass for purposes of applying those rules and, therefore, all full-time employees would be treated as one class to which either a traditional group health plan or an HRA could be offered, but not both.

(iv) *Example 4: Permissible second application of the special rule for new hires to the same class of employees*—(A) *Facts.* For 2021, Plan Sponsor D offers all of its full-time employees a traditional group health plan. For 2022, Plan Sponsor D applies the special rule for new hires and offers an HRA on the same terms to all employees hired on and after January 1, 2022, and continues to offer a traditional group health plan to full-time employees hired before that date. For 2025, Plan Sponsor D discontinues use of the special rule for new hires, and again offers all full-time employees a traditional group health plan. In 2030, Plan Sponsor D decides to apply the special rule for new hires to the full-time employee class again, offering an HRA to all full-time employees hired on and after January 1, 2030, on the same terms, while continuing to offer employees hired before that date a traditional group health plan.

(B) *Conclusion.* Plan Sponsor D has permissibly applied the special rule for new hires and is in compliance with the requirements of paragraphs (c)(2) and (3) of this section.

(v) *Example 5: Impermissible second application of the special rule for new hires to the same class of employees*—(A) *Facts.* The facts are the same as in paragraph (f)(2)(iv) of this section (*Example 4*), except that

for 2025, Plan Sponsor D discontinues use of the special rule for new hires by offering all full-time employees an HRA on the same terms. Further, for 2030, Plan Sponsor D wants to continue to offer an HRA on the same terms to all full-time employees hired before January 1, 2030, and to offer all full-time employees hired on or after January 1, 2030, an HRA in a different amount.

(B) *Conclusion.* Plan Sponsor D may not apply the special rule for new hires for 2030 to the class of full-time employees being offered an HRA because the special rule for new hires may only be applied to a class that is being offered a traditional group health plan.

(vi) *Example 6: New full-time employees offered different HRAs in different rating areas*—(A) *Facts.* Plan Sponsor E has work sites in rating area 1, rating area 2, and rating area 3. For 2021, Plan Sponsor E offers its full-time employees a traditional group health plan. For 2022, Plan Sponsor E offers its full-time employees hired on or after January 1, 2022, in rating area 1 an HRA of $3,000, its full-time employees hired on or after January 1, 2022, in rating area 2 an HRA of $5,000, and its full-time employees hired on or after January 1, 2022, in rating area 3 an HRA of $7,000. Within each class offered an HRA, Plan Sponsor E offers the HRA on the same terms. Plan Sponsor E offers its full-time employees hired prior to January 1, 2022, in each of those classes a traditional group health plan. On the first day of the 2022 plan year, there is one new hire, full-time employee in rating area 1, three new hire, full-time employees in rating area 2, and 10 new hire-full-time employees in rating area 3.

(B) *Conclusion.* The same terms requirement of paragraph (c)(3) of this section is satisfied in this paragraph (f)(2)(vi) (*Example 6*) because, under the special rule for new hires in paragraph (d)(5) of this section, the full-time employees in each of the three rating areas newly hired on and after January 1, 2022, may be treated as three new hire subclasses and Plan Sponsor E offers the HRA on the same terms to all participants in the new hire subclasses. Further, the minimum class size requirement does not apply to the new hire subclasses.

(vii) *Example 7: New full-time employee class subdivided based on rating area*—(A) *Facts.* Plan Sponsor F offers its full-time employees hired on or after January 1, 2022, an HRA on the same terms and it continues to offer its full-time employees hired before that date a traditional group health plan. Plan Sponsor F offers no coverage to its part-time employees. For the 2025 plan year, Plan Sponsor F wants to subdivide the full-time new hire subclass so that those whose work site is in rating area 1 will be offered the traditional group health plan and those whose work site is in rating area 2 will continue to receive the HRA. Plan Sponsor F reasonably expects to employ 219 employees on January 1, 2025. As of January 1, 2025, Plan Sponsor F has 15 full-time employees whose work site in in rating area 2 and who were hired between January 1, 2022, and January 1, 2025.

(B) *Conclusion.* The same terms requirement of paragraph (c)(3) of this section is not satisfied in this paragraph (f)(2)(vii) (*Example 7*) because the new hire subclass has been subdivided in a manner that is subject to the minimum class size requirement, and the class offered the HRA fails to satisfy the minimum class size requirement. Specifically, once the new hire subclass is subdivided the general rules for applying the minimum class size requirement apply to the employees offered the HRA in the new hire subclass. In this case, because the subdivision of the new hire full-time subclass is based on rating areas; a class based on rating areas is an applicable class subject to the minimum class size requirement; and the employees in one rating area are to be offered the HRA, while the employees in the other rating area are offered the traditional group health plan, the minimum class size requirement would apply on and after the date of the subdivision. Further, the minimum class size requirement would not be satisfied, because the applicable class size minimum for Plan Sponsor F would be 20, and only 15 employees in rating area 2 would be offered the HRA.

(viii) *Example 8: New full-time employee class subdivided based on state*—(A) *Facts.* The facts are the same as in paragraph (f)(2)(vii) of this section (*Example 7*), except that for the 2025 plan year, Plan Sponsor F intends to subdivide the new hire, full-time class so that those in State 1 will be offered the traditional group health plan and those in State 2 will each be offered an HRA on the same terms.

(B) *Conclusion.* The same terms requirement of paragraph (c)(3) of this section is satisfied in this paragraph (f)(2)(viii) (*Example 8*) because even though the new hire subclass has been subdivided, it has been subdivided in a manner that is not subject to the minimum class size requirement as the subdivision is based on the entire state.

(ix) *Example 9: New full-time employees and part-time employees offered HRA*—(A) *Facts.* In 2021, Plan Sponsor G offers its full-time employees a traditional group health plan and does not offer coverage to its part-time employees. For the 2022 plan year, Plan Sponsor G offers its full-time employees hired on or after January 1, 2022, and all of its part-time employees, including those hired before January 1, 2022, and those hired on and after January 1, 2022, an HRA on the

≫→ *Caution: Reg. §54.9802-4, below, as added by T.D. 9867, applies to plan years beginning on or after January 1, 2020.*

same terms, and it continues to offer its full-time employees hired before January 1, 2022, a traditional group health plan.

(B) *Conclusion*. The minimum class size requirement applies to the part-time employees offered the HRA in 2022 because the class is being offered an HRA; the special rule for new hires does not apply (because this class was not previously offered a traditional group health plan) and so it is not a new hire subclass exempt from the minimum class size requirement; another class of employees (that is, full-time hired before January 1, 2022) are being offered a traditional group health plan; and the part-time employee class is generally an applicable classes that is subject to the minimum class size requirement. However, because the full-time, new hire subclass is based on the special rule for new hires, the minimum class size requirement does not apply to full-time new hires offered an HRA in 2022.

(g) *Applicability date*.—This section applies to plan years beginning on or after January 1, 2020. [Reg. §54.9802-4]

☐ [T.D. 9867, 6-13-2019.]

**[Reg. §54.9811-1]**

**§54.9811-1. Standards relating to benefits for mothers and newborns.**—(a) *Hospital length of stay*.—(1) *General rule*.—Except as provided in paragraph (a)(5) of this section, a group health plan that provides benefits for a hospital length of stay in connection with childbirth for a mother or her newborn may not restrict benefits for the stay to less than—

(i) 48 hours following a vaginal delivery; or

(ii) 96 hours following a delivery by cesarean section.

(2) *When stay begins*.—(i) *Delivery in a hospital*.—If delivery occurs in a hospital, the hospital length of stay for the mother or newborn child begins at the time of delivery (or in the case of multiple births, at the time of the last delivery).

(ii) *Delivery outside a hospital*.—If delivery occurs outside a hospital, the hospital length of stay begins at the time the mother or newborn is admitted as a hospital inpatient in connection with childbirth. The determination of whether an admission is in connection with childbirth is a medical decision to be made by the attending provider.

(3) *Examples*.—The rules of paragraphs (a)(1) and (2) of this section are illustrated by the following examples. In each example, the group health plan provides benefits for hospital lengths of stay in connection with childbirth and is subject to the requirements of this section, as follows:

*Example 1*. (i) *Facts*. A pregnant woman covered under a group health plan goes into labor and is admitted to the hospital at 10 p.m. on June 11. She gives birth by vaginal delivery at 6 a.m. on June 12.

(ii) *Conclusion*. In this *Example 1*, the 48-hour period described in paragraph (a)(1)(i) of this section ends at 6 a.m. on June 14.

*Example 2*. (i) *Facts*. A woman covered under a group health plan gives birth at home by vaginal delivery. After the delivery, the woman begins bleeding excessively in connection with the childbirth and is admitted to the hospital for treatment of the excessive bleeding at 7 p.m. on October 1.

(ii) *Conclusion*. In this *Example 2*, the 48-hour period described in paragraph (a)(1)(i) of this section ends at 7 p.m. on October 3.

*Example 3*. (i) *Facts*. A woman covered under a group health plan gives birth by vaginal delivery at home. The child later develops pneumonia and is admitted to the hospital. The attending provider determines that the admission is not in connection with childbirth.

(ii) *Conclusion*. In this *Example 3*, the hospital length-of-stay requirements of this section do not apply to the child's admission to the hospital because the admission is not in connection with childbirth.

(4) *Authorization not required*.—(i) *In general*.—A plan may not require that a physician or other health care provider obtain authorization from the plan, or from a health insurance issuer offering health insurance coverage under the plan, for prescribing the hospital length of stay specified in paragraph (a)(1) of this section. (See also paragraphs (b)(2) and (c)(3) of this section for rules and examples regarding other authorization and certain notice requirements.)

(ii) *Example*.—The rule of this paragraph (a)(4) is illustrated by the following example:

*Example*. (i) *Facts*. In the case of a delivery by cesarean section, a group health plan subject to the requirements of this section automatically provides benefits for any hospital length of stay of up to 72 hours. For any longer stay, the plan requires an attending provider to complete a certificate of medical necessity. The plan then makes a determination, based on the certificate of medical necessity, whether a longer stay is medically necessary.

(ii) *Conclusion*. In this *Example*, the requirement that an attending provider complete a certificate of medical necessity to obtain authorization for the period between 72 hours and 96 hours following a delivery by cesarean section is prohibited by this paragraph (a)(4).

(5) *Exceptions*.—(i) *Discharge of mother*.—If a decision to discharge a mother earlier than the period specified in paragraph (a)(1) of this section is made by an attending provider, in consultation with the mother, the requirements of paragraph (a)(1) of this section do not apply for any period after the discharge.

(ii) *Discharge of newborn*.—If a decision to discharge a newborn child earlier than the period specified in paragraph (a)(1) of this section is made by an attending provider, in consultation with the mother (or the newborn's authorized representative), the requirements of paragraph (a)(1) of this section do not apply for any period after the discharge.

(iii) *Attending provider defined*.—For purposes of this section, attending provider means an individual who is licensed under applicable state law to provide maternity or pediatric care and who is directly responsible for providing maternity or pediatric care to a mother or newborn child. Therefore, a plan, hospital, managed care organization, or other issuer is not an attending provider.

(iv) *Example*.—The rules of this paragraph (a)(5) are illustrated by the following example:

*Example*. (i) *Facts*. A pregnant woman covered under a group health plan subject to the requirements of this section goes into labor and is admitted to a hospital. She gives birth by cesarean section. On the third day after the delivery, the attending provider for the mother consults with the mother, and the attending provider for the newborn consults with the mother regarding the newborn. The attending providers authorize the early discharge of both the mother and the newborn. Both are discharged approximately 72 hours after the delivery. The plan pays for the 72-hour hospital stays.

(ii) *Conclusion*. In this *Example*, the requirements of this paragraph (a) have been satisfied with respect to the mother and the newborn. If either is readmitted, the hospital stay for the readmission is not subject to this section.

(b) *Prohibitions*.—(1) *With respect to mothers*.—(i) *In general*.—A group health plan may not—

(A) Deny a mother or her newborn child eligibility or continued eligibility to enroll or renew coverage under the terms of the plan solely to avoid the requirements of this section; or

(B) Provide payments (including payments-in-kind) or rebates to a mother to encourage her to accept less than the minimum protections available under this section.

(ii) *Examples*.—The rules of this paragraph (b)(1) are illustrated by the following examples. In each example, the group health plan is subject to the requirements of this section, as follows:

*Example 1*. (i) *Facts*. A group health plan provides benefits for at least a 48-hour hospital length of stay following a vaginal delivery. If a mother and newborn covered under the plan are discharged within 24 hours after the delivery, the plan will waive the copayment and deductible.

(ii) *Conclusion*. In this *Example 1*, because waiver of the copayment and deductible is in the nature of a rebate that the mother would not receive if she and her newborn remained in the hospital, it is prohibited by this paragraph (b)(1). (In addition, the plan violates paragraph (b)(2) of this section because, in effect, no copayment or deductible is required for the first portion of the stay and a double copayment and a deductible are required for the second portion of the stay.)

*Example 2*. (i) *Facts*. A group health plan provides benefits for at least a 48-hour hospital length of stay following a vaginal delivery. In the event that a mother and her newborn are discharged earlier than 48 hours and the discharges occur after consultation with the mother in accordance with the requirements of paragraph (a)(5) of this section, the plan provides for a follow-up visit by a nurse within 48 hours after the discharges to provide certain services that the mother and her newborn would otherwise receive in the hospital.

(ii) *Conclusion*. In this *Example 2*, because the follow-up visit does not provide any services beyond what the mother and her newborn would receive in the hospital, coverage for the follow-up visit is not prohibited by this paragraph (b)(1).

(2) *With respect to benefit restrictions*.—(i) *In general*.—Subject to paragraph (c)(3) of this section, a group health plan may not restrict the benefits for any portion of a hospital length of stay specified in paragraph (a) of this section in a manner that is less favorable than the benefits provided for any preceding portion of the stay.

(ii) *Example.*—The rules of this paragraph (b)(2) are illustrated by the following example:

*Example.* (i) *Facts.* A group health plan subject to the requirements of this section provides benefits for hospital lengths of stay in connection with childbirth. In the case of a delivery by cesarean section, the plan automatically pays for the first 48 hours. With respect to each succeeding 24-hour period, the participant or beneficiary must call the plan to obtain precertification from a utilization reviewer, who determines if an additional 24-hour period is medically necessary. If this approval is not obtained, the plan will not provide benefits for any succeeding 24-hour period.

(ii) *Conclusion.* In this *Example*, the requirement to obtain precertification for the two 24-hour periods immediately following the initial 48-hour stay is prohibited by this paragraph (b)(2) because benefits for the latter part of the stay are restricted in a manner that is less favorable than benefits for a preceding portion of the stay. (However, this section does not prohibit a plan from requiring precertification for any period after the first 96 hours.) In addition, the requirement to obtain precertification from the plan based on medical necessity for a hospital length of stay within the 96-hour period would also violate paragraph (a) of this section.

(3) *With respect to attending providers.*—A group health plan may not directly or indirectly—

(i) Penalize (for example, take disciplinary action against or retaliate against), or otherwise reduce or limit the compensation of, an attending provider because the provider furnished care to a participant or beneficiary in accordance with this section; or

(ii) Provide monetary or other incentives to an attending provider to induce the provider to furnish care to a participant or beneficiary in a manner inconsistent with this section, including providing any incentive that could induce an attending provider to discharge a mother or newborn earlier than 48 hours (or 96 hours) after delivery.

(c) *Construction.*—With respect to this section, the following rules of construction apply:

(1) *Hospital stays not mandatory.*—This section does not require a mother to—

(i) Give birth in a hospital; or

(ii) Stay in the hospital for a fixed period of time following the birth of her child.

(2) *Hospital stay benefits not mandated.*—This section does not apply to any group health plan that does not provide benefits for hospital lengths of stay in connection with childbirth for a mother or her newborn child.

(3) *Cost-sharing rules.*—(i) *In general.*—This section does not prevent a group health plan from imposing deductibles, coinsurance, or other cost-sharing in relation to benefits for hospital lengths of stay in connection with childbirth for a mother or a newborn under the plan or coverage, except that the coinsurance or other cost-sharing for any portion of the hospital length of stay specified in paragraph (a) of this section may not be greater than that for any preceding portion of the stay.

(ii) *Example.*—The rules of this paragraph (c)(3) are illustrated by the following examples. In each example, the group health plan is subject to the requirements of this section, as follows:

*Example 1.* (i) *Facts.* A group health plan provides benefits for at least a 48-hour hospital length of stay in connection with vaginal deliveries. The plan covers 80 percent of the cost of the stay for the first 24-hour period and 50 percent of the cost of the stay for the second 24-hour period. Thus, the coinsurance paid by the patient increases from 20 percent to 50 percent after 24 hours.

(ii) *Conclusion.* In this *Example 1*, the plan violates the rules of this paragraph (c)(3) because coinsurance for the second 24-hour period of the 48-hour stay is greater than that for the preceding portion of the stay. (In addition, the plan also violates the similar rule in paragraph (b)(2) of this section.)

*Example 2.* (i) *Facts.* A group health plan generally covers 70 percent of the cost of a hospital length of stay in connection with childbirth. However, the plan will cover 80 percent of the cost of the stay if the participant or beneficiary notifies the plan of the pregnancy in advance of admission and uses whatever hospital the plan may designate.

(ii) *Conclusion.* In this *Example 2,* the plan does not violate the rules of this paragraph (c)(3) because the level of benefits provided (70 percent or 80 percent) is consistent throughout the 48-hour (or 96-hour) hospital length of stay required under paragraph (a) of this section. (In addition, the plan does not violate the rules in paragraph (a)(4) or (b)(2) of this section.)

(4) *Compensation of attending provider.*—This section does not prevent a group health plan from negotiating with an attending

provider the level and type of compensation for care furnished in accordance with this section (including paragraph (b) of this section).

(d) *Notice requirement.*—See 29 CFR 2520.102-3(u) for rules relating to a disclosure requirement imposed under section 711(d) of ERISA (29 U.S.C. 1181) on certain group health plans that provide benefits for hospital lengths of stay in connection with childbirth.

(e) *Applicability in certain states.*—(1) *Health insurance coverage.*—The requirements of section 9811 and this section do not apply with respect to health insurance coverage offered in connection with a group health plan if there is a state law regulating the coverage that meets any of the following criteria:

(i) The state law requires the coverage to provide for at least a 48-hour hospital length of stay following a vaginal delivery and at least a 96-hour hospital length of stay following a delivery by cesarean section.

(ii) The state law requires the coverage to provide for maternity and pediatric care in accordance with guidelines that relate to care following childbirth established by the American College of Obstetricians and Gynecologists, the American Academy of Pediatrics, or any other established professional medical association.

(iii) The state law requires, in connection with the coverage for maternity care, that the hospital length of stay for such care is left to the decision of (or is required to be made by) the attending provider in consultation with the mother. State laws that require the decision to be made by the attending provider with the consent of the mother satisfy the criterion of this paragraph (e)(1)(iii).

(2) *Group health plans.*—(i) *Fully-insured plans.*—For a group health plan that provides benefits solely through health insurance coverage, if the state law regulating the health insurance coverage meets any of the criteria in paragraph (e)(1) of this section, then the requirements of section 9811 and this section do not apply.

(ii) *Self-insured plans.*—For a group health plan that provides all benefits for hospital lengths of stay in connection with childbirth other than through health insurance coverage, the requirements of section 9811 and this section apply.

(iii) *Partially-insured plans.*—For a group health plan that provides some benefits through health insurance coverage, if the state law regulating the health insurance coverage meets any of the criteria in paragraph (e)(1) of this section, then the requirements of section 9811 and this section apply only to the extent the plan provides benefits for hospital lengths of stay in connection with childbirth other than through health insurance coverage.

(3) *Preemption provisions under section 731(a) of ERISA.*—See 29 CFR 2590.711(e)(3) for a rule providing that the preemption provisions contained in section 731(a)(1) of ERISA and 29 CFR 2590.731(a) do not supersede a state law if the state law is described in paragraph (e)(1) of 29 CFR 2590.711 (which is substantially similar to paragraph (e)(1) of this section).

(4) *Examples.*—The rules of this paragraph (e) are illustrated by the following examples:

*Example 1.* (i) *Facts.* A group health plan buys group health insurance coverage in a state that requires that the coverage provide for at least a 48-hour hospital length of stay following a vaginal delivery and at least a 96-hour hospital length of stay following a delivery by cesarean section.

(ii) *Conclusion.* In this *Example 1*, the coverage is subject to state law, and the requirements of section 9811 and this section do not apply.

*Example 2.* (i) *Facts.* A self-insured group health plan covers hospital lengths of stay in connection with childbirth in a state that requires health insurance coverage to provide for maternity and pediatric care in accordance with guidelines that relate to care following childbirth established by the American College of Obstetricians and Gynecologists and the American Academy of Pediatrics.

(ii) *Conclusion.* In this *Example 2*, even though the state law satisfies the criterion of paragraph (e)(1)(ii) of this section, because the plan provides benefits for hospital lengths of stay in connection with childbirth other than through health insurance coverage, the plan is subject to the requirements of section 9811 and this section.

(f) *Effective/applicability date.*—This section applies to group health plans for plan years beginning on or after January 1, 2009. [Reg. § 54.9811-1.]

☐ [*T.D.* 9427, 10-17-2008.]

**[Reg. § 54.9812-1]**

**§ 54.9812-1. Parity in mental health and substance use disorder benefits.**—(a) *Meaning of terms.*—For purposes of this section, except where the context clearly indicates otherwise, the following terms have the meanings indicated:

*Aggregate lifetime dollar limit* means a dollar limitation on the total amount of specified benefits that may be paid under a group health plan (or health insurance coverage offered in connection with such a plan) for any coverage unit.

*Annual dollar limit* means a dollar limitation on the total amount of specified benefits that may be paid in a 12-month period under a group health plan (or health insurance coverage offered in connection with such a plan) for any coverage unit.

*Coverage unit* means coverage unit as described in paragraph (c)(1)(iv) of this section.

*Cumulative financial requirements* are financial requirements that determine whether or to what extent benefits are provided based on accumulated amounts and include deductibles and out-of-pocket maximums. (However, cumulative financial requirements do not include aggregate lifetime or annual dollar limits because these two terms are excluded from the meaning of financial requirements.)

*Cumulative quantitative treatment limitations* are treatment limitations that determine whether or to what extent benefits are provided based on accumulated amounts, such as annual or lifetime day or visit limits.

*Financial requirements* include deductibles, copayments, coinsurance, or out-of-pocket maximums. Financial requirements do not include aggregate lifetime or annual dollar limits.

*Medical/surgical benefits* means benefits with respect to items or services for medical conditions or surgical procedures, as defined under the terms of the plan or health insurance coverage and in accordance with applicable Federal and State law, but does not include mental health or substance use disorder benefits. Any condition defined by the plan or coverage as being or as not being a medical/surgical condition must be defined to be consistent with generally recognized independent standards of current medical practice (for example, the most current version of the International Classification of Diseases (ICD) or State guidelines).

*Mental health benefits* means benefits with respect to items or services for mental health conditions, as defined under the terms of the plan or health insurance coverage and in accordance with applicable Federal and State law. Any condition defined by the plan or coverage as being or as not being a mental health condition must be defined to be consistent with generally recognized independent standards of current medical practice (for example, the most current version of the Diagnostic and Statistical Manual of Mental Disorders (DSM), the most current version of the ICD, or State guidelines).

*Substance use disorder benefits* means benefits with respect to items or services for substance use disorders, as defined under the terms of the plan or health insurance coverage and in accordance with applicable Federal and State law. Any disorder defined by the plan as being or as not being a substance use disorder must be defined to be consistent with generally recognized independent standards of current medical practice (for example, the most current version of the DSM, the most current version of the ICD, or State guidelines).

*Treatment limitations* include limits on benefits based on the frequency of treatment, number of visits, days of coverage, days in a waiting period, or other similar limits on the scope or duration of treatment. Treatment limitations include both quantitative treatment limitations, which are expressed numerically (such as 50 outpatient visits per year), and nonquantitative treatment limitations, which otherwise limit the scope or duration of benefits for treatment under a plan or coverage. (See paragraph (c)(4)(ii) of this section for an illustrative list of nonquantitative treatment limitations.) A permanent exclusion of all benefits for a particular condition or disorder, however, is not a treatment limitation for purposes of this definition.

(b) *Parity requirements with respect to aggregate lifetime and annual dollar limits.*—This paragraph (b) details the application of the parity requirements with respect to aggregate lifetime and annual dollar limits. This paragraph (b) does not address the provisions of PHS Act section 2711, as incorporated in ERISA section 715 and Code section 9815, which prohibit imposing lifetime and annual limits on the dollar value of essential health benefits.

(1) *General.*—(i) *General parity requirement.*—A group health plan (or health insurance coverage offered by an issuer in connection with a group health plan) that provides both medical/surgical benefits and mental health or substance use disorder benefits must comply with paragraph (b)(2), (b)(3), or (b)(5) of this section.

(ii) *Exception.*—The rule in paragraph (b)(1)(i) of this section does not apply if a plan (or health insurance coverage) satisfies the requirements of paragraph (f) or (g) of this section (relating to exemptions for small employers and for increased cost).

(2) *Plan with no limit or limits on less than one-third of all medical/ surgical benefits.*—If a plan (or health insurance coverage) does not include an aggregate lifetime or annual dollar limit on any medical/ surgical benefits or includes an aggregate lifetime or annual dollar limit that applies to less than one-third of all medical/surgical benefits, it may not impose an aggregate lifetime or annual dollar limit, respectively, on mental health or substance use disorder benefits.

(3) *Plan with a limit on at least two-thirds of all medical/surgical benefits.*—If a plan (or health insurance coverage) includes an aggregate lifetime or annual dollar limit on at least two-thirds of all medical/surgical benefits, it must either—

(i) Apply the aggregate lifetime or annual dollar limit both to the medical/surgical benefits to which the limit would otherwise apply and to mental health or substance use disorder benefits in a manner that does not distinguish between the medical/surgical benefits and mental health or substance use disorder benefits; or

(ii) Not include an aggregate lifetime or annual dollar limit on mental health or substance use disorder benefits that is less than the aggregate lifetime or annual dollar limit, respectively, on medical/surgical benefits. (For cumulative limits other than aggregate lifetime or annual dollar limits, see paragraph (c)(3)(v) of this section prohibiting separately accumulating cumulative financial requirements or cumulative quantitative treatment limitations.)

(4) *Determining one-third and two-thirds of all medical/surgical benefits.*—For purposes of this paragraph (b), the determination of whether the portion of medical/surgical benefits subject to an aggregate lifetime or annual dollar limit represents one-third or two-thirds of all medical/surgical benefits is based on the dollar amount of all plan payments for medical/surgical benefits expected to be paid under the plan for the plan year (or for the portion of the plan year after a change in plan benefits that affects the applicability of the aggregate lifetime or annual dollar limits). Any reasonable method may be used to determine whether the dollar amount expected to be paid under the plan will constitute one-third or two-thirds of the dollar amount of all plan payments for medical/surgical benefits.

(5) *Plan not described in paragraph (b)(2) or (b)(3) of this section.*—(i) *In general.*—A group health plan (or health insurance coverage) that is not described in paragraph (b)(2) or (b)(3) of this section with respect to aggregate lifetime or annual dollar limits on medical/surgical benefits, must either—

(A) Impose no aggregate lifetime or annual dollar limit, as appropriate, on mental health or substance use disorder benefits; or

(B) Impose an aggregate lifetime or annual dollar limit on mental health or substance use disorder benefits that is no less than an average limit calculated for medical/surgical benefits in the following manner. The average limit is calculated by taking into account the weighted average of the aggregate lifetime or annual dollar limits, as appropriate, that are applicable to the categories of medical/surgical benefits. Limits based on delivery systems, such as inpatient/outpatient treatment or normal treatment of common, low-cost conditions (such as treatment of normal births), do not constitute categories for purposes of this paragraph (b)(5)(i)(B). In addition, for purposes of determining weighted averages, any benefits that are not within a category that is subject to a separately-designated dollar limit under the plan are taken into account as a single separate category by using an estimate of the upper limit on the dollar amount that a plan may reasonably be expected to incur with respect to such benefits, taking into account any other applicable restrictions under the plan.

(ii) *Weighting.*—For purposes of this paragraph (b)(5), the weighting applicable to any category of medical/surgical benefits is determined in the manner set forth in paragraph (b)(4) of this section for determining one-third or two-thirds of all medical/surgical benefits.

(c) *Parity requirements with respect to financial requirements and treatment limitations.*—(1) *Clarification of terms.*—(i) *Classification of benefits.*—When reference is made in this paragraph (c) to a classification of benefits, the term "classification" means a classification as described in paragraph (c)(2)(ii) of this section.

(ii) *Type of financial requirement or treatment limitation.*—When reference is made in this paragraph (c) to a type of financial requirement or treatment limitation, the reference to type means its nature. Different types of financial requirements include deductibles, copayments, coinsurance, and out-of-pocket maximums. Different types of quantitative treatment limitations include annual, episode, and lifetime day and visit limits. See paragraph (c)(4)(ii) of this section for an illustrative list of nonquantitative treatment limitations.

(iii) *Level of a type of financial requirement or treatment limitation.*—When reference is made in this paragraph (c) to a level of a type of financial requirement or treatment limitation, level refers to the magnitude of the type of financial requirement or treatment limitation. For example, different levels of coinsurance include 20 percent and 30 percent; different levels of a copayment include $15 and $20; different levels of a deductible include $250 and $500; and different levels of an episode limit include 21 inpatient days per episode and 30 inpatient days per episode.

(iv) *Coverage unit.*—When reference is made in this paragraph (c) to a coverage unit, coverage unit refers to the way in which a plan (or health insurance coverage) groups individuals for purposes of determining benefits, or premiums or contributions. For example, different coverage units include self-only, family, and employee-plus-spouse.

(2) *General parity requirement.*—(i) *General rule.*—A group health plan (or health insurance coverage offered by an issuer in connection with a group health plan) that provides both medical/surgical benefits and mental health or substance use disorder benefits may not apply any financial requirement or treatment limitation to mental health or substance use disorder benefits in any classification that is more restrictive than the predominant financial requirement or treatment limitation of that type applied to substantially all medical/surgical benefits in the same classification. Whether a financial requirement or treatment limitation is a predominant financial requirement or treatment limitation that applies to substantially all medical/surgical benefits in a classification is determined separately for each type of financial requirement or treatment limitation. The application of the rules of this paragraph (c)(2) to financial requirements and quantitative treatment limitations is addressed in paragraph (c)(3) of this section; the application of the rules of this paragraph (c)(2) to nonquantitative treatment limitations is addressed in paragraph (c)(4) of this section.

(ii) *Classifications of benefits used for applying rules.*—(A) *In general.*—If a plan (or health insurance coverage) provides mental health or substance use disorder benefits in any classification of benefits described in this paragraph (c)(2)(ii), mental health or substance use disorder benefits must be provided in every classification in which medical/surgical benefits are provided. In determining the classification in which a particular benefit belongs, a plan (or health insurance issuer) must apply the same standards to medical/surgical benefits and to mental health or substance use disorder benefits. To the extent that a plan (or health insurance coverage) provides benefits in a classification and imposes any separate financial requirement or treatment limitation (or separate level of a financial requirement or treatment limitation) for benefits in the classification, the rules of this paragraph (c) apply separately with respect to that classification for all financial requirements or treatment limitations (illustrated in examples in paragraph (c)(2)(ii)(C) of this section). The following classifications of benefits are the only classifications used in applying the rules of this paragraph (c):

(1) *Inpatient, in-network.*—Benefits furnished on an inpatient basis and within a network of providers established or recognized under a plan or health insurance coverage. See special rules for plans with multiple network tiers in paragraph (c)(3)(iii) of this section.

(2) *Inpatient, out-of-network.*—Benefits furnished on an inpatient basis and outside any network of providers established or recognized under a plan or health insurance coverage. This classification includes inpatient benefits under a plan (or health insurance coverage) that has no network of providers.

(3) *Outpatient, in-network.*—Benefits furnished on an outpatient basis and within a network of providers established or recognized under a plan or health insurance coverage. See special rules for office visits and plans with multiple network tiers in paragraph (c)(3)(iii) of this section.

(4) *Outpatient, out-of-network.*—Benefits furnished on an outpatient basis and outside any network of providers established or recognized under a plan or health insurance coverage. This classification includes outpatient benefits under a plan (or health insurance coverage) that has no network of providers. See special rules for office visits in paragraph (c)(3)(iii) of this section.

(5) *Emergency care.*—Benefits for emergency care.

(6) *Prescription drugs.*—Benefits for prescription drugs. See special rules for multi-tiered prescription drug benefits in paragraph (c)(3)(iii) of this section.

(B) *Application to out-of-network providers.*—See paragraph (c)(2)(ii)(A) of this section, under which a plan (or health insurance coverage) that provides mental health or substance use disorder benefits in any classification of benefits must provide mental health or substance use disorder benefits in every classification in which medical/surgical benefits are provided, including out-of-network classifications.

(C) *Examples.*—The rules of this paragraph (c)(2)(ii) are illustrated by the following examples. In each example, the group

health plan is subject to the requirements of this section and provides both medical/surgical benefits and mental health and substance use disorder benefits.

*Example 1.* (i) *Facts.* A group health plan offers inpatient and outpatient benefits and does not contract with a network of providers. The plan imposes a $500 deductible on all benefits. For inpatient medical/surgical benefits, the plan imposes a coinsurance requirement. For outpatient medical/surgical benefits, the plan imposes copayments. The plan imposes no other financial requirements or treatment limitations.

(ii) *Conclusion.* In this *Example 1,* because the plan has no network of providers, all benefits provided are out-of-network. Because inpatient, out-of-network medical/surgical benefits are subject to separate financial requirements from outpatient, out-of-network medical/surgical benefits, the rules of this paragraph (c) apply separately with respect to any financial requirements and treatment limitations, including the deductible, in each classification.

*Example 2.* (i) *Facts.* A plan imposes a $500 deductible on all benefits. The plan has no network of providers. The plan generally imposes a 20 percent coinsurance requirement with respect to all benefits, without distinguishing among inpatient, outpatient, emergency care, or prescription drug benefits. The plan imposes no other financial requirements or treatment limitations.

(ii) *Conclusion.* In this *Example 2,* because the plan does not impose separate financial requirements (or treatment limitations) based on classification, the rules of this paragraph (c) apply with respect to the deductible and the coinsurance across all benefits.

*Example 3.* (i) *Facts.* Same facts as *Example 2,* except the plan exempts emergency care benefits from the 20 percent coinsurance requirement. The plan imposes no other financial requirements or treatment limitations.

(ii) *Conclusion.* In this *Example 3,* because the plan imposes separate financial requirements based on classifications, the rules of this paragraph (c) apply with respect to the deductible and the coinsurance separately for—

(A) Benefits in the emergency care classification; and

(B) All other benefits.

*Example 4.* (i) *Facts.* Same facts as *Example 2,* except the plan also imposes a preauthorization requirement for all inpatient treatment in order for benefits to be paid. No such requirement applies to outpatient treatment.

(ii) *Conclusion.* In this *Example 4,* because the plan has no network of providers, all benefits provided are out-of-network. Because the plan imposes a separate treatment limitation based on classifications, the rules of this paragraph (c) apply with respect to the deductible and coinsurance separately for—

(A) Inpatient, out-of-network benefits; and

(B) All other benefits.

(3) *Financial requirements and quantitative treatment limitations.*—(i) *Determining "substantially all" and "predominant".*—(A) *Substantially all.*—For purposes of this paragraph (c), a type of financial requirement or quantitative treatment limitation is considered to apply to substantially all medical/surgical benefits in a classification of benefits if it applies to at least two-thirds of all medical/surgical benefits in that classification. (For this purpose, benefits expressed as subject to a zero level of a type of financial requirement are treated as benefits not subject to that type of financial requirement, and benefits expressed as subject to a quantitative treatment limitation that is unlimited are treated as benefits not subject to that type of quantitative treatment limitation.) If a type of financial requirement or quantitative treatment limitation does not apply to at least two-thirds of all medical/surgical benefits in a classification, then that type cannot be applied to mental health or substance use disorder benefits in that classification.

(B) *Predominant.*—(1) If a type of financial requirement or quantitative treatment limitation applies to at least two-thirds of all medical/surgical benefits in a classification as determined under paragraph (c)(3)(i)(A) of this section, the level of the financial requirement or quantitative treatment limitation that is considered the predominant level of that type in a classification of benefits is the level that applies to more than one-half of medical/surgical benefits in that classification subject to the financial requirement or quantitative treatment limitation.

(2) If, with respect to a type of financial requirement or quantitative treatment limitation that applies to at least two-thirds of all medical/surgical benefits in a classification, there is no single level that applies to more than one-half of medical/surgical benefits in the classification subject to the financial requirement or quantitative treatment limitation, the plan (or health insurance issuer) may combine levels until the combination of levels applies to more than one-half of medical/surgical benefits subject to the financial requirement or quantitative treatment limitation in the classification. The least restrictive level within the combination is considered the pre-

dominant level of that type in the classification. (For this purpose, a plan may combine the most restrictive levels first, with each less restrictive level added to the combination until the combination applies to more than one-half of the benefits subject to the financial requirement or treatment limitation.)

(C) *Portion based on plan payments.*—For purposes of this paragraph (c), the determination of the portion of medical/surgical benefits in a classification of benefits subject to a financial requirement or quantitative treatment limitation (or subject to any level of a financial requirement or quantitative treatment limitation) is based on the dollar amount of all plan payments for medical/surgical benefits in the classification expected to be paid under the plan for the plan year (or for the portion of the plan year after a change in plan benefits that affects the applicability of the financial requirement or quantitative treatment limitation).

(D) *Clarifications for certain threshold requirements.*—For any deductible, the dollar amount of plan payments includes all plan payments with respect to claims that would be subject to the deductible if it had not been satisfied. For any out-of-pocket maximum, the dollar amount of plan payments includes all plan payments associated with out-of-pocket payments that are taken into account towards the out-of-pocket maximum as well as all plan payments associated with out-of-pocket payments that would have been made towards the out-of-pocket maximum if it had not been satisfied. Similar rules apply for any other thresholds at which the rate of plan payment changes. (See also PHS Act section 2707(b) and Affordable Care Act section 1302(c), which establish limitations on annual deductibles for non-grandfathered health plans in the small group market and annual limitations on out-of-pocket maximums for all non-grandfathered health plans.)

(E) *Determining the dollar amount of plan payments.*—Subject to paragraph (c)(3)(i)(D) of this section, any reasonable method may be used to determine the dollar amount expected to be paid under a plan for medical/surgical benefits subject to a financial requirement or quantitative treatment limitation (or subject to any level of a financial requirement or quantitative treatment limitation).

(ii) *Application to different coverage units.*—If a plan (or health insurance coverage) applies different levels of a financial requirement or quantitative treatment limitation to different coverage units in a classification of medical/surgical benefits, the predominant level that applies to substantially all medical/surgical benefits in the classification is determined separately for each coverage unit.

(iii) *Special rules.*—(A) *Multi-tiered prescription drug benefits.*—If a plan (or health insurance coverage) applies different levels of financial requirements to different tiers of prescription drug benefits based on reasonable factors determined in accordance with the rules in paragraph (c)(4)(i) of this section (relating to requirements for nonquantitative treatment limitations) and without regard to whether a drug is generally prescribed with respect to medical/surgical benefits or with respect to mental health or substance use

disorder benefits, the plan (or health insurance coverage) satisfies the parity requirements of this paragraph (c) with respect to prescription drug benefits. Reasonable factors include cost, efficacy, generic versus brand name, and mail order versus pharmacy pick-up.

(B) *Multiple network tiers.*—If a plan (or health insurance coverage) provides benefits through multiple tiers of in-network providers (such as an in-network tier of preferred providers with more generous cost-sharing to participants than a separate in-network tier of participating providers), the plan may divide its benefits furnished on an in-network basis into sub-classifications that reflect network tiers, if the tiering is based on reasonable factors determined in accordance with the rules in paragraph (c)(4)(i) of this section (such as quality, performance, and market standards) and without regard to whether a provider provides services with respect to medical/surgical benefits or mental health or substance use disorder benefits. After the sub-classifications are established, the plan or issuer may not impose any financial requirement or treatment limitation on mental health or substance use disorder benefits in any sub-classification that is more restrictive than the predominant financial requirement or treatment limitation that applies to substantially all medical/surgical benefits in the sub-classification using the methodology set forth in paragraph (c)(3)(i) of this section.

(C) *Sub-classifications permitted for office visits, separate from other outpatient services.*—For purposes of applying the financial requirement and treatment limitation rules of this paragraph (c), a plan or issuer may divide its benefits furnished on an outpatient basis into the two sub-classifications described in this paragraph (c)(3)(iii)(C). After the sub-classifications are established, the plan or issuer may not impose any financial requirement or quantitative treatment limitation on mental health or substance use disorder benefits in any sub-classification that is more restrictive than the predominant financial requirement or quantitative treatment limitation that applies to substantially all medical/surgical benefits in the sub-classification using the methodology set forth in paragraph (c)(3)(i) of this section. Sub-classifications other than these special rules, such as separate sub-classifications for generalists and specialists, are not permitted. The two sub-classifications permitted under this paragraph (c)(3)(iii)(C) are:

(1) Office visits (such as physician visits), and

(2) All other outpatient items and services (such as outpatient surgery, facility charges for day treatment centers, laboratory charges, or other medical items).

(iv) *Examples.*—The rules of paragraphs (c)(3)(i), (c)(3)(ii), and (c)(3)(iii) of this section are illustrated by the following examples. In each example, the group health plan is subject to the requirements of this section and provides both medical/surgical benefits and mental health and substance use disorder benefits.

*Example 1.* (i) *Facts.* For inpatient, out-of-network medical/surgical benefits, a group health plan imposes five levels of coinsurance. Using a reasonable method, the plan projects its payments for the upcoming year as follows:

| Coinsurance rate | . 0 % | 10% | 15% | 20% | 30% | Total |
|---|---|---|---|---|---|---|
| Projected payments | $200x | $100x | $450x | $100x | $150x | $1,000x |
| Percent of total plan costs | 20% | 10% | 45% | 10% | 15% | |
| Percent subject to coinsurance level | N/A | 12.5% (100x/800x) | 56.25% (450x/800x) | 12.5% (100x/800x) | 18.75% (150x/800x) | |

The plan projects plan costs of $800x to be subject to coinsurance ($100x + $450x + $100x + $150x = $800x). Thus, 80 percent ($800x/$1,000x) of the benefits are projected to be subject to coinsurance, and 56.25 percent of the benefits subject to coinsurance are projected to be subject to the 15 percent coinsurance level.

(ii) *Conclusion.* In this *Example 1*, the two-thirds threshold of the substantially all standard is met for coinsurance because 80 percent of all inpatient, out-of-network medical/surgical benefits are subject to coinsurance. Moreover, the 15 percent coinsurance is the predominant level because it is applicable to more than one-half of

inpatient, out-of-network medical/surgical benefits subject to the coinsurance requirement. The plan may not impose any level of coinsurance with respect to inpatient, out-of-network mental health or substance use disorder benefits that is more restrictive than the 15 percent level of coinsurance.

*Example 2.* (i) *Facts.* For outpatient, in-network medical/surgical benefits, a plan imposes five different copayment levels. Using a reasonable method, the plan projects payments for the upcoming year as follows:

| Copayment amount | $0 | $10 | $15 | $20 | $50 | Total |
|---|---|---|---|---|---|---|
| Projected payments | $200x | $200x | $200x | $300x | $100x | $1,000x |
| Percent of total plan costs | 20% | 20% | 20% | 30% | 10% | |
| Percent subject to copayments | N/A | 25% (200x/800x) | 25% (200x/800x) | 37.5% (300x/800x) | 12.5% (100x/800x) | |

The plan projects plan costs of $800x to be subject to copayments ($200x + $200x +$300x + $100x = $800x). Thus, 80 percent ($800x/$1,000x) of the benefits are projected to be subject to a copayment.

(ii) *Conclusion.* In this *Example 2*, the two-thirds threshold of the substantially all standard is met for copayments because 80

percent of all outpatient, in-network medical/surgical benefits are subject to a copayment. Moreover, there is no single level that applies to more than one-half of medical/surgical benefits in the classification subject to a copayment (for the $10 copayment, 25%; for the $15 copayment, 25%; for the $20 copayment, 37.5%; and for the $50 copayment, 12.5%). The plan can combine any levels of copayment, including the highest levels, to determine the predominant level that can be applied to mental health or substance use disorder benefits. If the plan combines the highest levels of copayment, the combined projected payments for the two highest copayment levels, the $50 copayment and the $20 copayment, are not more than one-half of the outpatient, in-network medical/surgical benefits subject to a copayment because they are exactly one-half ($300x + $100x = $400x; $400x/$800x = 50%). The combined projected payments for the three highest copayment levels - the $50 copayment, the $20 copayment, and the $15 copayment - are more than one-half of the outpatient, in-network medical/surgical benefits subject to the copayments ($100x + $300x + $200x = $600x; $600x/$800x = 75%). Thus, the plan may not impose any copayment on outpatient, in-network mental health or substance use disorder benefits that is more restrictive than the least restrictive copayment in the combination, the $15 copayment.

*Example 3.* (i) *Facts.* A plan imposes a $250 deductible on all medical/surgical benefits for self-only coverage and a $500 deductible on all medical/surgical benefits for family coverage. The plan has no network of providers. For all medical/surgical benefits, the plan imposes a coinsurance requirement. The plan imposes no other financial requirements or treatment limitations.

(ii) *Conclusion.* In this *Example 3*, because the plan has no network of providers, all benefits are provided out-of-network. Because self-only and family coverage are subject to different deductibles, whether the deductible applies to substantially all medical/surgical benefits is determined separately for self-only medical/surgical benefits and family medical/surgical benefits. Because the coinsurance is applied without regard to coverage units, the predominant coinsurance that applies to substantially all medical/surgical benefits is determined without regard to coverage units.

*Example 4.* (i) *Facts.* A plan applies the following financial requirements for prescription drug benefits. The requirements are applied without regard to whether a drug is generally prescribed with respect to medical/surgical benefits or with respect to mental health or substance use disorder benefits. Moreover, the process for certifying a particular drug as "generic", "preferred brand name", "non-preferred brand name", or "specialty" complies with the rules of paragraph (c)(4)(i) of this section (relating to requirements for nonquantitative treatment limitations).

|  | Tier 1 | Tier 2 | Tier 3 | Tier 4 |
|---|---|---|---|---|
| Tier description | Generic drugs | Preferred brand name drugs | Non-preferred brand name drugs (which may have Tier 1 or Tier 2 alternatives) | Specialty drugs |
| Percent paid by plan | 90% | 80% | 60% | 50% |

(ii) *Conclusion.* In this *Example 4*, the financial requirements that apply to prescription drug benefits are applied without regard to whether a drug is generally prescribed with respect to medical/surgical benefits or with respect to mental health or substance use disorder benefits; the process for certifying drugs in different tiers complies with paragraph (c)(4) of this section; and the bases for establishing different levels or types of financial requirements are reasonable. The financial requirements applied to prescription drug benefits do not violate the parity requirements of this paragraph (c)(3).

*Example 5.* (i) *Facts.* A plan has two-tiers of network of providers: a preferred provider tier and a participating provider tier. Providers are placed in either the preferred tier or participating tier based on reasonable factors determined in accordance with the rules in paragraph (c)(4)(i) of this section, such as accreditation, quality and performance measures (including customer feedback), and relative reimbursement rates. Furthermore, provider tier placement is determined without regard to whether a provider specializes in the treatment of mental health conditions or substance use disorders, or medical/surgical conditions. The plan divides the in-network classifications into two sub-classifications (in-network/preferred and in-network/participating). The plan does not impose any financial requirement or treatment limitation on mental health or substance use disorder benefits in either of these sub-classifications that is more restrictive than the predominant financial requirement or treatment limitation that applies to substantially all medical/surgical benefits in each sub-classification.

(ii) *Conclusion.* In this *Example 5*, the division of in-network benefits into sub-classifications that reflect the preferred and participating provider tiers does not violate the parity requirements of this paragraph (c)(3).

*Example 6.* (i) *Facts.* With respect to outpatient, in-network benefits, a plan imposes a $25 copayment for office visits and a 20 percent coinsurance requirement for outpatient surgery. The plan divides the outpatient, in-network classification into two sub-classifications (in-network office visits and all other outpatient, in-network items and services). The plan or issuer does not impose any financial requirement or quantitative treatment limitation on mental health or substance use disorder benefits in either of these sub-classifications that is more restrictive than the predominant financial requirement or quantitative treatment limitation that applies to substantially all medical/surgical benefits in each sub-classification.

(ii) *Conclusion.* In this *Example 6*, the division of outpatient, in-network benefits into sub-classifications for office visits and all other outpatient, in-network items and services does not violate the parity requirements of this paragraph (c)(3).

*Example 7.* (i) *Facts.* Same facts as *Example 6*, but for purposes of determining parity, the plan divides the outpatient, in-network classification into outpatient, in-network generalists and outpatient, in-network specialists.

(ii) *Conclusion.* In this *Example 7*, the division of outpatient, in-network benefits into any sub-classifications other than office visits and all other outpatient items and services violates the requirements of paragraph (c)(3)(iii)(C) of this section.

(v) *No separate cumulative financial requirements or cumulative quantitative treatment limitations.*—(A) A group health plan (or health insurance coverage offered in connection with a group health plan) may not apply any cumulative financial requirement or cumulative quantitative treatment limitation for mental health or substance use disorder benefits in a classification that accumulates separately from any established for medical/surgical benefits in the same classification.

(B) The rules of this paragraph (c)(3)(v) are illustrated by the following examples:

*Example 1.* (i) *Facts.* A group health plan imposes a combined annual $500 deductible on all medical/surgical, mental health, and substance use disorder benefits.

(ii) *Conclusion.* In this *Example 1*, the combined annual deductible complies with the requirements of this paragraph (c)(3)(v).

*Example 2.* (i) *Facts.* A plan imposes an annual $250 deductible on all medical/surgical benefits and a separate annual $250 deductible on all mental health and substance use disorder benefits.

(ii) *Conclusion.* In this *Example 2*, the separate annual deductible on mental health and substance use disorder benefits violates the requirements of this paragraph (c)(3)(v).

*Example 3.* (i) *Facts.* A plan imposes an annual $300 deductible on all medical/surgical benefits and a separate annual $100 deductible on all mental health or substance use disorder benefits.

(ii) *Conclusion.* In this *Example 3*, the separate annual deductible on mental health and substance use disorder benefits violates the requirements of this paragraph (c)(3)(v).

*Example 4.* (i) *Facts.* A plan generally imposes a combined annual $500 deductible on all benefits (both medical/surgical benefits and mental health and substance use disorder benefits) except prescription drugs. Certain benefits, such as preventive care, are provided without regard to the deductible. The imposition of other types of financial requirements or treatment limitations varies with each classification. Using reasonable methods, the plan projects its payments for medical/surgical benefits in each classification for the upcoming year as follows:

| Classification | Benefits Subject to Deductible | Total Benefits | Percent Subject to Deductible |
|---|---|---|---|
| Inpatient, in-network | $1,800x | $2,000x | 90% |
| Inpatient, out-of-network | $1,000x | $1,000x | 100% |
| Outpatient, in-network | $1,400x | $2,000x | 70% |
| Outpatient, out-of-network | $1,880x | $2,000x | 94% |
| Emergency care | $300x | $500x | 60% |

Reg. §54.9812-1(c)(3)(v)(B)

(ii) *Conclusion.* In this *Example 4*, the two-thirds threshold of the substantially all standard is met with respect to each classification except emergency care because in each of those other classifications at least two-thirds of medical/surgical benefits are subject to the $500 deductible. Moreover, the $500 deductible is the predominant level in each of those other classifications because it is the only level. However, emergency care mental health and substance use disorder benefits cannot be subject to the $500 deductible because it does not apply to substantially all emergency care medical/surgical benefits.

(4) *Nonquantitative treatment limitations.*—(i) *General rule.*—A group health plan (or health insurance coverage) may not impose a nonquantitative treatment limitation with respect to mental health or substance use disorder benefits in any classification unless, under the terms of the plan (or health insurance coverage) as written and in operation, any processes, strategies, evidentiary standards, or other factors used in applying the nonquantitative treatment limitation to mental health or substance use disorder benefits in the classification are comparable to, and are applied no more stringently than, the processes, strategies, evidentiary standards, or other factors used in applying the limitation with respect to medical/surgical benefits in the classification.

(ii) *Illustrative list of nonquantitative treatment limitations.*— Nonquantitative treatment limitations include—

(A) Medical management standards limiting or excluding benefits based on medical necessity or medical appropriateness, or based on whether the treatment is experimental or investigative;

(B) Formulary design for prescription drugs;

(C) For plans with multiple network tiers (such as preferred providers and participating providers), network tier design;

(D) Standards for provider admission to participate in a network, including reimbursement rates;

(E) Plan methods for determining usual, customary, and reasonable charges;

(F) Refusal to pay for higher-cost therapies until it can be shown that a lower-cost therapy is not effective (also known as fail-first policies or step therapy protocols);

(G) Exclusions based on failure to complete a course of treatment; and

(H) Restrictions based on geographic location, facility type, provider specialty, and other criteria that limit the scope or duration of benefits for services provided under the plan or coverage.

(iii) *Examples.*—The rules of this paragraph (c)(4) are illustrated by the following examples. In each example, the group health plan is subject to the requirements of this section and provides both medical/surgical benefits and mental health and substance use disorder benefits.

*Example 1.* (i) *Facts.* A plan requires prior authorization from the plan's utilization reviewer that a treatment is medically necessary for all inpatient medical/surgical benefits and for all inpatient mental health and substance use disorder benefits. In practice, inpatient benefits for medical/surgical conditions are routinely approved for seven days, after which a treatment plan must be submitted by the patient's attending provider and approved by the plan. On the other hand, for inpatient mental health and substance use disorder benefits, routine approval is given only for one day, after which a treatment plan must be submitted by the patient's attending provider and approved by the plan.

(ii) *Conclusion.* In this Example 1, the plan violates the rules of this paragraph (c)(4) because it is applying a stricter nonquantitative treatment limitation in practice to mental health and substance use disorder benefits than is applied to medical/surgical benefits.

*Example 2.* (i) *Facts.* A plan applies concurrent review to inpatient care where there are high levels of variation in length of stay (as measured by a coefficient of variation exceeding 0.8). In practice, the application of this standard affects 60 percent of mental health conditions and substance use disorders, but only 30 percent of medical/surgical conditions.

(ii) *Conclusion.* In this *Example 2*, the plan complies with the rules of this paragraph (c)(4) because the evidentiary standard used by the plan is applied no more stringently for mental health and substance use disorder benefits than for medical/surgical benefits, even though it results in an overall difference in the application of concurrent review for mental health conditions or substance use disorders than for medical/surgical conditions.

*Example 3.* (i) *Facts.* A plan requires prior approval that a course of treatment is medically necessary for outpatient, in-network medical/surgical, mental health, and substance use disorder benefits and uses comparable criteria in determining whether a course of treatment is medically necessary. For mental health and substance use disorder treatments that do not have prior approval, no benefits will be paid; for medical/surgical treatments that do not have prior

approval, there will only be a 25 percent reduction in the benefits the plan would otherwise pay.

(ii) *Conclusion.* In this *Example 3*, the plan violates the rules of this paragraph (c)(4). Although the same nonquantitative treatment limitation—medical necessity—is applied both to mental health and substance use disorder benefits and to medical/surgical benefits for outpatient, in-network services, it is not applied in a comparable way. The penalty for failure to obtain prior approval for mental health and substance use disorder benefits is not comparable to the penalty for failure to obtain prior approval for medical/surgical benefits.

*Example 4.* (i) *Facts.* A plan generally covers medically appropriate treatments. For both medical/surgical benefits and mental health and substance use disorder benefits, evidentiary standards used in determining whether a treatment is medically appropriate (such as the number of visits or days of coverage) are based on recommendations made by panels of experts with appropriate training and experience in the fields of medicine involved. The evidentiary standards are applied in a manner that is based on clinically appropriate standards of care for a condition.

(ii) *Conclusion.* In this *Example 4*, the plan complies with the rules of this paragraph (c)(4) because the processes for developing the evidentiary standards used to determine medical appropriateness and the application of these standards to mental health and substance use disorder benefits are comparable to and are applied no more stringently than for medical/surgical benefits. This is the result even if the application of the evidentiary standards does not result in similar numbers of visits, days of coverage, or other benefits utilized for mental health conditions or substance use disorders as it does for any particular medical/surgical condition.

*Example 5.* (i) *Facts.* A plan generally covers medically appropriate treatments. In determining whether prescription drugs are medically appropriate, the plan automatically excludes coverage for antidepressant drugs that are given a black box warning label by the Food and Drug Administration (indicating the drug carries a significant risk of serious adverse effects). For other drugs with a black box warning (including those prescribed for other mental health conditions and substance use disorders, as well as for medical/surgical conditions), the plan will provide coverage if the prescribing physician obtains authorization from the plan that the drug is medically appropriate for the individual, based on clinically appropriate standards of care.

(ii) *Conclusion.* In this *Example 5*, the plan violates the rules of this paragraph (c)(4). Although the standard for applying a nonquantitative treatment limitation is the same for both mental health and substance use disorder benefits and medical/surgical benefits— whether a drug has a black box warning—it is not applied in a comparable manner. The plan's unconditional exclusion of antidepressant drugs given a black box warning is not comparable to the conditional exclusion for other drugs with a black box warning.

*Example 6.* (i) *Facts.* An employer maintains both a major medical plan and an employee assistance program (EAP). The EAP provides, among other benefits, a limited number of mental health or substance use disorder counseling sessions. Participants are eligible for mental health or substance use disorder benefits under the major medical plan only after exhausting the counseling sessions provided by the EAP. No similar exhaustion requirement applies with respect to medical/surgical benefits provided under the major medical plan.

(ii) *Conclusion.* In this *Example 6*, limiting eligibility for mental health and substance use disorder benefits only after EAP benefits are exhausted is a nonquantitative treatment limitation subject to the parity requirements of this paragraph (c). Because no comparable requirement applies to medical/surgical benefits, the requirement may not be applied to mental health or substance use disorder benefits.

*Example 7.* (i) *Facts.* Training and State licensing requirements often vary among types of providers. A plan applies a general standard that any provider must meet the highest licensing requirement related to supervised clinical experience under applicable State law in order to participate in the plan's provider network. Therefore, the plan requires master's-level mental health therapists to have post-degree, supervised clinical experience but does not impose this requirement on master's-level general medical providers because the scope of their licensure under applicable State law does require clinical experience. In addition, the plan does not require post-degree, supervised clinical experience for psychiatrists or PhD level psychologists since their licensing already requires supervised training.

(ii) *Conclusion.* In this *Example 7*, the plan complies with the rules of this paragraph (c)(4). The requirement that master's-level mental health therapists must have supervised clinical experience to join the network is permissible, as long as the plan consistently applies the same standard to all providers even though it may have a disparate impact on certain mental health providers.

*Example 8.* (i) *Facts.* A plan considers a wide array of factors in designing medical management techniques for both mental health and substance use disorder benefits and medical/surgical benefits, such as cost of treatment; high cost growth; variability in cost and quality; elasticity of demand; provider discretion in determining diagnosis, or type or length of treatment; clinical efficacy of any proposed treatment or service; licensing and accreditation of providers; and claim types with a high percentage of fraud. Based on application of these factors in a comparable fashion, prior authorization is required for some (but not all) mental health and substance use disorder benefits, as well as for some medical/surgical benefits, but not for others. For example, the plan requires prior authorization for: outpatient surgery; speech, occupational, physical, cognitive and behavioral therapy extending for more than six months; durable medical equipment; diagnostic imaging; skilled nursing visits; home infusion therapy; coordinated home care; pain management; high-risk prenatal care; delivery by cesarean section; mastectomy; prostate cancer treatment; narcotics prescribed for more than seven days; and all inpatient services beyond 30 days. The evidence considered in developing its medical management techniques includes consideration of a wide array of recognized medical literature and professional standards and protocols (including comparative effectiveness studies and clinical trials). This evidence and how it was used to develop these medical management techniques is also well documented by the plan.

(ii) *Conclusion.* In this *Example 8,* the plan complies with the rules of this paragraph (c)(4). Under the terms of the plan as written and in operation, the processes, strategies, evidentiary standards, and other factors considered by the plan in implementing its prior authorization requirement with respect to mental health and substance use disorder benefits are comparable to, and applied no more stringently than, those applied with respect to medical/surgical benefits.

*Example 9.* (i) *Facts.* A plan generally covers medically appropriate treatments. The plan automatically excludes coverage for inpatient substance use disorder treatment in any setting outside of a hospital (such as a freestanding or residential treatment center). For inpatient treatment outside of a hospital for other conditions (including freestanding or residential treatment centers prescribed for mental health conditions, as well as for medical/surgical conditions), the plan will provide coverage if the prescribing physician obtains authorization from the plan that the inpatient treatment is medically appropriate for the individual, based on clinically appropriate standards of care.

(ii) *Conclusion.* In this *Example 9,* the plan violates the rules of this paragraph (c)(4). Although the same nonquantitative treatment limitation—medical appropriateness—is applied to both mental health and substance use disorder benefits and medical/surgical benefits, the plan's unconditional exclusion of substance use disorder treatment in any setting outside of a hospital is not comparable to the conditional exclusion of inpatient treatment outside of a hospital for other conditions.

*Example 10.* (i) *Facts.* A plan generally provides coverage for medically appropriate medical/surgical benefits as well as mental health and substance use disorder benefits. The plan excludes coverage for inpatient, out-of-network treatment of chemical dependency when obtained outside of the State where the policy is written. There is no similar exclusion for medical/surgical benefits within the same classification.

(ii) *Conclusion.* In this *Example 10,* the plan violates the rules of this paragraph (c)(4). The plan is imposing a nonquantitative treatment limitation that restricts benefits based on geographic location. Because there is no comparable exclusion that applies to medical/surgical benefits, this exclusion may not be applied to mental health or substance use disorder benefits.

*Example 11.* (i) *Facts.* A plan requires prior authorization for all outpatient mental health and substance use disorder services after the ninth visit and will only approve up to five additional visits per authorization. With respect to outpatient medical/surgical benefits, the plan allows an initial visit without prior authorization. After the initial visit, the plan pre-approves benefits based on the individual treatment plan recommended by the attending provider based on that individual's specific medical condition. There is no explicit, predetermined cap on the amount of additional visits approved per authorization.

(ii) *Conclusion.* In this *Example 11,* the plan violates the rules of this paragraph (c)(4). Although the same nonquantitative treatment limitation—prior authorization to determine medical appropriateness—is applied to both mental health and substance use disorder benefits and medical/surgical benefits for outpatient services, it is not applied in a comparable way. While the plan is more generous with respect to the number of visits initially provided without pre-authorization for mental health benefits, treating all mental health conditions and substance use disorders in the same manner, while

providing for individualized treatment of medical conditions, is not a comparable application of this nonquantitative treatment limitation.

(5) *Exemptions.*—The rules of this paragraph (c) do not apply if a group health plan (or health insurance coverage) satisfies the requirements of paragraph (f) or (g) of this section (relating to exemptions for small employers and for increased cost).

(d) *Availability of plan information.*—(1) *Criteria for medical necessity determinations.*—The criteria for medical necessity determinations made under a group health plan with respect to mental health or substance use disorder benefits (or health insurance coverage offered in connection with the plan with respect to such benefits) must be made available by the plan administrator (or the health insurance issuer offering such coverage) to any current or potential participant, beneficiary, or contracting provider upon request.

(2) *Reason for any denial.*—The reason for any denial under a group health plan (or health insurance coverage offered in connection with such plan) of reimbursement or payment for services with respect to mental health or substance use disorder benefits in the case of any participant or beneficiary must be made available by the plan administrator (or the health insurance issuer offering such coverage) to the participant or beneficiary in accordance with this paragraph (d)(2).

(i) *Plans subject to ERISA.*—If a plan is subject to ERISA, it must provide the reason for the claim denial in a form and manner consistent with the requirements of 29 CFR 2560.503-1 for group health plans.

(ii) *Plans not subject to ERISA.*—If a plan is not subject to ERISA, upon the request of a participant or beneficiary the reason for the claim denial must be provided within a reasonable time and in a reasonable manner. For this purpose, a plan that follows the requirements of 29 CFR 2560.503-1 for group health plans complies with the requirements of this paragraph (d)(2)(ii).

(3) *Provisions of other law.*—Compliance with the disclosure requirements in paragraphs (d)(1) and (d)(2) of this section is not determinative of compliance with any other provision of applicable Federal or State law. In particular, in addition to those disclosure requirements, provisions of other applicable law require disclosure of information relevant to medical/surgical, mental health, and substance use disorder benefits. For example, ERISA section 104 and 29 CFR 2520.104b-1 provide that, for plans subject to ERISA, instruments under which the plan is established or operated must generally be furnished to plan participants within 30 days of request. Instruments under which the plan is established or operated include documents with information on medical necessity criteria for both medical/surgical benefits and mental health and substance use disorder benefits, as well as the processes, strategies, evidentiary standards, and other factors used to apply a nonquantitative treatment limitation with respect to medical/surgical benefits and mental health or substance use disorder benefits under the plan. In addition, 29 CFR 2560.503-1 and 29 CFR 2590.715-2719 set forth rules regarding claims and appeals, including the right of claimants (or their authorized representative) upon appeal of an adverse benefit determination (or a final internal adverse benefit determination) to be provided upon request and free of charge, reasonable access to and copies of all documents, records, and other information relevant to the claimant's claim for benefits. This includes documents with information on medical necessity criteria for both medical/surgical benefits and mental health and substance use disorder benefits, as well as the processes, strategies, evidentiary standards, and other factors used to apply a nonquantitative treatment limitation with respect to medical/surgical benefits and mental health or substance use disorder benefits under the plan.

(e) *Applicability.*—(1) *Group health plans.*—The requirements of this section apply to a group health plan offering medical/surgical benefits and mental health or substance use disorder benefits. If, under an arrangement or arrangements to provide medical care benefits by an employer or employee organization (including for this purpose a joint board of trustees of a multiemployer trust affiliated with one or more multiemployer plans), any participant (or beneficiary) can simultaneously receive coverage for medical/surgical benefits and coverage for mental health or substance use disorder benefits, then the requirements of this section (including the exemption provisions in paragraph (g) of this section) apply separately with respect to each combination of medical/surgical benefits and of mental health or substance use disorder benefits that any participant (or beneficiary) can simultaneously receive from that employer's or employee organization's arrangement or arrangements to provide medical care benefits, and all such combinations are considered for purposes of this section to be a single group health plan.

(2) *Health insurance issuers.*—The requirements of this section apply to a health insurance issuer offering health insurance coverage for mental health or substance use disorder benefits in connection with a group health plan subject to paragraph (e)(1) of this section.

(3) *Scope.*—This section does not—

(i) Require a group health plan (or health insurance issuer offering coverage in connection with a group health plan) to provide any mental health benefits or substance use disorder benefits, and the provision of benefits by a plan (or health insurance coverage) for one or more mental health conditions or substance use disorders does not require the plan or health insurance coverage under this section to provide benefits for any other mental health condition or substance use disorder;

(ii) Require a group health plan (or health insurance issuer offering coverage in connection with a group health plan) that provides coverage for mental health or substance use disorder benefits only to the extent required under PHS Act section 2713 to provide additional mental health or substance use disorder benefits in any classification in accordance with this section; or

(iii) Affect the terms and conditions relating to the amount, duration, or scope of mental health or substance use disorder benefits under the plan (or health insurance coverage) except as specifically provided in paragraphs (b) and (c) of this section.

(4) *Coordination with EHB requirements.*—Nothing in paragraph (f) or (g) of this section changes the requirements of 45 CFR 147.150 and 45 CFR 156.115, providing that a health insurance issuer offering non-grandfathered health insurance coverage in the individual or small group market providing mental health and substance use disorder services, including behavioral health treatment services, as part of essential health benefits required under 45 CFR 156.110(a)(5) and 156.115(a), must comply with the provisions of 45 CFR 146.136 to satisfy the requirement to provide essential health benefits.

(f) *Small employer exemption.*—(1) *In general.*—The requirements of this section do not apply to a group health plan (or health insurance issuer offering coverage in connection with a group health plan) for a plan year of a small employer. For purposes of this paragraph (f), the term *small employer* means, in connection with a group health plan with respect to a calendar year and a plan year, an employer who employed an average of at least two (or one in the case of an employer residing in a State that permits small groups to include a single individual) but not more than 50 employees on business days during the preceding calendar year. See section 9831(a) and § 54.9831-1(b), which provide that this section (and certain other sections) does not apply to any group health plan for any plan year if, on the first day of the plan year, the plan has fewer than two participants who are current employees.

(2) *Rules in determining employer size.*—For purposes of paragraph (f)(1) of this section—

(i) All persons treated as a single employer under subsections (b), (c), (m), and (o) of section 414 are treated as one employer;

(ii) If an employer was not in existence throughout the preceding calendar year, whether it is a small employer is determined based on the average number of employees the employer reasonably expects to employ on business days during the current calendar year; and

(iii) Any reference to an employer for purposes of the small employer exemption includes a reference to a predecessor of the employer.

(g) *Increased cost exemption.*—(1) *In general.*—If the application of this section to a group health plan (or health insurance coverage offered in connection with such plans) results in an increase for the plan year involved of the actual total cost of coverage with respect to medical/surgical benefits and mental health and substance use disorder benefits as determined and certified under paragraph (g)(3) of this section by an amount that exceeds the applicable percentage described in paragraph (g)(2) of this section of the actual total plan costs, the provisions of this section shall not apply to such plan (or coverage) during the following plan year, and such exemption shall apply to the plan (or coverage) for one plan year. An employer or issuer may elect to continue to provide mental health and substance use disorder benefits in compliance with this section with respect to the plan or coverage involved regardless of any increase in total costs.

(2) *Applicable percentage.*—With respect to a plan or coverage, the applicable percentage described in this paragraph (g) is—

(i) 2 percent in the case of the first plan year in which this section is applied to the plan or coverage; and

(ii) 1 percent in the case of each subsequent plan year.

(3) *Determinations by actuaries.*—(i) Determinations as to increases in actual costs under a plan or coverage that are attributable to implementation of the requirements of this section shall be made and certified by a qualified and licensed actuary who is a member in good standing of the American Academy of Actuaries. All such determinations must be based on the formula specified in paragraph (g)(4) of this section and shall be in a written report prepared by the actuary.

(ii) The written report described in paragraph (g)(3)(i) of this section shall be maintained by the group health plan or health insurance issuer, along with all supporting documentation relied upon by the actuary, for a period of six years following the notification made under paragraph (g)(6) of this section.

(4) *Formula.*—The formula to be used to make the determination under paragraph (g)(3)(i) of this section is expressed mathematically as follows:

$$[(E_1 - E_0)/T_0] - D > k$$

(i) $E_1$ is the actual total cost of coverage with respect to mental health and substance use disorder benefits for the base period, including claims paid by the plan or issuer with respect to mental health and substance use disorder benefits and administrative costs (amortized over time) attributable to providing these benefits consistent with the requirements of this section.

(ii) $E_0$ is the actual total cost of coverage with respect to mental health and substance use disorder benefits for the length of time immediately before the base period (and that is equal in length to the base period), including claims paid by the plan or issuer with respect to mental health and substance use disorder benefits and administrative costs (amortized over time) attributable to providing these benefits.

(iii) $T_0$ is the actual total cost of coverage with respect to all benefits during the base period.

(iv) k is the applicable percentage of increased cost specified in paragraph (g)(2) of this section that will be expressed as a fraction for purposes of this formula.

(v) D is the average change in spending that is calculated by applying the formula $(E_1 - E_0)/T_0$ to mental health and substance use disorder spending in each of the five prior years and then calculating the average change in spending.

(5) *Six month determination.*—If a group health plan or health insurance issuer seeks an exemption under this paragraph (g), determinations under paragraph (g)(3) of this section shall be made after such plan or coverage has complied with this section for at least the first 6 months of the plan year involved.

(6) *Notification.*—A group health plan or health insurance issuer that, based on the certification described under paragraph (g)(3) of this section, qualifies for an exemption under this paragraph (g), and elects to implement the exemption, must notify participants and beneficiaries covered under the plan, the Secretary, and the appropriate State agencies of such election.

(i) *Participants and beneficiaries.*—(A) *Content of notice.*—The notice to participants and beneficiaries must include the following information:

(1) A statement that the plan or issuer is exempt from the requirements of this section and a description of the basis for the exemption.

(2) The name and telephone number of the individual to contact for further information.

(3) The plan or issuer name and plan number (PN).

(4) The plan administrator's name, address, and telephone number.

(5) For single-employer plans, the plan sponsor's name, address, and telephone number (if different from paragraph (g)(6)(i)(A)(3) of this section) and the plan sponsor's employer identification number (EIN).

(6) The effective date of such exemption.

(7) A statement regarding the ability of participants and beneficiaries to contact the plan administrator or health insurance issuer to see how benefits may be affected as a result of the plan's or issuer's election of the exemption.

(8) A statement regarding the availability, upon request and free of charge, of a summary of the information on which the exemption is based (as required under paragraph (g)(6)(i)(D) of this section).

(B) *Use of summary of material reductions in covered services or benefits.*—A plan or issuer may satisfy the requirements of paragraph (g)(6)(i)(A) of this section by providing participants and beneficiaries (in accordance with paragraph (g)(6)(i)(C) of this section) with a summary of material reductions in covered services or benefits consistent with 29 CFR 2520.104b-3(d) that also includes the information specified in paragraph (g)(6)(i)(A) of this section. However, in all cases, the exemption is not effective until 30 days after notice has been sent.

(C) *Delivery.*—The notice described in this paragraph (g)(6)(i) is required to be provided to all participants and beneficiaries. The notice may be furnished by any method of delivery that satisfies the requirements of section 104(b)(1) of ERISA (29 U.S.C. 1024(b)(1)) and its implementing regulations (for example, first-class mail). If the notice is provided to the participant and any beneficiaries at the participant's last known address, then the requirements of this paragraph (g)(6)(i) are satisfied with respect to the participant and all beneficiaries residing at that address. If a beneficiary's last known address is different from the participant's last known address, a separate notice is required to be provided to the beneficiary at the beneficiary's last known address.

(D) *Availability of documentation.*—The plan or issuer must make available to participants and beneficiaries (or their representatives), on request and at no charge, a summary of the information on which the exemption was based. (For purposes of this paragraph (g), an individual who is not a participant or beneficiary and who presents a notice described in paragraph (g)(6)(i) of this section is considered to be a representative. A representative may request the summary of information by providing the plan a copy of the notice provided to the participant under paragraph (g)(6)(i) of this section with any personally identifiable information redacted.) The summary of information must include the incurred expenditures, the base period, the dollar amount of claims incurred during the base period that would have been denied under the terms of the plan or coverage absent amendments required to comply with paragraphs (b) and (c) of this section, the administrative costs related to those claims, and other administrative costs attributable to complying with the requirements of this section. In no event should the summary of information include any personally identifiable information.

(ii) *Federal agencies.*—(A) *Content of notice.*—The notice to the Secretary must include the following information:

(1) A description of the number of covered lives under the plan (or coverage) involved at the time of the notification, and as applicable, at the time of any prior election of the cost exemption under this paragraph (g) by such plan (or coverage);

(2) For both the plan year upon which a cost exemption is sought and the year prior, a description of the actual total costs of coverage with respect to medical/surgical benefits and mental health and substance use disorder benefits; and

(3) For both the plan year upon which a cost exemption is sought and the year prior, the actual total costs of coverage with respect to mental health and substance use disorder benefits under the plan.

(B) *Reporting with respect to church plans.*—A church plan (as defined in section 414(e)) claiming the exemption of this paragraph (g) for any benefit package, must provide notice to the Department of the Treasury. This requirement is satisfied if the plan sends a copy, to the address designated by the Secretary in generally applicable guidance, of the notice described in paragraph (g)(6)(ii)(A) of this section identifying the benefit package to which the exemption applies.

(C) *Reporting with respect to ERISA plans.*—See 29 CFR 2590.712(g)(6)(ii) for delivery with respect to ERISA plans.

(iii) *Confidentiality.*—A notification to the Secretary under this paragraph (g)(6) shall be confidential. The Secretary shall make available, upon request and not more than on an annual basis, an anonymous itemization of each notification that includes—

(A) A breakdown of States by the size and type of employers submitting such notification; and

(B) A summary of the data received under paragraph (g)(6)(ii) of this section.

(iv) *Audits.*—The Secretary may audit the books and records of a group health plan or a health insurance issuer relating to an exemption, including any actuarial reports, during the 6 year period following notification of such exemption under paragraph (g)(6) of this section. A State agency receiving a notification under paragraph (g)(6) of this section may also conduct such an audit with respect to an exemption covered by such notification.

(h) *Sale of nonparity health insurance coverage.*—A health insurance issuer may not sell a policy, certificate, or contract of insurance that fails to comply with paragraph (b) or (c) of this section, except to a plan for a year for which the plan is exempt from the requirements of this section because the plan meets the requirements of paragraph (f) or (g) of this section.

(i) *Applicability dates.*—(1) *In general.*—Except as provided in paragraph (i)(2) of this section, this section applies to group health plans and health insurance issuers offering group health insurance coverage on the first day of the first plan year beginning on or after July 1, 2014.

(2) *Special effective date for certain collectively-bargained plans.*—For a group health plan maintained pursuant to one or more collective bargaining agreements ratified before October 3, 2008, the requirements of this section do not apply to the plan (or health insurance coverage offered in connection with the plan) for plan years beginning before the date on which the last of the collective bargaining agreements terminates (determined without regard to any extension agreed to after October 3, 2008). [Reg. § 54.9812-1.]

☐ [T.D. 9640, 11-8-2013.]

>>>→ *Caution: Reg. §54.9815-1251, below, as added by T.D. 9744, is applicable to group health plans and health insurance issuers beginning on the first day of the plan year (or, in the individual market, the first day of the first policy year) beginning on or after January 1, 2017.*

**[Reg. § 54.9815-1251]**

**§54.9815-1251. Preservation of right to maintain existing coverage.**—(a) *Definition of grandfathered health plan coverage.*—(1) *In general.*—(i) *Grandfathered health plan coverage* means coverage provided by a group health plan, or a health insurance issuer, in which an individual was enrolled on March 23, 2010 (for as long as it maintains that status under the rules of this section). A group health plan or group health insurance coverage does not cease to be grandfathered health plan coverage merely because one or more (or even all) individuals enrolled on March 23, 2010 cease to be covered, provided that the plan or group health insurance coverage has continuously covered someone since March 23, 2010 (not necessarily the same person, but at all times at least one person). In addition, subject to the limitation set forth in paragraph (a)(1)(ii) of this section, a group health plan (and any health insurance coverage offered in connection with the group health plan) does not cease to be a grandfathered health plan merely because the plan (or its sponsor) enters into a new policy, certificate, or contract of insurance after March 23, 2010 (for example, a plan enters into a contract with a new issuer or a new policy is issued with an existing issuer). For purposes of this section, a plan or health insurance coverage that provides grandfathered health plan coverage is referred to as a grandfathered health plan. The rules of this section apply separately to each benefit package made available under a group health plan or health insurance coverage. Accordingly, if any benefit package relinquishes grandfather status, it will not affect the grandfather status of the other benefit packages.

(ii) *Changes in group health insurance coverage.*—Subject to paragraphs (f) and (g)(2) of this section, if a group health plan (including a group health plan that was self-insured on March 23, 2010) or its sponsor enters into a new policy, certificate, or contract of insurance after March 23, 2010 that is effective before November 15, 2010, then the plan ceases to be a grandfathered health plan.

(2) *Disclosure of grandfather status.*—(i) To maintain status as a grandfathered health plan, a plan or health insurance coverage must include a statement that the plan or coverage believes it is a grandfathered health plan within the meaning of section 1251 of the Patient Protection and Affordable Care Act, and must provide contact information for questions and complaints, in any summary of benefits provided under the plan.

(ii) The following model language can be used to satisfy this disclosure requirement:

This [group health plan or health insurance issuer] believes this [plan or coverage] is a "grandfathered health plan" under the Patient Protection and Affordable Care Act (the Affordable Care Act). As permitted by the Affordable Care Act, a grandfathered health plan can preserve certain basic health coverage that was already in effect when that law was enacted. Being a grandfathered health plan means that your [plan or policy] may not include certain consumer protections of the Affordable Care Act that apply to other plans, for example, the requirement for the provision of preventive health services without any cost sharing. However, grandfathered health plans must comply with certain other consumer protections in the Affordable Care Act, for example, the elimination of lifetime dollar limits on benefits.

Questions regarding which protections apply and which protections do not apply to a grandfathered health plan and what might cause a plan to change from grandfathered health plan status can be directed to the plan administrator at [insert contact information]. [For ERISA plans, insert: You may also contact the Employee Benefits Security Administration, U.S. Department of Labor at 1-866-444-3272 or www.dol.gov/ebsa/healthreform. This Web site has a table summariz-

»»→ *Caution: Reg. §54.9815-1251, below, as added by T.D. 9744, is applicable to group health plans and health insurance issuers beginning on the first day of the plan year (or, in the individual market, the first day of the first policy year) beginning on or after January 1, 2017.*

ing which protections do and do not apply to grandfathered health plans.] [For individual market policies and nonfederal governmental plans, insert: You may also contact the U.S. Department of Health and Human Services at www.healthcare.gov.]

(3)(i) *Documentation of plan or policy terms on March 23, 2010.*—To maintain status as a grandfathered health plan, a group health plan, or group health insurance coverage, must, for as long as the plan or health insurance coverage takes the position that it is a grandfathered health plan—

(A) Maintain records documenting the terms of the plan or health insurance coverage in connection with the coverage in effect on March 23, 2010, and any other documents necessary to verify, explain, or clarify its status as a grandfathered health plan; and

(B) Make such records available for examination upon request.

(ii) *Change in group health insurance coverage.*—To maintain status as a grandfathered health plan, a group health plan that enters into a new policy, certificate, or contract of insurance must provide to the new health insurance issuer (and the new health insurance issuer must require) documentation of plan terms (including benefits, cost sharing, employer contributions, and annual dollar limits) under the prior health coverage sufficient to determine whether a change causing a cessation of grandfathered health plan status under paragraph (g)(1) of this section has occurred.

(4) *Family members enrolling after March 23, 2010.*—With respect to an individual who is enrolled in a group health plan or health insurance coverage on March 23, 2010, grandfathered health plan coverage includes coverage of family members of the individual who enroll after March 23, 2010 in the grandfathered health plan coverage of the individual.

(b) *Allowance for new employees to join current plan.*—(1) *In general.*—Subject to paragraph (b)(2) of this section, a group health plan (including health insurance coverage provided in connection with the group health plan) that provided coverage on March 23, 2010 and has retained its status as a grandfathered health plan (consistent with the rules of this section, including paragraph (g) of this section) is grandfathered health plan coverage for new employees (whether newly hired or newly enrolled) and their families enrolling in the plan after March 23, 2010. Further, the addition of a new contributing employer or new group of employees of an existing contributing employer to a grandfathered multiemployer health plan will not affect the plan's grandfather status.

(2) *Anti-abuse rules.*—(i) *Mergers and acquisitions.*—If the principal purpose of a merger, acquisition, or similar business restructuring is to cover new individuals under a grandfathered health plan, the plan ceases to be a grandfathered health plan.

(ii) *Change in plan eligibility.*—A group health plan or health insurance coverage (including a benefit package under a group health plan) ceases to be a grandfathered health plan if—

(A) Employees are transferred into the plan or health insurance coverage (the transferee plan) from a plan or health insurance coverage under which the employees were covered on March 23, 2010 (the transferor plan);

(B) Comparing the terms of the transferee plan with those of the transferor plan (as in effect on March 23, 2010) and treating the transferee plan as if it were an amendment of the transferor plan would cause a loss of grandfather status under the provisions of paragraph (g)(1) of this section; and

(C) There was no bona fide employment-based reason to transfer the employees into the transferee plan. For this purpose, changing the terms or cost of coverage is not a bona fide employment-based reason.

(iii) *Illustrative list of bona fide employment-based reasons.*—For purposes of paragraph (b)(2)(ii)(C) of this section, bona fide employment-based reasons include—

(A) When a benefit package is being eliminated because the issuer is exiting the market;

(B) When a benefit package is being eliminated because the issuer no longer offers the product to the employer;

(C) When low or declining participation by plan participants in the benefit package makes it impractical for the plan sponsor to continue to offer the benefit package;

(D) When a benefit package is eliminated from a multiemployer plan as agreed upon as part of the collective bargaining process; or

(E) When a benefit package is eliminated for any reason and multiple benefit packages covering a significant portion of other employees remain available to the employees being transferred.

(3) *Examples.*—The rules of this paragraph (b) are illustrated by the following examples:

*Example 1.* (i) *Facts.* A group health plan offers two benefit packages on March 23, 2010, Options *F* and *G*. During a subsequent open enrollment period, some of the employees enrolled in Option *F* on March 23, 2010 switch to Option *G*.

(ii) *Conclusion.* In this *Example 1*, the group health coverage provided under Option *G* remains a grandfathered health plan under the rules of paragraph (b)(1) of this section because employees previously enrolled in Option *F* are allowed to enroll in Option *G* as new employees.

*Example 2.* (i) *Facts.* A group health plan offers two benefit packages on March 23, 2010, Options *H* and *I*. On March 23, 2010, Option *H* provides coverage only for employees in one manufacturing plant. Subsequently, the plant is closed, and some employees in the closed plant are moved to another plant. The employer eliminates Option *H* and the employees that are moved are transferred to Option *I*. If instead of transferring employees from Option *H* to Option *I*, Option *H* was amended to match the terms of Option *I*, then Option *H* would cease to be a grandfathered health plan.

(ii) *Conclusion.* In this *Example 2*, the plan has a bona fide employment-based reason to transfer employees from Option *H* to Option *I*. Therefore, Option *I* does not cease to be a grandfathered health plan.

(c) *General grandfathering rule.*—(1) Except as provided in paragraphs (d) and (e) of this section, subtitles A and C of title I of the Patient Protection and Affordable Care Act (and the amendments made by those subtitles, and the incorporation of those amendments into ERISA section 715 and Internal Revenue Code section 9815) do not apply to grandfathered health plan coverage. Accordingly, the provisions of PHS Act sections 2701, 2702, 2703, 2705, 2706, 2707, 2709 (relating to coverage for individuals participating in approved clinical trials, as added by section 10103 of the Patient Protection and Affordable Care Act), 2713, 2715A, 2716, 2717, 2719, and 2719A, as added or amended by the Patient Protection and Affordable Care Act, do not apply to grandfathered health plans. (In addition, *see* 45 CFR 147.140(c), which provides that the provisions of PHS Act section 2704, and PHS Act section 2711 insofar as it relates to annual dollar limits, do not apply to grandfathered health plans that are individual health insurance coverage.)

(2) To the extent not inconsistent with the rules applicable to a grandfathered health plan, a grandfathered health plan must comply with the requirements of the PHS Act, ERISA, and the Internal Revenue Code applicable prior to the changes enacted by the Patient Protection and Affordable Care Act.

(d) *Provisions applicable to all grandfathered health plans.*—The provisions of PHS Act section 2711 insofar as it relates to lifetime dollar limits, and the provisions of PHS Act sections 2712, 2714, 2715, and 2718, apply to grandfathered health plans for plan years beginning on or after September 23, 2010. The provisions of PHS Act section 2708 apply to grandfathered health plans for plan years beginning on or after January 1, 2014.

(e) *Applicability of PHS Act sections 2704, 2711, and 2714 to grandfathered group health plans and group health insurance coverage.*—(1) The provisions of PHS Act section 2704 as it applies with respect to enrollees who are under 19 years of age, and the provisions of PHS Act section 2711 insofar as it relates to annual dollar limits, apply to grandfathered health plans that are group health plans (including group health insurance coverage) for plan years beginning on or after September 23, 2010. The provisions of PHS Act section 2704 apply generally to grandfathered health plans that are group health plans (including group health insurance coverage) for plan years beginning on or after January 1, 2014.

(2) For plan years beginning before January 1, 2014, the provisions of PHS Act section 2714 apply in the case of an adult child with respect to a grandfathered health plan that is a group health plan only if the adult child is not eligible to enroll in an eligible employer-sponsored health plan (as defined in section 5000A(f)(2) of the Internal Revenue Code) other than a grandfathered health plan of a parent. For plan years beginning on or after January 1, 2014, the provisions of PHS Act section 2714 apply with respect to a grandfathered health plan that is a group health plan without regard to whether an adult child is eligible to enroll in any other coverage.

(f) *Effect on collectively bargained plans—In general.*—In the case of health insurance coverage maintained pursuant to one or more collective bargaining agreements between employee representatives and

>>>→ *Caution: Reg. §54.9815-1251, below, as added by T.D. 9744, is applicable to group health plans and health insurance issuers beginning on the first day of the plan year (or, in the individual market, the first day of the first policy year) beginning on or after January 1, 2017.*

one or more employers that was ratified before March 23, 2010, the coverage is grandfathered health plan coverage at least until the date on which the last of the collective bargaining agreements relating to the coverage that was in effect on March 23, 2010 terminates. Any coverage amendment made pursuant to a collective bargaining agreement relating to the coverage that amends the coverage solely to conform to any requirement added by subtitles A and C of title I of the Patient Protection and Affordable Care Act (and the amendments made by those subtitles, and the incorporation of those amendments into ERISA section 715 and Internal Revenue Code section 9815) is not treated as a termination of the collective bargaining agreement. After the date on which the last of the collective bargaining agreements relating to the coverage that was in effect on March 23, 2010 terminates, the determination of whether health insurance coverage maintained pursuant to a collective bargaining agreement is grandfathered health plan coverage is made under the rules of this section other than this paragraph (f) (comparing the terms of the health insurance coverage after the date the last collective bargaining agreement terminates with the terms of the health insurance coverage that were in effect on March 23, 2010).

(g) *Maintenance of grandfather status.*—(1) *Changes causing cessation of grandfather status.*—Subject to paragraphs (g)(2) and (3) of this section, the rules of this paragraph (g)(1) describe situations in which a group health plan or health insurance coverage ceases to be a grandfathered health plan. A plan or coverage will cease to be a grandfathered health plan when an amendment to plan terms that results in a change described in this paragraph (g)(1) becomes effective, regardless of when the amendment was adopted. Once grandfather status is lost, it cannot be regained.

(i) *Elimination of benefits.*—The elimination of all or substantially all benefits to diagnose or treat a particular condition causes a group health plan or health insurance coverage to cease to be a grandfathered health plan. For this purpose, the elimination of benefits for any necessary element to diagnose or treat a condition is considered the elimination of all or substantially all benefits to diagnose or treat a particular condition. Whether or not a plan or coverage has eliminated substantially all benefits to diagnose or treat a particular condition must be determined based on all the facts and circumstances, taking into account the items and services provided for a particular condition under the plan on March 23, 2010, as compared to the benefits offered at the time the plan or coverage makes the benefit change effective.

(ii) *Increase in percentage cost-sharing requirement.*—Any increase, measured from March 23, 2010, in a percentage cost-sharing requirement (such as an individual's coinsurance requirement) causes a group health plan or health insurance coverage to cease to be a grandfathered health plan.

(iii) *Increase in a fixed-amount cost-sharing requirement other than a copayment.*—Any increase in a fixed-amount cost-sharing requirement other than a copayment (for example, deductible or out-of-pocket limit), determined as of the effective date of the increase, causes a group health plan or health insurance coverage to cease to be a grandfathered health plan, if the total percentage increase in the cost-sharing requirement measured from March 23, 2010 exceeds the maximum percentage increase (as defined in paragraph (g)(4)(ii) of this section).

(iv) *Increase in a fixed-amount copayment.*—Any increase in a fixed-amount copayment, determined as of the effective date of the increase, and determined for each copayment level if a plan has different copayment levels for different categories of services, causes a group health plan or health insurance coverage to cease to be a grandfathered health plan, if the total increase in the copayment measured from March 23, 2010 exceeds the greater of:

(A) An amount equal to $5 increased by medical inflation, as defined in paragraph (g)(4)(i) of this section (that is, $5 times medical inflation, plus $5); or

(B) The maximum percentage increase (as defined in paragraph (g)(4)(ii) of this section), determined by expressing the total increase in the copayment as a percentage.

(v) *Decrease in contribution rate by employers and employee organizations.*—(A) *Contribution rate based on cost of coverage.*—A group health plan or group health insurance coverage ceases to be a grandfathered health plan if the employer or employee organization decreases its contribution rate based on cost of coverage (as defined in paragraph (g)(4)(iii)(A) of this section) towards the cost of any tier of coverage for any class of similarly situated individuals (as described in §54.9802(d)) by more than 5 percentage points below the

contribution rate for the coverage period that includes March 23, 2010.

(B) *Contribution rate based on a formula.*—A group health plan or group health insurance coverage ceases to be a grandfathered health plan if the employer or employee organization decreases its contribution rate based on a formula (as defined in paragraph (g)(4)(iii)(B) of this section) towards the cost of any tier of coverage for any class of similarly situated individuals (as described in §54.9802(d)) by more than 5 percent below the contribution rate for the coverage period that includes March 23, 2010.

(vi) *Changes in annual limits.*—(A) *Addition of an annual limit.*—A group health plan, or group health insurance coverage, that, on March 23, 2010, did not impose an overall annual or lifetime limit on the dollar value of all benefits ceases to be a grandfathered health plan if the plan or health insurance coverage imposes an overall annual limit on the dollar value of benefits. (But see §54.9815-2711, which prohibits all annual dollar limits on essential health benefits for plan years beginning on or after January 1, 2014).

(B) *Decrease in limit for a plan or coverage with only a lifetime limit.*—A group health plan, or group health insurance coverage, that, on March 23, 2010, imposed an overall lifetime limit on the dollar value of all benefits but no overall annual limit on the dollar value of all benefits ceases to be a grandfathered health plan if the plan or health insurance coverage adopts an overall annual limit at a dollar value that is lower than the dollar value of the lifetime limit on March 23, 2010. (But see §54.9815-2711, which prohibits all annual dollar limits on essential health benefits for plan years beginning on or after January 1, 2014).

(C) *Decrease in limit for a plan or coverage with an annual limit.*—A group health plan, or group health insurance coverage, that, on March 23, 2010, imposed an overall annual limit on the dollar value of all benefits ceases to be a grandfathered health plan if the plan or health insurance coverage decreases the dollar value of the annual limit (regardless of whether the plan or health insurance coverage also imposed an overall lifetime limit on March 23, 2010 on the dollar value of all benefits). (But see §54.9815-2711, which prohibits all annual dollar limits on essential health benefits for plan years beginning on or after January 1, 2014).

(2) *Transitional rules.*—(i) *Changes made prior to March 23, 2010.*—If a group health plan or health insurance issuer makes the following changes to the terms of the plan or health insurance coverage, the changes are considered part of the terms of the plan or health insurance coverage on March 23, 2010 even though they were not effective at that time and such changes do not cause a plan or health insurance coverage to cease to be a grandfathered health plan:

(A) Changes effective after March 23, 2010 pursuant to a legally binding contract entered into on or before March 23, 2010;

(B) Changes effective after March 23, 2010 pursuant to a filing on or before March 23, 2010 with a State insurance department; or

(C) Changes effective after March 23, 2010 pursuant to written amendments to a plan that were adopted on or before March 23, 2010.

(ii) *Changes made after March 23, 2010 and adopted prior to issuance of regulations.*—If, after March 23, 2010, a group health plan or health insurance issuer makes changes to the terms of the plan or health insurance coverage and the changes are adopted prior to June 14, 2010, the changes will not cause the plan or health insurance coverage to cease to be a grandfathered health plan if the changes are revoked or modified effective as of the first day of the first plan year (in the individual market, policy year) beginning on or after September 23, 2010, and the terms of the plan or health insurance coverage on that date, as modified, would not cause the plan or coverage to cease to be a grandfathered health plan under the rules of this section, including paragraph (g)(1) of this section. For this purpose, changes will be considered to have been adopted prior to June 14, 2010 if:

(A) The changes are effective before that date;

(B) The changes are effective on or after that date pursuant to a legally binding contract entered into before that date;

(C) The changes are effective on or after that date pursuant to a filing before that date with a State insurance department; or

(D) The changes are effective on or after that date pursuant to written amendments to a plan that were adopted before that date.

(3) *Special rule for certain grandfathered high deductible health plans.*—With respect to a grandfathered group health plan or group health insurance coverage that is a high deductible health plan

⫸→ *Caution: Reg. §54.9815-1251, below, as added by T.D. 9744, is applicable to group health plans and health insurance issuers beginning on the first day of the plan year (or, in the individual market, the first day of the first policy year) beginning on or after January 1, 2017.*

within the meaning of section 223(c)(2), increases to fixed-amount cost-sharing requirements made effective on or after June 15, 2021 that otherwise would cause a loss of grandfather status will not cause the plan or coverage to relinquish its grandfather status, but only to the extent such increases are necessary to maintain its status as a high deductible health plan under section 223(c)(2)(A).

(4) *Definitions.*—(i) *Medical inflation defined.*—For purposes of this paragraph (g), the term *medical inflation* means the increase since March 2010 in the overall medical care component of the Consumer Price Index for All Urban Consumers (CPI-U) (unadjusted) published by the Department of Labor using the 1982-1984 base of 100. For purposes of this paragraph (g)(4)(i), the increase in the overall medical care component is computed by subtracting 387.142 (the overall medical care component of the CPI-U (unadjusted) published by the Department of Labor for March 2010, using the 1982-1984 base of 100) from the index amount for any month in the 12 months before the new change is to take effect and then dividing that amount by 387.142.

(ii) *Maximum percentage increase defined.*—For purposes of this paragraph (g), the term *maximum percentage increase* means:

(A) With respect to increases for a group health plan and group health insurance coverage made effective on or after March 23, 2010, and before June 15, 2021, medical inflation (as defined in paragraph (g)(4)(i) of this section), expressed as a percentage, plus 15 percentage points; and

(B) With respect to increases for a group health plan and group health insurance coverage made effective on or after June 15, 2021, the greater of:

(1) Medical inflation (as defined in paragraph (g)(4)(i) of this section), expressed as a percentage, plus 15 percentage points; or

(2) The portion of the premium adjustment percentage, as defined in 45 CFR 156.130(e), that reflects the relative change between 2013 and the calendar year prior to the effective date of the increase (that is, the premium adjustment percentage minus 1), expressed as a percentage, plus 15 percentage points.

(iii) *Contribution rate defined.*—For purposes of paragraph (g)(1)(v) of this section:

(A) *Contribution rate based on cost of coverage.*—The term *contribution rate based on cost of coverage* means the amount of contributions made by an employer or employee organization compared to the total cost of coverage, expressed as a percentage. The total cost of coverage is determined in the same manner as the applicable premium is calculated under the COBRA continuation provisions of section 604 of ERISA, section 4980B(f)(4) of the Internal Revenue Code, and section 2204 of the PHS Act. In the case of a self-insured plan, contributions by an employer or employee organization are equal to the total cost of coverage minus the employee contributions towards the total cost of coverage.

(B) *Contribution rate based on a formula.*—The term *contribution rate based on a formula* means, for plans that, on March 23, 2010, made contributions based on a formula (such as hours worked or tons of coal mined), the formula.

(5) *Examples.*—The rules of this paragraph (g) are illustrated by the following examples:

*Example 1.* (i) *Facts.* On March 23, 2010, a grandfathered health plan has a coinsurance requirement of 20% for inpatient surgery. The plan is subsequently amended to increase the coinsurance requirement to 25%.

(ii) *Conclusion.* In this *Example 1*, the increase in the coinsurance requirement from 20% to 25% causes the plan to cease to be a grandfathered health plan.

*Example 2.* (i) *Facts.* Before March 23, 2010, the terms of a group health plan provide benefits for a particular mental health condition, the treatment for which is a combination of counseling and prescription drugs. Subsequently, the plan eliminates benefits for counseling.

(ii) *Conclusion.* In this *Example 2*, the plan ceases to be a grandfathered health plan because counseling is an element that is necessary to treat the condition. Thus the plan is considered to have eliminated substantially all benefits for the treatment of the condition.

*Example 3.* (i) *Facts.* On March 23, 2010, a grandfathered group health plan has a copayment requirement of $30 per office visit for specialists. The plan is subsequently amended to increase the copayment requirement to $40, effective before June 15, 2021. Within the 12-month period before the $40 copayment takes effect, the greatest value of the overall medical care component of the CPI-U (unadjusted) is 475.

(ii) *Conclusion.* In this *Example 3*, the increase in the copayment from $30 to $40, expressed as a percentage, is 33.33% (40–30 = 10; 10 ÷ 30 = 0.3333; 0.3333 = 33.33%). Medical inflation (as defined in paragraph (g)(4)(i) of this section) from March 2010 is 0.2269 (475–387.142 = 87.858; 87.858 ÷ 387.142 = 0.2269). The maximum percentage increase permitted is 37.69% (0.2269 = 22.69%; 22.69% + 15% = 37.69%). Because 33.33% does not exceed 37.69%, the change in the copayment requirement at that time does not cause the plan to cease to be a grandfathered health plan.

*Example 4.* (i) *Facts.* Same facts as *Example 3* of this paragraph (g)(5), except the grandfathered group health plan subsequently increases the $40 copayment requirement to $45 for a later plan year, effective before June 15, 2021. Within the 12-month period before the $45 copayment takes effect, the greatest value of the overall medical care component of the CPI-U (unadjusted) is 485.

(ii) *Conclusion.* In this *Example 4*, the increase in the copayment from $30 (the copayment that was in effect on March 23, 2010) to $45, expressed as a percentage, is 50% (45–30 = 15; 15 ÷ 30 = 0.5; 0.5 = 50%). Medical inflation (as defined in paragraph (g)(4)(i) of this section) from March 2010 is 0.2527 (485–387.142 = 97.858; 97.858 ÷ 387.142 = 0.2527). The increase that would cause a plan to cease to be a grandfathered health plan under paragraph (g)(1)(iv) of this section is the greater of the maximum percentage increase of 40.27% (0.2527 = 25.27%; 25.27% + 15% = 40.27%), or $6.26 (5 × 0.2527 = $1.26; $1.26 + $5 = $6.26). Because 50% exceeds 40.27% and $15 exceeds $6.26, the change in the copayment requirement at that time causes the plan to cease to be a grandfathered health plan.

*Example 5.* (i) *Facts.* Same facts as *Example 4* of this paragraph (g)(5), except the grandfathered group health plan increases the copayment requirement to $45, effective *after* June 15, 2021. The greatest value of the overall medical care component of the CPI-U (unadjusted) in the preceding 12-month period is still 485. In the calendar year that includes the effective date of the increase, the applicable portion of the premium adjustment percentage is 36%.

(ii) *Conclusion.* In this *Example 5*, the grandfathered health plan may increase the copayment by the greater of: medical inflation, expressed as a percentage, plus 15 percentage points; or the applicable portion of the premium adjustment percentage for the calendar year that includes the effective date of the increase, plus 15 percentage points. The latter amount is greater because it results in a 51% maximum percentage increase (36% + 15% = 51%) and, as demonstrated in *Example 4* of this paragraph (g)(5), determining the maximum percentage increase using medical inflation yields a result of 40.27%. The increase in the copayment, expressed as a percentage, is 50% (45–30 = 15; 15 ÷ 30 = 0.5; 0.5 = 50%). Because the 50% increase in the copayment is less than the 51% maximum percentage increase, the change in the copayment requirement at that time does not cause the plan to cease to be a grandfathered health plan.

*Example 6.* (i) *Facts.* On March 23, 2010, a grandfathered group health plan has a copayment of $10 per office visit for primary care providers. The plan is subsequently amended to increase the copayment requirement to $15, effective before June 15, 2021. Within the 12-month period before the $15 copayment takes effect, the greatest value of the overall medical care component of the CPI-U (unadjusted) is 415.

(ii) *Conclusion.* In this *Example 6*, the increase in the copayment, expressed as a percentage, is 50% (15–10 = 5; 5 ÷ 10 = 0.5; 0.5 = 50%). Medical inflation (as defined in paragraph (g)(4)(i) of this section) from March 2010 is 0.0720 (415.0–387.142 = 27.858; 27.858 ÷ 387.142 = 0.0720). The increase that would cause a group plan to cease to be a grandfathered health plan under paragraph (g)(1)(iv) of this section is the greater of the maximum percentage increase of 22.20% (0.0720 = 7.20%; 7.20% + 15% = 22.20%), or $5.36 ($5 × 0.0720 = $0.36; $0.36 + $5 = $5.36). The $5 increase in copayment in this *Example 6* would not cause the plan to cease to be a grandfathered health plan pursuant to paragraph (g)(1)(iv) of this section, which would permit an increase in the copayment of up to $5.36.

*Example 7.* (i) *Facts.* Same facts as *Example 6* of this paragraph (g)(5), except on March 23, 2010, the grandfathered health plan has no copayment ($0) for office visits for primary care providers. The plan is subsequently amended to increase the copayment requirement to $5, effective before June 15, 2021.

(ii) *Conclusion.* In this *Example 7*, medical inflation (as defined in paragraph (g)(4)(i) of this section) from March 2010 is 0.0720 (415.0–387.142 = 27.858; 27.858 ÷ 387.142 = 0.0720). The increase that would cause a plan to cease to be a grandfathered health plan under paragraph (g)(1)(iv)(A) of this section is $5.36 ($5 × 0.0720 = $0.36; $0.36 + $5 = $5.36). The $5 increase in copayment in this *Example 7* is less than the amount calculated pursuant to paragraph (g)(1)(iv)(A) of this section of $5.36. Thus, the $5 increase in copayment does not cause the plan to cease to be a grandfathered health plan.

⫸→ *Caution: Reg. §54.9815-1251, below, as added by T.D. 9744, is applicable to group health plans and health insurance issuers beginning on the first day of the plan year (or, in the individual market, the first day of the first policy year) beginning on or after January 1, 2017.*

*Example 8.* (i) *Facts.* On March 23, 2010, a self-insured group health plan provides two tiers of coverage—self-only and family. The employer contributes 80% of the total cost of coverage for self-only and 60% of the total cost of coverage for family. Subsequently, the employer reduces the contribution to 50% for family coverage, but keeps the same contribution rate for self-only coverage.

(ii) *Conclusion.* In this *Example 8*, the decrease of 10 percentage points for family coverage in the contribution rate based on cost of coverage causes the plan to cease to be a grandfathered health plan. The fact that the contribution rate for self-only coverage remains the same does not change the result.

*Example 9.* (i) *Facts.* On March 23, 2010, a self-insured grandfathered health plan has a COBRA premium for the 2010 plan year of $5,000 for self-only coverage and $12,000 for family coverage. The required employee contribution for the coverage is $1,000 for self-only coverage and $4,000 for family coverage. Thus, the contribution rate based on cost of coverage for 2010 is 80% (($5,000–1,000)/5,000) for self-only coverage and 67% (($12,000–4,000)/12,000) for family coverage. For a subsequent plan year, the COBRA premium is $6,000 for self-only coverage and $15,000 for family coverage. The employee contributions for that plan year are $1,200 for self-only coverage and $5,000 for family coverage. Thus, the contribution rate based on cost of coverage is 80% (($6,000–1,200)/6,000) for self-only coverage and 67% (($15,000–5,000)/15,000) for family coverage.

(ii) *Conclusion.* In this *Example 9*, because there is no change in the contribution rate based on cost of coverage, the plan retains its status as a grandfathered health plan. The result would be the same if all or part of the employee contribution was made pre-tax through a cafeteria plan under section 125.

*Example 10.* (i) *Facts.* A group health plan not maintained pursuant to a collective bargaining agreement offers three benefit packages on March 23, 2010. Option *F* is a self-insured option. Options *G* and *H* are insured options. Beginning July 1, 2013, the plan increases coinsurance under Option *H* from 10% to 15%.

(ii) *Conclusion.* In this *Example 10*, the coverage under Option *H* is not grandfathered health plan coverage as of July 1, 2013, consistent with the rule in paragraph (g)(1)(ii) of this section. Whether the coverage under Options *F* and *G* is grandfathered health plan coverage is determined separately under the rules of this paragraph (g).

*Example 11.* (i) *Facts.* A group health plan that is a grandfathered health plan and also a high deductible health plan within the meaning of section 223(c)(2) had a $2,400 deductible for family coverage on March 23, 2010. The plan is subsequently amended after June 15, 2021 to increase the deductible limit by the amount that is necessary to comply with the requirements for a plan to qualify as a high deductible health plan under section 223(c)(2)(A), but that exceeds the maximum percentage increase.

(ii) *Conclusion.* In this *Example 11*, the increase in the deductible at that time does not cause the plan to cease to be a grandfathered health plan because the increase was necessary for the plan to continue to satisfy the definition of a high deductible health plan under section 223(c)(2)(A). [Reg. § 54.9815-1251.]

☐ [*T.D. 9744, 11-13-2015. Amended by T.D. 9928, 12-11-2020*]

⫸→ *Caution: Temporary Reg. §54.9815-1251T, below, was removed by T.D. 9744 and is inapplicable under Code Sec. 7805(e)(2). However, until final Reg. §54.9815-1251 is applicable on the first day of the plan or policy year beginning after January 1, 2017, taxpayers may comply with the corresponding interim final regulation at 29 CFR part 2590 that is substantially similar to the temporary reg below.*

**[Reg. §54.9815-1251T]**

**§54.9815-1251T. Preservation of right to maintain existing coverage (temporary).**—(a) *Definition of grandfathered health plan coverage.*—(1) *In general.*—(i) *Grandfathered health plan coverage.*— Grandfathered health plan coverage means coverage provided by a group health plan, or a health insurance issuer, in which an individual was enrolled on March 23, 2010 (for as long as it maintains that status under the rules of this section). A group health plan or group health insurance coverage does not cease to be grandfathered health plan coverage merely because one or more (or even all) individuals enrolled on March 23, 2010 cease to be covered, provided that the plan has continuously covered someone since March 23, 2010 (not necessarily the same person, but at all times at least one person). In addition, subject to the limitation set forth in paragraph (a)(1)(ii) of this section, a group health plan (and any health insurance coverage offered in connection with the group health plan) does not cease to be a grandfathered health plan merely because the plan (or its sponsor) enters into a new policy, certificate, or contract of insurance after March 23, 2010 (for example, a plan enters into a contract with a new issuer or a new policy is issued with an existing issuer). For purposes of this section, a plan or health insurance coverage that provides grandfathered health plan coverage is referred to as a grandfathered health plan. The rules of this section apply separately to each benefit package made available under a group health plan or health insurance coverage.

(ii) *Changes in group health insurance coverage.*—Subject to paragraphs (f) and and (g)(2) of this section, if a group health plan (including a group health plan that was self-insured on March 23, 2010) or its sponsor enters into a new policy, certificate, or contract of insurance after March 23, 2010 that is effective before November 15, 2010, then the plan ceases to be a grandfathered health plan.

(2) *Disclosure of grandfather status.*—(i) To maintain status as a grandfathered health plan, a plan or health insurance coverage must include a statement, in any plan materials provided to a participant or beneficiary describing the benefits provided under the plan or health insurance coverage, that the plan or coverage believes it is a grandfathered health plan within the meaning of section 1251 of the Patient Protection and Affordable Care Act and must provide contact information for questions and complaints.

(ii) The following model language can be used to satisfy this disclosure requirement:

This [group health plan or health insurance issuer] believes this [plan or coverage] is a "grandfathered health plan" under the Patient Protection and Affordable Care Act (the Affordable Care Act). As permitted by the Affordable Care Act, a grandfathered health plan can preserve certain basic health coverage that was already in effect when that law was enacted. Being a grandfathered health plan means that your [plan or policy] may not include certain consumer protections of the Affordable Care Act that apply to other plans, for example, the requirement for the provision of preventive health services without any cost sharing. However, grandfathered health plans must comply with certain other consumer protections in the Affordable Care Act, for example, the elimination of lifetime limits on benefits.

Questions regarding which protections apply and which protections do not apply to a grandfathered health plan and what might cause a plan to change from grandfathered health plan status can be directed to the plan administrator at [insert contact information]. [For ERISA plans, insert: You may also contact the Employee Benefits Security Administration, U.S. Department of Labor at 1-866-444-3272 or *www.dol.gov/ebsa/healthreform*. This website has a table summarizing which protections do and do not apply to grandfathered health plans.] [For individual market policies and nonfederal governmental plans, insert: You may also contact the U.S. Department of Health and Human Services at *www.healthreform.gov*.]

(3)(i) *Documentation of plan or policy terms on March 23, 2010.*—To maintain status as a grandfathered health plan, a group health plan, or group health insurance coverage, must, for as long as the plan or health insurance coverage takes the position that it is a grandfathered health plan -

(A) Maintain records documenting the terms of the plan or health insurance coverage in connection with the coverage in effect on March 23, 2010, and any other documents necessary to verify, explain, or clarify its status as a grandfathered health plan; and

(B) Make such records available for examination upon request.

(ii) *Change in group health insurance coverage.*—To maintain status as a grandfathered health plan, a group health plan that enters into a new policy, certificate, or contract of insurance must provide to the new health insurance issuer (and the new health insurance issuer must require) documentation of plan terms (including benefits, cost sharing, employer contributions, and annual limits) under the prior health coverage sufficient to determine whether a change causing a cessation of grandfathered health plan status under paragraph (g)(1) of this section has occurred.

(4) *Family members enrolling after March 23, 2010.*—With respect to an individual who is enrolled in a group health plan or health insurance coverage on March 23, 2010, grandfathered health plan coverage includes coverage of family members of the individual who enroll after March 23, 2010 in the grandfathered health plan coverage of the individual.

(b) *Allowance for new employees to join current plan.*—(1) *In general.*—Subject to paragraph (b)(2) of this section, a group health plan (including health insurance coverage provided in connection with the group health plan) that provided coverage on March 23, 2010 and has retained its status as a grandfathered health plan (consistent with the rules of this section, including paragraph (g) of this section) is

⟫⟫→ *Caution: Temporary Reg. §54.9815-1251T, below, was removed by T.D. 9744 and is inapplicable under Code Sec. 7805(e)(2). However, until final Reg. §54.9815-1251 is applicable on the first day of the plan or policy year beginning after January 1, 2017, taxpayers may comply with the corresponding interim final regulation at 29 CFR part 2590 that is substantially similar to the temporary reg below.*

grandfathered health plan coverage for new employees (whether newly hired or newly enrolled) and their families enrolling in the plan after March 23, 2010.

(2) *Anti-abuse rules.*—(i) *Mergers and acquisitions.*—If the principal purpose of a merger, acquisition, or similar business restructuring is to cover new individuals under a grandfathered health plan, the plan ceases to be a grandfathered health plan.

(ii) *Change in plan eligibility.*—A group health plan or health insurance coverage (including a benefit package under a group health plan) ceases to be a grandfathered health plan if—

(A) Employees are transferred into the plan or health insurance coverage (the transferee plan) from a plan or health insurance coverage under which the employees were covered on March 23, 2010 (the transferor plan);

(B) Comparing the terms of the transferee plan with those of the transferor plan (as in effect on March 23, 2010) and treating the transferee plan as if it were an amendment of the transferor plan would cause a loss of grandfather status under the provisions of paragraph (g)(1) of this section; and

(C) There was no bona fide employment-based reason to transfer the employees into the transferee plan. For this purpose, changing the terms or cost of coverage is not a bona fide employment-based reason.

(3) *Examples.*—The rules of this paragraph (b) are illustrated by the following examples:

*Example 1.* (i) *Facts.* A group health plan offers two benefit packages on March 23, 2010, Options F and G. During a subsequent open enrollment period, some of the employees enrolled in Option F on March 23, 2010 switch to Option G.

(ii) *Conclusion.* In this *Example 1*, the group health coverage provided under Option G remains a grandfathered health plan under the rules of paragraph (b)(1) of this section because employees previously enrolled in Option F are allowed to enroll in Option G as new employees.

*Example 2.* (i) *Facts.* Same facts as *Example 1*, except that the plan sponsor eliminates Option F because of its high cost and transfers employees covered under Option F to Option G. If instead of transferring employees from Option F to Option G, Option F was amended to match the terms of Option G, then Option F would cease to be a grandfathered health plan.

(ii) *Conclusion.* In this *Example 2*, the plan did not have a bona fide employment-based reason to transfer employees from Option F to Option G. Therefore, Option G ceases to be a grandfathered health plan with respect to all employees. (However, any other benefit package maintained by the plan sponsor is analyzed separately under the rules of this section.)

*Example 3.* (i) *Facts.* A group health plan offers two benefit packages on March 23, 2010, Options H and I. On March 23, 2010, Option H provides coverage only for employees in one manufacturing plant. Subsequently, the plant is closed, and some employees in the closed plant are moved to another plant. The employer eliminates Option H and the employees that are moved are transferred to Option I. If instead of transferring employees from Option H to Option I, Option H was amended to match the terms of Option I, then Option H would cease to be a grandfathered health plan.

(ii) *Conclusion.* In this *Example 3*, the plan has a bona fide employment-based reason to transfer employees from Option H to Option I. Therefore, Option I does not cease to be a grandfathered health plan.

(c) *General grandfathering rule.*—(1) Except as provided in paragraphs (d) and (e) of this section, subtitles A and C of title I of the Patient Protection and Affordable Care Act (and the amendments made by those subtitles, and the incorporation of those amendments into section 9815 and ERISA section 715) do not apply to grandfathered health plan coverage. Accordingly, the provisions of PHS Act sections 2701, 2702, 2703, 2705, 2706, 2707, 2709 (relating to coverage for individuals participating in approved clinical trials, as added by section 10103 of the Patient Protection and Affordable Care Act), 2713, 2715A, 2716, 2717, 2719, and 2719A, as added or amended by the Patient Protection and Affordable Care Act, do not apply to grandfathered health plans. (In addition, see 45 CFR 147.140(c), which provides that the provisions of PHS Act section 2704, and PHS Act section 2711 insofar as it relates to annual limits, do not apply to grandfathered health plans that are individual health insurance coverage.)

(2) To the extent not inconsistent with the rules applicable to a grandfathered health plan, a grandfathered health plan must comply with the requirements of the Code, the PHS Act, and ERISA applica-

ble prior to the changes enacted by the Patient Protection and Affordable Care Act.

(d) *Provisions applicable to all grandfathered health plans.*—The provisions of PHS Act section 2711 insofar as it relates to lifetime limits, and the provisions of PHS Act sections 2712, 2714, 2715, and 2718, apply to grandfathered health plans for plan years beginning on or after September 23, 2010. The provisions of PHS Act section 2708 apply to grandfathered health plans for plan years beginning on or after January 1, 2014.

(e) *Applicability of PHS Act sections 2704, 2711, and 2714 to grandfathered group health plans and group health insurance coverage.*—(1) The provisions of PHS Act section 2704 as it applies with respect to enrollees who are under 19 years of age, and the provisions of PHS Act section 2711 insofar as it relates to annual limits, apply to grandfathered health plans that are group health plans (including group health insurance coverage) for plan years beginning on or after September 23, 2010. The provisions of PHS Act section 2704 apply generally to grandfathered health plans that are group health plans (including group health insurance coverage) for plan years beginning on or after January 1, 2014.

(2) For plan years beginning before January 1, 2014, the provisions of PHS Act section 2714 apply in the case of an adult child with respect to a grandfathered health plan that is a group health plan only if the adult child is not eligible to enroll in an eligible employer-sponsored health plan (as defined in section 5000A(f)(2)) other than a grandfathered health plan of a parent. For plan years beginning on or after January 1, 2014, the provisions of PHS Act section 2714 apply with respect to a grandfathered health plan that is a group health plan without regard to whether an adult child is eligible to enroll in any other coverage.

(f) *Effect on collectively bargained plans.*—In the case of health insurance coverage maintained pursuant to one or more collective bargaining agreements between employee representatives and one or more employers that was ratified before March 23, 2010, the coverage is grandfathered health plan coverage at least until the date on which the last of the collective bargaining agreements relating to the coverage that was in effect on March 23, 2010 terminates. Any coverage amendment made pursuant to a collective bargaining agreement relating to the coverage that amends the coverage solely to conform to any requirement added by subtitles A and C of title I of the Patient Protection and Affordable Care Act (and the amendments made by those subtitles, and the incorporation of those amendments into section 9815 and ERISA section 715) is not treated as a termination of the collective bargaining agreement. After the date on which the last of the collective bargaining agreements relating to the coverage that was in effect on March 23, 2010 terminates, the determination of whether health insurance coverage maintained pursuant to a collective bargaining agreement is grandfathered health plan coverage is made under the rules of this section other than this paragraph (f) (comparing the terms of the health insurance coverage after the date the last collective bargaining agreement terminates with the terms of the health insurance coverage that were in effect on March 23, 2010).

(g) *Maintenance of grandfather status.*—(1) *Changes causing cessation of grandfather status.*—Subject to paragraph (g)(2) of this section, the rules of this paragraph (g)(1) describe situations in which a group health plan or health insurance coverage ceases to be a grandfathered health plan.

(i) *Elimination of benefits.*—The elimination of all or substantially all benefits to diagnose or treat a particular condition causes a group health plan or health insurance coverage to cease to be a grandfathered health plan. For this purpose, the elimination of benefits for any necessary element to diagnose or treat a condition is considered the elimination of all or substantially all benefits to diagnose or treat a particular condition.

(ii) *Increase in percentage cost-sharing requirement.*—Any increase, measured from March 23, 2010, in a percentage cost-sharing requirement (such as an individual's coinsurance requirement) causes a group health plan or health insurance coverage to cease to be a grandfathered health plan.

(iii) *Increase in a fixed-amount cost-sharing requirement other than a copayment.*—Any increase in a fixed-amount cost-sharing requirement other than a copayment (for example, deductible or out-of-pocket limit), determined as of the effective date of the increase, causes a group health plan or health insurance coverage to cease to be a grandfathered health plan, if the total percentage increase in the cost-sharing requirement measured from March 23, 2010 exceeds the

>>→ *Caution: Temporary Reg. §54.9815-1251T, below, was removed by T.D. 9744 and is inapplicable under Code Sec. 7805(e)(2). However, until final Reg. §54.9815-1251 is applicable on the first day of the plan or policy year beginning after January 1, 2017, taxpayers may comply with the corresponding interim final regulation at 29 CFR part 2590 that is substantially similar to the temporary reg below.*

maximum percentage increase (as defined in paragraph (g)(3)(ii) of this section).

(iv) *Increase in a fixed-amount copayment.*—Any increase in a fixed-amount copayment, determined as of the effective date of the increase, causes a group health plan or health insurance coverage to cease to be a grandfathered health plan, if the total increase in the copayment measured from March 23, 2010 exceeds the greater of:

(A) An amount equal to $5 increased by medical inflation, as defined in paragraph (g)(3)(i) of this section (that is, $5 times medical inflation, plus $5), or

(B) The maximum percentage increase (as defined in paragraph (g)(3)(ii) of this section), determined by expressing the total increase in the copayment as a percentage.

(v) *Decrease in contribution rate by employers and employee organizations.*—(A) *Contribution rate based on cost of coverage.*—A group health plan or group health insurance coverage ceases to be a grandfathered health plan if the employer or employee organization decreases its contribution rate based on cost of coverage (as defined in paragraph (g)(3)(iii)(A) of this section) towards the cost of any tier of coverage for any class of similarly situated individuals (as described in § 54.9802-1(d)) by more than 5 percentage points below the contribution rate for the coverage period that includes March 23, 2010.

(B) *Contribution rate based on a formula.*—A group health plan or group health insurance coverage ceases to be a grandfathered health plan if the employer or employee organization decreases its contribution rate based on a formula (as defined in paragraph (g)(3)(iii)(B) of this section) towards the cost of any tier of coverage for any class of similarly situated individuals (as described in § 54.9802-1(d)) by more than 5 percent below the contribution rate for the coverage period that includes March 23, 2010.

(vi) *Changes in annual limits.*—(A) *Addition of an annual limit.*—A group health plan, or group health insurance coverage, that, on March 23, 2010, did not impose an overall annual or lifetime limit on the dollar value of all benefits ceases to be a grandfathered health plan if the plan or health insurance coverage imposes an overall annual limit on the dollar value of benefits.

(B) *Decrease in limit for a plan or coverage with only a lifetime limit.*—A group health plan, or group health insurance coverage, that, on March 23, 2010, imposed an overall lifetime limit on the dollar value of all benefits but no overall annual limit on the dollar value of all benefits ceases to be a grandfathered health plan if the plan or health insurance coverage adopts an overall annual limit at a dollar value that is lower than the dollar value of the lifetime limit on March 23, 2010.

(C) *Decrease in limit for a plan or coverage with an annual limit.*—A group health plan, or group health insurance coverage, that, on March 23, 2010, imposed an overall annual limit on the dollar value of all benefits ceases to be a grandfathered health plan if the plan or health insurance coverage decreases the dollar value of the annual limit (regardless of whether the plan or health insurance coverage also imposed an overall lifetime limit on March 23, 2010 on the dollar value of all benefits).

(2) *Transitional rules.*—(i) *Changes made prior to March 23, 2010.*—If a group health plan or health insurance issuer makes the following changes to the terms of the plan or health insurance coverage, the changes are considered part of the terms of the plan or health insurance coverage on March 23, 2010 even though they were not effective at that time and such changes do not cause a plan or health insurance coverage to cease to be a grandfathered health plan:

(A) Changes effective after March 23, 2010 pursuant to a legally binding contract entered into on or before March 23, 2010;

(B) Changes effective after March 23, 2010 pursuant to a filing on or before March 23, 2010 with a State insurance department; or

(C) Changes effective after March 23, 2010 pursuant to written amendments to a plan that were adopted on or before March 23, 2010.

(ii) *Changes made after March 23, 2010 and adopted prior to issuance of regulations.*—If, after March 23, 2010, a group health plan or health insurance issuer makes changes to the terms of the plan or health insurance coverage and the changes are adopted prior to June 14, 2010, the changes will not cause the plan or health insurance coverage to cease to be a grandfathered health plan if the changes are revoked or modified effective as of the first day of the first plan year (in the individual market, policy year) beginning on or after September

ber 23, 2010, and the terms of the plan or health insurance coverage on that date, as modified, would not cause the plan or coverage to cease to be a grandfathered health plan under the rules of this section, including paragraph (g)(1) of this section. For this purpose, changes will be considered to have been adopted prior to June 14, 2010 if:

(A) The changes are effective before that date;

(B) The changes are effective on or after that date pursuant to a legally binding contract entered into before that date;

(C) The changes are effective on or after that date pursuant to a filing before that date with a State insurance department; or

(D) The changes are effective on or after that date pursuant to written amendments to a plan that were adopted before that date.

(3) *Definitions.*—(i) *Medical inflation defined.*—For purposes of this paragraph (g), the term *medical inflation* means the increase since March 2010 in the overall medical care component of the Consumer Price Index for All Urban Consumers (CPI-U) (unadjusted) published by the Department of Labor using the 1982 - 1984 base of 100. For this purpose, the increase in the overall medical care component is computed by subtracting 387.142 (the overall medical care component of the CPI-U (unadjusted) published by the Department of Labor for March 2010, using the 1982 - 1984 base of 100) from the index amount for any month in the 12 months before the new change is to take effect and then dividing that amount by 387.142.

(ii) *Maximum percentage increase defined.*—For purposes of this paragraph (g), the term *maximum percentage increase* means medical inflation (as defined in paragraph (g)(3)(i) of this section), expressed as a percentage, plus 15 percentage points.

(iii) *Contribution rate defined.*—For purposes of paragraph (g)(1)(v) of this section:

(A) *Contribution rate based on cost of coverage.*—The term *contribution rate based on cost of coverage* means the amount of contributions made by an employer or employee organization compared to the total cost of coverage, expressed as a percentage. The total cost of coverage is determined in the same manner as the applicable premium is calculated under the COBRA continuation provisions of section 4980B(f)(4), section 604 of ERISA, and section 2204 of the PHS Act. In the case of a self-insured plan, contributions by an employer or employee organization are equal to the total cost of coverage minus the employee contributions towards the total cost of coverage.

(B) *Contribution rate based on a formula.*—The term *contribution rate based on a formula* means, for plans that, on March 23, 2010, made contributions based on a formula (such as hours worked or tons of coal mined), the formula.

(4) *Examples.*—The rules of this paragraph (g) are illustrated by the following examples:

*Example 1.* (i) *Facts.* On March 23, 2010, a grandfathered health plan has a coinsurance requirement of 20% for inpatient surgery. The plan is subsequently amended to increase the coinsurance requirement to 25%.

(ii) *Conclusion.* In this *Example 1*, the increase in the coinsurance requirement from 20% to 25% causes the plan to cease to be a grandfathered health plan.

*Example 2.* (i) *Facts.* Before March 23, 2010, the terms of a group health plan provide benefits for a particular mental health condition, the treatment for which is a combination of counseling and prescription drugs. Subsequently, the plan eliminates benefits for counseling.

(ii) *Conclusion.* In this *Example 2*, the plan ceases to be a grandfathered health plan because counseling is an element that is necessary to treat the condition. Thus the plan is considered to have eliminated substantially all benefits for the treatment of the condition.

*Example 3.* (i) *Facts.* On March 23, 2010, a grandfathered health plan has a copayment requirement of $30 per office visit for specialists. The plan is subsequently amended to increase the copayment requirement to $40. Within the 12-month period before the $40 copayment takes effect, the greatest value of the overall medical care component of the CPI-U (unadjusted) is 475.

(ii) *Conclusion.* In this *Example 3*, the increase in the copayment from $30 to $40, expressed as a percentage, is 33.33% (40 - 30 = 10; 10 ÷ 30 = 0.3333; 0.3333 = 33.33%). Medical inflation (as defined in paragraph (g)(3)(i) of this section) from March 2010 is 0.2269 (475 - 387.142 = 87.858; 87.858 ÷ 387.142 = 0.2269). The maximum percentage increase permitted is 37.69% (0.2269 = 22.69%; 22.69% + 15% = 37.69%). Because 33.33% does not exceed 37.69%, the change in the copayment requirement at that time does not cause the plan to cease to be a grandfathered health plan.

>>>→ *Caution: Temporary Reg. §54.9815-1251T, below, was removed by T.D. 9744 and is inapplicable under Code Sec. 7805(e)(2). However, until final Reg. §54.9815-1251 is applicable on the first day of the plan or policy year beginning after January 1, 2017, taxpayers may comply with the corresponding interim final regulation at 29 CFR part 2590 that is substantially similar to the temporary reg below.*

*Example 4.* (i) *Facts.* Same facts as *Example 3*, except the grandfathered health plan subsequently increases the $40 copayment requirement to $45 for a later plan year. Within the 12-month period before the $45 copayment takes effect, the greatest value of the overall medical care component of the CPI-U (unadjusted) is 485.

(ii) *Conclusion.* In this *Example 4*, the increase in the copayment from $30 (the copayment that was in effect on March 23, 2010) to $45, expressed as a percentage, is 50% (45 - 30 = 15; 15 ÷ 30 = 0.5; 0.5 = 50%). Medical inflation (as defined in paragraph (g)(3)(i) of this section) from March 2010 is 0.2527 (485 - 387.142 = 97.858; 97.858 ÷ 387.142 = 0.2527). The increase that would cause a plan to cease to be a grandfathered health plan under paragraph (g)(1)(iv) of this section is the greater of the maximum percentage increase of 40.27% (0.2527 = 25.27%; 25.27% + 15% = 40.27%), or $6.26 ($5 × 0.2527 = $1.26; $1.26 + $5 = $6.26). Because 50% exceeds 40.27% and $15 exceeds $6.26, the change in the copayment requirement at that time causes the plan to cease to be a grandfathered health plan.

*Example 5.* (i) *Facts.* On March 23, 2010, a grandfathered health plan has a copayment of $10 per office visit for primary care providers. The plan is subsequently amended to increase the copayment requirement to $15. Within the 12-month period before the $15 copayment takes effect, the greatest value of the overall medical care component of the CPI-U (unadjusted) is 415.

(ii) *Conclusion.* In this *Example 5*, the increase in the copayment, expressed as a percentage, is 50% (15 - 10 = 5; 5 ÷ 10 = 0.5; 0.5 = 50%). Medical inflation (as defined in paragraph (g)(3) of this section) from March 2010 is 0.0720 (415.0 - 387.142 = 27.858; 27.858 ÷ 387.142 = 0.0720). The increase that would cause a plan to cease to be a grandfathered health plan under paragraph (g)(1)(iv) of this section is the greater of the maximum percentage increase of 22.20% (0.0720 = 7.20%; 7.20% + 15% = 22.20), or $5.36 ($5 × 0.0720 = $0.36; $0.36 + $5 = $5.36). The $5 increase in copayment in this *Example 5* would not cause the plan to cease to be a grandfathered health plan pursuant to paragraph (g)(1)(iv)this section, which would permit an increase in the copayment of up to $5.36.

*Example 6.* (i) *Facts.* The same facts as *Example 5*, except on March 23, 2010, the grandfathered health plan has no copayment ($0) for office visits for primary care providers. The plan is subsequently amended to increase the copayment requirement to $5.

(ii) *Conclusion.* In this *Example 6*, medical inflation (as defined in paragraph (g)(3)(i) of this section) from March 2010 is 0.0720 (415.0 - 387.142 = 27.858; 27.858 ÷ 387.142 = 0.0720). The increase that would cause a plan to cease to be a grandfathered health plan under paragraph (g)(1)(iv)(A) of this section is $5.36 ($5 × 0.0720 = $0.36; $0.36 + $5 = $5.36). The $5 increase in copayment in this *Example 6* is less than the amount calculated pursuant to paragraph (g)(1)(iv)(A)

of this section of $5.36. Thus, the $5 increase in copayment does not cause the plan to cease to be a grandfathered health plan.

*Example 7.* (i) *Facts.* On March 23, 2010, a self-insured group health plan provides two tiers of coverage — self-only and family. The employer contributes 80% of the total cost of coverage for self-only and 60% of the total cost of coverage for family. Subsequently, the employer reduces the contribution to 50% for family coverage, but keeps the same contribution rate for self-only coverage.

(ii) *Conclusion.* In this *Example 7*, the decrease of 10 percentage points for family coverage in the contribution rate based on cost of coverage causes the plan to cease to be a grandfathered health plan. The fact that the contribution rate for self-only coverage remains the same does not change the result.

*Example 8.* (i) *Facts.* On March 23, 2010, a self-insured grandfathered health plan has a COBRA premium for the 2010 plan year of $5000 for self-only coverage and $12,000 for family coverage. The required employee contribution for the coverage is $1000 for self-only coverage and $4000 for family coverage. Thus, the contribution rate based on cost of coverage for 2010 is 80% ((5000 - 1000)/5000) for self-only coverage and 67% ((12,000 - 4000)/12,000) for family coverage. For a subsequent plan year, the COBRA premium is $6000 for self-only coverage and $15,000 for family coverage. The employee contributions for that plan year are $1200 for selfonly coverage and $5000 for family coverage. Thus, the contribution rate based on cost of coverage is 80% ((6000 -1200)/6000) for self-only coverage and 67% ((15,000 - 5000)/15,000) for family coverage.

(ii) *Conclusion.* In this *Example 8*, because there is no change in the contribution rate based on cost of coverage, the plan retains its status as a grandfathered health plan. The result would be the same if all or part of the employee contribution was made pre-tax through a cafeteria plan under section 125 of the Internal Revenue Code.

*Example 9.* (i) *Facts.* A group health plan not maintained pursuant to a collective bargaining agreement offers three benefit packages on March 23, 2010. Option F is a selfinsured option. Options G and H are insured options. Beginning July 1, 2013, the plan increases coinsurance under Option H from 10% to 15%.

(ii) *Conclusion.* In this *Example 9*, the coverage under Option H is not grandfathered health plan coverage as of July 1, 2013, consistent with the rule in paragraph (g)(1)(ii) of this section. Whether the coverage under Options F and G is grandfathered health plan coverage is determined separately under the rules of this paragraph (g).

(h) *Expiration date.*—This section expires on or before June 14, 2013. [Temporary Reg. § 54.9815-1251T.]

☐ [*T.D. 9489*, 6-14-2010. *Amended by T.D. 9506*, 11-15-2010. *Removed by T.D. 9744*, 11-13-2015.]

>>>→ *Caution: Reg. §54.9815-2704, below, as added by T.D. 9744, is applicable to group health plans and health insurance issuers beginning on the first day of the plan year (or, in the individual market, the first day of the first policy year) beginning on or after January 1, 2017.*

**[Reg. § 54.9815-2704]**

**§ 54.9815-2704. Prohibition of preexisting condition exclusions.**—(a) *No preexisting condition exclusions.*—A group health plan, or a health insurance issuer offering group health insurance coverage, may not impose any preexisting condition exclusion (as defined in § 54.9801-2).

(b) *Examples.*—The rules of paragraph (a) of this section are illustrated by the following examples (for additional examples illustrating the definition of a preexisting condition exclusion, *see* § 54.9801-3(a)(2)):

*Example 1.* (i) *Facts.* A group health plan provides benefits solely through an insurance policy offered by Issuer *P*. At the expiration of the policy, the plan switches coverage to a policy offered by Issuer *N*. *N's* policy excludes benefits for oral surgery required as a result of a traumatic injury if the injury occurred before the effective date of coverage under the policy.

(ii) *Conclusion.* In this *Example 1*, the exclusion of benefits for oral surgery required as a result of a traumatic injury if the injury occurred before the effective date of coverage is a preexisting condition exclusion because it operates to exclude benefits for a condition

based on the fact that the condition was present before the effective date of coverage under the policy. Therefore, such an exclusion is prohibited.

*Example 2.* (i) *Facts.* Individual *C* applies for individual health insurance coverage with Issuer *M*. *M* denies *C's* application for coverage because a pre-enrollment physical revealed that *C* has type 2 diabetes.

(ii) *Conclusion.* See *Example 2* in 45 CFR 147.108(a)(2) for a conclusion that *M's* denial of *C's* application for coverage is a preexisting condition exclusion because a denial of an application for coverage based on the fact that a condition was present before the date of denial is an exclusion of benefits based on a preexisting condition. Therefore, such an exclusion is prohibited.

(c) *Applicability date.*—The provisions of this section are applicable to group health plans and health insurance issuers for plan years beginning on or after January 1, 2017. Until the applicability date for this regulation, plans and issuers are required to continue to comply with the interim final regulations promulgated by the Department of Labor at 29 CFR part 2590, contained in the 29 CFR, parts 1927 to end, edition revised as of July 1, 2015. [Reg. § 54.9815-2704.]

☐ [*T.D. 9744*, 11-13-2015.]

>>>→ *Caution: Temporary Reg. §54.9815-2704T, below, was removed by T.D. 9744 and is inapplicable under Code Sec. 7805(e)(2). However, until final Reg. §54.9815-2704 is applicable on the first day of the plan or policy year beginning after January 1, 2017, taxpayers may comply with the corresponding interim final regulation at 29 CFR part 2590 that is substantially similar to the temporary reg below.*

**[Reg. § 54.9815-2704T]**

**§ 54.9815-2704T. Prohibition of preexisting condition exclusions (temporary).**—(a) *No preexisting condition exclusions.*—(1) *In general.*—A group health plan, or a health insurance issuer offering group health insurance coverage, may not impose any preexisting condition exclusion (as defined in § 54.9801-2).

(2) *Examples.*—The rules of this paragraph (a) are illustrated by the following examples (for additional examples illustrating the definition of a preexisting condition exclusion, see § 54.9801-3(a)(1)(ii)):

*Example 1.* (i) *Facts.* A group health plan provides benefits solely through an insurance policy offered by Issuer P. At the expiration of the policy, the plan switches coverage to a policy offered by Issuer N.

⟫⟫→ *Caution: Temporary Reg. §54.9815-2704T, below, was removed by T.D. 9744 and is inapplicable under Code Sec. 7805(e)(2). However, until final Reg. §54.9815-2704 is applicable on the first day of the plan or policy year beginning after January 1, 2017, taxpayers may comply with the corresponding interim final regulation at 29 CFR part 2590 that is substantially similar to the temporary reg below.*

N's policy excludes benefits for oral surgery required as a result of a traumatic injury if the injury occurred before the effective date of coverage under the policy.

(ii) *Conclusion*. In this *Example 1*, the exclusion of benefits for oral surgery required as a result of a traumatic injury if the injury occurred before the effective date of coverage is a preexisting condition exclusion because it operates to exclude benefits for a condition based on the fact that the condition was present before the effective date of coverage under the policy.

*Example 2*. (i) *Facts*. Individual C applies for individual health insurance coverage with Issuer M. M denies C's application for coverage because a pre-enrollment physical revealed that C has type 2 diabetes.

(ii) *Conclusion*. See *Example 2* in 45 CFR 147.108(a)(2) for a conclusion that M's denial of C's application for coverage is a preexisting condition exclusion because a denial of an application for coverage based on the fact that a condition was present before the date of denial is an exclusion of benefits based on a preexisting condition.

(b) *Effective/applicability date*.—(1) *General applicability date*.—Except as provided in paragraph (b)(2) of this section, the rules of this section apply for plan years beginning on or after January 1, 2014.

(2) *Early applicability date for children*.—The rules of this section apply with respect to enrollees, including applicants for enrollment, who are under 19 years of age for plan years beginning on or after September 23, 2010.

(3) *Applicability to grandfathered health plans*.—See §54.9815-1251T for determining the application of this section to grandfathered health plans (providing that a grandfathered health plan that is a group health plan or group health insurance coverage must comply with the prohibition against preexisting condition exclusions).

(4) *Example*.—The rules of this paragraph (b) are illustrated by the following example:

*Example*. (i) *Facts*. Individual F commences employment and enrolls F and F's 16-yearold child in the group health plan maintained by F's employer, with a first day of coverage of October 15, 2010. F's child had a significant break in coverage because of a lapse of more than 63 days without creditable coverage immediately prior to enrolling in the plan. F's child was treated for asthma within the six-month period prior to the enrollment date and the plan imposes a 12-month preexisting condition exclusion for coverage of asthma. The next plan year begins on January 1, 2011.

(ii) *Conclusion*. In this *Example*, the plan year beginning January 1, 2011 is the first plan year of the group health plan beginning on or after September 23, 2010. Thus, beginning on January 1, 2011, because the child is under 19 years of age, the plan cannot impose a preexisting condition exclusion with respect to the child's asthma regardless of the fact that the preexisting condition exclusion was imposed by the plan before the applicability date of this provision.

(c) *Expiration date*.—This section expires on June 21, 2013. [Temporary Reg. §54.9815-2704T.]

☐ [T.D. 9491, 6-22-2010. *Removed by T.D.* 9744, 11-13-2015.]

**[Reg. §54.9815-2705]**

**§54.9815-2705. Special rules for certain church plans.**—(a) *In general*.—A group health plan and a health insurance issuer offering group health insurance coverage must comply with the requirements of §54.9802-1.

(b) *Applicability date*.—This section is applicable to group health plans and health insurance issuers offering group health insurance coverage for plan years beginning on or after January 1, 2014. [Reg. §54.9815-2705.]

☐ [T.D. 9620, 5-29-2013.]

**[Reg. §54.9815-2708]**

**§54.9815-2708. Prohibition on waiting periods that exceed 90 days.**—(a) *General rule*.—A group health plan, and a health insurance issuer offering group health insurance coverage, must not apply any waiting period that exceeds 90 days, in accordance with the rules of this section. If, under the terms of a plan, an individual can elect coverage that would begin on a date that is not later than the end of the 90-day waiting period, this paragraph (a) is considered satisfied. Accordingly, in that case, a plan or issuer will not be considered to have violated this paragraph (a) solely because individuals take, or are permitted to take, additional time (beyond the end of the 90-day waiting period) to elect coverage.

(b) *Waiting period defined*.—For purposes of this part, a waiting period is the period that must pass before coverage for an individual who is otherwise eligible to enroll under the terms of a group health plan can become effective. If an individual enrolls as a late enrollee (as defined under §54.9801-2) or special enrollee (as described in §54.9801-6), any period before such late or special enrollment is not a waiting period.

(c) *Relation to a plan's eligibility criteria*.—(1) *In general*.—Except as provided in paragraphs (c)(2) and (c)(3) of this section, being otherwise eligible to enroll under the terms of a group health plan means having met the plan's substantive eligibility conditions (such as, for example, being in an eligible job classification, achieving job-related licensure requirements specified in the plan's terms, or satisfying a reasonable and bona fide employment-based orientation period). Moreover, except as provided in paragraphs (c)(2) and (c)(3) of this section, nothing in this section requires a plan sponsor to offer coverage to any particular individual or class of individuals (including, for example, part-time employees). Instead, this section prohibits requiring otherwise eligible individuals to wait more than 90 days before coverage is effective. *See also* section 4980H of the Code and its implementing regulations for an applicable large employer's shared responsibility to provide health coverage to full-time employees.

(2) *Eligibility conditions based solely on the lapse of time*.—Eligibility conditions that are based solely on the lapse of a time period are permissible for no more than 90 days.

(3) *Other conditions for eligibility*.—Other conditions for eligibility under the terms of a group health plan are generally permissible under PHS Act section 2708, unless the condition is designed to avoid compliance with the 90-day waiting period limitation, determined in accordance with the rules of this paragraph (c)(3).

(i) *Application to variable-hour employees in cases in which a specified number of hours of service per period is a plan eligibility condition*.—If a group health plan conditions eligibility on an employee regularly having a specified number of hours of service per period (or working full-time), and it cannot be determined that a newly-hired employee is reasonably expected to regularly work that number of hours per period (or work full-time), the plan may take a reasonable period of time, not to exceed 12 months and beginning on any date between the employee's start date and the first day of the first calendar month following the employee's start date, to determine whether the employee meets the plan's eligibility condition. Except in cases in which a waiting period that exceeds 90 days is imposed in addition to a measurement period, the time period for determining whether such an employee meets the plan's eligibility condition will not be considered to be designed to avoid compliance with the 90-day waiting period limitation if coverage is made effective no later than 13 months from the employee's start date plus, if the employee's start date is not the first day of a calendar month, the time remaining until the first day of the next calendar month.

(ii) *Cumulative service requirements*.—If a group health plan or health insurance issuer conditions eligibility on an employee's having completed a number of cumulative hours of service, the eligibility condition is not considered to be designed to avoid compliance with the 90-day waiting period limitation if the cumulative hours-of-service requirement does not exceed 1,200 hours.

(iii) *Limitation on orientation periods*.—To ensure that an orientation period is not used as a subterfuge for the passage of time, or designed to avoid compliance with the 90-day waiting period limitation, an orientation period is permitted only if it does not exceed one month. For this purpose, one month is determined by adding one calendar month and subtracting one calendar day, measured from an employee's start date in a position that is otherwise eligible for coverage. For example, if an employee's start date in an otherwise eligible position is May 3, the last permitted day of the orientation period is June 2. Similarly, if an employee's start date in an otherwise eligible position is October 1, the last permitted day of the orientation period is October 31. If there is not a corresponding date in the next calendar month upon adding a calendar month, the last permitted day of the orientation period is the last day of the next calendar month. For example, if the employee's start date is January 30, the last permitted day of the orientation period is February 28 (or February 29 in a leap year). Similarly, if the employee's start date is August 31, the last permitted day of the orientation period is September 30.

(d) *Application to rehires*.—A plan or issuer may treat an employee whose employment has terminated and who then is rehired as newly eligible upon rehire and, therefore, required to meet the plan's eligibility criteria and waiting period anew, if reasonable under the circumstances (for example, the termination and rehire cannot be a subterfuge to avoid compliance with the 90-day waiting period limitation).

(e) *Counting days.*—Under this section, all calendar days are counted beginning on the enrollment date (as defined in §54.9801-2), including weekends and holidays. A plan or issuer that imposes a 90-day waiting period may, for administrative convenience, choose to permit coverage to become effective earlier than the 91st day if the 91st day is a weekend or holiday.

(f) *Examples.*—The rules of this section are illustrated by the following examples:

*Example 1.* (i) *Facts.* A group health plan provides that full-time employees are eligible for coverage under the plan. Employee *A* begins employment as a full-time employee on January 19.

(ii) *Conclusion.* In this *Example 1*, any waiting period for *A* would begin on January 19 and may not exceed 90 days. Coverage under the plan must become effective no later than April 19 (assuming February lasts 28 days).

*Example 2.* (i) *Facts.* A group health plan provides that only employees with job title *M* are eligible for coverage under the plan. Employee *B* begins employment with job title *L* on January 30.

(ii) *Conclusion.* In this *Example 2*, *B* is not eligible for coverage under the plan, and the period while *B* is working with job title *L* and therefore not in an eligible class of employees, is not part of a waiting period under this section.

*Example 3.* (i) *Facts.* Same facts as in *Example 2*, except that *B* transfers to a new position with job title *M* on April 11.

(ii) *Conclusion.* In this *Example 3*, *B* becomes eligible for coverage on April 11, but for the waiting period. Any waiting period for *B* begins on April 11 and may not exceed 90 days; therefore, coverage under the plan must become effective no later than July 10.

*Example 4.* (i) *Facts.* A group health plan provides that only employees who have completed specified training and achieved specified certifications are eligible for coverage under the plan. Employee *C* is hired on May 3 and meets the plan's eligibility criteria on September 22.

(ii) *Conclusion.* In this *Example 4*, *C* becomes eligible for coverage on September 22, but for the waiting period. Any waiting period for *C* would begin on September 22 and may not exceed 90 days; therefore, coverage under the plan must become effective no later than December 21.

*Example 5.* (i) *Facts.* A group health plan provides that employees are eligible for coverage after one year of service.

(ii) *Conclusion.* In this *Example 5*, the plan's eligibility condition is based solely on the lapse of time and, therefore, is impermissible under paragraph (c)(2) of this section because it exceeds 90 days.

*Example 6.* (i) *Facts.* Employer *V*'s group health plan provides for coverage to begin on the first day of the first payroll period on or after the date an employee is hired and completes the applicable enrollment forms. Enrollment forms are distributed on an employee's start date and may be completed within 90 days. Employee *D* is hired and starts on October 31, which is the first day of a pay period. *D* completes the enrollment forms and submits them on the 90th day after *D*'s start date, which is January 28. Coverage is made effective 7 days later, February 4, which is the first day of the next pay period.

(ii) *Conclusion.* In this *Example 6*, under the terms of *V*'s plan, coverage may become effective as early as October 31, depending on when *D* completes the applicable enrollment forms. Under the terms of the plan, when coverage becomes effective depends solely on the length of time taken by *D* to complete the enrollment materials. Therefore, under the terms of the plan, *D* may elect coverage that would begin on a date that does not exceed the 90-day waiting period limitation, and the plan complies with this section.

*Example 7.* (i) *Facts.* Under Employer *W*'s group health plan, only employees who are full-time (defined under the plan as regularly averaging 30 hours of service per week) are eligible for coverage. Employee *E* begins employment for Employer *W* on November 26 of Year 1. *E*'s hours are reasonably expected to vary, with an opportunity to work between 20 and 45 hours per week, depending on shift availability and *E*'s availability. Therefore, it cannot be determined at *E*'s start date that *E* is reasonably expected to work full-time. Under the terms of the plan, variable-hour employees, such as *E*, are eligible to enroll in the plan if they are determined to be a full-time employee after a measurement period of 12 months that begins on the employee's start date. Coverage is made effective no later than the first day of the first calendar month after the applicable enrollment forms are received. *E*'s 12-month measurement period ends November 25 of Year 2. *E* is determined to be a full-time employee and is notified of *E*'s plan eligibility. If *E* then elects coverage, *E*'s first day of coverage will be January 1 of Year 3.

(ii) *Conclusion.* In this *Example 7*, the measurement period is permissible because it is not considered to be designed to avoid compliance with the 90-day waiting period limitation. The plan may use a reasonable period of time to determine whether a variable-hour employee is a full-time employee, provided that (a) the period of time is no longer than 12 months; (b) the period of time begins on a date between the employee's start date and the first day of the next calendar month (inclusive); (c) coverage is made effective no later than 13 months from *E*'s start date plus, if the employee's start date is not the first day of a calendar month, the time remaining until the first day of the next calendar month; and (d) in addition to the measurement period, no more than 90 days elapse prior to the employee's eligibility for coverage.

*Example 8.* (i) *Facts.* Employee *F* begins working 25 hours per week for Employer *X* on January 6 and is considered a part-time employee for purposes of *X*'s group health plan. *X* sponsors a group health plan that provides coverage to part-time employees after they have completed a cumulative 1,200 hours of service. *F* satisfies the plan's cumulative hours of service condition on December 15.

(ii) *Conclusion.* In this *Example 8*, the cumulative hours of service condition with respect to part-time employees is not considered to be designed to avoid compliance with the 90-day waiting period limitation. Accordingly, coverage for *F* under the plan must begin no later than the 91st day after *F* completes 1,200 hours. (If the plan's cumulative hours-of-service requirement was more than 1,200 hours, the requirement would be considered to be designed to avoid compliance with the 90-day waiting period limitation.)

*Example 9.* (i) *Facts.* A multiemployer plan operating pursuant to an arms-length collective bargaining agreement has an eligibility provision that allows employees to become eligible for coverage by working a specified number of hours of covered employment for multiple contributing employers. The plan aggregates hours in a calendar quarter and then, if enough hours are earned, coverage begins the first day of the next calendar quarter. The plan also permits coverage to extend for the next full calendar quarter, regardless of whether an employee's employment has terminated.

(ii) *Conclusion.* In this *Example 9*, these eligibility provisions are designed to accommodate a unique operating structure, and, therefore, are not considered to be designed to avoid compliance with the 90-day waiting period limitation, and the plan complies with this section.

*Example 10.* (i) *Facts.* Employee *G* retires at age 55 after 30 years of employment with Employer *Y* with no expectation of providing further services to Employer *Y*. Three months later, *Y* recruits *G* to return to work as an employee providing advice and transition assistance for *G*'s replacement under a one-year employment contract. *Y*'s plan imposes a 90-day waiting period from an employee's start date before coverage becomes effective.

(ii) *Conclusion.* In this *Example 10*, *Y*'s plan may treat *G* as newly eligible for coverage under the plan upon rehire and therefore may impose the 90-day waiting period with respect to *G* for coverage offered in connection with *G*'s rehire.

*Example 11.* (i) *Facts.* Employee *H* begins working full time for Employer *Z* on October 16. *Z* sponsors a group health plan, under which full time employees are eligible for coverage after they have successfully completed a bona fide one-month orientation period. *H* completes the orientation period on November 15.

(ii) *Conclusion.* In this *Example 11*, the orientation period is not considered a subterfuge for the passage of time and is not considered to be designed to avoid compliance with the 90-day waiting period limitation. Accordingly, plan coverage for *H* must begin no later than February 14, which is the 91st day after *H* completes the orientation period. (If the orientation period was longer than one month, it would be considered to be a subterfuge for the passage of time and designed to avoid compliance with the 90-day waiting period limitation. Accordingly it would violate the rules of this section.)

(g) *Special rule for health insurance issuers.*—To the extent coverage under a group health plan is insured by a health insurance issuer, the issuer is permitted to rely on the eligibility information reported to it by the employer (or other plan sponsor) and will not be considered to violate the requirements of this section with respect to its administration of any waiting period, if both of the following conditions are satisfied:

(1) The issuer requires the plan sponsor to make a representation regarding the terms of any eligibility conditions or waiting periods imposed by the plan sponsor before an individual is eligible to become covered under the terms of the plan (and requires the plan sponsor to update this representation with any changes), and

(2) The issuer has no specific knowledge of the imposition of a waiting period that would exceed the permitted 90-day period.

(h) *No effect on other laws.*—Compliance with this section is not determinative of compliance with any other provision of State or Federal law (including ERISA, the Code, or other provisions of the Patient Protection and Affordable Care Act). *See e.g.*, §54.9802-1, which prohibits discrimination in eligibility for coverage based on a health factor and section 4980H, which generally requires applicable large employers to offer coverage to full-time employees and their dependents or make an assessable payment.

(i) *Applicability date.*—The provisions of this section apply for plan years beginning on or after January 1, 2015. *See* section 1251 of the Affordable Care Act, as amended by section 10103 of the Affordable Care Act and section 2301 of the Health Care and Education Reconciliation Act, and its implementing regulations providing that the prohibition on waiting periods exceeding 90 days applies to all group health plans and group health insurance issuers, including grandfathered health plans. [Reg. §54.9815-2708.]

□ [*T.D. 9656, 2-20-2014. Amended by T.D. 9671, 6-20-2014.*]

**[Reg. §54.9815-2711]**

§54.9815-2711. No lifetime or annual limits.—(a) *Prohibition.*—(1) *Lifetime limits.*—Except as provided in paragraph (b) of this section, a group health plan, or a health insurance issuer offering group health insurance coverage, may not establish any lifetime limit on the dollar amount of essential health benefits for any individual, whether provided in-network or out-of-network.

(2) *Annual limits.*—(i) *General rule.*—Except as provided in paragraphs (a)(2)(ii) and (b) of this section, a group health plan, or a health insurance issuer offering group health insurance coverage,

may not establish any annual limit on the dollar amount of essential health benefits for any individual, whether provided in-network or out-of-network.

(ii) *Exception for health flexible spending arrangements.*—A health flexible spending arrangement (as defined in section 106(c)(2) of the Internal Revenue Code) offered through a cafeteria plan pursuant to section 125 of the Internal Revenue Code is not subject to the requirement in paragraph (a)(2)(i) of this section.

(b) *Construction.*—(1) *Permissible limits on specific covered benefits.*—The rules of this section do not prevent a group health plan, or a health insurance issuer offering group health insurance coverage, from placing annual or lifetime dollar limits with respect to any individual on specific covered benefits that are not essential health benefits to the extent that such limits are otherwise permitted under applicable Federal or State law. (The scope of essential health benefits is addressed in paragraph (c) of this section).

(2) *Condition-based exclusions.*—The rules of this section do not prevent a group health plan, or a health insurance issuer offering group health insurance coverage, from excluding all benefits for a condition. However, if any benefits are provided for a condition, then the requirements of this section apply. Other requirements of Federal or State law may require coverage of certain benefits.

⋙→ *Caution: Reg. §54.9815-2711(c), as added by T.D. 9744, is generally applicable to plan years beginning on or after January 1, 2017, and before January 1, 2020.*

(c) *Definition of essential health benefits.*—The term "essential health benefits" means essential health benefits under section 1302(b) of the Patient Protection and Affordable Care Act and applicable regulations. For this purpose, a group health plan or a health insurance issuer that is not required to provide essential health benefits under section 1302(b) must define "essential health benefits" in a manner that is consistent with—

(1) One of the EHB-benchmark plans applicable in a State under 45 CFR 156.110, and includes coverage of any additional required benefits that are considered essential health benefits consistent with 45 CFR 155.170(a)(2); or

(2) One of the three Federal Employees Health Benefits Program (FEHBP) plan options as defined by 45 CFR 156.100(a)(3), supplemented, as necessary, to meet the standards in 45 CFR 156.110.

⋙→ *Caution: Reg. §54.9815-2711(c), as amended by T.D. 9867, is generally applicable to plan years beginning on or after January 1, 2020.*

(c) *Definition of essential health benefits.*—The term "essential health benefits" means essential health benefits under section 1302(b) of the Patient Protection and Affordable Care Act and applicable regulations. For the purpose of this section, a group health plan or a health insurance issuer that is not required to provide essential health benefits under section 1302(b) must define "essential health benefits" in a manner that is consistent with the following:

(1) For plan years beginning before January 1, 2020, one of the EHB-benchmark plans applicable in a State under 45 CFR 156.110, and including coverage of any additional required benefits that are considered essential health benefits consistent with 45 CFR 155.170(a)(2), or one of the three Federal Employees Health Benefits

Program (FEHBP) plan options as defined by 45 CFR 156.100(a)(3), supplemented as necessary, to satisfy the standards in 45 CFR 156.110; or

(2) For plan years beginning on or after January 1, 2020, an EHB-benchmark plan selected by a State in accordance with the available options and requirements for EHB-benchmark plan selection at 45 CFR 156.111, including an EHB-benchmark plan in a State that takes no action to change its EHB-benchmark plan and thus retains the EHB-benchmark plan applicable in that State for the prior year in accordance with 45 CFR 156.111(d)(1), and including coverage of any additional required benefits that are considered essential health benefits consistent with 45 CFR 155.170(a)(2).

⋙→ *Caution: Reg. §54.9815-2711(d), as added by T.D. 9744, is generally applicable to plan years beginning on or after January 1, 2017, and before January 1, 2020.*

(d) *Special rule for health reimbursement arrangements (HRAs) and other account-based plans.*—(1) *In general.*—If an HRA or other account-based plan is integrated with other coverage under a group health plan and the other group health plan coverage alone satisfies the requirements in paragraph (a)(2) of this section, the fact that the benefits under the HRA or other account-based plan are limited does not mean that the HRA or other account-based plan fails to meet the requirements of paragraph (a)(2) of this section. Similarly, if an HRA or other account-based plan is integrated with other coverage under a group health plan and the other group health plan coverage alone satisfies the requirements in PHS Act section 2713 and section 54.9815-2713(a)(1), the HRA or other account-based plan will not fail to meet the requirements of PHS Act section 2713 and §54.9815-2713(a)(1).

(2) *Integration requirements.*—An HRA or other account-based plan is integrated with a group health plan for purposes of paragraph (a)(2) of this section if it meets the requirements under either the integration method set forth in paragraph (d)(2)(i) of this section or the integration method set forth in paragraph (d)(2)(ii) of this section. Integration does not require that the HRA (or other account-based plan) and the group health plan with which it is integrated share the same plan sponsor, the same plan document, or governing instruments, or file a single Form 5500, if applicable. The term "excepted benefits" is used throughout the integration methods; for a definition of the term "excepted benefits" see Code section 9832(c), ERISA section 733(c), and PHS Act section 2791(c).

(i) *Integration Method: Minimum value not required.*—An HRA or other account-based plan is integrated with another group health plan for purposes of this paragraph if:

(A) The plan sponsor offers a group health plan (other than the HRA or other account-based plan) to the employee that does not consist solely of excepted benefits;

(B) The employee receiving the HRA or other account-based plan is actually enrolled in a group health plan (other than the HRA or other account-based plan) that does not consist solely of excepted benefits, regardless of whether the plan is offered by the same plan sponsor (referred to as non-HRA group coverage);

(C) The HRA or other account-based plan is available only to employees who are enrolled in non-HRA group coverage, regardless of whether the non-HRA group coverage is offered by the plan sponsor of the HRA or other account-based plan (for example, the HRA may be offered only to employees who do not enroll in an employer's group health plan but are enrolled in other non-HRA group coverage, such as a group health plan maintained by the employer of the employee's spouse);

(D) The benefits under the HRA or other account-based plan are limited to reimbursement of one or more of the following—co-payments, co-insurance, deductibles, and premiums under the non-HRA group coverage, as well as medical care (as defined under section 213(d) of the Code) that does not constitute essential health benefits as defined in paragraph (c) of this section; and

(E) Under the terms of the HRA or other account-based plan, an employee (or former employee) is permitted to permanently opt out of and waive future reimbursements from the HRA or other account-based plan at least annually and, upon termination of employment, either the remaining amounts in the HRA or other account-based plan are forfeited or the employee is permitted to permanently opt out of and waive future reimbursements from the HRA or other account-based plan.

(ii) *Integration Method: Minimum value required.*—An HRA or other account-based plan is integrated with another group health plan for purposes of this paragraph if:

(A) The plan sponsor offers a group health plan (other than the HRA or other account-based plan) to the employee that provides

➤➤➤ *Caution: Reg. §54.9815-2711(d), as added by T.D. 9744, is generally applicable to plan years beginning on or after January 1, 2017, and before January 1, 2020.*

minimum value pursuant to Code section 36B(c)(2)(C)(ii) (and its implementing regulations and applicable guidance);

(B) The employee receiving the HRA or other account-based plan is actually enrolled in a group health plan that provides minimum value pursuant to section 36B(c)(2)(C)(ii) of the Code (and applicable guidance), regardless of whether the plan is offered by the plan sponsor of the HRA or other account-based plan (referred to as non-HRA MV group coverage);

(C) The HRA or other account-based plan is available only to employees who are actually enrolled in non-HRA MV group coverage, regardless of whether the non-HRA MV group coverage is offered by the plan sponsor of the HRA or other account-based plan (for example, the HRA may be offered only to employees who do not enroll in an employer's group health plan but are enrolled in other non-HRA MV group coverage, such as a group health plan maintained by an employer of the employee's spouse); and

(D) Under the terms of the HRA or other account-based plan, an employee (or former employee) is permitted to permanently opt out of and waive future reimbursements from the HRA or other account-based plan at least annually, and, upon termination of employment, either the remaining amounts in the HRA or other account-based plan are forfeited or the employee is permitted to permanently opt out of and waive future reimbursements from the HRA or other account-based plan.

(3) *Forfeiture.*—For purpose of integration under paragraphs (d)(2)(i)(E) and (d)(2)(ii)(D) of this section, forfeiture or waiver occurs even if the forfeited or waived amounts may be reinstated upon a fixed date, a participant's death, or the earlier of the two events (the reinstatement event). For this purpose coverage under an HRA or other account-based plan is considered forfeited or waived prior to a reinstatement event only if the participant's election to forfeit or waive is irrevocable, meaning that, beginning on the effective date of the election and through the date of the reinstatement event, the participant and the participant's beneficiaries have no access to amounts credited to the HRA or other account-based plan. This means that upon and after reinstatement, the reinstated amounts

under the HRA or other account-based plan may not be used to reimburse or pay medical expenses incurred during the period after forfeiture and prior to reinstatement.

(4) *No integration with individual market coverage.*—A group health plan, including an HRA or other account-based plan, used to purchase coverage on the individual market is not integrated with that individual market coverage for purposes of paragraph (a)(2) of this section (or for purposes of the requirements of PHS Act section 2713).

(5) *Integration with Medicare parts B and D.*—For employers that are not required to offer their non-HRA group health plan coverage to employees who are Medicare beneficiaries, an HRA or other account-based plan that may be used to reimburse premiums under Medicare part B or D may be integrated with Medicare (and deemed to comply with PHS Act sections 2711 and 2713) if the following requirements are satisfied with respect to employees who would be eligible for the employer's non-HRA group health plan but for their eligibility for Medicare (and the integration rules under paragraphs (d)(2)(i) and (ii) of this section continue to apply to employees who are not eligible for Medicare):

(i) The plan sponsor offers a group health plan (other than the HRA or other account-based plan and that does not consist solely of excepted benefits) to employees who are not eligible for Medicare;

(ii) The employee receiving the HRA or other account-based plan is actually enrolled Medicare part B or D;

(iii) The HRA or other account-based plan is available only to employees who are enrolled in Medicare part B or D; and

(iv) The HRA or other account-based plan complies with paragraphs (d)(2)(i)(E) and (d)(2)(ii)(D) of this section.

(6) *Account-based plan.*—An account-based plan for purposes of this section is an employer-provided group health plan that provides reimbursements of medical expenses other than individual market policy premiums with the reimbursement subject to a maximum fixed dollar amount for a period. An HRA is a type of account-based plan.

➤➤➤ *Caution: Reg. §54.9815-2711(d), as amended by T.D. 9867, is generally applicable to plan years beginning on or after January 1, 2020.*

(d) *Health reimbursement arrangements (HRAs) and other account-based group health plans.*—(1) *In general.*—If an HRA or other account-based group health plan is integrated with another group health plan or individual health insurance coverage and the other group health plan or individual health insurance coverage, as applicable, separately is subject to and satisfies the requirements in PHS Act section 2711 and paragraph (a)(2) of this section, the fact that the benefits under the HRA or other account-based group health plan are limited does not cause the HRA or other account-based group health plan to fail to satisfy the requirements of PHS Act section 2711 and paragraph (a)(2) of this section. Similarly, if an HRA or other account-based group health plan is integrated with another group health plan or individual health insurance coverage and the other group health plan or individual health insurance coverage, as applicable, separately is subject to and satisfies the requirements in PHS Act section 2713 and §54.9815-2713(a)(1) of this chapter, the fact that the benefits under the HRA or other account-based group health plan are limited does not cause the HRA or other account-based group health plan to fail to satisfy the requirements of PHS Act section 2713 and §54.9815-2713(a)(1) of this chapter. For the purpose of this paragraph (d), all individual health insurance coverage, except for coverage that consists solely of excepted benefits, is treated as being subject to and complying with PHS Act sections 2711 and 2713.

(2) *Requirements for an HRA or other account-based group health plan to be integrated with another group health plan.*—An HRA or other account-based group health plan is integrated with another group health plan for purposes of PHS Act section 2711 and paragraph (a)(2) of this section if it satisfies the requirements under one of the integration methods set forth in paragraph (d)(2)(i) or (ii) of this section. For purposes of the integration methods under which an HRA or other account-based group health plan is integrated with another group health plan, integration does not require that the HRA or other account-based group health plan and the other group health plan with which it is integrated share the same plan sponsor, the same plan document or governing instruments, or file a single Form 5500, if applicable. An HRA or other account-based group health plan integrated with another group health plan for purposes of PHS Act section 2711 and paragraph (a)(2) of this section may not be used to purchase individual health insurance coverage unless that coverage consists solely of excepted benefits, as defined in 45 CFR 148.220.

(i) *Method for integration with a group health plan: Minimum value not required.*—An HRA or other account-based group health

plan is integrated with another group health plan for purposes of this paragraph (d) if:

(A) The plan sponsor offers a group health plan (other than the HRA or other account-based group health plan) to the employee that does not consist solely of excepted benefits;

(B) The employee receiving the HRA or other account-based group health plan is actually enrolled in a group health plan (other than the HRA or other account-based group health plan) that does not consist solely of excepted benefits, regardless of whether the plan is offered by the same plan sponsor (referred to as non-HRA group coverage);

(C) The HRA or other account-based group health plan is available only to employees who are enrolled in non-HRA group coverage, regardless of whether the non-HRA group coverage is offered by the plan sponsor of the HRA or other account-based group health plan (for example, the HRA may be offered only to employees who do not enroll in an employer's group health plan but are enrolled in other non-HRA group coverage, such as a group health plan maintained by the employer of the employee's spouse);

(D) The benefits under the HRA or other account-based group health plan are limited to reimbursement of one or more of the following — co-payments, co-insurance, deductibles, and premiums under the non-HRA group coverage, as well as medical care expenses that do not constitute essential health benefits as defined in paragraph (c) of this section; and

(E) Under the terms of the HRA or other account-based group health plan, an employee (or former employee) is permitted to permanently opt out of and waive future reimbursements from the HRA or other account-based group health plan at least annually and, upon termination of employment, either the remaining amounts in the HRA or other account-based group health plan are forfeited or the employee is permitted to permanently opt out of and waive future reimbursements from the HRA or other account-based group health plan (see paragraph (d)(3) of this section for additional rules regarding forfeiture and waiver).

(ii) *Method for integration with another group health plan: Minimum value required.*—An HRA or other account-based group health plan is integrated with another group health plan for purposes of this paragraph (d) if:

(A) The plan sponsor offers a group health plan (other than the HRA or other account-based group health plan) to the employee

>>>→ *Caution: Reg. §54.9815-2711(d), as amended by T.D. 9867, is generally applicable to plan years beginning on or after January 1, 2020.*

that provides minimum value pursuant to section 36B(c)(2)(C)(ii) (and its implementing regulations and applicable guidance);

(B) The employee receiving the HRA or other account-based group health plan is actually enrolled in a group health plan (other than the HRA or other account-based group health plan) that provides minimum value pursuant to section 36B(c)(2)(C)(ii) (and applicable guidance), regardless of whether the plan is offered by the plan sponsor of the HRA or other account-based group health plan (referred to as non-HRA MV group coverage);

(C) The HRA or other account-based group health plan is available only to employees who are actually enrolled in non-HRA MV group coverage, regardless of whether the non-HRA MV group coverage is offered by the plan sponsor of the HRA or other account-based group health plan (for example, the HRA may be offered only to employees who do not enroll in an employer's group health plan but are enrolled in other non-HRA MV group coverage, such as a group health plan maintained by an employer of the employee's spouse); and

(D) Under the terms of the HRA or other account-based group health plan, an employee (or former employee) is permitted to permanently opt out of and waive future reimbursements from the HRA or other account-based group health plan at least annually, and, upon termination of employment, either the remaining amounts in the HRA or other account-based group health plan are forfeited or the employee is permitted to permanently opt out of and waive future reimbursements from the HRA or other account-based group health plan (see paragraph (d)(3) of this section for additional rules regarding forfeiture and waiver).

(3) *Forfeiture.*—For purposes of integration under paragraphs (d)(2)(i)(E) and (d)(2)(ii)(D) of this section, forfeiture or waiver occurs even if the forfeited or waived amounts may be reinstated upon a fixed date, a participant's death, or the earlier of the two events (the reinstatement event). For the purpose of this paragraph (d)(3), coverage under an HRA or other account-based group health plan is considered forfeited or waived prior to a reinstatement event only if the participant's election to forfeit or waive is irrevocable, meaning that, beginning on the effective date of the election and through the date of the reinstatement event, the participant and the participant's beneficiaries have no access to amounts credited to the HRA or other account-based group health plan. This means that upon and after reinstatement, the reinstated amounts under the HRA or other account-based group health plan may not be used to reimburse or pay medical care expenses incurred during the period after forfeiture and prior to reinstatement.

(4) *Requirements for an HRA or other account-based group health plan to be integrated with individual health insurance coverage or Medicare Part A and B or Medicare Part C.*—An HRA or other account-based group health plan is integrated with individual health insurance coverage or Medicare Part A and B or Medicare Part C (and treated as complying with PHS Act sections 2711 and 2713) if the HRA or other account-based group health plan satisfies the requirements of §54.9802-4(c) of this chapter (as modified by §54.9802-4(e), for HRAs or other account-based group health plans integrated with Medicare Part A and B or Medicare Part C).

(5) *Integration with Medicare Part B and D.*—For employers that are not required to offer their non-HRA group health plan coverage to employees who are Medicare beneficiaries, an HRA or other account-based group health plan that may be used to reimburse premiums under Medicare Part B or D may be integrated with Medicare (and deemed to comply with PHS Act sections 2711 and 2713) if the following requirements are satisfied with respect to employees who would be eligible for the employer's non-HRA group health plan but for their eligibility for Medicare (and the integration rules under paragraphs (d)(2)(i) and (ii) of this section continue to apply to employees who are not eligible for Medicare):

(i) The plan sponsor offers a group health plan (other than the HRA or other account-based group health plan and that does not consist solely of excepted benefits) to employees who are not eligible for Medicare;

(ii) The employee receiving the HRA or other account-based group health plan is actually enrolled in Medicare Part B or D;

(iii) The HRA or other account-based group health plan is available only to employees who are enrolled in Medicare Part B or D; and

(iv) The HRA or other account-based group health plan complies with paragraphs (d)(2)(i)(E) and (d)(2)(ii)(D) of this section.

(6) *Definitions.*—The following definitions apply for purposes of this section.

(i) *Account-based group health plan.*—An account-based group health plan is an employer-provided group health plan that provides reimbursements of medical care expenses with the reimbursement subject to a maximum fixed dollar amount for a period. An HRA is a type of account-based group health plan. An account-based group health plan does not include a qualified small employer health reimbursement arrangement, as defined in section 9831(d)(2).

(ii) *Medical care expenses.*—Medical care expenses means expenses for medical care as defined under section 213(d).

>>>→ *Caution: Reg. §54.9815-2711(e), as added by T.D. 9744, is generally applicable to plan years beginning on or after January 1, 2017, and before January 1, 2020.*

(e) *Applicability date.*—The provisions of this section are applicable to group health plans and health insurance issuers for plan years beginning on or after January 1, 2017. Until the applicability date for this regulation, plans and issuers are required to continue to comply with the interim final regulations promulgated by the Department of Labor at 29 CFR part 2590, contained in the 29 CFR, parts 1927 to end, edition revised as of July 1, 2015.

>>>→ *Caution: Reg. §54.9815-2711(e), as amended by T.D. 9867, is generally applicable to plan years beginning on or after January 1, 2020.*

(e) *Applicability date.*—The provisions of this section are applicable to group health plans and health insurance issuers for plan years beginning on or after January 1, 2020. Until the applicability date for this section, plans and issuers are required to continue to comply with the corresponding sections of 26 CFR part 54, contained in the 26 CFR, subchapter D, revised as of April 1, 2018. [Reg. §54.9815-2711.]

☐ [*T.D. 9744*, 11-13-2015. *Amended by T.D. 9791*, 10-28-2016 *and T.D. 9867*, 6-13-2019.]

>>>→ *Caution: Temporary Reg. §54.9815-2711T, below, was removed by T.D. 9744 and is inapplicable under Code Sec. 7805(e)(2). However, until final Reg. §54.9815-2711 is applicable on the first day of the plan or policy year beginning after January 1, 2017, taxpayers may comply with the corresponding interim final regulation at 29 CFR part 2590 that is substantially similar to the temporary reg below.*

**[Reg. §54.9815-2711T]**

**§54.9815-2711T. No lifetime or annual limits (temporary).**— (a) *Prohibition.*—(1) *Lifetime limits.*—Except as provided in paragraph (b) of this section, a group health plan, or a health insurance issuer offering group health insurance coverage, may not establish any lifetime limit on the dollar amount of benefits for any individual.

(2) *Annual limits.*—(i) *General rule.*—Except as provided in paragraphs (a)(2)(ii), (b), and (d) of this section, a group health plan, or a health insurance issuer offering group health insurance coverage, may not establish any annual limit on the dollar amount of benefits for any individual.

(ii) *Exception for health flexible spending arrangements.*—A health flexible spending arrangement (as defined in section 106(c)(2)) is not subject to the requirement in paragraph (a)(2)(i) of this section.

(b) *Construction.*—(1) *Permissible limits on specific covered benefits.*— The rules of this section do not prevent a group health plan, or a health insurance issuer offering group health insurance coverage,

from placing annual or lifetime dollar limits with respect to any individual on specific covered benefits that are not essential health benefits to the extent that such limits are otherwise permitted under applicable Federal or State law. (The scope of essential health benefits is addressed in paragraph (c) of this section).

(2) *Condition-based exclusions.*—The rules of this section do not prevent a group health plan, or a health insurance issuer offering group health insurance coverage, from excluding all benefits for a condition. However, if any benefits are provided for a condition, then the requirements of this section apply. Other requirements of Federal or State law may require coverage of certain benefits.

(c) *Definition of essential health benefits.*—The term "essential health benefits" means essential health benefits under section 1302(b) of the Patient Protection and Affordable Care Act and applicable regulations.

(d) *Restricted annual limits permissible prior to 2014.*—(1) *In general.*—With respect to plan years beginning prior to January 1, 2014, a group health plan, or a health insurance issuer offering group health

>>>→ *Caution: Temporary Reg. §54.9815-2711T, below, was removed by T.D. 9744 and is inapplicable under Code Sec. 7805(e)(2). However, until final Reg. §54.9815-2711 is applicable on the first day of the plan or policy year beginning after January 1, 2017, taxpayers may comply with the corresponding interim final regulation at 29 CFR part 2590 that is substantially similar to the temporary reg below.*

insurance coverage, may establish, for any individual, an annual limit on the dollar amount of benefits that are essential health benefits, provided the limit is no less than the amounts in the following schedule:

(i) For a plan year beginning on or after September 23, 2010, but before September 23, 2011, $750,000.

(ii) For a plan year beginning on or after September 23, 2011, but before September 23, 2012, $1,250,000.

(iii) For plan years beginning on or after September 23, 2012, but before January 1, 2014, $2,000,000.

(2) *Only essential health benefits taken into account.*—In determining whether an individual has received benefits that meet or exceed the applicable amount described in paragraph (d)(1) of this section, a plan or issuer must take into account only essential health benefits.

(3) *Waiver authority of the Secretary of Health and Human Services.*—For plan years beginning before January 1, 2014, the Secretary of Health and Human Services may establish a program under which the requirements of paragraph (d)(1) of this section relating to annual limits may be waived (for such period as is specified by the Secretary of Health and Human Services) for a group health plan or health insurance coverage that has an annual dollar limit on benefits below the restricted annual limits provided under paragraph (d)(1) of this section if compliance with paragraph (d)(1) of this section would result in a significant decrease in access to benefits under the plan or health insurance coverage or would significantly increase premiums for the plan or health insurance coverage.

(e) *Transitional rules for individuals whose coverage or benefits ended by reason of reaching a lifetime limit.*—(1) *In general.*—The relief provided in the transitional rules of this paragraph (e) applies with respect to any individual—

(i) Whose coverage or benefits under a group health plan or group health insurance coverage ended by reason of reaching a lifetime limit on the dollar value of all benefits for any individual (which, under this section, is no longer permissible); and

(ii) Who becomes eligible (or is required to become eligible) for benefits not subject to a lifetime limit on the dollar value of all benefits under the group health plan or group health insurance coverage on the first day of the first plan year beginning on or after September 23, 2010, by reason of the application of this section.

(2) *Notice and enrollment opportunity requirements.*—(i) If an individual described in paragraph (e)(1) of this section is eligible for benefits (or is required to become eligible for benefits) under the group health plan — or group health insurance coverage — described in paragraph (e)(1) of this section, the plan and the issuer are required to give the individual written notice that the lifetime limit on the dollar value of all benefits no longer applies and that the individual, if covered, is once again eligible for benefits under the plan. Additionally, if the individual is not enrolled in the plan or health insurance coverage, or if an enrolled individual is eligible for but not enrolled in any benefit package under the plan or health insurance coverage, then the plan and issuer must also give such an individual an opportunity to enroll that continues for at least 30 days (including written notice of the opportunity to enroll). The notices and enrollment opportunity required under this paragraph (e)(2)(i) must be provided beginning not later than the first day of the first plan year beginning on or after September 23, 2010.

(ii) The notices required under paragraph (e)(2)(i) of this section may be provided to an employee on behalf of the employee's dependent. In addition, the notices may be included with other enrollment materials that a plan distributes to employees, provided the statement is prominent. For either notice, if a notice satisfying the requirements of this paragraph (e)(2) is provided to an individual, the obligation to provide the notice with respect to that individual is satisfied for both the plan and the issuer.

(3) *Effective date of coverage.*—In the case of an individual who enrolls under paragraph (e)(2) of this section, coverage must take effect not later than the first day of the first plan year beginning on or after September 23, 2010.

(4) *Treatment of enrollees in a group health plan.*—Any individual enrolling in a group health plan pursuant to paragraph (e)(2) of this section must be treated as if the individual were a special enrollee, as provided under the rules of §54.9801-6(d). Accordingly, the individual (and, if the individual would not be a participant once enrolled in the plan, the participant through whom the individual is otherwise eligible for coverage under the plan) must be offered all the benefit packages available to similarly situated individuals who did not lose

coverage by reason of reaching a lifetime limit on the dollar value of all benefits. For this purpose, any difference in benefits or cost-sharing requirements constitutes a different benefit package. The individual also cannot be required to pay more for coverage than similarly situated individuals who did not lose coverage by reason of reaching a lifetime limit on the dollar value of all benefits.

(5) *Examples.*—The rules of this paragraph (e) are illustrated by the following examples:

*Example 1.* (i) *Facts.* Employer Y maintains a group health plan with a calendar year plan year. The plan has a single benefit package. For plan years beginning before September 23, 2010, the plan has a lifetime limit on the dollar value of all benefits. Individual B, an employee of Y, was enrolled in Y's group health plan at the beginning of the 2008 plan year. On June 10, 2008, B incurred a claim for benefits that exceeded the lifetime limit under Y's plan and ceased to be enrolled in the plan. B is still eligible for coverage under Y's group health plan. On or before January 1, 2011, Y's group health plan gives B written notice informing B that the lifetime limit on the dollar value of all benefits no longer applies, that individuals whose coverage ended by reason of reaching a lifetime limit under the plan are eligible to enroll in the plan, and that individuals can request such enrollment through February 1, 2011 with enrollment effective retroactively to January 1, 2011.

(ii) *Conclusion.* In this *Example 1*, the plan has complied with the requirements of this paragraph (e) by providing a timely written notice and enrollment opportunity to B that lasts at least 30 days.

*Example 2.* (i) *Facts.* Employer Z maintains a group health plan with a plan year beginning October 1 and ending September 30. Prior to October 1, 2010, the group health plan has a lifetime limit on the dollar value of all benefits. Individual D, an employee of Z, and Individual E, D's child, were enrolled in family coverage under Z's group health plan for the plan year beginning on October 1, 2008. On May 1, 2009, E incurred a claim for benefits that exceeded the lifetime limit under Z's plan. D dropped family coverage but remains an employee of Z and is still eligible for coverage under Z's group health plan.

(ii) *Conclusion.* In this *Example 2*, not later than October 1, 2010, the plan must provide D and E an opportunity to enroll (including written notice of an opportunity to enroll) that continues for at least 30 days, with enrollment effective not later than October 1, 2010.

*Example 3.* (i) *Facts.* Same facts as *Example 2*, except that Z's plan had two benefit packages (a low-cost and a high-cost option). Instead of dropping coverage, D switched to the low-cost benefit package option.

(ii) *Conclusion.* In this *Example 3*, not later than October 1, 2010, the plan must provide D and E an opportunity to enroll in any benefit package available to similarly situated individuals who enroll when first eligible. The plan would have to provide D and E the opportunity to enroll in any benefit package available to similarly situated individuals who enroll when first eligible, even if D had not switched to the low-cost benefit package option.

*Example 4.* (i) *Facts.* Employer Q maintains a group health plan with a plan year beginning October 1 and ending September 30. For the plan year beginning on October 1, 2009, Q has an annual limit on the dollar value of all benefits of $500,000.

(ii) *Conclusion.* In this *Example 4*, Q must raise the annual limit on the dollar value of essential health benefits to at least $750,000 for the plan year beginning October 1, 2010. For the plan year beginning October 1, 2011, Q must raise the annual limit to at least $1.25 million. For the plan year beginning October 1, 2012, Q must raise the annual limit to at least $2 million. Q may also impose a restricted annual limit of $2 million for the plan year beginning October 1, 2013. After the conclusion of that plan year, Q cannot impose an overall annual limit.

*Example 5.* (i) *Facts.* Same facts as *Example 4*, except that the annual limit for the plan year beginning on October 1, 2009 is $1 million and Q lowers the annual limit for the plan year beginning October 1, 2010 to $750,000.

(ii) *Conclusion.* In this *Example 5*, Q complies with the requirements of this paragraph (e). However, Q's choice to lower its annual limit means that under §54.9815-1251T(g)(1)(vi)(C), the group health plan will cease to be a grandfathered health plan and will be generally subject to all of the provisions of PHS Act sections 2701 through 2719A.

(f) *Effective/applicability date.*—The provisions of this section apply for plan years beginning on or after September 23, 2010. See §54.9815-1251T for determining the application of this section to grandfathered health plans (providing that the prohibitions on lifetime and annual limits apply to all grandfathered health plans that

**⋙→ Caution:** *Temporary Reg. §54.9815-2711T, below, was removed by T.D. 9744 and is inapplicable under Code Sec. 7805(e)(2). However, until final Reg. §54.9815-2711 is applicable on the first day of the plan or policy year beginning after January 1, 2017, taxpayers may comply with the corresponding interim final regulation at 29 CFR part 2590 that is substantially similar to the temporary reg below.*

are group health plans and group health insurance coverage, including the special rules regarding restricted annual limits).

**⋙→ Caution:** *Reg. §54.9815-2712, below, as added by T.D. 9744, is applicable to group health plans and health insurance issuers beginning on the first day of the plan year (or, in the individual market, the first day of the first policy year) beginning on or after January 1, 2017.*

### [Reg. §54.9815-2712]

**§54.9815-2712. Rules regarding rescissions.**—(a) *Prohibition on rescissions.*—(1) A group health plan, or a health insurance issuer offering group health insurance coverage, must not rescind coverage under the plan, or under the policy, certificate, or contract of insurance, with respect to an individual (including a group to which the individual belongs or family coverage in which the individual is included) once the individual is covered under the plan or coverage, unless the individual (or a person seeking coverage on behalf of the individual) performs an act, practice, or omission that constitutes fraud, or makes an intentional misrepresentation of material fact, as prohibited by the terms of the plan or coverage. A group health plan, or a health insurance issuer offering group health insurance coverage, must provide at least 30 days advance written notice to each participant who would be affected before coverage may be rescinded under this paragraph (a)(1), regardless of whether the coverage is insured or self-insured, or whether the rescission applies to an entire group or only to an individual within the group. (The rules of this paragraph (a)(1) apply regardless of any contestability period that may otherwise apply.)

(2) For purposes of this section, a rescission is a cancellation or discontinuance of coverage that has retroactive effect. For example, a cancellation that treats a policy as void from the time of the individual's or group's enrollment is a rescission. As another example, a cancellation that voids benefits paid up to a year before the cancellation is also a rescission for this purpose. A cancellation or discontinuance of coverage is not a rescission if—

(i) The cancellation or discontinuance of coverage has only a prospective effect;

(ii) The cancellation or discontinuance of coverage is effective retroactively to the extent it is attributable to a failure to timely pay required premiums or contributions (including COBRA premiums) towards the cost of coverage;

(iii) The cancellation or discontinuance of coverage is initiated by the individual (or by the individual's authorized representative) and the sponsor, employer, plan, or issuer does not, directly or indirectly, take action to influence the individual's decision to cancel or discontinue coverage retroactively or otherwise take any adverse action or retaliate against, interfere with, coerce, intimidate, or threaten the individual; or

(iv) The cancellation or discontinuance of coverage is initiated by the Exchange pursuant to 45 CFR 155.430 (other than under paragraph (b)(2)(iii)).

(3) The rules of this paragraph (a) are illustrated by the following examples:

*Example 1.* (i) *Facts.* Individual A seeks enrollment in an insured group health plan. The plan terms permit rescission of coverage with respect to an individual if the individual engages in fraud or makes an intentional misrepresentation of a material fact. The plan requires A to complete a questionnaire regarding A's prior medical history, which affects setting the group rate by the health insurance issuer. The questionnaire complies with the other requirements of this part. The questionnaire includes the following question: "Is there anything else relevant to your health that we should know?" A inadvertently fails to list that A visited a psychologist on two occasions, six years previously. A is later diagnosed with breast cancer and seeks benefits under the plan. On or around the same time, the issuer receives information about A's visits to the psychologist, which was not disclosed in the questionnaire.

(ii) *Conclusion.* In this *Example 1*, the plan cannot rescind A's coverage because A's failure to disclose the visits to the psychologist was inadvertent. Therefore, it was not fraudulent or an intentional misrepresentation of material fact.

*Example 2.* (i) *Facts.* An employer sponsors a group health plan that provides coverage for employees who work at least 30 hours per week. Individual B has coverage under the plan as a full-time employee. The employer reassigns B to a part-time position. Under the terms of the plan, B is no longer eligible for coverage. The plan mistakenly continues to provide health coverage, collecting premiums from B and paying claims submitted by B. After a routine audit, the plan discovers that B no longer works at least 30 hours per week. The plan rescinds B's coverage effective as of the date that B changed from a full-time employee to a part-time employee.

(ii) *Conclusion.* In this *Example 2*, the plan cannot rescind B's coverage because there was no fraud or an intentional misrepresentation of material fact. The plan may cancel coverage for B prospectively, subject to other applicable Federal and State laws.

(b) *Compliance with other requirements.*—Other requirements of Federal or State law may apply in connection with a rescission of coverage.

(c) *Applicability date.*—The provisions of this section are applicable to group health plans and health insurance issuers for plan years beginning on or after January 1, 2017. Until the applicability date for this regulation, plans and issuers are required to continue to comply with the interim final regulations promulgated by the Department of Labor at 29 CFR part 2590, contained in the 29 CFR, parts 1927 to end, edition revised as of July 1, 2015. [Reg. §54.9815-2712.]

☐ [T.D. 9744, 11-13-2015.]

**⋙→ Caution:** *Temporary Reg. §54.9815-2712T, below, was removed by T.D. 9744 and is inapplicable under Code Sec. 7805(e)(2). However, until final Reg. §54.9815-2712 is applicable on the first day of the plan or policy year beginning after January 1, 2017, taxpayers may comply with the corresponding interim final regulation at 29 CFR part 2590 that is substantially similar to the temporary reg below.*

### [Reg. §54.9815-2712T]

**§54.9815-2712T. Rules regarding rescissions (temporary).**—(a) *Prohibition on rescissions.*—(1) A group health plan, or a health insurance issuer offering group health insurance coverage, must not rescind coverage under the plan, or under the policy, certificate, or contract of insurance, with respect to an individual (including a group to which the individual belongs or family coverage in which the individual is included) once the individual is covered under the plan or coverage, unless the individual (or a person seeking coverage on behalf of the individual) performs an act, practice, or omission that constitutes fraud, or unless the individual makes an intentional misrepresentation of material fact, as prohibited by the terms of the plan or coverage. A group health plan, or a health insurance issuer offering group health insurance coverage, must provide at least 30 days advance written notice to each participant who would be affected before coverage may be rescinded under this paragraph (a)(1), regardless of whether the coverage is insured or self-insured, or whether the rescission applies to an entire group or only to an individual within the group. (The rules of this paragraph (a)(1) apply regardless of any contestability period that may otherwise apply.)

(2) For purposes of this section, a rescission is a cancellation or discontinuance of coverage that has retroactive effect. For example, a cancellation that treats a policy as void from the time of the individual's or group's enrollment is a rescission. As another example, a cancellation that voids benefits paid up to a year before the cancella-

tion is also a rescission for this purpose. A cancellation or discontinuance of coverage is not a rescission if—

(i) The cancellation or discontinuance of coverage has only a prospective effect; or

(ii) The cancellation or discontinuance of coverage is effective retroactively to the extent it is attributable to a failure to timely pay required premiums or contributions towards the cost of coverage.

(3) The rules of this paragraph (a) are illustrated by the following examples:

*Example 1.* (i) *Facts.* Individual A seeks enrollment in an insured group health plan. The plan terms permit rescission of coverage with respect to an individual if the individual engages in fraud or makes an intentional misrepresentation of a material fact. The plan requires A to complete a questionnaire regarding A's prior medical history, which affects setting the group rate by the health insurance issuer. The questionnaire complies with the other requirements of this part. The questionnaire includes the following question: "Is there anything else relevant to your health that we should know?" A inadvertently fails to list that A visited a psychologist on two occasions, six years previously. A is later diagnosed with breast cancer and seeks benefits under the plan. On or around the same time, the issuer receives information about A's visits to the psychologist, which was not disclosed in the questionnaire.

(ii) *Conclusion.* In this *Example 1*, the plan cannot rescind A's coverage because A's failure to disclose the visits to the psychologist

**⫸→ Caution:** *Temporary Reg. §54.9815-2712T, below, was removed by T.D. 9744 and is inapplicable under Code Sec. 7805(e)(2). However, until final Reg. §54.9815-2712 is applicable on the first day of the plan or policy year beginning after January 1, 2017, taxpayers may comply with the corresponding interim final regulation at 29 CFR part 2590 that is substantially similar to the temporary reg below.*

was inadvertent. Therefore, it was not fraudulent or an intentional misrepresentation of material fact.

*Example 2.* (i) *Facts.* An employer sponsors a group health plan that provides coverage for employees who work at least 30 hours per week. Individual B has coverage under the plan as a full-time employee. The employer reassigns B to a part-time position. Under the terms of the plan, B is no longer eligible for coverage. The plan mistakenly continues to provide health coverage, collecting premiums from B and paying claims submitted by B. After a routine audit, the plan discovers that B no longer works at least 30 hours per week. The plan rescinds B's coverage effective as of the date that B changed from a full-time employee to a part-time employee.

(ii) *Conclusion.* In this *Example 2*, the plan cannot rescind B's coverage because there was no fraud or an intentional misrepresentation of material fact. The plan may cancel coverage for B prospectively, subject to other applicable Federal and State laws.

(b) *Compliance with other requirements.*—Other requirements of Federal or State law may apply in connection with a rescission of coverage.

(c) *Effective/applicability date.*—The provisions of this section apply for plan years beginning on or after September 23, 2010. See §54.9815-1251T for determining the application of this section to grandfathered health plans (providing that the rules regarding rescissions and advance notice apply to all grandfathered health plans).

(d) *Expiration date.*—This section expires on June 21, 2013. [Temporary Reg. §54.9815-2712T.]

☐ [*T.D. 9491, 6-22-2010. Removed by T.D. 9744, 11-13-2015.*]

### [Reg. §54.9815-2713]

**§54.9815-2713. Coverage of preventive health services.**—(a) *Services.*—(1) *In general.*—Beginning at the time described in paragraph (b) of this section and subject to §54.9815-2713A, a group health plan, or a health insurance issuer offering group health insurance coverage, must provide coverage for and must not impose any cost-sharing requirements (such as a copayment, coinsurance, or a deductible) for—

(i) Evidence-based items or services that have in effect a rating of A or B in the current recommendations of the United States Preventive Services Task Force with respect to the individual involved (except as otherwise provided in paragraph (c) of this section);

(ii) Immunizations for routine use in children, adolescents, and adults that have in effect a recommendation from the Advisory Committee on Immunization Practices of the Centers for Disease Control and Prevention with respect to the individual involved (for this purpose, a recommendation from the Advisory Committee on Immunization Practices of the Centers for Disease Control and Prevention is considered in effect after it has been adopted by the Director of the Centers for Disease Control and Prevention, and a recommendation is considered to be for routine use if it is listed on the Immunization Schedules of the Centers for Disease Control and Prevention);

(iii) With respect to infants, children, and adolescents, evidence-informed preventive care and screenings provided for in comprehensive guidelines supported by the Health Resources and Services Administration; and

(iv) With respect to women, such additional preventive care and screenings not described in paragraph (a)(1)(i) of this section as provided for in comprehensive guidelines supported by the Health Resources and Services Administration for purposes of section 2713(a)(4) of the Public Health Service Act, subject to 45 CFR 147.131, 147.132, and 147.133.

(2) *Office visits.*—(i) If an item or service described in paragraph (a)(1) of this section is billed separately (or is tracked as individual encounter data separately) from an office visit, then a plan or issuer may impose cost-sharing requirements with respect to the office visit.

(ii) If an item or service described in paragraph (a)(1) of this section is not billed separately (or is not tracked as individual encounter data separately) from an office visit and the primary purpose of the office visit is the delivery of such an item or service, then a plan or issuer may not impose cost-sharing requirements with respect to the office visit.

(iii) If an item or service described in paragraph (a)(1) of this section is not billed separately (or is not tracked as individual encounter data separately) from an office visit and the primary purpose of the office visit is not the delivery of such an item or service, then a plan or issuer may impose cost-sharing requirements with respect to the office visit.

(iv) The rules of this paragraph (a)(2) are illustrated by the following examples:

*Example 1.* (i) *Facts.* An individual covered by a group health plan visits an in-network health care provider. While visiting the provider, the individual is screened for cholesterol abnormalities, which has in effect a rating of A or B in the current recommendations of the United States Preventive Services Task Force with respect to the individual. The provider bills the plan for an office visit and for the laboratory work of the cholesterol screening test.

(ii) *Conclusion.* In this *Example 1*, the plan may not impose any cost-sharing requirements with respect to the separately-billed laboratory work of the cholesterol screening test. Because the office visit is billed separately from the cholesterol screening test, the plan may impose cost-sharing requirements for the office visit.

*Example 2.* (i) *Facts.* Same facts as *Example 1* of this section. As the result of the screening, the individual is diagnosed with hyperlipidemia and is prescribed a course of treatment that is not included in the recommendations under paragraph (a)(1) of this section.

(ii) *Conclusion.* In this *Example 2*, because the treatment is not included in the recommendations under paragraph (a)(1) of this section, the plan is not prohibited from imposing cost-sharing requirements with respect to the treatment.

*Example 3.* (i) *Facts.* An individual covered by a group health plan visits an in-network health care provider to discuss recurring abdominal pain. During the visit, the individual has a blood pressure screening, which has in effect a rating of A or B in the current recommendations of the United States Preventive Services Task Force with respect to the individual. The provider bills the plan for an office visit.

(ii) *Conclusion.* In this *Example 3*, the blood pressure screening is provided as part of an office visit for which the primary purpose was not to deliver items or services described in paragraph (a)(1) of this section. Therefore, the plan may impose a cost-sharing requirement for the office visit charge.

*Example 4.* (i) *Facts.* A child covered by a group health plan visits an in-network pediatrician to receive an annual physical exam described as part of the comprehensive guidelines supported by the Health Resources and Services Administration. During the office visit, the child receives additional items and services that are not described in the comprehensive guidelines supported by the Health Resources and Services Administration, nor otherwise described in paragraph (a)(1) of this section. The provider bills the plan for an office visit.

(ii) *Conclusion.* In this *Example 4*, the service was not billed as a separate charge and was billed as part of an office visit. Moreover, the primary purpose for the visit was to deliver items and services described as part of the comprehensive guidelines supported by the Health Resources and Services Administration. Therefore, the plan may not impose a cost-sharing requirement with respect to the office visit.

(3) *Out-of-network providers.*—(i) Subject to paragraph (a)(3)(ii) of this section, nothing in this section requires a plan or issuer that has a network of providers to provide benefits for items or services described in paragraph (a)(1) of this section that are delivered by an out-of-network provider. Moreover, nothing in this section precludes a plan or issuer that has a network of providers from imposing cost-sharing requirements for items or services described in paragraph (a)(1) of this section that are delivered by an out-of-network provider.

(ii) If a plan or issuer does not have in its network a provider who can provide an item or service described in paragraph (a)(1) of this section, the plan or issuer must cover the item or service when performed by an out-of-network provider, and may not impose cost-sharing with respect to the item or service.

(4) *Reasonable medical management.*—Nothing prevents a plan or issuer from using reasonable medical management techniques to determine the frequency, method, treatment, or setting for an item or service described in paragraph (a)(1) of this section to the extent not specified in the relevant recommendation or guideline. To the extent not specified in a recommendation or guideline, a plan or issuer may rely on the relevant clinical evidence base and established reasonable medical management techniques to determine the frequency, method, treatment, or setting for coverage of a recommended preventive health service.

(5) *Services not described.*—Nothing in this section prohibits a plan or issuer from providing coverage for items and services in addition to those recommended by the United States Preventive Services Task Force or the Advisory Committee on Immunization Practices of the Centers for Disease Control and Prevention, or provided for by guidelines supported by the Health Resources and

Services Administration, or from denying coverage for items and services that are not recommended by that task force or that advisory committee, or under those guidelines. A plan or issuer may impose cost-sharing requirements for a treatment not described in paragraph (a)(1) of this section, even if the treatment results from an item or service described in paragraph (a)(1) of this section.

(b) *Timing.*—(1) *In general.*—A plan or issuer must provide coverage pursuant to paragraph (a)(1) of this section for plan years that begin on or after September 23, 2010, or, if later, for plan years that begin on or after the date that is one year after the date the recommendation or guideline is issued.

(2) *Changes in recommendations or guidelines.*—(i) A plan or issuer that is required to provide coverage for any items and services specified in any recommendation or guideline described in paragraph (a)(1) of this section on the first day of a plan year must provide coverage through the last day of the plan year, even if the recommendation or guideline changes is or is no longer described in paragraph (a)(1) of this section, during the plan year.

(ii) Notwithstanding paragraph (b)(2)(i) of this section, to the extent a recommendation or guideline described in paragraph (a)(1)(i) of this section that was in effect on the first day of a plan year is downgraded to a "D" rating, or any item or service associated with any recommendation or guideline specified in paragraph (a)(1) of this section is subject to a safety recall or is otherwise determined to pose a significant safety concern by a federal agency authorized to regulate the item or service during a plan year, there is no requirement under this section to cover these items and services through the last day of the plan year.

(c) *Recommendations not current.*—For purposes of paragraph (a)(1)(i) of this section, and for purposes of any other provision of law, recommendations of the United States Preventive Services Task Force regarding breast cancer screening, mammography, and prevention issued in or around November 2009 are not considered to be current.

(d) *Effective/applicability date.*—April 16, 2012. [Reg. §54.9815-2713.]

☐ [*T.D.* 9578, 2-10-2012. *Amended by T.D.* 9624, 6-28-2013, *T.D.* 9726, 7-10-2015, *T.D.* 9827, 10-6-2017, *T.D.* 9840, 11-7-2018 *and T.D.* 9841, 11-7-2018.]

**[Reg. §54.9815-2713T]**

**§54.9815-2713T. Coverage of preventive health services (temporary).**—(a) *Services.*—(1) *In general.*—Beginning at the time described in paragraph (b) of this section and subject to §54.9815-2713A, a group health plan, or a health insurance issuer offering group health insurance coverage, must provide coverage for and must not impose any cost-sharing requirements (such as a copayment, coinsurance, or a deductible) for –

(i) Evidence-based items or services that have in effect a rating of A or B in the current recommendations of the United States Preventive Services Task Force with respect to the individual involved (except as otherwise provided in paragraph (c) of this section);

(ii) Immunizations for routine use in children, adolescents, and adults that have in effect a recommendation from the Advisory Committee on Immunization Practices of the Centers for Disease Control and Prevention with respect to the individual involved (for purposes of this paragraph (a)(1)(ii), a recommendation from the Advisory Committee on Immunization Practices of the Centers for Disease Control and Prevention is considered in effect after it has been adopted by the Director of the Centers for Disease Control and Prevention, and a recommendation is considered to be for routine use if it is listed on the Immunization Schedules of the Centers for Disease Control and Prevention);

(iii) With respect to infants, children, and adolescents, evidence-informed preventive care and screenings provided for in comprehensive guidelines supported by the Health Resources and Services Administration;

(iv) With respect to women, such additional preventive care and screenings not described in paragraph (a)(1)(i) of this section as provided for in comprehensive guidelines supported by the Health Resources and Services Administration for purposes of section 2713(a)(4) of the Public Health Service Act, subject to 45 CFR 147.131, 147.132, and 147.133; and

(v) Any qualifying coronavirus preventive service, which means an item, service, or immunization that is intended to prevent or mitigate coronavirus disease 2019 (COVID-19) and that is, with respect to the individual involved –

(A) An evidence-based item or service that has in effect a rating of A or B in the current recommendations of the United States Preventive Services Task Force; or

(B) An immunization that has in effect a recommendation from the Advisory Committee on Immunization Practices of the Centers for Disease Control and Prevention (regardless of whether the immunization is recommended for routine use). For purposes of this paragraph (a)(1)(v)(B), a recommendation from the Advisory Committee on Immunization Practices of the Centers for Disease Control and Prevention is considered in effect after it has been adopted by the Director of the Centers for Disease Control and Prevention.

(2) *Office visits.*—(i) If an item or service described in paragraph (a)(1) of this section is billed separately (or is tracked as individual encounter data separately) from an office visit, then a plan or issuer may impose cost-sharing requirements with respect to the office visit.

(ii) If an item or service described in paragraph (a)(1) of this section is not billed separately (or is not tracked as individual encounter data separately) from an office visit and the primary purpose of the office visit is the delivery of such an item or service, then a plan or issuer may not impose cost-sharing requirements with respect to the office visit.

(iii) If an item or service described in paragraph (a)(1) of this section is not billed separately (or is not tracked as individual encounter data separately) from an office visit and the primary purpose of the office visit is not the delivery of such an item or service, then a plan or issuer may impose cost-sharing requirements with respect to the office visit.

(iv) The rules of this paragraph (a)(2) are illustrated by the following examples:

(A) *Example 1.*—(1) *Facts.* An individual covered by a group health plan visits an in-network health care provider. While visiting the provider, the individual is screened for cholesterol abnormalities, which has in effect a rating of A or B in the current recommendations of the United States Preventive Services Task Force with respect to the individual. The provider bills the plan for an office visit and for the laboratory work of the cholesterol screening test.

(2) *Conclusion.* In paragraph (a)(2)(iv)(A)(1) of this section, the plan may not impose any cost-sharing requirements with respect to the separately-billed laboratory work of the cholesterol screening test. Because the office visit is billed separately from the cholesterol screening test, the plan may impose cost-sharing requirements for the office visit.

(B) *Example 2.*—(1) *Facts.* Same facts as in paragraph (a)(2)(iv)(A)(1) of this section (*Example 1*). As the result of the screening, the individual is diagnosed with hyperlipidemia and is prescribed a course of treatment that is not included in the recommendations under paragraph (a)(1) of this section.

(2) *Conclusion.* In paragraph (a)(2)(iv)(B)(1) of this section, because the treatment is not included in the recommendations under paragraph (a)(1) of this section, the plan is not prohibited from imposing cost-sharing requirements with respect to the treatment.

(C) *Example 3.*—(1) *Facts.* An individual covered by a group health plan visits an in-network health care provider to discuss recurring abdominal pain. During the visit, the individual has a blood pressure screening, which has in effect a rating of A or B in the current recommendations of the United States Preventive Services Task Force with respect to the individual. The provider bills the plan for an office visit.

(2) *Conclusion.* In paragraph (a)(2)(iv)(C)(1) of this section, the blood pressure screening is provided as part of an office visit for which the primary purpose was not to deliver items or services described in paragraph (a)(1) of this section. Therefore, the plan may impose a cost-sharing requirement for the office visit charge.

(D) *Example 4.*—(1) *Facts.* A child covered by a group health plan visits an in-network pediatrician to receive an annual physical exam described as part of the comprehensive guidelines supported by the Health Resources and Services Administration. During the office visit, the child receives additional items and services that are not described in the comprehensive guidelines supported by the Health Resources and Services Administration, nor otherwise described in paragraph (a)(1) of this section. The provider bills the plan for an office visit.

(2) *Conclusion.* In paragraph (a)(2)(iv)(D)(1) of this section, the service was not billed as a separate charge and was billed as part of an office visit. Moreover, the primary purpose for the visit was to deliver items and services described as part of the comprehensive guidelines supported by the Health Resources and Services Administration. Therefore, the plan may not impose a cost-sharing requirement with respect to the office visit.

(3) *Out-of-network providers.*—(i) Subject to paragraphs (a)(3)(ii) and (iii) of this section, nothing in this section requires a plan or issuer that has a network of providers to provide benefits for items or

services described in paragraph (a)(1) of this section that are delivered by an out-of-network provider, or precludes a plan or issuer that has a network of providers from imposing cost-sharing requirements for items or services described in paragraph (a)(1) of this section that are delivered by an out-of-network provider.

(ii) If a plan or issuer does not have in its network a provider who can provide an item or service described in paragraph (a)(1) of this section, the plan or issuer must cover the item or service when performed by an out-of-network provider, and may not impose cost-sharing with respect to the item or service.

(iii) A plan or issuer must provide coverage for and must not impose any cost-sharing requirements (such as a copayment, coinsurance, or a deductible) for any qualifying coronavirus preventive service described in paragraph (a)(1)(v) of this section, regardless of whether such service is delivered by an in-network or out-of-network provider. For purposes of this paragraph (a)(3)(iii), with respect to a qualifying coronavirus preventive service and a provider with whom the plan or issuer does not have a negotiated rate for such service (such as an out-of-network provider), the plan or issuer must reimburse the provider for such service in an amount that is reasonable, as determined in comparison to prevailing market rates for such service.

(4) *Reasonable medical management.*—Nothing prevents a plan or issuer from using reasonable medical management techniques to determine the frequency, method, treatment, or setting for an item or service described in paragraph (a)(1) of this section to the extent not specified in the relevant recommendation or guideline. To the extent not specified in a recommendation or guideline, a plan or issuer may rely on the relevant clinical evidence base and established reasonable medical management techniques to determine the frequency, method, treatment, or setting for coverage of a recommended preventive health service.

(5) *Services not described.*—Nothing in this section prohibits a plan or issuer from providing coverage for items and services in addition to those recommended by the United States Preventive Services Task Force or the Advisory Committee on Immunization Practices of the Centers for Disease Control and Prevention, or provided for by guidelines supported by the Health Resources and Services Administration, or from denying coverage for items and services that are not recommended by that task force or that advisory committee, or under those guidelines. A plan or issuer may impose cost-sharing requirements for a treatment not described in paragraph (a)(1) of this section, even if the treatment results from an item or service described in paragraph (a)(1) of this section.

(b) *Timing.*—(1) *In general.*—A plan or issuer must provide coverage pursuant to paragraph (a)(1) of this section for plan years that begin on or after September 23, 2010, or, if later, for plan years that begin on or after the date that is one year after the date the recommendation or guideline is issued, except as provided in paragraph (b)(3) of this section.

(2) *Changes in recommendations or guidelines.*—(i) A plan or issuer that is required to provide coverage for any items and services specified in any recommendation or guideline described in paragraph (a)(1) of this section on the first day of a plan year, or as otherwise provided in paragraph (b)(3) of this section, must provide coverage through the last day of the plan or policy year, even if the recommendation or guideline changes or is no longer described in paragraph (a)(1) of this section, during the applicable plan or policy year.

(ii) Notwithstanding paragraph (b)(2)(i) of this section, to the extent a recommendation or guideline described in paragraph (a)(1)(i) of this section that was in effect on the first day of a plan year, or as otherwise provided in paragraph (b)(3) of this section, is downgraded to a "D" rating, or any item or service associated with any recommendation or guideline specified in paragraph (a)(1) of this section is subject to a safety recall or is otherwise determined to pose a significant safety concern by a Federal agency authorized to regulate the item or service during a plan or policy year, there is no requirement under this section to cover these items and services through the last day of the applicable plan or policy year.

(3) *Rapid coverage of preventive services for coronavirus.*—In the case of a qualifying coronavirus preventive service described in paragraph (a)(1)(v) of this section, a plan or issuer must provide coverage for such item, service, or immunization in accordance with this section by the date that is 15 business days after the date on which a recommendation specified in paragraph (a)(1)(v)(A) or (B) of this section is made relating to such item, service, or immunization.

(c) *Recommendations not current.*—For purposes of paragraph (a)(1)(i) of this section, and for purposes of any other provision of law, recommendations of the United States Preventive Services Task Force regarding breast cancer screening, mammography, and preven-

tion issued in or around November 2009 are not considered to be current.

(d) *Applicability date.*—The provisions of paragraphs (a)(1)(i) through (iv), (a)(2), (a)(3)(i) and (ii), (a)(4) through (5), (b)(1) and (2), and (c) of this section are applicable as of April 16, 2012.

(e) *Sunset date.*—The provisions of paragraphs (a)(1)(v), (a)(3)(iii), and (b)(3) of this section will not apply with respect to a qualifying coronavirus preventive service furnished on or after the expiration of the public health emergency determined on January 31, 2020, to exist nationwide as of January 27, 2020, by the Secretary of Health and Human Services pursuant to section 319 of the Public Health Service Act, as a result of COVID-19, including any subsequent renewals of that determination.

☐ [*T.D.* 9931, 11-2-2020.]

## [Reg. § 54.9815-2713A]

**§ 54.9815-2713A. Accommodations in connection with coverage of preventive health services.**—(a) through (f)(a) *Eligible organizations for optional accommodation.*—An eligible organization is an organization that meets the criteria of paragraphs (a)(1) through (4) of this section.

(1) The organization is an objecting entity described in 45 CFR 147.132(a)(1)(i) or (ii), or 45 CFR 147.133(a)(1)(i) or (ii);

(2) Notwithstanding its status under paragraph (a)(1) of this section and under 45 CFR 147.132(a) or 147.133(a), the organization voluntarily seeks to be considered an eligible organization to invoke the optional accommodation under paragraph (b) or (c) of this section as applicable; and

(3) [Reserved]

(4) The organization self-certifies in the form and manner specified by the Secretary of Labor or provides notice to the Secretary of the Department of Health and Human Services as described in paragraph (b) or (c) of this section. To qualify as an eligible organization, the organization must make such self-certification or notice available for examination upon request by the first day of the first plan year to which the accommodation in paragraph (b) or (c) of this section applies. The self-certification or notice must be executed by a person authorized to make the certification or provide the notice on behalf of the organization, and must be maintained in a manner consistent with the record retention requirements under section 107 of ERISA.

(5) An eligible organization may revoke its use of the accommodation process, and its issuer or third party administrator must provide participants and beneficiaries written notice of such revocation, as specified herein.

(i) *Transitional rule.*—If contraceptive coverage is being offered on the date on which these final rules go into effect, by an issuer or third party administrator through the accommodation process, an eligible organization may give 60-days notice pursuant to section 2715(d)(4) of the PHS Act and § 54.9815-2715(b), if applicable, to revoke its use of the accommodation process (to allow for the provision of notice to plan participants in cases where contraceptive benefits will no longer be provided). Alternatively, such eligible organization may revoke its use of the accommodation process effective on the first day of the first plan year that begins on or after 30 days after the date of the revocation.

(ii) *General rule.*—In plan years that begin after the date on which these final rules go into effect, if contraceptive coverage is being offered by an issuer or third party administrator through the accommodation process, an eligible organization's revocation of use of the accommodation process will be effective no sooner than the first day of the first plan year that begins on or after 30 days after the date of the revocation.

(b) *Optional accommodation—self-insured group health plans.*— (1) A group health plan established or maintained by an eligible organization that provides benefits on a self-insured basis may voluntarily elect an optional accommodation under which its third party administrator(s) will provide or arrange payments for all or a subset of contraceptive services for one or more plan years. To invoke the optional accommodation process:

(i) The eligible organization or its plan must contract with one or more third party administrators.

(ii) The eligible organization must provide either a copy of the self-certification to each third party administrator or a notice to the Secretary of the Department of Health and Human Services that it is an eligible organization and of its objection as described in 45 CFR 147.132 or 147.133 to coverage of all or a subset of contraceptive services.

(A) When a copy of the self-certification is provided directly to a third party administrator, such self-certification must include notice that obligations of the third party administrator are set forth in 29 CFR 2510.3-16 and this section.

(B) When a notice is provided to the Secretary of Health and Human Services, the notice must include the name of the eligible organization; a statement that it objects as described in 45 CFR 147.132 or 147.133 to coverage of some or all contraceptive services (including an identification of the subset of contraceptive services to which coverage the eligible organization objects, if applicable), but that it would like to elect the optional accommodation process; the plan name and type (that is, whether it is a student health insurance plan within the meaning of 45 CFR 147.145(a) or a church plan within the meaning of section 3(33) of ERISA); and the name and contact information for any of the plan's third party administrators. If there is a change in any of the information required to be included in the notice, the eligible organization must provide updated information to the Secretary of the Department of Health and Human Services for the optional accommodation process to remain in effect. The Department of Labor (working with the Department of Health and Human Services) will send a separate notification to each of the plan's third party administrators informing the third party administrator that the Secretary of the Department of Health and Human Services has received a notice under paragraph (b)(1)(ii) of this section and describing the obligations of the third party administrator under 29 CFR 2510.3-16 and this section.

(2) If a third party administrator receives a copy of the self-certification from an eligible organization or a notification from the Department of Labor, as described in paragraph (b)(1)(ii) of this section, and is willing to enter into or remain in a contractual relationship with the eligible organization or its plan to provide administrative services for the plan, then the third party administrator will provide or arrange payments for contraceptive services, using one of the following methods—

(i) Provide payments for the contraceptive services for plan participants and beneficiaries without imposing any cost-sharing requirements (such as a copayment, coinsurance, or a deductible), premium, fee, or other charge, or any portion thereof, directly or indirectly, on the eligible organization, the group health plan, or plan participants or beneficiaries; or

(ii) Arrange for an issuer or other entity to provide payments for the contraceptive services for plan participants and beneficiaries without imposing any cost-sharing requirements (such as a copayment, coinsurance, or a deductible), premium, fee, or other charge, or any portion thereof, directly or indirectly, on the eligible organization, the group health plan, or plan participants or beneficiaries.

(3) If a third party administrator provides or arranges payments for contraceptive services in accordance with either paragraph (b)(2)(i) or (ii) of this section, the costs of providing or arranging such payments may be reimbursed through an adjustment to the federally facilitated Exchange user fee for a participating issuer pursuant to 45 CFR 156.50(d).

(4) A third party administrator may not require any documentation other than a copy of the self-certification from the eligible organization or notification from the Department of Labor described in paragraph (b)(1)(ii) of this section.

(5) Where an otherwise eligible organization does not contract with a third party administrator and files a self-certification or notice under paragraph (b)(1)(ii) of this section, the obligations under paragraph (b)(2) of this section do not apply, and the otherwise eligible organization is under no requirement to provide coverage or payments for contraceptive services to which it objects. The plan administrator for that otherwise eligible organization may, if it and the otherwise eligible organization choose, arrange for payments for contraceptive services from an issuer or other entity in accordance with paragraph (b)(2)(ii) of this section, and such issuer or other entity may receive reimbursements in accordance with paragraph (b)(3) of this section.

(6) Where an otherwise eligible organization is an ERISA-exempt church plan within the meaning of section 3(33) of ERISA and it files a self-certification or notice under paragraph (b)(1)(ii) of this section, the obligations under paragraph (b)(2) of this section do not apply, and the otherwise eligible organization is under no requirement to provide coverage or payments for contraceptive services to which it objects. The third party administrator for that otherwise eligible organization may, if it and the otherwise eligible organization choose, provide or arrange payments for contraceptive services in accordance with paragraphs (b)(2)(i) or (ii) of this section, and receive reimbursements in accordance with paragraph (b)(3) of this section.

(c) *Optional accommodation—insured group health plans.*—(1) *General rule.*—A group health plan established or maintained by an eligible organization that provides benefits through one or more group health insurance issuers may voluntarily elect an optional accommodation under which its health insurance issuer(s) will pro-

vide payments for all or a subset of contraceptive services for one or more plan years. To invoke the optional accommodation process—

(i) The eligible organization or its plan must contract with one or more health insurance issuers.

(ii) The eligible organization must provide either a copy of the self-certification to each issuer providing coverage in connection with the plan or a notice to the Secretary of the Department of Health and Human Services that it is an eligible organization and of its objection as described in 45 CFR 147.132 or 147.133 to coverage for all or a subset of contraceptive services.

(A) When a self-certification is provided directly to an issuer, the issuer has sole responsibility for providing such coverage in accordance with § 54.9815-2713.

(B) When a notice is provided to the Secretary of the Department Health and Human Services, the notice must include the name of the eligible organization; a statement that it objects as described in 45 CFR 147.132 or 147.133 to coverage of some or all contraceptive services (including an identification of the subset of contraceptive services to which coverage the eligible organization objects, if applicable) but that it would like to elect the optional accommodation process; the plan name and type (that is, whether it is a student health insurance plan within the meaning of 45 CFR 147.145(a) or a church plan within the meaning of section 3(33) of ERISA); and the name and contact information for any of the plan's health insurance issuers. If there is a change in any of the information required to be included in the notice, the eligible organization must provide updated information to the Secretary of Department of Health and Human Services for the optional accommodation process to remain in effect. The Department of Health and Human Services will send a separate notification to each of the plan's health insurance issuers informing the issuer that the Secretary of the Department Health and Human Services has received a notice under paragraph (c)(2)(ii) of this section and describing the obligations of the issuer under this section.

(2) If an issuer receives a copy of the self-certification from an eligible organization or the notification from the Department of Health and Human Services as described in paragraph (c)(2)(ii) of this section and does not have its own objection as described in 45 CFR 147.132 or 147.133 to providing the contraceptive services to which the eligible organization objects, then the issuer will provide payments for contraceptive services as follows—

(i) The issuer must expressly exclude contraceptive coverage from the group health insurance coverage provided in connection with the group health plan and provide separate payments for any contraceptive services required to be covered under § 54.9815-2713(a)(1)(iv) for plan participants and beneficiaries for so long as they remain enrolled in the plan.

(ii) With respect to payments for contraceptive services, the issuer may not impose any cost-sharing requirements (such as a copayment, coinsurance, or a deductible), or impose any premium, fee, or other charge, or any portion thereof, directly or indirectly, on the eligible organization, the group health plan, or plan participants or beneficiaries. The issuer must segregate premium revenue collected from the eligible organization from the monies used to provide payments for contraceptive services. The issuer must provide payments for contraceptive services in a manner that is consistent with the requirements under sections 2706, 2709, 2711, 2713, 2719, and 2719A of the PHS Act, as incorporated into section 9815 of the PHS Act. If the group health plan of the eligible organization provides coverage for some but not all of any contraceptive services required to be covered under § 54.9815-2713(a)(1)(iv), the issuer is required to provide payments only for those contraceptive services for which the group health plan does not provide coverage. However, the issuer may provide payments for all contraceptive services, at the issuer's option.

(3) A health insurance issuer may not require any documentation other than a copy of the self-certification from the eligible organization or the notification from the Department of Health and Human Services described in paragraph (c)(1)(ii) of this section.

(d) *Notice of availability of separate payments for contraceptive services - self-insured and insured group health plans.*—For each plan year to which the optional accommodation in paragraph (b) or (c) of this section is to apply, a third party administrator required to provide or arrange payments for contraceptive services pursuant to paragraph (b) of this section, and an issuer required to provide payments for contraceptive services pursuant to paragraph (c) of this section, must provide to plan participants and beneficiaries written notice of the availability of separate payments for contraceptive services contemporaneous with (to the extent possible), but separate from, any application materials distributed in connection with enrollment (or re-enrollment) in group health coverage that is effective beginning on the first day of each applicable plan year. The notice must specify that the eligible organization does not administer or fund contraceptive benefits, but that the third party administrator or issuer, as applicable, provides or arranges separate payments for contraceptive services, and must provide contact information for questions and complaints. The following model language, or substantially similar language, may be used to satisfy the notice requirement of this paragraph (d): "Your employer has certified that your group health plan qualifies for an accommodation with respect to the federal requirement to cover all Food and Drug Administration-approved contraceptive services for women, as prescribed by a health care provider, without cost sharing. This means that your employer will not contract, arrange, pay, or refer for contraceptive coverage. Instead, [name of third party administrator/health insurance issuer] will provide or arrange separate payments for contraceptive services that you use, without cost sharing and at no other cost, for so long as you are enrolled in your group health plan. Your employer will not administer or fund these payments. If you have any questions about this notice, contact [contact information for third party administrator/health insurance issuer]."

(e) *Reliance—insured group health plans.*—(1) If an issuer relies reasonably and in good faith on a representation by the eligible organization as to its eligibility for the accommodation in paragraph (c) of this section, and the representation is later determined to be incorrect, the issuer is considered to comply with any applicable requirement under §54.9815-2713(a)(1)(iv) to provide contraceptive coverage if the issuer complies with the obligations under this section applicable to such issuer.

(2) A group health plan is considered to comply with any applicable requirement under §54.9815-2713(a)(1)(iv) to provide contraceptive coverage if the plan complies with its obligations under paragraph (c) of this section, without regard to whether the issuer complies with the obligations under this section applicable to such issuer.

(f) *Definition.*—For the purposes of this section, reference to "contraceptive" services, benefits, or coverage includes contraceptive or sterilization items, procedures, or services, or related patient education or counseling, to the extent specified for purposes of §54.9815-2713(a)(1)(iv).

(g) *Severability.*—Any provision of this section held to be invalid or unenforceable by its terms, or as applied to any person or circumstance, shall be construed so as to continue to give maximum effect to the provision permitted by law, unless such holding shall be one of utter invalidity or unenforceability, in which event the provision shall be severable from this section and shall not affect the remainder thereof or the application of the provision to persons not similarly situated or to dissimilar circumstances. [Reg. §54.9815-2713A.]

☐ [*T.D.* 9624, 6-28-2013. *Amended by T.D.* 9690, 8-22-2014, *T.D.* 9726, 7-10-2015, *T.D.* 9827, 10-6-2017, *T.D.* 9840, 11-7-2018 *and T.D.* 9841, 11-7-2018.]

**⫸→ Caution:** *Reg. §54.9815-2714, below, as added by T.D. 9744, is applicable to group health plans and health insurance issuers beginning on the first day of the plan year (or, in the individual market, the first day of the first policy year) beginning on or after January 1, 2017.*

### [Reg. §54.9815-2714]

**§54.9815-2714. Eligibility of children until at least age 26.**—(a) *In general.*—(1) A group health plan, or a health insurance issuer offering group health insurance coverage, that makes available dependent coverage of children must make such coverage available for children until attainment of 26 years of age.

(2) The rule of this paragraph (a) is illustrated by the following example:

*Example.* (i) *Facts* For the plan year beginning January 1, 2011, a group health plan provides health coverage for employees, employees' spouses, and employees' children until the child turns 26. On the birthday of a child of an employee, July 17, 2011, the child turns 26. The last day the plan covers the child is July 16, 2011.

(ii) *Conclusion* In this *Example*, the plan satisfies the requirement of this paragraph (a) with respect to the child.

(b) *Restrictions on plan definition of dependent.*—(1) *In general.*—With respect to a child who has not attained age 26, a plan or issuer may not define dependent for purposes of eligibility for dependent coverage of children other than in terms of a relationship between a child and the participant. Thus, for example, a plan or issuer may not deny or restrict dependent coverage for a child who has not attained age 26 based on the presence or absence of the child's financial dependency (upon the participant or any other person); residency with the participant or with any other person; whether the child lives, works, or resides in an HMO's service area or other network service area; marital status; student status; employment; eligibility for other coverage; or any combination of those factors. (Other requirements of Federal or State law, including section 609 of ERISA or section 1908 of the Social Security Act, may require coverage of certain children.)

(2) *Construction.*—A plan or issuer will not fail to satisfy the requirements of this section if the plan or issuer limits dependent child coverage to children under age 26 who are described in section 152(f)(1). For an individual not described in section 152(f)(1), such as a grandchild or niece, a plan may impose additional conditions on eligibility for dependent child health coverage, such as a condition that the individual be a dependent for income tax purposes.

(c) *Coverage of grandchildren not required.*—Nothing in this section requires a plan or issuer to make coverage available for the child of a child receiving dependent coverage.

(d) *Uniformity irrespective of age.*—The terms of the plan or health insurance coverage providing dependent coverage of children cannot vary based on age (except for children who are age 26 or older).

(e) *Examples.*—The rules of paragraph (d) of this section are illustrated by the following examples:

*Example 1.* (i) *Facts.* A group health plan offers a choice of self-only or family health coverage. Dependent coverage is provided under family health coverage for children of participants who have not attained age 26. The plan imposes an additional premium surcharge for children who are older than age 18.

(ii) *Conclusion.* In this *Example 1*, the plan violates the requirement of paragraph (d) of this section because the plan varies the terms for dependent coverage of children based on age.

*Example 2.* (i) *Facts.* A group health plan offers a choice among the following tiers of health coverage: self-only, self-plus-one, self-plus-two, and self-plus-three-or-more. The cost of coverage increases based on the number of covered individuals. The plan provides dependent coverage of children who have not attained age 26.

(ii) *Conclusion.* In this *Example 2*, the plan does not violate the requirement of paragraph (d) of this section that the terms of dependent coverage for children not vary based on age. Although the cost of coverage increases for tiers with more covered individuals, the increase applies without regard to the age of any child.

*Example 3.* (i) *Facts.* A group health plan offers two benefit packages — an HMO Option and an indemnity option. Dependent coverage is provided for children of participants who have not attained age 26. The plan limits children who are older than age 18 to the HMO option.

(ii) *Conclusion.* In this *Example 3*, the plan violates the requirement of paragraph (d) of this section because the plan, by limiting children who are older than age 18 to the HMO option, varies the terms for dependent coverage of children based on age.

Example 4. (i) *Facts.* A group health plan sponsored by a large employer normally charges a copayment for physician visits that do not constitute preventive services. The plan charges this copayment to individuals age 19 and over, including employees, spouses, and dependent children, but waives it for those under age 19.

(ii) *Conclusion.* In this *Example 4*, the plan does not violate the requirement of paragraph (d) of this section that the terms of dependent coverage for children not vary based on age. While the requirement of paragraph (d) of this section generally prohibits distinctions based upon age in dependent coverage of children, it does not prohibit distinctions based upon age that apply to all coverage under the plan, including coverage for employees and spouses as well as dependent children. In this *Example 4*, the copayments charged to dependent children are the same as those charged to employees and spouses. Accordingly, the arrangement described in this *Example 4* (including waiver, for individuals under age 19, of the generally applicable copayment) does not violate the requirement of paragraph (d) of this section.

(f) *Applicability date.*—The provisions of this section are applicable to group health plans and health insurance issuers for plan years beginning on or after January 1, 2017. Until the applicability date for this regulation, plans and issuers are required to continue to comply with the interim final regulations promulgated by the Department of Labor at 29 CFR part 2590, contained in the 29 CFR, parts 1927 to end, edition revised as of July 1, 2015. [Reg. §54.9815-2714.]

☐ [*T.D.* 9744, 11-13-2015.]

>>>→ *Caution: Temporary Reg. §54.9815-2714T, below, was removed by T.D. 9744 and is inapplicable under Code Sec. 7805(e)(2). However, until final Reg. §54.9815-2714 is applicable on the first day of the plan or policy year beginning after January 1, 2017, taxpayers may comply with the corresponding interim final regulation at 29 CFR part 2590 that is substantially similar to the temporary reg below.*

**[Reg. §54.9815-2714T]**

**§54.9815-2714T. Eligibility of children until at least age 26 (temporary).**—(a) *In general.*—(1) A group health plan, or a health insurance issuer offering group health insurance coverage, that makes available dependent coverage of children must make such coverage available for children until attainment of 26 years of age.

(2) The rule of this paragraph (a) is illustrated by the following example:

*Example.* (i) *Facts.* For the plan year beginning January 1, 2011, a group health plan provides health coverage for employees, employees' spouses, and employees' children until the child turns 26. On the birthday of a child of an employee, July 17, 2011, the child turns 26. The last day the plan covers the child is July 16, 2011.

(ii) *Conclusion.* In this *Example*, the plan satisfies the requirement of this paragraph (a) with respect to the child.

(b) *Restrictions on plan definition of dependent.*—With respect to a child who has not attained age 26, a plan or issuer may not define dependent for purposes of eligibility for dependent coverage of children other than in terms of a relationship between a child and the participant. Thus, for example, a plan or issuer may not deny or restrict coverage for a child who has not attained age 26 based on the presence or absence of the child's financial dependency (upon the participant or any other person), residency with the participant or with any other person, student status, employment, or any combination of those factors. In addition, a plan or issuer may not deny or restrict coverage of a child based on eligibility for other coverage, except that paragraph (g) of this section provides a special rule for plan years beginning before January 1, 2014 for grandfathered health plans that are group health plans. (Other requirements of Federal or State law, including section 609 of ERISA or section 1908 of the Social Security Act, may mandate coverage of certain children.)

(c) *Coverage of grandchildren not required.*—Nothing in this section requires a plan or issuer to make coverage available for the child of a child receiving dependent coverage.

(d) *Uniformity irrespective of age.*—The terms of the plan or health insurance coverage providing dependent coverage of children cannot vary based on age (except for children who are age 26 or older).

(e) *Examples.*—The rules of paragraph (d) of this section are illustrated by the following examples:

*Example 1.* (i) *Facts.* A group health plan offers a choice of self-only or family health coverage. Dependent coverage is provided under family health coverage for children of participants who have not attained age 26. The plan imposes an additional premium surcharge for children who are older than age 18.

(ii) *Conclusion.* In this *Example 1*, the plan violates the requirement of paragraph (d) of this section because the plan varies the terms for dependent coverage of children based on age.

*Example 2.* (i) *Facts.* A group health plan offers a choice among the following tiers of health coverage: self-only, self-plus-one, self-plus-two, and self-plus-three-or-more. The cost of coverage increases based on the number of covered individuals. The plan provides dependent coverage of children who have not attained age 26.

(ii) *Conclusion.* In this *Example 2*, the plan does not violate the requirement of paragraph (d) of this section that the terms of dependent coverage for children not vary based on age. Although the cost of coverage increases for tiers with more covered individuals, the increase applies without regard to the age of any child.

*Example 3.* (i) *Facts.* A group health plan offers two benefit packages — an HMO option and an indemnity option. Dependent coverage is provided for children of participants who have not attained age 26. The plan limits children who are older than age 18 to the HMO option.

(ii) *Conclusion.* In this *Example 3*, the plan violates the requirement of paragraph (d) of this section because the plan, by limiting children who are older than age 18 to the HMO option, varies the terms for dependent coverage of children based on age.

(f) *Transitional rules for individuals whose coverage ended by reason of reaching a dependent eligibility threshold.*—(1) *In general.*—The relief provided in the transitional rules of this paragraph (f) applies with respect to any child—

(i) Whose coverage ended, or who was denied coverage (or was not eligible for coverage) under a group health plan or group health insurance coverage because, under the terms of the plan or coverage, the availability of dependent coverage of children ended before the attainment of age 26 (which, under this section, is no longer permissible); and

(ii) Who becomes eligible (or is required to become eligible) for coverage under a group health plan or group health insurance coverage on the first day of the first plan year beginning on or after September 23, 2010 by reason of the application of this section.

(2) *Opportunity to enroll required.*—(i) If a group health plan, or group health insurance coverage, in which a child described in paragraph (f)(1) of this section is eligible to enroll (or is required to become eligible to enroll) is the plan or coverage in which the child's coverage ended (or did not begin) for the reasons described in paragraph (f)(1)(i) of this section, and if the plan, or the issuer of such coverage, is subject to the requirements of this section, the plan and the issuer are required to give the child an opportunity to enroll that continues for at least 30 days (including written notice of the opportunity to enroll). This opportunity (including the written notice) must be provided beginning not later than the first day of the first plan year beginning on or after September 23, 2010.

(ii) The written notice must include a statement that children whose coverage ended, or who were denied coverage (or were not eligible for coverage), because the availability of dependent coverage of children ended before attainment of age 26 are eligible to enroll in the plan or coverage. The notice may be provided to an employee on behalf of the employee's child. In addition, the notice may be included with other enrollment materials that a plan distributes to employees, provided the statement is prominent. If a notice satisfying the requirements of this paragraph (f)(2) is provided to an employee whose child is entitled to an enrollment opportunity under this paragraph (f), the obligation to provide the notice of enrollment opportunity under this paragraph (f)(2) with respect to that child is satisfied for both the plan and the issuer.

(3) *Effective date of coverage.*—In the case of an individual who enrolls under paragraph (f)(2) of this section, coverage must take effect not later than the first day of the first plan year beginning on or after September 23, 2010.

(4) *Treatment of enrollees in a group health plan.*—Any child enrolling in a group health plan pursuant to paragraph (f)(2) of this section must be treated as if the child were a special enrollee, as provided under the rules of §54.9801-6(d). Accordingly, the child (and, if the child would not be a participant once enrolled in the plan, the participant through whom the child is otherwise eligible for coverage under the plan) must be offered all the benefit packages available to similarly situated individuals who did not lose coverage by reason of cessation of dependent status. For this purpose, any difference in benefits or cost-sharing requirements constitutes a different benefit package. The child also cannot be required to pay more for coverage than similarly situated individuals who did not lose coverage by reason of cessation of dependent status.

(5) *Examples.*—The rules of this paragraph (f) are illustrated by the following examples:

*Example 1.* (i) *Facts.* Employer Y maintains a group health plan with a calendar year plan year. The plan has a single benefit package. For the 2010 plan year, the plan allows children of employees to be covered under the plan until age 19, or until age 23 for children who are full-time students. Individual B, an employee of Y, and Individual C, B's child and a full-time student, were enrolled in Y's group health plan at the beginning of the 2010 plan year. On June 10, 2010, C turns 23 years old and loses dependent coverage under Y's plan. On or before January 1, 2011, Y's group health plan gives B written notice that individuals who lost coverage by reason of ceasing to be a dependent before attainment of age 26 are eligible to enroll in the plan, and that individuals may request enrollment for such children through February 14, 2011 with enrollment effective retroactively to January 1, 2011.

(ii) *Conclusion.* In this *Example 1*, the plan has complied with the requirements of this paragraph (f) by providing an enrollment opportunity to C that lasts at least 30 days.

*Example 2.* (i) *Facts.* Employer Z maintains a group health plan with a plan year beginning October 1 and ending September 30. Prior to October 1, 2010, the group health plan allows children of employees to be covered under the plan until age 22. Individual D, an employee of Z, and Individual E, D's child, are enrolled in family coverage under Z's group health plan for the plan year beginning on October 1, 2008. On May 1, 2009, E turns 22 years old and ceases to be eligible as a dependent under Z's plan and loses coverage. D drops coverage but remains an employee of Z.

(ii) *Conclusion.* In this *Example 2*, not later than October 1, 2010, the plan must provide D and E an opportunity to enroll (including written notice of an opportunity to enroll) that continues for at least 30 days, with enrollment effective not later than October 1, 2010.

⟫→ *Caution: Temporary Reg. §54.9815-2714T, below, was removed by T.D. 9744 and is inapplicable under Code Sec. 7805(e)(2). However, until final Reg. §54.9815-2714 is applicable on the first day of the plan or policy year beginning after January 1, 2017, taxpayers may comply with the corresponding interim final regulation at 29 CFR part 2590 that is substantially similar to the temporary reg below.*

*Example 3.* (i) *Facts.* Same facts as *Example 2*, except that D did not drop coverage. Instead, D switched to a lower-cost benefit package option.

(ii) *Conclusion.* In this *Example 3*, not later than October 1, 2010, the plan must provide D and E an opportunity to enroll in any benefit package available to similarly situated individuals who enroll when first eligible.

*Example 4.* (i) *Facts.* Same facts as *Example 2*, except that E elected COBRA continuation coverage.

(ii) *Conclusion.* In this *Example 4*, not later than October 1, 2010, the plan must provide D and E an opportunity to enroll other than as a COBRA qualified beneficiary (and must provide, by that date, written notice of the opportunity to enroll) that continues for at least 30 days, with enrollment effective not later than October 1, 2010.

*Example 5.* (i) *Facts.* Employer X maintains a group health plan with a calendar year plan year. Prior to 2011, the plan allows children of employees to be covered under the plan until the child attains age 22. During the 2009 plan year, an individual with a 22-year old child joins the plan; the child is denied coverage because the child is 22.

(ii) *Conclusion.* In this *Example 5*, notwithstanding that the child was not previously covered under the plan, the plan must provide the child, not later than January 1, 2011, an opportunity to enroll (including written notice to the employee of an opportunity to enroll the child) that continues for at least 30 days, with enrollment effective not later than January 1, 2011.

(g) *Special rule for grandfathered group health plans.*—(1) For plan years beginning before January 1, 2014, a group health plan that qualifies as a grandfathered health plan under section 1251 of the Patient Protection and Affordable Care Act and that makes available dependent coverage of children may exclude an adult child who has not attained age 26 from coverage only if the adult child is eligible to enroll in an eligible employer-sponsored health plan (as defined in section 5000A(f)(2)) other than a group health plan of a parent.

(2) For plan years beginning on or after January 1, 2014, a group health plan that qualifies as a grandfathered health plan under section 1251 of the Patient Protection and Affordable Care Act must comply with the requirements of paragraphs (a) through (f) of this section.

(h) *Applicability date.*—The provisions of this section apply for plan years beginning on or after September 23, 2010. *See* §54.9815-1251T for determining the application of this section to grandfathered health plans.

(i) *Expiration date.*—This section expires on or before May 10, 2013. [Temporary Reg. §54.9815-2714T.]

☐ [T.D. 9482, 5-10-2010. *Amended by T.D. 9489, 6-14-2010. Removed by T.D. 9744, 11-13-2015.*]

**[Reg. §54.9815-2715]**

**§54.9815-2715. Summary of benefits and coverage and uniform glossary.**—(a) *Summary of benefits and coverage.*—(1) *In general.*—A group health plan (and its administrator as defined in section 3(16)(A) of ERISA)), and a health insurance issuer offering group health insurance coverage, is required to provide a written summary of benefits and coverage (SBC) for each benefit package without charge to entities and individuals described in this paragraph (a)(1) in accordance with the rules of this section.

(i) *SBC provided by a group health insurance issuer to a group health plan.*—(A) *Upon application.*—A health insurance issuer offering group health insurance coverage must provide the SBC to a group health plan (or its sponsor) upon application for health coverage, as soon as practicable following receipt of the application, but in no event later than seven business days following receipt of the application. If an SBC was provided before application pursuant to paragraph (a)(1)(i)(D) of this section (relating to SBCs upon request), this paragraph (a)(1)(i)(A) is deemed satisfied, provided there is no change to the information required to be in the SBC. However, if there has been a change in the information required, a new SBC that includes the changed information must be provided upon application pursuant to this paragraph (a)(1)(i)(A).

(B) *By first day of coverage (if there are changes).*—If there is any change in the information required to be in the SBC that was provided upon application and before the first day of coverage, the issuer must update and provide a current SBC to the plan (or its sponsor) no later than the first day of coverage.

(C) *Upon renewal, reissuance, or reenrollment.*—If the issuer renews or reissues a policy, certificate, or contract of insurance for a succeeding policy year, or automatically re-enrolls the policyholder or its participants and beneficiaries in coverage, the issuer must provide a new SBC as follows:

(1) If written application is required (in either paper or electronic form) for renewal or reissuance, the SBC must be provided no later than the date the written application materials are distributed.

(2) If renewal, reissuance, or reenrollment is automatic, the SBC must be provided no later than 30 days prior to the first day of the new plan or policy year; however, with respect to an insured plan, if the policy, certificate, or contract of insurance has not been issued or renewed before such 30-day period, the SBC must be provided as soon as practicable but in no event later than seven business days after issuance of the new policy, certificate, or contract of insurance, or the receipt of written confirmation of intent to renew, whichever is earlier.

(D) *Upon request.*—If a group health plan (or its sponsor) requests an SBC or summary information about a health insurance product from a health insurance issuer offering group health insurance coverage, an SBC must be provided as soon as practicable, but in no event later than seven business days following receipt of the request.

(ii) *SBC provided by a group health insurance issuer and a group health plan to participants and beneficiaries.*—(A) *In general.*—A group health plan (including its administrator, as defined under section 3(16) of ERISA), and a health insurance issuer offering group health insurance coverage, must provide an SBC to a participant or beneficiary (as defined under sections 3(7) and 3(8) of ERISA), and consistent with the rules of paragraph (a)(1)(iii) of this section, with respect to each benefit package offered by the plan or issuer for which the participant or beneficiary is eligible.

(B) *Upon application.*—The SBC must be provided as part of any written application materials that are distributed by the plan or issuer for enrollment. If the plan or issuer does not distribute written application materials for enrollment, the SBC must be provided no later than the first date on which the participant is eligible to enroll in coverage for the participant or any beneficiaries. If an SBC was provided before application pursuant to paragraph (a)(1)(ii)(F) of this section (relating to SBCs upon request), this paragraph (a)(1)(ii)(B) is deemed satisfied, provided there is no change to the information required to be in the SBC. However, if there has been a change in the information that is required to be in the SBC, a new SBC that includes the changed information must be provided upon application pursuant to this paragraph (a)(1)(ii)(B).

(C) *By first day of coverage (if there are changes).*—(1) If there is any change to the information required to be in the SBC that was provided upon application and before the first day of coverage, the plan or issuer must update and provide a current SBC to a participant or beneficiary no later than the first day of coverage.

(2) If the plan sponsor is negotiating coverage terms after an application has been filed and the information required to be in the SBC changes, the plan or issuer is not required to provide an updated SBC (unless an updated SBC is requested) until the first day of coverage.

(D) *Special enrollees.*—The plan or issuer must provide the SBC to special enrollees (as described in §54.9801-6) no later than the date by which a summary plan description is required to be provided under the timeframe set forth in ERISA section 104(b)(1)(A) and its implementing regulations, which is 90 days from enrollment.

(E) *Upon renewal, reissuance, or reenrollment.*—If the plan or issuer requires participants or beneficiaries to renew in order to maintain coverage (for example, for a succeeding plan year), or automatically re-enrolls participants and beneficiaries in coverage, the plan or issuer must provide a new SBC, as follows:

(1) If written application is required for renewal, reissuance, or reenrollment (in either paper or electronic form), the SBC must be provided no later than the date on which the written application materials are distributed.

(2) If renewal, reissuance, or reenrollment is automatic, the SBC must be provided no later than 30 days prior to the first day of the new plan or policy year; however, with respect to an insured plan, if the policy, certificate, or contract of insurance has not been issued or renewed before such 30-day period, the SBC must be provided as soon as practicable but in no event later than seven business days after issuance of the new policy, certificate, or contract of insurance, or the receipt of written confirmation of intent to renew, whichever is earlier.

(F) *Upon request.*—A plan or issuer must provide the SBC to participants or beneficiaries upon request for an SBC or summary information about the health coverage, as soon as practicable, but in no event later than seven business days following receipt of the request.

(iii) *Special rules to prevent unnecessary duplication with respect to group health coverage.*—(A) An entity required to provide an SBC under this paragraph (a)(1) with respect to an individual satisfies that requirement if another party provides the SBC, but only to the extent that the SBC is timely and complete in accordance with the other rules of this section. Therefore, for example, in the case of a group health plan funded through an insurance policy, the plan satisfies the requirement to provide an SBC with respect to an individual if the issuer provides a timely and complete SBC to the individual. An entity required to provide an SBC under this paragraph (a)(1) with respect to an individual that contracts with another party to provide such SBC is considered to satisfy the requirement to provide such SBC if:

(1) The entity monitors performance under the contract;

(2) If the entity has knowledge that the SBC is not being provided in a manner that satisfies the requirements of this section and the entity has all information necessary to correct the noncompliance, the entity corrects the noncompliance as soon as practicable; and

(3) If the entity has knowledge the SBC is not being provided in a manner that satisfies the requirements of this section and the entity does not have all information necessary to correct the noncompliance, the entity communicates with participants and beneficiaries who are affected by the noncompliance regarding the noncompliance, and begins taking significant steps as soon as practicable to avoid future violations.

(B) If a single SBC is provided to a participant and any beneficiaries at the participant's last known address, then the requirement to provide the SBC to the participant and any beneficiaries is generally satisfied. However, if a beneficiary's last known address is different than the participant's last known address, a separate SBC is required to be provided to the beneficiary at the beneficiary's last known address.

(C) With respect to a group health plan that offers multiple benefit packages, the plan or issuer is required to provide a new SBC automatically to participants and beneficiaries upon renewal or reenrollment only with respect to the benefit package in which a participant or beneficiary is enrolled (or will be automatically re-enrolled under the plan); SBCs are not required to be provided automatically upon renewal or reenrollment with respect to benefit packages in which the participant or beneficiary is not enrolled (or will not automatically be enrolled). However, if a participant or beneficiary requests an SBC with respect to another benefit package (or more than one other benefit package) for which the participant or beneficiary is eligible, the SBC (or SBCs, in the case of a request for SBCs relating to more than one benefit package) must be provided upon request as soon as practicable, but in no event later than seven business days following receipt of the request.

(D) Subject to paragraph (a)(2)(ii) of this section, a plan administrator of a group health plan that uses two or more insurance products provided by separate health insurance issuers with respect to a single group health plan may synthesize the information into a single SBC or provide multiple partial SBCs provided that all the SBC include the content in paragraph (a)(2)(iii) of this section.

(2) *Content.*—(i) *In general.*—Subject to paragraph (a)(2)(iii) of this section, the SBC must include the following:

(A) Uniform definitions of standard insurance terms and medical terms so that consumers may compare health coverage and understand the terms of (or exceptions to) their coverage, in accordance with guidance as specified by the Secretary;

(B) A description of the coverage, including cost sharing, for each category of benefits identified by the Secretary in guidance;

(C) The exceptions, reductions, and limitations of the coverage;

(D) The cost-sharing provisions of the coverage, including deductible, coinsurance, and copayment obligations;

(E) The renewability and continuation of coverage provisions;

(F) Coverage examples, in accordance with the rules of paragraph (a)(2)(ii) of this section;

(G) With respect to coverage beginning on or after January 1, 2014, a statement about whether the plan or coverage provides minimum essential coverage as defined under section 5000A(f) and whether the plan's or coverage's share of the total allowed costs of benefits provided under the plan or coverage meets applicable requirements;

(H) A statement that the SBC is only a summary and that the plan document, policy, certificate, or contract of insurance should be consulted to determine the governing contractual provisions of the coverage;

(I) Contact information for questions;

(J) For issuers, an Internet web address where a copy of the actual individual coverage policy or group certificate of coverage can be reviewed and obtained;

(K) For plans and issuers that maintain one or more networks of providers, an Internet address (or similar contact information) for obtaining a list of network providers;

(L) For plans and issuers that use a formulary in providing prescription drug coverage, an Internet address (or similar contact information) for obtaining information on prescription drug coverage; and

(M) An Internet address for obtaining the uniform glossary, as described in paragraph (c) of this section, as well as a contact phone number to obtain a paper copy of the uniform glossary, and a disclosure that paper copies are available.

(ii) *Coverage examples.*—The SBC must include coverage examples specified by the Secretary in guidance that illustrate benefits provided under the plan or coverage for common benefits scenarios (including pregnancy and serious or chronic medical conditions) in accordance with this paragraph (a)(2)(ii).

(A) *Number of examples.*—The Secretary may identify up to six coverage examples that may be required in an SBC.

(B) *Benefits scenarios.*—For purposes of this paragraph (a)(2)(ii), a benefits scenario is a hypothetical situation, consisting of a sample treatment plan for a specified medical condition during a specific period of time, based on recognized clinical practice guidelines as defined by the National Guideline Clearinghouse, Agency for Healthcare Research and Quality. The Secretary will specify, in guidance, the assumptions, including the relevant items and services and reimbursement information, for each claim in the benefits scenario.

(C) *Illustration of benefit provided.*—For purposes of this paragraph (a)(2)(ii), to illustrate benefits provided under the plan or coverage for a particular benefits scenario, a plan or issuer simulates claims processing in accordance with guidance issued by the Secretary to generate an estimate of what an individual might expect to pay under the plan, policy, or benefit package. The illustration of benefits provided will take into account any cost sharing, excluded benefits, and other limitations on coverage, as specified by the Secretary in guidance.

(iii) *Coverage provided outside the United States.*—In lieu of summarizing coverage for items and services provided outside the United States, a plan or issuer may provide an Internet address (or similar contact information) for obtaining information about benefits and coverage provided outside the United States. In any case, the plan or issuer must provide an SBC in accordance with this section that accurately summarizes benefits and coverage available under the plan or coverage within the United States.

(3) *Appearance.*—(i) A group health plan and a health insurance issuer must provide an SBC in the form, and in accordance with the instructions for completing the SBC, that are specified by the Secretary in guidance. The SBC must be presented in a uniform format, use terminology understandable by the average plan enrollee, not exceed four double-sided pages in length, and not include print smaller than 12-point font.

(ii) A group health plan that utilizes two or more benefit packages (such as major medical coverage and a health flexible spending arrangement) may synthesize the information into a single SBC, or provide multiple SBCs.

(4) *Form.*—(i) An SBC provided by an issuer offering group health insurance coverage to a plan (or its sponsor), may be provided in paper form. Alternatively, the SBC may be provided electronically (such as by email or an Internet posting) if the following three conditions are satisfied—

(A) The format is readily accessible by the plan (or its sponsor);

(B) The SBC is provided in paper form free of charge upon request; and

(C) If the electronic form is an Internet posting, the issuer timely advises the plan (or its sponsor) in paper form or email that the documents are available on the Internet and provides the Internet address.

(ii) An SBC provided by a group health plan or health insurance issuer to a participant or beneficiary may be provided in paper form. Alternatively, the SBC may be provided electronically (such as by email or an Internet posting) if the requirements of this paragraph (a)(4)(ii) are met.

**Reg. §54.9815-2715(a)(4)(ii)**

(A) With respect to participants and beneficiaries covered under the plan or coverage, the SBC may be provided electronically as described in this paragraph (a)(4)(ii)(A). However, in all cases, the plan or issuer must provide the SBC in paper form if paper form is requested.

(1) In accordance with the Department of Labor's disclosure regulations at 29 CFR 2520.104b-1;

(2) In connection with online enrollment or online renewal of coverage under the plan; or

(3) In response to an online request made by a participant or beneficiary for the SBC.

(B) With respect to participants and beneficiaries who are eligible but not enrolled for coverage, the SBC may be provided electronically if:

(1) The format is readily accessible;

(2) The SBC is provided in paper form free of charge upon request; and

(3) In a case in which the electronic form is an Internet posting, the plan or issuer timely notifies the individual in paper form (such as a postcard) or email that the documents are available on the Internet, provides the Internet address, and notifies the individual that the documents are available in paper form upon request.

(5) *Language.*—A group health plan or health insurance issuer must provide the SBC in a culturally and linguistically appropriate manner. For purposes of this paragraph (a)(5), a plan or issuer is considered to provide the SBC in a culturally and linguistically appropriate manner if the thresholds and standards of 29 CFR 2590.715-2719(e) are met as applied to the SBC.

(b) *Notice of modification.*—If a group health plan, or health insurance issuer offering group health insurance coverage, makes any material modification (as defined under section 102 of ERISA) in any of the terms of the plan or coverage that would affect the content of the SBC, that is not reflected in the most recently provided SBC, and that occurs other than in connection with a renewal or reissuance of coverage, the plan or issuer must provide notice of the modification to enrollees not later than 60 days prior to the date on which the modification will become effective. The notice of modification must be provided in a form that is consistent with the rules of paragraph (a)(4) of this section.

(c) *Uniform glossary.*—(1) *In general.*—A group health plan, and a health insurance issuer offering group health insurance coverage, must make available to participants and beneficiaries the uniform glossary described in paragraph (c)(2) of this section in accordance with the appearance and form and manner requirements of paragraphs (c)(3) and (4) of this section.

(2) *Health-coverage-related terms and medical terms.*—The uniform glossary must provide uniform definitions, specified by the Secretary in guidance, of the following health-coverage-related terms and medical terms:

(i) Allowed amount, appeal, balance billing, co-insurance, complications of pregnancy, co-payment, deductible, durable medical equipment, emergency medical condition, emergency medical transportation, emergency room care, emergency services, excluded services, grievance, habilitation services, health insurance, home health care, hospice services, hospitalization, hospital outpatient care, in-network co-insurance, in-network co-payment, medically necessary, network, non-preferred provider, out-of-network co-insurance, out-of-network co-payment, out-of-pocket limit, physician services, plan, preauthorization, preferred provider, premium, prescription drug coverage, prescription drugs, primary care physician, primary care provider, provider, reconstructive surgery, rehabilitation services, skilled nursing care, specialist, usual customary and reasonable (UCR), and urgent care; and

(ii) Such other terms as the Secretary determines are important to define so that individuals and employers may compare and understand the terms of coverage and medical benefits (including any exceptions to those benefits), as specified in guidance.

(3) *Appearance.*—A group health plan, and a health insurance issuer, must provide the uniform glossary with the appearance specified by the Secretary in guidance to ensure the uniform glossary is presented in a uniform format and uses terminology understandable by the average plan enrollee.

(4) *Form and manner.*—A plan or issuer must make the uniform glossary described in this paragraph (c) available upon request, in either paper or electronic form (as requested), within seven business days after receipt of the request.

(d) *Preemption.*—State laws that conflict with this section (including a state law that requires a health insurance issuer to provide an SBC that supplies less information than required under paragraph (a) of this section) are preempted.

(e) *Failure to provide.*—A group health plan that willfully fails to provide information required under this section to a participant or beneficiary is subject to a fine of not more than $1,000 for each such failure. A failure with respect to each participant or beneficiary constitutes a separate offense for purposes of this paragraph (e). The Department will enforce this section using a process and procedure consistent with section 4980D of the Code.

(f) *Applicability to Medicare Advantage benefits.*—The requirements of this section do not apply to a group health plan benefit package that provides Medicare Advantage benefits pursuant to or 42 U.S.C. Chapter 7, Subchapter XVIII, Part C.

(g) *Applicability date.*—(1) This section is applicable to group health plans and group health insurance issuers in accordance with this paragraph (g). (See 29 CFR 2590.715-1251(d), providing that this section applies to grandfathered health plans.)

(i) For disclosures with respect to participants and beneficiaries who enroll or re-enroll through an open enrollment period (including re-enrollees and late enrollees), this section applies beginning on the first day of the first open enrollment period that begins on or after September 1, 2015; and

(ii) For disclosures with respect to participants and beneficiaries who enroll in coverage other than through an open enrollment period (including individuals who are newly eligible for coverage and special enrollees), this section applies beginning on the first day of the first plan year that begins on or after September 1, 2015.

(2) For disclosures with respect to plans, this section is applicable to health insurance issuers beginning September 1, 2015. [Reg. § 54.9815-2715.]

☐ [*T.D. 9575, 2-9-2012. Amended by T.D. 9724, 6-12-2015.*]

### [Reg. § 54.9815-2715A1]

**§ 54.9815-2715A1. Transparency in coverage - definitions.**— (a) *Scope and definitions.*—(1) *Scope.*—This section sets forth definitions for the price transparency requirements for group health plans and health insurance issuers offering group health insurance coverage established in this section and §§ 54.9815-2715A2 and 54.9815-2715A3.

(2) *Definitions.*—For purposes of this section and §§ 54.9815-2715A2 and 54.9815-2715A3, the following definitions apply:

(i) *Accumulated amounts* means:

(A) The amount of financial responsibility a participant or beneficiary has incurred at the time a request for cost-sharing information is made, with respect to a deductible or out-of-pocket limit. If an individual is enrolled in other than self-only coverage, these accumulated amounts shall include the financial responsibility a participant or beneficiary has incurred toward meeting his or her individual deductible or out-of-pocket limit, as well as the amount of financial responsibility that all the individuals enrolled under the plan or coverage have incurred, in aggregate, toward meeting the other than self-only deductible or out-of-pocket limit, as applicable. Accumulated amounts include any expense that counts toward a deductible or out-of-pocket limit (such as a copayment or coinsurance), but exclude any expense that does not count toward a deductible or out-of-pocket limit (such as any premium payment, out-of-pocket expense for out-of-network services, or amount for items or services not covered under the group health plan or health insurance coverage); and

(B) To the extent a group health plan or health insurance issuer imposes a cumulative treatment limitation on a particular covered item or service (such as a limit on the number of items, days, units, visits, or hours covered in a defined time period) independent of individual medical necessity determinations, the amount that has accrued toward the limit on the item or service (such as the number of items, days, units, visits, or hours the participant or beneficiary, has used within that time period).

(ii) *Beneficiary* has the meaning given the term under section 3(8) of the Employee Retirement Income Security Act of 1974 (ERISA).

(iii) *Billed charge* means the total charges for an item or service billed to a group health plan or health insurance issuer by a provider.

(iv) *Billing code* means the code used by a group health plan or health insurance issuer or provider to identify health care items or services for purposes of billing, adjudicating, and paying claims for a covered item or service, including the Current Procedural Terminology (CPT) code, Healthcare Common Procedure Coding System (HCPCS) code, Diagnosis-Related Group (DRG) code, National Drug Code (NDC), or other common payer identifier.

(v) *Bundled payment arrangement* means a payment model under which a provider is paid a single payment for all covered items and services provided to a participant or beneficiary for a specific treatment or procedure.

(vi) *Copayment assistance* means the financial assistance a participant or beneficiary receives from a prescription drug or medical supply manufacturer towards the purchase of a covered item or service.

(vii) *Cost-sharing liability* means the amount a participant or beneficiary is responsible for paying for a covered item or service under the terms of the group health plan or health insurance coverage. Cost-sharing liability generally includes deductibles, coinsurance, and copayments, but does not include premiums, balance billing amounts by out-of-network providers, or the cost of items or services that are not covered under a group health plan or health insurance coverage.

(viii) *Cost-sharing information* means information related to any expenditure required by or on behalf of a participant or beneficiary with respect to health care benefits that are relevant to a determination of the participant's or beneficiary's cost-sharing liability for a particular covered item or service.

(ix) *Covered items or services* means those items or services, including prescription drugs, the costs for which are payable, in whole or in part, under the terms of a group health plan or health insurance coverage.

(x) *Derived amount* means the price that a group health plan or health insurance issuer assigns to an item or service for the purpose of internal accounting, reconciliation with providers, or submitting data in accordance with the requirements of 45 CFR 153.710(c).

(xi) *Historical net price* means the retrospective average amount a group health plan or health insurance issuer paid for a prescription drug, inclusive of any reasonably allocated rebates, discounts, chargebacks, fees, and any additional price concessions received by the plan or issuer with respect to the prescription drug. The allocation shall be determined by dollar value for non-product specific and product-specific rebates, discounts, chargebacks, fees, and other price concessions to the extent that the total amount of any such price concession is known to the group health plan or health insurance issuer at the time of publication of the historical net price in a machine-readable file in accordance with § 54.9815-2715A3. However, to the extent that the total amount of any non-product specific and product-specific rebates, discounts, chargebacks, fees, or other price concessions is not known to the group health plan or health insurance issuer at the time of file publication, then the plan or issuer shall allocate such rebates, discounts, chargebacks, fees, and other price concessions by using a good faith, reasonable estimate of the average price concessions based on the rebates, discounts, chargebacks, fees, and other price concessions received over a time period prior to the current reporting period and of equal duration to the current reporting period, as determined under § 54.9815-2715A3(b)(1)(iii)(D)(3).

(xii) *In-network provider* means any provider of any item or service with which a group health plan or health insurance issuer, or a third party for the plan or issuer, has a contract setting forth the terms and conditions on which a relevant item or service is provided to a participant or beneficiary.

(xiii) *Items or services* means all encounters, procedures, medical tests, supplies, prescription drugs, durable medical equipment, and fees (including facility fees), provided or assessed in connection with the provision of health care.

(xiv) *Machine-readable file* means a digital representation of data or information in a file that can be imported or read by a computer system for further processing without human intervention, while ensuring no semantic meaning is lost.

(xv) *National Drug Code* means the unique 10- or 11-digit 3-segment number assigned by the Food and Drug Administration, which provides a universal product identifier for drugs in the United States.

(xvi) *Negotiated rate* means the amount a group health plan or health insurance issuer has contractually agreed to pay an in-network provider, including an in-network pharmacy or other prescription drug dispenser, for covered items and services, whether directly or indirectly, including through a third-party administrator or pharmacy benefit manager.

(xvii) *Out-of-network allowed amount* means the maximum amount a group health plan or health insurance issuer will pay for a covered item or service furnished by an out-of-network provider.

(xviii) *Out-of-network provider* means a provider of any item or service that does not have a contract under a participant's or beneficiary's group health plan or health insurance coverage to provide items or services.

(xix) *Out-of-pocket limit* means the maximum amount that a participant or beneficiary is required to pay during a coverage period for his or her share of the costs of covered items and services under his or her group health plan or health insurance coverage, including for self-only and other than self-only coverage, as applicable.

(xx) *Plain language* means written and presented in a manner calculated to be understood by the average participant or beneficiary.

(xxi) *Prerequisite* means concurrent review, prior authorization, and step-therapy or fail-first protocols related to covered items and services that must be satisfied before a group health plan or health insurance issuer will cover the item or service. The term prerequisite does not include medical necessity determinations generally or other forms of medical management techniques.

(xxii) *Underlying fee schedule rate* means the rate for a covered item or service from a particular in-network provider, or providers that a group health plan or health insurance issuer uses to determine a participant's or beneficiary's cost-sharing liability for the item or service, when that rate is different from the negotiated rate or derived amount.

(b) [Reserved] [Reg. § 54.9815-2715A1.]

☐ [*T.D.* 9929, 11-3-2020.]

### [Reg. § 54.9815-2715A2]

**§ 54.9815-2715A2. Transparency in coverage - required disclosures to participants and beneficiaries.**—(a) *Scope and definitions.*—(1) *Scope.*—This section establishes price transparency requirements for group health plans and health insurance issuers offering group health insurance coverage for the timely disclosure of information about costs related to covered items and services under a group plan or health insurance coverage.

(2) *Definitions.*—For purposes of this section, the definitions in § 54.9815-2715A1 apply.

(b) *Required disclosures to participants and beneficiaries.*—At the request of a participant or beneficiary who is enrolled in a group health plan, the plan must provide to the participant or beneficiary the information required under paragraph (b)(1) of this section, in accordance with the method and format requirements set forth in paragraph (b)(2) of this section.

(1) *Required cost-sharing information.*—The information required under this paragraph (b)(1) is the following cost-sharing information, which is accurate at the time the request is made, with respect to a participant's or beneficiary's cost-sharing liability for covered items and services:

(i) An estimate of the participant's or beneficiary's cost-sharing liability for a requested covered item or service furnished by a provider or providers that is calculated based on the information described in paragraphs (b)(1)(ii) through (iv) of this section.

(A) If the request for cost-sharing information relates to items and services that are provided within a bundled payment arrangement, and the bundled payment arrangement includes items or services that have a separate cost-sharing liability, the group health plan or health insurance issuer must provide estimates of the cost-sharing liability for the requested covered item or service, as well as an estimate of the cost-sharing liability for each of the items and services in the bundled payment arrangement that have separate cost-sharing liabilities. While group health plans and health insurance issuers are not required to provide estimates of cost-sharing liability for a bundled payment arrangement where the cost-sharing is imposed separately for each item and service included in the bundled payment arrangement, nothing prohibits plans or issuers from providing estimates for multiple items and services in situations where such estimates could be relevant to participants or beneficiaries, as long as the plan or issuer also discloses information about the relevant items or services individually, as required in paragraph (b)(1)(v) of this section.

(B) For requested items and services that are recommended preventive services under section 2713 of the Public Health Service Act (PHS Act), if the group health plan or health insurance issuer cannot determine whether the request is for preventive or non-preventive purposes, the plan or issuer must display the cost-sharing liability that applies for non-preventive purposes. As an alternative, a group health plan or health insurance issuer may allow a participant or beneficiary to request cost-sharing information for the specific preventive or non-preventive item or service by including terms such as "preventive", "non-preventive" or "diagnostic" as a means to request the most accurate cost-sharing information.

(ii) Accumulated amounts.

(iii) In-network rate, comprised of the following elements, as applicable to the group health plan's or health insurance issuer's payment model:

(A) Negotiated rate, reflected as a dollar amount, for an in-network provider or providers for the requested covered item or service; this rate must be disclosed even if it is not the rate the plan or issuer uses to calculate cost-sharing liability; and

(B) Underlying fee schedule rate, reflected as a dollar amount, for the requested covered item or service, to the extent that it is different from the negotiated rate.

(iv) Out-of-network allowed amount or any other rate that provides a more accurate estimate of an amount a group health plan or health insurance issuer will pay for the requested covered item or service, reflected as a dollar amount, if the request for cost-sharing information is for a covered item or service furnished by an out-of-network provider; provided, however, that in circumstances in which a plan or issuer reimburses an out-of-network provider a percentage of the billed charge for a covered item or service, the out-of-network allowed amount will be that percentage.

(v) If a participant or beneficiary requests information for an item or service subject to a bundled payment arrangement, a list of the items and services included in the bundled payment arrangement for which cost-sharing information is being disclosed.

(vi) If applicable, notification that coverage of a specific item or service is subject to a prerequisite.

(vii) A notice that includes the following information in plain language:

(A) A statement that out-of-network providers may bill participants or beneficiaries for the difference between a provider's billed charges and the sum of the amount collected from the group health plan or health insurance issuer and from the participant or beneficiary in the form of a copayment or coinsurance amount (the difference referred to as balance billing), and that the cost-sharing information provided pursuant to this paragraph (b)(1) does not account for these potential additional amounts. This statement is only required if balance billing is permitted under state law;

(B) A statement that the actual charges for a participant's or beneficiary's covered item or service may be different from an estimate of cost-sharing liability provided pursuant to paragraph (b)(1)(i) of this section, depending on the actual items or services the participant or beneficiary receives at the point of care;

(C) A statement that the estimate of cost-sharing liability for a covered item or service is not a guarantee that benefits will be provided for that item or service;

(D) A statement disclosing whether the plan counts copayment assistance and other third-party payments in the calculation of the participant's or beneficiary's deductible and out-of-pocket maximum;

(E) For items and services that are recommended preventive services under section 2713 of the PHS Act, a statement that an in-network item or service may not be subject to cost-sharing if it is billed as a preventive service if the group health plan or health insurance issuer cannot determine whether the request is for a preventive or non-preventive item or service; and

(F) Any additional information, including other disclaimers, that the group health plan or health insurance issuer determines is appropriate, provided the additional information does not conflict with the information required to be provided by this paragraph (b)(1).

(2) *Required methods and formats for disclosing information to participants and beneficiaries.*—The methods and formats for the disclosure required under this paragraph (b) are as follows:

(i) *Internet-based self-service tool.*—Information provided under this paragraph (b) must be made available in plain language, without subscription or other fee, through a self-service tool on an internet website that provides real-time responses based on cost-sharing information that is accurate at the time of the request. Group health plans and health insurance issuers must ensure that the self-service tool allows users to:

(A) Search for cost-sharing information for a covered item or service provided by a specific in-network provider or by all in-network providers by inputting:

(1) A billing code (such as CPT code 87804) or a descriptive term (such as "rapid flu test"), at the option of the user;

(2) The name of the in-network provider, if the user seeks cost-sharing information with respect to a specific in-network provider; and

(3) Other factors utilized by the plan or issuer that are relevant for determining the applicable cost-sharing information (such as location of service, facility name, or dosage).

(B) Search for an out-of-network allowed amount, percentage of billed charges, or other rate that provides a reasonably accurate estimate of the amount a group health plan or health insurance issuer will pay for a covered item or service provided by out-of-network providers by inputting:

(1) A billing code or descriptive term, at the option of the user; and

(2) Other factors utilized by the plan or issuer that are relevant for determining the applicable out-of-network allowed amount or other rate (such as the location in which the covered item or service will be sought or provided).

(C) Refine and reorder search results based on geographic proximity of in-network providers, and the amount of the participant's or beneficiary's estimated cost-sharing liability for the covered

item or service, to the extent the search for cost-sharing information for covered items or services returns multiple results.

(ii) *Paper method.*—Information provided under this paragraph (b) must be made available in plain language, without a fee, in paper form at the request of the participant or beneficiary. In responding to such a request, the group health plan or health insurance issuer may limit the number of providers with respect to which cost-sharing information for covered items and services is provided to no fewer than 20 providers per request. The group health plan or health insurance issuer is required to:

(A) Disclose the applicable provider-per-request limit to the participant or beneficiary;

(B) Provide the cost-sharing information in paper form pursuant to the individual's request, in accordance with the requirements in paragraphs (b)(2)(i)(A) through (C) of this section; and

(C) Mail the cost-sharing information in paper form no later than 2 business days after an individual's request is received.

(D) To the extent participants or beneficiaries request disclosure other than by paper (for example, by phone or e-mail), plans and issuers may provide the disclosure through another means, provided the participant or beneficiary agrees that disclosure through such means is sufficient to satisfy the request and the request is fulfilled at least as rapidly as required for the paper method.

(3) *Special rule to prevent unnecessary duplication.*—(i) *Special rule for insured group health plans.*—To the extent coverage under a group health plan consists of group health insurance coverage, the plan satisfies the requirements of this paragraph (b) if the plan requires the health insurance issuer offering the coverage to provide the information required by this paragraph (b) in compliance with this section pursuant to a written agreement. Accordingly, if a health insurance issuer and a plan sponsor enter into a written agreement under which the issuer agrees to provide the information required under this paragraph (b) in compliance with this section, and the issuer fails to do so, then the issuer, but not the plan, violates the transparency disclosure requirements of this paragraph (b).

(ii) *Other contractual arrangements.*—A group health plan or health insurance issuer may satisfy the requirements under this paragraph (b) by entering into a written agreement under which another party (such as a pharmacy benefit manager or other third-party) provides the information required by this paragraph (b) in compliance with this section. Notwithstanding the preceding sentence, if a group health plan or health insurance issuer chooses to enter into such an agreement and the party with which it contracts fails to provide the information in compliance with this paragraph (b), the plan or issuer violates the transparency disclosure requirements of this paragraph (b).

(c) *Applicability.*—(1) The provisions of this section apply for plan years beginning on or after January 1, 2023 with respect to the 500 items and services to be posted on a publicly available website, and with respect to all covered items and services, for plan years beginning on or after January 1, 2024.

(2) As provided under §54.9815-1251, this section does not apply to grandfathered health plans. This section also does not apply to health reimbursement arrangements or other account-based group health plans as defined in §54.9815-2711(d)(6) or short-term, limited-duration insurance as defined in §54.9801-2.

(3) Nothing in this section alters or otherwise affects a group health plan's or health insurance issuer's duty to comply with requirements under other applicable state or Federal laws, including those governing the accessibility, privacy, or security of information required to be disclosed under this section, or those governing the ability of properly authorized representatives to access participant or beneficiary information held by plans and issuers.

(4) A group health plan or health insurance issuer will not fail to comply with this section solely because it, acting in good faith and with reasonable diligence, makes an error or omission in a disclosure required under paragraph (b) of this section, provided that the plan or issuer corrects the information as soon as practicable.

(5) A group health plan or health insurance issuer will not fail to comply with this section solely because, despite acting in good faith and with reasonable diligence, its internet website is temporarily inaccessible, provided that the plan or issuer makes the information available as soon as practicable.

(6) To the extent compliance with this section requires a group health plan or health insurance issuer to obtain information from any other entity, the plan or issuer will not fail to comply with this section because it relied in good faith on information from the other entity, unless the plan or issuer knows, or reasonably should have known, that the information is incomplete or inaccurate.

(d) *Severability.*—Any provision of this section held to be invalid or unenforceable by its terms, or as applied to any person or circumstance, or stayed pending further agency action, shall be severable from this section and shall not affect the remainder thereof or the application of the provision to persons not similarly situated or to dissimilar circumstances. [Reg. §54.9815-2715A2.]

☐ [T.D. 9929, 11-3-2020.]

### [Reg. §54.9815-2715A3]

**§54.9815-2715A3. Transparency in coverage - requirements for public disclosure.**—(a) *Scope and definitions.*—(1) *Scope.*—This section establishes price transparency requirements for group health plans and health insurance issuers offering group health insurance coverage for the timely disclosure of information about costs related to covered items and services under a group plan or health insurance coverage.

(2) *Definitions.*—For purposes of this section, the definitions in §54.9815-2715A1 apply.

(b) *Requirements for public disclosure of in-network provider rates for covered items and services, out-of-network allowed amounts and billed charges for covered items and services, and negotiated rates and historical net prices for covered prescription drugs.*—A group health plan or health insurance issuer must make available on an internet website the information required under paragraph (b)(1) of this section in three machine-readable files, in accordance with the method and format requirements described in paragraph (b)(2) of this section, and that are updated as required under paragraph (b)(3) of this section.

(1) *Required information.*—Machine-readable files required under this paragraph (b) that are made available to the public by a group health plan or health insurance issuer must include:

(i) An in-network rate machine-readable file that includes the required information under this paragraph (b)(1)(i) for all covered items and services, except for prescription drugs that are subject to a fee-for-service reimbursement arrangement, which must be reported in the prescription drug machine-readable file pursuant to paragraph (b)(1)(iii) of this section. The in-network rate machine-readable file must include:

(A) For each coverage option offered by a group health plan or health insurance issuer, the name and the 14-digit Health Insurance Oversight System (HIOS) identifier, or, if the 14-digit HIOS identifier is not available, the 5-digit HIOS identifier, or if no HIOS identifier is available, the Employer Identification Number (EIN);

(B) A billing code, which in the case of prescription drugs must be an NDC, and a plain language description for each billing code for each covered item or service under each coverage option offered by a plan or issuer; and

(C) All applicable rates, which may include one or more of the following: negotiated rates, underlying fee schedule rates, or derived amounts. If a group health plan or health insurance issuer does not use negotiated rates for provider reimbursement, then the plan or issuer should disclose derived amounts to the extent these amounts are already calculated in the normal course of business. If the group health plan or health insurance issuer uses underlying fee schedule rates for calculating cost sharing, then the plan or issuer should include the underlying fee schedule rates in addition to the negotiated rate or derived amount. Applicable rates, including for both individual items and services and items and services in a bundled payment arrangement, must be:

(1) Reflected as dollar amounts, with respect to each covered item or service that is furnished by an in-network provider. If the negotiated rate is subject to change based upon participant or beneficiary-specific characteristics, these dollar amounts should be reflected as the base negotiated rate applicable to the item or service prior to adjustments for participant or beneficiary-specific characteristics;

(2) Associated with the National Provider Identifier (NPI), Tax Identification Number (TIN), and Place of Service Code for each in-network provider;

(3) Associated with the last date of the contract term or expiration date for each provider-specific applicable rate that applies to each covered item or service; and

(4) Indicated with a notation where a reimbursement arrangement other than a standard fee-for-service model (such as capitation or a bundled payment arrangement) applies.

(ii) An out-of-network allowed amount machine-readable file, including:

(A) For each coverage option offered by a group health plan or health insurance issuer, the name and the 14-digit HIOS identifier, or, if the 14-digit HIOS identifier is not available, the 5-digit HIOS identifier, or, if no HIOS identifier is available, the EIN;

(B) A billing code, which in the case of prescription drugs must be an NDC, and a plain language description for each billing code for each covered item or service under each coverage option offered by a plan or issuer; and

(C) Unique out-of-network allowed amounts and billed charges with respect to covered items or services, furnished by out-of-network providers during the 90-day time period that begins 180 days prior to the publication date of the machine-readable file (except that a group health plan or health insurance issuer must omit such data in relation to a particular item or service and provider when compliance with this paragraph (b)(1)(ii)(C) would require the plan or issuer to report payment of out-of-network allowed amounts in connection with fewer than 20 different claims for payments under a single plan or coverage). Consistent with paragraph (c)(3) of this section, nothing in this paragraph (b)(1)(ii)(C) requires the disclosure of information that would violate any applicable health information privacy law. Each unique out-of-network allowed amount must be:

(1) Reflected as a dollar amount, with respect to each covered item or service that is furnished by an out-of-network provider; and

(2) Associated with the NPI, TIN, and Place of Service Code for each out-of-network provider.

(iii) A prescription drug machine-readable file, including:

(A) For each coverage option offered by a group health plan or health insurance issuer, the name and the 14-digit HIOS identifier, or, if the 14-digit HIOS identifier is not available, the 5-digit HIOS identifier, or, if no HIOS identifier is available, the EIN;

(B) The NDC and the proprietary and nonproprietary name assigned to the NDC by the Food and Drug Administration (FDA) for each covered item or service that is a prescription drug under each coverage option offered by a plan or issuer;

(C) The negotiated rates which must be:

(1) Reflected as a dollar amount, with respect to each NDC that is furnished by an in-network provider, including an in-network pharmacy or other prescription drug dispenser;

(2) Associated with the NPI, TIN, and Place of Service Code for each in-network provider, including each in-network pharmacy or other prescription drug dispenser; and

(3) Associated with the last date of the contract term for each provider-specific negotiated rate that applies to each NDC; and

(D) Historical net prices that are:

(1) Reflected as a dollar amount, with respect to each NDC that is furnished by an in-network provider, including an in-network pharmacy or other prescription drug dispenser;

(2) Associated with the NPI, TIN, and Place of Service Code for each in-network provider, including each in-network pharmacy or other prescription drug dispenser; and

(3) Associated with the 90-day time period that begins 180 days prior to the publication date of the machine-readable file for each provider-specific historical net price that applies to each NDC (except that a group health plan or health insurance issuer must omit such data in relation to a particular NDC and provider when compliance with this paragraph (b)(1)(iii)(D) would require the plan or issuer to report payment of historical net prices calculated using fewer than 20 different claims for payment). Consistent with paragraph (c)(3) of this section, nothing in this paragraph (b)(1)(iii)(D) requires the disclosure of information that would violate any applicable health information privacy law.

(2) *Required method and format for disclosing information to the public.*—The machine-readable files described in this paragraph (b) must be available in a form and manner as specified in guidance issued by the Department of the Treasury, the Department of Labor, and the Department of Health and Human Services. The machine-readable files must be publicly available and accessible to any person free of charge and without conditions, such as establishment of a user account, password, or other credentials, or submission of personally identifiable information to access the file.

(3) *Timing.*—A group health plan or health insurance issuer must update the machine-readable files and information required by this paragraph (b) monthly. The group health plan or health insurance issuer must clearly indicate the date that the files were most recently updated.

(4) *Special rules to prevent unnecessary duplication.*—(i) *Special rule for insured group health plans.*—To the extent coverage under a group health plan consists of group health insurance coverage, the plan satisfies the requirements of this paragraph (b) if the plan requires the health insurance issuer offering the coverage to provide the information pursuant to a written agreement. Accordingly, if a health insurance issuer and a group health plan sponsor enter into a written agreement under which the issuer agrees to provide the information required under this paragraph (b) in compliance with this section, and the issuer fails to do so, then the issuer, but not the plan, violates the transparency disclosure requirements of this paragraph (b).

(ii) *Other contractual arrangements.*—A group health plan or health insurance issuer may satisfy the requirements under this paragraph (b) by entering into a written agreement under which another party (such as a third-party administrator or health care claims clearinghouse) will provide the information required by this paragraph (b) in compliance with this section. Notwithstanding the preceding sentence, if a group health plan or health insurance issuer chooses to enter into such an agreement and the party with which it contracts fails to provide the information in compliance with this paragraph (b), the plan or issuer violates the transparency disclosure requirements of this paragraph (b).

(iii) *Aggregation permitted for out-of-network allowed amounts.*— Nothing in this section prohibits a group health plan or health insurance issuer from satisfying the disclosure requirement described in paragraph (b)(1)(ii) of this section by disclosing out-of-network allowed amounts made available by, or otherwise obtained from, an issuer, a service provider, or other party with which the plan or issuer has entered into a written agreement to provide the information, provided the minimum claim threshold described in paragraph (b)(1)(ii)(C) of this section is independently met for each item or service and for each plan or coverage included in an aggregated Allowed Amount File. Under such circumstances, health insurance issuers, service providers, or other parties with which the group health plan or issuer has contracted may aggregate out-of-network allowed amounts for more than one plan or insurance policy or contract. Additionally, nothing in this section prevents the Allowed Amount File from being hosted on a third-party website or prevents a plan administrator or issuer from contracting with a third party to post the file. However, if a plan or issuer chooses not to also host the file separately on its own website, it must provide a link on its own public website to the location where the file is made publicly available.

(c) *Applicability.*—(1) The provisions of this section apply for plan years beginning on or after January 1, 2022.

(2) As provided under §54.9815-1251, this section does not apply to grandfathered health plans. This section also does not apply to

health reimbursement arrangements or other account-based group health plans as defined in §54.9815-2711(d)(6) or short term limited duration insurance as defined in §54.9801-2.

(3) Nothing in this section alters or otherwise affects a group health plan's or health insurance issuer's duty to comply with requirements under other applicable state or Federal laws, including those governing the accessibility, privacy, or security of information required to be disclosed under this section, or those governing the ability of properly authorized representatives to access participant, or beneficiary information held by plans and issuers.

(4) A group health plan or health insurance issuer will not fail to comply with this section solely because it, acting in good faith and with reasonable diligence, makes an error or omission in a disclosure required under paragraph (b) of this section, provided that the plan or issuer corrects the information as soon as practicable.

(5) A group health plan or health insurance issuer will not fail to comply with this section solely because, despite acting in good faith and with reasonable diligence, its internet website is temporarily inaccessible, provided that the plan or issuer makes the information available as soon as practicable.

(6) To the extent compliance with this section requires a group health plan or health insurance issuer to obtain information from any other entity, the plan or issuer will not fail to comply with this section because it relied in good faith on information from the other entity, unless the plan or issuer knows, or reasonably should have known, that the information is incomplete or inaccurate.

(d) *Severability.*—Any provision of this section held to be invalid or unenforceable by its terms, or as applied to any person or circumstance, or stayed pending further agency action, shall be severable from this section and shall not affect the remainder thereof or the application of the provision to persons not similarly situated or to dissimilar circumstances. [Reg. §54.9815-2715A3.]

☐ [*T.D.* 9929, 11-3-2020.]

⟫⟫→ *Caution: Reg. §54.9815-2719, below, as added by T.D. 9744, is applicable to group health plans and health insurance issuers beginning on the first day of the plan year (or, in the individual market, the first day of the first policy year) beginning on or after January 1, 2017.*

**[Reg. §54.9815-2719]**

**§54.9815-2719. Internal claims and appeals and external review processes.**—(a) *Scope and definitions.*—(1) *Scope.*—This section sets forth requirements with respect to internal claims and appeals and external review processes for group health plans and health insurance issuers that are not grandfathered health plans under §54.9815-1251. Paragraph (b) of this section provides requirements for internal claims and appeals processes. Paragraph (c) of this section sets forth rules governing the applicability of State external review processes. Paragraph (d) of this section sets forth a Federal external review process for plans and issuers not subject to an applicable State external review process. Paragraph (e) of this section prescribes requirements for ensuring that notices required to be provided under this section are provided in a culturally and linguistically appropriate manner. Paragraph (f) of this section describes the authority of the Secretary to deem certain external review processes in existence on March 23, 2010 as in compliance with paragraph (c) or (d) of this section.

(2) *Definitions.*—For purposes of this section, the following definitions apply

(i) *Adverse benefit determination.*—An *adverse benefit determination* means an adverse benefit determination as defined in 29 CFR 2560.503-1, as well as any rescission of coverage, as described in §54.9815-2712(a)(2) (whether or not, in connection with the rescission, there is an adverse effect on any particular benefit at that time).

(ii) *Appeal (or internal appeal).*—An *appeal* or *internal appeal* means review by a plan or issuer of an adverse benefit determination, as required in paragraph (b) of this section.

(iii) *Claimant.*—Claimant means an individual who makes a claim under this section. For purposes of this section, references to claimant include a claimant's authorized representative.

(iv) *External review.*—External review means a review of an adverse benefit determination (including a final internal adverse benefit determination) conducted pursuant to an applicable State external review process described in paragraph (c) of this section or the Federal external review process of paragraph (d) of this section.

(v) *Final internal adverse benefit determination.*—A *final internal adverse benefit determination* means an adverse benefit determination that has been upheld by a plan or issuer at the completion of the internal appeals process applicable under paragraph (b) of this section (or an adverse benefit determination with respect to which the

internal appeals process has been exhausted under the deemed exhaustion rules of paragraph (b)(2)(ii)(F) of this section).

(vi) *Final external review decision.*—A *final external review decision* means a determination by an independent review organization at the conclusion of an external review.

(vii) *Independent review organization (or IRO).*—An *independent review organization* (or *IRO*) means an entity that conducts independent external reviews of adverse benefit determinations and final internal adverse benefit determinations pursuant to paragraph (c) or (d) of this section.

(viii) *NAIC Uniform Model Act.*—The *NAIC Uniform Model Act* means the Uniform Health Carrier External Review Model Act promulgated by the National Association of Insurance Commissioners in place on July 23, 2010.

(b) *Internal claims and appeals process.*—(1) *In general.*—A group health plan and a health insurance issuer offering group health insurance coverage must implement an effective internal claims and appeals process, as described in this paragraph (b).

(2) *Requirements for group health plans and group health insurance issuers.*—A group health plan and a health insurance issuer offering group health insurance coverage must comply with all the requirements of this paragraph (b)(2). In the case of health insurance coverage offered in connection with a group health plan, if either the plan or the issuer complies with the internal claims and appeals process of this paragraph (b)(2), then the obligation to comply with this paragraph (b)(2) is satisfied for both the plan and the issuer with respect to the health insurance coverage.

(i) *Minimum internal claims and appeals standards.*—A group health plan and a health insurance issuer offering group health insurance coverage must comply with all the requirements applicable to group health plans under 29 CFR 2560.503-1, except to the extent those requirements are modified by paragraph (b)(2)(ii) of this section. Accordingly, under this paragraph (b), with respect to health insurance coverage offered in connection with a group health plan, the group health insurance issuer is subject to the requirements in 29 CFR 2560.503-1 to the same extent as the group health plan.

(ii) *Additional standards.*—In addition to the requirements in paragraph (b)(2)(i) of this section, the internal claims and appeals processes of a group health plan and a health insurance issuer offering group health insurance coverage must meet the requirements of this paragraph (b)(2)(ii).

**➤➤➤ Caution:** *Reg. §54.9815-2719, below, as added by T.D. 9744, is applicable to group health plans and health insurance issuers beginning on the first day of the plan year (or, in the individual market, the first day of the first policy year) beginning on or after January 1, 2017.*

(A) *Clarification of meaning of adverse benefit determination.*— For purposes of this paragraph (b)(2), an "adverse benefit determination" includes an adverse benefit determination as defined in paragraph (a)(2)(i) of this section. Accordingly, in complying with 29 CFR 2560.503-1, as well as the other provisions of this paragraph (b)(2), a plan or issuer must treat a rescission of coverage (whether or not the rescission has an adverse effect on any particular benefit at that time) as an adverse benefit determination. (Rescissions of coverage are subject to the requirements of §54.9815-2712.)

(B) *Expedited notification of benefit determinations involving urgent care.*—The requirements of 29 CFR 2560.503-1(f)(2)(i) (which generally provide, among other things, in the case of urgent care claims for notification of the plan's benefit determination (whether adverse or not) as soon as possible, taking into account the medical exigencies, but not later than 72 hours after the receipt of the claim) continue to apply to the plan and issuer. For purposes of this paragraph (b)(2)(ii)(B), a claim involving urgent care has the meaning given in 29 CFR 2560.503-1(m)(1), as determined by the attending provider, and the plan or issuer shall defer to such determination of the attending provider.

(C) *Full and fair review.*—A plan and issuer must allow a claimant to review the claim file and to present evidence and testimony as part of the internal claims and appeals process. Specifically, in addition to complying with the requirements of 29 CFR 2560.503-1(h)(2) —

(1) The plan or issuer must provide the claimant, free of charge, with any new or additional evidence considered, relied upon, or generated by the plan or issuer (or at the direction of the plan or issuer) in connection with the claim; such evidence must be provided as soon as possible and sufficiently in advance of the date on which the notice of final internal adverse benefit determination is required to be provided under 29 CFR 2560.503-1(i) to give the claimant a reasonable opportunity to respond prior to that date; and

(2) Before the plan or issuer can issue a final internal adverse benefit determination based on a new or additional rationale, the claimant must be provided, free of charge, with the rationale; the rationale must be provided as soon as possible and sufficiently in advance of the date on which the notice of final internal adverse benefit determination is required to be provided under 29 CFR 2560.503-1(i) to give the claimant a reasonable opportunity to respond prior to that date. Notwithstanding the rules of 29 CFR 2560.503-1(i), if the new or additional evidence is received so late that it would be impossible to provide it to the claimant in time for the claimant to have a reasonable opportunity to respond, the period for providing a notice of final internal adverse benefit determination is tolled until such time as the claimant has a reasonable opportunity to respond. After the claimant responds, or has a reasonable opportunity to respond but fails to do so, the plan administrator shall notify the claimant of the plan's benefit determination as soon as a plan acting in a reasonable and prompt fashion can provide the notice, taking into account the medical exigencies.

(D) *Avoiding conflicts of interest.*—In addition to the requirements of 29 CFR 2560.503-1(b) and (h) regarding full and fair review, the plan and issuer must ensure that all claims and appeals are adjudicated in a manner designed to ensure the independence and impartiality of the persons involved in making the decision. Accordingly, decisions regarding hiring, compensation, termination, promotion, or other similar matters with respect to any individual (such as a claims adjudicator or medical expert) must not be made based upon the likelihood that the individual will support the denial of benefits.

(E) *Notice.*—A plan and issuer must provide notice to individuals, in a culturally and linguistically appropriate manner (as described in paragraph (e) of this section) that complies with the requirements of 29 CFR 2560.503-1(g) and (j). The plan and issuer must also comply with the additional requirements of this paragraph (b)(2)(ii)(E).

(1) The plan and issuer must ensure that any notice of adverse benefit determination or final internal adverse benefit determination includes information sufficient to identify the claim involved (including the date of service, the health care provider, the claim amount (if applicable), and a statement describing the availability, upon request, of the diagnosis code and its corresponding meaning, and the treatment code and its corresponding meaning).

(2) The plan and issuer must provide to participants and beneficiaries, as soon as practicable, upon request, the diagnosis code and its corresponding meaning, and the treatment code and its corresponding meaning, associated with any adverse benefit determination or final internal adverse benefit determination. The plan or issuer must not consider a request for such diagnosis and treatment information, in itself, to be a request for an internal appeal under this paragraph (b) or an external review under paragraphs (c) and (d) of this section.

(3) The plan and issuer must ensure that the reason or reasons for the adverse benefit determination or final internal adverse benefit determination includes the denial code and its corresponding meaning, as well as a description of the plan's or issuer's standard, if any, that was used in denying the claim. In the case of a notice of final internal adverse benefit determination, this description must include a discussion of the decision.

(4) The plan and issuer must provide a description of available internal appeals and external review processes, including information regarding how to initiate an appeal.

(5) The plan and issuer must disclose the availability of, and contact information for, any applicable office of health insurance consumer assistance or ombudsman established under PHS Act section 2793 to assist individuals with the internal claims and appeals and external review processes.

(F) *Deemed exhaustion of internal claims and appeals processes.*—(1) In the case of a plan or issuer that fails to strictly adhere to all the requirements of this paragraph (b)(2) with respect to a claim, the claimant is deemed to have exhausted the internal claims and appeals process of this paragraph (b), except as provided in paragraph (b)(2)(ii)(F)(2) of this section. Accordingly the claimant may initiate an external review under paragraph (c) or (d) of this section, as applicable. The claimant is also entitled to pursue any available remedies under section 502(a) of ERISA or under State law, as applicable, on the basis that the plan or issuer has failed to provide a reasonable internal claims and appeals process that would yield a decision on the merits of the claim. If a claimant chooses to pursue remedies under section 502(a) of ERISA under such circumstances, the claim or appeal is deemed denied on review without the exercise of discretion by an appropriate fiduciary.

(2) Notwithstanding paragraph (b)(2)(ii)(F)(1) of this section, the internal claims and appeals process of this paragraph (b) will not be deemed exhausted based on *de minimis* violations that do not cause, and are not likely to cause, prejudice or harm to the claimant so long as the plan or issuer demonstrates that the violation was for good cause or due to matters beyond the control of the plan or issuer and that the violation occurred in the context of an ongoing, good faith exchange of information between the plan and the claimant. This exception is not available if the violation is part of a pattern or practice of violations by the plan or issuer. The claimant may request a written explanation of the violation from the plan or issuer, and the plan or issuer must provide such explanation within 10 days, including a specific description of its bases, if any, for asserting that the violation should not cause the internal claims and appeals process of this paragraph (b) to be deemed exhausted. If an external reviewer or a court rejects the claimant's request for immediate review under paragraph (b)(2)(ii)(F)(1) of this section on the basis that the plan met the standards for the exception under this paragraph (b)(2)(ii)(F)(2), the claimant has the right to resubmit and pursue the internal appeal of the claim. In such a case, within a reasonable time after the external reviewer or court rejects the claim for immediate review (not to exceed 10 days), the plan shall provide the claimant with notice of the opportunity to resubmit and pursue the internal appeal of the claim. Time periods for re-filing the claim shall begin to run upon claimant's receipt of such notice.

(iii) *Requirement to provide continued coverage pending the outcome of an appeal.*—A plan and issuer subject to the requirements of this paragraph (b)(2) are required to provide continued coverage pending the outcome of an appeal. For this purpose, the plan and issuer must comply with the requirements of 29 CFR 2560.503-1(f)(2)(ii), which generally provides that benefits for an ongoing course of treatment cannot be reduced or terminated without providing advance notice and an opportunity for advance review.

(c) *State standards for external review.*—(1) *In general.*—(i) If a State external review process that applies to and is binding on a health insurance issuer offering group health insurance coverage includes at a minimum the consumer protections in the NAIC Uniform Model Act, then the issuer must comply with the applicable State external review process and is not required to comply with the Federal external review process of paragraph (d) of this section. In such a case, to the extent that benefits under a group health plan are provided through health insurance coverage, the group health plan is not required to comply with either this paragraph (c) or the Federal external review process of paragraph (d) of this section.

(ii) To the extent that a group health plan provides benefits other than through health insurance coverage (that is, the plan is self-

>>>→ *Caution: Reg. §54.9815-2719, below, as added by T.D. 9744, is applicable to group health plans and health insurance issuers beginning on the first day of the plan year (or, in the individual market, the first day of the first policy year) beginning on or after January 1, 2017.*

insured) and is subject to a State external review process that applies to and is binding on the plan (for example, is not preempted by ERISA) and the State external review process includes at a minimum the consumer protections in the NAIC Uniform Model Act, then the plan must comply with the applicable State external review process and is not required to comply with the Federal external review process of paragraph (d) of this section. Where a self-insured plan is not subject to an applicable State external review process, but the State has chosen to expand access to its process for plans that are not subject to the applicable State laws, the plan may choose to comply with either the applicable State external review process or the Federal external review process of paragraph (d) of this section.

(iii) If a plan or issuer is not required under paragraph (c)(1)(i) or (c)(1)(ii) of this section to comply with the requirements of this paragraph (c), then the plan or issuer must comply with the Federal external review process of paragraph (d) of this section, except to the extent, in the case of a plan, the plan is not required under paragraph (c)(1)(i) of this section to comply with paragraph (d) of this section.

(2) *Minimum standards for State external review processes.*—An applicable State external review process must meet all the minimum consumer protections in this paragraph (c)(2). The Department of Health and Human Services will determine whether State external review processes meet these requirements.

(i) The State process must provide for the external review of adverse benefit determinations (including final internal adverse benefit determinations) by issuers (or, if applicable, plans) that are based on the issuer's (or plan's) requirements for medical necessity, appropriateness, health care setting, level of care, or effectiveness of a covered benefit.

(ii) The State process must require issuers (or, if applicable, plans) to provide effective written notice to claimants of their rights in connection with an external review for an adverse benefit determination.

(iii) To the extent the State process requires exhaustion of an internal claims and appeals process, exhaustion must be unnecessary where the issuer (or, if applicable, the plan) has waived the requirement; the issuer (or the plan) is considered to have exhausted the internal claims and appeals process under applicable law (including by failing to comply with any of the requirements for the internal appeal process, as outlined in paragraph (b)(2) of this section); or the claimant has applied for expedited external review at the same time as applying for an expedited internal appeal.

(iv) The State process provides that the issuer (or, if applicable, the plan) against which a request for external review is filed must pay the cost of the IRO for conducting the external review. Notwithstanding this requirement, a State external review process that expressly authorizes, as of November 18, 2015, a nominal filing fee may continue to permit such fees. For this purpose, to be considered nominal, a filing fee must not exceed $25; it must be refunded to the claimant if the adverse benefit determination (or final internal adverse benefit determination) is reversed through external review; it must be waived if payment of the fee would impose an undue financial hardship; and the annual limit on filing fees for any claimant within a single plan year must not exceed $75.

(v) The State process may not impose a restriction on the minimum dollar amount of a claim for it to be eligible for external review. Thus, the process may not impose, for example, a $500 minimum claims threshold.

(vi) The State process must allow at least four months after the receipt of a notice of an adverse benefit determination or final internal adverse benefit determination for a request for an external review to be filed.

(vii) The State process must provide that IROs will be assigned on a random basis or another method of assignment that assures the independence and impartiality of the assignment process (such as rotational assignment) by a State or independent entity, and in no event selected by the issuer, plan, or the individual.

(viii) The State process must provide for maintenance of a list of approved IROs qualified to conduct the external review based on the nature of the health care service that is the subject of the review. The State process must provide for approval only of IROs that are accredited by a nationally recognized private accrediting organization.

(ix) The State process must provide that any approved IRO has no conflicts of interest that will influence its independence. Thus, the IRO may not own or control, or be owned or controlled by a health insurance issuer, a group health plan, the sponsor of a group health plan, a trade association of plans or issuers, or a trade association of health care providers. The State process must further provide that the IRO and the clinical reviewer assigned to conduct an external review may not have a material professional, familial, or financial

conflict of interest with the issuer or plan that is the subject of the external review; the claimant (and any related parties to the claimant) whose treatment is the subject of the external review; any officer, director, or management employee of the issuer; the plan administrator, plan fiduciaries, or plan employees; the health care provider, the health care provider's group, or practice association recommending the treatment that is subject to the external review; the facility at which the recommended treatment would be provided; or the developer or manufacturer of the principal drug, device, procedure, or other therapy being recommended.

(x) The State process allows the claimant at least five business days to submit to the IRO in writing additional information that the IRO must consider when conducting the external review, and it requires that the claimant is notified of the right to do so. The process must also require that any additional information submitted by the claimant to the IRO must be forwarded to the issuer (or, if applicable, the plan) within one business day of receipt by the IRO.

(xi) The State process must provide that the decision is binding on the plan or issuer, as well as the claimant except to the extent the other remedies are available under State or Federal law, and except that the requirement that the decision be binding shall not preclude the plan or issuer from making payment on the claim or otherwise providing benefits at any time, including after a final external review decision that denies the claim or otherwise fails to require such payment or benefits. For this purpose, the plan or issuer must provide benefits (including by making payment on the claim) pursuant to the final external review decision without delay, regardless of whether the plan or issuer intends to seek judicial review of the external review decision and unless or until there is a judicial decision otherwise.

(xii) The State process must require, for standard external review, that the IRO provide written notice to the issuer (or, if applicable, the plan) and the claimant of its decision to uphold or reverse the adverse benefit determination (or final internal adverse benefit determination) within no more than 45 days after the receipt of the request for external review by the IRO.

(xiii) The State process must provide for an expedited external review if the adverse benefit determination (or final internal adverse benefit determination) concerns an admission, availability of care, continued stay, or health care service for which the claimant received emergency services, but has not been discharged from a facility; or involves a medical condition for which the standard external review time frame would seriously jeopardize the life or health of the claimant or jeopardize the claimant's ability to regain maximum function. As expeditiously as possible but within no more than 72 hours after the receipt of the request for expedited external review by the IRO, the IRO must make its decision to uphold or reverse the adverse benefit determination (or final internal adverse benefit determination) and notify the claimant and the issuer (or, if applicable, the plan) of the determination. If the notice is not in writing, the IRO must provide written confirmation of the decision within 48 hours after the date of the notice of the decision.

(xiv) The State process must require that issuers (or, if applicable, plans) include a description of the external review process in or attached to the summary plan description, policy, certificate, membership booklet, outline of coverage, or other evidence of coverage it provides to participants, beneficiaries, or enrollees, substantially similar to what is set forth in section 17 of the NAIC Uniform Model Act.

(xv) The State process must require that IROs maintain written records and make them available upon request to the State, substantially similar to what is set forth in section 15 of the NAIC Uniform Model Act.

(xvi) The State process follows procedures for external review of adverse benefit determinations (or final internal adverse benefit determinations) involving experimental or investigational treatment, substantially similar to what is set forth in section 10 of the NAIC Uniform Model Act.

(3) *Transition period for external review processes.*—(i) Through December 31, 2017, an applicable State external review process applicable to a health insurance issuer or group health plan is considered to meet the requirements of PHS Act section 2719(b). Accordingly, through December 31, 2017, an applicable State external review process will be considered binding on the issuer or plan (in lieu of the requirements of the Federal external review process). If there is no applicable State external review process, the issuer or plan is required to comply with the requirements of the Federal external review process in paragraph (d) of this section.

(ii) An applicable State external review process must apply for final internal adverse benefit determinations (or, in the case of simultaneous internal appeal and external review, adverse benefit

»»→ *Caution: Reg. §54.9815-2719, below, as added by T.D. 9744, is applicable to group health plans and health insurance issuers beginning on the first day of the plan year (or, in the individual market, the first day of the first policy year) beginning on or after January 1, 2017.*

determinations) provided on or after January 1, 2018. The Federal external review process will apply to such internal adverse benefit determinations unless the Department of Health and Human Services determines that a State law meets all the minimum standards of paragraph (c)(2) of this section. Through December 31, 2017, a State external review process applicable to a health insurance issuer or group health plan may be considered to meet the minimum standards of paragraph (c)(2) of this section, if it meets the temporary standards established by the Secretary in guidance for a process similar to the NAIC Uniform Model Act.

(d) *Federal external review process.*—A plan or issuer not subject to an applicable State external review process under paragraph (c) of this section must provide an effective Federal external review process in accordance with this paragraph (d) (except to the extent, in the case of a plan, the plan is described in paragraph (c)(1)(i) of this section as not having to comply with this paragraph (d)). In the case of health insurance coverage offered in connection with a group health plan, if either the plan or the issuer complies with the Federal external review process of this paragraph (d), then the obligation to comply with this paragraph (d) is satisfied for both the plan and the issuer with respect to the health insurance coverage. A Multi State Plan or MSP, as defined by 45 CFR 800.20, must provide an effective Federal external review process in accordance with this paragraph (d). In such circumstances, the requirement to provide external review under this paragraph (d) is satisfied when a Multi State Plan or MSP complies with standards established by the Office of Personnel Management.

(1) *Scope.*—(i) *In general.*—The Federal external review process established pursuant to this paragraph (d) applies to the following:

(A) An adverse benefit determination (including a final internal adverse benefit determination) by a plan or issuer that involves medical judgment (including, but not limited to, those based on the plan's or issuer's requirements for medical necessity, appropriateness, health care setting, level of care, or effectiveness of a covered benefit; its determination that a treatment is experimental or investigational; its determination whether a participant or beneficiary is entitled to a reasonable alternative standard for a reward under a wellness program; or its determination whether a plan or issuer is complying with the nonquantitative treatment limitation provisions of Code section 9812 and § 54.9812, which generally require, among other things, parity in the application of medical management techniques), as determined by the external reviewer. (A denial, reduction, termination, or a failure to provide payment for a benefit based on a determination that a participant or beneficiary fails to meet the requirements for eligibility under the terms of a group health plan or health insurance coverage is not eligible for the Federal external review process under this paragraph (d)); and

(B) A rescission of coverage (whether or not the rescission has any effect on any particular benefit at that time).

(ii) *Examples.*—The rules of paragraph (d)(1)(i) of this section are illustrated by the following examples:

*Example 1.* (i) *Facts.* A group health plan provides coverage for 30 physical therapy visits generally. After the 30th visit, coverage is provided only if the service is preauthorized pursuant to an approved treatment plan that takes into account medical necessity using the plan's definition of the term. Individual *A* seeks coverage for a 31st physical therapy visit. *A*'s health care provider submits a treatment plan for approval, but it is not approved by the plan, so coverage for the 31st visit is not preauthorized. With respect to the 31st visit, *A* receives a notice of final internal adverse benefit determination stating that the maximum visit limit is exceeded.

(ii) *Conclusion.* In this *Example 1*, the plan's denial of benefits is based on medical necessity and involves medical judgment. Accordingly, the claim is eligible for external review under paragraph (d)(1)(i) of this section. Moreover, the plan's notification of final internal adverse benefit determination is inadequate under paragraphs (b)(2)(i) and (b)(2)(ii)(E)(3) of this section because it fails to make clear that the plan will pay for more than 30 visits if the service is preauthorized pursuant to an approved treatment plan that takes into account medical necessity using the plan's definition of the term. Accordingly, the notice of final internal adverse benefit determination should refer to the plan provision governing the 31st visit and should describe the plan's standard for medical necessity, as well as how the treatment fails to meet the plan's standard.

*Example 2.* (i) *Facts.* A group health plan does not provide coverage for services provided out of network, unless the service cannot effectively be provided in network. Individual *B* seeks coverage for a specialized medical procedure from an out-of-network provider because *B* believes that the procedure cannot be effectively

provided in network. *B* receives a notice of final internal adverse benefit determination stating that the claim is denied because the provider is out-of-network.

(ii) *Conclusion.* In this *Example 2*, the plan's denial of benefits is based on whether a service can effectively be provided in network and, therefore, involves medical judgment. Accordingly, the claim is eligible for external review under paragraph (d)(1)(i) of this section. Moreover, the plan's notice of final internal adverse benefit determination is inadequate under paragraphs (b)(2)(i) and (b)(2)(ii)(E)(3) of this section because the plan does provide benefits for services on an out-of-network basis if the services cannot effectively be provided in network. Accordingly, the notice of final internal adverse benefit determination is required to refer to the exception to the out-of-network exclusion and should describe the plan's standards for determining effectiveness of services, as well as how services available to the claimant within the plan's network meet the plan's standard for effectiveness of services.

(2) *External review process standards.*—The Federal external review process established pursuant to this paragraph (d) is considered similar to the process set forth in the NAIC Uniform Model Act and, therefore satisfies the requirements of paragraph (d)(2), if such process provides the following.

(i) *Request for external review.*—A group health plan or health insurance issuer must allow a claimant to file a request for an external review with the plan or issuer if the request is filed within four months after the date of receipt of a notice of an adverse benefit determination or final internal adverse benefit determination. If there is no corresponding date four months after the date of receipt of such a notice, then the request must be filed by the first day of the fifth month following the receipt of the notice. For example, if the date of receipt of the notice is October 30, because there is no February 30, the request must be filed by March 1. If the last filing date would fall on a Saturday, Sunday, or Federal holiday, the last filing date is extended to the next day that is not a Saturday, Sunday, or Federal holiday.

(ii) *Preliminary review.*—(A) *In general.*—Within five business days following the date of receipt of the external review request, the group health plan or health insurance issuer must complete a preliminary review of the request to determine whether:

(1) The claimant is or was covered under the plan or coverage at the time the health care item or service was requested or, in the case of a retrospective review, was covered under the plan or coverage at the time the health care item or service was provided;

(2) The adverse benefit determination or the final adverse benefit determination does not relate to the claimant's failure to meet the requirements for eligibility under the terms of the group health plan or health insurance coverage (e.g., worker classification or similar determination);

(3) The claimant has exhausted the plan's or issuer's internal appeal process unless the claimant is not required to exhaust the internal appeals process under paragraph (b)(1) of this section; and

(4) The claimant has provided all the information and forms required to process an external review.

(B) Within one business day after completion of the preliminary review, the plan or issuer must issue a notification in writing to the claimant. If the request is complete but not eligible for external review, such notification must include the reasons for its ineligibility and current contact information, including the phone number, for the Employee Benefits Security Administration. If the request is not complete, such notification must describe the information or materials needed to make the request complete, and the plan or issuer must allow a claimant to perfect the request for external review within the four-month filing period or within the 48 hour period following the receipt of the notification, whichever is later.

(iii) *Referral to Independent Review Organization.*—(A) *In general.*—The group health plan or health insurance issuer must assign an IRO that is accredited by URAC or by similar nationally-recognized accrediting organization to conduct the external review. The IRO referral process must provide for the following:

(1) The plan or issuer must ensure that the IRO process is not biased and ensures independence;

(2) The plan or issuer must contract with at least three (3) IROs for assignments under the plan or coverage and rotate claims assignments among them (or incorporate other independent, unbiased methods for selection of IROs, such as random selection); and

(3) The IRO may not be eligible for any financial incentives based on the likelihood that the IRO will support the denial of benefits.

➤➤➤ *Caution: Reg. §54.9815-2719, below, as added by T.D. 9744, is applicable to group health plans and health insurance issuers beginning on the first day of the plan year (or, in the individual market, the first day of the first policy year) beginning on or after January 1, 2017.*

*(4)* The IRO process may not impose any costs, including filing fees, on the claimant requesting the external review.

*(B) IRO contracts.*—A group health plan or health insurance issuer must include the following standards in the contract between the plan or issuer and the IRO:

*(1)* The assigned IRO will utilize legal experts where appropriate to make coverage determinations under the plan or coverage.

*(2)* The assigned IRO will timely notify a claimant in writing whether the request is eligible for external review. This notice will include a statement that the claimant may submit in writing to the assigned IRO, within ten business days following the date of receipt of the notice, additional information. This additional information must be considered by the IRO when conducting the external review. The IRO is not required to, but may, accept and consider additional information submitted after ten business days.

*(3)* Within five business days after the date of assignment of the IRO, the plan or issuer must provide to the assigned IRO the documents and any information considered in making the adverse benefit determination or final internal adverse benefit determination. Failure by the plan or issuer to timely provide the documents and information must not delay the conduct of the external review. If the plan or issuer fails to timely provide the documents and information, the assigned IRO may terminate the external review and make a decision to reverse the adverse benefit determination or final internal adverse benefit determination. Within one business day after making the decision, the IRO must notify the claimant and the plan.

*(4)* Upon receipt of any information submitted by the claimant, the assigned IRO must within one business day forward the information to the plan or issuer. Upon receipt of any such information, the plan or issuer may reconsider its adverse benefit determination or final internal adverse benefit determination that is the subject of the external review. Reconsideration by the plan or issuer must not delay the external review. The external review may be terminated as a result of the reconsideration only if the plan decides, upon completion of its reconsideration, to reverse its adverse benefit determination or final internal adverse benefit determination and provide coverage or payment. Within one business day after making such a decision, the plan must provide written notice of its decision to the claimant and the assigned IRO. The assigned IRO must terminate the external review upon receipt of the notice from the plan or issuer.

*(5)* The IRO will review all of the information and documents timely received. In reaching a decision, the assigned IRO will review the claim de novo and not be bound by any decisions or conclusions reached during the plan's or issuer's internal claims and appeals process applicable under paragraph (b). In addition to the documents and information provided, the assigned IRO, to the extent the information or documents are available and the IRO considers them appropriate, will consider the following in reaching a decision:

*(i)* The claimant's medical records;

*(ii)* The attending health care professional's recommendation;

*(iii)* Reports from appropriate health care professionals and other documents submitted by the plan or issuer, claimant, or the claimant's treating provider;

*(iv)* The terms of the claimant's plan or coverage to ensure that the IRO's decision is not contrary to the terms of the plan or coverage, unless the terms are inconsistent with applicable law;

*(v)* Appropriate practice guidelines, which must include applicable evidence-based standards and may include any other practice guidelines developed by the Federal government, national or professional medical societies, boards, and associations;

*(vi)* Any applicable clinical review criteria developed and used by the plan or issuer, unless the criteria are inconsistent with the terms of the plan or coverage or with applicable law; and

*(vii)* To the extent the final IRO decision maker is different from the IRO's clinical reviewer, the opinion of such clinical reviewer, after considering information described in this notice, to the extent the information or documents are available and the clinical reviewer or reviewers consider such information or documents appropriate.

*(6)* The assigned IRO must provide written notice of the final external review decision within 45 days after the IRO receives the request for the external review. The IRO must deliver the notice of the final external review decision to the claimant and the plan or issuer.

*(7)* The assigned IRO's written notice of the final external review decision must contain the following:

*(i)* A general description of the reason for the request for external review, including information sufficient to identify the claim (including the date or dates of service, the health care provider, the claim amount (if applicable), and a statement describing the availability, upon request, of the diagnosis code and its corresponding meaning, the treatment code and its corresponding meaning, and the reason for the plan's or issuer's denial);

*(ii)* The date the IRO received the assignment to conduct the external review and the date of the IRO decision;

*(iii)* References to the evidence or documentation, including the specific coverage provisions and evidence-based standards, considered in reaching its decision;

*(iv)* A discussion of the principal reason or reasons for its decision, including the rationale for its decision and any evidence-based standards that were relied on in making its decision;

*(v)* A statement that the IRO's determination is binding except to the extent that other remedies may be available under State or Federal law to either the group health plan or health insurance issuer or to the claimant, or to the extent the health plan or health insurance issuer voluntarily makes payment on the claim or otherwise provides benefits at any time, including after a final external review decision that denies the claim or otherwise fails to require such payment or benefits;

*(vi)* A statement that judicial review may be available to the claimant; and

*(vii)* Current contact information, including phone number, for any applicable office of health insurance consumer assistance or ombudsman established under PHS Act section 2793.

*(viii)* After a final external review decision, the IRO must maintain records of all claims and notices associated with the external review process for six years. An IRO must make such records available for examination by the claimant, plan, issuer, or State or Federal oversight agency upon request, except where such disclosure would violate State or Federal privacy laws.

*(iv) Reversal of plan's or issuer's decision.*—Upon receipt of a notice of a final external review decision reversing the adverse benefit determination or final adverse benefit determination, the plan or issuer immediately must provide coverage or payment (including immediately authorizing care or immediately paying benefits) for the claim.

*(3) Expedited external review.*—A group health plan or health insurance issuer must comply with the following standards with respect to an expedited external review:

*(i) Request for external review.*—A group health plan or health insurance issuer must allow a claimant to make a request for an expedited external review with the plan or issuer at the time the claimant receives:

*(A)* An adverse benefit determination if the adverse benefit determination involves a medical condition of the claimant for which the timeframe for completion of an expedited internal appeal under paragraph (b) of this section would seriously jeopardize the life or health of the claimant or would jeopardize the claimant's ability to regain maximum function and the claimant has filed a request for an expedited internal appeal; or

*(B)* A final internal adverse benefit determination, if the claimant has a medical condition where the timeframe for completion of a standard external review would seriously jeopardize the life or health of the claimant or would jeopardize the claimant's ability to regain maximum function, or if the final internal adverse benefit determination concerns an admission, availability of care, continued stay, or health care item or service for which the claimant received emergency services, but has not been discharged from the facility.

*(ii) Preliminary review.*—Immediately upon receipt of the request for expedited external review, the plan or issuer must determine whether the request meets the reviewability requirements set forth in paragraph (d)(2)(ii) of this section for standard external review. The plan or issuer must immediately send a notice that meets the requirements set forth in paragraph (d)(2)(ii)(B) for standard review to the claimant of its eligibility determination.

*(iii) Referral to independent review organization.*—(A) Upon a determination that a request is eligible for expedited external review following the preliminary review, the plan or issuer will assign an IRO pursuant to the requirements set forth in paragraph (d)(2)(iii) of this section for standard review. The plan or issuer must provide or transmit all necessary documents and information considered in making the adverse benefit determination or final internal adverse benefit determination to the assigned IRO electronically or by telephone or facsimile or any other available expeditious method.

*(B)* The assigned IRO, to the extent the information or documents are available and the IRO considers them appropriate, must

⋙➤ *Caution: Reg. §54.9815-2719, below, as added by T.D. 9744, is applicable to group health plans and health insurance issuers beginning on the first day of the plan year (or, in the individual market, the first day of the first policy year) beginning on or after January 1, 2017.*

consider the information or documents described above under the procedures for standard review. In reaching a decision, the assigned IRO must review the claim de novo and is not bound by any decisions or conclusions reached during the plan's or issuer's internal claims and appeals process.

(iv) *Notice of final external review decision.*—The plan's or issuer's contract with the assigned IRO must require the IRO to provide notice of the final external review decision, in accordance with the requirements set forth in paragraph (d)(2)(iii)(B) of this section, as expeditiously as the claimant's medical condition or circumstances require, but in no event more than 72 hours after the IRO receives the request for an expedited external review. If the notice is not in writing, within 48 hours after the date of providing that notice, the assigned IRO must provide written confirmation of the decision to the claimant and the plan or issuer.

(4) *Alternative, Federally-administered external review process.*—Insured coverage not subject to an applicable State external review process under paragraph (c) of this section may elect to use either the Federal external review process, as set forth under paragraph (d) of this section or the Federally-administered external review process, as set forth by HHS in guidance. In such circumstances, the requirement to provide external review under this paragraph (d) is satisfied.

(e) *Form and manner of notice.*—(1) *In general.*—For purposes of this section, a group health plan and a health insurance issuer offering group health insurance coverage are considered to provide relevant notices in a culturally and linguistically appropriate manner if the plan or issuer meets all the requirements of paragraph (e)(2) of this section with respect to the applicable non-English languages described in paragraph (e)(3) of this section.

(2) *Requirements.*—(i) The plan or issuer must provide oral language services (such as a telephone customer assistance hotline) that includes answering questions in any applicable non-English language and providing assistance with filing claims and appeals (including external review) in any applicable non-English language;

(ii) The plan or issuer must provide, upon request, a notice in any applicable non-English language; and

(iii) The plan or issuer must include in the English versions of all notices, a statement prominently displayed in any applicable non-English language clearly indicating how to access the language services provided by the plan or issuer.

(3) *Applicable non-English language.*—With respect to an address in any United States county to which a notice is sent, a non-English language is an applicable non-English language if ten percent or more of the population residing in the county is literate only in the same non-English language, as determined in guidance published by the Secretary.

(f) *Secretarial authority.*—The Secretary may determine that the external review process of a group health plan or health insurance issuer, in operation as of March 23, 2010, is considered in compliance with the applicable process established under paragraph (c) or (d) of this section if it substantially meets the requirements of paragraph (c) or (d) of this section, as applicable.

(g) *Applicability date.*—The provisions of this section are applicable to group health plans and health insurance issuers for plan years beginning on or after January 1, 2017. Until the applicability date for this regulation, plans and issuers are required to continue to comply with the interim final regulations promulgated by the Department of Labor at 29 CFR part 2590, contained in the 29 CFR, parts 1927 to end, edition revised as of July 1, 2015. [Reg. §54.9815-2719.]

☐ [T.D. 9744, 11-13-2015.]

⋙➤ *Caution: Temporary Reg. §54.9815-2719T, below, was removed by T.D. 9744 and is inapplicable under Code Sec. 7805(e)(2). However, until final Reg. §54.9815-2719 is applicable on the first day of the plan or policy year beginning after January 1, 2017, taxpayers may comply with the corresponding interim final regulation at 29 CFR part 2590 that is substantially similar to the temporary reg below.*

**[Reg. §54.9815-2719T]**

**§54.9815-2719T. Internal claims and appeals and external review processes (temporary).**—(a) *Scope and definitions.*—(1) *Scope.*—This section sets forth requirements with respect to internal claims and appeals and external review processes for group health plans and health insurance issuers that are not grandfathered health plans under §54.9815-1251T. Paragraph (b) of this section provides requirements for internal claims and appeals processes. Paragraph (c) of this section sets forth rules governing the applicability of State external review processes. Paragraph (d) of this section sets forth a Federal external review process for plans and issuers not subject to an applicable State external review process. Paragraph (e) of this section prescribes requirements for ensuring that notices required to be provided under this section are provided in a culturally and linguistically appropriate manner. Paragraph (f) of this section describes the authority of the Secretary to deem certain external review processes in existence on March 23, 2010 as in compliance with paragraph (c) or (d) of this section. Paragraph (g) of this section sets forth the applicability date for this section.

(2) *Definitions.*—For purposes of this section, the following definitions apply -

(i) *Adverse benefit determination.*—An *adverse benefit determination* means an adverse benefit determination as defined in 29 CFR 2560.503-1, as well as any rescission of coverage, as described in §54.9815-2712T(a)(2) (whether or not, in connection with the rescission, there is an adverse effect on any particular benefit at that time).

(ii) *Appeal (or internal appeal).*—An *appeal* or *internal appeal* means review by a plan or issuer of an adverse benefit determination, as required in paragraph (b) of this section.

(iii) *Claimant.*—*Claimant* means an individual who makes a claim under this section. For purposes of this section, references to claimant include a claimant's authorized representative.

(iv) *External review.*—*External review* means a review of an adverse benefit determination (including a final internal adverse benefit determination) conducted pursuant to an applicable State external review process described in paragraph (c) of this section or the Federal external review process of paragraph (d) of this section.

(v) *Final internal adverse benefit determination.*—A *final internal adverse benefit determination* means an adverse benefit determination that has been upheld by a plan or issuer at the completion of the internal appeals process applicable under paragraph (b) of this sec-

tion (or an adverse benefit determination with respect to which the internal appeals process has been exhausted under the deemed exhaustion rules of paragraph (b)(2)(ii)(F) of this section).

(vi) *Final external review decision.*—A *final external review decision*, as used in paragraph (d) of this section, means a determination by an independent review organization at the conclusion of an external review.

(vii) *Independent review organization (or IRO).*—An *independent review organization* (or IRO) means an entity that conducts independent external reviews of adverse benefit determinations and final internal adverse benefit determinations pursuant to paragraph (c) or (d) of this section.

(viii) *NAIC Uniform Model Act.*—The *NAIC Uniform Model Act* means the Uniform Health Carrier External Review Model Act promulgated by the National Association of Insurance Commissioners in place on [INSERT DATE OF PUBLICATION IN THE FEDERAL REGISTER].

(b) *Internal claims and appeals process.*—(1) *In general.*—A group health plan and a health insurance issuer offering group health insurance coverage must implement an effective internal claims and appeals process, as described in this paragraph (b).

(2) *Requirements for group health plans and group health insurance issuers.*—A group health plan and a health insurance issuer offering group health insurance coverage must comply with all the requirements of this paragraph (b)(2). In the case of health insurance coverage offered in connection with a group health plan, if either the plan or the issuer complies with the internal claims and appeals process of this paragraph (b)(2), then the obligation to comply with this paragraph (b)(2) is satisfied for both the plan and the issuer with respect to the health insurance coverage.

(i) *Minimum internal claims and appeals standards.*—A group health plan and a health insurance issuer offering group health insurance coverage must comply with all the requirements applicable to group health plans under 29 CFR 2560.503-1, except to the extent those requirements are modified by paragraph (b)(2)(ii) of this section. Accordingly, under this paragraph (b), with respect to health insurance coverage offered in connection with a group health plan, the group health insurance issuer is subject to the requirements in 29 CFR 2560.503-1 to the same extent as the group health plan.

(ii) *Additional standards.*—In addition to the requirements in paragraph (b)(2)(i) of this section, the internal claims and appeals

>>>→ *Caution: Temporary Reg. §54.9815-2719T, below, was removed by T.D. 9744 and is inapplicable under Code Sec. 7805(e)(2). However, until final Reg. §54.9815-2719 is applicable on the first day of the plan or policy year beginning after January 1, 2017, taxpayers may comply with the corresponding interim final regulation at 29 CFR part 2590 that is substantially similar to the temporary reg below.*

processes of a group health plan and a health insurance issuer offering group health insurance coverage must meet the requirements of this paragraph (b)(2)(ii).

(A) *Clarification of meaning of adverse benefit determination.*—For purposes of this paragraph (b)(2), an "adverse benefit determination" includes an adverse benefit determination as defined in paragraph (a)(2)(i) of this section. Accordingly, in complying with 29 CFR 2560.503-1, as well as the other provisions of this paragraph (b)(2), a plan or issuer must treat a rescission of coverage (whether or not the rescission has an adverse effect on any particular benefit at that time) as an adverse benefit determination. (Rescissions of coverage are subject to the requirements of § 54.9815-2712T.)

(B) *Expedited notification of benefit determinations involving urgent care.*—The requirements of 29 CFR 2560.503-1(f)(2)(i) (which generally provide, among other things, in the case of urgent care claims for notification of the plan's benefit determination (whether adverse or not) as soon as possible, taking into account the medical exigencies, but not later than 72 hours after receipt of the claim) continue to apply to the plan and issuer. For purposes of this paragraph (b)(2)(ii)(B), a claim involving urgent care has the meaning given in 29 CFR 2560.503-1(m)(1), as determined by the attending provider, and the plan or issuer shall defer to such determination of the attending provider.

(C) *Full and fair review.*—A plan and issuer must allow a claimant to review the claim file and to present evidence and testimony as part of the internal claims and appeals process. Specifically, in addition to complying with the requirements of 29 CFR 2560.503-1(h)(2) —

(1) The plan or issuer must provide the claimant, free of charge, with any new or additional evidence considered, relied upon, or generated by the plan or issuer (or at the direction of the plan or issuer) in connection with the claim; such evidence must be provided as soon as possible and sufficiently in advance of the date on which the notice of final internal adverse benefit determination is required to be provided under 29 CFR 2560.503-1(i) to give the claimant a reasonable opportunity to respond prior to that date; and

(2) Before the plan or issuer can issue a final internal adverse benefit determination based on a new or additional rationale, the claimant must be provided, free of charge, with the rationale; the rationale must be provided as soon as possible and sufficiently in advance of the date on which the notice of final internal adverse benefit determination is required to be provided under 29 CFR 2560.503-1(i) to give the claimant a reasonable opportunity to respond prior to that date.

(D) *Avoiding conflicts of interest.*—In addition to the requirements of 29 CFR 2560.503-1(b) and (h) regarding full and fair review, the plan and issuer must ensure that all claims and appeals are adjudicated in a manner designed to ensure the independence and impartiality of the persons involved in making the decision. Accordingly, decisions regarding hiring, compensation, termination, promotion, or other similar matters with respect to any individual (such as a claims adjudicator or medical expert) must not be made based upon the likelihood that the individual will support the denial of benefits.

(E) *Notice.*—A plan and issuer must provide notice to individuals, in a culturally and linguistically appropriate manner (as described in paragraph (e) of this section) that complies with the requirements of 29 CFR 2560.503-1(g) and (j). The plan and issuer must also comply with the additional requirements of this paragraph (b)(2)(ii)(E).

(1) The plan and issuer must ensure that any notice of adverse benefit determination or final internal adverse benefit determination includes information sufficient to identify the claim involved (including the date of service, the health care provider, the claim amount (if applicable), and a statement describing the availability, upon request, of the diagnosis code and its corresponding meaning, and the treatment code and its corresponding meaning).

(2) The plan and issuer must provide to participants and beneficiaries, as soon as practicable, upon request, the diagnosis code and its corresponding meaning, and the treatment code and its corresponding meaning, associated with any adverse benefit determination or final internal adverse benefit determination. The plan or issuer must not consider a request for such diagnosis and treatment information, in itself, to be a request for an internal appeal under this paragraph (b) or an external review under paragraphs (c) and (d) of this section.

(3) The plan and issuer must ensure that the reason or reasons for the adverse benefit determination or final internal ad-

verse benefit determination includes the denial code and its corresponding meaning, as well as a description of the plan's or issuer's standard, if any, that was used in denying the claim. In the case of a notice of final internal adverse benefit determination, this description must include a discussion of the decision.

(4) The plan and issuer must provide a description of available internal appeals and external review processes, including information regarding how to initiate an appeal.

(5) The plan and issuer must disclose the availability of, and contact information for, any applicable office of health insurance consumer assistance or ombudsman established under PHS Act section 2793 to assist individuals with the internal claims and appeals and external review processes.

(F) *Deemed exhaustion of internal claims and appeals processes.*—(1) In the case of a plan or issuer that fails to adhere to all the requirements of this paragraph (b)(2) with respect to a claim, the claimant is deemed to have exhausted the internal claims and appeals process of this paragraph (b), except as provided in paragraph (b)(2)(ii)(F)(2) of this section. Accordingly, the claimant may initiate an external review under paragraph (c) or (d) of this section, as applicable. The claimant is also entitled to pursue any available remedies under section 502(a) of ERISA or under State law, as applicable, on the basis that the plan or issuer has failed to provide a reasonable internal claims and appeals process that would yield a decision on the merits of the claim. If a claimant chooses to pursue remedies under section 502(a) of ERISA under such circumstances, the claim or appeal is deemed denied on review without the exercise of discretion by an appropriate fiduciary.

(2) Notwithstanding paragraph (b)(2)(ii)(F)(1) of this section, the internal claims and appeals process of this paragraph (b) will not be deemed exhausted based on *de minimis* violations that do not cause, and are not likely to cause, prejudice or harm to the claimant so long as the plan or issuer demonstrates that the violation was for good cause or due to matters beyond the control of the plan or issuer and that the violation occurred in the context of an ongoing, good faith exchange of information between the plan and the claimant. This exception is not available if the violation is part of a pattern or practice of violations by the plan or issuer. The claimant may request a written explanation of the violation from the plan or issuer, and the plan or issuer must provide such explanation within 10 days, including a specific description of its bases, if any, for asserting that the violation should not cause the internal claims and appeals process of this paragraph (b) to be deemed exhausted. If an external reviewer or a court rejects the claimant's request for immediate review under paragraph (b)(2)(ii)(F)(1) of this section on the basis that the plan met the standards for the exception under this paragraph (b)(2)(ii)(F)(2), the claimant has the right to resubmit and pursue the internal appeal of the claim. In such a case, within a reasonable time after the external reviewer or court rejects the claim for immediate review (not to exceed 10 days), the plan shall provide the claimant with notice of the opportunity to resubmit and pursue the internal appeal of the claim. Time periods for re-filing the claim shall begin to run upon claimant's receipt of such notice.

(iii) *Requirement to provide continued coverage pending the outcome of an appeal.*—A plan and issuer subject to the requirements of this paragraph (b)(2) are required to provide continued coverage pending the outcome of an appeal. For this purpose, the plan and issuer must comply with the requirements of 29 CFR 2560.503-1(f)(2)(ii), which generally provides that benefits for an ongoing course of treatment cannot be reduced or terminated without providing advance notice and an opportunity for advance review.

(c) *State standards for external review.*—(1) *In general.*—(i) If a State external review process that applies to and is binding on a health insurance issuer offering group health insurance coverage includes at a minimum the consumer protections in the NAIC Uniform Model Act, then the issuer must comply with the applicable State external review process and is not required to comply with the Federal external review process of paragraph (d) of this section. In such a case, to the extent that benefits under a group health plan are provided through health insurance coverage, the group health plan is not required to comply with either this paragraph (c) or the Federal external review process of paragraph (d) of this section.

(ii) To the extent that a group health plan provides benefits other than through health insurance coverage (that is, the plan is self-insured) and is subject to a State external review process that applies to and is binding on the plan (for example, is not preempted by ERISA) and the State external review process includes at a minimum the consumer protections in the NAIC Uniform Model Act, then the

➤➤➤ *Caution: Temporary Reg. §54.9815-2719T, below, was removed by T.D. 9744 and is inapplicable under Code Sec. 7805(e)(2). However, until final Reg. §54.9815-2719 is applicable on the first day of the plan or policy year beginning after January 1, 2017, taxpayers may comply with the corresponding interim final regulation at 29 CFR part 2590 that is substantially similar to the temporary reg below.*

plan must comply with the applicable State external review process and is not required to comply with the Federal external review process of paragraph (d) of this section.

(iii) If a plan or issuer is not required under paragraph (c)(1)(i) or (c)(1)(ii) of this section to comply with the requirements of this paragraph (c), then the plan or issuer must comply with the Federal external review process of paragraph (d) of this section, except to the extent, in the case of a plan, the plan is not required under paragraph (c)(1)(i) of this section to comply with paragraph (d) of this section.

(2) *Minimum standards for State external review processes.*—An applicable State external review process must meet all the minimum consumer protections in this paragraph (c)(2). The Department of Health and Human Services will determine whether State external review processes meet these requirements.

(i) The State process must provide for the external review of adverse benefit determinations (including final internal adverse benefit determinations) by issuers (or, if applicable, plans) that are based on the issuer's (or plan's) requirements for medical necessity, appropriateness, health care setting, level of care, or effectiveness of a covered benefit.

(ii) The State process must require issuers (or, if applicable, plans) to provide effective written notice to claimants of their rights in connection with an external review for an adverse benefit determination.

(iii) To the extent the State process requires exhaustion of an internal claims and appeals process, exhaustion must be unnecessary where the issuer (or, if applicable, the plan) has waived the requirement, the issuer (or the plan) is considered to have exhausted the internal claims and appeals process under applicable law (including by failing to comply with any of the requirements for the internal appeal process, as outlined in paragraph (b)(2) of this section), or the claimant has applied for expedited external review at the same time as applying for an expedited internal appeal.

(iv) The State process provides that the issuer (or, if applicable, the plan) against which a request for external review is filed must pay the cost of the IRO for conducting the external review. Notwithstanding this requirement, the State external review process may require a nominal filing fee from the claimant requesting an external review. For this purpose, to be considered nominal, a filing fee must not exceed $25, it must be refunded to the claimant if the adverse benefit determination (or final internal adverse benefit determination) is reversed through external review, it must be waived if payment of the fee would impose an undue financial hardship, and the annual limit on filing fees for any claimant within a single plan year must not exceed $75.

(v) The State process may not impose a restriction on the minimum dollar amount of a claim for it to be eligible for external review. Thus, the process may not impose, for example, a $500 minimum claims threshold.

(vi) The State process must allow at least four months after the receipt of a notice of an adverse benefit determination or final internal adverse benefit determination for a request for an external review to be filed.

(vii) The State process must provide that IROs will be assigned on a random basis or another method of assignment that assures the independence and impartiality of the assignment process (such as rotational assignment) by a State or independent entity, and in no event selected by the issuer, plan, or the individual.

(viii) The State process must provide for maintenance of a list of approved IROs qualified to conduct the external review based on the nature of the health care service that is the subject of the review. The State process must provide for approval only of IROs that are accredited by a nationally recognized private accrediting organization.

(ix) The State process must provide that any approved IRO has no conflicts of interest that will influence its independence. Thus, the IRO may not own or control, or be owned or controlled by a health insurance issuer, a group health plan, the sponsor of a group health plan, a trade association of plans or issuers, or a trade association of health care providers. The State process must further provide that the IRO and the clinical reviewer assigned to conduct an external review may not have a material professional, familial, or financial conflict of interest with the issuer or plan that is the subject of the external review; the claimant (and any related parties to the claimant) whose treatment is the subject of the external review; any officer, director, or management employee of the issuer; the plan administrator, plan fiduciaries, or plan employees; the health care provider, the health care provider's group, or practice association recommending the treatment that is subject to the external review; the facility at which the recommended treatment would be provided; or the devel-

oper or manufacturer of the principal drug, device, procedure, or other therapy being recommended.

(x) The State process allows the claimant at least five business days to submit to the IRO in writing additional information that the IRO must consider when conducting the external review and it requires that the claimant is notified of the right to do so. The process must also require that any additional information submitted by the claimant to the IRO must be forwarded to the issuer (or, if applicable, the plan) within one business day of receipt by the IRO.

(xi) The State process must provide that the decision is binding on the plan or issuer, as well as the claimant, except to the extent other remedies are available under State or Federal law, and except that the requirement that the decision be binding shall not preclude the plan or issuer from making payment on the claim or otherwise providing benefits at any time, including after a final external review decision that denies the claim or otherwise fails to require such payment or benefits. For this purpose, the plan or issuer must provide benefits (including by making payment on the claim) pursuant to the final external review decision without delay, regardless of whether the plan or issuer intends to seek judicial review of the external review decision and unless or until there is a judicial decision otherwise.

(xii) The State process must require, for standard external review, that the IRO provide written notice to the claimant and the issuer (or, if applicable, the plan) of its decision to uphold or reverse the adverse benefit determination (or final internal adverse benefit determination) within no more than 45 days after the receipt of the request for external review by the IRO.

(xiii) The State process must provide for an expedited external review if the adverse benefit determination (or final internal adverse benefit determination) concerns an admission, availability of care, continued stay, or health care service for which the claimant received emergency services, but has not been discharged from a facility; or involves a medical condition for which the standard external review time frame would seriously jeopardize the life or health of the claimant or jeopardize the claimant's ability to regain maximum function. As expeditiously as possible but within no more than 72 hours after the receipt of the request for expedited external review by the IRO, the IRO must make its decision to uphold or reverse the adverse benefit determination (or final internal adverse benefit determination) and notify the claimant and the issuer (or, if applicable, the plan) of the determination. If the notice is not in writing, the IRO must provide written confirmation of the decision within 48 hours after the date of the notice of the decision.

(xiv) The State process must require that issuers (or, if applicable, plans) include a description of the external review process in or attached to the summary plan description, policy, certificate, membership booklet, outline of coverage, or other evidence of coverage it provides to participants, beneficiaries, or enrollees, substantially similar to what is set forth in section 17 of the NAIC Uniform Model Act.

(xv) The State process must require that IROs maintain written records and make them available upon request to the State, substantially similar to what is set forth in section 15 of the NAIC Uniform Model Act.

(xvi) The State process follows procedures for external review of adverse benefit determinations (or final internal adverse benefit determinations) involving experimental or investigational treatment, substantially similar to what is set forth in section 10 of the NAIC Uniform Model Act.

(3) *Transition period for external review processes.*—(i) Through December 31, 2011, an applicable State external review process applicable to a health insurance issuer or group health plan is considered to meet the requirements of PHS Act section 2719(b). Accordingly, through December 31, 2011, an applicable State external review process will be considered binding on the issuer or plan (in lieu of the requirements of the Federal external review process). If there is no applicable State external review process, the issuer or plan is required to comply with the requirements of the Federal external review process in paragraph (d) of this section.

(ii) For final internal adverse benefit determinations (or, in the case of simultaneous internal appeal and external review, adverse benefit determinations) provided on or after January 1, 2012, the Federal external review process will apply unless the Department of Health and Human Services determines that a State law meets all the minimum standards of paragraph (c)(2) of this section.

(d) *Federal external review process.*—A plan or issuer not subject to an applicable State external review process under paragraph (c) of this section must provide an effective Federal external review process in accordance with this paragraph (d) (except to the extent, in the

»»→ *Caution: Temporary Reg. §54.9815-2719T, below, was removed by T.D. 9744 and is inapplicable under Code Sec. 7805(e)(2). However, until final Reg. §54.9815-2719 is applicable on the first day of the plan or policy year beginning after January 1, 2017, taxpayers may comply with the corresponding interim final regulation at 29 CFR part 2590 that is substantially similar to the temporary reg below.*

case of a plan, the plan is described in paragraph (c)(1)(i) of this section as not having to comply with this paragraph (d)). In the case of health insurance coverage offered in connection with a group health plan, if either the plan or the issuer complies with the Federal external review process of this paragraph (d), then the obligation to comply with this paragraph (d) is satisfied for both the plan and the issuer with respect to the health insurance coverage.

(1) *Scope.*—(i) *In general.*—Subject to the suspension provision in paragraph (d)(1)(ii) of this section and except to the extent provided otherwise by the Secretary in guidance, the Federal external review process established pursuant to this paragraph (d) applies to any adverse benefit determination or final internal adverse benefit determination (as defined in paragraphs (a)(2)(i) and (a)(2)(v) of this section), except that a denial, reduction, termination, or a failure to provide payment for a benefit based on a determination that a participant or beneficiary fails to meet the requirements for eligibility under the terms of a group health plan is not eligible for the Federal external review process under this paragraph (d).

(ii) *Suspension of general rule.*—Unless or until this suspension is revoked in guidance by the Secretary, with respect to claims for which external review has not been initiated before September 20, 2011, the Federal external review process established pursuant to this paragraph (d) applies only to:

(A) An adverse benefit determination (including a final internal adverse benefit determination) by a plan or issuer that involves medical judgment (including, but not limited to, those based on the plan's or issuer's requirements for medical necessity, appropriateness, health care setting, level of care, or effectiveness of a covered benefit; or its determination that a treatment is experimental or investigational), as determined by the external reviewer; and

(B) A rescission of coverage (whether or not the rescission has any effect on any particular benefit at that time).

(iii) *Examples.*—This rules of paragraph (d)(1)(ii) of this section are illustrated by the following examples:

*Example 1.* (i) *Facts.* A group health plan provides coverage for 30 physical therapy visits generally. After the 30th visit, coverage is provided only if the service is preauthorized pursuant to an approved treatment plan that takes into account medical necessity using the plan's definition of the term. Individual *A* seeks coverage for a 31st physical therapy visit. *A*'s health care provider submits a treatment plan for approval, but it is not approved by the plan, so coverage for the 31st visit is not preauthorized. With respect to the 31st visit, *A* receives a notice of final internal adverse benefit determination stating that the maximum visit limit is exceeded.

(ii) *Conclusion.* In this *Example 1*, the plan's denial of benefits is based on medical necessity and involves medical judgment. Accordingly, the claim is eligible for external review during the suspension period under paragraph (d)(1)(ii) of this section. Moreover, the plan's notification of final internal adverse benefit determination is inadequate under paragraphs (b)(2)(i) and (b)(2)(ii)(E)(3) of this section because it fails to make clear that the plan will pay for more than 30 visits if the service is preauthorized pursuant to an approved treatment plan that takes into account medical necessity using the plan's definition of the term. Accordingly, the notice of final internal adverse benefit determination should refer to the plan provision governing the 31st visit and should describe the plan's standard for medical necessity, as well as how the treatment fails to meet the plan's standard.

*Example 2.* (i) *Facts.* A group health plan does not provide coverage for services provided out of network, unless the service cannot effectively be provided in network. Individual *B* seeks coverage for a specialized medical procedure from an out-of-network provider because *B* believes that the procedure cannot be effectively provided in network. *B* receives a notice of final internal adverse benefit determination stating that the claim is denied because the provider is out-of-network.

(ii) *Conclusion.* In this *Example 2*, the plan's denial of benefits is based on whether a service can effectively be provided in network and, therefore, involves medical judgment. Accordingly, the claim is eligible for external review during the suspension period under paragraph (d)(1)(ii) of this section. Moreover, the plan's notice of final internal adverse benefit determination is inadequate under paragraphs (b)(2)(i) and (b)(2)(ii)(E)(3) of this section because the plan does provide benefits for services on an out-of-network basis if the services cannot effectively be provided in network. Accordingly, the notice of final internal adverse benefit determination is required to refer to the exception to the out-of-network exclusion and should describe the plan's standards for determining effectiveness of ser-

vices, as well as how services available to the claimant within the plan's network meet the plan's standard for effectiveness of services.

(2) *External review process standards.*—The Federal external review process established pursuant to this paragraph (d) will be similar to the process set forth in the NAIC Uniform Model Act and will meet standards issued by the Secretary. These standards will comply with all of the requirements described in this paragraph (d)(2).

(i) These standards will describe how a claimant initiates an external review, procedures for preliminary reviews to determine whether a claim is eligible for external review, minimum qualifications for IROs, a process for approving IROs eligible to be assigned to conduct external reviews, a process for random assignment of external reviews to approved IROs, standards for IRO decision-making, and rules for providing notice of a final external review decision.

(ii) These standards will provide an expedited external review process for —

(A) An adverse benefit determination, if the adverse benefit determination involves a medical condition of the claimant for which the timeframe for completion of an expedited internal appeal under paragraph (b) of this section would seriously jeopardize the life or health of the claimant, or would jeopardize the claimant's ability to regain maximum function and the claimant has filed a request for an expedited internal appeal under paragraph (b) of this section; or

(B) A final internal adverse benefit determination, if the claimant has a medical condition where the timeframe for completion of a standard external review pursuant to paragraph (d)(3) of this section would seriously jeopardize the life or health of the claimant or would jeopardize the claimant's ability to regain maximum function, or if the final internal adverse benefit determination concerns an admission, availability of care, continued stay, or health care service for which the claimant received emergency services, but has not been discharged from a facility.

(iii) With respect to claims involving experimental or investigational treatments, these standards will also provide additional consumer protections to ensure that adequate clinical and scientific experience and protocols are taken into account as part of the external review process.

(iv) These standards will provide that an external review decision is binding on the plan or issuer, as well as the claimant, except to the extent other remedies are available under State or Federal law, and except that the requirement that the decision be binding shall not preclude the plan or issuer from making payment on the claim or otherwise providing benefits at any time, including after a final external review decision that denies the claim or otherwise fails to require such payment or benefits. For this purpose, the plan or issuer must provide any benefits (including by making payment on the claim) pursuant to the final external review decision without delay, regardless of whether the plan or issuer intends to seek judicial review of the external review decision and unless or until there is a judicial decision otherwise.

(v) These standards may establish external review reporting requirements for IROs.

(vi) These standards will establish additional notice requirements for plans and issuers regarding disclosures to participants and beneficiaries describing the Federal external review procedures (including the right to file a request for an external review of an adverse benefit determination or a final internal adverse benefit determination in the summary plan description, policy, certificate, membership booklet, outline of coverage, or other evidence of coverage it provides to participants or beneficiaries).

(vii) These standards will require plans and issuers to provide information relevant to the processing of the external review, including, but not limited to, the information considered and relied on in making the adverse benefit determination or final internal adverse benefit determination.

(e) *Form and manner of notice.*—(1) *In general.*—For purposes of this section, a group health plan and a health insurance issuer offering group health insurance coverage are considered to provide relevant notices in a culturally and linguistically appropriate manner if the plan or issuer meets all the requirements of paragraph (e)(2) of this section with respect to the applicable non-English languages described in paragraph (e)(3) of this section.

(2) *Requirements.*—(i) The plan or issuer must provide oral language services (such as a telephone customer assistance hotline) that include answering questions in any applicable non- English language and providing assistance with filing claims and appeals (including external review) in any applicable non-English language;

⟫⟫→ *Caution: Temporary Reg. §54.9815-2719T, below, was removed by T.D. 9744 and is inapplicable under Code Sec. 7805(e)(2). However, until final Reg. §54.9815-2719 is applicable on the first day of the plan or policy year beginning after January 1, 2017, taxpayers may comply with the corresponding interim final regulation at 29 CFR part 2590 that is substantially similar to the temporary reg below.*

(ii) The plan or issuer must provide, upon request, a notice in any applicable non-English language; and

(iii) The plan or issuer must include in the English versions of all notices, a statement prominently displayed in any applicable non-English language clearly indicating how to access the language services provided by the plan or issuer.

(3) *Applicable non-English language.*—With respect to an address in any United States county to which a notice is sent, a non-English language is an applicable non-English language if ten percent or more of the population residing in the county is literate only in the same non-English language, as determined in guidance published by the Secretary.

(f) *Secretarial authority.*—The Secretary may determine that the external review process of a group health plan or health insurance issuer, in operation as of March 23, 2010, is considered in compliance with the applicable process established under paragraph (c) or (d) of this section if it substantially meets the requirements of paragraph (c) or (d) of this section, as applicable.

(g) *Applicability/effective date.*—The provisions of this section apply for plan years beginning on or after September 23, 2010. See §54.9815-1251T for determining the application of this section to grandfathered health plans (providing that these rules regarding internal claims and appeals and external review processes do not apply to grandfathered health plans).

(h) *Expiration date.*—The applicability of this section expires on July 22, 2013 or on such earlier date as may be provided in final regulations or other action published in the **Federal Register**. [Temporary Reg. §54.9815-2719T.]

☐ [T.D. 9494, 7-22-2010. *Amended by T.D.* 9532, 6-22-2011. *Removed by T.D.* 9744, 11-13-2015.]

⟫⟫→ *Caution: Reg. §54.9815-2719A, below, as added by T.D. 9744, is applicable to group health plans and health insurance issuers beginning on the first day of the plan year (or, in the individual market, the first day of the first policy year) beginning on or after January 1, 2017.*

### [Reg. §54.9815-2719A]

**§54.9815-2719A. Patient protections.**—(a) *Choice of health care professional.*—(1) *Designation of primary care provider.*—(i) *In general.*—If a group health plan, or a health insurance issuer offering group health insurance coverage, requires or provides for designation by a participant or beneficiary of a participating primary care provider, then the plan or issuer must permit each participant or beneficiary to designate any participating primary care provider who is available to accept the participant or beneficiary. In such a case, the plan or issuer must comply with the rules of paragraph (a)(4) of this section by informing each participant of the terms of the plan or health insurance coverage regarding designation of a primary care provider.

(ii) *Construction.*—Nothing in paragraph (a)(1)(i) of this section is to be construed to prohibit the application of reasonable and appropriate geographic limitations with respect to the selection of primary care providers, in accordance with the terms of the plan or coverage, the underlying provider contracts, and applicable State law.

(iii) *Example.*—The rules of this paragraph (a)(1) are illustrated by the following example:

*Example.* (i) *Facts.* A group health plan requires individuals covered under the plan to designate a primary care provider. The plan permits each individual to designate any primary care provider participating in the plan's network who is available to accept the individual as the individual's primary care provider. If an individual has not designated a primary care provider, the plan designates one until one has been designated by the individual. The plan provides a notice that satisfies the requirements of paragraph (a)(4) of this section regarding the ability to designate a primary care provider.

(ii) *Conclusion* In this *Example*, the plan has satisfied the requirements of paragraph (a) of this section.

(2) *Designation of pediatrician as primary care provider.*—(i) *In general.*—If a group health plan, or a health insurance issuer offering group health insurance coverage, requires or provides for the designation of a participating primary care provider for a child by a participant or beneficiary, the plan or issuer must permit the participant or beneficiary to designate a physician (allopathic or osteopathic) who specializes in pediatrics (including pediatric subspecialties, based on the scope of that provider's license under applicable State law) as the child's primary care provider if the provider participates in the network of the plan or issuer and is available to accept the child. In such a case, the plan or issuer must comply with the rules of paragraph (a)(4) of this section by informing each participant of the terms of the plan or health insurance coverage regarding designation of a pediatrician as the child's primary care provider.

(ii) *Construction.*—Nothing in paragraph (a)(2)(i) of this section is to be construed to waive any exclusions of coverage under the terms and conditions of the plan or health insurance coverage with respect to coverage of pediatric care.

(iii) *Examples.*—The rules of this paragraph (a)(2) are illustrated by the following examples:

*Example 1.* (i) *Facts.* A group health plan's HMO designates for each participant a physician who specializes in internal medicine to serve as the primary care provider for the participant and any beneficiaries. Participant *A* requests that Pediatrician *B* be designated as the primary care provider for *A*'s child. *B* is a participating provider in the HMO's network and is available to accept the child.

(ii) *Conclusion.* In this *Example 1*, the HMO must permit *A*'s designation of *B* as the primary care provider for *A*'s child in order to comply with the requirements of this paragraph (a)(2).

*Example 2.* (i) *Facts.* Same facts as *Example 1*, except that *A* takes *A*'s child to *B* for treatment of the child's severe shellfish allergies. *B* wishes to refer *A*'s child to an allergist for treatment. The HMO, however, does not provide coverage for treatment of food allergies, nor does it have an allergist participating in its network, and it therefore refuses to authorize the referral.

(ii) *Conclusion.* In this *Example 2*, the HMO has not violated the requirements of this paragraph (a)(2) because the exclusion of treatment for food allergies is in accordance with the terms of *A*'s coverage.

(3) *Patient access to obstetrical and gynecological care.*—(i) *General rights.*—(A) *Direct access.*—A group health plan, or a health insurance issuer offering group health insurance coverage, described in paragraph (a)(3)(ii) of this section may not require authorization or referral by the plan, issuer, or any person (including a primary care provider) in the case of a female participant or beneficiary who seeks coverage for obstetrical or gynecological care provided by a participating health care professional who specializes in obstetrics or gynecology. In such a case, the plan or issuer must comply with the rules of paragraph (a)(4) of this section by informing each participant that the plan may not require authorization or referral for obstetrical or gynecological care by a participating health care professional who specializes in obstetrics or gynecology. The plan or issuer may require such a professional to agree to otherwise adhere to the plan's or issuer's policies and procedures, including procedures regarding referrals and obtaining prior authorization and providing services pursuant to a treatment plan (if any) approved by the plan or issuer. For purposes of this paragraph (a)(3), a health care professional who specializes in obstetrics or gynecology is any individual (including a person other than a physician) who is authorized under applicable State law to provide obstetrical or gynecological care.

(B) *Obstetrical and gynecological care.*—A group health plan or health insurance issuer described in paragraph (a)(3)(ii) of this section must treat the provision of obstetrical and gynecological care, and the ordering of related obstetrical and gynecological items and services, pursuant to the direct access described under paragraph (a)(3)(i)(A) of this section, by a participating health care professional who specializes in obstetrics or gynecology as the authorization of the primary care provider.

(ii) *Application of paragraph.*—A group health plan, or a health insurance issuer offering group health insurance coverage, is described in this paragraph (a)(3) if the plan or issuer—

(A) Provides coverage for obstetrical or gynecological care; and

(B) Requires the designation by a participant or beneficiary of a participating primary care provider.

(iii) *Construction.*—Nothing in paragraph (a)(3)(i) of this section is to be construed to—

(A) Waive any exclusions of coverage under the terms and conditions of the plan or health insurance coverage with respect to coverage of obstetrical or gynecological care; or

(B) Preclude the group health plan or health insurance issuer involved from requiring that the obstetrical or gynecological provider notify the primary care health care professional or the plan or issuer of treatment decisions.

➤➤➤ *Caution: Reg. §54.9815-2719A, below, as added by T.D. 9744, is applicable to group health plans and health insurance issuers beginning on the first day of the plan year (or, in the individual market, the first day of the first policy year) beginning on or after January 1, 2017.*

(iv) *Examples.*—The rules of this paragraph (a)(3) are illustrated by the following examples:

*Example 1.* (i) *Facts.* A group health plan requires each participant to designate a physician to serve as the primary care provider for the participant and the participant's family. Participant *A*, a female, requests a gynecological exam with Physician *B*, an in-network physician specializing in gynecological care. The group health plan requires prior authorization from *A*'s designated primary care provider for the gynecological exam.

(ii) *Conclusion.* In this *Example 1*, the group health plan has violated the requirements of this paragraph (a)(3) because the plan requires prior authorization from *A*'s primary care provider prior to obtaining gynecological services.

*Example 2.* (i) *Facts.* Same facts as *Example 1* except that *A* seeks gynecological services from *C*, an out-of-network provider.

(ii) *Conclusion.* In this *Example 2*, the group health plan has not violated the requirements of this paragraph (a)(3) by requiring prior authorization because *C* is not a participating health care provider.

*Example 3.* (i) *Facts.* Same facts as *Example 1* except that the group health plan only requires *B* to inform *A*'s designated primary care physician of treatment decisions.

(ii) *Conclusion.* In this *Example 3*, the group health plan has not violated the requirements of this paragraph (a)(3) because *A* has direct access to *B* without prior authorization. The fact that the group health plan requires notification of treatment decisions to the designated primary care physician does not violate this paragraph (a)(3).

*Example 4.* (i) *Facts.* A group health plan requires each participant to designate a physician to serve as the primary care provider for the participant and the participant's family. The group health plan requires prior authorization before providing benefits for uterine fibroid embolization.

(ii) *Conclusion.* In this *Example 4*, the plan requirement for prior authorization before providing benefits for uterine fibroid embolization does not violate the requirements of this paragraph (a)(3) because, though the prior authorization requirement applies to obstetrical services, it does not restrict access to any providers specializing in obstetrics or gynecology.

(4) *Notice of right to designate a primary care provider.*—(i) *In general.*—If a group health plan or health insurance issuer requires the designation by a participant or beneficiary of a primary care provider, the plan or issuer must provide a notice informing each participant of the terms of the plan or health insurance coverage regarding designation of a primary care provider and of the rights—

(A) Under paragraph (a)(1)(i) of this section, that any participating primary care provider who is available to accept the participant or beneficiary can be designated;

(B) Under paragraph (a)(2)(i) of this section, with respect to a child, that any participating physician who specializes in pediatrics can be designated as the primary care provider; and

(C) Under paragraph (a)(3)(i) of this section, that the plan may not require authorization or referral for obstetrical or gynecological care by a participating health care professional who specializes in obstetrics or gynecology.

(ii) *Timing.*—The notice described in paragraph (a)(4)(i) of this section must be included whenever the plan or issuer provides a participant with a summary plan description or other similar description of benefits under the plan or health insurance coverage.

(iii) *Model language.*—The following model language can be used to satisfy the notice requirement described in paragraph (a)(4)(i) of this section:

(A) For plans and issuers that require or allow for the designation of primary care providers by participants or beneficiaries, insert:

[Name of group health plan or health insurance issuer] generally [requires/allows] the designation of a primary care provider. You have the right to designate any primary care provider who participates in our network and who is available to accept you or your family members. [If the plan or health insurance coverage designates a primary care provider automatically, insert: Until you make this designation, [name of group health plan or health insurance issuer] designates one for you.] For information on how to select a primary care provider, and for a list of the participating primary care providers, contact the [plan administrator or issuer] at [insert contact information].

(B) For plans and issuers that require or allow for the designation of a primary care provider for a child, add:

For children, you may designate a pediatrician as the primary care provider.

(C) For plans and issuers that provide coverage for obstetric or gynecological care and require the designation by a participant or beneficiary of a primary care provider, add:

You do not need prior authorization from [name of group health plan or issuer] or from any other person (including a primary care provider) in order to obtain access to obstetrical or gynecological care from a health care professional in our network who specializes in obstetrics or gynecology. The health care professional, however, may be required to comply with certain procedures, including obtaining prior authorization for certain services, following a pre-approved treatment plan, or procedures for making referrals. For a list of participating health care professionals who specialize in obstetrics or gynecology, contact the [plan administrator or issuer] at [insert contact information].

(b) *Coverage of emergency services.*—(1) *Scope.*—If a group health plan, or a health insurance issuer offering group health insurance coverage, provides any benefits with respect to services in an emergency department of a hospital, the plan or issuer must cover emergency services (as defined in paragraph (b)(4)(ii) of this section) consistent with the rules of this paragraph (b).

(2) *General rules.*—A plan or issuer subject to the requirements of this paragraph (b) must provide coverage for emergency services in the following manner—

(i) Without the need for any prior authorization determination, even if the emergency services are provided on an out-of-network basis;

(ii) Without regard to whether the health care provider furnishing the emergency services is a participating network provider with respect to the services;

(iii) If the emergency services are provided out of network, without imposing any administrative requirement or limitation on coverage that is more restrictive than the requirements or limitations that apply to emergency services received from in-network providers;

(iv) If the emergency services are provided out of network, by complying with the cost-sharing requirements of paragraph (b)(3) of this section; and

(v) Without regard to any other term or condition of the coverage, other than—

(A) The exclusion of or coordination of benefits;

(B) An affiliation or waiting period permitted under part 7 of ERISA, part A of title XXVII of the PHS Act, or chapter 100 of the Internal Revenue Code; or

(C) Applicable cost sharing.

(3) *Cost-sharing requirements.*—(i) *Copayments and coinsurance.*—Any cost-sharing requirement expressed as a copayment amount or coinsurance rate imposed with respect to a participant or beneficiary for out-of-network emergency services cannot exceed the cost-sharing requirement imposed with respect to a participant or beneficiary if the services were provided in network. However, a participant or beneficiary may be required to pay, in addition to the in-network cost sharing, the excess of the amount the out-of-network provider charges over the amount the plan or issuer is required to pay under this paragraph (b)(3)(i). A group health plan or health insurance issuer complies with the requirements of this paragraph (b)(3) if it provides benefits with respect to an emergency service in an amount at least equal to the greatest of the three amounts specified in paragraphs (b)(3)(i)(A), (B), and (C) of this section (which are adjusted for in-network cost-sharing requirements).

(A) The amount negotiated with in-network providers for the emergency service furnished, excluding any in-network copayment or coinsurance imposed with respect to the participant or beneficiary. If there is more than one amount negotiated with in-network providers for the emergency service, the amount described under this paragraph (b)(3)(i)(A) is the median of these amounts, excluding any in-network copayment or coinsurance imposed with respect to the participant or beneficiary. In determining the median described in the preceding sentence, the amount negotiated with each in-network provider is treated as a separate amount (even if the same amount is paid to more than one provider). If there is no per-service amount negotiated with in-network providers (such as under a capitation or other similar payment arrangement), the amount under this paragraph (b)(3)(i)(A) is disregarded.

(B) The amount for the emergency service calculated using the same method the plan generally uses to determine payments for

⋙→ *Caution: Reg. §54.9815-2719A, below, as added by T.D. 9744, is applicable to group health plans and health insurance issuers beginning on the first day of the plan year (or, in the individual market, the first day of the first policy year) beginning on or after January 1, 2017.*

out-of-network services (such as the usual, customary, and reasonable amount), excluding any in-network copayment or coinsurance imposed with respect to the participant or beneficiary. The amount in this paragraph (b)(3)(i)(B) is determined without reduction for out-of-network cost sharing that generally applies under the plan or health insurance coverage with respect to out-of-network services. Thus, for example, if a plan generally pays 70 percent of the usual, customary, and reasonable amount for out-of-network services, the amount in this paragraph (b)(3)(i)(B) for an emergency service is the total (that is, 100 percent) of the usual, customary, and reasonable amount for the service, not reduced by the 30 percent coinsurance that would generally apply to out-of-network services (but reduced by the in-network copayment or coinsurance that the individual would be responsible for if the emergency service had been provided in-network).

(C) The amount that would be paid under Medicare (part A or part B of title XVIII of the Social Security Act, 42 U.S.C. 1395 *et seq.*) for the emergency service, excluding any in-network copayment or coinsurance imposed with respect to the participant or beneficiary.

(ii) *Other cost sharing.*—Any cost-sharing requirement other than a copayment or coinsurance requirement (such as a deductible or out-of-pocket maximum) may be imposed with respect to emergency services provided out of network if the cost-sharing requirement generally applies to out-of-network benefits. A deductible may be imposed with respect to out-of-network emergency services only as part of a deductible that generally applies to out-of-network benefits. If an out-of-pocket maximum generally applies to out-of-network benefits, that out-of-pocket maximum must apply to out-of-network emergency services.

(iii) *Special rules regarding out-of-network minimum payment standards.*—(A) The minimum payment standards set forth under paragraph (b)(3) of this section do not apply in cases where State law prohibits a participant or beneficiary from being required to pay, in addition to the in-network cost sharing, the excess of the amount the out-of-network provider charges over the amount the plan or issuer provides in benefits, or where a group health plan or health insurance issuer is contractually responsible for such amounts. Nonetheless, in such cases, a plan or issuer may not impose any copayment or coinsurance requirement for out-of-network emergency services that is higher than the copayment or coinsurance requirement that would apply if the services were provided in network.

(B) A group health plan and health insurance issuer must provide a participant or beneficiary adequate and prominent notice of their lack of financial responsibility with respect to the amounts described under this paragraph (b)(3)(iii), to prevent inadvertent payment by the participant or beneficiary.

(iv) *Examples.*—The rules of this paragraph (b)(3) are illustrated by the following examples. In all of these examples, the group health plan covers benefits with respect to emergency services.

*Example 1.*(i) *Facts.* A group health plan imposes a 25% coinsurance responsibility on individuals who are furnished emergency services, whether provided in network or out of network. If a covered individual notifies the plan within two business days after the day an individual receives treatment in an emergency department, the plan reduces the coinsurance rate to 15%.

(ii) *Conclusion.* In this *Example 1*, the requirement to notify the plan in order to receive a reduction in the coinsurance rate does not violate the requirement that the plan cover emergency services without the need for any prior authorization determination. This is the result even if the plan required that it be notified before or at the time of receiving services at the emergency department in order to receive a reduction in the coinsurance rate.

*Example 2.* (i) *Facts.* A group health plan imposes a $60 copayment on emergency services without preauthorization, whether provided in network or out of network. If emergency services are preauthorized, the plan waives the copayment, even if it later determines the medical condition was not an emergency medical condition.

(ii) *Conclusion.* In this *Example 2*, by requiring an individual to pay more for emergency services if the individual does not obtain prior authorization, the plan violates the requirement that the plan cover emergency services without the need for any prior authorization determination. (By contrast, if, to have the copayment waived, the plan merely required that it be notified rather than a prior authorization, then the plan would not violate the requirement that the plan cover emergency services without the need for any prior authorization determination.)

*Example 3.* (i) *Facts.* A group health plan covers individuals who receive emergency services with respect to an emergency medical condition from an out-of-network provider. The plan has agree-

ments with in-network providers with respect to a certain emergency service. Each provider has agreed to provide the service for a certain amount. Among all the providers for the service: one has agreed to accept $85, two have agreed to accept $100, two have agreed to accept $110, three have agreed to accept $120, and one has agreed to accept $150. Under the agreement, the plan agrees to pay the providers 80% of the agreed amount, with the individual receiving the service responsible for the remaining 20%.

(ii) *Conclusion.* In this *Example 3*, the values taken into account in determining the median are $85, $100, $100, $110, $110, $120, $120, $120, and $150. Therefore, the median amount among those agreed to for the emergency service is $110, and the amount under paragraph (b)(3)(i)(A) of this section is 80% of $110 ($88).

*Example 4.* (i) *Facts.* Same facts as *Example 3*. Subsequently, the plan adds another provider to its network, who has agreed to accept $150 for the emergency service.

(ii) *Conclusion.* In this *Example 4*, the median amount among those agreed to for the emergency service is $115. (Because there is no one middle amount, the median is the average of the two middle amounts, $110 and $120.) Accordingly, the amount under paragraph (b)(3)(i)(A) of this section is 80% of $115 ($92).

*Example 5.* (i) *Facts.* Same facts as *Example 4.* An individual covered by the plan receives the emergency service from an out-of-network provider, who charges $125 for the service. With respect to services provided by out-of-network providers generally, the plan reimburses covered individuals 50% of the reasonable amount charged by the provider for medical services. For this purpose, the reasonable amount for any service is based on information on charges by all providers collected by a third party, on a zip code by zip code basis, with the plan treating charges at a specified percentile as reasonable. For the emergency service received by the individual, the reasonable amount calculated using this method is $116. The amount that would be paid under Medicare for the emergency service, excluding any copayment or coinsurance for the service, is $80.

(ii) *Conclusion.* In this *Example 5*, the plan is responsible for paying $92.80, 80% of $116. The median amount among those agreed to for the emergency service is $115 and the amount the plan would pay is $92 (80% of $115); the amount calculated using the same method the plan uses to determine payments for out-of-network services — $116 — excluding the in-network 20% coinsurance, is $92.80; and the Medicare payment is $80. Thus, the greatest amount is $92.80. The individual is responsible for the remaining $32.20 charged by the out-of-network provider.

*Example 6.* (i) *Facts.* Same facts as *Example 5.* The group health plan generally imposes a $250 deductible for in-network health care. With respect to all health care provided by out-of-network providers, the plan imposes a $500 deductible. (Covered in-network claims are credited against the deductible.) The individual has incurred and submitted $260 of covered claims prior to receiving the emergency service out of network.

(ii) *Conclusion.* In this *Example 6*, the plan is not responsible for paying anything with respect to the emergency service furnished by the out-of-network provider because the covered individual has not satisfied the higher deductible that applies generally to all health care provided out of network. However, the amount the individual is required to pay is credited against the deductible.

(4) *Definitions.*—The definitions in this paragraph (b)(4) govern in applying the provisions of this paragraph (b).

(i) *Emergency medical condition.*—The term *emergency medical condition* means a medical condition manifesting itself by acute symptoms of sufficient severity (including severe pain) so that a prudent layperson, who possesses an average knowledge of health and medicine, could reasonably expect the absence of immediate medical attention to result in a condition described in clause (i), (ii), or (iii) of section 1867(e)(1)(A) of the Social Security Act (42 U.S.C. 1395dd(e)(1)(A)). (In that provision of the Social Security Act, clause (i) refers to placing the health of the individual (or, with respect to a pregnant woman, the health of the woman or her unborn child) in serious jeopardy; clause (ii) refers to serious impairment to bodily functions; and clause (iii) refers to serious dysfunction of any bodily organ or part.)

(ii) *Emergency services.*—The term *emergency services* means, with respect to an emergency medical condition—

(A) A medical screening examination (as required under section 1867 of the Social Security Act, 42 U.S.C. 1395dd) that is within the capability of the emergency department of a hospital, including ancillary services routinely available to the emergency department to evaluate such emergency medical condition, and

⟫→ *Caution: Reg. §54.9815-2719A, below, as added by T.D. 9744, is applicable to group health plans and health insurance issuers beginning on the first day of the plan year (or, in the individual market, the first day of the first policy year) beginning on or after January 1, 2017.*

(B) Such further medical examination and treatment, to the extent they are within the capabilities of the staff and facilities available at the hospital, as are required under section 1867 of the Social Security Act (42 U.S.C. 1395dd) to stabilize the patient.

(iii) *Stabilize.*—The term *to stabilize,* with respect to an emergency medical condition (as defined in paragraph (b)(4)(i) of this section) has the meaning given in section 1867(e)(3) of the Social Security Act (42 U.S.C. 1395dd(e)(3)).

(c) *Applicability date.*—The provisions of this section are applicable to group health plans and health insurance issuers for plan years beginning on or after January 1, 2017. Until the applicability date for this regulation, plans and issuers are required to continue to comply with the interim final regulations promulgated by the Department of Labor at 29 CFR part 2590, contained in the 29 CFR, parts 1927 to end, edition revised as of July 1, 2015. [Reg. § 54.9815-2719A.]

☐ *[T.D. 9744, 11-13-2015.]*

⟫→ *Caution: Temporary Reg. §54.9815-2719AT, below, was removed by T.D. 9744 and is inapplicable under Code Sec. 7805(e)(2). However, until final Reg. §54.9815-2719A is applicable on the first day of the plan or policy year beginning after January 1, 2017, taxpayers may comply with the corresponding interim final regulation at 29 CFR part 2590 that is substantially similar to the temporary reg below.*

### [Reg. § 54.9815-2719AT]

**§54.9815-2719AT. Patient protections (temporary).**—(a) *Choice of health care professional.*—(1) *Designation of primary care provider.*—(i) *In general.*—If a group health plan, or a health insurance issuer offering group health insurance coverage, requires or provides for designation by a participant or beneficiary of a participating primary care provider, then the plan or issuer must permit each participant or beneficiary to designate any participating primary care provider who is available to accept the participant or beneficiary. In such a case, the plan or issuer must comply with the rules of paragraph (a)(4) of this section by informing each participant of the terms of the plan or health insurance coverage regarding designation of a primary care provider.

(ii) *Example.*—The rules of this paragraph (a)(1) are illustrated by the following example:

*Example.* (i) *Facts.* A group health plan requires individuals covered under the plan to designate a primary care provider. The plan permits each individual to designate any primary care provider participating in the plan's network who is available to accept the individual as the individual's primary care provider. If an individual has not designated a primary care provider, the plan designates one until one has been designated by the individual. The plan provides a notice that satisfies the requirements of paragraph (a)(4) of this section regarding the ability to designate a primary care provider.

(ii) *Conclusion.* In this *Example,* the plan has satisfied the requirements of paragraph (a) of this section.

(2) *Designation of pediatrician as primary care provider.*—(i) *In general.*—If a group health plan, or a health insurance issuer offering group health insurance coverage, requires or provides for the designation of a participating primary care provider for a child by a participant or beneficiary, the plan or issuer must permit the participant or beneficiary to designate a physician (allopathic or osteopathic) who specializes in pediatrics as the child's primary care provider if the provider participates in the network of the plan or issuer and is available to accept the child. In such a case, the plan or issuer must comply with the rules of paragraph (a)(4) of this section by informing each participant of the terms of the plan or health insurance coverage regarding designation of a pediatrician as the child's primary care provider.

(ii) *Construction.*—Nothing in paragraph (a)(2)(i) of this section is to be construed to waive any exclusions of coverage under the terms and conditions of the plan or health insurance coverage with respect to coverage of pediatric care.

(iii) *Examples.*—The rules of this paragraph (a)(2) are illustrated by the following examples:

*Example 1.* (i) *Facts.* A group health plan's HMO designates for each participant a physician who specializes in internal medicine to serve as the primary care provider for the participant and any beneficiaries. Participant A requests that Pediatrician B be designated as the primary care provider for A's child. B is a participating provider in the HMO's network.

(ii) *Conclusion.* In this *Example 1,* the HMO must permit A's designation of B as the primary care provider for A's child in order to comply with the requirements of this paragraph (a)(2).

*Example 2.* (i) *Facts.* Same facts as *Example 1,* except that A takes A's child to B for treatment of the child's severe shellfish allergies. B wishes to refer A's child to an allergist for treatment. The HMO, however, does not provide coverage for treatment of food allergies, nor does it have an allergist participating in its network, and it therefore refuses to authorize the referral.

(ii) *Conclusion.* In this *Example 2,* the HMO has not violated the requirements of this paragraph (a)(2) because the exclusion of treatment for food allergies is in accordance with the terms of A's coverage.

(3) *Patient access to obstetrical and gynecological care.*—(i) *General rights.*—(A) *Direct access.*—A group health plan, or a health insur-

ance issuer offering group health insurance coverage, described in paragraph (a)(3)(ii) of this section may not require authorization or referral by the plan, issuer, or any person (including a primary care provider) in the case of a female participant or beneficiary who seeks coverage for obstetrical or gynecological care provided by a participating health care professional who specializes in obstetrics or gynecology. In such a case, the plan or issuer must comply with the rules of paragraph (a)(4) of this section by informing each participant that the plan may not require authorization or referral for obstetrical or gynecological care by a participating health care professional who specializes in obstetrics or gynecology. The plan or issuer may require such a professional to agree to otherwise adhere to the plan's or issuer's policies and procedures, including procedures regarding referrals and obtaining prior authorization and providing services pursuant to a treatment plan (if any) approved by the plan or issuer. For purposes of this paragraph (a)(3), a health care professional who specializes in obstetrics or gynecology is any individual (including a person other than a physician) who is authorized under applicable State law to provide obstetrical or gynecological care.

(B) *Obstetrical and gynecological care.*—A group health plan or health insurance issuer described in paragraph (a)(3)(ii) of this section must treat the provision of obstetrical and gynecological care, and the ordering of related obstetrical and gynecological items and services, pursuant to the direct access described under paragraph (a)(3)(i)(A) of this section, by a participating health care professional who specializes in obstetrics or gynecology as the authorization of the primary care provider.

(ii) *Application of paragraph.*—A group health plan, or a health insurance issuer offering group health insurance coverage, is described in this paragraph (a)(3) if the plan or issuer—

(A) Provides coverage for obstetrical or gynecological care; and

(B) Requires the designation by a participant or beneficiary of a participating primary care provider.

(iii) *Construction.*—Nothing in paragraph (a)(3)(i) of this section is to be construed to—

(A) Waive any exclusions of coverage under the terms and conditions of the plan or health insurance coverage with respect to coverage of obstetrical or gynecological care; or

(B) Preclude the group health plan or health insurance issuer involved from requiring that the obstetrical or gynecological provider notify the primary care health care professional or the plan or issuer of treatment decisions.

(iv) *Examples.*—The rules of this paragraph (a)(3) are illustrated by the following examples:

*Example 1.* (i) *Facts.* A group health plan requires each participant to designate a physician to serve as the primary care provider for the participant and the participant's family. Participant A, a female, requests a gynecological exam with Physician B, an in-network physician specializing in gynecological care. The group health plan requires prior authorization from A's designated primary care provider for the gynecological exam.

(ii) *Conclusion.* In this *Example 1,* the group health plan has violated the requirements of this paragraph (a)(3) because the plan requires prior authorization from A's primary care provider prior to obtaining gynecological services.

*Example 2.* (i) *Facts.* Same facts as *Example 1* except that A seeks gynecological services from C, an out-of-network provider.

(ii) *Conclusion.* In this *Example 2,* the group health plan has not violated the requirements of this paragraph (a)(3) by requiring prior authorization because C is not a participating health care provider.

*Example 3.* (i) *Facts.* Same facts as *Example 1* except that the group health plan only requires B to inform A's designated primary care physician of treatment decisions.

(ii) *Conclusion.* In this *Example 3,* the group health plan has not violated the requirements of this paragraph (a)(3) because A has direct access to B without prior authorization. The fact that the group

**⫸→ Caution:** *Temporary Reg. §54.9815-2719AT, below, was removed by T.D. 9744 and is inapplicable under Code Sec. 7805(e)(2). However, until final Reg. §54.9815-2719A is applicable on the first day of the plan or policy year beginning after January 1, 2017, taxpayers may comply with the corresponding interim final regulation at 29 CFR part 2590 that is substantially similar to the temporary reg below.*

health plan requires notification of treatment decisions to the designated primary care physician does not violate this paragraph (a)(3).

*Example 4.* (i) *Facts.* A group health plan requires each participant to designate a physician to serve as the primary care provider for the participant and the participant's family. The group health plan requires prior authorization before providing benefits for uterine fibroid embolization.

(ii) *Conclusion.* In this *Example 4,* the plan requirement for prior authorization before providing benefits for uterine fibroid embolization does not violate the requirements of this paragraph (a)(3) because, though the prior authorization requirement applies to obstetrical services, it does not restrict access to any providers specializing in obstetrics or gynecology.

(4) *Notice of right to designate a primary care provider.*—(i) *In general.*—If a group health plan or health insurance issuer requires the designation by a participant or beneficiary of a primary care provider, the plan or issuer must provide a notice informing each participant of the terms of the plan or health insurance coverage regarding designation of a primary care provider and of the rights—

(A) Under paragraph (a)(1)(i) of this section, that any participating primary care provider who is available to accept the participant or beneficiary can be designated;

(B) Under paragraph (a)(2)(i) of this section, with respect to a child, that any participating physician who specializes in pediatrics can be designated as the primary care provider; and

(C) Under paragraph (a)(3)(i) of this section, that the plan may not require authorization or referral for obstetrical or gynecological care by a participating health care professional who specializes in obstetrics or gynecology.

(ii) *Timing.*—The notice described in paragraph (a)(4)(i) of this section must be included whenever the plan or issuer provides a participant with a summary plan description or other similar description of benefits under the plan or health insurance coverage.

(iii) *Model language.*—The following model language can be used to satisfy the notice requirement described in paragraph (a)(4)(i) of this section:

(A) For plans and issuers that require or allow for the designation of primary care providers by participants or beneficiaries, insert:

> [Name of group health plan or health insurance issuer]generally [requires/allows] the designation of a primary care provider. You have the right to designate any primary care provider who participates in our network and who is available to accept you or your family members. [If the plan or health insurance coverage designates a primary care provider automatically, insert: Until you make this designation, [name of group health plan or health insurance issuer] designates one for you.] For information on how to select a primary care provider, and for a list of the participating primary care providers, contact the [plan administrator or issuer] at [insert contact information].

(B) For plans and issuers that require or allow for the designation of a primary care provider for a child, add:

> For children, you may designate a pediatrician as the primary care provider.

(C) For plans and issuers that provide coverage for obstetric or gynecological care and require the designation by a participant or beneficiary of a primary care provider, add:

> You do not need prior authorization from [name of group health plan or issuer] or from any other person (including a primary care provider) in order to obtain access to obstetrical or gynecological care from a health care professional in our network who specializes in obstetrics or gynecology. The health care professional, however, may be required to comply with certain procedures, including obtaining prior authorization for certain services, following a pre-approved treatment plan, or procedures for making referrals. For a list of participating health care professionals who specialize in obstetrics or gynecology, contact the [plan administrator or issuer] at [insert contact information].

(b) *Coverage of emergency services.*—(1) *Scope.*—If a group health plan, or a health insurance issuer offering group health insurance coverage, provides any benefits with respect to services in an emergency department of a hospital, the plan or issuer must cover emer-

gency services (as defined in paragraph (b)(4)(ii) of this section) consistent with the rules of this paragraph (b).

(2) *General rules.*—A plan or issuer subject to the requirements of this paragraph (b) must provide coverage for emergency services in the following manner—

(i) Without the need for any prior authorization determination, even if the emergency services are provided on an out-of-network basis;

(ii) Without regard to whether the health care provider furnishing the emergency services is a participating network provider with respect to the services;

(iii) If the emergency services are provided out of network, without imposing any administrative requirement or limitation on coverage that is more restrictive than the requirements or limitations that apply to emergency services received from in-network providers;

(iv) If the emergency services are provided out of network, by complying with the costsharing requirements of paragraph (b)(3) of this section; and

(v) Without regard to any other term or condition of the coverage, other than -

(A) The exclusion of or coordination of benefits;

(B) An affiliation or waiting period permitted under part 7 of ERISA, part A of title XXVII of the PHS Act, or chapter 100 of the Internal Revenue Code; or

(C) Applicable cost sharing.

(3) *Cost-sharing requirements.*—(i) *Copayments and coinsurance.*—Any cost-sharing requirement expressed as a copayment amount or coinsurance rate imposed with respect to a participant or beneficiary for out-of-network emergency services cannot exceed the cost-sharing requirement imposed with respect to a participant or beneficiary if the services were provided in-network. However, a participant or beneficiary may be required to pay, in addition to the innetwork cost sharing, the excess of the amount the out-of-network provider charges over the amount the plan or issuer is required to pay under this paragraph (b)(3)(i). A group health plan or health insurance issuer complies with the requirements of this paragraph (b)(3) if it provides benefits with respect to an emergency service in an amount equal to the greatest of the three amounts specified in paragraphs (b)(3)(i)(A), (b)(3)(i)(B), and (b)(3)(i)(C) of this section (which are adjusted for in-network cost-sharing requirements).

(A) The amount negotiated with in-network providers for the emergency service furnished, excluding any in-network copayment or coinsurance imposed with respect to the participant or beneficiary. If there is more than one amount negotiated with in-network providers for the emergency service, the amount described under this paragraph (b)(3)(i)(A) is the median of these amounts, excluding any in-network copayment or coinsurance imposed with respect to the participant or beneficiary. In determining the median described in the preceding sentence, the amount negotiated with each in-network provider is treated as a separate amount (even if the same amount is paid to more than one provider). If there is no per-service amount negotiated with in-network providers (such as under a capitation or other similar payment arrangement), the amount under this paragraph (b)(3)(i)(A) is disregarded.

(B) The amount for the emergency service calculated using the same method the plan generally uses to determine payments for out-of-network services (such as the usual, customary, and reasonable amount), excluding any in-network copayment or coinsurance imposed with respect to the participant or beneficiary. The amount in this paragraph (b)(3)(i)(B) is determined without reduction for out-of-network cost sharing that generally applies under the plan or health insurance coverage with respect to out-of-network services. Thus, for example, if a plan generally pays 70 percent of the usual, customary, and reasonable amount for out-of-network services, the amount in this paragraph (b)(3)(i)(B) for an emergency service is the total (that is, 100 percent) of the usual, customary, and reasonable amount for the service, not reduced by the 30 percent coinsurance that would generally apply to out-of-network services (but reduced by the in-network copayment or coinsurance that the individual would be responsible for if the emergency service had been provided in-network).

(C) The amount that would be paid under Medicare (part A or part B of title XVIII of the Social Security Act, 42 U.S.C. 1395 *et seq.*) for the emergency service, excluding any in-network copayment or coinsurance imposed with respect to the participant or beneficiary.

(ii) *Other cost sharing.*—Any cost-sharing requirement other than a copayment or coinsurance requirement (such as a deductible or out-of-pocket maximum) may be imposed with respect to emer-

**➤➤➤ Caution:** *Temporary Reg. §54.9815-2719AT, below, was removed by T.D. 9744 and is inapplicable under Code Sec. 7805(e)(2). However, until final Reg. §54.9815-2719A is applicable on the first day of the plan or policy year beginning after January 1, 2017, taxpayers may comply with the corresponding interim final regulation at 29 CFR part 2590 that is substantially similar to the temporary reg below.*

gency services provided out of network if the cost-sharing requirement generally applies to out-of-network benefits. A deductible may be imposed with respect to out-of-network emergency services only as part of a deductible that generally applies to out-of-network benefits. If an out-of-pocket maximum generally applies to out-of-network benefits, that out-of-pocket maximum must apply to out-of-network emergency services.

(iii) *Examples.*—The rules of this paragraph (b)(3) are illustrated by the following examples. In all of these examples, the group health plan covers benefits with respect to emergency services.

*Example 1.* (i) *Facts.* A group health plan imposes a 25% coinsurance responsibility on individuals who are furnished emergency services, whether provided in network or out of network. If a covered individual notifies the plan within two business days after the day an individual receives treatment in an emergency department, the plan reduces the coinsurance rate to 15%.

(ii) *Conclusion.* In this *Example 1,* the requirement to notify the plan in order to receive a reduction in the coinsurance rate does not violate the requirement that the plan cover emergency services without the need for any prior authorization determination. This is the result even if the plan required that it be notified before or at the time of receiving services at the emergency department in order to receive a reduction in the coinsurance rate.

*Example 2.* (i) *Facts.* A group health plan imposes a $60 copayment on emergency services without preauthorization, whether provided in network or out of network. If emergency services are preauthorized, the plan waives the copayment, even if it later determines the medical condition was not an emergency medical condition.

(ii) *Conclusion.* In this *Example 2,* by requiring an individual to pay more for emergency services if the individual does not obtain prior authorization, the plan violates the requirement that the plan cover emergency services without the need for any prior authorization determination. (By contrast, if, to have the copayment waived, the plan merely required that it be notified rather than a prior authorization, then the plan would not violate the requirement that the plan cover emergency services without the need for any prior authorization determination.)

*Example 3.* (i) *Facts.* A group health plan covers individuals who receive emergency services with respect to an emergency medical condition from an out-of-network provider. The plan has agreements with in-network providers with respect to a certain emergency service. Each provider has agreed to provide the service for a certain amount. Among all the providers for the service: one has agreed to accept $85, two have agreed to accept $100, two have agreed to accept $110, three have agreed to accept $120, and one has agreed to accept $150. Under the agreement, the plan agrees to pay the providers 80% of the agreed amount, with the individual receiving the service responsible for the remaining 20%.

(ii) *Conclusion.* In this *Example 3,* the values taken into account in determining the median are $85, $100, $100, $110, $110, $120, $120, $120, and $150. Therefore, the median amount among those agreed to for the emergency service is $110, and the amount under paragraph (b)(3)(i)(A) of this section is 80% of $110 ($88).

*Example 4.* (i) *Facts.* Same facts as *Example 3.* Subsequently, the plan adds another provider to its network, who has agreed to accept $150 for the emergency service.

(ii) *Conclusion.* In this *Example 4,* the median amount among those agreed to for the emergency service is $115. (Because there is no one middle amount, the median is the average of the two middle amounts, $110 and $120.) Accordingly, the amount under paragraph (b)(3)(i)(A) of this section is 80% of $115 ($92).

*Example 5.* (i) *Facts.* Same facts as *Example 4.* An individual covered by the plan receives the emergency service from an out-of-network provider, who charges $125 for the service. With respect to services provided by out-of-network providers generally, the plan reimburses covered individuals 50% of the reasonable amount charged by the provider for medical services. For this purpose, the reasonable amount for any service is based on information on charges by all providers collected by a third party, on a zip-code-by-zip-code basis, with the plan treating charges at a specified percentile as reasonable. For the emergency service received by the individual, the reasonable amount calculated using this method is $116. The amount that would be paid under Medicare for the emergency service, excluding any copayment or coinsurance for the service, is $80.

(ii) *Conclusion.* In this *Example 5,* the plan is responsible for paying $92.80, 80% of $116. The median amount among those agreed to for the emergency service is $115 and the amount the plan would pay is $92 (80% of $115); the amount calculated using the same

method the plan uses to determine payments for out-of-network services — $116 — excluding the innetwork 20% coinsurance, is $92.80; and the Medicare payment is $80. Thus, the greatest amount is $92.80. The individual is responsible for the remaining $32.20 charged by the out-of-network provider.

*Example 6.* (i) *Facts.* Same facts as *Example 5.* The group health plan generally imposes a $250 deductible for in-network health care. With respect to all health care provided by out-ofnetwork providers, the plan imposes a $500 deductible. (Covered in-network claims are credited against the deductible.) The individual has incurred and submitted $260 of covered claims prior to receiving the emergency service out of network.

(ii) *Conclusion.* In this *Example 6,* the plan is not responsible for paying anything with respect to the emergency service furnished by the out-of-network provider because the covered individual has not satisfied the higher deductible that applies generally to all health care provided out of network. However, the amount the individual is required to pay is credited against the deductible.

(4) *Definitions.*—The definitions in this paragraph (b)(4) govern in applying the provisions of this paragraph (b).

(i) *Emergency medical condition.*—The term *emergency medical condition* means a medical condition manifesting itself by acute symptoms of sufficient severity (including severe pain) so that a prudent layperson, who possesses an average knowledge of health and medicine, could reasonably expect the absence of immediate medical attention to result in a condition described in clause (i), (ii), or (iii) of section 1867(e)(1)(A) of the Social Security Act (42 U.S.C. 1395dd(e)(1)(A)). (In that provision of the Social Security Act, clause (i) refers to placing the health of the individual (or, with respect to a pregnant woman, the health of the woman or her unborn child) in serious jeopardy; clause (ii) refers to serious impairment to bodily functions; and clause (iii) refers to serious dysfunction of any bodily organ or part.)

(ii) *Emergency services.*—The term *emergency services* means, with respect to an emergency medical condition—

(A) A medical screening examination (as required under section 1867 of the Social Security Act, 42 U.S.C. 1395dd) that is within the capability of the emergency department of a hospital, including ancillary services routinely available to the emergency department to evaluate such emergency medical condition, and

(B) Such further medical examination and treatment, to the extent they are within the capabilities of the staff and facilities available at the hospital, as are required under section 1867 of the Social Security Act (42 U.S.C. 1395dd) to stabilize the patient.

(iii) *Stabilize.*—The term *to stabilize,* with respect to an emergency medical condition (as defined in paragraph (b)(4)(i) of this section) has the meaning given in section 1867(e)(3) of the Social Security Act (42 U.S.C. 1395dd(e)(3)).

(c) *Effective/applicability date.*—The provisions of this section apply for plan years beginning on or after September 23, 2010. See §54.9815-1251T for determining the application of this section to grandfathered health plans (providing that these rules regarding patient protections do not apply to grandfathered health plans).

(d) *Expiration date.*—This section expires on June 21, 2013. [Temporary Reg. §54.9815-2719AT.]

☐ [T.D. 9491, 6-22-2010. *Removed by T.D. 9744, 11-13-2015.*]

**[Reg. §54.9831-1]**

**§54.9831-1. Special rules relating to group health plans.**—(a) *Group health plan.*—(1) *Defined.*—A group health plan means a plan (including a self-insured plan) of, or contributed to by, an employer (including a self-employed person) or employee organization to provide health care (directly or otherwise) to the employees, former employees, the employer, others associated or formerly associated with the employer in a business relationship, or their families.

(2) *Determination of number of plans.*—[Reserved.]

(b) *General exception for certain small group health plans.*—(1) Subject to paragraph (b)(2) of this section, the requirements of §§54.9801-1 through 54.9801-6, 54.9802-1, 54.9802-2, 54.9811-1, 54.9812-1, 54.9815-1251 through 54.9815-2719A, and 54.9833-1 do not apply to any group health plan for any plan year if, on the first day of the plan year, the plan has fewer than two participants who are current employees.

(2) The exception of paragraph (b)(1) of this section does not apply with respect to the following requirements:

(i) Section 54.9802-1(b), as such paragraph applies with respect to genetic information as a health factor.

(ii) Section 54.9802-1(c), as such paragraph applies with respect to genetic information as a health factor.

(iii) Section 54.9802-1(e), as such paragraph applies with respect to genetic information as a health factor.

(iv) Section 54.9802-3T(b).

(v) Section 54.9802-3T(c).

(vi) Section 54.9802-3T(d).

(vii) Section 54.9802-3T(e).

(c) *Excepted benefits.*—(1) *In general.*—The requirements of §§ 54.9801-1 through 54.9801-6, 54.9802-1, 54.9802-2, 54.9811-1, 54.9812-1, 54.9815-1251 through 54.9815-2719A, and 54.9833-1 do not apply to any group health plan in relation to its provision of the benefits described in paragraph (c)(2), (3), (4), or (5) of this section (or any combination of these benefits).

(2) *Benefits excepted in all circumstances.*—The following benefits are excepted in all circumstances —

(i) Coverage only for accident (including accidental death and dismemberment);

(ii) Disability income coverage;

(iii) Liability insurance, including general liability insurance and automobile liability insurance;

(iv) Coverage issued as a supplement to liability insurance;

(v) Workers' compensation or similar coverage;

(vi) Automobile medical payment insurance;

(vii) Credit-only insurance (for example, mortgage insurance);

(viii) Coverage for on-site medical clinics; and

(ix) Travel insurance, within the meaning of § 54.9801-2.

(3) *Limited excepted benefits.*—(i) *In general.*—Limited-scope dental benefits, limited-scope vision benefits, or long-term care benefits are excepted if they are provided under a separate policy, certificate, or contract of insurance, or are otherwise not an integral part of a group health plan as described in paragraph (c)(3)(ii) of this section. In addition, benefits provided under a health flexible spending arrangement (health FSA) are excepted benefits if they satisfy the requirements of paragraph (c)(3)(v) of this section; benefits provided under an employee assistance program are excepted benefits if they satisfy the requirements of paragraph (c)(3)(vi) of this section; benefits provided under limited wraparound coverage are excepted benefits if they satisfy the requirements of paragraph (c)(3)(vii) of this section; and benefits provided under a health reimbursement arrangement or other account-based group health plan, other than a health FSA, are excepted benefits if they satisfy the requirements of paragraph (c)(3)(viii) of this section.

(ii) *Not an integral part of a group health plan.*—For purposes of this paragraph (c)(3), benefits are not an integral part of a group health plan (whether the benefits are provided through the same plan or a separate plan) only if the following two requirements are satisfied—

(A) Participants must have the right to elect not to receive coverage for the benefits; and

(B) If a participant elects to receive coverage for the benefits, the participant must pay an additional premium or contribution for that coverage.

(ii) *Not an integral part of a group health plan.*—For purposes of this paragraph (c)(3), benefits are not an integral part of a group health plan (whether the benefits are provided through the same plan, a separate plan, or as the only plan offered to participants) if either paragraph (c)(3)(ii)(A) or (B) are satisfied.

(A) Participants may decline coverage. For example, a participant may decline coverage if the participant can opt out of the coverage upon request, whether or not there is a participant contribution required for the coverage.

(B) Claims for the benefits are administered under a contract separate from claims administration for any other benefits under the plan.

(iii) *Limited scope.*—(A) *Dental benefits.*—Limited scope dental benefits are benefits substantially all of which are for treatment of the mouth (including any organ or structure within the mouth).

(B) *Vision benefits.*—Limited scope vision benefits are benefits substantially all of which are for treatment of the eye.

(iv) *Long-term care.*—Long-term care benefits are benefits that are either—

(A) Subject to state long-term care insurance laws;

(B) For qualified long-term care services, as defined in section 7702B(c)(1), or provided under a qualified long-term care insurance contract, as defined in section 7702B(b); or

(C) Based on cognitive impairment or a loss of functional capacity that is expected to be chronic.

(v) *Health flexible spending arrangements.*—Benefits provided under a health flexible spending arrangement (as defined in section 106(c)(2)) are excepted for a class of participants only if they satisfy the following two requirements—

(A) Other group health plan coverage, not limited to excepted benefits, is made available for the year to the class of participants by reason of their employment; and

(B) The arrangement is structured so that the maximum benefit payable to any participant in the class for a year cannot exceed two times the participant's salary reduction election under the arrangement for the year (or, if greater, cannot exceed $500 plus the amount of the participant's salary reduction election). For this purpose, any amount that an employee can elect to receive as taxable income but elects to apply to the health flexible spending arrangement is considered a salary reduction election (regardless of whether the amount is characterized as salary or as a credit under the arrangement).

(vi) *Employee assistance programs.*—Benefits provided under employee assistance programs are excepted if they satisfy all of the requirements of this paragraph (c)(3)(vi).

(A) The program does not provide significant benefits in the nature of medical care. For this purpose, the amount, scope and duration of covered services are taken into account.

(B) The benefits under the employee assistance program are not coordinated with benefits under another group health plan, as follows:

(1) Participants in the other group health plan must not be required to use and exhaust benefits under the employee assistance program (making the employee assistance program a gatekeeper) before an individual is eligible for benefits under the other group health plan; and

(2) Participant eligibility for benefits under the employee assistance program must not be dependent on participation in another group health plan.

(C) No employee premiums or contributions are required as a condition of participation in the employee assistance program.

(D) There is no cost sharing under the employee assistance program.

(vii) *Limited wraparound coverage.*—Limited benefits provided through a group health plan that wrap around eligible individual health insurance (or Basic Health Plan coverage described in section 1331 of the Patient Protection and Affordable Care Act); or that wrap around coverage under a Multi-State Plan described in section 1334 of the Patient Protection and Affordable Care Act, collectively referred to as "limited wraparound coverage," are excepted benefits if all of the following conditions are satisfied. For this purpose, eligible individual health insurance is individual health insurance coverage that is not a grandfathered health plan (as described in section 1251 of the Patient Protection and Affordable Care Act and 29 CFR 2590.715-1251), not a transitional individual health insurance plan (as described in the March 5, 2014 Insurance Standards Bulletin Series – Extension of Transitional Policy through October 1, 2016), and does not consist solely of excepted benefits (as defined in paragraph (c) of this section).

(A) *Covers additional benefits.*—The limited wraparound coverage provides meaningful benefits beyond coverage of cost sharing under either the eligible individual health insurance, Basic Health Program coverage, or Multi-State Plan coverage. The limited wraparound coverage must not provide benefits only under a coordination-of-benefits provision and must not consist of an account-based reimbursement arrangement.

(B) *Limited in amount.*—The annual cost of coverage per employee (and any covered dependents, as defined in § 54.9801-2) under the limited wraparound coverage does not exceed the greater of the amount determined under either paragraph (c)(3)(vii)(B)(1) or (2) of this section. Making a determination regarding the annual cost of coverage per employee must occur on an aggregate basis relying on sound actuarial principles.

(1) The maximum permitted annual salary reduction contribution toward health flexible spending arrangements, indexed in the manner prescribed under section 125(i)(2). For this purpose, the cost of coverage under the limited wraparound includes both employer and employee contributions towards coverage and is determined in the same manner as the applicable premium is calculated under a COBRA continuation provision.

(2) Fifteen percent of the cost of coverage under the primary plan. For this purpose, the cost of coverage under the primary plan and under the limited wraparound coverage includes both employer and employee contributions towards the coverage and

each is determined in the same manner as the applicable premium is calculated under a COBRA continuation provision.

(C) *Nondiscrimination.*—All of the conditions of this paragraph (c)(3)(vii)(C) are satisfied.

(1) *No preexisting condition exclusion.*—The limited wraparound coverage does not impose any preexisting condition exclusion, consistent with the requirements of section 2704 of the PHS Act (incorporated by reference into section 9815) and 29 CFR 2590.715-2704.

(2) *No discrimination based on health status.*—The limited wraparound coverage does not discriminate against individuals in eligibility, benefits, or premiums based on any health factor of an individual (or any dependent of the individual, as defined in §54.9801-2), consistent with the requirements of section 9802 and section 2705 of the PHS Act (incorporated by reference into section 9815).

(3) *No discrimination in favor of highly compensated individuals.*—Neither the limited wraparound coverage, nor any other group health plan coverage offered by the plan sponsor, fails to comply with section 2716 of the PHS Act (incorporated by reference into section 9815) or fails to be excludible from income for any individual due to the application of section 105(h)(as applicable).

(D) *Plan eligibility requirements.*—Individuals eligible for the wraparound coverage are not enrolled in excepted benefit coverage under paragraph (c)(3)(v) of this section (relating to health FSAs). In addition, the conditions set forth in either paragraph (c)(3)(vii)(D)(1) or (2) of this section are met.

(1) *Limited wraparound coverage that wraps around eligible individual insurance for persons who are not full-time employees.*—Coverage that wraps around eligible individual health insurance (or that wraps around Basic Health Plan coverage) must satisfy all of the conditions of this paragraph (c)(3)(vii)(D)(1).

(i) For each year for which limited wraparound coverage is offered, the employer that is the sponsor of the plan offering limited wraparound coverage, or the employer participating in a plan offering limited wraparound coverage, offers to its full-time employees coverage that is substantially similar to coverage that the employer would need to offer to its full-time employees in order not to be subject to a potential assessable payment under the employer shared responsibility provisions of section 4980H(a), if such provisions were applicable; provides minimum value (as defined in section 36B(c)(2)(C)(ii)); and is reasonably expected to be affordable (applying the safe harbor rules for determining affordability set forth in §54.4980H-5(e)(2)). If a plan or issuer providing limited wraparound coverage takes reasonable steps to ensure that employers disclose to the plan or issuer necessary information regarding their coverage offered and affordability information, the plan or issuer is permitted to rely on reasonable representations by employers regarding this information, unless the plan or issuer has specific knowledge to the contrary. In the event that the employer that is the sponsor of the plan offering wraparound coverage, or the employer participating in a plan offering wraparound coverage, has no full-time employees for any plan year limited wraparound coverage is offered, the requirement of this paragraph (c)(3)(vii)(D)(1)(i) is considered satisfied.

(ii) Eligibility for the limited wraparound coverage is limited to employees who are reasonably determined at the time of enrollment to not be full-time employees (and their dependents, as defined in §54.9801-2), or who are retirees (and their dependents, as defined in §54.9801-2). For this purpose, full-time employees are employees who are reasonably expected to work at least an average of 30 hours per week.

(iii) Other group health plan coverage, not limited to excepted benefits, is offered to the individuals eligible for the limited wraparound coverage. Only individuals eligible for the other group health plan coverage are eligible for the limited wraparound coverage.

(2) *Limited coverage that wraps around Multi-State Plan coverage.*—Coverage that wraps around Multi-State Plan coverage must satisfy all of the conditions of this paragraph (c)(3)(vii)(D)(2). For this purpose, the term "full-time employee" as defined in §54.4980H-1(a)(21) who is not in a limited non-assessment period for certain employees (as defined in §54.4980H-1(a)(26)). Moreover, if a plan or issuer providing limited wraparound coverage takes reasonable steps to ensure that employers disclose to the plan or issuer necessary information regarding their coverage offered and contribution levels for 2013 or 2014 (as applicable), and for any year in which limited wraparound coverage is offered, the plan or issuer is permitted to rely on reasonable

representations by employers regarding this information, unless the plan or issuer has specific knowledge to the contrary. Consistent with the reporting and evaluation criteria of paragraph (c)(3)(vii)(E) of this section, the Office of Personnel Management may verify that plans and issuers have reasonable mechanisms in place to ensure that contributing employers meet these standards.

(i) The limited wraparound coverage is reviewed and approved by the Office of Personnel Management, consistent with the reporting and evaluation criteria of paragraph (c)(3)(vii)(E) of this section, to provide benefits in conjunction with coverage under a Multi-State Plan authorized under section 1334 of the Patient Protection and Affordable Care Act. The Office of Personnel Management may revoke approval if it determines that continued approval is inconsistent with the reporting and evaluation criteria of paragraph (c)(3)(vii)(E) of this section.

(ii) The employer offered coverage in the plan year that began in either 2013 or 2014 that is substantially similar to coverage that the employer would need to have offered to its full-time employees in order to not be subject to an assessable payment under the employer shared responsibility provisions of section 4980H(a), if such provisions had been applicable. In the event that a plan that offered coverage in 2013 or 2014 has no full-time employees for any plan year limited wraparound coverage is offered, the requirement of this paragraph (c)(3)(vii)(D)(2)(ii) is considered satisfied.

(iii) In the plan year that began in either 2013 or 2014, the employer offered coverage to a substantial portion of full-time employees that provided minimum value (as defined in section 36B(c)(2)(C)(ii)) and was affordable (applying the safe harbor rules for determining affordability set forth in §54.4980H-5(e)(2)). In the event that the plan that offered coverage in 2013 or 2014 has no full-time employees for any plan year limited wraparound coverage is offered, the requirement of this paragraph (c)(3)(vii)(D)(2)(iii) is considered satisfied.

(iv) For the duration of the pilot program, as described in paragraph (c)(3)(vii)(F) of this section, the employer's annual aggregate contributions for both primary and limited wraparound coverage are substantially the same as the employer's total contributions for coverage offered to full-time employees in 2013 or 2014.

(E) *Reporting.*—(1) *Reporting by group health plans and group health insurance issuers.*—A self-insured group health plan, or a health insurance issuer, offering or proposing to offer limited wraparound coverage in connection with Multi-State Plan coverage pursuant to paragraph (c)(3)(vii)(D)(2) of this section reports to the Office of Personnel Management (OPM), in a form and manner specified in guidance, information OPM reasonably requires to determine whether the plan or issuer qualifies to offer such coverage or complies with the applicable requirements of this section.

(2) *Reporting by group health plan sponsors.*—The plan sponsor of a group health plan offering limited wraparound coverage under paragraph (c)(3)(vii) of this section, must report to the Department of Health and Human Services (HHS), in a form and manner specified in guidance, information HHS reasonably requires.

(F) *Pilot program with sunset.*—The provisions of paragraph (c)(3)(vii) of this section apply to limited wraparound coverage that is first offered no earlier than January 1, 2016 and no later than December 31, 2018 and that ends no later than on the later of:

(1) The date that is three years after the date limited wraparound coverage is first offered; or

(2) The date on which the last collective bargaining agreement relating to the plan terminates after the date limited wraparound coverage is first offered (determined without regard to any extension agreed to after the date limited wraparound coverage is first offered).

(viii) *Health reimbursement arrangements (HRAs) and other account-based group health plans.*—Benefits provided under an HRA or other account-based group health plan, other than a health FSA, are excepted if they satisfy all of the requirements of this paragraph (c)(3)(viii). See paragraph (c)(3)(v) of this section for the circumstances in which benefits provided under a health FSA are excepted benefits. For purposes of this paragraph (c)(3)(viii), the term "HRA or other account-based group health plan" has the same meaning as "account-based group health plan" set forth in §54.9815-2711(d)(6)(i) of this part, except that the term does not include health FSAs. For ease of reference, an HRA or other account-based group health plan that satisfies the requirements of this paragraph (c)(3)(viii) is referred to as an excepted benefit HRA.

(A) *Otherwise not an integral part of the plan.*—Other group health plan coverage that is not limited to excepted benefits and that is not an HRA or other account-based group health plan must be made available by the same plan sponsor for the plan year to the participant.

(B) *Benefits are limited in amount.*—*(1) Limit on annual amounts made available.*—The amounts newly made available for each plan year under the HRA or other account-based group health plan do not exceed $1,800. In the case of any plan year beginning after December 31, 2020, the dollar amount in the preceding sentence shall be increased by an amount equal to such dollar amount multiplied by the cost-of-living adjustment. The cost of living adjustment is the percentage (if any) by which the C-CPI-U for the preceding calendar year exceeds the C-CPI-U for calendar year 2019. The term "C-CPI-U" means the Chained Consumer Price Index for All Urban Consumers as published by the Bureau of Labor Statistics of the Department of Labor. The C-CPI-U for any calendar year is the average of the C-CPI-U as of the close of the 12-month period ending on March 31 of such calendar year. The values of the C-CPI-U used for any calendar year shall be the latest values so published as of the date on which the Bureau publishes the initial value of the C-CPI-U for the month of March for the preceding calendar year. Any such increase that is not a multiple of $50 shall be rounded down to the next lowest multiple of $50. The Department of the Treasury and the Internal Revenue Service will publish the adjusted amount for plan years beginning in any calendar year no later than June 1 of the preceding calendar year.

(2) *Carryover amounts.*—If the terms of the HRA or other account-based group health plan allow unused amounts to be made available to participants and dependents in later plan years, such carryover amounts are disregarded for purposes of determining whether benefits are limited in amount.

(3) *Multiple HRAs or other account-based group health plans.*—If the plan sponsor provides more than one HRA or other account-based group health plan to the participant for the same time period, the amounts made available under all such plans are aggregated to determine whether the benefits are limited in amount, except that HRAs or other account-based group health plans that reimburse only excepted benefits are not included in determining whether the benefits are limited in amount.

(C) *Prohibition on reimbursement of certain health insurance premiums.*—The HRA or other account-based group health plan must not reimburse premiums for individual health insurance coverage, group health plan coverage (other than COBRA continuation coverage or other continuation coverage), or Medicare Part A, B, C, or D, except that the HRA or other account-based group health plan may reimburse premiums for such coverage that consists solely of excepted benefits. See also, paragraph (c)(3)(viii)(F) of this section.

(D) *Uniform availability.*—The HRA or other account-based group health plan is made available under the same terms to all similarly situated individuals, as defined in § 54.9802-1(d) of this part, regardless of any health factor (as described in § 54.9802-1(a)).

(E) *Notice requirement.*—See 29 CFR 2520.102-3(j)(2) and (3) and 29 CFR 2520.104b-2(a) for rules regarding the time, manner, and content for summary plan descriptions (including a description of conditions pertaining to eligibility to receive benefits; annual or lifetime caps or other limits on benefits under the plan; and a description or summary of the benefits) applicable to plans subject to Tile I of the Employee Retirement Income Security Act of 1974, as amended.

(F) *Special rule.*—The HRA or other account-based group health plan must not reimburse premiums for short-term, limited-duration insurance (as defined in § 54.9801-2 of this part) if the conditions of this paragraph (c)(3)(viii)(F) are satisfied.

(1) The HRA or other account-based group health plan is offered by a small employer (as defined in PHS Act section 2791(e)(4)).

(2) The other group health plan coverage offered by the employer pursuant to paragraph (c)(3)(viii)(A) of this section is either fully-insured or partially-insured.

(3) The Secretary of Health and Human Services (HHS) makes a finding, in consultation with the Secretaries of Labor and the Treasury, that the reimbursement of premiums for short-term, limited-duration insurance by excepted benefit HRAs has caused significant harm to the small group market in the state that is the principal place of business of the small employer.

(4) The finding by the Secretary of HHS is made after submission of a written recommendation by the applicable state authority of such state, in a form and manner specified by HHS. The written recommendation must include evidence that the reimbursement of premiums for short-term, limited-duration insurance by excepted benefit HRAs established by insured or partially-insured small employers in the state has caused significant harm to the state's small group market, including with respect to premiums.

(5) The restriction shall be imposed or discontinued by publication by the Secretary of HHS of a notice in the Federal Register and shall apply only prospectively and with a reasonable time for plan sponsors to comply.

(4) *Noncoordinated benefits.*—(i) *Excepted benefits that are not coordinated.*—Coverage for only a specified disease or illness (for example, cancer-only policies) or hospital indemnity or other fixed indemnity insurance is excepted only if it meets each of the conditions specified in paragraph (c)(4)(ii) of this section. To be hospital indemnity or other fixed indemnity insurance, the insurance must pay a fixed dollar amount per day (or per other period) of hospitalization or illness (for example, $100/day) regardless of the amount of expenses incurred.

(ii) *Conditions.*—Benefits are described in paragraph (c)(4)(i) of this section only if—

(A) The benefits are provided under a separate policy, certificate, or contract of insurance;

(B) There is no coordination between the provision of the benefits and an exclusion of benefits under any group health plan maintained by the same plan sponsor; and

(C) The benefits are paid with respect to an event without regard to whether benefits are provided with respect to the event under any group health plan maintained by the same plan sponsor.

(iii) *Example.*—The rules of this paragraph (c)(4) are illustrated by the following example:

*Example.* (i) *Facts.* An employer sponsors a group health plan that provides coverage through an insurance policy. The policy provides benefits only for hospital stays at a fixed percentage of hospital expenses up to a maximum of $100 a day.

(ii) *Conclusion.* In this *Example*, even though the benefits under the policy satisfy the conditions in paragraph (c)(4)(ii) of this section, because the policy pays a percentage of expenses incurred rather than a fixed dollar amount, the benefits under the policy are not excepted benefits under this paragraph (c)(4). This is the result even if, in practice, the policy pays the maximum of $100 for every day of hospitalization.

(5) *Supplemental benefits.*—(i) The following benefits are excepted only if they are provided under a separate policy, certificate, or contract of insurance—

(A) Medicare supplemental health insurance (as defined under section 1882(g)(1) of the Social Security Act; also known as Medigap or MedSupp insurance);

(B) Coverage supplemental to the coverage provided under Chapter 55, Title 10 of the United States Code (also known as TRICARE supplemental programs); and

(C) *Similar supplemental coverage provided to coverage under a group health plan.*—To be similar supplemental coverage, the coverage must be specifically designed to fill gaps in the primary coverage. The preceding sentence is satisfied if the coverage is designed to fill gaps in cost sharing in the primary coverage, such as coinsurance or deductibles, or the coverage is designed to provide benefits for items and services not covered by the primary coverage and that are not essential health benefits (as defined under section 1302(b) of the Patient Protection and Affordable Care Act) in the State where the coverage is issued, or the coverage is designed to both fill such gaps in cost sharing under, and cover such benefits not covered by, the primary coverage. Similar supplemental coverage does not include coverage that becomes secondary or supplemental only under a coordination-of-benefits provision.

(ii) The rules of this paragraph (c)(5) are illustrated by the following example:

*Example.* (i) *Facts.* An employer sponsors a group health plan that provides coverage for both active employees and retirees. The coverage for retirees supplements benefits provided by Medicare, but does not meet the requirements for a supplemental policy under section 1882(g)(1) of the Social Security Act.

(ii) *Conclusion.* In this *Example*, the coverage provided to retirees does not meet the definition of supplemental excepted benefits under this paragraph (c)(5) because the coverage is not Medicare supplemental insurance as defined under section 1882(g)(1) of the Social Security Act, is not a TRICARE supplemental program, and is not supplemental to coverage provided under a group health plan.

(d) *Treatment of partnerships.*—For purposes of this part:

(1) *Treatment as a group health plan.*—(See 29 CFR 2590.732(d)(1) and 45 CFR 146.145(d)(1), under which a plan providing medical care, maintained by a partnership, and usually not treated as an employee welfare benefit plan under ERISA is treated as a group health plan for purposes of Part 7 of Subtitle B of Title I of ERISA and Title XXVII of the PHS Act.)

(2) *Employment relationship.*—In the case of a group health plan, the term *employer* also includes the partnership in relation to any

bona fide partner. In addition, the term *employee* also includes any bona fide partner. Whether or not an individual is a bona fide partner is determined based on all the relevant facts and circumstances, including whether the individual performs services on behalf of the partnership.

(3) *Participants of group health plans.*—In the case of a group health plan, the term *participant* also includes any individual described in paragraph (d)(3)(i) or (ii) of this section if the individual is, or may become, eligible to receive a benefit under the plan or the individual's beneficiaries may be eligible to receive any such benefit.

(i) In connection with a group health plan maintained by a partnership, the individual is a partner in relation to the partnership.

(ii) In connection with a group health plan maintained by a self-employed individual (under which one or more employees are participants), the individual is the self-employed individual.

(e) *Determining the average number of employees.*—[Reserved.] [Reg. §54.9831-1.]

☐ [*T.D.* 9166, 12-29-2004 *(corrected* 4-25-2005). *Amended by T.D.* 9299, 12-12-2006; *T.D.* 9427, 10-17-2008; *T.D.* 9464, 10-1-2009; *T.D.* 9656, 2-20-2014, *T.D.* 9697, 9-26-2014, *T.D.* 9714, 3-16-2015, *T.D.* 9791, 10-28-2016 *and T.D.* 9867, 6-13-2019.]

**[Reg. §54.9833-1]**

**§54.9833-1. Applicability dates.**—Sections 54.9801-1 through 54.9801-6, 54.9831-1, and this section are applicable for plan years beginning on or after July 1, 2005. Notwithstanding the previous sentence, the definition of "short-term, limited-duration insurance" in §54.9801–2 applies October 2, 2018. [Reg. §54.9833-1.]

☐ [*T.D.* 9166, 12-29-2004. *Amended by T.D.* 9791, 10-28-2016 *and T.D.* 9837, 8-1-2018.]

**[The next page is 72,301.]**

# STATEMENT OF PROCEDURAL RULES
## (26 C.F.R., Part 601)
### Subpart A—General Procedural Rules

**§ 601.101. Introduction.**—(a) *General.*—The Internal Revenue Service is a bureau of the Department of the Treasury under the immediate direction of the Commissioner of Internal Revenue. The Commissioner has general superintendence of the assessment and collection of all taxes imposed by any law providing internal revenue. The Internal Revenue Service is the agency by which these functions are performed. Within an internal revenue district the internal revenue laws are administered by a district director of internal revenue. The Director, Foreign Operations District, administers the internal revenue laws applicable to taxpayers residing or doing business abroad, foreign taxpayers deriving income from sources within the United States, and taxpayers who are required to withhold tax on certain payments to nonresident aliens and foreign corporations, provided the books and records of those taxpayers are located outside the United States. For purposes of these procedural rules any reference to a district director or a district office includes the Director, Foreign Operations District, or the District Office, Foreign Operations District, if appropriate. Generally, the procedural rules of the Service are based on the Internal Revenue Code of 1939 and the Internal Revenue Code of 1954, and the procedural rules in this part apply to the taxes imposed by both Codes except to the extent specifically stated or where the procedure under one Code is incompatible with the procedure under the other Code. References to sections of the Code are references to the Internal Revenue Code of 1954, unless otherwise expressly indicated.

(b) *Scope.*—This part sets forth the procedural rules of the Internal Revenue Service respecting all taxes administered by the Service, and supersedes the previously published statement (26 CFR (1949 ed., Part 300-End) Parts 600 and 601) with respect to such procedural rules. Subpart A provides a descriptive statement of the general course and method by which the Service's functions are channeled and determined, insofar as such functions relate generally to the assessment, collection, and enforcement of internal revenue taxes. Certain provisions special to particular taxes are separately described in Subpart D of this part. Conference and practice requirements of the Internal Revenue Service are contained in Subpart E of this part. Specific matters not generally involved in the assessment, collection, and enforcement functions are separately described in Subpart B of this part. A description of the rulemaking functions of the Department of the Treasury with respect to internal revenue tax matters is contained in Subpart F of this part. Subpart G of this part relates to matters of official record in the Internal Revenue Service and the extent to which records and documents are subject to publication or open to public inspection. This part does not contain a detailed discussion of the substantive provisions pertaining to any particular tax or the procedures relating thereto, and for such information it is necessary that reference be made to the applicable provisions of law and the regulations promulgated thereunder. The regulations relating to the taxes administered by the Service are contained in Title 26 of the Code of Federal Regulations. The regulations administered by the Bureau of Alcohol, Tobacco and Firearms are contained in Title 27 of the Code of Federal Regulations. [Reg. § 601.101.]

☐ [38 FR 4955, Feb. 23, 1973 and 41 FR 20880, May 21, 1976, as amended at 45 FR 7251, Feb. 1, 1980; 49 FR 36498, Sept. 18, 1984; T.D. 8685, 61 FR 58008, Nov. 12, 1996.]

**§ 601.102. Classification of taxes collected by the Internal Revenue Service.**—(a) *Principal divisions.*—Internal Revenue taxes fall generally into the following principal divisions:

(1) Taxes collected by assessment.

(2) Taxes collected by means of revenue stamps.

(b) *Assessed taxes.*—Taxes collected principally by assessment fall into the following two main classes—

(1) Taxes within the jurisdiction of the United States Tax Court. These include:

(i) Income and profits taxes imposed by chapters 1 and 2 of the 1939 Code and taxes imposed by subtitle A of the 1954 Code, relating to income taxes.

(ii) Estate taxes imposed by chapter 3 of the 1939 Code and chapter 11 of the 1954 Code.

(iii) Gift tax imposed by chapter 4 of the 1939 Code and chapter 12 of the 1954 Code.

(iv) The tax on generation-skipping transfers imposed by chapter 13 of the 1954 Code.

(v) Taxes imposed by chapters 41 through 44 of the 1954 Code.

(2) Taxes not within the jurisdiction of the United States Tax Court. Taxes not imposed by chapter 1, 2, 3, or 4 of the 1939 Code or subtitle A or chapter 11 or 12 of the 1954 Code are within this class, such as—

(i) Employment taxes.

(ii) Miscellaneous excise taxes collected by return.

(3) The difference between these two main classes is that only taxes described in subparagraph (1) of this paragraph, i.e., those within the jurisdiction of the Tax Court, may be contested before an independent tribunal prior to payment. Taxes of both classes may be contested by first making payment, filing claim for refund, and then bringing suit to recover if the claim is disallowed or no decision is rendered thereon within six months. [Reg. § 601.102.]

☐ [32 FR 15990, Nov. 22, 1967, as amended at 35 FR 7111, May 6, 1970; 46 FR 26053, May 11, 1981; T.D. 8685, 61 FR 58008, Nov. 12, 1996.]

**§ 601.103. Summary of general tax procedure.**—(a) *Collection procedure.*—The Federal tax system is basically one of self-assessment. In general each taxpayer (or person required to collect and pay over the tax) is required to file a prescribed form of return which shows the facts upon which tax liability may be determined and assessed. Generally, the taxpayer must compute the tax due on the return and make payment thereof on or before the due date for filing the return. If the taxpayer fails to pay the tax when due, the district director of internal revenue or the director of the regional service center after assessment issues a notice and demands payment within 10 days from the date of the notice. In the case of wage earners, annuitants, pensioners, and nonresident aliens, the income tax is collected in large part through withholding at the source. Another means of collecting the income tax is through payments of estimated tax which are required by law to be paid by certain individual and corporate taxpayers. Neither withholding nor payments of estimated tax relieves a taxpayer from the duty of filing a return otherwise required. Certain excise taxes are collected by the sale of internal revenue stamps.

(b) *Examination and determination of tax liability.*—After the returns are filed and processed in internal revenue service centers, some returns are selected for examination. If adjustments are proposed with which the taxpayer does not agree, ordinarily the taxpayer is afforded certain appeal rights. If the taxpayer agrees to the proposed adjustments and the tax involved is an income, profits, estate, gift, generation-skipping transfer, or chapter 41, 42, 43, or 44 tax, and if the taxpayer waives restrictions on the assessment and collection of the tax (see § 601.105(b)(4)), the deficiency will be immediately assessed.

(c) *Disputed liability.*—(1) *General.*—The taxpayer is given an opportunity to request that the case be considered by an Appeals Office provided that office has jurisdiction (see § 601.106(a)(3)). If the taxpayer requests such consideration, the case will be referred to the Appeals Office, which will afford the taxpayer the opportunity for a conference. The determination of tax liability by the Appeals Office is final insofar as the taxpayer's appeal rights within the Services are concerned. Upon protest of cases under the jurisdiction of the Director, Foreign Operations District, exclusive settlement authority is vested in the Appeals Office having jurisdiction of the place where the taxpayer requests the conference. If the taxpayer does not specify a location for the conference, or if the location specified is outside the territorial limits of the United States, the Washington, D.C. Appeals Office of the Mid-Atlantic Region assumes jurisdiction.

(2) *Petition to the U.S. Tax Court.*—In the case of income, profits, estate, and gift taxes imposed by subtitles A and B, and excise taxes under chapters 41 through 44 of the 1954 Code, before a deficiency may be assessed a statutory notice of deficiency (commonly called a "90-day letter") must be sent to the taxpayer by certified mail or registered mail unless the taxpayer waives this restriction on assessment. See, however, §§ 601.105(h) and 601.109 for exceptions. The taxpayer may then file a petition for a redetermination of the proposed deficiency with the U.S. Tax Court within 90 days from the date of the mailing of the statutory notice. If the notice is addressed to a person outside the States of the Union and the District of Columbia, the period within which a petition may be filed in the Tax Court is 150 days in lieu of 90 days. In other words, the taxpayer has

the right in respect of these taxes to contest any proposed deficiency before an independent tribunal prior to assessment or payment of the deficiency. Unless the taxpayer waives the restrictions on assessment and collection after the date of the mailing of the statutory notice, no assessment or collection of a deficiency (not including the correction of a mathematical error) may be made in respect of these taxes until the expiration of the applicable period or, if a petition is filed with the Tax Court, until the decision of the Court has become final. If, however, the taxpayer makes a payment with respect to a deficiency, the amount of such payment may be assessed. See, however, § 601.105(h). If the taxpayer fails to file a petition with the Tax Court within the applicable period, the deficiency will be assessed upon the expiration of such period and notice and demand for payment of the amount thereof will be mailed to the taxpayer. If the taxpayer files a petition with the Tax Court, the entire amount redetermined as the deficiency by a final decision of the Tax Court will be assessed and is payable upon notice and demand. There are no restrictions on the timely assessment and collection of the amount of any deficiency determined by the Tax Court, and a notice of appeal of the Court's decision will not stay the assessment and collection of the deficiency so determined, unless on or before the time the notice of appeal is filed the taxpayer files with the Tax Court a bond in a sum fixed by the Court not exceeding twice the portion of the deficiency in respect of which the notice of appeal is filed. No part of an amount determined as a deficiency but disallowed as such by a decision of the Tax Court which has become final may be assessed or collected by levy or by proceeding in court with or without assessment.

(3) *Claims for refund.*—After payment of the tax a taxpayer may, within the applicable period of limitations, contest the assessment by filing with the district director a claim for refund of all or any part of the amount paid, except with respect to certain taxes determined by the Tax Court, the decision of which has become final. If the claim is allowed, the overpayment of tax and allowable interest thereon will be credited against other liabilities of the taxpayer, or will be refunded to the taxpayer. Generally, if the claim for refund is rejected in whole or in part, the taxpayer is notified of the rejection by certified mail or registered mail. The taxpayer may then bring suit in the United States District Court or in the United States Claims Court for recovery of the tax. Suit may not be commenced before the expiration of six months from the date of filing of the claim for refund, unless a decision is rendered thereon within that time, nor after the expiration of two years from the date of mailing by certified mail or registered mail to the taxpayer of a notice of the disallowance of the part of the claim to which the suit relates. Under the 1954 Code, the 2-year period of limitation for bringing suit may be extended for such period as may be agreed upon in a properly executed Form 907. Also, under the 1954 Code, if the taxpayer files a written waiver of the requirement that the taxpayer be sent a notice of disallowance, the 2-year period for bringing suit begins to run on the date such waiver is filed. See section 6532(a) of the Code. [Reg. § 601.103.]

☐ [32 FR 15990, Nov. 22, 1967, as amended at 38 FR 4955, Feb. 23, 1973; 43 FR 44497, Sept. 28, 1978; 45 FR 7251, Feb. 1, 1980; 46 FR 26053, May 11, 1981; 49 FR 36498, Sept. 18, 1984.]

### [Reg. § 601.104]

**§ 601.104. Collection functions.**—(a) *Collection methods.*—(1) *Returns.*—Generally, an internal revenue tax assessment is based upon a return required by law or regulations to be filed by the taxpayer upon which the taxpayer computes the tax in the manner indicated by the return. Certain taxpayers who choose to use the Optional Tax Tables may elect to have the Internal Revenue Service compute the tax and mail them a notice stating the amount of tax due. If a taxpayer fails to make a return it may be made for the taxpayer by a district director or other duly authorized officer or employee. See section 6020 of the Code and the regulations thereunder. Returns must be made on the forms prescribed by the Internal Revenue Service. Forms are obtainable at the principal and branch offices of district directors of internal revenue. Taxpayers overseas may also obtain forms from any United States Embassy or consulate. Forms are generally mailed to persons whom the Service has reason to believe may be required to file returns, but failure to receive a form does not excuse failure to comply with the law or regulations requiring a return. Returns, supplementary returns, statements or schedules, and the time for filing them, may sometimes be prescribed by regulations issued under authority of law by the Commissioner with the approval of the Secretary of the Treasury or the Secretary's delegate. A husband and wife may make a single income tax return jointly. Certain affiliated groups of corporations may file consolidated income tax returns. See section 1501 of the Code and the regulations thereunder.

(2) *Withholding of tax at source.*—Withholding at the source of income payments is an important method used in collecting taxes. For example, in the case of wage earners, the income tax is collected in large part through the withholding by employers of taxes on wages paid to their employees. The tax withheld at the source on wages is applied as a credit in payment of the individual's income tax liability for the taxable year. In no case does withholding of the tax relieve an individual from the duty of filing a return otherwise required by law. The chief means of collecting the income tax due from nonresident alien individuals and foreign corporations having United States source gross income which is not effectively connected with the conduct of a trade or business in the United States is the withholding of the tax by persons paying or remitting the income to the recipients. The tax withheld is allowed as a credit in payment of the tax imposed on such nonresident alien individuals and foreign corporations.

(3) *Payments of estimated tax.*—Any individual who may reasonably expect to receive gross income for the taxable year from wages or from sources other than wages, in excess of amounts specified by law, and who can reasonably expect his or her estimated tax to be at least $200 in 1982, $300 in 1983, $400 in 1984, and $500 in 1985 and later is required to make estimated tax payments. Payments of estimated tax are applied in payment of the tax for the taxable year. A husband and wife may jointly make a single payment which may be applied in payment of the income tax liability of either spouse in any proportion they may specify. For taxable years ending on or after December 31, 1955, the law requires payments of estimated tax by certain corporations. See section 6154 of the Code.

(b) *Extension of time for filing returns.*—(1) *General.*—Under certain circumstances the district directors or directors of service centers are authorized to grant a reasonable extension of time for filing a return or declaration. The maximum period for extensions cannot be in excess of 6 months, except in the case of taxpayers who are abroad. With an exception in the case of estate tax returns, written application for extension must be received by the appropriate director on or before the date prescribed by law for filing the return or declaration.

(2) *Corporations.*—On or before the date prescribed by law for filing its income tax return, a corporation may obtain an automatic 6-month extension of time (a 3-month extension in the case of taxable years ending before December 31, 1982) for filing the income tax return by filing Form 7004 and paying the full amount of the properly estimated unpaid tax liability. For taxable years beginning before 1983, however, the corporation must remit with Form 7004 an estimated amount not less than would be required as the first installment of tax should the corporation elect to pay the tax in installments.

(3) *Individuals.*—On or before the date prescribed for the filing of the return of an individual, such individual may obtain an automatic 4-month extension of time for filing his or her return by filing Form 4868 accompanied by payment of the full amount of the estimated unpaid tax liability.

(c) *Enforcement procedure.*—(1) *General.*—Taxes shown to be due on returns, deficiencies in taxes, additional or delinquent taxes to be assessed, and penalties, interest, and additions to taxes, are recorded by the district director or the director of the appropriate service center as "assessments." Under the law an assessment is prima facie correct for all purposes. Generally, the taxpayer bears the burden of disproving the correctness of an assessment. Upon assessment, the district director is required to effect collection of any amounts which remain due and unpaid. Generally, payment within 10 days from the date of the notice and demand for payment is requested; however, payment may be required in a shorter period if collection of the tax is considered to be in jeopardy. When collection of income tax is in jeopardy, the taxpayer's taxable period may be terminated under section 6851 of the Code and assessment of the tax made expeditiously under section 6201 of the Code.

(2) *Levy.*—If a taxpayer neglects or refuses to pay any tax within the period provided for its payment, it is lawful for the district director to make collection by levy on the taxpayer's property. However, unless collection is in jeopardy, the taxpayer must be furnished written notice of intent to levy no fewer than 10 days before the date of the levy. See section 6331 of the Code. No suit for the purpose of restraining the assessment or collection of an internal revenue tax may be maintained in any court, except to restrain the assessment or collection of income, estate, chapters 41 through 44, or gift taxes during the period within which the assessment or collection of deficiencies in such taxes is prohibited. See section 7421 of the Code. Property taken under authority of any revenue law of the United States is irrepleviable. 28 U.S.C. 2463. If the Service sells property, and it is subsequently determined that the taxpayer had no interest in the property or that the purchaser was misled by the Service as to the value of the taxpayer's interest, immediate action will be taken to refund any money wrongfully collected if a claim is made and the pertinent facts are present. The mere fact that a taxpayer's interest in property turns out to be less valuable than the purchaser expected

will not be regarded as giving the purchaser any claim against the Government.

(3) *Liens.*—The United States' claim for taxes is a lien on the taxpayer's property at the time of assessment. Such lien is not valid as against any purchaser, holder of a security interest, mechanic's lienor, or judgment lien creditor until notice has been filed by the district director. Despite such filing, the lien is not valid with respect to certain securities as against any purchaser of such security who, at the time of purchase, did not have actual notice or knowledge of the existence of such lien and as against a holder of a security interest in such security who, at the time such interest came into existence, did not have actual notice or knowledge of the existence of such lien. Certain motor vehicle purchases are similarly protected. Even though a notice of lien has been filed, certain other categories are afforded additional protection. These categories are: Retain purchases, casual sales, possessory liens, real property taxes and property assessments, small repairs and improvements, attorneys' liens, certain insurance contracts and passbook loans. A valid lien generally continues until the liability is satisfied, becomes unenforceable by reason of lapse of time or is discharged in bankruptcy. A certificate of release of lien will be issued not later than 30 days after the taxpayer furnishes proper bond in lieu of the lien, or 30 days after it is determined that the liability has been satisfied, has become unenforceable by reason of lapse of time, or has been discharged in bankruptcy. If a certificate has not been issued and one of the foregoing criteria for release has been met, a certificate of release of lien will be issued within 30 days after a written request by a taxpayer, specifying the grounds upon which the issuance of release is sought. The Code also contains additional provisions with respect to the discharge of specific property from the effect of the lien. Also, under certain conditions, a lien may be subordinated. The Code also contains additional provisions with respect to liens in the case of estate and gift taxes. For the specific rules with respect to liens, see subchapter C of chapter 64 of the Code and the regulations thereunder.

(4) *Penalties.*—In the case of failure to file a return within the prescribed time, a certain percentage of the amount of tax (or a minimum penalty) is, pursuant to statute, added to the tax unless the failure to file the return within the prescribed time is shown to the satisfaction of the district director or the director of the appropriate service center to be due to reasonable cause and not neglect. In the case of failure to file an exempt organization information return within the prescribed time, a penalty of $10 a day for each day the return is delinquent is assessed unless the failure to file the return within the prescribed time is shown to be due to reasonable cause and not neglect. In the case of failure to pay or deposit taxes due within the prescribed time, a certain percentage of the amount of tax due is, pursuant to statute, added to the tax unless the failure to pay or deposit the tax due within the prescribed time is shown to the satisfaction of the district director or the director of the appropriate service center to be due to reasonable cause and not neglect. Civil penalties are also imposed for fraudulent returns; in the case of income and gift taxes, for intentional disregard of rules and regulations or negligence; and additions to the tax are imposed for the failure to comply with the requirements of law with respect to the estimated income tax. There are also civil penalties for filing false withholding certificates, for substantial understatement of income tax, for filing a frivolous return, for organizing or participating in the sale of abusive tax shelters, and for aiding and abetting in the understatement of tax liability. See chapter 68 of the Code. A 50 percent penalty, in addition to the personal liability incurred, is imposed upon any person who fails or refuses without reasonable cause to honor a levy. Criminal penalties are imposed for willful failure to make returns, keep records, supply information, etc. See chapter 75 of the Code.

(5) *Informants' rewards.*—Payments to informers are authorized for detecting and bringing to trial and punishment persons guilty of violating the internal revenue laws. See section 7623 of the Code and the regulations thereunder. Claims for rewards should be made on Form 211. Relevant facts should be stated on the form, which after execution should be forwarded to the district director of internal revenue for the district in which the informer resides, or the Commissioner of Internal Revenue, Washington, D.C. 20224. [Reg. § 601.104.]

□ [32 FR 15990, Nov. 22, 1967, as amended at 32 FR 20645, Dec. 21, 1967; 33 FR 17234, Nov. 21, 1968; 34 FR 6424, Apr. 12, 1969; 35 FR 7112, May 6, 1970; 36 FR 7584, Apr. 22, 1971; 38 FR 4956, Feb. 23, 1973; 45 FR 7251, Feb. 1, 1980; 49 FR 36499, Sept. 18, 1984; 49 FR 40809, Oct. 18, 1984; T.D. 8685, 61 FR 58008, Nov. 12, 1996.]

**[Reg. § 601.105]**

**§ 601.105. Examination of returns and claims for refund, credit or abatement; determination of correct tax liability.**—(a) *Processing of returns.*—When the returns are filed in the office of the district director of internal revenue or the office of the director of a regional service center, they are checked first for form, execution, and mathe-

matical accuracy. Mathematical errors are corrected and a correction notice of any such error is sent to the taxpayer. Notice and demand is made for the payment of any additional tax so resulting, or refund is made of any overpayment. Returns are classified for examination at regional service centers. Certain individual income tax returns with potential unallowable items are delivered to Examination Divisions at regional service centers for correction by correspondence. Otherwise, returns with the highest examination potential are delivered to district Examination Divisions based on workload capacities. Those most in need of examination are selected for office or field examination.

(b) *Examination of returns.*—(1) *General.*—The original examination of income (including partnership and fiduciary), estate, gift, excise, employment, exempt organization, and information returns is a primary function of examiners in the Examination Division of the office of each district director of internal revenue. Such examiners are organized in groups, each of which is under the immediate supervision of a group supervisor designated by the district director. Revenue agents (and such other officers or employees of the Internal Revenue Service as may be designated for this purpose by the Commissioner) are authorized to examine any books, papers, records, or memoranda bearing upon matters required to be included in Federal tax returns and to take testimony relative thereto and to administer oaths. See section 7602 of the Code and the regulations thereunder. There are two general types of examination. These are commonly called "office examination" and "field examination". During the examination of a return a taxpayer may be represented before the examining officer by an attorney, certified public accountant, or other representative. See Subpart E of this part for conference and practice requirements.

(2) *Office examination.*—(i) *Adjustments by Examination Division at service center.*—Certain individual income tax returns identified as containing potential unallowable items are examined by Examination Divisions at regional service centers. Correspondence examination techniques are used. If the taxpayer requests an interview to discuss the proposed adjustments, the case is transferred to the taxpayer's district office. If the taxpayer does not agree to the proposed adjustments, regular appeals procedures apply.

(ii) *Examinations at district office.*—Certain returns are examined at district offices by office examination techniques. These returns include some business returns, besides the full range of nonbusiness individual income tax returns. Office examinations are conducted primarily by the interview method. Examinations are conducted by correspondence only when warranted by the nature of the questionable items and by the convenience and characteristics of the taxpayer. In a correspondence examination, the taxpayer is asked to explain or send supporting evidence by mail. In an office interview examination the taxpayer is asked to come to the district director's office for an interview and to bring certain records with the taxpayer in support of the return. During the interview examination, the taxpayer has the right to point out to the examining officer any amounts included in the return which are not taxable, or any deductions which the taxpayer failed to claim on the return. If it develops that a field examination is necessary, the examiner may conduct such examination.

(3) *Field examination.*—Certain returns are examined by field examination which involves an examination of the taxpayer's books and records on the taxpayer's premises. An examiner will check the entire return filed by the taxpayer and will examine all books, papers, records, and memoranda dealing with matters required to be included in the return. If the return presents an engineering or appraisal problem (e.g., depreciation or depletion deductions, gains or losses upon the sale or exchange of property, or losses on account of abandonment, exhaustion, or obsolescence), it may be investigated by an engineer agent who makes a separate report.

(4) *Conclusion of examination.*—At the conclusion of an office or field examination, the taxpayer is given an opportunity to agree with the findings of the examining officer. If the taxpayer does not agree, the examining officer will inform the taxpayer of the taxpayer's appeal rights. If the taxpayer does agree with the proposed changes the examining officer will invite the taxpayer to execute either Form 870 or another appropriate agreement form. When the taxpayer agrees with the proposed changes but does not offer to pay any deficiency or additional tax which may be due, the examining officer will also invite payment (by check or money order), together with any applicable interest or penalty. If the agreed case involves income, profits, estate, gift, generation-skipping transfer or chapter 41, 42, 43 or 44 taxes, the agreement is evidenced by a waiver by the taxpayer of restrictions on assessment and collection of the deficiency, or an acceptance of a proposed overassessment. If the case involves excise or employment taxes or 100 percent penalty, the agreement is evidenced in the form of a consent to assessment and collection of additional tax or penalty and waiver of right to file claim for abate-

ment, or the acceptance of the proposed overassessment. Even though the taxpayer signs an acceptance of a proposed overassessment the district director or the director of the regional service center remains free to assess a deficiency. On the other hand, the taxpayer who has given a waiver may still claim a refund of any part of the deficiency assessed against, and paid by, the taxpayer or any part of the tax originally assessed and paid by the taxpayer. The taxpayer's acceptance of an agreed overassessment does not prevent the taxpayer from filing a claim and bringing a suit for an additional sum, nor does it preclude the Government from maintaining suit to recover an erroneous refund. As a matter of practice, however, waivers or acceptances ordinarily result in the closing of a case insofar as the Government is concerned.

(5) *Technical advice from the National Office.*—(i) *Definition and nature of technical advice.*—(a) As used in this subparagraph, "technical advice" means advice or guidance as to the interpretation and proper application of internal revenue laws, related statutes, and regulations, to a specific set of facts, furnished by the National Office upon request of a district office in connection with the examination of a taxpayer's return or consideration of a taxpayer's return claim for refund or credit. It is furnished as a means of assisting Service personnel in closing cases and establishing and maintaining consistent holdings in the several districts. It does not include memorandums on matters of general technical application furnished to district offices where the issues are not raised in connection with the examination of the return of a specific taxpayer.

(b) The consideration or examination of the facts relating to a request for a determination letter is considered to be in connection with the examination or consideration of a return of the taxpayer. Thus, a district director may, in his discretion, request technical advice with respect to the consideration of a request for a determination letter.

(c) If a district director is of the opinion that a ruling letter previously issued to a taxpayer should be modified or revoked, and requests the National Office to reconsider the ruling, the reference of the matter to the National Office is treated as a request for technical advice and the procedures specified in subdivision (iii) of this subparagraph should be followed in order that the National Office may consider the district director's recommendation.

Only the National Office can revoke a ruling letter. Before referral to the National Office, the district director should inform the taxpayer of his opinion that the ruling letter should be revoked. The district director, after development of the facts and consideration of the taxpayer's arguments, will decide whether to recommend revocation of the ruling to the National Office. For procedures relating to a request for a ruling, see § 601.201.

(d) The Assistant Commissioner (Technical), acting under a delegation of authority from the Commissioner of Internal Revenue, is exclusively responsible for providing technical advice in any issue involving the establishment of basic principles and rules for the uniform interpretation and application of tax laws other than those which are under the jurisdiction of the Bureau of Alcohol, Tobacco, and Firearms. This authority has been largely redelegated to subordinate officials.

(e) The provisions of this subparagraph apply only to a case under the jurisdiction of a district director, but do not apply to the Employee Plans case under the jurisdiction of a key district director as provided in § 601.201(o) or to an Exempt Organization case under the jurisdiction of a key district director as provided in § 601.201(n). The technical advice provisions applicable to Employee Plans and Exempt Organization cases are set forth in § 601.201(n)(9). The provisions of this subparagraph do not apply to a case under the jurisdiction of the Bureau of Alcohol, Tobacco, and Firearms. They also do not apply to a case under the jurisdiction of an Appeals office, including a case previously considered by Appeals. The technical advice provisions applicable to a case under the jurisdiction of an Appeals office, other than Employee Plans and Exempt Organizations cases, are set forth in § 601.106(f)(10). A case remains under the jurisdiction of the district director even though an Appeals office has the identical issue under consideration in the case of another taxpayer (not related within the meaning of section 267 of the Code) in an entirely different transaction. Technical advice may not be requested with respect to a taxable period if a prior Appeals disposition of the same taxable period of the same taxpayer's case was based on mutual concessions (ordinarily with a Form 870-AD, Offer of Waiver of Restrictions on Assessment and Collection of Deficiency in Tax and of Acceptance of Overassessment). However, technical advice may be requested by a district director on issues previously considered in a prior Appeals disposition, not based on mutual concessions, of the same taxable periods of the same taxpayer with the concurrence of the Appeals office that had the case.

(ii) *Areas in which technical advice may be requested.*—(a) District directors may request technical advice on any technical or procedural question that develops during the audit or examination of a return,

or claim for refund or credit, of a taxpayer. These procedures are applicable as provided in subdivision (i) of this subparagraph.

(b) District directors are encouraged to request technical advice on any technical or procedural question arising in connection with any case of the type described in subdivision (i) of this subparagraph which cannot be resolved on the basis of law, regulations, or a clearly applicable revenue ruling or other precedent issued by the National Office. This request should be made at the earliest possible stage of the examination process.

(iii) *Requesting technical advice.*—(a) It is the responsibility of the district office to determine whether technical advice is to be requested on any issue before that office. However, while the case is under the jurisdiction of the district director, a taxpayer or his/her representative may request that an issue be referred to the National Office for technical advice on the grounds that a lack of uniformity exists as to the disposition of the issue, or that the issue is so unusual or complex as to warrant consideration by the National Office. This request should be made at the earliest possible stage of the examination process. While taxpayers are encouraged to make written requests setting forth the facts, law, and argument with respect to the issue, and reason for requesting National Office advice, a taxpayer may make the request orally. If, after considering the taxpayer's request, the examiner is of the opinion that the circumstances do not warrant referral of the case to the National Office, he/she will so advise the taxpayer. (See subdivision (iv) of this subparagraph for taxpayer's appeal rights where the examiner declines to request technical advice.)

(b) When technical advice is to be requested, whether or not upon the request of the taxpayer, the taxpayer will be so advised, except as noted in (g) of this subdivision. If the examiner initiates the action, the taxpayer will be furnished a copy of the statement of the pertinent facts and the question or questions proposed for submission to the National Office. The request for advice submitted by the district director should be so worded as to avoid possible misunderstanding, in the National Office, of the facts or of the specific point or points at issue.

(c) After receipt of the statement of facts and specific questions from the district office, the taxpayer will be given 10 calendar days in which to indicate in writing the extent, if any, to which he may not be in complete agreement. An extension of time must be justified by the taxpayer in writing and approved by the Chief, Audit Division. Every effort should be made to reach agreement as to the facts and specific point at issue. If agreement cannot be reached, the taxpayer may submit, within 10 calendar days after receipt of notice from the district office, a statement of his understanding as to the specific point or points at issue which will be forwarded to the National Office with the request for advice. An extension of time must be justified by the taxpayer in writing and approved by the Chief, Examination Division.

(d) If the taxpayer initiates the action to request advice, and his statement of the facts and point or points at issue are not wholly acceptable to the district officials, the taxpayer will be advised in writing as to the areas of disagreement. The taxpayer will be given 10 calendar days after receipt of the written notice to reply to the district official's letter. An extension of time must be justified by the taxpayer in writing and approved by the Chief, Examination Division. If agreement cannot be reached, both the statements of the taxpayer and the district official will be forwarded to the National Office.

(e)(1) In the case of requests for technical advice the taxpayer must also submit, within the 10-day period referred to in (c) and (d) of this subdivision, whichever applicable (relating to agreement by the taxpayer with the statement of facts submitted in connection with the request for technical advice), the statement described in (f) of this subdivision of proposed deletions pursuant to section 6110(c) of the Code. If the statement is not submitted, the taxpayer will be informed by the district director that such a statement is required. If the district director does not receive the statement within 10 days after the taxpayer has been informed of the need for such statement, the district director may decline to submit the request for technical advice. If the district director decides to request technical advice in a case where the taxpayer has not submitted the statement of proposed deletions, the National Office will make those deletions which in the judgment of the Commissioner are required by section 6110(c) of the Code.

(2) The requirements included in § 601.105(b)(5) with respect to submissions of statements and other material with respect to proposed deletions to be made from technical advice memoranda before public inspection is permitted to take place do not apply to requests made by the district director before November 1, 1976, or requests for any document to which section 6104 of the Code applies.

(f) In order to assist the Internal Revenue Service in making the deletions, required by section 6110(c) of the Code, from the text of technical advice memoranda which are open to public inspection pursuant to section 6110(a) of the Code, there must accompany requests for such technical advice either a statement of the deletions proposed by the taxpayer and the statutory basis for each proposed deletion, or a statement that no information other than names, addresses, and taxpayer identifying numbers need be deleted. Such statements shall be made in a separate document. The statement of proposed deletions shall be accompanied by a copy of all statements of facts and supporting documents which are submitted to the National Office pursuant to (c) or (d) of this subdivision, on which shall be indicated, by the use of brackets, the material which the taxpayer indicates should be deleted pursuant to section 6110(c) of the Code. The statement of proposed deletions shall indicate the statutory basis, under section 6110(c) of the Code, for each proposed deletion. The statement of proposed deletions shall not appear or be referred to anywhere in the request for technical advice. If the taxpayer decides to request additional deletions pursuant to section 6110(c) of the Code prior to the time the National Office replies to the request for technical advice, additional statements may be submitted.

(g) If the taxpayer has not already done so, the taxpayer may submit a statement explaining the taxpayer's position on the issues, citing precedents which the taxpayer believes will bear on the case. This statement will be forwarded to the National Office with the request for advice. If it is received at a later date, it will be forwarded for association with the case file.

(h) At the time the taxpayer is informed that the matter is being referred to the National Office, the taxpayer will also be informed of the right to a conference in the National Office in the event an adverse decision is indicated, and will be asked to indicate whether such a conference is desired.

(i) Generally, prior to replying to the request for technical advice, the National Office shall inform the taxpayer orally or in writing of the material likely to appear in the technical advice memorandum which the taxpayer proposed be deleted but which the Internal Revenue Service determined should not be deleted. If so informed, the taxpayer may submit within 10 days any further information, arguments or other material in support of the position that such material be deleted. The Internal Revenue Service will attempt, if feasible, to resolve all disagreements with respect to proposed deletions prior to the time the National Office replies to the request for technical advice. However, in no event shall the taxpayer have the right to a conference with respect to resolution of any disagreements concerning material to be deleted from the text of the technical advice memorandum, but such matters may be considered at any conference otherwise scheduled with respect to the request.

(j) The provisions of (a) through (i) of this subdivision, relating to the referral of issues upon request of the taxpayer, advising taxpayers of the referral of issues, the submission of proposed deletions, and the granting of conferences in the National Office, are not applicable to technical advice memoranda described in section 6110(g)(5)(A) of the Code, relating to cases involving criminal or civil fraud investigations and jeopardy or termination assessments. However, in such cases the taxpayer shall be allowed to provide the statement of proposed deletions to the National Office upon the completion of all proceedings with respect to the investigations or assessments, but prior to the date on which the Commissioner mails the notice pursuant to section 6110(f)(1) of the Code of intention to disclose the technical advice memorandum.

(k) Form 4463, Request for Technical Advice, should be used for transmitting requests for technical advice to the National Office.

(iv) *Appeal by taxpayers of determinations not to seek technical advice.*—(a) If the taxpayer has requested referral of an issue before a district office to the National Office for technical advice, and after consideration of the request the examiner is of the opinion that the circumstances do not warrant such referral, the examiner will so advise the taxpayer.

(b) The taxpayer may appeal the decision of the examining officer not to request technical advice by submitting to that official, within 10 calendar days after being advised of the decision, a statement of the facts, law, and arguments with respect to the issue, and the reasons why he believes the matter should be referred to the National Office for advice. An extension of time must be justified by the taxpayer in writing and approved by the Chief, Examination Division.

(c) The examining officer will submit the statement of the taxpayer through channels to the Chief, Examination Division, accompanied by a statement of his reasons why the issue should not be referred to the National Office. The Chief, Examination Division, will determine, on the basis of the statements submitted, whether technical advice will be requested. If he determines that technical advice is not warranted, he will inform the taxpayer in writing that he proposes to deny the request. In the letter to the taxpayer the Chief, Examination Division, will (except in unusual situations where such action would be prejudicial to the best interests of the Government) state specifically the reasons for the proposed denial. The taxpayer will be given 15 calendar days after receipt of the letter in which to notify the Chief, Examination Division, whether he agrees with the

proposed denial. The taxpayer may not appeal the decision of the Chief, Examination Division, not to request technical advice from the National Office. However, if he does not agree with the proposed denial, all data relating to the issue for which technical advice has been sought, including taxpayer's written request and statements, will be submitted to the National Office, Attention: Director, Examination Division, for review. After review in the National Office, the district office will be notified whether the proposed denial is approved or disapproved.

(d) While the matter is being reviewed in the National Office, the district office will suspend action on the issue (except where the delay would prejudice the Government's interests) until it is notified of the National Office decision. This notification will be made within 30 days after receipt of the data in the National Office. The review will be solely on the basis of the written record and no conference will be held in the National Office.

(v) *Conference in the National Office.*—(a) If, after a study of the technical advice request, it appears that advice adverse to the taxpayer should be given and a conference has been requested, the taxpayer will be notified of the time and place of the conference. If conferences are being arranged with respect to more than one request for advice involving the same taxpayer, they will be so scheduled as to cause the least inconvenience to the taxpayer. The conference will be arranged by telephone, if possible, and must be held within 21 calendar days after contact has been made. Extensions of time will be granted only if justified in writing by the taxpayer and approved by the appropriate Technical branch chief.

(b) A taxpayer is entitled, as a matter of right, to only one conference in the National Office unless one of the circumstances discussed in (c) of this subdivision exists. This conference will usually be held at the branch level in the appropriate division (Corporation Tax Division or Individual Tax Division) in the office of the Assistant Commissioner (Technical), and will usually be attended by a person who has authority to act for the branch chief. In appropriate cases the examining officer may also attend the conference to clarify the facts in the case. If more than one subject is discussed at the conference, the discussion constitutes a conference with respect to each subject. At the request of the taxpayer or his representative, the conference may be held at an earlier stage in the consideration of the case than the Service would ordinarily designate. A taxpayer has no "right" of appeal from an action of a branch to the director of a division or to any other National Office official.

(c) In the process of review of a holding proposed by a branch, it may appear that the final answer will involve a reversal of the branch proposal with a result less favorable to the taxpayer. Or it may appear that an adverse holding proposed by a branch will be approved, but on a new or different issue or on different grounds than those on which the branch decided the case. Under either of these circumstances, the taxpayer or his representative will be invited to another conference. The provisions of this subparagraph limiting the number of conferences to which a taxpayer is entitled will not foreclose inviting a taxpayer to attend further conferences when, in the opinion of National Office personnel, such need arises. All additional conferences of this type discussed are held only at the invitation of the Service.

(d) It is the responsibility of the taxpayer to furnish to the National Office, within 21 calendar days after the conference, a written record of any additional data, line of reasoning, precedents, etc., that were proposed by the taxpayer and discussed at the conference but were not previously or adequately presented in writing. Extensions of time will be granted only if justified in writing by the taxpayer and approved by the appropriate Technical branch chief. Any additional material and a copy thereof should be addressed to and sent to the National Office which will forward the copy to the appropriate district director. The district director will be requested to give the matter his prompt attention. He may verify the additional facts and data and comment upon it to the extent he deems it appropriate.

(e) A taxpayer or a taxpayer's representative desiring to obtain information as to the status of the case may do so by contacting the following offices with respect to matters in the areas of their responsibility:

| Official | Telephone Numbers (Area Code 202) |
|---|---|
| Director, Corporation Tax Division | 566-4504 or 566-4505 |
| Director, Individual Tax Division | 566-3767 or 566-3788 |

(vi) *Preparation of technical advice memorandum by the National Office.*—(a) Immediately upon receipt in the National Office, the technical employee to whom the case is assigned will analyze the file to ascertain whether it meets the requirements of subdivision (iii) of this subparagraph. If the case is not complete with respect to any requirement in subdivision (iii) (a) through (d) of this subparagraph, appropriate steps will be taken to complete the file. If any request for technical advice does not comply with the requirements of subdivision (iii) (e) of this subparagraph, relating to the statement of proposed deletions, the National Office will make those deletions from the technical advice memorandum which in the judgment of the Commissioner are required by section 6110(c) of the Code.

(b) If the taxpayer has requested a conference in the National Office, the procedures in subdivision (v) of this subparagraph will be followed.

(c) Replies to requests for technical advice will be addressed to the district director and will be drafted in two parts. Each part will identify the taxpayer by name, address, identification number, and year or years involved. The first part (hereafter called the "Technical Advice Memorandum") will contain (1) a recitation of the pertinent facts having a bearing on the issue; (2) a discussion of the facts, precedents, and reasoning of the National Office; and (3) the conclusions of the National Office. The conclusions will give direct answers, whenever possible, to the specific questions of the district office. The discussion of the issues will be in such detail that the district officials are apprised of the reasoning underlying the conclusion. There shall accompany the technical advice memorandum a notice pursuant to section 6110(f)(l) of the Code of intention to disclose the technical advice memorandum (including a copy of the version proposed to be open to public inspection and notations of third party communications pursuant to section 6110(d) of the Code) which the district director shall forward to the taxpayer at such time that the district director furnishes a copy of the technical advice memorandum to the taxpayer pursuant to (e) of this subdivision.

(d) The second part of the reply will consist of a transmittal memorandum. In the unusual cases it will serve as a vehicle for providing the district office administrative information or other information which, under the nondisclosure statutes, or for other reasons, may not be discussed with the taxpayer.

(e) It is the general practice of the Service to furnish a copy of the technical advice memorandum to the taxpayer after it has been adopted by the district director. However, in the case of technical advice memoranda described in section 6110(g)(5)(A) of the Code, relating to cases involving criminal or civil fraud investigations and jeopardy or termination assessments, a copy of the technical advice memorandum shall not be furnished the taxpayer until all proceedings with respect to the investigations or assessments are completed.

(f) After receiving the notice pursuant to section 6110(f)(1) of the Code of intention to disclose the technical advice memorandum, if the taxpayer desires to protest the disclosure of certain information in the technical advice memorandum, the taxpayer must within 20 days after the notice is mailed submit a written statement identifying those deletions not made by the Internal Revenue Service which the taxpayer believes should have been made. The taxpayer shall also submit a copy of the version of the technical advice memorandum proposed to be open to public inspection on which the taxpayer indicates, by the use of brackets, the deletions proposed by the taxpayer but which have not been made by the Internal Revenue Service. Generally, the Internal Revenue Service will not consider the deletion under this subparagraph of any material which the taxpayer did not, prior to the time when the National Office sent its reply to the request for technical advice to the district director, propose be deleted. The Internal Revenue Service shall, within 20 days after receipt of the response by the taxpayer to the notice pursuant to section 6110(f)(1) of the Code, mail to the taxpayer its final administrative conclusion with respect to the deletions to be made.

(vii) *Action on technical advice in district offices.*—(a) Unless the district director feels that the conclusions reached by the National Office in a technical advice memorandum should be reconsidered and promptly requests such reconsideration, his office will proceed to process the taxpayer's case on the basis of the conclusions expressed in the technical advice memorandum.

(b) The district director will furnish to the taxpayer a copy of the technical advice memorandum described in subdivision (vi) (c) of this subparagraph and the notice pursuant to section 6110(f)(1) of the Code of intention to disclose the technical advice memorandum (including a copy of the version proposed to be open to public inspection and notations of third party communications pursuant to section 6110(d) of the Code). The preceding sentence shall not apply to technical advice memoranda involving civil fraud or criminal investigations, or jeopardy or termination assessments, as described in subdivision (iii) (j) of this subparagraph or to documents to which section 6104 of the Code applies.

(c) In those cases in which the National Office advises the district director that he should not furnish a copy of the technical memorandum to the taxpayer, the district director will so inform the taxpayer if he requests a copy.

(viii) *Effect of technical advice.*—(a) A technical advice memorandum represents an expression of the views of the Service as to the application of law, regulations, and precedents to the facts of a specific case, and is issued primarily as a means of assisting district officials in the examination and closing of the case involved.

(b) Except in rare or unusual circumstances, a holding in a technical advice memorandum that is favorable to the taxpayer is applied retroactively. Moreover, since technical advice, as described in subdivision (i) of this subparagraph, is issued only on closed transactions, a holding in a technical advice memorandum that is adverse to the taxpayer is also applied retroactively unless the Assistant Commissioner (Technical) exercises the discretionary authority under section 7805(b) of the Code to limit the retroactive effect of the holding. Likewise, a holding in a technical advice memorandum that modifies or revokes a holding in a prior technical advice memorandum will also be applied retroactively, with one exception. If the new holding is less favorable to the taxpayer, it will generally not be applied to the period in which the taxpayer relied on the prior holding in situations involving continuing transactions of the type described in § 601.201(*l*)(7) and § 601.201(*l*)(8).

(c) Technical advice memoranda often form the basis for revenue rulings. For the description of revenue rulings and the effect thereof, see § 601.601(d)(2)(i)(a) and § 601.601(d)(2)(v).

(d) A district director may raise an issue in any taxable period, even though he or she may have asked for and been furnished technical advice with regard to the same or a similar issue in any other taxable period.

(c) *District procedure.*—(1) *Office examination.*—(i) In a correspondence examination the taxpayer is furnished with a report of the examiner's findings by a form letter. The taxpayer is asked to sign and return an agreement if the taxpayer accepts the findings. The letter also provides a detailed explanation of the alternatives available if the taxpayer does not accept the findings, including consideration of the case by an Appeals office, and requests the taxpayer to inform the district director, within the specified period, of the choice of action. An Appeals office conference will be granted to the taxpayer upon request without submission of a written protest.

(ii) If, at the conclusion of an office interview examination, the taxpayer does not agree with the adjustments proposed, the examiner will fully explain the alternatives available which include, if practicable, an immediate interview with a supervisor or an immediate conference with an Appeals Officer. If an immediate interview or Appeals office conference is not practicable, or is not requested by the taxpayer, the examination report will be mailed to the taxpayer under cover of an appropriate transmittal letter. This letter provides a detailed explanation of the alternatives available, including consideration of the case by an Appeals office, and requests the taxpayer to inform the district director, within the specified period, of the choice of action. An Appeals office conference will be granted to the taxpayer upon request without submission of a written protest.

(2) *Field examination.*—(i) If, at the conclusion of an examination, the taxpayer does not agree with the adjustments proposed, the examiner will prepare a complete examination report fully explaining all proposed adjustments. Before the report is sent to the taxpayer, the case file will be submitted to the district Centralized Services and, in some cases, Quality Review function for appropriate review. Following such review, the taxpayer will be sent a copy of the examination report under cover of a transmittal (30-day) letter, providing a detailed explanation of the alternatives available, including consideration of the case by an Appeals office, and requesting the taxpayer to inform the district director, within the specified period, of the choice of action.

(ii) If the total amount of proposed additional tax, proposed overassessment, or claimed refund (or, in an offer in compromise, the total amount of assessed tax, penalty, and interest sought to be compromised) does not exceed $2,500 for any taxable period, the taxpayer will be granted an Appeals office conference on request. A written protest is not required.

(iii) If for any taxable period the total amount of proposed additional tax including penalties, proposed overassessment, or claimed refund (or, in an offer in compromise, the total amount of assessed tax, penalty, and interest sought to be compromised) exceeds $2,500 but does not exceed $10,000, the taxpayer, on request, will be granted an Appeals office conference, provided a brief written statement of disputed issues is submitted.

(iv) If for any taxable period the total amount of proposed additional tax including penalties, proposed overassessment, or claimed refund (or, in an offer in compromise, the total amount of assessed tax, penalty, and interest sought to be compromised) exceeds $10,000, the taxpayer, on request, will be granted an Appeals office conference, provided a written protest is filed.

(d) *Thirty-day letters and protests.*—(1) *General.*—The report of the examiner, as approved after review, recommends one of four determinations:

(i) Acceptance of the return as filed and closing of the case;

(ii) Assertion of a given deficiency or additional tax;

(iii) Allowance of a given overassessment, with or without a claim for refund, credit, or abatement;

(iv) Denial of a claim for refund, credit, or abatement which has been filed and is found wholly lacking in merit.

When a return is accepted as filed (as in (i) above), the taxpayer is notified by appropriate "no change" letter. In an unagreed case, the district director sends to the taxpayer a preliminary or "30-day letter" if any one of the last three determinations is made (except a full allowance of a claim in respect of any tax). The 30-day letter is a form letter which states the determination proposed to be made. It is accompanied by a copy of the examiner's report explaining the basis of the proposed determination. It suggests to the taxpayer that if the taxpayer concurs in the recommendation, he or she indicate agreement by executing and returning a waiver or acceptance. The preliminary letter also informs the taxpayer of appeal rights available if he or she disagrees with the proposed determination. If the taxpayer does not respond to the letter within 30 days, a statutory notice of deficiency will be issued or other appropriate action taken, such as the issuance of a notice of adjustment, the denial of a claim in income, profits, estate, and gift tax cases, or an appropriate adjustment of the tax liability or denial of a claim in excise and employment tax cases.

(2) *Protests.*—(i) No written protest or brief written statement of disputed issues is required to obtain an Appeals office conference in office interview and correspondence examination cases.

(ii) No written protest or brief written statement of disputed issues is required to obtain an Appeals office conference in a field examination case if the total amount of proposed additional tax including penalties, proposed overassessment, or claimed refund (or, in an offer in compromise, the total amount of assessed tax, penalty, and interest sought to be compromised) is $2,500 or less for any taxable period.

(iii) A written protest is required to obtain an Appeals consideration in a field examination case if the total amount of proposed tax including penalties, proposed overassessment, or claimed refund (or, in an offer in compromise, the total amount of assessed tax, penalty, and interest sought to be compromised) exceeds $10,000 for any taxable period.

(iv) A written protest is optional (although a brief written statement of disputed issues is required) to obtain Appeals consideration in a field examination case if for any taxable period the total amount of proposed additional tax including penalties, proposed overassessment, or claimed refund (or, in an offer in compromise, the total amount of assessed tax, penalty, and interest sought to be compromised) exceeds $2,500 but does not exceed $10,000.

(v) Instructions for preparation of written protests are sent to the taxpayer with the transmittal (30-day) letter.

(e) *Claims for refund or credit.*—(1) After payment of the tax a taxpayer may (unless he has executed an agreement to the contrary) contest the assessment by filing a claim for refund or credit for all or any part of the amount paid, except as provided in section 6512 of the Code with respect to certain taxes determined by the Tax Court, the decision of which has become final. A claim for refund or credit of income taxes shall be made on Form 1040X, 1120X, or an amended income tax return, in accordance with § 301.6402-3. In the case of taxes other than income taxes, a claim for refund or credit shall be made on Form 843. The appropriate forms are obtainable from district directors or directors of service centers. Generally, the claim, together with appropriate supporting evidence, must be filed at the location prescribed in § 301.6402-2(a)(2). A claim for refund or credit must be filed within the applicable statutory period of limitation. In certain cases, a properly executed income tax return may operate as a claim for refund or credit of the amount of the overpayment disclosed by such return. (See § 301.6402-3.)

(2) When claims for refund or credit are examined by the Examination Division, substantially the same procedure is followed (including appeal rights afforded to taxpayers) as when taxpayers' returns are originally examined. But see § 601.108 for procedure for reviewing proposed overpayment exceeding $200,000 of income, estate, and gift taxes.

(3) As to suits for refund, see § 601.103(c).

(4) [Reserved.]

(5) There is also a special procedure applicable to applications for tentative carryback adjustments under section 6411 of the Code (consult Forms 1045 and 1139).

(6) For special procedure applicable to claims for payment or credit in respect of gasoline used on a farm for farming purposes, for certain nonhighway purposes, for use in commercial aircraft, or used by local transit systems, see sections 39, 6420, and 6421 of the Code and § 601.402(c)(3). For special procedure applicable to claims for payment or credit in respect of lubricating oil used otherwise than in a highway motor vehicle, see sections 39 and 6424 of the Code and § 601.402(c)(3). For special procedure applicable for credit or refund of aircraft use tax, see section 6426 of the Code and § 601.402(c)(4). For special procedure applicable for payment or credit in respect of

special fuels not used for taxable purposes, see sections 39 and 6427 of the Code and § 601.402(c)(5).

(7) For special procedure applicable in certain cases to adjustment of overpayment of estimated tax by a corporation see section 6425 of the Code.

(f) *Interruption of examination procedure.*—The process of field examinations and the course of the administrative procedure described in this section and in the following section may be interrupted in some cases by the imminent expiration of the statutory period of limitations for assessment of the tax. To protect the Government's interests in such a case, the district director of internal revenue or other designated officer may be required to dispatch a statutory notice of deficiency (if the case is within jurisdiction of United States Tax Court), or take other appropriate action to assess the tax even though the case may be in examination status. In order to avoid interruption of the established procedure (except in estate tax cases), it is suggested to the taxpayer that he execute an agreement on Form 872 (or such other form as may be prescribed for this purpose). To be effective this agreement must be entered into by the taxpayer and the district director or other appropriate officer concerned prior to the expiration of the time otherwise provided for assessment. Such a consent extends the period for assessment of any deficiency, or any additional or delinquent tax, and extends the period during which the taxpayer may claim a refund or credit to a date 6 months after the agreed time of extension of the assessment period. When appropriate, a consent may be entered into restricted to certain issues.

(g) *Fraud.*—The procedure described in this section does not apply in any case in which criminal prosecution is under consideration. Such procedure does obtain, however, in cases involving the assertion of the civil fraud penalty after the criminal aspects of the case have been closed.

(h) *Jeopardy assessments.*—If the district director believes that the assessment or collection of a tax will be jeopardized by delay, he/she is authorized and required to assess the tax immediately, together with interest and other additional amounts provided by law, notwithstanding the restrictions on assessment or collection of income, estate, gift, generation-skipping transfer or chapter 41, 42, 43, or 44 taxes contained in section 6213(a) of the Code. A jeopardy assessment does not deprive the taxpayer of the right to file a petition with the Tax Court. Collection of a tax in jeopardy may be immediately enforced by the district director upon notice and demand. To stay collection, the taxpayer may file with the district director a bond equal to the amount for which the stay is desired. The taxpayer may request a review in the Appeals office of whether the making of the assessment was reasonable under the circumstances and whether the amount assessed or demanded was appropriate under the circumstances. See section 7429. This request shall be made, in writing, within 30 days after the earlier of—

(1) The day on which the taxpayer is furnished the written statement described in section 7429(a)(1); or

(2) The last day of the period within which this statement is required to be furnished.

An Appeals office conference will be granted as soon as possible and a decision rendered without delay.

(i) *Regional post review of examined cases.*—Regional commissioners review samples of the examined cases closed in their district offices to ensure uniformity throughout their districts in applying Code provisions, regulations, and rulings, as well as the general policies of the Service.

(j) *Reopening of cases closed after examination.*—(1) The Service does not reopen any case closed after examination by a district office or service center to make an adjustment unfavorable to the taxpayer unless:

(i) There is evidence of fraud, malfeasance, collusion, concealment or misrepresentation of a material fact; or

(ii) The prior closing involved a clearly defined substantial error based on an established Service position existing at the time of the previous examination; or

(iii) Other circumstances exist which indicate failure to reopen would be a serious administrative omission.

(2) All reopenings are approved by the Chief, Examination Division (District Director in streamlined districts), or by the Chief, Compliance Division, for cases under his/her jurisdiction. If an additional inspection of the taxpayer's books of account is necessary, the notice to the taxpayer required by Code section 7605(b) will be delivered to the taxpayer at the time the reexamination is begun.

(k) *Transfer of returns between districts.*—When a request is received to transfer returns to another district for examination or the closing of a case, the district director having jurisdiction may transfer the case, together with pertinent records, to the district director of such other district. The Service will determine the time and place of the examination. In determining whether a transfer should be made, circumstances such as the following will be considered:

(1) Change of the taxpayer's domicile, either before or during examination.

(2) Discovery that taxpayer's books and records are kept in another district.

(3) Change of domicile of an executor or administrator to another district before or during examination.

(4) The effective administration of the tax laws.

(l) *Special procedures for crude oil windfall profit tax cases.*—For special procedures relating to crude oil windfall profit tax cases, see § 601.405. [Reg. § 601.105.]

☐ [32 FR 15990, Nov. 22, 1967, as amended at 33 FR 6819, May 4, 1968; 34 FR 6424, Apr. 12, 1969; 35 FR 7112, May 6, 1970; 35 FR 15916, Oct. 9. 1970; 36 FR 7584, Apr. 22, 1971; 38 FR 4956, Feb. 23, 1973; 38 FR 7458, Mar. 22, 1973; 38 FR 33300, Dec. 3, 1973; 41 FR 20880, May 21, 1976; 41 FR 48740, Nov. 5, 1976; 42 FR 34280, July 5, 1977; 43 FR 17817, Apr. 26, 1978; 43 FR 44497, Sept. 28, 1978; 43 FR 53029, Nov. 15, 1978; 45 FR 7252, Feb. 1, 1980; 46 FR 26053, May 11, 1981; 48 FR 15623, Apr. 12, 1983; 48 FR 24670, June 2, 1983; 49 FR 19649, May 9, 1984; 52 FR 38406, Oct. 16, 1987.]

### [Reg. § 601.106]

**§ 601.106. Appeals functions.**—(a) *General.*—(1)(i) There are provided in each region Appeals offices with office facilities within the region. Unless they otherwise specify, taxpayers living outside the United States use the facilities of the Washington, D.C., Appeals Office of the Mid-Atlantic Region. Subject to the limitations set forth in subparagraphs (2) and (3) of this paragraph, the Commissioner has delegated to certain officers of the Appeals offices authority to represent the regional commissioner in those matters set forth in subdivisions (ii) through (v) of this subparagraph. If a statutory notice of deficiency was issued by a district director or the Director, Foreign Operations District, the Appeals office may waive jurisdiction to the director who issued the statutory notice during the 90-day (or 150-day) period for filing a petition with the Tax Court, except where criminal prosecution has been recommended and not finally disposed of, or the statutory notice includes the ad valorem fraud penalty. After the filing of a petition in the Tax Court the Appeals office will have exclusive settlement jurisdiction, subject to the provisions of subparagraph(2) of this paragraph, for a period of 4 months (but no later than the receipt of the trial calendar in regular cases and no later than 15 days before the calendar call in S cases), over cases docketed in the Tax Court. Subject to the exceptions and limitations set forth in subparagraph(2) of this paragraph, there is also vested in the Appeals offices authority to represent the regional commissioner in his/her exclusive authority to settle (a) all cases docketed in the Tax Court and designated for trial at any place within the territory comprising the region, and (b) all docketed cases originating in the office of any district director situated within the region, or in which jurisdiction has been transferred to the region, which are designated for trial at Washington, D.C., unless the petitioner resides in, and his/her books and records are located or can be made available in, the region which includes Washington, D.C.

(ii) Certain officers of the Appeals offices may represent the regional commissioner in his/her exclusive and final authority for the determination of—

(a) Federal income, profits, estate (including extensions for payment under section 6161(a)(2)), gift, generation-skipping transfer or chapter 41, 42, 43, or 44 tax liability (whether before or after the issuance of a statutory notice of deficiency);

(b) Employment or certain Federal excise tax liability; and

(c) Liability for additions to the tax, additional amounts, and assessable penalties provided under chapter 68 of the Code.

in any case originating in the office of any district director situated in the region, or in any case in which jurisdiction has been transferred to the region.

(iii) The taxpayer must request Appeals consideration.

(a) An oral request is sufficient to obtain Appeals consideration in (1) all office interview or correspondence examination cases or (2) a field examination case if the total amount of proposed additional tax including penalties, proposed overassessment, or claimed refund (or, in an offer in compromise, the total amount of assessed tax, penalty, and interest sought to be compromised) is $2,500 or less for any taxable period. No written protest or brief statement of disputed issues is required.

(b) A brief written statement of disputed issues is required (a written protest is optional) to obtain Appeals consideration in a field examination case if the total amount of proposed additional tax including penalties, proposed overassessment, or claimed refund (or, in an offer in compromise, the total amount of assessed tax, penalty, and interest sought to be compromised) exceeds $2,500 but does not exceed $10,000 for any taxable period.

(c) A written protest is required to obtain Appeals consideration in a field examination case if the total amount of proposed additional tax including penalties, proposed overassessment, or claimed refund (or, in an offer in compromise, the total amount of assessed tax, penalty, and interest sought to be compromised) exceeds $10,000 for any taxable period.

(d) A written protest is required to obtain Appeals consideration in all employee plan and exempt organization cases.

(e) A written protest is required to obtain Appeals consideration in all partnership and S corporation cases.

(iv) Sections 6659(a)(1) and 6671(a) provide that additions to the tax, additional amounts, penalties and liabilities (collectively referred to in this subdivision as "penalties") provided by chapter 68 of the Code shall be paid upon notice and demand and shall be assessed and collected in the same manner as taxes. Certain chapter 68 penalties may be appealed after assessment to the Appeals office. This postassessment appeal procedure applies to all but the following chapter 68 penalties:

(a) Penalties that are not subject to a reasonable cause or reasonable basis determination (examples are additions to the tax for failure to pay estimated income tax under sections 6654 and 6655);

(b) Penalties that are subject to the deficiency procedures of subchapter B of chapter 63 of the Code (because the taxpayer has the right to appeal such penalties, such as those provided under section 6653(a) and (b), prior to assessment);

(c) Penalties that are subject to an administratively granted preassessment appeal procedure such as that provided in § 1.6694-2(a)(1) because taxpayers are able to protest such penalties prior to assessment;

(d) The penalty provided in section 6700 for promoting abusive tax shelters (because the penalty is subject to the procedural rules of section 6703 which provide for an extension of the period of collection of the penalty when a person pays not less than 15% of the amount of such penalty); and

(e) The 100 percent penalty provided under section 6672 (because the taxpayer has the opportunity to appeal this penalty prior to assessment).

The appeal may be made before or after payment, but shall be made before the filing of a claim for refund. Technical advice procedures are not applicable to an appeal made under this subdivision.

(v) The Appeals office considers cases involving the initial or continuing recognition of tax exemption and foundation classification. See § 601.201(n)(5) and (n)(6). The Appeals office also considers cases involving the initial or continuing determination of employee plan qualification under subchapter D of chapter 1 of the Code. See § 601.201(o)(6). However, the jurisdiction of the Appeals office in these cases is limited as follows:

(a) In cases under the jurisdiction of a key district director (or the National Office) which involve an application for, or the revocation or modification of, the recognition of exemption or the determination of qualification, if the determination concerning exemption is made by a National Office ruling, or if National Office technical advice is furnished concerning exemption or qualification, the decision of the National Office is final. The organization/plan has no right of appeal to the Appeals office or any other avenue of administrative appeal. See § 601.201(n)(5)(i), (n)(6)(ii)(b), (n)(9)(viii)(a), (o)(2)(iii), and (o)(6)(i).

(b) In cases already under the jurisdiction of an Appeals office, if the proposed disposition by that office is contrary to a National Office ruling concerning exemption, or to a National Office technical advice concerning exemption or qualification, issued prior to the case, the proposed disposition will be submitted, through the Office of the Regional Director of Appeals, to the Assistant Commissioner (Employee Plans and Exempt Organizations) or, in section 521 cases, to the Assistant Commissioner (Technical). The decision of the Assistant Commissioner will be followed by the Appeals office. See § 601.201(n)(5)(iii), (n)(6)(ii)(d), (n)(6)(iv), and (o)(6)(iii).

(2) The authority described in subparagraph (1) of this paragraph does not include the authority to:

(i) Negotiate or make a settlement in any case docketed in the Tax Court if the notice of deficiency, liability or other determination was issued by Appeals officials;

(ii) Negotiate or make a settlement in any docketed case if the notice of deficiency, liability or other determination was issued after appeals consideration of all petitioned issues by the Employee Plans/ Exempt Organizations function;

(iii) Negotiate or make a settlement in any docketed case if the notice of deficiency, liability or final adverse determination letter was issued by a District Director and is based upon a National Office ruling or National Office technical advice in that case involving a qualification of an employee plan or tax exemption and/or foundation status of an organization (but only to the extent the case involves such issue);

(iv) Negotiate or make a settlement if the case was docketed under Code sections 6110, 7477, or 7478;

(v) Eliminate the ad valorem fraud penalty in any case in which the penalty was determined by the district office or service center office in connection with a tax year or period, or which is related to or affects such year or period, for which criminal prosecution against the taxpayer (or related taxpayer involving the same transaction) has been recommended to the Department of Justice for willful attempt to evade or defeat tax, or for willful failure to file a return, except upon the recommendation or concurrence of Counsel; or

(vi) Act in any case in which a recommendation for criminal prosecution is pending, except with the concurrence of Counsel.

(3) The authority vested in the Appeals does not extend to the determination of liability for any excise tax imposed by subtitle E or by subchapter D of chapter 78, to the extent it relates to subtitle E.

(4) In cases under Appeals jurisdiction, the Appeals official has the authority to make and subscribe to a return under the provisions under section 6020 of the Code where taxpayer fails to make a required return.

(b) *Initiation of proceedings before the official Appeals.*—In any case in which the district director has issued a preliminary or "30-day letter" and the taxpayer requests Appeals consideration and files a written protest when required (see paragraph (c)(1) of § § 601.103, (c)(1) and (c)(2) of 601.105, and 601.507) against the proposed determination of tax liability, except as to those taxes described in paragraph (a)(3) of this section, the taxpayer has the right (and will be so advised by the district director) of administrative appeal to the Appeals organization. However, the appeal procedures do not extend to cases involving solely the failure or refusal to comply with the tax laws because of moral, religious, political, constitutional, conscientious, or similar grounds. Organizations such as labor unions and trade associations which have been examined by the district director to determine the amounts expended by the organization for purposes of lobbying, promotion or defeat of legislation, political campaigns, or propaganda related to those purposes are treated as "taxpayers" for the purpose of this right of administrative appeal. Thus, upon requesting appellate consideration and filing a written protest, when required, to the district director's findings that a portion of member dues is to be disallowed as a deduction to each member because expended for such purposes, the organization will be afforded full rights of administrative appeal to the Appeals activity similar to those rights afforded to taxpayers generally. After review of any required written protest by the district director, the case and its administrative record are referred to the Appeals. Appeals may refuse to accept a protested nondocketed case where preliminary review indicates it requires further consideration or development. No taxpayer is required to submit the case to the Appeals for consideration. Appeal is at the option of the taxpayer. After the issuance by the district director of a statutory notice of deficiency, upon the taxpayer's request, the Appeals may take up the case for settlement and may grant the taxpayer a conference thereon.

(c) *Nature of proceedings before Appeals.*—Proceedings before the Appeals are informal. Testimony under oath is not taken, although matters alleged as facts may be required to be submitted in the form of affidavits, or declared to be true under the penalties of perjury. Taxpayers may represent themselves or designate a qualified representative to act for them. See Subpart E of this part for conference and practice requirements. At any conference granted by the Appeals on a nondocketed case, the district director will be represented if the Appeals official having settlement authority and the district director deem it advisable. At any such conference on a case involving the ad valorem fraud penalty for which criminal prosecution against the taxpayer (or a related taxpayer involving the same transaction) has been recommended to the Department of Justice for willful attempt to evade or defeat tax, or for willful failure to file a return, the District Counsel will be represented if he or she so desires.

(d) *Disposition and settlement of cases before the Appeals.*—(1) *General.*—During consideration of a case, the Appeals office should neither reopen an issue as to which the taxpayer and the office of the district director are in agreement nor raise a new issue, unless the ground for such action is a substantial one and the potential effect upon the tax liability is material. If the Appeals raises a new issue, the taxpayer or the taxpayer's representative should be so advised and offered an opportunity for discussion prior to the taking of any formal action, such as the issuance of a statutory notice of deficiency.

(2) *Cases not docketed in the Tax Court.*—(i) If after consideration of the case by the Appeals a satisfactory settlement of some or all the issues is reached with the taxpayer, the taxpayer will be requested to sign Form 870-AD or other appropriate agreement form waiving restrictions on the assessment and collection of any deficiency and accepting any overassessment resulting from the agreed settlement. In addition, in partially unagreed cases, a statutory notice of deficiency will be prepared and issued in accordance with subdivision (ii) of this subparagraph with respect to the unagreed issue or issues.

(ii) If after consideration of the case by Appeals it is determined that there is a deficiency in income, profits, estate, generation-skipping transfer gift tax, or chapter 41, 42, 43, or 44 tax liability to which the taxpayer does not agree, a statutory notice of deficiency will be prepared and issued by Appeals. Officers of the Appeals office having authority for the administrative determination of tax liabilities referred to in paragraph (a) of this section are also authorized to prepare, sign on behalf of the Commissioner, and send to the taxpayer by registered or certified mail any statutory notice of deficiency prescribed in sections 6212 and 6861 of the Code, and in corresponding provisions of the Internal Revenue Code of 1939. Within 90 days, or 150 days if the notice is addressed to a person outside of the States of the Union and the District of Columbia, after such a statutory notice of deficiency is mailed (not counting Saturday, Sunday, or a legal holiday in the District of Columbia as the last day), the taxpayer may file a petition with the U.S. Tax Court for a redetermination of the deficiency. In addition, if a claim for refund is disallowed in full or in part by the Appelate Division and the taxpayer does not sign Form 2297, Appeals will prepare the statutory notice of claim disallowance and send it to the taxpayer by certified mail (or registered mail if the taxpayer is outside the United States), with a carbon copy to the taxpayer's representative by regular mail, if appropriate. In any other unagreed case, the case and its administrative file will be forwarded to the appropriate function with directions to take action with respect to the tax liability determined in Appeals. Administrative appeal procedures will apply to 100-percent penalty cases, except where an assessment is made because of Chief Counsel's request to support a third-party action in a pending refund suit. See Rev. Proc. 69-26.

(iii) Taxpayers desiring to further contest unagreed excise (other than those under chapters 41 through 44 of the Code) and employment tax cases and 100-percent penalty cases must pay the additional tax (or portion thereof of divisible taxes) when assessed, file claim for refund within the applicable statutory period of limitations (ordinarily three years from time return was required to be filed or two years from payment, whichever expires later), and upon disallowance of claim or after six months from date claim was filed, file suit in U.S. District Court or U.S. Claims Court. Suits for refund of taxes paid are under the jurisdiction of the Department of Justice.

(3) *Cases docketed in the Tax Court.*—(i) If the case under consideration in the Appeals is docketed in the Tax Court and agreement is reached with the taxpayer with respect to the issues involved, the disposition of the case is effected by a stipulation of agreed deficiency or overpayment to be filed with the Tax Court and in conformity with which the Court will enter its order.

(ii) If the case under consideration in Appeals is docketed in the Tax Court and the issues remain unsettled after consideration and conference in Appeals, the case will be referred to the appropriate district counsel for the region for defense of the tax liability determined.

(iii) If the deficiency notice in a case docketed in the Tax Court was not issued by the Appeals office and no recommendation for criminal prosecution is pending, the case will be referred by the district counsel to the Appeals office for settlement as soon as it is at issue in the Tax Court. The settlement procedure shall be governed by the following rules:

(a) The Appeals office will have exclusive settlement jurisdiction for a period of 4 months over certain cases docketed in the Tax Court. The 4-month period will commence at the time Appeals receives the case from Counsel, which will be after the case is at issue. Appeals will arrange settlement conferences in such cases within 45 days of receipt of the case. In the event of a settlement, Appeals will prepare and forward to Counsel the necessary computations and any stipulation decisions secured. Counsel will prepare any needed settlement documents for execution by the parties and filing with the Tax Court. Appeals will also have authority to settle less than all the issues in the case and to refer the unsettled issues to Counsel for disposition. In the event of a partial settlement, Appeals will inform Counsel of the agreement of the petitioner(s) and Appeals may secure and forward to Counsel a stipulation covering the agreed issues. Counsel will, if necessary, prepare documents reflecting settlement of the agreed issues for execution by the parties and filing with the Tax Court at the appropriate time.

(b) At the end of the 4-month period, or before that time if Appeals determines the case is not suceptible of settlement, the case will be returned to Counsel. Thereafter, Counsel will have exclusive authority to dispose of the case. If, at the end of the 4-month period, there is substantial likelihood that a settlement of the entire case can be effected in a reasonable period of time, Counsel may extend Appeals settlement jurisdiction for a period not to exceed 60 days, but not beyond the date of the receipt of a trial calendar upon which the case appears. Extensions beyond the 60-day period or after the event indicated will be granted only with the personal approval of regional counsel and will be made only in those cases in which the probability of settlement of the case in its entirety by Appeals clearly outweighs the need to commence trial preparation.

*(c)* During the period of Appeals jurisdiction, Appeals will make available such files and information as may be necessary for Counsel to take any action required by the Court or which is in the best interests of the Government. When a case is referred by Counsel to Appeals, Counsel may indicate areas of needed factual development or areas of possible technical uncertainties. In referring a case to Counsel, Appeals will furnish its summary of the facts and the pertinent legal authorities.

*(d)* The Appeals office may specify that proposed Counsel settlements be referred back to Appeals for its views. Appeals may protest the proposed Counsel settlements. If Counsel disagrees with Appeals, the Regional Counsel will determine the disposition of the cases.

*(e)* If an offer is received at or about the time of trial in a case designated by the Appeals office for settlement consultation, Counsel will endeavor to have the case placed on a motions calendar to permit consultation with and review by Appeals in accordance with the foregoing procedures.

*(f)* For issues in docketed and nondocketed cases pending with Appeals which are related to issues in docketed cases over which Counsel has jurisdiction, no settlement offer will be accepted by either Appeals or Counsel unless both agree that the offer is acceptable. The protest procedure will be available to Appeals and regional counsel will have authority to resolve the issue with respect to both the Appeals and Counsel cases. If settlement of the docketed case requires approval by regional counsel or Chief Counsel, the final decision with respect to the issues under the jurisdiction of both Appeals and Counsel will be made by regional counsel or Chief Counsel. See Rev. Proc. 79-59.

*(g)* Cases classified as "Small Tax" cases by the Tax Court are given expeditious consideration because such cases are not included on a Trial Status Request. These cases are considered by the Court as ready for placing on a trial calendar as soon as the answer has been filed and are given priority by the Court for trial over other docketed cases. These cases are designated by the Court as small tax cases upon request of petitioners and will include letter "S" as part of the docket number.

*(e) Transfer and centralization of cases.*—(1) An Appeals office is authorized to transfer settlement jurisdiction in a non-docketed case or in an excise or employment tax case to another region, if the taxpayer resides in and the taxpayer's books and records are located (or can be made available) in such other region. Otherwise, transfer to another region requires the approval of the Director of the Appeals Division.

(2) An Appeals office is authorized to transfer settlement jurisdiction in a docketed case to another region if the location for the hearing by the Tax Court has been set in such other region, except that if the place of hearing is Washington, D.C., settlement jurisdiction shall not be transferred to the region in which Washington, D.C., is located unless the petitioner resides in and the petitioner's books and records are located (or can be made available) in that region. Otherwise, transfer to another region requires the approval of the Director of the Appeals Division. Likewise, the Chief Counsel has corresponding authority to transfer the jurisdiction, authority, and duties of the regional counsel for any region to the regional counsel of another region within which the case has been designated for trial before the Tax Court.

(3) Should a regional commissioner determine that it would better serve the interests of the Government, he or she may, by order in writing, withdraw any case not docketed before the Tax Court from the jurisdiction of the Appeals office of the region, and provide for its disposition under his or her personal direction.

*(f) Conference and practice requirements.*—Practice and conference procedure before Appeals is governed by Treasury Department Circular 230 as amended (31 CFR Part 10) [¶ 44,500 et seq.], and the requirements of Subpart E of this part [¶ 44,408 et seq.]. In addition to such rules but not in modification of them, the following rules are also applicable to practice before Appeals:

(1) *Rule I.*—An exaction by the U.S. Government, which is not based upon law, statutory or otherwise, is a taking of property without due process of law, in violation of the Fifth Amendment to the U.S. Constitution. Accordingly, an Appeals representative in his or her conclusions of fact or application of the law, shall hew to the law and the recognized standards of legal construction. It shall be his or her duty to determine the correct amount of the tax, with strict impartiality as between the taxpayer and the Government, and without favoritism or discrimination as between taxpayers.

(2) *Rule II.*—Appeals will ordinarily give serious consideration to an offer to settle a tax controversy on a basis which fairly reflects the relative merits of the opposing views in light of the hazards which would exist if the case were litigated. However, no settlement

will be made based upon nuisance value of the case to either party. If the taxpayer makes an unacceptable proposal of settlement under circumstances indicating a good-faith attempt to reach an agreed disposition of the case on a basis fair both to the Government and the taxpayer, the Appeals official generally should give an evaluation of the case in such a manner as to enable the taxpayer to ascertain the kind of settlement that would be recommended for acceptance. Appeals may defer action on or decline to settle some cases or issues (for example, issues on which action has been suspended nationwide) in order to achieve greater uniformity and enhance overall voluntary compliance with the tax laws.

(3) *Rule III.*—Where the Appeals officer recommends acceptance of the taxpayer's proposal of settlement, or, in the absence of a proposal, recommends action favorable to the taxpayer, and said recommendation is disapproved in whole or in part by a reviewing officer in the Appeals, the taxpayer shall be so advised and upon written request shall be accorded a conference with such reviewing officer. The Appeals may disregard this rule where the interest of the Government would be injured by delay, as for example, in a case involving the imminent expiration of limitation or the dissipation of assets.

(4) *Rule IV.*—Where the Appeals official having settlement authority and the district director deem it advisable, the district director may be represented at any Appeals conferences on a non-docketed case. This rule is also applicable to the Director, Foreign Operations District, in the event his or her office issued the preliminary or "30-day letter."

(5) *Rule V.*—In order to bring an unagreed income, profits, estate, gift, or chapter 41, 42, 43, or 44 tax case in prestatutory notice status, an employment or excise tax case, a penalty case, an Employee Plans and Exempt Organization case, a termination of taxable year assessment case, a jeopardy assessment case, or an offer in compromise before the Appeals office, the taxpayer or the taxpayer's representative should first request Appeals consideration and, when required, file with the district office (including the Foreign Operations District) or service center a written protest setting forth specifically the reasons for the refusal to accept the findings. If the protest includes a statement of facts upon which the taxpayer relies, such statement should be declared to be true under the penalties of perjury. The protest and any new facts, law, or arguments presented therewith will be reviewed by the receiving office for the purpose of deciding whether further development or action is required prior to referring the case to the Appeals. Where the Appeals has an issue under consideration it may, with the concurrence of the taxpayer, assume jurisdiction in a related case, after the office having original jurisdiction has completed any necessary action. The Director, Appeals Division, may authorize the regional Appeals office to accept jurisdiction (after any necessary action by office having original jurisdiction) in specified classes of cases without written protests provided written or oral requests for Appeals consideration are submitted by or for each taxpayer.

(6) *Rule VI.*—A taxpayer cannot withhold evidence from the district director of internal revenue and expect to introduce it for the first time before the Appeals, at a conference in nondocketed status, without being subject to having the case returned to the district director for reconsideration. Where newly discovered evidence is submitted for the first time to the Appeals, in a case pending in nondocketed status, that office, in the reasonable exercise of its discretion, may transmit same to the district director for his or her consideration and comment.

(7) *Rule VII.*—Where the taxpayer has had the benefit of a conference before the Appeals office in the prestatutory notice status, or where the opportunity for such a conference was accorded but not availed of, there will be no conference granted before the Appeals office in the 90-day status after the mailing of the statutory notice of deficiency, in the absence of unusual circumstances.

(8) *Rule VIII.*—In cases not docketed in the United States Tax Court on which a conference is being conducted by the Appeals office, the district counsel may be requested to attend and to give legal advice in the more difficult cases, or on matters of legal or litigating policy.

(9) *Rule IX—Technical advice from the National Office.*—(i) *Definition and nature of technical advice.*—(a) As used in this subparagraph, "technical advice" means advice or guidance as to the interpretation and proper application of internal revenue laws, related statutes, and regulations, to a specific set of facts, furnished by the National Office upon request of an Appeals office in connection with the processing and consideration of a nondocketed case. It is furnished as a means of assisting Service personnel in closing cases and establishing and maintaining consistent holdings in the various regions. It does not include memorandum on matters of general

technical application furnished to Appeals offices where the issues are not raised in connection with the consideration and handling of a specific taxpayer's case.

(b) The provisions of this subparagraph do not apply to a case under the jurisdiction of a district director or the Bureau of Alcohol, Tobacco, and Firearms, to Employee Plans, Exempt Organization, or certain penalty cases being considered by an Appeals office, or to any case previously considered by an Appeals office. The technical advice provisions applicable to cases under the jurisdiction of a district director, other than Employee Plans and Exempt Organization cases, are set forth in §601.105(b)(5). The technical advice provisions applicable to Employee Plans and Exempt Organization cases are set forth in §601.201(n)(9). Technical advice may not be requested with respect to a taxable period if a prior Appeals disposition of the same taxable period of the same taxpayer's case was based on mutual concessions (ordinarily with a form 870-AD, Offer of Waiver of Restrictions on Assessment and Collection of Deficiency in Tax and of Acceptance of Overassessment). However, technical advice may be requested by a district director on issues previously considered in a prior Appeals disposition, not based on mutual concessions, of the same taxable periods of the same taxpayer with the concurrence of the Appeals office that had the case.

(c) The consideration or examination of the facts relating to a request for a determination letter is considered to be in connection with the consideration and handling of a taxpayer's case. Thus, an Appeals office may, under this subparagraph, request technical advice with respect to the consideration of a request for a determination letter. The technical advice provisions applicable to a request for a determination letter in Employee Plans and Exempt Organization cases are set forth in §601.201(n)(9).

(d) If an Appeals office is of the opinion that a ruling letter previously issued to a taxpayer should be modified or revoked and it requests the National Office to reconsider the ruling, the reference of the matter to the National Office is treated as a request for technical advice. The procedures specified in subdivision (iii) of this subparagraph should be followed in order that the National Office may consider the recommendation. Only the National Office can revoke a ruling letter. Before referral to the National Office, the Appeals office should inform the taxpayer of its opinion that the ruling letter should be revoked. The Appeals office, after development of the facts and consideration of the taxpayer's arguments, will decide whether to recommend revocation of the ruling to the National Office. For procedures relating to a request for a ruling, see §601.201.

(e) The Assistant Commissioner (Technical), acting under a delegation of authority from the Commissioner of Internal Revenue, is exclusively responsible for providing technical advice in any issue involving the establishment of basic principles and rules for the uniform interpretation and application of tax laws in cases under this subparagraph. This authority has been largely redelegated to subordinate officials.

(ii) *Areas in which technical advice may be requested.—* (a) Appeals offices may request technical advice on any technical or procedural question that develops during the processing and consideration of a case. These procedures are applicable as provided in subdivision (i) of this subparagraph.

(b) As provided in §601.105(b)(5)(ii)(b) and (iii)(a), requests for technical advice should be made at the earliest possible stage of the examination process. However, if identification of an issue on which technical advice is appropriate is not made until the case is in Appeals, a decision to request such advice (in nondocketed cases) should be made prior to or at the first conference.

(c) Subject to the provisions of (b) of this subdivision, Appeals Offices are encouraged to request technical advice on any technical or procedural question arising in connection with a case described in subdivision (i) of this subparagraph which cannot be resolved on the basis of law, regulations, or a clearly applicable revenue ruling or other precedent issued by the National Office.

(iii) *Requesting technical advice.—(a)* It is the responsibility of the Appeals Office to determine whether technical advice is to be requested on any issue being considered. However, while the case is under the jurisdiction of the Appeals Office, a taxpayer or his/her representative may request that an issue be referred to the National Office for technical advice on the grounds that a lack of uniformity exists as to the disposition of the issue, or that the issue is so unusual or complex as to warrant consideration by the National Office. While taxpayers are encouraged to make written requests setting forth the facts, law, and argument with respect to the issue, and reason for requesting National Office advice, a taxpayer may make the request orally. If, after considering the taxpayer's request, the Appeals Officer is of the opinion that the circumstances do not warrant referral of the case to the National Office, he/she will so advise the taxpayer. (See subdivision (iv) of this subparagraph for taxpayer's appeal rights where the Appeals Officer declines to request technical advice.)

(b) When technical advise is to be requested, whether or not upon the request of the taxpayer, the taxpayer will be so advised, except as noted in (j) of this subdivision. If the Appeals Office initiates the action, the taxpayer will be furnished a copy of the statement of the pertinent facts and the question or questions proposed for submission to the National Office. The request for advice should be so worded as to avoid possible misunderstanding, in the National Office, of the facts or of the specific point or points at issue.

(c) After receipt of the statement of facts and specific questions, the taxpayer will be given 10 calendar days in which to indicate in writing the extent, if any, to which he/she may not be in complete agreement. An extension of time must be justified by the taxpayer in writing and approved by the Chief, Appeals Office. Every effort should be made to reach agreement as to the facts and specific points at issue. If agreement cannot be reached, the taxpayer may submit, within 10 calendar days after receipt of notice from the Appeals Office, a statement of his/her understanding as to the specific point or points at issue which will be forwarded to the National Office with the request for advice. An extension of time must be justified by the taxpayer in writing and approved by the Chief, Appeals Office.

(d) If the taxpayer initiates the action to request advice, and his/her statement of the facts and point or points at issue are not wholly acceptable to the Appeals Office, the taxpayer will be advised in writing as to the areas of disagreement. The taxpayer will be given 10 calendar days after receipt of the written notice to reply to such notice. An extension of time must be justified by the taxpayer in writing and approved by the Chief, Appeals Office. If agreement cannot be reached, both the statements of the taxpayer and the Appeals Office will be forwarded to the National Office.

(e)(1) In the case of requests for technical advice, the taxpayer must also submit, within the 10-day period referred to in (c) and (d) of this subdivision, whichever is applicable (relating to agreement by the taxpayer with the statement of facts and points submitted in connection with the request for technical advice), the statement described in (f) of this subdivision of proposed deletions pursuant to section 6110(c) of the Code. If the statement is not submitted, the taxpayer will be informed by the Appeals Office that the statement is required. If the Appeals Office does not receive the statement within 10 days after the taxpayer has been informed of the need for the statement, the Appeals Office may decline to submit the request for technical advice. If the Appeals Office decides to request technical advice in a case where the taxpayer has not submitted the statement of proposed deletions, the National Office will make those deletions which in the judgment of the Commissioner are required by section 6110(c) of the Code.

(2) The requirements included in this subparagraph relating to the submission of statements and other material with respect to proposed deletions to be made from technical advice memoranda before public inspection is permitted to take place do not apply to requests for any document to which section 6104 of the Code applies.

(f) In order to assist the Internal Revenue Service in making the deletions required by section 6110(c) of the Code, from the text of technical advice memoranda which are open to public inspection pursuant to section 6110(a) of the Code, there must accompany requests for such technical advice either a statement of the deletions proposed by the taxpayer, or a statement that no information other than names, addresses, and taxpayer identifying numbers need be deleted. Such statements shall be made in a separate document. The statement of proposed deletions shall be accompanied by a copy of all statements of facts and supporting documents which are submitted to the National Office pursuant to (c) or (d) of this subdivision, on which shall be indicated, by the use of brackets, the material which the taxpayer indicates should be deleted pursuant to section 6110(c) of the Code. The statement of proposed deletions shall indicate the statutory basis for each proposed deletion. The statement of proposed deletions shall not appear or be referred to anywhere in the request for technical advice. If the taxpayer decides to request additional deletions pursuant to section 6110(c) of the Code prior to the time the National Office replies to the request for technical advice, additional statements may be submitted.

(g) If the taxpayer has not already done so, he/she may submit a statement explaining his/her position on the issues, citing precedents which the taxpayer believes will bear on the case. This statement will be forwarded to the National Office with the request for advice. If it is received at a later date, it will be forwarded for association with the case file.

(h) At the time the taxpayer is informed that the matter is being referred to the National Office, he/she will also be informed of the right to a conference in the National Office in the event an adverse decision is indicated, and will be asked to indicate whether a conference is desired.

(i) Generally, prior to replying to the request for technical advice, the National Office shall inform the taxpayer orally or in writing of the material likely to appear in the technical advice memorandum which the taxpayer proposed be deleted but which the

Internal Revenue Service determined should not be deleted. If so informed, the taxpayer may submit within 10 days any further information, arguments, or other material in support of the position that such material be deleted. The Internal Revenue Service will attempt, if feasible, to resolve all disagreements with respect to proposed deletions prior to the time the National Office replies to the request for technical advice. However, in no event shall the taxpayer have the right to a conference with respect to resolution of any disagreements concerning material to be deleted from the text of the technical advice memorandum, but such matters may be considered at any conference otherwise scheduled with respect to the request.

(j) The provisions of (a) through (i) of this subdivision, relating to the referral of issues upon request of the taxpayer, advising taxpayers of the referral of issues, the submission of proposed deletions, and the granting of conferences in the National Office, are not applicable to technical advice memoranda described in section 6110(g)(5)(A) of the Code, relating to cases involving criminal or civil fraud investigations and jeopardy or termination assessments. However, in such cases, the taxpayer shall be allowed to provide the statement of proposed deletions to the National Office upon the completion of all proceedings with respect to the investigations or assessments, but prior to the date on which the Commissioner mails the notice pursuant to section 6110(f)(1) of the Code of intention to disclose the technical advice memorandum.

(k) Form 4463, Request for Technical Advice, should be used for transmitting requests for technical advice to the National Office.

(iv) *Appeal by taxpayers of determinations not to seek technical advice.*—(a) If the taxpayer has requested referral of an issue before an Appeals Office to the National Office for technical advice, and after consideration of the request, the Appeals Officer is of the opinion that the circumstances do not warrant such referral, he/she will so advise the taxpayer.

(b) The taxpayer may appeal the decision of the Appeals Officer not to request technical advice by submitting to that official, within 10 calendar days after being advised of the decision, a statement of the facts, law, and arguments with respect to the issue, and the reasons why the taxpayer believes the matter should be referred to the National Office for advice. An extension of time must be justified by the taxpayer in writing and approved by the Chief, Appeals Office.

(c) The Appeals Officer will submit the statement of the taxpayer to the chief, Appeals Office, accompanied by a statement of the officer's reasons why the issue should not be referred to the National Office. The Chief will determine, on the basis of the statements submitted, whether technical advice will be requested. If the Chief determines that technical advice is not warranted, that official will inform the taxpayer in writing that he/she proposes to deny the request. In the letter to the taxpayer the Chief will (except in unusual situations where such action would be prejudicial to the best interests of the Government) state specifically the reasons for the proposed denial. The taxpayer will be given 15 calendar days after receipt of the letter in which to notify the Chief whether the taxpayer agrees with the proposed denial. The taxpayer may not appeal the decision of the Chief, Appeals Office not to request technical advice from the National Office. However, if the taxpayer does not agree with the proposed denial, all data relating to the issue for which technical advice has been sought, including the taxpayer's written request and statements, will be submitted to the National Office, Attention: Director, Appeals Division, for review. After review in the National Office, the Appeals Office will be notified whether the proposed denial is approved or disapproved.

(d) While the matter is being reviewed in the National Office, the Appeals Office will suspend action on the issue (except where the delay would prejudice the Government's interests) until it is notified of the National Office decision. This notification will be made within 30 days after receipt of the data in the National Office. The review will be solely on the basis of the written record and no conference will be held in the National Office.

(v) *Conference in the National Office.*—(a) If, after a study of the technical advice request, it appears that advice adverse to the taxpayer should be given and a conference has been requested, the taxpayer will be notified of the time and place of the conference. If conferences are being arranged with respect to more than one request for advice involving the same taxpayer, they will be so scheduled as to cause the least inconvenience to the taxpayer. The conference will be arranged by telephone, if possible, and must be held within 21 calendar days after contact has been made. Extensions of time will be granted only if justified in writing by the taxpayer and approved by the appropriate Technical branch chief.

(b) A taxpayer is entitled, as a matter of right, to only one conference in the National Office unless one of the circumstances discussed in (c) of this subdivision exists. This conference will usu-ally be held at the branch level in the appropriate division (Corporation Tax Division or Individual Tax Division) in the Office of the Assistant Commissioner (Technical), and will usually be attended by a person who has authority to act for the branch chief. In appropriate cases the Appeals Officer may also attend the conference to clarify the facts in the case. If more than one subject is discussed at the conference, the discussion constitutes a conference with respect to each subject. At the request of the taxpayer or the taxpayer's representative, the conference may be held at an earlier stage in the consideration of the case than the Service would ordinarily designate. A taxpayer has no "right" of appeal from an action of a branch to the director of a division or to any other National Office official.

(c) In the process of review of a holding proposed by a branch, it may appear that the final answer will involve a reversal of the branch proposal with a result less favorable to the taxpayer. Or it may appear that an adverse holding proposed by a branch will be approved, but on a new or different issue or on different grounds than those on which the branch decided the case. Under either of these circumstances, the taxpayer or the taxpayer's representative will be invited to another conference. The provisions of this subparagraph limiting the number of conferences to which a taxpayer is entitled will not foreclose inviting a taxpayer to attend further conferences when, in the opinion of National Office personnel, such need arises. All additional conferences of this type discussed are held only at the invitation of the Service.

(d) It is the responsibility of the taxpayer to furnish to the National Office, within 21 calendar days after the conference, a written record of any additional data, line of reasoning, precedents, etc., that were proposed by the taxpayer and discussed at the conference but were not previously or adequately presented in writing. Extensions of time will be granted only if justified in writing by the taxpayer and approved by the appropriate Technical branch chief. Any additional material and a copy thereof should be addressed to and sent to the National Office which will forward the copy to the appropriate Appeals Office. The Appeals Office will be requested to give the matter prompt attention, will verify the additional facts and data, and will comment on it to the extent deemed appropriate.

(e) A taxpayer or the taxpayer's representative desiring to obtain information as to the status of the case may do so by contacting the following offices with respect to matters in the areas of their responsibility:

| Official | Telephone Numbers (Area Code 202) |
|---|---|
| Director, Corporation Tax Division | 566-4504 or 566-4505 |
| Director, Individual Tax Division | 566-3767 or 566-3788 |

(vi) *Preparation of technical advice memorandum by the National Office.*—(a) Immediately upon receipt in the National Office, the technical employee to whom the case is assigned will analyze the file to ascertain whether it meets the requirements of subdivision (iii) of this subparagraph. If the case is not complete with respect to any requirement in subdivision (iii) (a) through (d) of this subparagraph, appropriate steps will be taken to complete the file. If any request for technical advice does not comply with the requirements of subdivision (iii)(e) of this subparagraph, relating to the statement of proposed deletions, the National Office will make those deletions from the technical advice memorandum which in the judgment of the Commissioner are required by section 6110(c) of the Code.

(b) If the taxpayer has requested a conference in the National Office, the procedures in subdivision (v) of this subparagraph will be followed.

(c) Replies to requests for technical advice will be addressed to the Appeals office and will be drafted in two parts. Each part will identify the taxpayer by name, address, identification number, and year or years involved. The first part (hereafter called the "technical advice memorandum") will contain (1) a recitation of the pertinent facts having a bearing on the issue; (2) a discussion of the facts, precedents, and reasoning of the National Office; and (3) the conclusions of the National Office. The conclusions will give direct answers, whenever possible, to the specific questions of the Appeals office. The discussion of the issues will be in such detail that the Appeals office is apprised of the reasoning underlying the conclusion. There shall accompany the technical advice memorandum a notice, pursuant to section 6110(f)(1) of the Code, of intention to disclose the technical advice memorandum (including a copy of the version proposed to be open to public inspection and notations of third party communications pursuant to section 6110(d) of the Code) which the Appeals office shall forward to the taxpayer at such time that it furnishes a copy of the technical advice memorandum to the taxpayer pursuant to (e) of this subdivision and subdivision (vii)(b) of this subparagraph.

(d) The second part of the reply will consist of a transmittal memorandum. In the unusual cases it will serve as a vehicle for providing the Appeals office administrative information or other information which, under the nondisclosure statutes, or for other reasons, may not be discussed with the taxpayer.

*(e)* It is the general practice of the Service to furnish a copy of the technical advice memorandum to the taxpayer after it has been adopted by the Appeals office. However, in the case of technical advice memorandums described in section 6110(g)(5)(A) of the Code, relating to cases involving criminal or civil fraud investigations and jeopardy or termination assessments, a copy of the technical advice memorandum shall not be furnished the taxpayer until all proceedings with respect to the investigations or assessments are completed.

*(f)* After receiving the notice pursuant to section 6110(f)(1) of the Code of intention to disclose the technical advice memorandum, the taxpayer, if desiring to protest the disclosure of certain information in the memorandum, must, within 20 days after the notice is mailed, submit a written statement identifying those deletions not made by the Internal Revenue Service which the taxpayer believes should have been made. The taxpayer shall also submit a copy of the version of the technical advice memorandum proposed to be open to public inspection on which the taxpayer indicates, by the use of brackets, the deletions proposed by the taxpayer but which have not been made by the Internal Revenue Service. Generally, the Internal Revenue Service will not consider the deletion of any material which the taxpayer did not, prior to the time when the National Office sent its reply to the request for technical advice to the Appeals office, propose be deleted. The Internal Revenue Service shall, within 20 days after receipt of the response by the taxpayer to the notice pursuant to section 6110(f)(1) of the Code, mail to the taxpayer its final administrative conclusion regarding the deletions to be made.

(vii) *Action on technical advice in Appeals offices..—(a)* Unless the Chief, Appeals Office, feels that the conclusions reached by the National Office in a technical advice memorandum should be reconsidered and promptly requests such reconsideration, the Appeals office will proceed to process the taxpayer's case taking into account the conclusions expressed in the technical advice memorandum. The effect of technical advice on the taxpayer's case is set forth in subdivision (viii) of this subparagraph.

*(b)* The Appeals office will furnish the taxpayer a copy of the technical advice memorandum described in subdivision (vi)*(c)* of this subparagraph and the notice pursuant to section 6110(f)(1) of the Code of intention to disclose the technical advice memorandum (including a copy of the version proposed to be open to public inspection and notations of third-party communications pursuant to section 6110(d) of the Code). The preceding sentence shall not apply to technical advice memorandums involving civil fraud or criminal investigations, or jeopardy or termination assessments, as described in subdivision (iii)*(j)* of this subparagraph (except to the extent provided in subdivision (vi)*(e)* of this subparagraph) or to documents to which section 6104 of the Code applies.

*(c)* In those cases in which the National Office advises the Appeals office that it should not furnish a copy of the technical advice memorandum to the technical advice memorandum to the taxpayer, the Appeals office will so inform the taxpayer if he/she requests a copy.

(viii) *Effect of technical advice.—(a)* A technical advice memorandum represents an expression of the views of the Service as to the application of law, regulations, and precedents to the facts of a specific case, and is issued primarily as a means of assisting Service officials in the closing of the case involved.

*(b)* Except in rare or unusual circumstances, a holding in a technical advice memorandum that is favorable to the taxpayer is applied retroactively. Moreover, since technical advice, as described in subdivision (i) of this subparagraph, is issued only on closed transactions, a holding in a technical advice memorandum that is adverse to the taxpayer is also applied retroactively unless the Assistant Commissioner or Deputy Assistant Commissioner (Technical) exercises the discretionary authority under section 7805(b) of the Code to limit the retroactive effect of the holding. Likewise, a holding in a technical advice memorandum that modifies or revokes a holding in a prior technical advice memorandum will also be applied retroactively, with one exception. If the new holding is less favorable to the taxpayer, it will generally not be applied to the period in which the taxpayer relied on the prior holding in situations involving continuing transactions of the type described in § 601.201(1)(7) and § 601.201(1)(8).

*(c)* The Appeals office is bound by technical advice favorable to the taxpayer. However, if the technical advice is unfavorable to the taxpayer, the Appeals office may settle the issue in the usual manner under existing authority. For the effect of the technical advice in Employee Plans and Exempt Organization cases see § 601.201(n)(9)(viii).

*(d)* In connection with section 446 of the Code, taxpayers may request permission from the Assistant Commissioner (Technical) to change a method of accounting and obtain a 10-year (or less) spread of the resulting adjustments. Such a request should be made prior to or at the first Appeals conference. The Appeals office has authority to allow a change and the resulting spread without referring the case to Technical.

*(e)* Technical advice memorandums often form the basis for revenue rulings. For the description of revenue rulings and the effect thereof, see § § 601.601(d)(2)(i)*(a)* and 601.601(d)(2)(v).

*(f)* An Appeals office may raise an issue in a taxable period, even though technical advice may have been asked for and furnished with regard to the same or a similar issue in any other taxable period.

(g) *Limitation on the jurisdiction and function of Appeals.—(1) Overpayment of more than $200,000.—*If Appeals determines that there is an overpayment of income, war profits, excess profits, estate, generation-skipping transfer or gift tax, or any tax imposed by chapters 41 through 44, including penalties and interest, in excess of $200,000, such determination will be considered by the Joint Committee on Taxation, See section 601.108.

(2) *Offers in compromise.—*For jurisdiction of Appeals with respect to offers in compromise of tax liabilities, see § 601.203.

(3) *Closing agreements.—*For jurisdiction of Appeals with respect to closing agreements under section 7121 of the Code relating to any internal revenue tax liability, see § 601.202.

(h) *Reopening closed cases not docketed in the Tax Court.—*(1) A case not docketed in the Tax Court and closed by Appeals on the basis of concessions made by both Appeals and the taxpayer will not be reopened by action initiated by the Service unless the disposition involved fraud, malfeasance, concealment or misrepresentation of material fact, or an important mistake in mathematical calculation, and then only with the approval of the Regional Director of Appeals.

(2) Under certain unusual circumstances favorable to the taxpayer, such as retroactive legislation, a case not docketed in the Tax Court and closed by Appeals on the basis of concessions made by both Appeals and the taxpayer may be reopened upon written application from the taxpayer, and only with the approval of the Regional Director of Appeals. The processing of an application for a tentative carryback adjustment or of a claim for refund or credit for an overassessment (for a year involved in the prior closing) attributable to a claimed deduction or credit for a carryback provided by law, and not included in a previous Appeals determination, shall not be considered a reopening requiring approval. A subsequent assessment of an excessive tentative allowance shall likewise not be considered such a reopening. The Director of Appeals may authorize, in advance, the reopening of similar classes of cases where legislative enactments or compelling administrative reasons require such advance approval.

(3) A case not docketed in the Tax Court and closed by Appeals on a basis not involving concessions made by both Appeals and the taxpayer will not be reopened by action initiated by the Service unless the disposition involved fraud, malfeasance, concealment or misrepresentation of material fact, an important mistake in mathematical calculation, or such other circumstance that indicates that failure to take such action would be a serious administrative omission, and then only with the approval of the Regional Director of Appeals.

(4) A case not docketed in the Tax Court and closed by Appeals on a basis not involving concessions made by both Appeals and the taxpayer may be reopened by the taxpayer by any appropriate means, such as by the filing of a timely claim for refund.

(i) *Special procedures for crude oil windfall profit tax cases.—*For special procedures relating to crude oil windfall profit tax cases, see § 601.405. [Reg. § 601.106.]

☐ [32 FR 15990, Nov. 22, 1967, as amended at 32 FR 20646, Dec. 21, 1967; 33 FR 6820, May 4, 1968; 34 FR 14600, Sept. 19, 1969; 35 FR 7113, May 6, 1970; 35 FR 15917, Oct. 9, 1970; 36 FR 7584, Apr. 22, 1971; 38 FR 4959, Feb. 23, 1973; 38 FR 33301, Dec. 3, 1973; 39 FR 8917, Mar. 7, 1974; 41 FR 20880, May 21, 1976; 41 FR 40103, Sept. 17, 1976; 42 FR 46519, Sept. 16, 1977; 42 FR 48336, Sept. 23, 1977; 43 FR 17817, Apr. 26, 1978; 43 FR 44498, Sept. 28, 1978; 43 FR 53029, Nov. 15, 1978; 45 FR 7253, Feb. 1, 1980; 46 FR 26053, May 11, 1981; 48 FR 24670, June 2, 1983; 49 FR 26499, Sept. 18, 1984; 52 FR 38406, Oct. 16, 1987.]

**[Reg. § 601.107]**

**§ 601.107. Criminal Investigation functions.—**(a) *General.—*Each district has a Criminal Investigation function whose mission is to encourage and achieve the highest possible degree of voluntary compliance with the internal revenue laws by: enforcing the statutory sanctions applicable to income, estate, gift, employment, and certain excise taxes through the investigation of possible criminal violations of such laws and the recommendation (when warranted) of prosecution and/or assertion of the 50 percent ad valorem addition to the tax; developing information concerning the extent of criminal violations of all Federal tax laws (except those relating to alcohol, tobacco, narcotics, and firearms); measuring the effectiveness of the investigation process; and providing protection of persons and of property and other enforcement coordination as required.

(b) *Investigative procedure.*—(1) A witness when questioned in an investigation conducted by the Criminal Investigation Division may have counsel present to represent and advise him. Upon request, a copy of an affidavit or transcript of a question and answer statement will be furnished a witness promptly, except in circumstances deemed by the Regional Commissioner to necessitate temporarily withholding a copy.

(2) A taxpayer who may be the subject of a criminal recommendation will be afforded a district Criminal Investigation conference when he requests one or where the Chief, Criminal Investigation Division, makes a determination that such a conference will be in the best interests of the Government. At the conference, the IRS representative will inform the taxpayer by a general oral statement of the alleged fraudulent features of the case, to the extent consistent with protecting the Government's interests, and, at the same time, making available to the taxpayer sufficient facts and figures to acquaint him with the basis, nature, and other essential elements of the proposed criminal charges against him.

(c) *Processing of cases after investigation.*—The Chief, Criminal Investigation Division, shall ordinarily notify the subject of an investigation and his authorized representative, if any, when he forwards a case to the Regional Counsel with a recommendation for prosecution. The rule will not apply if the case is with a United States Attorney. [Reg. § 601.107.]

□ [33 FR 17325, Nov. 21, 1968, as amended at 38 FR 9227, Apr. 12, 1973; 39 FR 8917, Mar. 7, 1974; 43 FR 53029, Nov. 15, 1978.]

**[Reg. § 601.108]**

**§ 601.108. Review of overpayments exceeding $200,000.**— (a) *General.*—Section 6405(a) of the Code provides that no refund or credit of income, war profits, excess profits, estate, or gift taxes, or any tax imposed by chapters 41 through 44, including penalties and interest, in excess of $200,000 may be made until after the expiration of 30 days from the date a report is made to the Joint Committee on Taxation. Taxpayers in cases requiring review by the Joint Committee are afforded the same appeal rights as other taxpayers. In general, these cases follow regular procedures, except for preparation of reports to and review by the Joint Committee.

(b) *Reports to Joint Committee.*—In any case in which no protest is made to Appeals and no petition docketed in the Tax Court, the report to the Joint Committee is prepared by a Joint Committee Coordinator, who is an Examination Division regional specialist. In cases in which a protest has been made, the report to the Joint Committee is prepared by an Appeals officer; in cases in which a petition is docketed, either an Appeals officer or a Counsel attorney prepares the report, depending on the circumstances.

(c) *Procedure after report to Joint Committee.*—After compliance with section 6405 of the Code, the case is processed for issuance of a certificate of overassessment, and payment or credit of any overpayment. If the final determination involves a rejection of a claimed overpayment in whole or in part, a statutory notice of disallowance will be sent by certified or registered mail to the taxpayer, except where the taxpayer has filed a written waiver of such notice of disallowance. [Reg. § 601.108.]

□ [32 FR 15990, Nov. 22, 1967, as amended at 42 FR 46519, Sept. 16, 1977; 43 FR 44503, Sept. 28, 1978; 43 FR 53030, Nov. 15, 1978; 45 FR 7255, Feb. 1, 1980.]

**[Reg. § 601.109]**

**§ 601.109. Bankruptcy and receivership cases.**—(a) *General.*— (1) Upon the adjudication of bankruptcy of any taxpayer in any liquidating proceeding, the filing or (where approval is required by the Bankruptcy Act) the approval of a petition of, or the approval of a petition against, any taxpayer in any other proceeding under the Bankruptcy Act or the appointment of a receiver for any taxpayer in any receivership proceeding before a court of the United States or of any State or Territory or of the District of Columbia, the assessment of any deficiency in income, profits, estate, or gift tax (together with all interest, additional amounts, or additions to the tax provided for by law) shall be made immediately. See section 6871 of the Code. In such cases the restrictions imposed by section 6213(a) of the Code upon assessments are not applicable. (In the case of an assignment for the benefit of creditors, the assessment will be made under section 6861, relating to jeopardy assessments. See § 601.105(h).) Cases in which immediate assessment will be made include those of taxpayers in receivership or in bankruptcy, reorganization, arrangement, or wage earner proceedings under chapters I to VII, section 77, chapters X, XI, XII, and XIII of the Bankruptcy Act. The term "approval of a petition in any other proceeding under the Bankruptcy Act" includes the filing of a petition under chapters XI to XIII of the Bankruptcy Act with a court of competent jurisdiction. A fiduciary in any proceeding under the Bankruptcy Act (including a trustee, receiver-debtor in possession, or other person designated by the court

as in control of the assets or affairs of a debtor) or a receiver in any receivership proceeding may be required, as provided in regulations prescribed under section 6036 of the Code, to give notice in writing to the district director of his qualification as such. Failure on the part of such fiduciary in a receivership proceeding or a proceeding under the Bankruptcy Act to give such notice, when required, results in the suspension of the running of the period of limitations on the making of assessments from the date of the institution of the proceeding to the date upon which such notice is received by the district director, and for an additional 30 days thereafter. However, in no case where the required notice is not given shall the suspension of the running of the period of limitations on assessment exceed 2 years. See section 6872 of the Code.

(2) Except in cases where departmental instructions direct otherwise, the district director will, promptly after ascertaining the existence of any outstanding Federal tax liability against a taxpayer in any proceeding under the Bankruptcy Act or receivership proceeding, and in any event within the time limited by appropriate provisions of law or the appropriate orders of the court in which such proceeding is pending, file a proof of claim covering such liability in the court in which the proceeding is pending. Such a claim may be filed regardless of whether the unpaid taxes involved have been assessed. Whenever an immediate assessment is made of any income, estate, or gift tax after the commencement of a proceeding, the district director will send to the taxpayer notice and demand for payment together with a copy of such claim.

(b) *Procedure in office of district director.*—(1) While the district director is required by section 6871 of the Code to make immediate assessment of any deficiency in income, estate, or gift taxes, such assessment is not made as a jeopardy assessment (see paragraph (h) of § 601.105), and the provisions of section 6861 of the Code do not apply to any assessment made under section 6871. Therefore, the notice of deficiency provided for in section 6861(b) will not be mailed to the taxpayer. Nevertheless, Letter 1005 (DO) will be prepared and addressed in the name of the taxpayer, immediately followed by the name of the trustee, receiver, debtor in possession, or other person designated to be in control of the assets or affairs of the debtor by the court in which the bankruptcy or receivership proceeding is pending. Such letter will state how the deficiency was computed, advise that within 30 days a written protest under penalties of perjury may be filed with the district director showing wherein the deficiency is claimed to be incorrect, and advise that upon request an Appeals office conference will be granted with respect to such deficiency. If, after protest is filed (in triplicate) and an Appeals office conference is held, adjustment appears necessary in the deficiency, appropriate action will be taken. Except where the interests of the Government require otherwise, Letters 1005 (DO) are issued by the office of the district director.

(2) The immediate assessment required by section 6871 of the Code represents an exception to the usual restrictions on the assessment of Federal income, estate, and gift taxes. Since there are no restrictions on the assessment of Federal excise or employment taxes, immediate assessment of such taxes will be made in any case where section 6871 of the Code would require immediate assessment of income, estate, or gift taxes.

(3) If after such assessment a claim for abatement is filed and such claim is accompanied by a request in writing for a conference, an Appeals office conference will be granted. Ordinarily, only one conference will be held, unless it develops that additional information can be furnished which has a material bearing upon the tax liability in which event the conference will be continued to a later date.

(c) *Procedure before the Appeals office.*—If an income, estate, or gift tax case is under consideration by an Appeals office (whether before or after issuance of a statutory notice of deficiency) at the time of either: (i) The adjudication of bankruptcy of the taxpayer in any liquidating proceeding; (ii) the filing with a court of competent jurisdiction or (where approval is required by the Bankruptcy Act) the approval of a petition of, or against, the taxpayer in any other proceeding under the Bankruptcy Act; or (iii) the appointment of any receiver, then the case will be returned to the district director for assessment (if not previously made), for issuance of the Letter 1005 (DO), and for filing proof of claim in the proceeding. Excise and employment tax cases pending in the Appeals office at such time will likewise be returned to the district director for assessment (if not previously made) and for filing proof of claim in the proceeding. A petition for redetermination of a deficiency may not be filed in the Tax Court after the adjudication of bankruptcy, the filing or (where approval is required by the Bankruptcy Act) the approval of a petition of, or the approval of a petition against, the taxpayer in any other bankruptcy proceeding, or the appointment of a receiver. See section 6871(b) of the Code. However, the Tax Court is not deprived of jurisdiction where the adjudication of bankruptcy, the filing or (where approval is required by the Bankruptcy Act) the approval of a petition of, or the approval of a petition against, the taxpayer in any other bankruptcy proceeding, or the appointment of a receiver, occurred after the filing of the petition. In such a case, the jurisdiction of the bankruptcy or receivership court and the Tax Court is concurrent.

(d) *Priority of claims.*—Under Section 3466 of the Revised Statutes and Section 3467 of the Revised Statutes, as amended, taxes are entitled to priority over other claims therein stated and the receiver or other person designated as in control of the assets or affairs of the debtor by the court in which the receivership proceeding is pending may be held personally liable for failure on his part to protect the priority of the Government respecting taxes of which he has notice. Under Section 64 of the Bankruptcy Act, taxes may be entitled to priority over other claims therein stated and the trustee, receiver, debtor in possession or other person designated as in control of the assets or affairs of the debtor by the court in which the bankruptcy proceeding is pending may be held personally liable for any failure on his part to protect a priority of the Government respecting taxes of which he has notice and which are entitled to priority under the Bankruptcy Act. Sections 77(e), 199, 337(2), 455 and 659(6) of the Bankruptcy Act also contain provisions with respect to the rights of the United States relative to priority of payment. Bankruptcy courts have jurisdiction under the Bankruptcy Act to determine all disputes regarding the amount and the validity of tax claims against a bankrupt or a debtor in a proceeding under the Bankruptcy Act. A receivership proceeding or an assignment for the benefit of creditors does not discharge any portion of a claim of the United States for taxes and any portion of such claim allowed by the court in which the proceeding is pending and which remains unsatisfied after the termination of the proceeding shall be collected with interest in accordance with law. A bankruptcy proceeding under Chapters I through VII of the Bankruptcy Act does discharge that portion of a claim of the United States which became legally due and owing more than three years preceding bankruptcy, with certain exceptions [as] provided in the Bankruptcy Act, as does a proceeding under Section 77 or Chapter X of the Bankruptcy Act. Any taxes which are dischargeable under the Bankruptcy Act which remain unsatisfied after the termination of the proceeding may be collected only from exempt or abandoned property. [Reg. § 601.109.]

☐ [32 FR 15990, Nov. 22, 1967, as amended at 33 FR 6821, May 4, 1968; 35 FR 15917, Oct. 9, 1970; 43 FR 44503, Sept. 28, 1978; 45 FR 7255, Feb. 1, 1980.]

## Subpart B—Rulings and Other Specific Matters

### [Reg. § 601.201]

**§ 601.201. Rulings and determination letters.**—(a) *General practice and definitions.*—(1) It is the practice of the Internal Revenue Service to answer inquiries of individuals and organizations, whenever appropriate in the interest of sound tax administration, as to their status for tax purposes and as to the tax effects of their acts or transactions. One of the functions of the National Office of the Internal Revenue Service is to issue rulings in such matters. If a taxpayer's request for a ruling concerns an action that may have an impact on the environment, compliance by the Service with the requirements of the National Environmental Policy Act of 1969 (Public Law 91-190) may result in delay in issuing the ruling. Accordingly, taxpayers requesting rulings should take this factor into account. District directors apply the statutes, regulations, Revenue Rulings, and other precedents published in the Internal Revenue Bulletin in the determination of tax liability, the collection of taxes, and the issuance of determination letters in answer to taxpayers' inquiries or requests. For purposes of this section any reference to district director or district office also includes, where appropriate, the office of the Director, Office of International Operations.

(2) A "ruling" is a written statement issued to a taxpayer or his authorized representative by the National Office which interprets and applies the tax laws to a specific set of facts. Rulings are issued only by the National Office. The issuance of rulings is under the general supervision of the Assistant Commissioner (Technical) and has been largely redelegated to the Director, Corporation Tax Division and Director, Individual Tax Division.

(3) A "determination letter" is a written statement issued by a district director in response to a written inquiry by an individual or an organization that applies to the particular facts involved, the principles and precedents previously announced by the National Office. A determination letter is issued only where a determination can be made on the basis of clearly established rules as set forth in the statute, Treasury decision, or regulation, or by a ruling, opinion, or court decision published in the Internal Revenue Bulletin. Where such a determination cannot be made, such as where the question presented involves a novel issue or the matter is excluded from the jurisdiction of a district director by the provisions of paragraph (c) of this section, a determination letter will not be issued. However, with respect to determination letters in the pension trust area, see paragraph (o) of this section.

(4) An "opinion letter" is a written statement issued by the National Office as to the acceptability of the form of a master or prototype plan and any related trust or custodial account under sections 401 and 501(a) of the Internal Revenue Code of 1954.

(5) An "information letter" is a statement issued either by the National Office or by a district director which does no more than call attention to a well-established interpretation or principle of tax law, without applying it to a specific set of facts. An information letter may be issued when the nature of the request from the individual or the organization suggests that it is seeking general information, or where the request does not meet all the requirements of paragraph (e) of this section, and it is believed that such general information will assist the individual or organization.

(6) A "Revenue Ruling" is an official interpretation by the Service which has been published in the Internal Revenue Bulletin. Revenue Rulings are issued only by the National Office and are published for the information and guidance of taxpayers, Internal Revenue Service officials, and others concerned.

(7) A "closing agreement," as the term is used herein, is an agreement between the Commissioner of Internal Revenue or his delegate and a taxpayer with respect to a specific issue or issues entered into pursuant to the authority contained in section 7121 of the Internal Revenue Code. Such a closing agreement is based on a ruling which has been signed by the Commissioner or his delegate and in which it is indicated that a closing agreement will be entered into on the basis of the holding of the ruling letter. Closing agreements are final and conclusive except upon a showing of fraud, malfeasance, or misrepresentation of material fact. They may be entered into where it is advantageous to have the matter permanently and conclusively closed, or where a taxpayer can show good and sufficient reasons for an agreement and the Government will sustain no disadvantage by its consummation. In appropriate cases, taxpayers may be required to enter into a closing agreement as a condition to the issuance of a ruling. Where in a single case, closing agreements are requested on behalf of each of a number of taxpayers, such agreements are not entered into if the number of such taxpayers exceeds 25. However, in a case where the issue and holding are identical as to all of the taxpayers and the number of taxpayers is in excess of 25, a Mass Closing Agreement will be entered into with the taxpayer who is authorized by the others to represent the entire group. See, for example, Rev. Proc. 78-15, 1978-2 C.B. 488, and Rev. Proc. 78-16, 1978-2 C.B. 489.

(b) *Rulings issued by the National Office.*—(1) In income and gift tax matters and matters involving taxes imposed under Chapter 42 of the Code, the National Office issues rulings on prospective transactions and on completed transactions before the return is filed. However, rulings will not ordinarily be issued if the identical issue is present in a return of the taxpayer for a prior year which is under active examination or audit by a district office, or is being considered by a branch office of the Appellate Division. The National Office issues rulings involving the exempt status of organizations under section 501 or 521 of the Code, only to the extent provided in paragraph (n) of this section, Revenue Procedure 72-5, Internal Revenue Bulletin No. 1972-1, 19, and Revenue Procedure 68-13, C.B. 1968-1, 764. The National Office issues rulings as to the foundation status of certain organizations under sections 509(a) and 4942(j)(3) of the Code only to the extent provided in paragraph (r) of this section. The National Office issues rulings involving qualification of plans under section 401 of the Code only to the extent provided in paragraph (o) of this section. The National Office issues opinion letters as to the acceptability of the form of master or prototype plans and any related trusts or custodial accounts under sections 401 and 501(a) of the Code only to the extent provided in paragraphs (p) and (q) of this section. The National Office will not issue rulings with respect to the replacement of involuntarily converted property, even though replacement has not been made, if the taxpayer has filed a return for the taxable year in which the property was converted. However, see paragraph (c)(6) of this section as to the authority of district directors to issue determination letters in this connection.

(2) In estate tax matters, the National Office issues rulings with respect to transactions affecting the estate tax of a decedent before the estate tax return is filed. It will not rule with respect to such matters after the estate tax return has been filed, nor will it rule on matters relating to the application of the estate tax to property or the estate of a living person.

(3) In employment and excise tax matters (except taxes imposed under Chapter 42 of the Code), the National Office issues rulings with respect to prospective transactions and to completed transactions either before or after the return is filed. However, the National

Office will not ordinarily rule with respect to an issue, whether related to a prospective or a completed transaction, if it knows or has reason to believe that the same or an identical issue is before any field office (including any branch office of the Appellate Division) in connection with an examination or audit of the liability of the same taxpayer for the same or a prior period.

(4) The Service will not issue rulings to business, trade, or industrial associations or to other similar groups relating to the application of the tax laws to members of the group. However, rulings may be issued to such groups or associations relating to their own tax status or liability provided such tax status or liability is not an issue before any field office (including any branch office or the Appellate Division) in connection with an examination or audit of the liability of the same taxpayer for the same or a prior period.

(5) Pending the adoption of regulations (either temporary or final) that reflect the provisions of any Act, consideration will be given to the issuance of rulings under the conditions set forth below.

   (i) If an inquiry presents an issue on which the answer seems to be clear from an application of the provisions of the statute to the facts described, a ruling will be issued in accordance with usual procedures.

   (ii) If an inquiry presents an issue on which the answer seems reasonably certain but not entirely free from doubt, a ruling will be issued only if it is established that a business emergency requires a ruling or that unusual hardship will result from failure to obtain a ruling.

   (iii) If an inquiry presents an issue that cannot be reasonably resolved prior to the issuance of regulations, a ruling will not be issued.

   (iv) In any case in which the taxpayer believes that a business emergency exists or that an unusual hardship will result from failure to obtain a ruling, he should submit with the request a separate letter setting forth the facts necessary for the Service to make a determination in this regard. In this connection, the Service will not deem a "business emergency" to result from circumstances within the control of the taxpayer such as, for example, scheduling within an inordinately short time the closing date for a transaction or a meeting of the board of directors or the shareholders of a corporation.

(c) *Determination letters issued by district directors.*—(1) In income and gift tax matters, and in matters involving taxes imposed under Chapter 42 of the Code, district directors issue determination letters in response to taxpayers' written requests submitted to their offices involving completed transactions which affect returns over which they have audit jurisdiction, but only if the answer to the question presented is covered specifically by statute, Treasury Decision or regulation, or specifically by a ruling, opinion, or court decision published in the Internal Revenue Bulletin. A determination letter will not usually be issued with respect to a question which involves a return to be filed by the taxpayer if the identical question is involved in a return or returns already filed by the taxpayer. District directors may not issue determination letters as to the tax consequence of prospective or proposed transactions, except as provided in subparagraphs (5) and (6) of this paragraph.

(2) In estate and gift tax matters, district directors issue determination letters in response to written requests submitted to their offices affecting the estate tax returns of decedents that will be audited by their offices, but only if the answer to the questions presented are specifically covered by statute, Treasury decision or regulation, or by a ruling, opinion, or court decision published in the Internal Revenue Bulletin. District directors will not issue determination letters relating to matters involving the application of the estate tax to property or the estate of a living person.

(3) In employment and excise tax matters (except excise taxes imposed under Chapter 42 of the Code), district directors issue determination letters in response to written requests from taxpayers who have filed or who are required to file returns over which they have audit jurisdiction, but only if the answers to the questions presented are covered specifically by statute, Treasury decision or regulation, or a ruling, opinion, or court decision published in the Internal Revenue Bulletin. Because of the impact of these taxes upon the business operation of the taxpayer and because of special problems of administration both to the Service and to the taxpayer, district directors may take appropriate action in regard to such requests, whether they relate to completed or prospective transactions or returns previously filed or to be filed.

(4) Notwithstanding the provisions of subparagraphs (1), (2), and (3), of this paragraph, a district director will not issue a determination letter in response to an inquiry which presents a question specifically covered by statute, regulations, rulings, etc., published in the Internal Revenue Bulletin, where (i) it appears that the taxpayer has directed a similar inquiry to the National Office, (ii) the identical issue involving the same taxpayer is pending in a case before the Appellate Division, (iii) the determination letter is requested by an industry, trade association, or similar group, or (iv) the request involves an industrywide problem. Under no circumstances will a

district director issue a determination letter unless it is clearly indicated that the inquiry is with regard to a taxpayer or taxpayers who have filed or are required to file returns over which his office has or will have audit jurisdiction. Notwithstanding the provisions of subparagraph (3), of this paragraph, a district director will not issue a determination letter on an employment tax question when the specific question involved has been or is being considered by the Central Office of the Social Security Administration. Nor will district directors issue determination letters on excise tax questions if a request is for a determination of a constructive sales price under section 4216(b) or 4218(e) of the Code. However, the National Office will issue rulings in this area. See paragraph (d)(2) of this section.

(5) District directors issue determination letters as to the qualification of plans under sections 401 and 405(a) of the Code, and as to the exempt status of related trusts under section 501 of the Code, to the extent provided in paragraphs (o) and (q) of this section. Selected district directors also issue determination letters as to the qualification of certain organizations for exemption from Federal income tax under sections 501 and 521 of the Code, to the extent provided in paragraph (n) of this section. Selected district directors also issue determination letters as to the qualification of certain organizations for foundation status under sections 509(a) and 4942(j)(3) of the Code, to the extent provided in paragraph (r) of this section.

(6) District directors issue determination letters with regard to the replacement of involuntarily converted property under section 1033 of the Code even though the replacement has not been made, if the taxpayer has filed his income tax return for the year in which the property was involuntarily converted.

(7) A request received by a district director with respect to a question involved in an income, estate, or gift tax return already filed will, in general, be considered in connection with the examination of the return. If response is made to such inquiry prior to an examination or audit, it will be considered a tentative finding in any subsequent examination or audit of the return.

(d) *Discretionary authority to issue rulings and determination letters.*—(1) It is the practice of the Service to answer inquiries of individuals and organizations, whenever appropriate in the interest of sound tax administration, as to their status for tax purposes and the tax effect of their acts or transactions.

(2) There are, however, certain areas where, because of the inherently factual nature of the problem involved, or for other reasons, the Service will not issue rulings or determination letters. A ruling or determination letter is not issued on alternative plans of proposed transactions or on hypothetical situations. A specific area or a list of these areas is published from time to time in the Internal Revenue Bulletin. Such list is not all inclusive since the Service may decline to issue rulings or determination letters on other questions whenever warranted by the facts or circumstances of a particular case. The National Office and district directors may, when it is deemed appropriate and in the best interest of the Service, issue information letters calling attention to well-established principles of tax law.

(3) The National Office will issue rulings in all cases on prospective or future transactions when the law or regulations require a determination of the effect of a proposed transaction for tax purposes, as in the case of a transfer coming within the provisions of sections 1491 and 1492 of the Code, or an exchange coming within the provisions of section 367 of the Code. The National Office will issue rulings in all cases involving the determination of a constructive sales price under section 4216(b) or 4218(e) of the Code.

(e) *Instructions to taxpayers.*—(1) A request for a ruling or determination letter is to be submitted in duplicate if (i) more than one issue is presented in the request or (ii) a closing agreement is requested with respect to the issue presented. There shall accompany the request a declaration in the following form: "Under penalties of perjury, I declare that I have examined this request, including accompanying documents, and to the best of my knowledge and belief, the facts presented in support of the requested ruling or determination letter are true, correct, and complete". The declaration must accompany requests that are postmarked or hand delivered to the Internal Revenue Service after October 31, 1976. The declaration must be signed by the person or persons on whose behalf the request is made.

(2) Each request for a ruling or a determination letter must contain a complete statement of all relevant facts relating to the transaction. Such facts include names, addresses and taxpayer identifying numbers of all interested parties; the location of the district office that has or will have audit jurisdiction over the return or report of each party; a full and precise statement of the business reasons for the transaction; and a carefully detailed description of the transaction. In addition, true copies of all contracts, wills, deeds, agreements, instruments, and other documents involved in the transaction must be submitted with the request. However, relevant facts reflected in documents submitted must be included in the taxpayer's state-

ment and not merely incorporated by reference, and must be accompanied by an analysis of their bearing on the issue or issues, specifying the pertinent provisions. (The term "all interested parties" is not to be construed as requiring a list of all shareholders of a widely held corporation requesting a ruling relating to a reorganization, or a list of employees where a large number may be involved in a plan.) The request must contain a statement whether, to the best of the knowledge of the taxpayer or his representative, the identical issue is being considered by any field office of the Service in connection with an active examination or audit of a tax return of the taxpayer already filed or is being considered by a branch office by the Appellate Division. Where the request pertains to only one step of a larger integrated transaction, the facts, circumstances, etc., must be submitted with respect to the entire transaction. The following list contains references to revenue procedures for advance ruling requests under certain sections of the Code.

(i) For ruling requests under section 103 of the Code, see Rev. Proc. 79-4, 1979-1 C.B. 483, as amplified by Rev. Proc. 79-12, 1979-1 C.B. 492. Revenue Procedure 79-12 sets forth procedures for submitting ruling requests to which sections 103 and 7478 of the Code apply.

(ii) For ruling requests under section 367 of the Code, see Rev. Proc. 68-23, 1968-1 C.B. 821, as amplified by Rev. Proc. 76-20, 1976-1 C.B. 560, Rev. Proc. 77-5, 1977-1 C.B. 536, Rev. Proc. 78-27, 1978-2 C.B. 526, and Rev. Proc. 78-28, 1978-2 C.B. 526. Revenue Procedure 68-23 contains guidelines for taxpayers and their representatives in connection with issuing rulings under section 367. Revenue Procedure 76-20 explains the effect of Rev. Rul. 75-561, 1975-2 C.B. 129, on transactions described in section 3.03(1)(c) of Rev. Proc. 68-23. Revenue Procedure 77-5 sets forth procedures for submitting ruling requests under section 367, and the administrative remedies available to a taxpayer within the Service after such rulings have been issued. Revenue Procedure 78-27 relates to the notice requirement set forth in the section 367(b) temporary regulations. Revenue Procedure 78-28 relates to the timely filing of a section 367(a) ruling request.

(iii) For ruling requests under section 351 of the Code, see Rev. Proc. 73-10, 1973-1 C.B. 760, and Rev. Proc. 69-19, 1969-2 C.B. 301. Revenue Procedure 73-10 sets forth the information to be included in the ruling request. Revenue Procedure 69-19 sets forth the conditions and circumstances under which an advance ruling will be issued under section 367 of the Code that an agreement which purports to furnish technical know-how in exchange for stock is a transfer of property within the meaning of section 351.

(iv) For ruling requests under section 332, 334(b)(1), or 334(b)(2) of the Code, see Rev. Proc. 73-17, 1973-2 C.B. 465. Revenue Procedure 73-17 sets forth the information to be included in the ruling request.

(v) See Rev. Proc. 77-30, 1977-2 C.B. 539, and Rev. Proc. 78-18, 1978-2 C.B. 491, relating to rules for the issuance of an advance ruling that a proposed sale of employer stock to a related qualified defined contribution plan of deferred compensation will be a sale of the stock rather than a distribution of property.

(vi) For ruling requests under section 302 or section 311 of the Code, see Rev. Proc. 73-35, 1973-2 C.B. 490. Revenue Procedure 73-35 sets forth the information to be included in the ruling request.

(vii) For ruling requests under section 337 of the Code (and related section 331) see Rev. Proc. 75-32, 1975-2 C.B. 555. Revenue Procedure 75-32 sets forth the information to be included in the ruling request.

(viii) For ruling requests under section 346 of the Code (and related sections 331 and 336), see Rev. Proc. 73-36, 1973-2 C.B. 496. Revenue Procedure 73-36 sets forth the information to be included in the ruling request.

(ix) For ruling requests under section 355 of the Code, see Rev. Proc. 75-35, 1975-2 C.B. 561. Revenue Procedure 75-35 sets forth the information to be included in the ruling request.

(x) For ruling requests under section 368(a)(1)(E) of the Code, see Rev. Proc. 78-33, 1978-2 C.B. 532. Revenue Procedure 78-33 sets forth the information to be included in the ruling request.

(xi) For ruling requests concerning the classification of an organization as a limited partnership where a corporation is the sole general partner, see Rev. Proc. 72-13, 1972-1 C.B. 735. See also Rev. Proc. 74-17, 1974-1 C.B. 438, and Rev. Proc. 75-16, 1975-1 C.B. 676. Revenue Procedure 74-17 announces certain operating rules of the Service relating to the issuance of advance ruling letters concerning the classification of organizations formed as limited partnerships. Revenue Procedure 75-16 sets forth a checklist outlining required information frequently omitted from requests for rulings relating to classification of organizations for Federal tax purposes.

(xii) For ruling requests concerning the creditability of a foreign tax under section 901 or 903 of the Code, see Rev. Rul. 67-308, 1967-2 C.B. 254, which sets forth requirements for establishing that translations of foreign law are satisfactory as evidence for purposes of determining the creditability of a particular foreign tax. Original documents should not be submitted because documents and exhibits become a part of the Internal Revenue Service file which cannot be returned. If the request is with respect to a corporate distribution, reorganization, or other similar or related transaction, the corporate balance sheet nearest the date of the transaction should be submitted. (If the request relates to a prospective transaction, the most recent balance sheet should be submitted.) In the case of requests for rulings or determination letters, other than those to which section 6104 of the Code applies, postmarked or hand delivered to the Internal Revenue Service after October 31, 1976, there must accompany such requests a statement, described in subparagraph (5) of this paragraph, of proposed deletions pursuant to section 6110(c) of the Code. Such statement is not required if the request is to secure the consent of the Commissioner with respect to the adoption of or change in accounting or funding periods or methods pursuant to section 412, 442, 446(e), or 706 of the Code. If, however, the person seeking the consent of the Commissioner receives from the Internal Revenue Service a notice that proposed deletions should be submitted because the resulting ruling will be open to public inspection under section 6110, the statement of proposed deletions must be submitted within 20 days after such notice is mailed.

(3) As an alternative procedure for the issuance of rulings on prospective transactions, the taxpayer may submit a summary statement of the facts he considers controlling the issue, in addition to the complete statement required for ruling requests by subparagraph (2) of this paragraph. Assuming agreement with the taxpayer's summary statement, the Service will use it as the basis for the ruling. Any taxpayer wishing to adopt this procedure should submit with the request for ruling:

(i) A complete statement of facts relating to the transaction, together with related documents, as required by subparagraph (2) of this paragraph; and

(ii) A summary statement of the facts which he believes should be controlling in reaching the requested conclusion.

Where the taxpayer's statement of controlling facts is accepted, the ruling will be based on those facts and only this statement will ordinarily be incorporated in the ruling letter. It is emphasized, however, that:

(a) This procedure for a "two-part" ruling request is elective with the taxpayer and is not to be considered a required substitute for the regular procedure contained in paragraphs (a) through (m) of this section;

(b) Taxpayers' rights and responsibilities are the same under the "two-part" ruling request procedure as those provided in paragraphs (a) through (m) of this section;

(c) The Service reserves the right to rule on the basis of a more complete statement of facts it considers controlling and to seek further information in developing facts and restating them for ruling purposes; and

(d) The "two-part" ruling request procedure will not apply where it is inconsistent with other procedures applicable to specific situations such as: requests for permission to change accounting method or period; application for recognition of exempt status under section 501 or 521; or rulings on employment tax status.

(4) If the taxpayer is contending for a particular determination, he must furnish an explanation of the grounds for his contentions, together with a statement of relevant authorities in support of his views. Even though the taxpayer is urging no particular determination with regard to a proposed or prospective transaction, he must state his views as to the tax results of the proposed action and furnish a statement of relevant authorities to support such views.

(5) In order to assist the Internal Revenue Service in making the deletions, required by section 6110(c) of the Code, from the text of rulings and determination letters, which are open to public inspection pursuant to section 6110(a) of the Code, there must accompany requests for such rulings or determination letters either a statement of the deletions proposed by the person requesting the ruling or determination letter and the statutory basis for each proposed deletion, or a statement that no information other than names, addresses, and taxpayer identifying numbers need be deleted. Such statement shall be made in a separate document. The statement of proposed deletions shall be accompanied by a copy of the request for a ruling or determination letter and supporting documents, on which shall be indicated, by the use of brackets, the material which the person making such request indicates should be deleted pursuant to section 6110(c) of the Code. The statement of proposed deletions shall indicate the statutory basis, under section 6110(c) of the Code, for each proposed deletion. The statement of proposed deletions shall not appear or be referred to anywhere in the request for a ruling of determination letter. If the person making the request decides to request additional deletions pursuant to section 6110(c) of the Code prior to the time the ruling or determination letter is issued, additional statements may be submitted.

(6) If the request is with respect to the qualification of a plan under section 401 or 405(a) of the Code, see paragraphs (o) and (p) of this section. If the request is with respect to the qualification of an

organization for exemption from Federal income tax under section 501 or 521 of the Code, see paragraph (n) of this section, Revenue Procedure 72-5, Internal Revenue Bulletin No. 1972-1, 19 [1972-1 C.B. 709], and Revenue Procedure 68-13, C.B. 1968-1, 764.

(7) A request by or for a taxpayer must be signed by the taxpayer or his authorized representative. If the request is signed by a representative of the taxpayer, or if the representative is to appear before the Internal Revenue Service in connection with the request, he must either be:

(i) An attorney who is a member in good standing of the bar of the highest court of any State, possession, territory, Commonwealth, or the District of Columbia, and who files with the Service a written declaration that he is currently qualified as an attorney and he is authorized to represent the principal,

(ii) A certified public accountant who is duly qualified to practice in any State, possession, territory, Commonwealth, or the District of Columbia, and who files with the Service a written declaration that he is currently qualified as a certified public accountant and he is authorized to represent the principal, or

(iii) A person, other than an attorney or certified public accountant, enrolled to practice before the Service, and who files with the Service a written declaration that he is currently enrolled (including in the declaration either his enrollment number or the expiration date of his enrollment card) and that he is authorized to represent the principal. (See Treasury Department Circular No. 230, as amended, C.B. 1966-2, 1171, for the rules on who may practice before the Service. See § 601.503(c) for the statement required as evidence of recognition as an enrollee.)

(8) A request for a ruling or an opinion letter by the National Office should be addressed to the Commissioner of Internal Revenue, Attention: T:PP:T, Washington, D.C. 20224. A request for a determination letter should be addressed to the district director of internal revenue whose office has or will have audit jurisdiction of the taxpayer's return. See also paragraphs (n) through (q) of this section.

(9) Any request for a ruling or determination letter that does not comply with all the provisions of this paragraph will be acknowledged, and the requirements that have not been met will be pointed out. If a request for a ruling lacks essential information, the taxpayer or his representative will be advised that if the information is not forthcoming within 30 days, the request will be closed. If the information is received after the request is closed, the request will be reopened and treated as a new request as of the date of the receipt of the essential information. Priority treatment of such request will be granted only in rare cases upon the approval of the division director.

(10) A taxpayer or his representative who desires an oral discussion of the issue or issues involved should indicate such desire in writing when filing the request or soon thereafter in order that the conference may be arranged at that stage of consideration when it will be most helpful.

(11) Generally, prior to issuing the ruling or determination letter, the National Office or district director shall inform the person requesting such ruling or determination letter orally or in writing of the material likely to appear in the ruling or determination letter which such person proposed be deleted but which the Internal Revenue Service determines should not be deleted. If so informed, the person requesting the ruling or determination letter may submit within 10 days any further information, arguments or other material in support of the position that such material be deleted. The Internal Revenue Service will attempt, if feasible, to resolve all disagreements with respect to proposed deletions prior to the issuance of the ruling or determination letter. However, in no event shall the person requesting the ruling or determination letter have the right to a conference with respect to resolution of any disagreements concerning material to be deleted from the text of the ruling or determination letter, but such matters may be considered at any conference otherwise scheduled with respect to the request.

(12) It is the practice of the Service to process requests for rulings, opinion letters, and determination letters in regular order and as expeditiously as possible. Compliance with a request for consideration of a particular matter ahead of its regular order, or by a specified time, tends to delay the disposition of other matters. Requests for processing ahead of the regular order, made in writing in a separate letter submitted with the request or subsequent thereto and showing clear need for such treatment, will be given consideration as the particular circumstances warrant. However, no assurance can be given that any letter will be processed by the time requested. For example, the scheduling of a closing date for a transaction or a meeting of the Board of Directors or shareholders of a corporation without due regard to the time it may take to obtain a ruling, opinion letter, or determination letter will not be deemed sufficient reason for handling a request ahead of its regular order. Neither will the possible effect of fluctuation in the market price of stocks on a transaction be deemed sufficient reason for handling a request out of order. Requests by telegram will be treated in the same manner as requests by letter. Rulings, opinion letters, and determination letters ordina-

rily will not be issued by telegram. A taxpayer or his representative desiring to obtain information as to the status of his case may do so by contacting the appropriate division in the office of the Assistant Commissioner, Technical).

(13) The Director, Corporation Tax Division, has responsibility for issuing rulings in areas involving the application of Federal income tax to taxpayers; those involving income tax conventions or treaties with foreign countries; those involving depreciation, depletion, and valuation issues; and those involving the taxable status of exchanges and distributions in connection with corporate reorganizations, organizations, liquidations, etc.

(14) The Director, Individual Tax Division, has responsibility for issuing rulings with respect to the application of Federal income tax to taxpayers (including individuals, partnerships, estates and trusts); areas involving the application of Federal estate and gift taxes including estate and gift tax conventions or treaties with foreign countries; areas involving certain excise taxes; the provisions of the Internal Revenue Code dealing with procedure and administration; and areas involving employment taxes.

(15) A taxpayer or the taxpayer's representative desiring to obtain information as to the status of the taxpayer's case may do so by contacting the following offices with respect to matters in the areas of their responsibility:

| Official | Telephone Numbers (Area Code 202) |
|---|---|
| Director, Corporation Tax Division | 566-4504 or 566-4505 |
| Director, Individual Tax Division | 566-3767 or 566-3788 |

(16) After receiving the notice pursuant to section 6110(f)(1) of the Code of intention to disclose the ruling or determination letter (including a copy of the version proposed to be open to public inspection and notations of third-party communications pursuant to section 6110(d) of the Code), if the person requesting the ruling or determination letter desires to protest the disclosure of certain information in the ruling or determination letter, such person must within 20 days after the notice is mailed submit a written statement identifying those deletions not made by the Internal Revenue Service which such person believes should have been made. Such person shall also submit a copy of the version of the ruling or determination letter proposed to be open to public inspection on which such person indicates, by the use of brackets, the deletions proposed by the taxpayer but which have not been made by the Internal Revenue Service. Generally, the Internal Revenue Service will not consider the deletion under this subparagraph of any material which the taxpayer did not, prior to the issuance of the ruling or determination letter, propose be deleted. The Internal Revenue Service shall, within 20 days after receipt of the response by the person requesting the ruling or determination letter to the notice pursuant to section 6110(f)(1) of the Code, mail to such person its final administrative conclusion with respect to the deletions to be made.

(17) After receiving the notice pursuant to section 6110(f)(1) of the Code of intention to disclose (but no later than 60 days after such notice is mailed), the person requesting a ruling or determination letter may submit a request for delay of public inspection pursuant to either section 6110(g)(3) or section 6110(g)(3) and (4) of the Code. The request for delay shall be submitted to the office to which the request for a ruling or determination letter was submitted. A request for delay shall contain the date on which it is expected that the underlying transaction will be completed. The request for delay pursuant to section 6110(g)(4) of the Code shall contain a statement from which the Commissioner may determine that good cause exists to warrant such delay.

(18) When a taxpayer receives a ruling or determination letter prior to the filing of his return with respect to any transaction that has been consummated and that is relevant to the return being filed, he should attach a copy of the ruling or determination letter to the return.

(19) A taxpayer may protest an adverse ruling letter, or the terms and conditions contained in a ruling letter, issued after January 30, 1977, under section 367(a)(1) of the Code (including a ruling with respect to an exchange described in section 367(b) which begins before January 1, 1978) or section 1042(e)(2) of the Tax Reform Act of 1976, not later than 45 days after the date of the ruling letter. (For rulings issued under these sections prior to January 31, 1977, see section 4.01 of Revenue Procedure 77-5.) The Assistant Commissioner (Technical) will establish an ad hoc advisory board to consider each protest, whether or not a conference is requested. A protest is considered made on the date of the postmark of a letter of protest or the date that such letter is hand delivered to any Internal Revenue Service office, including the National Office. The protest letter must be addressed to the Assistant Commissioner (Technical), Attention: T:FP:T. The taxpayer will be granted one conference upon request. Whether or not the request is made the board may request one or more conferences or written submissions. The taxpayer will be notified of the time, date, and place of the conference, and the names of the members of the board. The board will consider all materials

submitted in writing by the taxpayer and oral arguments presented at the conference. Any oral arguments made at a conference by the taxpayer, which have not previously been submitted to the Service in writing, may be submitted to the Service in writing if postmarked not later than seven days after the day of the conference.

The Board will make its recommendation to the Assistant Commissioner (Technical) and the Assistant Commissioner will make the decision. The taxpayer will be informed of the decision of the Assistant Commissioner by certified or registered mail. The specific procedures to be used by a taxpayer in protesting an adverse ruling letter, or the terms and conditions contained in a ruling letter, under section 367 will be published from time to time in the Internal Revenue Bulletin (see, for example, Revenue Procedure 77-5).

(f) *Conferences in the National Office.*—(1) If a conference has been requested, the taxpayer will be notified of the time and place of the conference. A conference is normally scheduled only when the Service deems it will be helpful in deciding the case or an adverse decision is indicated. If conferences are being arranged with respect to more than one request for a ruling involving the same taxpayer, they will be so scheduled as to cause the least inconvenience to the taxpayer.

(2) A taxpayer is entitled, as a matter of right, to only one conference in the National Office unless one of the circumstances discussed in subparagraph (3) of this paragraph develops. This conference will usually be held at the branch level of the appropriate division in the office of the Assistant Commissioner (Technical) and will usually be attended by a person who has authority to act for the branch chief. (See § 601.201(a)(2) for the divisions involved.) If more than one subject is to be discussed at the conference, the discussion will constitute a conference with respect to each subject. In order to promote a free and open discussion of the issues, the conference will usually be held after the branch has had an opportunity to study the case. However, at the request of the taxpayer or his representative, the conference may be held at an earlier stage in the consideration of the case than the Service would ordinarily designate. No taxpayer has a "right" to appeal the action of a branch to a division director or to any other official of the Service, nor is a taxpayer entitled, as a matter of right, to a separate conference in the Chief Counsel's office on a request for a ruling.

(3) In the process of review in Technical of a holding proposed by a branch, it may appear that the final answer will involve a reversal of the branch proposal with a result less favorable to the taxpayer. Or it may appear that an adverse holding proposed by a branch will be approved, but on a new or different issue or on different grounds than those on which the branch decided the case. Under either of these circumstances, the taxpayer or his representative will be invited to another conference. The provisions of this section limiting the number of conferences to which a taxpayer is entitled will not foreclose the invitation of a taxpayer to attend further conferences when, in the opinion of National Office personnel, such need arises. All additional conferences of the type discussed in this paragraph are held only at the invitation of the Service.

(4) It is the responsibility of the taxpayer to add to the case file a written record of any additional data, lines of reasoning, precedents, etc., which are proposed by the taxpayer and discussed at the conference but which were not previously or adequately presented in writing.

(g) *Referral of matters to the National Office.*—(1) Requests for determination letters received by the district directors that, in accordance with paragraph (c) of this section, may not be acted upon by a district office, will be forwarded to the National Office for reply and the taxpayer advised accordingly. District directors also refer to the National Office any request for a determination letter that in their judgment warrants the attention of the National Office. See also the provisions of paragraphs (o), (p), and (q) of this section, with respect to requests relating to qualification of a plan under sections 401 and 405(a) of the Code, and paragraph (n) of this section, Revenue Procedure 72-5, Internal Revenue Bulletin No. 1972-1, 19, and Revenue Procedure 68-13, C.B. 1968-1, 764, with respect to application for recognition of exempt status under section 501 and 521 of the Code.

(2) If the request is with regard to an issue or an area with respect to which the Service will not issue a ruling or a determination letter, such request will not be forwarded to the National Office, but the district office will advise the taxpayer that the Service will not issue a ruling or a determination letter on the issue. See paragraph (d)(2) of this section.

(h) *Referral of matters to district offices.*—Requests for rulings received by the National Office that, in accordance with the provisions of paragraph (b) of this section, may not be acted upon by the National Office will be forwarded for appropriate action to the district office that has or will have audit jurisdiction of the taxpayer's return and the taxpayer advised accordingly. If the request is with respect to an issue or an area of the type discussed in paragraph

(d)(2) of this section, the taxpayer will be so advised and the request may be forwarded to the appropriate district office for association with the related return or report of the taxpayer.

(i) *Review of determination letters.*—(1) Determination letters issued with respect to the types of inquiries authorized by paragraph (c)(1), (2), and (3) of this section are not generally reviewed by the National Office as they merely inform a taxpayer of a position of the Service which has been previously established either in the regulations or in a ruling, opinion, or court decision published in the Internal Revenue Bulletin. If a taxpayer believes that a determination letter of this type is in error, he may ask the district director to reconsider the matter. He may also ask the district director to request advice from the National Office. In such event, the procedures in paragraph (b)(5) of § 601.105 will be followed.

(2) The procedures for review of determination letters relating to the qualification of employers' plans under section 401(a) of the Code are provided in paragraph (o) of this section.

(3) The procedures for review of determination letters relating to the exemption from Federal income tax of certain organizations under sections 501 and 521 of the Code are provided in paragraph (n) of this section.

(j) *Withdrawals of requests.*—The taxpayer's request for a ruling or a determination letter may be withdrawn at any time prior to the signing of the letter of reply. However, in such a case, the National Office may furnish its views to the district director whose office has or will have audit jurisdiction of the taxpayer's return. The information submitted will be considered by the district director in a subsequent audit or examination of the taxpayer's return. Even though a request is withdrawn, all correspondence and exhibits will be retained in the Service and may not be returned to the taxpayer.

(k) *Oral advice to taxpayers.*—(1) The Service does not issue rulings or determination letters upon oral requests. Furthermore, National Office officials and employees ordinarily will not discuss a substantive tax issue with a taxpayer or his representative prior to the receipt of a request for a ruling, since oral opinions or advice are not binding on the Service. This should not be construed as preventing a taxpayer or his representative from inquiring whether the Service will rule on a particular question. In such cases, however, the name of the taxpayer and his identifying number must be disclosed. The Service will also discuss questions relating to procedural matters with regard to submitting a request for a ruling, including the application of the provisions of paragraph (e) to the particular case.

(2) A taxpayer may, of course, seek oral technical assistance from a district office in the preparation of his return or report, pursuant to other established procedures. Such oral advice is advisory only and the Service is not bound to recognize it in the examination of the taxpayer's return.

(l) *Effect of rulings.*—(1) A taxpayer may not rely on an advance ruling issued to another taxpayer. A ruling, except to the extent incorporated in a closing agreement, may be revoked or modified at any time in the wise administration of the taxing statutes. See paragraph (a)(6) of this section for the effect of a closing agreement. If a ruling is revoked or modified, the revocation or modification applies to all open years under the statutes, unless the Commissioner or his delegate exercises the discretionary authority under section 7805(b) of the Code to limit the retroactive effect of the revocation or modification. The manner in which the Commissioner or his delegate generally will exercise this authority is set forth in this section. With reference to rulings relating to the sale or lease of articles subject to the manufacturers excise tax and the retailers excise tax, see specifically subparagraph (8) of this paragraph.

(2) As part of the determination of a taxpayer's liability, it is the responsibility of the district director to ascertain whether any ruling previously issued to the taxpayer has been properly applied. It should be determined whether the representations upon which the ruling was based reflected an accurate statement of the material facts and whether the transaction actually was carried out substantially as proposed. If, in the course of the determination of the tax liability, it is the view of the district director that a ruling previously issued to the taxpayer should be modified or revoked, the findings and recommendations of that office will be forwarded to the National Office for consideration prior to further action. Such reference to the National Office will be treated as a request for technical advice and the procedures of paragraph (b)(5) of § 601.105 will be followed. Otherwise, the ruling is to be applied by the district office in its determination of the taxpayer's liability.

(3) Appropriate coordination with the National Office will be undertaken in the event that any other field official having jurisdiction of a return or other matter proposes to reach a conclusion contrary to a ruling previously issued to the taxpayer.

(4) A ruling found to be in error or not in accord with the current views of the Service may be modified or revoked. Modification or revocation may be effected by a notice to the taxpayer to

whom the ruling originally was issued, or by a Revenue Ruling or other statement published in the Internal Revenue Bulletin.

(5) Except in rare or unusual circumstances, the revocation or modification of a ruling will not be applied retroactively with respect to the taxpayer to whom the ruling was originally issued or to a taxpayer whose tax liability was directly involved in such ruling if (i) there has been no misstatement or omission of material facts, (ii) the facts subsequently developed are not materially different from the facts on which the ruling was based, (iii) there has been no change in the applicable law, (iv) the ruling was originally issued with respect to a prospective or proposed transaction, and (v) the taxpayer directly involved in the ruling acted in good faith in reliance upon the ruling and the retroactive revocation would be to his detriment. To illustrate, the tax liability of each employee covered by a ruling relating to a pension plan of an employer is directly involved in such ruling. Also, the tax liability of each shareholder is directly involved in a ruling related to the reorganization of a corporation. However, the tax liability of members of an industry is not directly involved in a ruling issued to one of the members, and the position taken in a revocation or modification of ruling to one member of an industry may be retroactively applied to other members of that industry. By the same reasoning, a tax practitioner may not obtain the nonretroactive application to one client of a modification or revocation of a ruling previously issued to another client. Where a ruling to a taxpayer is revoked with retroactive effect, the notice to such taxpayer will, except in fraud cases, set forth the grounds upon which the revocation is being made and the reasons why the revocation is being applied retroactively.

(6) A ruling issued to a taxpayer with respect to a particular transaction represents a holding of the Service on that transaction only. However, the application of that ruling to the transaction will not be affected by the subsequent issuance of regulations (either temporary or final), if the conditions specified in subparagraph (5) of this paragraph are met. If the ruling is later found to be in error or no longer in accord with the holding of the Service, it will afford the taxpayer no protection with respect to a like transaction in the same or subsequent year, except to the extent provided in subparagraphs (7) and (8) of this paragraph.

(7) If a ruling is issued covering a continuing action or a series of actions and it is determined that the ruling was in error or no longer in accord with the position of the Service, the Assistant Commissioner (Technical) ordinarily will limit the retroactivity of the revocation or modification to a date not earlier than that on which the original ruling was modified or revoked. To illustrate, if a taxpayer rendered service or provided a facility which is subject to the excise tax on services or facilities, and in reliance on a ruling issued to the same taxpayer did not pass the tax on to the user of the service or the facility, the Assistant Commissioner (Technical) ordinarily will restrict the retroactive application of the revocation or modification of the ruling. Likewise, if an employer incurred liability under the Federal Insurance Contributions Act, but in reliance on a ruling made

to the same employer neither collected the employee tax nor paid the employee and employer taxes under the Act, the Assistant Commissioner (Technical) ordinarily will restrict the retroactive application of the revocation or modification of the ruling with respect to both the employer tax and the employee tax. In the latter situation, however, the restriction of retroactive application ordinarily will be conditioned on the furnishing by the employer of wage data, or of such corrections of wage data as may be required by §31.6011(a)-1(c) of the Employment Tax Regulations. Consistent with these provisions, if a ruling relates to a continuing action or a series of actions, the ruling will be applied until the date of issuance of applicable regulations or the publication of a Revenue Ruling holding otherwise, or until specifically withdrawn. Publication of a notice of proposed rulemaking will not affect the application of any ruling issued under the procedures set forth herein. (As to the effective date in cases involving revocation or modification of rulings or determination letters recognizing exemption, see paragraph (n)(1) of this section.)

(8) A ruling holding that the sale or lease of a particular article is subject to the manufacturers excise tax or the retailers excise tax may not revoke or modify retroactively a prior ruling holding that the sale or lease of such article was not taxable, if the taxpayer to whom the ruling was issued, in reliance upon such prior ruling, parted with possession or ownership of the article without passing the tax on to his customer. Section 1108(b), Revenue Act of 1926.

(9) In the case of rulings involving completed transactions, other than those described in subparagraphs (7) and (8) of this paragraph, taxpayers will not be afforded the protection against retroactive revocation provided in subparagraph (5) of this paragraph in the case of proposed transactions since they will not have entered into the transactions in reliance on the rulings.

(m) *Effect of determination letters.*—A determination letter issued by a district director in accordance with this section will be given the same effect upon examination of the return of the taxpayer to whom the determination letter was issued as is described in paragraph (l) of this section, in the case of a ruling issued to a taxpayer, except that reference to the National Office is not necessary where, upon examination of the return, it is the opinion of the district director that a conclusion contrary to that expressed in the determination letter is indicated. A district director may not limit the modification or revocation of a determination letter but may refer the matter to the National Office for exercise by the Commissioner or his delegate of the authority to limit the modification or revocation. In this connection see also paragraphs (n) and (o) of this section.

(n) *Organization claiming exemption under section 501 or 521 of the Code.*—(1) *Filing applications for exemption.*—(i) An organization seeking recognition of exempt status under section 501 or section 521 of the Code is required to file an application with the key district director for the Internal Revenue district in which the principal place of business or principal office of the organization is located. Following are the 19 key district offices that process the applications and the Internal Revenue districts covered by each:

| Key District(s) | IRS Districts Covered |
|---|---|
| **Central Region** | |
| Cincinnati | Cincinnati, Louisville, Indianapolis. |
| Cleveland | Cleveland, Parkersburg. |
| Detroit | Detroit. |
| **Mid-Atlantic Region** | |
| Baltimore | Baltimore (which includes the District of Columbia and Office of International Operations), Pittsburgh, Richmond. |
| Philadelphia | Philadelphia, Wilmington. |
| Newark | Newark. |
| **Midwest Region** | |
| Chicago | Chicago. |
| St. Paul | St. Paul, Fargo, Aberdeen, Milwaukee. |
| St. Louis | St. Louis, Springfield, Des Moines, Omaha. |
| **North-Atlantic Region** | |
| Boston | Boston, Augusta, Burlington, Providence, Hartford, Portsmouth. |
| Manhattan | Manhattan. |
| Brooklyn | Brooklyn, Albany, Buffalo. |
| **Southeast Region** | |
| Atlanta | Atlanta, Greensboro, Columbia, Nashville. |
| Jacksonville | Jacksonville, Jackson, Birmingham. |
| **Southwest Region** | |
| Austin | Austin, New Orleans, Albuquerque, Denver, Cheyenne. |
| Dallas | Dallas, Oklahoma City, Little Rock, Wichita. |
| **Western Region** | |
| Los Angeles | Los Angeles, Phoenix, Honolulu. |
| San Francisco | San Francisco, Salt Lake City, Reno. |
| Seattle | Seattle, Portland, Anchorage, Boise, Helena. |

(ii) A ruling or determination letter will be issued to an organization provided its application and supporting documents establish that it meets the particular requirements of the section under which exemption is claimed. Exempt status will be recognized in advance of operations if proposed operations can be described in sufficient detail to permit a conclusion that the organization will meet the particular requirements of the section under which exemption is claimed. A mere restatement of purposes or a statement that proposed activities will be in furtherance of such purposes will not satisfy these requirements. The organization must fully describe the activities in which it expects to engage, including the standards, criteria, procedures, or other means adopted or planned for carrying out the activities; the anticipated sources of receipts; and the nature of contemplated expenditures. Where the Service considers it warranted, a record of actual operations may be required before a ruling or determination letter will be issued.

(iii) Where an application for recognition of exemption does not contain the required information, the application may be returned to the applicant without being considered on its merits with an appropriate letter of explanation. In the case of an application under section 501(c)(3) of the Code, the applicant will also be informed of the time within which the completed application must be resubmitted in order for the application to be considered as timely notice within the meaning of section 508(a) of the Code.

(iv) A ruling or determination letter recognizing exemption will not ordinarily be issued if an issue involving the organization's exempt status under section 501 or 521 of the Code is pending in litigation or on appeal within the Service.

(2) *Processing applications.*—(i) Under the general procedures outlined in paragraphs (a) through (m) of this section, key district directors are authorized to issue determination letters involving applications for exemption under sections 501 and 521 of the Code, and requests for foundation status under sections 509 and 4942(j)(3).

(ii) A key district director will refer to the National Office those applications that present questions the answers to which are not specifically covered by statute, Treasury decision or regulation, or by a ruling, opinion, or court decision published in the Internal Revenue Bulletin. The National Office will consider each such application, issue a ruling directly to the organization, and send a copy of the ruling to the key district director. Where the issue of exemption under section 501(c)(3) of the Code is referred to the National Office for decision under this subparagraph, the foundation status issue will also be the subject of a National Office ruling. In the event of a conclusion unfavorable to the applicant, it will be informed of the basis for the conclusion and of its rights to file a protest and to a conference in the National Office. If a conference is requested, the conference procedures set forth in subparagraph (9)(v) of this paragraph will be followed. After reconsideration of the application in the light of the protest and any information developed in conference, the National Office will affirm, modify, or reverse the original conclusion, issue a ruling to the organization, and send a copy of the ruling to the key district director.

(iii) Key district directors will issue determination letters on foundation status. All adverse determinations issued by key district directors (including adverse determinations on the foundation status under section 509(a) of the Code of nonexempt charitable trusts described in section 4947(a)(1)) are subject to the protest and conference procedures outlined in subparagraph (5) of this paragraph. Key district directors will issue such determinations in response to applications for recognition of exempt status under section 501(c)(3). They will also issue such determinations in response to requests for determination of foundation status by organizations presumed to be private foundations under section 508(b), requests for new determinations of foundation status by organizations previously classified as other than private foundations, and, subject to the conditions set forth in subdivision (vi) of subparagraph (6) of this paragraph, requests to reconsider status. The requests described in the preceding sentence must be made in writing. For information relating to the circumstances under which an organization presumed to be a private foundation under section 508(b) may request a determination of its status as other than a private foundation, see Revenue Ruling 73-504, 1973-2 C.B. 190. All requests for determinations referred to in this paragraph should be made to the key district director for the district in which the principal place of business or principal office of the organization is located.

(iv) If the exemption application or request for foundation status involves an issue which is not covered by published precedent or on which there may be nonuniformity between districts, or if the National Office had issued a previous contrary ruling or technical advice on the issue, the key district director must request technical advice from the National Office. If, during the consideration of its

application or request by a key district director, the organization believes that the case involves an issue with respect to which referral for technical advice is appropriate, the organization may ask the district director to request technical advice from the National Office. The district director shall advise the organization of its right to request referral of the issue to the National Office for technical advice. The technical advice provisions applicable to these cases are set forth in subparagraph (9) of this paragraph. The effect on an organization's appeal rights of technical advice or a National Office ruling issued under this subparagraph are set forth in § 601.106(a)(1)(iv) (*a*) and in subparagraph (5)(i) of this paragraph.

(3) *Effect of exemption rulings or determination letters.*—(i) A ruling or determination letter recognizing exemption is usually effective as of the date of formation of an organization, if its purposes and activities during the period prior to the date of the ruling or determination letter were consistent with the requirements for exemption. However, with respect to organizations formed after October 9, 1969, applying for recognition of exemption under section 501(c)(3) of the Code, the provisions of section 508(a) apply. If the organization is required to alter its activities or make substantive amendments to its enabling instrument, the ruling or determination letter recognizing its exemption will be effective as of the date specified therein.

(ii) A ruling or determination letter recognizing exemption may not be relied upon if there is a material change inconsistent with exemption in the character, the purpose, or the method of operation of the organization.

(iii)(*a*) When an organization that has been listed in IRS Publication No. 78, "Cumulative List of Organizations described in Section 170(c) of the Internal Revenue Code of 1954," as an organization contributions to which are deductible under section 170 of the Code subsequently ceases to qualify as such, and the ruling or determination letter issued to it is revoked, contributions made to the organization by persons unaware of the change in the status of the organization generally will be considered allowable until (*1*) the date of publication of an announcement in the Internal Revenue Bulletin that contributions are no longer deductible, or (*2*) a date specified in such an announcement where deductibility is terminated as of a different date.

(*b*) In appropriate cases, however, this advance assurance of deductibility of contributions made to such an organization may be suspended pending verification of continuing qualification under section 170 of the Code. Notice of such suspension will be made in a public announcement by the Service. In such cases allowance of deductions for contributions made after the date of the announcement will depend upon statutory qualification of the organization under section 170.

(*c*) If an organization, whose status under Section 170(c)(2) of the Code is revoked, initiates within the statutory time limit a proceeding for declaratory judgment under section 7428, special reliance provisions apply. If the decision of the court is adverse to the organization, it shall nevertheless be treated as having been described in section 170(c)(2) for purposes of deductibility of contributions from other organizations described in section 170(c)(2) and individuals (up to a maximum of $1,000), for the period beginning on the date that notice of revocation was published and ending on the date the court first determines that the organization is not described in section 170(c)(2).

(*d*) In any event, the Service is not precluded from disallowing any contributions made after an organization ceases to qualify under section 170 of the Code where the contributor (*1*) had knowledge of the revocation of the ruling or determination letter, (*2*) was aware that such revocation was imminent, or (*3*) was in part responsible for, or was aware of, the activities or deficiencies on the part of the organization which gave rise to the loss of qualification.

(4) *National Office review of determination letters.*—The National Office will review determination letters on exemption issued under sections 501 and 521 of the Code and foundation status under sections 509(a) and 4942(j)(3) to assure uniformity in the application of the established principles and precedents of the Service. Where the National Office takes exception to a determination letter the key district director will be advised. If the organization protests the exception taken, the file and protest will be returned to the National Office. The referral will be treated as a request for technical advice and the procedures of subparagraph (9) of this paragraph will be followed.

(5) *Protest of adverse determination letters.*—(i) Upon the issuance of an adverse determination letter, the key district director will advise the organization of its right to protest the determination by requesting Appeals office consideration. However, if the determination was made on the basis of National Office technical advice the organization may not appeal the determination to the Appeals office.

See § 601.106(a)(1)(iv)(*a*). To request Appeals consideration, the organization shall submit to the key district director, within 30 days from the date of the letter, a statement of the facts, law, and arguments in support of its position. The organization must also state whether it wishes an Appeals office conference. Upon receipt of an organization's request for Appeals consideration, the key district director will, if it maintains its position, forward the request and the case file to the Appeals office.

(ii) Except as provided in subdivisions (iii) and (iv) of this subparagraph, the Appeals office, after considering the organization's protest and any additional information developed, will advise the organization of its decision and issue an appropriate determination letter. Organizations should make full presentation of the facts, circumstances, and arguments at the initial level of consideration, since submission of additional facts, circumstances, and arguments at the Appeals office may result in suspension of Appeals procedures and referral of the case back to the key district for additional consideration.

(iii) If the proposed disposition by the Appeals office is contrary to a National Office technical advice or ruling concerning tax exemption, issued prior to the case, the proposed disposition will be submitted, through the Office of the Regional Director of Appeals, to the Assistant Commissioner (Employee Plans and Exempt Organizations) or, in a section 521 case, to the Assistant Commissioner (Technical). The decision of the Assistant Commissioner will be followed by the Appeals office. See § 601.106(a)(1)(iv)(*b*).

(iv) If the case involves an issue that is not covered by published precedent or on which there may be nonuniformity between regions, and on which the National Office has not previously ruled, the Appeals office must request technical advice from the National Office. If, during the consideration of its case by Appeals, the organization believes that the case involves an issue with respect to which referral for technical advice is appropriate, the organization may ask the Appeals office to request technical advice from the National Office. The Appeals office shall advise the organization of its right to request referral of the issue to the National Office for technical advice. If the Appeals office requests technical advice, the decision of the Assistant Commissioner (Employee Plans and Exempt Organizations) or, in a section 521 case, the decision of the Assistant Commissioner (Technical), in a technical advice memorandum is final and the Appeals office must dispose of the case in accordance with that decision. See subparagraph (9)(viii)(*a*) of this paragraph.

(6) *Revocation or modification of rulings or determination letters on exemption and foundation status.*—(i) An exemption ruling or determination letter may be revoked or modified by a ruling or determination letter addressed to the organization, or by a revenue ruling or other statement published in the Internal Revenue Bulletin. The revocation or modification may be retroactive if the organization omitted or misstated a material fact, operated in a manner materially different from that originally represented, or engaged in a prohibited transaction of the type described in subdivision (vii) of this subparagraph. In any event, revocation or modification will ordinarily take effect no later than the time at which the organization received written notice that its exemption ruling or determination letter might be revoked or modified.

(ii)(*a*) If a key district director concludes as a result of examining an information return, or considering information from any other source, that an exemption ruling or determination letter should be revoked or modified, the organization will be advised in writing of the proposed action and the reasons therefor. If the case involves an issue not covered by published precedent or on which there may be nonuniformity between districts, or if the National Office had issued a previous contrary ruling or technical advice on the issue, the district director must seek technical advice from the National Office. If the organization believes that the case involves an issue with respect to which referral for technical advice is appropriate, the organization may ask the district director to request technical advice from the National Office. The district director shall advise the organization of its right to request referral of the issue to the National Office for technical advice.

(*b*) The key district director will advise the organization of its right to protest the proposed revocation or modification by requesting Appeals office consideration. However, if National Office technical advice was furnished concerning revocation or modification under (*a*) of this subdivision, the decision of the Assistant Commissioner in the technical advice memorandum is final and the organization has no right of appeal to the Appeals office. See § 601.106(a)(1)(iv)(*a*). To request Appeals consideration, the organization must submit to the key district director, within 30 days from the date of the letter, a statement of the facts, law, and arguments in support of its continued exemption. The organization must also state whether it wishes an Appeals office conference. Upon receipt of an organization's request for Appeals consideration, the key district office, will, if it maintains its position, forward the request and the case file to the Appeals office.

(*c*) Except as provided in (*d*) and (*e*) of this subdivision, the Appeals office, after considering the organization's protest and any additional information developed, will advise the organization of its decision and issue an appropriate determination letter. Organizations should make full presentation of the facts, circumstances, and arguments at the initial level of consideration, since submission of additional facts, circumstances, and arguments at the Appeals office may result in suspension of Appeals procedures and referral of the case back to the key district for additional consideration.

(*d*) If the proposed disposition by the Appeals office is contrary to a National Office technical advice or ruling concerning tax exemption, issued prior to the case, the proposed disposition will be submitted, through the Office of the Regional Director of Appeals, to the Assistant Commissioner (Employee Plans and Exempt Organizations) or, in a section 521 case, to the Assistant Commissioner (Technical). The decision of the Assistant Commissioner will be followed by the Appeals office. See § 601.106(a)(1)(iv)(*b*).

(*e*) If the case involves an issue that is not covered by published precedent or on which there may be nonuniformity between regions, and on which the National Office has not previously ruled, the Appeals office must request technical advice from the National Office. If the organization believes that the case involves an issue with respect to which referral for technical advice is appropriate, the organization may ask the Appeals office to request technical advice from the National Office. The Appeals office shall advise the organization of its right to request referral of the issue to the National Office for technical advice.

(iii) A ruling or determination letter respecting private foundation or operating foundation status may be revoked or modified by a ruling or determination letter addressed to the organization, or by a revenue ruling or other statement published in the Internal Revenue Bulletin. If a key district director concludes, as a result of examining an information return or considering information from any other source, that a ruling or determination letter concerning private foundation status (including foundation status under section 509(a)(3) of the Code of a nonexempt charitable trust described in section 4947(a)(1)) or operating foundation status should be modified or revoked, the procedures in subdivision (iv) or (v) of this subparagraph should be followed depending on whether the revocation or modification is adverse or non-adverse to the affected organization. Where there is a proposal by the Service to change foundation status classification from one particular paragraph of section 509(a) to another paragraph of that section, the procedures described in subdivision (iv) of this subparagraph will be followed to modify the ruling or determination letter.

(iv) If a key district director concludes that a ruling or determination letter concerning private foundation or operating foundation status should be revoked or modified, the organization will be advised in writing of the proposed adverse action, the reasons therefor, and the proposed new determination of foundation status. The procedures set forth in subdivision (ii) of this subparagraph apply to a proposed revocation or modification under this subdivision. Unless the effective date of revocation or modification of a ruling or determination letter concerning private foundation or operating foundation status is expressly covered by statute or regulations, the effective date generally is the same as the effective date of revocation or modification of exemption rulings or determination letters as provided in subdivision (i) of this subparagraph.

(v) If the key district director concludes that a ruling or determination letter concerning private foundation or operating foundation status should be revoked or modified and that such revocation or modification will not be adverse to the organization, the key district director will issue a determination letter revoking or modifying foundation status. The determination letter will also serve to notify the organization of its foundation status as redetermined. A nonadverse revocation or modification as to private foundation or operating foundation status will ordinarily be retroactive if the initial ruling or determination letter was incorrect.

(vi) In cases where an organization believes that it received an incorrect ruling or determination letter as to its private foundation or operating foundation status, the organization may request a key district director to reconsider such ruling or determination letter. Except in rare circumstances, the key district director will only consider such requests where the organization had not exercised any protest or conference rights with respect to the issuance of such ruling or determination letter. If a key district director decides that reconsideration is warranted, the request will be treated as an initial request for a determination of foundation status, and the key district director will issue a determination on foundation status or operating foundation status under the procedures of subparagraph (2) of this paragraph. If a nonadverse determination is issued, it will also inform the organization that the prior ruling or determination letter is revoked or modified. Adverse determinations are subject to the procedures set out in subparagraph (5) of this paragraph. If the key district director decides that reconsideration is not warranted, the organization will be notified accordingly. The organization does not have a right to protest the key district director's decision not to reconsider.

(vii) If it is concluded that an organization that is subject to the provisions of section 503 of the Code entered into a prohibited transaction for the purpose of diverting corpus or income from its exempt purpose, and if the transaction involved a substantial part of the corpus or income of the organization, its exemption is revoked effective as of the beginning of the taxable year during which the prohibited transaction was commenced.

(viii) The provisions of this subparagraph relating to protests, conferences, and the rights of organizations to ask that technical advice be requested before a revocation (or modification) notice is issued are not applicable to matters where delay would be prejudicial to the interests of the Internal Revenue Service (such as in cases involving fraud, jeopardy, the imminence of the expiration of the period of limitations, or where immediate action is necessary to protect the interests of the Government).

(7) *Declaratory judgments relating to status and classification of organizations under section 501(c)(3) of the Code.*—(i) An organization seeking recognition of exempt status under section 501(c)(3) of the Code must follow the procedures of subparagraph (1) of this paragraph regarding the filing of Form 1023, Application for Recognition of Exemption. The 270-day period referred to in section 7428(b)(2) will be considered by the Service to begin on the date a substantially completed Form 1023 is sent to the appropriate key district director. A substantially completed Form 1023 is one that:

(a) Is signed by an authorized individual;

(b) Includes an Employer Identification Number (EIN) or a completed Form SS-4, Application for Employer Identification Number;

(c) Includes a statement of receipts and expenditures and a balance sheet for the current year and the three preceding years or the years the organization was in existence, if less than four years (if the organization has not yet commenced operations, a proposed budget for two full accounting periods and a current statement of assets and liabilities will be acceptable);

(d) Includes a statement of proposed activities and a description of anticipated receipts and contemplated expenditures;

(e) Includes a copy of the organizing or enabling document that is signed by a principal officer or is accompanied by a written declaration signed by an officer authorized to sign for the organization certifying that the document is a complete and accurate copy of the original; and

(f) If the organization is a corporation or unincorporated association and it has adopted bylaws, includes a copy that is signed or otherwise verified as current by an authorized officer.

If an application does not contain all of the above items, it will not be further processed and may be returned to the applicant for completion. The 270-day period will not be considered as starting until the date the application is remailed to the Service with the requested information, or, if a postmark is not evident, on the date the Service receives a substantially completed application.

(ii) Generally, rulings and determination letters in cases subject to declaratory judgment are issued under the procedures outlined in this paragraph. In National Office exemption application cases, proposed adverse rulings will be issued by the rulings sections in the Exempt Organizations Technical Branch. Applicants shall appeal these proposed adverse rulings to the Conference and Review Staff of the Exempt Organizations Technical Branch. In those cases where an organization is unable to describe fully its purposes and activities (see subparagraph (1)(ii) of this paragraph), a refusal to rule will be considered an adverse determination for which administrative appeal rights will be afforded. Any oral representation of additional facts or modification of the facts as represented or alleged in the application for a ruling or determination letter must be reduced to writing.

(iii) If an organization withdraws in writing its request for a ruling or determination letter, the withdrawal will not be considered by the Service as either a failure to make a determination within the meaning of section 7428(a)(2) of the Code or as an exhaustion of administrative remedies within the meaning of section 7428(b)(2).

(iv) Section 7428(b)(2) of the Code requires that an organization must exhaust its administrative remedies by taking timely, reasonable steps to secure a determination. Those steps and administrative remedies that must be exhausted within the Internal Revenue Service are:

(a) The filing of a substantially completed application Form 1023 pursuant to subdivision (i) of this subparagraph, or the filing of a request for a determination of foundation status pursuant to subparagraph (2) of this paragraph;

(b) The timely submission of all additional information requested to perfect an exemption application or request for determination of private foundation status; and

(c) Exhaustion of all administrative appeals available within the Service pursuant to subparagraphs (5) and (6) of this paragraph, as well as appeal of a proposed adverse ruling to the Conference and Review Staff of the Exempt Organizations Technical Branch in National Office original jurisdiction exemption application cases.

(v) An organization will in no event be deemed to have exhausted its administrative remedies prior to the completion of the steps described in subdivision (iv) of this subparagraph and the earlier of:

(a) The sending by certified or registered mail of a notice of final determination; or

(b) The expiration of the 270-day period described in section 7428(b)(2) of the Code, in a case in which the Service has not issued a notice of final determination and the organization has taken, in a timely manner, all reasonable steps to secure a ruling or determination.

(vi) The steps described in subdivision (iv) of this subparagraph will not be considered completed until the Internal Revenue Service has had a reasonable time to act upon the appeal or request for consideration, as the case may be.

(vii) A notice of final determination to which section 7428 of the Code applies is a ruling or determination letter, sent by certified or registered mail, which holds that the organization is not described in section 501(c)(3) or section 170(c)(2), is a private foundation as defined in section 509(a), or is not a private operating foundation as defined in section 4942(j)(3).

(8) *Group exemption letters.*—(i) *General.*—(a) A group exemption letter is a ruling issued to a central organization recognizing on a group basis the exemption under section 501(c) of the Code of subordinate organizations on whose behalf the central organization has applied for exemption in accordance with this subparagraph.

(b) A central organization is an organization which has one or more subordinates under its general supervision or control.

(c) A subordinate is a chapter, local, post, or unit of a central organization. It may or may not be incorporated. A central organization may be a subordinate itself, such as a state organization which has subordinate units and is itself affiliated with a national organization.

(d) A subordinate included in a group exemption letter should not apply separately for an exemption letter, unless it no longer wants to be included in the group exemption letter.

(e) A subordinate described in section 501(c)(3) of the Code may not be included in a group exemption letter if it is a private foundation as defined in section 509(a) of the Code. Such an organization should apply separately for exempt status under the procedures outlined in subparagraph (1) of this paragraph.

(ii) *Requirements for inclusion in a group exemption letter.*—(a) A central organization applying for a group exemption letter must establish its own exempt status.

(b) It must also establish that the subordinates to be included in the group exemption letter are:

(1) Affiliated with it;

(2) Subject to its general supervision or control;

(3) Exempt under the same paragraph of section 501(c) of the Code, though not necessarily the paragraph under which the central organization is exempt; and

(4) Not private foundations if application for a group exemption letter involves section 501(c)(3) of the Code.

(c) Each subordinate must authorize the central organization to include it in the application for the group exemption letter. The authorization must be signed by a duly authorized officer of the subordinate and retained by the central organization while the group exemption letter is in effect.

(iii) *Filing application for a group exemption letter.*—(a) A central organization seeking a group exemption letter for its subordinates must obtain recognition of its own exemption by filing an application with the District Director of Internal Revenue for the district in which is located the principal place of business or the principal office of the organization. For the form of organization see section 1.501(a)-1 of the Income Tax Regulations. Any application received by the National Office or by a district director other than as provided above will be forwarded, without any action thereon, to the appropriate district director.

(b) If the central organization has previously established its own exemption, it must indicate its employer identification number, the date of the exemption letter, and the Internal Revenue Office that issued it. It need not resubmit documents already submitted. However, if it has not already done so, it must submit a copy of any amendments to its governing instruments or internal regulations as well as any information regarding any change in its character, purposes, or method of operation.

(c) In addition to the information required to establish its own exemption, the central organization must submit to the district director the following information, in duplicate, on behalf of those subordinates to be included in the group exemption letter:

(1) A letter signed by a principal officer of the central organization setting forth or including as attachments;

(i) Information verifying the existence of the relationships required by subdivision (ii)(b) of this subparagraph;

(ii) A description of the principal purposes and activities of the subordinates;

(iii) A sample copy of a uniform governing instrument (charter, trust indenture, articles of association, etc.), if such an instrument has been adopted by the subordinates; or, in the absence of a uniform governing instrument, copies of representative instruments;

(iv) An affirmation to the effect that, to the best of his knowledge, the subordinates are operating in accordance with the stated purposes;

(v) A statement that each subordinate to be included in the group exemption letter has furnished written authorization to the central organization as described in subdivision (ii)(c) of this subparagraph; and

(vi) A list of subordinates to be included in the group exemption letter to which the Service has issued an outstanding ruling or determination letter relating to exemption.

(vii) If the application for a group exemption letter involves section 501(c)(3) of the Code, an affirmation to the effect that, to the best of his knowledge and belief, no subordinate to be included in the group exemption letter is a private foundation as defined in section 509(a) of the Code.

(2) A list of the names, mailing addresses (including Postal ZIP Codes), and employer identification numbers (if required for group exemption letter purposes by (e) of this subdivision) of subordinates to be included in the group exemption letter. A current directory of subordinates may be furnished in lieu of the list if it includes the required information and if the subordinates not to be included in the group exemption letter are identified.

(d) If the central organization does not have an employer identification number, it must submit a completed Form SS-4, Application for Employer Identification Number, with its exemption application. See Rev. Rul. 63-247, C.B. 1963-2, 612.

(e) Each subordinate required to file an annual information return, Form 990 or 990-A, must have its own employer identification number, even if it has no employees. The central organization must submit with the exemption application a completed Form SS-4 on behalf of each subordinate not having a number. Although subordinates not required to file annual information returns, Form 990 or 990-A, need not have employer identification numbers for group exemption letter purposes, they may need such numbers for other purposes.

(iv) *Information required annually to maintain a group exemption letter.*—(a) The central organization must submit annually within 45 days after the close of its annual accounting period the information set out below to the Philadelphia Service Center, 11601 Roosevelt Boulevard, Philadelphia, Pennsylvania 19155, Attention: EO:R Branch:

(1) Information regarding all changes in the purposes, character, or method of operation of subordinates included in the group exemption letter.

(2) Lists of (i) subordinates which have changed their names or addresses during the year, (ii) subordinates no longer to be included in the group exemption letter because they have ceased to exist, disaffiliated, or withdrawn the authorization to the central organization, and (iii) subordinates to be added to the group exemption letter because they are newly organized or affiliated or they have newly authorized the central organization to include them. A separate list must be submitted for each of the three categories set out above. Each list must show the names, mailing addresses (including Postal ZIP Codes), and employer identification numbers of the affected subordinates. An annotated directory of subordinates will not be acceptable for this purpose. If there were none of the above changes, the central organization must submit a statement to that effect.

(3) The information required by subdivision (iii)(c)(1) of this subparagraph, with respect to subordinates to be added to the group exemption letter. However, if the information upon which the group exemption letter was based is applicable in all material respects to such subordinates, a statement to this effect may be submitted in lieu of the information required by subdivision (iii)(c)(1)(i) through (v) of this subparagraph.

(b) Submission of the information required by this subdivision does not relieve the central organization or any of its subordinates of the duty to submit such additional information as a key district director may require to enable him to determine whether the conditions for continued exemption are being met. See sections 6001 and 6033 of the Code and the regulations thereunder.

(v) *Termination of a group exemption letter.*—(a) Termination of a group exemption letter will result in non-recognition of the exempt status of all included subordinates. To reestablish an exempt status in such cases, each subordinate must file an exemption application under the procedures outlined in subparagraph (1) of this paragraph, or a new group exemption letter must be applied for under this subparagraph.

(b) If a central organization dissolves or ceases to exist, the group exemption letter will be terminated, notwithstanding that the subordinates continue to exist and operate independently.

(c) Failure of the central organization to submit the information required by subdivision (iv) of this subparagraph, or to file a required information return, Form 990 or 990-A, or to otherwise comply with section 6001 or 6033 of the Code and the regulations thereunder, may result in termination of the group exemption letter on the grounds that the conditions required for the continuance of the group exemption letter have not been met. See Rev. Rul. 59-95, C.B. 1959-1, 627.

(d) The dissolution of a subordinate included in a group exemption letter will not affect the exempt status of the other included subordinates.

(e) If a subordinate covered by a group exemption letter fails to comply with section 6001 or 6033 of the Code and the regulations thereunder (for example, by failing to file a required information return) and the Service terminates its recognition of the subordinate's status, a copy of the termination letter to the subordinate will be furnished to the central organization. The group exemption letter will no longer be applicable to such subordinate, but will otherwise remain in effect. (It should be noted that if Form 990 is required to be filed, failure to file such return on time may also result in the imposition of a penalty of $10 for each day the return is late, up to a maximum of $5,000. See section 6652 of the Code and the regulations thereunder.)

(vi) *Revocation of a group exemption letter.*—(a) If the Service determines, under the procedures described in subparagraph (6) of this paragraph, that a central organization no longer qualifies for exemption under section 501(c) of the Code, the group exemption letter will be revoked. The revocation will result in nonrecognition of the exempt status of all included subordinates. To reestablish an exempt status in such cases, each subordinate must file an exemption application under the procedures outlined in subparagraph (1) of this paragraph or a new group exemption letter must be applied for under this subparagraph.

(b) If the Service determines, under the procedures described in subparagraph (6) of this paragraph, that a subordinate included in a group exemption letter no longer qualifies for exemption under section 501(c) of the Code, the central organization and the subordinate will be notified accordingly, and the group exemption letter will no longer apply to such subordinate, but will otherwise remain in effect.

(c) Where a subordinate organization has been disqualified for inclusion in a group exemption letter as described in (b) of this subdivision, and thereafter wishes to reestablish its exempt status, the central organization should, at the time it submits the information required by subdivision (iv) of this subparagraph, submit detailed information relating to the subordinate's qualification for reinclusion in the group exemption letter.

(vii) *Instrumentalities or agencies of political subdivisions.*—An instrumentality or agency of a political subdivision that exercises control or supervision over a number of organizations similar in purposes and operations, each of which may qualify for exemption under the same paragraph of section 501(c) of the Code, may obtain a group exemption letter covering those organizations in the same manner as a central organization. However, the instrumentality or agency must furnish evidence that it is a qualified governmental agency. Examples of organizations over which governmental agencies exercise control or supervision are Federal credit unions, State chartered credit unions, and Federal land bank associations.

(viii) *Listing in cumulative list of organizations to which charitable contributions are deductible.*—If a central organization to which a group exemption letter has been issued is eligible to receive deductible charitable contributions as provided in section 170 of the Code, it will be listed in Publication No. 78, Cumulative List—Organizations Described in Section 170(c) of the Internal Revenue Code of 1954. The names of the subordinates covered by the group exemption letter will not be listed individually. However, the identification of the central organization will indicate whether contributions to its subordinates are also deductible.

(9) *Technical advice from the National Office.*—(i) *Definition and nature of technical advice.*—(a) As used in this subparagraph, "technical advice" means advice or guidance as to the interpretation and proper application of internal revenue laws, related statutes, and regulations, to a specific set of facts, in Employee Plans and Exempt

Organization matters, furnished by the National Office upon request of a key district office or Appeals office in connection with the processing and consideration of a nondocketed case. It is furnished as a means of assisting Service personnel in closing cases and establishing and maintaining consistent holdings. It does not include memorandums on matters of general technical application furnished to key district offices or to Appeals offices where the issues are not raised in connection with the consideration and handling of a specific case.

(b) The provisions of this subparagraph only apply to Employee Plans and Exempt Organization cases being considered by a key district director or Appeals office. They do not apply to any other case under the jurisdiction of a district director or Appeals office or to a case under the jurisdiction of the Bureau of Alcohol, Tobacco, and Firearms. The technical advice provisions applicable to cases under the jurisdiction of a district director, other than Employee Plans and Exempt Organization cases, are set forth in § 601.105(b)(5). The technical advice provisions applicable to cases under the jurisdiction of an Appeals office, other than Employee Plans and Exempt Organization cases are set forth in § 601.106(f)(10).

(c) A key district director or an Appeals office may, under this subparagraph, request technical advice with respect to the consideration of a request for a determination letter. If the case involves certain Exempt Organization issues that are not covered by published precedent or on which there may be nonuniformity, requesting technical advice is mandatory rather than discretionary. See subparagraphs (2)(iv) and (5)(iii) of this paragraph.

(d) If a key district director is of the opinion that a National Office ruling letter or technical advice previously issued should be modified or revoked and it requests the National Office to reconsider the ruling or technical advice, the reference of the matter to the National Office is treated as a request for technical advice. The procedures specified in subdivision (iii) of this subparagraph should be followed in order that the National Office may consider the recommendation. Only the National Office can revoke a National Office ruling letter or technical advice. Before referral to the National Office, the key district director should inform the plan/organization of its opinion that the ruling letter or technical advice should be revoked. The key district director, after development of the facts and consideration of the arguments, will decide whether to recommend revocation of the ruling or technical advice to the National Office.

(e) The Assistant Commissioner (Employee Plans and Exempt Organizations) and, in section 521 cases, the Assistant Commissioner (Technical), acting under a delegation of authority from the Commissioner of Internal Revenue, are exclusively responsible for providing technical advice in any issue involving the establishment of basic principles and rules for the uniform interpretation and application of tax laws in cases under this subparagraph. This authority has been largely redelegated to subordinate officials.

(ii) *Areas in which technical advice may be requested.*—(a) Key district directors and Appeals offices may request technical advice on any technical or procedural question that develops during the processing and consideration of a case. These procedures are applicable as provided in subdivision (i) of this subparagraph.

(b) Key district directors and Appeals offices are encouraged to request technical advice on any technical or procedural question arising in connection with any case described in subdivision (i) of this subparagraph which cannot be resolved on the basis of law, regulations, or a clearly applicable revenue ruling or other precedent issued by the National Office. However, in Exempt Organization cases concerning qualification for exemption or foundation status, key district directors and Appeals offices must request technical advice on any issue that is not covered by published precedent or on which nonuniformity may exist. Requests for technical advice should be made at the earliest possible stage of the proceedings.

(iii) *Requesting technical advice.*—(a) It is the responsibility of the key district office or the Appeals office to determine whether technical advice is to be requested on any issue before that office. However, while the case is under the jurisdiction of the key district director or the Appeals office, an employee plan/organization or its representative may request that an issue be referred to the National Office for technical advice on the grounds that a lack of uniformity exists as to the disposition of the issue, or that the issue is so unusual or complex as to warrant consideration by the National Office. This request should be made at the earliest possible stage of the proceedings. While plans/organizations are encouraged to make written requests setting forth the facts, law, and argument with respect to the issue, and reason for requesting National Office advice, a plan/organization may make the request orally. If, after considering the plan's/organization's request, the examiner or the Appeals Officer is of the opinion that the circumstances do not warrant referral of the case to the National Office, he/she will so advise the plan/organization. (See subdivision (iv) of this subparagraph for a plan's/organiza-

tion's appeal rights where the examiner or Appeal Officer declines to request technical advice.)

(b) When technical advice is to be requested, whether or not upon the request of the plan/organization, the plan/organization will be so advised, except as noted in (j) of this subdivision. If the key district office or the Appeals office initiates the action, the plan/organization will be furnished a copy of the statement of the pertinent facts and the question or questions proposed for submission to the National Office. The request for advice should be so worded as to avoid possible misunderstanding, in the National Office, of the facts or of the specific point or points at issue.

(c) After receipt of the statement of facts and specific questions, the plan/organization will be given 10 calendar days in which to indicate in writing the extent, if any, to which it may not be in complete agreement. An extension of time must be justified by the plan/organization in writing and approved by the Chief, Employee Plans and Exempt Organizations Division (in the district office) or the Chief, Appeals Office, as the case may be. Every effort should be made to reach agreement as to the facts and specific points at issue. If agreement cannot be reached, the plan/organization may submit, within 10 calendar days after receipt of notice from the key district director or the Appeals office, a statement of its understanding as to the specific point or points at issue which will be forwarded to the National Office with the request for advice. An extension of time must be justified by the plan/organization in writing and approved by the Chief, Employee Plans and Exempt Organizations Division or the Chief, Appeals Office.

(d) If the plan/organization initiates the action to request advice, and its statement of the facts and point or points at issue are not wholly acceptable to the key district office or the Appeals office, the plan/organization will be advised in writing as to the areas of disagreement. The plan/organization will be given 10 calendar days after receipt of the written notice to reply to such notice. An extension of time must be justified by the plan/organization in writing and approved by the Chief, Employee Plans and Exempt Organizations Division or the Chief, Appeals Office. If agreement cannot be reached, both the statements of the plan/organization and the key district office or the Appeals office will be forwarded to the National Office.

(e)(1) In the case of requests for technical advice subject to the disclosure provisions of section 6110 of the Code, the plan/organization must also submit, within the 10-day period referred to in (c) and (d) of this subdivision, whichever applicable (relating to agreement by the plan/organization with the statement of facts and points submitted in connection with the request for technical advice) the statement described in (f) of this subdivision of proposed deletions pursuant to section 6110(c) of the Code. If the statement is not submitted, the plan/organization will be informed by the key district director or the Appeals office that the statement is required. If the key district director or the Appeals office does not receive the statement within 10 days after the plan/organization has been informed of the need for the statement, the key district director or the Appeals office may decline to submit the request for technical advice. If the key district director or the Appeals office decides to request technical advice in a case where the plan/organization has not submitted the statement of proposed deletions, the National Office will make those deletions which in the judgment of the Commissioner are required by section 6110(c) of the Code.

(2) The requirements included in this subparagraph, relating to the submission of statements and other material with respect to proposed deletions to be made from technical advise memoranda before public inspection is permitted to take place, do not apply to requests made by the key district director before November 1, 1976, or requests for any document to which section 6104 of the Code applies.

(f) In order to assist the Internal Revenue Service in making the deletions, required by section 6110(c) of the Code, from the text of technical advice memoranda which are open to public inspection pursuant to section 6110(a) of the Code, there must accompany requests for such technical advice either a statement of the deletions proposed by the plan/organization, or a statement that no information other than names, addresses, and identifying numbers need be deleted. Such statements shall be made in a separate document. The statement of proposed deletions shall be accompanied by a copy of all statements of facts and supporting documents which are submitted to the National Office pursuant to (c) or (d) of this subdivision, on which shall be indicated, by the use of brackets, the material which the plan/organization indicates should be deleted pursuant to section 6110(c) of the Code. The statement of proposed deletions shall indicate the statutory basis for each proposed deletion. The statement of proposed deletions shall not appear or be referred to anywhere in the request for technical advice. If the plan/organization decides to request additional deletions pursuant to section 6110(c) of the Code prior to the time the National Office replies to the request for technical advice, additional statements may be submitted.

(g) If the plan/organization has not already done so, it may submit a statement explaining its position on the issues, citing precedents which it believes will bear on the case. This statement will be forwarded to the National Office with the request for advice. If it is received at a later date, it will be forwarded for association with the case file.

(h) At the time the plan/organization is informed that the matter is being referred to the National Office, it will also be informed of the right to a conference in the National Office in the event an adverse decision is indicated, and will be asked to indicate whether a conference is desired.

(i) Generally, prior to replying to the request for technical advice, the National Office shall inform the plan/organization orally or in writing of the material likely to appear in the technical advice memorandum which the plan/organization proposed be deleted but which the Internal Revenue Service determined should not be deleted. If so informed, the plan/organization may submit within 10 days any further information, arguments, or other material in support of the position that such material be deleted. The Internal Revenue Service will attempt, if feasible, to resolve all disagreements with respect to proposed deletions prior to the time the National Office replies to the request for technical advice. However, in no event shall the plan/organization have the right to a conference with respect to resolution of any disagreements concerning material to be deleted from the text of the technical advice memorandum, but such matters may be considered at any conference otherwise scheduled with respect to the request.

(j) The provisions of (a) through (i) of this subdivision, relating to the referral of issues upon request of the plan/organization, advising plans/organizations of the referral of issues, the submission of proposed deletions, and the granting of conferences in the National Office, are not applicable to technical advice memoranda described in section 6110(g)(5)(A) of the Code, relating to cases involving criminal or civil fraud investigations and jeopardy or termination assessments. However, in such cases the plan/organization shall be allowed to provide the statement of proposed deletions to the National Office upon the completion of all proceedings with respect to the investigations or assessments, but prior to the date on which the Commissioner mails the notice pursuant to section 6110(f)(1) of the Code of intention to disclose the technical advice memorandum.

(k) Form 4463, Request for Technical Advice, should be used for transmitting requests for technical advice to the National Office.

(iv) *Appeal by plans/organizations of determinations not to seek technical advice.*—(a) If the plan/organization has requested referral of an issue before a key district office or an Appeals office to the National Office for technical advice, and after consideration of the request the examiner or the Appeals Officer is of the opinion that the circumstances do not warrant such referral, he/she will so advise the plan/organization.

(b) The plan/organization may appeal the decision of the examiner or the Appeals Officer not to request technical advice by submitting to the relevant official, within 10 calendar days after being advised of the decision, a statement of the facts, law, and arguments with respect to the issue, and the reasons why the plan/organization believes the matter should be referred to the National Office for advice. An extension of time must be justified by the plan/organization in writing and approved by the Chief, Employee Plans and Exempt Organizations Division of the Chief, Appeals Office.

(c) The examiner or the Appeals Officer will submit the statement of the plan/organization to the Chief, Employee Plans and Exempt Organizations Division or the Chief, Appeals Office, accompanied by a statement of the official's reasons why the issue should not be referred to the National Office. The Chief will determine, on the basis of the statements submitted, whether technical advice will be requested. If the Chief determines that technical advice is not warranted, that official will inform the plan/organization in writing that he/she proposes to deny the request. In the letter to the plan/organization the Chief will (except in unusual situations where such action would be prejudicial to the best interests of the Government) state specifically the reasons for the proposed denial. The plan/organization will be given 15 calendar days after receipt of the letter in which to notify the Chief whether it agrees with the proposed denial. The plan/organization may not appeal the decision of the Chief, Employee Plans and Exempt Organizations Division, or of the Chief, Appeals Office, not to request technical advice from the National Office. However, if the plan/organization does not agree with the proposed denial, all data relating to the issue for which technical advice has been sought, including the plan's/organization's written request and statements, will be submitted to the National Office, Attention: Director, Exempt Organizations or Employee Plans Division or Actuarial Division or, in a section 521 case, Attention: Director, Corporation Tax Division for review. After review in the

National Office, the submitting office will be notified whether the proposed denial is approved or disapproved.

(d) While the matter is being reviewed in the National Office, the key district office or the Appeals office will suspend action on the issue (except where the delay would prejudice the Government's interests) until it is notified of the National Office decision. This notification will be made within 30 days after receipt of the data in the National Office. The review will be solely on the basis of the written record and no conference will be held in the National Office.

(v) *Conference in the National Office.*—(a) If, after a study of the technical advice request, it appears that advice adverse to the plan/organization should be given and a conference has been requested, the plan/organization will be notified of the time and place of the conference. If conferences are being arranged with respect to more than one request for advice involving the same plan/organization, they will be so scheduled as to cause the least inconvenience to the plan/organization. The conference will be arranged by telephone, if possible, and must be held within 21 calendar days after contact has been made. Extensions of time will be granted only if justified in writing by the plan/organization and approved by the appropriate branch chief.

(b) A plan/organization is entitled, as a matter of right, to only one conference in the National Office unless one of the circumstances discussed in (c) of this subdivision exists. This conference will usually be held at the branch level in the appropriate division in the Office of the Assistant Commissioner (Employee Plans and Exempt Organizations) or, in section 521 cases, in the Office of the Assistant Commissioner (Technical), and will usually be attended by a person who has authority to act for the branch chief. In appropriate cases the examiner or the Appeals Officer may also attend the conference to clarify the facts in the case. If more than one subject is discussed at the conference, the discussion constitutes a conference with respect to each subject. At the request of the plan/organization or its representative, the conference may be held at an earlier stage in the consideration of the case than the Service would ordinarily designate. A plan/organization has no "right" of appeal from an action of a branch to the director of a division or to any other National Office official.

(c) In the process of review of a holding proposed by a branch, it may appear that the final answer will involve a reversal of the branch proposal with a result less favorable to the plan/organization. Or it may appear that an adverse holding proposed by a branch will be approved, but on a new or different issue or on different grounds than those on which the branch decided the case. Under either of these circumstances, the plan/organization or its representative will be invited to another conference. The provisions of this subparagraph limiting the number of conferences to which a plan/organization is entitled will not foreclose inviting the plan/organization to attend further conferences when, in the opinion of National Office personnel, such need arises. All additional conferences of this type discussed are held only at the invitation of the Service.

(d) It is the responsibility of the plan/organization to furnish to the National Office; within 21 calendar days after the conference, a written record of any additional data, line of reasoning, precedents, etc., that were proposed by the plan/organization and discussed at the conference but were not previously or adequately presented in writing. Extensions of time will be granted only if justified in writing by the plan/organization and approved by the appropriate branch chief. Any additional material and a copy thereof should be addressed to and sent to the National Office which will forward the copy to the appropriate key district director or Appeals office. The key district director or the Appeals office will be requested to give the matter prompt attention, will verify the additional facts and data, and will comment on it to the extent deemed appropriate.

(e) A plan/organization or its representative desiring to obtain information as to the status of its case (other than a section 521 case) may do so by contacting the following offices with respect to matters in the areas of their responsibility:

| Official | Telephone Numbers (Area Code 202) |
|---|---|
| Chief, Employee Plans Technical Branch | 566-3871 |
| Chief, Exempt Organizations Technical Branch | 566-3856 or 566-3593 |
| Director, Actuarial Division | 566-4311 |

An organization or its representative desiring to obtain information as to the status of its section 521 case may do so by contacting the Director, Corporation Tax Division (202-566-4504 or 566-4505).

(vi) *Preparation of technical advice memorandum by the National Office.*—(a) Immediately upon receipt in the National Office, the employee to whom the case is assigned will analyze the file to ascertain whether it meets the requirements of subdivision (iii) of this subparagraph. If the case is not complete with respect to any requirement in subdivision (iii)(a) through (d) of this subparagraph, appropriate steps will be taken to complete the file. If any request for technical advice does not comply with the requirements of subdivision (iii)(e) of this subparagraph, if applicable, relating to the statement of proposed deletions, the National Office will make those deletions from the technical advice memorandum which in the judgment of the Commissioner are required by section 6110(c) of the Code.

(b) If the plan/organization has requested a conference in the National Office, the procedures in subdivision (v) of this subparagraph will be followed.

(c) Replies to requests for technical advice will be addressed to the key district director or to the Appeals office and will be drafted in two parts. Each part will identify the plan/organization by name, address, identification number, and year or years involved. The first part (hereafter called the "technical advice memorandum") will contain (1) a recitation of the pertinent facts having a bearing on the issue; (2) a discussion of the facts, precedents, and reasoning of the National Office; and (3) the conclusions of the National Office. The conclusions will give direct answers, whenever possible, to the specific questions of the key district director or the Appeals office. The discussion of the issues will be in such detail that the key district director or the Appeals office is apprised of the reasoning underlying the conclusion. There shall accompany the technical advice memorandum, where applicable, a notice, pursuant to section 6110(f)(1) of the Code, of intention to disclose the technical advice memorandum (including a copy of the version proposed to be open to public inspection and notations of third party communications pursuant to section 6110(d) of the Code) which the key district director or the Appeals office will forward to the plan/organization at such time that it furnishes a copy of the technical advice memorandum to the plan/organization pursuant to (e) of this subdivision and subdivision (vii)(b) of this subparagraph.

(d) The second part of the reply will consist of a transmittal memorandum. In the unusual cases it will serve as a vehicle for providing the key district office or Appeals office administrative information or other information which, under the nondisclosure statutes, or for other reasons, may not be discussed with the plan/organization.

(e) It is the general practice of the Service to furnish a copy of the technical advice memorandum to the plan/organization after it has been adopted by the key district director or the Appeals office. However, in the case of technical advice memoranda described in section 6110(g)(5)(A) of the Code, relating to cases involving criminal or civil fraud investigations and jeopardy or termination assessments, a copy of the technical advice memorandum shall not be furnished the plan/organization until all proceedings with respect to the investigations or assessments are completed.

(f) After receiving the notice, pursuant to section 6110(f)(1) of the Code, of intention to disclose the technical advice memorandum (if applicable), the plan/organization, if desiring to protest the disclosure of certain information in the memorandum, must, within 20 days after the notice is mailed, submit a written statement identifying those deletions not made by the Internal Revenue Service which the plan/organization believes should have been made. The plan/organization shall also submit a copy of the version of the technical advice memorandum proposed to be open to public inspection on which it indicates, by the use of brackets, the deletions proposed by the plan/organization but which have not been made by the Internal Revenue Service. Generally, the Internal Revenue Service will not consider the deletion of any material which the plan/organization did not, prior to the time when the National Office sent its reply to the request for technical advice to the key district director or the Appeals office, propose be deleted. The Internal Revenue Service shall, within 20 days after receipt of the response by the plan/organization to the notice pursuant to section 6110(f)(1) of the Code (if applicable), mail to the plan/organization its final administrative conclusion regarding the deletions to be made.

(vii) *Action on technical advice in key district offices and in Appeals offices.*—(a) Unless the key district director or the Chief, Appeals office, feels that the conclusions reached by the National Office in a technical advice memorandum should be reconsidered and promptly requests such reconsideration, the key district office or the Appeals office will proceed to process the case on the basis of the conclusions expressed in the technical advice memorandum. The effect of technical advice on the plan's/organization's case once the technical advice memorandum is adopted is set forth in subdivision (viii) of this subparagraph.

(b) The key district director or the Appeals office will furnish the plan/organization a copy of the technical advice memorandum described in subdivision (vi)(c) of this subparagraph and the notice pursuant to section 6110(f)(1) of the Code (if applicable) of intention to disclose the technical advice memorandum (including a copy of the version proposed to be open to public inspection and notations of third party communications pursuant to section 6110(d) of the Code). The preceding sentence shall not apply to technical advice memoranda involving civil fraud or criminal investigations, or jeopardy or termination assessments, as described in subdivision

(iii)(j) of this subparagraph (except to the extent provided in subdivision (vi)(e) of this subparagraph) or to documents to which section 6104 of the Code applies.

(c) In those cases in which the National Office advises the key district director or the Appeals office that it should not furnish a copy of the technical advice memorandum to the plan/organization, the key district director or the Appeals office will so inform the plan/organization if it requests a copy.

(viii) *Effect of technical advice.*—(a) A technical advice memorandum represents an expression of the views of the Service as to the application of law, regulations, and precedents to the facts of a specific case, and is issued primarily as a means of assisting Service officials in the examination and closing of the case involved. In cases under this subparagraph concerning a plan's/organization's qualification or an organization's status, the conclusions expressed in a technical advice memorandum are final and will be followed by the key district office or the Appeals office.

(b) Unless otherwise stated, a holding in a technical advice memorandum will be applied retroactively. Moreover, where the plan/organization had previously been issued a favorable ruling or determination letter (whether or not it was based on a previous technical advice memorandum) concerning that transaction, its purpose, or method of operation, the holding in a technical advice memorandum that is adverse to the plan/organization is also applied retroactively unless the Assistant Commissioner or Deputy Assistant Commissioner (Employee Plans and Exempt Organizations) or, in a section 521 case, the Assistant Commissioner or Deputy Assistant Commissioner (Technical) exercises the discretionary authority under section 7805(b) of the Code to limit the retroactive effect of the holding as illustrated, in the case of rulings, in paragraph (1)(5) of this section.

(c) Technical advice memoranda often form the basis for revenue rulings. For the description of revenue rulings and the effect thereof, see §§ 601.601 (d)(2)(i)(a) and 601.601 (d)(2)(v).

(d) A key district director or an Appeals office may raise an issue in a taxable period, even though technical advice may have been asked for and furnished with regard to the same or a similar issue in any other taxable period. However, if the proposal by the key district director or the Appeals office is contrary to a prior technical advice or ruling issued to the same plan/organization, the proposal must be submitted to the National Office. See § 601.106(a)(1)(iv)(b) and subdivision (i)(d) of this subparagraph.

(o) *Employees' trusts or plans.*—(1) *In general.*—Paragraph (o) provides procedures relating to the issuance of determination letters with respect to the qualification of retirement plans. Paragraph (o)(2) of this section sets forth the authority of key district directors to issue determination letters. Paragraph (o)(3) provides instructions to applicants, including which forms to file, where such forms must be filed, and requirements for giving notice to interested parties. Paragraph (o)(5) describes the administrative remedies available to interested parties and the Pension Benefit Guaranty Corporation. Paragraph (o)(6) describes the administrative appeal rights available to applicants. Paragraph (o)(7) provides for the issuance of notice of final determination. Paragraph (o)(8) describes the documents which will make up the administrative record. Paragraph (o)(9) describes the notice of final determination. Paragraph (o)(10) sets forth the actions that will be necessary on the part of applicants, interested parties, and the Pension Benefit Guaranty Corporation in order for each to exhaust the administrative remedies within the meaning of section 7476(b)(3) of the Code.

(2) *Determination letters.*—(i) The district directors of the key district offices (described in paragraph (o)(4) of this section) shall have the authority to issue determination letters involving the provisions of sections 401, 403(a), 405, and 501(a) of the Internal Revenue Code of 1954 with respect to:

(a) Initial qualification of stock bonus, pension, profit-sharing, annuity, and bond purchase plans;

(b) Initial exemption from Federal income tax under section 501(a) of trusts forming a part of such plans, provided that the determination does not involve application of section 502 (feeder organizations) or section 511 (unrelated business income), or the question of whether a proposed transaction will be a prohibited transaction under section 503;

(c) Compliance with the applicable requirements of foreign situs trusts as to taxability of beneficiaries (section 402(c)) and deductions for employer contributions (section 404(a)(4)) in connection with a request for a determination letter as to the qualification of a retirement plan;

(d) Amendments, curtailments, or terminations of such plans and trusts.

(ii) Determination letters authorized by paragraph (o)(2)(i) of this section do not include determinations or opinions relating to other inquiries with respect to plans or trusts. Thus, except as specically provided in paragraph (o)(2)(i) of this section, key district directors may not issue determination letters relating to issues under other sections of the Code, such as sections 72, 402 through 404, 412, 502, 503, and 511 through 515, unless such determination letters are otherwise authorized under paragraph (c) of this section.

(iii) If, during the consideration of a case described in paragraph (o)(2)(i) of this section by a key district director, the applicant believes that the case involves an issue with respect to which referral for technical advice is appropriate, the applicant may ask the district director to request technical advice from the National Office. The district director shall advise the applicant of its right to request referral of the issue to the National Office for technical advice. The technical advice provisions applicable in these cases are set forth in paragraph (n)(9) of this section. If technical advice is issued, the decision of the National Office is final and the applicant may not thereafter appeal the issue to the Appeals office. See § 601.106(a)(1)(iv)(a) and paragraph (o)(6) of this section.

(3) *Instructions to taxpayers.*—(i) If an applicant for a determination letter does not comply with all the provisions of this paragraph, the district director, in his discretion, may return the application and point out to the applicant those provisions which have not been met. If such a request is returned to the applicant, the 270 day period described in section 7476(b)(3) will not begin to run until such time as the provisions of this paragraph are complied with.

(ii) An applicant requesting a determination letter must file with the appropriate district director specified in paragraph (o)(3)(xii) of this section the application form required by paragraphs (o)(3)(iii) through (x) of this section including all information and documents required by such form. (See section 6104 and the regulations thereunder for provisions relating to the extent to which information submitted to the Internal Revenue Service in connection with the application for determination may be subject to public inspection.) However, before filing such application, the applicant must comply with the provisions of paragraphs (o)(3)(xiv) through (xx) of this section (relating to notification of interested parties). (See paragraph (o)(5)(vi) of this section with respect to the effective date of paragraphs (o)(3)(xiv) through (xx) of this section.)

(iii) Paragraphs (o)(3)(iv)-(vi), (viii), and (ix) apply only to applications for determinations in respect of plan years to which section 410 of the Code does not apply. Paragraph (o)(3)(x) applies only to applications for determinations in respect of plan years to which section 410 applies. Paragraph (o)(3)(vii) applies whether or not the application is for a determination in respect of plan years to which section 410 applies. For this purpose, section 410 will be considered to apply with respect to a plan year if an election has been made under section 1017(d) of the Employee Retirement Income Security Act of 1974 to have section 410 apply to such plan year, whether or not the election is conditioned upon the issuance by the Commissioner of a favorable determination. For purposes of this paragraph (o)(3), in the case of an organization described in section 410(c)(1), section 410 will be considered to apply to a plan year of such organization for any plan year to which section 410(c)(2) applies to such plan.

(iv) If the request relates to the initial qualification of an individually designed plan, a subsequent amendment thereto, or compliance with the requirements for a foreign situs trust, the employer should (a) if the plan does not include self-employed individuals, file Form 4573, Application for Determination—Individually Designed Plan (not covering self-employed individuals), or (b) if the plan includes self-employed individuals, file Form 4574, Application for Determination—Individually Designed Plan Covering Self-Employed Individuals, except that where a bond purchase plan includes a self-employed individual, file Form 4578, Application for Approval of Bond Purchase Plan. (See paragraph (o)(3)(iii) for plan years to which this paragraph (o)(3)(iv) applies.)

(v) If the request involves a curtailment or termination of the plan (or complete discontinuance of contributions), the applicant should file Form 4576, Application for Determination—Termination or Curtailment of Plan. This form will also be applicable to the termination of a plan that includes self-employed individuals. (See paragraph (o)(3)(iii) of this section for plan years to which this paragraph (o)(3)(v) applies.)

(vi) An association of employers or a board of trustees should file Form 4577, Application for Determination—Industry-Wide Plan and Trust, if the request relates to the initial qualification or subsequent amendments of an industry-wide or area-wide union negotiated plan. (See paragraph (o)(3)(iii) of this section for plan years to which this paragraph (o)(3)(vi) applies.)

(vii) If the request relates to the qualification of a bond purchase plan, which includes self-employed individuals, the applicant should file, in duplicate, Form 4578, Application for Approval of Bond Purchase Plan that includes Self-Employed Individuals. When properly completed, Form 4578 will constitute a bond purchase plan. (See paragraph (o)(3)(iii) for plan years to which this section (o)(3)(vii) applies.)

(viii) An employer who desires a determination letter on his adoption of a master or prototype plan which is designed to satisfy section 401(a) or 403(a) but which is not designed to include self-employed individuals within the meaning of section 401(c)(1) must file Form 4462, Employer Application—Determination as to Qualification of Pension, Annuity, or Profit-Sharing Plan and Trust, and furnish a copy of the adoption agreement or other evidence of adoption of the plan and such additional information as the district director may require. (See paragraph (o)(3)(iii) of this section for plan years to which this paragraph (o)(3)(viii) applies.)

(ix) An applicant who amends his adoption agreement under a master or prototype plan may request a determination letter as to the effect of such amendment by filing Form 4462 with his district director, together with a copy of the amendment and a summary of the changes. However, in the event an applicant desires to amend his adoption agreement under a master or prototype plan, and such amendment is not contemplated or permitted under the plan, then such amendment will in effect substitute an individually designed plan for the master or prototype plan. (See paragraph (o)(3)(iii) of this section for plan years to which this paragraph (o)(3)(ix) applies.)

(x) An applicant requesting a determination letter relating to a defined contribution plan, other than a letter on the qualification of a bond purchase plan, shall file in duplicate, Form 5301, Application for Determination of Defined Contribution Plan, and Form 5302, Employee Census. Those forms are to be filed in accordance with the instructions therefor and accompanied by any schedules or additional material prescribed in those instructions. (See paragraph (o)(3)(iii) of this section for plan years to which this paragraph (o)(3)(x) applies.)

(xi) When, in connection with an application for a determination on the qualification of the plan, it is necessary to determine whether an organization (including a professional service organization) is a corporation or an association classified as a corporation under § 301.7701-2 of this chapter of the Regulations on Procedure and Administration, and whether an employer-employee relationship exists between it and its associates, the district director will make such determination. In such cases, the application with respect to the qualification of the plan should be filed in accordance with the provisions herein set forth and should contain the information and documents specified in the application. It should also be accompanied by such information and copies of documents as the organization deems appropriate to establish its status. The Service may, in addition, require any further information that is considered necessary to determine the status of the organization, the employment status of the individuals involved, or the qualification of the plan. After the taxable status of the organizations and the employer-employee relationship have been determined, the key district director may issue a determination letter as to the qualification of the plan.

(xii) Requests for determination letters on matters authorized by paragraph (o)(2) of this section, and the necessary supporting data, are to be addressed to the district director (whether or not such district director is the director of a key district) specified below (determined without regard to the application of section 414(b) or (c) to the plan):

(a) In the case of a plan for a single employer, the request shall be addressed to the district director for the district in which such employer's principal place of business is located.

(b) In the case of a single plan for a parent company and its subsidiaries, the request shall be addressed to the district director for the district in which the principal place of business of the parent company is located, whether separate or consolidated returns are filed.

(c) In the case of a plan established or proposed for an industry by all subscribing employers whose principal places of business are located within more than one district, the request shall be addressed to the district director for the district in which is located the principal place of business of the trustee, or if more than one trustee, the usual meeting place of the trustees.

(d) In the case of a pooled fund arrangement (individual trusts under separate plans pooling their funds for investment purposes through a master trust), the request on behalf of the master trust shall be addressed to the district director for the district where the principal place of business of such trust is located. Requests on behalf of the participating trusts and related plans will be addressed as otherwise provided herein.

(e) In the case of a plan of multiple employers (other than a master or prototype plan) not otherwise herein provided for, the request shall be addressed to the district director for the district in which is located the principal place of business of the trustee, or if not trusteed or if more than one trustee, the principal or usual meeting place of the trustees or plan supervisors.

(xiii) The applicant's request for a determination letter may be withdrawn by a written request at any time prior to appealing the proposed determination to the regional office as described in paragraph (o)(6) of this section. In the case of such a withdrawal the

Service will not render a determination of any type. A failure to render a determination as a result of such a withdrawal will not be considered a failure of the Secretary or his delegate to make a determination within the meaning of section 7476. In the case of a withdrawal the district director may consider the information submitted in connection with the withdrawn request in a subsequent audit or examination.

(xiv) In the case of an application for a determination for plan years to which section 410 applies (see paragraph (o)(5)(vi) of this section), notice that an application for an advance determination regarding the qualification of plans described in section 401(a), 403(a), or 405(a) is to be made must be given to all interested parties in the manner set forth in the regulations under section 7476 of the Code.

(xv) When the notice referred to in paragraph (o)(3)(xiv) of this section is given in the manner set forth in § 1.7476-2(c) of this chapter, such notice must be given not less than 10 days nor more than 24 days prior to the date the application for a determination is made. See paragraph (o)(3)(xxi) of this section for determining when an application is made. If, however, an application is returned to the applicant for failure to adequately satisfy the notification requirement with respect to a particular group or class of interested parties, the applicant need not cause notice to be given to those groups or classes of interested parties with respect to which the notice requirement was already satisfied merely because, as a result of the resubmission of the application, the time limitations of this paragraph (o)(3)(xv) would not be met.

(xvi) The notice referred to in paragraph (o)(3)(xiv) of this section shall be given in the manner prescribed in § 1.7476-2 of this chapter and shall contain the following information:

(a) a brief description identifying the class or classes of interested parties to whom the notice is addressed (*e.g.,* all present employees of the employer, all present employees eligible to participate);

(b) the name of the plan, the plan identification number, and the name of the plan administrator;

(c) the name and taxpayer identification number of the applicant;

(d) that an application for a determination as to the qualified status of the plan is to be made to the Internal Revenue Service, stating whether the application relates to an initial qualification, a plan amendment or a plan termination, and the address of the district director to whom the application will be submitted;

(e) a description of the class of employees eligible to participate under the plan;

(f) whether or not the Service has issued a previous determination as to the qualified status of the plan;

(g) a statement that any person to whom the notice is addressed is entitled to submit, or request the Department of Labor to submit, to the district director described in paragraph (o)(3)(xvi)(d) of this section, a comment on the question of whether the plan meets the requirements for qualification under part I of Subchapter D of Chapter 1 of the Internal Revenue Code of 1954; that two or more such persons may join in a single comment or request; and that if such a person or persons request the Department of Labor to submit a comment and that department declines to do so in respect of one or more matters raised in the request, the person or persons so requesting may submit a comment to the district director in respect of the matters on which the Department of Labor declines to comment;

(h) that a comment to the district director or a request of the Department of Labor must be made according to the following procedures:

(1) a comment to the district director must be received on or before the 45th day (specified by date) after the day on which the application for determination is received by the district director;

(2) or if the comment is being submitted on a matter on which the Department of Labor was first requested but declined to comment, on or before the later of such 45th day or the 15th day after the day on which the Department of Labor notifies such person or persons that it declines to comment, but in no event later than the 60th day (specified by date) after the day the application is received by the district director; and

(3) a request of the Department of Labor to submit such a comment must be received by such department on or before the 25th day (specified by date) (or if the person or persons requesting the Department of Labor to submit such a comment wish to preserve their right to submit a comment to the district director in the event the Department of Labor declines to comment, on or before the 15th day (specified by date)) after the day the application is received by the district director;

(i) except to the extent there is included in the notice the additional informational materials which paragraphs (o)(3)(xviii), (xix), and (xx) of this section require be made available to interested parties, a description of a reasonable procedure whereby such addi-

tional informational material will be made available to them (see paragraph (o)(3)(xvii) of this section).

(xvii) The procedure referred to in paragraph (o)(3)(xvi)(i) of this ection whereby the additional informational material required by paragraphs (o)(3)(xviii), (xix), and (xx) of this section will (to the extent not included in this notice) be made available to interested parties, may consist of making such material available for inspection and copying by interested parties at a place or places reasonably accessible to such parties, or supplying such material by using a method of delivery or a combination thereof that is reasonably calculated to ensure that all interested parties will have access to the materials. The procedure referred to in paragraph (o)(3)(xvi)(i) of this section must be immediately available to all interested parties and must be designed to supply them with such additional informational material in time for them to pursue their rights within the time period prescribed, and must be available until the earlier of the filing of a pleading commencing a declaratory judgment action under section 7476 with respect to the qualification of the plan or the ninety-second day after the day the notice of final determination is mailed to the applicant.

(xviii) Unless provided in the notice, the following materials shall be made available to interested parties under a procedure described in paragraph (o)(3)(xvii) of this section:

(a) An updated copy of the plan and the related trust agreement (if any);

(b) The application for determination;

provided, however, that if there would be less than 26 participants in the plan, as described in the application (including, as participants, retired employees and beneficiaries of deceased employees who have a nonforfeitable right to benefits under the plan and employees who would be eligible to participate upon making mandatory employee contributions, if any), then in lieu of making such materials available to interested parties who are not participants (as described above), there may be made available to such interested parties a document containing the following information: a description of the plan's requirements respecting eligibility for participation and benefits; a description of the provisions providing for nonforfeitable benefits; a description of the circumstances which may result in ineligibility, or denial or loss of benefits; a description of the source of financing of the plan and the identity of any organization through which benefits are provided; whether the applicant is claiming in his application that the plan meets the requirements of section 410(b)(1)(A) of the Code, and, if not, the coverage schedule required by the application in the case of plans not meeting the requirements of such section. However, once such an interested party or his designated representative receives a notice of final determination, the applicant must, upon request, make available to such interested party (regardless of whether or not the interested party is a participant in the plan and regardless of whether or not the plan has less than 26 participants) an updated copy of the plan and related trust agreement (if any) and the application for determination. Information of the type described in section 6104(a)(1)(D) of the Code should not be included in the application, plan, or related trust agreement submitted to the Internal Revenue Service. Accordingly, such information should not be included in any of the materials required by this paragraph (o)(3) to be available to interested parties. There may be excluded from such material information contained in Form 5302 (Employee Census). However, information showing the number of individuals covered and not covered in the plan, listed by compensation range, shall not be excluded.

(xix) Unless provided in the notice, there shall be made available to interested parties under a procedure described in paragraph (o)(3)(xvii) of this section, any additional document dealing with the application which is submitted by or for the applicant to the Internal Revenue Service, or furnished by the Internal Revenue Service to the applicant; provided, however, if there would be less than 26 participants in the plan as described in the application (including, as participants, retired employees and beneficiaries of deceased employees who have a nonforfeitable right to benefits under the plan and employees who would be eligible to participate upon making mandatory employee contributions, if any), such additional documents need not be made available to interested parties who are not participants (as described above) until they or their designated representative, receive a notice of final determination. The applicant may also withhold from such inspection and copying, information described in section 6104(a)(1)(C) and (D) of the Code which may be contained in such additional documents.

(xx) Unless provided in the notice, there shall be made available to all interested parties under a procedure described in paragraph (o)(3)(xvii) of this section, material setting forth the following information:

(a) the rights of interested parties described in paragraph (o)(5)(i) of this section; and

(b) the information provided in paragraph (o)(5)(ii), (iii), (iv) and (v) of this section.

(xxi) An application for an advance determination, a comment to the district director, or a request to the Department of Labor, shall be deemed made when it is received by the district director, or the Department of Labor. The notice to interested parties required by paragraph (o)(3)(xiv) of this section shall be deemed given when it is given in person, posted as prescribed in the regulations under section 7476 or received through the mail. In any case where such an application, request, comment, or notice is sent by mail, it shall be deemed received as of the date of the postmark (or if sent by certified or registered mail, the date of certification or registration), if it is deposited in the mail in an envelope, or other appropriate wrapper first class postage prepaid, properly addressed. However, if such an application, request or comment is not received within a reasonable period from the date of postmark, the immediately preceding sentence shall not apply.

(4) *Key district offices.*—Following are the 19 key district offices that issue determination letters and the area covered:

| Key District(s) | IRS Districts Covered |
| --- | --- |
| **Central Region** | |
| Cincinnati | Cincinnati, Louisville, Indianapolis |
| Cleveland | Cleveland, Parkersburg |
| Detroit | Detroit |
| **Mid-Atlantic Region** | |
| Baltimore | Baltimore (which includes the District of Columbia and Office of International Operations), Pittsburgh, Richmond |
| Philadelphia | Philadelphia, Wilmington |
| Newark | Newark |
| **Midwest Region** | |
| Chicago | Chicago |
| St. Paul | St. Paul, Fargo, Aberdeen, Milwaukee |
| St. Louis | St. Louis, Springfield, Des Moines, Omaha |
| **North-Atlantic Region** | |
| Boston | Boston, Augusta, Burlington, Providence, Hartford, Portsmouth |
| Manhattan | Manhattan |
| Brooklyn | Brooklyn, Albany, Buffalo |
| **Southeast Region** | |
| Atlanta | Atlanta, Greensboro, Columbia, Nashville |
| Jacksonville | Jacksonville, Jackson, Birmingham |
| **Southwest Region** | |
| Austin | Austin, New Orleans, Albuquerque, Denver, Cheyenne |
| Dallas | Dallas, Oklahoma City, Little Rock, Wichita |
| **Western Region** | |
| Los Angeles | Los Angeles, Phoenix, Honolulu |
| San Francisco | San Francisco, Salt Lake City, Reno |
| Seattle | Seattle, Portland, Anchorage, Boise, Helena |

(5) *Administrative remedies of interested parties and the Pension Benefit Guaranty Corporation.*—(i) With respect to plan years to which section 410 applies (see paragraph (o)(5)(vi) of this section), persons who qualify as interested parties under the regulations issued under section 7476 and the Pension Benefit Guaranty Corporation shall have the following rights:

(a) To submit to the district director for the district where an application for determination is filed, by the 45th day after the day on which the application is received by the district director, a written comment on said application, with respect to the qualification of the plan under subchapter D of chapter 1 of the Internal Revenue Code.

(b) To request the Administrator of Pension and Welfare Benefit Programs, Department of Labor, 200 Constitution Avenue, N.W., Washington, D.C. 20210, to submit to such district director such a written comment under the provisions of section 3001(b)(2) of the Employee Retirement Income Security Act of 1974. Such a request, if made by an interested party or parties, must be received by such department on or before the 25th day after the day said application is received by the district director. However, if such party or parties requesting the Department of Labor to submit such a comment wish to preserve their rights to submit a comment to the district director in the event the Department of Labor declines to comment (pursuant to paragraph (o)(5)(i)(c) of this section), such request must be received by such department on or before the 15th day after the day the application is received by the district director.

(c) If a request described in paragraph (o)(5)(i)(b) of this section is made and the Department of Labor notifies the interested party or parties making the request that it declines to submit a comment on a matter concerning qualification of the plan which was raised in such request, to submit a written comment to the district director on such matter by the later of the 45th day after the day the application for determination is received by the district director or the 15th day after the day on which the Department of Labor notifies such party or parties that it declines to submit a comment on such matter, but, in no event later than the 60th day after the application for determination was received. (See paragraph (o)(5)(iii) of this section for determining when notice that the Department of Labor declines to comment is received by an interested party or parties.)

Such a comment must comply with the requirements of paragraph (o)(5)(ii) of this section, and include a statement that the comment is being submitted on matters raised in a request to the Department of Labor on which that department declined to comment.

(ii) A comment submitted by an interested party or parties to the district director must be in writing, signed by such party or parties or by an authorized representative of such party or parties (as provided in paragraph (e)(6) of this section), be addressed to the district director described in paragraph (o)(3)(xvi)(d) of this section, and contain the following:

(a) The name or names of the interested party or parties making the comment;

(b) The name and taxpayer identification number of the applicant making the application;

(c) The name of the plan and the plan identification number;

(d) Whether the party or parties submitting the comments are—

(1) Employees eligible to participate under the plan,

(2) Former employees or beneficiaries of deceased former employees who have a vested right to benefits under the plan, or

(3) Employees not eligible to participate under the plan;

(e) The specific matter or matters raised by the interested party or parties on the question of whether the plan meets the requirements for qualification under Part I of Subchapter D of the Code, and how such matter or matters relate to the interests of such party or parties making such comment.

(f) The address of the interested party submitting the comment to which all correspondence, including a notice of the Internal Revenue Service's final determination with respect to qualification, should be sent. (See section 7476(b)(5) of the Code.) If more than one interested party submits the comment, they must designate a representative for receipt of such correspondence and notice on behalf of all interested parties submitting the said comment, and state the address of such representative. Such representative shall be one of the interested parties submitting the comment or the authorized representative.

(iii) For purposes of paragraph (o)(3)(xvi)(h) and (o)(5)(i)(c), notice by the Department of Labor that it declines to comment shall be deemed given to the interested party designated to receive such notice when received by him.

(iv) A request of the Department of Labor to submit a comment to the district director must be in writing, signed, and in addition to the information prescribed in paragraph (o)(5)(ii) of this section must also contain the address of the district director to whom the application was, or will be, submitted. The address designated for notice by the Internal Revenue Serivce will be used by the Department of Labor in communicating with the party or parties submitting the request.

(v) The contents of written comments submitted by interested parties to the Internal Revenue Service pursuant to paragraphs (o)(5)(i)(a) and (c) will not be treated as confidential material and may be inspected by persons outside the Internal Revenue Service, including the applicant for the determination. Accordingly, designations of material as confidential or not to be disclosed, contained in such comments, will not be accepted. Thus, a person submitting a written comment should not include therein material that he considers to be confidential or inappropriate for disclosure to the public. It will be presumed by the Internal Revenue Service that every written comment submitted to it is intended by the party or parties submitting it to be subject in its entirety to public inspection and copying.

(vi)(a) Paragraphs (o)(3)(xiv) through (xxi) and (o)(5) of this section apply to an application for an advance determination in respect of a plan year or years to which section 410 applies to the plan, whether or not such application is received by the district director before the first date on which such section applies to the plan.

(b) For purposes of paragraph (o)(5)(vi)(a) of this section, section 410 shall be considered to apply to a plan year if an election has been made under section 1017(d) of the Employee Retirement Income Security Act of 1974 to have section 410 apply to such plan year, whether or not the election is conditioned upon the issuance by the Commissioner of a favorable determination.

(c) For purposes of paragraph (o)(5)(vi)(a) of this section, in the case of an organization described in section 410(c)(1), section 410 will be considered to apply to a plan year of such organization for any plan year to which section 410(c)(2) applies to such plan.

(vii) The Internal Revenue Service will provide to the applicant a copy of all comments on the application submitted pursuant to paragraph (o)(5)(i) (a), (b) or (c) of this section. In addition, the Internal Revenue Service will provide to the applicant a copy of all correspondence in respect of a comment between the Internal Revenue Service and a person submitting the comment.

(6) *Reference of matters to the Appeals office.*—(i) Where issues arise in a district director's office on matters within the contemplation of paragraph (o)(2)(i) of this section, and the key district director issues a notice of proposed determination which is adverse to the applicant, the applicant may appeal the proposed determination to the Appeals office. However, the applicant may not appeal a determination that is based on a National Office technical advice. See §601.106(a)(1)(iv)(a) and paragraph (o)(2)(iii) of this section. The applicant shall notify the key district director that it intends to request Appeals office consideration by submitting the request, in writing, to the key district director within 30 days from issuance of the notice of proposed determination. The key district director will forward the request and the administrative record to the Appeals office and will so notify the applicant in writing. A failure by the applicant to request Appeals office consideration will constitute a failure to exhaust available administrative remedies as required by section 7476(b)(3) and will thus preclude the applicant from seeking a declaratory judgment as provided under section 7476. (See paragraph (o)(10)(i)(c) of this section.)

(ii) The request for Appeals office consideration must show the following:

(a) Date of application for determination letter;

(b) Name and address of the applicant and the name and address of the representative, if any, who has been authorized to represent the applicant as provided in paragraph (c)(6) of this section;

(c) The key district office in which the case is pending;

(d) Type of plan (pension, annuity, profit-sharing, stock bonus, bond purchase, and foreign situs trusts), and type of action involved (initial qualification, amendment, curtailment, or termination);

(e) Date of filing this request with the key district director and the date and symbols of the letter referred to in paragraph (o)(6)(i) of this section;

(f) A complete statement of the issues and a presentation of the arguments in support of the applicant's position; and

(g) Whether a conference is desired.

(iii) After receipt of the administrative record in the Appeals office, the applicant will be afforded the opportunity for a conference, if a conference was requested. After full consideration of the entire administrative record, the Appeals office will notify the applicant in writing of the proposed decision and the reasons therefor and will issue a notice of final determination in accordance with the decision. However, if the proposed disposition by the Appeals office is con-

trary to a National Office technical advice concerning qualification, issued prior to the case, the proposed disposition will be submitted to the Assistant Commissioner (Employee Plans and Exempt Organizations) and the decision of that official will be followed by the Appeals office. See §601.106(a)(1)(iv)(b). Additionally, if the applicant believes that the case involves an issue with respect to which referral for technical advice is appropriate, the applicant may ask the Appeals office to request technical advice from the National Office. The Appeals office shall advise the applicant of its right to request referral of the issue to the National Office for technical advice. The technical advice provisions applicable to these cases are set forth in paragraph (n)(9) of this section. If technical advice is issued, the decision of the National Office will be followed by the Appeals office. See paragraph (n)(9)(viii)(a) of this section.

(iv) Applicants are advised to make full presentation of the facts, circumstances, and arguments at the initial level of consideration, since submission of additional facts, circumstances, and arguments at the Appeals office may result in suspension of Appeals procedures and referral of the case back to the key district for additional consideration.

(7) *Issuance of the notice of final determination.*—The key district director or Appeals office will send notice of the final determination to the applicant. The key district director will send notice of the final determination to the interested parties who have previously submitted comments on the application to the Internal Revenue Service pursuant to paragraph (o)(5)(i)(a) or (c) of this section (or to the persons designated by them to receive such notice), to the Department of Labor in the case of a comment submitted by that department upon the request of interested parties or the Pension Benefit Guaranty Corporation pursuant to paragraph (o)(5)(i)(b) of this section, and to the Pension Benefit Guaranty Corporation if it has filed a comment pursuant to paragraph (o)(5)(i)(a) of this section.

(8) *Administrative record.*—(i) In the case of a request for an advance determination in respect of a retirement plan, the determination of the district director or Appeals office on the qualification or nonqualification of the retirement plan shall be based solely on the facts contained in the administrative record. Such administrative record shall consist of the following:

(a) The request for determination, the retirement plan and any related trust instruments, and any written modifications or amendments thereof made by the applicant during the proceedings within the Internal Revenue Service;

(b) All other documents submitted to the Internal Revenue Service by or on behalf of the applicant in respect of the request for determination;

(c) All written correspondence between the Internal Revenue Service and the applicant in respect of the request for determination and any other documents issued to the applicant from the Internal Revenue Service;

(d) All written comments submitted to the Internal Revenue Service pursuant to paragraphs (o)(5)(i)(a), (b), and (c) of this section, and all correspondence in respect of comments submitted between the Internal Revenue Service and persons (including the Pension Benefit Guaranty Corporation and the Department of Labor) submitting comments pursuant to paragraphs (o)(5)(i)(a), (b), and (c) of this section;

(e) In any case in which the Internal Revenue Service makes an investigation regarding the facts as represented or alleged by the applicant in his request for determination or in comments submitted pursuant to paragraphs (o)(5)(i)(a), (b), and (c) of this section, a copy of the official report of such investigation;

(ii) The administrative record shall be closed upon the earlier of the following events:

(a) The date of mailing of a notice of final determination by the Internal Revenue Service in respect of the application for determination; or

(b) The filing of a petition with the United States Tax Court seeking a declaratory judgment in respect of the retirement plan. Any oral representation or modification of the facts as represented or alleged in the application for determination or in a comment filed by an interested party, which is not reduced to writing and submitted to the Service shall not become a part of the administrative record and shall not be taken into account in the determination of the qualified status of the retirement plan by the district director or Appeals office.

(9) *Notice of final determination.*—For purposes of this paragraph (o), the notice of final determination shall be—

(i) In the case of a final determination which is favorable to the applicant, the letter issued by the key district director or Appeals office (whether or not by certified or registered mail) which states that the applicant's plan satisfies the qualification requirements of the Internal Revenue Code.

(ii) In the case of a final determination which is adverse to the applicant, the letter issued by certified or registered mail by the key district director or Appeals office, subsequent to a letter of proposed determination, stating that the applicant's plan fails to satisfy the qualification requirements of the Internal Revenue Code.

(10) *Exhaustion of administrative remedies.*—For purposes of section 7476(b)(3), a petitioner shall be deemed to have exhausted the administrative remedies available to him in the Internal Revenue Service upon the completion of the steps described in paragraph (o)(10)(i), (ii), or (iii) of this section, subject, however, to paragraphs (o)(10)(iv) and (v) of this section. If an applicant, interested party, or the Pension Benefit Guaranty Corporation does not complete the applicable steps described below, such applicant, interested party, or the Pension Benefit Guaranty Corporation will not have exhausted available administrative remedies as required by section 7476(b)(3) and will thus be precluded from seeking a declaratory judgment under section 7476 except to the extent that paragraph (o)(10)(iv)(*b*) or (v) of this section applies.

(i) The administrative remedies of an applicant with respect to any matter relating to the qualification of a plan are:

(*a*) Filing a completed application with the appropriate district director pursuant to paragraphs (o)(3)(iii) through (xii) of this section;

(*b*) Compliance with the requirements pertaining to notice to interested parties as set forth in paragraphs (o)(3)(xiv) through (o)(3)(xxi) of this section; and

(*c*) An appeal to the Appeals office pursuant to paragraph (o)(6) of this section, in the event of a notice of proposed adverse determination from the district director.

(ii) The administrative remedy of an interested party with respect to any matter relating to the qualification of the plan is submission to the district director of a comment raising such matter in accordance with paragraph (o)(5)(i)(*a*) of this section or requesting the Department of Labor to submit to the district director a comment with respect to such matter in accordance with paragraph (o)(5)(i)(*b*) of this section, and, if such department declines to comment, submission of such a comment in accordance with paragraph (o)(5)(i)(*c*) of this section, so that such comment may be considered by the Internal Revenue Service through the administrative process.

(iii) The administrative remedy of the Pension Benefit Guaranty Corporation with respect to any matter relating to the qualification of the plan is submission to the district director of a comment raising such matter in accordance with paragraph (o)(5)(i)(*a*) of this section or requesting the Department of Labor to submit to the district director a comment with respect to such matter in accordance with paragraph (o)(5)(i)(*b*) of this section, and, if such department declines to comment, submission of such a comment to the Internal Revenue Service directly, so that such comment may be considered by the Internal Revenue Service through the administrative process.

(iv) An applicant, or an interested party, or the Pension Benefit Guaranty Corporation shall in no event be deemed to have exhausted his (its) administrative remedies prior to the earlier of:

(*a*) The completion of all the steps described in paragraph (o)(11)(i), (ii), or (iii) of this section, whichever is applicable, subject, however, to paragraph (o)(11) (v), or

(*b*) The expiration of the 270 day period described in section 7476(b)(3), in a case where the completion of the steps referred to in paragraph (o)(10)(iv)(*a*) of this section shall not have occurred before the expiration of such 270 day period because of the failure of the Internal Revenue Service to proceed with due diligence.

The step described in paragraph (o)(10)(i)(*c*) of this section will not be considered completed until the Internal Revenue Service has had a reasonable time to act upon the appeal. In addition, the administrative remedies described in paragraphs (o)(10)(ii) and (iii) will not be considered completed until the Internal Revenue Service has had a reasonable time to consider the comments submitted pursuant to such paragraphs at each step of the Administrative process described in paragraph (o)(10)(i).

(v) The administrative remedy described in paragraph (o)(10)(i)(*c*) of this section will not be available to an applicant with respect to any issue on which technical advice from the National Office has been obtained.

(p) *Pension plans of self-employed individuals.*—(1) *Rulings, determination letters, and opinion letters.*—(i) The National Office of the Service, upon request, will furnish a written opinion as to the acceptability (for the purpose of sections 401 and 501(a) of the Code) of the form of any master or prototype plan designed to include groups of self-employed individuals who may adopt the plan, where the plan is submitted by a sponsor that is a trade or professional association, bank, insurance company, or regulated investment company as defined in section 851 of the Code. Each opinion letter will bear an identifying plan serial number. If the trustee or custodian has been designated at the time of approval of a plan as to form, a ruling will be issued as to the exempt status of such trust or custodial account which forms part of the master or prototype plan. As used

here, the term "master plan" refers to a standardized form of plan, with a related trust or custodial agreement, where indicated, administered by the sponsoring organization for the purpose of providing plan benefits on a standardized basis. The term "prototype plan" refers to a standardized form of plan, with or without a related form of trust or custodial agreement, that is made available by the sponsoring organization, for use without change by employers who wish to adopt such a plan, and which will not be administered by the sponsoring organization that makes such form available. The degree of relationship among the separate employers adopting either a master plan or a prototype plan or to the sponsoring organization is immaterial.

(ii) Since a determination as to the qualification of a particular employer's plan can be made only with regard to facts peculiar to that employer, a letter expressing the opinion of the Service as to the acceptability of the form of a master or prototype plan will not constitute a ruling or determination as to the qualification of a plan as adopted by any individual employer or as to the exempt status of a related trust or custodial account. However, where an employer adopts a master or prototype plan and any related prototype trust or custodial account previously approved as to form, and observes the provisions thereof, such plan and trust or custodial account will be deemed to satisfy the requirements of sections 401 and 501(a) of the Code, provided the eligibility requirements and contributions on benefits under the plan for owner-employees are not more favorable than for other employees, including those required to be covered under plans of all businesses controlled by such owner-employees.

(iii) Although district directors no longer make advance determinations on plans of self-employed individuals who have adopted previously approved master or prototype plans, they will continue, upon request, to issue determination letters as to the qualification of individually designed plans (those not utilizing a master or prototype plan) and the exempt status of a related trust or custodial account, if any, in accordance with the procedures set forth in paragraph (o) of this section.

(2) *Determination letters as to qualified bond purchase plans.*—A determination as to the qualification of a bond purchase plan will, upon request, be made by the appropriate district director. Form 4578, Application for Approval of Bond Purchase Plan, must be used for this purpose. When properly completed, this form will constitute a bond purchase plan.

(3) *Instructions to sponsoring organizations and employers.*—(i) A sponsoring organization of the type referred to in subparagraph (1)(i) of this paragraph, that desires a written opinion as to the acceptability of the form of a master or prototype plan (or as to the exempt status of a related trust or custodial account) should submit its request to the National Office. Copies of all documents, including the plan and trust instruments and all amendments thereto, together with specimen insurance contracts (where applicable) must be submitted with the request. The request must be submitted to the Commissioner of Internal Revenue Service, Washington, D.C. 20224, Attn: T:MS:PT. Form 3672, Application for Approval of Master or Prototype Plan for Self-Employed Individuals, is to be used for this purpose.

(ii) If, subsequent to obtaining approval of the form of a master or prototype plan, an amendment is to be made, the procedure will depend on whether the sponsor is authorized to act on behalf of the subscribers.

(*a*) If the plan provides that each employer has delegated to the sponsor the power to amend the plan and that each employer shall be deemed to have consented thereto, the plan may be amended by the sponsor. If the plan contains no specific provision permitting the sponsor to amend such plan, but all employers consent in writing to permit such amendment, the sponsor may then amend the plan. However, where a sponsor is unable to secure the consent of each employer, the plan cannot be amended by the sponsor. In such cases, any change will have to be effected by the adoption of a new plan and the submission of a new Form 3672. The new plan will be complete and separate from the old plan and individual employers may, if they desire, substitute the new plan for the old plan.

(*b*) In the first two instances mentioned above, where the plan has been properly amended, the sponsor must submit Form 3672, a copy of the amendment and, if required, copies of the signed consent of each participating employer.

(*c*) Upon approval of the amendment by the Service, an opinion letter will be issued to the sponsor containing the serial number of the original plan followed by a suffix: "A-1" for the first amendment, "A-2" for the second amendment, etc. Employers adopting the form of plan subsequent to the date of the amendment will use the revised serial number.

(*d*) If a new plan is submitted, together with form 3672 and copies of all documents evidencing the plan, an opinion letter bearing a new serial number will be issued to the sponsor and all employers who adopt the new plan shall use the new serial number.

Employers who adopted the old plan will continue to use the original serial number.

(4) *Applicability.*—The general procedures of paragraphs (a) through (m) and paragraph (o) of this section, relating to the issuance of rulings and determination letters, are applicable to requests relating to the qualification of plans covering self-employed individuals under sections 401 and 405(a) of the Code and the exempt status of related trusts or custodial accounts under section 501(a), to the extent that the matter is not covered by the specific procedures and instructions contained in this paragraph.

(q) *Corporate master and prototype plans.*—(1) *Scope and definitions.*—(i) The general procedures set forth in this paragraph pertain to the issuance of rulings, determination letters, and opinion letters relating to master and prototype pension, annuity, and profit-sharing plans (except those covering self-employed individuals) under section 401(a) of the Code, and the status for exemption of related trusts or custodial accounts under section 501(a). (A custodial account described in section 401(f) of the Code is treated as a qualified trust for purposes of the Code.) These procedures are subject to the general procedures set forth in paragraph (o) of this section, and relate only to master plans and prototype plans that do not include self-employed individuals and are sponsored by trade or professional associations, banks, insurance companies, or regulated investment companies. These plans are further identified as "variable form" and "standardized form" plans.

(ii) A "master plan" is a form of plan in which the funding organization (trust, custodial account, or insurer) is specified in the sponsor's application, and a "prototype plan" is a form of plan in which the funding organization is specified in the adopting employer's application.

(iii) A "variable form" plan is either a master or prototype plan that permits an employer to select various options relating to such basic provisions as employee coverage, contributions, benefits, and vesting. These options must be set forth in the body of the plan or in a separate document. Such plan, however, is not complete until all provisions necessary for qualification under section 401(a) of the Code are appropriately included.

(iv) A "standardized form" plan is either a master or prototype plan that meets the requirements of subparagraph (2) of this paragraph.

(2) *Standardized form plan requirements.*—A standardized form plan must be complete in all respects (except for choices permissible under subdivisions (i) and (iv) of this subparagraph) and contain among other things provisions as to the following requirements:

(i) *Coverage.*—The percentage coverage requirements set forth in section 401(a)(3)(A) of the Code must be satisfied. Provisions may be made, however, for an adopting employer to designate such eligibility requirements as are permitted under that section.

(ii) *Nonforfeitable rights.*—Each employee's rights to or derived from the contributions under the plan must be nonforfeitable at the time the contributions are paid to or under the plan, except to the extent that the limitations set forth in § 1.401(a)(4)-5 of this chapter, regarding early termination of a plan, may be applicable.

(iii) *Bank trustee.*—In the case of a trusteed plan, the trustee must be a bank.

(iv) *Definite contribution formula.*—In the case of a profit-sharing plan, there must be a definite formula for determining the employer contributions to be made. Provision may be made, however, for an adopting employer to specify his rate of contribution.

(3) *Rulings, determination letters, and opinion letters.*—(i) A favorable determination letter as to the qualification of a pension or profit-sharing plan and the exempt status of any related trust or custodial account, is not required as a condition for obtaining the tax benefits pertaining thereto. However, paragraph (c)(5) of this section authorizes district directors to issue determination letters as to the qualification of plans and the exempt status of related trusts or custodial accounts.

(ii) In addition, the National Office upon request from a sponsoring organization will furnish a written opinion as to the acceptability of the form of a master or prototype plan and any related trust or custodial account, under sections 401(a) and 501(a) of the Code. Each opinion letter will bear an identifying plan serial number. However, opinion letters will not be issued under this paragraph as to (*a*) plans of a parent company and its subsidiaries, (*b*) pooled fund arrangements contemplated by Revenue Ruling 56-267, C.B. 1956-1, 206, (*c*) industry-wide or area-wide union negotiated plans, (*d*) plans that include self-employed individuals, (*e*) stock bonus plans, and (*f*) bond purchase plans.

(iii) A ruling as to the exempt status of a trust or custodial account under section 501(a) of the Code will be issued to the trustee

or custodian by the National Office where such trust or custodial account forms part of a plan described in subparagraph (1) of this paragraph and the trustee or custodian is specified on Form 4461, Sponsor Application—Approval of Master or Prototype Plan. Where not so specified, a determination letter as to the exempt status of a trust or custodial account will be issued by the district director for the district in which is located the principal place of business of an employer who adopts such trust or custodial account after he furnishes the name of the trustee or custodian.

(iv) Since a determination as to the qualification of a particular employer's plan can be made only with regard to facts peculiar to such employer, a letter expressing the opinion of the Service as to the acceptability of the form of a master or prototype plan will not constitute a ruling or determination as to the qualification of a plan as adopted by any individual employer nor as to the exempt status of a related trust or custodial account.

(v) A determination as to the qualification of a plan as it relates to a particular employer will be made by the district director for the district in which each employer's principal place of business is located, if the employer has adopted a master or prototype plan that has been previously approved as to form. An employer who desires such a determination must file Form 4462, Employer Application—Determination as to Qualification of Pension, Annuity, or Profit-Sharing Plan and Trust, and furnish a copy of the adoption agreement or other evidence of adoption of the plan and such additional information as the district director may require.

(vi) Where master or prototype plans involve integration with Social Security benefits, it is impossible to determine in advance whether in an individual case a particular restrictive definition of the compensation (such as basic compensation) on which contributions or benefits are based would result in discrimination in contributions or benefits in favor of employees who are officers, shareholders, persons whose principal duties consist in supervising the work of other employees, or highly compensated employees. See Revenue Ruling 69-503 C.B. 1969-2, 94. Accordingly, opinion letters relating to master or prototype plans that involve integration with Social Security benefits will not be issued except for those plans where annual compensation, for the purposes of § § 3.01, 5.02, 6.02, 6.03, 13.01, 13.02, and 14.02 of Revenue Ruling 69-4, C.B. 1969-1, 118, is defined to be all of each employee's compensation that would be subject to tax under section 3101(a) of the Code without the dollar limitation of section 3121(a)(1) of the Code.

(4) *Request by sponsoring organizations and employers.*—(i) The National Office will consider the request of a sponsoring organization desiring a written opinion as to the acceptability of the form of a master or prototype plan and any related trust or custodial account. Such request is to be made on Form 4461 and filed with the Commissioner of Internal Revenue, Washington, D.C. 20224, attention T:MS:PT. Copies of all documents, including the plan and trust or custodial agreement, together with specimen insurance contracts, if applicable, are to be submitted with the request. In making its determination, the National Office may require additional information as appropriate.

(ii) Each district director, in whose jurisdiction there are employers who adopt the form of plan, must be furnished a copy of the previously approved form of plan and related documents by the sponsoring organization. The sponsoring organization must also furnish such district director a copy of all amendments subsequently approved as to form by the National Office.

(iii) The sponsoring organization must furnish copies of opinion letters as to the acceptability of the form of plan, including amendments (see subparagraph (5) of this paragraph), to all adopting employers.

(5) *Amendments.*—(i) Subsequent to obtaining approval of the form of a master or prototype plan, a sponsoring organization may wish to amend the plan. Whether a sponsoring organization may effect an amendment depends on the plan's administrative provisions.

(ii) If the plan provides that each subscribing employer has delegated authority to the sponsor to amend the plan and that each such employer shall be deemed to have consented thereto, the plan may be amended by the sponsor acting on behalf of the subscribers. If the plan does not contain such provision but all subscribing employers consent in a collateral document to permit amendment, the sponsor, acting on their behalf, may amend the plan. However, where a sponsor is unable to secure the consent of each such employer, the plan cannot be amended. In such cases any change can only be effected by the establishment of a new plan and the submission of a new Form 4461 by the sponsor. The new plan must be complete and separate from the old plan, and individual employers may, if they desire, substitute the new plan for the old plan.

(iii) Where the plan has been amended pursuant to subdivision (ii) of this subparagraph, the sponsor is to submit an application, Form 4461, a copy of the amendment, a description of the changes, and a statement indicating the provisions in the original plan authorizing amendments, or a statement that each participating employer's consent has been obtained.

(iv) Upon approval of the amendment by the National Office, an opinion letter will be issued to the sponsor containing the serial number of the original plan, followed by a suffix: "A-1" for the first amendment, "A-2" for the second amendment, etc. Employers adopting the form of plan subsequent to the date of the amendment must use the revised serial number.

(v) If a new plan is submitted, together with Form 4461 and copies of all documents evidencing the plan, an opinion letter bearing a new serial number will be issued to the sponsor, and all employers who adopt the new plan are to use the new serial number. Employers who adopted the old plan continue to use the original serial number. However, any employer who wishes to change to the new plan may do so by filing with his district director a new Form 4462, indicating the change.

(vi) An employer who amends his adoption agreement may request a determination letter as to the effect of such amendment by filing Form 4462 with his district director, together with a copy of the amendment and a summary of the changes. However, in the event an employer desires to amend his adoption agreement under a master or prototype plan, and such amendment is not contemplated or permitted under the plan, then such amendment will in effect substitute an individually designed plan for the master or prototype plan and the amendment procedure described in paragraph (o) of this section will be applicable.

(6) *Effect on other plans.*—Determination letters previously issued by district directors specified in paragraph (o)(2)(viii) of this section are not affected by these procedures even though the plans covered by the determination letters were designed by organizations described in subparagraph (1)(i) of this paragraph. However, such organizations may avail themselves of these procedures with respect to any subsequent action regarding such plans if they otherwise come within the scope of this paragraph.

(r) *Rulings and determination letters with respect to foundation status classification.*—(1) *Rulings and determination letters on private and operating foundation status.*—The procedures relating to the issuance of rulings and determination letters on private foundation status under section 509(a), and operating foundation status under section 4942(j)(3), of organizations exempt from Federal Income Tax under section 501(c)(3) of the Code will be published from time to time in the Internal Revenue Bulletin (see for example, Rev. Proc. 76-34, 1976-2 C.B. 656, as modified by Rev. Proc. 80-25, 1980-1 C.B. 667. These procedures apply in connection with notices filed by the organizations on Form 4653, Notification Concerning Foundation Status, or with applications for recognition of exempt status under section 501(c)(3) of the Code. Such notices and statements are filed by organizations in accordance with section 508(a) of the Code in order for an organization to avoid the presumption of private foundation status or to claim status as an operating foundation. In addition, these procedures also relate to National Office review of determination letters on foundation status under sections 509(a) and 4942(j)(3) of the Code and protest of adverse determination letters regarding foundation status.

(2) *Nonexempt charitable trusts claiming nonprivate foundation status under section 509(a)(3) of the Code.*—A trust described in section 4947(a)(1) of the Code is one that is not exempt from tax under section 501(a) of the Code, has all of its unexpired interests devoted to one or more of the purposes described in section 170(c)(2)(B) of the Code, and is a trust for which a charitable deduction was allowed. These trusts are subject to the private foundation provisions (Part II of subchapter F of chapter 1 and chapter 42 of the Code) except section 508(a), (b), and (c) of the Code. The procedures to be used by nonexempt charitable trusts to obtain determinations of their foundation status under section 509(a)(3) of the Code will be published from time to time in the Internal Revenue Bulletin (see, for example, Rev. Proc. 72-50, 1972-2 C.B. 830).

(s) *Advance rulings or determination letters.*—(1) *General.*—It is the practice of the Service to answer written inquiries, when appropriate and in the interest of sound tax administration, as to the tax effects of acts or transactions of individuals and organizations and as to the status of certain organizations for tax purposes prior to the filing of returns or reports as required by the Revenue laws.

(2) *Exceptions.*—There are, however, certain areas where because of the inherently factual nature of the problems involved or for other reasons, the Service will not issue advance rulings or determination letters. Ordinarily, an advance ruling or determination letter is not issued on any matter where the determination requested is primarily one of fact (e.g., market value of property), or on the tax effect of any transaction to be consummated at some indefinite future time or of any transaction or matter having as a major purpose the reduction of Federal taxes. A specific area or a list of these areas is published from

time to time in the Internal Revenue Bulletin (see, for example, Rev. Proc. 80-22, 1980-1 C.B. 654). Such list is not all inclusive. Whenever a particular item is added to or deleted from the list, however, appropriate notice thereof will be published in the Internal Revenue Bulletin. The authority and general procedures of the National Office of the Internal Revenue Service and of the offices of the district directors of internal revenue with respect to the issuance of advance rulings and determination letters are outlined in paragraphs (b) and (c) of this section.

(t) *Alternative method of depletion.*—(1) *In general.*—Section 1.613-4(d)(1)(i) of the regulations, adopted by T.D. 7170, March 10, 1972, provides that, in those cases where it is impossible to determine a representative market or field price under the provisions of §1.613-4(c), gross income from mining shall be computed by use of the proportionate profits method set forth in §1.613-4(d)(4).

(2) *Exception.*—An exception is provided in §1.613-4(d)(1)(ii) where, upon application, the Office of the Assistant Commissioner (Technical) approves the use of an alternative method that is more appropriate than the proportionate profits method or the alternative method being used by the taxpayer.

(3) *Procedure.*—The procedure for making application for approval to compute gross income from mining by use of an alternative method, other than the proportionate profits method; the conditions for approval and use of an alternative method; changes in an approved method; and other pertinent information with respect thereto, will be published from time to time in the Cumulative Bulletin (see, for example, Rev. Proc. 74-43, 1974-2 C.B. 496).

(u) *Conditions for issuing rulings involving bonuses and advanced royalties of lessors under §631(c) of IRC of 1954.*—(1) *In general.*—Rev. Proc. 77-11, 1977-1 C.B. 568, provides that the tax liability of a lessor who received a bonus or an advance royalty is required to be recomputed for the taxable year or years in which such payment or payments were received if the right to mine coal or iron ore under the lease expires, terminates, or is abandoned before (with respect to bonuses) any coal or iron ore has been mined; or (with respect to advance royalties) the coal or iron ore that has been paid for in advance is mined. In such recomputation, the lessor is required to treat the bonus payment or payments or any portion of the advance royalty payment or payments attributable to unmined coal or iron ore, as ordinary income and not as received from the sale of coal or iron ore under section 631(c) of the Code.

(2) *Condition for issuing rulings.*—Prior to issuing a ruling to lessors who request a ruling that they may treat bonuses or advance royalties received under a lease for coal or iron ore as received from a sale of coal or iron under section 631(c) of the Code, the Internal Revenue Service will require that the lessor enter a closing agreement in which the lessor agrees that—

(i) If the lease under which the lessor received a bonus or an advance royalty expires, terminates, or is abandoned before (with respect to a bonus) any coal or iron ore has been mined or (with respect to an advance royalty) the coal or iron ore that has been paid for in advance is mined, the tax liability of the lessor will be recomputed for the taxable year or years of receipt of (A) the bonus by treating the bonus payment or payments as ordinary income or (B) the advance royalty by treating any portion of the advance royalty payment or payments attributable to unmined coal or iron ore as ordinary income;

(ii) If the recomputation described in paragraph (u)(2)(i) of this section is required, the lessor will pay the additional amount, if any, of all federal income tax finally determined as due and payable by the lessor for the taxable year or years of the receipt of the bonus or advance royalty; and

(iii) If any of the described events has occurred, the lessor will notify the appropriate district director of such event in writing within 90 days of the close of the taxable year in which the lease expires, terminates, or is abandoned. [Reg. §601.201.]

☐ [32 FR 15990, Nov. 22, 1967, as amended at 33 FR 6821, May 4, 1968; 33 FR 17236, Nov. 21, 1968; 34 FR 6425, Apr. 12, 1969; 34 FR 14601, Sept. 19, 1969; 35 FR 7114, May 6, 1970; 35 FR 15918, Oct. 9, 1970; 36 FR 7585, Apr. 22, 1971; 38 FR 4960, Feb. 23, 1973; 38 FR 33301, Dec. 3, 1973; 39 FR 8917, Mar. 7, 1974; 40 FR 32323, Aug. 1, 1975; 41 FR 20881, 20884, May 21, 1976; 41 FR 48741, Nov. 5, 1976; 42 FR 34280, July 5, 1977; 42 FR 46519, Sept. 16, 1977; 42 FR 48336, Sept. 23, 1977; 43 FR 17817, Apr. 26, 1978; 43 FR 44504, Sept. 28, 1978; 45 FR 7255, Feb. 1, 1980; 46 FR 26053, May 11, 1981; 48 FR 15624, Apr. 12, 1983; T.D. 8685, 61 FR 58008, Nov. 12, 1996; T.D. 9006, July 18, 2002 and T.D. 9849, 3-11-2019.]

**[Reg. §601.202]**

**§601.202. Closing agreements.**—(a) *General.*—(1) Under section 7121 of the Code and the regulations and delegations thereunder, the Commissioner, or any officer or employee of the Internal Revenue

Service authorized in writing by the Commissioner, may enter into and approve a written agreement with a person relating to the liability of such person (or of the person or estate for whom he acts) in respect of any internal revenue tax for any taxable period. Such agreement, except upon a showing of fraud or malfeasance, or misrepresentation of a material fact, shall be final and conclusive.

(2) Closing agreements under section 7121 of the Code may relate to any taxable period ending prior or subsequent to the date of the agreement. With respect to taxable periods ended prior to the date of the agreement, the matter agreed upon may relate to the total tax liability of the taxpayer or it may relate to one or more separate items affecting the tax liability of the taxpayer. A closing agreement may also be entered into in order to provide a "determination", as defined in section 1313 of the Code, and for the purpose of allowing a deficiency dividend deduction under section 547 of the Code. But see also sections 547(c)(3) and 1313(a)(4) of the Code and the regulations thereunder as to other types of "determination" agreements. With respect to taxable periods ending subsequent to the date of the agreement, the matter agreed upon may relate to one or more separate items affecting the tax liability of the taxpayer. A closing agreement with respect to any taxable period ending subsequent to the date of the agreement is subject to any change in or modification of the law enacted subsequent to the date of the agreement and applicable to such taxable period, and each such closing agreement shall so recite. Closing agreements may be entered into even though under the agreement the taxpayer is not liable for any tax for the period to which the agreement relates. There may be a series of agreements relating to the tax liability for a single period. A closing agreement may be entered into in any case in which there appears to be an advantage in having the case permanently and conclusively closed, or where good and sufficient reasons are shown by the taxpayer for desiring a closing agreement and it is determined by the Commissioner or his representatives that the Government will sustain no disadvantage through consummation of such an agreement.

(b) *Use of prescribed forms.*—In cases in which it is proposed to close conclusively the total tax liability for a taxable period ending prior to the date of the agreement, Form 866, Agreement as to Final Determination of Tax Liability, generally will be used. In cases in which agreement has been reached as to the disposition of one or more issues and a closing agreement is considered necessary to insure consistent treatment of such issues in any other taxable period Form 906, Closing Agreement as to Final Determination Covering Specific Matters, generally will be used. A request for a closing agreement which determines tax liability may be submitted and entered into at any time before the determination of such liability becomes a matter within the province of a court of competent jurisdiction and may thereafter be entered into in appropriate circumstances when authorized by the court (e.g., in certain bankruptcy situations). The request should be submitted to the district director of internal revenue with whom the return for the period involved was filed. However, if the matter to which the request relates is pending before an office of the Appellate Division, the request should be submitted to that office. A request for a closing agreement which relates only to a subsequent period should be submitted to the Commissioner of Internal Revenue, Washington, D.C. 20224.

(c) *Approval.*—(1) Closing agreements relating to alcohol, tobacco, and firearms taxes in respect of any prospective transactions or completed transactions affecting returns to be filed may be entered into and approved by the Director, Bureau of Alcohol, Tobacco and Firearms.

(2) Closing agreements relating to taxes other than those taxes covered in subparagraph (1) of this paragraph in respect of any prospective transactions or completed transactions affecting returns to be filed may be entered into and approved by the Assistant Commissioner (Technical).

(3) Closing agreements for a taxable period or periods ended prior to the date of agreement and related specific items affecting other taxable periods (including those covering competent authority determinations in the administration of the operating provisions of the tax conventions of the United States) may be entered into and approved by the Assistant Commissioner (Compliance).

(4) Regional commissioners, assistant regional commissioners (appellate), assistant regional commissioners (examination), district directors (including the Director, Foreign Operations District), chiefs and assistant chiefs of appellate branch offices may enter into and approve closing agreements on cases under their jurisdiction (but excluding cases docketed before the U.S. Tax Court) for a taxable period or periods which end prior to the date of agreement and related specific items affecting other taxable periods.

(5) Regional commissioners, assistant regional commissioners (examination) and (appellate), chiefs and assistant chiefs of appellate branch offices are authorized to enter into and approve closing agreements in cases under their jurisdiction docketed in the U.S. Tax

Court but only in respect to related specific items affecting other taxable periods.

(6) Closing agreements providing for the mitigation of economic double taxation under section 3 of Revenue Procedure 64-54, C.B. 1964-2, 1008, or under Revenue Procedure 69-13, C.B. 1969-1, 402 or for such mitigation and relief under Revenue Procedure 65-17, C.B. 1965-1, 833, may be entered into and approved by the Director, Foreign Operations District.

(7) Closing agreements in cases under the jurisdiction of a district director providing that the taxability of earnings from a deposit or account of the type described in Revenue Procedure 64-24, C.B. 1964-1 (Part 1), 693, opened prior to November 15, 1962, will be determined on the basis that earnings on such deposits or accounts are not includible in gross income until maturity or termination, whichever occurs earlier, and that the full amount of earnings on the deposit or account will constitute gross income in the year the plan matures, is assigned, or is terminated, whichever occurs first, may be entered into and approved by such district director.

(d) *Applicability of ruling requirements.*—The requirements relating to requests for rulings (see § 601.201) shall be applicable with respect to requests for closing agreements pertaining to prospective transactions or completed transactions affecting returns to be filed (see paragraph (c)(2) of this section). [Reg. § 601.202.]

☐ [32 FR 15990, Nov. 22, 1967, as amended at 32 FR 20647, Dec. 21, 1967; 33 FR 17237, Nov. 21, 1968; 34 FR 14601, Sept. 19, 1969; 35 FR 15920, Oct. 9, 1970; 38 FR 4967, Feb. 23, 1973; 42 FR 46520, Sept. 16, 1977; 43 FR 53030, Nov. 15, 1978; 49 FR 36499, Sept. 18, 1984; T.D. 8685, 61 FR 58008, Nov. 12, 1996.]

## [Reg. § 601.203]

**§ 601.203. Offers in compromise.**—(a) *General.*—(1) The Commissioner may compromise, in accordance with the provisions of section 7122 of the Code, any civil or criminal case arising under the internal revenue laws prior to reference to the Department of Justice for prosecution or defense. Certain functions of the Commissioner with respect to compromise of civil cases involving liability of $100,000 or more, based solely on doubt as to liability, have been delegated to regional commissioners and, for cases arising in the District Office, Foreign Operations District, to the Assistant Commissioner (Compliance). The authority concerning liability of $100,000 or more based on doubt as to collectibility or doubt as to both collectibility and liability has been delegated to the Director, Collection Division, and regional commissioners. The authority with respect to compromise of civil cases involving liability under $100,000, and of certain specific penalties has been delegated to district directors, assistant district directors, and (including the District Director and Assistant District Director, Foreign Operations District), regional directors of Appeals, and chiefs and associate chiefs, Appeals offices. The authority concerning offers in compromise of penalties based solely on doubt as to liability, if the liability is less than $100,000, has also been delegated to service center directors and assistant service center directors. In civil cases involving liability of $500 or over and in criminal cases the functions of the General Counsel are performed by the Chief Counsel for the Internal Revenue Service. These functions are performed in the District Counsel, Regional Counsel, or National Office as appropriate. (See also paragraph (c) of this section.) In cases arising under chapters 51, 52, and 53 of the Code, offers are acted upon by the Bureau of Alcohol, Tobacco and Firearms.

(2) An offer in compromise of taxes, interest, delinquency penalties, or specific penalties may be based on either inability to pay or doubt as to liability. Offers in compromise arise usually when payments of assessed liabilities are demanded, penalties for delinquency in filing returns are asserted, or specific civil or criminal penalties are incurred by taxpayers. A criminal liability will not be compromised unless it involves only the regulatory provisions of the Internal Revenue Code and related statutes. However, if the violations involving the regulatory provisions are deliberate and with intent to defraud, the criminal liabilities will not be compromised.

(b) *Use of prescribed form.*—Offers in compromise are required to be submitted on Form 656, properly executed, and accompanied by a financial statement on Form 433 (if based on inability to pay). Form 656 is used in all cases regardless of whether the amount of the offer is tendered in full at the time the offer is filed or the amount of the offer is to be paid by deferred payment or payments. Copies of Form 656 and Form 433 may be obtained from district directors. An offer in compromise should be filed with the district director or service center director.

(c) *Consideration of offer.*—(1) An offer in compromise is first considered by the director having jurisdiction. Except in certain penalty cases, an investigation of the basis of the offer is required. The examining officer makes a written recommendation for acceptance or rejection of the offer. If the director has jurisdiction over the processing of the offer he or she will:

(i) Reject the offer, or

(ii) Accept the offer if it involves a civil liability under $500, or

(iii) Accept the offer if it involves a civil liability of $500 or more, but less than $100,000, or involves a specific penalty, and the District Counsel concurs in the acceptance of the offer, or

(iv) Recommend to the National Office the acceptance of the offer if it involves a civil liability of $100,000 or over.

(2)(i) If the district director does not have jurisdiction over the entire processing of the offer, the offer is transmitted to the appropriate District Counsel if the case is one in which:

(a) Recommendations for prosecution are pending in the Office of the Chief Counsel, the Department of Justice, or in an office of a United States attorney, including cases in which criminal proceedings have been instituted but not disposed of and related cases in which offers in compromise have been submitted or are pending;

(b) The taxpayer is in receivership or is involved in a proceeding under any provision of the Bankruptcy Act;

(c) The taxpayer is deceased; in joint liability cases, where either taxpayer is deceased;

(d) A proposal is made to discharge property from the effect of a tax lien or to subordinate the lien or liens;

(e) An insolvent bank is involved;

(f) An assignment for the benefit of creditors is involved;

(g) A liquidation proceeding is involved; or

(h) Court proceedings are pending, except Tax Court cases.

(ii) The District Counsel considers and processes offers submitted in cases described in paragraph (c)(2)(i)(a) through (h) of this section and forwards those offers to the district director, service center director, Regional Counsel, or Office of Chief Counsel in Washington, as appropriate.

(iii) In those cases described in (a) of subdivision (i) of this subparagraph no investigation will be made unless specifically requested by the office having jurisdiction of the criminal case.

(iv) In those cases described in (b) through (h) of subdivision (i) of this subparagraph the district director retains the duplicate copy of the offer and the financial statement for investigation. After investigation, the district director transmits to the appropriate District Counsel for consideration and processing his or her recommendation for acceptance or rejection of the offer together with the examining officer's report of the investigation.

(3) The district directors, assistant district directors (including the District Director and Assistant District Director, Foreign Operations District), service center directors, assistant service center directors, Regional Directors of appeals, and Chiefs and Associate Chiefs, Appeals Offices are authorized to reject any offer in compromise referred for their consideration. Unacceptable offers considered by the District Counsel, Regional Counsel, or Office of Chief Counsel in Washington, or the Appeals office are also rejected by the district directors (including the Director, Foreign Operations District) as applicable. If an offer is not acceptable, the taxpayer is promptly notified of the rejection of that offer. If an offer is rejected, the sum submitted with the offer is returned to the proponent, unless the taxpayer authorizes application of the sum offered to the tax liability. Each Regional Commissioner will perform a post review of offers accepted, rejected, or withdrawn by the district director's office if the offer covers liabilities of $5,000 or more. The post review will cover a sampling of cases processed by the Collection function and all cases processed by the Examination function.

(4) If an offer involving unpaid liability of $100,000 or more is considered acceptable by the office having jurisdiction over the offer, a recommendation for acceptance is forwarded to the National Office or Regional Office, as appropriate, for review. If the recommendation for acceptance is approved, the offer is forwarded to the Regional Counsel or Office of Chief Counsel in Washington, as appropriate, for approval. After approval by the Regional Counsel or Office of Chief Counsel in Washington, as appropriate, it is forwarded to the Assistant Commissioner (Compliance), Director, Collection Division, or Regional Commissioner, as appropriate, for acceptance. The taxpayer is notified of the acceptance of the offer in accordance with its terms. Acceptance of an offer in compromise of civil liabilities does not remit criminal liabilities, nor does acceptance of an offer in compromise of criminal liabilities remit civil liabilities.

(d) *Conferences.*—Before filing a formal offer in compromise, a taxpayer may request a meeting in the office which would have jurisdiction over the offer to explore the possibilities of compromising unpaid tax liability. After all investigations have been made, the taxpayer may also request a meeting in the office having jurisdiction of the offer to determine the amount which may be accepted as a compromise. If agreement is not reached at such meeting and the district director has processing jurisdiction over the offer, the taxpayer will be informed that the taxpayer may request consideration of the case by an Appeals office. The request may be in writing or oral. If the tax, penalty, and assessed (but not accrued) interest sought to be compromised exceeds $2,500 for any return, taxable year

or taxable period, a written protest is required. Taxpayers and their representatives are required to comply with the applicable conference and practice requirements. See subpart E of this part. [Reg. § 601.203.]

☐ [32 FR 15990, Nov. 22, 1967, as amended at 33 FR 17238, Nov. 21, 1968; 35 FR 7116, May 6, 1970; 35 FR 15920, Oct. 9, 1970; 43 FR 44510, Sept. 28, 1978; 45 FR 7255, Feb. 1, 1980; 46 FR 26054, May 11, 1981; 49 FR 36499, Sept. 18, 1984; T.D. 8685, 61 FR 58008, Nov. 12, 1996.]

### [Reg. § 601.204]

**§ 601.204. Changes in accounting periods and in methods of accounting.**—(a) *Accounting periods.*—A taxpayer who changes his accounting period shall, before using the new period for income tax purposes, comply with the provisions of the income tax regulations relating to changes in accounting periods. In cases where the regulations require the taxpayer to secure the consent of the Commissioner to the change, the application for permission to change the accounting period shall be made on Form 1128 and shall be submitted to the Commissioner of Internal Revenue, Washington, D.C. 20224, within the period of time prescribed in such regulations. See section 442 of the Code and regulations thereunder. If the change is approved by the Commissioner, the taxpayer shall thereafter make his returns and compute his net income upon the basis of the new accounting period. A request for permission to change the accounting period will be considered by the Corporation Tax Division. However, in certain instances, Form 1128 may be filed with the Director of the Internal Revenue Service Center in which the taxpayer files its return. See, for example, Rev. Proc. 66-13, 1966-1 C.B. 626; Rev. Proc. 66-50, 1966-2 C.B. 1260, and Rev. Proc. 68-41, 1968-2 C.B. 943. With respect to partnership adoption, see § 1.706-1(b) of the Income Tax Regulations.

(b) *Methods of accounting.*—A taxpayer who changes the method of accounting employed in keeping his books shall, before computing his income upon such method for purposes of income taxation, comply with the provisions of the income tax regulations relating to changes in accounting methods. The regulations require that, in the ordinary case, the taxpayer secure the consent of the Commissioner to the change. See section 446 of the Code and the regulations thereunder. Application for permission to change the method of accounting employed shall be made on Form 3115 and shall be submitted to the Commissioner of Internal Revenue, Washington, D.C. 20224, during the taxable year in which it is desired to make the change. Permission to change the method of accounting will not be granted unless the taxpayer and the Commissioner agree to the terms and conditions under which the change will be effected. The request will be considered by the Corporation Tax Division. However, in certain instances, Form 3115 may be filed with the Director of the Internal Revenue Service Center. See, for example, Rev. Proc. 74-11, 1974-1 C.B. 420.

(c) *Verification of changes.*—Written permission to a taxpayer by the National Office consenting to a change in his annual accounting period or to a change in his accounting method is a "ruling." Therefore, in the examination of returns involving changes of annual accounting periods and methods of accounting, district directors must determine whether the representations upon which the permission was granted reflect an accurate statement of the material facts, and whether the agreed terms, conditions, and adjustments have been substantially carried out as proposed. An application, Form 3115, filed with the Director of the Internal Revenue Service Center is also subject to similar verification.

(d) *Instructions to taxpayers.*—The person seeking to secure the consent of the Commissioner with respect to a change of accounting periods or methods pursuant to section 442 or 446(e) of the Code need not submit the statement of proposed deletions described in § 601.201(e)(5) at the time the request is made. If, however, the person seeking the consent of the Commissioner receives from the National Office a notice that proposed deletions should be submitted because the resulting ruling will be open to public inspection under section 6110, the statement of proposed deletions must be submitted within 20 days after such notice is mailed. [Reg. § 601.204.]

☐ [41 FR 20882, May 21, 1976, as amended at 41 FR 48742, Nov. 5, 1976; 42 FR 34280, July 5, 1977; T.D. 8719, May 15, 1997; T.D. 8742, Dec. 30, 1997.]

### [Reg. § 601.205]

**§ 601.205. Tort claims.**—Claims for property loss or damage, personal injury, or death caused by the negligent or wrongful act or omission of any employee of the Service, acting within the scope of his office or employment, filed under the Federal Tort Claims Act, as amended, must be prepared and filed in accordance with Treasury Department regulations entitled "Central Office Procedures" and "Claims Regulations" (31 CFR, Parts 1 and 3). Such regulations contain the procedural and substantive requirements relative to such claims, and set forth the manner in which they are handled. The claims should be filed with the Commissioner of Internal Revenue,

Washington, D.C. 20224, and must be filed within two years after the accident or incident occurred. [Reg. § 601.205.]

☐ [32 FR 15990, Nov. 22, 1967.]

**[Reg. § 601.206]**

**§ 601.206. Certification required to obtain reduced foreign tax rates under income tax treaties.**—(a) *Basis of certification.*—Most of the income tax treaties between the United States and foreign countries provide for either a reduction in the statutory rate of tax or an exemption from tax on certain types of income received from sources within the foreign treaty country by citizens, domestic corporations, and residents of the United States. Some of the treaty countries reduce the withholding tax on such types of income or exempt the income from withholding tax after the claimant furnishes evidence that he is entitled to the benefits of the treaty. Other countries initially withhold the tax at statutory rates and refund the excess tax withheld after satisfactory evidence of U.S. residence has been accepted. As part of the proof that the applicant is a resident of the United States and thus entitled to the benefits of the treaty, he must usually furnish a certification from the U.S. Government that he has filed a U.S. income tax return as a citizen, domestic corporation, or resident of the U.S.

(b) *Procedure for obtaining the certification.*—Most of the treaty countries which require certification have printed special forms. The forms contain a series of questions to be answered by the taxpayer claiming the benefits of the treaty, followed by a statement which the foreign governments use for the U.S. taxing authority's certification. This certification may be obtained from the office of the district director of the district in which the claimant filed his latest income tax return. Some certification forms are acceptable for Service execution; however, others cannot be executed by the Service without revision. In these instances the office of the district director will prepare its own document of certification in accordance with internal instructions. This procedure has been accepted by most treaty countries as a satisfactory substitute.

(c) *Obtaining the official certification forms.*—The forms may be obtained from the foreign payor, the tax authority of the treaty country involved, or the District Office, Foreign Operations District. [Reg. § 601.206.]

☐ [34 FR 14601, Sept. 19, 1969, as amended at 49 FR 36500, Sept. 18, 1984.]

# Subpart C—[Reserved]

# Subpart D—Provisions Special to Certain Employment Taxes

**[Reg. § 601.401]**

**§ 601.401. Employment taxes.**—(a) *General.*—(1) *Description of taxes.*—Federal employment taxes are imposed by Subtitle C of the Internal Revenue Code. Chapter 21 (Federal Insurance Contributions Act) imposes a tax on employers of one or more individuals and also a tax on employees, with respect to "wages" paid and received. Chapter 22 (Railroad Retirement Tax Act) imposes (i) an employer tax and employee tax with respect to "compensation" paid and received,(ii) an employee representative tax with respect to "compensation" received, and (iii) a supplemental tax on employers, measured by man-hours for which "compensation" is paid. Chapter 23 (Federal Unemployment Tax Act) imposes a tax on employers of one or more individuals with respect to "wages" paid. Chapter 24 (collection of income tax at source on wages) requires every employer making payment of "wages" to deduct and withhold upon such wages the tax computed or determined as provided therein. The tax so deducted and withheld is allowed as a credit against the income tax liability of the employee receiving such wages.

(2) *Applicable regulations.*—The descriptive terms used in this section to designate the various classes of taxes are intended only to indicate their general character. Specific information relative to the scope of each tax, the forms used, and the functioning of the Service with respect thereto is contained in the applicable regulations. Copies of all necessary forms, and instructions as to their preparation and filing, may be obtained from the district director of internal revenue.

(3) *Collection methods.*—Employment taxes are collected by means of returns and by withholding by employers. Employee tax must be deducted and withheld by employers from "wages" or "compensation" (including tips reported in writing to employers) paid to employees, and the employer is liable for the employee tax whether or not it is so deducted. For special rules relating to tips see § § 31.3102-3 and 31.3402(k)-1. Rev. Proc. 81-48, 1981-2 C.B. 623, provides guidelines for determining wages when the employer pays the employee tax imposed by chapter 21 without deducting the amount from the employee's pay. Employee representatives (as defined in the Railroad Retirement Tax Act) are required to file returns. Employment tax returns must be filed with the district director or, if so provided in instructions applicable to a return, with the service center designated in the instructions. The return of the Federal unemployment tax is required to be filed annually on Form 940 with respect to wages paid during the calendar year. All other returns of Federal employment taxes (with the exception of returns filed for agricultural employees) are required to be filed for each calendar quarter except that if pursuant to regulations the district director so notifies the employer, returns on Form 941 are required to be filed on a monthly basis. In the case of certain employers required to report withheld income tax but not required to report employer and employee taxes imposed by chapter 21 (for example, state and local government employers), Form 941E is prescribed for reporting on a quarterly basis. The employer and employee taxes imposed by chapter 21 (other than the employer and employee taxes on wages paid for agricultural labor) and the tax required to be deducted and withheld upon wages by chapter 24 are combined in a single return on Form 941. In the case of wages paid by employers for domestic service performed in a private home not on a farm operated for profit, the return of both the employee tax and the employer tax imposed by chapter 21 is on Form 942. However, if the employer is required to file a return for the same quarter on Form 941, the employer may elect to include the taxes with respect to such domestic service on Form 941. The employer and employee taxes imposed by chapter 21 with respect to wages paid for agricultural labor are required to be reported annually on Form 943. Under the Railroad Retirement Tax Act, the return required of the employer is on Form CT-1, and the return required of each employee representative is on Form CT-2. An employee is not required to file a return of employee tax, except that the employee must include in his or her income tax return (as provided in the applicable instructions) any amount of employee tax (i) due with respect to tips that the employee failed to report to the employer or (ii) shown on the employee's Form W-2 as "Uncollected Employee Tax on Tips".

(4) *Receipts for employees.*—Employers are required to furnish each employee a receipt or statement, in duplicate, showing the total wages subject to income tax withholding, the amount of income tax withheld, the amount of wages subject to tax under the Federal Insurance Contributions Act, and the amount of employee tax withheld. See section 6051 of the Code.

(5) *Use of authorized commercial banks and trust companies in connection with payment of Federal employment taxes.*—Most employers are required to deposit employment taxes either on a monthly basis, a semimonthly basis or a quarter-monthly period basis as follows:

(i) *Quarter-monthly period deposits.*—With respect to wages paid after January 31, 1971, (March 31, 1971 in the case of wages paid for agricultural labor), if at the close of any quarter-monthly period (that ends on the 7th, 15th, 22nd, or the last day of any month) the aggregate amount of undeposited taxes, exclusive of taxes reportable on Form 942, is $2,000 or more, the employer shall deposit such taxes within 3 banking days after the close of such quarter-monthly period.

(ii) *Monthly deposits.*—With respect to employers not required to make deposits under subdivision (i) of this subparagraph, if after January 31, 1971 (March 31, 1971, in the case of income tax withheld from wages paid for agricultural labor) (a) during any calendar month, other than the last month of a calendar quarter, the aggregate amount of the employee tax deducted and the employer tax under chapter 21 and the income tax withheld at source on wages under chapter 24, exclusive of taxes reportable on Form 942, exceeds $200, or (b) at the end of any month or period of 2 or more months and prior to December 1 of any calendar year, the total amount of undeposited taxes imposed by chapter 21, with respect to wages paid for agricultural labor, exceeds $200, it is the duty of the employer to deposit such amount within 15 days after the close of such calendar month.

(iii) *Quarterly and year-end deposits.*—Whether or not an employer is required to make deposits under subdivisions (i) and (ii) of this subparagraph, if the amount of such taxes reportable on Form 941 or 943 (reduced by any previous deposits) exceeds $200, the employer shall, on or before the last day of the first calendar month following the period for which the return is required to be filed, deposit such amount with an authorized financial institution. However, if the amount of such taxes (reduced by any previous deposits) does not exceed $200, the employer may either include with his return a direct remittance for the amount of such taxes or, on or before the last day of the first calendar month following the period for which the return is required to be filed, voluntarily deposit such amount with an authorized financial institution.

(iv) *Additional rules.*—Deposits under subdivisions (i), (ii) and (iii) of this subparagraph are made with an authorized financial institution. The remittance of such amount must be accompanied by a Federal Tax Deposit form. Each employer making deposits shall report on the return for the period with respect to which such deposits are made information regarding such deposits in accordance with the instructions applicable to such return and pay therewith (or deposit by the due date of such return) the balance, if any, of the taxes due for such period.

(v) *Employers under chapter 22 of the Code.*—Depositary procedures similar to those prescribed in this subparagraph are prescribed for employers as defined by the Railroad Retirement Tax Act, except that railroad retirement taxes are not requested to be deposited semimonthly or quarter-monthly. Such taxes must be deposited by using a Federal Tax Deposit form.

(vi) *Employers under chapter 23 of the Code.*—Every person who is an employer as defined by the Federal Unemployment Tax Act shall deposit the tax imposed under chapter 23 on or before the last day of the first calendar month following the quarterly period in which the amount of such tax exceeds $100.

(6) *Separate accounting.*—If an employer fails to withhold and pay over income, social security, or railroad retirement tax due on wages of employees, the employer may be required by the district director to collect such taxes and deposit them in a separate banking account in trust for the United States not later than the second banking day after such taxes are collected.

(b) *Provisions special to the Federal Insurance Contributions Act.*— (1) *Employers' identification numbers.*—For purposes of the Federal Insurance Contributions Act each employer who files Form 941 or Form 943 must have an identification number. Any such employer who does not have an identification number must secure a Form SS-4 from the district director of internal revenue or from a district office of the Social Security Administration and, after executing the form in accordance with the instructions contained thereon, file it with the district director or the district office of the Social Security Administration. At a subsequent date the district director will assign the employer a number which must appear in the appropriate space on each tax return, Form 941 or Form 943, filed thereafter. The requirement to secure an identification number does not apply to an employer who employs only employees who are engaged exclusively in the performance of domestic service in the employer's private home not on a farm operated for profit.

(2) *Employees' account numbers.*—Each employee (or individual making a return of net earnings from self-employment) who does not have an account number must file an application on Form SS-5), a copy of which may be obtained from any district office of the Social Security Administration or from a district director of internal revenue. The form, after execution in accordance with the instructions thereon, must be filed with the district office of the Social Security Administration, and at a later date the employee will be furnished an account number. The employee must furnish such number to each employer for whom the employee works, in order that such number may be entered on each tax return filed thereafter by the employer.

(3) *Reporting of wages.*—Forms 941, 942, and 943 each require, as a part of the return, that the wages of each employee paid during the period covered by the return be reported thereon. Form 941a is available to employers who need additional space for the listing of employees. Employers who meet the requirements of the Social Security Administration may, with the approval of the Commissioner of Internal Revenue, submit wage information on reels of magnetic tape in lieu of Form 941a. It is necessary at times that employers correct wage information previously reported. A special form, Form 941c, has been adopted for use in correcting erroneous wage information or omissions of such wage information on Forms 941, 942, or 943. Instructions on Forms 941, 941c, 942, and 943 explain the manner of preparing and filing the forms. Any further instructions should be obtained from the district director.

(c) *Adjustments by employers.*—(1) *Undercollections and underpayments.*—(i) *Employer tax or employee tax.*—If a return is filed by an employer under the Federal Insurance Contributions Act or the Railroad Retirement Tax Act, and the employer reports and pays less than the correct amount of employer tax or employee tax, the employer is required to report and pay the additional amount due. The reporting will be an adjustment without interest only if the employer reports and pays the additional amount on or before the last day on

which the return is required to be filed for the return period in which the error is ascertained. The employer may so report theadditional amount either on the return for that period or on a supplemental return for the period for which the underpayment was made. If the employer fails to report the additional amount due within the time so fixed for making an interest-free adjustment, the employer nevertheless is required to report the additional amount in the same manner, but interest will be due. No adjustment of an underpayment may be made under this section or § 31.6205-1(b)(2) if the employer is sent a notice and demand for payment of the additional tax.

(ii) *Income tax withholding.*—If an employer files a return reporting and paying less than the correct amount of income tax required to be withheld from wages paid during the return period, the employer is required to report and pay the additional amount due, either (*a*) on a return for any return period in the calendar year in which the wages were paid, or (*b*) on a supplemental return for the return period in which the wages were paid. The reporting will be an adjustment without interest only if the employer reports and pays the additional amount on or before the last day on which the return is required to be filed for the return period in which the error was ascertained. If an employer reports and pays less than the correct amount of income tax required to be withheld in a calendar year, and the employer does not correct the underpayment in the same calendar year, the employer should consult the district director of internal revenue as to the manner of correcting the error.

(2) *Overcollections from employees.*—(i) *Employee tax.*—If an employer collects from an employee more than the correct amount of employee tax under the Federal Insurance Contributions Act or the Railroad Retirement Act, and the error is ascertained within the applicable period of limitation on credit or refund, the employer is required either to repay the amount to the employee, or to reimburse the employee by applying the amount of the overcollection against employee tax which otherwise would be collected from the employee after the error is ascertained. If the overcollection is repaid to the employee, the employer is required to obtain and keep the employee's written receipt showing the date and amount of the repayment. In addition, if the employer repays or reimburses an employee in any calendar year for an overcollection which occurred in a prior calendar year, the employer is required to obtain and keep the employee's written statement (*a*) that the employee has not claimed refund or credit of the amount of the overcollection, or if so, such claim has been rejected, and (*b*) that the employee will not claim refund or credit of such amount.

(ii) *Income tax withholding.*—If, in any return period in a calendar year, an employer withholds more than the correct amount of income tax, and pays over to the Internal Revenue Service the amount withheld, the employer may repay or reimburse the employee in the excess amount in any subsequent return period in the same calendar year. If the amount is so repaid, the employer is required to obtain and keep the employee's written receipt showing the date and amount of the repayment.

(3) *Employer's claims for credit or refund of overpayments.*— (i) *Employee tax.*—If an employer repays or reimburses an employee for an overcollection of employee tax, as described in subparagraph (2)(i) of this paragraph, the employer may claim credit on a return in accordance with the instructions applicable to the return. In lieu of claiming credit the employer may claim refund by filing Form 843, but the employer may not thereafter claim credit for the same overpayment.

(ii) *Income tax withholding.*—If an employer repays or reimburses an employee for an excess amount withheld as income tax, as described in subparagraph (2)(ii) of this paragraph, the employer may claim credit on a return for a return period in the calendar year in which the excess amount was withheld. The employer is not otherwise permitted to claim credit or refund for any overpayment of income tax that the employer deducted or withheld from an employee.

(d) *Special refunds of employee social security tax.*—(1) An employee who receives wages from more than one employer during a calendar year may, under certain conditions, receive a "special refund" of the amount of employee social security tax (*i.e.,* employee tax under the Federal Insurance Contributions Act) deducted and withheld from wages that exceed the following amounts: calendar years 1968 through 1971, $7,800; calendar year 1972, $9,000; calendar year 1973, $10,800; calendar year 1974, $13,200; calendar years after 1974, an amount equal to the contribution and benefit base (as determined under section 230 of the Social Security Act) effective with respect to that year. An employee who is entitled to a special refund of employee tax with respect to wages received during a calendar year, and who is required to file an income tax return for such calendar year (or for his last taxable year beginning in such calendar year), may obtain the benefits of such special refund only by claiming credit for such special refund on such income tax return in the same manner as if such special refund were an amount deducted and withheld as income tax at source on wages.

(2) The amount of the special refund allowed as a credit shall be considered as an amount deducted and withheld as income tax at source on wages. If the amount of such special refund when added to amounts deducted and withheld as income tax under chapter 24 exceeds the income tax imposed by chapter 1, the amount of the excess constitutes an overpayment of income tax, and interest on such overpayment is allowed to the extent provided under section 6611 of the Code upon an overpayment of income tax resulting from a credit for income tax withheld at source on wages.

(3) If an employee entitled to a special refund of employee social security tax is not required to file an income tax return for the year in which such special refund may be claimed as a credit, the employee may file a claim for refund of the excess social security tax on Form 843. Claims must be filed with the district director of internal revenue for the district in which the employee resides.

(4) Employee taxes under the Federal Insurance Contributions Act and the Railroad Retirement Tax Act include a percentage rate for hospital insurance. If in 1968 or any calendar year thereafter employee taxes under both Acts are deducted from an employee's wages and compensation aggregating more than $7,800, the "special refund" provisions may apply to the portion of the tax that is deducted for hospital insurance. The employee may take credit on Form 1040 for the amount allowable, in accordance with the instructions applicable to that form. [Reg. § 601.401.]

☐ [32 FR 15990, Nov. 22, 1967, as amended at 33 FR 6825, May 4, 1968; 33 FR 17239, Nov. 21, 1968; 36 FR 7586, Apr. 22, 1971; 38 FR 4970, Feb. 23, 1973; 39 FR 8918, Mar. 7, 1974; 41 FR 20883, May 21, 1976; 45 FR 7257, Feb. 1, 1980; 49 FR 19648, 19649, May 9, 1984; 49 FR 25239, June 20, 1984; 49 FR 36500, Sept. 18, 1984; 66 FR 33830, June 26, 2001.]

# Subpart E—Conference and Practice Requirements

**[Reg. § 601.501]**

**§ 601.501. Scope of rules; definitions.**—(a) *Scope of rules.*—The rules prescribed in this subpart concern, among other things, the representation of taxpayers before the Internal Revenue Service under the authority of a power of attorney. These rules apply to all offices of the Internal Revenue Service in all matters under the jurisdiction of the Internal Revenue Service and apply to practice before the Internal Revenue Service (as defined in 31 CFR 10.2(a) and 10.7(a)(7)). For special provisions relating to alcohol, tobacco, and firearms activities, see §§ 601.521 through 601.527. These rules detail the means by which a recognized representative is authorized to act on behalf of a taxpayer. Such authority must be evidenced by a power of attorney and declaration of representative filed with the appropriate office of the Internal Revenue Service. In general, a power of attorney must contain certain information concerning the taxpayer, the recognized representative, and the specific tax matter(s) for which the recognized representative is authorized to act. (See § 601.503(a).) A "declaration of representative" is a written statement made by a recognized representative that he/she is currently eligible to practice before the Internal Revenue Service and is authorized to represent the particular party on whose behalf he/she acts. (See § 601.502(c).)

(b) *Definitions.*—(1) *Attorney-in-fact.*—An agent authorized by a principal under a power of attorney to perform certain specified act(s) or kinds of act(s) on behalf of the principal.

(2) *Centralized Authorization File (CAF) system.*—An automated file containing information regarding the authority of a person appointed under a power of attorney or designated under a tax information authorization.

(3) *Circular No. 230.*—Treasury Department Circular No. 230 codified at 31 CFR part 10, which sets forth the regulations governing practice before the Internal Revenue Service.

(4) *Declaration of representative.*—(See § 601.502(c).)

(5) *Delegation of authority.*—An act performed by a recognized representative whereby authority given under a power of attorney is delegated to another recognized representative. After a delegation is made, both the original recognized representative and the recognized representative to whom a delegation is made will be recognized to represent the taxpayer. (See § 601.505(b)(2).)

(6) *Form 2848, "Power of Attorney and Declaration of Representative."*—The Internal Revenue Service power of attorney form which may be used by a taxpayer who wishes to appoint an individual to represent him/her before the Internal Revenue Service. (See § 601.503(b)(1).)

(7) *Matter.*—The application of each tax imposed by the Internal Revenue Code and the regulations thereunder for each taxable period constitutes a (separate) matter.

(8) *Office of the Internal Revenue Service.*—The office of each district director, the office of each service center, the office of each compliance center, the office of each regional commissioner, and the National Office constitute separate offices of the Internal Revenue Service.

(9) *Power of attorney.*—A document signed by the taxpayer, as principal, by which an individual is appointed as attorney-in-fact to perform certain specified act(s) or kinds of act(s) on behalf of the principal. Specific types of powers of attorney include the following—

(i) *General power of attorney.*—The attorney-in-fact is authorized to perform any or all acts the taxpayer can perform.

(ii) *Durable power of attorney.*—A power of attorney which specifies that the appointment of the attorney-in-fact will not end due to either the passage of time (i.e., the authority conveyed will continue until the death of the taxpayer) or the incompetency of the principal (e.g., the principal becomes unable or is adjudged incompetent to perform his/her business affairs).

(iii) *Limited power of attorney.*—A power of attorney which is limited in any facet (i.e., a power of attorney authorizing the attorney-in-fact to perform only certain specified acts as contrasted to a general power of attorney authorizing the representative to perform any and all acts the taxpayer can perform).

(10) *Practice before the Internal Revenue Service.*—Practice before the Internal Revenue Service encompasses all matters connected with presentation to the Internal Revenue Service or any of its personnel relating to a taxpayer's rights, privileges, or liabilities under laws or regulations administered by the Internal Revenue Service. Such presentations include the preparation and filing of necessary documents, correspondence with and communications to the Internal Revenue Service, and the representation of a taxpayer at conferences, hearings, and meetings. (See 31 CFR 10.2(a) and 10.7(a)(7).)

(11) *Principal.*—A person (i.e., taxpayer) who appoints an attorney-in-fact under a power of attorney.

(12) *Recognized representative.*—An individual who is recognized to practice before the Internal Revenue Service under the provisions of § 601.502.

(13) *Representation.*—Acts performed on behalf of a taxpayer by a representative in practice before the Internal Revenue Service. (See § 601.501(b)(10).) Representation does not include the furnishing of information at the request of the Internal Revenue Service or any of its officers or employees (See 31 CFR 10.7(c).)

(14) *Substitution of representative.*—An act performed by an attorney-in-fact whereby authority given under a power of attorney is transferred to another recognized representative. After a substitution is made, only the newly recognized representative will be considered the taxpayer's representative. (See § 601.505(b)(2).)

(15) *Tax information authorization.*—A document signed by the taxpayer authorizing any individual or entity (e.g., corporation, partnership, trust or organization) designated by the taxpayer to receive and/or inspect confidential tax information in a specified matter. (See section 6103 of the Internal Revenue Code and the regulations thereunder.)

(c) *Conferences.*—(1) *Scheduling.*—The Internal Revenue Service encourages the discussion of any Federal tax matter affecting a taxpayer. Conferences may be offered only to taxpayers and/or their recognized representative(s) acting under a valid power of attorney. As a general rule, such conferences will not be held without previous arrangement. However, if a compelling reason is shown by the taxpayer that an immediate conference should be held, the Internal Revenue Service official(s) responsible for the matter has the discretion to make an exception to the general rule.

(2) *Submission of information.*—Every written protest, brief, or other statement the taxpayer or recognized representative wishes to be considered at any conference should be submitted to or filed with the appropriate Internal Revenue Service official(s) at least five business days before the date of the conference. If the taxpayer or the representative is unable to meet this requirement, arrangement

should be made with the appropriate Internal Revenue Service official for a postponement of the conference to a date mutually agreeable to the parties. The taxpayer or the representative remains free to submit additional or supporting facts or evidence within a reasonable time after the conference. [Reg. § 601.501.]

☐ [56 FR 24003, May 28, 1991; amended at 57 FR 27356, June 19, 1992.]

### [Reg. § 601.502]

**§ 601.502. Recognized representative.**—(a) A recognized representative is an individual who is

(1) Appointed as an attorney-in-fact under a power of attorney, and a

(2) Member of one of the categories described in § 601.502(b) and who files a declaration of representative, as described in § 601.502(c).

(b) *Categories.*—(1) *Attorney.*—Any individual who is a member in good standing of the bar of the highest court of any state, possession, territory, commonwealth, or the District of Columbia;

(2) *Certified public accountant.*—Any individual who is duly qualified to practice as a certified public accountant in any state, possession, territory, commonwealth, or the District of Columbia;

(3) *Enrolled agent.*—Any individual who is enrolled to practice before the Internal Revenue Service and is in active status pursuant to the requirements of Circular No. 230;

(4) *Enrolled actuary.*—Any individual who is enrolled as an actuary by and is in active status with the Joint Board for the Enrollment of Actuaries pursuant to 29 U.S.C. 1242.

(5) *Other individuals.*—(i) *Temporary recognition.*—Any individual who is granted temporary recognition as an enrolled agent by the Director of Practice (31 CFR 10.5(c)).

(ii) *Practice based on a relationship or special status with a taxpayer.*—Any individual authorized to represent a taxpayer with whom/which a special relationship exists (31 CFR 10.7(a)(1)-(6)). (For example, an individual may represent another individual who is his/her regular full-time employer or a member of his/her immediate family; an individual who is a bona fide officer or regular full-time employee of a corporation or certain other organizations may represent that entity.)

(iii) *Unenrolled return preparer.*—Any individual who signs a return as having prepared it for a taxpayer, or who prepared a return with respect to which the instructions or regulations do not require that the return be signed by the preparer. The acts which an unenrolled return preparer may perform are limited to representation of a taxpayer before revenue agents and examining officers of the Examination Division in the offices of District Director with respect to the tax liability of the taxpayer for the taxable year or period covered by a return prepared by the unenrolled return preparer (31 CFR 10.7(a)(7)).

(iv) *Special appearance.*—Any individual who, upon written application, is authorized by the Director of Practice to represent a taxpayer in a particular matter (31 CFR 10.7(b)).

(c) *Declaration of representative.*—A recognized representative must attach to the power of attorney a written declaration (e.g., Part II of Form 2848) stating the following—

(1) I am not currently under suspension or disbarment from practice before the Internal Revenue Service or other practice of my profession by any other authority;

(2) I am aware of the regulations contained in Treasury Department Circular No. 230 (31 C.F.R., part 10), concerning the practice of attorneys, certified public accountants, enrolled agents, enrolled actuaries, and others);

(3) I am authorized to represent the taxpayer(s) identified in the power of attorney; and

(4) I am an individual described in § 601.502(b).

If an individual is unable to make such declaration, he/she may not engage in representation of a taxpayer before the Internal Revenue Service or perform the acts described in § § 601.504(a)(2) through (6). [Reg. § 601.502.]

☐ [56 FR 24004, May 28, 1991; amended at 57 FR 27356, June 19, 1992.]

### [Reg. § 601.503]

**§ 601.503. Requirements of power of attorney, signatures, fiduciaries and Commissioner's authority to substitute other requirements.**—(a) *Requirements.*—A power of attorney must contain the following information—

(1) name and mailing address of the taxpayer;

(2) identification number of the taxpayer (i.e., social security number and/or employer identification number);

(3) employee plan number (if applicable);

(4) name and mailing address of the recognized representative(s);

(5) description of the matter(s) for which representation is authorized which, if applicable, must include—

(i) the type of tax involved;

(ii) the Federal tax form number;

(iii) the specific year(s)/period(s) involved; and

(iv) in estate matters, decedent's date of death; and

(6) a clear expression of the taxpayer's intention concerning the scope of authority granted to the recognized representative(s).

(b) *Acceptable power of attorney documents.*—(1) *Form 2848.*—A properly completed Form 2848 satisfies the requirements for both a power of attorney (as described in § 601.503(a)) and a declaration of representative (as described in § 601.502(c)).

(2) *Other documents.*—The Internal Revenue Service will accept a power of attorney other than Form 2848 provided such document satisfies the requirements of § 601.503(a). However, for purposes of processing such documents onto the Centralized Authorization File (see § 601.506(d)), a completed Form 2848 must be attached. (In such situations, Form 2848 is not the operative power of attorney and need not be signed by the taxpayer. However, the Declaration of Representative must be signed by the representative.)

(3) *Special provision.*—The Internal Revenue Service will not accept a power of attorney which fails to include the information required by § § 601.503(a)(1) through (5). If a power of attorney fails to include some or all of the information required by such section, the attorney-in-fact can cure this defect by executing a Form 2848 (on behalf of the taxpayer) which includes the missing information. Attaching a Form 2848 to a copy of the original power of attorney will validate the original power of attorney (and will be treated in all circumstances as one signed and filed by the taxpayer) provided the following conditions are satisfied—

(i) The original power of attorney contemplates authorization to handle, among other things, Federal tax matters (e.g., the power of attorney includes language to the effect that the attorney-in-fact has the authority to perform any and all acts).

(ii) The attorney-in-fact attaches a statement (signed under penalty of perjury) to the Form 2848 which states that the original power of attorney is valid under the laws of the governing jurisdiction.

(4) *Other categories of powers of attorney.*—Categories of powers of attorney not addressed in these rules (e.g., durable powers of attorney and limited powers of attorney) will be accepted by the Internal Revenue Service provided such documents satisfy the requirements of § 601.503(b)(2) or (3).

(c) *Signatures.*—Internal Revenue Service officials may require a taxpayer (or such individual(s) required or authorized to sign on behalf of a taxpayer) to submit appropriate identification or evidence of authority. Except when Form 2848 (or its equivalent) is executed by an attorney-in-fact under the provisions of § 601.503(b)(3), the individual who must execute a Form 2848 depends on the type of taxpayer involved—

(1) *Individual taxpayer.*—In matter(s) involving an individual taxpayer, a power of attorney must be signed by such individual.

(2) *Husband and wife.*—In matters involving a joint return the following rules apply—

(i) *Joint representation.*—In the case of any matter concerning a joint return in which both husband and wife are to be represented by the same representative(s), the power of attorney must be executed by both husband and wife.

(ii) *Individual representation.*—In the case of any matter concerning a joint return in which both husband and wife are not to be represented by the same recognized representative(s), the power of attorney must be executed by the spouse who is to be represented. However, the recognized representative of such spouse cannot perform any act with respect to a tax matter that the spouse being represented cannot perform alone.

(3) *Corporation.*—In the case of a corporation, a power of attorney must be executed by an officer of the corporation having authority to legally bind the corporation, who must certify that he/she has such authority.

(4) *Association.*—In the case of an association, a power of attorney must be executed by an officer of the association having authority to legally bind the association, who must certify that he/she has such authority.

(5) *Partnership.*—In the case of a partnership, a power of attorney must be executed by all partners, or if executed in the name of the partnership, by the partner or partners duly authorized to act for the partnership, who must certify that he/she has such authority.

(6) *Dissolved partnership.*—In the case of a dissolved partnership, each of the former partners must execute a power of attorney. However, if one or more of the former partners is deceased, the following provisions apply—

(i) The legal representative of each deceased partner(s) (or such person(s) having legal control over the disposition of partnership interest(s) and/or the share of partnership asset(s) of the deceased partner(s)) must execute a power of attorney in the place of such deceased partner(s). (See § 601.503(c)(6)(ii).)

(ii) Notwithstanding § 601.503(c)(6)(i), if the laws of the governing jurisdiction provide that such partner(s) has exclusive right to control or possession of the firm's assets for the purpose of winding up its affairs, the signature(s) of the surviving partner(s) alone will be sufficient. (If the surviving partner(s) claims exclusive right to control or possession of the firm's assets for the purpose of winding up its affairs, Internal Revenue Service officials may require the submission of a copy of or a citation to the pertinent provisions of the law of the governing jurisdiction upon which the surviving partner(s) relies.)

(d) *Fiduciaries.*—In general, when a fiduciary is involved in a tax matter, a power of attorney is not required. Instead Form 56, "Notice Concerning Fiduciary Relationship," should be filed. Types of taxpayer for which fiduciaries act are—

(1) *Dissolved corporation.*—(i) *Appointed trustee.*—In the case of a dissolved corporation, Form 56, "Notice Concerning Fiduciary Relationship," should be filed by the liquidating trustee(s), if one or more have been appointed, or by the trustee(s) deriving authority under a law of the jurisdiction in which the corporation was organized. If there is more than one trustee, all must join unless it is established that fewer than all have authority to act in the matter under consideration. Internal Revenue Service officials may require the submission of a properly authenticated copy of the instrument and/or citation to the law under which the trustee derives his/her authority. If the authority of the trustee is derived under the law of a jurisdiction, Internal Revenue Service officials may require a statement (signed under penalty of perjury) setting forth the facts required by the law as a condition precedent to the vesting of authority in said trustee and stating that the authority of the trustee has not been terminated.

(ii) *No appointed trustee.*—If there is no appointed trustee, a Form 56, "Notice Concerning Fiduciary Relationship," should be filed by the stockholder(s) holding a majority of the voting stock of the corporation as of the date of dissolution. Internal Revenue Service officials may require submission of a statement showing the total number of outstanding shares of voting stock as of the date of dissolution, the number of shares held by each signatory to a power of attorney, the date of dissolution, and a representation that no trustee has been appointed.

(2) *Insolvent taxpayer.*—In the case of an insolvent taxpayer, Form 56, "Notice Concerning Fiduciary Relationship," should be filed by the trustee, receiver, or attorney appointed by the court. Internal Revenue Service officials may require the submission of a certified order or document from the court having jurisdiction over the insolvent taxpayer which shows the appointment and qualification of the trustee, receiver, or attorney and that his/her authority has not been terminated. In cases pending before a court of the United States (e.g., U.S. District Court or U.S. Bankruptcy Court), an authenticated copy of the order approving the bond of the trustee, receiver, or attorney will meet this requirement.

(3) *Deceased taxpayers.*—(i) *Executor, personal representative or administrator.*—In the case of a deceased taxpayer, a Form 56, "Notice Concerning Fiduciary Relationship," should be filed by the executor, personal representative or administrator if one has been appointed and is responsible for disposition of the matter under consideration. Internal Revenue Service officials may require the submission of a short-form certificate (or authenticated copy of letters testamentary or letters of administration) showing that such authority is in full force and effect at the time the Form 56, "Notice Concerning Fiduciary Relationship," is filed.

(ii) *Testamentary trustee(s).*—In the event that a trustee is acting under the provisions of the will, a Form 56, "Notice Concerning Fiduciary Relationship," should be filed by the trustee, unless the executor, personal representative or administrator has not been discharged and is responsible for disposition of the matter. Internal Revenue Service officials may require either the submission of evidence of the discharge of the executor and appointment of the trustee or other appropriate evidence of the authority of the trustee.

(iii) *Residuary legatee(s).*—If no executor, administrator, or trustee named under the will is acting or responsible for disposition of the matter and the estate has been distributed to the residuary legatee(s), a Form 56, "Notice Concerning Fiduciary Relationship," should be filed by the residuary legatee(s). Internal Revenue Service officials may require the submission of a statement from the court certifying that no executor, administrator, or trustee named under the will is acting or responsible for disposition of the matter, naming the residuary legatee(s), and indicating the proper share to which each is entitled.

(iv) *Distributee(s).*—In the event that the decedent died intestate and the administrator has been discharged and is not responsible for disposition of the matter (or none was ever appointed), a Form 56, "Notice Concerning Fiduciary Relationship," should be filed by the distributee(s). Internal Revenue Service officials may require the submission of evidence of the discharge of the administrator (if one had been appointed) and evidence that the administrator is not responsible for disposition of the matter. It also may require a statement(s) signed under penalty of perjury (and such other appropriate evidence as can be produced) to show the relationship of the individual(s) who sign the Form 56, "Notice Concerning Fiduciary Relationship," to the decedent and the right of each signer to the respective shares of the assets claimed under the law of the domicile of the decedent.

(4) *Taxpayer for whom a guardian or other fiduciary has been appointed.*—In the case of a taxpayer for whom a guardian or other fiduciary has been appointed by a court of record, a Form 56, "Notice Concerning Fiduciary Relationship," should be filed by the fiduciary. Internal Revenue Service officials may require the submission of a court certificate or court order showing that the individual who executes the Form 56, "Notice Concerning Fiduciary Relationship," has been appointed and that his/her appointment has not been terminated.

(5) *Taxpayer who has appointed a trustee.*—In the case of a taxpayer who has appointed a trustee, a Form 56, "Notice Concerning Fiduciary Relationship," should be filed by the trustee. If there is more than one trustee appointed, all should join unless it is shown that fewer than all have authority to act. Internal Revenue Service officials may require the submission of documentary evidence of the authority of the trustee to act. Such evidence may be either a copy of a properly executed trust instrument or a certified copy of extracts from the trust instruments, showing—

(i) The date of the instrument;

(ii) That it is or is not of record in any court;

(iii) The names of the beneficiaries;

(iv) The appointment of the trustee, the authority granted, and other information as may be necessary to show that such authority extends to Federal tax matters; and

(v) That the trust has not been terminated and the trustee appointed therein is still legally acting as such.

In the event that the trustee appointed in the original trust instrument has been replaced by another trustee, documentary evidence of the appointment of the new trustee must be submitted.

(e) *Commissioner's authority to substitute other requirements for power of attorney.*—Upon application of a taxpayer or a recognized representative, the Commissioner of Internal Revenue may substitute a requirement(s) other than provided herein for a power of attorney as evidence of the authority of the representative. [Reg. § 601.503.]

☐ [56 FR 24005, May 28, 1991; 57 FR 27356, June 19, 1992.]

**[Reg. § 601.504]**

**§ 601.504. Requirements for filing power of attorney.**—(a) *Situations in which a power of attorney is required.*—Except as otherwise provided in § 601.504(b), a power of attorney is required by the Internal Revenue Service when the taxpayer wishes to authorize a recognized representative to perform one or more of the following acts on behalf of the taxpayer—

(1) *Representation.*—(See § § 601.501(b)(10) and 601.501(b)(13).)

(2) *Waiver.*—Offer and/or execution of either (i) a waiver of restriction on assessment or collection of a deficiency in tax, or (ii) a waiver of notice of disallowance of a claim for credit or refund.

(3) *Consent.*—Execution of a consent to extend the statutory period for assessment or collection of a tax.

(4) *Closing agreement.*—Execution of a closing agreement under the provisions of the Internal Revenue Code and the regulations thereunder.

(5) *Check drawn on the United States Treasury.*—The authority to receive (but not endorse or collect) a check drawn on the United States Treasury must be specifically granted in a power of attorney. (The endorsement and payment of a check drawn on the United States Treasury are governed by Treasury Department Circular No.

21, as amended, 31 CFR part 240. Endorsement and payment of such check by any person other than the payee must be made under one of the special types of powers of attorney prescribed by Circular No. 21, 31 CFR Part 240. For restrictions on the assignment of claims, see Revised Statute section 3477, as amended (31 U.S.C. 3727).)

(6) *Signing tax returns.*—The filing of a power of attorney does not authorize the recognized representative to sign a tax return on behalf of the taxpayer unless such act is both—

(i) permitted under the Internal Revenue Code and the regulations thereunder (e.g., the authority to sign income tax returns is governed by the provisions of §1.6012-1(a)(5) of the Income Tax Regulations); and

(ii) specifically authorized in the power of attorney.

(b) *Situations in which a power of attorney is not required.*—(1) *Disclosure of confidential tax information.*—The submission of a tax information authorization to request a disclosure of confidential tax information does not constitute practice before the Internal Revenue Service. (Such procedure is governed by the provisions of §6103 of the Internal Revenue Code and the regulations thereunder.) Nevertheless, if a power of attorney is properly filed, the recognized representative also is authorized to receive and/or inspect confidential tax information concerning the matter(s) specified (provided the power of attorney places no limitations upon such disclosure).

(2) *Estate matter.*—A power of attorney is not required at a conference concerning an estate tax matter if the individual seeking to act as a recognized representative presents satisfactory evidence to Internal Revenue Service officials that he/she is—

(i) an individual described in §601.502(b); and

(ii) the attorney of record for the executor, personal representative, or administrator before the court where the will is probated or the estate is administered.

(3) *Bankruptcy matters.*—A power of attorney is not required in the case of a trustee, receiver, or an attorney (designated to represent a trustee, receiver, or debtor in possession) appointed by a court having jurisdiction over a debtor. In such a case, Internal Revenue Service officials may require the submission of a certificate from the court having jurisdiction over the debtor showing the appointment and qualification of the trustee, receiver, or attorney and that his/her authority has not been terminated. In cases pending before a court of the United States (e.g., U.S. District Court or U.S. Bankruptcy Court), an authenticated copy of the order approving the bond of the trustee, receiver, or attorney will meet this requirement.

(c) *Administrative requirements of filing.*—(1) *General.*—Except as provided in this section, a power of attorney (including the declaration of representative and any other required statement(s)) must be filed in each office of the Internal Revenue Service in which the recognized representative desires to perform one or more of the acts described in §601.504(a).

(2) *Regional offices.*—If a power of attorney (including the declaration of representative and any other required statement(s)) is filed with the office of a district director or with a service center which has the matter under consideration, it is not necessary to file a copy with the office of a regional commissioner which subsequently has the matter under consideration unless requested.

(3) *National Office.*—In case of a request for a ruling or other matter to be considered in the National Office, a power of attorney, including the declaration of representative and any other required statement(s), must be submitted with each request or matter.

(4) *Copy of power of attorney.*—The Internal Revenue Service will accept either the original or a copy of a power of attorney. A copy of a power of attorney received by facsimile transmission (FAX) also will be accepted.

(d) *Practice by correspondence.*—If an individual desires to represent a taxpayer through correspondence with the Internal Revenue Service, such individual must submit a power of attorney, including the declaration of representative and any other required statement(s), even though no personal appearance is contemplated. [Reg. §601.504.]

☐ [56 FR 24007, May 28, 1991; 57 FR 27356, June 19, 1992.]

**[Reg. §601.505]**

**§601.505. Revocation, change in representation and substitution or delegation of representative.**—(a) *By the taxpayer.*—(1) *New power of attorney filed.*—A new power of attorney revokes a prior power of attorney if it is granted by the taxpayer to another recognized representative with respect to the same matter. However, a new power of attorney does not revoke a prior power of attorney if it contains a clause stating that it does not revoke such prior power of attorney and there is attached to the new power of attorney either—

(i) a copy of the unrevoked prior power of attorney; or

(ii) a statement signed by the taxpayer listing the name and address of each recognized representative authorized under the prior unrevoked power of attorney.

(2) *Statement of revocation filed.*—A taxpayer may revoke a power of attorney without authorizing a new representative by filing a statement of revocation with those offices of the Internal Revenue Service where the taxpayer has filed the power of attorney to be revoked. The statement of revocation must indicate that the authority of the first power of attorney is revoked and must be signed by the taxpayer. Also, the name and address of each recognized representative whose authority is revoked must be listed (or a copy of the power of attorney to be revoked must be attached).

(b) *By the recognized representative.*—(1) *Revocation of power of attorney.*—A recognized representative may withdraw from representation in a matter in which a power of attorney has been filed by filing a statement with those offices of the Internal Revenue Service where the power of attorney to be revoked was filed. The statement must be signed by the representative and must identify the name and address of the taxpayer(s) and the matter(s) from which the representative is withdrawing.

(2) *Substitution or delegation of recognized representative.*—Any recognized representative appointed in a power of attorney may substitute or delegate authority under the power of attorney to another recognized representative if substitution or delegation is specifically permitted under the power of attorney. Unless otherwise provided in the power of attorney, a recognized representative may make a substitution or delegation without the consent of any other recognized representative appointed to represent the taxpayer in the same matter. A substitution or delegation is effected by filing the following items with offices of the Internal Revenue Service where the power of attorney has been filed—

(i) *Notice of substitution or delegation.*—A Notice of Substitution or Delegation is a statement signed by the recognized representative appointed under the power of attorney. The statement must contain the name and mailing address of the new recognized representative and, if more than one individual is to represent the taxpayer in the matter, a designation of which recognized representative is to receive notices and other written communications;

(ii) *Declaration of representative.*—A written declaration which is made by the new representative as required by §601.502(c); and

(iii) *Power of attorney.*—A power of attorney which specifically authorizes the substitution or delegation.

An employee of a recognized representative may not be substituted for his/her employer with respect to the representation of a taxpayer before the Internal Revenue Service unless the employee is a recognized representative in his/her own capacity under the provisions of §601.502(b). However, even if such employee is not a recognized representative in his/her own capacity under the provisions of §601.502(b), that individual may be authorized by the taxpayer under a tax information authorization to receive and/or inspect confidential tax information under the provisions of section 6103 of the Internal Revenue Code and the regulations thereunder. [Reg. §601.505.]

☐ [56 FR 24007, May 28, 1991, amended at 57 FR 27356, June 19, 1992.]

**[Reg. §601.506]**

**§601.506. Notices to be given to recognized representative; direct contact with taxpayer; delivery of a check drawn on the United States Treasury to recognized representative.**—(a) *General.*—Any notice or other written communication (or a copy thereof) required or permitted to be given to a taxpayer in any matter before the Internal Revenue Service must be given to the taxpayer and, unless restricted by the taxpayer, to the representative according to the following procedures—

(1) If the taxpayer designates more than one recognized representative to receive notices and other written communications, it will be the practice of the Internal Revenue Service to give copies of such to two (but not more than two) individuals so designated.

(2) In a case in which the taxpayer does not designate which recognized representative is to receive notices, it will be the practice of the Internal Revenue Service to give notices and other communications to the first recognized representative appointed on the power of attorney.

(3) Failure to give notice or other written communication to the recognized representative of a taxpayer will not affect the validity of any notice or other written communication delivered to a taxpayer. Unless otherwise indicated in the document, a power of attorney other than Form 2848 will be presumed to grant the authority to receive notices or other written communication (or a copy thereof)

required or permitted to be given to a taxpayer in any matter(s) before the Internal Revenue Service to which the power of attorney pertains.

(b) *Cases where taxpayer may be contacted directly.*—Where a recognized representative has unreasonably delayed or hindered an examination, collection or investigation by failing to furnish, after repeated request, nonprivileged information necessary to the examination, collection or investigation, the Internal Revenue Service employee conducting the examination, collection or investigation may request the permission of his/her immediate supervisor to contact the taxpayer directly for such information.

(1) *Procedure.*—If such permission is granted, the case file will be documented with sufficient facts to show how the examination, collection or investigation was being delayed or hindered. Written notice of such permission, briefly stating the reason why it was granted, will be given to both the recognized representative and the taxpayer together with a request of the taxpayer to supply such nonprivileged information. (See 7521(c) of the Internal Revenue Code and the regulations thereunder.)

(2) *Effect of direct notification.*—Permission to by-pass a recognized representative and contact a taxpayer directly does not automatically disqualify an individual to act as the recognized representative of a taxpayer in a matter. However, such information may be referred to the Director of Practice for possible disciplinary proceedings under Circular No. 230, 31 CFR Part 10.

(c) *Delivery of a check drawn on the United States Treasury.*—(1) *General.*—A check drawn on the United States Treasury (e.g., a check in payment of refund of internal revenue taxes, penalties, or interest, see §601.504(a)(5)) will be mailed to the recognized representative of a taxpayer provided that a power of attorney is filed containing specific authorization for this to be done.

(2) *Address of recognized representative.*—The check will be mailed to the address of the recognized representative listed on the power of attorney unless such recognized representative notifies the Internal Revenue Service in writing that his/her mailing address has been changed.

(3) *Authorization of more than one recognized representative.*—In the event a power of attorney authorizes more than one recognized representative to receive a check on the taxpayer's behalf, and such representatives have different addresses, the Internal Revenue Service will mail the check directly to the taxpayer, unless a statement (signed by all of the recognized representatives so authorized) is submitted which indicates the address to which the check is to be mailed.

(4) *Cases in litigation.*—The provisions of §601.506(c) concerning the issuance of a tax refund do not apply to the issuance of a check in payment of claims which have been either reduced to judgment or settled in the course (or as a result) of litigation.

(d) *Centralized Authorization File (CAF) system.*—(1) *Information recorded onto the CAF system.*—Information from both powers of attorney and tax information authorizations is recorded onto the CAF system. Such information enables Internal Revenue Service personnel who do not have access to the actual power of attorney or tax information authorizations to—

(i) determine whether a recognized representative or an appointee is authorized by a taxpayer to receive and/or inspect confidential tax information;

(ii) determine, in the case of a recognized representative, whether that representative is authorized to perform the acts set forth in §601.504(a); and

(iii) send copies of computer generated notices and communications to an appointee or recognized representative so authorized by the taxpayer.

(2) *CAF number.*—A Centralized Authorization File (CAF) number will generally be issued to

(i) a recognized representative who files a power of attorney and a written declaration of representative; or

(ii) an appointee authorized under a tax information authorization.

The issuance of a CAF number does not indicate that a person is either recognized or authorized to practice before the Internal Revenue Service. Such determination is made under the provisions of Circular No. 230, 31 CFR Part 10. The purpose of the CAF number is to facilitate the processing of a power of attorney or a tax information authorization submitted by a recognized representative or an appointee. A recognized representative or an appointee should include the same CAF number on every power of attorney or tax information authorization filed. However, because the CAF number is not a substantive requirement (i.e., as listed in §601.503(a)), a tax information authorization or power of attorney which does not include such number will not be rejected based on the absence of a CAF number.

(3) *Tax matters recorded on CAF.*—Although a power of attorney or tax information authorization may be filed in all matters under the jurisdiction of the Internal Revenue Service, only those documents which meet each of the following criteria will be recorded onto the CAF system—

(i) *Specific tax period.*—Only documents which concern a matter(s) relating to a specific tax period will be recorded onto the CAF system. A power of attorney or tax information authorization filed in a matter unrelated to a specific period (e.g., the 100% penalty for failure to pay over withholding taxes imposed by §6672 of the Internal Revenue Code, applications for an employer identification number, and requests for a private letter ruling request pertaining to a proposed transaction) cannot be recorded onto the CAF system.

(ii) *Future three-year limitation.*—Only documents which concern a tax period that ends no later than three years after the date on a power of attorney is received by the Internal Revenue Service will be recorded onto the CAF system. For example, a power of attorney received by the Internal Revenue Service on August 1, 1990, which indicates that the authorization applies to Form 941 for the quarters ended December 31, 1990 through December 31, 2000, will be recorded onto the CAF system for the applicable tax periods which end no later than July 31, 1993 (i.e., three years after the date of receipt by the Internal Revenue Service).

(iii) *Documents for prior tax periods.*—Documents which concern any tax period which has ended prior to the date on which a power of attorney is received by the Internal Revenue Service will be recorded onto the CAF system provided that matters concerning such years are under consideration by the Internal Revenue Service.

(iv) *Limitation on representatives recorded onto the CAF system.*—No more than three representatives appointed under a power of attorney or three persons designated under a tax information authorization will be recorded onto the CAF system. If more than three representatives are appointed under a power of attorney or more than three persons designated under a tax information authorization, only the first three names will be recorded onto the CAF system.

The fact that a power of attorney or tax information authorization cannot be recorded onto the CAF system is not determinative of the (current or future) validity of such document. (For example, documents which concern tax periods that end more than three years from the date of receipt by the IRS are not invalid for the period(s) not recorded onto the CAF system, but can be resubmitted at a later date.) [Reg. §601.506.]

☐ [56 FR 24008, May 28, 1991.]

### [Reg. §601.507]

**§601.507. Evidence required to substantiate facts alleged by a recognized representative.**—The Internal Revenue Service may require a recognized representative to submit all evidence, except that of a supplementary or incidental character, over a declaration (signed under penalty of perjury) that the recognized representative prepared such submission and that the facts contained therein are true. In any case in which a recognized representative is unable or unwilling to declare his/her own knowledge that the facts are true and correct, the Internal Revenue Service may require the taxpayer to make such a declaration under penalty of perjury. [Reg. §601.507.]

☐ [56 FR 24009, May 28, 1991.]

### [Reg. §601.508]

**§601.508. Dispute between recognized representatives of a taxpayer.**—Where there is a dispute between two or more recognized representatives concerning who is entitled to represent a taxpayer in a matter pending before the Internal Revenue Service (or to receive a check drawn on the United States Treasury), the Internal Revenue Service will not recognize any party. However, if the contesting recognized representatives designate one or more of their number under the terms of an agreement signed by all, the Internal Revenue Service will recognize such designated recognized representatives upon receipt of a copy of such agreement according to the terms of the power of attorney. [Reg. §601.508.]

☐ [56 FR 24009, May 28, 1991.]

### [Reg. §601.509]

**§601.509. Power of attorney not required in cases docketed in the Tax Court of the United States.**—The petitioner and the Commissioner of Internal Revenue stand in the position of parties litigant before a judicial body in a case docketed in the Tax Court of the United States. The Tax Court has its own rules of practice and procedure and its own rules respecting admission to practice before it. Accordingly, a power of attorney is not required to be submitted by an attorney of record in a case which is docketed in the Tax Court. Correspondence in connection with cases docketed in the Tax Court will be addressed to counsel of record before the Court. However, a power of attorney is required to be submitted by an individual other than the attorney of record in any matter before the Internal Revenue Service concerning a docketed case. [Reg. § 601.509.]

☐ [56 FR 24009, May 28, 1991.]

### Requirements for Alcohol, Tobacco, and Firearm Activities

**[Reg. § 601.521]**

**§ 601.521. Requirements for conference and representation in conference.**—Any person desiring a conference in the office of the regional regulatory administrator in the Bureau of Alcohol, Tobacco, and Firearms of his region or of the Director, Bureau of Alcohol, Tobacco, and Firearms, in Washington, DC, relative to any matter arising in connection with his operations, will be accorded such a conference upon request. No formal requirements are prescribed for such conference. Where an industry member or other person is to be represented in conference, the representative must be recognized to practice as provided in paragraph (b) of § 601.502. When a representative presents himself on behalf of an industry member or other person for the initial meeting in the office of a regional regulatory administrator in the Bureau of Alcohol, Tobacco, and Firearms or of the Director, Bureau of Alcohol, Tobacco, and Firearms, he must submit evidence of recognition; or he should state in his first letter or other written communication with such office whether he is recognized to practice, and should enclose evidence of such recognition. In the case of a qualified attorney or a qualified certified public accountant, the filing of the applicable written declaration described in paragraphs (b)(1) (i) and (ii) of § 601.502 shall constitute evidence of recognition. In the case of an enrollee, the filing of a notification, stating that he is enrolled to practice and giving his enrollment number or the expiration date of his enrollment card, shall constitute evidence of recognition. [Reg. § 601.521.]

☐ [34 FR 6432, Apr. 12, 1969, as amended at 45 FR 7259, Feb. 1, 1980.]

**[Reg. § 601.522]**

**§ 601.522. Power of attorney.**—Except as otherwise provided in this section, a power of attorney, or copy thereof, will be required for a representative of a principal (a) to perform the acts specified in paragraph (c)(1) of § 601.502; or (b) to sign any application, bond, notice, return, report, or other document required by, or provided for in, regulations issued pursuant to chapter 51 (Distilled Spirits, Wines, and Beer), Chapter 52 (Cigars, Cigarettes, and Cigarette Papers and Tubes), and chapter 53 (Machine Guns, Destructive Devices, and Certain Other Firearms), Internal Revenue Code, title 1 of the Gun Control Act of 1968, or the Federal Alcohol Administration Act, which is filed with or acted on by (1) the office of a regional regulatory administrator in the Bureau of Alcohol, Tobacco, and Firearms, or (2) the Director, Bureau of Alcohol, Tobacco, and Firearms. The power of attorney may be executed on Form 1534, copies of which may be obtained from the regional regulatory administrator in the Bureau of Alcohol, Tobacco, and Firearms. A power of attorney will not be required for a person authorized to sign on behalf of the principal by articles of incorporation, bylaws, or a board of directors, where an acceptable copy of such authorization is on file in the office of the regional regulatory administrator or of the Director. A power of attorney filed under the provisions of this section may cover one or more acts for which a power of attorney is required and will continue in effect with respect to such acts until revoked as provided in § 601.526. The exceptions to the requirements for a power of attorney contained in paragraph (c) (3) and (4) of § 601.502 are applicable to powers of attorney under this section. [Reg. § 601.522.]

☐ [34 FR 14603, Sept. 19, 1969, as amended at 45 FR 7259, Feb. 1, 1980.]

**[Reg. § 601.523]**

**§ 601.523. Tax information authorization.**—Where any of the acts specified in paragraph (c)(2)(i) of § 601.502 are to be performed by a representative, and a power of attorney for such representative has not been filed, a tax information authorization, or copy thereof, will be required. The authorization may be executed on Form 1534-A, copies of which may be obtained from the regional regulatory administrator in the Bureau of Alcohol, Tobacco, and Firearms. Such authorization may cover one or more of the acts for which a tax information authorization is required and will continue in effect with respect to such acts until revoked as provided in § 601.526. The exceptions to the requirements for a tax information authorization, provided in paragraphs (c) (3) and (4) of § 601.502, are applicable to such authorizations under this section. [Reg. § 601.523.]

☐ [34 FR 6432, Apr. 12, 1969.]

**[Reg. § 601.524]**

**§ 601.524. Execution and filing powers of attorney and tax information authorizations.**—(a) *Time of filing.*—A copy of the power of attorney must be filed in each office (that is, office of a regional regulatory administrator and Office of the Director, Bureau of Alcohol, Tobacco, and Firearms), in which a document specified in § 601.522, covered by the power of attorney, is required to be filed, or in which the representative desires to perform one or more of the acts enumerated in paragraph (c)(1) of § 601.502. If a power of attorney covering an act otherwise requiring the filing of a tax information authorization has not been filed, a copy of the tax information authorization must be filed in each office in which the representative inspects or receives confidential information, or, where acts requiring a power of attorney or a tax information authorization are handled by correspondence, the representative should enclose a copy of the power or authorization with the initial correspondence. However, where a power of attorney or tax information authorization is on file with the regional regulatory administrator in the Bureau of Alcohol, Tobacco, and Firearms, an additional copy thereof will not be required in the office of the regional counsel of the same region.

(b) *Execution.*—The power of attorney required by § 601.522, or tax information authorization required by § 601.523, shall be executed in the manner prescribed in paragraph (b) of § 601.504; shall indicate all acts to which it relates; should contain the mailing address of the representative; and, if more than one representative is authorized to perform the same acts on behalf of the industry member or other person, a designation as to which representative is to receive notices and other written communications. For rules relating to the mailing of notices or other written communications to a representative, see § 601.506.

(c) *Attestation and corporate seal.*—In the case of a corporation, a power of attorney filed with an officer of the Bureau of Alcohol, Tobacco, and Firearms must be attested by the secretary and the corporate seal must be affixed. If the officer who signs the power of attorney is also the secretary, another officer of the corporation, preferably the president, vice president, or treasurer, must also sign the power of attorney so that two different individuals' signatures appear thereon. If the corporation has no seal, a certified copy of a resolution duly passed on by the board of directors of the corporation authorizing the execution of powers of attorney should be attached.

(d) *Acknowledgment.*—A power of attorney filed with an office of the Bureau of Alcohol, Tobacco, and Firearms must be acknowledged, witnessed, or certified as provided in paragraph (d) of § 601.504. [Reg. § 601.524.]

☐ [32 FR 15990, Nov. 22, 1967, as amended at 34 FR 6432, Apr. 12, 1969; 45 FR 7259, Feb. 1, 1980.]

**[Reg. § 601.525]**

**§ 601.525. Certification of copies of documents.**—The provisions of paragraph (e) of § 601.504 with respect to certification of copies are applicable to a power of attorney or a tax information authorization required to be filed under § 601.522 or § 601.523. [Reg. § 601.525.]

**[Reg. § 601.526]**

**§ 601.526. Revocation of powers of attorney and tax information authorizations.**—The revocation of the authority of a representative covered by a power of attorney or tax information authorization filed in an office of the Bureau of Alcohol, Tobacco, and Firearms shall in no case be effective prior to the giving of written notice to the proper official that the authority of such representative has been revoked. [Reg. § 601.526.]

☐ [34 FR 6432, Apr. 12, 1969, as amended at 45 FR 7259, Feb. 1, 1980.]

**[Reg. § 601.527]**

**§ 601.527. Other provisions applied to representation in alcohol, tobacco, and firearms activities.**—The provisions of paragraph (b) of § 601.505, and of §§ 601.506 through 601.508 of this subpart, as applicable, shall be followed in offices of the Bureau of Alcohol, Tobacco, and Firearms. [Reg. § 601.527.]

☐ [34 FR 6433, Apr. 12, 1969, as amended at 34 FR 14604, Sept. 19, 1969; 45 FR 7259, Feb. 1, 1980.]

## Subpart F—Rules, Regulations, and Forms

**[Reg. § 601.601]**

**§ 601.601. Rules and regulations.**—(a) *Formulation.*—(1) Internal Revenue rules take various forms. The most important rules are issued as regulations and Treasury decisions prescribed by the Commissioner and approved by the Secretary or his delegate. Other rules may be issued over the signature of the Commissioner or the signature of any other official to whom authority has been delegated.

Regulations and Treasury decisions are prepared in the Office of the Chief Counsel. After approval by the Commissioner, regulations and Treasury decisions are forwarded to the Secretary or his delegate for further consideration and final approval.

(2) Where required by 5 U.S.C. 553 and in such other instances as may be desirable, the Commissioner publishes in the FEDERAL REGISTER general notice of proposed rules (unless all persons subject thereto are named and either personally served or otherwise have actual notice thereof in accordance with law). This notice includes (i) a statement of the time, place, and nature of public rule-making proceedings; (ii) reference to the authority under which the rule is proposed; and (iii) either the terms or substance of the proposed rule or a description of the subjects and issues involved.

(3)(i) This subparagraph shall apply where the rules of this subparagraph are incorporated by reference in a notice of hearing with respect to a notice of proposed rule making.

(ii) A person wishing to make oral comments at a public hearing to which this subparagraph applies shall file his written comments within the time prescribed by the notice of proposed rule making (including any extensions thereof) and submit the outline referred to in subdivision (iii) of this subparagraph within the time prescribed by the notice of hearing. In lieu of the reading of a prepared statement at the hearing, such person's oral comments shall ordinarily be limited to a discussion of matters relating to such written comments and to questions and answers in connection therewith. However, the oral comments shall not be merely a restatement of matters the person has submitted in writing. Persons making oral comments should be prepared to answer questions not only on the topics listed in his outline but also in connection with the matters relating to his written comments. Except as provided in paragraph (b) of this section, in order to be assured of the availability of copies of such written comments or outlines on or before the beginning of such hearing, any person who desires such copies should make such a request within the time prescribed in the notice of hearing and shall agree to pay reasonable costs for copying. Persons who make such a request after the time prescribed in the notice of hearing will be furnished copies as soon as they are available, but it may not be possible to furnish the copies on or before the beginning of the hearing. Except as provided in the preceding sentences, copies of written comments regarding the rules proposed shall not be made available at the hearing.

(iii) A person who wishes to be assured of being heard shall submit, within the time prescribed in the notice of hearing, an outline of the topics he or she wishes to discuss, and the time he or she wishes to devote to each topic. An agenda will then be prepared containing the order of presentation of oral comments and the time allotted to such presentation. A period of 10 minutes will be the time allotted to each person for making his or her oral comments.

(iv) At the conclusion of the presentations of comments of persons listed in the agenda, to the extent time permits, other persons may be permitted to present oral comments provided they have notified, either the Commissioner of Internal Revenue (Attention: CC:LR:T) before the hearing, or the representative of the Internal Revenue Service stationed at the entrance to the hearing room at or before commencement of the hearing, of their desire to be heard.

(v) In the case of unusual circumstances or for good cause shown, the application of rules contained in this subparagraph, including the 10-minute rule in subdivision (iii), above, may be waived.

(vi) To the extent resources permit, the public hearings to which this subparagraph applies may be transcribed.

(b) *Comments on proposed rules.*—(1) *In general.*—Interested persons are privileged to submit any data, views, or arguments in response to a notice of proposed rule making published pursuant to 5 U.S.C. 553. Further, procedures are provided in paragraph (d)(9) of § 601.702 for members of the public to inspect and to obtain copies of written comments submitted in response to such notices. Designations of material as confidential or not to be disclosed, contained in such comments, will not be accepted. Thus, a person submitting written comments in response to a notice of proposed rule making should not include therein material that he considers to be confidential or inappropriate for disclosure to the public. It will be presumed by the Internal Revenue Service that every written comment submitted to it in response to a notice of proposed rule making is intended by the person submitting it to be subject in its entirety to public inspection and copying in accordance with the procedures of paragraph (d)(9) of § 601.702. The name of any person requesting a public hearing and hearing outlines described in paragraph (a)(3)(iii) of this section are not exempt from disclosure.

(2) *Effective date.*—This paragraph (b) applies only to comments submitted in response to notices of proposed rule making of the Internal Revenue Service published in the Federal Register after June 5, 1974.

(c) *Petition to change rules.*—Interested persons are privileged to petition for the issuance, amendment, or repeal of a rule. A petition

for the issuance of a rule should identify the section or sections of law involved; and a petition for the amendment or repeal of a rule should set forth the section or sections of the regulations involved. The petition should also set forth the reasons for the requested action. Such petitions will be given careful consideration and the petitioner will be advised of the action taken thereon. Petitions should be addressed to the Commissioner of Internal Revenue, Attention: CC:LR:T, Washington, D.C. 20224. However, in the case of petitions to amend the regulations pursuant to subsection (c)(4)(A)(viii) or (5)(A)(i) of section 23 or former section 44C, follow the procedure outlined in paragraph (a) of § 1.23-6.

(d) *Publication of rules and regulations.*—(1) *General.*—All internal revenue regulations and Treasury decisions are published in the FEDERAL REGISTER and in the Code of Federal Regulations. See paragraph (a) of § 601.702. The Treasury decisions are also published in the weekly Internal Revenue Bulletin and the semi-annual Cumulative Bulletin. The Internal Revenue Bulletin is the authoritative instrument of the Commissioner for the announcement of official rulings, decisions, opinions, and procedures, and for the publication of Treasury decisions, Executive orders, tax conventions, legislation, court decisions, and other items pertaining to internal revenue matters. It is the policy of the Internal Revenue Service to publish in the Bulletin all substantive and procedural rulings of importance or general interest, the publication of which is considered necessary to promote a uniform application of the laws administered by the Service. Procedures set forth in Revenue Procedures published in the Bulletin which are of general applicability and which have continuing force and effect are incorporated as amendments to the Statement of Procedural Rules. It is also the policy to publish in the Bulletin all rulings which revoke, modify, amend, or affect any published ruling. Rules relating solely to matters of internal practices and procedures are not published; however, statements of internal practices and procedures affecting rights or duties of taxpayers, or industry regulation, which appear in internal management documents, are published in the Bulletin. No unpublished ruling or decision will be relied on, used, or cited by any officer or employee of the Internal Revenue Service as a precedent in the disposition of other cases.

(2) *Objectives and standards for publication of Revenue Rulings and Revenue Procedures in the Internal Revenue Bulletin.*—(i)(a) A "Revenue Ruling" is an official interpretation by the Service that has been published in the Internal Revenue Bulletin. Revenue Rulings are issued only by the National Office and are published for the information and guidance of taxpayers, Internal Revenue Service officials, and others concerned.

(b) A "Revenue Procedure" is a statement of procedure that affects the rights or duties of taxpayers or other members of the public under the Code and related statutes or information that, although not necessarily affecting the rights and duties of the public, should be a matter of public knowledge.

(ii)(a) The Internal Revenue Bulletin is the authoritative instrument of the Commissioner of Internal Revenue for the publication of official rulings and procedures of the Internal Revenue Service, including all rulings and statements of procedure which supersede, revoke, modify, amend, or affect any previously published ruling or procedure. The Service also announces in the Bulletin the Commissioner's acquiescences and non-acquiescences in decisions of the United States Tax Court (other than decisions in memorandum opinions), and publishes Treasury decisions, Executive orders, tax conventions, legislation, court decisions, and other items considered to be of general interest. The Assistant Commissioner (Technical) administers the Bulletin program.

(b) The Bulletin is published weekly. In order to provide a permanent reference source, the contents of the Bulletin are consolidated semiannually into an indexed Cumulative Bulletin. The Bulletin Index-Digest System provides a research and reference guide to matters appearing in the Cumulative Bulletins. These materials are sold by the Superintendent of Documents, U.S. Government Printing Office, Washington, D.C. 20402.

(iii) The purpose of publishing revenue rulings and revenue procedures in the Internal Revenue Bulletin is to promote correct and uniform application of the tax laws by Internal Revenue Service employees and to assist taxpayers in attaining maximum voluntary compliance by informing Service personnel and the public of National Office interpretations of the internal revenue laws, related statutes, treaties, regulations, and statements of Service procedures affecting the rights and duties of taxpayers. Therefore, issues and answers involving substantive tax law under the jurisdiction of the Internal Revenue Service will be published in the Internal Revenue Bulletin, except those involving:

(a) Issues answered by statute, treaty, or regulations;

(b) Issues answered by rulings, opinions, or court decisions previously published in the Bulletin;

(c) Issues that are of insufficient importance or interest to warrant publication;

(d) Determinations of fact rather than interpretations of law;

*(e)* Informers and informers' rewards; or

*(f)* Disclosure of secret formulas, processes, business practices, and similar information.

Procedures affecting taxpayers' rights or duties that relate to matters under the jurisdiction of the Service will be published in the Bulletin.

(iv) [Reserved].

(v)*(a)* Rulings and other communications involving substantive tax law published in the Bulletin are published in the form of Revenue Rulings. The conclusions expressed in Revenue Rulings will be directly responsive to and limited in scope by the pivotal facts stated in the revenue ruling. Revenue Rulings arise from various sources, including rulings to taxpayers, technical advice to district offices, studies undertaken by the Office of the Assistant Commissioner (Technical), court decisions, suggestions from tax practitioner groups, publications, etc.

*(b)* It will be the practice of the Service to publish as much of the ruling or communication as is necessary for an understanding of the position stated. However, in order to prevent unwarranted invasions of personal privacy and to comply with statutory provisions, such as 18 U.S.C. 1905 and 26 U.S.C. 7213, dealing with disclosure of information obtained from members of the public, identifying details, including the names and addresses of persons involved, and information of a confidential nature are deleted from the ruling.

*(c)* Revenue Rulings, other than those relating to the qualification of pension, annuity, profit-sharing, stock bonus, and bond purchase plans, apply retroactively unless the Revenue Ruling includes a specific statement indicating, under the authority of section 7805(b) of the Internal Revenue Code of 1954, the extent to which it is to be applied without retroactive effect. Where Revenue Rulings revoke or modify rulings previously published in the Bulletin the authority of section 7805(b) of the Code ordinarily is invoked to provide that the new rulings will not be applied retroactively to the extent that the new rulings have adverse tax consequences to taxpayers. Section 7805(b) of the Code provides that the Secretary of the Treasury or his delegate may prescribe the extent to which any ruling is to be applied without retroactive effect. The exercise of this authority requires an affirmative action. For the effect of Revenue Rulings on determination letters and opinion letters issued with respect to the qualification of pension, annuity, profit-sharing, stock bonus, and bond purchase plans, see paragraph (o) of § 601.201.

*(d)* Revenue Rulings published in the Bulletin do not have the force and effect of Treasury Department Regulations (including Treasury decisions), but are published to provide precedents to be used in the disposition of other cases, and may be cited and relied upon for that purpose. No unpublished ruling or decision will be relied on, used, or cited, by an officer or employee of the Service as a precedent in the disposition of other cases.

*(e)* Taxpayers generally may rely upon Revenue Rulings published in the Bulletin in determining the tax treatment of their own transactions and need not request specific rulings applying the principles of a published Revenue Ruling to the facts of their particular cases. However, since each Revenue Ruling represents the conclusion of the Service as to the application of the law to the entire state of facts involved, taxpayers, Service personnel, and others concerned are cautioned against reaching the same conclusion in other cases unless the facts and circumstances are substantially the same. They should consider the effect of subsequent legislation, regulations, court decisions, and revenue rulings.

*(f)* Comments and suggestions from taxpayers or taxpayer groups on Revenue Rulings being prepared for publication in the Bulletin may be solicited, if justified by special circumstances. Conferences on Revenue Rulings being prepared for publication will not be granted except where the Service determines that such action is justified by special circumstances.

(vi) Statements of procedures which affect the rights or duties of taxpayers or other members of the public under the Code and related statutes will be published in the Bulletin in the form of Revenue Procedures. Revenue Procedures usually reflect the contents of internal management documents, but, where appropriate, they are

also published to announce practices and procedures for guidance of the public. It is Service practice to publish as much of the internal management document or communication as is necessary for an understanding of the procedure. Revenue Procedures may also be based on internal management documents which should be a matter of public knowledge even though not necessarily affecting the rights or duties of the public. When publication of the substance of a Revenue Procedure in the Federal Register is required pursuant to 5 U.S.C. 552, it will usually be accomplished by an amendment of the Statement of Procedural Rules (26 CFR Part 601).

(vii)*(a)* The Assistant Commissioner (Technical) is responsible for administering the system for the publication of Revenue Rulings and Revenue Procedures in the Bulletin, including the standards for style and format.

*(b)* In accordance with the standards set forth in subdivision (iv) of this subparagraph, each Assistant Commissioner is responsible for the preparation and appropriate referral for publication of Revenue Rulings reflecting interpretations of substantive tax law made by his office and communicated in writing to taxpayers or field offices. In this connection, the Chief Counsel is responsible for the referral to the appropriate Assistant Commissioner, for consideration for publication as Revenue Rulings, of interpretations of substantive tax law made by his Office.

*(c)* In accordance with the standards set forth in subdivision (iv) of this subparagraph, each Assistant Commissioner and the Chief Counsel is responsible for determining whether procedures established by any office under his jurisdiction should be published as Revenue Procedures and for the initiation, content, and appropriate referral for publication of such Revenue Procedures.

(e) *Foreign tax law.*—(1) The Service will accept the interpretation placed by a foreign tax convention country on its revenue laws which do not affect the tax convention. However, when such interpretation conflicts with a provision in the tax convention, reconsideration of that interpretation may be requested.

(2) Conferences in the National Office of the Service will be granted to representatives of American firms doing business abroad and of American citizens residing abroad, in order to discuss with them foreign tax matters with respect to those countries with which we have tax treaties in effect. [Reg. § 601.601.]

☐ [32 FR 15990, Nov. 22, 1967, as amended at 33 FR 6826, May 4, 1968; 35 FR 16593, Oct. 24, 1970; 38 FR 4971, Feb. 23, 1973; 39 FR 15755, May 6, 1974; 41 FR 13611, Mar. 31, 1976; 41 FR 20883, May 21, 1976; 43 FR 17821, Apr. 26, 1978; 47 FR 56333, Dec. 16, 1982; 48 FR 15624, Apr. 12, 1983; 52 FR 26673, July 16, 1987.]

### [Reg. § 601.602]

**§ 601.602. Tax forms and instructions.**—(a) *Tax return forms and instructions.*—The Internal Revenue Service develops forms and instructions that explain the requirements of the Internal Revenue Code and regulations. The Service distributes the forms and instructions to help taxpayers comply with the law. The tax system is based on voluntary compliance, and the taxpayers complete and return the forms with payment of any tax owed.

(b) *Other forms and instructions.*—In addition to tax return forms, the Internal Revenue Service furnishes the public copies of other forms and instructions developed for use in complying with the laws and regulations. These forms and instructions lead the taxpayer step-by-step through data needed to accurately report information required by law.

(c) *Where to get forms and instructions.*—The Internal Revenue Service mails tax return forms to taxpayers who have previously filed returns. However, taxpayers can call or write to district directors or directors of service centers for copies of any forms they need. These forms are described in Publication 676 *Catalog of Federal Tax Forms, Form Letters, and Notices,* which the public can buy from the Superintendent of Documents, U.S. Government Printing Office, Washington, D.C. 20402. [Reg. § 601.602.]

☐ [46 FR 26055, May 11, 1981.]

## Subpart G—Records

**§ 601.702. Publication, public inspection, and specific requests for records.**—(a) *Publication in the Federal Register.*—(1) *Requirement.*—(i) Subject to the application of the exemptions and exclusions described in the Freedom of Information Act, 5 U.S.C. 552(b)

and (c), and subject to the limitations provided in paragraph (a)(2) of this section, the IRS is required under 5 U.S.C. 552(a)(1), to state separately and publish currently in the Federal Register for the guidance of the public the following information—

(A) Descriptions of its central and field organization and the established places at which, the persons from whom, and the methods whereby, the public may obtain information, make submittals or requests, or obtain decisions, from the IRS;

(B) Statement of the general course and method by which its functions are channeled and determined, including the nature and requirements of all formal and informal procedures which are available;

(C) Rules of procedure, descriptions of forms available or the places at which forms may be obtained, and instructions as to the scope and contents of all papers, reports, or examinations;

(D) Substantive rules of general applicability adopted as authorized by law, and statements of general policy or interpretations of general applicability formulated and adopted by the IRS; and

(E) Each amendment, revision, or repeal of matters referred to in paragraphs (a)(1)(i)(A) through (D) of this section.

(ii) Pursuant to the foregoing requirements, the Commissioner publishes in the Federal Register from time to time a statement, which is not codified in this chapter, on the organization and functions of the IRS, and such amendments as are needed to keep the statement on a current basis. In addition, there are published in the Federal Register the rules set forth in this Part 601 (Statement of Procedural Rules), such as those in paragraph E of this section, relating to conference and practice requirements of the IRS; the regulations in Part 301 of this chapter (Procedure and Administration Regulations); and the various substantive regulations under the Internal Revenue Code of 1986, such as the regulations in Part 1 of this chapter (Income Tax Regulations), in Part 20 of this chapter (Estate Tax Regulations) and, in Part 31 of this chapter (Employment Tax Regulations).

(2) *Limitations.*—(i) *Incorporation by reference in the Federal Register.*—Matter which is reasonably available to the class of persons affected thereby, whether in a private or public publication, shall be deemed published in the Federal Register for purposes of paragraph (a)(1) of this section when it is incorporated by reference therein with the approval of the Director of the Office of the Federal Register. The matter which is incorporated by reference must be set forth in the private or public publication substantially in its entirety and not merely summarized or printed as a synopsis. Matter, the location and scope of which are familiar to only a few persons having a special working knowledge of the activities of the IRS, may not be incorporated in the Federal Register by reference. Matter may be incorporated by reference in the Federal Register only pursuant to the provisions of 5 U.S.C. 552(a)(1) and 1 CFR Part 20.

(ii) *Effect of failure to publish.*—Except to the extent that a person has actual and timely notice of the terms of any matter referred to in paragraph (a)(1) of this section which is required to be published in the Federal Register, such person is not required in any manner to resort to, or be adversely affected by, such matter if it is not so published or is not incorporated by reference therein pursuant to paragraph (a)(2)(i) of this section. Thus, for example, any such matter which imposes an obligation and which is not so published or incorporated by reference shall not adversely change or affect a person's rights.

(b) *Public inspection and copying.*—(1) *In general.*—(i) Subject to the application of the exemptions described in 5 U.S.C. 552(b) and the exclusions described in 5 U.S.C. 552(c), the IRS is required under 5 U.S.C. 552(a)(2) to make available for public inspection and copying or, in the alternative, to promptly publish and offer for sale the following information:

(A) Final opinions, including concurring and dissenting opinions, and orders, if such opinions and orders are made in the adjudication of cases;

(B) Those statements of policy and interpretations which have been adopted by the IRS but are not published in the Federal Register;

(C) Its administrative staff manuals and instructions to staff that affect a member of the public; and

(D) Copies of all records, regardless of form or format, which have been released to any person under 5 U.S.C. 552(a)(3) and which, because of the nature of their subject matter, the IRS determines have become or are likely to become the subject of subsequent requests for substantially the same records. The determination that records have become or may become the subject of subsequent requests shall be based on the following criteria:

(1) The subject matter is clearly of interest to the public at large or to special interest groups from which more than one request is expected to be received; or

(2) When more than four requests for substantially the same records have already been received.

(ii) The IRS is also required by 5 U.S.C. 552(a)(2) to maintain and make available for public inspection and copying current indexes identifying any matter described in paragraphs (b)(1)(i)(A) through (C) of this section which is issued, adopted, or promulgated after July 4, 1967, and which is required to be made available for public inspection or published. In addition, the IRS shall also promptly publish, quarterly or more frequently, and distribute (by sale or otherwise) copies of each index or supplements thereto unless it determines by order published in the Federal Register that the publication would be unnecessary and impracticable, in which case the IRS shall nonetheless provide copies of such indexes on request at a cost not to exceed the direct cost of duplication. No matter described in paragraphs (b)(1)(i)(A) through (C) of this section which is required by this section to be made available for public inspection or published may be relied upon, used, or cited as precedent by the IRS against a party other than an agency unless such party has actual and timely notice of the terms of such matter or unless the matter has been indexed and either made available for inspection or published, as provided by this paragraph (b). This paragraph (b) applies only to matters which have precedential significance. It does not apply, for example, to any ruling or advisory interpretation issued to a taxpayer or to a particular transaction or set of facts which applies only to that transaction or set of facts. Rulings, determination letters, technical advice memorandums, and Chief Counsel advice are open to public inspection and copying pursuant to 26 U.S.C. 6110. This paragraph (b) does not apply to matters which have been made available pursuant to paragraph (a) of this section.

(iii) For records required to be made available for public inspection and copying pursuant to 5 U.S.C. 552(a)(2) and paragraphs (b)(1)(i)(A) through (D) of this section, which are created on or after November 1, 1996, the IRS shall make such records available on the Internet within one year after such records are created.

(iv) The IRS shall make the index referred to in paragraph (b)(1)(ii) of this section available on the Internet.

(2) *Deletion of identifying details.*—To prevent a clearly unwarranted invasion of personal privacy, the IRS shall, in accordance with 5 U.S.C. 552(a)(2), delete identifying details contained in any matter described in paragraphs (b)(1)(i)(A) through (D) of this section before making such matter available for inspection or publication. Such matters shall also be subject to any applicable exemption set forth in 5 U.S.C. 552(b). In every case where identifying details or other matters are so deleted, the justification for the deletion shall be explained in writing. The extent of such deletion shall be indicated on the portion of the record which is made available or published, unless including that indication would harm an interest protected by the exemption in 5 U.S.C. 552(b) under which the deletion is made. If technically feasible, the extent of the deletion shall be indicated at the place in the record where the deletion was made.

(3) *Freedom of Information Reading Room.*—(i) *In general.*—The Headquarters Disclosure Office of the IRS shall provide a reading room where the matters described in paragraphs (b)(1)(i)(A) through (D) of this section which are required to be made available for public inspection, and the current indexes to such matters, shall be made available to the public for inspection and copying. The Freedom of Information Reading Room shall contain other matters determined to be helpful for the guidance of the public, including a complete set of rules and regulations (except those pertaining to alcohol, tobacco, firearms, and explosives) contained in this title, any Internal Revenue matters which may be incorporated by reference in the Federal Register (but not a copy of the Federal Register so doing) pursuant to paragraph (a)(2)(i) of this section, a set of Cumulative Bulletins, and copies of various IRS publications. The public shall not be allowed to remove any record from the Freedom of Information Reading Room.

(ii) *Location of Freedom of Information Reading Room.* The location of the Headquarters Disclosure Office Freedom of Information Reading Room is: IRS, 1111 Constitution Avenue, N.W., Room 1621, Washington, D.C.

(iii) *Copying facilities.* The Headquarters Disclosure Office shall provide facilities whereby a person may obtain copies of material located on the shelves of the Freedom of Information Reading Room.

(c) *Specific requests for other records.*—(1) *In general.*—(i) Subject to the application of the exemptions described in 5 U.S.C. 552(b) and the exclusions described in 5 U.S.C. 552(c), the IRS shall, in conformance with 5 U.S.C. 552(a)(3), make reasonably described records available to a person making a request for such records which conforms in every respect with the rules and procedures set forth in this section. Any request or any appeal from the initial denial of a request that does not comply with the requirements set forth in this section shall not be considered subject to the time constraints of paragraphs (c)(9), (10), and (11) of this section, unless and until the request or appeal is amended to comply. The IRS shall promptly advise the requester in what respect the request or appeal is deficient so that it may be resubmitted or amended for consideration in accordance with this section. If a requester does not resubmit a perfected request or appeal within 35 days from the date of a communication from the IRS, the request or appeal file shall be closed. When the resubmitted request or appeal conforms with the requirements of this section, the time constraints of paragraphs (c) (9), (10), and (11) of this section shall begin.

(ii) Requests for the continuing production of records created or for records created after the date of receipt of the request shall not be honored.

(iii) Specific requests under paragraph (a) (3) for material described in paragraph (a) (2) (A) through (C) and which is in the Freedom of Information Reading Room shall not be honored.

(2) *Electronic format records.*—(i) The IRS shall provide the responsive record or records in the form or format requested if the record or records are readily reproducible by the IRS in that form or format. The IRS shall make reasonable efforts to maintain its records in forms or formats that are reproducible for the purpose of disclosure. For purposes of this paragraph, the term *readily reproducible* means, with respect to electronic format, a record or records that can be downloaded or transferred intact to a floppy disk, computer disk (CD), tape, or other electronic medium using equipment currently in use by the office or offices processing the request. Even though some records may initially be readily reproducible, the need to segregate exempt from nonexempt records may cause the releasable material to be not readily reproducible.

(ii) In responding to a request for records, the IRS shall make reasonable efforts to search for the records in electronic form or format, except where such efforts would significantly interfere with the operation of the agency's automated information system(s). For purposes of this paragraph (c), the term *search* means to locate, manually or by automated means, agency records for the purpose of identifying those records which are responsive to a request.

(iii) Searches for records maintained in electronic form or format may require the application of codes, queries, or other minor forms of programming to retrieve the requested records.

(3) *Requests for records not in control of the IRS.*—(i) Where the request is for a record which is determined to be in the possession or under the control of a constituent unit of the Department of the Treasury other than the IRS, the request for such record shall immediately be transferred to the appropriate constituent unit and the requester notified to that effect. Such referral shall not be deemed a denial of access within the meaning of these regulations. The constituent unit of the Department to which such referral is made shall treat such request as a new request addressed to it and the time limits for response set forth in paragraphs (c)(9) and (c)(10) of this section shall commence when the referral is received by the designated office or officer of the constituent unit. Where the request is for a record which is of a type that is not maintained by any constituent unit of the Department of the Treasury, the requester shall be so advised.

(ii) Where the record requested was created by another agency or constituent unit of the Department of the Treasury and a copy thereof is in the possession of the IRS, the IRS official to whom the request is delivered shall refer the request to the agency or constituent unit which originated the record for direct reply to the requester. The requester shall be informed of such referral. This referral shall not be considered a denial of access within the meaning of these regulations. Where the record is determined to be exempt from disclosure under 5 U.S.C. 552, the referral need not be made, but the IRS shall inform the originating agency or constituent unit of its determination. Where notifying the requester of its referral may cause a harm to the originating agency or constituent unit which would enable the originating agency or constituent unit to withhold the record under 5 U.S.C. 552, then such referral need not be made. In both of these circumstances, the IRS official to whom the request is delivered shall process the request in accordance with the procedures set forth in this section.

(iii) When a request is received for a record created by the IRS (*i.e.*, in its possession and control) that includes information originated by another agency or constituent unit of the Department of the Treasury, the record shall be referred to the originating agency or constituent unit for review, coordination, and concurrence prior to being released to a requester. The IRS official to whom the request is delivered may withhold the record without prior consultation with the originating agency or constituent unit.

(4) *Form of request.*—(i) Requesters are advised that only requests for records which fully comply with the requirements of this section can be processed in accordance with this section. Requesters shall be notified promptly in writing of any requirements which have not been met or any additional requirements to be met. Every effort shall be made to comply with the requests as written. The initial request for records must—

(A) Be made in writing and signed by the individual making the request;

(B) State that it is made pursuant to the Freedom of Information Act, 5 U.S.C. 552, or regulations thereunder;

(C) Be addressed to and mailed to the office of the IRS official who is responsible for the control of the records requested

(see paragraph (h) of this section for the responsible officials and their addresses), regardless of where such records are maintained. Generally, requests for records pertaining to the requester, or other matters of local interest, should be directed to the office servicing the requester's geographic area of residence. Requests for records maintained in the Headquarters of the IRS and its National Office of Chief Counsel, concerning matters of nationwide applicability, such as published guidance (regulations and revenue rulings), program management, operations, or policies, should be directed to the Headquarters Disclosure Office. If the person making the request does not know the official responsible for the control of the records being requested, the person making the request may contact, by telephone or in writing, the disclosure office servicing the requester's geographic area of residence to ascertain the identity of the official having control of the records being requested so that the request can be addressed, and delivered, to the appropriate responsible official. Misdirected requests that otherwise satisfy the requirements of this section shall be immediately transferred to the appropriate responsible IRS official and the requester notified to that effect. Such transfer shall not be deemed a denial of access within the meaning of these regulations. The IRS official to whom the request is redirected shall treat such request as a new request addressed to it and the time limits for response set forth in paragraphs (c)(9) and (c)(11) of this section shall commence when the transfer is received by the designated office;

(D) Reasonably describe the records in accordance with paragraph (c)(5)(i) of this section;

(E) In the case of a request for records the disclosure of which is limited by statute or regulations (as, for example, the Privacy Act of 1974 (5 U.S.C. 552a) or section 6103 and the regulations thereunder), establish the identity and the right of the person making the request to the disclosure of the records in accordance with paragraph (c)(5)(iii) of this section;

(F) Set forth the address where the person making the request desires to be notified of the determination as to whether the request shall be granted;

(G) State whether the requester wishes to inspect the records or desires to have a copy made and furnished without first inspecting them;

(H) State the firm agreement of the requester to pay the fees for search, duplication, and review ultimately determined in accordance with paragraph (f) of this section, or, in accordance with paragraph (c)(4)(ii) of this section, place an upper limit for such fees that the requester is willing to pay, or request that such fees be reduced or waived and state the justification for such request; and

(I) Identify the category of the requester and, with the exception of "other requesters," state how the records shall be used, as required by paragraph (f)(3) of this section.

(ii) As provided in paragraph (c)(4)(i)(H) of this section, rather than stating a firm agreement to pay the fee ultimately determined in accordance with paragraph (f) of this section or requesting that such fees be reduced or waived, the requester may place an upper limit on the amount the requester agrees to pay. If the requester chooses to place an upper limit and the estimated fee is deemed to be greater than the upper limit, or where the requester asks for an estimate of the fee to be charged, the requester shall be promptly advised of the estimate of the fee and asked to agree to pay such amount. Where the initial request includes a request for reduction or waiver of the fee, the IRS officials responsible for the control of the requested records (or their delegates) shall determine whether to grant the request for reduction or waiver in accordance with paragraph (f) of this section and notify the requester of their decisions and, if their decisions result in the requester being liable for all or part of the fee normally due, ask the requester to agree to pay the amount so determined. The requirements of this paragraph shall not be deemed met until the requester has explicitly agreed to pay the fee applicable to the request for records, if any, or has made payment in advance of the fee estimated to be due. If the requester has any outstanding balance of search, review, or duplication fees, the requirements of this paragraph shall not be deemed met until the requester has remitted the outstanding balance due.

(5) *Reasonable description of records; identity and right of the requester.*—(i) The request for records must describe the records in reasonably sufficient detail to enable the IRS employees who are familiar with the subject matter of the request to locate the records without placing an unreasonable burden upon the IRS. While no specific formula for a reasonable description of a record can be established, the requirement shall generally be satisfied if the requester gives the name, taxpayer identification number (*e.g.*, social security number or employer identification number), subject matter, location, and years at issue, of the requested records. If the request seeks records pertaining to pending litigation, the request shall indicate the title of the case, the court in which the case was filed, and the nature of the case. It is suggested that the person making the request furnish any additional information which shall more clearly identify

the requested records. Where the requester does not reasonably describe the records being sought, the requester shall be afforded an opportunity to refine the request. Such opportunity may involve a conference with knowledgeable IRS personnel at the discretion of the disclosure officer. The reasonable description requirement shall not be used by officers or employees of the Internal Revenue as a device for improperly withholding records from the public.

(ii) The IRS shall make a reasonable effort to comply fully with all requests for access to records subject only to any applicable exemption set forth in 5 U.S.C. 552(b) or any exclusion described in 5 U.S.C. 552(c). In any situation in which it is determined that a request for voluminous records would unduly burden and interfere with the operations of the IRS, the person making the request shall be asked to be more specific and to narrow the request, or to agree on an orderly procedure for the production of the requested records, in order to satisfy the request without disproportionate adverse effect on IRS operations.

(iii) *Statutory or regulatory restrictions.*—(A) In the case of records containing information with respect to particular persons the disclosure of which is limited by statute or regulations, persons making requests shall establish their identity and right to access to such records. Persons requesting access to such records which pertain to themselves may establish their identity by—

(1) The presentation of a single document bearing a photograph (such as a passport or identification badge), or the presentation of two items of identification which do not bear a photograph but do bear both a name and signature (such as a credit card or organization membership card), in the case of a request made in person,

(2) The submission of the requester's signature, address, and one other identifier (such as a photocopy of a driver's license) bearing the requester's signature, in the case of a request by mail, or

(3) The presentation in person or the submission by mail of a notarized statement, or a statement made under penalty of perjury in accordance with 28 U.S.C. 1746, swearing to or affirming such person's identity.

(B) Additional proof of a person's identity shall be required before the requests shall be deemed to have met the requirement of paragraph (c)(4)(i)(E) of this section if it is determined that additional proof is necessary to protect against unauthorized disclosure of information in a particular case. Persons who have identified themselves to the satisfaction of IRS officials pursuant to this paragraph (c) shall be deemed to have established their right to access records pertaining to themselves. Persons requesting records on behalf of or pertaining to another person must provide adequate proof of the legal relationship under which they assert the right to access the requested records before the requirement of paragraph (c)(4)(i)(E) of this section shall be deemed met.

(C) In the case of an attorney-in-fact, or other person requesting records on behalf of or pertaining to other persons, the requester shall furnish a properly executed power of attorney, Privacy Act consent, or tax information authorization, as appropriate. In the case of a corporation, if the requester has the authority to legally bind the corporation under applicable state law, such as its corporate president or chief executive officer, then a written statement or tax information authorization certifying as to that person's authority to make a request on behalf of the corporation shall be sufficient. If the requester is any other officer or employee of the corporation, then such requester shall furnish a written statement certifying as to that person's authority to make a request on behalf of the corporation by any principal officer and attested to by the secretary or other officer (other than the requester) that the person making the request on behalf of the corporation is properly authorized to make such a request. If the requester is other than one of the above, then such person may furnish a resolution by the corporation's board of directors or other governing body which provides that the person making the request on behalf of the corporation is properly authorized to make such a request, or shall otherwise satisfy the requirements set forth in section 6103(e). A person requesting access to records of a partnership or a subchapter S Corporation shall provide a notarized statement, or a statement made under penalty of perjury in accordance with 28 U.S.C. 1746, that the requester was a member of the partnership or subchapter S corporation for a part of each of the years included in the request.

(6) *Requests for expedited processing.*—(i) When a requester demonstrates compelling need, a request shall be taken out of order and given expedited treatment. A compelling need involves—

(A) Circumstances in which the lack of expedited treatment could reasonably be expected to pose an imminent threat to the life or physical safety of an individual;

(B) An urgency to inform the public concerning actual or alleged Federal government activity, if made by a person primarily engaged in disseminating information. A person primarily engaged in disseminating information, if not a fulltime representative of the news media, as defined in paragraph (f)(3)(ii)(B) of this section, must establish that he or she is a person whose main professional activity or occupation is information dissemination, though it need not be his or her sole occupation. A person primarily engaged in disseminating information does not include individuals who are engaged only incidentally in the dissemination of information. The standard of urgency to inform requires that the records requested pertain to a matter of current exigency to the American public, beyond the public's right to know about government activity generally, and that delaying a response to a request for records would compromise a significant recognized interest to and throughout the American general public;

(C) The loss of substantial due process rights.

(ii) A requester who seeks expedited processing must submit a statement, certified to be true and correct to the best of his or her knowledge and belief, explaining in detail why there is a compelling need for expedited processing.

(iii) A request for expedited processing may be made at the time of the initial request for records or at any later time. For a prompt determination, requests for expedited processing must be submitted to the responsible official of the IRS who maintains the records requested except that a request for expedited processing under paragraph (c)(6)(i)(B) of this section shall be submitted directly to the Director, Communications Division, whose address is Office of Media Relations, CL:C:M, Internal Revenue Service, Room 7032, 1111 Constitution Avenue, N.W., Washington, D.C. 20224.

(iv) Upon receipt by the responsible official in the IRS, a request for expedited processing shall be considered and a determination as to whether to grant or deny the request shall be made, and the requester notified, within ten days of the date of the request, provided that in no event shall the IRS have less than five days (excluding Saturdays, Sundays, and legal public holidays) from the date of the responsible official's receipt of the request for such processing. The determination to grant or deny a request for expedited processing shall be made solely on the information initially provided by the requester.

(v) An appeal of an initial determination to deny expedited processing must be made within ten days of the date of the initial determination to deny expedited processing, and must otherwise comply with the requirements of paragraph (c)(10) of this section. Both the envelope and the appeal itself shall be clearly marked, "Appeal for Expedited Processing."

(vi) IRS action to deny or affirm denial of a request for expedited processing pursuant to this paragraph, and IRS failure to respond in a timely manner to such a request shall be subject to judicial review, except that judicial review shall be based on the record before the IRS at the time of the determination. A district court of the United States shall not have jurisdiction to review the IRS's denial of expedited processing of a request for records after the IRS has provided a complete response to the request.

(7) *Date of receipt of request.*—(i) Requests for records and any separate agreement to pay, final notification of waiver of fees, or letter transmitting payment, shall be promptly stamped with the date of delivery to or dispatch by the office of the IRS official responsible for the control of the records requested. A request for records shall be considered to have been received on the date on which a complete request containing the information required by paragraphs (c)(4)(i)(A) through (I) has been received by the IRS official responsible for the control of the records requested. A determination that a request is deficient in any respect is not a denial of access, and such determinations are not subject to administrative appeal.

(ii) The latest of such stamped dates shall be deemed for purposes of this section to be the date of receipt of the request, provided that the requirements of paragraphs (c)(4)(i)(A) through (I) of this section have been satisfied, and, where applicable—

(A) The requester has agreed in writing, by executing a separate contract or otherwise, to pay the fees for search, duplication, and review determined due in accordance with paragraph (f) of this section, or

(B) The fees have been waived in accordance with paragraph (f) of this section, or

(C) Payment in advance has been received from the requester.

(8) *Search for records requested.*—(i) Upon the receipt of a request, search services shall be performed by IRS personnel to identify and locate the requested records. Search time includes any and all time spent looking for material responsive to the request, including page-by-page or line-by-line identification of material within records. Where duplication of an entire record would be less costly than a line-by-line identification, duplication should be substituted for this kind of search. With respect to records maintained in computerized form, a search shall include services functionally analogous to a search for records which are maintained on paper.

(ii) In determining which records are responsive to a request, the IRS official responsible for the control of the records requested shall include only those records within the official's possession and control as of the date of the receipt of the request by the appropriate disclosure officer.

(9) *Initial determination.*—(i) *Responsible official.*—(A) The Associate Director, Personnel Security or delegate shall have the sole authority to make initial determinations with respect to requests for records under that office's control.

(B) The Director of the Office of Governmental Liaison and Disclosure or delegate shall have the sole authority to make initial determinations with respect to all other requests for records of the IRS maintained in the Headquarters and its National Office of the Chief Counsel. For all other records within the control of the IRS, the initial determination with respect to requests for records may be made either by the Director, Office of Governmental Liaison and Disclosure, or by the IRS officials responsible for the control of the records requested, or their delegates (see paragraph (h) of this section).

(ii) *Processing of request.*—The appropriate responsible official or delegate shall respond in the approximate order of receipt of the requests, to the extent consistent with sound administrative practice. In any event, the initial determination shall be made and notification thereof mailed within twenty days (excepting Saturdays, Sundays, and legal public holidays) after the date of receipt of the request, as determined in accordance with paragraph (c)(7) of this section, unless the responsible official invokes an extension pursuant to paragraph (c)(11) of this section, the requester otherwise agrees to an extension of the twenty day time limitation, or the request is an expedited request.

(iii) *Granting of request.*—If the request is granted in full or in part, and if the requester wants a copy of the records, a statement of the applicable fees, if there are any, shall be mailed to the requester either at the time of the determination or shortly thereafter. In the case of a request for inspection, the records shall be made available promptly for inspection, at the time and place stated, normally at the appropriate office where the records requested are controlled. If the person making the request has expressed a desire to inspect the records at another office of the IRS, a reasonable effort shall be made to comply with the request. Records shall be made available for inspection at such reasonable and proper times so as not to interfere with their use by the IRS or to exclude other persons from making inspections. In addition, reasonable limitations may be placed on the number of records which may be inspected by a person on any given date. The person making the request shall not be allowed to remove the records from the office where inspection is made. If, after making inspection, the person making the request desires copies of all or a portion of the requested records, copies shall be furnished upon payment of the established fees prescribed by paragraph (f) of this section.

(iv) *Denial of request.*—If it is determined that some records shall be denied, the person making the request shall be so notified by mail. The letter of notification shall specify the city or other location where the requested records are situated, contain a brief statement of the grounds for not granting the request in full including the exemption(s) relied upon, the name and any title or position of the official responsible for the denial, and advise the person making the request of the right to appeal to the Commissioner in accordance with paragraph (c)(10) of this section.

(A) In denying a request for records, in whole or in part, the IRS shall include the date that the request was received in the appropriate disclosure office, and shall provide an estimate of the volume of the denied matter to the person making the request, unless providing such estimate would harm an interest protected by an exemption in 5 U.S.C. 552(b) or (c) pursuant to which the denial is made; and

(B) The amount of information deleted shall be indicated on the released portion of the record, unless including that indication would harm an interest protected by an exemption in 5 U.S.C. 552(b) under which the deletion is made. If technically feasible, the amount of the information deleted and the asserted exemption shall be indicated at the place in the record where such deletion is made.

(v) *Inability to locate and evaluate within time limits.*—Where the records requested cannot be located and evaluated within the initial twenty day period or any extension thereof in accordance with paragraph (c)(11) of this section, the search for the records or evaluation shall continue, but the requester shall be notified, and advised that the requester may consider such notification a denial of the request for records. The requester shall be provided with a statement of judicial rights along with the notification letter. The requester may also be invited, in the alternative, to agree to a voluntary extension of time in which to locate and evaluate the records. Such voluntary

extension of time shall not constitute a waiver of the requester's right to appeal or seek judicial review of any denial of access ultimately made or the requester's right to seek judicial review in the event of failure to comply with the time extension granted.

(10) *Administrative appeal.*—(i) The requester may submit an administrative appeal to the Commissioner of Internal Revenue by letter that is postmarked within 35 days after the later of the date of any letter of notification described in paragraph (c)(9)(iv) of this section, the date of any letter of notification of an adverse determination of the requester's category described in paragraph (f)(3) of this section, the date of any letter of notification of an adverse determination of the requester's fee waiver or reduction request described in paragraph (f)(2) of this section, the date of any letter determining that no responsive records exist, or the date of the last transmission of the last records released. An administrative appeal for denial of a request for expedited processing must be made to the Commissioner of Internal Revenue by letter that is postmarked within ten days after the date of any letter of notification discussed in paragraph (c)(6)(iv) of this section.

(ii) The letter of appeal shall

(A) Be made in writing and signed by the requester;

(B) Be addressed to the Commissioner and mailed to IRS Appeals, 6377A Riverside Avenue, Suite 110, Riverside, California 92506-FOIA Appeal;

(C) Reasonably describe the records requested to which the appeal pertains in accordance with paragraph (c)(5)(i) of this section;

(D) Set forth the address where the appellant desires to be notified of the determination on appeal;

(E) Specify the date of the request, the office to which the request was submitted, and where possible, enclose a copy of the initial request and the initial determination being appealed; and

(F) Ask the Commissioner to grant the request for records, fee waiver, expedited processing, or favorable fee category, as applicable, or verify that an appropriate search was conducted and the responsive records were either produced or an appropriate exemption asserted. The person submitting the appeal may submit any argument in support of the appeal in the letter of appeal.

(iii) Appeals shall be stamped promptly with the date of their receipt in the Office of Appeals, and the later of this stamped date or the stamped date of a document submitted subsequently which supplements the original appeal so that the appeal satisfies the requirements set forth in paragraphs (c)(10)(ii)(A) through (F) of this section shall be deemed by the IRS to be the date of receipt of the appeal for all purposes of this section. The Commissioner or a delegate shall acknowledge receipt of the appeal and advise the requester of the date of receipt and the date a response is due in accordance with this paragraph. If an appeal fails to satisfy any of the requirements of paragraph (c)(10)(ii)(A) through (F) of this section, the person making the request shall be advised promptly in writing of the additional requirements to be met. Except for appeals of denials of expedited processing, the determination to affirm the initial denial (in whole or in part) or to grant the request for records shall be made and notification of the determination shall be mailed within twenty days (exclusive of Saturdays, Sundays, and legal public holidays) after the date of receipt of the appeal unless extended pursuant to paragraph (c)(11)(i) of this section. Appeals of initial determinations to deny expedited processing must be made within ten calendar days of the determination to deny the expedited processing. If it is determined that the appeal from the initial denial is to be denied (in whole or in part), the requester shall be notified in writing of the denial, the reasons therefor, the name and title or position of the official responsible for the denial on appeal, and the provisions of 5 U.S.C. 552(a)(4) for judicial review of that determination.

(11) *Time extensions.*—(i) *Unusual circumstances.*—(A) In unusual circumstances, the time limitations specified in paragraphs (c)(9) and (10) of this section may be extended by written notice from the official charged with the duty of making the determinations to the person making the request or appeal setting forth the reasons for this extension and the date on which the determination is expected to be sent. As used in this paragraph, the term *unusual circumstances* means, but only to the extent reasonably necessary to the proper processing of the particular request:

(1) The need to search for and collect the requested records from field facilities or other establishments that are separate from the office processing the request;

(2) The need to search for, collect, and appropriately examine a voluminous amount of separate and distinct records which are demanded in a single request;

(3) The need for consultation, which shall be conducted with all practicable speed, with another agency having a substantial interest in the determination of the request or among two or more constituent units of the Department of the Treasury having substantial subject matter interest therein; and

(4) The need for consultation with business submitters to determine the nature and extent of proprietary information in accordance with this section.

(B) Any extension or extensions of time for unusual circumstances shall not cumulatively total more than ten days (exclusive of Saturday, Sunday and legal public holidays). If additional time is needed to process the request, the IRS shall notify the requester and provide the requester an opportunity to limit the scope of the request or arrange for an alternative time frame for processing the request or a modified request. The requester shall retain the right to define the desired scope of the request, as long as it meets the requirements contained in this section.

(ii) *Aggregation of requests.*—If more than one request is received from the same requester, or from a group of requesters acting in concert, and the IRS believes that such requests constitute a single request which would otherwise satisfy the unusual circumstances specified in subparagraph (c)(11)(i) of this section, and the requests involve clearly related matters, the IRS may aggregate these requests for processing purposes. Multiple requests involving unrelated matters shall not be aggregated.

(12) *Failure to comply.*—If the IRS fails to comply with the time limitations specified in paragraphs (c)(9), (10), or paragraph (c)(11)(i) of this section, any person making a request for records satisfying the requirements of paragraphs (c)(4)(i)(A) through (I) of this section, shall be deemed to have exhausted administrative remedies with respect to such request. Accordingly, this person may initiate suit in accordance with paragraph (c)(13) of this section.

(13) *Judicial review.*—If an administrative appeal pursuant to paragraph (c)(10) of this section for records or fee waiver or reduction is denied, or if a request for expedited processing is denied and there has been no determination as to the release of records, or if a request for a favorable fee category under paragraph (f)(3) of this section is denied, or a determination is made that there are no responsive records, or if no determination is made within the twenty day periods specified in paragraphs (c)(9) and (10) of this section, or the period of any extension pursuant to paragraph (c)(11)(i) of this section, or by grant of the requester, respectively, the person making the request may commence an action in a United States district court in the district in which the requester resides, in which the requester's principal place of business is located, in which the records are situated, or in the District of Columbia, pursuant to 5 U.S.C. 552(a)(4)(B). The statute authorizes an action only against the agency. With respect to records of the IRS, the agency is the IRS, not an officer or an employee thereof. Service of process in such an action shall be in accordance with the Federal Rules of Civil Procedure (28 U.S.C. App.) applicable to actions against an agency of the United States. Delivery of process upon the IRS shall be directed to the Commissioner of Internal Revenue, Attention: CC:PA, 1111 Constitution Avenue, N.W., Washington, D.C. 20224. The IRS shall serve an answer or otherwise plead to any complaint made under this paragraph within 30 days after service upon it, unless the court otherwise directs for good cause shown. The district court shall determine the matter *de novo*, and may examine the contents of the IRS records in question *in camera* to determine whether such records or any part thereof shall be withheld under any of the exemptions described in 5 U.S.C. 552(b) and the exclusions described in 5 U.S.C. 552(c). The burden shall be upon the IRS to sustain its action in not making the requested records available. The court may assess against the United States reasonable attorney fees and other litigation costs reasonably incurred by the person making the request in any case in which the complainant has substantially prevailed.

(14) *Preservation of records.*—All correspondence relating to the requests received by the IRS under this chapter, and all records processed pursuant to such requests, shall be preserved, until such time as the destruction of such correspondence and records is authorized pursuant to Title 44 of the United States Code. Under no circumstances shall records be destroyed while they are the subject of a pending request, appeal, or lawsuit under 5 U.S.C. 552.

(d) *Rules for disclosure of certain specified matters.*—Requests for certain specified categories of records shall be processed by the IRS in accordance with other established procedures.

(1) *Inspection of tax returns and attachments or transcripts.*—The inspection of returns and attachments is governed by the provisions of the internal revenue laws and regulations thereunder promulgated by the Secretary of the Treasury. *See* section 6103 and the regulations thereunder. Written requests for a copy of a tax return and attachments or a transcript of a tax return shall be made using IRS Form 4506, "Request for Copy or Transcript of Tax Form." A reasonable fee, as the Commissioner may from time to time establish, may be charged for such copies.

(2) *Record of seizure and sale of real estate.*—Subject to the rules on disclosure set forth in section 6103, Record 21, Part 2, "Record of seizure and sale of real estate", is available for public inspection in the local IRS office where the real estate is located. Copies of Record 21, Part 2 shall be furnished upon written request. Members of the public may call the toll-free IRS Customer Service number, 1-800-829-1040, to obtain the address of the appropriate local office. Record 21 does not list real estate seized for use in violation of the internal revenue laws (*see* section 7302).

(3) *Public inspection of certain information returns, notices, and reports furnished by certain tax-exempt organizations and certain trusts.*—Subject to the rules on disclosure set forth in section 6104: Information furnished on any Form 990 series or Form 1041-A returns, pursuant to sections 6033 and 6034, shall be made available for public inspection and copying, upon written request; information furnished by organizations exempt from tax under section 527 on Forms 8871, Political Organization Notice of Section 527 Status, and Forms 8872, Political Organization Report of Contributions and Expenditures, are available for public inspection and copying from the IRS website at *www.eforms.irs.gov*. In addition, Forms 8871 and 8872 shall be made available for public inspection and copying, upon written request; and information furnished by organizations exempt from tax under section 527 on Form 1120-POL pursuant to section 6012(a)(6) shall be made available for public inspection and copying upon written request. Written requests to inspect or obtain copies of any of the information described in this paragraph (d)(3) shall be made using Form 4506-A, "Request for Public Inspection or Copy of Exempt or Political Organization IRS Form," and be directed to the appropriate address listed on Form 4506-A.

(4) *Public inspection of applications and determinations of certain organizations for tax exemption.*—Subject to the rules on disclosure set forth in section 6104, applications, including Forms 1023 and 1024, and certain papers submitted in support of such applications, filed by organizations described in section 501(c) or (d) and determined to be exempt from taxation under section 501(a), and any letter or other document issued by the IRS with respect to such applications, shall be made available for public inspection and copying, upon written request. Written requests to inspect or obtain copies of this information shall be made using Form 4506-A, "Request for Public Inspection or Copy of Exempt or Political Organization IRS Form" and be directed to the appropriate address listed on Form 4506-A.

(5) *Public inspection of applications and annual returns with respect to certain deferred compensation plans and accounts and employee plans.*—Subject to the rules on disclosure set forth in section 6104; forms, applications, and papers submitted in support of such applications, with respect to the qualification of a pension, profit sharing, or stock bonus plan under sections 401(a), 403(a), or 405(a), an individual retirement account described in section 408(a), an individual retirement annuity described in section 408(b), or with respect to the exemption from tax of an organization forming part of such a plan or account, and any document issued by the IRS dealing with such qualification or exemption, shall be open to public inspection and copying upon written request. This paragraph shall not apply with respect to plans with no more than 25 plan participants. Written requests to inspect or obtain copies of such material shall be directed to IRS Customer Service—Tax Exempt & Government Entities Division (TEGE), P.O. Box 2508, Room 2023, Cincinnati, Ohio 45201; and information furnished on the Form 5500 series of returns, pursuant to section 6058, shall be made available for public inspection and copying upon written request. Except for requests for Form 5500-EZ, written requests to inspect or to obtain a copy of this information shall be directed to the Department of Labor, Public Disclosure, Room N-5638, 200 Constitution Avenue, N.W., Washington, D.C. 20210. Written requests to inspect or to obtain a copy of Form 5500-EZ shall be directed to the Internal Revenue Service Center, P.O. Box 9941, Stop 6716, Ogden, Utah 84409.

(6) *Publication of statistics of income.*—Statistics with respect to the operation of the income tax laws are published annually in accordance with section 6108 and § 301.6108-1.

(7) *Comments received in response to a notice of proposed rulemaking, a solicitation for public comments, or prepublication comments.*—Written comments received in response to a notice of proposed rulemaking, a solicitation for public comments, or prepublication comments, may be inspected, upon written request, by any person upon compliance with the provisions of this paragraph. Comments may be inspected in the Freedom of Information Reading Room, IRS, 1111 Constitution Avenue, N.W., Room 1621, Washington, D.C. The request to inspect comments must be in writing and signed by the person making the request and shall be addressed to the Commissioner of Internal Revenue, Attn: CC:ITA:RU, P.O. Box 7604, Ben Franklin Station, Washington, D.C. 20044. The person submitting the written request may inspect the comments that are the subject of the request during regular business hours. If the requester wishes to inspect the docu-

ments, the requester shall be contacted by IRS Freedom of Information Reading Room personnel when the documents are available for inspection. Copies of comments may be made in the Freedom of Information Reading Room by the person making the request or may be requested, in writing, to the Commissioner of Internal Revenue, Attn: CC:ITA:RU, P.O. Box 7604, Ben Franklin Station, Washington, D.C. 20044. The IRS shall comply with requests for records under the paragraph within a reasonable time. The provisions of paragraph (f)(5)(iii) of this section, relating to fees for duplication, shall apply with respect to requests made in accordance with this paragraph.

(8) *Accepted offers in compromise.*—For one year after the date of execution, a copy of the Form 7249, "Offer Acceptance Report," for each accepted offer in compromise with respect to any liability for a tax imposed by Title 26 shall be made available for inspection and copying in the location designated by the Compliance Area Director or Compliance Services Field Director within the Small Business and Self-Employed Division (SBSE) of the taxpayer's geographic area of residence.

(9) *Public inspection of written determinations.*—Certain rulings, determination letters, technical advice memorandums, and Chief Counsel advice are open to public inspection pursuant to section 6110.

(e) *Other disclosure procedures.*—For procedures to be followed by officers and employees of the IRS upon receipt of a request or demand for certain internal revenue records or information the disclosure procedure for which is not covered by this section, see §301.9000-1.

(f) *Fees for services.*—(1) *In general.*—Except as otherwise provided, the fees to be charged for search, duplication, and review services performed by the IRS, with respect to the processing of Freedom of Information Act requests, shall be determined and collected in accordance with the provisions of this subsection. A fee shall not be charged for monitoring a requester's inspection of records which contains exempt matter. The IRS may recover the applicable fees even if there is ultimately no disclosure of records. Should services other than the services described in this paragraph be requested and rendered, which are not required by the Freedom of Information Act, fees shall be charged to recover the actual direct cost to the IRS.

(2) *Waiver or reduction of fees.*—(i) The fees authorized by this paragraph may be waived or reduced on a case-by-case basis in accordance with this subsection by any IRS official who is authorized to make the initial determination pursuant to paragraph (c)(9) of this section. Fees shall be waived or reduced by such official when it is determined that disclosure of the requested information is in the public interest because it is likely to contribute significantly to public understanding of the operations or activities of the IRS and is not primarily in the commercial interest of the requester. Such officials shall consider several factors, including, but not limited to, paragraphs (f)(2)(i) through (vi), in determining requests for waiver or reduction of fees—

(A) Whether the subject of the releasable records concerns the agency's operations or activities;

(B) Whether the releasable records are likely to contribute to an understanding of the agency's operations or activities;

(C) Whether the releasable records are likely to contribute to the general public's understanding of the agency's operations or activities (*e.g.*, how will the requester convey the information to the general public);

(D) The significance of the contribution to the general public's understanding of the agency's operations or activities (*e.g.*, is the information contained in the releasable records already available to the general public);

(E) The existence and magnitude of the requester's commercial interest, as that term is used in paragraph (f)(3)(i)(A) of this section, being furthered by the releasable records; and

(F) Whether the magnitude of the requester's commercial interest is sufficiently large in comparison to the general public's interest.

(ii) Requesters asking for reduction or waiver of fees must state the reasons why they believe disclosure meets the standards set forth in paragraph (f)(2)(ii) of this section in a written request signed by the requester.

(iii) The indigence of the requester shall not be considered as a factor to determine if the requester is entitled to a reduction or waiver of fees.

(iv) Normally, no charge shall be made for providing records to federal, state, local, or foreign governments, or agencies or offices thereof, or international governmental organizations.

(v) The initial request for waiver or reduction of fees shall be addressed to the official of the IRS to whose office the request for disclosure is delivered pursuant to paragraph (c)(4)(i)(C) of this section. Appeals from denials of requests for waiver or reduction of

fees shall be decided by the Commissioner's delegate in accordance with the criteria set forth in paragraph (f)(2)(ii) of this section. Appeals shall be received by the Commissioner's delegate within 35 days of the date of the letter of notification denying the initial request for waiver or reduction and shall be decided promptly. See paragraph (c)(10)(ii)(B) of this section for the appropriate address. Upon receipt of the determination on appeal to deny a request for waiver of fees, the requester may initiate an action in a United States district court to review the request for waiver of fees. In such action, the court shall consider the matter *de novo*, except that the court's review of the matter shall be limited to the record before the IRS official to whose office the request for waiver is delivered. In such action, the court shall consider the matter under the arbitrary and capricious standard.

(3) *Categories of requesters.*—(i) *Attestation.*—A request for records under this section shall include an attestation as to the status of the requester for use by the IRS official to whose office the request is delivered in determining the appropriate fees to be assessed. No attestation is required for a requester who falls within paragraph (f)(3)(ii)(E) (an "other requester").

(ii) *Categories.*—(A) *Commercial use requester.*—Any person who seeks information for a use or purpose that furthers the commercial, trade, or profit interests of the requester or the person on whose behalf the request is made.

(B) *News media requester.*—Any person actively gathering news for an entity that is organized and operated to publish or broadcast news (*i.e.*, information about current events or of current interest to the public) to the public. News media entities include, but are not limited to, television or radio stations broadcasting to the public at large, publishers of periodicals, to the extent they disseminate news, who make their periodicals available for purchase or subscription by the general public, computerized news services and telecommunications. Free lance journalists shall be included as media requesters if they can demonstrate a solid basis for expecting publication through a qualifying news entity (*e.g.*, publication contract, past publication record). Specialized periodicals, although catering to a narrower audience, may be considered media requesters so long as they are available to the public generally, via newsstand or subscription.

(C) *Educational institution requester.*—Any person who, on behalf of a preschool, public or private elementary or secondary school, institution of undergraduate or graduate higher education, institution of professional or vocational education, which operates a program or programs of scholarly research, seeks records in furtherance of the institution's scholarly research and is not for a commercial use. This category does not include requesters wanting records for use in meeting individual academic research or study requirements.

(D) *Noncommercial scientific institution requester.*—Any person on behalf of an institution that is not operated on a commercial basis, that is operated solely for the purpose of conducting scientific research whose results are not intended to promote any particular product or industry.

(E) *Other requester.*—Any requester who does not fall within the categories described in paragraphs (f)(3)(ii)(A) through (D).

(iii) *Determination of proper category.*—Where the IRS has reasonable cause to doubt the use to which a requester shall put the records sought, or where that use is not clear from the record itself, the IRS shall seek additional clarification from the requester before assigning the request to a specific category. In any event, a determination of the proper category of requester shall be based upon a review of the requester's submission and may also be based upon the IRS' own records.

(iv) *Allowable charges.*—(A) *Commercial use requesters.*—Records shall be provided to commercial use requesters for the cost of search, duplication, and review (including doing all that is necessary to excise and otherwise prepare records for release) of records. Commercial use requesters are not entitled to two hours of free search time or 100 pages of free duplication.

(B) *News media, educational institution, and noncommercial scientific institution requesters.*—Records shall be provided to news media, educational institution, and noncommercial scientific institution requesters for the cost of duplication alone, excluding fees for the first 100 pages.

(C) *Other requesters.*—Requesters who do not fit into any of the above categories shall be charged fees that shall cover the full actual direct cost of searching for and duplicating records, except that the first two hours of search time and first 100 pages of duplication shall be furnished without charge. Requests from individuals for records about themselves maintained in the IRS's systems of records shall continue to be treated under the fee provisions of the Privacy Act of 1974, which permits fees only for duplication after the first 100 pages are furnished free of charge.

(4) *Avoidance of unexpected fees.*—(i) In order to protect requesters from unexpected fees, all requests for records shall state the agreement of the requesters to pay the fees determined in accordance with paragraph (f)(5) of this section or state the upper limit they are willing to pay to cover the costs of processing their requests.

(ii) When the fees for processing requests are estimated by the IRS to exceed the upper limit agreed to by a requester, or when a requester has failed to state a limit and the costs are estimated to exceed $250, and the IRS has not then determined to waive or reduce the fees, a notice shall be sent to the requester. This notice shall—

(A) Inform the requester of the estimated costs;

(B) Extend an offer to the requester to confer with agency personnel in an attempt to reformulate the request in a manner which shall reduce the fees and still meet the needs of the requester;

(C) If the requester is not amenable to reformulation, which would reduce fees to under $250, then advance payment of the estimated fees shall be required; and

(D) Inform the requester that the time period, within which the IRS is obliged to make a determination on the request, shall not begin to run, pending a reformulation of the request or the receipt of advance payment from the requester, as appropriate.

(5) *Fees for services.*—The fees for services performed by the IRS shall be imposed and collected as set forth in this paragraph. No fees shall be charged if the costs of routine collecting and processing the fees allowable under 5 U.S.C. 552(a)(4)(A) are likely to equal or exceed the amount of the fee.

(i) *Search services.*—Fees charged for search services are as follows:

(A) *Searches for records other than computerized records.*—The IRS shall charge for search services at the salary rate(s) (*i.e.*, basic pay plus 16 percent) of the employee(s) making the search. An average rate for the range of grades typically involved may be established. Fees may be charged for search time as prescribed in this section even if the time spent searching does not yield any records, or if records are denied.

(B) *Searches for computerized records.*—Actual direct cost of the search, including computer search time, runs, and the operator's salary. The fee for computer output shall be actual direct costs. For requesters in the "other requester" category, the charge for the computer search shall begin when the cost of the search (including the operator time and the cost of operating the computer) equals the equivalent dollar amount of two hours of the salary of the person performing the search.

(C) *Searches requiring travel or transportation.*—Shipping charges to transport records from one location to another, or for the transportation of an employee to the site of requested records when it is necessary to locate rather than examine the records, shall be at the rate of the actual cost of such shipping or transportation.

(ii) *Review Services.*—(A) *Review defined.*—Review is the process of examining records in response to a commercial use requester, as that term is defined in paragraph (f)(3)(i)(A), upon initial consideration of the applicability of an exemption described in 5 U.S.C. 552(b) or an exclusion described in 5 U.S.C. 552(c) to the requested records, be it at the initial request or administrative appeal level, to determine whether any portion of any record responsive to the request is permitted to be withheld. Review includes doing all that is necessary to excise and otherwise prepare the records for release. Review does not include the time spent on resolving general legal or policy issues regarding the applicability of exemptions to the requested records.

(B) *Fees charged for review services.*—The IRS shall charge commercial use requesters for review of records at the initial determination stage at the salary rate(s) (*i.e.*, basic pay plus 16 percent) of the employee(s) making the review. An average rate for the range of grades typically involved may be established by the Commissioner.

(iii) *Duplication other than for tax returns and attachments.*—(A) Duplication fees charged for copies of paper records shall be a reasonable fee, as the Commissioner may from time to time establish.

(B) The actual direct cost of duplication for photographs, films, videotapes, audiotapes, compact disks, and other materials shall be charged.

(C) Records may be provided to a private contractor for copying and the requester shall be charged for the actual cost of duplication charged by the private contractor.

(D) When other duplication processes not specifically identified above are requested and provided pursuant to the Freedom of Information Act, their actual direct cost to the IRS shall be charged.

(E) Where the condition of the record does not enable the IRS to make legible copies, the IRS shall not attempt to reconstruct it. The official having jurisdiction over the record shall furnish the best copy that is available and advise the requester of this fact.

(iv) *Charges for copies of tax returns and attachments, and transcripts of tax returns.*—A charge shall be made for each copy of a tax return and its attachments, and transcripts of tax returns, supplied in response to a Form 4506, "Request for Copy of Tax Form." The amount of the charge shall be a reasonable fee as computed by the Commissioner from time to time, and as set forth on Form 4506.

(v) *Other services.*—Other services and materials requested (*e.g.*, certification, express mailing) which are not specifically covered by this part and/or not required by the Freedom of Information Act are provided at the discretion of the IRS and are chargeable at the actual direct cost to the IRS.

(6) *Printed material.*—Certain relevant government publications which shall be placed on the shelves of the Freedom of Information Reading Room shall not be sold at that location. Copies of pages of these publications may be duplicated on the premises and a fee for such service may be charged in accordance with paragraph (f)(5)(iii) of this section. A person desiring to purchase the complete publication, for example, an Internal Revenue Bulletin, should contact the Superintendent of Documents, U.S. Government Printing Office, Washington, D.C. 20402.

(7) *Search, duplication, and deletion services with respect to records open to public inspection pursuant to section 6110.*—Fees charged for searching for, making deletions in, and copies of records subject to public inspection pursuant to section 6110 only upon written request shall be at the actual cost, as the Commissioner may from time to time establish.

(8) *Form of payment.*—Payment shall be made by check or money order, payable to the order of the Treasury of the United States.

(9) *Advance payments.*—(i) If previous fees have not been paid in a timely fashion, as defined in paragraph (f)(10) of this section, or where the estimated fees exceed $250, the IRS shall require payment in full of any outstanding fees and all estimated fees prior to processing a request. Additionally, the IRS reserves the right to require payment of fees after a request is processed and before any records are released to a requester. For purposes of this paragraph, a requester is the individual in whose name a request is made; however, where a request is made on behalf of another individual, and previous fees have not been paid within the designated time period by either the requester or the individual on whose behalf the request is made, then the IRS shall require payment in full of all outstanding fees and all estimated fees before processing the request.

(ii) When the IRS acts pursuant to paragraph (f)(9) (i) of this section, the administrative time limits prescribed in paragraphs (c)(9) and (10) of this section, plus permissible extensions of these time limits as prescribed in paragraph (c)(11)(i) of this section, shall begin only after the IRS official to whom the request is delivered has received the fees described above in paragraph (f)(9)(i) of this section.

(10) *Interest.*—Interest shall be charged to requesters who fail to pay the fees in a timely fashion; that is, within 30 days following the day on which the statement of fees as set forth in paragraph (c)(9)(i) of this section was sent by the IRS official to whom the request was delivered. Whenever interest is charged, the IRS shall begin assessing interest on the 31st day following the date the statement of fees was mailed to the requester. Interest shall be at the rate prescribed in 31 U.S.C. 3717. In addition, the IRS shall take all steps authorize by the Debt Collection Act of 1982, including administrative offset, disclosure to consumer reporting agencies, and use of collection agencies, as otherwise authorized by law to effect payment.

(11) *Aggregating requests.*—When the IRS official to whom a request is delivered reasonably believes that a requester or group of requesters is attempting to break down a request into a series of requests for the purpose of evading the assessment of fees, the IRS shall aggregate such requests and charge accordingly, upon notification to the requester and/or requesters.

(g) *Business information and contractor proposal procedures.*—(1) *In general.*—Business information provided to the IRS by a business submitter shall not be disclosed pursuant to a Freedom of Information Act request except in accordance with this section.

(2) *Definition.*—Business information is any trade secret or other confidential financial or commercial (including research) information.

(3) *Notice to business submitters.*—Except where it is determined that the information is covered by paragraph (g)(9), the official having control over the requested records, which includes business information, shall provide a business submitter with prompt written

notice of a request encompassing its business information whenever required in accordance with paragraph (g)(4) of this section. Such written notice shall either describe the exact nature of the business information requested or provide copies of the records or portions thereof containing the business information.

(4) *When notice is required.*—(i) For business information submitted to the IRS prior to October 13, 1987, the official having control over the requested records shall provide a business submitter with notice of a request whenever—

(A) The business information was submitted to the IRS upon a commitment of confidentiality; or

(B) The business information was voluntarily submitted and it is of a kind that would customarily not be released to the public by the person from whom it was obtained; or

(C) The official has reason to believe that disclosure of the information may result in commercial or financial injury to the business submitter.

(ii) For business information submitted to the IRS on or after October 13, 1987, the IRS shall provide a business submitter with notice of a request whenever—

(A) The business submitter has designated the information as commercially or financially sensitive information; or

(B) The official has reason to believe that disclosure of the information may result in commercial or financial injury to the business submitter.

(iii) The business submitter's designation that the information is commercially or financially sensitive information should be supported by a statement or certification by an officer or authorized representative of the business providing specific justification that the information in question is, in fact, confidential commercial or financial information and has not been disclosed to the public.

(iv) Notice of a request for business information falling within paragraph (g)(4)(ii)(A) of this section shall be required for a period of not more than ten years after the date of submission unless the business submitter requests, and provides acceptable justification for, a specific notice period of greater duration.

(5) *Opportunity to object to disclosure.*—Through the notice described in paragraph (g)(3) of this section, the official having control over the requested records shall afford a business submitter ten days (excepting Saturdays, Sundays and legal public holidays) within which to provide the official with a detailed statement of any objection to disclosure. Such statement shall specify all grounds for withholding any of the information, with particular attention to why the information is claimed to be trade secret or commercial or financial information that is privileged and confidential. Information provided by a business submitter pursuant to this paragraph may itself be subject to disclosure under 5 U.S.C. 552.

(6) *Notice of intent to disclose.*—The IRS shall consider a business submitter's objections and specific grounds for nondisclosure prior to determining whether to disclose business information. Whenever the official having control over the requested records decides to disclose business information over the objection of a business submitter, the official shall forward to the business submitter a written notice which shall include—

(i) A statement of the reasons for which the business submitter's disclosure objections were not sustained;

(ii) A description of the business information to be disclosed; and

(iii) A specified disclosure date, which is ten days (excepting Saturdays, Sundays and legal public holidays) after the notice of the final decision to release the requested records has been mailed to the submitter. Except as otherwise prohibited by law, a copy of the disclosure notice shall be forwarded to the requester at the same time.

(7) *Judicial review.*—(i) *In general.*—The IRS' disposition of the request and the submitter's objections shall be subject to judicial review under paragraph (c)(14) of this section. A requester is not required to exhaust administrative remedies if a complaint has been filed under this paragraph by a business submitter of the information contained in the requested records. Likewise, a business submitter is not required to exhaust administrative remedies if a complaint has been filed by the requester of these records.

(ii) *Notice of FOIA lawsuit.*—Whenever a requester brings suit seeking to compel disclosure of business information covered by paragraph (g)(4) of this section, the official having control over the requested records shall promptly provide the business submitter with written notice thereof.

(iii) *Exception to notice requirement.*—The notice requirements of this paragraph shall not apply if—

(A) The official having control over the records determines that the business information shall not be disclosed;

(B) The information lawfully has been published or otherwise made available to the public; or

(C) Disclosure of the information is required by law (other than 5 U.S.C. 552).

(8) *Appeals.*—Procedures for administrative appeals from denials of requests for business information are to be processed in accordance with paragraph (c)(10) of this section.

(9) *Contractor Proposals.*—(i) Pursuant to 41 U.S.C. 253b(m), the IRS shall not release under the Freedom of Information Act any proposal submitted by a contractor in response to the requirements of a solicitation for a competitive proposal, unless that proposal is set forth or incorporated by reference in a contract entered into between the IRS and the contractor that submitted the proposal. For purposes of this paragraph, the term *proposal* means any proposal, including a technical, management, or cost proposal, submitted by a contractor in response to the requirements of a solicitation for a competitive proposal.

(ii) A copy of the FOIA request for information protected from disclosure under this paragraph shall be furnished to the contractor who submitted the proposal.

(h) *Responsible officials and their addresses.*—For purposes of this section, the IRS officials in the disclosure offices listed below are responsible for the control of records within their geographic area. In the case of records of the Headquarters Office (including records of the National Office of the Office of Chief Counsel), except as provided in paragraph (c)(9)(i)(A), the Director, Office of Governmental Liaison and Disclosure, or delegate, is the responsible official. Requests for these records should be sent to:

IRS FOIA Request
Headquarters Disclosure Office
CL:GLD:D
1111 Constitution Avenue, N.W.
Washington, D.C. 20224

(1) For Personnel Background Investigation Records, the address of the responsible official is:

Internal Revenue Service
Attn: Associate Director, Personnel Security
Room 4244, A:PS:PSO
1111 Constitution Avenue N.W.
Washington, D.C. 20224

(2) For records of the Office of Chief Counsel other than those located in the Headquarters or Division Counsel immediate offices, records shall be deemed to be under the jurisdiction of the local area Disclosure Office. Requesters seeking records under this section should send their requests to the local area Disclosure Office address listed for the state where the requester resides or any activity associated with the records occurred (for states with multiple offices, the request should be sent to the nearest office):

**Alabama**
IRS FOIA Request
New Orleans Disclosure Office
Mail Stop 40
600 S. Maestri Place
New Orleans, LA 70130

**Alaska**
IRS FOIA Request
Oakland Disclosure Office
1301 Clay Street, Suite 840-S
Oakland, CA 94612-5210

**Arkansas**
IRS FOIA Request
Nashville Disclosure Office
MDP 44
801 Broadway, Room 480
Nashville, TN 37203

**Arizona**
IRS FOIA Request
Phoenix Disclosure Office
Mail Stop 7000 PHX
210 E. Earll Drive
Phoenix, AZ 85012

**California**
IRS FOIA Request
Laguna Niguel Disclosure Office
24000 Avila Road, M/S 2201
Laguna Niguel, CA 92677-0207
IRS FOIA Request
Los Angeles Disclosure Office
Mail Stop 1020
300 N. Los Angeles Street
Los Angeles, CA 90012-3363
IRS FOIA Request
Oakland Disclosure Office

1301 Clay Street, Suite 840-S
Oakland, CA 94612
IRS FOIA Request
San Jose Disclosure Office
Mail Stop HQ-4603
55 South Market Street
San Jose, CA 95113
**Colorado**
IRS FOIA Request
Denver Disclosure Office
Mail Stop 7000 DEN
600 17th Street
Denver, CO 80202-2490
**Connecticut**
IRS FOIA Request
Hartford Disclosure Office
William R. Cotter F.O.B.
Mail Stop 140
135 High Street
Hartford, CT 06103
**Delaware**
IRS FOIA Request
Baltimore Disclosure Office
George Fallon Fed. Bldg.
31 Hopkins Plaza, Room 1210
Baltimore, MD 21201
**District of Columbia**
IRS FOIA Request
Baltimore Disclosure Office
George Fallon Fed. Bldg.
31 Hopkins Plaza, Room 1210
Baltimore, MD 21201
**Florida**
IRS FOIA Request
Fort Lauderdale Disclosure Off.
Mail Stop 4030
7850 SW 6th Court, Rm. 260
Plantation, FL 33324-3202
IRS FOIA Request
Jacksonville Disclosure Office
MS 4030
400 West Bay Street
Jacksonville, FL 32202-4437
**Georgia**
IRS FOIA Request
Atlanta Disclosure Office
Mail Stop 602D, Room 1905
401 W. Peachtree Street, NW
Atlanta, GA 30308
**Hawaii**
IRS FOIA Request
Laguna Niguel Disclosure Office
24000 Avila Road, M/S 2201
Laguna Niguel, CA 92677-0207
**Idaho**
IRS FOIA Request
Seattle Disclosure Office
Mail Stop W625
915 2nd Avenue
Seattle, WA 98174
**Illinois**
IRS FOIA Request
Chicago Disclosure Office
Mail Stop 7000 CHI, Room 2820
230 S. Dearborn Street
Chicago, IL 60604
**Indiana**
IRS FOIA Request
Indianapolis Disclosure Office
Mail Stop CL 658
575 N. Penn. Street
Indianapolis, IN 46204
**Iowa**
IRS FOIA Request
St. Paul Disclosure Office
Stop 7000
316 N. Robert Street
St. Paul, MN 55101
**Kansas**
IRS FOIA Request
St. Louis Disclosure Office
Mail Stop 7000 STL
P.O. Box 66781
St. Louis, MO 63166
**Kentucky**
IRS FOIA Request

Cincinnati Disclosure Office
Post Office Box 1818, Rm. 7019
Cincinnati, OH 45201
**Louisiana**
IRS FOIA Request
New Orleans Disclosure Office
Mail Stop 40
600 S. Maestri Place
New Orleans, LA 70130
**Maine**
IRS FOIA Request
Boston Disclosure Office
Mail Stop 41150
Post Office Box 9112
JFK Building
Boston, MA 02203
**Maryland**
IRS FOIA Request
Baltimore Disclosure Office
George Fallon Fed. Bldg.
31 Hopkins Plaza, Room 1210
Baltimore, MD 21201
**Massachusetts**
IRS FOIA Request
Boston Disclosure Office
Mail Stop 41150
JFK Building
Post Office Box 9112
Boston, MA 02203
**Michigan**
IRS FOIA Request
Detroit Disclosure Office
Mail Stop 11
Post Office Box 330500
Detroit, MI 48232-6500
**Minnesota**
IRS FOIA Request
St. Paul Disclosure Office
Stop 7000
316 N. Robert Street
St. Paul, MN 55101
**Mississippi**
IRS FOIA Request
New Orleans Disclosure Office
Mail Stop 40
600 S. Maestri Place
New Orleans, LA 70130
**Missouri**
IRS FOIA Request
St. Louis Disclosure Office
Mail Stop 7000 STL
P.O. Box 66781
St. Louis, MO 63166
**Montana**
IRS FOIA Request
Denver Disclosure Office
Mail Stop 7000 DEN
600 17th Street
Denver, CO 80202-2490
**Nebraska**
IRS FOIA Request
St. Paul Disclosure Office
Stop 7000
316 N. Robert Street
St. Paul, MN 55101
**Nevada**
IRS FOIA Request
Phoenix Disclosure Office
Mail Stop 7000 PHX
210 E. Earll Drive
Phoenix, AZ 85012
**New Hampshire**
IRS FOIA Request
Boston Disclosure Office
Mail Stop 41150
Post Office Box 9112
JFK Building
Boston, MA 02203
**New Mexico**
IRS FOIA Request
Phoenix Disclosure Office
Mail Stop 7000 PHX
210 E. Earll Drive
Phoenix, AZ 85012
**New Jersey**
IRS FOIA Request

Springfield Disclosure Office
P.O. Box 748
Springfield, N.J. 07081-0748
**New York (Brooklyn, Queens, and the counties of Nassau and Suffolk)**
IRS FOIA Request
Brooklyn Disclosure Office
10 Metro Tech Center
625 Fulton Street
4th Floor, Suite 611
Brooklyn, N.Y. 11201-5404
**New York (Manhattan, Staten Island, the Bronx, and the counties of Rockland and Westchester)**
IRS FOIA Request
Manhattan Disclosure Office
110 W. 44th Street
New York, N.Y. 10036
**New York (all other counties)**
IRS FOIA Request
Buffalo Disclosure Office
111 West Huron St., Room 505
Buffalo, N.Y. 14202
**North Carolina**
IRS FOIA Request
Greensboro Disclosure Office
320 Federal Place, Room 409
Greensboro, N.C. 27401
**North Dakota**
IRS FOIA Request
St. Paul Disclosure Office
Stop 7000
316 N. Robert Street
St. Paul, MN 55101
**Ohio**
IRS FOIA Request
Cincinnati Disclosure Office
Post Office Box 1818, Rm. 7019
Cincinnati, OH 45201
**Oklahoma**
IRS FOIA Request
Oklahoma City Disclosure Office
Mail Stop 7000 OKC
55 N. Robinson
Oklahoma City, OK 73102
**Oregon**
IRS FOIA Request
Seattle Disclosure Office
Mail Stop W625
915 2nd Avenue
Seattle, WA 98174
**Pennsylvania**
IRS FOIA Request
Philadelphia Disclosure Office
600 Arch Street, Room 3214
Philadelphia, PA 19106
**Rhode Island**
IRS FOIA Request
Hartford Disclosure Office
William R. Cotter F.O.B.
Mail Stop 140
135 High Street
Hartford, CT 06103
**South Carolina**
IRS FOIA Request
Greensboro Disclosure Office
320 Federal Place, Room 409
Greensboro, N.C. 27401
**South Dakota**
IRS FOIA Request
St. Paul Disclosure Office
Stop 7000
316 N. Robert Street
St. Paul, MN 55101
**Tennessee**
IRS FOIA Request
Nashville Disclosure Office

MDP 44
801 Broadway, Room 480
Nashville, TN 37203
**Texas**
IRS FOIA Request
Austin Disclosure Office
Mail Stop 7000 AUS
300 East 8th Street, Room 262
Austin, TX 78701
IRS FOIA Request
Dallas Disclosure Office
Mail Stop 7000 DAL
1100 Commerce Street
Dallas, TX 75242
IRS FOIA Request
Houston Disclosure Office
Mail Stop 7000 HOU
1919 Smith Street
Houston, TX 77002
**Utah**
IRS FOIA Request
Denver Disclosure Office
Mail Stop 7000 DEN
600 17th Street
Denver, CO 80202-2490
**Vermont**
IRS FOIA Request
Boston Disclosure Office
Mail Stop 41150
Post Office Box 9112
JFK Building
Boston, MA 02203
**Virginia**
IRS FOIA Request
Richmond Disclosure Office
P.O. Box 10107
Richmond, VA 23240
**Washington**
IRS FOIA Request
Seattle Disclosure Office
Mail Stop 625
915 2nd Avenue
Seattle, WA 98174
**West Virginia**
IRS FOIA Request
Cincinnati Disclosure Office
Post Office Box 1818, Rm. 7019
Cincinnati, OH 45201
**Wisconsin**
IRS FOIA Request
Milwaukee Disclosure Office
Mail Stop 7000 MIL
310 W. Wisconsin Avenue
Milwaukee, WI 53203-2221
**Wyoming**
IRS FOIA Request
Denver Disclosure Office
Mail Stop 7000 DEN
600 17th Street
Denver, CO 80202-2490
**All APO and FPO addresses**
IRS FOIA Request
Headquarters Disclosure Office
CL:GLD:D
1111 Constitution Avenue, N.W.
Washington, D.C. 20224
[Reg. § 601.702.]

☐ [32 FR 15990, Nov. 22, 1967, as amended at 33 FR 6826, May 4, 1968; 34 FR 6433, Apr. 12, 1969; 34 FR 14604, Sept. 19, 1969; 35 FR 7117, May 6, 1970; 36 FR 7587, Apr. 22, 1971; 36 FR 8149, Apr. 30, 1970; 38 FR 4973, Feb. 23, 1973; 39 FR 15755, May 6, 1974; 41 FR 19937, May 14, 1976; 41 FR 24704, June 18, 1976; 41 FR 48472, Nov. 5, 1976; 43 FR 53030, Nov. 15, 1978; 45 FR 7259, Feb. 1, 1980; 48 FR 15624, Apr. 12, 1983; 49 FR 12702, Mar. 30, 1984; 49 FR 19651, May 9, 1984; 49 FR 36500, Sept. 18, 1984; 51 FR 7442, Mar. 4, 1986; 52 FR 30996, Aug. 18, 1987; 52 FR 37940, Oct. 13, 1987; 67 FR 69673, Nov. 19, 2002.]

# Subpart H—Tax Counseling for the Elderly

[Reg. § 601.801]

**§ 601.801. Purpose and statutory authority.**—(a) This Subpart H contains the rules for implementation of the Tax Counseling for the Elderly assistance program under Section 163 of the Revenue Act of 1978, Public Law 95-600, November 6, 1978 (92 Stat. 2810). Section 163 authorizes the Secretary of the Treasury, through the Internal Revenue Service, to enter into agreements with private or public nonprofit agencies or organizations for the purpose of providing training and technical assistance to prepare volunteers to provide tax counseling assistance for elderly individuals, age 60 and over, in the preparation of their Federal income tax returns.

(b) Section 163 provides that the Secretary may provide:

(1) Preferential access to Internal Revenue Service taxpayer service representatives for the purpose of making available technical information needed during the course of the volunteers' work;

(2) Publicity for making elderly persons aware of the availability of volunteer taxpayer return preparation assistance programs under this section; and

(3) Technical materials and publications to be used by such volunteers.

(c) In carrying out responsibilities under Section 163, the Secretary, through the Internal Revenue Service is also authorized:

(1) To provide assistance to organizations which demonstrate, to the satisfaction of the Secretary, that their volunteers are adequately trained and competent to render effective tax counseling to the elderly in the preparation of Federal income tax returns;

(2) To provide for the training of such volunteers, and to assist in such training, to ensure that such volunteers are qualified to provide tax counseling assistance to elderly individuals in the preparation of Federal income tax returns;

(3) To provide reimbursement to volunteers through such organizations for transportation, meals, and other expenses incurred by them in training or providing tax counseling assistance in the preparation of Federal income tax returns under this section, and such other support and assistance determined to be appropriate in carrying out the provisions of the section;

(4) To provide for the use of services, personnel, and facilities of Federal executive agencies and State and local public agencies with their consent, with or without reimbursement; and

(5) To prescribe rules and regulations necessary to carry out the provisions of the section.

(d) With regard to the employment status of volunteers, section 163 also provides that service as a volunteer in any program carried out under this section shall not be considered service as an employee of the United States. Volunteers under such a program shall not be subject to the provisions of law relating to Federal employment, except that the provisions relating to the illegal disclosure of income or other information punishable under Section 1905 of Title 18, United States Code, shall apply to volunteers as if they were employees of the United States. [Reg. § 601.801.]

☐ [44 FR 72113, Dec. 13, 1979.]

### [Reg. § 601.802]

**§ 601.802. Cooperative agreements.**—(a) *General.*—Tax Counseling for the Elderly programs will be administered by sponsor organizations under cooperative agreements with the Internal Revenue Service. Use of cooperative agreements is in accordance with the Federal Grant and Cooperative Agreement Act of 1977, Public Law 95-224, February 3, 1978 (92 Stat. 3, 41 U.S.C. 501-509). Cooperative agreements will be legally binding agreements in document form.

(b) *Nature and contents of cooperative agreements.*—Each cooperative agreement will provide for implementation of the program in specified geographic areas. Cooperative agreements will set forth:

(1) The functions and duties to be performed by the Internal Revenue Service and the functions and duties to be performed by the program sponsor,

(2) The maximum amount of the award available to the program sponsor,

(3) The services to be provided for each geographical area, and

(4) Other requirements specified in the application.

(c) *Entry into cooperative agreements.*—The Commissioner of Internal Revenue, the Director, Taxpayer Service Division, or any other individual designated by the Commissioner may enter into a cooperative agreement for the Internal Revenue Service.

(d) *Competitive award of cooperative agreements.*—Cooperative agreements will generally be entered into based upon competition among eligible applicants.

(1) To be eligible to enter into a cooperative agreement, an organization must be a private or public non-profit agency or organization with experience in coordinating volunteer programs. Federal, state, and local governmental agencies and organizations will not be eligible to become program sponsors.

(2) Eligible applicants will be selected to enter into cooperative agreements based on an evaluation by the Internal Revenue Service of material provided in their applications. The Service will set forth the evaluative criteria in the application instructions.

(3) Determinations as to the eligibility and selection of agencies and organizations to enter into cooperative agreements will be made solely by the Internal Revenue Service and will not be subject to appeal.

(e) *Noncompetitive award of cooperative agreements.*—If appropriations to implement the Tax Counseling for the Elderly program are received at a time close to when tax return preparation assistance must be provided or when other factors exist which make the use of competition to select agencies and organizations to enter into cooperative agreements impracticable, cooperative agreements will be entered into without competition with eligible agencies and organizations selected by the Internal Revenue Service. Determination of when the use of competition is impracticable will be made solely by the Internal Revenue Service and will not be subject to appeal.

(f) *Renegotiation, suspension, termination and modification.*

(1) Cooperative agreements will be subject to renegotiation (including the maximum amount of the award available to a sponsor), suspension, or termination if performance reports required by the cooperative agreement and/or other evaluations by or audits by the Internal Revenue Service or others indicate that planned performance goals or other provisions of the cooperative agreement, the regulations, or Section 163 of the Revenue Act of 1978 are not being satisfactorily met. The necessity for renegotiation, suspension, or termination, will be determined solely by the Internal Revenue Service and will not be subject to appeal.

(2) Cooperative agreements may be modified in writing by mutual agreement between the Internal Revenue Service and the program sponsor at any time. Modifications will be based upon factors such as an inability to utilize all funds available under a cooperative agreement, the availability of additional funds and an ability to effectively utilize additional funds, and interference of some provisions with the efficient operation of the program.

(g) *Negotiation.*—If the proposed program of an eligible applicant does not warrant award of an agreement, the Internal Revenue Service may negotiate with the applicant to bring the application up to a standard that will be adequate for award. If more than one inadequate application has been received for the geographic area involved, negotiation to bring all such applications up to standard will be conducted with all such applicants unless time does not permit negotiations with all. [Reg. § 601.802.]

☐ [44 FR 72113, Dec. 13, 1979.]

### [Reg. § 601.803]

**§ 601.803. Program operations and requirements.**—(a) *Objective.*—The objective of the Tax Counseling for the Elderly program is to provide free assistance in the preparation of Federal income tax returns to elderly taxpayers age 60 and over, by providing training, technical and administrative support to volunteers under the direction of non-profit agencies and organizations that have cooperative agreements with the Internal Revenue Service.

(b) *Period of program operations.*—Most tax return preparation assistance will be provided to elderly taxpayers during the period for filing Federal income tax returns, from January 1 to April 15 each year. However, the program activities required to ensure elderly taxpayers efficient and quality tax assistance will normally be conducted year round. Program operations will generally be divided into the following segments each year: October—recruit volunteers; November and December—set training and testing schedules for volunteers, identify assistance sites, complete publicity plans for sites; December and January—train and test volunteers, set volunteer assistance schedules; January through May—provide tax assistance, conduct publicity for sites; May and June—prepare final report and evaluate program; July and August—prepare for next year's program.

(c) *Assistance requirements.*—All tax return preparation assistance provided under Tax Counseling for the Elderly programs must be provided free of charge to taxpayers and must be provided only to elderly individuals. An elderly individual is an individual age 60 or over at the close of the individual's taxable year with respect to which tax return preparation assistance is to be provided. Where a joint return is involved, assistance may be provided where only one spouse satisfies the 60 year age requirement.

(d) *Training and testing of volunteers.*—Volunteers will normally be provided training and will normally be required to pass tests designed to measure their understanding of Federal tax subjects on which they will provide tax return assistance. Volunteers who do not receive a satisfactory score will not be eligible to participate in the program.

(e) *Confidentiality of tax information.*—Program sponsors must obtain written assurance from all volunteers and all other individuals involved in the program, to respect the confidentiality of income and financial information known as a result of preparation of a return or of providing tax counseling assistance in the preparation of Federal income tax returns. [Reg. § 601.803.]

☐ [44 FR 72113, Dec. 13, 1979.]

**[Reg. §601.804]**

**§601.804. Reimbursements.**—(a) *General.*—When provided for in cooperative agreements, the Internal Revenue Service will provide amounts to program sponsors for reimbursement to volunteers for transportation, meals, and other expenses incurred in training or providing tax return assistance and to program sponsors for reimbursement of overhead expenses. Cooperative agreements will establish the items for which reimbursements will be allowed and the method of reimbursement, e.g. stipend versus actual expenses for meals, as well as developing necessary procedures, forms, and accounting and financial control systems.

(b) *Direct, reasonable, and prudent expenses.*—Reimbursements will be allowed only for direct, reasonable, and prudent expenses incurred as a part of a volunteer's service or as a part of the program's sponsor's overhead.

(c) *Limitation.*—Total reimbursements provided to a program sponsor shall not exceed the total amount specified in the cooperative agreement. The Internal Revenue Service shall not be liable for additional amounts to program sponsors, volunteers, or anyone else.

(d) *Availability of appropriated funds.*—Expense reimbursements and other assistance to be provided by the Internal Revenue Service under cooperative agreements are contingent upon the availability of appropriated funds for the Tax Counseling for the Elderly program. [Reg. §601.804.]

☐ [44 FR 72113, Dec. 13, 1979.]

**[Reg. §601.805]**

**§601.805. Miscellaneous administrative provisions.**—(a) *Responsibilities and relationship of Internal Revenue and program sponsor.*—Substantial involvement is anticipated between the Internal Revenue Service and the program sponsors in conducting this program. Specific responsibilities and obligations of the Internal Revenue Service and the program sponsors will be set forth in each cooperative agreement.

(b) *Administrative requirements set forth in OMB and Treasury Circulars.*

(1) The basic administrative requirements applicable to individual cooperative agreements are contained in Office of Management and Budget Circular No. A-110, Grants and Agreements with Institutions of Higher Education, Hospitals and Other Nonprofit Organizations (41 F.R. 32016). All applicable provisions of this circular and any existing and further supplements and revisions are incorporated into these regulations and into all cooperative agreements entered into between the Internal Revenue Service and program sponsors.

(2) Additional operating procedures and instructions may be developed by the Internal Revenue Service to direct recipient organizations in carrying out the provisions of this subpart, such as instructions for using letters of credit. Any such operating procedures or instructions will be incorporated into each cooperative agreement.

(c) *Joint funding.*—Tax Counseling for the Elderly programs will not be eligible for joint funding. Accordingly, the Joint Funding Simplification Act of 1974, Public Law 93-510, December 5, 1974 (88 Stat. 1604, 42 U.S.C. 4251-4261) and Office of Management and Budget Circular No. A-111, Jointly Funded Assistance to State and Local Governments and Nonprofit Organizations (41 F.R. 32039), will not apply.

(d) *Discrimination.*—No program sponsor shall discriminate against any person providing tax return assistance on the basis of age, sex, race, religion or national origin in conducting program operations. No program sponsor shall discriminate against any person in providing such assistance on the basis of sex, race, religion or national origin. [Reg. §601.805.]

☐ [44 FR 72113, Dec. 13, 1979, as amended at 49 FR 36500, Sept. 18, 1984.]

**[Reg. §601.806]**

**§601.806. Solicitation of applications.**—(a) *Solicitation.*—The Commissioner of Internal Revenue or the Commissioner's delegate may, at any time, solicit eligible agencies and organizations to submit applications. Generally, applications will be solicited and accepted in June and July of each year. Deadlines for submitting applications and the schedule for selecting program sponsors will be provided with application documents.

(1) Before preparing and submitting an unsolicited application, organizations are strongly encouraged to contact the Internal Revenue Service at the address provided in (b)(2) of this section.

(2) A solicitation of an application is not an assurance or commitment that the Internal Revenue Service will enter into a cooperative agreement. The Internal Revenue Service will not pay any expenses or other costs incurred by the applicant in considering, preparing or submitting an application.

(b) *Application.*

(1) In the application documents, the Commissioner or the Commissioner's delegate will specify program requirements which the applicant must meet.

(2) Eligible organizations interested in participating in the Internal Revenue Service Tax Counseling for the Elderly program should request an application from the:

Program Manager
Tax Counseling for the Elderly
Taxpayer Service Division TX:T:I
Internal Revenue Service
1111 Constitution Ave., N.W.
Washington, D.C. 20224
(202) 566-4904

[Reg. §601.806.]

☐ [44 FR 72113, Dec. 13, 1979.]

# Subpart I—Use of Penalty Mail in the Location and Recovery of Missing Children

**[Reg. §601.901]**

**§601.901. Missing children shown on penalty mail.**—(a) *Purpose.*—To support the national effort to locate and recover missing children, the Internal Revenue Service (IRS) joins other executive departments and agencies of the Government of the United States in using official mail to disseminate photographs and biographical information on hundreds of missing children.

(b) *Procedures for obtaining and disseminating data.*—(1) The IRS shall publish pictures and biographical data related to missing children in domestic penalty mail containing annual tax forms and instructions, taxpayer information publications, and other IRS products directed to members of the public in the United States and its territories and possessions.

(2) Missing children information shall not be placed on the "Penalty Indicia," "OCR Read Area," "Bar Code Read Area," and "Return Address" areas of letter-size envelopes.

(3) The IRS shall accept photographic and biographical materials solely from the National Center for Missing and Exploited Children (National Center). Photographs that were reasonably current as of the time of the child's disappearance, or those which have been updated to reflect a missing child's current age through computer enhancement technique, shall be the only acceptable form of visual media or pictorial likeness used in penalty mail.

(c) *Withdrawal of data.*—The shelf life of printed penalty mail is limited to 3 months for missing child cases. The IRS shall follow those guidelines whenever practicable. For products with an extended shelf life, such as those related to filing and paying taxes, the IRS will not print any pictures or biographical data relating to missing children without obtaining from the National Center a waiver of the 3-month shelf-life guideline.

(d) *Reports and contact official.*—IRS shall compile and submit to OJJDP reports on its experience in implementing Public Law 99-87, 99 Stat. 290, as required by that office. The IRS contact person is: Chief, Business Publications Section (or successor office), Tax Forms and Publications Division, Technical Publications Branch, OP:FS:FP:P:3, Room 5613, Internal Revenue Service, 1111 Constitution Ave., N.W., Washington, DC 20224.

(e) *Period of applicability.*—This section is applicable December 13, 1999 through December 31, 2002. [Reg. §601.901.]

☐ [T.D. 8848, 12-10-99.]